Reference Encyclopedia

Reference Encyclopedia

Oxford New York

OXFORD UNIVERSITY PRESS

Oxford University Press, Great Clarendon Street, Oxford OX2 6DP

Oxford New York
Athens Auckland Bangkok Bogota Buenos Aires Calcutta
Cape Town Chennai Dar es Salaam Delhi Florence Hong Kong Istanbul
Karachi Kuala Lumpur Madrid Melbourne Mexico City Mumbai
Nairobi Paris São Paolo Singapore Taipei Tokyo Toronto Warsaw

and associated companies in
Berlin Ibadan

Oxford is a registered trade mark of Oxford University Press

British Library Cataloguing in Publication Data
Data available

Library of Congress Cataloging in Publication Data
Data available
ISBN 0-19-969073-1

10 9 8 7 6 5 4 3 2 1

Typeset by Market House Books Ltd
Printed in Great Britain by
Clays Ltd,
Bungay, Suffolk

Contents

Acknowledgements vi

Preface vii

Encyclopedia 1

Quick-Reference Appendices 1471
- *SI Units* 1471
- *Unit Conversion Tables* 1472
- *Periodic Table* 1473
- *Classification of the Animal Kingdom* 1474
- *Classification of the Plant Kingdom* 1475
- *Books of the Bible* 1475
- *Prime Ministers* 1476
- *Presidents of the United States of America* 1478
- *The British Monarchy* 1479
- *Scottish Monarchs* 1480
- *Nobel Prize Winners* 1481
- *Academy Award Winners* 1485
- *Booker Prize Winners* 1488
- *The Olympic Games Venues* 1489
- *Association Football: FIFA World Cup* 1489
- *Rugby Union* 1490
- *Cricket* 1491
- *Tennis: Grand Slam Championships — Singles* 1492
- *Tennis: International Team Competitions* 1495
- *Motor Racing: Formula One World Championship* 1496

Acknowledgements

Consultant editors

Michael Allaby
Ian Chilvers

MARKET HOUSE BOOKS LTD

Editors

Alan Isaacs
Elizabeth Martin
Jonathan Law
Peter Blair
John Clark
Amanda Isaacs

Computing and Keyboarding

John Daintith
Anne Stibbs
Jessica Scholes
Sandra McQueen

Illustrations

Picture Research
Linda Wells

Artwork:
Hardlines, Charlbury, Oxfordshire.
The Map Studio, Romsey, Hants.
Maps on pages 31 and 693 prepared using Maps in Minutes™ © RH Publications (1997).

Preface

This new encyclopedia has been prepared by the editors of Market House Books Ltd using the extensive resources of the databases set up over the years by Oxford University Press.

The aim has been to produce a comprehensive reference book suitable for a broad readership, for use at home, school, or the office. The alphabetical arrangement of the articles, and the extensive network of cross-references between them, makes the book extremely easy to use. It is ideal for homework, for example, especially in compiling cross-curricular projects; it also provides a fund of knowledge enabling all the members of a family to find factual and reliable answers to many of their questions.

The editors have attempted to cover all human preoccupations – not only science, technology, medicine, philosophy, politics, economics, religion, history, and the arts, but also sports and pastimes. Many entries are derived from the multi-volume *Oxford Illustrated Encyclopedia*. All the countries of the world have major entries giving for each an outline of its geography, economy, and history, plus useful statistical information. The world's main towns and cities have their own separate entries based on David Munro's *Oxford Dictionary of the World*. Generally, the criteria for including towns and cities are based on the size of their populations. However, some places with quite small populations are included if they have been the scene of some memorable historical event. The encyclopedia also has over 4,500 biographical entries, many drawn from the *Pocket Oxford Dictionary of Biography* (edited by Angus Stevenson). The entries cover not only historically important figures and those who have made their mark in politics and the arts and sciences, but also those who have achieved their fame in entertainment and sport. A quick reference section at the back of the book provides useful tables gathered together for ease of use.

The extensive use of cross-references in this book has made it self-indexing. Cross references are printed in small capital letters and are of three kinds. The first kind occurs at the end of an article and directs the reader to another article that will provide further information relevant to the article being read. In the second type, the entry itself is simply a cross-reference to another entry, indicating either that the word or name is an alternative or former name, or that the subject in question is best explained within a longer entry with related terms. In the latter case, the word is usually printed in a bold typeface within the text of the longer entry, in order to draw it to the reader's attention. In the third type of cross-reference, small capitals are used in the text of articles to indicate that the word or phrase so printed is itself an entry. Not all words that are entries are printed in small capitals, however; the editors have restricted the use of small capitals to words and phrases they think might provide additional relevant information.

We would be extremely grateful to readers who draw our attention to any errors in the encyclopedia, so that they can be corrected in subsequent editions.

A.I.

E.A.M.

1998

A

Aachen (French **Aix-la-Chapelle**) An industrial city and spa in the state of North Rhine-Westphalia, Germany. Close to the Belgian and Dutch borders, it is the most westerly city in Germany; pop. (1991) 244,440. The Springs of Grannus (Latin *Aquae Granni*) were named after the Celtic god of healing and later used by the Romans as public baths. The cathedral was built by Charlemagne who was born and buried in Aachen. From 946 (Otto I) to 1531 (Ferdinand I) monarchs of the Holy Roman Empire were crowned in Aachen.

Aalborg (or **Ålborg**) An industrial city and port in north Jutland, Denmark; pop. (1991) 155,000. Situated on the Limfjord, which links the Kattegat with the North Sea, Aalborg is the capital of Nordjylland district. Ship-building and the production of aquavit are important industries.

Aalesund (or **Ålesund**) A commercial seaport and fishing town in west Norway; pop. (1991) 35,900. Established in 1848, the town was destroyed by fire in 1904 but quickly rebuilt. The 8-km-long tunnels that link offshore islands with Aalesund are the longest submarine tunnels in Scandinavia.

Aalto, Alvar (1898–1976) Finnish architect, designer, sculptor, and painter. One of the most illustrious architects of the 20th century, Aalto was also a talented abstract sculptor and painter and an important furniture designer: more than anyone else he is responsible for Finland's high contemporary reputation in architecture and design. In the 1920s and 1930s much of his work was in the sleek vein of MODERNISM, but after World War II his style became more personal, original, and expressive. In the latter part of his career he employed white marble for major cultural buildings, such as the Finlandia Concert Hall in Helsinki (1962–75). As a designer he is renowned as the inventor of bent plywood furniture.

aardvark (or **Cape ant-eater**) An African mammal quite unrelated to the South American ant-eaters. It is found in all habitats except dense forest, from Ethiopia to the Cape of Good Hope. Growing up to 1.4 m (4.5 feet) in length, it has a round body, tapering tail, and short, thick legs with powerful claws. The long, narrow head has large, donkey-like ears, and an elongated snout. The aardvark digs extensive burrows, large enough for a small man to enter. Feeding at night, it quickly demolishes termite nests up to 1.8 m (6 feet) in height, and consumes the termites with its sticky tongue, which is 30 cm (12 inches) long.

Aarhus (or **Århus**) The capital of Århus county, east Jutland, Denmark, on Aarhus Bay, an arm of the Kattegat; pop. (1990) 261,440. Aarhus is the second-largest city in Denmark. It is a cultural centre with a cathedral, museums, a concert hall, and a university founded in 1934. Its industries include clothing, paper, and foodstuffs.

Aaron A biblical figure, the elder brother of Moses and leader of the Israelite tribe of Levi. Remembered as the traditional founder and head of the Jewish priesthood, with Moses he led the Israelites out of slavery in Egypt. He wielded a magic rod which brought ten plagues upon the Egyptians. During Moses' absence on Mount Sinai, Aaron erected a golden calf which was idolatrously worshipped by the people. In Islamic legend Moussa (Moses) and Hārūn (Aaron) ascended Mount Horeb, not knowing which of them was to die. The coffin they found fitted Hārūn and he was taken to heaven in it.

Aba An industrial city in Imo state, southern Nigeria, north-east of Port Harcourt, developed as an administrative centre by the British in the early 20th century; pop. (1995) 291,600. The Imo River gas field lies to the south of the city. Soap, oil palm, textiles, and beer are produced.

abacus An ancient CALCULATOR. The abacus probably originated in Mesopotamia around 3500 BC. It evolved from a simple grooved board with counters, to the wire frame carrying beads still used today in parts of the Middle East, Russia, Japan, and China. Demonstrations have proved that an abacus, expertly used, is faster than many early 20th-century calculating machines. The modern abacus uses a decimal number system, designating each bead wire as a multiple of ten; some wires can be reserved for storage of intermediate results. Addition and subtraction are performed directly; multiplication and division are repeated additions and subtractions.

Abadan A city on an island of the same name on the Shatt al-Arab waterway in western Iran; pop. (1986) 308,000. It developed from a small village after the discovery of oil in 1908 and is today a major port and oil-refining centre with petrochemical industries.

abalone A marine MOLLUSC of the genus *Haliotis*, related to limpets and snails. Abalones have flat, ear-shaped shells that have a series of holes to one side, providing the exit for the water currents that allow them to breathe. They live in shallow coastal waters. Abalones produce particularly good mother-of-pearl on the inner shell, hence their frequent use as ornamental ash-trays. They are also used as food in some areas.

abattoir (or **slaughterhouse**) A place in which animals are killed and prepared as carcasses of meat for supply to retailers. In the past many small butcher's shops ran their own abattoirs, but legislation on hygiene and animal welfare led to the process becoming more centralized. In modern abattoirs, animals are stunned, using either a special gun or an anaesthetic gas, before slaughter. Most commonly animals are killed by cutting a vein or artery in the neck. Recently the slaughtering of dirty animals has been implicated in the spread of *E. coli* infection.

Abbas I (known as **Abbas the Great**) (1557–1628) Shah of Persia 1588–1628. He ended an inherited war with the Ottomans by conceding territory (1590) in order to free himself to drive the Uzbek Turks from north-eastern Persia (1598). By 1618 he had strengthened his army by curbing the Turcoman chiefs who supplied his recruits, and by using foreign advisers, and had reconquered the lands ceded to the Ottomans, but he died before the end of a further war over Mesopotamia (1623–29).

Abbas, Ferhat (1899–1989) Algerian nationalist leader. After attempting to cooperate with the French in setting up an Algerian state, he became disenchanted and in 1956 joined the revolutionary Front de Libération Nationale (FLN). He was elected President of the provisional government of the Algerian republic (based in Tunisia) in 1958 and President of the constituent assembly of independent Algeria in 1962. In 1963 he was detained for opposing the FLN's proposed constitution, but was released the following year.

Abbasid A dynasty of caliphs ruling in Baghdad from 750 to 1258, claiming descent from Abbas, uncle of the prophet Muhammad. Some were outstanding patrons of culture such as Mamun (813–33). Their power ended with the fall of Baghdad to the Tartars in 1258.

Abbe, Ernst (1840–1905) German physicist. He worked with Carl Zeiss from 1866, and in 1868 invented the apochromatic lens. He also designed several optical instruments, including a light condenser for use in microscopes and a refractometer. He became sole owner of the Zeiss company in 1888.

Abbey Theatre A theatre in Abbey Street, Dublin, first opened in 1904, staging chiefly Irish plays. W. B. YEATS was associated with its foundation. In 1925 it became the first state-subsidized theatre in the English-speaking world. The earlier theatre burnt down in 1951 and was replaced by the present theatre in 1966.

ABC Islands An acronym for the Dutch islands of Aruba, Bonaire, and Curaçao which lie in the Caribbean Sea near the northern coast of Venezuela.

Abd el-Krim (1881–1963) Moroccan Berber resistance leader. In 1921 he roused the Rif Berbers, and defeated a Spanish army of 20,000. He held out until 1925, when a joint Franco-Spanish force took him prisoner. He was exiled to Réunion until 1947, when he was given permission to go to France. On the way he escaped to Cairo, where he set up the Maghrib Bureau, or Liberation Committee of the Arab West. After Moroccan independence (1956), he refused to return as long as French troops remained on African soil.

Abdication crisis See EDWARD VIII.

abdomen In vertebrates, the part of the body or trunk which lies between the thorax and the pelvic girdle, and contains the viscera. In mammals the abdomen contains the organs of DIGESTION, EXCRETION, and REPRODUCTION. It is separated from the thorax, containing the heart and lungs, by a muscular sheet called the diaphragm. The muscular walls of the mammalian abdomen are flexible, allowing for expansion of the intestines during feeding and for respiratory movements of the diaphragm. The membrane lining the abdomen is called the peritoneum.

In arthropods, such as insects, crabs, or spiders, the abdomen is one of three major subdivisions of the body, forming the posterior, and often largest, part of the animal. In common with most invertebrates, the arthropod abdomen is divided into segments as well as containing the organs of digestion, excretion, and reproduction.

Abdul Hamid II (known as 'the Great Assassin') (1842–1918) The last sultan of Turkey (1876–1909). An autocratic ruler, he suspended Parliament and the constitution and is remembered for the brutal massacres of Christian Armenians in 1894–96. In 1909 he was deposed after the revolt in the previous year of the Young Turks.

Abdullah, Sheikh Muhammad (known as 'the Lion of Kashmir') (1905–82) Kashmiri Muslim leader. In the 1930s he actively opposed the rule of the Hindu maharajah of Kashmir. After accepting Indian sovereignty (1947), he eventually won for Kashmir a form of autonomy within India, although he was imprisoned for much of the time

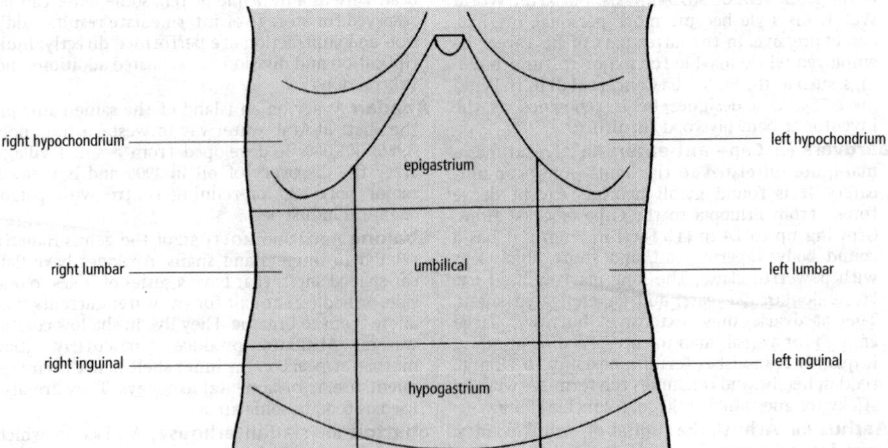

Abdomen Regions of the human abdomen.

between 1953 and 1968 on suspicion of seeking its full independence.

Abdullah ibn Hussein (1882–1951) King of Jordan 1946–51. He served as emir of Transjordan (1921–46), becoming Jordan's first king on independence in 1946. He was assassinated.

Abdul Rahman, Tunku (1903–90) Malayan statesman, Prime Minister of Malaya 1957–63 and of Malaysia 1963–70. A skilled negotiator, he secured Malayan independence from Britain (1957) and was one of the architects of modern Malaysia (1963).

Abel A biblical figure, the second son of Adam and Eve. Abel, a shepherd, was killed by his brother, CAIN, who was jealous that God had accepted Abel's sacrifice whereas his own had been rejected. In Christian tradition Abel is regarded as the first martyr. The story of Ḥabil (Abel) and Kabil (Cain) is also elaborated upon in Islamic legend.

Abel, Niels Henrik See ABELIAN GROUP.

Abelard, Peter (1079–1142) French scholar, theologian, and philosopher. His independence of mind brought him into frequent conflict with the authorities and led to his being twice condemned for heresy. He lectured in Paris until 1118 and his tragic love affair with his pupil Héloïse, niece of Fulbert, a canon of Notre-Dame. Abelard was castrated at Fulbert's instigation; he entered a monastery, and made Héloïse become a nun. Abelard continued his controversial teaching, applying reason to questions of faith, notably to the doctrine of the Trinity. In the early 1130s he and Héloïse put together a collection of their love letters and other correspondence, which was published in 1616. Abelard and Héloïse are buried together in Paris.

Abelian group (in mathematics) A group that, in addition to satisfying the conditions necessary for a mathematical group, is commutative (see COMMUTATIVITY). For example, the set of REAL NUMBERS under the operation of multiplication forms an Abelian group, as do VECTORS under addition. Abelian groups are named after the Norwegian mathematician, Niels Henrik Abel (1802–29).

Aberbrothock See ARBROATH.

Aberdeen A city, seaport, and council area in north-east Scotland, situated between the rivers Dee (south) and Don (north); pop. (1991) 201,100. Known to the Romans as Devena, or the 'town of the two waters', it is the third-largest city in Scotland, a cultural centre, fishing port, and a centre of the offshore North Sea oil industry. In modern times Aberdeen has been named the 'Granite City' after its fine grey granite buildings. The city received its charter from William the Lion in 1179. In 1860 King's College (founded in 1494) united with Marischal College (founded by the Earl Marischal of Scotland in 1593) to form the modern University of Aberdeen. The Robert Gordon University (formerly the Robert Gordon Institute of Technology) was established in 1992. Historic buildings also include St Machar's Cathedral, Robert Gordon's College, Provost Skene's House (the oldest domestic dwelling house in Aberdeen).

Aberdeen, George Hamilton Gordon, 4th Earl of (1784–1860) British statesman. He was Foreign Secretary during 1828–30 and again from 1841 to 1846, when he concluded the Webster–Ashburton and Oregon Boundary treaties, which settled boundary disputes between the USA and Canada. As a leader of those Conservatives who campaigned for free trade, he supported Sir Robert Peel in repealing the CORN LAWS (1846). As Prime Minister (1852–55) of the 'Aberdeen Coalition', he reluctantly involved his country in the CRIMEAN WAR and was subsequently blamed for its mismanagement. He resigned in 1855.

Aberdeenshire A council area of north-east Scotland, on the North Sea; area 6,318 sq km (2,439 sq miles); pop. (1993) 223,600. Its administrative centre is Aberdeen. In 1975 the historic county of Aberdeenshire was absorbed into Grampian Region. It became an independent unitary authority in 1996 (with Aberdeen City forming a separate council area). The main economic activities are fishing and fish processing, agriculture (especially stock raising), tourism, whisky distilling, and the North Sea oil industries.

Aberfan A village in Merthyr Tydfil county borough, south Wales, on the River Taff, where, in 1966, a slag-heap collapsed and mining waste overwhelmed houses and a school, killing 28 adults and 116 children.

aberration The difference between the observed direction of a star and its true direction. Aberration is due to the combined effect of the Earth's orbital motion and the finite speed of light. The effect was discovered by BRADLEY in 1725. To correct for aberration, a telescope has to be tilted in the direction of the Earth's motion in its orbit about the Sun; otherwise, by the time the light from the star has passed through the telescope, the Earth will have moved sufficiently in its orbit to make the star appear to be at a different position. A star's apparent direction can be as much as 20.5 arc seconds from its true position. The effect is analogous to the passenger's view of rain falling at an angle past the side window of a moving vehicle. A smaller effect, **diurnal aberration**, is due to the Earth's rotation about its axis and amounts to at most 0.32 arc seconds.

Chromatic aberration is the production, by a simple lens, of an image with coloured edges. These coloured fringes arise because the focal length of the lens is different at different wavelengths of light. See also ACHROMATIC LENS.

Spherical aberration is caused by the rays from an object coming to a focus in slightly different positions as a result of the curvature of a lens or mirror. A diaphragm is used with a lens to correct it and parabolic rather than spherical mirrors are used.

Aberystwyth A resort town on Cardigan Bay, in Ceredigion, west Wales, at the mouth of the Ystwyth and Rheidol rivers; pop. (1991) 11,154. The town, which was built around a fortress of Edward I, is home to a University College (founded in 1872) and the National Library of Wales.

Abidjan The former capital, commercial centre, and chief port of Côte d'Ivoire, on the Ebrié Lagoon; pop. (1988) 1,929,079. It is the largest port in West Africa and the principal transit point for goods to and from the West African Sahel. Settled by the French at the end of the 19th century, Abidjan first owed its development to the building of the Ocean–Niger railway line (begun in 1903). In the 1920s the city became a seaport with the opening of the Vridi Canal that links the Ebrié Lagoon to the Gulf of Guinea, and in 1935 Abidjan became the administrative centre of the French Ivory Coast. It has many light industries.

Abiola, Moshood (Kashimawo Olawale) (1937–) Nigerian politician. The leader of the Social Democratic Party, he declared himself President-elect in June 1993 after election results showed him to be on the way to a comfortable victory. The election was annulled by the military regime; a year later Abiola again declared himself President, but was placed under house arrest.

Abkhazia A territory on the Black Sea coast of the Republic of Georgia; area 8,600 sq km (3,320 sq miles); pop. (1990) 537,500. Its capital is the resort of Sukhumi. Identified with the ancient province of Colchis, the region was captured by the Romans, Byzantines, Arabs, and Ottoman Turks before coming under Russian protection in 1810. Under Russian occupation, large numbers of Muslim Abkhazis moved to Turkish territory. In 1921 the region was constituted as the Abkhazian Autonomous Soviet Socialist Republic and in 1992, following the breakup of the former Soviet Union, the local parliament unilaterally declared itself an independent state, launching the region into armed conflict with the government of Georgia. In 1993 Abkhazian forces expelled the Georgian National Army from Abkhazia. The political situation remains unresolved.Tobacco, tea, and fruit are the chief crops.

Åbo The Swedish name for the city of TURKU in Finland.

abolitionists Militant opponents of slavery in 19th-century USA. In the first two decades of the 19th century, there was only a handful of individual abolitionists, but thereafter, fired by religious revivalism, the abolition movement became a strong political force. Prominent as writers and orators were the Boston newspaper-owner William Lloyd Garrison, the author Harriet Beecher Stowe (whose anti-slavery novel *Uncle Tom's Cabin* sold 1.5 million copies within a year of its publication in 1852), and the ex-slave Frederick Douglass. The abolitionist cause at first found little support in Congress or the main political parties, except among a few individuals such as Charles Sumner, but it played an increasing part in precipitating the political division which led to the AMERICAN CIVIL WAR.

Aborigines The aboriginal inhabitants of Australia comprising several physically distinct groups of dark-skinned hunter-gatherers who arrived in prehistoric times and brought with them the dingo. Before the arrival of Europeans they were scattered through the whole continent, including Tasmania. In 1788 the population was estimated to stand at around 250,000–300,000 Aborigines who were divided into more than 500 linguistic groups. Today nearly 1.5 per cent of the people of Australia are Aborigine. Although over 65 per cent now live in towns and cities, the cultural heritage of the Aborigines has been protected in recent years by changes in Australian federal and state laws that have established land rights, community development programmes, and educational assistance.

abortion The termination of pregnancy before the foetus is able to survive outside the mother or is considered legally viable. Spontaneous abortion (miscarriage) may occur during the first three months of pregnancy, and is commonly caused by foetal abnormalities. Spontaneous abortion later in the pregnancy may be caused by maternal factors such as reproductive system disorders. Vaginal bleeding during the pregnancy is referred to as threatened abortion; inevitable abortion refers to contractions in addition to vaginal bleeding and abortion occurs shortly after the symptoms. Missed abortion describes retention of the products of conception for a prolonged time after the foetus has died. Therapeutic abortion is the termination of pregnancy by choice. In many countries, the legalization of abortion has been fairly recent. In some it is restricted to cases where the continued pregnancy would endanger the life of the mother, and in others (such as the Republic of Ireland and Iran) it is still illegal. The official Roman Catholic position (not shared by the mainstream Protestant Church) is that the embryo at all stages deserves the full protection which would be afforded to any human being; others who oppose abortion make a similar argument. Those who support abortion argue that women have the right to choose whether to bear a child, and that legal abortion makes the procedure safer. Improved medical techniques, making a foetus viable from a younger age, undermine the currently accepted 24-week limit for abortion.

Aboukir Bay (or **Abukir**, **Abu Qir**) A bay on the Mediterranean coast of Egypt, lying between Alexandria and the Rosetta mouth of the Nile. Nelson defeated the French fleet under Brueys at the Battle of the Nile which was fought in the bay on 1–2 August 1798. Sir Ralph Abercromby's expedition landed near the village of Aboukir and defeated the French in 1801.

Abraham First of the patriarchs of Israel, from whom the Israelites traced their descent. He is revered by Jews, Christians, and Muslims. According to the book of Genesis (the first book of the Old Testament) Abraham lived in the middle of the 2nd millennium BC at Haran in northern Mesopotamia. He was divinely called to leave his home and family and go to a new land, Canaan. God made a covenant with him, promising him a multitude of descendants to whom he would give Canaan for ever, provided that he and all his male descendants were circumcised. Accordingly, Abraham's wife Sarah, although aged over 90, gave birth to a son, Isaac. God subsequently tested Abraham's faith by asking him to sacrifice Isaac to him. When Abraham showed his readiness to do this, a ram was substituted for the sacrifice and God confirmed his covenant. Through Ishmael, his son by Hagar, the maidservant of Sarah, Abraham (Ibrahim) is considered by Muslims an ancestor of the Arabs.

Abraham, Plains of See PLAINS OF ABRAHAM.

Abrahams, Harold (Maurice) (1899–1978) British athlete. In 1924 he became the first Briton to win the 100 metres in the Olympic Games. His story was the subject of the film *Chariots of Fire* (1981).

abrasion (in geomorphology) The scouring action that occurs when rock particles rub together. It is caused by rock debris embedded in bases of glaciers, bedloads of rivers, and sand and shingle carried by wind or waves.

abrasive A material used to wear away the surfaces of other, softer materials. Abrasives are used in manufacturing industries to shape surfaces accurately and as a finishing treatment, for example in polishing. Highly brittle materials such as CERAMICS, GLASS, and CERMETS (ceramic metals) can be machined to shape only through the use of abrasives. Abrasives must be hard, and natural materials such as FLINT and sand (forms of silicon dioxide, SiO_2, pumice (hardened lava foam), ALUMINA and emery (forms of aluminium oxide, Al_2O_3), and DIAMOND meet this requirement. Flint is used in the manufacture of sandpaper, and sand in sand blasting; pumice is not so hard and finds application in metal polishes. Alumina and emery are used to some extent on abrasive papers and grinding wheels, but for most industrial purposes synthetic materials such as SILICON CARBIDE (carborundum) and synthetic diamond are used. Abrasive powders are also added to most household cleaning agents, to supplement the action of the soap or detergent.

Abruzzi A mountainous region on the Adriatic coast of east-central Italy, between the Tronto and Trigno rivers; area 10,795 sq km (4,168 sq miles); pop. (1993) 1,255,549; capital, L'Aquila. The Abruzzi Apennines include the highest peaks in the Italian peninsula: Gran Sasso d'Italia (2,912 m, 9,553 ft), the Maiella (2,793 m, 9,163 ft), and Mt. Laga (2,458 m, 8,064 ft). Abruzzi National Park, which extends over 400 sq km (155 sq miles) in the Upper Sangro Valley, was established in 1922 to protect beech forests.

Absalom A biblical figure, the third and favourite son of DAVID, king of Judah. Exiled for the murder of his half-brother Amnon and eventually forgiven, Absalom later led a rebellion against his father. During the battle, Absalom was found by his cousin, Joab, caught by his hair in an oak tree; despite David's command that he should not be harmed, Joab killed him.

abscess A localized collection of pus in the body surrounded by inflamed tissue. The usual cause is the presence of harmful bacteria, which the white blood cells have failed to destroy. Pus consists of dead white blood cells and a mixture of living and dead bacteria. An abscess can cause illness until it works its way to a surface and discharges, or is surgically drained. Healing usually follows adequate drainage and antibiotic treatment.

absolute magnitude See MAGNITUDE.

absolute zero The lowest temperature theoretically possible (equivalent to −273.15°C). According to the KINETIC THEORY, the temperature of a substance is a measure of the average kinetic energy which its molecules possess and absolute zero is the temperature at which molecules would have no energy, and molecular motion would cease. However, according to QUANTUM THEORY, atoms and molecules still have some energy, the ZERO-POINT ENERGY, at absolute zero. It is not possible to reach absolute zero experimentally, though substances have been cooled to within a few millionths of a degree of it.

ABS plastic See POLYMER.

abstract art Any art that does not represent recognizable objects, especially those forms of MODERN ART in which the traditional European conception of art as the imitation of nature is abandoned. KANDINSKY is usually credited with having made the first entirely non-representational picture in about 1910, and since then modern abstract art has developed into many different movements and 'isms'. Two broad tendencies are, however, recognizable within it: the reduction of natural appearances to radically simplified forms, exemplified in the work of BRANCUSI; and the construction of art objects from non-representational (often geometric) forms, as in Ben NICHOLSON's reliefs.

Abstract Expressionism A movement in US painting that developed in New York in the 1940s. The painters whose work is embraced by the term (among them POLLOCK, DE KOONING, and ROTHKO) varied considerably in style, being linked rather by a similarity of outlook, which called for freedom from traditional aesthetic and social values, and abandoned the naturalism that had dominated 20th-century US painting in favour of spontaneous freedom of expression. Traditional technical procedures were sometimes replaced by those of ACTION PAINTING. Abstract Expressionism made a strong impact in several European countries in the 1950s and 1960s; it was the first American movement to do so, marking the fact that New York had replaced Paris as the world centre of avant-garde art.

abstract music See PROGRAMME MUSIC.

Absurd, Theatre of the Theatrical movement originating in France in the early 1950s. It is characterized by outlandish characters, behaving without motivation, and preposterous (or non-existent) plots. Its exponents include Eugène IONESCO and Samuel BECKETT, whose *Waiting for Godot* (1953) is an aimless dialogue between two tramps. Outside France, other playwrights who have been classed as 'absurdist' for the illogical or unexpected action of their plays include Harold PINTER and Edward ALBEE.

Abu Bakr (*c.*573–634) First CALIPH of Islam (632–34). He was one of the earliest converts to Islam and a close companion of the Prophet MUHAMMAD, who married his daughter Aisha. When he succeeded to Muhammad's position as temporal leader of the Muslim community, this pious and gentle man was chiefly concerned to reaffirm the allegiance of those Arabian tribes who had withdrawn it at the time of the Prophet's death. These 'wars of apostasy' initiated the ARAB CONQUESTS.

Abu Dhabi ▶**1** The largest of the seven member-states of the United Arab Emirates, lying to the south of Dubai, between the Sultanate of Oman and the Gulf coast; area 67,600 sq km (26,101 sq miles); pop. (1995) 928,360. Although most of the emirate comprises desert or *sabkhah* salt flats, it has two main centres of population at Abu Dhabi on the coast and Al Ain on the frontier with Oman. The economy is largely based on the production of oil and on petrochemical industries. The sheikdom of Abu Dhabi became a British Protectorate in 1892 and joined the federation of the United Arab Emirates in 1971. Oil was discovered in the early 1960s. ▶**2** Its capital city, which is also the federal capital of the United Arab Emirates; pop. (1989) 363,432. It is one of the region's most modern cities with little left of its old town.

Abuja A newly built city at the geographical centre of Nigeria, designated in 1982 to replace Lagos as the national capital; pop. (1991) 378,670. Designed by Kenzo Tange, the city is modelled on Milton Keynes in England.

Abukir Bay See ABOUKIR BAY.

Abū Nuwās, al-Hasan ibn Hani' (*c.*750–*c.*814) Arab poet. It is not certain when he moved to Baghdad, but he was soon recognized as the leading poet of his time. His particular excellence lay in lyrical compositions: amatory pieces and, above all, wine poems, which he developed into a separate genre. His lyrics had immense influence on later generations, particularly in Muslim Spain.

Abu Simbel (or **Ipsambul**) A former village in southern Egypt, site of two rock-cut temples built by Rameses II (13th century BC), a monument to the greatest of the pharaohs and a constant reminder to possibly restive Nubian tribes of Egypt's might. The great temple, with its façade (31 m, 103 ft, high) bearing four colossal seated statues of Rameses, faces due east, and is dedicated to Amun-Ra and other principal state gods of the period; the small temple is dedicated to Hathor and Nefertiti, first wife of Rameses. In 1963 an archaeological salvage operation was begun, comparable in scale to the original construction of the temples, in which engineers sawed up the monument and carried it up the hillside to be rebuilt, with its original orientation, well above the rising waters of Lake

Nasser, whose level was affected by the building of the High Dam at Aswan.

Abydos ▶**1** A town of ancient Mysia in Asia Minor, situated on a hill overlooking the Dardanelles, north-east of the modern Turkish city of Çanakkale. Abydos was the scene of the story of Hero and Leander and the place where the Persian King Xerxes constructed his bridge of boats over the Hellespont in 480 BC. ▶**2** A town in ancient Egypt and burial place of the first pharaohs, situated on the left bank of the Nile near modern El Balyana.

abyssal plain A flat or very gently sloping area of the ocean basin floor, reaching to depths of between 2,200 and 5,500 m (7,200 and 18,000 ft). Abyssal plains lie between the foot of a CONTINENTAL RISE and a MID-OCEANIC RIDGE. They result from the blanketing of an originally uneven surface of oceanic crust by fine-grained sediments, mainly clay and silt. Much of this sediment is deposited from turbidity currents which have been channelled from the continental margins along submarine canyons down into deeper water. The remainder of the sediment comprises chiefly dust (clay particles) blown out to sea from land, and the remains of small marine plants and animals (PLANKTON), which have sunk from the surface. Abyssal plains are less common in the Pacific than in other major ocean basins, because sediments from turbidity currents are trapped in the submarine trenches which border the Pacific.

abyssal zone The deepest region of the oceans, below depths of 1,000 m (3,300 ft) or, in geological terms, an area of igneous rock which has consolidated at a great depth.

Abyssinia A former name of ETHIOPIA.

acacia (or **wattle**) A tropical and subtropical tree, bush or climber of the genus *Acacia*. Acacias are particularly common in the drier regions of Africa, Australia, and South America, and there are about 1,100 species. Many of them are armed with hooks or large spines, and in some the thorns have an inflated base inhabited by ants, which deter other insects and also climbing plants. Wind blowing over the ants' entrance holes on certain African species gives rise to an eerie whistling noise.

Acacias yield timber, gum arabic, tanning materials, the dye for the original khaki cloth, and flowers used in perfumery. The florists' mimosa, or silver wattle, *A. dealbata*, has yellow heads of tiny flowers typical of the genus. The true *Mimosa* is a separate genus which includes the SENSITIVE PLANT. The false acacia is a species of *Robinia*.

Académie française An organization founded by Cardinal RICHELIEU in 1635, its original purpose being to regulate the French language. To this end it compiled a dictionary (1694) which originally included only words acceptable in polite society. Now in its ninth edition, this continues to be an authoritative work. During the 17th century in particular the Académie also acted as an arbiter of literary norms.

Academy The school established at Athens by PLATO in the 380s BC, probably intended to prepare men to serve the city-state. It was as a philosophical centre that it became celebrated, its students including ARISTOTLE, EPICURUS, and ZENO OF CITIUM. Much of its history is obscure, but it survived until its closure by Justinian in 529 AD.

Academy of Motion Picture Arts and Sciences (AMPAS) Organization formed in the USA in 1927 to improve artistic standards in the film industry and encourage cooperation in the technical and cultural fields. The Academy is best known for its annual Academy Awards, known as Oscars, for achievement in various categories.

Acadia (French **Acadie**) A name given to Nova Scotia in Canada prior to the establishment of the first French settlement there in 1604. The name, from which the term Cajun derives, was later applied to the territory between the St Lawrence River and the Atlantic Ocean that now forms the south-east part of Quebec, east Maine, New Brunswick, Nova Scotia, and Prince Edward Island.

acanthocephalan See SPINY-HEADED WORM.

acanthus A perennial herb of the genus *Acanthus*, comprising about 50 species, chiefly native to the Mediterranean region. The generic name comes from the Greek *acantha* (thorn) in allusion to their spiny leaves and bracts. They belong to the family Acanthaceae, which also includes black-eyed Susan, *Thunbergia alata*. The shapely leaves of the acanthus were the inspiration for certain ornaments in classical architecture, including the capital of the Corinthian column. Some species, notably *A. spinosus* and *A. mollis*, are grown as garden plants for their spikes of white, pink, or purple flowers.

Acapulco (fully **Acapulco de Juárez**) A port and holiday resort in the south of Mexico, on the Pacific coast; pop. (1990) 592,290. Established in 1530, Acapulco was the only Mexican port authorized to receive Spanish trading galleons from the Orient. When Mexico severed its trade links with Spain in 1821 Acapulco declined as a port city and remained isolated until linked to Mexico City by a road built in 1927.

ACAS Acronym for Advisory, Conciliation, and Arbitration Service, a British government body set up by parliament in 1975 to arbitrate in disputes between employers and trade unions. See INDUSTRIAL RELATIONS.

acceleration The rate of change of VELOCITY with time. It is a VECTOR quantity with the symbol a and in SI UNITS is measured in units of m/s^2. If v is the velocity vector then dv/dt, the DERIVATIVE with respect to time, is the acceleration. When the movement is in a straight line then v and dv/dt can be treated as SCALARS, but when the object is travelling along a curved path there will be two acceleration components, one along the tangent to the curve at the point and the other along the normal to the curve. Angular acceleration is the rate of change of angular velocity with time.

Acceleration of free fall (formerly called acceleration due to gravity) is the downward acceleration of an object falling freely under the influence of gravity. Denoted by the symbol g, its value near the Earth's surface is 9.8 m/s^2. The measured value of g varies slightly from one point to another around the Earth.

accelerometer An instrument for measuring acceleration, especially in connection with the measurement of vibration. Older (linear or angular) accelerometers depend on a mass which is free to move in one direction against the constraint of a spring. In modern accelerometers used in INERTIAL NAVIGATION systems, the force produced by the acceleration is applied to a PIEZOELECTRIC crystal, which generates a voltage proportional to the acceleration.

accent The part of DIALECT that refers to pronunciation. Although they are usually difficult to separate, regional accents identify the speaker's place of origin (for example, Scotland, southern USA), and social accents identify the speaker's cultural and educational background. Alternative ways of pronouncing sounds may be good indicators of class membership. In British English the accent which is not associated with any particular region is RP (received pronunciation).

accentor A sparrow-sized bird making up the subfamily Prunellidae, which contains 13 species. Accentors are typically brownish, streaked with black, although some species have touches of pink, red, or yellow, and are confined to the Old World, North Africa, and the Middle East. Almost all species live in rocky or mountainous areas. The dunnock or hedge sparrow, *Prunella modularis*, is atypical in being widespread at low altitudes.

accordion A free-reed musical instrument strapped to the player's body. The right hand plays a short piano keyboard, or on some continental European models several rows of buttons. The left hand, which is responsible for the bellows, also controls rows of buttons which produce bass notes or chords. The more elaborate accordions also have 'register' keys, which can add higher and lower octaves. A simpler version, the melodeon, produces two notes from each key, one on pushing and the other on pulling the bellows, and has fewer bass and chord keys.

Accra The capital of Ghana, a port on the Gulf of Guinea; pop. (latest estimate) 867,450. Greater Accra, which extends over an area of 2,030 sq km (784 sq miles), has a population of 1,431,100. Originally the capital of the Ga kingdom, the city developed around three trading posts at Jamestown, Crèvecœur, and Christianborg established respectively by Britain, France, and Denmark in the 17th century. In 1850 and 1871 the French and Danish posts were ceded to Britain and in 1875 it became the capital of the Gold Coast Colony.

accretion disc A disc of hot gas sometimes found surrounding the smaller member of a binary star. Between the two members of a binary star there is a LAGRANGIAN POINT of zero gravity where the stars' gravitational attractions pull equally in both directions. If one member is very much larger than the other and extends beyond this point of zero gravity so that it overfills its Roche lobe, matter is drawn away from the larger companion. This material is drawn towards the smaller star at supersonic velocity and grows into a disc which surrounds the smaller star. The disc forms under the combined effects of gravitational forces, the orbital motion of the system, and the rotation of the two stars.

accumulator A secondary or storage BATTERY, in particular the rechargeable lead–acid battery. All batteries contain electrochemical cells that change chemical energy into electrical energy during discharge. In an accumulator, this process can be reversed. A current is passed through the cell in the direction opposite to the discharge flow, and the original chemicals are regenerated. Thus an accumulator can store electrical energy. The modern lead–acid accumulator is a direct development of Gaston Plante's 1859 invention. The negative electrode is spongy lead, the positive electrode is lead dioxide on a lead support, and the electrolyte is sulphuric acid. During discharge, the surface materials of both electrodes are converted to lead sulphate, and the electrolyte becomes more dilute. Accumulators provide the large currents required for starting petrol and diesel engines. Electrical GENERATORS, powered by the engine, keep the accumulators charged. They are also used to power electric cars, for which purpose more sophisticated accumulators are being developed.

ACE See COMPUTER, HISTORY OF.

acetic acid See ETHANOIC ACID.

acetone See PROPANONE.

acetylene See ETHYNE.

Achaea (or **Achaia**; Greek **Akhaïa**) ►**1** A region of ancient Greece on the north coast of the Peloponnese, first achieving political unity with the formation of the **Achaean League** of 12 cities which allied itself with Athens against Sparta. Powerful after the death of Alexander the Great, the League was eventually dissolved by the Romans who occupied Achaea as an imperial province between 146 BC

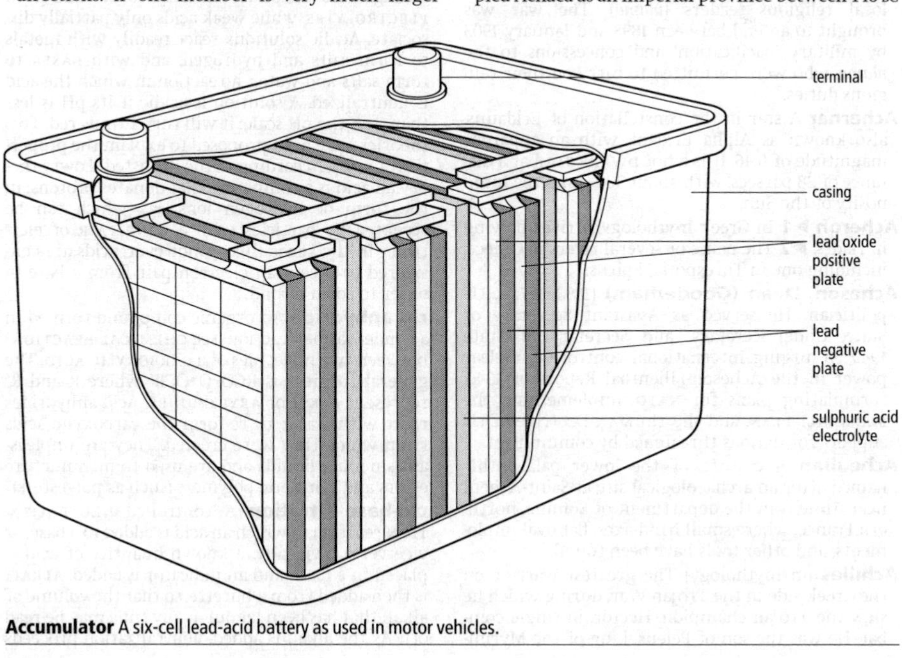

Accumulator A six-cell lead-acid battery as used in motor vehicles.

and the 4th century AD. ▶2 A department of the Peloponnese region of south-west Greece; area 3,271 sq km (1,263 sq miles); pop. (1991) 297,320; capital, Patras.

Achaemenid The dynasty established by CYRUS THE GREAT in the 6th century BC and named after his ancestor Achaemenes. Cyrus' predecessors ruled Parsumash, a vassal state of the Median empire, but he overthrew their king Astyages and incorporated the MEDES within his Persian empire, which by his death in 530 BC extended from Asia Minor to the River Indus. His successor Cambyses II (529–521 BC) added Egypt. DARIUS I instituted a major reorganization of the administration and finances of the empire, establishing twenty provinces ruled by Satraps. Both he and XERXES failed in their attempts to conquer Greece in the early 5th century. By the time ALEXANDER III (the Great) invaded with his Macedonian army (334 BC) the empire was much weakened. Darius III, defeated at Issus and Gaugamela, was killed by his own men in 330 BC. Achaemenid rule was tolerant of local customs, religions, and forms of government. The construction of a major road system, centred on Susa, facilitated trade and administration. The magnificent remains of PERSEPOLIS provide a glimpse of Achaemenid wealth and power.

Achebe, Chinua (born Albert Chinualumgu) (1930–) Nigerian novelist, poet, short-story writer, and essayist. His novels, all written in English, show traditional African society in confrontation with European customs and values. They include *Things Fall Apart* (1958), *A Man of the People* (1966), and *Anthills of the Savannah* (1987).

Acheh War (1873–1903) A conflict in north Sumatra between the Dutch and the Achehnese. Trade rivalry and attempts by the sultan of Acheh to obtain foreign assistance against Dutch domination of north Sumatra caused the dispatch of an abortive Dutch expeditionary force in 1871. Although a larger force, sent later in the year, captured the sultan's capital, the Dutch met with fierce resistance in the interior, organized by the local religious leaders (*ulama*). The war was brought to an end between 1898 and January 1903 by military 'pacification' and concessions to the *ulama*, who were permitted to carry on their religious duties.

Achernar A star in the constellation of Eridanus, also known as Alpha Eridani, with an apparent magnitude of 0.46. It is a hot DWARF STAR at a distance of 38 parsecs, with about 300 times the luminosity of the Sun.

Acheron ▶1 In Greek mythology, a river flowing in Hades. ▶2 The name of several rivers in Greece, including one in Threspotía, Epirus.

Acheson, Dean (Gooderham) (1893–1971) , US politician. He served as Assistant Secretary of State, Under-Secretary, and Secretary of State 1949–53, urging international control of nuclear power in the Acheson-Lilienthal Report of 1946, formulating plans for NATO, implementing the MARSHALL PLAN, and the TRUMAN Doctrine of US support for nations threatened by communism.

Acheulian A culture of the lower palaeolithic named after an archaeological site at Saint-Acheul near Amiens in the department of Somme, northern France, where small hand-axes, flat oval implements, and other tools have been found.

Achilles (in mythology) The greatest warrior on the Greek side in the Trojan War, during which he slew the Trojan champion, Hector, in single combat. He was the son of Peleus, king of the Myrmidons, and Thetis, a sea-nymph. His mother dipped him in the River Styx to make him immune to wounds, but the heel by which she held him remained vulnerable and he was killed by an arrow, shot by Paris, that struck him there.

Achilles (in astronomy) A member of the Trojan group of ASTEROIDS discovered in 1906 by the German astronomer Max Wolf. It is 70 km in diameter and was the first of the Trojan group to be discovered.

Achilles tendon The tendon of the muscles of the calf of the human leg. It lies at the back of the ankle and is attached to the heel bone (calcaneus). It is named after ACHILLES from Greek mythology.

Acholi (or **Acoli**, **Gang**, **Shuli**) A distinct ethnolinguistic group of northern Uganda and southern Sudan.

achondrite See CHONDRITE.

achromatic lens (or **achromat**) A combination of LENSES, used in most optical instruments, that reduces image blurring due to chromatic ABERRATION. This aberration occurs with simple lenses, which refract (bend) the different colours in white light by different amounts, resulting in images with coloured fringes. The achromat was invented in about 1733. The simplest type combines a concave and a convex lens with different dispersions (dispersion measures the amount of colour separation). It reduces blurring by bringing together red and blue light. Image quality can be further improved using achromats with more lenses or combinations, in contact or separated.

acid Any chemical compound of a class, the members of which commonly have a sour taste, and are mostly poisonous and corrosive. Those acids that derive from mineral sources (mineral acids) are almost always stronger than acids derived from organic sources (carboxylic acids). Corrosive acids such as nitric acid and sulphuric acid are mineral acids; weaker acids such as citric acid, found in citrus fruits, and formic acid, found in some insects, are carboxylic acids. Acids are soluble in water; strong acids dissociate entirely to become good ELECTROLYTES, while weak acids only partially dissociate. Acidic solutions react readily with metals to form salts and hydrogen, and with BASES to form salts and water, a reaction in which the acid is neutralized. A solution is acidic if its pH is less than 7 on the pH scale: it will turn litmus red. Two theories have been proposed to explain the properties of acids. According to the Brønsted–Lowry theory an acid is a compound that donates protons, in the form of hydrogen ions, H^+, which can be accepted by particles with a LONE PAIR of electrons. In the Lewis theory, however, acids are considered to accept an electron pair from a base in order to form a bond.

acid anhydride An organic compound formed in a condensation reaction (see CHEMICAL REACTION) between two molecules of a CARBOXYLIC ACID. The general formula is RCO–O–OCR′ where R and R′ represent ALKYL or ARYL GROUPS. Acid anhydrides react with water to re-form the carboxylic acids from which they were created. They are unpleasant-smelling liquids and are used to manufacture esters and synthetic polymers (such as polyesters).

acid-base titration A controlled NEUTRALIZATION reaction in which an acid is added to a base, or vice versa. Typically, a known quantity of acid is placed in a flask, and an indicator is added. ALKALI is then added from a burette, so that the volume of alkali that has been let out at any time may be read off. As the alkali is added, neutralization proceeds and the pH of the solution rises. When neutralization is complete, the end-point of the titration is indicated by the change in colour of the indicator. Acid-base titrations can be put to several uses. For example, if the concentration of the acid is unknown, it can be determined by titration against alkali of known concentration. Or if, in the preparation of a SALT, it is desired to ensure that complete neutralization occurs, this can be done by carrying out a titration and stopping as soon as the end-point is reached. The solution will then contain neither excess alkali nor acid, but only the salt and water.

acid rain The deposition of chemical pollutants either as dry particles or as acidified rain, hail, snow, or fog. Motor vehicles, industrial processes, and the burning of fossil fuels in power-stations create pollution, chiefly in the form of sulphur dioxide, nitrogen oxide, and hydrocarbons all of which react with water and sunlight to form dilute sulphuric acid, nitric acid, ammonium salts, and other mineral acids. These fall to Earth, often long distances from their source, causing corrosion, health risks, tree death, and the detrimental acidification of water and soil.

Aconcagua ▶1 A snow-capped extinct volcano rising to a height of 6,960 m (22,834 ft) in the Andes of South America, on the frontier between Chile and Argentina. First climbed by Edward A. Fitzgerald's expedition in 1897, it is the highest mountain in the Western Hemisphere. **▶2** A river rising at the north-west foot of Mt Aconcagua, central Chile. It flows 193 km (120 miles) west, entering the Pacific Ocean north of Valparaiso.

aconite A widely distributed plant of the genus *Aconitum*, part of the buttercup family. All aconites contain the very poisonous alkaloid aconitine, once used to poison wolves, a quality from which the common name of wolfsbane was derived. The name monkshood for *A. napellus* indicates the shape of the attractive blue flower. As a decorative herbaceous plant, *A. napellus* has long been grown in European gardens. The yellow-flowered winter aconite, *Eranthis hyemalis*, is also a member of the buttercup family.

acorn worm A soft-bodied, worm-like animal, closely related to vertebrates, named for its acorn-like proboscis. Acorn worms form a class within the phylum Hemichordata and are usually 9–45 cm (4–18 inches) long, although a Brazilian species, *Balanoglossus gigas*, can reach 1.5 m (5 ft) in length. They live in sandy sea-beds, with only the front of the body emerging to feed; and for this they use gill-slits, acting as filters.

acoustics See SOUND.

ACP States Countries in Africa, the Caribbean, and the Pacific which signed the Lomé Conventions establishing cooperation with the European Community in trade and industrial development.

Acre (or **'Akko**; French **Saint-Jean-d'Acre**) An industrial seaport of Israel, on the Bay of Haifa; pop. (latest estimate) 37,000. Known to the Phoenicians as Ptolemaïs, Acre was taken by the Arabs in 683 and used as a supply port for Damascus. Captured by the Crusaders in the 12th century, it became part of the Kingdom of Jerusalem and later a residence of the Knights of St John. It fell into Muslim hands again in 1291 and was eventually taken by the Ottoman Turks in 1517. Captured by British forces in 1918, Acre was assigned to the Arabs in the proposed 1948 partition of Palestine but was subsequently absorbed into the new State of Israel.

acropolis The citadel of an ancient Greek city, most notably of Athens. The Athenian citadel was destroyed by the invading Persians in 480 BC, but PERICLES instituted a rebuilding programme. The Parthenon, built 447–432, was a Doric temple containing a gold and ivory statue of Athena. This was followed by the gateway or Propylaea, the temple of Athena Nike (commemorating victory over the Persians), and the Erectheum, which housed the shrines of various cults. See also ELGIN, 7TH EARL OF.

Acrux A first-magnitude BINARY STAR in the constellation of Crux and also known as Alpha Crucis. It comprises a hot subgiant and a hot dwarf star; the orbital period is very long. The brighter component is a spectroscopic binary whose components orbit each other every 76 days. The combined luminosity of Acrux is about 6,000 times that of the Sun, and its distance is 160 parsecs. It is a member of the Scorpius-Centaurus stellar association, a large moving group which also includes Antares and Becrux.

acrylic fibre A synthetic fibre POLYMER composed of macromolecules of recurring acrylonitrile ($CH_2{=}CH.C.N$) groups. The fibres have a wool-like feel and are used extensively as a substitute for WOOL. The fibre is seldom used as continuous filament, but is cut into short lengths for spinning

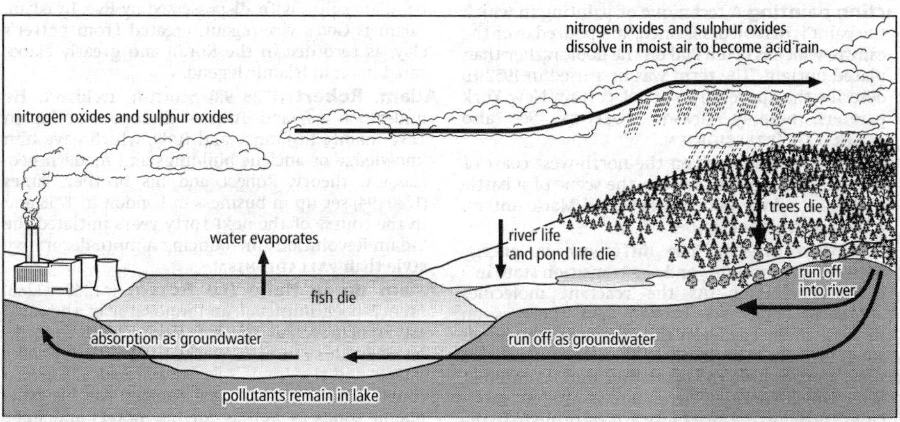

Acid rain Oxides of sulphur and nitrogen produced by the combustion of fossil fuels in industry (especially in power stations) react with rain to form dilute sulphuric and nitric acids, which enter the water cycle causing widespread pollution.

into yarn. Because acrylonitrile is highly flammable, various additions to the basic synthetic material are used to reduce flammability; such low fire-risk fibres are referred to as modacrylics.

acrylic paint (acrylic vinyl polymer emulsion paint) A synthetic paint combining some of the properties of OIL PAINT and WATER-COLOUR. It is soluble in water, quick-drying, and can be applied to virtually any painting base. The surface it produces can be matt or gloss, and in texture it can range from thin washes to rich impasto. It was first used by artists in the 1940s and has become a serious rival to oil paint.

Actaeon In Greek mythology, a young hunter who inadvertently saw the goddess Artemis bathing naked and in punishment was turned by her into a stag and killed by his own dogs.

actinide Any metallic element of a series in the PERIODIC TABLE with atomic numbers from 89 (actinium) to 103 (lawrencium). The first four members of the series, actinium to uranium, occur naturally. All the actinides generally resemble each other and the lanthanides. They form a range of IONIC COMPOUNDS, such as sulphates, nitrates, and chlorides, in which the metal shows a valency of 3 but higher valencies are found, for example, thorium (4) and uranium (4, 5, and 6). The actinides are radioactive, and those with atomic numbers greater than 92, the TRANSURANIC ELEMENTS, are formed by bombardment of heavy nuclei. They are very unstable, and several have been produced only in tiny quantities.

action and reaction (in physics) Force and its counterpart in the opposite direction. The force itself is the 'action'. As described by the third of NEWTON'S LAWS OF MOTION, for every action there is an equal and opposite 'reaction'. This reaction is a force that is always in opposite direction to the original force. All rockets and jet engines use this principle; burning gases are ejected with tremendous force from the rear end and as a consequence there is a reaction that propels them forwards.

Action Française An extreme right-wing group in France during the first half of the 20th century, and also the name of the newspaper published to promote its views. Founded by the poet and political journalist Charles Maurras, it aimed at overthrowing the parliamentary republic and sought to restore the monarchy. Strongly nationalist, it became discredited for its overt FASCISM and association with the VICHY government in 1940–44.

action painting A technique of painting in which the paint is dribbled, splashed, and poured over the canvas, which is often laid on the floor, rather than placed upright. The term was first used in 1952 to describe the approach to art of certain New York painters, notably Jackson POLLOCK. See also ABSTRACT EXPRESSIONISM.

Actium A promontory on the north-west coast of Acarnania in western Greece, the scene of a battle in 31 BC at which Octavian defeated Mark Antony to become ruler of Rome.

activation energy The difference in energy between the reactants and the transition state in a chemical reaction. As the reactant molecules approach, bonds are broken, and there is an increase in energy, even though some new bonds start to form. The increase in energy continues until a maximum, the transition state, is reached, after which energy is given out as product molecules form (or the reactants are reformed). If the reactant molecules have enough energy to reach the transition state, they will react to form products. The energy required to do so is called the activation energy, and it varies from one reaction to another, as does the amount of energy that is liberated or absorbed.

activity series A series of elements or compounds listed in order of their reactivity with respect to a particular type of reaction. For example, the halogens can act as oxidizing agents. Their reactivity in this capacity can be summarized in the following activity series, the strongest oxidizing agent being listed first: fluorine, chlorine, bromine, iodine, and astatine. The ELECTROCHEMICAL SERIES is another example of an activity series.

Act of Union See UNION, ACTS OF.

actuary An insurance professional who is concerned with the calculation of risk involved in underwriting ASSURANCE and INSURANCE policies. Actuarial work relies on past trends and statistics relating to the event to be insured. If a person wishes to take out a term insurance policy, the actuarial calculations will be concerned with an examination of life expectancy to determine the probability of death within the insured period. This probability will be used to calculate the premium to be paid.

acupuncture A form of therapy originating in ancient Chinese medicine, which supports the belief that a life-force is essential to good health, and that an energy flow (called *chi*) flows along well-defined pathways in the body called meridians. Interruption of the energy flow is considered to impair body function and result in disease. Acupuncture attempts to restore this energy flow by inserting thin needles at specific points along the meridians. In therapies related to acupuncture, pressure or heat may be used instead of needles. Acupuncture is well accepted in Western medicine, although the way in which it works is unknown, and it is not effective in everybody. It is thought that acupuncture may induce ANAESTHESIA by activating sensory nerves that stimulate the pituitary gland and hypothalamus to release the body's natural painkillers (endorphins), although a psychological belief that it will work may also be a contributory factor.

Adam According to traditional Jewish, Christian, and Islamic belief, the first man and consort of Eve. In the account given in the Book of Genesis he was created on the sixth day in the image and likeness of God, commanded to multiply, and given dominion over the Earth. In the Talmud, Lilith is said to be Adam's first wife, dispossessed by Eve. In Islam, Adam is God's vice-regent, created from potter's clay, as recorded in the Koran and greatly elaborated upon in Islamic legend.

Adam, Robert (1728–92) Scottish architect. He undertook a Grand Tour of Europe, starting in 1754, mainly in France and Italy, which gave him knowledge of ancient buildings and modern neoclassical theory. Robert and his brother James (1730–94) set up in business in London in 1758 and in the course of the next forty years initiated the 'Adam Revolution', introducing a more decorative style than PALLADIANISM.

Adam de la Halle (Le Bossu) (*c.*1240–*c.*1288) French poet, musician, and innovator of the earliest French secular theatre. He is chiefly remembered for his dramatic works the *Jeu de la feuillée* (*c.*1262) and the *Jeu de Robin et Marion* (*c.*1283). As a court musician he became famous for his polyphonic songs as well as for his motets and stage productions on topical themes.

Adams, Ansel (Easton) (1902–84) US photographer. In the 1930s he developed the use of large-format cameras and small apertures to produce sharp images with maximum depth of field, very different from the fashionable soft-focus work of the time. Many of Adams's collections, such as *My Camera in the National Parks* (1950) and *This is the American Earth* (1960), depict the American wilderness.

Adams, Henry (Brooks) (1838–1918) US historian, essayist, and novelist. After completing two novels, *Democracy* (1880) and *Esther* (1884), he travelled extensively, completed a nine-volume history of the USA under Thomas Jefferson and James Madison (1889–91), and wrote *Mont-Saint-Michel and Chartres* (1904) about medieval France. His autobiography, *The Education of Henry Adams* (1907), describes the failure of his education.

Adams, John (1735–1826) US Federalist statesman, 2nd President of the USA 1797–1801. He was a key figure in the drafting of the Declaration of Independence (1776), and was minister to Britain (1785–88).

Adams, John Couch (1819–92) British astronomer. In 1843 he postulated the existence of an eighth planet from perturbations in the orbit of Uranus. Similar calculations performed almost simultaneously by Le Verrier resulted in the discovery of Neptune three years later.

Adams, John Quincy (1767–1848) US Republican statesman, 6th President of the USA 1825–29. The eldest son of President John Adams, he was minister to Britain (1809–14). As Secretary of State (1817–24) he helped to shape the Monroe doctrine, the principle of US foreign policy that any intervention by external powers in the politics of the Americas is a potentially hostile act against the US. After leaving office he was prominent in the campaign against slavery.

Adams, Richard (1920–) British writer. While still in the British civil service he wrote his international bestseller *Watership Down* (1972). Ostensibly a children's book about a colony of rabbits, it has also attracted a large adult readership. His other books include *Shardik* (1974); *The Plague Dogs* (1977), an indictment of the use of animals for research; *The Girl in a Swing* (1980); and *Traveller* (1989).

Adams, Samuel (1722–1803) American patriot, the leader of resistance to Britain in Massachusetts between 1763 and 1776. He founded the Sons of Liberty in Boston and organized riots, propaganda, and boycotts against tax-raising. He attended the CONTINENTAL CONGRESS and signed the DECLARATION OF INDEPENDENCE. He later served as governor of Massachusetts and was drafter of its constitution (1780).

adaptation In nature, the process by which plants and animals have evolved to operate efficiently in a particular ecological NICHE. It ensures that an organism will be able to develop, feed and reproduce successfully within its normal environment. To this end, adaptation may involve modification of structure, function, and, in animals, behaviour.

Adaptation arises through NATURAL SELECTION, which acts upon inheritable variation within a species (arising from MUTATION) to remove less effective individuals, and to increase the reproductive success of those individuals with improved characteristics. Thus, the species as a whole may become increasingly well designed to fit its particular role or niche. For example, plants in dry habitats have evolved extensive roots and mechanisms to reduce water loss and store water.

In a similar way, adaptive 'radiation' can occur, whereby new species evolve from one common ancestor to fit a range of micro-habitats.

ad-Dajjāl (Arabic, 'the deceiver' or 'imposter') The Muslim antichrist. According to Islamic tradition there will be a number of false prophets in history, but the last and greatest will be the red-faced and one-eyed al-Masih ad-Dajjāl, who will appear in a time of great turmoil and seek to lead people astray. He will be destroyed by Jesus or the Mahdi, and the Day of Resurrection and Judgement will follow.

adder A snake, *Vipera bera*, that belongs to the VIPER family, Viperidae, and is widely distributed in Europe. It is found in a variety of habitats, including marshes, heaths, moors, hedgerows, and open woodland. It is Britain's only poisonous snake and, although venomous, its bite is not fatal to humans. Adults grow up to 65 cm (2.2 ft) in length. Males tend to be greyish in colour, and females brown or reddish; both sexes generally have a dark zigzag stripe down the back, but some entirely black individuals occur.

Addington, Henry, 1st Viscount Sidmouth (1757–1844) British Tory statesman, Prime Minister 1801–04. As Home Secretary (1812–21), he introduced harsh legislation to suppress the Luddites and other protest groups.

Addis Ababa (or **Adis Abeba**) The capital city of Ethiopia, situated at an altitude of *c.*2,440 m (8,000 ft) in the highlands of Shewa province; pop. (1994) 2,316,400. Founded by King Menelik II in 1887, Addis Ababa replaced Intotto as capital of Abyssinia two years later. In 1917 an 800-km (500-mile) rail link with the port of Djibouti was completed. It is the headquarters of the Organization of African Unity and the United Nations Economic Commission for Africa and the trade centre for coffee, Ethiopia's chief export.

Addison, Joseph (1672–1719) British poet, dramatist, essayist, and Whig politician. In 1711 he founded the *Spectator* with Sir Richard Steele. His tragedy *Cato* (1713) was an immediate success. He is notable for his simple unornamented prose style, marking the end of the florid writing of the 17th century.

Addison, Thomas (1793–1860) British physician. He described the disease now named after him, ascribing it correctly to defective functioning of the adrenal glands. Distinguished for his zeal in the investigation of disease, Addison had a great reputation as a clinical teacher.

addition reaction See CHEMICAL REACTION.

Addled Parliament (5 April–7 June 1614) The nickname given to JAMES I of England's second Parliament. In the absence of effective guidance from crown or councillors, those opposed to the king's policies were able to divert the House of Commons to discussion of grievances, including church reform, import duties, and court interference at the elections. The king dissolved the Parliament before it had passed any legislation – hence the term 'addled' meaning empty or muddled – and ruled without one until 1621.

Adelaide The capital and chief port of South Australia, at the mouth of the Torrens River, between the Mount Lofty Ranges and the Gulf of St Vincent; pop. (1990) 1,049,870. Founded in 1836, Adelaide was named after the wife of William IV. It is the oldest city in the state and was in 1840 the first Australian settlement to be incorporated into a municipal government. Its historic buildings include its Town Hall, Government House, and Parliament House. Its principal industries are vehicle assembly, railway workshops, and electrical and household appliances.

Adélie Land (or **Adélie Coast**; French **Terre Adélie**) A section of the Antarctic continent lying south of the 60th parallel, between Wilkes Land and King George V Land. Placed under French sovereignty in 1938, the Adélie Coast was discovered in 1840 by the naval explorer Dumont d'Urville who named it after his wife.

Aden A port commanding the entrance to the Red Sea, the commercial capital of the Republic of Yemen and former capital of South Yemen (1967–90); pop. (1993) 400,800. A trading centre since Roman times, it was formerly under British rule, first as part of British India (from 1839), then from 1935 as a Crown Colony. It has an oil refinery and building materials industries.

Adenauer, **Konrad** (1876–1967) German statesman, first Chancellor of the Federal Republic of Germany (1949–63). He co-founded the Christian Democratic Union in 1945. As Chancellor, he is remembered for the political and economic transformation of his country. He secured the friendship of the USA and was an advocate of strengthening political and economic ties with Western countries.

adenoids Part of a ring of lymphoid tissue surrounding the openings of the mouth and nose into the gullet. The adenoids are found in all mammals and protect against the entrance of infection. In humans, they are larger in children than in adults, and may either grow to restrict the passage of air through the nose, or block the tubes taking air to the middle ear, causing deafness. In such cases they have to be removed surgically.

adenosine triphosphate See ATP.

adhesive A material, usually a liquid, used to join together solid materials. A thin layer of adhesive is applied to each of the components to be joined, which are then brought together. The adhesive solidifies by a combination of chemical reaction and evaporation of solvent to form a bond: it may bond chemically to the solid surfaces, or interlock mechanically with surface roughnesses. Adhesives were first manufactured from natural sources using starch and animal protein (bones and hoofs). Today a wide range of adhesives is available. Adhesives are used extensively in the manufacture of plastic and wooden articles, and are increasingly being used for joining metals. They are of particular importance in the aerospace industry.

adiabatic change Any physical change occurring when no heat either enters or leaves the system in which it occurs. Experiments on a material contained in a vacuum flask, for example, would be under adiabatic conditions because the inside of the flask is well insulated. When air rises it expands adiabatically as atmospheric pressure falls. This causes its temperature to decrease, the rate of fall being given by a lapse rate. Compare ISOTHERMAL CHANGE.

Adige (German **Etsch**) A river in north-east Italy, which rises in the Rhaetian Alps and flows 408 km (255 miles) southwards to meet the Adriatic Sea between Venice and the mouth of the River Po. The Adige is Italy's second-longest river.

Adi Granth (Punjabi, 'first book') The most important sacred book of SIKHISM. The original compilation was made under the direction of Guru Arjan (1563–1606), the fifth Sikh GURU. Written in the Gurmukhi script, the *Adi Granth* consists of the preachings of the first five Gurus, but also includes Muslim and Hindu hymns. The work was completed by the tenth Guru, GOBIND SINGH, who declared that hence-forward there would be no more Gurus: his successor would be the *Adi Granth*, now given the honorific title Guru Granth Sahib ('Holy Book Guru'). For this reason, the *Adi Granth* is treated with great respect: the throne holding the book forms the focus of worship in a Sikh temple.

Adler, **Alfred** (1870–1937) Austrian psychologist and psychiatrist. At first a disciple of Sigmund FREUD, he came to disagree with Freud's idea that mental illness was caused by sexual conflicts in infancy, arguing that society and culture were equally, if not more, significant factors. In 1907 he introduced the concept of the inferiority complex, asserting that the key to understanding both personal and mass problems was the sense of inferiority and the individual's striving to compensate for this. In 1911 he and his followers formed their own school to develop the ideas of individual psychology, and in 1921 he founded the first child guidance clinic, in Vienna.

Admiralty Islands An island group of Papua New Guinea in the western Pacific Ocean. In 1884 the islands became a German protectorate, but after 1920 they were administered as an Australian mandate. Lorengau on Manus Island is the chief settlement.

adobe A sun-dried mixture of silt and clay used to make reddish-brown bricks for mud building. The mixture was deposited under water in what are now flat desert basins, where it lies in thick sheets. It has been used extensively in South America, the south-western USA, and Africa.

Adonis (in Greek mythology) An extremely beautiful youth with whom the goddess APHRODITE fell in love. While hunting he was killed by a wild boar, but because of Aphrodite's grief he was restored to life for part of each year.

Adonis (in astronomy) An APOLLO-AMOR OBJECT discovered by the Belgian astronomer Eugene Delporte in 1936. That year it passed within 2 million km of the Earth, a near miss by astronomical standards. Unfortunately it was lost soon afterwards, but was rediscovered in 1977 by the US astronomer Charles Kowal.

adoption The legal transfer of an individual from his or her biological family to another family. In Western countries, adoption is a way of meeting the needs both of children whose parents cannot care for them and of infertile couples. In Japan, adults as well as children may be adopted in order, for example, to inherit a family business or to ensure care for the adoptive couple in later life. In some parts of the world, adoption is little used, children either being absorbed into the 'extended' family or left to institutional care. Research shows that adoptions of children are generally successful, as strong mutual attachment develops; nevertheless, adoptees often retain a sense of separate identity, and some as adults seek to contact their biological families. In some economically developed countries the use of contraception and abortion has so sharply reduced the number of local babies for adoption that the great majority of adoptees are brought in from developing countries, primarily in Latin America and parts of Asia. While inter-country adoption may offer the hope of a better life, there is concern that some children are kidnapped or sold for adoption.

Adorno, **Theodor Wiesengrund** (born Theodor Wiesengrund) (1903–69) German philosopher, sociologist, and musicologist. Director of the Frankfurt Institute for Social Research (1958–69), he was a leading figure in the Frankfurt School of philosophy, which reappraised Marxism in terms of modern industrial society. He is known for such works as *Dialectic of Enlightenment* (1947, written with Max Horkheimer) and *Negative Dialectics* (1966).

Adowa, Battle of (1 March 1896) A decisive defeat of the Italians by the Ethiopian Emperor Menelik II. Italy had established a protectorate in Ethiopia in 1889. In 1895 there was a rebellion, and at Adowa an Italian force of 10,000 was routed, losing 4,500 dead and 300 prisoners. In the resulting Treaty of Addis Ababa the Italians recognized the independence of Ethiopia and restricted themselves to the colony of Eritrea. The battle ensured Ethiopian survival as an independent kingdom in Africa.

adrenal gland In mammals, one of a pair of small ENDOCRINE GLANDS found near the kidneys. Each gland has two parts, the inner medulla and the outer cortex. The outer cortex releases aldosterone, a steroid HORMONE that regulates an animal's fluid and salt content, and glucocorticoids, hormones that assist in coordinating the daily patterns of sugar and fat usage. The inner part of the gland is formed of tissue specialized to produce and store large amounts of noradrenalin and adrenalin: hormones that increase the breakdown of body fat and increase the blood sugar level. Their actions raise the blood pressure by increasing the rate of the heartbeat and regulating the diameter of blood vessels. In other vertebrate groups, the adrenal gland is a diffuse organ which is located among the other body contents.

Adrian IV (born Nicholas Breakspear) (*c.*1100–59) Pope 1154–59. The only Englishman to have held this office, he assisted Henry II of England to gain control of Ireland and opposed Frederick I's (Barbarossa's) claims to power.

Adrianople, Battle of (9 August 378 AD) . The Roman city of Adrianople, 480 km (300 miles) west of Constantinople, was the scene of the defeat of the Roman forces by the VISIGOTHS. Emperor Valens, who had hoped to prevent the Gothic invasion of the Roman empire, was killed.

Adrianople, Treaty of (1829) A peace treaty between Russia and the Ottoman empire. It terminated the war between them (1828–29) and gave Russia minor territorial gains in Europe, including access to the mouth of the Danube, and substantial gains in Asia Minor. The treaty also confirmed the autonomy of Serbia, promised autonomy for Greece, and guaranteed free passage for merchant ships through the Dardanelles.

Adriatic Sea An arm of the Mediterranean Sea between the Balkans and the Italian peninsula. Extending a distance of 720 km (450 miles) from the Gulf of Otranto in the south to the coast of Istria in the north, the Adriatic has an area of some 135,200 sq km (52,220 sq miles).

adult education See CONTINUING EDUCATION.

Advaita Hinduism (Sanskrit, 'non-duality') One of the VEDANTA philosophical schools in Hinduism, based on the teaching of Shankara (*c.*700). Shankara systematized the basic principles of the UPANISHADS (part of the VEDAS, the Hindu sacred texts) into a coherent philosophy, according to which there is an essential oneness between ultimate spiritual reality, BRAHMAN, and the human soul, ATMAN. The realization of this identity between Brahman and atman, which leads to spiritual liberation (MOKSHA), cannot be achieved through ritual action, but only through meditation. Advaita Hinduism is only one of the branches of Vedanta, but it has become well known in Western countries through its modern exponents, in particular the Ramakrishna Mission, founded in Calcutta by Vivekananda in 1897.

advanced gas-cooled reactor See NUCLEAR REACTOR.

advection The horizontal transport of heat or cold, either in the atmosphere by the large-scale movement of air or in the oceans by currents of seawater. In both cases a major example is the transport of cold masses from the polar regions to lower latitudes. Vertical transport is more localized and is known as CONVECTION.

advection fog A type of fog that is formed when warm air passes horizontally over cold land or sea, generally occurring in mid-latitudes during winter.

Advent (from Latin *adventus*, coming) The season in the Christian year preceding CHRISTMAS, first mentioned by the Council of Tours (567). The length of the Advent season varies: in the West it commences on the Sunday nearest to St Andrew's Day (30 November): in the East it lasts forty days. Although lacking the strictness of LENT, it is traditionally a penitential season of fasting in anticipation both of Christmas and of the expected Second Coming of Christ.

Adventists Various Protestant groups, originating in the USA in 1831 as the Evangelical Adventists, who believe in an imminent Second Coming of Christ. There are now about two million full members, including two major groups: the 'Second Advent Christians', and the 'Seventh-day Adventists', who strictly observe the sabbath on the seventh day (Saturday) and require adult baptism and abstinence from alcohol. See also ESCHATOLOGY; MILLENARIANISM.

adversarial procedure A legal procedure found in countries with COMMON LAW SYSTEMS, in which the two parties to a legal case confront one another in court. According to the procedure, the burden of presenting evidence falls on each of the parties. (In a criminal trial, these are the PROSECUTION and the defence.) Evidence is presented in turn by the parties or their representatives, and there is an opportunity for each side to question the other through cross-examination. The role of the JUDGE is to act as an umpire to ensure that the trial is conducted according to correct legal procedure, and to evaluate the evidence presented by each side. The adversarial procedure lays emphasis on the oratorical skills of the ADVOCATE, in contrast to the inquisitorial procedure, found in civil law jurisdictions.

advertising The use of MASS MEDIA to carry paid messages for a commercial purpose or to advance a cause, institution, or political candidate. Advertising has become an integral element in free-market economies; it influences the pricing, packaging, design, display, and sales incentives of a product. Most advertising is channelled through national agencies, which employ copy-writers, art directors, jingle writers, video producers, production specialists, MARKET RESEARCHERS, public relations officers, and a media department. Their task is to build a 'brand image' or 'personality' that dovetails with the psychological profile of a product, person, or cause. In many countries, government is a major advertiser on behalf of state-owned industries and enterprises. In authoritarian regimes, political advertising is co-opted into the PROPAGANDA machine, but it also plays an important role in democratic countries through its involvement in the electoral process.

advocate (in law) One whose profession it is to plead for another in court. The title is used in those countries, such as France and Scotland, whose legal systems are based on ROMAN LAW. The Faculty of Advocates is the collective body of Scottish advocates, whose members may appear before any court in Scotland and before the House of Lords. The Lord Advocate is the principal law officer in Scotland. In the USA, the term advocate is sometimes used synonymously with attorney, counsel, or lawyer.

Adygea (or **Adygey**) ▶**1** A republic of the Russian Federation lying between the Caucasus and the Kuban River; area 7,600 sq km (2,934 sq miles); pop. (1995) 450,000; capital, Maikop. Peopled by Circassians who were converted to Islam in the 17th century, Adygea was established as an autonomous region of the USSR in 1922. It was given the status of a republic in 1992 after the breakup of the Soviet Union. It produces timber and cattle. ▶**2** A language spoken in the northern Caucasus region.

Adzharia (or **Adjaria**, **Adzharistan**) An autonomous republic on the Black Sea coast of the Republic of Georgia populated by Muslim Georgians; area 3,000 sq km (1,160 sq miles); pop. (1993) 386,700; capital, Batumi. Formerly held by the Ottoman Turks, the agricultural and predominantly Muslim Adzharia region became an autonomous republic of the Soviet Union in 1921.

Aegean civilization See MYCENAEAN CIVILIZATION.

Aegean Sea That part of the Mediterranean Sea lying between Greece and Turkey, bounded to the south by the islands of Crete and Rhodes. It is linked to the Black Sea by the Dardanelles, the Sea of Marmara, and the Bosporus and takes its name from the legendary Aegeus who drowned himself in the belief that his son Theseus had been killed by the minotaur. The prehistoric Aegean civilization flourished in this region *c.*3,000–1,000 BC.

Aelfric (*c.*955–*c.*1020) Anglo-Saxon monk, writer, and grammarian. His chief works are the *Catholic Homilies* (990–92) and the *Lives of the Saints* (993–96), both written in Old English. His Latin grammar earned him the name 'Grammaticus'.

Aeneas In Roman mythology, a Trojan prince, son of the goddess Aphrodite and Anchises. He played a prominent role in the defence of TROY against the Greeks, but when the city fell, he escaped to Carthage. There he fell in love with Dido, the widowed queen, but abandoned her in order to found the state of Rome.

aeolian harp A stringed musical instrument sounded by the wind, invented by Athanasius Kircher in 1650 in Rome, and popular into the 19th century. The commonest form is a long rectangular box, with a number of strings running along it, which is wedged in a partly open window so that the draught, passing across the strings, makes them vibrate and sound. Other versions were designed to hang in trees and other places out of doors. Although the strings are all the same length, they differ in thickness and thus produce different pitches.

aerial See ANTENNA.

aerial perspective A way of producing a sense of depth in a painting by imitating the atmospheric effect that makes objects look paler and bluer the further away they are from the viewer. The term was invented by Leonardo DA VINCI, but the effect was exploited by painters much earlier – for example, the mural painters of Roman times. Generally, aerial perspective has been most subtly exploited in northern Europe, most notably by TURNER; in some of his late paintings the atmosphere is virtually the subject of the painting. See also PERSPECTIVE.

aerodynamics The study of the movement of air or other gaseous fluids relative to bodies immersed in them, and the forces produced. One of the major tools in aerodynamics is testing in a WIND-TUNNEL. A knowledge of aerodynamics is essential for applications ranging from low-speed air-flow around buildings to the prediction of the behaviour of aeroplanes, rockets, and missiles. See also FLIGHT, PRINCIPLES OF MANNED; FLUID MECHANICS; SUPERSONIC FLIGHT.

aerofoil (US **airfoil**) A structure whose cross-section is shaped to produce a desired aerodynamic reaction (such as lift) by its motion through air. Aircraft examples include wings, control surfaces, tail fins, PROPELLERS, turbine blades, and HELICOPTER rotor blades. Other examples include sails, some windmill blades, and racing-car aerofoils.

aeronautics See FLIGHT, PRINCIPLES OF MANNED.

aeroplane (US **airplane**) A power-driven, heavier-than-air aircraft with fixed wings. Before the 1930s aeroplanes had wooden, wire-braced airframes covered by fabric, but with a few exceptions (e.g. the Mosquito of the 1940s) modern aircraft are constructed as a shell of thin metal sheeting strengthened by ribs and longitudinal members. The commonest aircraft structural materials are aluminium ALLOYS, which are strong and light. Alloys of TITANIUM, and COMPOSITE materials, such as FIBRE-REINFORCED PLASTICS, are increasingly used for structural components because of their lightness.

The basic components of an aeroplane are the fuselage, wings, engines, tail assembly (empennage), and undercarriage. The fuselage carries the passengers, crew, and cargo. The shape of the fuselage relates to the aircraft's operating speed. Low-speed aircraft have little STREAMLINING, while the shapes of high-speed subsonic and supersonic aircraft are shaped to minimize drag. Most modern aeroplanes are monoplanes, with only one pair of wings. Wing shape varies with function. Most aeroplanes are powered by piston engines and propellers, by turboprops, or by turbojet engines (see JET ENGINE). The tail unit consists of a horizontal stabilizer, usually projecting from the mid-line of the rear fuselage, and a vertical tail fin. Pneumatic-tyred undercarriages are fitted on virtually all modern aeroplanes. On older aircraft, and on some light aircraft, the main wheels are located well forward, with a smaller wheel or skid on the tail, but most aeroplanes now use a 'tricycle' undercarriage, with the main wheels behind the centre of gravity and a smaller wheel at the nose. Undercarriages are often retractable, as this greatly improves flight performance. Aeroplane controls comprise a control column or wheel for operating ailerons and elevators, a rudder bar moved by the feet, and the engine ignition and throttle. Computers are often used to monitor aircraft functions, or actually to control the aeroplane. See also FLIGHT, PRINCIPLES OF MANNED; FLIGHT, HISTORY OF MANNED; and individual aircraft types.

aerosol A dispersion of finely divided solid or liquid particles in a gas, for example fog or smoke (see COLLOID). Aerosols can be natural, such as fog, or manufactured, such as smoke. Aerosols are used in industry in canisters containing a propellant gas to spray paint and insecticides. Consumer aerosols include paints, polishes, perfumes, cleaners, deodorants, shaving cream, and whipped cream. Some medications for respiratory complaints are taken via dosage-controlled aerosols.

Aeschines (*c*.390–*c*.314 BC) Athenian orator and statesman. He opposed DEMOSTHENES' efforts to unite the Greek city-states against Macedon, with which he attempted to make peace. Aeschines was tried for treason in 343 but acquitted, and left Athens for Rhodes in 330 after failing to defeat Demosthenes.

Aeschylus (*c*.525–*c*.456 BC) Greek dramatist. The earliest writer of Greek tragic drama whose works survive, he is best known for his trilogy the *Oresteia* (458), consisting of *Agamemnon*, *Choephoroe*, and *Eumenides*. These tell the story of Agamemnon's murder at the hands of his wife Clytemnestra and the vengeance of their son Orestes. Aeschylus departed from tradition by giving more weight to dialogue than to choral song and in adding a second actor to the existing one plus chorus.

Aesop (6th century BC) Greek storyteller. The moral animal fables associated with him were probably collected from many sources, and initially communicated orally; they were later popularized by the Roman poet Phaedrus (1st century BC), who translated some of them into Latin. Aesop is said to have lived as a slave on the island of Samos.

Aesthetic Movement An English art movement of the later 19th century, characterized by an exaggerated belief in the doctrine of 'art for art's sake' – the view that art need have no ulterior moral, political, or religious purpose. Central figures of the movement included WHISTLER, WILDE, and Beardsley. It was frequently ridiculed for its tendency towards affectation, most notably in Gilbert and Sullivan's opera *Patience* (1881).

aesthetics The philosophical study of art and the values, concepts, and kinds of experience associated with art, such as taste, beauty, and the sublime. In being concerned with conceptual questions, aesthetics is to be distinguished sharply from psychology; and in seeking to say what is common to all aesthetic experience rather than describe the meaning of particular works of art, it is also distinguished from criticism and interpretation. In classical philosophy, two important discussions are PLATO's criticism of art, as in some sense promoting illusion, in *The Republic* (*c*.350 BC) and ARISTOTLE's account of tragedy in his *Poetics* (*c*.340 BC) as a vital function to purge the emotions. KANT's *Critique of Judgement* (1790) is the outstanding modern work of aesthetics.

Afars and Issas, French Territory of the The former name of DJIBOUTI between 1946 and 1977.

affenpinscher See DOG.

Afghan hound See DOG.

Afghani, Jamal al-Din al- (1839–97) Muslim revivalist of Iranian origin. He advocated social and political reforms within Muslim countries and Pan-Islamism. Afghani was active as a teacher in Egypt during the 1870s, edited a newspaper (*al-Urwa al-Wuthqa*, 'the Unbreakable Link') in Paris during the 1880s, and played a part in the protest in Iran in 1891–92.

Afghanistan A mountainous, land-locked country in south-central Asia, bounded on the west by Iran, on the south and east by Pakistan, and on the north by Turkmenistan, Uzbekistan, and Tajikistan.

Physical. Afghanistan's eastern region is dominated by the vast mountain range of the Hindu Kush, and most of the country is high plateau. In winter much of it is under snow; but in spring grass appears, soon to be scorched dry and swept by the dust storms of summer.

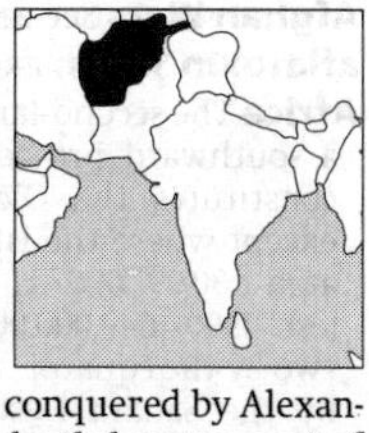

Economy. Agriculture, mainly sheep-raising and subsistence farming, is the mainstay of the economy, which has been devastated by the civil war.

History. Afghanistan was conquered by Alexander the Great, and after his death became part of the Bactrian state. A succession of foreign overlords was followed by Arab conquest from the 7th century. The territory was converted to Islam, and the most important Muslim ruler was Mahmud of Ghazna. The country was overrun by Mongols in 1222, only becoming united under an Afghan leader in 1747, when Ahmad Shah founded the Durrani dynasty at Kandahar. In the 19th and early 20th centuries Afghanistan was the focal point of conflicting Russian and British interests. A British attempt to replace the Kabul ruler Dost Muhammad was repulsed in the First ANGLO-AFGHAN WAR, but Afghan foreign policy came under British control in 1879 by the Treaty of Gandamak, when Britain gained control of the Khyber Pass. In 1880 Abdurrahman Khan became amir, establishing a strong central government; his heirs achieved some modernization and social reform. In 1953 General Mohammad Daoud Khan seized power and was Prime Minister until 1963, during which time he obtained economic and military assistance from the Soviet Union. There were border disputes with Pakistan, but it was Daoud's policy to maintain 'non-alignment' between the two super-power blocs. In 1964 Afghanistan became a parliamentary democracy, but a military coup in 1973 overthrew the monarchy and Daoud reasserted control. In 1977 he issued a constitution for a one-party state. Within a year, however, he had been assassinated and the Democratic Republic of Afghanistan proclaimed, headed by a revolutionary council, whose first President was Nur Mohammad Taraki. The new regime embarked on reforms, causing some rural unrest. In February 1979 the US ambassador was killed and one month later Taraki was assassinated by supporters of the deputy Prime Minister, Ha'zullah Amin, who sought US support. In December 1979 Soviet troops entered the country. Amin was killed and replaced by Babrak Karmal. Guerrilla Mujahidin forces, equipped with US arms, then waged a *jihad* or holy war against government troops armed and supported by Soviet forces. Some six million refugees fled to Iran and Pakistan. In 1987 the Soviet Union began to disengage, all troops being withdrawn by 1989, when the pro-Soviet government of Mohammad Najibullah was replaced by an Islamic state. However, civil conflict between both rival Mujahidin factions and other militant groups continued. In 1995–96 the Taleban militia, an army of young Islamic militants, gained control of southern Afghanistan, including Kabul, and imposed strict Islamic law.

Capital: Kabul
Area: 652,225 sq km (251,825 sq mi)
Population: 16,600,000 (1991)
Currency: 1 afghani = 100 puls
Religions: Sunni Muslim 93.0%; Shiite Muslim 7.0%
Ethnic Groups: Pathan (Pashto) 52.3%; Tajik 20.3%; Uzbek 8.7%; Hazara 8.7%; Chahar Aimak 2.9%; Turkmen 2.0%; Baluchi 1.0%
Languages: Pashto, Dari (Persian) (both official); minority languages
International Organizations: UN; Colombo Plan; Non-Aligned Movement

Afghan Wars See ANGLO-AFGHAN WARS.

aflatoxin See ASPERGILLUS.

Africa The second-largest of the world's continents, a southward projection of the land mass which constitutes the Old World, surrounded by sea except where the isthmus of Suez joins it to Asia; area *c.*30,097,000 sq km (11,620,451 sq miles); pop. (est. 1990) 642,000,000. Divided almost exactly in two by the equator, the northern half is dominated by the Sahara Desert, while southern Africa is dominated by a central plateau comprising a southern tableland with a mean altitude of 1,070 m (3,000 ft) that falls northwards to a lower plain at *c.*400 m (1,300 ft). The highest peak is Mt. Kilimanjaro (5,895 m, 19,340 ft) and the lowest point is Lake Assal in the Afar Depression of Djibouti (−153 m, −502 ft). Principal physical features include the Great Rift Valley in the east, the Atlas Mountains in the north-west, the Kalahari, Namib, and Karoo deserts in the south and the Nile, Congo, Niger, Zambezi, Limpopo, Volta, and Orange rivers. On either side of the equator a belt of dry savanna known as the Sahel stretches across the entire continent. Over 30 per cent of the world's minerals, including more than 50 per cent of the world's diamonds and 47 per cent of its gold, are mined in Africa. With a growth rate of 3 per cent (ten times greater than Europe) Africa's population has more than doubled since 1960 when it stood at 278 million. Food shortages in Africa, especially in the 1980s, have been the direct result of war, drought, and population growth. Over 1,000 languages are spoken. Egypt in the north-east was one of the world's earliest centres of civilization, and the Mediterranean coast has been subject to European influence since classical times, but much of the continent remained unknown to the outside world until voyages of discovery along the coast between the 15th and 17th centuries. The continent was explored and partitioned by European nations in the second half of the 19th century. Since World War II most of the former colonies have secured independence, but decolonization has left a legacy of instability.

African Charter on Human and People's Rights A charter adopted by the ORGANIZATION OF AFRICAN UNITY in 1981 and ratified by 35 of its members. The Charter reaffirms the duty of African states to eliminate colonialism, apartheid, and ZIONISM, and stresses that civil and political

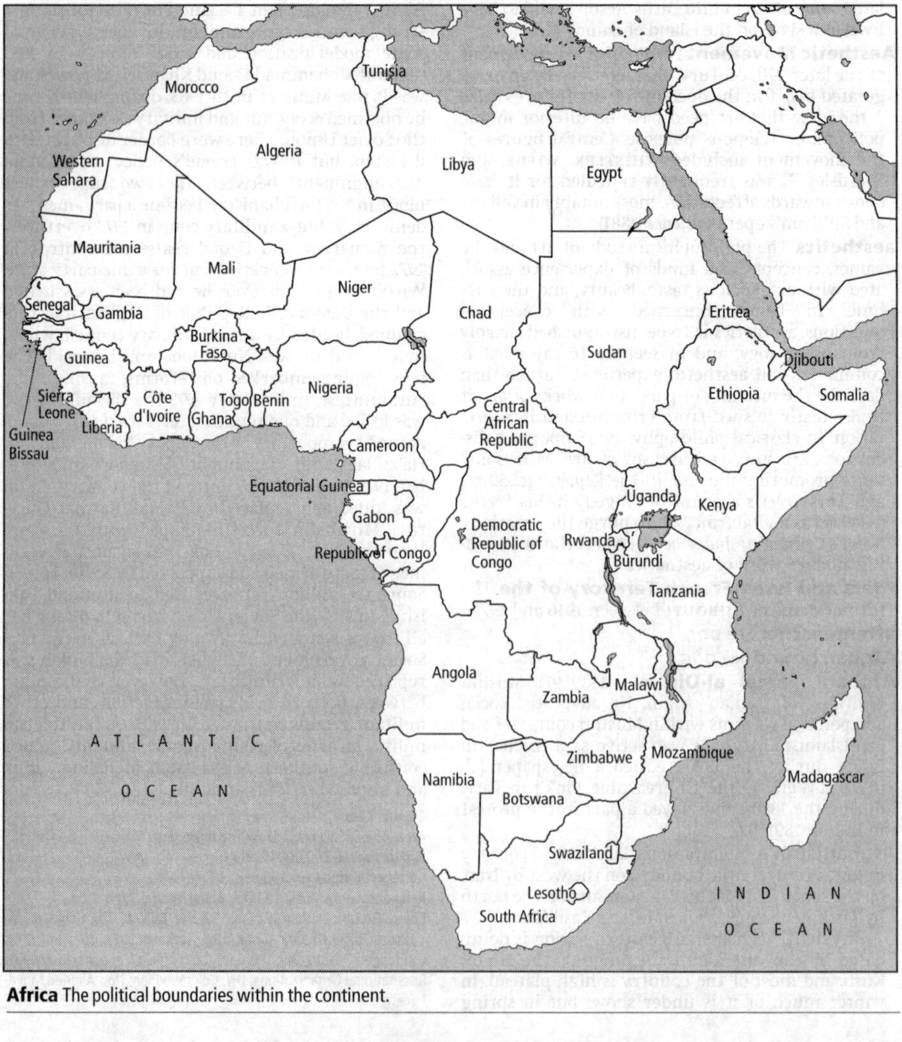

Africa The political boundaries within the continent.

rights cannot be dissociated from economic, social, and cultural rights. The Charter concurs with the Universal Declaration of Human Rights, and emphasizes the rights of 'peoples'. It established the African Commission on Human and People's Rights, based in Dakar, Senegal, a body intended to promote HUMAN RIGHTS, as well as to investigate complaints from individuals. However, in many African countries habitual abuse of human rights continues.

African languages See BERBER LANGUAGES; CHADIC LANGUAGES; CUSHITIC LANGUAGES; KHOISAN LANGUAGES; NIGER-CONGO LANGUAGES; NILO-SAHARAN LANGUAGES; SEMITIC LANGUAGES.

African lily See LILY.

African National Congress (ANC) A South African political party. It was established in Bloemfontein in 1912 as the South African Native National Congress by a Zulu Methodist minister, J. W. Dube. In 1914 he led a deputation to Britain protesting against the Native Land Act (1913), which restricted the purchase of land by Black Africans. In 1926 the ANC established a united front with representatives of the Indian community, which aimed to create a racially integrated, democratic southern Africa. It sought to achieve racial equality by non-violent means, as practised by GANDHI in India, and from 1952 until 1967 was led by the Natal chieftain Albert LUTHULI. Together with the more militant break-away movement, the Pan-Africanist Congress (PAC), it was declared illegal by the South African government in 1960. Confronted by Afrikaner intransigence on racial issues, the ANC saw itself forced into a campaign of violence. Maintaining that APARTHEID should be abolished, and every South African have the vote, it formed a liberation army, 'Umkhonto Wesizwe' (Spear of the Nation). In 1962 its vice-president, Nelson MANDELA and some of his colleagues were convicted of sabotage and jailed for life. The exiled wing of the ANC maintained a campaign of violence during the 1980s, but following the election of President DE KLERK (1989) the party was legalized and Mandela was released from prison in 1990. The ANC subsequently entered into talks with the government and participated in the drafting of a new constitution, which gave the vote to all South African adults. The first multi-racial elections, held in 1994, were won by the ANC and Mandela became President.

Afrikaans A language that is one of the 11 official languages of the Republic of South Africa; from 1925 to 1994 it was one of only two official languages (the other being English). It is a development of 17th-century Dutch brought to South Africa by settlers from Holland. It is spoken by 4 million people – 2 million White Afrikaners and about 2 million people of mixed race.

Afrikaners (or **Boers**) The white Afrikaans-speaking population of South Africa, especially the descendants of the families that emigrated from the Netherlands, Germany, and France before 1806. The AFRIKAANS language and the Christian Calvinist tradition, out of which arose the concept of APARTHEID, are unifying factors.

Afro-Asiatic languages See BERBER LANGUAGES; CHADIC LANGUAGES; CUSHITIC LANGUAGES; SEMITIC LANGUAGES.

afterlife The belief that the human spirit or soul survives physical death and passes through to a new mode of existence, which is often determined by a person's conduct during life, or by the rituals surrounding death. Conceptions of the afterlife are a common feature of many religions. The veneration of ancestral spirits, which implies belief in an afterlife, is common to many religions. In Judaic, Christian, and Islamic thought, the human soul is consigned to HEAVEN or to HELL, depending on God's judgement. Roman Catholicism teaches furthermore that most souls require purification in purgatory before entry into heaven. Many Roman Catholics also believe in a state called limbo, the abode of unbaptized but otherwise innocent souls (such as infants). According to Hinduism, the soul or ATMAN is constantly reborn through a variety of lives until ultimate enlightenment or MOKSHA occurs, and the cycle of rebirth ceases. Buddhists reject the notion of the individual soul, but they too believe in an endless cycle of REINCARNATION until the attainment of NIRVANA. See also ANCESTOR WORSHIP.

Agade See AKKAD.

Agadir A southern seaport and resort town on the Atlantic coast of Morocco; pop. (1993) 137,000. The city was rebuilt and developed as a tourist resort after a devastating earthquake in 1960.

Aga Khan The title of the imam or leader of the Nizari sect of Ismaili Muslims. The first Aga Khan was given his title in 1818 by the shah of Persia, subsequently moving with the majority of the Nizaris to the Indian subcontinent. The present (4th) Aga Khan (Karim Al-Hussain Shah (1937–), born in Geneva) inherited the title from his grandfather in 1957. The title of Aga Khan (which comes from the Turkish words for master and ruler) carries with it responsibility for various services and welfare provisions for members of the Nizari community.

Agamemnon In Greek mythology, king of Mycenae and the commander-in-chief of the Greeks during the Trojan War. To get fair winds for sailing to TROY he sacrificed his daughter Iphigenia to Artemis. After his return from the war he was murdered by his wife, Clytemnestra, and avenged by his son, Orestes, who was urged on by his sister, Electra.

agamid A LIZARD of the family Agamidae, comprising about 300 species. Some forms resemble lizards of the iguana family in external appearance and habits, but the two families occur in different parts of the world. Agamids occur in warmer parts of the Old World, including Australia. They are typical lizards, having well-developed limbs, and most species have a fairly long tail. Their life-styles are diverse; terrestrial, rock-dwelling, and tree-dwelling forms occur – flying lizards and frilled lizards are included within the last category. They include species such as the bearded lizard, *Amphibolorus barbatus*, and the frilled lizard, *Chlamydosaurus kingii*.

agaric (or **gill fungus**) A FUNGUS belonging to the order Agaricales within the phylum Basidiomycota. Agarics produce MUSHROOMS or toadstools as their spore-bearing structures; examples are blewits, death cap, fly agaric, and the cultivated mushroom. The spores are produced in millions from gills underneath the cap and are carried away in air currents. The cap of an agaric, left overnight on clean paper, will leave a 'spore print'. Most are SAPROPHYTES and play an important part in the breakdown of dead wood and leaves.

Agartala The capital of the state of Tripura in north-east India; pop. (1991) 157,640. Rice, tea, cotton, and mustard are produced locally.

Agassi, André (1970–) US tennis player, who by the age of 18 was ranked third in the world. Noted for his unconventional on-court appearance and impetuous behaviour, Agassi clashed repeatedly with the tennis establishment. On winning the Wimbledon men's singles title in 1992, however, he was awarded honorary membership of the All-England Club.

Agassiz, (Jean) Louis (Rodolphe) (1807–73) Swiss-born geologist and palaeontologist who in 1840 introduced the idea of the ICE AGE, a period when glaciers and ice-sheets covered most of the Northern Hemisphere. The concept not only caused an enormous popular sensation but also provided a vital key to the scientific study of much of the Earth's landscape. In 1846 he moved to the USA, where he dominated palaeontology and geology until his death. His *Contributions to the Natural History of the US* (four volumes, 1857–62) firmly rejected the views of LYELL and Darwin's theory of natural selection.

agate A form of CHALCEDONY, a variety of quartz, formed in the steam cavities found in the lavas of volcanic rock. It is always striped or banded due to impurities of iron and manganese, the shape of the bands depending on that of the cavity. The colour varies too, onyx (white or grey) and cornelian (red) being among those prized as semiprecious stones. The best agates come from Brazil and Uruguay.

agave (or **century plant**) A monocotyledon of the genus *Agave*, comprising some 700 species native to Central and South America. Their common name alludes to the long period of up to seventy years before the plant is mature enough to flower, after which it dies. The fleshy, sword-like leaves form large rosettes – in some species up to 3 m (10 ft) across – which are expended in the production of a flowering stem often several metres in height. *A. sisalana* produces the fibre sisal, while the Mexican liquors pulque and tequila are distilled from the sap obtained by cutting away the developing flower stem of *A. americana*.

ageing See SENESCENCE.

age of the Earth From radioisotope studies, the Earth's oldest crustal rocks must be at least 3.8 billion years old. There is evidence that the Earth formed with the other members of the SOLAR SYSTEM some 4.6 billion years ago.

age of the Solar System Studies of rock samples from the Earth, Moon, and meteorites, together with conclusions drawn from the dynamics of the solar system's bodies, suggest that the Solar System formed 4.6 billion years ago.

age of the Universe If the BIG BANG THEORY of the origin of the Universe is accepted the Universe had a beginning. Theories of cosmology and the observed value of HUBBLE's constant (estimated to be 55 km/s per megaparsec) give the age of the Universe as about 15 billion years.

agglomerate (in geology) A deposit, produced by a volcano, that consists of a mixture of volcanic fragments and ash. Agglomerates are usually deposited as part of a volcanic cone, but may also be found in the necks of volcanoes. They generally show a roughly layered structure.

aggradation (in geomorphology) A process that occurs whenever rivers, glaciers, winds, or waves deposit the sediment they carry. The deposits raise the surface and may steepen the local slope of the ground. Much of the High Plains of the USA results from aggradation by rivers draining eastwards from the Rocky Mountains.

aggregate A building material used to provide bulk, particularly in CONCRETE and MORTAR. For most concrete work the aggregates used are gravels or crushed rock and sand. Lightweight aggregates are commonly used for their thermal resistance in cavity walls, or when a reduced load is required on a structure. Shielding against ionizing radiation requires high-density aggregates of barium sulphate or iron pellets.

aggression (in psychology) Unprovoked and intentional injury of another, or the motivation and feelings behind such action. In a wide sense aggression may include assertiveness and competitiveness at one extreme and predation at the other. A restricted sense is violence and threat against members of the aggressor's own species. Biological theories of the origin of aggression rely on studies which show that animals can easily be bred for aggression. Doses of the male hormone testosterone increase aggression in adult males of many species. Social learning theory provides the other main explanatory hypotheses. An early version, put forward in the 1940s by psychologists held that frustration of goal-directed behaviour causes aggression. Later social learning theorists, especially the Canadian Albert Bandura in the 1970s, showed that frustration is unnecessary, for children imitate adults' aggression without frustration or any other form of distress.

Agincourt, Battle of (25 October 1415) The village of Agincourt in northern France was the scene of the defeat of a large French force by an English army led by HENRY V. Henry's force invaded Normandy in 1415, captured Harfleur, but was intercepted by a large French army after a long march north towards Calais. The English troops, mainly archers and foot soldiers, dug in behind wooden stakes between thickly wooded ground. The next day the French cavalry advanced on a narrow front across muddy ground only to be killed by English archers and infantry. A dozen French notables, including the Constable of France, died, together with perhaps 1,500 knights and 4,500 men-at-arms. English casualties were light but included the Duke of York and the Earl of Suffolk. The battle was fought on St Crispin's day.

Agnesi, Maria Gaetana (1718–99) Italian mathematician and philosopher. She is regarded as the first female mathematician of the Western world, though she worked on a variety of scientific subjects. Her major work, which appeared in two volumes in 1748, was a comprehensive treatment of algebra and analysis.

Agni The Indo-Aryan god of fire and of priests, and the bearer of the oblation to the gods in the smoke of the sacrifice. Born from a lotus created by BRAHMA, Agni was also regarded as the protector and friend of mankind, the giver of rain, and the bestower of immortality, who cleansed man from sin after death.

Agnon, Shmuel Yosef (born Samuel Josef Czaczkes) (1888–1970) Hebrew novelist and short-story writer. His work reflects life in the East European *shtetl* (village), (*A Guest for the Night*, 1938), the early settlement in Palestine (*Yesterday and the Day Before*, 1945), and life in modern Jerusalem. He also described the sense of loss following the breakdown of Jewish orthodox tradition, and expressed the life of the unconscious in collections of stories such as *The Book of Deeds*. He received the Nobel Prize for Literature (shared with the poet Nelly Sachs) in 1966.

agnosticism (from Greek *agnostos*, 'unknown') A term coined in 1869 by T. H. Huxley (1825–95), the British biologist and supporter of DARWIN's theories of evolution, to indicate his position with regard to orthodox religious belief. Influenced by modern scientific thought, the agnostic holds that phenomena which cannot be proved or disproved by material means (such as the existence of God) cannot be the subjects of belief or disbelief. The term should not be confused with ATHEISM, which is the denial of the existence of God or any supernatural being.

Agostini, Giacomo (1944–) Italian racing motorcyclist. Between 1966 and 1975 he won a record fifteen world titles, and held the 500 cc. title eight times, also a record. Among his other wins were the Isle of Man TT (ten times, between 1966 and 1975). He retired in 1975 and subsequently became manager of the Yamaha racing team.

agouti A RODENT that looks like a large, long-legged guinea-pig, with hoof-like claws and a short or rudimentary tail. Agoutis make up a genus, *Dasyprocta*, of 11 species, native to South and Central America. They are characterized by long, coarse hair on the rump, which is often conspicuously coloured. The hairs are erected when the animal is alarmed. Agoutis live on the floor of tropical evergreen forests or in savannah. They feed on fruit, roots, seeds, and succulent plants. They make up the family Dasyproctidae together with two species of acuchis (*Myoprocta* species) and are distinct from the family Agoutidae, which includes the two species of PACA.

Agra A city on the River Jumna in Uttar Pradesh state, northern India; pop. (1991) 899,195. Founded by Akbar in 1566, Agra was capital of the Mogul empire until 1658. Its most famous building is the Taj Mahal, a white marble mausoleum built by the Emperor Shah Jahan for his favourite wife who died in 1629. The city is noted for its shoes, glass, and handicrafts.

Agricola, Georgius (born Georg Bauer) (1494–1555) German pioneer of chemical and mining technology. He published several critiques of the methods used at the time to mine and extract metals, but his greatest work was *De Re Metallica* ('On Metals') (1556), a comprehensive treatise in Latin, profusely illustrated with fine woodcuts.

Agricola, Gnaeus Julius (40–93 AD) Governor of Roman Britain 78–84. He served with Paulinus against the Iceni queen BOUDICCA (61) and commanded the Twentieth Legion in the north-west (70–73). As governor he subjugated the Ordovices of north Wales and extended the frontier north to the rivers Forth and Clyde, defeating the Caledonians in the process. His successes irritated Emperor Domitian who recalled him to Rome in 84. His career is described in his *Life* by TACITUS, his son-in-law.

Agricultural Revolution The agricultural changes that occurred in Britain during the 18th century. Some historians stress that agriculture was already undergoing evolutionary change, but that this was speeded up by ENCLOSURE, particularly the parliamentary enclosures of the 18th century. The medieval economy rested on the manorial system and open-field cultivation in strips which hampered change. The Agricultural Revolution saw this replaced by large-scale farming in consolidated units, the extension of arable farming over heaths and commons, the adoption of intensive livestock husbandry, the conversion of a largely self-subsistent peasantry into a community of agricultural labourers, and considerable attention to the improvement of agricultural techniques like CROP ROTATION, new crops, for example turnips and potatoes, and improved grasses. Viscount Townshend (1674–1738) and Thomas Coke, Earl of Leicester (1752–1842) were notable for their adoption and promotion of crop rotation; Jethro Tull (1674–1741) for his seed drills; and Robert Bakewell (1725–95) was the most famous of the livestock improvers.

agriculture Cultivation of the soil, including the allied pursuits of gathering crops and rearing livestock. The 'Neolithic revolution', the change from an economy based on hunting and gathering to one based on settled agriculture, is thought to have begun in many independent centres around the world, at very roughly the same time (*c.*9000 BC): changes in climate and population growth may have stimulated this process. Archaeological evidence suggests at least three independent centres of origin for agriculture based on grain crops (the Near East, the Far East, and meso-America), plus other sites (for example, Peru and Indonesia) where root vegetables formed the main crops. The most complete evidence has come from the Near East, where domesticated barley and emmer wheat strains have been found which date from about 8000 BC. Domesticated animals (e.g. sheep and goats) were reared in large numbers from at least 7000 BC, and there is evidence for the use of the ox-drawn wooden plough from 5000 BC. In the early civilizations of Babylonia, Egypt, the Indus Valley, and China (from *c.*3000 BC), large-scale IRRIGATION systems were developed.

Agricultural practices spread gradually from the different centres to other parts of the world, and were adapted to local conditions; many different field systems evolved. In Europe and the Mediterranean, practices, once established, remained basically unchanged for many years. Roman farmers used an ox-drawn, wheelless plough with iron shares or blades. They sowed seed by hand, harvested using a curved sickle, threshed grain with a hand flail, and winnowed it by throwing it into the air and letting the wind carry away the chaff. By the 4th century AD, high labour input, the transplanting of seedlings, and use of FERTILIZERS were producing cereal yields in China not matched elsewhere until the 19th century. In the Americas, maize was the main crop in some areas, the potato in others. The llama was domesticated as a beast of burden, while the alpaca was kept for its wool, and the guinea-pig for meat. In medieval Europe, slow improvements were made in agricultural practice, particularly in northern areas. From the 5th to the 12th centuries, agricultural land was created by forest clearance, or was reclaimed from marshland and the sea. From the late 13th to the early 15th centuries, much arable land fell into disuse due to the effects of floods, famine, plague, and wars. Recovery began slowly in the 15th century.

In the 17th and 18th centuries several different developments led to improvements in crop yields and in livestock production. In particular, the AGRICULTURAL REVOLUTION of 18th-century Britain introduced new, more efficient practices into farming. Principal among these was the Norfolk four-course system, in which grain and fodder or grazing crops were grown in a four-year rotation. The effects of this system were cumulative: grazing animals manured the land and increased its fertility, while the growing of winter fodder and summer grazing crops meant that animals were better fed, and more productive. In the 18th century selective breeding was introduced, and the Rotherham plough (the forerunner of the modern plough) was developed, along with a variety of simple machines for threshing, chopping animal feed, hoeing, and seed drilling. However, it was not until the mid-19th century that agricultural machinery, for example the reaper and the TRACTION-ENGINE, began to be adopted by farmers.

The 19th century also saw the development of agricultural science, with the introduction of the earliest chemical and synthetic fertilizers, and the opening of agricultural research stations in several countries. During this period large areas of the USA, Canada, South America, and Australia were settled: huge sheep and cattle ranches were established, and large areas were given over to wheat farming. In colonial countries, plantation farming of beverage crops, rubber, and SUGAR CANE expanded tremendously, although these developments had little effect on indigenous agricultural practices. Much of the cheap food generated by the opening up of these new areas was exported to Europe.

The 20th century has seen far-reaching changes in FARMING practices. The internal-combustion engine has replaced steam-power for agricultural machinery, and improved transport has led to the development of a world market for some agricultural products. The GREEN REVOLUTION saw increased crop production in developing countries. From 1965 to the early 1990s, world cereal production increased by over 70 per cent. Thus India, for example, which formerly suffered regularly from FAMINE and was forced to spend scarce foreign exchange on food imports is now self-sufficient in food although its population has doubled since independence in 1947. AGROCHEMICALS were being used in huge quantities by the 1960s, but since that time the hazards of indiscriminate pesticide use have led to the development of other strategies such as the breeding of disease-resistant plant strains and the use of biological methods of pest control favoured by ORGANIC FARMERS. Genetic development of plant strains and intensive ANIMAL BREEDING have greatly increased the productivity of croplands and livestock in developed countries.

Agrippa, Marcus Vipsanius (63–12 BC) Roman general. Augustus' adviser and son-in-law, he played an important part in the naval victories over Mark Antony, and held commands in western and eastern provinces of the empire.

agrochemical A chemical produced specifically for use in farming. Agrochemicals include FERTILIZERS to increase plant growth, and INSECTICIDES and HERBICIDES to control agents that cause plant disease or damage crops during growth or storage. Agrochemicals are also used to control such physical processes as fermentation in the making of SILAGE. There is public concern over the widespread use of agrochemicals because many are toxic to humans, they persist in the food chain, and they can cause build-up of high concentrations of phosphates, nitrates, and other potentially harmful substances in water supplies.

Aguascalientes **▶1** A state of central Mexico that takes its name from the numerous hot springs that exist; area 5,471 sq km (2,217 sq miles); pop. (1990) 719,650. The economy of the state is largely based on its ranches, vineyards, and orchards. **▶2** Its capital, a health resort in the Sierra Madre Occidental north-east of Guadalajara; pop. (1990) 506,380. The town is noted for its catacombs which were built before the arrival of the Spanish in 1522.

Aguinaldo, Emilio (1869–1964) Filipino nationalist leader. He became active in the nationalist movement in the early 1890s and led an armed uprising against Spanish rule (1895–96). He returned during the Spanish–American War (1898) and organized another guerrilla campaign, but, after the US victory, his nationalist aspirations resulted in war with American forces (1899–1901). Finally accepting US rule, he waged a peaceful campaign for independence for the next four decades before collaborating with the Japanese during World War II. Briefly imprisoned by the Americans in 1945, he retired from active politics after his release.

Agulhas, Cape The southernmost tip of the African continent, its name (derived from the Portuguese for 'needles') describing the sharp-edged reefs and sunken rocks extending from the shore. It defines the official boundary between the Atlantic and Indian Oceans and marks the northern end of the Agulhas Plateau, a major submarine ridge. It also lends its name to the Agulhas Current, a warm surface current that is part of the westerly-moving South Equatorial Current. Offshore the Agulhas Banks provide good fishing grounds.

Ahab (9th century BC) Second king of the Omri dynasty in northern Israel *c.*869–*c.*850 BC. He campaigned in alliance with Syria against Assyria, but was defeated at the Battle of Qarqar (853 BC). Three years later he allied with Jehoshaphat, King of Judah, to regain Transjordan from the Syrians. Although temporarily uniting the kingdoms, Ahab was defeated and killed. His wife Jezebel was a Phoenician from Tyre. While the marriage brought political advantage, it introduced Phoenician traditions into Hebrew life and religion, and Ahab was publicly denounced by the prophet ELIJAH for attempting to unite the Canaanites and Israelites in the worship of Phoenician gods.

ahimsā (Sanskrit, 'not-desiring-violence') An important Indian concept which encourages respect for all life. It is most commonly expressed through VEGETARIANISM. Jain practice prohibits any activity (such as farming) which may cause harm. Buddhist doctrine condemns killing and encourages compassion for all life. Many Buddhists still eat meat, however; meat or fish may be eaten as long as there was no intent on the part of the eater to kill the animal. *Ahimsā* formed the basis of Mahatma Gandhi's policy of non-violent non-cooperation or *satyagraha.*

Ahmadabad (or **Ahmedabad**) An industrial city in the state of Gujarat in western India, on the River Sabarmati; pop. (1991) 2,873,000. Founded in 1411 by Ahmed Shah, Ahmadabad has developed into one of the leading industrial cities of India, specializing in textiles.

Ahmadnagar (or **Ahmednagar**) A commercial and industrial city in Maharashtra state, west-central India, on the River Sina, between Pune and Aurangabad; pop. (1991) 221,700.

Ahriman (or **Angra Mainyu**) In the *Avesta,* the sacred book of the Zoroastrians, the destructive, evil spirit and opponent of the spirit of wisdom, Ahura Mazda, by whom, after 9,000 years, it is believed he will eventually be overcome. Ahriman and his followers, the malevolent *devas,* whom he created as counterparts to Ahura Mazda's good spirits, the *amesha spentas,* are considered the source of all evil, death, suffering, and destruction in the world. Ahriman's principal epithet is *Druj* (Ancient Persian 'the lie').

Ahura Mazda (or **Ormazd**) The creator god of ancient Iran, in particular of Zoroastrianism. Elevated to a supreme position by the Achaemenian dynasty (*c.*550–330 BC), Ahura Mazda was considered to be the creator of the Universe and the cosmic order who, according to the prophet Zoroaster (7th–6th century BC), created the twin spirits of Spenta Mainyu, who chose truth, light, and life, and Angra Mainyu (see AHRIMAN), who chose the lie, darkness, and death. The Earth is the battleground between the two.

Ahvenanmaa Islands The Finnish name for the ÅLAND ISLANDS in the Gulf of Bothnia.

Aidan, St (died 651) Irish missionary. While a monk in the monastery at Iona, he was assigned the mission of Christianizing Northumbria by the Northumbrian king Oswald (*c.*604–41). Aidan founded a church and monastery at Lindisfarne in 635 and became its first bishop; he also established a school for training missionaries of the Celtic Church. He later founded further churches and monasteries in Northumbria.

Aids (*a*cquired *i*mmune *d*eficiency *s*yndrome) The complex of conditions that arise as a result of infection by the human immunodeficiency virus (HIV). There are two types of HIV: HIV-1, which has been shown to be the primary cause of Aids in Western countries, and HIV-2, which is more common in Africa. HIV destroys cells of the immune system (see IMMUNOLOGY), notably helper T cells (which manufacture antibodies), and macrophages (which engulf bacteria and other foreign bodies), causing progressively diminished IMMUNITY (IMMUNODEFICIENCY). HIV is a retrovirus: its genetic material is RNA (see DNA), from which it makes DNA within the host cell by means of the enzyme reverse transcriptase. This viral DNA is then incorporated into the host cell chromosomes, where it may lie dormant for many years before being activated to make new copies of the virus. Following initial infection, mild feverish illness may occur, which is commonly mistaken for influenza or glandular fever, and patients may recover completely. HIV-antibodies are formed at this stage, and are used to diagnose the presence of HIV-infection. Patients may then remain symptom-free for months or years, during which the virus remains latent. Thereafter, reactivation and progressive immunodeficiency leads to the development of the so-called Aids-related complex (ARC), which includes weight loss, swollen lymph nodes, fever, night sweats, and persistent diarrhoea. Further progression may lead to the complete spectrum of conditions associated with Aids. These include opportunistic infections, such as *Pneumocystis carinii* pneumonia and TUBERCULOSIS; types of cancer, such as Kaposi's sarcoma; and brain disease, such as MENINGITIS.

The mean period between first infection and the development of Aids itself is ten years in North America and Europe, but only three to four years in developing countries, probably because of the different diseases prevalent in different countries and the availability of drugs to treat them. The HIV virus is spread primarily by infected blood and blood products, cervical secretions, occasionally breast milk, and by semen. The syndrome was first recognized in 1981, when a common pattern of symptoms was observed among a small number of homosexual men who had died in the USA. The World Health Organization (WHO) estimates that between 1981 and 1991 about 1.5 million Aids cases occurred. By the year 2000 it is predicted that 40 million people will be infected with the HIV virus and that the number of victims of full-blown Aids will probably approach 10 million, of whom 90 per cent will be from developing countries. In industrialized countries, most cases of Aids in the early years of the epidemic were the result of homosexual contact or the sharing of needles by intravenous drug users; men far outnumbered women with the disease. The transmission of the virus is increasingly through heterosexual contact and the number of HIV-positive women is growing. In developing countries reporting high numbers of cases, SEXUALLY-TRANSMITTED DISEASES and poorer general health are thought to be contributing factors to the epidemic spread of Aids among the heterosexual urban population. The countries of central and eastern Africa are hardest hit. In Rwanda, Tanzania, and Uganda 5 to 20 per cent of the sexually active age-group is infected with the HIV virus and in certain risk groups, such as prostitutes, the rate can exceed 80 per cent. The other major transmission route in certain developing countries with a high number of infected women, is via the placenta, from an infected mother to her unborn baby, during childbirth, or during breastfeeding.

Until a cure or a vaccine for Aids can be found, the main strategies for prevention and control are information, counselling, and education, all of which imply major changes in sexual behaviour and drug-injecting practices. A combination of zidovudine (AZT) and other antiviral drugs slows the progression of HIV infection to the complete spectrum of Aids, although supportive care and treatment of opportunistic infections constitutes the main part of treatment.

aikido See MARTIAL ARTS.

Ailey, Alvin (1931–89) US dancer, choreographer, and director. He trained with Horton and then with GRAHAM and Holm, going on to form a company in 1958 to perform his own works. He blended primitive, modern, and JAZZ elements of dance with a concern for black rural America, as in his signature work *Revelations* (1960).

Ailsa Craig A small rocky island in the Firth of Clyde, opposite the town of Girvan in south-west Scotland. Its granite rock has been used to make curling stones.

Ain A river that rises in the Jura Mountains of eastern France and flows 194 km (120 miles) southwards to meet the Rhône above Lyon.

Aintree A suburb of Liverpool, in Merseyside, site of a racecourse over which the Grand National steeplechase has been run since 1839.

Ainu A non-Mongoloid people inhabiting the Japanese archipelago whose physical characteristics (light skin colour, round eyes, and exceptionally thick, wavy hair) set them apart dramatically from the majority population of the islands and have stimulated much speculation as to their possible Caucasoid origin, although recent studies suggest close relations with some of the neighbouring Tungusic, Altaic, and Uralic populations of Siberia. Archaeological evidence suggests that the Ainu were resident in the area as early as 5,000 BC, thereby predating the great Mongoloid migrations. Forced by Japanese expansion to retreat to the northernmost islands (i.e. Hokkaido, Sakhalin, and the Kurile Islands) the Ainu are on the verge of cultural extinction and now number *c.*25,000. Of these, only about 10 per cent are 'pure' Ainu.

air-brake A mechanical brake applied by means of the pressure of compressed air; the term is also used for extendible flaps that provide a braking effect on AEROPLANES. Compressed-air brakes are common on lorries and on some railway rolling stock. An engine-driven COMPRESSOR charges an air tank to provide a reservoir of high-pressure air that can be applied to the brake pistons or diaphragms when needed. When this air pressure is released there is a characteristic hiss. Another form of air-brake is a PARACHUTE attached to the tail of an aircraft, which is opened on landing to slow the vehicle.

air brush An instrument for spraying paint or varnish in a fine mist by means of compressed air, patented in 1893. An air brush looks rather like an outsize fountain pen and is operated in a similar fashion, the pressure of the forefinger on a lever regulating the air supply. It can be controlled so as to give large areas of flat colour, delicate gradations of tone, or a fairly fine line.

air conditioning Environmental control of the interior of a building (or other enclosed space such as a car) by the mechanical circulation of air at the desired temperature and relative humidity. An air conditioning plant includes a chiller, heater, humidifier and dehumidifier, air filters, and circulation fans. The air is distributed through the building via ducts above ceilings or under raised floors; stale air is returned to the air-conditioning plant for recycling via a further duct system. The interior of the building is sealed against the external atmosphere (having no openable windows). In hot climates, solar heat-gain through windows and CURTAIN WALLS is considerable, and large amounts of energy are required to keep the internal environment comfortable. Recently, problems have arisen from bacterial contamination of air-conditioning, and it has been suggested that these systems are responsible for 'sick-building syndrome', a high incidence of illness in office workers, attributed to the immediate working environment.

aircraft See AEROPLANE; HELICOPTER; MILITARY AIRCRAFT.

aircraft carrier A WARSHIP designed to operate aircraft at sea. Carriers are usually fitted with a flight-deck for launching and landing, and have hangars below for stowage and servicing of aircraft. The first aircraft carriers, before World War I, were converted merchant ships or warships carrying seaplanes; later some CRUISERS were converted, by the addition of a flight-deck over the foredeck. Towards the end of World War I, carriers were built with a flight-deck running the whole length of the ship, capable of handling the faster and heavier aircraft being developed. They were fitted with arrester wires (often spring-loaded) to enable the aircraft's momentum on landing to be absorbed within the length of the deck. With the introduction of jet-engined aircraft an angled deck was developed, and a steam catapult permitted more efficient and faster handling of aircraft during operations. The most modern carriers have a displacement of around 90,000 tonnes and accommodate over 100 aircraft. The development of VTOL AIRCRAFT and the increasing use of HELICOPTERS have now reduced the need for long flight-decks.

air-cushion vehicle See HOVERCRAFT.

Airdrie An industrial town in central Scotland, 18 km (11 miles) east of Glasgow; pop. (1981) 45,750.

Airedale The upper valley of the River Aire which rises in the West Yorkshire Pennines, northern England, and flows 123 km (70 miles) south-eastwards through Leeds to meet the River Ouse near Goole.

Airedale terrier See DOG.

airforce The armed service concerned with attack and defence in the air. Aircraft were first used in World War I to locate targets for artillery on the Western Front, but from 1916 onwards they were developed for bombing, while rival fighter aircraft engaged in aerial dogfights both in France and in the Mesopotamian Campaign, where aircraft were also invaluable for reconnaissance. Airships were also constructed, especially by Germany, which used Zeppelin airships for bombing attacks against civilian targets. After disastrous crashes in the 1930s, however, airships lost popularity. Very rapid development in aircraft design between the wars meant that World War II began with both sides possessing formidable bomber and fighter capability. During the war dive-bombing techniques as well as heavily armed bombers for massed high altitude air raids (BOMBING OFFENSIVES) were developed, while the invention of radar assisted defenders in locating attacking aircraft. Large troop-carrying planes were also introduced, together with the helicopter, which became a key weapon in later wars in Korea, Vietnam, and Afghanistan. The Cold War, from the late 1940s to 1990, saw the deployment by the superpowers of strategic nuclear bombers and intercontinental ballistic missiles (ICBMs). With the advent of supersonic flight, the high costs of increasingly sophisticated aircraft since World War II have led to the design of aircraft that each fulfil several roles, often jointly developed by a consortium of nations. Air power was decisive in the GULF WAR of 1991. This saw the first large-scale use of several innovations, such as laser-guided bombs and computer-guided cruise missiles, that were able to pinpoint and destroy specific targets. A further development was the use of the Stealth bomber, which was designed to evade and destroy radar defences.

airlock A two-door chamber separating spaces of differing air pressures. When someone enters from one pressure region, the door on that side is sealed and the pressure in the chamber is changed, allowing access to the other pressure region with minimal loss of air. Airlocks are used in buildings in which parts of the interior are kept slightly above atmospheric pressure in order to maintain extremely clean environments, for example when making electronic components. Some laboratories are kept slightly below atmospheric pressure to prevent the escape of dangerous organisms. Other important uses of airlocks are in DEEP-SEA AND DIVING TECHNOLOGY and in SPACE EXPLORATION.

air pollution Pollution caused by the release into the atmosphere of gases, or finely dispersed solid or liquid particles, at rates too great to dissipate or to be incorporated into the land or water. Natural causes of air pollution include dust storms, forest or grass fires, and volcanic activity. Air pollution caused by human activity comes from a variety of sources. Motor vehicle emissions are responsible for major urban air pollution, in particular smog (smoke plus fog), and lead pollution arising from the addition of LEAD TETRAETHYL to petrol. The burning of FOSSIL FUELS in power stations is also a major source of air pollution. One of the main problems arising from the combustion of fossil fuels is the GREENHOUSE EFFECT resulting mainly from the production of carbon dioxide. Pesticides have been discovered in Antarctica, where they have never been used, indicating that the atmosphere can carry pollutants over large distances. Radioactive pollution is a continual threat.

Efforts are being made to reduce air pollution from some sources. Air pollution from volatile hydrocarbons may be reduced by the development of solvent-free PAINTS. Devices such as the CATALYTIC CONVERTER are used to reduce carbon monoxide and hydrocarbon levels in vehicle exhaust emissions, and the use of lead-free petrol is mandatory in some countries and strongly encouraged in others. Low-pollution methods for burning fossil fuels are encouraged, such as the elimination of sulphur gases (ACID RAIN), although a more radical shift to less polluting forms of power generation – WIND and SOLAR POWER, for example – could be used to reduce air pollution significantly if it were possible to produce sufficient power for modern needs by these methods.

airport A defined area on land or water for the take-off and landing of aircraft, with facilities for their shelter, servicing, and repair, and for passengers and cargo. While some airports are quite small and serve the requirements of perhaps only one company (for example, at an oilfield), others operate to deal with the requirements of international airlines. Such large international airports cover vast areas: London's Heathrow Airport, for example, covers 1,141 ha (2,819 acres). The main runways are positioned to face the prevailing winds, with a cross-runway interconnecting them in many cases. The control tower, which supervises the landing and take-off of aircraft as well as the movement of aircraft and vehicles on the runways, taxi-ways, and aprons, is sited so as to overlook the majority of the airport (although AIR-TRAFFIC CONTROL relies heavily on RADAR). Around the airport are positioned servicing hangars, passenger terminals, and cargo facilities. These have to be easily accessible by road and rail.

airship A power-driven, lighter-than-air aircraft developed from the BALLOON. Practicable designs for steerable, cigar-shaped airships were first produced in 1784 by the French military engineer J.-B.-M.-C. Meusnier de la Place. GIFFARD, another Frenchman, developed the first airship actually to fly (1852). In 1894 the French government financed a more successful, electric-powered airship, but it was not until the advent of the internal-combustion engine that airship developments really began. Early airships had non-rigid, gas-filled fabric envelopes. Later developments were the semi-rigid design, with a structural fore-and-aft keel; and rigid airships comprising an external skeleton covered by light fabric surrounding a series of internal gas-filled cells. Large, rigid airships with light-alloy frames were developed principally in Germany by von ZEPPELIN. They were successfully used for military and passenger purposes between 1900 and 1930, but a series of disasters in the 1930s, attributable to the highly flammable nature of the hydrogen-filled envelope, led to their decline. Airships using non-flammable helium were used on the east coast of the USA for early warning until 1961, and have found applications since the 1970s in advertising and aerial photography. Since 1987 the US Coast Guard has operated sophisticated airships for coastal patrol. See also FLIGHT, HISTORY OF MANNED.

air-traffic control A system for controlling the safe, orderly, and speedy movement of aircraft at take-off and landing, during flight, and while on the ground at an AIRPORT. Once an aircraft takes off, its flight is controlled by the local air traffic control centre. The pilot flies a prearranged course and height, which is monitored by RADAR, and progress reports are made by the pilot at regular intervals. At some point *en route* the pilot will be handed on to the next air traffic control centre, and this process continues until the aircraft reaches its destination, where the pilot will receive detailed landing instructions.

Airy, Sir George Biddell (1801–92) British astronomer and geophysicist. He investigated the diffraction pattern of a point source of light and devised cylindrical lenses to correct for astigmatism. In geophysics, he proposed the concept of isostasy to account for the gravitational anomalies associated with mountain masses, and gave an improved estimate of the Earth's density. Airy was Astronomer Royal for forty-six years.

Aisne A river that rises in the Argonne area of north-east France and flows 240 km (150 miles) west and north-west to meet the River Oise near Compiègne.

Aitken, William Maxwell See BEAVERBROOK.

Aix-en-Provence An ancient cultural and commercial city of Provence in southern France, 30 km (19 miles) north of Marseille; pop. (1990) 126,850. Founded in 123 BC by the Roman Consul Caius Sextius, the city has long been famous for its thermal springs. A major centre of Provençal culture, it has many 17th- and 18th-century buildings, an 11th-century cathedral and a university founded in 1409. Aix-en-Provence was the home of the painter Paul Cezanne (1839–1906). Its industries include food processing, wine-making and electrical equipment, and tourism.

Aix-la-Chapelle The French name for the German town of AACHEN.

Aix-la-Chapelle, Treaty of (1748) The treaty that concluded the War of the AUSTRIAN SUCCESSION. It restored conquered territory to its original owners, with a few exceptions. The terms were drawn up by the British and French and reluctantly accepted by Empress MARIA THERESA of Austria, who had to abandon Silesia to FREDERICK II of Prussia. In Italy Don Philip, the younger son of Philip V of Spain, received Parma. This treaty was a temporary truce in the Anglo-French conflict in India and North America. In North America colonists unwillingly ceded the French fortress of Louisburg, in order to secure the return of Madras to Britain. Prussia's rise to the rank of a great power was strongly resented by Austria. The treaty left many issues of conflict unresolved and war (the SEVEN YEARS WAR) broke out again eight years later.

Aix-les-Bains A spa town in the Savoy, south-east France, situated on the southeast shore of Lake Bourget; pop. (1990) 24,830.

Ajaccio A seaport on the west coast of Corsica, overlooking the Bay of Ajaccio; the capital of Corse-du-Sud department; pop. (1990) 59,320. Napoleon I was born here on 15 August 1769.

Ajanta Caves A series of 29 caves in the state of Maharashtra, south-central India, containing Buddhist frescoes and sculptures of the 1st century BC–7th century AD, with the finest examples belonging to the Gupta period (5th–6th century AD). The caves are cut into the steep rock-face of a gorge on a bend of the River Waghore.

Ajax In Greek mythology, a warrior at the Trojan War, second in prowess on the Greek side only to Achilles. After Achilles' death, Ajax coveted his armour, and when this was awarded to Odysseus he went mad with resentment and killed himself.

Ajman The smallest of the seven emirates of the United Arab Emirates; area 250 sq km (96 sq miles); pop. (1985) 64,320; capital, Ajman. Ajman comprises territory on the south-west coast of the Persian Gulf and exclaves at Masfut, in the Hajar Mts. to the south-east, and Manama, east of Ajman town. Fishing, pearling, and dhow building are traditional industries that survive alongside oilfield service industries such as engineering and ship repair.

Ajmer An industrial city in the state of Rajasthan,

north-west India; situated by Ana Sagar, an artificial lake created by the damming of the River Luni in the 12th century; pop. (1991) 402,000. Ajmer was the capital of the former state of the same name which was merged with Rajasthan in 1956. The Dargah tomb, burial place of a Sufi saint who came to Ajmer in 1192, is an important place of Muslim pilgrimage. It has large railway workshops and many light industries.

Akali (Punjabi, 'worshipper of the Timeless One') A militaristic order of Sikh ascetics. The sect dates from before the formation of the KHALSA by GOBIND SINGH in 1699, but Akalis became its most militant adherents, skilled in fighting and greatly feared. They were at their most prominent under Ranjit Singh (1790–1839), who set up a powerful Sikh kingdom in the Punjab. The name was revived in the 1920s during the struggle to regain control of the GURDWARAS, or Sikh temples. The *Akali Dal* ('Immortal Army') assisted in the return of *Gurdwara* custodianship to the Sikhs, and since then has played a part in the politics of the Punjab, becoming more sectarian and militant in recent years.

Akbar, Jalaludin Muhammad (known as **Akbar the Great**) (1542–1605) Mogul emperor of India 1556–1605. Akbar expanded the Mogul empire to incorporate northern India, and established administrative efficiency and a coherent commercial system. He was the first ruler of India to promote religious and racial toleration. Akbar abolished slavery, prohibited the practice of suttee, legitimized the remarriage of widows, and banned polygamy except in cases of infertility.

Akhenaten (or **Akhenaton**, **Ikhnaton**) (14th century BC) Egyptian pharaoh of the 18th dynasty, reigned 1379–1362 BC. The husband of Nefertiti, he came to the throne as Amenhotep IV, and after six years introduced the monotheistic solar cult of Aten, the Sun disc, with the king as sole intermediary, changing his name to Akhenaten. The capital of Egypt was moved from Thebes to his newly built city of Akhetaten (now Tell el-Amarna). He was succeeded by his son-in-law, Tutankhamen, who abandoned the new religion early in his reign.

Akhmatova, Anna (pseudonym of Anna Andreevna Gorenko) (1889–1966) Russian poet. A member of the Acmeist group of poets with Osip Mandelstam, Akhmatova favoured concrete detail, direct expression, and precision of language as a reaction against the mysticism of contemporary symbolist poetry. The personal and Christian tone of *Anno Domini* (1922), however, contributed to her official disfavour, which was to last for over thirty years. Her works include *Poem without a Hero* (1940–62) and *Requiem* (1940).

Akkad (or **Agade**) A city on the Euphrates (as yet undiscovered) which gave its name to an ancient northern Semitic kingdom, traditionally founded by Sargon (2334–2279 BC) in north-central Mesopotamia (modern Iraq). Its power extended over Babylonia, Assyria, and Syria, and even penetrated into Asia Minor, until it was overwhelmed by invading tribes from the east *c.*2150 BC. The Akkadian language, used in Mesopotamia from about 3,000 BC and known from cuneiform inscriptions, is the oldest recorded Hamito-Semitic language. Two dialects of Akkadian, Assyrian and Babylonian, were spoken in the Middle East for the next 2,000 years before they gave way to Aramaic.

Akmola See AQMOLA.

Akola A cotton-manufacturing city in the state of Maharashtra, central India; pop. (1991) 327,900. It is also a major grain-trading centre.

Akron The county seat of Summit county, north-eastern Ohio, USA, on the Little Cuyahoga River; pop. (1990) 223,000. Once described as the 'rubber capital of the world', Akron was for many years a major centre of the rubber and tyre industry after the opening of the first factory in 1870; it now has numerous light industries.

Aksum (or **Axum**) A town in the province of Tigré in northern Ethiopia. It was a religious centre and the capital of a powerful kingdom during the 1st–6th centuries AD. According to ancient Aksumite tradition their kings were descended from Menelik (legendary son of Solomon and Sheba) who brought to the country the Ark of the Covenant containing the original Tablets of the Law given to Moses.

Aksyonov, Vasily (Pavlovich) (1932–) Russian novelist. He was the foremost among the 'young prose' writers who revitalized the short story during the Khrushchev thaw (1956–64). Increasingly in conflict with the authorities, especially because his novel *The Burn* (published abroad 1979) was denied publication, he left the Soviet Union in 1981 and became a US citizen.

Aktyubinsk The former name of AQTÖBE in Kazakhstan.

Akureyri A fishing port in Nordurland region, Iceland, at the head of Eyja Fjord; pop. (1990) 14,170. Founded in the late 1700s by a Danish trader, Akureyri is now the largest settlement in northern Iceland. Its shipyard is the largest in the country. The Icelandic poet laureate and dramatist Matthías Jochumsson (1835–1920), author of Iceland's national anthem, lived in Akureyri.

Alabama A state in the south-eastern USA bordering on the Gulf of Mexico; area 133,915 sq km (51,705 sq miles); pop. (1990) 4,040,587; capital, Montgomery. The largest cities are Birmingham, Mobile, Montgomery, and Huntsville. Alabama is also known as the Yellowhammer State, the Heart of Dixie, and the Camellia State. Visited by Spanish explorers in the mid-16th century, and later settled by the French, it passed to Britain in 1763 and to the USA in 1783, becoming the 22nd state of the USA in 1819. Its chief products are lumber, pulp, paper, electronics, chemicals, textiles, motor tyres, fabricated metals, cement, and processed food. Alabama is divided into 67 counties.

alabaster A fine-grained, banded variety of the mineral GYPSUM. White or pale reddish-brown in colour, it is formed by direct precipitation from salt-rich waters, often from hot volcanic springs. The alabaster of the ancient world, called 'oriental alabaster' or onyx marble, occurs both in spring deposits and in cave formations. The ease with which alabaster can be carved and polished has led to its widespread use in sculpture and the decorative arts.

Alain-Fournier (pseudonym of Henri-Alban Fournier) (1886–1914) French novelist. A literary columnist, he completed only one novel before he was killed in action in World War I. The book, *Le Grand Meaulnes* (1913), is a lyrical semi-autobiographical narrative set in the countryside of Alain-Fournier's adolescence.

Alamein, El, Battle of (October–November 1942) A critical battle in Egypt in World War II. In June 1942, the British took up a defensive position in Egypt. One flank rested on the Mediterranean at El Alamein and the other on the salt marshes of the Qattara Depression. In August, General MONTGOMERY was appointed to command the defending 8th Army. He launched an offensive in which, after a heavy artillery preparation, about 1,200 tanks advanced, followed by infantry, against the German Afrika Korps commanded by General ROMMEL. Rommel was handicapped by a grave fuel shortage and had only about 500 tanks. The outnumbered Germans never regained the initiative. Rommel managed to withdraw most of his men back into Libya, but this battle marked the beginning of the end of the NORTH AFRICAN CAMPAIGN for Germany.

Alamo, the A mission fort in San Antonio, Texas, and scene of a siege during the Texas Revolution against Mexico of 1836. A Mexican army of 3,000 led by Santa Anna besieged the fort held by fewer than 200 men, under the joint command of William B. Travis and James Bowie. The siege lasted from 24 February to 6 March, when the Mexicans finally breached the walls. Travis, Bowie, Davy CROCKETT, and all their men were killed. The defence of the Alamo became the symbol of Texan resistance.

Alanbrooke, Alan Francis Brooke, 1st Viscount (1883–1963) British field-marshal. He served with distinction during World War I, and in the 1930s was noted as an artillery expert. In World War II he was a corps commander during the withdrawal from DUNKIRK. Later, as Chief of the Imperial General Staff and Chairman of the Chiefs of Staff Committee (1941–46), he represented the service chiefs in discussions with Churchill. As Churchill's chief adviser on military strategy, he accompanied him to all his conferences with Roosevelt and Stalin.

Åland Islands (Finnish **Ahvenanmaa**) A group of islands in the Gulf of Bothnia forming an autonomous region of Finland; area 1,552 sq km (600 sq miles); pop. (1990) 24,600. The group includes more than 6,500 islands and rocky islets of which only 80 are inhabited. The only town is the capital, Mariehamn (Maarianhamina). Swedish is the main language. In 1809 the islands became part of Russia, eventually becoming a demilitarized zone under the Treaty that ended the Crimean War. In 1921 they were assigned to Finland by the League of Nations. Shipping, tourism, and agriculture are the chief industries.

Alania The name adopted in 1994 by the Caucasian Republic of North Ossetia in Russia. See OSSETIA.

Alarcón, Pedro Antonio de (1833–91) Spanish novelist and short-story writer. His best-known work, the humorous short story *The Three-Cornered Hat* (1874), was the source for Manuel de Falla's ballet and Hugo Wolf's opera, both of the same name.

Alarcón y Mendoza See RUIZ DE ALARCÓN Y MENDOZA.

Alaric I (*c*.370–410) King of the VISIGOTHS. He commanded THEODOSIUS' Gothic allies and helped put down the Western usurper emperor Eugenius. On Theodosius' death the Eastern and Western Roman empires were formally divided. Alaric revolted against the rule of CONSTANTINOPLE and moved with his people in search of homelands. He invaded Italy in 401. Twice defeated by Stilicho, the Roman general, he entered a treaty of alliance with him. After the execution of Stilicho by Emperor Honorius, Alaric repudiated the pact and ravaged Italy, laying siege to Rome three times. The city fell in 410. That same year he planned invasions of Sicily and Africa, but his fleet was destroyed by storms. He died at Cosenza.

Alaska The largest state of the USA, in the extreme north-west of North America, with coasts in the Arctic Ocean, Bering Sea, and North Pacific; area 1,530,700 sq km (591,004 sq miles); pop. (1990) 550,000; capital, Juneau. The largest settlements are Anchorage, Kenai, and Fairbanks. About one-third of Alaska lies within the Arctic Circle. It was discovered by Russian explorers (under Vitus Bering) in 1741, and further explored by Cook, Vancouver, and others during the last quarter of the 18th century. The territory was purchased from Russia in 1867 for the sum of $2 million and in 1896 the famous Gold Rush began. Alaska became the 49th state of the USA in 1959. Oil, gas, timber, fishing, and tourism are the principal industries.

Alaska Current A warm current that flows northwards then westwards in the Gulf of Alaska.

Alaska Highway A road, originally known as the Alcan Highway (ALaska–CANada), that links the Canadian town of Dawson Creek in British Columbia with Fairbanks, Alaska, passing through Fort St John, Fort Nelson, and Whitehorse. Built as a military supply route by US Army engineers in 1942, the highway was later improved and realigned with a total length of 2,450 km (1,523 miles).

Alaska Purchase (1867) The purchase by the USA of Alaska from Russia for $200,000 (less than five cents a hectare) arranged by William H. Seward. It remained an unorganized territory until 1884. Despite extensive copper and gold discoveries there was little population growth.

Alawites (or **Alawi**, **Nusairis**) An offshoot of the Shiite Islamic faith with beliefs that include elements of Christianity and ancient eastern cults. In Syria, where they took power in 1966, Alawites account for an estimated 8–9 per cent of the population.

Alba, Fernando Alvarez de Toledo, Duke of (*c*.1507–82) Spanish statesman and general. He rose to prominence in the armies of Emperor Charles V. A stickler for discipline and a master of logistics, he contributed significantly to the defeat of the German Protestants at the battle of Mühlberg (1547). Philip II sent him as governor-general to deal with unrest in the Netherlands in 1567, but his notorious 'Council of Blood' executed or banished over a thousand men, and was responsible for sparking off the Dutch Revolts against Spanish rule. He was recalled to Spain at his own request in 1573, and in 1580 Philip gave him command of the forces which conquered Portugal.

Albacete Capital of Albacete province, south-east Spain, an agricultural centre once noted for the manufacture of knives; pop. (1991) 134,584.

albacore See TUNA.

Alba Iulia A marketing city in west-central Romania, to the north of the Transylvanian Alps; pop. (1989) 72,330. Founded by the Romans in the 2nd century AD, it was the capital of Transylvania and for a short time (1599–1601) capital of the united principalities of Transylvania, Moldavia, and Walachia. It is the centre for a wine-making region.

Alban, St (3rd century) The first British Christian martyr. A pagan of Verulamium (now St Albans, Herts.), he was converted and baptized by a fugitive priest whom he sheltered. When soldiers searched his house, he put on the priest's cloak and was arrested and condemned to death. Feast day, 22 June.

Albania A small country in south-eastern Europe, on the Adriatic coast of the Balkan Peninsula, with Montenegro, Kosovo, and Macedonia to its north and east, and Greece to its south.

Physical. Its coastal plain is marshy in the north but mostly fertile. Inland are rugged mountains,

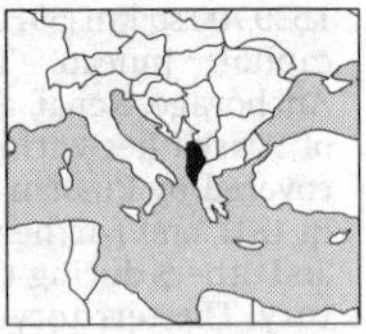

forested hills, and fast-flowing rivers. It also has the shores of three large lakes within its frontiers. In winter the BORA blows cold from the north and in summer the SIROCCO blows Saharan dust over the crops. Rainfall is generally moderate.

Economy. Formerly a centrally PLANNED ECONOMY under communism, since 1992 Albania has undertaken economic reforms, which include the privatization of farmland, state enterprises, and housing; the abolition of price subsidies; and the liberalization of trade. The economy is primarily agricultural, but crude oil is exported, and petroleum-refining is an important industry. The main crops are wheat, maize, potatoes, sugar-beet, citrus fruits, grapes, olives, and tobacco. Chromite (chromium ore), copper, nickel, and coal are mined. Up to 80 per cent of Albania's power is hydroelectric, although the drought in the 1990s has affected both power supplies and agriculture. Industry, which is limited, is in great need of modernization and has suffered from a ban on foreign investment.

History. As part of the Ottoman empire from the 15th century, Albania was noted for the military dictatorship of Ali Pasha (*c.*1744–1822), whose court was described by the English poet Byron in *Childe Harold*. Nationalist resistance was crushed in 1831, but discontent persisted and a national league was created during the Russo-Turkish War of 1877–78. It became an independent state as a result of the BALKAN WARS in 1912, and after a brief period as a republic became a monarchy under King ZOG in 1928. Invaded by Italy in 1939, it became a Communist state under Enver Hoxha after World War II. Under the strong influence of the Soviet Union until a rift in 1958, it became closely aligned with China until MAO ZEDONG's death in 1976. Albania was expelled from the WARSAW PACT in 1968, but remained Stalinist in policy and outlook until the death of Hoxha in 1985. From then on its isolationism began to ease, with cautious steps to restore democracy in 1990. The Communists (renamed the Socialist Party) held power in the first free elections in 1991, but were defeated by the Democratic Party in 1992. Elections in 1996 saw the return of the Democratic Party, but were widely suspected of being held under fraudulent conditions. Early in 1997 the collapse of several companies involved in pyramid investment schemes triggered anti-government protests and rioting. A state of emergency was declared, the government resigned, and a Socialist-led coalition came to power after elections in July 1997.

Capital: Tirana
Area: 28,748 sq km (11,100 sq mi)
Population: 3,300,000 (1991)
Currency: 1 lek = 100 qindars
Religions: Non-religious 55.4%; Muslim 20.5%; atheist 18.7%; Eastern Orthodox 5.4%
Ethnic Groups: Albanian, with Greek and gypsy minorities
Languages: Albanian (official); Greek; Macedonian; Romany
International Organizations: UN; CSCE; North Atlantic Co-operation Council

Albanian language An INDO-EUROPEAN LANGUAGE spoken by 3 million people in Albania and southern Yugoslavia; there are also small groups of speakers in Greece and southern Italy. It is not closely related to any other language, though it may be connected with the ancient language spoken in Dacia (present-day Romania) before the coming of Latin speakers to the area. The earliest Albanian document dates from the late 15th century, and there is no real literature until the 18th century. An official Roman alphabet has been in use since 1909. There are two distinct dialect groups, Gheg in the north and Tosk in the south, separated by the River Shkumbin. These are not on the whole mutually intelligible, except for less extreme forms. The official standard language in Albania is based on Tosk.

Albany ▶1 A seaport and resort on the south coast of the state of Western Australia, on the Ataturk Entrance of King George Sound; pop. (1991) 18,830. Originally named Frederickstown after the Duke of York and Albany, it was founded as a penal colony in 1826. **▶2** The capital of New York State, on the Hudson River; pop. (1990) 101,080. Combined with Shenectady and Troy it forms a metropolitan area with a population of 874,300. It was settled by the Dutch in 1614 and surrendered to the British in 1664. The city grew with the development of the Champlain and Erie canals in the 1820s. Today it is an administrative and cultural centre with many old buildings. It is also an important river port and transshipment centre with oil tanks, machine shops, foundries, breweries, and numerous light industries.

albatross A long-winged oceanic bird that has a wingspan of 2–3.5 m (6–12 feet), and a distinctive gliding and soaring flight. The albatross family, Diomedeidae, contains nine species of the Southern Hemisphere, inhabiting temperate and Antarctic waters, and three tropical species of the central Pacific. They all feed on surface-caught fish and squid. They breed on windswept islands, laying single eggs, like their closest relatives the petrels.

albedo The proportion of light or radiation reflected by a surface. Generally, white objects reflect more than dark ones. The mean albedo or reflectivity of the Earth's surface is about 30 per cent, varying from up to 95 per cent on fresh clean snow to 10 per cent on dark peaty soil.

Albee, Edward (Franklin) (1928–) US dramatist. The leading American representative of the Theatre of the ABSURD, he first came to public attention with the short works *The Zoo Story* (1959), *The Death of Bessie Smith* (1960), and *The American Dream* (1961). His best-known work, *Who's Afraid of Virginia Woolf?* (1962), is a three-act play in which a college professor, his wife, and a second couple eventually achieve catharsis through the verbal torturing of one another. He found success more elusive after the early 1960s, although both *A Delicate Balance* (1966) and *Seascape* (1975) won Pulitzer Prizes. *Marriage Play* (1986) was more abstract than his earlier works.

Albemarle, George, 1st Duke of See MONCK.

Albéniz, Isaac (Manuel Francisco) (1860–1909) Spanish composer and pianist. He perfected his piano technique with Liszt, but gave up his concert career in 1890, to concentrate on teaching and composition. Apart from the comic opera *The Magic Opal* (1893), his most important works are for the piano. The mature examples use Spanish folk music as their inspiration; their Impressionist qualities influenced Debussy and Ravel.

Alberoni, Giulio (1664–1752) Italian cardinal and statesman. In 1713 he arranged the marriage of the Duke of Parma's niece Elizabeth Farnese with Philip V of Spain. He became effective ruler of Spain in 1715 and strengthened royal power in Spain at the expense of the nobles. His chief aims were to strengthen Spain, nullify the Peace of

UTRECHT, and crush HABSBURG power in Italy. He was doubtful about the wisdom of declaring war on Austria in July 1717 and it proved to be a disastrous decision, mainly because of British and French intervention against Spain, and resulted in his dismissal by Philip in 1719. He retired to Rome.

Albers, Josef (1888–1976) German-born American artist, designer, and teacher. He was a teacher at the Bauhaus from 1923 to 1933, then emigrated to the USA, where he played an important role in disseminating Bauhaus ideas, notably at Black Mountain College, North Carolina (1933–49) and at Yale University (1950–59). His best-known paintings are his severely abstract *Homage to the Square* series (begun in 1950) in which he experimented with colour juxtaposition.

Albert, Prince (1819–61) Consort to Queen Victoria. First cousin of the queen and prince of Saxe-Coburg-Gotha, he revitalized the British court in the first twenty years of his wife's reign. He was one of the driving forces behind the Great Exhibition of 1851; its profits allowed the construction of the Royal Albert Hall (1871) and of museum buildings in South Kensington. In 1861, just before his premature death from typhoid fever, his moderating influence was crucial in keeping Britain out of the American Civil War.

Alberta The westernmost of the three prairie provinces of Canada, bounded on the south by the USA and on the west by the Rocky Mountains; area 661,190 sq km (255,287 sq miles); pop. (1991) 2,522,300; capital, Edmonton. Largest cities, Edmonton, Calgary, Lethbridge, Red Deer, Medicine Hat. Highest peak, Mount Columbia (3,747 m, 12,293 ft). Southern Alberta was once the domain of the Blackfoot nation, settlement by people of European descent taking place largely between 1896 and 1914. Named after the fourth daughter of Queen Victoria, it became a province of Canada in 1905. Coal, oil, gas, timber, grain, and livestock are the chief products, Alberta's greatest period of growth following the development of the petroleum industry after 1947. Among the province's leading tourist attractions are the Calgary Stampede and Banff and Jasper national parks.

Albert Canal A canal in north-east Belgium linking the Meuse and Scheldt rivers, connecting the industrial city of Liège with the port of Antwerp. Built in the 1930s and named after King Albert I, the canal is 128 km (80 miles) long.

Alberti, Leon Battista (1404–72) Italian architect, humanist, painter, and art critic. He wrote the first account of the theory of perspective in the Renaissance in his *Della Pittura* (1435). He is also credited with reawakening interest in Roman architecture, after the publication of his *De Re Aedificatoria* (1485). His own architecture, classical in style, includes the façade of the church of Santa Maria Novella in Florence and San Francesco in Rimini.

Alberti, Rafael (1902–) Spanish poet. His upbringing in an impoverished family and his Jesuit education provided the themes for his major works, and his autobiographical *The Lost Grove* (1959) helps explain many of the allusions in his poems. His early works, *A Sailor Ashore* (1924), *The Lover* (1925), and *The Last Duke of Alba* (1925–26) are inspired by traditional songs and folklore. This soon gives way to a poetry of crisis, first *Tightly Constructed* (1926–27), with its dual influence of Luis de Góngora and the Generation of '27, and then his major work *Concerning the Angels* (1927–28), in which angels represent different forces in the poet's tortured psyche.

Albertus Magnus, St (known as 'Doctor Universalis') (*c*.1200–80) Dominican theologian, philosopher, and scientist. A teacher of St Thomas Aquinas, he was a pioneer in the study of Aristotle and contributed significantly to the comparison of Christian theology and pagan philosophy. His particular interest in the physical sciences, including alchemy, earned him a reputation for magical powers. Feast day, 15 November.

Albi An industrial town in the Midi-Pyrénées region of southern France, on the River Tarn; pop. (1990) 48,700. Its huge Gothic cathedral is famous for its many paintings, and an annual summer pageant recalls the 13th-century suppression of the Albigensian heretics. The artist Henri de TOULOUSE-LAUTREC was born in Albi. Agribusiness and the manufacture of glass, chemicals, and textiles, and tourism are the chief industries.

Albigensians (or **Albigenses**) Followers of a form of the CATHAR heresy; they took their name from the town of Albi in Languedoc in southern France. There and in northern Italy the sect acquired immense popularity. The movement was condemned at the Council of Toulouse in 1119 and by the Third and Fourth LATERAN councils in 1179 and 1215, which opposed it not only as heretical but because it threatened the family and the state. St BERNARD and St DOMINIC were its vigorous opponents. Between 1209 and 1228 the wars known as the **Albigensian Crusade** were mounted, led principally by Simon de MONTFORT. By 1229 the heretics were largely crushed and the Treaty of Meaux delivered most of their territory to France.

albinism An inherited condition of humans and animals in which the individual (albino) has an abnormally pale skin, pink or light-blue irises, and very fair hair. It is caused by an absence of the enzyme tyrosinase, which is required for the formation of the brown pigment MELANIN. Human sufferers need to protect their skin and eyes from direct sunlight and often require spectacles to correct visual defects, which can occur as a result of albinism.

Albinoni, Tomaso (1671–1751) Italian composer. He wrote more than fifty operas, but is now best known for his melodic instrumental music. Several of his many concertos have seen a revival, but the *Adagio in G* with which he is popularly associated was in fact composed by the Italian musicologist Remo Giazotto, based on a fragment of manuscript.

Ålborg An industrial, transportation and cultural centre on the Lim Fjord, north Jutland, Denmark; pop. (1990) 155,000. The city, which is capital of Nordjylland county, is linked by bridge and tunnel to Nørresundby on the north side of the Lim Fjord, and has many historic buildings and a world-famous art gallery. It has large cement plants and distilleries.

Albuquerque The largest city in the state of New Mexico, USA; pop. (1990) 384,740. Founded in 1706 by the governor of New Mexico, the original settlement or 'Old Town' was named after the Duke of Alburquerque, Viceroy of New Spain. After 1880 the 'New Town' of Albuquerque developed further east alongside the Santa Fe Railroad. The University of New Mexico (1889), the Bataan Lovelace Medical Center, and the Sandia nuclear and solar research laboratories are located in the city which is also a centre for the livestock trade and the production of electronics.

Albuquerque, Alfonso de (known as **Albuquerque the Great**) (1453–1515) Portuguese colonial statesman. He first travelled east in 1502, and, after being appointed viceroy of the Portuguese Indies four years later, conquered Goa and made it the capital of the Portuguese empire in the east. Albuquerque made further conquests in Ceylon, Malacca, Ormuz, the Sunda Islands, and the Malabar Coast, but was relieved of office as a result of a court intrigue at home and died on the passage back to Portugal.

Albury A market town on the north bank of the Murray River, New South Wales, Australia; pop. (1991) 63,610 (with Wodonga). Wine, wool, and food-processing are the chief industries.

Alcaeus (*c.*620–*c.*580 BC) Greek lyric poet. His most important contribution was a new form of lyric metre in four-line stanzas, the alcaic; he also wrote political odes, drinking-songs, and love-songs. His works were an important model for the Roman poet HORACE as well as for French and English verse of the Renaissance.

Alcatraz A rocky island in San Francisco Bay, California, named after its pelicans (Spanish *álcatraces*). It was the site of a top-security federal prison (1933–63). Since 1972, the island has been part of the Golden Gate National Recreation Area.

alcázar (Arabic *al-kasr*, 'the palace') A type of fortress in Spain, built by the Christians during their 14th- and 15th-century wars against the MOORS. It was usually rectangular with great corner towers, and contained an open space or patio, surrounded by chapels, hospitals, and salons. The most renowned is the Alcázar of Seville, built by King Pedro the Cruel (1334–69). The most splendid Muslim fortress-palace in Spain is the Alhambra ('the red'), built by the Moorish monarchs of Granada, chiefly between 1238 and 1358.

Alcestis In Greek mythology, the wife of King Admetus of Thessaly. She was a paragon of wifely love and virtue and offered to take her husband's place when he was about to die. However, Hercules (Hercules) followed her to the Underworld and rescued her.

alchemy A pseudo-science originating independently in China, Greece, and India in about the 3rd century BC, concerned with the possible transmutation of all matter, most famously the transmutation of base metals such as lead into gold. The transmutation was variously an end in itself, a means by which to make an elixir of life, and a route to the creation of a panacea, or universal medicine. Early alchemy degenerated into superstition and mysticism, but the art flourished once again in the 8th century AD in Arab countries. Translations of Arabic alchemical texts led in the 12th century to a second revival of alchemy in Europe, notably in Prague. It attracted such medieval scholars as Roger BACON and ALBERTUS MAGNUS, and was patronized by princes and emperors. The influential Swiss writer Paracelsus (16th century) was primarily concerned with its medical application to his search for a chemical therapy for disease; his followers developed specialized chemical medicines and sought a universal elixir which they dreamed would prolong life and restore youth. During the Renaissance alchemy fell into disrepute, but the chemical experience accumulated by alchemists over many centuries became the basis upon which the modern science of chemistry was built.

Alchera (or **Altjira**, **Altjiranga**, **Alcheringa**, **Wongar**, **Djugurba**) (Australian Aboriginal, 'Dream time') In Australian Aboriginal belief, a mythological period of time during which the natural environment was shaped and mythic beings began to walk the Earth. Some were responsible for creating human life, which shares a common life force with its creators and with all nature. The dream time has no foreseeable end, and the mythic beings, transsubstantiated and metamorphosed into natural features such as rocks, water holes, or ritual objects, are eternal.

Alcibiades (*c.*450–404 BC) Athenian general and statesman. Educated in the household of Pericles, he became the pupil and friend of Socrates. In the PELOPONNESIAN WAR he sponsored the unsuccessful Athenian expedition against Sicily, but fled to Sparta after being recalled for trial on a charge of sacrilege. He later held commands for Athens against Sparta and Persia, before his enemies finally forced him from Athens and had him murdered in Phrygia.

Alcock, Sir John William (1892–1919) British aviator. Together with Sir Arthur Whitten Brown, he made the first non-stop transatlantic flight (16 hours 27 minutes) on 14–15 June 1919, from Newfoundland to Clifden, Ireland, in a converted Vickers Vimy bomber.

alcohol Any of a large group of organic compounds containing one or more hydroxyl (–OH) groups. In the common series of alcohols, the hydroxyl group is bonded to an ALKYL GROUP. If the alkyl group is denoted by R, the formula of an alcohol is ROH. The simplest of these alkyl alcohols are METHANOL (CH_3OH) and ETHANOL (C_2H_5OH). Ethanol is a colourless volatile liquid, the intoxicant present in wine, beer, and spirits. Alcohols are important organic chemicals, with a variety of industrial applications both in the manufacture of other materials (such as detergents and plastics), and in their own right as fuels and SOLVENTS.

alcohol abuse The habitual, compulsive, and excessive consumption of alcohol, to the extent that health or social interaction are adversely affected. Alcohol dependence is common in cases of a daily consumption of more than 100 g (3.5 ounces), which is equivalent to 1 litre (1.75 pints) of wine, half a bottle of spirits, or 4 litres (7 pints) of beer. Figures indicate that alcohol abuse is increasing, especially among women. Excessive alcohol consumption can adversely affect the liver, leading to cirrhosis or liver cancer; it can contribute to HEART DISEASE, high blood pressure, stroke, gastric ulcers, and renal failure; and in pregnancy it can lead to foetal abnormalities. Withdrawal symptoms for those addicted to alcohol include shaking, sweating, and nausea. Alcohol is also a major factor in CRIME, domestic problems, such as marital breakdown and child abuse; work problems, such as absenteeism; and accidents, particularly in cars. There is disagreement about treatment: many experts consider that a cure can only be brought about by total abstinence, whereas others believe that controlled consumption can be achieved. Treatment for alcohol dependence may involve a period of detoxification, followed by individual COUNSELLING or GROUP THERAPY. For many people dependent on alcohol, successful treatment is achieved through attending self-help groups, such as Alcoholics Anonymous (AA).

Alcott, Louisa May (1832–88) US novelist. From an early age she published sketches and stories to support her family, including *Hospital Sketches* (1863), which recounted her experiences as a nurse in the Civil War. Her most popular novel is *Little Women* (1868–69), a largely autobiographical work about a New England family, written for adolescent girls.

Alcuin (*c.*735–804) English scholar and theologian.

In 782 was employed by Emperor CHARLEMAGNE as head of his palace school at Aachen, where his pupils included many of the outstanding figures in the 'Carolingian Renaissance'. Alcuin played a central role in fostering this cultural revival. In 796 he became abbot of St Martin at Tours, where he continued his work until his death.

Aldabra A coral-island group in the Indian Ocean, north-west of Madagascar, comprising the island of Aldabra and the smaller atolls of Assomption, Astove, and Cosmoledo. From 1963 to 1976 it was part of the British Indian Ocean Territory. Noted for its giant land tortoises, it has been administered as a nature reserve since 1976, when it became a dependency of the Seychelles.

Aldebaran A first-magnitude variable star in the constellation of Taurus, and also known as Alpha Tauri. It is a RED GIANT star at a distance of 18 parsecs, with about 100 times the luminosity of the Sun. A thirteenth-magnitude red dwarf companion has the same PROPER MOTION, and the pair may form a binary star of very long period.

Aldeburgh A resort town on the coast of Suffolk, England, home of the composer Benjamin Britten who died there in 1976; pop. (est. 1981) 3,000. The annual Aldeburgh Music Festival is held at Snape Maltings near the head of the Alde estuary to the west of the town. The pioneer woman physician Elizabeth Garrett ANDERSON, who lived at Alde House, was the first woman mayor in England (1908).

aldehyde Any of a group of organic compounds with a general formula RCHO in which a carbon atom forms a double bond with an oxygen atom and is also bonded to a hydrogen atom and another group denoted by R, which can be a second hydrogen atom, an ALKYL GROUP, or an ARYL GROUP. Aldehydes undergo addition and condensation reactions, and are rapidly oxidized to form carboxylic acids, unlike the related group of compounds, the KETONES. Short-chain aldehydes, such as methanal (formaldehyde, HCHO), and ethanal (acetaldehyde, CH_3CHO), are unpleasant-smelling liquids widely used in the chemical industry, whereas aromatic aldehydes frequently have pleasant smells and are used as flavourings and perfumes; benzenecarbaldehyde (benzaldehyde, C_6H_5CHO), for example, smells of bitter almonds.

alder A deciduous tree or shrub of the genus *Alnus*, comprising about 35 species native to north temperate zones and the Andes. Alders form part of the BIRCH family, along with hazels and hornbeams. They are readily distinguished from the allied birches, *Betula* species, as they have small, woody cones which persist after the seeds have been dispersed. The common alder, *A. glutinosa*, of Eurasia and North Africa, is a plant of wet places in woods and on stream-sides, and its seeds attract SISKINS in winter. The wood of the North American red alder, *A. rubra*, has been used for furniture. The common alder has a soft, light timber used in the production of charcoal and plywood.

alderfly An insect with two pairs of delicate wings, each with a net-like arrangement of veins. Alderflies are unrelated to true flies and are part of the order Megaloptera, which, with the SNAKE-FLIES, includes some 200 species worldwide. Adult alderflies are found near still or slow-moving water. The larvae are predatory and aquatic, with strong, biting jaws and seven pairs of feathery gills fringing the tapering abdomen. A North American alderfly, *Corydalis* species, is known as the Dobson fly. The adult can have a wingspan of up to 16 cm (6 inches) and has larvae up to 7.5 cm (3 inches) long.

alderman (Old English *ealdorman*, 'elderman') A title dating from the Anglo-Saxon period when ealdormen, nobles by birth, exercised considerable powers. They were initially appointed by the crown to administer the shire system (particularly the shire moot or assembly and fyrd). By the 10th century their influence extended beyond the shire, and in the early 11th century their title evolved into 'earl'. Under the Norman kings the senior shire official was the sheriff, and the title alderman later came to apply to those who held municipal office.

Aldermaston A village in Berkshire, England, site of an atomic weapons research establishment. The Campaign for Nuclear Disarmament (CND) held an anti-nuclear protest march (the Aldermaston March) from London to Aldermaston and back each year at Easter from 1958 to 1963.

Alderney The third-largest and northernmost of the Channel Islands; area 8 sq km (3 sq miles); pop. (1986) 2,130. The chief town is St Anne's. The island gives its name to a breed of cattle that is more generally known as the Guernsey.

Aldershot A town in Hampshire, southern England, site of a military training centre established in 1854; pop. (1981) 54,360.

Aldiss, Brian W(ilson) (1925–) British novelist and critic. Known primarily for his works of science fiction such as *Frankenstein Unbound* (1973) and *Moreau's Other Island* (1980), he has done much to promote the cause of science fiction as a literary genre, including writing a history of the subject, *Billion Year Spree* (1973).

Aldrin, Edwin Eugene (known as 'Buzz' Aldrin) (1930–) US astronaut. Originally an airforce pilot, he became an astronaut in 1963, and walked in space for 5 hours 37 minutes during the 1966 Gemini 12 mission. In 1969 he took part in the first Moon landing, the Apollo 11 mission, becoming the second person to set foot on the Moon, after Neil ARMSTRONG.

aleatory music The deliberate inclusion of chance elements as part of a composition or performance of music. Thus no two performances will be alike, and indeterminacy can be seen as a reaction against the over-organization of SERIALISM. Aleatoric experiments began in the 1940s and have involved such composers as CAGE, BOULEZ, STOCKHAUSEN, and XENAKIS. Computers are sometimes used to generate 'random music'.

Alembert, Jean le Rond d' (1717–83) French mathematician, physicist, and philosopher. His most famous work was the *Traité de dynamique* (1743), in which he developed his own laws of motion. From 1746 to 1758 he was Diderot's chief collaborator on the *Encyclopédie*, a seminal text of the Age of Enlightenment.

Alençon The capital of the department of Orne in the Basse-Normandie region of northwest France; pop. (1990) 31,140. The town, which lies on a bend of the River Sarthe, produces lace and household appliances. Alençon was the birthplace of Thérèse Martin (1873–97), who was canonized St Thérèse in 1927.

Aleppo (Arabic **Halab**) An ancient city in north-west Syria, the second-largest in the country; pop. (1993) 1,494,000. Occupied by the Hittites, Assyrians, Persians, and Seleucids, Aleppo developed as a commercial centre on the caravan route between the Mediterranean and the countries of the East, particularly after the fall of Palmyra in 273 AD, but declined in importance after the advent of sea-trade with the Far East in the late 19th century. The city prospered again after 1921 under French control and continued to develop after Syrian independence in 1941. Grain, fruit, and cotton are grown in the surrounding semidesert region.

Alessandri, Arturo (1868–1950) Chilean statesman. In 1920 he was elected President on a liberal policy, but, finding his attempts at reform blocked, he went into voluntary exile in 1924. The following year he was brought back by the army when a new constitution was adopted. He extended the suffrage, separated church and state while guaranteeing religious liberty, and made primary education compulsory. He resigned again in October 1925 and went to Italy. On his return he was re-elected President (1932–38). He reorganized the nitrate industry, developed schools, and improved conditions in agriculture and industry.

Alessandria A city on the River Tanaro in the Piedmont region of north-west Italy, capital of the province of Alessandria; pop. (1990) 93,350. The city is named after the warrior-pope Alexander III, who led the local people against the Emperor Frederick Barbarossa in the 12th century. During the 19th century Alessandria was an important military stronghold. It is now a market and industrial centre with light industries including clothing, furniture, and machinery.

Ålesund See AALESUND.

Aletschhorn A mountain in the Bernese Alps, Switzerland, rising to a height of 4,195 m (13,763 ft). The Aletsch glacier is among the largest in Europe.

Aleut A native of the Aleutian Islands, Alaska, USA. Closely related to the Inuit, the Aleuts comprise two linguistic subgroups, the Unalaskans of the Alaskan Peninsula and the eastern Aleutian Islands, and the Atkans of the western Aleutians.

Aleutian Islands (or **Aleutians**) A chain of virtually treeless volcanic islands in US possession, extending *c.*1,930 km (1,200 miles) west-south-west from the tip of the Alaska Peninsula. Separating the Bering Sea from the Pacific Ocean, the Aleutians comprise five main groups: Fox Islands, Islands of the Four Mountains, Andrean of Islands, Rat Islands, and Near Islands. The main settlement is the town of Dutch Harbor on Unalaska Island. There are several active volcanoes, the highest of which (Shishaldin) rises to 2,856 m (9,370 ft) on Unimak. The islands with their indigenous population of Aleuts were discovered by the Danish explorer Vitus Bering in 1741. Exploited by Russian trappers and fur traders, the Aleutians were later incorporated into the USA following the Alaska purchase of 1867. Their proximity to the Soviet Union gave them a strategic significance during the Cold War.

Alexander I *c.*1078–1124 King of Scotland 1107–24. He succeeded his brother Edgar although the regions of Strathclyde, Lothian, and Cumbria were ruled with Anglo-Norman support by his younger brother (later DAVID I). Educated in England, Alexander encouraged the feudalization of his country while still retaining its independence of England. After crushing a Celtic revolt (*c.*1115) he was styled 'the Fierce' although he was a pious man, founding Augustinian houses at Scone (1115) and Inchcolm.

Alexander I (1777–1825) Emperor of Russia 1801–25. The son of Paul I (in whose murder he may indirectly have assisted), he set out to reform Russia and correct many of the injustices of the preceding reign. His private committee (Neglasny Komitet) introduced plans for public education, but his reliance on the nobility made it impossible for him to abolish serfdom. At first a supporter of the coalition against NAPOLEON, his defeats by the latter at AUSTERLITZ (1805) and Friedland (1807) resulted in the Treaties of Tilsit (1807) with France and in his support of the CONTINENTAL SYSTEM against the British. His wars with Persia (1804–13) and Turkey (1806–12) brought territorial gains, including the acquisition of Georgia. His armies helped to defeat Napoleon's *grande armée* at LEIPZIG, after its retreat from Moscow (1812). In an effort to uphold Christian morality in Europe he formed a HOLY ALLIANCE of European monarchs. He supported METTERNICH in suppressing liberal and national movements, and gave no help to the Greeks in rebellion against the Ottoman Turks, although they were Orthodox Christians like himself. He was reported to have become a hermit.

Alexander I (1888–1934) King of Yugoslavia 1921–34. Of the Karageorgević dynasty of Serbia, he tried to overcome the ethnic, religious, and regional rivalries in his country by means of a personal dictatorship (1929), supported by the army. In the interest of greater unity, he changed the name of his kingdom, which consisted of Serbs, Croats, and Slovenes, to 'YUGOSLAVIA' in 1929. In 1931 some civil rights were restored, but they proved insufficient to quell rising political and separatist dissent. He was assassinated by a Croatian terrorist.

Alexander II (1198–1249) King of Scotland 1214–49. He succeeded William the Lion. After supporting the English barons in the first Barons' War against King JOHN he had to suppress revolts in Moray (1221), Argyll (1222), Caithness (1222), and Galloway (1224). His campaigns against England and the Norse in the Western Isles (1249) were motivated by territorial ambitions.

Alexander II (1818–81) Emperor of Russia 1855–81. Known as the 'Tsar Liberator', he was the eldest son of NICHOLAS I and succeeded to the throne when the CRIMEAN WAR had revealed Russia's backwardness. His Emancipation Act of 1861 freed millions of serfs and led to an overhaul of Russia's archaic administrative institutions. Measures of reform, however, did not disguise his belief in the need to maintain autocratic rule and his commitment to military strength, as witnessed by the introduction of universal conscription in 1874. His reign saw great territorial gains in the Caucasus, Central Asia, and the Far East, to offset the sale of ALASKA to the USA (1867). The growth of secret revolutionary societies such as the NIHILISTS and Populists, culminating in an assassination attempt in 1862, completed his conversion to conservatism. After further assassination attempts, he was mortally wounded (1881) by a bomb, thrown by a member of the People's Will Movement.

Alexander III (the Great) (356–323 BC) Son of Philip II, king of Macedon 336–323. He was a pupil of Aristotle. After his succession he invaded Persia, liberating the Greek cities in Asia Minor, and then defeating the Persians in Egypt, Syria, and Mesopotamia. While in Egypt he founded Alexandria (332 BC), his first and best-known city. He went on to extend his conquests eastwards, taking Bactria and the Punjab. He died of a fever at Babylon, and his empire quickly fell apart after his death. Regarded as a god in his lifetime, he became a model for many subsequent imperialist conquerors of antiquity, and the subject of many legends. See map p. 31.

Alexander III (1241–86) King of Scotland 1249–86. He defeated Haakon of Norway at the Battle of Largs (1263) and received the Hebrides by the

Treaty of Perth. Despite close ties with England (his father-in-law was HENRY III), Alexander resisted English claims to the Scottish kingdom. The early death of his children left the succession to his granddaughter Margaret of Norway.

Alexander III (1845–94) Emperor of Russia 1881–94. Following the assassination of his father ALEXANDER II he rejected all plans of liberal reform, suppressing Russian NIHILISTS and Populists, extending the powers of nominated landed proprietors over the peasantry, and strengthening the role of landowners in local government. Autocratic in attitude, he was, however, genuinely interested in the principles of administration and his reign saw the abolition of the poll tax, the creation of a Peasant Land Bank, and tentative moves towards legalization of trade unions. Alexander's concept of *naradnost* (belief in the Russian people) led to the Russian language being imposed as the single language of education throughout the empire. Although he resented the loss of the Russian Balkans imposed by the Congress of BERLIN, he nevertheless continued to support Bismarck's League of the Three Emperors, the Dreikaiserbund, until 1890, when the aggressive attitudes of the new German emperor WILLIAM II led to its replacement by an alliance with France.

Alexander, Harold (Rupert Leofric George), 1st Earl Alexander of Tunis (1891–1969) British Field Marshal and Conservative statesman. In World War II he supervised the evacuation from DUNKIRK, the withdrawal from Burma, and the victorious campaigns in North Africa (1943), Sicily, and Italy (1943–45). After the war he became Governor-General of Canada (1946–52) and British Minister of Defence (1952–54).

Alexander Archipelago A group of *c.*1,100 US islands in the Gulf of Alaska, forming the remnants of a submerged mountain system. Rugged and densely forested, the largest islands are Baranof, Chichagof, Prince of Wales, Admiralty, Kuiu, Kupreanof, and Revillagigedo. Sitka, Hoonah, Petersburg, and Ketchikan are the chief settlements.

Alexander Nevsky (*c.*1220–63) Russian soldier, Grand Duke of Vladimir 1252–63. Born in Vladimir, son of the Grand Duke Jaroslav II of Novgorod, he acquired his second name after his defeat of the Swedish army on the banks of the River Neva in 1240. Wars against the Germans and Lithuanians culminated in a battle with the TEUTONIC KNIGHTS on the frozen Lake Peipus which he won decisively. After his death he was canonized as a saint of the Russian Orthodox Church.

Alexander the Great See ALEXANDER III (THE GREAT).

Alexandria (Arabic **El Iskandarîya**) The chief port and second-largest city of Egypt, on the Mediterranean coast, northwest of Cairo; pop. (1990) 3,170,000. Founded in 332 BC by Alexander the Great, after whom it is named, it became a major centre of Hellenistic and Jewish culture, with renowned libraries, and was the capital city until the Arab invasions *c.*641 AD. On an island off the coast was the Pharos lighthouse (3rd century BC), often considered one of the Seven Wonders of the World. It is a modern industrial city with tanneries, oil refinery, chemical plants, and vehicle-assembly plants. Its deep-water docks handle three-quarters of Egypt's overseas trade.

alexandrine A verse line of 12 syllables adopted by poets since Ronsard as the standard verse-form of French poetry, especially dramatic and narrative. The division of the line into two groups of six syllables in the age of Racine was later challenged by Hugo and other 19th-century poets, who preferred three groups of four.

alfalfa One of the most important forage crops in the world, *Medicago sativa*, cultivated widely in temperate and warm temperate areas, principally in the USA. Known as 'lucerne' in Europe, South Africa, and Australia, this protein-rich LEGUME, originating in the Middle East, was the principal fodder of Roman cavalry- and chariot-horses. It is a perennial, deep-rooting, bushy plant with purple, sometimes yellow, flowers; the young leaves are used as a vegetable in China and elsewhere.

al-Farabī (*c.*873–950) Islamic philosopher. He commented on the logical works of ARISTOTLE and the political works of PLATO, combining ideas from both in his principal work, *The Ideal City*. This hierarchical society would be headed by a philosopher-prophet, from whom lower ranks would derive their authority.

Alfieri, Vittorio, Count (1749–1803) Italian poet and tragedian. Alfieri travelled widely and found in England the political liberty that was to become

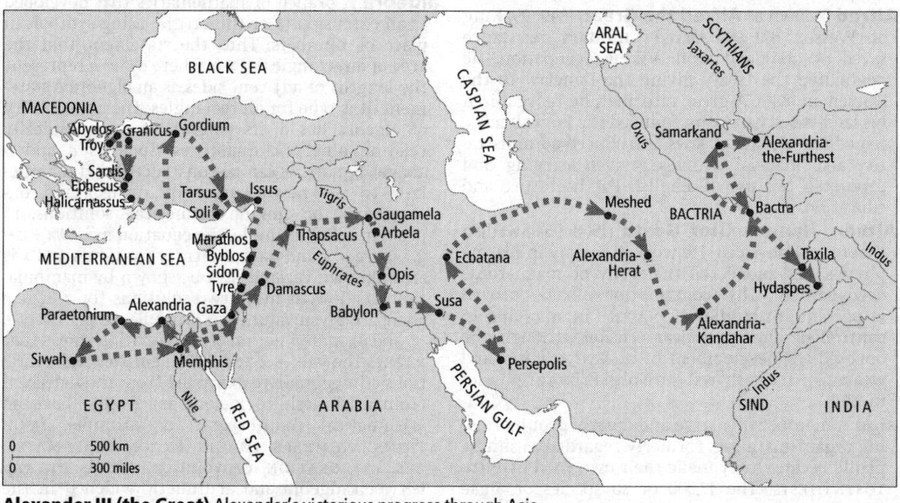

Alexander III (the Great) Alexander's victorious progress through Asia.

his ideal; on his return he settled in Florence. Considered the herald of the RISORGIMENTO, he wrote nineteen TRAGEDIES (1775–89) expressing his hatred of tyranny. His rugged heroes, reflecting his own blunt, vehement, and uncompromising nature, caught the Italian imagination. Besides his tragedies, he wrote SONNETS, satires (among them 'The Anti-Gaul' (1793–99), on the excesses of the French revolution), and a notable autobiography.

alfisol A type of soil with a grey, brown, or red upper HORIZON, containing little organic matter and overlying a zone of clay accumulation. This clayey horizon is generally rich in exchangeable BASES, such as calcium and magnesium compounds. This, with the fact that they are usually moist for all but a small part of the year, makes these soils relatively good for agriculture. Alfisols are found in areas with humid and subhumid climates, particularly in central North America, southern Europe, and south-east Australia.

Alfonso V (the Magnanimous) (1396–1458) King of ARAGON 1416–58 and of NAPLES 1443–58. He pursued a foreign policy committed to territorial expansion, particularly in Italy. Joanna II, Queen of NAPLES, adopted him as her heir and on her death he transferred his court to Naples in 1443, which he developed as a centre of RENAISSANCE culture. His patronage earned the admiration of contemporary humanists.

Alfonso X (the Wise) (1221–84) King of CASTILE and León 1252–84. His reign was a contrast between the failure of his political ambitions and his scholarly success as a law-giver. He spent fruitless years trying to become Holy Roman Emperor and failed to complete his father's Crusade against the MOORS in southern Spain. His indecision caused his son, Sancho IV, to rebel and isolate him in Seville. Of real importance was his *Siete Partidas* (1256), a collection of constitutional, civil, and criminal law, the first such work to be written in Spanish.

Alfonso XIII (1886–1941) King of Spain 1886–1931. Alfonso ruled under the regency of his mother until 1902, during which time Spain lost her colonial possessions in the Philippines and Cuba to the USA. In 1923 he supported Miguel Primo de Rivera's assumption of dictatorial powers, but by 1931 Alfonso had agreed to elections. When these indicated the Spanish electorate's clear preference for a republic, the king was forced to abdicate.

Alfred (known as **Alfred the Great**) (849–99) King of Wessex 871–99. Alfred's military resistance saved SW England from Viking occupation. He negotiated the treaty giving the Danelaw to the Norsemen (886). A great reformer, he reorganized his land-based garrisons, founded the English navy, issued a new code of laws, introduced administrative and financial changes, revived learning, and promoted the use of English for literature and education.

Alfvén, Hannes Olof Gösta (1908–95) Swedish theoretical physicist. He worked mainly in plasma physics, and pioneered the study of magnetohydrodynamics. His contributions have proved important for studies of plasmas in stars and in controlled thermonuclear fusion, though he opposed the development of nuclear reactors and weapons. Alfvén shared the Nobel Prize for physics in 1970.

alga A member of a large and diverse group of living organisms, algae, formerly regarded as simple plants because they make their own food by PHOTOSYNTHESIS. The 17,000 or so species of algae include all the marine SEAWEEDS and also vast numbers of microscopic, single-celled species which are the major components of PLANKTON. Algae vary greatly in size from single-celled forms such as *Euglena*, through filamentous (thread-like) species such as *Spirogyra*, to KELPS which may reach 60 m (197 feet) in length. Algae are CRYPTOGAMS, and they reproduce by means of spores. In many species spores move with the use of tiny undulating hairs known as flagellae.

As planktonic organisms in both marine and freshwater habitats, algae often undergo spectacular outbursts of growth. These phases, known as algal blooms, occur in response to an increase in nutrient levels in their lake, river, or sea. The 'red tides' of some parts of the world are caused by blooms of algae which often have red or reddish photosynthetic pigments.

The classification of algae has always presented a problem to biologists as many algae have features in common with both animals and plants. Many species lack a cellulose cell wall, considered basic to all plant cells, while others possess the ability to photosynthesize, yet also ingest food particles. Thus algae have been grouped along with plants by some, or as a separate group by others. They are now regarded by many authorities as part of the kingdom PROTOCTISTA, which also includes slime moulds and protozoa; the term 'alga' now has no taxonomic status and is used only informally, the different types being assigned to several phyla. The organisms formerly known as blue-green algae are now accepted to be bacteria and are called CYANOBACTERIA. Plants are believed to have evolved from green algae because of the close structural and chemical similarities between them and some BRYOPHYTES.

Algarve, the (or **Faro**) The southern-most region of Portugal, on the Atlantic coast, stretching from Cape St Vincent in the west to the River Guadiana on the Spanish frontier; area 5,072 sq km (1,959 sq miles); pop. (1989) 344,900; capital, Faro. The hilly Upper Algarve (Alto Algarve) is sparsely populated while the scenic, rocky coast-line of the Lower Algarve (Baixo Algarve) has attracted tourism development. Coextensive with the administrative district of Faro, the irrigated plantations of the Algarve produce almonds, olives, figs, oranges, sugar-cane, cotton, and rice. (Arabic *al*, the + *gharb*, west).

algebra A branch of mathematics that developed as an extension of arithmetic by using symbols in place of numbers. Thus the statement that the area of a rectangle is $a \times b$, where a and b represent the lengths of adjacent sides, is an algebraic statement. It is true for all rectangles. The great utility of algebra lies in its potential for economically relating algebraic quantities (such as a and b above). Equations can be constructed and manipulated to yield new relationships, unsuspected consequences, or unique numerical solutions to problems. For example, the equation $ax^2 + bx + c = 0$, where a, b and c are arbitrary constants and x is an unknown variable, can be shown by manipulation to allow, at most, two solutions for x. If a, b and c are given values (for example, respectively 1, −5 and 6), manipulation of the equation shows that x takes the values 2 and 3. The entities and operations of algebra have expanded from those derived from arithmetic to include many that have no arithmetical counterpart, for example, IRRATIONAL NUMBERS, IMAGINARY NUMBERS, MATRICES, INTEGRATION, convolution, etc. As the gap between algebra and arithmetic widened in the 19th century, mathematicians increasingly viewed the rules and definitions of algebra as arbitrary. Alternative algebras were developed (for example, Boolean algebra, a symbolic LOGIC). Thus the study of abstract algebraic systems grew. These systems are SETS of elements with one or more operations. The real numbers, with the operations of addition and multiplication, are merely one example of one kind of system. The word algebra comes from the Arabic *al-jabr*, which refers to the transposition of terms in an equation.

Algeciras A city in the province of Cadiz, southern Spain, a ferry port and resort on the Bay of Algeciras, opposite Gibraltar; pop. (1991) 101,365.

Algeria A country extending from the North African coast southward across a large part of the Sahara, its narrow coastal strip being bounded by Morocco on the west and Tunisia on the east.

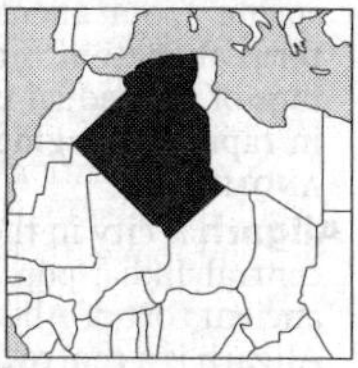

Physical. The coast has an equable Mediterranean climate well suited to agriculture. Inland the ground rises until it is mountainous, though here also the valleys are fertile. Plains and plateaux provide grazing, while many of the mountain slopes are forested. South is the desert – dry and with temperatures over 35°C (95°F) – and further south-east are more mountains with desolate plateaux and volcanic cones and craters.

Economy. Algerian industry, mainly state-owned, is based on oil-refining, but cement and steel are also produced. The country's main exports are crude oil, petroleum products, and natural gas. Agriculture is limited: the northern mountainous region is suited only to grazing and timber, and the south of the country is the Sahara Desert. Algeria imports much of its food, the EU being the major trading partner.

History. The indigenous population of Algeria were Berbers, but the coast was colonized by the Phoenicians in the 9th century BC. In the 2nd century BC the Romans incorporated the whole region into the province of Africa. In the 7th century AD the Romanized Berbers resisted the Arab invasion fiercely. Once conquered they were converted to Islam, and became members of the extreme Kharijite sect. From the 11th century they were repeatedly ravaged by the Banu Hilal and other Arabs, and ruled by a series of dynasties until conquest by the Ottoman empire in the 16th century. Throughout the 18th century, Algeria was notorious as a base for pirates raiding Mediterranean shipping. Conquered by France in the 1830s (when its present boundaries were established) and formally annexed in 1842, Algeria was 'attached' to metropolitan France and heavily settled by European Christians. The refusal of the European settlers to grant equal rights to the native population led to increasing instability, and in 1954 a war of national independence broke out which was characterized by atrocities on both sides. In 1962, in spite of considerable resistance in both France and white Algeria, President DE GAULLE negotiated an end to hostilities in the Evian Agreement, and Algeria was granted independence as the result of a referendum. In 1965 a coup established a left-wing government under Colonel Houari BOUMÉDIENNE and afterwards serious border disputes broke out with Tunisia, Morocco, and Mauritania. After Boumédienne's death in 1978, his successor Benjedid Chadli relaxed his repressive domestic policies and began to normalize Algeria's external relations. Algeria was a one-party state, ruled by the FLN (Front de Libération Nationale), from 1976 until 1989, when other political parties were legalized. The fundamentalist FIS (Front Islamique du Salut) party rapidly gained popular support. In 1992 the FIS seemed poised to win a general election but Chadli dissolved the government and resigned. A transitional military regime took over and cancelled the election. FIS supporters continued to wage a campaign of violence and terrorism; an estimated 60,000 people fell victim to political violence in the years 1992–97.

Capital: Algiers
Area: 2,381,741 sq km (919,595 sq mi)
Population: 25.800,000 (1991)
Currency: 1 Algerian dinar = 100 centimes
Religions: Sunni Muslim 99.1%; Roman Catholic 0.5%
Ethnic Groups: Arab 82.6%; Berber 17.0%; French 0.1%
Languages: Arabic (official); Berber; French
International Organizations: UN; Arab League; OAPEC; OPEC; Maghreb Union; Non-Aligned Movement; OAU

Algiers (French **Alger**; Arabic **El Djezair**) The capital of Algeria and one of the leading Mediterranean ports of North Africa, on the Bay of Algiers; pop. (1989) 1,722,000. Founded by the Phoenicians, the city was later known as Icosium by the Romans. It was re-established by the Arabs in the 10th century and later captured by the Turks in 1511. Thereafter it became a base for the Barbary pirates who preyed upon European shipping until French forces captured the port in 1830. During World War II Algiers was the headquarters of the French provisional government and of the Allied Forces. One of the oldest buildings in the city, the Sidi Abderrahman Mosque is a major centre of Muslim pilgrimage and there are many other fine mosques and museums. Wine, citrus fruit, iron ore, and cork are major exports and industries include oil refining, metallurgy, chemicals, engineering, and consumer goods.

alginate A high-molecular-weight carbohydrate obtained from seaweeds and other algae. Alginates are surfactants, which, by lowering the SURFACE TENSION of water, cause emulsions to form and become stable. This is their main use in the food, pharmaceutical, cosmetic, and textile industries.

Algol (or **Beta Persei**) A variable star at a distance of 29 parsecs in the constellation of Perseus. Its magnitude varies between 2.1 and 3.4 every 2.87 days. It is an ECLIPSING BINARY star, in which the brighter primary component, a hot dwarf star of about 100 times the luminosity of the Sun, is periodically eclipsed by its fainter secondary companion, a cool subgiant. The magnitude does not vary much except during the eclipses, which last nearly ten hours. A third star orbits the eclipsing pair every 1.86 years. The variations in brightness of Algol were discovered by Geminiano Montanari in 1667; the period of these variations was measured in 1782 by GOODRICKE, who also offered an explanation for them. Algol gives its name to the class of eclipsing binaries that behaves in this way.

ALGOL See COMPUTER LANGUAGE.

Algonquian (or **Algonkian**) ▶**1** A large group of North American Indian tribes speaking related languages, pushed northward and westward by colonial expansion in the 18th and 19th century. ▶**2** Any of their languages or dialects, forming one of the largest groups of American Indian languages and including Ojibwa, Cree, Blackfoot, Cheyenne, Fox, and Delaware, which are spoken mainly in the north Middle West of the USA, Montana, and south-central Canada. Many English and

American words have been adopted from this group, e.g. *moccasin, moose, pow-wow, squaw, toboggan.*

algorithm A procedure or set of instructions for carrying out a mathematical or symbolic operation in a finite number of steps. For example, an algorithm for dividing a whole number by a fraction might be: invert the fraction; multiply the number by that which is now the numerator; divide the result by the denominator. Computing is the automation and execution of algorithms, which are usually represented in some kind of formal notation such as a FLOW CHART and form the basis of all conventional computer PROGRAMS.

Al-Hudayda See HODEIDA.

Ali (*c.*600–661) The fourth caliph of Islam, cousin and son-in-law of the Prophet Muhammad through his marriage to the Prophet's daughter FATIMA, and father of Hasan and Husain from whom the progeny of Muhammad – the SAYYID DYNASTY – descends. Revered in particular by Shiite Muslims as the rightful successor to Muhammad, and as the first of their Imams, Ali is renowned throughout the Islamic world for his piety, courage, and learning. By some Muslim sects, rejected by orthodox Islam, Ali is regarded as the incarnation of Allah.

Ali, Muhammad See MUHAMMAD ALI.

Alicante The seaport capital of Alicante province, on the Mediterranean coast of south-east Spain; pop. (1991) 270,951. Known to the Romans as Lucentum and the Moors as Al-Lucant, Alicante is now an important centre for the shipping of wine, fruit, raisins, almonds, oil, esparto grass, and vegetables.

Alice Springs A railway terminus and supply centre, serving the outback of Northern Territory, Australia; pop. (1991) 20,450. European discovery was by William Whitfield Mills while surveying a route for the Overland Telegraph Line in 1871, the site was named after the wife of the South Australian Superintendent of Telegraphs. The Royal Flying Doctor Service is based in Alice Springs.

alicyclic compound Any of a class of organic compounds with the properties of ALIPHATIC COMPOUNDS and containing one or more rings of carbon atoms that are not BENZENE RINGS (with a benzene ring the compound would be classed as an AROMATIC COMPOUND). For example, the cycloalkanes have the general formula C_nH_{2n}, where *n* is a whole number, and, like the ALKANES, possess only single bonds between carbon atoms. Thus, cyclohexane, C_6H_{12}, consists of a hexagonal ring of carbon atoms which can adopt either the chair or boat CONFORMATION. In general, alicyclic compounds exhibit chemical properties similar to those of their non-cyclic counterparts. Thus, cycloalkenes, which contain a double bond between two carbon atoms, undergo addition reactions (see CHEMICAL REACTION), like the ALKENES.

al-Idrisi (*c.*1100–60) Arabian geographer in the service of Roger of Sicily. He collected descriptions of Africa, Asia, and Europe from his own travels and from Arabic works. His *Book of Roger* (1145) is the best account of the geography of the world as it was known at that time.

alienation (in sociology) Separation or estrangement from fellow human beings, society, or inner self. In his classic formulation in *The Economic and Philosophical Manuscripts of 1844*, MARX distinguished four principal forms: the worker's distancing from the process of work so that it became a commodity to be sold and lacked intrinsic satisfaction; the worker's lack of control over the product of his labour; detachment from fellow human beings; and estrangement from one's essential human nature. In the 20th century, work in mass production, such as automobile manufacture, has been seen as particularly alienating. The worker must work at the pace dictated by the assembly line, and may have a single repetitive task with no scope for initiative or interaction with others. The recognition of such alienating processes has led to changes in some factories so that workers operate in small groups or produce whole products. The delinquent behaviour of certain groups, for example football hooligans, is sometimes claimed to spring from alienation in a broader sense. The term alienation is also often used to signify feelings of individual powerlessness or disorientation in rapidly changing societies. A related concept is ANOMIE.

Aligarh A city in the state of Uttar Pradesh, north-central India; pop. (1991) 480,000. Comprising the ancient fort of Aligarh and the former city of Koil, Aligarh is a centre of agricultural trade and cotton milling. Its Muslim university (1921) was opened in 1875 as the Anglo-Oriental College.

Alighieri, Dante See DANTE (ALIGHIERI).

alimentary canal A muscular tube starting at the mouth and ending at the anus. It is concerned with the passage, digestion, and absorption of nutrients. It varies in complexity depending upon the animal and its food. In an earth-worm it is a straight tube. In birds it contains specialized parts, such as the crop and gizzard, in which food is broken up. In mammals the tract differs in herbivores, omnivores, and carnivores.

Ali Pasha, Mehmed Emin (1815–71) Ottoman statesman and reformer. After service in the Foreign Ministry he became Grand Vizier in 1852. He became one of the leading statesmen of the Tanzimat reform movement, and was responsible for the Hatt-i Humayun reform edict of 1856. This guaranteed Christians security of life and property, opened civil offices to all subjects, abolished torture, and allowed acquisition of property by foreigners. He believed in autocratic rule and opposed the granting of a parliamentary constitution.

aliphatic compound Any of a class of organic compounds that do not possess a ring of carbon atoms of the type found in AROMATIC COMPOUNDS. They may be either straight-chain compounds where the carbon atoms are joined in one continuous line; or branched-chain compounds where the line of carbon atoms has one or more branches coming off it. Aliphatic compounds containing a ring of carbon atoms, as in cyclohexane, are classified as ALICYCLIC COMPOUNDS. Aliphatic compounds can be separately classified as saturated or unsaturated. Saturated compounds contain only single bonds: for example, the ALKANES contain carbon-hydrogen bonds and carbon-carbon single bonds. Unsaturated compounds, in contrast, contain at least one multiple bond: for example, ALDEHYDES contain a carbon-oxygen double bond.

Al Jizah The Arabic name for El GIZA.

alkali Any BASE that is soluble in water. Alkalis form caustic solutions, and include the hydroxides of the Group 1 and Group 2 metals of the PERIODIC TABLE. Solutions of alkalis turn litmus paper blue and have a HYDROGEN ION CONCENTRATION of more than 7 on the pH scale. They have a soapy feel, and neutralize acids forming salt, water and heat.

alkali metal Any of the elements found in Group 1

(formerly IA) of the PERIODIC TABLE: lithium, sodium, potassium, rubidium, caesium, and francium. They are soft, reactive metals that react readily with water and non-metals, and explosively with acids; their reactivity increases from lithium to francium. They are usually stored under oil for safety. Atoms of the alkali metals contain one valence electron, and they form ionic compounds in which the metal has a valency of 1; almost all their compounds are soluble in water. They are called the alkali metals because of the alkalinity of their hydroxides.

alkaline earth metal Any of the elements found in Group 2 (formerly IIA) of the PERIODIC TABLE: magnesium, calcium, strontium, barium, and radium. They are reactive metals, although less so than the ALKALI METALS; their reactivity increases as the elements become heavier, and barium is stored in oil for safety. They react readily with non-metals and acids, forming ionic compounds in which the metal has a valency of 2. Beryllium appears at the top of Group 2 but it differs quite markedly from other members of the group in chemical properties. The metals are sometimes incorrectly called the 'alkaline earths'; strictly, this refers to their oxides.

alkali soil A type of soil found in low-lying depressions in steppe or desert areas where evaporation greatly exceeds precipitation. It has a pH of more than 7. As a result of poor drainage and intense evaporation, mineral salts are carried up through the soil profile by capillary action and redeposited at or near the surface. This process is known as salinization. The two main types of alkali soils are known as solonchaks and solonetz.

alkaloid An organic nitrogen-containing compound, found in plants. Many alkaloids, such as morphine, cocaine, quinine, and caffeine, are valuable drugs which have useful pharmacological properties.

alkane Any of a series of saturated aliphatic HYDROCARBONS having the general formula C_nH_{2n+2}, where n is a whole number. They contain only single bonds between carbon atoms. Chemically they are fairly unreactive; reactions they undergo are mostly substitution reactions (see CHEMICAL REACTION), in which hydrogen atoms are replaced by other atoms.

alkene Any of a series of unsaturated aliphatic HYDROCARBONS containing a double bond and having the general formula C_nH_{2n}, where n is a whole number. This double bond is the part of the molecule where most reactions occur. The reactions are generally addition reactions (see CHEMICAL REACTION), in which one or more atoms are added to each carbon of the double bond, converting it to a single bond. Simple alkenes, such as ETHENE, (ethylene, C_2H_4) and propene (propylene,

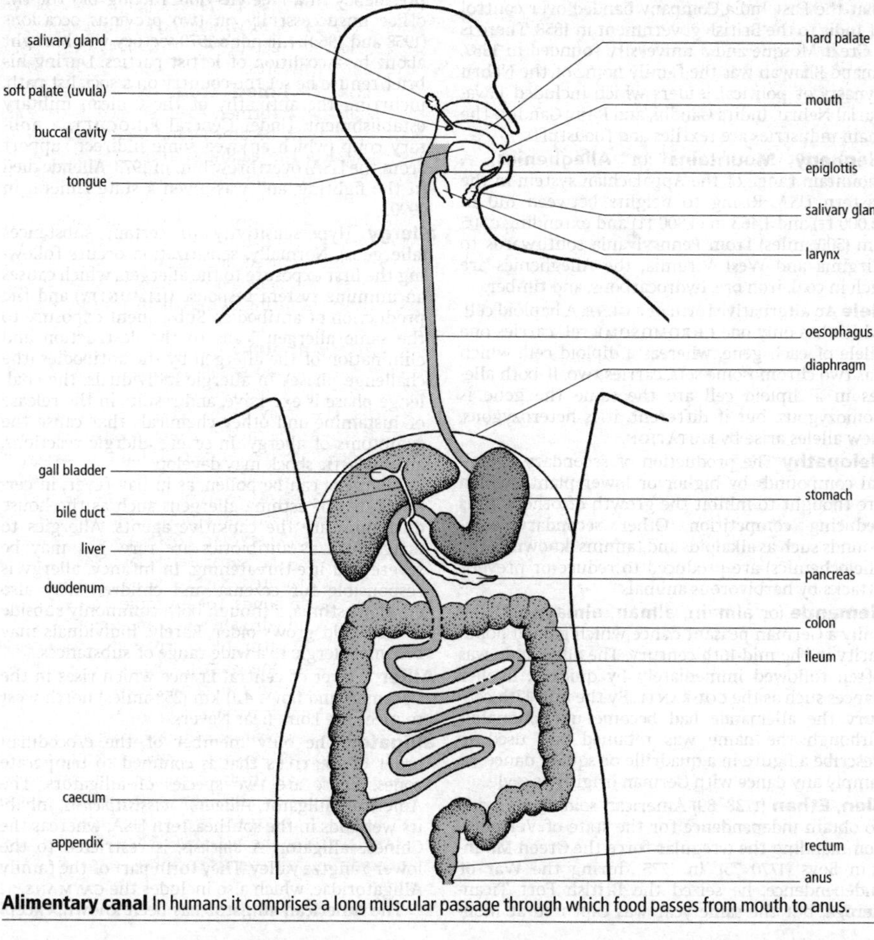

Alimentary canal In humans it comprises a long muscular passage through which food passes from mouth to anus.

C_3H_6) are widely used in the synthesis of polymers and other organic compounds.

Alkmaar A city and tourist centre in the province of North Holland, north-west Netherlands; pop. (1991) 90,780. Founded in the 10th century, it received its charter in 1254. The city is noted for its Edam cheese market, and has light industries.

alkyl group A group of atoms derived from an ALKANE by the removal of one hydrogen atom. Thus the general formula is C_nH_{2n+1}, where *n* is a whole number.

alkyne (or **acetylene**) Any of a series of unsaturated aliphatic HYDROCARBONS containing a triple bond and having the general formula C_nH_{2n-2}, where *n* is a whole number. They are unsaturated compounds, all containing a triple bond between two carbon atoms. As with the ALKENES, the multiple bond is the part of the molecule where most reactions occur. These reactions are generally addition reactions (see CHEMICAL REACTION). For example, in the presence of a catalyst, alkynes react with hydrogen to form the corresponding alkenes. ETHYNE (acetylene, C_2H_2), is the simplest alkyne and has many industrial applications.

Allahabad A city in the state of Uttar Pradesh, north-central India; pop. (1991) 806,000. Situated at the confluence of the sacred Jumna and Ganges rivers, Allahabad is a place of Hindu pilgrimage. The Ashoka Pillar dating from 232 BC stands inside the Moghul fort built by Akbar in 1583. It was here that the East India Company handed over control of India to the British government in 1858. There is a Great Mosque and a university founded in 1887. Anand Bhawan was the family home of the Nehru dynasty of political leaders which included Jawaharlal Nehru, Indira Gandhi, and Rajiv Gandhi. The main industries are textiles and foodstuffs.

Allegheny Mountains (or **Alleghenies**) A mountain range of the Appalachian system in the eastern USA. Rising to heights between 610 m (2,000 ft) and 1,463 m (4,800 ft) and extending *c.*805 km (500 miles) from Pennsylvania southwards to Virginia and West Virginia, the Alleghenies are rich in coal, iron ore, hydrocarbons, and timber.

allele An alternative form of a GENE. A haploid cell, which has only one CHROMOSOME set, carries one allele of each gene, whereas a diploid cell, which has two chromosome sets, carries two. If both alleles in a diploid cell are the same the gene is homozygous, but if different, it is heterozygous. New alleles arise by MUTATION.

allelopathy The production of secondary chemical compounds by higher or lower plants, which are thought to inhibit the growth of others, thus reducing competition. Other secondary compounds such as alkaloids and tannins (known as the allelochemics) are produced to reduce or prevent attacks by herbivorous animals.

allemande (or **almain**, **alman**, **almayne**) Originally a German peasant dance which gained popularity in the mid-16th century. The allemande was often followed immediately by quicker, livelier dances such as the COURANTE. By the mid-17th century the allemande had become unfashionable, although the name was retained and used to describe a figure in a quadrille or square dance, or simply any dance with German origins or style.

Allen, **Ethan** (1738–89) American soldier. He tried to obtain independence for the state of Vermont, commanding the irregular force the Green Mountain Boys (1770–75). In 1775, during the War of Independence, he seized the British Fort Ticanderoga, but the same year was captured at Montreal. On his release in 1778 he presented to Congress Vermont's claims to independence, which was achieved the following year.

Allen, **Woody** (born Allen Stewart Konigsberg) (1935–) US film director, writer, and actor. Allen stars in most of his own films, which humorously explore themes of neurosis and sexual inadequacy. Zany early comedies such as *Play it Again, Sam* (1972) and *Love and Death* (1975) were followed by the slightly graver *Annie Hall* (1977), for which he won three Oscars. His later films include *Hannah and her Sisters* (1986) and *Husbands and Wives* (1992). In 1993 he was involved in a much-publicized court case with his former partner Mia Farrow (1945–) over custody of their children, after he had embarked on an affair with Farrow's adopted daughter, whom he later married.

Allenby, **Edmund Henry Hynman**, **1st Viscount** (1861–1936) British soldier. A veteran of the Boer War, during World War I he commanded the First Cavalry Division and later the Third Army on the Western Front. In 1917 he led the Egyptian Expeditionary Force. Having captured Jerusalem in December 1917, he went on to defeat the Turkish forces in Palestine in 1918. He was promoted to Field Marshal and later served as High Commissioner in Egypt (1919–25).

Allende (Gossens), **Salvador** (1908–73) Chilean statesman. As President of Chile (1970–73), he was the first avowed Marxist to win a Latin American presidency in a free election. Having bid for the office unsuccessfully on two previous occasions (1958 and 1964), Allende's 1970 victory was brought about by a coalition of leftist parties. During his brief tenure he set the country on a socialist path, incurring the antipathy of the Chilean military establishment. Under General PINOCHET, a military coup (which enjoyed some indirect support from the USA) overthrew him in 1973. Allende died in the fighting, and was given a state funeral in 1990.

allergy Hypersensitivity to certain substances (allergens). Normally, sensitization occurs following the first exposure to the allergen, which causes an immune system response (IMMUNITY) and the production of antibodies. Subsequent exposure to the same allergen leads to the destruction and elimination of the allergen by the antibodies (the challenge phase). In allergic individuals, the challenge phase is excessive, and results in the release of histamine and other chemicals that cause the symptoms of allergy. In severe allergic reactions, anaphylactic shock may develop.

Allergens can be pollen, as in hay fever; in certain types of asthma allergens such as the house dust mite are the causative agents. Allergies to drugs such as antibiotics are rare, but may be severe and life-threatening. In infancy, allergy is responsible for eczema, and children may also develop asthma, although both commonly subside as the child grows older. Rarely, individuals may become allergic to a wide range of substances.

Allier A river of central France which rises in the Cévennes and flows 410 km (258 miles) north-west to meet the Loire near Nevers.

alligator The only member of the crocodilian order of REPTILES that is confined to temperate zones. There are two species of alligators. The American alligator, *Alligator mississipiensis*, inhabits wetlands in the southeastern USA, whereas the Chinese alligator, *A. sinensis*, is restricted to the lower Yangtze valley. They form part of the family Alligatoridae, which also includes the CAYMANS.

The American alligator has been known, exceptionally, to attain a length of 5.8 m (19.2 feet). The female deposits her eggs in a nest constructed of mud and rotting vegetation and guards them until they hatch. Although hunting and habitat loss have reduced the range of the American alligator, protective legislation has contributed to a recent recovery in numbers. The endangered Chinese alligator is smaller, secretive in its habits, and spends much of its time in burrows close to water. Alligators are distinguished from crocodiles by having the upper teeth lying outside the lower teeth when the mouth is closed. Their head is broader and shorter than that of most crocodiles.

alligator bug See LANTERN FLY.

Alloa A town in Clackmannan, central Scotland, on the River Forth; pop. (1981) 26,430. Textiles, brewing, distilling, and engineering are the chief industries.

allopathy The term used in HOMOEOPATHY to denote the conventional use of medicines that oppose, and therefore alleviate, symptoms caused by a disease or disorder.

allotrope Any of several different forms in which an element may exist. For example, carbon has three allotropes, graphite, buckminsterfullerene, and diamond, the physical properties of which are quite different because of different crystal structures. Oxygen has two allotropes: dioxygen, O_2, and ozone, O_3, which differ markedly in their chemical properties.

Alloway A small village just south of Ayr in south-west Scotland, birthplace of the poet Robert Burns (1759–96).

alloy A material that is formed by mixing METALS, sometimes with the addition of non-metals. This process causes significant changes to the crystal structure, and therefore the properties, of the metal. The result may be a harder, stronger, stiffer, more corrosion-resistant, or less dense material. The first alloys, BRONZE and BRASS, were probably formed accidentally by the chance SMELTING of mixed metal ores and have been known since about 3500 BC. Alloys of IRON began to be developed about 1000 BC. STEEL was made in small quantities in early times, but it was not until the mid-19th century that it was manufactured on a large scale in the IRON and steel industry. The commercial production of pure ALUMINIUM in about 1890 heralded a new range of alloys (such as Duralumin, an alloy of about 94 per cent aluminium, with small quantities of copper, manganese, magnesium, and silicon) that are both light and strong. NICKEL is frequently mixed with other metals for specialist purposes: 'silver' coinage in the UK is made from cupro-nickel (75 per cent copper, 25 per cent nickel), and constantan (60 per cent copper, 40 per cent nickel) is used for electrical resistance wire. Nickel silver (50–60 per cent copper, 20 per cent zinc, 20–30 per cent nickel) has the appearance of silver, but is more hard-wearing, and can serve as a cheaper substitute in jewellery and fine metal-work. Permalloy is a nickel-iron alloy that is magnetically soft (that is, the polarity of its magnetic field can be easily changed) and is used for TRANSFORMER cores. Monel metals contain about two parts nickel to one part copper, plus other elements. They are stronger than nickel and extremely corrosion-resistant, making them useful in handling FLUORINE. Electrum is a natural or artificial alloy of gold containing 15–45 per cent silver. It was used in the ancient world for coinage. Bismuth frequently forms part of alloys with low melting-points. Today, with increased metallurgical understanding, alloys can be designed for particular applications.

allspice See PIMENTO.

Allston, Washington (1779–1843) US landscape painter. He was the first major artist of the American romantic movement; his early works (for example *The Deluge*, 1804, and his vast, unfinished canvas, *Belshazzar's Feast*, 1817–43) exhibit a taste for the monumental, apocalyptic, and melodramatic, in the same vein as the English painters J. M. W. Turner and John Martin. More influential in America, however, were his later visionary and dreamlike paintings such as *Moonlit Landscape* (1819).

alluvial fan A cone-shaped deposit of cobbles, sand, gravel, silt, and clay, built up by rivers where the slope of the bed is sharply reduced and the speed of flow decreases. Alluvial fans are akin to arcuate DELTAS, but are built on land rather than underwater and have much steeper slopes. Most fans occur at junctions between mountains and plains, where the flow of steep upland rivers carrying coarse debris is checked by the change in gradient and the rivers are forced to deposit much of their load. Fans are common in arid and semi-arid areas. Some provide fertile soil for agriculture and they are usually reliable sources of GROUNDWATER, but they are treacherous places to build on.

alluvium A deposit of sand, silt, or gravel laid down by rivers, especially when in flood. An ALLUVIAL FAN is formed when a river opens out into a valley after following a constricted course.

Alma-Ata See ALMATY.

Almadén A town in the province of Ciudad Real, south-central Spain, in the Sierra Morena Mountains; pop. (1981) 15,000. Mercury has been mined locally since ancient times.

Almagest (Arabic 'The Greatest') The most important astronomical work of the 2nd-century Greek astronomer, geographer, and mathematician PTOLEMY (Claudius Ptolemaeus). The original title of the work was *The Mathematical Collection*, but it became known as *The Great Astronomer*, from which, via Arabic, comes the name *Almagest*. Most of the work's 13 books are devoted to an exposition of his GEOCENTRIC SYSTEM of the Universe, now known as the Ptolemaic system, and to the development of the methods of trigonometry and spherical geometry needed for predicting the motions and apparent changes in size of the Sun, Moon, and planets. It also includes a catalogue of over 1,000 stars, apparently based on an earlier one by HIPPARCHUS.

almanac A compilation of observational data for a particular interval of time, usually a year. The data, such as directions, distances, and brightnesses of astronomical objects, are listed at dates throughout the year. Examples are the *Astronomical Almanac* published jointly by the ROYAL GREENWICH OBSERVATORY and the Washington Naval Observatory, and the *Connaissance des Temps*, published by the Paris Observatory.

al-Masudi (died 957) Arab historian and traveller, born in Baghdad. More than twenty books have been attributed to him, but his major work (now lost) was *The History of Time* in thirty volumes. He later used this material in his most famous book, *The Meadows of Gold and the Mines of Gems*, half of which is devoted to the life of the Prophet Muhammad and the other half to a survey of the Islamic and the non-Islamic world of his day.

Alma-Tadema, Sir Lawrence (1836–1912) Dutch-born British painter. Influenced by a trip to Naples and Pompeii in 1863, he turned to lush genre scenes set in the ancient world, which earned him many imitators. His major paintings include *Pyrrhic Dance* (1869) and *Roses of Heliogabalus* (1888).

Almaty (formerly **Alma-Ata**) The former capital of Kazakhstan in Central Asia; pop. (1991) 1,515,300. Founded in 1854 as a military town and trading centre, and known as Verny until 1921, Almaty developed into an industrial and commercial city after becoming a terminus of the Turkestan–Siberia railroad. Following the breakup of the USSR, representatives of 11 former Soviet republics established the Commonwealth of Independent States at an historic meeting held in Almaty in December 1991 (Alma-Ata Declaration). In 1993 the government changed the city's name from Alma-Ata to Almaty. It trades in local agricultural products and manufactures machinery, railway equipment, leather, and timber. In 1997 the capital began to transfer to Aqmola.

Almelo A textile-manufacturing city in the province of Overijssel, east Netherlands; pop. (1991) 62,668.

Almeria The seaport capital of Almeria province; pop. (1991) 157,760. It exports grapes, esparto grass, and iron ore. It has refineries and processing plants.

Almodóvar, Pedro (1951–) Spanish film director. His films are outlandishly inventive and deal outrageously with sexual matters. *Women on the Verge of a Nervous Breakdown* (1988) is one of his most successful works, merging gaiety, violence, and tragedy. His other films include *Tie Me Up, Tie Me Down* (1990), *High Heels* (1991), and *Kika* (1993).

Almohad An Islamic dynasty that ruled in Morocco and Spain during the 12th and 13th centuries. The Almohads built many of the defensive monasteries or *ribats* of North Africa. They were defeated by the Portuguese and Spanish on the Iberian peninsula in 1228 and superseded by the Merenid dynasty in Morocco in 1269.

almond A deciduous, ornamental fruit tree, *Prunus amygdalis*, belonging to the CHERRY subfamily (Prunoideae). Almond trees grow up to 8 m (27 feet) tall, producing pink blossom in spring. Originating in the Near East, they are naturalized in southern Europe and introduced and cultivated in many other parts of the world, including California, South Australia, and South Africa. The bitter almond is a variety whose nuts, which contain prussic acid, are the chief source of almond oil. The sweet almond is the variety grown for its oval, edible nuts.

Almoravid An Islamic dynasty that ruled in Morocco and Spain in the 11th and 12th centuries until overthrown by the Almohads in 1147. It founded the city of Marrakesh.

almshouse A sanctuary for the reception and succour of the poor. Almshouses were originally those sections of medieval monasteries in which alms (food and money) were distributed. Most medieval foundations were made by clergymen. Privately financed dwellings, usually for the support of the old and infirm, have also been called almshouses. From the 16th century the charitable relief supplied by almshouses was supplemented by a series of POOR LAWS.

aloe An African succulent of the genus *Aloe* with fleshy leaves and, in some species, trunk-like stems up to 7 m (23 feet) in height. They belong to the lily family, Liliaceae. Bitter aloes is a pharmaceutical product of the plant sap. The flowers of aloes are bell-like, or tubular, and are produced on long stalks.

alopecia An absence of hair from areas of the skin on which it normally grows. It may be hereditary, as in the progressive loss of head hair in men, or it can be caused by disease and taking certain drugs. Alopecia areata consists of bald patches, which may regrow. It is an autoimmune disease.

alpaca A domesticated South American camelid which belongs to the same genus as the llama and guanaco, *Lama*. It has been known since 200 BC, but nothing precise is recorded about its domestication. It is bred as a beast of burden as well as for its wool and meat. Its long fleece, which often reaches to the ground, is of uniform black, reddish-brown, or white, or is sometimes piebald. It is sheared every two years, and may provide up to 5 kg (11 pounds) of wool each time.

The alpaca, *L. pacos*, thrives best when at altitudes of 4,000–4,800 m (13,000–16,000 feet) in the high Andes, and grows to about 90 cm (3 feet) tall at the shoulders. The female has a gestation period of eleven months and foals during the rainy season.

alphabet A phonological WRITING system with the graphs (letters) representing individual sounds of a LANGUAGE. In one category of alphabets, called 'consonantal', only the consonants are represented by the letters and the vowels are indicated with diacritics (marks such as dots, accents, and circles above or below the appropriate letters). Hebrew and Arabic are among the languages using scripts based on this principle. In the other category, letters represent both consonants and vowels. Since, however, the correspondence is rarely one-to-one, here too diacritics are often used. Most of the European languages and many others use this kind of alphabet. The wide variety of alphabets worldwide, except possibly for the Indian alphabets, evolved over 4,000 years from the consonantal Semitic script. One of its variants, Phoenician, was the source of the Roman alphabet via Greek. The transition from Phoenician to Greek occurred between *c.*1000 BC and *c.*800 BC; the shapes of the letters altered, and some Semitic consonants, not needed in the Greek phonological system, were now used as vowels. The spread of Christianity from Rome across western Europe was accompanied by the spread of the Roman alphabet. Greek missionaries took Christianity and the Greek alphabet to eastern Europe, which gave rise to the Cyrillic alphabet used for writing Russian. In India, the Devanagari alphabet in which Sanskrit was notated developed independently between the 7th

Alphabets The development of the modern alphabet from the Phoenician.

and the 9th centuries. Many modern Indian scripts are based on, and generically termed, Devanagari. In China, the Roman alphabet has been introduced since 1958 in a transliteration system called Pinyin to facilitate the pronunciation and comprehension of the Chinese characters, which are logograms.

Alpha Centauri (or **Rigil Kentaurus**) A nearby first-magnitude multiple star in the constellation of Centaurus. It is 1.3 parsecs away and comprises two DWARF STARS, each similar to the Sun, which orbit each other every eighty years. A third member of the system, PROXIMA CENTAURI, is the Sun's nearest known stellar neighbour; it takes about one million years to orbit the other two stars.

alpha particle The nucleus of a helium atom. Alpha particles are stable particles and consist of two protons and two neutrons. They are often emitted when a radioactive nucleus decays. Rays of alpha particles are called alpha radiation. Alpha radiation does not have great penetrating power and can be stopped by a sheet of paper, but intense ionization occurs along its track. Thus alpha radiation is a form of ionizing radiation.

alphorn A long trumpet usually made by splitting wood lengthways, hollowing it, and reuniting the halves. They vary from about 1 m (3 ft) to 4 m (12 ft) long, and allow up to twelve natural harmonics. Alphorns are used by herdsmen, especially in Switzerland and other mountainous regions, and sometimes for rituals.

alpine plant A plant adapted to habitats with low temperatures, seasonal snow cover, and strong winds. Alpine plants are found at various altitudes from sea-level in Arctic and Antarctic zones, to several thousand metres in the tropics and subtropics. Usually dwarf and compact in habit, they may be mat-forming species, shrubs, or bulbs. All are adapted to a short growing season, either by flowering after the snow melts, or by reproducing by vegetative means. Most are waxy or hairy so that water loss is minimized.

Alps One of the principal mountain systems of Europe extending through a series of ranges for a distance of 800 km (500 miles) in a wide curve from the Mediterranean coast of south-east France, through northern Italy, Switzerland, Liechtenstein, southern Germany, Austria, Slovenia, and Croatia. The principal ranges are divided into three groups: (1) the Western Alps (Ligurian, Maritime, Cottian, Dauphiné, Graian); (2) the Middle Alps (Pennine, Bernese, Glarner, Lepontine, Albula, Otztaler, Ortler, Trientine, Rhaetian, Silvretta); and (3) the Eastern Alps (Zillertaler, Kitzbühler, Noric, Carnic, Julian). The Mont Blanc Group (with 25 peaks over 4,000 m, 13,000 ft) rises to a height of 4,807 m (15,771 ft) at Mont Blanc which is the highest mountain in the Alps. There are numerous glaciers, amongst the largest of which is the Aletsch glacier in the Bernese Alps. The Alps are the source of many of Europe's greatest rivers including the Rhine, Rhône, Po, and Drava.

Alsace A region of north-east France between the Vosges Mts. and the Rhine; area 8,280 sq km (3,198 sq miles); pop. (1990) 1,624,370; capital, Strasbourg. Mulhouse is the chief centre of industry. The region comprises the departments of Bas-Rhin and Haut-Rhin. It was annexed with part of Lorraine (the annexed territory was known as Alsace-Lorraine) after the Franco-Prussian war of 1870, and restored to France after World War I. Its architecture and traditions reflect both German and French influence. It is a major industrial region with hydroelectric power from the Rhine and specializing in textiles and wine-making.

Alsace-Lorraine A French region west of the Rhine. Alsace and the eastern part of Lorraine were ceded to Germany after the FRANCO-PRUSSIAN WAR (1871) and held in common by all the German states. Rich in both coal and iron-ore, Lorraine enabled Germany to expand its naval and military power. The subsequent policy of Germanization of the region was resented by French nationalists, and the province was restored to France by the Treaty of VERSAILLES after World War I. In 1940 Nazi troops occupied the region and it reverted to Germany. In 1945 French and US troops recovered Alsace-Lorraine for France.

Alston, Richard (1948–) British dancer, choreographer, and director. He trained at the London School of Contemporary Dance and in 1972 formed Strider, one of the first British postmodern dance companies. After studying with CUNNINGHAM in the USA he returned to choreograph for modern dance and large-scale classical companies, notably the Royal Ballet and Royal Danish Ballet. He joined the Rambert Dance Company in 1981 as resident choreographer, becoming artistic director in 1986. His works include *Windhover* (1972), which uses a collage of bird-like sound, *Soda Lake* (1981), a silent work, and *Pulcinella* (1987), using the Stravinsky score.

Altai Mountains (or **Altai Shan**) A mountain system of central Asia that extends eastwards from Kazakhstan into west Mongolia and northern China with an average height between 2,000 and 3,000 m (6,500–10,000 ft) above sea-level. The Irtysh and Ob rivers rise in the Altai.

Altaic languages A family of central Asian languages comprising the Turkic, Mongolian, and Tungusic groups, whose common features include vowel harmony, with all the vowels of a word belonging to the same class (i.e. either front or back).

Altair A first-magnitude star in the constellation of Aquila, and also known as Alpha Aquilae. It is a hot dwarf star at a distance of 5 parsecs, with about ten times the luminosity of the Sun. It rotates very rapidly, and as a result its equatorial diameter may be nearly twice as large as its polar diameter.

Altamira The site of a cave with palaeolithic rock paintings, south of Santander in north-east Spain, discovered in 1879. The paintings are boldly executed polychrome figures of animals, including deer, wild boar, aurochs, and especially bison; they are dated to the upper Magdalenian period.

Altdorf The capital of the canton of Uri in central Switzerland, on the south-east shore of Lake Urner; pop. (1980) 8,200. There is a statue of William Tell on the site where he is alleged to have shot the apple on his son's head. Dating from 1581, the Capuchin monastery is the oldest in Switzerland.

Altdorfer, Albrecht (*c*.1485–1538) German painter and engraver. Inspired by travels along the Danube and in the Austrian Alps in 1511, he emerged as one of the first European landscape painters of modern history and principal artist of the Danube School. His romantic treatment of landscape and the emotional harmony of landscape and human action (as in *Saint George in the Forest*) epitomize the methods and sentiments of the school.

alternating current (a.c.) See ELECTRIC CURRENT; ELECTRICITY GENERATION AND SUPPLY.

alternation of generations See LIFE CYCLE.

alternative energy See ENERGY RESOURCES.

alternative medicine See COMPLEMENTARY MEDICINE.

alternative technology See APPROPRIATE TECHNOLOGY.

alternator See GENERATOR, ELECTRICAL.

Althusser, Louis (1918–90) French philosopher. His work in reinterpreting traditional Marxism in the light of structuralist theories had a significant influence on literary and cultural theory from the 1970s. He sought to reassert an anti-humanist approach to Marxism and develop it into a structural analysis of society. His most important works include *For Marx* (1965) and *Reading Capital* (1970). Found guilty of the murder of his wife, he spent his last years in a mental asylum.

altimeter An instrument used in aircraft for measuring altitude above land or sea. The pressure altimeter utilizes the fact that atmospheric pressure decreases with altitude by measuring pressure using an evacuated metal bellows similar to that in a BAROMETER, and converting this pressure reading into a height measurement. Radio altimeters measure height by transmitting a vertical radio signal and comparing the phase of the transmitted signal with that reflected back from the ground: they measure distance above ground rather than height above sea-level.

Altman, Robert (1925–) US film director. He made his name with *MASH* (1970), a black comedy about an army surgical hospital at the front in the Korean War. He has been nominated for an Oscar for best director four times, for *MASH*, *Nashville* (1975), *The Player* (1992), and *Short Cuts* (1993), which he also co-wrote.

altocumulus A cloud formation at medium altitude consisting of rounded masses with a level base.

altostratus A continuous and uniformly flat cloud formation at medium altitude.

Altrincham A market town in the borough of Trafford, Greater Manchester, England; pop. (1981) 39,641. Engineering and market gardening are important.

altruism Concern for other people, or unselfish or helpful actions. Most attempts to explain humans' altruism treat it as a form of covert selfishness, for natural selection (see DARWIN) must favour behaviour that increases the individual's own Darwinian fitness. Animals' altruism is therefore usually explained by positing mechanisms that ultimately help the altruist or the survival of its characteristic genes. One mechanism is reciprocal altruism, which promotes cooperative behaviour involving temporary sacrifices for longer-term pay-offs for the individuals involved. Another mechanism, 'kin selection', involves care given by parents, which increases the survival chances of the altruist's offspring and thereby of its genes.

alum (or **potassium aluminium sulphate**, $KAl(SO_4)_2.12H_2O$) A white crystalline compound used in the dyeing industry as a MORDANT, in water purification, in dressing leather, sizing paper, in waterproofing fabrics, in fireproofing, and in medicine as a styptic and astringent. It is manufactured by treating bauxite with sulphuric acid and then potassium sulphate. The name alum also refers to similar types of double sulphate salt.

alumina (or **aluminium oxide**, Al_2O_3) A white solid that is virtually insoluble in water. It is an AMPHOTERIC COMPOUND and reacts with both acids and bases. It occurs naturally as anhydrous aluminium oxide in the mineral CORUNDUM, or is obtained from BAUXITE, which is an impure hydrated form of the oxide, by heating to 90°C. The properties of the compound make it a versatile material and its applications are widespread. It is used as a catalyst in petrochemical processes, as an absorbent in chromatography, and, as bauxite, as the commercial source of aluminium. As it is a very hard CERAMIC material, it is used as an ABRASIVE and as an electrical insulator. Alumina ceramic fibres are used for high-temperature thermal insulation and as reinforcements in COMPOSITES. Many naturally occurring gemstones are composed of aluminium oxide crystals coloured by impurities. Artificial gemstones can be manufactured from alumina for various applications: for example, sapphire crystals are used as insulating substrates in electronics, while artificial rubies have applications in lasers. Alumina is also an important constituent of many pottery and porcelain compositions.

aluminium (US **aluminum**; symbol Al, at. no. 13, r.a.m. 26.98) A soft metallic element in Group 3 (formerly IIIA) of the PERIODIC TABLE, which in air has a thin, unreactive, and strongly adherent oxide coating that protects the metal from further oxidation and accounts for its apparently low reactivity. Articles made of aluminium can be coloured and given additional resistance to wear by ANODIZING. Aluminium is an excellent conductor of heat. This property, together with its resistance to corrosion and its low density, explains why it is used for cooking utensils and foil and, increasingly, in the canning industry. It is also a good conductor of electricity and is widely used in overhead CABLES. Aluminium powder is used in paints and in the thermite reaction (see WELDING). ALLOYS of aluminium, such as Duralumin, have high tensile strengths and are of considerable industrial importance, particularly in the aerospace industry. The most important ORE is the hydrated oxide, BAUXITE (approximately $Al_2O_3.2H_2O$). This is dissolved in hot sodium hydroxide, precipitated, and heated to form ALUMINA. Alumina is then reduced to aluminium by an electrolytic process developed by HALL and HÉROULT. Some aluminium compounds are important: aluminium chloride is used as a catalyst in organic chemistry and for CRACKING petroleum; ALUM is used in the purification of water and as a MORDANT for dyes.

aluminium-lithium alloys Extremely stiff, low-density alloys of aluminium and lithium. They were first manufactured in Germany in the 1920s, but significant development did not take place until the 1980s. The alloys have high strength and good fatigue-resistance due to the formation of small Al_3Li particles (precipitation hardening) within the alloy. Commercial alloys also contain small amounts of copper, magnesium, and zirconium. The weight of a large airliner is reduced by about 5 tonnes if aluminium–lithium alloys are used instead of conventional aluminium alloys.

Alvarez, Luis Walter (1911–88) US physicist. In particle physics, he discovered the phenomenon whereby an atomic nucleus can capture an orbiting electron, and made (with F. Bloch) the first measurement of the neutron's magnetic moment. He also developed the bubble chamber for detecting charged particles, for which he received the Nobel Prize for physics in 1968. In 1980 Alvarez and his son Walter, a geologist, discovered iridium in sediment from the Cretaceous–Tertiary boundary and proposed that this resulted from a catastrophic meteorite impact which caused a drastic climate change and resulted in the extinction of the dinosaurs.

Alzheimer's disease See DEMENTIA.

AM (amplitude modulation) See MODULATION.

Amagasaki An industrial city to the west of Osaka in the Kinki region of Honshu Island, Japan; pop. (1990) 499,000. It has iron and steel, chemical, and textile industries.

Amalfi A small resort town and ferry port on the coast of Campania, southern Italy, on the Gulf of Sorrento, 40 km (25 miles) south-east of Naples; pop. (1990) 5,900. During the 9th century Amalfi became the focal point of a tiny but wealthy maritime republic, but fell into decline in the 12th century after being sacked by Normans and Pisans. In 1343 a storm destroyed the greater part of the town which survived thereafter as a fishing settlement.

amalgam (in chemistry) A solution of a metal in MERCURY. Many metals dissolve in mercury to form amalgams, which may be liquid or solid. Gold in particular is highly soluble in mercury: this property has been exploited to extract small metallic gold particles from the insoluble (non-metallic) ore. The mercury is later driven off by heat. Amalgams containing tin, silver, gold, or other metals are used to make dental fillings.

Amalthea A satellite of JUPITER, discovered by the US astronomer Edward Barnard in 1892. Amalthea orbits at 181,300 km from the centre of Jupiter. It has an irregular shape with a mean diameter of about 200 km. The albedo is low (0.06) and the composition is probably rocky. Its reddish colour may be due to contamination by sulphur compounds coming from IO.

Amarillo A city in the panhandle of north-west Texas; pop. (1990) 157,615. Originally known as Ragtown when it was settled in 1887, it was later renamed Amarillo after the colour of a creek bank (Spanish *yellow*). The 'Yellow Rose of Texas' is a symbol of the city which lies at the centre of one of the world's largest cattle-producing areas. In addition to copper, oil and natural gas, nearly all of the world's supply of natural helium gas comes from within a 150-mile radius of Amarillo. It is also a centre of the nuclear-weapons industry.

Amarna, Tell el- The modern name of Akhetaten (the horizon of the Aten), the short-lived capital of ancient Egypt, founded by Akhenaten in the fifth year of his reign 450 km (280 miles) north of Thebes and dismantled by his successors. It is particularly famous for its lively and expressionistic art, which shows a conscious divergence from the old artistic conventions, and for the cuneiform tablets known as the Amarna Letters, discovered in 1887. These texts provide valuable insight into Near Eastern diplomacy of the 14th century BC.

amaryllis A plant of the genus *Amaryllis*, which has a single species. Related to the daffodil, the true amaryllis, *Amaryllis belladonna* (belladonna lily), is native to southern Africa. It has a bulb and a cycle of growth and rest. The large, sweetly scented, rose-pink flowers are produced at the end of the dry season and they are followed by strap-like leaves which grow during the rainy period. The name is wrongly applied to the South American bulbous plant *Hippeastrum*, which is often grown as an indoor plant.

Amati A family of Italian violin-makers. The three generations, all based in Cremona, included Andrea (*c*.1520–*c*.1580), his sons Antonio (1550–1638) and Girolamo (1551–1635), and, most notably, the latter's son Nicolò (1596–1684). From Nicolò's workshop came the violin-makers Antonio Stradivari and Andrea Guarneri (*c*.1626–98), uncle of Giuseppe Guarneri 'del Gesù'. The Amatis developed the proportions of the violin, viola, and cello.

Amazon A member of a mythical race of female warriors in Scythia and Asia Minor. Their name was explained by the ancient Greeks as meaning 'without a breast', in connection with the fable that they destroyed the right breast so as not to interfere with the use of the bow, but this is probably the popular etymology of an unknown word. Amazons appear as allies of the Trojans in the Trojan war, and their queen, Penthesilea, was killed by Achilles. One of the labours of Hercules was to obtain the girdle of Hippolyta, queen of the Amazons. In later years the name has been applied to groups of female warriors such as the Amazons of South America and the royal bodyguard of the former kings of Dahomey in Africa.

Amazon (Spanish **Río de las Amazonas**; Portuguese **Rio Amazonas**) A great river in South America, 6,570 km (4,080 miles) long, flowing through Peru, Colombia, and Brazil into the Atlantic Ocean on the north coast of Brazil. Its two principal headstreams in the Andes are the Marañon and Ucayali rivers. After the Nile, it is the second-longest river in the world. It drains two-fifths of the continent (7 million sq km, 2.8 million sq miles) and in terms of water-flow it is the largest river in the world with a mean annual discharge of 95,000 cu m of water per second. Northern tributaries, which include the Napo, Japurá, Negro, and Jari rivers, flood in June whereas southern tributaries, such as the Purus, Madeira, Tapajos, and Xingu rivers, flood in March. At its mouth, alluvial deposits and land submergence have created a large delta with many islands, the largest of which is Marajó. The Amazon bore various names after its discovery by Vincente Pinzón in 1500 and was finally named because of a tribe of female warriors believed to live somewhere on its banks. In 1541 the Spanish explorer Francisco de Orellana was the first person to travel the greater part of its full length from the Andes to the Atlantic. Ships with a draught of 4.3 m (14 ft) can reach as far upstream as Iquitos in Peru, *c*.3,700 km (2,300 miles) from the Atlantic.

Amazonian Indian An original American Indian inhabitant of the Amazonian rain forest in South America, a vast area which shows great linguistic and cultural diversity. The dominant form of social organization is one of semi-nomadic tribes of HUNTER-GATHERERS, who prior to the arrival of Europeans had no domestic animals except dogs. The population is dispersed in small tribal groupings such as the YANOMANI, unlike the confederations that were formed by some Plains Indians, for example. KINSHIP is based on a system of mostly patrilineal lineage groups, and elaborate puberty rituals are of central importance, while some tribes are also divided into totemic clans. The predominant religious beliefs are a form of spirit worship or ANIMISM, in which nature is considered to be inhabited by a variety of spirits, and tribal shamans are important in mediating between the spirit world and the world of the living. The shamans also function as healers, and frequently use hallucinogenic drugs as a means of entering the spirit world. Other forms of magical control may include body ornamentation, and some kinds of body painting and tattooing express magical beliefs. The mythology of the Amazonians is diverse, although the French anthropologist LÉVI-STRAUSS claims to have uncovered significant patterns of similarity among a large body of MYTH. Contact with Europeans has often produced drastic effects, in particular competing claims from the settlers and the Indians over land use, and the DEFORESTATION of the jungle.

Ambartzumyan, Viktor Amazaspovich (1908–96) Armenian astrophysicist who investigated the origin and evolution of stars and galaxies. After teaching at the University of Leningrad, he became head of the Byurakan Observatory and in 1955 he put forward his theory that the centres of galaxies were the scenes of enormous explosions that would account for many extragalactic radio waves. He also worked on a method for determining the masses of nebulae, and discovered a new type of star system, known as a star association, from which individual stars can escape.

amber A fossilized resin that has been formed from the gum exuded from conifers. It occurs in irregular masses in estuarine deposits that in geological terms are relatively young. It is found notably south of the Baltic. Insects are occasionally embedded in it. Brittle and easily broken, it is light in weight and warm to the touch. In colour it is typically orange or yellow, but ranges from white to darkish brown, and may be transparent or cloudy. Its use in Europe is now virtually confined to jewellery, but amber carving is still a living craft in China.

Ambler, Eric (1909–) British novelist. His suspense novels, written in the 1930s, include *The Dark Frontier* (1936) and *The Mask of Dimitrios* (1939). His later novels include *A Passage of Arms* (1959) and *In Case of Time* (1981).

Ambrose, St (*c.*339–97) Doctor of the Church. He was a Roman governor at Milan and a converted Christian, though not yet baptized, when he was elected bishop of Milan (374) and became a champion of orthodoxy. He was partly responsible for the conversion of St AUGUSTINE of Hippo. His knowledge of Greek enabled him to introduce much Eastern theology and liturgical practice into the West; Ambrosian (antiphonal) plainsong is associated with his name, and the Athanasian Creed has been attributed to him. Feast day, 7 December.

ambrosia beetle (or **pin-hole borer**) A small, dark, cylindrical BARK BEETLE. The young adults carry fruiting bodies of certain fungi into their egg tunnels, in which the developing hyphae form food for the beetles' larvae. There are two families of beetles which have species known as ambrosia beetles, the Scolytidae and a large tropical family, the Platypodidae.

Amenhotep (Greek **Amenophis**) Four Egyptian pharaohs of the 18th dynasty. **Amenhotep I** (16th century BC), son of Ahmose I (founder of the 18th dynasty), reigned 1546–1526. He fought wars in Nubia and raided Libya. **Amenhotep II** (15th century BC), son of Hatshepsut and Tuthmosis III, reigned 1450–1425. Brought up as a warrior, he fought successful campaigns in Syria and the Middle East; he completed some of the buildings begun by his father. **Amenhotep III** (15th–14th century BC), son of Tuthmosis IV, reigned 1417–1379. After early military campaigns, his reign was generally peaceful and prosperous; he embarked on an extensive building programme centred on his capital, Thebes, including the colossi of Memnon and the Luxor temple. **Amenhotep IV** See AKHENATEN.

America (or **the Americas**) A name sometimes applied specifically to the United States of America but more generally used to describe a continent of the New World or Western Hemisphere, consisting of two great land masses, North and South America, joined by the narrow isthmus of Central America. Human beings first arrived in the Americas *c.*30,000 BC; by 8,000 BC they had settled the whole continent. North America was probably visited by Norse seamen in the 8th or 9th century, but its European discovery is credited to Christopher Columbus, who reached the West Indies in 1492 and the South American mainland in 1498. America derives its name from *Americus Vespucius*, the Latin form of the name of the Italian navigator Amerigo Vespucci (1441–1512) who travelled along the coast of South America in search of a sea route to the Orient in 1501 and concluded that this was not a part of Asia. The name was first used by the German geographer Martin Waldseemüller in 1507 in an account of Vespucci's travels in the New World, and again in 1538 by Mercator.

American Association for the Advancement of Science (AAAS) A US scientific society. Derived from the Association of American Geologists and Naturalists (1840), it was founded as the AAAS in 1848, and modelled on the British Association for the Advancement of Science (1831). Like the latter, it aims to inform the public about the progress of science, mainly through a large annual meeting.

American Civil War (1861–65) A war between the Northern (Union) and Southern (CONFEDERACY) states of the USA. It was officially known as the War of the Rebellion and usually called the War between the States in the South. Economic divergence between the industrialized North and the agricultural, slave-based economy of the South was transformed into political rivalry by the ABOLITIONISTS, and by the dispute over the expansion of slavery into the western territories. By the late 1850s, all efforts at compromise had failed and violence had begun with John BROWN's armed descent on Harper's Ferry (1859). South Carolina seceded from the Union in December 1860 in the wake of Abraham LINCOLN's victory in the presidential election of that year. When the war began with the bombardment of FORT SUMTER (1861), the newly established Southern Confederacy increased to eleven states under the presidency of Jefferson DAVIS.

The war itself is best considered as three simultaneous campaigns. At sea, the North held the upper hand, but the blockade imposed in 1861 took a long time to become effective. Virtually no cotton was exported. Massive naval expansion produced a blockade which helped to cripple the Confederate war effort. On land a series of engagements took place in the Virginia Campaigns, where the close proximity of the Union and Confederacy capitals, Washington and Richmond, and the military genius of General LEE enabled the Confederacy to keep superior Union forces at bay for much of the war. In the more spacious western regions, after a series of abortive starts, the North managed to split the Confederacy in the Vicksburg Campaign, by gaining control of the Mississippi. From here General GRANT moved through Tennessee in the Chattanooga Campaign, opening the way for the drive by SHERMAN through Georgia to the sea. This ruthless strategy, together with Lee's surrender to Grant at APPOMATTOX, brought the war to an end in April 1865. Over 600,000 soldiers died in the Civil War. While the immediate results were the salvation of the union and the abolition of slavery, the challenges of revitalizing the South and promoting racial justice and equality persisted.

American Indian A member of a group of indigenous peoples of North and South America and the Caribbean Islands, called Indians by the error of Columbus and other Europeans in the 15th–16th centuries, who thought they had reached part of

India by a new route. They are characterized by certain blood-type features which are markedly different from those of the Mongoloid peoples whom they otherwise resemble and with whom they were formerly classified. The Amerindian population of North America is *c.*2 million, compared with a South American total of *c.*8 million.

American Revolution See INDEPENDENCE, AMERICAN WAR OF.

American Samoa An unincorporated overseas territory of the USA comprising a group of five volcanic islands and two coral atolls in the South Pacific Ocean, to the east of Western Samoa; area 197 sq km (76.2 sq miles); pop. (1990) 46,770;

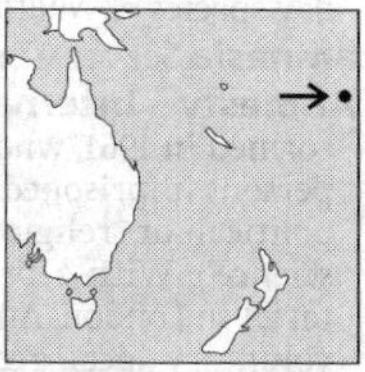

capital, Fagatogo. The principal inhabited islands are Aunu'u, Ofu, Olosega, Ta'u, and Tutuila. Rose Island is uninhabited and Swain's Island, with a population of 29 (1980), lies 334 km (210 miles) to the north-west. The largely Polynesian people of American Samoa mostly work for the US government or in the tuna fish canning industry. In 1899 the USA acquired rights to the islands by agreement with Germany and Britain, and in April 1900 the High Chiefs of Tutuila ceded the islands of Tutuila and Aunu'u to the USA. In 1904 the islands of the Manu'a group (Ofu, Olosega, Ta'u, and Rose) were handed over and in 1925 Swain's Island was added to the territory. American Samoa was administered by the US Department of Navy until 1951, when administrative responsibility was transferred to the Department of the Interior.

America's Cup A cup given to the winner of a sailing competition based at Cowes, on the Isle of Wight, in 1851. The cup is named after the US schooner *America*, owned by J. L. Stevens, which won this race. Subsequent periodical races in different venues have been won by New York Yacht Club except in 1983, when Australia won it, and 1989, when it went to New Zealand but was given back to America after a law suit. New Zealand won the cup in 1995.

americium (symbol Am, at. no. 95, r.a.m. 243) A strongly radioactive transuranic element synthesized by G. T. Seaborg in 1944 by bombarding plutonium with neutrons. Compounds known include the oxide AmO_2 and such trihalides as $AmCl_3$.

Amersfoort A commercial and industrial city in the province of Utrecht, central Netherlands, 20 km (13 miles) north-east of the city of Utrecht; pop. (1991) 101,970. After receiving its charter in 1279, it developed in association with brewing and the textile industry. Engineering, food processing, and the manufacture of chemicals are now important industries.

amethyst A form of QUARTZ found in IGNEOUS ROCK, notably in Brazil and Uruguay, and prized as a semi-precious gem. Transparent and violet to purple in colour, it must not be confused with the rarer oriental amethyst which is a variety of corundum (sapphire).

Amharic The official and commercial language of Ethiopia, spoken by about one-third of the population in the area of the capital, Addis Ababa, and the region to the north of it. It belongs to the Semitic language group but within the Ethiopic branch of this group it is directly descended from the ancient Classical Ethiopian or Ge'ez tongue.

AM Herculis stars A recently discovered class of variable stars that exhibit periodic variations in luminosity and POLARIZATION, both linear and circular. They appear to have a source of SYNCHROTRON RADIATION which is swept around the star as it rotates. This radiation is detectable by X-ray observations. AM Herculis stars are sometimes referred to as **polars** because of the large polarization changes that are observed.

Amherst, Jeffrey, Baron (1717–97) British general. He commanded the combined operation which captured Louisburg in 1758. On his appointment as commander-in-chief in America, he applied widespread pressure on the French. His own army advanced northward up the Hudson Valley, taking Ticonderoga and Crown Point in 1759 and Montreal in 1760, thus ending French control of Canada. He was then made governor of Virginia, but failed to contain PONTIAC's Indian Rebellion in 1763 and was recalled. He refused to fight against Americans in 1775, but advised on strategy.

Amiens The capital of Picardy (Picardie) in northern France, on the River Somme; pop. (1990) 136,230. A market town and textile centre since the Middle Ages, Amiens has been famous for its velvet since the 16th century and today has textile, clothing, tyres, and chemical industries. Its 13th-century Gothic cathedral is one of the largest in France.

Amin Dada, Idi (*c.*1925–) Ugandan head of state 1971–79. Possessed of only rudimentary education, Amin rose through the ranks of the army to become its commander. In 1971 he overthrew President OBOTE and seized power. His rule was characterized by the advancing of narrow tribal interests, the expulsion of non-Africans (most notably Ugandan Asians), and violence on a huge scale. He was overthrown with Tanzanian assistance in 1979 and went into exile in Saudi Arabia.

Amindivi Islands (or **Amindivis**) The northernmost group of islands in the Indian territory of Lakshadweep in the Indian Ocean.

amine An organic compound derived from ammonia, NH_3, by replacement of one or more hydrogen atoms by an ALKYL or ARYL GROUP. If these groups are represented by R, R′, and R″, a primary amine has the general formula RNH_2, a secondary amine RR′NH, and a tertiary amine RR′R″N. Like ammonia, amines are BASES; they dissociate in water (some very weakly) and react with acids to give salts and with acid anhydrides to form amides. Simple amines have a characteristic fishy smell. Amines have many uses, for example, as insecticides, dyestuffs (the best known being ANILINE), pharmaceuticals, and rust-inhibitors.

amino acid A natural organic compound. Amino acids are the subunits of PROTEINS: there are twenty different amino acids generally found in proteins, although some are less common than others, and a few specialized proteins contain amino acids different from the twenty. Many other amino acids which are not incorporated into proteins also occur in living organisms. Each amino acid molecule consists of a central carbon atom with four bonds attaching it to hydrogen (–H), amino ($-NH_2$), and carboxyl (–COOH) groups, and also to a variable group known as the '–R' group. The –R group has a different structure in each amino acid, and determines its individual chemical properties. Amino acids can be joined together like the coaches of a train by chemical bonds (peptide bonds) formed between the carboxyl group of one, and the amino group of the next. Short chains of two to twenty amino acids are called peptides; longer chains are called polypeptides. In proteins, the chains are twisted and folded to give a three-dimensional shape which is determined by the order of the individual amino acids.

In the human diet, nine of the twenty different types must be present. These nine are known as 'essential' amino acids. The remaining 'non-essential' types can be manufactured by the liver. Amino acids cannot be stored in the body for more than four hours, so all of the essential ones must be provided in the diet. Excess amino acids in the body, obtained from the digestion of proteins, are 'deaminated': the amino group is removed and converted into UREA (in man and most mammals) for excretion. In addition to their use in building proteins, amino acids are also used for making certain HORMONES, VITAMINS, COENZYMES, and transmitters of impulses between NEURONES.

Amirante Islands A group of coral islands in the Indian Ocean, forming part of the Seychelles.

Amis, Sir Kingsley (1922–95) British poet and novelist. He came to fame with his first novel, *Lucky Jim* (1954), whose hero, a lower-middle-class history lecturer at odds with conservative social attitudes, was hailed as an ANGRY YOUNG MAN; its provincial university setting was indicative of a new realism in fiction which Amis further developed in *That Uncertain Feeling* (1955) and *Take a Girl Like You* (1960). He is best known for his satiric comedies, including *One Fat Englishman* (1963), *Ending Up* (1974), *Jake's Thing* (1978), and *The Old Devils* (1986: Booker Prize).

Amis, Martin (1949–) British novelist, son of Kingsley Amis. His books include *The Rachel Papers* (1974) and *Money* (1984). The novels *London Fields* (1989) and *Time's Arrow* (1991) were well received.

Amish A strict US Mennonite sect that shuns most modern technical appliances. Centred in rural Pennsylvania, thousands of Amish moved to the Midwest during the mid-19th century. The sect is divided into 'Church Amish' or 'Amish Mennonites' and 'House Amish' or 'Old Order' who worship in their own homes.

Amman The capital of Jordan, on the River Zarqa; pop. (1991) 965,000. Noted for its coloured marble, Amman produces leather, textiles, tobacco, and tiles. Occupied since ancient times, the city lay on the desert highway linking Egypt with the Levant and Tigris-Euphrates basins. Described as Rabbath-Ammon in the Old Testament, Amman was known as Philadelphia throughout the Roman and Byzantine periods. It declined after the Arab conquest of 635 AD but was made capital of Trans-Jordan in 1921. After 1945 the city expanded rapidly, absorbing refugees from Palestine.

ammeter An instrument used to measure ELECTRIC CURRENT in a circuit. Ideal ammeters have negligible internal resistance and thus do not take any power from the circuit. The GALVANOMETER is a type of ammeter.

ammonia (or **nitrogen trihydride**, NH_3) A colourless gas with a characteristic pungent smell; it is readily soluble in water, giving an alkaline solution. It is also toxic, causing blindness and respiratory problems, although small quantities are administered via smelling salts to revive people who have fainted. Ammonia is manufactured, using the HABER–BOSCH PROCESS, in which nitrogen and hydrogen are mixed at high temperature and pressure in the presence of an iron catalyst. Solid compounds of ammonia, such as ammonium sulphate, ammonium nitrate, and urea, are important FERTILIZERS. Ammonia is also used in the manufacture of NITRIC ACID, explosives, and cleaning materials.

ammonite The fossil remains of a CEPHALOPOD mollusc, now extinct, but which flourished in the seas during the Mesozoic Era (245–66.4 million years ago). Ammonites consist of flat, tightly coiled shells which protected the animal and probably also contained air to help it to float. In some respects, these animals were probably like present-day species of *Nautilus* (PEARLY NAUTILUS).

amnesia See MEMORY DISORDER.

Amnesty International A pressure group formed in 1961, whose activities and aims focus on persons imprisoned or maltreated because of their political or religious beliefs ('prisoners of conscience'). With a professional international secretariat in London, Amnesty is based on a network of voluntary local groups and individual members throughout the world, who adopt prisoners of conscience and pursue their cases with the governments concerned or through international bodies; methods of investigation include monitoring, fact-finding missions, publicity, and individual correspondence. Amnesty is not associated with any single ideology, government, or political party, and impartiality is central to its Statute.

amniocentesis A technique in OBSTETRICS and gynaecology involving the removal and testing of a sample of the amniotic fluid surrounding the foetus in the womb. The sample is usually taken between the twelfth and eighteenth weeks of pregnancy, using a hollow needle inserted through the abdominal wall. The amniotic fluid contains foetal cells which can be examined cytologically and biochemically. Amniocentesis allows prenatal diagnosis of diseases caused by chromosomal abnormality, such as DOWN'S SYNDROME, and developmental disorders such as spina bifida.

amoeba A unicellular PROTOZOAN. Amoebae are usually highly asymmetric organisms that move by means of flowing pseudopodia (foot-like protrusions of the flexible cell MEMBRANE). Within the one-celled body a large nucleus and many microscopic organelles occur, yet there is usually little detail to be seen even in giant amoebae, which are up to 0.5 cm (0.2 inch) long. Amoebae live in seas, fresh water, and soils, or occasionally as parasites (causing amoebic dysentery). Amoebae are closely related to FORAMINIFERA and RADIOLARIA.

Amor group A collection of ASTEROIDS which have orbits that cross the orbit of Mars but not that of the Earth. The exact characteristics are that the semi-major axis is greater than 1.0 astronomical unit (a.u.), but the perihelion distance lies between 1.017 and 1.3 a.u. Apart from the asteroid Amor, the group contains Alinda, Betulia, Ivar, Quetzal-coatl, Cuyo, and Anza.

Amorites A group of semi-nomadic tribes, bearing Semitic personal names, from the east Syrian steppe and desert region. In the late 3rd and early 2nd millenium BC they founded a number of states and dynasties, including Mari on the Euphrates and the First Dynasty of Babylon, associated with Hammurabi I (died 1750 BC).

amortization The repayment of the capital value of a debt, usually by instalments. Amortization is also used to mean DEPRECIATION, the decline in value of a capital good during its working life.

Amos A Hebrew prophet in the reign of Jeroboam II (8th century BC). A herdsman, Amos prophesied the fate of the nations surrounding Israel and of Israel itself. He denounced the social abuses of his time, strongly supporting the poor and oppressed.

ampere (symbol A) The SI UNIT of electric current. It is named after the French physicist André Marie AMPÈRE. A current in a conductor is a flow of ELECTRIC CHARGE, usually in the form of electrons. A current of 1 A passing through a metal conductor is equivalent to a flow of about 10^{19} electrons per second. The ampere is defined in terms of the magnetic force produced by an electric current: a current of 1 A flowing in each of two infinitely long, straight, narrow wires 1 m apart in a vacuum produces a force between the two wires of 2×10^{-7} newton per metre length.

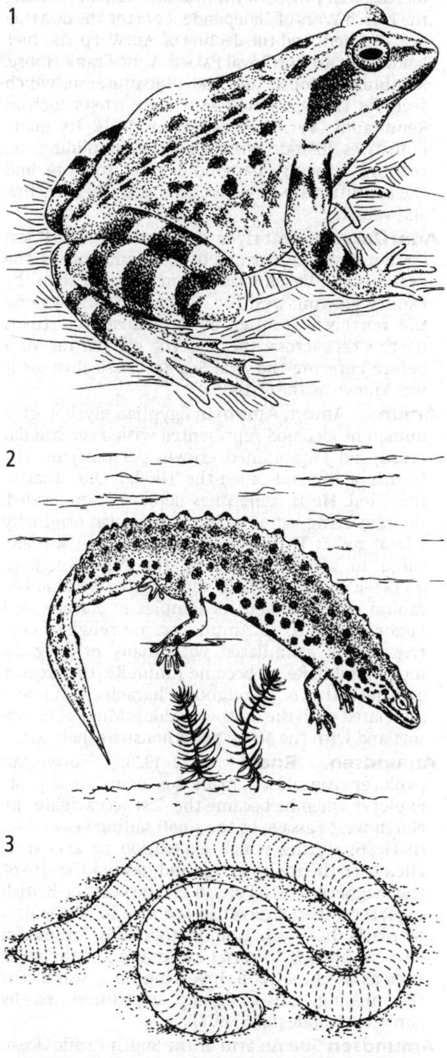

Amphibians (1) European common frog. This amphibian belongs to the order Anura, members of which are specialized for jumping by having long muscular legs and no tail. (2) Smooth or common newt. This is a typical member of the order Caudata, having a long body and tail and short limbs as adaptations to a largely aquatic existence. (3) American caecilian. This burrowing amphibian, like other members of its order, Gymnophiona, lacks limbs and superficially resembles a giant worm.

Ampère, André-Marie (1775–1836) French physicist, mathematician, and philosopher. He was a child prodigy who became one of the founders of electromagnetism and electrodynamics, and is best known for his analysis of the relationship between magnetic force and electric current. Ampère also developed a precursor of the galvanometer.

amphibian A member of a class of vertebrate animals, the Amphibia, which can live on land and in water, and commonly have eggs which are externally fertilized. The class includes frogs, toads, newts, salamanders, sirens, and caecilians. REPTILES, which do not need to breed in water, subsequently evolved from amphibians.

The skin is particularly important to an amphibian, since it acts as a respiratory (air-breathing) surface, although it needs to be kept moist to function in this way. The lungs, present in most though not all amphibians, are simple sac-like structures which connect via a tube to the oral cavity. An efficient excretory system removes the waste products of metabolism, while controlling salt and water losses from the body. Frogs and toads have a true EAR and a more complex heart than their fish ancestors. These features, which first appeared among vertebrates in the amphibians, together with a variety of further structural and behavioural adaptations, have enabled the amphibians to colonize a wide variety of habitats in most continents of the world, except Antarctica.

Modern amphibians (approximately 4,000 species) belong to three distinct major orders: the Caudata or Urodela, the tailed amphibians (newts, salamanders, and sirens); the Anura or tail-less amphibians (frogs and toads); and the Gymnophiona or Apoda (the limbless, worm-like caecilians).

amphibious vehicle A vehicle designed to be used on land or on water, for military, rescue, or agricultural purposes. By World War II several amphibious vehicles were being used by the military, including the US DUKW or 'Duck', the British 'Terrapin', and the German Volkswagen *Schwimmwagen*. Today, HOVERCRAFT and LOW-GROUND-PRESSURE VEHICLES are used in many amphibious applications.

amphiboles (from Greek, 'ambiguous') A common group of minerals found mainly in IGNEOUS ROCKS and METAMORPHIC ROCKS. They are characterized by a double chain structure of linked silicate tetrahedra. Iron, calcium, sodium, magnesium, aluminium, and other elements may be present: HORNBLENDE, a common rock-forming mineral, is the commonest member of the group. Certain amphiboles occur in fibrous form, and belong to the ASBESTOS group.

amphioxus See LANCELET.

amphipod A member of an order of CRUSTACEANS, Amphipoda, with over 4,600 species, including the very common sandhoppers, *Orchestia*, and the freshwater 'shrimps', such as *Gammarus pulex*, as well as many marine shrimp-like animals and the elongate 'skeleton shrimps', *Caprella*. Most amphipods are specialized to inhabit the bottom of ponds and streams or along sea-shores; they have different sets of legs for swimming, walking, and jumping. They are generally flattened laterally and look hunch-backed as they scavenge on mud or sand, sometimes even swimming on their sides. Some species are parasitic and have evolved bizarre body shapes. Any stream or pond should yield examples of the commonest freshwater species, *G. pulex*, often found in mating pairs.

amphisbaenid A REPTILE of the family Amphisbaenidae. Amphisbaenids resemble earthworms, being exceedingly specialized for a burrowing lifestyle. They are limbless, with the exception of three Mexican species which have forelimbs only. Their blunt heads and strong skulls are well adapted for ramming through soil. They comprise about 130 species and, in spite of sometimes being referred to as worm lizards, are quite distinct from both lizards and snakes. In the Americas they range from Florida to Patagonia; in the Old World they occur in Africa, western Asia, Spain, and Portugal.

amphitheatre A circular or oval unroofed building with tiers of seats rising outwards from a central open space or arena, used by the Romans for gladiatoral combats and similar spectacles. The earliest known amphitheatres date from the 1st century BC, and they later became common throughout the Roman empire. The largest and most famous example is the Colosseum in Rome, begun in about 75 AD. It held 50,000 spectators.

amphora A two-handled ancient Greek or Roman pottery jar with a pointed or knobbed bottom to facilitate its transport, used for the storage of wine and olive oil. Often located by marine archaeologists in wrecks, they provide valuable evidence of trade links.

amphoteric compound A compound, usually an oxide or hydroxide, that can behave as both an ACID and BASE. The elements whose oxides can show amphoteric character are the metals towards the right-hand side of the PERIODIC TABLE. For example, zinc oxide, ZnO, is amphoteric. It acts as a base by dissolving in aqueous acids to give solutions of zinc salts, and it acts as an acid by dissolving in aqueous alkali to form solutions of the zincate-ion, $Zn(OH)_4^{-2}$.

amplifier An electronic device or circuit that provides gain, using an external energy source to produce a signal output larger than the input. Amplifiers are used extensively to magnify weak signals from MICROPHONES, TRANSDUCERS, and tuning circuits, in order to provide a large enough signal to drive a LOUDSPEAKER, CATHODE-RAY TUBE, transmitter, or other device. If one amplifier unit alone provides insufficient amplification, several amplifiers may be joined together in stages. Excessive amplification, however, may cause malfunction or distortion. Although amplifiers were in the past made using THERMIONIC VALVES, the vast majority of modern amplifiers use TRANSISTORS or INTEGRATED CIRCUITS. The transistors are the devices that actually amplify the electrical signal. Many types of amplifier exist, their design depending on whether they amplify electrical voltage or current, and their application. They include audio-frequency amplifiers used for SOUND recording and reproduction, and radio-frequency amplifiers used to boost tuned radio and television receiver signals. Amplifiers may also be categorized as 'small signal' amplifiers, using relatively small input and output signals, or 'power' amplifiers, delivering enough signal to energize such devices as loudspeakers.

amplitude (in physics) A quantity that varies periodically, the maximum departure from a mean or base value. In the case of a vibration or oscillation it is half the total extent of the motion. Of waves, it is the greatest distance by which a wave departs from its mean position. The greater the energy of the wave, the larger is its amplitude.

Amritsar A city in the state of Punjab, north-west India; pop. (1991) 709,000. Founded in 1577 by Ram Das, fourth guru of the Sikhs, it became the centre of the Sikh faith and the site of its holiest temple, the Golden Temple. It was the scene of a riot in 1919 when British troops killed 400 people and in 1984 a Sikh leader was killed there during fighting between Sikh militants and the Indian Army. The city is famous for its crafts, particularly carpets and woollen cloths.

Amsterdam The capital and largest city of the Netherlands, one of the major ports and commercial centres of Europe, built on *c.*100 islands separated by the canals for which it is noted; pop. (1991) 702,440. Founded in the 13th century, the city increased in prosperity in the 16th century during the Dutch Wars of Independence after the destruction of Ghent and the decline of Antwerp. Its chief landmarks are the Royal Palace, Anne Frank House, Rembrandt House, and the Rijksmuseum, which features famous works by Dutch artists such as Rembrandt, Vermeer, and Frans Hals. Its many industries include engineering, shipbuilding, oil refining, brewing, diamond cutting, tourism, and the manufacture of petrochemicals, steel, textiles, and vehicles.

Amu Darya A great river of central Asia, *c.*2,541 km (1,578 miles) long, formed by the confluence of the Pyandzh and Vaksh headstreams which rise in the Pamirs. Flowing west for 270 km (170 miles) along the northern frontier of Afghanistan it turns north-west across the deserts of central Asia before entering the Aral Sea. In classical times it was known as the Oxus.

Amun (or **Amon, Amen**) In Egyptian mythology, a human-headed god represented with a ceremonial beard and two-plumed crown, personifying the breath of life and called the 'Hidden One', that is, the wind. He is sometimes depicted ram-headed, the ram being sacred to him. Amun was originally a local god at Thebes (modern Luxor), but was elevated to state god during the New Kingdom (*c.*1550–1050 BC), at which time Thebes became the capital of Egypt and its temples at Karnak and Luxor, dedicated to Amun, became religious centres. Amun assimilated with many other gods, most notably Re, to become Amun-Re, the creator god and father of all reigning Pharaohs. Amun was associated with the mother goddess Mut as his consort and with the Moon god Khonsu as their son.

Amundsen, Roald (1872–1928) Norwegian explorer. Amundsen made his name as a polar explorer when he became the first to navigate the North-west Passage in the small sailing vessel *Gjöa* (1903–06), during which expedition he also travelled over the ice by sledge and located the site of the magnetic North Pole. In 1911 he beat the British explorer Robert F. Scott in the race to be the first to reach the South Pole. In the 1920s Amundsen devoted himself to aerial exploration of the polar regions, eventually disappearing on a search for the missing Italian airship expedition led by Umberto Nobile (1885–1978).

Amundsen Sea An arm of the South Pacific Ocean in the seas of Antarctica, off the coast of Marie Byrd Land. It was explored and named by a Norwegian, Nils Larsen, in 1929.

Amur (Chinese **Hei Ho, Heilung Jiang**) A river of north-east Asia, forming for the greater part of its length the boundary between Russia and China before entering the Sea of Okhotsk via the Tatar Strait. Its length is 2,824 km (1,777 miles), but including its northern headstream, the Shilka River, its total length is 4,416 km (2,744 miles).

Amzirght The language of the Berber people of North Africa.

Anabaptism A Christian religious doctrine which centred on the baptism of believers, and held that people baptized as infants must be rebaptized as adults. Anabaptists or 'Re-baptists' formed part of the radical wing of the 16th-century REFORMATION. The sects originated mainly in Zürich in the 1520s, with the aim of restoring the spirit and institutions of the early Church. Their belief that the Church was not an earthly institution and that true earthly institutions were by their nature hopelessly corrupt, led them to a repudiation of the very basis of the authority of the civil power. Thus, though they were often law-abiding, they reserved the right in conscience to disobey the law, and for this they were feared and persecuted. They managed to establish centres in Saxony, Austria, Moravia, Poland, the Lower Rhine, and the Netherlands, but made almost no headway in the French-speaking world. In the 17th century the MENNONITES preserved some of the best of the Anabaptist traditions, which made a significant contribution to the religious history of modern Europe and America.

anabatic wind A meteorological term used to describe a wind caused by air that is drawn upwards by convection currents on mountain slopes.

anabolic steroid See STEROIDS AND STEROID TREATMENT.

anaconda A species of snake, *Eunectes murinus*, belonging to the boa family, that occurs in northern South America. It is the largest living snake; there are credible records of anaconda skins up to 11.4 m (37.4 feet) long. Anacondas are usually found basking in pools and streams, or sometimes in trees or bushes on an adjacent bank. It feeds mainly on mammals and birds that come to the water to drink, though it will also eat aquatic animals such as fishes, turtles, and small caymans. A smaller but closely related species, the southern anaconda, *E. notaeus*, occurs in Paraguay. Anacondas kill their prey by constriction, effectively suffocating their victims.

Anacreon (*c.*570–478 BC) Greek lyric poet. The surviving fragments of his work include iambic invectives and elegiac epitaphs, but he is most famous for his poetry written in celebration of love and wine.

anaemia The deficiency of red BLOOD cells, HAEMOGLOBIN, or both; the size and shape of red blood cells may also be altered. In anaemia, the oxygen-carrying capacity of the blood is reduced. Common symptoms include fatigue and generalized weakness and pallor, although in some cases no symptoms may be apparent. In severe cases, increased heart rate, chest pain, headache, breathlessness, and menstrual disturbances may occur.

Common causes of anaemia include iron, folic acid, or VITAMIN B_{12} deficiency, which result in reduced or defective production of red blood cells. Increased destruction of red blood cells is also a cause of anaemia (haemolytic anaemia), which is characteristic of certain inherited conditions such as sickle-cell anaemia and beta THALASSAEMIA.

anaesthesia Loss of feeling in all or a part of the body. Anaesthesia of part of the body may occur through injury to or disease in a nerve, but the term is more usually applied to the reduction or abolishing of surgical pain using drugs, or other methods such as ACUPUNCTURE or hypnosis. In the mid-19th century in the USA and Europe the anaesthetics ether, CHLOROFORM, and nitrous oxide were first used for pain relief during operations. Anaesthetic drugs act on the fatty membranes of nerve cells, disrupting the transmission of electrical impulses. Anaesthesia may be general, regional, or local. Local anaesthesia blocks nerve transmission at the site where the anaesthetic is administered, so that sensory signals do not reach the central nervous system. In regional anaesthesia, the anaesthetic is applied to large nerves whose branches supply a wide area of the body, or to an area around the spinal cord. Regional anaesthetic techniques have made surgery available to many patients too frail to undergo general anaesthesia. General anaesthesia relies on the initial injection of drugs that readily dissolve in nerve cells throughout the central nervous system, thus disrupting its function and leading to unconsciousness. The patient then breathes in inhalational anaesthetics to maintain anaesthesia. See also SURGERY.

Anaheim A city in Orange County, south-west California, USA, a part of the greater Los Angeles conurbation to the east of Long Beach; pop. (1990) 266,400. Founded by German settlers in 1857, Anaheim developed into an industrial centre, producing electronics, aircraft parts, and canned fruit. It is the site of the Disneyland amusement park which was opened in 1955.

analgesic A drug that reduces pain. NARCOTIC analgesics act on the brain: opium derivatives such as morphine are powerful, but easily produce addiction and their supply is strictly controlled by law. Non-narcotic analgesics, of which paracetamol and non-steroidal anti-inflammatories (such as aspirin and ibuprofen) are the most common, act peripherally by preventing the formation of pain-producing substances in injured or inflamed tissues. Although far less powerful than narcotic analgesics, they are effective for headaches and minor pains and usually have no serious side-effects. The anti-inflammatory analgesics are widely used for pain relief in rheumatic conditions. See also PHARMACOLOGY.

analog computer A COMPUTER that uses continuously variable (analog) quantities to represent numbers. Analog computers can perform complex arithmetical operations extremely quickly with very few components, but they are not very accurate. Digital computers have replaced them almost entirely except in signal processing, where the basic analog computing elements are still used very widely. Recent work suggests that analog computing techniques might have a significant future in NEURAL NETWORK computers.

analysis (in chemistry) The determination of the composition of a substance. This can be carried out by physical means: for example, the melting-point of an unknown substance can be measured, and a suggestion made as to its identity by comparison with a table of melting-points. An important branch is SPECTROSCOPY. Substances absorb and emit characteristic wavelengths of light in all regions of the visible spectrum. For example, salts of certain metals impart characteristic colours to a flame, and a flame test can be carried out to determine the presence of these metals. Analysis can also be carried out by chemical means, both qualitative and quantitative. Qualitative analysis establishes only the presence or absence of substances; it cannot determine their quantities or concentrations. This is the objective of quantitative analysis, which can be carried out in many ways. In gravimetric analysis, a precipitate is formed and is then weighed; and knowledge of its mass allows the original concentration to be determined. In volumetric analysis, a **titration** is carried out: the substance of unknown concentration is titrated against a substance of known concentration, which reacts specifically with it. By measuring the quantity required for complete reaction, the unknown concentration can be determined. Analysis has many practical applications, not least in forensic science.

In mathematics, analysis involves the study of infinite processes. These processes may proceed either by indefinite accretion (as when terms are added in an infinite SERIES) or by indefinite diminution (as when the separation of two points on a continuous line is allowed to contract indefinitely). Thus analysis encompasses the mathematics of CALCULUS, continuity, limits, series, and related topics.

analytical engine See BABBAGE; COMPUTER, HISTORY OF.

analytic philosophy A broad movement in 20th-century philosophy, influential chiefly in Austria, the UK, and the USA, which regards central philosophical problems as primarily demanding clarification or analysis of such notions as meaning, truth, and necessity. Although analytical philosophy is a loosely unified tradition, rather than a specific doctrine, there has been broad agreement on some specific matters. First, philosophy is a distinctive kind of enquiry, which employs methods different from those of the natural or social sciences; additionally, unlike, for instance, biology or economics, it is not addressed to any distinctive realm of facts. Philosophy does not seek to construct theories which build upon or add to our knowledge of the world, but to clarify the knowledge and beliefs we already have. Secondly, this clarification is to be achieved by analysis of the language in which our non-philosoical, common-sense, or scientific knowledge is expressed. This framework leaves ample room for internal divisions. There is, for instance, disagreement between RUSSELL's view that this kind of clarification will yield answers to the traditional questions of METAPHYSICS and EPISTEMOLOGY, and WITTGENSTEIN's contention that such questions are the products of confusions which the careful analysis of language will enable us to avoid. A related dispute concerns whether philosophical analysis can itself be conducted in a systematic way, using the tools and techniques of mathematical LOGIC, as the LOGICAL POSITIVISTS held, or whether resolution of philosophical problems demands piecemeal attention to specific areas of ordinary language (see LINGUISTIC PHILOSOPHY).

anamorphosis A picture (or a part of one) executed in such a way that it gives a distorted image of the object represented until it is seen from a particular angle or by means of a special lens or mirror, when it appears in lifelike aspect. Generally, the purpose of anamorphosis was to mystify or amuse.

Anand, Mulk Raj (1905–) Indian novelist. He made his name with the powerful protest novel *Untouchable* (1935), which was followed by other studies of the Indian poor in *Coolie* (1936) and *Two Leaves and a Bud* (1937). His Lalu Singh trilogy, *The Village* (1939), *Across the Black Waters* (1940), and *The Sword and the Sickle* (1942), follows the fortunes of a young Sikh during World War I. The best known of his later works is *The Private Life of an Indian Prince* (1953).

anarchism The belief that government and law should be abolished and society organized by voluntary means without resort to force or compulsion. The French social theorist Pierre Joseph PROUDHON first expounded the theory that equality and justice should be achieved through the abolition of the state and the substitution of free agreements between individuals. Other anarchist visions of the society of the future include the economic individualism, outlined in the American writer Benjamin Tucker's *Instead of a Book* (1893) and the communism envisaged by the Russian émigré Peter Kropotkin's work *The Conquest of Bread* (1906).

Groups of anarchists tried to find popular support in many European states in the 1860s and 1870s. They were hostile to MARXISM on the grounds that a seizure of state-power by the workers would only perpetuate oppression. The Russian anarchist Mikhail BAKUNIN founded a Social Democratic Alliance (1868), which attempted to wrest control of the workers International from MARX. Anarchists switched between strategies of spontaneous mutual association and violent acts against representatives of the state. The Presidents of France and Italy, the King of Italy, and the Empress of Austria were killed by anarchists between 1894 and 1901. Subsequently they tried to mobilize mass working-class support behind the Russian General Strike, which was a central feature of the RUSSIAN REVOLUTIONS of 1905 and 1917. Their influence in Europe declined after the rise of totalitarian states elsewhere. They were active in the SPANISH CIVIL WAR, and in the latter half of the 20th century anarchism attracted urban terrorists.

Anatolia (Turkish **Anadolu**) The western peninsula of Asia that now forms the greater part of Turkey. See ASIA MINOR.

Anatolian languages A group of INDO-EUROPEAN LANGUAGES spoken in Anatolia (modern Turkey) and Syria in the second and first millennia BC. The best attested is Hittite. The other languages, which are rather poorly attested, are Luwian, Lycian, Lydian, and Palaic. Hittite was written in cuneiform on clay tablets discovered in the early 20th century at Boğazköy (ancient Hattusa) in central Turkey. Cuneiform is a script made up of small wedge shapes, in which each character stands for a syllable, and was borrowed from Mesopotamia. The tablets date from the 17th to the 13th centuries BC, which makes Hittite the earliest known Indo-European language. As such it has been extremely valuable for the reconstruction of Indo-European.

anatomy The study of the shape, form, consistency, and organization of plants and animals. Comparative anatomy deals with differences in these aspects between humans and other animals and is important in the study of evolution.

Study of the external features of living organisms is called MORPHOLOGY and covers all external detail down to that visible only under an electron microscope. Anatomy embraces morphology, and applies also to the internal features of organs, skeletons, and even cellular detail. Anatomy has been studied by means of dissection, while modern non-destructive means of studying internal structures include body-scanners and X-RAYS. The study of tissues is known as HISTOLOGY, and that of cells as CYTOLOGY.

Anaxagoras (*c.*500–*c.*428 BC) Greek philosopher. He taught in Athens, where his pupils included Pericles. He believed that all matter was infinitely divisible and initially held together in a motionless, uniform mixture until put into a system of

circulation directed by Spirit or Intelligence, which created the sky and Earth, from which the Sun, Moon, and stars were formed.

Anaximander (*c.*610–*c.*545 BC) Greek scientist, who lived at Miletus. He is reputed to have drawn the earliest map of the inhabited world, to have introduced the sundial into Greece, and to have taught that life began in water and that man originated from fish. He believed that all phenomena result from vortical motion in the primordial substance, and that the Earth is cylindrical and poised in space.

Anaximenes (*c.*546 BC) Greek philosopher and scientist, who lived at Miletus. Anaximenes believed the Earth to be flat and shallow, and his view of astronomy was a retrograde step from that of Anaximander.

ANC See AFRICAN NATIONAL CONGRESS.

ancestor worship The worship of dead ancestors by the living, based on the belief that the spirits of the dead continue to have a close relation to their kin, and are capable of influencing their affairs. Ancestral spirits can be male or female, and can include all ancestors, those of a few generations, or indeed mythical ancestors. Worship takes many ritual forms, such as propitiatory prayers, offerings, sacrifice, and festivals of honour. Ancestor worship is found in many African traditional religions, where the spirits are called on to avert illness, help obtain good crops, or assure fertility. CHINESE RELIGIONS and SHINTO in Japan stress reverence for ancestors, although in modern China, as the importance of KINSHIP has declined, so has ancestor worship.

anchor A device for securing a ship to the sea-bed or river-bed. It is attached to the ship by a chain or cable, which hangs in a deep curve (catenary) in the water, thus improving the anchor's holding power. Originally, a heavy stone, or a basket of stones, was used, and stone anchors are still in use in some places. As ships grew larger, hooked anchors were introduced, later incorporating a stock or shaft at right angles to the hooks for improved holding power. When iron replaced wood as a shipbuilding material in the 19th century, ships' anchors increased considerably in size and weight. The anchor arms were developed into large flukes (blade-like projections), pivoted about the central shaft, and anchor chains replaced rope cables. In the 20th century several new anchor designs have been introduced.

Anchorage The largest city in the state of Alaska, USA, at the head of the Cook Inlet; pop. (1990) 226,340. Founded as a railway town in 1915, Anchorage developed into an important port, transportation hub, and centre of the oil, fishing, and gold-mining industries. The city was badly damaged during an earthquake in 1964.

anchovy Any one of the several species of slender fish of the family Engraulidae. Related to the herring, it has a clear green back, silvery sides, and a very long upper jaw. The European anchovy, *Engraulis encrasicolus*, forms large schools near the surface of the sea round European coasts. Other species of anchovy live in warm and temperate waters around the world; many are important commercial fishes.

ancien régime The political and administrative systems in France in the 17th and 18th centuries under the Bourbon kings, before the FRENCH REVOLUTION; it is also applied more widely to much of the rest of Europe. The monarch had (in theory) unlimited authority, including the right to imprison individuals without trial. There was no representative assembly. Privilege, above all, was the hallmark of the *ancien régime*: the nobility were privileged before the law, in matters of taxation, and in the holding of high offices. The French Revolution was an uprising by the underprivileged.

Ancona An Adriatic port and capital of the Marche region of central Italy; pop. (1990) 103,270. Founded near a sharp bend in the coast (Greek *ankon* elbow) by Greeks from Syracuse *c.*390 BC, it was named Dorica Ancon. Later as a Roman colony it was developed as a naval base by Caesar and Trajan. In the 9th century Ancona became a semi-independent maritime state which was in 1532 incorporated as part of the Papal States. There is a large naval and commercial port with ferry services to Greece and the Balkans. Industries include fishing, ship repairing, sugar refining, and the making of musical instruments.

Andalusia (Spanish **Andalucia**) The southernmost and largest of the regions of Spain, bordering on the Atlantic Ocean and the Mediterranean Sea; area 87,268 sq km (33,707 sq miles); pop. (1991) 6,940,520. It comprises the provinces of Almeria, Cadiz, Córdoba, Granada, Huelva, Jaén, Malaga, and Sevilla and includes the tourist resorts of the Costa del Sol and Spain's highest mountain, Mulhacén (3,482 m, 11,424 ft). The River Guadalquivir flows westwards through Andalusia to the Gulf of Cadiz. It is rich in minerals and grows olives, grapes, and citrus fruits.

Andaman and Nicobar Islands A Union Territory of India consisting of two groups of tropical islands in the Bay of Bengal; area 8,293 sq km (3,203 sq miles); pop. (1991) 279,110; capital, Port Blair. The 19 small islands of the Nicobar group lie to the south of the Andamans, which comprise the Great Andamans and Little Andaman. Peopled by Negrito aborigines, the islands export timber, coffee, fruit, and coconuts. They have served as a penal colony since the mid-19th century.

Andean Group A regional economic grouping comprising Colombia, Peru (suspended from 1992 to 1993), Bolivia, Chile (from 1969 to 1977), Venezuela, and Ecuador. Formally established by the Cartagena Agreement of 1969 – hence its official name, *Acuerdo de Cartagena* – it was an attempt to enhance the competitive edge of the member states in their economic relations with the more developed economies of the Latin American region. In 1987 members signed the Quito Protocol, which included a relaxation of the strict controls on foreign investors in the region, which had acted as a deterrent to investment. The Andean Group committed itself in 1989 to both regional and political integration. The Andean Pact of 1991 (the Caracas Declaration) agreed to the abolition of internal trade tariffs by 1995. In 1994 it agreed to form a free trade area with MERCOSUR, another South American economic group.

Andersen, Hans Christian (1805–75) Danish writer. The son of a poor shoemaker, he published several volumes of poetry and was acknowledged in Scandinavia as a novelist and travel writer before publishing the first of his fairy tales. These appeared from 1835 and include 'The Snow Queen', 'The Ugly Duckling', and 'The Little Match Girl'. Although deeply rooted in Danish folklore, the stories were also shaped by Andersen's own psychological alienation.

Anderson, Carl David (1905–91) US physicist. In 1932, while using a cloud chamber to investigate cosmic rays, he discovered the positron – the first antiparticle known. He shared the Nobel Prize for

physics for this in 1936, and also discovered the muon later the same year.

Anderson, Elizabeth Garrett (1836–1917) British physician. Debarred from entry to medical courses because of her sex, she studied privately and in 1865 obtained a licence to practise from the Society of Apothecaries. In 1866 she opened a dispensary for women and children in London, which later became a hospital; it was renamed the Elizabeth Garrett Anderson Hospital in 1918. In 1870 she received the degree of MD from Paris University, and in 1873 she became the first woman to be elected to the BMA. Her influence was considerable in securing the admission of women to professional medical bodies.

Anderson, Lindsay (Gordon) (1923–94) British film director. He made a number of documentary films during the 1950s, and won an Oscar for *Thursday's Children* (1955). His first feature film, the fiercely satirical *This Sporting Life* (1963), established him as a leading director in Britain. He went on to produce the bleak but blackly humorous trilogy *If...* (1968), *O Lucky Man* (1973), and *Britannia Hospital* (1982) and the more sentimental *The Whales of August* (1987).

Anderson, Marian (1902–93) US operatic contralto. Despite early recognition of her singing talents, racial discrimination meant that she was initially unable to give concerts in her native land. She gained international success from several European tours between 1925 and 1935, but it was not until after her New York début in 1936 that her American career flourished. In 1955 she became the first black singer to perform at the New York Metropolitan Opera.

Anderson, Philip Warren (1923–) US physicist. He made contributions to the study of solid-state physics, and research on molecular interactions has been facilitated by his work on the spectroscopy of gases. He also investigated magnetism and superconductivity, and his work is of fundamental importance for modern solid-state electronics. He shared the Nobel Prize for physics in 1977.

Andes A major mountain system running the length of the Pacific coast of South America, a distance of some 8,000 km (5,000 miles). It is the world's longest range of mountains with a continuous height of more than 3,000 m (10,000 ft). The mountains are of varying age, with ancient remnants dating back to the Palaeozoic. More recent uplift during the Tertiary period raised former coastlines to more than 1,000 m (3,000 ft) above present sea-levels. Tectonic activity continues throughout the length of the Andes, occasionally causing damage through earthquakes, hot ash, and mudslides. Aconcagua, the highest peak in the Western Hemisphere, reaches a height of 6,960 m (22,834 ft) on the border between Argentina and Chile, and Guallatiri in Chile (6,060 m, 19,882 ft) is the highest active volcano in the world. Throughout its length the Andes system breaks up into three or more parallel lines of mountain ranges (cordilleras) that are separated by high fertile basins. The largest of these intermontane basins is the altiplano of Peru and Bolivia. The headwaters of the River Amazon rise in the northern Andes and on the Chilean side of the southern Andes, low temperatures and heavy precipitation result in the presence of a discontinuous ice-cap of more than 10,000 sq km (3,850 sq miles). The Andes gives its name to ANDESITE.

andesite Fine-grained volcanic rock of intermediate composition (that is, with up to 60 per cent silica) containing PLAGIOCLASE feldspar, with BIOTITE, HORNBLENDE, or PYROXENE. Andesites are grey or grey-black in colour. Chemically more or less equivalent to DIORITES, they occur as DYKES and SILLS, and also as extrusive rocks at the surface.

Andhra Pradesh A state in south-east India, on the Bay of Bengal; area 276,814 sq km (106,919 sq miles); pop. (1991) 66,304,850; capital, Hyderabad. The principal language is Telugu. Andhra state was formed in 1953 out of territory separated from Madras. In 1956 and 1960 its boundaries were further altered to form the present-day state of Andhra Pradesh which produces forest-products, tobacco, textiles, paper, chemicals, and ships.

Andorra A small co-principality in the Pyrennes, between France and Spain.

Physical. Andorra has a landscape of valleys at around 900 m (3,000 feet) which rise to peaks at 2,900 m (9,600 feet). Bisected by the River Valira, it contains three distinct natural regions: the valleys of the north and east Valira, and that of the Gran Valira. The attractive mountain scenery is snow-covered for several months of the year.

Economy. Tourism is the main industry, employing 37 per cent of the labour-force, with commerce, forestry, and the construction industry also of importance.

History. According to tradition, Charlemagne granted independence to Andorra in 803 AD. Andorra came under the control of the Counts of Urgel and subsequently the Bishops of the diocese of Urgel. A dispute between the French and Spanish heirs of the Bishops and Counts in the late 13th century was resolved by making Andorra a co-principality, jointly ruled by a French and a Spanish prince. In 1993 Andorra adopted a democratic constitution which reduced the powers of the co-princes (who are now the President of France and the Spanish Bishop of Urgel), making them constitutional heads of state only, and which legalized political parties.

Capital: Andorra la Vella
Area: 468 sq km (181 sq mi)
Population: 61,600 (1993)
Currency: French francs, Spanish pesetas
Religions: Roman Catholic 94.2%; Jewish 0.4%; Jehovah's Witnesses 0.3%; Protestant 0.2%
Ethnic Groups: Spanish 55.1%; Andorran 27.5%; French 7.4%; Portuguese 4.1%; British 1.5%
Languages: Catalan (official); French; Spanish

andosol Dark-coloured soil that forms on certain types of volcanic deposits, including ashes and basic lava. In humid conditions these materials weather rapidly into clay-rich soils which are initially extremely fertile and often support luxuriant plant growth. The soils therefore tend to be rich in organic matter, but their natural fertility is rapidly destroyed under cultivation unless care is taken to replace the nutrients removed by crops. Important areas of andosols occur in New Zealand, Japan, Hawaii, and the north-west United States.

Andre, Carl (1935–) US minimalist sculptor. His most famous works are installations created by stacking or arranging ready-made units such as bricks, cement blocks, or metal plates according to a mathematically imposed modular system and without adhesives or joints. Andre's *Equivalent VIII* (1966), which consists of 120 bricks arranged two deep in a rectangle, was the subject of protests in

Britain at the alleged waste of public money when it was purchased by the Tate Gallery.

Andrea del Sarto (Andrea d'Agnolo di Francesco) (1486–1530) Italian painter. Apart from a visit to France from 1518 to 1519, he lived in Florence all his life. He was outstanding as a FRESCO decorator, as a painter of altar-pieces, and as a portraitist. Andrea's pupils included his biographer Vasari, who both made and marred his reputation by describing his works as 'faultless', but representing him as a weakling.

Andretti, Mario (Gabriele) (1940–) Italian-born US motor-racing driver. In the 1960s he won the Indy car championship three times (1965, 1966, 1969) and won the Indianapolis 500 in 1969. In 1968 he began Formula One racing, and won the world championship in 1978 before retiring from Formula One in 1982 and returning to Indy car racing; he won that sport's championship again in 1984.

Andrew, Prince (full name Prince Andrew Albert Christian Edward, Duke of York) (1960–) Second son of Elizabeth II. Educated at Gordonstoun School, Scotland and the Royal Naval College, Dartmouth, he gained a commission in the Royal Marines and in 1982 served as a helicopter pilot in the Falklands War. He married Sarah Ferguson (born 1959) in 1986; the couple formally separated in 1993 and divorced in 1996. They have two children, Princess Beatrice Elizabeth Mary (born 1988) and Princess Eugenie Victoria Helena (born 1990).

Andrew, St An Apostle, the brother of St Peter. An apocryphal work dating probably from the 3rd century describes his death by crucifixion; the X-shaped cross became associated with his name during the Middle Ages. Since *c.*750 he has been regarded as the patron saint of Scotland; he is also a patron saint of Russia. Feast day, 30 November.

Andrewes, Lancelot (1555–1626) English prelate, successively Bishop of Chichester (1605), Ely (1609), and Winchester (1619). A celebrated scholar and famous preacher, he was prominent at the courts of ELIZABETH I and JAMES I. He was a key figure at the HAMPTON COURT CONFERENCE (1603–04), and was closely involved in producing the Authorized Version of the English Bible (1611). He played an important part in developing the theology of the ANGLICAN COMMUNION.

Andrews, Julie (born Julia Elizabeth Wells) (1935–) British actress and singer. Early success in the British and American theatre, including her creation of the role of Eliza Doolittle in *My Fair Lady* on Broadway (1956), was followed by her film début in *Mary Poppins* (1964), for which she won an Oscar. Her wholesome appeal and talents as a singer were further displayed in *The Sound of Music* (1965). In her later films, such as *10* (1979), she moved away from her typecast prim image to play more diverse roles.

Andrić, Ivo (1892–1975) Yugoslav novelist, essayist, and short-story writer. A diplomat turned writer, he wrote his best-known novels while living under voluntary house arrest in German-occupied Belgrade. Set in his native Bosnia, these include *The Bridge on the Drina* (1945), whose narrative symbolically bridges past and present, as well as Western and Eastern cultures, and *Bosnian Chronicle* (1945). He was awarded the Nobel Prize for literature in 1961.

Androcles A mythical Roman slave who escaped into the African bush, where he removed a thorn from the paw of a lion. After recapture Androcles was thrown to the lions in the arena; however, the lion expected to destroy him turned out to be the limping lion Androcles had helped. When the lion refused to harm his benefactor, Emperor Tiberius freed them both. The story was originally told by Aulus Gellius (?125–?165 AD) and satirized by G. B. Shaw in his play *Androcles and the Lion* (1913).

Andromeda (in mythology) An Ethiopian princess who was chained to a rock as a sacrifice to a sea-monster. She was rescued by (and then married) Perseus, who turned the monster to stone with the Gorgon's head.

Andromeda (in astronomy) A CONSTELLATION of the Northern Hemisphere, one of the forty-eight constellations known to the Greeks. It represents the mythical Princess Andromeda, daughter of King Cepheus and Queen Cassiopeia of Ethiopia, who was chained to a rock in sacrifice to a sea monster, represented by CETUS. The brightest stars in Andromeda are of second magnitude, and the most celebrated feature in the constellation is the **Andromeda Galaxy**. The star Alpha Andromedae, known as Sirrah or Alpheratz, forms one corner of the Square of PEGASUS. Gamma Andromedae is an attractive double star for small telescopes, consisting of yellow and blue components of second and fifth magnitude.

Andromedids (or **Bielids**) A METEOR SHOWER associated with BIELA'S COMET, which used to return every 6.6 years. However, the comet split apart in 1846, and in 1872, 1885, 1892, and 1899 there were impressive displays of meteors when the Earth crossed the orbit of the vanished comet. On the night of 27 November 1885 the rate was estimated to be 75,000 meteors per hour. The shower is now very poor.

Andropov, Yuri (Vladimirovich) (1914–84) Soviet statesman, General Secretary of the Communist Party of the USSR 1982–84 and President 1983–84. Born in Russia, he served as ambassador to Hungary 1954–57, playing a significant role in the crushing of that country's uprising in 1956. He was appointed chairman of the KGB in 1967; its suppression of dissidents enhanced Andropov's standing within the Communist Party, and he gained the presidency on Brezhnev's death. While in office, he initiated the reform process carried through by Mikhail GORBACHEV, his chosen successor.

Andrzejewski, Jerzy (1909–83) Polish novelist. His work confronts sometimes controversial moral issues: the wartime stories *Night* (1945) deal with betrayal, the Jews, and Auschwitz; the novel *Ashes and Diamonds* (1948), describes the first confused days of peace. Later works include *The Inquisitors* (1956) and *The Gates of Paradise* (1960).

anemometer An instrument for measuring air speed, particularly wind-speed, used in meteorology and in wind-tunnels, ventilation shafts, and so on. There are two main types of anemometer, mechanical and hot-wire. In the former, the moving air rotates either a vertical shaft fitted with fan-like vanes or cups, or a propeller mounted on a horizontal shaft. The rate of rotation gives a measure of air-speed. In hot-wire anemometers, wind-speed is measured by its cooling effect on an electrically heated wire.

anemone A plant of the genus *Anemone*, mostly native to the Northern Hemisphere. They belong to the buttercup family and have either a tuberous corm or a fibrous root. Several species have been developed as garden plants, including *A. coronaria*, the cut-flower of the florist.

anemone, sea See SEA ANEMONE.

aneurysm A localized dilatation (widening) of an

artery following a weakening in its wall. Aneurysms are inherently unstable, and tend to enlarge until they rupture. They may occur in the aorta, the main artery of the body, and are a consequence of ARTERIOSCLEROSIS and high blood pressure; rarely, they may also be caused by syphilis, or by injury. Cerebral aneurysms occur in arteries supplying the brain; they are often multiple, and rupture results in STROKE.

Angara A river in south-east Siberia. It flows from the south-west end of Lake Baikal north-westwards then westwards for a distance of 1,779 km (1,039 miles) before meeting the River Yenisei just south of Yeniseysk. It is a major source of hydroelectric power.

Angarsk An industrial city in East Siberia in the Russian Federation, 50 km (31 miles) north-west of Irkutsk, at the junction of the Angara and Kitoi rivers; pop. (1990) 267,000. Founded in 1949, it is a centre for the production of petrochemicals, clothing, and building materials on the Trans-Siberian Railway.

angel (from Greek *angelos*, 'messenger') In Judaism, Christianity, and Islam, an immortal spirit, the messenger of God, and usually depicted in human form, with wings. In Jewish and Christian belief angels are regarded as intermediate between God and man. In Islam *malāika* (sing. *malak*), angels, are considered by some to be lower than man since in the Koran they were commanded to prostrate themselves before Adam. See also ARCHANGEL; CHERUBIM AND SERAPHIM; SATAN; IBLĪS; GABRIEL; MICHAEL; NAKIR AND MUNKAR.

Angel Falls A waterfall in the Guiana Highlands of south-east Venezuela. With an uninterrupted fall of 978 m (3,210 feet) it is the highest waterfall in the world. The falls were discovered in 1935 by the American aviator and prospector James Angel, after whom they are named.

angelfish A member of either one of two distinct and unrelated groups of fishes. The freshwater angelfishes, *Pterophyllum* species, are South American CICHLIDS with very deep bodies and long rays in the dorsal, anal, and pelvic fins. They are popular tropical aquarium fishes. Marine angelfishes, *Pomacanthus* species, live mainly on coral reefs in all tropical seas. They are brightly coloured and deep-bodied and all have a sharp, backwardly pointing spine on the lower edge of the gill cover. They belong to the same family, Chaetontidae, as the marine butterfly fishes.

angelica A large biennial herb of the genus *Angelica*, in the carrot family, Umbelliferae. It occurs naturally in northern Europe, Greenland, and Iceland, and is cultivated and naturalized in many parts of Europe. The young stem and leaf-stalk of *Angelica archangelica* are crystallized in sugar and used in confectionery as flavouring and decoration.

Angelic Doctor See AQUINAS, ST THOMAS.

Angelico, Fra (born Guido di Pietro; monastic name Fra Giovanni da Fiesole) (*c.*1400–55) Italian painter. He was a Dominican friar and his work was intended chiefly for contemplation and instruction. His simple and direct, mature style shows an awareness and understanding of contemporary developments in Renaissance painting, especially in his mastery of new ideas such as perspective. His most celebrated works are the frescos in the convent of San Marco, Florence (*c.*1438–47), and the *Scenes from the Lives of SS Stephen and Lawrence* (1447–49) in the private chapel of Pope Nicholas V in the Vatican.

Angelou, Maya (1928–) US novelist and poet. After working variously as a waitress, actress, teacher, and night-club singer, she became involved in the black civil-rights movement in the 1950s and 1960s. She received critical acclaim as a writer with the first volume of her autobiography, *I Know Why the Caged Bird Sings* (1970), which recounts her harrowing childhood experiences. More volumes of autobiography followed, as well as several volumes of poetry, including *Oh Pray My Wings Are Gonna Fit Me Well* (1975).

Angers A city in the Pays de la Loire region of western France, on the River Maine (Mayenne); pop. (1990) 146,160. Capital of the former province of Anjou, it is the present-day capital of Maine-et-Loire department and a centre for the production of wine and Cointreau liqueur.

angina pectoris Episodic chest pain, which may extend to the arms, back, and jaw. It may be accompanied by breathlessness, dizziness, and sweating. Angina pectoris is caused by narrowing of the arteries supplying the heart muscle (the coronary arteries); the heart is deprived of oxygen during increased demand. Typically, arteries become occluded (obstructed) as a result of a form of ARTERIOSCLEROSIS called atherosclerosis. Angina pectoris is brought on by exercise and stress, and relieved by rest. In some cases, angina pectoris may be caused by spasm of coronary arteries, and symptoms may appear while at rest.

angioplasty The surgical repair or reconstruction of narrowed or obstructed arteries. In **balloon angioplasty** an inflatable balloon attached to the tip of a catheter is passed to the diseased site and inflated to enlarge the passage. This frequently provides a permanent solution and is used in coronary, ileac, and femoral arteries.

angiosperm A member of the dominant group of plants in the world today, the flowering plants. Thus most trees, herbaceous plants, herbs, shrubs, all grasses, and some aquatic plants are angiosperms. They exhibit a diversity of form and ecology greater than any other group of plants has at any point in Earth's history. They probably arose in the Cretaceous Period from a group of seed ferns, and they differ from other seed-bearing plants in usually having closed carpels, which protect the seeds from desiccation and attacks from animals. They also have a unique form of fertilization whereby, in addition to the egg, other accessory cells are fertilized to give the endosperm, which later nourishes the developing plant embryo. The only other seed-bearing plants now living are the GYMNOSPERMS.

Angkor The capital of the ancient Khmer kingdom in north-west Cambodia, famous for its temples, especially Angkor Wat (early 12th century), decorated with relief sculptures. Abandoned in 1443, the site was overgrown with jungle when it was rediscovered in 1860.

angle of dip See DIP.

anglerfish A bony fish in which the first ray of the dorsal fin is modified to form a flexible 'fishing-rod' with a fleshy bait, used to lure fishes close to the mouth of the angler. Anglerfishes comprise the order Lophiiformes; they all have large jaws with very sharp and often long teeth, and feed almost entirely on fishes. They are all marine, and include the shallow-water angler, *Lophius piscatorius*, of the eastern Atlantic, and the North American goosefish, *L. americanus*.

Angles A Germanic tribe closely linked to the JUTES and SAXONS, thought to have originated in Schleswig-Holstein or Denmark. In the 5th century

they settled in eastern Britain in EAST ANGLIA and NORTHUMBRIA. Because of their presence, the land of the ANGLO-SAXONS later became known as 'Englaland' and thereby England.

Anglesey (Welsh **Yns Môn**) An island of north-west Wales, separated from the mainland by the Menai Strait; area 715 sq km (276 miles); pop. (1996) 70,000. Holyhead and Beaumaris are the chief towns.

Anglican Communion The body of PROTESTANT Churches around the world that claim descent from the Church in England as reformed in the 16th century. They all recognize the spiritual leadership of the Archbishop of Canterbury, though he does not have any jurisdiction over Anglicans outside England. There are 20 fully autonomous national member Churches, including the Church of England, the largest, with about 16 million full members; the Protestant Episcopal Church of America (the first diocese of which was formed in 1784); the Church of Wales; the Episcopal Church of Scotland; and Anglican and Episcopal Churches in former British colonies or areas of Anglican Missionary activity, for example Japan. There is little formal structure linking the Anglican Churches, but since 1867 their bishops have gathered every ten years at the Lambeth Conference in England, an occasion to affirm the unity of the Anglican Churches and to debate outstanding issues, though the resolutions of the conference have no binding authority. The Anglican Communion is distinguished by considerable diversity in both doctrine and LITURGY, but the Churches unite in acknowledging the three-fold ministry of bishops, priests, and deacons, the authority of the BIBLE, and a tradition of liturgical practice or form of worship inherited from the 16th-century Book of Common Prayer. In recent times various issues have strained the unity of the various Churches, and on some, such as the ordination of women, there has been an agreement to differ. There is also great divergence within some of the Anglican Churches. For example, two distinct traditions co-exist within the Church of England. The 'high' Church, which has its origins in the Oxford Movement of the 1830s, led by John Henry NEWMAN, claims historical continuity with the pre-Reformation Roman Catholic Church. By contrast, the 'low' Church (see EVANGELICALISM) is more Protestant in outlook, setting less store by the sacraments and tradition, and emphasizing the importance of the Bible as the basis of faith. The churches of the Anglican Communion each have individual membership of the WORLD COUNCIL OF CHURCHES, and have been active in the ecumenical movement.

angling See FISHING.

Anglo-Afghan Wars A series of wars between Afghan rulers and British India. The first occurred (1838–42) when Britain, concerned about Russian influence in AFGHANISTAN, sent an army to replace Dost Muhammad with a pro-British king, Shah Shuja al-Mulk. Resistance to Shuja's rule culminated in an uprising (1841) which led to the destruction of the British Indian forces in Kabul during their withdrawal to Jalalabad (1842). Kabul was reoccupied the same year, but British forces were withdrawn from Afghanistan. The second (1878–80) was also fought to exclude Russian influence. By the Treaty of Gandamak (1879) Britain acquired territory and the right to maintain a Resident in Kabul, but in September of the same year the Resident, Sir Louis Cavagnari, was killed in Kabul and further campaigns were fought before the British withdrawal. The third war was fought in 1919, when the new amir of Afghanistan, Amanullah, attacked British India and, although repulsed, secured the independence of Afghanistan through the Treaty of Rawalpindi (1919).

Anglo-Burmese Wars (1824–26, 1852–53, 1885) Conflicts between British India and Burma. In 1824 a threatened Burmese invasion of Bengal led to a British counter-invasion, which captured Rangoon and forced the cession to Britain of Arakan and Tenasserim, the payment of a large indemnity, and the renunciation of Burmese claims to Assam. After a period of relative harmony, hostile treatment of British traders led to a second invasion in 1852, as a result of which Rangoon and the Irrawaddy delta was annexed. In 1885, the alleged francophile tendencies of King Thibaw (1878–85) provoked a third invasion which captured the royal capital at Mandalay and led to Thibaw's exile. Upper Burma became a province of British India, although guerrilla resistance to British rule was not suppressed for another five years.

Anglo-Dutch Wars Three maritime wars, 1652–54, 1665–67, and 1672–74, fought between the United Provinces and Britain on grounds of commercial and naval rivalry. The Dutch navy was commanded by able admirals but the prevailing westerly winds gave the English sailors a significant advantage.

The first war began when the Dutch carrying-trade was undermined by the English Navigation Acts of 1651, and the Dutch refused to salute the English flag in the English Channel. Maarten Tromp defeated BLAKE off Dungeness in December 1652, but convoying Dutch merchant ships through the Channel proved difficult and the Dutch chief minister, Johan de Witt, settled for reasonable peace terms from Cromwell in 1654. The Dutch recognized English sovereignty in the English Channel, gave compensation for the massacre at Amboina, and promised not to assist the exiled Charles II. An encounter off the African coast began the second war, followed by the fall of New Amsterdam (renamed New York) to the English, who also defeated the Dutch off Lowestoft in June 1665. However in 1666 Charles II was in financial difficulties, Cornelius Tromp and Michiel de Ruyter won the Four Days War, and Ruyter made his celebrated raid on the English dockyards at Chatham. Peace was made at Breda in 1667. The Navigation Acts were modified in favour of the Dutch and territories gained during the war were retained, the Dutch keeping Surinam and the British, Delaware and New England. In 1672 Charles II, dependent on French subsidies, supported Louis XIV against the Dutch. The Dutch admirals had the advantage and the Treaty of Westminster signed in 1674 renewed the terms of Breda.

Anglo-Irish Agreement See NORTHERN IRELAND.

Anglo-Japanese Alliance (1902) A diplomatic agreement between Britain and Japan. It improved Britain's international position and consolidated Japan's position in north-east Asia at a time of increasing rivalry with Russia. The two powers agreed to remain neutral in any war fought by the other to preserve the *status quo* and to join the other in any war fought against two powers. Britain and Japan began to drift apart after World War I, and when the Washington Conference was summoned in 1921, Britain decided not to renew the alliance, which ended in 1923.

Anglo-Maori Wars A complex series of conflicts following the colonization of New Zealand. In the mid-1840s there were rebellions under the Maori chiefs Hone Heke and Te Rauparaha. In 1860 the Taranaki Wars began, but Wiremu Tamihana, a

leader of the KINGITANGA unity movement, negotiated an uneasy truce in 1861. Governor Browne was replaced by Sir George GREY in an attempt to secure peace. Grey and his advisers were reluctant to see the Kingitanga consolidated, for fear that British authority could not be asserted throughout New Zealand, and that land purchases would be halted. Fighting resumed in Taranaki in May 1863 and in July the Waikato was invaded. Fighting with the Kingitanga stopped in 1865 but was sustained by resistance from the Pai Marire (1864–65) and from Titokowaru in Taranaki and Te Kooti on the east coast (1868). London recalled Grey and the British regiments that year, but the pursuit of Titokowaru and Te Kooti, masters of guerrilla warfare, was carried on by settler militia and Maori auxiliaries. The last engagement was in 1872, after which Maori resistance gradually subsided.

Anglo-Saxon A person or language of the English Saxons, distinct from the Old Saxons and the Angles, a group of Germanic peoples who invaded and settled in Britain between the 5th and 7th centuries.

Anglo-Saxon Chronicle A collection of seven manuscripts written in Anglo-Saxon (Old English) that together provide a history of England from the beginning of the conversion to Christianity up to 1154. The major text (known as the *Parker Chronicle*) appears to have been written by one clerk until 891. Most of the copies end in the 11th century; after 1079 only the *Peterborough Chronicle* continued, breaking off abruptly with an unfinished entry for 1154. The *Chronicle* probably originated as notes inserted in the tables used by the Christian Church when calculating the date of Easter.

Angola (formerly **Portuguese West Africa**) A country of south-central Africa bounded by the Atlantic on the west, the Democratic Republic of Congo (formerly Zaïre) and Zambia on the north and east, and Namibia on the south. While most of Angola lies south of the Congo River, the Cabinda province lies north of the Congo and is separated from the rest of Angola by a section of Congo.

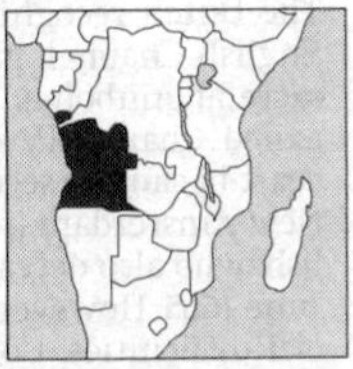

Physical. Most of the country lies on a high plateau; but there is a coastal plain which, starting near the mouth of the River Congo, is broad and fertile until, southward, it becomes drier and narrower as it approaches the Namib desert. The vast plateau is a region of SAVANNAH, watered by rivers that flow outwards from highlands near the centre and usually have swamps along their valleys.

Economy. Potentially Africa's richest country, Angola has a wealth of mineral deposits, including the oil produced offshore from Cabinda, on which the economy is heavily dependent, diamonds, and iron ore. Exports include crude oil, petroleum products, coffee, diamonds, and mahogany hardwoods. Agricultural crops include sugar-cane, bananas, palm oil, and tobacco. Industry is limited to food-processing and metal-refining. Electricity is generated mainly from hydroelectric dams. The economy has suffered major disruption from the civil war, which has caused widespread migration, famine, and destitution; it is badly in need of investment in infrastructure.

History. The coastal strip was colonized by the Portuguese in the 16th century, but it was not until the 19th century that, following wars with the Ovimbundu, Ambo, Humbo, and Kuvale, they began to exploit the mineral reserves of the hinterland. In 1951 Angola became an Overseas Province of Portugal. In 1954 a nationalist movement emerged, demanding independence. The Portuguese at first refused, but finally agreed in 1975 after a protracted guerrilla war, and 400,000 Portuguese were repatriated. Almost total economic collapse followed. Internal fighting continued between guerrilla factions. The ruling Marxist party, the Popular Movement for the Liberation of Angola (MPLA), was supported by Cuba, the Soviet Union, and East Germany, and its opponent, the National Union for the Total Independence of Angola (UNITA), by SOUTH AFRICA and the USA. Punitive South African raids took place from time to time, aimed at Namibian resistance forces operating from Angola. In 1988 there was a Geneva Accord between the various interested parties, aimed to end violence. UNITA leader Jonas Savimbi at first refused to accept its terms, but more moderate MPLA policies, committed to 'democratic Socialism', together with the withdrawal of South African aid, resulted in a peace treaty in 1991. In spite of violations of this, multi-party elections were held in 1992. The MPLA won the elections but UNITA disputed the results and fighting broke out again. In 1997 UNITA agreed to participate in a government of national reconciliation.

Capital: Luanda
Area: 1,246,700 sq km (481,354 sq mi)
Population: 10,301,000 (1991)
Currency: 1 kwanza = 100 lwei
Religions: Roman Catholic 68.7%; Protestant 19.8%; traditional beliefs 9.5%
Ethnic Groups: Ovimbundu 37.2%; Mbundu 21.6%; Kongo 13.2%; Portuguese and Mestizo
Languages: Portuguese (official); Umbundu; African Bantu languages
International Organizations: UN; OAU; Non-Aligned Movement; SADC

Angora The former name (until 1930) of ANKARA, capital of Turkey. Angora wool, a mixture of sheep's wool and rabbit hair takes its name from Angora.

Angostura The former name (1824–49) of the city of CIUDAD BOLIVAR in south-east Venezuela. The tonic known as Angostura Bitters was first made there by a physician in 1824.

Angoulême A commercial and industrial town in Poitou-Charentes region, west France, on the River Charente; pop. (1990) 46,190. Once a river port, it is now a major transport centre and capital of Charente department. Its paper industry dates from the 15th century. Known to the Romans as Iculisma, the fortified town of Angoulême was capital of the former province of Angoumois.

Angry Young Men A group of British playwrights and novelists of the 1950s, who held radical or anarchic views. It is sometimes said to derive from the title of the autobiography *Angry Young Man* (1951) by the Irish writer Leslie Paul. The phrase gained widespread popularity after the production of John OSBORNE's play, *Look Back in Anger* (1956). Other writers in the category include Kingsley AMIS, John WAIN, Colin WILSON, Alan SILLITOE, Arnold WESKER, and John BRAINE.

angström (symbol Å) A UNIT of length equal to 10^{-10} m (one ten-thousand millionth of a metre). Named after Anders Jonas ÅNGSTRÖM, the unit is used to measure lengths on an atomic scale. In SI UNITS, the nanometre (10^{-9} metre) is used.

Ångström, Anders Jonas (1814–1874) Swedish physicist. He wrote on terrestrial magnetism and the conduction of heat, but his most important work was in spectroscopy. He proposed a relation-

ship between the emission and absorption spectra of chemical elements, discovered hydrogen in the Sun's atmosphere, and published an atlas of the solar spectrum. He measured optical wavelengths in the unit later named in his honour.

Anguilla The most northerly of the Leeward Islands in the CARIBBEAN. Flat and scrub-covered, its area is only 91 sq km (35 sq mi) of coral formation with fine, sandy beaches, but it is flanked by many islets. The climate is dry and warm, and fresh water is scarce. Salt deposits are the main natural resources, and fish and lobster are the island's chief export. A British colony since 1650, Anguilla formed part of the Federation of the West Indies (1958–62) and subsequently received associated state status with St Kitts and Nevis. Anguilla declared independence in 1967 and two years later was occupied by British troops, who reduced the island to colonial status once again. In 1980 it became a British dependency with full self-government.

angular measure As part of a system of COORDINATES, a measure of the angles between the directions of celestial objects as well as their **angular diameter**. It is also used to measure changes in the directions and sizes of objects. If the angle is measured around a great circle, as for example, declination, the circle is usually divided into 360 degrees each of which is subdivided into 60 arc minutes. Each arc minute is further subdivided into 60 arc seconds. Degrees, arc minutes, and arc seconds are also used for right ascension, ECLIPTIC, and other longitudes. However, it is sometimes convenient for a full circle of right ascension to be divided into 24 hours, where each hour equals 60 minutes, or 3,600 seconds of time.

angular momentum A measure of the effect of MOMENTUM in a rotating system. It is a VECTOR and a conserved quantity. It is defined as the MOMENT OF INERTIA of the body about the axis of rotation, multiplied by the ANGULAR VELOCITY. Since angular momentum is conserved, a reduction in the moment of inertia leads to an increase in angular velocity. For example, if a spinning star shrinks in size after a SUPERNOVA explosion, the conservation of its angular momentum results in a very much smaller NEUTRON STAR which spins much more rapidly than the original star. The stability of spinning tops and gyroscopes illustrates the conservation of angular momentum.

angular velocity (symbol Ω) The rate at which an object rotates about an axis. It is normally measured in RADIANS per second. A complete revolution (360°) is equal to 2π radians – so an object rotating at 5 revolutions per second would have an angular velocity of 10π radians per second. If the axis is within the body then the body is said to be spinning; for example, the Earth spins on its axis once every day. If the axis is outside the body the whole of the body revolves about the axis; for example, the Earth moving in its orbit about the Sun takes a year to complete one revolution.

Angus A district of eastern Scotland, situated between the Sidlaw Hills and the Grampian Mountains; area 2,022 sq km (780 sq miles); pop. (1993) 111,000; administrative centre, Forfar. From the 16th century to 1928 it was the county of Forfarshire and from 1975 to 1996 it was an administrative district of Tayside region.

Anhui (or **Anhwei**) A province in eastern China in the middle and lower valleys of the Yangtze and Huai rivers; area 139,900 sq km (54,036 sq miles); pop. (1990) 56,181,000; capital, Hefei (Hofei). It was named after the first letters of the two cities of Anqing and Huizhou. The province is divided into three distinct regions by its leading rivers, namely, Huaibei, to the north of the River Huai, Huainan between the Huai and Yangtze rivers, and Wannan to the south of the Yangtze. Rich in mineral and agricultural resources, including coal, iron ore, rice, tea, bamboo, and timber, Anhui is noted for its paper, brushes, and ink sticks which are sought after by Chinese calligraphers and artists.

anhydrite An evaporite mineral consisting of anhydrous calcium sulphate, $CaSO_4$, white in colour with a pearly or vitreous lustre. It occurs in sedimentary rocks, commonly with its hydrated form, gypsum, and halite (rock salt), in various places. It is used as a fertilizer, in the manufacture of plaster, and as a raw material for making sulphuric acid.

anhydrous compound A compound containing no water, especially an inorganic salt. For example, anhydrous calcium chloride, $CaCl_2$, contains only the elements calcium and chlorine; on exposure to atmospheric moisture, the compound becomes hydrated, its formula now being $CaCl_2.2H_2O$. This capacity to absorb moisture means that anhydrous compounds can be used as drying agents. If the hydrated compound is heated, the water is given off and the anhydrous compound is reformed.

aniline (or **aminobenzene**, $C_6H_5NH_2$) An oily, colourless liquid, turning brown on oxidation. It is the starting material for the production of a wide range of chemicals, the most important being AZO DYES. Aniline is related to BENZENE: it is produced industrially by reacting nitrobenzene vapour with hydrogen gas over a copper CATALYST at a temperature of around 300°C.

animal An organism that relies upon preformed food, as distinct from an AUTOTROPHIC ORGANISM. One of the main distinguishing features of many species of animals is their ability to move freely through air or water. This mobility is effected by muscles. At a cellular level, animal cells are bounded by flexible membrane systems, unlike the rigid cellulose walls of plant cells.

With the exception of CNIDARIANS, such as jellyfish, and ECHINODERMS, most animals are bilaterally symmetrical. This means that their body can be divided into similar halves along a line drawn from head to tail. Associated with this body-plan is the development of a head (cephalization). This is the first part of a mobile animal to reach new stimuli in its environment, and hence contains a vast array of sensory organs. The high activity levels of most animals, and their large multicellular bodies, necessitated the evolution of efficient circulatory systems to move oxygen and food to the tissues, and remove waste products. Larger bodies also need good excretory and nervous systems.

Animals comprise one of the KINGDOMS of living organisms. The link between animals and other organisms is revealed in the basic chemical reactions which sustain life. Processes such as RESPIRATION, and the enzymes used in many similar biochemical pathways, are common to all kingdoms. See also Appendix.

animal behaviour See BEHAVIOUR.

animal breeding The deliberate selection of mating partners in domesticated animals to maximize the desirable characteristics of the species, for example meat, milk, or wool production, strength, stamina, or speed. Animal breeding has been practised for centuries, and a wide variety of animals have been bred for many different purposes, for example sheep, cattle, and pigs for food, dogs for hunting or herding, horses for racing or for pulling heavy loads, and mice and rats for scientific research. Animals are selected for breeding on their physical characteristics, the character of their parents and siblings, and on the results of progeny testing. Animals may be inbred (mated with closely related individuals) to maintain desirable characteristics, or crossbred (mated with different breeds) or outbred (mated with unrelated individuals) to increase the genetic pool of a particular line or strain. ARTIFICIAL INSEMINATION is particularly important in dairy cattle, and is becoming more so in beef cattle, sheep, and pigs.

animal husbandry See LIVESTOCK FARMING.

animal rights An extension to animals of the respect for life inherent in the concept of HUMAN RIGHTS. Those who advocate animal rights claim that because animals possess the capacity to feel pain, to fear, or to experience enjoyment or happiness, they have a basic right to be treated in ways that respect their independent value. The main areas in which human beings currently fail to observe animal rights are in intensive farming methods, commercial and sport hunting, the use of animals for scientific experimentation (vivisection), and in the destruction of their habitats (see ENDANGERED SPECIES). Frustrated by the continued abuse of animals, some organizations, such as the Animal Liberation Front, have taken extreme action by fire-bombing shops, raiding laboratories, and threatening scientists.

animals, domestication of The process by which wild animals are bred and reared under human control and adapted for such purposes as meat, milk, or wool production, and hunting. Domestication has only been achieved with a small number of the wild species available. In most cases the time and place of domestication remain obscure, but cattle, goats, sheep, pigs, and camels were certainly domesticated at least 7,000 years ago. More recent domestications have been confined to specialized animals, like the silkworm.

animation (on film) Photographing of individual drawings and replaying them in rapid succession to give the illusion of movement. Each drawing in an animated sequence is minutely different from the one before, and the camera stops after each has been photographed. Animation can also be achieved by filming puppets and silhouettes: Lotte Reiniger (1899–1981) adapted the techniques of shadow plays for this purpose. More recently, COMPUTER graphics techniques have been applied to animation.

animism The attribution of a living soul to all creatures, inanimate objects, and natural phenomena. In anthropology the term denotes the belief that the world is animated by spirits who are capable of harming or helping a person's interests. For example, Melanesian societies believed in an all-pervasive spirit called *mana*, which was capable of both good and evil. Animistic belief gives rise to all manner of ways in which the spirits may be propitiated or evil avoided, including TABOOS and magic charms or amulets.

anise (or **aniseed**) An annual herb, *Pimpinella anisum*, a member of the family Umbelliferae, that was introduced long ago from China to Europe, Asia, and North America. The small, greyish-brown, aromatic fruits are used for flavouring, giving the characteristic flavour to the liqueur 'anisette' as well as to various beverages, cakes, and sweets. Oil of anise, distilled from the fruits, is used in cough medicines and lozenges.

Anjou A former province of western France, on the Loire, now part of the department of Main-et-Loire. Henry II of England, as a Plantagenet, was Count of Anjou, but it was lost to the English Crown by King John in 1204. Its capital was the town of Angers.

Ankara (formerly **Angora**) An inland city of Asia Minor, the capital of Turkey since 1923; pop. (1990) 2,559,470. Known to the Hittites as Ankuwash and to the Romans as Ankyra, it prospered at the junction of east–west and north–south trade routes. Under Ottoman rule it later dwindled to insignificance until chosen by Kemal Atatürk in 1920 as his seat of government. Modern Ankara is a planned city with long, wide boulevards. Industries include the manufacture of cement, textiles, and leather products.

ankle See FOOT.

Ankylosaurus See DINOSAUR.

annals (from Latin *annus*, 'year') The yearly records kept by the priests in Rome from the earliest times. They noted ceremonies, state enactments, and the holders of office. The high priest (Pontifex Maximus) was responsible for maintaining the records in his official residence. The accumulated material (mainly dating from after 300 BC) was published in eighty books known as the *Annales Maximi c.*123 BC. The name came to be applied generally to the writing of history in strict chronological order.

Annam A former kingdom on the east coast of Indochina now lying largely in Vietnam. After driving out the Chinese in 939 AD, the Annamese maintained an independence that lasted until 1883 when the French established a protectorate. Its last ruler was deposed in 1955.

Annapolis The capital of the state of Maryland, USA, on the Severn River near its mouth on Chesapeake Bay; pop. (1990) 33,180. Settled in 1649 by Puritans from Virginia who named it Providence, the town later changed its name to Anne Arundel Town. In 1695 when it was planned and laid out as the state capital of Maryland it was renamed Annapolis in honour of Princess (later Queen) Anne. It is the home of the United States Naval Academy which was founded by George Bancroft in 1845. The Scottish-born American sailor John Paul Jones (1747–92) is buried in Annapolis.

Annapurna A ridge of the central Himalayas, in north-central Nepal. Its highest peak, rising to 8,078 m (26,503 ft), was first climbed in 1950 by a French expedition under Maurice Herzog.

Ann Arbor A city in the state of Michigan, USA, 50 km (32 miles) west of Detroit; pop. (1990) 109,600. First settled in 1823, the University of Michigan was moved here from Detroit in 1837. It is a centre of research and high technology.

Anne (1665–1714) Queen of England and Scotland (known as Great Britain from 1707) and Ireland 1702–14. The last of the Stuart monarchs, daughter of the Catholic James II (but herself a Protestant), she succeeded her brother-in-law William III to the throne, there presiding over the Act of Union, which completed the unification of Scotland and England. None of her five children born alive survived childhood, and by the Act of Settlement (1701) the throne passed to the House of Hanover on her death.

Anne, Princess (full name Anne Elizabeth Alice Louise, the Princess Royal) (1950–) Daughter of Elizabeth II. A skilled horsewoman, she rode for Great Britain in the 1976 Olympics. She has also been involved in the work of charitable organizations, notably as president of Save the Children

Fund since 1971. She was married to Captain Mark Philips (1948–) 1973–92. In December 1992 she married Commander Timothy Laurence. She has two children, Peter Mark Andrew Philips (1977–) and Zara Anne Elizabeth Philips (1981–).

Anne, St Traditionally the mother of the Virgin Mary, first mentioned by name in the apocryphal gospel of James (2nd century). The extreme veneration of St Anne in the late Middle Ages was attacked by Martin Luther and other reformers. She is the patron saint of Brittany and the province of Quebec in Canada. Feast day, 26 July.

annealing A heat treatment in which a material at high temperature is cooled slowly. In metalworking this is done to reverse changes such as work-hardening that have taken place during cold working, so that the metal once more becomes malleable and ductile (capable of being drawn out without cracking). Unlike TEMPERING, annealing is not a finishing process. Glass is annealed to avoid internal stresses, so that the cold glass does not shatter.

Annecy The capital of the department of Haute-Savoie, in the Rhône-Alpes region of south-east France, at the north-west end of Lake Annecy; pop. (1990) 51,140. In addition to producing paper, textiles, and precision instruments, the town is a popular tourist resort. There is a nuclear-research centre.

annelid A member of the Annelida, an advanced and diverse phylum of worms (over 8,700 species) which show segmentation, being built up from many similar ring-shaped body-sections. The annelids are divided into three main classes according to their pattern of body bristles, or appendages. The polychaetes, which are marine worms, form the bulk of the phylum with over 5,300 species, such as bristle worms and lugworms. The oligochaetes, which lack the segmental appendages of the polychaetes, include the common earthworm (which has stiff bristles on each segment) and live on land or in fresh water. Among the 3,100 species of oligochaete are the giant Australian earthworms, which reach 3 m (10 feet) in length. The final class is the Hirudinea, which contains over 500 species of smooth, segmented worms called leeches.

The annelid body is generally soft and cylindrical, with an outer wall and an inner gut, separated by the COELOM, which acts as the hydrostatic (fluid-filled) skeleton. Small bristles or longer appendages anchor the animal into sand or mud; in free-swimming predatory species these appendages are larger, supporting the lateral paddles that assist locomotion. Annelids also have a proper blood-system with a long, tubular, dorsal heart, unlike most other 'worms'. They also have a simple brain, and can show learned behaviour.

Anne of Austria (1601–66) Wife of Louis XIII of France, whom she married in 1615. She was the daughter of Philip III of Spain. Her friend Madame de Chevreuse was involved in plots against RICHELIEU, and she was accused of encouraging the advances of the Duke of BUCKINGHAM. When her 4-year-old son succeeded to the throne as LOUIS XIV in 1643 she was declared regent and gave her full support to MAZARIN during the FRONDE. She influenced her son until her death, though her regency ended in 1651.

Anne of Cleves (1515–57) Fourth wife of Henry VIII. Henry's marriage to her (1540) was the product of his minister Thomas Cromwell's attempt to forge a dynastic alliance with one of the Protestant German states. Henry, initially deceived by a flattering portrait of Anne painted by Holbein, took an instant dislike to his new wife and dissolved the marriage after six months.

Annigoni, Pietro (1910–88) Italian painter. One of the few 20th-century artists to practise the techniques of the Old Masters, he painted mainly in tempera, and his religious paintings include altarpieces and frescos. However, he is most famous for his portraits of Queen Elizabeth II (1955, 1970), President Kennedy (1961), and other prominent figures.

annihilation of matter A phenomenon that occurs when an ELEMENTARY PARTICLE interacts with its corresponding antiparticle (ANTIMATTER). Their combined mass is converted into electromagnetic radiation in accordance with the Einstein formula $E = mc^2$, where E represents the energy released, m the combined mass, and c the speed of light in a vacuum.

annuity A constant annual payment. The guarantee of the maintenance of such annual payments is also known as an annuity, and can usually be purchased from insurance companies. A 'certain' annuity is paid over a specified number of years, whereas a 'life' annuity is paid until the death of the named recipient. An annuity may be bought with a lump sum or through a series of contributions. Annuities may be 'immediate' or 'deferred', depending on whether payments to the recipient commence on purchase of the annuity or at a later specified date.

annual A plant that germinates from seeds, develops, flowers, and fruits within a single year. The field poppy is an example. Species that produce several short-lived generations in a year, such as groundsel, are called **ephemerals**.

anode The positive ELECTRODE, usually made of metal, in a THERMIONIC VALVE, CATHODE-RAY TUBE, or BATTERY. The anode attracts negative charges or electron current, and is the electrode by which electrons leave a system. See also ELECTRIC CURRENT; ELECTROLYSIS.

anodizing A process in which a tough, thin, adherent film of metal oxide is built up by ELECTROLYSIS on the surface of a metal to protect it from CORROSION and physical damage. Anodized aluminium appears white, but can be coloured with dyes.

anole A small LIZARD of the iguana family, ranging from 13 cm (5 inches) to 46 cm (18 inches) in length. There are 165 species in the genus *Anolis*. They range from the southeastern USA to Brazil, being particularly diverse in the Caribbean, and are sometimes misleadingly known as American chameleons (because of their ability to change colour). They live mainly in trees and bushes; their fingers and toes are adapted for climbing, bearing pads, rather like those of some geckos. Males DISPLAY by head-bobbing and by extending a gular flap (throat flap), which is often coloured bright red or yellow.

anomaly One of three angles used in calculating the position of a body P in an elliptical orbit about another body S. The **true anomaly** f and the **eccentric anomaly** E are related by the equation $\tan f/2 = \sqrt{[(1+e)/(1-e)]} \tan E/2$, where e is the orbital eccentricity. The **mean anomaly** M is the angle between SA and the direction of a fictitious body Q moving at a constant angular speed equal to the mean motion of the body P. The angles M and E are related by Kepler's equation $E - e \sin E = M$.

anomie (or **anomy**) The lack or weakness of the usual social or ethical standards in an individual or group. The sociologist DURKHEIM, taking the term from the Greek *anomia* (lawlessness), argued that anomie could result from rapid social change. Some US sociologists, in particular Robert K. Merton (1910–), have maintained that anomie can lead to deviance. Where an individual or group is prevented from achieving widely accepted goals, law-breaking may result. See also ALIENATION.

anorexia nervosa An eating disorder of unknown cause that results in a distorted perception of body image. Anorexia means loss of appetite, which is controlled by complex mechanisms. Anorexia nervosa is most common in girls of 16–17 years of age. Patients usually have an intense desire to lose weight, although they commonly have a body-weight 25 per cent below normal. They usually eat very little, and excessive exercise, induced vomiting, and use of laxatives is common. Marked weight loss is associated with menstrual periods stopping, loss of interest in sexual intercourse, and impotence; other features include constipation, low blood pressure, and reduced heart rate. Patients commonly have excessive downy hair on the body. Binge eating followed by induced vomiting or laxative misuse may also be a feature. See also BULIMIA NERVOSA.

Anouilh, Jean (1910–87) French dramatist. Anouilh's first success was *Traveller without Luggage* (1937), and he soon achieved widespread popularity. Works include romantic comedies such as *Ring Round the Moon* (1947), fantasies (*Thieves' Carnival*, 1932), historical dramas (*Beckett or The Honour of God*, 1959), and *Antigone* (1944), a reworking of the Greek myth with undertones of the situation in Nazi-occupied Paris.

Anschluss (German, 'connection') Hitler's annexation of Austria. The GERMAN SECOND EMPIRE did not include Austrian Germans, who remained in Austria-Hungary. In 1934 a coup by Austrian Nazis failed to achieve union with Germany. In February 1938 Hitler summoned Kurt von Schuschnigg, the Austrian Chancellor, to Berchtesgaden and demanded the admission of Nazis into his cabinet. Schuschnigg attempted to call a plebiscite on Austrian independence, failed, and was forced to resign. German troops entered Vienna and on 13 March 1938 the Anschluss was proclaimed. The majority of Austrians welcomed the union. The ban on an Anschluss, laid down in the Treaties of VERSAILLES and St Germain (1919), was reiterated when the Allied Powers recognized the second Austrian republic in 1946.

Anselm, St (*c*.1033–1109) Italian-born philosopher and theologian, Archbishop of Canterbury 1093–1109. A distinguished theologian and reformer who worked to free the Church from secular control, he preferred to defend the faith by intellectual reasoning rather than by basing arguments on scriptural and other written authorities. Feast day, 21 April.

Anshan A city in the province of Liaoning, northeast China; pop. (1990) 1,370,000. Situated close to iron ore deposits, Anshan has developed as one of China's largest integrated iron and steel complexes. Other industries include chemicals, tractors, and machinery.

Anson, George, Baron Anson (1697–1762) British admiral, remembered for his circumnavigation of the world, 1740–44. Due to shipwreck and scurvy among his crew he returned with only one of his original six ships though with almost £500,000 worth of Spanish treasure. In 1747, off Cape Finisterre, he captured six French enemy warships during the War of the AUSTRIAN SUCCESSION. Later, at the Board of Admiralty, he created the corps of marines, and by his reforms and effective planning, played a major part in securing Britain's naval successes in the SEVEN YEARS WAR.

ant An insect that belongs to the family Formicidae and to the same order as bees, wasps, and sawflies (Hymenoptera). Ants are found in almost all terrestrial habitats. There are about 14,000 species, most occurring in the tropics. Ants, whose sizes range from 1 mm to 4 cm (0.04 to 1.5 inches), live in colonies made up of different functional types, or castes. These include workers, soldiers, and reproductive castes. At certain seasons, winged males and females are produced synchronously by adjacent colonies of a species. These leave their nests in swarms and mate, after which the males die. The fertilized females shed their wings and usually start a new colony. Queens of some species join existing colonies, a few infiltrate colonies of different species and kill the queen, and others raise workers which raid nests of different species for 'slaves'. Colony cohesion and organization are maintained by the queen's PHEROMONES and by the exchange of regurgitated food and saliva.

Most ants excavate subterranean nests, but some build nests in the branches of trees, or excavate tree-trunks. Tailor or weaver ants, such as *Decophylla smaragdina*, use their silk-producing larvae to sew leaves into a chamber. The majority of ants are voracious predators, although some species also avidly eat sugary fluids, such as nectar and honeydew. A few store and eat seeds, and leaf-cutter ants of tropical America (*Atta* species) cut small sections off leaves and use these as a basis for fungal 'gardens', which are harvested for food.

Antakya (or **Hatay**; English **Antioch**) The capital of Hatay province, southern Turkey, and a marketing centre at the foot of Mount Habib Neccar in the alluvial plain of the River Asi (Orontes); pop. (1990) 123,871. Part of Syria until 1939, it was the ancient capital of the Seleucid kings of Syria who founded the city *c*.300 BC. It was a noted centre of commerce and culture in Hellenistic times and an early stronghold of Christianity. Its museum has an outstanding collection of Roman mosaics. After its destruction by the Mamelukes in 1266 it fell into decline and its harbour silted up. The city was devastated by earthquakes in 525 and 1872.

Antalya A Mediterranean seaport and resort on the Gulf of Antalya on the south coast of Turkey; pop. (1990) 378,200. The city is capital of Antalya province, and named after Attalus II, king of Pergamum who founded Antalya *c*.150 BC. Its industries are timber, food processing, and tourism.

Antananarivo The capital of Madagascar and its chief industrial centre, situated at an altitude of 1,200–1,500 m (4,000–5,000 ft) above sea-level overlooking the eastern coastal plains of the island; pop. (1990) 802,390. Until 1975 the city was known as Tananarive. It produces tobacco, processed foods, textiles, and leather goods.

Antar (fl. 6th century AD) In Arab legend, the black desert poet and warrior Antarah ibn Shaddād, the hero of the pre-Islamic collection of poems, *al-Mu'al-laqāt*, composed anonymously between the 8th and 12th centuries. The 'Romance of Antar' encompasses 500 years of Arab history, court life, and warrior-chivalry. Antarah was the son of King Shaddad of the Banu Abs and of the negro slave-girl Zabiba. His famed love for his cousin Abla enabled him to overcome all the obstacles set in the way of their eventual marriage.

Antarctica A continent centred on the South Pole, situated mainly within the Antarctic Circle and

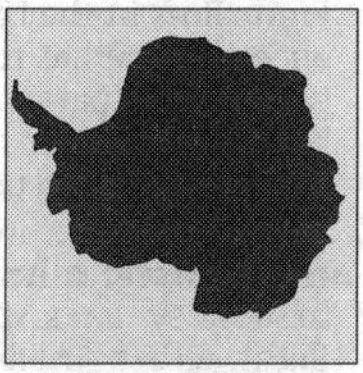

almost entirely covered by an ice sheet that has an average thickness of 1,880 m (6,170 ft) but in places reaches depths of 5,000 m (16,000 ft). With an area of 13.9 million sq km (5.4 million sq miles), the Antarctic continent occupies 10 per cent of the world's surface and contains 90 per cent of the world's ice and 70 per cent of its fresh water. It is divided by the Transantarctic Mountains into West Antarctica or Lesser Antarctica, which includes the mountainous Antarctic Peninsula, Palmer Land, and Ellsworth Land, and East Antarctica or Greater Antarctica, which includes Terre Adélie, Queen Maud Land, and Wilkes Land. Only a few patches of moss and lichen grow – too few to support land animals, but there is abundant life in the sea, including whales, seals, penguins, and other sea birds. Exploration at first concentrated on establishing the existence of a continent. Bransfield, Biscoe, Foster, Wilkes, Ross, and Dumont D'Urville all explored the coastline of Antarctica between 1820 and 1840. Later explorers concentrated on reaching the South Pole. SCOTT pioneered the way in 1902, followed by SHACKELTON in 1908; in 1911 AMUNDSEN was the first to reach the Pole, and Scott reached it a month later. The American aviator Richard BYRD flew over the South Pole in 1929. Although there is no permanent human habitation, Norway, Australia, France, New Zealand, and the UK claim sectors of the continent (Argentina and Chile claim parts of the British sector); its exploration and exploitation are governed by an international treaty (Antarctic Treaty) of 1959 renewed in 1991.

Antarctic Peninsula A mountainous peninsula extending northwards for a distance of *c.*1,900 km (1,200 miles) from west Antarctica. Explored by the British navigator Edward Bransfield in 1820, it was not confirmed to be a continuous part of the Antarctic continent until 1937.

Antares A variable first-magnitude BINARY STAR in the constellation of Scorpius, and also known as Alpha Scorpii. The bright component is a red SUPERGIANT star with about 10,000 times the luminosity of the Sun. It has a hot fifth-magnitude companion in a 900-year orbit, and is surrounded by a large reflection nebula. The estimated distance of Antares is 160 parsecs.

antbird A largely insectivorous bird. The typical antbirds, Thamnophilidae, contain 188 species, and the ground antbirds, Formicariidae, some 56 species. Some species follow columns of army ants and catch the insects which these flush out, hence their name. They are largely confined to South America, although about 35 occur in Central America. Ranging in size from that of a sparrow to that of a large thrush, they are mostly black, brown, and white. They live on or near the ground in scrub or tropical rain forest. They build a simple cup-shaped nest and lay two pale, speckled eggs.

anteater A relative of the sloth and armadillo. The four species of anteater are native to South and Central America. The giant anteater, *Myrmecophaga tridactyla*, is 1.8 m (6 feet) long with an enormously elongated face terminating in an extremely small mouth. It has a long hairy coat and a long bushy tail and lives in forests and savannah. The front legs have powerful claws, the middle one being much enlarged and sabre-like, used in tearing open ant nests or occasionally termite nests. As the insects swarm out they are collected by the long, smooth, whip-like tongue, which often extends 22 cm (9 inches) out of its mouth and is moistened with a sticky saliva. In captivity the giant anteater has lived for up to 26 years. A single offspring is born each year, the female carrying it on her back; the youngster is not fully independent for almost two years.

The remaining three species of anteater: the northern tamandua, *Tamandua mexicana*, southern tamandua, *T. tetradactyla*, and the silky anteater, *Cyclopes didactylus*, live in trees, where they climb and cling by their hind-legs, so leaving the forelegs free to dig for ants. The snout of the silky anteater is much shorter than that of the others. See also PANGOLIN.

antelope Any of various hoofed mammals of the family Bovidae, which also includes sheep, cattle, and goats. Antelopes are typically tall, slender, graceful, swift-moving animals with smooth hair and upward-pointing hollow horns. Examples of antelopes include gazelles, gnus (wildebeest), hartebeest, klipspringers, kudus, nilgai, oryxes, and springboks.

antenna (in communications) (or **aerial**) A device, usually a simple conductor, for the transmission or reception of ELECTROMAGNETIC RADIATION. If the transmitting antenna is vertical, the most effective reception antenna will also be vertical. The transmission effectiveness of an antenna system depends greatly on the signal FREQUENCY used. Any conductor may act as an antenna, although at microwave frequencies a simple slot cut in a WAVEGUIDE will suffice. However, the commonest type of antenna is the simple DIPOLE, more usually represented in refined form as the YAGI antenna used for UHF (ultra-high frequency) television reception.

antenna (in zoology) A long, jointed, mobile, paired appendage on the head of many arthropods. In insects, millipedes, and centipedes they are usually concerned with the senses of smell, touch, etc. In crustaceans the antennae are modified for swimming and for attachment.

anthem An elaborate hymn, the Anglican equivalent of the Roman Catholic MOTET. The first Elizabethan anthems were derived from metrical psalm settings and were therefore very simple. Gradually they became more elaborate and polyphonic, taking on the expressive qualities of the MADRIGAL. There developed verse anthems, which introduced passages for solo voices to contrast with the normal four- or five-part choir. The full anthem employed the choir only, with or without organ or instrumental accompaniment. During the Restoration period (after 1660) anthems often employed elaborate orchestral accompaniments and acquired something of the vocal display of OPERA. The great period of the anthem includes such composers as Byrd, Weelkes, Gibbons, Purcell, Blow, and Handel. The word is also used in the general sense of a special 'hymn', as in a NATIONAL ANTHEM.

Anthemius (known as **Anthemius of Tralles**) (6th century AD) Greek mathematician, engineer, and architect. His experiments included study of the effects of compressed steam, and he had a high reputation for both these and his artistic pursuits. In 532 he was chosen by Justinian to design the church of St Sophia in Constantinople.

Anthony, St (or **Antony**) (*c.*251–356) Egyptian hermit, the founder of monasticism. At the age of 20 he gave away his possessions and went to live as a hermit in the Egyptian desert, attracting a colony of followers. These he organized into a community which became the first to live under a monastic rule. During the Middle Ages the belief arose that praying to St Anthony would effect a cure for ergotism. Feast day, 17 January.

Anthony of Padua, St (or **Antony**) (1195–1231) Portuguese Franciscan friar. His charismatic preaching in the south of France and Italy made many converts. His devotion to the poor is commemorated by the alms known as St Anthony's bread; he is invoked to find lost articles. Feast day, 13 June.

anthracite A hard, shiny black metamorphic rock of the COAL family which is clean to handle and burns very hot, with a short flame and little or no smoke. It is an organic sedimentary rock that has been subjected to heat and pressure. Most anthracites were formed in the CARBONIFEROUS PERIOD. They are found most notably in huge deposits in eastern Pennsylvania, USA.

anthrax An infection of animals, particularly goats, sheep, and cattle, which can be transmitted to humans through infected animal meat, bones, hair, hides, and excrement. It is caused by a specific type of bacteria, *Bacillus anthracis,* which the animals swallow or inhale from the environment. The organism has the capacity to form spores, which may lie dormant in soil, but remain potentially infectious for many years. The disease attacks the skin in humans, although the lungs and gastrointestinal tract may also be affected by inhalation or ingestion of the bacteria, respectively.

anthropic principle The principle in cosmology that theories of the origin of the Universe are constrained by the necessity to allow individual human existence. There are several versions of this principle. The **weak anthropic principle** holds that fundamental constants, such as the gravitational constant, have to hold in the present epoch, because in no other epoch would there have been intelligent beings to measure them. The **strong anthropic principle** is concerned with whether or not intelligent life could exist in any other Universe. Anthropic principles are viewed with some scepticism by many physicists.

anthropology The study of humankind, especially of its societies and customs. Interest in the activities of other cultures is as old as written records, and anthropology traces its antecedents to the Greek travellers Xenophanes (6th century BC) and Herodotus. Travellers' reports (e.g. Marco Polo) continued to be a popular form of proto-anthropology in the Middle Ages and Renaissance. The philosophical debates on the nature of humankind during the Enlightenment stimulated further interest in other cultures, but it was not until the advances of Saint-Simon and Comte that the foundation for a 'science of man' was laid. Modern academic anthropology traces its origin to the evolutionary theories of Darwin, which stimulated European interest in the 'primitive' peoples of the world who were seen to provide a living laboratory to test theories of cultural evolution and diffusion. The second half of the 19th century saw an expansion of scholarly attention in and the quest for reliable information about the isolated and technologically less-developed peoples of the world. Initially ambitious comparative studies were undertaken on diverse topics including kinship systems, law, magic and religion, and culture, by a generation of library-bound scholars. At the beginning of the 20th century advances by Durkheim saw a retreat from these evolutionary beginnings and a shift to the study of the ways in which societies maintain themselves. The functionalist revolution occasioned by Bronislaw Malinowski and Alfred Radcliffe-Brown in Britain and Franz Boas in the USA saw an increasing emphasis on ethnographic fieldwork studies utilizing the technique of participant observation that has since become the single most important feature distinguishing anthropolgy from its sister discipline sociology.

anti-ballistic missile (ABM) A MISSILE designed to destroy BALLISTIC MISSILES or warheads in flight, either just before or after re-entering the atmosphere. Their numbers were limited as a result of the Strategic Arms Limitation Talks (SALT) (1969–79) and very few have been deployed. The Soviet Union had a screen of ABMs protecting Moscow, and the USA deployed Patriot ABMs in Saudi Arabia and Israel during the Gulf War (1991) to intercept Iraqi 'Scud' missiles. In both cases, the propaganda value of the ABMs far outweighed their potential or actual operational effectiveness. The problems involved in destroying the large numbers of warheads released by a MULTIPLE INDEPENDENTLY TARGETABLE RE-ENTRY VEHICLE just before they fall on the target has resulted in other anti-ballistic defence systems being investigated, such as the STRATEGIC DEFENSE INITIATIVE (SDT, or 'Star Wars') in the USA. SDI never became operational, and research was abandoned in 1993.

Antibes A fishing port on the French Riviera, in the Alpes-Martimes department of Provence-Alpes-Côte d'Azur, south-east France; pop. (1990) 70,690. It exports dried fruit, olives, tobacco, perfume, and wine. The town was established by the Greeks as a colony in the 4th century BC. Napoleon landed here on his return from Elba in 1815.

antibiotic Any substance produced by a living organism (such as a fungus), or made synthetically, that is capable of destroying or inhibiting the growth of microorganisms. Antibiotics are widely used in the CHEMOTHERAPY of microbial infections. The first antibiotic, PENICILLIN, was discovered by Alexander FLEMING in 1928 and developed for clinical use by FLOREY. Streptomycin was developed by WAKSMAN in 1944, and was later followed by tetracyclines, cephalosporins, and other compounds. Antibiotics differ from each other in their chemical structures and mode of action. Most are selective, in that they are effective against only a few types of organism, but synthetic derivatives have been produced with a wider range of activity, the so-called broad-spectrum antibiotics. Like other chemotherapeutic agents, antibiotics may be harmful to the host as well as killing the target microorganism. In addition, some patients develop an allergy which, in the case of penicillin, may be dangerous. The most serious problem is that the organism may become resistant to the antibiotic, making treatment ineffective. Despite their dangers and disadvantages, antibiotics remain powerful tools in human and veterinary medicine, and their use has contributed greatly to the dramatic fall in the death-rate from communicable diseases over the last 50 years.

antibody One of a group of important proteins known as immunoglobulins, which help to defend vertebrate animals against infection. Antibodies inactivate viruses and bacterial toxins and recruit various LEUCOCYTES (white blood cells) to kill and remove foreign material. Attached to the surfaces of lymphocytes (a type of leucocyte), antibodies bind themselves to molecules foreign to the body. These molecules are called **antigens**, and may be chemicals, or particles such as pollen grains. The highly selective reaction of an antigen with its antibody activates the parent lymphocyte to multiply into special cells able to produce very large quantities of soluble antibody protein and release them into the blood. The reaction forms an important component of IMMUNITY to specific diseases.

anticline A ridge or fold of stratified rock in which the strata slope down from the crest. The opposite is a syncline.

anticoagulant A substance that prevents clotting, especially of the blood. Anticoagulants such as heparin are added to blood that is to be stored before use in BLOOD TRANSFUSION and to specimens taken for laboratory examination. They are given to patients in CARDIOLOGY and cardiac surgery to reduce the risk of thrombosis (blood-clot formation) after heart operations.

Anti-Comintern Pact (25 November 1936) An agreement between Germany and Japan ostensibly to collaborate against international communism (the COMINTERN). Italy signed the pact (1937), followed by other nations in 1941.

Anti-Corn Law League A movement to bring about the repeal of the duties on imported grain in Britain known as the CORN LAWS. Founded in Manchester in 1839 under Richard COBDEN and John BRIGHT, the League conducted a remarkably successful campaign. A combination of bad harvests, trade depression, and the IRISH FAMINE strengthened the League's position and in 1846 the Prime Minister, Sir Robert PEEL, was persuaded to abolish the Corn Laws. The expected slump in agriculture did not take place.

anticyclone A system of winds rotating outwards from an area of high barometric pressure, clockwise in the Northern Hemisphere and anticlockwise in the Southern Hemisphere. Anticyclones are usually associated with dry, cold, and sometimes foggy weather in the winter and fine weather in the summer. At the centre of an anticyclone the weather is usually calm and settled.

antidepressant See PSYCHOTROPIC DRUG.

Antietam (Sharpsburg), Battle of (17 September 1862) A battle in the AMERICAN CIVIL WAR, fought in Maryland. After his victory at the second battle of Bull Run, General LEE invaded the North, but with only 30,000 men under his immediate command was attacked by a Union (Northern) army under General George McClellan at Sharpsburg on the Antietam Creek. Although the Confederates were badly mauled, they held their positions and made an orderly retreat on the following day. The casualties of 23,000 (divided almost equally between the two sides) were the worst of any single day of the war.

antifreeze Now almost always an approximately equal mixture of ethanediol (ethylene glycol, $CH_2OH.CH_2OH$) and deionized water to which rust inhibitors are added. Such formulations are used extensively to protect COOLING SYSTEMS such as car radiators, which rely on circulating water. Antifreezes give freeze protection down to −40°C and boil at about 116°C.

antigen See ANTIBODY; IMMUNITY.

Antigone In Greek mythology, the daughter of King Oedipus, whom she faithfully attended when he was blind and in exile. Her brother Polynices was killed fighting against Thebes, and her uncle, Creon, king of Thebes, forbade his burial. She was condemned to death for disobeying him, but killed herself.

Antigonus I (known as the 'One-eyed') (*c.*382–301 BC) An officer in the army of ALEXANDER III (the Great). After the latter's death (323), and that of the Macedonian regent, Antipater (319), he attempted to re-establish Alexander's empire under his own sole leadership, declaring himself king (306). His considerable success induced his rivals – Ptolemy, Seleucus, Cassander, and Lysimachus – to combine, defeat, and kill him at the 'battle of the kings' at Ipsus.

Antigua and Barbuda A country in the Leeward Island group of the CARIBBEAN, comprising the islands of Antigua, Barbuda, and Redonda (uninhabited).

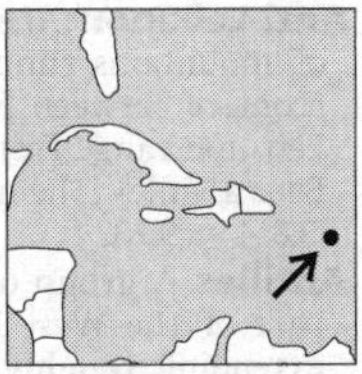

Physical. The main island, Antigua, comprises 280 sq km (108 sq mi) of fairly bare scrubland. Formed of volcanic rock in the south-west and coral in the north and east, it is moderately hilly, rising to 405 m (1,329 feet). The coastline is indented. The climate of the islands is dry and warm, although there are occasional hurricanes in summer. Water is scarce.

Economy. The mainstay of the economy is up-market tourism. Manufacturing industry includes clothing and the assembly of electrical components for re-export. Aside from some cultivation of sugar cane and cotton, agriculture has been neglected, resulting in dependence on food imports, which exacerbates the high foreign debt.

History. Antigua and Barbuda were colonized from the 17th century by the British, who brought slaves from Africa to work on the islands. From 1871 until 1956 the islands were part of the British colony of the Leeward Islands. Antigua and Barbuda joined the West Indian Federation, and in 1967 became an Associated State of Britain, gaining internal autonomy. The country became fully independent in 1981. The Antiguan Labour Party (ALP) has held power since 1976.

Capital: Saint John's
Area: 441.6 sq km (170.5 sq mi)
Population: 59,355 (1991)
Currency: 1 East Caribbean dollar = 100 cents
Religions: Anglican 44.5%; other Protestant (mainly Moravian, Methodist, and Seventh-day Adventist) 41.6%; Roman Catholic 10.2%; Rastafarian 0.7%
Ethnic Groups: Black 94.4%; Mixed 3.5%; White 1.3%
Languages: English (official); English creole
International Organizations: UN; Commonwealth; CARICOM

antihistamine A drug that inhibits the action of HISTAMINE in the body by blocking the receptors for histamine, of which there are two types: H_1 and H_2. When stimulated by histamine, H_1 receptors may produce such allergic reactions as hay fever, pruritus (itching), and urticaria (nettle rash). Antihistamines that block H_1 receptors, for example acrivastine, astemizole, azatadine, and chlorpheniramine, are used to relieve these conditions. Many of these drugs, especially cyclizine and promethazine, are also used to prevent motion sickness. Because a common side-effect of these drugs is drowsiness, they are sometimes used to promote sleep. H_2 receptors are found mainly in the stomach, where stimulation by histamine causes secretion of acid gastric juice. The drugs cimetidine and ranitidine block these receptors and so reduce gastric acid secretion; they are therefore used in the treatment of peptic ulcers.

antiknock A substance added to fuel to prevent uneven combustion in engines and thereby improve performance. Knock describes the characteristic noise in internal-combustion engines when uncontrolled combustion occurs. In petrol engines this may happen when the 'end gas', the last part of the mixture to burn, becomes over-heated and burns before the flame front has reached it, causing shock waves to strike the cylinder head and walls. Tetraethyl lead and 1,2-dibromoethane are used as antiknock agents in petrol. However, lead compounds formed in the exhaust gases cause AIR POLLUTION and are a health hazard.

Anti-Lebanon (Arabic **Jebel esh Sharqi**) A range of mountains running north to south along the frontier between Lebanon and Syria, east of the Lebanon range from which it is separated by the Beqa'a Valley. The highest point is Mount Hermon (2,814 m, 9,232 ft).

Antilles A group of islands forming the greater part of the West Indies. The **Greater Antilles**, extending roughly east to west, comprise Cuba, Jamaica, Hispaniola (Haiti and the Dominican Republic), and Puerto Rico; the **Lesser Antilles**, to the south-east, include the Virgin Islands, Leeward Island, Windward Islands, and various small islands to the north of Venezuela, including the NETHERLANDS ANTILLES.

Anti-Masonic Party A US political party of the 1820s and 1830s opposed to Freemasons. Formed in 1826 in the wake of the disappearance of William Morgan, a New York bricklayer alleged to have divulged lodge secrets, the Anti-Masonic Party was the product of hysteria, cleverly played upon by local politicians. It played an influential part in the politics of New York and surrounding states, and drew sufficient WHIG support away from Henry CLAY in the 1832 presidential election to help sweep President JACKSON back into office.

antimatter Matter composed of **antiparticles**. For each ELEMENTARY PARTICLE there is a corresponding antiparticle, which has the same properties as the particle itself but with the opposite electric charge (if it is charged) and the opposite SPIN and magnetic moment. If a particle meets its antiparticle they annihilate one another (see ANNIHILATION OF MATTER) and their combined mass is converted into electromagnetic radiation. Because there is a preponderance of matter in the Universe, antimatter particles are very short-lived as they are rapidly annihilated by particles of matter.

antimony (symbol Sb, at. no. 51, r.a.m. 121.75) A lustrous, silvery-white, brittle element, in Group 15 (formerly VB) of the PERIODIC TABLE, intermediate in properties between a non-metal and a metal. Reacting with non-metals and some metals rather slowly, it forms compounds in which it shows valencies 3 and 5. The principal ORE is stibnite, which occurs in China and South America. Antimony is obtained by heating the ore with iron, or by roasting it to form the oxide, followed by reduction with carbon. Antimony is added to germanium and indium in semiconductors. It is also alloyed with lead for bearings, storage-battery plates, and type metal. Antimony trisulphide is used in safety matches.

Antioch An alternative name for the city of ANTAKYA, southern Turkey.

Antiochus Eight Seleucid kings, notably Antiochus III and Antiochus IV. **Antiochus III** (known as Antiochus the Great) (*c*.242–187 BC) reigned 223–187 BC. He restored and expanded the Seleucid empire, regaining the vassal kingdoms of Parthia and Bactria and conquering Armenia, Syria, and Palestine. When he invaded Europe he came into conflict with the Romans, who defeated him on land and sea and severely limited his power. **Antiochus IV** Epiphanes (*c*.215–163 BC), son of Antiochus III, reigned 175–163 BC. His firm control of Judaea and his attempt to Hellenize the Jews resulted in the revival of Jewish nationalism and the Maccabean revolt.

antioxidant A compound that prevents reaction of a substance with OXYGEN from the air. Antioxidants are important in FOOD PRESERVATION, and are used in the formulation of paints and plastics and to prevent the formation of gum in the petrol for car engines. Natural antioxidants, such as vitamin E and beta-carotene, reduce damage to living cells caused by toxins.

antiparticle See ANTIMATTER.

Antipodes Islands An outlying island group of New Zealand in the South Pacific Ocean, lying 3° of latitude further south than the southern tip of New Zealand, comprising a central island and several islets.

antipope A person who claims or exercises the office of pope (PAPACY) in opposition to the true pope of the time. There have been about 35 antipopes in the history of the Catholic Church, the last being Felix V (1439–49). There have been two main causes. First, a disputed election, in which there was disagreement among the electors or other interested parties as to which person was elected pope. Secondly, the desire of various Holy Roman Emperors to have a more pliable person as pope, and their setting up of antipopes for this purpose. In some cases, especially during the GREAT SCHISM of 1378–1417, it is very difficult to say which person was the true pope and which was the antipope.

antirrhinum A plant of the genus *Antirrhinum*, commonly known as a snapdragon, in allusion to the shape of the flower. There are about 40 perennial, herbaceous species native to the Northern Hemisphere. They belong to the foxglove family and are related to figwort and speedwell. Many garden varieties in a large range of colours and sizes have been developed from *A. majus*.

anti-Semitism Hostility towards and discrimination against JEWISH PEOPLE. In the late 19th and early 20th centuries it was strongly evident in France, Germany, Poland, Russia, and elsewhere, many Jewish emigrants fleeing from persecution or POGROMS in south-east Europe to Britain and the USA. After World War I early Nazi propaganda in Germany encouraged anti-Semitism, alleging Jewish responsibility for the nation's defeat. By 1933 Jewish persecution was active throughout the country. The 'final solution' which Hitler worked for was to be a HOLOCAUST or extermination of the entire Jewish race; some six million Jews were killed in CONCENTRATION CAMPS before the defeat of Nazism in 1945. Anti-Semitism was a strong feature of society within the former Soviet Union, especially after World War II. Anti-Semitism remains a problem in eastern Europe and in the former Soviet republics, although Jewish people are now allowed to emigrate from these countries. During the early 1990s in western Europe, especially in France and Germany, there was an increase in racist violence by neo-Nazi groups.

antisepsis Prevention of the spread of disease-carrying microorganisms. Many surgeons of the 18th and 19th centuries noted that by observing strict cleanliness during operations they could significantly reduce the incidence of infection, though they were unable to explain why. Later, the work of PASTEUR and others identified the cause of these infections as bacteria. This led to the use, by LISTER and others, of carbolic acid (phenol) to eradicate them. Since then, other methods of killing bacteria and viruses have been introduced, including heat treatment (autoclaving) and ultraviolet light. See also ASEPSIS, STERILIZATION.

antitank gun An ARTILLERY weapon firing ammunition designed to destroy TANKS. The problem of piercing a tank's armour was at first solved by using solid shot at high velocities, so that at impact the round broke through the armour. During World War II, tank armour became too thick to be penetrated in this way, and the hollow charge shell was developed. This shell had a hollow metal nose, behind which was an explosive charge that detonated on impact. The detonation wave passed forwards, melting the hollow nose of the shell and directing a high-speed jet of molten metal and explosive gas against the target. Most modern antitank missiles also use hollow charges.

anti-trade winds Westerly winds in the atmosphere (above 2,000 m, 6,600 ft) blowing in the opposite direction to middle latitude surface winds known as trade winds.

Anti-Trust laws US laws restricting business monopolies. After twenty-five years' agitation against monopolies, the CONGRESS passed the Sherman Anti-Trust Act (1890) that declared illegal 'every contract, combination, or conspiracy in restraint of trade'. The Clayton Anti-Trust Act (1914), amended by the Robinson-Patman Act (1936), prohibited discrimination among customers and mergers of firms that would lessen competition. After World War II there was a further growth in giant multi-national corporations and the Celler-Kefauver Antimerger Act (1950) was intended to prevent oligarchic tactics, such as elimination of price competition, as being against the public interest.

antler One of a pair of horns belonging to deer. They are usually found only in the male, but are present in both sexes of the reindeer. They are bony outgrowths and are shed each year. After the old antlers are cast, new ones begin to grow almost immediately and, to satisfy its need for minerals, especially calcium phosphate, the animal will gnaw the shed antlers. In successive years, there is an increase in the size and complexity of the antlers, with progressively more branches (tines) as the animal grows older.

ant lion A dragonfly-like insect with a wing-span of up to 12.5 cm (5 inches), making up a family, Myrmeliontidae, containing some 1,200 species. Ant lions are mainly tropical insects, and part of the same insect order as the LACEWINGS (Neuroptera). Their larvae excavate conical pits in sand and lie at the bottom. When another insect, often an ant, passes over the top they flick sand at it to make it fall in. They have strong, sickle-shaped jaws with which they hold their prey, while sucking out its juices.

Antofagasta A port on the Pacific coast of northern Chile; pop. (1991) 218,750. Founded in 1870 as an outlet for copper and nitrates from the Atacama Desert, it is capital of Antofagasta province. It has large ore refineries and foundries.

Antonello da Messina (*c.*1430–79) Italian painter from Messina in Sicily. He was one of the first Italian painters to master the new technique of OIL PAINTING and he played a major role in popularizing it. Antonello painted religious subjects and portraits, and in his work he successfully combined the Netherlandish passion for exquisite detail with the Italian tradition of clarity and dignity of form.

Antonescu, Ion (1882–1946) Romanian military leader and fascist dictator. In 1940 he assumed dictatorial powers. He forced the abdication of King CAROL, and supported the Axis Powers. His participation in the Nazi invasion of the Soviet Union resulted, in 1944, in the fall of his regime as the Red Army entered Romania. In 1946 he was executed as a war criminal.

Antonines A Roman imperial dynasty beginning with Titus Aurelius Antoninus (86–161 AD). He succeeded HADRIAN in 137 and was entitled 'Pius' (Latin, 'the Devout') by the ROMAN SENATE. His reign was peaceful, by virtue of his respect for the traditional role of the Senate. The remains of a column and temple to his memory still exist in Rome. His nephew and son-in-law Marcus AURELIUS was named his adopted son and heir. Aurelius' son, Commodus, was technically the last of the dynasty; but Lucius Septimius SEVERUS adopted himself into the line. Severus' son 'Caracalla' and great-nephew Elagabalus continued to use the name and the title 'Pius'.

Antonine Wall A defensive fortification about 59 km (37 miles) long, built across the narrowest part of central Scotland between the Firth of Forth and the Firth of Clyde *c.*140 AD, in the time of Antoninus Pius. It was intended to mark the frontier of the Roman province of Britain, and consisted of a turf wall with a broad ditch in front and a counterscarp bank on the outer edge, with 29 small forts linked by a military road. The Romans, however, were unable to consolidate their position and in *c.*181 the wall was breached and the northern tribes forced a retreat from the Forth–Clyde frontier, eventually to that established earlier at Hadrian's Wall.

Antoninus Pius (86–161) Roman emperor 138–61. The adopted son and successor of Hadrian, he was the first of the Antonine emperors. His reign was generally peaceful and he ruled in harmony with the Senate, pursuing a policy of moderation and liberality. Although no great conqueror, he extended the empire; the frontier of Britain was temporarily advanced to the ANTONINE WALL.

Antonioni, Michelangelo (1912–) Italian film director. He won international acclaim with *L'avventura* (1960), and made his first colour film, *Il deserto rosso*, in 1964. His films concentrate on the study of character and illuminate such themes as suicide and humankind's alienation from the environment. His other films include *Blow-Up* (1966), *Zabriskie Point* (1970), and *The Passenger* (1975).

Antony of Padua, St See ANTHONY OF PADUA, ST.

Antrim ▶1 A historic county of Northern Ireland; area 2,831 sq km (1,093 sq miles). It is administered by several district councils. **▶2** A market town in County Antrim, Northern Ireland, on the north-east shore of Lough Neagh; pop. (1981) 22,340.

Antwerp (French **Anvers**; Flemish **Antwerpen**) A commercial and industrial seaport in Belgium, on the River Scheldt; pop. (1991) 467,520. It is capital of a province of the same name and was designated European City of Culture 1993. Founded as a small trading centre in the 8th century, Antwerp became a seat of the Counts of Flanders. By the 16th century it had eclipsed Bruges and Ghent to become one of Europe's leading commercial and financial centres and was a distribution centre for spices from the East Indies. Still one of Europe's busiest entrepôts, its 19th-century links with southern Africa have resulted in Antwerp becoming a major centre of diamond cutting for both jewellery and industry. It was the birthplace of Anthony Van Dyke and the home of Paul Peter Rubens.

Anubis The Egyptian dog or jackal god of cemeteries and of embalming, also depicted as a dog-headed man attending to a mummy or conducting the dead into the underworld Hall of Judgement to weigh their hearts in the presence of Osiris. Anubis' role in burial promoted him throughout Egypt, although his cult centre was in the 17th Upper Egyptian nome (district) near el-Qeis. In later times Anubis' role as a judge of the dead was supplanted by that of Osiris.

Anuradhapura The ancient capital of the Sinhalese kings of Sri Lanka from the 4th century BC to the 11th century AD when it was abandoned in the face of invading Hindu Tamils. The modern city is the capital of a district of the same name in north-central Sri Lanka; pop. (1981) 36,000. The sacred Botree brought as a sapling from the Buddha's original tree in Bodh Gaya in India over 2,000 years ago is alleged to be the oldest living tree in the world.

anus See ALIMENTARY CANAL.

anxiety A feeling of actual or anticipated unease, similar to fear, but more closely associated with uncertainty. It is associated with bodily changes, such as raised heart-rate and perspiration. Psychologists distinguish the state of being anxious from the trait of being an anxious person. Levels of trait anxiety appear to be major, and perhaps innate, differences between people. In PSYCHIATRY, anxiety occurs in many psychological disorders, both NEUROSES and PSYCHOSES. A notable exception is the PSYCHOPATHIC PERSONALITY, where it is precisely the absence of anxiety (failure to worry about the consequences of one's actions) that is the problem. In certain disorders, such as PHOBIAS, in which extreme anxiety is the main feature, the person is incapacitated by fear of, and hence driven to avoid, what in reality are harmless situations. Although drugs (tranquillizers) can be used in the treatment of abnormal anxiety, this may lead to dependence and does not relieve the underlying problem, which is better dealt with by PSYCHOTHERAPY or one of the newer instructional methods (BEHAVIOUR THERAPY), in which the patient is taught self-help techniques of anxiety management.

Anyang ▶**1** A city in the province of Henan, central China; pop. (1990) 480,670. Once known as Yin it was the last capital (1300–1066 BC) of the Shang (or Yin) dynasty and one of China's earliest centres of civilization. Ruins of the ancient city lie to the north-west of Anyang on the banks of the River Huan or Anyang, which is a tributary of the Yellow River. The *I Ching Book of Changes* was compiled here during the Zhou Dynasty (1122–221 BC). Modern Anyang is an industrial city manufacturing iron and steel, textiles, and light industry products. ▶**2** A city in the province of Kyonggi, north-west Korea; pop. (1990) 480,670.

ANZAC An acronym derived from the initials of the Australian and New Zealand Army Corps, which fought during World War I. Originally it was applied to those members of the Corps who took part in the GALLIPOLI campaign. The name came to be applied to all Australian and New Zealand servicemen. Anzac Day (25 April), commemorating the Gallipoli landing (and later contributions to other campaigns), has been observed since 1916.

Anzio A fishing port and resort on the coast of Latium, central Italy, situated on the Tyrrhenian Sea, 57 km (36 miles) south of Rome; pop. (1990) 34,680. It was the birthplace of the Emperor Nero. During World War II Allied troops landed on the beaches of Anzio (Jan. 1944).

ANZUS An acronym given to a tripartite Pacific security treaty between Australia, New Zealand, and the USA, signed at San Francisco in 1951. Known also as the Pacific Security Treaty, it recognizes that an armed attack in the Pacific Area on any of the Parties would be dangerous to peace and safety, and declares that it would act to meet the common danger, in accordance with its constitutional processes. Following New Zealand's anti-nuclear policy, which included the banning of nuclear-armed ships from its ports, the USA suspended its security obligations to New Zealand in 1986. ANZUS continues to govern security relations between Australia and the USA, and between Australia and New Zealand.

Aomori A port at the northern tip of Honshu Island, Japan, on Musu Bay; pop. (1990) 287,810. It is the leading port of north Japan, capital of a prefecture of the same name, and a centre of high-technology and biochemical industries, and the site of the Nebuto Festival held in early August each year.

aorta The main artery of the body, from which the others derive. It arises from the left ventricle, arches over the top of the heart, and descends in front of the backbone, giving off large and small branches and finally dividing to form the right and left iliac arteries. The part of the descending aorta from the aortic arch to the diaphragm is called the thoracic aorta; the part below the diaphragm is the abdominal aorta.

Apache A group of Plains Indians of the south-western USA. Traditionally, the Apache practised subsistence farming and hunting, and a system of matrilocal (at the home of the wife) residence. Their nomadic existence, using the dog-travois (sledge) in the central and southern Great Plains, gradually led them southwards into semi-desert regions during the 9th to the 15th centuries. They had a reputation as fierce fighters; they and the NAVAHO raided towns of the Anasazi as early as *c.*1275. Spanish explorers found them well established in Arizona, New Mexico, Texas, and northern Mexico in the late 16th century and regular contact with Spanish settlements was developed by the early 17th century. As they, and numerous other tribes on the eastern edges of the plains, acquired horses, competition for buffalo hunting became fierce and the COMANCHE eventually drove them off the Great Plains into the deserts by the mid-18th century. The Apache resisted domination by the Spanish and Mexicans until the mid-19th century, when their territory was incorporated into the USA. They were not finally subjugated, however, until the end of the 19th century, and many of their chiefs, such as Geronimo, entered into American folklore. They now live in the state of Arizona.

apartheid (Afrikaans, 'separateness') A racial policy in South Africa. It involved a strict segregation of black people from white people, in land ownership, residence, marriage and other social intercourse, work, education, religion, and sport. From 1985 certain restrictions began to be mitigated by creating subordinate parliamentary chambers for Indians and Coloureds (people of mixed descent), by relaxation of rules for sport and leisure, by abolishing the Pass Laws, and by modifying the Group Areas Act. Increasing internal unrest along with international pressure for its abolition eventually swayed the government, and in July 1991 President DE KLERK repealed all remaining apartheid legislation, including the Population Registration Act. In December 1991 a Convention for a Democratic South Africa (CODESA) was established. In 1993 a new transitional constitution, drafted by CODESA, was ratified by the government. The constitution gave the vote to all South African adults and the first multi-racial elections were held in 1994.

apatite A widely distributed calcium phosphate mineral that contains chlorine or fluorine and sometimes both. Crystalline in form, it is translucent, usually sea-green or yellowish green, but can be found in several other colours. Commercially it is used in phosphatic fertilizers.

Apatosaurus See BRONTOSAURUS.

ape Any PRIMATE of the family Pongidae. The living apes include chimpanzees and gorillas from Africa, and gibbons, siamangs, and orangutans from Asia. Instead of walking along the branches of trees as monkeys do, most apes swing by their powerful, muscular arms, which are longer than their legs. However, gorillas rarely swing by their arms owing to their large size. In all apes, both hands and feet are efficient grasping organs. Most of the apes are vegetarians, but chimpanzees occasionally eat meat.

The apes have highly developed social organization and systems of communication, except the orang-utan, which is solitary. The gestation period of apes is up to nine months in some species, and their life-span can be up to forty years in the case of chimpanzees, gorillas, and orang-utans.

Apeldoorn A town in the province of Gelderland, east-central Netherlands, 27 km (17 miles) north of Arnhem; pop. (1991) 148,200. The Het Loo Palace here has been a summer residence of the Dutch royal family since 1685. It is a light industrial and tourist centre.

Apelles (fl. 4th century BC) Greek painter, born at Colophon in Asia Minor. He was court painter to Philip of Macedon and his son Alexander the Great, and in antiquity he was considered the greatest of all painters, celebrated for his mastery of CHIAROSCURO and composition.

Apennines A mountain range 1,350 km (840 miles) long running the entire length of the Italian peninsula. The central division of the Apennines contains the highest mountains, including Monte Corno at 2,914 m (9,560 feet). Numerous rivers, providing hydroelectric power, fall steeply down the eastern slope to the Adriatic Sea and more gently to the western Tyrrhenian Sea. The Apennines contain crater lakes, mineral springs, and volcanic hills. Near Naples is a region subject to earthquakes where the active volcano Vesuvius is located. There is a variety of minerals, and in the north-west Apennines are the quarries of the renowned Carrara marble.

aperture (in photography) The opening through which light is allowed into a CAMERA. See EXPOSURE METER; AUTOMATIC EXPOSURE.

aperture synthesis In radio astronomy, a technique for achieving high angular resolution (image clarity) using INTERFEROMETRY. In its basic form, it requires two radio telescopes, one in a fixed location, and the other placed successively at a series of positions. In each of these positions, observations and measurements are made with both telescopes. The position of the movable telescope is changed every twenty-four hours. Computer analysis of the complete series of observations synthesizes essentially the same results as those that would have been obtained from a single telescope whose size is equal to the whole of the area covered by the movable telescope.

aphasia A speech disorder caused by brain damage from strokes, headwounds, or sometimes infectious disease. Two distinct kinds are recognized, named after their discoverers, the French physician Paul Broca (1824–80) and the German physician Carl Wernicke (1848–1905). They are caused by damage to different areas of the brain. Sufferers from Broca's or non-fluent aphasia speak telegraphically, without grammatical features such as prepositions and conjunctions. Sufferers from Wernicke's or fluent aphasia speak fluently and grammatically but have trouble finding the right words. Impairment of language does not necessarily imply loss of other faculties such as INTELLIGENCE and MEMORY. Most aphasic people, especially younger ones, spontaneously recover a good deal of speech in time.

aphelion The point in a planet's orbit round the Sun at which it is furthest from the Sun. The Earth is at its aphelion on 3 July. Compare PERIHELION.

aphid A small insect which belongs to the homopteran BUG family Aphididae, with over 3,000 species worldwide. Aphids all have sucking mouth-parts and feed on the sap of plants. Their life cycles are often extremely complex, including parthenogenetic and sexual generations, winged or wingless adults, and alternation of food plants. In the course of feeding, they excrete excess sugars as honeydew, which is farmed by ants. Many aphid species, commonly known as greenfly, blackfly, or plant lice, are important pests of crops.

Aphrodite The ancient Greek goddess of love, beauty, and fertility. She was said to be the daughter of Zeus or alternatively to have been born of the sea foam. Her husband was Hephaestos, but she had other lovers among both gods (notably Ares) and mortals (notably Adonis). See also PARIS.

Apia The capital of Western Samoa in the central Pacific, situated on the north coast of the island of Upolu; pop. (1992) 32,000. It was the home of Robert Louis Stevenson from 1888 until his death in 1894.

apiculture The care and breeding of bees to obtain honey and, to a lesser degree, beeswax and 'royal jelly' (food prepared by the bees for young queens). Although evidence exists for the tending of bees since 2400 BC, apiculture on a commercial scale became possible only with the invention of the modern framed hive, patented by the US clergyman L. L. Langstruth in 1852. Apiculture is also important for the pollination of seed and fruit crops. Great care must be exercised in the application of INSECTICIDES to avoid killing the pollinators. Although wild bees provide a source of honey worldwide, their mixing with hived stock is generally undesirable, as interbreeding between wild and domestic bees can affect the latter's productivity and docility.

Apis In Egyptian mythology, a god always depicted as a bull (symbolizing strength in war and in fertility), worshipped especially at Memphis, where he was recognized as a manifestation of Ptah, the city's patron, then of Ra (the solar disc was placed between his horns), and later of Osiris. A live bull, carefully chosen, was considered to be his incarnation and kept in an enclosure. When it died it was mummified and ceremonially interred, and a young black bull with suitable markings was installed in its place.

Apo, Mount An active volcano rising to 2,954 m (9,692 ft) on Mindanao Island in the Philippines, south-west of Davao. It is the highest peak in the Philippines.

apogee The point in the Moon's orbit round the Earth at which it is furthest from the Earth. The term is also used with reference to artificial Earth satellites. Compare PERIGEE.

Apollinaire, Guillaume (pseudonym of Wilhelm Apollinaris de Kostrowitzki) (1880–1918) French poet. He was born in Rome of Polish descent. In 1900 he moved to Paris and began writing collections of poetry, including *Les Alcools* (1913) and *Calligrammes* (1918). He coined the term *surrealist* and was acknowledged by the surrealist poets as their precursor.

Apollinaris (*c.*310–*c.*390) Bishop of Laodicea in Asia Minor. He upheld the heretical doctrine, condemned at the Council of Constantinople (381), which asserted that Christ had a human body and soul but no human spirit, this being replaced by the divine Logos.

Apollo (in mythology) One of the most important of the Greek gods, the son of Zeus and twin brother of Artemis. He was primarily the god of the Sun and light, but he was also particularly associated with the forces of civilization, notably music, poetry, and medicine.

Apollo (in astronomy) The first ASTEROID found to cross the Earth's orbit, discovered by the German astronomer Karl Reinmuth in 1932. That year it passed within 11 million kilometres of the Earth. This irregularly shaped S-type asteroid has a mean diameter of 1.4 km.

Apollo-Amor objects ASTEROIDS that cross the orbits of Mars and, in some cases, the Earth. They follow highly elliptical orbits which take them closer to the Sun than other asteroids in the main asteroid belt. Apollo-Amor asteroids are small and there has been considerable debate as to whether they are fragments produced by collisions between large main-belt asteroids, or are the remnants of cometary nuclei after all the ice has disappeared.

Apollonia The site of an ancient city of Illyria, situated near present-day Fier in Albania. Founded by Corinthians in the 7th century BC, its importance as a trading centre was later superseded by Vlorë.

Apollonius (known as **Apollonius of Rhodes**) (3rd century BC) Greek poet. The librarian at Alexandria, he was the author of many works on grammar. He is chiefly known for his epic poem *Argonautica*; written in Homeric style and dealing with the expedition of the Argonauts, it was the first such poem to place love (Medea's love for Jason) in the foreground of the action.

Apollo programme The US space programme conducted by NASA, announced by President John F. Kennedy in 1961, aimed at 'landing a man on the Moon and returning him safely to Earth'. After a number of ground tests and three unmanned flights, the first manned mission (*Apollo 7*) flew in 1968, powered by a *Saturn V* (see LAUNCH VEHICLE). Three further *Apollo* flights tested the equipment and techniques to be used in the Moon landing. Then in 1969 *Apollo 11* was launched to make the first manned Moon landing. The three astronauts travelled in the command module, which was docked during flight to both the lunar module and the service module, the latter carrying fuel and supplies. On reaching the Moon, the command and service modules remained in orbit with Michael Collins on board, while Neil Armstrong and Edwin ('Buzz') Aldrin landed on the Moon's surface in the lunar module. There, they set up the Apollo Lunar Surface Experiments Package (ALSEP). When they had completed their tasks, Armstrong and Aldrin took off from the Moon in the upper half of the lunar module and docked with the command module, which took the three astronauts safely back to Earth. Parachutes were used to land the command module in the ocean for recovery by ships and helicopters. There were five more successful missions to the Moon; for the last three the astronauts had a wheeled lunar roving vehicle to help them explore further. In all, *Apollo* astronauts took about fifty experiments to the Moon and brought over 380 kg (840 pounds) of rock back to Earth. Since the last Apollo mission in 1972, there have been no further manned flights to the Moon.

Apollo-Soyuz project Docking in space of Soviet and US spacecraft. The *Apollo* and *Soyuz* spacecraft could not be directly joined because they had different atmospheres, and so a docking module incorporating an airlock was built. In 1975 the two spacecraft were launched, *Apollo* carrying the docking module; they docked two days later. The two cosmonauts and three astronauts, who had trained together and learned each other's languages, each visited the other spacecraft and together they carried out joint experiments for two days.

apoptosis The process of cell death, which occurs naturally as part of the normal development, maintenance, and renewal of tissues. During embryonic development it plays a vital role in determining the final size and form of tissues and organs. For example, the fingers are sculpted on the spadelike embryonic hands by apoptosis of the cells between them. Cancer is associated with the suppression of apoptosis, which can occur when viruses infect cells. Apoptosis differs from cellular necrosis, in which the cell's death may be stimulated by a toxic substance or waste product.

Apostle (Greek, 'one who is sent') The official name in Christianity for the twelve disciples chosen by Jesus to be with him during his ministry, and to whom he entrusted the organization of the Church. They were James (the Great) and John, the sons of Zebedee; James (the Less), the son of Alpheus; Jude, thought to be the same as Judas Lebbaeus, surnamed Thaddeus; Simon who was renamed Peter, and his brother Andrew; Matthew; Thomas, also called Didymus; Simon the Canaanite; Philip; Bartholomew, thought to be the same as Nathanael. The twelfth, Judas Iscariot, was replaced by Matthias. Three of the Apostles, Peter, James, and John, formed an inner circle. Paul and Barnabas are also given the title of Apostle in the New Testament even though they were not among the Twelve.

Appalachian Mountains (or **Appalachians**) A mountain system of eastern North America which confined early European settlers to the eastern coastal belt. Stretching from the Gulf of St Lawrence to central Alabama it comprises a series of parallel ridges separated by wide valleys. The highest peak is Mt. Mitchell (2,037 m, 6,684 ft) in the Black Mts. of North Carolina.

appeal A request made to a higher court for an alteration of the decision of a lower court. In order to control the number of appeals, restrictions are often imposed, such as the necessity to obtain leave to appeal from the higher court. A defendant in a criminal case may also appeal for a reduction in his sentence; and in many countries, the PROSECUTION can seek a heavier sentence. In some jurisdictions there is a hierarchy of appellate courts, culminating in a court of ultimate appeal, such as the US Supreme Court, the French *Cour de Cassation*, or the UK House of Lords. Appeals can also be made to the European Court of Human Rights or EUROPEAN COURT OF JUSTICE.

appeasement The efforts by the British Prime Minister, Neville CHAMBERLAIN, and his French counterpart, Édouard Daladier, to satisfy the demands (1936–39) of the AXIS POWERS. Their policy of appeasement enabled Hitler to occupy the RHINELAND, to annex Austria, and to acquire the Sudetenland in Czechoslovakia after the MUNICH PACT of 1938. Appeasement ended when Hitler, in direct contravention of assurances given at Munich, invaded the rest of Czechoslovakia in March 1939. A policy of 'guarantees' was then instituted, by which Britain and France pledged themselves to protect Romania, Greece, and Poland should they be attacked by Germany or Italy. The German invasion of Poland five months later signalled the outbreak of World War II.

Appel, Karel (1921–) Dutch painter, sculptor, and graphic artist. An exponent of abstract expressionism, he is best known for his paintings, executed in impasto and bright colours and characteristically depicting swirling abstract images suggestive of human and animal forms or fantasy figures. He has also produced polychrome aluminium sculptures.

appendicitis Inflammation of the APPENDIX, which is a medical emergency. It can occur in all age groups, but is more common in children and young adults. Symptoms include moderate to severe central or right-side abdominal pain, loss of appetite, fever, and vomiting. Rupture may cause PERITONITIS, which is life-threatening, but can be prevented by early surgical removal of the inflamed appendix.

appendix A blind-ended tube, up to 10 cm (4 inches) long in humans, which protrudes from the inner side of the caecum, or the first part of the large INTESTINE. The appendix is often considered vestigial in humans, but it is also present in many other mammals. In herbivorous mammals it is a well-developed elongated organ which assists in the digestion of cellulose.

Appert, Nicolas François (1750–1841) French pioneer of food preservation by canning. The son of a hotelier, and resident chef in his father's hotel, he first experimented with the preservation of food by traditional methods such as pickling. He later discovered that food could be preserved indefinitely by prolonged heating and then sealing in the absence of air, anticipating PASTEUR's research on bacterial spoilage by fifty years. At first he used glass containers, but in about 1814 metal cans were introduced.

Appian Way (Latin **Via Appia**) The principal southward road from Rome in classical times, named after the censor Appius Claudius Caecus who began it in 312 BC. It originally stretched to Capua (*c*.210 km, 132 miles), but was later extended to Brindisi in Apulia.

apple A small tree of the genus *Malus*, growing up to 6 m (20 feet) tall, represented by some twenty-five species in north temperate regions. The wild or crab apple, *M. sylvestris*, has small sour fruits; breeding and selection from it has yielded thousands of varieties of cider, cooking, and dessert apples. Other species of *Malus* are grown as ornamental trees, especially for their colourful spring blossom, as are many of their relatives in the rose family. Some cultivated apples are self-fertile but most require POLLINATION by another compatible variety for good fruit production.

Appleton, Sir Edward Victor (1892–1965) British physicist. His investigation of the Heaviside or E layer of the atmosphere led him to the discovery of a higher region of ionized gases (the Appleton layer, now resolved into two layers F1 and F2), from which short-wave radio waves are reflected back to Earth. This work, for which he was awarded the Nobel Prize for physics in 1947, was important for long-range radio transmission and radar.

applications program A computer PROGRAM such as a SPREADSHEET designed to perform the functions required by the end-user, rather than being part of the OPERATING SYSTEM. An applications package is a suite of programs directed at some generic application (for example, word processing or computer GRAPHICS) that can be tailored to the needs of specific instances of that application.

applied mathematics A branch of mathematics that deals with the manipulation of experimental data and other information relating to real physical systems. It is used today throughout all aspects of the pure and applied sciences and technology. The solution of problems in mechanical, civil, electrical, and chemical ENGINEERING depends heavily on applied mathematics. Experimental data from real systems can be processed using calculations which lead to more generally applicable conclusions.

One of the most important research tools of applied mathematics is mathematical modelling, which is able to predict how an experimental system will behave without actually having to build it in reality. Computer simulation using mathematical models can, for example, enable medical students to experiment with different courses of treatment without any risk to real patients. Attempts by chemists and physicists to describe the structure and nature of matter have relied heavily on applied mathematics. Quantum mechanics is the applied mathematics of the subatomic world. At the other end of the scale, astronomers use Einstein's theories of relativity to describe the structure of the Universe and to interpret processes that occur in vast expanses of space and time.

Appomattox A village in Virginia, USA, scene of the surrender of the CONFEDERACY Army of Northern Virginia to the Union Army of the Potomac on 9 April 1865. The surrender terminated Confederate resistance in the east and marked the effective end of the AMERICAN CIVIL WAR.

appropriate technology (or **alternative technology, intermediate technology**) An approach to the development and use of technology, dating from the late 1960s, reflecting a concern for minimizing environmental damage. Attempts to apply this approach in the Third World have led to the development of an intermediate technology, using local skills and resources, as opposed to capital-intensive high technology, or indigenous low technology. Intermediate technology has made significant contributions to health care, agricultural practice and food production, manufacturing, and energy production. The organization of collective or cooperative groups has given many poorer people access to otherwise unaffordable technology, for example pumps for irrigation or to ensure water supplies. Somewhat similar concepts applied in Western countries have given rise to the term 'alternative technology', implying an alternative to existing forms of technology. The initial emphasis of alternative technology was on rural self-sufficiency, often using ORGANIC FARMING practices. Subsequently the Western alternative technology movement, along with the environmental movement, has emphasized renewable energy technology (for example, solar, WIND, OR TIDAL ENERGY); and conservation of energy and raw materials through such methods as improved building insulation and RECYCLING. In the 1980s commercial wind farms were developed in many countries, and research was undertaken worldwide into solar and GEOTHERMAL ENERGY, BIOFUEL energy crops, and other renewable energy sources.

apricot A tree, *Prunus armenaica*, cultivated mainly in California, China, Japan, and northern Africa, as it is susceptible to frosts in cooler climates. The medium-sized tree can grow up to 10 m (33 feet) tall, and produces white or occasionally pink blossom. As a member of the cherry subfamily, apricots produce edible fruit similar to that of the peach, both species originating from China. The wild apricot is the parent of all cultivated varieties.

a priori In EPISTEMOLOGY, denoting knowledge or concepts which can be gained independently of all experience. It is contrasted with *a posteriori* knowledge, in which experience plays an essential role. The extent of a priori knowledge is much debated. RATIONALISTS and others, including KANT, argue that we can have substantial a priori knowledge. Empiricist philosophies, though, generally limit a priori knowledge to that derivable from analytic truths. See also EMPIRICISM.

Apuleius (born *c.*123) Roman writer, born in Africa. Renowned as an orator, he wrote a variety of rhetorical and philosophical works, but is best known as the author of the *Metamorphoses* (*The Golden Ass*), a picaresque novel which recounts the adventures of a man who is transformed into an ass. Apuleius' writings are characterized by an exuberant and bizarre use of language.

Apulia (Italian **Puglia**) A region forming the south-eastern 'heel' of Italy and comprising the provinces of Bari, Brindisi, Foggia, Lecce, and Taranto; area 19,345 sq km (7,472 sq miles); pop. (1990) 4,081,540; capital, Bari. In medieval times the region was divided into the northern Capitanata covering the forested Gargano peninsula and the Tavoliere plain, the central Terra di Bari which consists of a series of plateaus, and the Terra di Otranto extending over the hilly southern peninsula of Salento. The Tremite Islands in the Adriatic are part of Apulia.

Aqaba A port and popular resort at the northern end of the Gulf of Aqaba, southern Jordan; pop. (est. 1983) 40,000. Developed after the Arab–Israeli war of 1948, it is Jordan's only seaport.

Aqmola (or **Akmola**) The capital (since 1997) of Kazakhstan, a city in the steppeland of north-central Kazakhstan, on the Ishim (Esil) River; pop. (1990) 281,400. It is capital of the so-called Virgin Lands, a major wheat-producing region, and its industries are agriculturally based. Formerly named Akmolinsk, the city was known as Tselinograd from 1961 to 1993.

Aqtöbe (formerly **Aktyubinsk**) An industrial city in Kazakhstan, in the southern foothills of the Urals, on the River Ilek; pop. (1990) 261,000. Founded in 1869, it developed after the building of the Trans-Caspian railway in 1905. Industries include heavy engineering, oil, and the manufacture of textiles.

aquaculture The growing of aquatic plants and animals under controlled conditions for commercial, scientific, and recreational purposes. Aquaculture has existed since about 500 BC, but has gained widespread commercial importance only in the past 40 years. FISH-FARMING provides fish for food, and also supplies stock for sporting waters and for ornamental use. Invertebrates such as shrimp, crayfish, lobsters, prawns, food and pearl oysters, mussels, and scallops are also reared in SHELLFISH farming. Edible seaweed is a traditional part of Japanese diet and is grown by aquaculture in sheltered coastal regions. Aquaculture also provides fish products for the pharmaceutical and chemical industries.

aquamarine A transparent and usually greenish-blue variety of the mineral BERYL. Yellow ('golden beryl'), pink ('morganite'), and green (EMERALD) varieties of beryl also occur. It is found in cavities in granite and pegmatite in the Ural Mountains and in Brazil, Sri Lanka, Madagascar, and the USA.

aqua regia A mixture of three volumes of concentrated hydrochloric acid (HCl) to one volume of concentrated nitric acid (HNO_3). It is a very strong oxidizing agent: for example, it will oxidize and thus dissolve gold, a reaction which none of the common acids can perform individually.

Aquarius The Waterbearer, a CONSTELLATION of the zodiac, representing a youth pouring water from an urn. The Sun passes through the constellation from late February to early March. Its brightest stars are of third magnitude. Aquarius contains two celebrated PLANETARY NEBULAE: NGC 7293, popularly known as the Helix Nebula, and NGC 7009, known as the Saturn Nebula because of its resemblance to that planet when seen through a telescope. The globular CLUSTER M2 (NGC 7089) is visible through binoculars.

aquatint An engraving process for producing prints from a metal plate invented in about the middle of the 18th century. An aquatint produces finely granulated tonal areas and resembles a brush drawing or water-colour. A metal plate is sprinkled with acid-resistant resin, which is fused to the plate by heating, and when the plate is immersed in an acid bath (as in ETCHING) the acid bites between the tiny particles of resin and produces an evenly granulated surface. The design is created by drawing on the plate with acid-resistant varnish. It has been much used for reproducing water-colours, but also as an original creative technique by artists such as GOYA and DEGAS.

aqueduct Often a BRIDGE that carries a water channel, but also, more generally, the system of CANALS, siphons, TUNNELS, and bridges forming the main distribution channel for domestic or industrial water supply, for irrigation, or for hydroelectric power generation. Water loss to the ground can be prevented by lining the canals with concrete or asphalt, while the risk of contamination to drinking-water supplies is reduced by covering over the channel. The aqueduct is built to a gradient of at least 1 in 6,000 so that water flows by gravity where the general slope of the terrain allows. In a pressure conduit the water may flow by gravity (as in an inverted siphon) or it may be pumped; it is confined within the closed conduit and exerts a bursting pressure upon its walls. To cope with this, conduits are commonly made from large-diameter welded steel or reinforced concrete, or are lined tunnels through solid rock. In hydroelectric schemes the water pressure in the penstocks (the pipes delivering water to the turbines) may be very high, on account of the fall between the reservoir and the turbines. Notable modern aqueducts include those serving Los Angeles and New York; the most extensive of the ancient systems are Roman aqueducts.

aquifer A layer of rock or soil able to hold or transmit water.

Aquila (Italian **L'Aquila**) The chief city of the Abruzzi region in east-central Italy, on the River Aterno; pop. (1990) 67,820. Founded in the 13th century, it was a century later the second city of southern Italy after Naples.

aquilegia A perennial herbaceous plant of the genus *Aquilegia*, from the mountains and temperate zones of the Northern Hemisphere. Aquilegias are relatives of the delphinium, clematis, and other members of the buttercup family. The common name columbine indicates the dove- or bird-like appearance of the flowers, which have long, nectar-bearing spurs attractive to bumble-bees.

Aquinas, St Thomas (known as 'the Angelic Doctor') (1225–74) Italian philosopher, theologian, and Dominican friar. Regarded as the greatest figure of scholasticism, he also devised the official Roman Catholic tenets as declared by Pope Leo XIII. His works include many commentaries on Aristotle as well as the *Summa Contra Gentiles* (intended as a manual for those disputing with Spanish Muslims and Jews). His principal achievement was to make the work of Aristotle acceptable in Christian western Europe; his own metaphysics, his account of the human mind, and his moral philosophy were a development of Aristotle's, and in his famous arguments for the existence of God ('the Five Ways') he was indebted to Aristotle and to Arabic philosophers. Feast day, 28 January.

Aquitaine ▶**1** An ancient province of south-west France, comprising at some periods the whole country from the Loire to the Pyrenees. By the marriage of Eleanor of Aquitaine to Henry II in 1152 it became one of the English possessions in France. It was held by the English Crown until 1453 when Charles VII took Bordeaux and united the region with France as the province of Aquitaine. ▶**2** A region of modern France comprising the departments of Dordogne, Gironde, Landes, Lot-et-Garonne, and Pyrénées-Atlantiques; area 41,308 sq km (15,955 sq miles); pop. (1990) 2,795,830; capital, Bordeaux.

Aquitaine, Eleanor of See ELEANOR OF AQUITAINE.

Arab A member of the Semitic people inhabiting originally the Arabian Peninsula and neighbouring countries, now also parts of the Middle East and North Africa. The Arabic language, with a script that is written from right to left, has spread as far east as Malaysia, Indonesia, and the Philippines, and as far west as Morocco. It is the language of some 120 million people and is the language of the Koran. Arabic numerals, which probably originated in India, were adopted by the people of Europe in the Middle Ages in place of Roman numerals.

Arab conquests Wars which, in the century after the death of MUHAMMAD in 632, created an empire stretching from Spain to the Indus valley. Beginning as a JIHAD (holy war) against the apostasy of the Arabian tribes that had renounced ISLAM they acquired a momentum of their own as the Arabs, inspired by the prospect of vast booty and the belief that death in battle would gain them instant admission to paradise, confronted the waning power of BYZANTIUM and Persia.

In Syria and Egypt the conquerors allowed both Christians and Jews to keep their faiths as *dhimmi* (protected peoples) upon payment of a discriminatory tax. Local resistance in Persia and North Africa made the conquests there slower. After the first civil war (656–61) the Arab capital was moved from Medina to Damascus by the UMAYYADS, and under the ABBASIDS to the new city of Baghdad where, with the encouragement of the caliphs HARUN AR-RASHID and al-Mamun, Islamic culture flowered. The political unity of this empire was short-lived – rival caliphates appeared in North Africa and Spain in the 9th and 10th centuries – but cultural coherence was maintained by the universality of the Arabic language and Islamic law (*shariah*), and by the traffic of traders, scholars, and pilgrims which these made possible.

Arabia The original homeland of the Arabs on the Arabian Peninsula of south-west Asia. Lying between the Red Sea and the Persian Gulf and bounded to the north by Jordan and Iraq, modern Arabia comprises the states of Saudi Arabia, Yemen, Oman, Bahrain, Kuwait, Qatar, and the United Arab Emirates. Mainly desert (An Nafud Desert in the north and the Empty Quarter in the south), it forms a large plateau of ancient crystalline rock covered by sedimentary sandstone and limestone. With an area of some 3,250,000 sq km (1,250,000 sq miles), Arabia is the largest peninsula in the world. During the 18th and 19th centuries Arabia was explored by European travellers including Burckhardt, Burton, Palgrave, Doughty, and the Blunts. During the 20th century travellers such as Lawrence, Philby, Thomas, Shakespear, and Thesiger have explored Arabia in the wake of the discovery of oil in the region.

Arabian Sea The north-western part of the Indian Ocean, between Arabia and India.

Arabic language See SEMITIC LANGUAGES.

Arabic numerals The numbers 0, 1, 2, 3, 4, 5, 6, 7, 8, 9, which are used throughout the world for all scientific and trade purposes. The system was developed in India in the 9th century, reaching Europe and the rest of the world through the Arab countries, where the place-value aspect of the system, with 10 as the base, developed. The use of zero and the place-values enabled the system to replace the ROMAN NUMERALS then in use. All forms of computation can be carried out efficiently using the Arabic system, whereas calculations using Roman numerals are extremely cumbersome.

arable farming The cultivation of large areas of land, as opposed to smaller-scale, more intensive horticultural cultivation. CEREALS are the major arable crops, accounting for over 50 per cent of all cultivated land worldwide; ROOT and FORAGE CROPS are also important. The first stage in crop production is to prepare the soil, which should have a structure of large pores for drainage and aeration, interspersed with smaller pores to retain moisture. Weeds must be cleared, and previous crop residues broken up. These objectives are achieved by tillage: initially the ground is ploughed, and then broken up further by HARROWS, land rollers, or CULTIVATORS. Weeds may be killed with HERBICIDES. In minimum-tillage farming this ground preparation is kept to a minimum, to preserve as much as possible the soil's natural structure. FERTILIZERS and other soil conditioners may be added at this stage, then the seed is sown using a seed drill. The developing crop is protected by PESTICIDES and other forms of pest management, and when ripe it is harvested by a COMBINE HARVESTER or other appropriate agricultural machinery. The types of crop grown on the same land year by year is known as the cropping system. Crops may be rotated, with a variety of crops being grown to maintain the nutrient balance of the soil, or the same crop may be grown each year (monoculture), with chemical fertilizers supplying nutrient deficiencies. Monoculture carries a potential threat of disease, and usually 'break' crops are grown at intervals to reduce this risk. Break crops may be animal forage, pulses, temporary pasture, or cash-crops such as oil-seed rape, sugar beet, sunflowers, tobacco, or cotton.

Aracajú A port in north-east Brazil, on the River Sergipe, capital of the state of Sergipe; pop. (1990) 404,830. Chosen as the new state capital (replacing São Cristóvão) in 1855, Aracajú was Brazil's first planned city. Sugar refining and cotton milling are the two chief industries.

arachnid A member of the Arachnida, one of the most numerous classes within the ARTHROPODS, being second in number only to the insects. It contains at least 60,000 species, including scorpions, spiders, mites, and ticks, which range in size from a fraction of a centimetre in some mites, to 18 cm (7 inches) in the African scorpion, *Pandinus imperator*. Arachnids succeed in all habitats from tundra to desert, mostly as carnivores, pursuing or trapping other small animals. Their body plan consists typically of two main parts: the front part, or 'head', bears eyes, jaws, PEDIPALPS, and eight walking legs, while the abdomen houses most of the organs.

Arachnid jaws cannot bite strongly, so poisons are used to subdue prey, or silk to enwrap it, before it is chewed. Being so aggressive, many spiders and scorpions have to be very careful when mating; males are usually smaller, and may be eaten by their mates. The males use ritual dancing during courtship, bring gifts of food to the female, or woo her with instinctive caresses. They deposit packages of sperm, generally within her body, and then retreat hastily. The females produce eggs which may be held inside the body until hatching, laid singly, or laid collectively in batches. Development and growth necessitate a series of skin changes, or moults.

Arad A commercial and industrial city in Transylvania, western Romania, on the River Mures; pop. (1989) 191,430. It is the capital of Arad county and a railway junction linking lines to Budapest, Bucharest, and Belgrade. It has a citadel built by the Empress Maria Theresa in the 18th century. Its industries include sawmilling, textiles, distilling, machine tools, and electrical goods.

Arafat, Yasser (1929–) Palestinian leader, chairman of the Palestine Liberation Organization from 1968. In 1956 he co-founded Al Fatah, the Arab group which came to dominate the PLO from 1967. In 1974 he became the first representative of a non-governmental organization to address the United Nations General Assembly. Despite challenges to his authority within the PLO, he has remained its leader. After the signing of a PLO–Israeli peace accord providing for limited Palestinian autonomy in the West Bank and the Gaza Strip, in July 1994 Arafat became leader of the new Palestine National Authority. The same year he shared the Nobel Peace Prize with Yitzhak Rabin and Shimon Peres. Arafat won a landslide victory in the first Palestinian presidential elections (1996).

Arafura Sea A shallow sea lying between northern Australia and the islands of east Indonesia. It is linked to the Indian Ocean by the Timor Sea and the Pacific Ocean by the Coral Sea.

Arago, (Dominique) François (Jean) (1786–1853) French physicist whose researches did much to establish (1838) the wave nature of light, according to which light should be retarded as it passes from a rarer to a denser medium. He was the first to discover that polarized light is twisted by certain types of crystal, and with Augustin FRESNEL, he proposed laws describing the behaviour of polarized light. Arago also discovered the principle of the production of magnetism by the rotation of a non-magnetic conductor. An active republican and liberal reformer, he became a government minister in 1848.

Aragon (Spanish **Aragón**) ▶**1** A former kingdom of north-east Spain, conquered by the Visigoths in the 5th century and then the Moors in the 8th century but later united with Catalonia (1137) and Castile (1479). ▶**2** An autonomous region of modern Spain, bounded on the north by the Pyrenees and on the east by Catalonia and Valencia; area 47,669 sq km (18,412 sq miles); pop. (1991) 1,188,820; capital, Saragossa (Zaragoza). It comprises the provinces of Huesca, Teruel, and Zaragoza.

Aragon, Catherine of See CATHERINE OF ARAGON.

aragonite (or **mother-of-pearl**) A calcium carbonate ($CaCO_3$) mineral. It can show attractive lustrous crystals of pointed shape. It tends to change into calcite, a more stable form of calcium carbonate, and it is therefore found only in younger deposits, as at Fort Collins, Colorado, USA. Another source of supply is from the shells of certain molluscs, of which it forms the lining. Delicate but very brittle, and white and grey in colour, it is widely used for ornament.

Araguaía A river rising in south-central Brazil on the frontier between Mato Grosso and Goiás. It flows a distance of *c.*2,100 km (1,300 miles) northwards to meet the River Tocantins west of Imperatriz. The island of Bananal which separates the river into two arms is one of the largest freshwater islands in the world.

Arakan (or **Rakhine**) A state of western Myanmar (Burma) facing onto the Bay of Bengal; pop. (1983) 2,045,900; capital. Sittwe. It is separated from the inland states of Chin, Magwe, Pegu, and Irrawaddy by the Arakan Yoma mountain range, which also forms a natural boundary between India and Myanmar. Arakan has a short border with Bangladesh to the north.

Aral Sea (Russian **Aral'skoye More**) An inland sea in the Central Asian states of Kazakhstan and Uzbekistan. Fed by the Amu Darya (Oxus) in the south and the Syr Darya in the north-east, it was at its full extent the fourth-largest lake in the world. The diversion for irrigation of water flowing into the Aral Sea led to waterlevel falling by 13 m (43 ft) and the area of the sea being reduced to two-thirds of its original size of 64,501 sq km (24,904 sq miles) between 1960 and 1990.

Aramaic A Semitic language of ancient Syria (whose Biblical name was Aram), which was used as the lingua franca in the Near East from the 6th century BC and gradually replaced Hebrew as the language of the Jews in those parts. It was supplanted by Arabic in the 7th century AD. A modern form of Aramaic is still spoken in small communities in Syria and Turkey. One of its most important descendants is Syriac; Aramaic was written in the Hebrew alphabet from which the various Syriac scripts developed.

aramid fibre See NYLON.

Aran Islands (Irish **Oileain Arann**) A group of three rugged and barren islands (Inishmore, Inishmaan, and Inisheer) in Galway Bay, off the west coast of the Republic of Ireland; pop. (1981) 1,381. Its chief settlement is Kilronan. The islands were immortalized by the playwright J. M. Synge.

Aranjuez A horticultural market town and former royal summer residence on the River Tagus, in the province of Madrid, central Spain; pop. (1991) 35,870.

Arapaho An Uto-Aztecan-speaking American Indian tribe of the Great Plains and prairies of eastern North Dakota and western Minnesota. In 1870 with the founding of the Arapaho Agency most settled on a reservation in Oklahoma.

arapaima A tropical South American fish, *Arapaima gigas*, the largest freshwater fish known, which grows up to a length of 4 m (13.2 feet). The arapaima is long and slender, with a flattened, scaleless head and low dorsal and anal fins. It has specialized palatal jaws which have a double bite, and a lung-like swim bladder which gives it a large breathing capacity. It is an important food-fish for the aboriginal inhabitants of the Amazon, but has become scarce in many areas. In Brazil, it is called pirarucu.

Ararat, Mount (Turkish **Agri Dagi**) Either of two volcanic peaks of the Armenian plateau in eastern Turkey, near the frontiers of Iran and Armenia, of which the higher (**Great Ararat**, 5,122 m, 16,804 ft) last erupted in 1840. **Little Ararat** to the south-east rises to a height of 3,896 m (12,782 ft). A site to the south is the traditional resting place of Noah's ark after the Flood (Genesis 8:4).

Araucanía A region of southern Chile, south of the River Bío-Bío; area 31,946 sq km (12,339 sq miles); pop. (1982) 692,920; capital, Temuco. A Frenchman (who is buried in Tortoirac, France), Orllie Antoine, declared himself King of Araucania and Patagonia in 1860.

Araucanian Indian A South American Indian people who were the original inhabitants of central Chile and parts of Argentina. They resisted both Spanish and Chilean rule until the late 19th century, their last revolt ending in a treaty signed in 1881.

Arawak An indigenous American people of the Greater Antilles and northern and western South America, speaking languages of the same linguistic family. They were forced out of the Antilles by the more warlike Carib Indians shortly before Spanish expansion in the Caribbean.

Arbil (or **Irbil**) ▶**1** A Kurdish province in northern Iraq;. area 14,428 sq km (5,573 sq miles); pop. (est. 1985) 742,700. In 1974 it joined with the provinces of Dohuk and Suleimaniya to form a Kurdish Autonomous Region. ▶**2** The capital of the province of Arbil, 80 km (50 miles) east of Mosul; pop. (est. 1985) 333,900. Alexander the Great defeated the Persians under Darius III near here in 331 BC.

arbitrage The simultaneous buying and selling of GOODS or assets in different MARKETS (which are separated in either space or time) in order to profit from differences in price. As the dealers buy and sell simultaneously, they are not exposed to risk from price movements, in contrast to speculators, who buy (or sell) in the expectation of a rise (or fall) in the relevant price. Arbitrage most commonly takes place in COMMODITY MARKETS, the foreign-exchange market, and the markets for BILLS OF EXCHANGE and BONDS. See also FUTURES MARKETS.

arbitration See INDUSTRIAL RELATIONS.

Arbroath (formerly **Aberbrothock**) A North Sea-fishing port on the Angus coast of east Scotland; pop. (1981) 24,100. At Arbroath Abbey (built in 1178) the Declaration of Arbroath asserting Scotland's independence from England was signed in 1320 by King Robert I.

Arbuthnot, John (1667–1735) Scottish physician and writer. He was the physician to Queen Anne and is known as the author of medical works as well as for his satirical writings. A friend of Jonathan Swift and acquainted with Alexander Pope and John Gay, he was the principal author of a satirical work entitled *Memoirs of Martinus Scriblerus* (c.1714). His *History of John Bull* (1712), a collection of pamphlets advocating the termination of the war with France, was the origin of John Bull, the personification of the typical Englishman.

Arcadia (Greek **Arkhadia**) A mountainous district in the Peleponnese of southern Greece; pop. (1991) 103,840; area 4,419 sq km (1,706 sq miles); capital, Tripolis. In ancient times Arcadia was the home of the god Pan and a noted centre of song and music. In poetic fantasy Arcadia is a rustic paradise, the idyllic pastoral home of song-loving shepherds.

arch (in architecture and STRUCTURAL ENGINEERING) An upward-curved or pointed arrangement of blocks of stone or other rigid materials used to span a gap and support a structure above it; the term is also applied to similar features used decoratively. In a traditional masonry arch the individual wedge-shaped blocks are called voussoirs and the central one is the keystone. The blocks support each other, and the downward pressure of the superstructure is partially converted into outward thrust, which requires substantial abutment from a wall or pillar; if this is not strong enough the arch collapses. With modern materials such as steel and reinforced concrete, however, the stresses can be so distributed that massive supports are not needed, even for very wide spans. The arch was known to many ancient peoples, but they used it mainly for utilitarian purposes such as drains, and the Romans were the first to exploit it as a major element of architectural design. They used it to cover much wider spans than were possible with the simple post and lintel constructional system (two uprights supporting a flat slab) favoured by the Greeks, and they made it a key element of the decorative vocabulary of their architecture. The semicircular arch of the Romans continued to be dominant in European architecture until it was superseded in the 12th century by the pointed Gothic arch, which was stronger structurally and more versatile aesthetically. See illustration p. 72.

Archaean (or **Archean**) A geological period of time relating to the earlier part of the PRECAMBRIAN ERA.

archaeology The study of the past of humankind, especially in the prehistoric period, and usually by excavation. Archaeological research includes four stages. The most obvious is recovery of material by excavation, chance find, surface survey, and observation from the air. Digging remains crucial because it alone can recover the precise context of finds, without which they lose much of their significance. It can take a wide variety of forms depending on the nature of the site – an isolated grave, a long-occupied cave, a wreck on the sea-bed, a standing building, a modern construction site, and many more. Then, finds have to be turned into evidence by analysis. Their form, composition, date, and associations all have information to impart. Typology (study of changes in forms) can link finds from different sites. A whole battery of scientific and mathematical aids can be brought to bear at this stage. Thirdly, the results have to be built into a coherent story to give an account of what happened when. Finally, and often the most difficult task, reasons must be sought for the processes of cultural change.

Archaeopteryx Formerly the oldest-known fossil bird, found in parts of Germany in rocks about 150 million years old. Seven fossil specimens exist.

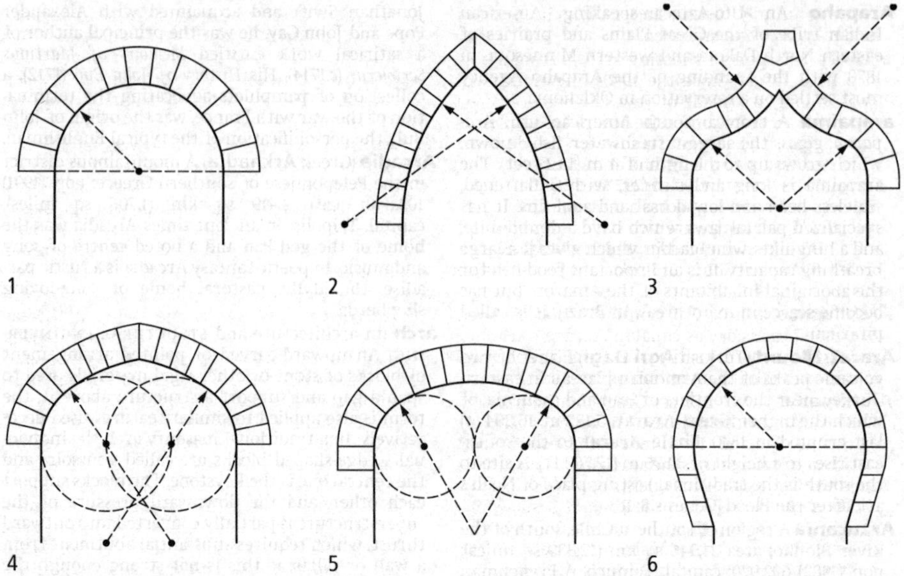

Arches (1) The semicircular Roman or Norman arch. (2) The Gothic lancet arch. (3) The Gothic ogee arch. (4) The Gothic Tudor arch. (5) The basket arch. (6) The Islamic horseshoe arch.

Archaeopteryx displays a mosaic of bird-like features, such as feathered wings and a 'wish-bone' or fused clavicles, and reptilian features, such as a long tail supported by vertebrae, separate clawed fingers, and teeth. Despite this unique mix of anatomical features, *Archaeopteryx* may now be 75 million years too young to be a true 'missing link' between birds and their dinosaurian ancestors. Bird-like fossils of *Protoavis* are also known from 225 million-year-old rocks in Texas, USA.

archangel An angel of the highest rank. In Jewish and Christian belief, Gabriel, Michael, Raphael, and Uriel are the four archangels who surround the throne of God. In Islam, Jibrīl, Mikāl, and Isrāfīl correspond to the first three, but the fourth is Azrael ('Izrā'īl), the Jewish and Islamic angel of death.

Archangel (Russian **Arkhangelsk**) A port of north-west European Russia, near the mouth of the North Dvina River where it meets the White Sea (Beloye More); pop. (1990) 419,000. Established in 1584 as Novo-Kholmogory, the port was renamed in 1613 after the monastery of the Archangel Michael. It was Russia's leading seaport until the building of St Petersburg in 1703, but regained its importance as a supply route with the completion of a rail link to Moscow in 1898. From December to April the port is usually icebound. Its principal exports are timber and timber products. Its factories produce pulp and paper, turpentine, resin, cellulose, and building materials. Fishing and shipbuilding are also important.

archer A soldier armed with bow and arrows. Archers have practised their deadly skill since prehistory in most parts of the world, for example, the Romans employed Scythian archers on horseback. In the Middle Ages the cumbrous but powerful crossbow was widely used in continental Europe, despite being forbidden against all save infidels by the Lateran Council of 1139. In England the potential of the longbow was discovered in the time of Edward I, but it was in Edward III's reign that full use was first made of it; nearly 2 m (6 ft) long, and made of yew, oak, or maple, it enabled accurate firing of arrows at a range of up to about 320 m (350 yards), and it gave England such victories as CRÉCY in 1346 and POITIERS in 1356. Archery became the English national sport; Roger Ascham, tutor to the future ELIZABETH I, published *Toxophilus*, a treatise on archery (1545). The musketeer superseded the archer in Europe from the later 16th century, but in 19th-century North America the Indians proved how devastating the mounted archer could be, even against men armed with rifles. See also ARCHERY.

Archer See SAGITTARIUS.

Archer, Jeffrey (Howard), Baron Archer of Weston-super-Mare (1940–) British writer and Conservative politician. Conservative MP for Louth from 1969 to 1974, he resigned his seat after being declared bankrupt. To pay his debts, he embarked on a career as a novelist, *Not a Penny More, Not a Penny Less* (1975) becoming the first of many best sellers. He was deputy chairman of the Conservative Party 1985–86, resigning after a libel case, and was created a life peer in 1992.

Archer, Thomas (*c*.1668–1743) English architect. His output was small, but his buildings are important in being the only ones by an English Baroque architect to show evidence of first-hand study of contemporary continental, particularly Italian, architecture. His finest works are the north front of Chatsworth, Derbyshire (1704–05), and the London churches of St Paul, Deptford (1713–30), and St John, Smith Square (1713–28).

archerfish A fish widespread in the lowland rivers and estuaries of south-east Asia and northern Australia. Archerfishes make up a family of four species, Toxotidae. The common archerfish, *Toxote jaculatrix*, has a relatively deep body, especially towards the tail, and a pointed snout. Inside the mouth, the palate has a lengthwise groove through which water can be ejected by sudden compression of the tongue and gill covers. By this means it can spit drops of water between 1 and 3 m (3–10 feet) away, accurately hitting insects, which then fall into the water and are eaten.

archery The sport of shooting arrows from a bow at a fixed target. Since the 1940s, the traditional English longbow, made of yew, has been replaced by a more accurate composite bow of wood, plastic, and fibreglass. The target stands with its centre 1.3 m (51 inches) above the ground at distances varying from 30 m (98 feet) to 90 m (295 feet). Under international rules, the target has a ten-zone face in five colours. At the centre are two bands of gold (scoring 10, 9 points for each hit), then two bands each of red (8, 7 points), blue (6, 5), black (4, 3), and white (2, 1).

Archilochus (8th or 7th century BC) Greek poet. Acclaimed in his day as equal in stature to Homer and Pindar, he wrote satirical verse and fables and is credited with the invention of iambic metre.

Archimedes (*c.*287–212 BC) Greek mathematician and inventor. Although best known as a brilliant mathematician and the founder of the sciences of statics and hydrostatics, he was also an ingenious engineer who applied his talents to a wide range of practical problems. When the Romans besieged his native Syracuse in 213 BC, he invented a range of ballistic weapons that considerably delayed the capture of the city. Archimedes also developed in detail the principle of the lever and of the multiple pulley. However, inventions such as the **Archimedean screw** (a screw mechanism used to raise water from lower levels) may have been wrongly ascribed to him. His principle, which states that a body immersed displaces a weight of fluid equal to its own apparent loss of weight, is applied to calculations of density, and in studies of flotation.

archipelago A group of islands or a sea with many islands, as in the MALAY ARCHIPELAGO.

Archipenko, Alexander (1887–1964) Russian-born sculptor, who became a US citizen in 1928. Archipenko was one of the most inventive of modern sculptors. He was one of the first to apply the principles of CUBISM to sculpture, analysing the human figure into geometrical forms and opening parts of it up with holes and concavities. In moving away from a sculpture of solid form towards one of space and light he influenced the course of modern art.

architecture The art of designing and constructing buildings that are both functionally and aesthetically satisfying. The factors principally influencing an architect are: the use to which the building will be put; the materials obtainable; the resources available in money and labour; and contemporary artistic taste. The earliest civilizations built on a monumental scale for their gods or the deified dead (see PYRAMID; ZIGGURAT). Secular architecture reflected the needs of local rulers for security, comfort, and – very important – display. The Greeks (see GREEK ART AND ARCHITECTURE) were the first to develop the concepts of proportion and harmony that still influence western architecture. Roman engineers greatly extended flexibility of design by their use of ARCHES and domes. Western European medieval architecture reached its zenith in the gothic cathedral (see GOTHIC ART AND ARCHITECTURE). The Renaissance brought a resurgence of interest in all types of building; the rediscovered principles of classical architecture dominated theory and practice until the GOTHIC REVIVAL in the 18th century. In the 20th century technical advances in the use of prestressed concrete opened the way to modern architecture; while the necessities of engineering increasingly determine a building's appearance, the best modern architects demonstrate that architecture can still survive as an art form although a great deal of modern architecture uses unsuitable materials in situations that cry out for more friendly buildings.

arc lamp A lamp invented by DAVY in 1805 that emits a brilliant light by the production of an electric spark, or arc, between two closely spaced carbon electrodes in air. Arc lamps have been largely superseded by INCANDESCENT LAMPS, but have been retained in applications that require an intense light, for example searchlights.

Arctic The region of the world surrounding the North Pole, largely comprising the Arctic Ocean but also including the northern reaches of Canada, Alaska, Russia, and Norway as well as Iceland, Greenland, and Svalbard. Pack ice, which reaches a maximum extent in February and a minimum in August, occupies almost the entire region from the North Pole to the coasts of North America and Eurasia. In spring the pack ice begins to break up into ice floes which are carried southwards to the Atlantic Ocean. The plants of the Arctic tundra (including lichens, mosses, grasses, shrubs, and perennial plants) spring into life for two months of the summer. Animals include polar bear, musk ox, reindeer, caribou, fox, hare, lemming, seal, and walrus. Exploration of Arctic regions began in the 16th century when northern European nations tried to find a way to the rich trade of China and the East Indies by way of a north-east or north-west passage across the Arctic Ocean at a time when the longer but easier routes round Africa and South America were secured by Portugal and Spain. John Davis, William Barents, Henry Hudson, and Vitus Bering searched for these routes in the period 1585–1740 and during the relatively ice-free years of the early 19th century John Ross, William Parry, David Buchan, John Franklin, and James Clark Ross renewed British interest in finding a north-west passage. The north-east passage was first navigated in 1878–79 by Nils Nordenskjöld in the *Vega*. In the late 19th century attention turned to reaching the North Pole over the floating sea-ice with the explorations of Frederic Nansen, Otto Sverdrup, and Roald Amundsen. In 1909 the American explorer R. E. Peary claimed to be the first man to reach the Pole and the aviator Richard Byrd claimed to have flown over the North Pole in 1926. The charting of Arctic regions by Vilhjalmur Stefansson, Rudolph Anderson, and Gino Watkins pioneered the way for the 'Great Circle' air routes over polar ice and in 1958–59 the US submarine *Nautilus* made the first crossing of the Arctic Ocean under the polar ice-cap, a distance of 1,600 km (1,000 miles) from the Pacific to the Atlantic. In 1969 Wally Herbert led the first surface crossing of the Arctic Ocean.

Arctic Ocean An ocean that surrounds the North Pole, entirely within the Arctic Circle. It is the world's smallest ocean with an area of 14 million sq km (5.4 million sq miles), but the ocean with the world's widest continental shelf. The Arctic Ocean, which deepens to 2,000 fathoms (3,660 m, 12,000 ft) at its centre, is largely covered with pack ice 2–4.3 m (6–14 ft) thick. It reaches a maximum depth of 5,450 m (17,880 ft) in an abyssal plain to the north of the Chukchi Sea. Connected to the Pacific Ocean by the Bering Sea, its chief link with the Atlantic Ocean is the Greenland Sea.

Arcturus A star in the constellation of Boötes, and also known as Alpha Boötis, with an apparent magnitude of −0.04. It is a red giant star at a distance of

10 parsecs, with about seventy times the luminosity of the Sun. Its large PROPER MOTION, 2.3 arc seconds per year, was first detected by HALLEY in 1718.

Arden, Forest of An area of Warwickshire, central England, that was formerly part of an extensive forest that stretched across the Midlands. It was possibly the setting of Shakespeare's *As You Like It*.

Arden, Elizabeth (born Florence Nightingale Graham) (*c*.1880–1966) Canadian-born US businesswoman. She trained as a nurse before going to New York, where she opened her own beauty salon on Fifth Avenue in 1909. An effective use of advertising gave her brand a select and elegant image and contributed to the success of her business; she ultimately owned more than 100 beauty salons in America and Europe and her range of cosmetics comprised over 300 products.

Ardennes ▶**1** A forested upland region of north-west Europe, rising to heights above 610 m (2,000 ft) and extending over parts of south-east Belgium, north-east France, and Luxembourg. It was the scene of the last great German offensive of World War II (the Battle of the Bulge, December 1944). ▶**2** A department in the Champagne-Ardenne region of north-east France; area 5,229 sq km (2,020 sq miles); pop. (1990) 296,360; capital, Charleville-Mézières.

arenaceous rock (or **arenite**) A sandy SEDIMENTARY ROCK composed of eroded fragments of pre-existing rocks. The individual particles are of about the same size as sand grains: from 0.05 to 2 mm (0.002 to 0.08 inches) is the usual definition. They thus include grits and siltstones as well as sandstones. Rocks of this type can be of marine, freshwater, terrestrial, or glacial origin. Quartz sandstone is the most common type, and the terms 'arenite' and 'sandstone' are often used interchangeably. Special types of arenaceous rocks include GREYWACKES, GREENSANDS, and ARKOSES.

Arendt, Hannah (1906–75) German-born US philosopher and political theorist. A pupil of Martin Heidegger, she established her reputation as a political thinker with *The Origins of Totalitarianism* (1951), one of the first works to propose that Nazism and Stalinism had common roots in the 19th century, sharing anti-Semitic, imperialist, and nationalist elements. In 1959 she became the first woman professor at Princeton University.

Ares The ancient Greek god of war, son of Zeus and Hera. He was widely disliked by the other gods because of his savagery, but he became the lover of Aphrodite.

Aretino, Pietro (1492–1556) Italian poet, prose writer, and dramatist. In addition to five vigorous comedies depicting lower-class life he left a unique dossier of letters which are of great biographical and topical interest. His tragedy, *The Horatii* (1545), is considered by some the best Italian tragedy of the 16th century.

Arezzo A city in Tuscany, north-central Italy, at the junction of the Arno and Chiana rivers, capital of the province of Arezzo; pop. (1990) 91,620. It was the birthplace of the Italian poets Francesco Petrarch (1304–74) and Pietro Aretino (1492–1557). The city is noted for its trade in antiques and olive oil.

argali The largest of the wild sheep of Eurasia, *Ovis ammon*, found on the central Asian plateau. It weighs around 158 kg (350 pounds) and has long horns with a 1.5 m (5 feet) curve. Herds live in the valleys in winter and graze up to 5,500 m (18,000 feet) or above in summer. It will strike the ground sharply if alarmed to warn other members of the herd. Individuals may live for up to six years.

Argand, Jean Robert (1768–1822) Swiss mathematician who was renowned for his development of a diagram representing COMPLEX NUMBERS geometrically, in the form $a + bi$, in which a and b are real numbers and i is the square root of –1. One axis represents the pure, imaginary numbers (those consisting of the bi portion only); the second represents the real numbers (a values only). This allows the complex numbers to be plotted as points in the field defined by the two axes.

Argenteuil An industrial north-western suburb of Paris in the department of Vald'Oise, on the River Seine; pop. (1990) 94,160. Its market gardens are noted for their asparagus and grapes. Textiles, vehicle parts, and electrical equipment are manufactured.

Argentina The second largest country of South America, occupying nearly the whole of the south-east of the continent, from the Andes to the Atlantic Ocean and from tropical Bolivia to the Southern Ocean, the latter being a distance of nearly 3,700 km (2,300 miles).

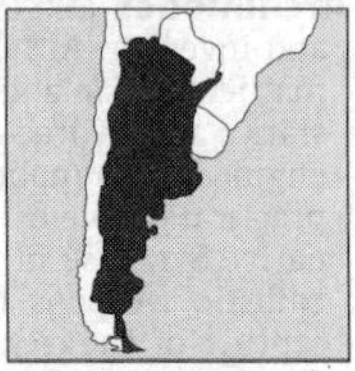

Physical. In the west the CORDILLERA, some of it volcanic, contains deposits of many minerals, copper, zinc, tungsten, and mica among them. The foothills are wooded, except in the south, and shelter valleys with vineyards and orchards. In the extreme north is the Gran Chaco, an area of subtropical forest and swamp, from which run tributaries of the Paraná. The Chaco yields hardwoods, and its southern part opens into land suitable for plantation crops. Southward, in the centre of the country, lie the PAMPAS – a vast region of high plains which supports some of the best agricultural and livestock farming in the world. Further south is Patagonia, a series of cold, infertile plateaux which are suitable only for sheep grazing.

Economy. Argentina's principal exports are agricultural products such as cereals, soya beans, and meat, but there is also a broad range of manufacturing industry, of which petroleum products and chemicals are significant exports. A high percentage of agricultural land is taken up by large cattle-raising estates. Argentina has some oil and natural gas deposits (notably in Patagonia) whose exploitation is important to the development of industry. There is also a long-standing programme to develop nuclear technology. In recent years government policies, including extensive privatization, have successfully reduced very high rates of inflation.

History. Argentina was colonized by the Spanish from 1515 onwards, with settlers dedicating themselves to stock raising on the fertile pampas and agriculture in the areas of Salta, Jujuy, and Cordoba. In 1776 Argentina was incorporated into the viceroyalty of La Plata, with its capital in Buenos Aires; in addition to Argentina, the viceroyalty of La Plata comprised Uruguay, Paraguay, and Bolivia. The independence of the country, as the 'United Provinces of South America', was declared at the Congress of Tucuman in 1816. Divisional differences produced a series of conflicts between unitarios (centralists) and federales (federalists) which characterized much of the 19th century. The lack of political or constitutional legitimacy saw the emergence of the age of the CAUDILLOS until the promulgation of the National Constitution in

1853. The second half of the 19th century witnessed a demographic and agricultural revolution. The fertile plains (pampas) in the interior were transformed by means of foreign and domestic capital, while immigrant workers (principally from Spain and Italy), an extensive railway network, and the introduction of steamships and refrigeration vastly increased the export of cattle and grain. The influx of immigrants between 1870 and 1914 contributed to an increase in the national population from 1.2 million in 1852 to 8 million in 1914. Argentina's export-orientated economy proved vulnerable to the fluctuations of the international market, and the Great DEPRESSION saw a drop of 40 per cent in the nation's exports. The military coup of 1930 saw the emergence of the armed forces as the arbiter of Argentinian politics. The failure of civilian democratic government and of achieving sustained economic growth has led to frequent military intervention. This was true even in the case of Peronism, the populist movement created with the support of trade unions by Juan Domingo PERÓN (1946–55). Peron was re-elected as President in 1973 after an eighteen-year exile. His death in 1974 was followed by another period of military dictatorship (1976–83) in a particularly bitter and tragic period of authoritarian rule, as a result of which an estimated 20,000 Argentinians lost their lives in the 'dirty war' waged by the junta against opposition groups. In 1982 the armed forces suffered a humiliating defeat in the war with Britain over the FALKLAND ISLANDS (Malvinas), and in 1983 a civilian administration was elected under President Raul Alfonsin of the Radical Party. The process of redemocratization in Argentina faced severe problems, most notably a virtually bankrupt economy and the political sensitivity of the armed forces to reform. The Perónist Justicialist Party came to power in 1989 with Carlos Menem as President. Diplomatic relations with Britain were restored and the economy deregulated. The constitution was amended in 1994, allowing the President to hold office for two terms. Menem triumphed again in presidential elections in 1995.

Capital: Buenos Aires
Area: 2,780,092 sq km (1,073,399 sq mi)
Population: 32,646,000 (1991)
Currency: 1 peso = 100 centavos
Religions: Roman Catholic 92.0%; Protestant 3.0%; Jewish 2.0%
Ethnic Groups: White, mainly Spanish and Italian extraction 85.0%; Mestizo, Amerindian and other 15.0%
Languages: Spanish (official); Italian; Amerindian languages
International Organizations: UN; OAS; Non-Aligned Movement

argentite The main ore of silver, consisting of silver sulphide (Ag_2S), often found together with other silver minerals. It is soft, very dense, and has an opaque, bright lustre. Argentite is formed at high temperatures, deep underground in veins. There are deposits in many places, and sizeable ones in Nevada and Colorado, USA, and in Peru.

argillaceous rock (or **argillite**) A clayey SEDIMENTARY ROCK of fine-grained sediments composed of particles that are less than 0.0625 mm (0.002 inch) in size. Mudstones, clays, shales, marls, and silts are all examples. Most argillaceous rocks contain material of two types: clay minerals and rock flour, the latter consisting of very fine particles of quartz, feldspar, and other rock-forming minerals. The great majority of argillaceous rocks have been deposited in water, whether in the sea, in estuaries, or in lakes. There are also terrestrial deposits in this category, such as LOESS and clays of glacial origin.

argon (symbol Ar, at. no. 18, r.a.m. 39.9) A gaseous element found in minute proportions (*c*.1 per cent) in the Earth's atmosphere. A colourless gas, argon is one of the NOBLE GASES and forms no chemical compounds. It is obtained from the FRACTIONAL DISTILLATION of air. It is used in gas-discharge lamps, to provide an inert atmosphere in electric light bulbs, and create a non-oxidizing atmosphere in modern arc-welding equipment. Most argon has arisen from the decay of radioactive potassium-40.

Argonauts In Greek mythology, the 50 heroes who sailed with JASON in his ship *Argo* in search of the Golden Fleece. The ship was named after the craftsman, Argos, who built it. Hercules was the most famous of the Argonauts, but he parted company from his companions when he tarried to search for his page Hylas, who had been carried off by water-nymphs.

Argos A city in the north-east Peleponnese of Greece; pop. (1981) 20,700. One of the oldest cities of ancient Greece, it was in the 7th century the dominant city of the Peleponnese and the western Aegean.

Argyll and Bute A unitary authority of western Scotland; area 6,497 sq km (2,509 sq miles); pop. (1991) 66,990; capital, Lochgilphead. It includes the island of Bute, whose chief town is Rothesay, and part of historic Argyllshire.

Argyllshire A former county on the west coast of Scotland. It is now divided between Argyll and Bute and Highland.

Århus See AARHUS.

Ariadne In Greek mythology, the daughter of Minos, king of Crete. She fell in love with Theseus and helped him in his most famous exploit, giving him a ball of string by means of which he was able to retrace his steps from the Minotaur's maze after slaying the monster. They left Crete together, but Theseus deserted her on the island of Naxos. She was consoled by Dionysos, whom she married.

Ariane See LAUNCH VEHICLE.

Arianism The teaching of Arius (250–336 AD), a Libyan priest living in Alexandria, who preached a Christian heresy. He declared JESUS CHRIST was not divine, simply an exceptional human being. In 325 the Council of NICAEA excommunicated and banished him. After CONSTANTINE'S death the Roman empire was divided on the issue, and another condemnation was issued at Constantinople in 381. Germanic invaders of the empire generally adopted Arianism as it was simpler than orthodox Christianity. It spread throughout western Europe and persisted in places until the 8th century.

Arica A Pacific port in the Tarapacá region of northern Chile, situated close to the border with Peru and north of the Atacama Desert; pop. (1991) 195,000. Formerly (until 1929) part of Peru, it is linked by rail to La Paz in Bolivia. Over 50 per cent of Bolivia's foreign trade passes through Arica.

aridisol A type of soil which forms in semi-desert or desert areas, where water is only available for plant growth during limited periods. Under such conditions vegetation is restricted to ephemeral grasses or drought-resistant shrubs, so these soils contain little organic matter. Soluble salts such as calcium carbonate and gypsum often accumulate as distinct HORIZONS, which are sometimes cemented to form HARDPANS. Some aridisols, known as argids, also have a clay-rich horizon. As clay accumulation is generally produced by LEACHING, such horizons are thought to be a relic of moister conditions in the past.

Aries The Ram, a CONSTELLATION of the zodiac. In Greek mythology it represented the ram whose golden fleece was sought by Jason and the Argonauts. Over 2,000 years ago this constellation contained the vernal EQUINOX, known also as the FIRST POINT OF ARIES, but this point has since moved into neighbouring PISCES because of the effect of PRECESSION. Alpha Arietis is the brightest star in the constellation, at second magnitude; it is also known as Hamal, an Arabic name meaning 'sheep'. Gamma Arietis is an attractive pair of fifth-magnitude stars for small telescopes.

Ariosto, Ludovico (1474–1533) Italian poet. His *Orlando Furioso* (final version 1532), about the exploits of Roland (Orlando) and other knights of Charlemagne, was the greatest of the Italian romantic epics; Spenser used its narrative form as a model for his *Faerie Queene*.

Aristarchus (known as **Aristarchus of Samothrace**) (*c.*217–145 BC) Greek scholar. The librarian at Alexandria, he is regarded as the originator of scientific literary scholarship, and is noted for his editions of the writings of Homer and other Greek authors, as well as for commentaries and treatises on their works.

Aristarchus of Samos (*c.*310–*c.*230 BC) Greek astronomer. Aristarchus is the first known astronomer to have suggested that the stars and the Sun remain fixed in position, while the Earth moves about the Sun in a circular orbit whose size is infinitesimal in comparison with the distance of the fixed stars. His work was largely ignored by his contemporaries, but was known to COPERNICUS who revived the HELIOCENTRIC SYSTEM. A prominent lunar crater, 40 km (23 miles) in diameter, is named after Aristarchus. The brightest feature on the Moon, it is a site of suspected transient lunar phenomena.

Aristides (known as **Aristides the Just**) (5th century BC) Athenian statesman and general. In the Persian Wars he commanded the Athenian army at the battle of Plataea in 479 BC, and was subsequently prominent in founding the Delian League, an alliance of Greek city-states that joined against Persians in 478–447 BC and constituted the Athenian empire.

Aristippus (known as **Aristippus the Elder**) (late 5th century BC) Greek philosopher. He was a native of Cyrene and pupil of Socrates, and is generally considered the founder of the Cyrenaic school, holding that pleasure is the highest good and that virtue is to be equated with the ability to enjoy. His grandson Aristippus the Younger further developed his philosophy.

aristocracy (from Greek, 'the rule of the best') Originally a form of government, but now usually a hereditary social élite. From PLATO and ARISTOTLE onwards, it was commonly assumed that political power was best placed in the hands of those who, through education, occupation, or social position, had shown their capacity to exercise it. This assumption was challenged by the democratic sentiments nurtured by the American and French Revolutions (1776 and 1789). The aristocracy now describes a hereditary SOCIAL CLASS, normally based on landed property.

Aristophanes (*c.*450–*c.*385 BC) Greek dramatist. His eleven surviving comedies, characterized by inventive situations and exuberant language, are largely occupied with topical themes; Aristophanes satirizes politicians and intellectuals (such as Socrates), and parodies contemporary poets such as Aeschylus and Euripides. Much use is made of political and social fantasy, as exemplified by the city of the birds ('Cloud-cuckoo-land') in the *Birds*, and by the women's sex-strike for peace in *Lysistrata*.

Aristotle (384–322 BC) Greek philosopher and scientist. A pupil of Plato and tutor to Alexander the Great, in 335 BC he founded a school and library (the Lyceum) outside Athens. His surviving written works constitute a vast system of analysis, including logic, physical science, zoology, psychology, metaphysics, ethics, politics, and rhetoric. In reasoning, he established the inductive method. In metaphysics, he rejected Plato's doctrine of forms or ideals; for him form and matter were the inseparable constituents of all existing things. His empirical approach to science is most notable in the field of biology, where he analysed and described the stomach of ruminants and the development of the chick embryo. His work on the classification of animals by means of a scale ascending to man (without implying evolution) was not fully appreciated until the 19th century: Darwin acknowledged a debt to him. In astronomy, his proposal that the stars and the planets are composed of a perfect incorruptible element (ether), carried on revolving spheres centred on the Earth, was a serious handicap to later thinking.

Arizona A state in south-west USA, on the Mexican frontier, between California and New Mexico; area 295,260 sq km (114,000 sq miles); pop. (1990) 3,665,230; capital, Phoenix. The largest cities are Phoenix, Tucson, and Mesa. Arizona is also known as the Grand Canyon State. It was acquired from Mexico in 1848 and 1853 (Gadsden Purchase) and became the 48th state of the USA in 1912. The chief products of the state are copper, electrical equipment, aeronautical parts, and agricultural produce. Major tourist attractions include the Grand Canyon, Petrified Forest, Hoover Dam, Fort Apache, and the reconstructed London Bridge at Lake Havasu City. Arizona has the largest Indian population in the USA, with more than 14 tribes represented on 19 reservations. The state is divided into 15 counties.

Arjuna Pandava In Hindu mythology, the son of Indra, and boyhood friend of Krishna. Arjuna is the principal hero of the Hindu philosophical poem the *Bhagavadgita*. Arjuna's first wife was Draupadi, whom he won in an archery contest and who became the wife of all five Pandava brothers. He later married Krishna's sister, Subhadra.

Arkansas A state in south-central USA, bounded by the Mississippi River on the east and Oklahoma to the west; area 137,754 sq km (53,187 sq miles); pop. (1990) 2,350,725; capital, Little Rock. The largest cities are Little Rock, Fort Smith, North Little Rock, and Pine Bluff. Arkansas is also known as the 'Land of Opportunity'. In 1803 it was acquired by the USA as part of the Louisiana purchase and became the 25th state in 1836. Arkansas is a major producer of bauxite and such agricultural produce as cotton, rice, and soybeans. Major attractions include the radioactive mineral waters of Hot Springs National Park and the Buffalo National River in the Ozarks. The state is divided into 75 counties.

Arkansas A river that rises in the Rocky Mountains of central Colorado, USA, and flows 2,333 km (1,450 miles) south-east across the Great Plains of Colorado, Kansas, Oklahoma, and Arkansas before it joins the Mississippi south of Memphis.

Ark of the Covenant The sacred chest in which the Israelites, after their departure from Egypt, carried the two tablets of the law given to Moses by God, a pot of manna, and Aaron's rod. Symbolic of the divine presence, the Ark was eventually placed in Solomon's Temple, but after the fall of Jerusalem (587 BC) it was hidden in a cave, and its fate remains unknown.

arkose A category of ARENACEOUS ROCK, a SANDSTONE that is usually reddish in colour and made up chiefly of quartz and feldspar. It is formed typically by the disintegration of granites or similar rocks.

Arkwright, Sir Richard (1732–92) British inventor and industrialist. A pioneer of mechanical cotton-spinning, in 1767 he patented a water-powered spinning machine (known as a 'water frame'), the first such machine to produce yarn strong enough to be used as warp. He also improved the preparatory processes, including carding. He established spinning mills in Lancashire, Derbyshire, and Scotland, and became rich and powerful, despite disputes with rivals over patents and opposition to his mechanization of the industry.

Arles A marketing and tourist city in the Bouche-du-Rhône department of Provence-Alpes-Côte d'Azur region in south-east France, at the head of the Camargue delta on the River Rhône; pop. (1990) 52,590. It was capital of Provence and the medieval kingdom of Arles and has been an important centre of communication since Roman times. Constantine I convoked a synod at Arles in AD 314 in order to condemn the revolutionary Donatist Christian movement in North Africa. It has a large Roman arena (now used for bullfighting), a Roman theatre, and a Provençal museum. Arles has attracted many artists including Gaugin and Van Gogh who spent his last and most productive years (1888–90) in the city.

Arlington A county in north Virginia, USA, forming a residential suburb of Washington on the opposite side of the Potomac River; pop. (1990) 170,936. The Pentagon, which is one of the largest office buildings in the world, and the Arlington National Cemetery (1864) are located here.

arm One of a pair of limbs peculiar to humans and other primates, held by muscles to the shoulder-bones (scapulae), which in turn are held by muscles to the sides of the chest wall. The collar-bones (clavicles) hold the joints of the shoulder-bone and the arm from the side of the body, forming shoulders, and allow the arms to be far more mobile than the fore-limbs of all other mammals. Strictly speaking, arms consist of the humerus, a bone stretching from shoulder to elbow which joins the forearms. The forearms stretch from the elbows to the wrists. Each forearm contains two bones: the ulna, which is hinged to the elbow, and the radius, which rotates round it so that the wrist can be moved.

Armada See SPANISH ARMADA.

armadillo An armoured mammal in the family Dasypodidae, of which there are 20 species, found in South and Central America and southern parts of North America. The largest, the giant armadillo, *Priodontes maximus*, reaches 1.5 m (5 feet) in length, while the lesser fairy armadillo, *Chlamyphorus truncatus*, is only 12 cm (5 inches) long. The armour takes the form of horny bands and plates, which are modifications of the skin, connected by flexible tissue. The narrow flexible bands on the back serve to break the rigidity, and the number of these bands is given in the common names of the species such as the Brazilian three-banded armadillo, *Tolypeutes tricinctus*, and the nine-banded, or common long-nosed armadillo, *Daspypus novemcinctus*. Many can draw their legs and feet beneath the shell and a few can roll into a ball. They dig burrows with their powerful claws, which are also used when foraging for insects, arachnids, eggs, worms, and small reptiles, or leaves and shoots. Armadillos exhibit polyembryony, which is the production of two or more genetically identical offspring (CLONES) from a single fertilized egg. Most species have four young, but up to twelve may be produced.

Armageddon (Hebrew *har megiddon*, 'hill of Megiddo') An archaeological site in Israel on the plain of Esdraelon to the south of Haifa. In the New Testament Armageddon is the name given to the last battle between good and evil before the Day of Judgement (Revelations 16:16). See MEGIDDO.

Armagh ▶**1** A historic county in Northern Ireland, lying to the south of Lough Neagh; area 1,254 sq km (484 sq miles). It is administered by several district councils. ▶**2** A city in Co. Armagh; pop. (1991) 14,640. The seat of the kings of Ulster from *c*.400 BC to AD 333, it became the religious centre of Ireland in AD 445 when St Patrick was made archbishop.

Armani, Giorgio (1935–) Italian fashion designer. After studying medicine at university he worked as a window-dresser before becoming a designer for Nino Cerruti in 1961. He then worked for several designers until 1975, when he established his own company and rapidly became one of Italy's best-known ready-to-wear designers for both men and women.

armature The rotating assembly of coils and windings on a core (usually of soft iron or other similar magnetic material) that forms the rotor of an ELECTRIC MOTOR or GENERATOR. The term is also used to describe the component in an ELECTROMAGNET or SOLENOID that moves in response to the electromagnetic field.

Armenia, Republic of A country in west Asia, formerly a constituent republic of the Soviet Union.

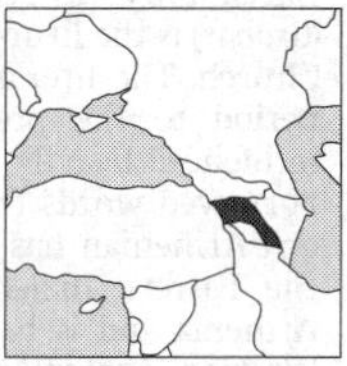

Physical. The Republic of Armenia comprises the north-eastern part of the historic kingdom of Armenia, the rest of this region forming part of Turkey.

Economy. Mineral resources include copper, lead, and zinc, and there has been rapid industrial expansion, particularly in mechanical engineering, chemicals production, and mining. Agriculture, which includes cotton, rice, tobacco, fruit, and viticulture, remains important. There is considerable hydroelectric potential, but Armenia is dependent on imports for its other energy requirements.

History. An independent Armenian republic was proclaimed in 1920, but in 1922 this was reunited with its former partners, Georgia and Azerbaijan, as the Transcaucasian Soviet Socialist Republic. This split in 1936 and the Soviet Socialist Republic of Armenia was proclaimed. In 1989 ethnic violence erupted over the status of the Armenian region of Nagorno Karabagh (Christian) within AZERBAIJAN (Shiite Muslim). Armenia became independent in 1991, having declared itself no longer part of the Soviet Union. Sporadic violence in Nagorno Karabagh has continued, despite a cease-fire agreement (1994), and Armenia temporarily withdrew from peace talks in 1995. In 1996 the region unilaterally declared independence. Attempts to broker a permanent peace settlement have continued. Armenia's first parliamentary elections since independence were held in 1995 and a new constitution was approved by a referendum.

Armenia is a member of the COMMONWEALTH OF INDEPENDENT STATES.

Capital: Yerevan
Area: 29,766 sq km (11,490 sq mi)
Population: 3,360,000 (1991)
Currency: 1 dram = 100 lumas
Religions: Armenian Orthodox and Catholic Churches; minority faiths
Ethnic Groups: Armenian 93.0%; Azeri 2.0%; Russian and Kurdish minorities
Languages: Armenian (official); Russian; minority languages
International Organizations: UN; Commonwealth of Independent States; CSCE; North Atlantic Co-operation Council

Armenian Apostolic Church One of the Monophysite CHRISTIAN CHURCHES. The Armenian Apostolic Church was founded by St Gregory the Illuminator in *c.*300 AD; the Armenian kingdom thereby became the first state to adopt Christianity as an official religion. The Church is headed by the Catholicates (supreme ecclesiastical office) of Etchmiadzen, in Armenia, and of Sis (Cilicia) in Turkey (now resident in Lebanon), and the patriarchates of Jerusalem and Istanbul. The Armenian Church is unique in celebrating the birth of Christ as part of the EPIPHANY (6 January) and having no separate feast of CHRISTMAS. There are about 2 million members, principally in Armenia and the USA. There is also an Armenian Catholic rite with its own patriarch in Beirut, which is in communion with the POPE.

Armenian language An INDO-EUROPEAN LANGUAGE spoken by nearly 6 million people in Armenia, Turkey, Iran, and (as a result of emigration) in Europe and the USA. The earliest documents go back to the 5th century AD, but the language was certainly established in the south Caucasus area before this date. A 38-letter alphabet was developed around AD 400 following the introduction of Christianity to the area. Classical Armenian (*Grabar*) is the liturgical language of the Armenian Church. The literary tradition extends from this period to the present day. The language was influenced heavily by Persian and Greek, and also borrowed words from Arabic and Aramaic. Modern Armenian has two standard literary dialects: the Eastern dialect is the official language of Armenia and is based on the dialect of Yerevan; Western Armenian is generally used elsewhere, and is based on the dialect spoken in Istanbul.

Armentières An industrial town in the Nord department of north-west France, to the west of Lille on the River Lys; pop. (1990) 26,240. It has foundries, breweries, and textile factories, but is best known through the World War I song *Mademoiselle from Armentières*.

Armidale A city in New South Wales, south-east Australia, situated between Sydney and Brisbane at the centre of a rich agricultural region in the New England plateau; pop. (1991) 21,605. The University of New England (1954) lies north-west of the city.

armillary sphere A hollow three-dimensional model of the Solar System and the CELESTIAL SPHERE, the armillary sphere is the earliest known astronomical device, used from at least the 2nd century BC for observations of the heavens. It usually consists of two circular hoops that link the celestial poles, one representing the PRIME MERIDIAN and the other the prime vertical. These are intersected by an equatorial and an ecliptic hoop and smaller ones representing the two tropics. The sphere contains a series of rings or arms that show the positions of the planets.

Arminius (*c.*18 BC–19 AD) Leader of the Germanic resistance to Roman colonization. Son of a noble family, he served as an officer in the Roman auxiliary forces and became a Roman citizen. But he turned against Rome, and in AD 9 annihilated Quinctilius Varus and his three legions, thereby wrecking AUGUSTUS' German policy; and again in 16 he thwarted the attempt of TIBERIUS' nephew Germanicus to renew the conquest. However, he failed to unite the fragmented Germanic tribes; in 19 his own aspirations to kingship encountered popular opposition, and he was murdered.

Arminius, Jacobus (born Jakob Harmensen) (1560–1609) Dutch theologian, the founder of the theological movement known as Arminianism. He studied at Utrecht, Leiden, Basle, and Geneva before being ordained in 1588. The last six years of his life were spent as professor of theology at Leiden University. Arminianism subsequently gave rise to the Dutch Remonstrant movement and in England it influenced Archbishop LAUD.

armoured vehicle An armed, motorized military vehicle protected from enemy fire by armour plating. TANKS are the principal type of armoured vehicle; other examples include armoured cars, armoured personnel carriers, self-propelled guns, AMPHIBIOUS VEHICLES, and specialized vehicles such as armoured bulldozers and bridge-layers. In the early part of World War I some automobile chassis were converted into armoured cars, and later the purpose-built armoured car (a wheeled vehicle with the main armament in a gun turret) was developed. Experiments were made with half-track vehicles, which have wheels at the front but tracks at the rear, but they proved inadequate for the terrain. World War II saw the development of two new vehicle types: the self- propelled gun, providing much greater mobility for ARTILLERY; and the armoured personnel carrier, now probably the most important armoured vehicle after the battle tank. Originally, armoured personnel carriers were intended to carry troops into battle with more protection than in an unarmoured lorry, but since the 1960s they have been used for fighting as well as for transport. Purpose-built vehicles of this sort are known as MICVs (mechanized infantry combat vehicles). Generally, they carry a gun turret and perhaps a machine-gun or other weaponry, plus provision for its occupants to fire their own weapons from within.

arms and armour Personal weapons and protective clothing used in combat or for ceremonial purposes, being regarded both as objects of beauty as well as of practical use. In Europe armourers have invariably been workers in metal, but in other parts of the world materials such as wickerwork, bone, and coconut fibre have been used. Outside Europe, the richest traditions of arms and armour have been in the Japanese and Indo-Persian cultures, in which metal (in the form of both mail and plate) is combined with leather and padded and studded textiles. European armour reached its highest peak of development in the 15th and 16th centuries, when plate armour, which had gradually replaced mail, encased the whole body in an ingeniously articulated suit. The finest armours were made in Germany and Milan, and the main English centre of production was Greenwich, where Henry VIII established workshops. Henry's own armours, however, were intended more for the tournament than the battlefield, because by the 16th century firearms were becoming so effective that armour could not be made proof against bullets without being excessively heavy. Cavalry continued to wear breast and back plates until the early 18th century, however. Among weapons, the sword occupies pride of place as the symbol of knighthood, justice, and power. Certain towns – notably Toledo in Spain in the 16th and 17th centuries – have been famous for their production, and in Japan the blades of the great swordsmiths are regarded with an almost religious veneration.

arms control The attempts made to manage and regulate the arms race, by reducing and controlling armed forces and weapons. The term is particularly used in connection with NUCLEAR WEAPONS, and should be distinguished from DISARMAMENT, which implies the reduction or elimination of existing forces and weapons. Efforts had been made to bring about arms control as well as disarmament before and after World War I (for example, the Washington Naval Agreement (1922), which limited the warships of the major powers). In 1952 a Disarmament Commission of the United Nations was set up, and helped to bring about the Non-Proliferation Treaty (1968), covering nuclear weapons. Most of the important negotiations on arms control, however, have taken place in direct talks between the USA, the Soviet Union, and other powers. A NUCLEAR TEST-BAN TREATY limiting nuclear testing was signed by the USA, the Soviet Union, and Britain in 1963, while direct STRATEGIC ARMS LIMITATIONS TALKS (SALT) between the USA and the Soviet Union (1969–79) led to some limitation of strategic nuclear weapons. Member states of NATO and the WARSAW PACT have met in Vienna since 1973 in the Mutual and Balanced Force Reduction (MBFR) talks, concerned with limiting conventional ground forces in central Europe. Soviet and US negotiations on strategic nuclear weapons restarted in 1982 under the title of STRATEGIC ARMS REDUCTION TALKS (START). These eventually led to the signing of a treaty in 1991, in which the parties agreed to reduce the number of strategic missiles and limit other nuclear weaponry. In 1987 a treaty on eliminating intermediate-range nuclear forces (INF) was agreed between the superpowers. In 1990 there were treaties on the destruction of chemical weapons and on conventional forces in Europe. In 1993 the USA and Russia signed START II, a treaty in which they agreed to reduce nuclear warheads to 3,500 each by the year 2003. In 1995 the nuclear Non-Proliferation Treaty was extended indefinitely.

Armstrong, Edwin Howard (1890–1954) US electrical engineer. He was the inventor of the superheterodyne radio receiver and the frequency modulation (FM) system in radio. During the 1930s Armstrong developed the FM system, which removed the static that had ruined much early broadcasting, but the radio industry was very slow to accept it.

Armstrong, (Daniel) Louis (known as 'Satchmo', an abbreviation of 'Satchelmouth') (1900–71) US jazz musician. He learned the cornet in the Waifs' Home in New Orleans, later switching to the trumpet. He played on Mississippi river-boats before forming his own small groups, with which he made some sixty recordings in 1925–28. He later led various big bands, toured internationally, and appeared in many films, including *The Birth of the Blues* (1941).

Armstrong, Neil (Alden) (1930–) US astronaut. A former fighter pilot and test pilot, he began training as an astronaut in 1962, being appointed to command the Apollo 11 mission, during which he became the first man to set foot on the Moon (20 July 1969).

army An organized force of men or women armed for fighting on land. Armies came into existence with the earliest states, and underpinned the great empires of antiquity: Egypt, Babylon, and Assyria. The essential components of armies in early history were infantry, with some chariots, and cavalry. In ancient Greece the tendency towards greater professionalism reached its climax with the Macedonian army of Alexander the Great. From this time on, the development of siege techniques was an important part of military practice. The generals of Carthage, especially HANNIBAL, hired mercenaries to great effect in their forces, but it was the armies of Rome, gradually evolving into fully professional standing forces, which dominated Europe from the 2nd century BC to the 5th century AD. Less organized but swiftly moving armies then came to the fore in the DARK AGES, from those of ATTILA THE HUN to the Mongols. In Europe in the Middle Ages the limitations of the heavily armoured mounted knight were finally exposed by Swiss infantry armed with pikes or halberds and English infantry armed with longbows. The use of mercenaries (see CONDOTTIERE) became commonplace.

The major advances of the 15th and 16th centuries were the invention of gunpowder and the development of cannon. Organization, discipline, and further advances in weaponry led to the creation of highly efficient armies, most notably those of FREDERICK I (the Great) of Prussia. In the late 18th century European armies were mainly of mercenaries recruited (often under pressure) and trained by a professional officer class. The first conscript armies were recruited in France to fight the REVOLUTIONARY and NAPOLEONIC WARS. During the 19th century most European countries adopted a system of conscription of young men to train and serve for about two years. (Britain only enforced conscription in 1916–18, and again between 1939 and 1959.) European armies played an essential role in 19th- and early 20th-century IMPERIALISM, their superior fire-power enabling them to dominate the peoples of Africa and Asia. The AMERICAN CIVIL WAR 1861–65 saw large armies of the Union (the North) and the Confederacy (the South) engaged in a struggle in which railways were crucial for movement of troops, and new infantry weapons, such as the breech-loading rifle and the repeating carbine, were developed. By the time of the FRANCO-PRUSSIAN WAR in 1870–71 heavy artillery was developing, but infantry and cavalry tactics remained little changed until World War I, when motor transport and heavier artillery developed. Even then, armies were slow to adapt to armoured vehicles, and the massed infantry attacks of its battles still used rifle, bayonet, and hand-grenade as their basic weapons, now pitched against machine-guns. By World War II armies were fully motorized, and tanks played a major part in the NORTH AFRICAN CAMPAIGN and at the Eastern Front. This mobility required large back-up fuel and maintenance services. Basic infantry tactics still remained essential (even though the rifle was being replaced by the semiautomatic or automatic submachine gun), especially in the jungle warfare of the BURMA CAMPAIGN. They remained so for later campaigns in Korea, Vietnam, and the Falklands. In the COLD WAR balance of power, large armies of NATO and the WARSAW PACT continued to face one another in Europe, armed with both conventional weapons and missiles. Allied victory in the GULF WAR was achieved through massive tank deployment. Since the end of the Cold War the armies of UN member nations have increasingly been combined to form multi-national peacekeeping and 'rapid reaction' forces.

army worm The caterpillar of one of several species of moths of the family Noctuidae (OWLET MOTHS), which move *en masse* in search of food-plants when their previous supply is exhausted. Species such as the African army worm, *Spodoptera exempta*, are migratory as adult moths and can occur in most tropical parts of the world. Army worms are usually pests of crops such as cereals, tobacco, maize, cotton, and potatoes.

Arne, Thomas (1710–78) British composer. He is remembered for his distinctive contribution to 18th-century theatrical music, especially with his settings of Shakespearian songs such as 'Blow, Blow Thou Winter Wind', and for his operas *Artaxerxes* (1762) and *Love in a Village* (1762). His famous song 'Rule, Britannia' (with words attributed to James Thomson) was composed for the masque *Alfred* (1740).

Arnhem The capital of the province of Gelderland, in the east Netherlands, situated on the Rhine near its junction with the IJssel; pop. (1991) 131,700. Founded in the 13th century, it prospered in the Middle Ages as a river trading port. In September 1944 British airborne troops made a famous landing on the nearby Veluwe moorland but were overwhelmed by superior German forces.

Arnhem Land A peninsula in Northern Territory, Australia, situated to the west of the Gulf of Carpentaria and inhabited by Aborigines for over 40,000 years; area *c.*80,776 sq km (31,200 sq miles); pop. (est. 1985) 96,000. The chief town is Nhulunbuy. In 1976 Arnhem Land was declared Aboriginal Land.

Arno A river of northern Italy, which rises on Monte Falterona in the Apennines and flows 240 km (150 miles) north-westwards through Florence to meet the Ligurian Sea near Pisa.

Arnold, Benedict (1741–1801) American soldier and traitor. He was a hero of the early stages of the War of INDEPENDENCE, serving with conspicuous valour at Ticonderoga, the invasion of Canada, and SARATOGA SPRINGS. After 1778, possibly persuaded by his loyalist wife, he began plotting with Clinton to deliver West Point to the British. When his courier, Major André, was captured, he fled to the British, for whom he fought thereafter. He died, neglected, in England.

Arnold, Sir Malcolm (Henry) (1921–) British composer and trumpet-player. His skill as a craftsman is as evident in his many film scores (including that for *The Bridge on the River Kwai*) as in his orchestral output, which includes seven symphonies and numerous concertos. His style is basically tonal and rejoices in lively rhythms, brilliant orchestration, and an unabashed tunefulness.

Arnold, Matthew (1822–88) British poet, essayist, and social critic. Author of 'The Scholar Gipsy' (1853), 'Dover Beach' (1867) and 'Thyrsis' (1867), he held the post of professor of poetry at Oxford (1857–67) and published several works of literary and social criticism, including *Culture and Anarchy* (1869). This established him as an influential social and cultural critic, who, in his views on religion, education, and the arts, criticized the Victorian age in terms of its materialism, philistinism, and complacency.

aromatic compound Any of a group of organic compounds that contain in their molecule the BENZENE RING or a ring with similar characteristics. Strictly, an aromatic compound is defined as one that has $(4n + 2)$ electrons shared over its ring, where n is an integer, and aromaticity refers to the structural and chemical properties common to these compounds. It is the distribution of electrons in the aromatic ring that determines the type of chemical reactions they undergo. Reagents with high electron density (nucleophiles) are repelled and thus do not react. On the other hand, reagents with regions of high positive charge (electrophiles) are attracted by the aromatic ring. Most reactions of aromatic compounds are electrophilic substitutions in which the electrophilic reagent displaces another electrophile, normally the hydrogen ion, H^+, from the molecule. Examples of aromatic compounds include benzene, C_6H_6; thiophen, C_4H_4S; and borazole, $B_3N_3H_6$. An example of an electrophile is the nitronium ion, NO_2^+. This reacts with benzene, displacing a hydrogen ion and forming nitrobenzene, $C_6H_5NO_2$.

Arp, Jean (Hans) (1887–1966) French sculptor, painter, and poet. In 1912 in Munich he exhibited with the BLAUE REITER group, and in 1915 in Zurich he was one of the founders of the DADA movement. During the 1920s, living at Meudon near Paris, he was associated with the SURREALISTS. In the 1930s he turned to sculpture and produced what are now his best-known and most admired works.

Arran An island in the Firth of Clyde, Scotland, situated between the Mull of Kintyre and the Ayrshire coast; area 430 sq km (166 sq miles). It chief town is the port of Brodick. A popular tourist island, its attractions include Goat Fell (874 m, 2,867 ft), the Machrie Moor stone circles, and Brodick Castle.

Arras The capital of Pas-de-Calais department in north-west France, between Lille and Amiens; pop. (1990) 42,715. Known as Nemetocenna in Gallo-Roman times, the town became an important trading and commercial centre during the Middle Ages, but was devastated during a war between France and Burgundy which ended in 1435 with the signing of the Treaty of Arras. Noted for its Flemish architecture which has been restored after further devastation in World War I, Arras gives its name to a fabric used to make a rich tapestry.

Arrau, Claudio (1903–91) Chilean pianist. A child prodigy whose first public performance was at the age of five, he became a renowned interpreter of the works of Chopin, Liszt, Beethoven, Mozart, Schumann, and Brahms. An unostentatious pianist, he built his reputation on the meticulous musicianship and intellectual penetration which accompanied his virtuoso technique.

Arrau turtle See GREAVED TURTLE.

Arrhenius, Svante August (1859–1927) Swedish chemist. One of the founders of modern physical chemistry, he was the first Swede to win the Nobel Prize for chemistry, which was awarded in 1903 for his work on electrolytes.

arrow-poison frog A frog used by the Choco Indians of Colombia to poison their blow-gun darts. One species, *Phyllobates terribilis*, described in 1978, is so toxic that the Indians need only to rub the dart tip along the back of the living frog to obtain the poison. Approximately 76 species of arrow-poison frogs are known, most of them highly coloured and restricted to the tropical regions of South and Central America. They are an interesting family of frogs as the male guards the fertilized eggs, and eventually carries the tadpoles on his back until they are ready to be released in a pool and lead independent lives. The poison, which is produced by its skin glands, protects the frog from its predators, and its bright colouring acts as a warning to them.

arrowroot A tropical, herbaceous perennial, *Maranta arundinacea*, whose swollen rhizomes (underground stems) yield a highly digestible fine-grained starch, particularly useful in infant and invalid diets. The name is also used for other fine-starch yielding plants. The commercial cultivation of the arrowroot is essentially limited to the Caribbean island of St Vincent, although the plant is native to northern South America. It is also a source of the coating of carbonless paper, used for computer printouts.

arrow worm A member of the phylum Chaetognatha, which contains some 65 species of marine planktonic animals, with dart-like bodies, only 1–5 cm (0.5–2 inches) long. Adult arrow worms are swift, predatory creatures, their heads bearing eyes, tiny teeth, and spines. They are stabilized by their lateral fins, and swim by rapid muscle contractions in pursuit of other plankton. The developmental stages of their embryo show them to be part of the same major group of animals as the vertebrates, despite the somewhat worm-like appearance of the adults.

arroyo (or **wash**, **dry wash**, **coulee**; Arabic **wadi**; French **oued**) Originally the bed of an ephemeral stream; a gully or flat-floored, steep-sided valley common in semi-arid regions such as south-western USA, Australia, and northern Africa. Arroyos form in areas where the general slope of the ground is gentle and where there are deposits of fine-grained sediment. The streams which cut the arroyos usually flow only after thunderstorms or when snow is melting, and they frequently exhibit BRAIDING across the valley floors. Many arroyos caused by poor land management have been formed since the 19th century, destroying grazing land and causing flooding and AGGRADATION in larger river valleys.

Ars Antiqua, **Ars Nova** Latin terms meaning 'ancient art' and 'new art' in music, used by French and Italian theorists in the 14th century to distinguish between the notational systems and composition practices of the 12th and 13th centuries and the technical advances of the 14th century. The Ars Antiqua style was based upon PLAINSONG and ORGANUM, and restricted itself to triple metres. The Ars Nova style, as exemplified by such composers as Machaut, explored a greater variety of rhythm and independent part-writing.

arsenic (symbol As, at. no. 33, r.a.m. 74.92) A METALLOID in Group 15 (formerly VB) of the PERIODIC TABLE; the most common and stable of its ALLOTROPES is a grey metallic substance. It reacts with concentrated acids, non-metals, and some metals, forming compounds in which it shows valencies 3 and 5. Arsenic is used in alloys (e.g. lead shot) as a hardening agent; in combination with GALLIUM it is widely used in SEMICONDUCTOR DEVICES. Many arsenic compounds are poisonous, and have been used as insecticides, wood preservatives, and weedkillers. The oxide, As_4O_6, is often sold as 'white arsenic'. The main sources of arsenic are sulphide ores.

Arta ▶**1** A department in Epirus, western Greece; area 1,662 sq km (642 sq miles); pop. (1991) 78,880. ▶**2** Its capital, on the River Arta (Arakhthos); pop. (1981) 18,280. It was known as Ambracia to the Corinthians who founded the city in the 7th century BC. Pyrrhus, king of Epirus made his capital here in 295 BC and much later in Byzantine times a new town named Arta was established.

Artaud, **Antonin** (1896–1948) French actor, director, and poet. Influenced by Balinese dancing and oriental drama, he sought to return drama to its symbolic and ritualistic roots, developing the concept of the non-verbal **Theatre of Cruelty**, which concentrated on the use of sound, mime, and lighting. He expounded his theory in a series of essays published as *Le Théâtre et son double* (1938), but his only play to be based on it was *Les Cenci* (1935).

Artaxerxes II (*c.*436–358 BC) King of Persia 404–358, the son of Darius II. He crushed the rebellion of his younger brother CYRUS THE YOUNGER at Cunaxa in 401. By the peace of Antalcidas, made with the Spartans in 386, he recovered the Greek cities of Asia Minor, but he was unsuccessful in his attempts to repossess Egypt, and he put down the satraps' revolt of 366–358 only with difficulty. His son, Artaxerxes III, killed his brothers and crushed two rebellious satraps in order to establish his power. In 343 he finally forced Egypt back into the empire, but his reign was one of terror and he was murdered by his minister Bagoas in 338.

art deco A style in the decorative arts defined by the Exposition Internationale des Arts Décoratifs et Industriels held in Paris in 1925. Although applied principally to the decorative arts and interior design of the 1920s and 1930s the term can be extended to analogous styles in architecture and painting. Concentrating on stylishness tuned to domestic use and popular consumption, it is characterized by geometric patterning, sharp edges, and flat, bright colours, and often involved the use of enamel, chrome, bronze, and highly polished stone. The simplicity of the style can be seen as classicizing in spirit, attested by the Egyptian and Greek motifs which were often adopted (for example, the schematized Egyptian scarab). Although it led to a re-confirmation, in both Europe and the USA, of the role of the craftsman-designer, popularization of the style often resulted in the mass production of less refined objects.

Artemis In Greek mythology, goddess of hunting and the Moon. She was the daughter of Zeus and the twin sister of Apollo. Although she was herself a virgin, she was the helper of women in childbirth.

artemisia An aromatic shrub or herb of the genus *Artemisia*, part of the sunflower family. There are many species in the genus, mainly from the Northern Hemisphere, and most possess hairy, silvery leaves, rendering the plants very tolerant of arid conditions. The flower-heads are small, yellow, and button-shaped. Some species have medicinal properties and yield stimulants and worming compounds (hence the common name wormwood for *A. absinthium*). The shrub *A. abrotanum* is known as southernwood.

arteriosclerosis The hardening and loss of elasticity of the arteries, which also occurs normally as a result of ageing. A form of arteriosclerosis, called atherosclerosis, is caused by the occlusion (narrowing) of arteries by deposition of fatty plaques (atheroma) in their walls. THROMBOSIS may occur and atherosclerosis in arteries supplying the heart can cause ANGINA PECTORIS and myocardial infarction (a 'heart attack'); in arteries supplying the brain, atherosclerosis may cause a STROKE. Arteriosclerosis is the major cause of death in developed countries. Among the risk factors implicated are smoking, high blood pressure, obesity, and lack of exercise; genetic factors and stress may be contributory elements.

artery A blood vessel with an elastic, muscular wall, which in vertebrates carries blood away from the heart. The pulmonary artery carries blood to the lungs, where it is oxygenated; other arteries carry

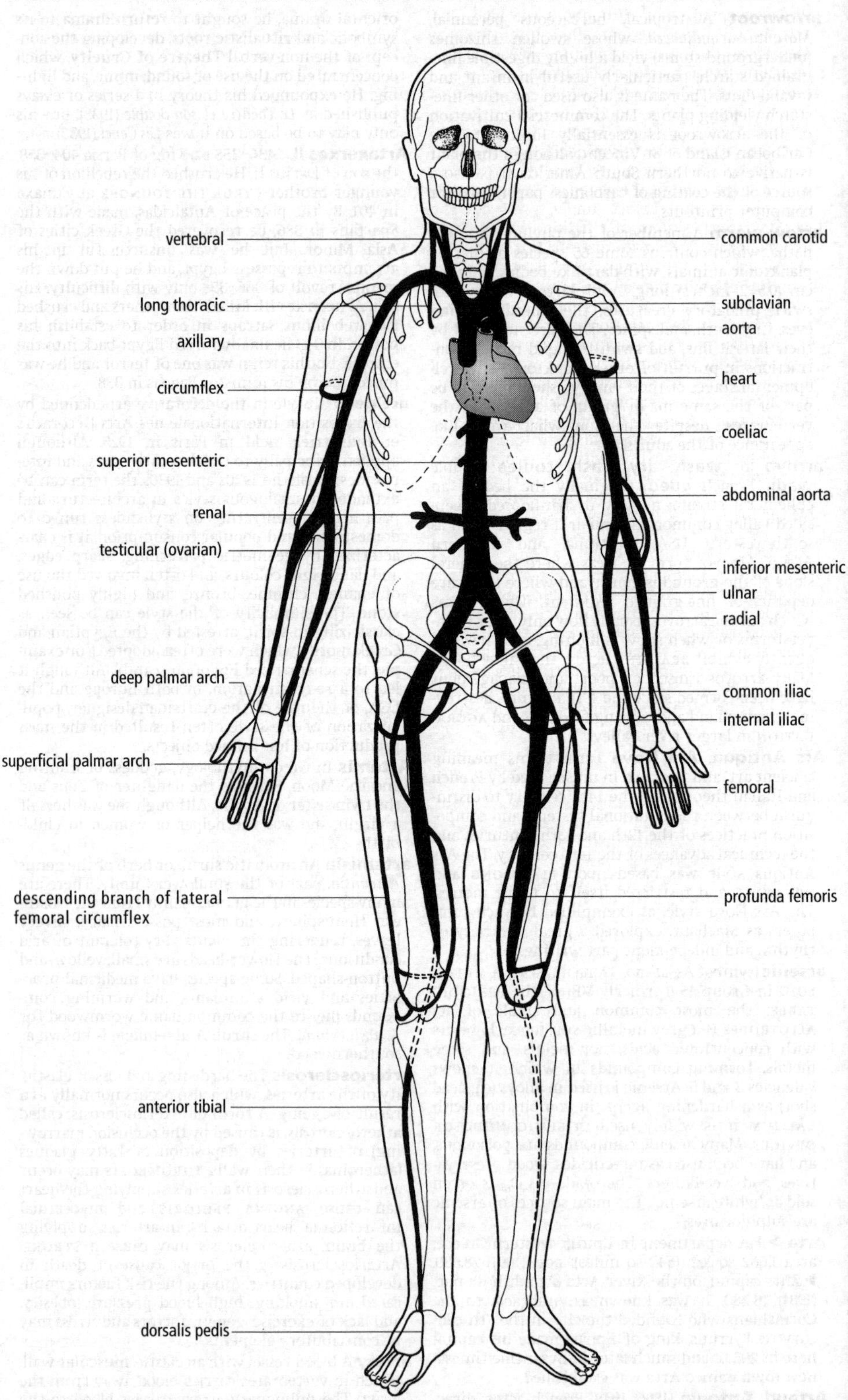

Artery The principal arteries of the human body.

the oxygenated blood throughout the body, and oxygen and other nutrients diffuse into the tissues from thin-walled capillaries. Blood vessels returning to the heart are called VEINS.

artesian well A discharge of water under pressure from an AQUIFER. The aquifer is a water-bearing stratum that is confined between impermeable strata above and below it. Provided that the difference in height between its highest and lowest parts is large enough, the water in the lower parts may rise to the surface under pressure. The world's largest system of this kind is the Great Artesian Basin of eastern Australia. Artesian wells are named from the famous Artois Basin in France.

arthritis Inflammation of the joints. It may be a result of infection, but it is more commonly a response to a degeneration of the CARTILAGE (osteoarthritis) or a lapse in IMMUNITY (rheumatoid arthritis). Osteoarthritis is predominantly a disorder of later life, whereas rheumatoid arthritis may affect younger people as well. Both conditions are common causes of disability, and neither is well understood. Rheumatoid arthritis is characterized by the production within the joints of an ANTIBODY which is active against part of other antibodies, the ensuing interaction being responsible for the inflammation. Many diseases can cause arthritis: a disease of the metabolism of uric acid leads to the form known as gout.

arthropod A member of the largest phylum of animals, the Arthropoda, comprising several million species. Although enormously diverse in form and habits, arthropods are quite easy to recognize. They share two critical features: a tough segmented covering or EXOSKELETON (forming a waterproof cuticle in insects and spiders, or a thick shell in crabs), and a number of jointed legs (usually one pair per segment) used for swimming, walking, or food-handling.

Arthropods can be found in every conceivable habitat. CRUSTACEANS live mainly in the seas and fresh water. On land, ARACHNIDS (such as spiders and mites), MYRIAPODS (such as centipedes), and INSECTS abound. Winged insects also thrive in aerial habitats. Arthropod success in all these ecological NICHES is due to several features: the protective exoskeleton and its associated sense organs; speedy and nimble locomotion, legs being mechanically superior to the hydrostatic system of many other invertebrates; diversity of cuticular mouthparts, which can exploit almost any food; and (on land especially) elaborate courtship and mating strategies and the production of resistant eggs. The small size of arthropods (necessitated by the cuticle) is also useful, as it allows them to inhabit small spaces among vegetation, within crevices, or in soils, which are unavailable to larger creatures.

Arthur Traditionally king of Britain, historically perhaps a 5th- or 6th-century Romano-British chieftain or general. His life and court have become the focus for many romantic legends in various languages, including the exploits of adventurous knights and the quest for the Holy Grail. The stories were developed and recounted by Malory, Chrétien de Troyes, and others; the Norman writer Wace (12th century) mentions the 'Round Table', which enabled the knights to be seated in such a way that none had precedence. Arthur's court was at Camelot, a place variously located by writers and historians in Wales, Somerset, Cornwall, and Winchester.

Arthur, Chester Alan (1830–86) US Republican statesman, 21st President of the USA 1881–85. He was appointed Garfield's Vice-President in 1881 and became President after Garfield's assassination. During his term of office, he was responsible for improving the strength of the US navy.

Arthur's Pass A mountain pass through the Otira Gorge in the Southern Alps of central South Island, New Zealand. Opened in 1866, the 17-km (10.7-mile) highway through the pass links the townships of Otira and Arthur's Pass. Beneath the pass runs the 8.5-km (5.3-mile) Otira Rail Tunnel which was completed in 1923 and is the only rail link across South Island.

ārtī (from Sanskrit *ārātrika*) A ceremony of light, which, in HINDUISM, constitutes one of the basic elements of PUJA or worship. A tray, upon which are placed items symbolizing the elements, including a lamp with five small candles, is waved before the shrine of a god, and then passed around the worshippers so that they can receive the god's blessing.

artichoke Either the globe artichoke, *Cynara scolymus*, an edible thistle of Mediterranean origin; or the Jerusalem artichoke, *Helianthus tuberosus*, a member of the sunflower family, Compositae. The fleshy flower-heads of the globe artichoke have been used as a vegetable since ancient Greek and Roman times. The Jerusalem artichoke of North America is a tall plant up to 2 m (6.5 feet) in height and is a close relative of the sunflower (hence the designation Jerusalem, a corruption of French *giresol*, sunflower). It is grown for its sweet-fleshed underground tubers.

artificial horizon An instrument used in conjunction with a SEXTANT to measure the altitude (angle above the horizon) of a celestial body when the real horizon is obscured. Several types of artificial horizon are in use, but all provide a horizontal line or plane parallel to the plane of the true horizon, from which readings can be taken. This may be a spirit-level bubble or, more usually in aircraft, a horizontal reference provided by a spinning GYROSCOPE.

artificial insemination (AI) The injection of semen into the female reproductive tract by other than natural means. Semen for insemination can be diluted, treated, and stored frozen for a considerable period. It is therefore possible to produce a large number of offspring from one sire. In animal breeding, progeny testing is used to ensure the development of animals with desirable characteristics. Artificial insemination may also be used in humans if conception by natural means is not possible.

artificial intelligence (AI) 'The science of making machines do things that would require intelligence if done by humans' as defined in 1968 by Marvin Minsky of the Massachusetts Institute of Technology, USA. Sensing, reasoning, pattern recognition, speech recognition, and problem-solving are among such tasks. The degree of sophistication that constitutes AI tends to be revised upwards with each new generation of computers. At its most ambitious level AI has the goal of creating computers and robots capable of reproducing a broad range of human behaviour. Doubts remain, however, about whether such systems are theoretically or practically possible, because of the vast complexity of the human brain. However, one important result of AI research is the development of systems known as NEURAL NETWORKS, which can be 'taught' to solve problems. These show promise for a number of different AI applications, particularly those involving pattern recognition. The demands of AI have also stimulated the development of COMPUTER LANGUAGES, such as

PROLOG and LISP, which are better suited to represent and process symbolic structures than more conventional languages.

'Pseudo-intelligence' is one term for computer applications being developed in translation systems, semi-automatic offices in which human speech and instructions are turned into a properly laid-out document, in linguistic and PSYCHOLINGUISTIC studies, and in ROBOTICS – replacing human actions by those of a robot, on the production line or in an artificial limb, for example. Robot sensing is used in weapons guidance systems and in product quality control. The impact of such developments is likely to be huge.

artificial satellite See SATELLITE, ARTIFICIAL.

Artigas, José Gervasio (1764–1850) National hero of Uruguay. He led the Uruguyan movement for independence from Spain during the years 1811–13 and maintained this in the face of the territorial ambitions of Argentina in 1814. Uruguay also had to contend with Portuguese expansionists from Brazil, and Portuguese troops captured Montevideo in 1817. Artigas was unable to dislodge them. He conducted guerrilla warfare against them for three years but in 1820 was forced to retreat to Argentina, and never returned to Uruguay.

artillery War engines or FIREARMS too large to be managed by a single soldier. Ballistas, onagers, and CATAPULTS were early examples of artillery. Their use was largely restricted to siege warfare, and it was in such operations that CANNON came to replace them. Modern artillery functions in the same way as all firearms, but fires larger projectiles over longer distances. Muzzle-loaders, common from the 15th to the 19th century, had their explosive charge and ammunition loaded from the front of the barrel. Breech-loaders, used in the 15th and 16th centuries and reintroduced on a large scale in the mid-19th century, have the charge and shot loaded at the rear. Modern categories of artillery fire solid shot, SHRAPNEL, or explosive SHELLS. They include field guns, which fire with a flat trajectory, howitzers and MORTARS, which have arching trajectories, ANTITANK GUNS, firing high-velocity shot, and self-propelled guns. Since 1918 there has been a decline in the importance of heavy artillery as missiles, bomber aircraft, and armed helicopters have taken over many of their roles, while mortars have taken over many light artillery roles.

art nouveau Decorative style flourishing in most of western Europe and the USA from about 1890 to World War I. It was a deliberate attempt to create a new style in reaction to the academic 'historicism' of much 19th-century art, its most characteristic theme being the use of sinuous asymmetrical lines based on plant forms. Primarily an art of ornament, its most typical manifestations occurred in applied art, decoration, and illustration, but its influence can also be seen in the work of many painters and sculptors. The style takes its name from a gallery called L'Art Nouveau opened in Paris in 1895. However, the roots of the style were in Britain, where the ARTS AND CRAFTS MOVEMENT had established a tradition of vitality in the applied arts, and it spread to the Continent of Europe chiefly from London. The style was truly international, the most celebrated exponents ranging from BEARDSLEY in Britain to MUCHA, a Czech whose most characteristic work was done in Paris, and TIFFANY in the USA. Leading art nouveau architects included MACKINTOSH in Scotland, GAUDÍ in Spain, Guimard in France, and HORTA in Belgium.

Artois A former province in north-west France between Picardy and Flanders. Known in Roman times as Artesium, the area gave its name to the artesian well which was first sunk here in the 12th century.

Artois, Charles, Comte d' See CHARLES X.

Arts and Crafts Movement British social and aesthetic movement of the latter half of the 19th century that aimed to reassert the importance of craftsmanship in the face of increasing mechanization and mass production. It had its basis in the ideas of PUGIN and RUSKIN, but it was left to William MORRIS to translate their ideas into practical activity. His hand-made products (books, furniture, textiles, wall-paper, and so on) were successful aesthetically, but his ideal of producing art for the masses failed. Nevertheless, in the early years of the 20th century the ideals of the Arts and Crafts Movement spread abroad, notably to Germany, Austria, the Low Countries, and Scandinavia, where the Danish silver designer George Jensen was one of the key figures. After World War I the movement was transformed by the acceptance of modern industrial methods, but it has had an enduring legacy on 20th-century design.

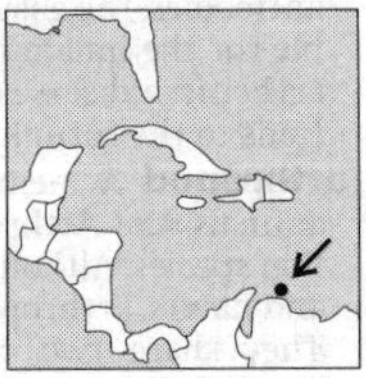

Aruba A Dutch island in the Caribbean Sea 24 km (15 miles) north of the Venezuelan coast. Formerly part of the Netherlands Antilles, it separated from that group in 1986 in advance of gaining full independence; area 193 sq km (74 sq miles); pop. (est. 1991) 60,000; chief town, Oranjestad. The economy is based on the refining of crude oil imported from Venezuela.

arum A plant of the genus *Arum*, part of the Araceae, a family with a distinctive floral structure usually consisting of a petal-like sheath, the spathe, enclosing a club-like column, the spadix, with male and female flowers attached to its base. The family includes arum lilies, monsteras, and philodendrons; some species smell of carrion and attract flies, which pollinate them.

Arunachal Pradesh A mountainous state of north-east India, bounded to the north by Tibet, to the east by Burma and to the west by Bhutan; area 83,578 sq km (32,282 sq miles); pop. (1991) 858,350; capital, Itanagar. Formerly the North East Frontier Agency of Assam in British India, Arunachal Pradesh became the 24th state of India in 1986. Nearly two-thirds of the state is under forest, the chief products being coffee, rice, rubber, fruits, and spices. There are over 80 tribal groups speaking 50 different dialects.

Arundel A market town in West Sussex, southern England, on the River Arun; pop. (1981) 2,500. Nearby is the 12th-century Arundel Castle, seat of the dukes of Norfolk.

Arvand The Iranian name for the SHATT AL-ARAB waterway between Iraq and Iran.

Aryabhata (476–*c.*550) Indian astronomer and mathematician. He wrote two works, one of which is now lost. The surviving work, the *Aryabhatiya* (499), has sections dealing with mathematics, the measurement of time, planetary models, the sphere, and eclipses. India's first space satellite was named after him.

Aryan A member of the peoples (not to be regarded as a race) speaking any of the languages of the Indo-European (esp. Indo-Iranian) family. The idea current in the 19th century of an Aryan race corresponding to a definite Aryan language was taken up by nationalistic, historical, and romantic writers. It was given especial currency by M. A. de Gobineau, who linked it with the theory of the essential inferiority of certain races. The term 'Aryan race' was later revived and used for purposes of political propaganda in Nazi Germany.

aryl group A group of atoms derived from an AROMATIC COMPOUND by the removal of one hydrogen atom from the aromatic ring. The simplest aromatic compound is benzene, C_6H_6, and the simplest aryl group is therefore the phenyl group, C_6H_5–. When aryl groups bond to FUNCTIONAL GROUPS, they give rise to the corresponding aryl compounds. For instance, if the functional group is a halogen atom, the resulting compound is an aryl halide, of which chlorobenzene, C_6H_5Cl, is an example.

asbestos A fibrous variety of AMPHIBOLES and several other silicate minerals containing SiO_4 groups linked into chains. Asbestos minerals occur in metamorphic and basic IGNEOUS ROCKS. Different varieties are found in Canada, South Africa, Cyprus, and elsewhere. The fibres are released from the rock by crushing followed by blowing. Only those fibres at least 1 cm (0.4 inch) in length are suitable for SPINNING into yarn. Shorter fibres are used for such products as paper, millboard, and asbestos–cement building materials. Spun products usually contain 10–25 per cent of a rough-surfaced fibre such as cotton to facilitate the spinning of the smooth, brittle fibres. It is the non-flammable nature of asbestos fibre that gives it its industrial importance. Applications include brake linings, building materials, electrical equipment, and thermal insulation materials. Asbestos fabrics are used for FIRE-FIGHTING suits, safety apparel, and fire curtains. Since the early 1970s there has been growing concern about the effect of short asbestos fibres on human health. The short fibres are thought to cause asbestosis, a lung disorder leading to progressively greater breathing difficulties plus concomitant heart strain, and mesothelioma, a rapidly fatal form of lung cancer. This has led to a limitation in its use and to elaborate procedures for its safe removal from public buildings.

ascarid A ROUNDWORM of the genus *Ascaris*, an intestinal parasite of man, dogs, cats, pigs, and many other vertebrates. The human ascarid, *Ascaris lumbricoides*, is similar in appearance to a smooth, pale earthworm and feeds as an adult on the host's intestinal contents. The adult female can reach 35 cm (14 inches) in length, and her eggs pass out in faeces to be transmitted to new hosts in contaminated food or drink. Infestation is very common in tropical and subtropical regions, and damage is caused by the migration of *Ascaris* larvae into other organs of the host body.

Ascension A major Christian festival celebrated forty days after Easter Sunday, which commemorates Jesus being taken into heaven. The Ascension constitutes the last of Jesus Christ's resurrection appearances, and signifies his exaltation as Lord of heaven and Earth. It is mentioned in the New Testament and Apostles' CREED and was widely celebrated by the end of the 4th century, with processions to the traditional location of the Ascension, the Mount of Olives.

Ascension Island A small island in the South Atlantic, incorporated with St Helena with which it is a dependency of the UK; area 88 sq km (34 sq miles); pop. (1988) 1,007. It was discovered by the Portuguese, traditionally on Ascension Day in 1501, but remained uninhabited until a small British garrison was stationed there on the arrival of Napoleon for imprisonment on St Helena in 1815. It is now a British telecommunications centre and a US air base.

asceticism (from Greek *askeo*, 'to exercise' or 'to train') A system of austere religious practices designed to combat the natural passions and inclinations in order to strengthen spiritual life. The word has its origins in strict regimes of training for athletes, but the idea has formed part of religions and philosophies throughout history. Ascetic cults are found in CHRISTIANITY, HINDUISM, and ISLAM.

Aschaffenburg A city in the German state of Bavaria, on the River Main, south-east of Frankfurt; pop. (1991) 64,470. Its river port is a major outlet for coal, timber, textiles, wine, and scientific equipment. It manufactures precision and optical instruments and machinery.

Ascham, Roger (*c*.1515–68) English humanist scholar and writer. His posts included that of tutor to the future Elizabeth I and Latin secretary to Queen Mary and later to Elizabeth. He is noted for his treatise on archery, *Toxophilus* (1545), and *The Scholemaster* (1570), a practical and influential treatise on education.

ASCII (American Standard Code for Information Interchange) The commonest way of representing text characters using BINARY code in digital computer systems. The code covers the numbers 0 to 9, the alphabet, punctuation marks, and other special characters. Each number or letter is assigned a unique binary number: thus the character 'A' is 01000001 and '?' is 00111111. Each character is usually stored in one BYTE. In computing terminology an ASCII file refers to a file that consists only of text or data without any special characters for controlling PERIPHERALS. Another common data communication code is EBCDIC ('ebbseedik', Extended Binary Coded Decimal Interchange Code), which can code for 256 different characters, as opposed to the 128 codes available in ASCII. A new character set, called Unicode, represents characters with 16-bit rather than 8-bit 'words', and can therefore code for 27,000 different characters. This makes it possible to represent most letters, ideographs, and symbols of the world's main languages in Unicode.

Asclepius In Greek mythology, the patron of healing. In some accounts he is a god – the son of Apollo. In others he is mortal and is killed by Zeus, who feared that his healing powers would save humans from death. His emblem was a snake; the sloughing of its skin symbolized the regenerative power of healing.

Ascoli Piceno A tourist resort and the capital of a province of the same name in the Marche region of east-central Italy, 25 km (16 miles) from the Adriatic coast at the junction of the Tronto and Castellano rivers; pop. (1990) 52,625. The original Roman town was built on a salt-trading route.

Ascot A racecourse near Windsor in Berkshire, England. It is the scene of an annual race-meeting in June (Ascot Week), founded by Queen Anne in 1711.

ASDIC See SONAR.

ASEAN See ASSOCIATION OF SOUTH-EAST ASIAN NATIONS.

asepsis The modern practice of rendering all equipment in contact with surgical or other wounds free from microbiological material which may lead to infection. Asepsis was combined with ANTISEPSIS in the late 19th century, and largely replaced antisepsis in the 20th. Whereas antisepsis attempted chemically to disinfect instruments and especially wounds, aseptic techniques rely on heat or other physical methods for the STERILIZATION of equipment and so minimize the chances of wound contamination.

Asgard In Scandinavian mythology, a region at the centre of the Universe inhabited by the gods.

ash Any of several of the 70 tree species of *Fraxinus* native to the Northern Hemisphere. They belong to the same family as olive and lilac and have pinnate or, more rarely, simple leaves and winged fruits. The common ash of Europe, *F. excelsior*, has very strong, pale wood, long used for tool handles, bows, and hockey sticks. Its flowers generally have no petals, though those of the manna ash of southern Europe, *F. ornus*, have slender whitish petals. A few unrelated trees, such as the rowan, are sometimes called ash.

ash, volcanic Tiny, unconsolidated fragments of lava emitted from volcanoes. The ejection of ash is usually caused by an obstruction in the vent or inner wall of the crater. Huge quantities enter the atmosphere at the time of eruptions, sometimes in a NUÉE ARDENTE. Suspended in the air as dust it can be carried round the globe by high-level winds. After precipitation, soil resulting from its decomposition becomes extremely fertile, and as a result, settlements grow around volcanoes in spite of dangers.

Ashanti (or **Asante**) A region of central Ghana inhabited by the Ashanti, one of Ghana's principal ethnic groups; area 25,123 sq km (9,700 sq miles); pop. (1984) 2,089,700. The regional capital, Kumasi, was the capital of the former **Ashanti Confederation**, a tribal union (covering a wider area) that was forged in the 17th century. After a series of wars the area was formally annexed by Britain on 1 January 1902 and became part of the British colony of the Gold Coast. The Ashanti people speak a dialect of the Kwa group within the Niger-Kordofanian family of African languages.

Ashcan School A group of US painters active from about 1908 until World War I who painted urban realist subjects. It was inspired largely by Robert Henri; other artists associated with the movement included George Wesley Bellows and Edward HOPPER. They often painted slum life and outcasts, but they were interested more in the picturesque aspects of their subjects than in the social issues involved.

Ashcroft, Dame Peggy (full name Edith Margaret Emily Ashcroft) (1907–91) British actress. She played a number of Shakespearian roles including Desdemona to Paul Robeson's Othello (1930) and Juliet in John Gielgud's production of *Romeo and Juliet* (1935). Other outstanding performances included the title role in Ibsen's *Hedda Gabler* (1954), for which she received a royal award. She won an Oscar for best supporting actress in the film *A Passage to India* (1984).

Ashdown, Paddy (full name Jeremy John Durham Ashdown) (1941–), British Liberal Democrat politician, born in India. Formerly a Liberal MP (1983–88), he became the first leader of the Liberal Democrats (originally the Social and Liberal Democrats) in 1988.

Ashe, Arthur (Robert) (1943–93) US tennis player. He won the US Open championship in 1968 and Wimbledon in 1975, and was the first black male player to achieve world rankings. He died of Aids, having contracted HIV from a blood transfusion.

Ashes A trophy, consisting of an urn containing the ashes of a burnt cricket stump, presented to the winning side in Test Matches between Australia and England. It was made in 1883 as a joke and given to the victorious England captain. Australia's victory in the previous year had prompted an advertisement in the *Sporting Times* stating that the body of English cricket would be cremated and the ashes taken to Australia.

Ashford A market town in Kent, south-east England, on the Great Stour River; pop. (1981) 45,962. It is the site of a terminus of the Channel Tunnel.

Ashkenazi (pl. **Ashkenazim**) An East European Jew or a Jew of East European ancestry.

Ashkenazy, Vladimir (Davidovich) (1937–) Russian-born pianist and conductor. A child prodigy, he made his Moscow début in 1945 and went on to win several international awards, including sharing the first prize in the 1962 Moscow Tchaikovsky Piano Competition with John Ogdon (1937–89). Ashkenazy left the Soviet Union the following year, settling in Iceland and then Switzerland.

Ashley, Laura (1925–85) British fashion and textile designer. In the 1960s her clothes, in traditional floral patterns and reflecting romantic Victorian and Edwardian styles, became highly popular, as did the range of furnishing fabrics and wallpapers which her company (founded with her husband Bernard) introduced. The chain of shops under Laura Ashley's name spread through Britain and later to Europe, America, Australia, and Japan.

Ashley Cooper, Anthony See SHAFTESBURY.

Ashmole, Elias (1617–92) English antiquary. Ashmole showed an insatiable desire for knowledge, studying such diverse topics as alchemy, astrology, Hebrew, and mathematics. In 1677 he presented to Oxford University his collection of rarities, which he had inherited from John Tradescant and which formed the nucleus of the Ashmolean Museum.

Ashmore and Cartier Islands An external territory of Australia in the Indian Ocean, comprising the uninhabited Ashmore Reef and Cartier Islands; area *c.*3 sq km (1 sq mile). Part of Australia since 1931, the islands were administered by Northern Territory from 1938 to 1978. A national nature reserve was established in 1983.

ashram (from Sanskrit, 'hermitage') A monastery or retreat centre for spiritual seekers within Hinduism. Visitors are taught YOGA exercises and meditation under the supervision of a *swami*, or teacher, and regular worship also takes place. In an environment of peace, prayer, work, and community life, the seeker after truth develops his or her own inner life.

Ashton, Sir Frederick (William Mallandaine) (1904–88) British ballet-dancer, choreographer, and director. He became chief choreographer and principal dancer of the Vic-Wells Ballet in 1935, remaining with the company when it became the Sadler's Wells and finally the Royal Ballet, of which he was director 1963–70. As a choreographer, Ashton established a lyrical and fluid style of classical ballet, creating successful new works as well as making popular adaptations of historical ballets.

Ashton-under-Lyne An industrial suburb of Tameside borough in Greater Manchester, north-west England, on the River Tame.

Ashurbanipal King of Assyria *c.*668–627 BC. The grandson of Sennacherib, he was responsible for the sacking of the Elamite capital Susa and the suppression of a revolt in Babylon. However, he is chiefly recognized for his patronage of the arts; he established a library of more than 20,000 clay tablets at Nineveh, which included literary, religious, scientific, and administrative documents.

Ash Wednesday The first day of Lent, 40 weekdays before Easter Day. Its name comes from the former practice of Christians who put ashes on their heads as a sign of penitence.

Asia The largest of the world's continents, constituting nearly one-third of the land mass, lying in the eastern hemisphere, entirely north of the equator except for some south-east Asian islands. It stretches from Cape Chelyubinsk on the Arctic coast to Cape Piai at the southern tip of the Malay peninsula, and from Cape Baba in western Turkey through more than 165° of longitude to Cape Dezhnev in north-east Siberia. The world's highest mountain (Mount Everest), lowest elevation (the Dead Sea), greatest area of coniferous forest (the taiga of Siberian Russia), and largest inland sea (Caspian) are all located in Asia. The continent is connected to Africa by the Isthmus of Suez, and generally divided from Europe (which forms part of the same land mass) by a line running through the Ural Mountains and the Caspian Sea; area 44 million sq km (17 million sq miles); pop. (est. 1990) 3,113 million. The principal cities are Tokyo, Shanghai, Beijing, Seoul, Calcutta, Bombay, Jakarta, Tehran, Delhi, Bangkok, Tianjin, and Karachi. Major rivers include the Yangtze, Yellow River, Ob-Irtysh, Amur, Lena, Mekong, Yenisei, Indus, Ganges, Brahmaputra, Tigris, Euphrates, Amu Darya, and Irrawaddy. Extensive areas of desert include the Gobi, Takla Makan, Kara-Kum, Syrian Desert, Arabian Desert, and the Negev. Over 90 per cent of the world's rice, rubber, jute, flax, cotton, and tobacco comes from Asia. It is also the world's leading source of tropical timber.

Asia Minor (or **Anatolia**) The westernmost part of Asia now comprising Asiatic Turkey. The first major civilization established there was that of the Hittites in the 2nd millenium BC. The Greeks colonized the western coast, while the kingdoms of Lydia and Phrygia developed independently. The land was subjugated by various invaders, including Cyrus of Persia (546 BC) and Alexander the Great (333 BC). It was subsequently the Roman province of Asia and then part of the Byzantine empire. Conquered by the Turks, it became part of the Ottoman empire from the end of the 13th century until the establishment of modern Turkey after World War I.

asiento de negros A contract made between Britain and Spain in 1713 for the sale of slaves to the Spanish American colonies. In the Peace of UTRECHT (1713) Spain granted Britain a monopoly of the supply of slaves to the Spanish American colonies of 144,000 slaves at 4,800 a year for thirty years, with other privileges. They were the origin of the speculation which resulted in the SOUTH SEA BUBBLE. They led to endless disputes, and to the War of JENKINS'S EAR between England and Spain in 1739. The treaty was ended by agreement in 1750.

Asimov, Isaac (1920–92) Soviet-born US writer and scientist. He was a distinguished biochemist, but is more widely known as the author of many works of science fiction, books on science for non-scientists, and essays on a wide variety of subjects.

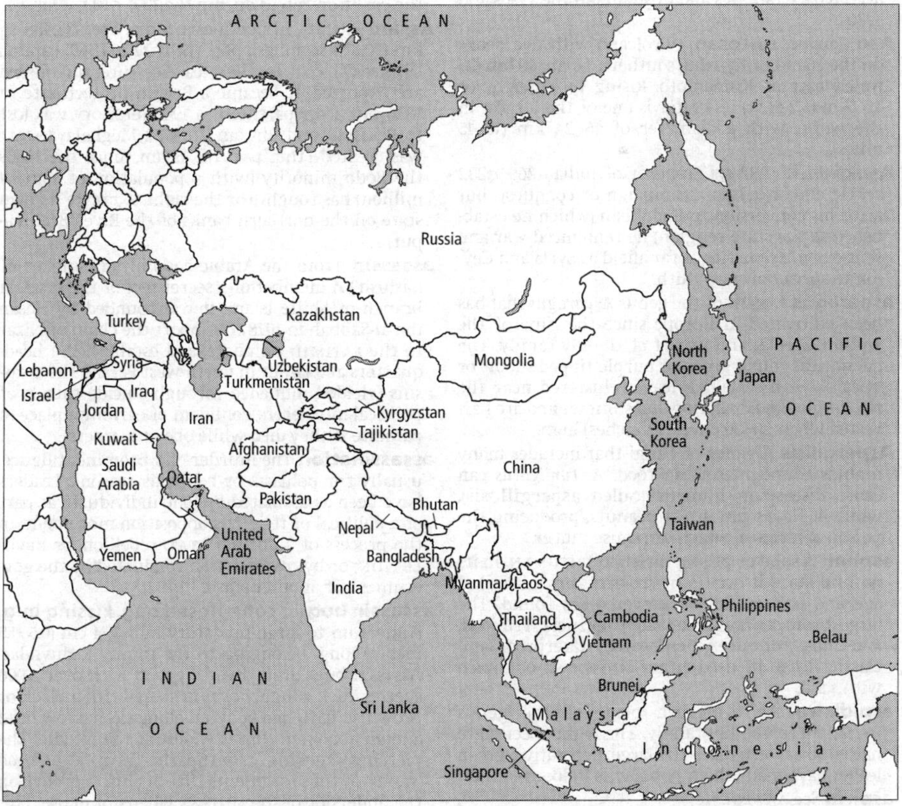

Asia The political boundaries within the continent.

Among his best-known science fiction is *I, Robot* (1950) and the *Foundation* trilogy (1951–53). Building on Karel ČAPEK's concept of the robot, in 1941 Asimov coined the term *robotics*.

Askey, Arthur (Bowden) (1900–82) British comedian and actor. Having made his professional début in 1924, he was always in demand after his highly popular radio show *Band Waggon* (1938–39), and appeared in a great number of pantomimes, West End musicals, films, and television programmes.

Askia Muhammad I (died 1528) Emperor of SONGHAY in West Africa 1493–1528. Originally named Muhammad Turé, he was Sonni Ali's best general. He usurped Songhay from Ali's son in 1493, thus founding a new dynasty, and took the title Askia. He was a convert to Islam, but tolerant towards pagans, and made the pilgrimage to MECCA, meeting many notable men, especially the great Muslim teacher al-Maghili. He had close political and commercial relationships with Morocco and Egypt, organized an efficient administration, and an army and a navy on the River Niger, and made TIMBUKTU the capital of the SONGHAI empire and an important intellectual and religious centre.

Asmara (or **Asmera**) The capital of Eritrea in East Africa, situated at an altitude of 2,350 m (7,710 ft) on the Hamasen plateau; pop. (1991) 367,300. In 1900 Asmara became the capital of the Italian colony of Eritrea and in the 1930s it was developed as an Italian base from which the invasion of Ethiopia was launched in 1935. The USA built a large military communications centre here in the 1950s. Today it has numerous light industries but was severely affected by famines and droughts in the 1970s and 1980s.

Aso (Japanese **Asosan**) A volcano with five peaks on the island of Kyushu, southern Japan, 40 km (25 miles) east of Kumamoto. Rising to a height of 1,592 m (5,222 ft) its crater is one of the largest in the world with a diameter of 16–24 km (10–15 miles).

Asoka (died *c.*232 BC) Emperor of India *c.*269–*c.*232 BC. He embarked on a campaign of conquest, but after his conversion to Buddhism (which he established as the state religion) he renounced war and sent out missionaries as far afield as Syria and Ceylon to spread his new faith.

asparagus A plant of the genus *Asparagus* that has been cultivated in Europe since the time of the ancient Greeks, and is part of the lily family. The cylindrical young green or purple-tipped shoots or 'spears', with scale-like leaves clustered near the tip, develop in late spring and summer and are harvested when 20–30 cm (8–12 inches) high.

Aspergillus A genus of fungi that includes many moulds found in rotting food. *A. fumigatus* can cause disease in humans (called **aspergillosis**), while *A. flavus* can infect peanuts, producing the poison **aflatoxin**, which can cause cancer.

asphalt A solid or plastic variety of BITUMEN. In its natural state it occurs in rocks of any geological age and particularly wherever oil is found. The largest sources are in Canada, Venezuela, Trinidad, and Cuba. Adhesive when heated, waterproof, and elastic, it can be used either on its own or mixed with sand.

aspidistra An evergreen plant of the genus *Aspidistra* in the lily family. The eight species are native to eastern Asia. The large, decorative, green leaves have made them popular as indoor plants.

aspirin See ANALGESIC.

Asplund, Gunnar (1885–1940) The outstanding Swedish architect of the 20th century. He was a pioneer of MODERNISM in his country. His style was noble and graceful, and his finest work, the Woodland Crematorium at Stockholm South Cemetery (1935–40), is one of the undisputed masterpieces of modern architecture.

Asquith, Herbert Henry, 1st Earl of Oxford and Asquith (1852–1928) British Liberal statesman, Prime Minister 1908–16. In the years before the World War I he introduced the third bill for Irish Home Rule, while also contending with the challenge posed by the women's suffrage movement and outrage from the House of Lords over LLOYD GEORGE's People's Budget (1909). In 1915 Asquith brought the Conservatives into a coalition government, but his failure to consult his colleagues divided the Liberals; he was displaced as Prime Minister by Lloyd George the following year, but retained the party leadership.

ass A member of the same genus as the horse. Both species of wild asses – the African, *Equus africanus*, and Asiatic, *E. hemionus* – live in steppes, semideserts, and even in the deserts of eastern Africa and Asia. The largest is the kiang, a subspecies of the Asiatic ass, of Tibet and the Himalayas. The Asiatic asses live in herds of up to fifteen females and foals; stallions are territorial. Foals are born during the summer months. The DONKEY is the domesticated form.

Assad, Hafiz al- (1928–) Syrian Baath statesman, President since 1971. While in office he has ensured the strengthening of Syria's oil-based economy and suppressed political opposition such as the uprising of Muslim extremists (1979–82). He supported the coalition forces during the 1991 GULF WAR.

Assam A state in north-east India; area 88,438 sq km (30,673 sq miles); pop. (1991) 22,294,560; capital, Dispur. Oil, coal, textiles, tea, rice, jute, and oilseed are exported. It became a British protectorate in 1826 but after partition in 1947 territory was lost to Pakistan and Bhutan. In 1972 Meghalaya state was created from part of Assam. Since the 1960s the Bodo minority (with a population of some 4 million) has fought for the right to create its own state on the northern banks of the River Brahmaputra.

assassin (from the Arabic *hashishiyun*, 'smoker of hashish') A member of a secret sect of the ISMAILI branch of Shiite Islam. It was founded by Hasan ibn al-Sabbah in 1078 to support the claim of Nizar to the FATIMID caliphate, and established a headquarters at Alamut in north-west Persia. The assassins wielded influence through suicide squads of political murderers, confident of earning a place in paradise if they died while obeying orders.

assassination The murder of a prominent figure, usually for political or religious reasons. Leaders have been assassinated by lone individuals; as part of a political or religious opposition movement; in the process of a COUP D'ÉTAT, rebellion, or REVOLUTION; or by covert action conducted by the government of another state.

assassin bug (or **cone-nosed bug**, **kissing bug**) A medium to large predatory BUG 1–4 cm (0.5–1.5 inches) long, belonging to the family Reduviidae. Assassin bugs are a diverse group with over 3,000 species, each roughly oval in shape with a black or brownish flattened body, an elongate, narrow head and an abdomen that is widest at the middle. The piercing, sucking mouthparts form a pointed 'snout' of three segments that fits into a groove on the underside of the THORAX when not in use. This is used to pierce and suck out the juices of prey,

using a pair of sliding needles, or stylets. A few species are bloodsuckers that inflict painful bites on humans, and several American species of *Triatoma* are VECTORS of the trypanosome (parasite) that causes Chagas' disease (see TRYPANOSOMIASIS).

assembly language A computer language that represents MACHINE CODE programs in a form people can read. Each machine code instruction is represented by a short mnemonic code. MEMORY registers and storage addresses may be referred to by symbolic names rather than numeric codes, and labels and comments can be used to improve legibility. Assembly language programs have to be translated into machine code by a special program called an assembler before they can be run on a computer.

assembly line A method of manufacturing a complicated product by means of a series of operations performed by people or machines, each operation adding one or more parts. The method has largely superseded traditional manufacturing methods in which one person built a complete unit from constituent parts. Frequently the assembly line is formed around a moving belt or a railed track along which the product is moved either continuously or intermittently. This method was pioneered for motor-car assembly by FORD in 1913; it enabled him to use semi-skilled labour to produce cars cheaply and in quantity. An assembly line is appropriate for manual assembly of parts, but is equally applicable to AUTOMATION, where parts are made and assembled by machines. The assembly line is a major concern of production engineering; its success depends on careful planning and design, mechanical handling of parts, continuous supply of material, inspection, maintenance, and control. In some fields, linear assembly lines are being replaced by cellular assembly, in which small teams of workers are responsible for a particular stage of production, for example preparation and painting of a car's bodywork. See also MASS PRODUCTION; ROBOTICS.

Assiniboine A river in southern Canada that rises in south-eastern Saskatchewan and flows 1,070 km (673 miles) south-east then east through Manitoba to meet the Red River of the North at Winnipeg. Its chief headstreams are the Souris and the Qu'Appelle. The valley of the Assiniboine was the route to the plains followed by colonists from the Red River valley.

Assisi A historic medieval town of Umbria in central Italy, situated in the Apennines in the province of Perugia; pop. (1990) 24,790. St FRANCIS OF ASSISI, who lived and died there, founded an order in Assisi that bears his name. The saint's tomb is located beneath two churches that form the Basilica of St Francis. During an earthquake in 1997 the Basilica was seriously damaged and subsequently looted.

Assisi, Clare of See CLARE OF ASSISI, ST.

Assisi, Francis of See FRANCIS OF ASSISI, ST.

Association of Caribbean States An association of 25 Caribbean basin countries formed in 1994 for the purpose of promoting regional integration, economic cooperation, and a common approach to regional political problems.

Association of South-East Asian Nations (ASEAN) A regional organization formed by Indonesia, Malaysia, the Philippines, Singapore, and Thailand through the Bangkok Declaration of 1967. Brunei joined the organization in 1984, Vietnam joined in 1995, and Myanmar (Burma) and Laos joined in 1997. ASEAN aims to accelerate and to promote regional stability. In 1992 it agreed to create the ASEAN Free Trade Area (AFTA) as the first step towards the creation of an ASEAN common market. Since ASEAN members have historically given more priority to external than intra-ASEAN trade, one of its principal roles has been to negotiate with other countries and with organizations such as the EUROPEAN UNION. From its inception ASEAN opposed communist regimes in other Asian countries such as North Vietnam and, subsequently, Laos and Cambodia.

assurance (in commerce) A (life) assurance policy is an arrangement providing for the payment of a sum of money to a named individual on a specific date (a term or endowment assurance) or at death (a whole-life assurance), in exchange for earlier payments to the insurance fund known as premiums. The sum assured is specified in advance, but, for a higher premium, may also include a proportion of the PROFITS of the assurance company.

Assyria An ancient country in what is now northern Iraq. It was originally centred on Ashur, a city-state on the west bank of the Tigris, which first became prominent and expanded its borders in the 14th century BC. From the 8th to the late 7th century BC Assyria was the dominant Near-Eastern power and created an empire which stretched from the Persian Gulf to Egypt. Its capital city was Nineveh near modern Mosul, Iraq. The state fell in 612 BC, defeated by a coalition of Medes and Chaldeans.

Astaire, Fred (born Frederick Austerlitz) (1899–1987) US dancer, singer, and actor. He danced in music halls from an early age, before starring in a number of film musicals, including *Top Hat* (1935), *Follow the Fleet* (1936), and *Shall We Dance?* (1937), in a successful partnership with Ginger Rogers. After his partnership with Rogers ended he continued to appear in films such as *Easter Parade* (1948) with Judy Garland.

Astarte The Greek name for Ashtoreth, the Phoenician goddess of the Moon, fertility, and sexual love. In the Bible her worship is linked to that of the Canaanite Baal. The cult of Astarte, in various forms, was widespread in the eastern Mediterranean world. In Egypt she was identified with Isis, in Greece with Aphrodite, and in Babylonia with Ishtar.

astatine (symbol At, at. no. 85, r.a.m. 210) The heaviest member of the HALOGENS. All its isotopes are strongly radioactive; the most stable is astatine-210 with a HALF-LIFE of eight hours. The element is made by bombarding bismuth with alpha particles; its chemistry is similar to that of IODINE.

asteroid A minor planet with a near-circular orbit close to the plane of the ECLIPTIC that lies between the orbits of Mars and Jupiter. Asteroids are numbered in approximate order of the date of discovery and the establishment of an orbit accurate enough for them to be rediscovered. In 1796 the French astronomer Joseph Jerome le Français de Lalande had instigated a search for the 'missing' planet between Mars and Jupiter, this planet being predicted by BODE'S LAW. The Italian astronomer Giuseppe Piazzi found CERES on New Year's Day 1801. The German scientist Karl Gauss calculated the orbit. Soon four more asteroids were discovered: PALLAS in 1802, JUNO in 1804, VESTA in 1807, and Astraea in 1845. A hundred asteroids had been found by 1868, 200 by 1879, and now the list contains around 3,500. Ceres, Pallas, and Vesta have radii of 512, 304, and 290 km, respectively; the rest are smaller. It is estimated that there are about 100

million asteroids in the main belt and the total mass is 1.1×10^{22} kg, about 15 per cent the mass of the Moon. The present-day asteroids are fragments of what was a much larger group of Moon-sized minor planets.

asthma The difficulty experienced in breathing due to excessive contraction of the involuntary muscle in the walls of bronchial tubes leading into the lungs, with consequent narrowing of the tubes. The muscle reacts excessively to a wide range of stimuli such as infections, exertion, and, most importantly, allergens, the substances that cause ALLERGIES. If the attack is prolonged it is complicated by plugging of the small airways by abnormal secretion, and it is this that can make asthma a threat to life. Asthma commonly starts in childhood, and about half those affected improve or recover around puberty. The condition can be alleviated by drug treatment.

Asti (Latin **Asta Pompaeia**, **Asta Colonia**) The capital of Asti province in the Piedmont region of north-west Italy, at the junction of the Borbore and Tanaro rivers; pop. (1990) 74,500. It has several medieval monuments and is noted for its sparkling wine.

Aston, Francis William (1877–1945) British physicist. Aston worked in Cambridge with J. J. THOMSON, inventing the mass spectrograph. With this he eventually discovered many naturally occurring isotopes of non-radioactive elements, announcing in 1919 the whole-number rule governing their masses. He was awarded the Nobel Prize for chemistry in 1922.

Astor, John Jacob (1763–1848) US fur trader and financier. He entered the American fur trade and by 1800 had established the beginnings of a commercial empire, with chartered ships plying both the Atlantic and the Pacific. His American Fur Company, formed in 1808, dominated the fur trade in the prairies and mountains within a decade. In 1834 he sold his interest in the fur trade and spent his remaining years managing his highly profitable property holdings.

Astor, Nancy Witcher Langhorne, Viscountess (1879–1964) US-born British Conservative politician. She became the first woman to sit in the House of Commons when she succeeded her husband as MP for Plymouth in 1919. She supported causes about which she had deep convictions, such as temperance and women's rights, rather than following the party line.

Astrakhan A market city and port in southern Russia at the head of the River Volga delta near the Caspian Sea; pop. (1993) 507,700. It was capital of a Tatar khanate before being taken by Ivan IV for Russia in the 16th century. The Astrakhan fur which comes from further east in Turkistan takes its name from the city. Its industries include fishing, shipbuilding, cotton, and the processing of lambskins.

astrolabe An instrument usually consisting of a disc and pointer, formerly used to make astronomical measurements, especially of the altitudes of celestial bodies, and as an aid in navigation. Its form and structure varied with the progress of astronomy and the purpose for which it was intended. In its earliest form (which dates from classical times) it consisted of a disc with the degrees of the circle marked round its edge, and a pivoted pointer along which a heavenly body could be sighted. From late medieval times it was used by mariners for calculating latitude, until replaced by the SEXTANT.

astrology A pseudo-science that attempts to make predictions about worldly events and people's lives through interpreting the supposed influences of the position and motion of celestial bodies, principally the Sun, Moon, and planets. Developed in Mesopotamia in the 2nd millennium BC, it interpreted astronomical and meteorological phenomena as astral omens, the phenomena being indications of the gods' intentions for kings and kingdoms. In time the nature of astrology changed and in Hellenistic times the horoscope was devised, which gives the fortune of an individual from the positions of celestial bodies at the moment of birth. Astrology reached Christian Europe via the Arabs. Different systems flourished in China, India, and elsewhere. The ancient division of the ECLIPTIC into the twelve signs of the ZODIAC, first designated *c.*2,000 years ago, is basic to astrology and it is claimed that the configurations of Sun, Moon, and planets within those signs are crucial in forecasting influences and trends occurring at any moment in the individual's life.

Although astrology is now discredited, it still enjoys a lingering popularity.

astrometry The high-precision measurement of the positions of stars and other celestial bodies on the CELESTIAL SPHERE. The fundamental instrument of optical astrometry is the meridian circle, which is a telescope that is free to move only in the MERIDIAN, or north-south plane. The elevation of the telescope above the horizon as a star passes through the meridian can be related to the star's declination, and the time of passage is linked to the star's right ascension. In addition, astrometric measurements in limited areas of the sky are made with more conventional telescopes, especially long-focal-length refractors, such as the one at the YERKES OBSERVATORY. In recent times the use of photography has largely replaced the meridian circle in astrometry. High-quality positional information is also produced by certain radio telescopes.

astronautics The science of manned space flight, in contrast to aeronautics. Pioneers of astronautics include Robert H. Goddard (1882–1945), a US physicist; Robert Esnault-Pelterie (1881–1957), a French engineer; and Constantin Tsiolkovsky (1857–1935), a Russian schoolteacher. Goddard and Esnault-Pelterie were experimenters and theoreticians while Tsiolkovsky published a dozen influential theoretical works on astronautics. Rapid progress in rocketry took place during and after World War II when rocket and space flight enthusiasts such as the German Wernher von Braun developed powerful intercontinental ballistic missiles, enabling artificial satellites to be orbited. Sputnik 1, the first artificial Earth satellite, was launched by the Soviet Union on 4 October 1957. A month later, Sputnik 2, with the dog Laika on board, was put into orbit. The first human to orbit the Earth was Yuri Gagarin, of the Soviet Air Force; he was launched on 12 April 1961. John H. Glenn, launched on 20 February 1962, was the first American to orbit the Earth. Many men and women have now been placed in orbit for long periods of time. The successful US APOLLO PROGRAMME took astronauts to the Moon. In the last thirty years, progress in astronautics has continued, culminating in the establishment in Earth orbit of prototype space stations such as the US Skylab and the Soviet MIR, in which crews of scientists can remain for months at a time carrying out a wide range of scientific, technological, and biological experiments.

Astronomer Royal Originally, the chief astronomer in the UK. The post of Astronomer

Royal has been filled by eminent astronomers since 1675 when FLAMSTEED was appointed first Astronomer Royal by King Charles II. Before 1971, the post of director of the ROYAL GREENWICH OBSERVATORY was also held by the Astronomer Royal but since that year they have been separate appointments. All Astronomers Royal from Airy onwards have been knighted. The post is currently held by Sir Martin Rees. A special post of Astronomer Royal for Scotland has existed since 1834, being held by the director of the Royal Observatory, Edinburgh.

astronomical clock A highly accurate clock keeping either sidereal TIME or GREENWICH MEAN TIME (Universal Time). The former is based on the time between passages across the observer's MERIDIAN of the vernal EQUINOX (First Point of Aries); the latter is essentially based on the time between passages of the mean Sun across the observer's meridian. Both are therefore related to the rotation of the Earth. Nowadays the Earth is seen to be an irregular timekeeper and atomic clocks are used.

astronomical units The distances between the Sun and planets can be calculated as multiples of the distance between the Sun and Earth, the **astronomical unit** (a.u.), and was first done by KEPLER in the 17th century, but the a.u. was not accurately measured until 1930–31, following a worldwide concerted effort to measure the PARALLAX of EROS. Its currently accepted value is 149,600,000 km.

The distances of stars are usually given in PARSECS. The LIGHT-YEAR, the distance that light travels in one year (95×10^{12} km, about 1/3 parsec), is used in most popular articles about astronomy but is rarely used by astronomers. In RADIO ASTRONOMY the amount of power received at the Earth's surface from a radio source is measured in Janskys, where one Jansky is 10^{-26} W m^{-2} Hz^{-1}.

astronomy The study and understanding of the Universe beyond the Earth. As early as the 3rd millennium BC, Prehistoric astronomy recognized the connection between the yearly cycle of the positions of the rising and setting of the Sun and the cycle of the seasons; in Egyptian astronomy the coincidence of the time of the heliacal rising of the bright star Sirius and the annual inundation of the Nile Valley, with its life-giving waters, was observed. The Chinese people had astrological schools as early as 2000 BC which contributed to the development of Chinese astronomy. The astronomer-priests of the Sumero–Akkadian civilizations of the Middle East spent many centuries recording the movements of the Sun, Moon, and planets against the rotating stellar background, attaching astrological significance to their patterns and to the occurrence from time to time of eclipses of the Sun and Moon. Many of the hundreds of clay tablets recovered from the ruins of Nineveh and other once powerful Babylonian cities are astronomical EPHEMERIDES of the Sun, Moon, and planets strongly reminiscent of the astronomical almanacs published today.

In GREEK ASTRONOMY a much clearer understanding of the nature of the Universe arose during the flowering of Greek genius in the 1st millennium BC. ARISTARCHUS of Samos taught a heliocentric theory of the Solar System with the planets, including the Earth, orbiting the Sun. Philolaus also believed that the Earth moved through space. ERATOSTHENES in *c.*250 BC measured the circumference of the Earth. HIPPARCHUS, probably the most outstanding of Greek astronomers, discovered the precession of the equinoxes, measured the Sun's distance, and provided theories of the motion of the Sun and Moon. Ptolemy, in his great work, the ALMAGEST, published *c.*140 AD, collected the whole corpus of Greek astronomical knowledge. This work survived the Dark Ages of Europe and influenced astronomical thought right up to the 17th century. During these Dark Ages, Islamic astronomy flourished, with Ptolemy's *Almagest* being held in high esteem. The influence of Muslim astronomers on astronomical thought was profound. The awakening of Europe from its sleep of ignorance brought a new revolution in astronomy. Tycho BRAHE's highly accurate observations of the planetary positions, coupled with COPERNICUS's heliocentric theory of the Solar System, provided KEPLER with the data and perspective necessary to formulate his three laws of planetary motion. The invention of the telescope and its use by GALILEO to observe the heavens provided crucial discoveries regarding the enormous scale of the Universe, as well as the nature of planets. The final step was taken by NEWTON. The application of his law of universal gravitation and his three laws of motion to the dynamics of the Moon and the planets integrated the works of Copernicus, Kepler, and Galileo. During the next two centuries there flowed two main streams of development in astronomy. The first was the exploration of wider and wider regions of the Universe by means of the bigger and better telescopes built in that era. The second was the successful application of Newtonian dynamics to the motions of the planets and their satellites, to comets and asteroids, and to the increasing number of binary systems of stars discovered. Everything obeyed Newton's law of gravitation, its culminating triumph being the discovery of a new planet by ADAMS and LE VERRIER from their mathematical investigations of the orbit of Uranus.

The last half of the 19th century saw three further torrents of discovery with the application of the camera and spectroscope to astronomy and the measurement of the distances of an increasing number of stars. Spectroscopic analysis of celestial objects such as the Sun, stars, and nebulae revealed their composition and the conditions within them, and the measurement of stellar distances confirmed the immense scale of the Universe. Developments in atomic physics in the 20th century enabled the US physicist Hans Bethe and the German physicist Carl Friedrich von Weizsäcker to produce a breakthrough in astronomers' understanding of the major problems of the source of stellar energy, the ages of stars and star clusters, their creation and evolution, and the observed relationships between stellar luminosities, sizes, and masses. The development of radar and rockets during and after World War II provided two new major branches of astronomy: radio astronomy and space research. Radio astronomy's discovery that celestial objects such as supernovae and galaxies give out radiation in the radio region of the electromagnetic spectrum is matched in its importance by the discovery of hitherto unsuspected objects such as pulsars and quasars. The greater penetrating power of the most powerful radio telescopes and their high resolution produced by interferometric arrays has been found to be of relevance in distinguishing between cosmological models such as the BIG BANG and the Steady State theories. The ability of the rocket to place packages of scientific instruments in orbit above the atmosphere surrounding our planet has opened the whole of the electromagnetic spectrum to man's scrutiny. Thus gamma-ray, X-ray, ultravio-

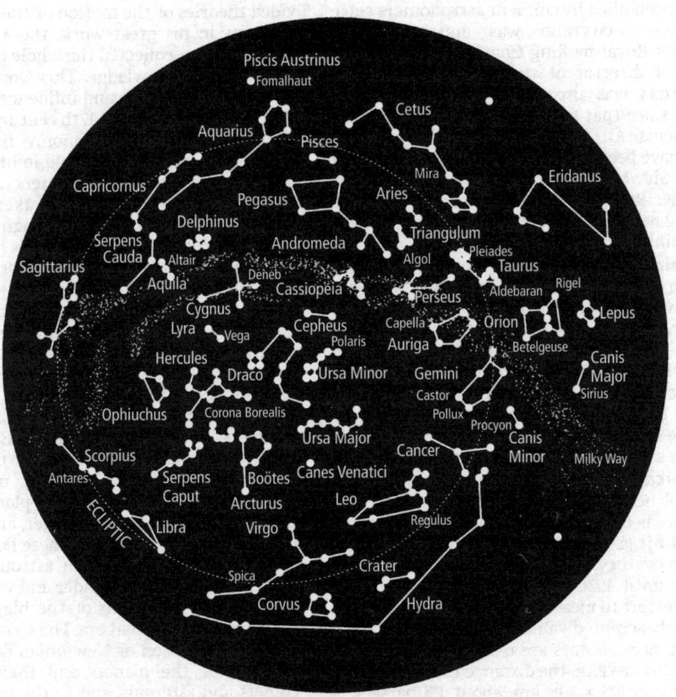

1

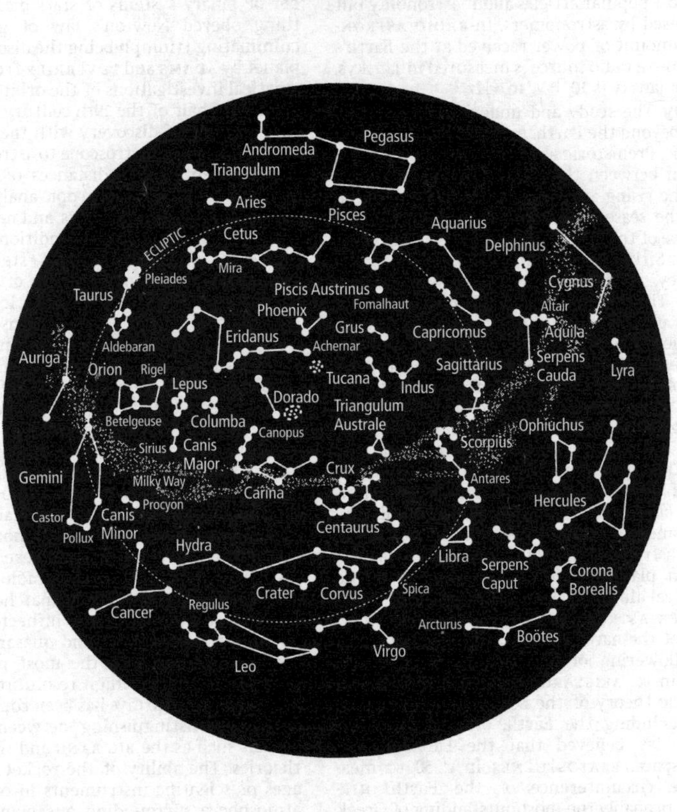

2

Astronomy (1)The Northern sky at night. (2) The Southern sky.

let, infrared, and millimetre astronomy has been born and the exciting discovery has been made that there exist in space many objects radiating in these regions. Exotic objects such as black holes are being looked for; these are thought to be regions of matter so dense that not even light itself is fast enough to achieve escape velocity in their gravitational fields. Packages of instruments have also been sent to fly past, orbit, or land upon the planets, in particular Mars, where the search for extraterrestrial life goes on.

astrophysics The study of the physical nature of astronomical objects, especially stars. Astrophysics has developed mainly in the 20th century and complements the traditional domains of astronomy such as ASTROMETRY, stellar dynamics and kinematics, and CELESTIAL MECHANICS. Observational astrophysics interprets the electromagnetic radiation emitted by celestial objects. Theoretical astrophysics is concerned with understanding these observations in terms of mathematical models. These models are constructed from the known laws of physics, and may occasionally result in the discovery of new laws under extreme astrophysical conditions. Physics is applied to astronomy in areas such as the understanding of the spectra of stellar atmospheres; the nuclear energy processes which fuel the stars; and the structure of PULSARS and NEUTRON STARS.

Asturias An autonomous region and former principality of north-west Spain, co-extensive with the province of Oviedo; area 10,565 sq km (4,080 sq miles); pop. (1991) 1,093,940; capital, Oviedo. Prince of Asturias is the title of the eldest son of the king of Spain. Coal, zince, fluorspar, and iron are mined in the region.

Asturias, Miguel Ángel (1899–1974) Guatemalan novelist and poet. He is best known for his experimental novel *The President* (1946), which deals with the disintegration of human relationships under a repressive dictatorship. Later novels, such as *Mulata* (1963), draw more extensively on his knowledge of Mayan myth and history. He was awarded the Nobel Prize for literature in 1967.

Asunción The capital and chief port of Paraguay, on the River Paraguay near its junction with the Pilcomayo; pop. (1992) 637,740. Founded in 1538 by the Spanish, it was the first permanent European settlement in the La Plata region of South America. It is Paraguay's only large city and has textile and agricultural processing industries, especially meat packing.

Aswan A city in southern Egypt on the right bank of the Nile, 16 km (10 miles) north of Lake Nasser; pop. (1991) 215,000. It is situated close to two dams across the Nile. The first was built in 1898–1902 to regulate the flooding of the Nile and control the supply of water for irrigation and other purposes. It is now superseded by the high dam, built in 1960–70 with Soviet aid, about 3.6 km (2.25 miles) long and 111 m (364 ft) high. The controlled release of water from Lake Nasser behind it produces the greater part of Egypt's electricity. Aswan has long been a winter resort and commercial centre. It has steel and textile industries.

Asyut (ancient Greek **Lycopolis**) A commercial city on the west bank of the Nile, 380 km (240 miles) south of Cairo; pop. (1991) 313,000. It is the largest city in Upper Egypt. Carpets, camels, cotton, and grain are its chief trading commodities. The Asyut Barrage was built across the Nile in the late 19th century in order to regulate the flow of water into the Ibrahimya Canal and provide irrigation water.

Atacama Desert The most arid region of South America, extending for a distance of some 965 km (600 miles) southwards into Chile from the Peruvian border. Nitrate, iodine, and borax are extracted from salt basins.

Atahualpa (died 1533) The last ruler of the INCA empire, son of Huayna Capac. Ruling from 1525 in QUITO, he defeated Huáscar, his half-brother and co-ruler in CUZCO, whom he killed after the battle of Huancavelica in 1530. In 1532 he marched against PIZARRO and remnants of the Huáscar faction, who had allied themselves to the Spaniards; at Cajamarca he was drawn into an ambush, captured, and held for ransom. He ordered a room to be filled with gold and silver objects while another army secretly marched to free him, but was murdered when Pizarro learned of it. Shortly thereafter Pizarro captured Cuzco and within a few years Spain ruled the lands of the Incas.

Atalanta In Greek mythology, a huntress who was a remarkably swift runner. She declared that she would marry only a man who could overtake her in a race; suitors who tried and failed were killed. Finally she was outstripped by Hippomenes, who was helped by Aphrodite: she had given him three golden apples, which he dropped during the race, and Atalanta paused to pick them up while Hippomenes raced past her.

Atatürk, Kemal (or **Kemal Pasha**; born Mustafa Kemal) (1881–1938) Turkish general and statesman, President 1923–38. Leader of the postwar Turkish Nationalist Party, he was elected President of a provisional government in 1920. With the official establishment of the Turkish republic in 1923, he was elected its first President, taking the name of Atatürk (Turkish for 'father of the Turks') in 1934. During his presidency he introduced many political and social reforms, including the abolition of the caliphate, the adoption of the Roman alphabet for writing Turkish, and other policies designed to make Turkey a modern secular state.

Aten, the (or **Aton**) The supreme god and creative principle of Ancient Egypt worshipped during the reign of the heretic king Amenhotep, who changed his name to AKHENATEN (*c.*1353–1335 BC). He is symbolized in the Sun's disc, depicted with rays ending in hands which offer the ankh-sign of life to the king. Formerly an aspect of Re, during the Amarna Period (Akhenaten's reign) the Aten was worshipped to the exclusion of all other gods, whose temples were closed. As his son, Akhenaten was the sole intercessor between the Aten and mankind. He built a new city for himself and the god, naming it Akhetaten. After his death, Tutankhamen brought the court back to Thebes, and Aten-worship ceased.

Atget, Eugene (1856–1927) French architectural photographer. Atget became a photographer at the age of 41, taking pictures of Parisian life and architecture as reference material for painters. Discovered by Berenice Abbott, his pictures came to be recognized as far more than mere documents.

Athabasca, Lake Canada's fourth longest lake, straddling the Alberta–Saskatchewan boundary on the Canadian Shield in a thin crescent some 320 km (200 miles) long. In the south-west it receives the Peace and Athabasca Rivers, discharging northward by the Slave River into the Great Slave Lake, which connects it with the Mackenzie River system. Because of ice, it is navigable only in summer.

Athanasius, St (*c.*296–373) Greek theologian. As bishop of Alexandria he was a consistent upholder

of Christian orthodoxy, especially against Arianism. He aided the ascetic movement in Egypt and introduced knowledge of monasticism to the West. Feast day, 2 May.

atheism (from Greek *a theos*, 'not god') The denial of the existence of any GOD or supernatural being. It should not be confused with AGNOSTICISM, which holds that as the existence of god cannot be proved or disproved, it should not be subject to belief or disbelief. The atheist maintains, on the other hand, that the very notion of god is meaningless, a view also subscribed to by some Asian religious traditions such as THERAVADA Buddhism. In the 19th century MARX based his atheism on MATERIALISM, and argued for the abolition of religion, which he saw as upholding an unjust socio-economic order. Communist theory, developed from Marxism, is strictly atheist. NIETZSCHE proclaimed the 'death of god' and encouraged man to seek for the meaning of life in himself alone, a position also taken by 20th-century Existentialists such as HEIDEGGER and SARTRE. The modern philosophical school of LOGICAL POSITIVISM is also atheist, arguing that religious speculation is logically ill-founded, since knowledge can only be derived from observation and experience.

Athelstan (895–939) King of England 925–39. Effectively the first king of all England, Athelstan came to the thrones of Wessex and Mercia in 924 before becoming king of all England a year later. He successfully invaded both Scotland and Wales and inflicted a heavy defeat on an invading Danish army.

Athena (or **Athene**) The ancient Greek goddess of wisdom and of the arts and crafts. Represented as a woman of severe beauty, in armour, she was the daughter of Zeus, springing from his forehead, which Hephaestus (or Prometheus) had opened with an axe. Like Apollo, she exerted a benevolent, civilizing influence (she was a patron of war, but in its just rather than its savage aspects). Her most famous temple is the Parthenon, built on the Acropolis at Athens (447–432 BC) by Pericles to honour her as the city's patron goddess.

Athenian democracy A form of popular government established in Athens by Cleisthenes in the last decade of the 6th century BC. The principal organ of democracy was the popular assembly (*ekklesia*), which was open to all Athenian male citizens aged over 18. All members had the right to speak, and it was the assembly that decided all legislative and policy matters. The council of 500 (*boule*), elected by lot for a year from Athenian male citizens over the age of 30, was an executive body which prepared business for the assembly and then saw that its decisions were carried out. Pericles dominated the democracy until his death in 429, but none of the 'demagogues' who followed him achieved the same level of influence.

Athenian empire The cities and islands mainly in the Aegean area that paid tribute to Athens in the 5th century BC. It developed out of the DELIAN LEAGUE as Athens, by virtue of its great naval superiority, imposed its will on its allies. A significant step was the transference of the League's treasury from Delos to Athens probably in 454 BC, since this ensured for Athens absolute control of the tribute. Inscriptions and literary sources reveal the means by which Athens controlled its subjects: the installation of garrisons; the establishment of clenruchies (colonies) of Athenian citizens in important or rebellious areas; the encouragement of local democracies; the referral of important judicial cases to Athens; the imposition of Athian weights and measures throughout the empire; and officials to keep an eye on subject cities.

As long as it had a strong navy, Athens could crush revolts and enforce its will throughout the Aegean, but the empire died with Athens' final defeat in the PELOPONNESIAN WAR. Nevertheless it did establish the Second Athenian Confederacy in 377 BC, trying to avoid the mistakes of the 5th century.

Athens (Greek **Athínai**) The capital city of Greece, lying 6 km (nearly 4 miles) from its port Piraeus; pop. (1991) 784,110. It was a flourishing city-state from early times in ancient Greece, and by the mid-5th century BC was established as leader of a league of Greek states from whom it exacted tribute. Under Pericles it became a cultural centre, and many of its best-known buildings (e.g. the Parthenon and Erechtheum) date from the extensive rebuilding that he commissioned. Athens recovered only slowly from defeat in the PELOPONNESIAN WAR (404 BC). In 146 BC it became subject to Rome, but in the early Roman Empire it enjoyed imperial favour and was still the cultural centre of the Greek world. Gothic invaders captured and sacked Athens in 267 AD, and its importance declined as power and wealth were transferred to Constantinople. After its capture by the Turks in 1456 it declined to the status of a village until chosen as the capital of a newly independent Greece in 1834 after the successful revolt against Turkish rule. Today the traffic of its noisy busy streets creates pollution problems for humans and ancient monuments alike. It is the main commercial and communications centre of Greece. Greater Athens (pop. 3,096,775), which includes the port of PIRAEUS, has industries ranging from steel, shipbuilding, and chemicals to the manufacture of consumer goods of all kinds. Tourism is a major earner of foreign currency.

athletics The sports of running, jumping, and throwing, also known as track and field events. Many are modelled on the OLYMPIC GAMES of the ancient Greeks, though the development of modern athletics did not begin until about 1850. Athletics meetings are held in summer in a field or stadium, with an oval 400 m (438 yards) running-track laid out in six or more lanes around the perimeter. Within the oval are the various approach runways, pits, and enclosures for the non-track events. In winter, indoor meetings take place on banked tracks with a shorter circuit of, usually, 200 m (219 yards); sprint events are shortened to 50–60 m (55–66 yards), and there are no long-throwing events. At a full outdoor athletics meeting, there may be events for track: sprinting, hurdles, middle- and long-distance running, steeplechase, relays; field: high jump, long jump, triple jump, pole vault, shotput, and throwing events – hammer, discus, javelin; mixed events: decathlon (men) and heptathlon (women); road events: marathon and race walking, which begin and end in the stadium. The women's programme, once fairly restricted, is now almost as broad as the men's, and only the decathlon, hammer, and steeplechase are excluded.

Athos, Mount (Greek **Pangaíon Oros**) A mountainous peninsula projecting into the Aegean Sea from the coast of Macedonia, an autonomous district of Greece since 1927; area 336 sq km (130 sq miles); pop. (1991) 1,557. It is inhabited by monks of the Eastern Orthodox Church in twenty monasteries; the earliest monastic settlement dates from 962. A curious rule of the monks forbids women,

or even female animals, to set foot on the peninsula.

Atkinson, Sir Harry (Albert) (1831–92) New Zealand statesman, Prime Minister 1876–77, 1883–84, and 1887–91. Born in Britain, he emigrated to New Zealand in 1853 and became a member of the House of Representatives in 1861, also serving as a commander in the Maori Wars in the early 1860s. During his first term as Prime Minister he passed a bill abolishing the colony's provincial governments. He later served as colonial treasurer (1879–82; 1882–83) and is chiefly remembered for the austere economic policy that he pursued throughout the 1880s to boost New Zealand's recovery from economic depression.

Atlanta The capital and largest city of the state of Georgia, USA; pop. (1990) 394,000. Founded at the end of a railroad line in 1837, the city was originally called Terminus; in 1843 it was incorporated as Marthasville, and in 1845 its name was finally changed to Atlanta. Vehicles, aircraft parts, and soft drinks (it is the headquarters of the Coca-Cola company) are produced. The city was the venue of the 1996 summer Olympics.

Atlantic, Battle of the The name given to a succession of sea-operations in World War II.

Atlantic Charter A joint declaration of principles to guide a post-World War II peace settlement. It resulted from a meeting at sea between CHURCHILL and F. D. ROOSEVELT on 14 August 1941. It stipulated freely chosen governments, free trade, freedom of the seas, and disarmament of current aggressor states, and it condemned territorial changes made against the wishes of local populations. A renunciation of territorial ambitions on the part of Britain and the USA was also prominent. In the following month other states fighting the AXIS POWERS, including the USSR, declared their support for these principles. The Atlantic Charter provided the ideological base for the UNITED NATIONS.

Atlantic City A beach-resort town on the Atlantic coast of south-east New Jersey, USA, on a sand bar at Absecon Beach; pop. (1990) 37,986. It is known for its conventions, gambling casinos, and its 60-foot-wide boardwalk which extends along 8 km (5 miles) of beaches. The board game Monopoly was originally based on Atlantic City and the Miss America pageant has been held here annually since 1921.

Atlantic Ocean (or **the Atlantic**) The ocean lying between Europe and Africa to the east and North and South America to the west. The Atlantic is divided by the equator into the North Atlantic and South Atlantic oceans; area 82.4 million sq km (31.5 million sq miles). It has an average depth of 3 km (2 miles), falling to 9,220 m (30,249 ft) in the Milwaukee Depth in the Puerto Rico Trench. A submarine ridge known as the Mid-Atlantic Ridge runs down the centre from north to south. On either side lie deep basins which include the North American, Guyana, Brazil, and Argentina basins to the west and the North-east Atlantic, Canary, Cape Verde, Guinea, Angola, and Cape basins to the east.

Atlantis A legendary island said to have been submerged following an earthquake nearly 12,000 years ago.

Atlas (in Greek mythology) A giant, one of the Titans who revolted against Zeus. As a punishment for this he was condemned to support the heavens on his shoulders. Perseus turned him to stone with the Gorgon's head and he thus became the ATLAS MOUNTAINS in northwest Africa.

Atlas (in astronomy) A small shepherding satellite of Saturn. Atlas is approximately spherical with a mean diameter of 30 km, moving in a circular orbit of radius 137,670 km from Saturn in a period of orbital revolution of 0.602 days.

atlas moth A member of a genus of silk moths (see SILKWORM) found only in east and south-east Asia. The atlas moth, *Attacus atlas*, and Edwards' atlas moth, *A. edwardsi*, are among the largest moths in the world, with wing-spans of up to 30 cm (12 inches). They have hooked wing-tips and bold brown and cream markings, and in some countries are protected by law. Their caterpillars, which feed on the leaves of a wide range of trees and which may reach 10 cm (4 inches) in length, are green and brown with large tubercules on each segment.

Atlas Mountains A range of mountains in North Africa extending from Morocco to Tunisia in a series of folded mountain chains which include the Anti-Atlas, High Atlas, Middle Atlas, Rif Mountains, Tell Atlas, and Sahara Atlas. The highest peak in the Atlas Mountains and in North Africa is Djebel Toubkal which rises to 4,166 m (13,664 ft) in the High Atlas south of Marrakech.

atman (from Sanskrit *ātman*, 'essence') The Hindu concept that describes the pure, immortal, spiritual essence or soul of human beings and animals. The *jwatman* is the inner self or personality of a human being, the essence of all his or her past experiences. It is this *jwatman* that undergoes REINCARNATION, or rebirth, through the processes of SAMSARA, into a new body after physical death, and which continues to manifest itself in human form according to its conduct in each life. In philosophical discourse, it is represented as the self, the source of awareness and the subject of 'I'-thoughts (*ahampratyaya*), which is distinguished from the objects of awareness.

atmosphere The envelope of air surrounding the Earth. In its lowest layer (the troposphere, bounded by the tropopause) it comprises oxygen (21%), nitrogen (78%), carbon dioxide, water vapour, and other gases. It is in this layer that most weather phenomena are generated. The upper layers of the atmosphere include the stratosphere, immediately above the tropopause; the ionosphere, which enables radio waves to be reflected back to the Earth's surface over long distances; a hot layer known as the thermosphere; and an ozone layer that shields the Earth's surface from lethal doses of ultraviolet radiation.

atoll A ring-shaped coral reef that appears above the surface of the water enclosing a lagoon. The word is derived from the Maldivian 'atolu' or atoll, of which there are 26 in the Maldives. The central Pacific island of Kwajalein in the Marshall Islands is the world's largest atoll.

atom The smallest particle that can be differentiated in chemical tests. Atoms of hydrogen are the simplest and lightest, and atoms of uranium are the heaviest to occur naturally. All atoms consist of a central core called the NUCLEUS, which possesses a certain number of units of positive charge, and is surrounded by a cloud of ELECTRONS, each of which has unit negative charge. Their total negative charge is exactly equal to the positive charge on the nucleus; hence the atom as a whole is electrically neutral. The nucleus is composed of two types of particle which have almost the same mass. These are protons, each of which carries one unit of positive charge, and neutrons, which are uncharged. The electrons are very light, each having a mass only about 1/1,836 of that of the proton;

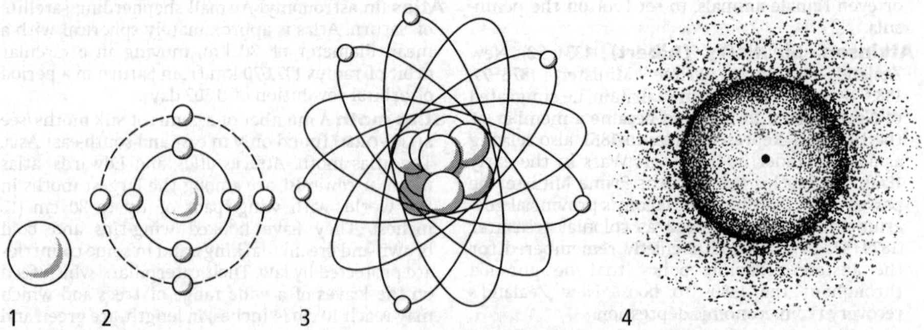

1 2 3 4

Atoms (1) In the 19th century atoms were thought of as miniature billiard balls. (2) In the first 15 years of the 20th century they were visualized as a central nucleus with orbiting electrons in fixed circular orbits. (3) In 1916 Sommerfeld's quantum theory refinements led to a model with spinning electrons in elliptical precessing orbits. (4) By 1926 wave mechanics had reduced the electron orbits to a much vaguer haze of probabilities that an electron would occur in a particular position.

and so nearly all the mass of an atom is concentrated in the nucleus. The arrangement of the electrons is described by Niels BOHR's atomic theory and by QUANTUM MECHANICS. Atoms of the various elements are characterized by the charge on the nucleus, (the ATOMIC NUMBER). The number of neutrons associated with the protons in the nucleus can vary, and therefore a range of atomic masses (ISOTOPES) is possible for a single element. This gives the element a characteristic RELATIVE ATOMIC MASS (r.a.m.). Chemical reactions occur through interaction and redistribution of electrons in the outer layer (shell) of the atom. Electricity and magnetism are also properties of the electrons of an atom. Atoms can react by losing electrons to form positively charged IONS, by gaining electrons to form negatively charged ions, or by sharing electrons to form covalent molecules. NUCLEAR ENERGY is derived from the splitting (FISSION) or FUSION of atomic nuclei. See also PERIODIC TABLE.

atomic bomb See NUCLEAR WEAPON.

atomic energy See FISSION, NUCLEAR; FUSION, NUCLEAR.

atomic number The number of protons in the NUCLEUS of a particular element, being therefore equal to the positive charge on the nucleus. It is the basis for the classification of elements in the PERIODIC TABLE.

atomic pile The world's first NUCLEAR REACTOR, built under a squash court at Chicago University in 1942 by FERMI. Rods of URANIUM fuel were interspersed in a 'pile' of graphite blocks: the graphite acted as a moderator (see FISSION, NUCLEAR), slowing down neutrons to speeds at which they were effective in splitting further uranium atoms. Rods of cadmium were used to control the reactor. The pile was activated only long enough to achieve a self-sustaining CHAIN REACTION: it was then shut down. The atomic pile demonstrated that controlled nuclear fission was feasible, and it provided the basis for early nuclear reactor designs.

atomic weight See RELATIVE ATOMIC MASS.

atomism The philosophical view that complex items and phenomena are to be understood as composed of some few types of basic, simple constituents, and that the intrinsic features and manner of combination of these simple constituents explain the properties and behaviour of all complexes formed from them. Atomism may be a metaphysical view of all reality, as when it was first proposed by the Greek philosopher Democritus (*c.*460–370 BC), or a stance towards some particular subject area, such as HUME's psychological atomism of 'impressions' and 'ideas'. Atomism contrasts with **holism**, according to which the properties of constituents are regarded as abstractions from the complex phenomena in which they figure.

atonality The absence of a readily identifiable musical KEY, music in which all twelve notes of the chromatic SCALE are used without reference to a tonal centre. The first truly atonal works were written by Schoenberg, in about 1908–09. Other early atonal composers were his pupils Webern and Berg. The search for a structural justification for atonality, to replace that developed over the centuries for tonal music, led to SCHOENBERG's proposal of the twelve-note serial technique in about 1920–21. See also TONALITY.

atonement In Christianity, reconciliation between God and humanity, achieved through the life and death of JESUS CHRIST. This concept is rooted in Jewish thought, where atonement was closely linked with animal sacrifice and later with righteous living and martyrdom (see YOM KIPPUR). There is no formal doctrine of the atonement within Christianity, and interpretations have varied throughout Christian history. The idea of Christ's death as a sacrifice, delivering mankind from SIN, is found in the New Testament and has remained a predominant theme in both Roman Catholic and Reformation Churches. Another understanding of the atonement based on scripture stresses the triumph of Christ's life and death over the forces of evil, or, in some contemporary interpretations, the overcoming of ALIENATION. Other interpretations focus on the exemplary nature of Christ's life and death, or on the powers of God's love revealed in him to transform believers.

ATP (adenosine triphosphate) A compound found in all living CELLS, important for its role as an energy carrier. The formation of ATP from ADP or AMP (adenosine di- or monophosphate) is an endergonic (energy-requiring) reaction: ATP is a major product of RESPIRATION and FERMENTATION, the biological processes that release energy from food molecules. The breakdown of ATP to ADP and inorganic phosphate is exergonic (energy-releasing). The energy of this breakdown is used to provide the chemical energy for other processes – for example, to drive endergonic reactions such as the synthesis of proteins and other complex molecules; to do mechanical work (movement), as in muscle fibres; to provide heat (maintenance of body temperature); or to produce light (the glow of fireflies). Thus ATP serves as a form of energy 'currency' within the cell.

Attenborough, Sir David (Frederick) (1926–) British naturalist and broadcaster. In 1952 he joined the BBC, where he developed the concept of filming animals in their natural habitats for the series *Zoo Quest* (1954–64). He became a household name with his documentary film series *Life on Earth* (1979), *The Living Planet* (1983), and *The Trials of Life* (1990). He is the brother of Richard Attenborough.

Attenborough, Richard (Samuel), Baron Attenborough of Richmond-upon-Thames (1923–) British film actor, producer, and director. From 1942 onwards he appeared in a number of war films and comedies, and extended his repertoire into character roles such as that of Pinkie in *Brighton Rock* (1947). The films he has directed include *Oh! What a Lovely War* (1969), *Gandhi* (1982, for which he won an Oscar), *Cry Freedom* (1987), and *Shadowlands* (1993). He is the brother of David Attenborough.

Attica (Greek **Attikí**) A triangular promontory, constituting the easternmost part of central Greece which, with the Saronic Gulf islands, forms a department of Greece; area 3,381 sq km (1,306 sq miles); pop. (1991) 426,000 (excluding Athens).

Attila (406–53) King of the Huns 434–53. From his base in Hungary he ravaged vast areas between the Rhine and the Caspian Sea between 445 and 450, inflicting great devastation on the Eastern Roman Empire. Attila then invaded the Western Empire but was defeated by the joint forces of the Roman army and the Visigoths at Châlons in 451. He and his army were the terror of Europe during his lifetime, and he earned the nickname 'Scourge of God'.

Attila Line (or **Sahin Line**) The frontier line dividing Greek from Turkish Cyprus following the Turkish invasion of 1974. The invasion, which was likened to the action of Attila the Hun, put into effect Turkey's scheme for the partition of Cyprus (the Attila Plan). It stretches from Morphou Bay in the west to Famagusta in the east.

Attlee, Clement Richard, 1st Earl Attlee (1883–1967) British Labour statesman, Prime Minister 1945–51. He became Labour Party leader in 1935, and deputy Prime Minister in 1942 in Churchill's coalition government. Following his party's landslide election victory in 1945, Attlee became the first Labour Prime Minister to command an absolute majority in the House of Commons. His term saw the creation of the modern welfare state and a wide programme of nationalization of major industries (including coal, gas, and electricity). Foreign policy initiatives included a progressive withdrawal from colonies and support for NATO.

Atwood, Margaret (Eleanor) (1939–) Canadian novelist, poet, critic, and short-story writer. She made her name with the novel *The Edible Woman* (1969), which was championed by the resurgent women's movement of the time. Her novels explore the question of women finding and asserting their identities, and include *The Handmaid's Tale* (1986), her dystopian vision of a patriarchal state, *Cat's Eye* (1989), and *Alias Grace* (1996).

Aube ▶**1** A department in the Champagne-Ardenne region of north-east France; area 6,004 sq km (2,319 sq miles); pop. (1990) 289,200; capital, Troyes. It is the centre of the Champagne wine-producing area. ▶**2** A river of north-east France that rises in the Langres plateau, Haute-Marne department, and flows 248 km (154 miles) northwestwards to meet the River Seine near Romilly-sur-Seine.

aubergine (or **egg plant**) *Solanum melongena*, a relative of the tomato and potato that originated in tropical Asia. The aubergine is a herbaceous, branched perennial plant with an edible fruit cultivated widely in India (where it is known as brinjal), the West Indies, USA, and Mediterranean countries. It is a somewhat spiny plant with large leaves, and it bears large, smooth, egg- or sausage-shaped fruits which are up to 15 cm (6 inches) in length. These fruits vary in colour from the more common deep purple to green, red, or white.

aubretia (or **aubrieta**) A trailing evergreen plant of the genus *Aubretia*, named in honour of Claude Aubriet, a French flower-painter. About 15 species are known; they are mostly alpine and are distributed from Italy to Asia Minor. They are close relatives of the wallflower and other species of the mustard family. *Aubrieta deltoidea* is the parent of many garden varieties, mostly with purple, lilac, or pink flowers.

Aubrey, John (1626–97) English antiquarian and author. He was a pioneer of field archaeology, most of his researches being centred on the earthworks and monuments in Wiltshire (particularly Avebury and Stonehenge), and became one of the first Fellows of the Royal Society in 1663. As an author, he is chiefly remembered for the lively and anecdotal collection of biographies of eminent persons, such as John Milton and Francis Bacon, known as *Brief Lives*, a bowdlerized edition of which was first published in 1813.

Auch (Latin **Elimberrum, Augusta Auscorum**) The capital of the department of Gers in Gascony, south-west France, on the River Gers; pop. (1990) 24,730. It was capital of Gascony in the 17th century and Armagnac during the 10th century.

Auchinleck, Sir Claude John Eyre (1884–1981) British field-marshal. He served with distinction in World War I. He commanded the land forces at Narvik in the ineffectual Norwegian campaign in April–May 1940, was commander-in-chief in India (1940–41) and from mid-1941 he commanded in North Africa. He led the advance in Libya, but was driven back by stronger German forces in 1942. When TOBRUK surrendered, he took personal command of the troops, establishing the key defensive line at El ALAMEIN. Churchill then replaced him with MONTGOMERY and he returned to India as commander-in-chief.

Auckland ▶**1** A local government region at the northern end of North Island, New Zealand created in 1989 and comprising the cities of Auckland, North Shore, Waitakere, and Manukau, and districts of Rodney, Papakura, and part of Franklin; pop. (1991) 953,980. ▶**2** The largest city and chief seaport of New Zealand, at the northern end of North Island; pop. (1991) 315,670. The port, which was established in 1840 on land purchased from the Maoris, handles 60 per cent of the country's trade. Its industries include engineering, vehicle assembly, metals, textiles, chemicals, and food processing. Founded by Captain William Hobson, Lieutenant-Governor of New Zealand, it was named after the 1st Earl of Auckland who, as First Lord of the Admiralty, had given Hobson the command of the ship that brought him to New Zealand in 1837. The first immigrants from Scotland arrived in 1842 and in 1854 the first parliament of New Zealand was opened in Auckland. The capital was transferred to a more central location at Wellington in 1865.

auction A sale (normally public) in which articles or livestock are sold to the highest bidder. A reserve price may be set by the seller, below which the article will not be sold. Works of art, antiques, houses, commodities, and foreign currencies may be sold by auction.

Auden, W(ystan) H(ugh) (1907–73) British-born poet. *Look, Stranger!* (1936) is the collection of poems that secured his position as a leading left-wing poet. He supported the Republicans in the Spanish Civil War, and wrote *Spain* (1937). Auden also collaborated with Christopher Isherwood on several Brechtian verse dramas, notably *The Ascent of F6* (1936). After emigrating to the USA in 1939, he became a US citizen and continued to publish volumes of poetry, including *The Age of Anxiety* (1947), which was awarded the Pulitzer Prize. He also worked on several opera libretti, such as Stravinsky's *The Rake's Progress* (1951).

Audenarde The French name for OUDENARDE.

audiometer A device used to measure acuteness of hearing. The most common type, the pure tone audiometer, comprises an adjustable-frequency OSCILLATOR, an amplifier, and a precision volume control. Signals from the audiometer are played through headphones to subjects being tested, who indicate the lowest sound intensity that they can detect at a range of frequencies. The results are then compared with established standards of normal hearing.

audit An examination of the financial records of an organization by an independent body, usually a firm of chartered accountants. Public and private limited companies are required by law to publish annual accounts which have been audited by independent qualified auditors. Increasingly, large companies make use of computerized financial records, which can help to simplify the auditing process.

Audubon, John James (1785–1851) US naturalist and artist. He is chiefly remembered for his great illustrated work *The Birds of America* (1827–38), which was compiled during his travels through America. He portrayed even the largest birds life-size, and painted them not in conventionally formal postures but in dramatic and sometimes violent action. The National Audubon Society is a North American organization for the study and protection of birds, founded in 1886.

Auer, Carl, Baron von Welsbach (1858–1929) Austrian chemist. Working at Heidelberg under Bunsen, he discovered in 1885 that the so-called element didymium was actually a mixture of two rare-earth elements, neodymium and praseodymium. In the same year Auer patented the incandescent gas mantle for which he is remembered today. He also discovered the cerium–iron alloy that is used for flints in cigarette and gas lighters.

Augean Stables In Greek mythology, the stables of Augeas, king of Elis, which housed an immense herd of cattle and had not been cleaned for thirty years. As one of his Twelve Labours, Hercules had to cleanse them in a day, which he accomplished by diverting a river through them.

augite One of the chief members of the PYROXENE group of minerals. Essentially it is a calcium magnesium iron aluminosilicate. Its physical properties vary but crystals are usually hard, dense, and opaque. Black or greenish black in colour, it is a common mineral of igneous and metamorphic rocks.

Augsburg A city in south Bavaria, Germany, at the junction of the Lech and Wertach rivers; pop. (1991) 259,880. In 15 BC the Emperor Augustus founded a Roman colony known as Augusta Vindelicorum. During the Middle Ages Augsburg was a prosperous centre of commerce on the trade route to Italy and in the Reformation the Augsburg Confession was a statement of the Lutheran position approved by Luther before being presented to Charles V at Augsburg on 25 June 1535. The Peace of Augsburg in 1555 allowed princes of the Holy Roman Empire to impose a religion on their subjects. Augsburg was the birth-place of the artist Hans Holbein (1497–1543), the engineer Rudolf Diesel (1858–1913), Willy Messerschmitt (1898–1978), and Bertolt Brecht (1898–1956). The city's cathedral dates from the 9th century and has the world's oldest stained glass. Augsburg has an old-established textile industry now superseded by engineering.

Augusta ▶**1** A resort town in east Georgia, USA, at the head of navigation on the Savannah River; pop. (1990) 44,640. A former tobacco town and river trading post, Augusta was named by James Oglethorpe in 1735 after the mother of George III. It now produces fertilizers, cotton goods, and kaolin bricks and tiles. Nearby is the Fort Gordon military base and training school. The annual Masters golf tournament is played at Augusta. ▶**2** The state capital of Maine, USA, on the Kennebec River; pop. (1990) 21,325. It was founded as a trading post in 1628 by settlers from Plymouth. Manufactures include textiles, steel, and processed food.

Augustan Age (English and French) The early and mid-18th century, when such writers as POPE, ADDISON, SWIFT, and STEELE admired and imitated their Roman counterparts who flourished under the Emperor Augustus (27 BC–14 AD). This period was notable for the perfection of the HEROIC COUPLET, a preference for wit and elegance, and for intellectual rather than emotional satisfaction. The tradition survived in Britain throughout the greater part of the 18th century, notably in the writings of JOHNSON, SHERIDAN, and GOLDSMITH, who wrote in the weekly periodical the *Bee* an 'Account of the Augustan Age in England' (1759). In French literature the term is applied to the period of CORNEILLE, RACINE, and MOLIÈRE.

Augustine, St (known as **St Augustine of Hippo**) (354–430) Doctor of the Church. Born in North Africa of a pagan father and a Christian mother, he underwent a series of spiritual crises in his early life, described in his *Confessions*. While in Milan he was influenced by the bishop, Ambrose, adopting his Neoplatonic understanding of Christianity and being baptized by him in 386. Augustine henceforth lived a monastic life, becoming bishop of Hippo in North Africa in 396. His episcopate was marked by his continual opposition to the heresies of the Pelagians, Donatists, and Manichees. Of his extensive writings, perhaps his best-known work is the *City of God*. His theology has dominated all later Western theology, with its psychological insight, its sense of man's utter dependence on grace (expressed in his doctrine of predestination), and its conception of the Church and the sacraments. Feast day, 28 August.

Augustine of Canterbury, St (died *c*.605) The first Archbishop of Canterbury. He was chosen (596) by Pope GREGORY the Great to convert the English to Christianity. With forty monks Augustine came first to Kent (597) and converted King Ethelbert, whose wife was already a Christian. Consecrated archbishop (597), Augustine organized the church into twelve dioceses (598) but failed at a meeting with the Celtic bishops in 603 to resolve

the differences between the Roman and Celtic churches, although these differences were resolved at the Synod of WHITBY (664). Augustine's work was instrumental in the re-establishment of Christianity in England.

Augustus (known until 27 BC as **Octavian**) (63 BC–14 AD) The first Roman emperor. Originally called Gaius Octavianus, he took the name Gaius Julius Caesar Octavianus when he was adopted by the will of his great-uncle Julius Caesar in 44 BC. He established his position as one of the triumvirate of 43 BC, gaining supreme power by his defeat of Antony in 31 BC. A constitutional settlement in 27 BC in theory restored the republic but in practice regularized his sovereignty; in the same year he was given the title Augustus (Latin for 'venerable'). His rule was marked abroad by a series of expansionist military campaigns and at home by moral and religious reforms intended to restore earlier Roman values disrupted during previous civil wars.

Augustus II (known as **Augustus the Strong**) (1670–1733) King of Poland 1696–1733. He was Elector of Saxony from 1694 and succeeded JOHN III (John Sobieski) as King of Poland in 1696. He joined Russia and Denmark against CHARLES XII of Sweden without Polish support but was defeated. Charles had him banished and Stanislaus Leszczynski elected king in his place. Augustus recovered his position after Charles's defeat at Poltava (1709) and for the rest of his reign brought some economic prosperity to Saxony and Poland, although renewed war with Sweden lasted until 1718. A ruler of considerable extravagance, supposed to be the most dissolute monarch in Europe, he was a patron of the arts and gave special support to the Dresden and Meissen china factories.

auk A member of a family, Alcidae, of some 23 species of mainly black and white Northern Hemisphere seabirds with distinctive whirring flight. The family includes razor-bills, little auks, great auks (now extinct), guillemots, auklets, murres, and puffins. Auks nest in colonies, mainly on high cliffs and steep-sided islands. Some make burrows. They dive and swim powerfully under water using their webbed feet and short wings, and feed on fish, molluscs, and crustaceans. Most species lay one or two eggs. In some species the young birds leave the nests before they can fly, and swim to their feeding grounds.

Aung San (1914–47) Burmese nationalist leader. A leader of the radicals from his student days, during World War II he accepted Japanese assistance and secret military training for his supporters. Returning to Burma in 1942 he became leader of the Japanese-sponsored Burma National Army, which defected to the Allies in the closing weeks of the war in the Pacific. As leader of the postwar Council of Ministers, in January 1947 he negotiated a promise of full self-government from the British; in July of that year he and six of his colleagues were assassinated by political rivals during a meeting of the Council.

Aung San Suu Kyi (1945–) Burmese political leader. Daughter of Aung San, she became the co-founder and leader of the National League for Democracy (NLD), the country's main opposition party, in 1988. Although she was placed under house arrest in 1989 and not allowed to stand as a candidate, the NLD won 80 per cent of the seats in the democratic elections of 1990; the ruling military government refused to recognize the NLD's victory. A supporter of political reform through non-violent public protest and democratic processes, she was awarded the Nobel Peace Prize in 1991. She was released from house arrest in 1995.

Aurangzeb (1618–1707) Mogul emperor of Hindustan 1658–1707. Having usurped the throne from his father, Aurangzeb assumed the title Alamgir (Conqueror of the World). His expansionist policies increased the Mogul empire to its widest extent, and it experienced a period of great wealth and splendour, but constant rebellions and wars greatly weakened the empire and it declined sharply after his death.

Aurelian (full name Lucius Domitius Aurelianus) (*c.*215–75) Roman emperor 270–75. Originally a common soldier, he rose through the ranks and was elected emperor by the army. By a series of military campaigns, including the defeat of Queen Zenobia at Palmyra (272), he successfully quelled rebellions and repelled barbarian invaders; he also built new walls round Rome, and established the state worship of the Sun. He was assassinated by his own army officers.

Aurelius, Marcus (full name Caesar Marcus Aurelius Antoninus Augustus) (121–80) Roman emperor 161–80. The adopted successor of Antoninus Pius, he was occupied for much of his reign with wars against Germanic tribes invading the empire from the north. He was by nature a philosophical contemplative; his *Meditations* are a collection of aphorisms and reflections based on a Stoic outlook and written down for his own guidance.

Auric, Georges (1899–1983) French composer. While studying music in Paris, he met Erik Satie and Jean Cocteau, under whose influence he and five other composers formed the anti-romantic group Les Six. His works include operas, ballets (notably Diaghilev's *Les Matelots*, 1925), orchestral works, and songs, but he is probably best known for film music such as the scores for *The Lavender Hill Mob* (1951) and *Moulin Rouge* (1952).

auricula See PRIMROSE.

Auriga The Charioteer, a CONSTELLATION of the northern sky, one of the 48 constellations known to the Greeks. It is usually said to represent Erichthonius, a legendary king of Athens who was a champion charioteer, but sometimes it is identified as Myrtilus, charioteer of King Oenomaus of Elis. The brightest star in Auriga is CAPELLA, representing a goat carried by the charioteer. Its two kids are represented by the stars Eta and Zeta Aurigae. Epsilon Aurigae is a supergiant star that is eclipsed every twenty-seven years by a dark companion; this companion is now thought to be a close binary surrounded by a disc of dust. The last eclipse was in 1983. Auriga contains three star CLUSTERS visible through binoculars: M36, M37, and M38.

Aurignacian See CRO-MAGNON.

aurochs (pl. **aurochs** or **aurochsen**) A now extinct type of wild ox, *Bos primigenius*, which was the ancestor of domestic cattle. It first appeared about 230,000 years ago and became extinct in the Bronze Age, 3,600–1,000 years ago. It occurred across much of Europe and western Asia. Its decline was probably due to persecution by humans. A number of Stone Age cave paintings depict this animal, showing its importance to early people.

aurora A luminous phenomenon caused by solar radiation interacting with the upper atmosphere, seen as streamers of light in the sky above the northern (aurora borealis) or southern (aurora australis) magnetic pole.

Auschwitz (Polish **Oswieecim**) A town near Cra-

cow in southern Poland that was the site of one of the largest Nazi concentration camps of World War II.

Ausgleich (1867; German, 'compromise') A constitutional compromise between Hungary and the AUSTRIAN EMPIRE following the defeat of Austria in Italy and Germany. It was drawn up by Francis Deák, and ratified by the Austrian emperor FRANCIS JOSEPH, granting Hungary its own parliament and constitution but retaining Francis Joseph as King of Hungary. A dual monarchy, AUSTRIA-HUNGARY, was created, in which the Magyars were permitted to dominate their subject peoples, and the Austrians the remaining seventeen provinces of the empire.

Austen, Jane (1775–1817) British novelist. The youngest of seven children of a Hampshire rector, she was greatly stimulated by her extended and affectionate family. Her major novels are *Sense and Sensibility* (1811), *Pride and Prejudice* (1813), *Mansfield Park* (1814), *Emma* (1815), *Northanger Abbey* (1818), and *Persuasion* (1818). They are notable for skilful characterization and penetrating social observation.

Austerlitz, Battle of (2 December 1805) A battle fought by Austria and Russia against France, near the town of Austerlitz in Moravia. Alexander I of Russia persuaded FRANCIS I of Austria to attack before reinforcements arrived. Their complicated plan to encircle the French allowed NAPOLEON to split their army and defeat each half. It was a decisive battle; the Russian army had to withdraw from Austria, and Austria signed the Treaty of Pressburg (1805), in which it recognized Napoleon as King of Italy, and ceded territories in northern Italy, the Alpine regions, and on the Adriatic coast.

Austin ▶**1** A city in south-east Minnesota, USA, on the Cedar River; pop. (1990) 21,910. Named after a pioneer settler, Austin is a trading and processing centre for livestock, grain, and vegetables from the surrounding farm land. ▶**2** The state capital of Texas, USA, on the Colorado River; pop. (1990) 465,620. The first settlement of 1839 was named after Stephen F. Austin, son of Moses Austin, leader of the first Texas colony. The University of Texas at Austin was founded in 1883. Seven hydroelectric dams across the nearby Colorado River create a series of reservoirs known as the Highland Lakes. It is the market for a major agricultural region and a convention, education, and manufacturing centre. Many electronic research firms are located here.

Austin, Herbert, 1st Baron Austin of Longbridge (1866–1941) British motor manufacturer. Having joined the Wolseley Sheep Shearing Machine Company in 1893, Austin persuaded the company to embark on the manufacture of cars. He produced vehicles with them until 1905, when he opened his own works near Birmingham. The output of the factory steadily increased, especially following the launch of the Austin Seven (known as 'the Baby Austin') in 1921; 300,000 models of this car were produced before 1939.

Austin, John (1790–1859) British jurist. Regarded as the founder of analytical jurisprudence, he was greatly influenced by the utilitarianism of his friend Jeremy Bentham, as can be seen from his work *The Province of Jurisprudence Determined* (1832). An important influence on the English legal system, Austin is significant for his strict delimitation of the sphere of law and its distinction from that of morality, as well as his examination of the connotations of such common legal terms and ideas as right, duty, liberty, injury, and punishment.

Austin, John Langshaw (1911–60) British philosopher. A lecturer and later professor of moral philosophy at Oxford University (1952–60), he was a careful and witty exponent of the linguistic school of philosophy, seeking to elucidate philosophical problems by analysis of the words in which they are expressed. Two of his courses of lectures were published posthumously in 1962: *Sense and Sensibilia* discusses perception, while *How to Do Things with Words* distinguishes 'performative' utterances (in which something is done, such as promising or making marriage vows) from utterances that convey information.

Australasia The region that comprises Australia, New Zealand, New Guinea, and the neighbouring islands of the Pacific.

Australia An island country and continent in the Southern Hemisphere in the south-west Pacific Ocean. Surrounding it are numerous islands, the largest being Tasmania, and off its east coast lies the GREAT BARRIER REEF.

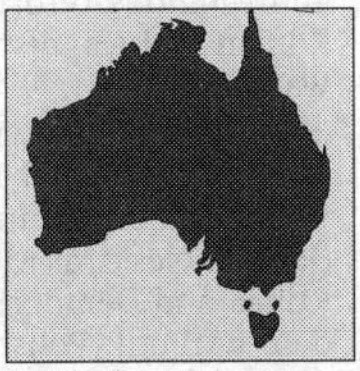

Physical. Much of the continent has a hot, dry climate, and a large part of the central area is desert or semi-desert; the most fertile areas are on the eastern coastal plains and in the south-west corner of Western Australia. The south-western coastal areas are undulating, their hills supporting forests of hardwood trees. They rise to a low plateau of ancient rocks, and this gives way in turn to the Great Sandy and Gibson Deserts. In the centre of the continent are the MacDonnell ranges, beyond which the land falls away to the Simpson Desert and Lake Eyre before gradually rising again to the Sturt Desert. The Murray–Darling basin is the country's largest water catchment area; its water supply for irrigation was greatly increased with the diversion of the Snowy River (1974) from its natural south-eastward course into the Murray River. Eastwards, the land rises to the GREAT DIVIDING RANGE and then falls sharply to the sea. Moderate rain brought by depressions from the Southern Ocean is sufficient to support dense, evergreen forests and the cultivation of fruit and vegetables.

Economy. Australia's economy is based on mining, agriculture, and industry. Agricultural land, which is periodically devastated by drought, accounts for 64 per cent of Australia's territory, almost all of this devoted to cattle and sheep. Australia is the world's leading wool producer and largest beef exporter, as well as being an important wheat producer. Paramount in mineral production, Australia is the world's leading exporter of iron ore and aluminium, and highly important in producing coal, nickel, zinc, and other metals. Australia's energy resources, which include high quality black coal, oil, natural gas, and uranium, constitute 18 per cent of global reserves. Domestic crude oil meets 70 per cent of domestic needs and is also exported. Manufacturing industry is aimed principally at domestic markets, and is comparatively undeveloped and vulnerable to competition from Asian neighbours. Japan and the USA are Australia's main trading partners, to which raw materials are supplied. Although Australia's trading relationship with countries of the Pacific Rim and Asia is well established, the formation of European and American trading blocs is viewed with

concern; there is also recurrent concern over the servicing of a sizeable foreign debt.

History. Australia was first inhabited by ABORIGINES thought to have migrated from south-east Asia 50,000–40,000 years ago. Although the first known European discoveries of the continent were those made in the early 17th century, there may have been earlier Portuguese discoveries. It was visited by an Englishman, William Dampier, in 1688 and 1699. Captain James Cook claimed British possession of the eastern part of the continent in 1770, naming it New South Wales. The British penal colony of New South Wales was founded in 1788. Immigration of free settlers from 1820 onwards aided the colony's development, as did exploration, which opened pastures for the wool industry. Squatter settlement of much of eastern Australia led to conflict with the Aborigines, resulting in events such as the Myall Creek Massacre (1838). Van Diemen's Land (from 1855 Tasmania), settled in 1803, became a separate colony in 1825. Moreton Bay, founded as a penal settlement in 1824, became the colony of Queensland in 1859. The colony of Western Australia was founded in 1829. The Port Phillip District, settled illegally in 1834, became the colony of Victoria in 1851. South Australia, founded as a province in 1834, became a crown colony in 1842. All of the colonies except Western Australia were granted responsible government during the 1850s. The GOLD RUSHES of the 1850s and 1860s brought many changes. The White Australia Policy can be traced back to that period. Demands for land to be opened for selectors increased. Western Australia, granted responsible government in 1890, developed more slowly than the other colonies. In 1901 the six colonies were federated as self-governing states to form the Commonwealth of Australia in 1901. Powers were distributed between the Commonwealth and state governments, and with the crown through its representative, the governor-general, retaining (until 1931) overall responsibility for defence and foreign affairs. State legislators would have full responsibility for internal state affairs. BARTON, who had been prominent in the federation movement, was the first Prime Minister. The Northern Territory was transferred from South Australia to the Commonwealth in 1911. In the same year land was transferred to the Commonwealth from New South Wales, for the creation of the Australian Capital Territory, Canberra. (Jervis Bay was added to the Australian Capital Territory in 1915.) The Commonwealth Parliament met in Melbourne until 1927, when it was transferred to Canberra. In the 1930s reserves were established for the ABORIGINES, and in 1981 the Pitjantjara Aborigines were granted freehold titles to land in Southern Australia. Australia fought with the Allies in both WORLD WARS and with the USA in VIETNAM. After World War II ties with Britain diminished, and Australia joined the ANZUS and SEATO powers. The Labor governments of the 1970s and 1980s, led by Gough WHITLAM and Robert HAWKE, strengthened trade ties with the non-communist Far East, but a deteriorating economy in

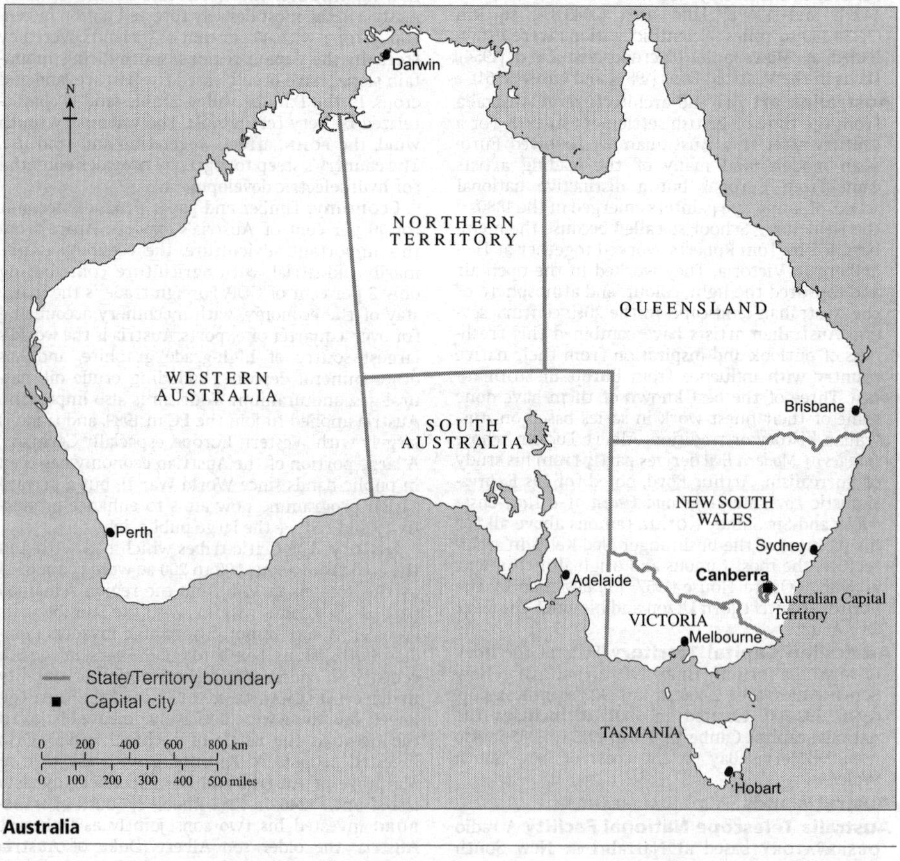

Australia

the 1980s led to labour unrest and in 1991 to the replacement of Bob Hawke (Prime Minister since 1983) by his deputy Paul Keating. In response to increasing support for Australia becoming a republic, Queen Elizabeth II in 1993 announced that she would agree to such a constitutional change if the Australian people wanted it. In 1995 Paul Keating announced that a referendum on the issue would be held by the end of 1999. However, Keating's Labor Party suffered a heavy electoral defeat by a Liberal-National Party coalition in 1996. Liberal leader John Howard was appointed Prime Minister.

Capital: Canberra
Area: 7,682,300 sq km (2,966,200 sq mi)
Population: 17,500,000 (1991)
Currency: 1 Australian dollar = 100 cents
Religions: Anglican 26.1%; Roman Catholic 26.0%; other Protestant 20.8%; Eastern Orthodox, Muslim, Jewish, and Buddhist minorities
Ethnic Groups: native-born 78.2 (of which 1.5 Aboriginal); country of origin of foreign-born: UK 7.2%; Asia and Middle East 3.9%; New Zealand 1.9%; Italy 1.6%; Africa and Americas 1.5%; Yugoslavia 1.0%; Greece 1.0%
Languages: English (official); minority and Aboriginal languages
International Organizations: UN; OECD; Colombo Plan; ANZUS Pact; South Pacific Commission; Commonwealth

Australian Alps The south-eastern and highest section of the Great Dividing Range of eastern Australia in the states of Victoria and New South Wales. It includes the highest peak in Australia, Mt. Kosciusko (2,228 m, 7,310 ft).

Australian Antarctic Territory Territory in Antarctica claimed by Australia and lying between 142°E and 136°E; land area 6,043,852 sq km (2,334,435 sq miles). Scientific stations were established at Mawson in Macrobertson Land (1954), Davis in the Vestfold Hills (1957), and Casey (1961).

Australian art Art and architecture in Australia from the time of British settlement in 1788. For a century after this, Australian art followed European models (and many of the leading artists came from Europe), but a distinctive national school of landscape painters emerged in the 1880s – the Heidelberg School, so called because the members, led by Tom Roberts, worked together at Heidelberg in Victoria. They worked in the open air and captured the light, colour, and atmosphere of the Australian landscape. In the 20th century several Australian artists have combined this freshness of outlook and inspiration from their native country with influence from European MODERNISM. Three of the best known of them have done some of their finest work in series based on Australian history or tradition: Albert Tucker, whose *Images of Modern Evil* derives partly from his study of Surrealism; Arthur Boyd, noted for his Expressionistic *Love, Marriage and Death of a Half-Caste* cycle; and Sir Sidney NOLAN, famous above all for his pictures of the bushranger Ned Kelly. In architecture, the most famous and original monument is Sydney Opera House (1957–73), designed by the Danish architect Jorn Utzon and his chief engineer Ove Arup.

Australian Capital Territory Federal territory of Australia forming (since 1911) an enclave in New South Wales; area 2,400 sq km (927 sq miles); pop. (1991) 292,700. Created in 1901, it includes the national capital, Canberra. From 1915 to 1988 it also included Jervis Bay on the coast of New South Wales.

Austral Islands See TUBUAI ISLANDS.

Australia Telescope National Facility A radio OBSERVATORY based at Narrabri in New South Wales. Officially opened in 1988 as part of the Australian bicentenary celebrations, it has the most powerful radio INTERFEROMETRY system in the Southern Hemisphere. The instrument combines the features of several different RADIO TELESCOPES. The Compact Array consists of five telescopes which can be moved along a 3 km (1.9 miles) railway track, and a sixth telescope which is fixed. The dishes are 22 m (72 feet) in diameter. Their high surface accuracy enables measurements to be made at radio wavelengths of less than 1 cm. The Long Baseline Array links the Compact Array with other radio telescopes in Australia by the satellite AUSSAT for VLBI observations.

australopithecines Early members of the human line of evolution, living between 4 and 1 million years ago. The first australopithecine fossil was discovered at Taung in southern Africa in 1924 and named *Australopithecus africanus* ('southern ape of Africa'). Since then, australopithecine fossils have been found in southern and eastern Africa but the relationships between the different forms is still far from clear. See EVOLUTION; FOSSIL HOMINID.

Austria A country in central Europe, bounded by Italy, Slovenia, and Croatia to the south, Hungary and Slovakia to the east, the Czech Republic and Germany to the north, and Liechtenstein and Switzerland to the west.

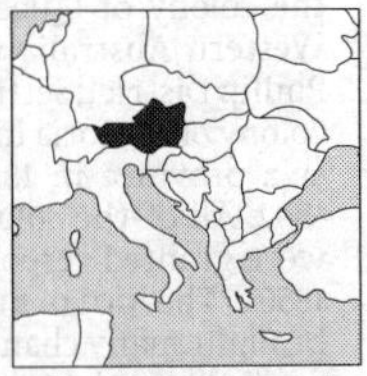

Physical. Much of Austria is mountainous, with the River Danube flowing through the north-east of the country. Austria is the most densely forested nation in central Europe, with 40 per cent of its land covered by trees. In the Alpine regions, south-facing mountain slopes have been cleared for pasture land and crops. In the Danube valley, arable land is characterized by very fertile soils. The warm, dry south wind, the FÖHN, affects vegetation and land use. The country's steep topography provides potential for hydroelectric development.

Economy. Timber and paper products account for 10 per cent of Austria's exports. Apart from this important silviculture, the economy is primarily industrial, with agriculture contributing only 3 per cent of GDP. Foreign trade is the mainstay of the economy, with machinery accounting for over a quarter of exports. Austria is the world's largest source of high-grade graphite, and has other mineral deposits, including crude oil, natural gas, and uranium. Tourism is also important. Austria applied to join the EC in 1989, and trade is largely with Western Europe, especially Germany. A large portion of the Austrian economy has been in public hands since World War II, but a privatization programme now aims to enhance productivity and reduce the large public debt.

History. The Celtic tribes which had settled in the area from about 500 to 200 BC were conquered by the Romans in 14 BC, and the region remained part of the ROMAN EMPIRE, with the Danube as its frontier. A succession of Germanic invaders (Vandals, Goths, Huns, Lombards, and Avars) in the 5th century AD ended with a short period of stability under CHARLEMAGNE. MAGYAR invaders then followed, but these were decisively defeated by OTTO the Great at the Battle of Lechfeld in 955. Otto invested Leopold of Babenberg with the title of Margrave of Austria, and the Babenberg dynasty lasted until 1246. In 1282 Rudolf I, Count of HABSBURG invested his two sons jointly as Dukes of Austria, the older son Albert (Duke of Austria 1282–1308) founding a dynasty which survived into

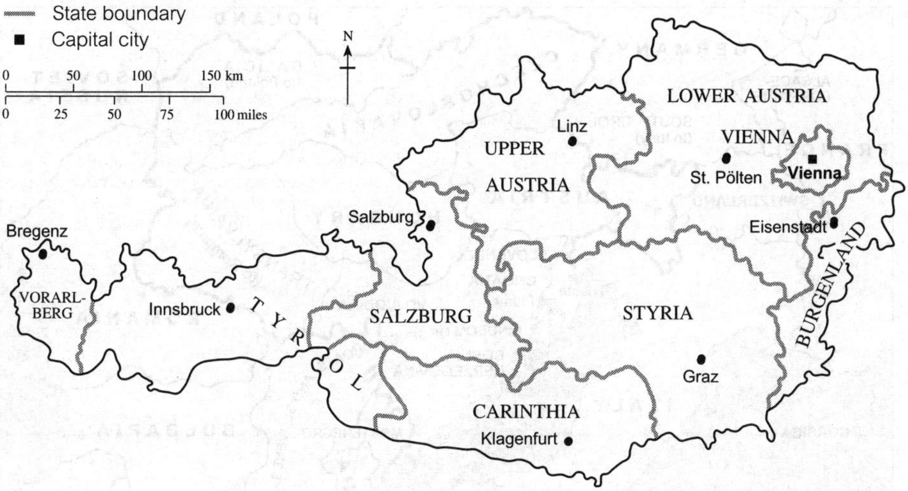

Austria

the 20th century. The first Habsburg Holy Roman Emperor was Frederick III (1452–93) and perhaps the greatest CHARLES V (1530–56). From Vienna, the Habsburgs ruled the vast empire which, before its dissolution in 1918, included Hungary, Bohemia, Moravia, Burgundy, Tuscany, Piedmont, Croatia, Bosnia-Hercegovina, Bukovina, Slovenia, parts of Serbia, of Romania, and of Spanish America, Silesia, Spain, Luxembourg, The Netherlands, Venetia, and Naples. In 1575 the court moved from Vienna to Prague, where it remained until 1621. Vienna withstood a Muslim siege in 1529 and again in 1683, when the Polish army forced the OTTOMAN retreat. The War of the AUSTRIAN SUCCESSION brought the conflict over supremacy in the German orbit to a head, and the SEVEN YEARS' WAR confirmed Prussia as a power of equal weight. The end of the 18th century saw almost continuous conflict, with Austrians fighting against the French revolutionary armies in The Netherlands, the Rhineland, and northern Italy. The unification of Germany by Prussia in 1866–71 excluded the AUSTRIAN EMPIRE from German affairs and destroyed hopes for the creation of a union of all the German-speaking peoples. Austria was forced to make concessions to the Hungarians by forming AUSTRIA-HUNGARY. Austrian diplomats, however, retained links with the new GERMAN SECOND EMPIRE, and tried to gain German support for their ambitions against Russia in the Balkans through an alliance system. During World War I the Austrian Imperial Army was virtually under German military control. Defeat and revolution destroyed the monarchy in 1918, and the first Austrian republic which followed it was only a rump of the former state. This was destabilized by the Nazis, who in 1934 murdered DOLLFUSS and staged an abortive coup. They were more successful in achieving ANSCHLUSS in 1938, when Hitler's army invaded the country without opposition. Defeated in World War II, Austria was invaded by Soviet troops, and divided into separate occupation zones, each controlled by an Allied Power. In 1955 a treaty between the Allies and Austria restored full sovereignty to the country. The treaty prohibited the possession of major offensive weapons and required Austria to pay heavy reparations to the USSR, as well as to give assurances that it would ally itself with neither East nor West Germany, nor restore the Habsburgs. It remained neutral, democratic, and increasingly prosperous under a series of socialist regimes. Extreme right-wing candidates won a number of seats in elections in 1994, but the socialists were re-elected in general elections in 1995, the year in which Austria also joined the EUROPEAN UNION.

Capital: Vienna
Area: 83,857 sq km (32,377 sq mi.)
Population: 7,700,000 (1991)
Currency: 1 Schilling = 100 Groschen
Religions: Roman Catholic 84.3%; non-religious and atheist 6.0%; Evangelical 5.6%; Muslim, Jewish, and other minorities
Ethnic Groups: Austrian 96.1%; Yugoslav 1.7%; Turkish 0.8%; German 0.5%
Languages: German (official) and other minority languages
International Organizations: UN; OECD; EU; Council of Europe; CSCE

Austria-Hungary (or **Austro-Hungarian Empire**) The 'Dual Monarchy', established by the Austrian emperor Francis Joseph after Austria's defeat by Prussia in 1866 in which Austria and Hungary became autonomous states under a common sovereign. The dualist system came under increasing pressure from the other subject nations, including Croatians, Serbs, Slovaks, Romanians, and Czechs, and failure to resolve these nationalistic aspirations was one of the causes of World War I. After their victory the Allies gave support to the emergent nations, and the Austro-Hungarian Empire was dissolved by the Versailles peace settlement (1919). See map p. 104.

Austrian empire (1806–67) Those territories and peoples from whom the Habsburg emperors in Vienna demanded allegiance. Following the dissolution of the Holy Roman Empire (1806), Emperor Francis II continued to rule as FRANCIS I (1804–35), Emperor of Austria and of the hereditary Habsburg lands of Bohemia, Hungary, Croatia and Transylvania, Galicia (once a province of Poland), and much of northern Italy (Venetia and Lombardy). He ruled by means of a large bureaucracy, a loyal army, the Roman Catholic Church, and an elaborate police force. His chief minister was Chancellor METTERNICH. Nationalist feelings were emerging, and during the reign of his successor Ferdinand I (1835–48), liberal agitation for reform developed. Vienna was becoming rapidly industrialized and in March 1848, at a time of economic depression, riots

Austria-Hungary The empire and its successor states.

in the capital led to Metternich's resignation. The emperor abolished censorship and promised a constitution. This, published in April, was not democratic enough for radical leaders, who organized a popular protest on 15 May 1848. The emperor fled to Innsbruck and later abdicated. His 18-year-old nephew FRANCIS JOSEPH succeeded. There were movements for independence among all the peoples of the empire, including the Hungarians led by KOSSUTH, the Czechs, Slovaks, Serbs, Croats, Romanians, and Italians. A Pan-Slav conference met (1848) in Prague. But the opposition to the government in Vienna was divided and the Prime Minister, Felix Schwarzenberg and Francis Joseph were able to regain control. The army crushed the reform movements in Prague and Vienna and with the help of Russia, subjugated Budapest. Alexander Bach, the new Minister of the Interior, greatly strengthened the centralized bureaucracy, and the empire regained some stability, until its defeat by France and Piedmont at MAGENTA and Solferino, which ended Austrian rule in Italy. In an effort to appease nationalist feeling the emperor proposed a new federal constitution, but it came too late and after a further defeat at Sadowa he agreed to the AUSGLEICH (Compromise) of 1867 and the creation of AUSTRIA-HUNGARY.

Austrian Succession, War of the (1740–48) A complicated European conflict in which the key issue was the right of MARIA THERESA of Austria to succeed to the lands of her father, Emperor Charles VI, and that of her husband Francis of Lorraine to the imperial title. Francis's claims (in spite of the Pragmatic Sanction) were disputed by Charles Albert, Elector of Bavaria, supported by Frederick II of Prussia and Louis XV of France. Additionally Philip V of Spain and Maria Theresa were in dispute over who should have control of Italy, and Britain was challenging France and Spain's domination of the Mediterranean (War of JENKINS'S EAR), and fighting for control of India and America (King George's War).

After the death of Charles VI in 1740 war was precipitated by Frederick II of Prussia, who seized Silesia. The war began badly for Austria: the French seized Prague, a Spanish army landed in north Italy, Charles Albert was elected Holy Roman Emperor, and Silesia was ceded by treaty to Frederick II in 1742. Britain now supported Austria by organizing the so-called Pragmatic Army (Britain, Austria, Hanover, and Hesse) and under the personal command of George II it defeated the French at DETTINGEN in 1743. Savoy joined Austria and Britain (Treaty of Worms, September 1743) and the tide of war began to turn in Austria's favour. In 1744–45 Frederick II re-entered the war, determined to retain Silesia. Meanwhile Charles Albert died and Francis was elected Holy Roman Emperor in exchange for the return of the lands of Bavaria to the Elector's heir. Frederick II won a series of victories against Austria, and the Treaty of Dresden (1745) confirmed his possession of Silesia.

The struggle between France and Britain intensified. The French supported the Jacobite invasion of Britain (the FORTY-FIVE) and in India the French captured the British town of Madras (1746). The British won major victories at sea: off Cape Finisterre, Spain and Belle-Ile, France in 1747.

By 1748 all participants were ready for peace, which was concluded at AIX-LA-CHAPELLE. The war had been a long and costly effort by Maria Theresa to keep her Habsburg inheritance intact and in this she largely succeeded. But Austria was weakened and Prussia, which held Silesia, consolidated its position as a significant European power.

Austro-Asiatic languages A group of languages spoken in south-east Asia ('austro-' means 'south') in an area stretching from north-eastern India across to Vietnam and Malaysia. The family consists of three unequal branches; Nicobarese, Munda, and Mon-Khmer. Nicobar is spoken by a very small number of people on the Nicobar Islands in the Bay of Bengal. It is closely related to Mon-Khmer, and some scholars think that it does not deserve a sub-group to itself. Munda is spoken by nearly 7 million people in north-east India. Two languages account for the vast majority of speakers: these are Mundari (1.5 million) and Santali (5 million). Mon-Khmer, the third and largest branch, contains three important languages: Mon, Khmer, and Vietnamese. Mon and Khmer are closely akin to one another, while Vietnamese has developed separately. Mon (*Taliang* in Myanmar (Burma)) is spoken by small groups in Myanmar and Thailand. Khmer is the official language of Cambodia, where it has around 8 million speakers. Vietnamese is by far the largest language in the group, with over 64 million speakers in Vietnam, Laos, and Cambodia. Some scholars have made a controversial attempt to link Austro-Asiatic with AUSTRONESIAN and TAI LANGUAGES to create a super-family called Austric.

Austro-Hungarian Empire See AUSTRIA-HUNGARY.

Austronesian languages A large group of languages spread over a huge area in the Indian and Pacific oceans. The central area in which they are spoken is Indonesia, Malaysia, and the Philippines; they extend west to Madagascar, and east to New Zealand and the Pacific islands ('Austronesian' means 'southern islands'). Despite the large distances involved the languages are all remarkably similar to each other, which makes internal subgrouping difficult. However, it is clear that the Austronesian languages spoken on Taiwan (now almost submerged by Chinese) stand outside the main group. This group, sometimes called Malayo-Polynesian, can be split into a western area and an eastern area by a dividing line which runs through the eastern tip of Papua New Guinea. Although the number of languages on each side of this line is roughly the same (estimated at 300–400 each), almost all the speakers (over 180 million) are found on the western half. The eastern, or Oceanic, languages have around 2 million speakers. They include New Zealand Maori, and languages of Polynesia (such as Samoan, Tahitian, Tongan, and Hawaiian, which is close to extinction), Melanesia, and Micronesia. The largest western language is Javanese, which has over 60 million speakers. However, Malay is the most important language in the area. Forms of Malay are official languages in Indonesia (160 million speakers), Malaysia (15 million), and Singapore (3 million). The official language of the Philippines, Filipino, is based on Tagalog, an indigenous language of the Philippines. There are around 10 million native speakers of Tagalog, and Filipino is spoken by most of the population as a second language.

Austro-Prussian War (or **Seven Weeks War**) (June–August 1866) A war fought between Prussia, allied with Italy, and Austria, allied with Bavaria and other, smaller German states. War had become inevitable after BISMARCK challenged Austria's supremacy in the German Confederation. Hostilities finally broke out when Bismarck, having gained France's neutrality and the support of Italy, proposed that the German Confederation should be abolished. Prussian troops forced the Austrians out of Schleswig-Holstein, but the Austrians defeated the Italian army at Custozza. However, the Prussian army, better trained and equipped, crushed the main Austrian army at Sadowa. Seven weeks later the Austrians signed the Treaty of Prague, by which the German Confederation was dissolved. Austria ceded Venetia to Italy, while Prussia annexed the smaller states into the new North German Confederation. Austria, excluded from its territories in the south and from political influence to the north, turned towards the east, accepting the Hungarian AUSGLEICH and forming AUSTRIA-HUNGARY.

authoritarian state A state in which political authority is exercised by a person or group who are not responsible to the people they control, and in which there is no legal and orderly method of changing governments. Such systems may be either of the Right or of the Left, and may be either military or civilian in composition. Elections may be held in such states, but are commonly organized on a one-party basis; coups of one kind or another, along with ASSASSINATIONS, are one method of bringing about political change in authoritarian states. Examples of authoritarian regimes include those of certain Latin American rulers, such as Alfredo Stroessner of Paraguay (1954–89), and Augusto Pinochet of Chile (1973–90), and the regime of Saddam Hussein in Iraq (1979–).

autism A rare infantile disorder characterized by apparent pensive self-absorption and failure to develop normal relationships, obsessive insistence on sameness which leads to distress if the physical environment or routine is disrupted, and language abnormalities such as monotonous repetition of what others say. There are disagreements about diagnosis, and estimates of incidence vary from four per 10,000 to one per 25,000. About 75 per cent show some mental retardation, but high abilities in arithmetic, memory, music, and sometimes art are quite common. Prognosis is relative to degree of retardation and language ability. The cause is unknown.

autofocus A mechanism on a camera for automatically moving the lens-film distance in order to focus an image on the film. This can be achieved by measuring the distance to the photographic subject. A pulse of infrared rays or ULTRASOUND emitted by the camera bounces off the subject and returns to a detector in the camera. The time delay between sending and receiving the pulse is a measure of the distance between camera and subject. An electric motor moves the lens to the correct focal position on the basis of this measurement. Another type of autofocus adjusts the lens for maximum image contrast, which is achieved when the image is sharply focused.

autogyro (US **autogiro**) An AEROPLANE propelled by a conventionally mounted engine and propeller, which obtains most of its lift from an unpowered rotor similar to that of a HELICOPTER. The rotor spins in the airstream generated by the aircraft's forward motion, thus providing the required lift First developed by the Spanish engineer Juan de la Cierva in 1923, the autogyro was popular during the early 1930s because of its short take-off and landing capabilities. Development ceased with the advent of the helicopter.

automatic exposure An electronic system in a CAMERA that automatically selects the correct

APERTURE and SHUTTER settings to give a correct film exposure in different lighting conditions. There are three main types of automatic exposure control. In aperture priority, the photographer chooses the aperture setting and the camera selects the appropriate shutter speed. With shutter priority, the photographer selects a suitable shutter speed, and the camera automatically sets the correct aperture. In programmed selection, both aperture and shutter speed are chosen automatically according to a pre-programmed system.

automatic landing (US **autoland**) A method whereby, especially in conditions of poor visibility, an aeroplane fitted with appropriate equipment can approach an airport and receive high-precision signals from an instrument landing system. It is automatically guided down on to the runway, has its engines throttled back, and its brakes applied, all without the aid of the pilot. Now fitted to many airliners, the system was first tried experimentally in 1964, and first used commercially in 1965.

automatic pilot (or **autopilot**, **autohelmsman**) An electronic device in an AEROPLANE, spacecraft, or SHIP which automatically steers and keeps the vehicle on a pre-set course and at a pre-set speed. The steering vane used by single-handed yachtsmen is perhaps the simplest type of automatic pilot: the vane is set to the wind, and keeps the vessel on a constant course as long as the wind stays constant. Complex automatic pilots note deviations on GYROSCOPES within GYROCOMPASSES and ACCELEROMETERS and automatically stabilize a vehicle about its three axes of yaw, pitch, and roll (see FLIGHT, PRINCIPLES OF MANNED). They also restore it to the pre-set course and speed if there is any divergence, and can be programmed to alter the vehicle's direction and speed automatically. On many long-distance air journeys an automatic pilot is used to cut down crew workload. On MILITARY AIRCRAFT the device can also receive signals from sensing and weapon-aiming systems to direct the aircraft towards a target. AUTOMATIC LANDING devices for aircraft are a form of autopilot.

automatic train control A system to ensure that the instructions from trackside railway signals are not ignored by the driver. Where there are very intensive services, such as on London's underground railway, the system automatically halts the train in the event of the driver over-running a stop signal. On main-line services a more flexible train control system, such as the UK's Automatic Warning System (AWS), is needed. A magnetic device between the tracks, some 200 m (650 feet) before the signal, sounds a horn in the driver's cab if the signal shows danger. If the driver does not acknowledge the horn, the train's brakes are applied automatically. A more recent development is fully automatic train operation (ATO). This not only provides for safe operation of trains but controls their speed throughout the route and stops the train in a controlled manner at each station.

automatic transmission A replacement for the manually controlled GEARBOX on a motor vehicle, which adjusts itself automatically to conditions of speed, acceleration, and gradient. There are three main types: the earliest, a semi-automatic fluid drive, used a hydraulic coupling with epicyclic GEARS, and enabled gear changes to be made by simply pressing a pedal. Later a hydraulic torque converter was developed, for use with or without an epicyclic gearbox. The latest type is a continuously variable transmission (CVT), using a steel or rubber belt running between 'vee' pulleys of variable spacing. All automatic transmissions aim to match the power and TORQUE available from the engine to the demands of the vehicle.

automation The use of automatic machinery and systems, particularly those manufacturing or data-processing systems which require little or no human intervention in their normal operation. During the 19th century a number of machines such as looms and lathes became increasingly self-regulating. At the same time transfer-machines were developed, whereby a series of machine-tools, each doing one operation automatically, became linked in a continuous production line by pneumatic or hydraulic devices transferring components from one operation to the next. In addition to these technological advances in automation, the theory of 'scientific management', which was based on the early time-and-motion studies of Frederick Winslow Taylor in Philadelphia, USA, in the 1880s was designed by Taylor to enhance the efficiency and productivity of workers and machines. In the early 20th century, with the development of electrical devices and time-switches, more processes became automatically controlled, and a number of basic industries such as oil-refining, chemicals, and food-processing were increasingly automated. The development of computers after World War II enabled more sophisticated automation to be used in manufacturing industries, for example iron and steel.

The most familiar example of a highly automated system is perhaps an assembly plant for automobiles or other complex products. Such a plant might involve the automatic machining, welding, transfer, and assembly of parts, using equipment and techniques such as numerically controlled machine-tools, automatically controlled robot arms, and guided vehicles, automated warehousing, materials handling, stock control, and so on. Over the last few decades automation has evolved from the comparatively straightforward mechanization of tasks traditionally carried out by hand, through the introduction of complex automatic control systems, to the widespread automation of information collection and processing. Whereas in the past automation has involved a high degree of standardization and uniformity in production, the increasing use of INFORMATION TECHNOLOGY has now made it possible to develop more flexible manufacturing systems.

automatism A method of producing paintings or drawings in which the artist suppresses conscious control over the movements of the hand, allowing the subconscious mind to take over. Although the idea was anticipated by some earlier artists, automatism in its fully developed form is associated particularly with SURREALISM and ABSTRACT EXPRESSIONISM, especially ACTION PAINTING.

autonomic nervous system The part of the nervous system that controls the vegetative functions of the body such as the circulation of the blood, intestinal activity and secretion, and the production of chemical 'messengers', HORMONES, that circulate in the blood. The system is subdivided into the sympathetic and parasympathetic nervous systems. Each is controlled by areas within the central nervous system, which lie in the brain and/or spinal cord, and are linked to organs under involuntary control by NERVES. The outflow from the autonomic centres is not under direct conscious control, although it can be influenced by deliberate relaxation or meditation. The separate systems tend to have opposite effects: the parasympathetic vagus nerve acts to slow heart-rate, while the sympathetic nerves speed it up. Sympathetic nervous activity increases in response to fear, producing increases in heart-rate and blood pressure, diversion of blood flow to the muscles in readiness for action, and increasing energy production. See illustration overleaf)

autopsy See POSTMORTEM.

autotrophic organism An organism that manufactures complex organic molecules, such as carbohydrates and proteins, from simple inorganic substances, including water, carbon dioxide, and mineral salts. The most common and important autotrophs are the green PLANTS, which use the

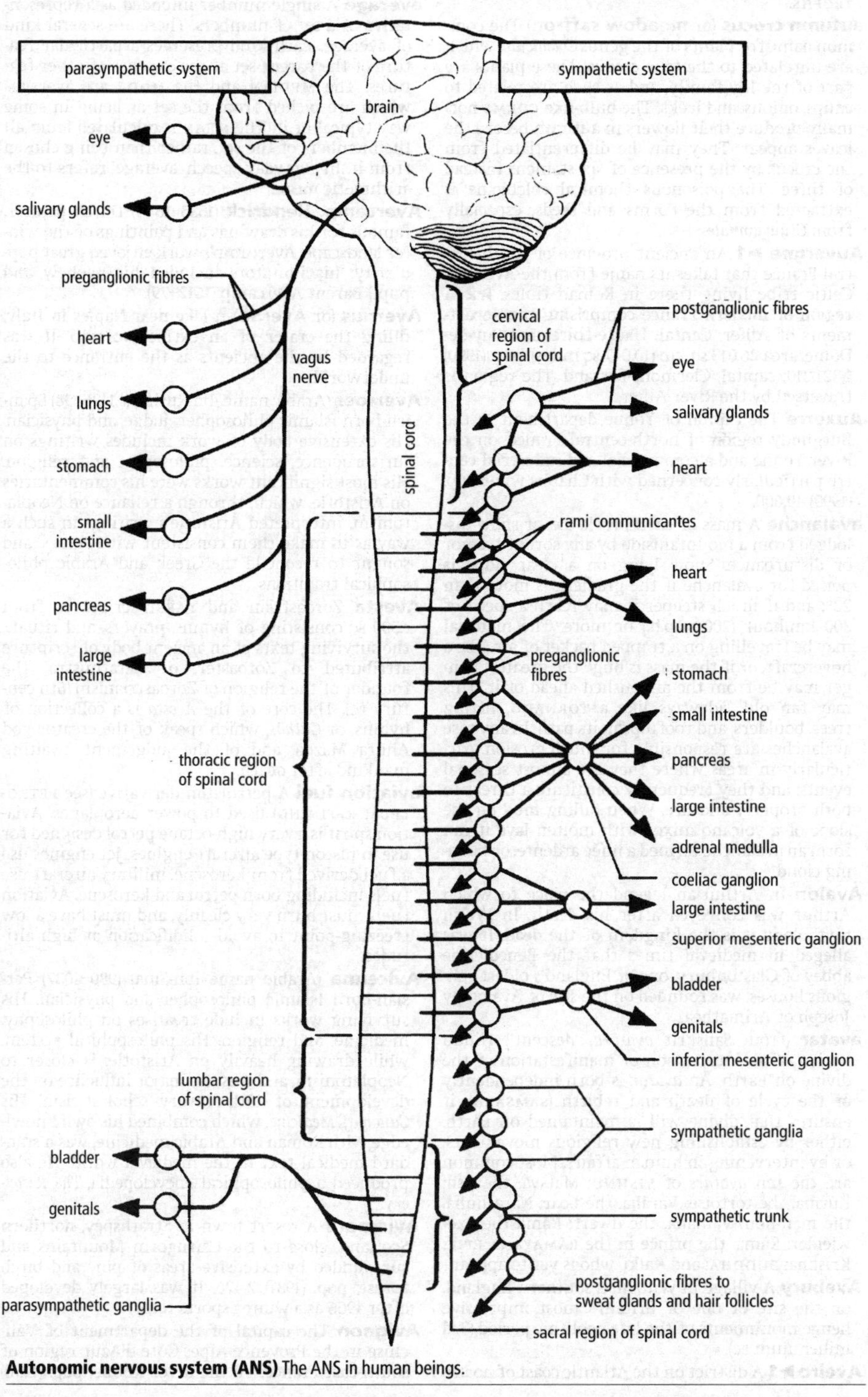

Autonomic nervous system (ANS) The ANS in human beings.

Sun's energy to fuel the manufacturing process, PHOTOSYNTHESIS. Other autotrophs, mostly bacteria, make use of energy released by various chemical reactions to convert inorganic molecules into food. This process is known as chemosynthesis. Non-autotrophic organisms are termed HETEROTROPHS.

autumn crocus (or **meadow saffron**) The common name for plants of the genus *Colchicum*, which are unrelated to the true crocus. These plants are part of the lily family, and as such are related to tulips, onions, and leeks. The bulb-like CORMS normally produce their flowers in autumn before the leaves appear. They may be differentiated from the crocus by the presence of six stamens instead of three. The poisonous chemical colchicine is extracted from the corms and seeds, especially from *C. autumnale*.

Auvergne ►**1** An ancient province of south-central France that takes its name from the Averni, a Celtic tribe living there in Roman times. ►**2** A region of modern France comprising the departments of Allier, Cantal, Haute-Loire, and Puy-de-Dôme; area 26,013 sq km (10,047 sq miles); pop. (1990) 1,321,210; capital, Clermont-Ferrand. The region is traversed by the River Allier.

Auxerre The capital of Yonne department in the Burgundy region of north-central France, on the River Yonne and a commercial and industrial centre particularly concerned with Chablis wine; pop. (1990) 40,600.

avalanche A mass of earth, rock, ice, or snow dislodged from a mountainside by any sort of tremor or disturbance. Snow lying on a clear slope is poised for avalanche if the gradient is more than 22°; and if much steeper it may reach a speed of 300 km/hour (200 m.p.h.) or more. The material may be travelling on a trapped packet of air, like a hovercraft, or if the mass is huge the greatest danger may be from the air pushed ahead of it. This may fan out sideways like a TORNADO, lifting trees, boulders, and rooftops in its path. In any case avalanches are responsible for much erosion, particularly in areas where they are almost seasonal events; and they frequently constitute a threat to both property and life. When falling mud on the slope of a volcano mixes with molten lava it can form an avalanche termed a nuée ardente, or burning cloud.

Avalon In Arthurian legend the place to which Arthur was conveyed after his death. In Welsh mythology it is the kingdom of the dead. It was alleged in medieval times that the Benedictine abbey of Glastonbury, one of England's oldest religious houses, was founded on the site of Avalon by Joseph of Arimathea.

avatar (from Sanskrit *avatāra*, 'descent') Hindu notion of an incarnation or manifestation of the divine on Earth. An *avatar* is born independently of the cycle of death and rebirth (SAMSARA); it ensures that divine will is maintained on Earth, either by establishing new religious movements, or by intervening in human affairs. Most common are the ten *avatars* of VISHNU: Matsya, the fish; Kūrma, the tortoise; Varāha, the boar; Narasimha, the man-lion; Vāmana, the dwarf; Rāma the axe-wielder; Rāma, the prince in the RAMAYANA EPIC; Krishna; BUDDHA; and Kalki, who is yet to appear.

Avebury A village in Wiltshire, southern England, on the site of one of Britain's most impressive henge monuments of the late neolithic period (3rd millennium BC).

Aveiro ►**1** A district on the Atlantic coast of north-west Portugal; area 2,708 sq km (1,046 sq miles); pop. (est. 1989) 674,400. ►**2** Its capital on the Aveiro lagoon to the south of Oporto; pop. (1991) 35,250. A former fishing port of the Newfoundland cod-bank fishers, Aveiro now has salt-pans, ceramic factories, and a seaweed fishing industry.

average A single number intended as a representative of a set of numbers. There are several kind of average. Each kind preserves a particular feature of the parent set at the expense of other features. The MEDIAN and the MODE are averages which are picked from the set as being in some way typical of it. The MEAN is calculated from all the members of the set, rather than being chosen from it. In everyday speech 'average' refers to the arithmetic mean.

Avercamp, Hendrick (1585–1634) Dutch painter, famous for his drawings and paintings of the winter landscape. Avercamp's work enjoyed great popularity; his imitators included his nephew and pupil Barent Avercamp (1612–79).

Avernus (or **Averno**) A lake near Naples in Italy, filling the crater of an extinct volcano. It was regarded by the ancients as the entrance to the underworld.

Averroës (Arabic name ibn-Rushd) (*c*.1126–98) Spanish-born Islamic philosopher, judge, and physician. His extensive body of work includes writings on jurisprudence, science, philosophy, and religion. His most significant works were his commentaries on Aristotle, which, through a reliance on Neoplatonism, interpreted Aristotle's writings in such a way as to make them consistent with Plato's, and sought to reconcile the Greek and Arabic philosophical traditions.

Avesta Zoroastrian and PARSI scriptures from *c*.500 BC consisting of hymns, prayers, and rituals, the surviving texts of an ancient body of scripture attributed to Zoroaster, or Zarathustra, the founder of the religion of Zoroastrianism (6th century BC). The core of the *Avesta* is a collection of hymns, or *Gāthās*, which speak of the creator god Ahura Mazdā, and of the judgement awaiting mankind after death.

aviation fuel A petroleum derivative (see PETROLEUM REFINING) used to power aeroplanes. Aviation spirit is a very high-octane petrol designed for use in piston-type aircraft engines. Jet engines use a fuel derived from kerosene: military aircraft use fuels including both petrol and kerosene. Aviation fuels must burn very cleanly, and must have a low freezing-point to avoid solidification at high altitudes.

Avicenna (Arabic name ibn-Sina) (980–1037) Persian-born Islamic philosopher and physician. His surviving works include treatises on philosophy, medicine, and religion. His philosophical system, while drawing heavily on Aristotle, is closer to Neoplatonism, and was the major influence on the development of 13th-century scholasticism. His *Canon of Medicine*, which combined his own knowledge with Roman and Arabic medicine, was a standard medical text in the medieval world. He also produced a philosophical encyclopedia, *The Recovery*.

Aviemore A resort town in Strathspey, northern Scotland, close to the Cairngorm Mountains and surrounded by extensive areas of pine and birch forest; pop. (1981) 2,426. It was largely developed after 1966 as a winter sports resort.

Avignon The capital of the department of Vaucluse in the Provence-Alpes-Côte d'Azur region of south-east France; on the River Rhône; pop. (1990)

89,440. From 1309 until 1377 it was the residence of the popes during their exile from Rome, and became papal property by purchase in 1348. After the papal court had returned to Rome two antipopes re-established a papal court in Avignon. The second of these was expelled in 1408, but the city remained in papal hands until the French Revolution and the Palace of the Popes still stands. Today it is a centre of commerce and tourism with varied manufactures. John Stuart Mill is buried in the city's cemetery.

Avila ▶**1** A province in the Castilla-León region of north-central Spain; area 8,048 sq km (3,108 sq miles); pop. (1991) 174,380. ▶**2** (or **Avila de los Caballeros**) Its capital, an ancient walled city of Old Castile at the foot of the Sierra de Guadarrama; pop. (1991) 49,870. It was the birth-place of St Teresa (1515–82) and Queen Isabella of Castile (1451–1504).

avionics Usually, electronics as applied to aircraft, spacecraft, or missiles, although ground-based equipment may sometimes be included. Electronic instrumentation onboard aircraft has reached a high level of sophistication. For example, after take-off a MILITARY AIRCRAFT such as a fighter plane can be flown automatically to the target area by computer control of the AUTOMATIC PILOT. RADAR systems can then search for and locate a target, guide the aircraft towards it, and fire weapons at the optimum moment, all without pilot aid. Modern navigational systems offer a high degree of accuracy, and head-up displays avoid the pilot having to glance down at critical moments by projecting vital information directly on to the aircraft windscreen. See also FLY-BY-WIRE SYSTEMS.

avocado A small to medium-sized tropical evergreen tree, *Persea americana,* belonging to the family Lauraceae, which also includes bay laurel and cinnamon. The green, pear-shaped fruit is a rich source of energy in tropical diets, as it contains protein- and fat-rich creamy flesh that is rich in vitamins A, B, and E. Cultivated for at least 9,000 years in its Central American homeland, it has only relatively recently been grown widely in tropical and subtropical areas; it is now an important cash crop in Florida, California, Hawaii, Israel, and tropical Australia and South America. The old name of 'alligator pear' refers to the thick, rough skin.

avocet A WADING BIRD of the family Recurvirostridae, with a slender, upcurved beak which it sweeps from side to side in the shallow water when feeding. The pied Palearctic avocet, *Recurvirostra avosetta,* now breeds in Britain after a century's absence. Three other species inhabit North America, the Andes, and Australia. STILTS are members of the same family.

Avogadro, Amedeo (1776–1856) Italian chemist and physicist. He is best known for his hypothesis (formulated in 1811), that equal volumes of all gases, at the same temperature and pressure, contain the same number of molecules, from which it became relatively simple to derive both molecular weights and a system of atomic weights. See also MOLE.

avoirdupois measure A system of UNITS commonly, but decreasingly, used for measuring MASS. (The pound is the most familiar example.) The term is derived from the Old French *aveir de peis* meaning 'goods of weight', though in the strict scientific sense it is mass rather than weight which the units measure. Their abbreviations and relationships are as follows: 16 drachms = 1 ounce (oz.); 16 ounces = 1 pound (lb.); 14 pounds = 1 stone; 28 pounds = 1 quarter; 112 pounds = 4 quarters = 1 hundredweight (cwt.); 2,240 pounds = 20 hundredweight = 1 ton. The units are all based on the grain. By definition, 1 pound = 7,000 grains.

Avon A former county of south-west England. Formed in 1974 from the parts of Somerset and Gloucestershire surrounding Bristol and Bath, in 1996 it was abolished and administrative powers were devolved to four unitary authorities.

Avon ▶**1** A river in central England. It flows 154 km (96 miles) south-west from Northamptonshire to the River Severn at Tewkesbury. ▶**2** A river in south-west England flowing 120 km (75 miles) east, south, and then north-west from the Gloucestershire–Wiltshire border through Bath and Bristol to the Severn. ▶**3** A river in southern England flowing 96 km (60 miles) south from Wiltshire to the English Channel at Christchurch, Dorset.

Avon, Anthony Eden, 1st Earl of See EDEN.

AWACS (Airborne Warning And Control System) A term used to describe an aeroplane carrying a large RADAR capable of detecting distant enemy aircraft, missiles, and occasionally ships. By flying the radar at altitude, its range and early-warning capability are greatly increased compared to ground-based radar. The AWACS can transmit information to a ground- or ship-based control centre, or deal with the threat itself by calling up fighter aircraft, missiles, or ships. The first aircraft designated AWACS was the Lockheed RC-121C in 1954, part of the US Early Warning and Control Squadron.

Axholme, Isle of A low-lying area of Lincolnshire in east England, to the west of the River Trent. It was drained and settled by Dutch and Flemish immigrants in the early 17th century. The evangelist brothers Charles and John Wesley were born at Epworth.

axiom (in mathematics) A basic statement on which a mathematical theory is built. Axioms are assumptions to be neither proved nor disproved, but taken as defining properties or self-evident truths.

axis of the Earth An imaginary straight line through the Earth's centre and both poles, about which it rotates. This is not at right angles to the plane of the Earth's orbit round the Sun, the ECLIPTIC, but at an angle of 66° 33′; and its direction relative to the stars is not fixed since it rotates very slowly round the perpendicular to the orbit plane, completing a revolution once every 26,000 years, and causing the PRECESSION of the equinoxes. Other minor deviations in its direction, and thus in the precise locations of the poles, are constantly being observed by astronomers all over the world, notably at the South Pole.

Axis Powers An alliance of fascist states fighting with Germany during WORLD WAR II. The term was used in an agreement (October 1936) between Hitler and Mussolini proclaiming the creation of a Rome–Berlin 'axis round which all European states can also assemble'. Japan joined the coalition on signing the ANTI-COMINTERN PACT (November 1936). A full military and political alliance between Germany and Italy (the Pact of Steel) followed in 1939. The Tripartite Pact between the three powers in 1940 cemented the alliance, and, by subsequently joining it, Hungary, Romania, and Bulgaria, as well as the Nazi-created states of Slovakia and Croatia, became members.

Axminster A town in Devon, south-west England, on the River Axe, famous in the 18th and 19th centuries for its carpets.

axolotl A well-known species of MOLE SALAMANDER, *Ambystoma mexicanum,* from Mexico, which remains a feathery-gilled larva all of its life in the natural state. The axolotl is capable of reproducing, as it becomes sexually mature in the larval state, a condition known as NEOTENY. Two types are known, a black form and a white form with pink gills. They resemble newts and feed upon aquatic invertebrates such as insect larvae, worms, and crustaceans, but they may also attack small, wounded fishes.

Axum See AKSUM.

Ayacucho A city in the Andes, capital of the department of Ayacucho in Peru; pop. (1990) 101,600. The modern city was founded by Pizarro in 1539. The last great battle in the war of independence against Spain was fought here in 1824. The Shining Path guerrilla movement first emerged in this part of Peru in 1980. The city is the commercial centre of a rich mining region; tourism is also important.

Ayala A strong warm wind that blows in the Massif Central of France.

āyātollāh (from Arabic, 'sign of God') Title given to Shi'ite, usually Iranian, religious leaders. The title has been in use since the early 20th century in Iran. It may be used for any established *mujtahid,* one who has the right to interpret the law of Islam according to changing conditions. In Sunni Islam, however, the 'gate of *ijtihād*', or legal interpretation, has been regarded as closed since the end of the 9th century.

Ayatollah Khomeini See KHOMEINI, RUHOLLAH.

Ayckbourn, Alan (1939–) British dramatist. *Relatively Speaking* (1967) was his first major success, and was followed by the domestic farce *Absurd Person Singular* (1973) and the trilogy *The Norman Conquests* (1974). A prolific and successful writer of comedies dealing with suburban and middle-class life, in his later plays he often explores darker themes and blurs the distinction between farce and tragedy. Other works include *Way Upstream* (1982) and *A Chorus of Disapproval* (1985). Most of his plays are premièred at Scarborough's Stephen Joseph Theatre in the Round, where he became artistic director in 1971.

Aydin ▶1 A province of western Turkey on the Aegean Sea; area 8,007 sq km (3,093 sq miles); pop. (1990) 824,820. Drained by the Menderes (Meander) and Akcay rivers, Aydin has a wide range of mineral deposits including iron, copper, magnesite, antimony, and emery. **▶2** Its capital, on the River Menderes, to the south-east of Izmir (Smyrna); pop. (1990) 107,000. Formerly known as Tralles, it was an important trading centre of ancient Lydia.

aye-aye A species of small PRIMATE, *Daubentonia madagascariensis,* related to LEMURS, but forming its own unique family, the Daubentoniidae. In common with lemurs, the aye-aye is found only in Madagascar. It has a body length of 40 cm (16 inches) with an additional 55 cm (22 inches) of bushy tail. It has large, forward-facing eyes, large bat-like ears, a fairly small snout, and a thick, dark brown coat. A nocturnal animal, it inhabits coastal rain forests, where it lives high in the larger branches of the trees. Unlike lemurs, the aye-aye has specialized as an insect feeder; the large upper and lower incisor teeth grow continuously throughout its life, like those of rodents, and its third finger is exceptionally thin and elongated, enabling it to dig out insect larvae from trees; it also occasionally eats fruit. It builds nests in the forks of trees and produces one offspring at each birth. Once thought to be extinct, it has recently been rediscovered and rescued by the establishment of a reserve.

Ayer, Sir A(lfred) J(ules) (1910–89) British philosopher. In Vienna in 1932, he attended the meetings of the group of philosophers, scientists, and mathematicians known as the Vienna Circle, becoming a notable proponent of logical positivism; his book *Language, Truth, and Logic* (1936) was one of the most successful philosophical works of the 20th century.

Ayers Rock (Aboriginal **U luru**) An inselberg or rock mound in Northern Territory, Australia, rising 348 m (1,143 feet) in isolation above the flat, sandy desert. It has a long, rounded summit and measures over 8 km (5 miles) round the base. The Rock is composed of CONGLOMERATE interbedded with layers of red sandstone, both tilted vertically. Parallel gutters show the erosional characteristics of the different rocks. It is between 400 and 600 million years old and is one of the largest rock mounds in the world. To several of the country's Aboriginal tribes it is a sacred place.

Aylesbury The county town of Buckinghamshire in southern England, to the north of the Chiltern Hills; pop. (est. 1985) 50,000. The town gives its name to a breed of large white domestic ducks. Insurance and food processing are its main industries.

Aylward, Gladys (May) (1902–70) British missionary. In 1932 she bought a railway ticket to northern China with her savings, and helped found an inn in Yangsheng (later portrayed in the 1959 film *The Inn of the Sixth Happiness*). During the Sino-Japanese war she made a perilous journey to lead a hundred children to safety, and in 1949 returned to England to great acclaim. She later settled in Taiwan as head of an orphanage.

Aymara An indigenous American Indian people mainly inhabiting the plateau lands of Bolivia and Peru near Lake Titicaca.

Ayr A resort town and fishing port on the south-west coast of Scotland, at the mouth of the River Ayr where it meets the Firth of Clyde; pop. (1981) 49,500. Its well-known racecourse lies to the east of the town.

Ayrshire A former Scottish county in south-west Scotland, on the Firth of Clyde. It became part of Strathclyde Region in 1975.

Ayub Khan, Muhammad (1907–74) Pakistani soldier and statesman, President 1958–69. After independence he became the first Commander-in-Chief of the country's army (1951–58) and served as Minister of Defence 1954–55, taking over the presidency shortly after the declaration of martial law. His term of office saw the introduction of a new constitution and the lifting of martial law in 1962, but civil liberties were curtailed. Opposition to his foreign policy with regard to India and his increasingly repressive style of government led to widespread disorder and he was ultimately forced to resign.

Ayurvedic medicine (from Sanskrit *āyur,* 'life' and *veda,* 'knowledge') The traditional medical system of Sri Lanka and India, derived in part from the Hindu sacred texts, the VEDAS, and from later texts of the 5th and 2nd centuries BC. As well as promoting physical health, Ayurvedic medicine encompasses moral, religious, and social education. The Ayurvedic system aims for a balance of the influence of the five elements (air, water, earth, fire, ether) on the five senses of the body. Treatment involves herbal remedies and touch. In 1970 the Indian Parliament passed legislation drawing up a register of qualified Ayurvedic practitioners.

Ayutthaya A market and tourist town, the capital of a province of the same name in south-central Thailand, on the River Chao Phraya, noted for its early Siamese royal palace, temples, and pagodas; pop. (1990) 61,185. Built on the site of a Khmer settlement, Ayutthaya became the capital of a Thai kingdom in the mid-14th century. It was destroyed by the Burmese in 1559, rebuilt by the Siamese and later laid waste again by the Burmese in 1767.

azalea See RHODODENDRON.

Azande (or **Zande**) An agricultural people living in southern Sudan, the Democratic Republic of Congo (formerly Zaïre), and the Central African Republic. They consist of numerous patrilineal CLANS, which are totemic: when a man dies, it is believed that one of his two souls becomes a totemic animal of his clan. The Azande are best known for their belief in witchcraft In *Witchcraft, Oracles and Magic among the Azande* (1937), the anthropologist EVANS-PRITCHARD showed how apparently irrational beliefs may be as logical as 'scientific' thinking. In recent years the Azande have suffered greatly in civil war and natural disasters such as famine in the region.

azeotrope (in chemistry) A mixture of two liquids whose boiling-point remains unchanged as the mixture vaporizes during distillation. The distillate has the same composition as the liquid, so the components cannot be separated by distillation. Ethanol and water form an azeotrope containing 95.6 per cent ethanol by mass, which boils at 78.2°C (172.8°F). If the liquids are mixed in any other proportion, the composition and boiling-point both approach these values as evaporation proceeds.

Azerbaijan A region of north-western Iran forming the southern part of the historic Transcaucasian region of Azerbaijan. It is divided into the two provinces of East and West Azerbaijan; area 105,952 sq km (40,924 sq miles); pop. (1986) 6,085,760. The provincial capitals are Tabriz and Orumiyeh. Iranian Azerbaijan is separated from the former Soviet Republic of Azerbaijan by the River Araks.

Azerbaijan, Republic of A country in western Asia, in the Caucasus. Situated on the west coast of the Caspian Sea, Azerbaijan is bordered by Armenia to the west, Georgia and Russia to the north, and Iraq to the south.

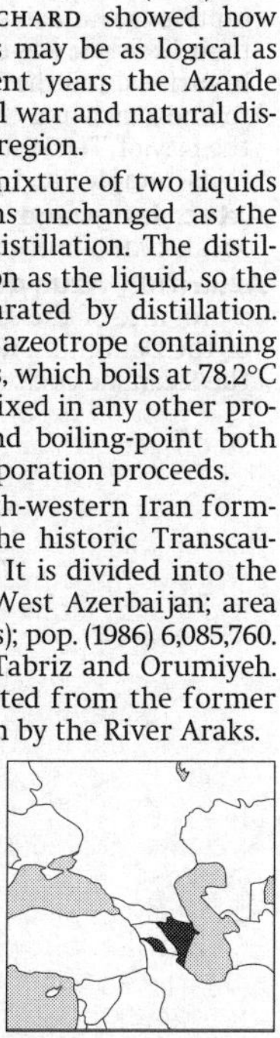

Physical. The Apsheron Peninsula in the north contains the long-established Baku oilfields. The hot and arid Kura valley runs towards the south-east below the Caucasian foothills, cotton and tobacco being cultivated along the river banks. The Caspian coastal plain with a subtropical climate is more naturally fertile; and round it lie well-wooded hills with deep valleys. The mountainous south-west contains the large and scenic Lake Gyoygyol and numerous deposits of copper, iron, and lead.

Economy. Azerbaijan was the world's leader in petroleum production at the beginning of the 20th century, and has rich mineral resources, including petroleum, gas, and metal ores. Industry concentrates on power, manufacturing, and chemicals production. Cotton and tobacco are the main crops; viticulture is also important.

History. The country comprises the part of the Azerbaijan area that was conquered by Russia in the 18th and 19th centuries (the remainder of the traditional Azerbaijan area is now incorporated in Iran). By 1914 it was the largest oil-producing area in the world, centred on Baku. After the Bolshevik Revolution in Russia of 1917, it declared its independence, but in 1920 was conquered by the Red Army. The Azerbaijan Soviet Socialist Republic was created, which in 1922 was linked with Armenia and Georgia as the Transcaucasian Soviet Federated Socialist Republic. This split in 1936 into three separate republics as members of the Soviet Union. The autonomous region of Nakhichevan formed an exclave within Armenia, while a second area, that of Nagorno Karabagh, inhabited by Christian Armenians and claimed by Armenia, lay within the Republic. Severe violence erupted over the latter, with military intervention by the Soviet Union in 1989. In 1991 Azerbaijan declared its independence, as a Shi'ite Muslim state. The autonomous region of Nakhichevan allegedly received aid from Iran during 1992 in a bid for its own independence. Fighting in Nagorno Karabagh and Nakhichevan has continued, despite several cease-fire agreements, including one made in 1994. Nagorno Karabagh declared itself to be independent in 1996, and attempts to negotiate peace have continued. In 1993 President Elchibey was ousted in a military coup; President Geidar Aliyev took over, his position being ratified in elections. The government agreed to several oil exploitation deals with foreign companies in 1994. Parliamentary elections in 1995 were won by Aliyev's party.

Capital: Baku
Area: 88,606 sq km (33,430 sq mi)
Population: 7,525,000 (1995)
Currency: 1 manat = 100 gopik
Religions: Shiite Muslim; minority religions
Ethnic Groups: Azeri 83.0%; Armenian 6.0%; Russian 6.0%
Languages: Azeri Turkish (official); Armenian, Russian, and other minority languages
International Organizations: UN; Commonwealth of Independent States; CSCE; North Atlantic Co-operation Council

Azikiwe, (Benjamin) Nnamdi (1904–96) Nigerian statesman, President 1963–66. Azikiwe founded (1944) the anti-colonial National Council of Nigeria and the Cameroons, a gathering of forty political, labour, and educational groups. He was the first Governor-General of an independent Nigeria (1960–63) and its first President when it became a republic. When his civilian government was ousted by a military coup in 1966, Azikiwe joined the Biafran secessionist government. In 1978, after the reunification of Nigeria, he founded the Nigerian People's Party and was its leader until 1983.

azimuth ▶**1** The angular distance from a north or south point of the horizon to the intersection with the horizon of a vertical circle passing through a given celestial body. ▶**2** The horizontal angle or direction of a compass bearing.

azo dye Any member of a group of DYES produced from a diazonium salt (formed by the reaction of ANILINE, or a derivative, and nitrous acid at low temperature) and a PHENOL or amine. The linking group between the atoms of the salt and the coupling agent is called an 'azo' group (–N=N–). Varying the nature of the aniline derivative and the reacting phenol or amine produces different colours. Azo dyes are used to dye cloth, and also as food colouring (see FOOD ADDITIVES). The first azo dye (aniline yellow) was made in the 19th century by Griess. Materials can be dyed by soaking in a solution of the phenol or amine, drying, and subsequently reacting with a diazonium salt solution; by this method the dye is formed within the fibres.

azonal soil A relatively young soil developed on recently laid down sediments, on rock which is very resistant to weathering, or on steep slopes where erosion removes most of the unconsolidated material. It has therefore only been exposed to the influence of the active factors of soil formation, such as climate and vegetation, for a relatively short time. As a result it has had insufficient time to develop the characteristics typical of zonal soil at the same latitudes. It tends to be shallow and to lack well-defined HORIZONS. LITHOSOLS and REGOSOLS are types of azonal soils.

Azores (Portuguese **Ilhas dos Açores**) A group of volcanic islands in the North Atlantic, 1,287 km (800 miles) west of Portugal, in Portuguese possession, but partially autonomous; pop. (1991) 241,590; chief port and capital, Ponta Delgada (on São Miguel). The nine largest islands lie in three distinct groups, Santa Maria and São Miguel to the south-east, Corvo and Flores to the north-west, and Faial, Pico, Graciosa, Terceira, and São Jorge in the middle. Portugal's highest mountain rises to 2,351 m (7,714 ft) on the island of Pico. Known to the Phoenicians and the Norse, the islands were not settled until they were rediscovered by the Portuguese during the early 15th century. Used as a port of call by navigators on voyages of exploration, the islands were developed as strategic naval and air bases during both world wars. In summer the islands are exposed to the trade winds blowing from the north-east and in winter strong winds blow in from the south-west.

Azov, Sea of (Russian **Azovskoye More**) A shallow inland sea between the Russian Federation and Ukraine, separated from the Black Sea by the Crimea and communicating with it by a narrow strait; area 37,555 sq km (14,500 sq miles). It is fed by the Don and Kuban rivers and is an important source of fish. Zhdanov, Taganrog, and Kerch are the chief ports.

Azrael See ARCHANGEL.

AZT (azidothymidine) US name for the drug zidovudine, used to treat HIV infection (see AIDS).

Aztec The indigenous people dominant in Mexico before the Spanish conquest of the 16th century (also called *Mexica* or *Tenochca*) who arrived in the central valley of Mexico after the collapse of the Toltec civilization in the 12th century. By the early 15th century they had risen to dominance of the area, and a century later commanded a territory that covered most of the central and southern part of present-day Mexico, exacting tribute from their subjects. They were a warring people who slew captives as human sacrifices to their chief god, but their life-style was comfortable and (for the rulers) luxurious, and the Spaniards under Cortés arrived to find a rich and elaborate civilization centred on the city of Tenochtitlán, which boasted vast pyramids, temples, and palaces.

Aztec language See MEXICAN AND CENTRAL AMERICAN INDIAN LANGUAGES.

Azua (fully **Azua de Compostella**) The capital of a province of the same name near the south coast of the Dominican Republic, at the southern end of the Sierra de Ocoa; pop. (1986) 71,800.

B

Baade, Walter (1893–1960) German-born US astronomer who proposed the existence of two STELLAR POPULATIONS. He deduced this from photographs taken of the satellites of the Andromeda Galaxy (M31). Young stars belonging to the spiral arms of galaxies he called Population I stars and the old stars associated with the more central regions he called Population II stars. Baade reinvestigated the PERIOD-LUMINOSITY LAW for variable stars which can be used to measure the distances of nearby galaxies. In 1952 he proposed a revision of the law which meant that the estimated distances of these galaxies had to be doubled.

Baader-Meinhof gang Byname of the West German anarchist terrorist group, Red Army Faction. Its leaders were Andreas Baader (1943–77) and Ulrike Meinhof (1934–76). The group set itself to oppose the capitalist organization of German society and the presence of US armed forces by engaging in murders, bombings, and kidnappings. The leaders were arrested in 1972, and their trial and deaths (by suicide) received considerable publicity. The group continued its terrorist activities until 1998, forming a number of splinter cells.

Baal The Phoenician god of fertility, the storm, and winter rains, whose annual struggle with Mot, the god of harvesting crops, symbolized for Phoenicians the renewal of the Earth's vegetation each spring. The name Baal, as a general title meaning 'lord', came to be applied to any of the male fertility gods whose sacrificial cult, so often condemned by the Hebrew prophets, was widespread in ancient Phoenician and Canaanite lands.

Baalbek A town in eastern Lebanon at the foot of the Anti-Lebanon Mountains, site of the ancient city of Heliopolis (Greek, 'city of the sun') associated in Phoenician times with the worship of the Sun-god BAAL. Its principal surviving monuments date from the Roman period, and include the Corinthian temples of Jupiter and Bacchus, and private houses with important mosaics.

Ba'athism An Arab political doctrine that combines elements of socialist thinking with pan-Arabism. Ba'athism originated in Syria, where the first Ba'ath Party was founded in 1953. Ba'athists have held power in Syria since 1963 and Iraq since 1968, although the two branches of the movement are deeply divided. While the Iraqi leader Saddam Hussein employed the slogans of pan-Arabism to justify his invasion of Kuwait in 1990, the Ba'ath Party in Iraq has been reduced to an instrument of state power.

Babbage, Charles (1791–1871) British mathematician, inventor, and pioneer of machine computing. His interest in the compilation of accurate mathematical and astronomical tables led to his design for a mechanical computer or 'difference engine' (in which he was assisted by Byron's daughter, Ada LOVELACE), which would both perform calculations and print the results. Because of practical and financial difficulties neither this machine nor a subsequent **analytical engine** was finished in Babbage's lifetime (although a difference engine was constructed in London for the bicentenary of Babbage's birth).

Babbitt, Milton (Byron) (1916–) US composer and mathematician. His compositions developed from the twelve-note system of Schoenberg and Webern; his first twelve-note work was *Composition for Orchestra* (1941). He later pioneered the use of synthesizers in composition; his works using synthesizers include *Philomel* (1964) and *Canonic Form* (1983).

babbler A bird making up a large family, Timaliidae, of about 233 species which occur throughout the warmer areas of Asia, some of the species extending to Africa and Australia. Ranging from sparrow-sized to jay-sized, they are a very diverse family. Most species are brown, but some have brightly coloured patches. Most are insectivorous, catching their food with a long, thin beak. Some of the tree-babblers have strongly curved beaks which they use for probing into soft wood and leaves. Many species live in groups of six to twelve and defend a joint territory.

Babel The Hebrew name for Babylon. According to the biblical account in the Book of Genesis, the Babylonians tried to rebel against God by building a tower to reach the heavens. Their plan was frustrated by God causing linguistic confusion amongst its builders. The many languages of the world were accounted for in this way.

Babel, Isaak (Emmanuilovich) (1894–1941) Russian writer. His early short stories, collected in *Red Cavalry* (1926), present, with concentrated economy, the brutality and heroism of the post-revolutionary Russian Civil War as observed by an alienated intellectual. Babel was arrested in 1939 and died in a prison camp in Siberia.

Babeuf, François Noël (1760–97) French Revolutionary who called himself 'Caius-GRACCHUS, tribune of the people'. A domestic servant before the French Revolution, he moved to Paris in 1794. There he started to publish the *Journal de la liberté de la presse*, in which he argued that the Revolution should go further than establishing political equality. He formed a small group (the Equals) of discontented artisans and soldiers and campaigned for the equal ownership of property by all. This idea thrived in the turmoil following ROBES-

PIERRE's execution but secret agents learnt of his plans for an armed rising on 11 May 1796. He was captured and executed.

Babington Plot (1586) A conspiracy to coordinate a Spanish invasion of England with a rising of English Catholics, to assassinate ELIZABETH I, and to replace her on the throne with MARY, Queen of Scots. Sir Anthony Babington (1561–86) was the go-between in the secret preparations. WALSINGHAM monitored Babington's correspondence with the captive Queen Mary until he had enough evidence of her treasonable intentions to have her tried and executed in 1587, Babington having been executed after torture at Tyburn.

Bábism The doctrines of a Muslim messianic Shiite sect. Founded in 1844 by the Persian Sayyid Ali Muhammad of Shiraz (1819–50) known as the *Báb ed-Din* (the gate or intermediary between man and God), who declared himself to be the long-awaited Mahdi. For inciting insurrection the Báb was arrested in 1848 by the government and executed in 1850, his remains being interred (1909) on Mt Carmel, Palestine. In 1863 Baha'ullah and his son Abdul Baha declared themselves the new leaders, and their followers became known as the BAHA'IS.

Babits, Mihály (1883–1941) Hungarian poet, novelist, and essayist. His poetry is concerned mainly with the role of the individual in a confused world, while his novels such as *The Children of Death* (1927) explore psychological problems.

Babol (or **Babul**) A commercial city in northern Iran just south of the Caspian Sea in the province of Mazandaran; pop. (1983) 96,000. It has textiles and food-processing industries. Babol was founded during the 16th century on the site of the ancient city of Mamter. Its port on the Caspian Sea is Babol Sar.

baboon Any one of seven species of Old World monkey in the genus *Papio* that have evolved from tree-dwelling ancestors to become terrestrial, walking on all four limbs. Typical open-country monkeys, they are found all over the savannah, semi-desert, and lightly forested regions of Africa south of the Sahara Desert. (The species of baboons known as the MANDRILL and the drill, however, live in more forested habitats.) The face is elongated and rather dog-like, and the jaw carries a long row of grinding molar teeth. Baboons feed on the ground, eating seeds, tubers, grass, insects, and small animals, and this makes them vulnerable to predators. Troops of baboons will often associate with a herd of ungulates (hoofed mammals) such as impala, which are alert and will give warning of approaching predators. The association is of mutual benefit, as baboons are powerful animals and give protection to the impala from smaller predators.

The hamadryas baboon, *Papio hamadryas*, is 76 cm (30 inches) tall with a tail 61 cm (24 inches) long; the females have brown hair and the males have grey hair with a long mane. They live in highly organized societies of 25–30 animals, and occasionally in groups of up to 200.

Babur (1483–1530) The first MOGUL Emperor of India 1526–30. He was born in Ferghana, Central Asia, in a princely family of mixed Mongol and Turkish blood. Failure to recover his father's lands caused him to turn reluctantly south-east, for India seemed to present the last hope for his ambitions. Defeat of Ibrahim Lodi, the Afghan ruler of Delhi, at the Battle of Panipat in 1526 initiated 200 years of strong Mogul rule in India. Having conquered much of northern India, Babur ruled by force, lacking any civil administration. In addition to his military genius, he possessed a love of learning and wrote his own memoirs.

Babylon An ancient city in Mesopotamia, first prominent under Hammurabi who made it capital of the kingdom of BABYLONIA. The city (now in ruins) lay on the Euphrates 88 km (55 miles) south of present-day Baghdad and was noted for its luxury, its fortifications, and particularly for the 'Hanging Gardens', which were one of the Seven Wonders of the World.

Babylonia The ancient name for southern Mesopotamia (earlier called Sumer), which first became a political entity when an Amorite dynasty united Sumer and Akkad in the first half of the 2nd millenium BC. At this period its power ascended over Assyria and part of Syria. After *c.*1530 BC first the Hittites then other invaders, the Kassites, dominated the land, and it became part of the Assyrian empire. With the latter's decline Babylonia again became prominent under the Chaldeans (625–538 BC), only to fall to Cyrus the Great, whose entry into BABYLON ended its power for ever.

Babylonian art The art and architecture of BABYLONIA, the ancient Near East kingdom controlled by Babylon. The city first became the centre of a great empire in the 18th century BC under HAMMURABI. The Babylonians were great traders and were renowned for their love of luxury. Their buildings were often ambitious in scale, but because building materials were poor (mainly Sun-dried brick) very little of them survives above ground. An example is the famous ziggurat (tiered temple) of Babylon of which only the foundations survive. The best idea of the splendour of Babylonian architecture can be gained from Babylon's Ishtar Gate (*c.*575 BC), a sumptuous structure of coloured glazed bricks, reconstructed in the Pergamon Museum, Berlin. The other Babylonian arts were much influenced by the Sumerians and included terracotta plaques, cylinder seals, ivories, and, where the material was available, stone carvings.

Bacchus The Roman god of wine and ecstasy, identified with DIONYSOS in Greek mythology.

Bach, Carl Philipp Emanuel (1714–88) German composer and harpsichordist. The second and most famous surviving son of J. S. BACH, he was taught by his father, but also undertook extensive law studies and only settled to music in 1738, when he was engaged by the future King Frederick the Great of Prussia as accompanist to the royal chamber music. By 1768 he was the most famous keyboard-player and teacher in Europe and left Berlin to become director of music in Hamburg's five principal churches.

Bach, Johann Christian (1735–82) German composer, the youngest son of J. S. BACH. He was taught by his father and, after 1750, by his brother Carl Philipp Emanuel BACH. From 1754 to 1762 he studied and worked in Italy, becoming organist (1760) at Milan Cathedral and gaining success as an opera composer. It was in this capacity that he came in 1762 to London where he became music-master to the British royal family and where, apart from a period (1772–78) when he worked concurrently in Mannheim, he remained for the rest of his life.

Bach, Johann Sebastian (1685–1750) German composer. His compositions range from violin concertos, suites, and the six Brandenburg Concertos (1720–21) to many clavier works and more than 250 sacred cantatas. His large-scale choral works include *The Passion according to St John* (1723), *The Passion according to St Matthew* (1729), and the *Mass in B minor* (1733–38); through these and other liturgical works Bach expressed his devout Protestant faith in the Lutheran tradition. Of his 20 children, three became famous composers: Carl Philipp Emanuel BACH, Johann Christian BACH, and his eldest son, Wilhelm Friedemann Bach (1710–84), who became an organist and composer.

Bacharach, Burt (1929–) US writer of popular songs. With lyricist Hal David (1921–) he became an acclaimed songwriter in the 1960s with songs like 'Walk On By' (1961), 'Alfie' (1966), and 'Do You Know the Way to San José?' (1968), many of which were performed by the singer Dionne Warwick. Bacharach also composed scores for several films, notably *Casino Royale* (1967) and *Butch Cassidy and the Sundance Kid* (1969).

backgammon A board-game in which two players race their pieces or stones around a board divided into four sections or tables. Each section is marked with six long triangular points, and a line called the bar divides the board into inner and outer tables. Moves are dictated by throwing two dice. Each player has fifteen stones (black or white) and 'makes' a point by landing two or more stones on the point. The object is to get all stones into the home or inner table and then move them off the board.

background radiation Low intensity ionizing radiation that is always present in the environment. Most background radiation comes from natural sources, such as cosmic rays and some types of rocks (for example granite in the Earth's crust); the rest – about 13 per cent – comes from artificial sources.

backwash The flow of water down a beach under the influence of gravity after the breaking of a wave and its associated swash. As this water returns to the breaker zone it carries beach material with it. Steep waves, which break almost vertically on to a beach, have an extremely powerful backwash and move much material out to sea. Backwash contributes to longshore drift.

Bacolod The chief city on the island of Negros in the central Philippines; pop. (1990) 364,180. Situated on the north-west coast of the island, it is a major port and processing centre for sugar-cane. The city, which is capital of Negros Occidental province, is also a leading producer of ceramics.

Bacon, Francis (1909–92) British painter. In 1945 he became the most controversial painter in post-war Britain when his *Three Studies for Figures at the Base of a Crucifixion* (1944) was exhibited in London. The impact of his pictures derives not only from their subject-matter – usually single figures in isolation or despair – but also on his handling of paint, by means of which he smudges and twists faces and bodies into ill-defined jumbled protuberances suggestive of formless, slug-like creatures.

Bacon, Francis, 1st Baron Verulam, Viscount St Albans (1561–1626) English statesman and philosopher. He became a barrister in 1582 and entered Parliament two years later. In the 1590s he prospered as a member of the ESSEX faction at court, and published his first edition of witty, aphoristic *Essays* (1597). Under James I he had to compete with COKE for high legal office, but when Coke began to oppose the crown, Bacon was taken up by VILLIERS and rose to be Lord Chancellor (1618). In 1621 he was impeached by Parliament for accepting bribes and his political career was ruined. In retirement he devoted himself to literary and philosophical work.

Bacon, Roger (*c.*1219–*c.*1292) English scholar, educational reformer, and monk. Based at Oxford and Paris, he introduced the study of Aristotle in the West, as well as of languages, optics, and alchemy. He elucidated the principles of REFRACTION, REFLECTION, and spherical aberration, and described spectacles, which soon thereafter came into use. He developed many mathematical results concerning lenses, proposed mechanically propelled ships, carriages, and flying machines, and used a camera obscura to observe eclipses of the Sun.

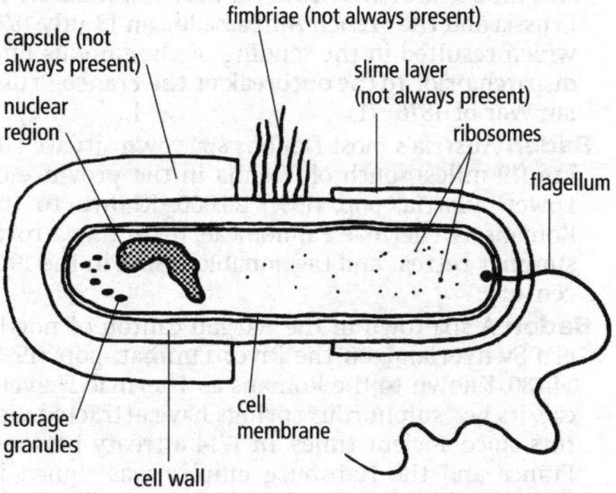

Bacteria A generalized bacterial cell. The capsule protects the bacterium against desiccation and makes ingestion by phagocytes more difficult; the fimbriae have a role in sexual reproduction.

bacteria A large group of microorganisms, mainly unicellular, that constitute one of the five major groupings (KINGDOMS) of living organisms, the Prokaryotae (or Monera). They are characterized by a nuclear region without a bounding membrane, a single CHROMOSOME formed into a ring, and the lack of MITOCHONDRIA. Bacterial cells may be spherical, rod-like, or spiral, or individual cells may collect as filamentous colonies. Each cell is enclosed in a complex cell wall formed largely of a polysaccharide. Each bacterium is microscopic, between 0.0005 and 0.005 mm (up to 0.0002 inch) in size. They reproduce rapidly by simple division of cells to form large colonies or by sexual REPRODUCTION.

Bacteria are essential in the decomposition of organic matter, and in soil formation. They are also necessary for the breakdown of sewage, and are used in the production of certain fermented foods. They may also be used in the future to break up oil slicks in a technique known as bioremediation. In biotechnological applications, bacteria are cultured on a large scale to produce chemical products such as vitamins and enzymes in industrial quantities. A minority of bacteria cause diseases, such as cholera, typhoid, and tuberculosis, often through the manufacture of toxins. The control of such bacteria is important in FOOD PRESERVATION, and in many medical situations. Bacteria are also used as tools in GENETIC ENGINEERING.

Bactria The ancient name for a country that included the northern part of modern Afghanistan and parts of the central Asian republics. Its capital was Bactra (present-day Balkh in northern Afghanistan). Traditionally the home of Zoroaster and the Zend-Avesta, it was the seat of a powerful Indo-Greek kingdom in the 3rd and 2nd centuries BC.

Badajoz ▶**1** A province in the Extremadura region of western Spain; area 21,657 sq km (8,365 sq miles); pop. (1991) 650,390. It is the largest Spanish province. ▶**2** Its capital on the River Guadiana; pop. (1991) 129,737. Known to the Romans as Colonia Pacensis, the Aftasside Moors made it the capital of a small kingdom that was eventually captured by Alfonso IX of León in 1229. It is the marketing centre of a fertile region and has food-processing industries.

Bad Ems (or **Ems**) A resort town in the German state of Rhineland-Palatinate, on the River Lahn. It was the scene of an encounter between the King of Prussia and the French Ambassador on 13 July 1870 which resulted in the sending of the famous Ems dispatch prior to the outbreak of the Franco-Prussian War of 1870–71.

Baden Austria's most famous spa town situated 30 km (19 miles) south of Vienna in the province of Lower Austria; pop. (1991) 24,000. Known to the Romans as Thermae Pannonicae, it became a royal summer retreat and fashionable resort in the 19th century.

Baden A spa town in the Aargau canton of northern Switzerland, on the River Limmat; pop. (1990) 14,780. Known to the Romans as Thermae Helveticae, its hot sulphurous springs have attracted visitors since ancient times. In 1714 a treaty between France and the Habsburg empire was signed in Baden during the War of Spanish Succession.

Baden-Baden A spa town with hot mineral springs in the state of Baden-Württemberg, southwest Germany, in the Black Forest; pop. (1991) 52,520. Known to the Romans as Aquae Aureliae, Baden-Baden became a fashionable watering place in the 19th century.

Badenoch and Strathspey A district in the Highland Region of northern Scotland from 1975 to 1996, situated between the Cairngorm and Monadhliath mountains and extending over part of the upper valley of the River Spey.

Baden-Powell, Robert (Stephenson Smyth), 1st Baron Baden-Powell of Gilwell (1857–1941) British soldier and founder of the Boy Scout movement. He became a national hero after his successful defence of Mafeking (1899–1900) in the Boer War. The Boy Scout movement, which he founded in 1908, and the Girl Guide movement, which he founded together with his sister Agnes and his wife Olave in 1910, grew to become important international youth movements.

Baden-Württemberg A state of south-west Germany; area 35,751 sq km (13,809 sq miles); pop. (est. 1990) 9,619,000; capital, Stuttgart.

Bader, Sir Douglas (Robert Steuart) (1910–82) British airman. Despite having lost both legs in a flying accident in 1931, he rejoined the RAF in 1939 and saw action as a fighter pilot during the evacuation from Dunkirk (1940) and in the Battle of Britain (1940–41), becoming a national hero.

badger A large, stocky mammal belonging to the family Mustelidae, related to weasels, skunks, otters, and the ratel. The eight species of badger are found throughout Eurasia and North America. They include the Eurasian badger, *Meles meles*; the American badger, *Taxidea taxus*; and three species of Asian ferret badgers, *Melogale* (*Helictis*) species. All badgers burrow and have similar omnivorous habits, though the American badger is more carnivorous than other species.

Bad Homburg A spa town at the foot of the Taunus Mts. in the German state of Hesse, to the north-east of Wiesbaden; pop. (1983) 50,600. The first Homburg felt hats for men were made here.

badlands (in geomorphology) Areas of bare ground that have been intensely eroded by running water into a maze of miniature canyons and steep slopes. Common on clays and shales in areas where the climate is semi-arid, they occur also on the tip-heaps of mines, especially of china-clay workings, in areas where the climate is wetter.

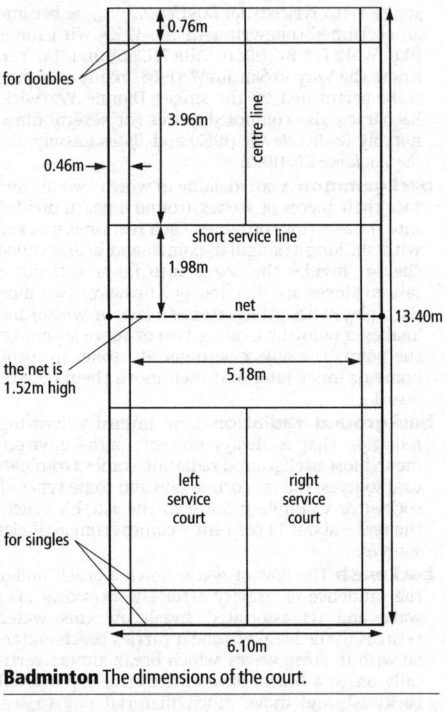

Badminton The dimensions of the court.

badminton An indoor serve-and-volley racket game played over a net, 1.52 m (5 feet) at the centre. The missile is a shuttle, either cork-based with white goosefeathers fixed to it or made of nylon in one piece. Rackets have whippy handles and small heads 21 cm (8 inches) wide. The court is 13.4 m (44 feet) long overall, 6.1 m (20 feet) wide for doubles play and 5.18 m (17 feet) for singles. Players serve or receive as in TENNIS, but only the serving side can score a point. Matchplay is usually up to fifteen points in each game, the best of three games deciding the winner.

Badoglio, Pietro (1871–1956) Italian general and Prime Minister. By 1925 he was chief of staff; Mussolini appointed him governor of Libya (1929) and sent him (1935) to rescue the faltering Italian campaign in ETHIOPA. He captured Addis Ababa and became governor. When Mussolini was deposed in 1943, he was chosen to head the new non-fascist government. He made peace with the advancing Allies, declared war against Germany, but resigned soon afterwards.

Badrinath A mountain peak in the Garwhal Himalayas of Uttar Pradesh, northern India. It is one of four important Hindu holy sites (Yamunotri, Gangotri, and Kedarnath are the others) near the sources of the great rivers that flow down from the mountains.

Baedeker, Karl (1801–59) German publisher. In

1827 he started his own publishing firm in Koblenz. He is remembered chiefly for the series of guide-books to which he gave his name and which are still published today.

Baekeland, Leo Hendrik (1863–1944) Belgian-born US chemist who invented **Bakelite**, the first industrially important plastic. He emigrated to the USA in 1889. There he made a fortune from his development of Velox photographic paper, an invention which he sold to EASTMAN (pioneer of the Kodak camera) in 1899. In 1905, he began exploring the thermosetting plastic product resulting from the reaction between phenol and formaldehyde, and in 1909 he patented Bakelite (a PHENOL-FORMALDEHYDE resin), which he began to manufacture in 1911.

Baer, Karl Ernest von (1792–1876) German biologist. His discovery that ova were particles within the ovarian follicles was his chief contribution to embryology. He also formulated the principle that in the developing embryo general characters appear before special ones, and his studies were used by Darwin in the theory of evolution.

Baeyer, Adolph Johann Friedrich Wilhelm von (1835–1917) German organic chemist. He prepared the first barbiturates, and investigated dyes, synthesizing indigo and determining its structural formula. His work pioneered the study of ring structures and stimulated the synthetic dye industry. He was awarded the Nobel Prize for chemistry in 1905.

Baez, Joan (1941–) US folk-singer. From the late 1950s she was a prominent figure in the American folk revival; she is best known for her performances at civil-rights demonstrations of the early 1960s. Albums include *Any Day Now* (1968) and *Diamonds and Rust* (1975).

Baffin, William (*c.*1584–1622) English navigator and explorer. The pilot of several expeditions in search of the North-west Passage (1612–16) he discovered the largest island of the Canadian Arctic in 1616; this and the strait between it and Greenland are named after him.

Baffin Bay The strait between Baffin Island and Greenland, linked to the North Atlantic Ocean by the Davis Strait and to the Arctic Ocean by the Nares Strait and the Lancaster and Jones Sounds. Baffin Bay is largely ice-bound in winter and in summer navigation is made more dangerous by the presence of icebergs brought down by the Labrador current. The bay is named after William BAFFIN who explored the area with Robert Bylot.

Baffin Island The largest island in the Canadian Arctic, and the fifth-largest island in the world, situated at the mouth of Hudson Bay; area 507,451 sq km (195,928 sq miles). The west coast is covered largely by tundra vegetation while the east is dominated by snow-covered mountains with extensive glaciers and snow-fields. Coastal fishing stations include Frobisher Bay, Cape Dyer, and Cape Dorset.

Baganda A group of settled farmers in Uganda. The Baganda constituted a kingdom in the 19th century, in which the king was seen as the supreme ruler who exercised his power through a system of district chiefs. The Baganda consist of fifty exogamous (based on marriage outside the group) clans, each distinguished by totemic symbols. Originally practitioners of a form of ANCESTOR WORSHIP, they are now predominantly Christian.

bagatelle A short, lightweight instrumental piece in music, usually for keyboard: a mere trifle. The term is first found in 1717 in one of Couperin's keyboard suites. Beethoven's three sets of keyboard bagatelles (not all of which are 'trifling') gave the term greater currency. Webern wrote Six Bagatelles for string quartet (1913).

Bagehot, Walter (1826–77) British economist and journalist. He worked as a banker before becoming editor of the *Economist* in 1860, a post which he held until his death. His insight into economic and political questions is shown in his books *The English Constitution* (1867), *Lombard Street* (1873), and *Economic Studies* (1880).

Baghdad The capital of Iraq, on the River Tigris; pop. (est. 1985) 4,648,600. Under Caliph Harun-al-Rashid (died 809) it became one of the greatest cities of Islam until its destruction at the hands of the Mongols in 1258, Tamerlane in 1400, and the Persians in 1524. During the Gulf War of 1991 the city was badly damaged by bombing. The rich brocade known as baldachin derives its name from Baldacco, the Italian name for Baghdad. The city is rich in ancient walls, gates, and bazaars, as well as having a 13th-century university and 14th-century *khan* or inn. It is a commercial and industrial centre with mainly light industries including carpets and textiles.

bagpipe A reed musical instrument blown via a bag, which may be inflated either by mouth or by means of bellows. There are two basic varieties: those with a conical shawm chanter or melody pipe, and those with a cylindrical (clarinet ancestor) chanter. The former are usually loud outdoor instruments; many of the European examples of the latter are quiet indoor instruments. DRONE pipes are often added and a few bagpipes have more than one chanter.

Baguio A mountain resort and summer capital of the Philippines, on the island of Luzon; pop. (1990) 183,140. First settled by the Spanish, the modern city was laid out by the Americans in 1909. The city lends its name to the tropical storms that occur in the Philippines during July–November.

bagworm moth One of some 800 species of MOTHS in the family Psychidae. Their name comes from their caterpillars, each of which encloses itself in a silken bag, often incorporating fragments of leaves and twigs. Adult male moths have dull unmarked wings, up to 25 mm (1 inch) across, and are swift-flying; females are wingless, never leaving the bag, and in many species lack legs, antennae, eyes, and mouthparts.

Baha'i A monotheistic religion founded in Persia in the 19th century by Baha-ullah (1817–92) and his son Abdul Baha (1844–1921). The seat of its governing body, the Universal House of Justice, is in Haifa, Israel, adjacent to the golden-domed shrine of the Bab where his bones were buried in 1909 after freedom was granted to religious minorities in the Ottoman empire.

Bahamas, The Commonwealth of The A country in the CARIBBEAN, consisting of a group of islands in the western Atlantic Ocean, set between Florida and Hispaniola.

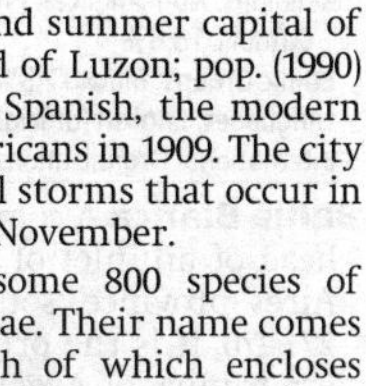

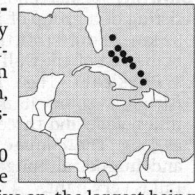

Physical. Of the 700 mainly coral islands some thirty are large enough to live on, the largest being the Grand Bahama and New Providence islands. The climate is very warm in winter and also in summer, which is the rainy season.

Economy. Tourism makes a large contribution to the economy, while exports are dominated by petroleum products, refined from imported crude oil. A favourable system of taxation has led to the Bahamas becoming an important financial centre. There is some industry, and shipping has expanded since free-flag status was established in 1976.

History. The earliest known inhabitants of the Bahamas were Arawak Indians. According to most historians, Guanahani was the site of Columbus's first landing in the Americas in 1492. The Spanish subsequently raided the islands, attacking and enslaving the Arawaks, but did not settle there. In 1629 the Bahamas were included in the British Carolina colonies, but actual settlement did not begin until 1648, with settlers from BERMUDA. By this time all the Arawaks had died out. Possession was disputed by Spain, but was acknowledged in 1670 under the Treaty of Madrid. The Bahamas became a British Crown Colony in 1717. Of major strategic importance, they were captured by the Spanish in 1782, but returned to Britain in 1783. There were also frequent raids by pirates. Many Africans were brought to the islands to work as slaves in the sugar plantations. A civil-rights movement led to the creation of the Progressive Liberal Party (PLP) in 1953. The PLP advocated parliamentary representation for the black majority, and independence for the Bahamas. Internal self-government was achieved in 1964, the PLP were elected in 1967, and independence was gained in 1973. In 1992 the Free National Movement (FNM) won elections, ending 25 years of PLP government; the FNU was returned to power in elections in 1997.

Capital: Nassau
Area: 13,939 sq km (5,382 sq mi)
Population: 276,000 (1995)
Currency: 1 Bahamian dollar = 100 cents
Religions: Non-Anglican Protestant 55.2%; Anglican 20.1%; Roman Catholic 18.8%
Ethnic Groups: Black 72.3%; Mixed 14.2%; White 12.9%
Languages: English (official); English creole; French (Haitian) creole
International Organizations: UN; OAS; Commonwealth; CARICOM

Bahía Blanca A commercial centre and port at the head of an inlet of the Atlantic Ocean in Buenos Aires province, south-east Argentina; pop. (1991) 271,470. It is the principal port serving the southern pampas of Argentina and ships grain and fruit.

Bahmani A dynasty of sultans of the DECCAN plateau in central India 1347–1518. The dynasty was founded by Ala-ud-din Bahman Shah, who in 1347 rebelled against his Delhi suzerain. His successors expanded over the west-central Deccan, reaching a peak in the late 15th century under Mahmud Gawan, who successfully held encroaching Hindu and Muslim powers at bay. During the early 16th century the Hindu empire of Vijayanagar to the south expanded at the Bahmanis' expense, and between 1490 and 1518 the sultanate gradually dissolved into five successor Muslim states, Bijapur, Ahmadnagar, Golconda, Berar, and Bidar.

Bahrain A sheikhdom consisting of a group of islands 32 km (20 miles) off the Arabian coast of the Gulf.

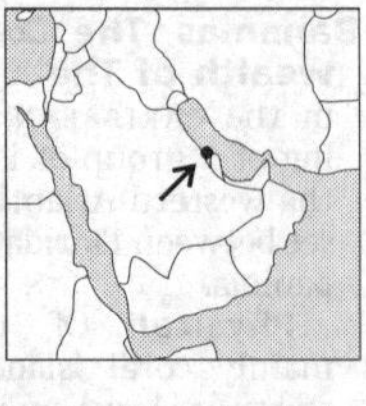

Physical. The largest island is some 16 km (10 miles) wide and three times as long. The climate is hot and humid, although rainfall is very light.

Economy. The country's exports are dominated by crude oil and petroleum products from a large oil refinery on Bahrain Island. An aluminium smelter constitutes the largest non-oil industry in the Gulf; there is also a growing banking and communications sector. Shipbuilding and repair in dry docks are also significant. Islam is the state religion. There is an array of social services: medical care is free, as is schooling to technical college level.

History. Iran, which ruled Bahrain from 1602 to 1783, was expelled by the al-Khalifas, who still reign. British political control dates from 1820. Oil was discovered in 1932, when the Bahrain National Oil Company was formed. After the withdrawal of Britain in 1971 and the abandonment by Iran of its claims, the country joined the Arab League. Tension between Shiite and Sunni communities increased, leading to the suspension of the National Assembly in 1975. Together with other members of the Gulf Co-operation Council (Saudi Arabia, Kuwait, Qatar, and Oman), Bahrain repeatedly called for an end to the IRAN–IRAQ WAR (1980–88), while retaining its neutrality then and in the GULF WAR (1991). Its economy became increasingly diversified as oil reserves dwindled. Increasing opposition to the government and demands for the restoration of the National Assembly led to rising civil unrest in the mid-1990s.

Capital: Manama
Area: 691 sq km (267 sq mi)
Population: 579,000 (1995)
Currency: 1 Bahrain dinar = 1,000 fils
Religions: Shiite Muslim 60.0%; Sunni Muslim 40.0%; Christian minority
Ethnic Groups: Bahraini Arab 68.0%; Iranian, Indian, and Pakistani 24.7%; other Arab 4.1%; European 2.5%
Languages: Arabic (official) and minority languages
International Organizations: UN; Arab League; OAPEC; OPEC; GCC

Bahrām Gūr (ruled 420–38) In Persian mythology, the legendary Sassanian king, renowned as a hunter and lover, credited with the invention of poetry, and a frequent figure in Persian poetry and iconography.

Bai A minority nationality of southern China, mostly found in Yunnan where the Bai people number *c*.1.1 million.

Baia Mare (Hungarian **Nagybánya**) The capital town of Maramureş county in north-west Romania; pop. (1989) 150,460. Founded by Saxon immigrants in the 12th century, it was originally known as Neustadt. It is situated in a region where lead, zinc, and copper are mined, and has food-processing, machine-building, and chemical industries.

Baikal, Lake (Russian **Ozero Baykal**) A large lake in southern Siberia, the largest freshwater lake in Asia and the deepest lake in the world; area 31,494 sq km (12,160 sq miles); max. depth 1,743 m (5,714 ft). Fed by the Barguzin and Selenga rivers, its only outlet is the River Angara.

Baikonur A coal-mining town in Kazakhstan, north-east of the Aral Sea. Nearby is the Baikonur Cosmodrome from which the world's first satellite (1957) and first manned space flight (1961) were launched. A major centre of Russia's space programme, it continued in use as a space centre after the breakup of the Soviet Union, Russia agreeing in 1994 to rent the site for 20 years.

bail Permission for an arrested person's release from custody, often subject to the pledge of money or property as security, until his or her return to court to stand trial. The word may also refer to the money or property so pledged.

Bailey bridge See BRIDGE.

bailiff The estate manager of the lord of the manor in England from the 11th century. The word 'bailiff' gradually shifted its meaning, and in the later Middle Ages, when lords more commonly let out their manors to farmers, the bailiff was one of the lesser officials of the sheriff. Farmers and urban landlords also employed him as a rent-collector, knowing that his legal skills could be drawn on in cases of non-payment.

Baird, John Logie (1888–1946) British pioneer of television. He started his work in the early 1920s, gave a demonstration in London in 1926, and made the first transatlantic transmission and demonstration of colour television in 1928. Baird used a mechanical system of picture scanning, which was soon displaced in television development by an electronic system developed by V. K. ZWORYKIN and others in the 1930s.

Baja California ▶**1** (or **Lower California**) An arid mountainous peninsula in north-west Mexico that separates the Gulf of California from the Pacific Ocean. It stretches *c.*1,225 km (760 miles) southwards from the US state of California. Tourism is developing along its Pacific coastlands. ▶**2** (or **North Baja**) A state of north-west Mexico comprising that part of the Baja California (Lower California) peninsula lying to the north of the 28th parallel; area 69,921 sq km (27,007 sq miles); pop. (1990) 1,657,930; capital, Mexicali. It was formerly known as Baja California Norte.

Bakelite See BAEKELAND, LEO HENDRIK; PHENOL-FORMALDEHYDE RESIN.

Baker, Dame Janet (Abbott) (1933–) British mezzo-soprano singer. Although extremely versatile, her operatic repertoire stretching from Monteverdi to Kate in Britten's *Owen Wingrave*, Baker is perhaps most associated with roles in 18th-century opera, notably by Handel and Rameau. An intense and intelligent singer, Baker was an impressive interpreter of *Lieder*, British and French song, and oratorio.

Baker, Sir Samuel White (1821–93) British explorer who traced the Nile tributaries in Ethiopia (1861–62). In 1864, despite the opposition of Arab slave traders, he located the Nile source in Lake Albert Nyanza.

bakery A place in which BREAD and cakes are made, and sometimes also sold. In all bakeries, the processes involved in bread-making are essentially similar, but large modern bakeries are usually highly mechanized. Often a sponge dough process is used for leavened bread, in which all the yeast and some of the flour are mixed and left to ferment, then the rest of the flour is added to form the final dough. After the second mixing the dough is divided up and rounded by machine, then left to 'proof' or rise: this intermediate proofing restores elasticity, pliability, and volume to the dough. A moulder then flattens the dough and rolls it into cylinders before it is put into loaf tins and left to proof a second time. Bread ovens may be of various types, but the most common for large-scale production is the tunnel oven, in which the loaves travel on a metal belt through a connected series of baking chambers. After baking, the bread may be sliced and packaged before distribution to retail outlets.

Bakewell, Robert (1725–95) British pioneer in scientific methods of livestock breeding and husbandry. He produced pedigree herds of sheep and cattle from his Leicestershire farm; irrigation of the grassland gave four cuts a year, and feeding and selective breeding greatly increased the meat production from his animals.

Bakhchisarai A town on the Crimean peninsula of southern Ukraine, south-west of Simferopol. The palace of the khans, built in 1519 and destroyed in 1736, was restored by Field Marshall Potemkin in 1787 four years after he had annexed Crimea and become its governor.

Bakhtaran See KERMANSHAH.

baking powder A mixture of sodium hydrogencarbonate and tartaric acid (or cream of tartar) used in baking because it produces carbon dioxide gas on heating or wetting, which makes dough rise.

Bakker, Robert T. (1945–) US palaeontologist. He proposed, and vigorously defends, the controversial idea that dinosaurs were both active and warm-blooded, citing three lines of supporting evidence: the ability to live in cold climates, the lack of growth rings in bone, and the low ratios of predator to prey.

Bakony Mountains A forested range of mountains to the north of Lake Balaton in the Transdanubian Highlands of western Hungary. Mt. Köris (702 m, 2,303 ft) is the highest peak.

Bakst, Léon (born Lev Semuilovich Rosenberg) (1866–1924) Russian painter and set designer. Associated with DIAGHILEV's magazine *The World of Art* from 1899, he became one of the most influential members of the Diaghilev circle and a leading designer for the Ballets Russes.

Bakunin, Mikhail (1814–76) Russian revolutionary, leading exponent of ANARCHISM and founder-member of the Russian Populist movement. He served in the emperor's army until his dismissal in 1835. After taking part in the REVOLUTIONS OF 1848 he was exiled to Siberia. He escaped in 1861 and went to London, which was used as a headquarters for militant anarchists and communists. The first International Workingmen's Association, founded in 1864, was marred by the conflict between MARX and Bakunin.

Baku The capital of Azerbaijan, on the Caspian Sea; pop. (1990) 1,779,500. It is an industrial port and has been a major centre of the oil industry since 1872 with oil refineries, oilfield equipment manufacturing, chemicals, and shipbuilding.

Balabalagan Islands (or **Little Paternosters**) An archipelago of *c.*30 low-lying Indonesian coral islands in the Makassar (Ujungpandang) Strait between Borneo and the Celebes (Sulawesi).

Balaclava (or **Balaklava**) A village on the south-west coast of the Crimean peninsula in southern Ukraine, scene of a battle (1854) in the Crimean War during which the famous Charge of the Light Brigade took place.

Balakirev, Mily See FIVE, THE.

balalaika A Russian folk instrument with three strings and a triangular body, played like a BANJO. It has a long neck with frets on the fingerboard. The belly is flat and the back is made from several flat pieces of wood, each meeting at an angle. In the 19th century a full family was created, with sizes down to double bass, and balalaika orchestras became popular in Russia and elsewhere.

balance of payments A record of all transactions occurring in a period of time between the residents of a country and the rest of the world. It consists of a current account, a capital account, and a balancing item (for estimated accounting errors). The current account records the money inflows and outflows arising from trade in GOODS ('visibles') and services ('invisibles'). The capital account records investment and financial asset flows, including inter-government loans and other international transactions by government. The capital and current accounts combined are said to be in surplus if the money inflows exceed the money outflows or in deficit if the reverse applies; surpluses or deficits imply rises or falls respectively in official external reserves. A negative balance of payments may lead to severe depreciation or DEVALUATION of the home currency, although this will often be avoided by official government financing to support the currency. See also BALANCE OF TRADE.

balance of power (in international relations) A term meaning that international order is preserved by maintaining an equilibrium of power among different states; it can also refer to the deliberate policy of achieving this equilibrium. After World War I there was a movement towards a system characterized by cooperation (see COLLECTIVE SECURITY) rather than the use of force to maintain equilibrium.

balance of trade The record of money inflows and outflows on the current account of the BALANCE OF PAYMENTS. The term is used sometimes to refer to GOODS ('visibles') only and sometimes to refer to the balance on goods and services ('invisibles') combined. In either case, it signifies the net receipts from abroad resulting from exports after the value of imports has been deducted. A trade gap is said to exist when the payments for imports exceed receipts from exports.

balance sheet A tabular account of a company's (or other economic agent's) WEALTH at a specific moment of time. Commonly it consists of two columns: liabilities on one side and assets on the other. A balance sheet contrasts with a profit-and-loss account, which records a company's expenditure and income during a period of time.

Balanchine, George (born Georgi Melitonovich Balanchivadze) (1904–83) Russian-born US ballet-dancer and choreographer. He worked as chief choreographer of Diaghilev's Ballets Russes during the 1920s. In 1934 he co-founded the company which later became the New York City Ballet, where he choreographed many ballets and revivals.

Balaton, Lake A lake in west-central Hungary, situated in a leading resort and wine-producing region to the south of the Bakony Mountains. It is the largest and shallowest lake in central Europe; area 596 sq km (230 sq miles).

Balboa, Vasco Núñez de (1475–1519) Spanish explorer. Having settled in the new Spanish colony of Hispaniola in 1501, in 1511 Balboa joined an expedition to Darien (in Panama) as a stowaway, but rose to command it after a mutiny. He founded a colony in Darien and continued to make expeditions into the surrounding areas. In 1513 he reached the western coast of the isthmus after an epic twenty-five-day march, thereby becoming the first European to see the Pacific Ocean.

Balcon, Sir Michael (1896–1977) British film producer. He was responsible for several early Hitchcock films but is mainly remembered for his long association with Ealing Studios, during which he produced famous comedies.

Balder In Norse and Germanic mythology, the Aesir Sun-god, the favourite of the gods, representing joy, goodness, beauty, and wisdom. The son of Odin and Frigga, Balder was killed by a branch of mistletoe, the only thing that would hurt him, thrown by his blind brother, Hoder, but guided by Loki, who alone hated him.

Baldwin I (*c.*1058–1118) King of Jerusalem 1100–18. On the death of his brother, Godfrey of Bouillon, he was crowned first King of Jerusalem. He foiled the ambitions of the Patriarch Daimbert and ensured that Jerusalem would become a secular kingdom with himself as its first monarch. His control of the Levantine ports secured vital sea communications with Europe, and by asserting his suzerainty over other Crusader principalities he consolidated the primacy of the Latin Kingdom of Jerusalem.

Baldwin, James Arthur (1924–87) US novelist, short-story writer, dramatist, and essayist. With his first novel, *Go Tell It On The Mountain* (1953), he was hailed as the successor to Richard Wright as the leading black American novelist. *Giovanni's Room* (1956) and other novels reinforced this reputation.

Baldwin, Robert (1804–58) Canadian statesman. Born in York (renamed Toronto in 1834), he was elected to the Assembly of Upper Canada in 1829, and became one of the leaders of the campaign for reformed government which would give more say to elected representatives. After the Act of Union (1840) he was elected for Canada West and in 1842–43 led a reformist ministry with La Fontaine.

Baldwin, Stanley, 1st Earl Baldwin of Bewdley (1867–1947) British statesman. A Conservative Member of Parliament (1908–37), he was a member of LLOYD GEORGE's coalition (1918–22) but led the Conservative rebellion against him. He was Chancellor of the Exchequer under Bonar LAW and was chosen as Prime Minister in preference to Curzon when Law resigned in 1923. He lost the 1923 election in an attempt to introduce tariffs but returned to office in 1924. His premiership was marked by the return to the GOLD STANDARD, the GENERAL STRIKE, Neville CHAMBERLAIN's social legislation, and the Trades Dispute Act of 1927. He lost the 1929 election, but served under Ramsay MACDONALD in the coalition caused by the 1931 crisis, succeeding him as Prime Minister in 1935. His last ministry had to deal with the Abdication crisis (see EDWARD VIII), which he handled skilfully. In 1935 he approved the Hoare-Laval pact which allowed fascist Italy to annex Ethiopia. Although international relations continued to deteriorate with the German occupation of the Rhineland and the outbreak of the SPANISH CIVIL WAR, Baldwin opposed rearmament, believing that the public would not support it.

Balearic Islands A Spanish archipelago in the western Mediterranean Sea comprising three large islands and several smaller ones. The largest, Majorca, has the best climate. Minorca is unprotected from the north and has cold winds, while Ibiza, the third in size, sometimes suffers from the SIROCCO which blows up from the North African coast. Pop. (1986) 754,800.

baler A machine used on high-volume crops, such as hay, to make tightly packed bundles, convenient for transport and storage. The crop is forced into a chamber by a ram, and then tied. Modern rotary balers use plastic twine or tape for tying, and roll the crop into high-density bales weighing around half a tonne.

Balewa, Alhaji Sir Abubakar Tafawa (1912–66) Nigerian statesman. He entered politics in 1946, and became a member of the Central Legislative Council in 1947. The first Prime Minister of the Federation of Nigeria, he retained his office when the country became independent (1960) until he was killed in an army coup.

Balfour, Arthur James, 1st Earl of Balfour (1848–1930) British Conservative statesman, Prime Minister 1902–05. His premiership saw the formation of the Committee of Imperial Defence and the creation of the *entente cordiale* with France (1904), but the party split over the issue of tariff reform, forcing Balfour's resignation, although he remained as party leader until 1911. In 1917, in his capacity as Foreign Secretary during World War I, Balfour issued the declaration in favour of a Jewish national home in Palestine that came to be known as the **Balfour Declaration.**

Bali A mountainous island of Indonesia, lying between Java to the west and Lombok to the east; area 5,561 sq km (2,148 sq miles); pop. (est. 1993) 2,856,000; chief town, Denpasar. Bali is dominated by the volcanic peaks of Mt. Agung ('Holy Mountain'), which rises to a height of 3,142 m (10,308 ft) and Mt. Batur (1,740 m, 5,700 ft). In the north, rice, vegetables, and copra are grown by islanders. Tourist resorts have developed on the south coast at Sanur, Kuta, and Nusa Dua. The predominant religion is a form of Hindu known as Agama-Hindu.

Balkan Mountains (Bulgarian **Stara Planina**) A range of mountains stretching eastwards across Bulgaria from the Serbian frontier to the Black Sea. Its highest point is Botev Peak (2,375 m, 7,793 ft).

Balkans (or **Balkan States**) The countries occupying the Balkan peninsula of south-eastern Europe, lying south of the Danube and Sava rivers, between the Adriatic and Ionian seas in the west, the Aegean and Black seas in the east, and the Mediterranean in the south. It is the home of various peoples including Albanians, Vlachs, Greeks, Serbs, Bulgars, and Turks. From the 3rd to 7th century the Balkan peninsula, nominally ruled by the Byzantine emperors, was invaded by successive migrations of Slavs; later, parts of it were conquered by Venice and other states. In 1356 the Ottoman invasion began. Constantinople fell to the Turks in 1453, and by 1478 most of the peninsula was in their power; the subject nations, though largely retaining their languages and religions, did not recover independence until the 19th century. In 1912–13 Turkey was attacked and defeated by other Balkan peoples in alliance, then the former allies fought over their gains. After World War I the peninsula was divided between Greece, Albania, Bulgaria, and Yugoslavia, with Turkey retaining only Constantinople and the surrounding land. The area was in turmoil from 1991 to 1995 as Yugoslavia disintegrated into its constituent republics and a savage ethnic conflict developed in Bosnia-Hercegovina.

Balkan Wars (1912–13) Two short wars, fought between Serbia, Montenegro, Greece, Romania, Turkey, and Bulgaria for the possession of remaining European territories of the OTTOMAN EMPIRE. In 1912 Greece, Serbia, Bulgaria, and Montenegro formed the Balkan League. In October 1912 the League armies captured all but Constantinople (now Istanbul). European ambassadors intervened to re-draw the Balkans map to the advantage of Bulgaria and detriment of Serbia in the Treaty of London (May 1913). A month later, Bulgaria launched a pre-emptive attack on the Serbs and Greeks, who coveted Bulgaria's gains, but was defeated. In the Treaty of Bucharest (August 1913) Greece and Serbia partitioned Macedonia, and Romania gained part of Bulgaria. Albania, which had been under Turkish suzerainty, was made an independent Muslim principality. A 'big Serbia' now presented a considerable threat to Austria-Hungary. Russia promised to support Serbia in its nationalist struggle, and Germany to give military aid to Austria-Hungary. The assassination of the Austrian heir apparent, Archduke Francis Ferdinand, at Sarajevo (1914) gave Austria-Hungary the pretext to invade Serbia, leading to the outbreak of World War I six weeks later.

Balkhash, Lake A shallow salt lake with no outlet in Kazakhstan, Central Asia; area 18,428 sq km (7,115 sq miles). It is fed by the River Ili which flows north-westwards into the lake from the Tien Shan range. The copper-mining town and fishing port of Balkhash lies on its northern shore. Like the Aral Sea it has been shrinking in size owing to the extraction of water upstream on the River Ili.

Ball, John (died 1381) English rebel. Ball was a Wycliffite priest who preached an egalitarian social message. He was excommunicated and imprisoned for heresy, but released in June 1381 during the Peasants' Revolt. He was later captured, tried, and hanged as a traitor.

Balla, Giacomo (1871–1958) Italian painter and sculptor, one of the leading artists of the Futurist movement. After World War I Balla stayed true to the ideals of FUTURISM when his colleagues abandoned them, but he turned to a more conventional style in the 1930s.

ballad A folk song, generally with a repeated melody, that tells in a direct and dramatic manner some story usually derived from a tragic incident in local history or legend. In Britain, ballads emerged in Scotland and England from the 14th century, and have been imitated since the 18th century by poets outside the folk-song tradition; notably by Coleridge in 'The Rime of the Ancient Mariner'.

ballade An Old French lyric verse form, usually consisting of three 8-line STANZAS with an additional half-stanza, each ending with the same line as a refrain. In music, the term can refer either to a folk-song (*ballade* being the German word for BALLAD) or to a kind of composition for piano in a narrative style, as in some works by Chopin, Brahms, and others.

Ballance, John (1839–93) New Zealand statesman. In the 1890 elections the Liberals emerged as the first party in New Zealand politics, broadly united on a programme of radical reform, and Ballance became Premier (1891–93). Ballance and his Liberal successors established the tradition of using the state to regulate the economy and protect poorer groups, laying the foundations of basic stability in New Zealand society.

Ballantyne, R(obert) M(ichael) (1825–94) Scottish writer. In 1856 he published his first adventure story, *The Young Fur Traders*. This and other early stories draw on his experiences in North Canada, where he worked as a clerk before returning to Edinburgh in 1848. After the success of *The Coral Island* (1857), his best-known work, he became an acclaimed writer of stories for boys.

Ballarat A mining and sheep-farming centre in the state of Victoria, Australia; pop. (1991) 64,980. The largest gold reserves in Australia were discovered here in 1851. There is a memorial to the Eureka Stockade, site of an armed rebellion by gold miners in 1854.

Ballard, J(ames) G(raham) (1930–) British novelist and short-story writer, born in China. His early work consists of dystopian science-fiction novels and stories such as his first novel, *The Drowned World* (1962). In 1984 he published the autobiographical novel *Empire of the Sun*, which heralded a movement away from science fiction.

ballerina A woman BALLET dancer, especially one

taking leading roles in classical ballet. The prima ballerina is the star dancer of a company. Prime examples of technical virtuosity and expressive power were Marie Camargo (1710–70) and Marie Sallé (1707–56) and ethereal lyricism and sensual dramatic qualities were displayed by Marie Taglioni (1804–84) and Fanny Elssler (1810–84). In the 20th century prominent interpreters of both Romantic and Classical works, often emerging from DIAGHILEV's Ballets Russes revival, have been the Russian dancer Anna PAVLOVA, who toured with her own company; Tamara Karsavina (1885–1978), famous in the Ballets Russes; Alexandra Danilova (1903–97), a member of Russian and US companies; Galina ULANOVA of the Bolshoi Ballet; Alicia MARKOVA, attached to British companies; Margot FONTEYN of the Royal Ballet; and Alicia Alonso (1917–) of the American Ballet Theater and Cuban Ballet. Natalia MAKAROVA has, like so many of her predecessors, crossed the boundaries between Russia and Western Europe, and Suzanne Farrell (1945–) of New York City Ballet is a notable exponent of the US tradition.

Ballesteros, Severiano (1957–) Spanish golfer. In 1979 he became the youngest player in the 20th century to win the British Open (also taking the title in 1984 and 1988), and the following year was the youngest-ever winner of the US Masters.

ballet A theatrical form of dance typically combining dance steps with music, sets, and costumes in an integrated whole. The dance is usually based on a narrative (in which case it might include MIME) or on the movements typical of the genre (the *danse d'école*). The lavish, and extremely long, Italian court spectacles of the Renaissance were often based on allegorical sources. They developed into the French BALLET DE COUR under Louis XIV to the music of composers such as Lully and Rameau. By establishing the first dance academy in 1661 and the Paris Opera Ballet in 1669, Louis XIV was responsible for encouraging the acceptance of dance as a professional art. In the early to mid-18th century *ballet d'action* attempted to unite the story-telling function with an increasingly codified vocabulary of mime and movement in a more realistic portrayal of events. John Weaver in London and NOVERRE in Stuttgart and Vienna were the chief exponents in a Europe-wide development which culminated in Taglioni's *Robert le Diable* in 1831 and BOURNONVILLE's *La Sylphide* in 1836. Initially the dance movement was restricted to small steps and graceful gestures of the arms with the emphasis on intricate floor patterns and groupings. The steps were formalized by Carlo Blasis in the early 1800s through an analysis of the five positions of the feet, and the positions for arms, trunk, and head; these remain the basis of the *danse d'école* (the academic school style of classic ballet) and of ballet in the 20th century. The development of ballet from this point might be roughly divided into the mid-19th-century romantic ballets, the Russian classics of the latter part of the 19th century, and the Ballets Russes of DIAGHILEV, which act as a bridge to the modern and postmodern ballets of the 20th century. The romantic ballets have characteristics common to ROMANTICISM across the arts, of the creation of an ethereal, idealized world. Dancing on point and the use of gauzy white floating fabric helped to create this illusion. Its highest point was undoubtedly reached in the Paris Opéra productions of the 1830s, while Copenhagen developed its own brand of middle-class ballet romanticism and London actively participated in the international ballet boom. Russian ballet owes its origins both to a romantic use of the folk or character dances of the 19th century and to the techniques of ballet. It flourished under Tsarist patronage and, with the arrival of the choreographer PETIPA in 1847, the Imperial Ballet developed the Classical form to perfection. Extraordinary precision, fleetness of foot, and lightness of movement typify CLASSICISM in dance. The major development under Petipa was the refinement and perfection of the technique in solos and *pas de deux* (duets) and in manipulating a large *corps de ballet* through complex geometric designs. Exotic settings and fantastical themes continued to be common, allowing mime to develop further its own code of gestures. *The Sleeping Beauty* (1890) is one of the archetypal works of dance Classicism. The Western European revival of ballet in the 20th century is credited to the Russian impresario Diaghilev through the Ballets Russes dance company, which first toured Europe in 1909. His ability to bring major choreographers (FOKINE, MASSINE, NIJINSKY, Nijinska) together with composers (STRAVINSKY, FAURÉ, PROKOFIEV, SATIE) and painters (Benois, BAKST, Roerich, Picasso) to collaborate on works such as *The Firebird*, *Petrushka*, and *The Rite of Spring* heralded a new age. Colourful Russian and oriental spectacles were set alongside works reflective of experimental modern art in what were sometimes seen as outrageous avant-garde programmes.

Although the Ballets Russes performed in London it was not until the middle of the 20th century that a distinctive style emerged in Britain. In the 1920s the formation of schools and companies by RAMBERT (Ballet Rambert, now Rambert Dance Company) and DE VALOIS (the ROYAL BALLET and Sadler's Wells Royal Ballet) was the start of a development based initially on Ballets Russes works. Later, revivals of ballets from the Romantic and Classical periods joined the repertoire, but always with new or 'modern' choreographies. Some of these new works owed allegiance to Romantic inspiration, perhaps seen particularly in ASHTON's treatment of themes, just as much as to modern movements in art. Modernism in dance, however, is reflected in works such as Antony Tudor's *Dark Elegies*, which reveal universal emotions in an Expressionist manner through movement, rather than facial expression. MACMILLAN is the British choreographer who continues this development within the Royal Ballet company repertoire through psychological studies, sometimes of historical characters. Bournonville took the French Romantic ballet to Denmark and established a repertoire which has remained intact. Classicism in ballet shows direct continuation from Petipa to BALANCHINE, the Ballets Russes choreographer who established an American style of ballet. Balanchine's Neoclassical works, often using STRAVINSKY scores, for example *Apollo* (1928) and *Agon* (1957), became the hallmarks of American ballet. Balanchine (with the writer Lincoln Kirstein) founded NEW YORK CITY BALLET in 1948 to perform his own works. His dances, produced over a long career, range from the austere to the Romantic, from Neoclassical abstraction to Broadway MUSICALS. Balanchine's interest in the development of musical theatre in the USA was shared by many other choreographers: Agnes DEMILLE and Jerome ROBBINS contributed *Oklahoma* (1943) and *West Side Story* (1957) to the genre. This eclecticism, revealed in the incorporation of jazz dance elements into ballet, continued later with MODERN

DANCE. Some of the characteristics of this newer genre are now seen in modern ballet, for example in MacMillan's *Gloria* (1980), which deals with the horrors of war. See also DANCE NOTATION.

ballet de cour A form of court entertainment, performed exclusively by aristocratic amateurs, which had its greatest flowering between 1580 and 1660. Derived from the intermedii of the Italian Renaissance, the *ballets de cour* consisted of spectacles produced in the private theatres and sometimes the grounds of royal palaces, in which the king and his court performed before invited audiences. The *ballet* consisted of a series of mythological one-act dramas in dance form, accompanied by instrumental music. The costumes and décor were sumptuous and the stage machinery created spectacular technical effects.

Ballet Rambert See RAMBERT, DAME MARIE.

Ballets Russes See DIAGHILEV, SERGEI.

Balliol, Edward (died *c.*1364) King of Scotland 1332–36, son of John Balliol. In 1332 he landed in Fife to reclaim the throne his father had given up. He defeated the Scots at Dupplin and was crowned at Scone. Within three months he was forced to flee but returned with the help of EDWARD III of England after his victory at Halidon Hill. In 1341 Balliol was again expelled from Scotland and in 1356 he resigned his claim to the Scottish throne.

Balliol, John (*c.*1240–1314) King of Scotland 1292–96. He was descended through his maternal grandmother from DAVID I of Scotland, and in 1291–92 his claim to the crown was upheld in a trial between him and Robert Bruce, Lord of Annandale. The trial was arranged by EDWARD I of England, and less than a month after his coronation (30 November 1292) Balliol grudgingly did homage to Edward as his superior. In 1295 he attempted to ally with France, which resulted in an English invasion of Scotland. Balliol was forced to give up his kingdom to Edward and was taken as a captive to England, before retiring to his estates in France.

ballista An early form of mechanical ARTILLERY. The earliest Greek version, dating from the first half of the 4th century BC, used a large BOW laid across one end of a grooved batten. A refined model, developed by the Romans, replaced the bow with two vertical springs made from bundles of animal sinews, each with an arm passing through it. The arms were connected by a bowstring, which functioned as a catapult.

ballistic missile A MISSILE that, after launching, follows a trajectory determined by speed and gravity only. Strictly speaking, spears and shells are ballistic missiles, but today the term refers chiefly to long-range nuclear missiles, which make most of their flight outside the Earth's atmosphere. Modern ballistic missiles are accelerated to high velocities by ROCKET MOTORS for approximately 3–5 minutes, but after burn-out they follow an unpowered, ballistic trajectory. The largest ballistic missiles are the inter-continental ballistic missiles (ICBMs), which have a range of over 10,000 km (6,000 miles). The latest types can launch a MULTIPLE INDEPENDENTLY TARGETABLE RE-ENTRY VEHICLE (MIRV), striking separate targets over a wide area. See also ANTI-BALLISTIC MISSILE; STRATEGIC DEFENSE INITIATIVE.

balloon A lighter-than-air aircraft with no propulsive power. It usually consists of a large, rounded bag (the envelope) inflated with hot air from a propane gas burner or a light gas such as helium or hydrogen. It may have instruments or a passenger basket suspended beneath it. Descent is controlled by releasing air or gas from the balloon, off-loading sand ballast from the basket, and using a rope drag-line as an anchor. A small hot-air balloon was demonstrated in Lisbon in 1709, but attracted little attention. The first free flight by humans was made in a hot-air balloon, built by the MONTGOLFIER brothers, in 1783. Balloons developed quickly in the 19th century, but with the advent of AIRSHIPS and AEROPLANES, interest died for a time. However, balloons became an important tool for taking meteorological measurements and in upper atmospheric research in the 1930s, and during World War II balloon barrages were used extensively in the UK to protect cities, ports, and important installations from low-flying aircraft. Ballooning as a sport remains popular today. See also FLIGHT, PRINCIPLES OF MANNED; FLIGHT, HISTORY OF MANNED.

ballroom dancing See SAMBA; WALTZ.

Ballymena (Gaelic **An Baile Meánach**) A market town in County Antrim, north-east Northern Ireland; pop. (1981) 18,150. It has textile and engineering industries.

Balmaceda, José Manuel (1840–91) Chilean statesman and liberal reformer. He was first elected to the Chilean Congress as a Liberal in 1864. As leader of the anti-clerical group he was sent to Argentina in 1878 to persuade that country not to enter the War of the Pacific. He became a member of the cabinet of President Santa Maria (1881–86) and was himself then elected president (1886–91). Despite national prosperity, tension arose between President and Congress, which Balmaceda increasingly ignored. In January 1891 this resulted in civil war. Balmaceda took refuge in the Argentinian Embassy, where, rather than face trial, he shot himself.

Balmer, Johann (1825–98) Swiss physicist, who analysed the light emitted by hot hydrogen and discovered that the most prominent wavelengths in the SPECTRUM are linked by a simple formula. These wavelengths are seen as a series of lines, now known as the Balmer series. His formula is basic to the subsequent development of atomic theory and to the field of atomic spectroscopy.

Balmoral Castle A holiday residence of the British royal family on the River Dee near Braemar in north-east Scotland. The estate was bought in 1847 by Prince Albert who rebuilt the castle.

balsa An evergreen tree, *Ochroma pyramidale*, native to Central and South America. It grows some 12 m tall and is valuable for its extremely light wood, used for aircraft models, corks, floats, etc.

Baltic Entente (1934) A mutual defence pact between Estonia, Latvia, and Lithuania. Soon after World War I there were negotiations for an alliance between all the countries which had recently broken away from the Russian empire, that is, Poland, Finland, Estonia, Latvia, and Lithuania, but these collapsed. Latvia and Estonia did however make an agreement in 1923, which Lithuania joined in 1934.

Baltic languages A branch of the INDO-EUROPEAN LANGUAGES quite closely related to Slavic. The two surviving languages are spoken in the Baltic states of Latvia and Lithuania; in Estonia a form of Finno-Ugric is spoken (see URALIC). A third language, Old Prussian, became extinct around 1700, having been submerged by German. The Baltic languages are written in a modified Latin script. Lithuanian is spoken by 3 million people, and is first attested in written form in 1547. There are two distinct dialects, East and West Lithuanian, each of which has several sub-dialects. A standard written language based on West Lithuanian was adopted at the end of the 19th century. Latvian (Lettish) has 2 million speakers, and is first attested in 1585. There are three main dialects: Central, West, and East. The standard language, which was developed at the end of the 19th century, is based on the Central dialect.

Baltic literatures Literature of Estonia, Latvia, and Lithuania. The first known printed vernacular books in all three Baltic states were the Lutheran and Catholic catechisms of the 16th century. In the 19th century an upsurge in patriotic feeling, similar to that expressed in Finnish literature, inspired the strongly nationalistic Romantic poetry of writers such as Friedrich Reinhold Kreutzwald (1803–82), Lydia Koidula (1843–86), and Antanas Baranauskas (1834–1902). This trend merged into a period of Realist writing in the plays of August Kitzberg (1856–1927), and the short stories of Rudolfs Blaumanis (1863–1908). Neo-romanticism and Symbolism in the writings of Jānis Rainis (1865–1929); and Vydūnas (Vilius Storasta; 1868–1953) respectively, were established forms at the turn of the century, and developed further in the wake of the 1905 revolution by members of the Young Estonia group such as Gustav Suits (1885–1956). The Nazi occupation and annexation of the states by the Soviet Union in 1944 drove many writers into exile. Initially writers at home, constrained by the dogmas of socialist realism, could only discuss certain aspects of political life, but gradually they began to look at a wider range of social subjects. Under the influence of *perestroika* émigré writings began to appear officially within the three states. Growing nationalist feeling (and eventual independence in 1991) led the three countries to re-establish single national literatures. There has also been a move away from novels to the more immediate essay form, and to accounts of recent history such as *The Tellings of the Truth* (1988), by the Lithuanian Stasys Kašauskas. Among younger writers there has been a return to idealist, Christian principles, for example *Memoirs of a Young Man* by the Lithuanian Ričardas Gavelis.

Baltic Sea An almost land-locked shallow sea in northern Europe, connected with the North Sea by the Kattegat and Skagerrak straits and by the Kiel Canal across the Jutland peninsula, and bordered by Sweden, Finland, Russia, the Baltic States, Poland, Germany, and Denmark. Its chief ports include Copenhagen, Stockholm, Turku, Helsinki, Tallinn, Riga, Klaipeda, Kaliningrad, Gdansk, and Rostock.

Baltic states ▶1 The independent states of Lithuania, Latvia, and Estonia. **▶2** The littoral states of the Baltic, as in the 10-member Council of Baltic States established in 1992 (Denmark, Estonia, Finland, Germany, Latvia, Lithuania, Norway, Poland, Russia, and Sweden).

Baltimore A commercial city and industrial seaport in north Maryland, USA, on the Patapsco River; pop. (1990) 736,000. First settled in the 1660s, it was named after Lord Baltimore (1606–75), the English proprietor of territory that later became the state of Maryland. During the 19th century it was a noted centre of shipbuilding. Johns Hopkins University (1876), Morgan State University (1867), and the University of Maryland at Baltimore are important centres of education. Coal, grain, and iron, steel, and copper products are exported. Industries include shipbuilding, oil refining, steel, chemicals, aerospace equipment, and food processing.

Baltistan (or **Little Tibet**) A region of Pakistani-held Kashmir in the Karakoram range of the Himalayas, to the south of Mt. K2, western Ladakh. It is the home of the Baltis, a Muslim tribe of Tibetan origin. The chief town is Skardu.

Baluchistan ▶1 A mountainous and arid region of western Asia that includes part of south-east Iran, south-west Afghanistan, and west Pakistan. **▶2** A province of west Pakistan, bounded in the south by the Arabian Sea, the north by Afghanistan, and the west by Iran; area 347,190 sq km (134,102 sq miles); pop. (1981) 4,332,000; capital, Quetta.

Balzac, Honoré de (1799–1850) French novelist. He is chiefly remembered for his series of ninety-one coordinated and interconnected novels and stories known collectively as *La Comédie humaine*, which appeared in a collected edition 1842–48, and includes *Eugénie Grandet* (1833) and *Le Père Goriot* (1835).

Bamako The capital and commercial centre of the African state of Mali, on the River Niger; pop. (est. 1990) 600,000. It is the country's main cattle and kola nut market, and has light industries.

bamboo An evergreen woody-stemmed plant belonging to the GRASS family. The 200 or so species of bamboo, which are widely distributed, are grouped into several genera. They may vary in height from a few centimetres (a few inches) to 30 m (100 feet) or more. The hard-skinned stems are very durable and have many uses, including building, furniture making, basketry, and as garden canes. The flowering of bamboos is very unusual. It usually occurs at indefinite and lengthy intervals of up to 120 years, and often results in the death of the plant.

Banaba (or **Ocean Island**) An island in the Pacific Ocean just south of the equator; area 5 sq km (2 sq miles); pop. (1990) 284. Now part of the Kiribati group, Banaba was the capital of the former British colony of Gilbert and Ellice.

banana A large-leaved perennial herbaceous plant, reaching up to 10 m (33 feet) in height. Banana plants originated in south-east Asia from two wild species, *Musa acuminata* and *M. balbisiana*, and are now grown throughout the tropics, predominantly in the humid lowland areas. They produce the most widely consumed tropical fruit, with an estimated world yield of 35,000,000 tonnes (38,580,000 US tons) per annum. Central America and the West Indies export large quantities of the sweet, dessert types to North America and Europe. A cooking type known as plantain, *M.* × *paradisiaca*, with a higher starch content and flesh too hard and indigestible to be eaten raw, is used for local consumption. Cultivated banana plants are sterile, ensuring seedless fruits, and are propagated vegetatively from suckers.

Bancroft, Edward (1744–1821) US traitor. Born in Massachusetts, he studied medicine in London. He met Benjamin FRANKLIN, and during the War of Independence was a friend of Arthur Lee and Silas Dean. Bancroft was actually an agent for England at an annual fee of £500 and a life pension and it was almost a century before his activities as a British agent were discovered.

Banda, Hastings Kamuzu (1906–97) Malawian statesman, Prime Minister 1964–94 and President 1966–94. He studied medicine in the USA and practised in Britain before returning to lead his country (formerly Nyasaland) to independence. As the first President of the Republic of Malawi he created an autocratic and paternalistic one-party state; a pragmatist, he was the first black African leader to visit South Africa (1970) and later established trading links with it. Banda was defeated in Malawi's first multi-party elections in 1994; the following year he was acquitted on charges of murdering four political opponents.

Banda Islands A group of ten volcanic islands in the Indonesian Moluccas, to the south-east of the island of Seram. It comprises Great Banda, Bandanaira, Agung Api, and seven small islands which were discovered by the Portuguese in 1512. In 1619 the islands were taken over by the Dutch who exterminated the indigenous population in order to gain control of the nutmeg trade. The chief port is Bandanaira.

Bandaranaike, Sirimavo Ratwatte Dias (1916–) Sinhalese stateswoman, Prime Minister of Sri Lanka 1960–65, 1970–77, and since 1994. The world's first woman Prime Minister, she succeeded her husband, S. W. R. D. BANDARANAIKE, after his assassination. Opposition to her policies and continuing ethnic conflict resulted in an overwhelming defeat in the 1977 elections. She was charged with misuse of power in 1980, stripped of her civil rights for six years, and expelled from Parliament. Her daughter, **Chandrika Bandaranaike Kumaratunga** (1945–), became Prime Minister and then President in 1994, being succeeded as Prime Minister by her mother.

Bandaranaike, S(olomon) W(est) R(idgeway) D(ias) (1899–1959) Sinhalese statesman. He formed the Maha Sinhala Party in the 1920s. In 1931 he was elected to the new State Council and after independence he assumed ministerial power. In 1952 he founded the Sri Lanka Freedom Party (SLFP), which was the leading partner in the coalition which won the 1956 elections, attracting left-wing and Buddhist support. As Prime Minister (1956–59) Bandaranaike pursued a policy of promoting the Sinhalese language, Buddhism, socialism, and neutrality. His policy alienated the Tamils. After his assassination in September 1959 by a dissident Buddhist monk, his widow, Mrs Sirimavo BANDARANAIKE, succeeded him as Prime Minister.

Bandar Seri Begawan (formerly **Brunei Town**) The capital of the sultanate of Brunei on the island of Borneo; pop. (1991) 46,000. A deep-water port was opened in 1972 at nearby Muara. There is a vast new royal palace and the largest mosque in south-east Asia.

Bandello, Matteo Maria (1485–1562) Italian short-story writer. He wrote a collection of 214 *Novelle* (Novels), which made him the most popular short-story writer of his day. His stories were a frequent inspiration to English, French, and Spanish dramatists, notably to Shakespeare.

bandicoot An Australian marsupial in the family Permelidae. The 17 species of bandicoots are about the size of rabbits, which they resemble in their reproductive rate and elongated hind-legs. With their long, flexible, rodent-like muzzles, they root in the soil for their insect food. The pouch opens towards the tail. Once widespread and numerous, some are now very rare.

bandkeramik The German term for a kind of pottery (decorated with incised ribbon-like ornament) which was characteristic of the first NEOLITHIC settlers in central Europe and which gives its name to their culture. These peoples spread up from the Balkans *c.*5000 BC. They occupied small plots of land on fertile soil near rivers, where they built wooden longhouses for themselves and their livestock, and cultivated cereals which they introduced to this area. They formed the basis of later Neolithic populations.

Bandung The capital of the province of West Java, Indonesia, situated at an altitude of 715 m (2,346 ft); pop. (1990) 2,056,900. Founded by the Dutch in 1810, it was the capital of the Dutch East Indies. It is the third-largest city in Indonesia and the chief centre of the Sundanese people of western Java. Textiles, tea, and quinine are produced.

Bandung Conference (1955) A conference of Asian and African states at Bandung in Java, Indonesia. Organized on the initiative of President SUKARNO and other leaders of the Non-Aligned Movement, the Bandung Conference brought together twenty-nine states in an attempt to form a non-aligned bloc opposed to colonialism and the 'imperialism' of the superpowers. The five principles of non-aggression, respect for sovereignty, non-interference in internal affairs, equality, and peaceful co-existence were adopted, but the subsequent emergence of the non-aligned movement was hamstrung by the deterioration of relations between India and China, and by the conflicting forces set loose by decolonization.

bandwidth A range of FREQUENCIES needed to transmit a signal. A telephone signal requires a bandwidth of 4 kHz, whereas a television picture is much more complex, requiring over 5 MHz. In computing, bandwidth refers to the number of BITS per second transmitted between two digital devices. The bandwidth between a microcomputer and its hard disk is around 10 Mbit (10 million bits) per second; between a supercomputer and its memory the bandwidth could be around 100,000 Mbit.

Banffshire A former county of north-east Scotland which formed part of a district (with Buchan) in Grampian Region (1975–96). The former county town was the resort and fishing port of Banff.

Bangalore The capital of the state of Karnataka in central India; pop. (1991) 2,651,000. Under British rule it was formerly the administrative centre of the state of Mysore. It is now a prosperous industrial city with aircraft, electronics, machine tools, agricultural implements, paper, and textile industries.

Bangkok The capital and chief port of Thailand, on the River Chao Phraya, 40 km (25 miles) upstream from its outlet into the Gulf of Thailand; pop. (1990) 5,876,000. Rice, rubber, tin, and timber are the chief exports. Originally a small port serving Ayutthaya the former capital of Siam, Bangkok became capital in 1782 when the founder of the Chakri dynasty, King Rama I, built his palace there. The city is rich in Thai culture and is a popular tourist destination. Its principal modern industries include rice mills, oil refineries, sawmills, shipyards, and textile factories. There is also a famous trade in jewellery.

Bangla See INDO-IRANIAN LANGUAGES.

Bangladesh A tropical low-lying country of the Indian subcontinent.

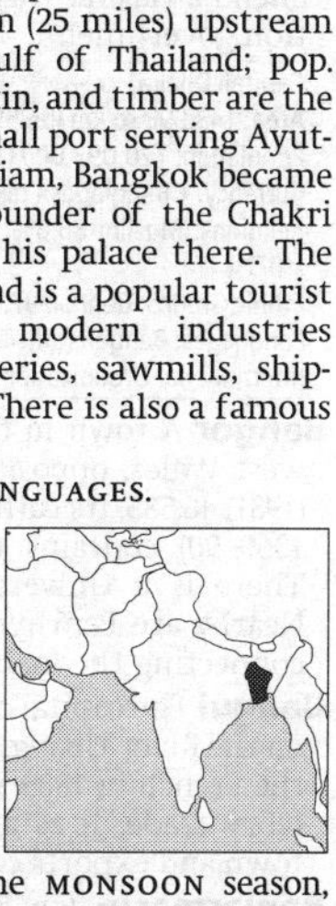

Physical. Situated at the head of the Bay of Bengal, Bangladesh is mainly occupied by the deltas of the Ganges and the Brahmaputra. It is a land of rivers, which flood regularly in the MONSOON season, leaving fertile soil on their banks. The south-west delta area, the Sundarbans, is mainly swamp and jungle; the region is subject to frequent CYCLONES which are funnelled up the Bay of Bengal and exacerbated by large-scale deforestation, thus causing immense damage and loss of life and crops.

Economy. The country grows 70 per cent of the world's supply of jute, and jute products are an important export, despite falling world demand. Other exports include clothing, shrimp, and leather goods. Industry is limited; the economy is primarily agrarian, with rice the most important food crop. There are substantial undeveloped reserves of oil, coal, and natural gas. The country is one of the world's poorest and most densely populated, and relies heavily on foreign aid.

History. Bangladesh was established in 1971 from territories which had previously formed the eastern part of Pakistan. Evidence of discontent in East Pakistan first appeared in the 1952 Bengali-language agitation and became much stronger after the 1965 INDO-PAKISTAN WAR. In 1966 the Awami League put forward a demand for greater autonomy which it proposed to implement after its victory in the 1970 elections. In March 1971, when this demand was rejected by the military government of Pakistan, civil war began, leading to a massive exodus of refugees to India. India sent help to the East Pakistan guerrillas (the Mukti Bahini). In the war of December 1971, Indian troops defeated the Pakistan forces in East Pakistan. The independence of Bangladesh was proclaimed in 1971 and recognized by Pakistan in 1974. The first Prime Minister, Mujibur Rahman, was murdered in 1975 and a period of political chaos, ethnic riots, floods, and famine followed, Bangladesh being declared the world's poorest country in 1987. In 1990 the military leader President Ershad was forced to resign, was arrested, and imprisoned for corruption. Elections in 1991 restored civilian rule under Prime Minister Begum Zia. The presidential form of government was replaced in 1991 when a parliamentary constitution was adopted. Abdur Rahman Biswas was elected to the Presidency, which had become primarily a ceremonial office. From 1995 Zia's government was troubled by strikes and mass protests against privatization and other policies. The political crisis deepened after elections held in February 1996 were boycotted by the opposition and much of the electorate. Following a second election in June 1996 Sheikha Hasina Wajed became the head of a coalition government.

Capital: Dhaka
Area: 143,998 sq km (55,598 sq mi)
Population: 120,093,000 (1995)
Currency: 1 Bangladesh taka = 100 paisa
Religions: Muslim 86.6%; Hindu 12.1%; Buddhist 0.6%; Christian 0.3%
Ethnic Groups: Bengali 97.7%; Bihari 1.3%; minority tribes 1.0%
Languages: Bengali (official) 99.0%; Urdu; Bihari; Hindi
International Organizations: UN; Commonwealth; Colombo Plan

Bangor A town in the county of Gwynedd, northwest Wales, opposite the island of Anglesey; pop. (1981) 46,585. Its cathedral (built *c*.1500 and restored 1869–90) contains tombs of the Welsh princes. There is a University College founded in 1884. Nearby are Penrhyn Castle and the Menai Bridge connecting the mainland with Anglesey.

Bangui The capital of the Central African Republic, on the River Ubangi, pop. (1988) 576,780. Founded by the French in 1889, it was formerly a centre of the ivory trade. It is a market and university (1970) town and exports cotton and timber.

Banjarmasin (or **Bandjarmasin**) A deep-water port and capital of the Indonesian province of South Kalimantan situated on a delta island near the junction of the Martapura and Barito rivers close to the south coast of the island of Borneo; pop. (1990) 480,740. It is the centre of a fertile agricultural region and a fishing port.

banjo A plucked stringed musical instrument of Afro-American origin with a drum-like resonator, the belly of which is made of skin or plastic. Banjos were first made by slaves on American plantations, possibly on the model of instruments such as the West African *banja*, remembered from their homelands. The earliest banjos had no frets, but fretted fingerboards are now normal. The standard banjo has five strings.

Banjul (name until 1973 **Bathurst**) The capital of the Gambia, on St Mary's Island at the mouth of the Gambia River, where it meets the Atlantic Ocean; pop. (1983) 44,536. It was founded by the British in 1816 as a trading station and base for suppressing the slave trade, and was named after the 3rd Earl of Bathurst (1762–1834) who was Secretary of State for the Colonies (1812–28). It is the Gambia's commercial centre and has groundnuts processing plants. The tourist industry has also recently developed with new hotels being built for European sunseekers.

bank A financial institution that deals in money, principally by accepting deposits and making loans. Customers' deposits are a bank's liabilities, and loans are its assets. Typically, a bank makes a profit by charging a higher rate of INTEREST for loans than it pays on deposits. The two main types of banks are commercial and CENTRAL BANKS. In the UK the BANK OF ENGLAND is the central bank. Commercial banks include clearing banks and merchant banks (see CLEARING HOUSE). In recent years financial institutions such as BUILDING SOCIETIES have challenged the banks by offering banking facilities to their private (but not commercial) customers. Some building societies have actually changed their status and become banks. In the UK, discount houses, which borrow and lend in the short-term money market (usually by buying and selling Treasury Bills and BILLS OF EXCHANGE), are also part of the commercial banking system. Merchant banks are banks whose main business is the provision of long-term credit, and financing for trading enterprises. They perform a variety of services for clients, such as sales of new issues, the acceptance of bills of exchange, and portfolio management. A main concern is to provide advice to firms concerning mergers and take-overs, and to supply finance for new businesses.

Bankhead, Tallulah (1903–68) US actress. Making her stage début in New York in 1918, Bankhead became noted for her uninhibited public persona, rich laugh, and harsh drawl. her most successful film appearance was in Alfred Hitchcock's *Lifeboat* (1944).

Bank of England The British CENTRAL BANK, popularly known as the 'Old Lady of Threadneedle Street', where its London office stands. It was founded in 1694 as an undertaking by 1268 shareholders to lend £1,200,000 to the government of William III to finance his wars against France. In return it received 8 per cent interest and the right to issue notes against the security of the loan. These privileges were confirmed in 1708 when its capital was doubled, and it was given a monopoly of joint-stock banking which lasted until 1826, thus preventing rival banks from having large numbers of shareholders.

The bank is controlled by the Governor of the

Bank of England and a court of 16 directors, appointed by the Crown. Its responsibilities include acting as banker to the government and as its agent in the issue of treasury bills; functioning as lender of last resort to the clearing banks, enabling it to control the amount of money in circulation; issuing the country's stock of money through its subsidiary, the Royal Mint; acting as registrar for government stocks; managing, on behalf of the Treasury, the money market and exchange equalization account; and determining the interest-rate structure of the economy.

bank rate (or **official discount rate**) The rate of INTEREST at which a CENTRAL BANK will lend to commercial banks and (sometimes) other financial institutions. Even when no central bank lending is taking place, bank rate will normally be a major influence on short-run interest rates. Changes in bank rate, by affecting market interest rates, may affect the domestic economy by altering consumption and investment plans. In addition, a change in short-run interest rates may affect the flow of internationally mobile funds into and out of a country. See also BALANCE OF PAYMENTS.

Banks, Sir Joseph (1743–1820) British naturalist and explorer, who brought back many plants and insects from his first expedition to Labrador and Newfoundland. Banks accompanied Captain James Cook in the voyage of the *Endeavour*, sent by the Royal Society to observe the transit of Venus in 1769, which set a pattern for geographical and scientific exploration of the Pacific. Banks helped to establish the Botanic Gardens at Kew, near London, not only as a repository of thousands of living specimens from all over the world, but as a centre for the introduction of plants to new regions, including BREADFRUIT and tea. He also imported merino sheep from Spain and sent them on to Australia.

banksia See PROTEA.

bank vole A species of VOLE, *Clethrionomys glareolus*, that occurs over much of Europe and western Asia in most vegetation types, provided there is sufficient cover. The tail is long for a vole, being about half the length of the 9 cm (4 inch) long body, giving it some resemblance to a mouse. It is mainly nocturnal, breeding throughout the summer and, if food is abundant, sometimes throughout much of the year. Predators of the bank vole include hawks, owls, weasels, and stoats. The genus *Clethrionomys* includes a further six species commonly called red-backed voles, native to North America and Asia.

Bann The principal river of Northern Ireland. It rises in the Mourne Mountains and flows 103 km (65 miles) northwards through Lough Neagh and Lough Beg before meeting the Atlantic Ocean beyond Coleraine.

Bannister, Sir Roger (Gilbert) (1929–) British middle-distance runner and neurologist. While still a medical student, in May 1954 he became the first man to run a mile in under 4 minutes, with a time of 3 minutes 59.4 seconds. He retired from athletics in the same year and went on to a distinguished medical career.

Bannockburn, Battle of (24 June 1314) A major battle fought between EDWARD II of England and ROBERT the Bruce at Bannockburn, about 4.5 km (2 miles) from Stirling in Scotland. Edward's large invading army, perhaps 20,000 strong, was outmanoevred and forced into the Bannock burn (or river) and adjacent marshes; it was a disastrous defeat for the English, and Edward was lucky to be able to flee to safety.

banshee A supernatural being in Celtic folklore whose wail or keening outside a house is believed to portend death within.

Banská Bystrica The chief town of central Slovakia, in the Low Tatras, at the confluence of the Hron and Bystrica rivers; pop. (1991) 177,578. Noted in medieval times for its copper and silver mines, Banská Bystrica is now a leading cultural and economic centre.

Bantam (or **Bantĕn**) A port in Java, commanding the Sunda Straits. At its height, Bantam's control extended over the major pepper-growing areas of southern Sumatra. In 1604 the English built a trading post and the subsequent Dutch conquest of Malacca (1641) and Macassar (1667–68) increased the importance of Bantam. After a rebellion in 1752 Bantam became a vassal of the DUTCH EAST INDIA COMPANY. Its sultanate was finally suppressed in 1832.

Banting, Sir Frederick Grant (1891–1941) Canadian physiologist and surgeon. Banting initiated research into the secretion of the pancreas in a laboratory provided by J. J. R. Macleod. A series of experiments with dogs, carried out with C. H. Best's assistance, led to the discovery of insulin in 1921–22. They then purified the extracts of insulin and used them to treat diabetes, which had previously been an incurable and fatal disease. Banting and Macleod shared a Nobel Prize in 1923.

Bantry Bay An inlet of the Atlantic Ocean in County Cork on the south coast of the Republic of Ireland.

Bantu A large group of Negroid peoples of south and central Africa speaking some 300 languages (with 100 million speakers) within the Niger-Kordofanian family of languages including Bemba, Ganda, Kikuyu, Kongo, Lingala, Luba, Makua, Mbundu, Ruanda, Rundi, Shona, Sotho, Swahili, Thonga, Xhosa, and Zulu. Of these, Swahili is the most important. Originally Arab traders introduced their Arabic script, which was used for Swahili along the coast, but elsewhere the Roman alphabet has been used, sometimes with additional characters. The Bantu people migrated to southern Africa, through the lake region of East Africa, by the 3rd century AD. It is believed that the Bantu introduced iron metallurgy to southern Africa at the time of their entry.

Bantu language See NIGER-CONGO LANGUAGES.

Bantustan One of the former 'homelands' reserved for black Africans in the Republic of South Africa. Ten Bantustans were created by the Bantu Self-Government Act of 1959. The Bantu Homelands Constitution Act (1971) established them as Separate Development Self-Governing Areas and envisaged eventual 'independence'. This was in fact granted to four of the homelands, their non-residents automatically becoming citizens of the new states: Transkei, chiefly Xhosa people, in 1976; Bophuthatswana, chiefly Tswana, in 1977; Venda in 1979; and Ciskei in 1981. Only South Africa recognized them. The homelands were regarded by many as the clearest manifestation of the policy of APARTHEID. All the Bantustans were abolished following South Africa's adoption of a multi-racial constitution in 1994 and South African nationality was restored to all their citizens.

banyan A species of FIG, *Ficus benghalensis*, which is a sacred tree in India. It is notable for its long aerial roots which develop on the trunk and branches and then take root in the ground, forming pillars which make an extensive thicket.

baobab A species of deciduous tree, *Adansonia digitata*, which grows in arid environments in tropical and southern Africa. A characteristic feature is its massive, barrel-shaped trunk, growing up to 30 m (100 feet) in circumference and reaching a height of 17 m (56 feet). This huge trunk is adapted for water storage. The baobab is part of the family Bombacaceae, which also includes the balsa, silk cotton or kapok, and durian trees in tropical regions.

Bao Dai (1913–) Emperor of Vietnam 1926–45. His initial aim to reform Vietnam did not receive French colonial support. During World War II he collaborated with the Japanese and in 1945 he was forced to abdicate by the VIETMINH. In 1949 he renounced his title and returned to Saigon as head of the state of Vietnam within the French Union. In 1955, after the partition of Vietnam at the Geneva Conference, he was once again deposed when power in the new republic of South Vietnam passed to Ngo Din Diem. He then went into exile, living mainly in France.

Baotou An industrial city in Inner Mongolia, northern China, on the Yellow River; pop. (1990) 1,200,000. Iron, steel, chemicals, and textiles are produced.

Baptism See SACRAMENT.

Baptist Church A Christian Protestant movement distinguished by its stress on baptism of adults by total immersion in water and the autonomy of local congregations. In the 16th century various religious groups in Europe (ANABAPTISM) established the ritual of adult baptism. The modern Baptist movement dates its beginnings from the English church established in Amsterdam in 1609 by John Smyth (1554–1612) and the church in London under Thomas Helwys (1612). They were 'General' or Arminian Baptists, as opposed to 'Particular' or Calvinist Baptists, who evolved between 1633 and 1638. After the RESTORATION they moved closer to the PRESBYTERIANS and Independents and were recognized as dissenters from the Anglican Church. The USA's first Baptist church was probably the one established at Providence, Rhode Island, with the help of Roger Williams (1639). From 1740, under the influence of the Great Awakening, the movement made considerable headway, especially in the southern states.

In both Britain and the USA Baptist churches grew in the late 18th century. Baptist missionaries first went to India in 1792 and in the 19th century were active all over the world including in Russia. In 1813 the Baptist Union of Great Britain was organized and Baptist churches became very popular, especially in towns. In the USA in 1845, the Southern Baptist Convention was formed and split from the Northern (later National) Convention. Black Baptist Churches grew after 1865 and contributed significantly to black culture. In 1905 the Baptist World Alliance was formed. By 1990 it included 144 churches with about 30 million full members in the USA, and a further 6 million in Africa, Asia, and elsewhere. Baptists constituted the largest Protestant group in the former Soviet Union, where many ministers were imprisoned. During the 1980s and 1990s, especially in the USA, there was a rise in the number of fundamentalist and militant Baptist groups. Many Baptist preachers have turned to such modern methods of communication as television and the Internet to spread their views to a wide audience.

Barabbas A New Testament figure, the bandit whom Pilate released instead of Jesus at the request of the Jews.

Barbados An island country in the south-east Caribbean.

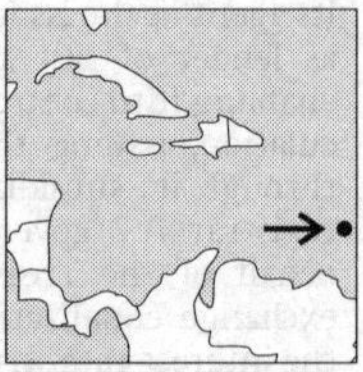

Physical. Barbados is the most easterly of the Windward Islands in the Caribbean Sea. Of coral formation, it is about 34 km (21 miles) long by 22 km (14 miles) wide and rises in gentle stages to some 336 m (1,100 feet). The climate is very warm with heavy rain watering the sugar cane, from which molasses is produced.

Economy. The principal economic activity is tourism, but agriculture, with sugar cane the main crop, remains important; a limited manufacturing industry includes food-processing, clothing, and assembly work. Offshore petroleum and natural gas reserves make an important contribution to the economy, and there is a developing services sector.

History. Barbados may have been visited by the conquistador Rodrigo de Bastidas in 1501; however the island that he called Isla Verde (because of its luxuriant vegetation) could have been Grenada rather than Barbados. The earliest inhabitants were thought to have been Arawak Indians, and later also some Carib Indians, but they had disappeared by the time British settlers began to colonize the island in 1627. Barbados became a British Crown colony in 1652. The British brought a large number of Africans to Barbados to work as slaves on sugar plantations. When slavery was abolished in 1834 six-sevenths of the population was black. Cane sugar remained the principal product of the island throughout the 17th, 18th, and 19th centuries. Barbados was also a strategic port for the British navy. In 1958 Barbados joined the West Indies Federation and in 1966 became fully independent within the Commonwealth. The Democratic Labour Party (DLP) was in power from 1961 until 1976 and from 1986 until 1994, when the Barbados Labour Party (BLP) won general elections.

Capital: Bridgetown
Area: 430 sq km (166 sq mi)
Population: 265,000 (1995)
Currency: 1 Barbados dollar = 100 cents
Religions: Anglican 39.7%; non-religious 17.5%; Pentecostal 7.6%; Methodist 7.1%; Roman Catholic 4.4%
Ethnic Groups: Black 80.0%; Mixed 16.0%; White 4.0%
Languages: English (official)
International Organizations: UN; OAS; CARICOM; Commonwealth

Barbarossa See FREDERICK I.

Barbarossa (Turkish **Khayr ad-Din Pasha**) (*c*.1483–1546) A famous CORSAIR, and later grand admiral of the OTTOMAN fleet. He and his brother Aruj first came to fame for their success against Christian vessels in the eastern Mediterranean. Aruj was killed fighting in 1518, and his brother Khayr ad-Din diplomatically ceded Algiers and its territory to the Ottoman sultan. He served as viceroy until 1533, when he was made grand admiral. In 1534 he took Tunis, but Charles V expelled him in 1535. After a number of minor engagements he retired in 1544.

barbary ape A species of MACAQUE monkey, *Macaca sylvanus*, which is found in northwest Africa and in a small colony on the Rock of Gibraltar. It is sociable and lives in small groups which travel through rocky woodland searching for their food of fruit, leaves, roots, and insects.

Barbary Coast The Mediterranean coast of North Africa from Morocco to Egypt, noted in the 16th–18th centuries for its pirates.

barbel A fish, *Barbus barbus*, of the CARP family, with a wide distribution in Europe. It prefers deep water with moderate currents, and lives close to the river-bed. Related species in the same genus, also often called barbels, live in Europe, Asia, and Africa; in the last two continents there are many small, brightly coloured species known as barbs, which are often kept as aquarium fishes. Barbels have four fleshy, threadlike, sensory structures (also called 'barbels') near the mouth.

Barber, Samuel (1910–81) US composer. He travelled extensively in Europe and developed a style based on romanticism allied to classical forms; his music includes operas, ballets, choral works, and orchestral and chamber music. His best-known works include the *Adagio for Strings* (1936) and the opera *Vanessa* (1958).

barberry A shrub of the genus *Berberis* in the family Berberidaceae, distributed in temperate regions of the Northern Hemisphere and of South America. There are around 450 species, both evergreen and deciduous, the leaves of the latter turning to bright colours in autumn. All species bear small yellow or orange flowers, which are followed by red, yellow, blue, or black fleshy berries, according to species. The common barberry, *B. vulgaris*, found in Europe and northern Asia, and introduced to North America, is the host at a stage in the life cycle of wheat black-rust disease.

barbet A bird making up three families allied to the toucans and woodpeckers. There are 26 Asian barbets (Megalaimidae), 42 African species (Lybiidae), and 14 New World barbets (Capitonidae). They vary in length from about that of a sparrow to that of a largish thrush, and are stocky, large-headed, stout-beaked birds. Most are brightly coloured with patches of red, blue, and yellow on a basic plumage of bright green, brown, or black. They live in wooded areas of the tropics feeding on fruits and insects, and are non-migratory. They nest in holes, usually in trees, but sometimes in the ground, and lay two to four white eggs.

Barbican A part of London near the ancient city walls, to the north-east of St Paul's Cathedral. It is noted for its post-war apartment blocks and the Barbican Centre, a complex of theatres, cinemas, and galleries (opened in 1982).

Barbirolli, Sir John (born Giovanni Battista Barbirolli) (1899–1970) British conductor, of Franco-Italian descent. Originally a cellist, he began his conducting career in 1924. He subsequently became conductor of several major opera companies and orchestras, including Covent Garden in Britain and the New York Philharmonic in the USA. In 1943 he returned to England as conductor of the Hallé Orchestra, Manchester, where he was responsible for rebuilding the orchestra's reputation.

barbiturate Any member of a group of drugs derived from barbituric acid, which are used for their action on the brain. Barbiturates can be injected intravenously before an operation to induce ANAESTHESIA. At one time they were taken orally for sleeplessness or anxiety, but since they produce dependence they have now been largely superseded by TRANQUILLIZERS. They are still used in the treatment of epilepsy.

Barbizon A village in the forest of Fontainebleau, Seine-et-Marne department, north-central France; pop. (1982) 1,270. It gave its name to the Barbizon school of French landscape painters who came together here in the 1840s. Théodore Rousseau (1812–67) was the leader of the group, which included Daubigny, Diaz, Millet, and Dupré.

Barbour, John (*c.*1320–95) Scottish poet and prelate. He was Archdeacon of Aberdeen (1357–95) and probably taught at Oxford and Paris. The only poem ascribed to him with certainty is *The Bruce*, a verse chronicle relating the deeds of Robert the Bruce and his follower James Douglas.

Barbuda See ANTIGUA AND BARBUDA.

barcarole A piece of music that imitates the songs sung by Venetian gondoliers. The form is found in operas (such as Offenbach's *Les Contes d'Hoffmann*) and in purely instrumental works, such as Mendelssohn's *Songs without Words*.

Barcelona The second-largest city of Spain and chief city of the region of Catalonia, situated on the Mediterranean coast of north-east Spain between the Llobregat and Bésos rivers; pop. (1991) 1,653,175. It is also the largest seaport and industrial city in Spain, producing vehicles, textiles, petrochemicals, and electrical equipment. Allegedly founded by the Phoenicians, Barcelona was held by Carthaginians, Romans, and Visigoths before falling to the Moors in the 8th century. It was taken by Charlemagne in 801 and during the succeeding two centuries became part of the independent Spanish March held by the counts of Barcelona who freed most of Catalonia from Arab rule. Noted as a centre of radical politics, it was the seat of the Spanish Loyalist government during 1938–39. Barcelona, a leading cultural centre of Spain, hosted the 1992 Olympic Games. Antonio Gaudí (1852–1926) studied architecture here and notable buildings include the 14th–15th-century cathedral of Santa Eulalia, the Pedralbes Palace, and Gaudi's Church of the Holy Family.

barchan A dune of sand or snow blown by wind into crescent shapes, with the horns trailing downwind on each side of a steep, downwind lee side.

Bar Cochba (or, in Jewish sources, **Simeon bar Kosiba**) Jewish leader of a rebellion in 132 AD against Hadrian's intention to rebuild Jerusalem as a non-Jewish city. His claim to be the Messiah was accepted by some. A number of letters in his handwriting have been found in archaeological excavations near the Dead Sea in Israel.

bar code An identification system that can be processed by a computer. Though there are several variations, they all consist of printed patterns of lines and spaces which record information such as price and batch number as a binary code. A computer-based CASH REGISTER or point-of-sale system can read bar codes optically.

bard A poet of the ancient Celts whose role it was to celebrate national events, especially heroic victories. The bards occupied a separate social status with hereditary privileges which, in Wales, were codified into distinct grades in the 10th century. They became extinct in Gaul relatively early but continued in Ireland and Scotland until the 18th century and in Wales and Cornwall to the present day, occupying a central position in the contest of poetry and music known as the Eisteddfod.

Bardeen, John See SHOCKLEY, WILLIAM BRADFORD.

Bardo (or **Le Bardo**) A town in northern Tunisia forming a north-western suburb of the city of Tunis. The National Museum of the Bardo, founded in 1882 and located in a palace of the former beys of Tunis, features one of the world's largest collections of mosaics.

Bardot, **Brigitte** (born Camille Javal) (1934–) French actress. She made her film début in 1952, but it was *And God Created Woman* in 1956 that established her reputation as an international sex symbol. Subsequent films include *Love is My Profession* (1959) and *A Very Private Affair* (1962). After retiring from acting she became an active supporter of animal welfare.

Barebones Parliament The assembly summoned by Oliver CROMWELL in July 1653, after he had dissolved the RUMP PARLIAMENT. It consisted of 140 members chosen partly by the army leaders and partly by congregations of 'godly men'. Known initially as the Parliament of Saints, it was later nicknamed after 'Praise-God' Barbon, or Barebones (*c*.1596–1679), one of its excessively pious leaders. Its attacks on the Court of Chancery and on the Church of England alarmed both Cromwell and its more moderate members. The dissolution of this Parliament was followed by the Instrument of Government and the proclamation of CROMWELL as Lord Protector.

Bareilly (or **Bareli**) An industrial city in the state of Uttar Pradesh, northern India; pop. (1991) 583,000. It was a capital of the Afghan region of Rohilkand until taken by the British in 1801, and a leading centre of disaffection during the Indian Mutiny of 1857.

Barenboim, **Daniel** (1942–) Israeli pianist and conductor, born in Argentina. Barenboim was musical director of the Orchestre de Paris 1975–88 and then of the Chicago Symphony Orchestra from 1991. In 1967 he married the cellist Jacqueline DU PRÉ.

Barents, **Willem** (*c*.1550–97) Dutch explorer and leader of several expeditions in search of a NORTH-EAST PASSAGE to Asia, south of the Arctic Ocean. He discovered Spitsbergen and reached the Novaya Zemlya archipelago north of European Russia. His accurate charting and valuable meteorological data make him one of the most important of the early Arctic explorers. The BARENTS SEA is named after him.

Barents Sea (or **Murmean Sea**) A part of the Arctic Ocean to the north of Russia, bounded by Spitsbergen, Franz Josef Land, and Novaya Zemlya. Navigation in the north is restricted by pack-ice; but the NORTH ATLANTIC DRIFT is just sufficient to keep the southern coasts clear. The underlying sea-bed is believed to be rich in oil. A southern arm, more frequently frozen, is known as the White Sea.

barge Most commonly a flat-bottomed freight vessel used chiefly on inland waterways and in shallow coastal waters. Early barges were sailing vessels, but with the construction of CANALS, animal and later mechanical haulage became common using narrow barges (narrowboats). In the late 19th and early 20th centuries steam-powered, and later diesel-engined barges were introduced. On suitable river navigations, such as the Mississippi (USA) and the Rhine (Europe), powered barges are used to tow assemblies of up to forty unpowered (dumb) barges.

Bari An industrial seaport on the Adriatic Sea in the Apulia region of south-east Italy; pop. (1990) 353,030. It is capital of the province of Bari. The Romanesque basilica (1087–1197) with relics of St Nicholas of Bari is a place of pilgrimage. In addition to traditional industries such as shipbuilding and the manufacture of textiles, Bari is the site of Italy's first atomic power station, and an important centre of the petrochemical industry.

Baring crisis (July 1890) A financial crisis in ARGENTINA. The London merchant bank of Baring Brothers was the country's financial agent in Europe, where a crisis of confidence occurred over the inflationary policy of President Juarez Celman (1886–90). The President gave way to his deputy Carlos Pellegrini, who had to stabilize the currency and adopt the GOLD STANDARD before London would give any more credit. One result was heavy urban unemployment, although the refrigerated beef and corn industries continued to expand. Approximately a century later (1995) Barings Bank collapsed as a result of unmonitored loss-making speculation by a futures dealer, Nick Leeson, on the Singapore markets.

barite (or **barytes**) Barium sulphate ($BaSO_4$), the chief ore of barium occurring in mineral veins with lead and zinc minerals. It is usually colourless with a vitreous or pearly lustre. Barite is used in paint manufacture and in paper-making as well as drilling for oil.

barium (symbol Ba, at. no. 36, r.a.m. 137.33) A soft, silvery-white metallic element, one of the ALKALINE EARTH METALS. It is a reactive element, which ignites spontaneously in moist air and reacts with non-metals, water, and acids to form ionic salts. Barium is obtained by the ELECTROLYSIS of fused barium chloride or by reduction of the metal oxide with aluminium in a vacuum furnace. It is used in alloys, and in fireworks to give a green flame. Barium compounds are generally toxic, but barium sulphate, which is insoluble, can be ingested, and is widely used in medicine as a contrast medium for RADIOLOGY of the gut.

bark The outer part of stems and roots, referring especially to the tissue outside the wood (XYLEM) of woody plants. Bark consists of PHLOEM and any outer tissue. In most trees, new tissue with CORK cells is produced as the wood expands and crushes the outer layers. The stem or root thus continues to be protected by a waterproof layer, and often contains preservatives which are exploited for tannin and in medicine.

bark beetle A small beetle of the family Scolytidae or Curculionidae. The larvae feed on the wood of rotting trees and also on living plants. The young adult males bore through the bark and make tunnels for the females to lay eggs in. The larvae make tunnels at right angles to the egg tunnel; they pupate at the end of their tunnels, and the newly emerged adults bore their way out. The larvae of AMBROSIA BEETLES feed on species of fungi brought in by their parents. Other members of the Scolytidae family are responsible for the spreading of Dutch elm disease, because they carry a fungus which blocks the vessels of the trees.

Barker, **George (Granville)** (1913–91) British poet. A self-styled 'Augustinian anarchist', he displays in his works a penchant for puns, distortion, and abrupt changes of tone. In his *True Confession of George Barker* (1950, augmented 1965), he presented himself as both irreverent and guilt-ridden.

Bar-le-Duc A market town in the Meuse department of Lorraine, north-east France, on the River Ornain; pop. (1982) 20,029. Formerly capital of the Duchy of Bar, it has many houses with fine 16th–18th century façades. Surrounded by a rich dairy-farming region, Bar-le-Duc is now one of the largest cheese depots in Europe.

barley An annual grass of temperate regions, first cultivated in western Asia at least 9,000 years ago. It provides the most important grain (malting barley) used in brewing beer; grain not used for this purpose is fed to livestock. The two commonly cultivated species are the six-row barley, *Hordeum vulgare*, and the two-row type, *H. distichon*. Although typically associated with light soils, both species are grown in a wide range of areas and about 10,000,000 hectares (38,000 square miles) per annum are cultivated worldwide. Europe is the largest producer, and Britain achieves the highest yields. Like wheat, barley can be sown in temperate countries in the autumn or spring. Pearl barley is produced by grinding away the outer husk of the grains.

bar mitzvah (Aramaic, 'son of the commandment') Jewish rite of passage commemorating male initiation into adulthood and full religious responsibility. *Mitzvah*, commandment, refers to the legally obligatory rituals and rule for living which mark the Jewish way of life, and are adhered to more or less strictly by the different branches of Judaism. The ceremony may be celebrated on the Sabbath, Monday, or Thursday (the other days on which readings from the Torah are held) following the day after the boy's 13th birthday. It includes reading from the TORAH, and the presentation of a prayer shawl (*tallith*) and prayer book. Orthodox, conservative, and other Jews also present phylacteries, small leather-covered boxes containing verses from the Torah. Girls come of age at 12, and this may or may not be marked by a ceremony (*bat mitzvah*), depending on the branch of Judaism. Different rules apply to women, some less onerous or prohibitive.

Barnabas, St A Cypriot Levite and Apostle. He introduced St Paul to the Apostles and accompanied him on the first missionary journey to Cyprus and Asia Minor, returning to Cyprus after they disagreed and separated (Acts 4–15). The traditional founder of the Cypriot Church, he is said to have been martyred in Cyprus in 61 AD. Feast day, 11 June.

barnacle A clinging CRUSTACEAN with stiff, jointed legs, but a calcified, mollusc-like shell; a familiar sight on rocky seashores worldwide. Barnacles are sessile, sitting upside-down within the shell and kicking food particles into their mouths. Most of the 900 or so species, which comprise the subclass Cirripedia, live cemented onto rocks or other animals' shells, but some (the goose barnacles) have stalks and a few are parasitic. Barnacle larvae are an important component of PLANKTON.

barnacle goose A GOOSE, *Branta leucopsis*, easily distinguished from other types by its white face contrasting with a black neck and breast. Barnacle geese breed in colonies on Arctic cliffs and rocks, and winter in northwestern Europe. They are similar in many respects to Canada geese, *Branta canadensis*.

Barnard, Christiaan (Neethling) (1922–) South African surgeon. A pioneer in the field of human heart transplantation, he performed the first operation of this kind in December 1967.

Barnardo, Thomas John (1845–1905) Irish-born doctor and philanthropist. He went to London in 1866 and while still a student of medicine, he founded the East End Mission for destitute children (1867), the first of many such homes. Now known as Dr Barnardo's Homes, they cater chiefly for those with physical and mental disabilities.

Barnard's star A tenth-magnitude BINARY STAR in the constellation of Ophiuchus. It was discovered by the US astronomer Edward Barnard in 1916 and is noted for its large PROPER MOTION of 10.3 arc seconds per year with respect to the Sun. It is the second-nearest star to the Sun, only 1.8 parsecs distant.

Barnaul The capital of Altai in eastern Russia, on the River Ob in southern Siberia; pop. (1990) 603,000. Founded in the 18th century as a silver-smelting town, Barnaul is now a major railway junction and commercial centre serving an agricultural region that produces cotton, grain, and sugar-beets.

Barnet, Battle of (14 April 1471) . A battle in the Wars of the ROSES fought between the Lancastrian forces, led by Richard Neville, Earl of WARWICK ('the Kingmaker') and the Yorkist troops of EDWARD IV. Both sides suffered heavy losses, but Warwick was slain and Edward's recovery of his throne was made almost certain.

barn owl A member of the family Tytonidae, which contains 17 species of closely related OWLS with distinctive pale, heart-shaped faces and slender legs. All species, including the widely distributed common barn owl, *Tyto alba*, are nocturnal predators of rodents and other small mammals, and have acute hearing. They often nest in barns and other farm buildings.

Barnum, P(hineas) T(aylor) (1810–91) US showman. He became famous in the mid-19th century for his extravagant advertising and exhibition of freaks at his American Museum in New York. He billed his circus, opened in 1871, as 'The Greatest Show on Earth'; ten years later he joined forces with his former rival Anthony Bailey (1847–1906) to found the Barnum and Bailey circus.

Barocci, Federico (c.1535–1612) Italian painter. Barocci is generally considered the greatest and most individual painter of his time in central Italy, the freshness and vigour of his work setting him apart from the prevailing MANNERISM and heralding BAROQUE ART.

barometer A device for measuring atmospheric pressure. In the traditional instrument, devised by Evangelista Torricelli in 1644, the pressure of the atmosphere is balanced against a column of mercury: the height of the column is a measure of the pressure. Standard atmospheric pressure is defined as 760 mm (30 inches) of mercury (Hg) at mean sea-level. In meteorology the bar is often used: 1 bar = 750.07 mm Hg. The aneroid barometer depends on the tiny movement of the surface of an evacuated metal capsule in response to pressure changes. The movement is mechanically transmitted to a pointer pivoted at the centre of a circular dial. The same principle is used in barometric ALTIMETERS.

baron A member of the lowest rank of the English peerage. The title was introduced in England with the Norman Conquest and signified the vassal of a lord. Its limitation to those who held land directly from the king in return for military service occurred early. MAGNA CARTA (1215) made the distinction between the lesser baronage, summoned to the Great Council (Parliament) by general writ, and the greater baronage, called by personal writ, which was regarded as having conferred a hereditary peerage on the recipient.

Baroque art The dominant style in European art between the MANNERIST and ROCOCO styles, that is, from about 1600 to the early years of the 18th century. From the Mannerist style the Baroque inherited movement and fervent emotion, and from the RENAISSANCE style solidity and grandeur. When the style spread outside Italy, it took root most deeply in other Catholic countries.

In painting, two great Italian artists stand at the head of the Baroque tradition – CARAVAGGIO and Annibale CARRACCI. In architecture, the most important figure in the creation of the Baroque in Rome was Carlo Maderna (1556–1629), who broke away from Mannerism to create a style of great lucidity and forcefulness. The major figure in the development of Baroque sculpture was Gianlorenzo BERNINI, whose first masterpieces in the new style date from around 1620. His Cornaro Chapel (1645–52) in the church of Santa Maria della Vittoria blends painting, sculpture, and architecture in a way that is considered quintessentially Baroque. In the 17th century Rome was the artistic capital of the world, attracting artists from all over Europe, and the Baroque style soon spread outwards from it. In some areas it became more extravagant (notably in Spain and Latin America, where a lavish style of architectural ornamentation called CHURRIGUERESQUE developed), and in others it was toned down to suit more conservative tastes. In Roman Catholic Flanders it had one of its finest flowerings in the work of RUBENS. However, in neighbouring Holland, a Protestant country, the Baroque had less impact, although REMBRANDT, for example, went through a distinctively Baroque phase in his early maturity. In France Louis XIV was a lavish patron and he realized the importance of the arts as a propaganda medium in promoting the idea of his regal glory. His adviser in artistic matters was Charles LEBRUN, who led the army of artists and decorators who worked on Louis's palace at Versailles. Baroque art favoured the theatrical effect created by the dramatic use of lighting, false perspective, and trick painting used for stage production. It made little appeal to sober British taste. In English architecture the Baroque spirit flourished briefly and idiosyncratically in the work of VANBRUGH and HAWKSMOOR in the early 18th century, and some of WREN's later work (including St Paul's Cathedral) comes close to this style.

Baroque music (*c*.1600–*c*.1750) Music of the period that corresponded with BAROQUE ART. Music composed from about 1600 to the death of J. S. BACH in 1750 has one simple feature in common: it was built on a continuo line, a bass that was used by players to generate an essentially improvised accompaniment. This allowed a freedom of expression that was particularly important to both composers and performers. It made possible the rise of OPERA, which took root, at Venice in the late 1630s: throughout the Baroque era, a very large part of the opera repertory was written merely as a melody line and continuo bass. Although only the operas of MONTEVERDI, CAVALLI, and HANDEL have been widely performed in modern times, opera was the most prominent music in the Baroque period. Instrumental music, and particularly the rise of the CONCERTO, similarly benefited from the virtuosity and freedom of this *stile moderno*; but they drew just as strongly on the church tradition, the *stile antico* inherited from Renaissance POLYPHONY.

Barossa Valley Australia's most famous wine-making area, situated to the north of Adelaide in South Australia. First settled in 1842 by predominantly German colonists, the area was named (with incorrect spelling) after Barrosa in Spain.

barque (US **bark**) A small sailing ship. Around the beginning of the 19th century, the term referred to a way of rigging a three-masted ship, with a square-rig on the fore and main masts, and fore-and-aft rigging on the mizen or rear mast. A variation was the barquentine, square-rigged only on the foremast.

Barquisimeto The capital of the state of Lara in northern Venezuela, on the Trans-Andean highway at the centre of a rich coffee, cacao, and cattle-ranching region; pop. (1991) 602,620.

Barra An island at the southern end of the Outer Hebrides off the west coast of Scotland, separated from South Uist by the Sound of Barra and named after St Finnbar; area 91 sq km (35 sq miles); pop. (est. 1984) 1,200. The chief town is Castlebay near which is Kisimul Castle, seat of the Clan Macneil.

barracouta See SNOEK.

barracuda A marine fish of tropical and warm temperate seas, including the southern Mediterranean. Barracudas make up a family, Sphyraenidae, of 20 species. They are long and slender-bodied, with a pointed head, with large, fang-like teeth. They live in shallow coastal waters and in lower estuaries. They are voracious predators, eating all kinds of fishes, which they capture with a high-speed charge. The largest species, the great barracuda, *Sphyraena barracuda*, found in the western Atlantic, reaches 1.8 m (5.75 feet). It occasionally attacks bathers, especially in the West Indies.

barramundi An Asiatic or Australian fish related to the ARAPAIMA. The spotted barramundi, *Scleropages formosus*, is found in south-east Asia and the Fitzroy river system of Australia, and the northern barramundi, *S. leichardti*, in northern Australia and New Guinea. They live in slow-flowing rivers and creeks, feeding on fishes, frogs, crustaceans, and insects, and grow to about 1 m (3.25 feet) in length. The name barramundi is also used to describe the giant perch, *Lates calcifer*, of the Indo-Pacific region.

Barranquilla The leading industrial seaport of Colombia, at the mouth of the River Magdalena, on the Caribbean coast of Atlantico department; pop. (1992) 1,018,700. Founded in 1629, Barranquilla was the site of the first air terminal to be built in South America. It has ship-building, chemical, textile, and food industries.

Barrault, Jean-Louis (1910–94) French actor and director. Barrault appeared in a number of acclaimed films, including *Les Enfants du paradis* (1945) and *The Longest Day* (1962).

barred spiral galaxy A GALAXY in which the nucleus is crossed by a bar of dust, gas, and stars with the spiral arms emerging from the ends of the bar. These types of galaxies have the HUBBLE CLASSIFICATIONS SBa to SBc.

barrel-fish A species of the family Centrolophidae, known by this name because the young fishes swim in company with floating wood at the surface of the sea. They also accompany jellyfishes and salps. The barrel-fish *Hyperoglyphe perciforma*, found throughout the North Atlantic, grows to 90 cm (3 feet) long, and lives in deep water when adult.

Barrett, Elizabeth See BROWNING, ELIZABETH BARRETT.

Barrie, Sir J(ames) M(atthew) (1860–1937) British dramatist and novelist. His most successful adult plays are his sentimental comedy *Quality Street* (1901), and *The Admirable Crichton* (1902). Barrie is best remembered for his celebrated children's play *Peter Pan* (1904) about a boy who would not grow up.

barrier island An accumulation of sand or a shingle forming a bar roughly parallel to the coast but separated from it by a shallow stretch of water, or lagoon.

barrier reef A large mass of coral that lies parallel to a coast or encircles an island but is separated from the land by channels or LAGOONS, often of considerable depth and width. Most of the reef is shallowly submerged, but extensive coral sandflats may accumulate above sea-level. The GREAT BARRIER REEF is the most extensive; others exist elsewhere in tropical waters.

barrister In England, Wales, and Northern Ireland, a legal practitioner who has been 'called to the Bar' by one of the INNS OF COURT. Barristers are appointed by SOLICITORS to represent their clients in court hearings and to provide specialist advice (opinions) on legal matters. Until 1990 barristers had an exclusive right to practise in the superior courts, but SOLICITORS are now eligible to do so in some circumstances. Junior barristers sit outside the Bar of the court, with solicitors and members of the public, whereas senior barristers, called QUEEN'S COUNSEL (or King's Counsel if the sovereign is male), sit within the Bar of the court with the bench. Queen's Counsel (QCs) wear silk gowns and the process of becoming a QC is called 'taking silk'.

barrow (or **tumulus**) An earthen mound raised over a grave (if of stone, 'cairn' is the usual term). Grave-mounds of this type were characteristic throughout Europe and parts of central and southern Asia during the NEOLITHIC and BRONZE AGES, and in places much later. They occurred less frequently in other parts of the world.

Barrow-in-Furness An industrial seaport on the Cumbrian coast of north-west England, on the Furness peninsula; pop. (1991) 48,947. Shipbuilding, steel, offshore gas, engineering, paper making, and chemical production are important industries.

Barry, Sir Charles (1795–1860) British architect. In 1836 he won a competition to design the new Houses of Parliament after the old buildings had been destroyed by fire. Work on the building began in 1840 with the assistance of Augustus PUGIN, who was responsible for the interior design, and continued after Charles Barry's death, his son **Edward Middleton Barry** (1830–80) completing the project.

Barry, James (1741–1806) Irish painter who moved to London in 1764, influenced by the great masters of the Renaissance. His most important work, the series of paintings on *The Progress of Human Culture* (1777–83) shows, however, that his ambitions outstripped his talent.

Barrymore A US family of actors. **Lionel** (1878–1954) withdrew from a successful career in the theatre in 1925 and devoted himself to films; these included *A Free Soul* (1931), for which he won an Oscar, and *Grand Hotel* (1932). His sister, **Ethel** (1879–1959), was also an actress; she gave notable stage performances in *The Second Mrs Tanqueray* (1924) and *The Corn is Green* (1942), and won an Oscar for her part in the film *None But the Lonely Heart* (1944). Their brother, **John** (1882–1942), was a light comedian as well as a serious actor; his most celebrated role was on stage as Hamlet, both in New York (1922) and in London (1925).

Barsac An area to the south of Bordeaux in the department of Gironde, south-west France noted for its sweet white wine. It is one of five locations bearing the Sauternes appellation.

Barsisa In Islamic legend, the ascetic who, tempted by the devil, continuously seduced and then killed women. Agreeing to worship the devil if his life were spared, Barsisa was then mocked by his adversary with words from the Koran.

Bart, Lionel (1930–) British composer and lyricist. Bart wrote the music and lyrics for *Fings Ain't Wot They Used T'Be* (1959), which together with *Lock Up Your Daughters* (1959) contributed to the revival of the English musical. *Oliver!* (1960) achieved 2,618 performances, setting a new record for a musical. *Twang!* (1965), however, was an expensive failure and seriously harmed Bart's career in the theatre.

barter The direct exchange of one (non-monetary) GOOD or service for another. In a barter economy, to exchange one specified good for another requires that there be someone willing to swap the good being offered for that which is wanted. Otherwise, it is necessary to go through a number of intermediate transactions. Barter is, therefore, not nearly as efficient a system of exchange as using MONEY.

Barth, Heinrich (1821–65) German explorer and geographer. The most influential of 19th-century European observers of West African life, Barth was a member of a British-sponsored expedition which left Tripoli in 1850 to explore the hinterland to the south. His five-volume account of his explorations, *Travels and Discoveries in North and Central Africa* (1857–58), contains much valuable anthropological, historical, and linguistic data.

Barth, John (Simmons) (1930–) US novelist and short-story writer. He is known as a writer of complex, elaborate, experimental novels, including *The Sot-Weed Factor* (1960) and *Giles Goat-Boy* (1966). *Letters* (1979) consists of correspondence exchanged by characters from his previous novels.

Barth, Karl (1886–1968) Swiss Protestant theologian. Under the shadow of World War I he was led to a radical questioning of contemporary religious thought and in 1919 published his seminal work *Epistle to the Romans*. A rebuttal of liberal 19th-century Protestant theology, the book established a neo-orthodox or theocentric approach. His work had its greatest impact in the 1930s, but it exerts a continuing influence on Protestant theology today.

Barthes, Roland (1915–80) French writer and critic. Barthes was a leading exponent of structuralism in literary criticism and cultural analysis. In the 1950s and 1960s, he spearheaded the *nouvelle critique*, which challenged the traditional approach of literary criticism. His iconoclastic work *On Racine* (1963) is still a subject of controversy amongst literary critics. Barthes was increasingly drawn to the theory of semiotics after *Mythologies* (1957), his critique of contemporary culture, proceeding to define the theory in further detail in *Elements of Semiology* (1964). Later works, such as the essay 'The Death of the Author' (1968) and *S/Z* (1970), which stress the role of the reader in constructing a text.

Bartholdi, Frédéric-Auguste (1834–1904) French sculptor. He is known for his colossal figures, especially the Statue of LIBERTY (*Liberty Enlightening the World*), which was presented to the USA in 1886.

Bartholomew, St An Apostle. He is said to have been flayed alive in Armenia, and is hence regarded as the patron saint of tanners. Feast day, 24 August.

Bartók, Béla (1881–1945) Hungarian composer. While his early work reflects the influence of Romantic composers, he later developed an original musical language; his music is often percussive and owes much to Hungarian folk music, which he began to record, notate, and classify in 1904. His work includes six string quartets (1908–39), three piano concertos (1926; 1930–31; 1945), *Concerto for Orchestra* (1943), and an opera, *Duke Bluebeard's Castle* (1911).

Bartolommeo, Fra (born Baccio della Porta) (*c.*1472–1517) Italian painter. A Dominican friar, he worked chiefly in Florence and made visits to Venice and Rome, where he was much impressed with the work of Raphael and Michelangelo. Notable works are *The Vision of St Bernard* (1507) and *The Mystic Marriage of St Catherine* (1511).

Barton, Sir Edmund (1849–1920) Australian statesman and jurist, first Prime Minister of Australia 1901–03. He helped to draft the proposed Commonwealth constitution and went to England in 1900 (accompanied by Alfred Deakin) to see the bill through Parliament. He resigned as Prime Minister in 1903 to become a senior judge in the High Court of Australia, serving until 1920.

Bartram, John and William Father and son, pioneering US botanists. John (1699–1777) gathered specimens for his Philadelphia gardens during his travels from the Catskills to Florida and from Pennsylvania to Ontario. By exchanging seeds and bulbs with European botanists, and by cross-fertilizing, he developed many new HYBRIDS. His son William (1739–1823) accompanied him and described his father's botanical journeys in *Travels* (1791), a book which attracted European attention.

Baruch, Bernard (Mannes) (1870–1965) US industrialist and financier, the respected adviser of presidents from Wilson to Eisenhower. In World War I he served on the Council of National Defense and was the successful Chairman of the War Industries Board. In the 1940s he acted as special adviser on war mobilization and post-war planning. He was appointed to the UN Atomic Energy Commission, which proposed (1946) a World Atomic Authority.

baryon An elementary particle which undergoes reactions due to the strong force. It consists of three QUARKS, and has a half-integral spin (1/2, 3/2, and so on). Baryons are one group of HADRONS (the MESONS are the other). Protons and neutrons are baryons.

Baryshnikov, Mikhail (Nikolaevich) (1948–) US ballet-dancer, born in Latvia of Russian parents. In 1974 he defected to the West while touring with the Kirov Ballet. He then danced with the American Theater Ballet and the New York City Ballet, where roles were devised for him by Jerome Robbins (*Opus 191/The Dreamer*, 1979) and Sir Frederick Ashton (*Rhapsody*, 1980). He was artistic director of the American Theater Ballet 1980–90.

barysphere (or **centrosphere**) The dense interior of the Earth, including the mantle and core, enclosed by the lithosphere.

barytes See BARITE.

baryton A stringed musical instrument, with six bowed strings tuned like a bass VIOL, and many sympathetic strings behind the neck that could be plucked by the left thumb to accompany the bowed melody.

basalt A dark, fine-grained rock, the most common of the extrusive IGNEOUS ROCKS, composed essentially of PLAGIOCLASE feldspar and PYROXENE. Under the sea, basalt flows are very extensive, being found along MID-OCEANIC RIDGES as a product of upwelling lava; they solidify in pillow-like structures called pillow lavas. Most sea mounts and oceanic islands (for example, the Azores, and Hawaii) are formed of basalts erupted from submarine volcanoes. The largest basalt flows on the Earth's surface are in the Deccan, India, and on the Columbia–Snake River plateau, USA, but extensive flows thousands of metres thick are also found in Greenland, Brazil, and Iceland. On cooling, basalts often shrink into polygonal pillars and can produce locally spectacular scenery; one of the most famous of these sites is the GIANT'S CAUSEWAY, County Antrim, Northern Ireland.

bascule bridge A BRIDGE with a pivoted, counterbalanced floor (deck) which can be raised at one end. This is used to span waterways with a low clearance height between the deck and the water, while still allowing the passage of shipping below. London's Tower Bridge over the River Thames, built in 1886–94, uses two bascules to span 61 m (200 feet).

base Any of a class of chemical compounds that can neutralize an ACID to give a salt and water. Typically bases are metal hydroxides, oxides, and carbonates. Like acids, bases can be poisonous and corrosive; strong bases such as sodium hydroxide (caustic soda) have to be handled with great care. An alkali is a base that is soluble in water. A basic solution has a HYDROGEN ION CONCENTRATION greater than 7 on the pH scale, and will turn litmus blue. Strong bases will completely dissociate and have high pH values. According to the Brønsted–Lowry theory a base is a substance which will accept protons in the form of hydrogen ions, H^+. In the Lewis theory a base is a substance that can donate electron pairs; thus ammonia can be regarded as a Lewis base because it contains a LONE PAIR of electrons.

baseball A field-game played chiefly in the USA between two teams of nine players, using a bat, ball, and gloves. The focus of play is the diamond, a square with sides of 27 m (90 feet) and a base at each corner. After three outs (an inning), the batting team and the fielding team switch, each team batting in rotation through nine innings. The object is to score more runs than the opposing side. The batter stands at the home-plate facing the pitcher who throws the ball from a mound 18 m (60 feet) away. A fair ball (strike) must pass through the strike-zone, the area above the home-plate between the batter's armpits and knees. If

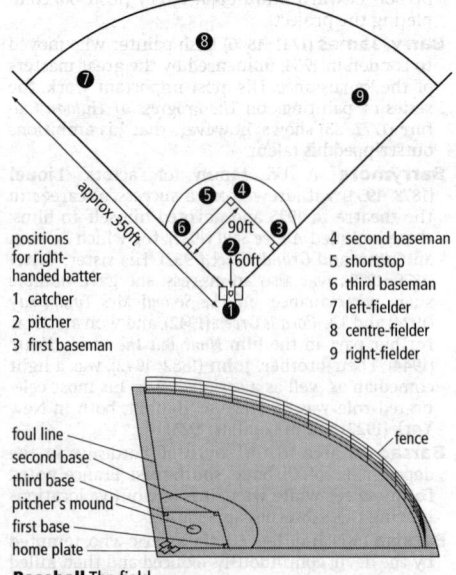

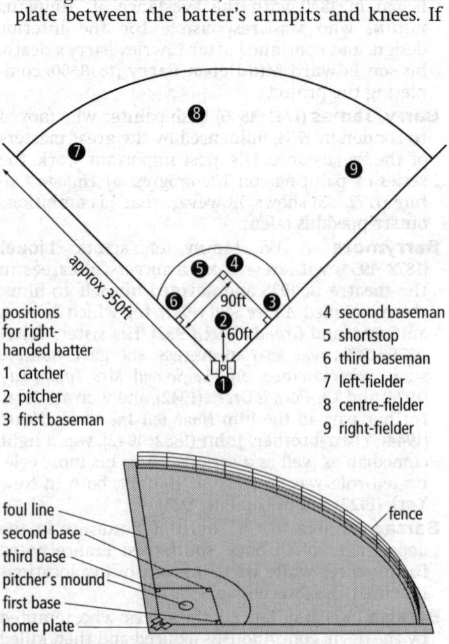

Baseball The field.

the pitcher throws three strikes, the batter is out. If he throws four 'balls' outside the strike zone, the batter walks to first base. The batter tries to hit the ball away and run to first base or further. If he hits it over the outfield fence, he automatically scores a home run. When the batter reaches base, a teammate succeeds him at the home-plate. Fielders guard the bases and the outfield and try to put batters out by catching a hit on the fly or volley, tagging a base-runner, or touching the base, ball-in-hand, before the runner reaches it.

basenji See DOG.

Bashkir A member of a people, the majority of whom live in the southern Urals. Some 70 per cent are to be found in the republic of Bashkortostan where they account for about one quarter of the population. They are Sunni Muslims of the Hanafi school. The northern and western Bashkirs are descended from Finnish-speaking tribes whereas the southern and eastern Bashkirs are the descendants of Turkic nomadic tribes.

Bashkortostan (formerly **Bashkiria**) A republic of the Russian Federation to the south-east of the Udmurt and Tartar republics in western Russia and to the west of the Urals; area 143,600 sq km (55,465 sq miles); pop. (1990) 3,964,000; capital, Ufa. Annexed to the Russian empire in 1557, it was constituted as an Autonomous Soviet Socialist Republic in 1919. Following the breakup of the Soviet Union it changed its name to Bashkortostan and was given federal republic status. It is an important centre of oil, coal, timber, paper, steel, and chemical production.

Bashō (or **Matsuo Bashō**) (1644–94) Japanese poet and travel-writer. He was a major influence on the development of HAIKU, but is also well known for his travel essays beginning with *Records of a Weather-Exposed Skeleton* (1684), written after his first journey west to Kyoto and Nara. The most famous, *Narrow Road to the Deep North* (1694), records a trip to the backward northern region of the main Japanese island, Honshū.

BASIC See COMPUTER LANGUAGE.

basic oxygen process (in steel-making) See IRON AND STEEL INDUSTRY.

Basie, Count (born William Basie) (1904–84) US jazz pianist, organist, and band-leader. In 1935 he formed his own big band, which became known as the Count Basie Orchestra. One of the best-known bands of the swing era, with its strong rhythm section and employment of some of the top instrumentalists and vocalists of the day, it enjoyed great success for many years.

basil A slightly hairy, aromatic annual, *Ocimum basilicum*, 40 cm (1.4 feet) tall. It is a member of the mint family, Labiatae, and is grown as a culinary herb in many areas of the world.

Basil, St (known as **St Basil the Great**) (*c*.330–79) Doctor of the Church. The brother of St Gregory of Nyssa, he was a staunch opponent of the heresy of Arianism, which denied Christ's divinity. He lived as a hermit until 370, when he was appointed bishop of Caesarea in Cappadocia.

basilica Originally, a large meeting hall used by the Romans in public business. Such halls were often rectangular in shape, with long colonnades dividing the interior into a central 'nave' flanked by an 'aisle' on each side. The name 'basilica' was adopted for early Christian churches that imitated this arrangement.

basilisk ▶**1** A lizard of the IGUANA family, Iguanidae, found in forests of Central America and northern South America. Basilisks live in trees and bushes overhanging rivers. When disturbed they plunge into the water and may rear up on to their hind-legs and run away across the water's surface. ▶**2** A legendary serpent of ancient Greece and Rome with a lethal glance.

Baskerville, John (1706–75) British printer. He designed the typeface that bears his name, and from 1757 onwards produced editions of authors such as Virgil, Milton, and Horace which were notable for their quality of type and paper.

basketball A game played worldwide between two teams of five on a hard rectangular court 26 m (85 feet) long and 14 m (46 feet) wide. At each end of the court is a basket, its ring 3 m (10 feet) above the floor and secured to a backboard. The team in possession tries to score a goal by throwing the ball into the basket, and the defending team tries to prevent it and secure possession. Players advance the ball by dribbling (bouncing and tapping it) and passing and may not carry it more than one pace. Only the hands may be used. The team in possession must try a shot at goal within thirty seconds of gaining possession and may shoot from any position on the court. After a goal is scored (two points), the other team puts the ball back in play by passing it in from behind the end-line. Body contact is not allowed, and body-contact fouls are penalized by a free throw from behind the foul-line, drawn 5 m (15 feet) from the backboard. If the player fouled was in the act of shooting and scores, he or she gets the goal plus one free throw; if the shot misses, he or she gets two free throws.

basket-makers A group of North American Indians in Colorado and neighbouring areas who developed out of the DESERT cultures in the last centuries BC. They adopted farming from MEXICO. The baskets they used instead of pottery have been preserved in the dry climatic conditions of their territory.

basket star See BRITTLE STAR.

basket-work Articles made from the plaiting or inter-weaving of such materials as osiers (willow shoots), reeds, cane, and split bamboo. Since antiquity, people have used basket-work to make dwellings, furniture, screens, boats, and containers. The raw material is first softened and then manipulated to form the complete article.

basking shark The second-largest species of fish, *Cetorhinus maximus*, (the largest is the whale shark), which can be 11 m (36 feet) in length. It is a member of the family Cetorhinidae, and lives in cool, temperate seas, and in summer swims near the surface, feeding on plankton which it sieves from the water with its gill rakers. Its teeth are numerous but minute. In winter it migrates to warmer areas or may simply live inactive close to the seabed of the cool, temperate sea.

Basle (German **Basel**) A commercial, cultural, and industrial city on the Rhine in north-east Switzerland; pop. (1990) 171,000. It has many museums and art galleries and Switzerland's oldest university (1459). It is a world centre of the pharmaceutical industry and also has textile and publishing industries.

Basque A member of a people living in the western Pyrenees on both sides of the French-Spanish border. They possess a distinctive culture and language. Although the BASQUE COUNTRY is divided between France and Spain, the Basques have maintained an identity separate from both states. In response to what they consider attempts to suppress their culture by the imposition of centralized authority, many Basques in Spain have campaigned for an independent Basque state, some violently in the military wing of the Basque movement ETA (Basque Fatherland and Liberty).

Basque Country (French **Pays Basque**; Spanish **Pais Vasco**; Basque **Euskadi**) That part of France and Spain on both sides of the western Pyrenees occupied by the Basque people. It comprises the Basque Provinces of northern Spain and the greater part of Pyrénées-Atlantiques department in the Aquitaine region of south-west France.

Basque language (or **Euskara**) The language of the BASQUE people of the north-west Pyrenees. Four-fifths of the speakers live in the Spanish part of the BASQUE COUNTRY; the others live in the French part. The number of speakers is estimated at slightly under a million, though virtually all are bilingual. The language is also spoken by some people, mostly in the USA, who left Spain after the Civil War (1936–39). Basque consists of a large number of quite diverse dialects, all mutually intelligible. It is related to no known language and is probably a remnant of the pre-INDO-EUROPEAN LANGUAGES of Europe.

Basque Provinces (Spanish **Provincias Vascongadas**) An autonomous region of northern Spain comprising the three provinces of Alava, Guipúzcoa, and Vizcaya; area 7,261 sq km (2,804 sq miles); pop. (1991) 2,104,040. The chief cities are Bilbao and San Sebastian.

Basra An oil port of Iraq, on the Shatt al-Arab waterway; pop. (est. 1985) 616,700. Severely damaged during the Iran–Iraq and Gulf wars, it is one of only two shipping outlets to the Persian Gulf from Iraq.

bas relief See RELIEF.

Bas-Rhin A department in the region of Alsace, north-east France, between the River Rhine and the eastern slopes of the Vosges Mountains; area 4,787 sq km (1,849 sq miles); pop. (1990) 953,050; capital, Strasbourg.

bass Either of two major groups of fishes. The sea bass family, Serranidae, contains some 400 species, typified by the torpedo-shaped fish *Dicentrarchus labrax*, which has strong first dorsal fin spines, a green-grey back, and brilliant silvery sides. It lives in the coastal waters of Europe, often in turbulent water near reefs, and in the breakers, but it also swims up estuaries. In North America a similar species, the striped bass, *Morone saxatilis*, is native to the Atlantic coast and has been successfully introduced to the Pacific coast.

The second group of bass comprises six species of the genus *Micropterus*, which are part of the largely North American sunfish family.

Bassano, Jacopo (*c*.1517–92) The most illustrious member of a family of Italian painters. Apart from a period training in Venice in the 1530s, Jacopo worked in Bassano, his home town near Venice, all his life. He specialized in religious paintings, but he often treated biblical themes in the manner of rural genre scenes. He was the son of a painter and had four painter sons himself, the best known being **Leandro** (1577–1622), who was an accomplished portraitist.

Basseterre The capital of St Kitts-Nevis in the Leeward Islands, on the island of St Kitts; pop. (est. 1994) 12,600.

basset horn A tenor CLARINET with an extended range. Modern instruments are straight, with an upturned bell. Because the bore diameter is hardly any larger than that of the clarinet, the extra length gives it a rather hollow tone colour, much liked by Mozart.

bassoon A bass double-reed musical instrument, one of the orchestral WOODWIND family. It is over 1.5 m (5 ft) long with the reed placed on a curving metal 'crook'. Down to the end of the butt (the thick part at the bottom) it functions like any other woodwind instrument. The tube then comes up again to the bell as an extension. The first bassoons, invented in France in the late 17th century, had three keys, but by 1800 six keys were standard.

Bass Rock A rocky islet with a lighthouse and large numbers of sea birds at the mouth of the Firth of Forth, east Scotland. Of volcanic origin, it rises to a height of 95 m (313 ft) above sea-level. It has been used on various occasions as a prison.

Bass Strait A channel separating the island of Tasmania from the Australian mainland. It is named after the English explorer George Bass, who discovered the strait in 1798.

Bastet The Egyptian cat goddess, also depicted as a cat-headed woman. She was the daughter of Re, and her most important cult centre was at Bubastis, where a vast cemetery of mummified cats sacred to her have been found. As a fertility goddess she is sometimes assimilated with Hathor, and with other feline goddesses such as Sekhmet and Pakhet.

Bastia The chief port of the French island of Corsica in the Mediterranean, situated on the north-east corner of the island; pop. (1990) 38,730. The port is dominated by the Genoese fortress (*bastaglia*) that gives the town its name. It has fishing and commercial harbours.

Bastille A fortified prison built on the city wall of Paris, France, between 1370 and 1382 in the reign of Charles V. Used by Cardinal Richelieu, Louis XIII's Minister, it became an infamous state prison in the 17th century. During the French Revolution it was completely demolished after being stormed on 14 July 1789. The prison is remembered in the name of a huge square, the Place de la Bastille, and a national holiday (Bastille Day) held annually on 14 July.

Basutoland The former name (until 1966) of LESOTHO in southern Africa.

bat The only mammal that is capable of true flight as opposed to gliding. The wings are formed by skin which stretches between the fingers, and the flight surface is often extended between the hind-legs. Bats hang by their feet while at rest, with the wings wrapped around the body. Most of the 942 species are nocturnal and spend the day roosting in large numbers in trees, caves, or old buildings.

Among mammals, bats are second only to rodents in the number of species. The order Chiroptera, to which bats belong, is divided into two groups: the large Old World suborder Megachiroptera, containing a single family, Pteropodidae, of FLYING FOXES, with around 173 species, and the smaller but more numerous insectivorous bats, which comprise 18 families in the suborder Microchiroptera. The latter use ultrasound to locate their insect prey in flight, rather like human sonar. The folds of skin around the snout and the huge ears, which give such a bizarre appearance to the insectivorous bats, serve to receive the 'sonar' signals. Most bats hibernate in winter. Mating occurs in the autumn, but the sperm is stored within the female's body and fertilization does not take place until the following spring.

Batan Islands The most northerly islands of the Philippines, lying between the Babuyan Islands and Taiwan. Batan, Sabtang, and Itbayat are the principal islands and Basco (on Batan Island) is the chief town.

Batavia The former name (until 1949) of JAKARTA in Indonesia.

Batavian Republic The name given to the Netherlands by the French who occupied that country from 1795 until 1806 when Napoleon installed his brother Louis as King of Holland.

Batdambang See BATTAMBANG.

bateleur A long-winged African harrier-EAGLE, *Terathopius ecaudatus*, distinguished by its short tail and scavenging habit. Mostly carrion feeders, bateleurs soar over the plains in search of dead mammals, and descend either to feed directly or to harry other birds into disgorging food.

Bateman, H(enry) M(ayo) (1887–1970) Australian-born British cartoonist. From 1904 Bateman developed an exclusively visual style of cartoon strip which was used in several periodicals, including *Tatler* and *Punch*. His best-known series of cartoons, entitled 'The Man Who...', ran from 1912 and illustrated social gaffes resulting from snobbery.

Bates, H(erbert) E(rnest) (1905–74) British novelist and short-story writer. His many short stories appeared in several collected volumes, including *The Beauty of the Dead* (1940). Of his novels, perhaps the best known is *The Darling Buds of May* (1958), which gained wide popularity in Britain when dramatized for television (1990–92).

Bates, Henry Walter (1825–92) British entomologist and naturalist who explored the upper Amazon region of South America (1848–59), collecting and describing over 8,000 new animal species. His travels are recounted in his classic book *Naturalist on the Amazon* (1863). He first described what is now known as Batesian MIMICRY.

Bateson, William (1861–1926) British geneticist. He continued the work of MENDEL in his study of discontinuity in variation through the experimental breeding of animals and plants. He ascribed these deviations from the laws of heredity to the interaction of genes, and was the first to use the term genetics. He published a classic book on genetics, *Materials for the Study of Variation* (1894).

Bath A spa town in the county of Somerset, south-west England; pop. (1991) 79,900. Known to the Romans as Aquae Sulis or Aquae Calidae, Bath has long been famous for its hot springs. The remains of Roman baths, a 15th–16th-century abbey church, and notable 18th-century Georgian crescents and squares are features of the town, which is the site of the University of Bath (1966). It was the birthplace of the Arctic explorer Sir William Parry (1790–1855). It has light industries and tourism is important.

batholith A very large IGNEOUS ROCK mass that has been injected upwards, while still molten, into the surrounding country rock. Some of the largest batholiths are more than 1,000 km (600 miles) long. They are steep-sided, generally cutting across any sedimentary structures, and are commonly aligned along mountain ranges associated with crustal plate activity (see PLATE TECTONICS) as with, for example, the Coast Range batholith of western USA and the Andean batholith of South America. Composed usually of granite, they are the source of many minerals, which are generally in workable deposits.

Bathsheba A biblical figure, the mistress and then wife of David, king of Israel. Seeking to conceal his guilt at taking Bathsheba as his mistress, David sent her husband Uriah to his death in the front line of battle. This act and his subsequent marriage to Bathsheba was denounced by the prophet Nathan. Bathsheba persuaded David to appoint their sole surviving son, Solomon, as his successor.

Bathurst The former name (until 1973) of BANJUL, capital of the Gambia. It is one of several places named after Earl Bathurst who was British Colonial Secretary from 1812 to 1828.

Bathurst A town in New South Wales, Australia, on the River Macquarie, 209 km (131 miles) west of Sydney; pop. (1991) 24,680. It is a former gold-mining town, now situated at the centre of a pastoral, fruit, and grain-growing region.

bathysphere A spherical steel vessel, forerunner of the modern SUBMERSIBLE, designed by the US zoologist BEEBE for deep-sea exploration. In 1934 Beebe and Otis Barton were lowered in it to a depth of 923 m (3,028 feet), then a record for deep-sea diving. Lateral movement was provided by a support ship on the surface, from which the bathysphere was slung. A development from the bathysphere was the bathyscaphe, an electrically powered deep-sea observation vessel that descended in 1960 to a depth of 11,000 m (36,000 feet).

batik A method of textile dyeing originating in south-east Asia. The areas of fabric that are not to be dyed are covered with melted wax, which is later removed by immersion in boiling water. The process can be repeated to produce multicoloured or blended effects.

Batistá y Zaldívar, Fulgencio (1901–73) Cuban statesman. He was President of Cuba 1933–44 and 1952–58, having come to national prominence in 1933 when, as a sergeant in the army, he led a successful revolt against President Gerardo Machado y Morales. He established a strong, efficient government, but increasingly used terrorist methods to achieve his aims. He amassed fortunes for himself and his associates, and the dictatorial excesses of his second term abetted CASTRO's revolution, which drove Batistá from power in December 1958.

Batlle y Ordóñez, José (1856–1929) Uruguayan statesman. He was President of Uruguay 1903–07 and 1911–15, and initiated legislation to increase public welfare. He believed that the Swiss Bundesrat or federal council was well suited to his own country's needs and during his second term he tried to have the office of president eliminated altogether. His political opponents compromised by agreeing to an executive branch in which power was shared between a president and a nine-man council. This decentralization of power placed Uruguay on a unique path in the 20th century.

Batoni, Pompeo (1708–87) Italian painter, the last great Italian artist in the history of painting in Rome. His early success was as a painter of religious and mythological works, but he is now famous above all for his portraits.

Baton Rouge The capital of the state of Louisiana, USA, on the east bank of the Mississippi; pop. (1990) 219,530. It is a major transportation centre with oil-refining, gas, petrochemical, engineering, and food-processing industries. Founded in 1719 by French settlers, the city was named after a red post that marked the boundary between the lands of two Indian tribes.

Battambang (or **Batdambang**) The capital of Battambang province in western Cambodia; pop. (1981) 551,860. Situated on the main supply route to Phnom Penh, it is the second-largest city in Cambodia and a centre for the milling of rice and production of textiles.

Batten, Jean (1909–82) New Zealand aviator. She was the first woman to fly from England to Australia and back (1934–35), breaking Amy Johnson's record for the England to Australia journey by nearly five days. In 1936, she made the first direct solo flight from England to New Zealand in a time of 11 days 45 minutes.

Battenberg A village in the state of Hesse, western Germany, a seat of aristocracy whose title was revived in 1851 for a branch of the German royal family. Members of the British royal household bearing this name renounced it in 1917, assuming the surname Mountbatten.

Battenberg, Prince Louis (1854–1921) British admiral. Of Polish-German descent, he became a naturalized British subject in 1868 and joined the navy, becoming First Sea Lord in 1912 in the critical period before the outbreak of World War I. His decision, criticized by some, not to disperse the naval squadrons gathered for exercises at Portsmouth at the time of the assassination of the Archduke FRANCIS FERDINAND at Sarajevo in 1914, assisted Britain's readiness for war. Anti-German hysteria in the early months of the war forced his resignation in October 1914. He became a marquis in 1917, giving up his German titles, and adopting the equivalent English name of Mountbatten. He married Princess Alice, granddaughter of Queen Victoria, in 1884. The younger of their two sons was Lord Louis Mountbatten, later Earl MOUNTBATTEN of Burma, and one grandson became Prince Philip, Duke of Edinburgh.

Battersea A district of the Inner London borough of Wandsworth, England, on the south bank of the River Thames. It is noted for its Dogs' Home (established in 1860) and its power-station (now being redeveloped) designed by Sir Giles Gilbert Scott.

battery Commonly, a single voltaic cell, but more correctly, two or more such cells connected together. A voltaic cell is a device that changes chemical energy directly into electrical energy. The first battery was constructed by VOLTA in 1800. Similar principles but differing constructions were used for the DANIELL cell (1836) and the LECLANCHÉ cell (1868), which developed into the universal dry battery. Such primary cells are not rechargeable and are used as portable sources of electrical energy in torches and communications equipment. Secondary cells (ACCUMULATORS), for example nickel–cadmium and lead–acid accumulators, can be discharged and recharged.

All voltaic cells contain two ELECTRODES, which are of different materials and are separated by, but are in contact with, an ELECTROLYTE. When the electrodes are joined by an external wire, a current flows through the wire. The electromotive force (e.m.f.) of a single electric cell is the maximum voltage that it can generate, that is the voltage across the cell when it is supplying no current. The value of the e.m.f. depends on the substances that comprise the electrodes and electrolyte. It is rarely greater than 2 volts, but cells can be connected in a series to make batteries that have higher voltages.

The electrolyte contains mobile ions and may be a solution, a paste, a molten salt, or a solid. It frequently contains a depolarizer which inhibits the formation of insulating gas bubbles on the electrodes. See also ENERGY STORAGE; FUEL CELL.

battery farming See FACTORY FARMING.

Battle A town in East Sussex, south-east England, to the north of Hastings. It takes its name from the Battle of Hastings, which was fought here in 1066.

battleship A class of warship carrying the heaviest armour and the largest guns. Perhaps the first true battleship (though not so called) was the British 9,210-tonne *HMS Warrior*, launched in 1860. With the development of efficient breech-loading guns mounted in turrets and the introduction of a reliable steam-engine, the battleship achieved its fully developed form. In the early 1900s both the UK and the USA designed a new type of battleship, with a main armament of at least eight large-calibre guns. The ships were called dreadnoughts after the first vessel to be commissioned, HMS *Dreadnought*. Their appearance stimulated other navies to copy the design, but by the end of World War I dreadnoughts were in decline. Battleships continued to be important until the end of World War II, after which there was a decline in their use due to their vulnerability to attack by submarines, aircraft and, later, missiles. By the early 1990s very few were in service.

Bauchi ▶**1** A state in north-east Nigeria; area 64,605 sq km (24,954 sq miles); pop. (1991) 4,294,400. Known as the 'land of slaves', the Bauchi plateau was a former Fulani kingdom. Tin and columbite are mined and cattle, groundnuts, cereals, and cotton are the chief agricultural products. ▶**2** Its capital; pop. (1981) 186,000. Founded in 1809, it was formerly named Yakoba. It grew rapidly with the demand for tin during World War I.

Baudelaire, Charles (Pierre) (1821–67) French poet and critic. An associate and champion of the painters Manet and Delacroix, he began his literary career writing art criticism and reviews, but is now largely known for *Les Fleurs du mal* (1857), a series of 101 lyrics in a variety of metres. He died in poverty and obscurity, and it was only in the later years of the 19th century that his importance to the symbolist movement was recognized.

baud rate The unit which measures the rate of data transmission in computer communication systems, named after J.-M.-E. Baudot (1845–1903), a French telegraph engineer. Usually 1 baud is defined as a rate of 1 BIT of information per second.

Bauhaus (German, 'building house') A school of architecture and design, founded in Weimar in 1919 by Walter GROPIUS and closed by the Nazis in 1933. Although short-lived, the Bauhaus was enormously important in establishing the relationship between design and industrial techniques. Gropius envisaged a unity of all the visual arts, fostering the idea of the artist as craftsman and forming a close relationship with industry. The characteristic Bauhaus style was impersonal, geometric, and severe, but with a refinement of line and shape that came from a strict economy of means and a close study of the nature of materials. Several of the most illustrious artists of the 20th century taught at the Bauhaus, notably MIES VAN DER ROHE (director 1930–33), KANDINSKY, and KLEE. The emigration of staff and students caused by Nazism ensured the international spread of Bauhaus ideas. See also FUNCTIONALISM.

Bausch, Pina (1940–) German dancer, choreographer, and director. She performed with German and American dance companies before founding the Wuppertal Dance Theatre in 1973.

bauxite A mineral consisting of aluminium oxides. The chief commercial source of aluminium, it is soft, light, and earthy. Bauxite is produced by the weathering of rocks containing aluminium in hot climates where there are both wet seasons, when LEACHING occurs, and long, dry periods when the aluminium ions are drawn back to the surface by capillary action. Constant repetition of this tropical weathering process removes other elements from the rocks and enables the bauxite to be formed. Regions in which such conditions occur are widespread, but exist notably in Jamaica, eastern Europe, the Balkans, and Hungary.

Bavaria (German **Bayern**) A state of southern Germany; area 70,553 sq km (27,251 sq miles); pop. (1990) 11,221,000; capital, Munich. It was until 1918 a kingdom of the German empire. Watered by the Main and Danube rivers, Bavaria is bounded to the south by the Bavarian Alps. The heartland of Bavaria, which has its own distinctive culture, is confined to the regions of Upper and Lower Bavaria. Industries are concentrated in the major cities of MUNICH and NUREMBERG. Forestry, agriculture, and tourism are also important.

Bax, Sir Arnold (Edward Trevor) (1883–1953) British composer. He achieved fame through a series of highly romantic, Impressionistic tone-poems based on Celtic folklore: *In the Faery Hills* (1909), *The Garden of Fand* (1916), and *Tintagel* (1919). Between 1922 and 1939 he wrote seven symphonies as well as three string quartets and four piano sonatas. He was knighted in 1937 and appointed Master of the King's Music in 1942.

Baxter, James K(eir) (1926–72) New Zealand poet, dramatist, and critic. His early lyric poetry focuses on the New Zealand landscape and its influence on its inhabitants. A convert to Roman Catholicism, in *Jerusalem Sonnets* (1970) he develops a fluid sonnet form to express his spirituality; *Autumn Testament* (1972) reflects his humanistic socialism. His criticism includes *Aspects of Poetry in New Zealand* (1967).

Baxter, Richard (1615–91) English Puritan minister. He was ordained as an Anglican clergyman, but rejected belief in episcopacy and became a NONCONFORMIST. In 1645 he became chaplain to a ROUNDHEAD regiment. He published the first of some 150 pamphlets in 1649 and in 1650 *The Saints' Everlasting Rest*, an important devotional work. During the Commonwealth period, his appeals for tolerance did not succeed. At the Restoration he became a royal chaplain but refused a bishopric. The 1662 Act of Uniformity forced his resignation, and in about 1673 he took out a licence as a Nonconformist minister. In 1685 he was imprisoned and fined by Judge JEFFREYS for 'libelling the Church'.

bay A curving indentation of the coastline between two promontories or headlands. Usually bays are wider at their seaward end than they are long. In general, therefore, they are a different shape from GULFS; they are also generally smaller, although larger than coves. The term is sometimes also used for a recess in a mountain range.

Bayard, Pierre du Terrail, Chevalier de (1473–1524) French soldier. He served under several French monarchs, including Louis XII, and became known as the knight 'sans peur et sans reproche' (fearless and above reproach).

bay duck The name used in North America for diving ducks such as the redhead (*Athya americana*), canvasback (*A. valisineria*), scaup (*A. marila*), and goldeneyes (*Bucephala* species). Although bay ducks frequent freshwater habitats in summer, they commonly winter in estuaries and sheltered coastal bays. In Europe some of these species are called POCHARDS.

Bayer letters A sequence of Greek letters used to identify the brightest stars in a constellation. The system was introduced by Johann Bayer (1572–1625), a German astronomer, on his star atlas *Uranometria* published in 1603. Bayer assigned the Greek letters to stars usually in order of brightness, although in some cases where there were several stars of similar apparent brightness, such as in Ursa Major, the letters were assigned in order of right ascension.

Bayern The German name for BAVARIA.

Bayeux A market and tourist town in the department of Calvados, Basse-Normandie region, northwest France; pop. (1982) 15,240. It has a 13th-century Gothic cathedral and the William the Conqueror Cultural Centre houses the famous BAYEUX TAPESTRY. Bayeux was the first town in Europe to be liberated by Allied Forces during World War II.

Bayeux Tapestry A celebrated piece of embroidered linen fabric (not a tapestry) depicting the Norman Conquest of England in 1066. It is about 70 m (231 ft) long – the last section is lost – and 50 cm (19½ in) wide, and is arranged with one episode succeeding another in more than seventy scenes. Perhaps made to the order of William the Conqueror's half-brother, Bishop Odo of Bayeux in Normandy, it was displayed for centuries in the cathedral at Bayeux and is now housed in the former Bishop's Palace there.

Bayezid I (1347–1403) Ottoman sultan 1389–1402, known as Yildirim ('Thunderbolt'). He succeeded his father Murad I and absorbed rival Turkish principalities in western Asia Minor, took Trnovo in Bulgaria (1393), and Thessaloniki in Greece (1394), blockaded Constantinople (1394–1401), and defeated a Christian army at Nicopolis in 1396. His thrust into eastern Asia Minor, however, brought him to disaster at Ankara in 1402, and he died a captive of his conqueror, TAMERLANE.

Bayezid II (*c.*1447–1512) Ottoman sultan 1481–1512. He wrested the throne from his brother Jem on the death of their father Mehmed, fought inconclusively with the MAMELUKES (1485–91), gained Greek and Adriatic territories from Venice, and was faced with the emerging power of Ismail Safavi. He abdicated a month before his death in favour of his youngest son, Selim.

Bay Islands (Spanish **Islas de la Bahia**) A group of Caribbean islands lying *c.*48 km (30 miles) north of the coast of Honduras; area 261 sq km (100 sq miles); pop. (1988) 22,060. Roatán, Guanaja, and Utila are the principal islands. Christopher Columbus landed on Guanaja in 1502 and throughout the 17th century the islands were frequented by British pirates and logwood cutters. The islands, which form a department of Honduras, are dependent on tourism, fishing, fruit, and timber.

bay laurel (or **sweet bay, laurel**) A white-flowered evergreen tree, *Laurus nobilis*, indigenous to the Mediterranean and growing to 20 m (65 feet) in height. Its aromatic leaves are used in cooking for flavouring. Bay leaves were woven into wreaths and used to crown victors in ancient Mediterranean civilizations.

Bayle, Pierre (1647–1706) French philosopher and critic. He argued that religion and morality were independent of one another, and championed the cause of universal religious toleration. His most famous work was a historical and analytical dictionary, the *Dictionnaire historique et critique* (1696).

Baylis, Lilian Mary (1874–1937) British theatre manager. She assisted in the running of the Royal Victoria Coffee Music Hall, a temperance hall housed in the Royal Victoria Theatre (the Old Vic). Under her management from 1912, the Old Vic acquired a reputation as the world's leading house for Shakespearian productions. Her initiative in reopening the old Sadler's Wells Theatre in 1931 led to the development of the Royal Ballet and the English National Opera.

Bay of Pigs (or **Cochinos Bay**) A bay on the southern coast of the island of Cuba in the Caribbean Sea, the scene of an unsuccessful invasion attempt in April 1961 by US-backed Cuban exiles seeking to oust the Communist government of Fidel Castro.

Bay of Plenty A region of North Island, New Zealand, stretching in a curve eastwards from the Coromandel Peninsula to Cape Runaway on the opposite side of the bay of the same name. Created in 1989, it comprises the districts of Tauranga, Western Bay of Plenty, Kawerau, Whakatane, Opotoki, and parts of Rotorua and Taupo; pop. (1991) 208,160.

Bayonne (Roman **Lapurdum**) A port in the department of Pyrénées-Atlantiques, part of the Basque region of south-west France, at the junction of the Adour and Nive rivers; pop. (1990) 41,850. In addition to exporting sulphur, phosphates, grain, and cement, it is a centre of the chemical and aeronautical industries.

Bayreuth A town in Bavaria, southern Germany; pop. (1991) 72,780. The composer Richard WAGNER made his home in Bayreuth from 1874 and is buried here. Festivals of his operas are held regularly in a theatre (Festspielhaus) specially built (1872–76) to house performances of *Der Ring des Nibelungen*. Textiles and cigarettes are local industries together with tourism.

bay rum tree A tree from which oil of bay is distilled, belonging to the family Myrtaceae which includes myrtles, eucalypts, and cloves. The principal species from which bay oil is extracted, *Pimenta racemosa*, is a tropical tree indigenous to the West Indies.

Bayswater A residential district of west London, England, between Paddington Station and the north side of Kensington Gardens. It is named after Baynard's Water the former name of the Westbourne which flows into the Serpentine.

Bazalgette, Sir Joseph William (1819–91) British civil engineer who rebuilt London's drainage system. Two major outbreaks of cholera in 1849 and 1853–54 made it clear that London's drainage system was totally inadequate for a city with a population of 7.5 million. In 1855 Bazalgette was appointed chief engineer to the Metropolitan Board of Works and within 20 years he had created a radically new drainage system. This involved construction of 160 km (100 miles) of large-diameter sewers and was the first large-scale use of concrete made with Portland cement, 70,000 tonnes of which were used.

BBC (British Broadcasting Corporation) The provider of non-commercial RADIO and TELEVISION services in the UK and a pioneer in public service broadcasting. The BBC was founded in 1922 and became an independent public corporation in 1927, operating under a royal charter and financed by licence fees collected by the government and payable initially on all domestic radio receivers, but currently on television sets only. The BBC World Service, financed by government grant and founded in 1932, broadcasts in English and other languages (37 in 1991) on radio. It started an English language satellite television service in 1991. In 1996 major structural reforms were proposed that would integrate the World Service more closely with the rest of the corporation.

beach A narrow area along a coast (or along a shore of a lake or inland sea) where loose, unconsolidated material, particularly shingle and sand, has accumulated, particularly in the zone between low water mark and the highest point reached by storm waves. These loose sediments, which are derived either from the weathering of the adjacent areas of cliffs and headlands or from the erosion of material from the sea floor, are underlain by shore platforms of solid rock.

beach flea See SANDHOPPER.

Beachy Head A high chalk cliff headland on the coast of East Sussex, southern England, between Seaford and Eastbourne; height, 162 m (535 ft). The French defeated a combined English and Dutch fleet in a naval encounter off Beachy Head in 1690.

beaded lizard See GILA MONSTER.

beaked whale A TOOTHED WHALE belonging to a family, Ziphidae, containing 18 species. Its snout is elongated into a beak, hence its name. There are usually only one or two pairs of functional teeth at the tip of the lower jaw; in some species there are a number of small teeth which never break through the gums. Among the best-known members of the family are Cuvier's beaked (also known as goose-beaked), *Ziphius cavirostris*, northern bottle-nosed, *Hyperoodon planifrons*, and Sowerby's, *Mesoplodon bidens*. They are between 4 and 12 m (13 and 40 feet) long and feed on squid and fishes.

Beaker cultures The people in many parts of western Europe at the end of the NEOLITHIC period (*c*.2600–2200 BC) who made and used a particular type of decorated pottery drinking-vessel. It was shaped like an inverted bell, with or without handles, and ornamented with zones of stamped impressions. These pots were valuable to their owners, and are often found as grave-goods in male burials, along with weapons such as a copper dagger or the remains of archery equipment. Their wide distribution, from the western Mediterranean to northern Germany, led earlier investigators to postulate a 'Beaker Folk' spreading northwards from Portugal, or perhaps from central Europe. They are now seen more simply as part of a general trend to ostentatious display of personal wealth, introduced at that time from central Europe.

Beale, Dorothea (1831–1906) Pioneer, together with her friend Frances Mary BUSS, in higher education for women in Britain. In 1858 she was appointed principal of the recently established Cheltenham Ladies' College, a position she was to hold until her death. She founded (1885) St Hilda's College, Cheltenham, for women teachers and lent her support to the establishment of St Hilda's Hall (later College), Oxford, in 1893. She was also an enthusiastic advocate of women's suffrage.

beam-engine (or **lever engine**) The earliest form of STEAM-ENGINE, invented by NEWCOMEN in 1712 for pumping water from mines. Chains were attached to either end of a rocking beam: one chain led to a piston enclosed in a cylinder, the other to the pump-rod down the mine-shaft. Steam from a BOILER entered the cylinder and pushed up the piston; the steam was then condensed by a spray of cold water, causing the piston to depress again, raising the pump-rod and delivering water. In 1765 WATT greatly improved the EFFICIENCY of the engine by using a separate condenser, and in 1782 he produced a double-acting engine in which the chains were replaced by rods to provide a push–pull action. Beam-engines are still used in a few water-pumping stations.

bean An extremely important LEGUME. Beans are grown principally as annual plants in the warm temperate and subtropical areas of the world for their large, protein-rich seeds and/or immature seed pods. The genus *Phaseolus*, particularly *P. vulgaris*, is native to South and Central America and is known to have been, together with maize, the staple diet of the indigenous Indians from at least 3000 BC. The protein of these beans complements that of the maize to form a full and balanced human diet.

The haricot, snap, string, green, and French or kidney beans are all varieties of *P. vulgaris*. The seeds, or 'beans', of this species differ markedly in colour according to the variety. The white haricot bean is particularly well known as the basis of the commercial 'baked beans'. The green immature pods of the French or kidney bean are a popular vegetable in Europe, as are those of the vigorous, climbing, scarlet runner bean, *P. coccineus*. A close relative, *P. lunatus*, the butter or Lima bean, has the largest seeds of the group. The coloured types of bean can contain poisonous glycosides that liberate prussic acid when chewed. Indeed, the wild varieties of all of this group contain these substances, but the process of selective breeding has largely eliminated them from cultivated varieties. Cultivated beans of other genera include BROAD BEANS and SOYA BEANS.

bear A large terrestrial mammal of the family Ursidae, characterized by its size and heavy build. Bears have thick limbs, a diminutive tail, small ears and eyes, a large black nose, and a somewhat dog-like head. The bears and dogs arose from the same ancestors in the Miocene Period of geological time. The thick, coarse fur is dark in colour in all except the polar bear. They have large feet, the entire soles of which rest on the ground with each step they walk, giving a slow, ponderous gait.

The eight species of bears are widely distributed in the Northern Hemisphere but only three species extend into the Southern Hemisphere. One of these, the spectacled bear, *Tremarctos ornatus*, is found beyond the Andes as far south as Bolivia. Most of the bears reach a length of 1.77 m (5.8 feet), while the grizzly of Alaska, Canada, and western North America is the largest, reaching 2.87 m (9.4 feet) and weighing up to 770 kg (1,700 pounds).

Bears have the reputation of being particularly ferocious, but most species are usually timid and peaceful, becoming formidable only when wounded or disturbed suddenly. They are omnivores, eating both animals and vegetables with the obvious exception of the POLAR BEAR. Some will kill large terrestrial mammals, others will kill seals or scoop fish from streams; fruit and grass are also eaten. The spectacled bear feeds only on grass, fruit, and roots. The sun bear, *Ursus malayanus*, occurs in forests of south-east Asia, where it eats fruit, bees, and termites, as well as rodents, birds, and eggs. The gestation period lasts six to nine months in most bear species, and the cubs when born are very small, perhaps between 0.45 and 1.8 kg (1 and 4 pounds).

beard-fish A deep-water fish found in the Atlantic, North Pacific, and parts of the Indian oceans. The Atlantic species, *Polymixia nobilis*, has been found at Madeira, and from Newfoundland to the Caribbean. It grows to 25 cm (10 inches) in length and lives at depths of about 500 m (1,625 feet). Its long chin-barbels suggest that it feeds on the ocean floor. There are thought to be six or so species, but these may all be subspecies of a single true species.

Beardmore Glacier One of the world's largest glaciers moving from the Queen Maude Mts. towards the Ross Sea Ice Shelf in Antarctica; length, 418 km (260 miles). It was discovered by Ernest Shackleton in 1908.

Beardsley, Aubrey (1872–98) British illustrator. Although he died young of tuberculosis, he was prolific and had already become a well-known, controversial figure in the art world. He had little formal training and his style was highly original, using vivid contrasts of black and white and grotesque figures to create a sense of menacing decay and depravity. Some of his work was frankly pornographic, and like WILDE – whose *Salome* he illustrated (1894) – he was regarded as a leading figure of the 'decadent' AESTHETIC MOVEMENT of the 1890s. The linear sophistication of his draughtsmanship also places him among the masters of ART NOUVEAU.

bearing A support used in almost all machines to reduce friction and wear between moving surfaces, and to dissipate heat. The commonest use of bearings is to support a rotating shaft. In a journal bearing, the shaft fits closely within a smooth cylindrical sleeve made of a low-friction material such as brass, tin-based alloy, or a plastic. Lubrication is achieved by pumping LUBRICATING OIL into the interface between shaft and sleeve. Some bearings are self-lubricating, being coated with a layer of powdered copper or bronze impregnated with oil or graphite. In rolling bearings, polished chromium steel balls or cylinders are used between the moving surfaces, replacing the sliding action with a rolling one. Tilting-pad thrust bearings, used in ships, have pads between the moving surfaces, and oil is forced between pad and surface by a wedging action. Dental drills and centrifuges have air bearings, in which the moving surfaces are separated by a film of air.

bear's breeches See ACANTHUS.

Beas A river of northern India that rises in the Himalayas and flows through Himachal Pradesh to join the River Sutlej in the state of Punjab. It is the easternmost of the 'five rivers' that give the Punjab its name. In ancient times, called the Hyphasis, it marked the eastern limit of Alexander the Great's conquests.

beatification See SAINT.

Beatles, The (1956–70) British pop group. Formed in Liverpool in the late 1950s by John Lennon (1940–80), Paul McCartney (1942–), and George Harrison (1943–), The Beatles were joined in 1962 by the drummer Ringo Starr (Richard Starkey) (1940–). In the same year they achieved national then international popularity under the management of Brian Epstein (1935–67). Their songs, mostly by Lennon and McCartney, initially blending rhythm and blues and rock and roll, became increasingly sophisticated. Paul McCartney was knighted in 1996.

Beat Movement A group of US writers, usually based in San Francisco or New York, which included the novelist Jack KEROUAC and the poets Allen GINSBERG, Gregory Corso (1930–), and Lawrence Ferlinghetti (1920–). William BURROUGHS, though older and frequently living abroad, had strong links with the Beats. Their writing first received national attention with the publication of Ginsberg's book *Howl and Other Poems* (1956) and Kerouac's autobiographical *On the Road* (1957), which remain the Movement's most famous works. Reacting against the middle-class values of the 'tranquillized Fifties', they celebrated states of ecstasy achieved with the aid of sex, drugs, jazz, or danger. They were influenced by existentialism, but often had leanings towards oriental mysticism. Rejecting an impersonal, academic literature, they returned the personal statement to the centre of the work, and wrote in a free and hectic vernacular style. Walt WHITMAN and Henry MILLER were predecessors they admired.

Beaton, Sir Cecil (Walter Hardy) (1904–80) British photographer. During the 1930s he worked with *Vogue* magazine and quickly earned international fame for his fashion features and portraits of celebrities; he is especially remembered today for his many portraits of the British royal family. After World War II he diversified into costume and set design for films, ballet, and the theatre; he won two Oscars for his design and costumes for the film *My Fair Lady* (1964).

Beaton, David (or **Bethune**) (1494–1546) Scottish churchman. He worked for the preservation of the Catholic religion, leading the anti-Protestant faction at court, and favouring the 'Auld Alliance' with France. Created cardinal in 1538, he succeeded his uncle as Archbishop of St Andrews in 1539 and was made Chancellor in 1543. His harsh persecution of Protestant preachers culminated in the execution of George Wishart, and Beaton was assassinated by Protestant nobles.

Beatty, David, 1st Earl (1871–1936) British admiral. He earned rapid promotion for his daring leadership in campaigns in Egypt and the Sudan, and in the BOXER RISING in China. Winston Churchill, First Lord of the Admiralty, secured for him in 1913 command of the battlecruiser squadrons. Beatty gained minor victories over German cruisers off Heligoland (1914) and the Dogger Bank (1915), and played a major role in the battle of JUTLAND. He was commander-in-chief of the Grand Fleet (1916–19) and First Sea Lord (1919–27).

Beau Brummell See BRUMMELL.

Beaufort An English family descended from three illegitimate sons of John of GAUNT (fourth son of Edward III) and Katherine Swynford. The children were legitimated in 1407 but with the exclusion of any claim to the crown. Their father and their half-brother HENRY IV made them powerful and wealthy: **Thomas** (died 1427) became Duke of Exeter, **John** (*c*.1371–1410) was made Lord High Admiral and Earl of Somerset, and **Henry** (died 1447) was Bishop of Winchester and later a cardinal. As a court politician he led the so-called constitutional party against Humphrey, Duke of Gloucester. The YORKISTS had no love for the Beauforts, and by 1471 all three of the Earl of Somerset's grandsons had been killed in battle or executed. The male line thus ended, but their niece Margaret Beaufort (1443–1509), daughter of John, Duke of Somerset, who married Edmund TUDOR, enjoyed a life of charity and patronage of learning after her son became king as HENRY VII.

Beaufort scale A system for estimating wind speeds with reference to the behaviour of certain standard subjects, such as smoke, trees, and the surface of the sea. Devised by the British hydrographer, Francis Beaufort (1774–1857), it grades wind force on a scale 0–12. A breeze is in the range 2–6; a strong wind or gale is 7–9; and storm to hurricane conditions, with wind speeds of 48 to over 65 knots (88 to over 120 km/h, 55 to over 75 m.p.h.), are 10–12.

Beaujolais A notable wine-making area in the Rhône-Alpes region of south-east France, on the north-eastern edge of the Massif Central, to the west of the River Saône and to the south of Mâcon. Formerly a part of the ancient province of Lyonnais, its chief town is Villefranche.

Beaulieu A village in Hampshire, southern England, on the edge of the New Forest, 9 km (6 miles) south-west of Southampton; pop. (est. 1985) 1,200. The remains of a Cistercian abbey, founded here *c*.1204 by King John, is in the grounds of Palace House, the home of Lord Montagu of Beaulieu alongside the National Motor Museum.

Beauly Firth An inlet of the North Sea forming a continuation of the Moray Firth on the north-east coast of Scotland, to the west of Inverness. It is spanned by the Kessock Bridge which was completed in 1982.

Beaumarchais, Pierre Augustin Caron de (1732–99) French dramatist. An important comic dramatist, he is chiefly remembered for his comedies *The Barber of Seville* (1775) and *The Marriage of Figaro* (1784); although still popular in France, they are best known in Britain as the inspiration for operas by Rossini and Mozart.

Beaumont, Sir Francis (1584–1616) English dramatist. He was educated at Oxford and entered the Inner Temple in 1600. He became an associate of Ben Jonson and John Fletcher, and collaborated

Beaufort number	description of wind	wind speed knots	wind speed metres per second
0	calm	<1	0.0–0.2
1	light air	1–3	0.3–1.5
2	light breeze	4–6	1.6–3.3
3	gentle breeze	7–10	3.4–5.4
4	moderate breeze	11–16	5.5–7.9
5	fresh breeze	17–21	8.0–10.7
6	strong breeze	22–27	10.8–13.8
7	near gale	28–33	13.9–17.1
8	gale	34–40	17.2–20.7
9	strong gale	41–47	20.8–24.4
10	storm	48–55	24.5–28.4
11	violent storm	56–63	28.5–32.6
12	hurricane	⩾64	⩾32.7

Beaufort scale

with the latter in *Philaster* (1609), *The Maid's Tragedy* (1610–11), and many other plays. *The Knight of the Burning Pestle* (*c.*1607) is attributed to Beaumont alone.

Beaumont, William (1785–1853) US army surgeon who pioneered gastric physiology. In 1822 at a frontier post he tended and studied a young soldier with a gastric fistula, a gunshot wound in the stomach which refused to close. His exhaustive report of his findings, *Experiments and Observations on the Gastric Juice and the Physiology of Digestion* (1833), remains a classic in its field.

Beau Nash See NASH.

Beaune A town in the department of Côte-d'Or, Burgundy, eastern France, centre of the Burgundy vineyards; pop. (1990) 22,170. There is a medieval infirmary that was used continuously from its founding in 1443 until 1971.

Beauregard, Pierre Gustave Toutant (1818–93) US general. He served as an engineer during the MEXICAN-AMERICAN WAR and was appointed superintendent of West Point in 1860, but he resigned at the outbreak of the AMERICAN CIVIL WAR to join the CONFEDERACY. As commander at Charleston, he ordered the first shot of the war against the Union-held FORT SUMTER. Beauregard was the field commander in the Confederate victory at the first battle of Bull Run (1861) before being promoted to full general and sent to the western theatre, where, after the battle of Shiloh (1862), he commanded the Army of Tennessee.

Beauvais (Roman **Caesaromagnus** or **Bellovacum**) A town in the department of Oise, in the Ile-de-France region of north-central France, to the north of Paris; pop. (1990) 56,280. The Gothic cathedral, begun in 1247 but never completed, is the tallest in France (68 m, 223 ft) and has the highest choir in the world.

Beauvoir, Simone de (1908–86) French novelist and essayist. From 1929 she was the companion of Jean-Paul SARTRE and her writing gives expression to the existentialist philosophy which they shared. She reached a wide public with her book on women's rights, *Le Deuxième Sexe* (1949), and *Les Mandarins* (1954), a novel describing existentialist circles in post-war Paris.

Beaux-Arts, École des The chief official art school of France, established as a separate institution in 1795. It dominated the teaching, practice, and criticism of art in France throughout the 19th century and into the 20th century, controlling the path to traditional success with its awards and state commissions. Teaching remained conservative until after World War II. Architecture was taught at the École des Beaux-Arts from 1819, and the term 'Beaux-Arts style' is applied to buildings expressing its official taste. Essentially this was academic and grandiose, and as with Victorian architecture, Beaux-Arts architecture was long condemned as stuffy and pretentious.

beaver An aquatic RODENT, one of two species: *Castor canadensis*, found in North America, and *C. fiber*, found in much lower numbers, in Europe and Asia. Most American, but few Eurasian, beavers construct nests or lodges made of sticks, often plastered with mud, which freezes in the winter into a hard roof, strong enough to deter predators. The entrance to the lodge is under water and so remains open if the pond, which forms upstream from the lodge, freezes. The pond is usually formed or enlarged by damming the exit streams with stones or branches taken from trees felled by the beaver with its strong front teeth.

For most of the year beavers feed on plants or tree herbage, but in the winter they rely upon branches stored under water during the summer. A family of beavers, consisting of parents and several generations of young, shares the lodge, and shows a social life which is unique among rodents. Beavers can radically alter their habitat but their activities are generally beneficial in improving the diversity of the vegetation.

Beaverbrook, (William) Max(well) Aitken, 1st Baron (1879–1964) Canadian-born British Conservative politician and newspaper proprietor. He made his fortune in Canadian business before coming to Britain and winning election to Parliament in 1910. However, it is for his activities as a newspaper proprietor that he is best known; he bought the *Daily Express* in 1916 and made it the daily newspaper with the world's largest circulation. He launched the *Sunday Express* in 1918 and acquired the *Evening Standard* in 1923, thus consolidating his substantial newspaper empire. As Minister of Aircraft Production in Churchill's Cabinet (1940), Beaverbrook made an important contribution to victory in the Battle of Britain.

Bebington A borough town in Merseyside, England, on the Wirral Peninsula to the south of Birkenhead; pop. (1981) 64,170. The nearby model village of Port Sunlight was built in 1888 to house workers at the Lever Bros. (later Unilever) soap and margarine factory.

Beche, Sir Henry Thomas de la (1796–1855) British geologist who established the Geological Survey of Great Britain in 1835. His early work in Devon and Cornwall resulted in the description and illustration for the first time of the Jurassic and Cretaceous strata of those regions. He supervised the drawing up of a geological map of England, the first large scale methodological geological survey.

Bechstein, Friedrich Wilhelm Carl (1826–1900) German piano-builder. His name is used to designate a piano manufactured by him or by the firm which he founded in 1856.

Bechuanaland The former name (until 1966) of BOTSWANA.

Becker, Boris (1967–) German tennis player. He became the youngest man to win the men's singles championship at Wimbledon in 1985, the first time that the title had been won by an unseeded player. He won at Wimbledon again in 1986 and 1989 and also won the US Open (1989) and the Australian Open (1991).

Becket, St Thomas à (*c.*1118–70) English prelate and statesman. A close and influential friend of Henry II, he served as his Chancellor and in 1162 became Archbishop of Canterbury, a position Becket accepted with reluctance, foreseeing the inevitable conflict of interests between the king and the Church. He soon found himself in open opposition to Henry, first on a matter of taxation and later over the coronation of Henry's son, and the king in anger uttered words which led four knights to assassinate Becket in his cathedral on 29 December. The murder aroused indignation throughout Europe, miracles were soon reported at his tomb, and Henry was obliged to do public penance there. The shrine became a major centre of pilgrimage until its destruction under Henry VIII (1538). Feast day, 29 December.

Beckett, Samuel (Barclay) (1906–89) Irish dramatist, novelist, and poet. A permanent resident in France from the mid-1930s, he is best known for his plays, especially *Waiting for Godot* (1952). A seminal work in the Theatre of the Absurd, the play was highly influential during the postwar period, especially because of Beckett's use of dramatic narrative and symbolism. His later works were increasingly short and enigmatic. Beckett was awarded the Nobel Prize for literature in 1969.

Beckford, William (1759–1844) British writer and collector. He inherited a large fortune from his father, which he spent lavishly. He travelled in Europe, collected works of art and curios, and commissioned the building of Fonthill Abbey in Wiltshire, a Gothic folly, where he lived in seclusion 1796–1822. He is remembered as the author of the fantastic oriental romance *Vathek* (1786, originally written in French).

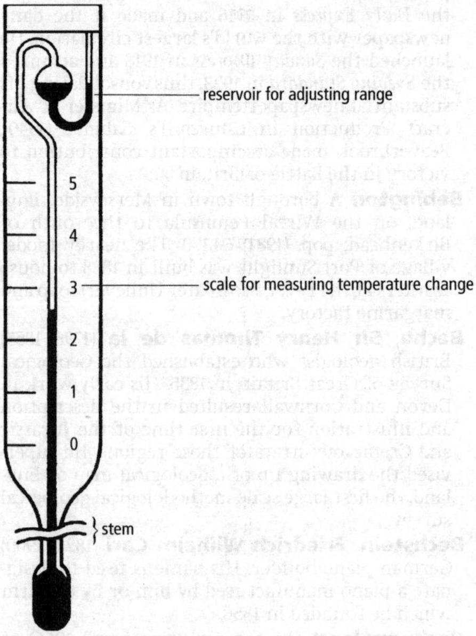

Beckmann thermometer

Beckmann, Ernst Otto (1853–1923) German chemist. Beckmann devised a method of determining a compound's molecular weight by measuring the rise in boiling-point of a solvent containing the compound. For this he designed an accurate thermometer (the **Beckmann thermometer**) with an adjustable range. He also discovered a rearrangement reaction important in organic synthesis.

Beckmann, Max (1884–1950) German painter and graphic artist. Beckmann was an expressionist and his paintings typically reflect his first-hand experience of human evil during World War I; a characteristic work is *The Night* (1919), a torture scene in which contemporary social conditions are portrayed with powerful symbolism. Beckmann was dismissed from his teaching post in Frankfurt by the Nazis in 1933; the same year he painted *Robbery of Europe*. In 1937 his work was denounced as 'degenerate' and he fled to Holland, before going to the USA in 1947.

becquerel (symbol Bq) The SI UNIT of radioactivity. The activity of a source is the number of nuclear disintegrations it undergoes per unit time. The unit is named after Henri BECQUEREL.

Becquerel, (Antoine) Henri (1852–1908) French physicist. He shared the 1903 Nobel Prize for physics with Marie and Pierre Curie for his discovery of natural radioactivity in uranium salts, which he proceeded to investigate. Initially, the rays emitted by radioactive substances were named after him.

Becrux A first-magnitude VARIABLE STAR in the constellation of CRUX and also known as Beta Crucis. It is a hot giant star at a distance of 140 parsecs, with about 6,000 times the luminosity of the Sun. It is a member of the Scorpius-Centaurus stellar association, a large moving group which also includes Acrux and Antares.

bedbug An oval, flattened insect of the BUG order which hides by day in beds and in crevices in furnishings and walls, emerging at night to suck the blood of vertebrates, including humans. A common species throughout Europe and North America is *Cimex lectularius*; its close relative *C. rotundatus* is found in southern Asia and Africa. They produce a characteristic smell and their bites are irritating, but they transmit no disease. Related species are parasites of birds and bats.

Bede, St (known as the **Venerable Bede**) (*c*.673–735) English monk, theologian, and historian. He lived and worked at the monastery in Jarrow, on Tyneside. Often regarded as 'the Father of English History', he wrote a number of historical works including *The Ecclesiastical History of the English People* (completed in 731). This is considered a primary source for early English history; it has vivid descriptions and is based on careful research, separating fact from hearsay and tradition. Feast day, 27 May.

Bedford The county town of Bedfordshire in southern England, on the River Ouse; pop. (est. 1983) 89,200. John Bunyan wrote *The Pilgrim's Progress*, *Grace Abounding*, and other works while imprisoned in the county jail from 1660 to 1672 for preaching without a licence. The town gives its name to Bedford cord, a tough woven fabric similar to corduroy. It is the site of the Cranfield Institute of Technology (1969).

Bedford, John, Duke of (1389–1435) Regent of France (1422–35). He was the third son of HENRY IV. While his brother HENRY V was in France, Bedford was appointed Guardian of England on several occasions between 1415 and 1421, and on Henry's death in 1422, he was made governor of Normandy and Regent of France. He succeeded in retaining England's French territories, despite the campaign of JOAN OF ARC and insufficient funds; by his first marriage, to Anne of Burgundy, daughter of Duke John the Fearless, he cemented England's crucial Burgundian alliance.

Bedfordshire A county of southern England; area 1,235 sq km (477 sq miles); pop. (1991) 514,200; county town, Bedford.

Bedlam The popular name of the Hospital of St Mary of Bethlehem, founded as a priory in 1247 at Bishopsgate, London, and by the 14th century a mental hospital. In 1675 a new hospital was built at Moorfields, and this in turn was replaced by a building in the Lambeth Road in 1815 (now the Imperial War Museum), and transferred to Beckenham in Kent in 1931.

Bedlington terrier See DOG.

Bedouin A nomadic Arab people of the deserts of Arabia and North Africa. Until the early 20th century the Bedouin supplied pack camels to the caravan trade and provided military protection to caravan cities and trade routes. The decline in the use of camels to transport cargo and the development of independent nation states has forced the Bedouin to adopt a more settled way of life.

bedrock The solid rock that lies below loose sand, gravel, or soil. Where visible it is seen as an outcrop protruding through the superficial cover.

bee An insect of the order Hymenoptera, which also includes ants, wasps and sawflies. Bees, which comprise some 2,000 species in the superfamily Apoidea, have a body covered with feathery hairs, two pairs of wings, the hind pair of which are smaller and linked to the front pair with a row of hooks, and mouthparts adapted for collecting pollen and sucking nectar. Most bees are solitary; only a few, the HONEYBEES and BUMBLEBEES and their relatives, are social, with a worker caste collecting food for their colonies. The solitary bees include species that construct nests in hollow stems, or dig their own nest burrows in wood or soil. Only females build, provision, and occasionally tend their nests; males, or drones, live only to mate. The cells of a nest can be formed from plant material, mud, or wax secreted by glands on the underside of the body. Each cell contains one or more eggs and, before being sealed, is provisioned with pollen and honey, which is nectar matured in the mother's honey stomach. The young of some species are fed as they grow, whereas others are parasitic on other kinds of bees.

Beebe, Charles William (1877–1962) US naturalist and pioneer of underwater exploration. As director of tropical research for the New York Zoological Society from 1919, he led scientific expeditions to many parts of the world; these are described in such books as *Jungle Days* (1925). In 1930 he invented and constructed the BATHYSPHERE, a spherical diving-vessel for use in underwater observations. In 1934 he and Otis Barton reached a depth of 923 m (3,028 feet) near Bermuda, a feat described in his *Half Mile Down* (1934). Later dives reached depths of around 1.5 km (nearly 1 mile).

beech The common name for two distinct genera of trees: the ten species of deciduous *Fagus* of the north temperate zone and Mexico, and the 36 species, both evergreen and deciduous, of *Nothofagus* (known as southern beeches) of the Southern Hemisphere. They all belong to the family Fagaceae along with oaks and sweet chestnuts. Beeches cast a dense shade, permitting little undergrowth to flourish. They produce good timber, that of the European common beech being used for furniture. The nuts, or mast, are edible and yield an oil. The copper or purple beeches are variants with dark red leaves and are now planted as ornamental trees.

Beecham, Sir Thomas (1879–1961) British conductor and impresario. He was associated with most of the leading British orchestras, founding the London Philharmonic in 1932 and the Royal Philharmonic in 1947; he was also artistic director of the Royal Opera House in the 1930s. He did much to stimulate interest in new and neglected music; a champion of Delius, he was also responsible for introducing Diaghilev's Ballets Russes and the work of Sibelius and Richard Strauss to the British public.

Beecher, Henry Ward (1813–87) US clergyman, orator, and writer. He was ordained as a Congregationalist in 1837 and ten years later accepted the pulpit of the Plymouth Church of Brooklyn. There he won fame as one of the greatest orators of his day, attacking political corruption and slavery in an emotional, florid style.

Beeching, Richard, Baron (1913–85) British businessman and engineer. Chairman of the British Railways Board (1963–65), Beeching is best remembered for the 'Beeching axe', the plan which proposed the closure of a substantial proportion of the British rail network. Much of the plan was rapidly carried out, although a change of government prevented its completion. Beeching was created a life peer in 1965 and became deputy chairman of ICI the same year.

bee-eater A brilliantly coloured, small bird of the family Meropidae. Many, but not all, of the 26 species are bright green in colour with patches of red, blue, or yellow. All have longish, slightly curved beaks. They are largely confined to the warmer areas of the Old World. The European bee-eater, *Merops apiaster*, is strongly migratory, spreading in summer from the tropics into Europe and temperate Asia. All species feed on large insects such as dragonflies and bees, often swooping down on them from perches. They nest in holes in banks or in the ground, laying two to four white eggs.

bee-fly A true FLY with over 2,000 species in the family Bombyliidae. Most are tropical species; they all have a long proboscis, and are often stout and hairy, with a superficial resemblance to small bumble-bees. Their larvae parasitize and ultimately kill developmental stages of mining bees, parasitic wasps and flies, caterpillars, or grasshopper eggs, depending upon species.

bee-keeping See APICULTURE.

Beelzebub The Greek form of Baalzebub, a god of Ekron, a Philistine town in Canaan. In Hebrew, the name means 'lord of the flies', though it may originally have been a corruption of Baal-zebul, 'exalted Lord'. In New Testament times and subsequently both forms have been used as epithets for 'the prince of evil spirits', that is, the Devil.

beer See BREWING.

Beerbohm, Sir (Henry) Max(imilian) (1872–1956) British caricaturist, essayist, and critic. A central figure of the Aesthetic Movement, from 1894 he contributed to the quarterly periodical *The Yellow Book*. He was well placed to comment on the avant-garde tendencies of the period, which he did in collections of essays and caricatures. His one completed novel, *Zuleika Dobson* (1911), is a fantasized distillation of the atmosphere of *fin-de-siècle* Oxford. From 1935 onwards he achieved success in the new medium of radio; some of his broadcasts were published in *Mainly on the Air* (1946).

Beersheba A town in southern Israel on the northern edge of the Negev Desert; pop. (est. 1993) 138,000. In Old Testament times it marked the southern limit of Israelite territory (Judges 20; see also Daniel 3).

beeswax A WAX secreted from glands under the abdomen of a worker bee, from which it constructs honey-comb. Beeswax is commercially extracted by melting the honeycomb after the removal of the honey, then straining and pressing the wax to rid it of impurities. It is soft to brittle in texture and consists mainly of fatty acids and esters, which are insoluble in water but dissolve in organic SOLVENTS. It melts at about 70°C and is used to make candles, polishes, inks, cosmetics, and ointments.

Beethoven, Ludwig van (1770–1827) German composer. Pre-eminently an instrumental composer, he reinvigorated the forms of sonata, symphony, and concerto that had matured during the latter part of the 18th century, reshaping them and expanding their terms of reference. Despite increasing deafness, he was responsible for a prodigious musical output; his work includes nine symphonies (including the *Eroica* of 1804, originally dedicated to his hero Napoleon), five piano concertos and one violin concerto, 32 piano sonatas, 16 string quartets, the opera *Fidelio* (1814), and the Mass in D (the *Missa Solemnis* of 1823). In the piano sonatas of 1816–22 and the string quartets of 1824–26 the old structural forms are merely implicit; in his Ninth Symphony (1824) he broke with precedent altogether in the finale by introducing voices to sing Schiller's *Ode to Joy*. With his expansion of 18th-century forms and techniques in his earlier work, and the personal emotion and individuality of his later works, he is often seen as bridging the classical and romantic movements.

beetle An INSECT of the order Coleoptera. The front two wings are thickened and hardened, forming protective covers (elytra) for the delicate, folded hind pair, and for much of the abdomen. The elytra are extended in flight but give little more than lift, the hind-wings giving most lift and thrust. All beetles go through a complete METAMORPHOSIS between egg and adult.

There are more described species of beetle than of any other order of insects, with some 300,000 species known. The smallest is smaller than the largest single-celled animal at 0.25 mm (0.01 inch), and the largest, such as the HERCULES BEETLE, is larger than the smallest mammal. The great number of species is due to the variety of life-styles followed, especially by the larvae. Beetles occur worldwide except in oceans and near the poles. Most species live on land, although there are many in fresh water and a few on the seashore. All have biting mouthparts. Some, such as the ground beetles, are carnivorous both as adults and as larvae. The majority of species feed on plants, including fungi, with many having special adaptations for feeding on leaves, fruit, seeds, and living or dead wood. Consequently many are pests of agriculture and forestry. These include weevils, leaf beetles, and longhorns.

Beeton, Mrs Isabella Mary (1836–65) British writer on cookery. Her best-selling *Book of Cookery and Household Management* (1861), first published serially in a women's magazine, contained over 3,000 recipes and articles, as well as sections giving advice on legal and medical matters.

beetroot A variety of *Beta vulgaris*, which also includes sugar-beet, mangel-wurzels, spinach beet, and seakale beet. The characteristic swollen, red root of beetroot is grown as an annual for a vegetable or as a perennial for fodder.

Begin, Menachem (Wolfovitch) (1913–92) Israeli statesman. Active in the ZIONIST movement throughout the 1930s, he was sent with the Polish army-in-exile to Palestine (1942), where he joined the militant IRGUN. On the creation of ISRAEL (1948) the Irgun regrouped as the Herut (Freedom) Party and elected Begin as its head. He was leader of the Opposition in the Knesset (Parliament) until 1967, when he joined the National Unity government. In 1970 he served as joint chairman of the Likud (Unity) coalition, and after its electoral victory in 1977 became Prime Minister (1977–83). He negotiated a peace treaty with President SADAT of Egypt at CAMP DAVID, but remained opposed to the establishment of a Palestinian state.

begonia A plant of the genus *Begonia* with a wide distribution in subtropical and tropical areas of the world. The 750 or so species belong to the family Begoniaceae and most have rather succulent, jointed stems; many are tuberous rooted or rhizomatous, a few are climbers with aerial roots, and others have woody stems. All species have leaves that are asymmetrical in shape, and male and female flowers (both on the same plant) which differ in appearance. Several species have been hybridized and selectively bred for either showy red, yellow, pink, or white flowers, or ornamental foliage in reds, greens, or silver. Some species contain medically valuable drugs.

Behan, Brendan (Francis) (1923–64) Irish dramatist and poet. A committed supporter of Irish nationalism, he spent periods in Borstal and in prison for his involvement in terrorist activities; his period of Borstal training is described in his autobiographical novel *Borstal Boy* (1958). His play *The Quare Fellow* (1956), set in an Irish prison and evoking the horror and humour prevailing on the eve of a hanging, is based on the time he spent in Dublin's Mountjoy prison (1942–46); the work became a key text in the contemporary anti-hanging debate.

behaviour The way an individual animal acts in response to its environment and to members of its own and other species. The behaviour of an animal, like its physiology or MORPHOLOGY, may be subject to the influence of NATURAL SELECTION, and may be important in providing survival value. Behaviour can be inherited or learned. Even simple organisms show complex inherited behaviour patterns: these are often referred to as instinctive behaviour. They may facilitate feeding, as in the web-building of many spiders, or ensure successful reproduction, as in COURTSHIP behaviour. Inherited behaviour may provide communication between social animals, such as the waggle-dance of hive BEES, which tells the closely related nest mates of the whereabouts of food. Inherited behaviour patterns tend to be relatively inflexible and usually consist of a series of actions, each of which requires a particular signal or reaction from another individual.

More sophisticated organisms, such as mammals, also show inherited behaviour, for example when human infants cling instinctively to their mothers. In addition, the actions of many organisms are modified by experience, allowing an animal's behaviour to be better suited to a complex and changing environment. Lion cubs, for example, learn to hunt by watching and copying their parents, while many insectivorous birds learn to avoid eating unpalatable prey through trial and error. The well-developed brain of humans and other animals, such as elephants, allows them to learn a wide range of complex behaviour patterns. These include complex social, manipulative, and mental skills, and in humans, speech. The study of animal behaviour in the wild was transformed into a science by such biologists as Konrad LORENZ and Nikolaas TINBERGEN, and is called ETHOLOGY.

behaviourism (in philosophy) A doctrine in the philosophy of mind formulated in response to dissatisfaction with introspection as a means of investigating the mind. Introspective investigation of the mind can be engaged in only by the subject and is notoriously unreliable. Behaviourists believe that the characterization of mental states (such as wanting to get home or being in pain) in terms of patterns of behaviour renders them publicly observable and so scientifically investigable. Being in pain, for a behaviourist, is a matter of behaving in a certain way, as is believing that it is raining. Among philosophical objections to behaviourism is the intuition that to be in pain is more than to behave in a certain way. Objections arise also from within psychology, whose theories need to consider relations between mental states, in addition to relations between mental states and behaviour. Such difficulties led to reformulations of behaviourist theories and to FUNCTIONALISM.

behaviour therapy (or **behaviour modification**) Clinical treatment to change maladaptive patterns of behaviour using techniques that derive from experiments on LEARNING. It is based on the view that neurotic behaviour is learnt in the same way as normal behaviour and may be eliminated by a manipulation of surroundings, which allows the subject to learn new and better responses. It developed in the 1950s from WATSON and SKINNER's ideas about therapeutic applications of CONDITIONING. The classic text was Joseph Wolpe's *Psychotherapy by Reciprocal Inhibition* (1958). He described how he had made cats fearful and then cured them by inducing them to eat closer and closer to the source of their fear. Behaviour therapy has become popular, in the form of desensitization, for treating PHOBIAS and OBSESSIONS, and has been used with some success for sexual problems and alcohol and drug abuse. It has also been used to try to 'modify' anti-social activities in classrooms. Generally, however, the cooperation of the patient seems necessary. More recent approaches, focus on patients' beliefs about what they are able to do.

Behn, Aphra (1640–89) English novelist and dramatist. Regarded as the first professional woman writer in England, she is best known for her philosophical novel *Oroonoko, or the History of the Royal Slave* (1688). Based on her trip to Suriname in 1663, the novel deplores the slave trade and Christian attitudes towards it, and encourages respect for its African hero. Of her fifteen plays, perhaps the best known is her Restoration comedy *The Rover* (1678).

Behrens, Peter (1868–1940) German architect and designer. A versatile artist who began his career as a painter, he joined the firm of AEG in 1907 and designed everything from factories to stationery. This marks the beginning of industrial design as a specialist field, showing a desire to humanize technology. As an architect Behrens was a pioneer of MODERNISM in Germany; his most famous work is the AEG Turbine Factory in Berlin (1908–09), a massive, bold structure of concrete, iron, and glass. Behrens was an influential figure, and his pupils included GROPIUS, LE CORBUSIER, and MIES VAN DER ROHE.

Behring, Emil Adolf von (1854–1917) German bacteriologist and one of the founders of immunology. He discovered in 1890 that animals can produce substances in the blood which counteract the effects of bacterial toxins. Behring applied this knowledge to the curing of diphtheria and tetanus, injecting patients with blood serum taken from animals previously exposed to the disease. He was awarded a Nobel Prize in 1901.

Beiderbecke, Bix (born Leon Bismarck Beiderbecke) (1903–31) US jazz musician and composer. A self-taught cornettist and pianist, he was one of a handful of white musicians who profoundly influenced the development of jazz. During a career abruptly terminated by his death from alcoholism, Beiderbecke played with Louis ARMSTRONG and American band-leader Paul Whiteman (1890–1967).

Beijing (or **Peking**) The capital of China; pop. (1990) 10,819,000. The city, whose name means 'northern capital', developed from Kublai Khan's capital built in the late 13th century and was the capital of China, except for brief periods, from 1421. At its centre lies the 'Forbidden City', a walled area containing a number of buildings including the imperial palaces of the emperors of China (1421–1911), entry to which was forbidden to all except the imperial family and servants. Tiananmen Square outside the Forbidden City was the scene of demonstrations in June 1989 that resulted in the deaths of hundreds of people. Beijing is the political, cultural, financial, educational, and transportation centre of China. It is also a major industrial centre with iron and steelworks, textile mills, machine and repair shops, chemical plants, and numerous other heavy and light industries.

Beilstein, Friedrich Konrad (1838–1906) Chemist born in St Petersburg of German parents, best known as the first editor of the *Handbuch der Organischen Chemie*, commonly referred to as 'Beilstein'. This major reference work, kept up to date by periodic supplements, is a compendium of all known organic compounds and now occupies more than a hundred volumes.

Beira A deep-water seaport on the east coast of Mozambique; pop. (1990) 299,300. It was founded in 1891 by the Portuguese Mozambique Company which administered that part of Africa until 1942. A railway, road, and oil-pipeline along the so-called 'Beira Corridor' link landlocked Zimbabwe with the port of Beira.

Beirut The capital and chief port of Lebanon, on the Mediterranean Sea; pop. (1989) 1,500,000. A major commercial centre since Phoenician times, Beirut became famous under the Romans for its trade in linen and wine and for its school of Roman law. It was captured by the Arabs in 635 AD, taken by the Crusaders in 1110, and from the early 16th century controlled by the Druses under Ottoman Rule. In 1918 Beirut was captured by the French and two years later made capital of Lebanon under French mandate. Once a prominent financial and cultural centre, the city was ravaged by the civil war that began in 1975 and has driven away its thriving tourist industry. Beirut has four universities, is a free port, and small-scale industries continue.

Beit, Sir Alfred (1853–1906) South African financier and philanthropist. Of German origin, he settled in Kimberley as a diamond merchant in 1875, and became a close friend of Cecil RHODES. His interest in gold greatly contributed to the development of the Rand and the British South African Company, and later of RHODESIA. He made benefactions to scholarship and the arts.

Bejaïa (formerly **Bougie**) A port on the Mediterranean coast of north-east Algeria; pop. (1989) 124,000. Capital of the Vandals in the 5th century, the city was rebuilt by the Berbers in the 11th century and was an important cultural and commercial centre. It later became a stronghold of the Barbary pirates and in the 20th century developed as a seaport trading in oil, minerals, grain, and fruit.

Béjart, Maurice (1927–) French dancer, choreographer, and company director. He trained in Paris and London, danced with several European companies, and in 1953 started his own company which became the Ballet of the Twentieth Century in 1959. He developed a popular expressionistic form of modern ballet, tackling vast themes. His works include *Firebird* (1970), *Kabuki* (1986), and *Nijinsky, Clown and God* (1990).

Belarus, Republic of A land-locked country in eastern Europe, formerly a constituent republic of the Soviet Union. It is bounded on the west by Poland, on the north-west by Latvia and Lithuania, on the north and east by Russia, and on the south by Ukraine.

Physical. Gentle hills run through a series of low plains which are forested with conifer, oak, lime, and ash. Cold in winter and warm in summer, the climate is predominantly wet, and many rivers drain the land into the vast area of the Pripet Marshes.

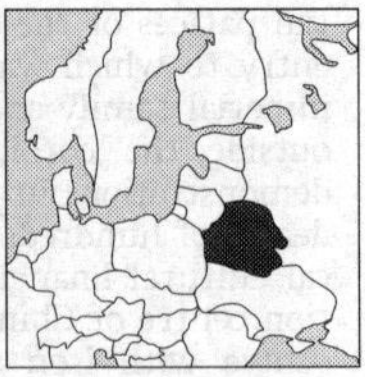

Economy. The rich plains of Belarus support agriculture and animal husbandry on a wide scale. Petroleum reserves in the south of the country are exploited, but other mineral resources are meagre. Belarus was the major Soviet supplier of heavy engineering equipment, transport and agricultural equipment, electronic and consumer goods, chemicals, timber, and textiles. However, much industry was dependent on processing raw materials from other parts of the former Soviet Union and after independence the country's inability to pay market prices for supplies led to severe recession. In 1994 Belarus entered into monetary union with Russia, enabling it to obtain cheap Russian raw materials.

History. Belarus (once referred to as White Russia) had been part of Lithuania and later Poland until conquered by Russia under Catherine the Great. Heavy fighting took place during and after World War I, before the Treaty of Riga (1921) which divided the area between Poland and the newly declared Soviet Socialist Republic of Belorussia, which joined the Soviet Union. In 1939 the latter occupied all the area as far as the River Bug, and heavy fighting took place after the German invasion in 1941. In 1945 the Belorussian SSR. was granted a seat in the UN National Assembly, and Poland abandoned its claim to western Belorussia, its Polish population being transferred to Poland. The rich steppe lands in the south of the republic suffered heavy pollution from the Chernobyl disaster of 1986. In April 1991 the Belorussian SSR. declared its independence from the Soviet Union, renaming itself the Republic of Belarus. Multiparty politics were adopted, but the communists have continued to dominate politics and the centrally planned economy has been maintained. A presidential constitution was adopted in 1994 and Aleksander Lukashenko (1954–) was elected President later that year. In four referendums in 1995 Belarussians voted in favour of establishing even greater political, economic, and cultural links with Russia than had existed during the Soviet era. A union treaty establishing joint economic, foreign, and defence policies between the two countries, was signed in 1996. Lukashenko's increasingly authoritarian style of leadership has provoked some concern about the future of democracy in Belarus.

Capital: Minsk
Area: 207,600 sq km (80.134 sq mi)
Population: 10,332,000 (1995)
Currency: 1 rouble = 100 kopeks
Religions: Eastern Orthodox Church
Ethnic Groups: Belorussian 78.0%; Russian 13.0%; Ukrainian, Polish, and Jewish minorities
Languages: Belorussian (official); Russian (official); minority languages
International Organizations: UN; Commonwealth of Independent States; CSCE; North Atlantic Co-operation Council

Belau (formerly **Palau**) A group of islands in the western Pacific Ocean, formerly held by Spain, Germany, and Japan, but part of the US Trust Territory of the Pacific Islands from 1947 until achieving independence as a self-governing state in 1994; area 488 sq km (188 sq miles); pop. (est. 1994) 18,000; official languages, English and Palauan; provisional capital, Koror (capital designate, Babelthuap). The group comprises 26 islands and over 300 small islets, the largest island being Babelthuap. The islands were the last to be held under UN Trusteeship and now maintain a compact of free association with the USA. The republic has a bicameral legislature comprising a Senate and a House of Delegates.

Belaúnde, Terry Fernando (1912–) Peruvian statesman. He was elected to the Chamber of Deputies (1945–48). In 1956 he helped to found the moderate Popular Action Party and in 1963 was elected President with the support of both Popular Action and Christian Democrats in opposition to Haya de la Torre, the candidate for APRA (Alianja Popular Revolucionaria Americana). His first term of office (1963–68) is remembered for its social, educational, and land reforms, as well as for industrial development and the construction of a vast highway system across the Andes. He was a strong supporter of the US Alliance for Progress programme, but his economic policies resulted in high inflation. He was deposed by the army and fled to the USA. He returned briefly to PERU in 1970, but was deported. He returned again in 1976 and was again President (1980–85). During his second term inflation grew worse and he was unable to counter the terrorist activities of the Sendero Luminoso (the Shining Path organization).

bel canto (Italian, 'beautiful song') A style of singing favoured by Italian OPERA, in particular in the work of BELLINI and DONIZETTI, in the 18th and early 19th centuries that was fluid and lyrical, beautiful in tone and flawless in technique. Now cultivated by singers who wish to do justice to the music of this period.

Belém (or **Pará**) A city and port at the mouth of the Amazon, 120 km (75 miles) from the Atlantic, the chief commercial centre of northern Brazil and capital of the mineral-rich state of Pará; pop. (1991) 1,245,000. The Portuguese landed here in 1616 and established a colony that united with Brazil in 1775 and developed a prosperous trade in cacao, vanilla, cinnamon, and cassia. During the 19th century rubber became an important export and the city grew towards a population of *c*.100,000. It processes and exports rubber, nuts, timber, fish, and vegetable oils.

belemnite The fossilized shell of an extinct CEPHALOPOD mollusc of the Mesozoic Era (245–66.4 million years ago). Belemnites are shaped like bullets and are actually reduced shells that lay entirely within the body of the animal and are equivalent to the cuttle-bone of the present-day cuttlefish. They may have been air-filled to assist buoyancy.

Belfast The capital of Northern Ireland, a port at the mouth of the River Lagan where it flows into Belfast Lough; pop. (1991) 280,970. Chartered by King James in 1613, Belfast grew after the arrival of Huguenot linen weavers in 1685. After the Act of Union in 1800 it expanded into an industrial centre with world-famous shipyards. Queen's University was founded in 1849. Belfast became a city in 1888 and capital of Northern Ireland in 1920. The Port of Belfast has seven miles of quays approached by a deep-water channel. Engineering, particularly aircraft manufacture, is a major industry and there are numerous light industries.

Belgae An Iron Age Celtic people of north-west Europe occupying part of ancient Gaul to the north of the Seine and Marne rivers. They were defeated by Julius Caesar in 57 BC.

Belgian Congo The former name (1908–60) of the Democratic Republic of CONGO.

Belgium A country in north-west Europe on the North Sea. It is bounded inland by The Netherlands, Germany, Luxembourg, and France.

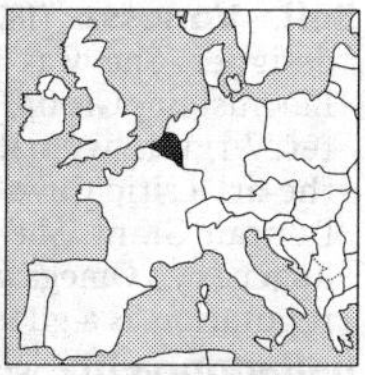

Physical. The coastal area comprises broad, sandy beaches backed by dunes. Inland, most of the rivers run across the flat, fertile Flanders Plain, north-eastward to The Netherlands. In the south-east the land rises from the Sambre–Meuse valley to the highlands of the Ardennes. Here the soil is poor, and the land generally forested. The Campine coalfield is in the east. The climate is cool and wet, with warm summers.

Economy. Manufacturing industries such as steel, textiles, engineering, and chemicals dominate the economy, but service industries are of increasing importance due to the location of the EU's headquarters in Brussels. Other than coal, Belgium has no natural resources, and processes imported raw materials. Major exports include steel, chemicals, motor vehicles, and foodstuffs. Agriculture is limited to production for the domestic market.

History. Belgium takes its name from the BELGAE, one of the peoples of ancient Gaul, but by the 5th century immigrations from the north had resulted in a large settled German population. After several centuries under the Franks the region split into independent duchies and, especially in FLANDERS, free merchant cities. In the 15th century all of what is now Belgium became part of the duchy of BURGUNDY, but the Low Countries (which included Belgium) in 1477 passed by marriage to the Habsburg empire of Maximilian I. They were later absorbed into the Spanish empire, and in 1713 passed to AUSTRIA. Belgium was occupied by France in 1795 during the French Revolutionary wars.

Following the defeat of Napoleon, Belgium became one of the provinces of the kingdom of The NETHERLANDS in 1815. However, in 1830 it separated from The Netherlands following a national revolution, and Prince Leopold of Saxe-Coburg was elected king. After an unsuccessful Dutch invasion, an international treaty was drawn up guaranteeing Belgian neutrality in 1839. In the later 19th century Belgium's King Leopold II (1865–1909) headed an international Association of the Congo (1876), following the exploration of the River Congo by H. M. STANLEY. This association was recognized at the Berlin Conference (1884) as the Congo Free State, with Leopold as its unrestrained sovereign. As the Congo was opened for trade, appalling atrocities against Africans were committed, leading to its transfer from Leopold's personal control to the Belgian Parliament (1908). Independence was granted to the Congo in June 1960, but was immediately followed by violence and bloodshed.

In 1914 Germany's invasion of Belgium precipitated Britain's entry into World War I. The country was occupied by the Germans, against whom Albert I (1908–34) led the Belgian army on the Western Front. When Germany invaded again in 1940 Leopold III (1901–83) at once surrendered. However, a government-in-exile in London continued the war, organizing a strong resistance movement. After the war Leopold was forced to abdicate (1951) in favour of his son Baudouin (1930–93). After World War II the main task for Belgium was to unite the Flemish-speaking northerners with the French-speaking Walloons of the south. In 1977 the Pact of Egmont, introduced by the Prime Minister, Leo Tindemans, recognized three semi-autonomous regions: that of the Flemings in the north, the Walloons in the south, and Brussels. The regions of Flanders, Wallonia, and Brussels were given greater autonomy by a constitution, adopted in 1993, that defines Belgium as a federal nation. Following his death in 1993, King Baudouin was succeeded by his younger brother, Albert II (1934–).

Capital: Brussels
Area: 30,518 sq km (11,783 sq mi)
Population: 10,064,000 (1995)
Currency: 1 Belgian franc = 100 centimes
Religions: Roman Catholic 90.0%; Muslim 1.1%; Protestant 0.4%
Ethnic Groups: Belgian 91.1%; Italian 2.8%; Moroccan 1.1%; French 1.1%; Dutch, Turkish, and other minorities
Languages: Flemish, French, German (all official); Italian
International Organizations: UN; EU; NATO; OECD; Council of Europe; CSCE

Belgorod An industrial city on the North Donets River, 72 km (45 miles) north of Kharkov, western Russia; pop. (1990) 306,000. The surrounding region has one of the world's largest deposits of iron ore and extensive areas of chalk and limestone which are used to manufacture cement and building materials.

Belgrade (Serbo-Croat **Beograd**) The capital of Serbia, at the junction of the River Sava with the Danube; pop. (1991) 1,168,450. Belgrade occupies a strategic location on the trade route between central Europe and the Balkans. It was an important river port to the Romans who called it Singidinum and was occupied by Huns, Goths, Franks, and Bulgars before becoming capital of Serbia in the 12th century. In 1521 it fell to the Ottoman Turks who made it their leading fortress town in Europe and from 1929 to 1991 it was capital of the Socialist Federal Republic of Yugoslavia. Its university was founded in 1860 and it has an outstanding national museum. Its industries include oil refining, metal manufactures, textiles, chemicals, electrical goods, and machine tools.

Belgravia A district of London, England, to the south of Knightsbridge, laid out between 1825 and 1830 by the builder Thomas Cubitt (1788–1855) who was also responsible for the east front of Buckingham Palace.

Belisarius (505–65 AD) Roman general under JUSTINIAN. He was instrumental in halting the collapse of the Roman empire, if only temporarily. In 530 he defeated the Persians in the east, although they quickly reasserted themselves in Syria. Six years later he conquered Vandal North Africa, capturing its king. In 535–40 he took back Italy from the OSTROGOTHS, advancing as far north as Ravenna, taking their king prisoner, and followed it with a second Italian campaign a few years later. He took Rome in 549 but was dismissed and even charged with conspiracy by a jealous Justinian, though reinstated in 564.

Belize A small tropical country lying at the south of the Yucatán Peninsula in Central America. It is bounded by Guatemala to the west and the Caribbean Sea to the east.

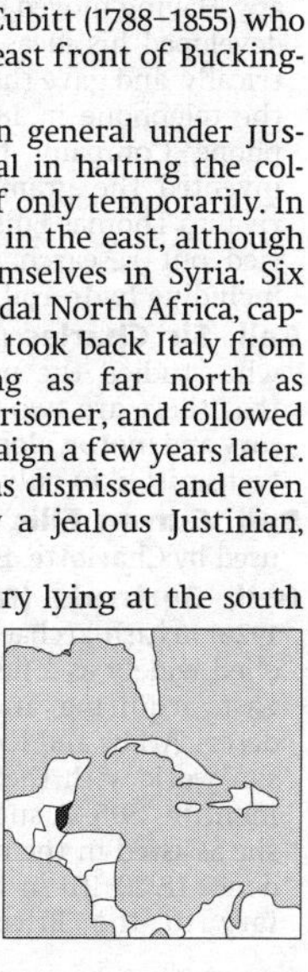

Physical. Belize is mainly low-lying and covered with rain forest; only in the south does it rise to pine forest and savannah. Sea breezes from the Caribbean temper the hot and humid climate. It is near an earthquake belt and is occasionally subject to hurricanes.

Economy. Belize has a predominantly agricultural economy. Industry is limited mainly to food-processing, and the chief exports are processed sugar, clothing, and citrus products. Tourism is another important source of revenue.

History. The British settled Belize in the 17th century, proclaiming the area (as British Honduras) a crown colony in 1862. Subject to the jurisdiction of the governor of Jamaica, the colony sustained itself with little direct support from the British government. Grudging acceptance by its Latin American neighbours in the 19th century led to treaties recognizing its permanent boundaries. In 1964 the colony gained complete internal self-government. It adopted the name Belize in 1973, and in 1981 became an independent state within the COMMONWEALTH OF NATIONS. However, Guatemala continued its long-standing claim to the territory on the basis of old Spanish treaties. In 1991 Guatemala recognized Belize's independence, the two countries having reached a provisional agreement on mutual fishing rights. In 1993 Britain decided to withdraw almost all its troops from Belize as a Guatemalan invasion was no longer thought likely.

Capital: Belmopan
Area: 22,965 sq km (8,867 sq mi)
Population: 216,000 (1995)
Currency: 1 Belize dollar = 100 cents
Religions: Roman Catholic 62.0%; Anglican 12.0%; Methodist 6.0%
Ethnic Groups: Creole (predominantly Black) 40.0%; Mestizo (Mayo-Spanish) 33.0%; Garifuna 8.0%; Maya 7.0%; European 4.0%; Ketchi 3.0%; East Indian 2.0%
Languages: English (official); English creole; Spanish; Mayan; Garifuna
International Organizations: UN; Commonwealth; CARICOM

Belize City The largest town and chief port of Belize in Central America, at the mouth of the Belize River; pop. (1991) 46,000. It was the capital of Belize until 1970.

Bell, Alexander Graham (1847–1922) Scottish-born US scientist and inventor. Bell studied sound waves, the mechanics of speech, and speech therapy. Having moved to the USA in the early 1870s, he developed his ideas for transmitting speech electrically, and gave the first public demonstration of the telephone in 1876; he founded the Bell Telephone Company the following year. He also invented the gramophone (1897) as a successful rival to Thomas Edison's phonograph. He later carried out research in a number of other areas, including hydrofoil speedboats and aeronautics.

Bell, Sir Charles (1774–1842) Scottish anatomist who studied the nervous system. He discovered that there are two types of NERVE filaments, sensory and motor, along which nerve impulses can be transmitted in only one direction.

Bell, Currer, Ellis, and **Acton** The pseudonyms used by Charlotte, Emily, and Anne BRONTË.

Bell, Gertrude (Margaret Lowthian) (1868–1926) British archaeologist and traveller. She travelled widely as a field archaeologist in the Middle East, acquiring an extensive knowledge of the desert Arabs and local politics, and undertook liaison work with the Arabs for the British government in 1915. A supporter of Arab independence, she assisted in the negotiations for Iraq's independence (1920–21) in her capacity as Oriental Secretary to the British High Commissioner. Her writings include a description of her travels in Syria, *The Desert and the Sown* (1907).

Bell, Vanessa (1879–1961) British painter and designer. She was a prominent member of the Bloomsbury Group, together with her younger sister Virginia WOOLF. In 1913 she left her husband the art critic Clive Bell to live with fellow artist Duncan Grant. She was a regular contributor to Roger Fry's Omega workshops (1913–19), and built a reputation as a gifted artist.

belladonna lily See AMARYLLIS.

bell-bird A bird of the genus *Procnias*, belonging to the COTINGA family, Cotingidae. The four species are confined to South and Central America. About the size of a largish thrush, the males of two species are almost completely white, and in both of the others have large amounts of white in their plumage. The females of all four species are yellowish-green. The birds live in rain forest and are famous for the powerful, bell-like calls given by the males. The single egg is laid in a very flimsy nest built on a tiny branch, presumably to make it difficult for predators to reach it. The female looks after the egg and young by herself. The Australian birds, the crested bell-bird, *Oreoica guttaralis*, and the bell-miner, *Manorina melanophrys*, are not related.

Bellerephon A hero in Greek mythology. After being falsely accused of trying to seduce the queen of Proteus, king of Argos, Bellerephon was given a number of seemingly impossible tasks, all of which he carried out successfully. The most famous was slaying the Chimaera. He was aided by the winged horse Pegasus, but later offended the gods by trying to ride Pegasus to heaven, and ended his life a lonely outcast.

bellflower See CAMPANULA.

bell founding The process by which bells are cast. The mould consists of an inner 'core' and an outer 'cope', with a void between them of the exact shape desired for the bell. The sides of the mould are insulated with loam or sand to prevent rapid cooling. Molten metal, usually BRONZE, is poured into the mould, which is tamped as the metal is poured to release any gases formed and to ensure that the void is completely filled. Cooling is regulated to prevent the outer surface from cooling faster than the inner, which would result in the formation of cracks. Large bells take up to two weeks to cool. After removal of the mould, the rough casting is sand-blasted and polished. If a certain pitch is required, small amounts of metal may be machined from the bell's inner surface.

Bellingshausen, Fabian Gottlieb von (1778–1852) Estonian-born Russian admiral who was the first to circumnavigate Antarctica. His discovery of islands within the Antarctic Circle (1821) was the first sighting of land there, and the Bellingshausen Sea was named after him.

Bellini A family of Italian painters. **Jacopo** (*c.*1400–70) was trained by Gentile da Fabriano: his elder son **Gentile** (*c.*1429–1507) was prominent as a portraitist and narrative painter. Jacopo's younger son **Giovanni** (*c.*1430–1516) is the most famous of the family; he had a large workshop of pupils and assistants and transformed the family's native Venice into a major centre of Renaissance painting.

Bellini, Vincenzo (1801–35) Italian composer. Of his 11 operas, the most famous are *La Sonnambula* (1831), *Norma* (1831), and *I Puritani* (1835). His work is typically dramatic and lyrical, displays a close relationship between the music and libretto, and is characterized by long, elegant melodies, such as 'Casta Diva' from *Norma*.

bell magpie An alternative name for three species of Australian magpies of the genus *Strepera* and belonging to the family Cracticidae, now usually referred to as currawongs. They are crow-sized and shiny black with patches of white in the tail, at the base of the tail, or in the wings; all have striking, yellow eyes. Their powerful beaks are used in taking small animals (including baby birds), fruits, and seeds. In winter many move out of forests and into parks and gardens in their search for food.

Bello, Alhaji Sir Ahmadu (1906–66) Nigerian statesman. He became leader of the Northern People's Congress, and, in 1952, the first elected minister in Northern Nigeria, and in 1954 Premier. When Nigeria became independent in 1960, his party combined with AZIKIWE's National Council of Nigeria and the Cameroons (NCNC) to control the federal Parliament. Bello's deputy in the NPC, Abubakar Tafawa BALEWA, became federal Prime Minister, while Bello himself remained to lead the party in the north. In 1966, when the army seized power, Bello was among the political leaders who were assassinated.

Belloc, (Joseph) Hilaire (Pierre René) (1870–1953) French-born British writer, historian, and poet, of French–British descent. A devout Roman Catholic, he collaborated with his friend G. K. Chesterton in works often critical of modern industrial society and socialism, notably in *The Servile State* (1912). His writings include biographies of Napoleon and Oliver Cromwell, but he is now best known for his light verse, such as *The Bad Child's Book of Beasts* (1896) and *Cautionary Tales* (1907).

Bellotto, Bernardo (1720–80) Italian painter, the nephew, pupil, and assistant of CANALETTO and his most skilful follower. In 1747 he left his native Venice and spent the rest of his life working at various European courts, notably Dresden and Warsaw. He called himself Canaletto and this caused confusion (perhaps deliberate) between his work and his uncle's, particularly in views of Venice.

Bellow, Saul (1915–) Canadian-born US novelist, of Russian Jewish descent. A leading figure in mid-20th century US fiction, he has written novels as diverse as the comic *The Adventures of Augie March* (1953) and the more sombre and semi-autobiographical *Herzog* (1964). His other works include the collection of short stories *Him with His Foot in His Mouth* (1984). His fiction is both ironic and optimistic in its treatment of the human condition. He was awarded the Nobel Prize for literature in 1976.

Belmopan The capital of Belize, Central America. Founded in 1970 in the interior of Belize, it is one of the smallest capital cities in the world; pop. (1991) 3,850.

Belo Horizonte A city in eastern Brazil, capital of the state of Minas Gerais, situated at the centre of a rich mining and agricultural region; pop. (1991) 2,020,160. Built in 1895–97, it was Brazil's first planned modern city. Its industries include steel, vehicles, electric trains, textiles, and cement.

Belorussia See BELARUS.

Belsen A village in Lower Saxony, north-west Germany, which was the site of a German concentration camp in World War II.

Belshazzar (6th century BC) Son of Nebuchadnezzar and last king of Babylon. According to Dan. 5, he was killed in the sack of the city and his doom was foretold by writing which appeared on the walls of his palace at a great banquet. In inscriptions and documents from Ur, however, he was perhaps the grandson of Nebuchadnezzar and the son of Nabonidos, last king of Babylon, and did not himself reign.

beluga See TOOTHED WHALE.

Bemba One of the largest ethnic groups in Zambia. Their Bantu language (see NIGER-CONGO LANGUAGES) has become the LINGUA FRANCA of the country. They were traditionally agriculturalists, living off their staple, millet, and shifting their villages every four or five years because of poor soil. The Bemba live in matrilineal CLANS, and their traditional religion includes the worship of ancestral spirits. Nowadays many Bemba men spend periods away from their home villages working in Zambia's copper mines, or in South Africa.

Benares See VARANASI.

Benbecula A flat boggy island with a deeply indented coastline in the Western Isles of Scotland between North and South Uist; area 93 sq km (36 sq miles). There are the remains of medieval church sites at Balivanich and Nunton.

Ben Bella, (Muhammad) Ahmed (1916–) Algerian statesman, Prime Minister 1962–63 and President 1963–65. In 1952 he founded the Front de Libération Nationale (FLN), which instigated the Algerian War of Independence (1954–62). He was elected Prime Minister of a provisional government shortly before the end of the war, becoming the first President of an independent Algeria the following year. As President he initiated social and economic reform and encouraged closer links with other Arab nations. Overthrown in a military coup, he was kept under house arrest until 1979 and lived in exile until 1990, when he returned to Algeria to lead the opposition to the ruling regime.

Benbow, John (1653–1702) English admiral. He was prominent in sea battles against the French for control of the English Channel during the early 1690s. He served in the West Indies for most of the period 1698–1702, where in his last engagement his daring plans for pursuing the retreating French were defied by his own captains. He died of his wounds in Jamaica, leaving a reputation for vigour, toughness, and bravery.

bench-mark A surveyor's mark cut in a wall, pillar, building or similar structure, and used as a reference point in measuring altitudes. In computing a benchmark is a task to be performed in a computer system, to measure the performance of the system under certain conditions, or undertaking certain classes of work.

Bendigo A former gold-mining town in the Central Uplands of the state of Victoria, Australia; pop. (1991) 57,430. Originally called Sandhurst, the town was renamed after a local boxer who adopted the nickname of a well-known English prize-fighter William Thompson (1811–89). Although gold is no longer mined, Bendigo now lies at the centre of a prosperous agricultural and wine-producing region.

Benedict, St (*c.*480–*c.*550) Italian hermit. A hermit from the age of 14, he attracted many followers by his piety; of these he chose the most devoted to form twelve small monastic communities, ultimately establishing a monastery at Monte Cassino (*c.*540). His *Regula Monachorum* (known as the Rule of St Benedict), austere but tempered by moderation, formed the basis of Western monasticism. Feast day, 11 July (formerly 21 March).

Benedictine A monk or nun of an order following the rule of St BENEDICT. From the original Benedictine foundations at Subiaco and Monte Cassino in Italy the number of monastic houses in Europe grew to many thousands. The order reached its peak of prestige and influence in the 10th and 11th centuries, with the abbey of CLUNY in Burgundy its most prestigious foundation. The basic concept of Benedictine monasticism was that it should encourage a way of life separated from the world, within which monks could achieve a life devoted to prayer.

benefit of clergy The privilege entitling a cleric, on being accused of a crime, to be exempted from trial by a secular court, and to be subject only to the church courts, which usually dealt with him more leniently. It was a system open to abuse, especially when clerics were numerous and difficult to identify with certainty, as was the case in the Middle Ages. Indeed the mere ability to read was often accepted as proof of clerical status. In England it was a principal issue in the controversy between Archbishop Thomas à BECKET and HENRY II and the privilege was largely conceded by the crown in the aftermath of Becket's murder in 1170; later its application was limited by various Acts of Parliament and it was finally abolished in 1827.

Benelux A collective name for Belgium, the Netherlands, and Luxembourg, especially with reference to their economic cooperation established in 1948.

Benevento (Roman **Beneventum**) The capital of the province of Benevento in Campania, southern Italy, 57 km (32 miles) north-east of Naples; pop. (1990) 64,690. Originally known as Maleventum (= ill wind), its name was changed to Beneventum (= fair wind) by the Romans who defeated Pyrrhus, King of Epirus, near the town in 275 BC. The Strega liqueur is produced in Benevento.

Beneš, Edvard (1884–1948) Czechoslovak statesman, Prime Minister 1921–22, President 1935–38 and 1945–48. A founder (with Tomáš Masaryk) of modern Czechoslovakia, he served as Masaryk's Minister of Foreign Affairs 1919–35, during which time he championed the League of Nations (he served as its chairman six times) and established close ties with France and the Soviet Union. He resigned as President over the Munich Agreement, and during World War II came to London as head of the Czechoslovakian government in exile (1941–45). In 1945 he returned to his country to regain the presidency, but resigned after the 1948 Communist coup.

Bengal A former province of British India divided in 1947 into the predominantly Hindu West Bengal, which became a state of India, and the largely Muslim East Bengal, which became part of East Pakistan and ultimately the independent nation of Bangladesh in 1971. The Bengali or Bangla language is a descendant of Sanskrit, written in a version of the Sanskrit Devanagari script. It is spoken by some 125 million people and is the official language of Bangladesh.

Bengal, Bay of An arm of the Indian Ocean bounded west by India and Sri Lanka, north by Bangladesh, and east by Burma and Thailand. It is separated from the Andaman Sea by the Andaman and Nicobar Islands. Calcutta, Madras, Chittagong, and Trincomalee are the chief ports.

Bengali See INDO-IRANIAN LANGUAGES.

Benghazi A Mediterranean port in Cyrenaica, north-east Libya; pop. (1984) 485,000. The Greeks founded the colony of Hesperides here in the 7th century BC. Later renamed Berenice after the wife of Ptolemy III of Egypt, it was conquered by Romans, Vandals, Arabs, Ottoman Turks, and Italians before Libya gained full independence in 1951. It was the co-capital (with Tripoli) of Libya from 1951 to 1972. Benghazi is an administrative and commercial centre with diverse light industries.

Benguela A port and railway terminal on the Atlantic coast of Angola, to the south of Lobito; pop. (1983) 155,000. The Benguela railway line provides a link with the interior coppermining regions of Zambia and Zaire. The town has food-processing plants.

Benguela current A cold ocean current that flows northwards from Antarctica along the coast of south-west Africa before meeting the warmer equatorial current at a latitude of 15°S. Its waters are rich in fish and plankton.

Ben-Gurion, David (1886–1973) Israeli statesman, Prime Minister 1948–53 and 1955–63. Born in Poland, he emigrated to Palestine in 1906, where he became an active Zionist. He was elected leader of the predominant socialist faction (the Mapai Party) of the Zionist movement in 1930. When the state of Israel was established in 1948, he became the country's first Prime Minister and Minister of Defence. After expulsion from the Labour Party in 1965 he formed a new party with Moshe Dayan.

Benidorm A popular Mediterranean resort town in the province of Alicante, eastern Spain, on the Costa Blanca; pop. (1991) 74,900.

Benin, kingdom of West African kingdom based on BENIN CITY, now in southern Nigeria, probably founded in about the 13th century. Its iron work and bronze and ivory sculptures rank with the finest art of Africa. It developed by trading in ivory, pepper, cloth, metals, and, from the 15th century, slaves. The kingdom achieved its greatest power under Oba Equare, who ruled from about 1440 to 1481. With his powerful army he conquered Yoruba lands to the west and Lower Niger to the east. He initiated administrative reforms, established a sophisticated bureaucracy, and ensured that the Portuguese, who arrived on the coast in 1472, did not establish control over Benin. The kingdom expanded further in the 16th century but by the 18th century its power waned with the growing strength of Oyo and other Yoruba states. Its extent declined further in the 19th century. Continuing slave-trading and the use of human sacrifice in religious rituals precipitated a British military expedition in 1897, which was massacred, whereupon a British force razed Benin city. The kingdom of Benin was incorporated into the new protectorate of southern NIGERIA in 1900. The republic of DAHOMEY subsequently took the name Benin.

Benin, Republic of A West African country lying between Togo and Nigeria on the Gulf of Guinea.

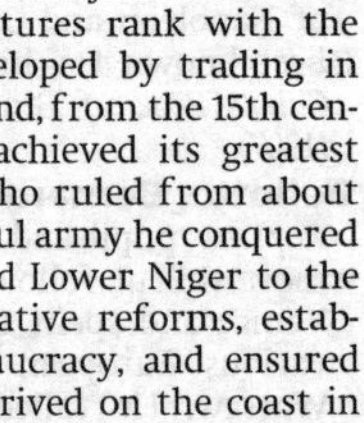

Physical. Benin has a southern coastline of only 125 km (78 miles) but extends inland for 700 km (460 miles) to Niger. The coast is sandy with large lagoons and is hot and wet. Inland there is a fertile clay plain with thick tropical forest that rises to a sandy plateau with SAVANNAH vegetation. In the north the land falls away to the middle Niger River valley.

Economy. Benin has an agricultural economy, with exports of cocoa, cotton, and palm products. There is some light industry, especially food-processing, brewing, and palm-oil processing. There are mineral deposits of off-shore oil, chromium, and phosphates; oil production began in 1982, but has disappointed expectations.

History. Formerly known as Dahomey, this region was ruled by kings of Yoruba origin until the French occupied it in 1892. It was constituted a territory of French West Africa in 1904. As Dahomey, it became an independent republic within the FRENCH COMMUNITY in 1960, after which periods of civilian government alternated with military rule. In 1972 it was declared a Marxist–Leninist state, and its name was altered (1975) to Benin. Under the leadership of Mathieu Kérékou (President 1972–91), Benin achieved greater domestic stability and international standing. In the country's first free elections, held in 1991, Kérékou was defeated by his Prime Minister Nicéphore Soglo, whose government moved towards a free-market economy with the support of the IMF. Legislative elections in 1995 were contested by 31 political parties and a coalition government was formed. However, presidential elections held in 1996 saw a surprise victory for the former dictator Kérékou.

Capital: Porto Novo
Area: 112,600 sq km (43,450 sq mi)
Population: 5,409,000 (1995)
Currency: 1 CFA franc = 100 centimes
Religions: Traditional beliefs 61.4%; Roman Catholic 18.5%; Muslim 15.2%; Protestant 2.8%
Ethnic Groups: Fon-Ewe 55.5%; Bargu 22.5%; Yoruba 13.6%
Languages: French (official); Fon-Ewe; Bargu; Yoruba
International Organizations: UN; OAU; Non-Aligned Movement; ECOWAS; Franc Zone

Benin City The capital of the state of Edo in southern Nigeria; pop. (1981) 183,000. Early trade with Portuguese was in slaves and ivory; now Benin City is a market for palm oil and rubber. It is also a centre of handicrafts.

Benjamin A biblical figure, the youngest and favourite son of the Hebrew patriarch Jacob and his wife Rachel. His only other full brother, Joseph, had been sold into slavery in Egypt, where he soon rose to a position of power. Jacob's ten other sons by his first wife Leah migrated to Egypt during a famine in Israel, where they and their father, together with Benjamin, were eventually reunited with Joseph. Benjamin's descendants formed one of the twelve tribes of Israel.

Ben Macdhui A peak in the Cairngorm Mountains of Scotland. At 1,309 m (4,296 ft), it is the second-highest mountain in the British Isles.

Benn, Tony (born Anthony Neil Wedgwood Benn) (1925–) British Labour politician. He became a Labour MP in 1950, but was debarred from the House of Commons on succeeding to the title of Viscount Stansgate in 1960. He renounced his title in 1963 and was re-elected the same year, going on to hold several government posts, including Secretary of State for Industry (1974–75) and Secretary for Energy (1975–79). He made unsuccessful bids for the party leadership in 1976 and 1988, but continued to be active on the left of the party.

Bennett, Alan (1934–) British dramatist and actor. He achieved fame with the revue *Beyond the Fringe* (1960) and the satirical comedy *Forty Years On* (1969), lampooning the Bloomsbury Group and other cult figures. Other plays in the same vein followed, including *Getting On* (1972), a political satire about a Labour MP. His play *The Madness of George III* (1991) was made into a film, for which he wrote the screenplay, in 1995.

Bennett, (Enoch) Arnold (1867–1931) British novelist, dramatist, and critic. He began his literary career in London writing stories for periodicals and editing the journal *Woman*; in Paris (1902–12) he was greatly influenced by the French realists and wrote several successful plays. However, his fame rests on the novels and stories set in the Potteries ('the Five Towns') of his youth, notably *Anna of the Five Towns* (1902), *The Old Wives' Tale* (1908), and the *Clayhanger* series (1902–08), in which he portrays provincial life and culture in documentary detail.

Bennett, Richard Rodney (1936–) British composer. He studied in Paris with Pierre Boulez (1956–58), then settled in London. He is known for his film scores, notably those for *Far from the Madding Crowd* (1967) and *Murder on the Orient Express* (1974). His concert works include operas, such as *The Mines of Sulphur* (1965), concertos, and chamber pieces, and his later work pays increasing attention to internal rhythmic structure.

Ben Nevis The highest mountain in the British Isles rising to 1,343 m (4,406 ft) near Fort William in western Scotland. At its summit, amidst massive boulders, are the ruins of an observatory built in 1883 and in use until 1904.

Bentham, Jeremy (1748–1832) British philosopher, the founder of the Utilitarian school of ethics and political thought. He promoted the idea that the morality of an action could be measured by its effects on people: the greatest happiness of the greatest number should be the goal, and human institutions judged by the extent to which they contributed to that happiness. He supported much humanitarian reform and provided the inspiration for the founding of London University.

benthic See BOUNDARY LAYER.

Bentinck, William Henry Cavendish, 3rd Duke of Portland (1738–1809) British statesman. As leader of the Whig Party he was briefly Prime Minister at the end of the American War of Independence in 1783. Later he supported the government of William PITT in its opposition to the French Revolution. He became Pitt's Home Secretary (1794–1801) and greatly assisted in the passing of the Act of UNION in 1801. After Pitt's death (January 1806) and the failure of the so-called 'Ministry of All the Talents' (1806–07), he was persuaded (1807) to take office again as Prime Minister. Then an old man, he failed to prevent internal dissension in his government, which led to the duel between CANNING and CASTLEREAGH, on news of which he resigned.

Bentley, Edmund Clerihew (1875–1956) British journalist and novelist. Examples of his comic verse-form, the CLERIHEW, were first published along with some sketches by his friend G. K. Chesterton in *Biography for Beginners* (1905). More clerihews appeared in volumes such as *Clerihews Complete* (1951). He was a successful journalist, and is also remembered for his detective novel *Trent's Last Case* (1913).

Benz, Karl Friedrich (1844–1929) German engineer and motor manufacturer. One of the pioneers of the motor car, in 1883 he formed a company to develop the internal-combustion engine, and in 1885 he built the first vehicle to be driven by such an engine. Benz's company was merged with Daimler in 1926.

benzene (C_6H_6) A clear, colourless, volatile liquid, highly toxic whether inhaled or absorbed through the skin. The benzene molecule consists of a hexagonal ring of six carbon atoms, with a hydrogen atom attached to each carbon of the BENZENE RING. Benzene was discovered by FARADAY in 1825,

1

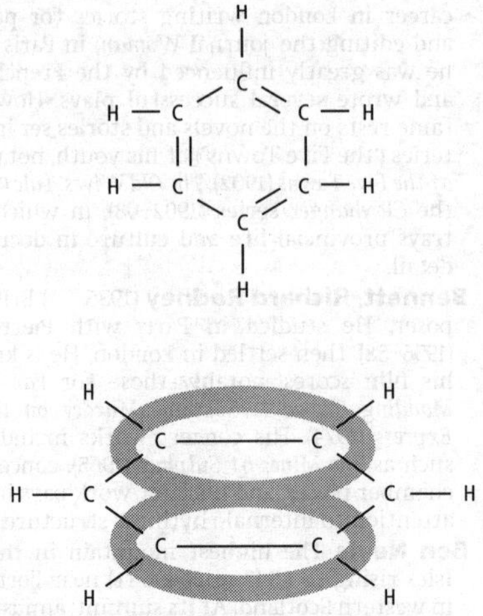

2

Benzene (1) The conventional Kekulé formula. (2) Modern explanation showing a delocalized orbital above and below the ring, within which the six valency electrons are free to move.

and is the simplest of the aromatic hydrocarbons, all of which are characterized by one or more benzene rings. It was originally produced by the fractional distillation of coal-tar, but is now obtained from certain petroleum fractions by catalytic REFORMING. Benzene and its derivatives are widely used in the manufacture of dyes, pharmaceuticals, explosives, and plastics.

benzene ring The characteristic feature of most AROMATIC COMPOUNDS, of which the prototype is BENZENE itself. Its structure consists of a hexagon of carbon atoms, to each of which is bonded a hydrogen atom. All twelve atoms lie in the same plane. The bonding in this hexagon, the benzene ring, is as follows: within the plane of the ring are localized sigma electrons, and above and below the plane of the ring are two identical clouds of delocalized pi electrons (see DELOCALIZED ELECTRONS). The effect of delocalization is to reduce the repulsions between electrons and thus to lower the energy of the molecule; for this reason, there are many naturally occurring compounds containing benzene rings. Moreover, benzene rings undergo reactions in which this delocalization is retained, namely substitution reactions, rather than those in which it is destroyed, namely addition reactions (see CHEMICAL REACTION).

benzodiazepines A group of compounds used as tranquillizers, sedatives, and sleeping pills. The group includes diazepam (Valium), chlordiazepoxide (Librium), and nitrazepam (Mogadon). Some are thought to be habit-forming.

Beowulf The most important epic in Old English literature and the first major poem in a European vernacular language. It survives in a 10th-century manuscript but is generally dated to the 8th century when Anglo-Saxon England was being won over from paganism to Christianity. The poem, which represents the fusion of Norse legend and history and Christian belief, describes two major events in the life of the Scandinavian hero Beowulf (see GRENDEL). The poem is over 3,000 lines long and is written in strongly accentual alliterative verse.

Berber (Berber **Tamazirght**) A Muslim Hamito-Semitic people of the Maghreb region of North Africa, now largely to be found in the Atlas Mountains of Morocco and Algeria. Speaking a language which they call Amzirght, the Berbers have a largely oral culture.

Berber languages A group of over 20 languages in North Africa, spoken by about 12 million BERBERS in scattered groups across Morocco, northern Algeria, Libya, and western Egypt, and in a large central-Saharan area in Niger, Mali, and southern Algeria. Berber languages originally covered most of North Africa, but after the 7th century AD were driven back or assimilated by the Arab invasions. As a result of this influence there are many Arabic loan-words in Berber, as well as Phoenician and Latin words which had been borrowed at an earlier date. The earliest attested (but poorly known) language in this family is Numidian (ancient Libyan), which is found written in a unique consonantal script in inscriptions dating from the time of the Roman Empire. A modified version of this script is still in use among the Saharan TUAREG. The other Berber languages are written in the Arabic script when they are written at all. There is virtually no literature. Scholars have not yet finally decided the internal sub-groupings of the Berber languages. Important groups beside Tuareg include Kabyle (Algeria), Riff (Morocco), and Schluh (Morocco and Mauritania). Berber languages are part of Afro-Asiatic, a larger group which includes CHADIC, CUSHITIC, and SEMITIC LANGUAGES.

Berchtesgaden A town in south-east Bavaria, southern Germany, in the Bavarian Alps, 16 km (10 miles) south of Salzburg. Salt has been continuously mined in the area since 1517. Nearby is the site of a villa built as a retreat for Adolf Hitler.

Berenice (3rd century BC) Egyptian queen, wife of Ptolemy III. She dedicated her hair as a votive offering for the safe return of her husband from an expedition. The hair was stolen and (according to legend) placed in the heavens. She is commemorated in the name of the constellation Coma Berenices (*Berenice's hair*).

Berent, Wacław (1873–1940) Polish novelist. Though a marine biologist, he devoted himself to writing, influenced by Nietzsche, whom he translated. He experimented with narrative and time, reconstructing the past in *Rotten Wood* (1903) and *Living Stones* (1918), set in the Middle Ages. *Winter Wheat* (1911) describes one night in Warsaw in 1904, when war is announced.

Berg, Alban (Maria Johannes) (1885–1935) Austrian composer. A pupil of Schoenberg, he was one of the leading exponents of twelve-note composition. He is best known for the Violin Concerto (1935), composed as a memorial after the death of the 18-year-old daughter of Alma and Walter GROPIUS, and for his two operas, *Wozzeck* (1914–21) and *Lulu* (1928–35).

Bergama (Roman **Pergamum**) A market town in the province of Izmir, western Turkey; pop. (1990) 101,421. Nearby are the ruins of ancient Pergamum which was capital of the Mysian kingdom of Pergamum and later the Roman province of Asia. The city, which developed under Eumenes II (197–159 BC), was famous for its library which rivalled the great collection of manuscripts at Alexandria.

Bergamo The capital of the province of Bergamo in Lombardy, northern Italy, at the foot of the Bergamo Alps; pop. (1990) 117,890. The upper walled town contains historic buildings; the lower town is commercial and industrial. The town gives its name to an oily perfume (bergamot) extracted from the rind of the fruit of the citrus tree *Citrus bergamia*, a dwarf variety of the Seville orange tree. Gaetano Donizetti (1797–1848) the Italian composer spent his whole life in Bergamo.

Bergen A seaport and capital of Hordaland county in south-west Norway; pop. (1991) 213,344. Founded in 1070 by King Olaf Kyrre it has developed into Norway's third-largest city as an important centre of the fishing and North Sea oil industries.

Bergen See MONS.

Berger, Hans (1873–1941) German psychiatrist. He attempted to correlate mental activity with brain physiology, detecting electric currents in the exposed cortex in 1924. Finding that these could also be detected through the intact skull, Berger went on to develop encephalography, which has since been used extensively to diagnose neurological conditions.

Bergerac See CYRANO DE BERGERAC.

Bergeron, Tor (1891–1977) Swedish meteorologist, best known for his work on cloud physics. He was the first meteorologist to take into account the upper atmospheric phenomena and their effect on climate. He demonstrated that raindrops can form in the upper parts of clouds, which contain little liquid water, through the growth of ice crystals. This happens at temperatures between −10°C and −30°C (14°F and −22°F) and is known as the Bergeron process.

Bergius, Friedrich Karl Rudolf (1884–1949) German industrial chemist. He is best known for his process for producing petroleum and other hydrocarbons from coal dust, using hydrogen and a catalyst under high pressure. He also made a type of coal by carbonizing peat, achieved the complete hydrolysis of cellulose, and developed industrial processes for synthesizing phenol and ethylene glycol. Bergius shared the Nobel Prize for chemistry in 1931.

Bergman, (Ernst) Ingmar (1918–) Swedish film and theatre director. His work is characterized by his use of haunting imagery and a symbolism often derived from Jungian dream analysis. He came to international fame with the film *Smiles of a Summer Night* (1955) and achieved further worldwide success with *The Seventh Seal* (1956) and *Wild Strawberries* (1957). An important theatre director, he has directed many of his players in both media.

Bergman, Ingrid (1915–82) Swedish actress. She made her name on stage and screen in Sweden before embarking on an international career in Hollywood in the 1930s. Probably her best-known film was *Casablanca* (1942), with Humphrey Bogart. Other notable films include *For Whom the Bell Tolls* (1943) and *Anastasia* (1956); she received an Oscar for the latter, as well as for her role in *Murder on the Orient Express* (1974).

Bergson, Henri (Louis) (1859–1941) French philosopher. His philosophy is dualistic, dividing the world into life (or consciousness) and matter. In his most famous work, *Creative Evolution* (1907), he attacked scientific materialism and rejected the Darwinian theory of evolution. He proposed instead that life possesses an inherent creative impulse (*élan vital*), the continuous operation of which as it seeks to impose itself upon matter leads to the production of new forms. He was awarded the Nobel Prize for literature in 1927.

berg wind A dry wind that blows from the interior to the coastal districts of South Africa and Namibia, particularly during the winter season.

Beria, Lavrenti (Pavlovich) (1899–1953) Soviet politician and head of the secret police (NKVD and MVD) 1938–53. Born in Georgia, he rose to prominence within the Soviet Communist Party under Stalin's patronage. As head of the secret police Beria was directly involved in the infamous 'purge trials' in which Stalin's opponents were eliminated; he was also responsible for the deportation of thousands to forced labour camps. After Stalin's death he was rumoured to be planning to seize power; feared by rival politicians, he was arrested. Although his fate is not certain, it was officially announced that he had been tried and shot as a traitor.

Bering, Vitus (Jonassen) (1681–1741) Danish navigator and explorer. At the instigation of Peter the Great he led several Russian expeditions aimed at discovering whether Asia and North America were connected by land. He sailed along the coast of Siberia and in 1741 reached Alaska from the east. On the return journey his ship was wrecked and he died on an island which now bears his name. Also named after him are the Bering Sea and Bering Strait.

Bering Glacier A glacier in the Chugach-St Elias Mountains, southern Alaska. It is the largest glacier in North America.

Bering Sea An arm of the north Pacific lying between Siberia and Alaska and bounded to the south by the Aleutian Islands. It is linked to the Arctic Ocean via the Bering Strait and Chukchi Sea, and takes its name from the Danish explorer Vitus BERING.

Berio, Luciano (1925–) Italian composer. A serialist, he often adopted an experimental approach to groupings of instruments and singers, the use of electronic sound, and the combination of live and pre-recorded music. His works include *Circles* (1960), for singer, harp, and percussion, a series of *Sequences* (1958–75) for virtuoso solo instruments, and the opera *Un Re in Ascolto* (1984).

Berkeley, Busby (1895–1976) US director and choreographer. He was known for his flamboyant stagings of dances in Hollywood films, sometimes using the camera to move among the dancers. He was famous on BROADWAY in the 1920s and then in the 1930s in HOLLYWOOD for such films as *Gold Diggers of 1933* and *Lady be Good* (1941).

Berkeley, George (1685–1753) Irish philosopher and bishop. His idealist philosophy is set out in his major works *A Treatise Concerning the Principles of Human Knowledge* (1710) and *Three Dialogues between Hylas and Philonous* (1713). He denied the existence of matter, holding that there are only minds and mental events; material objects exist solely by being perceived. To the objection that objects would leap in and out of existence according to whether they were being looked at, he replied that God perceives everything, and that this gives objects – ideas in the mind of God – a continuous existence. He held this to be a sound argument for the existence of God.

Berkeley, Sir Lennox (Randall Francis) (1903–89) British composer. He studied in Paris 1927–32, and his compositions display a distinct French influence. His works, which are noted for their intensity of feeling and technical elegance, include four operas, among them *Nelson* (1953) and *Ruth* (1956), four symphonies, music for ballet and film, and sacred choral music.

berkelium (symbol Bk, at. no. 97, r.a.m. 247) A synthetic transuranic element synthesized by G. T. Seaborg in 1949 by bombarding americium with helium ions. Visible quantities of the trihalide $BkCl_3$ have been produced.

Berkoff, Steven (1937–) British dramatist, director, and film actor. His first original play, *East*, a work in blank verse about his East End boyhood, was presented at the 1975 Edinburgh Festival. Among Berkoff's other plays are *Greek* (1979), a modern version of the Oedipus myth, and *The Murder of Jesus Christ* (1981).

Berkshire (or **Royal Berkshire**) An inland county of southern England; area 1,259 sq km (486 sq miles); pop. (1991) 716,500; county town, Reading. The county council is due for abolition in 1998, when administrative powers will be devolved to six unitary authorities.

Berlin The capital of Germany; pop. (1991) 3,446,000. Founded in the 13th century it was a seat of the royal Hohenzollerns, capital of Brandenburg, then capital of Prussia. From World War II until the reunification of Germany in 1990 it was divided into two parts: West Berlin (a state of the Federal Republic of Germany, forming an enclave within the German Democratic Republic) and East Berlin (the zone of the city that was Soviet-occupied at the end of the war, and later became capital of the German Democratic Republic). The Soviets blockaded West Berlin in 1949 (see BERLIN AIRLIFT). A fortified wall separating the two sectors was erected in 1961 by the Communist authorities to curb the flow of refugees to the West. Long regarded as a symbol of the East-West division of Europe, it was opened in November 1989 after the collapse of the Communist regime in East Germany, and subsequently dismantled. Berlin is a commercial, educational, and industrial centre. It has three airports, two universities (1810, 1946), the Academy of Sciences (1700), and numerous museums. Its diverse industries include chemicals, electronic and electrical equipment, machinery, textiles, and publishing.

Berlin, Congress of (1878) A conference of European powers. It revised the Treaty of San Stefano (1878) which had ended the war between the OTTOMAN EMPIRE and Russia (1877–78). Under the chairmanship of the German chancellor, Otto von BISMARCK, the congress limited Russian naval expansion; gave Montenegro, Serbia, and Romania independence; allowed Austro-Hungary to occupy Bosnia and Hercegovina; reduced BULGARIA to one-third of its size; and placed Cyprus under temporary occupation by the British. The congress left Russian nationalists and Pan-Slavs dissatisfied, and the aspirations of Greece, Serbia, and Bulgaria unfulfilled. Bismarck's handling of the congress antagonized Russia, and the claim of DISRAELI, that it had achieved 'peace with honour', proved unfounded.

Berlin, Irving (born Israel Baline) (1888–1989) Russian-born US songwriter. He had no formal musical training, but began writing songs when he was 16; in 1911 he had a hit with 'Alexander's Ragtime Band'. Thereafter he contributed to many musical shows, revues, and films, including *Annie Get Your Gun* (1946) and *Holiday Inn* (1942); the latter contained the song 'White Christmas'. Berlin also wrote 'God Bless America' (1939), which became the unofficial national anthem of the USA.

Berlin Airlift (1948–49) A measure undertaken by the US and British governments to counter the Soviet blockade of Berlin. In June 1948 the USA, Britain, and France announced a currency reform in their zones of occupied Germany. The Soviet Union, fearing this was a prelude to the unification of these zones, retaliated by closing all land and water communication routes from the western zones to Berlin. The western Allies in turn responded by supplying their sectors of Berlin with all necessities by cargo aircraft. The siege lasted until May 1949, when the Russians reopened the surface routes. The blockade confirmed the division of Berlin, and ultimately of Germany, into two administrative units.

Berlioz, (Louis-)Hector (1803–69) French composer. He was one of the most original composers of his time and a major exponent of 19th-century programme music. His *Symphonie fantastique* (1830) reflects his unhappy passion for Harriet Smithson, an Irish actress, whom he later married. His other major works include the five-act opera *Les Troyens* (1856–59) and the cantata *La Damnation de Faust* (1846).

Bermuda A self-governing British colony consisting of some 150 tiny coral islands in the western Atlantic Ocean (latitude 32° N).

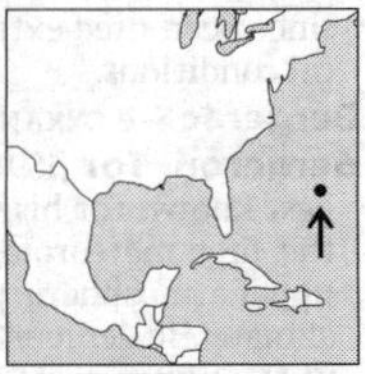

Physical. The islands are composed of a layer 60 m (200 feet) thick of limestone, polyps, coral, and other marine organisms, capping an extinct and submerged volcanic mountain range rising 4,200 to 4,500 m (14,000 to 15,000 feet) above the ocean floor.

Economy. Tourism is the most important industry, while medical products account for over half of total exports. International finance and insurance flourish due to low levels of taxation and well-developed communications systems. Over 10 per cent of Bermuda's land is occupied by US military and naval bases.

History. The first European to visit the islands was the Spaniard, Juan de Bermundez (1515). First settled in 1609 by the Virginia Company, they have the oldest parliament in the New World, dating to 1620. A flourishing slave economy, based mainly on tobacco production, existed until 1834 when slavery was abolished. By the 20th century two-thirds of the population was of African or Indian descent. Strategically important to the British navy, Bermuda grew rich on trade and tourism, with close ties with the USA. US naval and air-bases were granted in 1940. Universal adult suffrage was introduced in 1944 and the present constitution in 1967, granting the colony considerable self-government. Political activity developed in the 1960s and there were sporadic and bitter race-riots in the 1970s. In a referendum in 1995 Bermudans rejected independence from Britain.

Capital: Hamilton
Area: 54 sq km (21 sq mi)
Population: 60,075 (1994)
Currency: 1 Bermuda dollar = 100 cents
Religions: Anglican 37.3%; Methodist 16.3%; Roman Catholic 13.8%; non-religious 7.8%
Ethnic Groups: Black 61.3%; White 37.3%
Languages: English (official)
International Organizations: Commonwealth

Bermuda Triangle An area of the western Atlantic between Bermuda and Florida, credited since the mid-19th century with a number of unexplained disappearances of ships and aircraft.

Bernadette, St (born Marie Bernarde Soubirous) (1844–79) French peasant girl. Her visions of the Virgin Mary in Lourdes in 1858 led to the town's establishment as a centre of pilgrimage. Bernadette later became a nun and she was canonized in 1933. Feast day, 18 February.

Bernadotte, Folke, Count (1895–1948) Swedish

international mediator. The nephew of Gustav V, he entered the Swedish army as a young man. During World War II he worked for the Swedish Red Cross and in 1948 was appointed as UN mediator to supervise the implementation of the partition of PALESTINE and the creation of ISRAEL. He was murdered by Israeli terrorists.

Bernadotte, Jean Baptiste Jules (1763–1844) French soldier, king of Sweden (as CHARLES XIV) 1818–44. One of Napoleon's marshals, he was adopted by Charles XIII of Sweden in 1810 with Napoleon's support and became king in 1818, thus founding Sweden's present royal house.

Bernard, Claude (1813–78) French physiologist. Bernard used animal experiments to show the role of the pancreas in digestion, the method of regulation of body temperature, and the function of nerves supplying the internal organs. He realized that the constant composition of the body fluids was essential for the optimal functioning of the body, discovered the biological importance of glycogen, and investigated the action of curare.

Bernard, St (*c.*996–*c.*1081) French monk. He founded two hospices to aid travellers in the Alps. The St Bernard passes, where the hospices were situated, and St Bernard dogs, once kept by the monks and trained to aid travellers, are named after him. Feast day, 28 May.

Bernard of Clairvaux, St (1090–1153) French theologian and abbot. He was the first abbot of Clairvaux in France; his monastery there became one of the chief centres of the Cistercian order. He was noted for his asceticism, severity, and eloquence; his preaching at the council of Vézelay in 1146 instigated the Second Crusade; he had the French theologian Peter Abelard condemned for heresy. Feast day, 20 August.

Berne (or **Bern**) A city on the River Aar, founded in 1191 and the capital of Switzerland since 1848; pop. (1990) 134,620. It is the administrative centre of Switzerland and has national museums and libraries. The 'old town', which is largely unspoilt, has medieval and 18th-century buildings. Berne has light industries including watch-making and tourism. It is the headquarters of the Universal Postal Union which was founded in 1874.

Bernese Alps (German **Berner Alpen**) A northern range of the central Alps in the Swiss cantons of Bern and Valais. It is divided into the West Bernese Alps, a ridge running parallel to the Rhône valley from Lake Geneva to the Gemmi Pass, and the East Bernese Alps or Bernese Oberland, which forms the main group of the Bernese range. Finsteraarhorn (4,274 m, 14,022 ft) is the highest peak, although the most prominent mountains are the Jungfrau and the Eiger. The Aletsch glacier north of the Rhône is one of the largest in Europe.

Bernhardt, Sarah (1845–1923) French actress and theatre producer, renowned for her beautiful voice. Her outstanding performances included the title roles in Racine's *Phèdre* and Shakespeare's *Hamlet* (in which she played the prince). She also managed several theatres, including the Théâtre Sarah-Bernhardt, was an accomplished painter, and wrote poetry and plays.

Bernini, Gian Lorenzo (1598–1680) Italian sculptor, painter, and architect. An outstanding figure of the Italian Baroque, Bernini is notable for the vigour, movement, and dramatic and emotional power of his works. Using a variety of materials, including stucco, stone, and marble, he fused sculpture, architecture, and painting into a decorative whole. Working chiefly in Rome, he became architect to St Peter's in 1629, for which his work included the great canopy over the high altar and the colonnade round the piazza in front of the church. One of his most famous sculptures is *The Vision of St Teresa* (1644–67) in the church of Santa Maria della Vittoria in Rome.

Bernoulli Family of Belgian origin that settled in Switzerland and produced many prominent mathematicians within three generations. **Jacob** (or **Jacques**) **Bernoulli** (1654–1705) was a founder of PROBABILITY theory and the calculus of variations, while his brother **Johannes** (or **Jean**) **Bernoulli** (1667–1748) developed many applications of the CALCULUS to physics. **Daniel Bernoulli** (1700–82) made important contributions to HYDRODYNAMICS and propounded a version of the KINETIC THEORY of gases. He outlined the principle, now known by his name, that the pressure in a fluid is inversely proportional to its speed. Three further members of the family became professors of mathematics and a fourth became Astronomer Royal at Berlin.

Bernstein, Leonard (1918–90) US composer, pianist, and conductor. In 1943 a concert with the New York Philharmonic launched a spectacular conducting career that took him all over the world. His music, which combines jazz and classical techniques with great effect, includes the ballets *Fancy Free* (1944) and *On the Town* (1944), and the musicals *Candide* (1956) and *West Side Story* (1957), as well as 'serious' works such as the 'Jeremiah' Symphony (1943) and *Mass* (1971).

Berry, Chuck (born Charles Edward Berry) (1931–) US rock and roll singer, guitarist, and songwriter. One of the first rock and roll stars with a large teenage following, he first had a hit with 'Maybellene' (1955); this was followed by 'Johnny B Goode' and 'Sweet Little Sixteen' (both 1958). His recording career was interrupted by a period of imprisonment (1962–64); although he continued to release albums throughout the 1970s and 1980s, his only major hit single during that time was 'My Ding A Ling' (1972).

berry A fleshy FRUIT containing seeds, which are not encased in a tough layer, or endocarp. The fruits of tomatoes, papayas, bananas, and oranges are berries. However, 'berry' is the word commonly used to describe any small juicy fruit, irrespective of its precise structure. The strawberry is not a berry, but a 'false' fruit, and the mulberry is not strictly a berry, but a coalescence of the stalks of many flowers and their fruits. The blackberry, raspberry, and related species have fruits which are clusters of DRUPES. Berries are often brightly coloured and sweetly flavoured, making them attractive to birds and mammals, which disperse the seeds, usually in their droppings.

Berthelot, (Pierre Eugène) Marcelin (1827–1907) French chemist and statesman. He was one of the founders of thermochemistry, measuring the heats of reactions and devising a method for determining the LATENT HEAT of steam. He also synthesized a number of organic compounds using inorganic materials, thereby refuting the classical division between organic and inorganic chemistry. A prominent statesman, he was appointed foreign minister of France in 1895.

Berthollet, Claude Louis, Comte (1748–1822) French chemist who discovered potassium chlorate and, although this did not provide the substitute for saltpetre in gunpowder that he had sought, it did enable the manufacture of coloured fireworks. In 1785 he demonstrated that chlorine can act as a bleaching agent. He was the first scientist to note that the completeness of chemical reactions depends in part on the masses of the reacting substances, and his work led to the law of definite proportions.

Bertillon, Alphonse (1853–1914) French criminologist. He devised a system of body-measurements for the identification of criminals, which was widely used in France and other countries until superseded by the technique of finger-printing at the beginning of the 20th century.

Bertolucci, Bernardo (1940–) Italian film director. He made his début as a director in 1962. Critical acclaim came in 1964 with *Before the Revolution* and later with *The Spider's Stratagem* (1970), but it was with the box-office success of the sexually explicit *Last Tango in Paris* (1972) that he first gained a wide audience. His film *The Last Emperor* (1988), which dealt with the fall of the imperial dynasty in China, won nine Oscars.

Berwick, Treaty of Three treaties were named after Berwick-upon-Tweed, a town in Northumberland, sited on the border between England and Scotland. The first (3 October 1357) arranged for the release from captivity of David II of Scotland in return for a large ransom to be paid to Edward III of England, but this debt was never fully discharged. The second (27 February 1560) committed the English to send the Scottish Protestants military aid to help overthrow the Roman Catholic regent Mary of Guise. The third (18 June 1639) ended the first BISHOPS' WAR between Charles I and Scottish Covenanters, although it did not fully resolve the conflict and was regarded as unsatisfactory by both parties.

Berwickshire A former county of Scotland and from 1975 to 1996 a district in the Borders Region. In 1966 this district was abolished, when it became part of the new unitary authority Scottish Borders.

beryl A silicate of beryllium and aluminium that occurs in igneous rocks in the form of massive hexagonal crystals which are very hard but fracture readily. Its main use is as the source of beryllium, although two of its coloured forms, EMERALD and AQUAMARINE, are valued as gemstones.

beryllium (symbol Be, at. no. 4, r.a.m. 9.01) A grey, light metallic element in Group 2 (formerly IIA) of the PERIODIC TABLE. The element is usually obtained by ELECTROLYSIS of a fused mixture of beryllium fluoride and sodium fluoride. It reacts with acids and alkalis, showing valency 2 in its compounds, but is resistant to OXIDATION because of the formation of a protective oxide layer. It is used in certain beryllium–copper alloys, which have a range of uses depending on their strength, corrosion resistance, and electrical and thermal conductivity. The pure metal transmits X-rays because of its low atomic number and is used for windows in X-ray tubes. Beryllium metal dust and beryllium compounds are highly toxic, causing lung diseases and dermatitis.

Berzelius, Jöns Jakob, Baron (1779–1848) Swedish analytical chemist. Berzelius studied about 2,000 compounds and by 1818 had determined the atomic weights of most of the then known elements. He discovered three new elements (cerium, selenium, and thorium), suggested the basic principles of modern chemical notation, and introduced the terms *isomerism*, *polymer*, *protein*, and *catalysis*.

Besançon (Roman **Besontium**) The capital of the department of Doubs in the Franche-Comté region of north-east France, on the River Doubs; pop. (1990) 119,190. The world's first factory producing artificial fibres was established here in 1890. It has textile and watch-making industries, and a world-famous 'watch school'.

Besant, Annie (1847–1933) British social reformer and theosophist. She became a Fabian, a trade-union organizer (including the match girls' strike of 1888), and a propagandist for birth control. She became a leading exponent of the religious movement of theosophy, and founded the Hindu University in India, helping to form, in 1916, the All India Home Rule League. She was President of the Indian National CONGRESS 1918–19, one of only three Britons to have held this office.

Bessarabia A region in eastern Europe between the Dniester and Prut rivers. It chose to become part of Romania in 1918 but was forced to cede to the Soviet Union in 1940. Most of it now forms part of the Republic of Moldova (Moldavia); the remainder is in the Ukraine.

Bessel, Friedrich Wilhelm (1784–1846) German astronomer and mathematician. Self-taught in navigation and astronomy, he rose to become director of the new observatory in Königsberg. He determined the positions of some 75,000 stars, and was the first to obtain accurate measurements of stellar distances using the parallax resulting from the Earth's changing position. Bessel worked intensively on the orbits of planets and binary stars, developing mathematical functions that are named after him. Following a study of the orbit of Uranus he predicted the existence of an eighth planet.

Bessemer, Sir Henry (1813–98) British engineer and inventor. Bessemer is best known for the steel-making process that bears his name. At the time of the Crimean War in the 1850s, his proposals for the redesign of guns received little encouragement in Britain but a great deal from Napoleon III. The material available for gun construction was inadequate, however, so Bessemer then worked on a series of experiments and patents in the search for stronger material.

Best, Charles Herbert (1899–1978) US-born Canadian physiologist. His employer, Professor J. J. R. Macleod, placed him with F. G. Banting to assist in his research on pancreatic extracts. The research team announced the discovery of insulin in 1922. Unlike the others, Best was not awarded a Nobel Prize in 1923, but Banting shared half the prize money with him. He succeeded Banting as director of the Banting and Best Department of Medical Research at the University of Toronto in 1941, a post which he retained until 1967.

Best, George (1946–) Northern Irish footballer. He joined Manchester United after leaving school and later played for Northern Ireland. He was the leading scorer in the First Division in the 1967–68 season; he won a European Cup winners' medal and was named European Footballer of the Year in 1968. Unable to overcome a succession of personal problems in the late 1960s, his career came to a premature end.

beta-blocker A drug that acts on the sympathetic nervous system (a subdivision of the autonomic nervous system that controls the body's involuntary muscles). Beta-blockers block sympathetic (beta) receptors, which accelerate the heartbeat and dilate the bronchi in the lungs. Thus, blockers acting specifically on receptors in the heart slow its rate, and may be used in CARDIOLOGY to treat disordered cardiac rhythm. They also reduce the force of cardiac contraction and are therefore sometimes used to treat high blood pressure. Since their actions reduce the amount of work required of the heart, beta-blockers are also used to treat angina.

Beta Centauri A first-magnitude BINARY STAR in the constellation of Centaurus, and also known as Agena or Hadar. It comprises a hot bright giant star with about 5,000 times the luminosity of the Sun, with a fourth-magnitude companion, in an orbit of very long period. The distance of Beta Centauri is 100 parsecs.

Beta Lyrae stars A class of ECLIPSING BINARY in which, unlike ALGOL, the magnitude varies continuously even when eclipses are not taking place. Usually the component of greater surface brightness, the primary, fills its Roche lobe and is not spherical, so that the visible surface area changes as the system revolves. Beta Lyrae itself varies between magnitudes 3.3 and 4.4 in a period of 12.94 days; its changes were discovered by GOODRICKE in 1784. Matter is rapidly being transferred from the bright component to the smaller but more massive faint one via an ACCRETION DISC, and the period is slowly increasing.

beta particle The negatively charged electron emitted from some atomic nuclei during radioactive decay. Rays of beta particles are called beta radiation, and are ionizing radiation. Beta particles have a greater penetrating power than ALPHA PARTICLES.

betatron See PARTICLE ACCELERATOR.

Betelgeuse A first-magnitude red SUPERGIANT semi-regular VARIABLE STAR in the constellation of Orion, and also known as Alpha Orionis. Its magnitude changes between 0.0 and 1.3 in a varying period of about six years, with shorter changes of between seven and thirteen months. The variations were discovered by John HERSCHEL in 1836. If it is a member of the Orion stellar association at a distance of 400 parsecs, its mean luminosity is some 60,000 times that of the Sun.

Bethal (Hebrew, 'house of God') A town north of Jerusalem, of importance in biblical times. The site where Abraham first pitched his tent and built an altar, and where Jacob experienced the revelation from God, it became for a time the chief sanctuary of the Israelite tribes.

Bethany A village near Jerusalem on the eastern slopes of the Mount of Olives. It was the home of three close friends of Jesus, Martha, Mary, and Lazarus, and also of Simon the Leper. It was near Bethany that Jesus' ascension into heaven traditionally took place.

Bethe cycle See CARBON-NITROGEN CYCLE.

Bethesda (Hebrew, 'house of mercy') The site of a pool, outside one of the gates of Jerusalem, where the sick came to be healed in biblical times. It was traditionally here that Jesus cured a man who had been waiting for thirty-eight years.

Bethlehem (Arabic **Bayt Lahm**) A small town 8 km (5 miles) south of Jerusalem in the Israeli-occupied West Bank of the Jordan, first mentioned in Egyptian records of the 14th century BC; pop. (est. 1980) 14,000. The native city of King David and reputed birthplace of Jesus Christ, it contains a church built by Constantine in 330 over the supposed site of Christ's birth.

Bethune, Henry Norman (1890–1939) Canadian surgeon. He invented or improved a number of surgical instruments, but became disillusioned with medicine in Canada following his experiences of the surgical treatment of tuberculosis in his country. Bethune joined the Communist Party in 1935 and served in the Spanish Civil War against the Fascists, organizing the first mobile blood-transfusion service. Finally, he joined the Chinese army in their war against Japan as a surgeon, becoming a hero in the People's Republic; he died from septicaemia while in China.

Betjeman, Sir John (1906–84) British poet. His poems, as seen in collections such as *New Bats in Old Belfries* (1945), are self-deprecating, witty, and gently satirical; using traditional verse forms, they capture the spirit of his age. He also published a verse autobiography, *Summoned by Bells*, in 1960. His collection of architectural essays *Ghastly Good Taste* (1933) reflects his interest in the preservation of Victorian and Edwardian buildings. He was appointed Poet Laureate in 1972.

Betti, Ugo (1892–1953) Italian dramatist, poet, and short-story writer. He practised as a judge in Rome (1930–43); his writing did not gain wide recognition until just before his death, when *Crime on Goat Island* (1950) was produced in Paris.

Beuys, Joseph (1921–86) German artist. He is regarded as one of the most influential figures of avant-garde art in Europe in the 1970s and 1980s. His work consisted of 'assemblages' of various articles of rubbish, and he also directed a number of 'happenings'. In 1979 he co-founded the German Green Party.

Bevan, Aneurin (known as 'Nye') (1897–1960) British Labour politician. A brilliant though often abrasive orator, he was MP for Ebbw Vale 1929–60. His most notable contribution was the creation of the National Health Service (1948) during his time as Minister of Health 1945–51. He resigned from the government in protest against the introduction of health-service charges. The leader of the left wing of the Labour Party, he was defeated by Hugh Gaitskell in the contest for the party leadership in 1955.

Bevan, Edward John See CROSS, CHARLES FREDERICK.

Beveridge, William Henry, 1st Baron (1879–1963) British economist and social reformer, born in India. His most notable achievement was as chairman of the committee that prepared the Beveridge Report (Social Insurance and Allied Services, 1942); this recommended the establishment of a comprehensive scheme of social insurance and formed the basis of much subsequent social legislation establishing the welfare state in the UK.

Beverly Hills An affluent and largely residential city in southern California, surrounded by the city of Los Angeles; pop. (1990) 31,970. It gained city status in 1913 after which it became famous as the home of Hollywood film stars.

Bevin, Ernest (1881–1951) British Labour statesman and trade unionist. He was one of the founders of the Transport and General Workers' Union, serving as its first General Secretary (1921–40), and was a leading organizer of the General Strike (1926). He later entered Parliament, serving as Minister of Labour in Churchill's war Cabinet. As Foreign Secretary (1945–51), he helped form the Organization for European Economic Co-operation (1948) and NATO (1949). Unable to find a solution to the problem of Palestine, he surrendered the British mandate to the United Nations in 1947.

Bewick, Thomas (1753–1828) British artist and wood engraver. His best works are the shrewdly observed and expressive animal studies, which illustrate such books as his *A History of British Birds* (1797, 1804).

Bewick's swan A European swan, *Cygnus colum-*

bianus bewickii, resembling the whooper swan, but smaller and shorter in the neck and less vocal. It breeds in Siberia, wintering in central Asia and Europe, and takes its name from Thomas BEWICK. Their New World cousins are the WHISTLING SWANS, *C. c. columbianus*.

Bhagavadgita (Sanskrit, 'Song of the Lord') A Hindu philosophical poem inserted into the sixth book of the MAHABHARATA. The poem, which is the most famous religious text of HINDUISM, consists of 700 Sanskrit verses divided into 18 chapters. It was probably written in the 1st or 2nd century AD. The Pandava prince Arjuna, revolted by the prospect of killing his kinsmen in battle, seeks guidance from Krishna, disguised as his charioteer. Krishna urges Arjuna to fulfil his caste duties as a warrior selflessly and, revealing his divinity, preaches absolute devotion (*bhakti*) to the all-loving Supreme Being incarnated from age to age to save mankind. This is the first clear presentation of this doctrine in Hindu texts, and represents a move away from the priestly sacrificial cult of the VEDAS to a devotional Hinduism open to all.

Bhakti literature Medieval Indian writing inspired by devotion (*bhakti*) to the Hindu god Vishnu, a way of salvation first propounded in the BHAGAVADGITA. Bhakti literature began in southern India with the mystical Tamil hymns of the Alvār saint-poets (7th–10th centuries AD), but by 1500 had permeated all the Indian vernacular literatures. Poets like Kabīr (1430–1518) and the Sikh Guru Nanak (1469–1539) preached devotion to a universal God neither Hindu nor Muslim. Most Bhakti literature, however, concerned Vishnu's incarnations as Rama and Krishna. The greatest Rama devotee-poet was Tulsi Das (1532–1627), writing in Hindi. Krishna devotion was more widespread in northern and eastern India, from the Bengali poet Chandidas (15th century) to the Hindi poetess Mīrābāī (1498–*c*.1573), who expressed intense longing for God. In western India the most important Bhakti poets were the Marathis Nāmdev (*c*.15th century) and Tukaram (1608–49), and the Gujarati Narsimha Mehta (*c*.1500–80).

Bharat The Hindi name for INDIA.

Bharata-nāṭyam Important solo dance tradition from south India, especially amongst Tamils, performed by women. The programme consists of seven items, proceeding from the simple *alārippu*, an invocation to the deity and audience, through complex virtuoso dances, to the concluding *śloka*, a recitation of a short Sanskrit verse. Accompaniment is provided by a singer, a drum, a wind instrument, and a dance-master: the latter recites rhythmic compositions. This style was formerly performed by temple dancers: women who were dedicated to the service of the deity. It is said to follow the precepts of the earliest Indian treatise on music and dance, the *Nāṭyaśāstra* (early centuries AD), attributed to Bharata, after whom the style is named.

Bhava-chakra (Sanskrit, 'wheel of life') An iconographical representation of the cycle of existence in Tibetan Buddhism. The Bhava-chakra is depicted as a wheel, held by the god of the underworld, Yama, and divided into six segments representing the main types of worldly existences depicting the realms of the gods, demons, human beings, animals, rapacious ghosts, and hell. The centre of the wheel contains the animals representing the causes of the cycle: the cockerel (desire), the pig (ignorance), and the serpent (aggression or hate). Forming the outer rim of the wheel are the twelve nidānas or interrelated phases in the cycle of existence: a blind woman (ignorance), a potter (power of formation), a monkey (consciousness), two men in a boat (name and form, or mind and body), a six-windowed house (the six senses), a couple embracing (contact), an arrow piercing an eye (sensation), a person drinking (craving), a man gathering fruit (grasping, attachment), copulation (becoming), a woman in labour (birth), and a man carrying a corpse (death).

Bhave, Vinoba (1895–1982) Indian leader. A follower of GANDHI from 1916, he was active in attempts to re-vitalize Indian village life. Imprisoned by the British (1940–44) for defying wartime regulations, Bhave was, after Gandhi's assassination (1948), widely regarded as the leading exponent of Gandhism. He founded (1948) the Sarvodaya Samaj to work among refugees. In 1951 he began the BHOODAN or land-gift movement, and led the Shanti Sena movement for peace and economic and social reform.

Bhoodan A movement in India begun in 1951 by Vinoba BHAVE with the object of acquiring land for redistribution to landless villagers. At first the object was to acquire individual plots, but from the late 1950s an attempt was made to transfer ownership of entire villages to village councils. The movement had a measure of success in Bihar state.

Bhopal An industrial city in central India, the capital of the state of Madhya Pradesh; pop. (1991) 1,064,000. The city is said to have derived its name from its 11th-century founder Raja Bhoj who created lakes by building dams or *pals*. It has heavy electrical equipment industries. In December 1984 leakage of poisonous gas from a US-owned pesticide factory caused the death of about 2,500 people and thousands suffered injury in the world's worst industrial disaster.

Bhubaneswar The capital of the state of Orissa in east India, south of the Mahanadi River; pop. (1991) 412,000. It is noted for its Hindu temples of which it is said there were once 7,000. Of the 500 temples that remain, the great Lingaraj Temple dedicated to Bhubaneswar ('Lord of the Three Worlds') is one of the finest in India. Nearby are the ancient Udayagiri and Khandagiri Buddhist and Jain caves. It has an agricultural and technological university.

Bhutan, Kingdom of A small country in south Asia, lying in the Himalayas between China in the north and India in the south.

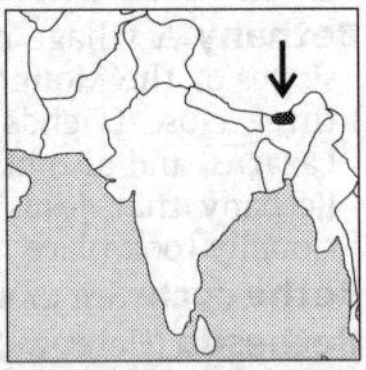

Physical. Northern Bhutan is entirely mountainous with spectacular peaks rising to 7,300 m (nearly 24,000 feet). Deep valleys with fast-flowing rivers lead to warmer and lower land in the south, which is forested and offers soil for cultivation.

Economy. Tourism is significant in a largely agricultural economy with some light industry. Only about 9 per cent of Bhutan's territory is cultivated; the chief crops are rice, maize, and fruit. Principal exports are electricity and wood products. Limestone and gypsum are present in large quantities. India, the major export destination, provides an annual subsidy.

History. Bhutan existed as a political unit by the end of the 17th century. The country is referred to in earlier monastic texts, but its early history is not clear. The first rulers of Bhutan were religious and political leaders, but the functions were later divided between a spiritual leader, the Dharma Raja, and an administrator, the Deb Raja.

The Deb Raja was in theory elected by the regional governors, but in practice the strongest governor claimed the position. During the 19th century there were frequent wars between rival governors. The Dharma Raja was succeeded by a person traditionally regarded as a reincarnation of him. The office ceased to exist in the early 20th century when no reincarnation of the last Dharma Raja could be agreed. In 1907 a powerful regional governor was elected as the first hereditary maharaja, or king, who is called the Druk Gyalpo. His great-grandson Jigme Singye Wangchuk became king in 1972.

In 1774 Bhutan and the EAST INDIA COMPANY signed a treaty of cooperation. This was replaced in 1865 by a treaty with Britain, which allowed Britain to supervise Bhutan's external affairs. This role was transferred to British India in 1910, and to the newly independent Indian government in 1949. During the 1950s and 1960s the king liberalized Bhutanese customs, abolishing slavery and the caste system and improving the status of women. He established a National Assembly in 1953. In 1969 a more democratic constitution was adopted, but political parties remain illegal. The country has received large numbers of Tibetan refugees and Nepalese immigrants. In 1990 ethnic conflict broke out in southern Bhutan, with many Nepalese demanding greater recognition and protesting against government measures aimed at preserving Bhutanese culture and language.

Capital: Thimphu
Area: 47,000 sq km (18,150 sq mi)
Population: 600,000 (est 1994)
Currency: 1 ngultrum = 100 chetrum (Indian rupee also legal tender)
Religions: Buddhist 69.6%; Hindu 24.6%; Muslim 5.0%
Ethnic Groups: Bhutia 62.5%; Gerung 15.5%; Assamese 13.2%
Languages: Dzongkha (a Tibetan dialect) (official); Gurung; Assamese
International Organizations: UN; Colombo Plan; Non-Aligned Movement

Bhutto, Benazir (1953–) Pakistani stateswoman, Prime Minister 1988–90 and 1993–96. The daughter of Zulfikar Ali BHUTTO and an opponent of the existing regime, she became joint leader in exile of the Pakistan People's Party (1984), returning to Pakistan in 1986 to campaign for open democratic elections. Following President Zia ul-Haq's death she became the first woman Prime Minister of a Muslim country. She took her country back into the Commonwealth and promised radical social reform, but failed to win widespread support from other parties. She was dismissed as Prime Minister and defeated in the ensuing election, re-elected as head of a coalition government in 1993, and dismissed again in 1996. In 1997 she was defeated in the elections.

Bhutto, Zulfikar Ali (1928–79) Pakistani statesman, President 1971–73 and Prime Minister 1973–77. As Pakistan's Foreign Minister (1963–66) he instigated a rapprochement with China and became known as an outspoken defender of his country's interests. He formed the Pakistan People's Party in 1967, coming to power as Pakistan's first civilian President in 1971 and later (after constitutional changes) serving as Prime Minister. While in office, he did much to strengthen national morale and introduced social, constitutional, and economic reforms. He was ousted by a military coup and executed for conspiring to murder a political rival.

Biafra A state proclaimed in 1967 when part of eastern Nigeria, inhabited chiefly by the Ibo people, sought independence from the rest of the country. In the ensuing civil war the new state's troops were overwhelmed by numerically superior forces, and by 1970 it had ceased to exist.

Biafra, Bight of An eastern bay of the Gulf of Guinea extending from the mouth of the River Niger to Gabon.

Bialik, Chaim Nahman (1873–1934) Hebrew poet. He was born in Volhyina, a region historically joined to Lithuania, Poland, and finally Russia. Regarded as the poet of the Jewish national renaissance, Bialik castigated his people for their helplessness in the face of persecution ('In the City of Slaughter', 1904). He was a noted essayist and storyteller, and translated major works from European languages.

Biarritz A seaside resort and fishing port in Pyrénées-Atlantiques department, south-west France, on the Bay of Biscay; pop. (1990) 28,890. It became a fashionable resort in the 1850s after Napoleon III's wife Eugénie built a villa there.

Bible The sacred book of Christianity. All Christian Churches accept two sections of the Bible: the Hebrew scriptures, known as the Old Testament, and specifically Christian writings, known as the New Testament. In addition, some Churches, including the Roman Catholic Church, accept a third section called the Apocrypha, found in the Greek version of the Old Testament (Septuagint). Each section consists of a number of separate books, written at different times by different authors. However, most Christians consider them to be endowed with unique divine authority.

The Old Testament contains 39 books. The first five books ('the Law', the TORAH, or Pentateuch) describe the origins of the Jewish people. 'The Prophets' give a history of the settlement in CANAAN, the period of the kingdom of ISRAEL, and prophetic commentaries. 'The Writings' consist of the remainder of the books including the Psalms, Job, and Daniel. The final content of the Hebrew Old Testament was probably agreed *c.*100 AD. The New Testament consists of 27 books. The four Gospels (meaning 'good news'), attributed to Matthew, Mark, Luke, and John, record the life, death, and resurrection of JESUS CHRIST. The Acts of the Apostles traces the development of the early Christian Church and the Epistles (or Letters), notably those of St PAUL, contain advice on worship, conduct, and organization for the first Christian communities. The Book of Revelation gives a prophetic description of the end of the world. Most of these books were acknowledged as canonical (accepted as sacred and genuine) by the middle of the 2nd century. The Apocrypha (Greek, 'hidden things') is the name given to a collection of 12 books written between 300 BC and 100 AD. They were included in the Septuagint, a Greek translation of the Old Testament of the 3rd and 2nd centuries BC that was used by the early Christian Church. These books do not appear in the Hebrew Old Testament and are not accepted by all Christian Churches. See also Appendix.

The Bible was originally written in Hebrew, Aramaic, and Greek. The first translation of the whole book was the Vulgate (405 AD) of St JEROME. The first translation into English was undertaken by John WYCLIF and his followers (1382–88). The development of PRINTING stimulated the production of vernacular editions. Martin LUTHER translated the New Testament into German in 1522 and William TYNDALE into English in 1525–26. William Coverdale's edition of the Bible, drawing heavily on Tyndale's work, was first published in 1535 and revised as the Great Bible in 1539. The Authorized or King James Version (1611), named after JAMES I who agreed to a new translation at the HAMPTON COURT CONFERENCE, was produced by about fifty scholars and remained for centuries the Bible of every English-speaking country. There are now translations of all or part of the Bible in over 1760 languages.

bicarbonate of soda See SODIUM HYDROGEN-CARBONATE.

biceps A muscle with two distinct points of origin, present in each arm and thigh of most vertebrates. In humans the biceps in the arm is attached at one end to the shoulder-bone, and at its lower end to the top of the radius bone of the forearm. The biceps both flexes the forearm and twists it to allow the back of the hand to face forwards.

Bichat, Marie François Xavier (1771–1802) French anatomist and physiologist, one of the pioneers of HISTOLOGY. Without using a microscope, he examined body tissues, dividing them into 21 different types. He proposed that tissues rather than organs were the elementary biological units for study.

bichir (or **polypterid**) A primitive fish of the genus *Polypterus*, which, with the reedfishes (*Erpetoichthys*), belongs to an unusual group of ray-finned BONY FISHES. Bichirs diverged from the vast majority of this group some 370 million years ago, and consequently, like the living COELACANTH, are often referred to as living fossils. They retain many of the features of the earliest bony fishes: thick, enamelled, bony scales, a paired lung-like swim bladder, and muscular lobes at the base of the paired fins at the front of the body. Like the LUNGFISHES, their young resemble tadpoles, and have external gills. The several species of *Polypterus* and *Erpetoichthys* are known to live in freshwater rivers, lakes and swamps of Africa, but little is known of their behaviour.

bicycle A human-powered vehicle comprising two WHEELS, one behind the other, connected by a frame. A precursor of the pedal-powered cycle was the hobby-horse, which was pushed along with the feet. The first pedal-operated bicycle was invented in 1839 by Kirkpatrick Macmillan, a British blacksmith, but he built only one or two of his foot-treadle-operated machines. In 1863 the brothers Pierre and Ernest Michaux invented the 'velocipede', essentially a hobby-horse with pedals attached directly to the front wheel. The Michaux concept was widely copied and improved, and the 'bone-shaker' cycle became a popular plaything for the rich. During the 1870s the bicycle's front wheel was gradually enlarged, enabling the cyclist to go further for each revolution of the pedals. This trend culminated around 1880 in the 'Ordinary' or 'Penny-farthing' cycle, invented by the British engineer James Starley, with a front-wheel diameter of up to 127 cm (50 inches). The first chain-driven cycle was designed by H. J. Lawson in 1879, but the first successful design was the Rover safety cycle. This was the forerunner of the modern bicycle, built in 1885 by John Starley, nephew of James. In 1889 pneumatic TYRES were introduced. By the beginning of the 20th century the bicycle had become a cheap form of personal transport for work and leisure. Since the 1960s there has been a resurgence of interest in bicycles because they are pollution-free and often faster than a car in urban traffic. Lightweight racing and touring models and more recently BMX (Bicycle Moto-Cross) and mountain bicycles (see TRANSPORT) have become popular for commuting, sport, and leisure.

Bidault, Georges (1899–1982) French statesman and journalist. After serving in World War I he became professor of history in Paris. During World War II he became a distinguished leader of the French RESISTANCE MOVEMENT. He was a founder-member and leader (1949) of the Mouvement Républicaine Populaire. Bidault was Foreign Minister in several administrations of the Fourth Republic (1944, 1947, 1953–54) and Prime Minister (1946, 1949–50, 1958). He subsequently became bitterly opposed to Algerian independence: he became President of the National Resistance Council in 1962, was charged with plotting against the state, and went into exile in Brazil. He returned to France in 1968.

Biela's Comet A COMET first seen by the French astronomer Jacques Montaigne in 1772 and then by Jean-Louis Pons in 1805 but whose orbit was calculated accurately only after it was rediscovered by the Austrian Wilhelm von Biela in 1826. The comet returned every 6.6 years and its orbit intersected the Earth's orbit. When the comet returned in 1846 it was found to have split in two. By 1852 the two components were separated by 2.4 million km and the comet has not been seen since.

biennial A plant, for example a foxglove, that takes two growing seasons to complete its life-cycle, from seed germination and growth in the first year to flowering and fruiting in the second.

Bierce, Ambrose (Gwinnett) (1842–*c*.1914) US writer. He served in the American Civil War (1861–65) and later became a prominent journalist in California, London, and Washington. He is best known for his realistic and sardonic short stories, strongly influenced by Edgar Allan Poe and including *Cobwebs from an Empty Skull* (1874) and *In the Midst of Life* (1898), and for the wickedly witty *The Devil's Dictionary* (1911). In 1913 he travelled to Mexico and mysteriously disappeared.

Biffen, Sir Rowland Henry (1874–1949) British botanist who made important contributions to the improvement of crop plants, notably cereals. Using the rudimentary principles of genetics discovered by Gregor MENDEL, he improved cultivated plants by hybridization. His first major success was to demonstrate that susceptibility to yellow rust in wheat results from a single, dominant factor. He was responsible for producing two important new wheat varieties.

bifocal lens See SPECTACLES.

Big Bang theory The most generally accepted theory in COSMOLOGY, which states that the Universe began in a primordial explosion about 15 billion years ago. The MICROWAVE background radiation found in 1965 by the US physicists Arno Penzias and Robert Wilson is a remnant of that earliest phase. Various versions of the Big Bang theory, such as the inflation theory, have been proposed recently to account for a number of observational features of the Universe. These include the distribution of matter, the types of celestial object, and the microwave background radiation at various distances. Physicists are now beginning to simulate, on a subatomic scale, the conditions that prevailed during the Big Bang. The STEADY STATE THEORY, once the principal alternative to the Big Bang theory, does not agree with current observational results.

Big Crunch In some cosmological models, the end of the Universe when the present expansion is reversed and the Universe contracts under its own gravitation. Oscillating Universe models suggest that the Big Crunch is followed by a new BIG BANG, producing another expanding Universe.

Big Dipper See PLOUGH.

bighorn sheep A wild SHEEP, found in the mountains of western North America, whose large horns often form more than one full turn. The record length of horns is 1.25 m (4.1 feet); the ewes have smaller horns, 37 cm (15 inches) long. The species *Ovis canadensis* is swift and agile, and there are few cliffs that it will not surmount, often at a gallop; its feet have pads to absorb the shock of its bouncing gait. The sexes live in separate herds except during the mating season. Another species, the snow sheep, *O. nivicola*, is sometimes known as the Siberian bighorn sheep.

Bihar A region in India comprising the middle Ganges plains and the Chota Nagpur plateau in north-eastern India. The region had its 'golden age' during the evolution of early Indian civilization. Among its ancient kingdoms was Magadha, where both Gautama BUDDHA and the Jain seer, Mahavira, preached. Its capital, Pataliputra (now Patna), was adopted by several notable empire builders, including the Mauryas and the GUPTAS. About 1200 it came under Muslim influence and remained subservient to the DELHI sultans until becoming a province of the MOGUL empire in the 16th century. In 1765 British victories resulted in its amalgamation with Bengal and the introduction of indigo plantations.

Bihar A state in north-east India, bounded north by Nepal, east by West Bengal, south by Orissa, and west by Uttar Pradesh and Madhya Pradesh. It has many coal-mines and steel plants. Wheat and rice are grown but food also has to be imported; area 173,877 sq km (57,160 sq miles); pop. (1991) 86,338,850; capital, Patna.

Bihari A group of three closely related languages, descended from Sanskrit, spoken principally in BIHAR. The three languages are Bhojpuri with 20 million speakers in western Bihar and eastern Uttar Pradesh, Maithili with 15 million speakers in northern Bihar and Nepal, and Magahi with 5 million speakers in central Bihar.

Bihzād, Kamāl al-Dīn (*c.*1455–1535/6) Persian painter. There is little firm information about his career and few certain works survive, but he is regarded as marking the highpoint of the great tradition of Islamic miniature painting. He worked mainly in Herat (famous for its miniaturists), but after the city was captured by the Safavids in 1510 he moved to Tabriz and perhaps Bukhara.

Bijapur A city and former state on the Deccan plateau, south-western India. It was the capital of a Muslim kingdom, founded by the Yadava dynasty in the 12th century. It fell under the control of the BAHMANI Muslims in the 14th century. Its era of independent splendour was from 1489 to 1686 when the Adil Shahi sultans made it their capital and were responsible for Islamic architecture of outstanding quality. In 1686 the Mogul emperor AURANGZEB defeated Bijapur, but was unable to exert firm control and the region soon fell under MARATHA sway, from which it passed into East India Company hands in the early 19th century.

Bikaner A walled city in the state of Rajasthan, north-west India, on the edge of the Thar Desert; pop. (1991) 415,000. Once capital of the Rajput state of Bikaner and an important trading post on the great caravan trade routes, it was merged with Rajasthan in 1949. The city is noted for its textile products and its camels which are bred locally.

Bikini Atoll An atoll in the MARSHALL ISLANDS, west central Pacific. It was the site for 23 US nuclear bomb tests (1946–58). Despite expectations that it would be fit again for human habitation in 1968, the atoll remains too contaminated for the return of the Bikinians, who have been relocated on surrounding islands. In 1985 the USA agreed to decontaminate the atoll, a process that would take 10–15 years.

Biko, Stephen (known as 'Steve') (1946–77) South African radical leader. While a medical student, he founded and became president of the South African Students Organization (1968). In 1972 he co-founded the Black People's Convention, a coalition of organizations which aimed to raise awareness of oppression in the black community and develop a sense of pride. He was banned from political activity in 1973 and his freedom of speech and association were severely restricted; detained several times in the last years of his life, he died in police custody, becoming a symbol of resistance to apartheid in black townships and beyond.

Bilbao A seaport and capital of the Basque Province of Vizcaya in northern Spain, on the Nervión estuary; pop. (1991) 372,200. It stands at the centre of a large industrial and coal-mining area. Greater Bilbao includes all the towns between Basauri and Galdakao. For centuries a wool port for Castile, Bilbao is now Spain's largest port as well as a major centre for oil-refining and shipbuilding.

bilberry (or **whortleberry**) A low shrub, *Vaccinium myrtillus*, within the heather family; the genus also includes the cranberry and the blueberry. The bilberry grows on heaths and moors of Europe and northern Asia and is known for its round, juicy, bluish-black fruits. The raw fruit is too acid to be palatable.

Bildungsroman A novel that follows the development of the hero or heroine from childhood or adolescence into adulthood, through a troubled quest for identity. The term ('formation-novel') comes from Germany, where Goethe's *Wilhelm Meister's Apprenticeship* (1795–96) set the pattern for later *Bildungsromane*.

bile An alkaline fluid containing yellow pigments derived from the breakdown of HAEMOGLOBIN. It also contains salts, acids, and CHOLESTEROL, and is produced continuously by liver cells in most vertebrates. During digestion of food, the bile flows directly into the small intestine; at other times it accumulates in the gall bladder. The stored bile is expelled from the gall bladder by a hormone released when food enters the intestine from the stomach. The bile salts aid the digestion and absorption of fat.

bilharzia (or **schistosomiasis**) A tropical disease caused by blood flukes of the genus *Schistosoma* whose free-swimming larvae (cercariae) penetrate the skin and migrate through the veins to the liver. Cercariae are released into fresh water by snails. In the liver, adult worms mature, and eventually male and female worms migrate along the liver veins to the intestines until the veins become smaller and their progression is halted. They remain lodged and produce large numbers of eggs, which must leave the body to facilitate the infection of snails and for the life-cycle to be continued in fresh water. Eggs penetrate the intestine to leave with the faeces, or the bladder wall to leave with the urine. Tissue damage gives rise to symptoms of bilharzia.

bill Draft or proposed legislation put before a legislative body. Bills may be introduced by a minister, by an ordinary member of the LEGISLATURE, or in some countries by public petition. Passage of a bill normally involves an opportunity for interested opinion to be represented, and for the measure to be discussed, possibly amended, or even rejected in the course of general debate, detailed consideration by committee, and legislative voting. In the UK, bills are often preceded by documents outlining the government's intentions on an issue. Green Papers (so-called because they have green covers) are consultative documents intended to elicit public debate, while White Papers set out the government's proposals, as a preliminary to the drawing up of the bill itself. If approved by the legislature, a bill becomes an act of parliament.

billiards A family of table-games played with various numbers of balls and a cue. English billiards is played with three balls – plain white, spot-white, and red – and six pockets. Players score by pocketing a ball other than their cue-ball, by their cue-ball going in a pocket off another ball, and by cannons, that is, striking the other two balls with the cue-ball. See also SNOOKER.

Billingsgate A fish market originally near London Bridge, London, England, on the site of a Roman river-wall. Dating from the 16th century it has long been known for the invective traditionally ascribed to its fish-porters. In 1982 the market moved to the Isle of Dogs.

bill of exchange A form of CREDIT used mainly in international trade. It is a promise to pay a certain sum on a specified future date by the drawer of the bill to the holder of the bill. If a bill is 'accepted' or guaranteed (usually by an acceptance house), it can be traded in the money markets. If it is accepted by a bank it is known as a bank bill; if by a trader, as a trade bill. In the USA bills are known as 'notes'.

bill of lading A document used in international trade giving details of the contents of a shipment, the ship carrying the goods, the sender (or consignor), and expected recipient (or consignee). Copies are held by the consignor, by the ship's captain, and by the consignee, who must present the document before being given the goods. A similar document in air transport is an air waybill.

bill of rights A constitutional or legal provision guaranteeing to citizens of a particular state fundamental CIVIL RIGHTS such as free speech, freedom of assembly and worship, and freedom from arbitrary arrest. It is usually part of a constitutional revolution or resettlement. The United States Bill of Rights (1791) consists of the first ten amendments to the US Constitution. The idea of making the bill of rights part of the constitution has been widely followed elsewhere: many Caribbean and African states, Canada, France, Germany, and India, for example, now have constitutional bills of rights under various names. Some of these countries allow JUDICIAL REVIEW of legislation for inconsistency with the bill of rights. The UK, Australia, and New Zealand as yet have no constitutional bill of rights.

Billy the Kid (born William H. Bonney) (1859–81) US outlaw. He arrived in New Mexico in 1868. A frequenter of saloons, he moved effortlessly into robbery and murder. In 1878 he became prominent in a cattle war, killing the local sheriff, Jim Brady. The territorial governor, Lew Wallace, was unable to persuade Billy to cease his activities. Sheriff Pat Garrett captured him in 1880, but he escaped, only to be shot by Garrett at Fort Sumner, New Mexico.

Bilqis See SHEBA, QUEEN OF.

bimetallic strip A strip formed of two different metals welded together. By using metals of very different coefficients of thermal expansion, such as steel and brass, the strip will curve when heated. A bimetallic strip in the form of a spiral can be used as a thermometer: a pointer is fixed to the centre of the spiral, and moves across a calibrated scale in response to movements of the strip. Some THERMOSTATS also employ bimetallic strips. A further use of bimetallic strips is for the protection of electric motors from thermal overload. In this context the circuit-breaker may be a bimetallic domed disc, which suddenly changes shape from concave to convex when a critical temperature is reached.

binary (in arithmetic) A way of representing numbers using only two different digits, 0 and 1. In ordinary decimal notation, a number such as 736 means 7 hundreds (10^2) + 3 tens (10^1) + 6 units. In a binary number powers of 2 are used; so, for example, 101 means 1×4 ($= 2^2$) $+ 0 \times 2 + 1 \times 1$, that is, 5. The first eight binary numbers in order are: 1, 10, 11, 100, 101, 110, 111, 1000. Binary code is especially suitable for use by digital computers because it uses just two numbers – 0 and 1 – represented in the computer as the absence or presence of an electrical signal (see MACHINE CODE) or stored as a magnetized or unmagnetized area on a magnetic disk. Values greater than 1 can be represented as a sequence of binary digits, known as BITS. Most computer systems use fixed-length 'words' which are multiples of 8 bits (a BYTE). Thus a small word-length of 8 bits can code for only 256 different numbers or characters: a 16-bit word can code for over 65,000 characters, and larger words can code for an extremely large number of characters. Frequently, slightly modified versions of basic binary code are used to allow the representation of negative numbers or decimal fractions.

binary form A simple two-part musical form consisting of two balancing sections of an AB structure. The first section generally modulates to a closely related KEY, while the balancing section makes the return journey.

binary pulsar A PULSAR that is one component of a BINARY STAR. The best known is PSR 1913+16 in the constellation of Aquila, discovered in 1974, whose pulse period is 0.059 seconds. It is in an elliptical orbit with an unseen companion thought to be a WHITE DWARF OR A NEUTRON STAR that emits no radio signals. The pulsar's orbital motion can be measured by the DOPPLER effect on the arrival time of its radio pulses. It completes an orbit every 7 hours 40 minutes. The strong gravitational field provides a sensitive test of the general theory of RELATIVITY, which predicts that the periastron should advance at almost exactly the observed rate of 4.2 degrees per year.

binary star A pair of stars in orbit about their common centre of gravity under their mutual gravitational attraction. Binary stars are sometimes called **double stars** and the individual stars in the system are called its **components**. Such pairs of stars, of which there are several types, are exceedingly common. A **visual binary** appears as a distinct pair of stars when viewed through a telescope with their separation and orientation changing slowly over the years. In an ECLIPSING BINARY each star regularly eclipses the other resulting in periodic variations in the total brightness. A **spectroscopic binary** contains members that are too close together to be seen as separate stars. As a star orbits its companion, it will periodically be moving towards and away from the Earth. By examining its spectrum, the DOPPLER effect can be used to measure the changes in its motion. A **polarization binary** displays periodic changes in the POLARIZATION of its light. In such binaries, as the stars orbit they illuminate gas and dust in the space between them, and the angle at which their light strikes this matter changes periodically. In this way the scattered light is polarized. Accurate measurement of these effects enables the orbits to be calculated, giving information about the relationship between the stars' masses, sizes, velocities, and separation. For example, if a star is both an eclipsing and spectroscopic binary, the masses of each star may be determined, together with the inclination of the orbit. Details of the way the light changes at the times of the eclipses give the relative sizes of the stars and allow the structure of their atmospheres to be studied. A binary star that emits X-RAYS is known as an X-ray binary.

In a number of cases a binary star reveals itself under extended observation to be a triple star with the third star in orbit about the centre of mass of the binary components, or it may be discovered that one of the components of the binary is itself a double star as in the case of ACRUX. Whereas the close binary components of the triple star may have a period of a few days, the more distant third component may orbit the centre of mass of the closer pair in a period of time measured in hundreds or even thousands of years.

bindweed The common name for the widely distributed, scrambling, climbing and non-climbing plants of the genera *Convolvulus* and *Calystegia*. They belong to the same family (Convolvulaceae) as morning glory and sweet potato. The common or field bindweed, *Convolvulus arvensis*, and its related species, are persistent and troublesome weeds of gardens. They spread by means of whitish rhizomes, of which the smallest portions will produce new plants. Some *Convolvulus* species, however, are grown as garden plants for their large trumpet-shaped flowers. The name bindweed is also used for a member of the rhubarb family known as black bindweed, *Fallopia convolvulus*.

Binet, Alfred (1857–1911) French psychologist and pioneer of modern intelligence testing. He was requested to devise a test that would detect intellectually slow schoolchildren, and together with the psychiatrist Théodore Simon (1873–1961) he produced tests (now known as the **Binet**, **Binet-Simon**, or **Stanford-Binet Scale**) intended to examine general reasoning capacities rather than perceptual-motor skills. Believing that bright and dull schoolchildren were simply advanced or retarded in their mental growth, Binet devised a mental age scale to describe performance in relation to the average performance of students of the same physical age.

binoculars A pair of refracting TELESCOPES, joined together for use with both eyes, giving stereoscopic viewing. Binoculars differ from simple telescopes in the inclusion of a pair of prisms between the objective and eyepiece LENSES in each telescope. These prisms invert and reverse the image from the objective lens so that the final image corresponds with the original object. They also increase the internal light path, increasing the magnification obtainable in a short tube, although some compact modern binoculars have a straight-through prism. Binoculars usually have a wider field of view than a telescope. Each eyepiece can be focused separately, or both can be moved together by a screw adjustment, to focus for different distances. Magnification and light-gathering power are given numerically – 6 × 30 denotes a magnification factor of six and an objective lens aperture 30 mm (1.17 inches) in diameter.

binomial expansion An algebraic expression giving the POWER of a sum of two elements in terms of powers of the individual elements. For example, $(x + y)^2 = x^2 + 2xy + y^2$. For any whole number n, $(x + y)^n = x^n + nx^{n-1}y + [n(n-1)/2!]\, x^{n-2}y^2 + \ldots + y^n$. (The term 2! means FACTORIAL 2.) The same form of expansion is valid for fractional or negative powers, but then the result is an infinite series rather than a finite number of terms and questions of convergence (see CONVERGENT SERIES) arise. If y/x is less than 1, the series converges and so the expansion can be used to obtain numerical approximations for such quantities as square roots and reciprocals.

binturong See CIVET.

biochemistry The study of the chemical processes taking place in living organisms. Individual cells contain thousands of different chemicals, and sophisticated techniques are needed for their identification and study. Such techniques show that the cells of all organisms contain four groups of very large molecules, or macromolecules. These are the two nucleic acids, DNA and RNA, PROTEINS, CARBOHYDRATES, and LIPIDS. Biochemistry has also shown that all organisms share the same basic molecules of life.

biodiversity The great variety and exceptional biological variety in living plants and animals throughout the world. The great centres of the Earth's biodiversity are the wetlands and especially the RAIN FORESTS. These areas are increasingly threatened by development, and conservationists from all over the world are eager to protect them and the organic life which inhabits them.

bioengineering The application of engineering techniques to biological processes. It describes the design, manufacture, and fitting of devices such as artificial limbs, heart valves and PACEMAKERS, or HEARING AIDS. Such devices, known as prostheses, are required to replace or aid body parts that have been removed or are defective. Bioengineering is also the design, manufacture, and use of medical monitoring or treatment devices, such as haemodialysis machines (used to remove toxic wastes from the blood), electrocardiographs, and heart–lung machines.

biofuel A source of energy based on biomass, the natural material of living organisms, including vegetable matter (from algae to trees), animal tissue, and manure. Biomass can be burned directly, or chemically or biologically processed into more convenient solid, liquid, or gaseous fuels. Forestry has provided wood as a biofuel over many centuries. Wood, other plant materials, and dried dung are still used in non-industrialized areas of the world for heating water and for cooking. Waste materials from agriculture and forestry can serve as biofuels for furnaces and boilers. Heating wood or other vegetable matter in the absence of air produces a gas with a high proportion of METHANE, together with an oily tar and a solid carbon or charcoal residue. All three products can be used as biofuels, although the tar requires further processing. Methane gas is also produced as a biofuel – biogas – by the bacterial fermentation of wastes with a high water content, such as human waste, animal manure, and crop residues. This process, which is used in China and India among other countries, also converts the wastes into nitrogen-rich fertilizer. Sewage works in the UK generate most of the heat and power they require by burning the methane gas produced from sewage FERMENTATION.

biogeochemical cycle The cyclical system in which chemical elements are transferred between biotic (living) and abiotic (non-living) parts of the biosphere (the global ECOSYSTEM). The major divisions of this process are the HYDROLOGICAL CYCLE, involving water, gaseous cycles, such as the OXYGEN, CARBON and NITROGEN CYCLES, and sedimentary cycles, which involve elements such as phosphorus. Modern environmental problems, such as the 'greenhouse effect' and EUTROPHICATION in marine and freshwater environments, are largely due to the overloading of these cycles.

biogeography The study of the geographical distribution of living things, which includes phytogeography (plants) and zoogeography (animals). Its first object was to collect information about plant and animal distribution, and to identify distinct patterns. Phytogeographers and zoogeographers have each divided the terrestrial world into major regions, generally continents or groups of continents considered to possess a characteristic flora or fauna. These two sets of regions do not have precisely the same boundaries.

The faunal system based on the divisions proposed by A. R. WALLACE and P. L. Sclater is probably the best known. In this system six faunal realms are recognized: Nearctic (most of North America); Neotropical (South and Central America); Palearctic (Europe and Asia north of the tropics, and parts of northern Africa); Ethiopian (Africa, except its northern fringe); Oriental (tropical Asia and its associated islands); and Australasian (Australasia, New Guinea, Oceania, and parts of south-east Asia). The Nearctic and Palearctic regions are sometimes combined to form the Holarctic. The divisions used by phytogeographers are more concerned with continental regions, although using the major division of the world into the New World (the Americas) and the Old World (mainly Europe, Asia, and Africa).

Geographical isolation can also influence evolution. The theory of island biogeography is an important concept in ECOLOGY, and postulates that the number of species in any isolated community is determined by the balance between the rate of arrival of new species, and the rate of extinction of existing ones.

Bioko An island of Equatorial Guinea, in the eastern part of the Gulf of Guinea; area 2,017 sq km (779 sq miles). Its chief town is Malabo (capital of Equatorial Guinea) and its main products are coffee, cocoa, and copra. It was known as Fernando Póo until 1973 and Macias Nguema Bijogo 1973–79.

biological pest control The use of living organisms to control agricultural or other pests. In Indonesia, for example, measures designed to encourage the natural predators of the brown planthopper, a notorious rice pest, improved rice yields and greatly reduced PESTICIDE use within three years. Another strategy is to introduce an organism from another country (an exotic species). In Australia in the 1920s, the Argentinian moth *Cactoblastis cactorum* was used to control the widespread growth of the prickly pear, a cactus of the genus *Opuntia*. Parasitic flies and wasps have proved useful in biological control, and one such wasp, *Encarsia formosa*, has been introduced to control the glasshouse whitefly, which became a pest in British greenhouses. This type of control can be highly species-specific and has few adverse environmental effects. However, such methods do not always work: over 200 pest species have been tackled in this way, but half of the attempts have failed completely.

Modern methods of biological control include spraying with fatal doses of HORMONES; releasing large numbers of sterile males of the pest species in order to reduce the breeding rate of females; spraying with a biological pesticide, a living organism (usually a BACTERIUM or a FUNGUS) that is toxic to a particular pest species; and breeding disease-resistant varieties of crops. This last method can involve the introduction of foreign genes for disease resistance by genetic engineering techniques. Environmental manipulation, such as destroying habitats where pests such as mosquitoes breed, also reduces the pest impact.

biology The science of living things. It is divided into specialist fields according to the kinds of organism studied: botany for plants, entomology for insects, and so on. It is further split into levels of study, ranging from molecular biology, the subject matter of BIOCHEMISTRY, to whole communities of plants and animals, which form the subject-matter of ECOLOGY. Biology also includes the history and evolution of life on Earth.

bioluminescence See PHOSPHORESCENCE.

biomass The total weight of living organisms in any given area, or their equivalent in energy. In animal and plant ECOLOGY, biomass refers to the organisms' numbers times their unit weight, often called standing crop biomass, or peak standard crop biomass in seasonal habitats such as grassland. In environmental development, it can refer to the generation of products, such as alcohol, firewood, food or wastes (wastes produce biogas). See also BIOFUEL.

biome A major geographical area defined by the flora and fauna characteristic of it. Authorities vary in the number of biomes recognized, but most include tropical rain forest, tropical seasonal forest, temperate forest, boreal forest, temperate grassland, tropical grassland, chaparral, desert, mountains, tundra, oceans, and fresh water.

biophysics The application of the theories and techniques of physics to biology. It can refer to the study of natural phenomena, such as the electrical conduction of nerve impulses, which are related to topics studied in physics itself. It can also refer to the investigation of any aspect of biology using complicated physical techniques.

biopsy The removal of a small amount of a patient's tissue for diagnostic purposes. Sections of tissue are stained and examined under a microscope for abnormal cells, which may indicate the presence of disease. Biopsies are obtained through the skin, using hollow needles and syringes (as in renal or liver biopsy), in exploratory operations, by ENDOSCOPY, or by scraping off surface cells. Specialized techniques include the use of vacuum capsules to examine the intestinal lining.

biosensor A miniature device incorporating a biochemical substance and electronic circuitry, which can monitor biochemical reactions in the laboratory or substances in body fluids. Biosensors recognize specific molecules in solutions or mixtures and produce electrical signals which indicate their concentration. Results are obtained far more quickly using biosensors than by traditional chemical analysis. At present, applications of biosensors, mainly in BIOTECHNOLOGY and FOOD TECHNOLOGY, are still at the research or development stage.

biotechnology Technology in which biological processes are involved. This traditionally includes brewing, cheesemaking, and all other processes involving fermentation. In the 1940s the field of biotechnology was broadened to include sterile fermentation to produce ANTIBIOTICS from moulds. Since the development of GENETIC ENGI-

NEERING, biotechnology has been broadened again to include the manufacture of more complicated medical products, such as hormones, vaccines, and monoclonal antibodies.

biotite A common rock-forming mineral, a member of the MICA group. It is found as dark brown plate-like crystals or as grains in both igneous and metamorphic rocks. It has a complex chemical formula (potassium magnesium iron aluminium silicate).

Biot–Savart law The result of investigations by two 19th-century French scientists, Jean-Baptiste Biot and Félix Savart, into the magnetic field produced by an ELECTRIC CURRENT. Measuring the strength of the field at various distances from a long, straight, current-carrying wire, they found (1820) that the field strength was, first, in direct proportion to the current and, second, in inverse proportion to the distance from the wire.

biplane An AEROPLANE or GLIDER with two sets of wings, one above the other. The first powered flight was made by the WRIGHT brothers in a biplane, and during World War I the biplane configuration was generally adopted for most aircraft (although some triplane designs were successful). The performance advantages of the biplane arose from its greater lift and lower stalling speeds. In the 1930s increased engine power and better aircraft design led to higher airspeeds; maximizing lift became less important, and the reduced drag and lighter weight of the monoplane predominated. Biplanes still find applications in aerobatics and crop-spraying, where their greater manœuvrability and low flying speeds are advantageous.

birch A tree or shrub of the genus *Betula* (40 species), of the north temperate zone and Arctic region. Together with ALDERS (*Alnus*), HAZELS (*Corylus*), and hornbeams (*Carpinus*), they make up the birch family, Betulaceae. They reach the polar limits of flowering plants, and several species are important constituents of TAIGA and TUNDRA. In lower latitudes, birches are colonist trees, invading herbaceous or shrubby vegetation and growing rapidly. They are shortlived and after death are replaced by other species. The pale wood is used mainly for charcoal and plywood. An oil extracted from the trees is used in tanning Russian leather. The bark often peels off in long, pale strips, and that of the paper birch, *B. papyrifera*, was used in the construction of canoes, tents, and huts by North American Indians.

bird A vertebrate of the class Aves, thought to be a descendant of small DINOSAURS. About 9,000 living species are known. The earliest known animals with bird-like features are those found in fossils from rocks as old as 225 million years. Fossils of the ARCHAEOPTERYX, from rocks about 150 million years old, show two obvious characteristics of birds: feathers, and the ability to fly. The power of flight has enabled birds to reach most parts of the world, and to migrate to and from breeding-grounds as the seasons change.

Birds range in weight from about 2 g (0.07 ounce) in the case of the vervain hummingbird, *Mellisuga minima*, to 90 kg (200 pounds) in the case of the ostrich. The largest birds are flightless, the upper limit to the weight of flying birds being about 15–20 kg (35–45 pounds). Many of the characteristics of birds reflect the great need to minimize weight in order to make flight as energetically economic as possible. These adaptations include loss of teeth, hollowed bones, and the fusing of many parts of the skeleton. The large breast muscles provide the source of the power needed to flap the wings. The main senses used by birds are vision and hearing, in contrast to many mammals, for whom vision may be much less important and sense of smell much more important. The largest order of birds – and the most advanced in evolutionary terms – comprises the **passerines**, or perching birds, of which there are about 5,000 species. Their feet are specialized for gripping branches by having the first toe directed backwards. This order includes the songbirds, in which the vocal organ (syrinx) is highly developed (see BIRD SONG).

Birds have been used widely by man, especially for the production of eggs and meat. They have also been popular as cage-birds on account of their beautiful songs; for sport, whether as prey or hunter (as in falconry); and, in the case of pigeons, for carrying messages. See illustration p. 168.

bird of paradise A bird of the family Paradisaeidae. This includes 45 species, most of which are found in New Guinea, although a few occur in eastern Australia and other nearby areas. Noted for their brilliant colours and ornamentation, the males display communally; the females come to the display grounds for mating, and look after the eggs and young by themselves. The feathers were once much valued for ladies' hats and are still used for local tribal headdresses.

bird of paradise flower A plant, *Strelitzia reginae*, related to the banana, and native to South Africa. It bears flowers with spikes of yellow and purple, each shaped like a bird's head, and is pollinated by the feet of nectar-seeking birds.

Birdseye, Clarence (1886–1956) US businessman and inventor. A former fur-trader, he had observed food preservation techniques practised by local people in Labrador; this led him to develop a process of rapid freezing of foods in small packages suitable for retail selling, creating a revolution in eating habits.

bird's nest fern A FERN, *Asplenium nidus*, native to the Old World tropics; it grows as an epiphyte with a rosette of fronds, each up to 1.4 m (4.6 feet) in length. The plant forms a nest-like structure which traps detritus, from which its roots obtain nourishment.

bird song The sounds produced by birds through a complex structure in the TRACHEA called the syrinx. Song is mainly used by male birds, particularly during the breeding season, and is thought to serve two main functions: to defend a territory against rival males by announcing the owner's presence; and to attract potential mates. Songs of each species tend to be characteristic, enabling the experienced ornithologist to identify a species without seeing it. Bird songs vary from quite simple vocalizations to very complex displays consisting of a large repertoire of different songs, as in the song thrush. Many species may sing most vociferously at dawn or dusk when it is too dark to gather food efficiently, or when it is most important for the male to be attentive. Some species mimic the calls of others in their song, and in a few species, the male and female may produce different parts of the same song (antiphonal singing, or duetting), their split-second synchronization making it almost impossible for a listener to realize that more than one bird is involved.

birdwing butterfly One of the largest and most beautiful butterflies, some of which are protected by law. Found in south-east Asia and Australasia, the 31 species in the genera *Triodes*, *Trogonoptera*, and *Ornithoptera* are known as birdwings on account of their size and brilliant colours. Those

Birds (1) Barn owl. (2) Baya weaver. (3) Calliope hummingbird. (4) Hoopoe. (5) Golden eagle. (6) Pied avocet. (7) Northern shoveller. (8) Emperor penguin and chick.

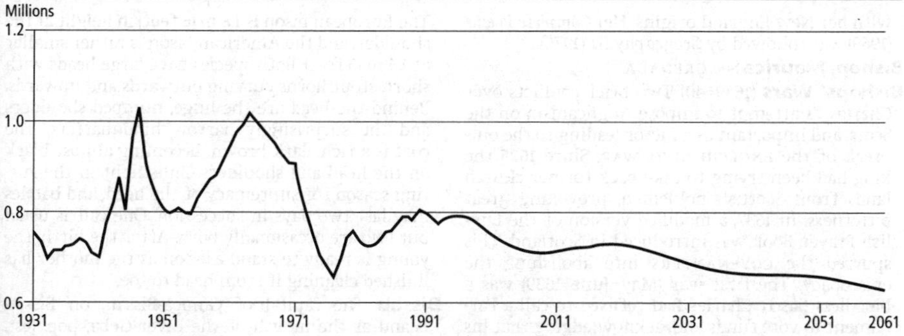

Birth rate The birth rate in the UK. The post-war baby boom of 1947 was followed by a similar peak in 1964. The figures for 1992–2061 are projections.

species such as the Rajah Brooke's birdwing, *Trogonoptera brookiana*, are strikingly patterned green and black. This probably advertises the toxicity of the adult, as its caterpillars feed on the poisonous Aristolochiaceae plants, like other members of the swallowtail family. The largest known butterfly is Queen Alexandra's birdwing, *Ornithoptera alexandrae*, of New Guinea, the female of which has a wing-span of up to 28 cm (11 inches).

Birgitta, St See BRIDGET, ST (of Sweden).

Birkeland, Kristian Olaf Bernhard (1867–1917) Norwegian physicist who, with fellow Norwegian Samuel Eyde, devised the first commercially successful process for the fixation of atmospheric NITROGEN. The process involved passing nitrogen and oxygen through an electric arc fanned out by electromagnets, and its economic viability depended on cheap electricity, available to Birkeland from hydroelectric installations. The process was used in Norway from 1905 until the early 1920s, but was later displaced by the more efficient HABER–BOSCH PROCESS.

Birkenhead A port and industrial town on the south bank of the River Mersey, England, on the Wirral peninsula, opposite Liverpool to which it is connected by the Queensway road tunnel (1934) and the Mersey rail tunnel (1886); pop. (1991) 116,000. Shipbuilding and engineering have been important to the development of Birkenhead.

Birkenhead, F(rederick) E(dwin) Smith, 1st Earl of (1872–1930) British politician and lawyer. He entered Parliament as a Conservative MP in 1906, becoming Attorney General (1915–19) and subsequently Lord Chancellor (1919–22), when he introduced several major land law reforms. His last government post was Secretary for India (1924–28).

Birla Indian commercial and industrial family of the Marwari or Hindu merchant caste. The best known member of the family was Ghanshyam Das Birla, who became GANDHI's principal financial backer, paying most of the cost of the *ashram* (retreat), the Harijan organizations, the peasant uplift campaign, and the national language movement, as well as supporting many other Gandhian welfare projects. It was at Birla House, New Delhi, that Gandhi was killed. The Birla family has continued to manage a successful business empire.

Birmingham A city in the West Midlands of central England; pop. (1991) 934,900. It is the second-largest city in Britain and a major centre of industries which include the manufacture of vehicles, chemicals, plastics, machine tools, aerospace components, and electrical equipment. For many years it was a noted centre for the manufacture of swords and later firearms. Birmingham is the site of the National Exhibition Centre and a cultural city with its own symphony orchestra. It is the home of the University of Birmingham (1900), Aston University (1966) and the University of Central England in Birmingham (formerly Birmingham Polytechnic) which was established in 1992.

Birr Castle The home of Lord Rosse in Ireland, where he built his giant 72-inch (1.8 m) REFLECTING TELESCOPE between 1842 and 1845. He mounted it between massive masonry walls. With it he was able to detect the spiral nature of a number of nebulae now known to be spiral galaxies. In 1844 he also named the famous nebula in Taurus the CRAB NEBULA because of its filamentary structure.

birth rate The ratio of births to a given population in a specified period. The most common measure, called the 'crude birth rate', is usually calculated as the annual number of births per thousand people. Between 1950 and 1955 and 1985 and 1990 crude birth rates fell from 20 to 13 in Europe, from 43 to 28 in Asia, from 42 to 29 in South America and from 49 to 45 in Africa. The UN expects the falls to continue in all continents and to accelerate in Africa. Despite falls in birth rates and FERTILITY RATES, world POPULATION growth is expected to be unavoidable, primarily because the numbers of women of child-bearing age will increase substantially.

Birtwistle, Sir Harrison (1934–) British composer. He was a member (1952–60) of the New Manchester Group, formed to study and perform advanced types of contemporary music. His music often has strong ritualistic aspects and is sometimes very violent. Such works as *The Triumph of Time* (1972) and the operas *The Mask of Orpheus* (1983) and *Gawain* (1991) have placed him in the forefront of British 20th-century music.

Biscay, Bay of (French **Golfe de Gascogne**; Spanish **Golfo de Vizcaya**) Part of the North Atlantic between the north coast of Spain and the west coast of France, noted for its strong currents and storms.

Bishkek The capital city of Kyrgyzstan in Central Asia; pop. (1990) 625,000. From 1926 to 1991 the city was named Frunze, after the Red Army general Mikhail Vasilyevich Frunze (1885–1925). Before 1926 it was known as Pishpek. It has metal, electrical, machinery, textile, and food industries.

Bishop, Elizabeth (1911–79) US poet. Bishop's first two collections, *North and South* (1946) and *A Cold Spring* (1955), received the Pulitzer Prize when published as a combined edition in 1955. She lived in Brazil from 1952 to 1967 and her formal, structured poetry contrasts her experiences in South America with her New England origins. Her *Complete Poems* (1969) was followed by *Geography III* (1976).

Bishop, Maurice See GRENADA.

Bishops' Wars (1639–40) Two brief conflicts over Charles I's attempt to impose Anglicanism on the Scots, and important as a factor leading to the outbreak of the ENGLISH CIVIL WAR. Since 1625 the king had been trying to take back former church lands from Scottish noblemen, provoking great bitterness. In 1637, a modified version of the English Prayer Book was introduced in Scotland. This spurred the COVENANTERS into abolishing the episcopacy. The first war (May–June 1639) was a bloodless fiasco. Charles had refused to call a Parliament to vote funds and, acknowledging that his new recruits were no match for the Covenanters, he made peace at Berwick. For the second war (August–September 1640), refused supplies by the English 'Short Parliament', he obtained money from the Irish Parliament, but his army was routed by the Covenanters at Newburn, near Newcastle upon Tyne. With the Scots occupying Northumberland and Durham, Charles was forced to make peace at Ripon, and to call the LONG PARLIAMENT.

Bismarck The capital of North Dakota, USA, on the Missouri River; pop. (1990) 49,256. It developed first as a steamboat port and then as a terminus of the Northern Pacific Railway, taking the name of the German Chancellor in order to attract German capital for railroad building. It is a trade and distribution centre for a large agricultural and oil-reserves region.

Bismarck, Otto (Eduard Leopold) von, Prince of Bismarck, Duke of Lauenburg (known as 'the Iron Chancellor') (1815–98) German statesman. As Minister-President and Foreign Minister of Prussia under Wilhelm I from 1862, Bismarck was the driving force behind the unification of Germany, orchestrating wars with Denmark (1864), Austria (1866), and France (1870–71) in order to achieve this end. As Chancellor of the new German Empire (1871–90), he continued to dominate the political scene, passing legislation intended to break the influence of the Catholic Church at home and consolidating Germany's position as a European power by creating a system of alliances. Bismarck was forced to resign in 1890 after a policy disagreement with Wilhelm II.

Bismarck Sea An arm of the Pacific Ocean north-east of New Guinea and north of New Britain. The Admiralty Islands and other islands of the Bismarck Archipelago were part of a German dependency that existed 1884–1919.

bismuth (symbol Bi, at. no. 83, r.a.m. 208.98) A lustrous, hard, brittle metallic element with a reddish tint in Group 15 (formerly VB) of the PERIODIC TABLE. It forms compounds in which it shows valencies 3 and 5, but is not very reactive. It is mixed with other low-melting metals to form fusible alloys, which are used in safety plugs in boilers and in automatic sprinkler systems. Bismuth alloys expand on solidification, and are used for intricate metal castings. The metal is a good absorber of gamma rays and is used as a gamma-ray filter.

bison Either of two species of large CATTLE. The American bison, *Bison bison*, once roamed the plains of North America; a larger subspecies, the wood bison, still does so in a remote region of Canada. The European bison, *B. bonasus*, once lived in the forests of Europe and Asia but is now restricted to captivity; wild populations became extinct in 1919. The European bison is 1.8 m (6 feet) in height at the shoulder, and the American bison is rather smaller at 1.5 m (5 feet). Both species have large heads with short, stout horns curving outwards and upwards. Behind the head are the huge, humped shoulders and the surprisingly narrow hindquarters. The coat is a rich, dark brown, becoming almost black on the head and shoulders. Bulls fight in the rutting season for supremacy of the herd, and battles may last two days in succession. One calf is usual but two are occasionally born. After the birth, the young is ready to stand as soon as the mother has finished cleaning it from head to toe.

Bissau The capital of Guinea-Bissau, on Bissau Island at the mouth of the River Geba; pop. (est. 1994) 125,000. It was established as a slave trading port in 1687 and developed as a free port after 1869. It is the country's main commercial centre and handles most of its trade. There is a massive Roman Catholic cathedral.

bistre A transparent brown pigment made by boiling the soot of burned wood. It was used, particularly in the 17th century, for pen-and-ink drawings or as a wash for water-colours. Rembrandt and Claude are among the artists who used it most successfully. The greenish tinge of bistre distinguishes it from the more reddish sepia.

bit (*bi*nary digi*t*) The smallest item of information that can be stored in a digital COMPUTER. A single bit exists in one of two states, labelled 0 or 1, and is usually represented in the computer as an electrical signal that is either absent or present. Groups of bits form a BINARY code to represent numerical and other data.

biting housefly See STABLE FLY.

biting louse (or **bird louse**) A small, wingless, flattened insect, the 2,800 species of which comprise the order Mallophaga. The majority are external parasites of birds, although some species occur on mammals. They feed on dead cells and, in heavy infestations, may damage feathers or hair. Some are active runners; others move slowly. As some species are confined to certain parts of the body, a given host may carry several species at any one time. The eggs are attached to the feathers or hairs and the young resemble the adults.

Bitola (or **Bitolj**; Turkish **Monastir**) The second-largest town in the Balkan republic of Macedonia; pop. (1981) 137,835. It processes local agricultural products and has many light industries including carpets and clothing.

bitonality The simultaneous use of two KEYS in musical performance (more than two constitutes polytonality). Brief examples of bitonality can be found in the music of Stravinsky, Holst, and many 20th-century composers. Milhaud and Ives, however, took the practice to greater and more consistent lengths.

Bitter Lakes Two lakes in north-east Egypt, situated in depressions to the north of Suez and traversed by the Suez Canal.

bittern A marsh bird belonging to the same family as the heron, the Ardeidae. There are 12 species in the two genera *Botaurus* and *Ixobrychus*, which are found throughout the world, and all of them frequent reed-beds. When disturbed, bitterns will thrust their head and neck upwards to face the danger, so that their elongated shape and streaky plumage merge in with the appearance of the reeds and they become difficult to see. The males' booming calls in the breeding season are audible up to 5 km (3 miles) away. These medium-sized birds construct a nest of vegetation in reed-beds and incubate between four and six eggs.

bitumen A thick, dark, flammable, water-resistant mineral substance composed of hydrocarbons. Bitumens range from viscous oils to waxy substances or brittle solids, depending on their hydrocarbon composition. An example is asphalt, which occurs in natural deposits such as the Athabasca Tar Sands of Canada and the Trinidad Pitch Lake. Sometimes, as at Rancho El Brea in California, USA, it contains the relics of animals of the Pleistocene Epoch (10,000 to 2,500,000 years ago), trapped in it. Bitumens can also be obtained as a by-product of PETROLEUM REFINING. Bitumen-impregnated felt is widely used for roof coverings and for DAMP-PROOF COURSES. Bituminous paint provides an inexpensive protection for ferrous products which may corrode. Bitumen is also used as an adhesive. When mixed with AGGREGATE it is used as a road surface. In ancient times it was used as a cement in building. See also COAL.

bivalve A MOLLUSC with a two-piece hinged shell, a member of the class Pelecypoda (formerly Bivalvia), which includes many familiar sea-shore animals. Clams, scallops, cockles, mussels, and oysters all belong to this group. Most of the 20,000 or so species are specialized as sedentary, often burrowing, filter-feeders. Within the valves (the two halves of the shell) are large flattened gills covered with tiny, beating cilia; these create water currents supplying oxygen, and carrying countless PLANKTON, which are filtered out and eaten. Burrowing bivalves have tubular siphons to carry water in and out. They leave tell-tale depressions on sandy beaches. Bivalves are among the commonest molluscs, often forming enormous beds in estuaries and shallow seas. They are renowned as edible-shellfish, for pearl manufacture, and sometimes as destructive burrowers into rock (piddocks) or into the wood of boats, or other man-made marine items (shipworms).

Biwa, Lake (Japanese **Biwako**) A lake in the Kinki region of central Honshu Island, Japan, 8 km (5 miles) north-east of Kyoto. With an area of 676 sq km (261 sq miles) it is the largest lake in Japan. Its only natural outlet is the River Seta.

Bizet, Georges (Alexandre César Léopold) (1838–75) French composer. He completed his first important opera, *Les Pêcheurs de perles*, in 1863, but his second, *La Jolie Fille de Perth* (1866), enjoyed a greater success. *Carmen*, the last and finest of his seven completed operas, failed when it was first produced in 1875, probably because its story was considered too improper by the audiences of the day. It was the first *opéra comique* (i.e. with a spoken dialogue) to portray an anti-heroine and to have a tragic ending.

Bjerknes, Vilhelm Friman Koren (1862–1951) Norwegian meteorologist and physicist, who pioneered the science of dynamical meteorology, applying mathematics to describe motions in the atmosphere. His best known work was on the origin and characteristics of DEPRESSIONS and on methods of weather forecasting. His son, **Jakob Aall Bonnevie Bjerknes** (1897–1975), was also a meteorologist. He discovered that depressions form, develop, and decay along the polar front.

Björling, Jussi (1911–60) Swedish tenor singer. After his Stockholm debut in 1930 as the Lamplighter in Puccini's *Manon Lescaut*, Björling's warm and appealing voice soon secured him the role of Ottavio in Mozart's *Don Giovanni*. Throughout Europe, and as a member of the New York Metropolitan company for almost twenty years, Björling sang the Italian, French, and Russian opera repertory with excellent taste.

Björnson, Björnstjerne (1832–1910) Norwegian playwright, novelist, and poet. His early prose work depicts Norwegian peasant life with unprecedented realism (*Synnøve Solbakken*, 1857; *The Fisher Girl*, 1868), and he achieved early and lasting success as a dramatist, overshadowing his contemporary Ibsen for much of his life. A poem of his became the National Anthem, and he won the Nobel Prize for Literature (1903).

Black, Sir James Whyte (1924–) British pharmacologist who designed new drugs to treat high blood pressure and weak hearts. Hormones such as adrenaline excite the muscles of the heart causing them to weaken. Black realized that by blocking the effect of the hormones he could protect the heart: drugs which act in this way are known as BETA-BLOCKERS. Sir James has also designed drugs to treat stomach ulcers by blocking gastric acid production. He received the Nobel Prize for physiology and medicine in 1988.

Black, Joseph (1728–99) Scottish chemist who studied the chemistry of gases and formulated the concepts of LATENT HEAT and HEAT CAPACITY. He developed accurate techniques for following chemical reactions by weighing reactants and products. In studying the chemistry of ALKALIS he isolated a gas which he termed 'fixed air' (now known to be CARBON DIOXIDE) and investigated its chemistry, including its characteristic reaction with LIME WATER.

Black-and-Tans An auxiliary force of the Royal Irish Constabulary. The demands of the Irish Republicans for a free IRELAND led in 1919 to violence by the Irish Republican Army against the Royal Irish Constabulary, an armed police force. Many of the policemen resigned, so the British government in 1920 reinforced the RIC with British ex-soldiers. Their distinctive temporary uniforms gave them their nickname of Black-and-Tans. They adopted a policy of harsh reprisals against republicans, many people being killed in raids and property destroyed. Public opinion in Britain and the USA was shocked and the Black-and-Tans were withdrawn after the Anglo-Irish truce in 1921.

black beetle See COCKROACH.

blackberry A shrub of the rose family that falls within the general species name of *Rubus fruticosus*, although blackberries are a highly variable and complex species-group, or aggregate. The varieties grown commercially, or in gardens, are derived from plants indigenous to Britain and other temperate countries. The fruit is really a cluster of small, black DRUPES, and is sweetly flavoured. Most individual kinds are prickly, climbing or sprawling plants that produce long, arching canes, capable of rooting and producing new plants where their tips reach the soil. Thornless plants have been developed in recent years, including the variety Oregon.

blackbird In the Old World, any of certain thrushes of the genus *Turdus*, especially *Turdus merula*, a common species that occurs throughout most of Europe and eastern Asia. About 25 cm (10 inches) long, the male is completely black with a bright yellow eye-ring and yellow beak, whereas the female and the young are brown. They build cup-shaped nests in bushes and lay three to five eggs, which are blue with brownish speckles. The parents may raise three broods in a season. Blackbirds feed primarily on earthworms and other invertebrates, and many of those breeding in the northern parts of the Northern Hemisphere migrate to milder areas for winter.

Certain New World orioles with dark plumage are called blackbirds.

black body (in physics) A hypothetical body that is able to absorb all the radiant energy falling on it. A black body is a perfect absorber of radiation and also a perfect emitter. The radiation emitted from such a body, known as **black-body radiation**, has a characteristic spectrum that depends only on the temperature of the body and not on other properties. In practice, a perfect black body cannot be constructed, but a good approximation is an enclosure at constant temperature with a small hole in the enclosure wall. The spectral distribution of black-body radiation can be calculated using quantum mechanics, and is called PLANCK's law. For a black body of a particular temperature, the emission peaks at a particular wavelength. This peak moves to shorter wavelengths for hotter temperatures, as given by Wien's displacement law. The total power emitted per unit surface area of a black body is given by STEFAN's law, and increases exceedingly rapidly with increasing temperature.

black box (in aviation) See FLIGHT RECORDER.

blackcap See WARBLER.

Black Churches Christian congregations of African-Americans found largely in the USA. They may be of any Protestant denomination, especially Baptist, Methodist, or Pentecostal. Originating among black slaves, Black Churches have a strong awareness of political and social injustice, and played an important part in the US Civil Rights Movement of the 1960s and 1970s. Black theology, like LIBERATION THEOLOGY, emphasizes the freedom of the oppressed and God's identification with the victims in society. Worship in Black Churches is often informal, with spontaneous singing, shouting, and dancing. Preaching is central, and the minister may also be active in community activities and politics.

blackcock See GROUSE.

blackcurrant A common garden and commercially-grown bushy shrub, *Ribes nigrum*, belonging to the family Grossulariaceae, along with redcurrants and gooseberries. The purplish-black fruit is used in jam and tarts and is rich in vitamin C. It is a European native, growing wild over a wide area, although many improved varieties have been produced, differing in fruit size, flavour, and season of ripening. Established plants can become infected by a virus spread by mites, causing big-bud disease.

Black Death (1347–50) The most virulent epidemic of bubonic and pneumonic plague ever recorded. It reached Europe from the TARTAR armies, fresh from campaigning in the Crimea, who besieged the port of Caffa (1347). Rats carrying infected fleas swarmed aboard trading vessels, thus transmitting the plague to southern Europe. By 1348 it reached France, Spain, and England; a year later Germany, Russia, and Scandinavia. Numbers of dead cannot be exact but up to 25,000,000 may have died in Europe; perhaps one-third of the population in England.

black earth See CHERNOZEM.

Blackett, Patrick Maynard Stuart, Baron (1897–1974) British physicist. During World War II he was involved in operational research in the U-boat war and was a member of the Maud Committee, which dealt with the development of the atom bomb. He modified the cloud chamber for the study of cosmic rays, and was awarded the Nobel Prize for physics in 1948.

black-eyed Susan See ACANTHUS; CONEFLOWER.

black fly (or **buffalo gnat**) A small, dark, thickset FLY of the family Simuliidae, occurring in all parts of the world, especially the north temperate and sub-Arctic regions. Female black flies have a vicious bite and feed on the blood of vertebrates; they are often so abundant as to be serious pests, even causing deaths of livestock and occasionally of man. In Central America and Africa they are potential vectors for a nematode worm that causes onchocerciasis or RIVER BLINDNESS. The larvae live in running water, attached to stones or to other animals by a sucker, filtering their food out of the water. Control measures include the addition of specific insecticides to the head-waters of streams.

Blackfoot A North American Indian tribe of the Great Plains and prairies of northern Montana and southern Alberta. Divided into Blackfoot Proper, Blood Blackfoot, and Piegan subgroups, the Blackfoot are among the westernmost of the Algonquian-speaking Indians. They were formerly almost entirely dependent on buffalo and other large game. The principal Blackfoot city is Browning, Montana, which is home to the Museum of the Plains Indians.

Black Forest (German **Schwarzwald**) A hilly wooded region of south-west Germany lying to the east of the Rhine valley. The spa town of Baden-Baden lies in the Black Forest and the highest point is the Feldberg (1,493 m, 4,898 ft). It is a popular tourist and holiday area and is famous for its clocks and toys. Lumbering is an important industry.

Blackfriars A district of London on the north bank of the Thames named after a Black Friar or Dominican priory founded there in 1238. The buildings of the district were mostly destroyed during the Great Fire of 1666.

Black Hand Symbol and name for a number of secret societies that flourished in the 19th and early 20th centuries. It was the name adopted by a Serbian terrorist organization, founded in 1911 by Colonel Dimitrijevic largely from army officers, to liberate Serbs still under Habsburg or Turkish rule. It organized the assassination at Sarajevo of Archduke FRANCIS FERDINAND (1914), an event that contributed to the outbreak of World War I. The name and symbol were adopted by organizations controlled by the MAFIA in the USA and Italy, which used intimidation and murder to gain their ends.

Black Hills A range of mountains in east Wyoming and west South Dakota, USA, so called because the densely forested slopes look dark from a distance. The highest point is Harney Peak (2,207 m, 7,242 ft) and on the granite face of Mt. Rushmore (1,890 m, 6,200 ft) are sculpted the giant heads of Presidents Washington, Lincoln, Jefferson, and Theodore Roosevelt.

black hole A possible final state of a star, when its mass, and hence its gravitational pull, is so large that the star undergoes catastrophic gravitational collapse inwards, completely overwhelming the stabilizing forces within it. The matter becomes more and more compressed during this process which ultimately results in an object of zero size and infinite density. Indeed according to Einstein's theory of general RELATIVITY a space-time SINGULARITY is formed where the gravitational forces become infinite. As this inward collapse proceeds, the gravitational field on the surface of the star increases so much that it becomes more and more difficult for particles and light emitted from the star to escape. Eventually all of the star is hidden inside a one-way membrane or EVENT HORIZON through which no light can escape. The collapsing star has now become a black hole and all that can be felt from the outside is the gravitational pull of the original star; the star is otherwise completely invisible. The radius of the event horizon is called the SCHWARZSCHILD RADIUS after the German astronomer Karl Schwarzschild, who, in 1916, discovered the correct solution of Einstein's equations. This solution describes an isolated non-rotating black hole. In 1963 the corresponding solution for a rotating black hole was discovered by the New Zealand physicist Roy Kerr. The Schwarzschild radius of a black hole can be very small. A star three times the Sun's mass will probably form a black hole with a Schwarzschild radius of only 9 km. Astronomers believe that many black holes are to be found in the Milky Way. Indeed many believe that X-rays coming from Cygnus X-1, a binary star system in the constellation of Cygnus, are due to the presence of a black hole which forms one component of the binary system. Gas drawn from the surface of the ordinary visible star in the system is swept around into an ACCRETION DISC surrounding the apparently invisible member of the system, that is, the black hole. This swirling disc of gas is believed to be heated by friction to temperatures of tens of millions of degrees. Such a hot gas would emit X-rays which are probably those seen during satellite observations of this system.

Some astronomers have suggested that very large black holes may also be found at the centres of some galaxies including, perhaps, our own. It has also been suggested that very small black holes may have been formed during the highly compressed initial phase of the Universe. If these black holes are within a Schwarzschild radius comparable to the size of an atom then quantum mechanics must be considered. From the point of view of Einstein's theory of gravitation, the event horizon represents an absolutely impenetrable barrier. However, when we try to harmonize quantum mechanics with gravitation theory, we discover that the matter inside black holes can 'tunnel' out, rather like a kind of radioactive decay. The quantum decay of black holes takes an enormously long time, unless the black hole is very small. Indeed a tiny black hole, the mass of an average mountain, but whose Schwarzschild radius is as small as an atomic nucleus, would decay explosively. It is possible that such an explosion could give rise to gamma rays.

Black Hole of Calcutta A prison room at Fort William, Calcutta, India, so called after the alleged suffocation there in 1756 of some English prisoners. They had been incarcerated by the nawab, Siraj ud-Daula, in retaliation for extending the fort against previous agreements. The incident has an important place in British imperial mythology, for British accounts grossly exaggerated both the smallness of the room and the number of prisoners, thus suggesting an act of barbarism on the nawab's part.

Black Isle A peninsula in Highland Region, northern Scotland, between the Cromarty Firth to the north and the Beauly and Moray Firths to the south and east. The fishing port of Cromarty was the birthplace of the Scottish geologist and writer Hugh Miller (1802–56).

blackmail The extraction of unwarranted payment in return for not carrying out a threat (sometimes called demanding money with menaces). Such menaces include the threat of violence or the exposure of past misconduct. In law, it is an essential requirement that the blackmail should concern economic as opposed to any other sort of gain, since the offence is concerned with the invasion of economic interests.

Blackmore, R(ichard) D(oddridge) (1825–1900) British novelist and poet. He published several collections of poetry before turning to fiction; his fame rests almost entirely on his popular romantic novel *Lorna Doone* (1869), set on 17th-century Exmoor.

Black Mountains In the USA, a part of the Appalachians in western North Carolina, rising to 2,037 m (6,684 feet) at Mount Mitchell, the highest point east of the Rocky Mountains. The Black Mountains in South Wales are part of the Brecon Beacons National Park, rising to 811 m (2,661 feet).

Black Muslim Movement An Islamic organization in the USA. It was founded in 1930 and led by Elijah Muhammad from 1934 until his death in 1975. The Movement expanded greatly in the 1950s when MALCOLM X became one of its spokesmen; by the 1960s, at the height of the BLACK POWER MOVEMENT, it probably had over 100,000 members. With the suspension of Malcolm X from the Movement and his assassination in 1965, it lost some of its influence to the Black Panthers, but continued to establish separate black enterprises and to provide a source of inspiration for thousands of black Americans. Elijah Muhammad was succeeded in 1975 by his son, Wallace D. Muhammad, who advocated a more moderate form of Islam and racial integration. This led to disagreements within the Movement and in 1976 it split into the American Muslim Mission and the radical Nation of Islam, led by Louis Farrakhan.

Blackpool A seaside resort on the coast of Lancashire, north-west England; pop. (1991) 144,500. It is the largest and most popular holiday resort in northern England with famous autumn illuminations and a 173-m (568-ft) observation tower built in 1894 and modelled on the Eiffel Tower in Paris.

Black Power Movement A term used among black people in the USA in the mid-1960s. The movement aimed at a more militant approach towards securing CIVIL RIGHTS, and stressed the need for action by blacks alone, rather than in alliance with white liberals. Many blacks felt that the civil rights movement had done little to alter their lives, and under such leaders as Stokeley Carmichael they proposed that black Americans should concentrate in their own communities to establish their own political and economic power. In 1966 a Student Non-Violent Co-ordinating Committee (SNCC) was formed by Carmichael to activate black college students, and at the same time the BLACK MUSLIM MOVEMENT was advocating Islam as the black salvation. Others, like the Black Panthers, emphasized violence and militancy, but all were concerned to stress the value of black culture and all things black. The riots in the cities in the middle and late 1960s seemed to herald new waves of black militancy, but the intensity of the Black Power Movement tended to decline in the early 1970s, when many blacks began cooperating with white organizations against the VIETNAM WAR.

Black Prince See EDWARD THE BLACK PRINCE.

Black Sea (or **Euxine Sea**; Russian **Chernoye More**; Turkish **Karadeniz**) A tideless virtually landlocked sea bounded by Ukraine, Russia, Georgia, Turkey, Bulgaria, and Romania, and connected to the Mediterranean Sea through the Bosporus and the Sea of Marmara; area 413,365 sq km (159,662 sq miles). It reaches a maximum depth of 2,246 m (7,369 ft) and receives a number of rivers including the Danube, Volga, Dniester, and Dnieper, which give its upper layers a low salt content.

Black September Palestinian terrorist organization. It emerged after the defeat of the Palestinian guerrilla organizations in Jordan in September 1970, from which event it took its name. It was claimed to be an independent organization, but was apparently a cover for al-Fatah operations, the most atrocious of which was the massacre of Israeli athletes at the Munich Olympics in September 1972. Shortly after that event the organization became inactive.

Blackshirt The colloquial name given to the *Squadre d'Azione* (Action Squad), the national combat groups, founded in Italy in 1919. Organized along paramilitary lines, they wore black shirts and patrolled cities to fight socialism and communism by violent means. In 1921 they were incorporated into the Fascist Party (see FASCISM) as a national militia. The SS in Nazi Germany and the followers of Oswald MOSLEY's British Union of Fascists in the 1930s were also known as Blackshirts.

Blackstone, Sir William (1723–80) British jurist. His major work was the *Commentaries on the Laws of England* (1765–69), based on lectures given at Oxford University; setting out English legal structure and principles, it became a highly influential exposition of English law, forming the basis of legal education in England and the USA.

blackthorn (or **sloe**) A deciduous, spiny shrub, *Prunus spinosa*, of hedgerows and forest edges in Europe. It is related to the cherry, and has small, white flowers and blue-black fruits which have a sour, astringent taste. In Britain, these are used in preserves and in flavouring a kind of gin, and the wood is used for walking-sticks. The fruits are eaten by birds, badgers, and foxes, which disperse the seeds in their droppings.

Blackwell, Elizabeth (1821–1910) US physician. She was the first woman to gain a degree in medicine in the USA. Born in Bristol, England, she emigrated with her family to the USA in 1832. After her father's death she supported her family by teaching, and began studying medicine privately. Rejected by various medical schools, she was finally accepted by the Geneva Medical College, New York, graduating in 1849. She practised in New York but later lived in England, becoming professor of gynaecology at the London School of Medicine for Women (1875–1907).

black widow spider A SPIDER of the genus *Latrodectus*, especially *L. mactans*, found in many parts of the world. Black widows are among the few spiders whose venom affects the nerves, producing muscular spasms and respiratory difficulty. They often have a red hourglass mark on the back of their nearly spherical abdomen, build rather untidy webs, and hang beneath them, wrapping their catches up in silk trusses. Females carry large egg-cases at certain times of the year.

Blackwood, Algernon (Henry) (1869–1951) British writer. He was sent to Canada by his parents at the age of 20, and his ten struggling years spent there and in the USA were later described in his vivid autobiography *Episodes Before Thirty* (1923). He then worked as a journalist before returning to England to write ghost stories, such as *Tales of the Uncanny and Supernatural* (1949).

bladder The muscular bag into which urine passes from the kidneys via tubes called ureters. This organ is found in the majority of vertebrates with the exception of birds. It swells up as it fills with urine, and urination occurs when the ring of muscle, or sphincter, guarding its outlet relaxes. This is under voluntary control in adult mammals, but in the young voiding occurs automatically, being dependent on the amount of urine to be secreted and the speed at which the bladder fills. The duct through which urine passes from the bladder is the urethra. In the male, the sphincter is surrounded by the PROSTATE GLAND, which tends to enlarge in old age and interfere with its action causing incontinence.

bladderwort The common name for 120 species of *Utricularia*, a genus of CARNIVOROUS PLANTS which trap small aquatic animals such as *Daphnia* and use them as a food source. They may be rootless aquatics or marginal bog-plants found throughout most of the world. The traps are small bladders produced on the leaves and runners, which are triggered by contact, sucking in their prey with a rush of water. They give their name to the bladderwort family, Lentibulariaceae, which also includes BUTTERWORTS.

Blaine, James Gillespie (1830–93) US politician He was Secretary of State to President GARFIELD (1881), and to President William Henry HARRISON (1889–91). As leader of the so-called 'Half Breeds Republicans (those committed to a conciliatory policy towards the South and to civil-service reform), he helped three lesser men (Hayes Garfield, Harrison) attain the presidency but was denied the prize himself in the 1884 election against CLEVELAND.

Blair, Tony (full name Anthony Charles Lynton Blair) (1953–) British politician, Labour Prime Minister since 1997. Blair, a lawyer before entering politics, was elected as a Labour Member of Parliament in 1983 and became a member of the shadow cabinet in 1984. A 'modernizer', he took part in negotiations to end the 'closed shop' TRADE UNION monopoly over certain jobs, and insisted that the LABOUR PARTY should support private enterprise As shadow spokesman for Home Affairs (1992–94 he emphasized the need to tackle the underlying social causes of crime. He became Leader of the Opposition following the death of John Smith in 1994 and led 'New Labour' to an overwhelming victory in the general election of 1997.

Blake, Peter (1932–) British painter. In the late 1950s and early 1960s he was prominent in the pop art movement in the UK. One of his most famou creations is the cover design for the Beatles album *Sergeant Pepper's Lonely Hearts Club Band* (1967).

Blake, Robert (1599–1657) English admiral. He wa a member of the LONG PARLIAMENT and fough for the ROUNDHEADS during the ENGLISH CIVI WAR. He achieved successes against the Royalist (1649–51), the Dutch (1652–54), and Spain (1656–57 His involvement in the preparation of the *Fightin Instructions* and *Articles of War* was crucial to th developing professionalism of the English navy, a was his association with the building of large heavily armed vessels.

Blake, William (1757–1827) British painte engraver, and poet. His poems mark the beginnin of romanticism and a rejection of the Age o Enlightenment; they include *Songs of Innocenc* (1789) and *Songs of Experience* (1794). The short poen known as 'Jerusalem', which later became a popu lar hymn, appears in *Milton* (1804–08). His majo prose work, *The Marriage of Heaven and He* (*c*.1790–93), is a collection of paradoxical and revo lutionary aphorisms. His watercolours and engravings, like his writings, were only fully appreciated after his death.

Blanc, Louis (1811–82) French politician and historian. In 1839 he published *The Organization of Labour* in which he outlined his ideal of a new social order based on the principle 'from each according to his abilities, to each according to his needs'. In 1848 he headed a commission of workers' delegates to find solutions to problems of exploitation and unemployment. The suppression of the workers' revolt later that year forced him to flee to Britain and he did not return until 1871.

Blanchard, Jean Pierre François (1753–1809) French balloonist. Together with American John Jeffries (1744–1819) he made the first crossing of the English Channel by air, flying by balloon from Dover to Calais on 7 January 1785, and was the first to fly a balloon in the USA. Blanchard was among the earliest to experiment with parachuting, using animals in his demonstrations; he was killed making a practice jump by parachute from a balloon.

blank verse Unrhymed lines usually of iambic PENTAMETER: 'Was this the face that launch'd a thousand ships, And burnt the topless towers of Ilium?' (Marlowe). It is a very flexible English verse-form which can attain rhetorical grandeur while echoing the natural rhythms of speech. First used in about 1540 by Henry Howard, Earl of Surrey, it soon became both the required metre for dramatic poetry and a widely used form for narrative and meditative poems. Much of the finest verse in English – by Shakespeare, Milton, Wordsworth, and Tennyson – has been written in blank verse.

Blanqui, Louis Auguste (1805–81) French radical thinker and revolutionary leader. He launched an attack on the Paris Hotel de Ville in 1839. Sentenced to death, his sentence was later commuted to life imprisonment. A brief period of freedom allowed him to lead the republicans in the REVOLUTION OF 1848. He remained in prison until 1859, was re-arrested in 1861, and escaped to Belgium in 1865, where he organized the extremist republican opposition to NAPOLEON III. He was imprisoned in 1871, after attempting to overthrow the French provisional government. His influence over the Commune of PARIS was considerable. He died in 1881, two years after being finally released from prison.

Blarney A village in County Cork, southern Ireland, 8 km (5 miles) north-west of Cork; pop. (1981) 1,500. Those who kiss the Blarney stone at Blarney Castle are said to be conferred with a cajoling tongue.

blasphemy A speech, thought, or action regarded as derogatory to God or to sacred institutions. What is considered blasphemous varies between societies and religions, but it may be regarded as an indicator of what a society and its religious institutions believe must be protected in order to maintain morality and religious integrity. In JUDAISM, blasphemy was punishable by death; Jesus was accused of blasphemy because he claimed to be God. In many countries, blasphemy is still regarded as an offence punishable by law. In the UK, the blasphemy laws currently apply only to slanders against Christianity, although there are calls for them to be extended to other religions. Penalties for blasphemy in ISLAM are interpreted differently by the four schools of law, but it may be a capital offence.

blast-furnace A chamber in which IRON is extracted from iron ore, an essential process in the IRON AND STEEL INDUSTRY. The furnace is filled from the top with a charge of iron ore, COKE, and limestone; the major ore used is haematite (Fe_2O_3). Blasts of hot air introduced near the base of the furnace burn the coke and melt the iron oxide in the material around the lower edges of the furnace. The burning of the coke gives off carbon monoxide, which is the main reducing agent for converting the iron oxide to iron. As it is formed, the iron melts and runs down to collect in a pool at the bottom of the furnace, while the molten slag floats on the surface. The iron and slag can then be tapped off. The furnace is built of steel and lined with heat-resistant bricks. Once started, it runs continuously for two or more years, until the lining begins to fail.

Blaue Reiter, Der (German, 'The Blue Rider') A loosely organized group of Expressionist artists, formed in Germany in 1911, and with Die BRÜCKE the leading modern art movement in Germany before 1914. The name derives from the title of a picture by KANDINSKY; other leading members of the group included Paul KLEE and Franz Marc. Though its members differed widely in artistic outlook, they shared a desire to express spiritual values in their work. The group disintegrated with the outbreak of World War I.

Blavatsky, Helena (Petrovna) (known as **Madame Blavatsky**; née Hahn) (1831–91) Russian spiritualist, born in Ukraine. She went to the USA in 1873, and in 1875 founded the Theosophical Society in New York together with the American Henry Steel Olcott (1832–1907). The movement was based on Hindu and Buddhist teachings and taught of the transmigration of souls and universal fellowship; in 1878 Blavatsky and Olcott transferred the society's headquarters to India.

bleach A chemical used to whiten coloured materials. The active ingredient (usually CHLORINE) reacts with coloured material to form colourless substances. Bleaches are used extensively to treat wood-pulp for paper manufacture, in the textile industry to treat cotton and linen, and domestically for cleaning stained surfaces. Originally, textiles were bleached by exposure to sunlight in 'bleach fields'. Later industrial bleaching used bleaching powder, a mixture of chlorine with calcium hydroxide first manufactured by TENNANT in 1799. However, as new techniques for handling chlorine have been developed, bleaching powder has been largely replaced by liquid chlorine. Bleaching powder is still used for domestic cleaning, although liquid bleaches are now more common. Some of these contain sodium hypochlorite solution as the active ingredient. Some washing powders also contain mild bleaches. Sulphur dioxide gas is used to bleach materials such as straw, which would be damaged by the action of chlorine. HYDROGEN PEROXIDE is sometimes used to bleach hair.

Blenheim, Battle of (13 August 1704) . A Bavarian village on the north bank of the River Danube gave its name to a major battle of the War of the SPANISH SUCCESSION. John Churchill, 1st Duke of Marlborough, commanded a British and Austrian army that defeated the French forces of Louis XIV. **Blenheim Palace**, the Duke's seat at Woodstock in Oxfordshire, England, was named after this victory. Begun in 1705, the building was designed by the English architects Sir John Vanbrugh and Nicholas Hawksmoor. The park was laid out by 'Capability' Brown.

blenny A mostly marine fish that lives in tropical and subtropical seas; a few live in fresh water.

Fishes of several families are called blennies, including the comb-tooth blennies of the family Blennidae, the clinids (Clinidae), pricklebacks (Stichaediae), and gunnels (Pholididae). Their bodies are scaleless, the head is usually blunt, and the jaws have numerous, closely packed, small teeth. They have two long, slender rays in each pelvic fin, and often have flaps of skin above the eyes or elsewhere on the head. They usually live in shallow water, sometimes inhabiting shore pools. There are over 500 species within the family groups known as blennies.

Blériot, Louis (1872–1936) French aviation pioneer. Trained as an engineer, he built one of the first successful monoplanes in 1907. On 25 July 1909 he became the first to fly the English Channel (Calais to Dover) in a monoplane. Later he became an aircraft manufacturer, building more than 800 aeroplanes of 40 different types between 1909 and 1914.

blewit See AGARIC.

Bligh, William (1754–1817) British admiral. He accompanied Captain Cook on his second voyage (1772–75). On a further visit to the South Pacific islands in 1788, his irascible temper and overbearing conduct provoked the BOUNTY MUTINY. Returning to Britain, he served under Nelson at Copenhagen (1801) and in 1805 was appointed governor of New South Wales. Conflict with the New South Wales Corps culminated in the RUM REBELLION of 1808. Settling in England in 1810, he was promoted to the rank of vice-admiral.

blind fish A type of fish, found over a wide geographical range, which is mostly associated with caves and underground systems, although there are a few marine species. In all blind fishes the eyes are much reduced in size, being covered with skin but rarely totally absent. Blind fishes also lack all pigment in the skin and are pink in colour. Several deep-sea fishes which live in the dark have greatly reduced eyes and some are virtually blind. Blind fishes occur in a variety of families, but are mainly catfishes, cyprinids (carp family), or cave fishes (five North American species in the family Characidae). Most belong to groups in which there are abundant alternative sense organs. The catfishes, for example, all have well-developed barbels, and the cave fishes have highly elaborate sense organs on the head and body. The blind characin, *Anoptichthys jordani*, from Mexico, has a normally coloured and sighted relative, *A. mexicanus*, in the surrounding rivers, with which it will interbreed.

blindness Partial or complete loss of vision that cannot be corrected by ordinary glasses. It may be due to damage to that part of the brain involved with vision, or to the optic nerve, but much more commonly it is due to the eyes themselves. It has been estimated that there are about ten million people in the world without effective vision, and that for most of them the loss of sight could have been prevented. A major cause of blindness, particularly in the developing world, is infectious disease, such as trachoma (a form of chronic CONJUNCTIVITIS), SEXUALLY TRANSMITTED DISEASE, measles, meningitis, diphtheria, leprosy, and onchocerciasis (RIVER BLINDNESS). Dietary deficiency also plays a role. In developed countries the causes are more commonly GLAUCOMA, diabetes, and hereditary and congenital conditions. Restoration of sight is possible only when blindness is due to clouding of the translucent lens (cataract) or cornea. In that case, removal of the lens or corneal grafting is effective. Facilities to help the blind and partially sighted minimize their DISABILITY, include training in the use of a long white cane or a guide dog to help with mobility; special education and training for jobs; books, textbooks, and other material written in BRAILLE; and braille computer terminals.

blind snake Any of about 200 burrowing species of snake in the family Typhlopidae, distributed worldwide in tropical and subtropical regions. They are completely harmless to man and rather small, although a few species are known to exceed 61 cm (2 feet) in length. Their eyes are tiny and probably capable only of distinguishing between light and dark. Their bodies are covered with smooth, shiny scales which have the property of resisting soil adhesion. Their diet consists mainly of ants, termites, and other small soil creatures and they have a markedly reduced dentition; the upper jaw bears teeth, whereas the lower jaw is toothless. Snakes of the unrelated Leptotyphlopidae family are also known as blind snakes.

Bliss, Sir Arthur (Drummond) (1891–1975) British composer. After active service throughout World War I, Bliss became known as a very 'advanced' composer, much influenced by Stravinsky and Ravel. Such works as *A Colour Symphony* (1922) and the choral symphony *Morning Heroes* (1930) confirmed his importance, as did a series of lively ballets, beginning with *Checkmate* (1937). Later works, such as the opera *The Olympians* (1949), were more romantic in manner. He was appointed MASTER OF THE QUEEN'S MUSIC in 1953.

blister beetle A mostly blackish and soft-bodied BEETLE up to 2 cm (0.75 inch) long. If these beetles are crushed and rubbed on human skin, a chemical in their blood, cantharidin, causes blisters, a characteristic which has led to their use in medicine as counter-irritants. Their larvae are parasitic, mostly on solitary bees. Along with the OIL BEETLES, they form the family Meloidae.

Blitzkrieg (German, 'lightning war') A military tactic employed by the Germans in World War II, which was especially successful in campaigns against Poland, France, Greece, and the Soviet Union. It employed fast-moving tanks and motorized infantry, supported by dive-bombers, to throw superior but slower enemy forces off balance and thereby win crushing victories rapidly and with small expenditure of men and materials. In Britain, where it was known as 'the Blitz', it consisted of an air assault on British cities in 1940. After 1941, Germany's enemies were better prepared and new battlefields in the Soviet Union and Africa were less suited to the technique.

Blixen, Karen (Christentze), Baroness Blixen-Finecke (née Dinesen; also known by the pseudonym **Isak Dinesen**) (1885–1962) Danish novelist and short-story writer in English. Blixen married her second cousin in 1914 and moved to Kenya. Despite divorcing in 1921 she stayed on to run their coffee plantation, becoming deeply involved with the country and people. She returned to Denmark in 1931 and published her first major work, *Seven Gothic Tales*, in 1934. Her autobiography *Out of Africa* (1937) was made into a successful film in 1985.

blizzard A storm with temperatures below 0°C (32°F), heavy snowfalls, and strong winds, which keep drifting snow in suspension and reduce the visibility to less than 200 m (220 yards). The snow is driven by the wind, often at speeds in excess of 56 km/h (35 m.p.h.) and will form new drifts when meeting any obstacle. In the USA a blizzard is defined slightly differently, i.e. a temperature below −6.7°C (19.94°F) and visibility reduced by falling or blowing snow to less than 400 m (440 yards).

Bloch, Ernest (1880–1959) Swiss-born US composer, of Jewish descent. Before he settled in the USA in 1916, his opera *Macbeth* (1910) was produced in Paris to great acclaim. His musical language derives from the late 19th-century romanticism of Liszt and Richard Strauss; the influence of Jewish musical forms can be seen in the *Israel Symphony* (1912–16), *Solomon* (1916), and numerous other orchestral compositions.

block mountains (or **fault-block mountains**) Large uplifted land masses (HORSTS) bordered on two or more sides by faults. The Great Basin of western USA is broken by many of them, some rising to more than 3,000 m (9,800 feet). Mountains of this type (where a tilted block is bounded by a steep scarp on one side and a gentle slope on the other) have evidently been formed by vertical movements in the Earth's crust, but the exact mechanism involved is still debated.

Bloemfontein The capital of the Free State province and judicial capital of the Republic of South Africa; pop. (1991) 300,150. Founded in 1846, it was the venue (in 1909) for the final negotiations that led to the formation of the Union of South Africa in 1910. It is a commercial centre with light industries.

Blok, Aleksandr (Aleksandrovich) (1880–1921) Russian poet, the most important poet of Russian Symbolism. Loss of faith in his ideal, disillusionment following the Russo-Japanese War, and disappointment in the failure of the 1905 revolution are all reflected in Blok's later verse.

Blondin, Charles (born Jean-François Gravelet) (1824–97) French acrobat. He is renowned for walking across a tightrope suspended over Niagara Falls in 1859; on subsequent occasions he performed the same feat blindfold, with a wheelbarrow, and carrying a man on his back.

blood A fluid containing cells that circulates in the bodies of all animals with the exception of a few phyla of lower invertebrates. It supplies tissues with oxygen and foodstuffs and transports waste products, which are removed from the body by the excretory system. See CIRCULATION.

Mammalian blood consists mainly of ERYTHROCYTES (red cells), LEUCOCYTES (white cells, including lymphocytes, granulocytes, and monocytes), and PLATELETS suspended in PLASMA. Some of the white blood cells combat infections directly; other white cells manufacture ANTIBODIES and strengthen the body's immunity towards unwanted foreign proteins. Red blood cells convey oxygen to tissues and remove carbon dioxide to the lungs. The plasma conveys foodstuffs to tissues and also takes away waste products. In adult vertebrates, blood is manufactured in the BONE marrow. See also HAEMATOLOGY.

Blood, Thomas (*c.*1618–80) Irish colonel and adventurer. He lost his estates at the RESTORATION in 1660 and hoped to persuade the authorities to return them by his attack on Dublin castle in 1663. His most famous exploit was the theft of the English crown jewels from the Tower of London in 1671. Charles II, who examined Blood personally after his arrest, was so impressed with his audacity that he was pardoned and his estates restored.

blood fluke A FLUKE belonging to the genus *Schistosoma*. Blood flukes are parasites of terrestrial vertebrates, including man, throughout Africa and Asia. There are several species, each capable of causing the disease BILHARZIA.

blood groups Systems for the typing and characterization of human blood for transfusion; incompatible blood transfusion can result in severe reactions. The two most important systems are the ABO and rhesus factor (Rh), used together to type blood for transfusion. The ABO system identifies the presence of antigens A and B on the surfaces of red blood cells, and the presence of antibodies, anti-A and anti-B, to these antigens. Blood group A has antigen A and anti-B antibodies and vice versa for blood group B; blood group AB has A and B antigens and neither anti-A nor anti-B antibodies; blood group O has neither A nor B antigens and both anti-A and anti-B antibodies. In the rhesus system, 85 per cent of people possess the rhesus antigen on the red cell surface and are referred to as being rhesus positive (Rh+); the remainder are rhesus negative (Rh–).

blood pressure Pressure resulting from the force driving the blood round the closed system of blood vessels supplying an animal's body. At each beat of the heart, blood is pumped into the arteries, creating a brief peak of high pressure. The pressure declines between beats to about two-thirds of this high peak of pressure. The difference between these values is a useful indicator of the condition of the heart and arteries. A raised blood pressure (hypertension) may lead to heart disease. Blood

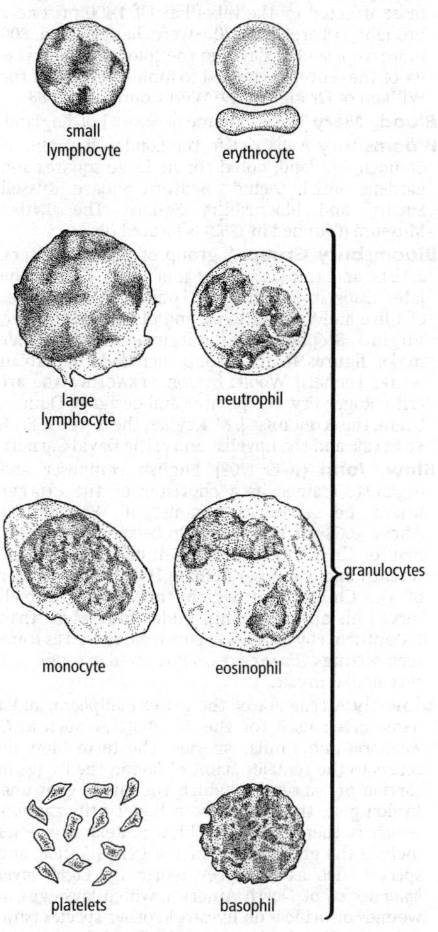

Blood Types of blood cell.

pressure can be estimated in the limb arteries of humans using a SPHYGMOMANOMETER.

Blood River, Battle of (16 December 1838) Fought between Voortrekkers and ZULUS, led by DINGAAN, near a tributary of the Buffalo River, subsequently called Blood River after its waters reddened with the blood of some 3,000 Zulus, killed to avenge the slaughter of about 500 BOERS earlier in the year. The Zulu defeat enabled the Boers to establish the Republic of NATAL.

blood transfusion The injection of blood previously taken from a healthy person into the veins of a patient. In early transfusions serious mishaps occurred due to blood incompatibility: blood from the donor agglutinated (clotted) on being transfused, due to the presence of antigens in the donor blood that caused an immune response in the patient (see IMMUNOLOGY). In 1900 LANDSTEINER devised the ABO BLOOD GROUP system. In 1935 a process for freezing and drying blood plasma for later use was developed. During World War II, blood banks were established for the storage and management of blood and plasma.

bloodworm See MIDGE.

Bloody Assizes A series of trials held in 1685 to punish those who took part in MONMOUTH'S REBELLION, conducted by Judge JEFFREYS, the Lord Chief Justice, in those centres of western England most affected by the rebellion. Of 1,400 prisoners brought before him, 300 were hanged and 800 more were sold as slaves in the colonies. The severity of the sentences helped to mobilize support for William of Orange in the West Country in 1688.

Bloody Mary The nickname of MARY I of England.

Bloomsbury A district in the London borough of Camden, England, noted for its large squares and gardens which include Bedford Square, Russell Square, and Bloomsbury Square. The British Museum (founded in 1753) is located here.

Bloomsbury Group A group of British writers, artists, and thinkers. They met from 1905 to the later 1930s, in Bloomsbury, London, at the houses of Clive and Vanessa BELL, and of Vanessa's sister, Virginia Stephen, later Virginia WOOLF. Other major figures in the group included the Fabian writer Leonard Woolf, Lytton STRACHEY, the art critic Roger Fry, the painter and designer Duncan Grant, the economist J. M. Keynes, the novelist E. M. FORSTER, and the novelist and critic David Garnett.

Blow, John (1649–1708) English composer and organist. Trained as a chorister of the CHAPEL ROYAL, he served as organist of Westminster Abbey (1668–79, 1695–1708). On becoming a Gentleman of the Chapel Royal (1674) he succeeded the lutenist and composer Pelham Humfrey as Master of the Children, at which time Henry Purcell served his apprenticeship under him. More than 100 anthems by Blow have survived, as well as fourteen settings for services, some secular songs, and ceremonial music.

blow fly A true FLY of the genus *Calliphora*, and a name often used for the 'bluebottles' such as *C. vomitoria* and similar species. The term blow fly refers to the females' habit of laying their eggs in carrion or excrement which the larvae consume. In doing so, the larvae often liquefy the carrion, which is then known as 'blown'. Related species include the greenbottles of the genus *Lucilia*, and species such as the screw-worm fly, *Cochliomyia homnivorax*, of North America, which lays eggs in wounds or orifices on livestock; other species parasitize nestling birds and toads. Blow fly maggots have been used medically to clean wounds. Adult blow flies feed indiscriminately on excrement or sweet substances which they liquefy with saliva and regurgitated food. As a consequence they may contaminate food with pathogens causing dysentery, typhoid, or cholera.

Blücher, Gebhard Leberecht von (1742–1819) Prussian field-marshal, whose victories were due more to dash and energy than to military tactics. Forced to surrender to the French in 1806, he helped to re-create his country's opposition to NAPOLEON, and was commander-in-chief of the armies in their victory at LEIPZIG in 1813. The following year he led the invasion of France, gaining a major victory at Laon, which led to the overthrow of Napoleon. He retired to Silesia, only to be recalled when Napoleon returned. His intervention at a late stage of the battle of WATERLOO was decisive.

blue A butterfly belonging to a family of some 6,000 species. This family, Lycaenidae, which is predominantly tropical, also includes the HAIRSTREAKS and COPPERS. The upperside of the male is blue, sometimes brilliantly so, that of the female more often being brown. Several species have caterpillars that feed on the grubs of ants, while some, including the Australian mistletoe butterflies, *Orygis* species, are protected by ants. The caterpillar of the Chinese blue butterfly, *Gerydus chinensis*, eats aphids. Many lycaenids feed on the leaves of tropical trees and shrubs. Their larvae are typically woodlouse- or slug-shaped, unlike the normal shape of a caterpillar.

bluebell See CAMPANULA; HYACINTH.

blueberry The fruit of several shrubs of the genus *Vaccinium* that are native to North America, where they are grown commercially. Blueberries are related to the European BILBERRY, but bear larger, sweeter fruit. The bluish-black berries are about 1 cm (0.5 inch) across. The high-bush blueberries may grow as tall as 4.5 m (15 feet); the hardier low-bush species are only about 30 cm (12 inches) tall.

bluebird Any of three species of the thrush family, Turdidae, belonging to the genus *Sialia*. All occur in North America and Mexico. They are rather larger in size than a sparrow, and the males of all species are bright blue on top. The mountain bluebird, *S. currucoides*, is entirely blue, whereas the other species are rusty red underneath. The females of all species are dull grey in colour. All inhabit open woodlands or orchards and nest in holes in trees, laying four to six blue eggs. They eat a wide range of insects and fruits.

bluebottle See BLOW FLY.

blue chip An EQUITY (or ordinary SHARE) in a large, stable, and well-known company, which is likely to prove a more reliable investment than a share in a less reputable enterprise. Pension funds, insurance companies, and other such institutions are likely to invest in blue chips for the majority of their portfolios.

blue-green bacteria (formerly **blue-green algae**) See CYANOBACTERIA.

Blue Mosque (or **Sultan Ahmet Mosque**) An Islamic mosque with six minarets in Istanbul, Turkey, said to be one of the finest in the world. Built by Sultan Ahmet I in 1609–16, its dome is 43 m (141 ft) high and 23.5 m (77 ft) in diameter.

Blue Mountains A section of the Great Dividing Range in New South Wales, Australia. The mountains appear blue because the fine droplets of oil that are dispersed from the Eucalyptus trees cause the blue light rays of the Sun to be scattered more effectively. Now a popular resort area, the range was first traversed in 1813 by Blaxland, Lawson, and Wentworth.

Blue Nile One of the two principal headwaters of the River Nile. It rises in Lake Tana in the Ethiopian Highlands and flows *c.*1,600 km (1,000 miles) south through Ethiopia then northwestwards into Sudan where it meets the White Nile at Khartoum. The Roseires Dam close to the Ethiopian frontier supplies the greater part of Sudan's hydroelectric power.

Blue Ridge Mountains A range of the Appalachian Mountains in the eastern USA, stretching 1,040 km (650 miles) from south Pennsylvania to north Georgia. Mt. Mitchell (2,039 m, 6,684 ft) is the highest peak.

blues A type of black American song, taken up by jazz musicians in the 1920s but with much older folk roots, and an ancestry going back to African origins. Words and music were originally improvised on a simple, fixed-harmonic, twelve-bar basis. Characteristic of the music are the 'blue' notes, in which the third, the seventh, and (more rarely) the fifth notes of the SCALE are slightly lowered or 'bent', giving the music its distinctive bittersweet quality. The pitch or intonation of blue notes is not fixed precisely, but varies according to the instinct of the performer. Blues structures and formulae have also been developed as purely instrumental music, just as the words and music of the sung blues has been developed by professional composers and lyricists. The true blues is a state of mind: cynical, disillusioned, but defiant in the face of adversity. The singing style can be harsh with raw emotion, as in the work of such remarkable blues singers as Bessie Smith and Billie Holiday. The so-called 'country' blues is quieter and more meditative than the harsh 'city' blues.

blue whale *Balaenoptera musculus*, a species of WHALEBONE WHALE in the family Balaenopteridae. The blue whale is the largest animal that has ever lived, and can grow up to a length of 33 m (109 feet) and weigh some 120 tonnes (132 US tons). It is distributed worldwide and migrates between high and low latitudes, swimming at speeds of up to 36 km/hour (22 miles per hour). In contrast with its size, the blue whale's food consists of krill (EUPHAUSID SHRIMP). This is collected on the fibrous fringe of the baleen plates, which hang in its mouth; the efficiency of this system is indicated by the discovery of 2 tonnes of krill in the stomach of a single whale.

Pairing is thought to occur in June and July and the gestation period lasts ten or eleven months. The young are born in the comparatively warm waters of lower latitudes and may be as long as 7.5 m (24.5 feet) and weigh up to 2,790 kg (6,150 pounds) at birth. The young grow rapidly on the rich milk, increasing from 7 to 15 m (23 to 50 feet) in length in seven months. Females conceive every two or three years and pregnant females of 30 years of age have been found. Blue whales may live for as long as 65 years. Populations of the blue whale have been severely reduced by over-fishing and it is now an endangered species. Two subspecies are recognized: the blue whale *Balaenoptera musculus musculus*, and the pygmy blue whale *B. m. brevicauda*.

bluetit A European woodland sparrow-sized TIT, *Parus caeluleus*, now also seen in urban surroundings. It is a distinctive bird with a blue crown and wings, a yellow breast, and a white face.

Blum, Léon (1872–1950) French statesman, Prime Minister 1936–37, 1938, 1946–47. A lawyer and literary critic, he was drawn into politics by the Dreyfus affair of 1894; he joined the Socialist Party in 1902 and became its leader in opposition in 1925. During the 1930s he led the Popular Front, being elected France's first socialist and Jewish Prime Minister in 1936. He introduced significant labour reforms, but was forced to resign the following year. Interned in Germany during World War II, he returned to France to head a socialist caretaker Cabinet, and retained the party leadership until his death.

Blumenbach, Johann Friedrich (1752–1840) German physiologist and anatomist. He is regarded as the founder of physical anthropology, though his approach has since been much modified. He classified modern humans into five broad categories (Caucasian, Mongoloid, Malayan, Ethiopian, and American), based mainly on cranial measurements.

Blumlein, Alan (1903–42) British inventor. In 1931 he conceived the idea of stereo recording, and by 1933 he had begun to make test recordings, though stereo systems were not commercially adopted until 1958. In 1935–36 he developed a 405-line electronic TELEVISION system, which replaced BAIRD's photomechanical system in the early BBC television transmissions.

Blunden, Edmund (Charles) (1896–1974) British poet and critic. His prose work *Undertones of War* (1928) is a sensitive account of his experiences in World War I. His poetry reveals his deep love of the English countryside, as can be seen in *Pastorals* (1916) and *The Waggoner and Other Poems* (1920).

blunderbus (from Dutch *donderbus*, 'thunder gun') A gun ranging in size from a pistol to a small artillery piece, with a smooth base and a bell-shaped muzzle. It fired small balls over a short range and was in use from the 17th to the 19th centuries.

Blunt, Anthony (Frederick) (1907–83) British art historian and Soviet spy. He was one of the leading figures in establishing art history as an academic discipline in Britain. In 1964 he confessed that he had passed secret information to the Soviet Union during World War II (when he had worked for MI5) and had facilitated the escape of the spies Guy Burgess and Donald Maclean in 1951. These facts were made public in 1979, and he was subsequently stripped of the knighthood he had been awarded in 1956.

Blyton, Enid (1897–1968) British writer of children's fiction. Her best-known creation for young children was the character Noddy, who first appeared in 1949; her books for older children included the series of *Famous Five* and *Secret Seven* adventure stories.

boa A SNAKE of the family Boidae, which resembles the python in many respects, but occurs in some areas, such as the Americas and Madagascar, where pythons are absent. Some small species are found in the Old World (sand boas), and dwarf boas occur in New Guinea and some South Pacific islands. Like some other primitive snakes, they retain vestiges of a pelvic girdle; their hind limbs are retained in the form of claw-like cloacal spurs. All boas suffocate their prey by constriction. There are records of the American boa constrictor reaching 5.6 m (18.5 feet) in length.

Boadicea See BOUDICCA.

boar A member of the PIG family, Suidae. The word 'boar' has two meanings: it is used of all uncastrated male pigs, and also refers universally to the five species of the genus *Sus*, including the European wild boar, *S. scrofa*, which still ranges over a wide area of the forested regions of Europe, and east into Asia. Other members of the genus are found throughout Asia and south into New Guinea. The European wild boar may stand 90 cm (3 feet) at the shoulder, and is almost 150 cm (5 feet) long. Dusky or greyish-brown to black, its coat is of long coarse hair with scattered bristles. It has large, sharp, strong tusks that may be 30 cm (1 foot) long. The sow often has two litters per year, each of four to six young.

Boas, Franz (1858–1942) German-born US anthropologist. A pioneer of modern anthropology, he developed the linguistic and cultural components of ethnology. He did much to overturn the theory that Nordic peoples constitute an essentially superior race; his writings were burnt by the Nazis.

boat See CANOE; CORACLE; DINGHY; SAILING SHIPS AND BOATS.

boat-billed heron (or **boatbill**) A species of bird, *Cochlearius cochlearius*, found in Central and South America, similar to night herons, but with a beak which is flat and broad and which is used to catch and eat reptiles and small mammals. This species is largely nocturnal and solitary in habit.

boat fly See WATER BOATMAN.

bobcat See WILD CAT.

bobolink A sparrow-sized bird, *Dolichonyx oryzivorus*, a member of the New World ORIOLE group. Bobolinks breed in the northern half of North America in open grassy areas, and feed on insects. They spend the northern winter in central South America after migrating across the Gulf of Mexico, a distance of 1,900–2,400 km (1,200–1,500 miles).

Boccaccio, Giovanni (1313–75) Italian storywriter, poet, and humanist, son of a Florentine merchant. He was a friend and admirer of DANTE and endeavoured, apparently with little success, to interest PETRARCH in his fellow poet. In 1348 he witnessed the Black Death in Florence. His most famous work, the *Decameron* (1348–58), is a collection of tales supposedly told by a group of ten young people fleeing from the pestilence.

Boccherini, Luigi (1743–1805) Italian composer and cellist. A prolific composer, chiefly of chamber music, he is especially known for his cello concertos and sonatas.

Boccioni, Umberto (1882–1916) Italian painter, sculptor, and art theorist, the most energetic artist of the Futurist group. He believed that objects have a kind of personality of their own, revealed by 'force lines' with which the object reacts to its environment.

Bodensee See CONSTANCE, LAKE.

Bode's Law (or **Titius-Bode Law**) A mathematical sequence that described the relative sizes of the orbits of the planets known in the 18th century. It was Johann Titius von Wittenberg who in 1766 found such a sequence. His publication was not widely read and it was the better-known German astronomer Johann Bode (1747–1826) who made the law famous. The law states that if 4 is added to the sequence 0, 3, 6, 12, 24, 48, 96, 192 and the totals divided by 10, the result is the average distance of the planets from the Sun (in ASTRONOMICAL UNITS). The modern view is that the 'law', which does not hold for Neptune and Pluto, is a coincidence.

Bodhidharma (6th century AD) Indian Buddhist, who is credited with the founding of ZEN Buddhism. Born in Conjeeveram, near Madras, he moved in about 520 to China, where he taught a form of meditation called *dhyana* (or *zen* in Japanese, *ch'an* in Chinese).

bodhisattva (Sanskrit, 'a being for enlightenment') A central ideal within the MAHAYANA Buddhist tradition, describing both living and transcendent beings who are accorded much respect. Heavenly or transcendent bodhisattvas have achieved enlightenment and freedom from rebirth through the cultivation of various virtues, such as generosity, morality, patience, diligence, meditation, and wisdom, but they renounce NIRVANA in order to benefit humanity. Earthly bodhisattvas seek both personal and communal enlightenment through exemplary learning and compassion. The term bodhisattva is also used more generally to describe the historical BUDDHA before his enlightenment, or other individuals destined to become Buddhas.

Bodin, Jean (1530–96) French political philosopher and economist. In 1576 he published his great work on limited monarchy, *Les Six Livres de la République* ('Six Books of the Commonwealth'). Its argument that sovereignty arose from human needs rather than divine institution influenced the later English philosopher Thomas HOBBES.

Bodleian Library The library of Oxford University in England. The first library was founded in the 14th century and benefited from the manuscript collections donated by Humphrey, duke of Gloucester (1391–1447). It was refounded by Sir Thomas Bodley (1545–1613), diplomat and scholar, for the use both of the University of Oxford and the 'republic of the learned', and opened in 1602. In 1610 the Stationers' Company agreed to give the library a copy of every book printed in England, and by various Copyright Acts it is now one of the six libraries entitled to receive on demand a copy of every book published in the UK.

Bodley, Sir Thomas (1545–1613) English scholar and diplomat. He expended a great amount of money enlarging the Oxford University library, which was opened in 1602, being renamed the BODLEIAN LIBRARY by King James I in 1604.

body language See NON-VERBAL COMMUNICATION.

Boeotia (Greek **Voíotía**) A department in central Greece, to the north of the Gulf of Corinth; area 2,952 sq km (1,140 sq miles); pop. (1991) 134,000; capital, Levádhia. Hesiod, Pindar, and Plutarch were natives of ancient Boeotia.

Boer (from Dutch, 'farmer') A South African of Dutch descent. See AFRIKANERS.

Boerhaave, Hermann (1668–1738) A Dutch physician who made Leiden the centre of European medical teaching in his time. He wrote several comprehensive medical textbooks which were widely accepted and translated into several languages.

Boer Wars (or **South African Wars**, **Anglo-Boer Wars**, **First and Second Wars of Freedom**) (1880–81, 1899–1902) Wars fought between Britain and Transvaal and between Britain and Transvaal and the Orange Free State. The first arose from the British annexation of the Transvaal in 1877 and the incompetent administration that followed. In 1880 it was thought that the GLADSTONE government would grant independence, or at least self-government; when hopes were dashed, KRUGER, Joubert, and PRETORIUS took power as a triumvirate. British disasters at the battles of Laing's Nek, Ingogo, and Majuba Hill forced peace upon Gladstone, who granted self-government. The second war (1899–1902) was caused by multiple grievances. The Boers, under the leadership of Kruger, resented the imperialist policies of Joseph

CHAMBERLAIN, which they feared would deprive the Transvaal of its independence. The refusal of political rights to Uitlanders aggravated the situation, as did the aggressive attitude of Lord Milner, British High Commissioner. For Britain, control of the Rand goldfield was all-important. In 1896 the Transvaal and the Orange Free State formed a military alliance. The Boers, equipped by Germany, never mustered more than 88,000 men, but defeated Britain in numerous initial engagements, for example, Spion Kop. British garrisons were besieged in Ladysmith, Kimberley, and Mafeking. In 1900 the British, under KITCHENER and Roberts, landed with reinforcements. The Boers were gradually defeated, despite the brilliant defence of the commandos. Kitchener adopted a scorched-earth policy, interning the civil population in CONCENTRATION CAMPS, and systematically destroying farms. Peace was offered in 1901, but terms that included the loss of Boer independence were not agreed until the Peace of Vereeniging in 1902.

Boethius, Anicius Manlius Severinus (*c*.480–524) Roman statesman and philosopher. He is best known for *The Consolation of Philosophy*, a work written in a mixture of prose and verse while he was in prison for treason. In this he argued that the soul can attain happiness in affliction by realizing the value of goodness and meditating on the reality of God. While drawing upon Stoicism and Neoplatonism, his work echoed Christian sentiments and exercised considerable influence throughout the Middle Ages.

bog A flat area in which the surface layers of the ground contain large quantities of water, either seasonally or all the year round. The mixture of soil, vegetation, and water is spongy and treacherous. It contains so much water and so little oxygen that the decomposition of vegetation is slowed down, allowing the development of peat. Other organic remains (including those of humans and their settlements) are also well preserved, so bogs provide information about climate and historical changes.

Bogarde, Sir Dirk (born Derek Niven van den Bogaerde) (1921–) British actor and writer, of Dutch descent. He became famous in the 'Doctor' series of comedy films (including *Doctor in the House*, 1953). His later films include *The Servant* (1963), *Death in Venice* (1971), and *A Bridge Too Far* (1977). He has also published a number of volumes of autobiography and several novels.

Bogart, Humphrey (DeForest) (1899–1957) US actor. His acting career began on the stage in 1922; his success as a ruthless gangster in the play *The Petrified Forest* was repeated in the screen version of 1936. Many memorable gangster films followed, including *They Drive by Night* (1940). His best-known films are probably *Casablanca* (1942), *The Big Sleep* (1946, in which he played opposite his fourth wife Lauren Bacall), and *The African Queen* (1951).

bogie A sub-frame of a locomotive, carriage, or freight wagon that carries a set of wheels (usually on two axles) and which is pivoted with respect to the main frame of the vehicle to facilitate the negotiation of sharp curves.

Bognor Regis A resort town in West Sussex on the south coast of England, east of Chichester; pop. (1991) 56,744. The word *Regis* (Latin, 'of the king') was added to its name after King George V went to recuperate there in 1929.

Bogotá The capital and largest city of Colombia, situated in the eastern Andes at *c*.2,610 m (8,560 ft); pop. (est. 1994) 4,921,200. Founded by the Spanish in 1538 on the site of a pre-Columbian centre of the Chibcha culture, it was originally known as Santa Fe de Bogotá. It is the political, social, financial, and marketing centre of the republic; it has several universities. Its industries include textiles, vehicles, chemicals, engineering, and food processing.

Bohemia A region in central Europe, now the north-western part of the Czech Republic; pop. (1991) 6,288,350.

Physical. Bohemia is a dissected plateau rising to 1,602 m (5,256 feet) and composed of crystalline rock with rounded features that provides subdued highland scenery. Bounded by the Ore Mountains or Kru né Hory (German, Erzgebirge) in the north-west and the Bohemian–Moravian heights in the south-east, it is drained by the Labe (ELBE) and its chief tributaries, the Vltava (Moldau), Jizera, and Ohře Rivers.

History. Bohemia was established as a duchy by the Premyslid dynasty in the 9th century, but as a result of the rising power of the Ottonians was forced to accept the suzerainty of the German Holy Roman Emperors in the following century. Having incorporated the neighbouring region of Moravia as a province, Bohemia remained under the Pre-myslids until 1306, becoming a kingdom in 1198. At the height of its power, under Ottakar II, it also controlled the duchies of Austria. In the later Middle Ages Bohemia was ruled by a number of families, most notably the German Luxemburgs and the Polish Jagiellons, and played a central role in the turbulent politics of the empire and papacy. In the early 15th century the martyrdom of the Prague religious reformer John HUSS (1415) solidified the identification of religious reform with an emerging popular nationalism; the Hussite wars of 1420–33 marked the departure of Bohemia from the German orbit and its assumption of a more overtly Slavic identity. In 1526 the kingdom was inherited by the imperial HABSBURG dynasty, but in the 17th century it was once again at the centre of politico-religious upheaval within the empire, Protestantism and resurgent nationalism helping precipitate a revolt against imperial power which led to the THIRTY YEARS WAR (1618–48).

In 1848, a Slav Congress demanding greater autonomy assembled in Prague under the leadership of Palacký Austrian domination was forcibly restored in 1849, and Moravia was made into a separate crown land. Concessions made to the Czechs by Vienna after 1867 served only to disconcert the Germans living in Bohemia. Independence as part of the republic of CZECHOSLOVAKIA, incorporating Bohemia, Moravia, Slovakia, and Austrian Silesia, was achieved after the collapse of AUSTRIA-HUNGARY in 1918. In 1938, having earmarked Bohemia and Moravia for German colonization, Hitler invaded the SUDETENLAND and annexed the rest of the region in the following year. A lasting shift of population was effected by the expulsion by the Czechoslovak government of three million Germans, mainly from Bohemia and Moravia, after World War II. From 1948 until 1989 Czechoslovakia was under communist control. On the break-up of Czechoslovakia in 1993, Bohemia and Moravia together formed the Czech Republic.

Bohemond I (*c*.1056–1111) Norman Prince of Antioch, the eldest son of Robert Guiscard. He fought for Guiscard against the Byzantine emperor, Alexius COMNENUS; after his father's death he joined the First CRUSADE and played a prominent part in the capture of the Syrian city of Antioch. He established himself as prince in Antioch but was captured by the TURKS and imprisoned for two years. In 1107 he led an expedition against the BYZANTINE EMPIRE and was defeated by Alexius, making peace at the Treaty of Devol (1108).

Bohr, Niels Henrik David (1885–1962) Danish physicist who successfully applied the QUANTUM THEORY to Ernest RUTHERFORD's model of the atom to produce a model known as the Bohr atom, and was able to explain how atoms emit light. Using PLANCK's theory that energy exists only in 'packets' or quanta, he suggested that electrons orbit the nucleus of an atom at set distances or 'energy levels', changing level only when a quantum of energy is lost or gained, and emitting or absorbing radiation in the process. Many of his concepts are included in the theory of quantum mechanics. He was awarded the Nobel Prize for physics in 1922.

Boileau, Nicholas (born Nicholas Boileau-Despréaux) (1636–1711) French critic and poet. He gained wide recognition as the legislator and model for French neoclassicism with his didactic poem *Art poétique* (1674); based on Horace's *Ars Poetica*, it establishes canons of taste and defines principles of composition and criticism.

boiler A device for producing steam from water. The major use of large-scale boilers is to provide steam for electricity generation (see POWER-STATION). Large-scale boilers use a water-tube design developed in the USA: water is passed through small-diameter tubes, over which the hot furnace gases are passed. A very high rate of heat transfer is achieved. The major fuels for boilers are coal, oil, gas, and nuclear power. In large-scale water-tube boilers the fuel is usually pulverized or atomized and blown into the furnace in a current of air. Coal-fired FLUIDIZED-BED FURNACES use larger fragments.

Domestic water- and space-heating systems also use boilers, heated by natural gas or oil, to raise the temperature of water without raising steam.

boiling-point The temperature at which the VAPOUR PRESSURE of a liquid is equal to the pressure of its surroundings. Thus at high altitudes, where the air is thinner, boiling occurs with a lower vapour pressure and, therefore, at a lower temperature.

boiling-water reactor See PRESSURIZED-WATER REACTOR.

Bois de Boulogne A park in the centre of Paris, France, to the south of the Avenue Charles de Gaulle; area 865 hectares (2,137 acres). Once part of a royal hunting ground, it developed a reputation as the resort of duellists and robbers before being laid out in 1852 with lakes, avenues, and gardens.

Boise The capital and largest city of Idaho, USA, on the Boise River; pop. (1990) 125,738. Established as a gold-mining town in 1862, the area was originally named *Les Bois* (= the woods) by French fur trappers. Electronics, steel fabrication, and the construction of mobile homes are the chief industries.

Bokassa, Jean Bédel (1921–96) Central African Republic statesman and military leader, President 1972–76, emperor 1976–79. He led a successful coup in 1966, from which time he steadily increased his personal power, becoming President for life and later self-styled emperor of his country, which he renamed the Central African Empire. He was held responsible for many deaths and was ousted in 1979; in 1987 he was tried for his crimes and sentenced to death, but the sentence was eventually commuted.

bolas A throwing weapon from South America. It consists of two or more balls or stones connected together by strong cord, which are swung round the head before being thrown. Once thrown, the cord wraps itself around the legs of the quarry.

Boldrewood, Rolf (pseudonym of Thomas Alexander Browne) (1826–1915) Australian novelist. His most enduring work was *Robbery Under Arms* (first published as a serial in 1882–83), a narration of the life and crimes of a bushranger under sentence of death.

Boleyn, Anne (1507–36) Second wife of Henry VIII and mother of Elizabeth I. Although the king had fallen in love with Anne, and had divorced Catherine of Aragon in order to marry her (1533), she fell from favour when she failed to provide him with a male heir. She was eventually executed because of alleged infidelities.

Bolger, James B(rendan) (1935–) New Zealand statesman, Prime Minister 1990–97. He was leader of the National Party, which won elections in 1990 and 1993. He formed a coalition government after the elections of 1996 but resigned the following year.

Bolingbroke, Henry Henry IV of England. See HENRY (kings of England).

Bolingbroke, Henry St John, 1st Viscount (1678–1751) English politician. He entered Parliament as a Tory in 1701, became Secretary of State following the Tory triumph of 1710, and was responsible for negotiating the Peace of UTRECHT in 1713. Dismissed by George I in 1714, and impeached by the Whig Parliament of 1715, he fled to France, where he joined James Edward Stuart, but soon became disillusioned with the PRETENDER's cause. In 1723 he was pardoned by George I and allowed back into England.

Bolívar, Simón (known as 'the Liberator') (1783–1830) Venezuelan patriot and statesman. Bolívar was active in the Latin-American independence movement from 1808 onwards. Although his military career was not without its failures, he succeeded in driving the Spanish from Venezuela, Colombia, Peru, and Ecuador; Upper Peru was named Bolivia in his honour.

Bolivia A landlocked country of central South America. It is bounded by Brazil and Paraguay to the north and east, Argentina to the south, and Peru and Chile to the west.

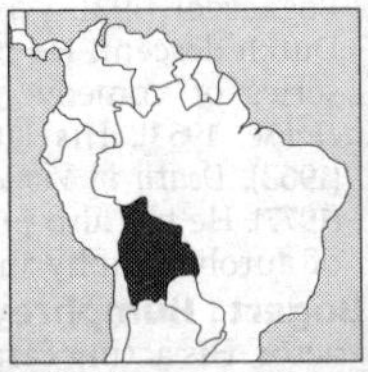

Physical. In the south-west is a great plateau, the Altiplano, some 800 km (500 miles) long and 3,660 m (12,000 feet) high, set between two even loftier ranges of the Andes. At its northern end is the southern shore of a huge mountain lake, Titicaca, while in the south there are vast salt pans. The north-east by contrast has low plains with hot, wet rain forest and several navigable rivers. Here and in the Gran Chaco to the east, the soil is fertile and suitable for sugar cane, rice, coffee, coca, and cotton. Southward the ground rises to plains which are covered with lighter woodland and grass.

Economy. The mountains of Bolivia offer large deposits of minerals: mining is the principal industry, and the country is developing its capacity to smelt mineral ore. Other industry includes chemicals, textiles, and food-processing. Natural gas accounts for 60 per cent of exports, while tin, of which Bolivia is one of the world's largest producers, provides another 30 per cent. Bolivia produces enough petroleum for internal consumption.

Agriculture is the mainstay of the economy despite periodic droughts and floods. Principal crops are sugar cane, potatoes, and maize. The coca plant, from the leaves of which the drug cocaine is produced, grows freely; it is smuggled to Colombia for processing. Bolivia's economy has suffered from protracted political instability, fluctuating commodity prices, a large external debt, high inflation, and lack of investment.

History. The area became an important Ayamará Indian state between 600 and 1000 AD but was conquered by the growing INCA state *c*.1200. Some Ayamará continued to resist, however, and were not completely subdued until the late 15th century. Spanish conquest followed six years after PIZARRO's landing in Peru in 1532, and in 1539 the capital at Charcas (modern Sucre) was founded. The discovery of silver deposits in the Potosí mountains in 1545 led to the establishment of the Audiencia (a high court with a political role) of Charcas, under the viceroyalty of Peru. Revolutionary movements against Spain occurred here earlier than anywhere else in South America – at La Paz in 1661, Cochabamba in 1730, and Charcas, Cochabamba, La Paz, and Oruro in 1776–80 – but all failed.

Independence was finally won under José de Sucre, at the battle of Ayacucho (1824). A National Assembly declared Upper Peru independent, and named it Bolivia after Simón BOLÍVAR. A short-lived Peru-Bolivian Confederation was formed (1825–39). Control of the Atacama coast region, where rich guano nitrate deposits were found, was challenged by Chile in 1842 and finally lost in 1884 in the disastrous War of the Pacific. A series of military dictatorships (1839–80) was succeeded by more liberal regimes, with Liberal and Republican Parties alternating. In 1930 a popular revolution elected a reforming President, Daniel Salamanca. In 1936, following the disastrous CHACO WAR, military rule returned. In 1952 the Bolivian National Revolution overthrew the dictatorship of the junta, and Paz Estenssoro, leader of the MNR (Movimento Nacionalista Revolucionario) Party returned from exile and was installed as President. Tin mines were nationalized, adult suffrage introduced, and a bold programme of social reforms begun. Paz was re-elected in 1960 but overthrown in 1964 by a military coup. In 1967 a communist revolutionary movement, led by Ché GUEVARA, was defeated. Military regimes followed each other quickly. Not all were right-wing, and that of General Juan José Torres (1970–71) sought to replace Congress by workers' soviets. Democratic elections were restored in 1978, when the first woman President, Lydia Guelier Tejada, briefly held office. There was another military coup in 1980 and a state of political tension continued until 1982, when civilian rule was restored. Paz Estenssoro resumed the presidency (1985–89) but faced extreme economic difficulties. His successor Jaime Paz Zamora, President from 1989 to 1993, initiated a campaign against the drug traffic. In 1993 Gonzalo Sánchez de Lozada was elected President. He continued the campaign against illegal drugs and pursued policies of free-market reforms, despite widespread civil unrest. Disputes with Chile over the issue of access to the Pacific Coast have continued.

Capital: La Paz (administrative); Sucre (judicial)
Area: 1,098,581 sq km (424,164 sq mi)
Population: 6,420,800 (1992)
Currency: 1 boliviano = 100 centavos
Religions: Roman Catholic 92.5%; Baha'i 2.6%
Ethnic Groups: Mestizo 31.0%; Quechua 25.0%; Aymara 17.0%; White (mainly Spanish extraction) 15.0%
Languages: Spanish, Aymara, Quechua (all official)
International Organizations: UN; OAS; Andean Group

Böll, Heinrich (Theodor) (1917–85) German novelist and short-story writer. His years in the German army (1938–44) provided the material for his earliest work, including the novel *Adam, Where Art Thou?* (1951). His later work concerns aspects of postwar German society and is frequently critical of the prevailing political and business ethos. He was awarded the Nobel Prize for literature in 1972.

Bologna An historic city in north Italy, capital of Emilia-Romagna; pop. (1990) 411,800. Its university, which dates from the 11th century, is one of the oldest in Europe. Engineering, electrical equipment, and food-processing are the main industries.

bolometer An electrical instrument for measuring radiant heat energy. In one form, the heat is directed at a blackened platinum strip, which forms one arm of a WHEATSTONE bridge circuit. The change in the strip's resistance (compared with a similar unheated strip) is a measure of the amount of heat falling on it.

Bolshevik (Russian, 'a member of the majority') The wing of the Social Democratic Party in Russia which, from 1903, and under the leadership of LENIN, favoured revolutionary tactics. Their opponents, the Mensheviks ('members of the minority'), led by Martov and Georgi Plekhanov, favoured a loosely organized mass labour party, in which workers had more influence, and which was prepared to collaborate with the liberal bourgeoisie against the Tsarist autocracy. After the abortive RUSSIAN REVOLUTION of 1905 Bolshevik leaders fled abroad, having made little appeal to the peasantry, and it was the Mensheviks led by KERENSKY who joined the Provisional Government, following the February RUSSIAN REVOLUTION in 1917. The infiltration by Bolsheviks into soviets and factory committees contributed to the success of the October Revolution. During the RUSSIAN CIVIL WAR the Bolsheviks succeeded in seizing control of the country from other revolutionary groups. In 1918 they changed their name to the Russian Communist Party. The Mensheviks were formally suppressed in 1922.

Bolshoi Ballet Company One of the two major Russian ballet companies, based at the Bolshoi Theatre in Moscow. Ballets were staged at the theatre from 1776, but the present company developed after the Revolution (1917). Until the late 1940s it was secondary to the KIROV BALLET, but the dancer Galina Ulanova and choreographer Leonid Lavrovsky were seconded there and the Bolshoi school started producing its own great dancers. When it appeared in the West in 1956 its acrobatic, dramatic style caused a sensation. Yuri Grigorovich became director in 1976, bringing ballets like *Spartacus* (1956) into the Bolshoi's repertoire.

Bolt, Robert (Oxton) (1924–95) British dramatist and screenwriter. He taught in Somerset 1950–58 before devoting himself to writing after the success of his first play, *Flowering Cherry* (1958). His other plays include his acclaimed *A Man for All Seasons* (1960), which was filmed in 1967. His screenplay for this won an Oscar, as did that for *Dr Zhivago* (1965). He also wrote screenplays for *Lawrence of Arabia* (1962) and *The Mission* (1986).

Bolton A town in Greater Manchester, England, north-west of Manchester; pop. (1991) 253,300. Formerly a major centre of wool and cotton production, engineering, and the manufacture of chemicals, textiles, and paper are now the chief industries.

Boltzmann, Ludwig Eduard (1844–1906) Austrian physicist who made a fundamental contribution to THERMODYNAMICS and the KINETIC THEORY of gases. He applied a statistical approach to give the MAXWELL–BOLTZMANN DISTRIBUTION for a large number of particles among the different energy states accessible to them. The Boltzmann constant ($k = 1.381 \times 10^{-23}$ joule/kelvin) is a universal constant equal to the ratio of the GAS CONSTANT to the Avogadro number.

Boltzmann distribution See MAXWELL–BOLTZMANN DISTRIBUTION.

Bolzano (German **Bozen**) ▶**1** An autonomous, largely German-speaking province in the Trentino-Alto Adige region of north Italy; area 7,400 sq km (2,858 sq miles); pop. (1990) 441,670. The province includes the Dolomite and Ortler ranges. ▶**2** Its capital, on the River Isarco south of the Brenner Pass; pop. (1990) 100,380. It is a cultural centre with numerous museums, libraries, and institutions.

Bombay (official name **Mumbai**) A city and port on the west coast of India, the country's second-largest city and a commercial centre long noted for its textile industry; pop. (1991) 9,990,000. It is capital of the state of Maharashtra. Ceded to Portugal by the Sultan of Gujarat, Bombay was given in 1661 as a wedding gift to King Charles I who married the daughter of the Portuguese king. It was the headquarters of the British East India Company from 1685 to 1708 and developed as the 'Gateway to India' after the opening of the Suez Canal in 1869. Its principal public buildings are built in Victorian styles, and Bombay is considered to be the most 'westernized' of Indian cities. It is also a major cultural, financial, and industrial centre with oilrefining, chemical, textile, and vehicle industries plus all kinds of consumer goods. Tourism is also important. It has two universities and is the centre of the considerable Hindi film industry.

Bombay duck (or **bummalo**) A marine and brackish water BONY FISH of the family Harpadontidae. It has a torpedo-shaped body and a compressed head with small eyes and a large mouth. There are five species widespread in the Indian Ocean, some of which, such as *Harpadon nehereus*, are of commercial value. Bombay ducks belong to the same order as lanternfish, the Myctophiformes.

bomber A MILITARY AIRCRAFT primarily designed and equipped to carry bombs against enemy targets. Bombs are usually carried in an internal bomb bay and released through a bomb door, but they can also be carried on special external wing racks. An early light bomber of World War I was the De Havilland DH9A, which could carry a 200-kg (450-pound) load under its wings. By World War II bombers were carrying much greater loads; Lancaster bombers could carry a 10,000-kg (22,000-pound) load of bombs by the end of the War. Dive-bombers were designed to drop their bomb loads at the bottom of a steep dive in order to obtain pin-point accuracy. Land- and submarine-based intercontinental BALLISTIC MISSILES have lessened the importance of long-range strategic bombers, although both the USA and the Soviet Union continued to develop such aircraft.

bombing offensives (in World War II) Attacks by bomber aircraft on military and civilian targets. As part of his BLITZKRIEG tactics, Hitler deployed dive-bombers in the offensives in Poland (1939) and western Europe (1940). In August 1940 the first major German offensive was launched against Britain, a series of daylight attacks by bombers, many of which were destroyed by fighter aircraft of the Royal Air Force in the Battle of BRITAIN. A German night-bombing offensive on civilian targets then began which lasted until May 1941. The Allied air offensive against Germany and the occupied countries grew in intensity throughout the war. The development of radar to intercept aircraft and direct gunfire revolutionized the Allied bombing offensive. Increasing resources were made available to the British Bomber Command under Air Marshal Sir Arthur Harris, and daylight raids by the US Air Force, combined with British night-bombing, endeavoured to obliterate key German cities. Meanwhile the bulk of German bombing power was turned to the Eastern Front, where fighter-bombers supported the army, attacking besieged cities, such as Leningrad and Stalingrad. Pilotless flying bombs (V1s) and rocket missiles (V2s), launched against southern England during 1944 and 1945, did relatively little damage. In the Far East a massive bomber offensive was launched by US forces against Japanese cities in October 1944. On 6 and 9 August 1945 respectively, US aircraft dropped the world's first atomic bombs on the Japanese cities of HIROSHIMA and NAGASAKI, bringing the war against Japan to a close.

Bonaparte (Italian **Buonaparte**) See NAPOLEON.

Bonaventura, St (born Giovanni di Fidanza; known as 'the Seraphic Doctor') (1221–74) Franciscan theologian. Appointed minister general of his order in 1257, he was made cardinal bishop of Albano in 1273. He wrote the official biography of St Francis and had a lasting influence as a spiritual writer. Feast day, 15 (formerly 14) July.

bond (in finance) A SECURITY giving a fixed-interest return issued by firms or governments wishing to borrow long-term funds. In the USA DEBENTURES are also known as bonds. Most bonds are redeemable: at a date stated on the bond the cash amount specified on the bond will be paid by the issuer to the holder of the bond. Some bonds are irredeemable and the only return on them will be the nominal (or coupon) interest paid. Both redeemable and irredeemable bonds can be traded on the STOCK EXCHANGE.

bond (in chemistry) See CHEMICAL BOND.

Bond, Edward (1934–) British dramatist. His first play, *The Pope's Wedding* (1962), was followed by *Saved* (1965). Notable works include *Narrow Road to the Deep North* (1968), *Restoration* (1981), and *September* (1990).

bone Tissue that forms the vertebrate ENDOSKELETON, giving it structural strength, while acting as an attachment point for muscle tendons, and providing storage places for mineral salts. Bones are made of a relatively soft, flexible material called collagen, reinforced by calcium carbonate and phosphates. The hard outer shell is called compact bone, whereas the interior is made up of a network of bony plates, called spongy bone. Cavities help to lighten bones (in birds, bones have particularly large cavities, which are supported by struts), and provide a sight for the storage of **bone marrow**.

In adult mammals, bones are 80 per cent calcium salts, which are deposited in the collagen matrix secreted by cells called osteoblasts. These eventually become embedded in the bone as osteocytes (bone cells). Bones are living structures, and as they grow, they are constantly being changed in shape and form. This occurs by the interaction of osteoblasts, which build them up, with osteoclasts, which eat them away. The myeloid tissue of marrow in some bones, such as the femur and sternum, produces ERYTHROCYTES (red blood cells). The non-functional marrow of other bones consists of fat, the level of which is an indicator of body condition.

bone carving The art of carving or incising various types of animal bone. Bone can be used for some of the same kinds of work as ivory, but allows little more than surface treatment because of its large soft core. It is associated mainly with prehistoric and primitive peoples, but there are some fine examples of Anglo-Saxon carving in whalebone, and Japanese NETSUKE are often carved in bone.

bone china A type of PORCELAIN made with the addition of bone ash (the powdery remains of burnt bones) to the clay. The ash gives bone china a pure white colour that is considered desirable in porcelain and it became popular within a short period of the technique being devised. The first patent was taken out in 1748 by Thomas Frye, co-founder of the Bow porcelain factory, and the process was used at the French Sèvres factory shortly afterwards. It was perfected in about 1800 by Josiah Spode II, son of the founder of one of the most famous Staffordshire pottery works.

bone marrow See BONE.

bongos A pair of small drums played with the fingers and used predominantly in Latin American music. Cylindrical in shape and with a single head or skin (nowadays often of plastic), they are fixed together and usually held between the knees, or sometimes fixed to a stand.

Bonhoeffer, Dietrich (1906–45) German Lutheran theologian. An active opponent of Nazism, he signed (1934) the Barmen Declaration in protest against attempts by German Christians to synthesize Nazism with Christianity. He was forbidden by the government to teach, and in 1937 his seminary at Finkenwalde was closed. In 1942 he tried to form a link between the Germans opposed to Hitler and the British government. Arrested in 1943, he was sent to Buchenwald concentration camp, where he was hanged in 1945.

Boniface, St (born Wynfrith; known as 'the Apostle of Germany') (680–754) Anglo-Saxon missionary. Sent to Frisia and Germany to spread the Christian faith, he laid the foundations of a settled ecclesiastical organization there and made many converts. He was appointed Primate of Germany in 732, and in 741 was given authority to reform the whole Frankish Church. He was martyred in Frisia. Feast day, 5 June.

Boniface VIII (1235–1303) Pope 1294–1303. He was a papal diplomat and lawyer who travelled widely. He succeeded Pope Celestine V. He quarrelled disastrously with Philip IV of France when he asserted papal authority to challenge Philip's right to tax the clergy. In response Philip had him siezed in 1303. The shock hastened the pope's death and contributed towards the transfer of the papacy from Italy to Avignon in France.

Bonington, Sir Chris(tian) John Storey (1934–) British mountaineer and author. He finally reached the summit of Everest in 1985, having previously led the 1970 Annapurna I expedition and made the first British ascent of the north face of the Eiger in 1962.

Bonington, Richard Parkes (1802–28) British painter, active mainly in France, where his family moved when he was 15. Although he died young of tuberculosis, his work (mainly landscapes) was highly regarded and influential in France.

bonito A small member of the TUNA or mackerel family, Scombridae. In the eastern Atlantic the name is used for both the skipjack tuna, *Katsuwonus pelamis*, and Atlantic bonito, *Sarda sarda*. The Atlantic bonito ranges across the Atlantic from Scandinavia to Nova Scotia and South Africa to Brazil, and is an open-sea predator which swims in small schools, feeding on fishes and squids near the surface. It is relatively slender in appearance, with a pointed head, and a steel-blue back with numerous oblique, black lines across it. It grows to 90 cm (3 feet) in length.

Bonn A city in North Rhine-Westphalia, western Germany; pop. (1991) 296,240. Founded by the Romans in the 1st century AD, it later became the seat of the electors of Cologne (1238–1794) whose Baroque-style palace is now one of the main buildings of a university founded in 1786. From 1949 until the reunification of Germany in 1990 Bonn was the capital of the Federal Republic of Germany.

Bonnard, Pierre (1867–1947) French painter and graphic artist. A member of a group of painters called the Nabi Group, he produced ornamental screens and lithographs before concentrating on painting from about 1905. His works continue and develop the impressionist tradition.

Bonnet, Charles (1720–93) Swiss naturalist who made many contributions to entomology and botany, despite being virtually blind and deaf from an early age. He was one of the first to study PHOTOSYNTHESIS, and he discovered parthenogenesis (reproduction without fertilization).

Bonneville Flats The salt flats surrounding the Great Salt Lake in Utah, USA, scene of several attempts to break the world land-speed record.

Bonney, William H. See BILLY THE KID.

Bonnie Prince Charlie See STUART, CHARLES EDWARD.

bony fish A member of the largest class of fishes, Osteichthyes, which includes more than 34,000 species of marine and freshwater forms. They have a bone-based internal skeleton, in contrast to the CARTILAGINOUS FISHES and JAWLESS FISHES. They are subdivided into two main groups: the ray-finned fishes (actinopterygians) and the lobe-finned fishes (sarcopterygians). Lobe-finned fishes are represented today by the LUNGFISHES and the COELACANTH. The largest group by far are the ray-finned fishes, of which the vast majority are teleosts.

booby A large seabird of the family Sulidae, which has a sharp, conical bill, and plunges into the sea to catch squid and small fish at the ocean surface. Boobies are tropical equivalents of the GANNET and belong to the genus *Sula*, which contains six species. Three species are wide-ranging, two (the white booby, *S. dactylatra*, and the red-footed booby, *S. sula*) occurring in all tropical oceans. The remaining three species have restricted ranges over parts of South America.

bookbinding The process of making a book by joining together written or printed sheets inside a cover that identifies and protects them. Leaves of manuscript were bound inside covers well before the advent of printing in the 15th century. Binding single leaves was achieved originally by side-sewing, but such books could not open flat. Later, pages were produced in pairs on each side of a sheet that folded to form a four-page folio. Inserting folios one into another made a section that could be sewn together by looping threads through the spine. Several sections could then be joined by passing threads from one section to the next. This method of sewing produced a more flexible book-block (the book prior to adding a cover). Sewing of sections (saddle-stitching) is now mechanized, and is complemented by cutting, folding, and gathering machines, which convert printed sheets into sections (usually of sixteen or thirty-two pages) and collate them into order. However, unsewn methods of binding can now continuously convert bundles of loose sections directly into book-blocks, usually by cutting off the folded spines and gluing the cut edges together with plasticized adhesive (perfect binding). Most cheaper editions are produced this way. Book covers were originally two pieces of leather-covered wood attached by thongs round the spine. Following the introduction of printing to Europe (*c.*1450), many more book covers were required. While individual leather-bound covers were still produced, many covers (cases) were made from substitute materials. Today cases are made from heavy card-board covered with cloth or paper. Case-making runs parallel with book-block manufacture, as does the printing of paperback covers. Combining book-blocks and covers is now done automatically on lines of casing-in or bookbinding machines. Modern adhesives have helped speed up production times from a few hundred per hour to between 1,500 and 6,000 per hour for hard-cased books, and 2,500 to 10,000 or more per hour for paperbacks.

book illustration The art of adorning printed books with pictures and decorative motifs. The earliest printed books were modelled closely on illuminated manuscripts, with spaces left blank for illustrations to be added by hand, but by the end of the 15th century woodcut illustrations – particularly in Italy – had attained a high level of mastery. Copper ENGRAVING, though it required a separate printing process, allowed greater detail, and it became the standard method of book illustration from about the mid-16th century to the end of the 18th century. Colour printing first became common in the 18th century. In the 1790s Thomas BEWICK popularized wood engraving, which became the most common method until it was superseded by various photo-mechanical processes at the end of the 19th century, although LITHOGRAPHY and AQUATINT were used for more expensive publications. In recent years the growth of computer graphics has added a new dimension to the illustration of books. In many modern books the illustrations are scanned and held in digitized form on computer disk or tape, which enables them to be merged with text, captions, and annotations when the pages are typeset by, for example, a desk-top page-make-up program.

bookkeeping The recording of all financial transactions in an organization, usually recorded as 'debits' or 'credits' depending on whether they represent outflows or inflows of money. Double-entry bookkeeping uses the principle of balance so that, for example, every sale results in an inflow of money and an outflow of product. In this way the accuracy of the records is easily checked. Most bookkeeping is now handled by computer.

book louse A minute, wingless, pale yellow insect, around 1 mm (0.04 inch) in length, found in house dust and often in old books. Book lice comprise over 2,000 species in the order Psocoptera, and feed by scraping the surface of their foodstuff, causing much damage if they are numerous. They occur on tree trunks and fungi, under bark, and in other places where fragments of vegetable matter collect. Some species have winged females or, more rarely, males, which can swarm under certain conditions.

Boole, George (1815–64) British mathematician. Professor at Cork in Ireland from 1849, Boole wrote important works on differential equations and other branches of mathematics, but is remembered chiefly for the algebraic description of reasoning now known as Boolean algebra. The study of mathematical or symbolic logic developed mainly from his ideas.

boomerang A flat, curved wooden projectile that spins in flight, used for hunting and warfare. It is commonly associated with the Australian Aborigines, but boomerang-type weapons have also long been used by peoples of North America, India, and Africa. War boomerangs have sharp edges and are slightly convex on one side, and can be designed to swerve to the left or right.

Boone, Daniel (*c.*1734–1820) US pioneer. Moving west from his native Pennsylvania, Boone made trips into the unexplored area of Kentucky from 1767 onwards, organizing settlements and successfully defending them against hostile Indians. He later moved further west to Missouri, being granted land there in 1799. As a hunter, trail-blazer, and fighter against the Indians he became a legend in his own lifetime.

Boötes The Herdsman, a CONSTELLATION of the Northern Hemisphere, one of the 48 constellations known to the Greeks. In mythology it represents Arcas, son of the god Zeus and the nymph Callisto. Boötes is often depicted as a man driving the great bear around the pole. The constellation's brightest star is the red giant ARCTURUS. A celebrated double star is Epsilon Boötis, also known as Izar or Pulcherrima, consisting of a close pair of orange and blue stars of third and fifth magnitude that make a beautiful colour contrast in telescopes.

booth A portable theatre that during the Middle Ages provided travelling companies with an adequate stage, supplanting the adapted inn-yards, barns, or makeshift rooms, which were at first the only places available for theatrical productions. Booths consisted originally of tents housing a small stage on which were presented short sketches interspersed with juggling and rope dancing. Portable buildings, easily dismantled and re-erected, later made their appearance, becoming more elaborate as time went on. Some of the more successful showmen contrived to build up a front of gaudily painted canvas flats, sometimes with a platform outside on which the performers could appear to tempt the audience in. The booths lasted longest for the accommodation of puppet shows, and the portable stage of the Punch and Judy show is a vestigial remnant of this.

Booth, Charles (1840–1916) British social researcher. As the author of *Life and Labour of the People in London* (1891–1903) he presented an exhaustive study of poverty in London, showing its extent, causes, and location. Aided by Beatrice WEBB, his methods, based on observation and on searches into public records, pioneered an approach to social studies which has been influential ever since. His special interest in the problems of old age accelerated the Old Age Pensions Act (1908).

Booth, John Wilkes (1838–65) US assassin of President LINCOLN. Brother of the tragic actor Edwin Booth, and sympathizer with the CONFEDERACY, he participated during the closing stages of the

AMERICAN CIVIL WAR in a small conspiracy to overthrow the victorious Lincoln government. On 14 April 1865 he mortally wounded Lincoln in Ford's Theatre in Washington and escaped to Virginia, but was discovered and killed on 26 April. Four of his fellow conspirators were hanged.

Booth, William (1829–1912) British religious leader and founder of the SALVATION ARMY (1878). Originally a Methodist preacher, Booth, assisted by his wife, Catherine, preached in the streets, and made singing, uniforms, and bands a part of his evangelical mission. He used his organizational gifts to inspire similar missions in other parts of the world.

bootlace worm See RIBBON WORM.

bootstrap The sequence of start-up instructions executed by a COMPUTER when it is initially switched on. It may include loading all the relevant systems programs into computer memory (called 'booting' the computer), or simply loading a program to make sure that all the parts of the CENTRAL PROCESSING UNIT are put into a specific state (initialized), ready for the main OPERATING SYSTEM and other programs to function correctly.

Bophuthatswana A former independent homeland of the Tswana people of South Africa, created in 1977 and comprising seven separate territories, now part of North-West Province and Mpumalanga. Its capital was Mmabatho. The territory is one of the world's major producers of platinum as well as an important source of minerals such as chrome, copper, asbestos, coal, diamonds, nickel, and gold.

bora A strong cold dry north-easterly wind blowing in the upper Adriatic, particularly during winter and spring.

borage See FORGET-ME-NOT.

borax (or **sodium borate**, $Na_2B_4O_7.10H_2O$) A white crystalline solid, the chief mineral source of BORON and boric acid. In its natural state it is usually massive, white, greasy to the touch, soft, and very light; and it has a sweet taste. It occurs in evaporites found in salt-pans, and is particularly abundant in those of Death Valley, California, USA. Since the Middle Ages, borax has been used as a flux to remove oxides from metal surfaces in soldering and brazing. Modern uses include the manufacture of specialist borosilicate glass and enamel, and in the sizing of paper. It is also used medicinally as a mild antiseptic and astringent.

bord-and-pillar mining A MINING technique in which chambers of ore are excavated, leaving pillars of material in place to support the roof. This method of excavation, known as partial extraction, is favoured when mining beneath surface buildings or under seas and lakes. The pillars are left in position to minimize movement of the ground at the surface. If conditions permit, the pillars are later excavated working back towards the mine entrance, causing the roof to collapse.

Bordeaux An inland port on the River Garonne in south-west France; pop. (1990) 213,270. It is capital of the department of Gironde and a major commercial centre for the Aquitaine region. Oil-refining, shipbuilding, and the manufacture of chemicals and aeronautical equipment are the chief industries of the city. The surrounding area is noted for its wines, notably those in the regions of Médoc, St Emilion, Pomerol, Graves, Barsac, Sauternes, and Entre-Deux-Mers. Bordeaux was held by the English for three centuries before falling to the French in 1453. It has a Gothic cathedral dating from the 11th century, a university founded in 1441, and several medieval churches.

Borden, Sir Robert Laird (1854–1937) Canadian statesman. He was chosen as leader of the Conservative Party in 1901. In the general election of 1911 he defeated the Liberals and succeeded LAURIER as Prime Minister of Canada. Knighted in 1914, he remained in office throughout World War I, leading a coalition government after 1917 and joining the imperial war cabinet. He retired from political life in 1920.

Borders A former local government region in southern Scotland created in 1975 from the counties of Berwick, Roxburgh, Peebles, Selkirk, and part of Midlothian. In 1996 it became a unitary authority and was renamed **Scottish Borders**.

Bordet, Jules (1870–1961) Belgian bacteriologist and immunologist. He discovered the heat-sensitive complement system found in blood serum, and demonstrated its role in antibody–antigen reactions and bacterial lysis. He also isolated a number of pathogenic bacteria, and developed a vaccine for whooping cough. Bordet was awarded a Nobel Prize in 1919.

boreal Describing cold northern regions, derived from the name of the Greek god of the wind, *Boreas*. The northern coniferous forest of Eurasia and North America is known as the boreal forest.

Borg, Björn (1956–) Swedish tennis player. His first major titles were the Italian and French championships (1974); he then went on to win five consecutive men's singles titles at Wimbledon (1976–80), beating the record of three consecutive wins held by Fred Perry. He retired in 1983, returned in 1991, and retired again in 1993.

Borges, Jorge Luis (1899–1986) Argentinian poet, short-story writer, and essayist. His first three collections of poetry (1923–29) explore the themes of time and identity that are later treated in his fiction. His first volume of short stories, *A Universal History of Infamy* (1935, revised 1954), recounting the lives of real and fictitious criminals and exploring the relationships between fiction, truth, and identity, is regarded as a founding work of magic realism. His fiction also includes *The Aleph and Other Stories* (1949). *Labyrinths* (1962) is an anthology of some of his best-known works.

Borgia, Cesare (*c.*1476–1507) Italian statesman. The illegitimate son of Cardinal Rodrigo Borgia (later Pope Alexander VI) and brother of Lucrezia BORGIA, he became a cardinal in 1493. He succeeded his brother Juan, possibly through murder, as captain-general of the papal army in 1499. Through two campaigns he became master of a large portion of central Italy, but after the death of his father (1502) his enemies rallied and he was defeated at Naples in 1504.

Borgia, Lucrezia (1480–1519) Italian noblewoman. The illegitimate daughter of Cardinal Rodrigo Borgia (later Pope Alexander VI), she married three times, according to the political alliances useful to her father and to her brother, Cesare BORGIA. Always associated with the scandals of her birth and marriages, after her third marriage in 1501 she established herself as a patron of the arts and became increasingly religious.

Boris Godunov (*c.*1551–1605) Tsar of Russia 1598–1605. He began his career of court service under IVAN the Terrible, became virtual ruler of Muscovy during the reign of his imbecile son Fyodor (1584–98), and engineered his own elevation to the Tsardom. He conducted a successful war against Sweden (1590–95), promoted foreign trade, and dealt ruthlessly with those BOYAR families which opposed him. In 1604 boyar animosity combined with popular dissatisfaction ushered in the 'Time of Troubles' – a confused eight-year dynastic and political crisis, Boris having died suddenly in 1605.

Bormann, Martin (1900–*c.*1945) German politician. Bormann was appointed to Hitler's personal staff in 1928 and succeeded Hess as Party chancellor in 1941. Bormann was considered to be Hitler's closest collaborator, but remained the most obscure of the top Nazis and disappeared at the end of World War II. He was sentenced to death *in absentia* at the Nuremberg trials in 1945 and was formally pronounced dead in 1973 after identification of a skeleton exhumed in Berlin.

Born, Max (1882–1970) German physicist who was instrumental in extending the QUANTUM THEORY to take account of the results of wave mechanics. In particular he introduced the concept of probability to describe the position of an electron in an ORBITAL to replace the fixed orbits of the BOHR model of the atom. He also undertook extensive research into the properties of crystals. In 1933 he was forced to leave Germany and settled in Britain until 1953, when he returned to his homeland. He was awarded the Nobel Prize for physics in 1954.

Borneo A large densely forested and mountainous island of the Malay archipelago, comprising Kalimantan (a region of Indonesia), Sabah and Sarawak (now parts of Malaysia), and Brunei. It is the second-largest non-continental island in the world; area 751,100 sq km (290,000 sq miles).

Bornholm A detached Danish island in the Baltic Sea, south-east of Sweden; 588 sq km (227 sq miles); pop. (1990) 46,100; chief town and ferry port, Rønne. Fishing, agriculture, handicrafts, and tourism are the chief occupations.

Borno (or **Bornu**) A state in northeast Nigeria; pop. (1991) 2,596,600; capital, Maiduguri. From the 9th to the 19th century the much larger kingdom of Borno extended to the west and south of Lake Chad in parts of present day Niger, Nigeria, and Cameroon. Converted to Islam in the 11th century, the Borno empire reached the peak of its power in the 15th–18th centuries before being absorbed into British, French, and German colonies.

Bornu See KANEM-BORNU.

Borobudur A Buddhist monument in central Java, built *c.*800, abandoned *c.*1000, and restored in 1907–11 and again in the 1980s. Designed for the purpose of worship, veneration, and meditation, it consists of five square successively smaller terraces, one above the other, surmounted by three concentric galleries with open stupas culminating in a supreme closed stupa. It is the largest religious monument in south-east Asia.

Borodin, Aleksandr (Porfirevich) (1833–87) Russian composer. He began to compose music at the age of nine, but trained as a chemist before undertaking formal musical studies in 1862. A member of the group known as 'The Five' or 'The Mighty Handful' (the others were Mily (Alekseevich) Balakirev (1837–1910), César (Antonovich) Cui (1835–1918), MUSSORGSKY, and RIMSKY-KORSAKOV), he composed symphonies, string quartets, songs, and piano music, but is best known for the epic opera *Prince Igor* (completed after his death by Rimsky-Korsakov and GLAZUNOV).

Borodino, Battle of (7 September 1812) A battle fought between Russia and France, about 110 km (70 miles) west of Moscow. Here KUTUZOV chose to take his stand against NAPOLEON's army. The Russian position was centred upon a well-fortified hill. After twelve hours of fierce combat, a terrific artillery bombardment and a decisive cavalry charge split the Russian forces. They were forced to withdraw and Napoleon, claiming victory, marched on an undefended Moscow. Over 80,000 men were lost in the most bloody battle of the NAPOLEONIC WARS.

boron (symbol B, at. no. 5, r.a.m. 10.81) A yellow-brown, non-metallic element of Group 3 (formerly IIIB) of the PERIODIC TABLE. It occurs as the ore orthoboric acid $B(OH)_3$ and as borates such as BORAX. Pure boron is produced from the oxide B_2O_3 by reaction with magnesium followed by chlorination and reduction with hydrogen. Crystalline boron is transparent, brittle, a non-conductor, and nearly as hard as diamond. Treating the surface of STEEL with boron makes it very hard. The boron-10 isotope is used in the control rods of nuclear reactors because it is a strong neutron absorber. Chemically, boron does not resemble the other Group 3 elements closely; it reacts with the halogens, concentrated acids, and oxygen, forming covalent compounds. Its most important compounds are the borates, which are derived from boric oxide (B_2O_3); they are used in glasses, enamels, and glazes. Sodium borohydride ($NaBH_4$) is an important reducing agent in organic chemistry.

borough A town in England, enjoying particular privileges. The boroughs evolved from the Anglo-Saxon *burhs* and from the 12th century benefited from royal and noble grants of charters. Their representatives attended Parliament regularly from the 14th century, having first been summoned in 1265 when Simon de MONTFORT called two representatives from each city and borough. The Scottish equivalent of the English borough was the BURGH.

Borromini, Francesco (1599–1667) Italian architect. He worked in Rome for most of his life, first as a mason at St Peter's and subsequently on the Palazzo Barberini (1620–31) as the chief assistant to his rival BERNINI. Borromini's own buildings include the churches of San Carlo alle Quattro Fontane (1641) and San Ivo della Sapienza (1643–60).

Borrow, George (Henry) (1803–81) British writer. His travels in England, Europe, Russia, and the Far East, sometimes in the company of gypsies, provided material for his picaresque narrative *Lavengro* (1851) and its sequel *The Romany Rye* (1857). In these books he combines fiction with a factual account of his travels. He also wrote *Wild Wales* (1862).

Boscawen, Edward (1711–61) British admiral, known as 'Old Dreadnought'. He served in the West Indies during the War of JENKINS'S EAR and the War of the AUSTRIAN SUCCESSION, and was in charge of naval operations at the siege of Louisburg, Nova Scotia, in 1758, where his success opened the way for the conquest of Canada. His most famous exploit was the destruction of the French Mediterranean fleet off the Portuguese coast at Lagos in 1759, which helped to establish British naval supremacy in the SEVEN YEARS WAR.

Bosch, Carl (1874–1940) German industrial chemist who transformed HABER's ammonia synthesis into a workable large-scale process (see HABER–BOSCH PROCESS). After reading chemistry at Leipzig, Bosch joined the Badische Anilinund Soda-Fabrik (BASF) in 1899. In 1908 Haber told BASF about his ammonia synthesis, and Bosch was made responsible for its industrial development. After World War I Bosch cooperated with BERGIUS in making petroleum from coal, and in 1931 shared the Nobel Prize for Chemistry with him.

Bosch, Hieronymus (*c*.1450–1516) Dutch painter. His highly detailed works are typically crowded with creatures of fantasy, half-human half-animal, and grotesque demons, and are interspersed with human figures in non-realistic settings that are often representations of sin and folly. His style is distinctly unlike that of mainstream Dutch painting of the period, and the elements of the grotesque and fantasy in his work prefigure the style of the surrealists.

Bosch, Juan (1909–) Dominican statesman. He founded the leftist Partido Revolucionario Dominicano (PRD) in 1939, and was exiled during the dictatorship of Rafael TRUJILLO. After the latter's assassination he returned (1961) to the Dominican Republic and was elected President (1962–63) in the first free elections for nearly forty years. He introduced sweeping liberal and democratic reforms, but after nine months in office was overthrown by rightist military leaders with the backing of the Church, of landowners, and of industrialists. His supporters launched their revolt in 1965, a movement which prompted a military intervention by the USA. In 1966 he was defeated for the presidency by Joaquin Balaguer, who had heavy US backing.

Bose, Sir Jagdis Chandra (1858–1937) Indian physicist and plant physiologist. He investigated the properties of very short radio waves, wireless telegraphy, and radiation-induced fatigue in inorganic materials. His physiological work involved comparative measurements of the responses of plants exposed to stress.

Bose, Satyendra Nath (1894–1974) Indian physicist. He contributed to statistical mechanics, quantum statistics, and unified field theory, and derived Planck's black-body radiation law without reference to classical electrodynamics. With Einstein, he described fundamental particles that later came to be known as BOSONS. The statistical mechanics that these particles obey is called **Bose-Einstein statistics**. Bose also worked on X-ray crystallography and the electromagnetic properties of the ionosphere.

Bose, Subhas Chandra (1897–1945) Indian nationalist politician. With Jawaharlal NEHRU he founded the Indian Independence League in 1928. He became President of the Indian National CONGRESS Party (1938–39) but quarrelled with other leaders. He escaped from virtual house arrest (1941), went to Germany but failed to secure Nazi support and in 1943 went to Japan and Singapore. There he assumed command of the Indian National Army, recruited from Indian prisoners-of-war, and formed a provisional Indian government.

Bosnia-Hercegovina A country in south-east Europe, in the Balkan Peninsula. It is bordered by Croatia to the north and west, Serbia to the east, and Montenegro to the south-east.

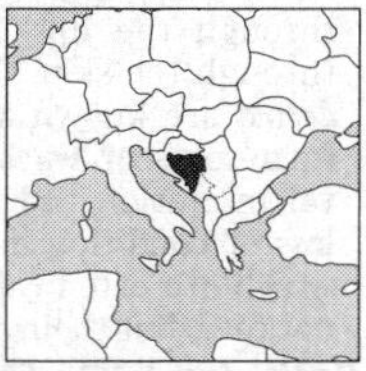

Physical. The country is mostly mountainous and wooded. It has a short Adriatic coastline.

Economy. The poorest of the former Yugoslav republics, Bosnia-Hercegovina has suffered severe economic disruption from the civil war of 1992 to 1995. It has a variety of mineral resources, including coal, iron, copper, chrome, manganese, cinnabar, zinc, and mercury. Livestock and sheep are raised, and the principal crops are cereals, fruits, citrus, and tobacco. Industry comprises mining, steelworks, and oil refineries. Many Bosnians are migrant workers in Western Europe.

History. First inhabited by the Illyrians, the region became part of the Roman province of Illyricum. SLAVS settled in the 7th century and, in 1137, it came under Hungarian rule. The Ottomans invaded in 1386 and after much resistance made it a province in 1463. They governed through Bosnian nobles, many of whom became Muslim, though much of the population became rebellious as Ottoman power declined. During the early 18th century Austrian forces began to push the Turks back. The rise of Pan-Slavonic nationalism provoked revolts in 1821, 1831, and 1837. A revolt in 1875 brought Austrian occupation, which was consolidated by formal annexation into AUSTRIA-HUNGARY in 1908. This provoked protest from Serbia and Russia. An international crisis only subsided when Germany threatened to intervene. Serbs continued to protest and to indulge in terrorist activity, culminating in the assassination of the Archduke FRANCIS FERDINAND and his wife in the capital Sarajevo in 1914. This sparked off World War I, after which Bosnia was integrated into the new Kingdom of Serbs, Croats, and Slovenes, later renamed YUGOSLAVIA. During World War II the two provinces were incorporated into the German puppet state of Croatia, and were the scene of much fighting by the Yugoslav partisans. After the war they were integrated into TITO's communist Yugoslavia.

Alija Izetbegović (1925–) became President in 1990. In 1992, as Yugoslavia disintegrated, the mainly Muslim population of Bosnia-Hercegovina voted to become an independent country in a referendum. Although most Western countries recognized this decision, areas occupied mainly by the Serb and Croat minorities proclaimed themselves independent of the Muslim-dominated government and all three groups began fighting for territory. Attempts by the UN and the European Community to mediate in the ensuing ferocious civil war made little headway. The three main factions agreed in principle to Bosnia-Hercegovina being a federal nation with regions based on ethnic groupings but failed to agree on the borders of the proposed regions. (In 1993 a fourth faction emerged when the mainly Muslim area around Bihac in the west of the country also proclaimed itself independent.)

In April 1992 the Serbs besieged Sarajevo; by the end of that year they had taken possession of over two-thirds of the country despite the intervention of a UN peace-keeping force. Although the UN declared it would defend certain areas, making them 'safe areas' for Muslims fleeing from Serb attacks and from 'ethnic cleansing', it was unable to prevent thousands of civilians from being massacred. In February 1994 NATO shot down four Serb fighter planes that were flying in the UN-established 'no-fly zone' and subsequently bombed Serb ground targets. These were NATO's first aggressive military actions since it was founded (1949). In 1994 Bosnian Muslims and Bosnian Croats agreed to form an alliance, and by mid-1995, with support from the Croatian army, they had recaptured a large amount of territory from the Serbs. Further NATO air strikes led to the lifting of the siege of Sarajevo in September 1995. In December 1995, the Dayton Accord, a US-brokered peace deal, was signed. This stated that although Bosnia-Hercegovina would remain a single state with unchanged borders, it would henceforth be divided into a Bosnian–Croat Federation in the West and a Bosnian Serb Republic in the north and east. Although there has been no resumption of full-scale violence, a number of serious problems remain – notably the resettlement of many thousands of refugees and the capture and prosecution of war criminals on all sides. In 1996 Izetbegović was re-elected as the chairman of a new tripartite presidency, serving alongside a Serb and a Croat. However, there were allegations that the electoral process had been marred by intimidation and corruption.

Capital: Sarajevo
Area: 51,129 sq km (19,741 sq mi)
Population: 3,459,000 (1995)
Currency: dinar
Religions: Muslim 44.0%; Eastern Orthodox 31.0%; Roman Catholic 17.0%
Ethnic Groups: Muslim Slav 44.0%; Serb 31.0%; Croat 17.0%
Languages: Serbo-Croat (official)

boson An ELEMENTARY PARTICLE that has zero or integral number SPIN. Photons and alpha particles are bosons. They are named after Satyendra Nath BOSE, who, together with Albert EINSTEIN, provided the statistical description of their behaviour known as Bose-Einstein statistics.

Bosporus (or **Bosphorus**; Turkish **Karadeniz Boğazi**) A strait, *c.*32 km (20 miles) in length, connecting the Black Sea and the Sea of Marmara, with Istanbul at its south end. It separates Europe from Asia Minor which are linked by two bridges completed in 1973 and 1988.

Boston The state capital of Massachusetts, USA, on Boston Bay; pop. (1990) 574,283; metropolitan area (1990) 2,870,670. Founded *c.*1630 as the principal settlement of the Massachusetts Bay Company, Boston was an early centre of New England Puritanism. Faneuil Hall Marketplace, bequeathed to the city as a public meeting-hall and market place in 1742, is known as the 'Cradle of Liberty'. The Hall was the scene of mass protest meetings held before the American War of Independence, which broke out near here in 1775. Boston is the home of Boston University (1839), Harvard Medical School, numerous colleges, institutions, and museums. Harvard University and the Massachusetts Institute of Technology are located at nearby Cambridge. Its Symphony Orchestra is world-renowned. Its industries include electronics, machinery, publishing, and food processing.

Boston A market town on the River Witham, Lincolnshire, east England; pop. (est. 1985) 27,000. John Cotton led a party of Puritans who sailed from Boston to Massachusetts Bay in 1633. St Botolph's Church is said to be England's largest parish church.

Boston fern A houseplant, one of several subspecies of the sword fern, *Nephrolepis exaltata*, a native of tropical regions. The name is derived from the fact that it was first discovered in a shipment of ferns sent to Boston. The Boston fern, *N. e. bostoniensis*, and other members of its genus, are unusual among ferns in being able to reproduce vegetatively by means of runners.

Boswell, James (1740–95) Scottish author and biographer. He first met Samuel Johnson in London (1763) and Boswell's *Journal of a Tour to the Hebrides* (1785) describes their travels together in 1773. He is now best known for his celebrated biography *The Life of Samuel Johnson* (1791), which gives a vivid and intimate portrait of Johnson and an invaluable panorama of the age and its personalities.

Bosworth Field, Battle of (22 August 1485) A battle fought close to the English town of Bosworth in Leicestershire, its outcome was to establish HENRY VII and the Tudor dynasty on the English throne. Just over a fortnight after Henry had landed on the Welsh coast, he and his army of Welsh followers were met in battle by RICHARD III's larger army. The issue was uncertain when Lord Stanley arrived and with his followers went over to Henry's side; Henry was victorious, Richard was killed, and at the end of the day Stanley placed Richard's crown on Henry's head.

botanical garden A type of garden first planted in Italy – at Pisa in 1543 and Padua in 1545 – which began as a centre of teaching at a time when plants were the main source of medicinal drugs. The first English botanical garden was founded in Oxford in 1621, the first North American one, the Elgin Botanic Garden in New York, in 1801. The purpose of these gardens did not restrict their contents, for any new plant was considered worthy of study in case it turned out to be useful. A flood of plants, new to European gardens, came from sea voyages of exploration from the late 17th century onwards. By the mid-19th century the Royal Botanic Gardens at Kew had become the main channel for the introduction of new plants to English gardens. Kew also became an important centre for the transfer of food and other economic plants from their native lands to similar habitats elsewhere.

botany The study of plants. The origins of botany go back to around 300 BC, when Theophrastus wrote about the form and functions of plants. This early interest in plants was largely a result of their use as food and in medicine. Plant anatomy developed in the 17th century, aided by the invention of the microscope, whereas physiology, the study of processes essential to life, began a century later. Botany now covers all aspects of the biology of plants, and traditionally also includes the study of FUNGI and microorganisms.

Botany Bay An inlet of the Tasman Sea on the coast of New South Wales, south-east Australia, just south of Sydney. In 1770 Captain James Cook landed here naming the bay after the large variety of plants collected by Sir Joseph BANKS. Chosen as the site for a penal settlement in 1787, it proved to be unsuitable and a location at nearby Sydney Cove was selected.

bot fly (or **warble fly**) A member of a family of large FLIES, Oestridae, which are often bee-like. As larvae they parasitize hoofed mammals. The fat, spiny larvae develop in the gut of horses, in the throat and windpipe of deer, and in the nasal cavities and sinuses of sheep. The eggs are deposited around the mouth or nostrils, or attached to body hairs. The larvae then enter their host's body through the lips or nostrils, or by burrowing through the skin. The species of the genus *Hypoderma* are known as warble flies, as their larvae form sores, or 'warbles', on the backs of cattle. Larval migration and feeding inside the host cause loss of condition in the livestock. The adult flies, which are often called gadflies or breeze flies, do not feed, but their presence distresses the animals.

Both, Jan (*c.*1618–52) Dutch landscape painter. He lived in Italy from about 1637 to 1641 and became one of the best-known exponents of the type of Italianate landscape painting that was highly popular in his lifetime and (especially with British collectors) in the 18th century.

Botha, Louis (1862–1919) South African soldier and statesman, first Prime Minister of the Union of

South Africa 1910–19. One of the most successful Boer leaders in the Boer War, Botha became Commander-in-Chief in 1900 and waged guerrilla warfare against the British forces. As Transvaal's first Prime Minister he played a leading role in the National Convention (1908–09), which was responsible for drafting the constitution for the Union of South Africa; he became its Prime Minister a year later. Botha supported the Allies in World War I, gaining recognition for his annexation of German South West Africa in 1915.

Botha, P(ieter) W(illem) (1916–) South African statesman, Prime Minister 1978–84, State President 1984–89. He joined the National Party in 1936 and was involved in party organization, particularly in Cape Province, until his election as Prime Minister. An authoritarian leader, he continued to enforce apartheid, but in response to pressure introduced limited reforms, including a new constitution (1984) giving certain classes of non-whites a degree of political representation. His resistance to more radical change ultimately led to his fall from power.

Botham, Ian (Terence) (1955–) British cricketer. An all-rounder, he made his county début for Somerset in 1973 and his test début against Australia in 1977 and was admired for his bold attacking style of batting and skill as a medium-fast bowler. In 1978 he became the first player to score 100 runs and take eight wickets in a single test match; in 1982 he also achieved the record of 3,000 runs and 250 wickets in test matches overall. He retired from first-class cricket in 1993.

Bothwell, James Hepburn, 4th Earl of (1536–78) Scottish Protestant nobleman, the third husband of MARY, QUEEN OF SCOTS. He was a supporter and adviser of Mary, while she was married to DARNLEY. In 1567 he was acquitted of Darnley's murder but then his swift divorce, promotion to the dukedom of Orkney and Shetland, and marriage to Mary caused the Scottish lords to rise against him. He fled from Scotland after the battle of Carberry Hill (June 1567), when Mary's forces were defeated. He turned to piracy, but was captured in Norway, and died in a Danish prison.

Botswana A landlocked country in southern Africa. It is bordered by Namibia to the west and north, Zimbabwe to the east, and South Africa to the south.

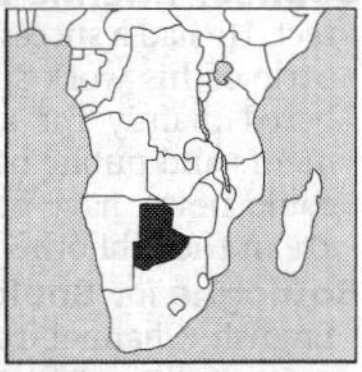

Physical. Botswana lies in the hot, dry central region of southern Africa. The north-west, which has 600 mm (24 inches) of rain a year, drains into a swampy basin, the Okavango, the only surface water in the country. The centre and west is covered by the Kalahari Desert, while in the east is a large salt-pan, the Makgadikgadi.

Economy. Diamonds are the chief export, producing revenues which have supported a high growth rate, the world's fastest growing economy. In recent years a deterioration in the diamond market has caused severe economic difficulties. It is thought that further mineral wealth awaits discovery; other exports are copper-nickel matte and beef. Agriculture is mainly pastoral, but recent droughts have decimated cattle herds. A large proportion of the work-force is employed in South African mines. Landlocked, Botswana depends on South Africa for much of its trade and imports.

History. Botswana was formerly known as Bechuanaland. British missionaries visited the southern Tswana people in 1801, and in 1817 the London Missionary Society settled at Kuruman. David LIVINGSTONE and other missionaries operated from here during the second quarter of the 19th century. In 1885 the British protectorate of Bechuanaland was declared, to be administered from Mafeking. The success of the cattle industry led the Union of South Africa to seek to incorporate Botswana, along with Basutoland (Lesotho) and Swaziland, but this was rejected by the British government in 1935; no transfer would be tolerated until the inhabitants had been consulted and an agreement reached. The dominant tribe was the Ngwato, whose chief Seretse KHAMA was banned from the country from 1948 until 1956 for marrying an Englishwoman. By now a nationalist movement had begun, which culminated in a democratic constitution in 1965 followed by independence on 30 September 1966, as the republic of Botswana, with Seretse Khama as President. He was succeeded on his death in 1980 by the vice-president Quett Masire, who was re-elected in 1989 and again in 1994.

Capital: Gaborone
Area: 581,730 sq km (224,607 sq mi)
Population: 1,549,000 (1995)
Currency: 1 pula = 100 thebe
Religions: Traditional beliefs 49.2%; Protestant 29.0%; African Christian 11.8%; Roman Catholic 9.4%
Ethnic Groups: Tswana 97.0%; Shona, !Kung San (Bushmen), Khoikhoin (Hottentot), and Ndebele minorities
Languages: Tswana, English (both official); Shona and local languages
International Organizations: UN; OAU; SADC; Non-Aligned Movement; Commonwealth

Böttger, Johann Friedrich (1682–1719) German alchemist to the Elector of Saxony and the first potter in Europe to make true hard-paste PORCELAIN, previously imported from China. In 1708 he made a hard red stoneware by mixing the normally infusible local clay with alabaster, and shortly afterwards perfected a white porcelain using kaolin (a type of clay) from Aue, Germany. On the basis of these technological advances he founded the Meissen porcelain works with the mathematician E. W. von Tschirnhausen.

Botticelli, Sandro (born Alessandro di Mariano Filipepi) (1444/45–1510) Italian painter. A pupil of Filippo Lippi, he had his own studio in Florence and enjoyed the patronage of the Medici. His reputation rests largely on his mythological paintings such as *Primavera* (*c*.1478) and *The Birth of Venus* (*c*.1480). His work was neglected until the second half of the 19th century, when it was re-evaluated by John Ruskin and Walter Pater.

bottlebrush An evergreen small tree or shrub of the genus *Callistemon*, which is native to Australia and New Caledonia. Bottlebrushes belong to the family Myrtaceae, which also includes myrtles, *Eucalyptus*, and cloves. All 12 or so species of bottlebrushes have narrow, leathery leaves and colourful red or yellow flowers in dense, cylindrical clusters round the stem. The stamens protrude well beyond the petals and give the flowers the appearance of the spiky brushes once used to clean bottles – hence their common name.

botulism A rare and life-threatening form of food poisoning caused by the bacterial toxin of *Clostridium botulinum*. The organism produces spores that are not destroyed by cooking and can multiply and produce the toxin in canned foods, which is ingested and responsible for most cases. The toxin causes nausea, vomiting, and diarrhoea initially, which may be followed by generalized PARALYSIS, urinary retention, and constipation; double and blurred vision and difficulty in breathing may also occur.

Boucher, François (1703–70) French painter and decorative artist, one of the foremost artists of the Rococo style in France. His output ranged from large decorative paintings of mythological scenes to popular engravings, *fêtes galantes*, and tapestry design. Significant paintings include *The Rising of the Sun* (1753) and *Summer Pastoral* (1749).

Boucher de Perthes, Jacques (1788–1868) French archaeologist. He discovered some of the first evidence of man-made stone tools near the bones of extinct (Pleistocene) animals in the valley of the River Somme in northern France. In the decade following 1837 he argued that these tools (and their makers) belonged to a remote pre-Celtic 'antediluvian' age, but it was not until the 1850s, when geologists supported his claims, that his findings were accepted.

Boudicca (or **Boadicea**) (died 62 AD) A queen of the Britons, ruler of the Iceni tribe in eastern England. When Rome broke the treaty made with King Prasutagus (her husband) after his death in AD 60, Boudicca led her forces in revolt against the Romans and sacked Colchester, St Albans, and London before being completely defeated by the Roman governor Suetonius Paulinus. She committed suicide soon after her defeat, but her name became a symbol of native resistance to the Roman occupation.

Boudin, Eugène (1824–98) French painter. He was the son of a sailor and lived mainly near the coast of northern France, his work consisting principally of beach scenes and seascapes. A strong advocate of direct painting from nature, he is regarded as a link between the generation of COROT and the Impressionists.

Bougainville A volcanic island in the South Pacific Ocean at the north-west end of the Solomon Islands. With the island of Buka it forms a province of Papua New Guinea; area 10,050 sq km (3,880 sq miles); pop. (est. 1990) 128,000. Named after the French explorer Louis de BOUGAINVILLE who visited the island in 1768, Bougainville became part of German New Guinea in 1884 while the rest of the Solomons came under British rule. Under Australian mandate after 1920, it became part of independent Papua New Guinea in 1975. It is one of the world's largest producers of copper and potentially one of the greatest producers of gold outside South Africa. In 1989 Melanesian nationalists declared unilateral independence at the height of a guerrilla war that forced the island's mines to close down.

Bougainville, Louis Antoine de (1729–1811) French explorer. Between 1766 and 1769 he led the first successful French circumnavigation of the globe, visiting many of the islands of the South Pacific and compiling a scientific record of his findings. The largest of the Solomon Islands is named after him, as is the tropical plant BOUGAINVILLAEA.

bougainvillea A climbing shrub, or LIANA, native to South America, the 18 species of which form the genus *Bougainvillea*. They have been hybridized and are widely grown as garden ornamentals in the tropics and warm temperate zones. Each of the 'flowers' consists of a group of three inconspicuous blossoms surrounded by three large, showy bracts, which are white, bluish, lilac, or orange in colour. Bougainvillea forms part of the chiefly tropical family Nyctaginaceae.

Bougie See BEJAÏA.

Boulanger, Georges Ernest (1837–91) French general and politician. He won increasing popular support for his campaign for revenge on Germany after the FRANCO-PRUSSIAN WAR (1870–71). In 1886 he became Minister of War but forfeited the support of moderate republicans who feared that he might provoke another war with Germany. Forced from his ministry in 1887, he became the focus of opposition to the government and won a series of by-elections. He failed to seize this opportunity to make himself President, and his popularity waned. The government prepared to have him tried for treason but he fled into exile.

Boulanger, Nadia (1887–1979) French conductor and teacher of music. After studying with Fauré at the Paris Conservatoire she gained a considerable reputation as a conductor and champion of early music (particularly Monteverdi), finally becoming famous as a teacher of composition. Her pupils include Aaron Copland, Virgil Thomson, Lennox Berkeley, and Jean Françaix. Her sister **Lili Boulanger** (1893–1918) was a talented composer.

boulder clay A glacial deposit typically consisting of an unsorted mixture of boulders in a matrix of stiff clay. The material, which can range from large boulders to fine rock flour, is unstratified: it shows no layered structure.

Boulez, Pierre (1925–) French composer and conductor. His first publicly acclaimed work was *Le Marteau sans maître* (1954, revised 1957); other more recent compositions include *Répons* (1981–86). He was principal conductor with the New York Philharmonic Orchestra (1971–78).

Boulle, André-Charles (1642–1732) French furniture-maker and designer, the most famous of Louis XIV's reign. A fine craftsman in wood and metal and a versatile designer, he was appointed royal cabinet-maker in 1672 and created much of the sumptuous furniture for the palace of Versailles, ending the domination of foreign furniture-makers at the French court. He perfected the use of tortoiseshell and brass MARQUETRY, which became known as Boulle (or Buhl) work.

Boullée, Etienne-Louis (1728–99) French architect. He had a successful career as an architect, but little of his work survives and he is now remembered mainly for a series of designs for monuments and public buildings on a scale so vast they could never have been constructed (the drawings are in the Bibliothèque Nationale, Paris).

Boulogne (or **Boulogne-sur-Mer**) A fishing and English Channel ferry port on the north-west coast of France, at the mouth of the River Liane; pop. (1990) 44,240. Julius Caesar set out from here to invade England in 55 BC. The town, which is a leading European fishing port, is France's principal fish-processing centre.

Boult, Sir Adrian (Cedric) (1889–1983) British conductor. Noted especially for his championship of British composers, he was music director of the BBC (1930–49) and trained and conducted the BBC Symphony Orchestra (1931–50). He was also principal conductor of the London Philharmonic Orchestra (1950–57) and continued to conduct until two years before his death.

Boulting, John and Roy British film producers and directors. Twin brothers, John (1913–85) and Roy (1913–) alternated roles as producer and director. They made a number of memorable films, including *Brighton Rock* (1947) and *Seven Days to Noon* (1950). From the late 1950s their main output was comedy and farce, including *Private's*

Progress (1956), *I'm All Right Jack* (1959), and *There's a Girl in My Soup* (1970).

Boulton, Matthew (1728–1809) British engineer and manufacturer. With his partner James Watt he pioneered the manufacture of steam engines, which they began to produce in 1774. Under Boulton's influence the engines began to enjoy widespread commercial success.

Boumédienne, Houari (1925–78) Algerian statesman. In the early 1950s he joined a group of expatriate Algerian nationalists in Cairo which included BEN BELLA, and in 1955 he joined resistance forces in ALGERIA operating against the French. He became chief-of-staff of the exiled National Liberation Front in Tunisia (1960–62). In March 1962 his forces occupied Algiers for Ben Bella after which a peace treaty was signed with France. He displaced Ben Bella in a coup in 1965, ruling until his death in 1978.

boundary layer A layer of flowing air or water whose characteristics are affected by the surface over which the fluid is flowing. In the atmosphere, the boundary layer defines the altitude at which airflow is affected by the ground. The greatest height at which airflow is affected by frictional drag and turbulence, 550 m (1,600 feet), is called the planetary boundary layer. At the other end of the scale is the surface boundary layer, below 50 m (160 feet).

In oceanography, the boundary layer (or benthic) defines the height above the sea-bed at which bottom currents cease to be affected by frictional drag and turbulence. The benthic boundary layer is typically of the order of 50 m (160 feet) thick and is best developed in the oceans and deeper waters of the CONTINENTAL SHELF. It is also more turbid than waters above, because of suspended bottom sediment stirred up by the turbulence. In shallow waters nearer shore, the benthic boundary layer, stirred by tidal currents, merges with the wind-mixed surface layer. The part of the atmosphere immediately above the ocean, and the uppermost part of the ocean, are referred to as the atmosphere-ocean boundary layers.

Bounty mutiny (1789) A British mutiny that occurred near the Tongan Islands on HMS *Bounty*, under the command of Captain BLIGH. Some of the crew, resenting Bligh's harsh authority, rebelled under the leadership of Fletcher Christian. Bligh and 18 others were cast off in a small, open boat with no chart. Thanks to Bligh's navigational skill and resource, they covered a distance of 5,822 km (3,618 miles), arriving in Timor about six weeks later. Some of the mutineers surrendered and others were captured and court martialled in England. Fletcher Christian and some of the other mutineers, with a number of Tahitian men and women, settled on Pitcairn Island in 1790. Their descendants moved to Norfolk Island in 1856.

Bourbaki, Nicolas The pseudonym under which a group of mathematicians, mainly French, attempted in the mid-1930s to publish an encyclopedic survey of pure mathematics. Their approach was highly abstract and strictly axiomatic in style and spirit, intending to lay bare the structure of the entire field. Volumes in different areas of mathematics began appearing in 1939 and were highly influential among mathematicians, not least in rendering Bourbaki's non-standard notation the norm. This approach also influenced the widespread reforms in school mathematics which took place during the 1960s.

Bourbon A great European ruling dynasty, founded when **Robert of Clermont** (1256–1317), the sixth son of Louis IX of France, married the heiress to the lordship of Bourbon. The first duke was their son, **Louis I** (1279–1341). In 1503 the title passed to the Montpensier branch of the family, but in 1527 headship of the house of Bourbon passed to the line of Marche-Vendôme. **Antoine de Bourbon** (1518–62), Duc de Vendôme, became King Consort of NAVARRE, while his brother Louis (1530–69) was made Prince of CONDÉ. On the death of the last VALOIS king in 1589, Antoine's son became King of France as HENRY IV (ruled 1589–1610). His heirs ruled France uninterruptedly until 1792: Louis XIII (ruled 1610–43), Louis XIV (ruled 1643–1715), Louis XV (ruled 1715–74) and Louis XVI (ruled 1774–92). The latter was overthrown during the FRENCH REVOLUTION, and Louis XVII (titular king 1793–95) died without reigning; Louis XVI's brothers Louis XVIII (ruled 1814–24) and Charles X (ruled 1824–30) both ruled after the Bourbon restoration. Louis-Philippe (ruled 1830–48), the last Bourbon King of France, was a member of the cadet ORLÉANS branch of the family.

In 1700 Louis XIV's second grandson became Philip V (ruled 1700–46) of Spain, thus setting in train the War of the SPANISH SUCCESSION. His successors have held the Spanish throne ever since (excepting the republican period, 1931–75).

Bourgogne See BURGUNDY.

Bourguiba, Habib ibn Ali (1903–) Tunisian nationalist and statesman, President 1957–87. Having negotiated the settlement that led to his country's autonomy, he was its first Prime Minister after independence in 1956 and was chosen as its first President when the country became a republic in 1957. A moderate socialist, he embarked on a reform programme intended to improve Tunisia's economy and to establish democratic government. He was deposed following continuing political unrest.

Bourke-White, Margaret (1906–71) US photojournalist. As a staff photographer with *Life* magazine in 1937 she took photographs of the effects of the Depression among the rural poor in the southern USA. During World War II she was the first female photographer to be attached to the US armed forces, at the end of the war accompanying the Allied forces when they entered the concentration camps. Later assignments included the Korean War (1950–53) and work in India and South Africa.

Bournemouth A resort town on Poole Bay, an inlet on the Dorset coast of southern England; pop. (1991) 154,400. Bournemouth University (formerly Bournemouth Polytechnic) was established in 1992. Bournemouth has its own orchestra.

Bournonville, August (1805–79) Danish dancer, choreographer, and director. He trained at the Royal Danish Ballet School and later danced in Paris, partnering Taglioni, the archetypal Romantic BALLERINA. He returned to Copenhagen in 1830 as director, and presented *La Sylphide* in 1836 in a version that has endured to the present day.

Bourse (fully **Palais de la Bourse**) The Paris stock exchange in the Rue Vivienne, Paris, France. Built in the style of a Graeco-Roman temple in 1808–27 by the architect A.-Th. Brongniart, it was later enlarged in 1902–03.

Boussingault, Jean-Baptiste Joseph Dieudonné (1802–87) French chemist who was one of the first to apply chemical principles to AGRICULTURE. He recognized that NITROGEN was necessary for the growth of plants and that soil was able to fix atmospheric nitrogen; he suggested that this was due to the presence of microorganisms. He developed a process for making OXYGEN from barium oxide, and with his compatriot J.-B.-A. Dumas determined the relative proportions of gases in the atmosphere.

Boutros-Ghali, Boutros (1922–) Egyptian diplomat and politician, Secretary-General of the United Nations 1992–96. He served as Egyptian minister of state for foreign affairs from 1971 to 1991.

bouzouki A plucked stringed instrument used in Greek café music. During the Ottoman period, the Turks introduced the *bozuk* into Greece, a medium sized saz (long-necked lute) with three pairs or courses of strings. It is thus an urban instrument rather than a folk instrument common to the whole country. Since the late 1940s it has acquired a fourth course of strings and it now resembles a MANDOLIN with a very long neck and geared tuning pegs.

bovine spongiform encephalopathy (BSE) A degenerative and ultimately fatal brain disease of cattle, popularly known as 'mad cow disease', characterized by a staggering gait and behavioural changes. The first outbreaks of the disease were recorded in Britain in the mid-1980s; it is thought to have been transmitted in cattle feed containing brain tissue of sheep infected with SCRAPIE and from infected cows to their calves. BSE, scrapie, and CREUTZFELDT-JAKOB DISEASE (CJD), a degenerative brain disease that affects humans, appear to be caused by the same type of highly resistant infective agent, and outbreaks of a new variant form of CJD affecting mainly young people in Britain in the 1990s have been linked with the consumption of meat and meat products from BSE-infected cattle. Because of this, in 1996 the European Union imposed a worldwide ban on exports of British beef and beef products, to remain in place until measures to eradicate BSE (by the slaughter of selected animals from infected herds) had been implemented.

bow (in archery) A device for shooting arrows, consisting in its simplest form (the longbow) of a single piece of flexible wood with a piece of string under tension fastened to its two ends. The arrow is propelled by the energy stored in the bow when the string is drawn back. The arrow is a piece of wood with a point, sometimes made of metal, at one end and a notch cut at the other. The string fits in the notch when the arrow is to be fired. Arrows usually have two or three feathers glued to the end of the shaft; these act as a tailplane, making the arrow fly straighter. More powerful bows are made from several pieces of wood (the built bow), wood, horn, and sinew (the composite bow), or, for modern target-shooting bows, fibreglass. The CROSSBOW is a mechanical weapon.

bow (in music) A band of horsehair attached to both ends of a stick, drawn across strings to make them sound; rosin makes the hair sticky, so that it grips the string. Early bows in about AD 1000 were curved like the archer's and thus held the hair taut. As bows became straighter, methods of keeping the hair taut and away from the stick changed, culminating in the screw frog, a block between the stick and the hair at the handle, tightened with a screw.

Bow The name of several locations in London, England. ▶**1** (or **Stratford-le-Bow**) A district in Tower Hamlets, east London, named after the bows of a bridge built during the reign of Queen Matilda. ▶**2** The City parish church of St Mary-le-Bow in Cheapside, within earshot of which the true cockney is supposed to be born. ▶**3** Bow Street in the Covent Garden area of Westminster in which the Royal Opera House stands. See also BOW STREET RUNNERS.

Bowen, Elizabeth (Dorothea Cole) (1899–1973) British novelist and short-story writer, born in Ireland. Her writing is distinguished by delicate characterization and acute observation, especially of emotions and the relationships between her chiefly upper-middle-class characters. Among her best-known novels are *The Death of the Heart* (1938) and *The Heat of the Day* (1949).

bowel See INTESTINE.

bower-bird A bird of the family Ptilonorhyncidae, which contains 20 species. Bower-birds occur in New Guinea and Australia, and range in size from that of a thrush to that of a small crow. Although a few are brightly coloured, many are brownish, with colourful, erectile crown or neck feathers. They have a stout beak for feeding on fruits, berries, and large insects. They are particularly famous for their display grounds or bowers, which are built by the males. These are intricately woven walls of twigs, decorated with flowers, berries and leaves. Some of the gardener bower-birds, *Amblyornis* species, may concentrate their decorations around the base of a small sapling. The females come to the display grounds for mating and subsequently care for the eggs and young by themselves.

Bowery, The A street in lower Manhattan, New York City, USA. Once the road to the farm or *bouwerie* of Peter Stuyvesant, it became part of the mail road to Boston in the 1670s. It later gained a reputation for its theatres, saloons, drunks, and down-and-outs.

bowfin A species of ancient freshwater fish, *Amia calva*, of eastern North America, which lives in sluggish or still waters. It can breathe air, using its swim bladder as a lung. It breeds in spring, when the male makes a saucer-shaped hollow in the lake or river-bed in which the eggs are laid. The bowfin grows to 90 cm (3 feet) in length, and weighs up to 6 kg (13 pounds).

Bowie, David (born David Robert Jones) (1947–) British rock singer, songwriter, and actor. His first hit single, 'Space Oddity' (1969), was followed by a number of other hit singles and albums such as *Hunky Dory* (1971), *Ziggy Stardust* (1972), and *Aladdin Sane* (1973); later albums include *Let's Dance* (1985). He became known for his theatrical performances and unconventional stage personae, involving the use of elaborate costumes and make-up. He also acted in a number of films, especially in the 1980s.

Bowie, James (known as 'Jim') (1799–1836) US frontiersman. In 1828 he moved from Georgia to Texas and became a leader among the American settlers who opposed Mexican rule. He shared command of the garrison that resisted the attack on the Alamo, where he died.

Bowles, Paul (Frederick) (1910–) US writer and composer. In the 1930s he lived in Europe and North Africa, studying music and working as a music critic and composer; in 1941 he was funded to write the opera *The Wind Remains*. Bowles's first novel, *The Sheltering Sky* (1949), was published to widespread acclaim. His other books include *Let It Come Down* (1952) and *The Spider's House* (1966).

bowling A game derived from skittles. In its most popular form – tenpin bowling – players compete to roll a ball and knock down ten pins set in a triangle 18 m (60 feet) away at the far end of a lane made of polished wood. Balls weigh up to 7 kg (16 pounds) and are fitted with one thumb-hole and two finger-holes. An earlier 19th-century version, called ninepins, was taken by settlers from Europe to North America, where the tenth pin was added, and the game evolved into a popular, highly organized indoor sport. In another game, known as road bowling, played chiefly in Ireland, two players compete in bowling iron balls along a public road; the winner completes the course in fewer throws than his opponent.

bowls A group of games in which opposing individuals or teams seek to roll their bowls or woods closer to the jack (a small white ball) than their opponents' bowls. The bowl, made of wood, rubber, or composition, weighs up to 1.6 kg (3.5 pounds) and is flattened slightly on one side to impart bias, so that it travels in a curved path. Lawn bowls is played internationally on a level green. In crown-green bowls, played in northern England, the centre of the green is higher than the boundaries.

Bow Street Runners The first organized police force, based at BOW Street Magistrates' Court in London, recruited by the magistrate (and novelist) Henry Fielding from the 1740s to augment the forces at his disposal. Their functions included serving writs and acting as detectives. They gained a reputation for efficiency and were much feared and respected by criminals. The formation of the London Metropolitan Police Force in 1829 brought their separate existence to an end.

box An evergreen shrub or small tree of the genus *Buxus*, native to northern temperate regions and Central America. There are about 30 species, three of which are found in Europe. The common box, *B. sempervirens*, is a slow-growing, bushy, evergreen tree of western Europe. It is most widely grown as a hedging plant and as an edging plant for flower beds. The finely grained, hard, yellow wood is valued for inlay work, rules, and fine carving.

boxer See DOG.

Boxer Rising (1899–1900) A popular anti-western movement in China. The secret society of Righteous and Harmonious Fists, which was opposed to foreign expansion and the Manchu court, claimed that by training (including ritual boxing) its members could become immune to bullets. The movement began in Shandong province and had its roots in rural poverty and unemployment, blamed partly on western imports. It was pushed westwards and missionaries, Chinese Christians, and people handling foreign goods were attacked. The movement was backed by the empress dowager CIXI and some provincial governors. In 1900 the Boxers besieged the foreign legations in Beijing for two months until they were relieved by an international force which occupied and looted the capital; Cixi and the emperor fled in disguise. The foreign powers launched punitive raids in the Beijing region and negotiated heavy reparations in the Boxer Protocol (1901). The rising greatly increased foreign interference in China, and further reduced the authority of the QING dynasty.

box-fish See TRUNK FISH.

box-girder A thin-walled hollow girder of steel, timber, or concrete. It has a rectangular or trapezoidal cross-section, which, compared with the more traditional 'I' section, gives increased stiffness and resistance to torsion (twisting). Internal transverse diaphragms prevent buckling of the box-girder walls. Prefabrication of long girders is common in bridges, where steel or pre-cast concrete box-sections can be progressively added by forming a cantilever from an abutment or a pier.

boxing An international sport in which two opponents attack each other with gloved fists and attempt to win by a knockout (opponent floored for ten seconds) or on points awarded by a referee or judges – according to rules devised by the Marquess of Queensberry in 1865. Modern boxing is highly organized worldwide at professional and amateur levels, and boxers compete in a series of weight divisions from flyweight to heavyweight. A bout takes place in a three-roped boxing ring and is divided into a series of rounds, each of three minutes for professionals and senior amateurs. The sport is opposed by lobbies who claim it is too dangerous. Other versions include Chinese, Thai, and French boxing.

boyar A member of the highest non-princely class of medieval Russian society. In the 10th to 12th centuries the boyars formed the senior levels of the princes' retinues. They received large grants of land, and exercised considerable independent power during the period of decentralization after the 13th-century Mongol conquest; but as the grand princes of Muscovy consolidated their own power, they managed to curb boyar independence.

From the 15th to the 17th centuries Muscovite boyars formed a closed aristocratic class drawn from about 200 families. They retained a stake in princely affairs through their membership of the boyar *duma* or council. IVAN the Terrible (ruled 1547–84) reduced their power significantly by relying on favourites and locally elected officials. Their social and political importance continued to decline throughout the 17th century, and PETER I eventually abolished the rank and title.

Boyce, William (1711–79) British composer and organist. His compositions include songs, overtures, church anthems and services, and eight symphonies; one of his most famous songs is 'Hearts of Oak'. He is noted also for his *Cathedral Music* (1760–73), an anthology of English sacred music of the 16th to 18th centuries.

boycott A refusal to have dealings with a person, group, or nation, or to handle its goods (from Captain BOYCOTT, a land agent in Ireland, so treated in 1880). A boycott of a country whose policies are disapproved of may in its practical effects differ little from the imposition of SANCTIONS.

Boycott, Charles Cunningham (1832–97) British land agent in Ireland. When, at the direction of the Land League, Irish tenants on the estate of Lord Erne in County Mayo asked for rent reductions and refused to pay their full rents, Boycott ordered their eviction (1880). PARNELL urged everyone to refuse all communication with Boycott and to ostracize his family. The policy was successful and Boycott was forced to leave. The practice of non-communication became known as boycotting.

Boyd, Arthur (Merric Bloomfield) (1920–) Australian painter, potter, etcher, and ceramic artist. His first paintings were influenced by expressionism and surrealism; later works, such as *The Mockers* (1945), show the influence of Rembrandt, Bosch, and Bruegel. He became famous for his large ceramic totem pole erected in Melbourne and for his series of twenty pictures inspired by his travels among the Aboriginals of central Australia.

Boyd, Martin A'Beckett (1893–1972) Australian novelist. His novels examine ironically the tensions between old and new cultures among upper-class Anglo-Australians; some are based on his upbringing in Melbourne. He shows a strong interest in character in his family sagas, which include *The Montfords* (1928), *Lucinda Brayford* (1946), and *The Cardboard Crown* (1952).

Boyle, Robert (1627–91) Irish-born physicist, chemist, and founder member of the Royal Society who was largely responsible for establishing CHEMISTRY as a serious scientific subject. He did much to advance the theory that matter consists of 'corpuscles', now identified as ATOMS, and was the first to distinguish between mixtures and compounds. He made detailed studies of the behaviour of gases, performed experiments using the air pump, demonstrated that air has weight and, in 1663, published the law which now bears his name (see GAS).

Boylston, Zabdiel (1679–1766) Boston physician, who introduced the practice of inoculation into America against bitter opposition during the smallpox epidemic of 1721. A violent mob threatened his life; but only six of his 245 inoculated patients died, and in the next epidemic (1729) other doctors adopted the practice.

Boyne, Battle of the (1 July 1690) A major defeat for the Stuart cause which confirmed WILLIAM III's control over Ireland. It took place near Drogheda, where the recently deposed JAMES II and his Irish and French forces were greatly outnumbered by the Protestant army led by William III. When William attacked across the River Boyne James's troops broke and fled. He returned to exile in France, and William's position as King of England, Scotland, and Ireland was immeasurably strengthened. The victory is still commemorated annually by the Orange Order, a political society founded in 1795 to support Protestantism in Ireland.

Boys, Sir Charles Vernon (1855–1944) British physicist and prolific inventor, who developed a simple method of measuring the REFRACTIVE INDEX (bending power) of the glass in a lens. Another of his achievements was a sensitive detector of radiation from hot objects called a radiomicrometer.

Boz The pseudonym used by Charles DICKENS in his *Pickwick Papers* and contributions to the *Morning Chronicle.*

brachiopod See LAMP SHELL.

bracken A widespread species of FERN, belonging to the genus *Pteridium*, which spreads by means of underground stems called rhizomes. These enable it to invade existing plant communities and spread over large areas, particularly on acid soils. Its fronds grow up to 4 m (12 feet) long, and it is a particular nuisance on hill farms, where it replaces grass and is poisonous to livestock. If eaten by cattle or horses, it causes bone-marrow damage with associated internal bleeding and fever.

bracket fungi The spore-bearing structures of many saprophytic and parasitic fungi, which appear on trunks and stumps of infected trees or timber. The hemispherical brackets are supplied with food by microscopic fungal threads (hyphae) growing in the wood. They belong to the fungal order Aphyllophorales, often called polypores, and occur throughout much of the northern temperate zone. Familiar species in both Europe and North America include the birch bracket, *Piptoporus betulinus*, dryad's saddle, *Polyporus squamosus*, and beefsteak fungus, *Fistulina hepatica*.

Bradbury, Malcolm (Stanley) (1932–) British novelist, critic, and academic. His first three novels (including *The History Man*, 1975) are satires of university campus life; *Rates of Exchange* (1983) recounts the experiences of an academic on a lecture tour of an eastern European country. His critical works include studies of Evelyn Waugh (1962) and Saul Bellow (1982).

Bradbury, Ray (Douglas) (1920–) US writer of science fiction. He is best known for his collections of short stories, such as *The Martian Chronicles* (1950) and *The Golden Apples of the Sun* (1953). His novels include *Fahrenheit 451* (1951), a depiction of a future totalitarian state.

Bradford An industrial city in West Yorkshire; pop. (1991) 289,376. It developed in medieval times as a wool and cloth-manufacturing town. Since the decline of the textile industry in the 1970s engineering, printing, and the manufacture of electronics have become important. The University of Bradford was founded in 1966.

Bradford, William (1590–1657) Pilgrim leader. He was born in Yorkshire and escaped to Holland with the Scrooby separatists. After the *Mayflower* reached PLYMOUTH, he was elected governor and guided the colony until his death. He pacified the American Indians, achieved financial independence from the London merchants, and wrote his *History of Plimmoth Plantation.*

Bradlaugh, Charles (1833–91) British social reformer. A republican and keen supporter of reform movements, he was tried, with Annie BESANT, in 1877–78 for printing a pamphlet on birth control. The charge failed and contraceptives could thereafter be openly advertised.

Bradley, James (1693–1762) English astronomer. Bradley was appointed Savilian professor of astronomy at Oxford in 1721 and Astronomer Royal in 1742. His attempt to measure the distance of stars from the Earth by means of stellar parallax resulted in his discovery of the aberration of light, which he ascribed correctly to the combined effect of the velocity of light and the Earth's annual orbital motion. He also observed the oscillation of the Earth's axis, which he termed *nutation.*

Bradley, Omar Nelson (1893–1981) US general. In WORLD WAR II he commanded a corps in the North African and Sicilian campaigns. He commanded US land forces in the NORMANDY CAMPAIGN, and later, following the ARDENNES campaign, went beyond Eisenhower's orders to link up with the Soviet forces on the Elbe in 1945. He was instrumental in building up NATO, formulating US global defence strategy in the post-war years, and in committing US troops to fight in the KOREAN WAR.

Bradman, Sir Donald George (1908–) Australian cricketer. An outstanding batsman who dominated the sport in his day, he began his career in 1927 with New South Wales and played for his country from 1928 until his retirement in 1949. He scored 117 centuries in first-class cricket, 29 of them in test matches.

Braemar A Deeside village in northeast Scotland. Situated near Balmoral Castle, its Braemar Gathering is the most famous of the Highland Games held every summer. The standard for the first Jacobite Rising of 1715 was raised at Braemar by the 6th Earl of Mar whose family seat was at Braemar Castle.

Braganza The ruling dynasty of Portugal 1640–1910. Alfonso, an illegitimate son of John I of Portugal, was made first Duke of Braganza (1442). His descendants became the wealthiest nobles in the kingdom, and, by marriage into the royal family, had a claim to the Portuguese throne before the Spaniards took control of the country in 1580. When the Portuguese threw off Spanish rule in 1640, the 8th Duke of Braganza ascended the throne as John IV. The title of Duke of Braganza was thenceforth borne by the heir to the throne.

Bragg, Sir William Henry (1862–1942) British physicist, a founder of solid-state physics. His early work was concerned with X-rays and ionizing radiation, but in 1912 he began to collaborate with his son, **Sir (William) Lawrence Bragg** (1890–1971), in developing the technique of X-ray diffraction for determining the atomic structure of crystals; for this they shared the 1915 Nobel Prize for physics. He later established a research school for crystallography at University College, London, and became director of the Royal Institution in 1923. His son was appointed head of the same establishment in 1953. Their diffraction studies of organic crystals were of fundamental importance in molecular biology.

Brahe, Tycho (1546–1601) Danish astronomer. A nobleman, he built his own observatory, which he equipped with new instruments for determining planetary motions and star positions with great precision, making due allowance for atmospheric refraction. He was regarded as the leading observational astronomer of his day; his observations of comets, published in the book *De Nova Stella* (1577), demonstrated that they followed regular Sun-centred paths, but despite this he adhered to a geocentric picture of the orbits of the planets. A 'new star' which he observed in 1572 is now known to have been a supernova. From the 1590s he corresponded with Kepler, who later assisted him in his work.

Brahma In Hindu belief, the creator god of the triad with Vishnu, the 'preserver', and Shiva, the 'destroyer'. Brahma's consort is Sarasvati, goddess of wisdom and of learning (and, according to tradition, the inventor of the Sanskrit language). He is often depicted as appearing from a lotus flower that grows in the navel of the sleeping Vishnu. When he emerges, he creates many worlds, of which this is only one. He is often shown with four heads and arms. His vehicle is the goose, symbol of the creative principle. Brahma, originally a minor Vedic god, became the personification of the impersonal Supreme Principle (BRAHMAN) in the transition of Hinduism to monotheism. Nevertheless, his importance was soon eclipsed by that of Vishnu and Shiva and his cult is practically non-existent in modern times.

Brahman A central theological notion within HINDUISM, particularly VEDANTA. It signifies the ultimate holy power, the all-pervading soul or spiritual reality of the Universe; eternal, uncreated, and infinite; the source of all things animate and inanimate. The doctrine of Brahman is particularly explored in the UPANISHADS, which are the last part of the HINDU SACRED TEXTS, or VEDAS. While Brahman is recognized as the source and purpose of the Universe, it is conceptualized impersonally. Within Vedānta, ADVAITA HINDUISM takes the reality of Brahman to be language-transcendent, a reality which cannot be captured by the attribution of qualities, and which can only be capable of being experienced (rather than described) as identical with the self; Vishishtādvaita (or qualified non-dualism) holds Brahman to be language-transcendent in terms of logic and possessed of qualities in terms of a devotee's understanding of Brahman as a personal deity, and thinks of Brahman both as consisting of individual souls and being more than their aggregation (as a black cow cannot lack colour but is more than black); Dvaita (dualist Vedānta) holds that Brahman is clearly identifiable as the creator God, a personal deity separate from the souls of individual devotees.

Brahmaputra (Bengali **Jamuna**; Chinese **Yarlung Zangbo**) A river of southern Asia, which rises in Tibet and flows 2,735 km (1,700 miles) through the Himalayas and north-east India to join the Ganges at its delta (in Bangladesh) on the Bay of Bengal.

Brahminism The complex sacrifical religion that emerged in post-Vedic India (*c.*900 BC) under the influence of the dominant priesthood (Brahmans). It was as a reaction to Brahman orthodoxy that heterodox sects such as Buddhism and Jainism were formed.

Brahmo Samaj (Hindu, 'Society of God') Indian religious movement. It was a development of a Hindu social reform movement founded in Bengal in 1828 by Ram Mohan Roy and revived as a purely religious movement in 1842 by Maharshi Devendranath Tagore (1817–1905). Following the latter's repudiation of the vedic scriptures in 1850 the movement divided between a religious group, the Adi Brahmo Samaj, and the social reformers, Brahmo Samaj of India (under Keshab Chandra Sen (1838–84)). The latter sponsored a temperance movement and campaigned for women's education and social rights. Brahmo Samaj had a powerful influence on 20th-century Hindu society.

Brahms, Johannes (1833–97) German composer and pianist. He lived for most of the last 35 years of his life in Vienna and owed much of his early success to the friendship and patronage of Schumann, whom he first met in 1853. Firmly opposed to the 'New German' school of Liszt and the young Wagner, he eschewed programme music and opera and concentrated his energies on 'pure' and traditional forms. He wrote four symphonies, two piano concertos, a violin concerto (1879) and the Double Concerto (1887), chamber and piano music, choral works including the *German Requiem* (1857–68), and nearly 200 songs.

braiding (in geomorphology) A process that occurs when a river channel becomes divided into two or more branches, with small islands or channel bars between them. Indeed, the subchannels may weave a wide and intricate basketwork pattern all over the valley floor. The phenomenon is usually caused by a combination of large, seasonal river flows, steep slopes, and large amounts of coarse-grained sediment such as sand or gravel.

Braille, Louis (1809–52) French educationist. In 1819 he entered the Institute des Jeunes Aveugles in Paris, having been blind from the age of 3. By the age of 15 he had developed his own system of raised-point reading and writing (known as **Braille**). Each letter of the alphabet is represented by a different pattern of six dots in a 3 × 2 matrix. Special patterns are used for common words and 'contractions' (commonly occurring groups of letters). Other signs correspond to numbers, punctuation marks, and musical notes. See illustration p. 198.

brain The part of the central NERVOUS SYSTEM of humans and other vertebrates that is within the skull. Brain tissue is composed of NEURONES and their supporting cells, the glia; the human brain contains more than ten billion nerve cells. Within the brain each nerve cell is connected to many others, up to sixty thousand in the case of humans, and has links to and from the rest of the nervous system. The human brain has a very complex structure and can be divided into three main parts: the hindbrain, the midbrain, and the forebrain.

The hindbrain includes the cerebellum which, in man and other vertebrates, is responsible for the unconscious muscular control of balance. The midbrain is part of the brainstem, an area through which nerves enter and leave the brain; it connects the brain to the top of the spinal cord. The forebrain, or cerebrum, is the largest portion of the human brain and consists of a left and a right hemisphere. Each hemisphere includes 'grey matter', where the nerve cells are situated, and 'white matter', where the nerve fibres lie. The outer cortex of grey matter has a crucial role in higher intellectual functions, sensory perception, and voluntary movement. The motor and sensory cortex of one hemisphere is connected with the opposite side of the body. The dominant hemisphere, usually the left, controls most aspects of language.

Brain, **Dennis** (1921–57) British player of the French horn. Brain was principal horn with the Royal Philharmonic and Philharmonia Orchestras. A frequent concerto soloist, the subtlety of his musicianship evident in his performances of Mozart and Strauss, Brain was regarded as the finest virtuoso of his day. Britten composed the *Serenade for Tenor, Horn, and Strings* (1943) for him.

Braine, **John (Gerard)** (1922–86) British novelist. His first novel, *Room at the Top* (1957), was an instant success, its opportunistic hero being hailed as a representative example of an 'angry young man'. Braine's later novels express less radical views and include *Finger of Fire* (1977) and *One and Last Love* (1981).

brake-van (US **caboose**) A vehicle at the end of a freight train that provides braking, as well as accommodation for the train guard. Continuous BRAKING SYSTEMS on all vehicles of a train were introduced in the mid-19th century. Before this, brake-vans provided the only braking other than that on the locomotive.

braking system A device used to retard or stop

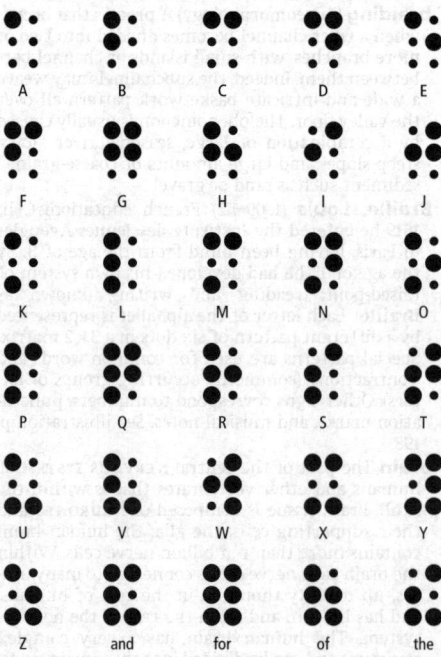

Braille The embossed dots of the letters of the alphabet.

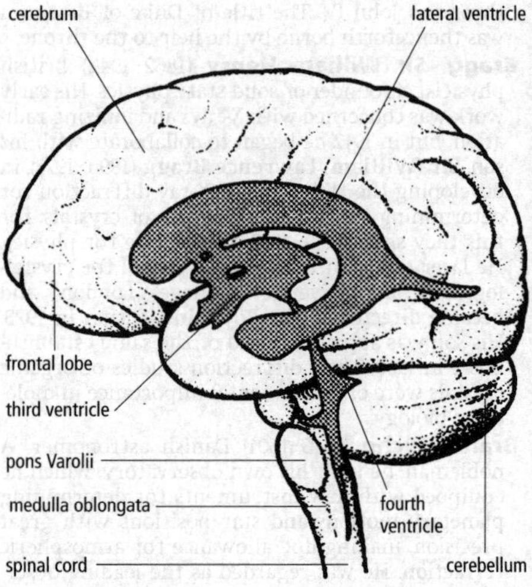

Brain The human brain.

the motion of a vehicle or machine. Carts use simple brake-blocks pressed against the wheel-rim; BICYCLES also most commonly use rim brakes with callipers to press rubber or leather blocks against both sides of the rim. Early motor cars used band brakes, in which a metal band lined with friction material was wrapped around a brake wheel. These had a tendency to 'lock' (seize solidly) and were supplanted by drum brakes, in which, when the brake pedal is depressed, two pivoted brake shoes are forced apart at their free ends to press against the inside of a brake drum. Much heat is dissipated in braking and may cause 'brake fade' through reduced friction between brake drum and shoe at higher temperatures. For this reason most cars and some MOTOR CYCLES use disc brakes, at least on the front wheels. Brake pads are applied to both sides of a cast-iron disc by means of hydraulic cylinders held in a calliper. The disc is open to the atmosphere except where it passes through the calliper, so cooling is very effective. With disc brakes a larger brake force is needed, and the pedal action is therefore usually augmented by a SERVO-MECHANISM. Pressure hydraulic brakes, which use a hydraulic system with a pump and microprocessor anti-lock control, are becoming common in cars. They are known as ABS (anti-lock braking systems).

Bramah, **Joseph** (1748–1814) British inventor. One of the most influential engineers of the Industrial Revolution, Bramah is best known for his hydraulic press, used for heavy forging; he also patented a successful lock. His other inventions included milling and planing machines and other machine tools, a beer-engine, a machine for numbering banknotes, and a water-closet.

Bramante, **Donato (di Angelo)** (1444–1514) Italian architect. Strongly influenced by the architecture of ancient Rome, his work often typifies the Renaissance spirit striving for the ideal of classical perfection as exemplified by the Tempietto in the cloister of San Pietro in Montorio (*c.*1502). As architect to Pope Julius II he designed works at the Vatican as well as the new St Peter's (begun in 1506); his floor-plan for the latter, in the form of a Greek cross crowned with a central dome, was the starting-point for subsequent work on the basilica.

Bran Legendary king of Britain. According to a myth recounted in the medieval Welsh *Mabino-*

gion, Bran was a deity of gigantic stature. After being severely wounded fighting the Irish, he requested his followers to cut off his head. It retained its independent life and continued to provide them with marvellous entertainment on their voyages, until it was laid to rest in London.

Branagh, Kenneth (Charles) (1960–) British actor, producer, and director. In 1984 he joined the Royal Shakespeare Company, where he attracted critical acclaim for roles such as Henry V; in 1989 he played the same part in the film of *Henry V*, which he also directed. He has starred in and directed several other films, such as *Peter's Friends* (1992) and *Mary Shelley's Frankenstein* (1994). He married Emma THOMPSON in 1989; the couple separated in 1995.

Brancusi, Constantin (1876–1957) Romanian sculptor, who spent most of his working life in France. His sculpture represents an attempt to move away from a representational art and to capture the essence of forms by reducing them to their ultimate, almost abstract, simplicity. His subjects, often executed in marble and polished bronze, were frequently repeated and refined several times in his quest for simplicity, as can be seen in his series of 28 'bird' sculptures (*c*.1911–36).

Brandenburg ►**1** A former region of north-west Europe whose Hohenzollern rulers became kings of Prussia and emperors of Germany. Its eastern part was ceded to Poland after World War II. ►**2** A state of Germany, part of East Germany 1952–90; area 29,060 sq km (11,224 sq miles); pop. (est 1990) 2,799,000; capital, Potsdam.

Brandenburg Gate The only one of the city gates of Berlin to survive. It was built in 1788–91 by Carl Langhans (1732–1808), chief architect to Frederick William II of Prussia, in neoclassical style, and surmounted by the Quadriga of Victory, a chariot drawn by four horses. After the construction of the Berlin Wall (1961) it stood in East Berlin, a conspicuous symbol of a divided city; it was reopened on 21 December 1989.

Brando, Marlon (1924–) US actor. An exponent of method acting, he first attracted critical acclaim in the stage production of *A Streetcar Named Desire* (1947); he starred in the film version four years later. Other notable early films included *The Wild One* (1953) and *On the Waterfront* (1954), for which he won an Oscar. His later career included memorable roles in *The Godfather* (1972) and *Apocalypse Now* (1979).

Brandt, Bill (born Hermann Wilhelm Brandt) (1904–83) German-born British photographer. He studied in Paris with Man Ray before moving to London in 1932. He portrayed English social conditions in several books and journals, and was commissioned by the government to record conditions in the London Blitz during World War II. He is best known for his almost abstract treatment of the nude, on which he published a number of books, including *Perspectives of Nudes* (1961).

Brandt, Willy (born Karl Herbert Frahm) (1913–92) German statesman, Chancellor of West Germany 1969–74. He was mayor of West Berlin 1957–66 and in 1964 he became chairman of the West German Social Democratic Party. He achieved international recognition for his policy of détente and the opening of relations with the former Communist countries of the Eastern bloc in the 1960s. A pragmatist, he encouraged the negotiation of joint economic projects and a policy of non-aggression. He also chaired the Brandt Commission on the state of the world economy, the report on which was published in 1980 (see BRANDT REPORT). He was awarded the Nobel Peace Prize in 1971.

Brandt Report A report, entitled *North-South: A Programme for Survival* (1980), by an international commission on the state of the world economy. Convened by the United Nations, it met from 1977 to 1979 under the chairmanship of Willy BRANDT. It recommended urgent improvement in the trade relations between the rich Northern Hemisphere and poor Southern for the sake of both. Governments in the north were reluctant to accept the recommendations. Members of the commission therefore reconvened to produce a second report, *Common Crisis North-South: Co-operation for World Recovery* (1983), which perceived 'far greater dangers than three years ago', forecasting 'conflict and catastrophe' unless the imbalances in international finance could be solved.

brandy An alcoholic drink distilled from wine. The best grape brandies are matured in oak casks and are known as Cognacs or Armagnacs, after the French districts in which they are made. The highest quality of French brandy – very superior old pale (or VSOP) – is usually stored for at least 20 years. Brandy is also made in other countries and from the fermented juice of fruits other than the grape.

Braque, Georges (1882–1963) French painter. A co-founder of the cubist movement with Picasso in 1908, Braque was influenced by Cézanne's geometrical simplification of forms. His collages were the first stage in the development of synthetic cubism. He continued to paint during the postwar period in an essentially cubist style, gradually introducing brighter and brighter colours into his work, at the same time becoming noted for his highly individual treatment of still life.

Brasilia The capital (since 1960) of Brazil; pop. (1991) 1,601,100. Designed by Lucio Costa (1902–63) it was built in an unpopulated region, on a site at the geographical centre of the country, chosen (in 1956) in an unsuccessful attempt to draw commerce away from the crowded coastal areas. It was laid out in the shape of an aeroplane with the most impressive buildings, designed by the Brazilian architect Oscar Niemeyer, at its 'nose'.

brass Originally an ALLOY of copper and zinc. Brass was first made in the 1st millennium BC. It is suitable for CASTING, resists corrosion, and is stronger, harder, and tougher than copper alone. There are two main types of brass: one with more than 64 per cent copper, which can be worked cold (such as pinchbeck, or gilding metal, containing 7–11 per cent zinc and used for decorative metalwork); the other with less copper, which must be worked hot. Other metals can be added to give desirable properties: the addition of manganese increases strength, and adding nickel gives high-tensile brass.

brass, memorial A funerary monument consisting of an engraved brass sheet mounted on a stone slab. Brasses, which were cheaper than sculptured tombs, were probably first introduced during the early 13th century, and had their greatest popularity in England, where more than seven thousand survive from the late 13th to the late 16th centuries.

brass band A combination of musical instruments found throughout Europe, especially popular in Germany and central Europe. In Britain it normally consists of cornets, tubas, tenor horns, baritones, flugelhorn, euphonium, and trombones, with percussion. The history of the British brass band derives partly from the old city 'waits' or street singers and partly from the military wind-band. Competitions began in about 1818 and now centre around Manchester's British Open Championship (founded in 1853) and London's National Brass Band Championship (1860). Much of the brass band material consists of arrangements of light classics, but original works by Elgar (*Severn Suite*) and Holst (*Moorside Suite*) are commensurate with the exceptional skills of the top bands.

Brassey, Thomas (1805–70) British engineer and railway contractor. He built more than 10,000 km (6,500 miles) of railways worldwide and during one period employed an estimated 75,000 workers.

brassica A member of the MUSTARD family, Cruciferae. The genus *Brassica* includes a number of familiar and valuable vegetables, such as the cabbage, cauliflower, Brussels sprout, turnip, and swede. Some species, such as rape, are grown for their oil-rich seeds; some, such as mustard, are used as condiments. Brassicas are native to Europe and the Mediterranean region, and the large number of local races within each species makes their classification very difficult. They tend to be either annual or biennial and to have a strong taproot. Some biennial species, such as the swede and the turnip, develop a swollen root in their first year and are food for humans and cattle. Kohlrabi develops a swollen stem base, which is also used as a vegetable.

brass instruments Wind instruments formerly made of brass though now sometimes other metals are used. They do not include instruments formerly of wood but now sometimes of metal (e.g. flute), nor metal instruments with reed mouthpieces (e.g. saxophone). Each instrument has a cup- or funnel-shaped mouthpiece to be pressed against the player's lips, which vibrate within it something like the double reed of the OBOE. The shape of the mouthpiece affects the quality of the tone, a deep funnel-shaped mouthpiece (such as the HORN's) giving more smoothness, and a cup-shaped mouthpiece (such as the TRUMPET's) giving more brilliance. The shape of the bell at the end of the tube also affects the character of the tone, as does the nature of the tube's bore, cylindrical or conical. Brass instruments sound only the natural HARMONICS of their tube-length, and can thus only play melodies in the high register; in the lower registers they are limited to fanfares, unless equipped with some device to alter their tube-length. The tube may be shortened by opening finger-holes (cornett and serpent) or lengthened by a slide (TROMBONE) or valves. Valves were introduced in the early 19th century. By depressing or turning the valve the column of air is diverted into auxiliary tubing and lengthened sufficiently to lower the pitch by a musical interval so that a further harmonic series becomes available. Brass instruments have been included in the orchestra since the earliest days. In the classical period the orchestral brass usually included merely two horns and two trumpets. Later Beethoven includes either two or three trombones, and up to four horns.

Brathwaite, Edward Kamau (1930–) West Indian poet and historian. His trilogy written in the 1960s and published as *The Arrivants: A New World Trilogy* (1973) explores the Caribbean sense of identity from its African roots, blending oral, written, and musical traditions. A second trilogy on his native Barbados comprises *Mother Poem* (1977), *Sun Poem* (1982), and *X-Self* (1987).

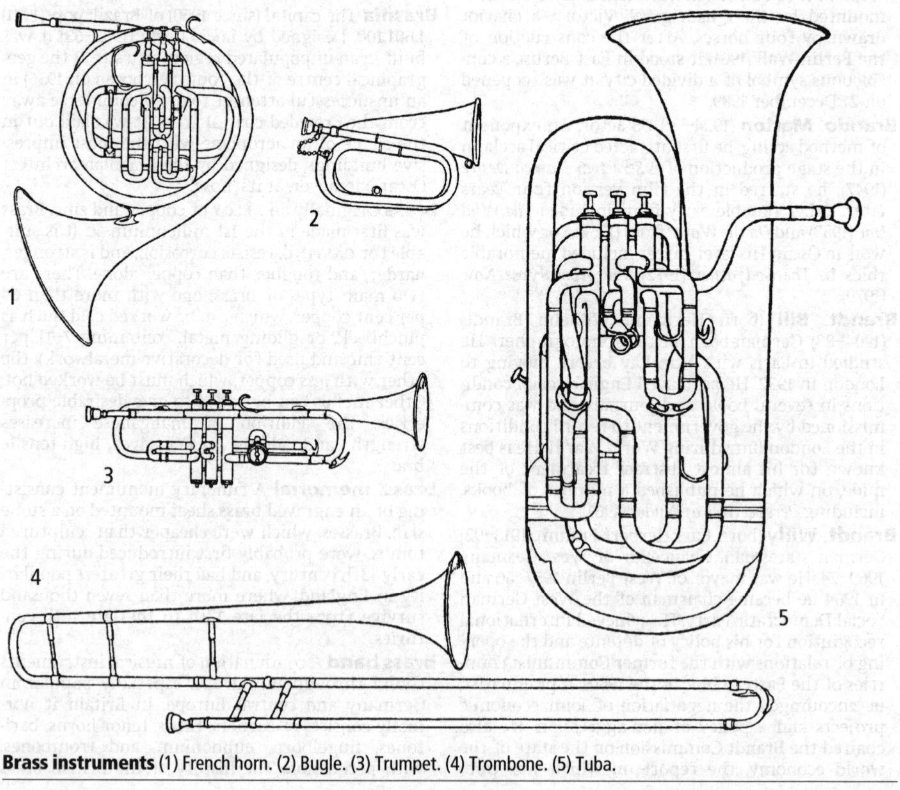

Brass instruments (1) French horn. (2) Bugle. (3) Trumpet. (4) Trombone. (5) Tuba.

Bratislava (German **Pressburg**) A port on the Danube, the capital city of Slovakia; pop. (1991) 441,453. In the Middle Ages it was a frontier town of the Magyar state and from 1536 to 1784 was the capital of Hungary. Its university was founded in 1467. It was incorporated into Czechoslovakia in 1918, becoming capital of the Slovak Socialist Republic in 1969 and capital of independent Slovakia in 1992. Its industrial suburbs produce chemicals, oil, rubber, electrical and engineering goods.

Brattain, Walter Hauser See SHOCKLEY, WILLIAM BRADFORD.

Braun, Eva (1910–45) German wife of Adolf Hitler. Secretary to Hitler's staff photographer, Braun became Hitler's mistress in the 1930s. Hitler and Braun married during the fall of Berlin, shortly before committing suicide together in the air-raid shelter of his Berlin headquarters.

Braun, Karl Ferdinand (1850–1918) German physicist. Braun contributed to wireless telegraphy and to the development of the cathode ray tube. He discovered the rectification properties of certain crystals and invented the coupled system of radio transmission. His demonstration that a beam of electrons could be deflected by an electric field or by a magnetic field led to the development of the Braun tube, the forerunner of the cathode-ray tube. He shared the Nobel Prize for physics in 1909.

Braun, Wernher Magnus Maximilian von (1912–77) German-born US rocket engineer. An enthusiast for space travel from boyhood, Braun began to develop rockets in the 1930s. His work received support from the German army, his team being responsible for the V-2 rockets used by Germany in World War II. After the war he moved to the USA, leading the efforts which eventually resulted in successful launches of satellites, interplanetary missions, and the landing of men on the Moon in 1969.

Bravo, Manuel Alvarez (1902–) Mexican photographer. Bravo taught himself to take photographs in 1920, soon receiving encouragement from Edward Weston. At first a Pictorialist, he was soon influenced by SURREALISM, exploring intuitively, poetically, and compassionately the metaphorical symbols beneath the stark religious and political contrasts of his native land.

Brazil The largest country in South America. Brazil borders ten countries, has a coastline 7,400 km (4,600 miles) long, and straddles the equator from latitude 4° N to past latitude 33° S.

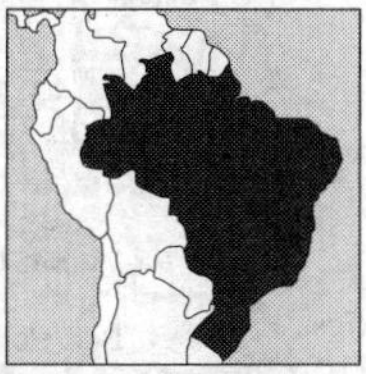

Physical. The whole of the northern region lies in the vast Amazon basin with its tributary rivers. South of this are the Mato Grosso with its grassland plateau and the *campos*, mountain plateaux intersected by deep river valleys. In the region of great lakes the climate becomes suited to coffee-growing. Southward the land drops away to a vast plain suitable for livestock and plantation farming. The destruction in recent decades of up to 12 per cent of the vast Amazonian rain forest is a cause for worldwide concern.

Economy. A huge newly industrialized country, Brazil has the eighth largest economy in the world. Industry is concentrated in the centre and south, while the drought-prone north and north-east remain undeveloped. Only about 7 per cent of Brazil's land area is considered arable. While agriculture has been neglected in favour of industry and food imports have increased, crops such as sugar and cocoa and exports such as coffee, soya beans, and orange concentrates remain important. Brazil is rich in minerals: it has the third largest reserves of bauxite in the world, the largest reserves of columbium, high-grade iron ore, one of the largest reserves of beryllium, as well as gold, manganese and tin in large quantities. Tin, iron ore, machinery, and other industrial products now account for more than half of all exports. Brazil also has one of the world's largest capacities for hydroelectric power production. High inflation, a massive foreign debt, and extreme inequalities in wealth distribution have restricted economic growth and led to severe social problems including an estimated 3 million street children.

History. Brazil is the only South American country originally established as a Portuguese colony, having been awarded to the Portuguese crown by the Treaty of Tordesillas (1494). Settlement began in 1532 with the foundation of São Vicente by Martim Afonso de SOUSA. During the first half of the 16th century twelve captaincies were established. No centralized government was established until 1549 when Thomé de Sousa was named governor-general and a capital was established at Salvador (Bahia). The north-eastern coast was lost to the Dutch briefly in the 17th century but was regained.

By 1800 the prosperity of the colony had outstripped that of Portugal. As a result of the NAPOLEONIC WARS, the Portuguese court was transferred to Rio de Janeiro, which was transformed into the centre of the Portuguese empire. When John VI returned to Lisbon in 1821, his son Pedro remained behind as regent. In 1822 he became Emperor Pedro I of Brazil in an almost bloodless coup, and established an independent empire which lasted until the abdication of his son Pedro II in 1889. Brazil's neo-colonial economy based upon agricultural exports such as coffee and wild rubber produced upon the fazenda (estate), and dependent on slave labour, remained virtually intact until the downfall of the country's two predominant institutions – slavery (1888), and the monarchy (1889). In 1891 Brazil became a republic with a federal constitution. The fraudulent elections of 1930 and the effects of the Great DEPRESSION prompted the intervention of the military and the appointment of Getúlio VARGAS as provisional president. Vargas was to remain in power until he was deposed in 1945. He remained a powerful force in international politics until his suicide in 1954. Vargas' successor, Juscelino Kubitschek (1956–61) embarked upon an ambitious expansion of the economy, including the construction of a futuristic capital city at BRASILIA, intended to encourage development of the interior. President João Goulart (1961–64) had to face the consequent inflation and severe balance-of-payments deficit. In rural areas peasant leagues mobilized behind the cause of radical land reform. Faced with these threats, Brazil's landowners and industrialists backed the military coup of 1964 and the creation of a series of authoritarian regimes which sought to attract foreign investment. President Figueiredo (1978–84) re-established civilian rule and democracy, and under his successor José Sarne (1985–89) a new constitution was approved. Rapid industrialization, together with urbanization, had greatly increased inequalities of income. In the early 1990s very high inflation, together with an economic recession, challenged the government of President Collor de Mello, who himself was faced with allegations of corruption, and resigned in 1992. Itamar Franco then served as President until 1995, when Fernando Cardoso (elected in 1994) succeeded him. Cardoso pursued privatization policies but the economy has remained weak.

Capital: Brasília
Area: 8,511,965 sq km (3,286,488 sq mi)
Population: 155,822,000 (1995)
Currency: 1 cruzeiro = 100 centavos
Religions: Roman Catholic 87.8%; Protestant 6.1%
Ethnic Groups: Mulatto 22.0%; Portuguese 15.0%; Mestizo 12.0%; Italian 11.0%; Black 11.0%; Spanish 10.0%; German 3.0%; Japanese 0.8%; Amerindian 0.1%
Languages: Portuguese (official); German; Japanese; Italian; Amerindian languages
International Organizations: UN; OAS

Brazil nut tree A tree, *Bertholletia excelsa*, which can grow up to 40 m (130 feet), and is a native of South American rain forests. It is a member of the family Lecythidaceae, with some 450 species spread throughout the tropics, and produces large, round, woody fruits, up to 15 cm (6 inches) in diameter, inside which are up to 24 Brazil 'nuts'. These are really SEEDS, rich in oil, and not true NUTS in the botanical sense.

brazing The joining of two metals by heating, using BRASS as a filler. The surfaces of the two metals to be joined are placed next to each other and cleaned by heating with a FLUX. When both pieces are at red heat the brass (sometimes called spelter) is introduced. It melts and flows between the two surfaces. On cooling, the brass solidifies and the two pieces are held firmly together. Only those metals with a melting-point significantly above that of brass can be joined in this way. The joint is not as strong as one made by WELDING, although it is stronger than a soldered joint.

Brazzaville The capital and a major port of the Republic of the Congo, at the lowest navigable point on the River Congo; pop. (est. 1995) 2,936,000. It was founded in 1880 by the French explorer Savorgnan de Brazza and was capital of French Equatorial Africa from 1910 to 1958. The city developed after World War II when it was used as a base for the Free French forces in Africa as a trans-shipment point of goods for other Central African countries. Its university was founded in 1972. Industries include railway repair works, shipyards, and consumer goods.

bread A staple food made by baking a dough composed principally of meal or flour mixed with water. Leavened bread is made with yeast, which causes the dough to rise, while unleavened bread uses no yeast and produces a flat bread. Types of

Brazil

unleavened bread include Mexican tortillas, made from a special type of corn flour, and Indian chapatis and Greek pitta bread, both made from wheat flour. Leavened bread is nearly always made with wheat, as it is unique in forming an elastic, springy dough when kneaded with water. This elastic texture is due to a protein, gluten, present in the wheat. For bread-making, flour that is high in protein is generally used, derived from bread wheat (*Triticum aestivum*). The milled grain is mixed to a dough with water and yeast. Bakers' yeast, *Saccharomyces cerevisiae*, is used commercially. The dough is left for a period to rise: during this time the yeast reacts with sugars in the dough to form carbon dioxide gas, the raising agent, and ETHANOL, which is vaporized during baking and contributes to the smell of the freshly baked bread. Other fermentation products add to the texture or flavour of the final bread. Although the simplest breads (such as the French baguette or Italian-style bread) use only white flour, salt, and yeast, other breads have added ingredients. Different flours, such as wholewheat (milled from whole grains), rye, and potato flour, produce breads with different colours, flavours, and textures. Small amounts of shortening (fat or oil) can be added to soften the bread, and sugar may sometimes be added for sweetening and in order to increase the amount of material available for fermentation.

breadfruit (or **jackfruit**) A tropical tree, *Artocarpus altilis*, native to parts of south-east Asia. Breadfruits belong to the economically important family Moraceae, also including figs and mulberries. Although native to eastern Malaysia, the breadfruit is cultivated throughout south-east Asia, the Pacific islands, and parts of South America. Its oval green fruits, each around 20 cm (8 inches) in diameter, consist of 30–40 per cent carbohydrate; the bread-like flesh of this fruit forms the staple diet in some areas. Other species of the genus include the giant jackfruit, *A. scortechinii*.

Breakspear, Nicholas See ADRIAN IV.

bream A species of fish in the CARP family, *Abramis brava*, widely distributed in Europe. It is a deep-bodied fish with an exceptionally long anal fin, and thrives in slow-flowing deep rivers, canals, and lowland lakes. It feeds, often in schools, in a head-down posture. Its prey are mainly bottom-living invertebrates, which burrow into the mud, from which the bream's protrusible mouthparts are well equipped to extract them.

Bream, Julian (Alexander) (1933–) British guitarist and lute-player. He made his London début in 1950 and benefited from an early involvement with Andrés Segovia. He formed the Julian Bream Consort for the performance of early consort music and has revived and edited much early music. Britten, Walton, and others composed works for him.

Brearley, Harold (1871–1948) British metallurgist responsible for the commercial development of stainless STEEL. The latter part of the 19th century saw intense interest in the development of alloy STEELS for use with machine-tools, and for manufacturing the teeth of power shovels and other equipment subject to severe abrasion. In 1912, while investigating the use of high-chromium steel for rifle barrels, Brearley noted its exceptional resistance to CORROSION and suggested its use in cutlery.

breathalyser A simple, portable apparatus that estimates the concentration of alcohol in the blood by testing alcohol levels in the breath, usually by noting the colour change in crystals of potassium dichromate. It is commonly used to determine whether or not drivers have exceeded permitted levels of alcohol intake. A positive breathalyser test will usually be followed up by a more accurate breath test, and tests of blood or urine alcohol levels.

breccia Rocks comprising mixtures of angular rock fragments cemented within a finer-grained deposit. These fragments may be sedimentary, igneous, or organic in origin, but by definition they must be angular; if they are rounded, the rock is called a CONGLOMERATE.

Brecht, (Eugen) Bertolt (Friedrich) (1898–1956) German dramatist, producer, and poet. His interest in combining music and drama led to a number of successful collaborations with Kurt Weill, the first of these being *The Threepenny Opera* (1928), an adaptation of John Gay's *The Beggar's Opera*. In his later drama, which was written in exile after Hitler's rise to power and includes *Mother Courage* (1941) and *The Caucasian Chalk Circle* (1948), Brecht experimented with his ideas of a Marxist 'epic theatre'.

Breckinridge, John Cabell (1821–75) US politician and general. He served as a Democrat member of the House of Representatives (1851–55), before being elected as BUCHANAN's Vice-President in 1856. When the Democratic Party split in 1860, he ran for President against Abraham LINCOLN as the candidate of the Southern Democrats. From November 1861, he saw extensive service as a major-general in the army of the Confederacy Party before becoming Secretary of State for War under Jefferson DAVIS in 1865.

Breckland A tract of heathland with thicket in east England on the border between Norfolk and Suffolk.

Brecon Beacons An area of the Welsh countryside dominated by the two highest peaks in south Wales – Pen y Fan (886 m, 2,906 ft) and Corn Dû (873 m, 2,863 ft). The Brecon Beacons National Park (1957) stretches from the Tywi valley in the west to the Black Mountains in the east, covering an area of 1,344 sq km (519 sq miles).

Breda A manufacturing town in the province of North Brabant, south-west Netherlands, at the junction of the Mark and Aa rivers; pop. (1991) 124,800. It is remembered for the Compromise of Breda (1866), a protest against Spanish rule; the manifesto of Charles II (who lived there in exile), stating his terms for accepting the throne of Britain (1660); and the Treaty of Breda, which ended the Anglo-Dutch war of 1665–67. Its industries include textiles, chocolate, and metal goods.

Breitenfeld, Battles of Two battles during the THIRTY YEARS WAR, which take their name from a village near Leipzig. The first was fought on 17 September 1631, between Count Johannes Tilly's Catholic forces and the Protestant army of GUSTAVUS ADOLPHUS of Sweden. Despite an early advantage, Tilly's traditional infantry squares were overwhelmed by the Swedes' flexible linear tactics. Gustavus's victory was the first major Protestant success of the war, and it announced the arrival of Sweden as a power on the European stage. The second battle, on 2 November 1642, ended in another Swedish victory.

Bremen ▶**1** A state of Germany surrounded on all sides by Lower Saxony; area 404 sq km (156 sq miles); pop. (1991) 552,750. ▶**2** An industrial city and port on the River Weser; pop. (1989) 537,600. It is the capital of Bremen state and a major trade outlet to the North Sea with oil refineries, shipbuilding, textiles, vehicles, electronics, and food processing.

Bremerhaven A port in Lower Saxony, on the North Sea coast of Germany, north of Bremen; pop. (1991) 130,940. Fishing, engineering, and shipbuilding are the main industries. Founded in 1827, the first regular shipping service between continental Europe and the USA began here in 1847.

bremsstrahlung (in physics) The ELECTROMAGNETIC RADIATION produced by a change in velocity of a charged particle. Typically, bremsstrahlung occurs in an X-ray tube when high-energy electrons are slowed down on impact with a metal target, hence the name, which is German for 'braking radiation'. The radiation shows a continuous range of wavelengths down to a minimum, which depends on the velocity of the charged particles. Another example of bremsstrahlung emission is in secondary COSMIC RAYS, in which high-energy electrons and positrons passing close to the nuclei of atoms lose energy with the production of gamma radiation. In the above examples, the charged particles change their velocity in the electric fields of atomic nuclei. A related effect is **magneto bremsstrahlung**, also known as **synchrotron radiation**, which is radiation produced when charged particles change their direction in passing through magnetic fields. This occurs in cyclic PARTICLE ACCELERATORS and is one of the causes of energy loss in the electron synchrotron. The radiation produced has a definite wavelength, which depends on the magnetic field and is usually in the ultraviolet or X-ray region of the electromagnetic spectrum. Synchrotron radiation of this type is a useful research tool.

Brendan, St (*c*.486–*c*.575) Irish abbot. The legend of the 'Navigation of St Brendan' (*c*.1050), describing his voyage with a band of monks to a promised land (possibly Orkney or the Hebrides), was widely popular in the Middle Ages. Feast day, 16 May.

Brentano, Franz (1838–1917) German philosopher, celebrated for his emphasis on intentionality as a defining characteristic of mental acts. The idea was introduced in his best-known book, *Psychology from an Empirical Standpoint* (1874).

brent goose See GOOSE.

Bresson, Robert (1907–) French film director. His most notable films, most of which feature unknown actors, include *Diary of a Country Priest* (1951), *The Trial of Joan of Arc* (1962), and *The Devil, Probably* (1977).

Brest A commercial port, arsenal, and naval base on the Atlantic coast of Brittany in north-west France; pop. (1990) 153,100. Originally a Roman military outpost, Brest was developed as a major French port by Cardinal Richlieu in the 1630s. It has shipyards, engineering, and chemical factories as well as a Naval School, Maritime Museum, Oceanographic Research Centre, and university. Brest has been largely rebuilt after the devastation of World War II when it was a German submarine base.

Brest (or **Brest-Litovsk**; Polish **Brzescnad Bugiem**) A port and industrial city in western Belarus, situated close to the Polish border at the junction of the Bug and Mukhavets rivers; pop. (1990) 268,800. A treaty of peace between Germany and Russia was signed here in 1918. It was the birthplace of the Israeli prime minister Menachem Begin. Its industries include engineering, sawmilling, textiles, and food processing.

Brest-Litovsk, Treaty of (1918) An agreement between Soviet Russia, Germany, and Austria-Hungary, signed in the town of that name in Poland. The conference opened in December 1917 in order to end Soviet participation in World War I. TROTSKY skilfully prolonged discussions in the hope of Allied help for the RUSSIAN REVOLUTION or of a socialist uprising of German and Austro-Hungarian workers. Neither happened. LENIN capitulated and ordered his delegates to accept the German terms. By the treaty, Russia surrendered nearly half of its European territory: Finland, the Baltic provinces, Belorussia (now Belarus), Poland, the Ukraine, and parts of the Caucasus. The German armistice in the west (November 1918) annulled the treaty, but at VERSAILLES Russia only regained the Ukraine.

Brétigny, Treaty of (1360) Treaty concluded between Edward III of England, and John II of France following John's defeat and capture at POITIERS. It released John on payment of a ransom of three million crowns, brought the HUNDRED YEARS WAR temporarily to a halt, and saw the English renounce claims to Anjou and Normandy while retaining Gascony and Guyenne. It was never fully implemented, and Anglo-French hostilities broke out again in 1369.

Breton (or **Brezhoneg**) A native of Brittany in north-west France. The language of the Bretons belongs to the Brythonic branch of the Celtic language group. It is the only Celtic language now spoken on the European mainland, representing the modern development of the language brought from Cornwall and south Wales in the 5th and 6th centuries by Britons fleeing from the Saxon invaders. Until the 20th century it was widely spoken in Brittany, but official encouragement of the use of French contributed to its decline, although there has recently been some revival of the language.

Breton, André (1896–1966) French poet, essayist, and critic. Influenced by the work of Sigmund Freud and the poet Paul Valéry, Breton was first involved with Dadaism, co-founding the movement's review *Littérature* in 1919. When Dada collapsed in the early 1920s, Breton launched the surrealist movement; its chief theorist, he first outlined the movement's philosophy in his manifesto of 1924. His creative writing is characterized by surrealist techniques such as 'automatic' writing and the startling juxtaposition of images, as in his famous poetic novel *Nadja* (1928).

Bretton Woods Conference (1944) A United Nations monetary and financial conference. Representatives from 44 nations met at Bretton Woods, New Hampshire, USA, to consider the stabilization of world currencies and the establishment of credit for international trade in the post-war world. They drew up a project for an International Bank for Reconstruction and Development (WORLD BANK) which would make long-term capital available to states urgently needing such aid, and a plan for an INTERNATIONAL MONETARY FUND (IMF) to finance short-term imbalances in international trade and payments. The Bank and the Fund continue as specialized agencies of the United Nations.

Breughel See BRUEGEL.

brewing The process by which beers, ales, and lagers are made. In the West the basic ingredient of beer is barley, while in Africa millet or maize may be used, and rice beer is made in Japan. In beer-making the barley or other grain is germinated, and the young seedlings are then dried to produce malt. The malt is ground, and placed in a mash tub with water and cereal, where enzymes in the malt convert the starch into fermentable sugars. The resulting liquid, called wort, is transferred to a brewing kettle, where flavourings, particularly hops, are added, and the mixture is boiled. The mixture is then filtered, and FERMENTATION is stimulated by the introduction of yeast. Traditionally, the liquid at this stage is filtered again and placed in wooden barrels, where fermentation continues. Ales and stouts are usually fermented at 15–20°C, while lagers are fermented at 6–8°C for longer periods. In keg beers and lagers, fermentation is stopped after only a short period by placing the liquid in sealed metal barrels and introducing carbon dioxide.

Brewster, Sir David (1781–1868) Scottish physicist. He is best known for his work on the laws governing the polarization of light, and for his invention of the kaleidoscope. Brewster also worked extensively on the optical classification of crystals and minerals, and on the use of spectroscopy for chemical analysis.

Brezhnev, Leonid (Ilich) (1906–82) Soviet statesman, General Secretary of the Communist Party of the USSR 1966–82 and President 1977–82. Born in Russia, he held offices within the Soviet Communist Party (CPSU) before and after World War II, rising to become Chairman of the Presidium in 1960. In 1964 he and Aleksei Kosygin forced Nikita Khrushchev to resign and Brezhnev eventually became General Secretary of the Party. His period in power was marked by intensified persecution of dissidents at home and by attempted détente followed by renewed cold war in 1968. He was largely responsible for the decision to invade Czechoslovakia in 1968.

Brezhoneg See BRETON.

Brian Boru (*c.*926–1014) The last High King of Ireland (1011). He had previously made himself ruler of Munster and Limerick in southern Ireland. In doing so Brian, ruler of the Dal Cais dynasty of Munster, overcame the influence of the powerful Uú Néill dynasty which had dominated Ireland for three centuries. In 1012 the men of Leinster, and supported by the Norse settlers of Dublin, rose in revolt. The battle of CLONTARF brought victory to Brian's forces, though he was killed in the fighting.

Briand, Aristide (1862–1932) French statesman. He was 11 times Premier, and Foreign Minister in fourteen successive governments. He entered Parliament in 1903, a strong socialist and an impressive orator. In 1905 he took a leading part in the separation of Church from state and by 1909 had become Premier. In the 1920s he was a powerful advocate of peace and international cooperation, and supported the League of Nations. The cabinet he headed in 1921 fell because of his criticism of France's harsh treatment of Germany after the Treaty of VERSAILLES. Working closely with Austen CHAMBERLAIN and Gustav Stresemann, the British and German Foreign Ministers, his greatest achievements were the LOCARNO Pact (1925) and the KELLOGG–BRIAND PACT (1928).

brick A rectangular manufactured block of dried or fired clay, small enough to be lifted and placed with one hand, used in building. Bricks are CERAMICS, and were first made by drying mixtures of mud and straw (adobe), and such bricks are still used in hot, dry climates. KILN-fired bricks were first made in Mesopotamia in about 3200–2800 BC. Firing made the bricks harder and resistant to rain erosion. Brick-making remains essentially the same today: clay or shale is blended to a plastic consistency with water, then moulded to shape. In large-scale production the clay is either extruded and then cut to size by wires, or moulded under high pressure in steel moulds. The bricks are then fired in kilns. REFRACTORY bricks are made from special clays with high concentrations of silica or ALUMINA.

bricklaying The process of arranging BRICKS in a wall. Bonding (overlapping the bricks in successive courses) ensures strength and stability. Different bonding patterns result from different arrangements of stretchers (bricks with the long axis parallel to the wall) and headers (bricks with the long axis at right angles to the wall). In CAVITY WALLS, the two walls (leaves) are laid in stretcher bond and linked with metal ties across the cavity. For solid walls, various bonds are used, with the headers tying the wall across its width. The bricks are laid in MORTAR; where the brickwork is visible in the finished building, clean and regular jointing between the bricks is important.

Bride, St See BRIDGET, ST (of Ireland).

bridge (in construction) A structure, usually built over a river, road, or railway, enabling road or rail vehicles or pedestrians to cross. One type of primitive bridge is the clapper bridge, in which large stone slabs are supported on stone piers. The

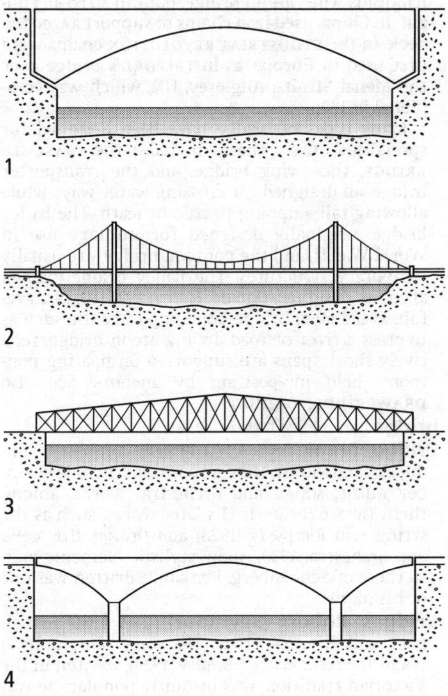

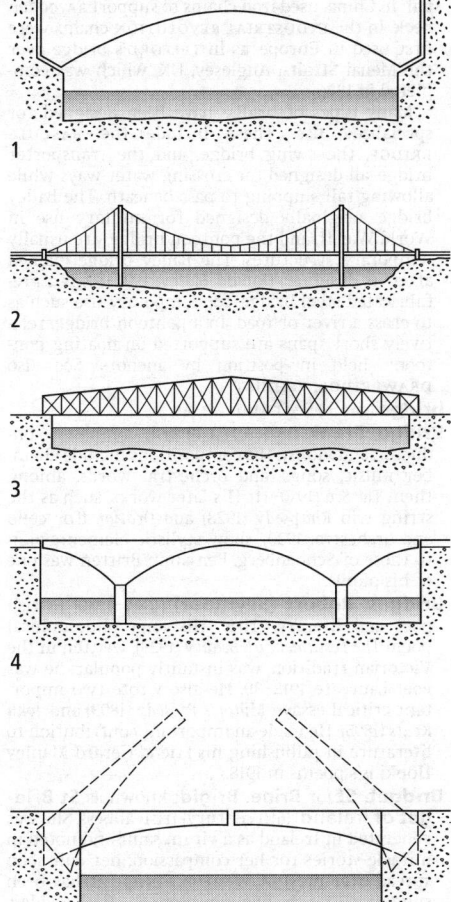

Bridges (1) Arch bridge. (2) Suspension bridge. (3) Girder bridge. (4) Cantilever bridge. (5) Bascule bridge.

Romans were the first to use the masonry arch in bridge-building. The Romans also used timber to build bridges. Roman arches were invariably semicircular, but in China flatter, segmental-arch bridges were built, which could span greater distances than the semicircular arch. Arched bridges of this type were first built in Europe in the 14th century.

In 1779 the Coalbrookdale **iron bridge** heralded a new era of iron and steel arch bridges. Cast iron was soon replaced by wrought iron because of its greater strength under bending loads. The use of wrought iron reached its peak in 1885 with the completion of the Luiz I bridge at Oporto in Portugal, which spanned 173 m (566 feet). Since then, several steel arch bridges have been built with spans of over 500 m (1,650 feet). The Forth Bridge, in Scotland, UK, built between 1882 and 1889, was the first long-span CANTILEVER bridge and has two spans, each of 520 m (1,710 feet). The concrete arch of the Gladesville Bridge in Sydney, built in 1964, spans 305 m (1,000 feet). The earliest SUSPENSION BRIDGES, which were widespread geographically, had three ropes which hung from anchorages on each side and formed a V-shaped walkway with handrails. The Lan Jin Bridge, built in AD 65 at Yunnan in China, used iron chains to support a wooden deck. In the INDUSTRIAL REVOLUTION chains were first used in Europe, as in TELFORD's bridge over the Menai Straits, Anglesey, UK, which was completed in 1826.

Many types of bridge have been designed for specialized use. These include the BASCULE BRIDGE, the swing bridge, and the transporter bridge, all designed for crossing water-ways while allowing tall shipping to pass beneath. The Bailey bridge, originally designed for military use in World War II, and the pontoon bridge, are usually temporary structures. The Bailey bridge (named after its designer, Donald Bailey, 1901–85) is a prefabricated steel bridge, for temporary use such as to cross a river or road. In a pontoon bridge, relatively short spans are supported on floating pontoons, held in position by anchors. See also DRAWBRIDGE; VIADUCT.

bridge (game) See CARD-GAMES.

Bridge, Frank (1879–1941) British composer, conductor, and violist. His compositions include chamber music, songs, and orchestral works, among them *The Sea* (1910–11). His later works, such as the string trio *Rhapsody* (1928) and *Oration* (for cello and orchestra, 1930), show stylistic elements akin to those of Schoenberg. Benjamin Britten was one of his pupils.

Bridges, Robert (Seymour) (1844–1930) British poet and literary critic. His long philosophical poem *The Testament of Beauty* (1929), written in the Victorian tradition, was instantly popular; he was Poet Laureate 1913–30. He also wrote two important critical essays, *Milton's Prosody* (1893) and *John Keats* (1895). He made an important contribution to literature in publishing his friend Gerard Manley Hopkins's poems in 1918.

Bridget, St (or **Bride, Brigid**; known as **St Bridget of Ireland**) (6th century) Irish abbess. She was venerated in Ireland as a virgin saint and noted in miracle stories for her compassion; her cult soon spread over most of western Europe. It has been suggested that she may represent the Irish goddess Brig. Feast day, 1 February.

Bridget, St (or **Birgitta**; known as **St Bridget of Sweden**) (*c*.1303–73), Swedish nun and visionary. She experienced her first vision of the Virgin Mary at the age of 7. After her husband's death she was inspired by further visions to devote herself to religion and she founded the Order of Bridgettines (*c*.1346) at Vadstena in Sweden. Feast day, 23 July.

Bridgetown The capital of Barbados, a port on the south coast; pop. (1990) 6,720.

Bridgewater, Francis Egerton, 3rd Duke of (1736–1803) British landowner, pioneer of canal construction. His estates included coal-mines and to move his coal cheaply, he financed the cutting of the Bridgewater canal from Worsley to Manchester. James Brindley (1716–72) was the gifted engineer he employed for this project, completed in 1772, which not only caused a dramatic reduction in the price of coal there, but introduced new methods of canal construction and inaugurated the great era of English canal-building in the 1770s and 1780s.

Bridgman, Percy Williams (1882–1961) US physicist. He worked mainly on the properties of liquids and solids under very high pressures, and designed an apparatus that achieved a fluid pressure of 30,000 atmospheres. His techniques were later used in making artificial diamonds and other minerals, and he became involved in the Manhattan Project, which was set up in 1942 to develop an atom bomb. He was awarded the Nobel Prize for physics in 1946.

brig A small two-masted sailing vessel square-rigged on both masts, widely used in the days of sail on short sea routes and for coastal trading. A brigantine is similar but is fore-and-aft rigged on the mainmast. A hermaphrodite brig has the usual square-rigged foremast combined with the mainmast of a SCHOONER, a rig designed to increase speed with the wind abeam (from the side). The marine steam-engine made brigs obsolete, although some are still used by navies for sail training.

Brigantes The Celtic inhabitants of northern Britain between the Humber and the Tyne, known as the 'mountain folk'. After the Roman invasion in 43 AD, Emperor Claudius formed an alliance with their queen Cartimandua. Roman troops helped suppress at least three revolts against her; she also handed over the refugee CARATACUS. During the ROMAN civil wars 68–69 she was expelled by her anti-Roman husband. Petilius Cerealis was made governor (legatus) of Britain by Vespasian; he advanced north *c*.71–74 AD, and established Eboracum (York) as a permanent legionary fortress for the Ninth Legion in this former tribal territory.

Briggs, Henry (1561–1630) English mathematician. He was renowned for his work on logarithms, in which he introduced the decimal base, made the thousands of calculations necessary for the tables, and popularized their use. Briggs also devised the usual method used for long division.

Bright, John (1811–89) British Liberal politician and reformer. A noted orator, Bright was the leader, along with Richard Cobden, of the campaign to repeal the Corn Laws. He was also a vociferous opponent of the Crimean War (1854) and was closely identified with the 1867 Reform Act.

brightening agent A fluorescent substance added to soapless detergents (for example washing powders) which absorbs ultraviolet light and emits blue light, thereby counteracting the yellowing of white fabrics caused by repeated washings. They are also used to enhance the appearance of new fabrics.

brightness See LUMINOSITY.

Brighton A residential town and resort on the south coast of England, in East Sussex; pop. (1991) 133,400. It was patronized by the Prince of Wales (later George IV) from *c.*1780 to 1827, and has much Regency architecture and a royal pavilion rebuilt for him by John Nash in Oriental style. The University of Sussex at nearby Lewes was founded in 1961 and the University of Brighton (formerly Brighton Polytechnic) was established in 1992.

Brigid, St See BRIDGET, ST (of Ireland).

brill A species of FLATFISH with a thickset, large head and both eyes on the left side. Native to the seas around Europe, it is most common on sandy bottoms, from the shoreline down to 70 m (230 feet). It feeds on fishes such as sand eels and whiting, and less often on crustaceans.

brimstone butterfly A bright yellow butterfly of the genus *Gonopteryx* (six species), found mainly in Europe and temperate Asia, and belonging to the WHITE butterfly family, Pieridae. Their colour may be the source of the name 'butterfly'.

Brindisi An Adriatic port and capital of Brindisi province, Apulia, on the 'heel' of south-east Italy; pop. (1991) 93,290. The Romans developed a harbour here at the southern end of the Appian Way. It was later used as a point of departure for Crusaders during the 12th–13th century, and as a naval base during World War I. There is a ferry link with Greece and a petrochemicals industry.

Brindley, James (1716–72) Pioneer British canal builder. He began with the Bridgwater canal near Manchester, which included an aqueduct that was a wonder of the age. He designed some 600 km (375 miles) of waterway, connecting most of the major rivers of England. Brindley believed in building contour canals with the minimum of locks, embankments, cuttings, or tunnels, at the expense of greater lengths, and such canals have proved to be the longest to survive.

brine Water saturated or nearly saturated with salt. It is used (now less often than previously) to preserve vegetables, fish, and meat. Sea water, particularly that of the DEAD SEA, is regarded as brine – as is that which penetrates freshwater rivers and lakes. Brine lakes develop as a result of high evaporation, the salt being derived either from the rock or from airborne sea-salt. Some of the most extensive occur in continental interiors, the Great Salt Lake in Utah, USA, being an example.

Brink, André (1935–) South African novelist, short-story writer, and dramatist. Brink, who writes in Afrikaans and translates his work into English, gained international recognition with his seventh novel *Looking on Darkness* (1973), an open criticism of apartheid which became the first novel in Afrikaans to be banned by the South African government. Subsequent novels include *A Dry White Season* (1979), *A Chain of Voices* (1982), *On the Contrary* (1993), and *Imaginings of Sand* (1995).

briquetting A process in which fine coal is compressed into a briquette or block, sometimes with the use of a binder. Coal briquettes were first made in the 1840s and 1850s in Germany. Coal was mixed with a medium-soft tar or asphaltic pitch, heated with steam, and then compressed. Substances now used as binders include inorganic materials such as Portland cement, silica, soda, limestone, and clay; and organic materials such as resins, pitch, molasses, and starch. Binderless briquettes are also produced by carbonizing the coal (see COKE) at about 450°C and then briquetting the resulting char. See also WASTE MANAGEMENT.

Brisbane A port on the east coast of Australia, on the Brisbane River, the capital and largest city of Queensland; pop. (1991) 1,145,540. Founded in 1824 as a penal colony, it is named after Sir Thomas BRISBANE. Its university was founded in 1909 and the city has oil-refining, shipbuilding, textiles, and agricultural machinery industries.

Brisbane, Sir Thomas Makdougall (1773–1860) Scottish soldier and astronomer. In 1790 he joined the army and served with distinction, becoming major-general in 1813. From 1821 until 1825 he was appointed governor of New South Wales. He became an acclaimed astronomer. Brisbane was named after him.

bristle fly (or **tachinid fly**) A stout, true FLY, the size of a housefly or larger. The 1,500 or so species make up the family Tachinidae. Although at first glance bristle flies resemble houseflies, unlike them they have many strong, black bristles, particularly on the abdomen. The cylindrical larvae develop as internal parasites of arthropods, usually other insects, and particularly in the larvae of moths, butterflies, sawflies, and beetles. A single host may have one or several maggots within it, and is ultimately destroyed by these parasites. The adults most commonly feed from flowers.

bristletail See SILVERFISH.

bristleworm A member of the class of ANNELID worms called polychaetes. In narrower usage, bristleworms are species of the subclass Errantia, which includes free-swimming predatory worms and a few parasitic species. They are generally found on sandy sea-shores and species such as the ragworms (*Nereis*) or lugworms (*Arenicola*) are used as fishing bait. Most are flat, bristly, and 5–10 cm (2–4 inches) long. The predatory species have many lateral paddles to help them swim and have eyes and jaws as an aid to catching small invertebrate prey. Many show bright coloration, especially greens and reds, and some are iridescent. When sexually mature, in many bristleworms the rear segments grow large nuptial paddles, allowing them to swim strongly to seek mates.

Bristol A city in south-west England, at the junction of the Avon and Frome rivers; pop. (1991) 370,300. Formerly the county town of Avon (now abolished), since 1996 it has been an independent unitary authority. A leading port and commercial centre since the 12th century, Bristol was the second most important town in England between the 15th and 18th centuries. It was given the status of a county by Edward III in 1373. It developed as one of the 'corners' of the triangular colonial trade which included the shipping of slaves from Africa to the Americas. It is particularly rich in old churches: its cathedral dates back to the 12th century and St Mary Redcliffe to the 13th and 14th centuries. It is the site of the University of Bristol (1909) and the University of the West of England, Bristol (formerly Bristol Polytechnic), which was established in 1992. The city has many light industries; its suburb of Filton has a major aerospace complex. Clifton has BRUNEL's suspension bridge, completed after his death.

Bristol Channel An extension of the River Severn estuary separating England and Wales.

Britain (in full **Great Britain**) The island containing England, Wales, and Scotland, and including the small adjacent islands. After the Old English period 'Britain' was used only as an historical term until about the time of Henry VIII and Edward VI, when it came into practical politics in connection with the efforts made to unite England and Scotland. In 1604 James I was proclaimed 'King of Great Britain', and this name was adopted for the United Kingdom at the Union of 1707, after which 'South Britain' and 'North Britain' were frequent in Acts of Parliament for England and Scotland respectively.

Britain, Battle of (August–October 1940) A series of air battles between Britain and Germany fought over Britain. After the fall of France, German aircraft launched a BOMBING OFFENSIVE against British coastal shipping with the aim of attracting and then destroying British fighter aircraft, as a prelude to a general invasion of Britain. This action (July–August 1940) resulted in heavy German dive-bomber losses. Attacks were then made on southern England, but German losses were again heavy. In late August and early September mass bombing raids took place on British aircraft factories, radar installations, and fighter airfields; these caused heavy British losses, but Hitler ordered the offensive to be diverted to British cities just as RAF Fighter Command was exhausting its reserves of machines and pilots. Hitler's priority of the day bombing of London gave time for Fighter Command to recover. On 1 October day-bombing of major cities was replaced by night-bombing, but by this time it was clear that the major German objective, to destroy British air power, had failed. On 12 October Hitler postponed indefinitely his plan to invade Britain. Though heavily outnumbered by the Germans, the British lost 900 aircraft against 1,700 German losses. Radar, used by the British for the first time in battle, made a significant contribution.

British Antarctic Territory That part of Antarctica claimed by Britain. Designated in 1962 from territory formerly administered as part of the Falklands Islands Dependencies, it includes some 388,500 sq km (150,058 sq miles) of the continent of Antarctica as well as adjacent South Orkney Islands and South Shetland Islands in the South Atlantic. Also in 1962 the former Falklands Islands Dependencies Survey, which had established its first shore-stations in 1944, became the British Antarctic Survey.

British Columbia A province of Canada on the west coast of North America, formed in 1866 by the union of Vancouver Island (a British colony from 1849) and the mainland area which was then called New Caledonia; area 947,800 sq km (365,947 sq miles); pop. (1991) 3,282,060; capital, Victoria. British Columbia is Canada's westernmost and third-largest province. Off its 7,022-km (4,419-mile) Pacific coast lie Vancouver Island and Queen Charlotte Islands. It is a largely mountainous province, with the Rocky Mountains in the south-east, the Coast Mountains along the Pacific coast, and the Stikine Mountains in the north-west. Its highest peak is Fairweather Mountain (4,663 m, 15,298 ft). There are over two million hectares of lakes and waterways which support fishing, farming, recreation, and the generation of hydroelectric power, the largest river being the Fraser River. Commercial forest covers more than half of the province which contains 50 per cent of Canada's softwood timber. Coal, oil, gas, copper, zinc, and molybdenum are the most important mineral resources.

British Commonwealth (fully **British Commonwealth of Nations**) The former name of the COMMONWEALTH or Commonwealth of Nations.

British Empire Lands throughout the world once linked by a common allegiance to the British crown. In 1800, although Britain had lost its 13 American colonies, it still retained Newfoundland, thinly populated parts of Canada, many West Indian islands, and other islands useful for trading purposes. It held Gibraltar from Spain and in 1788 had created a convict settlement in New South Wales, Australia. During the NAPOLEONIC WARS Britain acquired further islands, for example Malta, Mauritius, the Maldives, and also Ceylon and Cape Colony, which was particularly valuable for fresh food supplies for ships on the way to the East. Most of these belonged to the EAST INDIA COMPANY, which was steadily developing and exploiting its trade monopoly in India and beyond. All such acquisitions were seen as part of the development of British commerce, as was to be the seizure of Hong Kong in 1841. From the 1820s, a new colonial movement began, with British families taking passages abroad to develop British settlements. In 1857 the INDIAN MUTINY obliged the British government to take over from the East India Company the administration of that vast sub-continent; in January 1877 Queen Victoria was proclaimed Empress of India. New tropical colonies were competed for in the 'SCRAMBLE FOR AFRICA' and in the Pacific. In 1884 an Imperial Federation League was formed, seeking some form of political federation between Britain and its colonies. The scheme soon foundered, being rejected by the colonial Premiers when they gathered in London for the two Colonial Conferences of 1887 and 1897. Strategically, the key area was seen to be southern Africa, and it was the dream of Cecil RHODES and Alfred Milner to create a single Cape-to-Cairo British dominion, linked by a railway, and acting as the pivot of the whole empire, a dream which faded with the Second BOER WAR. Another result of the Boer War was the creation of the permanent Committee of Imperial Defence (1902), whose function was to be the coordination of the defence of the empire, and which was to continue until 1938. The empire reached its zenith *c.*1920, when German and Ottoman mandates were acquired, and over 600 million people were ruled from London. In the later 19th century movements for home-rule had begun in all the white colonies. Starting in Canada, but spreading to Australasia and South Africa, such moves resulted in 1931 in DOMINION status for these lands. Although the Indian National CONGRESS had been founded in 1885, success by the non-white peoples of the empire for similar self-government proved more difficult. It was only after 1945 that the process of decolonization began, which by 1964 was largely complete. Most former colonies remained members of the COMMONWEALTH OF NATIONS after becoming independent. Britain has 13 remaining dependent territories including GIBRALTAR, the FALKLAND ISLANDS, and BERMUDA, which rejected independence in a referendum in 1995. HONG KONG was handed back to China in 1997.

British Expeditionary Force (BEF) British army contingents sent to France at the outbreak of WORLD WAR I. Following the army reforms of Richard HALDANE a territorial reserve army had been created. This was immediately mobilized when war was declared on 4 August 1914 and, together with regular troops, sent to France under Sir John FRENCH. An expeditionary force was again mobilized and sent to France in September 1939 but, after failing to halt the German advance across the Low Countries and France, had to be rescued in the DUNKIRK evacuation.

British Film Institute Organization founded in 1933 to foster the development and appreciation of film as an art. It operates the National Film Theatre in London, which offers members a daily selection of the world's films on its two screens,

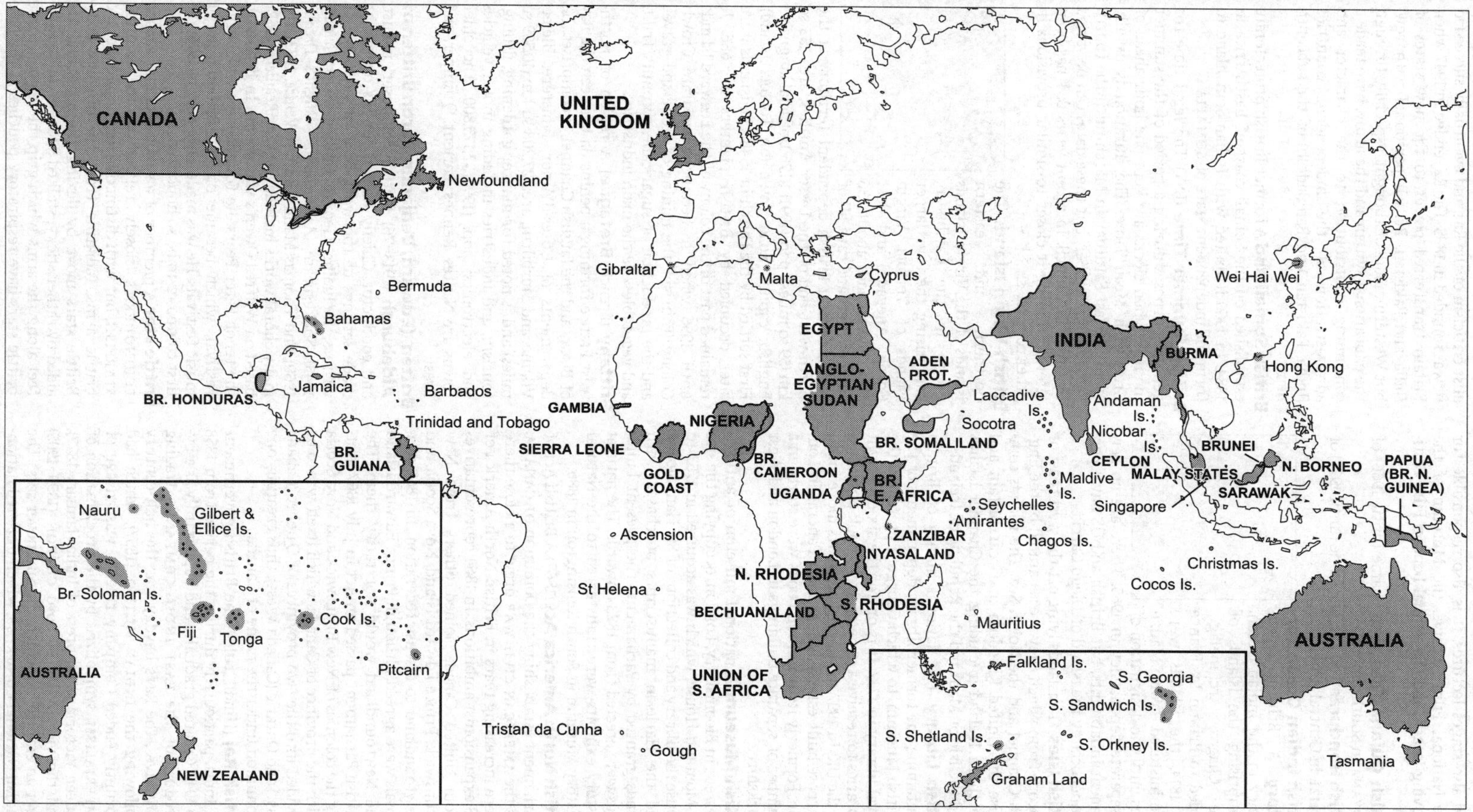

British Empire The Empire in 1914.

and also stages lectures. It is also responsible for the National Film Archive, the Museum of the Moving Image, and the annual London Film Festival.

British Guiana The former name (until 1966) of GUYANA in South America.

British Honduras The former name (until 1973) of BELIZE in Central America.

British Indian Ocean Territory A British dependency in the Indian Ocean, comprising the islands of the Chagos Archipelago. Ceded to Britain by France in 1814, the islands were administered from Mauritius until the designation of a separate dependency in 1965. There are no permanent inhabitants, but British and US naval personnel occupy the island of Diego Garcia.

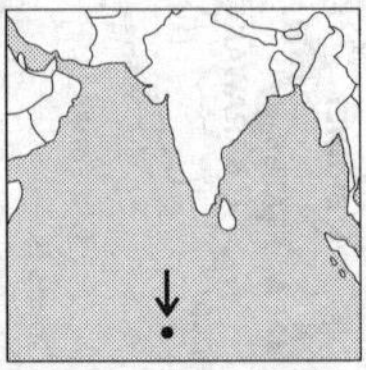

British Isles The islands lying off the west coast of Europe from which they are separated by the English Channel and the North Sea. The islands comprise the United Kingdom of Great Britain and Northern Ireland (including the Channel Islands and the Isle of Man) and the Republic of Ireland.

British Library The national library of Britain containing the former library departments of the British Museum, to which George II presented the royal library in 1757. It is one of the six copyright libraries to receive a copy of every book published in the UK. In 1997 the library began its move into a purpose-built establishment in St Pancras in London. Formerly its 18 million books were stored in a number of separate buildings in London and West Yorkshire.

British Museum A national museum of antiquities, etc. in Bloomsbury, London, occupying the site of Montagu House, which was acquired in 1753 to house the library and collections of Sir Hans Sloane and the Harleian manuscripts purchased with funds granted by Parliament. The present buildings were erected from 1823 onwards. The natural history exhibits were transferred to the Natural History Museum in South Kensington in 1880.

British North America Act (1867) A British Act of Parliament establishing the Dominion OF CANADA. As the AMERICAN CIVIL WAR drew to a close there were increasing fears in British North America of US expansionist ambitions. In 1864 representatives from United Canada joined others from New Brunswick, Prince Edward Island, Nova Scotia, and Newfoundland to discuss federation. In 1867 proposals were agreed, although Prince Edward Island and Newfoundland would not ratify them. The British Parliament passed an Act in July 1867 uniting the colonies of New Brunswick and Nova Scotia with the province of Canada, which itself was to be divided into the two provinces of Quebec (Canada East) and Ontario (Canada West), thus creating 'one Dominion under the name of Canada'.

British Raj (Hindi, 'rule') The British government in India, particularly during the period from 1858 to 1947. Created gradually and haphazardly as a by-product of the EAST INDIA COMPANY's trading objectives, the Raj's heyday was the half-century following the INDIAN MUTINY (1857), which had abruptly ended Company rule. It was an age of IMPERIALISM, symbolized by the proclamation of Queen Victoria as Empress of India (January 1877), and the viceroyalty of Lord CURZON (1899–1905) over an empire 'on which the Sun never sets'. The Indian National CONGRESS, which initiated nationalist criticism of the Raj, and eventually succeeded it, was founded in 1885. The Raj ended in 1947 when Britain transferred power to the new states of India and Pakistan. British personnel withdrew, but Western modes of thought, especially through the educational system and the army, have made a continuing contribution to the character and administration of the independent countries (India, Pakistan, and Bangladesh) of the subcontinent.

British Somaliland A former British protectorate established on the Somali coast of East Africa in 1884. In 1960 it united with Italian Somaliland to form the independent state of SOMALIA.

British Summer Time (BST) The legal time for general purposes during a period of the summer months, when clocks are kept one hour ahead of Greenwich Mean Time. The duration is usually from the last Saturday in March until the fourth Saturday in October, but these dates can be varied by Order in Council. In recent years BST has been altered to bring it closer to similar provisions in other countries.

British Virgin Islands The northern and eastern islands of the Virgin Islands group in the Caribbean, comprising the four larger islands of Tortola, Virgin Gorda, Anegada, and Jost Van Dyke, and about 36 smaller islets and cays, all of which form a British dependent territory at the north-west end of the Lesser Antilles; area 153 sq km (59 sq miles); pop. (1991) 16,750; official language, English; capital, Road Town (on Tortola Island). First settled by the Dutch in 1648, the islands were later occupied by British planters in 1666. It remained part of the colony of the Leeward Islands until 1956 when it became a separate Crown Colony. Tourism, the mining of stone and gravel, and the production of sugar-cane, coconuts, fruit, and vegetables are the main industries.

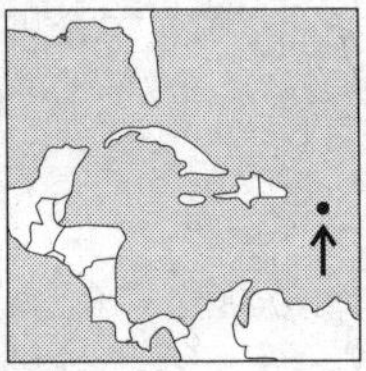

Brittany (French **Bretagne**) A region of north-west France forming a peninsula between the Bay of Biscay and the English Channel. It comprises the departments of Côtes-d'Amor, Finistère, Ille-et-Vilaine, and Morbihan; area 27,208 sq km (10,509 sq miles) and is noted for market gardening, fishing, tourism, and industries including motor vehicles and electronics; pop. (1990) 2,175,800. The chief towns are Nantes, Rennes, Lorient, Quimper, and Brest.

Britten, (Edward) Benjamin, Baron Britten of Aldeburgh (1913–76) British composer, pianist, and conductor. Chiefly known for his operas, he made settings of the work of a varied range of writers, including George Crabbe (*Peter Grimes*, 1945), Shakespeare (*A Midsummer Night's Dream*, 1960), and Thomas Mann (*Death in Venice*, 1973). His many choral works include the *War Requiem* (1962), based on Wilfred Owen's war poems. In 1948, with the tenor Peter Pears, he founded the Aldeburgh Festival, which became one of Britain's major music festivals. He was made a life peer in 1976, the first composer to be so honoured.

brittle star A member of a subclass of star-shaped ECHINODERMS closely related to the familiar STARFISH, but with distinctive longer, mobile, and brittle arms, radiating from the disc-like body. Brittle stars move by flexing the arms and are aided by rather sticky, stalked suckers called tube-feet along the arms which grip the sea-bed. Some brittle stars have respiratory pouches at the base of each arm, which are also used to brood the young. They are the most numerous echinoderms, with some 2,000 species occurring worldwide. A group of species known as basket-stars have arms that branch to form a circular mass of tendrils.

Brno (German **Brünn**) An industrial city of South Moravia in the Czech Republic, situated at the junction of the Svratka and Svitava rivers; pop. (1991) 387,990. Founded in the 10th century and later capital of the Austrian Crownland of Moravia, it is now the second-largest city in the country. As well as armaments, the city has textile, chemical, and machinery industries.

broad bean A plant that belongs to the genus *Vicia*, unlike other beans, and which is far hardier. Broad beans have been cultivated in the Old World, particularly the Mediterranean region, since ancient times. Small-seeded varieties, commonly called horse beans and tick beans, are used to feed livestock.

broadbill A member of a family of some 14 species of squat, brightly coloured birds, the Eurylaimidae, which occur in Africa and south-east Asia. Mainly bright green and sparrow- to thrush-sized, broadbills live in forests and open woodland. Their beaks are broad, blunt, and partially covered in feathers, and are used for eating a wide range of fruits, insects, and other small animals. They build hanging nests of leaves and grass, often suspended over water.

broadcast database A system of data transmission that broadcasts information in the form of text and graphic displays to viewers at home. Teletext systems, such as the BBC's Ceefax or the IBA's Oracle in the UK, transmit 'pages' of graphic and textual information to television screens as an electronic newspaper or directory. Such systems are one-way; on the other hand, viewdata or videotex systems, such as Prestel in the UK or Minitel in France, have an interactive capacity for users: they give home shoppers and small businesses low-cost on-line access to computerized databanks via a telephone line and a television set with a decoder modem.

broadcasting The transmission of RADIO and TELEVISION programmes for public reception. The first radio broadcast was made in 1906, when a broadcast in the USA by FESSENDEN was received by numerous ships' wireless operators. The first commercial radio station began broadcasting from Pittsburgh, USA, in 1920. By 1931 television broadcasting was technically feasible, and a complete high-definition broadcasting system was first used for public broadcasts by the BBC in 1935. Television broadcasting in the USA followed in 1939, but other countries did not begin wide-scale broadcasts until the 1950s. By the early 1960s COMMUNICATIONS SATELLITES made it possible to link the television networks of Europe and the USA, and by the early 1970s satellite links could be made to nearly all parts of the world. In recent decades broadcasting has been revolutionized by developments in CABLE TELEVISION, SATELLITE BROADCASTING, digital and stereophonic transmission and narrowcasting to audience 'segments' and individual subscribers.

The PROPAGANDA potential of radio was demonstrated in World War II and during the cold war, and since television became pre-eminent in the 1950s and 1960s, debates about the ownership, regulation, and underlying philosophy of broadcasting have intensified. Wider access to the airwaves has been demanded by sections of the public in both industrialized and developing countries as demands for a New International Information Order emerged in the 1970s (see UNITED NATIONS EDUCATIONAL, SCIENTIFIC AND CULTURAL ORGANIZATION). However, in the 1980s, commercial pressure for DEREGULATION and PRIVATIZATION of broadcasting services increased everywhere. Concentration of media ownership continued, yet the number of radio and television stations proliferated. Both radio and television are important elements of DISTANCE EDUCATION.

Broads, The The part of East Anglia in England typified by shallow freshwater lakes that are created by the broadening out of slow-moving rivers. The largest of the lakes is Hickling Broad and there are over 320 km (200 miles) of navigable waterways.

Broadway A street traversing the length of Manhattan Island, New York City, USA. One of the longest streets in the world, it extends for about 21 km (13 miles), and is famous for its theatres, which formerly made its name synonymous with show-business.

broccoli See CABBAGE.

Broch, Hermann (1886–1951) Austrian novelist and essayist of Jewish parentage, living in the USA from 1938. The trilogy *The Sleepwalkers* (1930–32) records the disintegration of values in late 19th- and early 20th-century Germany. Political developments after 1918 are indirectly reflected in *The Guiltless* (1950) and *The Tempter* (1952). Broch's best-known work is *The Death of Virgil* (1945).

Brocken The highest peak (1,143 m, 3,747 ft) in the Harz Mountains in northern Germany, reputed to be the scene of witches' Walpurgis-night revels. It gives its name to the *Brocken spectre*, a magnified shadow of the spectator thrown on a bank of cloud in high mountains when the Sun is low, and often encircled by rainbow-like bands.

Brodsky, Joseph (born Iosif Aleksandrovich Brodsky) (1940–96) Soviet-born US poet. He wrote in both Russian and English, and his poetry is preoccupied with themes of loss and exile. Brodsky is most famous for his collection *The End of a Beautiful Era* (1977). He was awarded the Nobel Prize for literature in 1987.

Broken Hill ▶**1** A town in New South Wales, Australia; pop. 23,260 (1991). It is a centre of lead, silver, and zinc mining. ▶**2** The former name (1904–65) for KABWE.

bromeliad A monocotyledonous plant of the pineapple family (Bromeliaceae), distributed from southern North America to central South America. Some species are small, terrestrial shrubs with functional root systems; species of the Andean *Puya*, for example, may reach 3 m (10 feet) in height. Most bromeliads, however, are short-stemmed EPIPHYTES with stiff, usually spiny leaves with coloured bases. The leaves form a rosette which creates a funnel or tank in which water accumulates. The adventitious roots are used mainly for attaching the plant to its support, rather than for nutrient gathering. The flowers are typically adapted for insect or bird pollination and are carried in the axils of coloured bracts, making species such as *Aechmea*, *Bilbergia*, and *Bromelia* attractive pot plants.

bromine (symbol Br, at. no. 35, r.a.m. 79.90) A dense, deep reddish-brown liquid element belonging to the HALOGENS. It readily vaporizes to form a reddish brown vapour. It occurs as bromide in seawater, from which it is extracted commercially, and in salt deposits. Its main application has been as 1,2-dibromoethane ($C_2H_4Br_2$), an additive to leaded petrol, but since the introduction of lead-free petrol this application has declined. It is also used in the manufacture of silver bromide for photographic emulsions, in fire-extinguishing and flame-retardant agents, in fumigants, and in chemical synthesis. Chemically, it reacts with most metals and non-metals.

Bronowski, Jacob (1908–74) Polish-born British scientist, writer, and broadcaster. Bronowski qualified in mathematics, worked from 1942 to 1963 with various UK government bodies, and spent the last ten years of his life in a research post in California. He was a great popularizer of science and the history of intellectual thought, writing such books as *The Common Sense of Science* (1951) and presenting the 1970s television documentary series *The Ascent of Man*.

Brontë sisters British novelists. Motherless and largely educated at home, **Charlotte** (1816–55), **Emily** (1818–48), and **Anne** (1820–49) led a lonely childhood in the village of Haworth in a remote part of Yorkshire. All died young, Emily of tuberculosis after the publication (but before the success) of her masterpiece *Wuthering Heights* (1847). Anne also died of tuberculosis, after publishing *Agnes Grey* (1845) and *The Tenant of Wildfell Hall* (1847). Charlotte died during pregnancy, when she was already famous for her romantic tour-de-force *Jane Eyre* (1847) and for *Shirley* (1849) and *Villette* (1853). Their works were published under the pseudonyms Currer, Ellis, and Acton Bell.

brontosaurus (literally 'thunder lizard') A member of the sauropod group of reptile-hipped DINOSAURS. It is more correctly called *Apatosaurus*. Like other sauropods, such as *Diplodocus*, it reached enormous size: about 20 m (66 feet) in length and 30 tonnes (33 US tons) in weight. It had a small skull, a very long neck and tail, and four massive legs. *Apatosaurus* is known from 150 million-year-old rocks in North America and Europe. Their small peg-like teeth and huge barrel-shaped bodies suggest that sauropods were herbivores.

Bronx, The A borough of New York City, USA, north-east of the Harlem River; area 109 sq km (42 sq miles); pop. (1990) 1,203,790. It was named after a Dutch settler Jonas Bronck, who purchased land here in 1641. It is a crowded residential area with factories, warehouses, and a vast wholesale produce market. It has New York's zoo and botanical gardens, Yankee Stadium, and many educational institutions.

bronze Originally an ALLOY of copper and tin, known since *c*.3500 BC. It is harder than copper and has a lower melting-point, making it suitable for CASTING. Varying the ratio of copper to tin gives alloys with different properties. Bell metal contains 20–25 per cent tin and is remarkable for its sonorous quality, whereas statuary bronze has only 10 per cent tin, plus a little zinc to increase hardness. Adding phosphorus (around 0.5 per cent) greatly increases the strength, and phosphor bronzes are used for pump plungers and valves. Most 'copper' coins are made from bronze with added zinc to prevent wear. The term bronze is sometimes used for other copper alloys, containing no tin. Aluminium bronzes contain copper with up to 10 per cent aluminium and occasionally silicon, manganese, iron, nickel, and zinc. They are lightweight, very strong, and resistant to corrosion, so are used in engines for crankcases and connecting-rods.

Bronze Age The prehistoric period during which BRONZE was the principal material used for tools and weapons. The transition from the COPPER AGE is difficult to fix, as is that to the IRON AGE which followed. It is now accepted that the technological advance to bronze was made on several separate occasions between 3500 and 3000 BC in the Near East, the Balkans, and south-east Asia, and not until the 15th century AD among the Aztecs of Mexico. Knowledge of the new alloy spread slowly, mainly because of the scarcity of tin, so the Bronze Age tends to have widely different dates in different parts of the world. Indeed sub-Saharan Africa and Australasia, nearly all of America, and much of Asia never experienced a Bronze Age at all.

Although much more metal came into circulation in Bronze Age cultures, the high cost of tin led to two significant results. International trade increased greatly in order to secure supplies, and greater emphasis on social stratification is noticeable practically everywhere following the introduction of bronze, as those able to produce or obtain it strengthened their power over those without it. In the Middle East the Bronze Age developed into the Iron Age from about 1200 BC, in southern Europe from about 1000 BC, and in northern Europe from about 500 BC.

Bronze Age art The art produced when bronze was first used regularly in making artefacts. This phase of human development began and ended at widely differing times in various parts of the world. In Crete the Bronze Age had begun by about 3200 BC, and bronze artefacts seem to have been made even earlier in Thailand. In some areas the Bronze Age coincided with the development of great civilizations, notably in China, Egypt, the Mediterranean, and the Middle East, and apart from metalwork the arts of the time included architecture on a grandiose scale, stone sculpture, and painting. However, in other areas, for example Britain, Bronze Age culture was much less advanced. Early bronze technology began in Britain *c*.1800 BC, and may be associated with immigrants named the Beaker folk (after the shape of their drinking vessels). See BEAKER CULTURES.

Bronzino, Agnolo (1503–72) Italian painter. A pupil of Pontormo, who adopted him, Bronzino spent most of his career in Florence as court painter to Cosimo de' Medici. Bronzino's mannerist work influenced the course of European court portraiture for a century. His paintings also include religious scenes and the allegorical *Venus, Cupid, Folly, and Time* (*c*.1546).

Brook, Peter (Stephen Paul) (1925–) British theatre director. Appointed co-director of the Royal Shakespeare Company in 1962, he earned critical acclaim with *King Lear* (1963) and *A Midsummer Night's Dream* (1970). In 1971 he founded the International Centre for Theatre Research in Paris, developing new acting techniques drawn from mime and other cultures.

Brooke, Sir James (1803–68) British adventurer and ruler of SARAWAK (1841–68). Arriving in Borneo in 1839 he helped one of the Brunei princes to put down a revolt and was rewarded with the governorship of Kuching in 1841. He established himself as an independent ruler (the 'White Raja') governing as a benevolent autocrat and extending his rule over much of Sarawak. Renowned for his legal reforms (which successfully adapted local custom) he resisted external attacks by Chinese opponents in 1857. Sarawak was effectively ruled by the Brooke family until the Japanese occupation of 1942–45.

Brooke, Rupert (Chawner) (1887–1915) British poet. His works include 'Tiara Tahiti' and other poems, but he is most famous for his wartime poetry *1914 and Other Poems* (1915) and for his lighter verse, such as 'The Old Vicarage, Grantchester'. He died of blood-poisoning while on naval service in the Mediterranean in World War I.

Brooklyn A borough of New York City, USA, at the south-west corner of Long Island; area 182 sq km (70 sq miles); pop. (1990) 2,292,160. The **Brooklyn Bridge** (1883), Manhattan Bridge, and **Brooklyn Battery Tunnel** (the longest vehicular tunnel in the USA) link Brooklyn with Lower Manhattan and the Verrazano-Narrows Bridge (1964) links Brooklyn with Staten Island. It is both a residential and industrial borough with machinery, paper, chemical, and textile industries. It has notable museums and libraries, and many educational institutions, as well as botanical gardens, old churches, and the New York Aquarium.

Brookner, Anita (1928–) British novelist and art historian. She has written studies of Jacques-Louis David (1981) and Watteau (1968). Her career as a novelist began in 1981 with *A Start in Life*; three years later she won the Booker Prize for *Hotel du Lac* (1984). Her novels are characterized by their pervading atmosphere of melancholy and their use of allusion.

Brooks, Cleanth (1906–94) US teacher and critic. A leading proponent of the New Criticism movement, he edited *The Southern Review*, a journal that advanced the movement's ideas, from 1935 to 1942. He taught at Yale University 1947–75 and wrote a number of critical works such as *Modern Poetry and Tradition* (1939) and *The Well-Wrought Urn* (1947). He was cultural attaché at the US Embassy in London between 1964 and 1966.

broom A shrubby, yellow-flowered member of the PEA family with reduced leaves. Common broom, *Cytisus scoparius*, is native to western and central Europe but widely cultivated. It and related species are short-lived perennials bearing yellow, white, or purple flowers, and are poisonous to livestock.

broomrape An annual and perennial parasitic plant of the family Orobanchaceae, without leaves or chlorophyll. Broomrapes form a widely distributed genus, *Orobanche*, of about 90 species of plant. They have normal flowers and produce light, windblown seeds. The seedlings attach themselves to the root-systems of suitable host plants by means of suckers and draw sustenance from them. They may have a wide host range or be specific to one particular host.

Brougham, Henry Peter, 1st Baron Brougham and Vaux (1778–1868) British lawyer and statesman. A notable legal reformer, he, as Attorney-General, successfully defended Queen Caroline at her trial in 1820. An enthusiast for education, in 1828 he helped to found London University. As Lord Chancellor (1830–34) he was responsible for the setting up of the Central Criminal Court and the Judicial Committee of the Privy Council. He also helped to secure the passage of the 1832 Reform Bill through the House of Lords and the Act of 1833 abolishing slavery in the British Empire. However, his somewhat autocratic and eccentric behaviour made him enemies and, although he lived on until 1868, he never again held high office. He is also remembered as the designer of the four-wheeled light horse-drawn carriage that bears his name.

Brouwer, Adriaen (*c*.1605–38) Flemish painter. He was based in Haarlem, where he probably studied with Frans Hals; he provides an important link between Dutch and Flemish genre painting. His most typical works represent peasant scenes in taverns; they are characterized by a delicate use of colour, which contrasts with the coarseness of the subject-matter.

brown (or **satyr**) A butterfly belonging to the subfamily Satyrinae and including some 1,100 species found worldwide in many types of habitat. The upperside of most species is a shade of brown, often with a few white-centred eye-spots; the underside often has prominent eye-spots, especially near the wing margins. A few species, such as the marbled white, *Melanargia galathea*, are very differently coloured. Flight in some species is feeble, and tropical species are more active towards dusk or fly in the shade of forests. Their eye-spots act as deflection marks to protect their vulnerable bodies from attacks by birds. A few tropical species have wet- and dry-season forms or mimic unpalatable butterflies. The caterpillars feed on grasses and related plants. The browns are often given family status, but modern classification places them as part of the BRUSH-FOOTED BUTTERFLIES.

Brown, Sir Arthur Whitten (1886–1948) Scottish aviator. He made the first transatlantic flight in 1919 with Sir John William Alcock.

Brown, Ford Madox (1821–93) British painter. He became a friend of and influence on the Pre-Raphaelites, and a number of his paintings, including *Chaucer at the Court of Edward III* (1851) and *The Last of England* (1855), were inspired by the ideals of the Brotherhood. In 1861 he became a founder member of William Morris's company, for which he designed stained glass and furniture. In later life he designed a cycle of twelve frescos in Manchester Town Hall (1878–93).

Brown, John (1800–59) US abolitionist. The leader of an unsuccessful uprising in Virginia in 1859, he was captured and executed after raiding the government arsenal at Harpers Ferry, intending to arm runaway black slaves and start a revolt. Brown became a hero of the American abolitionists in the subsequent American Civil War. He is commemorated in the popular marching-song 'John Brown's Body'.

Brown, Lancelot (known as **Capability Brown**) (1716–83) British landscape gardener. He evolved an English style of landscape parks, made to look natural by serpentine waters, clumps of trees, and other artifices. Famous examples of his work are to be found at Blenheim Palace in Oxfordshire, Chatsworth House in Derbyshire, and Kew Gardens. He earned his nickname by telling his patrons that their estates had 'great capabilities'.

Brown, Robert (1773–1858) Scottish botanist, appointed as naturalist on Flinders's voyage to Australia (1801) by Sir Joseph BANKS. He returned with thousands of species new to science, and in classifying them noted the main differences between GYMNOSPERMS and ANGIOSPERMS. He gave the cell nucleus its name and in 1827 gave his own name to Brownian motion, which describes the molecular movement of liquids which moves small particles suspended in it, though he did not then understand the cause of this movement.

Browne, Robert (*c*.1550–1633) English Protestant Nonconformist, founder of a religious sect, the 'Brownists'. His followers were the first to separate from the Anglican Church after the Reformation. His treatise *Reformation without Tarrying for Any* (1582) called for immediate separatism and doctrinal reform. Mental instability undermined his leadership, and by 1591 he was reconciled to the Anglican Church. He is seen by English and American CONGREGATIONALISTS as the founder of their principles of church government.

brown earth (or **brown forest soil**) A rich type of soil found in temperate latitudes, in areas that were once covered with deciduous woodland. Most of these areas have been cultivated for a long time and the original forests have been cut down; nevertheless, the soil is often rich in organic matter and very fertile. The upper HORIZONS are grey-brown and often some LEACHING takes place because of the high rainfall. The B-horizon is thick, dark brown in colour and generally clayey. Brown earths are found in the north-east USA, northern China, and north-west Europe.

Brownian motion See BROWN, ROBERT.

Browning, Elizabeth Barrett (1806–61) British poet. After first becoming known with *The Seraphim* (1838), she established her reputation with *Poems* (1844), which was so well received that she was seriously considered as a possible successor to William Wordsworth as Poet Laureate. In 1845 Robert Browning began his passionate correspondence with her. The pair met and were secretly married the following year, eloping to Italy to escape the wrath of Elizabeth Barrett's domineering father. She is best known for the love poems *Sonnets from the Portuguese* (1850), the experimental verse novel *Aurora Leigh* (1857), and the posthumous *Last Poems* (1862).

Browning, Robert (1812–89) British poet. In 1842 he established his name as a poet with the publication of *Dramatic Lyrics*, containing such poems as 'The Pied Piper of Hamelin' and 'My Last Duchess'. *Dramatic Romances and Lyrics* (1845), which included 'Home Thoughts from Abroad', built on this success. In 1846 he eloped to Italy with Elizabeth Barrett, and a highly creative period followed: *Men and Women* (1855) and *The Ring and the Book* (1868–69), a series of dramatic monologues, were among the important works completed during this time.

Brownshirt Member of an early Nazi paramilitary organization, the *Sturmabteilung* or SA ('assault division'). The Brownshirts, recruited from various rough elements of society, were founded by Adolf HITLER in Munich in 1921. Fitted out in brown uniforms reminiscent of Mussolini's BLACKSHIRTS, they figured prominently in organized marches and rallies. Their violent intimidation of political opponents and of Jews played a key role in Hitler's rise to power. From 1931 the SA was led by a radical anti-capitalist, Ernst Röhm. By 1933 it numbered some two million, double the size of the army, which was hostile to them. Röhm's ambition was that the SA should achieve parity with the army and the Nazi Party, and serve as the vehicle for a Nazi revolution in state and society. For Hitler the main consideration was to ensure the loyalty to his regime of the German establishment, and in particular of the German officer corps. Consequently, he had more than 70 members of the SA, including Röhm, summarily executed by the SS in the 'Night of the Long Knives', after which the revolutionary period of Nazism may be said to have ended.

brown soil A light- or greyish-brown type of soil containing little humus. Brown soils occur under sparse bunch grass or scrub vegetation in the semi-arid mid-latitude steppes of North America and Asia where rainfall is less than 350 mm (14 inches) a year. They are closely related to CHESTNUT SOILS, which form where rainfall is a little higher. Brown soils form marginal agricultural lands, suitable only for livestock grazing, in areas such as the Colorado piedmont, USA; central Turkey, and eastern Mongolia.

Brubeck, David Warren (known as 'Dave') (1920–) US jazz pianist, composer, and bandleader. Brubeck studied composition under Arnold Schoenberg and Darius Milhaud before forming the Dave Brubeck Quartet in 1951. He gained a reputation as an experimental musician and won international recognition with the album *Time Out*, which included the immensely popular 'Take Five' (1959). Brubeck continued to record with small groups throughout the 1980s and 1990s.

Bruce, Christopher (1945–) British dancer and choreographer. He trained at the Rambert School, joining the company in 1963. He has choreographed for the Rambert Dance Company and other European companies. His works blend MODERN DANCE and ballet styles. They deal with emotional relationships (*George Frideric*, 1969), are sometimes intensely theatrical (*Cruel Garden*, 1977, with Lindsay Kemp), or emphasize social and political themes (*Ghost Dances*, 1981). Several recent works, notably *The Dream is Over* (1987) and *Moonshine* (1993), are based on rock music.

Bruce, James (1730–94) Scottish explorer in Africa and discoverer (1770) of the source of the Blue Nile at Lake Tana in Ethiopia. His *Travels to Discover the Source of the Nile* (1790) was for many years the best European source of information about Ethiopia, and remains one of the epics of African adventure literature.

Bruce, Lenny (born Leonard Alfred Schneider) (1925–66) US comedian. Bruce gained notoriety as a nightclub comedian whose satire and 'sick' humour flouted the bounds of respectability. Bruce was imprisoned for obscenity in 1961 and in 1963 was refused entry to Britain and banned in Australia. He was convicted of illegal possession of drugs the same year and in 1966 was found dead in Hollywood following an accidental drugs overdose.

Bruce, Robert See ROBERT.

Bruce, Stanley Melbourne, Viscount Bruce of Melbourne (1883–1967) Australian statesman. A member of the House of Representatives, he represented the Nationalists and the United Australia Party. He became Prime Minister and Minister for External Affairs in the so-called Bruce–Page government. His government's policies were summed up in the slogan 'Men, Money, and Markets'. He served in the British War Cabinet and Pacific War Council (1942–45). He chaired the World Food Council (1947–51) and the British Finance Corporation for Industry (1947–57).

brucellosis (or **undulant fever**) A chronic disease of farm animals caused by bacteria of the genus *Brucella*. It can be transmitted to humans by contact with an infected animal or by drinking unpasteurized contaminated milk. Symptoms include fever, sickness, and weakness but the disease responds to treatment with antibiotics.

Bruch, Max (Karl August) (1838–1920) German composer. In 1891 he became Professor of Composition at the Berlin Academy, where he remained until his retirement in 1910. Though once admired as the composer of large-scale choral works (*Odysseus*, 1872), he is now chiefly remembered for his Violin Concerto in G minor (1868) – a work of singular beauty in the MENDELSSOHN tradition.

Brücke, Die (German, 'The Bridge') A group of German Expressionist artists founded in 1905 by Ernst KIRCHNER in Dresden. Its members sought to achieve 'freedom of life and action against established and older forces' (the name, Die Brücke, indicated their faith in the art of the future, towards which their own work was to serve as a bridge);

their aims, however, remained vague. Their most lasting achievement was the revival of graphic arts, in particular the woodcut with its characteristically strong contrasts of black and white, bold cutting, and simplified forms. The group moved to Berlin in 1910 and broke up in 1913.

Bruckner, Anton (1824–96) Austrian composer and organist. After dividing his time for several years between teaching and organ-playing, he turned to composition, writing ten symphonies between 1863 and his death, together with four masses and a *Te Deum* (1884). Bruckner was often persuaded by well-meaning friends to alter his scores; for the most part, though, editors have been able to trace his original intentions.

Bruegel (or **Breughel**, **Brueghel**) A family of Flemish artists. **Pieter** (*c*.1525–69, known as **Pieter Bruegel the Elder**) joined the Antwerp guild in 1551, but produced the bulk of his famous work in Brussels, where he moved in 1563. He worked successfully in a variety of genres, including landscapes, religious allegories, and satires of peasant life. His major works include *The Procession to Calvary* (1564), *The Blind Leading the Blind* (1568), and *The Peasant Dance* (1568). Both of his sons also worked as painters, chiefly in Antwerp. **Pieter ('Hell') Bruegel the Younger** (1564–1638) is known primarily as a very able copyist of his father's work; he is also noted for his paintings of devils (hence his diabolic nickname). **Jan ('Velvet') Bruegel** (1568–1623) was a celebrated painter of flower, landscape, and mythological pictures.

Bruges (Flemish **Brugge**) An historic and commercial city in north-west Belgium, capital of the province of West Flanders; pop. (1991) 117,000. In medieval times Bruges was the chief city of the Hanseatic League and a major centre of the textile industry. Its trade declined in the 15th century in the face of competition with Antwerp and the silting-up of the River Zwyn which linked it to the North Sea. The well-preserved medieval buildings make it a popular tourist destination. Other industries include chemicals, textiles, and electronics.

Brummell, George Bryan (known as **Beau Brummell**) (1778–1840) British dandy. He was the arbiter of British fashion for the first decade and a half of the 19th century, owing his social position to his close friendship with the Prince of Wales (later George IV). Brummell quarrelled with his patron and fled to France to avoid his creditors in 1816, eventually dying penniless in a mental asylum in Caen.

Brundtland, Gro Harlem (1939–) Norwegian Labour politician. After serving as Environment Minister in the Labour government, in February 1981 she became Norway's first woman Prime Minister, but only held office until October of that year. During her second premiership (1986–89) she chaired the World Commission on Environment and Development (known as the Brundtland Commission), which produced the report *Our Common Future* in 1987. In 1992, during her third term of office (1990–96), Norway's application to join the EU was accepted by Europe but voted down in a referendum (1994).

Brunei A small country on the north-west coast of Borneo, comprising two enclaves surrounded by SARAWAK Malaysia.

Physical. A narrow coastal plain of alluvium and peat changes inland to rugged hill country of infertile lateritic soils, the highest point being Bukit Belalong at 913 m (2,997 feet) in the south-east. The coast is noted for its oil and natural gas, found both on shore and off-shore. The climate is tropical.

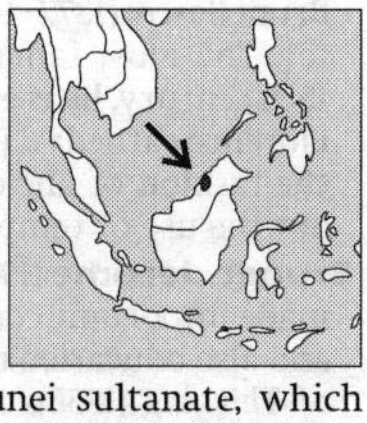

Economy. The economy is almost entirely dependent on oil and natural gas, with one of the world's largest gas liquefaction plants.

History. By 1800 the Brunei sultanate, which had once controlled all of Borneo, had been reduced to Sarawak and SABAH. Control of Sarawak was lost to Sir James BROOKE and his successors after 1841, and in 1888 further incursions drove the sultan to accept a British protectorate, which in 1906 was extended through the appointment of a British resident. The Brunei economy was revolutionized by the discovery of substantial onshore oil deposits in 1929 and offshore oil and gas fields in the early 1960s. The sultanate was put under pressure to join the newly formed Federation of MALAYSIA, provoking a brief rebellion in 1962 of Bruneians opposed to joining Malaysia. Brunei did not join, however, partly because of its natural resources. It achieved internal self-government in 1971 and de facto independence from Britain in 1983 but did not become formally independent until 1994. A state of emergency has been in force since 1962, allowing the sultan to rule by decree. During the 1990s the level of unemployment and social unrest rose. In 1991 the sultan banned the import of alcohol and the celebration of Christmas, measures designed to encourage the population to adopt strict Islamic codes of behaviour.

Capital: Bandar Seri Begawan
Area: 5,765 sq km (2,226 sq mi)
Population: 291,000 (1995)
Currency: 1 Brunei dollar = 100 cents
Religions: Muslim 63.4%; Buddhist 14.0%; Christian 9.7%
Ethnic Groups: Malay 68.8%; Chinese 18.3%; Indian and other 7.9%; other indigenous 5.0%
Languages: Malay, English (both official); Chinese; minority languages
International Organizations: UN; Commonwealth; ASEAN

Brunei Town The former name (until 1970) of BANDAR SERI BEGAWAN, capital of Brunei.

Brunel, Isambard Kingdom (1806–59) British engineer. Son of Sir Marc Isambard Brunel, he was equally versatile, designing the famous Clifton suspension bridge in Bristol (1829–30), then in 1833 becoming chief engineer of the Great Western Railway, for which he surveyed more than a thousand miles of line (originally laid with broad gauge track, which he favoured) and designed many engineering works. He turned to steamship construction with the *Great Western* (1838), the first successful transatlantic steamship. His *Great Eastern* (1858) remained the world's largest ship until 1899. A little-known but remarkable achievement was Brunel's design in 1855 for a prefabricated hospital for the Crimean War.

Brunel, Sir Marc Isambard (1769–1849) French-born British engineer. He came to England in 1799 and persuaded the government to adopt his designs for mass-production machinery for making pulley blocks at Portsmouth dockyard, an early example of automation. He also designed other machines for woodworking, boot-making, knitting, and printing. A versatile civil engineer, he built bridges, landing stages, and the first tunnelling shield, which he used to construct the first tunnel under the Thames (1825–43).

Brunelleschi, Filippo (born Filippo di Ser

Brunellesco) (1377–1446) Italian architect and sculptor. The most famous Florentine architect of the 15th century, he is especially noted for the dome of Florence cathedral (1420–61), which he raised, after the fashion of ancient Roman construction, without the use of temporary supports.

Bruner, Jerome (1915–) US psychologist who has made important contributions to social, cognitive, and also educational and child psychology. *A Study of Thinking* (1956), with J. Goodnow and G. Austin, focused on the sequence of decisions made in thinking through a problem. It is usually regarded as one of the main contributions to the development of cognitive psychology. In the 1960s Bruner stressed the participation of the pupil in the educational process. Bruner's argument that language development depends on a set of non-linguistic skills contrasts with that of CHOMSKY and is described in *Child's Talk: Learning to Use Language* (1983).

Brunhild In the Germanic epic poem *Nibelungenlied* (*c.*1205), the beautiful, imposing Icelandic princess who became the wife of Gunther, king of the Burgundians. Brunhild was wooed and won by Siegfried on behalf of Gunther, king of the Burgundians. Later, in the guise of Gunther, Siegfried took her ring and girdle and gave it to the Burgundian princess Kriemhild. When Brunhild discovered the deception, she had Siegfried killed in revenge.

Brunhilda (died 534–613) Visigothic queen of the MEROVINGIAN kingdom of Austrasia. After her husband's assassination she tried to rule in the name of her son Childebert II but, faced with internal revolts and the opposition of the King of Neustria, she fled to Burgundy. In old age she claimed Burgundy and Austrasia in the name of her great-grandson, but Chlothar of Neustria defeated her. She is alleged to have been executed by being dragged to death by wild horses.

Brüning, Heinrich (1885–1970) German statesman. As leader of the Weimar Republic's Catholic Centre Party, he was Chancellor and Foreign Minister, 1930–32. He attempted to solve Germany's economic problems by unpopular deflationary measures such as higher taxation, cuts in government expenditure, and by trying to reduce REPARATION payments. But after the elections of 1930 he lost support in the Reichstag and ruled by emergency decrees. He was forced to resign in 1932 by President Hindenburg, whose confidence he had lost. He escaped the 1934 purge and emigrated to the USA.

Bruno, Giordano (1548–1600) Italian philosopher. After a period in the Dominican order, he became a follower of the magical tradition of Hermes Trismegistus. He was a supporter of the heliocentric Copernican view of the Solar System, envisaging an infinite Universe of numerous worlds moving in space. He was tried by the Inquisition for heresy and later burned at the stake.

Bruno, St (*c.*1032–1101) German-born French churchman. After withdrawing to the mountains of Chartreuse in 1084, he founded the Carthusian order at La Grande Chartreuse in SE France in the same year. Feast day, 6 October.

Brunswick (German **Braunschweig**) An industrial city in Lower Saxony, north-west Germany, on the Oker River; pop. (1991) 259,130. Henry the Lion (d. 1195), Emperor Otto IV (d. 1218) and the philosopher Gotthold Lessing (1729–81) are buried in Brunswick. Manufactures include pianos, computers, vehicle parts, and cameras.

brush-footed butterfly (or **nymphalid**) A BUTTERFLY of the family Nymphalidae, which contains over 5,600 species. The name is applied to all species in which the front pair of legs is useless for walking, being short, held close to the body, and, in the male, clothed in long brush-like hairs. This family contains some of the most colourful butterflies from several subfamilies, including Heliconiinae, Acraeinae, Charaxinae, as well as the MORPHOS and BROWNS. They range in size from 2.5 cm (1 inch) in wing-span, in the Central American *Dynamine theseus*, to over 20 cm (8 inches) in *Morpho hecuba*. Among the more familiar species are the tortoiseshell butterflies and the Camberwell beauty or mourning cloak, *Nymphalis antiopa*, both of Eurasia and North America.

Brusilov, Aleksky (1853–1926) Russian general. He won a brilliant campaign against Austro-Hungary (1916) in south-west Russia, which, although it cost Russia at least a million lives, forced Germany to divert troops from the SOMME and encouraged Romania to join the Allies. After the fall of the Russian emperor he sided with the BOLSHEVIKS and directed the war against Poland.

Brussels (French **Bruxelles**; Flemish **Brüssel**) A city on the River Senne, the capital of Brabant since the 14th century and of Belgium since it achieved independence in 1830; pop. (1991) 954,000. It was an important textile city in medieval times and was the seat of the dukes of Burgundy and the governors of the Spanish Netherlands. The North Atlantic Treaty Organization (NATO) and the Commission of the European Communities have their headquarters here. Brussels is a major administrative, commercial, cultural, and industrial centre. It has many medieval and Renaissance-style buildings, churches, art galleries, and museums. Its cathedral dates from the 13th century and its university from 1834. Industries, largely in the suburbs, include electronic and electrical equipment, textiles, chemicals, machinery, rubber, brewing, and food processing.

Brussels sprout A variety of CABBAGE and a valuable garden and commercial vegetable in temperate regions. Brussels sprouts arose as a mutant strain of *Brassica oleracea* in Belgium and are characterized by the large number of swollen buds, resembling miniature cabbages, that develop, tightly packed, on the tall, main stem.

Brussels tapestries TAPESTRIES woven at factories in Brussels, which, during the 16th and 17th centuries, was one of the most important centres in Europe for this art. The industry was well established by the late 15th century, and the technical excellence of Brussels craftsmen was reflected in Pope Leo X's decision to send Raphael's cartoons of the Acts of the Apostles there to be woven into tapestries for the Sistine Chapel (1516–19). This marked a turning-point in the history of the art, for henceforth the designer of the tapestry was accorded greater status than its weavers. After the reorganization of the GOBELINS factory in 1662 the leadership in tapestry production moved to Paris, though Brussels continued to produce large numbers of tapestries during most of the 18th century.

Brutalism An architectural style characterized by the late massive work LE CORBUSIER and of his contemporaries in the 1950s, which was widely copied in many parts of the world until the end of the 1960s. The most characteristic feature of the style is the use of *béton brut* (French, 'concrete in the raw'), that is, concrete that is left just as it is after the removal of the shuttering (the framework into which it is poured). Sometimes wood with a pronounced grain was used for the shuttering to emphasize the sense of toughness.

Bruton, John (Gerard) (1947–) Irish Fine Gael statesman, Taoiseach (Prime Minister) 1994–97.

Brutus, Marcus Junius (85–42 BC) Roman senator. With Cassius he was a leader of the conspirators who assassinated Julius Caesar in the name of the Republic in 44. He and Cassius were defeated by Caesar's supporters Antony and Octavian at the battle of Philippi in 42, after which he committed suicide.

bryony Either of two unrelated plants. The **white bryony**, *Bryonia cretica*, and other *Bryonia* species are annual and perennial herbs climbing by means of tendrils and bearing male and female flowers on separate plants. They belong to the PUMPKIN family. **Black bryony**, *Tamus communis*, is a twining climber native to Europe and the Mediterranean region. The sexes are separate, and the female plant bears red berries, which are very poisonous. It belongs to the YAM family.

bryophyte A member of the Bryophyta, a phylum of CRYPTOGAM plants including the MOSSES and LIVERWORTS. About 35,000 species of bryophyte are known. They possess chlorophyll and multicellular sex organs, but lack true roots. They have a heteromorphic alternation of generations (see LIFE CYCLE), with sexual (gametophyte) plant and a nonsexual (sporophyte) type typically in the form of a capsule (usually stalked), which is partly or wholly parasitic on the gametophyte.

bryozoan See MOSS ANIMAL.

Brythonic The southern group of the Celtic languages, including Welsh, Cornish, and Breton. It grew from the language spoken by the Britons at the time of the Roman invasion, and borrowed a number of Latin words during the Roman occupation. When in the 5th century Britain was invaded by Germanic-speaking peoples the language of the Britons died out in most parts but survived in the mountainous and more remote parts of Wales, Cumberland, the Scottish lowlands, and Cornwall, and was carried by British emigrants across the Channel, where it survives as the BRETON language in Brittany.

BSE See BOVINE SPONGIFORM ENCEPHALOPATHY.

BST See BRITISH SUMMER TIME.

Buber, Martin (1878–1965) Israeli religious philosopher, born in Austria. A supporter of Hasidism and a committed Zionist, he settled in Palestine in 1938 after fleeing the Nazis. His most famous work *I and Thou* (1923) sums up much of his religious philosophy, comparing mutual and reciprocal relationships with objective or utilitarian ones. His other important publications include *Between Man and Man* (1946) and *Eclipse of God* (1952).

buccaneer A pirate or privateer who preyed on Spanish shipping and settlements in the Caribbean and South America in the 17th century. Mainly of British, French, and Dutch stock, buccaneers made their headquarters first on Tortuga Island off Haiti and then on Jamaica. In wartime they formed a mercenary navy for Spain's enemies, fighting with reckless bravery. Their triumphs included the sackings of Porto Bello, Panama, Chagres, New Segovia, and Maracaibo. Henry MORGAN was their most famous commander. After 1680 they penetrated to the Pacific coast of South America. Their power and prosperity rapidly declined in the early 18th century.

Buchan An area of north-east Scotland to the north of the River Ythan. The **Buchan Ness** headland south of Peterhead is the easternmost point of Scotland and the **Bullers of Buchan** is a rocky hollow on the Buchan coast.

Buchan, Alexander (1829–1907) Scottish meteorologist. He proposed that at certain times of the year the temperature regularly deviated from the normal, though it is now thought that such cold spells are probably distributed at random. As well as writing a standard textbook on meteorology, he produced maps and tables of atmospheric circulation, and of ocean currents and temperatures, based largely on information gathered on the voyage of HMS *Challenger* in 1872–76.

Buchan, John, 1st Baron Tweedsmuir (1875–1940) Scottish novelist. Although he wrote several non-fictional works, he is remembered for his adventure stories, which often feature recurring heroes such as Richard Hannay. These include *The Thirty-Nine Steps* (1915), *Greenmantle* (1916), and *The Three Hostages* (1924). Buchan was also active in public life, serving as MP for the Scottish Universities (1927–35) and as Governor-General of Canada (1935–40).

Buchanan, James (1791–1868) US Democratic statesman, 15th President of the USA 1857–61. He consistently leaned towards the pro-slavery side in the developing dispute over slavery. Towards the end of his term the issue grew more fraught and he retired from politics in 1861.

Bucharest (Romanian **Bucureşti**) A city on the River Dambovita, capital of Romania; pop. (1993) 2,343,800. Founded in the 14th century on the trade route between Europe and Constantinople, Bucharest became capital of the principality of Walachia in 1698 and of Romania in 1861. It is a cultural centre with theatres, museums, galleries, and old churches. Engineering, oil refining, food processing, and the manufacture of textiles and chemicals are the chief industries.

Buchenwald A village in central Germany near Weimar in Thuringia, site of a Nazi concentration camp in World War II.

Buchner, Eduard (1860–1917) German organic chemist. He discovered that intact yeast cells were not necessary for alcoholic fermentation, which could be carried out by an active extract that he called *zymase*. Buchner investigated the chain of reactions involved in fermentation, identifying various other enzymes. He won the Nobel Prize for chemistry in 1907.

Buck, Pearl S(ydenstricker) (1892–1973) US writer. Her earliest novels, including the Pulitzer Prize-winning *The Good Earth* (1931), were inspired by her experiences in China, where she was brought up and worked as a missionary and teacher. She continued to write on her return to America in 1935, producing novels such as *Dragon Seed* (1942) as well as several short stories, children's books, and essays. She won the Nobel Prize for literature in 1938.

Buckingham, George Villiers, 1st Duke of (1592–1628) English statesman, favourite of James I and Charles I. His personal extravagance, promotion of Archbishop LAUD, and political incompetence combined to tarnish the reputation of the court. He accompanied Charles, Prince of Wales, to Madrid in 1623 in the hopes of arranging a marriage for him with the Spanish Infanta, an expedition that served only to fuel hostile rumours of Charles's conversion to the Catholic faith. After Charles's accession in 1625 Buckingham remained the king's policy-maker, ignored Parliament's hostility towards war, and insisted on a costly campaign against Spain which ended with a disastrous expedition to Cadiz in 1625. Parliament attempted to impeach him, charging him with corruption and financial mismanagement, but the king dissolved Parliament and Buckingham pursued campaigns against both France and Spain, personally leading an unsuccessful expedition to the relief of the HUGUENOTS at La Rochelle. In 1628 he was murdered by a soldier aggrieved by the mismanagement of the war.

Buckingham Palace The London residence of the British sovereign since 1837, adjoining St James's Park, Westminster. It was built for the Duke of Buckingham in the early 18th century, bought by George III in 1761, and redesigned by John Nash for George IV in 1825; the façade facing the Mall was redesigned in 1913. Nash's triumphal main gateway to the palace, Marble Arch, was built in 1828 and moved to its present position as the northern entrance to Hyde Park in 1851. Certain parts of the Palace were opened to the public in 1993.

Buckinghamshire A southern county of England, situated to the north of the Chiltern Hills; area 1,883 sq km (727 sq miles); pop. (1991) 619,500; county town, Aylesbury.

Buckland, William (1784–1856) British geologist. He taught at Oxford, later becoming dean of Westminster. He helped to redefine geology, linking type of deposit with local dynamic conditions and using the associated fossils to establish former habitats and climate. He was the first to describe and name a dinosaur (*Megalosaurus*), in 1824. Buckland supported the idea of a past catastrophic event, first interpreting this as being the biblical flood and later moving to the idea of an ice age.

buckminsterfullerene A form of CARBON composed of ball-shaped clusters of 60 carbon atoms covalently bonded together in a symmetrical structure. The carbon atoms are located at the vertices of a polyhedron with hexagonal and pentagonal faces, which are arranged in the same way as the panels on a modern football. The name of the C_{60} molecule comes from the US architect Richard Buckminster Fuller, and is an allusion to its resemblance to one of Fuller's geodesic domes. This form of carbon, also known as **fullerene**, was discovered in 1985 by directing a high-power laser at a graphite target. It can be made in quantity by striking an electric arc between graphite electrodes in an inert atmosphere.

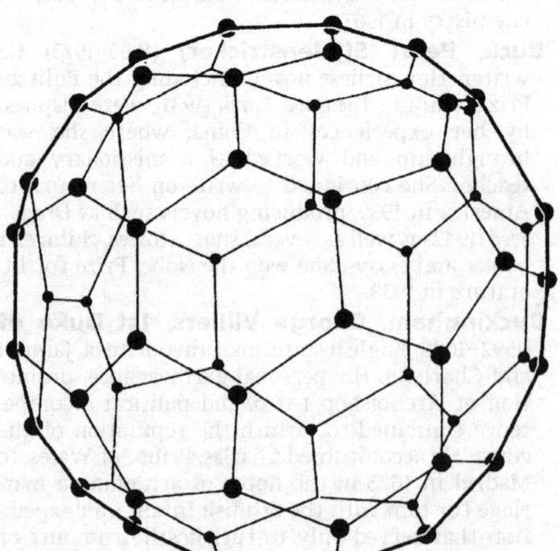

Buckminsterfullerene A carbon molecule containing 60 carbon atoms in the ball-like structure, known as a buckyball.

buckthorn A deciduous, evergreen shrub belonging to the family Rhamnaceae, native to north temperate regions. Buckthorns include species of the genus *Rhamnus*, such as the common or purging buckthorn, *R. cathartica*, of Eurasia, and *R. purshiana* of North America, which is the source of the purgative cascara sagrada. A close relative, once considered part of the genus *Rhamnus*, is the alder buckthorn, *Frangula alnus*. In addition to the buckthorns, the family includes the jujube or Chinese date, *Ziziphus jujuba*, the Californian lilacs, *Ceanothus* species, and the spiny *Paliurus spina-christi*, which is supposed to have been used to make Christ's crown of thorns. The sea buckthorns of the genus *Hippophae* are unrelated, and belong to the oleaster family, Elaeagnaceae.

buckwheat A member of the same family as rhubarb and sorrel, the Polygonaceae, and not a cereal. The common buckwheat, *Fagopyrum esculentum*, is an erect, fast-growing annual from central Asia. Cultivated in southern China for over 1,000 years, it is now also grown to a limited extent in cool, temperate regions, especially in the former Soviet Union, and occasionally in parts of the tropics. The greyish-brown, three-cornered, angular seeds resemble minute beechnuts. Despite being 40 per cent husk by weight, the seeds yield a flour that can be used to make bread, pancakes, or a kind of porridge. Useful also as fodder for stock, the crop's main advantage is its ability to grow well in soils of low fertility, as it is particularly efficient at extracting phosphorus from the soil.

Budapest The capital of Hungary, formed in 1873 by the union of the hilly Buda on the right bank of the Danube with the low-lying Pest on the left bank (they are connected by several bridges including the Chain Bridge built by British engineers (1839–49), and modelled on that across the Thames at Marlow, Bucks.); pop. (1989) 2,000,000. Its old town is a mixture of Romanesque, Gothic, and Baroque buildings. Its principal landmarks are Buda Castle, the 13th-century Matthias Church, the Fisherman's Bastion, the neo-Gothic Parliament, the remains of the Roman town of Aquincum, the Liberation Monument on Gellért Hill, and the Hungarian National Museum. The city is associated with the composers Béla Bartók, Zoltán Kodály, and Franz Liszt, and was the birth-place in 1885 of the literary historian Georg Lukács. Its international airport is at Ferihegy, 14 km (9 miles) south-east of the city centre. It is the economic, political, and cultural centre of Hungary and produces nearly half of its industrial products. Its suburban industries include oil refining, chemicals, pharmaceuticals, textiles, engineering, and foodstuffs.

Buddha A title given to successive teachers (past and future) of Buddhism, although it usually denotes the founder of Buddhism, Siddhartha Gautama (*c.*563 BC–*c.*480 BC). Although born an Indian prince (in what is now Nepal), he renounced his kingdom, wife, and child to become an ascetic, taking religious instruction until he attained enlightenment (nirvana) through meditation beneath a bo tree in the village of Bodhgaya. He then taught all who wanted to learn, regardless of sex, class, or caste, until his death. 'Buddha' means 'enlightened' in Sanskrit.

Buddhism A widespread Asian religion or philosophy, founded by Siddhartha Gautama, entitled the Buddha, in north-east India in the 5th century BC as a reaction against the sacrificial religion of orthodox Brahminism. It is a religion without a god, in which human mistakes and human doom are linked in a relentless chain of cause and effect. There are two major traditions, namely: THERAVADA (often called *Hinayana*), and MAHAYANA; and emerging from the latter, *Vajrayana*. The basic teachings of Buddhism are contained in the 'four noble truths': all existence is suffering; the cause of suffering is desire; freedom from suffering is nirvana; and the means of attaining nirvana is prescribed in the 'eightfold path' that combines ethical conduct, mental discipline, and wisdom. Central to this religious path are the doctrine of 'no self' (*anatta*) and the practice of meditation. The three 'jewels' of Buddhism are the Buddha, the doctrine (*dharma*), and the sangha. There are approximately 300 million adherents of Buddhism worldwide. Buddhism was made the national religion in India by the emperor ASOKA in the 3rd century BC, and from India it spread over much of Asia. It is still a major force in many parts of the continent, but ironically there are now few Buddhists in India, where the religion barely survived the Muslim invasions in the 13th century.

Buddhist art Art and architecture in the service of Buddhism. Buddhism attracted a strong following among wealthy merchants, who erected STUPAS to venerate the BUDDHA's memory, and this became one of the most characteristic forms of architecture throughout the Buddhist world. Other typical forms of Buddhist architecture are the rock-cut shrine (as at the AJANTA CAVES), hollowed out of the side of a mountain or cliff, often with elaborate façades and pillared halls, and the monastery, which in India took on a fairly standard form, with small cells arranged around a courtyard

Initially there was reluctance to depict the physical form of the Buddha, his presence being indicated by symbols such as his footprints. However, at Gandhāra and Mathurā, at about the same time (*c*.100 AD), he was first shown in human form, and the statue of the Buddha, ranging in size from colossal figures carved from the living rock to small bronzes, became one of the most characteristic forms of Buddhist art. He is generally shown standing or seated in the lotus position and is often in monastic garb. As well as the Buddha himself, BODHISATTVAS were frequently represented; these were people who had attained enlightenment, but refrained from remaining in a state of NIRVANA (absolute blessedness) so as to help others to attain it. There were also many minor 'gods' in the Buddhist pantheon, some borrowed from Hindu mythology, so Buddhist iconography can be exceedingly complex, not least when Buddhism mingled with native religions, as for example in Tibetan art. There were various schools of Buddhist thought, of which Zen Buddhism was particularly influential in China and Japan.

Buddhist festivals Festivals in the Buddhist religious year. This is based on a lunar calendar, which varies in different Buddhist countries, and festivals generally fall on new or full moons. The three major events of the BUDDHA's life, his birth, enlightenment, and entry into NIRVANA, are celebrated in all Buddhist countries, but not necessarily at the same time. In THERAVADA countries, all three events are commemorated in the festival of WESAK (Vesak), which usually takes place in April. Magha-Puja, celebrating the Buddha's teaching of the rules of monastic life, takes place in February. Another important festival, largely confined to Theravada countries, is the rainy season retreat of Vassa, which brings monks and other followers together for prayer, meditation, and important ordination and initiation ceremonies. It ends with Kathina, a joyous celebration during which monks are presented with robes and other gifts. In MAHAYANA countries, the three events in Buddha's life are celebrated separately. In China and Japan, there are in addition important festivals commemorating the dead (Ullambana in China, Bon in Japan), which take place in August/September. Mahayana countries also celebrate the anniversaries connected with the founders of particular sects. New Year is widely and colourfully celebrated, particularly in Tibet.

buddleia A small deciduous or evergreen tree or shrub of the genus *Buddleia*, forming part of the family Loganiaceae along with strychnine, *Strychnos* species. Buddleias are native to South America, South Africa, and parts of Asia. Most species have stems that are angular in cross-section, and have leaves with downy surfaces. The butterfly bush, *B. davidii*, from central and western China, has spikes of fragrant, lilac flowers, which are much visited by butterflies. This popular garden shrub has become naturalized in many parts of the world.

budgerigar Possibly the world's best known parrot, a member of the family Psittacidae. Budgerigars are now bred in a wide range of colours, including blue, yellow, white, grey, and green. The wild budgerigar, *Melopsittacus undulatus*, is green underneath and has a mottled grey-green back and a yellow face. It is about 20 cm (8 inches) in length, including the long tail. The wild birds are restricted to the drier areas of Australia, being absent from the wetter coastal districts, and sometimes occur in flocks of many thousands. They are nomadic, their migrations prompted in part by the effect of rain upon the supply of seeds. They nest in hollow trees, laying four to six white eggs.

Buenos Aires The capital city, chief port, commercial, industrial, and cultural centre of Argentina, on the south bank of the River Plate; pop. (1991) 2,960,980; metropolitan area pop. (1991) 11,256,000. The first permanent settlement was established here by the Spanish in 1580 and in 1776 it was made capital of the new viceroyalty of the Río de la Plata. In 1862 it became capital of a united Argentina. The subsequent construction of railways attracted large numbers of immigrants to the surrounding pampas and the city developed as a major outlet and processing centre for cattle, grain, and dairy products. Its industries include motor vehicles, engineering, oil, chemicals, textiles, paper, and food processing with large meat-packing and refrigeration plants. It is a major cultural centre with several universities, The National Library, and a world-famous opera house.

buffalo A member of the CATTLE family, Bovidae. There are two distinctive species: the water buffalo of Asia, *Bubalus arnee* (*bubalis*), and the African buffalo, *Syncerus caffer*. Related species include the anoas, *B. depressicornis* and *B. quarlesi*, and tamarau, *B. mindorensis*, of the islands of Sulawesi and the Philippines respectively (placed in the separate genus *Anoa* by some). Buffaloes have a rounded forehead, horns which drop and sweep widely outwards before curving upwards, and large, horizontally held ears. Short hair leaves the skin almost naked. Their coat is black, sometimes a little brownish. All of them wallow in mud; this protects them against ticks and other insects.

The African buffalo is found all over the African continent; the largest subspecies is the Cape buffalo, which is some 2.75 m (9 feet) long. It is a carrier of the blood parasite that causes sleeping sickness in man, and which is transmitted by tsetse flies. The water buffalo is a native of India and Sri Lanka. Although a dangerous beast, it has been successfully domesticated and is used as a draught animal. It provides rich milk and butter and the dark meat is eaten; the skin makes a very strong leather. The name buffalo is also used when referring to the North American and European BISON.

Buffalo An industrial city and major port of the St Lawrence Seaway at the eastern end of Lake Erie, in north-west New York State, USA; pop. (1990) 328,120. It is the second-largest city in the state of New York and one of the largest railroad centres in the USA. The National Center for Earthquake Research is located at the State University of New York at Buffalo (1846). Its industries include steel, chemicals, grain milling, and feedstuffs.

Buffalo Bill (born William Frederick Cody) (1846–1917) US showman. A former US army scout and dispatch-bearer, Cody gained his nickname for killing 4,280 buffalo in eight months to feed the Union Pacific Railroad workers. He subsequently devoted his life to show business, particularly his Wild West Show, which travelled all over Europe and the USA. These dramatics more than any real frontier exploits made Cody a national figure; his death in 1917 was widely seen as symbolizing the end of an era.

buffalo gnat See BLACK FLY.

buffalo weaver A bird belonging to the same family as sparrows and other weavers, the Ploceidae. There are three species in the subfamily to which buffalo weavers belong: the white-billed buffalo weaver, *Bubalornis albirostris*, and the red-billed buffalo weaver, *B. niger*, which are both black, and the white-headed buffalo weaver, *Dinemellia dinemelli*, which is predominantly white, with a brown back and red under and above the tail. All occur in tropical Africa and are the size of large sparrows. They are particularly noted for their communal nests.

buffer solution A solution in which the hydrogen ion concentration (pH) is relatively insensitive to the addition of an acid or base. The pH changes only gradually and hence reactions take place at a known pH. Natural buffers play an important part in the chemistry of living organisms, where the reactions are sensitive to change in pH; in the laboratory they are usually prepared from the salts of a weak acid in the presence of the acid itself. In the case of sodium ethanoate, CH_3COONa, with ethanoic acid, CH_3COOH, the pH (or hydrogen ion concentration) is given by the equilibrium constant,

$$K = [H^+]\,[CH_3COO^-]/[CH_3COOH],$$

and it will change only slowly on the addition of hydrogen ions: the CH_3COONa is fully dissociated and serves as a source of ethanoate ions; it will mop up the extra hydrogen ions. Similarly, the salt of a weak base in the presence of the base will act as a buffer solution, which is insensitive to added alkali.

Buffon, Georges Louis Leclerc, Comte de (1707–88) French naturalist who compiled the forty-four volume *Histoire naturelle* (1749–1804), which was completed by his contemporaries after his death. This work, and especially its volumes on the animal kingdom, had great influence on the study of natural history.

bug Popularly any sort of insect, but correctly bugs are the 68,000 or so species in the order Hemiptera, characterized by modification of the mouthparts into a piercing and sucking beak, which is usually held horizontally beneath the body when not in use. Typically, they have two pairs of wings, but these are absent in BEDBUGS, many APHIDS, and other species. METAMORPHOSIS is incomplete, the young, or nymphs, being miniatures of the adults, though without wings. Although some are predatory animals, the majority feed on plants, and these include many agricultural pests, which not only inflict direct damage but also transmit viruses.

The order is divided into two suborders. In the Heteroptera, the tips of the fore-wings are flexible, the bases leathery. When at rest, the fore-wings lie flat over the folded membranous hind-wings. The beak, or rostrum, rises from the front of the head. Some members of this group, such as shieldbugs, feed on plants; others, such as assassin bugs, are predatory; and many, such as WATER BOATMEN, are aquatic. The second suborder is the Homoptera, which includes CICADAS and SCALE INSECTS; they are all plant-feeders. The fore-wings are uniform in texture, though they may be stiff, and at rest they are held roof-like over the body. The beak is underneath the head.

Buganda See UGANDA.

Bugis Muslim mercenaries and traders of south-east Asia. They were enterprising seamen and traders living in villages in Sulawesi (Celebes). When Macassar fell to the Dutch (1667) they lost their livelihood. Thereafter they sought employment as mercenaries and engaged in piracy in Borneo, Java, Sumatra, and Malaya. They fought for and against the Dutch. They suffered a reverse when their leader Raja Haji was killed while assaulting MALACCA (1784), but went on to found states, such as Selangor and Riao, on the Malay peninsula.

bugle (in botany) A perennial creeping plant with short spikes of blue or purple flowers. It belongs to the genus *Ajuga*, which is part of the mint family. There are several species, spread over northern temperate areas. The kinds with variegated leaves are grown in gardens as ground-cover plants.

bugle (in music) A brass musical instrument without valves used for military signalling. The modern instrument, closely folded twice round, was in use by the time of the Crimean War. In 1810 Joseph Haliday patented a bugle with five keys, capable of playing any melody, and the key bugle remained popular to the end of the century.

building society A form of savings bank in the UK. It takes in deposits from customers, on which INTEREST is paid. It then lends these funds to borrowers, mainly in the form of MORTGAGE loans for the buying of houses. The US equivalents of building societies are savings-and-loan associations. Originally building societies were non-profit-making COOPERATIVES, but some have now entered the mainstream banking system, after converting to public limited companies. While the former building societies, of which some still exist, were owned by their subscribing members, those that have converted to banks are owned by their shareholders. Since the 1980s they have competed more intensely with BANKS, introducing their own banking services, such as cheque books and cash-point cards.

Bujumbura The capital and largest city of Burundi, on the Ruzizi Plain at the north-east corner of Lake Tanganyika; pop. (1990) 235,400. Formerly known as Usumbura (until 1962), the modern city developed after 1899 when it became a military post of German East Africa. After World War I it became the administrative centre of the Belgian mandate of Ruanda-Urundi.

Bukharin, Nikolai (Ivanovich) (1888–1938) Russian revolutionary activist and theorist. Editor of *Pravda* (1918–29), a member of the Politburo (1924–29), and chairman of Comintern from 1926, he initially supported Stalin but was later denounced by him and expelled from the Politburo. After working as editor of the official government newspaper *Izvestia* (1934–37), he became one of the victims of Stalin's purges and was arrested, convicted, and executed.

Bulawayo An industrial city and transportation centre in western Zimbabwe, the administrative and commercial capital of Matabeleland North and South; pop. (1992) 620,940. Formerly the capital of the Matabele chiefs, the city developed into the country's second-largest city after 1893 when it was occupied by the British South Africa Company as a mining settlement. Its industries include motor vehicles, metals, machinery, textiles, tyres, building materials, and food processing.

bulb The underground storage organ of a plant. Bulbs are composed of fleshy leaves, usually acting to carry the plant through times of climatic stress, such as winter and hot summers. Many provide food for animals including man, especially onions in the Old World and quamash (*Camassia* species) in America. Some other swollen underground organs, such as CORMS and RHIZOMES, are commonly called bulbs, although this is botanically incorrect.

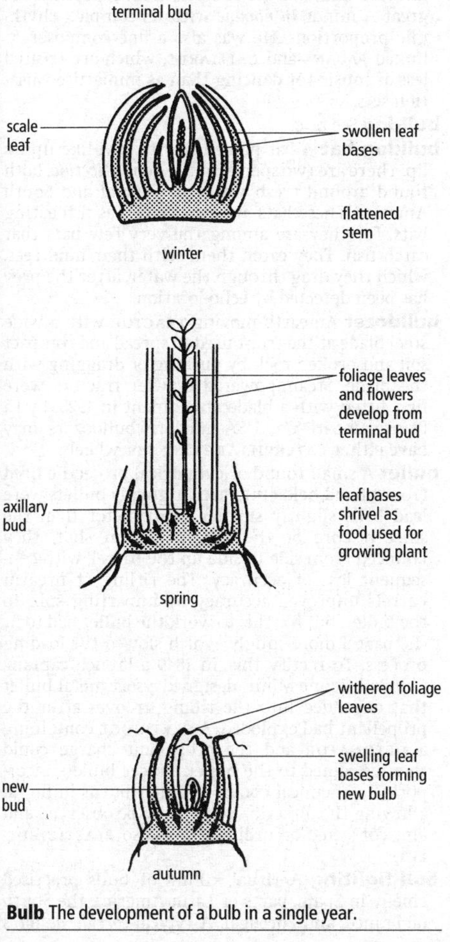

Bulb The development of a bulb in a single year.

bulbul A member, with the greenbul, of a large family of 137 species of sparrow- to thrush-sized birds, the Pycnonotidae. Bulbuls are mostly brown, grey, or olive-green, though some have brightly coloured patches of yellow or red under the tail. They are found in Africa and throughout most of the warmer areas of Asia, occurring primarily in wooded country, usually in small flocks. They eat mainly fruits, but also take insects.

Bulgakov, Mikhail (Afanasyevich) (1891–1940) Russian dramatist, novelist, and short-story writer. He became a professional writer with the success of his early short stories, some of which are autobiographical (*A Young Doctor's Notes*, 1925–26), whereas others use elements of the fantastic to explore ethical problems (*The Heart of a Dog*, published in the Soviet Union 1988). His Civil War novel *The White Guard* (1925–27) explores the post-revolutionary predicament of the intelligentsia and professional classes; it formed the basis of his play *Days of the Turbins* (1926). In the 1930s Bulgakov encountered increasing difficulties during the Sovietization of cultural life. He worked on his most original novel, *The Master and Margarita*, from 1929 until his death; it was published in the Soviet Union only in 1966.

Bulganin, Nikolai (Aleksandrovich) (1895–1975) Soviet statesman, Chairman of the Council of Ministers (Premier) 1955–58. Born in Russia, he succeeded Stalin as Minister of Defence in 1946, and was appointed Vice-Premier in the government of Georgi Malenkov in 1953. Following Malenkov's resignation in 1955, Bulganin became Premier, sharing power with Nikita Khrushchev, who replaced him.

Bulgar An ancient Finnish tribe that conquered the Slavs of the lower Danube area in the 7th century AD and settled in what is now Bulgaria, becoming Slavonic in language.

Bulgaria A country of the Balkan Peninsula in south-east Europe. It is bordered by Romania to the north, Serbia and Macedonia to the west, Greece and Turkey to the south, and the Black Sea.

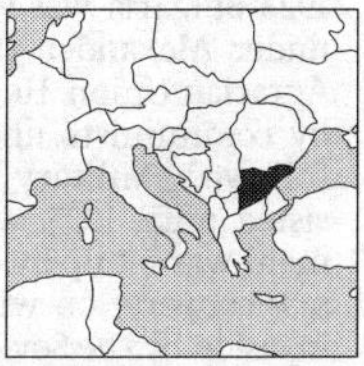

Physical. The northern boundary of Bulgaria is formed by the River Danube, except in the north-east; about 80 km (50 miles) to the south the long Planina range of Balkan Mountains runs parallel to the river, dividing the country laterally. Further south the Rhodope ranges cut the country off from the mild climate of the Mediterranean Sea. Although its summers are very warm, winters are cold with snow and frost.

Economy. Until 1989 Bulgaria was a communist republic closely allied to the Soviet Union. An economic reform programme was introduced in 1991 with the support of the IMF; this involved the return of collectivized land to former owners and the privatization of small businesses. The removal of subsidies from food and other basic commodities caused considerable hardship and further reform stalled until 1994, when a mass privatization programme was launched. In 1996 the country was engulfed by an acute financial crisis when the national currency, the lev, collapsed. Bulgaria's mineral resources include coal, iron ore, copper, lead, zinc, and petroleum from the Black Sea. Agricultural products include wheat, maize, barley, sugar-beet, grapes, and tobacco, which are exported along with wine and spirits. Manufacturing industry specializes in electrical and transport equipment, steel, and chemicals. Tourism is a significant source of revenue.

History. Bulgaria was settled by central Asian tribesmen in the 5th century, colonized by the Romans, and then invaded by SLAV Bulgars. They killed Emperor Nicephorus in AD 811, and captured ADRIANOPLE in 813. Christianity was introduced in the 9th century. Greek and MAGYAR threats were repulsed but rebellion, and incursions by Greeks, Russians, and Serbs resulted in the kingdom being divided into three in the 11th century. It was annexed by the OTTOMAN EMPIRE in 1396 and ruled by the Turks for nearly five centuries.

In the 19th century Bulgarian nationalism led to a series of insurrections against the Ottoman Turks culminating in 1876, when several thousand Bulgars were massacred. Russia gave its support to Bulgaria, and war between Russia and Turkey followed. This was ended by the Treaty of San Stefano (March 1878) which created a practically independent Bulgaria covering three-fifths of the Balkan Peninsula. Britain, however, now feared that the new state would become a puppet of Russia. The Treaty of BERLIN (1878) therefore split the country into Bulgaria and Eastern Roumelia, which remained nominally under Turkish rule. In 1879 a democratic constituent assembly elected the German Prince, Alexander of Battenburg, as ruling prince and in 1885 Alexander incorporated Eastern Roumelia into Bulgaria. For this he was kidnapped by Russian officers and forced to abdicate. His successor was another German prince, Ferdinand of Saxe-Coburg (1887–1918). Taking advantage of the YOUNG TURK movement Ferdinand formally proclaimed full independence from Turkish rule in 1908, and was crowned king. Participation in World War I on the side of Germany led to invasion by the Allies (1916), and the loss of territory through the VERSAILLES PEACE SETTLEMENT. Between 1919 and 1923 Bulgaria was virtually a peasant-dictatorship under Alexander Stamboliyski, the leader of the Agrarian Union. He was murdered and an attempt by communists under DIMITROV to seize power followed. Military and political instability persisted until 1935, when an authoritarian government was set up by Boris III (1918–43). World War II saw cooperation with Nazi Germany, followed by invasion by the Soviet Union. In 1946 the monarchy was abolished and a communist state proclaimed, Bulgaria becoming the most consistently pro-Soviet member of the WARSAW PACT countries. In 1989 the communist leader Todor Zhivkov, who had been in office since 1954, was ousted from power. Free elections followed, with a new constitution in 1990. The introduction of privatization and other economic reforms has proved particularly painful in Bulgaria. After elections in 1994 a coalition government was formed (1995), led by the former Communist Party (renamed the Bulgarian Socialist Party, BSP). The BSP was defeated by the Union of Democratic Forces in elections in 1997.

Capital: Sofia
Area: 110,994 sq km (42,855 sq mi)
Population: 8,351,000 (1995)
Currency: 1 lev = 100 stotinki
Religions: atheist 64.5%; Eastern Orthodox 26.7%; Muslim 7.5%; Protestant 0.7%; Roman Catholic 0.5%
Ethnic Groups: Bulgarian 85.3%; Turkish 8.5%; gypsy 2.6%; Macedonian 2.5%; Armenian 0.3%; Russian 0.2%
Languages: Bulgarian (official); Turkish; Romany; Macedonian; minority languages
International Organizations: UN; CSCE; North Atlantic Co-operation Council

Bulge, Battle of the See ARDENNES.

bulimia nervosa An eating disorder related to ANOREXIA NERVOSA, in which sufferers indulge in compulsive bouts of binge eating followed by induced vomiting. As is the case with anorexia, sufferers are mostly young women for whom slimming is an obsession. Most bulimia sufferers have a less damaging psychological disorder than anorexia and treatment is usually more effective.

bulk carrier Any merchant ship designed to carry cargoes in bulk, either dry (for example, grain, mineral ores, and coal), or liquid (such as oil, liquefied gas, and wine). Those fitted to carry liquid cargoes are more generally described as TANKERS, but are still part of the family of bulk carriers. The largest dry carriers hold up to 120,000 tonnes.

bulkhead A vertical partition dividing the hull of a ship into watertight compartments, first seen in the Chinese JUNK. Main bulkheads, across the whole hull, are normally made watertight to limit flooding should the hull be holed. A collision bulkhead is a watertight bulkhead near the bows of a ship, which is intended to prevent extensive flooding after a collision.

Bull, John (*c*.1562–1628) English composer, organist, and organ-builder. He joined the Children of the CHAPEL ROYAL in 1574, returning to his native Hereford as cathedral organist in 1582. His interest in COUNTERPOINT is shown in a set of 120 canons, most of them on the plainsong *Miserere*. This skill informs many of his compositions, especially the great A minor *In nomine* with its complex rhythmic proportions. He was also a fine composer of linked PAVANS and GALLIARDS, which are treated less as music for dancing than as miniature variation sets.

bulldog See DOG.

bulldog bat A bat named for its jowl-like upper lip. There are two species in the genus *Noctilio*, both found around fresh water in Central and South America. These bats are also known as fish-eating bats, for they are among the very few bats that catch fish. They catch them with their hind feet, which they drag through the water, after the prey has been detected by echo-location.

bulldozer An earth-moving TRACTOR with a wide steel blade at the front used to spread and compact soil and broken rock by pushing or dragging with the blade. Steam-powered crawler tractors were first fitted with a blade attachment in 1923, by La Plante Choate Co., USA. Modern bulldozers may have either CATERPILLAR TRACKS or wheels.

bullet A small round or cylindrical projectile fired from a hand-held FIREARM. Originally bullets were lead balls slightly smaller in diameter than the smooth bore of the firearm. When shot, they bounced from side to side up the barrel, with consequent loss of accuracy. The rifling of firearm barrels improved accuracy by imparting spin to the bullet, but for this to work the bullet had to fit the barrel more snugly, which slowed the loading process. To rectify this, in 1849 a French captain, Claude-Etienne Minié, designed a soft metal bullet that expanded into the rifling grooves after the propellant had exploded. A CARTRIDGE containing a DETONATOR and the propellant charge could then be joined to the bullet. Tracer bullets incorporate a chemical compound that burns in flight, allowing the direction of flight to be observed and aim corrected accordingly. See also PLASTIC BULLET.

bull-fighting A ritual killing of bulls practised chiefly in Spain, parts of Latin America, the South of France, and Portugal. A typical *corrida de toros* (literally, running of the bulls) features six fighting bulls. Three *cuadrillos* (teams), each led by a *matador* (killer), taking two bulls each, put them to death in a traditional sequence of moves using capes, lances, and pairs of barbed sticks. In the final phase, the *matador* plays the bull with his *muleta* (red cloth) and kills it with a climactic sword thrust. In other versions of the sport, the bull may be killed by a mounted bull-fighter (Spanish, *rejoneo*) or grappled with by teams of catchers (Portuguese, *forcado*).

bullfinch A bird making up six species of the genus *Pyrrhula* belonging to the FINCH family, Fringillidae. All occur in the Old World. They are sparrow-sized birds, 15 cm (6 inches) long. The best-known species is the common bullfinch, *Pyrrhula pyrrhula*, which occurs over a wide area of Europe and Asia. The male is grey above, with a white rump, and bright red below; the female is olive-green, also with a white rump. They live in open wooded country, feeding on seeds. In spring, when these are scarce, the birds take flower buds and can be a considerable pest in orchards.

bullfrog Any moderate to large frog that has a loud or noisy call. The American bullfrog, *Rana catesbiana*, is native to the USA, although introduced elsewhere. It has an unmistakable 'jug o' rum' call. The African bullfrog, *Pyxicephalus adspersus*, grows up to 20 cm (8 inches) long, and is capable of eating full-grown mice.

bullhead (or **sculpin**) A marine and freshwater fish, mainly confined to the Northern Hemisphere. Bullheads are most abundant in the North Pacific and in fresh water in North America, but also occur in Europe and northern Asia. The name bullhead is used in Europe to cover the family Cottidae with 130 species, but in North America fish in this family are known as sculpins. Usually not longer than 30 cm (12 inches), they are squat, heavy-headed fishes with numerous spines on the head, and scaleless bodies, although the skin has prickles in it.

The freshwater bullhead, or miller's thumb, *Cottus gobio*, is common in Britain and northern Europe. It lives mainly in rivers with a moderate current and stony bed, usually hiding beneath stones or among dense plant cover. Active mostly at night, it feeds on crustaceans and bottom-living insect larvae. Its broad, flattened head is said to resemble the shape of a miller's thumb developed from constantly assessing the fineness of ground meal. The name bullhead is used in North America to describe a group of small catfish of the genus *Ictalurus*.

bull-roarer (or **thunderstick**, **whizzer**, etc.) An ancient musical instrument comprising a flat piece of wood, typically about 15–30 cm (6–12 in) long, tied, through a hole at one end, to a long piece of string; when whirled above the head it produces a roaring or screaming sound. It is still used by various peoples throughout the world and is often used in important rituals.

Bülow, Bernard, Prince von (1849–1920) German statesman. He served in the FRANCO-PRUSSIAN WAR and the German Foreign Service before becoming German Foreign Minister (1897–1900) and then Chancellor (1900–09) under WILLIAM II. Following the BOER WAR, when William openly supported the Boers, von Bülow improved relations with Britain, who suggested in 1900 that Germany might assist to support the decaying regime of Abdul Aziz in Morocco. France was also interested and following the *entente* with Britain (1904) the latter supported its claim. At first von Bülow retaliated by sending the emperor on a provocative visit to Tangier (1905), when Franco-German tension developed. He then, however, helped to convene the Algeciras Conference (1906) and in 1909 agreed that France be the protector of Morocco. He supported the Austrian annexation of BOSNIA-HERCEGOVINA, a move which was to help to precipitate WORLD WAR I. Von Bülow retired when he lost the support of the Reichstag in 1909.

Bultmann, Rudolf (Karl) (1884–1976) German Lutheran theologian. He held that the Gospels were a patchwork of traditional elements and insisted on the need for demythologizing the whole Gospel story. His important works include *The History of the Synoptic Tradition* (1921), *Jesus Christ and Mythology* (1960), and *Existence and Faith* (1964).

Bulwer-Lytton See LYTTON.

bumblebee (or **humblebee**) A large social BEE of the genus *Bombus*, of the Northern Hemisphere and the mountains of some tropical regions. Bumblebees are often colourful, in a combination of blacks, browns, whites, and yellows. Nests are built underground, or, in the case of carder bees, on the surface, and are lined with grass or moss. Bumblebees form highly organized colonies, with non-reproductive females acting as 'workers' to provision and maintain the nest. In autumn some grubs develop as males (drones) and females; these mate and the potential queen then hibernates over winter. Bumblebees are unusual in that they can raise their body temperature by 'shivering'; they function best at around 30°C (80°F).

Bunche, Ralph (1904–71) US administrator and diplomat. During World War II, he served with the joint chiefs-of-staff and the State Department. In 1946 he joined the secretariat of the United Nations and served on the UN Palestine Commission in 1947. After Count BERNADOTTE was assassinated in 1948, he carried on negotiations between the warring Arabs and Jews with such skill that he was able to arrange an armistice between them. For this achievement he was awarded (1950) the Nobel Peace Prize, the first awarded to a black American.

Bunin, Ivan (Alekseevich) (1870–1953) Russian poet and prose-writer. An opponent of modernism, he made peasant life and love the most prominent themes in his prose works, which include the novel *The Village* (1910), the short-story collection *The Gentleman from San Francisco* (1914), and an autobiography, *The Well of Days* (1910). He opposed the October Revolution and left Russia in 1918, eventually reaching France and remaining in permanent exile. In 1933 he became the first Russian to be awarded the Nobel Prize for literature.

Bunker Hill, Battle of (17 June 1775) A battle in the American War of INDEPENDENCE ending in a British victory. Thomas GAGE, the British commander besieged in Boston, sent 2,400 troops (redcoats) to take the heights occupied by 1,600 Americans under William Prescott. Only after three bloody uphill assaults, costing 1,000 British against 400 American casualties, were they successful.

bunraku See PUPPETRY.

Bunsen, Robert Wilhelm Eberhard (1811–99) German chemist. Bunsen was a pioneer of chemical spectroscopy and photochemistry. During his early research he lost the use of his right eye in an explosion. With G. Kirchhoff he developed spectroscopy, using it to detect new elements (caesium and rubidium) and to determine the composition of substances and of the Sun and stars. Bunsen designed numerous items of chemical apparatus, and championed the **Bunsen Burner** for which he is best known. This is used for heating laboratory equipment and chemicals and was probably devised in 1855 by Bunsen's assistant, Peter Desdega, based on a design by FARADAY.

bunting A member of the subfamily Emberizinae, which contains 156 sparrow-sized birds in the bunting family, Emberizidae (or in the FINCH family according to some authorities). The name also refers to the six *Passerina* species of the cardinaline tribe. In most species the females are dull brown, though often with white edges to their tails. The males in breeding plumage may be strikingly coloured, with black and white patterned heads and yellow underparts. The male snow bunting, *Plectrophenax nivalis*, is largely white with black wing-tips. Most of the species occur in the Old World and only a few in North America. They live in a wide variety of habitats, from open country, such as grassland and reed-beds, to open forest. Many species migrate long distances. They have smallish, stout beaks and eat seeds, although they may catch and eat insects in the summer.

Buñuel, Luis (1900–83) Spanish film director. Profoundly influenced by surrealism, he wrote and directed his first film *Un Chien andalou* (1928) jointly with Salvador Dali. After the banning of his early work, he left Spain and worked on dubbing US films for fifteen years before re-establishing his reputation in Mexico with *Los Olvidados* (1950). Among the notable films that followed were *Belle de jour* (1967) and *The Discreet Charm of the Bourgeoisie* (1972).

Bunyan, John (1628–88) English writer. He served with the Parliamentary army during the Civil War, an experience which possibly inspired his allegory *The Holy War* (1682). In 1653 he joined the Nonconformist Church at Bedford, where he preached and clashed with the Quakers. He was put under arrest in 1660 for unlicensed preaching and spent most of the next twelve years in prison, where he wrote his spiritual autobiography *Grace Abounding* (1666) and a number of other works; during a later period of imprisonment, he began his major work *The Pilgrim's Progress* (1678–84), an allegory recounting the spiritual journey of its hero Christian.

buoy A fixed, floating mark, anchored to the seabed, to assist navigation by marking fairways and indicating under-water dangers such as sandbanks. Buoys are known to have been in use from the Middle Ages, but are probably much older. Through the centuries national buoyage systems developed into two types: 'lateral' buoys, marking the sides of shipping lanes, and 'cardinal' buoys, indicating the direction of hazards. In 1987 agreement was reached on an international system of both lateral and cardinal buoys. Buoys usually carry lights to allow recognition at night. Different types are recognized by differences in shape, colour, and top marking.

Burakumin A social minority group in Japan with a total population of *c.*3 million, most of whom live in Buraku communities throughout the country. Over 40 per cent of all Burakumin, Japan's largest minority group, are found in the Kinki region of central Japan. Originally of outcaste status, the Burakumin have a long history of political militancy designed to combat discrimination.

buran The Russian name for a strong, cold north-easterly wind that blows in Central Asia. A winter blizzard of this kind is known as a *white buran* or *poorga*.

Buraq In Islamic legend, the miraculous steed brought to the Prophet MUHAMMAD by the archangel Gabriel for his Night Journey (*isrā*) from Mecca to Jerusalem. Also said to have been used by Ibrahim (Abraham) to visit his son Ishmael in Mecca, Buraq is described as 'smaller than a mule, larger than an ass' and white.

Burbage, Richard (*c.*1567–1619) English actor. He was the creator of most of Shakespeare's great tragic roles – Hamlet, Othello, Lear, and Richard III. He was also associated with the building of the Globe Theatre.

burbot The only fish of the cod family to live in fresh water, *Lota lota*. It is distributed across the cold and temperate land masses of the Northern Hemisphere, from the Netherlands to the North American Great Lakes, but is extinct in Britain. It lives in lowland rivers and lakes, and feeds, at dawn and dusk, mainly on other bottom-living fishes, insect larvae, and crustaceans.

burette A thin, cylindrical, graduated glass tube commonly of 50 ml capacity, open at one end and with a stopcock at the other, which allows measured amounts of liquid to be run out. It is a standard piece of laboratory equipment used for volumetric analysis.

Burges, William (1827–81) British architect and designer, one of the most original exponents of the GOTHIC REVIVAL. His masterpieces are the 'restorations' (in fact reconstructions) of Cardiff Castle (1868–81) and the nearby Castell Coch (1875–81), undertaken for the immensely wealthy 3rd Marquess of Bute, who shared Burges's medievalist vision.

Burgess, Anthony (pseudonym of John Anthony Burgess Wilson) (1917–93) British novelist and critic. His experiences as an education officer in Malaya and Borneo (1954–60) inspired his first novels *The Malayan Trilogy* (1956–59). One of his best-known novels is *A Clockwork Orange* (1962), a disturbing, futuristic vision of juvenile delinquency, violence, and high technology. His many other works include the best-selling novel *Earthly Powers* (1980).

Burgess, Guy (Francis de Moncy) (1911–63) British Foreign Office official and spy. Acting as a Soviet agent from the 1930s, he worked for MI5 while ostensibly employed by the BBC. After the war, he served the Foreign Office and became Second Secretary at the British Embassy in Washington, DC, under Kim Philby. Alerted to impending charges of espionage in 1951, he fled to the USSR with Donald Maclean.

burgh Any town in Scotland that has been granted a charter giving it special privileges as a royal burgh, ecclesiastical burgh, or burgh of barony.

Burghley, William Cecil, 1st Baron (1520–98) English statesman. Secretary of State to Queen Elizabeth I 1558–72 and Lord High Treasurer 1572–98, Burghley was the queen's most trusted councillor and minister and the driving force behind many of her government's policies.

Burgos Spanish city on the River Arlanzón; pop. (1991) 169,279. Founded in the 9th century, it was the capital of Castile during the 11th century and the burial place in 1099 of the Spanish hero El Cid. Its 13th-century cathedral is regarded as one of Europe's finest Gothic buildings. During the Spanish Civil War (1936–39) it was General Franco's capital city. It has numerous light industries.

Burgoyne, John (known as 'Gentleman Johnny') (1722–92) British general and dramatist. He is largely remembered for surrendering to the

Americans at Saratoga (1777) in the War of American Independence. His plays include the comedies *The Maid of the Oaks* (1774) and *The Heiress* (1786).

Burgundian school Artists and musicians of the Burgundy region of eastern France, especially during its golden age in the late 14th and early 15th centuries. Burgundy's period of greatest importance began in 1363 when Philip the Bold was created Duke of Burgundy. Under Philip and his successors, Burgundy acquired large areas of north-eastern France and the Low Countries. Its capital, Dijon, was one of the most thriving cultural centres in Europe, attracting artists such as the great Netherlandish sculptor Claus Sluter (died 1406), almost all of whose surviving work can still be seen there. Sluter led the way from the INTERNATIONAL GOTHIC style, which had one of its finest flowerings in Burgundy, to a more solid, naturalistic style that formed the basis of much Flemish art in the 15th century. Choir schools flourished in the major cities, attracting such major composers as DUFAY and Gilles Binchois (*c.*1400–1460). Sophisticated CHANSONS were composed by the church musicians, lending their work a characteristically warm style that distinguished it from the more intellectual ARS NOVA.

Burgundy (French **Bourgogne**) A former kingdom, now a region of east-central France, comprising the departments of Côte-d'Or, Nièvre, Saône-et-Loire, and Yonne; area 31,582 sq km (12,198 sq miles); pop. (1990) 1,609,650. Dijon is the chief town. It is a notable wine-producing region.

Buriat See BURYATIA.

Burke, Edmund (1729–97) British man of letters and Whig politician. Burke was a prolific writer on the issues of political emancipation and moderation, supporting proposals for relaxing the laws against Roman Catholics in Britain and protesting against the harsh handling of the American colonies. He was a fierce opponent of the radical excesses of the French Revolution, calling on European leaders to resist the new regime in the influential *Reflections on the Revolution in France* (1790).

Burke, John (1787–1848) Irish genealogical and heraldic writer. He compiled *Burke's Peerage* (1826), the first reference guide of peers and baronets in alphabetical order.

Burke, Robert O'Hara (1820–61) Irish explorer. He emigrated to Australia in 1853 and led a successful expedition from south to north across Australia in the company of William Wills and two other men – the first white men to make this journey. On the return journey, however, Burke, Wills, and a third companion died of starvation.

Burkina Faso A landlocked country in West Africa surrounded by Mali, Niger, Benin, Togo, Ghana, and Côte d'Ivoire.

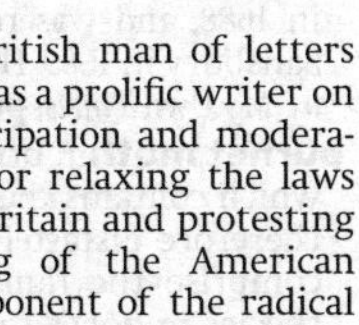

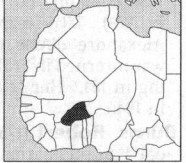

Physical. Burkina Faso lies on a plateau, rising highest in the west and cut in the centre by the north–south route of the Volta River. The soils are mostly coarse and sandy, based on hard rock; the climate is hot and arid, and the natural vegetation except in the river valleys is thornscrub and thin SAVANNAH.

Economy. Burkina Faso is one of the poorest countries in the world, heavily dependent on western aid. The economy is mainly agricultural and vulnerable to drought, with most of the population engaged in subsistence agriculture. The major exports are cotton and gold. There is some industry, mostly state-owned, with largely unexploited mineral deposits of gold, manganese, and zinc. Many Burkinabé seek employment abroad.

History. Before French colonization in the 19th century the region was ruled by a number of Mossi states. It was a French protectorate from 1898, originally as part of French Sudan (now Mali) and later as Haute Volta (Upper Volta). It became an autonomous republic within the FRENCH COMMUNITY in 1958 and independent in 1960. Following a military coup in 1970, a new constitution was adopted in 1977. A series of military governments followed, including those of Captain Thomas Sankara, who was assassinated in 1987, and of Blaise Compaore. The latter ended military rule in June 1991 and held multi-party elections, for which there were 44 eligible political parties. Compaore's Popular Front won these, and he became President. However, the opposition parties had withdrawn their candidates and there was a widespread boycott of the elections because of alleged corruption. Legislative elections, held in 1992, were won by supporters of Compaore.

Capital: Ouagadougou
Area: 274,200 sq km (105,869 sq mi)
Population: 10,324,000 (1995)
Currency: 1 CFA franc = 100 centimes
Religions: Traditional beliefs 65.0%; Muslim 25.0%; Roman Catholic 9.8%; Protestant 2.4%
Ethnic Groups: Mossi 47.9%; Mande 8.8%; Fulani 8.3%; Lobi 6.9%; Bobo 6.8%; Senufo 6.0%; Grunshi 5.0%; Bunasi 5.0%; Gurma 4.5%
Languages: French (official); Mossi; Dyula; Fulani; Lobi; local languages
International Organizations: UN; OAU; Non-Aligned Movement; Franc Zone; ECOWAS

burlesque A comic parody that ridicules some serious literary work either by treating its solemn subject in an undignified style, or by applying its elevated style to a trivial subject, as in Pope's 'mock epic' *The Rape of the Lock* (1712). Often used in the theatre, burlesque appears in Shakespeare's *A Midsummer Night's Dream*, mocking theatrical interludes in the Pyramus and Thisbe play, while *The Beggar's Opera* (1728) by Gay burlesques Italian opera. In the USA a burlesque is a sex-and-comedy entertainment originally intended for men only. See also VAUDEVILLE.

Burlington, Richard Boyle, 3rd Earl of (1694–1753) English architect and patron. He was the leading figure of PALLADIANISM, promoting it through his own buildings, his publication of the designs of PALLADIO and Inigo JONES, and his patronage of artists such as his friend William KENT. Burlington's masterpiece is Chiswick House (*c.*1723–29), a villa he built for himself.

Burma See MYANMAR.

Burma Campaigns (January 1942–August 1945) In 1942 two Japanese divisions advanced into Burma (now MYANMAR), accompanied by the Burma National Army of AUNG SAN, capturing Rangoon, and forcing the British garrison to begin the long evacuation west. The Japanese reached Lashio at the southern end of the 'Burma Road', thus cutting off the supply link from India to Nationalist China. They captured Mandalay (May 1942) and the British forces under General ALEXANDER withdrew to the Indian frontier. During 1943 there were attempts to reassert control over the Arakan, but these failed, although General WINGATE with his Chindit units organized effective guerrilla activity behind Japanese lines, where an originally pro-Japanese population was becoming increasingly disillusioned. Early in the spring of 1944 heavy fighting took place in defence of Imphal, when an attempted Japanese invasion of Assam/Northern India was deflected in a series of bloody battles, of which Kohima was the most important. In October a three-pronged offensive was launched by British, Commonwealth, US, and Chinese Nationalist troops, and in January 1945 the **Burma Road** was re-opened. By now a discontented Aung San had contacted MOUNTBATTEN and in March his troops joined the Allies. Rangoon was finally captured on 1 May 1945.

Burmese art The art and architecture of Burma (known since 1989 as MYANMAR). Myanmar is bordered by India and China, but it is cut off from them by formidable mountain ranges; consequently, although there has been influence from both countries, Burmese art has a distinctive cultural and artistic tradition. BUDDHISM (adopted from India in about the 5th century AD) has been the main religious force, but there has also been widespread worship of nature-spirits (*nats*). Several distinct peoples have influenced Burmese art, notably the Mon of lower Burma, the Pyu of central Burma, and the Burmese (or Burmans) of upper Burma. The earliest artistic survivals of Burma are extensive remains of brick architecture near Prome, built by the Pyu from about the 6th century AD. The central artistic impulse came from the Burmans, however. By the 9th century they controlled the strategic city of Pagan, and in the 11th, 12th, and 13th centuries it was the centre of a great architectural flowering, stimulated by widespread conversion to Buddhism. Pagan grew rapidly and the remains of over 5,000 temples can be traced today scattered over a 41 sq km (16 sq mile) site east of the Irrawaddy River. The temples were richly decorated in stucco and glazed tiles on the exterior, with mural painting on the interiors. Sculpture, although important at Pagan, appears to have played a subordinate role. Large-scale images were typically constructed of brick with a stucco render and were rarely of the quality seen in contemporary bronzes or mural painting. In the small bronzes which survive can be seen the contending influences of the indigenous Mon and Indian Pala styles. The standard representation of the Buddha is in the 'earth touching' attitude, a posture which allows little scope for invention. Examples of Burmese ceramics survive from at least the 9th century, and excavations of Pagan period temples (11th–13th centuries) have revealed terracotta and glazed wares. Glazed tiles, including reliefs depicting Buddhist stories, are an important part of Pagan architecture, and kilns for the production of glazed wares have been discovered there. In 1287 Burma was invaded by the Mongols and building activity at Pagan largely ceased, although descendants of the Pagan rulers continued to govern. In the south the Mons established an independent state at Pegu and under King Dhammaceti (reigned 1472–92) built a temple complex richly decorated with glazed ceramic tiles. Kilns for producing glazed wares were found at Pegu and it is also associated with the trade in the large glazed storage jars (*martabans*), famous from the middle of the 14th century. The emergence of the courts of Amarapura and Mandalay (1783–1885) stimulated the production of decorative arts such as fine goldwork and elaborately carved teak, often lacquered and gilded, and a flamboyant style of wooden architecture. After three Anglo-Burmese wars in the 19th century, Burma became a province of British India from 1887 to 1937 and achieved independence in 1948. Decorative arts have continued to flourish in the 20th century. Mandalay and other centres continued to produce low-fired glazed wares for both domestic and temple use into modern times.

burn A tissue injury from heat, electricity, or chemicals. They may be partial or involve the full depth of skin, depending on whether the germinal layer is destroyed. A severe burn may be less painful than a superficial burn because sensitive nerve endings have been destroyed. The severity depends on the percentage of body surface area burned, 50 per cent resulting in a 50 per cent chance of death. Even a 10–15 per cent burn causes massive fluid loss and collapse or shock, requiring immediate transfusion and specialized hospital care to prevent infection and promote healing with minimal scarring and skin contracture. Deep burns may also require skin grafts.

Burne-Jones, **Sir Edward (Coley)** (1833–98) British painter and designer. A founder member of William Morris's business venture, he created many tapestry and stained-glass window designs for Morris & Company. Major works include the tapestry *The Adoration of the Magi* in Exeter College Chapel, Oxford, and the paintings *The Golden Stairs* (1880) and *The Mirror of Venus* (1898–99).

Burnet, **Gilbert** (1643–1715) Scottish churchman and historian. He sought advancement in England from 1674, but moved to the Continent on the accession of James II. He became adviser to William of Orange, accompanying him to England in 1688, and was rewarded with the bishopric of Salisbury in 1689. His greatest work was *The History of My Own Times*, published after his death.

burnet moth A brightly coloured day-flying moth which contains chemicals similar to cyanide and is therefore distasteful to predators. Burnet moths comprise the family Zygaenidae with some 100 species in north temperate regions. Most are patterned blue and red, but the foresters, such as *Adscita* species, are brilliant metallic green. These bright colours are equalled by the yellow and black of their caterpillars (which are also poisonous).

Burnett, **Frances (Eliza) Hodgson** (1849–1924) British-born US novelist. She is remembered chiefly for her novels for children, including *Little Lord Fauntleroy* (1886), *The Little Princess* (1905), and *The Secret Garden* (1911).

Burney, **Frances** (known as 'Fanny') (1752–1840) British novelist. Her first novel, the satire *Evelina* (1778), brought her fame and the patronage of Dr Johnson. Her second novel *Cecilia* (1782) was also a success. However, her father exhorted her to accept a post serving Queen Charlotte at court in 1786. Unhappy, Burney sought permission to retire in 1791. Two years later she married General Alexandre d'Arblay (1753–1818), with whom she was interned in France by Napoleon, finally returning in 1812. Her *Letters and Diaries* were published in 1846.

Burns, **Robert** (1759–96) Scottish poet. He developed an inclination for literature at an early age; his *Poems, Chiefly in the Scottish Dialect* (1786) was an immediate success. The satire 'The Jolly Beggars' (1786) and the narrative poem 'Tam o' Shanter' (1791) are among his most important poems. Approached in 1786 to collect old Scottish songs for *The Scots Musical Museum* (1787–1803), he responded with over 200 songs, including the famous lyrics 'Auld Lang Syne' and 'Ye Banks and Braes'. Burns was a firm patriot, and his popularity with the Scots is reaffirmed annually in the Burns Night celebrations held worldwide on his birthday, 25 January.

Burr, Aaron (1756–1836) US Democratic Republican statesman. After losing the presidential election to Jefferson in 1800, Burr was elected Vice-President. He was defeated in the contest for the governorship of New York in 1804, largely through the campaign of his rival Alexander Hamilton. Later the same year Burr killed Hamilton in a duel.

Burra, Edward (1905–76) British painter. He was fascinated by low-life and seedy subjects, as paintings such as *Harlem* (1934) attest. In the mid-1930s he became interested in the bizarre and fantastic (*Dancing Skeletons*, 1934), and in the 1950s and 1960s he turned to landscape.

Burroughs, Edgar Rice (1875–1950) US novelist and writer of science fiction. He is remembered principally for his adventure stories about Tarzan, who first featured in *Tarzan of the Apes* (1914).

Burroughs, William S(eward) (1914–97) US novelist. In the 1940s he became addicted to heroin and also became associated with figures who were later prominent members of the beat generation. His best-known writing deals in a unique, surreal style with life as a drug addict (*Junkie*, 1953; *The Naked Lunch*, 1959).

bursa A sac-like cavity of fibrous tissue which contains a thick lubricating fluid (synovial fluid). Bursae are found in parts of the bodies of vertebrates, including humans, where friction between skin, muscle, or ligaments and bone occurs, and they help to reduce this friction. Typically they are found around joints, or where tendons pass over bones of the legs or arms. Infection or injury can lead to inflammation of the bursa, bursitis, which can result in complaints such as housemaid's knee and tennis elbow.

burster A stellar source of X-rays exhibiting a sudden fluctuation in the strength of its X-ray emission several times a day. The X-rays may be emitted by gas being transferred to a NEUTRON STAR from a companion star. The short bursts are thought to be created by the enormous accelerations and collisions of the gas as it is transferred.

Burt, Cyril Lodowic (1883–1971) British psychologist. He worked chiefly on the study of intelligence and attempted to determine whether it is inherited. Burt claimed to show a high degree of correlation between pairs of identical twins, but subsequent accusations that some of his data was fabricated have caused his work to remain controversial.

Burton, Richard (born Richard Jenkins) (1925–84) Welsh actor. He played a number of Shakespearian roles and performed in the radio adaptation of Dylan Thomas's *Under Milk Wood* (1954), before becoming well known in such films as *The Spy Who Came in from the Cold* (1966) and *Who's Afraid of Virginia Woolf* (1966). He often co-starred with Elizabeth TAYLOR (whom he twice married and twice divorced).

Burton, Sir Richard (Francis) (1821–90) British explorer, anthropologist, and translator. He joined the Indian Army in 1842; subsequent travels took him to Mecca disguised as a Pathan, and to Brazil, Damascus, and Trieste as consul. With John Hanning Speke, he became the first European to discover Lake Tanganyika (1858). As a translator, he is best known for his unexpurgated versions of the *Kama Sutra* (1883), the *Arabian Nights* (1885–8), *The Perfumed Garden* (1886), and other works of Arabian erotica.

Burton, Robert (1577–1640) British writer and clergyman. Apart from a few minor works in Latin he left only one work, *Anatomy of Melancholy* (1621), which is structured to resemble a medical work but in effect is an affectionate satire on the inefficacy of human learning and endeavour.

Burundi A small landlocked country on the east side of Lake Tanganyika in east central Africa. It is bounded to the north by Rwanda, to the east and south by Tanzania and to the west by the Democratic Republic of Congo.

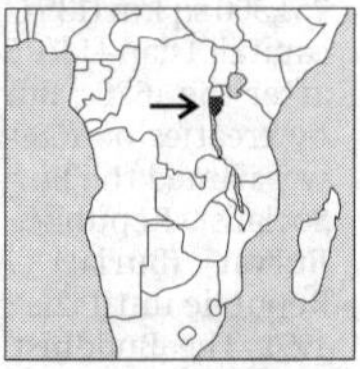

Physical. Burundi straddles the watershed of the Congo and the Nile rivers, while the Ruzizi River in the west flows along the Great Rift Valley.

Economy. Burundi's economy depends heavily on coffee exports, with cotton and tea as subsidiary exports. The biggest sector of employment is subsistence agriculture. There are large unexploited nickel deposits, and uranium, vanadium, and gold. Industry is limited. Since the late 1980s the economy has been disrupted by endemic ethnic violence and an acute refugee problem.

History. Burundi was ruled as a monarchy in the 19th century by *Bami* (kings) of the Tutsi tribe, who dominated a population of Hutu. Germany annexed it as part of German East Africa in the 1890s and from 1914 it was administered by Belgium, which obtained a League of Nations mandate and ruled it as a part of Ruanda-Urundi. In 1962 it became independent and in 1964 its union with Ruanda (now Rwanda) was dissolved. Burundi became a republic after a coup in 1966, but tribal rivalries and violence obstructed the evolution of central government. There were military coups in 1976 and 1987, and renewed ethnic violence in 1988 that left 5,000 Hutu dead. In 1991 a referendum voted to restore the constitution with 'democracy within the single party'. President Pierre Buyoya (a Tutsi) increased the Hutu membership of his Council of Ministers, but violence continued with many seeking refuge in Zaire and Rwanda. In 1992 a multi-party constitution was adopted. The first Hutu head of state, Melchior Ndadaye, was elected in 1993, along with a Hutu majority in the National Assembly, ending political dominance by the Tutsi. Tutsi army officers staged an unsuccessful coup six days after Ndadaye's election, but in a second coup a few months later killed Ndadaye and many other Hutu politicians. The coup triggered fierce ethnic violence and massacres throughout Burundi and over a million refugees fled their homes, many going to neighbouring countries. Ndadaye's successor, another Hutu, was killed in a plane crash in 1994. Violence and instability have continued, with ethnic killings reaching an average of 1,000 a month in 1996. In July of that year a Tutsi-led military coup ousted President Sylvestre Ntibantunganya and installed Pierre Buyoya in his place.

Capital: Bujumbura
Area: 27,834 sq km (10,747 sq mi)
Population: 5,936,000 (1995)
Currency: 1 Burundi franc = 100 centimes
Religions: Roman Catholic 62.0%; traditional beliefs 32.0%; Protestant 5.0%; Muslim 1.0%
Ethnic Groups: Rundi 96.4% (Hutu 81.9%; Tutsi 13.5%; Twa Pygmy 1.0%)
Languages: Rundi, French (both official); Swahili
International Organizations: UN; OAU

Bury A town in Greater Manchester, north-west England, on the River Irwell; pop. (1991) 62,633. Cotton spinning and weaving as well as papermaking are the main industries.

Buryatia A republic of the Russian Federation in Siberia, between Lake Baikal and the Yablonovy Mountains on the frontier with Mongolia; area 351,300 sq km (135,600 sq miles); pop. (1990) 1,049,000; capital, Ulan-Udé. Settled by Russians during and after the 1620s, Buryatia was annexed from China by treaties of 1689 and 1727. From 1923 to 1958 it was named the Buryat-Mongol Autonomous Soviet Socialist Republic. Thereafter it was styled the Buryat (Buriat) Autonomous Soviet Socialist Republic until the break-up of the Soviet Union in 1991. The Buddhist and shamanist Buryat people rear sheep, cattle, and reindeer.

burying beetle (or **sexton beetle**) A medium-sized CARRION BEETLE, often with red and black wing-covers. Burying beetles are attracted by smell to the corpses of small birds and mammals, and a male and female will dig the earth from under the corpse so that the female may lay her eggs there. Some species show parental care by guarding the eggs, and the female may even feed the young larvae until they are old enough to fend for themselves.

bus (in computing) The channel that carries signals within a COMPUTER and sometimes also from the computer to PERIPHERALS. Conventional computers use two main kinds of bus: the address bus and the data bus. The address bus locates in MEMORY the data that the CENTRAL PROCESSING UNIT needs to access; the data bus is the pathway by which this data is entered or extracted. The width of the bus is measured as the number of BITS that can be transmitted simultaneously, usually 8, 16, 32, or 64 bits. A wide bus can greatly increase the performance of a computer.

buses and coaches Public-service road vehicles for the use of fare-paying passengers, usually operating along fixed routes and often running to a timetable. Motor coaches tend to be used for longer-distance routes. The word 'bus', a shortening of *omnibus* (Latin, for all), was probably first used of horse-drawn vehicles in Paris around 1827. The first self-propelled buses were steam-powered vehicles. The first internal-combustion-engined bus, designed by BENZ, came into service in Germany in 1895. By the early years of this century, buses were much improved. Before 1920 buses were built on lorry chassis, but later buses were designed as specialist vehicles, with improved comfort. DIESEL-ENGINED buses were introduced in 1938; the diesel engine gave greater reliability and longevity. Since the 1920s, London has been known for its red double-decker buses, which since the mid 1990s have been privatized. The modern long-distance inter-city or international touring coach has evolved separately from the urban bus and can now give the passenger a range of facilities such as air-conditioning and on-board toilets.

Bush, George (Herbert Walter) (1924–) US Republican statesman, 41st President of the USA 1989–93. He was director of the CIA from 1976 to 1977, and President Reagan's Vice-President from 1981 to 1988. In 1989 Bush became President. While in office he negotiated further arms reductions with the Soviet Union and organized international action to liberate Kuwait following the Iraqi invasion in 1990.

bushbaby (or **galago**) Any of six species of primates of the genus *Galago*, belonging to the loris family, which includes the pottos. Bushbabies live in the forests and bushland of Africa south of the Sahara. The smallest, the dwarf bushbaby, *G. demidovii*, is mouse-sized, and the largest, the thick-tailed bushbaby, *G. crassicaudatus*, is the size of a domestic cat. They have thick woolly fur and a bushy tail. The head is round, and the very large eyes, which face forwards, are brown. Their long, slender fingers and toes have pads that act like suction cups, allowing the animal to run up a tree without using its claws. Bush babies are agile and can leap some 6 m (20 feet) from tree to tree. On the ground, they leap like kangaroos. They are nocturnal and emerge at sunset to rush around in search of food; their food is insects, fruits, seeds, and birds' eggs.

bush cricket See LONGHORN GRASSHOPPER.

bush dog A species of dog, *Speothos venaticus*, found in the tropical regions of South and Central America, where it lives in holes on river banks. Its shape resembles that of a weasel more than a dog, with a long body, short legs and webbed feet. The body, legs, and short tail are dark brown in colour, whereas the large head and shoulders and small ears are yellowish, white, or buff. It will feed on any animal that it can catch and kill, sometimes hunting in packs of up to ten.

bushido (Japanese, 'way of the warrior') The strict codes of behaviour, duties, and training of the samurai, the traditional ruling warrior class of Japan. The *bushido* code was influenced by SHINTO, ZEN Buddhism, and CONFUCIANISM, but its predominant ideals were martial skills, including swordsmanship; duty to the emperor and feudal lords; and a strong emphasis on honour, which dominated everything from speech to ritual suicide or *seppuku* (less correctly termed HARA-KIRI).

Bushmen A nomadic people speaking a Khoisan or Click language and, before the coming of the Bantu and the Europeans, found throughout southern Africa, but now largely found in Namibia and Botswana in the neighbourhood of the Kalahari Desert.

bush pig (or **red river hog**) A species of pig, *Potamochoerus porcus*, found south of the Sahara Desert. It has a subspecies on the island of Madagascar, where it is the only even-toed, hoofed mammal native to that island. An inhabitant of dense bush, reed-beds, and heavily forested regions, the bush pig is seldom seen. Though a wary animal, it is fierce and tough, and does great damage to crops. It stands about 60 cm (2 feet) high at the shoulder and weighs some 90 kg (200 pounds). It has a coat of reddish-brown hair, with white face patches. It has small eyes, pointed ears ending with tufts of hair, and a pair of warts in front of the eyes and another, smaller pair behind.

bushranger Law-breaker who lived in the Australian bush. The term came into use in the early 19th century and the first bushrangers were escaped convicts such as John Donahoe. They often operated in well-organized gangs and attacked both white settlers and ABORIGINES.

bushveld A South African term for savanna or open country consisting largely of bush.

busing (or **bussing**) An educational policy introduced in the USA in the 1960s. Children were taken by bus from black, white, or hispanic neighbourhoods, usually to suburban schools, in order to secure racially integrated schooling. The desegregation movement had mainly affected the southern states, where busing was first introduced, against strong opposition from white families. *De facto* segregation also existed in many northern cities, since the central areas were often inhabited entirely by blacks. In 1971 the Supreme Court approved the principle of busing. In 1972 Congress ordered that further schemes should be delayed. Busing remained a controversial issue and its use steadily declined as a means of racial integration.

Busoni, Ferruccio (Benvenuto) (1866–1924) Italian composer, conductor, and pianist. A child prodigy, Busoni began performing at the age of 9 and went on to become an international concert pianist. As a composer he is best known for his works for piano, and for his unfinished opera *Doktor Faust* (1925).

Buss, Frances Mary (1827–94) British educationist. At the age of 18 she was in charge of her own school, which in 1850 became known as the North London Collegiate School for Ladies (which remains one of the premier girls' independent schools in the UK). She was to remain headmistress there until 1894 and was the first to use the title headmistress. In 1886 she co-founded a training college for women teachers in Cambridge. With her friend Dorothea BEALE, she also campaigned for higher education for women.

Bustamante, Sir (William) Alexander (1884–1977) Jamaican statesman. He was a labour leader and founder of the Jamaican Labour Party, and became his country's first Prime Minister (1962–65) after independence from Britain in 1962. During this time he initiated an ambitious five-year plan which embraced major public works projects, agrarian reform, and social welfare.

Bustamante, Anastasio (1780–1853) Mexican statesman. As President of Mexico (1830–32, 1837–41) Bustamante posed as a champion of constitutionalism while violating Mexico's constitutions of 1824 and 1836. His regime was troubled by revolution and conflict with the French, who blockaded Vera Cruz (1838) as a means of obtaining compensation for damages suffered by French nationals.

bustard A chicken- to turkey-sized bird, the males often larger than the females, making up the 25 species of the family Otidae. Most are light brown and grey on top, and may have pale-coloured or black undersides. Some have black and white patterns on the head, and a few are crested. Bustards have longish necks and long, powerful legs; being ground-dwelling birds, they tend to run rather than fly when disturbed. All occur in open country in Africa, southern Europe, southern Asia, and Australia. Many species have been severely reduced in number by humans, and several are endangered. The nest is a small depression in the ground, and most species lay just two eggs. These hatch into well-feathered young, which leave the nest within a few hours.

butane A gaseous HYDROCARBON (C_4H_{10}), obtained either from natural gas or from PETROLEUM REFINING. It exhibits structural ISOMERISM: normal butane has the structure $CH_3CH_2CH_2CH_3$, while its isomer, 2-methylpropane, formerly called isobutane, has the structure $(CH_3)_3CH$. Butane is readily liquefied by the application of pressure. In pressurized containers it is widely used for domestic and industrial purposes, and in cigarette lighters. It is also used in the manufacture of synthetic rubber.

butcher bird A member of the six species of the genus *Cracticus*, and the family Cracticidae, from New Guinea and Australia. In the same family as the bell magpies, butcher birds are crow-sized with black, black and white, or black-grey and white markings. They have stout, powerful beaks with a hooked tip, and feed mainly upon small animals and other birds, although they also eat fruit. The name 'butcher bird' is also given to some SHRIKES (*Lanius* species) which, like the true butcher birds, impale their prey on thorns for later use.

butcher's broom A small shrub, *Ruscus aculeatus*, belonging to the LILY family. It is native to Europe and the Mediterranean region, and forms thickets of dark green stems up to 75 cm (30 inches) in height. It is botanically interesting because of its leaf-like spiny branches, which bear small green flowers, usually of one sex, on the upper surfaces.

Bute, John Stuart, 3rd Earl of (1713–92) Scottish courtier and Tory statesman, Prime Minister 1762–63. His influence with George III ensured his appointment as Premier, but he was widely disliked and soon fell out of favour with the king.

Buthelezi, Chief Mangosuthu (Gatsha) (1928–) South African politician. In 1953 he was appointed assistant to the Zulu king Cyprian, a position he held until 1968. He was elected leader of Zululand (later KwaZulu) in 1970 and was responsible for the revival of the Inkatha movement, of which he became leader in 1975. He was appointed Minister of Home Affairs in Nelson Mandela's Cabinet (1994).

Butler, R(ichard) A(usten), Baron Butler of Saffron Walden (1902–82) British politician. During 1941–45 he was President of the Board of Education and was responsible for the Education Act of 1944, which laid down the framework for the post-war English free secondary education system and introduced the '11-plus' examination for the selection of grammar school children. He was an important influence in persuading the Conservative Party to accept the principles of the WELFARE STATE. Butler held several ministerial posts between 1951 and 1964, including Chancellor of the Exchequer (1951–55), but was defeated in the contest for the leadership of the Conservative Party by Harold MACMILLAN in 1957 and again by Sir Alec DOUGLAS-HOME in 1963.

Butler, Samuel (1835–1902) British novelist. Emigrating in 1859, he became a successful sheep farmer in New Zealand, before returning to England in 1864. Turning to literature, he published his satirical anti-utopian novel *Erewhon* (1872) and its sequel *Erewhon Revisited* (1901), both of which challenged aspects of Darwinism. His semi-autobiographical *The Way of All Flesh* (1903) parodies child–parent relations and the effects of inherited family traits.

butte A residual hill formed by the erosion of a mesa (a flat-topped steep-sided hill). Characteristically found in desert or semi-desert areas, the classic butte has a flat top of resistant rock overlying steep cliffs of softer rock; and the cliffs stand above straight and gentle slopes which fall away to the surrounding plains. It has little vegetation cover.

butter A DAIRY PRODUCT made by removing water from cream by mechanical means. Cream will rise to the surface of milk left to stand, and the cream can then be skimmed off with a ladle. A centrifugal cream separator, developed by LAVAL in the 19th century, speeded up this process, extracting the cream more efficiently and hygienically. The cream is composed of 35 per cent fat globules in 65 per cent water: when agitated in a churn, the fat globules combine to form butter, which is 15 per cent water suspended in 85 per cent fat. The excess water is squeezed out of the butter as it is formed into pats or slabs. MARGARINE is a synthetic butter-like spread.

buttercup A member of a group of plants belonging to the genus *Ranunculus*. About 200 species of buttercup are known; they are distributed throughout the temperate and alpine zones of the Northern Hemisphere, including North America and Africa. Buttercups are chiefly plants of arable lands, often preferring damp places. The flowers are generally yellow but may also be white or red. The common names of several species, such as mountain, bulbous, creeping, and meadow buttercup, indicate the plant's habitat or its other characteristics. The buttercup family, Ranunculaceae, also includes clematis, delphiniums, and many other ornamental garden species. The whole family contains some 1,800 species which are concentrated mainly in the Northern Hemisphere.

Butterfield, William (1814–1900) British architect. Butterfield was one of the most individual exponents of the Gothic revival. His mature style uses hard, angular forms and patterned, coloured brickwork, thereby breaking with the historicist approach of his contemporaries, such as PUGIN. Keble College, Oxford (1870) is probably his best-known building.

butterfly A usually brightly coloured INSECT that flies by day and rests with the wings held together. With the moths, butterflies comprise the order Lepidoptera; they can be distinguished from moths by their antennae, which typically end in a knob. Like moths, they feed by sucking nectar and other liquids through a long proboscis, which is coiled when not in use. They are distributed worldwide, but the majority of the 20,000 species occur in the tropics. Among the more familiar families are the BLUES, BROWNS, BRUSH-FOOTED BUTTERFLIES, SWALLOWTAIL BUTTERFLIES, and WHITES.

Butterflies have complex life-histories, which include complete METAMORPHOSIS. The ovum (egg) hatches into a larva (caterpillar), which develops into a pupa (chrysalis) from which the adult butterfly emerges. Butterflies range in size from the tiny blues, which are only 1.5 cm (just over half an inch) in wing-span, to the birdwing butterflies from New Guinea, which have a large wing-span of 28 cm (11 inches). The two pairs of wings have a powdery covering of scales, which may contain pigments, or be so structured microscopically that they either reflect light of a certain wavelength or break white light into its constituent colours by interference. The conspicuous compound eyes and the striking wing patterns are used in sexual recognition and often as protection. Many species that are toxic or unpalatable are vividly coloured, while other species use CAMOUFLAGE or some form of eye-spot, flash coloration, or MIMICRY in their wing patterns to disguise themselves from predators.

butterfly bush See BUDDLEIA.

butterfly fish A marine fish of the family Chaetodontidae, found mainly in the tropical Indo-Pacific, but also in the Caribbean. Their bright coloration merges with the background colour, and many of the 150 known species have an eyespot near the tail, which confuses predators. Their deep, disc-shaped bodies enable them to slip between the crevices of the coral, and their long snouts and minute teeth are designed for feeding among the coral. The family also includes species known as marine angelfishes. The name butterfly fish is also used to refer to freshwater fishes of the family Pantodontidae. The only species in this family, *Pantodon buchholzi*, is capable of jumping and gliding above water using its strong pectoral fins.

butternut Either of two trees and their seeds: the white walnut, *Juglans cinerea*, of eastern North America, and the Brazilian *Caryocar nuciferum* and allied species. The first resembles the common walnut; the second has a DRUPE with two to four hard-shelled seeds within. Both trees are a source of oils. The timber of *Caryocar nuciferum* is valued in shipbuilding.

butterwort A small CARNIVOROUS PLANT of the genus *Pinguicula*, belonging to the family Lentibulariaceae, found in boggy places. They are often rootless, with rosettes of sticky-surfaced leaves to which insects are attracted, before being trapped and utilized as a food source. About 40 species are known, chiefly from the Northern Hemisphere but also extending along the Andes in the Southern Hemisphere. They are close relatives of the BLADDERWORTS.

button quail A bird that resembles a tiny partridge. Button quails are brown, grey, and black in colour and well camouflaged. They form the family Turnicidae, containing 17 species in the two genera *Turnix* and *Ortyxelos*, and occur in Africa, south-east Asia, and Australia. They lay two to four eggs in a grassy nest built on the ground, and the young leave the nest soon after hatching.

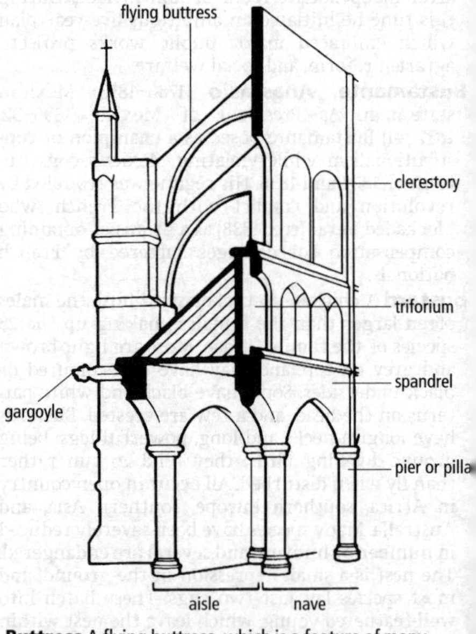

Buttress A flying buttress, which is a feature of many Gothic structures.

buttress A structure, usually of stone or brick, projecting from or built against a wall to strengthen the wall or counteract pressure from a vault. At its simplest the buttress is merely a pile of masonry, but in Gothic architecture buttresses were often as aesthetically striking as they were structurally sophisticated. Many French Gothic cathedrals, in particular, feature a rich array of flying buttresses; in this form, an ARCH (or segment of an arch) of masonry springs from the upper part of a main wall and leads outward to a vertical buttress rising against and above the side aisles. Flying buttresses were often enriched with tracery and other decoration.

Buxar, Battle of (22 October 1764) A decisive battle at the town of Buxar in north-east India, which confirmed the EAST INDIA COMPANY's control of Bengal and Bihar. Facing the Company were the combined forces of the MOGUL emperor (Shah Alam), the governor of Oudh (Shuja ad-Daula), and the dispossessed governor of Bengal (Mir Qasim). The Company's victory achieved recognition of its predominance in the region, demonstrated by the transfer of the *diwani* (revenue collecting powers) to the Company's agents in 1765.

Buxtehude, Dietrich (*c*.1637–1707) Danish organist and composer. He worked as an organist in Lübeck from 1668 until his death, turning the traditional Sunday evening concerts there into celebrated occasions for the performance of his vocal, organ, and chamber music. His toccatas, preludes, fugues, and choral variations give some idea of his mastery of the instrument as well as of his gifts as a composer.

Buys Ballot, Christoph Hendrik Didericus (1817–90) Dutch meteorologist who formulated a law for locating areas of low pressure from the wind's direction. Buys Ballot's law states that, in the Northern Hemisphere, if one stands with one's back to the wind, low pressure lies to the left and high pressure to the right, whereas the reverse is true in the Southern Hemisphere. The effect is due to the CORIOLIS FORCE.

buzzard The name given in Europe to large HAWKS of the genus *Buteo*. In the USA the same name is applied to certain vultures and falcons. The genus *Buteo* is widely distributed throughout Eurasia and the New World and includes 27 species. Buzzards are large-winged, slow-flying diurnal predators; although capable of soaring, they usually hunt from spotting-posts on rocks or trees, dropping swiftly on to their prey. They often occur on marshy or open ground, but may also hunt along the forest edge or in the canopy of a rain forest.

Byatt, A(ntonia) S(usan) (1936–) British novelist and literary critic. Her fiction is noted for its use of literary and historical allusion and pastiche. Major novels include *The Virgin in the Garden* (1978), set largely in the coronation year of 1953, with complex allegorical references to Spenser, Shakespeare, and Raleigh; *Possession* (1990), a romance and satire of the literary biography industry, which won the Booker Prize; and *Babel Tower* (1997). She is the elder sister of the novelist Margaret DRABBLE.

Byng, George, Viscount Torrington (1663–1733) English admiral. He received promotion for his loyalty to William of Orange, and gained a great reputation for his successes in the War of the SPANISH SUCCESSION. His most famous battle was in 1718 at Cape Passaro, when he sank a Spanish fleet which was attempting to take Sicily. His son **John** (1704–57) owed his rapid and somewhat undeserved promotion to his father's influence. He was sent with an inadequate force in 1756 to save Minorca, then under siege by the French, and to protect Gibraltar, but returned to England having failed to do either. He was court-martialled for negligence and sentenced to death.

Byrd, Richard E(velyn) (1888–1957) US explorer, naval officer, and aviator. He claimed to have made the first aeroplane flight over the North Pole in 1926, although his actual course has been disputed. He was the first to fly over the South Pole in 1929 and led further scientific expeditions to the Antarctic in 1933–34 and 1939–41.

Byrd, William (1543–1623) English composer. Joint organist of the Chapel Royal with Tallis, he is often held to be one of the finest Tudor composers. As a Roman Catholic under the Anglican Elizabeth I, he wrote for both Churches and is most famous for his Latin masses for three, four, and five voices and his Anglican Great Service. He composed a great quantity of music for virginals in addition to much consort music, including more than forty consort songs.

Byron, George Gordon, 6th Baron (1788–1824) British poet. His first literary success was *Childe Harold's Pilgrimage* (1812–18). In 1815 an incestuous relationship with his half-sister led to the birth of a daughter, Medora; his wife left him the following year, and debts associated with his ancestral home increased. Ostracized and embittered, he left England permanently and stayed with Shelley in Geneva, finally settling in Italy. In *Beppo* (1818) he found a new ironic colloquial voice, which he fully developed in his epic satire *Don Juan* (1819–24). Though criticized on moral grounds, Byron's poetry exerted considerable influence on the Romantic movement, particularly on the Continent. In 1824 he joined the fight for Greek independence, but died of malaria at Missolonghi before seeing serious battle. His legitimate daughter Augusta Ada Byron, who became Countess of LOVELACE, was a mathematician involved with early computers. The programming language ADA is named after her.

byte A group of eight BITS. Computer information is usually transferred or stored as BINARY code in byte-sized groups. One byte can represent the integer numbers between 0 and 255, two bytes together represent 0 to over 64,000, and so on. One-byte groups can represent numbers, letters, punctuation characters, or other specified data.

Byzantine art The art and architecture produced in or under the influence of the Eastern Roman (Byzantine) Empire. CONSTANTINOPLE (on the site of the ancient city of Byzantium) was founded in AD 330 by Constantine, and remained Christian until taken by the Ottoman Turks in 1453. Byzantine art extended beyond the political or geographical boundaries of the empire, penetrating into the Slav countries; in certain areas, for example Russia, where the Eastern Orthodox Church flourished, its tradition continued long after the collapse of the empire. In architecture the Byzantines evolved a new style for churches from two types of ROMAN building: the three-aisled, flat-roofed BASILICA, and the domed and vaulted buildings such as the pantheon. The Byzantines produced a cruciform plan, and then placed a DOME above the central crossing. They completed the transformation by rounding the east end to form either a single apse or, more often, three apses. Most Byzantine churches are comparatively small, but the finest of them all, the great church of Hagia Sophia, in Constantinople, erected by Justinian in the 6th century, is vast. The interiors of Byzantine churches were often sumptuous: the lower parts of the walls were panelled with rare marbles, and the upper parts were covered with MOSAICS and wall-paintings. Apart from churches, the most imposing works of Byzantine architecture are immense subterranean cisterns and defence works designed to withstand sieges. The cisterns were vaulted and domed, the roofs supported by great columns surmounted by capitals. During a siege Constantinople depended on them for its water supply. Byzantine religious paintings were governed by clearly defined rules, each scene being allotted its particular place in the decorative scheme. The pose and gesture, even the colour of the vestments, was also exactly prescribed. The artists, generally monks, were expected to remain anonymous. Innovation was forbidden, and artistic genius was concentrated on the emotional and symbolic as well as the decorative use of colour, and on the intensity of feeling expressed in the work. The Byzantines developed the art of religious pictures or icons, painted on panels, for either devotional or ritualistic use. The style of these was much the same as in the wall paintings, with figures arranged frontally and flat. Much fine painting is also to be found in illuminated manuscripts, sumptuously bound, either in tooled leather, carved boards, or ivory panels, or in worked metal ornamented by jewels, CLOISONNÉ enamel, or carved ivory plaques. Elaborately and finely carved ivory was used for caskets, mounts, and figures. Metal-work varied from vast metal doors set up in the sanctuaries, to crosses, reliquaries, ecclesiastical plate, and a great variety of secular jewellery. The Byzantines excelled in cloisonné enamel, outlined by tiny gold wire threads. Their woven silks and brocades, bearing fiercely vital animals facing each other in stylized design, intricate geometric patterns, or exuberant floral motifs, rank with the finest in the medieval world. The splendid embroideries in gold thread and coloured silks, their ceramics and glass, and other minor arts carry the vivid stamp of their genius.

Byzantine empire The eastern half of the Roman empire. Emperor CONSTANTINE (306–34) had reunited the two halves, divided by Diocletian (284–305), and had refounded the Greek city of Byzantium as his eastern capital, calling it CONSTANTINOPLE (330). At his death in 395 Emperor THEODOSIUS divided the empire between his sons. After the fall of Rome to the OSTROGOTHS (476) Constantinople was the capital of the empire and was famous for its art, architecture, and wealth. While barbarian invaders overran the Western empire, the Byzantine emperors always hoped to defeat them and reunite the empire. Emperor JUSTINIAN reconquered North Africa and part of Italy, making Ravenna the western capital, but his success was shortlived.

After MUHAMMAD's death (632) Muslim Arab forces swept through Persia and the Middle East, across North Africa, and into Spain. By 750 only the Balkans and Asia Minor remained unconquered. From the 9th century CHARLEMAGNE's Frankish empire dominated the West. In the 8th and 9th centuries religious disunity, notably the ICONCLASTIC CONTROVERSY, weakened the empire. Theological and political differences between Rome and Constantinople led to the EAST-WEST SCHISM between Latin and Orthodox Christianity. (1054). The vigorous emperor Alexius COMNENUS (1081–1118) defeated barbarian attacks from the north and appealed to the Franks for help against the SELJUK Turks. In the 12th century, some reconquests were made in Asia Minor and the period was one of achievement in literature and art, only brought to an end by the Frankish sack of Constantinople in 1204. The failure to achieve any united Christian opposition to the Turks and the growing independence of the Balkan princedoms weakened the empire. Ottoman incursions in the 14th and 15th centuries culminated in the capture of Constantinople in 1453 and the end of the empire.

Byzantium An ancient Greek city on the European side of the south end of the Bosporus, founded in the 7th century BC and refounded as CONSTANTINOPLE by Constantine in AD 330. It became capital of the Eastern Roman or BYZANTINE EMPIRE, which survived until the city was captured by the Turks in 1453. See ISTANBUL.

C

cabal A group or association of political intriguers. In England in the 17th century it was a precursor of the English CABINET, but in modern times the term is applied to any political group which pursues its aims by underhand methods.

Caballé, Montserrat (1933–) Spanish operatic soprano. Caballé made her operatic début in 1956. In addition to her concert repertoire, Caballé has earned an international reputation in a wide variety of stage roles, especially in operas by Donizetti and Verdi.

cabbage A BRASSICA cultivated for its greatly enlarged terminal bud with a large number of tightly packed leaves which form the familiar cabbage 'head'. A range of varieties exist, each being distinguished by its shape (round-headed or conical), colour (red, white, or green), and season of use (spring, summer or winter).

Cabbages, along with Brussels sprouts, broccoli, calabrese, cauliflower, kale, and kohlrabi, are derived from a single species known as the sea cabbage, *Brassica oleracea*, that grows on cliffs of northwest Europe and the Mediterranean region.

cabbage white Either of two species of WHITE butterfly with black wing-tips. The most cosmopolitan species is the small white, *Pieris rapae*, which although native to Eurasia has been introduced into North America and Australia. As caterpillars they all feed on cruciferous plants, particularly brassicas, so they are regarded as pests. Caterpillars of the large whites, *P. brassicae*, are black and yellow, and gregarious; those of small whites are green, and solitary.

Cabeza de Vaca, Álvar Núñez (*c.*1490–*c.*1557) Spanish soldier. He pursued a military career, serving in Europe before joining Pánfilo de Narváez in an expedition to Florida in 1527. When it failed, he and three other survivors spent ten years trekking 6,000 miles through the south of North America and back to New Spain. He hoped to command another expedition, but delays in returning to Spain lost him the opportunity. Instead he was made governor of Rio de La Plata, and led two 1,000-mile expeditions through the jungles and up the Rio Paraguay in 1541 and 1542. Arrested in 1543 by jealous colleagues, he was returned to Spain in chains. His sentence of eight years' exile in Africa was annulled, however, and a royal pension enabled him to write his *Commentarios* on his South American treks.

Cabinda An exclave of Angola at the mouth of the River Congo, separated from the rest of Angola by a wedge of the Democratic Republic of Congo: area 7,270 sq km (2,808 sq miles); pop. (1991) 163,000. Rich oilfields lie off the coast of Cabinda which claims independence from Angola on the basis of the legitimacy of the 1885 Simulambuco Treaty which first linked Cabinda and Angola.

cabinet The group of ministers responsible for implementing government policy. The cabinet may make collective decisions, as it does in the UK and most European democracies, or it may have only an advisory status, as in the case of the President's cabinet in the USA. The size and membership of cabinets vary, but the holders of the major offices of state, such as the ministers responsible for finance, defence, and foreign affairs, are always included.

cable A thick strong rope of hemp, wire, or other material; an anchor chain; or a nautical measure of length: one-tenth of a nautical mile, 185 m (607 feet). Apart from nautical uses, cables are much used for engineering purposes: modern suspension bridges use cables made from many parallel strands of strong steel wire bound tightly together. Cables are also used for CABLE-CARS, for haulage of passenger trains and of mining cars underground, and for passenger lifts and mining hoists.

An electrical cable is an insulated, wire-based conductor or bundle of metallic conductors made of copper or aluminium. An INSULATOR normally sheathes the conductor completely. Cables may be used to carry electrical signals or power. Most cable conductors are built up from individual fine strands of conductor braided together. The braiding provides increased mechanical strength, flexibility, and superior current-carrying capacity. COAXIAL CABLES possess an additional outer, earthed, braiding. OPTICAL-FIBRE cables are made up of fine glass fibres rather than copper strands. Cables are specified by maximum current capacity (determined by total conductor cross-sectional area), capacitance (tendency of the cable to store charge), and resistance. See also ELECTRICITY GENERATION AND SUPPLY.

cable-car A method of transporting passengers and goods across terrain over which it would be difficult and expensive to build a railway. Passenger-carrying cars or goods hoppers are suspended from a steel CABLE and hauled by another cable. Various suspension and haulage systems are used: the cables may be continuous, passing around large pulleys; or a balanced pair of cars may operate on two separate suspension ropes joined by a haulage cable, as in a funicular. Aerial ropeways for transporting minerals from mining sites may run for as much as 10 km (6 miles), carrying 500 tonnes per hour, while cableways may operate at heights of over 1 km (0.6 mile) with up to 100 passengers on board.

cable-ship A vessel specially fitted for laying or repairing underwater telegraph or telephone CABLES. A cable-ship has a large hold to carry the coils of cable and to allow the cable to run freely when it is being laid; and a large roller built out over the bow (and sometimes also over the stern) to pay out the cable evenly when laying. The roller also serves for taking in an existing cable when lifting it for repairs. Although satellite communication seemed at one stage likely to render cables obsolete, cables for OPTICAL FIBRES are now proving cheap and reliable.

cable television A system enabling TELEVISION signals to be transmitted to receiving sets via cables rather than through radio-frequency broadcasting. Cable television was developed in the 1950s to re-transmit broadcasts in regions of the USA with poor 'off-air' reception. It was first used in rural areas, where a hilltop receiving station would pick up and amplify weak broadcast signals, which were then cabled to houses in the area. A similar system was developed for hotels and apartment buildings, where one aerial could serve all the receivers in the building. Cable News Network (CNN) was founded by the US entrepreneur Ted Turner (1938–) in 1980. It carries round-the-clock all-news television which can rival network viewing figures. Cable networks in the USA and elsewhere now connect subscribers directly to transmitting stations. The spread of video film rentals and SATELLITE BROADCASTING, together with the high cost of cabling, slowed the spread of cable television. The full potential of multi-channel cable systems by which 'one wire' (a fibre-optic cable) brings telephone, television, BROADCAST DATABASES, and other facilities has yet to be realized, but such systems are planned for some areas by the end of the 1990s.

Cabot, John (Italian name Giovanni Caboto) (*c.*1450–*c.*1498) Italian explorer and navigator. He and his son Sebastian (*c.*1475–1557) sailed from Bristol in 1497 with letters patent from Henry VII of England in search of Asia, but in fact discovered the mainland of North America. The site of their arrival is uncertain (it may have been Cape Breton Island, Newfoundland, or Labrador). John Cabot returned to Bristol and undertook a second expedition in 1498. Sebastian made further voyages of exploration after his father's death, most notably to Brazil and the River Plate (1526).

cabotage The reservation to a country of traffic (especially air) operation within its territory.

Cabral, Amilcar (1924–73) Guinean revolutionary. He founded a clandestine liberation organization against Portuguese rule. From 1963 to 1973 he led a successful guerrilla campaign which had gained control of much of the interior before he was assassinated, supposedly by a Portuguese agent. In the following year Portuguese Guinea became independent as GUINEA-BISSAU.

Cabrillo, Juan Rodriguez (died *c.*1543) Portuguese captain in the employ of Spain, one of the *conquistadors* of what is now Guatemala, El Salvador, and Nicaragua. In 1542 he discovered California. He sailed up the west coast of Mexico, hoping to open a route to the East Indies through Spanish waters, and entered San Diego and Monterey bays.

cacao (or **cocoa**) A small, spreading, evergreen tree, *Theobroma cacao*, up to 8 m (26 feet) tall, from the South and Central American rain forests. One of 30 species in its genus, the cacao is now cultivated principally in Ghana, Nigeria, and Côte d'Ivoire (Ivory Coast) and is the source of cocoa and chocolate. The large, oval pods, which grow up to 30 cm (12 inches) long, are borne on the trunk and contain 20–60 seeds embedded in a pink pulp. These are scooped out, fermented naturally, and then dried in the Sun to produce brown cocoa beans. Fifty to sixty per cent of the cocoa bean consists of a pale yellow fat, cocoa butter, which is used as a base for chocolate manufacture. The residue, after extraction of the butter, is used to make cocoa powder.

CACM See CENTRAL AMERICAN COMMON MARKET.

cacomistle See RING-TAILED CAT.

cactus A prickly plant belonging to the family Cactaceae, members of which are mostly spiny, and some bear short-lived flowers. The family includes more than 2,000 species. Cacti are found chiefly in the semi-desert regions of North, Central, and South America, but some occur in other places, where they flourish as weeds. They vary in shape and size, lacking leaves and photosynthesizing in fleshy green stems and branches. The reduction of leaves is an adaptation for conserving water. Many cacti have extensive root systems, allowing them to collect water from near the surface. Some species produce edible fruit, notably the prickly pear, *Opuntia*; others are grown as house plants.

Cadbury, George (1839–1922) British cocoa and chocolate manufacturer and social reformer. He and his brother Richard (1835–99) took over their father's business in 1861 and established Cadbury Brothers. Committed Quakers, they greatly improved working conditions and in 1879 George Cadbury moved the works to a new factory on a rural site (which he called Bournville) outside Birmingham, where he subsequently built a housing estate intended primarily for his workers.

caddis fly A hairy-winged insect (not a true fly) with aquatic larvae. Caddis flies comprise the order Trichoptera, which has a worldwide distribution; there are some 5,000 species. They have a complete METAMORPHOSIS, the eggs normally being laid in water and surrounded by a jelly-like mass. The larva breathes by gills and is generally herbivorous, though some are carnivorous. Many species build a protective case with bits of twig, shell, stone, and weed, which they bind together with silk. The pupa is unusual among insects in having movable jaws and legs. When the time comes for it to emerge, it bites its way out of the larval case and crawls or swims upwards to the surface of the water.

The wings of the adults can be dark or pale and occasionally patterned, and are usually moth-like. Most species cannot eat, as they have no jaws, but some can sip fluids such as nectar. A bright light from a window will attract them.

Cade, John (known as 'Jack') (died 1450) Irish rebel. In 1450 he assumed the name of Mortimer and led the Kentish rebels against Henry VI. They occupied London for three days and executed both the treasurer of England and the sheriff of Kent. When many of the rebels accepted an offer of pardon, Cade fled, but died of a wound received in an attempt to capture him.

cadence A harmonic progression in music involving two chords that acts as a method of punctuating the progress of a composition by marking its end, or the end of a section or phrase. There are four cadences in common use: two, the perfect and plagal cadences, have a feeling of finality; the other two, as their names suggest, are less conclusive: the interrupted and imperfect cadences imply that more is to follow.

Cader Idris (Welsh, 'the chair of Idris') A mountain ridge in north-west Wales that rises to 892 m (2,926 ft) at Pen-y-Gader.

Cadiz A city and port on the Andalusian coast of south-west Spain; pop. (1991) 156,558. It is the capital of a province of the same name. Originally a Phoenician settlement, it reached its highest importance in the 16th–18th centuries as the headquarters of the Spanish naval fleets. In 1587 Sir Francis Drake burnt the ships of Philip II at anchor here. There are ferry links with Casablanca and the Canary Islands. Shipbuilding and the export of sherry, salt, fish, and olives are the chief economic activities, together with tourism.

cadmium (symbol Cd, at. no. 48, r.a.m. 112.41) An unreactive silvery TRANSITION METAL occurring in the rare mineral greenockite, but extracted as a by-product of ZINC production. It is used in alloys of low melting-point, in metals for BEARINGS, in nuclear reactor control rods, nickel–cadmium BATTERIES, and in ELECTROPLATING to protect and embellish more relative metals. Cadmium sulphide is a yellow paint pigment. Many cadmium compounds are toxic.

Cadwalader (or **Cadwallon**) (died 633) King of Gwynedd, north Wales. His hatred of the Anglo-Saxon kingdom of NORTHUMBRIA intensified when his attempts at invasion (629) failed and he was forced to flee to Ireland. Although a Christian, he next allied with the heathen King Penda of Mercia. Their victory at Hatfield Chase (632) over Edwin of Northumbria was followed by the devastation of Northumbria. Thereafter Northumbrian fortunes recovered and Cadwalader was killed in battle by Edwin's nephew Oswald at Heavenfield, near Hexham.

caecilian A type of limbless AMPHIBIAN that looks more like a worm, having a series of ring-like folds in the skin. Caecilians possess rudimentary eyes, sensory tentacles beneath the eyes, and a shark-like mouth with jaws and teeth. Some species have minute scales embedded in the skin. Approximately 170 species are known; they inhabit the wet tropical forest areas of South America, Africa, and Asia. Most of them burrow in soft earth, though one South American group is apparently largely aquatic. Some lay eggs; others give birth to live young.

Caedmon (7th century) English poet and monk. According to Bede he was an illiterate herdsman, who received in a vision the power of song and was called to sing in praise of the Creation. He then joined the monastery at Whitby and later wrote English poetry inspired by biblical themes.

Caelum The Chisel, a small, faint, Southern Hemisphere CONSTELLATION, introduced in the 1750s by the French astronomer Nicolas Louis de Lacaille. Located near ORION, it represents a sculptor's chisel.

Caen A port, commercial, and industrial city on the coast of Normandy in north-west France, on the River Orne; pop. (1990) 115,620. It is capital of the department of Calvados in the Basse-Normandie region. William the Conqueror is buried in the abbey church of St Etienne and Beau Brummel died here in the pauper lunatic asylum in 1840. Manufactures include steel and electronics.

Caernarvon (Welsh **Caernarfon**) The county town and tourist centre of Gwynedd in north-west Wales, on the shore of the Menai Strait; pop. (1991) 9,695. The seat of the native princes of Wales until the 9th century, its 13th-century castle (built by Edward I) was the birthplace of Edward II, the first English Prince of Wales. Nearby are the remains of the Roman fort of Segontium. It was the administrative centre of the former county of Caernarvon until 1974.

Caerphilly A market town in Mid Glamorgan, south Wales, 10 km (7 miles) north-west of Cardiff. It gives its name to a kind of mild white cheese made in the area. Caerphilly Castle, built in the 13th century by Edward I, is said to be the second-largest castle in England and Wales.

Caesar, (Gaius) Julius (100–44 BC) Roman general and dictator. Born into a patrician family, he became Pontifex Maximus (High Priest) in 63 BC as part of a deal with POMPEY and CRASSUS, the so-called 'First Triumvirate'; as consul in 59 he obtained the provinces of Illyricum and Cisalpine and Transalpine GAUL. A superb general, able to inspire loyalty in his soldiers, he subjugated Gaul, crossed the River Rhine, and made two expeditions to Britain. He refused to surrender command until he had secured a second consulship for 48 BC, which would render him immune from prosecution by his enemies, by now including Pompey. When the Senate delivered an ultimatum in January 49, he crossed the RUBICON, took Rome, and defeated Pompey at Pharsalus in 48. He demonstrated clemency by permitting those who wished to do so to return to Italy. After campaigns in Asia Minor, Egypt, Africa, and Spain he returned to Rome in 45.

He governed Rome as dictator, finally as 'perpetual' dictator. His wide-ranging programme of reform, which included the institution of the Julian CALENDAR, reveals his breadth of vision, but he flaunted his ascendancy and ignored republican traditions. A conspiracy was formed, led by BRUTUS and Cassius, and he was assassinated on the Ides (15th) of March 44.

Caesarea (formerly **Caesarea Palestinae**) A seaport on the Mediterranean coast of Israel midway between Haifa and Tel Aviv. Originally founded by Phoenicians in the 4th century BC, it was later occupied by the Greeks. In 22 BC Herod the Great founded a new port that became one of the chief cities of Roman Palestine and named it after Caesar Augustus. After its capture by the Arabs in 637 AD it lost its importance and the harbour silted up.

Caesarea Philippi An ancient city of Palestine on the site of the modern village of Baniyas in the Israeli-occupied Golan Heights. Formerly known as Paneas, it was an important Hellenistic shrine to the god Pan before being rebuilt by Herod the Great and named in honour of the Roman emperor Augustus.

Caesars A branch of the aristocratic Roman Julia clan, the name of which passed from its most famous member Julius CAESAR to become an imperial title. All succeeding Roman emperors adopted it, conferring the title on their designated heirs so that it came signify a 'prince'. The name and title was used in the Eastern empire as 'Kaisaros'. From this were later derived the imperial Russian and German titles Tsar and Kaiser.

caesium (US **cesium**, symbol Cs, at. no. 55, r.a.m. 132.91) A soft silvery metallic element, one of the ALKALI METALS. It reacts vigorously with non-metals and water; and its compounds closely resemble potassium compounds. It is used in photoelectric cells and in the caesium atomic clock.

Caetano, Marcello José das Neves Alves (1904–81) Portuguese statesman. He was Prime Minister from 1968 to 1974. He was ousted from power by General Spinola in 1974 in a *putsch* which brought to an end half a century of dictatorship in Portugal, established by Caetano's predecessor, SALAZAR.

Cage, John (Milton) (1912–92) US composer, pianist, and writer. A pupil of Schoenberg, he is notable for his experimental approach to music, including the use of silence and the role of chance. He was a pioneer of aleatory music, in which the composition or performance is randomly determined, for example by use of a computer or dice. Cage experimented with musical instruments, inventing the 'prepared piano' (with pieces of metal, rubber, etc., inserted between the strings to alter the tone), and also used electronic instruments and various sound-effects.

Cagney, James (1899–1986) US actor. He is chiefly remembered for his parts as a gangster in films, such as *The Public Enemy* (1931) and *Angels with Dirty Faces* (1938). Also a skilled dancer and comedian, he received an Oscar for his part in the musical *Yankee Doodle Dandy* (1942).

Caiaphas A biblical figure, the Jewish high priest of the Temple (*c.*18–37 AD) who presided over the Sanhedrin when it tried Jesus, and handed him over to the Romans for crucifixion.

Cain According to Jewish, Christian, and Muslim belief, the eldest son of Adam and Eve. Cain, a farmer, became jealous that God had accepted the sacrifice of his brother Abel, a shepherd, in preference to his own. He murdered Abel and was condemned by God to wander over the face of the Earth. According to Islamic tradition, Cain and Abel (Kabil and Ḥabil) each had twin sisters, Aklima and Labuda. It was Kabil's refusal to marry Ḥabil's twin sister, Labuda, that caused Allah to reject Kabil's sacrifice and accept Ḥabil's, the latter having obeyed Adam's wish that he marry Aklima. In a fit of rage Kabil killed his brother, but not knowing what to do with the body, he wandered with it over the face of the Earth for many years.

Caine, Michael (born Maurice Micklewhite) (1933–) British film actor. He had his first major role in *Zulu* (1963), and soon established a reputation for laconic, anti-heroic roles, for example as a spy in *The Ipcress File* (1965) and as a streetwise cockney in *Alfie* (1966). Since then, he has appeared in a wide variety of films, such as *Educating Rita* (1983) and *Hannah and Her Sisters* (1986), for which he won an Oscar.

Cainozoic Era (or **Cenozoic**) (from the Greek, 'new animal') The most recent of the four eras of the GEOLOGICAL TIMESCALE, comprising the TERTIARY and QUATERNARY PERIODS. It represents the period of time covering the last 66 million years to the present day. The Cainozoic was very much the age of mammals, which became dominant in the Tertiary Period. Great changes took place in the world's temperature, which increased and then decreased during the Tertiary and led to the Pleistocene ice ages of the Quaternary Period.

Cairngorms A group of mountains forming part of the Grampian system of central Scotland, rising to 1,309 m (4,296 feet) at Ben Macdui. The name Cairngorm is given to a form of QUARTZ that is yellow or wine-coloured and prized as a semi-precious stone.

Cairns A resort town on the north-east coast of Queensland, Australia, on Trinity Bay; pop. (1991) 64,430. An embarkation point for tours of the Barrier Reef, it is also a trading centre for agricultural produce, sugar, timber, fish, and minerals.

Cairo (Arabic **El Qâhira**) The capital of Egypt, a port on the Nile near the head of the delta, and the largest city in Africa; pop. (1991) 6,663,000. Founded by the Fatamid dynasty in 969 it was later fortified against the Crusaders by Saladin, whose citadel (built *c.*1179) still survives. Cairo's mosques include that of Al Azhar (972), housing an Islamic university said to be the oldest in the world and the leading centre of Koranic studies. Islamic Cairo has been designated a world heritage site by UNESCO. Cairo has many light industries including tourism.

Cairo Conference (22–26 November 1943) A World War II meeting, attended by ROOSEVELT, CHURCHILL, and CHIANG KAI-SHEK, to decide on post-war policy for the Far East. Unconditional surrender by Japan was its prerequisite; Manchuria was to be returned to China, and Korea to its own people. At a second conference Roosevelt and Churchill met President Inönü of Turkey, and confirmed that country's independence. The TEHERAN CONFERENCE was held immediately afterwards.

caisson A bottomless, reinforced CONCRETE box or cylindrical structure used for building foundations in unstable and waterlogged ground. It is built upwards from ground level, and when it reaches the required height, soil is removed from inside and the caisson sinks under its own weight until foundation level is reached. A pneumatic caisson is sealed at the top and water is excluded by compressed air. Caissons are also used in DRY DOCKS.

Caithness A former county in the far north of Scotland, now part of Highland local government area.

calabrese See CABBAGE.

Calais A Channel ferry-port in the department of Pas-de-Calais, north-west France; pop. (1990) 75,840. Captured by Edward III in 1347 after a long siege, it was saved from destruction by the surrender of six burghers (commemorated in Rodin's sculpture), and remained an English possession until retaken by the French in 1558 in the reign of Mary. The French terminal of the Channel Tunnel is at Fréthun, to the south of Calais.

calamine See SMITHSONITE.

calamite (or **giant horsetail**) A fossil plant of the genus *Calamites*, an important tree-like plant in the swamps of the Carboniferous Period, 360–286 million years ago. Like their smaller living relatives the HORSETAILS, *Equisetum*, they bore branches and leaves in whorls around a jointed stem. The most common fossil is the grooved internal cast of the stem, but coaly compressions of leaves are sometimes also found in the shales above coal seams.

Calamity Jane (born Martha Jane Cannary) (*c.*1852–1903) US frontierswoman. A colourful character noted for her skill at shooting and riding, she dressed as a man and lived for a time in Wyoming, where she became known for her wild behaviour and heavy drinking. She later joined Buffalo Bill's Wild West Show.

calceolaria (or **slipper flower**) Any of about 200 species of plant in the genus *Calceolaria*, which belongs to the foxglove family. They are chiefly New World plants from Central and South America and New Zealand. Several species are popular garden and glasshouse plants.

calcite A form of calcium carbonate that is a common mineral and the main constituent of limestone rocks. Semi-hard and white or colourless, although it can be coloured by impurities, it occurs in several forms: crystalline, massive concretionary as in STALACTITES, and spheroidal as OOLITE. It can form by precipitation from sea water, by evaporation, or in veins by recrystallization. As limestone and in various other forms calcite is used as building stone and in the manufacture of cement.

calcium (symbol Ca, at. no. 20, r.a.m. 40.08) A silvery white metal, the fifth most abundant element in the Earth's crust. It occurs in many minerals: as calcium carbonate in, for example, limestone, chalk, and marble, as calcium fluoride in fluorite, and as calcium sulphate in gypsum. It also occurs in seawater, and as calcium phosphate in bones and teeth. The HARDNESS OF WATER is due chiefly to calcium compounds. Calcium is one of the ALKALINE EARTH METALS. It is a reactive metal; on treatment with non-metals, water, and acids it gives ionic compounds in which the metal has a valency of 2. The metal is obtained by the ELECTROLYSIS of molten calcium chloride (produced in the manufacture of SODIUM CARBONATE), followed by distillation under high vacuum or in ARGON to obtain the pure metal. Calcium is used as a dehydrating agent for organic solvents and to remove gases from molten metals prior to casting. It is also used as a hardening agent in lead for cable covering, for making storage battery grids and bearings, and, alloyed with silicon, in steel.

calcium bicarbonate See CALCIUM HYDROGENCARBONATE.

calcium carbonate ($CaCO_3$) A white solid that occurs widely in nature as calcite, chalk, Iceland spar, limestone, and marble. It is insoluble in pure water, but dissolves in water containing carbon dioxide, a process which causes the formation of caves. It reacts with acids, and gives off carbon dioxide on heating; it is used in blast furnaces and for making mortar and cement.

calcium hydrogencarbonate (or **calcium bicarbonate**, $Ca(HCO_3)_2$) A compound that is formed when calcium carbonate reacts with a solution of carbon dioxide in water. Water containing calcium hydrogencarbonate is hard, the calcium forming a scum when soap is added; the hardness is temporary, and is removed by boiling, when carbon dioxide is driven off and insoluble calcium carbonate (familiar as the fur in kettles) is precipitated.

calcium hydroxide (or **slaked lime**, $Ca(OH)_2$) A white crystalline powder formed from the action of water on calcium oxide. It is slightly soluble in water, and in solution is known as LIME WATER. Mixed with sand and water it makes mortar.

calcium oxide (or **quicklime**, CaO) A white solid which is formed industrially by heating limestone, $CaCO_3$. It combines readily with water giving calcium hydroxide; it is used to make mortar and cement, and (as lime) as a cheap BASE. When heated it gives out a bright white light; this was once used for lighting in theatres – called 'limelight'.

calcium sulphate ($CaSO_4$) A white crystalline solid. It occurs naturally as ANHYDRITE and GYPSUM; on heating it loses water and becomes plaster of Paris, $CaSO_4.½H_2O$. When mixed with water the plaster can be moulded before it sets hard, as $CaSO_4.2H_2O$ re-forms. Calcium sulphate is found in some water supplies, and causes permanent HARDNESS OF WATER. It is used in paint- and paper-making.

calcrete (or **caliche**, **hardpan**) A hard crust of calcium carbonate occurring in desert and semidesert regions. Usually white, although sometimes stained pinkish, yellowish, or brownish, it often has a rubble-like appearance. The material is extremely resistant to attack by weathering in dry environments and is largely impermeable to water movement, so calcretes develop only very thin soils and present a barren, inhospitable surface to vegetation. All calcretes are formed by a concentration of lime resulting from evaporation.

calc tufa See TUFA.

calculator A device that performs arithmetical calculations. An early aid to calculation was the ABACUS, a bead frame still used in parts of the Arab world, Russia, south-east Asia and China.

The first half of the 20th century saw a great demand for adding machines, typically desk-top mechanical devices, hand-operated by a lever. For more specialized work, engineers began to explore methods of programming desk calculators, research which ultimately led to the modern digital computer (see COMPUTER, HISTORY OF). The calculating machine itself evolved into the present-day hand-held electronic calculator, in which a small number of INTEGRATED CIRCUITS replace the gears of the mechanical calculator. Data and commands are entered through a simple key-pad and are usually read from a seven-segment display. Frequently, a MEMORY is used to store partial or temporary results. A programmable calculator resembles a simple computer system in that a complex PROGRAM involving many calculation steps may be entered into memory and executed on different data each time the program is run.

calculus The branch of mathematics concerned with the rates of change of dependent quantities relative to variations in other quantities. Calculus was developed independently by Isaac NEWTON and Gottfried LEIBNIZ in the 17th century, primarily to solve problems of motion. Calculus is divided into two fields. Differential calculus is used for solving problems involving the rates at which processes occur and for obtaining maximum and minimum values for continuously varying quantities. Integral calculus, which was initially concerned with the calculation of irregular areas and volumes by dividing them into regular fragments, is also used to solve other problems involving the summation of infinitesimals. Differential and integral calculus are connected by the processes of DIFFERENTIATION and INTEGRATION, which are the reverse of each other.

Calcutta The capital of the state of West Bengal in north-east India, on the east bank of the Hugli River; pop. (1991) 10,916,000. It is a major port and the largest city of India. Founded *c.*1690 by the East India Company, it was the capital of British India from 1833 until 1912 when it was replaced by Delhi. Calcutta is a major commercial and industrial centre with jute mills, and textile, chemical, metal, and paper industries. Other industries lie across the Hugli at Haora and at Haldia, a new outport developed because of the silting of the river. See also BLACK HOLE OF CALCUTTA.

Caldecott, Randolph (1846–86) British graphic artist and watercolour painter. He is best known for his illustrations for children's books, such as those for *The House that Jack Built* (1878). A medal awarded annually for the illustration of US children's books is named after him.

Calder, Alexander (1898–1976) US sculptor and painter. He was one of the first artists to introduce movement into sculpture, from the early 1930s, making mobiles incorporating abstract forms and often using wire. His static sculptures (such as *The Red Crab*, 1962) are known by contrast as 'stabiles'.

caldera A large volcanic depression left after the removal of a mountain peak by immense volcanic activity.

Calder Hall reactor The world's first commercially operating nuclear power-station, which opened in the UK in 1956. It was the first of a series of 18 MAGNOX REACTORS built over the next 15 years, which gave the UK an early lead in electricity generation using NUCLEAR POWER. It is still in operation.

Calderón de la Barca, Pedro (1600–81) Spanish dramatist and poet. He wrote some 120 plays, more than 70 of them religious dramas for outdoor performance on the festival of Corpus Christi. His secular dramas include *El Alcalde de Zalamea* (*c.*1643).

Caldwell, Erskine (Preston) (1903–87) US novelist and short-story writer. *Tobacco Road* (1932), his best-known work, was adapted for the stage and ran for more than seven years on Broadway. His other books include *God's Little Acre* (1933), *Georgia Boy* (1943), and *Close to Home* (1962).

Caledonia A Roman name for the northern part of Britain that is now Scotland.

Caledonian Canal A system of lochs and man-made canals in Scotland stretching for nearly 100 km (63 miles) from Inverness south-westwards to Fort William, linking the North Sea with the Atlantic Ocean. The work of Thomas Telford, it was opened in 1822.

Caledonian folds (or **Caledonian orogeny**) The north-east to south-west alignment of folds, faults, and mountains created in Europe during the late Silurian and early Devonian periods of geological time.

calendar Any system for fixing the beginning, length, order, and subdivisions of the year. Calendrical systems have been used by societies since the earliest times, nearly all of them based on one of two astronomical cycles: the cycle of the phases of the Moon (the synodic month or lunation), often of major ritual and religious significance, and the cycle of the seasons (the period of the Earth's orbit around the Sun), of importance in agriculture. The two cycles are incompatible in that the synodic month has a period of about 29.5 days, giving a lunar year (12 months) of just over 354 days, over 11 days shorter than the mean solar year of 365.2422 days.

The JULIAN CALENDAR was introduced to the Roman Empire by Julius CAESAR in 46 BC. It was developed from the traditional Roman lunar calendar, as is evident from its division into 12 months. However, the months no longer corresponded to lunations, as days were added to give a total year length of 365 days. Almost exact correspondence with the mean solar year was maintained by the intercalation of a **leap year** containing an extra day, on 29 February, every four years. The average length of the year was therefore 365.25 days which is only slightly longer than the length of the mean solar year. The GREGORIAN CALENDAR, first introduced in 1582 by Pope Gregory XIII and in almost universal civil use today, superseded, with only slight modification, the Julian calendar. The Gregorian reform of 1582 omitted ten days from the calendar that year, the day after 4 October becoming 15 October. This restored the vernal equinox to 21 March and, to maintain this, three leap years are now suppressed every 400 years, centurial years ceasing to be leap years unless they are divisible by 400. The average length of the calendar year is now reduced to 365.2425 days, so close to the mean solar year that no adjustment will be required before 5000 AD.

Other calendrical systems continue to be used, particularly for religious purposes, alongside the Gregorian system. The present JEWISH CALENDAR uses the 19-year Metonic cycle made up of 12 common years and 7 leap years. The common years have 12 months, each of 29 or 30 days, while the leap years have an additional month. The rules governing the detailed construction of the calendar are very complicated but the year begins on the first day of Tishri, an autumn month. Years are reckoned from the era of creation (*anno mundi*) for which the epoch adopted is 7 October 3761 BC. The ISLAMIC CALENDAR is wholly lunar, the year always containing 12 months without intercalation. This means that the Muslim New Year occurs seasonally about 11 days earlier each year. The months have alternately 30 and 29 days and are fixed in length, except for the twelfth month (Dulheggia) which has one intercalatory day in 11 years out of a cycle of 30 calendar years.

calendering See PAPER MANUFACTURE.

Calgary A commercial and industrial city in southern Alberta, south-west Canada, situated to the east of the Rocky Mountains, on the edge of a rich agricultural and stock-raising area; pop. (1991) 754,030 (metropolitan area). It is the centre of Alberta's oil business with oil-refining, timber-processing, and flour-milling industries. The Calgary Stampede, inaugurated in 1912, is an annual rodeo.

Calhoun, John Caldwell (1782–1850) US statesman. He was elected to Congress in 1811. As a leader of the 'War Hawks', Calhoun committed the USA to the WAR OF 1812. He served as Secretary of War under President MONROE (1817–25), and as Vice-President to both John Quincy Adams (1825–29) and JACKSON (1829–32). Calhoun was the spokesman of Southern interests who saw a North-South confrontation as inevitable. He served briefly as Secretary of State under TYLER (1844–45) before returning to the Senate.

caliche A lime-rich cemented deposit commonly found in the surface sediments and soils of semi-arid regions, especially under conditions of sparse rainfall. It is formed by the drawing of lime-rich waters to the surface by capillary action and the subsequent deposition of calcium carbonate in the pore spaces in the sediment when the water evaporates. Well-hardened caliches are known as CALCRETES.

Calicut (or **Kozhikode**) A seaport in the state of Kerala, south-west India, on the Malabar Coast; pop. (1991) 420,000. This was Vasco da Gama's first port of call when he visited India in 1498. It subsequently developed as a European trading town which gave its name to the cotton cloth known as calico. It manufactures ropes and nets and exports tea, coffee, spices, and timber.

California A state on the Pacific coast of the USA, bounded north by Oregon, east by Nevada, south-east by Arizona, and south by Mexico; area 411,049 sq km (158,706 sq miles); pop. (1990) 29,760,000; capital, Sacramento. The largest cities are Los Angeles, San Diego, San José, and San Francisco. California is also known as the Golden State. It was ceded by Mexico in 1847, a year before the discovery of gold that brought large numbers of settlers to the territory. In 1850 it became the 31st state of the union. By 1964 it had become not only the most populous US state but the state with the greatest per capita income and expenditure. The chief products are timber, natural gas, petroleum, electronics, transportation equipment, and food. Major tourist attractions include Disneyland, the Golden Gate Bridge, and Yosemite, Sequoia, and Kings Canyon National Parks.

California, Gulf of An arm of the Pacific Ocean separating the Baja California peninsula from mainland Mexico. It stretches for about 1,125 km (700 miles) and has a width of 80–210 km (50–130 miles). Deepening from north to south, the gulf reaches a depth of *c.*2,595 m (8,500 ft).

California current A cold ocean current of the eastern Pacific that flows south along the west coast of North America.

Californian poppy See ESCHSCHOLZIA.

californium (symbol Cf, at.no. 98, r.a.m. 251) A strongly radioactive transuranic element synthesized by G. T. Seaborg in 1950, it is an intense source of neutrons making it useful in activation analysis.

Caligula (born Gaius Julius Caesar Germanicus) (12–41 AD) Roman emperor 37–41. Brought up in a military camp, he gained the nickname Caligula (Latin for 'little boot') as an infant on account of the miniature military boots he wore. Caligula's brief reign as emperor, which began when he succeeded Tiberius and ended with his assassination, became notorious for its tyrannical excesses.

caliph (from Arabic, 'successor' or 'representative') Title given to the heads of the Muslim community following the death of Muhammad in 632 AD, and used in the KORAN, meaning 'successor' or 'viceregent' of God. SUNNI Muslims accept the authority of the first four 'rightly guided' caliphs: Abu Bakr (632–4), immediate successor to Muhammad; Umar (634–44); Uthman (644–56); and ALI. Shiite Muslims accept authority as passing directly from Muhammad to Ali. The caliphate was abolished with the demise of the Ottoman Empire in 1922, but Islamic fundamentalists have called for its restitution in recent years.

Callaghan, (Leonard) James, Baron Callaghan of Cardiff (1912–) British Labour statesman, Prime Minister 1976–79. He became Prime Minister following Harold Wilson's resignation; the leader of a minority government, he was forced in 1977 to negotiate an agreement with the Liberal Party (known as the Lib–Lab Pact) to stay in power. After widespread strikes in the so-called 'winter of discontent' (1978–79), Callaghan received a vote of no confidence; the Labour Party was defeated by the Conservatives in the subsequent election.

Callas, Maria (born Maria Cecilia Anna Kalageropoulos) (1923–77) US-born operatic soprano, of Greek parentage. She was a coloratura soprano whose bel canto style of singing especially suited her to early Italian opera; a number of works by Rossini, Bellini, and Donizetti were revived for her.

Calles, Plutarco Elías (1877–1945) Mexican statesman. He achieved prominence as a military leader during the Mexican Revolution (1910–40). As President of Mexico (1924–28), Calles implemented Mexico's constitution (1917) by supporting agrarian reform, organized labour, economic nationalism, and education.

Callicrates (5th century BC) Greek architect. He was the leading architect in Periclean Athens, and with Ictinus designed the Parthenon (447–438 BC). Many other structures are attributed to him, including the Ionic temple of Athena Nike on the Acropolis (448–after 421 BC).

calligraphy The art of producing beautiful handwriting. Usually the term refers to writing in ink or similar materials, but it is sometimes extended to certain types of epigraphy (inscriptions on durable materials, particularly stone). The earliest surviving examples of calligraphy are in Egyptian papyri of the third millennium BC, and the art has been practised in most civilizations since then. With the invention of printing the need for skilled handwriting declined, but professional writing masters flourished from the 16th to the 19th century, producing many instructional manuals. Often these included drawings of animals, specimens of ornament, and so on, composed of penstrokes and flourishes. This tradition came to an end in about the middle of the 19th century, but there was a revival of interest in calligraphy in the early 20th century, spearheaded by the British designer and teacher Edward Johnston, whose *Writing and Illuminating, and Lettering* (1906) was highly influential.

Callimachus (*c.*305–*c.*240 BC) Greek poet and scholar. As head of the library at Alexandria, he compiled a critical catalogue of the existing Greek literature of his day. As a poet he is best known for his short or episodic poetry, especially hymns and epigrams.

Calliope In Greek mythology, the Muse of epic poetry.

Callisto A GALILEAN SATELLITE of Jupiter, discovered by Galileo in 1610. Callisto has a nearly circular orbit above Jupiter's equator at 1.883 million km from the planet's centre. Its diameter is 4,800 km. Its composition is probably a mixture of water ice and rocks. VOYAGER images have shown that its icy surface is heavily cratered.

calorie The quantity of energy needed to raise the temperature of 1 gram of water by 1°C. The kilocalorie (kcal) is equal to 1,000 calories, and is sometimes referred to as the large calorie when indicating the energy value of foods. For scientific purposes the calorie has now been largely replaced by the JOULE as the unit of work and energy (1 cal = 4.2 joules).

calorimeter An instrument for measuring the heat energy changes taking place in a chemical reaction, or the heat required to melt a solid, or the heat capacity of a substance. It consists of a closed vessel in which the reaction takes place. The vessel is either heavily insulated, in which case the temperature change during the reaction is measured; or the heat is transferred to a known amount of water, and the temperature rise in the water is measured. For liquids, a continuous-flow type of calorimeter can be used. Measurements on combustion reactions are carried out in bomb calorimeters, sealed vessels containing oxygen under pressure.

Caloris Basin An impact crater with a diameter of 1,300 km, the largest feature on MERCURY. It was formed relatively recently. The impact produced a series of mountain ranges, the 3 km high, 40 km wide Calores Montes being a typical example, and also a region known as the weird terrain.

calotype See PHOTOGRAPHY.

Calpe An ancient name for the Rock of Gibraltar.

Calvados A low-lying department on the English Channel in the Basse-Normandie region of northwest France; area 5,548 sq km (2,143 sq miles); pop. (1990) 618,480; capital, Caen. Textiles, dairy produce, and the Calvados liqueur are the chief products of the area. Tourism is also important.

Calvary (Hebrew **Golgotha**) A place just outside the city of Jerusalem where the crucifixion of Jesus took place. Although its location is uncertain, it is traditionally taken to be the site of the present Church of the Holy Sepulchre.

Calvin, John (1509–64) French Protestant theologian and reformer. He began his theological career in France, but was forced to flee to Basle in Switzerland after embracing Protestantism in the early 1530s. He attempted a re-ordering of society on reformed Christian principles, with strong and sometimes ruthless control over the private lives of citizens. From 1541 he lived in Geneva, where he established the first Presbyterian government. He exerted an important influence on the development of Protestant thought; his theological system, Calvinism, was further developed by his followers, notably Theodore Beza (1519–1605).

Calvin, Melvin (1911–97) US biochemist. He investigated the metabolic pathways involved in photosynthesis, discovering the cycle of reactions which is named after him, and attempting to duplicate them synthetically. He was awarded the Nobel Prize for chemistry in 1961.

Calvino, Italo (1923–85) Italian novelist and short-story writer, born in Cuba. His first novel *The Path to the Nest of Spiders* (1947) is considered a significant example of neo-realism, whereas his later works increasingly use fantasy, allegory, and innovative narrative structures and have been associated with magic realism; his later novels include *Invisible Cities* (1972) and *If on a Winter's Night a Traveller* (1979).

Calypso In Greek mythology, a nymph, a daughter of Atlas. Odysseus was shipwrecked on her island, Ogygia, and she promised to make him immortal if he would stay with her. After seven years, she let him go at the command of Zeus.

calypso A type of West Indian popular song, originating in Trinidad and Tobago. It is a form of folk-song whose words comment on newsworthy topics in a humorous and, if necessary, critical way, and whose music is typically played by STEEL BANDS. Calypso music is syncopated and repetitious.

cam A projecting part of a wheel or rotating shaft designed to impart an alternating or variable motion to another mechanism, such as a valve or oscillating shaft. In a PETROL ENGINE the valves are operated in sequence by a series of cams on the camshaft, which rotates at half engine speed. Each cam is circular for about three-quarters of its periphery, the rest forming a curved nose which lifts the valve at a specific point in the rotation of the camshaft.

Camargue, the The area of the Rhône delta in south-east France, characterized by numerous shallow salt lagoons. The region is known for its white horses and as a nature reserve for migratory birds.

Camberley A residential town in Surrey, south-east England, near Aldershot; pop. (1981) 45,700. The Royal Staff College is located here.

Camberwell beauty See BRUSH-FOOTED BUTTERFLY.

Cambodia A tropical country in south-east Asia flanked by Thailand, Laos, and Vietnam.

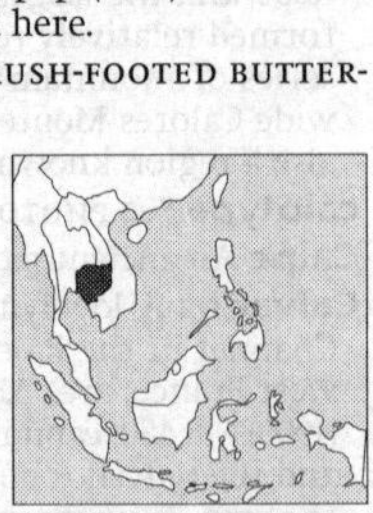

Physical. Through it from the north flows the Mekong, while westward is a large lake, the Tonlé Sap. The climate is tropical monsoon, and most of the land marshy or forested, providing good crops of rice and timber. A short coastline faces south-west on the Gulf of Thailand.

Economy. Cambodia's economy is overwhelmingly agricultural, and rubber is a major export. There is limited light industry. The prolonged civil war and the Khmer Rouge regime's policies of enforced resettlement decimated agriculture, and caused a sharp drop in productivity of rice, the staple crop. The economy is being rebuilt with the help of foreign aid donations.

History. Cambodia was occupied from the 1st to the 6th century AD by the Hindu kingdoms of Funan, and subsequently Chenla. The KHMER people overthrew the Hindu rulers of Chenla and established a Buddhist empire, centred around the region of ANGKOR. The classical, or Angkorean, period lasted from 802 to 1432, with the Kmer empire reaching its peak during the 12th century. After 1432 the empire went into decline and suffered frequent invasions from Vietnam and Thailand. Continuing foreign domination forced Cambodia to seek French protection in 1863, and from 1884 it was treated as part of FRENCH INDO-CHINA, although allowed to retain its royal dynasty. After Japanese occupation in World War II, King Norodom SIHANOUK achieved independence within the French Union (1949) and full independence in 1953. Sihanouk abdicated in 1955 to form a broad-based coalition government. Cambodia was drawn into the VIETNAM WAR in the 1960s, and US suspicions of Sihanouk's relations with communist forces led to his overthrow by the army under Lon Nol in 1970, following a US bombing offensive (1969–70) and invasion. The Lon Nol regime renamed Cambodia the Khmer Republic. The regime soon came under heavy pressure from the communist KHMER ROUGE. Following the fall of Phnom Penh in 1975, the Khmer Rouge under POL POT renamed the country Democratic Kampuchea and launched a bloody reign of terror, which is estimated to have resulted in as many as two million deaths, or nearly a third of the population. Border tensions led to an invasion of the country by Vietnam in 1978, and the overthrow of the Pol Pot regime two weeks later. The Vietnamese installed a client regime under an ex-Khmer Rouge member, Heng Samrin, who proclaimed a new People's Republic of Kampuchea, but conflict with Khmer Rouge guerrillas continued. International relief organizations were active in Cambodia from 1980. A government in exile comprising anti-Vietnamese factions and led by Son Sann, the Coalition Government of Democratic Kampuchea (CGDK), was recognized by the United Nations in 1983. Civil war lasted until 1987, when inconclusive peace talks were held in Paris. These later moved to Jakarta, and in 1990 a peace agreement ended 13 years of civil strife. A UN Transitional Authority enforced a ceasefire and installed an interim Supreme Council, under Prince Norodom Sihanouk as head of state. The Council included representatives of the former government, the Cambodian People's Party (CPP) led by Hun Sen, and the three former guerrilla movements: the Party of Democratic Kampuchea (the former Khmer Rouge); the Khmer People's National Liberation Front, led by Son Sann; and the National United Front (NUF), led by Norodom Ranariddh, son of Prince Sihanouk. Multi-party elections were held in 1993, and UN peace-keepers supervised the process and helped to repatriate and rehabilitate some half million refugees and released prisoners. No party won a clear majority of seats, but a democratic monarchist constitution was adopted; Sihanouk became king and a coalition government headed by the CPP and NUF was formed, their leaders becoming co-premiers (1993). The Khmer Rouge refused to participate in the elections and continued to launch guerrilla attacks. In 1997 the NUF leader, Prince Ranariddh, was ousted by Hun Sen's forces.

Capital: Phnom Penh
Area: 181,035 sq km (69,898 sq mi)
Population: 9,610,000 (1995)
Currency: 1 riel = 100 sen
Religions: Buddhist 88.4%; Muslim 2.4%
Ethnic Groups: Khmer 88.1%; Chinese 4.6%; Vietnamese 4.6%
Languages: Khmer (official); Chinese; Vietnamese; French
International Organizations: UN; Colombo Plan

Cambrai, League of (1508) An alliance of the PAPACY, the HOLY ROMAN EMPIRE, France, and Spain against VENICE. In 1529 the 'Ladies' Peace (the Peace of Cambrai) temporarily halted the Habsburg–Valois wars.

Cambrian Mountains A high and rugged plateau running from north to south along the length of the interior of Wales. The tallest peaks are in the north: Aran Fawddwy rises to 905 m (2,970 feet). There are numerous deep lakes and valleys, and the mountains contain the sources of many rivers, including the Severn and the Wye. The word Cambria is the medieval Latin name for Wales.

Cambrian Period The oldest GEOLOGICAL TIME period of the PHANEROZOIC AGE, extending from 570 to 505 million years ago. Rocks of this age were first recognized in Wales (Cambria). The Cambrian Period was one of widespread seas. Cambrian rocks are the oldest in which FOSSILS can be used for geological dating. They contain trilobites (marine arthropods, now extinct), molluscs, and other marine invertebrates. Cambrian rocks are today exposed most notably in North Wales and Scotland, Norway, Spain, south-east Australia, and in the Appalachians and along the Saint Lawrence River in North America.

Cambridge (Latin **Cantabrigia**) A city in Cambridgeshire, England, on the River Cam, the seat of a major English university organized as a federation of colleges; pop. (1991) 101,000. The first historical trace of Cambridge as a University (*studium generale*) is in 1209: a number of scholars migrated from Oxford to Cambridge in 1209–14 after a conflict with townsmen during which two or three students were hanged. The first college, Peterhouse, was founded in 1284 and another nine followed in the 14th and 15th centuries, but the university did not achieve real eminence until the 16th-century Reformation when it produced Tyndale, Coverdale, Cranmer, and Latimer. After a prolonged period of stagnation, Cambridge was revived by its growth as a centre of scientific research in the late 19th and early 20th century. Women's colleges were founded in the mid-19th century, but women did not receive full academic status until 1948. Cambridge also processes agricultural produce, and has computer-based high-tech industries.

Cambridge An industrial and educational city in eastern Massachusetts, USA, on the Charles River opposite Boston; pop. (1990) 95,800. Harvard University (the oldest college in the USA) was established here in 1636 and four years later in 1640 the first printing press in the USA was set up. Cambridge is also the home of the distinguished Massachusetts Institute of Technology.

Cambridgeshire A county of eastern England; area 3,401 sq km (1,314 sq miles); pop. (1991) 640,700; county town, Cambridge. The former county of Cambridge was united with the Isle of Ely in 1965 and part of Huntingdonshire in 1974.

camcorder See VIDEO CAMERA.

Camden An inner borough of London, England; pop. (1991) 170,500. Situated to the north of the City of Westminster, it includes the suburbs of Bloomsbury, Hampstead, St Pancras, Highgate, and Holborn. It is named after Sir Charles Pratt, 1st Earl Camden (1713–94), who was Lord Chancellor from 1766 to 1770.

Camden Town Group A group of British painters including Harold Gilman (1876–1919), Spencer Gore (1878–1914), and Robert Bevan (1865–1925). Formed in 1911, it took its name from the drab working-class area of London made popular as a subject by SICKERT, their prime inspiration. The group merged with a number of smaller groups in 1913 to form an exhibiting society called the London Group. The group helped to introduce Post-Impressionism to British art.

camel A RUMINANT of the family Camelidae, which is among the largest of the even-toed ungulates (hoofed mammals). Camels form a family of six species which includes the two species of 'camel' as well as the LLAMA, ALPACA, GUANACO, and VICUÑA. The two species commonly called camels, the dromedary, *Camelus dromedarius*, and the Bactrian camel, *C. bactrianus*, can be as tall as 2.3 m (7.5 feet) at the shoulder. The long head is set on an arched neck. The eyes have long lashes to keep sand out, the ears are small, and the nostrils are set high above the fleshy lips. The legs are long and slender and the feet have two toes united by a web of skin, allowing the toes to spread sideways, thus enabling the animal to walk on soft sand.

Camels can survive for six to eight days in the desert and can travel for 1,000 km (620 miles) without drinking. When water does become available they can drink up to 90 litres (23 US gallons) to rehydrate their tissues. The large hump of fat provides an energy store when food is in short supply. The thick, dense fur acts as a substantial barrier to heat. By allowing their body temperature to rise during the day, camels reduce the need to sweat, thus preventing water loss. Another aid to water conservation is the concentrated nature of their urine.

camellia An evergreen shrub native to the Far East and widely cultivated since ancient times by the Chinese, and latterly by Europeans, for its showy spring flowers. There are about 80 species in the genus *Camellia*, which belongs to a family of trees and shrubs confined to the tropics and subtropics. *C. sinensis* is the tea plant.

Camelopardalis The Giraffe, a CONSTELLATION in the north polar region of the sky, introduced in 1613 by the Dutchman Petrus Plancius. It represents the animal on which Rebecca rode into Canaan for her marriage to Isaac. Its brightest stars are of only fourth magnitude.

Camelot The mythical court of the Celtic hero King Arthur. It was from here that the Knights of the Round Table set off on their many quests. Camelot is variously identified with sites in Cornwall, Somerset, Hampshire, and Caerleon in Wales.

Camembert A village of Normandy in north-west France, situated near Falaise in the department of Orne in the Basse-Normandie region. It gives its name to a kind of soft creamy cheese with a strong flavour.

cameo A small carving (often a portrait) cut in relief on a gemstone, shell, or similar surface. Often a banded or multicoloured stone, such as agate, is used, so as to exploit the different layers of colour – with, for example, one colour for the background and another for the carving. The cameo was highly popular among the Greeks and

Romans, particularly for jewellery; it was revived during the Renaissance, and again in Victorian times.

camera An instrument for producing a photographic image. All cameras, including CINE CAMERAS used in cinematography, share the same basic design: a light-tight compartment with a LENS at one end, through which light can pass to form an image on a light-sensitive film surface at the other. The amount of light entering the camera is controlled by the SHUTTER and an APERTURE, so that only enough light is admitted to produce a satisfactory exposure. A focusing mechanism adjusts the position of the lens so that a sharp image can be recorded of a subject at any distance from the lens. A viewfinder enables the user to aim the camera accurately at the subject. Modern cameras for amateur use have evolved into a number of basic types. Direct-viewfinder cameras are designed for general snapshot photography. The subject is observed through a viewfinder lens, separate from the lens system used to expose the film. 'Compact' cameras taking 35-mm film fall into this category. Single-lens reflex (SLR) cameras use the same lens for the viewfinder as for film exposure, so the photographer sees the subject framed exactly as it will be on the photograph. A variety of interchangeable lenses and accessories is available for SLR cameras, making them highly versatile. Twin-lens reflex (TLR) cameras use two lenses of the same focal length, mounted one above the other and sharing a common focusing mechanism. The top lens acts as a viewing lens, forming an image reflected by a mirror on to a viewing screen on the top of the camera, while the bottom lens is used for exposing the film, and is fitted with a shutter and diaphragm. See also TELEVISION; VIDEO CAMERA.

camera obscura A darkened room or box with a lens or small hole in one side, through which light can enter and form an inverted image on a screen of the scene outside. The Islamic scholar Alhazen (*c.*965–1039) first proposed the use of the camera obscura for observing solar eclipses. In the 16th century the introduction of a lens and a diaphragm improved the image obtained, and a concave mirror was used to correct the reversal of the image. The camera obscura became a photographic camera when light-sensitive material was used to make a permanent record of the image.

Cameron, Charles (*c.*1743–1812) British Neoclassical architect. Born in Scotland, he was active mainly in Russia, where he settled in about 1778 and remained for the rest of his life.

Cameron, Julia Margaret (1815–79) British photographer. Although she did not take up photography until the age of 48, she quickly gained acclaim for her portraits of prominent figures, such as Alfred Tennyson, Charles Darwin, and Thomas Carlyle.

Cameroon A country in West Africa, with Nigeria and Chad to its west and north, the Central African Republic to its east, and Gabon and Congo to the south.

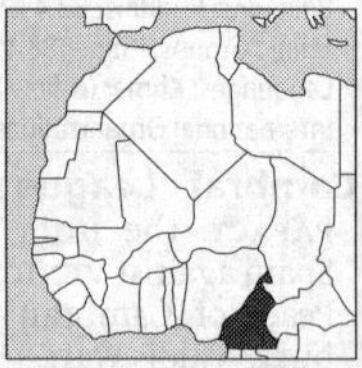

Physical. Most of the coastline is low, with creeks, lagoons, and swamps, although near Mount Cameroon, an active volcano, there are steep cliffs. The coastal plain is hot and very wet and covered with thick rain forest. Inland this becomes open woodland and then SAVANNAH as the ground rises to the plateau that makes up most of the country.

Economy. Crude oil is the largest export, followed by cocoa and coffee. Mineral deposits include oil and natural gas, gold, uranium, bauxite, nickel, and cobalt. Industries include aluminium smelting (from imported bauxite and alumina), food-processing, and brewing. Fifty per cent of land is under forest, but poor transportation has restricted its development.

History. The Portuguese and other Europeans who explored Cameroon in the 15th and 16th centuries found that it was mainly uninhabited, but it was believed to be the original home of the BANTU. About 1810 King Mbwé-Mbwé walled his capital, Fomban, against the FULANI EMPIRE OF SOKOTO. Other peoples set up small kingdoms. Germans began trading *c.*1860, and signed protectorate treaties in 1884. The German Protectorate of Kamerun was confirmed by the Franco-German Treaty of 1911, but in 1916 Anglo-French forces occupied it. From 1919 it was administered under LEAGUE OF NATIONS (later UN) trusteeship, having been divided into British and French mandates. In 1960 the French Cameroons became an independent republic, to be joined in 1961 by part of the British Cameroons, the remainder becoming part of Nigeria. The French and British territories in 1972 merged as the United Republic of Cameroon, later renamed the Republic of Cameroon. It was from 1972 a one-party republic ruled by the Cameroon People's Democratic Movement, from 1982 under President Paul Biya. Legislation providing for multi-party government was adopted in 1990 and, following strikes, demonstrations, and unrest through 1991, President Biya finally held

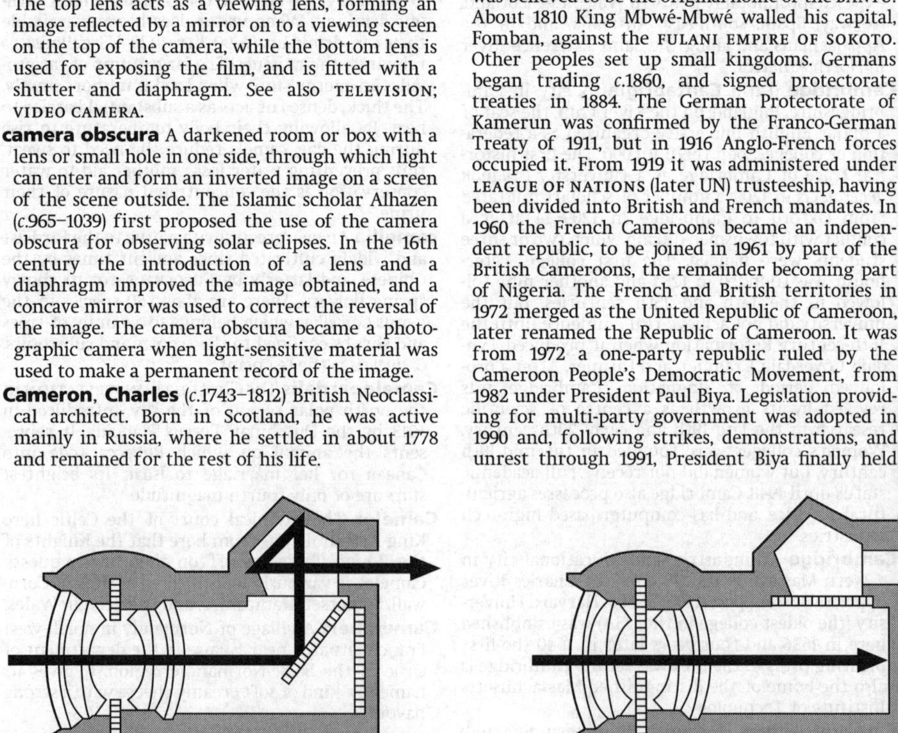

1 2

Camera In the single-lens reflex (SLR) camera, the photographer views the scene through the lens that takes the picture. This is achieved by means of a reflex mirror (1), which swings out of the way when the film is being exposed (2).

elections in 1992. His party failed to win an overall majority and a coalition government was formed. Biya was re-elected in presidential elections (also held in 1992) but the result was rejected by opponents, who alleged that fraud had taken place. Political unrest continued. In 1993 Cameroon applied to join the COMMONWEALTH OF NATIONS and was accepted in 1995.

Capital: Yaoundé
Area: 475,458 sq km (179,714 sq mi)
Population: 13,233,000 (1995)
Currency: 1 CFA franc = 100 centimes
Religions: Roman Catholic 35.0%; traditional religions 25.0%; Muslim 22.0%; Protestant 18.0%
Ethnic Groups: Bamileke 27.0%; Beti-Pahonin 18.0%; Kirdi 15.0%; Fulani 9.5%; Bassa Bakoko 8.0%; Baya Mbum 6.0%
Languages: French, English (both official); Bati-Pahonin, Bamileke, and almost one hundred other languages and dialects
International Organizations: UN; OAU; Non-Aligned Movement; Franc Zone

Camisards French Protestants, who in 1702 defied LOUIS XIV in the Cévennes, a mountainous region of southern France with a strong tradition of independence. The loss of their leaders in 1704 was followed by a period of savage persecution, but the rebels were bought off rather than defeated.

Camlan An unidentified location in England (but possibly near Camelford in Cornwall) where King Arthur is said to have died in battle in 537.

Camões, Luis (Vaz) de (or **Camoëns**) (*c*.1524–80) Portuguese poet. His most famous work, *The Lusiads* (1572), describes Vasco da Gama's voyage and discovery of the sea route to India and celebrates the golden age of Portuguese discovery.

camomile See CHAMOMILE.

camouflage (in animals) The ways in which animals use their surface coloration and form to conceal themselves from their enemies. Thus the mottled fore-wing patterns of many cryptic moths, such as the UNDERWING MOTHS, make the insects hard to spot even to the trained eye. Colour can also be used to break up outlines, or to provide counter-shading. Many fishes have a dark upperside and a paler underside to counteract the effect of light from above. Some creatures, such as the chameleon, have evolved a mechanism which changes their colour to match their background, thus allowing them to live a more flexible lifestyle. The stripes of the tiger help it to blend into the shadows and sun-spots of its natural background, but in this case it is using camouflage to evade detection by its prey. Other animals achieve crypsis (concealment) using strange outgrowths from their bodies, such as the sea-dragon, a relative of the SEA HORSE, which is covered with membranous streamers which conceal it beautifully in seaweed. Camouflage can also be achieved by special resemblance of other objects in the environment. Thus, stick insects can look just like twigs, aligning themselves to enhance the effect, and the leaf-like patterns of leaf insects and some butterflies can be meticulous copies right down to the fine detail of the leaf's midrib or curled-up edge.

camouflage (in warfare) The disguising of military equipment, vehicles and personnel by making them blend with their surroundings. Camouflage has been used by armies from very early times, but the term camouflage came into general use only during World War I, when ground troops used camouflage as a protection from aerial reconnaissance and it provided effective cover for snipers. Much greater use of camouflage was made in World War II; troops, vehicles, and installations were disguised to avoid air bombardment, and elaborate dummy harbours, manufacturing plants, and even cities were constructed to protect vital sites.

Campaign for Nuclear Disarmament (CND) A British pressure group pledged to nuclear disarmament, and to the abandonment of British nuclear weapons. CND was created in 1958 with the philosopher Bertrand Russell as President. Frustration at the lack of progress led to the creation of a splinter-group, the Committee of 100, led by Russell and pledged to civil disobedience. From 1963 to 1980 CND was in eclipse. It revived in 1980–84 mainly as a protest against the deployment of US cruise missiles at Greenham Common. In 1980 European Nuclear Disarmament (END) was formed, linking closely with dissident groups in Eastern Europe. Similar movements developed in France, Germany, Australasia, and the USA, campaigning after the Cold War against nuclear proliferation.

Campania A region of west-central Italy comprising the provinces of Caserta, Benevento, Napoli, Avellino, and Salerno; area 13,598 sq km (5,252 sq miles); pop. (1991) 5,853,900; capital, Naples. The ancient cities of Pompeii, Herculaneum, Paestum, and Velia are located in the fertile Campania region which produces, grain, fruit, wine, tobacco, and vegetables.

campanula A plant often called a bell-flower in allusion to the bell-like shape of the flower. At least 250 species are known in the genus *Campanula*, mostly from the Mediterranean region, Europe, Asia, and the Caucasus. They give their name to the family Campanulaceae, which contains over 600 species. Campanulas range from tiny alpine plants to herbaceous species over 2 m (6.5 feet) in height. The attractive flowers, which are chiefly blue or white, make the frost-hardy species valuable as garden plants; *C. medium*, the Canterbury bell, is an example. *C. rotundifolia*, which is found throughout Europe, is commonly known as harebell; but in Scotland this species is often called 'bluebell'.

Campbell, Colen (1676–1729) Scottish architect, one of the key figures of PALLADIANISM. In 1715 he published the first volume (two more followed in 1717 and 1725) of his lavishly illustrated *Vitruvius Britannicus*; this was ostensibly a review of modern British architecture, but it was heavily biased against the 'affected and licentious' Baroque style and in favour of 'antique simplicity'. Campbell's most important work was Wanstead House, Essex (*c*.1714–20, destroyed), the prototype of the large Palladian country house. His best surviving building is Mereworth Castle, Kent (1722–25), closely based on PALLADIO's Villa Rotonda.

Campbell, Donald (Malcolm) (1921–67) British motor-racing driver and holder of world speed records. Following in the footsteps of his father Sir Malcolm Campbell, he broke a number of world speed records in boats and cars named *Bluebird*. In 1964 he achieved a speed of 276.33 m.p.h. (445 k.p.h.) on water and 403 m.p.h. (649 k.p.h.) on land, both in Australia. He was killed in an attempt to achieve a water speed of 300 m.p.h. (483 k.p.h.) on Coniston Water in England.

Campbell, Sir Malcolm (1885–1948) British motor-racing driver and holder of world speed records. In 1935 he became the first man to exceed a land speed of 300 m.p.h. (483 k.p.h.), driving his car *Bluebird* on Bonneville Flats in Utah in the USA, a record which was not broken until 1950. He also achieved a water-speed record of 141.74 m.p.h. (228 k.p.h.) in his boat of the same name in 1939.

Campbell, Mrs Patrick (née Beatrice Stella Tanner) (1865–1940) British actress. Renowned for her wit and beauty, she created the part of Paula in Pinero's *The Second Mrs Tanqueray* (1893) and also gave notable performances in roles ranging from Shakespeare to Ibsen. George Bernard Shaw wrote the part of Eliza Doolittle in *Pygmalion* (1914) for her.

Campbell, (Ignatius) Roy(ston Dunnachie) (1901–57) South African poet. His works include *The Flaming Terrapin* (1924), an allegorical narrative of the Flood, and *The Wayzgoose* (1928), a satire on South African life. His first autobiography *Broken Record* (1934) and the long poem *Flowering Rifle* (1939) show strong right-wing sympathies.

Campbell, Thomas (1777–1844) Scottish poet. He published *The Pleasures of Hope* (1799) and *Gertrude of Wyoming* (1809) among other volumes of verse, and is now chiefly remembered for his patriotic lyrics such as 'The Battle of Hohenlinden' and 'Ye Mariners of England'.

Campbell-Bannerman, Sir Henry (1836–1908) British Liberal statesman, Prime Minister 1905–08. He was first elected to Parliament as MP for the Stirling burghs in 1868 and became leader of his party in 1899. His premiership, which ended with his resignation only a few days before his death, saw the grant of self-government to the defeated Boer republics of Transvaal (1906) and the Orange River Colony (1907), the passing of the important Trade Disputes Act (1906), which exempted trade unions from certain liabilities in connection with strikes, and the entente with Russia (1907).

Camp David Accord (1978) A Middle East peace agreement. It was named after the official country house of the US President in Maryland, where President CARTER met President SADAT of Egypt and Prime Minister BEGIN of Israel to negotiate a settlement of the disputes between the two countries. Peace was made between Egypt and Israel after some 30 years of conflict, and provisions were agreed for an Israeli withdrawal from Egyptian territory. This agreement did not bring about peace with the other Arab countries. Instead it led increasingly to Egypt being isolated from its Arab neighbours.

Camperdown, Battle of (11 October 1797) A naval battle fought off the coast of Holland in which the British fleet destroyed the Dutch fleet. The Dutch tried to lure the British commander on to the shoals, but he accepted the risk, chased them, and captured nine ships.

campion One of several plant species in the genus *Silene*, of which the white campion, *S. latifolia*, and the red campion, *S. dioica*, are the best known in Europe. Both are biennial or short-lived perennial herbs belonging to the pink family, Caryophyllaceae. Both species bear male and female flowers on different plants and, where they grow together, hybrids occur between them with intermediate characteristics. Garden plants in the genus *Lychnis* are sometimes called campions.

Campion, Edmund, St (1540–81) English JESUIT scholar and Catholic martyr. He was ordained in the Church of England in 1568. In 1571 he left England for Douai in the Low Countries, where he joined the Roman Catholic Church; in Rome, two years later, he became a Jesuit. In 1580 he participated in the first secret Jesuit mission to England. He was arrested, tortured, tried, and executed for treason.

Campion, Jane (1954–) New Zealand film director and screenwriter. Campion's films reflect her interest in awkward, shy, or marginalized young women who possess great strength of character and inner tranquillity. Among them are *An Angel at My Table* (1990), *The Piano* (1993), for which Campion received an Oscar for best screenplay, and *The Portrait of a Lady* (1997).

Camus, Albert (1913–60) French novelist, dramatist, and essayist. He joined the French resistance during World War II and became co-editor (with Jean-Paul Sartre) of the left-wing daily *Combat* (1944–47). His essay *The Myth of Sisyphus* (1942) and his first novel *The Outsider* (1942) gained him international respect. Other notable works include the novel *The Plague* (1947) and the essay *The Rebel* (1951). He was awarded the Nobel Prize for literature in 1957.

Cana A small town in Galilee in northern Israel, north-east of Nazareth, where Christ is said to have performed his first miracle by changing water into wine during a marriage feast (John 2: 1–11).

Canaan Ancient Palestine, but more specifically the land lying between the River Jordan and the Mediterranean. Occupied in the 3rd millenium BC by the Canaanites, a Semitic-speaking people, it was conquered and occupied during the latter part of the 2nd millenium BC by the Israelites who described it as their 'Promised Land' (Exodus 3:8).

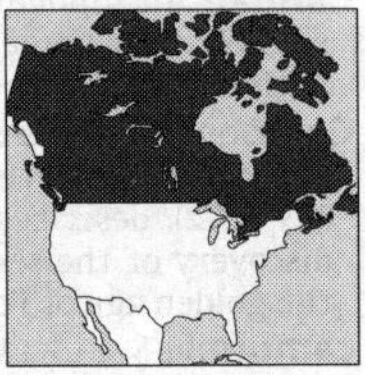

Canada The second largest country of the world, occupying the whole of the northern part of North America except for Alaska and bounded by three oceans: the Pacific on the west, the Arctic on the north, and the Atlantic on the east. Canada is a federation of ten North American provinces (Alberta, British Columbia, Manitoba, New Brunswick, Newfoundland, Nova Scotia, Ontario, Prince Edward Island, Quebec, Saskatchewan), the Yukon Territory, and the Northwest Territories.

Physical. Canada's southern boundary crosses the Rocky Mountains and continues eastward on latitude 49° N. to the Great Lakes and the Saint Lawrence, and then crosses the northern Appalachian Mountains to join the sea along the Saint Croix River. While the Saint Lawrence is Canada's most important river, the Mackenzie in the north-west is the longest and the Fraser in the south-west the most beautiful. Northern Canada is a land of lakes, wide and winding rivers, low tundra vegetation, and dark coniferous forests. Snow lies for six to nine months in the year and there is much PERMAFROST, making building and mining difficult and agriculture impossible. The west coast, with its mild climate and salmon rivers, is scored by fiords and over-hung by snow-capped mountains. Inland, the main Rocky Mountain chain yields rich mineral deposits, and its deep, sheltered valleys with hot, dry summers produce crops of vines and peaches. Through its eastern foothills, a major area of cattle-ranching and oil production, the land falls gently eastward to the prairies. This is the heart of the country and a vast grain-growing region, despite a harsh climate of very cold winters and very warm but short summers. Huge mineral deposits exist here too. To the east lies the lowland of the CANADIAN SHIELD, also rich in minerals and covered by a mosaic of lakes and forest. Eastward again, between Lakes Huron, Erie, and Ontario, are rich farming lands. The land becomes more hilly in Quebec and the easternmost maritime provinces, and farmers concentrate on orchard crops. Fishing is an important activity as the waters of the North Atlantic Ocean are well stocked: this coast is less rugged than the west, but the cool, damp climate and poor, rocky ground limit agriculture. To the north are the plateaux of Labrador, and its huge deposits of iron ore and other minerals.

Economy. A leading industrial nation, Canada depends on the neighbouring USA, with whom it signed a free-trade agreement in 1989, for about 75 per cent of its trade. Major exports include motor vehicles (assembled from imported components), machinery, crude oil, timber, natural gas, non-ferrous metals, chemicals, and newsprint. Canada is the world's largest producer of zinc, nickel, and uranium and is rich in many other minerals. A little more than half the country's electricity comes from hydroelectric generation. Canadian agriculture is diverse, with extensive grain, dairy, and fruit-farming as well as ranching and fur-farming.

History. Originally inhabited by NORTH AMERICAN INDIANS and by Inuit in the far north, in the 10th century VIKINGS established a settlement at L'Anse aux Meadows. John CABOT landed in Labrador, Newfoundland, or Cape Breton Island, in 1497 and in 1534 Jacques CARTIER claimed the land for France. The first French settlement was begun by fur traders in ACADIA in 1604. In 1608 Samuel de CHAMPLAIN founded QUEBEC on the St Lawrence River. Governor Frontenac defended Quebec against Sir William Phips (1691) and led a successful campaign against the hostile IROQUOIS (1696). Explorers followed the routes of the Great Lakes and the Mississippi Valley – LA SALLE reached the mouth of the Mississippi in 1682 – and the name Canada came to be used interchangeably with that of NEW FRANCE, which referred to all French possessions in North America. Conflict between Britain and France was mirrored in Canada in the FRENCH and Indian wars. By the Peace of UTRECHT (1713) France gave up most of Acadia, Newfoundland, and Hudson Bay. The remainder of New France was conquered by Britain and ceded in 1763. During or immediately after the American War of INDEPENDENCE some 40,000 United Empire Loyalists arrived in Nova Scotia (formerly Acadia) and present-day Ontario. St John's Island was renamed Prince Edward Island in 1799 and Cape Breton Island was joined to Nova Scotia in 1820. In 1791 Quebec was divided into Upper and Lower Canada, but following the Act of Union of 1840 the two were reunited to form the Province of Canada. Two frontier agreements were made with the USA: the Webster–Ashburton Treaty (1842) and a treaty ending the Oregon boundary dispute (1846). Fears of US expansion led to the British North America Act (1867), creating the Dominion of Canada. The new dominion acquired full responsibility for home affairs. In 1870 the Hudson's Bay Company's lands around the Red River were formed into the Province of Manitoba, while the Northwest Territories passed from control of the Company to the federal government. In 1873 Prince Edward Island joined the Confederation, British Columbia, including Vancouver Island, having done so in 1871. This had been on the promise of a Canadian Pacific Railway, which was completed in 1885, enabling prairie wheat to flow east for export. Britain gave Canada title to the arctic islands in 1880. In 1896 the Yukon boomed briefly with the Klondike GOLD RUSH. In 1905 Alberta and

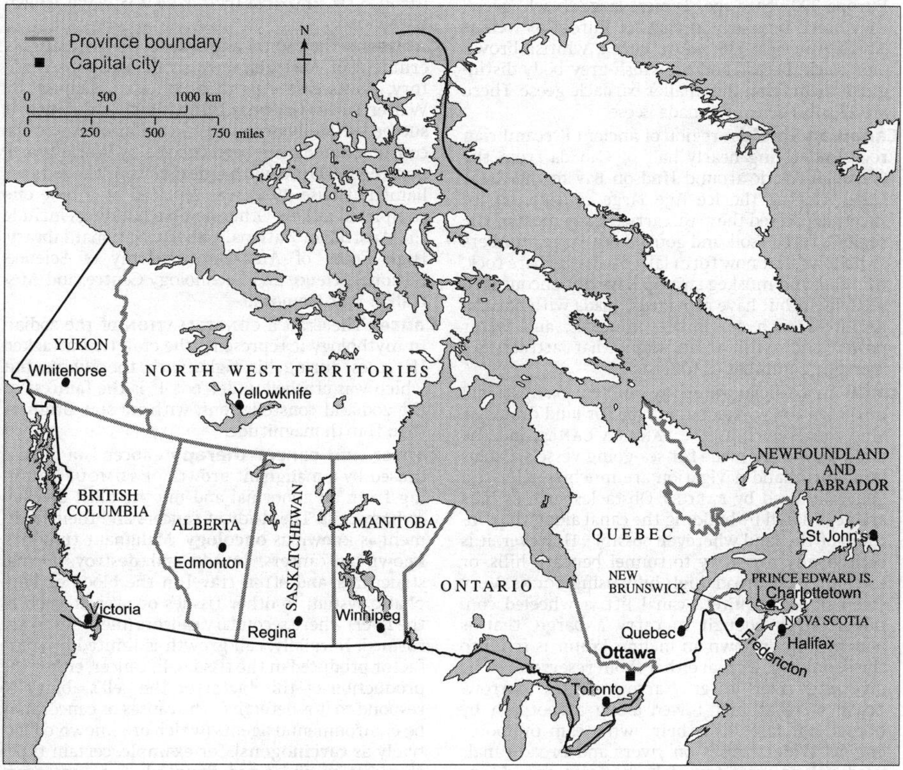

Canada

Saskatchewan became federated provinces. Newfoundland joined the dominion in 1949. The Hudson's Bay Company gradually ceded all the lands for which it was responsible, but as a corporation it has retained a significant place in the Canadian economy. As the provinces developed, so did their strength *vis-à-vis* the central federal government, a strongly centralized political system being resisted. In 1982 the British Parliament accepted the 'patriation' of the British North America Act to Canada, establishing the complete national sovereignty of Canada, although it retained allegiance to the British crown as well as membership of the COMMONWEALTH OF NATIONS. Constitutional disputes continued through the 1980s and 1990s, with Newfoundland, Manitoba, and Quebec all rejecting proposed solutions, the latter insisting on 'distinct society' status, but rejecting independence in provincial referendums in 1980 and 1995. In 1992 Canada signed the NORTH AMERICAN FREE TRADE AGREEMENT.

Capital: Ottawa
Area: 9,970,610 sq km (3,849,675 sq mi)
Population: 29,463,000 (1995)
Currency: 1 Canadian dollar = 100 cents
Religions: Roman Catholic 46.5%; Protestant 41.2%; non-religious 7.4%; Eastern Orthodox 1.5%; Jewish 1.2%; Muslim 0.4%; Hindu 0.3%; Sikh 0.3%
Ethnic Groups: (by origin) British 34.4%; French 25.7%; German 3.6%; Italian 2.8%; Ukrainian 1.7%; Amerindian and Inuit (Eskimo) 1.5%; Chinese 1.4%; Dutch 1.4%
Languages: English, French (both official)
International Organizations: UN; Commonwealth; OECD; NATO; OAS; CSCE

Canada goose A North American species of GOOSE, *Branta canadensis*, which was introduced to Europe 300 years ago. Typical large 'black' geese, they breed regularly in parts of Europe as well as North America. The white cheek, whitish-brown (not black) breast, and brownish-grey body distinguish them from the smaller barnacle geese. There are 12 subspecies of Canada geese.

Canadian Shield A region of ancient Precambrian rock underlying nearly half of Canada from the Canadian Arctic around Hudson Bay to the Great Lakes. During the Ice Age large continental ice sheets depressed the area, carried away most of the region's fertile soil, and gouged out large numbers of hollows that now form lake basins. Its bare rock, thin soil, and muskeg swamp have not encouraged settlement but have provided Canada with natural resources such as timber, minerals, and water power and with a landscape that attracts an increasing number of tourists.

canal An artificial waterway built for navigational purposes, for WATER SUPPLY, or for land drainage. Ship canals such as the PANAMA CANAL and the SUEZ CANAL are made for sea-going vessels. Canals built for inland navigation are much smaller and generally used by BARGES. Obstacles such as hills are negotiated by building the canal along the contours of the land wherever possible. However, it is occasionally necessary to tunnel beneath hills, or to climb over broad, high hills using LOCKS. Very steep slopes require a canal lift: a wheeled container, large enough to carry a barge, that is winched up or down an incline. Water is fed into the summit of a canal either from reservoirs or by diverting river water. Narrow barges (narrowboats) were at first towed along a footpath by horses, but later had their own steam or motor engine. Wider barges on rivers and broad canals used sail or were towed by a steam tug. At its height, canal-building employed thousands of labourers known as navigators (navvies), but with the advent of the railways during the first half of the 19th century, canal-building virtually ceased.

Canaletto (born Giovanni Antonio Canale) (1697–1768) Italian painter. Working chiefly in his native city of Venice, he was especially popular with the English aristocracy, who commissioned his paintings of Venetian festivals and scenery as mementoes of their grand tour. His early work is dramatic and freely handled, reflecting his training as a theatrical scene painter, but from *c.*1730 he changed to the more precise style for which he is mainly remembered, aided by his use of the camera obscura. His works include *Scene in Venice: The Piazzetta Entrance to the Grand Canal* (*c.*1726–28).

Canaries current A cold ocean current in the North Atlantic that flows south-westwards from Spain to meet equatorial waters near the Canary Islands.

canary Any of the ten species of the genus *Serinus* of the finch family, Fringillidae. The common canary, *S. canaria*, was first brought to Europe from the Canary Islands (its native country) in the 15th century. This small bird, which in its natural habitat is greenish above and yellow below, is the ancestor of all of the domestic strains of this very common cage-bird.

canary creeper See NASTURTIUM.

Canary Islands A group of seven islands in Spanish possession, and volcanic in origin, which rise from the Atlantic Ocean floor some 108 km (67 miles) off the west coast of Africa at latitude 28° N. Their average temperature ranges from 10°C to 35°C (50 to 95°F) and the rainfall is moderate. The main physical feature is the conical peak of Tenerife, at 3,717 m (12,195 feet), which is often ringed with cloud.

Canberra The capital and seat of the federal government of Australia in Australian Capital Territory, south-east Australia. It was planned by Walter Burley Griffin, a US architect, and in 1927 it succeeded Melbourne as the capital of Australia, construction having been delayed by World War I; pop. (1991) 299,890 (with Queanbeyan). The old Parliament House (1927) was replaced by a new one completed in 1988. Other notable buildings include the Australian National Gallery, National Library, High Court of Australia, Academy of Science, National Science and Technology Centre, and Australian War Memorial.

Cancer The Crab, a CONSTELLATION of the zodiac. In mythology it represents the crab that attacked Hercules during his fight with the Hydra, but which was crushed underfoot. It is the faintest of the zodiacal constellations, with no star brighter than fourth magnitude.

cancer and cancer therapy Cancer is a disease caused by a malignant growth or TUMOUR resulting from an abnormal and uncontrolled division of body cells. The study of cancers and their treatment is known as **oncology**. Malignant tumours, known as cancers, invade and destroy normal structures, and often travel in the blood or lymphatic system to other tissues or organs (such as the liver) where secondary cancers (metastases) are formed. Normally, cell growth is limited by some factor produced in the tissues. In cancer, either the production of this factor or the cell's ability to respond to it is defective. The causes of cancer may be environmental agents (which are known collectively as **carcinogens**), for example, certain types of radiation and some chemicals (e.g. those contained in tobacco smoke); VIRUSES; or genetic elements, but the molecular mechanism by which these factors result in cancer is not yet fully understood. Smoking has been positively linked to the development of lung cancer and ultraviolet radiation to skin cancer. Age is the single most important predictive factor for a majority of cancers, because exposure to risk factors accumulates. Cancers may cause death, partly because of their tendency to invade other tissues and interfere with their normal function, but also because they alter the body's metabolism in some way to produce very profound weight loss (cachexia): even a high-protein diet cannot reverse this process.

Therapy is directed at reducing the primary tumour, for example by surgical excision where this is practicable; this may be supplemented by treatment to limit the growth of metastatic tumours, and to destroy any stray cells left behind after the surgery. Cancer chemotherapy aims to destroy malignant cells without harming normal tissues. This was originally achieved by means of cytotoxic drugs, which were toxic to all cells, but particularly affected rapidly growing cells such as cancer cells. Since rapidly growing normal cells (for example, in the bone marrow) were often also affected, these drugs produced many unpleasant side-effects. The development of MONOCLONAL ANTIBODIES specific to cancer cells has more recently permitted more selective cytotoxic therapy. RADIOTHERAPY uses radiation to destroy localized tumours; it is often used as an adjunct to surgical and chemical cancer therapy. Techniques such as CERVICAL SCREENING aim to detect pre-cancerous changes in the body.

candela (symbol cd) The SI UNIT of luminous intensity. It is defined as the luminous intensity emitted in a given direction from a source that emits monochromatic radiation of frequency 540 × 10^{12} hertz and has a radiant intensity in that direction of 1/683 watt per steradian.

Candela, Félix (1910–) Spanish-born architect who settled in Mexico in 1939 after fighting on the losing Republican side in the Spanish Civil War (1936–39). The buildings on which he has worked include the Church of Santa Maria Miraculosa (1954–55) and the Olympic Stadium (1968), both in Mexico City.

Candolle, Augustin Pyrame de (1778–1841) Swiss botanist. His prolific writings in taxonomy and botany were highly influential, particularly his belief that taxonomy should be based on morphological characters, and his scheme of classification prevailed for many years.

CANDU reactor (*Can*adian *D*e*u*terium) A type of thermal NUCLEAR REACTOR that uses heavy water as both a coolant and a moderator (see FISSION, NUCLEAR), and natural URANIUM as a fuel. Such reactors were first developed in Canada between 1945 and 1947, with the help of French and UK scientists. Heavy-water reactors find military application in the production of tritium, a radioactive form of hydrogen used in experimental FUSION reactors.

candytuft An annual plant, *Iberis amara*, up to 30 cm (12 inches) high, with heads of small white flowers, native to western Europe. It belongs to the mustard family, Cruciferae, and is related to plants such as the cabbage, wall-flower, and charlock.

cane rat Either of two species of African RODENT that belong to the family Thryonomyidae and are related to porcupines and guinea-pigs; they resemble a rat because of their long, scaly tail. Both species are strictly vegetarian, as the alternative name of grass-cutter indicates. They are widely used as food, particularly in West Africa, and experiments have shown that they can be domesticated. The larger of the two species, *Thryonomys swinderianus*, can reach a body length of 60 cm (2 feet) and weigh 9 kg (20 pounds).

Canes Venatici The Hunting Dogs, a CONSTELLATION of the northern celestial hemisphere, introduced by the Polish astronomer Johannes Hevelius (1611–87). It represents a pair of dogs held on a leash by Boötes. Alpha Canum Venaticorum, of third magnitude, is also known as COR CAROLI.

Canetti, Elias (1905–94) Bulgarian-born British writer. Although he lived in England from 1938, he continued to write in German. His novel *Auto-da-Fé* (1936) concentrates on the doomed attempt of the aloof, narrow-minded intellectual to avoid contamination by the material world. *Crowds and Power* (1960), a behavioural study of crowds and dictators, is his other most important work. He was awarded the Nobel Prize for literature in 1981.

Canis Major The Greater Dog, a prominent CONSTELLATION of the Southern Hemisphere of the sky, one of the 48 constellations known to the Greeks. It represents one of the two dogs of Orion and contains SIRIUS, the brightest star in the sky, popularly known as the Dog Star.

Canis Minor The Lesser Dog, a Northern Hemisphere CONSTELLATION on the celestial equator. It is one of the 48 constellations known to the Greeks and represents the smaller of the two dogs following Orion. Its only prominent feature is the bright star PROCYON, a visual binary star.

cannabis A tall annual plant, *Cannabis sativa*, cultivated for its stem fibre, HEMP, and for its oil-rich seeds; the name is also used for the narcotic, otherwise known as marijuana or hashish, that is derived from the leaves, stems, and particularly the flowers of this species. Deliberate cultivation for this purpose is prohibited in most countries (see DRUG ABUSE). Certain varieties grown in India yield the powerful narcotic, ganja, from the dried female flowers, and this is used medicinally.

The seed may contain up to 22 per cent protein and 32 per cent oil, the latter being a substitute for linseed oil in paints. The seeds are a useful livestock feed, particularly for poultry.

Cannae, Battle of (216 BC) A battle fought at the village of Cannae in southern Italy, which was one of the classic victories in military history. The Carthaginian general HANNIBAL, his infantry considerably outnumbered, but stronger in cavalry, stationed his troops in a shallow crescent formation. The densely-packed Roman legionaries, under the consuls Aemilius Paullus and Terentius Varro, charged Hannibal's centre, forced it back, but failed to break it. As it slowly and deliberately gave ground, and the Romans pushed deeper, Hannibal effected his brilliant double-encirclement: his cavalry, having defeated the opposing right and left wings, closed the trap and assaulted the Romans from flanks and rear. Out of some 50,000 men the Romans lost 35,000 killed or captured, Hannibal only 5,700. Rome's hold on Italy was imperilled, and many of its allies in central and southern Italy defected to Hannibal.

Cannes A coastal resort on the Riviera in the Alpes-Maritimes department of southern France, made fashionable in the 19th century by visiting royalty and aristocracy; pop. (1990) 69,360. An important international film festival is held here annually.

canning A FOOD PRESERVATION process in which the food is sealed into airtight metal containers and then sterilized using heat. A similar process is heat sterilization combined with aseptic packaging, in which the food is sterilized before being sealed in the can. Cans can also be filled with precooked foods in aseptic conditions. The can is usually made of tin plate or, increasingly, of aluminium, with a coating of inert enamel on the inside to prevent reaction between food and container.

Canning, Charles John, 1st Earl Canning (1812–62) British statesman. The son of George CANNING, he was governor-general of India at the time of the INDIAN MUTINY, and played a notable part in the work of reconciliation which followed it. He was subsequently first viceroy of India (1858–62), and was known as 'Clemency Canning' for his policy of no retribution.

Canning, George (1770–1827) British Tory statesman, Prime Minister 1827. Foreign Secretary from 1807, he resigned in 1809 after a disagreement with his rival Castlereagh over a disastrous expedition in the Napoleonic Wars, but returned to office following Castlereagh's suicide in 1822. During this ministry he presided over a reversal of Britain's hitherto conservative foreign policy, being particularly responsible for the support of nationalist movements in various parts of Europe. He succeeded Lord Liverpool as Prime Minister in 1827, but died shortly afterwards.

Cannizzaro, Stanislao (1826–1910) Italian chemist. He is chiefly remembered for his revival of Avogadro's hypothesis, using it to distinguish clearly between atoms and molecules, and introducing the unified system of atomic and molecular weights. Cannizzaro also discovered a reaction (named after him) in which an aldehyde is converted into an acid and an alcohol in the presence of a strong alkali.

cannon A large, heavy gun installed on a carriage or mounting, the earliest class of gunpowder ARTILLERY. The earliest cannon were developed in Europe during the first half of the 14th century, soon after the introduction of GUNPOWDER. Cannon were mounted on two-wheeled carriages, with a balancing trail projecting behind the axle. Cylindrical projections (trunnions) on either side of the barrel provided pivot points by which the cannon could be mounted on the carriage, allowing the barrel to be raised or lowered for aiming. Naval cannon at first had the same appearance as land cannon. However, during the 1530s the four-wheeled truck carriage was developed by the English and later became standard in other navies, remaining so until turret mountings were introduced in the late 19th century. Cannon is also used as a term for a heavy MACHINE-GUN, of a calibre greater than 20 mm (0.78 inches).

Cano, Alonso (1601–67) Spanish sculptor, painter, and architect. His career was spent mainly in his native Granada, in Seville, and in Madrid, where he worked for Philip IV. His work tends to be serene, and it is best represented in Granada Cathedral, which has several examples of his painting and his superb painted wooden statue of the *Immaculate Conception* (1655). Cano also designed the façade of the cathedral, one of the most original works of Spanish Baroque architecture.

canoe A light, narrow craft with pointed or square ends, powered by paddles or sails. The dug-out, a type of canoe made by hollowing out a tree trunk, was one of the earliest types of boat. Modern dug-outs are often powered by outboard motors. Other types of canoe include the outrigger canoe (with a log fixed parallel to the canoe to stabilize it), used particularly in the Pacific islands; light, portable canoes made of birch bark stitched to a bent-ash frame, developed in Canada; and the Arctic kayak, which was originally made of skins and had a watertight cover to improve its chances of righting after a capsize. Canadian canoes and kayaks have been developed into modern sport canoes, usually made of glass-FIBRE-REINFORCED PLASTIC and used for sport and leisure in many parts of the world. There are three kinds of **canoeing** competition: slalom, wild water or down-river racing, and racing over short-and long-distance courses.

canon In music, a device in COUNTERPOINT that occurs when a melody in one voice (or part) is imitated exactly in another voice, or voices. Thus the voices overlap and the melody is made to echo itself. Imitations may occur at any PITCH, and can be 'strict' (exact) or 'free'. Simple infinite canons for popular singing are known as rounds or catches.

canonization See SAINT.

canon law The rules and laws made by ecclesiastical authority by which a Church and its members are governed. Historically, canon law was the universal law of the western Roman Catholic Church; it has been codified and repromulgated many times in the history of the Church, with the last major revision in 1917. The canon law of the ANGLICAN COMMUNION has been separate since the 16th-century Reformation. Canon law today is the internal law of a Church governing matters such as the regulation of the clergy, and administration of the sacraments, for example marriage.

Canopus A first-magnitude star in the constellation of Carina and also known as Alpha Carinae. It is the second-brightest star in the sky after Sirius. Of whitish hue, Canopus is a hot luminous SUPERGIANT or GIANT STAR twenty-five times the Sun's diameter and 1,200 times its luminosity. It is a young Population I star in the disc of the Galaxy, and lies some 23 parsecs from the Sun. Because of its great brightness, satellite star trackers often use Canopus for orientation.

Canossa A castle in the Apennines, in Italy, where, in the winter of 1077, the German emperor HENRY IV waited for three days until Pope GREGORY VII granted absolution and removed a ban of EXCOMMUNICATION from him. Henry had been at odds with the papacy over ultimate control within the Holy Roman Empire. His penance greatly strengthened his hand against the German princes who threatened him, for they had been allies of the pope and when Henry was absolved the princes withdrew their support for Gregory.

Canova, Antonio (1757–1822) Italian sculptor. His most famous works range from classical subjects such as *Cupid and Psyche* (1792) and *The Three Graces* (1813–16) to funeral monuments and life-size busts; highly regarded in his day, he executed commissions for papal and royal monuments and for Napoleon and his family.

cantaloupe See MELON.

cantata A musical work that is 'sung', as opposed to one that is 'sounded' by instruments (the SONATA). In the 17th century the cantata was a short work for several voices: a series of arias and recitatives, linked by a common dramatic theme and with an instrumental accompaniment. Those that dealt with secular subjects were known as chamber cantatas (*cantata da camera*). Church sonatas (*cantata da chiesa*) dealt with sacred matters. By the 18th century the chamber cantata had become more operatic in style and content. Church cantatas had become more like miniature ORATORIOS and were of particular importance to the Protestant composers of Germany, such as Schütz and J. S. Bach. In their hands the use of the CHORALE as a basis of cantata composition became of prime importance.

Canterbury (Latin **Durovernum** or **Cantuaria**) An historic city in Kent, south-east England; pop. (1981) 39,700. It was St Augustine's centre for the conversion of England to Christianity, now the seat of the Anglican archbishop, 'Primate of All England'. The 11th–15th-century cathedral was the scene of the murder of Thomas à Becket in 1170 and became thereafter a centre of pilgrimage. Chaucer stayed here in 1360–61 as part of the Royal Household and subsequently wrote his *Canterbury Tales*. The University of Kent at Canterbury was founded here in 1965. The city is a major tourist destination.

Canterbury bell See CAMPANULA.

Canterbury Plains A region on the central east coast of South Island, New Zealand, stretching southwards for 193 km (121 miles) from the Banks Peninsula. The lower parts of the plain contain the widest area of flat land in New Zealand, while the northern and southern extremities merge into rolling downs.

canticle The musical setting of words from the Bible, other than the psalms, used as part of the liturgy or fixed form of public worship used in churches.

cantilever bridge A BRIDGE in which a central span is supported by outer spans, each of which forms a cantilever. The outer spans are usually anchored at the abutments and project over piers into the central space.

Canton See GUANGZHOU.

Canton and Enderbury Two Pacific islands in the Phoenix group, Kiribati, administered from 1939 to 1980 as a joint UK-USA condominium.

cantor (in Judaism) A man, expert in prayer and ritual matters, who leads the congregation of a SYNAGOGUE, especially in incantation. The role of the cantor is particularly important within ORTHODOX JUDAISM, which forbids musical instruments as being inappropriate and as involving a form of work not permitted on the Sabbath.

Cantor, Georg (1845–1918) Russian-born German mathematician. Cantor's work on numbers laid the foundations of the theory of sets. He introduced the concept of transfinite numbers, and his work stimulated 20th-century exploration of number theory and the logical foundation of mathematics.

cantus firmus See PLAINSONG.

Canute (or **Cnut**, **Knut**) (died 1035) Son of Sweyn I, Danish king of England 1017–35, Denmark 1018–35, and Norway 1028–35. After Edmund Ironside's murder in 1016, Canute became king of England, ending a prolonged struggle for the throne. As king, he presided over a period of relative peace. He is most commonly remembered for demonstrating to his fawning courtiers that, contrary to their expectations, he was unable to command the tide to stop rising.

canvas A strong cloth, usually of plain weave, originally made from hemp. Later, flax replaced hemp, and canvas became widely used for making sails. Today, there is no standard specification: canvas may be made from flax, cotton, or SYNTHETIC FIBRE yarns and is used as a general-purpose strong cloth.

Canvey Island An island on the north side of the Thames estuary, south-east England, to the west of Southend.

canyon A spectacularly deep valley with almost vertical sides. For a canyon rather than a broad valley to be formed, a river must be powerful, the rocks resistant, and the climate so dry or so cold that little soil accumulates and the valley sides stay steep and angular. Moreover, the area must lie a long way above base level, so that the river is able to cut a very deep vertical trench. Some canyons, such as that at Yosemite, USA, have also been occupied by glaciers; but glaciated valleys are usually much wider than true canyons. Canyons also occur underwater as submarine canyons.

canzona A musical term used in the 16th century to describe a type of Italian vocal composition similar to the MADRIGAL, but simpler in style. The term also describes a type of instrumental composition of the same period, which either transcribes the vocal composition directly or imitates its general characteristics. The term is also used in 18th- and 19th-century opera to describe a short aria.

Cao Cao (or **Ts'ao Ts'ao**) (155–220) Chinese general. One of China's greatest soldiers, he unified much of northern China after the collapse of the HAN dynasty. His conquests enabled his son to found the Wei kingdom, one of the three kingdoms. His campaigns and adventures are recorded in one of the classics of Chinese literature, *The Romance of the Three Kingdoms*.

Cao Yu (1910–) Chinese dramatist. Cao Yu was one of the first Chinese playwrights to produce Western-influenced spoken drama rather than traditional opera and his *Thunderstorm* (1933) and *Sunrise* (1935) were popular.

Capa, Robert (Andor Friedmann) (1913–64) Hungarian photo-journalist. Capa's most famous picture shows a soldier being killed in the Spanish Civil War (often said to be staged rather than real). He went on to cover four more wars, eventually being killed by a landmine on assignment in Indo-China.

Capability Brown See BROWN, LANCELOT.

Capablanca, José Raúl (1888–1942) Cuban chess player. As world champion 1921–27 he made a considerable impact on the game, particularly on opening theory.

capacitance and capacitors Capacitance is the property of an electrical system of conductors and insulators that enables it to store charge. The greater the potential, the greater the amount of charge that can be stored. For a charge of magnitude Q and a potential difference of V, the ratio Q/V is the capacitance, which is a constant for that capacitor, measured in farads. The FARAD is a very large unit: in practice, values range between 10^{-12} and 10^{-6} farad.

A typical capacitor consists of two parallel conductors consisting of metal plates or electrodes separated by an INSULATOR or dielectric. A capacitor presents an extremely high resistance to a direct current (d.c.): no current will flow in a d.c. circuit containing a capacitor. However, alternating current (a.c.) is allowed to pass much more easily, and the higher the FREQUENCY of the a.c. signal, the less opposition the capacitor presents. Because of this ability to separate a.c. and d.c. signals, capacitors are frequently employed in both filters and power supplies. Several types of capacitor exist. Ceramic capacitors are used in radio-frequency circuits, while capacitors made from polyester and polycarbonate plastics have general application.

Cape Breton See NOVA SCOTIA.

Cape Canaveral A cape on the east coast of Florida, USA, known as Cape Kennedy from 1963 until 1973. It is the location of the John F. Kennedy Space Center which has been the principal US launching site for manned space flights since 1961.

Cape Cod A sandy peninsula in south-east Massachusetts USA, which forms a wide curve enclosing Cape Cod Bay. The Pilgrim Fathers landed on the northern tip of Cape Cod in November 1620.

Cape Finisterre A point on the north-west coast of Spain, in the province of La Coruña.

Cape Horn The southernmost point of South America, on an island south of Tierra del Fuego, belonging to Chile. It was discovered by the Dutch navigator Schouten in 1616 and named after Hoorn, his birthplace. The ocean region is notorious for storms, and until the opening of the Panama Canal in 1914 lay on a sea route between the Atlantic and Pacific Oceans.

Cape hunting dog See HUNTING DOG.

Čapek, Karel (1890–1938) Czech novelist and dramatist. He wrote several plays with his brother Josef (1887–1945), including *The Insect Play* (1921), a satire on human society and totalitarianism. Čapek's best-known independent work was *R.U.R.* (*Rossum's Universal Robots*) (1920), a cautionary drama about the dangers of mechanization set 'on a remote island in 1950–60'. The title introduced the word *robot* to the English language.

Capella A BINARY STAR in the constellation of Auriga, and also known as Alpha Aurigae, with an apparent magnitude of 0.08. Two GIANT STARS with temperatures similar to that of the Sun move in a 104-day orbit. A distant twelfth-magnitude companion, itself a binary comprising two red DWARF STARS, has the same PROPER MOTION, and the two pairs may form a binary of very long period. Capella's distance is 13 parsecs, and its combined luminosity is about sixty times that of the Sun.

Cape of Good Hope (Afrikaans **Kaap die Goeie Hoop**) A mountainous promontory near the southwestern extremity of Africa, south of Cape Town. It was sighted towards the end of the 15th century by the Portuguese explorer Bartholomew Diaz and named Cape of Storms, and was rounded for the first time by Vasco da Gama in 1497.

Cape Province (Afrikaans **Kaapprovinsie**) A former province of the Republic of South Africa; area 641,379 sq km (247,332 sq miles); pop. (1985) 5,041,100. Its capital was Cape Town. Ceded to the British by the Dutch in 1814, it joined the Union of South Africa in 1910 and in 1994 was divided into the provinces of Eastern Cape, Western Cape, and Northern Cape.

caper A plant of the genus *Capparis* and a member of the Capparaceae, a family which includes over 700 species of herbaceous plants, trees, shrubs, and some lianas, distributed throughout the tropics and subtropics. The common caper, *C. spinosa*, whose pickled flower buds are used as a condiment, is native to the Mediterranean regions. It is a small, spiny shrub with conspicuous white or lilac flowers, each with a large number of long stamens.

capercaillie Either of two species of grouse, *Tetrao parvirostris* and, particularly, the Eurasian species *T. urogallus*, a bird found primarily in the conifer belt across Europe and west and central Asia. The turkey-sized male is dusky grey with a glossy blue-green sheen on the neck and breast, and has a shaggy 'beard' of loose feathers. The female is much smaller, and is speckled brown with pale underparts. They are herbivores, feeding on a wide range of leaves, pine needles, seeds, and berries. Because of their large size and tasty flesh they are hunted over large parts of their range. They were exterminated in Scotland and Ireland in the late 1700s, but a massive programme of reintroduction with Swedish stock in the mid-1800s led to their re-establishment.

Capernaum (Hebrew **Kefar Naḥum**) The site of an ancient village on the northern shores of the Sea of Galilee, Israel. It was the centre of Jesus' ministry in Galilee, where he healed the servant of the centurion who had built a synagogue (Luke 7: 1–10), and where he found his first disciples Simon and Andrew casting their nets into the water (Matthew 4: 19).

Cape St Vincent, Battle of (14 February 1797) A naval battle off the south-west coast of Portugal in which NELSON and JERVIS defeated a combined French and Spanish fleet of twenty-seven ships. The British were outnumbered almost two to one, but the disorder of the Spanish fleet cancelled out its advantage in numbers. After this victory the British fleet was able to continue its blockade of Cadiz and to re-enter the Mediterranean in pursuit of Napoleon in Egypt.

Capet, Hugh (or **Hugo**) (938–96) King of France 987–96. His election as king in 987 marked the foundation of the CAPETIAN dynasty, which survived until 1328.

Capetians (987–1328) The dynasty of French kings who succeeded the CAROLINGIANS. It was not until the reign of Louis VI (1108–1137), that the dynasty established firm control over its own territories around Paris and began the slow process of gaining real power in France. By the end of the reign of Philip IV (1285–1314) France had achieved a great degree of stability and acquired many of the legal and governmental systems which were to survive up to the French Revolution. On the death of Charles IV in 1328 the throne passed to the House of VALOIS who, together with the later BOURBONS, could claim indirect descent from Hugh Capet, the first of the line.

Cape Town (Afrikaans **Kaapstad**) The legislative capital of the Republic of South Africa and administrative capital of the Western Cape Province, situated on Table Bay at the foot of Table Mountain (1,080 m, 3,543 ft); pop. (1985) 776,600. Founded as a victualling station by the Dutch East India Company in 1652, Cape Town was eventually occupied by the British in 1795. Capital of the Western Cape since 1994, it was capital of the former Cape Province. Its castle (1666) is South Africa's oldest building; the Dutch Reformed church dates from 1699. Groote Schuur, the former estate of Cecil Rhodes, contains the University of Cape Town, the Rhodes Memorial, a hospital, and museum. The National Botanic Gardens (1913) contain a famous collection of South African flora. Cape Town is the chief port, commercial, and industrial centre for the surrounding region. Its industries include food processing, wine making, clothing, printing, and tourism.

Cape Verde A country comprising an archipelago of volcanic islands in the Atlantic Ocean, 563 km (350 miles) west of Cape Verde Peninsula, Senegal, the most westerly point of Africa.

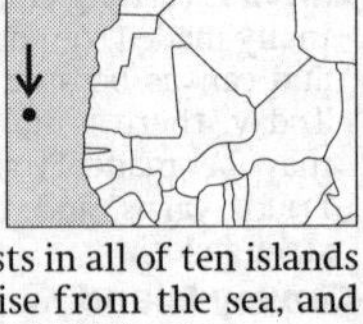

Physical. The archipelago is in two groups, Windward and Leeward, and consists in all of ten islands and five islets. Sheer cliffs rise from the sea, and the inland slopes present a jagged landscape as a result of erosion by wind-blown sand. The prevailing winds are north-easterly trades, and the temperate maritime climate provides little temperature variation throughout the year. A dense haze containing Saharan sand often occurs.

Economy. Agriculture and fishing are the main productive sectors, with fish and salt dominating exports. The domestic economy relies heavily on remittances from Cape Verdeans working overseas.

History. The islands were uninhabited until they were colonized by the Portuguese from 1462, and were used as a base for the Portuguese slave trade. In 1951 Cape Verde became an overseas province of Portugal and its residents were given Portuguese citizenship in 1961. An independence movement for Cape Verde and GUINEA-BISSAU gained strength during the 1950s and 1960s, and later became the African Party for the Independence of Cape Verde and Guinea-Bissau (PAICVGB). Cape Verde gained full independence in 1975, but remained linked with Guinea-Bissau as the PAICVGB was the only legal political party in both countries. In 1980 the PAICVGB in Guinea-Bissau was ousted in a coup and the party in Cape Verde dropped the reference to Guinea-Bissau from its name. A multi-party constitution was adopted in 1991, and elections were won in the same year (and again in 1995) by the newly created Movement for Democracy Party.

Capital: Praia
Area: 4,033 sq km (1,557 sq mi)
Population: 392,000 (1995)
Currency: Escudo Caboverdiano = 100 centavos
Religions: Roman Catholic 80.0%; Protestant and other 2.2%
Ethnic Groups: Mixed 71.0%; Black 28.0%; White 1.0%
Languages: Portuguese (official); Portuguese creole (crioulo)
International Organizations: UN; OAU; ECOWAS; Non-Aligned Movement

capillarity The process in which liquids rise in very fine tubes (capillaries) or networks of fibre above the level of liquid in the main reservoir. It is responsible for the rise of the molten wax in the wick of a candle and for the action of blotting paper. It is caused by the attractive force between the molecules of the liquid and those on the surface of the capillaries. Liquids which have a high SURFACE TENSION show a large capillary effect.

capital (in architecture) The crowning feature of a column, forming a transition between the shaft of the column and the member it supports. Capitals are often more or less elaborately carved with figurative or decorative elements (and sometimes painted) and in classical architecture the various types of capitals mark the most obvious distinctions between the different ORDERS OF ARCHITECTURE.

capital (in economics) GOODS whose part in the production process is to assist in producing other goods and services rather than being available for consumption. The production of capital implies foregone CONSUMPTION, that is, saving, because resources have been used to produce capital goods rather than consumer goods. Capital is commonly classified into fixed capital and working capital. Fixed capital, such as buildings and machinery, lasts beyond the production process. Working capital (circulating capital or inventories) comprises INTERMEDIATE GOODS which are used up in the production process. An increase in the stock of capital in any period is termed investment. Skilled labour is often classified as human capital. Gross investment less DEPRECIATION leaves net investment. In common usage the word capital may also refer to stocks of personal wealth or money. See also FACTORS OF PRODUCTION.

capitalism A system of economic organization, based on market competition, under which the means of production, distribution, and exchange are privately owned and directed by individuals or corporations. All human production requires both LABOUR and CAPITAL. In a capitalist system, capital is supplied either by the single owner of a firm, or by shareholders in the case of a JOINT-STOCK COMPANY. Labour is supplied separately by employees who receive a wage or salary. The residual PROFIT of the firm after wages and costs have been paid accrues to the owners of capital. Firms compete with one another to sell to customers in what is primarily a FREE MARKET. In its most developed form capitalism, which is based on the principle that economic decisions should be taken by private individuals, restricts the role of the state in economic policy to the minimum. It thus stands for FREE TRADE. In the 20th century capitalist societies have been modified in various ways: often a capitalist economy is accompanied by the development of a WELFARE STATE and is therefore known as 'welfare capitalism' as in western Europe. Another development is the MIXED ECONOMY, in which the production of certain goods or services is nationalized, while the rest of the economy remains in private ownership. A trend in 20th-century capitalism, particularly since World War II, has been the growth of multi-national companies operating across national frontiers, often controlling greater economic resources than small- or medium-sized states.

capital punishment The infliction of death by an authorized public authority as punishment for a CRIME. In most jurisdictions where it remains, its use is limited to those who have been convicted of murder, although in some countries where its use is more frequent it is imposed as a penalty for other offences, such as armed robbery (in certain African countries), large-scale embezzlement of state property (the former Soviet Union), RAPE and gang-fighting (China), and drug-trafficking (Thailand). A UN survey in 1990 revealed that 43 countries had abolished the death penalty entirely, 17 had retained it but only for exceptional crimes such as treason, 24 had retained it but not used it for at least ten years, and 97 were still using it.

Capitol The seat of the US Congress in Washington DC. Its site was chosen by George Washington, who laid the first stone in 1793.

Capodimonte A village near Naples in Italy, which lends its name to a type of porcelain first produced there in the mid-18th century.

Capone, Al(phonse) (1899–1947) US gangster, of Italian descent. He was notorious for his domination of organized crime in Chicago in the 1920s; his earnings from liquor, prostitution, gambling, and other rackets were estimated to be $30 million per year. Although indirectly responsible for many murders, including those of the St Valentine's Day Massacre (1929), he was never tried for any of them; it was for federal income-tax evasion that he was eventually imprisoned in 1931.

Caporetto, Battle of (24 October 1917) A battle fought north of Trieste when Austro-Hungarian and German forces overwhelmed the Italian army. General Cadorna withdrew his demoralized troops north of Venice, where his new line held, eventually strengthened by British and French reinforcements. Some 300,000 Italian prisoners-of-war were taken and Italy was temporarily out of the war, and a German offensive for March 1918 on the Western Front could now be planned.

Capote, Truman (born Truman Streckfus Persons) (1924–84) US writer. His works range from the light-hearted novella *Breakfast at Tiffany's* (1958) to the grim and meticulous re-creation of a brutal multiple murder in *In Cold Blood* (1966).

Capp, Al (born Alfred Gerald Caplin) (1909–79) US cartoonist. He began his career as an assistant on a number of cartoon strips for the Associated Press. In 1934 his own comic strip 'Li'l Abner' appeared in the *New York Mirror*. The strip featured a number of social caricatures including the protagonist, Li'l Abner, a shy and awkward rustic. The strip was hugely popular and ran until Capp's retirement in 1977.

Cappadocia The ancient name for the region in the centre of Asia Minor, now in modern Turkey, between Lake Tuz and the Euphrates, north of Cilicia. During the 3rd century BC it became a kingdom that maintained its independence until annexed by Rome in 17 AD. It was an important centre of early Christianity.

cappella (Italian, 'chapel') In choral music *a cappella* means 'in a church style' (that is to say, unaccompanied), and *maestro di cappella* means 'director of church music'. The German equivalents are Kapelle and Kapellmeister. 'Chapel', as in CHAPEL ROYAL, can also refer to the salaried musicians serving a church or noble household.

Capra, Frank (1897–1991) Italian-born US film director. His reputation rests on the film comedies which he made in the 1930s and early 1940s, such as *It Happened One Night* (1934), *Mr Deeds Goes to Town* (1936), and *Arsenic and Old Lace* (1944). He won six Oscars for his films.

Capri, Isle of An island off the west coast of Italy in the Bay of Naples. Its chief towns are Capri and Anacapri. The Swedish writer Axel Munthe (1857–1949) lived at the Villa of San Michele.

capriccio (Italian, 'caprice') In music a light, fanciful vocal or instrumental piece. It is also used of certain 16th-century Italian MADRIGALS and, later, such keyboard pieces as employ fugal imitation.

In art, any fantasy subject, but most commonly used of a type of townscape in which real buildings are combined with imaginary ones or are shown with their locations rearranged. Such pictures were particularly popular in the 18th century.

Capricornus The Sea Goat, a CONSTELLATION of the zodiac. In Greek mythology Capricornus represents the god Pan who jumped into a river on the approach of the monster Typhon and was turned into a fish. The star Alpha Capricorni, sometimes called Algedi or Giedi, both names from the Arabic meaning 'kid', consists of a pair of fourth-magnitude stars separable by the naked eye or through binoculars.

Caprivi Strip A narrow strip of Namibia that extends towards Zambia from the north-east corner of Namibia and reaches the River Zambezi. It was part of German South West Africa until after World War I, having been ceded by Britain in 1893 in order to give the German colony access to the Zambezi, and is named after Leo Graf von Caprivi, German imperial chancellor 1890–94.

Capsian The palaeolithic industry of North Africa and southern Europe (*c.*8,000–4,500 BC) noted for its microliths. The Capsian culture takes its name from the town of GAFSA in Tunisia.

capsicum A plant of the genus *Capsicum*, including some ten species native to tropical America and the West Indies. Although capsicums are commonly referred to as peppers (for example, red, paprika, chilli, green, cayenne, and SWEET PEPPERS), the true PEPPER is a completely different plant, native to India. Capsicums are members of the potato family, Solanaceae, and are related to the aubergine, the tomato, and tobacco. They were first cultivated in the Americas in pre-Columbian times.

capsid See MIRID BUG.

capstan A cylindrical barrel, vertically mounted on the decks of larger ships, for heavy lifting when working ANCHORS and CABLES. A ratchet-and-pawl mechanism below the barrel prevents back-slipping when lifting heavy loads. Smaller ships use a windlass, which is similar to a capstan but is mounted horizontally.

capuchin monkey Perhaps the best known of the New World MONKEYS, with the four species being found in Central and South America. Common and conspicuous, they live in fairly large troops of up to thirty individuals, feeding mostly on fruit. They are medium-sized: 38–53 cm (15–21 inches) long, with a long prehensile tail covered in hair; both this and the body hair is short and brown. The name of these monkeys comes from the 'cowl' of thick hair on the crown of the head. The most distinctive species is the tufted, or brown, capuchin, *Cebus apella*, which has tufts of hair on the forehead.

capybara The largest RODENT in the world, weighing up to 45 kg (99 pounds) and measuring over 1 m (3.25 feet) in length. The capybara, *Hydrochaeris hydrochaeris*, has several subspecies throughout South America in marshy areas, one of which, the so-called Panama capybara, may be a true species or simply a subspecies of *H. hydrochaeris*. Capybaras are semi-aquatic and leave the water only to graze. They make up one, or possibly two, species, and are related to porcupines and guinea-pigs.

car See MOTOR CAR.

Caracalla (born Septimius Bassanius; later called Marcus Aurelius Severus Antoninus Augustus) (188–217) Roman emperor 211–17. He spent much of his reign campaigning in Germany and in the East, where he hoped to repeat the conquests of Alexander the Great, but was assassinated in Mesopotamia. By an edict of 212 he granted Roman citizenship to all free inhabitants of the Roman Empire.

caracara A HAWK belonging to the falcon family, Accipitridae. All nine species are confined to South and Central America except one, the common caracara, *Polyborus plancus*, which extends into North America. They are medium-sized birds of prey, 60 cm (24 inches) long, and are brown or black with white markings. Several species have stout, powerful beaks which are used in their role of scavengers to tear carcasses. Non-scavenging species hunt their prey by stalking it on the ground. Two, the yellow-throated caracara, *Daptrius ater*, and the red-throated caracara, *D. americanus*, take quite small prey, such as frogs and wasp larvae, and also eat fruits.

Caracas The capital and largest city of Venezuela; pop. (1991) 1,824,890; 3,435,795 (metropolitan area). Founded in 1567 as Santiago de León de Caracas, the city developed rapidly during the oil boom of the 1950s. It was the birthplace in 1783 of the revolutionary leader Simón Bolívar who is buried in the Panteón Nacional and whose home has been reconstructed as a museum. The cathedral dates from 1614, and the city is a contrasting mixture of skyscrapers and shanty towns. Main industries are oil refining, textiles, vehicle assembly, chemicals, and food processing.

Caratacus (or **Caractacus**) (1st century AD) British chieftain, son of Cunobelinus. He took part in the resistance to the Roman invasion of 43 AD, and when defeated fled to Yorkshire, where he was handed over to the Romans in 51 AD.

Caravaggio, Michelangelo Merisi da (1571–1610) Italian painter. An important figure in the transition from late mannerism to Baroque, he reinvigorated religious art and had a far-reaching influence on later artists. The characteristic features of his work include naturalistic realism (achieved partly by the use of ordinary people as models for biblical characters) and dramatic use of light and shade.

caravel A small Mediterranean trading ship, used in the 14th–17th centuries. It had a LATEEN RIG on two or sometimes three masts. Late in the 15th century, Spain and Portugal adapted the three-masted caravel for exploration and trade, square-rigged on the two forward masts and lateen-rigged on the mizen. The *Santa Maria*, in which Christopher COLUMBUS reached the West Indies in 1492, was a 29 m (95 ft) caravel.

carbine See FIREARM.

carbohydrate A natural organic compound of one of the major classes, which typically has the general formula $C_n(H_2O)_n$ The simplest carbohydrates are SUGARS, such as ribose and GLUCOSE. These are called monosaccharides because their molecular structure is based upon a single ring or chain of carbon atoms: five for ribose, for example, or six for glucose. Monosaccharides are the basic units from which all other carbohydrates are built. When two of these simple sugars are bonded together, they form compounds called disaccharides; these include sucrose (common table sugar) and maltose (malt sugar). Compounds known as polysaccharides are formed by joining together ten or more monosaccharides (often hundreds). These are very important biological compounds and include storage substances such as starch and GLYCOGEN, and structural molecules such as cellulose and chitin.

All carbohydrates are formed from simple sugars (especially glucose), which are produced by plants during PHOTOSYNTHESIS. Once produced, the simple sugars are converted into disaccharides and move from the leaves (translocation) to be used elsewhere or stored. Carbohydrates are an essential component of the diet of animals and may be used as a source of energy (RESPIRATION) or may be modified by being combined with fats or proteins. These more complex compounds include glycoproteins (sugar + protein), which form some enzymes and the rigid cell walls of bacteria, and glycolipids (sugar + fat), which include the insulating material (myelin) of nerves.

carbolic acid See PHENOL.

carbon (symbol C, at. no. 6, r.a.m. 12.01) A non-metallic element in Group IV of the PERIODIC TABLE. It exists in three ALLOTROPES: diamond is extremely hard, colourless, and an insulator; graphite is a soft, black solid which conducts heat and electricity; BUCKMINSTERFULLERENE is a yellow crystalline compound containing C_{60} molecules. COKE, produced by the destructive distillation of coal, is almost pure carbon, and CHARCOAL is a form of carbon made from wood or bones. CARBON FIBRES are long chains of pure carbon formed by heat treatment of acrylic fibres. Although carbon is rather unreactive at low temperatures, on heating it reacts with oxygen, sulphur, and some metals. Carbon atoms can bond together in chains and rings, and carbon forms more compounds than any other element. Because many of them were first discovered in living organisms, their chemistry is called ORGANIC CHEMISTRY, but there is no fundamental distinction between organic and other compounds. All life forms are based on carbon chemistry. Diamonds are used as jewellery and for cutting and grinding; graphite is used as a lubricant, in pencil leads, in nuclear reactors and as electrodes. Charcoal is used to absorb gases, as a decolorizer, and in paints and gunpowder; coal and coke are important fuels. Carbon has a radioactive isotope, carbon-14, which is formed in the upper atmosphere from nitrogen and then incorporated into living things; radiocarbon (or carbon) dating is based on the decay of the carbon-14 isotope after the death of an animal or plant (see RADIOMETRIC DATING). Carbon forms two common oxides: CARBON DIOXIDE and CARBON MONOXIDE.

Carbonari (Italian, 'charcoal burners') Secret revolutionary society formed in Italy, and active in France, and the Iberian Peninsula. It was formed in the kingdom of Naples during the reign of Joachim Murat (1808–15) and its members plotted to free the country from foreign rule. The society was influential in the revolt in Naples in 1820 which resulted in the granting of a constitution to the Kingdom of the Two Sicilies. Similar revolts took place in Spain and Portugal (1820), Piedmont (1821), Romagna and Parma (1831), all in turn being suppressed. It was supplanted in Italy by the more broadly based YOUNG ITALY movement. Meanwhile the French movement, after mutinies in 1821–22, also declined.

carbonate Any of a class of basic compounds which contain the ion CO_3^{2-}. Carbonates are formed from the reaction of oxides with carbon dioxide; they give off carbon dioxide on addition of strong acids, and form hydrogencarbonates when treated with carbon dioxide in water. They occur widely in nature: calcite, dolomite, and magnesite are all carbonate minerals.

carbon-black A fine black powder obtained by burning NATURAL GAS or liquid HYDROCARBONS in a limited supply of air. It is insoluble and chemically inactive, and so it is used to make permanent INKS, CARBON-PAPER, and printer ribbons. It is also added to RUBBER to make it tougher and more resistant to sunlight.

carbon cycle One of the most important BIOGEOCHEMICAL CYCLES, in which the element carbon circulates between living organisms and the non-living environment. Carbon dioxide forms 0.04 per cent of the atmosphere and is used by plants for PHOTOSYNTHESIS, during which they 'lock' carbon into CARBOHYDRATES. These compounds can be stored by the plant or used in respiration, releasing some of the carbon back into the atmosphere as carbon dioxide. The remaining carbon is trapped in the plants' tissue until it either dies or is eaten. Animals use carbon compounds obtained from plants both for respiration and for building up their own tissues until they too die or are eaten.

The carbon compounds in dead plants and animals are broken down by decomposers such as bacteria or fungi. These organisms degrade the complex carbon compounds into simple ones, which they then use in respiration or fermentation, ultimately releasing carbon dioxide or methane (CH_4). Under certain chemical or physical conditions, some of the organic material escapes the action of decomposers and forms FOSSIL FUELS, such as coal or oil. The carbon they contain is returned to the atmosphere in the form of car-

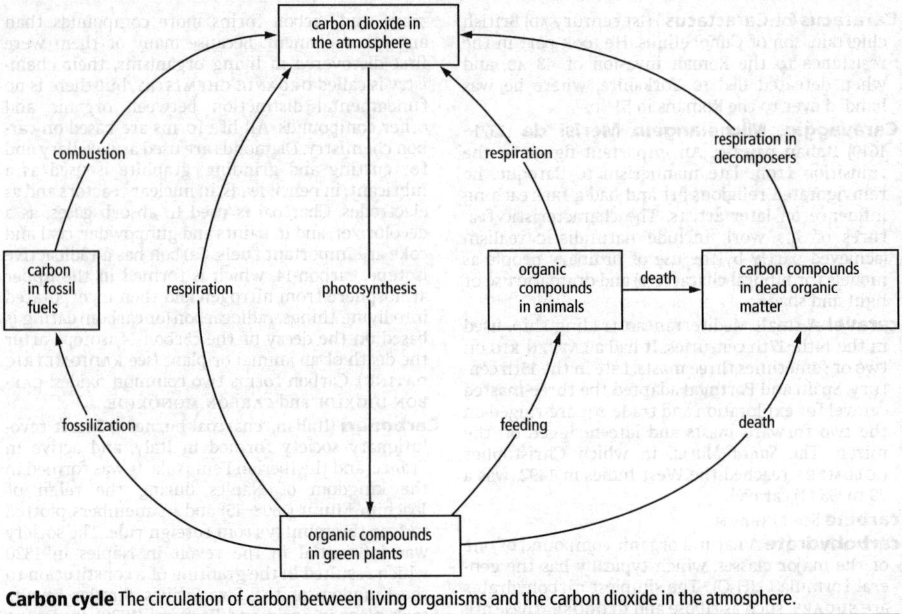

Carbon cycle The circulation of carbon between living organisms and the carbon dioxide in the atmosphere.

bon dioxide by natural erosion of the deposits or by their combustion (see GREENHOUSE EFFECT). The carbon contained in organisms whose bodies have been incorporated in sedimentary rock, such as LIMESTONE, is released by erosion or volcanoes.

carbon dating See RADIOCARBON DATING.

carbon dioxide (CO_2) A colourless gas which is denser than air. It forms 0.04 per cent of the atmosphere by volume; this has an important effect on the Earth's temperature, as the carbon dioxide allows heat energy from the Sun to pass through it to the Earth, but absorbs energy radiated from the Earth's surface (this is known as the GREENHOUSE EFFECT). Carbon dioxide is formed by the combustion of organic matter and carbon, by heating carbonates, by the addition of acids to carbonates, and in fermentation. Mammals breathe out carbon dioxide, but plants absorb it during photosynthesis. Carbon dioxide is quite unreactive although it is reduced to carbon monoxide by reactive metals, hydrogen, and carbon and it reacts with ammonia to form urea, which is used in the manufacture of fertilizers and plastics. It dissolves slightly in water, forming carbonic acid; fizzy drinks all contain carbon dioxide dissolved under pressure. Because it does not support combustion, it is commonly used in fire extinguishers; and liquid and solid carbon dioxide (DRY ICE) are used as refrigerants.

carbon fibre A filament of pure carbon. Carbon fibres achieve extremely high strength and stiffness because the strong axis of the crystalline structure is aligned along the fibre axis. However, they lack tensile strength, which has limited their engineering applications. They were first manufactured in the 1960s, from acrylic fibres. These fibres were stretched to align their carbon chains and then converted to graphite at high temperatures. Currently, carbon fibres are made from a number of different textile fibres and also from pitch, a by-product of petroleum refining. Carbon fibres are the stiffest engineering materials in common use, being over twice as stiff as steel. They are used in FIBRE-REINFORCED PLASTICS to make strong, low-density materials, which find application in aircraft wing and fuselage age sections, and for a wide range of sports and specialist engineering equipment.

Carboniferous Period The fifth period of the PALAEOZOIC ERA in the GEOLOGICAL TIMESCALE, extending from 360 to 286 million years ago, so named because of the wide occurrence in rocks of this age of carbon, in the form of coal. Seed-bearing plants first appeared during the Carboniferous Period. Corals were widespread and extensive limestone deposits were formed. Rivers formed deltas and luxuriant vegetation developed on coastal swamps. This vegetation was later drowned and buried under mud and sand to form successive layers of PEAT, which subsequently became coal. Rocks of Carboniferous age yield not only coal but also oil and iron ores. In the USA the Carboniferous Period is divided into the MISSISSIPPIAN PERIOD (Lower Carboniferous, or Dinantian) and the PENNSYLVANIAN PERIOD (Upper Carboniferous).

carbon monoxide (CO) A colourless, poisonous gas produced by the combustion of carbon in an inadequate supply of oxygen. It burns with a characteristic blue flame to give carbon dioxide and acts as a reducing agent. A component of domestic gas produced from coal (but not of natural gas), it is also produced when incomplete combustion of carbon compounds occurs, hence the dangers of car exhaust fumes and the need for adequate ventilation with paraffin stoves, gas fires, and similar heating appliances. As little as 0.1 per cent by volume in air can be fatal. Haemoglobin (the carrier of oxygen in the blood) has a much higher affinity for carbon monoxide than for oxygen and rapidly forms carbonmonoxyhaemoglobin, which is useless as an oxygen carrier, thus depriving the body of oxygen.

carbon-nitrogen cycle The dominant nuclear fusion reaction in main-sequence stars whose central temperature is above 1.8×10^7 K. The cycle, also known as the **Bethe cycle**, is a six-stage reaction in which hydrogen is converted to helium via the nuclei of carbon, nitrogen, and oxygen which exist in small quantities in stellar interiors. Gamma rays and NEUTRINOS are also produced in this cycle. Stars such as the Sun whose central temperature is less than 1.8×10^7 K are dominated by the PROTON–PROTON REACTION. See FUSION, NUCLEAR.

carbon-paper A thin paper or plastic sheet coated on one side with a mixture of mineral colour (usually CARBON-BLACK) and a waxy substance, used for making copies. Typing or writing on a top sheet of paper is copied (through pressure transfer) by the carbon-paper on to an underlying sheet of paper. The widespread availability of PHOTOCOPIERS and the development of carbonless transfer papers have greatly reduced the use of carbon-paper.

carbon tetrachloride (or **tetrachloromethane**, CCl_4) A colourless volatile liquid, which is a versatile organic solvent. It has been used in dry cleaning and in fire extinguishers, although it is toxic and is now being replaced by less hazardous chemicals.

carbonyl group A carbon atom and an oxygen atom joined by a double bond. Such groups occur in aldehydes and ketones, and in carboxylic acids and their derivatives.

carborundum See ABRASIVE; SILICON CARBIDE.

carboxylic acid An organic compound containing a carboxyl group (–COOH) bonded to either hydrogen, an ALKYL GROUP, or an ARYL GROUP. If the latter group is denoted by R, the formula of a carboxylic acid can be represented by RCOOH. Carboxylic acids dissolve in water to form acidic solutions. The hydroxyl group can be replaced, resulting in a series of acid derivatives. These include acid chlorides (RCOCl), amides, ACID ANHYDRIDES, and ESTERS. Many carboxylic acids occur naturally, and they are formed by mild oxidation of most organic compounds.

carburettor A device used in some petrol engines to charge air with a spray of liquid fuel. At the heart of the carburettor is the VENTURI, a constriction in the air passage through the carburettor. This constriction creates an area of faster-moving, low-pressure air, and the lowered pressure draws petrol into the air-stream from a jet nozzle on the side of the venturi. Petrol is supplied to the jet from a small reservoir in the carburettor, the float tank. The flow of the petrol–air mixture from the carburettor into the engine cylinders is controlled by the throttle butterfly valve, which allows more or less mixture into the cylinder depending on the power needed. The choke controls the petrol-air mixture by increasing or decreasing the air supply, while in the variable-jet carburettor, the petrol supply is adjusted. In most modern car engines there is no carburettor, and a fuel injection system is used. In this, a throttle butterfly regulates the amount of air passing into the cylinder, while the petrol is injected under pressure directly into the cylinder, the timing and amount of petrol injected being controlled electronically.

carcinogen See CANCER AND CANCER THERAPY.

cardamom A tropical, perennial shrub, *Elettaria cardamomum*, native to Sri Lanka and India. It is a member of the ginger family, Zingiberaceae, and has aromatic seeds that are highly flavoured and have been prized for chewing in those countries for centuries. It is best known as a spice, being a constituent of curry powder.

cardboard Any thick and stiff paper or paper-like substance especially for making cards or boxes. Originally, it was used to describe pasteboard, that is, a form of board made from a straw or other coarse base material on to which paper had been pasted to imitate thick, smooth card.

Cárdenas, Lázaro (1895–1970) Mexican statesman. As President of Mexico (1934–40), he carried the {Mexican Revolution} to the left during his administration. He redistributed land, encouraged organized labour through support of the Confederación de Trabajadores de Mexico (CTM), and nationalized the property of the foreign-owned oil companies in 1938. Himself a mestizo (of mixed American Indian and European descent), he won the support of the Indian and Mexican working classes.

card-games Games usually played with a pack (or packs) of 52 cards derived from the picture cards of the Tarot to which numeral cards were added. Packs may differ in their details; in some countries, packs of 56 cards are common. The modern 52 card pack is divided into four suits – spades, hearts, diamonds, and clubs – each consisting of an ace, king, queen, jack, and nine numeral cards numbered 10 to 2. While the chief function of Tarot cards is fortune-telling, most modern card-games are played either for amusement, albeit competitively, or as a vehicle for gambling. The principal solo games are variations of solitaire or patience, in which the player lays out a number of key cards and tries to build the remaining cards on them in an agreed sequence. In games based on rank, such as whist, players are dealt a hand of cards face down and then lay them out in sequence, trying to defeat other players' cards and collect tricks. Bidding, or declaring in advance how many tricks the player expects to win, produced the modern game of contract bridge. Other games, such as poker, are based on combinations of cards; players bet on their hands and seek to win through a blend of good cards and bluffing.

Cardiff (Welsh **Caerdydd**) The capital of Wales, an administrative and commercial centre on the Bristol Channel at the mouth of the Taff, Ely, and Rhymney rivers; pop. (1991) 272,600. Among its chief industries are the manufacture of steel, engineering, and food processing, and among its principal landmarks are Llandaff Cathedral, Cardiff Castle, the National Museum of Wales, and the Welsh National Folk Museum. The administrative headquarters of Mid Glamorgan and South Glamorgan are in Cardiff at Cathays Park and Atlantic Wharf. Its University Colleges were founded in 1884 and 1893. Cardiff Arms Park rugby stadium is world famous and the Royal Mint is near Cardiff at Llantrisant.

Cardiganshire A former county of west Wales stretching from the River Dovey in the north to the River Teifi in the south. It became part of Dyfed in 1974, but was reinstated as a unitary authority under its Welsh name, **Ceredigion**, in 1996. Area, 1,793 sq km (692 sq miles); pop. (1996) 63,700; administrative centre, Aberystwyth.

Cardin, Pierre (1922–) French couturier. He was the first designer in the field of *haute couture* to show a collection of clothes for men as well as women (1960). He is also noted for his ready-to-wear clothes and accessories.

cardinal Any bird of the genera *Paroaria*, *Cardinalis*, and *Pyrrhuloxia*, all of which belong to the family Fringillidae. The best known is the red or common cardinal, *Cardinalis cardinalis*, of North and Central America. This species is about 20 cm (8 inches) long; the male is a striking red with a red crest and a black mark around the beak, and the female is olive-green with a full red tail and crest.

It breeds in thick cover, and builds an untidy cup-shaped nest of grasses and thin twigs, in which are laid three to four pale eggs speckled with dark brown and grey.

cardinal beetle A beetle of the family Pyrochroidae, comprising 100 species, occurring mainly in northern temperate regions. They have long antennae and are often bright red – hence their name. The larvae of all species live under bark; the adults of some species visit flowers.

cardinal fish A fish of the family Apogonidae, found in shallow tropical and subtropical seas. About 170 species are known, most of them growing only up to 10 cm (4 inches) in length. Many are uniformly reddish; others have lengthwise black lines along the body. They are most numerous on coral reefs, where many are nocturnal, spending daylight hours in crevices in the coral. The males of many species incubate the eggs in their mouth.

carding machine A device for disentangling and aligning textile fibres preparatory to SPINNING. Carding is applied to almost all natural fibres and to many manufactured ones. Layers of fibre are passed between moving, parallel surfaces densely covered with fine sharp spikes. Originally, this was done manually in small batches. Modern rotary carding machines accept a continuous layer of randomly oriented fibres and automatically deliver parallel fibres as a soft rope or 'sliver' 1–2 cm (0.4–0.8 inches) in diameter.

cardiology and cardiac surgery Cardiology is the study of the heart and the vascular (blood) system, and of diseases affecting them. Heart (cardiac) failure is a failure of the heart to pump an adequate flow of blood round the body. This may result from a decreased contractile force in the muscle fibres, which can be treated with containing substances such as digoxin, which slows the heart rate and strengthens its contraction. Cardiac failure can also result from a failure of coordination between the individual heart-muscle fibres (fibrillation). These two conditions usually result from narrowing of the coronary arteries, from leaking or narrowed valves within the heart, or from an overgrowth (hypertrophy) of the heart muscle itself, usually in response to high blood pressure (hypertension). Echocardiography uses ULTRASOUND to provide a real-time picture of the heart, aiding the diagnosis of valvular and muscular abnormalities. Narrowing ('hardening') of the arteries (atherosclerosis) is common in affluent societies. It may affect any arteries: coronary atherosclerosis produces angina pectoris (pain in the chest resulting from a fall in oxygen supply to the heart), heart attack (sudden, and usually complete loss of cardiac function due to failure of the blood supply to part of the heart muscle), or heart failure (a chronic heart condition with symptoms of breathlessness, weakness, and lethargy). Atherosclerosis may be treated by a surgical procedure (coronary bypass) in which a vein (usually taken from the leg) is grafted around the obstruction. An alternative technique (coronary angioplasty) that avoids open-heart surgery involves the passing of a balloon-ended catheter into the narrowed artery: the balloon is then inflated for a few seconds, breaking the calcified tissue and effectively removing the obstruction. Blood clots can be treated with fibrinolytic drugs, such as streptokinase (an enzyme isolated from bacteria), which soften the clots. See also ELECTROCARDIOGRAPH.

cardiovascular system See CIRCULATION (of the blood).

Carducci, Giosuè (1835–1907) Italian poet and literary critic. Born in Tuscany, he was Professor of Italian Literature at Bologna from 1860 to 1904. In 1906 he was awarded the Nobel Prize for Literature. In *Iambs and epodes* (1867–69), *Barbarian Odes* (1877–89), and *New Rhymes* (1861–67), his poetry, when not over-rhetorical, beautifully evokes place and mood.

Cardwell, Edward, Viscount (1813–86) British statesman. A supporter of Sir Robert PEEL, he served as Secretary to the Treasury (1845–46) and as Secretary for War in GLADSTONE'S ministry of 1868–74. British incompetence in the CRIMEAN WAR (1853–56) and the efficiency of the German army in the European wars of the 1860s were the background to Cardwell's military reforms.

Carey, George (Leonard) (1935–) British Anglican churchman, Archbishop of Canterbury from 1991. He was formerly a theology lecturer and comes from a broadly evangelical background. The controversial introduction of women priests into the Church of England was finally approved under his leadership.

car ferry A ship designed to carry vehicles and passengers, usually on short-haul crossings. Early vehicle ferries were passenger ships with a specially adapted hold: vehicles were hoisted in and out by derricks and carried secured to the deck. Roll-on roll-off (ro-ro) ferries for trains appeared in the mid-19th century; ro-ro car ferries appeared in the 1920s. With these, vehicles can drive on one end of the ferry and drive off the other without turning. Wide, hydraulically operated ramps or doors, usually at bow and stern, can be manœuvred against purpose-built matching ramps at the shore-side sites being served. The large vehicle decks with no bulkheads make car ferries prone to rapid capsizing if holed. Regulations introduced by the International Maritime Organization in 1990 require increased clearance between the cargo doors and the water-line.

cargo cults MILLENNARIAN movements originally found in Melanesian societies. The charismatic leaders of such cults claim that when the new millennium arrives, the ancestors, or a god, will return, bringing the cargo (Western trade goods) that rightfully belongs to the people, having been stolen by white men. The use of the term 'cargo' results from the contact of the Melanesian people with European traders, and the cults can be seen as anti-colonial protest movements. Cult followers often build storehouses, jetties, and airstrips, or adopt European dress and habits in a form of RITUAL that anticipates the arrival of cargo. When this fails to materialize, the cult may decline.

Carib A member of the pre-Columbian American Indian inhabitants of the Lesser Antilles and parts of the neighbouring South American coast, or of their descendants. A fearsome maritime people, the Caribs forced the peaceful Arawak-speaking peoples of the Antilles to migrate to South America to escape their depredations. Still expanding at the time of the Spanish conquest the Caribs were supplanted, in turn, by European colonialism and have all but disappeared in the West Indies (where only a few hundred still remain on the island of Dominica). On mainland South America Carib-speaking groups occupy territory in the north-east and Amazon regions, living in small autonomous communities. Peculiarly, the Carib language was spoken only by men; their women, who were captured in raids on other tribes, spoke only Arawak.

Caribbean A sea (see CARIBBEAN SEA) and its islands on the Atlantic side of Central America. The **Caribbean Islands** (see also WEST INDIES) form an archipelago bordered on the west by Central America and on the south by South America. The islands sweep like a hook round the north and east, forming a barrier against the Atlantic Ocean. They consist of: the BAHAMAS, the Greater Antilles, and the Lesser Antilles. The Bahamas are a string of some 500 islands running south-west off Florida, USA. The Greater Antilles is a chain of mostly large islands running roughly east-west and consisting of CUBA, JAMAICA, Hispaniola (shared by HAITI and the DOMINICAN REPUBLIC), PUERTO RICO, and a few off-shore and small islands, notably the CAYMAN ISLANDS (a British colony and tax-haven). The Lesser Antilles are grouped into the Leeward and Windward Islands, running roughly north-south, and consisting of numerous small islands colonized in the 17th century by the Spanish, British, French, Dutch, and Danish. They include the US VIRGIN ISLANDS, about 50 small islands bought by the USA in 1917 from Denmark for strategic reasons and since developed for tourism; the British Virgin Islands, a smaller group, that retain colonial status with increasing self-government; MONTSERRAT; MARTINIQUE and GUADELOUPE, overseas dependencies of France; Curaçao (part of the NETHERLANDS ANTILLES) and ARUBA, which retained the status of self-governing colonies; TRINIDAD AND TOBAGO, and a string of now independent Commonwealth states which were colonized by the British.

Caribbean Community and Common Market (CARICOM) An organization formed in 1973 to promote unity among the many small nations of the Caribbean. The main purpose of the organization is to promote the economic integration of its 14 members by means of a Caribbean Common Market, replacing the former Caribbean Free Trade Association (CARIFTA). Member nations also cooperate on other projects in areas such as health, education, and agricultural development. A summit meeting in 1984 agreed to create a single market, but many issues were unresolved. At subsequent annual summit meetings disagreements were gradually settled and in 1995 the members decided to remove all internal trade tariffs by the end of the year. Its headquarters are in Georgetown, Guyana.

Caribbean music Music of the islands of the Caribbean. The music of the islands thus results from nearly five centuries of fusion of peoples and cultures of European, African, and Asian descent. The call and response patterning of much Caribbean music and its pervasive use in ritual, work, and play, is typical of sub-Saharan Africa; but the textures of Caribbean polyphony and the roles of individual composers and of solo performances seem to be different.

Among contemporary dance forms, limbo dancing is said to date from the time of slavery, while the quadrille was imported into the Caribbean from Europe during the same period. Cuban dances such as the *danzón* and rumba are akin to Latin American dances in their combination of Spanish and African elements; early in the 20th century they were exported to ballrooms in the USA and Europe. The most common carnival music forms are Trinidadian CALYPSO and STEEL BAND music, and Jamaican reggae.

Caribbean Sea An arm of the Atlantic Ocean lying between the Antilles and the mainland of Central and South America. It reaches a depth of 7,680 m (25,197 ft) in the Cayman Trench between Cuba and Jamaica.

caribou See REINDEER.

caricature A form of art, usually portraiture, in which characteristic features of the subject represented are distorted or exaggerated for comic effect. Its invention is usually credited to Annibale CARRACCI, who flourished in the late 16th and early 17th centuries, although other forms of grotesque or ludicrous representation were known earlier (and are sometimes loosely called caricature). Political caricature developed in the last three decades of the 18th century, James Gillray and ROWLANDSON being great exponents at this time in Britain, and DAUMIER some years later in France. George CRUIKSHANK produced gentler, less satirical caricatures in the early Victorian period in the UK, while the weekly *Punch* cartoon institutionalized political caricature for the middle-class home. Most newspapers now carry a daily political caricature (or cartoon).

CARICOM See CARIBBEAN COMMUNITY AND COMMON MARKET.

carillon A chime of bells so arranged that melodies can be played on it. Originating in the Low Countries but also popular elsewhere, it is played either by a *carillonneur* using a 'keyboard' of rods struck with the fist, or mechanically by a pinned barrel. Recently, electronic imitations have been introduced.

Carina The Keel, a CONSTELLATION of the southern skies. It is one of the three parts into which the ancient Greek constellation of Argo Navis was dismembered by the 18th-century French astronomer Nicolas Louis de Lacaille. Its brightest star is CANOPUS. Its most celebrated feature is the nebula NGC 3372, known as the Keyhole Nebula, visible to the naked eye, which contains the unusual variable star Eta Carinae. In 1843 Eta Carinae temporarily became the second brightest star in the sky but now lies around sixth magnitude. Eta Carinae is thought to be an unstable SUPERGIANT that may one day explode as a SUPERNOVA.

Carling, Will(iam David Charles) (1965–) British Rugby Union player. He made his England début in 1988 and was appointed captain the same year. He led England to the Five Nations championship in 1991, 1992, 1995, and 1996, and to the World Cup Final in 1991. He is the most-capped England centre and holds the world record for international appearances as captain, a position he retired from in 1996. He retired from club rugby in 1997.

Carlisle The county town and market centre of Cumbria in north-west England, at the junction of the Eden, Caldew, and Petteril rivers; pop. (1991) 99,800. It was the site of the Roman camp of Luguvallum at the western end of Hadrian's Wall. Its cathedral dates from the 12th century. Carlisle changed hands frequently between Scots and English in the Middle Ages. It manufactures textiles, metal products, and biscuits.

Carlist A conservative who supported the claims of Don Carlos (1788–1855) and his descendants to the throne of Spain. Don Carlos's religious orthodoxy and belief in the divine right of kings made him the natural leader of these traditionalists. After unsuccessful claims to the throne for nearly a century, the Carlists emerged as a strong force with popular support after the establishment of a republic in 1931. In the SPANISH CIVIL WAR the Carlists sided with the nationalists, and for many years obstructed Franco's aim to restore the Bourbon dynasty. In 1969 Franco overcame Carlist objections and named the grandson of Alfonso XIII, Juan Carlos, as his successor.

Carlow (Gaelic **Ceatharlach**) A county in the province of Leinster in the Republic of Ireland; area 896 sq km (346 sq mi); pop. (1991) 40,946; county town Carlow. Arable farming is important.

Carlsbad The German name for KARLOVY VARY.

Carlson, Chester Floyd (1906–68) US physicist and developer of the process of xerography (see PHOTOCOPIER). He developed between 1934 and 1938 a practical xerographic copying process, though it was not until 1944 that he was able to obtain funding for further development. In 1947 he sold the commercial rights for his invention to the Haloid Company (later the Xerox Corporation).

Carlyle, Thomas (1795–1881) Scottish historian and political philosopher. He worked as a teacher before starting to write articles for the *Edinburgh Encyclopedia* and critical works on German literature in the 1820s. His first major philosophical work was *Sartor Resartus* (1833–34), which dealt with social values and is written in a mannered prose style. He established his reputation as a historian with his *History of the French Revolution* (1837). Carlyle's influence on the development of social and political ideas in Britain during the 19th century was considerable.

Carmarthen The administrative centre of Carmarthenshire, south Wales; pop. (1991) 54,800. It is a dairying centre and cattle market.

Carmarthenshire A county of Wales, which became part of Dyfed in 1974 and was reinstated in 1996. Area 2,380 sq km (919 sq miles); pop. (1996) 163,200; administrative centre Carmarthen.

Carmelite A monk or nun who is a follower of the Order of Our Lady of Mount Carmel. Carmelites obey the strict monastic 'rule' of St Albert of Jerusalem. They originated in PALESTINE *c*.1154 but came to western Europe when Palestine was conquered by the Muslims. Their order was approved by Pope Honorius III in 1226. In 1452 the Carmelite Sisters was formed. In 1594 a reformed group of the order was established, the Discalced Carmelites, but it remained essentially similar in organization and objectives.

Carmichael, Hoagy (born Howard Hoagland Carmichael) (1899–1981) US jazz pianist, composer, and singer. His best-known songs include 'Stardust' (1929), 'Two Sleepy People' (1938), and 'In the Cool, Cool, Cool of the Evening' (1951).

Carmina Burana ('Songs of Beuern') A collection of late 12th-century Latin and German lyrics discovered in Munich in 1803 among documents from the Bavarian Benediktbeuern monastery. They represent a reaction against the medieval ascetic ideal of the church. Some were set to music in 1937 by the Bavarian composer Carl ORFF, in a secular choral cantata.

Carnaby Street A street in the West End of London, England, made famous in the 1960s as a centre of the teenage fashion industry.

Carnac A town in Brittany, France, near a major centre of ritual activity between the 5th and 3rd millennia BC. A peninsula is marked off by rows of MEGALITHS, presumably as some sort of sanctuary. There are numerous megalithic tombs in the area and nearby, at Locmariaquer, is the largest known MENHIR, originally standing 20 m (65 ft) high.

Carnap, Rudolf (1891–1970) German-born US philosopher. One of the originators of logical positivism, he was a founder and the most influential member of the Vienna Circle and was noted for his contributions to logic, the analysis of language, the theory of probability, and the philosophy of science. His emphasis on scientific method in philosophy and the need to verify statements through observation marked a turning-point in philosophical enquiry and the rejection of traditional metaphysics. His major works include *The Logical Structure of the World* (1928) and *The Logical Foundations of Probability* (1950).

carnation See PINK.

Carné, Marcel (1909–96) French film director. He held a dominant position among film-makers of the 1930s and 1940s, gaining his reputation in particular for the films he made with the poet and scriptwriter Jacques Prévert (1900–77). Characterized by a fatalistic outlook and a masterly evocation of atmosphere, they include *Quai des brumes* (1938), *Le Jour se lève* (1939), and *Les Enfants du paradis* (1945).

Carnegie, Andrew (1835–1919) Scottish-born US industrialist and philanthropist. He built up a considerable fortune in the steel industry in the USA, then retired from business in 1901 and devoted his wealth to charitable purposes on both sides of the Atlantic, supporting many educational institutions, libraries, and the arts. One of his most notable achievements was the creation of the Carnegie Peace Fund to promote international peace.

carnival (from Italian, 'farewell to meat') The festival period before LENT, celebrated in Roman Catholic countries and communities. Festivities, a succession of parades, masked balls, and theatrical performances in public places, occur between Epiphany (6 January) and Shrove Tuesday, the last day before Lent. Mardi Gras in New Orleans is one of the most famous carnivals. In North America, carnival also means a travelling fun-fair.

carnivore Broadly speaking, a flesh-eating animal, though the term is used more specifically to describe an order of mammals, the Carnivora. Although principally predators, some also eat plant material; only one member of the order, the giant panda, is wholly herbivorous. There are seven distinct families, of which four are dog-like and three cat-like. They are Ursidae (bears), Canidae (dogs, foxes), Procyonidae (racoons), Mustelidae (stoats, badgers, otters), Viverridae (mongooses, genets), Hyaenidae (hyenas), and Felidae (cats). The seals, sea lions, and walruses used to be included among the carnivores, but now they are placed in a separate order. Distinctive features of carnivores include the pointed canine teeth and the scissor-like cheek teeth (carnassials). The claws may be blunt, as in bears and dogs, or very sharp, as in cats. All carnivores are covered with fur, which preserves their body heat.

Carnivores tend only to take prey that are about their own size, unless several animals band together in packs so that they can overpower much larger prey. The large cats usually kill their prey by suffocation; the smaller carnivores tend to have a killing bite; but many, such as the WOLF and the HYENA, kill by tearing their prey to pieces. Many of the small carnivores are also insectivorous or eat fruit. All carnivores scavenge and some, such as the hyenas, are specialized scavengers.

carnivorous plant (or **insectivorous plant**) A plant that depends upon animal tissue for its sustenance. Carnivorous plants include some 450 species spread over several plant families and genera. Their distribution is worldwide and their habitats range from acid bog lands to semi-deserts. They attract and ensnare a range of insects and other invertebrates by means of traps. These may be of the pitfall (or passive) kind, or active and able to move as an aid to the capture of prey. The prey items provide the plant with nutrients, such as nitrogen, which are deficient in their habitats. The most active trappers include the VENUS's fly-trap and the SUNDEWS, while the passive kinds are typified by the PITCHER PLANT of North and South America.

Certain species of fungi catch and digest eelworms by means of a noose of fungal filaments (hyphae).

Carnot, Lazare Nicolas Marguerite (1753–1823) French general and military tactician. He entered the French army in 1784 and two years later published his influential *Essay on the Use of Machines in Warfare*. In 1791, after the FRENCH REVOLUTION, he was elected to the National Assembly and, as a republican, voted for the execution of Louis XVI. He was a member of the COMMITTEE OF PUBLIC SAFETY, was in charge of the war department, and between 1795 and 1797 was a member of the DIRECTORY. He fled to Germany, falsely accused of treason in 1797, following the royalist victory in the elections. He returned to become Minister of War (1800) and continued with his administrative reforms for a year under NAPOLEON BONAPARTE, but resigned in 1801.

Carnot, Nicolas Léonard Sadi (1796–1832) French scientist. An army officer for most of his life, Carnot became interested in the principles of operation of steam engines, and analysed the efficiency of such engines using the notion of a cycle of reversible temperature and pressure changes of the gases, known as a **Carnot cycle**. Carnot's work was recognized after his death as being of crucial importance to the theory of thermodynamics. **Carnot's theorem** states that no engine can have a greater efficiency than a reversible engine working between the same temperatures.

Caro, Sir Anthony (1924–) British sculptor. In 1951–53 he was assistant to Henry MOORE, but after meeting David SMITH in 1959, he began making sculpture using prefabricated metal elements, painted in rich colours. His work has been highly influential on younger sculptors.

carob The seed-pod of *Ceratonia siliqua*, a tree legume native to the Mediterranean region. Carobs are rich in sugars and gums, and are sometimes used as a substitute for chocolate. A second species of *Ceratonia* has recently been discovered in Arabia.

Carol I (1839–1914) First King of Romania 1881–1914. A German-born prince and Prussian officer, he was elected in 1866 to succeed Alexander John Cuza as Prince of Romania. His pro-German sympathies made him unpopular during the FRANCO-PRUSSIAN WAR, but skill in manipulating politicians and elections saved him from abdication. As a result of his military leadership in the Russo-Turkish War, he gained full independence for Romania at the Congress of BERLIN and declared a Romanian kingdom in 1881.

Carol II (1893–1953) King of Romania 1930–40. The great-nephew of CAROL I, he was exiled in 1925 for his scandalous domestic life. In 1930 he returned as king, and established a royal dictatorship inspired by intense admiration of MUSSOLINI. In 1940 he was forced to cede large parts of his kingdom to the AXIS POWERS, and to abdicate in favour of his son, Michael.

carole (or **carol**) An early dance form and the type of song deriving from it. Most carols have religious texts, though some, such as the 'Agincourt Song' sung after the 1415 victory, were purely secular. When the Christmas season developed as a public holiday in the 19th century, new carols (Christmas hymns) were written as part of the festivities.

Caroline Islands (or **Carolines**) A group of islands in the western Pacific Ocean, north of the equator, forming (with the exception of Palau and some smaller islands) the Federated States of MICRONESIA.

Caroline of Ansbach (1683–1737) German princess, Queen consort of GEORGE II, whom she married in 1705. She was a popular queen, and during the king's absences in Hanover, she was four times appointed 'Guardian of the Realm'. She was responsible for enclosing 121 ha. (300 acres) of London's Hyde Park to form Kensington Gardens.

Carolingian art The art and architecture of the reign of Charlemagne (800–14), the first Holy Roman Emperor, and of his successors until about 900. The most important Carolingian building to survive largely intact is his Palatine (imperial palace) Chapel at Aachen (792–805), which shows the sturdiness of Carolingian architecture and its dependence on early Christian precedents. There is no surviving large-scale sculpture, but Carolingian ivory carving and metalwork (on book covers, for example) reached a high level. Carolingian art had great influence on Ottonian and ROMANESQUE art.

Carolingian Empire The collection of territories in Western Europe ruled by the family of CHARLEMAGNE (768–814 AD) from whom the dynasty took its name. Under Charlemagne, the empire covered modern-day France, part of Spain, Germany to the River Elbe, and much of Italy. Charlemagne was crowned Emperor of the West by Pope Leo III in 800 and made his court a centre of learning (the 'Carolingian Renaissance'). After the division of the empire by the Treaty of Verdun in 843, civil war among the Carolingians, VIKING raids, and the ambitions of rival families subjected the empire to intolerable strains. Nevertheless, Carolingians reigned in Germany until 911 and in France until 987 and they left behind a prestige which later kings of the Middle Ages sought to emulate.

Carothers, Wallace Hume (1896–1937) US industrial chemist. He took up the study of long-chain molecules, now called polymers, and developed the first successful synthetic rubber, neoprene, and the first synthetic fibre able to be spun from a melt, Nylon.

carp A fish that gives its name to the large family of freshwater fish, the Cyprinidae, which includes some 1,500 species. They all lack teeth; two pairs of barbels protruding from their lips help them to find food. Carp are omnivorous, eating mainly plants and also insect larvae and snails. The European carp, *Cyprinus carpio*, is native to the Danube and the rivers of the Black Sea basin. It has been introduced to many parts of the world and is used as a food-fish in Europe. It is now also kept as an angling and as an ornamental fish. Carp prefer to live in deep, slow-flowing rivers and in lakes, especially well-vegetated ones.

Carpaccio, Vittore (*c*.1455–1525) Italian painter. He is noted especially for his paintings including details of Venice and for his lively narrative cycle of paintings *Scenes from the Life of St Ursula* (1490–95).

carpal See HAND.

Carpathian Mountains (or **Carpathians**) A mountain system extending in an arc south-eastwards from southern Poland and the Czech Republic into Romania and the Ukraine. They are divided into the White Carpathians (Bílé Karpaty) in the Czech Republic, the Little Carpathians (Malé

Karpaty) in Slovakia, the Beskids (Beskydy) in southern Poland, the High Tatra (Vysoké Tatry) and Low Tatra (Nizké Tatry) of southern Poland and Slovakia, the Transylvanian Carpathians (Carpatii Meridionali), and the Eastern or Romanian Carpathians (Carpatii Orientali). The highest peak is Gerlachovsky which rises to 2,655 m (8,711 ft) in the Tatra Mountains of Slovakia.

Carpentaria, Gulf of A large bay indenting the eastern part of the north coast of Australia, between Arnhem Land and Cape York Peninsula. Discovered by Abel Tasman in 1606, it was named after Pieter Carpentier, Governor-General of the Dutch East Indies.

carpenter bee A large, blue-black, solitary BEE belonging to the family Xylocopidae. Carpenter bees resemble dark bumble-bees and they have a loud, deep buzz. The queens dig long tunnels into living timber with their jaws, and build their cells of leaves, laying a single egg in each cell. They are mostly tropical, although a few species do occur in Europe.

carpenter worm See GOAT MOTH.

carpetbaggers (in the USA) Northerners who moved into the post-Civil War American South. In the wake of the RECONSTRUCTION ACTS of 1867, large numbers of Northern entrepreneurs, educators, and missionaries arrived in the South to share in the rebuilding of the former states of the CONFEDERACY. Some carpetbaggers (so called because it was said that they could transport their entire assets in a carpetbag) hoped to help the black ex-slave population, but others were interested only in making a quick profit.

carpet manufacture Most carpets and rugs consist of a base fabric supporting a more-or-less upright pile. The pile may be inserted into an already existing base fabric, or pile and fabric may be formed integrally during weaving.

In modern tufted carpets, the insertion of pile into the base fabric occurs at high speed using a battery of hollow needles, the pile then being held in place by the application of latex or similar ADHESIVE. Such carpets predominate in world markets. Woven carpets, in which the pile and base fabric are formed integrally, are of two main types. In Wilton carpets, the pile yarns are raised above the backing or base fabric during weaving. In Axminster carpet, the rows of pile are fed to the structure by devices which grip the pile (spools or grippers). In spool Axminster, tufts are cut at the weaving point; in gripper Axminster, tufts are cut from the yarn supply before being inserted into the fabric by the grippers. A wide range of colours and patterns may be used. Patterning is controlled by Jacquard mechanisms. Other types of textile floor-covering include felted, needled, melt-bonded, and other nonwoven structures. Wool, the traditional fibre for the pile of woven carpets, is now usually blended with NYLON, ACRYLIC, or polypropylene fibres. Most tufted carpets are made from bulked continuous filament (BCF) yarns of nylon or, increasingly, polypropylene.

carpet moth A moth of the family Geometridae, whose caterpillars are sometimes called LOOPERS or inch worms. Carpet moths belong to a number of genera, and are distributed worldwide. Most have mottled, marbled, or intricately barred fore-wings, and rest by day with their wings pressed flat against tree-trunks or walls.

The name is often associated with the genus *Xanthorhoe*, which includes the garden carpet moth, *X. fluctuata*, common throughout Eurasia and North Africa. Its fore-wings are white, dark at the base, and with variable dark markings in the centre.

carpet shark A member of a family of CARTILAGINOUS FISHES, Orectolobidae, containing about 25 species of small sharks, rarely longer than 4 m (13 feet). Most of them live in the tropical Indo-Pacific, but one, the nurse shark, *Ginglymostoma cirratum*, occurs in the tropical Atlantic. Carpet sharks are thickset and heavy-bodied with rather broad fins, and they have a pair of large barbels in front of the mouth. They are often boldly patterned with dark markings. All are bottom-living and feed on invertebrates; they are harmless to man.

Carr, Emily (1871–1945) Canadian painter and writer. Her paintings, inspired by the wilderness of British Columbia, often drew on the motifs of American Indian folk art. From 1927 she came into contact with the group of Canadian landscape painters known as the Group of Seven and produced such expressionist works as *Forest Landscape II* and *Sky* (both 1934–35).

Carr, John (known as **Carr of York**) (1723–1807) British architect. His work, essentially Palladian in style, was unoriginal but assured, and he had high standards of craftsmanship (he was a stone-mason by training). Late in his career he was influenced by the elegant style of Robert ADAM in his interiors.

Carrà, Carlo (1881–1966) Italian painter. He was a prominent member of the Futurists (whom he joined in 1909), and visits to Paris in 1911 and 1912 introduced CUBISM into his work. In 1915 he met de CHIRICO and turned to metaphysical painting, although his work was generally without de Chirico's sinister feeling. Carrà broke with de Chirico in 1918 and abandoned Metaphysical painting, devoting himself to trying to recapture the monumental grandeur of early Italian painters such as GIOTTO and MASACCIO and becoming an influential teacher.

Carracci A family of Italian painters. **Ludovico** (1555–1619) is remembered chiefly as a distinguished teacher; with his cousins he established an academy at Bologna which was responsible for training many important painters. His cousin **Annibale** (1560–1609) is the most famous of the family, especially for his work in Rome, such as the ceiling of the Farnese Gallery (1597–1600). He is also remembered for his invention of the caricature. Annibale's brother **Agostino** (1557–1602) was chiefly an engraver, but he also worked with his brother in the Farnese Gallery.

carrack See SAILING SHIPS AND BOATS.

Carrantuohill (or **Carrauntoohill**) The highest mountain, at 1041 m (3414 ft), in Ireland, in Macgillicuddy's Reeks, County Kerry, in the Republic of Ireland.

Carranza, Venustiano (1859–1920) Mexican statesman. As President of Mexico (1917–20), he played a minor role in the revolution against Porfirio DÍAZ but a major role in shaping the course of the Mexican Revolution from 1913 to 1920. A voice for moderation during the violent decade of revolutionary politics, he defeated his rival Pancho VILLA and reluctantly accepted the leftist constitution of 1917. Driven from office before his presidential term expired, he was assassinated in the village of Tlaxcalantongo on his way into exile.

Carrel, Alexis (1873–1944) French surgeon and biologist. He developed improved techniques for suturing arteries and veins, and carried out some of the first organ transplants. He also succeeded in keeping organs alive outside the body by perfusion, using a glass pump devised with the aid of Charles Lindbergh. Carrel, who spent much of his career in the USA, received a Nobel Prize in 1912.

Carreras, José (1946–) Spanish operatic tenor. Since his operatic début in his native city of Barcelona (1970), he has given many performances in opera houses worldwide. Noted for his soft voice in the upper register, he has had great success in the operas of Verdi, Puccini, and Donizetti. In the 1990s he enlarged his career to include conducting.

carriages and coaches Horse-drawn vehicles designed to carry passengers. Four-wheeled vehicles carried fare-paying paying passengers in Roman times. In medieval Europe, passenger-carrying wagons fell out of use because of the poor state of the roads, and land travel was mainly on horseback or on foot. In Hungary in the 15th century, light, covered, four-wheeled vehicles began to be built, which were suspended between the axles rather than resting on them. These early coaches spread throughout Europe during the 16th century. Initially such coaches were available only for the very rich, but in the 17th century various two- and four-wheeled designs arose – from large coaches carrying up to six people inside, to light, two-wheeled gigs for two people. Hackney carriages for hire were introduced in London in 1625, and **stage-coaches** for longer-distance travel in 1640. During the 18th and 19th centuries, carriage types proliferated, with many variations according to purpose, locality, and available materials. Small carriages were generally owner-driven: larger vehicles could either be driven by a coachman, or by a rider (postilion) on the horses.

Carrickfergus (Gaelic **Carraig Fhearghais**) A port in County Antrim. Northern Ireland, on the north shore of Belfast Lough; pop. (1981) 17,600. Its Norman castle is built on Fergus's rock where legend has it that the progenitor of the royal house of Scotland was drowned. William II landed here before the battle of the Boyne in 1690.

carrier wave See MODULATION.

Carrington, Dora (de Houghton) (1893–1932) British painter. She became involved with the Bloomsbury Group and in particular Lytton Strachey, with whom she continued a relationship despite her marriage in 1921. In 1932 she committed suicide.

carrion beetle A beetle that, as larva or adult, feeds on dead animal material. Carrion beetles may belong to one of several different groups, but the name is used specifically for the 200 or so species of the family Silphidae, which are most common in northern temperate regions. These include roving carrion beetles, such as *Silpha*, and BURYING BEETLES, such as *Necrophorus*.

carrion crow A species of crow, *Corvus corone*, which has two main subspecies. The common carrion crow, *C. c. corone*, is black all over, with a glossy blue sheen; the so-called hooded crow, *C. c. cornix*, has a grey rather than black back and underparts. The common form occurs in Europe, whereas the hooded form also extends over much of Asia. The birds are about 50 cm (20 inches) long. They build bulky nests of twigs in the tops of trees or on rock ledges and eat a wide range of food, varying from carrion to other birds and mammals, and to fruits and seeds.

Carroll, Lewis (born Charles Lutwidge Dodgson) (1832–98) British writer. He worked as a mathematics lecturer at Oxford University 1855–81; after a boat trip with Alice Liddell, the daughter of the dean of his college, he was inspired to write *Alice's Adventures in Wonderland* (1865) and *Through the Looking Glass* (1871). Both books tell the story of a child's fantastic dream adventures; illustrated by John Tenniel, they became classics of children's literature. Carroll also wrote nonsense verse, notably *The Hunting of the Snark* (1876), and experimented in portrait photography.

carrot A vegetable of the family Umbelliferae, most members of which are characterized by large, disc-shaped heads of tiny white, pink, or yellow flowers. This family contains 3,000 species of herbs, shrubs, and trees, some of which are poisonous. Examples include parsnips, angelica, fennel, celery, and hemlock. The cultivated carrot is derived from the European wild carrot, *Daucus carota*, which produces a white or purplish, rather woody tap-root and flowers in its second year. The edible roots of cultivated carrots may be cylindrical or conical, and vary in length. They contain the orange pigment carotene, which is a rich source of vitamin A.

carrying capacity The maximum number of individuals of a particular species that a HABITAT is able to support. This is an important concept in ECOLOGY and is determined by a number of factors, including the availability of food, space, and light, and the degree of competition, disease, predation, and accumulation of wastes. Such factors inhibit the population of a species from increasing beyond a certain point within the habitat, and when it reaches that point it stabilizes, fluctuating in numbers within narrow limits.

Carson, Edward Henry, Baron (1854–1935) Anglo-Irish statesman. Elected to the British Parliament in 1892, he opposed the third HOME RULE Bill (1912) and organized a private army of ULSTER VOLUNTEERS, threatening that Ulster would set up a separate provisional government if the Bill proceeded. In 1914 he reluctantly agreed to Home Rule for southern Ireland but insisted that NORTHERN IRELAND, including the predominantly Catholic counties of Tyrone and Fermanagh, should remain under the British crown.

Carson, Rachel (Louise) (1907–64) US zoologist. Remembered as a pioneer ecologist and popularizer of science, she wrote *The Sea Around Us* (1951) and *Silent Spring* (1963), an attack on the indiscriminate use of pesticides and weed-killers.

Carson, William Hunter Fisher (known as 'Willie') (1942–) Scottish jockey. In 1972 he became the first Scotsman to be champion jockey and also had his first Classic success in the 2,000 Guineas. His first Derby win came seven years later, and he won again in 1980 and 1989.

Carson City The capital of the US state of Nevada, near Lake Tahoe; pop. (1990) 40,443. Founded as a trading post in 1851 on the route from Salt Lake City to California, it is now a commercial centre at the heart of a mining and agricultural region. Named after the US frontiersman Kit Carson, it became state capital in 1864.

cartel A group of producers (firms or countries) that attempts to fix the price of its common product or products, usually through restriction of output by cartel members, often by operating a QUOTA system.

Carter, Angela (1940–92) British novelist and short-story writer. Her fiction is characterized by fantasy, black humour, and eroticism, while her second novel *The Magic Toyshop* (1967) established her as a major exponent of magic realism. Later novels, such as *The Passion of New Eve* (1977), offer a strong feminist perspective on capitalism and

Western society. Her exploration of the symbolic function of myth and folklore in the unconscious is reflected in short stories such as 'The Company of Wolves' (1979), which formed the basis for a film in 1984.

Carter, Elliott (Cook) (1908–) US composer. He is noted for his innovative approach to metre and eclectic choice of sources as diverse as modern jazz and Renaissance madrigals.

Carter, Howard (1874–1939) British archaeologist. In 1922 he achieved fame when, studying the Valley of the Kings at Thebes, he discovered the tomb of Tutankhamen. His work, under the patronage of Lord Carnarvon, gave a great boost to public interest in archaeology.

Carter, James Earl (known as 'Jimmy') (1924–) US Democratic statesman, 39th President of the USA 1977–81. A progressive and reformist governor of Georgia (1970–74), he was elected President on a manifesto of civil rights and economic reform. Although his administration was notable for achieving the Panama Canal Treaty (1977) and the Camp David agreements (1978), he failed to resolve the crisis caused by the seizure of US hostages in Iran.

Cartesian coordinates The most commonly used coordinate system for specifying numerically the location of points in a plane or in space, devised by the French philosopher and mathematician René Descartes. The basis of the system is a pair of lines at right angles to one another; they are called the coordinate axes. To give the Cartesian coordinates of any point, its perpendicular distances to the vertical line (y-axis) and the horizontal line (x-axis) are stated. These numbers, placed in an ordered pair (x, y) are the Cartesian coordinates of that point. Each point has a unique pair of Cartesian coordinates. Many curves have simple Cartesian descriptions, that is, sets of points satisfying some algebraic equation which facilitates the study of their geometric properties. For example, a PARABOLA is $y^2 = 4ax$: the (x, y) coordinates of every point on a parabola satisfy this equation. This system of reference can be extended to three dimensions (x, y, z) or, in mathematics, to spaces of higher dimensions. POLAR COORDINATES are another way of specifying the location of a point.

Carthage The ruins of an ancient city on the north coast of Africa in Tunisia, situated to the west of Tunis. Traditionally founded by Phoenicians from Tyre (in modern Lebanon) in 814 BC, it became a major centre of the Mediterranean, with interests in North Africa, Spain, and Sicily which brought it into conflict with Greece until the 3rd century BC and then with Rome in the Punic Wars, until the Romans finally destroyed it in 146 BC.

Carthusian A member of the monastic order founded by St BRUNO of Cologne at Chartreuse in France in 1084. Their 'rule' is extremely severe, requiring solitude, abstinence from meat, regular fasting, and silence except for a few hours each week. Nuns affiliated to the order may eat together and, uniquely within the Roman Catholic Church, are allowed to become deaconesses. Lay brothers and sisters tend their needs and provide the minimum necessary contact with the outside world. They are governed by the general chapter, consisting of the priors of all houses together with the community of La Grande Chartreuse itself.

Cartier, Sir George-Etienne (1814–73) French-Canadian statesman. His involvement in 1837 in the Papineau Rebellion forced him into brief exile in the USA. In 1848 he was elected as a Conservative to the Canadian Legislative Assembly, holding a seat there, and later in the Canadian House of Commons, until his death.

Cartier, Jacques (1491–1557) French explorer. The first to establish France's claim to North America, he made three voyages to Canada between 1534 and 1541, sailing up the St Lawrence River as far as present-day Montreal and building a fort at Cap Rouge (a few miles upstream of what is now Quebec City).

Cartier-Bresson, Henri (1908–) French photographer and film director. Intent on capturing the 'decisive moment' of a scene or event, he travelled widely, recording the lives of ordinary people without artificial composition and establishing a reputation as a humane and perceptive observer. His collections of photographs include *The Decisive Moment* (1952).

cartilage A structural material found in animals which exists in three forms: articular, elastic, and fibrous. Articular cartilage is the gristle at the ends of bones, forming movable joints. It has a translucent, smooth surface which, lubricated by synovial fluid, allows the ends of the bones to glide

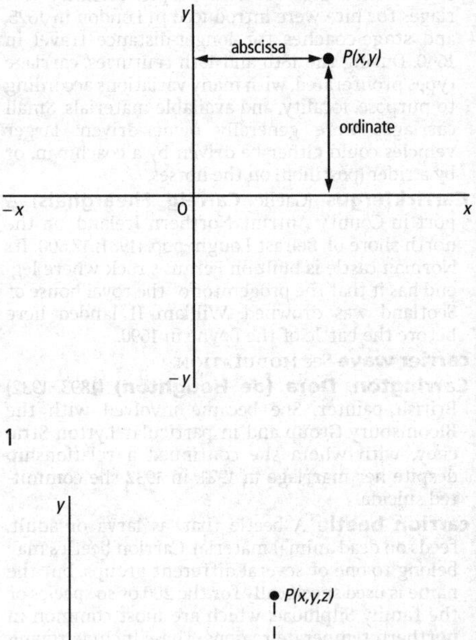

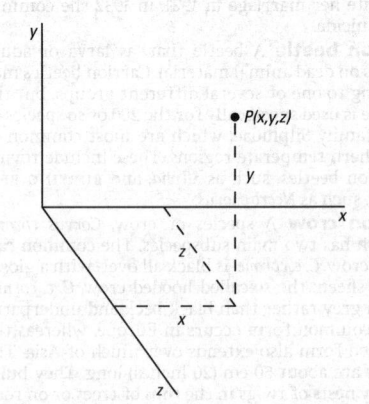

Cartesian coordinates (1) The coordinates of any point P in a two-dimensional plane are given by the values of x (called the abscissa) and y (the ordinate). (2) In a three-dimensional space, the position of P is given by the three coordinates x, y, and z.

smoothly over one another. Elastic cartilage forms much of the skeleton of the larynx, epiglottis, and the external ear. It contains numerous elastic fibres and is a springy, rubber-like material. Fibrous cartilage forms discs between the spinal vertebrae, and between other bones that move only slightly over one another.

cartilaginous fish A member of one of the three main classes of fishes, including all those species that lack true bone in their skeleton. Instead, they have a skeleton made of cartilage, hardened by the deposition of calcium but still partly flexible. Their skin is covered in tooth-like (placoid) SCALES, and they lack the swim bladder of the BONY FISHES. The cartilaginous fishes are subdivided into three orders: the sharks; the skates, rays, and allied families; and the ratfishes, or chimaeras. The sharks, skates, and rays are sometimes classed together as the elasmobranchs.

Cartland, Dame (Mary) Barbara (Hamilton) (1901–) British writer. A prolific author, she specializes in light romantic fiction; her popular romances include *Bride to a Brigand* (1983) and *A Secret Passage to Love* (1992).

cartography The science and art of making maps, by establishing and presenting in a suitable form the locations, shapes, and sizes of the features being mapped. (Normally these are features on the Earth's surface; but the term includes mapping geological strata, the surface of the Moon, and even nebulae with radio telescopes.) Cartographic presentation requires drawing with carefully designed and uniform lines, symbols, and lettering, and conversion to transparent film, printing plates, or digital tapes, from which copies can be made.

cartoon A full-size drawing made for the purpose of transferring a design to a painting or tapestry. Cartoons were an essential part of the process of making stained glass, and were used in painting by the early 15th century. In the 19th century proposed designs for frescos in the Houses of Parliament in London were parodied in the magazine *Punch*; thereafter the word came to mean a humorous drawing or parody. See also CARICATURE.

cartridge A container for the propellant charge used in FIREARMS. First developed at the end of the 16th century, cartridges became standard military equipment in the early 19th century. The development of breech-loading firearms enabled the cartridge and BULLET to be combined, as they are in modern weapons. The breech-loader's firing pin strikes a percussion cap at the centre of the cartridge base. The percussion cap contains a DETONATOR, which ignites the propellant charge within the cartridge.

Cartwright, Edmund (1743–1823) British engineer, inventor of the power loom. Initially a clergyman, he became interested in textile machinery, and despite financial failures continued to innovate, developing machines for wool-combing and rope-making and an alcohol engine.

Caruso, Enrico (1873–1921) Italian operatic tenor. He had his greatest successes in operas by Verdi, Puccini, and Jules Massenet (1842–1912). The first major tenor to be recorded on gramophone records, he became a household name even among those who never attended operatic performances.

Carver, John (*c.*1576–1621) Pilgrim leader. He had been deacon of the separatist church in Leiden and led the migration in the *Mayflower* in 1620. Elected first governor of Plymouth Plantation, he died shortly afterwards and was succeeded by William BRADFORD.

Cary, (Arthur) Joyce (Lunel) (1888–1957) British novelist. His major works constitute two trilogies; the first is concerned with art and includes *The Horse's Mouth* (1944), a memorable portrait of an outrageous artist, whereas the second deals with political life and includes *Not Honour More* (1955).

caryatid A carved female figure clad in long robes and serving as a column. Caryatids were first used in Greek architecture, the most famous examples being on the Erechtheum in Athens (*c.*421–407 BC), and again came into prominence with the Greek Revival of the 19th century.

Casablanca A seaport and commercial centre on the Atlantic coast of north-west Africa, the largest city of Morocco; pop. (1993) 2,943,000. It was founded in 1515 by the Portuguese who had in 1468 destroyed the older city of Anfa. Casablanca is a mixture of old Muslim quarter, modern European city, and outlying shanty towns. The King Hassan Mosque, completed in 1993, is the world's largest mosque. Casablanca handles three-quarters of the country's commerce and has textile, glass, and tourist industries.

Casablanca Conference (14–24 January 1943) A meeting in Morocco between CHURCHILL and F. D. ROOSEVELT to determine Allied strategy for the continuation of World War II. Plans were made to increase bombing of Germany, invade Sicily, and transfer British forces to the Far East after the collapse of Germany.

Casals, Pablo (1876–1973) Spanish cellist, conductor, composer, and pianist. Starting his career in Barcelona cafés, Casals performed as a soloist throughout Europe from the late 1890s, and from 1901, when he toured the USA, was regarded as the world's greatest cellist. Forming a notable trio with the pianist Alfred Cortot (1877–1962) and the violinist Jacques Thibaud (1880–1953), Casals was forced to leave Spain in 1936, and refused to return after the Spanish Civil War. His compositions include the oratorio *The Manger* (1943–60).

Casanova, Giovanni Giacomo (1725–98) Italian adventurer. He is famous for his memoirs (first published in French 1828–38), describing his adventures in Europe and especially his sexual encounters.

Cascade Range A range of mountains to the east of the Coast Range on the Pacific coast of North America, running north-south from the Canadian frontier to northern California. The range, which includes Crater Lake and volcanic peaks such as Mt. St Helens, Mt. Hood, Mt. Shasta, and Mt. Adams, rises to 4,392 m (14,409 ft) at Mt. Rainier.

case-bearer moth A tiny moth of the family Coleophoridae, whose caterpillars enclose themselves in characteristically shaped cases about 6 mm (0.25 inch) long. The 400 or so species are commonest in the Northern Hemisphere. *Coleophora* species have long, narrow, fringed wings. Young larvae are leaf-miners; older ones feed on leaves or seeds from within their attached cases, which are made of hollowed-out seeds or of silk, incorporating fragments of leaves and other plant debris. One common species, introduced to the USA from Europe, eats clover and is a minor pest.

case law A legal system in which the reasoning employed by judges in reaching decisions in cases litigated before them constitutes a source of law by creating a PRECEDENT. Legal systems that operate in this way, such as those in England and Wales and the USA, are sometimes called COMMON LAW

SYSTEMS and can be distinguished from code-based or CIVIL LAW systems such as are to be found in France and Germany, in which a judge's decision as to the scope of a principle in the code is incapable, on its own, of authoritatively defining or amending the principle for the future. Nevertheless, most systems have elements of both case law and codes.

Casement, Sir Roger (David) (1864–1916) Irish nationalist. He served with the British consular service in Africa until his retirement in 1912, when he joined the Irish nationalist cause. Shortly after the outbreak of World War I, he visited Germany to seek support for an Irish uprising. He was captured on his return to Ireland before the Easter Rising of 1916, and subsequently hanged by the British for treason. His diaries, which reveal his homosexuality, were not released for publication until 1959.

Casey, Richard Gardiner, Baron (1890–1976) Australian diplomat and statesman. He was a United Australia Party Member of the House of Representatives (1931–40). He was Australia's first Minister to the USA (1940–42), joined the British war cabinet (1942–43), and was governor of Bengal (1944–46). On returning to the House of Representatives (1949–60), representing the Liberal Party, Casey held various portfolios including that of External Affairs (1951–60). He was governor-general of the Commonwealth of Australia (1965–69).

Cash, Johnny (1932–) US country music singer and songwriter. The poverty and hardship of his childhood are reflected in his early songs, which tend to feature outlaws, prisoners, or characters who are unlucky in life or love. He formed a brief association with Bob Dylan in the 1960s; during the 1970s he turned increasingly to gospel music. His most famous hits include 'I Walk the Line' (1956) and 'A Boy Named Sue' (1969).

cash crop See SHIFTING CULTIVATION.

cashew nut A small, evergreen tree of the family Anacardiaceae, *Anacardium occidentale*, which is related to the mango and native to Central and South America. It is now widely cultivated throughout the world, often growing on soils too poor to support other crops. The 'nuts', which are really SEEDS, are unusual in that they are not formed within the fruit, which is called the cashew apple, but are attached to it at one end and hang beneath it. They contain up to 50 per cent oil and 20 per cent protein.

cash register An electromechanical or electronic device for recording retail financial transactions. Cash registers evolved directly from mechanical CALCULATORS and proved to be a major business innovation. The modern cash register is known as a point-of-sale terminal.

Casimir III (known as **Casimir the Great**) (1310–70) King of Poland 1333–70. He consolidated the achievements of his predecessor, Wladyslaw I, reorganizing the country's administration, codifying the law, and acquiring territory through diplomacy. Links with Lithuania, Hesse, Silesia, Brandenburg, and the Holy Roman Empire were forged through marriage. He successfully fought against RUSSIA, the TEUTONIC KNIGHTS, and the BOHEMIANS.

Caspian Sea A land-locked salt lake enclosed by Russia, Kazakhstan, Turkmenistan, Azerbaijan, and Iran. It is the world's largest body of inland water with an area of *c.*370,992 sq km (143,524 sq miles). Its surface lies 28 m (92 ft) below sea-level.

Cassandra In Greek mythology, a daughter of Priam, king of Troy, and his wife Hecuba. Apollo gave her the gift of prophecy, but because she rejected his love, he ordained that none of her predictions would be believed. Thus her warning to the Trojans about the Wooden Horse of the Greeks was disregarded. After the sack of Troy, Cassandra was taken to Greece as the prize of Agamemnon and was murdered by his wife, Clytemnestra.

Cassatt, Mary (1844–1926) US painter. Cassatt worked mostly in Paris and was persuaded to exhibit with the impressionists by Degas. She was noted for her draughtsmanship, etching, and drypoint studies. Her paintings, including *Lady at the Tea Table* (1885), display a close interest in everyday subject matter.

cassava A woody shrub of the genus *Manihot*, belonging to the SPURGE family, Euphorbiaceae, and growing to 3 m (9.75 feet) in height. It is also known as manioc. It originated in South and Central America, but in the last few hundred years it has been introduced throughout the tropics. The large, starchy, underground tubers of cassava contain a certain amount of cyanide compounds. The bitter types, which are the most nutritious, are cut into pieces, boiled, and squeezed to expel the poisonous sap. The bitterness of all parts of the plant makes it virtually immune to locust attack and even to the ravages of baboons. Apart from its use as a food crop in the tropics, cassava starch enters world trade as tapioca, a form that can be stored and exported after heat treatment.

Cassegrain telescope See TELESCOPE.

Cassian Way (Latin **Via Cassia**) An ancient Roman road linking Florence with Rome.

Cassini family The four generations of Cassini who managed and directed the Paris Observatory from its inception in 1667 until around 1793. **Giovanni Domenico Cassini** (1625–1712) (also known as Cassini I) was an Italian-born French astronomer and a precise and systematic observer. He used long-focus telescopes to observe the surfaces of planets and made accurate measurements of the spin periods of Jupiter and Mars. He discovered four satellites of Saturn and the division in SATURN's rings that is named after him. He was the first to maintain records of the zodiacal light. His son **Jacques Cassini** (1677–1756) (Cassini II) managed the observatory from 1710. Under his directorship the observatory began measuring the shape of the Earth, and the determination of the arc of the meridian between Dunkirk and Perpignan was completed in 1718. **César-François Cassini** (1714–84) (Cassini III) continued the work of his father. He was also a cartographer and was instrumental in producing the first modern map of France. **Jacques-Dominique Cassini** (1748–1845) (Cassini IV) directed the observatory from 1784 but had to abandon his plans of restoring and equipping it after his imprisonment during the French Revolution.

Cassino A town of Latium in west-central Italy, in the province of Frosinone 130 km (80 miles) south-east of Rome; pop. (1990) 34,590. An important centre of learning in the Middle Ages, the Benedictine abbey of Monte Cassino on a hill above the town was founded by St Benedict of Nursia in 529. Cassino was rebuilt after being completely destroyed during World War II. See also MONTE CASSINO.

Cassiopeia A CONSTELLATION of the northern sky, one of the forty-eight constellations known to the ancient Greeks. It represents Queen Cassiopeia, the vain wife of King Cepheus of Ethiopia; she is depicted sitting in a chair, circling the north celestial pole. The five brightest stars of the constellation form a distinctive W-shape. The centre star of the W, called Gamma Cassiopeiae, is an unpredictable variable known as a shell star. In 1572 the Danish astronomer Tycho Brahe observed a brilliant supernova in Cassiopeia, now known as Tycho's star. Also in Cassiopeia lies the strong radio source Cassiopeia A, the remains of a supernova that erupted around the year 1600 but which went unnoticed at the time.

cassiterite (or **tin oxide**, SnO_2) An ore of TIN. It is a hard and dense but brittle mineral, very dark brown or black in colour. Many of the deposits are alluvial and are found in river and marine sands, although it originally formed in veins associated with igneous rocks.

Cassius (Longinus), Gaius (died 42 BC) Roman general. With Brutus he was one of the leaders of the conspiracy in 44 BC to assassinate Julius Caesar. He and Brutus were defeated by Caesar's supporters Antony and Octavian at the battle of Philippi in 42 BC, in the course of which he committed suicide.

Casson, Sir Hugh (Maxwell) (1910–) British architect. Casson was professor of Interior Design at the Royal College of Art (1953–75). His directorship of architecture at the Festival of Britain (1948–51) ensured the site's success as a piece of organized townscape. Casson was president of the Royal Academy from 1976 to 1984.

cassowary A large, heavily built, flightless bird of the genus *Casuarius*, which occurs in New Guinea and Australia. Large individuals stand 1.5 m (5 feet) high. They are mainly covered with hair-like greyish-black plumage. The neck and head, which are featherless, are often coloured bright blue or red. They live mainly in forest and can run swiftly through the undergrowth. The head has a heavy shield, or casque, which may protect it while the bird is running. The female lays three to eight eggs in a scrape on the ground and leaves the male to incubate them. They eat mainly fruits and berries.

castanets Wooden clappers, a pair for each hand, characteristic of Spanish music, and of orchestral music with a Spanish flavour, where traditionally they are made of chestnut wood or *castaña*. The left-hand pair is lower pitched than the right. The two shells of each pair are linked together with cord, tightened round the thumb so that the shells are sprung apart and can be struck together with the fingers. In orchestras, one pair of shells is attached to a handle, with a plate between them, which makes playing easier.

caste system A means of stratification, that groups people according to specific social rank. Variations of caste are found in all Indian religious communities, not only Hindu but also Jain, Buddhist, Muslim, and Christian communities. All stem from the tripartite social division of the Aryans, who invaded northern India *c.*1500 BC. However, only Hindus developed theological and legal rationales for caste. The three divisions or *varnas* consisted of Brahmins (priests and professionals), Kshatriyas (rulers, warriors, and administrators), and Vaishyas (farmers and merchants). Later a fourth *varna* developed, the Shūdras (artisans and labourers). Each *varna* classifies many *jātis* or castes, traditionally determined by occupation, but often linked through geographical locality, marriage, or dietary customs. One of the preoccupations of the caste system is the notion of purity and pollution: varying degrees of defilement result from a *jāti*'s occupation, dietary habits, or customs. Those who carried out the most polluting tasks became known as 'untouchables'. Untouchables are outside the *varna* system, although still part of the caste system. Mahatma Gandhi, desiring to improve their status, renamed them *Harijans*, 'Children of God', a title subsequently rejected by them in favour of the name *dalit*, 'depressed'. They remain the most oppressed members of Indian society, despite legislation to reserve government jobs, education places, and parliamentary seats for them. Despite the attempts of Gandhi and subsequent leaders to abolish the caste system, discrimination on the basis of caste persists.

Castile The central plateau of the Iberian peninsula, a former Spanish kingdom. Castile became an independent Spanish kingdom in the 10th century and, with Aragon to the east, dominated the Spanish scene during the Middle Ages. The marriage of Isabella of Castile to Ferdinand of Aragon in 1469 effectively unified Spain into a single country.

Castilian (Spanish **Castellano**) The language of Castile which is the standard spoken and literary Spanish.

Castilla, Ramón (1797–1867) Peruvian statesman. As President (1845–51, 1855–62), he encouraged railway development and telegraphic communication, and supported the commercial use of the guano (the nitrogen-rich droppings of fish-eating seabirds) as a fertilizer. He developed the nitrate industries by establishing government monopolies and leasing them to private individuals. He abolished slavery, and freed the Peruvian Indian from tribute payments.

casting A process for making objects, in which molten material is poured into a mould, where it hardens. Casting is used both industrially, as a method of manufacturing objects, and by artists. A mould made from a statue or similar object can be used to reproduce the original in a material, such as BRONZE or plaster of Paris that can be shaped into the mould. Casting may be used to make a copy of a finished work or to create the permanent version of a work that the sculptor has modelled in some fragile material such as clay.

castle A fortified building for the defence of a town or district, doubling as the private residence of a BARON in the Middle Ages. Although also called 'castles', Celtic hill-forts, Roman camps, and Saxon burhs were designed to provide refuge for whole populations; archaeological evidence suggests that in England fortified private residences date from the 9th century. The 'motte and bailey' design of the 11th century comprised a palisaded 'motte' (a steep-sided earthen mound) and a 'bailey' (an enclosure or courtyard) separated from the motte by a ditch. Both were surrounded by a second ditch. Initially timber-built, and often prefabricated for rapid assembly, many were later rebuilt in stone. Design modifications in the 12th century included stone tower keeps to replace the motte. The keep (the rounded form was called a shell keep) combined strong defence with domestic quarters. The need to extend these quarters meant that the courtyard had to be protected by a line of towers joined by 'curtain' walls. In the 12th century the concentric castle (one ring of defences enclosing another) was developed from the model of the castles built by the Crusaders, who themselves had copied the Saracens. At the end of the 13th century, EDWARD I of England, following a policy of subduing north Wales, built a series of castles, including those at Caernarvon, Conway, Harlech, and Beaumaris. Design improvements saw the further development of rounded towers, which were more difficult to undermine, machicolations, which enabled objects to be dropped or poured on the besiegers, massive gatehouses, and refinements to the battlements, or crenellations, along the walls. The invention of cannon had made castles obsolete for defensive purposes by the middle of the 16th century.

Castle, Barbara (Anne), Baroness Castle of Blackburn (1911–) British Labour politician. Castle became Labour MP for Blackburn in 1945 and remained in the House for 34 years. She held a number of government posts, including chairman of the Labour Party (1958–59) and, controversially, Minister of Transport (1965–68), introducing the 70 m.p.h. speed limit and the breathalyser test. Castle was elected to the European Parliament in 1979, and was created a life peer in 1990.

Castlereagh, Robert Stewart, Viscount (1769–1822) British Tory statesman. Born in Ulster, he began his political career as a Whig in the Irish Parliament and continued to concern himself with Irish affairs after becoming a Tory in 1795. He became Foreign Secretary in 1812, and in this capacity represented his country at the Congress of Vienna (1814–15), playing a central part in reviving the Quadruple Alliance (whereby Britain, Russia, Austria, and Prussia united to defeat Napoleon). He committed suicide, apparently as a result of mental strain owing to pressure of work.

Castner–Kellner cell An apparatus for producing SODIUM HYDROXIDE. A direct electric current is passed through brine (salt solution), using a mercury cathode (negative electrode) and a graphite anode (positive electrode). CHLORINE is released at the anode, while SODIUM is released at the cathode and combines with the mercury to form an amalgam. This amalgam is treated with water to produce sodium hydroxide solution. The by-products of the process (chlorine and hydrogen) are also valuable, and make the process economically viable.

Castor A second-magnitude MULTIPLE STAR in the constellation of Gemini, and also known as Alpha Geminorum. Two hot DWARF STARS move in a 500-year orbit, and each component is a spectroscopic BINARY STAR. A third, distant member of the system is the ninth-magnitude ECLIPSING BINARY YY Geminorum, in which both components are FLARE STARS. Thus Castor is a system of six stars. Castor's distance is 15 parsecs, and its combined luminosity is about fifty times that of the Sun.

Castor and Pollux In Greek mythology, twin sons of Zeus. Their mother was Leda, queen of Sparta; Zeus came to her in the form of a swan, and from their union, the twins were hatched from an egg. Great warriors and inseparable companions, Castor and Pollux were among the Argonauts. After their deaths they became the constellation Gemini.

castor bean tick See SHEEP-TICK.

castrato A type of male soprano or contralto voice achieved by castration before puberty, in great demand in Italy for opera in the 17th and 18th centuries. Castrati parts were written as late as 1824 (Meyerbeer's *The Crusader in Egypt*) and the voice survived in the Vatican Chapel well into the late 19th century. The practice of castration for this purpose was finally banned by the Vatican in 1903.

Castries A seaport in the Caribbean, capital of the island of St Lucia; pop. (1994) 14,055. Built on the shores of an almost-landlocked harbour and named in 1758 after Marechal de Castries, a Minister of the French Navy and the Colonies, its strategic position at the centre of the Eastern Caribbean has attracted shipping.

Castro, Fidel (1927–) Cuban statesman, Prime Minister 1959–76 and President since 1976. He forced President Batista from power in 1959, setting up a Communist regime which he has led ever since. The abortive US-backed invasion attempt by Cuban exiles at the Bay of Pigs in 1961 boosted his popularity, as did his successful survival of the Cuban Missile Crisis of 1962. He became leader of the Non-Aligned Movement in 1979, in spite of Cuba's reliance on the USSR for economic aid. Since the collapse of the Soviet bloc Castro has strictly maintained Communism in Cuba.

casuarina Any one of about 45 species of very unusual tree of the genus *Casuarina*, confined to south-east Asia and to Australia, where they are known as she-oaks. Their slender green branchlets have tiny scale leaves, thereby resembling HORSETAILS. They are adapted to survive in very dry, hot conditions, and the shoots have been used as emergency fodder for animals. One species, *C. equisetifolia*, is common on sea-shores and makes good firewood. The wood of many species is very hard.

cat A CARNIVORE belonging to the family Felidae, which includes pumas, ocelots, leopards, lions, tigers, and jaguars. The cats are the most specialized of the carnivores, and are well adapted to a hunting life. The ears, eyes, whiskers, and nose are well developed as organs of sense. The teeth are of the specialized carnivore pattern; even some of the rear molars (the carnassials) have developed into cutting blades.

In order to pursue prey, cats make use of scent, sight, and even such obscure clues as footmarks. They are masters in the art of leaping; from a running, walking, standing, or sitting position they can catapult into the air to hit their prey with stunning impact. They land with jaws wide open, teeth bared, and claws extended ready to sink into the throat and flesh of their prey. Cats have the sharpest claws of all mammals, claws that can be withdrawn into a sheath by all species except the cheetah. In this way, the claws are protected and the cat can move silently on its pads. Some of the patterns of behaviour associated with hunting may be observed in the play of kittens.

The domestic cat is believed to be descended from interbreeding European WILD CATS (*Felis sylvestris sylvestris*) and North African wild cats (*F. s. libyca*). Many breeds of the domestic cat have been developed with long or short coats.

catabolism See METABOLISM.

cataclysmic variable A VARIABLE STAR that undergoes outbursts when it may brighten by several magnitudes. Most such objects are very close BINARY STARS in which a cool star fills its Roche lobe and loses material in the direction of a WHITE DWARF companion. The mass may form a bright ACCRETION DISC or, if the white dwarf has a strong magnetic field, as in the AM HERCULIS STARS, may land directly on one or both of its magnetic poles. In NOVAE, the outbursts are due to the nuclear fusion of hydrogen on the surface of the white dwarf. In **dwarf novae**, which may have outbursts every few weeks, the outbursts are the release of gravitational energy in the form of light and heat, triggered by an instability in the accretion disc. Binary stars with a similar structure may be included among the cataclysmic variables even though no outbursts have been detected; they resemble ex-novae and are called **nova-like variables**. Some authorities also include the symbiotic stars and SUPERNOVAE as cataclysmic variables.

catacomb An underground burial gallery, especially in early Christian Rome. Catacombs were

Cats (1) Tiger. (2) Leopard. (3) Lion. (4) European wild cat. (5) Puma. (6) Cheetah. These species are members of the cat family, Felidae. They range in size from the tiger, the largest of all the felids, which can attain a length (including the metre-long tail) of 3.8 m (12.5 ft), to the wild cat, 63 cm (2 ft) long, including the 35-cm (14-inch) tail. Like the domestic cat, all these species except the cheetah have retractile claws.

named after the best known example, St Sebastian in the Hollow (*ad Catacumbas*). Forty such subterranean chambers are known in Rome, tunnelled through soft rock outside the ancient city boundaries. The anniversaries of MARTYRS were celebrated at the graves. Looted by barbarians and subject to collapse, they were virtually forgotten until their accidental rediscovery in the 16th century. Similar ones are also found as far apart as Salzburg and Malta.

Catalan A Romance language most closely related to Provençal. Traditionally it is the language of Catalonia, but it is also spoken in Andorra, the Balearic Islands, and some parts of southern France.

Catalaunian Fields (or **Plains**) The site of a major battle in 451 AD reputedly near Châlons-sur-Marne in France, but placed by some nearer Troyes. The Roman general Aetius with a combined force of Romans, Goths, and Burgundians defeated ATTILA the Hun, forcing his retreat from Gaul. He was expelled from Italy the following year.

Catalonia (Catalan **Catalunya**; Spanish **Cataluña**) An autonomous region of north-east Spain, comprising the provinces of Barcelona, Gerona, Lérida, and Tarragona; area 31,932 sq km (12,334 sq miles); pop. (1991) 6,059,450; capital, Barcelona. The region includes the Mediterranean resorts of the Costa Brava.

catalpa (or **Indian bean tree**) A deciduous tree legume of the genus *Catalpa*, native to eastern Asia, North America, and the Caribbean. All 11 species have very large leaves and long bean-like pods, some up to 45 cm (18 inches) long, containing winged seeds. Most widely planted as an ornamental is *C. bignonioides* of the south-eastern USA: its timber is valued as well as its showy, scented white flowers.

catalyst A substance that changes the rate of a chemical reaction without undergoing permanent chemical change itself. Positive catalysts increase the rate of reaction; negative catalysts (inhibitors) decrease the rate of reaction. Catalysts make it possible for the reaction to proceed by an alternative pathway with a different ACTIVATION ENERGY, such as at lower temperatures or at lower pressures. Catalysts play an important part in many biochemical and industrial reactions. ENZYMES are biochemical catalysts that enable specific reactions to take place.

catalytic converter A device used to promote combustion of pollutant gases in a motor-car exhaust. One type of converter comprises an insulated chamber containing a bed of metal oxide CATALYST pellets. Hot exhaust gases are passed through the chamber, and carbon monoxide and hydrocarbon residues in the exhaust are further oxidized. Three-way converters, using rhodium catalysts, are also used – these are capable of reducing the nitrogen oxides by up to 62 per cent, while the CO and hydrocarbons are reduced by 85 per cent.

catamaran Most commonly, a twin-hulled craft, first developed by the Polynesians but now also a type of YACHT. Catamarans may also be rafts of two or more logs lashed together, used as fishing craft in South India, as well as the rectangular float used in dockyards to hold a ship clear of quayside obstructions.

catapult A forked stick (or piece of metal) with elastic for shooting small stones, or a large military machine worked by levers and ropes, for firing bolts, spears, stones, or gunpowder projectiles. Catapult-type devices were used as grenade launchers in World War I. Devices known as catapults are used to assist the launch of aircraft from AIRCRAFT CARRIERS, using hydraulic pressure, tension, or other force.

cataract (of the eye) A restriction to vision brought about by loss of translucency of the eye lens. There are many causes but the most common is an age-related change in one of the special lens proteins. Clear sight may be restored by removal of the lens. A strong spectacle lens, or plastic contact lens, is then required to achieve focus; alternatively, a plastic lens can be implanted in the eye to replace the natural lens.

cataract See WATERFALL.

catastrophe theory The mathematical description of dynamical systems that undergo discontinuities, that is abrupt jumps or breaks in which a continuous evolution or development in one PARAMETER gives rise to a discontinuous effect, such as a sudden change. The theory has application in pure mathematics and in a surprisingly dissimilar array of applications in the real world. These include problems in physics (for example, phase transition), in engineering (the buckling and failure of beams and bridges), in cell biology, and in the social sciences (the instability leading to prison riots or the instability of a commodities market).

A quite unrelated theory of catastrophes attempts to describe the effect of violent astronomical events on the biosphere of the Earth. For example, the impact of an enormous meteorite, either an APOLLO-AMOR OBJECT or a comet, has been proposed as the cause of the extinction of many species, including all the dinosaurs, at the end of the Cretaceous geological period.

catbird A member of three separate groups of birds. The first comprises two species of mocking bird: the catbird, *Dumetella carolinensis*, and the black catbird, *Melanoptila glabrirostris*, both of which occur in Central and North America. The second group is that of the babblers, with the Abyssinian catbird, *Parophasma galinieri*, found in high mountains in Ethiopia. The third group is that of the bower-birds from Australia and New Guinea, which has three species of *Ailuroedus* called catbirds, and one species of *Scenopoectes*.

catch See CANON.

catchment area A drainage basin or area from which water flows into a river. The term is also used to describe an area served by a business or public facility such as a school or a hospital.

catena A related sequence of soils that occur in a regular succession as a result of changing conditions down a hillside. Even where the underlying bedrock is the same, environmental factors change dramatically as one goes down a hill. On top of the hill, soils are relatively stable and well drained. zonal soils are typically found here. On steep upper slopes, where erosion is pronounced, soil material is stripped away and soils tend to be shallow. Eroded material is carried downslope and redeposited to form thick soils which are comparatively young. At the base of the slope drainage is poor, and waterlogged or peaty soils form.

catenary The curve assumed by a flexible, inelastic chain when suspended freely from two points, and allowed to hang under the influence of gravity on its own weight. The wires that hold up the overhead current-carrying conductor of an electric tramway or railway are also called catenaries.

caterpillar The larva of a butterfly, moth, or sawfly. In shape, caterpillars resemble segmented worms but possess several pairs of legs, and strong jaws. They are adapted to a life of eating, and store food in preparation for the development of the adult insect. Some moths do not feed as adults and rely entirely upon the foodstores laid down as fat by the caterpillar.

The caterpillar's skin is covered with hairs, sometimes long and sometimes so short that the body looks bare. Moulting occurs at regular intervals, usually four to six times in the life of the caterpillar, allowing room for growth. Most caterpillars move slowly, and rely on PROTECTIVE COLORATION for defence. Some have unpleasant scent organs or spray poison; others carry large horns or spines, while others live in a protective casing.

caterpillar track A flexible belt of steel plates running around the wheels of a vehicle, used to give increased traction and to spread the weight of the vehicle over a larger area. Caterpillar tracks were originally evolved for the heavy agricultural tractor, but are now used principally for heavy earth-moving equipment, bulldozers, and tanks.

catfish A fish that typically possesses several whisker-like barbels around the mouth. Some 2,000 species are known; most of them are freshwater fishes, but about 50, in two families, are sea fishes. They are widely distributed in all tropical and temperate continents. Most of them have scaleless skins but many South American species have a covering of hard, large scales. Catfishes range in size from the South American candiru, *Vandellia cirrhosa*, only 2.5 cm (1 inch) long, to the European wels, *Silurus glanis*, which is 3 m (10 feet) long.

Cathar (from Greek *katharos*, 'pure') A member of a medieval sect seeking to achieve a life of great purity. Cathars believed in a 'dualist' heresy. Their basic belief was that if God, being wholly good, had alone created the world it would have been impossible for evil to exist within it, and that another, diabolical, creative force must have taken part. They held that the material world and all within it were irredeemably evil. The heresy originated in Bulgaria and appeared in western Europe in the 1140s. In southern France the followers of this Christian heresy were called ALBIGENSIANS.

Cathay (or **Khitai**) The name by which China was known to medieval Europe, the Khitans being a people of Manchu race, to the north-east of China, who established an empire over northern China during the two centuries ending in 1123.

Cather, Willa (Sibert) (1873–1947) US novelist and short-story writer. She used her knowledge of the lives of the immigrant families of the Midwest as the basis for a series of novels, beginning with *O Pioneers!* (1913), *The Song of the Lark* (1915), *My Ántonia* (1918), and *One of Ours* (1922). Later novels like *Death Comes for the Archbishop* (1927) and *Shadows on the Rock* (1931) reflect her interest in history and religion.

Catherine I (*c*.1684–1727) Empress of Russia 1725–27. She was a Lithuanian servant girl who was first the mistress and then the second wife of PETER I. On his death she was proclaimed ruler with the support of her husband's favourite, Menshikov, and the guards regiments. Menshikov became the effective head of government, working through the newly established Privy Council, but fell from power on Catherine's death. Her daughter ELIZABETH became empress (1741–62).

Catherine II (known as **Catherine the Great**) (1729–96) Empress of Russia 1762–96. A German princess, she was made empress following a plot which deposed her husband Peter III (1728–62). Her attempted social and political reforms were impeded by entrenched aristocratic interests, and in later years her reign became increasingly conservative. Under Catherine Russia played an important part in European affairs, participating in the three partitions of Poland and forming close links with Prussia and Austria, while to the south and east further territorial advances were made at the expense of the Turks and Tartars.

Catherine, St (known as **St Catherine of Alexandria**) (died *c*.307) Early Christian martyr. Traditionally, she opposed the persecution of Christians under the Roman emperor Maxentius, debated with 50 scholars sent to undermine her position, and refused to recant or to marry the emperor. She is then said to have been tortured on a spiked wheel and beheaded when it broke. The Catherine wheel subsequently became her emblem. Feast day, 25 November.

Catherine de' Medici (1519–89) Queen of France. The wife of Henry II of France, Catherine ruled as regent 1560–74 during the minority reigns of their three sons, Francis II (reigned 1559–60), Charles IX (reigned 1560–74), and Henry III (reigned 1574–89). She proved unable or unwilling to control the confused situation during the French Wars of Religion, and it was on her instigation that Huguenots were killed in the Massacre of St Bartholomew (1572).

Catherine of Aragon (1485–1536) Spanish princess, the first wife of HENRY VIII of England to whom she was married in 1509. She bore him a daughter, the future MARY I, but no male heir survived; the importance of the Spanish alliance diminished, and by 1527 Henry, infatuated with Anne BOLEYN, sought a papal annulment, claiming that Catherine's marriage in 1501 to his elder brother Arthur rendered his own marriage invalid. The pope was uncooperative, and CRANMER annulled the king's marriage in 1533. Thereafter Catherine lived in seclusion in England.

Catherine of Braganza (1638–1705) Portuguese princess and Queen consort of Charles II of England, whom she married in 1662, bringing Tangier and Bombay as part of her dowry. The marriage was childless and she had to tolerate the king's infidelities. As a Roman Catholic, she was unpopular and there were attempts to implicate her in the POPISH PLOT. In 1692, as a widow, she returned to Portugal, where she died.

catheter A tube of small diameter that is temporarily or permanently inserted into a body cavity or vessel to introduce or remove fluid. Catheters to drain the bladder, introduced into the urethra, have been known since ancient times. Originally made of metal, especially silver, the rigid catheter was largely replaced during this century by flexible rubber designs and, more recently, by plastic catheters. New materials have greatly expanded the use of catheters, allowing fine-bore tubes to be threaded into the vascular system for diagnostic or therapeutic purposes. Since the 1970s OPTICAL-FIBRE instruments have facilitated such processes as cardiac catheterization, in which catheters inserted into the arms or legs are manipulated into the heart chambers.

cathode The negative electrode of a THERMIONIC VALVE, CATHODE-RAY TUBE, BATTERY, or electrolytic cell. The cathode is the electrode by which electrons enter a system: they are emitted by, or flow from, the cathode. In ELECTROLYSIS cations gain electrons at the cathode.

cathode ray See ELECTRONS.

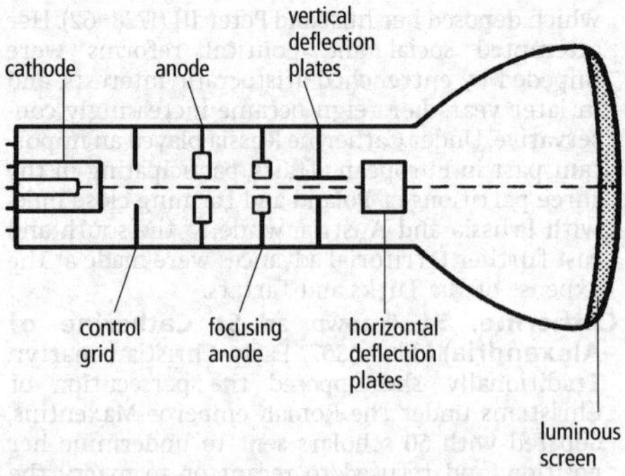

Cathode-ray tube Electrons emitted by the cathode are focused into a beam by the anode; after passing through vertical and horizontal deflection plates the beam causes a spot of light to appear where it strikes the luminous screen. As the beam moves across the screen a full moving display is created.

cathode-ray tube (CRT) A funnel-shaped electron tube that converts electrical signals into a visible form that can be displayed on a screen. CRTs are used widely in TELEVISION RECEIVERS, visual display units (monitors) for computers, and in displays for oscilloscopes. They consist primarily of an electron beam traversing the length of the tube, the intensity of which varies according to an input signal containing the visual information to be displayed. Acting on this electron beam are several sets of electrodes and magnetic coils, which together confine and direct the beam and enable it to be moved back and forth across (scan) a phosphor coat on the back of the screen inside the tube. When the electron beam strikes the phosphor, a spot of light is produced, the intensity of which is proportional to the intensity of the beam. As the beam scans the screen, a full screen display is formed.

Catholic Church See ROMAN CATHOLIC CHURCH.

Catholic emancipation The granting of full political and civil liberties to British and Irish Roman Catholics. Partial religious toleration had been achieved in Britain by the late 17th century, but the TEST ACTS limited holders of public office to communicant Anglicans and placed additional disabilities on members of other churches. Until 1745 the JACOBITE threat seemed to justify continued discrimination against Roman Catholics, and fears of Catholic emancipation led to the GORDON RIOTS in 1780. By the late 18th century many reformists were agitating for total religious freedom. In Ireland, where a majority were Catholics, concessions were made from 1778 onwards, culminating in the Relief Act of 1793, passed by the Irish Parliament and giving liberty of religious practice and the right to vote in elections, but not to sit in Parliament or hold public office. William PITT had become convinced of the need for full Catholic emancipation by 1798, and promises were made to the Irish Parliament when it agreed to the Act of UNION in 1800. Protestant landlords as well as George III resisted emancipation and Pitt resigned. Daniel O'CONNELL took up the cause for emancipation and founded the Catholic Association in 1823, dedicated to peaceful agitation. In 1828 O'Connell won a parliamentary election for County Clare, but as a Catholic could not take his seat. The Prime Minister, WELLINGTON, reluctantly introduced a Relief Bill to avoid civil war. The 1829 Act removed most civil restrictions; the only one to survive to the present is that no British monarch may be a Roman Catholic.

cation A positively charged ion, so called because it is attracted by the cathode (negative electrode) in ELECTROLYSIS. Cations are formed from neutral atoms or molecules by the loss of one or more electrons. For example, the sodium atom loses one electron to form the sodium cation, Na^+.

catkin A stalkless, simple flower, making up spikes, which are separated by bracts; typically the inflorescences of trees such as birches, willows, and poplars. Most catkins have no scent and are wind-pollinated, but willow catkins are insect-pollinated and produce nectar.

Cato, **Marcus Porcius** (known as **Cato the Elder**) (*c*.234–149 BC) Roman statesman. As consul in 195 Cato suppressed revolt in former Carthaginian Spain with severity; as censor in 184 he was equally severe against private extravagance. Cato prosecuted SCIPIO for corruption.

Cato, Marcus Porcius (known as **Cato the Younger**) (95–46 BC) The great-grandson of Cato the Elder. He was known posthumously as 'Uticensis' after the place of his death. A conservative republican, he long opposed POMPEY, but finally sided with him against Julius CAESAR. He committed suicide at Utica in northern Africa after Caesar's victory at Thapsus rather than seek Caesar's pardon.

Cato Street Conspiracy (1820) A plot to assassinate members of the British government. Under the leadership of Arthur Thistlewood, a revolutionary extremist, the conspirators planned to murder Lord CASTLEREAGH and other ministers while they were at dinner, as a prelude to a general uprising. However, government spies revealed the plot and possibly also provoked the conspirators to take action. They were arrested at a house in Cato Street, off the Edgware Road, in London. Convicted of high treason, Thistlewood and four others were executed, the rest being sentenced to transportation for life.

CAT scan See COMPUTERIZED TOMOGRAPHY.

cat's-eye A stud embedded in the road that acts as a guide to drivers in bad light by reflecting back the vehicle's headlights. Glass prisms are set in a rubber moulding mounted in a box which projects slightly above the road surface, usually in the centre of the road. When a vehicle drives over a cat's-eye, the prisms are pressed down into the rubber moulding, thus wiping off any dirt. They were invented in 1934 by Percy Shaw, a US inventor.

Catskill Mountains A northern arm of the Appalachian Mountains in south-east New York State, USA, to the west of the Hudson River. Rising to 1,282 m (4,206 ft) at Mt. Slide, the wooded rolling mountains of this dissected plateau are a popular resort area.

cattle RUMINANT mammals adapted to feed on grasses by having the teeth of the upper jaw fused into a pad. Cattle lack incisor or canine teeth, and those of the lower jaw work with a grinding motion against the pad of the upper jaw. All cattle have cloven hooves; that is, they are even-toed, and both sexes have horns, which are never shed. They are one of the most economically important groups in the animal kingdom. The subfamily Bovinae has 12 species, which include bison, buffalo, and yak, as well as all the domesticated breeds. This subfamily includes the genus *Bos*, which comprises five species of so-called 'true' cattle, such as the yak, gaur, and the cow of domestication.

Domesticated cattle, *Bos primigenius*, are derived from the now extinct AUROCHS, and have been part of agricultural life for thousands of years. Some breeds have become draught animals; others provide humans with milk, used to make cream and cheese, as well as with meat, hide, horn, and bone. Females mature at 18 months to three years and are referred to as heifers until the first calf is born, after which they are called cows. A cow will continue to breed for more than ten years; she will normally produce milk only when her calf is small, but lactation can be prolonged by showing her calf to her and by the act of milking. Many cows can produce over 9,000 litres (2,000 US gallons) per year. Much food is needed to maintain this output: a cow will eat about 70 kg (150 pounds) of grass in a day, eight hours being spent eating and the remaining 16 hours resting and chewing the cud.

cattle farming The rearing of cattle for milk or beef, or as draught animals. Most modern cattle breeds are specialized for beef or DAIRY FARMING, although there are some dual- or general-purpose breeds. Most breeds of domestic cattle are derived from those domesticated in the Near East around 8000 BC (see AGRICULTURE), but the water-buffalo is kept for draught purposes, for milk, and for beef in warmer areas of Asia and the Middle East, and in parts of Europe. The yak is farmed in parts of Asia. See also LIVESTOCK FARMING.

Catullus, Gaius Valerius (*c.*84–*c.*54 BC) Roman poet. His one book of verse contains poems in a variety of metres on a range of subjects; he is best known for his poems to a married woman addressed as 'Lesbia', although he also wrote a number of longer mythological pieces. His importance for later Latin poetry lies both in the impetus he gave to the development of the love-elegy and in his cultivation of an Alexandrian refinement and learning.

Caucasian languages Around 40 languages spoken by 5 million people in the Caucasus area between the Black Sea and the Caspian Sea. There are two distinct groups, Northern Caucasian and Southern Caucasian, and though they are distantly related, it is doubtful whether they are descended from the same parent language. Southern Caucasian (or Kartvelian) includes Georgian, the most important Caucasian language. Georgian has nearly 3.5 million speakers, and is the official language of Georgia. The Northern family has two sub-groups, North-West (Abkhazo-Adyghian) and North-East (Nakho-Dagestanian). These two groups are rather different from each other grammatically. The Caucasian languages were influenced by Arabic and Persian in the past; in recent years, the main source of new vocabulary has been Russian.

Caucasoids Fair-skinned 'European' people, named after the Caucasus Mountains between the Black and Caspian seas. They occupy Europe, Africa as far south as the Sahara, the Middle East, and the Indian subcontinent; in the past five centuries they have spread worldwide. In parts of Central Asia they were replaced in historic times by MONGOLOIDS. There was always admixture with, and incomplete differentiation from, neighbouring races, making a coherent story of the origin and dispersal of Caucasoids difficult.

Caucasus (or **Caucasia**) A region of south-east Europe in Russia, Georgia, Armenia, and Azerbaijan, lying between the Black Sea and the Caspian Sea. It is dominated by the mountain ranges of the **Great Caucasus** (Russian **Bolshoy Kavkaz**) and **Little Caucasus** (Russian **Maly Kavkaz**). Mt. Elbrus in the Great Caucasus (5,642 m, 18,480 ft) is the highest mountain in Europe.

Cauchy, Augustin Louis, Baron (1789–1857) French mathematician. His numerous textbooks and writings introduced new standards of criticism and rigorous argument in calculus, from which grew the field of mathematics known as analysis. He transformed the theory of complex functions by discovering his integral theorems and introducing the calculus of residues. Cauchy also founded the modern theory of elasticity, produced fundamental new ideas about the solution of differential equations, and contributed substantially to the founding of group theory.

caudillo (Spanish, 'leader', 'hero') Military dictator in a Spanish-speaking country. In Latin American politics caudillos have tended to circumvent constitutions, and rule by military force.

cauliflower A variety of CABBAGE. It is grown for its succulent, immature flower-head, which is a large, roundish mass of white, creamy-white or green flower-buds.

causation (in philosophy) The apparently necessary connection between one event (the cause) and another (the effect). Philosophical discussions of the concept are mainly concerned with analysing what the causal relation actually is, what sort of things are linked by causation (is it objects, events, states, or processes?), and how we can know when one thing causes another (what distinguishes a genuine causal connection from an accidental correlation?). Other questions raised are whether causation is a necessary relation (could a cause operate but its effect fail to occur?), and whether causal relations have a unique temporal direction (can an effect precede its cause? Can a cause be instantaneous with its effect?). Recent developments in theoretical physics have somewhat diminished the importance of causation, though they seem to support a non-necessary, probabilistic interpretation.

caustic soda See SODIUM HYDROXIDE.

Cavafy, Constantine (Peter) (born Konstantinos Petrou Kavafis) (1863–1933) Greek poet. Cavafy's poems refer mainly to the Hellenistic and Graeco-Roman period of his native Alexandria, and are suffused with an ironic awareness of the instability of life and the limits of human knowledge. His first volume of poems was privately printed in 1904. Cavafy's posthumous reputation grew rapidly and his poetry has exerted a considerable influence on modern Greek verse.

Cavalcanti, Guido (*c.*1260–1300) Italian poet. Born in Florence, he was a close friend of DANTE, and the leader of the *dolce stil nuovo* ('sweet new style') school of poets, characterized by the dominant theme of love, the idolization of woman, by a propensity to philosophy, and by a stylistic grace and directness of diction. The passion in Cavalcanti's verse anticipates PETRARCH.

Cavalier Parliament (or **Long Parliament of the Restoration**) (1661–79) The first Parliament in Charles II's reign to be elected by royal writ. Strongly Royalist and Anglican in composition, it contained 100 members from the LONG PARLIAMENT of Charles I. Its long duration enabled the Commons to claim a large part in affairs, despite being in session for only 60 months of the 18 years. Its early years were marked by harsh laws against Roman Catholics and Protestant Dissenters. As its membership changed it became increasingly critical of royal policy.

Cavalier Poets A group of English poets in the time of Charles I, noted for their lyrical poetry and courtly behaviour. It included Thomas Carew (*c*.1594–1640), Richard LOVELACE, Sir John Suckling (1609–42), Edmund Waller (1606–87), and Robert HERRICK (who was not a courtier). Their lyrics, similar in tone and style, were distinguished by short lines, fluent and idiomatic diction, and urbane and graceful wit. Typical themes were love, honour, the transience of beauty, loyalty to the king, and gallantry.

Cavaliers (from French *chevalier*, 'horseman') The name of the Royalist party before, during, and after the English CIVIL WAR. Opponents used the word from about 1641 as a term of abuse: later it acquired a romantic aura in contrast to the image of puritanical ROUNDHEADS. The party, made up of all social classes, but dominated by the country gentry and landowners, was defined by loyalty to the crown and the Anglican Church. The Restoration brought the Royalists back to power – the Parliament of 1661–79 is called the CAVALIER PARLIAMENT.

Cavalli, (Pietro) Francesco (1602–76) Italian composer, organist, and singer. An advantageous marriage, and an appointment as one of the organists to St Mark's (for which he composed a number of motets, settings for masses, duets and trios, and a requiem), encouraged him to attempt OPERA, and he soon became one of the most distingushed operatic composers of his day. Such works as *Ormindo* (1644) and *Calisto* (1652) have figured largely in the recent revival of interest in operas of this period.

Cavan (Gaelic **Cabhán**) An inland county of the Republic of Ireland, forming part of the province of Ulster; area 1,890 sq km (730 sq miles); pop. (1991) 52,756; county town, Cavan.

cave A large hollow in a cliff or in the ground of any shape or size, generally formed by the action of water. The most spectacular examples usually develop in regions with limestone rocks. Rain, mildly acid, attacks and dissolves the soft limestone; ever-widening cracks occur and the water streams in. As a river underground it cuts a gallery in the heart of the rock and sometimes vertical shafts or pipes through which it falls to make another gallery. Most of the action of the water is by now mechanical; but some is chemical, occasionally forming STALACTITES and STALAGMITES. River systems may remain within the complex, forming lakes; and if the roofs collapse, rugged gorges will result. Caves are also made by the action of seawater against cliffs. Fissures appear at first; incoming waves compress the air within them and then retreat, releasing the compressed air with explosive force. Volcanic caves are formed by lava flows; they often include large pockets of gas, which cause holes to be left when lava has cooled.

cave bear A bear that lived in Europe and Asia during the Pleistocene Epoch, becoming extinct about 12,000 years ago. Cave bears were much larger than any living brown bear, and had long front feet and a domed forehead. Huge quantities of their bones have been found in caves, where they seem to have lived in family groups. Remains of their teeth suggest that they were herbivores.

cave-dwellers The people who first used caves as shelters. This became widespread during the Middle and Upper PALAEOLITHIC periods, when humans penetrated for the first time into the northern tundra environments in front of the icesheets of the last glaciation.

cave fish See BLIND FISH.

cave lion An extinct member of the cat family, one-third larger than any living lion, which lived in Europe during the Middle and Upper Pleistocene Epoch (370,000–10,000 years ago). Cave paintings indicate that it had a shaggy coat but no mane or tuft at the end of the tail. Cave lions died out at the end of the last Ice Age.

Cavell, Edith (Louisa) (1865–1915) British nurse. In charge of the Berkendael Medical Institute in Brussels during World War I, she helped many Allied soldiers to escape from occupied Belgium. She was arrested by the Germans and brought before a military tribunal, where she openly admitted her actions and was sentenced to death. Her execution provoked widespread condemnation and she became famous as a heroine of the Allied cause.

Cavendish, Henry (1731–1810) British scientist who in 1785 discovered the constitution of atmospheric air by passing electric sparks through it, and identifying the products formed. He also discovered 'inflammable air', now known as hydrogen, and established that it and oxygen are the constituents of water. He investigated electricity, and determined the gravitational constant in order to measure the density of the Earth.

cave painting Painting executed on cave walls and roofs during the Palaeolithic (Old Stone Age) period. Almost all the known cave paintings are in south-western France and northern Spain. The paintings are often deep in the cave systems, away from the areas used as dwellings, and may have magical or religious significance, one theory being that the animals painted there (humans rarely appear) were depicted in connection with hunting rites. The best-known cave paintings are at Altamira in Spain (discovered 1879) and at LASCAUX in France (discovered 1940), dating from about 12,000 BC to 15,000 BC.

cavitation The formation of cavities (bubbles) in moving liquids caused by rapid pressure changes. When the bubbles collapse, shock waves are produced in the liquid. In ships and boats, cavitation occurs around the PROPELLER when it is rotating at too high a speed, or when a vessel is travelling very quickly through the water. It causes vibration in the vessel, and heavy erosion of the propeller blades. Poor hull design, or a small propeller, can contribute to the occurrence of cavitation.

cavity wall A wall built as two leaves, each about 100 mm (4 inches) thick, with a continuous void, typically 50 mm (2 inches) wide, between the leaves. The void is often filled with insulation to reduce heat loss.

Cavour, Camillo Benso, Conte di (1810–61) Italian statesman. He was the driving force behind the unification of Italy under Victor Emmanuel II, king of the kingdom of Sardinia. In 1847 Cavour founded the newspaper *Il Risorgimento* to further the cause of unification. As Premier of Piedmont (1852–59; 1860–61), he obtained international support by forming an alliance with France and participating in the Crimean and Franco-Austrian wars. In 1861 he saw Victor Emmanuel crowned king of a united Italy, and became Italy's first Premier.

cavy A small South American RODENT of the family Caviidae, which contains some 16 species of which the domestic GUINEA-PIG is the most familiar example. All members of the family are very similar in appearance and habits, although they live in a variety of habitats, including open grassland, forest edges, and rocky ground. Strictly herbivorous, they are mainly nocturnal and spend the day in burrows. Other species include the mara, or Patagonian hare, *Dolichotis patagonum*; the rock cavy, *Kerodon rupestris*; and the desert cavies, *Microcavia*.

Cawdor A village near Nairn in northern Scotland. Nearby Cawdor castle, home of the Earls of Cawdor, was alleged by Shakespeare to be the scene of the murder of King Duncan by Macbeth in 1040.

Cawnpore See KANPUR.

Caxton, William (*c*.1422–91) The first English printer. Having learned the art of printing on the Continent, Caxton printed his first English text in 1474, when living in Bruges, and after returning to London in 1476 went on to produce about 80 other texts, including editions of Malory's *Le Morte d'Arthur*, Chaucer's *Canterbury Tales*, and his own translations of French romances.

Cayenne The capital and chief port of French Guiana, on an island in the Atlantic coast at the mouth of the Cayenne River; pop. (1990) 41,660. It gives its name to a type of pepper.

Cayley, Arthur (1821–95) British mathematician and barrister. Cayley wrote almost a thousand mathematical papers in algebra and geometry. These include articles on determinants, the newly developing group theory, and the algebra of matrices. He also studied dynamics and physical astronomy. The Cayley numbers, a generalization of complex numbers, are named after him.

Cayley, Sir George (1773–1857) British engineer, the father of British aeronautics. He is best known for his understanding of the principles of flight, his model gliders, and the first man-carrying glider flight in 1853. Cayley's research, inventions, and designs covered schemes and devices for land reclamation, artificial limbs, theatre architecture, railways, lifeboats, finned projectiles, optics, electricity, hot-air engines, and what was later called the Caterpillar tractor. He was a founder of the original Polytechnic Institution (1838), and was an MP for a time.

cayman A tropical relative of the ALLIGATOR, with five species found from Mexico southward through Central and South America. They have bony plates in their belly skin. The black cayman, *Melanosuchus niger*, and the broad-nosed cayman, *Caiman crocodilus*, are commercially valuable because of their pliable skins, and they have been subject to overexploitation.

Cayman Islands A British dependency, comprising an archipelago in the Caribbean Sea.

Physical. The Cayman Islands lie south of Cuba, north and west of Jamaica, the main islands being Grand Cayman, Little Cayman, and Cayman Brac. They have rocky coasts and reefs, and sharks and other tropical fish inhabit the surrounding sea.

Economy. The soil is unable to sustain agriculture on the islands, and the main economic activities are tourism and finance. The Cayman Islands are a tax haven and in 1993 there were 534 banks and 29,298 companies registered there.

History. The islands were discovered by COLUMBUS in 1503 and (with Jamaica) were recognized as British by the Treaty of Madrid in 1670. Grand Cayman was settled in 1734 but the other islands were not settled until 1833. In 1959 the Cayman Islands became a British Crown Colony, and are now largely self-governing.

Capital: George Town
Area: 264 sq km (102 sq mi)
Population: 31,930 (est. 1994)
Currency: 1 Cayman Islands dollar = 100 cents
Religions: Protestant 85.0%; Roman Catholic 5.0%
Ethnic Groups: Mixed 50.0%; Black 25.0%; White 25.0%
Languages: English (official)
International Organizations: Commonwealth

CB radio (citizens' band radio) A system of local communication between individuals on special bands of radio frequencies. Following a decision in 1945 by the US government that its citizens should have this right, the US Federal Communication Commission allocated a FREQUENCY of 467 mHz FM for the General Mobile Radio Service, now known as CB. In 1958 extra, lower-frequency channels were introduced on AM to encourage use. But it was not until the 1970s, when technology had advanced to reduce costs, that the CB market prospered, US truckers being at the head of the boom.

CCD camera In astronomy, an instrument that creates an electronic image of a celestial object using a charge-coupled device (CCD). A CCD contains a light-sensitive semiconductor chip which is divided up into an array of elements called **pixels**. The light from a celestial object is focused by a telescope into an optical image on the chip. Electrical charge accumulates at each pixel in proportion to the amount of light that falls on it so that the optical image is represented by the distribution of charge across the array. At the end of the exposure the charge at each pixel is transferred from the chip into subsidiary electronic equipment where it is measured and its value stored in a computer for display and analysis. CCD cameras are now widely used in optical and near infrared astronomical work because of their high sensitivity and their great accuracy in measuring the intensity of light. Extremely faint objects require exposures of several hours' duration, so CCD cameras are usually cooled with liquid nitrogen in order to minimize unwanted thermal generation of charge in the chip. A CCD camera is often used as the detector in PHOTOMETRY.

CD See COMPACT DISC.

CD-ROM See COMPACT DISC.

Ceanannus Mór See KELLS.

Ceauşescu, Nicolae (1918–89) Romanian Communist statesman, first President of the Socialist Republic of Romania 1974–89. Noted for his independence of the USSR, for many years he fostered his own personality cult, making his wife Elena his deputy and appointing many other members of his family to high office. His regime became increasingly totalitarian, repressive, and corrupt; a popular uprising in December 1989 resulted in its downfall and in the arrest, summary trial, and execution of Ceauşescu and his wife.

Cecil, Robert, 1st Earl of Salisbury and 1st Viscount Cranborne (1563–1612) English statesman. The son of William Cecil, Lord Burghley, he succeeded his father as ELIZABETH I's chief minister in 1598. He was responsible for ensuring the succession of JAMES I in 1603. He was created Viscount Cranborne (1604) and Earl of Salisbury (1605). He was made Lord Treasurer in 1608 and was faced with crown debts of nearly a million pounds. He increased the king's income by introducing additional CUSTOMS DUTIES (impositions) and various other unpopular means.

Cecil, William, 1st Baron Burghley (1520–98) English statesman. He trained as a lawyer and held office under HENRY VIII, EDWARD VI, and finally as

ELIZABETH I's Secretary of State from 1558. Politically adept, he formulated the queen's policy at home and abroad and was rewarded by the offices of Master of the Courts of Wards and Liveries (1561) and Lord Treasurer (1572). He was created Lord Burghley in 1571.

For 40 years he ensured the stability of the Elizabethan regime. More Protestant in sympathy than the queen, he persuaded her to aid the French Huguenots (1567) and the Dutch Calvinists (1585). He exercised control of appointments to the universities of Oxford and Cambridge and was responsible for ordering the execution of MARY, QUEEN OF SCOTS, whose existence he perceived as a threat to the state. He encouraged new industries, particularly glass-making, and introduced financial reforms.

Cecilia, St (2nd or 3rd century) Roman martyr. According to legend, she took a vow of celibacy but was forced to marry a young Roman; she converted her husband to Christianity and both were martyred. She is frequently pictured playing the organ and is the patron saint of church music. Feast day, 22 November.

cedar Any one of four species of evergreen conifer of the genus *Cedrus*, extending from the Mediterranean region to the Himalayas. They have tufts of small needles, and cones consisting of papery scales which carry the seeds. The cedar of Lebanon, *C. libani*, native in the eastern Mediterranean region, is now very sparse, but the tree is widely planted elsewhere. Cedars are members of the pine family, and closely related to larches. The timber and the oil distilled from them are useful. However, at least 70 different timbers with similar qualities are called cedar, for example Spanish cedar, *Cedrela odorata*, which is used to make cigar boxes.

Celebes See SULAWESI.

Celebes Sea (or **Sulawesi Sea**) An arm of the western Pacific extending westwards as far as Borneo and separating the Philippines from the Celebes (Sulawesi). It is linked to the Java Sea by the Makassar Strait.

celery A member of the CARROT family, Umbelliferae. Wild celery, *Apium graveolens*, is locally distributed in Europe, western Asia, and Africa. Cultivated celery is a relatively new crop, selected for its edible, swollen, leaf bases. The traditional commercial types are grown in trenches in rich soils, as the leaves need to be blanched by covering them with earth. A vegetable also derived from the wild celery is celeriac, of which the swollen root-like base of the stem is the part eaten.

celesta A small upright keyboard instrument invented by Auguste Mustel in Paris in 1886. The hammers strike metal plates, the sound being amplified by a wooden resonating box behind each plate; there is a sustaining pedal like that of the piano.

celestial axis See CELESTIAL SPHERE.

celestial equator See CELESTIAL SPHERE.

celestial latitude See CELESTIAL SPHERE.

celestial longitude See CELESTIAL SPHERE.

celestial mechanics The branch of astronomy dealing with the orbits of planets, natural and artificial satellites, comets, meteors, asteroids, and binary or multiple stars under the action of GRAVITATION, and, in the case of some satellites, atmospheric drag and radiation pressure. These orbits are often subject to small changes, known as **perturbations**, caused by the gravitational influence of nearby celestial bodies. Begun by NEWTON and based on his Law of Gravitation and three Laws of Motion, celestial mechanics attempts to produce analytical theories to account for and to predict the movements of celestial objects.

celestial meridian See MERIDIAN.

celestial poles See CELESTIAL SPHERE.

celestial sphere The sky represented by a sphere of arbitrarily large radius centred on the observer, the celestial objects being projected on to this sphere. The position of any celestial object on this sphere at any moment will be defined by two angular arcs. For this purpose a fixed reference plane passing through the centre of the celestial sphere is chosen, intersecting the sphere in a **great circle**. The two points 90 degrees away from this great circle are its POLES (analogous to the equator and the north and south poles on Earth). The great circle through the poles and a chosen point on the reference plane's intersection with the sphere's surface provides the necessary second reference circle.

Various systems of COORDINATES are used based on ANGULAR MEASURE. The **alt-azimuth system** uses the HORIZON and vertical great circles from the zenith to the nadir, the poles of the horizon circle. A celestial object's **altitude** is the arc from horizon to object measured along the vertical great circle through the object. Its **azimuth** is the arc measured from the most northerly point of the horizon along the horizon in an easterly direction to the foot of the vertical through the object. The **equatorial system** uses the **celestial equator**, the great circle formed by the intersection of the celestial sphere by the extended plane of the Earth's equator. The **north** and **south celestial poles**, formed by extending the Earth's axis of rotation to pierce the celestial sphere, are also used, MERIDIANS being drawn on the sphere from the north to the south pole. The angular distance of an object from the north celestial pole measured along the meridian from the pole to the object is known as the **north polar distance**. The **zenith distance** of an object is its angular distance from the zenith and is equal to 90 degrees minus the object's altitude.

A third commonly used coordinate system uses the ECLIPTIC as reference circle. The vernal equinox also lies on the ecliptic, being one of the

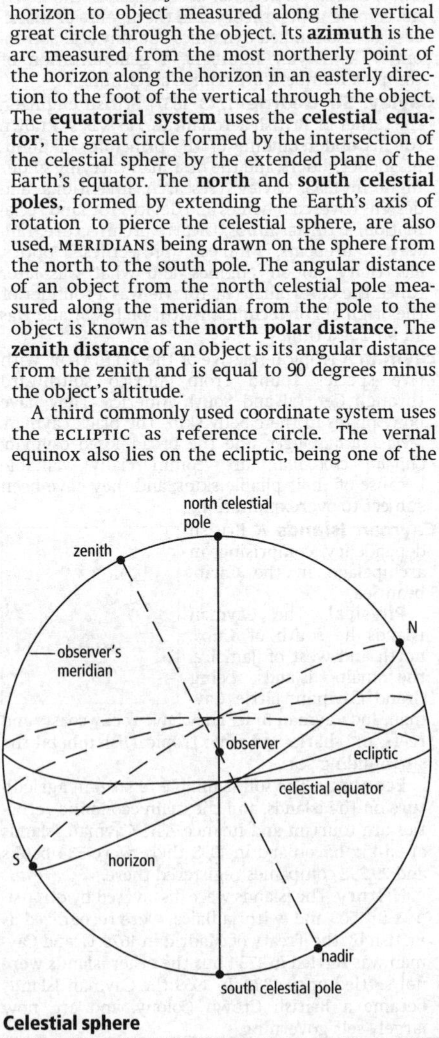

Celestial sphere

two points of intersection of the ecliptic and the equator. The half great circle through the poles of the ecliptic and the vernal equinox forms the other necessary circle. Then the **celestial** or **ecliptic latitude** of a celestial object is its angular distance north or south of the ecliptic, measured along the half circle through the object and the poles of the ecliptic. The **celestial** or **ecliptic longitude** of the object is the angular distance between Aries and the point of intersection of the latitude half circle through the object with the ecliptic. This distance is measured eastwards. Transformation from one coordinate system to another can be effected by the use of the formulae of spherical trigonometry.

cell (in biology) The basic unit of structure and function in all living things. Cytologists define cells as units of biological activity, each surrounded by a selectively permeable plasma MEMBRANE and capable of reproducing itself independently.

Cells are usually microscopic, though some, such as many PROTOZOANS and the ova of vertebrates, are considerably larger. Their shapes include spheres, discs, spindles, rods, and numerous other variations. Some cells are amoeboid: that is, they have the ability to locomote, like AMOEBAE. Although differing in magnitude and shape, all cells have a similar internal organization, consisting of CYTOPLASM and various structures known as organelles. In all cells except those of bacteria, the major organelle is the nucleus, which contains all the GENES, and thus controls all activities within the cell. Other vital organelles include MITOCHONDRIA and ribosomes (where proteins are synthesized).

The primitive cells of bacteria are called **prokaryotic cells** (see PROKARYOTE). The cells of all other organisms are called **eukaryotic cells** (see EUKARYOTE). The differences between cells arise because they have become adapted to perform specific functions. Photosynthetic cells, for example, contain CHLOROPHYLL, which is usually contained within organelles called chloroplasts, whereas ERYTHROCYTES are specialized cells containing HAEMOGLOBIN for oxygen transport.

cell (in physics) See BATTERY.

Cellini, Benvenuto (1500–71) Italian goldsmith and sculptor. His work is characterized by its elaborate virtuosity. After working in Rome and France, in 1545 he settled in Florence, where he cast the bronze *Perseus* (1545–54), regarded as his masterpiece. His autobiography is famous for its racy style and its vivid picture of Italian Renaissance life.

cello (or **violoncello**) Historically the bass of the VIOLIN family. Its vast range – in solo works the note C, for example, may be sounded in five different octaves – and its huge expressive powers render the cello the great solo instrument of the family after the violin itself. A little over twice the size of the violin, its great depth of body is nearly four times that of a violin. The strings are thicker than violin strings and under about twice the tension. They require a stouter BOW, about 25 mm (1 in) shorter and some 25 per cent heavier, with the band of hair wider to about the same degree. Though the cello, being held downwards, has its strings the opposite way round from those of the violin (that is, the top string to the left as the player sees it, not to the right) the principles of bowing are, broadly speaking, similar.

cellular telephone A mobile RADIO-TELEPHONE communications system. The basic system involves dividing the country into areas or cells, 2–13 km (1.25–8 miles) in radius, and employing different frequency bands in neighbouring cells to avoid interference. A mobile caller connects into the national telephone network via RADIO communication with the TELEPHONE EXCHANGE in his cell. The mobile units must be able to retune to a new frequency as they pass from one cell to another, a process that demands a highly sophisticated electronic switching system. A digitized network served by satellites is being introduced.

celluloid A transparent, flammable plastic made by the action on NITROCELLULOSE of a solution of camphor in ethanol. Celluloid was patented in 1870 by HYATT, who created the material while seeking a substitute for ivory in the manufacture of billiard balls. It was soon used in the USA for a range of household goods, and it was later used in sheet

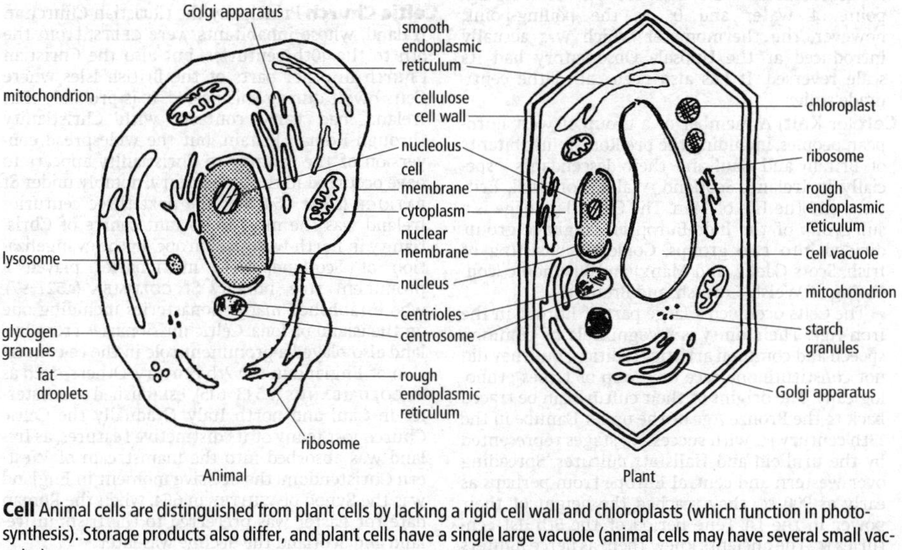

Cell Animal cells are distinguished from plant cells by lacking a rigid cell wall and chloroplasts (which function in photosynthesis). Storage products also differ, and plant cells have a single large vacuole (animal cells may have several small vacuoles).

form for making photographic FILM. In most applications it has now been replaced by less flammable materials.

cellulose $(C_6H_{10}O_5)_n$ A structural carbohydrate (a polysaccharide) found in the cell walls of all plants, many algae, and certain fungi: chemically it is a POLYMER of the sugar glucose. Its molecules, which comprise very long chains of glucose molecules, are insoluble in water, unlike most other carbohydrates. Typically, the cellulose chains lie parallel, forming tough microfibrils which may be embedded in lignin for greater strength, as in the wood of trees. The digestion of cellulose by all multicellular herbivores, from termites to ruminants, depends on the presence of certain types of bacteria or protozoa in the digestive system. These are the only organisms able to produce the enzymes necessary to digest cellulose. Cellulose is the main constituent of paper and many natural textiles such as COTTON and linen. For commercial use, cellulose is obtained mainly from wood pulp and cotton linters (cotton fibres too short for use in spinning). It is the principal raw material for PAPER MANUFACTURE, and both NITROCELLULOSE (cellulose nitrate) and CELLULOSE ACETATE are derived from it. Ethers of cellulose with methyl, ethyl, and benzyl alcohol are also of great industrial importance.

cellulose acetate Any of a family of non-flammable thermoplastics (see PLASTIC). Cellulose acetate is obtained by the action of acetic acid or acetic anhydride on purified cellulose (usually from short, waste-cotton fibres). Cellulose acetate was first manufactured by Cross and Bevan using a process patented in 1894. It was largely superseded after World War II by POLYTHENE and POLYSTYRENE, but it is still used for toys, spectacle frames, and packaging materials because of its impact resistance and ability to take colours.

cellulose nitrate See NITROCELLULOSE.

Celsius, Anders (1701–44) Swedish astronomer, best known for his THERMOMETER scale. He was professor of astronomy at Uppsala, and joined an expedition to measure a meridian in the north, which verified Newton's theory that the Earth is flattened at the poles. In 1742 he advocated a metric temperature scale with 100° as the freezing-point of water and 0° as the boiling-point; however, the thermometer which was actually introduced at the Uppsala Observatory had its scale reversed. It has also been called the centigrade scale.

Celt (or **Kelt**) A member of a group of west European peoples, including the pre-Roman inhabitants of Britain and Gaul and their descendants, especially in Ireland, Scotland, Wales, Cornwall, Brittany, and the Isle of Man. The Celtic language is a sub-group of the Indo-European language group, divided into two groups, Goidelic (consisting of Irish, Scots Gaelic, and Manx) and Brythonic (consisting of Welsh, Cornish, and Breton).

The Celts occupied a large part of Europe in the Iron Age. Their unity is recognizable by common speech and common artistic tradition, but they did not constitute one race or group of tribes ethnologically. The origins of their culture can be traced back to the Bronze Age of the upper Danube in the 13th century BC, with successive stages represented by the urnfield and Hallstatt cultures. Spreading over western and central Europe from perhaps as early as 900 BC, they reached the height of their power in the La Tène period of the 5th–1st centuries BC. The ancients knew them as fierce fighters and superb horsemen, with savage religious rites conducted by the Druid priesthood. They were farmers, who cultivated fields on a regular basis with ox-drawn ploughs in place of manual implements, revolutionary changes which permanently affected people's way of life. But Celtic political sense was weak, and the numerous tribes, continually warring against each other, were crushed between the migratory Germans and the power of Rome, to be ejected or assimilated by the former or conquered outright by the latter.

Celtic art The art of the CELTS, who in pre-Roman times inhabited much of Europe. A distinctive type of Celtic art, named after La Tène in Switzerland, first developed in the 5th century BC, expressed mainly in metalwork, a field in which the Celts showed extraordinary skill (see IRON AGE). Motifs were borrowed from many sources, but they were transformed by the Celtic genius for abstract ornament, which took delight in vigorous geometrical and spiral designs, often combined with stylized animal forms. The Roman conquest tended to submerge native forms in a provincial classicism, and the Celtic tradition survived most strongly in areas on the fringes of Europe, most notably Ireland, outside the Roman Empire. Metalwork skills declined, but with the Christianizing of Ireland Celtic art took on a new lease of life in manuscript ILLUMINATION, in which the written text is eclipsed by intricate latticework borders. After the Romans abandoned Britain in the 5th century, there was an influx of Celtic influence from Ireland, felt particularly in the north of England and most notably in the Lindisfarne Gospels, written and illuminated in the monastery at Lindisfarne, Northumbria, in about 700. In sculpture, Celtic art is most important for the free-standing stone cross, a type that seems to have been unique to Britain and Ireland. Their carving combines Christian subjects with pagan decorative motifs. Although much modified by Scandinavian influence, the Celtic tradition continued to flourish in Ireland until the 12th century, when, following the Anglo-Norman invasion of 1170, the country came much more into the mainstream of ROMANESQUE art. Vestiges of the Celtic style of ornamentation survived, however, into the 14th century.

Celtic Church Principally the Christian Church in Ireland, whose inhabitants were CELTS, from the 5th to the 10th centuries, but also the Christian Church in other parts of the British Isles where Celts dwelt during this period. It is probable that Ireland had early contacts with Christianity through Roman Britain, but the widespread conversion of the country to Christianity appears to have occurred in the 5th century, notably under St PATRICK (*c.*390–460). For the next three centuries Ireland was the most important centre of Christianity in north-western Europe. In the evangelization of Scotland, Irish missionaries played a prominent role, notably St COLUMBA (*c.*521–97), who established many monasteries including one on the island of Iona. Celtic missionaries from Ireland also played a prominent role in the re-conversion of England in the 7th century. Others, such as St COLUMBANUS (*c.*543–615), established monasteries in Gaul and north Italy. Gradually the Celtic Church lost many of its distinctive features, as Ireland was absorbed into the mainstream of Western Christendom: the decisive moment in England was the Synod of WHITBY in 664, when the Roman date for Easter was preferred to the Irish; in Ireland and Scotland the decline was later.

Celtic languages A group of INDO-EUROPEAN

LANGUAGES which includes Irish and Scots Gaelic, Manx, Welsh, Cornish, and Breton. There are now fewer than 3 million speakers, despite a linguistic and nationalistic revival in the 20th century. Celtic languages were originally spoken throughout Europe, from Spain to Asia Minor (present-day Turkey), but were submerged by other Indo-European languages, notably Romance languages. The Insular (island) languages fared better. These fall into two groups: Goidelic comprises Irish Gaelic, Scots Gaelic (Erse), and Manx, while Brythonic consists of Welsh, Cornish, and Breton. Irish is first attested, written in runic characters, in inscriptions of the 4th century AD. There was a great literary flowering in the 11th century, but after the 16th century the language began to retreat before English. It was adopted as the official language of the Irish Republic, where it is now spoken by roughly 31 per cent of the population. Scots Gaelic was imported from Ireland in the 5th century AD, and soon developed into a distinct dialect, although Irish remained as the literary language until the 17th century. Scots Gaelic is now spoken by under 100,000 people in the western Highlands and Islands of Scotland. Manx had become extinct as a mother-tongue by the mid-20th century. Welsh is attested from the 8th century, and has a rich medieval poetic tradition. It declined disastrously during the 19th century due to the Industrial Revolution, when thousands of English-speakers were moved to Wales to work in the factories and mines; by the beginning of the 20th century the Welsh-speakers were in a minority. The language has revived, however, since World War II and is now an official language of Wales, with over 750,000 speakers. Breton was introduced to Brittany from the British Isles in the 5th century AD. Its use was not generally encouraged in modern France until the 1950s, and the number of speakers has declined to around 500,000. Cornish became extinct at the beginning of the 19th century.

Celtic literature See IRISH LITERATURE; SCOTTISH-GAELIC LITERATURE; WELSH-LANGUAGE LITERATURE.

cement A powdered mixture of calcium silicates and aluminates, applied in a soft state to the surfaces of solid bodies to make them cohere firmly. The commonest cement is PORTLAND CEMENT. Hydraulic cements, first discovered by the Romans and reintroduced by Smeaton in the 1760s, set hard even under water. Cement forms CONCRETE when mixed with AGGREGATE and water, and with sand and water it forms MORTAR for masonry work or plastering. Other types of cement include rapid-hardening and sulphate-resisting cements. Mastic is a flexible cement used for sealing joints, for example between a window frame and the surrounding brickwork. The word cement is also used for certain ADHESIVES. Naturally occurring cements include CALCITE.

cementation The process of introducing a CEMENT into a loose mass of particles. Cementation increases the soil strength and reduces its compressibility, and may be carried out to hold back water in the ground when excavating. Tubes are inserted into the ground, and a mixture of cement and water (grout) is pumped through them. The mixture sets in the spaces between the soil particles. In finer soils, low-viscosity silicates and resins are used. Cementation is also a process in which iron packed with charcoal is heated to make STEEL. In naturally occurring cementation, particles are bound together by substances released by chemical reactions and flowing through the particulate material.

Cenozoic Era See CAINOZOIC ERA.

census An official count of a population or a class of things. Responsibility for population censuses, which supply information essential for planning, is usually taken by governments. Central to the concept of a census are regularity (the UN recommends censuses every ten years) and the complete coverage of all residents, although in some countries only a sample census is taken. Generally, a census yields information on the size and distribution of a population, and its breakdown by age, sex, and, sometimes, race or ethnicity. It may also cover such topics as occupation, housing conditions, and education.

Centaurs In Greek mythology, a tribe of creatures having the head, torso, and arms of a man, and the body and legs of a horse. Generally they are represented as barbarous, drunken, and lecherous, but Chiron – the best and wisest of them – was the tutor of Achilles, Castor and Pollux, Jason, and other heroes. After his death Chiron became the constellation Sagittarius.

Centaurus The Centaur, a prominent CONSTELLATION of the southern sky, one of the 48 constellations known to the ancient Greeks. It represents Chiron the centaur, a mythical beast with four legs like a horse but the torso, head, and arms of a human. Its two brightest stars are ALPHA CENTAURI (Rigil Kentaurus) and BETA CENTAURI (Hadar or Agena), representing the creature's front legs; they act as pointers to the Southern Cross, CRUX. Centaurus contains the largest and brightest globular CLUSTER in the sky, Omega Centauri, which appears like a fourth-magnitude fuzzy star covering an area greater than the full Moon; it lies approximately 5,000 parsecs away.

centaury In Europe, any of several representatives of the gentian family, including *Centaurium erythraea*, a small annual plant with pink or red flowers, which is often found at the edges of roads and on dryish grassy slopes. In America the name is applied to the related plant, the rose pink, *Sabatia angularis*.

centigrade See CELSIUS.

centipede A MYRIAPOD belonging to the class Chilopoda, which contains some 3,000 species, generally seen only when rocks or soils are disturbed. When disturbed, they scuttle to the nearest shelter, for they need cool, moist habitats, and are normally active only during the night. Centipedes have a single pair of jointed legs, of the typical ARTHROPOD type, on each segment; this distinguishes them from millipedes, which have two pairs per segment. They can also be distinguished from millipedes by the stout poison claws situated beneath the head, which are used for nocturnal predation. Usually centipedes are cryptically coloured, but some tropical forms reaching 26 cm (10 inches) long display brilliant coloration. Sperm is transferred, after courtship, in silken packages, and the females of many species brood over their eggs.

CENTO See CENTRAL TREATY ORGANIZATION.

Central A local government region of central Scotland from 1975 to 1996; it was replaced by the unitary authorities of Stirling, Clackmannanshire, and Falkirk.

Central African Federation (1953–63) A short-lived African federation, comprising the self-governing colony of Southern Rhodesia (ZIMBABWE) and the British protectorates of Northern Rhodesia

(ZAMBIA) and Nyasaland (MALAWI). In the 1920s and 1930s Europeans in both Rhodesias had pressed for union, but Britain had rejected the proposal because of its responsibilities towards Africans in Northern Rhodesia and Nyasaland. In 1953 the Conservative government in Britain allowed economic arguments to prevail, and a federal constitution was devised by which the federal government handled external affairs, defence, currency, intercolonial relations, and federal taxes. Riots and demonstrations by African nationalists followed (1960–61), and in 1962 Britain accepted in principle Nyasaland's right to secede. A meeting of the four concerned governments at the Victoria Falls Conference agreed to dissolve the Federation.

Central African Republic A land-locked country in Africa stretching west-to-east from Cameroon to the Sudan and south-to-north from humid equatorial forests bordering the Democratic Republic of Congo to the savannah plains of the Chad basin.

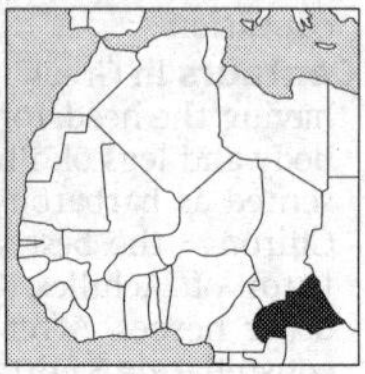

Physical. The rock formation mainly comprises ancient shields or platforms, forming low plateaux, with the highest point at 1,420 m (4,660 feet) in the west. There is high ground also in the north, and from it streams flow south to the Oubangi River, which forms the southern boundary. Upstream of about 50 km (30 miles) of rapids, the Oubangi is navigable for four months in the year. There is a dry season from December to March, and temperatures are very warm at all times.

Economy. The Central African Republic is one of Africa's poorer countries, with a largely agricultural economy. There are export crops of coffee, cotton, and hardwood timber, and subsistence crops such as maize, bananas, and cassava, which are often adversely affected by drought. Diamonds, followed by coffee and cotton, constitute the largest export commodity; some gold is mined and uranium extraction is planned. Light industry includes food-processing and the manufacture of cotton fabrics, footwear, and motorcycles.

History. Archaeological finds have shown that the area was inhabited from palaeolithic times (from about three million years ago), but there are no documentary records until the 19th century. The Central African Republic is thought to have been part of the empire of Gaoga, which flourished in the 16th century, and the region was raided for slaves during the 16th, 17th, and 18th centuries. The French began exploring the country in 1889 and by 1911 had taken full control of it. As the French colony of Ubangi Shari, it formed part of FRENCH EQUATORIAL AFRICA. In 1958 it became a republic within the FRENCH COMMUNITY, and fully independent in 1960. In 1976 its president, Jean Bedel Bokassa, declared it an empire, and himself emperor. Following allegations of atrocities, he was deposed in 1979, and the country reverted to a republic. Political instability persisted, and in 1981 General Kolingba seized power from the civilian government. This was restored in 1986 with Kolingba still President. There were demands for multi-party politics, and a new constitution was adopted in 1992. Elections were held in 1993: Ange-Félix Patasse became president and a coalition government was formed. In 1996 a military rebellion caused chaos for a week, but was suppressed with the help of French troops.

Capital: Bangui
Area: 622,436 sq km (240,324 sq mi)
Population: 3,141,000 (1995)
Currency: 1 CFA franc = 100 centimes
Religions: Traditional beliefs 60.0%; Roman Catholic 25.0%; Muslim 9.0%; Protestant 6.0%
Ethnic Groups: Banda 31.0%; Baya 29.0%; Mandjia 8.5%
Languages: French (official); Banda; Baya; Sango; local languages
International Organizations: UN; OAU; Non-Aligned Movement; Franc Zone

Central America The narrow strip of land to the south of Mexico, linking North and South America and including Guatemala, Belize, Honduras, El Salvador, Nicaragua, Costa Rica, and Panama.

Central American Common Market (CACM or ODECA) An economic organization comprising Guatemala, Honduras, El Salvador, Nicaragua, and Costa Rica. Beginning with a treaty signed by all five countries in 1960 the CACM sought to reduce trade barriers, stimulate exports, and encourage industrialization by means of regional cooperation. With a permanent secretariat at Guatemala City, its aim was cooperation with the member countries of the Latin American Free Trade Association (now called the Latin American Integration Association). During the 1970s, it somewhat lost impetus, owing to war, upheaval, international recession, and ideological differences among member states. A new tariff and customs agreement came into effect in 1986, when regional trade improved. In 1993 Panama agreed to implement full economic integration with the CACM nations.

Central Asian States An economic union involving the Central Asian republics of Kazakhstan, Uzbekistan, and Kyrgyzstan, created in 1994. Rich in mineral and energy resources, the union has a total population of some 48 million people.

central bank A BANK at the centre of a country's banking system. Most central banks, such as the Federal Reserve System in the USA, the Bank of England in the UK, and the Bundesbank in Germany, control the note issue and, by acting as lender of last resort to other financial institutions, guarantee the banking system against collapse. In the UK and some other countries, they license and regulate other banks within their jurisdiction. They are also responsible for the execution (and, in some countries, for the formulation) of monetary policy. Plans to amalgamate national EU currencies into a single European currency according to the plans laid down by Maastricht Treaty in 1991, include a plan for a single European Central Bank analogous to the US Federal Reserve Bank.

Central Intelligence Agency (CIA) A US government agency. It was established by Congress in 1947 and is responsible to the President through the National Security Council. Its work consists of gathering and evaluating foreign intelligence, undertaking counter-intelligence operations overseas, and organizing secret political intervention and psychological warfare operations in foreign areas. During the 1990s it sought to redefine its role following the end of the COLD WAR. See also INTELLIGENCE SERVICES.

Central Lancashire A development area in Lancashire, north-west England, incorporating the towns of Preston. Chorley, and Leyland. Established in 1970, it covers an area of 142 sq km (55 sq miles). The University of Central Lancashire (formerly Lancashire Polytechnic) was established in 1992.

Central Powers A Triple Alliance of Germany, Austria, and Hungary agreed in 1882.

central processing unit (CPU) The main operating unit of a digital COMPUTER. The CPU is the part of the hardware of a computer that performs instructions and controls the flow of data according to instructions provided by the computer SOFTWARE. The CPU of a conventional computer consists of two main components: a control unit and an arithmetic and logic unit (ALU), together with a limited number of local MEMORY locations, known as registers, which are used to store temporarily instructions, data, and results during the execution of a PROGRAM. The control unit interprets each MACHINE-CODE instruction sequentially and executes the appropriate operation, such as transferring data between the main memory and a register, or instructing the ALU to carry out a logical or arithmetical process. In older and larger computers the CPU consisted of many individual components, but now an entire CPU can be contained on a single silicon chip (see MICROPROCESSOR). Computers designed for parallel processing have multiple processors rather than a single CPU.

Central Treaty Organization (CENTO) (1955–79) A mutual security organization composed of representatives of Britain, Turkey, Iran, Pakistan, and Iraq. In 1956 the USA became an associate member. Formed as a result of the Baghdad Pact (1955), it was designed in part as a defence against the former Soviet Union and to consolidate the influence of Britain in the Arab world. Following the withdrawal of Iraq (1958), its headquarters were moved to Ankara. It became inactive after the withdrawal of Turkey, Pakistan, and Iran in 1979.

Centre National de la Recherche Scientifique (CNRS) A French government institution established to coordinate and promote research in the sciences and humanities; to give grants to university laboratories and research institutes; and to maintain its own laboratories. Policy is formulated by the Comité National de la Recherche Scientifique, which is organized into some 40 sections, each with 26 members.

centre of gravity The point at which the weight of a body (an object) appears to act. In a uniform gravitational field, it is the same as the CENTRE OF MASS.

centre of mass The point at which the entire mass of an object appears to be concentrated. In a uniform gravitational field, it is the same as the centre of gravity. The centre of mass does not have to be within the solid part of an object; for example, the centre of mass of a cup is located within the space inside it.

Centre Pompidou (or **Centre Beaubourg**; in full Centre National d'Art et de Culture Georges Pompidou; English, George Pompidou National Centre for Art and Culture) A modern exhibition centre housing the French National Gallery of Modern Art and the Centre for Industrial Design, situated between the Halles and Marais areas of Paris, France. Opened in 1977 and named after President POMPIDOU, the building was designed in glass and steel by Richard Rogers and Renzo Piano.

centrifugal force See CENTRIPETAL FORCE.

centrifuge A machine for separating solids from liquids, or separating immiscible liquids, using the CENTRIPETAL FORCE generated by rapid rotation. Centrifuging greatly accelerates processes that might eventually take place under the influence of normal gravity alone, for example the settling of suspended solids in liquids. A typical laboratory centrifuge creates a centripetal force about 1,000 times greater than that of gravity. Ultracentrifuges can create forces up to 750,000 times that of gravity, and are used to precipitate large biological molecules from solution. Gases can also be separated centrifugally. For example, uranium can be separated into its two isotopes, U-238 and U-235, by centrifuging the gaseous compound uranium hexafluoride (see NUCLEAR FUEL).

centripetal force The force that makes an object move in a circular path. If a body attached to a string is swung in a horizontal circle, even though its spread may remain constant its velocity (v) changes as result of its changing direction. This changing velocity creates a centripetal acceleration of v^2/r, where r is the length of the string. In this case the tension in the string, i.e. the centripetal force, is equal to mv^2/r, where m is the mass of the body. In the case of a satellite orbiting the Earth, the force pulling the satellite towards the Earth, is the gravitational force GmM/r^2, where M is the mass of the Earth, m is the mass of the satellite, r is the distance of the satellite from the centre of the Earth, and G is the gravitational constant. Therefore $GmM/r^2 = mv^2/r$, i.e. the gravitational force is the centripetal force.

It used to be said that the centripetal force is balanced by a centrifugal force. However, it is now recognized that the centrifugal force is fictitious. It is not that the satellite stays in orbit when the centrifugal force is equal to the gravitational force, rather that the gravitational force is the centripetal force.

centurion A professional middle-ranking officer of the Roman army. The title means 'leader of a hundred'. The rigorous discipline, leadership and experience of the centurions made them a vital factor in the success of the professional army.

century plant See AGAVE.

ceorl A free peasant farmer of Anglo-Saxon England. In status ceorls were above the SERFS but below the THANES (noblemen), with a wergild of usually 200 shillings. They were liable to military service in the fyrd and to taxation. Although they could own land, they were often forced by economic pressures and by reasons of security to place themselves in the control of the richer landowners. After the Norman Conquest their status diminished rapidly and the term 'churl' came to mean an ill-bred serf.

cephalochordate See LANCELET.

Cephalonia (Greek **Kefallinía**) A hilly Greek island in the Ionian Sea; area 781 sq km (302 sq mi); pop (1991) 29,400. Its capital is Argostólion.

cephalopod A marine MOLLUSC with many unique features, making up a class, Cephalopoda, of what are probably the most peculiar and most advanced of the INVERTEBRATES. Among the living 650 or so species are the familiar SQUID, OCTOPUS, CUTTLEFISH, and nautilus (see PAPER NAUTILUS; PEARLY NAUTILUS). They move by jet propulsion, squirting water from directed muscular jets. They have large, focusing eyes, complex brains, and a remarkable learning capacity. They use 'smoke-screens' of ink and extraordinary skin-colour changes to confuse predators, and they are active carnivores. The typical cumbersome molluscan shell is usually reduced or vestigial.

Cephalopod means 'head–foot', as the foot of other molluscs has evolved in cephalopods into a ring of tentacles around the mouth, bearing suckers to capture prey. Although the cephalopods are successful as intelligent marine carnivores, they have never adapted to other ways of life, and the modern species are only a fraction of the 7,500 fossil species which existed before the evolution of competing fish.

Cepheid variable stars An important class of highly luminous VARIABLE STARS named after Delta Cephei, which was the first of their type to be discovered, by GOODRICKE in 1784. They typically exhibit variations in luminosity, temperature, and radius with well-defined periods in the range 1–50 days. During their pulsation periods they rapidly rise to maximum brightness and slowly fade during expansion. The pulsations are caused by successive loss and recapture of electrons by helium. Observing Cepheids in the MAGELLANIC CLOUDS in 1912, the US astronomer Henrietta Leavitt discovered that their periods were uniquely related to their apparent magnitudes. It is now recognized that Cepheids fall into two types according to the STELLAR POPULATION in which they reside. Type I, the classical Cepheid of Population I, is more luminous than Type II, the W Virginis or cluster Cepheid, of the same period. The difference is attributed to the effect of their different chemical compositions on their oscillations.

Cepheus A CONSTELLATION of the north polar region of the sky, one of the forty-eight constellations known to the ancient Greeks. It represents King Cepheus of Ethiopia, husband of Cassiopeia and father of Andromeda. Its most celebrated star is Delta Cephei, prototype of the CEPHEID VARIABLE STARS. Delta Cephei is also a double star, consisting of a fourth-magnitude yellow star (the variable) and a sixth-magnitude blue-white companion. Mu Cephei is a red supergiant variable, called the Garnet Star by the British astronomer William HERSCHEL.

ceramic A material made from inorganic, nonmetallic chemicals, processed at high temperatures. Ceramics are one of the three main classes of engineering materials, the others being METAL and PLASTIC. In addition to traditional clay-based POTTERY, ceramics include BRICKS, CEMENT, and CONCRETE, GLASS, tiles, and modern engineering ceramics, such as ALUMINA and SILICON CARBIDE. Common features of ceramics are their hardness, brittleness and resistance to heat. Many are electrical insulators or have other electrical properties. Ceramics are made from raw materials with very high melting-points and are usually manufactured in the solid state from fine powders. Pottery is made from clay, a naturally occurring suspension of fine ceramic powder in water produced by the weathering of rock. Clays can be moulded to shape or mixed with water to form emulsified suspensions (slips). These slips can be cast in plaster moulds to form complicated shapes: the water from the slip is absorbed into the plaster. Once formed, the clay holds its shape before being fired in a kiln or furnace to harden it.

During firing, clays and other ceramic raw materials sinter (fuse without melting) to form a hard solid. Sintering is aided by small quantities of low-melting-point components, which melt during firing and help to bind the other material together. In pottery, this low-melting-point phase comprises small amounts of silica glass. Engineering ceramics are also sintered, but they require very high firing temperatures and are thus very expensive. It is very difficult to manufacture large components from ceramics and this is currently a limitation on their applications. Because of their extreme hardness, ceramics must be shaped by ABRASIVE techniques using diamond. Ceramics are used in high-temperature environments (for example, jet and diesel engines) and in articles that undergo high wear and require a long life (for example, artificial hip joints and teeth). The major limitation to their further use is their brittleness and the reduction in strength which occur if small cracks are present. Newer developments include tougher ceramics, such as ZIRCONIA and ceramic-matrix COMPOSITES. See also CHINESE CERAMICS; CREAMWARE; EARTHENWARE; MAIOLICA; WEDGWOOD.

Cerberus In Greek mythology, a monstrous three-headed dog that guarded the entrance to Hades, preventing the dead from escaping and the living from approaching the Underworld. Hercules – as his twelfth and final Labour – brought Cerberus up to Earth.

cereal An annual GRASS that flowers and seeds in its first year, and has been selected for its tough stems and seed heads that do not shed the grain, once ripe. Cereals belong to the very large family of grasses, Gramineae. Relatively few species have ever been cultivated, but these were probably the earliest cultivated crops (see AGRICULTURE), and now account for over 50 per cent of all ARABLE FARMING. Wheat, rice, maize, barley, oats, rye, millet, and sorghum are common cereals. Cereals are the staple food in many parts of the world. After harvesting, most cereals are threshed to separate the grain from the seed head. The grain may then be dried and stored, and is then milled or polished to produce whole grains, meal, flakes, or flour. Some cereals, such as WHEAT, have been selected to give naked grain, free of chaff.

cerebral palsy A group of disorders present at birth and arising from brain damage, which may be caused by lack of oxygen before or during childbirth, birth trauma, jaundice, and brain haemorrhage. Cerebral palsy may also be caused by prolonged convulsions or coma in infancy or severe disease such as meningitis. The effects of cerebral palsy are dependent on the site and extent of brain damage. Spastic PARALYSIS such as hemiplegia, diplegia, paraplegia, or quadriplegia is common; ataxia, muscle weakness, increased muscle tone, and contractures may also occur. Other symptoms include involuntary movements of the face, hands, and tongue; auditory and visual impairment; and persistent dribbling with difficulty in speaking and swallowing. The first sign is commonly the failure to achieve normal developmental milestones. Learning difficulties are common. Assessment of the intellectual ability of a child with cerebral palsy is of great importance, but is often rendered difficult by the child's difficulty in expressing itself.

Ceredigion See CARDIGANSHIRE.

Cerenkov radiation Radiation emitted by atomic particles when they pass through a transparent medium at a velocity greater than the SPEED OF LIGHT in that medium. It is named after the Russian physicist Pavel Cerenkov (1904–90), who discovered it in 1934 for which he was awarded a Nobel Prize in 1958.

Ceres (in astronomy) The largest ASTEROID and the first to be discovered (by the Italian astronomer Giuseppe Piazzi in 1801). About 1,023 km (639 miles) across, nearly spherical in shape, with an albedo of about 0.06 and a spin period of 9.075 hours, Ceres was probably a growing planetesimal when accretion was stopped in the primordial asteroid belt. Like the other large asteroids, it is likely to have retained its original size and rotational state, and its surface is probably covered by a thick REGOLITH layer of fragmented material.

Ceres (in mythology) The Roman goddess of corn, identified with the Greek Demeter.

cermet (or **ceramic metal**) A COMPOSITE material in which small particles of hard ceramics such as tungsten carbide or SILICON CARBIDE are combined with small amounts of a ductile metal such as cobalt. This produces a material with the hardness and wear-resistance of a ceramic but which is easier to fabricate because of the presence of the metal. Cermets are important for the manufacture of metal-cutting tools such as drill bits and lathe tools.

Cerne Abbas A village in Dorset, southern England, north-west of Dorchester, near which is the **Cerne Giant**, a prehistoric figure cut in the chalk hillside.

Cervantes (Saavedra), Miguel de (1547–1616) Spanish novelist and dramatist. His most famous work is *Don Quixote* (1605–15), a satire on chivalric romances. The character of Don Quixote had widespread appeal in many other countries and continues to inspire innumerable imitations; his name has passed into the English language as the adjective *quixotic*.

cervical screening A technique in OBSTETRICS and gynaecology involving the examination of cells from a woman's cervix (the neck of the womb) to detect early changes that may progress to CANCER. Such changes are treatable by a minor operation, whereas operations for more advanced cervical cancer are less successful. Since the 1950s, cervical screening has been widely employed as a routine preventive for healthy women. It consists of examining the cervix using a vaginal speculum. A few cells from the cervical opening are scraped off with a wooden spatula for microscopical examination. It is commonly called a 'pap' smear after its inventor, George Papanicolaou (1883–1962).

Césaire, Aimé (-Fernand) (1913–) French poet and dramatist. Born in the Caribbean colony of Martinique, which he later represented in the French National Assembly, he initiated (with Senghor) the black cultural self-awareness *négritude* movement in the 1930s. The movement opposed the French policy of assimilation, with its inherent assumption of European superiority. His collection of poems *Cahier d'un retour au pays natal* (1939) is a revolutionary landmark in modern black writing, influenced partly by {Surrealism}. His plays, which are polemical and rich in African imagery, include *Une saison au Congo* (1967).

cesium See CAESIUM.

cesspit See SEPTIC TANK.

cetane number See DIESEL OIL.

Cetshwayo (or **Cetewayo**) (*c.*1826–84) Zulu king. Cetshwayo became ruler of Zululand in 1873. He increased his army to defend his territory against the Boers and defeated the British at Isandhlwana in 1879. His capital, Ulundi, was captured eight months later, whereupon he was deposed and sent to London. In 1883 British efforts to restore him failed and he was driven out by an anti-royalist faction. See ZULU WARS.

Cetus The Whale, the fourth-largest CONSTELLATION. It lies across the celestial equator and was one of the 48 constellations known to the ancient Greeks. Cetus represents the sea monster to which Andromeda was to be sacrificed before her rescue by Perseus. It contains the long-period variable star Mira Ceti, also known as Omicron Ceti. Tau Ceti is a yellow dwarf star similar to the Sun. M77 (NGC 1068), at ninth magnitude, is the brightest example of a SEYFERT GALAXY.

Cévennes A mountain range on the south-eastern edge of the Massif Central in France, largely in the departments of Ardèche and Lozère. Its highest peak is Mt. Mézenc (1,754 m, 5,755 ft).

Ceylon The former name (until 1972) of SRI LANKA.

Cézanne, Paul (1839–1906) French painter. Although originally an impressionist, he later exemplified POST-IMPRESSIONISM and, through his use of geometrical shapes, influenced the development of cubism. His best-known works include landscapes, such as *Mont Sainte Victoire* (1904–06), and figure paintings such as *The Card Players* (1890–92) and *The Bathers* (1895–1905).

CFC See CHLOROFLUOROCARBON.

Chablis A village in the Yonne department of Burgundy in central France, noted for its dry white wine.

Chabrier, (Alexis-) Emmanuel (1841–94) French composer and pianist. Despite early proof of a talent for music, Chabrier was side-tracked into the study and practice of law and did not become a full-time musician until the end of 1880. Though WAGNER's music fired his imagination and ambitions (as in the opera *Gwendoline*, 1885), Chabrier retained a lighter touch; the *opéra comique Le roi malgré lui* (1887), the orchestral rhapsody *España* (1883), and *Joyeuse marche* (1888) have a sparkle and brilliance that are wholly French.

Chabrol, Claude See NOUVELLE VAGUE.

Chaco See GRAN CHACO.

chaconne (Italian **ciaccona**) A dance in triple time that originated in Latin America, was imported into Spain at the beginning of the 17th century, and came thence to the rest of Europe. The dance employed a traditional sequence of chords, the melodic outline of which was used in Italy as the basis for a set of variations – the bass melody was repeated over and over again while new material was added above.

Chaco War (1932–35) A conflict between Paraguay and Bolivia. The GRAN CHACO, an extensive lowland plain, had been an object of dispute between the two countries since the early 19th century, but Bolivia's final loss of its Pacific coast in 1929 (the Tacna–Arica settlement) prompted it to push its claims to the Chaco. Border clashes in the late 1920s led to outright war in 1932. Bolivia had the larger army and superior military equipment, but the Aymará and Quechua Indian conscripts from the Andean highlands did not fare well in the low, humid Chaco. The Paraguayan colonel José Félix Estigarribia drove the Bolivians west across the Chaco and forced his enemies to sue for peace in 1935. Paraguay gained most of the disputed territory, but the price was immense for both countries. More than 50,000 Bolivians and 35,000 Paraguayans had lost their lives. Economic stagnation was to plague both combatants for years to come.

Chad A land-locked country in north-Central Africa surrounded by Libya to the north, Sudan to the east, the Central African Republic to the south, and Niger, Nigeria, and Cameroon to the west.

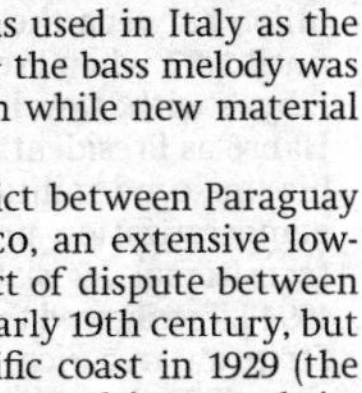

Physical. Out of the Sahara in its northern half rise the volcanic Tibesti Mountains, with reserves of tungsten, while in the east is the great depression surrounding Lake

CHAD, with deposits of natron (hydrated sodium carbonate). The south has moderate summer rains which produce a SAVANNAH and the seasonal Chari and Logone Rivers and their tributaries.

Economy. Chad is one of the poorest countries in Africa, with a mainly agricultural economy which is vulnerable to drought. Major exports include cotton and livestock products. The industrial sector is small, mostly comprising textiles and food-processing.

History. Northern Chad has been inhabited for about 10,000 years and southern Chad since about 500 BC. During the 8th century BERBER peoples moved into the area and founded the empire of Kanem. This empire expanded and in the 13th century merged with the kingdom of Bornu. The neighbouring kingdoms of Baguirmi and Ouaddaï grew more powerful during the 16th century. The three kingdoms fought during the 17th century until in the early 1890s all fell under the control of the Sudanese conqueror, Rabeh. French expeditions advanced into the region, and French sovereignty was recognized by the European powers. After confrontation with the British at Fashoda (1898) France declared a protectorate, and in 1908 Chad became part of French Equatorial Africa, though control was complete only in 1912. In 1920 Chad became a colony under French administration, its rich mineral deposits being rapidly exploited. In 1940 Chad was the first colony to declare for the FREE FRENCH. It became autonomous within the FRENCH COMMUNITY in 1958, and a fully independent republic in 1960, with François Tombalbaye as the first President. Since then the country has struggled to maintain unity between the Arabic-speaking Muslim peoples of the north and the more economically developed south and west. In 1980 Libya invaded, proposing union between the two countries. Civil war lasted until 1987, when French and US intervention led to Libya's withdrawal and the installation of Hissène Habré as President. Habré was deposed in 1990 by his one-time military commander Idriss Déby. A democratization process was agreed upon, and a transitional legislature was installed in 1993. In 1994 Libya agreed to hand back to Chad the Aouzou Strip, an area rich in minerals occupied by Libya since 1973. Armed rebels, based in the south of the country, agreed to a cease-fire in 1996 and a constitutional referendum, which had been postponed several times, was held. A new constitution was approved, establishing Chad as a unitary state.

Capital: Ndjamena
Area: 1,284,000 sq km (495,755 sq mi)
Population: 6,361,000 (1995)
Currency: 1 CFA franc = 100 centimes
Religions: Muslim 50.0%; traditional beliefs 45.0%; Christian 5.0%
Ethnic Groups: Arabic (Hassauna and Djoheina) 46.0%; Sudanic 28.0%; Nilotic 8.0%; Saharan 7.0%
Languages: Arabic, French (both official); Sara; Nilotic; Saharan
International Organizations: UN; OAU; Non-Aligned Movement; Franc Zone

Chad, Lake A shallow lake on the frontiers of Chad, Niger, and Nigeria in north-central Africa. Its size varies seasonally from *c.*10,360 sq km (4,000 sq miles) to *c.*25,900 sq km (10,000 sq miles).

Chadic languages A group of languages spoken in the region of Lake Chad in north-central Africa, of which the most important is Hausa.

Chadwick, Sir Edwin (1800–90) British public health reformer. A friend and disciple of Jeremy BENTHAM, he was the architect of the POOR LAW Amendment Act (1834). His report for the royal commission set up in 1833 to investigate the conditions of work of factory children resulted in the passing of the Ten Hours Act. During his term of office as Commissioner of the Board of Health (1848–54), he persuaded urban authorities to undertake major water, drainage, and slum clearance schemes to reduce disease.

Chadwick, Sir James (1891–1974) British physicist and pioneer of nuclear research who in 1932 discovered the NEUTRON, an uncharged particle from the NUCLEUS of the atom. He was awarded the Nobel Prize for physics in 1935. In World War II he was involved in the atomic bomb project, and afterwards stressed the importance of university research into nuclear physics.

chaetognathan See ARROW WORM.

chafer A BEETLE belonging to the family Scarabaeidae, especially of the subfamilies Cetoniinae (2,600 species) and Melolonthinae (9,000 species). The first group includes large beetles with metallic-coloured elytra (wing-cases) and characteristic fan-shaped antennae. The second group includes the cockchafer, *Melolontha melolontha*, whose subterranean larvae can do great damage to roots of plants. The majority of species are found in the tropics and are related to scarab beetles.

chaffinch Either of two species of bird of the genus *Fringilla* from the finch family, Fringillidae. Both are sparrow-sized and have conspicuous white wing-bars. The blue, or Canary Island, chaffinch, *F. teydea*, is confined to the Canary Islands; the male is a blue-grey colour, while the female is a duller, more greenish colour. The other species, the common chaffinch, *F. coelebs*, is widespread in Europe and western Asia. In some areas the females may migrate further than the males and, as a result, flocks of predominantly male or female birds may be found in some wintering areas.

Chagall, Marc (1887–1985) Russian-born French painter and graphic artist. Working chiefly in Paris, he was associated with the avant-garde circle of Delaunay, Modigliani, and Chaim Soutine. Inspired by fauvism and Russian folk art, he used rich emotive colour and dream imagery, as can be seen in paintings such as *Maternity* (1913); his early work had a significant influence on the development of surrealism. Other achievements came within theatre design (the costumes and decor for Stravinsky's *The Firebird*, 1945), stained-glass windows, and book illustrations.

Chagas' disease See TRYPANOSOMIASIS.

Chagos Archipelago An island group in the Indian Ocean, formerly a dependency of Mauritius and now part of the strategic BRITISH INDIAN OCEAN TERRITORY.

Chain, Sir Ernst Boris (1906–79) German-born British biochemist who, with FLOREY, developed PENICILLIN as a uniquely valuable antibiotic. Chain came to the UK as a Jewish refugee from Nazi persecution in 1933, and after working briefly with HOPKINS at Cambridge University, was invited by Florey to join him in Oxford. With E. P. Abraham, he established the initially controversial beta lactam formula for penicillin. He shared the Nobel Prize for physiology and medicine in 1945 with Florey and FLEMING.

chain-mail See ARMS AND ARMOUR.

chain reaction A self-sustaining nuclear reaction, for example nuclear FISSION, in which products of the reaction go on to induce the same nuclear reaction in other atoms. In one fission chain reaction a URANIUM-235 atom is split by a bombarding neutron. This splits the nucleus into two fragments, and also releases two, sometimes three, neutrons. Under the right conditions these neutrons will go on to split other nuclei, with the release of more neutrons, and so on. In a nuclear reactor, this chain reaction proceeds in a controlled manner; in a NUCLEAR WEAPON such as an atomic bomb the chain reaction is allowed to continue unchecked, with a resultant explosive release of enormous amounts of energy.

Chain reactions can also occur in chemical processes, especially those involving the production of free-radical intermediates. Combustion, explosions, and polymerizations take place through chain reactions.

chain-saw A power-driven saw in which the cutting action is achieved by means of a series of teeth attached to the links of an endless chain. The power is usually supplied by a compact petrol engine, or on some smaller models by an electric motor. In forestry, the chain-saw has largely replaced the axe.

Chaka See SHAKA.

Chalcedon (Turkish **Kadiköy**) A city in Asia Minor, on the Bosporus near present-day Istanbul, where the fourth ecumenical council of the Church was held in 451 AD, at which was drawn up the important statement of faith affirming the two natures, human and divine, united in the single person of Christ.

chalcedony A very finely crystalline (cryptocrystalline) variety of silica (SiO_2), found in various forms and colours, all with a wax-like lustre. Banded varieties (AGATE and ONYX) are common; so too are the reddish-brown (CORNELIAN), green (prase), and red (jasper) varieties; these are all regarded as semiprecious stones. Chalcedony occurs in sediments, in cavities in lavas, and in veins associated with igneous rocks.

chalcid A small or minute WASP with reduced veins on its wings, and usually black or metallic in colour. The larvae of most species are parasitic on the larvae of other insects, eventually killing the host. Other species are found in galls (abnormal growths of tissue on plants), being parasites on the larvae which have caused the gall to form, or even causing galls themselves. The chalcididae form one of the largest superfamilies of Hymenoptera (bees, wasps, and ants) and comprise an estimated 25,000 species. They include the smallest insects, fairyflies (Mymaridae), which have a body length of 0.2 mm (0.008 inch).

Chaldea The country of the Chaldeans, the southern part of Babylonia. The Chaldeans were a Semitic people originating from Arabia, who settled in the neighbourhood of Ur *c.*800 BC and ruled Babylonia 625–538 BC. They were famous as astronomers.

Chaliapin, Fyodor (Ivanovich) (1873–1938) Russian operatic bass. He made his début in St Petersburg, later going to Moscow, where he excelled in Russian opera, most notably in the title role of Mussorgsky's *Boris Godunov*. He left Russia after the Revolution and developed a successful international career, appearing in a wide range of operas in many different countries.

chalk A fine-grained limestone that is friable and porous. It is often pure white in colour and commonly contains up to 97 or 98 per cent of calcium carbonate in the form of CALCITE. This is generally composed of the shells of microscopic marine organisms, normally including foraminiferans such as *Globigerina*; algae known as coccoliths are also commonly present. Chalk is characteristically seen in the Upper CRETACEOUS period of western Europe and parts of North America. The most famous exposures are either side of the English Channel, where on the English side it forms the white cliffs of Dover. It contains FLINT, and it is used for burning into lime.

The stratigraphical name for rocks of Upper Cretaceous age in Europe is also chalk.

'Chalk' used to write on blackboards consists of calcium sulphate.

Challenger Deep The deepest part of the Mariana Trench in the Pacific Ocean (11,034 m, 36,197 ft), surveyed by and named after HMS *Challenger II* in 1948.

Châlons-sur-Marne The capital of the department of Marne in the Champagne-Ardenne region of north-east France, on the River Marne; pop. (1990) 51,530. Attila was defeated by the Romans here in 451 AD. Its industries include champagne-making, brewing, electrical engineering, and textiles.

Châlon-sur-Saône An industrial town in the department of Saône-et-Loire, Burgundy, east-central France, at the junction of the Saône and Loire rivers; pop. (1990) 56,260. It was the birthplace of the chemist and pioneer photographer Nicéphore Niepce (1765–1833). It is an inland port trading in grain and wine. Its industries include electrical equipment, barges, chemicals, metal products, and glass.

Chamaeleon A small and faint CONSTELLATION near the south celestial pole, representing a chameleon. It was introduced by the Dutch navigators Pieter Dirkszoon Keyser and Frederick de Houtman at the end of the 16th century. Its brightest stars are of only fourth magnitude. It lies near the conspicuous southern constellation CRUX (the Southern Cross).

Chamberlain, Sir Austen (1863–1937) British statesman. Son of Joseph CHAMBERLAIN, he entered Parliament in 1892 as a Liberal-Unionist. He was Chancellor of the Exchequer 1903–05 and Secretary of State for India 1915–17, resigning over alleged blunders in the Mesopotamia Campaign. He became Chancellor of the Exchequer again in 1919 and leader of the Conservative Party in 1921, but loyalty to LLOYD GEORGE led to his resignation in 1922. He was Foreign Secretary 1924–29, playing a major part in securing the Treaties of LOCARNO.

Chamberlain, Joseph (1836–1914) British Liberal statesman. He became a Liberal MP in 1876, but left the party in 1886 because of Gladstone's support of Irish Home Rule. The leader of the Liberal Unionists from 1891, in the coalition government of 1895 he served as Colonial Secretary, in which post he played a leading role in the handling of the Second Boer War.

Chamberlain, (Arthur) Neville (1869–1940) British Conservative statesman, Prime Minister 1937–40. The son of Joseph CHAMBERLAIN, he pursued a policy of appeasement towards Germany, Italy, and Japan as Prime Minister of a coalition government; in 1938 he signed the Munich Agreement ceding the Sudetenland to Germany, which he claimed would mean 'peace in our time'. Although the policy was primarily intended to postpone war until Britain had rearmed, it caused increasing discontent in his own party; he was forced to abandon it and prepare for war when Hitler invaded the rest of Czechoslovakia in 1939. He declared war on Germany in 1939 when Hitler invaded Poland. Chamberlain's leadership in World

War II proved inadequate and he was replaced by Winston Churchill.

Chamberlain, Owen (1920–) US physicist. He worked on the Manhattan Project for the development of the atom bomb during World War II, after which he investigated subatomic particles using a bevatron accelerator. He and E. G. Segrè discovered the antiproton in 1955, and four years later they shared the Nobel Prize for physics.

Chamberlin, Thomas Chrowder (1843–1928) US geologist who established the origin of LOESS. He also discovered beneath the ice of Greenland fossil forms which suggested an earlier, warmer climate, and he was one of the first to propose dating for the ice-sheets of the PLEISTOCENE EPOCH. Much of his life was spent in developing a theory of the Earth's origin, formation, and growth.

chamber music Originally the performance of music in the private salons of the nobility by a small group of instrumentalists or singers. It now refers to music for very small combinations of instrumentalists, regardless of where they are performing. Chamber music implies at least two instruments. The most honoured medium is that of the string quartet (two violins, viola, and cello). Other combinations include the string trio (violin, viola, and cello) and string quintet (usually two violins, two violas, and cello), together with similar combinations that involve an instrument other than strings, such as the piano trio (piano, violin, and cello), the piano quintet (piano, two violins, viola, and cello), and so on. Septets, octets and nonets tend to mix woodwind and strings.

chamber of commerce An association of businesses or business people located within a specified area who regularly meet together. Membership may be voluntary or, as in Germany and The Netherlands, compulsory. The function of the chamber is to assist its members in their business interests, chiefly through providing information, training, and representation.

Chambers, Sir William (1723–96) British architect. Travels in the Far East and studies in France and Italy helped to mould his eclectic but conservative neoclassical style. His most notable buildings include Somerset House in London (1776) and the pagoda in Kew Gardens (1757–62).

chameleon A lizard belonging to an Old World family, Chamaeleontidae, which contains about 80 species, the majority of which occur in Africa and Madagascar. Chameleons are adapted to life in trees. They have fingers and toes that grasp, and a prehensile tail which can be wrapped around twigs to stabilize them. They capture their food, such as insects, by shooting out their long tongue, which may be extended as far as the length of their body. Their well known ability to change colour is affected by light, temperature, and stress.

chamois A goat-like mountain-dweller, *Rupicapra rupicapra*, belonging to the same subfamily as the wild goat and sheep. It is found in the Alps, the Apennines, and east through the Carpathians into Asia Minor, living high above the tree-line. An elusive, swift-footed animal, it is recognized by its round, short horns (in both sexes) which rise perpendicularly from its head to turn backwards and downwards at the tip to form a hook. It is a slender animal, up to 81 cm (32 inches) tall at the shoulders, with a tawny-coloured coat in summer, changing to blackish-brown in winter.

chamomile (or **camomile**) A strongly scented herb of the genus *Chamaemelum*, which belongs to the sunflower family. They occur throughout Europe and south-west Asia. The daisy-like flowers of the prostrate species, such as *C. nobile*, are cropped for their medicinal properties as a tonic and to reduce fevers. These species, particularly the non-flowering varieties, are also used as a lawn-grass substitute on dry soils.

Chamonix A resort town in the department of Haute-Savoie, eastern France, on the River Arve near the Swiss frontier; pop. (1982) 9,255. It lies at the foot of Mont Blanc. The highest cable-car in the Alps rises from Chamonix to the summit of the Aiguille du Midi.

Champagne A province of north-eastern France adjoining Lorraine. International trade fairs were held there in the Middle Ages. In 1284 the marriage of Jeanne, daughter of Henry III, the last count, to PHILIP IV of France led to union with France. The discovery of the method of making its celebrated sparkling wine, champagne, is attributed to a Benedictine monk, Dom Perignon (1668–1715).

Champaigne, Philippe de (1602–74) Flemish-born painter who became a French citizen in 1629. He trained as a landscape painter and did many fine religious works, but his greatest fame is as a portrait painter. His early work shows influence from the Baroque style of RUBENS, but his style became more sober and classical in line with French artistic trends of the middle of the 17th century. His most famous work was painted to commemorate his daughter's miraculous recovery from paralysis (*Ex-Voto de 1662*). His nephew **Jean-Baptiste de Champaigne** (1631–81) was also a portrait and religious painter.

Champlain, Lake A lake close to sea-level in a long north–south valley in the Appalachians, which connects the middle Saint Lawrence and Hudson River valleys in south-east Canada and north-east USA. Only 10 km (6 miles) of its 172 km (107 miles) lie in Canada. Fed by Lake George to the south-west and by streams from the Green and Adirondack Mountains, to east and west, it drains north to the Saint Lawrence River.

Champlain, Samuel de (1567–1635) French explorer and colonial statesman. He made his first voyage to Canada in 1603, and between 1604 and 1607 explored the eastern coast of North America. In 1608 he was sent to establish a settlement at Quebec, where he developed alliances with the native peoples for trade and defence. He was appointed Lieutenant-Governor in 1612; much of his subsequent career was spent exploring the Canadian interior. After capture and imprisonment by the English (1629–32), he returned to Canada for a final spell as governor (1633–35).

Champs Elysées (in full **Avenue des Champs Elysées**) A celebrated avenue 1.88 km in length between the Place de la Concorde and the Arc de Triomphe in the city of Paris, France, built in open countryside (Elysian Fields) by André Le Nôtre (the landscape gardener of Versailles) after the completion of the Palace of the Tuileries in the 17th century. The upper part is flanked by luxury shops, hotels, restaurants, theatres, and pavement cafés.

Chancellor, Richard (died 1556) English navigator who, in seeking a NORTHEAST PASSAGE to China, reached the northern Russian coast. His visit to Moscow (1553–54) laid the foundations for English trade with Russia. He was pilot to an expedition under Hugh Willoughby, who in a storm found shelter in Vardø, Norway (1553). Chancellor, whose ship was separated from Willoughby's by the storm, went on into the White Sea and was taken overland to Moscow. On a second voyage two years later, he discovered that Willoughby and all his men had perished from the Arctic winter; Chancellor himself lost his life in a shipwreck off the coast of Scotland a few months later.

chancery (from the Latin *cancella*, 'screen', hence a screened-off place, or office) The writing-office attached to the court of a ruler – emperor, pope, or king. Since it supplied the writ necessary for a lawsuit to be heard by the king's judges, it came to be a law court itself, presided over by its head, the Chancellor.

Chandler, Raymond (Thornton) (1888–1959) US novelist. Of British descent and educated largely in England (1896–1912), Chandler is particularly remembered as the creator of the private detective Philip Marlowe and as one of the exponents of the tough, realistic style of hard-boiled detective fiction. His novels, which include *The Big Sleep* (1939), *Farewell, My Lovely* (1940), and *The Long Goodbye* (1953), are written in an ironic, terse, and fast-moving style; many were made into films, especially of the *film noir* genre, and Chandler himself worked on the screenplays.

Chandragupta Maurya (*c.*325–297 BC) Indian emperor. He founded the Mauryan empire, the first empire in India to extend over most of the subcontinent. From his capital at Paliputra he expanded westwards across the River Indus, annexing provinces deep into Afghanistan from Alexander's Greek successors. The empire continued to expand after his death, but ended in 185 BC.

Chandrasekhar, Subrahmanyan (1910–95) Indian-born US astronomer. He worked on stellar evolution, suggesting the process whereby some stars eventually collapse to form a dense white dwarf. He demonstrated that for this to happen the star's mass must not exceed 1.44 solar masses (the Chandrasekhar limit): stars above this mass collapse further to form neutron stars.

Chandrasekhar limit See CHANDRASEKHAR, SUBRAHMANYAN.

Chanel, Coco (born Gabrielle Chanel) (1883–1971) French fashion designer. She established her fashion house in 1924, quickly achieving success with her simple but sophisticated designs. Loose and comfortable, her garments were a radical departure from the dominant stiff corseted styles of the day. She also manufactured her own range of perfumes, costume jewellery, and textiles.

Chaney, Lon (born Alonso Chaney) (1883–1930) US actor. In a career that began in 1913 Chaney played a wide variety of deformed villains and macabre characters in more than 150 films. Chaney was especially known for his sympathetic portrayal of grotesques, such as Quasimodo in *The Hunchback of Notre Dame* (1923) and the musician in *The Phantom of the Opera* (1925).

Changamire (fl. *c.*1500) East African ruler, the name taken by Changa, son of Mwene Mutapa Matope, by adding the Arabic title *amir* (commander) to his given name. On his father's death he killed Nyahuma, the lawful successor. His own son fought Chikuyo, Nyahuma's son, until 1502. He began the dismemberment of the Rozvi empire. His kingdom was known also as Butwa, and lasted until the early 19th century, when the Nguni destroyed it. His successors built a number of stone monuments and added to the Great ZIMBABWE.

change-ringing A way of ringing church bells peculiar to Britain. A set of church bells is called a 'ring'. The number will vary, 12 being the usual maximum. The different orders of ringing are called 'changes'. With a ring of five bells, 120 changes are possible. With 12 bells the number of changes rises to nearly 480 million. Change-ringing is an art of timing and, if the changes are very long, can also be something of an athletic feat.

Chang Jiang The Chinese name for the YANGTZE RIVER.

Changsha The capital of Hunan province in south-east-central China, on the Xiang River; pop. (1990) 1,330,000. It is a river port and major distribution centre on the railway line linking Beijing and Canton (Guangzhou). A noted centre of education for a thousand years, Mao Zedong studied here 1912–18. It has a wide variety of light industries.

channel (in geomorphology) A clear, hollowed-out path cut by fresh or salt water, ice, or lava. Channels vary from shallow tracks of raindrops in a layer of dust to the huge dry channels in the Grand Coulée area, north-west USA, which were cut more than 10,000 years ago by the catastrophic draining of lakes dammed by glaciers. They are cut only when the force of flow (which increases with its depth and speed) exceeds the resistance of the surface. River channels have shallow, rather rectangular cross-sections, very curved courses and fairly regular pools and shallow sections along their long profiles, which fall in height as one travels downstream. Glacier channels resemble smooth parabolas in cross-section. They have few sharp curves but many very deep hollows and sharp rises along their course; and the outlet – as in the case of FIORDS – is often higher than the up-valley sections. Sea channels are much the most irregular in all dimensions, since flow directions vary with winds, currents, and tides; and frequent changes of sea-level in the PLEISTOCENE EPOCH have led to major differences in shapes and sizes.

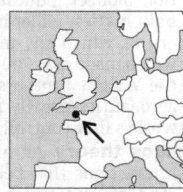

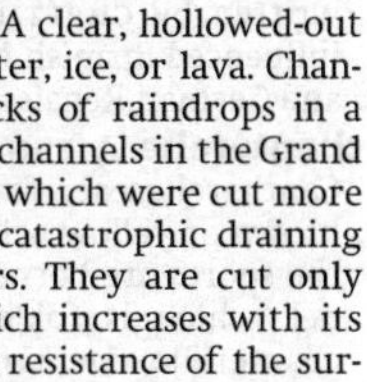

Channel Islands (French **Îles Normandes**) A group of islands in the English Channel off the north-west coast of France, of which the largest are Jersey, Guernsey, and Alderney; area 194 sq km (75 sq miles); pop. (1991) 146,000; chief towns, St Helier (Jersey), St Peter Port (Guernsey). Other smaller islands include Sark, Herm, Jethou, Brechou, Lihou, and the Minquiers. Divided administratively into the Bailiwicks of Jersey and Guernsey, they are the only portions of the former Duchy of Normandy that still owe allegiance to Britain, to which they have been attached since the Norman Conquest in 1066.

Channel Tunnel A TUNNEL beneath the English Channel providing a fixed link between the UK and France. The present tunnel was begun in 1986 and completed in 1994. It comprises two tunnels, each 7.6 m (25 feet) in diameter and 49.4 km (30.7 miles) long, 37.5 km (23.3 miles) of which is under water, and a service tunnel. The tunnels are, on average, 40 m (130 feet) below the sea-bed. They carry high-speed shuttle trains with vehicles and passengers on board between the UK and France. The journey time is about 35 minutes, enabling the centre of Paris to be reached from the centre of London in about four hours.

chanson (French, 'song') The polyphonic settings of a particular type of French verse written during the 14th to 16th centuries. The *chanson* was an ancestor of the MADRIGAL, though simpler in style and with greater emphasis placed upon the upper voice. Later examples, from the end of the 15th century, were no longer dependent on the original poetic form for their structure. Almost any kind of verse-repeating solo song of the 17th to 20th centuries is also called a chanson.

chanson de geste (French, 'song of deeds') Narrative poem recounting legendary heroic exploits of the time of Charlemagne (742–814). The poems (of which about 100 survive) date from the 11th to the 14th centuries, and were sung to short musical phrases, probably involving repetition, by *trouvères* (see MINSTREL). The most famous, *La Chanson de Roland* (early 12th century), recounts the death of Roland, one of Charlemagne's knights, with remarkable grandeur and pathos. The *chansons de geste* were predecessors of the verse romances written by CHRÉTIEN DE TROYES. They strongly influenced Spanish heroic poetry as well as Italian and German Renaissance epics.

chantarelle A FUNGUS belonging to the family Cantharellaceae, found in woodland. Most are brown or yellow, with funnel-shaped fruit bodies; the spores are borne on the underside of the funnel, which is folded into ridges. The common chanterelle, *Cantharellus cibarius*, is regarded as a delicacy, though the similar-looking but unrelated Jack o'lantern fungus, *Omphalotus olearia*, is poisonous.

Chantrey, Sir Francis (1781–1841) British sculptor. He succeeded Nollekens as the most successful sculptor of portrait busts in Britain, and his enormous workshop also executed statues and church monuments. Once he had become famous he did little of the actual marble cutting himself, leaving this to assistants. He became extremely wealthy, and left the bulk of his fortune to the Royal Academy for the purchase of works of art.

Chanute, Octave (1832–1910) French-born US aviation pioneer. Educated as a railway engineer, he built his first glider in 1896 and later produced others, of which the most successful was a biplane which made over 700 flights. His encouragement of the Wright brothers and of the serious study of aeronautics greatly assisted them in making the world's first controlled powered flight.

chaos theory An attempt to explain events or interactions that behave in a way which appears random, and which is different from what we would expect from calculation. The behaviour is not actually 'chaotic' in the usual sense of the word; it appears chaotic because it does not follow our prediction. If we knew everything about the initial conditions we could predict even chaotic behaviour – though, because it followed our prediction, the behaviour would then appear orderly. Weather forecasting is an example of an activity in which it is impossible to find all the information required to make accurate long-term predictions because weather is the result of complicated interactions between a number of different factors, although the system is, in principle, deterministic. An often-quoted illustration of the effects of chaos is the **butterfly effect**. Weather systems are so sensitive to small disturbances that it is said that a butterfly fluttering its wings on one side of the world could determine whether or not a tornado occurs on the other side.

chaparral A type of vegetation found in areas of low to moderate rainfall in the US states of California and Oregon. It is dominated by scrub or low-growing trees, the majority of which are drought-resistant evergreens.

Chapel Royal The musicians and clergy employed by the English monarch for religious services and, by extension, whatever building these services take place in. Records of the Chapel Royal go back as far as the first year (1135) of King Stephen's reign. The altos, tenors, and basses are known as Gentlemen of the Chapel Royal, and the boys as Children of the Chapel Royal. They are now based at St James's Palace, London.

Chaplin, Sir Charles Spencer (known as 'Charlie') (1889–1977) British film actor and director. Moving to Hollywood in 1914 he made many short comedies, mostly playing a little bowler-hatted tramp, a character that remained his trademark for more than 25 years. A master of mime who combined pathos with slapstick clowning, he was best suited to the silent medium; his most successful films include *The Kid* (1921) and *The Gold Rush* (1925). The director of all his films, he combined speech and mime in *Modern Times* (1936), while *The Great Dictator* (1940), a satire on Hitler, was his first proper sound film and his last appearance in his familiar bowler-hatted role.

Chapman, George (*c*.1560–1634) English poet and dramatist. Although acclaimed as a dramatist in his day, he is now chiefly known for his translations of Homer; twelve books of the *Iliad* were published in 1611 and the complete *Iliad* and *Odyssey* in 1616. They are commemorated in Keats's sonnet 'On First Looking into Chapman's Homer' (1817).

Chappe, Claude (1763–1805) French inventor who devised the visual SEMAPHORE telegraph system. Destined for the Church, Chappe had his career plans upset by the French Revolution of 1789, after which he turned his attention to developing signalling systems (see TELEGRAPHY). He finally settled on one in which movable wooden arms were pivoted on tall towers to represent letters of the alphabet and other symbols. In 1793 the government commissioned a telegraph line from Paris to Lille that involved fifteen relay stations. He completed the line in a year, and a second was commissioned, but he died before it was finished.

Chapultepec Conference (1945) An Inter-American conference, held in Mexico City. The Act of Chapultepec (1945), adopted by twenty republics, resolved to undertake joint action in repelling any aggression against an American state. This was formalized by the Inter-American Treaty of Reciprocal Assistance (the Rio Treaty, 1947), and constituted a significant step in the history of PAN-AMERICANISM.

characin A freshwater fish of the large family Characidae, with over 500 species occurring in both warm-temperate and tropical America and in tropical Africa. They include the predatory piranhas, *Serrasalmus* species, of South America and the tigerfish, *Hydrocynus goliath*, of Africa, as well as the aquarists' brightly coloured TETRAS. Characins are usually slender, with fully scaled bodies, a rayed dorsal fin, and an adipose dorsal fin. Their teeth are highly developed.

charango The treble GUITAR of the Andes with four or five double or triple courses, set of strings tuned to the same note. The back may be flat, but is often made of an armadillo shell, or of wood carved in that shape.

charcoal Black, brittle CARBON that results from the burning of organic material below 500°C in a limited supply of air. It comprises almost pure amorphous carbon, and burns with great heat and no flame. One tonne of wood yields 200–350 kg (450–750 pounds) of charcoal, together with turpentine, creosote, methanol, pitch, and flammable gases. Charcoal is a constituent of GUNPOWDER, and before the introduction of coke, it was used for SMELTING ores and forging metals. Because of its reactivity and highly porous structure it finds modern applications in RESPIRATORS and in removing impurities from liquids and gases.

As a drawing material its use dates back to Roman times and possibly much earlier. Charcoal is easily rubbed off the drawing surface unless a fixative is used, so it has been much favoured for preparatory work, for example for CARTOONS or for outlining a design that would be gone over with a more permanent medium. It has also been used for finished drawings, however, some artists finding its broad, soft-edged effects particularly suitable to their style.

Charcot, Jean-Martin (1825–93) French neurologist. Working at the Salpêtrière clinic in Paris, he established links between various neurological conditions and particular lesions in the central nervous system. He described several such diseases, some of which are named after him, and he is regarded as one of the founders of modern neurology. Charcot's work on hysteria was taken up by his pupil Sigmund FREUD.

Chardin, Jean-Baptiste-Simeon (1699–1779) French painter of still life and genre, in which fields he was one of the greatest masters of all time. He worked during the heyday of the elegant, lighthearted ROCOCO style, but his own paintings are completely different in spirit, having a feeling of deep seriousness in spite of the modest subjects he depicted. His genre scenes are also taken from domestic life and usually contain only one or two figures, presented without sentimentality. Late in life, when his sight was failing, he gave up painting in oils and turned to pastels, producing some penetrating portraits.

charge-coupled device (CCD) See CCD CAMERA.

Charing Cross A district in central London, England, in the City of Westminster at the west end of the Strand. In 1290 Edward I erected the last of 12 ELEANOR CROSSES here; each cross marked the resting place of Queen Eleanor's coffin on its journey from Nottinghamshire, where she died, to Westminster Abbey.

chariot A fast, two-wheeled, horse-drawn vehicle. They were originally designed for use in war, and developed from the battle-wagons used by the SUMERIANS *c.*2500 BC, which had four wheels, were drawn by onagers (wild asses), and served as mobile fighting platforms. The use of horses, and light two-wheeled vehicles adapted to them, was introduced to the Near East from the region between the Black Sea and the Caspian *c.*2000 BC. (Horses, which were only the size of ponies, were rarely used for riding.) Their crews consisted of two or three people, who were generally armed with BOWS or javelins. In northern Europe, however, the chariot was used to carry into battle soldiers who fought on foot. A popular tactic was to equip chariot wheels with scythe blades to hack at the legs of enemy soldiers.

charismatic movement A movement of spiritual renewal found in Roman Catholicism and Protestantism, but particularly associated with the PENTECOSTAL MOVEMENT. Known as 'charismatics', adherents believe that the experiences of the first disciples on receiving the Holy Spirit should be repeated in the present day. Particular emphasis is placed on 'baptism in the Holy Spirit', an experience equivalent to being 'born again' (reconverted to Jesus), often accompanied by 'spiritual gifts'. 'Speaking in tongues' – a highly charged, undeciphered syllabic language said to be directly transmitted by the Holy Spirit – is commonly practised among charismatics. The charismatic movement is strong in Latin America and among Black Churches and is increasingly popular elsewhere.

charity See VOLUNTARY ORGANIZATION.

Charlemagne (Latin *Carolus Magnus*, Charles the Great) (742–814) King of the Franks 768–814 and Holy Roman emperor (as Charles I) 800–14. He created an empire by conquering and Christianizing the Saxons (772–77; 782–85), Lombards (774), and Avars (791–99), and restoring areas of Italy to the pope. His coronation by Pope Leo III in Rome on Christmas Day, 800, is taken as having inaugurated the Holy Roman Empire. He gave government new moral drive and religious responsibility, and encouraged commerce and agriculture. A well-educated man, he promoted the arts and education, and under Alcuin his principal court at Aachen became a major centre of learning. The political cohesion of his empire did not last, but the influence of his scholars persisted in the Carolingian Renaissance.

Charles Two kings of England, Scotland, and Ireland. **Charles I** (1600–49), son of James I, reigned 1625–49. His reign was dominated by the deepening religious and constitutional crisis that eventually resulted in the English Civil War. His attempt to rule without Parliament (1629–40) eventually failed when he was obliged to recall Parliament to fund his war with Scotland; disputes with the new Parliament led to civil war in 1642. Charles surrendered to the Scots in 1646 and was handed over to Parliament in 1647. He escaped and made an alliance with the Scots in return for religious concessions, but the Royalist forces were defeated in 1648 and the Parliamentary army demanded Charles's death. He was tried by a special Parliamentary court and beheaded. **Charles II** (1630–85), son of Charles I, reigned 1660–85. After his father's execution in 1649 Charles was declared king in Scotland and then crowned there in 1651, but was forced into exile the same year, when his army attempted to invade England and was defeated by Cromwell's forces at Worcester. He remained in exile on the Continent for nine years before he was restored after the collapse of Cromwell's regime. Charles displayed considerable adroitness in handling the difficult constitutional situation, but continuing religious and political strife dogged his reign. Although he failed to produce a legitimate heir, he moved to ensure the Protestant succession by arranging the marriage of his niece Mary to William of Orange.

Charles Four kings of Spain. **Charles I** (1500–58), son of Philip I, reigned 1516–56, Holy Roman emperor (as Charles V) 1519–56. He united the Spanish and imperial thrones when he inherited the latter in 1519. His reign was characterized by the struggle against Protestantism in Germany, by rebellion in Castile, and by war with France (1521–44). Exhausted by these struggles, Charles handed Naples, the Netherlands, and Spain over to his son Philip II and the imperial crown (1556) to his brother Ferdinand, and retired to a monastery in Spain. **Charles II** (1661–1700) reigned 1665–1700. The last Habsburg to be king of Spain, he inherited a kingdom already in a decline which he was unable to halt. Childless, he chose Philip of Anjou, grandson of Louis XIV of France, as his successor; this ultimately gave rise to the War of the Spanish Succession. **Charles III** (1716–88) reigned 1759–88. He tried with some success to restore Spain's position as an international power through an increase in foreign trade, while at home his reforms brought Spain a brief cultural and economic revival. **Charles** IV (1748–1819) reigned 1788–1808. He was dominated by his wife Maria Luisa and her lover Manuel de Godoy (Prime Minister from 1792). During the Napoleonic Wars he suffered the loss of the Spanish fleet, destroyed along with that of France at Trafalgar in 1805. Following the French invasion of Spain in 1807, Charles was forced to abdicate. He died in exile in Rome.

Charles Seven Holy Roman emperors. **Charles** I See CHARLEMAGNE. **Charles** II (823–77) reigned 875–77. **Charles** III (839–88) reigned 881–87. **Charles** IV (1316–78), reigned 1355–78. **Charles** V (or Charles I of Spain) See CHARLES (kings of Spain). **Charles** VI (1685–1740) reigned 1711–40. His claim to the Spanish throne instigated the War of the Spanish Succession, but he was ultimately unsuccessful. He became emperor on the death of his elder brother; with no surviving male heirs, he drafted the Pragmatic Sanction in an attempt to ensure that his daughter Maria Theresa succeeded to the Habsburg dominions. The failure of this to be accepted by the whole of Europe triggered a struggle for power on Charles's death and the War of the Austrian Succession. **Charles** VII (1697–1745) reigned 1742–45.

Charles I (1226–85) King of Naples and Sicily 1266–85, son of Louis VIII of France. He acquired PROVENCE by marriage in 1246. Pope Urban IV was under severe threat from the HOHENSTAUFENS and gave him the kingdom of Sicily in order to curtail their power. He defeated and killed Manfred at Benevento, effectively ending Hohenstaufen influence, but then went on to take Naples as well as most of northern Italy, himself becoming a real threat to papal interests. His ambitions were ended by the uprising known as the SICILIAN VESPERS in which he was assassinated and the French expelled.

Charles II (known as **Charles the Bald**) (823–77) King of the West Franks 843–77, Emperor of Germany 875–77. He was the son of Emperor Louis the Pious. After the death of their father he and his brother, Louis the German, made war on their eldest brother Lothair, who had inherited the title of King of the West Franks. By the Treaty of Verdun in 843 Charles gained that kingdom. He and Louis divided Lothair's central kingdom between them in 870 by the Treaty of Mersen, and Charles gained the imperial title in 875. The internal conflicts of his reign were further complicated by VIKING incursions. He was a noted patron of scholarship and the arts.

Charles III (known as **Charles the Fat**) (832–88) King of the Franks 884–87, Emperor of Germany 882–88. He was the youngest son of Louis the German. He inherited Swabia and acquired both east and west Frankish kingdoms by 884 after his older brothers died. He was unsuccessful in repelling SARACEN invaders and was obliged to buy a respite from attacks by the VIKINGS and so was deposed in 887. His death marked the end of the Carolingian monopoly of kingship over the Franks.

Charles IV (1316–78) King of Bohemia 1346–78, Holy Roman Emperor 1347–78. He acquired authority over Austria and Hungary in 1364, and received the imperial crown from the pope, in Rome, in 1355. The Golden Bull (1356) issued in his reign formed the imperial constitution, regulating the duties of the seven ELECTORS. He was an intellectual, interested in the development of the German language, and founded the University of Prague in 1348.

Charles V (known as **Charles the Wise**) (1337–80) King of France 1364–80. He earned his nickname from his intellectual pursuits which included book-collecting and artistic patronage, his religious piety, and his cautious adoption of delaying and 'scorched-earth' tactics in fighting the English during the HUNDRED YEARS WAR. Assuming responsibility as Regent of France in 1356 when his father, John II was captured at POITIERS, he quelled revolt in Paris and from the Jacquerie and, aided by the Constable of France, Bertrand du Guesclin, was able to recover most of France from the invading English forces.

Charles VII (1403–61) King of France 1422–61. During his youth France was badly ruled by his father Charles the Mad and much territory was lost. Internal quarrels and war with England dominated his reign. At the time of his accession to the throne, much of northern France was under English occupation, including Reims, where he should have been crowned. After the intervention of JOAN OF ARC, however, the French experienced a dramatic military revival and Charles was crowned at Reims in 1429. He established greater control over the Church in the Pragmatic Sanction of Bourges of 1438, which upheld the right of the French Church to administer its property and nominate clergy to benefices, independently of the papacy. His reign eventually saw the defeat of the English and the end of the HUNDRED YEARS WAR. Having recovered most of the land his country had lost to the British, he modernized the administration of the army and did much to lay the foundations of French power in the following decades

Charles X (1757–1836) King of France 1824–30. As the Comte d'Artois, the dissolute and reactionary brother of Louis XVI, he was ordered by the king to leave France in 1789 and became the leader of the exiled royalists. He returned to France in 1814 and during the reign of his next brother, LOUIS XVIII, led the ultra-royalist party. His proclamation to rule by divine right and his choice of ministers who did not reflect liberal majorities in Parliament led to unrest. The defeat of an unpopular ministry in June 1830 prompted him to issue the July Ordinances, which established rigid control of the press, dissolved the newly elected chamber, and restricted suffrage. These measures enraged the populace and he was forced, in the JULY REVOLUTION, to abdicate. After the succession of LOUIS PHILIPPE, he returned to Britain.

Charles XII (1682–1718) King of Sweden 1697–1718. The story of his reign is reflected in the progress of the NORTHERN WAR. He was attacked by a coalition of enemies and won a series of victories; then in 1707 he invaded Russia and was defeated at Poltava. He took refuge in Turkish territory was imprisoned and escaped and was finally killed while on another military campaign. His wars left Sweden financially drained and no longer one of the great powers of Europe.

Charles XII (or **Karl XII**) (1682–1718) King of Sweden 1697–1718. Three years after his succession, he embarked on the Great Northern War against the encircling powers of Denmark, Poland-Saxony, and Russia. In the early years he won a series of victories, but in 1709 he embarked on an expedition deep into Russia which ended in the destruction of his army at Poltava and the internment of Charles until 1715. He resumed his military career after his return but was killed while besieging a fortress in Norway.

Charles XIV (born Jean Baptiste Jules Bernadotte) (1763–1844) King of Sweden and Norway 1818–44. A supporter of the French Revolution, he served brilliantly under NAPOLEON BONAPARTE in the Italian Campaign. At one time a rival to Napoleon, he nevertheless supported the latter when he proclaimed the empire in 1804. He fought at Austerlitz and Wagram and became governor of Hanover before being invited (1810) by the Swedish Riksdag (Parliament) to succeed the senile, childless Charles XIII. He accepted, becoming a member of the Lutheran Church. As crown prince he allied Sweden with Britain and Russia and played an important part in the defeat of Napoleon at the battle of Leipzig (1813). Having invaded Denmark, he obtained Danish agreement at the Treaty of Kiel (1814) for the transfer of NORWAY to Sweden. He succeeded Charles XIII in 1818. Autocratic in style and opposed to demands for a free press and more liberal government, he nevertheless maintained popular support throughout his reign. He was the founder of the present Swedish dynasty.

Charles, Jacques (1746–1823) French mathematician, physicist, and inventor who pioneered the use of hydrogen-filled balloons and, around 1787, discovered the gas law stating that a fixed mass of gas kept at constant pressure expands by a constant fraction of its volume at 0°C, for every degree its temperature is raised (see GAS).

Charles, Prince (full name Charles Philip Arthur George, Prince of Wales) (1948–) Heir apparent to Elizabeth II. Educated at Gordonstoun School in Scotland and Trinity College, Cambridge, he was invested as Prince of Wales in 1969. He served in the Royal Navy 1971–76, and married Lady Diana Spencer (see DIANA, PRINCESS OF WALES) in 1981. They had two children, Prince William Arthur Philip Louis (born 1982) and Prince Henry Charles Albert David ('Harry', born 1984). The couple publicly announced their separation in 1993 and divorced in 1996, a year before Diana was killed in a car crash.

Charles Martel (*c*.688–741) Frankish ruler of the eastern part of the Frankish kingdom from 715 and the whole kingdom from 719. He earned his nickname *Martel* ('the hammer') from his victory at Poitiers in 732, which effectively checked the Muslim advance into Europe. His rule marked the beginning of Carolingian power; Charlemagne was his grandson.

Charles the Bold (1433–77) Duke of BURGUNDY 1467–77. He was the greatest of the dukes of Burgundy, and almost succeeded in creating a kingdom independent of France. He tried to persuade the Holy Roman Emperor to grant him the title of king in 1473. He supported the League of the Public Weal against the French king, Louis XI, and, after 1467, concentrated with successful results on expansion into the Rhineland and Alsace. After 1475, war with the Swiss and defeat in battle culminated in his own death in battle. His realm was absorbed by the French and by Maximilian I.

Charleston A US ballroom dance of the 1920s, said to have originated among blacks in Charleston, South Carolina. It was in fast 4/4 time, with a characteristic syncopated RAGTIME rhythm and involved side kicking and swinging movements of the body.

Charlestown The chief town and port of the Caribbean island of Nevis in the federation of St Kitts-Nevis; pop. (1980) 1,243. Linked by ferry to Basseterre on St Kitts, it was the birthplace of Alexander Hamilton, architect of the US Constitution.

Charlotte Amalie The capital of the US Virgin Islands, on the south coast of the Caribbean island of St Thomas; pop. (1985) 52,660. Originally known to its Danish settlers as Tap Hus ('rum house'), it was renamed in 1730 after the wife of King Christian V of Denmark. From 1921 to 1937 it was named St Thomas. Its port is frequently visited by cruise ships.

Charlottetown The capital, chief port, and tourist centre of the Canadian province of Prince Edward Island; pop. (1991) 15,400. First settled by the French *c*.1720, it was laid out by the British in 1768. The town developed with the fishing and timber industries during the 19th century and was the venue in 1864 for the Charlottetown Conference of the Maritime Provinces which led to the eventual confederation of Canada. It is the smallest of Canada's provincial capitals.

Charlton, John (known as 'Jack') (1935–) British footballer and manager, brother of Bobby CHARLTON. A rugged defender, he played for Leeds United (1952–73) and was a member of the England side that won the World Cup in 1966. He later managed Middlesbrough, Sheffield Wednesday, and Newcastle United before taking over the management of the Republic of Ireland national team (1986–95).

Charlton, Sir Robert (known as 'Bobby') (1937–) British footballer, brother of Jack CHARLTON. An outstanding striker, he played for Manchester United 1954–73, appearing 751 times and scoring 245 goals, and for England (1957–73); he scored forty-nine goals for his country (a record for an England player) and was a member of the side that won the World Cup in 1966. After retiring as a player he managed Preston North End (1973–75) and became a director of Manchester United (from 1984).

charm (in particle physics) See QUARK.

Charon (in astronomy) The only known satellite of Pluto, discovered by the US astronomers James Christy and Robert Harrington in 1978. It is the only natural satellite in the Solar System whose orbital period is synchronous with the rotation period of its planet. It is also the largest satellite in the Solar System relative to its planet: its diameter of 1,200 km is about half that of Pluto. Its surface is probably covered by water ice. In 1985–90 its mutual eclipses with Pluto were observed by PHOTOMETRY, yielding the orbital elements of the system and a rough map of Pluto's surface.

Charon (in Greek mythology) The ferryman who carried the dead across the River Styx to Hades. The Greeks used to put a coin in the mouth of corpses as Charon's fee.

Charpentier, Marc-Antoine (*c*.1645–1704) French composer. A serious rival of LULLY in his lifetime, he was associated with MOLIÈRE's troupe (Comédie Française), writing incidental music for its productions until about 1686. It is for the variety and excellence of his sacred music that he is now remembered. This includes eleven settings of the mass, ten magnificat settings and over 200 MOTETS. He was master of a great variety of techniques, from the rich POLYPHONY of the old style to the harmonization of carol tunes in the well-known *Messe de minuit pour Noël*.

charr A species of fish of the salmon family, Salmonidae, distributed in cool, fresh waters of the Northern Hemisphere, and in Arctic seas. In the north it is migratory, feeding in the sea on crustaceans and fishes and returning to rivers to spawn. Elsewhere it is found in mountain lakes in which it has been isolated since the Ice Ages. In lakes it is very variable in size, coloration, and body form.

chart See MAPS AND CHARTS.

Charter 77 A Czechoslovak human rights movement. Named after a document initially signed in 1977 by 242 academics, intellectuals, and churchmen, the charter appealed to the Czech government to adjust the country's laws in conformity with the Universal Declaration of Human Rights enshrined in the United Nations covenants, and to respect in practice the agreements of the HELSINKI CONFERENCE. It failed to win widespread support, but some of its members, among them Václav HAVEL, became leading figures in post-communist CZECHOSLOVAKIA.

chartered company A form of trading company that developed from the European medieval trading guilds, and which was prominent in the late 16th and 17th centuries. The discovery by explorers of India and America stimulated individual merchants into forming groups, safe-guarded by royal charter in order to monopolize trade. Governments awarded exclusive trading rights in a particular area to a few rich merchants. Such companies were easy to control and, with their specially granted diplomatic, legislative, and military authority, they acted as virtual representatives of the crown. Since the companies were so restrictive, they could arouse considerable domestic opposition.

Chartism A popular movement in Britain for electoral and social reform (1836–48). The REFORM ACT of 1832 had left the mass of the population without any voice in the country's affairs, and widespread discontent was fuelled by a slump in the economy. The Chartist movement began with the formation of the London Working Men's Association, led by William Lovett and Francis Place, who drew up a programme of reform for the common people. In 1838 *The People's Charter* was launched at a meeting in Birmingham: it called for universal male suffrage, annual parliaments, vote by ballot, abolition of the property qualification for Members of Parliament, payment of Members of Parliament, and equal electoral districts. In 1839, the Chartists, now strongly influenced by the Irish radical Feargus O'CONNOR, met in London to prepare a petition to the House of Commons. The meeting revealed deep differences of opinion and after Parliament had rejected the petition, there was uncertainty about the movement's future. During that year there were riots in Birmingham and throughout the north of England; the Newport Rising took place in Monmouthshire, and several Chartist leaders were arrested and imprisoned. Reorganizing themselves, in 1842 the Chartists presented a second petition, signed by three million supporters, to Parliament, which again refused to listen to their claims. The plan for a final demonstration, to be held in London in 1848 for the purpose of presenting yet another petition, was called off after the government threatened military resistance, and the movement faded into insignificance, though many Chartists were later active in radical politics.

Chartres A historic, market town and the capital of Eure-et-Loire department in the Centre region of northern France, on the River Eure; pop. (1990) 41,850. It is noted for its vast twin-spired 12th–13th-century Gothic cathedral (a world heritage monument) in which Henry IV was crowned King of France in 1594. Its stained glass and carved portals are consummate works of art.

Charybdis In Greek legend, a dangerous whirlpool opposite the cave of Scylla in a narrow channel of the sea. It was later identified with Galofalo on the Strait of Messina near Cape Faro in Sicily.

chat Any of various unrelated birds. The Australian chats are four species of small birds of the genus *Ephthianura* that live in very dry areas in Australia. Chats are also groups of species in the thrush family, such as stonechats and whinchats, of the species *Saxicola*. Most of the latter are small, brightly coloured species which live in open country, but some are secretive and live among rocks or scrub. Four members of the family of New World WARBLERS are also called chats, the best known being the yellow-breasted chat, *Icteria virens*, which is a summer visitor to North America. It is a heavily built bird for a warbler, brown above, bright yellow below, and with a rather large bill.

Chateaubriand, François-René, Vicomte de (1768–1848) French writer and diplomat. An important figure in early French romanticism, he established his literary reputation with *Atala* (1801), but *Le Génie du christianisme* (1802), which contributed to the post-Revolution religious revival in France, won him his greatest fame. A supporter of the royalist cause during the French Revolution, he lived in exile in England (1793–1800), where he published his *Essai sur les révolutions* (1797). His autobiography, *Mémoires d'outre-tombe* (1849–50), gives an eloquent account of his life against a background of political upheaval.

Châteaugay (or **Châteauguay**) A town in southern Quebec, Canada, on the Châteaugay and St Lawrence rivers south-west of Montreal; pop. (1991) 60,500. It was the site in 1813 of a defeat of American forces attempting to invade Canada.

Châteauroux The capital of the department of Indre in the Centre region of northern France, on the River Indre; pop. (1990) 52,950. The French *Gitane* cigarettes are made here.

Château-Thierry A town in the department of Aisne in the Picardy region of northern France, on the River Marne; pop. (1982) 14,900. It was the birthplace of the writer of fables, Jean de la Fontaine (1621–95).

Châtellerault (or **Châtelherault**) An ancient trading port on the River Vienne in the Poitou-Charentes region of western France; pop. (1990) 3,690. The philosopher Descartes lived here.

Chatham A town with a former naval base on the estuary of the River Medway, 45 km (28 miles) east of London, England; pop. (1981) 66,100.

Chatham, 1st Earl of See PITT, WILLIAM (the Elder).

Chatham Islands An island group comprising the islands of Pitt (Rangihaute) and Chatham (Whairikauri), situated in the south-west Pacific Ocean to the east of New Zealand to which they belong; area 965 sq km (372 sq miles); pop. (1991) 769. The islands were discovered in 1791 by the British sailor Lt. William Broughton who named them after his ship, the *Chatham*.

Chattanooga An industrial city in the mountains of eastern Tennessee, USA, on the Tennessee River; pop. (1990) 152,470. Founded as a trading post in 1810, it was a centre for the shipping of salt and cotton before the introduction of the iron industry in the 1870s. After an increase in the generation of hydroelectric power was made possible by the Tennessee Valley Authority project in the 1930s, the city's manufacturing industries expanded. It manufactures textiles, metal products, primary metals, and chemicals.

chatterer The scaly chatterer, *Turdoides aylmeri*, a bird of the BABBLER family; it is greyish-brown with paler edgings to its feathers and occurs in East Africa. Other members of this family, such as *T. fulva* and *T. rubiginosa*, as well as COTINGAS,

WAXWINGS, and other species are also called chatterers.

Chatterton, Thomas (1752–70) British poet. He is chiefly remembered for his fabricated poems professing to be the work of Thomas Rowley, an imaginary 15th-century monk. Poverty and lack of recognition drove Chatterton to suicide at the age of 17. First published in 1777, the Rowley poems were eventually proved spurious in the philologist W. W. Skeat's 1871 edition.

Chaucer, Geoffrey (*c*.1343–1400) English poet. His writings develop from an early period of French influence (culminating in the *Book of the Duchess*, an allegorical lament, *c*.1370), through his middle period of both French and Italian influences (which includes the dream poems *House of Fame* (*c*.1374–85), *Parliament of Fowls*, and *Troilus and Criseyde* (*c*.1385) – one of the great poems on love in the English language), to the last period during which he produced most of his masterpiece, the *Canterbury Tales* (begun 1387). In his heroic COUPLETS, he established the iambic PENTAMETER as the standard English metre. Chaucer strongly influenced the development of Middle English, and his work is regarded by many as the starting-point of English literature.

Chauliac, Guy de (*c*.1300–68) French physician. Probably the most influential surgeon of the Middle Ages, he was private physician to three successive popes in Avignon from 1342. In his *Chirurgia Magna* (1363) Chauliac was the first to describe many surgical techniques, and it remained the standard work in Europe until at least the 17th century.

Chavín art See SOUTH AMERICAN INDIAN ART.

Chavín culture A civilization which flourished in Peru 1000–200 BC. The culture was based on the ceremonial centre of Chavín de Huantar, high in the Andes 280 km (175 miles) north of Lima. It united an area 800 km (500 miles) along the Peruvian coast in a common culture, and its influence spread almost as far again. The unifying force was probably religious rather than political, the most characteristic feature being figures, presumably gods, with jaguar fangs projecting from their lips. Notable advances included improved maize, the back-strap loom, and metallurgy. As its religious authority waned, regional groups appeared, that dominated Peru for the next thousand years.

Chechenya (or **Chechnya**, **Chechen Republic**) A republic of the Russian Federation, in the northern Caucasus; area 19,300 sq km (7,350 sq miles); pop. (1990) 1,290,000 (including Ingushetia); capital, Groznyy. Absorbed into the Russian empire during the 1850s, the Chechen and Ingush people maintained separate autonomous regions after the Russian Revolution, but were united in 1934 into a single autonomous republic. Large numbers of Chechens were moved into Central Asia by Stalin in 1944. Following the breakup of the Soviet Union in 1991 Chechenya and Ingushetia split apart again, declaring themselves unilaterally independent of the Russian Federation. This move eventually led to bloody conflicts with Russian troops which invaded Chechenya in 1994. Chief industries include engineering, oil production, food processing, and the manufacture of chemicals, building materials, and timber products.

Cheddar A village in the Mendip Hills of Somerset, south-west England, near the dramatic cliffs of the Cheddar Gorge. It gives its name to a firm smooth cheese originally made here.

Cheddar Gorge A narrow, rocky gorge 120 m (400 feet) deep in the Mendip Hills of south-west England. Erosion has exposed the grey limestones of the Lower Carboniferous Period. Water was the main agent of erosion, but the gorge is now dry. Numerous caves contain spectactular STALACTITES and stalagmites, and relics of Stone Age man have been discovered there.

cheese manufacture The production of the DAIRY PRODUCT cheese by separating milk into curd (mostly fat and the protein casein) and whey (sugars, some protein, water, and salts), pressing the curds to further remove moisture, and then ripening. This separation may be achieved by the addition to the milk of the ENZYME rennet; by the addition of a bacterial culture which acidifies the milk through fermentation; or by direct addition of acid. The milk is kept warm as it curdles; the curd is then cut and mildly heated to release the whey. The separated curd is pressed into moulds or hoops; most cheeses are then allowed to ripen, but some, like cottage cheese, may be sold fresh. In the ripening process, microorganisms, most commonly lactic-acid-producing bacteria, act on the cheese to produce the desired body and flavour. Control of temperature and moisture during ripening is critical in obtaining the desired cheese.

cheese-mite A tiny mite related to other MITE species, such as grain mites, that attack stored products. It is especially fond of foods with high fat and protein content, so that cheese is inevitably at risk. In some European countries they are deliberately introduced into ripening cheeses in order to impart a characteristic fragrance and appearance.

cheese-skipper A species of FLY, *Piophila casei*, whose larvae live in maturing and stored cheese. If disturbed, the larva takes its 'tail' in its mouth, tenses its body, and then suddenly releases the tail, resulting in a skipping movement. It belongs to a small family of true flies which normally breed in carrion.

cheetah A large CAT, *Acinonyx jubatus*, with long, slender legs; it is the fastest land animal on Earth, able to reach a speed of 72 km/hour (45 miles per hour) in two seconds from a standing start. The top speed of this cat is 112 km/hour (70 miles per hour); this pace, however, can only be maintained over some 450 m (1,500 feet) or so. It has for long been associated with humans and trained to hunt like a dog. Unlike many cats, it hunts during daylight, using sight rather than smell. In Asia it was once found from the Caspian Sea to Sumatra, but it is becoming a rarity; in Africa it is disappearing with the encroachment of man.

Cheever, John (1912–82) US short-story writer and novelist. He was contributing short stories regularly for the *New Yorker* by the age of 22. His stories frequently deal satirically with affluent New Englanders living in suburbia, and have been collected in such volumes as *The Housebreaker of Shady Hill* (1958). His novels include *The Wapshot Chronicle* (1957) and its sequel, *The Wapshot Scandal* (1964).

CHEKA Soviet secret police. An acronym for the All-Russian Extraordinary Commission for the Suppression of Counter-revolution and Sabotage, it was instituted by LENIN (1917) and run by Dzerzhinski, a Pole. Lenin envisaged the need for terror to protect his revolution and this was its purpose. Its headquarters, the Lubyanka prison in Moscow, contained offices and places for torture and execution. In 1922 the CHEKA became the GPU or secret police and later the OGPU (United State Political Administration). The OGPU was replaced in 1934 by the NKVD.

Chekhov, Anton (Pavlovich) (1860–1904) Russian dramatist and short-story writer. Chekhov studied medicine in Moscow, and combined his medical practice with writing short humorous stories for journals. He is best known as the author of such plays as *The Seagull* (1895), *Uncle Vanya* (1900), *The Three Sisters* (1901), and *The Cherry Orchard* (1904). First produced at the Moscow Art Theatre under Konstantin Stanislavsky, they established the theatre's reputation and style. Chekhov's work portrays upper-class life in pre-revolutionary Russia with a blend of naturalism and symbolism and almost imperceptible shifts from comedy to tragedy.

Chekiang See ZHEJIANG.

chelation The process by which metal atoms or ions are held by organic molecules that have two or more points at which they can link to the atom or ion (hence the name, from the Latin word *chele*, 'claw'). The metal atom thus becomes part of a ring of atoms. Chelation occurs naturally in soil, where organic compounds released by plants combine with metal ions, such as iron and aluminium. Chelation increases the rate of weathering and is thought to promote LEACHING, since the organometallic complexes, or chelates, tend to be more stable than the metal ions. Natural chelates are stable under acidic conditions but break down when the environment becomes more alkaline, releasing the metal ions.

Chelmsford The county town of Essex, south-east England; pop. (1991) 150,000. Its cathedral dates from 1424. It is the site of the Anglia University (1992).

Chelsea A district of London, England, on the north bank of the River Thames, associated with writers and artists. It gives its name to the Chelsea bun and to the 18th-century porcelain Chelseaware once made here. Chelsea pensioners are retired or disabled soldiers who live in the Chelsea Royal Hospital, designed by Christopher Wren.

Cheltenham A residential, commercial, and resort town in Gloucestershire, west-central England; pop. (1991) 85,900. Formerly noted as a spa town, its saline waters became fashionable after a visit by George III in 1788. It has many Georgian and Regency buildings. It is the headquarters of the UK electronic surveillance service (GCHQ), and at nearby Prestbury Park is a steeplechase course, scene of the annual Cheltenham Gold Cup.

chemical analysis See ANALYSIS.

chemical and biological warfare (CBW) The use of synthetic poisonous substances, or organisms such as disease germs, to kill or injure the enemy. They include chlorine, PHOSGENE, and MUSTARD GAS (first used in World War I), various NERVE GASES, defoliant agents, and viruses and bacteria (for example, anthrax). The use of chemical and biological weapons is prohibited by the GENEVA CONVENTION, but their production, possession, or transfer are not. Unlike their World War I counterparts, modern chemical weapons are sophisticated and may be delivered by long-range artillery, missile, or sprayed from aircraft. To be effective, the chemicals must be inhaled or come into contact with skin. The main defence against them is protective clothing – gas masks and special suits made of rubber or treated synthetic cloth. Biological weapons were banned under the Biological Weapons Convention of 1972, but research production was permitted for defensive purposes. Agreement regarding the limitation of chemical and biological weapons stands high on the agenda of the CONFERENCE ON DISARMAMENT, but many states, particularly in the developing world, are reluctant to give up possession of such weapons because they act as a form of deterrence.

chemical bond The state in which two atoms are held closely together by an attractive force. There are two principal types of bond between atoms, the ionic bond and the covalent bond, although these two represent the extremes, and many compounds exhibit bonding of an intermediate character. See also HYDROGEN BOND. In forming an ionic bond, one atom loses one or more electrons from its outer shell to form a cation, while the other atom gains electrons to form an anion. The resulting electrostatic attraction of the oppositely charged ions holds them together in an IONIC COMPOUND. Covalent bonding involves the sharing of electrons, rather than the complete transfer involved in ionic bonding. The reason that a bond forms is that the energy of the system is lowered by the process. The number of covalent bonds formed by an element is determined by the number of vacancies in its outer shell of electrons. Hydrogen, with one vacancy, can only form one covalent bond. Oxygen, on the other hand, has two vacancies in its outer shell and can thus form two covalent bonds. Thus, when oxygen reacts with hydrogen, the oxygen forms two covalent bonds, one to each hydrogen, forming water, H_2O. When two different atoms form a covalent bond, the resulting diatomic molecule possesses a DIPOLE moment, as the electrons in the bond are not shared equally. The greater the dipole moment, the more ionic the bond. In METALS a different form of bond occurs, called a metallic bond.

chemical engineering The practice of designing, building, operating, and maintaining chemical manufacturing plant. It embraces a wide range of disciplines: structural, electrical, and mechanical engineering, industrial and environmental chemistry, control and advanced manufacturing technologies, as well as financial and economic acumen. It is concerned primarily with the flow of materials and of energy throughout the plant and with maintaining safe operating conditions. Most industrial chemistry can be broken down into a series of unit processes, such as filtration, distillation, or drying, and it is on these processes that chemical engineering is based.

chemical equation A representation of the substances formed and used up in a chemical reaction, and the respective proportions of these. Each substance is represented by its chemical symbol; the equation is then balanced so that each element has the same number of atoms on each side, showing that no atom has been created or destroyed. Thus for the formation of sulphur trioxide from sulphur dioxide and oxygen the equation is: $2SO_2 + O_2 \rightarrow 2SO_3$. In this reaction the volumes of sulphur dioxide and oxygen used are in the ratio 2:1. Substances which are not used up in a reaction (such as CATALYSTS or solvents) are not normally included in the chemical equation.

chemical industry The major products of the chemical industry, called 'heavy' chemicals, are produced in quantities of millions of tonnes per year worldwide. Examples include sulphuric acid, hydrochloric acid, sodium carbonate, chlorine, hydrogen, ammonia, and organic chemicals such as benzene and ethene. Usually they are used in the manufacture of a wide variety of other products. The origins of the heavy chemical industry are to be found in the late 18th and early 19th centuries in the production of SODIUM CARBONATE, a chemical needed for the manufacture of SOAP and GLASS. The LEBLANC process, in which SULPHURIC ACID is reacted with sodium chloride (SALT) and then with LIMESTONE to produce sodium carbonate, was introduced to France in 1791 and to the UK in 1823. Sodium chloride was obtained by mining, but the sulphuric acid had to be manufactured, and the LEAD CHAMBER PROCESS for its production was another important early heavy chemical process. In the 1860s the SOLVAY process, in which sodium chloride solution is treated to produce sodium carbonate, was introduced to Belgium. The adoption of this process throughout Europe (in preference to the Leblanc process) would have led to a drop in demand for sulphuric acid, had the emerging dyeing industry not required it. However, the sulphuric acid required was of a higher concentration than could be produced by the lead chamber process, and therefore the CONTACT PROCESS (which had been known since 1831) was developed, and is still the major method of sulphuric acid production. At the same time, the development of electrical power generation in the late 19th century made electrolysis available to the chemical industry. The electrolysis of brine was used to produce SODIUM HYDROXIDE solution (using a CASTNER–KELLNER CELL) and SODIUM metal: this led to the decline of the less economic Solvay process.

The simultaneous production of chlorine and sodium hydroxide has led to this part of the chemical industry being known as the chlor–alkali sector. Large quantities of chlorine are used for bleaching and for purifying public water supplies. The main use of chlorine, however, is in making chemical compounds, including a wide range of metal chlorides and a variety of chlorinated organic compounds, such as vinyl chloride, used to make PVC.

The production of FERTILIZERS is dependent on several heavy chemicals – sulphuric acid, nitric acid, and ammonia – as well as such raw materials as phosphates, fossil fuels, and potassium salts. The phosphoric acid used in manufacturing fertilizers is obtained by treating phosphate rock with sulphuric acid. The ammonia is manufactured by the HABER–BOSCH PROCESS. Some of this ammonia is used to produce ammonium salts or urea for fertilizers, but the bulk is used to manufacture NITRIC ACID.

Until 1960 the term heavy chemical industry was employed to describe industrial chemistry based on inorganic chemicals. Since then, however, the production of such materials as BENZENE, ETHENE, and vinyl chloride has reached such proportions and has become of such significance in the production of other materials that they too have become known as heavy chemicals. The carbonization of coal to obtain coke for reducing metal ores did not produce enough benzene to meet requirements, and the chemical industry responded by developing methods to obtain benzene and related materials from PETROLEUM REFINING. Most of the hydrocarbons obtained from petroleum are simpler materials than benzene or other aromatics, but in addition to being used for fuels they can be 'cracked' to produce unsaturated hydrocarbons such as ethene, ethyne, propene, and butadiene, which, because of their reactivity, can be used as building blocks for a wide range of PETROCHEMICALS.

chemical reaction A change in which one or more substances (the reactants) are converted into new substances (the products). Chemical reactions can be classified into different categories. They include, for example, **synthesis reactions**, which involve elements or simple compounds being converted into larger, more complex, compounds; the reaction of aluminium and oxygen to form aluminium oxide, Al_2O_3, is a synthesis reaction. **Decomposition reactions** are the reverse, namely the breakdown of compounds into elements or simpler compounds: for example, when calcium carbonate, $CaCO_3$, is heated, it gives off carbon dioxide, CO_2, and leaves a solid residue of calcium oxide, CaO. **Neutralization reactions** involve the complete reaction of an acid and a base to form a salt: for example, hydrochloric acid, HCl, is neutralized by sodium hydroxide, NaOH, to form sodium chloride, NaCl, and water. **Precipitation reactions** involve the formation of a solid, the precipitate, from the reaction of solutions; if, for example, silver nitrate solution, $AgNO_3$, is added to sodium chloride solution, a precipitate of silver chloride, AgCl, is formed. Other categories of reactions include addition reactions, elimination reactions, condensation reactions, and substitution reactions.

Addition reactions are those in which one or more double or triple bonds in a molecule are converted to single bonds by the addition of further atoms or groups of atoms. They are the reverse of elimination reactions. The types of compounds that undergo these reactions are organic compounds, such as alkenes, alkynes, aldehydes, and ketones. **Condensation reactions** are usually between organic compounds, in which two molecules join with the elimination of the elements of a small molecule, such as water, from between them. **Elimination reactions** involve replacement of a single bond with a double or triple bond by the removal of atoms, or groups of atoms, from adjacent carbon atoms. **Substitution reactions** involve replacement of an atom, or group of atoms, in a molecule by another atom or group of atoms. There are two main types of substitution. For example, halocarbons undergo substitution involving NUCLEOPHILES, one nucleophile displacing another, whereas, AROMATIC COMPOUNDS undergo substitution involving electrophiles, in which one electrophile displaces another.

chemical symbol An internationally recognized abbreviation for the name of an element. The system now recognized, proposed by Jöns BERZELIUS in 1813, uses the initial letter of the Latin name of the element (usually followed by an additional letter for clarity). This use of Latin names means that some symbols are not immediately clear (for example, sodium is represented by Na [natrium] and gold by Au [aurum]); the symbols for more recently discovered elements are derived from their English names (see PERIODIC TABLE). A great advantage of symbols is that MOLECULAR FORMULAE can be shown by symbols which indicate both the elements present and the proportions in which they occur.

chemical warfare See CHEMICAL AND BIOLOGICAL WARFARE.

chemistry The scientific study of the elements and their compounds, and the reactions they undergo. Inorganic chemistry is concerned with the elements and all their compounds except those of carbon, which are the subject of ORGANIC CHEMISTRY. Physical chemistry studies their physical properties and structures and the relations between energy and physical and chemical change. Analytical chemistry is concerned with determining the composition of substances.

What began with the belief that earth, air, fire, and water combine to form all things, and proceeded through ALCHEMY to the scientific approach of Robert BOYLE in the 17th century, has now reached the point where elements can be made that are not found in nature. The discovery of RADIOACTIVITY and the electron, and theories such as those of VALENCY and the CHEMICAL BOND, have resulted in many chemical phenomena being explained in terms of atomic physics. The applications are wide. Industry, agriculture, medicine, are all supported by chemical research in specialist fields. Some 4 million chemicals have been identified, of which not more than 35,000 are in common use.

chemistry, cosmological The study of the chemical reactions taking place in the various bodies in the Universe and in the interplanetary, interstellar, and intergalactic mediums between them. Such studies provide information about the evolution and structure of planets, stars, and galaxies and demonstrate that chemical and physical laws operate universally. Many different types of molecules have been detected in interstellar space by the radio and infrared radiation they emit.

chemotherapy The treatment of diseases with drugs. Early examples are arsenic for syphilis and quinine for malaria, both of which have been in use in Europe since the 17th century. Modern chemotherapy was founded by EHRLICH. Some chemotherapeutic agents are extracted from moulds or fungi and are called ANTIBIOTICS, for example PENICILLIN and tetracyclines. Chemotherapy is also used to treat CANCER. See also PHARMACOLOGY.

Chenai The official name (since 1995) of MADRAS.

Chengchow See ZHENGZHOU.

chenier A beach ridge, usually composed of sand-sized material resting on clay or mud and formed by the reworking of these materials by waves. Muddy, marshy zones usually lie to the front and rear of the chenier.

Chénier, André (1762–94) Outstanding French poet. An early supporter of the French Revolution, he was executed when he protested against its excesses, and the bulk of his poetry was published posthumously. His best poems, which are imbued with a love of the poetry of ancient Greece, are odes and eclogues grouped under the title *Les Bucoliques*.

Cheops (Egyptian **Khufu**) (fl. early 26th century BC) Egyptian pharaoh of the 4th dynasty. He commissioned the building of the Great Pyramid at Giza.

Chequers A Tudor mansion in the Chiltern Hills near Princes Risborough, Buckinghamshire, central England, presented to the British nation in 1917 by Lord and Lady Lee of Fareham to serve as a country seat for the Prime Minister in office.

Cherbourg A seaport, naval base, and resort in the Manche department on the Normandy coast of north-west France; pop. (1990) 28,770. Developed by Vauban in the 17th century and by Napoleon over a century later, Cherbourg is linked by ferries to Portsmouth, Poole, and Weymouth in England.

Cherenkov, Pavel (Alekseevich) See CERENKOV RADIATION.

Chernenko, Konstantin (Ustinovich) (1911–85) Soviet statesman, General Secretary of the Communist Party of the USSR and President 1984–85. Born in Siberia, he became a full member of the Politburo in 1978 and was a close associate of Brezhnev from this time. Chernenko succeeded Yuri Andropov to the presidency, but died after only thirteen months in office. He was succeeded by Mikhail Gorbachev.

Chernobyl A city near Kiev in north-central Ukraine, where in April 1986 explosions at a nuclear power-station resulted in a serious escape of radioactivity which spread in the atmosphere to neighbouring republics of the former Soviet Union and a number of countries of Europe. The city, which had a population of 244,000 in 1985, was subsequently evacuated.

chernozem A fertile black soil rich in humus, found in semiarid regions, especially southern Russia and tapering to the east in Western Siberia and northern Kazakhstan. It is also called a black earth soil.

Cherokee A North American Iroquoian-speaking Indian tribe, one of the largest of the tribes of south-east USA, once occupying parts of Georgia, Tennessee, and the Carolinas and constituted as a Cherokee Nation from 1839 to 1914 following their forced removal to Oklahoma. They number 95,000 in Oklahoma and 10,000 in North Carolina.

cherry A small deciduous tree, typical of the subfamily Prunoideae, and part of the much larger rose family. The nearest relatives of the cherry include almonds, apricots, damsons, peaches, and plums. The cultivated cherry has originated from the wild cherry or gean, *Prunus avium*, found in woodlands in Europe and Asia, and also from the widely distributed sour cherry, *P. cerasus*. The fruits are borne in clusters on relatively long flower stalks and vary in colour from pale yellow to dark red. They are very susceptible to bird damage, and commercial orchards are concentrated in certain areas, such as Kent in England, to minimize losses. The genus *Prunus*, to which the cultivated cherry belongs, contains some 200 species growing in temperate regions worldwide; not all of them have edible fruits. Flowering cherry trees, first developed in Japan, include varieties with more clustered, white to pink single or double flowers.

chert A form of silica (SiO_2) that is cryptocrystalline, that is, the crystals are too small to be distinguished under the microscope at ordinary magnifications. Very dense and hard, it occurs in bands or nodules in limestone and other sedimentary rocks. Thicker deposits of chert also occur. They are thought to originate from the siliceous shells of marine organisms. FLINT is a dark-coloured variety of chert that when fractured shows a smoothly curved, shell-like surface (a conchoidal fracture).

cherubim and seraphim In Judaism, Christianity, and Islam, high-ranking ANGELS, the attendants of God, and classified in the early Christian Church as the highest orders of the celestial hierarchy. The six-winged seraphim are described in Isaiah's vision of God. The Old Testament cherubim are depicted as griffin-like creatures, probably derived from Babylonian beliefs, although in medieval Jewish folklore they were thought of as beautiful men. In post-medieval western European art they are usually depicted as *putti*: chubby, winged infants (cherubs).

Cherubini, Luigi (Carlo Zanobi Salvadore Maria) (1760–1842) Italian composer. He made his operatic debut in 1779, and scored his first great operatic success in 1782. He worked successfully in London (1784–86), but then settled in Paris under royal patronage. He survived the French Revolution and achieved his greatest operatic successes with *Médée* (1797) and *Les Deux Journées* (The Water Carrier) (1800). In addition to nearly forty operas,

Cherubini wrote much sacred music, including two requiem masses (1816, 1838).

Cherwell, Frederick Alexander Lindemann, 1st Viscount (1886–1957) German-born British physicist. He studied a wide variety of subjects, and a number of theories and items are named after him. These include a theory of specific heat, a theory of the upper atmosphere, a formula concerning the melting-point of crystals, an electrometer, and a type of glass for transmitting X-rays. He was Churchill's adviser on scientific and aeronautical matters during World War II.

Chesapeake Bay A large inlet of the Atlantic Ocean on the coast of the USA, 320 km (200 miles) in length, bordering on Virginia and Maryland.

Cheshire A north-west midlands county of England; area 2,333 sq km (901 sq miles); pop. (1991) 937,300; county town, Chester.

Cheshire, (Geoffrey) Leonard (1917–92) British airman and philanthropist. He served as a fighter pilot in World War II, was awarded the VC in 1944 for his one hundred bombing missions, and was an official observer of the atom bomb dropped on Nagasaki in 1945. From the late 1940s he founded the Cheshire Foundation Homes for the disabled and incurably sick; these spread to 45 countries. Cheshire married the philanthropist Sue Ryder in 1959.

Chesil Bank A shingle beach forming a spit of land that stretches for 25 km (17 miles) from Portland to Abbotsbury on the Dorset coast of England. Protecting a tidal lagoon noted for its wintering wildfowl, it is one of the longest storm beaches in Europe.

chess The best-known of all board-games and the archetype of war-games played out on a board or table. Two players, white and black, sit at either end of the chessboard, which is divided into 64 squares with eight vertical and eight horizontal rows. Each player has 16 men, which occupy prescribed places at the start of the game. Each piece has its own fixed type of movement. Players move one piece in turn, and the object of the game is to manœuvre and capture pieces until the opposing king is so cornered that it cannot avoid being captured. This state is called checkmate and ends the game.

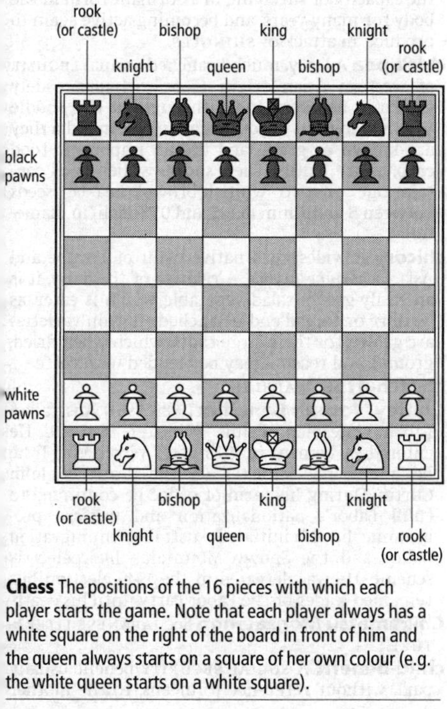

Chess The positions of the 16 pieces with which each player starts the game. Note that each player always has a white square on the right of the board in front of him and the queen always starts on a square of her own colour (e.g. the white queen starts on a white square).

Chester (Latin **Deva**) The county town and tourist city of Cheshire in the north midlands of England, on the River Dee; pop. (1991) 115,000. It is a well-preserved walled city with many ancient buildings including a Roman amphitheatre, a castle, a 12th-century cathedral, and fine medieval shops and houses. The conductor Sir Adrian Boult was born here in 1889.

Chesterfield A town in Derbyshire, central England; pop. (1991) 99,700. Its All Saints Church has an unusual twisted spire. The locomotive engineer George Stephenson (1781–1848) lies buried here.

Chesterton, G(ilbert) K(eith) (1874–1936) British essayist, novelist, and critic. He first came to prominence as a journalist for *The Speaker*, in which, with Hilaire Belloc, he took an anti-imperialist platform on the Boer War question. His best-known novel is his 'Merry England' fantasy *The Napoleon of Notting Hill* (1904), but he is also widely remembered for his creation of the character Father Brown, a priest with a talent for crime detection, who first appears in *The Innocence of Father Brown* (1911). Chesterton became a Roman Catholic in 1922; his other writings include biographies of St Francis of Assisi and St Thomas Aquinas.

chestnut soil A zonal soil found in the drier parts of the mid-latitude short-grass prairies where rainfall is about 350–500 mm (14–20 inches) a year. Although the low rainfall limits plant growth, the chestnut soils are fairly rich in humus. They are a characteristic dark brown colour, becoming paler with depth. The low rainfall also inhibits LEACHING and so they may be quite calcareous. Thus, although chestnut soils occur in regions subject to drought, they are fertile under conditions of adequate rainfall or irrigation.

chestnut tree Either of two distinct types of tree. The first, typified by the sweet or Spanish chestnut, *Castanea sativa*, contains 10–12 species native to southern Europe, Asia, and North America. The second type includes the horse chestnuts, or buckeyes (*Aesculus* species), of south-east Europe, North America, and northeast Asia. They include 25 species which are quite unrelated to the sweet chestnuts. The sweet chestnut has simple, toothed leaves, bears edible seeds, and is related to beech. It is widely planted for its excellent timber, and coppices well, producing wood for stakes and fencing. The common horse chestnut, *A. hippocastanum*, is related to litchi and is native to the Balkans. It has been much planted and its inedible seeds are the conkers of children's games. Other species and hybrids of *Aesculus* are cultivated for their flowers.

Chevalier, Maurice (1888–1972) French singer and actor. He gained an international reputation in the Paris music-halls of the 1920s, particularly in the Folies-Bergère, where he regularly partnered the French dancer Mistinguett (1874–1956). He went on to star in successful Hollywood musicals such as *Innocents of Paris* (1929), *Love Me Tonight* (1932), and *Gigi* (1958).

Cheviot Hills (or **Cheviots**) A range of hills on the border between Scotland and England, rising to 816 m (2,677 ft) in The Cheviot.

chevrotain (or **mouse deer**) Neither a mouse nor a deer, but an even-toed hoofed mammal, placed in a separate family, Tragulidae, in the order Artiodactyla. There are four species of these small animals; one species approaches a hare in size. The males have tusk-like upper canine teeth that project below the mouth. Most common in low country in rain forests and jungles, they may also live up in mountains. The Indian chevrotain or spotted mouse deer, *Tragulus meminna*, is the smallest species, and lives in Sri Lanka and India. There are two species of slightly larger Malayan chevrotain: the lesser mouse deer, *T. javanicus*, and larger mouse deer, *T. napu*. Both live in tropical rain forest. The African water chevrotain, *Hyemoschus aquaticus*, is somewhat larger and takes to the water at the least provocation. It occurs over West and Central Africa.

Cheyenne An Algonquian-speaking tribe of North American Indians that formerly lived on the Great Plains between the Missouri and Arkansas rivers. The majority (4,500) live in Montana, others live in Oklahoma.

Chiang Kai-shek (or **Jiang Jie Shi**) (1887–1975) Chinese statesman and general, President of China 1928–31 and 1943–49 and of Taiwan 1950–75. A prominent general in the army of Sun Yat-sen, in 1925 he became leader of the Kuomintang when Sun Yat-sen died, and launched a military campaign to unite China. In the 1930s he concentrated more on defeating the Chinese Communists than on resisting the invading Japanese, but he proved unable to establish order and was defeated by the Communists after the end of World War II. Forced to abandon mainland China in 1949, he set up a separate Nationalist Chinese State in Taiwan.

Chianti An area of Tuscany to the north-west of Siena in northern Italy, noted for its dry red wine. Gaiole, Radda, and Castellina are the chief towns.

chiaroscuro The effects of light and shade in a work of art, particularly when they are strongly contrasting. Although it is most commonly used in discussing paintings, it can also be applied to drawings or other works of graphic art.

Chicago A city in Illinois, on Lake Michigan, the third-largest city of the USA, known as the 'Windy City', and the original home of the skyscraper; pop. (1990) 2,783,726. Originally a trading post, then a military fort, Chicago first developed in the early 1800s after it was chosen as the terminal site of the Illinois and Michigan canal (completed in 1848). It became the largest grain market in the world and a major centre for iron and steel, electronics, food-processing and the transportation of livestock. Despite the Great Fire of 1871 which destroyed over 15,000 houses, the city continued to expand in the 20th century. It is a major Great Lakes port and its airport is the busiest in the world. The Sears Tower, built in 1974, was until 1996 the tallest inhabited building in the world at 443 m (1,454 ft), and the Union States Post Office is the largest in the world under one roof.

Chicago School (in architecture) The architects who in the late 19th and early 20th centuries made Chicago the most dynamic centre in the USA in the development of modern architecture, particularly the evolution of the skyscraper. William Le Baron Jenney was the first to use an iron and steel skeleton to construct a multi-storey building (the Home Insurance Building, 1883–85), but the central figure of the Chicago School was Louis SULLIVAN.

chicano A US citizen of Mexican origin.

Chichester The county town of West Sussex, near the south coast of England, east of Portsmouth; pop. (1991) 26,572. There are Roman remains at Fishbourne nearby and an 11th–12th-century cathedral.

Chichester, **Sir Francis (Charles)** (1901–72) British yachtsman. In 1960 he won the first solo transatlantic yacht race in his boat *Gipsy Moth III*. In 1966–67 he sailed alone round the world in *Gipsy Moth IV*, taking 107 days to sail from Plymouth to Sydney, and 119 days to make the return voyage. He was knighted on his return.

Chichimec A horde of invaders who entered the central valley of Mexico from the north-west *c.*950–1300, and came to be known as the Toltec after the founding of their capital, Tula, in 986.

chickadee See TIT.

Chickasaw A North American Indian tribe that inhabited the region of modern northern Alabama and Mississippi, and southern Tennessee, and were descendants of the late prehistoric MISSISSIPPI CULTURES.

chicken Any one of a wide variety of domesticated forms of the red jungle-fowl, *Gallus domesticus*, a member of the pheasant family and part of the order Galliformes. It occurs in its wild state in south-east Asia. This species was probably first domesticated in India, probably as early as 3000 BC, and was gradually transported to other parts of the world.

The modern POULTRY industry developed on a large scale in the late 19th century and led to a great proliferation of breeds of different sizes and colours. Many were developed for their egg-laying potential or for meat (see POULTRY FARMING), but some, such as the silkies and other bantams, were bred largely for decorative purposes.

chickenpox A highly infectious virus infection, producing a characteristic rash of small blisters. Most people are infected in childhood and suffer only a trivial illness, after which they are immune. Infection in adults can be more severe. The varicella-zoster virus, responsible for chickenpox, has the capacity of surviving in a dormant form in the body for many years, and becoming active again to produce an attack of SHINGLES.

chick-pea A leafy, much-branched annual LEGUME of western Asian origin, *Cicer arietinum*, widely grown in northern India, throughout the Middle East, and in parts of southern Europe. In India they are known as gram, and are an important food crop, as are lentils. Their short swollen pods contain one or two whitish-brown, beaked seeds between 5 and 7 mm (0.125 and 0.75 inch) in diameter.

chicory A widespread native plant of Europe and Asia, *Cichorium intybus*. A relative of the daisy, it is an easily-grown salad vegetable which is eaten as 'greens' or forced and balanched. Certain varieties are grown for their large roots, which when dried, ground, and roasted may be blended with coffee.

chiffchaff See WARBLER.

Chifley, **Joseph Benedict** (1885–1951) Australian Labor statesman, Prime Minister 1945–49. He entered Parliament in 1928; after World War II he became Prime Minister on the death of John Curtin. During his term of office he continued to fulfil Labor's nationalization and welfare programme; he also initiated Australia's immigration policy and the Snowy Mountains hydroelectric scheme. He was defeated in the 1949 election but remained leader of the Labor Party until his death.

Chikamatsu Monzaemon See JAPANESE LITERATURE.

child benefit A SOCIAL SECURITY benefit usually paid, without reference to means, to the mother for the maintenance of a child. First introduced in New Zealand in 1962, child-benefit schemes, which are financed from general taxation, are well established in the industrialized world and frequently found in developing countries.

Childers, (Robert) Erskine (1870–1922) Irish writer and political activist, born in England. His fame as a writer stems from his novel *The Riddle of the Sands* (1903), in which two amateur yachtsmen discover German preparations for an invasion of England. A supporter of Irish Home Rule from 1910, he settled in Ireland in 1920, became a Sinn Fein MP in 1921, and, in the same year, Minister of Propaganda. In 1922 he was court-martialled and shot for his involvement in the civil war following the establishment of the Irish Free State. His son **Erskine Hamilton Childers** (1905–74) was President of Ireland 1973–74.

child labour Work performed by children, often under compulsion and in violation of national and international labour standards, for the profit of others and their own sustenance. Before the INDUSTRIAL REVOLUTION children had frequently been compelled to work from an early age, but by 1800 their employment under dirty and dangerous conditions in the new mines and factories had become a cause for concern. In 1802 the British government enacted the first laws regulating child labour, but they proved ineffective. In 1833 a FACTORY ACT restricted working hours for children and provided for the appointment of inspectors. During the 19th century further factory acts and the introduction of compulsory education effectively limited child labour. Other western European countries, particularly Prussia after 1870, began to make legislation regulating the employment of children.

In developing countries the employment of children in factories, mines, and agriculture has remained widespread. Most child labourers, some as young as 4 years, are employed in agriculture, domestic service, or small, unregulated urban enterprises such as weavers' and mechanics' workshops or restaurants. In such societies, the child's contribution to the family's income may be vital to its survival. Child labour prevails where competition is strong, technologies are rudimentary, and production processes simple and routine. Children tend to be paid extremely low wages and some are bonded, working solely to pay off a debt. Many work long hours, frequently with no protection from toxic substances or dangerous machinery, no allowance being made for their physical vulnerability or developmental needs. The UNITED NATIONS Convention on the Rights of the Child contains articles requiring signatory states to take measures against child labour, and agencies such as UNICEF are committed to protecting child labourers.

Children's Crusade (1212) A pathetic episode in the CRUSADES, growing out of simple faith and fanatical zeal for the recapture of PALESTINE from the Saracens. Some 50,000 children, mainly from France and Germany, are said to have taken part in the expedition which probably included poor adults. It was doomed from the start. Those who did manage to embark from the ports of France and Italy were dispatched to Muslim slave markets. Very few ever returned to their homes.

children's literature Children and adults for a long time shared the ancient body of oral folk literature which was later written down and continues to be enjoyed today. The first literature specifically intended for children was educational, and alphabet books became popular with the invention of printing. The most successful of the didactic books inspired by the Puritan movement in Britain and North America was BUNYAN's *Pilgrim's Progress* (1678). This was followed by works written for adults but enjoyed by children, such as DEFOE's *Robinson Crusoe* (1719) and SWIFT's *Gulliver's Travels* (1726). In *c.*1765 a collection of nursery rhymes, *Mother Goose's Melody*, was published in England, possibly borrowing the title from Charles Perrault's fairy tales, *Contes de ma mère l'oye* (1697). German fairy tales collected by the brothers GRIMM and first published in 1812 were followed by stories composed by Hans Christian ANDERSEN in 1835, and Heinrich Hoffmann's surrealist tales in comic verse, *Struwwelpeter* in 1845. Charles KINGSLEY's *The Water Babies* (1863) touched on contemporary social problems, but Edward LEAR's *Book of Nonsense* (1846) and Lewis CARROLL's two *Alice* books (1865, 1872) were the first major writings designed for entertainment rather than self-improvement. A realistic portrayal of middle-class family life was recorded in Louisa M. Alcott's *Little Women* (1868), while Mark TWAIN's *Adventures of Tom Sawyer* (1876) and R. L. STEVENSON's *Treasure Island* (1883) introduced the adventure tale, and KIPLING's *Jungle Books* (1894–95) brought animal stories into the mainstream of children's literature. The first landmark in poems for children was Stevenson's *A Child's Garden of Verses* (1885). School and 'gang' stories evolved with Thomas HUGHES' *Tom Brown's Schooldays* (1857). Serial publications such as the *Boys' Own Paper* and the *Boys' Own Magazine* were launched in the latter half of the 19th century and were followed by similar publications for girls. Beatrix POTTER's *The Tale of Peter Rabbit* (1900) did much to establish the book in which pictures and text are of equal importance. The 20th century has seen the creation of memorable characters like Billy Bunter (F. Richardson), Dr Dolittle (H. Lofting), Winnie-the-Pooh (A. A. MILNE), Mary Poppins (P. L. Travers), Emil and the Detectives (Erich Kästner), the Moomintrolls (Tove Jansson), Pippi Longstocking (Astrid Lindgren), Tintin (Hergé), Asterix (Goscinny), and Tolkien's Hobbits. Among more recent leading writers are Roald Dahl, Leon Garfield, Maurice Sendak, Rosemary Sutcliffe, Tony Ross, Janet and Allan Ahlberg, Judy Blume, the Canadian Monica Hughes and the poets Roger McGough, Michael Rosen, and Ted Hughes. See also BOOK ILLUSTRATION.

child sexual abuse The exploitation of children by adults in sexual activities to which they are unable to give informed consent, and which violate social taboos. Such activities range from exhibitionism to fondling, INCEST, and RAPE. The offender is usually a family member or someone closely associated with the child, rather than a stranger. Pre-adolescent girls are the most frequent victims, but children of both sexes and all ages, even infants, are affected. Although the child may be physically harmed, the psychological injury may be even greater and can last a lifetime. Often the victims feel guilty, socially isolated, and humiliated, and because of the fear instilled by the offenders may either not confide in an adult, or if they do, may not be believed. In the case of incest, the whole family may collude to hide it in order to protect a family member. Sexual abuse of children is an emotive subject that has caused serious problems to the social services in the UK. Zealous over-reaction to ill-founded childish accusations, on the one hand, and an insensitive disregard of timid but truthful confessions, on the other, have led to several *causes célèbres* from which social workers have emerged with severely damaged reputations. Nevertheless, without extensive help (increasingly provided by professional helplines), some victims become abusers themselves in adult life, or are unable to form satisfactory relationships.

child sexual exploitation The use or trafficking of children in illicit sexual activities for the gratification and financial gain of adults. Those responsible include paedophiles and those who produce PORNOGRAPHY and organize PROSTITUTION and sex tourism. Although some children become involved as a result of their parents' desperation to supplement the family income, child runaways are most at risk, since it is often only by exchanging sexual services for money, food, and shelter that they can survive. The physical and psychological damage suffered by victims is similar to that suffered by victims of CHILD SEXUAL ABUSE, but the likelihood of contracting sexually transmitted diseases, and especially of becoming infected with the AIDS virus, or being subjected to violence is far greater.

Chile A long and narrow country on the west coast of South America, occupying some 4,600 km (2,860 miles) between Peru in the north and Cape Horn.

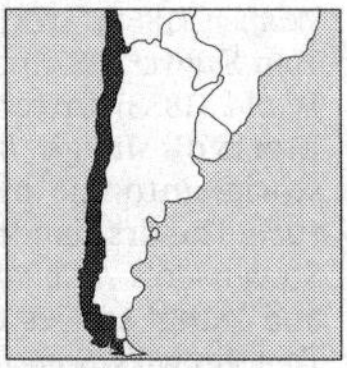

Physical. On average Chile is only 160 km (100 miles) in width from the Pacific to the high Andes, along which run the boundaries with Bolivia and Argentina. In the north is the arid Atacama Desert, while in the centre the climate is mild and conducive to most forms of agriculture. Here and in the south the lower slopes of the CORDILLERAS are well forested and there are short, fertile river valleys. Tierra del Fuego, in the extreme south, on the other hand is cold, very wet, and relatively barren, suitable only for sheep grazing. Inland, along the whole length of the country, stretch mountains.

Economy. Chile's economy is based largely on exploitation of substantial mineral reserves, and agriculture. Copper accounts for almost half of exports, with other minerals and fruit, fishmeal, and timber products of secondary importance. About 80 per cent of electricity is generated by hydroelectric power, and domestic oil production accounts for about half of total requirements. Manufacturing industry includes chemicals, brewing, wood-pulping, and tyre manufacture. The country has one of the best public education and social service systems in Latin America, although these suffered under military rule in the 1980s.

History. At the time of the first Spanish contact in 1536 the dominant Indian group, the Araucanians, were theoretically subject to the INCA empire, but in practice they retained considerable independence within the Inca realm. Though they resisted Spanish encroachments, the Araucanians were gradually pushed south of the Bío Bío River where they were more or less kept under control. Spanish colonization began with the foundation of Santiago in 1541. The colony grew moderately but did not prosper for the next two centuries as it was overshadowed by wealthier Peru. Politically Chile became part of the Spanish viceroyalty of Peru. Chilean independence from Spain was proclaimed in 1810 by O'HIGGINS; it was achieved after the South American liberator José de SAN MARTÍN crossed the Andes with an army of 3,200 men and defeated Spanish troops at the battles of Chacabuco (1817), and Maipo (1818). The discovery of rich copper deposits in the northern Atacama desert had a dramatic impact on economic life, with a railway system developing from 1851. Following war with BOLIVIA and PERU (1879–83), rich natural nitrate deposits were annexed in the north, leading to a fifty-year economic boom. By the 1920s synthetic nitrates were replacing saltpetre and dependence on copper exports placed Chile at the mercy of the world market. Political experiments after World War II failed to cope with a series of burgeoning social problems and prompted the election in 1970 of the Marxist democrat Salvador ALLENDE, the first avowed Marxist in world history to be elected President by popular vote. As the head of the Unidad Popular (a coalition of communists and socialists), Allende was faced with a majority opposition in Congress, and the hostility of the USA. He was increasingly frustrated in his attempts to implement his radical programme of nationalization and agrarian reform. Inflation, capital flight, and a balance-of-payments deficit contributed to an economic crisis in 1973. In September the army commander-in-chief PINOCHET led the military coup which cost Allende and 15,000 Chileans their lives, and prompted one-tenth of the population to emigrate. The military regime which replaced Chile's democracy brutally suppressed all labour unions and opposition groups, and pursued a free-market economy. Although inflation was dramatically reduced, so was demand, output, and employment. The economy continued on a downward spiral in the 1980s with the world's highest per-capita level of external debt. In 1988 Pinochet accepted a plebiscite decision for the 're-establishment' of 'workable democracy', and stepped down. In 1989 Patricio Aylwin was elected President and civilian rule was restored. Aylwin was succeeded in 1994 by Edúardo Frei Ruiz-Tagle, the son of the former president Edúardo FREI (MONTALVA). In 1994 Chile applied to join the NORTH AMERICAN FREE TRADE AGREEMENT.

Capital: Santiago
Area: 756,626 sq km (292,135 sq mi)
Population: 14,210,000 (1995)
Currency: 1 peso = 100 centavos
Religions: Roman Catholic 80.7%; atheist and non-religious 12.8%; Protestant 6.1%; Jewish 0.2%
Ethnic Groups: Mestizo 91.6%; Amerindian (mostly Araucarian) 6.8%; others (mainly European) 1.6%
Languages: Spanish (official); also Amerindian languages (mostly Araucarian)
International Organizations: UN; OAS

chilli A bushy perennial CAPSICUM, *Capsicum annuum*, with much smaller fruits than those of its close relative, the sweet pepper. The fruits can be as short as 1 cm (0.5 inch). There is a range of forms, with the red fruits differing in their pungency. All taste considerably hotter than the other capsicums, and some can cause irritation to the human skin. Chillies are a constituent of curry powder and tabasco sauce. Cayenne pepper is made from the powdered, dried fruits of some species.

Chiltern Hills (or **Chilterns**) A range of chalk hills in east-central England, north of the Thames, between the Berkshire Downs and the East Anglian Ridge. Coombe Hill (260 m, 853 ft) near Wendover is the highest point.

chimaera (or **ratfish**) A member of the family Chimaeridae, part of the class of CARTILAGINOUS FISHES. The family is widely distributed in the cooler regions of the North Atlantic, Indian, and Pacific oceans. They are allied to the sharks by their cartilaginous skeletons, but they have a single opening on each side for the gills, covered by a hard flap, similar to BONY FISHES. Many species live in deep oceans.

Chimaera In Greek mythology, a fearsome fire-breathing monster having a lion's head, a she-goat's body, and a serpent's tail. It was killed by Bellerephon.

Chimborazo An inactive volcano, the highest peak of the Andes in Ecuador, rising to a height of 6,310 m (20,487 ft) near Riobamba.

chimpanzee Either of the two smaller species of Old World APES living in Africa, the gorilla being the larger. The chimp, *Pan troglodytes*, is found from lowland forest up to altitudes of 3,300 m (11,000 feet), where the gorilla is absent. The bonobo, or pygmy chimp, *Pan panisus*, is only found in the Democratic Republic of Congo. Chimpanzees have a human-like face with long features and a prominent jaw. The ears are large and often pale. The rather sparse body hair is black, and the skin changes from flesh colour in juveniles to bronze and then black in adults. The forelimbs are longer than the hind-limbs, and the chimpanzee walks quadrupedally. Its time is spent equally between walking on the ground and climbing trees. Males are somewhat larger than females and can weigh up to 50 kg (110 pounds).

Chimpanzees are mainly fruit-eaters, but they also eat leaves, nuts, bark, ants, termites, and even meat. They are very sociable animals, with large and complex societies of up to eighty individuals. They communicate by a wide variety of sounds and gestures. The home range may occupy an area of 20 sq km (8 square miles) in rich forest land, but will be greater in more frugal places. The groups divide into smaller bands such as nursery, all-male, and mixed adults.

Chimú The most powerful state of the north coast of Peru between *c.*1000 AD and 1476, when it was conquered by the INCAS. Its capital was Chan Chan (near modern Trujillo), a vast city with ten large rectangular enclosures measuring 400 by 200 m. (1300 by 650 ft).

Chimú art See SOUTH AMERICAN INDIAN ART.

China The third-largest country in the world, occupying most of eastern Asia and bounded by North Korea, Kazakhstan and Mongolia on the north, Russia on the west, Afghanistan, Pakistan, India, Nepal and Bhutan on the south-west and Myanmar (Burma), Laos, and Vietnam on the south-east.

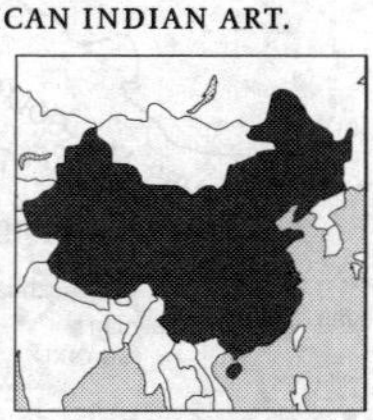

Physical. China's coastline adjoins the South and East China Seas and the Yellow Sea. In the north-west lies Xinjiang (Sinkiang), an area of mountains and desert, and in the south-west is the mountainous region of Tibet. The remainder of China is divided laterally by the Yangtze (Chang) River. To the north-west is the high LOESS region, supporting millet and wheat. The wind carries the loess eastward to the flat northern plain, while the eastward-flowing rivers carry yellow silt. The plain, with a monsoon climate of warm, wet summers and very cold, arid winters, is highly cultivable. In the north-east lies Manchuria, on higher ground and with many rivers and lakes. In the west are the mountains and plateaux surrounding the red clay basin of Sichuan, which is well watered and supports a mass of paddy fields. Huge lakes occupy low-lying land to the south of the Yangtze, while southward the terrain rises to many ranges of high hills. Here the climate is subtropical. The plateaux support tea plantations, many of the slopes are terraced for rice, and the deep valleys are full of natural forests of bamboo. The province of Gansu in the north-west region is the principal centre of earthquakes in China, where major earthquakes take place on an average of once every 65 years.

Economy. Since the late 1970s China has adopted pragmatic policies of liberalizing the economy. Four Special Economic Zones were established to attract foreign investment, direct state control of factories has been loosened, stockmarkets have been set up, and responsibility for agriculture switched from collective farms to individual households. China's economy is predominantly agricultural, with rice, wheat, and pigs the main products. Agriculture prospers, although there is a need for investment in irrigation and fertilizers. Mineral extraction is important: crude oil is refined and exported, there are large coal, tin, and iron ore deposits, and China leads the world in tungsten ore production. Several nuclear energy plants are under construction. Industry is targeted for expansion, and major industrial products include textiles and clothing, cement, chemicals, steel, and consumer electrical goods. Japan is the main trading partner. Tourism is also of increasing economic importance.

History. China has a recorded history beginning nearly 4,000 years ago, with the SHANG who settled in the Huang He (Yellow River) valley. Under the Eastern ZHOU, from the 6th century BC, CONFUCIUS and MENCIUS formulated ideas that became the frame-work of Chinese society. DAOISM appeared during the 3rd century BC. Gradually Chinese culture spread out from the Huang He valley. A form of writing with characters representing meanings rather than sounds – and required by Shi Huangdi, the first ruler of a unified China, to be written in a uniform style – bound together people divided by geography and different spoken dialects. From the QIN the concept of a unified empire prevailed, surviving periods of fragmentation and rule by non-Chinese dynasties such as the YUAN. Under strong dynasties such as the HAN and the TANG China's power extended far west into TURKISTAN and south into ANNAM. On its neighbours, particularly KOREA and Annam, it exercised a powerful influence. Barbarian invaders and dynasties usually adopted Chinese cultural traditions.

The ideas of BUDDHISM began to reach China from the 1st century AD and were gradually changed and assimilated into Chinese culture. The Chinese people, showing remarkable inventiveness, were ahead of the West in technology until about the end of the SONG dynasty. However, after the MONGOL conquest the country drew in on itself. Learning, in high esteem from early times, became rooted in the stereotyped study of the Confucian classics, for success in examinations based on the classics was for centuries the means to promotion in the civil service. In time, study of the classics had a deadening intellectual influence.

Throughout history, China, the 'Middle Kingdom', as it is called by the Chinese, regarded itself as superior to all others – a view shared by philosophers of the ENLIGHTENMENT. After the Manchu invasion of 1644, China was ruled by the QING dynasty, which was at its most powerful and prosperous in the 18th century. Western countries attempted to establish trading links with the Qing dynasty but with little success. As the power of the Qing dynasty weakened towards the end of the 18th century, Western pressure for change built up, leading to direct European involvement in China. Contact with the West precipitated crisis and decline. After the OPIUM WARS, treaty ports became the focus for both Western expansion and demands for modernization. Nineteenth-century rebellions, such as the TAIPING REBELLION, devastated the country and undermined imperial rule in spite of the Self-Strengthening Movement and the abortive Hundred Days Reform. Defeat in the SINO-JAPANESE WAR (1894–95) and the BOXER RISING stimulated reforms, but the dynasty ended in the CHINESE REVOLUTION of 1911. The Republic that followed SUN YAT-SEN's brief presidency degenerated into WARLORD regimes after Yuan Shikai's attempt to restore the monarchy. CHIANG KAI-SHEK united much of China after the Northern Expedition and ruled from Nanjing with his nationalist KUOMINTANG, but his Republic of China collapsed in the face of the Japanese invasion of 1937 and the civil war with the communists, and continued only on the island of TAIWAN after his retreat there in 1949. The CHINESE COMMUNIST PARTY under MAO ZEDONG won the civil war, established the People's Republic of China on the mainland, and set about revolutionizing and developing China's economy and society. In the 1950s, land reform led to the COMMUNES and the GREAT LEAP FORWARD, and urban industry was expanded and nationalized. Relations with the Soviet Union worsened and during 1966–76 the country was torn apart by the CULTURAL REVOLUTION, which ended only with Mao's death. During the 1980s DENG XIAOPING remained committed to economic reform, and to improving relations with the Soviet Union. Pressures for democratization grew, however, and a student demonstration in Beijing in June 1989 led to massacre in Tiananmen Square. Gradual moves towards a controlled market economy continue. In 1994 the USA decided to maintain special trade links with China despite its continued violations of human rights. Jiang Zemin (1926–), President since 1993, assumed the role of the country's leader after Deng's death in 1997.

Capital: Beijing
Area: 9,572,900 sq km (3,696,100 sq mi)
Population: 1,206,600,000 (1995)
Currency: 1 Renminbi (yuan) = 10 jiao = 100 fen
Religions: Non-religious 59.2%; Chinese traditional religions 20.1%; atheist 12.0%; Buddhist 6.0%; Muslim 2.4%; Christian 0.2%
Ethnic Groups: Han (Chinese) 93.3%; Chuang 1.33%; Hui 0.72%; Ughur 0.59%; Yi 0.54%; Miao 0.5%; Manchu 0.43%; Tibetan 0.39%; Mongolian 0.34%; Tuchia 0.28%; Puyi 0.21%; Korean 0.18%; Tung 0.14%; Yao 0.14%; Pai 0.11%; Hani 0.11%; Kasakh 0.09%; Tai 0.08%; Li 0.08%
Languages: Mandarin Chinese (official); six other dialects of Chinese; at least 41 other minority languages
International Organizations: UN

china clay One of the purest CLAYS, comprising a white powdery material arising from the decomposition of feldspar in granite. It is composed mainly of kaolin, the main constituent of which is **kaolinite**, a hydrous aluminium silicate. Known first in China and worked in Cornwall, UK, since 1746, china clay has long been used in the manufacture of fine porcelain. France and several places

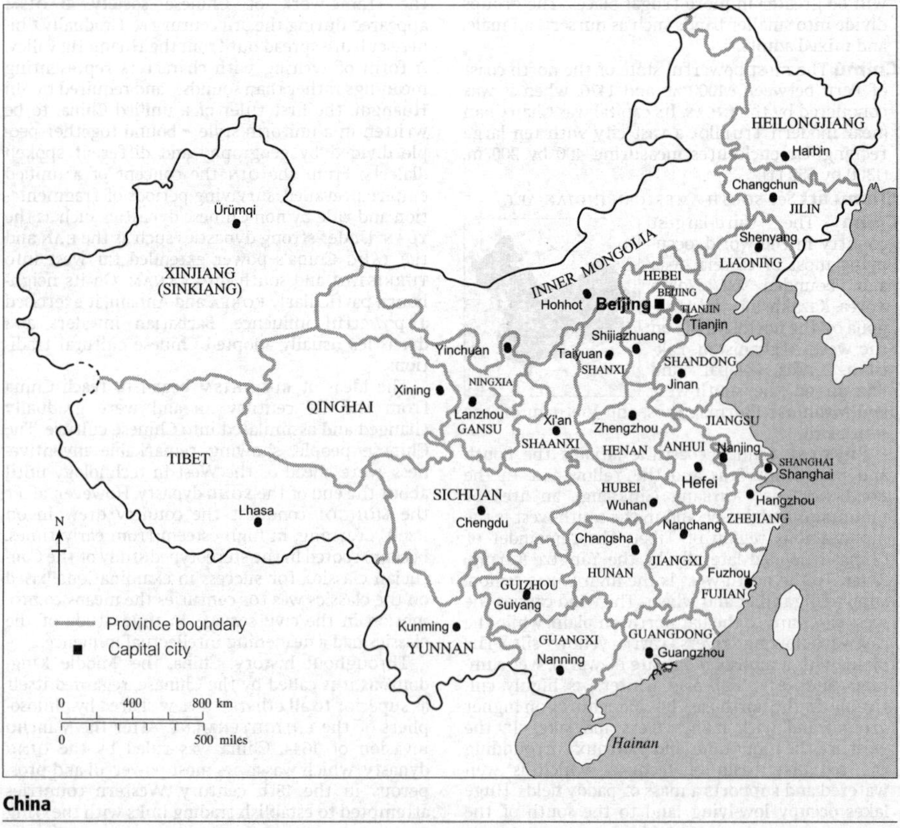

China

in the USA are other sources. It is also used as a filler in paint- and paper-making, and in plastics and fertilizers.

china-mark moth A small, delicately marked, brown and white moth. These moths, said to resemble porcelain, belong to two genera in the family Pyralidae. Their caterpillars are aquatic in their early stages, and feed on submerged or floating aquatic plants; some have gills on the sides, others trap a layer of air in body hairs. They construct webs or cases of silk, usually incorporating leaf fragments. The genus *Nymphula* contains several species of china-mark moths throughout the Northern Hemisphere. Several species of the genus *Paraponyx* are found worldwide.

China Sea The East and South China Seas, once known collectively as the China Seas. Divided by the island of Taiwan, they lie largely on the continental shelf to the east and south-east of Asia and are bounded by the Pacific along the arcs of the Ryukyu and Philippine Islands. They are both seas with weak tides. The East China Sea (Dong Hai) is the shallower, with a mean depth of 270 m (890 feet). The South China Sea (Nan Hai), which is connected to it by the Taiwan Strait, has a mean depth of 1,060 m (3,480 feet) but is much shallower in the south.

chinchilla Either of two species of South American RODENT characterized by long hind-legs, a bushy tail, and soft, luxuriant fur, which is highly valued in the fur trade. The chinchillas, *Chinchilla brevicaudata* and *C. lanigera*, inhabit the Andes of western South America, where they may now be almost extinct. They are still common in commercial fur farms. The family Chinchillidae also includes the VISCACHAS. All members of this family are herbivores, eating grasses and low-growing plants.

chinchilla rat Neither a chinchilla nor a rat, but either of the two species of cavy-like RODENT in the genus *Abrocoma*, from the Andes. They are rat-sized, and have soft, dense fur resembling that of chinchillas, whereas their large rounded ears, pointed snouts, and long tails give them the appearance of rats. They are colonial and live in underground burrows. Their diet is entirely herbivorous.

Chindwin The chief tributary of the River Irrawaddy in Myanmar (Burma). Rising in the hills of northern Myanmar, it flows southwards for 885 km (550 miles) before meeting the Irrawaddy 550 km (350 miles) north of Rangoon.

Chin dynasty See JIN.

Ch'in dynasty See QIN.

Chinese A member of the Sino-Tibetan language group, a tonal language with no inflexions, declensions, or conjugations. There are many dialects, including Mandarin (based on the pronunciation of Beijing), and Cantonese (spoken in the south-east and in Hong Kong). Written in Han characters, Chinese script is ideographic; the characters were in origin pictographic, with each sign standing for an object, and they gradually gave way to non-pictorial ideographs representing not only tangible objects but also abstract concepts. Despite its complexity the script makes written communication possible between people speaking mutually incomprehensible dialects. Examples of Chinese writing date back well beyond 1,000 BC. There are several systems of romanization, chief amongst these formerly being the Wade-Giles system which was used on official UK and US maps of China from 1942. A system of romanization known as *Pinyin* was officially adopted by China in 1958, but it was not fully accepted throughout the world until 1979.

Chinese art and architecture China has the longest cultural tradition in the world, with a continuous history of more than 3,000 years. Its art is significant not only because of its beauty and richness, but also because it has been a major source of inspiration for the entire Far East – Japan, Korea, Tibet, Mongolia, and Central Asia. Europe, too, owes many artistic impulses to China (see CHINOISERIE), as well as the introduction of various techniques, particularly in pottery and textiles (see CHINESE CERAMICS; SILK). The painter, instead of painting his pictures on canvas or wood in oil colours, usually worked on silk or paper in watercolours. The sculptor not only worked in stone, wood, or bronze, but also sometimes modelled or coated his statues in lacquer, an art-form that originated in China. PORCELAIN, also, was first made in China, more than a thousand years before the secret of its manufacture was discovered in Europe in the early 18th century. JADE is another material that is associated above all with China, being used for ritual objects, ceremonial weapons, jewellery, and small sculptures. In architecture, wood is the most important material. Houses are often of only one storey and spread over large areas, with gardens and courts between the various wings, though palaces, temples, and pagodas are higher. Roofs cover not only the types of buildings with which they are associated in the West; they are also put over gateways, bridges, walls, and monuments. Several roofs are often piled one on top of the other and the edges bent up in graceful curves, forming one of the most distinctive features of Chinese architecture. After a fairly obscure prehistoric period, the evolution of Chinese art can be divided into five long periods, for which, however, there are no very distinct boundary lines. Definite records date back to the second part of the Shang dynasty (1711–1066 BC), the most important surviving works from this time being bronze sacrificial vessels of severe form, decorated chiefly with animal motifs that have a religious significance. The second period begins when China was united in 221 BC under the Qin emperor Shi Huangdi, the builder of the Great Wall of China. Objects of bronze and jade are the most important examples of the art of the period; in addition, glazed earthenware vessels and tomb-figures have been found. One of the most important events of the Han period (206 BC–220 AD) was the introduction of Buddhism from India and Central Asia, for Buddhist temples and monasteries became great patrons and repositories of the arts. The best-preserved temples are those which, following Indian prototypes, were hewn into rock faces. They were decorated with sculpture and frescos. These cave temples belong to the third period of Chinese art, the climax of which is reached in the Sui (581–618) and Tang (618–907) dynasties, when China was united after a time of invasions and civil war and all branches of art flourished. The 10th century marks the beginning of the fourth period, which culminated in the Song dynasty (960–1279), when Chinese art reached its peak. The greatest achievement of these centuries was the evolution of pure landscape painting into a major art-form, long before Europe conceived of such a possibility. No less important, however, was the pottery of this period, unsurpassed for nobility of form and beauty of decoration. The last great period of traditional Chinese art covers the reign of the Ming emperors (1368–1644) and the last Chinese dynasty of the Manchu or Qing (1644–1911). Painting and pottery remained at a high level and new porcelain techniques were evolved. Outstanding skill was shown also in ivory and jade carving and in CLOISONNÉ enamel. In the 20th century a combination of Western influence and revolutionary upheaval undermined traditional Chinese art. Since the communist revolution of 1949 avant-garde movements have been branded as 'bourgeois formalism'. However, the revolution also brought a revival of traditional art-forms, with people being taught to value their artistic traditions.

Chinese ceramics The POTTERY and PORCELAIN of China. China has the greatest tradition of pottery-making in the world. The use of the word 'china' for any porcelain or porcelain-like products shows how closely the country is identified with ceramics. Pottery has been made in China from as early as the 3rd millennium BC, but it is only from the Han dynasty (206 BC–220 AD) that a continuous tradition begins, low-fired, lead-glazed EARTHENWARE being made in large quantities for use in tombs. High-fired wares were also made, developing into the Yue wares of the Six Dynasties (251–589) and Tang (618–907) periods. These were stoneware, fired to a temperature of about 1,200°C and covered in a green celadon-type GLAZE. The most important feature of Tang ceramics was the perfection of the fine pottery known in the West as porcelain in the 7th or 8th century. The Song dynasty (960–1279) was the golden age of Chinese ceramics, with famous kilns in both northern and southern China. Jingdezhen, in south-eastern China, became the most important ceramic centre from the Yuan dynasty (1279–1368) onwards. Underglaze cobalt painting started to be used at this time on the porcelain for which this area became famous. During the Ming dynasty (1368–1644), this 'blue and white' ware reached an unsurpassed level, particularly in the 15th century. Overglaze enamel colours were introduced in the 16th century, first in combination with underglaze blue (*doucai* or 'contending colours') and later on their own. During the Qing dynasty (1644–1911) 'famille verte' enamels became popular in the reign of Emperor Kangxi (1662–1722) and 'FAMILLE ROSE' in the reign of Emperor Yongzheng (1723–35). The pink used in 'famille rose' enamels was derived from colloidal or opaque gold and was probably introduced from the West by Jesuit monks at court. The ceramic complex at Jingdezhen was managed by able directors during the 18th century and enjoyed court patronage, notably that of the Emperor Qianlong (1736–95). Another important kiln site was in Dehua, Fujian province. This produced the fine white porcelain, left unpainted with a milky glaze, that came to be known as 'blanc de Chine' in the West and was very popular in Europe in the 17th and 18th centuries. Imperial wares of the 19th and early 20th century have recently begun to enjoy increased favour.

Chinese Civil War (1927–37; 1946–49) Conflicts between nationalist and communist Chinese forces. Hostilities broke out in 1927 during CHIANG KAI-SHEK's Northern Expedition, with anti-leftist purges of the KUOMINTANG and a series of abortive communist urban uprisings. Communist strength was thereafter most successfully established in rural areas and its supporters were able to utilize guerrilla tactics to neutralize superior nationalist strength. After a three-year campaign, Chiang finally managed to destroy the Jiangxi Soviet established by MAO ZEDONG, but after the LONG MARCH (1934–35), the communists were able to re-establish themselves in Yan'an, in the north of the country. Hostilities between the two sides were reduced by the Japanese invasion of 1937, and, until the end of World War II in 1945, an uneasy truce was maintained as largely separate campaigns were fought against the common enemy. Violence broke out briefly immediately the war ended, resuming on a widespread basis in April 1946 after the US general George MARSHALL had failed to arrange a lasting compromise settlement. During the first year of the renewed conflict, numerically superior nationalist troops made large territorial gains, including the communist capital of Yan'an. Thereafter Kuomintang morale began to crumble in the face of successful military operations by the communists, decreasing confidence in their administration, and by the end of 1947 a successful communist counter-offensive was well under way. In November 1948 LIN BIAO completed his conquest of Manchuria, where the nationalists lost half a million men, many of whom defected to the communists. In Central China the nationalists lost Shandong, and in January 1949 were defeated at the battle of Huai-Hai (near Xuzhou). Beijing fell in January, and Nanjing and Shanghai in April. The People's Republic of China was proclaimed (1 October 1949), and the communist victory was complete when the nationalist government fled from Chongqing to TAIWAN in December.

Chinese Communist Party (CCP) Chinese political party. Interest in communism was stimulated by the RUSSIAN REVOLUTION (1917) and the May Fourth Movement and promoted by Li Dazhao, librarian of Beijing University, and Chen Duxiu. They were co-founders of the Chinese Communist Party at its First Congress in Shanghai in July 1921. Under COMINTERN instructions, CCP members joined the KUOMINTANG and worked in it for national liberation. Early activities concentrated on trade union organization in Shanghai and other large cities, but a peasant movement was already being developed by Peng Pai. Purged by the Kuomintang in 1927 and forced out of the cities, the CCP had to rely on China's massive peasant population as its revolutionary base. It set up the Jiangxi Soviet in southern China in 1931, and moved north under the leadership of MAO ZEDONG in the LONG MARCH (1934–35). Temporarily at peace with the Kuomintang after the Xi'an Incident in 1936, the communists proved an effective resistance force when the Japanese invaded the country in 1937. After the end of World War II, the party's military strength and rural organization allowed it to triumph over the nationalists in the renewed civil war, and to proclaim a People's Republic in 1949. It has ruled China since 1949. Internal arguments over economic reform and political doctrine and organization led to the chaos of the CULTURAL REVOLUTION (1966–76), during which the CCP appeared to turn on itself. After the death of Mao Zedong and the purge of the GANG OF FOUR the CCP pursued a more stable political direction under the leadership of DENG XIAOPING; but allegations of corruption and demands for more open government led to a prolonged crisis in 1987–89, culminating in the Tiananmen Square massacre of an estimated 2,000 protesters in June 1989.

Chinese language See CHINESE; SINO-TIBETAN LANGUAGES.

Chinese literature One of the major literary heritages of the world, which has profoundly influenced the literary traditions of other Asian countries, particularly Japan, Korea, and Vietnam.

It has a virtually uninterrupted history of some 3,000 years, a timespan unequalled anywhere else in the world. The sheer quantity is also awe-inspiring: from the Tang dynasty (618–907 AD) alone, over 48,000 poems by more than 2,000 authors have survived. This body of literature has remained familiar to generations of Chinese scholars. The Chinese wrote their earliest preserved texts on bone and tortoise shell and in inscriptions on bronzes. Later they wrote on silk and wood. Paper was invented in about the 1st century AD, and China also developed (8th century AD) the first printing techniques in the world. Chinese literature has been divided into two streams: the classical or literary style, set by the ancient writers, and the vernacular, consisting of writings in the living tongue of the authors. Among the former are the CONFUCIAN scriptures, history, philosophy, and collected works of poetry and prose. All were written in the classical Chinese language, which was to be the vehicle for all recognized literature up to the 20th century.

Fiction was collected during the Ming dynasty, and it was during this period that the great Chinese novels such as *Water Margin*, with its tales of the daring deeds of an outlaw band, the magical satire *Monkey*, and *Romance of the Three Kingdoms* emerged. During the succeeding Qing dynasty (1644–1911) this fictional tradition saw its most sophisticated achievements, with *Dream of the Red Chamber* and *The Scholars*.

The literature of modern China began in the years leading up to the May Fourth Movement of 1919: the nationalist movement in which intellectuals grappled with Marxism and liberalism in their search for reform. Its authors committed themselves to write in the vernacular language rather than classical Chinese. They took a great interest in Western literature and made various attempts to copy Western styles, not always successfully. Soviet influence was quite marked in the 1920s. After Mao Zedong's 'Talks at the Yan'an Forum on Literature and Art' in 1942, in which he decreed that literature existed to serve politics and should be written for a proletarian readership, it became impossible for writers to separate politics from any literary genre. In the 1950s Chinese writers took Soviet Socialist Realism as their model. In 1956–57 there was a brief period of flowering of critical literature inspired by the Hundred Flowers Movement of self-criticism, but revolutionary romanticism took over with the Great Leap Forward of 1958, when culture became synonymous with industrial and agricultural expansion. By the time of the Cultural Revolution (1966–76) control over literary activities was complete. Traditional Chinese cultural expression was banned as bourgeois, while modernist writers and artists were purged as anti-socialist. The reform programme which began in 1978 has released great literary forces, beginning with the 'wound' literature from the generation damaged by the Cultural Revolution.

Chinese philosophy The essence of Chinese philosophy is humanism: people and their society have captivated the Chinese mind since antiquity. Although there have been comparatively few metaphysical speculations, the Chinese generally see a unity between the individual and the Universe. This harmonious relationship between the individual and the natural world characterizes the entire history of Chinese philosophy. During its 4,000 years of recorded history, Chinese philosophy has gone through four major periods. The first of these was the Classical Age, which culminated in the blossoming of the Hundred Schools during the Spring and Autumn (722–481 BC) and the Warring States (403–222 BC) Periods. It was followed by the Middle Period (206 BC–960 AD), when CONFUCIANISM first emerged supreme in the socio-political sphere, only to give way to Neo-DAOISM and BUDDHISM. The third period was the Neo-Confucian Stage (960–1850), during which Neo-Confucianism was the unchallenged state ideology. Last came the Modern Era, when MARXISM and Maoism ousted the indigeneous Chinese schools of thought. Chinese philosophy in the 20th century is still in a formative stage, engaged in a sometimes confusing and chaotic attempt to bring together the whole of the Western philosophical tradition with its own native developments.

Chinese religion Despite much regional diversity, linguistic, geographic, and religious, the people of China share one mutually intelligible written language and have traditionally adhered simultaneously to aspects of CONFUCIANISM, DAOISM, and BUDDHISM. The official cult of the imperial state was Confucianism, which dominated education. Confucianism and Daoism permeated intellectual life, and the monastic tradition of Buddhism and priesthood of Daoism played a significant role in social life. Co-existing with these three religions were a range of popular beliefs and practices. Primary among these, and indeed the single most important religious practice, is the belief in ANCESTOR WORSHIP, the veneration of ancestors in the father's line of descent. The importance attached to the family unit is underpinned by a belief in the holiness and interdependently sacred nature of all life. In popular religious belief there are many gods and goddesses who may be specific to a locality or have a wider following. They are symbols of order, spirits of the dead, who are part of a bureaucratic heavenly order and are subject to promotion and demotion according to their performance. The inferior counterparts of the gods are demons, who are symbols of disorder and hostile influences. The gods may be approached through food-offerings, special rituals, or charms, which may be offered or performed at popular religious temples, shrines, or holy spots in the landscape. Similarly, offerings are made at the tombs of the family's ancestors, particularly at the time of the annual Spring Festival. The other chief festival is New Year's Day, a festival for all when the powers of life are renewed. In the 20th century, religious practice in mainland China has declined because of government repression following the introduction of communism in 1949. It remains, however, a cogent influence on the Chinese world-view, for example in the importance attached to family life, and flourishes in Taiwan and Hong Kong, despite the influence of westernization.

Chinese Revolution of 1911 The overthrow of the Manchu QING dynasty and the establishment of a Chinese republic. After half a century of anti-Manchu risings, the imperial government began a reform movement which gave limited authority to provincial assemblies, and these became power bases for constitutional reformers and republicans. Weakened by provincial opposition to the nationalization of some major railways, the government was unable to suppress the republican Wuchang Uprising (10 October 1911). By the end of November fifteen provinces had seceded, and on 29 December 1911 provincial delegates proclaimed a republic, with SUN YAT-SEN as provisional President. In February 1912, the last Qing emperor PUYI was forced to abdicate and Sun stepped down to allow Yuan Shikai to become President. The Provisional Constitution of March 1912 allowed for the institution of a democratically elected parliament, but this was ignored and eventually dissolved by Yuan Shikai after the abortive Second Revolution of 1913 which challenged his authority. Yuan had himself proclaimed emperor in 1915, but by that time central government was ineffective, and China was controlled by provincial WARLORDS.

Ch'ing dynasty See QING.

chinoiserie The imitation or evocation of Chinese styles in Western art and architecture particularly in the 18th century, when pseudo-Chinese designs in a whimsical or fantastic vein accorded well with the prevailing lighthearted ROCOCO style. By the middle of the 18th century the enthusiasm for things Chinese affected virtually all the decorative arts, and there was also a vogue for Chinese-style buildings in garden architecture.

chinook A warm dry wind that blows from west to east across the Rocky Mountains in North America.

Chinook A North American Indian tribe originally inhabiting the region around the Columbus River in Oregon and Washington. Their livelihood was traditionally dependent on the king or Chinook salmon which spawned every year in the river.

chipmunk A GROUND SQUIRREL that occurs in North America and northern Asia, and belongs to one of two genera, *Tamias*, with one species, or *Eutamias*, which contains 22 species. They usually have alternate light and dark stripes running down the body. They are found in a variety of habitats from open grassland to mountain forests. They are noted for their habit of hoarding food, chiefly nuts and seeds, which they eat during the winter at intervals when they awake from hibernation. As they do not always find each store, this habit helps the germination of trees by the scattering of the seeds.

Chippendale, Thomas (1718–79) British furniture-maker and designer. He is one of the most famous names in the history of British furniture, mainly on account of his book *The Gentleman and Cabinet-maker's Director* (1754). This was the first comprehensive book of furniture designs and was immensely influential in Britain and the USA. Many of the designs are in a neoclassical vein, with elements of the French Rococo, chinoiserie, and Gothic revival styles.

Chippewa (or **Ojibwa**) A North American Algonquian-speaking Indian people, once the most powerful tribe in the Great Lakes region, now numbering *c.*80,000 and living in Canada and reservations in North Dakota, Wisconsin, and Minnesota.

Chirac, Jacques (René) (1932–) French statesman, Prime Minister 1974–76 and 1986–88 and President since 1995. He was elected mayor of Paris in 1977, a position he held for 18 years. The founder and leader of the right-wing RPR (Rally for the Republic) Party, Chirac headed the right's coalition in the National Assembly during the socialist government of 1981–86. When his coalition was victorious in the 1986 National Assembly elections, he was appointed Prime Minister by the socialist President François Mitterrand. After an unsuccessful bid for the presidency in 1988, Chirac was elected to succeed Mitterrand as President in 1995.

chirality (in chemistry) A property of a molecule lacking a centre or plane of symmetry and thus not superposable on its mirror image. In organic chemistry, this requires that a molecule contains a carbon atom, called the chiral centre, to which four different groups are bonded. Such a molecule exhibits optical ISOMERISM, and displays OPTICAL ACTIVITY; it occurs in two different forms called ENANTIOMERS. A molecule can possess more than one chiral centre. Thus, if there are two chiral centres there will be four isomers, divided into two sets of enantiomers.

Chirico, Giorgio de (1888–1978) Greek-born Italian painter. After 1910 he started painting disconnected and unsettling dream images, a style that became known as 'metaphysical painting'. His work exerted a significant influence on surrealism and he participated in the surrealist's Paris exhibition of 1925. Major works include *The Uncertainty of the Poet* (1913), portraying a bust with bananas, an arcade, and a distant train.

Chiron The most distant of the objects classified as ASTEROIDS, discovered by the US astronomer Charles Kowal in 1977. Its orbit lies mostly between Saturn and Uranus, resembling those of short-period comets. The discovery, in 1989, of a faint COMA around Chiron confirms that this object probably originated in the outer Solar System and perhaps came in recent times from the OORT-ÖPIK CLOUD.

chiropody The study of the care of feet. The paramedical specialists trained in chiropody treat minor foot ailments, such as corns, bunions, calluses, and ingrowing toenails.

chiropractic A system of COMPLEMENTARY MEDICINE, based on the belief that organic disease can be treated by manipulation of the spine and other joints. Conventional medicine takes the view that manipulation is one possible form of manual therapy, useful only in diseases originating in vertebral disorders or misalignment.

Chisinau (Russian **Kishinev**) The capital of the Republic of Moldova, on the River Byk; pop. (1990) 676,000. Founded in 1420 around a monastery, it became the chief town of Bessarabia under Russian rule and was part of Romania 1918–40. It has a 19th-century Orthodox cathedral and numerous light industries.

Chiswick A residential and commercial district of west London, England, on the north bank of the River Thames.

chitin The main structural component of the ENDOSKELETON of arthropods such as insects and crabs, and of the cell walls of FUNGI.

Chittagong A seaport in south-east Bangladesh, on the Bay of Bengal; pop. (1991) 1,566,070.

chivalry The code of behaviour practised in the Middle Ages, especially in the 12th and 13th centuries, by the mounted soldier or knight. The chivalric ethic represented the fusion of Christian and military concepts of conduct. A knight was to be brave, loyal to his lord, and the protector of women. The songs of the TROUBADOURS celebrated these virtues.

It was a system of apprenticeship: as boys, knights' sons became pages in the castles of other knights; from the age of 14 they learnt horsemanship and military skills, and were themselves knighted at the age of 21. The CRUSADES saw the apogee of the chivalric ideal, as new Christian orders of knights (KNIGHTS TEMPLARS; KNIGHTS HOSPITALLERS), waged war in PALESTINE against the Muslims. During times of peace, the tournament was the setting for displays of military and equestrian skill. The 15th century saw a decline in the real value of chivalry, and though new orders, such as the Order of the Golden Fleece (Burgundy) were created, tournaments survived merely as ritualized ceremonies.

chive A herb of the lily family, *Allium schoenoprasum*, closely related to the onion, garlic, and leek. Chives are widespread across the Northern Hemisphere and also occur in Asia Minor and the Himalayas. They produce dense tufts of bright green, tubular leaves, up to 25 cm (10 inches) long, which are used in salads, and bear attractive round purple or pink flower-heads.

chloride A compound which contains the element chlorine, Cl, showing valency 1; metal chlorides are ionic and contain the Cl^- ion, whereas non-metal chlorides are covalent. Metal chlorides are salts of hydrochloric acid. The most abundant chloride is SODIUM CHLORIDE, or common salt, which occurs in sea water and rock salt.

chlorine (symbol Cl, at. no. 17, r.a.m. 35.45) A yellow-green choking gas; it is a reactive non-metallic element in Group 17 (formerly VIIB), the HALOGENS, and in the free state consists of Cl_2 molecules. With metals it forms ionic compounds which contain the Cl^- ion, and with non-metals covalent compounds; it also forms compounds with oxygen in which it shows valencies 3, 5, and 7. It occurs as SODIUM CHLORIDE in seawater, from which it is obtained by electrolysis in, for example, a CASTNER-KELLNER CELL, and in rock salt. Widely used for disinfecting water supplies and swimming pools, large amounts are also used in BLEACHES for woodpulp in PAPER and TEXTILE manufacture. In reactions with HYDROCARBONS, chlorine is used to manufacture PVC, and a wide variety of other chemicals. Chlorine gas was used as a poison gas in World War I.

chlorite A silicate mineral mainly of green colour; it contains varying amounts of aluminium, magnesium, iron, and other metals in combination with water. It is formed by the alteration of MICAS in IGNEOUS ROCKS, and is common in low-grade METAMORPHIC ROCKS. Hard, dense, and plate-like in form, chlorites are of little commercial value and not much industrial use.

chlorofluorocarbon (CFC) Any of a family of non-flammable, non-toxic, non-corrosive, colourless, and nearly odourless gases or liquids, widely used as refrigerant liquids in domestic refrigerators since the 1930s and, more recently, as a propellant for aerosol sprays. Recently, there has been considerable concern over their effect on the environment. Exposure of CFCs to ultraviolet light in the upper atmosphere causes OZONE depletion. Their production and use is now forbidden in many countries.

chloroform ($CHCl_3$) Trichloromethane, a volatile, colourless, and non-flammable liquid that induces ANAESTHESIA. Discovered by the German chemist Justus von Liebig in 1831, it was first used as ananaesthetic by SIMPSON in 1847 but was eventually abandoned in the 1950s because of its toxicity.

chlorophyll Any one of several closely related pigments found in chloroplasts in plant and algal cells, and used by most plants and algae in PHOTOSYNTHESIS; they are responsible for the green colour of plants. During photosynthesis, chlorophyll absorbs energy from red and blue light. The molecules, 'excited' by the absorbed light, transfer electrons to energy-carrier substances in the cell, thus providing energy for making carbohydrates. Photosynthetic bacteria have a special type of chlorophyll called **bacteriochlorophyll**.

chocolate A food produced by grinding the shelled beans of CACAO. This produces a liquid known as chocolate liquor, containing fat-rich cocoa butter. Chocolate for CONFECTIONERY uses the full-fat liquor, mixed with DAIRY PRODUCTS and vegetable fats. The fat content may be reduced for drinking chocolates by applying pressure to the butter. The resulting press cake is then ground to produce cocoa powder. Cocoa butter is used in COSMETICS.

Choctaw A North American Algonquian-speaking Indian tribe originally inhabiting the lower Mississippi and known as the 'okla homa' ('red people'). There are nearly 39,000 Choctaw living in Oklahoma and Mississippi.

Choiseul, Étienne François, duc de (1719–85) French statesman. He concluded the Family Compact of 1761 with Charles III of Spain and, considering the weakness of the French position, was a successful negotiator at the Treaty of PARIS in 1763. He then tried to reform the army and navy, but was dismissed in December 1770 when he tried to persuade LOUIS XV to support Spain against Britain over the FALKLAND ISLANDS.

Chola A Tamil Hindu dynasty dominant in south India from the 9th to the 13th century. Their origins are uncertain, but they were influential from at least the 3rd century AD, becoming an imperial power on the overthrow of their Pallava neighbours in the late 9th century. Victory over the Pandyas followed, and then expansion into the Deccan, Orissa, and Sri Lanka. Their peak was during the reigns of Rajaraja I (985–1014) and Rajendra I (1014–44), when Chola armies reached the Ganges and the Malay archipelago. The dynasty remained the paramount power in south India until the mid-13th century, when HOYSALA and Pandya incursions and the rise of Vijayanagar eventually destroyed its claims.

cholera An acute communicable bacterial infection of the small intestine by *Vibrio cholerae*, derived almost exclusively from the ingestion of water or food contaminated with human sewage containing this microorganism. The bacterium produces a toxin which disrupts mechanisms that maintain cellular fluid and electrolyte levels. The result is the rapid onset of profuse, white, watery diarrhoea; muscle cramps and vomiting may also occur. Progressive fluid loss results in intense, life-threatening effects. Adequate fluid replacement is essential for complete recovery, which is attained in most cases; antibiotics may also be used.

cholesterol A fatty STEROID found in the blood and body tissues of animals. An essential component of their cell MEMBRANES, it modifies the physical properties of the water-repellent layers, and is found in high concentration in the myelin sheath that surrounds and insulates nerves. It also acts as the raw material on which steroid hormones and bile salts are based. Much of the body's cholesterol is made in the liver, and some can be absorbed from diets rich in animal fat. People with high levels of cholesterol in their blood are thought by some experts to be prone to circulatory diseases, such as ARTERIOSCLEROSIS.

Chomsky, (Avram) Noam (1928–) US theoretical linguist and political activist. His theory of transformational grammar is set out in *Syntactic Structures* (1957). A distinction is made between a speaker's linguistic competence, which is idealized, and actual performance; the theory sets out to account only for the former. Chomsky has revised the theory since 1957.

chondrite A stony METEORITE containing granules. The granules, known as **chondrules**, are solidified droplets of rock. Chondrites were formed at the birth of the Solar System 4.6 billion years ago and constitute the most ancient and chemically primitive material in the Solar System. There are three basic classes of chondrite: **carbonaceous**, which are thought to have a high carbon content; **enstatites**, which have an abundance of $MgSiO_3$; and ordinary chondrites, which are the most common. These three types were formed at progressively higher temperatures. Stony meteorites that have no chondrules are known as **achondrites**.

Chopin, Frédéric (François) (born Fryderyk Franciszek Szopen) (1810–49) Polish-born French composer and pianist. A concert pianist from the age of 8, he wrote almost exclusively for the piano. Inspired by Polish folk music, his mazurkas (55 in all) and polonaises (some 13) were to become his trademarks. He is also noted for his lyrical and poetic short piano pieces, including 19 nocturnes, 15 waltzes, and 24 preludes. As well as writing for solo piano, he wrote two piano concertos (1829; 1830). For some years Chopin was the lover of the French writer George Sand, but their affair ended two years before his death from tuberculosis.

chorale The simple congregational verse-hymn of the Lutheran Church. Chorales became an important means of spreading the Lutheran gospel. Chief among these compositions was the chorale prelude, in which the chorale melody is presented, either whole or in stages, in an elaborate web of organ POLYPHONY that is itself derived from the chorale.

chordate An animal of the phylum Chordata. Chordates are characterized by the development of a notochord (a flexible rod of vacuolated cells formed from mesoderm during development), gill pouches, and a dorsal, hollow, single nerve cord at some stage of their development. The phylum includes the VERTEBRATES, acraniates (animals which lack a skull), the ACORN WORMS, LANCELETS, and SEA SQUIRTS.

chorea See HUNTINGTON'S DISEASE; SYDENHAM.

choreography The process of arranging or designing dance. Choreographers almost never write a 'score' as a composer might, rather they create directly on the dancers, only writing the work down afterwards, if at all. Music was for hundreds of years the major inspiration for dance, and such 20th-century choreographers as BALANCHINE and ALSTON still start from a musical score. Many formal choreographic devices are analogous to those used in music, such as motif and development, canon, and repetition. Similarly, form may be derived from narrative or action, as in many BALLET works. In modern and postmodern choreography a new form may be devised for each individual work.

chorus In GREEK THEATRE, a group of actors who stand aside from the main action of the play and comment on it, often in general terms. On the Elizabethan stage the chorus was the speaker of an introductory prologue, a legacy from Euripides handed down via the Roman closet dramas of Seneca.

In the late 19th-century theatre the chorus was the troupe of supporting singers and dancers in musical comedy, VAUDEVILLE, and revue. By the 1920s chorus girls were wearing fewer clothes, and reached a high standard of precision dancing. The men in the chorus were often dispensed with at this time, but since World War II, under the influence of the US MUSICAL, both men and women now take a larger share in the plot.

Chou dynasty See ZHOU.

Chou En-lai See ZHOU ENLAI.

chough Either of two species of bird in the crow family. Both are about 38 cm (15 inches) long and have blue-black plumage and red legs. The red-beaked, or common, chough, *Pyrrhocorax pyrrhocorax*, has a long, sharply curved red beak; the alpine chough, *P. graculus*, has a shorter, straighter, yellow beak. Both species occur in Europe and southern parts of west and central Asia, the red-billed chough living primarily at low altitudes, the alpine chough at high altitudes. They feed on small insects and nest in cliff crevices.

Chrétien, (Joseph-Jacques) Jean (1934–) French-Canadian statesman. Before he entered politics in 1963, Chrétien had been a lawyer. He was appointed to nine successive cabinet posts, including Minister of Finance (1977–79), being the first French-Canadian to hold that post. As Minister of Justice (1980–82) he handled negotiations with Britain over revising Canada's constitution. In 1984 Chrétien became Deputy Prime Minister but resigned in 1986, returning to his law practice. In 1990 he resumed his political career and was elected leader of the Liberal Party, before becoming Prime Minister in 1993.

Chrétien de Troyes (12th century) French poet. The author of courtly romances, including some of the earliest on Arthurian themes, he is also thought to have written a romance about the legendary knight Tristram. Of his four extant volumes of romances, *Lancelot* (*c.*1177–81) is the most famous.

Christ See JESUS CHRIST.

Christadelphian A member of a Christian sect founded in America in 1848 by John Thomas, rejecting the beliefs and development associated with the term 'Christian', calling themselves 'Christadelphians' ('brothers of Christ') and claiming to return to the beliefs and practices of the earliest disciples. The core of their faith is that Christ will return in power to set up a worldwide theocracy beginning at Jerusalem, and that belief in this is necessary for salvation.

Christchurch The largest city in South Island, New Zealand, at the junction of the Heathcote and Avon rivers, at the southern end of Pegasus Bay; pop. (1991) 307,130. The city, which is the centre of administration and commerce for the Canterbury region, was founded in 1850 by English Anglican colonists whose leader, John Robert Godley, named it after his old university college of Christ Church, Oxford. Today it has numerous industries including woollen mills, carpets, furniture, fertilizers, and food processing.

Christian I (1426–81) King of Denmark and Norway 1448–81, and Sweden 1457–64, founder of the Oldenburg dynasty. Elected to power by the Danish Rigstad, and confirming his status by marriage to his predecessor's widow, he gained the Swedish throne after the war of 1451–57, but lost control to the Swedish nobility later. He also gained Schleswig and Holstein, and was at war with England (1469–74). Strongly Catholic, he founded the Catholic University of Copenhagen in 1479.

Christian, Fletcher (*c.*1764–*c.*1793) British seaman and mutineer. In 1787 he became master's mate under Captain William Bligh on HMS *Bounty*, a ship sailing for the West Indies. In April 1789 Christian seized the ship and cast Bligh adrift on account of his alleged tyranny. In 1790 the crew settled on Pitcairn Island, where Christian was probably killed by Tahitians.

Christian Church The collective body of all Christian believers, or any particular denomination of Christians. The Christian Church is divided into three main groups, the ROMAN CATHOLIC CHURCH, the ORTHODOX CHURCHES, and the PROTESTANT Churches, the most prominent of which are the ANGLICAN COMMUNION, the BAPTIST CHURCH, the LUTHERAN CHURCH, and the METHODIST Church. The variety of traditions within the present Christian Churches developed from the early church as it spread around the world. Divisions between Christians were often occasioned by doctrinal disagreements, though social and political factors also played a part. The major traditions of Christianity are broadly divided along geographical lines. The Roman Catholic Church is dominant in many countries of southern Europe and their former colonies in Central and South America, and in Poland and Ireland. Protestant Churches, which broke away from Roman Catholicism in the 16th century, are concentrated in northern Europe and the USA. Emigration and missionary work have established both traditions in Australasia, Africa, and elsewhere. The Orthodox Church, which finally separated from the Roman Catholic Church in the EAST-WEST SCHISM of the 11th century, is primary in Belarus, Bulgaria, Georgia, Greece, Moldova, Russia, Serbia, and parts of Ukraine, and is scattered throughout the Middle East. The Nestorian Church held that Christ united two persons, one divine and one human, while the Monophysites taught that Christ has only one divine nature. The Monophysites broke with the mainstream Church in the 6th century, eventually forming four important Churches, which accept each other's ministries and sacraments: the COPTIC, Ethiopian, ARMENIAN APOSTOLIC, and Syrian churches. These are sometimes known as the Oriental Orthodox Churches.

The 19th century saw great missionary activity, particularly by the Protestant Churches. Traditional Churches did not always serve growing urban areas, inspiring new Christian movements to grow, most notably the SALVATION ARMY. In the 20th century links between Church and state were further weakened, and after the communist revolutions in Russia and China, Churches were forcibly suppressed. In 1948 the need for greater unity between the many Churches was recognized with the establishment of the WORLD COUNCIL OF CHURCHES. Since then Church membership has been declining in Western Europe but continues to grow in many developing countries.

Christian Democrats A number of Centre-Right parties in post-war Europe, attempting to apply Christian principles to the management of industrial society. Arising in reaction both to classical LIBERALISM and to MARXISM, it sought to create social harmony in place of class divisions, and to use the state as a means of humanizing the capitalist economy. Its religious inspiration was predominantly, though not exclusively, Roman Catholic in character. Much stress was laid on strengthening the family, work associations, and other forms of community. In economic policy, Christian Democrats have tended to embrace CORPORATISM; in international relations they have advocated the protection of HUMAN RIGHTS, and been strong supporters of European integration.

Christianity A religion whose adherents believe in or follow the religion of JESUS CHRIST. At first Christianity was simply a Jewish sect which believed that Jesus of Nazareth was the Messiah (or 'Christ', 'anointed one'). Largely owing to the former Pharisee, Saul of Tarsus (later St Paul) it quickly became an independent, mainly gentile, organization. In the early centuries Christians experienced intermittent persecution by the state, though there was no clear legal basis for this until the reign of the Emperor Decius (250 AD). By the 3rd century, Christianity was widespread throughout the Roman Empire; in 313 Constantine ended persecution and in 380 Theodosius recognized it as the state religion. There were frequent disputes between Christians mainly over the status of Christ and the nature of the Trinity, and later over grace and Church organization. Division between East and West, in origin largely cultural and linguistic, intensified, culminating in the Schism of 1054, sealed by the Crusades. In the West the organization of the Church, focused on the Roman papacy, was fragmented by the Reformation of the 16th century. In the 20th century the ecumenical movement has sought to heal these ancient wounds. See also CHRISTIAN CHURCH.

Christian Science A religious movement founded in the USA by Mary Baker Eddy (1821–1910). In 1875 she published the first of many editions of the manual *Science and Health, with Key to the Scriptures*, and in 1879 she established the Church of Christ, Scientist. This teaches that God is divine mind. Only mind is real; matter, evil, sin, disease, and death are all unreal illusions. Centred in Boston, Massachusetts, it is found in all English-speaking countries. Membership has declined in North America and Europe since 1950, but there has been considerable growth in Africa and South America.

Christian Socialism A form of SOCIALISM based on Protestant Christian ideals. The term was first used in Britain in the 1840s by clergy, including Charles Kingsley, who opposed the social consequences of competitive business and unrestricted individualism, their aim being to improve the status of workers. Late 19th-century urban and industrial conditions stimulated further opposition to unrestricted capitalism, with the establishment in 1889 of the British Christian Social Union and the US Society of Christian Socialists. A belief that the established Churches were more sympathetic to the interests of capital than to the conditions of labour gave rise to the more radical Social Gospel movement.

Christie, Dame Agatha (1890–1976) British writer of detective fiction. Many of her novels feature the Belgian Hercule Poirot or the resourceful Miss Marple, her two most famous and successful creations. Among her best-known detective stories are *Murder on the Orient Express* (1934) and *Death on the Nile* (1937). She also wrote plays; *The Mousetrap* (1952) has had a record run of more than 45 years on the London stage.

Christie, Linford (1960–) Jamaican-born British sprinter. Having won Olympic silver medals in the 100 metres and 4 × 100 metres relay events in 1988, Christie took the individual 100-metre title in 1992. This was followed by the world championship title at this distance in 1993, and in 1994 he took the European 100-metre championship title for the third consecutive time.

Christina (1626–89) Queen of Sweden 1632–54. She was the daughter and successor of GUSTAVUS ADOLPHUS. During her minority, the kingdom was governed mainly by Chancellor Axel Oxenstierna. When she assumed power in 1644, she showed herself to be clever, restless, and headstrong. She attracted many foreign artists and scholars (including DESCARTES) to her court, but after a serious constitutional crisis in 1650, she abdicated in favour of her cousin, Charles X.

Christine de Pisan (1364–1430) French poet and prose writer. Her poems convey the sadness of her early widowhood, and continue a lyrical tradition based on courtly love, written in the new, rigidly determined BALLADE form which VILLON was to exemplify.

Christmas An annual Christian festival celebrating the birth of JESUS CHRIST. The date of Jesus' birth is unknown, but tradition celebrates Christmas Day on 25 December, a date first recorded in 336 AD. The importance of Christmas in the Christian year varies regionally: in the EASTERN ORTHODOX CHURCH, EPIPHANY is considered to be more important, whereas most Western Churches exalt EASTER.

Christmas Island ▶1 An Australian dependency in the Indian Ocean 350 km (200 miles) south of the western end of Java, renowned for its large stone statues; area 135 sq km (52 sq miles); pop. (1991) 1,275. Discovered on Christmas Day 1643 and annexed by the UK in 1888, the administration of the island was handed over to Australia in 1958. In 1991 It became subject to the laws of Western Australia. The island's income is mostly derived from the mining of rock phosphate. **▶2** (or **Kiritimati**) A Pacific island in the Line Islands group, Kiribati, the largest atoll in the world, area 578 sq km (223 sq miles); pop. (1990) 2,530. Fishing and the production of copra are important industries.

chromatic aberration See ACHROMATIC LENS.

chromatic scale See SCALE.

chromatography A technique for analysing or separating mixtures of compounds in which a mobile phase (liquid or gas) containing a mixture of substances flows over a stationary phase (solid or liquid). Each component in the mobile phase has a different tendency to adsorb on the stationary phase. Consequently, as the mixture moves over the stationary phase, the components of the mixture are separated into a series of single-substance 'bands' according to their retention on the stationary phase. Separation of certain mixtures can be improved by applying an electric potential difference across the stationary phase – a technique known as **electrophoresis**. This is used particularly in biochemistry.

chromium (symbol Cr, at. no. 24, r.a.m. 52.00) A hard, silvery-white metallic element; it is one of the TRANSITION METALS. Chromium resists corrosion and this, along with its metallic lustre, is the reason for its use in the ELECTROPLATING of steel and copper objects such as automobile trim and plumbing fixtures. The main ore is chromite ($FeCr_2O_4$), and reduction by carbon in an ELECTRIC-ARC FURNACE yields an ALLOY of iron and chromium which is used in making chromium and stainless STEEL. Chromium steels are very hard and strong and are used for armour plating, bank vaults, safes, cutting tools, and automobile parts. Its compounds are widely used as pigments; chromium oxide is green, and lead chromate yellow. Chromium salts are used for tanning leather and as MORDANTS for dyestuffs.

chromosome A structure consisting of DNA and PROTEINS, found in the nucleus of a cell, which carries the genetic information in living organisms. At certain stages in the cells of all higher organisms they are visible under a microscope.

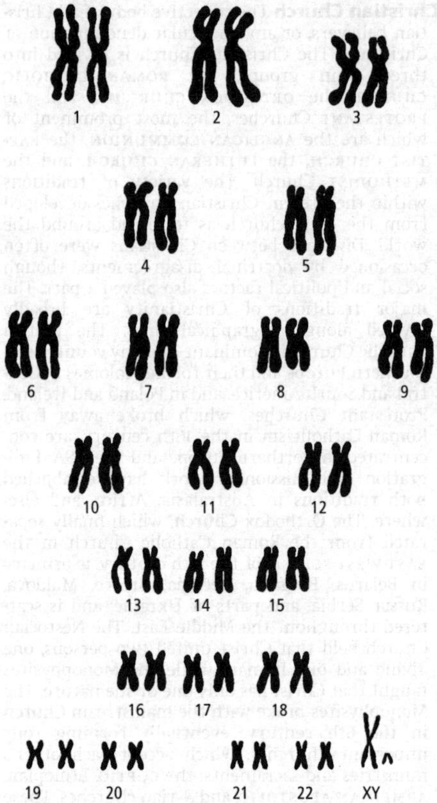

Chromosome A complete set of human male chromosomes. It consists of 23 matched pairs; 22 of these are each assigned a number, and the remaining pair, the sex chromosomes, are designated XY. The female set differs only in the sex chromosomes, which consist of two X chromosomes (XX).

Most species have more than one chromosome. The chromosome set in humans is represented by 23 different chromosomes. There are two chromosome sets (diploid) in every cell except gametes (sex cells) where there is one set (haploid). Chromosomal aberrations are a common form of mutation and may be an alteration of number, leading, for example, to DOWN'S SYNDROME, or of structure, in which pieces of chromosome are deleted, duplicated, inverted or translocated to other chromosomes (see TRANSLOCATION).

One pair of chromosomes, called the sex chromosomes, are involved in sex determination. In mammals the sex chromosomes are the X and Y chromosomes, and the presence or absence of the Y chromosome determines sex; thus XX individuals are female and XY male.

chromosphere The lowest layer of the Sun's tenuous atmosphere above the **reversing layer** and the PHOTOSPHERE. The chromosphere can be seen as a thin red band of light surrounding the Moon's disc during a total solar ECLIPSE.

chronic fatigue syndrome (or **postviral fatigue syndrome**; formerly **myalgic encephalomyelitis**, **ME**) A condition characterized by extremely disabling fatigue that has lasted for at least six months, is made worse by physical or mental exertion, does not resolve with bed rest, and cannot be attributed to other disorders, although it frequently follows glandular fever or some other serious viral infection. The fatigue is sometimes accompanied by muscle pain, sore throat, slight fever, painful lymph nodes, general malaise, and depression (a consequence and not a cause of the other symptoms). As the cause is unknown, treatment is limited to relieving the symptoms and providing psychological support.

chronometer A time-measuring instrument, especially one keeping accurate time in spite of movement or of variations in temperature, humidity, and air pressure. Modern chronometers use a quartz crystal kept in oscillation at a constant frequency by electronic means. Since the advent of radio time-signals the need for expensive marine chronometers scarcely exists.

chrysalis The PUPA of some butterflies, the term being also used occasionally for the pupae of moths and other insects. In a true chrysalis, the wings and legs are closely stuck to the body, and there may be a silken girdle round the middle that attaches it to a stick or plant, and sometimes there are patches of gold and silver colour. The chrysalids of some species can wriggle the abdomen section, but the rest is stationary. Chrysalids are not contained in a cocoon.

chrysanthemum An annual or perennial plant, chiefly of herbaceous habit but occasionally shrub-like. About 100 species are known within the genus *Chrysanthemum*. Their distribution includes Europe, Asia, America, and Africa. Several species have been developed as garden flowers, and the exhibition or florists' varieties are the result of centuries of selective breeding from early Chinese and Japanese kinds. Their flower shape reveals them as members of the sunflower family and relatives of the daisy.

Chrysostom, St John (*c.*347–407) Doctor of the Church, bishop of Constantinople. His name (Greek for 'golden-mouthed') is a tribute to the eloquence of his preaching. As patriarch of Constantinople, he attempted to reform the corrupt state of the court, clergy, and people; this offended many, including the Empress Eudoxia (died 404), who banished him in 403. Feast day, 27 January.

Chuang-tzu See ZHUANGZI.

chub (or **chubb**) A fish of the CARP family, typified by the European chub, *Leuciscus cephalus*, which grows up to 61 cm (22 inches) long. Most abundant in rivers but also living in lakes, they are schooling fishes when young, becoming solitary with age. There are some 17 species of North American chub belonging to the genus *Hybopsis*.

Chulalongkorn (1853–1910) King Rama V of Siam (Thailand) 1868–1910. Only 15 when his father Rama IV (Mongkut) died, Chulalongkorn was represented by a regent until he reached his majority in 1873 and used the intervening years to travel and study administrative practices abroad. He then continued his father's reformist policies, undertaking a massive modernization of his country.

church A building for Christian worship. Forms of worship vary greatly among the CHRISTIAN CHURCHES and this is reflected in the different structure and layout of church buildings. Many are cross-shaped, and most have a nave, where the congregation stand or sit, and a chancel with seats for a choir and the altar, which is sometimes in a small 'sanctuary' beyond the chancel. Most Western churches face east–west, with the altar at the eastern end. A church that is the seat of a bishop is known as a cathedral; many Protestant churches have rejected bishops and cathedrals although they are retained in the ANGLICAN COMMUNION.

Churches of Christ Autonomous conservative PROTESTANT Churches, mainly in the USA, which emerged from the 'Disciples of Christ' movement among early 19th-century PRESBYTERIANS. They consider the BIBLE to be all-sufficient and reject all human creeds and writings. There are about 2.5 million members.

Churchill, Caryl (1938–) British dramatist. She is best known for the satire *Serious Money* (1986); written in rhyming couplets, it deals with 1980s speculators and the ethics of high finance. Her other plays include *Top Girls* (1982) and *Mad Forest* (1990).

Churchill, Lord Randolph Henry Spencer (1849–94) British politician. Younger son of the Duke of Marlborough and father of Winston CHURCHILL, he was elected as Conservative MP in 1874. He became prominent in the 1880–85 Parliament, when he and a group of young Tories became known in opposition to the Liberals as 'the Fourth Party'. A gifted rhetorician, his comment in 1886 that 'Ulster will fight and Ulster will be right' became a slogan for those resisting HOME RULE for Ireland.

Churchill, Sir Winston (Leonard Spencer) (1874–1965) British statesman, Prime Minister 1940–45 and 1951–55. Originally a Conservative MP, he changed to the LIberal Party in 1904, serving as Home Secretary (1910–11) under the Liberals and First Lord of the Admiralty (1911–15), but lost this post after the unsuccessful Allied attack on the Turks in the Dardanelles. He returned to the Conservatives in 1929. In 1939, under Neville Chamberlain, he became First Lord of the Admiralty again, replacing Chamberlain as Prime Minister in May 1940. Serving as war leader of a coalition government until 1945, Churchill demonstrated rare qualities of leadership and outstanding gifts as an orator. Part of his contribution to victory was to maintain morale at home and to forge and maintain the Alliance, especially with the USA, which defeated the Axis Powers. After the victory he was defeated in the general election of 1945; elected Prime Minister for a second term in 1951, he retired from the premiership in 1955, but remained an MP until 1964. His writings include *The Second World War* (1948–53) and *A History of the English-Speaking Peoples* (1956–58); he was awarded the Nobel Prize for literature in 1953.

Church of England See ANGLICAN COMMUNION.

Churchward, George Jackson (1857–1933) British railway engineer. He spent most of his working life at the Swindon works of the Great Western Railway, rising to take effective control of rolling stock from 1899 to 1921. Churchward made Swindon the most modern locomotive works in the country, and is particularly remembered for the standard four-cylinder 4-6-0 locomotives that he introduced in 1903–11.

churl See CEORL.

Churrigueresque An extravagant style of architecture and decoration popular in Spain and Latin America in the 18th century, and sometimes used loosely to refer to the Late Baroque and Rococo period as a whole in Spanish architecture. The style, named after the Churriguera family of architects, particularly the Madrid architect José de Churriguera (1665–1725) is characterized by abundant use of barley-sugar columns and extremely florid surface ornamentation which sometimes runs riot to such an extent that it completely obscures the underlying structure.

Chuuk See TRUK.

Chuvashia (or **Chuvash Republic**) A republic in European Russia, in the valley of the River Volga; area 18,300 sq km (7,064 sq miles); pop. (1990) 1,340,000; capital, Cheboksary. Annexed by Russia in the 16th century, it became an autonomous region in 1920 and was a Soviet autonomous republic from 1925 until 1991 when it became an autonomous republic of Russia. About 70 per cent of the population are Chuvash people of Bulgar descent. Railway-repair industries, engineering, the manufacture of textiles and chemicals, and the production of grain and fruit are important.

CIA See CENTRAL INTELLIGENCE AGENCY; INTELLIGENCE SERVICES.

Ciano, **Count Galeazzo** (1903–44) Italian politician. A leading fascist, he married MUSSOLINI's daughter and from 1936 to 1943 was Foreign Minister. He was among those leaders who voted for the deposition of Mussolini, and for this he was tried and shot in Verona by the puppet government established by Mussolini in northern Italy.

Cibber, **Colley** (1671–1757) English actor, theatre manager, and dramatist. He excelled in comic roles and won recognition as a dramatist with his first comedy, *Love's Last Shift* (1696). He became joint manager of Drury Lane, where he spent most of his career, in 1711. After his much-ridiculed appointment as Poet Laureate in 1730 he wrote an *Apology for the Life of Mr Colley Cibber, Comedian* (1740).

cicada A large insect of the true BUG order, Hemiptera, often found in tropical regions. The adults feed on the sap of trees and shrubs, but the larvae live underground on roots, and may live for many years before completing their life cycle. The females are silent, but the males produce loud, high-pitched, persistent songs from organs on the underside of the body. Each buzzing song is characteristic of the species and is usually made by day.

Cicero, **Marcus Tullius** (106–43 BC) Roman statesman, orator, and writer. A supporter of Pompey against Julius Caesar, in the *Philippics* (43 BC) he attacked Mark Antony, who had him put to death. As an orator and writer, Cicero established a model for Latin prose.

cichlid A member of a very large family of freshwater fishes, Cichlidae, which live mostly in Africa and in South and Central America. A few species occur naturally as far north as Texas, and in parts of Asia, but many are found in the African Great Lakes. In general they are perch-like in body form, with spiny dorsal and anal fins, and the head and body are fully scaled. They have a single nostril each side. There are about 700 species, occupying a wide range of micro-habitats; some are even adapted to life in bodies of water that regularly dry out.

Cid, **El** (or **the Cid**) (born Rodrigo Díaz de Vivar) (*c.*1043–99) Spanish soldier. A champion of Christianity against the Moors, he also fought for the Moors in a tortuous military career that began in 1065; in 1094 he captured Valencia, which he went on to rule. He is immortalized in the Spanish *El cantar de mío Cid* (12th century) and in Corneille's play *Le Cid* (1637).

cigarette See TOBACCO.

Cilicia The ancient name for the eastern half of the south coast of Asia Minor. Between 1080 and the occupation of the region by Ottoman Turks in the 15th century, Cilicia was ruled first as an independent Armenian principality then as a kingdom known as Little Armenia.

Cimabue (born Cenni di Peppi) (*c.*1240–1302) Italian painter, his unflattering nickname meaning 'Oxhead'. Several major works are traditionally (and plausibly) attributed to him, including the majestic crucifix in Santa Croce in Florence, which was badly damaged in the Florentine flood of 1966.

Cimarosa, **Domenico** (1749–1801) Italian composer. In 1772 his first opera was produced in Naples, and by the mid-1780s he had become one of the most popular composers of *opera buffa* (comic opera) in Italy. He worked in Russia (1787–91), and Vienna (1791–93), where his masterpiece *The Secret Marriage* was performed (1792).

Cimarron A river of the USA that rises in northeast New Mexico and flows 1,123 km (698 miles) across Kansas into Oklahoma where it joins the Arkansas River.

cinchona An evergreen tree of South America, belonging to the gardenia family, Rubiaceae, related to coffee, and making up a genus of the same name containing some 40 species. They are the source of natural quinine, which is used in the treatment of malignant malaria and in flavouring tonic water and other drinks. The active principle is concentrated in the bark.

Cincinnati An industrial and commercial city in southern Ohio, USA, on the Ohio River; pop. (1990) 364,000. Founded near an Indian river-crossing in 1788–89, Cincinnati grew from three small frontier riverboat settlements (Columbia, North Bend, and Losantiville). After the opening of the Miami and Erie Canal in 1832 it became one of the largest cities in the USA, being described by the poet Longfellow as the 'Queen City of the West'. Its industries include machine tools, vehicles and aircraft engines, electronic and electrical equipment, and metal goods. It is also a cultural centre with the University of Cincinnati and several other institutions and museums.

Cincinnatus, **Lucius Quinctius** (*c.*519–438 BC) Roman republican hero famous for his devotion to the republic in times of crisis. Appointed dictator in 458 when a Roman army was trapped in battle by the Aequi tribe, he won a crushing victory and rescued the beleaguered troops. After this success, he resigned his command and returned to farm his small estate.

cinder cone A small volcanic cone built by explosive eruptions of clinkery fragments of lava and ash. The cinder (or scoria) is loosely packed and absorbs rainwater like a sponge, so that it is difficult for soil and vegetation to develop and the slopes stay steep and bare.

Cinderella A folktale found throughout the world but best known in Europe in Charles Perrault's version, 'Cendrillon' (1697). In this, Cinderella is mistreated by her stepmother and two stepsisters. With the help of a supernatural godmother, however, she attends a ball, dances with a prince who falls in love with her, and loses a glass slipper as she leaves in haste. After scouring his kingdom for the foot that will fit the slipper, the prince finds Cinderella and marries her.

cine camera A camera that takes motion pictures. Its basic elements are similar to those of a still CAMERA: a light-tight compartment for the film, a lens, and a shutter. A cine camera, however, has to be able to take a series of photographs in rapid succession at a steady speed. This is achieved by a film-transport mechanism, which moves the film intermittently, one frame at a time, past an opening or 'gate' through which the film is exposed. This intermittent motion is produced by a claw device that engages with perforations on the edge of the film and moves it on one frame. The film is then stationary for a brief interval as the claw engages farther along the film: it is in this stationary interval that the film is exposed. The cine camera's shutter is a rotating, partially cut-away disc that is geared to the intermittent mechanism. The opaque section of the disc prevents any light from reaching the film while it is moving. See also VIDEO CAMERA.

cinema See FILM.

cinéma-vérité Unscripted documentary style of film-making, which aspires to total truthfulness and spontaneity. Originating in the Soviet Union in the 1920s, it developed rapidly in the late 1950s and early 1960s, encouraged by the increase in location filming, the appetite of television for factual material, and the availability of lightweight cameras and sound-recording equipment.

cinnabar The chief ore of mercury, consisting of mercury sulphide, HgS. It has a distinctive cochineal red colour, and is soft, heavy, and fragile in crystal form. It is found in veins associated with igneous activity and is deposited by hot springs in volcanic regions. Important sources are Almaden (Spain), Monte Amiata (Italy), Idrija (Slovenia), and California (USA). The mineral pigment known as vermilion is prepared from cinnabar.

cinnamon A spice obtained from the dried bark of a species of evergreen trees, *Cinnamomum verum*, belonging to the laurel family. It is native to Sri Lanka, and its exploitation was the incentive for the successive Portuguese, Dutch, and British colonizations of that country. Cinnamon oil, used in medicine, is extracted from the bark residue, and an oil distilled from the green leaves is used as a substitute for clove oil. Camphor is obtained, in a similar manner to cinnamon oil, from *Cinnamomum camphora*, a closely related species.

Cinq, Les See FIVE, THE.

Cinque Ports A group of medieval ports in south-east England (originally five: Dover, Hastings, Hythe, Romney, and Sandwich; Rye and Winchelsea were added later) formerly allowed various trading privileges in exchange for providing the bulk of England's navy. Most of the old privileges were abolished in the 19th century and the Wardenship of the Cinque Ports is now a purely honorary post, currently held by Elizabeth The Queen Mother.

Cintra See SINTRA.

cipher A kind of code based on transposing letters of the ALPHABET used in intelligence, diplomacy, and elsewhere for protecting information from unauthorized people. Messages in cryptograms are encoded following patterns, called algorithms, and are decodable only by someone in possession of the key to a given pattern.

Circe In Greek mythology, a sorceress encountered by Odysseus and his companions on their return from the Trojan war. By means of a magic potion, she turned his companions into swine, but Odysseus himself – forewarned by Mercury – ate a herbal antidote, overcame her, and forced her to return them to their normal form.

Circinus The Compasses, a CONSTELLATION of the south celestial hemisphere, introduced by the 18th-century French astronomer Nicolas Louis de Lacaille. It represents a pair of drawing compasses or dividers used by draughtsmen and navigators. Circinus contains no objects of particular interest, the brightest star within it being of third magnitude.

circle A curve consisting of all the points lying in a plane at a fixed distance, called the radius (*r*), from a fixed point, called the centre. The diameter (*d*) of a circle is any straight line joining two points on the circumference that passes through the centre. In all circles the ratio of the circumference (*c*) to the diameter is equal to a fixed number, denoted by the Greek letter pi (π), which has the value 3.141,59..., i.e. $c = \pi d = 2\pi r$. The area of a circle is πr^2.

circuit-breaker A simple automatic safety switch used in electrical circuits that cuts off the current flow if it becomes too large and potentially damaging. The switch is usually magnetically operated, and, unlike a FUSE, it may be reset without replacement when the fault condition has been repaired. Circuit-breakers have replaced fuses in mains wiring for most domestic and industrial purposes.

circulation (in climatology) The global patterns of air movement in the TROPOSPHERE and of currents in the ocean. The oceanic circulation can be divided into surface currents driven primarily by winds, and the vertical or deep circulation which is density-driven. As the properties which determine the density of sea water are its temperature and salinity, this deep circulation is also known as the thermosaline circulation. Because they are deflected by land masses, and because they are acted upon by wind systems and the CORIOLIS FORCE, surface current systems tend to form GYRES. The subtropical gyres, which are driven by the mid-latitude anticyclones, are characterized by deeper, stronger currents along their western boundaries (for example, the GULF STREAM in the North Atlantic and the KUROSHIO in the North Pacific). By contrast, the eastern limbs of subtropical gyres tend to be wide, slow and diffuse currents; these eastern boundary currents are often associated with coastal upwelling. The main component of the deep circulation is cold, relatively saline water which sinks in polar regions and flows towards the equator at great depths in the ocean, but other water masses sink at regions of CONVERGENCE of surface water. All water which is carried downward in the deep circulation is eventually, after tens, hundreds or thousands of years, mixed up to the surface again. Along the Equator, and in the vicinity of 65° S., are zones of divergence of surface water and hence enhanced upwelling of deeper water.

Atmospheric circulation consists of horizontal wind systems and vertical airflows. The horizontal wind systems are governed by the way atmospheric pressure varies from place to place. The vertical airflows are caused partly by large-scale CONVECTION, partly by CONVERGENCE and DIVERGENCE at different levels, and partly by differences in the density of air masses. The driving forces are the atmospheric energy budget and the transfer of heat from the equatorial zone towards the poles. The seasonal migrations of the inter-tropical convergence zone north and south of the Equator is identified by areas of rising air and low pressure, which causes the monsoons. This rising air descends in the subtropics, giving areas of semi-permanent high pressure, and returns to the Equator in the TRADE WINDS. In the mid-latitudes WESTERLIES blow from the subtropical areas of high pressure towards the polar front, whose presence is marked by a westerly JET STREAM. In the mid-latitudes the airflow aloft is a series of atmospheric WAVES, while below it is dominated by cellular, migratory depressions and anticyclones. Temperatures over the South Pole are lower than over the North Pole, and consequently the thermal gradient and, therefore, the winds are strongest in the Southern Hemisphere, where the mid-latitude westerlies are termed the Roaring Forties.

circulation (of the blood) The flow of BLOOD through the body of an animal, enabling the transport of oxygen and nutrients to the tissues and the removal of waste products. Blood is pumped around the body by a HEART. Smaller animals, such as crabs and insects, have a tubular heart that pumps blood into the body cavity. The organs suspended within it thus come into direct contact with the blood and materials are exchanged by diffusion. This is described as an **open circulation**. With an increase in body size, diffusion is no longer efficient, and an active circulatory system is needed. The vertebrate cardiovascular system, with arteries, veins, and a powerful muscular heart, supplies this need. ARTERIES carry blood away from the heart, while VEINS return blood to the heart. Capillaries are the smallest blood vessels and form a branching network connecting arterioles (the fine end-branches of arteries) and venules. This type of circulation is called a **closed circulation**.

circumcision The practice of removing the foreskin of the male or the genital labia and/or the clitoris of the female for religious or ritual reasons, usually as a form of initiation or rite of passage. It is found in various traditional societies throughout the world, from Africa to Aboriginal Australia. Male circumcision is an important feature of Judaism and Islam. In Judaism the ceremony, known as *brit* in Hebrew, is performed by a professional *mohel* on the eighth day after birth, usually in the home, and circumcision is seen as a seal of the COVENANT between God and the Jewish people. Islamic circumcision, *khitan*, commonly left until early adolescence, follows the tradition or HADITH of Muhammad, although it is not demanded by the KORAN. Female circumcision, although less common than male, is also found within Arab, African, and other cultures, but some women's groups and those concerned with children's rights regard the practice as genital mutilation and are campaigning for its abolition in countries which still permit it. Female circumcision is rarely carried out in hygienic conditions and fatal infections are a serious risk. Many circumcised women suffer extreme pain associated with menstruation and sexual intercourse and run a greater risk of death due to complications during childbirth. The World Health Organization estimated in the 1990s that about 90 million women were circumcised. It is illegal in the UK.

circumpolar star A star whose proximity to the north celestial pole ensures that it never rises or sets but remains above the observer's horizon, cir-

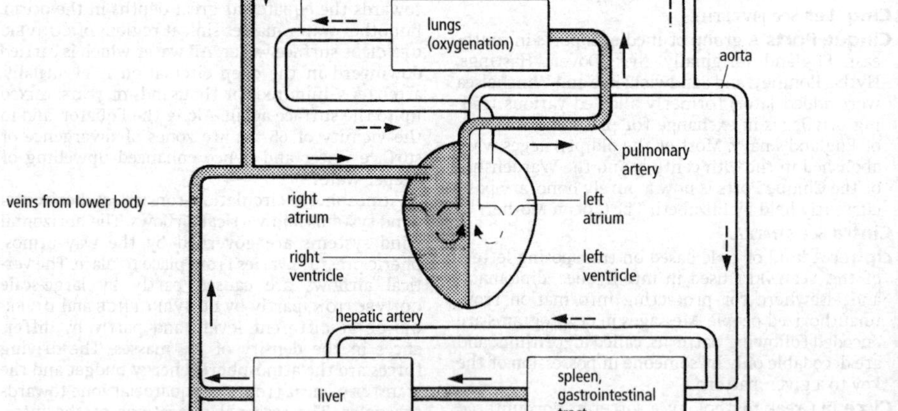

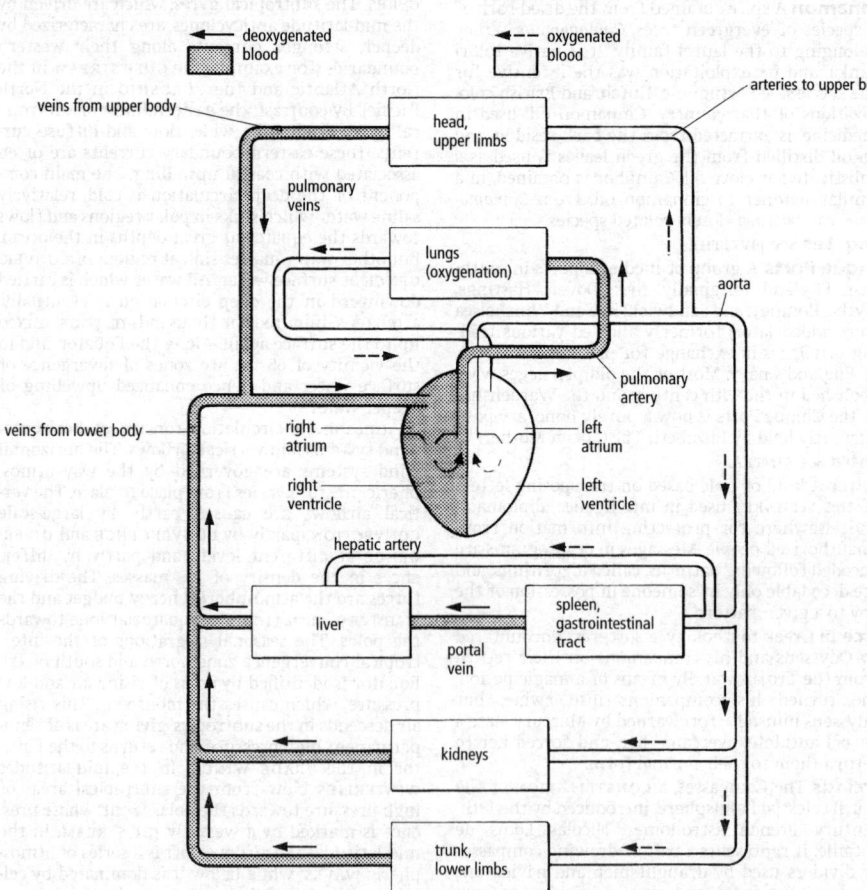

Circulation of the blood in a mammal. This type of system is described as double circulation as the blood passes through the heart twice during a complete circuit of the body.

cling the pole once every 24 sidereal hours. Stars so near the south celestial pole that they remain below the observer's horizon form a second group of circumpolar stars.

circumpolar vortex The two bands of mid-latitude westerly winds which encircle the poles in the middle and upper troposphere. The winds are strongest in winter, when there is the greatest temperature, and therefore pressure, difference between high and low latitudes. The westerlies of the middle latitudes are a manifestation of them at the Earth's surface.

Cirencester A market town in Gloucestershire, England on the River Churn; pop. (1981) 14,000. As Corinium Dobunorum it was an important road junction and the second-largest town in Roman Britain. It has a major museum with many locally found Roman artefacts.

cire-perdue (French, 'lost wax') A method of hollow metal CASTING used by sculptors, also called **investment casting**. A thin layer of wax corresponding to the shape of the final sculpture is encased within two layers of heat-resistant clay or plaster, melted and drained off, and then replaced with molten metal poured into the cavity that the 'lost wax' has created. The technique, found in every continent except Australasia, was used by the Egyptians, Greeks, and Romans, and is still the main means used for traditional bronze sculpture.

cirque (or **corrie**, **cwm**) A deep bowl-shaped hollow at the head of a valley or on a mountainside; formed during the Ice Age by high-level glaciers.

cirrhosis A progressive liver disease characterized by the destruction of liver cells, which is followed by the formation of nodules and fibrous strands. The liver blood flow and function are adversely affected, giving rise to symptoms, which include abdominal distension, pain, vomiting of blood, blood in the stools, generalized itching, jaundice, and fluid retention. Brain involvement (hepatic encephalopathy) may result in confusion, drowsiness, and coma (hepatic coma). In women, breast swelling, loss of libido, and menstrual disturbances may occur. The main cause in western countries is excessive alcohol consumption, although approximately 30 per cent of cases are of unknown cause; other causes include HEPATITIS and prolonged obstruction of the bile duct. Cirrhosis is incurable and irreversible, but progression can be halted particularly if the cause is alcohol.

cirrocumulus A form of usually high cloud consisting of small roundish fleecy clouds in contact with one another, known as 'mackerel sky'.

cirrostratus A thin usually high white cloud formation composed mainly of fine ice-crystals and producing halo phenomena.

cirrus A form of high altitude white wispy CLOUD.

CIS See COMMONWEALTH OF INDEPENDENT STATES.

cisalpine On the southern side of the Alps. The Cisalpine Republic was created by Napoleon in 1797 by uniting territory on either side of the River Po. With its capital at Milan, this territory formed part of the Kingdom of Italy created in 1805 but broken up ten years later in 1815.

Cistercian A religious order founded in 1098 at Cîteaux (Cistercium) near Dijon in France. Observing the Rule of St Benedict, Cistercian houses spread throughout Europe in the 12th–13th centuries.

citadel A key feature of a Greek city, being the stronghold around which large communities originally developed. When a city expanded, and a protective encircling wall was built to protect the citizens' houses, the citadel lessened in importance, though it often became a religious centre and housed the public treasury. The ACROPOLIS of Athens is the most famous example.

citizenship Membership of a political society, involving the possession of legal rights, which usually include the rights to vote and stand for political office. For many centuries citizenship was a privileged status extended only to those who fulfilled stipulated conditions such as owning fixed property, but in modern states citizens' rights are usually considered an aspect of nationality, granted to all those born in a particular country as well as to permanent settlers. Citizens, as opposed to mere subjects, enjoy legal protection against arbitrary decisions by their governments, and they are supposed to play an active role in influencing government policy. The Left tend to see citizenship as embracing social rights such as those provided by the WELFARE STATE, whereas the Right advance the idea of an active citizen as someone engaged in charitable work on behalf of the community.

Citlaltépetl (or **Pico de Orizaba**) The highest peak in Mexico, in the east of the country, north of the city of Orizaba after which it is sometimes named. It rises to a height of 5,610 m (18,405 ft) and is an extinct volcano, inactive since 1687. Its Aztec name means 'star mountain'.

citric acid A white crystalline hydroxycarboxylic acid that is present in citrus fruits. It is also an intermediate in KREBS' CYCLE in plant and animal cells. Synthetic citric acid is used as a food flavouring.

citronella A species of tropical grass, *Cymbopogon nardus*, that is grown extensively in Sri Lanka, Myanmar, and Java for distillation of the scented oil, much used in soap manufacture. It is not to be confused with the South American genus *Citronella*, which are small trees or bushes belonging to the family Icacinaceae.

citrus fruit The fruit from plants of the genus *Citrus*, which belong to the family Rutaceae. Also in this family are similar fruits, such as kumquats (*Fortunella*) and the inedible trifoliate orange *Poncirus trifoliata*. All, except the trifoliate orange, are evergreen trees with simple leaves, and usually with spines at the leaf axils of the younger shoots. The majority of citrus fruits are of Asian origin, although many hybrids, such as the CLEMENTINE, arose elsewhere. Citrus fruits were cultivated in China at least 5,000 years ago. Modern citrus crops are grown in tropical and subtropical climates, mostly in the Mediterranean region, Japan, and Central and North America. Plant breeding has concentrated on increasing fruit size, controlling acidity, and reducing the number of seeds. Oranges make up 75 per cent of citrus production, lemons and grapefruit each about 10 per cent. Other crops include limes, tangerines, mandarins, and pomelos (a type of grapefruit).

The fruits are a special type of berry called a hesperidium, with juice-filled segments surrounded by a white, spongy tissue, and a tougher, outer peel. All are typically orange- or lemon-shaped but vary in size from the massive SHADDOCK, up to 30 cm (12 inches) in diameter, to the lime, which is 4–6 cm (1.5–3.5 inches) in diameter. The sweetness of the juice, which is rich in vitamin C, varies according to its proportion of sugar to acid. Sweet orange has about 12 per cent sugar and 1 per cent citric acid, whereas lemons and limes contain 4 per cent and 6 per cent acid respectively.

cittern A plucked musical instrument that,

because it has wire strings, a strong construction, and a flat back, held its tuning much better than the lute. It could therefore be picked up and played without lengthy preliminary tuning and was popular for casual music-making from the 15th to 17th centuries.

Ciudad Bolivar A city in south-east Venezuela, capital of the state of Bolivar, on the Orinoco River; pop. (1991) 225,850. Its name was formerly ANGOSTURA ('narrows'), being changed in 1846 to honour the country's liberator Simón Bolívar. It is an inland port and commercial centre of a wide region.

civet A carnivore of the family Viverridae, found throughout Africa and tropical Asia. There are 19 species including the PALM CIVETS and 'true' civets. All are medium-sized animals, rather bigger than a large cat, with elongated bodies and snouts, long bushy tails, and short legs. They prey upon rodents, birds, and insects, and they also take fruit. They have well-developed anal scent glands whose secretions, although evil-smelling, can be refined for use in the perfume industry. The true civets are part of the same subfamily as genets and linsangs. The best-known and largest species of true civet is the African civet, *Civettictis civetta*, which occurs in a wide range of habitats, from tropical rain forest to arid grassland. The binturong of south-east Asia, *Arctictis binturong*, is an unusual civet in that it is one of the few mammals in the Old World to have a prehensile tail.

civil defence Activities designed to protect civilians in the event of an enemy attack. In the UK, for example, during World War II, civilians took on many roles, such as firefighters and air-raid wardens, in order to protect the population. After 1945, in the context of potential preparations for nuclear warfare, the term became associated with the development of shelters, warnings, and other means to evacuate and defend the civilian population in the event of an attack. In some countries there are elaborate provisions for civil defence in the event of a war. Examples are Switzerland and the former Soviet Union, where a comprehensive programme, including compulsory civilian training of a people's MILITIA, widespread public information, and regular alerts, was developed.

civil engineering The design and construction of engineering structures. It includes environmental, municipal, structural, and transportation engineering, and covers the design and construction of DAMS, BRIDGES, TUNNELS, large-scale earthworks, embankments, and cuttings; FLOOD CONTROL and COASTAL DEFENCES; ports and harbours, and offshore structures; roads; RAILWAYS; CANALS; the structure and foundations of large buildings; and land drainage, WATER SUPPLY, and SEWAGE treatment. Named to distinguish it from military engineering, civil engineering first became identified as a separate discipline in the late 18th century. The Institution of Civil Engineers was founded in London in 1818.

civil law The law governing the relations between private individuals or bodies, as opposed to criminal, administrative, or constitutional law (compare PUBLIC LAW). Areas covered by civil law include the principles governing commercial transactions, the settlement of disputes in the fields of TORT and CONTRACT, and matters involving family, property, and inheritance. In England, civil and criminal cases are heard in separate COURTS OF LAW.

Civil law systems are those in which ROMAN LAW has had a decisive influence on legal principles, methods, and terminology in the field of private law. They are to be found in Continental Europe, Latin America, and parts of Africa and Asia (in modified form). The great 6th-century codification of Roman law, the *Corpus Juris Civilis* ('Body of civil law'), forms the basis of such systems, which are therefore called civil law systems. The development of different nation-states in Europe led to the codification of laws into distinctive systems, most notably the CODE NAPOLÉON, adopted in France in 1804 (and in other European countries through Napoleonic expansion), and the *Bürgerliches Gesetzbuch*, the German Civil Code, which came into force in 1900. Civil law systems were subsequently exported through the process of colonial domination (for example, to some African countries and to Latin America) or imported out of respect for an intellectual tradition (for example, in Japan). An important characteristic of civil law codes is the division of private law into conceptual and organizational categories, such as the law of persons, property, obligations, and delict (tort), following the compilations of the Roman jurists. In principle, these codes require no interpretation, only application. In practice, interpretation and judicial development of the law are required. Judicial reasoning is marked by an economy of style, using logical deductions from the principles deemed to underlie the code. Although CASE LAW has acquired an important role as a source of law, there is no system of binding judicial PRECEDENT, as in COMMON LAW SYSTEMS.

civil rights Those rights which collectively safeguard political freedom and personal liberty. They are enumerated in the INTERNATIONAL COVENANT ON CIVIL AND POLITICAL RIGHTS (1966) and are generally taken to include FREEDOM OF EXPRESSION, association, movement, conscience, and religion; the right to liberty and to privacy, the right to vote, and the right to a fair trial. In many countries, civil rights are guaranteed to citizens through a BILL OF RIGHTS or the CONSTITUTION. Civil rights constitute a subset of HUMAN RIGHTS. The Civil Rights Movement was the movement in the USA in the 1960s for full legal and civil rights for black people.

civil service A body of officials employed by a state for the administration of civil affairs. Constitutionally subordinate to the government, the civil service is usually organized into departments with specific functions, such as finance, health care, agriculture, or trade and industry. Under parliamentary government, an elected minister is the head of each department, and responsible for it to the LEGISLATURE. Under presidential government, the PRESIDENT is administrator-in-chief; subordinate officials are appointed by and answerable to him. Civil servants operate within a hierarchical bureaucracy, with posts ranging from clerical grades to an administrative élite, which advises elected ministers. In countries which follow the Westminster system, the civil service is traditionally non-partisan and favours anonymity. By contrast, the civil service in France and Germany exhibits considerable *esprit de corps*, regarding itself as the embodiment of the state, above rather than beneath politics. In the USA, top civil servants are often political figures. Like all bureaucracies, the civil services are open to charges of cumbersomeness and abuse of power.

civil war (or **internal war**) A state of sustained, large-scale violent conflict between political, religious, ethnic, or ideological groups within a state. Such conflict can take place in order to overthrow the government, or to secede from the state. An example of the former is the civil war in Russia (1918–20), which followed the 1917 RUSSIAN REVOLUTION; an example of the latter is the American Civil War (1861–65), which resulted from the attempt at secession on the part of the Confederate States. Groups may resort to war if they feel their interests are not fairly reflected in government, or if they want to impose on the state an alternative ideology or political regime. Many wars since 1945 have been internal or civil wars, brought about by state boundaries fixed in the colonial period which ignore ethnic and religious diversity, resulting in post-colonial struggles for power and influence in the newly created states. Such civil wars have often been sustained and even escalated because of intervention by superpowers, neighbouring states, or other major powers who have acted to protect their own perceived interests or those of client groups within these conflicts. There have been more than 30 civil wars since 1945, including those in Angola, Cambodia, Nicaragua, El Salvador, Lebanon, Nigeria, Mozambique, Ethiopia, Pakistan, Yemen, and Yugoslavia.

Civil War, American See AMERICAN CIVIL WAR.

Civil War, English See ENGLISH CIVIL WAR.

civil wars, French See WARS OF RELIGION, FRENCH.

Cixi (or **Tz'u-hsi**) (*c.*1834–1908) Empress dowager of China 1862–1908. A Manchu, she became a concubine of the emperor Xianfeng (ruled 1851–61), giving birth to a son in 1856 who came to the throne in 1862 as the emperor Tongzhi. Cixi acted as Regent for twelve years, and after Tongzhi's death, resumed her position after the elevation of the latter's four-year-old cousin to the throne as the emperor Guangxu. She maintained her power through a combination of ruthlessness and corruption, until the last decade of the century, when the emperor attempted to reverse her conservative policies (Hundred Days Reform). Cixi responded by imprisoning Guangxu, and encouraging the BOXER RISING. Forced by foreign military forces to flee the capital, she returned in 1902, conceding some reforms, but still tried to delay the establishment of a constitutional monarchy.

Clackmannan A local government area in central Scotland, formerly the smallest county (Clackmannanshire) in Scotland, and from 1975 to 1996 a district of Central Region; area 907 sq km (350 sq miles); pop. (1991) 47,200; administrative centre, Alloa.

Clactonian The Lower Palaeolithic industries represented by the flint implements found at Clacton in Essex, south-east England, dated *c.*250,000–200,000 BC.

cladding A layer applied to an external or internal building surface to provide weather or fire-resistance or to improve appearance. For masonry or timber-frame walls, traditional claddings are weatherboarding and tiles or slates. Nowadays, in framed buildings, cladding describes a non-loadbearing external wall, usually thin-gauge metal sheeting, ribbed to improve stiffness, and supported on light 'rails' that span between main columns or beams. PRE-CAST CONCRETE cladding panels, with a range of decorative finishes, are commonly supported on edge beams and tied back to the structure.

Clair, René (born René Lucien Chomette) (1898–1981) French film director known for silent comedies. His early sound films included *Sous les toits de Paris* (1930), *Le Million* (1931), and *À nous la liberté* (1931). He later achieved wider success with *Les Belles de nuit* (1952). Clair was always involved in the scriptwriting for his films, which typically contain elements of surrealism, underpinned by satire.

clam Any of various BIVALVE molluscs, specifically the burrowing hard-shell molluscs (quahogs), such as *Mercenaria mercenaria*, and soft-shell molluscs (gapers), such as *Mya arenaria*, both of which are common beneath sandy and muddy beaches. Both groups include large, ovoid bivalves, but the soft-shell clam is endowed with long, stout siphons and can burrow down to 50 cm (20 inches). Other molluscs commonly called clams include the Venus clams (*Clausinella*), razor clams (*Ensis*), and giant clams (*Tridacna*) of the Indo-Pacific, which are over 1 m (3 feet) across and weigh 1,100 kg (1.2 US tons). All clams feed exclusively on tiny plankton.

clan A group of people within a wider society who claim descent from a common ancestor and are usually distinguished by a common clan name, as, for example, the Highland clans of Scotland. The term is rather a general one, and can refer to groups organized around different forms of lineage. In some societies, the ancestor from whom members claim descent may be a mythical figure or, as in forms of totemism, an animal or other non-human figure. Members of a clan have obligations towards each other, and their MARRIAGES are usually exogamous: that is, members must marry outside the clan.

Clans have always been politically significant in Scottish history and clan support was vital to the Scottish king, who often played upon clan rivalries to maintain his power. These rivalries, especially between the Highland and Lowland clans, intensified at the time of the Reformation. The Highland clans retained their Roman Catholic faith, they fought for the Royalists during the English Civil War, and their reluctance to accept William of Orange led to the Glencoe Massacre in 1692. They also took the lead in the Jacobite rebellions of 1715 and 1745, after which an attempt was made by the British government to break up the clans by banning the wearing of the kilt and by undermining the system of communal clan ownership of land. Since the 17th century the Highland clans have worn Highland dress, consisting of a kilt (wrap-over skirt) made of a **tartan** material. The tartan is a woollen cloth woven in different colours forming cross-meshed stripes, each clan having its own pattern.

In Ireland a clan-based social system prevailed until, after the 16th-century rebellions against English rule, their influence was progressively destroyed by military suppression and a policy of wholesale land confiscation.

Clapham A residential district in the London borough of Wandsworth, with a large common and major rail junction.

Clapton, Eric (1945–) British blues and rock guitarist, singer, and composer. He played in the Yardbirds and then formed his own group, Cream (1966–68), whose lengthy improvisations and experimental harmonies were influential in the development of rock music. The song 'Layla' (1972) is perhaps his best known; since then he has developed a restrained style that displays less of his instrumental virtuosity but has brought immense commercial success.

Clare (Gaelic **Chláir**) A county in the province of Munster in the Republic of Ireland, between the River Shannon and Galway Bay; area 3,188 sq km

(1,231 sq miles); pop. (1991) 90,800; county town, Ennis. The county is named after an Anglo-Norman family who settled here in the 13th century.

Clare, John (1793–1864) British poet. After working as a day labourer and gardener, he published *Poems Descriptive of Rural Life and Scenery* (1820). This was followed by *The Shepherd's Calendar* (1827), which has received renewed critical attention in recent years, along with *The Rural Muse* (1835) and other later poems. Clare's poetry is a simple man's celebration of the natural world; it is notable for its use of the poet's own dialect and grammar. In 1837 he was certified insane and spent the rest of his life in an asylum.

Clare election (1828) An event in Ireland that led to the passing of the Roman Catholic Relief Act by the British government in 1829. In 1828 Daniel O'CONNELL, an Irish lawyer, stood for election to Parliament in the County Clare constituency, winning a resounding victory over his opponent. However, O'Connell, as a Roman Catholic, could not take his seat. The Prime Minister, the Duke of Wellington, felt that if O'Connell were excluded there would be violent disorder in Ireland. Accordingly, despite furious opposition, the government pushed through a CATHOLIC EMANCIPATION measure allowing Catholics to sit in Parliament and hold public office.

Clarence, George Plantagenet, Duke of (1449–78) English prince, one of EDWARD IV's younger brothers. He intrigued with the Burgundians and fell out with both Edward and his other brother, Richard, Duke of Gloucester (RICHARD III); he was found guilty of high treason and is supposed to have been drowned in a butt of malmsey wine.

Clarence, Lionel, 1st Duke of (1338–68) The second surviving son of EDWARD III of England and Philippa of Hainault, known as Lionel of Antwerp from his birth in Antwerp. From about 1341 it was arranged that he would marry the Anglo-Irish heiress Elizabeth de Burgh (1332–63); he was created Earl of Ulster and in 1361 was sent to Ireland as governor, to reassert English rule there. In 1362 he was created Duke of Clarence, the title being derived from his wife's inheritance of the lordship of Clare in Suffolk. After her death another rich marriage was arranged for him, to Violante, the only daughter of Galeazzo Visconti, Lord of Pavia; he died only a few months after this wedding. The title of Clarence was revived in 1412 for **Thomas of Lancaster** (1389–1421), second son of HENRY IV of England and Mary de Bohun; it lapsed again after his death.

Clarendon, Constitutions of A document presented by HENRY II of England to a council convened at Clarendon, near Salisbury, in 1166. The king sought to define certain relationships between the state and the Church according to established usage. Churchmen, in particular Thomas à BECKET, saw it as state interference. The most controversial issue, BENEFIT OF CLERGY, concerned Henry's claim to try in his law courts clerics who had already been convicted in the ecclesiastical courts. After Becket's murder in 1170 Henry conceded the benefit of clergy, but not other points at issue.

Clarendon, Edward Hyde, Earl of (1609–74) English statesman and historian, chief adviser to Charles II 1660–67. He shifted his allegiance from the Roundheads to Charles I on the outbreak of the Civil War, becoming royal adviser and accompanying the king to Oxford. He was Chancellor of Oxford University (1660–67) and author of the prestigious *History of the Rebellion and Civil Wars in England*, which he began writing in 1646, but which was published posthumously (1702–04). A number of University and public buildings in Oxford are named after him.

Clare of Assisi, St (1194–1253) Italian saint and abbess. She joined St Francis in 1212 and together they founded the order of Poor Ladies of San Damiano, more commonly known as the 'Poor Clares', of which she was appointed abbess. She was canonized two years after her death and in 1958 Pope Pius XII declared her the patron saint of television, alluding to a story of her miraculously experiencing the Christmas midnight mass being held in the Church of St Francis in Assisi when on her deathbed. Feast day, 11 (formerly 12) August.

clarinet A single-reed musical instrument with a mainly cylindrical bore and the reed attached to a mouthpiece. It was almost certainly invented, as an improvement over the earlier chalumeau, by Johann Christoph Denner in about 1710. Early clarinets had only two keys, but by the mid-18th century five were normal, which, combined with the problems of the different fingering for the same note in different octaves, may explain why it did not become a standard orchestral instrument until around 1800. In the 19th century further keywork was devised, as with all the WOODWIND. From their early days, clarinets were made in a family of sizes, all of which, except for the BASSET HORN, had the written E below middle C as their lowest note. The family eventually ranged from a sopranino in Ab to a contrabass in Bb, two octaves below the normal size.

Clark, Alan (1928–) British politician, historian, and diarist. The son of Baron Clark, he first entered parliament as a Conservative in 1974, becoming Minister of State at the Ministry of Defence (1989–92), where he caused controversy over violations of the ban on selling arms to Iraq. His *Diaries* (1993, which were widely read, contained a number of indiscretions. He was re-elected to parliament in 1997. His other books include *The Fall of Crete* (1963) and *Aces High* (1973).

Clark, Kenneth, Baron (1903–83) British art historian. He became director of the National Gallery (1934–45) before becoming Slade Professor of Fine Art at Oxford (1946–50, 1961–62). He was subsequently Professor of Art History at the Royal Academy (1977–83). He reached a wide public with his television series *Civilization* (1969) and wrote a number of books, including *Leonardo da Vinci* (1939) and *The Nude* (1956). He was awarded an OM in 1976.

Clark, William (1770–1838) US explorer. With Meriwether Lewis, he jointly commanded the Lewis and Clark expedition (1804–06) across the North American continent.

Clarke, Sir Arthur C(harles) (1917–) British writer of science fiction. Originally a scientific researcher, he conceived the idea of communications satellites. He is better known as the writer of such novels as *Earthlight* (1955) and *The Fountains of Paradise* (1979). He also co-wrote (with Stanley Kubrick, the film's director) the screenplay for the film *2001: A Space Odyssey* (1968); Clarke and Kubrick collaborated in writing the novel of the same title, published in the year of the film's release.

Clarke, Jeremiah (*c.*1674–1707) English composer and organist. Little is known of his origins, but by 1685 Clarke was a chorister of the CHAPEL ROYAL. Clarke's work includes church music, songs, odes, incidental music for the theatre, and harpsichord pieces. The best of it has sometimes been mistaken for PURCELL's (including the 'Prince of Denmark's March', better known as the 'Trumpet Voluntary'). He also set to music John Dryden's poem *Alexander's Feast*.

Clarke, Kenneth (Harry) (1940–) British politician. First elected to parliament as a Conservative in 1970, he became Chancellor of the Exchequer (1993–97). His previous offices included Secretary of State for Health (1988–90), Secretary of State for Education (1990–92), and Home Secretary (1992–93). He failed to be elected as leader of the Conservative Party in 1997.

Clarke, Marcus (Andrew Hislop) (1846–81) British-born Australian writer. In 1863 he emigrated to Australia, where he worked on a sheep station before becoming a journalist. His fame is based on his novel *For the Term of his Natural Life* (1874) about an Australian penal settlement, as well as his shorter stories of Australian life, such as *Old Tales of a Young Country* (1871).

class (in biology) In the classification of living organisms, the group ranking below the PHYLUM and including orders of animals or plants. If the number of orders in a class is large, it may be divided into smaller units called subclasses, which are then divided into orders. Members of each class show characteristics indicating common evolutionary descent, but the limits which define the class are often the subject of disagreement among biologists.

class (in sociology) see SOCIAL CLASS; CLASS STRUGGLE.

classical economics The system of economic theory expounded in the writings of (mainly British) economists between Adam SMITH (whose *Wealth of Nations* was published in 1776) and J. S. MILL (whose *Principles of Political Economy* appeared in 1848). The principal contributors to classical economic theory were Smith, Jean-Baptiste Say (1767–1832), RICARDO, Robert MALTHUS, and Mill. The central idea in classical economics is that of competition. Although individuals behave solely to benefit themselves, competitive markets (Adam Smith's 'invisible hand') ensure that this is enough to lead to efficient allocation of RESOURCES and PRODUCTION, and no excess PROFITS. Government has a desirable economic role (above that of providing law and order) only in the context of market failure, that is, where competition does not exist. The supply of every good and every FACTOR OF PRODUCTION will be equal to demand. The equilibrating element in all markets is price, the price of labour being the wage. This was assumed by the classical economists to tend in the long run to subsistence level, any persistent wage above this level calling forth faster population growth. At the same time, Say's Law, that 'supply creates its own demand', was supposed to rule out persistent or involuntary unemployment of labour. The analysis of rent was another pre-occupation of classical economics because the need was felt to explain and justify the distribution of income among the owners of LABOUR, CAPITAL, and land. Ricardo argued that rent was equal to the surplus producible on more fertile land in competition with less fertile land. Classical economics assumes both savings and investment to be predominantly determined by INTEREST rates, one of the aspects disputed in the 20th century by KEYNES. The classical view of growth theory and economic development was that a stationary state was expected to materialize at some stage in the future. Following the new marginal analysis pioneered in the second half of the 19th century by the British economist William Stanley Jevons (1835–82), and the Austrian economist Carl Menger (1840–1921), classical economics developed into the neoclassical economics of Walras, Pareto, Marshall, and others. Neoclassical theory remains the scientific core of economic, especially microeconomic, analysis today.

Classicism in dance Periods in dance history in which ideas that derive from Ancient Greece are evident. Classicism represents economy and precision in movement, order and geometric design, grace and ease in performance, adherence to recognized rules and the values of symmetry, proportion, and restraint. The 16th- and 17th-century classical revival in the Italian *intermedii* and the French BALLETS DE COUR drew on classical imagery and themes, while NOVERRE brought a return to Greek myth in his *Orpheus* (1760). Greek characters and myths provide a rich seam throughout the history of Western theatre dance, recently in GRAHAM's *Clytemnestra* (1958) and David Bintley's *Choros* (1983). PETIPA, the arch-Classicist, showed the wealth of imaginative possibility in set steps and patterns and was known for the creation of sculptural 'tableaux'. The early 20th-century revival took many forms, from DUNCAN's *Iphigenia* (1904) to BALANCHINE's *Apollo* (1928), the latter demonstrating a spare neoclassical aesthetic based on Petipa but with distortions created by turned-in feet and hips and unexpected incidents.

classification (in biology) See NOMENCLATURE IN BIOLOGY; TAXONOMY. See also Appendix.

class struggle The theory of a permanent condition of social conflict between SOCIAL CLASSES. Such an idea emerged in the French Revolution (1789), but it was given its theoretical and ideological form by MARX and Friedrich Engels in the Communist Manifesto (1848), which asserted that 'the history of all society up to now is the history of class struggle'. According to Communist theory, the class struggle is to culminate in the victory of the working class, or proletariat, after which an ideal society based on shared resources would be established. The theory of conflict was underpinned by DIALECTICAL MATERIALISM, according to which the clashes of opposing systems result in positive progress. With the coming to power of the Bolsheviks in Russia (1917) and the Communists in China (1949), a focus on struggle and contradictions came to characterize not only domestic politics but also foreign policy in those countries and others influenced by them. The economic failure of socialism and communism, the collapse of Soviet control over Eastern Europe during the 1980s, and increased opportunities resulting from social change, industrialization, and enhanced legal rights, such as the right to form TRADE UNIONS, have undermined the idea of class struggle. In developing countries, where inequality and poverty may be extreme, notions of class struggle retain some appeal, but are often only loosely linked to those of Marx and Engels.

clastic sediments Fragments of various sizes, ranging from clay and silt to large stones and boulders, derived from pre-existing rocks, which may have been of any type. Normally they were transported to the place where they were deposited by wind, water, or gravity. The corresponding rocks range from clays and shales through sandstones to conglomerates and breccias.

Claude, Georges (1870–1960) French chemist and inventor. In 1897 he discovered that acetylene could be safely handled and transported by dissolving it in acetone. Five years later he perfected a process for liquefying air by compressing it and allowing it to expand through a valve, which could be used to make oxygen and nitrogen industrially. He also developed neon lighting and invented a synthetic ammonia process, similar to HABER's but operated at much higher pressures.

Claude Gellée (1604/5–82) French painter, one of the greatest of all landscape painters. He is often called Le Lorraine (in France) or Claude Lorraine (in Britain), after his birthplace, though he spent most of his life in Rome. Usually his pictures are inspired by the countryside around Rome (the Campagna), which he presents as a world of ideal order and tranquillity. Their ostensible subjects, taken usually from the Bible or Roman poets, are subordinate to the real theme, the mood of the landscape presented poetically in terms of light and colour. His style acquired great grandeur and formality in the 1640s and 1650s, but in his late work forms seem to lose their material solidity and melt into the magical atmosphere.

Claudel, Paul (1868–1955) French dramatist and poet. His conversion to Roman Catholicism in 1886 made a profound impression on his writing. In plays like *Partage de midi* (1906), *L'Otage* (1911), *L'Annonce faite à Marie* (1912), and *Le Soulier de satin* (1925–28), he creates a half-imaginary Universe impregnated by a divine presence which draws his characters on to perform deeds of self-sacrifice. His early association with the SYMBOLISTS is revealed in his use of imagery and the free-verse form in which he wrote both plays and poems (for example *Cinq grandes odes*, 1910). He also wrote an oratorio *Jeanne d'arc* (1938) with music by HONEGGER.

Claude Lorraine See CLAUDE GELLÉE.

Claudet, Antoine François Jean (1797–1867) French pioneer photographer. Director of a glass-manufacturing company, Claudet established a London warehouse twelve years before photography was first announced. Purchasing a licence to take daguerreotypes from DAGUERRE himself, he opened a portrait studio in 1841. A prolific inventor, Claudet reduced the early long exposures by chemical means, and obtained patents for a darkroom light, a light-meter, the use of artificial lighting and painted backgrounds in the studio, and several other devices – especially for stereo photography.

Claudius (full name Tiberius Claudius Drusus Nero Germanicus) (10 BC–54 AD) Roman emperor 41–54. He spent his early life engaged in historical study, prevented from entering public life by his physical infirmity; he was proclaimed emperor after the murder of Caligula. His reign was noted for its restoration of order after Caligula's decadence and for its expansion of the Roman Empire, in particular his invasion of Britain in the year 43, in which he personally took part. His fourth wife, Agrippina (15–59 AD), is said to have killed him with a dish of poisoned mushrooms.

Clausewitz, Karl von (1780–1831) Prussian general and military theorist. A Chief of Staff in the Prussian army (1815) and later a general (1818), he went on to write the detailed study *On War* (1833), which had a marked influence on strategic studies in the 19th and 20th centuries.

Clausius, Rudolf Julius Emanuel (1822–88) German physicist who established the mathematical explanation of the KINETIC THEORY of gases. He stated the second law of THERMODYNAMICS stressing the concept of entropy (dissipation of available energy), i.e. the entropy of the Universe tends towards a maximum.

clavichord The simplest and one of the most expressive of all keyboard instruments. When a key is depressed, a brass rod or blade (the tangent) mounted on its inner end rises and touches the string, making it sound. When the key is released, the tangent leaves the string and its vibration is stopped by a strip of felt (the listing) wound over the left-hand end of the strings. Thus the finger is in contact with the string while it sounds, and the sound can be varied by pressure on the key. The clavichord was invented *c.*1400 and was widely used, especially as a practice instrument, into the 19th century.

clavicle (or **collar-bone**) One of two bones jointed at their mid-point to the upper part of the breast bone and laterally to the shoulder bones above the shoulder joint. The clavicles keep the shoulder joints away from the chest wall and are longer and larger in humans than in any other mammal. The arrangement in humans permits a greater degree of movement of the arm at the shoulder joint than in other animals.

claw A keratinized epidermal structure of skin formed on the tips of the digits of VERTEBRATES, the simplest form of which may partly embrace the digit. Those of the cat can be retracted into a sheath, allowing it to approach its prey silently. Mammals may have nails or hooves in place of claws. In birds, large claws are called talons.

clay A SEDIMENTARY ROCK of very fine grain. The bulk of the microscopic particles of which it is composed are flaky. Their total surface area is correspondingly large, and they are able to take up relatively large amounts of water. When wet, the clay thus becomes plastic. The clay minerals that are the characteristic constituents of clays are hydrous aluminium silicates produced by the weathering of rocks. Some clays are rich in decayed plant and animal remains, which darken them; some contain iron and oxidize to brown colours when exposed to air. Residual clays are those that have formed in place by the weathering of rock. The sedimentary rocks termed clays are generally composed of material that has been transported, usually by water, and deposited elsewhere, often in a river estuary. Sometimes, when clay dries out, the surface cracks, peels off, and is carried away. Such flakes deposited in sand or other sediment are known as clay galls.

Clay, Cassius See MUHAMMAD ALI.

Clay, Henry (1777–1852) US statesman and orator. As Speaker of the House of Representatives (1811–14) he played a central role in the agitation leading to the WAR OF 1812, and was one of the commissioners responsible for the negotiation of the Treaty of GHENT which ended it. He was one of the architects of the Missouri Compromise and won support for his American System, a policy to improve national unity through a programme of economic legislation. His final political achievement lay in helping the passage of the Compromise of 1850 between the opposing free-soil and pro-slavery interests. His role in arranging major sectional compromises between North and South (1820, 1833, and 1850) earned him the title of 'the Great Compromiser'.

clearing house An institution for settling mutual debts. For example, the London Bankers' clearing house and the New York clearing house daily calculate the amounts owed by each member BANK to each other bank as a result of that day's cheque transactions by its customers. The debts are then settled by transferring commercial banks' balances at the CENTRAL BANK. The banks which are members of clearing houses are commercial banks (not merchant banks) and are known as clearing banks. Clearing houses also feature in commodity markets and derivative markets, in which the clearing house often acts as principal to contracts between members, thus minimizing the counterparty risk.

clearwing moth A member of a large family, Sesiidae, of small day-flying moths, which is distributed worldwide. They have extensive transparent patches on the wings, the scales from these areas having been shed on the first flight. Many species resemble wasps, bees, or ichneumon flies in shape and coloration, and are avoided by predators because of this resemblance. The maggot-like caterpillars of clearwings feed by burrowing in tree trunks, stems, or roots. The currant clearwing, *Synanthedon tipuliformis*, can be a pest of currant bushes in Europe and North America.

cleavage (in geology) The way in which a mineral or rock tends to split. In minerals, and particularly in crystalline materials, the natural lines of separation are determined by the internal arrangement, or lattice, of the atoms. There are planes of weakness in the atomic lattice, and the nature of the cleavage depends on the relative strengths of the bonds in these planes. In rocks, the cleavage is the result of partial or complete recrystallization during metamorphism. This produces a layered (foliated) structure that is independent of any original bedding.

Cleese, John (Marwood) (1939–) British comic actor and writer. He began his television writing and acting career in the 1960s, gaining widespread fame with *Monty Python's Flying Circus* (1969–74). He also co-wrote and starred in the situation comedy *Fawlty Towers* (1975–79). Cleese has also appeared in films, notably *A Fish Called Wanda* (1988), which he wrote.

cleft palate A birth defect which is caused by the failure of the tissues forming the roof of the mouth to join along the midpoint. It occurs in about one in a thousand births and can be associated with a cleft or hare lip. Undiagnosed, the baby has difficulty feeding and later with speech development. Treatment consists of plastic surgery at about one year of age, special dental care, and speech therapy.

cleg See HORSEFLY.

clematis A plant belonging to the genus *Clematis*, which includes some 250 species, most of them climbers, with opposite, usually compound leaves. They are members of the buttercup family Ranunculaceae. The climbing species attach themselves by bending their leaf-stalks round the support. The flowers are conspicuous because of their white or coloured sepals, there being no petals, while the fluffy fruits are single-seeded with a long fluffy 'parachute', which promotes wind-dispersal. Many species are cultivated, the most commonly seen being the large-flowered hybrids known collectively as *C. × jackmannii*.

Clemenceau, Georges (Eugène Benjamin) (1841–1929) French statesman, Prime Minister 1906–09 and 1917–20. A radical politician and journalist, he persistently opposed the government during the early years of World War I, before becoming Premier and seeing France through to victory in 1918. He presided at the Versailles peace talks, where he pushed hard for a punitive settlement with Germany, but failed to obtain all that he demanded (notably the River Rhine as a frontier). He founded the newspaper *L'Aurore*.

Clemens, Samuel Langhorne See TWAIN, MARK.

Clement, St (known as **St Clement of Rome**) (1st century AD) Pope *c*.88–*c*.97. Probably the third bishop of Rome after St Peter, he was the author of an epistle written *c*.96 to the Church at Corinth, insisting that certain deposed presbyters be reinstated. In later tradition he became the subject of a variety of legends; one held that he was martyred. Feast day, 23 November.

Clementi, Muzio (1752–1832) Italian-born British composer and pianist. He studied in Rome, where he became the protégé of Peter Beckford (cousin of the novelist William BECKFORD). On Beckford's Dorset estate Clementi was able to study (1766–73) and perfect his harpsichord technique. He moved to London in 1774, soon gaining great success as a composer, performer, teacher, and publisher, both in England and in Europe.

clementine A CITRUS FRUIT thought to be a hybrid between the mandarin and the sweet orange. It is intermediate between its parents in size, colour, and the looseness of peel. The most important areas for commercial production are in North Africa.

Clement of Alexandria, St (Latin name Titus Flavius Clemens) (*c*.150–*c*.215) Greek theologian. He was head of the catechetical school at Alexandria (*c*.190–202), but was forced to flee from Roman imperial persecution and was succeeded by his pupil Origen. Clement's main contribution to theological scholarship was to relate the ideas of Greek philosophy to the Christian faith. Feast day, 5 December.

Cleopatra (VII) (69–30 BC) Queen of Egypt 47–30. The last Ptolemaic ruler, she was restored to the throne by Julius Caesar, having been ousted by the guardians of her father Ptolemy Auletes (died 51). After her brief liaison with Caesar she forged a longer political and romantic alliance with Mark Antony, by whom she had three children. Their ambitions for the expansion of the Egyptian empire ultimately brought them into conflict with Rome, and she and Antony were defeated by Octavian at the battle of Actium in 31. She is reputed to have committed suicide by allowing herself to be bitten by an asp.

Cleopatra's Needles Two ancient obelisks erected at Heliopolis in the 15th century BC by Thothmes III and later transported by the Roman Emperor Augustus to Alexandria *c*.14 BC. One of the granite obelisks was removed to the Victoria Embankment, London, in 1878; the other was given to the USA in 1881 and erected in Central Park, New York.

clerihew A form of comic verse named after its inventor, Edmund Clerihew Bentley (1875–1956). It consists of two metrically awkward COUPLETS, and usually presents a ludicrously uninformative 'biography' of some famous person whose name appears as one of the rhymed words in the first couplet:

George the Third
Ought never to have occurred.
One can only wonder
At so grotesque a blunder.

Cleveland A former county in north-east England, on the North Sea coast, formed from parts of Durham and North Yorkshire in 1974 and abolished in 1996, when its administrative functions were devolved to four unitary authorities. Its county town was Middlesborough.

Cleveland A major port and industrial city in north-east Ohio, USA, situated on the southern shore of Lake Erie; pop. (1990) 505,600. Founded by Moses Cleaveland in 1796, Ohio developed rapidly after the opening (in 1827) of the Ohio Canal linking Lake Erie with the Ohio River. It is a leading iron and steel centre and has metal-manufacturing, oil-refining, chemical, vehicle, and electrical industries.

Cleveland, (Stephen) Grover (1837–1908) US Democratic statesman, 22nd and 24th President of the USA 1885–89 and 1893–97. His first term was marked by efforts to reverse the heavily protective import tariff, and his second by his application of the Monroe doctrine to Britain's border dispute with Venezuela (1895).

click beetle (or **skipjack**) One of a large family, Elateridae, of some 7,000 species of BEETLE found worldwide, including many species common in grassland. Most species are elongate and oval in shape. When they fall on their backs they can right themselves by a special mechanism on the thorax which throws them into the air with an audible click. The larvae of some species are known as wireworms, and these do tremendous damage to plant roots in some parts of the world. The wireworm larvae may take up to five years to develop fully.

cliff A steep, bare slope formed in rock, soil, LOESS, or ice. Cliffs may be small, simple features where rivers have cut away their banks, or large, complicated forms 1,000 m (3,000 feet) or more high, running for long distances along an escarpment, a canyon, or a coastline. The shape and size of cliffs depend on three things. The first is the strength of the material forming them: soil or clay cannot support high cliffs as well as cemented sandstones or granite can. The arrangement of layers of different materials in the cliff face is also important: weak rocks near the bottom cause the whole face to collapse. Secondly, for slopes to stay steep and bare it must be difficult or impossible for soil and vegetation to develop. This depends largely on climate: in wet tropical areas, plants may cover slopes of 80°, whereas in deserts, slopes of 45° are barren cliffs. Finally, material must be prevented from piling up, smothering the bare surface: the sea, a river, or a glacier has to be actively moving debris away from the foot and keeping the face clear.

climate The weather conditions experienced by a particular region over a long period. It includes extreme and variable conditions experienced, as well as average ones. The elements included, and recorded at weather stations, are: radiation, temperature, pressure, wind velocity, humidity, cloud types and amounts, precipitation, evaporation, hours of sunshine, and days with snow cover. It may refer to areas differing markedly in size, ranging from a small rural area or a town to a continent, or to the Earth as a whole. In any location the factors influencing the climatic conditions are latitude, altitude, topography, distance from the sea, ocean currents, type and density of vegetation, and soil conditions. Major CLIMATIC CHANGE occurs naturally over only very long periods, the last great ice age ending nearly 10,000 years ago; but there is evidence that modifications are being caused by human activity. Atmospheric pollution, urbanization, and denudation of the landscape are all contributing to this process.

climatic change A change caused by modifications to the Earth's atmospheric energy budget, which may be the result either of a fluctuation in the output of energy from the Sun or a change in the heat budget of the TROPOSPHERE. Radical changes brought about the last ice age, after which temperatures in mid-latitudes rose very rapidly, so that by 4000 BC summer temperatures were several degrees higher than at present. This relatively warm period was then followed by cooler, wetter conditions around 700 BC. Conditions had ameliorated by 1100 AD but a marked deterioration followed, producing the so-called Little Ice Age between 1550 and 1700. Subsequently instrumental records, which became available in Europe from the 17th century, have revealed a general upward trend in temperature. In the last hundred years or so increased concentrations of atmospheric pollutants have been released into the air. Carbon dioxide may have contributed to the GREENHOUSE EFFECT, and chlorofluorocarbons (CFCs) exposed to ultraviolet light in the upper atmosphere have led to OZONE depletion, cooling the stratosphere and warming the troposphere. However, short-term fluctuations on a global scale (such as those experienced during the last 7,000 years) may result more from an inherent instability in the atmospheric CIRCULATION, together with miscellaneous factors, such as an increase in atmospheric dust from volcanic activity.

climatic types The major kinds of climate that occur on the Earth. Classification enables the distribution of types to be described, although the boundaries are never sharply defined, since each type merges imperceptibly into its neighbours. While broad distinctions, as between desert, monsoon, and arctic climates, are easy to recognize, it is more useful to identify types in terms of biological response. Thus KÖPPEN recognized six major types on the basis of the relationship between temperature and plant growth, and Thornthwaite later identified five major types on the basis of the availability of soil moisture in each month of the year. Broadly it can be said that the various elements are covered in ten basic categories, as typical in the global pattern: equatorial, or tropical humid (as at Entebbe, Uganda); tropical monsoon (Calcutta, India); tropical wet/dry (Cuiabà, Brazil); hot desert (Aĭn Salah, Algeria); Mediterranean (Valparaiso, Chile); subtropical humid (New Orleans, USA); temperate maritime (London, Britain); temperate continental (Warsaw, Poland); boreal (Dawson City, USA), and polar (Mawson, Antarctica).

climatology The study of climates. It involves mean values and the long-term variations that occur in meteorological phenomena, such as precipitation and temperature, and their distribution over the Earth's surface. Synoptic climatology attempts to relate actual weather conditions to patterns of airflow, and palaeoclimatology examines climates in the geological past.

climbing fern A fern belonging to the genus *Lygodium*, which contains 25 species, mostly native to the tropics and subtropics. One species, *L. palmatum*, is native to the eastern USA. These ferns coil round other vegetation, using their leaf stalks to climb, and can reach 4.5 m (15 feet). They are used to make mats in Malaysia.

climbing perch A species of Asiatic freshwater fish, *Anabus testudineus*, which ranges from southern China to Sri Lanka. It lives in large rivers, canals, and ponds, often where oxygen levels are low, and it breathes air by means of respiratory organs in a cavity above each set of gills. It can travel overland from one patch of water to another, pulling itself slowly along by means of its pelvic fin spines and spiky gill covers, but its climbing ability has been much exaggerated.

climbing plant A plant which attaches itself to a support (often another plant) in order to grow towards the light to display its leaves, flowers, and fruits. Adaptations for climbing are numerous and include aerial roots, hooked prickles, twining leaf-stalks, branchlets modified as tendrils (often with the addition of adhesive discs), and leaf-tip tendrils. Moreover, climbers include simple scrambling plants, woody twining kinds, and the LIANAS.

Cline, Patsy (born Virginia Petterson Hensley) (1932–63) US country singer. She was discovered in 1957 when she sang 'Walkin' After Midnight' on a television show, and later had hits with 'Crazy' (1961) and 'Sweet Dreams of You' (1963). Just as she was becoming well known she was killed in an air crash. She was elected to the Country Music Hall of Fame in 1973.

clingfish A member of the family Gobiesocidae, which contains some 100 species. They are mostly small, scaleless fishes with a maximum length of 30 cm (12 inches), and with the pelvic fins adapted into a powerful sucking disc, by means of which they cling to rocks. They are mostly marine fishes of temperate and tropical shallow waters, but a few live in fresh water in Central America. The shore clingfish, *Lepadogaster lepadogaster*, is common on rocky shores in western Europe.

clinical linguistics The analysis and treatment of LANGUAGE disorders. These can occur at any level of linguistic organization, PHONETIC, phonological, grammatical, or SEMANTIC as deviance or delay in learning. A language disability can manifest itself either in spoken or in written language, and either at the production or the comprehension stage. There may be delays in learning language or difficulties in using it. Clinical linguistics uses the theories, methods, and findings of LINGUISTICS to elucidate the nature of pathological conditions in so far as these are manifested in language. See also APHASIA; DYSLEXIA.

clinical psychology The application of procedures derived from theory and research in PSYCHOLOGY to the assessment and treatment of mental and physical disorders. The term was first used in the 19th century to refer to methods of assessing physical and mental handicap. Assessment of clinical conditions such as brain damage developed during the two World Wars. After World War II clinical psychology also became important for procedures of rehabilitation and especially for the various PSYCHOTHERAPIES. Many of the latter derived initially from PSYCHOANALYSIS, but the research on which LEARNING theories were based gave rise to treatments which did not rely on drugs or make medical assumptions about abnormal behaviour being an 'illness'. These BEHAVIOUR THERAPIES have proved fairly successful in the treatment of PHOBIAS and some other disorders. Clinical psychologists are now likely to be eclectic rather than advocates of particular theoretical or therapeutic models. Nevertheless, the view that many abnormalities are at least partly caused by experience ('faulty learning') and can be improved by procedures akin to those of CONDITIONING remains fundamental to most clinical psychologists.

Clinton, Bill (born William Jefferson Clinton) (1946–) Forty-second President of the USA, inaugurated in 1993. Born in Arkansas, he was educated as a Rhodes Scholar at Oxford, and at Yale University. A Democrat, he succeeded BUSH on a programme to reduce the federal deficit by cutting military spending and reforming taxation, increasing investment in education, training, and public infrastructure. He appointed his wife Hillary to head the administration's health-care taskforce; her plans to provide health insurance for all Americans were rejected by Congress in 1994. Abroad, he pursued tighter controls against trading rivals while seeking to underpin Russia's reform economy. During 1994 Clinton agreed with Russian leader Boris YELTSIN not to keep their nuclear weapons constantly aimed at each other's countries and arranged the dismantling of many Ukrainian nuclear weapons in return for aid. He lifted the trade embargo on Vietnam, and pledged to work towards the creation of a trans-Pacific free-trade zone. He also decided to maintain trade links with China, despite its poor human rights record. Following mid-term elections in 1994, Clinton's position was weakened as the Democrats suffered such heavy losses that the Republicans gained control of the Senate. This allowed Congress to vote in favour of unilaterally ending the arms embargo against the former Yugoslavia, effectively agreeing to supply the Bosnian Muslims with weapons, despite the personal opposition of Clinton himself. He continued to support trade sanctions against Cuba and authorized the bombing of strategic targets in Iraq (1996) in response to Iraqi violations of a UN-imposed no-fly zone above Kurdish areas. He was re-elected in 1996.

Clio In Greek mythology, the MUSE of history.

clipper Certain types of very fast 19th-century sailing ship, long and low with a raked bow and overhanging stern. Fast, two-masted SCHOONERS and BRIGS, known as Baltimore clippers, were built in the USA in the early 19th century. In the mid-19th century three-masted, square-rig versions of these ships (the 'true' clippers) were built in both the USA and the UK. They were used for fast passages between Europe and California or Australia, carrying gold, or for carrying tea from China to London. Probably the best known of the tea clippers is the *Cutty Sark*, now preserved on the dockside at Greenwich in London. The opening of the SUEZ CANAL in 1869 removed the need for fast ships that could travel round the Cape of Good Hope, and heralded the end of the clipper era.

clitoris The female equivalent of the male penis, but which is not transversed by the urethra. It has a body ending in a conical head called a glans, all formed of erectile tissue. It is situated just below the pubis and above the opening of the urethra. Like the nipple, the clitoris is supplied with numerous nerves and is very sensitive to stimulation.

Clive, Robert, 1st Baron Clive of Plassey (known as **Clive of India**) (1725–74) British general and colonial administrator. In 1743 he joined the East India Company in Madras, becoming governor of Fort St David in 1755. Following the Black Hole of Calcutta incident, he commanded the forces that recaptured Calcutta from Siraj-ud-Dawlah (*c.*1729–57), nawab of Bengal, in 1757. Clive's victory at Plassey later that year made him virtual ruler of Bengal, helping the British to gain an important foothold in India. After a period in Britain 1760–65, he served as governor of Bengal until 1767, restructuring the administration of the colony and restoring discipline to the East India Company, whose reputation had been called into question. Clive was subsequently implicated in the company's corruption scandals; although officially exonerated, he committed suicide.

clock (in computers) The OSCILLATOR that determines the timing of operations within a computer's CENTRAL PROCESSING UNIT. The clock usually provides a sequence of square-wave electrical pulses, the edges of which trigger machine operation. Clock frequencies are necessarily high; MICROPROCESSOR clocks often operate at more than 100 MHz (100 million oscillations per second).

clocks and time measurement Among the earliest time-measuring devices was the shadow clock, known from around 1500 BC. This was later developed into the sundial. Other early clocks were the clepsydra or water clock (see CTESIBIUS), and the sand glass (still familiar as the egg-timer). Mechanical clocks were first made in China, where the escapement, a system of gears basic to all mechanical clocks, was developed in the 8th century AD by Yi Xing and Liang Lingzan. By the 11th century, the Chinese astronomer Su Sung was building elaborate astronomical clocks. Early European mechanical clocks from the 14th century were driven by the controlled fall of a weight, but they were only accurate to within about an hour per day, so had no minute hand. Spring-driven mechanisms appeared in the mid-15th century, and were used to manufacture WATCHES as well as clocks.

It was not until the 17th century, when the Dutch scientist Christiaan Huygens adopted the PENDULUM and the balance spring, that more accurate timekeeping became possible. In the mid-18th century accurate CHRONOMETERS, driven by balance springs, began to be used at sea for finding longitude.

Electrically driven clocks appeared in the 19th century. By the early 20th century pendulum clocks accurate to 0.01 second per day could be built, but in 1929 the quartz crystal clock was developed, capable of an accuracy of 0.0001 second per day. In a quartz clock, a crystal of quartz is stimulated by a small electric signal to vibrate at high frequency. The quartz crystal is PIEZOELECTRIC, and so this vibration induces a very precise, constant, high-frequency electrical signal. This signal is fed to an INTEGRATED CIRCUIT, which reduces the signal frequency to one pulse per second. This pulse is then used to drive the clock mechanism. In 1955 the first atomic clock was installed at the National Physical Laboratory in the UK, regulated by the extremely rapid, fixed oscillation rate of a specified energy transition in the nucleus of a caesium atom. Such atomic clocks vary by as little as one second every 3 million years. They are now internationally used as time standards.

clock star A star of precisely known right ascension used to measure the error of an observatory's sidereal clock. When the star is on the observer's MERIDIAN the local sidereal time equals the star's right ascension. The advent of highly accurate atomic clocks has diminished the need to use clock stars because atomic clocks are more accurate timekeepers than the Earth, whose rotation rate is subject to small but detectable changes.

cloisonné (from French *cloison*, 'partition') A technique in enamelwork in which thin strips of metal are attached to the background surface, forming a design made up of various little compartments that are filled with the vitreous enamel paste. The technique was known in the ancient Mediterranean world and has also been much used in China, but it is perhaps best associated with BYZANTINE ART. See also ENAMEL.

clone A group of organisms or cells that are genetically identical, having been produced from one parent by asexual REPRODUCTION. The individual organisms or cells are precise copies of the parent and genetically identical to it. Clones are found naturally among single-celled organisms (such as bacteria), a few invertebrates (such as corals), and some asexually reproducing plants (as in the production of runners by a strawberry plant). In agriculture, plant cloning can be used to replicate individuals with desirable properties, such as pest-resistance or high growth rates, without the unpredictable results associated with sexual reproduction. Artificial cloning of plants can be achieved by isolating and culturing cells from plant-growth regions (meristems); these cells are capable of growing into mature plants. The first successful artificial cloning of a higher animal was achieved in 1996, when the nucleus of a somatic (body) cell of a sheep was fused with an egg cell from another sheep from which the nucleus had been removed. This 'embryo' was implanted into the uterus of a third sheep, which eventually gave birth to a lamb (named 'Dolly') that was a clone of the first sheep. This achievement has caused concern about the possibilities of human cloning, which though feasible is regarded by many as ethically unacceptable.

In GENETIC ENGINEERING cloning refers to the copying of DNA molecules.

Clonmel The county town of Tipperary (South Riding) in the Republic of Ireland, on the River Suir; pop. (1991) 14,500.

Clontarf Site of a battle (1014), near Dublin, in which BRIAN BORU, High King of Ireland, defeated a large force of Danes. Brian was killed, but his victory ensured that subsequent Viking influence in Ireland was limited to seaports.

closed-circuit television (CCTV) A system in which television signals are transmitted to specific pre-selected television receivers. Transmission can be through cables over short distances, or by microwaves over longer distances: international transmission may be via SATELLITE communications. OPTICAL FIBRES offer another alternative for long-distance transmission. CCTV has several applications. As part of a security system it can provide general surveillance of a building or area. Scientifically it can be used to monitor hazardous situations. In conjunction with eidophors, sporting events can be relayed to large audiences. It can also be used for long-distance conferencing.

closed shop (in industrial relations) A workplace in which, by agreement or arrangement, only TRADE UNION members are employed; it may be a pre-entry or post-entry closed shop, depending on whether a worker must be a union member before being engaged. Pre-entry closed shops give the union control of entry to an occupation. The closed shop strengthens the union and may encourage orderly INDUSTRIAL RELATIONS. Opponents of the closed shop argue that it infringes the CIVIL RIGHTS of the individual worker and unduly restricts the freedom of the employer to hire and fire. Some developing countries, such as Mexico and the Philippines, have made legal provision for closed shops; elsewhere governments, as in the UK in the 1980s, have legislated to curb the practice.

closure (in mathematics) In set theory, the smallest closed set that contains a given set. The set of REAL NUMBERS is closed under addition, since the sum of any two real numbers is also a real number. Closure is one of the necessary conditions for a set and an operation to form a group.

clothes moth Any one of the small, dark-coloured moths whose caterpillars eat furs, woollen goods, and other textiles. In the wild, these moths are scavengers on carcasses and in birds' nests and mammal burrows, but some have spread worldwide in association with humans. They get insufficient nutrients from clean textiles, and prefer raw or soiled wool. Some species have become less abundant with the introduction of synthetic fibres; others eat these too, and chew through polythene. The common clothes moth, *Tineola bisselliella*, originated in warm countries but spread elsewhere with the efficient heating of houses. These moths are among the 2,400 or so species in the family Tineidae.

cloud A visible mass of water droplets or ice crystals in the air. The former occurs when the air is cooled to its DEW-point and the relative humidity reaches 100 per cent. The air can be chilled in two ways: ADVECTION over a colder land or sea surface, and expansion when raised to a greater height. The first leads to the formation of a low layer of cloud, the second to a layer or a heap, depending on atmospheric stability. Layers form when stable air is forced to rise either up a hillside or over colder, denser air at a FRONT; heaps form when the upper air is unstable and CONVECTION currents develop. Clouds exist only for as long as the condensation rate equals or is greater than the rate of evaporation of water droplets on their margins into the surrounding air. They are classified in two ways. The first is on the basis of their shape and structure: stratus is layered cloud in horizontal sheets; cumulus is heaped or lumpy, with a flat base and rounded top; cirrus is fibrous or feathery. The second way is according to the height of the cloud base: low means below 2,000 m (6,500 feet); medium means from there to 7,000 m (23,000 feet); and high may mean anything above 5,000 m (16,500 feet), for medium and high clouds are often lower in polar regions, and higher in tropical, than at the mid-latitudes. Cirrus cloud may occur at heights up to 13 km (8 miles). There are various combinations of form and height. Thus cirrostratus and cirrocumulus are both high clouds, altostratus (layered) and altocumulus (heaped) are medium-level clouds, and stratocumulus is a low, thick one. A nimbus cloud is a raincloud; nimbostratus is low and rain-bearing, while cumulonimbus towers up as a convectional thundercloud.

cloud cover The amount of sky obscured by clouds. It is measured in eighths, or oktas, of the sky observed; and observers give estimates for the total cloud cover and for each type of high, medium, and low cloud seen.

clouded leopard A species of large CAT, *Neofelis nebulosa*, some 90 cm (3 feet) in length. They are found in south-east Asia in the densest forests. The coat is of soft, thick fur and is decorated with spots and stripes. The canine teeth are relatively longer than those of other cats. These powerful animals are nocturnal hunters and can kill deer, though they usually prey upon smaller mammals.

Clouet, Jean (*c*.1485–1541) French painter. He worked as court painter to Francis I (1494–1547); the monarch's portrait in the Louvre is attributed to him. He was succeeded as court painter by his son **François Clouet** (*c*.1516–72), who as court painter is chiefly known for his undated portraits of Elizabeth of Austria and of Mary, Queen of Scots.

Clough, Arthur Hugh (1819–61) British poet. He is especially remembered for his longer poems: *The Bothie of Tober-na-Vuolich* (1848) is about a student reading party in Scotland; *Amours de Voyage* (1858) concerns a traveller's spiritual crisis in Rome; *Dipsychus* (1865) is a dialogue reminiscent of Faust and set in Venice.

clove The dried flower-bud of *Syzygium aromaticum*, a tree native to the Moluccas, which, together with nutmeg, was responsible for their being named the Spice Islands. The cloves are the unopened flower-buds, picked and dried in the Sun. They were used in China as long ago as 300 BC and were ordered to be used as breath-sweeteners by courtiers addressing the Emperor. Along with eucalyptus and allspice, they belong to the myrtle family.

clover A herbaceous annual or perennial LEGUME. The generic name of clovers, *Trifolium*, refers to the appearance of their leaves, each consisting of three leaflets. They are a vital component of pastures in temperate regions of the world; the creeping, white clover, *T. repens*, is valuable for sheep grazing, while the taller, red clover, *T. pratense*, is useful in hay meadows. Their vital role in agriculture is in maintaining soil fertility, the bacteria in their root nodules converting atmospheric nitrogen into a form suitable for plant growth.

Clovis (465–511) King of the Franks 481–511. He succeeded his father Childeric (died 481) as king of the Salian Franks at Tournai, and extended Merovingian rule to Gaul and Germany after victories at Soissons (486) and Cologne (496). After his conversion to Christianity, he championed orthodoxy against the Arian Visigoths, finally defeating them in the battle of Poitiers (507). He made Paris his capital.

Clovis culture A prehistoric culture in North America, characterized by lance-shaped stone points, 7–12 cm (3–5 in) long, fluted near the base. The tools are often found in association with bones of large mammals, such as bison and extinct mammoth, and are assumed to have been used as spear heads. Named after a town in western New Mexico, they are found at sites throughout the mid-west and south-west, USA from a period between 12,000 and 10,000 years ago. At one time, Clovis hunters were regarded as typifying the first American Indians, but there is increasing evidence that people were in the Americas long before, perhaps by 30,000 years ago.

clubmoss A CRYPTOGAM plant that bears spores in spore cases which are usually aggregated into club-like cones. Clubmosses are closely related to the ferns, and the 1,250 or so species are placed in the phylum Lycopodophyta (or, in traditional classifications, class Lycopsida of the division Pteridophyta); they include the genera *Lycopodium* and *Selaginella*, which are usually small plants with tufts of branching stems clothed with very small leaves. They have roots and woody tissue, and can be considered as perennial plants. Like horsetails, they once included giant tree-like forms which were most numerous in the Carboniferous Period, 300 million years ago, and contributed towards coal formation. The fossil clubmoss, *Lepidodendron*, appears to have been about 30 m (100 feet) high. Many present-day species are found among the ground flora of tropical rain forest, and some grow as EPIPHYTES. Some accumulate aluminium from the soil.

Cluny A town in the department of Saône-et-Loire in the Burgundy region of eastern France; pop. (1982) 4,700. A powerful monastery was founded here in 910 by the Duke of Aquitaine with the object of returning to the strict Benedictine rule. Other houses followed suit, and the order became centralized and influential in the 11th–12th centuries.

cluster, star A group of stars that are relatively close together and which move through space with the same velocity as each other. OPEN CLUSTERS or galactic clusters, such as the PLEIADES, typically contain between ten and a thousand young Population I stars and lie in the galactic disc. Open clusters are subject to disruption from the gravitational attractions of the galactic centre and interstellar clouds, and are generally short-lived entities (10^7–10^9 years). **Globular clusters** contain 10^5–10^6 densely packed Population II stars and are located in the GALACTIC HALO. These clusters all have ages of around 10^{10} years as indicated by the low stellar mass at the turn-off point where the giant branch leaves the main sequence of the HERTZSPRUNG–RUSSELL DIAGRAM. Because of their greater populations and position in the galactic halo, globular clusters are stable groups. The centres of some globular clusters are sources of X-rays, possibly due to the gravitational collapse of the inner core.

cluster-fly A true FLY, *Pollenia rudis*, that resembles the housefly, and belongs to the same family as the BLOW FLY. The adults hibernate and are sometimes found clustering in crevices or in the corners of attics. Their eggs are laid in soil, and the larvae are parasitic in earthworms, eventually killing their host.

clutch A device for connecting or disconnecting the drive between two rotating shafts. The simplest type is a dog or claw clutch, in which one shaft carries a castellated collar, which can be slid into contact with a matching collar on the other shaft. With the dog clutch, gear changes are sudden. For most purposes, especially vehicles, a friction clutch is used, which prevents jerking by allowing some slip at engagement. Common forms are cone (used for the synchromesh on a car GEARBOX), multi-plate, and single-plate clutches; the last is almost universal on modern manual gearbox cars. With AUTOMATIC TRANSMISSIONS hydraulic (fluid) clutches are used. Other types of clutch are used in some machine-tools.

Clwyd A former county in north-east Wales; area 2,428 sq km (937 sq miles); pop. (1991) 401,500; county town, Mold. Created in 1974, the county was divided into six districts. In 1996 it was replaced by the counties of Flintshire and Denbighshire (both of which were reinstated with redrawn borders).

Clyde A river in west-central Scotland that rises in the Southern Uplands and flows north and west for 170 km (106 miles) through Glasgow to the Firth of Clyde. The district of Clydebank on the north side of the river developed around the shipbuilding industry.

Clydesdale A district of central Scotland that gives its name to a breed of draught horse and a breed of terrier dog; pop. (1991) 57,000.

Clytemnestra In Greek mythology, the wife of Agamemnon and mother of Orestes and Electra. With her lover she murdered Agamemnon (and also Cassandra) and was in turn slain by Orestes.

cnidarian A member of the phylum Cnidaria, containing mainly marine animals, also known as coelenterates. They have radial symmetry, and examples include CORALS, JELLYFISHES, and SEA ANEMONES.

CN Tower (Canadian National Tower) The tallest free-standing man-made structure in the world, built during 1973–76 in Toronto, Canada. Its height to the top of the steel communication mast is 553 m (1,814 ft).

Cnut See CANUTE.

coal A hard, solid, opaque, black or blackish carbonaceous mineral of organic origin: an important FOSSIL FUEL. Coal is formed by the effect of pressure, temperature, and chemical processes on vegetable matter deposited millions of years ago. It consists mainly of carbonized plant tissue that originally accumulated in swamps where there was little oxygen. PEAT represents the first stage in the formation of coal. The quality of a coal depends on its carbon content, and the term 'rank' is used to designate this. Coals with a high carbon content are thus referred to as of high rank. Subsequent heating and the pressure of overlying deposits increase the carbon content. ANTHRACITE is the highest grade coal, with a carbon content of over 90 per cent and a high-temperature, smokeless flame. However, its relative scarcity limits it to mainly domestic use. Bituminous coal, dark shining coal containing 80–90 per cent carbon, is the most common type, used in a variety of applications. The lowest grade is LIGNITE, a soft, brown coal containing about 65 per cent carbon, which burns with a smoky flame. Lignite is used for power generation in some countries, and is often briquetted for transport (see BRIQUETTING). Most lignites are of late CRETACEOUS or TERTIARY age, and most black coals are of the CARBONIFEROUS PERIOD.

Coal was first used in China, Greece, and Italy over 2,000 years ago. It has been used for domestic heating and where high temperatures were required – for instance, by lime-burners, blacksmiths, and brickmakers. From the INDUSTRIAL REVOLUTION onwards, however, coal overtook wood as the principal domestic and industrial fuel. It was used in the manufacture of iron (instead of charcoal); for the generation of steam for engines; in the production of COAL-GAS; and later as a source of chemicals. Throughout this period, the UK was the largest producer of coal, but by 1900 it had been overtaken by the USA (total world production was then over 700 million tonnes per year). With strong competition from oil and nuclear energy, coal now provides only a quarter of the world's energy, but production in 1994 was still over 3,456 million tonnes, with the leading producer and consumer being China, producing 1,154 million tonnes; Australia was the world's leading exporter, shipping out 130 million tonnes; the USA produced 928.8 million tonnes.

The burning of coal has adverse environmental effects: sulphur and nitrogen oxides produced can lead to ACID RAIN, and the carbon dioxide emissions account for approximately 15 per cent of the GREENHOUSE EFFECT. However, coal technology is being improved, both to limit its environmental effects and to extend its range of uses, thus conserving less-plentiful reserves of PETROLEUM and NATURAL GAS. FLUIDIZED BED FURNACES are more efficient than conventional furnaces, and when combined with flue-gas desulphurization can largely eliminate emissions of sulphates and nitrates. Such furnaces can also be used to produce fuel-gas from coal, and for combined-cycle electricity generation. Another coal gasification process is used to produce synthesis gas (mostly carbon monoxide and hydrogen), from which a large range of products can be made, such as gaseous and liquid fuels, chemicals, fertilizers, and plastics. See also COAL-MINING.

Coalbrookdale Iron Bridge See BRIDGE.

coal-cutter Mechanized equipment for cutting coal from the seams. Jib coal-cutters were developed for underground COAL-MINING in the late 19th and early 20th centuries. The jib was a projecting horizontal arm carrying an endless chain to which cutter picks were fixed. In long-wall mining, the introduction of armoured flexible conveyors – a line of steel trays (pans) containing a continuous scraper chain – led to the evolution of machines able to cut the coal and then load it on to a conveyor. Other coal-cutters include the plough, a blade attached to an endless chain that cuts slices of coal up to 10 cm (4 inches) thick, and the shearer-loader, which has one or more horizontally pivoted rotating drums lined with cutting picks, and can extract a channel of coal up to 2 m (6.7 feet) high and 1 m (3.3 feet) deep.

coalescence (in meteorology) The process in which water droplets in a cloud combine to form larger drops. It occurs when large, free-falling, droplets, which have been produced by condensation, collide with and absorb smaller, slower, droplets lying in their path as they fall through the cloud.

coalfish A North Atlantic member of the cod family, *Pollachius virens*, known as the saithe pollack in North America. Its back and upper sides are very dark green in colour. It is a schooling fish that lives from the surface waters down to 200 m (650 feet) and feeds on small crustaceans and fishes. It is an important commercial fish.

coal-gas A valuable product of the manufacture of coke from COAL, containing largely hydrogen and methane, plus carbon oxides, ethene, and other gases. Coal-gas was used for GAS LIGHTING and for heating in Europe for over 150 years. It was replaced in the 1970s by natural gas. The presence in coal gas of carbon monoxide (which is absent in natural gas) makes it extremely toxic.

coalition government A government made up of two or more political parties. Coalitions are normally formed in parliamentary systems when no single party has a majority of seats in the LEGISLATURE. This is a frequent though not inevitable result of an election held under PROPORTIONAL REPRESENTATION. In TWO-PARTY SYSTEMS, coalitions are uncommon, because one party normally has a majority in the legislature. Coalitions normally have between two and five parties; many contain the fewest number of parties needed to gain a majority of seats.

coal-mining The excavation of COAL from the ground. The use and MINING of coal dates back to Roman times in Britain and to at least 200 BC in China. Until the 18th century, all coal was mined near surface outcrops by surface excavation, adit mining, or bell pits. During the INDUSTRIAL REVOLUTION, technology was introduced which eventually permitted shafts to be sunk as deep as 1,500 m (4,900 feet). New equipment was developed for pumping, ventilation, and the transport and cutting of coal. Today, the two main methods of mining coal underground are BORD-AND-PILLAR and long-wall mining. Both methods are now highly mechanized, using COAL-CUTTERS and hydraulic pit-props. Automation of coal production represents the next stage of technological advance. Presently, techniques are being introduced worldwide which allow remote control and automation of many mining operations and which should eventually lead to the full automation of underground coal production. Surface mining (strip or OPEN-CAST MINING) is undertaken where coal seams lie within about 200 m (650 feet) of the surface. The development of large earth-moving equipment in the last fifty years has resulted in surface mining replacing underground mining as the major source of coal worldwide. Since the 1950s other methods of mining coal have been tried. One of these is HYDRAULIC MINING; another is underground coal gasification, in which an air or oxygen–steam mixture is injected at high pressure as a gasifying agent down a borehole; the resultant fuel-gas is forced to another borehole, through which it flows to the surface. To date, neither of these methods has presented a serious challenge to conventional coal-mining methods.

coal-tar A thick, black, oily liquid by-product of the manufacture of gas and COKE from coal. It is a mixture of many different substances (mostly HYDROCARBONS), which are used to produce paraffin, naphtha, benzene, creosote, anthracene oil, and pitch by FRACTIONAL DISTILLATION. Pitch, a dark brown residue, is used in roofing tars and roofing felts. Tar was used from about 1781 to waterproof the hulls of wooden ships and in road construction, but it has largely been replaced by petroleum-based BITUMEN. In the latter half of the 19th century, the refining of tars and benzol products formed a large part of the world's organic chemical industry, notably in making the first synthetic aniline DYES. In the early 1900s over 3 million tonnes of coal-tar were produced annually in the UK alone, and several industries were entirely dedicated to making coal-tar products such as resins and plastics, explosives, solvents, wood preservatives, and disinfectants. However, the market for organic chemicals is now dominated by cheap petroleum feedstocks, and coal-tar production is much reduced.

coast The border of the land nearest the sea. Coasts may be flat and low-lying, with gentle BEACHES, LAGOONS, or MANGROVE swamps (as in the tropics), or they may be high with CLIFFS (as is often the case elsewhere); but they are constantly changing with time. Some are altered by ocean currents and winds or by slow land movement such as MOUNTAIN BUILDING. Others are added to by rivers depositing silt in the form of deltas and mudbanks. Yet others are subject to erosion by the sea. When a coast is flooded, the result will depend on whether the land has sunk, leaving only islets and low headlands, or whether the sea has risen over ridges into valleys beyond, leaving the ridges as long, narrow islands. Valleys running towards the sea, as in glacier regions, form fiords when flooded which may be deeper than the sea-bed off shore. Some coasts may be affected by volcanic action, while others (in the Pacific) have been altered by the growth of coral reefs, either as straight barriers or in the circular form of ATOLLS.

coastal defences Structures designed to resist the erosion of land by the sea. Banks and breakwaters (groynes) prevent the drifting of material along the shore by the daily tides. Earth embankments (dikes) protect low-lying coasts, and on the seaward side may need loose rocks (riprap) as additional protection against storm erosion. Where the shore is developed, sea-walls are built, usually of concrete. These often have curved profiles to deflect storm waves, and stepped bases to dissipate wave energy and prevent erosion of the ground under the seaward edge.

Coast Mountains A mountain range on the Pacific coast of north-west America extending northwards from the Cascade Range through British Columbia and into Alaska. It rises to 4,042 m (13,261 ft) at Mount Waddington in British Columbia.

coati Any one of four species of slim, long-tailed South American carnivores, related to the raccoon. Their most striking feature is the long, flexible snout with which they root for insects in the ground or in dead logs. They are omnivorous feeders, foraging by day in packs of up to a dozen animals. Males are more solitary and were once thought to be a separate species, the coatimundi ('solitary coati'), but join the pack when a female is on heat. The ring-tailed coati, *Nasua nasua*, grows up to 65 cm (25 inches) and, as its name implies, has a banded tail.

Coatlicue The Aztec Earth goddess, one of the wives of Mixcoatl, the cloud-serpent god of hunting. All land belonged to Coatlicue, a belief which upheld Aztec law that no one could own land. Celebrated in spring grain festivals, Coatlicue, who lived on human corpses, was depicted with clawed feet and hands, wearing a skirt of writhing serpents and a necklace of human hearts and hands from which a skull was suspended. Her son was Huitzilopochtli, god of the Sun, lightning, and storms, to whom a large number of human sacrifices were made.

coaxial cable A special type of CABLE used for carrying high-frequency or weak electrical signals. Coaxial cables consist of a central group of insulated conductors carrying the signal, surrounded by a sheath of braided conductor which is earthed. The whole cable is further insulated. The presence of the earthed braid substantially shields the signal from INTERFERENCE. Coaxial cable is widely used in electronics, and is commonly used for the ANTENNA (aerial) cable of domestic television receivers.

cobalt (symbol Co, at. no. 27, r.a.m. 58.93) A hard, grey metallic element; it is one of the TRANSITION METALS. Cobalt oxide is obtained mainly as a by-product in the extraction of nickel, copper, and iron ores. It is reduced to the metal with aluminium or hydrogen and then purified by ELECTROLYSIS. Chemically resembling iron and nickel, cobalt forms ionic compounds in which it shows valencies 2 and 3. It is commonly alloyed with other metals: with iron and nickel to make permanent magnets, and in steels to improve their cutting and wear resistance. The metal is also an industrial catalyst. Cobalt oxide is used in ceramics and glasses to give a blue colour and to neutralize the yellow from iron compounds. The radioactive isotope cobalt-60 is used as a tracer and in cancer therapy.

cobalt chloride ($CoCl_2.6H_2O$) A pale pink solid; on heating it loses WATER OF CRYSTALLIZATION and turns blue. The reverse change is used in anhydrous cobalt chloride papers, which are used to detect water.

Cobbett, William (1763–1835) British writer and political reformer. He started his political life as a Tory, but later became a radical; the change is reflected in *Cobbett's Political Register*, a periodical that he founded in 1802 and continued for the rest of his life. Cobbett was one of the leaders of the campaign for political and social reform after 1815, although he had already spent two years in prison for his outspoken criticism of flogging in the army (1810–12). A prolific writer, he published more than forty works in his lifetime, including *Rural Rides* (1830).

Cobden, Richard (1804–65) British political reformer. A Manchester industrialist, Cobden was one of the leading spokesmen of the free-trade movement in Britain. From 1838, together with John Bright, he led the Anti-Corn Law League in its successful campaign for the repeal of the Corn Laws (1846).

Coblenz (German **Koblenz**) A city at the junction of the Mosel and Rhine rivers, in the Rhineland-Palatinate, western Germany; pop. (1991) 109,050. It is an important wine-trading centre.

COBOL See COMPUTER LANGUAGE.

cobra A venomous SNAKE well known for its tendency, when alarmed, to rear up and spread a hood, which is formed in the neck region by loose skin. True cobras of the genus *Naja* occur in Africa, the Middle East, and Asia. The venom fangs of cobras are carried permanently erect within the mouth, in contrast to the foldable fangs of vipers. The discharge orifices of the fangs are modified in some species, such as the ringhales, *Hemachatus haemachatus*, and spitting cobra, *Naja nigricollis*, to enable them to spray venom into the eyes of an aggressor. This causes great pain and even temporary blindness if it reaches the eyes. The king cobra, or hamadryad, *Ophiophagus hannah*, is famous for preying on other snakes. The Indian cobra, *N. naja*, is one of the world's most dangerous snakes, killing a great many people every year.

Coburg A city in the state of Bavaria, southern Germany, on the River Itz; pop. (1991) 44,690. It alternated with Gotha as the capital of Saxe-Coburg-Gotha from 1826 to 1918 and its castle (Veste Coburg) is one of the largest in Germany. Coburg has associations with Martin Luther, the poet Friedrich Rückert, and the novelist Jean Paul. It has light industries including ceramics and toys.

Coburn, Alvin Langdon (1882–1966) British photographer born in the USA. He studied photogravure in London in 1906, publishing two books of atmospheric gravures: *London* (1909) and *New York* (1910). *Men of Mark* followed in 1913, with a second volume in 1922. He organized the influential 1917 exhibition of 'Old Masters of Photography' (all British) at the Albright Gallery, Buffalo, and two years later exhibited his first purely abstract photographs – 'Vorto-graphs' – in London alongside his paintings.

coca See COCAINE.

cocaine An alkaloid originally found in the leaves of the coca tree, *Erythroxylon coca*, native to Peru and also cultivated in other South American countries and in Java and Sri Lanka. The leaves have long been chewed in South America, the cocaine released relieving hunger and fatigue. Cocaine, largely produced synthetically was the first local anaesthetic to be used, but because it is addictive it is now replaced by safer drugs. Cocaine is also abused for the euphoric effects it is said to produce, especially in the form of a derivative known as crack, which is extremely addictive and when smoked can induce violence in habitual users.

coccyx The four fused vertebral bones lowermost on the spine of humans and other tail-less mammals. It is the bony part of an abbreviated tail which is not visible in man, and does not contain any part of the spinal cord. In old age it often fuses with the sacrum, the large triangular bone at the base of the spine.

Cochin See KERALA.

Cochin-China The former name for the southern region of what is now Vietnam. Part of French Indo-China from 1862, it became a French overseas territory in 1946 before merging officially with Vietnam in 1949. It gives its name to a breed of Asian fowl with feathery legs.

Cochinos Bay See BAY OF PIGS.

Cochise (*c.*1815–74) Apache Indian chief. Noted for his courage and military prowess, he gave his word in 1860 that he would not molest US mail riders passing through his Arizona territory in spite of war. In 1872 he made a peace treaty with the US government. He maintained both agreements, despite hostile acts from whites and Indians.

cochlea An organ of the inner EAR, consisting of a fluid-filled, spiral-shaped tube, inside which runs a membrane sensitive to sound. It is concerned with the breakdown of sound into its component frequencies before sending the information to the brain along the cochlear nerve. Sound waves pass along the cochlea and different frequencies cause vibrations to be set up in different parts of the cochlear membrane. This organ is best developed in mammals and is present in a non-spiral form in birds.

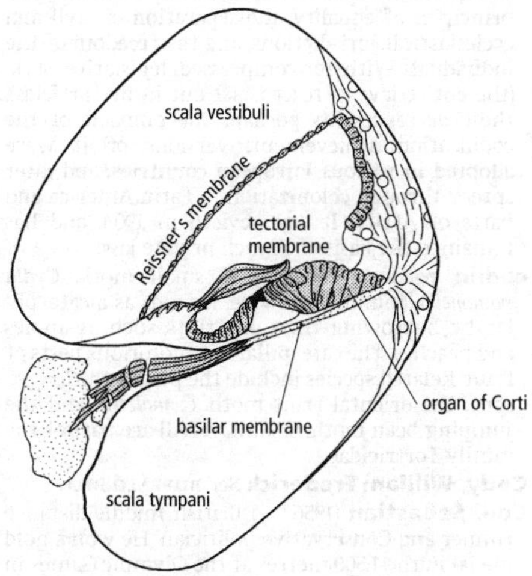

Cochlea A section through the cochlea. Vibration of the tectorial membrane, caused by sound waves passing through the cochlea, causes sensory cells in the organ of Corti to become distorted, which sends nerve impulses to the brain.

Cochran, Sir C(harles) B(lake) (1872–1951) British theatrical producer. Agent for Houdini and the French dancer Mistinguett (1874–1956), he is most famous for the musical revues which he produced from 1918 onwards at the London Pavilion, including Noël Coward's *Bitter Sweet* (1929) and *Cavalcade* (1931).

Cochran, Jacqueline (1910–80) US aviator. She made aviation history when she became the first woman to enter the trans-American Bendix Cup Air Race in 1935 and the first to win it in 1938. She achieved more than 200 speed, distance, and altitude records in her flying career, more than any of her contemporaries.

Cochrane, Thomas, 10th Earl of Dundonald (1775–1860) British naval officer. Elected to Parliament in 1806, he conducted a campaign against naval corruption, but was himself found guilty of fraud in 1814 and courtmartialled. After fruitless attempts to clear his name, in 1817 he took command of Chile's fleet during its struggle to win freedom from Spain. He subsequently commanded the navies of Brazil (1823–25) and of Greece (1827–28) when those countries were fighting for their independence. He was reinstated in the Royal Navy in 1832 with the rank of rear-admiral. Cochrane was one of the first to advocate the use of steam power in warships.

Cockaigne, Land of A mythical land of idle pleasure described in medieval English folklore.

cockatoo A bird belonging to the parrot family, Psittacidae, and occurring in Australia, New Guinea, and some adjacent islands. They are about 40–65 cm (16–26 inches) in length. All have powerful beaks; that of the palm cockatoo, *Probosciger aterrimus*, is exceptionally powerful and is used for opening large nuts. In plumage the 18 species of cockatoo are basically either black, like the red-tailed cockatoo, *Calyptorhyncus magnificus*, or white, like the sulphur-crested cockatoo, *Cacatua galerita*, though a few are pink, like the galah, *Eolophus roseicapillus*, which is grey above with deep pink underneath and a pale pink crown; all have erectile crests. Cockatoos are noisy, and live in groups ranging from a few to a large number of birds. They feed primarily on seeds, and the galah and the little corella, *Cacatua sanguinea*, sometimes do considerable damage to grain and rice crops. They nest in large holes in trees, laying two to three round white eggs. In captivity many of them live a very long time: fifty to sixty years having been recorded.

cockchafer See CHAFER.

Cockcroft, Sir John Douglas (1897–1967) British physicist who, with Ernest Walton, first brought about a nuclear disintegration ('splitting of the atom') by artificial means. In their classic experiment, performed in 1932, they used a high-voltage accelerator to speed up a beam of PROTONS (the nuclei of hydrogen atoms). The protons were directed at a plate of lithium metal, causing some of the lithium nuclei to break up into ALPHA PARTICLES (helium nuclei). For their experiment, the two scientists were awarded the 1951 Nobel Prize for physics.

Cockerell, Sir Christopher (1910–) British engineer who invented the HOVERCRAFT. He conceived the idea of a vessel which, by riding on a cushion of air, reduced the frictional resistance of the land or water over which it travelled. He took out a patent in 1955, and four years later launched his first experimental craft, which attained speeds of 100 km/h (62 m.p.h.). The first hovercraft crossing of the English Channel was made in 1959.

cock-fighting The sport of setting two gamecocks against each other in a circular cockpit where, in principle, they fight to the death. Banned in the UK and most of North America, flourishes in some Latin American countries, notably Haiti, Mexico, and Puerto Rico.

cockle A BIVALVE mollusc. Cockles live just below the surface of sandy beaches in vast numbers. The edible cockle, *Cardium edule*, can be found between tide-marks, filtering fine food particles from the sea through short siphons that barely protrude above the sand. Other species, such as the prickly cockle, *C. echinata*, live further down the beach, permanently covered by water. All cockles have rather plump shells, usually heavily ribbed, perhaps to improve anchorage in the sand.

cock-of-the-rock Either of two species of bird from the cotinga family, Cotingidae, belonging to the genus *Rupicola*. They are the Guianan cock-of-the-rock, *R. rupicola*, and the Andean cock-of-the-rock, *R. peruviana*. They live in tropical forests of northern South America. The males are a brilliant orange with black wings and tail; the orange feathers on the crown are stiffened to form a permanent crest. The females are olive-brown. The males display in communal groups, or leks, each bird having a separate court (an area of ground cleared of leaves). The females attend the leks for mating and then leave and look after the eggs and young by themselves.

cockroach A large brown or black insect that feeds on decaying vegetable material. Together with the PRAYING MANTIS, cockroaches make up the order Dictyoptera, which includes some 4,000 species. The adults have a flattened shape and the front wings (if present) are thickened and slippery to the touch. Cockroaches produce their eggs in a tough case called an ootheca, which the female usually carries around with her until the nymphs are ready to hatch. They show incomplete METAMORPHOSIS, and the young resemble the adults. Cockroaches are mainly tropical, but there are a few small species in temperate countries. The best known are common household pests, especially the black beetle or oriental cockroach, *Blatta orientalis*, and the German and American cockroaches, *Blattella germanica* and *Periplaneta americana*. In the tropics, a few species are colourful and live on flowers.

cockscomb See LOVE-LIES-BLEEDING.

cocoa See CACAO.

coconut A feathery-leaved tropical palm, *Cocos nucifera*, up to 24 m (80 feet) in height. Its nut consists of a single hard-shelled seed, surrounded by a thick, fibrous outer husk. The white-fleshed kernel has a central cavity containing coconut milk, which is a refreshing drink. Ripe nuts are harvested by climbing the tree (or by training monkeys to do so), or by allowing them to fall naturally.

The husk of the coconut (coir) is used to make mats, upholstery filling, and ropes, and the shells are useful as fuel. The dried, white flesh of the kernel is known as COPRA, now used in garden compost preparations.

coconut crab (or **robber crab**) A crab, *Birgus latro*, with an asymmetrical abdomen which reveals its relationship to the hermit crab. Unlike most hermit crabs, adult coconut crabs leave the sea to live on land. They use their stout, spiky claws to climb palm trees, though they have to descend backwards. They eat most types of vegetation, but are especially keen on fallen coconuts. Like all land CRABS, they nevertheless rely on the sea for spawning, and drink copiously to replace water lost by evaporation.

Cocos Islands (or **Keeling Islands**) A group of 27 small coral islands in the Indian Ocean, administered as an external territory of Australia since 1955; area 14 sq km (9 sq miles); pop. (1992) 586.

Cocteau, Jean (1889–1963) French dramatist, novelist, and film director. His plays include *La Machine infernale* (1934), based on the Oedipus legend, and *Orphée* (1926), which he made into a film in 1950. Among his other major films are *Le Sang d'un poète* (1930) and *La Belle et la bête* (1946), both of which mingle myth and reality. Also a prolific novelist, he is best known for *Les Enfants terribles* (1929).

cod A fish of the genus *Gadus*, which lives in the cool waters of the North Atlantic at depths ranging from near the shoreline to 600 m (1,950 feet). It is a schooling fish that prefers to swim at depths of 30–80 m (98–260 feet) above the sea-bed, although it feeds on the bottom. The individuals keep in contact with each other by means of sounds which are produced and amplified by the swim bladder. The cod feeds on a large variety of smaller fishes and crustaceans, and also eats molluscs and brittle stars. An immensely valuable food-fish, it is caught mainly by trawling, but many are taken on lines. The cod family, Gadidae, contains such fishes as haddock, *Melanogrammus aeglefinus*, and burbot, *Lota lota*, as well as the cod.

Code Napoléon (or **Code Civil**) The first modern codification of French civil law, issued between 1804 and 1810, which sought, under the direction of J. J. Cambacérès, to reorganize the French legal system. Napoleon himself presided over the commission drafting the laws, which drew on the philosophical heritage of the 18th-century Enlightenment, the articles of the laws representing a compromise between revolutionary principles and the ancient Roman (i.e. civil) law upon which much European law was based. The code enshrines the principles of equality, the separation of civil and ecclesiastical jurisdictions, and the freedom of the individual. With its compressed legislative style (the entire law of TORT is set out in five articles), the *Code* represents perhaps the pinnacle of the codification achievement; versions of it were adopted in various European countries, and later spread through colonization to Latin America and parts of Africa. It was revised in 1904, and has remained the basis of French private law.

codlin moth A species of small moth, *Cydia pomonella*, found worldwide. It feeds as a caterpillar by burrowing through fruits such as apples and peaches. The caterpillars are notorious pests of fruit. Related species include the pea moth, *C. nigricana*, the oriental fruit moth, *C. molesta*, and the jumping bean moth, *C. saltitans*. All are part of the family Tortricidae.

Cody, William Frederick See BUFFALO BILL.

Coe, Sebastian (1956–) British middle-distance runner and Conservative politician. He won a gold medal in the 1,500 metres at the Olympic Games in 1980 and 1984. In 1981 he created new world records in the 800 metres, 1,000 metres, and the mile. On retiring from athletics, Coe was an MP from 1992 to 1997.

coelacanth A species of fish, *Latimeria chalumnae*, that is the sole living representative of a group of lobefinned BONY FISHES which flourished from the Devonian to the end of the Cretaceous periods (408–66 million years ago). Coelacanths are well known as fossils, and were thought to be extinct, until December 1938, when a specimen was caught off the mouth of the Chalumna River, South Africa. Since then, many specimens have been caught around the Comoro Archipelago, near Madagascar. The living coelacanth grows to 1.9 m (6 feet) in length, and lives at depths of 150–400 m (500–1,300 feet) on near-vertical underwater cliffs. The coelacanth gives birth to live young (as did certain fossil forms), and their behaviour is currently being studied in their natural HABITAT.

coelenterate See CNIDARIAN.

coelom The fluid-filled body-cavity in animals that separates the skin from the gut, allowing organs to develop independently; it also provides a circulating fluid. Animals that lack a coelom are small and usually simple, while coelomate animals (such as annelids, arthropods, echinoderms, and chordates) are larger and more specialized. Those lacking stiff skeletons use their coelom for hydrostatic support, especially when their body is segmented, as in annelid worms.

coelostat A flat mirror fitted in a mount that is mechanically driven so that, as the Earth rotates on its axis, light from a chosen area of the sky can be continuously directed into an optical analysing instrument. Whereas a telescope is rotated by its mounting to keep the image within its field of view, this is not always practical for heavy optical analysing equipment. Therefore it is often simpler to keep the equipment fixed and to use a coelostat to follow the rotation of the celestial sphere, constantly guiding light into the main optical system. The HELIOSTAT performs a similar function for keeping an image of the Sun fixed.

coenzyme A relatively small, non-protein organic molecule essential for the correct functioning of some ENZYMES. The coenzyme fits into the active site of the enzyme along with the substance upon which the enzyme acts. The coenzyme is chemically changed after use and is converted back to its original form by further enzyme-controlled reactions. Among the most important examples are nicotinamide adenine dinucleotide (NAD) and coenzyme-A, which play an important role in KREBS' CYCLE. Many VITAMINS also act as coenzymes.

Coetzee, J(ohn) M(axwell) (1940–) South African novelist. In his major works, such as the two *Dusklands* novellas (1974), and the novels *In the Heart of the Country* (1977) and the Booker Prize-winning *Life and Times of Michael K* (1983), he explores the psychology and mythology of colonialism and racial domination. His recent output includes *White Writing* (1988), a collection of critical essays, and the novels *Age of Iron* (1990) and *The Master of Petersburg* (1994).

coffee A drink first brewed from the roasted and ground seeds of the small evergreen tree *Coffea arabica* by the Arabs of Yemen. A native of Ethiopia, this species grows up to 5 m (16 feet). It now provides most of the world's coffee, the bulk of it being grown in South and Central America, particularly Brazil, although it is also an important crop in parts of East Africa and the West Indies. The white, scented flowers produce red berries containing two grey-green seeds. These are separated from the pulp, washed repeatedly, fermented for one or two days, and Sun-dried for a week before the outer skin or parchment is removed to leave the well-known coffee bean. With bedstraws and gardenias the genus *Coffea* belongs to the Rubiaceae, one of the largest flowering plant families with over 7,000 species.

Most of the coffee produced in Africa is from *C. canephora*, native to the rain forests of central Africa. This 'robusta' coffee is cheaper to produce and is being increasingly used as a blend with 'arabica'. Robusta is also used extensively in the manufacture of instant coffee. A hardy, native species of Liberia, *C. liberica*, which is the least important of the cultivated species, produces an inferior coffee of bitter flavour.

coffee-house A public place of refreshment where the main beverage was coffee. Most of the cities of Europe had coffee-houses by the late 17th century, and the institution spread into the American colonies in 1689. They became centres where business was transacted, newspapers were read, and literary and political opinions were exchanged. In London Lloyd's coffee-house was the centre for marine insurance, and in New York the Merchants coffee-house, opened in 1737, became of major political importance in the years leading up to the American War of INDEPENDENCE.

Cognac A city in the department of Charente, western France, on the River Charente, noted for the production of high-quality brandy since the 17th century; pop. (1982) 23,000.

cognitive development A child's acquisition, organization, and use of knowledge from infancy to adulthood. The most influential theory was enunciated by PIAGET, who described a universal series of stages in intellectual development. During the sensorimotor period (from birth to 18 months), the infant acquires basic knowledge of objects, causes, space, and time; in the concrete operational period (up to about 11 years) the young child gradually acquires concepts of number, volume, classification, and measurement in specific contexts; in the formal operational stage (11 to adulthood) the adolescent becomes able to reason systematically about hypothetical propositions. Other theorists, notably BRUNER and the Russian psychologist Lev Vygotsky (1896–1934), have laid greater stress on the role of LANGUAGE development in cognitive growth. Another contemporary approach in COGNITIVE PSYCHOLOGY takes the computer as a model for the changing information-processing capacities of the child. This approach suggests that the basic differences between child and adult may be quantitative rather than qualitative and that development may reflect changes in information-processing capacity.

cognitive psychology The branch of PSYCHOLOGY dealing with the higher mental faculties: PERCEPTION, MEMORY, LANGUAGE, and thought. Cognitive psychologists are interested in how humans take in information through the senses (particularly in reading and speech), store it in MEMORY, and manipulate it during thinking and reasoning. Cognitive psychology has been one of two major developments in psychology since World War II (the other being SOCIAL PSYCHOLOGY). Its concern with internal mental life and human development contrasts with the weakness of BEHAVIOURISM in such areas. Child psychology and COGNITIVE DEVELOPMENT are areas of major concern. It includes the study of attention as an executive controller of mental activity. The computer has provided cognitive psychologists with a metaphor for looking at mental processes, using the language of computer programming and the concepts of information input, storage, retrieval, and processing to describe the brain as an information-processing machine. Cognitive psychology includes research in ARTIFICIAL INTELLIGENCE and the brain sciences, in particular neuropsychology. Recently the computer metaphor has been abandoned by some scientists, since the brain utilizes fundamentally different principles of computation. They suggest that modelling the electrical activity of large networks of nerve cells in the brain allows a more direct understanding of the brain's possibly unique methods of information-processing.

coherent radiation ELECTROMAGNETIC RADIATION that is always in phase, with peaks and troughs all occurring in the same place. Such a type of beam is produced by a laser. An ordinary beam of light, by contrast, consists of a series of wave pulses that begin and end in a random manner so that there is no regular wave pattern between one part of the beam and another.

Cohn, Ferdinand Julius (1828–98) German botanist, a founder of bacteriology. Noted for his studies of algae, bacteria, and other microorganisms, Cohn was the first to devise a systematic classification of bacteria into genera and species. It was Cohn who recognized the importance of the work of Robert Koch on anthrax.

coil (electrical) See IGNITION SYSTEM; INDUCTION; SOLENOID; TRANSFORMER.

coin collecting The hobby of collecting coins (or medals); also known as numismatics. Because coins have been struck by many nations since early times and therefore come in an enormous range, most collectors specialize, for example, in particular countries, designs, eras, or denominations. Gold coins, of course, have a substantial intrinsic value and are often treated as a form of investment.

coins Pieces of metal, usually discs, stamped by an authority, such as a monarch, as a guarantee of value and used as money. Early coins were stamped on only one side, but in about 560 BC the ruler of Athens, Pisistratus, had coins produced with a design on both sides. Until recently these were carved in INTAGLIO directly into the face of a metal die by a coin engraver, whose major problem was to produce an artistic and lifelike representation on such a small scale. One of the last coin types to be directly engraved was the well-known *St George and the Dragon* by Benedetto Pistrucci (1817). It has been used repeatedly on British coins for nearly 150 years and is an excellent energetic relief. Few mechanically produced coins are works of art due to the inflexibility of modern methods of coin production.

coir See FIBRE.

coke The solid residue left when coal is heated in the absence of air, or in a limited supply (carbonization). There is a limited domestic and industrial market for coke, and it is used primarily as a fuel or as a reducing agent in the iron and steel industry, most of it in BLAST-FURNACES. By-products of the coking process include COAL-GAS and COAL-TAR. DARBY was the first to use coke successfully for iron smelting early in the 18th century, an innovation which paved the way for the INDUSTRIAL REVOLUTION. Next to combustion, carbonization is the largest application of coal. A small amount of coke is also made from other feedstocks. Petroleum refinery residues, for example, yield a coke used to make arc-steel electrodes and anodes for aluminium smelting.

Coke, Sir Edward (1552–1634) English lawyer and politician. He rose to the position of Lord Chief Justice (1613), prosecuting such defendants as ESSEX (1601) and the GUNPOWDER PLOT conspirators (1606). In 1616 James I dismissed him, since, at first a supporter of the royal prerogative, Coke had become a defender of the common law against church and crown: as a Member of Parliament he led opposition to James I and Charles I. He was largely responsible for drafting the PETITION OF RIGHT (1628) and wrote commentaries on medieval and contemporary English law.

Coke, Thomas William, Earl of Leicester (1752–1842) British landowner who made many innovations in agricultural practice. In 1776 he inherited Holkham Hall in Norfolk and devoted himself to the improvement of its estates. Following Townshend, he introduced turnips as winter fodder; replaced rye with wheat; improved breeds of cattle, sheep, and pigs; and improved land by spreading clay (marling). He also introduced far-reaching changes in land tenure, granting long leases at fair rents to tenants, and encouraging them to discard old farming methods.

coke-oven A plant in which COAL is carbonized to produce COKE. The equipment consists of a battery of between 10 and 100 slot ovens which are ranged side by side and indirectly heated through the walls by the hot gases produced during carbonization. Each oven is generally about 14 m (50 feet) long, up to 6.5 m (20 feet) high, and 0.4–0.6 m (1.3–2.0 feet) wide. The ovens are each charged with over 20 tonnes of coal through holes in the oven top. Removable doors at each end are sealed to prevent air entering and gas leaking out. Coking is completed in 12–30 hours, depending on the coke type required, and the charge is then pushed by a ram into a quenching car.

Colbert, Claudette (born Lily Claudette Chauchoin) (1905–96) US film star, born in France. She won an Oscar for her appearance in CAPRA's *It Happened One Night* (1934); her subsequent appearances included *She Married Her Boss* (1935) and *The Egg and I* (1947). After retiring in 1961 to Barbados, she made several stage appearances in New York and appeared in a television series in 1987 at the age of 81.

Colbert, Jean Baptiste (1619–83) French statesman, chief minister to Louis XIV 1665–83. A vigorous reformer, he put order back into the country's finances, boosted industry and commerce, and established the French navy as one of the most formidable in Europe. His reforms, however, could not keep pace with the demands of Louis's war policies and extensive royal building programme, and by the end of Louis's reign the French economy was again experiencing severe problems.

Colchester A market town for grain and cattle in Essex, south-east England, on the River Colne; pop. (1991) 96,063. Claiming to be the oldest town in England, it retains well-preserved Roman walls and a Norman castle. The University of Essex was established here in 1964. It has engineering and food-processing industries.

cold An infection by one of a large number of related VIRUSES that cause inflammation of the mucous membranes of nasal passages and throat. The resulting illness is mild, but bacterial infection of nasal sinuses or bronchi may follow. Colds are transmitted through viral particles in the air after sneezing or coughing by the sufferer. There is at present no effective treatment of the viral infection, but bacterial complications respond to ANTIBIOTICS.

cold front The boundary between warm air and an advancing wedge of cold air.

Colditz A town in the state of Saxony, east Germany, south-east of Leipzig, noted for its castle, which was used as a top-security prison for Allied prisoners in World War II.

Cold War The struggle between the Soviet bloc countries and the Western countries from 1945 to 1990. The Soviet Union, the USA, and Britain had been wartime allies against Nazi Germany, but already before Germany was defeated they began to differ about the future of Germany and of Eastern Europe. Wartime summit meetings at YALTA and POTSDAM had laid down certain agreements, but as communist governments seized exclusive power in Eastern Europe, and Greece and Turkey were threatened with similar take-overs, the Western Powers became increasingly alarmed. From 1946 onwards popular usage spoke of a 'Cold War' (as opposed to an atomic 'hot war') between the two sides. The Western allies took steps to defend their position with the formation of the TRUMAN Doctrine (1947) and the MARSHALL PLAN (1947) to bolster the economies of Western Europe. In 1949 NATO was formed as a defence against possible attack. The communist bloc countered with the establishment of the Council for Mutual Aid and Assistance (COMECON, 1949), and the WARSAW PACT (1955). Over the following decades, the Cold War spread to every part of the world, and the USA sought containment of Soviet advances by forming alliances in the Pacific and south-east Asia. There were repeated crises (the KOREAN WAR,

Indo-China, HUNGARY, the CUBAN MISSILE CRISIS, and the VIETNAM WAR), but there were also occasions when tension was reduced as both sides sought DÉTENTE. The development of a nuclear arms race from the 1950s, only slightly modified by a NUCLEAR TEST-BAN TREATY in 1963 and STRATEGIC ARMS LIMITATION TALKS (1969–79), maintained tension at a high level. Tension intensified in the early 1980s with the installation of US Cruise missiles in Europe and the announcement of the US STRATEGIC DEFENSE INITIATIVE, and receded with an agreement in 1987 for limited ARMS CONTROL. It began to recede in 1985 with a resumption of START talks, followed by the INF Treaty (1987). Soviet forces withdrew from Afghanistan in 1989 and pacification in such troubled areas as Nicaragua and Angola followed. In December 1989 Presidents Bush and Gorbachev, at a summit meeting in Malta, declared the Cold War officially ended. By then the communist regimes of the Warsaw Pact countries were collapsing, and NATO began to change its role. NATO invited the former Soviet countries, including Russia, to join a 'partnership for peace' (inaugurated in 1994) as a first step towards granting them full NATO membership.

Cole, Nat King (born Nathaniel Adams Coles) (1917–65) US popular singer whose mellow vocal tones won him international recognition. In 1937 he formed the King Cole Trio (also known as the Fiddlers Three) and later became the first black man to have his own radio (1948–49) and television (1956–57) series. Cole recorded a number of major successes, including 'Mona Lisa' (1950), 'Too Young' (1951), and 'Ramblin' Rose' (1962).

Coleman, Ornette See JAZZ.

Coleridge, Samuel Taylor (1772–1834) British poet, critic, and philosopher. The ground-breaking collection *Lyrical Ballads* (1798), written with William WORDSWORTH, included Coleridge's famous poem 'The Rime of the Ancient Mariner' and marked the start of English literary romanticism. Coleridge's other well-known poems include the ballad 'Christabel' (1816), the opium-induced fantasy 'Kubla Khan' (1816), and the more pessimistic 'Dejection: an Ode' (1802). During his later years, while struggling with his life-long addiction to opium, Coleridge wrote little poetry, but contributed significantly to critical and philosophical literature, notably with his *Biographia Literaria* (1817).

Colette (born Sidonie Gabrielle Claudine) (1873–1954) French novelist. Her *Claudine* series (1900–03) was published by her husband, the novelist Henri Gauthier-Villars (1859–1931), who caused a scandal by inserting salacious passages. Colette made her name as a serious writer with her novels *Chéri* (1920) and *La Fin de Chéri* (1926), telling of a passionate relationship between a young man and an older woman. She was awarded the Legion of Honour in 1953.

Coligny, Gaspard de, Seigneur de Châtillon (1519–72) French nobleman of the House of Montmorency, appointed Admiral of France in 1552. He was captured by the Spaniards in 1557, and during his incarceration in prison he became a committed Calvinist. His high personal standing subsequently conferred respectability on the HUGUENOT cause in the first phase of the French WARS OF RELIGION. On CONDÉ's death he was elected commander-in-chief (1569), and then helped to engineer the favourable Peace of St Germain (1570). But his ascendancy over the youthful Charles IX alienated him from CATHERINE DE MEDICI, who almost certainly acquiesced in a plan to assassinate him. The ST BARTHOLOMEW'S DAY MASSACRE seems to have broken out spontaneously in the wake of his assassination.

colitis Inflammation of the colon. Amoebic colitis is caused by *Entamoeba histolytica*, and infective colitis by bacterial infection by a diverse range of microorganisms. Symptoms include abdominal pain and diarrhoea with, occasionally, blood and mucus in the stools. Ulcerative colitis is of unknown origin and results in widespread inflammation and ulceration; symptoms include diarrhoea containing blood and mucus, abdominal pain, cramps, fatigue, fever, loss of appetite, and weight loss. Ulcerative colitis is characterized by remissions and relapses. Ischaemic colitis is caused by disruption of the blood supply to the colon; symptoms include blood-stained stools, abdominal pain, nausea, and vomiting. See also CROHN'S DISEASE.

collage A pictorial technique in which photographs, newspaper cuttings, and other suitable objects are pasted on to a flat surface, often in combination with painted passages. It first became a serious artistic technique in the early 20th century, and the Cubists, Futurists, Dadaists, and Surrealists all made use of collage.

collar-bone See CLAVICLE.

collateral A marketable asset offered to a lender by a private borrower as a security for the loan. In the event of the borrower not repaying the loan at the time(s) specified, the lender has the right to take possession and dispose of the collateral, as specified in the loan agreement. In the case of a MORTGAGE, land or a building is the normal form of collateral.

collective bargaining (in INDUSTRIAL RELATIONS) Negotiations between management and employees' representatives, usually TRADE UNIONS, over pay and other conditions of employment. Collective bargaining is the major feature of industrial relations when the employer recognizes a trade union. When agreement cannot be reached, an industrial dispute arises, which may lead to conciliation, arbitration, or INDUSTRIAL ACTION. In some countries the unions coordinate their efforts, as in the 'spring offensive' each year in Japan.

collective ownership Ownership of land or of an enterprise in common, by all those who work on or in it (in the case of a COOPERATIVE), or by the state (as a consequence of NATIONALIZATION). (The terms public and social ownership are sometimes used in preference to nationalized property.) Collective ownership may date from the creation of a firm, or it may result from the buying out of a company's shareholders, or from their expropriation by the state. The principle of ownership by all is that all should benefit, rather than just the wealthy few. Land and industry are sometimes taken into collective ownership because they are underemployed or inefficiently run, or because the enterprise is bankrupt. Collective ownership, at least in theory, is a cardinal element of COMMUNISM, but with the decline of PLANNED ECONOMIES there are few countries where wholesale collective ownership is practised. In China, for example, collective farms have to some extent been replaced by farms run by individual households.

collective security A system of international security in which states unite with the agreed purpose of taking joint action to attack an aggressor state if one or more of them is attacked. It is often seen as an alternative to relying on the BALANCE OF POWER mechanism.

collectivism The view that society's affairs, and especially its economic life, should as far as possible be subject to collective control. It is typically opposed to individualism, private property, and the FREE MARKET. Collectivists believe that societies do best when they are consciously directed by some agency, usually but not necessarily the state, to achieve common ends. In the late 19th and early 20th centuries, many socialists described themselves as collectivists; now the term is almost entirely used by individualists to refer to policies and regimes of which they disapprove.

collectivization The creation of collective or communal farms. The policy was ruthlessly enforced in the Soviet Union by STALIN between 1929 and 1933 in an effort to overcome an acute grain shortage in the towns. The industrialization of the Soviet Union depended on cheap food and abundant labour. Bitter peasant resistance was overcome with brutality, but the liquidation of the kulaks and slaughter by peasants of their own livestock resulted in famine (1932–33). Gradually more moderate methods were substituted with the development of state farms. In the early 1990s collective farms accounted for about 67 per cent of the area of cultivated land, state farms about 30 per cent, and privately owned farms about 1.6 per cent. Private ownership of land was encouraged by GORBACHEV as part of his economic reforms. After 1945 a policy of collectivization was adopted in a number of socialist countries. The Soviet example was followed in China by MAO ZEDONG in his First Five Year Plan of 1953, but was only enforced by stages. China did not copy the ruthless subordination of agriculture to industry, preferring the peasant COMMUNE.

colligative properties The properties of a substance that depend on the number of particles present, rather than their nature. These include osmotic pressure of a solution, the lowering of the VAPOUR PRESSURE and the FREEZING-POINT of a solvent, and the raising of its BOILING-POINT. Thus, one MOLE of any solute lowers the freezing-point of a fixed mass of a given solvent by an equal amount. Therefore, knowing the mass of added solute and measuring the consequent decrease in freezing-point, one can determine the relative molecular mass (molecular weight) of the solute.

Collins, Joan (Henrietta) (1933–) British actress. She established a reputation as a sex symbol in her nine films of the 1950s, including the romantic comedy *Our Girl Friday* (1953). She continued to act in glamorous roles throughout the 1960s, 1970s, and 1980s, including that of Alexis in the US television soap opera *Dynasty* (1981–89). She is the sister of the novelist Jackie Collins.

Collins, Michael (1890–1922) Irish nationalist leader and politician. He took part in the EASTER RISING in 1916. Elected to Parliament as a member of SINN FEIN in 1919, he became Minister of Finance in the provisional government, at the same time directing the IRISH REPUBLICAN ARMY's guerrilla campaign against the British. He was one of the negotiators of the Anglo-Irish Treaty of 1921, and commanded the Irish Free State forces in the civil war that followed partition. On the death of Arthur GRIFFITH in 1922, he became head of state, but was shot in an ambush ten days later.

Collins, (William) Wilkie (1824–89) British novelist. Although he wrote in a number of genres, he is chiefly remembered as the writer of the first full-length detective stories in English, notably *The Woman in White* (1860) and *The Moonstone* (1868). These are striking for their use of multiple narrators and the complexity of their plots.

colloid A mixture in which fine particles (between 10^{-9} and 10^{-6} m in diameter) of one substance (the disperse phase) are spread throughout another substance (the continuous phase). The phases can be solid, liquid, or gas. Examples include emulsions (liquid dispersed in liquid) such as cosmetic creams; AEROSOLS (liquid or solid dispersed in gas) such as mist and smoke; and sols (solid dispersed in liquid) such as EMULSION PAINT. The properties of colloidal systems are unique and are not simply the sum of the properties of the two component substances. This is due to the large total surface area of the particles and the specific electrical interactions between them. In lyophobic colloids, the particles show a marked tendency to coagulate: for example, colloidal gold precipitates in the presence of certain metal ions. In contrast, in lyophilic colloids, there is a high affinity between the continuous phase and the disperse phase, with the result that the latter tends not to coagulate readily: an example is the protein albumen, found in egg-white. Because of their size, particles in the disperse phase frequently scatter light, a property known as the Tyndall effect, first observed by John TYNDALL. Particles in a colloid often carry a net charge and thus they can be coagulated by oppositely charged ions. For example, colloidal mud precipitates at a river mouth, where it encounters ions dissolved in sea water. Modern developments of colloid systems include surfactants (see SURFACE TENSION), colloidal graphite (used as a high-temperature lubricant), and colloidal solid fuels, used in FLUIDIZED BED FURNACES.

collotype printing A method used to make high-quality prints by LITHOGRAPHY. Using a printing surface of sensitized gelatine on a glass plate, it is capable of producing delicate tonal effects without the need for a HALF-TONE PROCESS. This process is now used mostly for printing limited numbers of fine-art reproductions.

colluvium Material loosened and moved by the various processes at work on hillsides, causing it to pile up at their feet. A mixture of particle sizes can be represented depending upon the processes at work. Avalanches, rock falls, and frost shattering produce coarse, angular material, whereas the action of earthworms, needle ice, and soil creep give layers of fine, crumbly silt and loam.

colobus See MONKEY.

Cologne (German **Köln**) An industrial and commercial city and transportation centre in the German state of North Rhine-Westphalia, on the west bank of the Rhine; pop. (1991) 956,690. Founded by the Romans, Cologne rose to prominence through the see established there, the Archbishop of Cologne becoming one of the most powerful German secular princes in the Middle Ages. The twin spires of its Gothic cathedral (which took 600 years to build) rise to 157 m (515 feet). Its university was founded in 1388. Cologne is a river port with heavy industries including iron and steel, machinery, and chemicals.

Colombia A country in the extreme north-west of the South American continent, the only South American country with coasts on both the Pacific and the Atlantic oceans, separated by the isthmus of Panama. To the east is Venezuela, and to the south Brazil, Peru, and Ecuador.

Physical. The northern end of the Andes occupies the north-western half of the country, here

breaking into three great CORDILLERAS which enclose high, cool plateaux. Running from them are several large rivers to water the hot northern coastal plains. South-east of the Andes, plains of rich pasture stretch away to the east and to the south, where the land falls in forested terraces towards the headstreams of the Amazon.

Economy. Colombia has a wide range of agricultural crops and is virtually self-sufficient in food production. About 5 per cent of Colombia's total area is arable, while 30 per cent is permanent pasture land. Colombia has large reserves of crude oil, coal, natural gas, gold, precious stones, platinum, bauxite, and copper. Coffee accounts for half of exports, and industrial products such as textiles, iron, chemicals, and petroleum products are also exported. Political instability has deterred much-needed foreign investment, and disrupted agriculture. Cannabis and coca are cultivated illicitly on a vast scale (73,000 hectares or about 180,000 acres of land) for the manufacture of illegal drugs.

History. Colombia was occupied by the Chibcha Indians before the Spanish conquest. The first permanent European settlements were made on the Caribbean coast, Santa Marta being founded in 1525 and Cartagena eight years later. Colonization of the interior was led by Gonzalo Jiménez de Quesada, who defeated the Chibchas and founded the city of Bogotá in 1538. The region was initially part of the viceroyalty of Peru, but a different political status came with the establishment of the viceroyalty of New Granada in the first half of the 18th century. The viceroy sitting in Bogotá was given jurisdiction over Colombia, but also over Venezuela, Ecuador, and Panama. Colombia remained a viceroyalty of Spain until the battle of Boyacá (1819) during the SPANISH–SOUTH AMERICAN WARS OF INDEPENDENCE, when, joined with Venezuela, it was named by Simón BOLÍVAR the United States of Colombia. In 1822 under his leadership New Granada, Panama, Venezuela, and Ecuador were united as the Republic of Gran Colombia, which collapsed in 1830. In 1832 a constitution for New Granada was promulgated by Francisco Santander, which was amended in 1858 to allow a confederation of nine states within the central republic now known as the Granadine Confederation. In 1863 the country was renamed the United States of Colombia. The constitution of 1886 abolished the sovereignty of the states and the presidential system of the newly named Republic of Colombia was established. The War of the Thousand Days (1899–1902), encouraged by the USA, led to the separation of Panama from Colombia (1903). Violence broke out again in 1948 and moved from urban to rural areas, precipitating a military government between 1953 and 1958. A semi-representative democracy was restored that achieved a degree of political stability, and Colombia's economy has recovered from the setbacks of the early 1970s as diversification of production and foreign investment have increased. Agriculture is the chief source of income in Colombia, but it is estimated that the country's illegal drugs trade supplies some 80 per cent of the world's cocaine market. During the 1980s Colombia achieved sustained economic growth and a successful record of external debt management, but the drug trade increasingly dominated both internal affairs and its relations with the USA. At the same time numerous extremist guerrilla groups, of both Left and Right, resorted to violence, including assassinations. In 1990 the ruling Liberal Party convened a Constitutional Assembly which produced a new constitution, followed by an agreement by some guerrillas (most notably the notorious M-19) to demobilize and take part in the political process, while several drug traffickers surrendered. However, violence has continued to be a major problem. In July 1991 a major new oilfield was discovered.

Capital: Bogotá
Area: 1,141,748 sq km (440,831 sq mi)
Population: 35,099,000 (1995)
Currency: 1 peso = 100 centavos
Religions: Roman Catholic 95%
Ethnic Groups: Mestizo 58.0%; White 20.0%; Mulatto 14.0%; Black 4.0%; mixed Black-Indian 3.0%; Amerindian 1.0%
Languages: Spanish (official); Amerindian languages
International Organizations: UN; OAS; Andean Group

Colombian Independence War See SPANISH–SOUTH AMERICAN WARS OF INDEPENDENCE.

Colombo The capital city and chief port of Sri Lanka; pop. (1990) 615,000. The government of the country has been based in the outer suburb of Sri-Jayawardenapura since 1983. Settled by the Portuguese and then the Dutch, the British took control in 1796. It was the location in 1950 of a Commonwealth conference that devised a plan for economic assistance of countries in Asia known as the COLOMBO PLAN. The city is a mixture of old colonial buildings, modern blocks, and shanty towns. It has three universities, an outstanding zoological gardens, temples, bazaars, and markets. It has many light and handicraft-based industries such as gem-cutting.

Colombo Plan (for Co-operative Economic Development in south and south-east Asia) An international organization of twenty-four countries, established to assist the development of member countries in the Asian and Pacific regions. Based on an Australian initiative at the meeting of COMMONWEALTH ministers in Colombo in January 1950, it was originally intended to serve Commonwealth countries of the region. The scheme was later extended to cover 26 countries, with the USA and Japan as major donors; Britain and Canada left in 1991 and 1992 respectively. In 1977 its title was changed to the 'Colombo Plan for Co-operative Economic and Social Development in Asia and the Pacific' following the withdrawal of several south-east Asian nations that had adopted communism.

colon The main part of the large INTESTINE in mammals. In humans the small intestine, which leads from the stomach, enters it just above the appendix, in the right lower part of the abdomen. The colon passes up towards the liver, crosses towards the spleen, and then drops down into the rectum. It is concerned chiefly with the absorption of water from digested food. In herbivores, bacteria break down cellulose in the colon and the resulting sugars are absorbed. See illustration p. 334. See also COLITIS.

Colón The chief port and a commercial centre of Panama, at the Caribbean end of the Panama Canal; pop. (1990) 140,900. Founded in 1850, it was originally named Aspinwall after the railway builder William Aspinwall. Its present name (since 1903) is the Spanish form of 'Columbus'; that of the neighbouring port Cristóbal is Spanish for 'Christopher'. It is the second-largest city in Panama and capital of a department of the same name, and has been a free-trade zone since 1953.

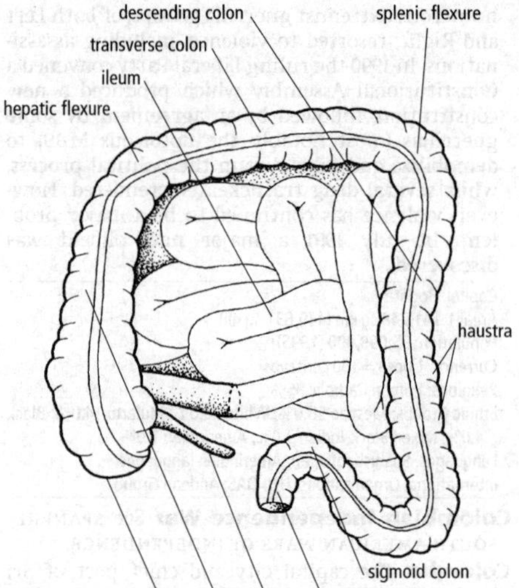

Colon The colon in humans.

colonialism See IMPERIALISM.

colony (or **dependency**, **protectorate**) A country or territory settled by and/or subject to the control of another, with supreme legislative and administrative power resting with the controlling country. The terms 'colony' and 'dependency' are often used interchangeably, while a protectorate, although subordinate to a 'protecting' power, may retain some autonomy.

Colorado A river that rises in the Rocky Mountains of north Colorado, USA, and flows 2,333 km (1,450 miles) south-west through the Grand Canyon and on into Mexico before entering the Gulf of California.

Colorado A state in central USA, named after the great Colorado River which rises there and flows into the Gulf of California; area 269,595 sq km (104,091 sq miles); pop. (1990) 3,294,400; capital, Denver. The largest cities are Denver, Colorado Springs, Boulder, and Fort Collins. Colorado is also known as the Centennial State. Part of it was acquired by the Louisiana Purchase in 1803 and the rest ceded by Mexico in 1848. It was organized as a territory in 1861 and became the 38th state in 1876. Traversed north-south by the Rocky Mountains, there are more than 1,000 peaks over 3,048 m (10,000 ft) high. Tourism, advanced technology, defence industries, gold mining, livestock, and grain production are important. The principal tourist attractions are the Rocky Mountain National Park, Mesa Verde National Park, and the Great Sand Dunes and Dinosaur National Monuments.

Colorado beetle A species of leaf beetle, *Leptinotarsa decemlineata*, up to 1 cm (0.4 inch) in length, oval in shape, and with striped yellow and black wing-covers. It is a serious pest of potato crops across North America and Europe. The beetle probably fed originally on wild species of potato in the Andes, but spread to the Rockies and, in the 20th century, invaded the potato-growing countries of the world. It is regularly accidentally introduced into Britain, and a great effort is made to prevent it from becoming established.

colorimetry See SPECTROSCOPY.

Colosseum The medieval name for the *Amphitheatre Flavium*, a vast amphitheatre in Rome begun by Vespasian *c.*75 AD and continued and completed by Titus and Domitian. It was capable of holding *c.*50,000 people, with seating in three tiers and standing-room above; an elaborate system of staircases served all parts. The arena, floored with timber and surrounded by a fence, was the scene of gladiatorial combats, fights between men and beasts, and large-scale mock battles.

Colossus See COMPUTER, HISTORY OF.

Colossus of Rhodes A huge bronze statue of the Sun-god Helios, one of the Seven Wonders of the World, said by Pliny to have been over 30 m (100 ft) high. Built *c.*292–280 BC, it commemorated the raising of the siege of Rhodes in 305–304 BC, and stood beside the harbour entrance at Rhodes for about 50 years but was destroyed in an earthquake in 224 BC.

colour (in optics) Light of different wavelengths as perceived and interpreted by the eye and brain. Visible light is ELECTROMAGNETIC RADIATION of wavelengths between about 400 and 750 nm (10^{-9} m). It can be split into a spectrum of colours (red, orange, yellow, green, blue, indigo, and violet), red having the longest wavelength and violet the shortest. White light, as emitted by the Sun, contains all these wavelengths. The colour of an opaque object corresponds to the wavelengths it reflects (it absorbs all other wavelengths). Its apparent colour also depends on the colour of the incident light – a blue object in red light will look black because there is no blue light to reflect. Coloured lights can be mixed to produce other colours. Red, blue, and green lights together produce white light; they are called primary colours. Such white light does not contain the full range of wavelengths present in sunlight, but it is perceived as white by the human eye. Different combinations and intensities of red, blue, and green light can produce almost any colour sensation in the eye: this principle is exploited in the colour TELEVISION RECEIVER, which produces a full range of colours using only red, blue, and green phosphors. The mixing of coloured lights is additive mixing, because the range of wavelengths reaching the eye is increased when colours are mixed. The situation with mixtures of coloured paints or dyes is, however, different. This is because the colour of a paint or dye pigment is determined by the wavelengths of light it reflects, all other wavelengths being absorbed: this is called subtractive mixing. Magenta, yellow, and cyan (green-blue) are often used as primary colours in PRINTING and PHOTOGRAPHY, where three superimposed layers, one in each of the primary colours, together with black, produce a full range of colours.

colour (in particle physics) A property possessed by QUARKS and GLUONS. The word 'colour' and the names of the colours are used in this context in a purely metaphorical way: the quarks and gluons are not coloured in the optical sense. Colour is analogous to electric charge but comes in three varieties – red, green and blue – rather than the two varieties of electric charge. Colour is believed to be the source of the STRONG FORCE, in the same way as electric charge is the source of the ELECTROMAGNETIC FORCE.

colour blindness A condition of the eye in which certain colours cannot be distinguished, most commonly inherited. About 8 per cent of European males and about 0.5 per cent of females may be affected. Total colour blindness is very rare. Cones (colour-sensitive receptors) containing single visual pigments selective for red, green, and blue light are present in the normal human eye. Disturbances of colour vision will occur if the amount of pigment per cone is reduced or if one or more of the three cone systems are absent. Problems in distinguishing reds and greens are the most common.

colour index A comparison of the MAGNITUDE of a star at two different wavelengths (colours) of light. The great utility of colour indices is that they relate to the relative amounts of light radiated at different wavelengths, not the actual light levels, because a difference of logarithmically defined magnitudes corresponds to a ratio of brightnesses. Furthermore, because it is a ratio, the colour index does not depend on the distance to the object.

colour-luminosity diagram See HERTZSPRUNG–RUSSELL DIAGRAM.

Colt, Samuel (1814–62) US inventor. He is remembered chiefly for the revolver named after him. Colt patented his invention in 1836, but had to wait ten years before its adoption by the US army after the outbreak of the war with Mexico. The revolver was highly influential in the 19th-century development of small arms.

Coltrane, John (William) (1926–67) US jazz musician. Once established as a jazz saxophonist, he played in groups led by Dizzy Gillespie and Miles Davis. In 1960 he formed his own quartet and soon became a leading figure in avant-garde jazz, bridging the transition between the harmonically dense jazz of the 1950s and the free jazz that was evolving in the 1960s.

colubrid snake A snake belonging to the family Colubridae, which includes about two-thirds of living SNAKE species. Colubrids form the main proportion of the snake species in all major regions of the world with the exception of Australia, where front-fanged (proteroglyphous) snakes predominate. Although most colubrids are non-venomous, many possess enlarged (often grooved) teeth on the rear of the upper jaw to enable toxic secretions to be introduced into the body of a prey or an enemy. These forms are generally not dangerous, but the African boomslang, *Dispholidus typhus*, and African twig snakes of the genus *Thelotornis*, are exceptions, and human deaths have resulted from their bites.

The family includes sand snakes, *Psammophis* species, whip snakes, *Coluber* species, tree snakes, *Chrysopelea* species, rat snakes, *Elaphe* species, and king snakes, *Lampropeltis* species.

colugo (or **flying lemur**) An insectivorous mammal of the order Dermoptera. In spite of their common name, the two species, the Malayan colugo, *Cynocephalus variegatus*, and Philippine colugo, *C. volans*, are not lemurs and cannot fly. They can, however, glide by means of a 'wing' or patagium. This is a membrane between the fore- and hindlimbs, and including the toes and tail, that allows it to move from tree to tree, often gliding for some 70 m (230 feet). The Malayan colugo lives in dense tropical forests and is found not only in Malaya but also in southern China, Indonesia, and neighbouring islands. A nocturnal animal, it sleeps by day, hanging by its feet from a branch. It wakes at dusk to forage for food. A single young is born and clings to its mother's breast or belly. The Philippine colugo, as its name suggests, is restricted to the forests of the Philippines.

Columba The Dove, a CONSTELLATION in the southern half of the sky, introduced by the Dutchman Petrus Plancius (1552–1622) from stars that the 2nd-century Greek astronomer Ptolemy had catalogued south of CANIS MAJOR. It represents Noah's dove, sent out to find dry land.

Columba, St (*c.*521–97) Irish abbot and missionary. After founding several churches and monasteries in his own country, he established the monastery at Iona in *c.*563, led a number of missions to mainland Scotland from there, and converted the Picts to Christianity. He is considered one of the leading figures of the Celtic missionary tradition in the British Isles and contributed significantly to the literature of Celtic Christianity. Feast day, 9 June.

Columbanus, St (*c.*543–615) Abbot and missionary, from his youth a monk at Bangor, Ireland. In about 590 he left for France and founded monasteries at Annegray and Luxeuil. His support for the practices of the CELTIC CHURCH, and especially for the Irish dating of Easter, upset Pope Gregory I and he was ordered back to Ireland (610). He promptly crossed the Alps to Lombardy in Italy and established an abbey at Bobbio (614). However, his austere monasticism lost its appeal before the more practical provisions of St BENEDICT.

Columbia The capital of South Carolina, USA, at the junction of the Broad and Saluda rivers which form the Congaree River; pop. (1990) 98,000. Founded in 1786, the city was reduced to ashes in 1865 by General William T. Sherman. It is the home of the University of South Carolina (1801) and the Fort Jackson US Army training centre.

Columbia, District of See DISTRICT OF COLUMBIA.

columbine See AQUILEGIA.

columbium See NIOBIUM.

Columbus The state capital of Ohio, USA, at the junction of the Scioto and Olentangy rivers; pop. (1990) 632,900. Founded in 1812, the growth of Columbus was stimulated first by stage-coach travel and then by the arrival of the railroad in 1850. It is the home of Ohio State University (1870). Printing, publishing, food-processing and the manufacture of transportation equipment, chemicals, and machinery are the chief industries.

Columbus, Christopher (Spanish name Cristóbal Colón) (1451–1506) Italian-born Spanish explorer. A Genoese by birth, Columbus persuaded the rulers of Spain, Ferdinand and Isabella, to sponsor an expedition to sail westwards across the Atlantic in search of Asia and prove that the world was round. Sailing with three small ships in 1492, he discovered the New World (in fact various Caribbean islands). He made three further voyages to the New World between 1493 and 1504, in 1498 discovering the South American mainland and finally exploring the coast of Mexico.

columnar jointing A feature formed when lava cools and shrinks. Contraction results in tension in a layer of cooling lava, and this produces fractures that are more or less evenly spaced and are in all directions. Polygonal columns form as a result. These usually have from four to eight sides and are often hexagonal. They are characteristic in BASALT; fine examples can be seen at the Giant's Causeway, in County Antrim, Northern Ireland, and the Devil's Postpile in the Sierra Nevada, USA.

coma (in astronomy) The almost spherical halo of gas and dust that surrounds a COMET when it is in the vicinity of the Sun. This dusty 'atmosphere' is continually being swept away by the SOLAR WIND and is replenished by gas and dust emitted by the nucleus. The coma can be about 100,000 km in diameter. The velocity of the escaping gas and dust is several kilometres per second relative to the nucleus and it disperses into the near vacuum of interplanetary space, some of it via the cometary tail.

coma (in medicine) A state of deep unconsciousness from which the patient cannot be aroused and does not respond fully to external stimuli. Reflexes may be affected and the degree of responsiveness is used to grade the depth of coma, which is particularly important in head injury. Coma can be precipitated by a wide range of causes, all of which affect brain function; recovery is dependent on intensive care and the underlying cause.

Coma Berenices A CONSTELLATION of the Northern Hemisphere of the sky, representing the hair of Queen Berenice of Egypt. The constellation consists mostly of a scattered cluster of faint stars. This group of stars was known to the Greeks, but was considered by them to be part of LEO. It was made into a separate constellation in 1551 by the Dutch cartographer Gerardus Mercator.

Comanche A North American Uto-Aztecan Indian people of the plains and prairies of Texas and Oklahoma. An offshoot of the Shoshone, they migrated to the plains from the Rocky Mountains to hunt buffalo. Their name is derived from the Spanish *camino ancho* ('wide trail').

Combination Acts Laws passed by the British Parliament in 1799 and 1800 in order to prevent the meeting ('combining together') of two or more people to obtain improvements in their working conditions. Flouting the law resulted in trial before a magistrate, and TRADE UNIONS were thus effectively made illegal. The Combination Acts were repealed in 1824 as a result of the skilful campaign by Francis Place and Joseph Hume, and were followed by an outbreak of strikes. In 1825 another Act was passed which resulted in trade union activity but limited the right to strike.

combined-cycle technology A system of ELECTRICITY GENERATION combining a GAS-TURBINE and a STEAM-TURBINE. The gas-turbine is powered by hot, high-pressure gas, obtained either by burning fuel-gas or from a FLUIDIZED BED FURNACE. The turbine in turn drives an electric generator, while the exhaust gases are used to heat water in a boiler to raise steam. The steam powers a steam-turbine to generate additional electricity. There are several advantages to this arrangement, despite it being considerably more expensive than traditional electricity-generation plant.

combined heat and power generation (or **CHP generation**; US **cogeneration**) The simultaneous production of heat and electricity. Heat production is inevitable when chemical or nuclear fuels are used to produce electricity. In conventional, electricity-only power-stations, achieving maximum generation efficiency means that the temperature of the heat produced is too low for it to be useful. CHP plants are designed to produce heat at a usefully high temperature. This usually involves a reduction in potential electricity output, but the overall conversion of fuel to useful energy output is much higher. The heat output can be in the form of hot water or steam for local industrial use or for DISTRICT HEATING.

combine harvester A mobile machine that combines harvest operations with the threshing and cleaning of grain. In 1838, only seven years after the appearance of MCCORMICK's mechanical reaper, a combine harvester built by the US inventor Hyram Moore was successfully operated in Michigan, USA. The combine had a cutting blade similar to that used on the reaper. Modern combine harvesters are used for cereals, legumes, and oil-seed crops. They can cut around 5.5 m (18 feet) at one pass, harvesting over 12 ha (30 acres) in a day's work. Electronics and hydraulics allow the driver to exercise fine control over the various operations, minimizing grain loss in the harvesting process.

comb jelly See SEA GOOSEBERRY.

combustion (or **burning**) The EXOTHERMIC REACTION of an element or compound usually with oxygen. For example, magnesium burns in oxygen with an intense white flame to form magnesium oxide (MgO). When a compound is burnt, each element is separately converted to its oxide; thus hydrocarbons give carbon dioxide (CO_2) and water (H_2O) on combustion. A large proportion of the energy we use is obtained in this way, by the combustion of FOSSIL FUELS, such as coal and oil. Some combustion takes place without the flame and heat associated with the process, such as when body tissues are oxidized to give energy.

COMECON (Council for Mutual Economic Assistance) The English name for an economic organization of Soviet-bloc countries. It was established by Stalin among the communist countries of eastern Europe in 1949 to encourage interdependence in trade and production as the second pillar, with the WARSAW PACT, of Soviet influence in Europe. It achieved little until 1962, when agreements restricting the satellite countries to limited production and to economic dependency on the Soviet Union were enforced. Its members were: Bulgaria, Cuba, Czechoslovakia, German Democratic Republic, Hungary, Mongolian People's Republic, Poland, Romania, the Soviet Union, and Vietnam (Yugoslavia had associate status). Albania was expelled in 1961. In 1987 it began to discuss cooperation with the EUROPEAN COMMUNITY, and it was dissolved in 1990, following the collapse of communist regimes in eastern Europe.

Comédie Française The French national theatre (used for both comedy and tragedy), in Paris, founded in 1680 by Louis XIV and reconstituted by Napoleon in 1803. It is organized as a cooperative society in which each actor holds a share or part-share.

comedy In the Western tradition, a literary composition, usually dramatic, written chiefly to amuse its audience. A comedy will normally be closer to everyday life than a TRAGEDY, and will explore common human failings rather than the tragedy's exalted passions and acts. Its ending will usually be happy for the leading characters, involving the downfall of any villains. In another sense, the term 'comedy' was applied in the Middle Ages to narrative poems which end happily: the title of DANTE's *Divine Comedy* (*c.*1310) carries this meaning. Comic elements can also appear in many kinds of non-dramatic writing; and comedy is an important genre in the cinema.

comet A ball of ice and dust that orbits the Sun. As the comet nears the Sun, it forms a COMA and a tail and the ball is referred to as the nucleus. The nucleus is frequently described as a dirty snowball and cometary nuclei are thought to be the remnants of the huge collection of icy planetesimals that were formed at the birth of the Solar System and which now reside in the OORT–ÖPIK CLOUD. An average cometary nucleus has a mass of 10^9–10^{11} kg, a diameter of 200–1,200 m, and a density of 200 kg per cubic metre, only one-fifth the density of water. The nucleus contains hollow regions, is fragile, and has about twice as much dust as ice. The ice is mainly water ice but is contaminated with other substances. Each time a comet passes close to the Sun the Sun's radiation causes the ice to give off gas which carries with it dust and dirty snowflakes. This material produces the spherical coma around the nucleus, and the long tail. The tail is in two parts, one of dust and the other of PLASMA, and generally points away from the Sun.

Comets are usually named after their discoverer and the year in which they were last seen. They divide naturally into short-period and long-period comets. Short-period comets orbit the Sun every few years. The average time is about eight years, and Encke's Comet, with a period of a little over three years, has the shortest period. By contrast, long-period comets take between 10,000 and a million years to orbit the Sun and at their aphelion they can be nearly one-third of the way towards the nearest stars. At present about 140 short-period and 800 long-period comets are known and around thirty new comets are being discovered each year. It is thought that the Sun actually has about a million million comets in orbit around it.

comfrey The common name for several species of perennial herbaceous plant of the genus *Symphytum*, which is part of the forget-me-not family, Boraginaceae. The common comfrey, *S. officinale*, has a fleshy, branching root-system and large, hairy leaves. The flowering stem, 30–120 cm (12–48 inches) high, bears drooping clusters of creamy-yellow or purplish blooms. It is native to temperate Asia and Europe. The leaves and roots have long been considered to have medicinal properties.

Cominform (Communist Information Bureau) An international communist organization to coordinate Party activities throughout Europe. Created in 1947, it assumed some of the functions of the INTERNATIONALS which had lapsed with the dissolution of the COMINTERN in 1943. After the quarrel of TITO and STALIN in 1948 Yugoslavia was expelled. The Cominform was abolished in 1956, partly as a gesture of renewed friendship with Yugoslavia and partly to improve relations with the West.

Comintern (Communist International) Organization of national communist parties for the propagation of communist doctrine with the aim of bringing about a world revolution. It was established by LENIN (1919) in Moscow at the Congress of the Third International with ZINOVIEV as its chairman. At its second meeting in Moscow (1920), delegates from 37 countries attended, and Lenin established the Twenty-one Points, which required all parties to model their structure on disciplined lines in conformity with the Soviet pattern, and to expel moderate ideologies. In 1943 STALIN dissolved the Comintern, though in 1947 it was revived in a modified form as the COMINFORM, to coordinate the activities of European communism. This, in turn, was dissolved in 1956.

command economy See PLANNED ECONOMY.

command module See APOLLO PROGRAMME.

commedia dell'arte The popular improvised Italian comedy of the 16th to 18th centuries, as opposed to the *commedia erudita*, written Italian drama of the time; *dell'arte* signifies that the actors were professionals – members of the *arte* or actors' guild. It was usually performed by companies of twelve to fifteen, who improvised while conforming to a pre-arranged skeleton scenario, with suggestions for acrobatics, singing, and dancing. Apart from the young lovers, all performers wore masks, each retaining his own mask (or character), though perhaps changing to an 'older' mask as he grew older. The lovers were opposed by the fathers or guardians, notably Pantalone, who became the English Pantaloon. Other characters included Dottore (Doctor), a pedant, and Capitano (Captain), a braggart. The servants (*zanni*) were a distinctive feature. Shrewd, opportunistic and greedy, they reappeared in various guises in European literature and theatre, providing several characters still familiar today, such as Arlecchino (Harlequin), Pulcinella (Punch), Colombina (Columbine), and Pedrolino (PIERROT). The tradition survived in PUPPETRY, the HARLEQUINADE, and PANTOMIME. See also MIME.

commensalism An association between organisms of different species in which one (the commensal) gains from the relationship, and the other (the host) neither benefits nor loses. A well-known example involves the hermit crab, whose adopted shell frequently has colonies of HYDRA-like hydroids attached to it. The hydroid gains food particles and a firm yet mobile anchorage from the crab. The crab receives nothing from the association, as far as we know. An association in which both partners benefit is called mutualism (see SYMBIOSIS).

commercial law In common law systems, the law of business, covering mercantile law, COMPANY LAW, competition law, insolvency, INTELLECTUAL PROPERTY, and PATENTS. Commercial law is not a separate branch of law in common law systems, but in civil law systems there is often a distinct body of law codified into a commercial code which contains definitions and applies to specified transactions.

Committee of Public Safety An emergency body set up in France in April 1793. It was the first effective executive government of the Revolutionary period and governed France during the most critical year of the Revolution. Its nine members (later twelve) were chiefly drawn from the JACOBINS and it contained some of the ablest men in France, dominated at first by DANTON and then by ROBESPIERRE. It successfully defeated France's external enemies but was largely responsible for the Reign of Terror, and its ruthless methods, at a time of growing economic distress, led to growing opposition. In March 1794 an attempt to overthrow it, led by Hébert, was quashed, but four months later the reaction which overthrew Robespierre marked the end of the Committee's power. It was restricted to foreign affairs until its influence was finally ended in October 1795.

commodity A GOOD; or any raw or semi-processed material that is usually traded internationally. Commodities are classified into agricultural products and minerals. Agricultural products are further classified into foods, which include tree crops, such as coffee, tea, and cocoa, and arable crops, such as wheat, rice, and soybeans, and non-foods, such as timber, natural rubber, or jute. Minerals comprise fossil fuels, such as oil, gas, and coal, and metals, such as copper, aluminium, and zinc.

commodity market A MARKET in a raw or semi-processed material. For many COMMODITIES there is a single world price, or a narrow range of prices, for a particular grade of product (for example, oil); and for many there is a single dominant market in which most deals take place. For example, some metals are bought and sold on the London Metal Exchange. Commodity stabilization agreements are sometimes made between producing and/or consuming countries to try to stabilize price.

These compare with occasional more ambitious attempts to control the long-term level of prices, such as the OPEC oil CARTEL. For a stabilization agreement to work, a central fund is necessary. It is used to support the market by buying up quantities of the commodity (thus reducing supply) to create a buffer stock when the price is below the desired level. These supplies can then be offered for sale to depress the market when the price is above the desired level. Fluctuations in the world prices of commodities may cause severe hardship, particularly to both the workers and the economies of developing countries, which tend to be dependent for foreign exchange on the export of a limited range of primary industry. See also FUTURES MARKETS.

common land (or **common**) Land that is subject to rights of common. These are rights to take the produce from land of which the right-holder is not the owner, for example a right of pasture. They are private rights, and need not be open to all. The right may be restricted, for example, to a portion of the year.

common law systems The family of legal systems deriving from the law as developed by the King's judges in England and Wales after the Norman conquest in 1066. These include English law and Irish law, and most legal systems in the USA and Commonwealth countries, with modifications where appropriate to local custom (for example, to Hindu law in India, and to African CUSTOMARY LAW in Africa). The common law was not systematically developed from a theoretical basis, as CIVIL LAW systems were, but evolved as a pragmatic response to specific disputes. It remained largely in the hands of a small group of professional practitioners, educated through an apprenticeship process; it was from their ranks that judges were appointed. Their professional solidarity meant that common law was largely resistant to ROMAN LAW influence, although this alone was taught in the universities until the famous lectures on English law by Sir William Blackstone (1723–80) at Oxford in the 1750s. As a result of the limited scope of the common law by the 16th century, the Chancellors of England had developed a body of principles and rules, known as EQUITY, which provided remedies in cases where the common law had failed to do so. Today, these equitable principles and remedies have been integrated into the mainstream of the common law. In common law systems, CASE LAW is still seen as a central source of law, even if frequently subject to the supreme authority of STATUTE. Common law procedures tend to maximize the role of ADVOCATES: the judge decides the issues on the basis of material presented in argument, rather than relying on abstract legal principles (see ADVERSARIAL PROCEDURE). In this way, common law has developed as a response to specific cases, and has been less shaped by the theorizing of legal scholars than has civil law.

common market A group of countries in which member states have no tariffs or other restrictions on trade or movements of resources such as labour or capital between each other, while maintaining common tariffs and restrictions against outside countries. The EUROPEAN UNION is an example of a common market which is endeavouring to move towards economic and monetary union.

Commonwealth The republican government of England between the execution of Charles I in 1649 and the restoration of Charles II in 1660. The RUMP PARLIAMENT claimed to 'have the supreme power in this nation', and ruled through a nominated forty-man Council of State. In 1650 an 'Engagement' to be faithful to the Commonwealth was imposed on all adult males. While Oliver CROMWELL was eliminating Royalist resistance in Ireland and then Scotland (1649–51), the Rump disappointed expectations of radical reform. Unpopular taxes had to be raised to finance the army's expeditions. Furthermore, the Navigation Acts sparked off the much-resented ANGLO-DUTCH WAR of 1652–54.

Cromwell expelled the Rump in April 1653. He hoped to reach a political and religious settlement through the BAREBONES PARLIAMENT (July–December 1653), but in December he accepted the necessity of taking the headship of state himself. The period of Cromwellian rule is usually known as the PROTECTORATE.

Commonwealth, British See COMMONWEALTH OF NATIONS.

Commonwealth of Independent States (CIS) A confederation of independent states, formerly among the constituent republics of the Soviet Union, established in 1991 following a summit in the Belorussian city of Brest at which the USSR was dissolved. The 12 member-states are Armenia, Azerbaijan, Belorussia (Belarus), Georgia, Kazakhstan, Kyrgyzstan, Moldova (Moldavia), Russia, Tajikistan, Turkmenistan, Ukraine, and Uzbekistan. The administrative headquarters of the CIS is in the Belorussian city of Minsk.

Commonwealth of Nations An international group of nations. It consists of the United Kingdom and former members of the BRITISH EMPIRE, all of whom are independent in every aspect of domestic and external affairs but who, for historical reasons, accept the British monarch as the symbol of the free association of its members and as such the head of the Commonwealth. The term British Commonwealth began to be used after World War I when the military help given by the DOMINIONS to Britain had enhanced their status. Their independence, apart from the formal link of allegiance to the crown, was asserted at the Imperial Conference of 1926, and given legal authority by the Statute of WESTMINSTER (1931). The power of independent decision by Commonwealth countries was evident in 1936 over the abdication of EDWARD VIII, and in 1939 when they decided whether or not they wished to support Britain in World War II. In 1945 the British Commonwealth consisted of countries where the white population was dominant. Beginning with the granting of independence to India, Pakistan, and Burma (now Myanmar) in 1947, its composition changed and it adopted the title of Commonwealth of Nations. A minority of countries have withdrawn from the Commonwealth, notably Burma in 1947, the Republic of Ireland in 1949, and Fiji in 1987. Pakistan left in 1972 but rejoined in 1989. SOUTH AFRICA withdrew in 1961 because of hostility to its apartheid policy, but was formally re-admitted in 1995. In 1993 Cameroon applied to join the Commonwealth, and was accepted in 1995. It is the first country that has never been wholly ruled by Britain to seek Commonwealth membership. Mozambique, which also has no historical links with Britain, was admitted as a special case in 1995. Nigeria was suspended from the Commonwealth in 1995 because of its violations of human rights.

commune (in China) A small district of local government; in China the basic unit of agricultural organization and rural local government from 1958 to about 1978. Cooperatives were formed when the mutual aid teams that emerged during the land reform of the early 1950s were merged as part of the 'high tide of socialism' of 1955–56. During the GREAT LEAP FORWARD these cooperatives were themselves combined to form large units known as communes which were responsible for planning local farming and for running public services. Commune power was gradually devolved to production brigades after the disastrous harvests of 1959–61. In the Four Modernizations movement communes were virtually abolished.

commune (in Europe) A medieval western European town which had acquired specific privileges by purchase or force. The privileges might include a charter of liberties, freedom to elect councils, responsibility for regulating local order, justice, and trade, and powers to raise taxes and tolls. The burghers initially swore an oath binding themselves together. The communes often pursued their own diplomatic policies as political alliances shifted. They flourished where central government was weak and became bastions of local power, and after the Reformation, of religious loyalties. The growth of strong national monarchies reduced them in the 16th and 17th centuries.

Commune of Paris See PARIS, COMMUNE OF.

communicable disease (or **contagious disease**, **infectious disease**) An INFECTION that can be transmitted from person to person. The individual with the infection is known as the carrier, who may or may not have the symptoms and manifestations of the infection. The modes of transmission are diverse, and include personal contact; inhalation of infected droplets derived from coughing or sneezing; ingestion of water or food contaminated with human sewage containing microorganisms that are capable of causing disease (PATHOGENS); sexual contact causing SEXUALLY-TRANSMITTED DISEASE; use of contaminated injection and surgical equipment; use of infected blood or blood products; and contact with inanimate objects that the carrier may have used (fomites). Communicable diseases may have to be reported to health authorities (notifiable diseases) for the purpose of initiating a rapid and effective response to contain the disease before widespread transmission. Infections that are notifiable include cholera, poliomyelitis, and tuberculosis.

communications An unprecedented advance in the speed of message transmission has taken place over the last two centuries. In 1794 the French army started to use semaphore to pass messages, and a hot-air balloon to observe the enemy. In 1837 Charles Wheatstone in Britain and Samuel Morse in the USA developed an electric telegraph, the latter sending electric signals by means of Morse code. Telegraph lines were erected between Washington and Baltimore in 1844, then across Europe, and in 1866 across the Atlantic. One of the effects of the telegraph was that it linked international banking; another was that newspapers could print up-to-date international news; thirdly, governments could exert much closer control, for example in war or in their distant colonies. With the telephone (1876) direct speech communication replaced the telegram, while radio (1899) removed the need for communicants to be linked by electric cables. Television (1926) enabled visual images to be transmitted, while satellites (from the 1970s) enabled the whole world to watch events of supranational interest, with English becoming increasingly the language of the world. In the 1980s information technology emerged as a computer-based means of storing and transmitting information using networks of computers linked together, especially for academic or business use. The networks were subsequently connected into a global system using fibre-optic cables and existing telephone channels. During the 1990s, the use of this system, known as the Internet, expanded dramatically with an increase in the ownership of personal computers. The Internet came to be used for transmitting electronic mail, accessing and exchanging information, electronic on-line publishing, and, to some extent, entertainment. Copies of documents can be transmitted from one place to another almost instantaneously using facsimile transmission (Fax).

communications satellite An artificial SATELLITE for worldwide telephone, television, and data communication, using microwaves (see ELECTROMAGNETIC RADIATION). Microwaves can carry vast amounts of information because of their large BANDWIDTH and suitability for multiplexing. They are, however, easily absorbed by solid objects, so transmitter and receiver need to be in line of sight. Satellites provide a method of achieving line-of-sight communication over long distances: worldwide coverage can be achieved using as few as three satellites. The first commercial geostationary satellite was *Early Bird* or *Intelsat 1*, launched in 1965 by the International Telecommunications Satellite Organization. Intelsat soon had three satellites over the Atlantic, Pacific, and Indian Oceans for worldwide coverage, and today numerous communications satellites orbit the Earth. Modern communications satellites can handle tens of thousands of telephone calls, plus radio and television broadcasts.

communism A social and political ideology advocating that authority and property be vested in the community, each member working for the common benefit according to capacity and receiving according to needs.

The ideal of communism has been embraced by many thinkers, including PLATO, the early Christians and the 16th-century humanist Thomas More (see UTOPIANISM), who saw it as expressing man's social nature to the highest degree. It became the basis of a revolutionary movement through the work of Karl MARX, who saw communism as the final outcome of the proletarian REVOLUTION that would overthrow CAPITALISM. According to the theories of Marx, a communist society will emerge after the transitional period of the dictatorship of the proletariat and the preparatory stage of SOCIALISM. In a fully communist society the state will, according to Marx, 'wither away' and all distinctions between social relations will disappear. Specifically communist parties did not emerge until after 1918, when extreme Marxists broke away from the SOCIAL DEMOCRATS. Marx's theories were the moving force behind LENIN and the BOLSHEVIKS and the establishment of the political system in the SOVIET UNION.

In the hands of LENIN and his successors in the Soviet Union, MARXISM was transformed into a doctrine justifying state control of all aspects of society. The doctrine had two main elements. The first was the leading role of the Communist Party, seen as representing the true interests of the working class. The party was to control the organs of the state, and was itself to be organized according to the principles of 'democratic centralism'. The second major element in communist doctrine was the social ownership of property and central planning of the economy (see PLANNED ECONOMY). In principle, all private ownership of the means of production and all elements of the market economy were to be abolished, and economic life was to be controlled by planning ministries, which would set production targets for factories and collective farms. Although this principle was never fully implemented, Soviet communism was a society whose every aspect was controlled by a small political élite (during the Stalinist period, 1928–53, by a single individual), and was thus the leading example of TOTALITARIANISM. Its economic and military achievements nevertheless inspired revolutionary movements in many other countries, and in some developing countries, such as China, Vietnam, North Korea, and Cuba, communist parties came to power and established regimes based more or less closely on the Soviet model. In Eastern Europe, communist governments were installed under Soviet influence at the end of World War II. But the communist model was increasingly criticized in the West, even by those sympathetic to Marxism, for its economic inefficiency, its lack of genuine democracy, and its denial of basic human freedoms. During the 1980s this questioning of orthodox communism spread to Eastern Europe and the Soviet Union, culminating in a remarkable series of largely peaceful revolutions, which removed communist parties from power and opened the way to liberal democracy and the market economy.

Following the collapse of the Soviet Union in 1991, the communist countries of eastern Europe adopted pluralist, democratic systems. Communism as practised in the USSR and its allied European states has clearly proved itself to be an unacceptable ideology. What will happen to it in other parts of the world remains to be seen.

Communism Peak (Russian **Pik Kommunizma**) A mountain rising to 7,495 m (24,590 ft) in the Pamirs of south-east Tajikistan. Known as Mt. Garmo until 1933 and Stalin Peak until 1962, it was the highest mountain in the former Soviet Union.

Communist Manifesto The primary source of the social and economic doctrine of COMMUNISM. It was written as *Das Manifest der Kommunistischen Partei* in 1848 by Karl MARX and Friedrich ENGELS to provide a political programme that would establish a common tactic for the working-class movement. The manuscript was adopted by the German Socialist League of the Just as its manifesto. It proposed that all history had hitherto been a development of class struggles, and asserted that the industrialized proletariat would eventually establish a classless society safeguarded by social ownership. It linked SOCIALISM directly with COMMUNISM and set out measures by which the latter could be achieved. It had no immediate impact and Marx suggested it should be shelved when the REVOLUTIONS OF 1848 failed. Nevertheless, it continued to influence worldwide communist movements throughout the 20th century.

community (in ecology) A natural assemblage of plants and animals living within a particular area or HABITAT. Although a community may comprise organisms in several habitats, the term usually refers to a specific habitat such as a woodland or grassland site. The organisms are usually interdependent, either directly, through FOOD CHAINS and webs, or indirectly, as one species modifies the environment to the advantage or detriment of others. In most communities, relatively few species are present in large numbers; rather, many species occur in small numbers. The community may be named after the predominant species, as in an oakwood community or a reed-bed community, and it may be either stable, persisting over many years, or changing through SUCCESSION.

community architecture An approach to architectural design in which stress is laid on the architect's responsibilities towards the users of his or her buildings, particularly housing. The idea of community architecture developed in the 1970s and became a recognizable movement in the 1980s, the Prince of Wales and his architectural adviser Rod Hackney being among the champions of the cause. It marked a reaction against the doctrinaire and dehumanizing attitude towards mass housing that had characterized much 20th-century building, encouraging instead consultation with the community, and the consideration of all relevant social conditions.

community care The policy of caring for people who need assistance because of MENTAL ILLNESS, MENTAL HANDICAP, physical DISABILITY, or old age in their own homes or in small residential units rather than in large institutions, such as hospitals. Since the sometimes damaging effects and expense of institutional care came to public attention in the 1950s, many countries have promoted community care. When working well, such policies enable some people who would otherwise be institutionalized to live in their own homes (specially adapted if necessary) with support from visiting nurses, social workers, or volunteers. Others may live in sheltered accommodation with resident staff.

community theatre A 20th-century movement in drama that seeks to involve the community. It began to flourish in Britain in the early 1970s and is closely allied to political theatre, usually with a socialist commitment, which may also embrace feminism and gay liberation. Community theatre groups, which usually perform in such non-theatrical places as working-men's clubs, public houses, village halls, streets, and open spaces, seek to relate their activities to a locality by presenting material of local interest and by creating a closer rapport with their audiences than is possible in a conventional theatre.

commutativity (in mathematics) A condition in set theory that occurs when, for any two elements a and b and an operation, $-$, $a - b = b - a$. REAL NUMBERS are commutative under addition $(3 + 7 = 7 + 3)$ and multiplication $(3 \times 7 = 7 \times 3)$. MATRICES are not, in general, commutative under multiplication.

commutator See GENERATOR, ELECTRICAL.

Comnenus, Alexius (1048–1118) Byzantine emperor 1081–1118. In the mid-11th century Byzantine politics were dominated by a military aristocracy and court officials; Alexius Comnenus was an army general who forged an alliance between his military supporters and a number of court officials and so won the throne for himself. He succeeded in checking the challenge from the NORMANS under Guiscard in the Mediterranean but was continually harassed by the threat of barbarian invasions. In 1095 he approached Pope Urban II for help in recruiting mercenaries, a call which led to the First CRUSADE which the pope hoped would save the empire from the Seljuk TURKS. The Crusade was to Alexius's advantage and he was able to leave his son John to inherit the Byzantine empire on his death.

Como, Lake A lake in the foothills of the Bernese Alps in Lombardy province north Italy, formed by a natural widening of the River Adda. The medieval resort town of Como lies on its south-west shore.

Comoros, Federal Islamic Republic of the A country made up of three main islands and several islets in the Indian Ocean.

Physical. The Comoro Islands are volcanic. They lie in the Mozambique Channel of the Indian Ocean, between the mainland of Africa and northern Madagascar. The chief islands are Great Comoro, Anjouan, and Mohéli. Great Comoro is well forested. Mayotte, geographically part of the archipelago, is a French dependency.

Economy. Exports are dominated by cloves, vanilla, and essential oils for perfume. Most foodstuffs are imported. France, the main trading partner, provides economic aid, while tourism is being developed by South African investors. There is high unemployment and the country suffers from lack of energy resources.

History. Arab peoples were living on the islands when the first Europeans encountered them in the 16th century. Since the 17th century the islands have been occupied by many different peoples, including Arab traders, Africans, Indonesians, and Madagascans. The islands became a French protectorate in 1886, a French overseas territory in 1947, and gained internal autonomy in 1961. In 1974 all the islanders voted for independence, except for those living on Mayotte, who voted to remain under French rule. The Comorian government declared the whole archipelago to be independent (1975) but France gave Mayotte the status of a 'special collectivity'. In 1978 European mercenaries, led by Bob Denard, overthrew the government and ruled until 1984 when democracy was restored. Denard returned from exile in 1995 to attempt another coup but French troops invaded and restored democracy.

Capital: Moroni
Area: 1,862 sq km (719 sq mi)
Population: 545,000 (1995)
Currency: 1 Comorian franc = 100 centimes
Religions: Sunni Muslim 99.7%; Christian 0.2%; Baha'i 0.1%
Ethnic Groups: Comorian (a mixture of Bantu, Arab, and Malagasy peoples) 96.9%; Makua 1.6%; French 0.4%
Languages: Arabic, French (both official); Comoran
International Organizations: UN; Non-Aligned Movement; Franc Zone; OAU

compact disc (CD) A small disc on which audio signals, video signals, or other data can be magnetically recorded in digital form (see DIGITIZATION). The disc comprises a clear plastic layer over a reflective aluminium surface. Data is stored on the disc in BINARY code, the 'ones' of the code being small pits in the plastic surface, the 'zeros' being the smooth plastic. When playing the disc, a LASER scans the disc surface: the beam is reflected back only by the 'zero' areas of the disc. The reflected pulses are picked up by a photodetector, which converts them into a digital electrical signal. The compact disc was first developed by Philips and Sony in the early 1980s. By the early 1990s it was the established medium for audio recordings. CD video applies the same technology to videos: discs can be replicated more quickly than videotape and it is easier to access a particular part of the recording. CDs are also used to store large amounts of computer information. CD-ROM (compact disc with read-only memory) is the most common format, but other forms of disc are available that allow data to be written on to the disc as well as read. Recent developments are the photo-CD, which records still images on a compact disc for viewing on a television screen or as hard copy, and the multimedia CD, which holds pictures, sound, and text on one CD and plays them back through a computer or television receiver and hi-fi equipment.

company A legally defined form of business organization. Although there are a very few unlimited companies, most companies are either private limited companies or public limited companies (PLCs). In both cases their owners, the shareholders, have the protection of LIMITED LIABILITY for the company's debts. A public limited company is one whose SHARES may be sold to the general public and then traded on the STOCK EXCHANGE (see JOINT-STOCK COMPANY). The sale of shares in private limited companies is restricted. In both cases, companies usually enjoy certain financial and tax advantages over partnerships and sole proprietorships. The establishment of companies and their operating practices are governed by COMPANY LAW.

company law Both CIVIL LAW and COMMON LAW SYSTEMS divide companies into two separate spheres of regulation: public limited companies and private limited companies. The concepts of LIMITED LIABILITY and the company as a separate legal entity, distinct from its members and able to sue and be sued as such are common to both systems. This distinction in alienability is achieved either by statute law (UK) or stock-market rules (for example, Germany). Harmonization of company law, such as accounting and auditing practices, within the EU is occurring gradually.

compass See GYROCOMPASS; MAGNETIC COMPASS.

compiler A computer PROGRAM that translates high-level COMPUTER LANGUAGES, such as FORTRAN, ALGOL, and C, into MACHINE CODE that can be executed directly on the computer. Unlike an interpreter, a compiler converts the whole program into machine code before running it, which is frequently more efficient.

complementarity (in physics) WAVE-PARTICLE DUALITY is a feature of QUANTUM MECHANICS: elementary particles behave as waves in some situations and as particles in others. The UNCERTAINTY PRINCIPLE is a mathematical statement of this dual nature. A consequence of the uncertainty principle is that there are some quantities, for example position and momentum, for which precision in the measurement of one precludes precision in the measurement of the other. According to the principle of complementarity, such pairs of quantities are complementary: that is, no possible measurement can determine them with greater accuracy than that allowed by the uncertainty principle.

complementary medicine (or **alternative medicine**) A variety of forms of health care that fall outside the official health sector. Such health care provides an alternative to Western or allopathic medicine, which complementary practitioners believe treats symptoms and diseases rather than individuals in their complex physical, emotional, and environmental contexts. Formalized traditional systems of medicine, such as Chinese and AYURVEDIC MEDICINE, or the practice of traditional healers in Africa, can be regarded as complementary, as well as newer therapies practised in the Western world, some of which are based on the theories or practices of traditional medicine. Such therapies include ACUPUNCTURE; homoeopathy; CHIROPRACTIC and **osteopathy** (forms of manipulation); and HERBAL MEDICINE. Some other diagnostic or therapeutic techniques that are regarded as fringe medicine. They include iridology (diagnosis from an examination of the eye); reflexology (treatment by massaging the foot in order to cure ailments in other parts of the body); and biofeedback (the use of monitoring equipment to help control involuntary processes, such as heart rate). Many forms of paranormal healing also come into the category of complementary medicine. Some doctors practise holistic medicine, which is the combination of conventional medicine with forms of complementary medicine, self-help skills, and PSYCHOTHERAPY, in an attempt to treat the whole person and not merely his or her physical symptoms. In general, however, mainstream medicine is based firmly on objective scientific principles, whereas alternative medicine is more subjective.

complex numbers Solutions of those quadratic equations that are insoluble in terms of REAL NUMBERS. They are defined as numbers of the form $a + ib$ where a and b are real numbers and $i = \sqrt{(-1)}$, a solution of the quadratic equation $x^2 + 1 = 0$. The real numbers can be seen as that subset of the complex numbers for which $b = 0$. Addition. subtraction, multiplication, and division of complex numbers can all be defined and obey the usual laws of arithmetic. The ARGAND diagram gives a representation of complex numbers as points in the plane with CARTESIAN COORDINATES (a, b). In terms of POLAR COORDINATES any complex number can be written equivalently as $r \cos \theta + ir \sin \theta$, where r is the length of the line from the point to the origin and θ the angle that this line makes with the horizontal axis.

Complex numbers have wide practical application in science and engineering. Electronics and quantum physics, for example, use complex numbers extensively.

components of a vector Any two VECTORS whose combined effect is equivalent to the original vector. Components do not have to be at right angles to each other, but for simplicity they are often chosen to be. A vector x at an angle θ to the horizontal has a horizontal component of $x \cos \theta$ and a vertical component of $x \sin \theta$.

composite A material consisting of two or more physically different solid constituents, each of which largely retains its original structure and identity. Composites are distinct from alloys in that their structure is engineered by mixing two materials in an intimate solid mixture, with one component being embedded in the other. A common feature of composite materials is the use of small quantities of a relatively expensive, strong, often fibrous material to reinforce the bulk of a cheap matrix material. The properties of the resulting composite are usually intermediate to those of the components from which it is made. However, certain properties, notably toughness or resistance to fracture, are much better than those of either of the components, giving composites with unique properties. The earliest composites were probably the Sun-dried adobe bricks used in the ancient civilizations of Egypt and Mesopotamia; these used straw to reinforce the brittle mud. reinforced CONCRETE is a somewhat analogous modern material, in which steel reinforcing rods are used to give concrete strength in tension. Cement can also be reinforced by thin fibres, traditionally ASBESTOS, but now more often glass, polymers or natural fibres. LAMINATES are also composite materials.

Since the 1960s the most important class of composite materials has been the FIBRE-REINFORCED PLASTICS: glass, carbon, or aramid (see NYLON) fibres in a plastic matrix. These composites can be used to make very light structures with good strength and stiffness. In the 1980s much interest has been shown in using metals to make metal-matrix composites (MMC). These use fibres of ceramics such as ALUMINA and SILICON CARBIDE to reinforce light metal alloys based on ALUMINIUM and TITANIUM. These materials are stiffer and lighter than their parent alloys and have high resistance to wear. They are, however, expensive to manufacture, a common feature of many fibre-reinforced composites. CERMETS are a second type of metal–ceramic composite. Composites with a ceramic matrix are another recent development, but new inert ceramic fibres usable at high temperatures are needed before the full potential of these materials can be realized.

compost A friable (easily crumbled) material, a natural product of the DECOMPOSITION of dead plant matter. The most familiar compost occurring naturally is that present in mature, deciduous woodland as leaf-mould on the forest floor. Compost is used by gardeners to provide a supply of HUMUS and nutrients for the garden and can be produced in quantity from vegetable peelings, grass cuttings, and dead leaves. Compost is produced via the action of microorganisms, which slowly degrade organic matter. Successful decomposition is dependent upon maintaining adequate aeration and controlling temperature. Potting composts used in HORTICULTURE are mixtures of composted plant material, loam, sand, and FERTILIZER. The term is often used to describe mixtures of rotted plant and animal waste or as a euphemism for manure.

compound A substance composed of molecules, formed when two or more elements combine chemically and in fixed ratios: for example, two molecules of hydrogen ($2H_2$) and one molecule of oxygen (O_2) react to give two molecules of water ($2H_2O$). The physical and chemical properties of a compound are different from those of its constituent elements. Water exhibits none of the characteristic properties of either hydrogen or oxygen: for example, it is a liquid at room temperature, while hydrogen and oxygen are both gases. In general terms, compound formation can be explained by considering the energy changes accompanying the process. In the formation of sodium chloride, sodium ions, Na^+, and chloride ions, Cl^-, have to be formed. In both cases, an input of energy is required. However, when these ions come together to form a crystal, the resulting attractions release so much energy as to outweigh the amount supplied in forming the ions. The formation of the compound is therefore accompanied by a net release of energy. Thus it is more favourable in energy terms for sodium and chlorine to exist as sodium chloride, rather than as the pure elements.

compound-engine See STEAM-ENGINE.

comprehensive education A system of education based on principles of inclusivity rather than selectivity for secondary schools. The model often taken is that of the US high school, which ideally admits all the young people of a neighbourhood and offers both vocational and academic courses. Most American schools have been co-educational (open to both sexes) since the end of the American Civil War (1861–65).

By contrast, in Europe and elsewhere, secondary schooling has historically been restricted to the few and has prepared this group to be the social and intellectual élite. Since World War II there has been a movement, which has often been accompanied by fierce debate, to transform selective systems into comprehensive systems as the need for a better educated labour-force has become apparent. The chief arguments for comprehensive education are that it promotes equal opportunity, that assessment at 11 – the common age for entry to selective schools – is too early in a child's development, and that a comprehensive system encourages flexible and efficient use of resources. Opponents, however, argue that it holds back the development of brighter children because the pace of teaching has to be determined by the weakest pupils in a class. On the other hand, the weaker children are forced to follow a curriculum designed for more able pupils. It is argued that comprehensive education confuses equality of ability with equality of opportunity. All pupils have a right to the latter, but this is not achieved by treating them as if they have equal ability.

In England and Wales, comprehensive schools became general as a result of policy changes introduced by the Labour governments of 1964–70. Previously there was a tripartite state system of grammar, secondary modern, and, often, junior technical schools with entry to grammar schools depending on success in the 'Eleven Plus' examination. However, in comprehensive schools the world over, 'streaming' into different ability groups continues. Furthermore, many countries have a two-stage secondary system that is comprehensive at junior level but has academic and vocational schools at senior level. In developing countries, where school enrolment is not universal, the concept of state comprehensive education is less applicable.

compression ratio The ratio between the maximum and minimum volumes of a cylinder fitted with a moving piston. It is of greatest importance in INTERNAL-COMBUSTION ENGINES. For spark-ignition engines the highest compression ratio that can be used with a particular fuel before the onset of KNOCK depends on many factors, including the bore (diameter) of the cylinder and the design of the cylinder head (it is usually in the range 8:1 to 9:1). As a general rule, high-performance, high-compression-ratio PETROL ENGINES require petrol of high OCTANE NUMBER, while low-compression-ratio engines can use lower-grade petrol. For compression-ignition engines (DIESEL ENGINES), the need to reach a high enough temperature to give rapid ignition of the fuel means that a minimum compression ratio of 14:1 is required.

compressor A pneumatic device for compressing air or other gases. Compressed air is widely used in industry and in mining as a safe source of power, for drilling and for operating rams. Gas compression, often to a very high pressure, is at the heart of many large-scale chemical processes, and compressors are essential to GAS-TURBINES. The simplest type of compressor is the reciprocating piston and cylinder, often used in successive stages, each giving pressure ratios of up to 7:1. Gas is greatly increased in temperature during compression, so cooling is necessary. A more compact compressor is the rotary type, of which there are many forms. Cooling is often achieved by spraying oil droplets into the air during compression and subsequently separating the oil. For the largest flows a high-speed turbo-compressor is used, either centrifugal or axial; no cooling is possible.

Compton, Arthur Holly (1892–1962) US physicist. He observed that the wavelength of X-rays increased when scattered by electrons (later known as the Compton effect). This demonstrated the dual particle and wave properties of electromagnetic radiation and matter predicted by quantum theory. Compton shared the 1927 Nobel Prize for physics, and during the war he contributed to work on the atom bomb by developing plutonium production for the Manhattan Project.

Compton-Burnett, Dame Ivy (1884–1969) British novelist. Her works include *Brothers and Sisters* (1929), *A Family and a Fortune* (1939), and *Manservant and Maidservant* (1947). Her novels typically portray life at the turn of the 19th century and are characterized by ironic wit and an emphasis on dialogue.

computer A device for storing and processing data, according to a program of instructions stored within the computer itself. The term computer normally refers to electronic digital computers, but ANALOG COMPUTERS also exist for use in specialist applications. Computers are 'universal' information-processing machines: any information-processing task that can be specified by an algorithm (a well-defined sequence of instructions) can, in principle, be performed by a computer. Unlike most other machines, it is not necessary to build a new computer for each new task. Computers can therefore perform a very large number of useful tasks, although limits do exist: it can be proved that some problems are incomputable. The mathematical study of what tasks are capable of being computed is known as compatibility, and complexity is the study of how hard it is to compute a task. Numerical analysis concerns the fastest and most accurate way to solve numerical problems.

A computer system can be regarded as being organized in a number of layers. The lowest layer is the HARDWARE (the physical components of the system, as opposed to the SOFTWARE, the programs and other operating information used by the computer). Both the information which is being processed (the DATA) and the processing instructions (the PROGRAM) are stored in the form of BITS of information in a MEMORY. The memory unit is connected by a BUS to the CENTRAL PROCESSING UNIT (CPU), which is the other essential hardware component. The CPU takes one instruction at a time from the memory, decodes it, and then performs the action specified by the instruction. Each instruction specifies a very simple operation, for example, multiplying together two numbers or checking that two pieces of information are identical. Other hardware items are PERIPHERAL devices, which include permanent data storage devices such as hard and floppy disks, input devices for feeding information into the system, and output devices through which results are fed out. A small layer of software above the hardware, called the microcode, allows the computer to execute a larger set of instructions than could be easily provided in hardware alone. The hardware and the microcode together execute MACHINE CODE.

The next layer in the computer's organization is a much larger body of software, the OPERATING SYSTEM. It interprets additional, very complex instructions which allow reading from and writing to FILES, input devices, and output devices. The layer above this is provided by the COMPILER or interpreter, which allows a programmer to write programs in a problem-orientated COMPUTER LANGUAGE, rather than in machine code or ASSEMBLY LANGUAGE. The programmer working with such a language needs to know nothing of the layers below, so that a FORTRAN programmer can regard any computer with a FORTRAN compiler as if it were a FORTRAN machine.

The final layer of software comprises the computer's APPLICATIONS PROGRAMS. Computing is about the correct design and implementation of useful applications programs from a given specification. Techniques of software engineering are being developed which make specification, design, and implementation a less error-prone process. Mathematics and formal reasoning are used to prove logically that the implementation of computer systems correspond to their specifications. Improving the reliability of programs is increasingly important as their use in safety-critical situations grows. Some large computer programs have many millions of instructions, each instruction being a separate 'working part' that must function correctly. On this basis, computer programs are the most complex artefacts built by humans. The major challenges of computing in the future are the development of software engineering techniques, very high-level computer languages, and parallel processing.

computer, history of Although the development of the computer has been largely played out during the 20th century, there is a long history of automatic calculation. HERO wrote in the 1st century AD of representing numbers using a train of gears, but little real progress seems to have been made until the early 17th century, when the first CALCULATORS were built, and the German mathematician Gottfried Leibniz speculated (1679) on the possibility of building a calculator using moving balls to represent numbers in BINARY code. The notion of storing a sequence of instructions mechanically is also very old and was incorporated into self-playing musical instruments and other automata even in ancient times. In 1725 Basile Bouchon invented a method of producing intricate woven patterns on a draw loom from instructions on a perforated paper tape. By 1800 this method had been refined by JACQUARD into a highly successful automatic loom controlled by punched cards. The idea of punched-card instructions was adapted by HOLLERITH to record and analyse the results of the 1890 US census in the earliest example of large-scale DATA PROCESSING.

In 1835 BABBAGE conceived of the basic idea of an **analytical engine** in which can be found most of the elements of a truly general-purpose computer. He drew together the ideas of mechanical calculation and a set of instructions recorded on perforated paper tape. Babbage's ideas were subsequently lost until the 1930s, when work on electromechanical computers was started independently in Germany and the USA. In 1941 Konrad Zuse in Germany built the world's first working stored-program computer. His Z_3 machine was based on electromechanical relays, and was used for military aircraft design. In the USA, the mathematician Howard Aiken, in association with IBM (International Business Machines), was working independently on a large electromechanical calculator that could be programmed using paper tape. The Automatic Sequence Controlled Calculator (ASCC), or Harvard Mark I, was completed in 1943; it was very similar in concept (although not in engineering realization) to Babbage's analytical machine.

Computers based on the electronic THERMIONIC VALVE were a major development, since they were much faster and more reliable than electromechanical computers. Among the earliest electronic computers were the Colossus series of special-purpose computers, developed secretly in the UK from 1943. They deciphered coded German messages produced on sophisticated mechanical systems called Enigma machines. An important member of the Colossus team was TURING, who in 1936 had published a paper that defined in abstract terms the generalized concept of a universal computer. The concept of the stored-program computer (an idea attributed to von NEUMANN), in which instructions for processing data are stored along with the data in the computer's own memory, proved to be very important, since it hugely enhanced the flexibility and potential of the computer. The earliest electronic stored-program computer was an experimental machine built under the leadership of Frederick Williams at Manchester University, UK, in 1948. This was followed by the Manchester Mark 1 computer in 1949 which, as the Ferranti Mark 1, was the first commercially available computer to be developed. Other notable early computers in the UK were **EDSAC** at Cambridge, later marketed as LEO, and Turing's **ACE** at the National Physical Laboratory.

MAUCHLY and Eckert at the University of Pennsylvania (USA) developed the ENIAC and EDVAC computers based on the highly influential ideas of von Neumann; they later developed the successful UNIVAC computer, which became commercially available in 1951. The development of the TRANSISTOR led to much cheaper, faster, and more reliable computers. The first transistorized computer was working at Manchester University in 1953, although the USA had a number of much larger computers operating within a few years. The first COMPILER was developed at Manchester in 1952, and in 1954 John Backus of IBM in the USA developed FORTRAN, the first internationally used COMPUTER LANGUAGE. A significant high point in this era was the joint development of the Atlas computer by Ferranti Ltd. and Manchester University. This was the world's first super-computer, and pioneered many aspects of computer architecture that are common today. After this, most major developments took place in the USA. Particularly crucial was the development of the INTEGRATED CIRCUIT (IC) in 1958 which allowed complete circuits to be manufactured on a tiny piece of silicon. In 1972 the Intel Corporation developed the world's first MICROPROCESSOR, the Intel 4004, which was very limited but was an immediate commercial success and led directly to the development of today's cheap, fast, and reliable MICROCOMPUTER as well as much more powerful mainframe computers. See also INFORMATION TECHNOLOGY.

computer-aided design (CAD) The use of computer systems in engineering and DESK-TOP PUBLISHING, for example to support the design of products. CAD complements the traditional design process, making it faster and more flexible, by providing an electronic drawing board for a design incorporating the required specifications. It usually employs a VISUAL DISPLAY UNIT and INPUT DEVICES such as enhanced keyboards and graphics pads. CAD systems typically use software libraries of previous designs and commonly used components, which can be included by the designer in the new specification. Sometimes simulation can be used to test the feasibility of several alternative designs without requiring them to be manufactured. The final design can then be plotted out as an engineering drawing or used in software to provide NUMERICAL CONTROL for machine-tools. See also COMPUTER-AIDED MANUFACTURE.

computer-aided manufacture (CAM) The use of computer-based systems to control the machinery in manufacturing processes. CAM is an extension of COMPUTER-AIDED DESIGN (CAD); CAM systems usually make use of detailed DATABASES produced by CAD systems. The databases (obtained either directly via a computer link, or from engineering drawings) are used to control machine-tool operation. Most engineered components require many machining operations to be carried out sequentially; CAD data must therefore be adapted to control each machine-tool. Complexes of numerically controlled machine-tools and handling equipment such as transfer machines form flexible manufacturing systems. CAM is advantageous particularly where a range of slightly different products is required, since changes can be implemented simply by modifying the SOFTWARE. ROBOTICS represents an extension of CAM, where a general-purpose machine can be programmed for a variety of different tasks. A further development has been COMPUTER-INTEGRATED MANUFACTURE, the integration of design and production with other disciplines such as planning, purchasing, and financial control.

computer graphics See GRAPHICS.

computer-integrated manufacture (CIM) The integration of design and production aspects of manufacturing with traditionally separate areas such as planning, purchasing, DATA PROCESSING, financial control, and management support. CIM has evolved out of earlier techniques such as COMPUTER-AIDED DESIGN (CAD), COMPUTER-AIDED MANUFACTURE (CAM), NUMERICAL CONTROL of machine-tools, ROBOTICS, flexible manufacturing systems (FMS), and automated materials handling, all of which have been made possible by the use of INFORMATION TECHNOLOGY and computer-based systems. As a result of the programmability and flexibility of the constituent processes, a CIM system can more easily be directed towards optimizing the effectiveness of the manufacturing operation as a whole, whereas earlier approaches to manufacturing often had to concentrate on maintaining or improving the efficiency of individual aspects only.

computerized tomography (CT) A diagnostic technique of producing images of 'slices' of the body using a specialized X-ray machine; it was formerly known as computerized axial tomography (CAT). The patient lies between an X-ray tube and an array of detectors, which receive different amounts of radiation according to the density of the tissue scanned by the X-ray beam. As the tube and detectors move round the patient, a series of readings is converted into numbers, and a computer calculates an image from these data. The technique has been particularly useful in imaging soft tissues, notably those of the brain. Moreover, the patient is exposed to a lower dose of X-rays than that received in a normal diagnostic X-ray. See also TOMOGRAPHY.

computer language A specialized, formal language used to write computer PROGRAMS. Computer languages were developed to relieve programmers of the arduous task of writing programs directly in MACHINE CODE. There are two broad classes of conventional programming languages: low-level languages, such as ASSEMBLY LANGUAGE, in which each instruction represents a single machine code operation, and high-level languages, in which each instruction may represent an operation involving many machine code instructions. In both cases a special program, either an assembler, a COMPILER, or an interpreter, must be used to translate the source code to machine code before the program can be run on a computer. A job-control language, or command language, is the usual interface between a computer and the OPERATING SYSTEM. It allows the user to describe what tasks, or jobs, are to be processed by the computer. The system interprets the user's commands and runs the required APPLICATIONS PROGRAMS.

The Swiss engineer Konrad Zuse is credited with the invention of the first programming language shortly after World War II. AUTOCODE, the first high-level language complete with translation program, was developed at Manchester University, UK, in the early 1950s. Since then hundreds of different programming languages have been designed, but only a few are in widespread use. The first two languages to be widely used (**FORTRAN** and **COBOL**) were released around 1957. Both languages dominated their respective fields for the next two decades and are still in widespread use. In 1958 **ALGOL** was developed by an international committee. Although ALGOL evolved over the next decade it had greater theoretical than practical significance. However, it did spawn **PASCAL**, one of today's most commonly used languages. **BASIC**, which was developed in the mid-1960s at Dartmouth College, USA, is the best-known language for programming MICROCOMPUTERS. Nowadays, the preferred language for much professional program development is **C**, designed at Bell Laboratories, USA, in 1971 to implement the UNIX OPERATING SYSTEM. Most ARTIFICIAL INTELLIGENCE applications use symbolic or logical languages, such as LISP and PROLOG, rather than conventional programming languages.

computer music Music in which computers are used either to work out the details arising out of whatever program is fed into them, or to produce electronic sound. Thus the computer might calculate the frequency and distribution of a series of events within the structure of a composition and then, in association with a SYNTHESIZER, simulate the required sounds. Computers are also beginning to find a place in publishing in the production of scores and instrumental parts, the notation having first been translated into a suitable code. During the 1980s and early 1990s digital recording and computing technology became widely available as personal computers, and in particular sequencers and samplers, fell in price. This led to a rapid increase in the use of computers to produce electronic popular and dance music. See also ALEATORY MUSIC.

Comte, Auguste (1798–1857) French philosopher, one of the founders of sociology. In his historical study of the progress of the human mind, he discerned three phases: the theological, the metaphysical, and the positive. He argued that only the last phase survives in mature sciences. Comte's positivist philosophy attempted to define the laws of social evolution and to found a genuine social science that could be used for social reconstruction. Major works include his *Cours de philosophie positive* (1830–42) and *Système de politique positive* (1851–54).

Conakry The capital and chief port of Guinea, established by the French in 1887 on Tombo Island; pop. (1992) 950,000. It exports iron ore, fruit, kola nuts, groundnuts, and coffee.

Conan Doyle See DOYLE.

concentration camp Originally a place in which non-combatants were accommodated, as instituted by Lord KITCHENER during the Second Boer War (1899–1902). The Boers, mainly women and children, were placed there for their own protection from Kitchener's 'scorched earth policy' in the Transvaal and Cape Colony, but mainly to prevent them from aiding the guerrillas. Some 20,000 detainees died, largely as a result of disease arising from unhygienic conditions.

During the NAZI regime in Germany (1933–45) concentration camps became places in which to intern unwanted persons, specifically JEWISH PEOPLE, but also Protestant and Catholic dissidents, communists, gypsies, trade unionists, homosexuals, and the handicapped. Described by GOEBBELS in August 1934 as 'camps to turn anti-social members of society into useful members by the most humane means possible', they in fact came to witness depraved acts of torture, slave labour, horror, and mass murder on a scale unprecedented in any country in any century. Some 200,000 had been through the camps before World War II began, when they were increased in size and number. The camps (Konzetrazionslager, or KZ), administered by the SS, were categorized into *Arbeitslager*, where prisoners were organized into labour battalions, and *Vernichtungslager*, set up for the extermination and incineration of men, women, and children. In eastern Europe prisoners were used initially in labour battalions or in the tasks of genocide, until they too were exterminated. In such camps as Auschwitz, gas chambers could kill and incinerate 12,000 people daily. In the west, Belsen, Dachau, and Buchenwald (a forced labour camp where doctors conducted medical research on prisoners) were notorious. An estimated six million Jews died in the camps (the HOLOCAUST), as well as some half million gypsies; in addition, millions of Poles, Soviet prisoners-of-war, and other civilians perished. After the war many camp officials were tried and punished, but others escaped. Maidanek was the first camp to be liberated (by the Red Army, in July 1944). After 1953 West Germany paid $37 billion in reparations to the surviving Jewish victims of Nazism.

In the Soviet Union, Lenin greatly enlarged (1919) the Tzarist forced labour camps, which were renamed Gulags (Russian acronym for the Main Administration of Corrective Labour Camps) in 1930. An estimated 15 million prisoners were confined to the Gulags during Stalin's purges, of whom many succumbed to disease, famine, or the firing squad.

conceptual art Various forms of art in which the idea for a work is considered more important than the finished product, if any. The notion goes back to Marcel DUCHAMP, but it was not until the 1960s that conceptual art became a major international phenomenon. Its manifestations have been diverse; most conceptual artists deliberately render their productions visually uninteresting in order to divert attention to the 'idea' they express. Exponents of conceptual art see it as posing questions about the nature of art and provocatively expanding its boundaries.

concertina A small free-REED INSTRUMENT held in the hands. The hexagonal or square end-plates, one for each hand, are separated by the bellows and carry several rows of buttons, whose function and number vary from model to model. The German, American, and Anglo-German concertinas produce two notes from each button, one when closing the bellows and the other on opening them. The English concertina produces a different note on each button, the same note on push and on pull. The Duet concertina is similar to the English with a larger bass range. The concertina was an enormously popular instrument from its invention in the early 19th century until it was gradually superseded by the piano ACCORDIAN following World War I. Since this time the instrument has again returned to favour, particularly with folk musicians.

concerto Literally, playing music together; towards the end of the 17th century the term was applied to a distinctive form, the CONCERTO GROSSO. During the second half of the 18th century the concerto grosso developed into a work for soloist and orchestra, usually in three movements. The great masters of the Classical concerto were Mozart and Beethoven. The gradual enlargement of orchestras, the rise of public concert-giving, and the increasing virtuosity of soloists all led to the Romantic concerto, in which the polite exchange of ideas between equals turned into something more passionate (as in the piano concertos of Tchaikovsky and Rakhmaninov) or more lyrical (as in the violin concertos of Mendelssohn and Bruch).

concerto grosso A musical work in several contrasted movements, in at least some of which a group of soloists (the concertino) was made to contrast with a full band of strings (the ripieno). The alternation between the two groups created the 'concerto style': a pattern of contrasts between soloists and orchestra, loud and soft sounds, lightness of texture and weight. The great masters of the concerto grosso include Corelli, J. S. Bach, Vivaldi, and Handel. From those examples in which the concertino group was reduced to a single instrument came the solo CONCERTO of the late 18th century.

conch A shell used as a trumpet, made in parts of Oceania and in East Africa by making a hole in the side, and elsewhere by removing the tip. In many areas it is a ritual instrument, for example in Fiji (where some have a finger-hole), India (where heroes of Hindu epics each have their own conch), Central and South America (where pottery copies are used), and Europe (where conches were used to avert thunderstorms: VIVALDI wrote a concerto imitating this use). It is also a signal instrument, particularly for fishermen.

Conchobar mac Nesse (or **King Conor**) Legendary Irish Gaelic king who held court at Emain Macha (near modern Armagh) with his Knights of the Red Branch, the greatest of whom was CUCHULAIN. A group of legends and tales, the Ulaid (Ulster) Cycle, recorded from oral tradition between the 8th and 11th centuries, is centred around him and the heroic exploits of his people, the Ulaids.

Conciliar Movement (1409–49) A Church movement centred on the three general (or ecumenical) councils of Pisa (1409), CONSTANCE (1414–18), and Basle (1431–49). Its original purpose was to heal the papal schism caused by there being two, and later three, popes at the same time (ANTIPOPE). The movement was successful, deposing or accepting the resignation of the popes concerned. It declared the superiority of a general council of the Church over the papacy, formulated in the decree *Haec Sancta* (sometimes called *Sacrosancta*) of 1415, and tried to make general councils a regular feature of the Western Church. It also dealt with various heresies, the council of Constance burning John HUSS and condemning John WYCLIF in 1415, and it initiated some reforms. The movement, in so far as it challenged papal authority, was eventually defeated by the papacy, but its long-term influence upon Christian Churches was considerable.

Concord The capital of the state of New Hampshire, USA, on the Merrimack River; pop. (1990) 36,000. The legislature that meets here every two years is the largest of any US state with 400 seats. There is a living museum of Shaker crafts, architecture, and inventions.

Concord See INDEPENDENCE, AMERICAN WAR OF.

Concordat Agreement between the Roman Catholic Church and a secular power. One of the most important was the Concordat of 1801 between Pius VII and Napoleon I which re-established the Catholic Church in France. Another concordat, in the form of the LATERAN Treaties of 1929, regulated the status of the papacy in Italy, which had been a source of contention since unification in 1870 abolished the temporal power of the pope. It gave the pope sovereignty over VATICAN CITY and restored the influence of the Catholic Church in Italy.

Concorde See SUPERSONIC FLIGHT.

concrete A mixture of a binder (usually CEMENT), AGGREGATE, and water that hardens to form a rock-like material. The Romans first used concrete on a large scale after discovering how to make LIME binder behave as a hydraulic cement by adding silica-rich volcanic earths (pozzolanas), found at Pozzuoli, Italy. In the following centuries, simple lime concretes were used only as fillings for walls because of their low strength and solubility in water. However, in the late 1700s, Smeaton investigated hydraulic cements, and this ultimately led to the development of PORTLAND CEMENT in 1824. Since then, the reliability of these cements and of the concrete made with them has improved. While resistance to compression is high, concrete has insufficient tensile strength to be used alone in structural members such as floors and beams, where bending occurs. In the mid-1800s patents were granted for reinforced concrete, in which ferrous bars or cables are placed in the tension zone of a member. The development of PRESTRESSED CONCRETE in 1929 led to much wider use of concrete in bridges and other structures, since it was stronger in tension than reinforced concrete and virtually maintenance-free. Pipes, covering panels, and other components are increasingly made from polymer and glass-fibre-reinforced concretes. Concrete behaves as a fluid when fresh, then sets, and subsequently hardens. All three stages can be modified by adding other substances (admixtures). Hardening can be retarded in hot weather to allow time for placing before setting, or accelerated in cold conditions to reduce the risk of the wet concrete freezing. A concrete can also be given specific properties by using special cements.

concrete mixer A machine in which water, CEMENT, and AGGREGATE are mixed together in a drum to form a homogeneous CONCRETE. In small mixers, the concrete is poured through a single opening by tilting the drum. Medium-capacity mixers have a drum that does not tilt but rotates in one direction for mixing; on reversing, fixed blades in the drum force the concrete through an opening. Large mixers have a fixed drum with rotating blades; materials are loaded from hoppers above, and the concrete is discharged through a flap to a vehicle below.

concrete painting Styles of modern painting that repudiate all figurative reference to an object and construct the composition from elementary pictorial elements, such as the rectangle or square. Many distinct movements in abstract art, including CONSTRUCTIVISM, SUPREMATISM, and Neo-Plasticism, are referred to as concrete painting.

concretion (in geology) A hard, compact, rounded nodule of mineral matter, which may be found in sedimentary rocks, unconsolidated deposits, and soils. Concretions are generally formed by localized precipitation of minor mineral constituents, such as manganese, or by a cementing material – for example, silica, calcite, or iron oxide – round a solid object such as a fossil. Concretions vary in size from small pellets to great spheroidal bodies as much as 3 m (10 feet) in diameter.

concussion Temporary loss of consciousness, from a few seconds to a few hours duration with, usually, complete recovery. Concussion is caused by a blow to the head, which affects centres that control consciousness, although brain damage is not evident. However, repeated concussion may result in brain damage.

Condé A junior branch of the French royal House of BOURBON. The name was first borne by Louis I de Bourbon (1530–69), prince de Condé, a military leader of the HUGUENOTS during the first phase of the French WARS OF RELIGION. A bitter enemy of the GUISE faction, he was killed at the battle of Jarnac. Henry I de Bourbon (1552–88) took over his father's leadership of the Huguenots. He briefly renounced his faith at the time of the ST BARTHOLOMEW'S DAY MASSACRE (1572), but subsequently embarrassed his cousin, the future HENRY IV, with his Protestant fanaticism.

Henry II de Bourbon (1588–1646) was brought up as a Catholic; he plotted during the regency of Marie de Medici, and distinguished himself only by fathering Louis II de Bourbon, his successor, known as the Great Condé. The latter married a niece of Cardinal RICHELIEU, and excelled as a military commander in the last phase of the THIRTY YEARS WAR. During the first FRONDE he sided with the court party; disagreements with MAZARIN led to his arrest and imprisonment (1650), and on the failure of his insurrection against the government (1651–52), he fled and took service in the Spanish armies in the Netherlands. When he was allowed to return to France in 1660, he conquered Franche-Comté for LOUIS XIV (1668), and held high command in the war against the United Provinces of the Netherlands (1672); but Louis never really forgave him for his part in the Fronde, and his treasonable defection to the Spaniards.

condensation of vapour A process that occurs when a gas is cooled so much that it liquefies – very often in tiny droplets. Vapour trails (or contrails) that appear to stream from the engines of high-flying jet aircraft are a result of this process. DEW is formed by the condensation of atmospheric water vapour on the surface of the ground. The reverse of condensation is EVAPORATION.

condensation reaction See CHEMICAL REACTION.

condenser (electrical) See CAPACITANCE AND CAPACITORS.

conditioning (in psychology) A change in behaviour due to association between events. It was the basis of LEARNING theories that dominated academic psychology from World War I to about 1960. Conditioning is usually divided into two kinds: classical or Pavlovian; and operant or instrumental. Both involve the pairing of an event with 'reinforcement', which may be 'positive' (rewards of food, drink, or sex) or 'negative' (punishment such as electric shock). In classical conditioning, which was discovered by PAVLOV, a light or sound is paired with a natural reinforcement. The response which was initially produced by the reinforcement becomes 'conditioned' so that it occurs to the light or sound even when no reinforcement is given. This is therefore a matter of learning an association between two stimuli (the reinforcement and the light or sound) and is referred to as S–S conditioning. Operant conditioning follows the US psychologist Edward Thorndike's (1874–1949) 'law of effect' (1911): that responses become more frequent if followed by satisfying consequences but less frequent if followed by aversive consequences. SKINNER showed that a rat which is rewarded when it 'operates on' its environment by pressing a lever will increase its number of lever-presses. It is therefore associating the stimulus (reinforcement) with its own behaviour (response). This is referred to as S–R conditioning. Psychologists dispute whether these two kinds of conditioning do really differ from each other. Most conditioning experiments have been done with animals. It is very doubtful whether all animal, let alone human, learning is due to conditioning. In 1920 WATSON showed that fears can be conditioned and thereby laid the foundations for BEHAVIOUR THERAPY treatments for PHOBIA.

condom See CONTRACEPTION.

condominium ▶**1** A territory administered jointly by two or more countries. For example, between 1906 and 1980 the New Hebrides (now Vanuatu) was governed as an Anglo-French condominium. ▶**2** The ownership of a building or estate by the residents who occupy it, especially in the USA.

condor Either of two species of American VULTURE. Andean condors, *Vultur gryphus*, with wings spanning almost 3 m (10 feet), occur mainly high up in the western mountains of South America, generally in the tropics, but are also widely distributed along the deserts and wooded cordilleras further south. Californian condors, *Gymnogyps californianus*, which are slightly smaller, have become extinct in the wild areas of inland California, but captive breeding for reintroduction is being pursued.

Condorcet, Antoine Nicolas, Marquis de (1743–94) French philosopher and politician. He was the only prominent French *philosophe* to play any real part in the events of the Revolution. As a GIRONDIN and a friend of Sieyès and BRISSOT he was elected to the National Convention. In October 1793 he was condemned by the Revolutionary Tribunal and eventually poisoned himself to avoid the guillotine.

Condor Legion A unit of the German airforce sent by HITLER to aid FRANCO in the SPANISH CIVIL WAR (1936) on condition that it remained under German command. It aided Franco in transporting troops from Morocco in the early days of the war, and played a major role in the bombing of rebel lines and civilian centres, notably the city of Guernica on 27 April 1937.

condottiere (Italian *condotta*, 'contract') The leader of a medieval mercenary band of soldiers. Mercenaries flourished in the climate of economic prosperity and inter-municipal warfare of 14th- and 15th-century Italy. The earliest such mercenaries were recruited from the unemployed mercenary 'free companies' of the 1360s and included Catalans, the Germans and Hungarians of the so-called Grand Company, and the English Sir John Hawkwood, leader of the White Company in the 14th century. The system was refined in the 15th century by the SFORZAS, although the condottieri were always motivated by self-interest, and changing of sides and loyalties was frequent. The system died out as a result of the Habsburg-Valois wars of the 16th century, which led to change in the financing and organization of armies.

conduction, electrical The flow of ELECTRIC CURRENT through matter. It occurs in three types of matter. In metals there is a bulk movement of electrons in the direction of an applied electric field. For a current to flow the electrons must be free to move and this occurs only if there are available energy levels just above the existing energy level of the electron; if these energy levels are too far above the existing levels then the material is an insulator. In SEMICONDUCTORS the ability of the material to conduct is much less than in metals, but unlike metals, it increases as the temperature rises. In solutions an electric current can be carried by electrolytes, as in ELECTROLYSIS.

conduction, thermal The flow of heat through matter. In order for it to flow from one point to another there must always be a temperature difference between the two points, the flow being from the higher to the lower temperature. The mechanism depends on the material. In metals the heat is transported by the same electrons that are responsible for electrical conductivity. In electrical insulators – that is, gases, some liquids, and non-metallic solids – no conduction electrons are available, and the heat is transferred from one atom to the next by the thermal vibration of the atoms. At room temperatures this mechanism is not as efficient as the transport of heat by electrons; and this is why metals tend to be much better conductors of heat than non-metals. In liquids and gases heat is transferred by direct collision between molecules, although this is less important than the bulk movement of fluid, CONVECTION. The measure of a material's ability to conduct heat is called its thermal conductivity.

conductor In music, the person who directs the performance of an orchestra or choir. The idea of a 'conductor', who indicates not only the basic beat but also the way in which the music is interpreted, is of comparatively recent date. It arose as a necessity alongside the development of the ORCHESTRA and the appearance of music that sought ever more subtle ways of being expressive and meaningful. The early orchestra could be directed from the keyboard by the continuo-player. Direction later passed to the first violin (still called the 'leader' in Britain and the 'concert master' in the USA), who would indicate with his bow, or by a mere inclination of the head, all that was needed. But by the 19th century orchestras had grown larger, the music was more expressive, and the art of orchestration had become an integral part of composition. The relative weight of sound produced by the different instruments now had to be 'balanced' if the music was to make its proper effect. Someone therefore had to take charge. Conducting with a baton began in Germany in the early part of the 19th century. The baton is mainly used to indicate the beat by a series of universally recognized movements. It can also be used to cue in instruments; to suggest (by amplitude of gesture) the required dynamics; and, by quality of gesture, to indicate the style of interpretation. The conductor's free hand can be used for additional or complementary indications and need not mirror the baton gestures.

coneflower A perennial, herbaceous member of the sunflower family, Compositae. They have showy flowers consisting of a ring of yellow ray-petals, surrounding a vertical cone of brown-to-purple tube-shaped florets. Those with dark disc florets are often called black-eyed Susan. They make up the 30 or so species of the genus *Rudbeckia*, which is native to North America.

Conegliano, Emmanuele See DA PONTE.

Coney Island A resort on the US Atlantic coast in Brooklyn, New York City, forming part of Long Island since the silting up of a creek. It has been developed as a pleasure ground since the 1840s but is now in decline.

confectionery Delicacies made with sweet ingredients. Confectioneries sweetened with honey were made in Egypt at least 3,000 years ago. In the Middle Ages the Persians developed confectionery made with refined cane sugar, and during the 18th century in Europe, machinery for confectionery manufacture was first developed. Boiled or hard sweets such as fruit drops and clear mints are made by boiling a flavoured solution of sugar and corn syrup until the sugar concentration reaches a high level. On cooling, a hard, glassy product is formed. Caramels and toffees are manufactured in a similar way, but the mixture includes condensed or evaporated milk. Fondant, the basis for the 'soft centres' of many CHOCOLATES, is made by rapidly beating a hot, concentrated sugar mixture so that minute crystals are formed: fudge can be made by similarly beating hot caramel. Agar, pectin, or gelatine is added to sugar syrup to form jellies and Turkish delight, while gums and pastilles are made by dissolving gum arabic in sugar syrup.

Confederacy The 11 southern US states that seceded from the Union of the United States in 1860–61. Seven states (Alabama, Florida, Georgia, Louisiana, Mississippi, South Carolina, and Texas) formed themselves into the Confederate States of America on 8 February 1861 at Montgomery, Alabama, with a constitution modelled on the US document but incorporating guarantees of states' rights and the institution of slavery. Jefferson DAVIS and Alexander H. Stephens were elected President and Vice-President. After the bombardment of FORT SUMTER, four further states joined the Confederacy (Arkansas, North Carolina, Tennessee, and Virginia). Although the Confederate flag contained thirteen stars, two represented Kentucky and Missouri, border states which in fact remained largely under federal control. Despite the relative weakness of its central government based at Richmond, Virginia, the Confederacy managed to sustain the civil war until its collapse in April 1865 after four years of war with most of its territory occupied, its armies defeated, and its economy in ruins. See AMERICAN CIVIL WAR.

confederation A weak form of political union between sovereign states, in order to secure some common purpose. Action by a confederal government requires unanimity among member states; the confederal government generally lacks its own means of taxation, law-making, and enforcement. The federal constitution of the USA was preceded by the Articles of Confederation of 1781 (see FEDERALISM). With the contemporary tendency to centralization, confederalism is not common: Switzerland is a confederation by name but in practice a federation. Confederal solutions were advocated, but not adopted, to resolve frictions in troubled federations such as Yugoslavia and the former Soviet Union, and some theorists compare the enhanced EUROPEAN UNION to a confederation.

Conference on Disarmament An organization within the framework of the UNITED NATIONS, comprising 40 member states, including the five declared nuclear-weapons states (the USA, the former Soviet Union, France, the UK, and China). Based in Geneva, it has contributed to discussions on the control of CHEMICAL AND BIOLOGICAL WARFARE, a nuclear test ban, the arms race in space, and new weapons of mass destruction. So far the Conference has failed to achieve significant positive results because of the reluctance of states to give up arms as deterrents, the problem of achieving significant reductions on both sides, and the difficulty of verification. See also ARMS CONTROL; DISARMAMENT.

Conference on Security and Co-operation in Europe See HELSINKI CONFERENCE.

configuration (in chemistry) The different spatial arrangements that are possible in molecules containing the same atoms. In this respect it is like CONFORMATION; the difference is that a change in configuration cannot occur by the simple rotation of a bond. Thus different configurations of a compound can be isolated. Cis- and trans-isomers are examples of compounds with different configurations (ISOMERISM).

conformation (in chemistry) The different spatial arrangements in a molecule that can occur by the twisting or rotation of single chemical bonds. Different conformations differ slightly in energy, and it is the one with the least energy that will tend to be the most stable form of the molecule. However, as it is relatively easy for a molecule to pass from one conformation to another, it is not usually possible to isolate one particular conformation of a compound.

conformity (in geology) The relationship shown by SEDIMENTARY ROCKS in which the successive beds rest on each other without any evidence of interruption in the process of deposition. Its opposite is **unconformity**.

conformity (in psychology) Aspects of a person's beliefs, feelings, or behaviour that are due to the influence of other people. Experimental findings about the power of such influence cast doubt on beliefs about the self-determination of individual behaviour. Conformity is distinguished from obedience by being imitation, often of equals. The conformer feels he or she is acting voluntarily, whereas obedience is a response to a superior's explicit command and therefore comparatively involuntary.

Confucianism A system of philosophical and ethical teachings founded by Confucius in the 6th century BC and developed by Mencius (Meng-tzu) in the 4th century BC, one of the two major Chinese ideologies (see taoism). The basic concepts are ethical ones: love for one's fellows, filial piety, decorum, virtue, and the ideal of the superior man. The publication in 1190 AD of the four great Confucian texts revitalized Confucianism throughout China. A second series of texts, the 'five classics', includes the *I Ching*. There are an estimated 5,800,000 followers of Confucianism in the world.

Confucian literature The body of Chinese literature founded in the 6th century BC and accepted as the basis for Confucian philosophical thought. The first acknowledged Confucian works were the Five Scriptures: the divination manual *Book of Changes* or *Yijing* (*I Ching*), the *Book of Documents*, which provided the ideological basis for Zhou dynasty rule to 256 BC, the *Book of Odes* or *Shijing*, a manual of *Ritual*, and the *Spring and Autumn Annals*, a chronicle of one of the early feudal states. In the Later Han dynasty (25–220 AD) the *Analects*, sayings of Confucius, the *Scripture of Filial Piety*, and the *Mencius*, by a disciple of Confucius, were added to the canon. Four Confucian works, the *Analects*, the *Great Learning*, the *Doctrine of the Mean*, and the *Mencius*, were selected for special use by Song dynasty (960–1279) educationists in 1190; they were known as the Four Books.

Confucius (Latinized name of K'ung Fu-tzu, 'Kong the master') (551–479 BC) Chinese philosopher. He spent much of his life as a moral teacher of a group of disciples, at first working for the government and later taking up the role of an itinerant sage. His ideas about the importance of practical moral values formed the basis of the philosophy of CONFUCIANISM. His teachings were collected by his pupils after his death in the *Analects*; later collections of Confucianist writings are probably only loosely based on his work.

conger eel A marine fish of the family Congridae, containing 100 species, which grow to a considerable size, up to 2.75 m (9 feet) in length. The European conger eel, *Conger conger*, is abundant on underwater wrecks and reefs, but also lives in deep shore-pools and in crevices in harbour walls. It feeds mainly on bottom-living crustaceans, octopuses, and fishes. A similar species, *C. oceanus*, lives on the Atlantic coast of North America, and about 20 other species occur in the Atlantic and Pacific oceans. Conger eels spawn in deep water, and their young, called leptocephalus larvae, are transparent and flattened, and drift towards the shore, where they change into tiny eels.

conglomerate (in economics) A group of firms operating in a disparate range of business activities, but all owned by the same parent or holding company. A conglomerate is usually established and built up by take-over or merger. The holding company may be small relative to the size of the group, but may claim to have the managerial talent to make the acquired firms more efficient.

conglomerate (in geology) A CLASTIC SEDIMENT composed of rounded pebbles or boulders cemented into a matrix of finer sediment. If the fragments are angular rather than rounded, the rock is called a BRECCIA.

Congo A major river of central Africa formed by the waters of the River Lualaba and its tributary, the River Luvua. It lies largely within the Democratic Republic of Congo (formerly Zaïre) and flows north, west, and south-west in a great curve for 4,374 km (2,718 miles) before emptying into the Atlantic Ocean. It was renamed the River Zaïre by the Zaïre government in 1971, but reverted to its original name in 1997. Its headwaters were explored by David Livingstone (1871) and later by Henry Stanley (1874–77) who proved that the Lualaba was the source of the Congo and not the Nile.

Congo, Belgian See CONGO, DEMOCRATIC REPUBLIC OF.

Congo, Democratic Republic of (name from 1971 to 1997 **Zaïre**) The largest country in equatorial Africa; it is bounded by nine other countries and has an outlet to the Atlantic Ocean at the mouth of the Congo.

Physical. Between the coast and the eastern mountains, annual rainfall varies from 1,000 mm (40 inches) to 1,800 mm (71 inches), while the temperature remains a fairly constant 25°C (77°F) except for cooler winters in the south. The Congo and its tributaries flow through the country. Thick forests cover the central districts and there is much swamp. In the south, however, are open highlands. The eastern boundary runs down the Great Rift Valley and includes the western shore of Lake Tanganyika.

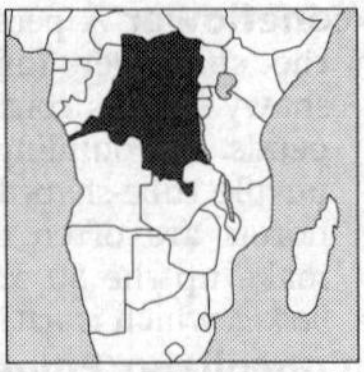

Economy. The country has substantial agricultural, mineral, and energy resources, whose development is impeded by corruption, smuggling, lack of infrastructure and investment, and falling world commodity prices. The main exports are copper, coffee, diamonds, crude petroleum, and cobalt; many of these minerals are mined in the open highlands of the south. Other mineral resources include manganese, zinc, uranium, and tin. Gold is found in the north-east of the country. Other than coffee, agriculture includes cash crops such as palm kernels, sugar, tea, cocoa, rubber, and cotton, livestock, forestry, and subsistence crops such as plantains and cassava. Coffee production is threatened by fungal disease. Industry includes textiles, cement, engineering, and food-processing.

History. The pre-colonial 19th-century history of the country was dominated by the Arab slave trade. LIVINGSTONE was the first European explorer of the country. In 1871 STANLEY undertook to sail down the River Congo. His reports prompted King LEOPOLD II of Belgium to found the International Association of the Congo (called the Congo Free State from 1885). Stanley began to open up its resources. Maladministration by Leopold's agents obliged him to hand the state over to the Belgian Parliament (1908), and it was renamed the Belgian Congo, but in the next 50 years little was done, except by Catholic mission schools, to prepare the country for self-government. The outbreak of unrest in 1959 led to the hasty granting of independence in the following year, but the regime of Patrice LUMUMBA was undermined by civil war, and disorder in the newly named Democratic Republic of Congo remained endemic until the coup of General MOBUTU Sese Seko in 1965. In 1967 the Union Minière, the largest copper-mining company, was nationalized and Mobutu achieved some measure of economic recovery. In 1971 the name of the country was changed to Zaïre. Falling copper prices and centralized policies undermined foreign business confidence, and two revolts followed in 1977 and 1978 in the province of Shaba (formerly Katanga), only put down with French military assistance. The 1980 constitution only recognized one political party, the Movement Populaire de la Révolution (MPR), and Mobutu was re-elected as sole candidate in 1977 and 1984. Multi-party elections were promised for 1991, during which the five main opposition parties all refused to support the president's nominated prime minister. Near economic collapse provoked riots, looting, and arson. In a confused situation, Mobutu cancelled elections for a renewal of his term of office in December 1991. During 1992 a national constitutional conference was convened by Mgr. Laurent Pasinya Monsengwo, Archbishop of Kisangani, which replaced the government with a High Council of the Republic. Political instability continued throughout 1993 and 1994, with the President and the High Council of the Republic appointing rival cabinets. An agreement was reached in 1994, when both cabinets were replaced by a new transitional legislature. The country's social and economic problems were increased in 1994 with the influx of over 1 million refugees from the civil war in neighbouring Rwanda. In August 1995, Zaïrean troops began the forcible repatriation of Rwandan refugees; however, after international condemnation, this policy was halted the following month. In April 1996 Hutu militiamen and Zaïrean soldiers launched a pogrom against Tutsis in Zaïre, driving hundreds of refugees into Rwanda. This led to civil war, with Zaïrean Tutsi rebels attacking government troops and gradually taking over more of the country. In June 1997 Mobutu fled, the rebels' leader, Laurent Kabila, became president, and the country reverted to its original name.

Capital: Kinshasa
Area: 2,345,000 sq km (905,446 sq mi)
Population: 43,901,000 (1995)
Currency: 1 zaïre = 100 makuta
Religions: Roman Catholic 48.4%; Protestant 29.0%; indigenous Christian 17.1%; traditional beliefs 3.5%; Muslim 1.4%
Ethnic groups: Luba 18.0%; Kongo 16.1%; Mongo 13.5%; Rwanda 10.3%; Azande 6.1%; Bangi and Ngale 5.8%; Rundi 3.8%; Teke 2.7%; Boa 2.3%; Chokwe 1.8%; Lugbara 1.6%; Banda 1.4%
Languages: French (official); Lingala; Kongo; Swahili; local languages
International Organizations: UN; OAU

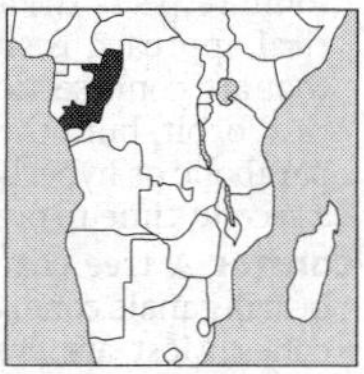

Congo, Republic of A country in western Africa, formerly called Congo (Brazzaville) after the French explorer de Brazza, whose eastern boundary is the Congo River; it is bounded by Cameroon and the Central African Republic on the north and Gabon on the west.

Physical. On its short stretch of Atlantic Ocean coast there are lagoons, large deposits of potash and oil. A small plain rises inland to a forest-covered escarpment, while most of the country comprises SAVANNAH-covered plateaux. The climate is hot and generally very wet, the river valleys inland being marshy forest.

Economy. Crude oil is the principal export, and oil revenues have funded a growing manufacturing base which includes food-processing, textiles, chemicals, and metalwork. Lead, copper, zinc, and gold ore are mined. Cassava, sugar-cane, and pineapples are the chief agricultural crops, and timber is an important export.

History. The Congo area is thought to have been uninhabited before the 15th century when Pygmies moved into the area from the north and Kongo (or Vili) people from the east. The two main kingdoms that flourished in pre-colonial times were the kingdoms of Loango and Teke, both of which prospered by supporting the slave trade. De Brazza began exploring the region in 1875 and he made the first of the series of treaties that brought it under French control in 1880. In 1888 it was united with Gabon, but was later separated from it as the Moyen Congo (Middle Congo). It was absorbed with Chad into French Equatorial Africa (1910–58). It became a member of the French Community as a constituent republic in 1958, and fully independent in 1960. In the 1960s and 1970s it suffered much from unstable governments, which alternated between civilian and military rule. Some measure of stability was achieved by the regime of Colonel Denis Sassou-Nguesso, who came to power in 1979 and was re-elected in 1989. Although a one-party Marxist state from 1970, Congo maintained links with Western nations, particularly France, from whom it gained economic assistance. In September 1990 it was agreed to adopt a multi-party political system. A new constitution was devised and accepted in a referendum in 1992. Elections held later that year produced no clear winner and a coalition was formed. The coalition collapsed and fresh elections were held in 1993. However, the results were disputed and fraud was alleged. A campaign of protest about the electoral process and results was launched by one political faction but it rapidly degenerated into fierce fighting between rival militias. Several cease-fire agreements were made and broken during 1994–97, but attempts to negotiate peace have continued.

Capital: Brazzaville
Area: 342,000 sq km (132,047 sq mi)
Population: 2,590,000 (1995)
Currency: 1 CFA franc = 100 centimes
Religions: Traditional religions 47.0%; Roman Catholic 33.0%; Protestant 17.0%; Muslim 2.0%
Ethnic Groups: Kongo 51.5%; Teke 17.3%; Mboshi 11.5%; Mbete 7.0%; Sanga 5.0%
Languages: French (official); Kongo; Teke; local languages
International Organizations: UN; OAU; Non-Aligned Movement; Franc Zone

congo eel An amphibian that makes up the smallest of the SALAMANDER families, Amphiumidae, comprising only three, mainly aquatic species, restricted to the southeastern USA. They are eel-like, although they have tiny, useless fore- and hind-limbs. Their larvae have external gills and metamorphose into adults that retain a pair of gill slits. Up to 200 eggs are laid by a single female in a shallow muddy depression, and are guarded by her.

Congregationalism PROTESTANT Churches based on local autonomy and the equality of all believers. Baptism and the Lord's Supper are the only SACRAMENTS accepted. As in other reformed Churches, there are ministers who carry out pastoral and liturgical duties. Their ordination rests with the congregation they serve; there is no formal hierarchy, though in practice senior ministers exercise over-sight in particular areas. The Congregational Church in England and Wales merged with the Presbyterian Church of England in 1972 to form the UNITED REFORMED CHURCH; in the USA the Congregational Christian Churches merged with the Evangelical and Reformed Church in 1957 to form the United Church of Christ.

Congregationalist A supporter of a form of church organization in which each local church is independent. The system derives from the belief that JESUS CHRIST is the sole head of his church, and it is held to represent the original form of the church's organization. Known at different times in England as Separatists or Independents, they can be traced back to the 16th century followers of Robert BROWNE, who broke with the Anglican Church. Driven underground by persecution, they resurfaced in 17th century Holland and America. They were among the PILGRIM FATHERS who sailed to the New World in 1620. Meanwhile in England, after figuring prominently in the NEW MODEL ARMY, they enjoyed freedom of worship under Oliver CROMWELL. This was abolished by the 1662 Act of Uniformity, then restored by the 1689 Toleration Act. In America they were allowed freedom of worship. Keen educationists, they played a major part in founding the universities of Harvard (1636) and Yale (1701).

Congress (of the USA) The legislative branch of the US federal government. Provided for in Article I of the US Constitution, Congress is divided into two constituent houses: the lower, the HOUSE OF REPRESENTATIVES, in which membership is based on the population of each state; and the upper, the SENATE, in which each state has two members. Representatives serve a two-year term and Senators a six-year term. Congressional powers include the collection of taxes and duties, the provision for common defence, general welfare, the regulation of commerce, patents and copyrights, the declaration of war, raising of armies, and maintenance of a navy, and the establishment of the post offices and federal courts. Originally, Congress was expected to hold the initiative in the federal government, but the emergence of the President as a national party leader has resulted in the continuous fluctuation in the balance of power between legislature and executive. Much of the effective work of Congress is now done in powerful standing committees dealing with major areas of policy

Congress, Indian National The principal Indian political party. It was founded in 1885 as an annual meeting of educated Indians desiring a greater share in government in cooperation with Britain. Later, divisions emerged between moderates and extremists, led by B. G. Tilak, and Congress split temporarily in 1907. Tilak died in 1920 and under the leadership of M. K. Gandhi Congress developed a powerful central organization, an elaborate branch organization in provinces and districts, and acquired a mass membership. It began to conduct major political campaigns for self-rule and independence. In 1937 it easily won the elections held under the Government of India Act (1935) in a majority of provinces. In 1939 it withdrew from government, and many of its leaders were imprisoned during the 1941 'Quit India' campaign. In 1945–47 Congress negotiated with Britain for Indian independence. Under Jawaharlal NEHRU it continued to dominate independent INDIA. After his death a struggle ensued between the Congress Old Guard (the Syndicate) and younger, more radical elements of whom Mrs Indira GANDHI assumed the leadership. In 1969 it split between these two factions but was quickly rebuilt under Mrs Gandhi's leadership. In 1977 it was heavily defeated by the Janata (People's) Alliance Party, led by Morarji Desai (1896–1995), who became Prime Minister (1977–79). In 1978 Mrs Gandhi formed a new party, the 'real' Indian National Congress, or Congress (I) (for Indira). In 1979 she led this faction to victory in elections and again became Prime Minister in 1980. After her assassination in October 1984 the splits between factions largely healed and leadership of the Congress (I) Party passed to her son Rajiv Gandhi (1944–91), who became Prime Minister (1984–89). He was assassinated in May 1991, during the run-up to a general election. The Congress (I) Party was re-elected under the leadership of P. V. Narasimha Rao (1921–), who became Prime Minister until 1996, when the Party lost the general election. Rao resigned as leader of the party later that year and was replaced by Sitaram Kesri.

Congreve, William (1670–1729) English dramatist. A close associate of Jonathan Swift, Alexander Pope, and Sir Richard Steele, he wrote plays such as *Love for Love* (1695) and *The Way of the World* (1700), which epitomize the wit and satire of Restoration comedy.

conic section A type of curve obtained by slicing a cone standing on a circular base with planes at various angles to its axis. Three distinct forms of conic section exist: ELLIPSE, PARABOLA, and HYPERBOLA, the circle being a special form of ellipse. Although the study of these curves tends nowadays to be based on a CARTESIAN COORDINATE description, in some respects the ancient Greeks' purely geometrical approach is simpler. Comets travel in orbits that are conic sections. Halley's comet has an elliptical orbit, but others, with greater speeds, follow parabolic or hyperbolic curves and so never return a second time to our Solar System.

conifer A tree characterized by its small, pollen-bearing male cones and larger seed-bearing female cones. Most are evergreen, the needle-like leaves living up to ten years, though a few species, such as the LARCH, are deciduous. Conifers are the dominant trees over large areas of the cool, temperate zones, but a few species, such as species of *Pinus*, *Araucaria*, and *Agathis*, are native to the tropics. They are the most widely used of plantation trees, important in the timber and paper industries, and a source of resin and turpentine. They include the tallest living trees, and about 520 species are known, comprising the majority of living GYMNOSPERMS.

conjunctivitis Inflammation of the membrane covering the white of the eye and lining the inside

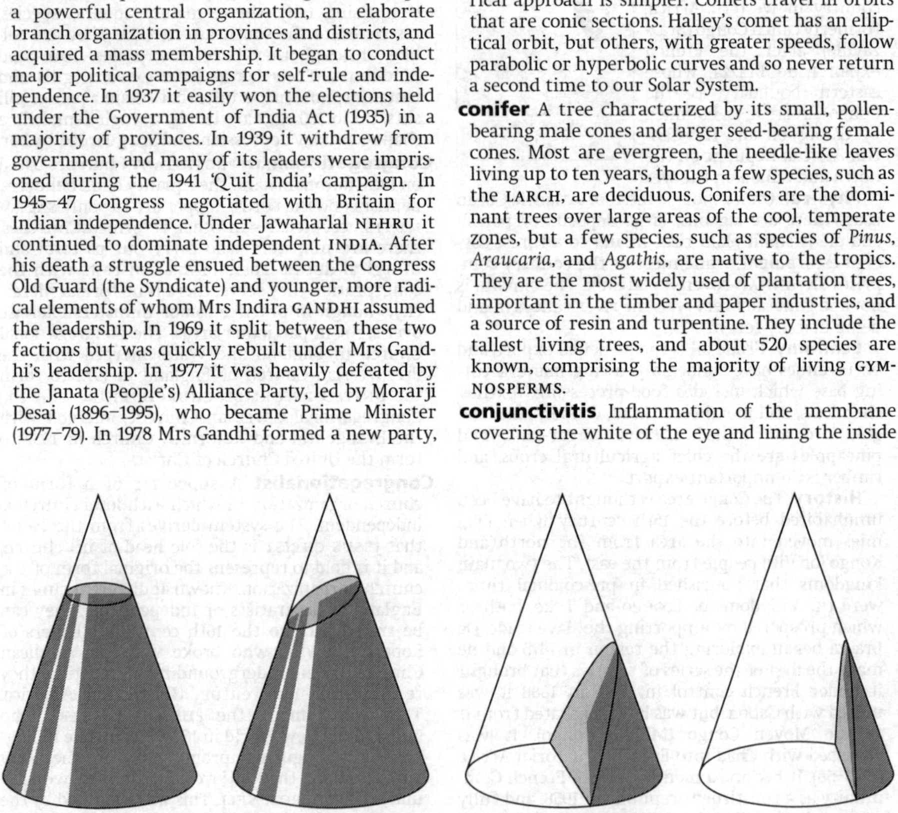

Conic sections The curve obtained by slicing a right circular cone with a plane. (1) If the plane is parallel to the base of the cone, a circle is formed. (2) If the plane is inclined but does not cut the base, an ellipse is formed. (3) If the inclined plane is parallel to a sloping side of the cone, the result is a parabola. (4) If the plane is more steeply inclined than the side of the cone, the resulting curve is a hyperbola.

of the lids. It may be caused by infection, or by exposure to irritant chemicals or ultraviolet light. It is not usually a serious condition, but trachoma, a specific chronic form, may damage the cornea and cause blindness.

Connacht (or **Connaught**) A province of the Republic of Ireland, comprising Galway, Leitrim, Mayo, Roscommon, and Sligo counties; area 17,121 sq km (6,613 sq miles); pop. (1991) 422,900.

Connecticut A state of north-east USA with the Atlantic to the south, Massachusetts to the north, Rhode Island to the east, and New York to the west; area 12,997 sq km (5,018 sq miles); pop. (1991) 3,287,100; capital, Hartford. The largest cities are Bridgeport, Hartford, New Haven, Waterbury, and Stamford. It is also known as the Constitution State or the Nutmeg State. Major products include hardware, vehicles, weapons, poultry, fruit, and dairy produce. A Puritan settlement in the 17th century, it was one of the original 13 states of the USA (1788).

Connemara A mountainous district of County Galway in the west of the Republic of Ireland.

Connery, Sean (born Thomas Connery) (1930–) Scottish actor. He is best known for his portrayal of James Bond in the films of Ian Fleming's spy thrillers. He played the part seven times from his first performance in *Dr No* (1962) to his last in *Never Say Never Again* (1984). He has also appeared in other films, such as *The Name of the Rose* (1986).

Connors, James Scott (known as 'Jimmy') (1952–) US tennis player. He established himself as one of the world's top players when he defeated the Australian Ken Rosewall (born 1934) in the 1974 Wimbledon and US Open championships. He won the US title again in 1976, 1978, 1982, and 1983 and Wimbledon in 1982.

conquistadores Spanish soldiers and adventurers in the 16th century. The most famous conquistadores were Hérnan CORTÉS, the conqueror of Aztec Mexico, and Francisco PIZARRO, the conqueror of Inca Peru; but there were many others. Their discoveries and conquests included the Caribbean, Latin America, southern and south-western USA, and the Philippines. Many would-be conquistadores explored immense areas but conquered nothing and founded no permanent settlements. As proper colonial administrations were established their activity diminished.

Conrad, Joseph (born Józef Teodor Konrad Korzeniowski) (1857–1924) Polish-born British novelist. Conrad's long career at sea (1874–94) inspired many of his most famous works, including his novel *Lord Jim* (1900). Much of Conrad's work, including *Heart of Darkness* (1902), *Nostromo* (1904), and *The Secret Agent* (1907), explores the darker side of human nature; however, the novel that initially brought him fame and success was *Chance* (1913), in which there is a romantic theme.

conscientious objection The opposition to the bearing of arms or to any type of military training on religious, philosophical, or moral grounds. Many ARMED FORCES are professional, but in cases where there is CONSCRIPTION it is likely that a minority will object to being called up, either on grounds of PACIFISM, or because of objections to a particular war. In most countries conscientious objection is treated as a breach of the law and is penalized.

conscription Compulsory call-up to take part in a country's ARMED FORCES. Citizens of a state are seen as having an obligation to defend that state by participating in military service. Conscription is generally used to mobilize national forces in times of war, but many countries still retain conscription in peacetime, young men and sometimes women being called up for a term of military service, followed by periodic refresher training. After active training, a conscript may be placed in the reserves. Conscription is retained in countries such as Israel and China (both men and women being called up), and Switzerland.

consequentialism The doctrine in ETHICS that the moral rightness or wrongness of an action is determined by its consequences. The kinds of consequences taken to be morally relevant typically include facts about the satisfaction or frustration of people's desires, with the result that there is a very intimate relation between consequentialism and UTILITARIANISM.

conservation The management of natural resources to avoid destruction of species and habitats. It involves maintaining and protecting habitats, controlling the harvesting of natural populations, and seeking to reduce pollution and other threats to other organisms resulting from human activity.

Conservation embraces all life and the environment that supports it. It may be concerned with the smallest pond, with sites of scientific interest or scenic beauty, with one of the planet's biomes, such as its rainforests, or with particular species of plants and animals. Some governments provide protected areas, such as wildlife parks and nature reserves, and impose bans on hunting endangered species. Many regulate their fishing industries, but several major fisheries have collapsed in recent years through overfishing. The reintroduction of captive-bred species may be used to rebuild a wild population, as in the case of the HAWAIIAN GOOSE. Conservation may include measures to protect clean air, water supplies, and land, or defend particular habitats against, for example, DEFORESTATION or DESERTIFICATION, or save ENDANGERED SPECIES. International conventions exist concerning the latter, but the preservation of vital habitats is the subject of fewer such agreements; the Convention on Wetlands of International Importance 1971 is one exception. To reach agreement on effective measures to combat ACID RAIN, the GREENHOUSE EFFECT, or OZONE depletion requires international collaboration to which the UN through its Environment Programme is directing increasing attention.

conservation laws Laws that relate the initial value of a physical quantity to its final value in a specific process. If the quantity is conserved, it will be the same before and after the process. The idea that mass (that is, the quantity of matter) is conserved during chemical processes – the total mass of the reagents equals the total mass of the products – was the starting point of the modern theories of chemical reactions. The principle of the conservation of energy is fundamental to classical physics. Energy cannot be created or destroyed: one form of energy can be converted into another – for example the chemical energy in petrol is converted to the kinetic energy of a moving car – but the total energy will be the same after the process as before it. These two principles – the conservation of energy and of mass – had to be modified in the light of EINSTEIN's proposition of the equivalence of mass and energy. In nuclear reactions, for example, mass and energy are considered together as a single quantity called the mass–energy: in such reactions it may be that mass and energy are not conserved, but, due to the conversion of one into the other, the overall result will be that mass–energy is conserved. Other quantities that are conserved include MOMENTUM; ANGULAR MOMENTUM; ELECTRIC CHARGE; and STRANGENESS.

conservatism A political outlook that values and seeks to conserve established institutions and is critical of proposals for radical social change. Conservatism first took shape as an ideology at the time of the French Revolution, when thinkers such as Edmund Burke (*Reflections on the Revolution in France*, 1790) and Joseph de Maistre (*Considerations on France*, 1796) denounced the revolutionary changes taking place in France as destructive of much that is valuable in society. Since then, conservatism has chiefly been opposed to LIBERALISM and SOCIALISM. Conservatives respect tradition as embodying the accumulated wisdom of the ages, and are correspondingly sceptical about untested plans and policies put forward by would-be reformers. Conservatives typically favour: constitutional government as a way of preserving democratic authority without allowing it to fall into the hands of a despot or dictator; an ordered society in which people know their places in the hierarchy; established religion, in order to integrate people into the fabric of society; and the family, the primary source of moral values and the place where responsible citizens are formed. Conservative economic attitudes have varied with time. Originally conservatives tended to support PROTECTIONIST policies in contrast to the LAISSEZ-FAIRE policies advocated by liberals, but in the 20th century they have increasingly turned to the FREE MARKET as the best means of organizing economic activity. This synthesis of conservative and classical liberal beliefs can be seen especially in the thinking of the NEW RIGHT. Political parties are rarely exclusively conservative, but politicians of a conservative disposition can be found in the Christian Democratic parties of Europe, in the US Republican Party, and in the Conservative Party in the UK.

Conservative Party (in Britain) A major political party in Britain. In 1830 it was suggested in the *Quarterly Review*, a Tory journal, that a better name for the old Tory Party might be Conservative, since the Party stood for the preservation of existing institutions. The idea was favoured by Sir Robert PEEL, whose Tamworth Manifesto brought him briefly to the premiership in 1834–35 and more firmly in 1841, but when in 1846 he was converted to FREE TRADE, the Party split. Peel's followers after a time joined the Liberals. The majority under Lord Derby and DISRAELI gradually adopted the title Conservative, although Tory continued to be used. Between 1846 and 1874 the Conservatives were a minority party though they were in office in 1867 and passed a Reform Bill. In 1867 they were the first party to create a national organization with the formation of the Central Office. In 1874, his government embarked on a programme of social reforms and increased the powers of central government. In 1886 those Liberals, led by Joseph CHAMBERLAIN, who rejected Gladstone's HOME RULE policy for Ireland, allied with the Party, whose full title then became the National Union of Conservative and Unionist Associations. The Party was strongly imperialist throughout the first half of the 20th century, although splitting in 1903 over the issue of free trade or empire preference. From 1915 until 1945 the Party either formed the government, except for 1924 and 1929–31, or joined a NATIONAL GOVERNMENT in coalition with the Labour Party (1931–35). Since World War II it has again been in office (1951–64, 1970–74, 1979–97). Before the 1970s the Party's policies tended to be pragmatic, accepting the basic philosophy of the WELFARE STATE and being prepared to adjust in response to a consensus of public opinion. Under the leadership of Margaret THATCHER, however, it moved towards the 19th-century liberal emphasis on individual free enterprise, challenging the need for state support and subsidy, while combining this with a strong assertion of state power against local authorities, a trend that continued under the leadership of John MAJOR. Many publicly owned companies, including British Airways, British Aerospace, British Gas, and British Telecom, were privatized by Thatcher's government. This initially raised a considerable amount of money for the government, and Major's government continued the policy, privatizing such organizations as British Rail and the water companies. By the mid-1990s the popularity of privatization was beginning to wane as criticism of the management of many of the newly privatized companies increased. With the growing crisis in NORTHERN IRELAND after 1968 the ULSTER UNIONISTS dissociated themselves from the Party. During the 1990s Major's government lost considerable credibility over its handling of Britain's departure from the Exchange Rate Mechanism in September 1992 and over its insistence that British beef was safe, during the 1996 BSE crisis. In addition, accusations of sleaze and sexual impropriety resulted in a landslide victory for Labour in the 1997 elections. The defeated and dispirited Conservative Party subsequently elected William HAGUE as its new leader, but were unable to agree a consistent opposition policy to integration into Europe.

consistence (of soil) The degree of cohesion between individual soil particles. It measures how easily the structure of the soil can be altered or destroyed, and is important in determining the shape and size of the peds. If consistence is poor, then cultivation, particularly ploughing, may lead to a loss of structure, making the soil more subject to erosion and destroying its natural fertility.

consort In music, an ensemble of voices and/or instruments. By extension the term also means the music played by such a group, and its performance in public. In Britain the term applies to chamber music from the early 16th to the early 18th century, and most frequently to the 'consort of viols'. A whole consort was one in which all the instruments were of the same family (all strings, all wind, all brass). A mixed group of instruments was known as a broken consort.

consortium A group of firms or nations cooperating for a specific purpose or project, such as a construction contract, in which different members of the consortium carry out different parts of the contract. The Channel tunnel linking France and the UK was constructed by a consortium. A consortium bank is a merchant bank set up by several banks, possibly from several countries, and typically involved in loan syndication (where the risk of a loan is shared by all the participating banks).

conspiracy An agreement between two or more persons to do something illegal or reprehensible. A conspiracy to do something illegal is a crime in many countries with COMMON LAW SYSTEMS, but is little known in countries with civil law systems. It is usually concerned with the preparation for the crime, not the crime itself.

Constable, John (1776–1837) British painter.

Among his best-known works are such paintings as *Flatford Mill* (1817) and *The Hay Wain* (1821), both inspired by the landscape of his native Suffolk. By the late 1820s and early 1830s, Constable had become fascinated by the painting of changing weather patterns, and in works such as *Sketch for 'Hadleigh Castle'* (*c*.1828–29) and *The Valley Farm* (1835) he focused on the transient effects of clouds and light, so breaking new ground in landscape painting.

Constance, Council of (1414–18) An ecclesiastical council held at Constance, in Germany, which was called to deal with reform and heresy within the Christian Church. It resolved the GREAT SCHISM, decreed the regular calling of councils, and presided over the trial and burning of John HUSS. It failed, however, to produce effective reform of outstanding abuses in clerical finance and conduct, or to curb papal independence.

Constance, Lake (German **Bodensee**) A lake on the north side of the Swiss Alps, at the meeting point of Germany, Switzerland, and Austria, forming part of the course of the River Rhine.

Constant, Benjamin (1767–1830) Franco-Swiss politician and novelist. He is best remembered for his novel *Adolphe* (1816), a forerunner of the modern psychological novel, which narrates the growth and decline of a passionate relationship which in many ways parallels his turbulent liaison with Mme de STAËL.

Constantine (known as **Constantine the Great**) (*c*.274–337) Roman emperor. The years from 305 until Constantine became sole emperor in 324 were marked by civil wars and continuing rivalry for the imperial throne. Constantine was the first Roman emperor to be converted to Christianity; he issued a decree of toleration towards Christians in the empire in 313. In 324 he made Christianity a state religion, although paganism was also tolerated. In 330 he moved his capital from Rome to Byzantium, renaming it Constantinopolis (Constantinople). His reign was marked by increasing imperial control of the Eastern Church and much church building, especially at the holy sites in Palestine. In the Orthodox Church he is venerated as a saint.

Constantinople A city (modern ISTANBUL) on the European side of the south end of the Bosporus, founded in 324 and inaugurated (330) as the second capital of the Roman Empire by Constantine the Great on the site of BYZANTIUM. Subsequently the seat of the Byzantine emperors, it was captured by the Ottoman Turks in 1453 and renamed Istanbul in 1930.

constellation One of the 88 areas into which the entire night sky is divided. Originally a constellation was simply a star pattern with no definite boundary, but in 1930 the International Astronomical Union adopted official boundaries to the constellations, drawn along lines of right ascension and declination for the epoch 1875.

Various civilizations have imagined their own patterns in the stars, but the constellations used internationally today stem from a group of forty-eight known to the ancient Greeks and listed by the 2nd-century Greek astronomer Ptolemy in the ALMAGEST. At the end of the 16th century two Dutch navigators, Pieter Dirkszoon Keyser (*c*.1540–96) and Frederick de Houtman (1571–1627), added twelve new constellations in the far southern part of the sky that was below the horizon to Greek astronomers.

The constellations of the northern sky were completed by eleven figures invented by the Polish astronomer Johannes Hevelius (1611–87).

constitution The rules regulating an association, and particularly the set of basic rules and principles governing the structure, organization, and powers of a state. A constitution is a fundamental law, specifying the sources, purposes, and uses of public power, and the restraints upon that power. It controls but also legitimizes the government organized under it and operating within it, which is accordingly known as a **constitutional government**. Nearly all constitutions have a wholly documentary basis, the constitution of the UK, which is unwritten, being a rare exception.

Constructivism A Russian movement in sculptural art founded in about 1913 by Vladimir Tatlin. He was later joined by the brothers Antoine PEVSNER and Naum GABO, who rejected the idea that art must serve a socially useful purpose and conceived a purely abstract art-form that explored the aesthetic use of modern machinery and technology and used industrial materials such as plastic or glass. Tatlin was among those who applied Constructivist principles to architecture and design. Pevsner and Gabo left Russia in 1922 after Constructivism had been condemned by the Soviet regime. They and other exiles had considerable influence throughout Europe and the USA.

consumer law Areas of law that include the provision of credit, the regulation of contract terms, and legislation covering specific aspects of consumer goods, for example the regulation of food labelling. All EU member states have different domestic laws covering these issues. In relation to the provision of consumer information each member state makes use of secondary committees; for example, in the UK marketing boards for each product impose and enforce certain standards, while in Germany quality marks are controlled by the owner of that label, who imposes and enforces certain standards.

consumption (in economics) Using a GOOD or service to satisfy some material demand of the population. Consumption is measured as the total expenditure in an economy upon goods and services classified as consumption goods, including durable goods such as motor vehicles, refrigerators, or clothing which are used over a number of years. Consumption is the largest component of national income, and can be divided into consumption by households and consumption by government. That by households is the larger part, and the term is often used to refer to this part alone.

contact lens A small plastic lens placed on the surface of the eye to correct faulty vision, used as an alternative to SPECTACLES. Each lens is shaped to fit the eye, and variations in thickness correct the focusing deficiencies that cause long or short sight. Contact lenses may be either hard or soft. Hard lenses cover the pupil and part of the cornea. Early designs were impermeable to gases and with prolonged use could starve the covered eye tissues of oxygen; they are being replaced by gas-permeable lenses, which allow oxygen to reach the cornea. Soft lenses are manufactured dry, then hydrated in saline solution. They cover the whole cornea and part of the sclera (white), and are more comfortable than hard lenses. However, they deteriorate more rapidly and are associated with a higher incidence of eye infection.

contact process The most important industrial process for the production of SULPHURIC ACID.

Sulphur dioxide (formed by burning sulphur) is first reacted with oxygen from the air to form sulphur trioxide; the reaction requires the presence of a vanadium CATALYST (usually vanadium oxide) and a temperature in excess of 400°C. The sulphur trioxide is dissolved in highly concentrated sulphuric acid to produce oleum (fuming sulphuric acid), which is subsequently diluted with water to produce 96 per cent sulphuric acid.

container ship A merchant ship specially designed and built for the carriage of cargo pre-packed in containers. The containers are of internationally standardized dimensions and holds and deck spaces are purpose-built to fit them, leading to greater ease and efficiency in stowage and minimization of the risk of the cargo shifting dangerously during heavy weather at sea.

contempt of court (in COMMON LAW) Disrespect for or disobedience to a COURT OF LAW. Civil contempt means disobeying an order of the court, for instance by breaking an INJUNCTION. Criminal contempt is conduct that tends to obstruct, prejudice, or abuse the administration of justice, either in a particular case or generally. The penalty for contempt of court, both civil and criminal, may be a fine or imprisonment.

continental climate Climatic conditions associated with continental rather than maritime areas, and characterized by marked contrasts between summer and winter.

Continental Congress (1774, 1775–89) The assembly that first met in Philadelphia to concert a colonial response to the 'Intolerable' Coercive Acts. At its first session, the radicals, led by delegates from Massachusetts, Virginia, and South Carolina, outmanoeuvred the moderates from New York and Pennsylvania and adopted the Suffolk County (Massachusetts) Resolves, rejecting the Acts as 'the attempts of a wicked administration to enslave America'. The second Congress, convened in the wake of Lexington and Concord, created a Continental Army under WASHINGTON and, as a result of British intransigence and radical pressure, moved gradually towards the DECLARATION OF INDEPENDENCE (1776). The Congress undertook the central direction of the War of INDEPENDENCE, and, under the Articles of Confederation (1781), the government of the USA.

continental drift Originally, the hypothesis that the continental masses (composed largely of SIAL) were floating on heavier oceanic material (SIMA) and were drifting relative to each other. It was proposed that before the CARBONIFEROUS PERIOD there was one vast continental land mass, PANGAEA, which split up into smaller land masses that drifted apart. This splitting occurred at different times to give the present configuration of continents and oceans. The lateral displacement idea is ascribed to F. B. Taylor and H. B. Baker in America (1908) but mostly to A. WEGENER in Germany (1910). The idea was, however, first published in 1858 by Antonio Snider-Pellegrini. Wegener published his theory in 1915, but gained little support in early years since no satisfactory mechanism or motive force could be found. When, however, SEA-FLOOR SPREADING and PLATE TECTONICS became established as theories in the 1960s the idea of continental drift became an accepted element of modern geological thought.

continental philosophy The tradition of modern philosophical thought that developed on the continent of Europe (principally France and Germany) as distinguished from the ANALYTIC PHILOSOPHY predominantly practised in the UK and the USA. The point at which the two traditions diverge is often identified with the rise of PHENOMENOLOGY, founded in Germany by Edmund Husserl (1859–1938) at the beginning of the 20th century. The distinctive feature of the phenomenological method has been its endeavour to describe the structures of consciousness, or, more broadly, the part played by the mind in the depiction of reality. The belief that the proper object of philosophical study is an area of being distinct from, and more fundamental than, the reality conceptualized by the natural sciences has been a hallmark of this tradition, which has not fought shy of making large claims about METAPHYSICS and existence (see ONTOLOGY). Phenomenology led to the EXISTENTIALISM of SARTRE and HEIDEGGER, and, supplemented by the influence of structuralist linguistics, to the post-structuralism of DERRIDA. By this route contemporary continental philosophy has come to accord a central place to the issues of language, communication, meaning, and reference, which currently dominate analytic philosophy.

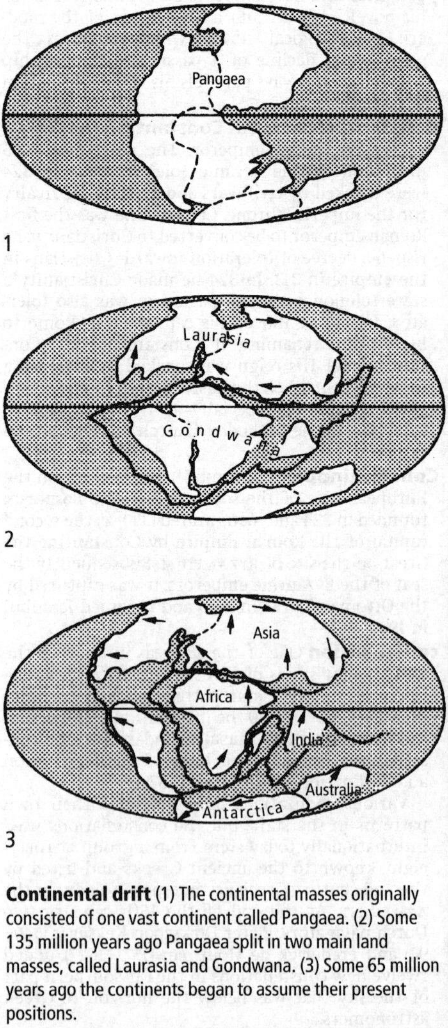

Continental drift (1) The continental masses originally consisted of one vast continent called Pangaea. (2) Some 135 million years ago Pangaea split in two main land masses, called Laurasia and Gondwana. (3) Some 65 million years ago the continents began to assume their present positions.

continental rise A feature on the ocean floor that marks the extreme edge of a continent. A moderately sloping region between the oceanic ABYSSAL PLAIN and the CONTINENTAL SLOPE. It takes the form of fans or aprons of sediment derived from the silts and clays of the continental shelf which have been carried downward by currents or under the influence of gravity.

continental shelf A gently sloping submarine plain stretching from the coastline of continents to the crest of the continental slope, which drops down steeply to the ocean depths of the abyssal plain. The continental shelf is covered by sedimentary deposits, which can be as deep as 3,650 m (12,000 ft) and can occasionally include deposits of oil.

continental slope The relatively steep slope that marks the end of a CONTINENTAL SHELF. It is generally about 20 km (12 miles) wide but can extend for up to 100 km (65 miles) and contain many long canyons. Generally covered in clay and silty sediments carried down from the continental shelf by currents or under the influence of gravity, it gradually becomes less steep at its seaward end until it merges into the CONTINENTAL RISE.

Continental System Economic strategy in Europe, intended to cripple Britain's economy. It was based upon the Berlin (1806) and Milan (1807) decrees of NAPOLEON, which declared Britain to be in a state of blockade and forbade either neutral countries or French allies to trade with it or its colonies. At Tilsit (1807) Russia agreed to the system and in 1808 Spain was obliged to join it. Britain responded by issuing Orders in Council which blockaded the ports of France and its allies and allowed them to trade with each other and neutral countries only if they did so via Britain. The restrictions contributed to the WAR OF 1812 with the USA over the right of neutral ships to trade with Europe. It gradually resulted in Napoleon losing support at home and being challenged abroad. His unsuccessful invasion of Russia in 1812 was provoked by Russian refusal to continue the system and it marked the beginning of his downfall.

continuing education Education for adults which replaces or supplements initial education in schools, colleges, and universities. Continuing adult education, often overlooked, has expanded to such an extent in recent years that in some countries more adults than children may be receiving education. It may take many forms, such as evening classes, on-the-job training, and correspondence courses (see DISTANCE EDUCATION). In developing countries, there is a strong demand for training schemes. Some focus closely on LITERACY, numeracy, and work-related skills, while other educators believe collective education of the poor will help them to overcome the problems they face.

continuo Short for 'basso continuo', a musical term meaning 'continuous bass'. In the 17th and 18th centuries instrumental music was provided with a 'figured bass' part: the lowest line of the music, complete with figures that indicated the chords to be supplied above. This was interpreted by such instruments as could play chords – harpsichords, organs, lutes, and so on – which usually worked with an instrument, such as the cello or bassoon, that could reinforce the bass line.

continuously variable transmission (CVT) See AUTOMATIC TRANSMISSION.

contour A mapping line along which all points are at the same height above sea-level. Contours can be surveyed on the ground or from aerial photographs. The width of space between contours indicates the degree of slope on the land: the closer the contours the steeper the slope. Round hills appear as concentric circles; long ridges or valleys as roughly parallel lines. The complete pattern depicts the relief, or configuration, of the land.

contraception The use of physical or chemical means to prevent unwanted pregnancy as a result of sexual intercourse. Many parents wish to plan the timing and number of children in a family, and most countries now aim to keep population growth in proportion to available resources. The Roman Catholic Church, however, remains firmly against the use of artificial means of contraception. Various methods of contraception are available.

The least effective is the rhythm method (encouraged by the Roman Catholic Church), in which couples abstain from intercourse during ovulation – the most fertile stage of the woman's menstrual cycle. Intercourse is restricted to 'safe periods' at the beginning and end of the menstrual cycle.

Barrier methods work by preventing sperm reaching the cervix or neck of the UTERUS. The oldest barrier contraceptive is the condom, or sheath. Originally of animal gut, it was used in earlier times chiefly to protect against disease. Modern condoms are made of thin rubber, and protect against sexually transmitted diseases, such as AIDS and hepatitis B, as well as providing contraception. Condoms for women are also available. Other barrier methods include rubber diaphragms and cervical caps, which, when worn in the vagina, cover the cervix to prevent sperm from entering the uterus. Chemical spermicide pessaries or creams kill sperm before fertilization occurs, but are more effective when used in conjunction with barrier methods. The intra-uterine device (IUD) is made of plastic, often with metal, and is inserted into the uterus. It is believed that it prevents the fertilized egg from attaching itself to the wall of the uterus.

The contraceptive pill, introduced in the 1960s, contains synthetic sex hormones (oestrogen and progestogen), which prevent ovulation. There has been some evidence that the contraceptive pill influences other bodily functions, in particular that it increases the risk of venous thrombosis (blood clotting), and thus carries the risk of strokes or heart attacks. To reduce this risk, a 'mini-pill' was devised, which contains progestogen but no oestrogen, and seems to have fewer associated side-effects. Some synthetic hormone preparations work over a longer period than the contraceptive pill. Depot-Provera, for example, is a synthetic progestogen preparation injected at three-monthly intervals, while Norplant and Norplant-2 are subdermal capsules implanted under the skin of the upper arm, which last five and two years, respectively. The current line of contraceptive research is aimed at developing a contraceptive vaccine. Sterilization, by vasectomy or ligature of the Fallopian tubes, is the most effective method of contraception. See also FAMILY PLANNING.

contract, law of The rules governing the formation, content, performance, and termination of contracts. A contract is a legally enforceable agreement between two or more persons. In COMMON LAW SYSTEMS, agreements will normally be enforceable only if one party has promised to do (or refrain from doing) specified acts in return for a promise by the other to do likewise. It is this notion of bargain which distinguishes legally binding promises from those which are morally or socially binding only: a contract requires performance by both parties. In CIVIL LAW systems, agreements may sometimes be enforceable in favour of a person who has not provided a reciprocal act. In both systems, failure to fulfil a contract without justification will entitle the innocent party to a remedy such as DAMAGES for loss suffered.

contracting-out The transfer of functions previously performed by government employees to voluntary or private agencies. The NEW RIGHT has recommended contracting-out as a way of reducing the size and power of the public sector and encouraging competitive pricing, greater efficiency, diversity of supply, and increased consumer choice. Public authorities may contract out practical services such as catering, cleaning, and refuse collection, or professional services such as computing and home nursing.

control system A system designed to cause a process or mechanism to conform to some specified behaviour under a set of given constraints. Control engineers often distinguish between regulators, designed to maintain a controlled variable at a constant set point (such as engine governors or central heating thermostats), and SERVO-MECHANISMS, designed to force the controlled variable to change with time in some specified way (such as robot arm or machine-tool control systems). Computer-based control systems for large industrial plants can involve the control of hundreds or even thousands of individual variables, together with extensive alarm handling and safety sub-systems. Recent developments in control engineering include self-tuning and adaptive control systems, in which the controller settings are modified automatically in response to changing process and/or disturbance conditions; and the application of NEURAL NETWORKS and ARTIFICIAL INTELLIGENCE techniques, which mimic the actions of skilled human operators.

convection A process of heat flow and transfer that occurs in fluids, and involves movement of the medium itself. As the lower part of a fluid gets warmer it expands and thus becomes less dense than the fluid above it. It therefore rises, its place being taken by colder fluid which in its turn is heated, expands, and rises. The process continues so that heat is transferred throughout the fluid.

convention (in politics) A form of international agreement between two or more countries intended to lay down certain obligations which are binding on its signatories. Such agreements may also be known as pacts, protocols, declarations, or TREATIES.

convergence Atmospheric convergence is a process which occurs whenever there is a net inflow of air into a region of the ATMOSPHERE. Such an inflow results in the accumulation of air and an accompanying increase in density. The increase is relieved by a vertical motion, and in the lower troposphere this means an upward movement of air away from the convergence. In the upper troposphere, however, some movement is downward because upward movement is limited above the tropopause, in the stratosphere. In such circumstances, convergence above is associated with DIVERGENCE below and a decrease in cyclonic vorticity. This encourages the development of anticyclones.

Oceanic convergences are found where surface waters are brought together and sink, as occurs in the centres of the subtropical oceanic GYRES under the influence of the mid-latitude anticyclonic wind systems. Convergence of water, and sinking, also occurs along oceanic FRONTS.

convergent series A number series such as $a_0 + a_1 + a_2 + a_3 + \ldots$, in which the successive partial sums obtained by taking more and more terms approach some fixed limit. For example, $3/10 + 3/100 + 3/1000 + \ldots + 3/10^n + \ldots$ is the series expansion of the decimal 0.333 ... and converges to 1/3, a third.

convertible issues See SHARES.

conveyor A mechanism for the continuous transfer of goods or materials during extraction, manufacture, or dispatch, especially in a factory. There are many forms: roller conveyors, a series of closely spaced rollers running freely or driven, are widely used for boxes and crates. Belt conveyors consist of an endless band of rubberized fabric passing over a driven roller at one end, across a series of idler rollers, then round another drum at the far end and back underneath. Other forms are bucket conveyors, used on DREDGERS, and vibrating conveyors for powders, in which vibration causes the grains to progress by jumping. Pneumatic conveyors are much used for flour and cement. In these conveyors, the powders are blown along a pipe by a current of air.

convolvulus See BINDWEED.

convoy system A system used in wartime to arrange for merchant vessels to sail in groups under the protection of an armed naval escort. In 1917 Germany's policy of unrestricted submarine (U-boat) warfare nearly defeated Britain. One ship in four leaving British ports was sunk; new construction only replaced one-tenth of lost tonnage. In the face of this crisis LLOYD GEORGE overruled the Admiralty's refusal to organize convoys, and by November 1918, 80 per cent of shipping, including foreign vessels, came in convoy. In World War II transatlantic convoys were immediately instituted in spite of a shortage of destroyers, using long-range aircraft for protection. During 1942 they were extended to the USA as the Allies were losing an average of 96 ships a month.

Conwy (or **Conway**) A market town in north Wales, on the River Conwy; pop. (1981) 12,950. There is a 13th-century castle. A suspension bridge built by Telford in 1826 and a railway bridge built by Stephenson in 1848 span the river here and since 1991 there has been a tunnel under the estuary.

cony See HYRAX; PIKA.

Cook, Captain James (1728–79) British explorer. He conducted an expedition to the Pacific (1768–71) in his ship *Endeavour*, charting the coasts of New Zealand and New Guinea as well as exploring the east coast of Australia and claiming it for Britain. He returned to the Pacific in 1772–75 to search for the fabled Antarctic continent, landing at Tahiti, the New Hebrides, and New Caledonia. Cook's final voyage (1776–79) to discover a passage round North America from the Pacific side ended in disaster when he was killed in a skirmish with native peoples in Hawaii.

Cook, Mount (Maori **Aorangi**, 'the cloud pieces') The highest mountain in New Zealand, situated in the Southern Alps of South Island. Surrounded by 22 peaks exceeding 3,000 m (10,000 feet), at 3,764 m (12,349 feet) it is permanently snow-capped. The snowfields feed glaciers, particularly the Tasman Glacier, the largest, which descends on the south-eastern side.

Cook, Thomas (1808–92) British founder of the travel firm Thomas Cook. In 1841 he organized the first publicly advertised excursion train in England, carrying 570 passengers from Leicester to Loughborough and back, to attend a temperance meeting, for the price of one shilling. The success of this induced him to organize further excursions both in Britain and abroad and to lay the foundations for the tourist and travel industry of the 20th century.

Cooke, Sir William Fothergill (1806–79) British inventor. He became interested in the application of electric telegraphy to alarm systems and railway signalling, and went into partnership with Charles Wheatstone in the 1830s. They took out a joint patent for a railway alarm system in 1837, when they set up the first practical telegraph between two stations in London, and they progressively improved the system over the next few years.

Cook Islands A group of 15 islands in the southwest Pacific Ocean between Tonga and French Polynesia with the status of a self-governing territory in free association with New Zealand; area 238 sq km (92 sq miles); pop. (est. 1992) 18,000; capital, Avarua. The islands have a tropical maritime climate with a hurricane season from November to April. Fruit and copra are the main exports.

Cookson, Dame Catherine (Anne) (1906–) British writer. A prolific author of light romantic fiction, she is best known for the Mary Ann series (1956–67), the Mallen trilogy (1973–74), and the Tilly Trotter series (1980–82).

Cook Strait A passage separating the North and South Islands of New Zealand. It was visited in 1642 by the Dutch explorer Abel Tasman, who believed it to be a bay; Captain Cook discovered in 1770 that it was in fact a strait.

coolabah See EUCALYPTUS.

Coolidge, (John) Calvin (1872–1933) US Republican statesman, 30th President of the USA 1923–29. Highly popular personally, he was seen as an embodiment of thrift, caution, and honesty in a decade when corruption in public life was common, even in his own administration. He was committed to reducing income taxes and the national debt, and was noted for his policy of non-interference in foreign affairs, which culminated in the signing of the Kellogg Pact in 1928.

Coolidge, William David (1873–1975) US innovator in the electrical industry. In 1908 he devised a process for drawing the very refractory metal tungsten into wires fine enough for use as filaments in electric light bulbs, thereby greatly increasing the bulb's efficiency. Another of his inventions was an improved X-ray tube, which he patented in 1916.

cooling system (in motor vehicles) The means of achieving the necessary cooling of a vehicle engine. Air cooling, widely used on small engines, motor cycles, and on some small cars, relies on air being blown across thin, closely spaced fins around the engine cylinders and cylinder heads. However, the majority of cars and commercial vehicles use water cooling. The cylinder and its head are double-walled; water is pumped through the jacket so formed and passed to a heat exchanger, the radiator, consisting of parallel passages surrounded by many thin fins. Air passing through the radiator cools the water by forced convection (not by radiation, as the name implies). The air-flow may be produced by the ram effect of the vehicle's motion, but when this is insufficient (as when the vehicle is stationary), a mechanically or electrically driven fan is used to blow air through the radiator. The cooling system is usually designed to work at a pressure above atmospheric, in order to avoid boiling of the water. Up to 50 per cent ANTIFREEZE is added to the radiator water to prevent it freezing in winter.

Cooper, Anthony Ashley See SHAFTESBURY.

Cooper, Gary (born Frank James Cooper) (1901–61) US actor. His performance in such westerns as *The Virginian* (1929) and *High Noon* (1952) established his reputation in cowboy roles. He also starred in other films, including *For Whom the Bell Tolls* (1943).

Cooper, Henry (1934–) British boxer. He won his first British heavyweight title in 1959. Two years later he beat Joe Erskine to claim his first Lonsdale belt, eventually becoming the only man to win one outright three times. In 1963 he knocked down Muhammad Ali (then Cassius Clay) in a non-title fight which Ali nevertheless went on to win, and was beaten by the same opponent in 1966 in his only world title fight. He retired in 1971.

Cooper, James Fenimore (1789–1851) US novelist. He is renowned for his tales of American Indians and frontier life, including *The Last of the Mohicans* (1826), *The Prairie* (1827), and *The Deerslayer* (1841). He also wrote novels inspired by his early career at sea, as well as historical studies.

cooperative A group of individuals or organizations engaged in economic activity on the basis of common ownership of facilities and profit sharing. Consumer cooperatives are engaged in wholesale and retail trade, and distribute profits (at least in part) to customers who register as members. The retail cooperative movement in the UK originated in the 19th century as a means of reducing the alleged exploitation of consumers in the capitalist system. Distribution and producer cooperatives, in both agriculture and manufacturing, are most common in developing countries and in industrialized countries with centrally planned economies. Cooperatives in industrial market economies include agricultural distribution cooperatives in France, the communal kibbutzim in Israel, and the agricultural and manufacturing cooperatives of Mondragon in the Basque country of northern Spain. In all of these the workers themselves or their representatives have final authority in the running of the enterprise.

Cooperative Movement An organization owned by and run for the benefit of its members. First developed in many of the new industrial towns in Britain at the end of the 18th century, the Cooperative Movement was largely an attempt to offer an alternative to competitive CAPITALISM. In the early 19th century the social reformer Robert OWEN made several attempts to set up his own cooperative communities, but it was with the founding of the Rochdale Pioneers in 1844 that the cooperative movement in Britain really got under way. In 1864 these came together in a federation known as the Cooperative Wholesale Society. In 1869 the Cooperative Union, an advisory and educational body, was formed. The Cooperative Wholesale Society developed as a manufacturer and wholesale trader, opening its first factories and developing its own farms. The Cooperative Party was established in 1917 to represent its members' interests in Parliament, and subsequently contested elections in alliance with the Labour Party. The movement spread rapidly to northern Europe. In the USA the first cooperatives were established at the end of the 18th and the beginning of the 19th centuries. In India and other developing countries, particularly in Africa after World War II, cooperatives have been an important factor in the growth of the economy.

co-orbital satellites Two of the small inner satellites of Saturn, JANUS and Epimetheus, which essentially share the same orbit. In fact, the orbits are only 50 km apart and although the two satellites do not collide, they do interact strongly at conjunction. The diameters of these satellites are about 200 km and 120 km, respectively. Their icy surfaces are rugged and heavily cratered.

coordinates (in mathematics) A means of specifying the location of points in space. Many different systems are possible, but the two most widely used systems in the plane are CARTESIAN COORDINATES and POLAR COORDINATES. The basis of any coordinate system is some collection of reference points or lines called axes. The coordinates of any point then reflect the distances or angles (or distances and angles) from it to the axes. Coordinate descriptions are usually ordered sets of numbers and contain the numerical information necessary to specify a particular point. On a sphere, such as the Earth, LATITUDE and longitude form one possible coordinate reference system.

In astronomy, a set of numbers (called coordinates) is used to fix the position of a point. Right ascension and declination are a coordinate system based on ANGULAR MEASURE for the points on the CELESTIAL SPHERE; the determination of such coordinates is usually performed by measuring the angular distance to some stars listed in a catalogue. Three perpendicular axes can be used to measure the coordinates for a point in ordinary space. To define such a coordinate system it is necessary to choose an origin (the point with zero coordinates), the direction of the three axes, and a unit of length. For the positions of the planets, the unit of length is usually the ASTRONOMICAL UNIT; the directions of the axes are defined by some **reference plane** such as the equator of the Earth or the ECLIPTIC, and by a reference direction such as the FIRST POINT OF ARIES, the direction of the ascending intersection of the ecliptic with the equator. Heliocentric coordinates use the Sun as the origin.

coot A RAIL with lobed toes. There are nine species of coot within the genus *Fulica*; with the exception of *F. atra*, most are South American. The Old World and Australian common coot, *F. atra*, is a stocky black bird, larger than a moorhen and with a white bill and forehead. Flocks of coots are often seen in winter with ducks, swimming and diving on open water.

Copeau, Jacques (1879–1949) French actor and director. In an effort to reverse the trend towards realism in the theatre he took over the Théâtre du Vieux-Colombier in 1913, presenting mainly Molière and Shakespeare.

Copenhagen (Danish **København**) The capital and chief port of Denmark, on the east coast of the island of Zealand and the northern part of Amager Island; pop. (1990) 466,700. Capital of Denmark since 1443, its airport (Kastrup) is a focal point of air travel in Scandinavia. Its principal attractions are the Tivoli amusement park, the Little Mermaid statue, Amalienborg Palace (home of the Danish royal family), Christiansborg Palace, and Rosenborg Castle. Its university was founded in 1497 and there are several major museums including the Toy Museum and Zoological Museum. Its industries include shipbuilding, furniture, clothing, silverware, and porcelain. It is a free port and popular tourist destination.

Copenhagen, First Battle of (1801) A naval engagement between the British and Danish fleets. The northern powers (Russia, Prussia, Denmark, and Sweden) formed a league of armed neutrality to resist the British right of search at sea. Without declaring war, a British fleet, commanded by Admiral Sir Hyde Parker, was sent to destroy the Danish fleet, anchored in Copenhagen. The British divided their fleet, NELSON attacking the Danes from the more protected south whilst Parker attacked from the north. Despite bad weather and the loss of three ships Nelson, ignoring Parker's signal to discontinue action by fixing the telescope to his blind eye, was able to sink or take all but three of the Danish ships. The Danes agreed to an armistice and the league was disbanded.

Copenhagen, Second Battle of (1807) A hostile incident between Denmark and Britain. The news that Denmark was about to join Napoleon's CONTINENTAL SYSTEM and to declare war on Britain, led the British government to challenge Denmark. When the Danes refused to surrender, the British landed troops and shelled Copenhagen.

Copernican system A heliocentric model of the Solar System introduced by COPERNICUS in 1543, which treated the Earth as one of the planets circling the Sun. The Moon revolved about the Earth as in the Ptolemaic system. Almost every known motion of the planets was accounted for by the Copernican model although he had to keep some epicycles in the system. According to Copernicus the apparent daily rotation of the heavens was due to the real diurnal rotation of the Earth, and the Earth actually moved along its own orbit about the Sun. The Copernican system had profound consequences, leading to a reassessment of the size of the Universe. Also, because objects had previously been assumed to fall to the centre of the Universe, that is, the Earth, ideas about gravity needed to be revised. This eventually resulted in NEWTON'S LAW OF GRAVITATION.

Copernicus, Nicolaus (born Mikołaj Kopernik) (1473–1543) Polish astronomer. Copernicus, canon of the cathedral at Frauenberg, first published his astronomical theories in outline in 1530, and more fully in *De Revolutionibus Orbium Coelestium* (1543). In order to avoid the complex system of epicycles required to explain planetary motions in Ptolemaic theory, he proposed a simpler model in which the planets orbited in perfect circles around the Sun. His work ultimately led to the overthrow of the established geocentric cosmology.

Copland, Aaron (1900–90) US composer, pianist, and conductor, of Lithuanian descent. He worked to establish a distinctive American style in music, borrowing from jazz in his *Music for the Theater* (1925), from Shaker music in *Appalachian Spring* (1944), and from other folk and traditional music in the ballet score *Rodeo* (1942).

Copley, John Singleton (1738–1815) US painter. A distinguished colonial portraitist, he sailed for England in 1774 and subsequently settled there. He made his mark with such paintings as *The Death of Chatham* (1779–80) and *The Death of Major Peirson* (1783), which are among the first large-scale paintings of contemporary events.

copper (in chemistry; symbol Cu, at. no. 29, r.a.m. 63.55) A reddish-yellow metallic element which is a good conductor of heat and electricity, and is corrosion-resistant. It is ductile (capable of being drawn into a wire) and malleable (able to be hammered or pressed without breaking). Copper is a member of the TRANSITION METALS and forms ionic compounds in which it shows valency 2, or more rarely 1. Rather an unreactive metal, it is unaffected by water and acids; on long exposure to air it acquires a green protective layer of basic copper carbonate: verdigris. Copper is chiefly used for electrical wiring, but also for tubes and pipes, cooking utensils, fermentation tanks, and sometimes as a roofing material. It can be combined with other metals to form alloys such as BRASS, BRONZE, and coinage metals. Copper salts, which are poisonous, are used as MORDANTS in dyeing; as FUNGICIDES, INSECTICIDES, and algicides; and in the production of pigments and plastics. The chief copper ORE is chalcopyrites ($CuFeS_2$), but other ores are also important, and the free element is found naturally. Major producers include the USA, Russia, Zambia, the Democratic Republic of Congo, and Chile.

copper (in natural history) A butterfly with metallic, coppery-coloured wings. Coppers are members of the family Lycaenidae, together with BLUES and HAIR-STREAKS. Most of the 500 or so species are north temperate in distribution. Often, only the male is truly copper-coloured, and it may have a purple, metallic sheen in addition.

Copper Age The stage of technological development between the introduction of copper and the manufacture of bronze (an alloy of copper and tin) in the BRONZE AGE. As copper was initially very scarce, the impact of metallurgy was often slight, and it was used only for ornaments and rare daggers or flat axes.

Copper appeared at very different dates in various parts of the world. In some cases there was no separate stage before the adoption of true bronze or even iron: in others, Andean South America for example, it was in use for very much longer.

copperhead A stout-bodied venomous snake, *Agkistrodon contortrix*, of the PIT VIPER group that occurs in the eastern and southern USA. Its common name derives from its head coloration, which is often coppery-red; the colour of the body is pinkish or coppery-orange with darker cross-bands. Maximum body length is about 1.4 m (4.5 feet). Its bite is painful but rarely fatal to man. The unrelated Australian copperhead, *Denisonia superba*, of south-eastern Australia, Tasmania, and some Bass Strait islands is also fairly stout-bodied; but the coloration ranges from reddish-brown to greyish or black and the maximum length is 1.7 m (5.6 feet). It is often found in marshy areas, particularly in thick grass and piles of stones. It is dangerously venomous, but human casualties are uncommon.

copper(II) oxide (CuO) A black solid that is insoluble in water. It is formed by heating copper in air, and by heating copper hydroxide, nitrate, or carbonate. One of its uses is in anti-fouling paints for ships' hulls.

copper(II) sulphate ($CuSO_4$) In its hydrated form ($CuSO_4 5H_2O$), a blue crystalline solid; on heating it loses water and turns white (becomes anhydrous). It is used in the electrolytic refining of copper, in ELECTROPLATING, in the manufacture of pigments, as a MORDANT for textiles, and to prevent growth of algae in swimming pools and reservoirs. Anhydrous copper sulphate is used to test for the presence of water.

copperwork Artefacts and decorative work made from copper, which was one of the first metals to be used by man, perhaps as early as the 5th millennium BC. As well as being attractive in colour, it is easy to hammer into shape, and its excellent conductivity of heat makes it a particularly useful material for cooking utensils. It can be cast as well as beaten, and has been used in this way for statuary (for example, in ancient Egypt), although it has proved more suitable for this purpose when alloyed with tin to form bronze. Other uses to which copper has been put in the arts include jewellery and architectural decoration.

Coppola, Francis Ford (1939–) US film director, writer, and producer. Coppola's reputation rests chiefly on *The Godfather* (1972) and its two sequels, a film trilogy charting the fortunes of a New York Mafia family over several generations; it earned him three Oscars as writer and director. Other films include *Apocalypse Now* (1979), a retelling of Joseph Conrad's story *Heart of Darkness* in the context of the Vietnam War, *The Cotton Club* (1984), and *Bram Stoker's Dracula* (1993).

copra A substance produced from the white, oil-rich (60–65 per cent) kernel of the coconut palm. Cup copra is produced when freshly harvested nuts are split open and either Sun- or kiln-dried. Coconut oil, used in the manufacture of soaps, cooking fats, and margarine is extracted from this copra. The major producers are the Philippines and Indonesia; lesser amounts come from India, Sri Lanka, and Mexico. Ball copra is produced when unhusked nuts are stored in the shade for up to twelve months.

Coptic Church (or **Egyptian Church**) One of the Monophysite CHRISTIAN CHURCHES, founded in 451. According to tradition, the **Copts** (Egyptian Christians) were converted by St Mark. The Coptic Church is led by the patriarch of Alexandria. Members observe five fasts each year: pre-Lent, Lent, pre-Assumption (the feast celebrating the Virgin Mary's ascension into heaven), post-Ascension, and Advent. Coptic was the EGYPTIAN LANGUAGE used from the 3rd to the 10th century; liturgies in the Coptic Church are still in Coptic, but a parallel Arabic text is provided. Outside Egypt, the Church has dioceses in Ethiopia, Jerusalem, Sudan, and South Africa; there are about 3.5 million full members. There are also a small number of Catholic Copts.

copyright The exclusive legal right to reproduce or authorize others to reproduce literary, artistic, or musical material, normally invested in the creator of such material or in his or her employer. This right lasts for the copyright holder's lifetime, and for an additional period of time after his or her death. In the European Union this was 50 years until 1995, when the additional period was extended to 70 years. Reproduction of the copyright work requires permission, and usually involves the payment of royalties for each copy made and sold, as well as protection against plagiarism or piracy. In the case of films and television programmes, fees are payable to the originators or their distribution companies for each public screening, while broadcasts of recorded music are covered by needle-time agreements that ensure payments to musicians, composers, and publishers. In some countries, authors can also claim lending rights for books borrowed from public libraries. See also INTELLECTUAL PROPERTY.

coracle A small and easily portable boat, occasionally circular but more often rectangular with rounded corners, constructed of wickerwork and made watertight. Coracles were originally made of hides but more recently of canvas covered in pitch. Coracles were used by the ancient Britons for river and coastal transport; today they are used by fishermen, mainly for salmon-fishing, on the rivers and lakes of Wales and Ireland. The bull-boat, similar in design and made of buffalo hides, was used by American Indians.

coral A tiny animal that belongs to the same class (Anthozoa) as SEA ANEMONES and SEA FANS; all corals are part of the phylum Cnidaria. Every individual secretes its own supporting skeleton, and in many species these join together as a coordinated structure. Tiny vulnerable animals thereby become massive colonies. There are two main groups of living corals: the stony corals, which may be solitary or colonial, and the octocorallian corals, which are always colonial.

Most stony corals have an external calcium-carbonate skeleton, deposited by photosynthesizing microorganisms. This dependence restricts them to depths to which light can penetrate. These corals form most of the large tropical reefs, their surfaces pitted with small cup-shaped cavities where the separate POLYPS live and feed, sharing nutrients through lateral cellular connections. The colony produces new polyps by budding, the specific pattern of budding determining whether the coral becomes branched (as in staghorn coral) or a massive and furrowed dome (as in brain coral). A few stony corals are solitary, especially in cold or deep waters. Octocorallian corals have a skeleton laid down within their own bodies, so the surface is living tissue; they include the soft corals and gorgonians. Such types always have eight feathery tentacles per polyp. The skeletons of certain corals, especially the red corals (*Corallium*) are used for making jewellery and ornaments.

Corals feed on small fish and invertebrate plankton, using stinging-cells on outstretched tentacles, often with mucous nets, to filter finer particles. As well as growing by budding, they also reproduce sexually, producing tiny planktonic larvae, which disperse and colonize new areas.

coral island An ATOLL, or reef comprising rock formed by the calcareous skeletons of myriad polyps, often building on a volcanic base. Because these coral animals can live only in clear, warm, and unpolluted water, the formations are found only between latitudes 30° N. and S. of the Equator, and generally in the Indian and Pacific Oceans, away from coastlines and river mouths. Once a formation is built up almost to the surface, waves break pieces off and pile them higher. Then Sun, wind, and marine borers help the water to split and grind the coral to sand. Seeds of plants and trees are carried by water, wind, or bird and take root; and, lastly, drifting flotsam arrives with insect life.

Coral Sea Part of the south-western Pacific Ocean, lying in a basin between the coast of Queensland, Australia, and an island arc comprising New Guinea, the Solomons, and Tuvalu. It has a mean depth of 2,390 m (7,850 feet) and contains many coral islets and reefs; the Great Barrier Reef runs along the Queensland coast. Its deeper northern part is known as the Solomon Sea.

coral snake A brightly coloured but usually secretive snake of the family Elapidae that occurs in Asia, Australia, southern Africa and the Americas. True coral snakes hunt at night and are inactive during the day. They normally eat lizards and other snakes. The true coral snakes are also poisonous, having cobra-style fangs; and their striking colours (which are often combinations of red, yellow, and black) apparently serve as a warning to would-be predators.

cor anglais (or **English horn**) A musical instrument, a tenor OBOE built a fifth lower, with a bulbous bell. The name is a mystery, for it is neither a horn nor English. The constricted bell opening gives the tone a hollow sound.

Cor Caroli A variable third-magnitude BINARY STAR in the constellation of CANES VENATICI, and also known as Alpha Canum Venaticorum. It comprises a hot DWARF STAR and another star somewhat hotter than the Sun, moving in an orbit of very long period. The distance of Cor Caroli is 40 parsecs, and its combined luminosity is about 110 times that of the Sun. The brighter component is a magnetic star with a variable spectrum.

Corcyra The former name of CORFU.

Corday d'Armont, **Charlotte** (1768–93) French noblewoman, the murderess of MARAT. After a lonely childhood in Normandy she began to attend the meetings of the GIRONDINS, where she heard of Marat as a tyrant and conceived the idea of assassinating him. She arrived in Paris in 1793 and on 13 July murdered Marat in his bath. A plea of insanity was overruled and she was sentenced to death on the guillotine.

cordillera A system or group of usually parallel mountain ranges together with intervening plateaux, applied originally by the Spaniards to the parallel chains of the Andes in Central America. The term is applied to the chain of mountain systems extending from Alaska to Nicaragua, including the Rocky Mountains, the ranges of the Great Basin, the Sierra Nevada, the Coast Ranges, and the Sierra Madre.

cordite See NITROCELLULOSE.

Córdoba A city in central Argentina, capital of Córdoba province; pop. (1990) 1,198,000. Its university has been one of the principal centres of learning in South America since it was founded in 1613.

Córdoba (or **Cordova**) A city in Andalusia, southern Spain, on the Guadalquivir River; pop. (1991) 309,200. It was founded by the Carthaginians and held by the Moors from 711 to 1236. As capital of the most powerful of the Arab Spanish states it flourished as a centre of learning, earning the title of the 'Athens of the West'. It began to decline after the overthrow of the caliphate in 1031. Textiles, olive oil and pharmaceuticals are produced.

Corelli, **Arcangelo** (1653–1713) Italian violinist and composer. His best-known works are his trio and solo sonatas for the violin (1681; 1685; 1689; 1694; 1700), and his concerti grossi (published posthumously in 1714), especially the 'Christmas' concerto, with its pastorale on the Nativity. Corelli's innovative use of harmony and attention to melody had an important influence on composers abroad, particularly Purcell, J. S. Bach, and Handel.

Correlli, **Marie** (pseudonym of Mary Mackay) (1855–1924) British novelist. A talented musician, she intended to become a concert pianist, but the success of her first novel, *A Romance of Two Worlds* (1886), encouraged her to become a full-time writer. She went on to write a series of other best-selling romantic novels, including *Thelma* (1887), *Barabbas* (1893), and *The Sorrows of Satan* (1895).

Corfu (formerly **Corcyra**; Greek **Kérkira**) One of the largest of the Ionian Islands, off the west coast of Greece; area 592 sq km (229 sq miles); pop. (1991) 105,350; chief town, Kérkira. It is a popular tourist resort.

Corinth (Greek **Kórinthos**) A city in the northeast Peloponnesus, capital of the prefecture of Corinth Greece, on the Gulf of Corinth; pop. (1991) 27,400. Rebuilt after earthquake damage in 1858 and again in 1928 and 1933, it is situated northeast of the ancient city of Corinth which dates from Homeric times. St Paul preached here and later wrote two epistles to the Corinthian church.

Corinth, Gulf of (or **Gulf of Lepanto**; Greek **Korinthiakos Kólpos**) An inlet of the Ionian Sea *c.*130 km (80 miles) long, separating the Peloponnese from mainland Greece.

Corinth, Isthmus of (Greek **Isthmos Korinthou**) A narrow neck of land linking the Peloponnese with central Greece and separating the Gulf of Corinth from the Saronic Gulf.

Corinth Canal A man-made channel across the Isthmus of Corinth, linking the Gulf of Corinth and the Saronic Gulf. Built between 1881 and 1893, it is 6.4 km (4 miles) long.

Coriolanus, Gaius (or **Gnaeus**) **Marcius** (5th century BC) Roman general. He earned his name by capturing the Volscian town of Corioli. He is said to have been banished from Rome in 491 BC after opposing the distribution of corn to the starving people and being charged with tyrannical conduct. He joined forces with the Volscians; according to legend, he led a Volscian army against Rome in 491 BC, and was turned back only by the pleas of his mother Veturia and his wife Volumnia. He was subsequently put to death by the Volscians. He is the subject of Shakespeare's play *Coriolanus* (*c.*1608).

Coriolis force A fictitious force used to explain the movement of objects in a rotating system, for example, the movement of an air mass or the path of a rocket over the surface of the Earth. It was first described by the French mathematician and engineer, Gaspard Gustave de Coriolis (1792–1843). A point on the Equator travels about 1,670 km (1,050 miles) in one hour as a result of the Earth's rotation. A parcel of air above such a point will move with the same speed, and will keep this speed as it travels north. However, the further north it travels, the smaller the distance that a point on the Earth beneath it moves in one hour. To an observer on the Earth therefore, it appears that the parcel of air is moving to the right. In this way wind and water currents are deflected to the right in the Northern Hemisphere and to the left in the Southern, an effect which explains BUYS BALLOT's law. The deflection is a direct result of the rotation of the Earth and not caused by any special force and is better called the Coriolis effect.

cork The outer part of BARK, consisting of layers of dead cells whose walls are impregnated with a waterproof substance. The cork of commerce is derived from the cork oak, *Quercus suber*, of southern Europe, which accumulates thick layers, and is harvested from the tree at intervals.

Cork (Gaelic **Corcaigh**) The largest county in the Republic of Ireland, in the province of Munster, on the Atlantic coast. Hills running east–west are broken by river valleys; area 7,459 sq km (2,880 sq mi); pop. (1991) 282,790; county town, Cork. Economic activities include agriculture and fishing. The famous BLARNEY Stone is housed at Blarney Castle.

Cork (Gaelic **Corcaigh**) The second largest city in the Republic of Ireland, capital of CORK county on the River Lee; pop. (1991) 127,000. St Finbarr is said to have founded an abbey here in the 7th century. It has both Catholic and Protestant cathedrals, and diverse light industries. Cork Harbour to the south of the city is a centre for offshore oil exploration.

corm An underground storage organ that carries plants through adverse growing conditions, such as winter or drought. Corms are derived from underground STEMS, bearing lateral buds, or small corms, and scale-like leaves. They occur in plants such as *Gladiolus* and *Crocus* and often last just one year. The flowering stem is produced from an apical bud with the exhaustion of the old corm, which, in turn, is replaced by one or more of the lateral ones. There is no sharp distinction to be drawn between corms and RHIZOMES or stem TUBERS.

cormorant A slender-billed coastal or riverine bird, usually dark brown or black. The 38 species of cormorants, comprising the family Phalocrocracidae, occur worldwide from the tropics to both polar regions. They are foot-swimmers and strong divers, with webbed feet and stout legs, and often hunt for fish, shrimps, and other aquatic food in small or large groups. Before diving they wet their plumage thoroughly, and after hunting they fly to a rock or branch to dry out, extending their wings in a characteristic pose. They breed colonially in untidy twig, seaweed, and guano nests, laying two to four eggs. The green cormorant, *Phalacrocorax aristotelis*, is also known as the shag.

corn A term used, as in peppercorn, to describe a grain or seed of a plant, particularly cereals. Alternatively, the growing cereal plant or crop can be referred to as 'corn'. In Britain, for example, all cereal crops are referred to loosely as 'corn'. In the USA it is a term used specifically to describe maize and hence is also used for its products, such as corn syrup, cornflour, and cornflakes.

corncrake See RAIL.

Corneille, Pierre (1606–84) French dramatist. He is generally regarded as the founder of classical French tragedy; his plays in this genre include *Le Cid* (1637), *Cinna* (1641), and *Polyeucte* (1643); the newly founded Académie française criticized *Le Cid* for moral laxity and performances of it were subsequently banned. He also wrote comedies such as *Mélite* (his first play, 1629) and *Le Menteur* (1642).

cornelian A red and white or reddish-brown agate, which is a form of CHALCEDONY and a variety of silica. Cornelians are prized as semiprecious stones and are also used for making seals.

cornet A brass musical instrument with three valves, similar in range to the TRUMPET but with the tubing narrowing more towards the mouthpiece, resulting in a rounder, less brilliant tone. In about 1825 valves were applied to the coiled continental POSTHORN, initially two, and later three, creating the *cornet à pistons*, which retained the posthorn's set of crooks and shanks (additional lengths of tubing, fitting between the mouthpiece and the instrument, to produce a lower pitch) from B♭ down to E. The cornet's main home today is in BRASS and military bands.

cornett A wind instrument combining a miniature trumpet mouthpiece with a wooden (or, occasionally, ivory) tube around ¾ metre (2 ft) long with finger-holes, the great virtuoso wind instrument of the Renaissance. It also played the treble line in support of choirs and the upper parts in *Turmmusik* or 'tower music', music played from a church, balcony, or town hall tower (a common practice in 16th- to 18th-century Germany).

cornflower A plant of the genus *Centaurea*, which also includes other members of the sunflower family, such as knapweeds and star thistles. The wild cornflower, *C. cyanus*, which is native to Europe, has deep blue flowers and is the parent of the many coloured garden varieties.

Corn Laws Regulations applied in Britain to the import and export of grain (mainly wheat) in order to control its supply and price. In 1815, following the end of the Napoleonic Wars, Parliament passed a law permitting the import of foreign wheat free of duty only when the domestic price reached 80 shillings per quarter (8 bushels). A sliding scale of duties was introduced in 1828 in order to alleviate the distress being caused to poorer people by the rise in the price of bread. A slump in trade in the late 1830s and a succession of bad harvest made conditions worse and strengthened the hand of the ANTI-CORN LAW LEAGUE. In 1846 the Corn Laws were repealed save for a nominal shilling. This split the Conservative Party, but agriculture in Britain did not suffer as had been predicted. The repeal of the Corn Laws came to symbolize the success of FREE TRADE and liberal political economy.

corn salad (or **lamb's lettuce**) An annual plant belonging to the valerian family, *Valerianella locusta*, with leaves like a forget-me-not. It is native to Europe, and is found in arable fields, on banks near hedges, and on roadsides. It is cultivated for its leaves, which are used in salads.

Cornwall A county occupying the extreme south-west peninsula of England; area 3,564 sq km (1,377 sq miles); pop. (1991) 469,300 (with the Isles of Scilly); county town, Truro. The ancient Celtic language of Cornwall, belonging to the Brythonic branch of the Celtic language group, was formerly spoken in Cornwall but gradually died out in the 17th-18th century.

Cornwallis, Charles, 1st Marquis (1738–1805) British general, who fought in the American War of INDEPENDENCE at Long Island and Brandywine. He took command of the southern campaign in 1780, defeating the Americans at Camden and Guildford Court House, but by his relentless pursuit into the interior he lost contact with Clinton and exhausted his troops. His choice of Yorktown as a base proved disastrous, and he was forced to surrender (1781). Later reinstated, he served as governor-general of India (1786–93, 1805) where he defeated Tipu Sultan and his Cornwallis Code reformed land tenure. He was also viceroy of Ireland (1798–1801) and negotiator of the Treaty of Amiens (1802).

corona The tenuous solar atmosphere seen as a ghostly halo of light which surrounds the Moon's disc during a total solar ECLIPSE. The corona is illuminated by light from the PHOTOSPHERE being scattered by electrons in the very hot (2×10^6 K) outer atmosphere of the Sun. The corona is now frequently observed using artificial eclipse instruments, known as coronagraphs, and by means of its own high-temperature X-ray emission. Such X-ray photographs reveal coronal holes, low-density regions from which the SOLAR WIND escapes. The name is also given to atmospheric effects in which a multi-coloured ring is seen round the Sun or Moon. This is caused by the DIFFRACTION of light passing through droplets in the water vapour in the Earth's atmosphere, the radius of the ring depending on the size of the droplets. The outside of the ring is red, and the inside blue.

Corona Australis The Southern Crown, a small CONSTELLATION of the Southern Hemisphere of the sky. It was known to the ancient Greeks, to whom it represented a crown or wreath of leaves at the foot of Sagittarius. Its brightest stars are of only fourth magnitude.

Corona Borealis The Northern Crown, a CONSTELLATION of the northern sky, one of the forty-eight constellations known to the Greeks. It represents the jewelled crown worn by Princess Ariadne of Crete when she married the god Dionysus. Fittingly, its brightest star is known as Gemma, Latin for 'jewel'.

coronary thrombosis The blockage or 'occlusion' by a blood clot of an artery supplying the heart. A common cause is a type of ARTERIOSCLEROSIS known as atherosclerosis, which results in the formation of patchy plaques (atheroma). A blood clot forms on the atheroma and blocks the artery, resulting in loss or diminished oxygen supply to the heart muscle. The effect is usually ANGINA PECTORIS or, more seriously, myocardial infarction, which is a heart attack with destruction of heart muscle. Prompt treatment to avoid a fatal outcome, and long-term preventive therapy, are essential.

Corot, (Jean-Baptiste) Camille (1796–1875) French painter. Trained in the neoclassical tradition, he worked in an essentially classical style despite his contact with the Barbizon School and his preference for taking preliminary studies outdoors. One of his most famous paintings is *La Danse des nymphes* (1850). Corot was a major influence on the impressionists, notably Camille Pissarro.

corporatism A political system in which economic and social policy is made through agreements between business associations, trade unions, and government. One effect of this is to lessen the scope of the FREE MARKET, and corporatist arrangements have therefore been criticized by the NEW RIGHT for hindering economic growth. All of the advanced capitalist societies display some corporatist features, but the degree of corporatism differs considerably, with countries such as Austria and Sweden near the top of the scale, and countries such as the USA and UK near the bottom.

corrasion (in geomorphology) The mechanical pounding, scraping, and battering action of water or ice carrying pieces of rock, which wears away the land surface. Indeed it is the main process of erosion nearly everywhere, although it gives way in deserts to abrasion by sand and rock carried by the wind, and in areas of soluble rocks such as limestone to the dissolving action of fresh or salt water, termed corrosion.

Correggio (born Antonio Allegri) (*c*.1489–1534) Italian painter, named after the small town in Emilia where he was born. He was one of the boldest and most inventive artists of the High RENAISSANCE, working mainly in Parma, where he painted two famous dome frescos, in the church of San Giovanni Evangelista (1520–21) and the cathedral (1526–30). These dome paintings were highly influential in BAROQUE ART, and other aspects of Correggio's art were equally forward-looking. The striking light effects that he often used in his altar-pieces again anticipate the Baroque, and his extraordinarily sensuous mythological paintings foreshadow the erotic works of such Rococo masters as Boucher.

Corregidor An island of the Philippines to the south of the Bataan Peninsula, Luzon Island. It divides the entrance to Manila Bay into two channels (Boca Chica and Boca Grande) and has been used as a fortification to protect the bay. It was the scene of heavy fighting during 1942 between Japanese and US Forces.

correlation (in statistics) The interdependence of sets of data. The correlation coefficient measures in some sense the similarity between two scores, independently of the units in which the data is presented. The coefficient is usually a number between −1 and +1. Positive values imply that as one score increases so does the other, negative coefficients indicate a decrease in one score compared with an increase in the other. Coefficients of −1 and +1 are said to exhibit perfect negative or positive correlation. A zero value indicates no correlation, although it does not imply that the data sets are necessarily independent.

Corrib The largest freshwater lough in the Republic of Ireland, a lake in Mayo and Galway counties; area 168 sq km (65 sq miles).

corrie See CIRQUE.

corrosion The wearing away of materials, particularly of metals, by chemical action. Corrosion usually involves the combined action of oxygen and water on a metal, forming a compound on the surface of the metal. The presence of such substances as salt, acids, or bases, or air pollutants like sulphur dioxide, can speed up the corrosion process. The most common corrosion product is metal oxide (for example RUST, which is iron oxide). In metals such as aluminium or copper, this oxide forms a tough surface layer, providing protection from further corrosion and merely tarnishing the surface. Attack by moisture on the other hand may cause electrolytic corrosion with pitting and weakening of the metal.

Many strategies are used to prevent or reduce corrosion. Most commonly, a surface coating of a non-corrosive metal (as in GALVANIZING or CHROMIUM plating) is applied, or a coating of paint, bitumen, plastic, or (for moving parts) grease. In aqueous environments, corrosion of steel structures is often prevented by cathodic protection. This involves electrically connecting 'sacrificial' anodes of aluminium or magnesium to the steel: the anodes are preferentially corroded, leaving the steel intact. Corrosion can also be reduced by controlling the surrounding environment. For example, oxygenating and neutralizing (see ACIDS and alkalis) the feed water in BOILERS can significantly reduce corrosion of boiler tubes.

corrugated iron Thin, mild-steel sheeting (often protected by GALVANIZING), folded so that it becomes stiffer and capable of supporting its own weight without significant deflection. It is structurally weak, but is used extensively for industrial roofing and cladding. Corrugated iron is now being superseded by polymer-based replacements which do not corrode so easily.

corsair A privateer of the Barbary Coast of North Africa, and especially Algiers. Piracy existed here in Roman times, but, after the Moorish expulsion from Spain, individuals (with government connivance) began attacks on Christian shipping. The early 17th century was the peak of their activity.

Corsica (French **Corse**) A mountainous island off the west coast of Italy, under French rule; area 8,680 sq km (3,353 sq miles); pop. (1990) 249,740; capital, Ajaccio. The highest peak on the island is Mont Cinto (2,710 m, 8,891 ft). Ajaccio was the birthplace of Napoleon I (who was known as 'the Corsican'). Since 1974 the island has been divided into the departments of **Corse-du-Sud** and **Haute-Corse**. It produces olive oil, wine, timber, wheat, cheese, and fish, and has many tourist resorts along its coasts.

Cort, Henry (1740–1800) British ironmaster. Initially a supplier of wrought iron for naval and ordnance use, he set up his own forge, and patented a process for producing iron bars by passing iron through grooved rollers to avoid the laborious business of hammering. He later patented the puddling process for refining molten pig-iron, which gave Britain a lead in the industry and earned Cort the nickname 'the Great Finer'.

Cortés, Hernando (or **Cortez**) (1485–1547) First of the Spanish conquistadores. Cortés overthrew the Aztec empire with a comparatively small army of adventurers; he conquered its capital city, Tenochtitlán, in 1519 and deposed the emperor, Montezuma. In 1521 he destroyed Tenochtitlán completely and established Mexico City as the new capital of Mexico (then called New Spain), serving briefly as governor of the colony.

corticosteroid See STEROIDS AND STEROID TREATMENT.

Cortona, Pietro da (1596–1669) Italian painter, architect, decorator, and designer: a major figure of BAROQUE ART in Rome. His most famous work as a painter is the huge fresco *Allegory of Divine Providence and Barberini Power* (1633–39) in the Palazzo Barberini in Rome. His masterpiece of architecture is the church of SS. Martina e Luca in Rome (1635–50), the first Baroque church designed and built as a complete unity.

corundum An aluminium oxide mineral occasionally found in the form of brilliantly coloured gemstone varieties such as RUBIES and SAPPHIRES. More commonly it occurs in opaque grey or brown crystalline form; crystals weighing upwards of 170 kg (375 pounds) have been found in South Africa. It occurs chiefly in shales and limestones that have been subjected to contact metamorphism and in veins associated with igneous rocks. Being extremely hard, it is ground for use as an abrasive powder (emery).

Corunna (Spanish **La Coruña**) A seaport in Galicia, north-west Spain, capital of La Coruña province; pop. (1991) 251,300. The Armada sailed from here to attack England in 1588, and the town was sacked by Francis Drake in 1589. It was the site of a battle (1809) in the Peninsular War. Sir John Moore, who died at the battle, is buried in San Carlos Gardens. There are car ferries to the Canary Islands. Its fisheries specialize in sardines and there are canning, cigar-making, textiles, and glass-making industries.

corvette Originally, a small sailing warship introduced in the 17th century. British copies of 18th-century French corvettes were known as SLOOPS. In the mid-19th century flush-decked steam corvettes with a single tier of guns were widely used in the UK. The name was revived briefly in the British Royal Navy at the start of World War II for a class of small anti-submarine convoy escorts.

Corvus The Crow, a CONSTELLATION lying just south of the celestial equator, one of the 48 constellations known to the ancient Greeks. In mythology it represents a crow sent by Apollo to fetch water in a cup; the cup is depicted by the neighbouring constellation of CRATER.

Cos (Greek **Kos**) A Greek island in the south-east Aegean Sea, in the Dodecanese group off the coast of Turkey; area 290 sq km (112 sq miles). The chief town is the port of Kos. In ancient times it was associated with Hippocrates and the Asklepius school of medicine.

Cosgrave, William Thomas (1880–1965) Irish statesman. Determined to gain Irish independence from Britain, he took part in the EASTER RISING (1916). Elected to the British Parliament in 1918 as a SINN FEIN member, he became Minister for Local Government in the provisional government of the Dáil Éireann in 1919. He reluctantly accepted the Anglo-Irish Treaty creating the IRISH FREE STATE. He was president of the Executive Council of the Free State from 1922 to 1932, during which time the international standing of the new state was greatly enhanced. He was Opposition Leader in the Dáil Eireann (1933–44). He was the father of **Liam Cosgrave** (1920–), who in turn became leader of the Fine Gael Party (1965–77) and later Taoiseach (Prime Minister) of the Republic of Ireland (1973–77).

cosmetic Any substance used to beautify, preserve, or alter the appearance of a person. The simplest cosmetics are powders dusted on to the skin: traditional Chinese and Japanese make-up uses a heavy application of rice powder to whiten the face, while *batikha*, an Arabic cosmetic powder, contains ground shells, borax, rice, lemon, and eggs. Many other cosmetics are pastes or creams: Western cosmetics use paraffin wax, carnauba wax, lanolin, and other fats or waxes as a base, to which are added pigments and (for lipstick) flavourings. Elsewhere coloured clays, ochres, charcoal, and various oils or greases are common ingredients of face or body paints. Eye make-up can be composed of many different ingredients. Arabic kohl is a mixture of soot, lead ore, burnt copper, rose water, and sandalwood. Mascara also uses soot, but mixed with paraffin and carnauba waxes to form a solid block. Among hair preparations are shampoos, based on DETERGENTS; conditioners; permanent-wave solutions to shape the hair; and dyes. See also PERFUME.

cosmic background radiation See MICROWAVE BACKGROUND RADIATION.

cosmic rays Radiation discovered by Victor Hess in 1912 when he found that the electrical conductivity of the atmosphere increased with altitude, so indicating a 'radiation from above'. Robert Millikan developed the hypothesis in the 1920s that this radiation was cosmic in origin and consisted of gamma rays; he gave it the name cosmic rays. However, with the development of charged particle detectors (in particular the Geiger–Müller counter) at the end of the decade came the discovery in 1930 by German physicists Walther Bothe and Werner Kölhorster that cosmic rays are high-energy charged particles. At the same time Bruno Rossi established that the radiation showed a small excess from the west which indicated that primary cosmic rays are influenced by the Earth's magnetic field; this implied not only that they were charged particles but that the charge was positive. It is now established that primary cosmic rays (those above the Earth's atmosphere) are the nuclei of atoms stripped of their electrons. Because of the preponderance of hydrogen in the Universe they are mainly protons, together with some alpha particles.

When primary cosmic rays interact with nitrogen and oxygen atoms in the Earth's atmosphere they produce cascades of secondary particles including elementary particles. At the Earth's surface the secondary cosmic rays consist mainly of muons, electrons, and photons with an intensity of about one particle per square centimetre per minute. During very large solar flares the Sun also accelerates particles to cosmic ray energies. These are often referred to as solar cosmic rays.

cosmogony The study of the origin and development of the Universe, or of a particular system in the Universe, such as a planetary system. The age of the Solar System has allowed sufficient time for all the planets to settle down into orbits that are in the same direction and in nearly the same plane. Its size, mass, and speed of rotation suggest that it condensed from a much more massive cloud of gas and dust. Stars are formed from clouds of gas and dust in the spaces between other stars, particularly in nebulae. A large or rapidly rotating cloud can condense into a double star. If the cloud is small or rotates slowly then all the mass is pulled into a single star. In between these extremes the condensing star is surrounded by a nebular cloud, parts of which may subsequently condense to form planets. It is now thought that the formation of planetary systems is common during the first stage of star formation and that about one in four of the stars in the Universe has a planetary system.

cosmography A description or mapping of general features of the Universe.

cosmology The science or theory of the creation and development of the Universe. Modern science debates whether an infinite and unchanging Universe is maintained by the continuous creation of matter from the void, or whether a big bang both created and dispersed matter in an expansion which continues today, and which may be reversed if the Universe is dense enough. The last of these interpretations is favoured by the detection of a radiation field permeating the Universe, believed to be the cool remnant of the initial fireball.

Cossack (from Turkish, 'adventurer' or 'guerrilla') A people in south Russia. They were descended from refugees from religious persecution in POLAND and Muscovy, and from peasants fleeing the taxes and obligations of the feudal system. Settling in mainly autonomous tribal groups around the rivers Don and Dnieper, they played an important role in the history of the Ukraine. A frontier life-style encouraged military prowess and horsemanship, males aged 16–60 years being obliged to bear arms. They were democratic, directly electing their leaders or *hetmen*. Their relations with Russia included military service and military alliance, especially against the Turks, but there were rebellions against Russia under the leaderships of Stenka Razin (1667–69), Iran Mazeppa (1709), and Yemelyan Pugachev (1773–74). Ukrainian Cossackdom experienced a revival following the breakup of the Soviet Union in 1991. There are 15,000 registered Cossacks in the Ukraine.

cost (in economics) Expenditure incurred in the process of production. In the short run, costs can be classified into fixed (or indirect) and variable (or direct) costs. Fixed costs, in some cases also known as overheads, are costs which vary with output. They have to be paid even when there is no output. Examples include rent, rates, service charges for capital GOODS, and INTEREST payments. Variable costs are those which vary with output, such as wages, raw material, and costs of intermediate goods. Unit costs are calculated by dividing total production costs by the number of units of output produced, thus arriving at the average cost per unit of output.

Costa, Lúcio (1902–63) French-born Brazilian architect, town planner, and architectural historian. He headed the group that designed the Ministry of Education in Rio de Janeiro (1937–43) and achieved a worldwide reputation with his plan for Brazil's new capital Brasilia, which was chosen by an international jury in 1956.

Costa Blanca (Spanish, 'white coast') A major resort region on the Mediterranean coast of south-east Spain.

Costa Brava (Spanish, 'wild coast') A major resort region to the north of Barcelona, on the Mediterranean coast of north-east Spain.

cost accounting The provision of cost information for management purposes. Cost information relates to the need to determine costs of production and to determine profitability and efficiency. Cost information is also necessary in planning and controlling budgets within the organization, usually on an annual cycle. Budget and cost control enables efficient cost standards to be maintained and involves a system of reporting to managers.

Costa del Sol (Spanish, 'coast of the Sun') A major resort region on the Mediterranean coast of south Spain. Marbella and Torremolinos are the principal resort towns.

Costa Dorada (Spanish, 'golden coast') A resort region on the Mediterranean coast of Spain to the south of Barcelona.

Costa Rica A small country on the Central American isthmus, between Nicaragua and Panama.

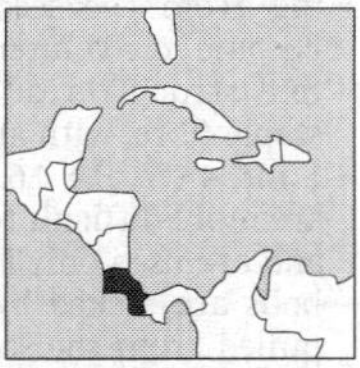

Physical. It has a Caribbean coast on its north-east and a Pacific coast on its south-west. While the coastal lowlands have a tropical climate, a range of volcanic mountains occupies the centre of the country, providing plateaux which have a mild climate. There are several peaks over 3,350 m (11,000 feet).

Economy. The soil is very fertile and supports livestock farming and some of the finest coffee in the world. Bananas are grown and cattle-rearing is important. The chemical and textile industries also contribute to the economy.

History. Costa Rica was discovered by COLUMBUS during his fourth voyage to the New World in 1502. Permanent settlement did not occur until 1564 when Juan Vásquez de Coronado, with settlers from Nicaragua, founded Cartago on the Meseta Central. The small Indian population fell victim to disease, leaving the ethnic make-up of the area mostly European. Costa Rica formed part of the captaincy-general of Guatemala until 1821, when it joined the independent Mexican empire (1821–23) and then the United Provinces of Central America (1823–38). In 1838 it became an independent republic. A policy of isolation and stability, together with agricultural fertility, brought considerable British and US investment in the 19th century. Apart from the brief dictatorship of Federico Tinoco Granados (1917–19), Costa Rica was remarkable in the late 19th and early 20th centuries for its democratic tradition. After World War II left-wing parties emerged, including the communist. The socialist Presidents Otilio Ulate (1948–53) and José Figueres (1953–58, 1970–74), tried to disband the army, nationalize banks, and curb US investment. A new constitution, granting universal suffrage and abolishing the armed forces, was introduced in 1949. Political tensions in the 1970s were aggravated by economic problems and by the arrival of many fugitives from neighbouring states. President Luis Alberto Monge (1982–86) had to impose severe economic restraint. In 1987 President Oscar Arias Sánchez (1986–90) put forward a peace-plan for Central America, to which President Reagan reacted by reducing US aid to the country. Severe economic difficulties continued under Presidents Rafael Calderón Fournier (1990–94) and José María Figueres (1994–), with an IMF-imposed austerity programme and widespread industrial unrest in the early 1990s.

Capital: San José
Area: 51,100 sq km (19,730 sq mi)
Population: 3,344,000 (1995)
Currency: 1 Costa Rican colón = 100 céntimos
Religions: Roman Catholic 88.6%; other (mostly Protestant) 11.4%
Ethnic Groups: European 87.0%; Mestizo 7.0%; Black/Mulatto 3.0%; East Asian (mostly Chinese) 2.0%; Amerindian 1.0%
Languages: Spanish (official); other minority languages
International Organizations: UN; OAS

cost–benefit analysis A method of appraising investment projects which takes into account not only the cash outflows and inflows expected to accrue to the investor, but the total economic impact by attempting to measure social consequences in money terms, and by including external (spillover) effects on other parts of the economy. The method is typically used by national and local government authorities in assessing whether major investment projects, public or private, should proceed.

cot death (medical name **sudden infant death syndrome, SIDS**) The sudden unexpected death of an infant less than two years old (peak occurrence between two and six months) from an unidentifiable cause. There appear to be many factors involved, the most important of which is the position in which the baby is laid to sleep: babies who sleep on their fronts (the prone position) have an increased risk. Other factors increasing the risk include parental smoking, overheating with bedding, prematurity, and a history of a cot death within the family. About half the affected infants will have had a viral upper respiratory tract infection within the 48 hours preceding their death. Since 1993, when these risk factors were identified, there has been a 55 per cent drop in cot deaths.

Côte d'Ivoire (formerly **Ivory Coast**) A tropical West African country, bounded on the west by Liberia and Guinea, on the north by Mali and Burkina Faso, and on the east by Ghana.

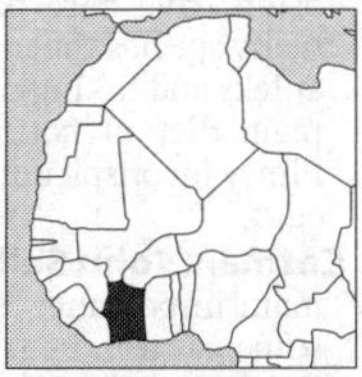

Physical. Its south-facing coastline is rocky in the west but elsewhere has sand-bars and lagoons. Three rivers run through the hot, rain-forested lowlands. In the central belt coffee is grown. In winter the drying HARMATTAN blows down from savannah-covered sandstone uplands. The Nimba Mountains in the west contain minerals, including iron.

Economy. The economy is primarily agricultural, with main exports including cocoa, coffee, cotton, tropical timber, and vegetable oils. Offshore oil reserves are exploited, but output does not meet domestic requirements. Industries, such as oil-refining, food-processing, textiles, and chemicals are well established, and there is a well-developed system of hydraulic electricity production from dams. Mineral deposits include iron, cobalt, bauxite, nickel, manganese, and diamonds.

History. There were scattered and isolated coastal settlements in the region when European slave traders arrived in the 15th century. The French had established trading posts in the area by the end of the 17th century and in the 19th century made treaties with local chiefs. France obtained rights on the coast in 1842, establishing a colony in 1893, which in 1904 became a territory of French West Africa. In 1933 most of the territory of Upper Volta was added to the Côte d'Ivoire, but in 1948 this area was returned to the reconstituted Upper Volta, today BURKINA FASO. The Côte d'Ivoire became an autonomous republic within the FRENCH COMMUNITY in 1958, and achieved full independence in 1960, becoming a one-party republic governed by the moderate Democratic

Party of the Côte d'Ivoire and with Félix Houphouët-Boigny its president. The country has large petroleum deposits and a developing industrial sector, but falling cocoa and coffee prices adversely affected the economy during the late 1980s. The resulting policy of economic austerity caused unrest and demonstrations. In the first multi-party elections in November 1990, the President's Democratic Party won all but 10 seats in the National Assembly. Following Houphouët-Boigny's death in 1993, Henri Konan Bedie (1934–) was elected President in 1995.

Capital: Abidjan (capital-designate, Yamoussoukro)
Area: 322,463 sq km (124,471 sq mi)
Population: 14,253,000 (1995)
Currency: 1 CFA franc = 100 centimes
Religions: Traditional beliefs 65.0%; Muslim 23.0%; Christian 12.0%
Ethnic Groups: Akan 27.0%; Mande 24.0%; Kru 18.0%; Senufo 12.0%; Lagoon 8.0%; Lobi 5.0%
Languages: French (official); Akan; Kru; local languages
International Organizations: ECOWAS; Non-Aligned Movement; OAU; UN; Franc Zone

cotinga A bird of the family Cotingidae, comprising about 70 species mostly native to rain forest in South and Central America. The group includes the bell bird (*Procnias* species), cock-of-the-rock (*Rupicola* species), and umbrella birds (*Cephalopterus* species). Although one or two species are only sparrow-sized, most are thrush- to crow-sized. The males of some species are dull brown or green, but most are strikingly coloured – red, purple, and blue being common colours; they often have bare patches of skin on the face. In many species the males are polygamous, displaying at leks and taking no part in raising the young. The main diet of cotingas is fruit. Most build very flimsy inconspicuous nests and lay only one or two eggs.

Cotman, John Sell (1782–1842) British painter. His main importance is as a watercolourist and landscape painter; he is regarded as one of the leading figures of the Norwich School. His early watercolours, including *Greta Bridge* (1805), are notable for their bold configurations of light and shade and have been compared in their flat areas of colour to Japanese painting. In the 1820s he developed a more richly coloured style, as in *The Drop Gate* (*c.*1826).

cotoneaster A deciduous, evergreen shrub or small tree, including a few climbers and scramblers. Cotoneasters are members of the rose family Rosaceae, like thorns and rowans, and form a genus with some 50 or so species. They are native to mountainous areas of the Old World temperate zone. Many are cultivated as ground-cover and wall plants, notably *Cotoneaster horizontalis* of Japan. Their seeds are dispersed by birds, attracted by the red or black colour of the fruits, which they eat.

Cotonou The largest city, chief port, and *de facto* capital of Benin, on the Guinea coast of West Africa; pop. (1992) 536,830. The National Assembly, Presidency, and foreign embassies are all located here due to the decline of PORTO NOVO. Light industries are developing to the east of the port.

Cotopaxi One of the highest active volcanoes in the world, rising to 5,897 m (19,347 ft) in the Andes of central Ecuador. Its Quechua name means 'shining peak'.

Cotswold Hills A range of limestone hills, largely in Gloucestershire, England, noted for its sheep pastures and its picturesque villages which were formerly centres of the woollen industry. The Cotswolds rise to 333 m (1,092 ft) at Cleeve Cloud near Cheltenham.

cotton A plant of the genus *Gossypium*, a relation of the mallow and hollyhock, and a member of the family Malvaceae. This rather complex genus of annual and perennial plants is grown throughout the world in subtropical regions for the valuable textile FIBRE it produces around the seeds.

Cotton accounts for almost 50 per cent (by weight) of world fibre production. The USA is the world's leading producer, followed by Russia, China, and India. The fruits are capsules known as bolls which split open when ripe, to reveal a mass of white fibres. This is largely 'lint', and consists of CELLULOSE hairs up to 50 mm (2 inches) long growing from the seed-coat. As the hairs dry, they become convoluted collapsed tubes, enabling a fine, strong thread to be spun. Cotton is a short-staple fibre, with an average fibre length between 1 and 4 cm (0.4–1.6 inches). The longer-fibre types are more difficult to grow, more expensive to buy, and are used only for the finest yarns. Usually the bolls are picked by hand and the lint is torn or pulled from the seed-coat by machines known as **cotton gins** (invented by WHITNEY in 1743); mechanical harvesters are common only in the USA. A fuzz of hairs, too short to be spun, is also extracted, and is used for cotton wool. Cotton is readily bleached and dyed; when blended with polyester fibre, it makes durable, easy-care fabrics.

A cooking or salad oil may be extracted from the seed, and the protein-rich seedcake is a valuable livestock food and can even be used as a nitrogenous fertilizer.

cotton spinner See SEA CUCUMBER.

cotton stainer See RED BUG.

cotyledon One of the first leaves of the plant embryo within a seed. Cotyledons are usually different in form from subsequent leaves, and DICOTYLEDONS have two, MONOCOTYLEDONS one. In some plants they remain within the seed, in others they come above ground at germination, turn green, and photosynthesize.

coucal (or **ground cuckoo**) A bird of the genus *Centropus*, which belongs to the cuckoo family Cuculidae. Coucals are found in parts of Africa, India, south-east Asia, some tropical islands, and Australia. Most of the nine species are brownish or black and are long-tailed and short-winged; they are weak fliers. Unlike many other members of the family, coucals do not parasitize other birds, but incubate their eggs and raise their own young. They build untidy, domed nests with a side entrance, usually fairly low down in thick vegetation. They eat insects and other small animals.

couch grass A particularly troublesome weed of cultivated ground. It is also known by several other names, such as scutch or twitch-grass, all applying to the species *Elymus repens*. It spreads rapidly by means of underground stems or rhizomes. Cultivation techniques, particularly with mechanical equipment, tend to divide and propagate the plant. As a wild grass species, it is widely distributed throughout Europe, northern Africa, Siberia, and North America. Other members of the genus *Agropyron* have couch as part of their common name.

coudé telescope See TELESCOPE.

cougar See PUMA.

coulomb (symbol C) The SI UNIT of ELECTRIC CHARGE. By definition, a charge of one coulomb passes any point in an electric circuit when a current of one ampere flows for one second. It is named in honour of the French physicist, Charles-Augustin de COULOMB.

Coulomb, Charles-Augustin de (1736–1806) French military engineer. He conducted research on structural mechanics, elasticity, friction, electricity, and magnetism. He is best known for **Coulomb's Law**, established with a sensitive torsion balance in 1785, according to which the forces between two electrical charges are proportional to the product of the sizes of the charges and inversely proportional to the square of the distance between them. See PERMITTIVITY.

Council of Europe An association of European states, independent of the European Community. It meets in Strasbourg. Founded in 1949, it is committed to the principles of freedom and the rule of law, and to safeguarding the political and cultural heritage of Europe. Its executive organ is the Committee of Ministers, and most of its conclusions take the form of international agreements (known as *European Conventions*) or recommendations to governments. One of the Council's principal achievements is the European Convention of Human Rights (1950) under which was established the European Commission and the European Court of Human Rights.

counselling (in psychology) Guidance offered in the form of discussion rather than any specific type of therapy. Counsellors may have a quantity of specialized knowledge on particular problems, possible solutions, and the potential pitfalls of different solutions, but often they see their role as assisting those who consult them to find their own solutions. Counselling may be available to help people adapt after physical injury, traumatic shock, bereavement, marriage break-up, when a family has been incapacitated by mental or physical injury, when a marriage is unhappy, when a child has been abused, or when career advice is needed. It may be offered by psychologists, doctors, social workers, or trained lay people. Counselling should be distinguished from PSYCHOTHERAPY, although there is some overlap. It is less intensive and sometimes more directive, and its clients may have a much wider range of concerns for which they require guidance.

counterglow See GEGENSCHEIN.

counter-intelligence services Government organizations dedicated to prevent the penetration and subversion of the intelligence services, and to maintain control of strategically important information, including technology. This defensive purpose can be allied to that of manipulating the adversary's intelligence services by penetration and subversion, through the use of double-agents or 'disinformation' (the planting of inaccurate or misleading intelligence).

counterpoint The art of combining two or more independent melodic lines in music. These may differ in rhythm and outline, yet in combination they make perfect sense. Music conceived contrapuntally requires the listener to take in the shape of each melody – to listen 'horizontally'. As the melodies pass one another they produce a vertical harmony. Until almost the end of the 19th century the degree of dissonance permitted in the resultant harmonies was strictly controlled. In 20th-century counterpoint the movement of parts is usually free of harmonic inhibitions.

Counter-Reformation A revival in the ROMAN CATHOLIC CHURCH between the mid-16th and mid-17th centuries. It had its origins in reform movements which were independent of the Protestant REFORMATION, but it increasingly became identified with, and took its name from, efforts to 'counter' the Protestant Reformation. There were three main ecclesiastical aspects. First a reformed papacy, with a succession of popes who had a notably more spiritual outlook than their immediate predecessors, and a number of reforms in the church's central government initiated by them. Secondly, the foundation of new religious orders, notably the Oratorians and in 1540 the Society of Jesus (JESUITS), and the reform of older orders, notably the Capuchin reform of the FRANCISCANS. Thirdly, the Council of TRENT (1545–63), which defined and clarified Catholic doctrine on most points in dispute with Protestants and instituted important moral and disciplinary reforms within the Catholic Church, including the provision of a better education for the clergy through theological colleges called seminaries. All this led to a flowering of Catholic spirituality at the popular level, but also to an increasingly anti-Protestant mentality. The movement became political through its links with Catholic rulers, notably PHILIP II of Spain, who sought to re-establish Roman Catholicism by force. The stalemate between Catholics and Protestants was effectively recognized by the Treaty of WESTPHALIA in 1648, which brought to an end the Thirty Years War and in a sense concluded the Counter-Reformation period.

counter-revolution The attempt to overturn or reverse the consequences of REVOLUTION, usually by subversion or military action. Many theories of revolution also contain the notion that the forces of conservatism or reaction, after initial defeat, will regroup and attempt to regain power. In this cause, they may be supported from outside the country.

country music Music with its roots in the rural South of the USA, derived from traditional oral music brought from Europe. The music was first recorded in the 1920s, when it was known as 'hillbilly music'. Initially there were many regional styles, but the nationwide spread of the music through records and the radio helped to forge a recognizable mainstream style. However, in the 1930s regional variations continued outside the mainstream: examples include cajun music (from French-speaking rural Louisiana), Western swing (a blend of hillbilly music with early jazz), honky tonk (an urban sound from Texas), and bluegrass (from the Appalachian mountains). Meanwhile, mainstream country and western continued to develop; in the 1950s and 1960s artists such as Jim Reeves, Johnny Cash, and Patsy Cline spread its appeal to (mainly white) urban communities. More recently, artists such as Glen Campbell, Dolly Parton, Garth Brooks, and k.d. lang have developed a style closer to that of popular music.

coup d'état The sudden overthrow of government, especially by military force. The resulting government may assume direct military rule (see MILITARY GOVERNMENT) or rule by a faction sponsored by the military (see JUNTA). In a coup, it is simply the government that undergoes sudden change; a REVOLUTION, on the other hand, involves a radical overturn of a country's entire political, social, and ideological system.

Couperin, François (1668–1733) French composer, organist, and harpsichordist. A composer at the court of Louis XIV, he is principally known for his harpsichord works, particularly those 220 pieces contained in his four books (1713; 1716–17; 1722; 1730). These pieces are characterized by extensive ornamentation and a blend of Italian and French styles.

couplet A pair of rhyming verse lines, usually of the same length. Chaucer established the use of couplets in English, notably in the *Canterbury Tales*, using rhymed iambic PENTAMETERS later known as 'heroic couplets', a form perfected in the 17th and 18th centuries by Dryden and Pope. Couplets of ALEXANDRINES were the standard verse-form of French drama in the age of Racine. A couplet may also stand alone as an epigram, or form part of a larger STANZA, or (as in Shakespeare) round off a SONNET or a dramatic scene.

coupling, railway A mechanism used to connect the vehicles of a train. On early trains a short chain transferred the pull from one vehicle to the next. Buffers enabled vehicles to be pushed against one another without damage. Chains were later replaced by screw couplings, which kept the vehicles in close contact, so minimizing 'snatch' and heavy contact when starting and stopping. Most vehicles throughout the world now use buckeye couplings, which may be connected or disconnected automatically. In modern designs the pipes and cables between vehicles may be integrated with the coupling.

courante A dance of French origin, popular in the 17th century. It was quick and in triple time, and was often used as a lively contrast to the ALLEMANDE. The courante appears in Italian sources as the *corrente* and in England as the coranto. It is one of the basic movements of the dance SUITE.

Courbet, Gustave (1819–77) French painter. A leader of the 19th-century realist school of painting, he favoured an unidealized choice of subject-matter that did not exclude the ugly or vulgar. Important works include *Burial at Ornans* (1850) and *Painter in His Studio* (1855).

courgette See MARROW.

courser A WADING BIRD of the family Glareoliae, closely related to PRATINCOLES. Coursers occur in the Old World, where they live in open, dryish country or deserts. The best known of the seven species is the cream-coloured courser, *Cursorius cursor*, of semi-desert in North Africa and the Middle East. This species is about 20 cm (8 inches) long, and pale sandy coloured, with a greyish crown and striking black and white stripes behind the eye. Coursers feed mainly on insects and lay their eggs (usually two) in a scrape on bare ground.

Courtauld, Samuel (1876–1947) British industrialist. He was a director of his family's silk firm and one of the earliest British collectors of French impressionist and post-impressionist paintings. He presented his collection to the University of London, endowing the Courtauld Institute of Art, and bequeathed to it his house in Portman Square, London.

court-martial A judicial court consisting of military officers with jurisdiction to try to punish those charged with military offences. The word also refers to the proceedings of such a court. Most countries have their own military codes of justice, and their own military courts, with the exception of Germany, where military personnel are tried in the civilian courts. In the UK, the court-martial usually consists of a group of serving officers, assisted by a legally qualified judge-advocate, who sums up the evidence and advises on the law.

court of law A place in which justice is administered. The function of the court is to decide disputes, award DAMAGES, impose punishments, authorize acts for which application has been made (such as divorce), and exercise other administrative functions. The jurisdiction and hierarchy of courts vary from country to country. One distinction may be between civil courts and criminal courts; another common distinction exists between courts of general jurisdiction, which deal with a variety of cases, and courts of special jurisdiction, confined to limited issues (such as COURTS-MARTIAL or JUVENILE COURTS). A further distinction exists between lower and higher courts: lower courts deal with less important matters, and may be presided over by a layman (such as a MAGISTRATE) rather than a JUDGE; more difficult or serious cases are heard by superior courts, often presided over by judges of higher status. An appeal against the decision of a lower court may be referred to an appellate court; there may be different levels of such appeal courts, culminating in a court of ultimate authority, such as the House of Lords in the UK, the French *Cour de Cassation* (subject to the EUROPEAN COURT OF JUSTICE), or the US Supreme Court.

Courtrai, Battle of (11 July 1302) Sometimes known as the 'battle of the Golden Spurs'. Philip IV of France had attempted to overrun FLANDERS but Flemish troops fought the French at Courtrai. Flemish burghers defeated the French nobility, and, in celebration of victory, hung their spurs in the churches of Bruges. The battle of Courtrai was one of the most significant defeats suffered by France in the 14th century. Charles VI of France avenged this insult by sacking Courtrai in 1382.

courtship (in biology) Behaviour that, in many animals, helps bring together opposite sexes of the same species at the right time and place, and in a suitable position for successful mating. Sound, scent, touch, and DISPLAY may all be used in courtship, and the pattern and combination of signals is unique to each species. This usually prevents individuals of different species from trying to mate.

A particularly important aspect of courtship is that it may contain features evolved through sexual selection, which help an individual select a good mate: one who is healthy and disease-free, good at defending a territory, or likely to be good at providing resources for the young.

Cousteau, Jacques-Yves (1910–97) French oceanographer and film director. A naval officer interested in underwater exploration, he began using a camera under water in 1939 and devised the scuba apparatus. Cousteau made three feature films and several popular series for television. In his last years he turned increasingly to biological research and marine conservation issues.

covalent bond See CHEMICAL BOND; COVALENT COMPOUND.

covalent compound A compound containing atoms joined by covalent bonds (see CHEMICAL BOND). If one pair of electrons is shared then a single bond is formed; with two pairs of electrons a double bond; and with three pairs of electrons a triple bond. In a molecular compound, such as carbon dioxide (CO_2), it may be possible to distinguish between individual molecules, since the distances between atoms in a given molecule are shorter than the distances between adjacent molecules. Molecular compounds tend to be soluble. Polar molecules, such as ethanol (CH_3OH), dissolve in polar solvents, such as water, whereas non-polar molecules, such as iodine (I_2), dissolve in non-polar solvents, such as hydrocarbons. In cases where compounds consist of covalent molecules bonded by intermolecular forces to form larger structures (such as silica, SiO_2), it is not possible to consider individual molecules; the entire crystal is composed of a 'giant molecule'. Such substances have high melting-points and boiling-points, and tend to be hard and insoluble.

covenant (in law) A promise made by one person to another in a formal document known as a deed. Such promises are often contained in the conveyancing deeds by which land is transferred, for example to restrict the purchaser's use of the land to residential purposes. In a commercial context, covenant is an agreement between a borrower and a lender. It specifies conditions of the loan which are legally binding on the borrower.

covenant (in theology) The central notion of Jewish belief and religious practice, and an important concept in Christian theology of God's commitment to his people. The Jewish covenant was originally offered to Noah by God, who promised to protect Noah's family and later generations from the great flood, and sealed his promise with a rainbow. An unquestioning obedience to God's will earned Abraham a covenant between God and the Jewish peoples: the gift of the land that was to be Israel and the blessing of descendants that were to become the Jewish nation. The practice of CIRCUMCISION (Hebrew, *brit*) seven days after birth, connects the individual Jewish male child to a larger covenant. The covenant was codified in the Ten Commandments, recalling God's deliverance of the Jews from Egypt. The ensuing rules govern life in minute detail and form the religious and cultural basis of Judaism. They include diet (see KOSHER), dress, morality, and religious ritual. The binding nature of the covenant was reasserted by the PROPHETS, who recognized their nation's disobedience towards God and demanded the people's return to righteousness. Some prophets referred to a 'new covenant', a notion later applied in Christianity by Christ to the imminent sacrifice of his life, which seals a renewed covenant between God and the new Israel, the Christian Church.

Covenanter Originally a Scot who opposed the ecclesiastical innovations of Charles I of England. Drawn from all parts of Scotland and all sections of society, Covenanters subscribed to the National Covenant of 1638. This was a revised version of a previous covenant (1581), which had been signed by James VI of Scotland. They swore to resist 'episcopal' (the church governed by bishops) religious changes, and, in the event of such changes, they set up a full PRESBYTERIAN system and defended it in the BISHOPS' WARS. They hoped to impose their system on England in 1643, by drawing up the SOLEMN LEAGUE AND COVENANT with the LONG PARLIAMENT. Disappointed in this, they turned in 1650 to Charles II, who signed the Covenant, but then abjured it at his RESTORATION (1660), condemning it as an unlawful oath. In Scotland in 1661 the episcopacy was re-established, and Covenanters were badly treated. In 1690, the Presbyterian Church of Scotland was established.

Covent Garden A district in central London, originally the convent garden of the Abbey of Westminster. It was the site for 300 years of London's chief fruit and vegetable market, which in 1974 was moved to Nine Elms, Battersea. The market site has now been developed as a large shopping area. The Royal Opera House is situated here (see COVENT GARDEN THEATRE).

Covent Garden Theatre The London theatre devoted since the mid-19th century to opera, now known as the Royal Opera House. It opened in 1732 as the Theatre Royal, sharing with DRURY LANE a monopoly of legitimate theatre in London until 1843. In 1773 it presented the first performance of Goldsmith's *She Stoops to Conquer*. Its dramatic heyday was the early 19th century, under the managements of KEMBLE and Macready. It was rebuilt twice after fires in 1808 and 1856. It is the current home of both the Royal Opera and the Royal Ballet Company. In 1997 it closed for two years for extensive rebuilding and refurbishment.

Coventry An industrial city in the West Midlands, central England; pop. (1991) 292,600. Formerly a centre of the clothing industry, Coventry now produces vehicles, machinery and telecommunications equipment in addition to man-made fibres. Its cathedral (1443), badly damaged during World War II, was replaced by a new cathedral designed by Sir Basil SPENCE and consecrated in 1962. It is the site of the University of Warwick (1965) and Coventry University (formerly Coventry Polytechnic) which was established in 1992.

Coverdale, Miles (1488–1568) English biblical scholar. He translated the first complete printed English Bible (1535), published in Zurich while he was in exile for preaching against confession and images. He also edited the Great Bible, brought out in 1539 by the printer Richard Grafton (*c*.1513–*c*.1572).

cow See CATTLE.

Coward, Sir Noël (1899–1973) British dramatist, composer, actor, and producer. His acting career began in 1911, his first popular song, 'Forbidden Fruit', dates from 1916, and his first play, *I'll Leave it to You*, from 1920. There followed successful comedies (*Hay Fever*, 1925), dramas (*The Vortex*, 1924), revues (*This Year of Grace*, 1928), and operettas (*Bitter Sweet*, 1929). Two comedies, *Private Lives* (1930) and *Blithe Spirit* (1942), are outstanding. His music, inextricably linked to his own brilliant lyrics, ranges from the delicately sentimental to the satirical. Coward was also active in film-making. Among his successes were the war film *In Which We Serve* (1942), of which he was producer, co-director, writer, and star, and *Brief Encounter* (1945), which he wrote and produced.

cowbird Any one of seven species of bird in the family Icteridae, which also includes the New World orioles or blackbirds. Cowbirds vary in size from that of a thrush to that of a small crow. Virtually all come from subtropical and tropical America. Some of the species are parasitic, laying their eggs in the nests of other birds. The brown-headed cowbird, *Molothrus ater*, parasitizes a wide range of small birds in North America, while the bay-winged cowbird, *Molothrus badius*, steals nests built by other species but raises its young itself.

cowboy Originally, a lawless marauder. The name was first applied to some pro-British gangs in the USA during the American War of Independence, who roamed the neutral ground of Westchester county in New York state (their Revolutionary counterparts were 'skinners'). By the 1870s, a cowboy described a herder of cattle on the Great Plains. The cattle industry spread across the Great Plains from Texas to Canada and westward to the Rocky Mountains. The introduction of barbed wire to fence in ranches rapidly encroached on the open ranges, and by 1895 railway expansion had made trail-driving uneconomical, and cowboys settled to work on the cattle ranches.

Cowes A town on the Isle of Wight, England, on the River Medina; pop. (1981) 16,300. It is internationally famous as a yachting centre and hosts the annual Cowes Week in August. Built by Henry VIII, Cowes Castle is the home of the Royal Yacht Squadron.

Cowley, Abraham (1618–67) English METAPHYSICAL POET and essayist. During the English Civil War he contributed to the Royalist cause with a satire, *The Puritan and the Papist* (1643). His other works include *The Mistress* (1647), love poems, 'Miscellanies' in *Poems* (1656), which contains the scriptural epic 'Davideis', and 'Pindarique Odes', which employ the irregular Pindaric ode that was to influence later poets. His prose works, which combine grace and simplicity with bright rhythmic discourse, include *A Proposition for the Advancement of Learning* (1661) and 'Essays' (1668).

Cowper, William (1731–1800) British poet. He wrote *Olney Hymns* (1779) with the evangelical minister John Newton (1725–1807), contributing 'Oh! for a Closer Walk with God' amongst other well-known hymns. His famous comic ballad *John Gilpin* appeared in 1782. Cowper is best known, however, for his long poem *The Task* (1785), notable for its intimate sketches of rural life.

cowrie (or **cowry**) A beautifully shaped and often brightly coloured gastropod MOLLUSC. The smooth outer shell is spiralled inside, just like that of related snails. The opening to the shell is toothed, and from this the soft body is extended in a fold over the top of the shell, most of it being covered by the living animal. Cowries feed upon colonial marine invertebrates such as bryozoans and sea squirts. Large tropical species may be spectacularly marked with spots and banding, and some are common enough for the shells to be used as currency in certain island communities.

cowslip See PRIMROSE.

Cox, David (1783–1859) British landscape painter, one of the best-known water-colourists of his period. In spite of a certain anecdotal homeliness, his style was broad and vigorous, and in 1836 he began to paint on a rough wrapping paper that was particularly suited to it. A similar paper was subsequently marketed as 'Cox Paper'. He wrote several treatises on landscape painting in water-colour, and frequently in oils.

coyote A species of wild canid, *Canis latrans*, confined to North America. It is very similar to a wolf in appearance but considerably smaller, being about 60 cm (24 inches) at the shoulder. Its distribution range overlaps that of wolves, but it can be distinguished from a wolf by the downward carriage of the tail when running, by the differing skull dimensions, and from the fact that the coyote does not form packs. It feeds on small mammals, birds, frogs, and fish, as well as carrion, but its favourite prey is rabbits and hares. Although not a serious pest, it is known as a sheep-killer in certain regions. Alterations of the habitat and the near extermination of wolves have led to a considerable extension of the coyote's range. In the eastern USA, it has hybridized with domestic dogs and wolves.

coypu A South American species of large RODENT, *Myocaster coypus*. Coypus look like huge rats but are related to guinea-pigs. They are aquatic but feed on waterside vegetation. Their soft, dense underfur, known as nutria, is of commercial value, and they were once farmed in Britain, USA, and elsewhere. Many escapes occurred and they are now widely established as a feral pest.

Cozens, Alexander (1717–86) British landscape draughtsman, the first major British artist to devote himself entirely to landscape. He worked almost exclusively in monochrome, and both his 'blot drawings' and his more formal compositions use intense lights and darks with masterly effect. His son, **John Robert Cozens** (1752–97), was also an outstanding landscape painter in water-colour.

CPU See CENTRAL PROCESSING UNIT.

crab Probably the best-known CRUSTACEAN, which is found throughout the shallow seas and tidal zone. Like other large crustaceans, such as prawns, crayfish, and lobsters, they are decapods: they have ten main walking-legs, the first pair of which are enlarged as pincers. Three front pairs of limbs are modified as mouthparts, giving a complex array of feeding structures. Crabs can be recognized by the large carapace (shell), which is expanded laterally to cover the respiratory gills; the remaining abdominal segments are tucked underneath this, giving the crab its squat, oval shape. Most are also characterized by sideways locomotion, some ghost crabs achieving 6.5 km/hour (4 miles per hour) over sand.

Crabs range from a few millimetres (tenths of an inch) long in such species as pea crabs, *Dissodactylus*, which live inside bivalves' shells, to the dimensions of spider crabs, *Macrocheira kaempferi*, the largest of all ARTHROPODS, which has a span across the legs of 4 m (13 feet). Crabs live in oceans, coastal waters, and rivers, and a few have been successful on land. Most are bottom-dwelling, though a few can swim powerfully. All crabs grow by casting, or shedding, their old EXOSKELETON, revealing a larger but temporarily soft new CUTICLE beneath.

Crab See CANCER.

crab apple See APPLE.

Crabbe, George (1754–1832) British poet. Crabbe's name is associated with grimly realistic narrative poems, such as *The Village* (1783) and *The Borough* (1810); the latter was based on his native Aldeburgh in Suffolk, and included tales of Peter Grimes and Ellen Orford. These later provided the subject-matter for Benjamin Britten's opera *Peter Grimes* (1945).

Crab Nebula A luminous gaseous NEBULA, in the constellation of Taurus. It has a filamentary structure and is expanding as a remnant of the SUPERNOVA of 1054. In 1948 it was found to emit radio waves (TAURUS A) and in 1964 it was found to be an X-ray source (Taurus X-1).

cracking A chemical process in which long-chain HYDROCARBON molecules, particularly those derived from PETROLEUM REFINING, are broken down into smaller, economically important molecules such as PETROL. The process is used particularly to increase the proportion of petrol produced from petroleum to as high as 80 per cent. Cracking is also used to produce raw materials for the chemical industry. Thermal cracking, the earliest system developed, was first used commercially in 1913. It involved distilling batches of fairly heavy gas oil at about 500°C, and pressures up to 25 bar. Catalytic cracking, used since the 1930s, produces more precise results than thermal cracking, and eliminates the need for high pressures. In the chemical industry, thermal cracking of ethane, PROPANE, naphtha, and gas oil is used to manufacture ETHENE and a variety of other compounds. Hydrocracking is basically catalytic cracking in a container pressurized by pumping in hydrogen gas. Valuable products are obtained without simultaneous formation of coke and gas, and the process is flexible enough to be applicable to many different oil fractions.

Cracow (Polish **Kraków**) An industrial and tourist city in southern Poland, at the head of navigation on the upper River Vistula; pop. (1990) 750,540. Originally an important commercial centre, Cracow was capital of Poland from 1302 to 1609. With the growth of Warsaw and the destruction of the city by the Swedes in 1655, the city went into decline but recovered in the 19th century when it developed into an industrial and railway centre. During the Communist period its industry was promoted by the building of a new town, Nova Huta, housing the Lenin steel works. It also has chemical, printing, and ceramic industries.

Craig, Edward Gordon (1872–1966) British stage designer and theorist. Originally an actor, he became an innovatory designer. His theory on acting, which involved the actor becoming the director's puppet, and on scenery (including movable screens), are collated in *On the Art of the Theatre* (1911), and had great influence in Europe and the USA.

Cranach, Lucas (known as **Cranach the Elder**) (1472–1553) German painter. A member of the Danube School, he is noted for his early religious pictures, in which landscape plays a prominent part, as in *The Rest on the Flight into Egypt* (1504). He also painted portraits, including several of his friend Martin Luther, and is regarded as the originator of the full-length secular portrait as a subject in its own right. His son **Lucas**, known as **Cranach the Younger** (1515–86), continued working in the same tradition.

cranberry The fruit of the evergreen species of the genus *Vaccinium*, part of the heather family. Cranberries are native to North America, Europe, and northern Asia, and are closely related to bilberries and blueberries. The low, creeping shrubs bear small, bright red berries, about 1 cm (0.5 inch) across, which are so acid that they need to be cooked before being eaten.

crane (in natural history) A ground-living bird that looks rather like a heron but is related to rails and bustards. Cranes make up a family, Gruidae, of some 14 species with representatives in most parts of the world; they include the demoiselle crane, *Anthropoides virgo*, and the Stanley crane *Tetrapteryx paradisea*. The largest are 1.5 m (5 feet) tall, and they all have long necks and legs but short beaks. They are mainly grey or white, with elongated wing-feathers trailing over their 'tails', and are well known for their resonant calls; the call of the common crane of Europe, *Grus grus*, is a trumpeting 'grooh'. They perform ceremonial dances, and possibly pair for life. Many species migrate in large flocks, flying in lines or wedge formations.

crane (in technology) A device for raising and moving heavy weights. There are two main types of crane: those with a revolving jib that can be rotated about a vertical post, and those that can traverse in two directions, so as to cover a rectangular area. The first type is typified by the derrick, in which the jib is pivoted at its base and supported by wire ropes from the top of a post. It can be raised or lowered and rotated to cover a circular area. Traversing cranes are typified by the overhead travelling crane and the gantry crane. Dockside cranes straddle the quayside road or railway and enable cargoes to be landed on the quayside or loaded into barges outboard of the ship. Heavy loads can be lifted by hammerhead cranes, in which the load is largely counterbalanced by the weight of the crane machinery, though sometimes weights are added. The hammerhead has evolved into the ubiquitous tower (cantilever) crane, to be seen on most building sites.

Crane, Stephen (1871–1900) US novelist. After working as a journalist in New York, he wrote *Maggie: A Girl of the Streets* (1893). His best-known book was *The Red Badge of Courage* (1895), an epic of the American Civil War. He also wrote short stories and poetry and worked as a war correspondent in Greece. He died prematurely of tuberculosis.

crane fly (or **daddy-long-legs**) A slender-bodied true FLY with very long legs and an elongated body. Most have simple thread-like antennae and a conspicuous pair of halteres (drumstick-like balancing organs which replace the hindwings of true flies). The elongated, cylindrical larvae, some of which are aquatic or found in damp wood, also include destructive leather-jackets, which eat the roots and lower stems of a variety of plants, especially grasses. The adults feed on nectar, if at all, and despite the sting-like appearance of the female's ovipositor, are harmless.

cranesbill Any species of the genus *Geranium*, a large group of perennial or occasionally annual plants, native to the temperate areas of the world. The leaves of most species are deeply lobed or dissected, and the flowers, which may be white, blue, pink, or red, are often large and attractive. When mature, the sections of the fruit split explosively, expelling the carpels and seeds. They are part of the family Geraniaceae, which has some 750 species distributed throughout temperate and subtropical regions.

Cranko, John (1927–73) South African dancer, choreographer, and director. He studied in South Africa and in London, and subsequently choreographed for both the Sadler's Wells and the Royal Ballet companies, his works including *Pineapple Poll* (1951). His choreography is notable chiefly for full-length dramatic works such as *Onegin* (1965) and Carmen (1971).

crankshaft A shaft in a machine or engine used to convert reciprocating into rotary motion, or vice versa. A shaft carries a crank-arm, which in turn carries a crankpin, a short length of shaft parallel to the main shaft and offset from it by a distance known as the throw. The reciprocating mechanism, such as a piston sliding in a cylinder, is linked to the crankpin by a connecting-rod so that each revolution of the crankshaft causes the piston to reciprocate through a distance, the stroke, of twice the throw. Multi-cylinder engines require a multi-throw crankshaft, with a series of crank-arms and crankpins interspersed by bearing to keep the crankshaft rigid.

Cranmer, Thomas (1489–1556) English cleric, a founding father of the English Protestant Church. He served HENRY VIII on diplomatic missions before becoming Archbishop of Canterbury in 1532. He annulled Henry's marriages to Catherine of Aragon, Anne Boleyn, and Anne of Cleves. During EDWARD VI's reign, he was chiefly responsible for liturgical reform including the First and Second English Prayer Books (1549 and 1552) and the Forty-Two Articles (1553). He supported Lady Jane GREY's succession in 1553; after Queen Mary's accession he was tried for high treason, then for heresy, and finally burnt at the stake in Oxford.

Crashaw, Richard (*c.*1612–49) English poet. He converted to Roman Catholicism in about 1645, at the time of Puritan rule in England, and spent the rest of his life in exile in France and Italy. His principal work, *Steps to the Temple* (1646) is a collection of religious poems influenced by Marino and the Spanish MYSTICS.

Crassus, Marcus Licinius (known as 'Dives') (*c.*115–53 BC) Roman politician. He defeated Spartacus in 71 BC, though Pompey claimed credit for the victory. Crassus joined Caesar and Pompey in the

First Triumvirate in 60. In 55 he was made consul and given a special command in Syria, where he hoped to regain a military reputation equal to that of his allies by a victory over the Parthians, but after some successes he was defeated and killed.

crater (in astronomy) An approximately circular feature found in large numbers on the Moon, Mercury, Mars, Venus, and most of the planetary satellites. Craters are caused either by volcanic activity or by the impact of bodies of various sizes, and they range in diameter from a few centimetres to more than 1,000 km. Many of the older ones have been partially obliterated by more recently formed ones. Most are now thought to be of impact origin rather than volcanic, the vast majority of the former being created in the early days of the Solar System when thousands of planetesimals, asteroids, and meteoroids existed and were swept up by the larger planets and satellites. Most craters of this kind on the Earth have been destroyed through erosion by wind, water, and geological processes except for those made in the last few hundred million years such as the Arizona meteor crater. See also VOLCANO.

Crater The Cup, a CONSTELLATION just south of the celestial equator, one of the 48 constellations known to the ancient Greeks. In mythology it represents the cup in which Corvus, the Crow, was supposed to bring water to Apollo. However, the crow was late with the water because he stopped along the way to eat figs. Apollo condemned the crow to a life of eternal thirst by placing it in the sky just out of reach of the water in the cup.

Crater Lake A lake with no inlet or outlet in a volcanic crater in the Cascade Range, south-west Oregon, USA. It is 9.5 km (6 miles) in diameter and at over 600 m (1,968 ft) deep is the deepest lake in the USA. Crater Lake lies within a 74,188-hectare (183,180-acre) national park created in 1902.

craton See SHIELD (in geology).

crawfish (or **spiny lobster**, **rock lobster**) A deep-water marine CRUSTACEAN of the family Palinuridae, rarely found inshore. Crawfish lack lobster-like pincers, and defend themselves instead with a very heavy and spiny carapace and by flailing sharp-edged antennae. They are caught for food in some countries.

Crawford, **Joan** (born Lucille le Sueur) (1906–77) One of Hollywood's leading film stars. A dancer in her early films, she later played the female lead in films, such as *Rain* (1932) and *Mildred Pierce* (1945), as well as mature roles, such as her part in the horror film *Whatever Happened to Baby Jane?* (1962).

crayfish A CRUSTACEAN that lives in fresh, flowing water, especially streams in chalk and limestone areas. Related to, and closely resembling, the LOBSTERS, crayfish have similar habits. They are mostly nocturnal, feeding on snails, tadpoles, and insect larvae, and generally hide beneath stones during the day. The female, which may live for 20 years, carries the eggs until they hatch in spring, and the youngsters cling on to her for some time while undergoing early moults. Most crayfish stay rather small, but some Australian species can reach 50 cm (20 inches) long.

Crazy Horse (Sioux name Ta-Sunko-Witko) (*c.*1849–77) Sioux chief. In 1876 he led a successful rearguard action of Sioux and Cheyenne warriors against invading US army forces in Montana. Shortly afterwards he and his men joined Sitting Bull at Little Bighorn, where Crazy Horse played an important strategic and military role in the massacre of US forces under General Custer. He surrendered in 1877 and was killed in custody in Nebraska a few months later.

creamware A type of pottery with a cream-coloured body containing flint. It was first made by the Staffordshire potter Enoch Booth in the mid-18th century, and an improved type called 'Queen's ware' was introduced by WEDGWOOD in 1765. Creamware was hardwearing and fairly cheap to produce, and it was well suited to painted, transfer-printed, or openwork (pierced) decoration. It soon became very popular in Britain and Europe, and as early as 1770 a factory for producing it was opened in South Carolina in the USA.

creationism See FUNDAMENTALISM.

creation myth A tale or MYTH recounting the origins of the natural world and human society. Myths about the creation of the world, whether they describe the operation of a creator GOD, the emergence of the world from primordial parents or a cosmic egg, sacrifice, or a primordial battle, have great importance within religious beliefs and associated RITUALS. Typical features include irreconcilable opposites, such as light and dark, or water and earth. Some creation myths refer to the origins of particular CLANS or lineages; these typically tell the story of descent from a single common ancestor or founder. Described by the anthropologist MALINOWSKI as a charter for legitimacy, myths of this kind often act to justify the authority of elders or chiefs, and may be an important component in the political organization of society.

Crécy, **Battle of** (26 August 1346) The village of Crécy in northern France was the site for the defeat of the French under Philip VI by the ARCHERS of the English king, Edward III. Edward's raiding army, anxious to avoid pitched battle, was trapped by a numerically superior French force. The English bowmen dug pits to impede advancing cavalry, while the knights dismounted and formed three supporting divisions, their right commanded by Edward's son and heir, EDWARD THE BLACK PRINCE. Over 1,500 of the French died, including the cream of the nobility, as against some 40 English dead. Edward was able to march north and besiege Calais. This was a decisive English victory at the outset of the HUNDRED YEARS WAR.

credit A debt incurred through the purchase of goods and services by delayed payment. A major form of credit is consumer credit. Bank credit is extended by a BANK (or similar institution) to its customers in the form of overdrafts and loans. Trade credit is allowed by one trader to another, in the course of business. Credit is vital in facilitating MARKET transactions, and is liable to have a significant effect on the general level of economic activity. A government wishing to reduce INFLATION may wish to limit credit (a credit squeeze) by raising INTEREST rates (and making credit more expensive since interest represents the price of borrowing) or by instituting more direct credit controls.

credit card A card issued to an individual, authorizing the purchase of goods or services on credit. A magnetic strip on the back of the credit card carries identifying information. Many retailers have machines from the credit company that immediately check the credit card's validity and automatically transfer payment from the customer's account. Recent increases in credit card fraud have led to the use of holograms on cards, to make them difficult to reproduce, and of encoding of information carried within the computer systems of banks and credit companies.

Cree An Algonquian-speaking Indian tribe of North America. Traditionally dependent on caribou and moose, they are the southernmost of the major subarctic tribes of Manitoba and Saskatchewan in Canada.

creed An authorized, formal statement of Christian belief, the most important being the Nicene Creed and the Apostles' Creed. In early Christianity, brief declarations of belief at baptism varied regionally, but usually made a threefold reference to God the Father, the Son, and the Holy Spirit. The Council of Nicaea (325) issued a formal creed for universal acceptance as a test of orthodoxy. This was later developed into the Nicene Creed, used today in both Western and Eastern Orthodox Eucharistic services. The Apostles' Creed, ascribed in legend to the twelve apostles, first mentioned *c.*390, and found in its present form *c.*700, is used only in the West. The Athanasian Creed is a 5th-century doctrinal statement wrongly attributed to Athanasius, a 4th-century bishop of Alexandria.

Creek A Muskogean North American Indian confederacy, originally one of the dominant groups of the mid-south. In the 18th century they were pushed westwards from the coasts of Carolina and Georgia, eventually settling in Indian Territory in Oklahoma where they number 50,000.

creep (in metallurgy) See METALLURGY AND METALWORKING.

creeper A member of any one of several unrelated groups of arboreal birds. The brown creeper, *Mohoua (finschia) novaeseelandiae*, a member of the family of Australian WARBLERS, is a small brown bird 13 cm (5 inches) long, which lives in the forests of the South Island, New Zealand. The Philippine group of creepers contains three species in the genus *Rhabdornis*, while the Hawaiian creeper, *Loxops maculata*, is a member of the family Drepanididae of Hawaiian honeycreepers. Other birds with 'creeper' as part of their name include the TREECREEPERS and WOODCREEPERS.

cremation Disposal of a corpse by burning it to ashes. The belief in the resurrection of the body meant that cremation was forbidden for Christians, except in cases of emergency, such as the 14th-century Black Death. Cremation became acceptable in the 19th century, largely because of the pressure for space in crowded churchyards. Protestant Churches, and since 1963 the Roman Catholic Church, allow cremation as an alternative to burial, but it is still forbidden in the Eastern Orthodox Christian Churches, and for Orthodox Jews and Muslims. In the East, cremation has always been the most general method of disposing of the dead, as a way of avoiding pollution from the corpse. In Buddhist, Hindu, and Sikh practice, bodies are usually burned on funeral pyres built close to flowing water, into which the ashes are cast. If possible, devout Hindus return the ashes of the dead to the River Ganges in India.

Creole See PIDGIN AND CREOLE LANGUAGES.

creosote See COAL-TAR.

cress A salad vegetable eaten in its seedling stage. If allowed to grow it develops into a short, strong-smelling annual with tiny white flowers. Cress, *Lepidium sativum*, originated in Asia and belongs to the MUSTARD family.

Cresta run A hazardously winding steeply banked channel of ice built each year as a tobogganing course at St Moritz, Switzerland, by the St Moritz Tobogganing Club, who draw up rules for racing on it. A run down the Cresta valley was first built in 1884.

crested swift A bird allied to the swifts, including four species that occur in south-east Asia and some Pacific islands. They are long-winged, short-tailed, and greyish to bronzy green, and they catch insects in flight. They build extremely small nests of bits of bark or moss, held together with saliva, and usually positioned on the side of small branches of trees. The female lays a single white egg. The nest is too frail to support her weight, so she perches on the branch while incubating.

Cretaceous Of or relating to the last period of the Mesozoic era, following the Jurassic and preceding the Tertiary, lasting from about 144 to 65 million years ago, during which time the climate was warm and the sea-level rose. It is characterized especially in north-west Europe by the deposition of chalk (whence its name). This period saw the emergence of the first flowering plants and the continued dominance of dinosaurs, although they died out at the end of it.

Crete (Greek **Kríti**; formerly **Candia**) A Greek island in the eastern Mediterranean, noted for remains of the Minoan civilization; area 8,336 sq km (3,220 sq miles); pop. (1981) 502,100; capital, Heraklion. The highest point on the island is Psiloríti (Mt. Ida) which rises to 2,456 m (8,058 ft). It fell to Rome in 67 BC and was subsequently ruled by Byzantines, Venetians, and Turks; it has been part of Greece since 1913. Fruit, olives, olive oil, raisins, and tourism are economically important.

Creutzfeldt-Jakob disease (CJD) A progressive degenerative neurological disease of humans that is related to SCRAPIE in sheep and BOVINE SPONGIFORM ENCEPHALOPATHY (BSE) in cattle. Typically affecting older people, it is characterized by DEMENTIA, which progresses rapidly, and sudden muscular spasms (myoclonus). The causative agent in CJD is believed to be the same as that which causes BSE and scrapie, namely, an abnormal prion protein that accumulates in the brain. However, the question of the transmission of these similar diseases between species remains highly controversial. The appearance of a new variant form of CJD in the mid-1990s, which affects younger people and shows marked similarities to BSE, has been linked to the consumption of beef or beef products from BSE-infected cattle. It is not yet clear whether or not these isolated cases are the forerunner of an epidemic. There is no cure for CJD, which invariably proves fatal. It is named after the German psychiatrists H. G. Creutzfeldt (1885–1964) and A. M. Jakob (1884–1931).

crevass A deep, gaping crack in a GLACIER or moving ice-sheet (although the term is also used to describe cracks in river banks, especially in the LEVEES of the lower Mississippi, USA). Crevasses are caused by stresses which build up within the ice as it meets obstacles and as different parts move at different rates. They open and close as it moves and may be hidden by crusts of snow, making travel on the ice both difficult and dangerous.

Crewe An industrial town and railway junction in Cheshire, England; pop. (1991) 63,351. It has important engineering industries.

crewel work A type of embroidery, distinguished by the two-ply worsted wool yarn called crewel, often on a twill foundation of linen warp and cotton weft, or sometimes on pure linen or cotton. It dates back to the 16th century, when it was used mainly for bed hangings and curtains. It had its greatest popularity in Britain, from the late 17th century, and then in the USA, where the vogue lasted throughout the 19th century. Crewel work most typically features bold tree designs, with curling leaves and exotic flowers, imitating embroidered hangings from India and China.

Crichton, James (known as 'the Admirable Crichton') (1560–*c.*1585) Scottish adventurer. Crichton was an accomplished swordsman, poet, and scholar. He travelled a great deal in Europe, serving in the French army and later making a considerable impression on French and Italian universities with his intellect and skills as a polyglot orator.

Crick, Francis Harry Compton (1916–) British biophysicist. Together with J. D. Watson he proposed the double helix structure of the DNA molecule, thus broadly explaining how genetic information is carried in living organisms and how genes replicate. He has since worked on the triplet code of bases in DNA, the processes of transcription into RNA and translation into amino acids, and the structure of other macromolecules and of viruses. He shared a Nobel Prize with Watson and M. H. F. Wilkins in 1962.

cricket (in natural history) A black or brown, flattened insect, which belongs to the same order (Orthoptera) as the grasshopper. Female crickets have large ovipositors and the males have sound-producing organs on their front wings. The house cricket, *Acheta domesticus*, which is pale brown, often lives with man in buildings, and sings mostly at night. Field crickets, such as the European *Gryllus campestris*, are black and live in burrows, the males singing by day at the mouths of the burrows. The related mole crickets, which belong to the family Gryllotalpidae, are almost entirely subterranean, and they cannot jump. There are some 2,300 species of true cricket distributed throughout the world, and some 50 species of mole cricket.

cricket (in sport) An eleven-a-side summer sport originating in England and now played at Test or top international level in the UK, Australia, New Zealand, the West Indies, India, Pakistan, Sri Lanka, Zimbabwe, and South Africa. The pitch is marked out at or near the centre of the field. It consists principally of two wickets (three stumps, 28 inches (71.12 cm) high, surmounted by two bails, each 4.37 inches (11.11 cm) long, which rest in grooves cut in the top of the stumps) set at a distance of 22 yards (20.12 m) from each other. 'Wicket' also refers to the playing pitch and, as in 'taking a wicket', the dismissal of a batsman. Each side has one or two innings (the time when one side or player is batting) of ten wickets each. Two players from the batting side go in against the fielding side. A bowler begins the first over of six – or (sometimes in Australia) eight – balls. Using an overarm action, the ball is delivered (bowled) from one end, and the batsman tries to defend the wicket at the other, if possible hitting the ball away into the field to score runs. As the fielders chase the ball and return it to the stumps, the two batsman may cross and score one or more runs. If the striking batsman hits the ball across the boundary line, four runs are scored if the ball bounces before crossing and six if it goes out on the full. A batsman may be dismissed in various ways, the most common being bowled (bowler's ball strikes the wicket and dislodges one or both bails), caught (fielder catches ball off bat), leg-before-wicket (batsman struck on leg by a ball, which would have hit stumps), and run out (batsman fails to make ground when running). The batting side tries to amass as many runs as possible and then to dismiss the opposing side for fewer runs. At test level, matches may last up to five days or longer.

crime A punishable act or conduct, prohibited by the CRIMINAL LAW. It is important to distinguish a criminal act from an immoral one; many crimes are immoral and harmful, but not all immoral or harmful actions are legally prohibited (lying, for example, is not illegal, except in certain circumstances, such as PERJURY). By definition, crime is socially determined: what constitutes crime can vary over time and between societies. However, certain categories of crime are recognized almost everywhere: violent crime, including assault and HOMICIDE; RAPE and other sexual offences; property crime, including theft and burglary; white-collar crime, such as fraud and embezzlement; and other crimes against society, such as DRUG OFFENCES. Crime is a public, as distinct from a private, wrong; it affects not only the victim but the community, which requires the punishment of the offender as a way of expressing public condemnation. Several countries have schemes to compensate victims of crime financially, the first being set up in New Zealand in 1964. In the fight against crime, the police use increasingly complex resources, such as computer records, forensic evidence, and international cooperation (see INTERPOL).

Crimea (Russian **Krym**) ▶1 A peninsula of the Ukraine lying between the Sea of Azov and the Black Sea. Settled successively by Goths, Huns, Khazars, Greeks, Tartars, Russians, and Ukrainians it became a khanate of the Turkic-speaking Tatar people in the 13th century. It was the scene of inconclusive but bloody fighting between Russia and Turkey, France and Britain during the CRIMEAN WAR of 1854–56 and in 1921 became an autonomous republic of the Russian republic.

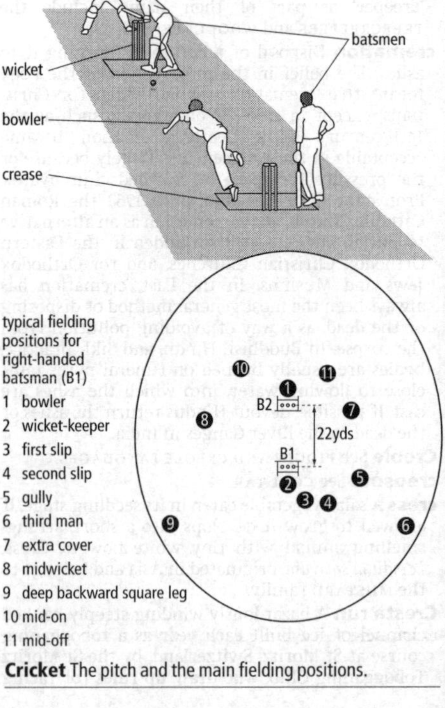

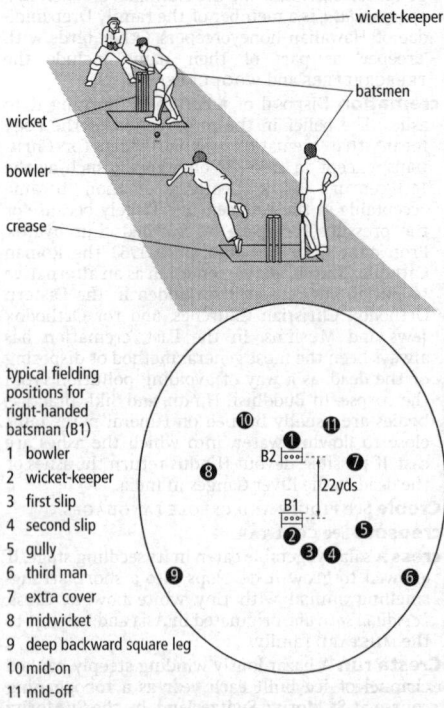

Cricket The pitch and the main fielding positions.

Under Stalin it was transferred to the Ukrainian Soviet Socialist Republic. Its resorts were much favoured by the Communist party élite. ►**2** An autonomous republic of Ukraine; area 26,990 sq km (10,425 sq miles); pop. (1989) 2,456,000; capital, Simferopol. Following the breakup of the Soviet Union in 1991 the Crimea became an autonomous republic of Ukraine, but its predominantly Russian-speaking population favour secession from the Ukraine and union with Russia.

Crimean War (1853–56) A war fought by Russia against Turkey, Britain, France, and Piedmont. The immediate cause was the dispute between France and Russia over the Palestinian holy places. War became inevitable after the Russians, having failed to obtain equal rights with the French, occupied territories of the OTTOMAN EMPIRE in July 1853. In a bid to prevent Russian expansion in the Black Sea area and to ensure existing trade routes, a conference was convened in Vienna. Turkey was pressed by the Powers to make some concessions to placate Russia, but it refused, and declared war. In November 1853 the Russians destroyed the Turkish fleet at Sinope, in the Black Sea. This forced the hand of Britain and France, who in March 1854 declared war, expecting, with their naval supremacy, a quick victory. Austria did not join the Allies but, by mobilizing its army, obliged the Russians to evacuate the provinces of Wallachia and Moldavia which they had occupied. The Allied forces were at first mustered at Varma, but in August 1854 they were transported to Eupatoria on the Crimea with Lord RAGLAN, commander-in-chief of an ill-prepared army which had been ravaged by cholera. They were able to defeat the Russian army, skilfully led by Menschikov, at the battle of the River Alma (20 September 1854) and began bombarding the strongly armed fort of Sevastopol. Following the battle of BALACLAVA, a long winter of siege warfare ensued, aggravated by lack of fuel, clothing, and supplies for the Allied armies. Public opinion in Britain became critical of the war after reading eyewitness reports in *The Times*, sent back by the Irishman W. H. Russell, the first journalist in history to write as a war correspondent using the telegraph. Florence NIGHTINGALE received permission to take nurses to the Crimea. Sevastopol fell on 8 September 1855; by that time the Russians, with a new emperor, ALEXANDER II, were already seeking peace. This was concluded at the Congress of PARIS in 1856.

criminal law That branch of the law concerned with wrongdoing against individuals, society, or the state, for which the state has power to seek punishment through the courts. The major goals of criminal law are deterrence and punishment, while that of CIVIL LAW is individual compensation. Criminal offences consist of two distinct elements; the physical act (the *actus reus*, 'guilty act') and the requisite mental state with which the act is done (the *mens rea*, 'guilty mind'). For example, in murder the *actus reus* is the unlawful killing of a person, while the *mens rea* is 'malice aforethought' (the intention to kill or cause grievous injury). The criminal law also details the defences that defendants may bring to lessen or negate their liability (CRIMINAL RESPONSIBILITY) and specifies the punishment that may be inflicted.

criminal responsibility A concept in CRIMINAL LAW that defines the degree of knowledge and intention with which an offender commits a crime. Ordinarily, an individual who commits a crime must be fully aware of the harmful nature of what he or she has done, and must have intended or foreseen the consequences or have acted with deliberate recklessness. A person who has not acted voluntarily, or is unaware of what he or she has done, is not normally regarded as criminally responsible, and neither are children under a certain age, an age which varies between societies. All legal systems recognize mental illness as a mitigating factor, though its definition can be problematic.

criminology The study of criminal behaviour and of the administration of the CRIMINAL LAW. Salient issues include the measurement, distribution, and causes of CRIME, and the operations of law-enforcement agencies. Criminological research has shown that official criminal statistics do not accurately measure crime: when members of the public are surveyed, their reports of their own criminal behaviour and of the crimes of which they have been victims indicate far higher levels. To investigate the distribution of crime and the characteristics of criminals, criminologists examine such factors as their age, sex, ethnic background, social class, and place of residence. Criminologists are also interested in the causes of crime. Criminologists also study law enforcement and such subjects as PLEA BARGAINING, sentencing, and punishment.

crinoid See SEA LILY.

Crippen, Hawley Harvey (1862–1910) US-born British murderer. Crippen poisoned his wife at their London home and sailed to Canada with his former secretary. His arrest in Canada was achieved through the intervention of radio-telegraphy, the first case of its use in apprehending a criminal. Crippen was later hanged.

Cripps, Sir (Richard) Stafford (1889–1952) British politician. During 1945–50 he served in ATTLEE's government successively as President of the Board of Trade and Chancellor of the Exchequer. In these posts he was responsible for the policy of austerity – a programme of rationing and controls introduced to adjust Britain to its reduced economy following the withdrawal of US lend-lease. He also directed a notable expansion of exports, especially after devaluation of the pound in 1949.

critical path method A management tool for controlling the progress of any large project where completion on time is important. The method works by breaking down the large project into activities or tasks each with a time allocation. These activities are then logically represented on a network showing their interrelationships in a chronological fashion. As each activity has a time allocation the completed network shows the critical path of activities which must be completed on time if the whole project is not to be delayed. It is also possible to identify the earliest and latest start times for each activity if the overall project is not to be delayed.

critical state The state of a fluid at which the properties of the liquid and gaseous phases become identical. It is defined by the fluid's critical temperature and critical pressure. The temperature above which it is impossible to liquefy a gas merely by compressing it is called the critical temperature, and the pressure which is necessary to produce liquefaction at this temperature is the critical pressure.

critical theory The radical social theory developed by members of the Institute for Social Research in Frankfurt, Germany (the FRANKFURT SCHOOL), during the 1930s and later. Following MARX, they criticized capitalist societies, believing that individuality and freedom were being destroyed, that social injustice was deepening, and that large corporations were eliminating competition and aggrandizing themselves. Through critical theory, they analysed these developments and sought to 'unmask' the discrepancies between the proclaimed goals of, for example, 'democratic' governments and 'free market' economies and the principles by which they in truth operated.

Croatia A country in south-eastern Europe, formerly a constituent republic of Yugoslavia.

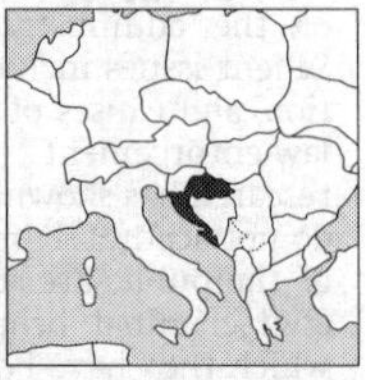

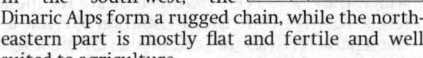

Physical. Croatia is bounded by Slovenia, Hungary, Bosnia-Hercegovina, Serbia, and the Adriatic Sea. In the south-west, the Dinaric Alps form a rugged chain, while the north-eastern part is mostly flat and fertile and well suited to agriculture.

Economy. Croatia has an industrialized economy in which mining, petroleum production, shipbuilding, and other heavy industry are important. Mineral resources include bauxite, petroleum, and natural gas. The civil war inflicted great damage on tourism, the principal earner of foreign exchange. The main agricultural products are grains, sugar-beet, and potatoes. Grapes are grown mainly on the off-shore islands.

History. Once the Roman province of Illyricum, the area suffered successive barbarian invasions, with the Slavs becoming the majority population. Conquered by CHARLEMAGNE, the first Croatian state was formed with its own knezes or princes when the Carolingian empire collapsed. With papal support Kneze Tomislav became the first king. Struggles between HUNGARY, VENICE, and the BYZANTINE EMPIRE resulted in rule by the Hungarian crown until 1301, when the House of Anjou took control. From 1381 there was a long period of civil war. The Battle of Mohács in 1526 brought most of the country under OTTOMAN rule with the remainder governed by the HABSBURGS. From 1809 to 1813 Croatia was part of Napoleon's Illyrian province, during which time Croatian nationalism emerged, strongly resisting both Habsburg imperialism and Hungarian control. In 1848 a revolution reasserted Croatian independence, ending serfdom, and proclaiming all citizens equal. In the following year Austria countered by proclaiming the nation an Austrian crownland. In 1868, following the establishment of AUSTRIA-HUNGARY, the territory was pronounced to be the autonomous Hungarian crownland of Croatia-Slovenia, apart from the coastline of Dalmatia, which was to remain an Austrian province. The Hungarian authorities tried to crush all manifestations of Croatian nationalism, with little success, and in October 1918 an independent Croatia was again proclaimed. This then joined the Kingdom of the Serbs, Croats, and Slovenes (1921), later renamed Yugoslavia. In 1941 it was once again declared an independent state under the fascist leader Ante Pavelič, whose brutal government provoked a guerrilla war. Croatia joined the new Federal Republic of Yugoslavia in 1945. A movement for Croatian independence re-emerged in the late 1980s and a non-communist government was formed in May 1990. By the end of the year anti-Serbian partisans were attacking enclaves of Serbian residents, who were then supported by units of the Serbian-dominated Yugoslav army. A confused military situation developed through 1991 with the ancient city of Dubrovnik being bombarded by Serbian artillery. Croatia was recognized as an independent country by the European Community in 1992, with Franjo TUDJMAN as President. Fighting continued in the region of Krajina, which had declared itself to be a Serbian republic, and UN peacekeepers were sent in (1992). Croatian forces attacked Krajina in 1993, and in 1995 launched an offensive that enabled them to regain possession of much of the region. From 1992 Croatian forces were involved in the civil war in BOSNIA-HERCEGOVINA, fighting Bosnian Serbs and, in some areas, Bosnian Muslims. Some Bosnian Croat nationalists even proclaimed themselves to be a separate republic. In 1994, however, the Croatians and the Bosnian government agreed to cooperate. Fighting with the Bosnian Serbs continued until late 1995, when the governments of Croatia, Serbia, and Bosnia accepted a US-brokered peace plan for the region.

Capital: Zagreb
Area: 56,537 sq km (21,829 sq mi)
Population: 4,495,000 (1995)
Currency: 1 kuna = 100 lipa
Religions: Roman Catholic 75.0%; Eastern Orthodox 12.0%
Ethnic Groups: Croat 75.0%; Serb 12.0%
Languages: Serbo-Croat (official)
International Organizations: CSCE

Croce, Benedetto (1866–1952) Italian philosopher. Croce presented his philosophical system in his major work *Filosofia dello spirito* (1902–17), which is notable for its denial of the physical reality of a work of art and its identification of philosophical endeavour with a methodological approach to history. Croce served as Minister of Education 1920–21, but opposed Mussolini and all forms of totalitarianism; he returned to political life and helped to rebuild democracy in Italy after the fall of Mussolini.

Crockett, David (known as 'Davy') (1786–1836) US frontiersman, soldier, and politician. He was a member of the House of Representatives 1827–35 and cultivated the image of a rough backwoods legislator. On leaving politics he returned to the frontier, where he took up the cause of Texan independence and was killed at the siege of the Alamo.

crocodile A member of the archosaurian group of REPTILES, apparently more closely related to birds and extinct groups, such as dinosaurs, than to other reptiles. Crocodiles have a number of adaptations for an aquatic life-style: their nostrils, for instance, are situated on top of the snout and can be closed by muscular action, and there are internal flaps in the throat which can be closed to prevent the lungs from flooding when the mouth is open under water.

There are three main categories of living crocodilians: true crocodiles; ALLIGATORS (together with caymans); and the GHARIAL. True crocodiles comprise some 13 species found in the tropical Americas, Africa, Asia, the East Indies, and Australasia. The largest living crocodilians belong to this group; they are the salt-water crocodiles, *Crocodylus porosus*, ranging from Asia to Australasia, of which there are reports of specimens up to 8.1 m (30 feet) long. At the other end of the scale is the Congo dwarf crocodile, *Osteolaemus* species, from West Africa, which reaches a maximum length of only 1.14 m (3.75 feet). Some crocodiles exhibit parental care: the female Nile crocodile, *C. niloticus*, once its eggs have incubated, digs open its nest and carries the hatchlings to the water.

crocus A small, monocotyledonous plant with underground CORMS and adventitious roots. There are about 80 species of crocus native to central and southern Europe, North Africa, and western Asia. They belong to the iris family and often grow at high altitudes. Crocuses have marked cycles of growth and rest, corresponding to wet and dry seasons. The attractive flowers open only in sunlight, or on bright days. The many colourful garden varieties are derived from any one of several species of *Crocus*. The yellow culinary dye, saffron, is produced from the stigmas of *C. sativus*.

Croesus King of LYDIA *c.*560–546 BC He expanded his domains to include all the Greek cities on the coast of Asia Minor, and the stories of his wealth indicate the extent of his power. However, he was unable to withstand CYRUS THE GREAT, and after his defeat Lydia entered the Persian empire of the Achaemenids.

Crohn's disease An inflammation of the intestinal tract, usually the terminal part of the ileum or the colon. It was discovered by the US physician B. B. Crohn (1884–1983). Symptoms include pain and diarrhoea; it often responds to treatment by steroids and sulpha drugs. The cause is unknown. In severe cases surgical removal of the affected part is required.

Cro-Magnon A hill of Cretaceous limestone in the Dordogne department of France, in a cave at the base of which skeletons of five individuals were found in 1868 among deposits of upper palaeolithic age. It had previously been supposed that modern man did not exist in palaeolithic times. The name is now applied in a more general sense to describe a particular race of modern man (*Homo sapiens*) that is associated with the Upper Palaeolithic Aurignacian industry found throughout western Europe and particularly south-west France from between *c.*34,000 and 29,000 years BC.

Cromarty Firth An inlet of the Moray Firth between the Black Isle and the mainland of Ross and Cromarty in Highland Region, northern Scotland. The principal settlements on its coastline are Invergordon, Dingwall, and Cromarty which was the birthplace of the geologist and writer Hugh Miller (1802–56).

Crome, John (1768–1821) British painter. Founder and leading member of the Norwich School, he was influenced by Dutch artists such as Hobbema and Ruisdael. He later developed a distinctive romantic style of his own, exemplified in such landscapes as *Slate Quarries* and *Moonrise on the Marshes of the Yare* (both undated).

Crompton, Richmal (pseudonym of Richmal Crompton Lamburn) (1890–1969) British writer. A classics teacher who wrote stories for magazines, she made her name with *Just William* (1922), a collection of stories for children about a mischievous schoolboy, William Brown. She published a further 37 collections based on the same character, as well as some 50 books for adults, during her writing career.

Crompton, Samuel (1753–1827) British inventor. Famed for his invention of the spinning mule, he lacked the means to obtain a patent and sold his rights to a Bolton industrialist for £67. The House of Commons subsequently gave him £5,000 in compensation.

Cromwell, Oliver (1599–1658) English general and statesman. He was the driving force in the revolutionary opposition to Charles I in the English Civil War, and was the leader of the Parliamentary forces (or Roundheads), winning decisive battles at Marston Moor and Naseby. After helping to arrange the trial and execution of Charles I, he returned to military command to suppress resistance to the Commonwealth in Ireland and Scotland, finally defeating a Scottish army at Worcester (1651). He styled himself Lord Protector of the Commonwealth (1653–58); although he called and dissolved a succession of Parliaments, he refused Parliament's offer of the crown in 1657. His rule was notable for its puritan reforms in the Church of England and for the establishment of the Commonwealth as the major Protestant power in the world.

Cromwell, Richard (1626–1712) Son of Oliver CROMWELL, whom he succeeded as Lord Protector of the Commonwealth of England 1658–59. He was more interested in country life than in politics and, incapable of reconciling the military and civilian factions in Parliament, he retired after a few months. At the RESTORATION he fled to the Continent, returning *c.*1689 to spend the rest of his life quietly in Hampshire.

Cromwell, Thomas (*c.*1485–1540) English statesman, chief minister to Henry VIII 1531–40. After serving Cardinal Wolsey from 1514, he succeeded him as the king's chief adviser. He presided over the king's divorce from Catherine of Aragon (1533) and his break with the Roman Catholic Church, as well as the dissolution of the monasteries and a series of administrative measures, such as the Act of Supremacy (1534), designed to strengthen the Crown. He fell from favour over Henry's marriage to Anne of Cleves and was executed on a charge of treason.

Cronin, A(rchibald) J(oseph) (1896–1981) Scottish novelist. His novels often reflect his early experiences as a doctor; they include *The Citadel* (1937), telling of the struggles of an idealistic young doctor, and *The Stars Look Down* (1935), about a mining community. Cronin's Scottish medical stories were successfully adapted for radio and television as *Dr Finlay's Casebook* in the 1960s and 1990s.

Cronus In pre-Hellenic and Greek mythology, the youngest son of Uranus (Heaven) and Gaea (Earth), leader of the Titans. By the advice of his mother he castrated his father, thus separating Heaven from Earth. He became ruler of the Earth, but was fated to be in turn deposed by one of his own children. He swallowed Hestia, Demeter, Hera, Hades, and Poseidon at birth. However, his wife Rhea (who was also his sister) substituted a stone wrapped in swaddling-clothes for Zeus, the last-born. Zeus eventually deposed his father and the other children were vomited up.

Crookes, Sir William (1832–1919) British physicist and chemist. Crookes combined private experimental research with business; he also edited several photographic and scientific journals. In 1861, shortly after the spectroscopic discoveries of Robert Bunsen and Gustav Kirchhoff, he discovered the element thallium. This led him indirectly to the invention of the radiometer in 1875. He later developed a vacuum tube (the precursor of the valve) and in 1903 invented the spinthariscope. His interest in spiritualism and psychic research led him into controversy.

crop rotation The practice of growing different crops in different years on the same land, in order to prevent the soil's nutrients from being exhausted and to reduce the risk of a build-up of diseases and pests specific to one crop. Crop rotation was widespread in Europe from the time of the ROMAN EMPIRE. Two-field rotation was practised by the ancient Greeks: one half of a farmer's land was planted in the spring or autumn of each year, while the other half was left fallow (i.e. not planted with crops), to allow the soil to 'rest'. The Romans developed the three-course rotation, which was in use from the Middle Ages until the 18th century. A three-year cycle was followed on each of three fields, with an autumn-sown crop such as rye or winter wheat, a spring-sown crop such as oats or beans, and a year of lying fallow. Two out of three fields were thus in cultivation every year. The three-field system succeeded only in countries with mild climates, such as England. With the AGRICULTURAL REVOLUTION and the acceleration of ENCLOSURES in the 18th century, more scientific methods were applied to crop rotation. A four-course rotation was adopted based on turnips, clover, barley, and wheat. The introduction of ROOT-CROPS (such as turnips) improved the soil and hence the quality of harvest and livestock; they also smother the weeds that have grown between plants of the previous crop. The replacement of the fallow with a leguminous crop, such as clover, peas, beans, or lentils, boosts the fertility of the soil since leguminous plants are able to 'fix' atmospheric nitrogen, which enriches the soil when they die (see LEGUME).

crop-spraying The process by which AGROCHEMICALS are applied to a crop for its protection or to influence its growth. Most crop-spraying equipment comprises three components: a storage tank, a pump, and a boom to which spray nozzles are attached. The crop-sprayer may be carried on, or towed by, a tractor, or mounted on an aircraft. Numerous variations exist on the basic design to accommodate spraying in specialized areas such as orchards. Crops are frequently sown leaving gaps ('tramlines') to allow access for spraying equipment. For all chemical applications calm weather is needed to avoid spray drift.

croquet A tactical lawn game, originating in France during the 17th century, played with four balls, six hoops, and mallets. The court measures approximately 32 by 26 m (35 by 28 yards), and players must hit their balls through the hoops in the correct sequence and finish on a central peg. Tactics include impeding an opponent's progress with devious manœuvres.

Crosby, **Bing** (born Harry Lillis Crosby) (1904–77) US singer and actor. His songs include 'Pennies from Heaven', 'Blue Skies', and in particular 'White Christmas' (from the film *Holiday Inn*, 1942), which has sold more than 30 million copies. He also starred in the series of *Road* films (1940–62) with Bob Hope and Dorothy Lamour (1914–96).

Crosland, **(Charles) Anthony (Raven)** (1918–77) British politician. He served as a Labour MP (1950–55, 1959–77). As Secretary of State for Education and Science (1964–67) his strongly held libertarian and egalitarian principles led to the closure of grammar schools, the establishment of a comprehensive state school system, and the growth of polytechnics. During 1965–70 and 1974–77 he held several cabinet posts, and was Foreign Secretary before his early death.

cross Any structure or symbol consisting of two main parts usually at right angles to each other. In Christianity the cross is a symbol of the wooden gallows on which JESUS CHRIST was crucified. The sign of the cross is used in Christian ceremonial as a benediction, dedication, profession of faith, or prayer. Crucifixes (crosses carrying representations of Christ), became popular within early Christianity and are still used in private prayer, especially in the Roman Catholic Church, as well as images of the Fourteen **Stations of the Cross**, showing Christ carrying his cross to the place of crucifixion. Representations of the cross include the Greek, with four equal arms; the Latin, with a long base; St Anthony's, in the form of the letter 'T' (also called a tau cross), and St Andrew's, which is diagonal.

Cross, **Charles Frederick** (1855–1935) British chemist who, with fellow-chemist E. J. Bevan, developed the viscose process for manufacturing RAYON. Cross and Bevan formed a partnership as consulting and analytical chemists in 1885. In 1892 they patented a process whereby cheap forms of cellulose, such as wood-pulp, were dissolved and then squirted through the fine holes of a spinneret (see SPINNING) into a coagulating bath to produce fibres, a process that became the basis of the rayon

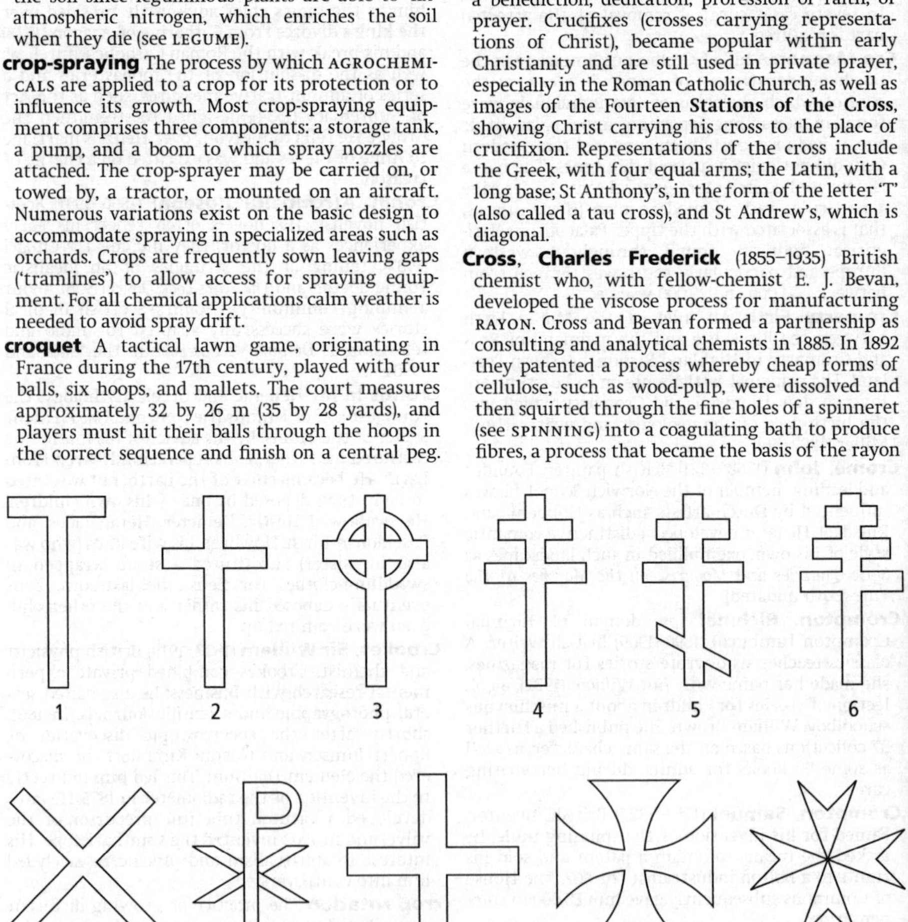

Crosses (1) T or tau cross. (2) Latin cross. (3) Celtic cross. (4) Cross of Lorraine. (5) Russian cross. (6) Papal cross. (7) St Andrew's cross. (8) Chi-Rho. (9) Greek cross. (10) Cross Paty. (11) Maltese cross.

industry. In 1894 they patented a process for making CELLULOSE ACETATE.

crossbill Any one of four species of bird of the genus *Loxia*, which in turn is part of the finch family, Fringillidae. Crossbills are native to the coniferous forests of the Northern Hemisphere. They are the size of large sparrows; the males are red, the females olive-green. Their most distinctive feature is that the two halves of the bills, or beaks, are elongated and twisted, crossing over each other at the tips, hence their name. This shape is adapted for levering up and twisting over the scales of conifer cones in order to extract the seeds, which form their staple diet.

crossbow A BOW that is attached horizontally across a stock and employs a mechanical firing action. In most cross-bows, the bowstring is gripped by a claw-like catch which is pulled back using a hand-winch. The arrow (called a bolt or quarrel) is fitted to the string, then fired by a trigger mechanism. The bowstring tension can be extremely high, allowing a heavier quarrel to be fired a greater distance than with a conventional bow.

cross-country running The winter sport of racing on foot over a country course containing natural obstacles, such as closed gates and water hazards. Championship courses for men are 12–14 km (7.5–9 miles) long in the UK, and shorter in Europe; women's races are usually over 3–5 km (2–3 miles). Races are contested by individuals and teams. The sport has its own specialists and is popular with distance track-runners, who use it to keep fit during their off-season. Some joggers move up to cross-country, but its rigours are not suitable for all.

cross-cultural psychology The comparison of people from different cultures to see if they think or feel differently. It is assumed that any differences in behaviour or performance in tests are probably due to culture, although racial factors or gross differences in physical surroundings might also play a part. Sometimes a researcher hopes to find no difference, thus indicating that a shared characteristic may be innate. Modern psychologists do not see cultural differences as signs of a more primitive stage in the same culture, but rather as signs of development of different appropriate 'tools of thought'.

Cross Fell The highest peak in the Pennine Chain, northern England, rising to 893 m (2,892 ft) in Cumbria.

cross-fertilization The fusion of GAMETES from two different organisms (FERTILIZATION). Most animals and some plants are dioecious, that is they have separate sexes. They can reproduce only by means of cross-fertilization, thus ensuring that GENES from different organisms mix, creating genetic variation (or individuality). Monoecious organisms, which include the majority of plants, have both male and female organs on the same individual and usually make use of physiological or anatomical mechanisms to increase the chances of cross-fertilization.

Crossman, Richard Howard Stafford (1907–74) British politician. He was assistant chief of the Psychological Warfare Division during World War II. He entered Parliament as a Labour MP in 1945. During the WILSON administrations he was successively Minister of Housing and Local Government, Leader of the House of Commons, and Secretary of State for Social Services. His posthumous *Diaries* (1975–77) provided revealing insights into the working of government.

cross-staff An instrument that came into general use for marine navigation during the 16th century, used for measuring the altitude (angle above the horizon) of a celestial body at sea; this measurement could be used to determine the latitude of a ship (see NAVIGATION). The cross-staff comprised a long wooden shaft with a movable cross-piece. The navigator sighted along the shaft, and moved the cross-piece until one end appeared to touch the horizon, the other the celestial body. The altitude could then be read from a scale on the shaft. The cross-staff could also be used for finding heights and distances in surveying.

crow A bird of the crow family, Corvidae, a large family containing about 103 species with a worldwide distribution, which includes many familiar birds, such as jays, rooks, jackdaws, magpies, ravens, choughs, and nutcrackers. They are medium to large birds, 30–40 cm (12–16 inches) long; a few, such as the magpies, are much larger than this because they have very long tails. The Chinese red-billed blue magpie, *Urocissa erythrorhyncha*, is 70 cm (28 inches) long, of which 40 cm (16 inches) is tail.

More narrowly, the word crow refers to the 39 species of the genus *Corvus*. Most of these species are black, and possess powerful black beaks which are used for scavenging, catching small animals, and opening seeds. The best-known species include the carrion crow, *C. corone*, the Indian house crow, *C. splendens*, and the North American crow, *C. brachyrhynchos*.

Crow and Hidatsa (or **Absaroke**) North American Indians who inhabited Montana and northern Wyoming. In prehistoric times they lived in permanent villages and practised a well-balanced agricultural economy with seasonal buffalo hunts. When they acquired horses in the 18th century, the Crow abandoned their villages for a nomadic life of full-time buffalo-hunting, trading meat for some of the crops of the farmer Hidatsa.

crow-bar An iron or steel rod, commonly 1.5–2 m (5–6.5 feet) in length, used as a lever. It is usually forked at one end, resembling a crow's foot. A closely allied tool is the case-opener, or wrecking bar. This is shaped like an elongated S, with a fork at one end and wedge-shape at the other.

crowd psychology The study and theory of the actions and emotions displayed by crowds or other masses of people. A primary controversy concerns the extent to which people in crowds cease to behave as individuals and give way to impulse or the power of the crowd. The French theorist Gustave Le Bon (1841–1931) set the agenda for most discussion in *La psychologie des foules* (1895). He held that important human thoughts and motives operate at an UNCONSCIOUS level. He argued that in a crowd people become 'suggestible' and lose conscious control of themselves just as someone under HYPNOSIS does; the mood of a crowd is 'contagious', and its anonymity and apparent power cause people to yield to dangerous INSTINCTS and disregard personal responsibility. Le Bon's ideas picture persons in a crowd as emotional, irrational, and violent in comparison with individuals alone. This can lead to heroism, but is usually destructive. Evidence from real crowd behaviour largely supports these views. Various events, including those in a wartime London Underground station and a collapsing British football stadium, led to an infectious panic in which anyone who fell was ruthlessly trampled to death. Lynch mobs, race riots, and *Kristallnacht* (a night of mob violence against Jews in Germany in 1938) are examples of crowd behaviour in which individual inhibitions against violence are discarded. On the other hand, the sombre and largely silent crowds that collected in London after the death of Diana, Princess of Wales, provided an example of the better aspects of crowd behaviour.

Crown The office of a sovereign, and acts performed in the name of the sovereign. The concept refers to the office and not the office-holder, usually an hereditary monarch who is the Crown personified. The whole of government in the UK is carried on in the name of the Crown, which is a legal entity representing the state and symbolizing its authority and continuity. In those Commonwealth countries that still acknowledge the UK monarch as head of state, the CROWN PREROGATIVE and immunities remain.

Crown Film Unit See DOCUMENTARY FILM.

crown jewels. The English collection of jewels kept in the Tower of London, made for the coronation of Charles II in 1661. It includes the sword of state, the royal sceptre (containing the Star of Africa, cut from the Cullinan diamond), the ampulla (the container for the holy oil used in anointing), the orb, and the anointing spoon.

crown of thorns starfish An ECHINODERM, *Acanthaster planci*, that takes its name from its particularly long spines. This starfish can occur in very large numbers, up to 15 adults per square metre (17 adults per square yard) in some parts of the Red Sea and off the Australian coast, where they seriously damage the reefs by eating CORALS. These numbers result from population explosions that seem to have a natural rhythm, and occur every 70 years or so. Under natural conditions they may be self-regulating before irrevocable destruction results; though the modification of the environment by humans may affect this balance. They belong to the order Spinulosida.

Crown prerogative (or **royal prerogative**) The legal pre-eminence enjoyed by the CROWN, comprising a range of actions that no other agent may lawfully carry out. Crown prerogatives are today almost all delegated to ministers by STATUTE or exercised by the monarch in accordance with the recommendations of elected ministers and appointed advisers.

Croydon A residential and commercial outer borough of Greater London, England, to the south of Lambeth; pop. (1991) 299,600. The Saxon market town of Crogedene ('valley of saffron') became a powerful medieval trading post, a home of the Archbishops of Canterbury, a London borough (1883), and in the 1960s the centre of south-east England's financial and insurance services. It was the site of London's first airport in 1915.

crucian carp A robust, rather deep-bodied fish, *Carassius carassius*, olive-green in colour, that, unlike the common carp, has no barbels around its mouth. Widely distributed in European lakes and the backwaters of slow-flowing rivers, it lives in heavily overgrown waters, can survive well where there is little oxygen, and can tolerate extreme cold. It feeds on plants and insect larvae, and spawns in May or June, the golden eggs adhering to plants.

crucible steel See IRON AND STEEL INDUSTRY; HUNTSMAN.

crucifixion A form of capital punishment used by various ancient peoples including the Persians, Carthaginians, and Romans for criminals, usually applicable only to slaves and other persons with no civil rights. The victim, nailed or roped to a crossbar, was hoisted on to an upright to form a 'T' or cross. SPARTACUS, with 6,000 rebels, was crucified in 71 BC, as was JESUS CHRIST (*c*.30 AD). Romans regarded the cross with horror. Only after Constantine abolished this form of penalty did Christians adopt the cross as a symbol.

Cruelty, Theatre of See ARTAUD, ANTONIN.

Cruft, Charles (1852–1939) British showman. In 1886 he initiated the first dog show in London. The Cruft's shows, held annually, have helped to raise standards in dog breeding and are now internationally known.

Cruikshank, George (1792–1878) British painter, illustrator, and caricaturist. The most eminent political cartoonist of his day, he was known for exposing the private life of the Prince Regent. His later work includes illustrations for Charles Dickens's *Sketches by Boz* (1836), as well as a series of etchings supporting the temperance movement.

cruise control A device designed to enable a motor vehicle to maintain a constant road speed irrespective of the road gradient or surface. The most obvious use of such a facility is in long-distance driving on a motorway. Cruise control is instantly overridable in the event of an emergency in which braking or other avoiding action has to be taken. 'Intelligent' cruise control, in which the car's speed is adjusted in relation to the distance between it and the car in front, began development in the early 1990s.

cruise missile Generally, a medium-range GUIDED MISSILE, carrying a nuclear or conventional warhead, that uses aerodynamic lift like an aeroplane. Cruise missiles are powered throughout their flight by conventional RAM-JET or JET ENGINES (unlike BALLISTIC MISSILES, which employ rocket motors for a short time only). Modern cruise missiles are guided by INERTIAL NAVIGATION systems, which are checked using astronomical readings or NAVIGATION SATELLITES, or are updated during flight by means of terrain-comparison programs and data stored in on-board computers. They are very versatile, because they can be launched from land, sea, or air. Compared with a ballistic missile, a cruise missile can carry a much heavier payload relative to its size. It is also much harder to detect by radar, since it is smaller and flies at a low altitude, though its subsonic speed may make it vulnerable to counter-attack if it is identified.

cruiser A large, fast WARSHIP with medium armament. In the 18th century all warships on detached service (not operating as part of a fleet) were called cruisers. During the last quarter of the 19th century the term began to mean a specific warship type, and was used to replace 'frigate' and 'corvette' as a description for vessels next in power to the battleship. Their role was to act as scouting vessels for battleships and to maintain command of a sea area after it had been taken by the fleet; they also raided commercial shipping. In the 1900s light cruisers for scouting appeared; after 1918 the larger cruisers were known as heavy cruisers. After World War II, the cruiser (mostly still gun-armed) was for a time the largest conventional warship. The term is still sometimes used to refer to the largest guided-missile vessels. A cruiser – usually in the form 'cabin cruiser' – is also a small yacht intended for cruising rather than racing.

crumhorn A reed musical instrument with a hook-shaped lower end used between about 1480 and about 1640 and now revived. It has a cylindrical bore and is played with a double reed inside a cap with a hole in the top to blow into. The sound is low-pitched and buzzing.

Crusades A series of expeditions (11th–14th century) to secure Christian rule over the Muslim-controlled holy places of PALESTINE. (The term is by extension used to describe any religious war or even moral or political movement.) The wealthy powerful orders of KNIGHTS HOSPITALLERS and KNIGHTS TEMPLAR were created by the Crusades. The First Crusade was called by Pope Urban II, and was provoked by the rise to power of the SELJUK Turks, which interfered with traditional PILGRIMAGE to Palestine. The pope promised spiritual benefits to warriors willing to fight under Christian banners. The Crusaders captured JERUSALEM in 1099 and massacred its inhabitants, establishing a kingdom there under Godfrey of Bouillon. The Second Crusade (1147–49) succeeded only in souring relations between the Crusader kingdoms, the Byzantines, and friendly Muslim rulers. The Third Crusade (1189–92), prompted by SALADIN's capture of Jerusalem, recaptured Acre but achieved little more. The Fourth (1202–04) was diverted by Venetian interests to Constantinople, which was sacked, making the gulf between Eastern and Western Churches unbridgeable, though some Crusaders benefited from the division of Byzantine territories known as the Latin empire of the East (1204–61). This briefly replaced the Greek empire at Constantinople until Michael VIII retook the city. Later expeditions concentrated on North Africa, but to little purpose. The fall of Acre in 1291 ended the Crusader presence in the Levant. All, except the peaceful Sixth Crusade (1228–29), were marred by greed and brutality: Jews and Christians in Europe were slaughtered by rabble armies on their way to the Holy Land. The papacy was incapable of controlling the immense forces at its disposal. However, the Crusades attracted such leaders as RICHARD I and LOUIS IX, greatly affected European CHIVALRY, and for centuries, its literature. While deepening the hostility between Christianity and Islam, they also stimulated economic and cultural contacts of lasting benefit to European civilization. See also CHILDREN'S CRUSADE.

crustacean A member of one of the three largest classes of ARTHROPODS (the others being insects and arachnids), which are particularly numerous in the sea. There are about 26,000 known species of crustaceans, which are distinguished from the other arthropods by having calcified EXOSKELETONS and two pairs of antennae (insects have one pair of antennae; arachnids have none).

Crustaceans have a three-part body: head, thorax, and abdomen, each made up of segments which bear a pair of limbs. The limbs have two parts, the upper part usually forming a gill. In primitive forms the limbs are all similar, and the lower part is used for swimming and simultaneous filter-feeding. The brine shrimps, fairy shrimps, and *Daphnia* (collectively called branchiopods) are of this type. Most of the familiar crustaceans, such as prawns, true shrimps, crabs, lobsters, and the like, are more advanced, and their legs are greatly modified. Some remain oar-like for swimming; others are specialized for crawling, grasping, jumping, sperm transfer, brooding eggs, or capturing and handling large food items.

Crustaceans are as ubiquitous in the sea as insects are on land, and some planktonic copepods, of which there are 7,500 species, may well be the single most abundant life-form, especially species such as *Calanus finmarchicus*. Some crustaceans also live in estuaries and fresh water (where AMPHIPODS and *Daphnia* are often dominant), and a few forms are amphibious (shore crabs) or fully terrestrial (COCONUT CRABS and WOODLICE).

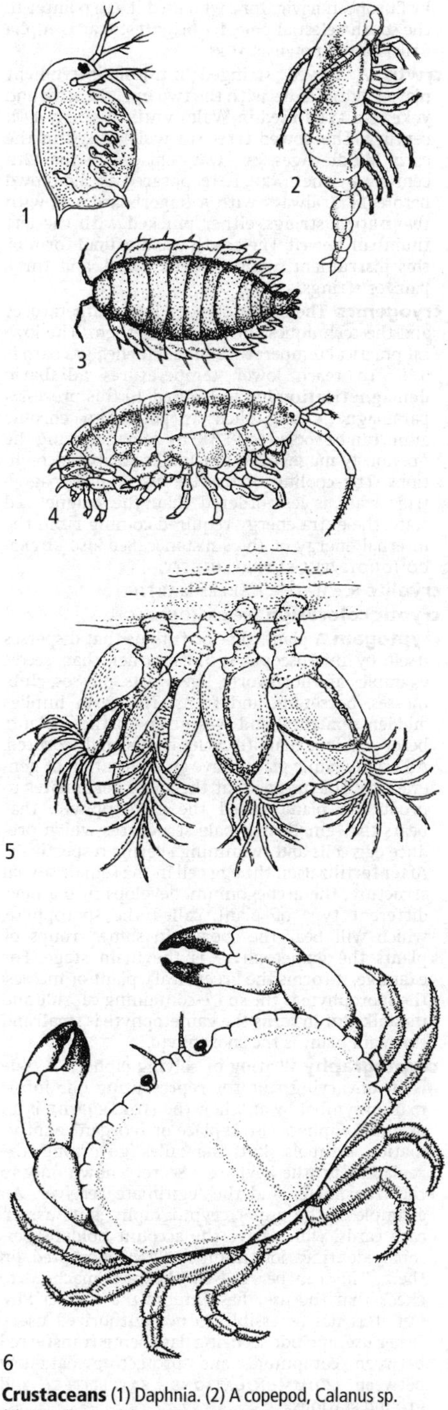

Crustaceans (1) Daphnia. (2) A copepod, Calanus sp. (3) Woodlouse. (4) Sandhopper. (5) Goose barnacles. (6) Edible crab.

Crux The Southern Cross, the smallest CONSTELLATION in the sky. The stars of Crux were known to the ancient Greeks, who regarded them as part of the hind legs of Centaurus, the Centaur. Crux was made a separate constellation in the 16th century by European navigators, who used it as a pointer to the south celestial pole. Its brightest star is Alpha Crucis, also known as ACRUX.

crwth A bowed stringed musical instrument played like a fiddle, with the two upright arms and yoke of a LYRE used in Wales until the early 19th century. The bowed lyre was widely used in the early Middle Ages, but was replaced in the 12th century by the HARP. It reappeared as the crowd before 1400, always with a fingerboard and with two DRONE strings, either plucked with the left thumb or bowed. The crwth was the final form of this instrument, with a finger board, and three pairs of strings.

cryogenics The study of very low temperatures and the techniques for producing them. The lowest practical temperature for a liquefied gas bath is 0.3K. To reach lower temperatures **adiabatic demagnetization** has to be used. In this process a paramagnetic salt, such as potassium chrome alum, can be cooled to 10^{-6} K, by demagnetizing the previously magnetized salt under adiabatic conditions. The cooling occurs because the demagnetized state is less ordered than the magnetized state, the extra energy required coming from the internal energy of the substance. See also SUPERCONDUCTIVITY; SUPERFLUIDITY.

cryolite See HALL, CHARLES MARTIN.

cryptic coloration See CAMOUFLAGE.

cryptogam A plant, alga, or fungus that disperses itself by microscopic SPORES rather than seeds; examples are hornworts, liverworts, mosses, club-mosses, horsetails, and ferns. The term implies 'hidden sexuality' and was given to these plants before their sexual life cycles had been discovered. All cryptogamic plants have an alternation of generations. This means that the spore germinates to produce a plant, called the gametophyte, that bears the female and male structures which produce egg cells and swimming sperms respectively. After fertilization the egg cell in the female sexual structure, the archegonium, develops into a new, different type of plant, called the sporophyte, which will bear the spores. In some groups of plants the gametophyte is the main stage. For example, it forms the green, leafy plant of mosses; the sporophyte is the spore-containing capsule and its stalk. But in ferns the gametophyte is small and the main plant is the sporophyte.

cryptography Writing or solving ciphers. A code is an unvarying rule for representing one information symbol by another: the MORSE CODE is an example. Ciphers also replace or reorganize information symbols, but the rules governing the replacement (the key) are a secret known only to the transmitter and the legitimate receiver. An example of the use of cryptography is its use on cash cards, which have the account holder's personal identification number (PIN) encrypted on them. This can be read by the cash machine to check that the user has entered the correct PIN, but it is not accessible to non-authorized users. Other uses include securing data being transferred between computers, and protecting data-flow between COMMUNICATIONS SATELLITES and ground stations.

crystal A solid three-dimensional form of a substance in which a regular internal atomic structure is expressed by a regular arrangement of plane (flat) faces. For each crystalline form of a substance the angles between particular crystal faces are always the same. The angles remain constant even when the growth of the crystal is distorted, as is often the case in nature. The crystal structure is one of the characteristic properties of a mineral identified by its X-ray diffraction pattern. All crystals can be assigned to one of the seven crystal systems, according to their degree of symmetry. Crystals may be described in terms of the groups of faces (forms) that bound the solid crystal. Well-formed crystals may be used for a variety of purposes. Some are used as gemstones; others, such as calcite or quartz, have commercial uses.

Crystal Palace A large building of iron and glass, resembling a giant greenhouse, designed by (Sir) Joseph Paxton as the centrepiece for the Great Exhibition of 1851 in Hyde Park, London. After the Exhibition it was re-erected at Sydenham near Croydon; it was accidentally burnt down in 1936.

crystal set See RADIO RECEIVER.

CSCE See HELSINKI CONFERENCE.

CS gas See TEAR-GAS.

ctenophoran See SEA GOOSEBERRY.

Ctesibius (fl. 250 BC) Alexandrian Greek inventor of a number of ingenious mechanical devices. Little is known of his life, and his writings are lost, but he is credited with the invention of the force PUMP and a hydraulic organ, and with making improvements to the clepsydra (see CLOCKS AND TIME MEASUREMENT). He also invented compressed-air weapons and a military catapult.

Ctesiphon An ancient city on the Tigris near Baghdad, Iraq, capital of the Parthian kingdom from *c*.224 and then of Persia under the Sassanian dynasty. It was taken by the Arabs in 636.

CT scanning See COMPUTERIZED TOMOGRAPHY.

Cuba An island country, the largest island in the CARIBBEAN Islands.

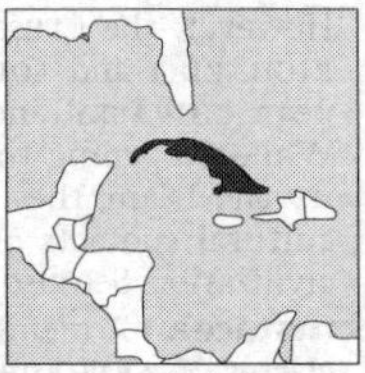

Physical. Cuba is long and narrow – about 1,280 km (795 miles) from west to east yet rarely more than 160 km (100 miles) from north to south. Most of it is flat, with plains rising southward to heights seldom greater than 90 m (295 feet), except in the south-east, where the Sierra Maestra reaches 2,000 m (6,560 feet) and more. The climate is tropical, with heavy rain and easterly winds which often become hurricanes.

Economy. The world's second largest producer of sugar, Cuba has a centrally planned economy. Exports have been heavily dependent on sugar (75 per cent in 1975, mainly to the Soviet Union), though nickel and petroleum products (based on the resale of imported Soviet crude oil) have also been important. Agriculture is highly mechanized, and most farms are cooperatively run on state-owned land. Tobacco is another major crop. Iron, nickel, and manganese are Cuba's main mineral resources. Compared to its neighbours, Cuba has a sizeable industrial sector and high standards of social services. The loss of Soviet aid and trade since the Soviet Union's disintegration in 1991 has had serious consequences on the economy, and social services have suffered.

History. Cuba was first settled by migrating hunter-gatherer-fisher people, the Ciboney from South America, by *c*.3000 BC. Migrations of agriculturist, pottery-making Arawak Indians from northern South America began to displace them in eastern Cuba after *c*.1000 BC, but the Ciboney remained in the west. Cuba was discovered by Columbus in 1492 but it was not realized that it was an island until it was circumnavigated in 1508. Spanish settlement began in 1511 when Diego Velásquez founded Havana and several other towns. The Arawak became virtually extinct by the end of the century from exploitation and European-introduced diseases. Black slaves were imported for the plantations (especially sugar and tobacco) from 1526. Britain seized the island in 1762–63 but immediately exchanged it with the Spanish for Florida. Slave importation ended in 1865, but slavery was not abolished until 1886. Various attempts were made by US interests to acquire the island and many Americans fought in the unsuccessful first War of Independence (1868–78). Large US investments were maintained in the sugar industry, which by now was producing one-third of the world's sugar. The second War of Independence (1895–1901) was joined by the USA (1898) after a well-orchestrated press campaign, and Cuba was occupied by US troops (1899–1901). In 1902 the Republic of Cuba was proclaimed. A series of corrupt and socially insensitive governments followed, culminating in the brutal, authoritarian regime of Gerardo Machado (1925–33), which prompted the abortive revolution of 1933–34, the island remaining under US 'protection' until 1934. Fulengio BATISTA was President 1940–44 and 1952–59. Although supported by the USA, his second government was notoriously corrupt and ruthless. In 1956 Fidel CASTRO initiated a guerrilla war which led to the establishment of a socialist regime (1959) under his leadership. He repulsed the invasion by Cuban exiles at Cochinos Bay, the BAY OF PIGS (April 1961), and survived the CUBAN MISSILE CRISIS of October 1962. The accomplishments of his one-party regime in public health, education, and housing are considerable though his record on human rights remains poor. Castro maintained a high profile abroad and although the espousal of world revolution was tempered under pressure from Moscow, Cuban assistance to liberation movements in Latin America and Africa was consistent. At home, after the political turbulence of the 1960s, the revolution stabilized with the establishment of more broadly based representative assemblies at municipal, provincial, and national levels. In economic terms, the initial hopes of diversification and industrialization were not realized, and Cuba continued to rely on the export of sugar as well as on substantial financial subsidy from the Soviet Union. Agricultural production in the socialist state was generally poor, and shortages and rationing continued. Frustrations with the regime led to an exodus of 125,000 Cubans in 1980. Yet the regime survived when COMECON and the Soviet Union collapsed in 1990 and 1991 respectively, and the country found itself faced with a grave economic situation. In October 1991 the fourth Congress of the Communist Party endorsed the policy of centralized control, but an opposition group, the Cuban Democratic Convergence, did emerge. In June 1992 a successful international conference for capital investment was held in Havana, in spite of the continuing US embargo on trade.

Capital: Havana
Area: 110,861 sq km (42,804 sq mi)
Population: 11,068,000 (1995)
Currency: 1 Cuban peso = 100 centavos
Religions: Non-religious 48.7%; Roman Catholic 39.6%; atheist 6.4%; Protestant 3.3%; Afro-Cuban syncretist 1.6%
Ethnic Groups: White 66.0%; Mixed 21.9%; Black 12.0%
Languages: Spanish (official)
International Organizations: UN; Non-Aligned Movement; suspended member of OAS

Cuban Missile Crisis (1962) An international crisis involving the USA and the Soviet Union. It was precipitated when US leaders learned that Soviet missiles with nuclear warheads capable of reaching the USA were being secretly installed in Cuba. President KENNEDY reinforced the US naval base at Guantanamo, ordered a naval blockade against Soviet military shipments to Cuba, and demanded that the Soviet Union remove its missiles and bases from the island. There seemed a real danger of nuclear war as the rival forces were placed on full alert, and the crisis sharpened as Soviet merchant vessels thought to be carrying missiles approached the island and the blockading US forces. However, the Soviet ships were ordered by KHRUSHCHEV to turn back, and the Soviet Union agreed to US demands to dismantle the rocket bases in return for a US pledge not to attack Cuba. An outcome of the crisis was the establishment of a direct, exclusive line of communication (the 'hot line') to be used in an emergency, between the President of the USA and the leader of the Soviet Union.

Cubism A movement in painting (and to a lesser extent sculpture) developed by PICASSO and BRAQUE from about 1907. Cubism made a radical break from the realistic depiction of nature that had dominated European painting and sculpture since the RENAISSANCE, for Picasso and Braque aimed to depict the permanent structure of objects rather than their appearance at a particular moment and place. They represented subjects from a multiplicity of angles, rather than showing them from a single, fixed viewpoint, so that many different aspects of the same object could be seen simultaneously. Influenced by African sculpture and the later paintings of CÉZANNE, Cubist work up to 1912 is called 'Analytical' Cubism: forms were analysed into predominantly geometrical structures and colour was extremely subdued. In a second phase, known as 'Synthetic' Cubism, colour became much stronger and shapes more decorative, and elements such as stencilled lettering and pieces of newspaper were introduced into paintings and made into COLLAGES. Juan GRIS was as important as Braque or Picasso in this phase of the movement. World War I brought an end to the collaboration of Braque and Picasso, but their work was a major influence on other movements, among them FUTURISM, ORPHISM, Purism, and VORTICISM. Certain forms of modern poetry, prose, and music have been called Cubist because of their multi-image structure.

cuchia A species of freshwater, eel-like fish that is widely distributed in southern and eastern India and Myanmar. It lives in swamps, ditches, and backwaters of rivers, and although these habitats are often oxygen-deficient, the cuchia survives by breathing air into lung-like sacs in the roof of its gill chamber. Locally, it is an important food-fish, which grows to 70 cm (28 inches) in length. Despite its body shape, it is not an eel, and belongs to a distinct order, Synbranchiformes, often called swamp eels.

Cuchulain (or **Cuchulainn**, **Cuchullain**, **Cú Chulainn**) Legendary Irish Gaelic warrior, the nephew of CONCHOBAR MAC NESSE, and the greatest of his Knights of the Red Branch. Among Cuchulain's ACHILLES-like feats was his single-handed defence of Ulster against the forces of Medb (Maeve), queen of Connaught. He is the central figure of the literary Ulaid (Ulster) Cycle, recorded from oral tradition between the 8th and 11th centuries.

cuckoo A bird that is widespread in both Old and New Worlds. Cuckoos belong to the family Cuculidae. Varying from sparrow-sized to crow-sized, they are mostly coloured grey, brown, and black, though some of the smaller ones are bronze-green. Although many of them build an ordinary cup nest and raise their young themselves, some lay their eggs in the nests of other birds and allow the host species to raise the young cuckoos. Most famous of these is the European cuckoo, *Cuculus canorus*, whose females lay eggs of various colours. Those of each female closely resemble those of the particular species which they parasitize. The young cuckoo hatches before the eggs of the host hatch, and ejects them from the nest, so leaving itself as the only mouth to feed. Other groups in the family include anis, ROADRUNNERS, and COUCALS. The cuckoo order, Cuculiformes, encompasses some 143 species.

cuckoo bee A small, yellow and black bee, belonging to the same superfamily as the true bees. They have no pollen baskets and some species resemble wasps in appearance. The females lay their eggs in the cells of other bees, where their larvae feed on the pollen stored for the host's larvae.

cuckoo-shrike A bird that occurs throughout the warmer areas of Africa, India, south-east Asia, Australia, and many Pacific islands, and is neither a shrike nor a cuckoo. The 49 species are all members of the genus *Coracina* in the oriole tribe of the family Corvidae. They vary in size from that of a sparrow to that of a large thrush. Cuckoo-shrikes tend to be brownish, grey, or black, often with pale or white underparts. Minivets, also part of the same family, are usually more brightly coloured, with glossy blue-black upperparts and bright red or yellow underparts. The cuckoo-shrike feeds on insects and small fruits and builds a very small cup nest in twigs at the tip of a branch.

cuckoo-spit See FROGHOPPER.

cuckoo wasp (or **ruby tail**) A WASP belonging to the family Chrysididae, with a body of metallic red, blue, or green, and a conspicuous ovipositor. The females lay their eggs in the cells of solitary wasps or bees, where the young feed on the larvae of the hosts and sometimes on food stored for them. They are a large family including over 1,000 species in the genus *Chrysis*. This includes the widespread European species *C. ignita*.

cucujo A species of CLICK BEETLE of the tropical New World that is the brightest, most luminous animal known. The adults produce light from spots on the thorax as well as from the tip of the abdomen. The eggs and the larvae are also luminous.

cucumber A plant, *Cucumis sativus*, belonging to the pumpkin family, most closely related to melons. Thought to be of Asian origin, cucumbers have been cultivated for centuries throughout Europe, being known to the ancient Greeks and Romans. The fruit of the plant is edible, usually eaten raw. A relative, the gherkin, *Cucumis anguria*, native to tropical and subtropical America, produces smaller, prickly fruits. Both are trailing or climbing plants with large, angular, toothed leaves and separate male and female flowers. The squirting cucumber, *Ecballium elaterium*, is a related plant whose ripe fruits explode when they fall, ejecting a fluid containing seeds.

Cudlipp, Hugh, Baron Cudlipp of Aldingbourne (1913–) British newspaper editor. The features editor on the *Daily Mirror* from 1935 and (after World War II) its editorial director, he was a pioneer of tabloid journalism. He conceived the formula of the sensationalized presentation of sex and crime together with populist politics that later proved a basis for other tabloids; this dramatically increased the paper's circulation. He gives an account of his career in *Publish and Be Damned* (1953).

Cugnot, Nicolas-Joseph (1725–1804) French pioneer of steam traction. In 1769 he was encouraged by the French Minister of War to develop a steam-propelled gun-carriage, the first ever steam-powered road vehicle. The following year he built a steam tricycle capable of carrying four passengers at walking pace.

Cui, César See FIVE, THE.

Culbertson, Ely (1891–1955) US bridge player. An authority on contract bridge, he revolutionized the game by formalizing a system of bidding. This, together with his other activities in the early 1930s, such as well-publicized challenge matches with high stakes, helped to establish this form of the game in preference to auction bridge.

Culloden, Battle of (16 April 1746) A battle, fought on a bleak moor in Scotland to the east of Inverness, in which the JACOBITE forces of Charles Edward Stuart, largely drawn from the Highland clans, were routed during a sleet storm by the English and German troops led by the Duke of CUMBERLAND. The battle was followed by ruthless slaughter of the Jacobite wounded and prisoners, with survivors hunted down and killed, earning Cumberland the nickname 'Butcher'. Culloden ended the FORTY-FIVE rebellion and virtually destroyed the Jacobite cause. It was the last land battle fought in Britain.

culmination The two points on the CELESTIAL SPHERE in the 24-hour circuit (the DIURNAL MOTION) of a celestial body when it is on the observer's meridian. For an object that rises and sets, upper culmination is its highest altitude above the horizon, lower culmination being below the horizon and therefore unseen. For a CIRCUMPOLAR STAR, both upper and lower culminations are observable.

Culpeper, Nicholas (1616–54) English physician and herbalist, wrote many books on medicine and astrology, including an English translation of the College of Physicians' Latin pharmacopoeia; chiefly remembered for his *English Physician* (1652), later revised and enlarged, which became known as 'Culpeper's Herbal'.

cultivar A plant variety bred from a wild species that differs from the wild species as a result of that breeding. The difference is maintained by inbreeding within the new variety, and by selection of offspring that most closely resemble the parent.

cultivator A machine that converts the surface of a field carrying plant remains into an environment tailored to the sowing of the next crop. The term thus encompasses ploughs, rotary cultivators, cultivators with spring tines or teeth, HARROWS, and land rollers.

Cultural Revolution (1966–76) A decade of chaos and political upheaval in China with its roots in a factional dispute over the future of Chinese socialism. Oblique criticisms of MAO ZEDONG in the early 1960s prompted him to retaliate against this threat to his ideology-led position from more pragmatic and bureaucratic modernizers with ideas closer to the Soviet Union. Unable to do so in the Communist Party, he utilized discontented students and young workers as his RED GUARDS to attack local and central party officials, who were then replaced by his own supporters and often had army backing. LIU SHAOQI, State Chairman of China since 1959 and Mao's heir-apparent, lost all his government and party posts and LIN BIAO became the designated successor. The most violent phase of the Cultural Revolution came to an end with the Ninth Party Congress in 1969, but its radical policies continued until Mao's death in 1976.

Cumberland A former county of north-west England united with Westmorland and part of Lancashire in 1974 to form the country of Cumbria.

Cumberland, William Augustus, Duke of (1721–65) Third son of George II, British military commander. He gained great notoriety (and his nickname 'the Butcher') for the severity of his suppression of the Jacobite clans in the aftermath of his victory at the Battle of CULLODEN.

Cumbernauld A New Town in central Scotland established in 1955, the administrative centre of Cumbernauld and Kilsyth District, Strathclyde Region from 1975 to 1996; pop. (1991) 48,760.

Cumbria A county of north-west England formed in 1974 from the former counties of Cumberland, Westmorland, and part of Lancashire; area 6,824 sq km (2,636 sq miles); pop. (1991) 486,900; county town, Carlisle. Separated from Northumberland by the Pennine Range, the county is dominated by the Cumbrian Mountains and the Lake District.

cummings, e. e. (born Edward Estlin Cummings) (1894–1962) US poet. His first published poetry was written in a relatively conventional style, but in *&* (1925) and *is 5* (1926) he started to adopt the techniques he is best known for: vernacular language, tricks of typography and spelling (including lower case for his own name), hybrid verse-forms, and word plays. His verse, collected in *Complete Poems* (1968), celebrates individual vision and experience in a modern age of mass culture and uniformity.

cumulonimbus A form of cloud consisting of a tall dense mass, present during thunderstorms.

cumulus A cloud formation consisting of round masses heaped on each other above a horizontal base.

Cunard, Sir Samuel (1787–1865) Canadian-born British shipowner. One of the pioneers of the regular transatlantic passenger service, he founded the steamship company which still bears his name with the aid of a contract to carry the mail between Britain and Canada. The first such voyage for the company was made in 1840.

cuneiform A family of scripts, developed in the Middle East as a result of using split reeds for writing on soft clay. Incised free-hand signs were turned into groups of impressed triangles (cuneiform means wedge-shaped) by the Sumerians *c.*2500 BC. Thereafter it was adapted for other languages, including Akkadian and Assyrian. The forms were rigidly maintained, even when inscriptions were carved on stone. About 1500 BC in Persia, alphabets of cuneiform signs were invented, eventually to be replaced by derivatives of the Phoenician alphabet.

Cunningham, Andrew Browne, Viscount Cunningham of Hyndhope (1883–1963) British admiral. At the beginning of World War II he was commander-in-chief, Mediterranean. Here he was faced with an Italian fleet that was numerically superior to his own. However, he asserted British domination by his air attack on the Italian base of Taranto in 1940, and at Cape Matapan in 1941, where his victory effectually neutralized the Italian fleet for the rest of the war. As First Sea Lord from 1943 he was responsible for naval strategy and attended the meetings of Allied heads of government.

Cunningham, Merce (1919–) US dancer and choreographer. He danced with Martha GRAHAM's company (1939–45) then, after a period as a solo dancer, started his own company in 1952. His many experimental abstract ballets are influenced by the music of John CAGE, with whom Cunningham has often collaborated. They include *How to Pass, Kick, Fall and Run* (1965), *Walkaround Time* (1968), *Travelogue* (1977), *Duets* (1980), and *Ocean* (1994).

Cunobelinus See CYMBELINE.

cupellation An ancient method of extracting SILVER from its ores. The silver is alloyed with lead and then heated in a porous ceramic dish called a cupel. The lead is oxidized and most of the oxide is swept away in an air blast. Any residual oxide is absorbed by the cupel, leaving behind pure silver.

Cupid The Roman god of love, identified with the Greek Eros.

cuprite A red copper oxide (Cu_2O) mineral found in very hard, dense masses and as crystals. It is produced in copper vein deposits where the copper becomes oxidized from weathering. Such deposits occur in many localities, including Chessey (France), Cornwall (UK), and Arizona (USA). It is an important source of copper, and as perfect crystals it is prized as a semiprecious gemstone.

cupro-nickel See ALLOY.

Curaçao The largest island of the Netherlands Antilles, situated in the Caribbean Sea 60 km (37 miles) north of the Venezuelan coast; area 444 sq km (171 sq miles); pop. (1992) 144,100; chief town, Willemstad. Curaçao's economy is based on refining of crude oil imported from Venezuela, and on tourism.

curare A substance extracted from certain plants growing in tropical South America, and used as an arrow poison. The active ingredient, D-tubocurarine, prevents nerve impulses from reaching the muscles, thus causing paralysis, but it does not affect sensation. In controlled doses it can be used during ANAESTHESIA to obtain muscular relaxation.

curassow A bird belonging to the family Cracidae, some of which are called guans. Related to other gamebirds, curassows are large, 50–90 cm (20–36 inches) long, somewhat turkey-like birds. They are glossy black or brown, often with white areas on the body. Primarily South American, some occur in Central America, and one, the chachalaca, *Ortalis vetula*, is found in the southern United States. They build flimsy nests of twigs on the branches of trees and lay two or three white eggs. In appearance they resemble the ARCHAEOPTERYX.

Curia The papal court and government departments of the Vatican City in Rome. It was also the name of an ancient Roman tribe, the senate house in Rome, and a feudal court of justice.

Curie, Marie (1867–1934) Polish-born French physicist. Marie and her husband, **Pierre Curie** (1859–1906), were pioneers of radioactivity. Pierre's early researches were on piezoelectricity and on the effects of temperature on magnetism. The two scientists married in 1895. Working together on the mineral pitchblende, they discovered the elements polonium and radium, for which they shared the 1903 Nobel Prize for physics with A.-H.

Becquerel. Marie succeeded to her husband's chair of physics at the Sorbonne after his accidental death, receiving another Nobel Prize (for chemistry) in 1911 for her isolation of radium. She also studied radioactive decay and the applications of radioactivity to medicine, pioneered mobile X-ray units, headed the French Radiological Service during World War I, and afterwards worked in the new Radium Institute. She died of leukaemia, undoubtedly caused by prolonged exposure to radioactive materials.

curium (symbol Cm, at. no. 96, r.a.m. 247) A strongly radioactive transuranic element synthesized by G. T. Seaborg in 1944 and named after Pierre and Marie CURIE. Compounds known include the oxides CmO_2 and Cm_2O_3, and such trihalides as CmF_3 and $CmCC_3$.

Curitiba A city in south-east Brazil, capital of Paraná state; pop. (1997) 1,315,035. Paper, textiles, and chemicals are produced.

curlew A large, streaky brown, buff, and white WADING BIRD with a long, downcurved beak. Curlews are members of the family Scolopacidae, closely related to the sandpipers and phalaropes. The eight species of their genus (*Numenius*) include the whimbrel, *N. phaeopus*, and the Eskimo curlew, *N. borealis*, but this last species may be extinct. The curlew, *N. arquata*, has a loud, ringing call, 'courlee', and a remarkable bubbling song.

Curragh, The A plain in County Kildare in the Republic of Ireland, noted for the breeding of racehorses. The Irish Derby is run annually on its racecourse.

currant A hardy, deciduous shrub, belonging to the Grossulariaceae family, especially BLACKCURRANTS and RED CURRANTS. The term currant is also applied to the small black fruit of a dessert grape, *Vitis vinifera*, which is grown in Greece.

currawong See BELL MAGPIE.

current, electric See ELECTRIC CURRENT; ELECTRICITY AND MAGNETISM.

current, ocean See OCEAN CURRENT; CIRCULATION.

curtain wall ▶**1** The outer wall of a medieval castle. It surrounds the castle and often has towers and bastions along its length. ▶**2** A lightweight, non-load-bearing wall in which a metal or timber framework is supported in front of the building frame on brackets at the floor edges. The spaces within the framework are filled either with glass or with other thin sheet material, backed with thermal insulation.

Curtin, John (Joseph Ambrose) (1885–1945) Australian Labor statesman, Prime Minister 1941–45. He led the Labor party from 1935 to 1945. As Premier during World War II, he mobilized Australian resources to meet the danger of Japanese invasion, laid down the groundwork for the postwar economy, and introduced various welfare measures. Curtin died while in office.

Curtiss, Glenn (Hammond) (1878–1930) US air pioneer and aircraft designer. He built his his first aeroplane in 1909, and invented the aileron and demonstrated the first practical seaplane two years later. In 1908 Curtiss made the first public US flight of 1.0 km (0.6 miles), and won the James Gordon Bennett Cup in 1909 for a flight in his own aeroplane at 46.6 m.p.h.

curvature In cosmology, the modification of SPACE-TIME in the presence of matter. Light will always travel by the shortest route, known as a **geodesic**, between two points. Usually this is a straight line. However, in the presence of a large amount of matter, such as in the vicinity of a very massive star or a BLACK HOLE, the light will appear to follow a curved path. In fact the light has still followed a geodesic, but it is space–time that has been curved by the massive body. According to the general theory of RELATIVITY, the gravitational field of a massive body is then an effect of the curvature of space–time.

Curzon, George Nathaniel, 1st Marquis Curzon of Kedleston (1859–1925) British statesman. As viceroy of India (1899–1905) he achieved reforms in administration, education, and currency, and set up the North-West Frontier province (1901). He was instrumental in the partitioning of Bengal in 1901, incurring thereby the ill-feeling of the Hindus. A strong supporter of imperialism, he resigned in 1905 in a dispute with KITCHENER. LLOYD GEORGE included him in his coalition war cabinet (1916–18). He became Foreign Secretary in 1919. Lloyd George's tendency to conduct foreign affairs himself irritated Curzon, who joined the Conservative rebellion in 1922 against the coalition government. Bonar LAW became Prime Minister and made Curzon his Foreign Secretary in 1922. As Foreign Secretary he gave his name to the frontier line proposed (1920) by Lloyd George, between Poland and Russia. The broad outline of the frontier became (1939) the boundary between the Soviet and German spheres of occupied Poland. It was imposed (1945) on Poland by the Allies as the definitive frontier between itself and the Soviet Union.

cuscus See PHALANGER.

Cushing, Harvey Williams (1869–1939) US surgeon. He introduced techniques that greatly increased the likelihood of success in neurosurgical operations, and described the hormonal disorder that was later named after him.

Cushing, Peter (1913–94) British actor. Cushing was known particularly for his roles in horror films, especially those made by Hammer Films; these include *Dracula* (1958) and *Frankenstein Must Be Destroyed* (1969). Making his début in 1939, he appeared in more than a hundred films; he played Sherlock Holmes in *The Hound of the Baskervilles* (1959), and also appeared in *Star Wars* (1977).

cushion star See STARFISH.

Cushitic languages A group of east African languages of the Hamitic type, spoken mainly in Ethiopia and Somalia.

custard apple See SOURSOP.

Custer, George (Armstrong) (1839–76) US cavalry general. He served with distinction in the American Civil War but led his men to their deaths in a clash (popularly known as Custer's Last Stand) with the Sioux at Little Bighorn in Montana. Controversy over his conduct in the final battle still continues.

customary law Unwritten rules generally accepted as binding by a community as a result of long use. All legal systems recognize custom as a source of law, although the authority ascribed to it and the extent to which it is recognized in legislative measures and CASE LAW varies. In English law, custom is at the root of much of the COMMON LAW, but it is rarely recognized by case law today, whereas in Japan, where the adoption of codified laws is very recent, courts have given effect to older customs (relating, for example, to marriage), even where they conflict with the civil code.

customs and excise Duties charged on goods (both home-produced and imported) to raise revenue for governments. In England customs date from the reign of EDWARD I, when duties were raised on wool and leather. Tunnage and poundage was introduced under EDWARD II. Excise was first introduced in 1643 to finance the parliamentary armies in the ENGLISH CIVIL WAR and was a tax on alcoholic beverages, mainly beer and ale. At the RESTORATION Charles II was granted excise duties for life by Parliament. Customs duties are tariffs paid on goods entering (or occasionally leaving) a country. Customs duties between members of the European Union were abolished in 1992. Excise duties are paid on the domestic sale of certain goods and activities, such as alcohol, tobacco, motor fuel, and betting. In the UK the Board of Customs and Excise is also responsible for collecting such indirect taxes as value-added tax.

customs union A group of countries forming an economic union that allows member-states to trade freely with each other while applying a common tariff to goods from outside the union.

Cuthbert, St (died 687) English monk. He travelled in the north of England as a missionary before living as a hermit on Farne Island and later becoming bishop of Lindisfarne. Feast day, 20 March.

cuticle The outer layer of some animals and plants, which acts to prevent water loss. In a plant it consists of a waxy layer which covers the stems and leaves. The cuticle of arthropods is secreted by the underlying epidermal cells and acts as a protective, supportive and waterproof EXOSKELETON.

cut-off river See OX-BOW LAKE.

cutter A type of mercantile sailing ship, adopted as a small warship in the mid-18th century. It was single-masted with a gaff (fore-and-aft) mainsail, a square topsail, and two foresails, armed with up to twenty light guns. From the 18th century, a cutter was also a SHIP's boat, with one or two masts and carrying eight to fourteen oars. The term is now usually used for a sailing YACHT with a mainsail and two foresails, or for a motor vessel used in the USA for coastguard, ice, and weather patrol duties.

cuttlefish A CEPHALOPOD mollusc belonging to the order Sepioidea, with an internal chambered shell known as the cuttlebone containing gas to provide buoyancy, lateral fins for gentle swimming, and jet propulsion for escaping. The skin of cuttlefish undergoes remarkably rapid colour and pattern changes, especially when they are mating. Eight arms and two longer tentacles are used for feeding, mainly on crustaceans. Male cuttlefish (like other male cephalopods) have one arm modified as a sperm-transferring organ when mature.

cutworm The destructive caterpillar of certain species of OWLET MOTHS. Cutworms feed by night on roots and shoots, and by day hide in soil or beneath stones. Many species, such as the dark swordgrass, or black cutworm, *Agrotis ipsilon*, which feed on crops and grasses, are serious pests.

Cuvier, Georges Léopold Chrétien Frédéric Dagobert, Baron (1769–1832) French naturalist. Cuvier carried out a study of fossil elephants which in effect founded the science of palaeontology. Pioneering also in comparative anatomy, he was the first to classify the lower invertebrates. He realized that each species could be derived from another by small changes in structure, which proved crucial in the emergence of evolutionary theory. However, he believed resolutely in the creationist view and quarrelled publicly with the early proponents of evolution, notably Lamarck.

Cuyp Family of Dutch painters, three members of which gained distinction. **Jacob Gerritsz Cuyp** (1594–*c*.1651) excelled as a portraitist, his depictions of children being particularly charming. His half-brother **Benjamin Gerritsz Cuyp** (1612–52) is noted for his biblical and genre scenes, which use light and shadow effects in a manner akin to the early work of REMBRANDT. The most illustrious member of the family is **Aelbert Cuyp** (1620–91), the son and probably the pupil of Benjamin Gerritsz. Aelbert painted many subjects, but he is now remembered as one of the greatest Dutch landscape painters. His finest works – typically river scenes and landscapes with placid, dignified-looking cows – show great serenity and masterly handling of glowing light.

Cuzco A historic city in the Andes of southern Peru that was the capital of the Inca empire and the beginning of the 'Inca Trail' to MACHU PICCHU until the Spanish conquest (1533); pop. (1990) 275,300. It is capital of a department of the same name. It has a magnificent Baroque cathedral and church built in 1668, and holds both Catholic and Inca festivals. It was heavily damaged by a severe earthquake in 1950 but the major buildings have been restored.

CVD See VAPOUR DEPOSITION.

cwm See CIRQUE.

Cwmbran A town in South Wales, on the Afon Lywel north-west of Newport; pop. (1991) 46,021. Established in 1949 as a New Town to accommodate steel workers, it is now the administrative centre of Monmouthshire.

cyanide A molecule containing the CN group or CN^- ion. Organic cyanides are called NITRILES and have the general formula R–CN, where R is an ALKYL or ARYL GROUP. All cyanides are extremely poisonous because the cyanide ion is able to coordinate with the ion in haemoglobin and so block the uptake of oxygen.

cyanobacteria (or **blue-green bacteria**; formerly **blue-green algae**) Unicellular, filamentous (thread-like), or colonial BACTERIA that carry out PHOTOSYNTHESIS, usually with the production of oxygen (unlike other photosynthetic bacteria, which carry out photosynthesis in the absence of air and without the production of oxygen). They are probably among the first living organisms to evolve on Earth; their fossilized remains have been discovered in Precambrian rocks 1,500 million years old. Early cyanobacteria are believed to have been responsible for generating the oxygen in the Earth's atmosphere. Cyanobacteria are found in both terrestrial and aquatic habitats, and often cause blue-green-coloured 'blooms' or 'mats'. They reproduce by cell division (binary or multiple fission) or, rarely, by budding. Other (now historic) names for the cyanobacteria include Cyanophyceae and Myxophyceae.

cybernetics (from Greek *kubernētēs*, 'steersman') The study of communication and control systems in machines, animals, and organizations. The discipline developed immediately after World War II, when CONTROL SYSTEMS and systems-engineering techniques were applied successfully to certain neurological problems. Cybernetics is characterized by a concentration on the flow of information (rather than energy or material) within a system, and on the use of FEEDBACK or 'goal-directed activity' in both technological artefacts and living organisms. Major areas of cybernetic study have been biological control systems, AUTOMATION, animal communication, and ARTIFICIAL INTELLIGENCE (AI).

cycad A tree that makes up a group, Cycadophyta, of some 100 species of GYMNOSPERM. They look quite unlike conifers and resemble palms in their stout-stemmed habit and large, fern-like leaves. Present-day cycads are classified into three families, largely according to the vein pattern of the leaves: one includes about 20 species of *Cycas* from Madagascar and tropical Asia; the second is made up of a single species of *Stangeria* native to southern Africa; and the third family comprises some 80 species in eight genera native to tropical and warm, temperate zones. These are relics of a formerly much more widespread and numerous group, which reached its zenith 100–150 million years ago. The pith of some *Cycas* species is made into sago in Asia.

Cyclades (Greek **Kikládhes**) A group of Greek islands in the Aegean Sea, regarded in antiquity as circling around the sacred island of Delos. They are the site of a Bronze Age civilization noted for developments in metallurgy and for angular figurines in white marble. The Cyclades form a department of modern Greece; pop. (1991) 100,100.

cyclamen A species of plant belonging to the primrose family. The 19 known species of the genus *Cyclamen* are Mediterranean in origin and all bear attractive pinkish or white flowers with upturned petals. *C. persicum* is the species from which the large-flowered varieties grown as pot plants are derived. In Italy and southern France, the tuberous rootstocks or corms are eaten by pigs, hence the common name sowbread.

cycling The recreation of riding a bicycle and the various branches of cycle-racing. Several sports can be adapted for playing on bicycles, such as hockey, POLO, and cycleball (a mounted version of football, using the wheels to propel the ball). Cycle-racing is basically divided into stadium events and road-racing; there is also cyclo-cross, a blend of cycle-racing and CROSS-COUNTRY RUNNING held over rough, hilly terrain. Cycle-stadia have steeply banked tracks for sprint events in which skilful manœuvring for position is important. Professional road-racing is established worldwide, but is most popular in Europe, where victory in the Tour de France is the sport's highest prize. The race-circuit, varied from year to year, consists of a gruelling series of stage-races and time-trials, lasting three weeks and covering some 4,828 km (3,000 miles).

Cyclops In Greek mythology, one of a race of savage giants who had one eye in the middle of the forehead. They were reputedly descended from three one-eyed Titans who made thunderbolts for Zeus. Polyphemus was the most famous of the Cyclopes.

cyclotron See PARTICLE ACCELERATOR.

Cygnus The Swan, a CONSTELLATION of the northern sky, one of the forty-eight constellations known to the ancient Greeks. In mythology it represents the swan as which Zeus disguised himself to seduce Queen Leda of Sparta. Cygnus is popularly known as the Northern Cross because of its distinctive shape. Its brightest star is DENEB. At the foot of the cross lies Beta Cygni, known as Albireo, a beautiful coloured double star for small telescopes, consisting of orange and green components of third and fifth magnitude. Cygnus lies in a rich part of the Milky Way where it is bisected by a dark dust cloud known as the Cygnus Rift. Near Deneb lies the NORTH AMERICA NEBULA.

Cygnus A One of the brightest radio sources in the sky, and the first RADIO GALAXY to be discovered. The galaxy was identified as a result of accurate radio position measurements made at Cambridge, UK, in the early 1950s by Francis Graham-Smith, later to become Astronomer Royal. The galaxy is 300 million parsecs away, and its radio output is millions of times greater than that of a normal galaxy.

cylinder snake (or **pipe snake**) A harmless, rather primitive, burrowing snake of the family Aniliidae, which occurs in tropical areas of Asia (nine species) and northern South America (one species). The New World form, *Anilius*, has very reduced eyes and is a CORAL SNAKE mimic, with a pattern of red and black bands. The Malaysian pipe snake has a bright red underside to its tail, which it displays when threatened.

cymbals Bronze plates, either clashed together in pairs, or used singly and struck with a drumstick. Small cymbals were used in the ancient world (the origin of the orchestral 'antique' cymbals), sometimes on the ends of thongs; they were also used in the Middle Ages. Medium-sized instruments came into military bands in the late 18th century with Turkish music, and were occasionally used orchestrally. Larger instruments were used from the mid-19th century.

Cymbeline (or **Cunobelinus**) (died *c*.42 AD) British chieftain. He was a powerful ruler whose tribe occupied a wide area from Northamptonshire to SE England. He made Camulodunum (Colchester) his capital, and established a mint there. He was the subject of a medieval fable used by Shakespeare for his play *Cymbeline* (*c*.1610).

Cymru The Welsh name for WALES.

Cynewulf (late 8th–9th centuries) Anglo-Saxon poet. Of the many poems that have been attributed to him in the past, modern scholarship restricts attribution to four: *Juliana*, *Elene*, *The Fates of the Apostles*, and *Christ II*. Each of these is inscribed with his name in runes in Anglo-Saxon collections.

Cynic In ancient times a member of a sect of philosophers popularly thought to have been established by DIOGENES, though his mentor, Antisthenes of Athens, should perhaps be accorded the title of founder. The Cynic philosophy flourished through the 3rd century BC, and the beggar-philosopher, knapsack on his back and stick in hand, became a familiar sight in Greece. A steady decline thereafter was reversed by a temporary revival in the 1st century AD, though the Cynics' readiness to criticize the conduct of the emperors led to many expulsions from Rome. The last recorded beggar-philosopher lived at the end of the 5th century.

cypress An evergreen conifer of the tree genera *Cupressus* and *Chamaecyparis*, though trees in other genera may also be called cypresses. For example, the tree known as swamp cypress (*Taxodium*) is a relative of the REDWOODS. In *Cupressus*, found in temperate and subtropical regions of the world, the leaves are reduced to tiny scales pressed close to the shoots. The Monterey cypress, *Cupressus macrocarpa*, is a familiar example since it is widely planted for timber and shade. *Chamaecyparis*, found only in North America and Japan, has larger leaves, and this genus includes Lawson's cypress, *C. lawsoniana*, which produces a useful timber. The Leyland cypress is a fast-growing hybrid between these two genera, and is widely used for hedging.

Cyprian, St (died 258) Carthaginian bishop and martyr. The author of a work on the nature of true unity in the Church in its relation to the episcopate, he was martyred in the reign of the Roman emperor Valerian. Feast day, 16 or 26 September.

Cyprus An island country in the north-east corner

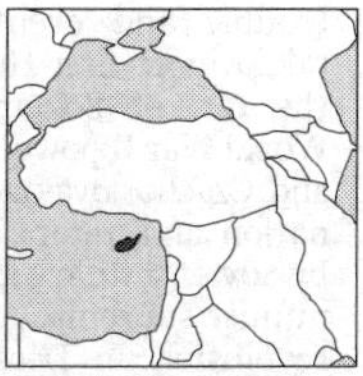

of the Mediterranean, with Turkey to the north and Syria to the east.

Physical. Cyprus is 225 km (140 miles) long and 97 km (60 miles) in breadth at its widest point. The Kyrenia coast on the north has a range of steep limestone mountains along most of its length. South of that is a treeless plain, hot and arid in summer, while further south still are igneous mountains rising to 1,950 m (6,400 feet). Here seasonally heavy rainfall has caused erosion, for winter torrents rush down unchecked. Lack of consistent rainfall is ameliorated by a high water-table which allows the use of wells.

Economy. In the south, exports of manufactured goods such as clothing, and agricultural products, together with the successful development of tourism, contribute to a thriving economy. Vineyards and orchards flourish, and sheep and goats graze the hills. Cyprus (Greek, 'copper') still has some copper, as well as iron pyrites and asbestos. The north, by contrast, is primarily agricultural and is dependent on Turkish aid.

History. A Mycenaean colony in the 14th century BC, it was ruled successively by the Assyrian, Persian, Roman, and Byzantine empires. RICHARD I of England conquered it in 1191 and sold it to the French Crusader Guy de Lusignan under whom it became a feudal monarchy. An important base for the CRUSADES, it eventually came under the control of Italian trading states, until in 1571 it fell to the OTTOMAN EMPIRE. It remained part of the Ottoman empire until 1879, when it was placed under British administration. It was formally annexed by Britain in 1914 and in 1925 declared a crown colony. From the outset there was rivalry between Greek- and Turkish-speaking communities, the former, the majority, desiring union (enosis) with Greece. After World War II there was much civil violence in which the Greek Cypriot terrorist organization EOKA played the leading role. In 1959 independence within the Commonwealth was granted under the presidency of Archbishop MAKARIOS, but by 1964 the government was in chaos and a United Nations peace-keeping force intervened. In 1974 a Greek Cypriot coup overthrew the president and Turkish forces invaded, gaining virtual control over most of the island. The Greek national government which had backed the revolt, collapsed. Talks in Geneva between Britain, Turkey, Greece, and the two Cypriot communities failed, and, although Makarios was able to resume the presidency in 1975, the Turkish Federated State of Cyprus was formed in northern Cyprus, comprising some 35 per cent of the island, with its own president. In 1983 it proclaimed itself the **Turkish Republic of Northern Cyprus**. Britain retained an important RAF base, which was also a key intelligence centre. In the early 1990s the presidents of the two communities held talks on uniting the island, but no agreement was reached.

Capital: Nicosia
Area: 9,251 sq km (3,572 sq mi) (south: 5,896 sq km (2,276 sq mi)) (north: 3,355 sq km (1,295 sq mi))
Population: 806,000 (combined; 1995) 651,000 (south) 155,000 (north)
Currency: south: 1 Cyprus pound = 100 cents; north: 1 Turkish lira = 100 kurush
Religions: south: predominantly Greek Orthodox; north: predominantly Muslim
Ethnic Groups: south: Greek 99.2%; north: Turkish 98.7%
Languages: south: Greek; north: Turkish (both official)
International Organizations: south: Council of Europe; UN; Commonwealth; Non-Aligned Movement; CSCE; the north is recognized only by Turkey

Cyrano de Bergerac, Savinien (1619–55) French soldier, duellist, and writer. He wrote comedies and satire, but is now chiefly remembered for the large number of duels that he fought (many on account of his proverbially large nose); this aspect of his life is immortalized in a play by Edmond Rostand (*Cyrano de Bergerac*, 1897).

Cyril, St (826–69) Greek missionary. The invention of the Cyrillic alphabet is ascribed to him. He and his brother St Methodius (*c*.815–85) became known as the 'Apostles to the Slavs'. Sent to Moravia, they taught in the vernacular, which they adopted also for the liturgy, and circulated a Slavonic version of the Scriptures. Feast day (in the Eastern Church) 11 May; (in the Western Church) 14 February.

Cyrillic alphabet See ALPHABET.

Cyril of Alexandria, St (died 444) Doctor of the Church and patriarch of Alexandria. A champion of orthodox thought, he is best known for his opposition to the views of Nestorius (whose condemnation he secured at the Council of Ephesus in 431). His writings include theological treatises, sermons, and letters. Feast day, 9 February.

Cyrus the Great (died *c*.530 BC) King of Persia 559–530 BC and founder of the Achaemenid dynasty. He became ruler of the Median empire after the capture of King Astyages in 550 BC, and went on to conquer Asia Minor, Babylonia, Syria, Palestine, and most of the Iranian plateau. A moderate and wise ruler, he maintained good relations with the Jews (whom he freed from the Babylonian Captivity) and the Phoenicians.

Cyrus the Younger (died 401 BC) Persian prince, second son of Darius II. On the death of his father (405 BC), Cyrus led an army of mercenaries against his elder brother, who had succeeded to the throne as Artaxerxes II; his campaign is recounted by the historian Xenophon, who had enlisted in his army. Cyrus was killed in battle north of Babylon.

cyst A small sac or closed cavity filled with a fluid. Cysts may be caused by a blockage preventing secretion from a gland, or may form part of a tumour. Parasitic cysts are part of the life cycle of certain worms.

cystic fibrosis An inherited disease affecting infants, children, and young adults characterized by the production of abnormal viscid mucus, which results in impaired pancreas and lung function. Respiratory complications are disabling and include obstruction, recurrent infection, and difficulty in breathing. The cystic fibrosis gene is recessive, so that both parents must possess the gene as carriers to result in a one in four probability of cystic fibrosis in their children.

cytology The microscopic study of CELLS that are either living or that have been killed and 'fixed' to preserve their structure. As with HISTOLOGY, there is a variety of methods for identifying and localizing different organelles or molecules. For example, the site of enzyme activity can be located by linking its substrate to a dye; such staining methods are known as cytochemistry. In immunocytochemistry antibodies are labelled with a fluorescent dye as part of the staining procedure.

cytoplasm The content of a CELL, excluding the nucleus. It is a complex, gel-like material containing soluble proteins and small molecules, that is supported by filamentous proteins which constitute the cytoskeleton. Also included are membrane-bound organelles, such as mitochondria,

Golgi bodies, and other structures essential to the functioning of the cell.

cytotoxic drug See CANCER AND CANCER THERAPY.

Czech literature The beginning of vernacular Czech writing dates to the 9th century, when the greater part of the Bible was translated into literary Slavonic (now known as Old Church Slavonic). The *Legends* that recount the life of St Wenceslas (10th century) are written partly in Czech. Until the late 14th century Czech literature consisted mainly of Latin chronicles such as the *History of Bohemia* by Cosmas of Prague, and Czech hymns, courtly literature such as the *Alexandreis*, and verse satire. The best and most original works of the religious reformer Jan Hus were written in the vernacular, laying the foundation for a new uniformity in Czech orthography and grammar. The defeat of the Czech nobility in the Thirty Years War (1618–48) resulted in a suppression of the Czech language, while its literature survived mainly in ballads and folk tales. The radical Protestant and egalitarian ideas of Peter Chelčicky (*c.*1390–*c.*1460) inspired scholars to translate the Kralice Bible (1579–93), whose language became the model for classical Czech. In the 17th century the educational reformer and religious thinker Comenius published, while in exile, one of the supreme achievements of Czech prose literature, the *Labyrinth of the World and Paradise of the Heart* (1631), as well as the first illustrated children's book in any language, *The Visible World in Pictures* (1658). In the 18th century the scholar Josef Dobrovský led a revival of older Czech literature and codified the language. In the 19th century Slavophilism, also expressed in Slovak literature, inspired the work of the greatest poet of Czech ROMANTICISM, Mácha. A reaction against this were the satirical writings of Karel Havlíček Borovskí (1821–56) and the realist novels of Božena Němcová (1820–62). The most internationally influential writer of this period was Franz KAFKA, most of whose works were published posthumously between 1912 and 1926. After independence in 1918 the plays and novels of ČAPEK achieved world renown, as did HAŠEK's satire on war, *The Good Soldier Schweik*. After the Communist take-over in 1948, Socialist Realism prevailed, but this was superseded by the introspective plays of writers such as HAVEL and Hrabal who chose to remain in their country after the 'Prague Spring' of 1968, and the novels of others such as Milan KUNDERA who chose exile after 1968. After 1969 the works of many playwrights, poets, and novelists were banned and were published instead by the underground press. An alternative culture was thus created, which proved to be culturally more influential than the official one. After the political upheaval of 1989 censorship restrictions on writers were removed.

Czechoslovakia (Czech **Ceskoslovensko**) A former state of central Europe comprising the Czech Republic and Slovakia, which separated and became independent republics in 1993; area 127,896 sq km (49,399 sq miles); pop. (1991) 15,567,600; capital, Prague. Czechoslovakia was created out of the northern part of the old Austro-Hungarian empire after the latter's collapse at the end of World War I. It incorporated the Czechs (who had enjoyed freedom within their own state of Bohemia until the rise of Habsburg power in the 16th and 17th centuries) of Bohemia and Moravia with the Slovaks of Slovakia. Czech history between the two World Wars represents a brave and enlightened attempt at integration, undermined by economic trouble and eventually crushed by the Nazi takeover of first the Sudetenland (1938) and then the rest of Bohemia and Moravia (1939). After World War II power was seized by the Communists and Czechoslovakia remained under Soviet domination, an attempt at liberalization being crushed by Soviet military intervention in 1968, until Communist supremacy was overthrown in a peaceful revolution in December 1989, followed by the introduction of democratic reforms and the eventual separation of Slovakia and the Czech Republic into independent states in 1993.

Czech Republic A landlocked country in central Europe, formerly part of CZECHOSLOVAKIA.

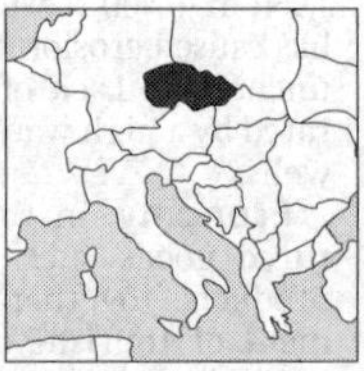

Physical. The Czech Republic comprises Bohemia and Moravia. It is bordered on the west by Germany, on the south by Austria, on the east by Slovakia, and on the north and east by Silesian Poland. The country lies in the headwater area of the main European watershed; the Labe–Vlatava (Moldau–Elba) river system flows in the Bohemian basin towards the North Sea, and the Odra (Oder) flows northwards towards the Baltic. Rich alluvial soils alongside river courses are characteristic. The country is rich in mineral springs. The Bohemian highlands form a large elevated basin encircled by mountain ranges that at Sněžka reach an altitude of 1,602 m (5,256 feet). South of the central Sudety (Sudeten) Mountains, which border on Germany, is found the spectacular Moravian karst. A moderate climate prevails.

Economy. The main mineral resources are brown coal, lignite, copper, and zinc, and large gold deposits have been found. Agriculturally, the country is to some extent reliant on imports, although wheat, barley, sugar-beet, and hops are grown, and there is an extensive timber industry. Industry is in urgent need of modernization, and is hampered by the need to import energy, as the potential for hydroelectric power has not yet been exploited. Motor vehicles, glass, beer, ceramics, footwear, and textiles are the main exports.

History. The Czech Republic came into existence on 1 January 1993; it was, until then, part of Czechoslovakia, but an increasingly strong Slovakian independence movement led to plans to separate the two states. The separation process was set in motion in June 1992 and went so smoothly that it was referred to as the 'velvet divorce'. Václav HAVEL, formerly President of Czechoslovakia, was elected President of the Czech Republic (1993).

Capital: Prague
Area: 78,864 sq km (30,442 sq mi)
Population: 10,346,000 (1995)
Currency: 1 koruna = 100 haléřů
Religions: Roman Catholic 39.3%; non-religious 39.7%; Protestant 4.1%; Orthodox 0.2%; other 0.5%
Ethnic Groups: Czech 94.0%; Slovak 4.1%; Hungarian 3.8%; other 1.7%
Languages: Czech, Slovak (both official); Hungarian; Romany; other minority languages
International Organizations: UN; CSCE; Council of Europe

Czerny, Karl (1791–1857) Austrian pianist, teacher, and composer. A pupil of Beethoven and the teacher of Liszt, he was active at a time when the piano was undergoing important structural developments; the bulk of his output is made up of more than 1,000 exercises and studies for this instrument, many of which are still used as exercizes by piano students.

D

dab A species of small FLATFISH, *Pleuronectes limanda*, extremely common in shallow coastal waters around Europe at depths of 2–40 m (6–130 feet). It prefers to live on sandy bottoms, but is also found on mud, and in estuaries. Its upperside is warm brown in colour, and its scales have rough edges.

dabchick An alternative name for the little grebe, *Tachybaptus ruficollis*, and a few other small GREBES. Little grebes are the commonest European species, distinguished by having a thicker neck than other species, and in their colour, which is brown and chestnut, without the crest or ear-tufts that many grebes have in summer. They nest on ponds, lakes, and rivers.

Dacca See DHAKA.

dace A small, silvery, freshwater fish, *Leuciscus leuciscus*, of wide distribution in Britain and Eurasia. Related to the CHUB and other members of the carp family, Cyprinidae, it is more slender and has a concave anal fin. It lives in rivers with a moderately fast current, feeding on insects at the surface and in the water. It spawns in early spring on shallow, gravelly bottoms. The name dace is also used for several North American freshwater fishes of the genus *Lepidomedea*.

Dacian wars Campaigns fought by successive Roman emperors over territory corresponding roughly to modern Romania and part of Hungary. The Dacians threatened the lands south of the River Danube which Rome regarded as a natural frontier. Under Emperor Domitian peace was agreed and considerable financial aid given to the Dacians. Then Emperor TRAJAN stopped payments, crossed the Lower Danube, and fought two campaigns 101 AD and 105–6 that were commemorated on Trajan's column in Rome, which is still standing today. Dacia became a Roman province, until Emperor Aurelian abandoned it to the Goths in 270.

dactyl A metrical unit (foot) of verse, having one stressed syllable followed by two unstressed syllables, as in the word 'barbarous'; or (in Greek and Latin verse) one long syllable and two short ones. Dactylic HEXAMETERS were used in Greek and Latin epic poetry.

Dada (French, 'hobby-horse') A movement in European and US art characterized by violent revolt against traditional values. It was founded in Zurich in 1915, arising from the mood of disillusionment engendered by World War I. Emphasis was given to the illogical and the absurd, and the importance of chance in artistic creation was exaggerated.

Dadd, Richard (1817–86) British painter. In 1842–43 he toured Europe and the Middle East before experiencing a mental breakdown and killing his father. He was confined in asylums for the rest of his life.

daddy-long-legs See CRANE FLY; HARVESTMAN.

Daedalus In Greek mythology, a great craftsman and inventor. He was held captive by King Minos of Crete, for whom he constructed the labyrinth that housed the monstrous Minotaur. To escape captivity he made wings for himself and his son Icarus out of wax and feathers, but Icarus flew too near the Sun, the wax melted, and he fell to his death.

daffodil A bulbous plant, *Narcissus pseudonarcissus*, whose petals are fused or united into a large tube or trumpet. The genus also includes narcissus and jonquil. Selective breeding, particularly since the late nineteenth century, has resulted in the introduction of many fine varieties of daffodils with a range of colour and shape of flower. They belong to the same family, Amaryllidaceae, as snowdrop and amaryllis. This contains some 1,100 species native to warm, temperate or subtropical regions.

da Gama, Vasco (*c.*1469–1524) Portuguese explorer. He led the first European expedition round the Cape of Good Hope in 1497, sighting and naming Natal on Christmas Day before crossing the Indian Ocean and arriving in Calicut in 1498. The Portuguese king Manuel I (1469–1521) chose him to lead a second expedition to Calicut in 1502. Da Gama forced the raja of Calicut (who had massacred Portuguese settlers from an earlier expedition) to make peace, also establishing colonies on the coast of Mozambique.

Dagda The ancient Irish deity of life and death, chief of the Tuatha Dé Dannan. Also known as Aed, 'fire', he held among his sacred possessions an inexhaustible cauldron and ever-laden fruit trees. His daughter was Brigid, goddess of fire, fertility, cattle, and poetry.

Daguerre, Louis-Jacques-Mandé (1789–1851) French physicist, painter, and inventor of the first practical photographic process. While working as a painter he co-invented the diorama, and he later went into partnership with Joseph-Nicéphore Niépce (1765–1833) to improve the latter's heliography process. Daguerre greatly reduced the exposure time, and in 1839 he presented to the French Academy of Sciences his daguerreotype process, which produced positive images directly on silvered copper plates.

Dahl, Roald (1916–90) British writer, of Norwegian descent. The short-story collection *Tales of the Unexpected* (1979) is characteristic of his fiction and drama, which typically include macabre plots and unexpected outcomes. Dahl is also widely known for his stories and poems for children; they include

Charlie and the Chocolate Factory (1964), *The BFG* (1982), and *Revolting Rhymes* (1982).

dahlia A tuberous-rooted perennial, chiefly of herbaceous habit. About 12 species are known, all of Mexican origin, including the tree-like *Dahlia imperialis*, which will grow to a height of 6–7 m (19–23 feet). The development of the many decorative garden varieties began with the introduction to Europe of the first plants from Mexico in 1789. Today they are among the most popular of garden plants because of the variety of plant size and the colour range of their flowers. They belong to the SUNFLOWER family, along with plants such as daisies, chrysanthemums, and many other familiar species.

Dahomey The former name (until 1975) of BENIN.

Dáil (in full **Dáil Eireann**) The lower house of parliament in the Republic of Ireland, composed of 166 members elected on a basis of proportional representation. It was first established in 1919 when the Irish republicans elected to Westminster in the 1918 election proclaimed an Irish State.

Daimler, Gottlieb (1834–1900) German engineer and motor manufacturer. An employee of Nikolaus Otto, he produced a small engine using the Otto cycle in 1884 and made it propel a bicycle in 1886, using petrol vapour. He founded the Daimler motor company in 1890, naming the cars 'Mercedes' after his daughter.

dairy farming The husbandry of animals for the supply of milk and DAIRY PRODUCTS. In the West, milk comes predominantly from dairy cows, but elsewhere the milk of sheep, goats, and water-buffalo is also consumed. The primary requirement for successful dairying is high-quality grassland. In New Zealand and some other countries, pastures support cows throughout the year. Elsewhere, where grass growth is seasonal, dairy cattle herds are housed over winter and fed on stored SILAGE, hay, or processed foods. The availability of concentrated cattle feeds, allowing herds to be enlarged without pressurizing land resources, and the use of milking machines have greatly increased dairy farm productivity in the West. By contrast, dairy farming is almost completely absent from tropical regions, due to the lack of native breeds that produce sufficient milk.

dairy product Any food derived from milk. Almost half the milk consumed is drunk as fresh or skimmed milk; in the West this milk undergoes PASTEURIZATION to reduce bacterial levels and improve keeping qualities. Sweetened, condensed milk is popular in many tropical countries, as it has excellent keeping qualities, even without refrigeration. Sterilized and UHT (ultra heat treated) milk are other long-life forms of milk. BUTTER and CHEESE are the most common products made from milk: originally, they were made as a way of preserving the milk. In hot countries, yoghurt, a semi-fluid, fermented milk food with a slightly sour taste due to the presence of lactic acid, is also made to preserve milk. Ice-cream is a dairy product that has become popular since the late 19th century, when mechanical REFRIGERATION was first developed. Freezing is also used as a way of preserving cream and concentrated milk for use in the food industry. Many dairy products such as skimmed and full-cream milk are dried to prolong life and to save weight and storage space. These dried products are used in the commercial manufacture of many foods. Milk whey (essentially the aqueous portion of the milk) and the milk protein casein are dairy industry by-products with high nutritive value.

daisy A flower sometimes identified by prefixes, such as dog, ox-eye, Michaelmas, and Swan River. All are members of the SUNFLOWER family, the Compositae, which includes many familiar garden plants, such as asters, calendulas, pyrethrums, and ragworts. *Bellis perennis* is the daisy which occurs as a lawn weed in Europe. Its American counterpart is *B. integrifolia*.

Dakar The capital of Senegal, a port on the Atlantic coast of West Africa; pop. (est. 1994) 1,641,350. It was founded by the French in 1857 on the site of a fishing village. It has a naval base and a railway link to the River Senegal. It is one of the largest industrial centres of West Africa with oil refining, sugar refining, groundnut crushing, textiles, fertilizer manufacturing, fishing, and tourism.

Dakota Indians The largest division of a North American Indian group of seven related tribes, commonly known as the Sioux, who inhabit areas of Nebraska, Montana, the woodlands of Minnesota, and the eastern Dakotas on the fringe of the northern Great Plains. In common with other Plains Indians, the Dakota were nomadic buffalo hunters, who gathered in tribes during the summer, and dispersed into family groups during the winter.

Dalai Lama (Tibetan, 'Ocean of wisdom and compassion') Title bestowed upon the head of the Yellow Hat monks, the dominant sect in TIBETAN BUDDHISM, by the Mongol ruler Altan Khan in 1578. The Dalai Lama himself is said to be the reincarnation of the important BODHISATTVA Avalokiteshvara. The position of Dalai Lama carries full state and religious responsibilities. The present, fourteenth, Dalai Lama, Tenzin Gyatso (1935–), was forced into exile in 1959, but his spiritual and political influence remains authoritative for Tibetans.

Dalcroze, Jaques See JAQUES-DALCROZE.

Dale, Sir Henry Hallett (1875–1968) British physiologist and pharmacologist. He worked first on the physiological action of ergot, going on to investigate the role of histamine in anaphylactic shock and allergy. He discovered the role of acetylcholine as a neurotransmitter, which led to a clearer understanding of the chemical transmission of nerve impulses. Dale later held the most senior posts in British medical research, and shared a Nobel Prize in 1936.

Dales, the A series of river valleys in northern England whose rivers drain the Pennine Hills through Yorkshire to the North Sea. Valleys include Teesdale, Swaledale, Wensleydale, Wharfedale, Nidderdale, and Airedale.

Dalhousie, James Andrew Broun Ramsay, 1st Marquess of (1812–60) British colonial administrator. As Governor-General of India (1847–56) he was responsible for a series of reforms and innovations, notably the introduction of railways and telegraphic communications, as well as the drafting of legislation against slavery, suttee, and female infanticide. He considerably expanded British territory in India, taking Punjab and Pegu and annexing Oudh and Nagpur.

Dali, Salvador (1904–89) Spanish painter, who joined the surrealists in 1928 and became one of the most prominent members of the movement. Like many surrealists, he was much influenced by Sigmund Freud's writings on dreams; many of his paintings portray subconscious or dream images painted with almost photographic realism against backgrounds of arid Catalan landscapes. Expelled from the surrealist group in 1939 because of his repudiation of its Marxist politics, he subsequently settled in the USA; after becoming a Roman Catholic he devoted much of the latter part of his life to symbolic religious paintings. His most famous pictures include *The Persistence of Memory* (1931) and *Christ of St John of the Cross* (1951). He also produced surrealist writings and collaborated with Luis Buñuel in the production of *Un chien andalou* (1928) and other films.

Dallapiccola, Luigi (1904–75) Italian composer. Influenced by the serial technique of Schoenberg and Webern, he further developed the twelve-note system in a variety of compositions, including songs, opera, ballet music, and a piano concerto. Among his best-known works is *Songs of Prison* (1938–41).

Dallas An industrial, commercial, and cultural city in north-east Texas, on the Trinity River, noted as a major centre of banking and the oil, aerospace, and fashion industries; pop. (1990) 1,006,900. Founded as a trading post in 1841, Dallas was settled in 1855 by French, Swiss, and Belgians seeking to found a Utopian colony. President John F. Kennedy was assassinated here on 22 November 1963.

Dalmatia A region of Croatia comprising mountains and a narrow lowland plain that stretches down the east coast of the Adriatic Sea from Rijeka (Fiume) to the Montenegrin frontier. Split and Dubrovnik are two of its chief centres. Dalmatia is noted for its scenic beauty, its resort towns, and its offshore islands.

Dalriada An ancient Gaelic kingdom in northern Ireland whose people (known as *Scoti*) established a colony in south-west Scotland from about the late 5th century. By the 9th century Irish Dalriada had declined but the people of Scottish Dalriada gradually acquired dominion over the whole of Scotland, giving that country its present name.

Dalton, John (1766–1844) British chemist, the father of modern atomic theory. His study of gases led to his formulation of the law of partial pressures (Dalton's law), according to which the total pressure of a mixture of gases is equal to the sum of the pressures that each gas would exert separately. He then worked on the solubility of gases, producing fundamental work on atomic theory. Dalton's Atomic Theory defines an atom as the smallest part of a substance that can participate in a chemical reaction, and assumes that elements are composed of atoms which combine in definite proportions. Dalton produced the first table of comparative atomic weights. He also gave the first detailed description of colour-blindness, based on his own inability to distinguish green from red.

dam A barrier to hold back water, often forming a lake or reservoir behind. Dams may be used to store water for irrigation, to aid flood control, for hydroelectric power, or for a combination of these purposes. The coffer-dam is normally a temporary dam used in building or excavation works. Many dams, however, are massive engineering structures, often built across valleys, with overflow channels (spillways) to prevent the impounded water from escaping over the top of the dam. Water is prevented from seeping under the dam by a cut-off, a deep trench dug beneath and filled with impermeable material such as clay or concrete to form a watertight barrier.

damages Compensation in the form of an award of money by a court, constituting the main remedy for loss caused by breach of CONTRACT or the commission of a TORT (that is, a breach of duty other than contractual, such as negligent driving). In COMMON LAW SYSTEMS, contractual damages are intended to give the victim the benefit of the bargain which has not been performed, while tortious damages are intended to put the victim in the position he or she would have been in if the tort had not been committed. Damages may generally be reduced if the plaintiff has contributed in part to the loss.

damascening The technique of ornamenting a metal (often steel or brass) by inlaying it with a design in another metal or metals (usually gold or silver).

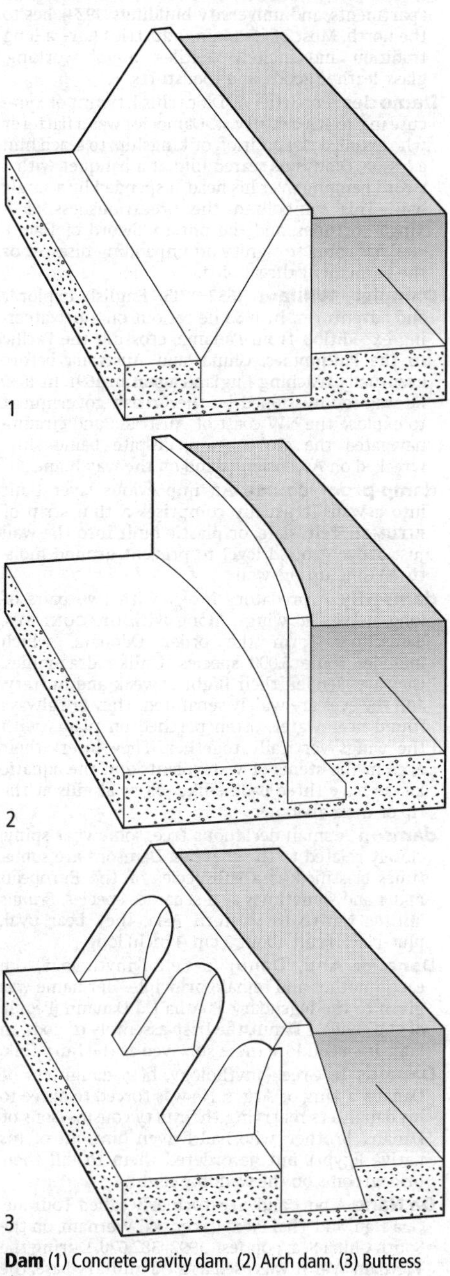

Dam (1) Concrete gravity dam. (2) Arch dam. (3) Buttress dam.

Damascus (Arabic **Dimashq**) The capital city of Syria since the country's independence in 1946; pop. (est. 1993) 1,497,000. Situated immediately east of the Anti-Lebanon Mts. on the Barada River, it has existed as a city for over 4,000 years. Under Roman rule it flourished as a commercial centre noted for its grain and its woven fabric which came to be known throughout the world as damask. Today it is Syria's administrative, financial, and communications centre. The old walled city, which contains Christian churches as well as the Great Mosque built in 708, lies south of the river, while the modern city, with its office blocks, apartments, and university buildings (1924), lies to the north. Most of its main industries have a long tradition and include textiles, metal working, glass, leather goods, and foodstuffs.

Damocles A courtier of Dionysius I, tyrant of Syracuse in the 4th century BC. Damocles was a flatterer who extolled the position of kingship; to teach him a lesson, Dionysius seated him at a banquet with a sword hanging over his head suspended by a single hair. This symbolized the precariousness of a king's fortunes, and the phrase 'Sword of Damocles' has come to signify an impending disaster or the permanent threat of it.

Dampier, William (1652–1715) English explorer and adventurer. In 1683 he set out on a privateering expedition from Panama, crossing the Pacific to the Philippines, China, and Australia before eventually reaching England again in 1691. In 1699 he was commissioned by the British government to explore the NW coast of Australia and circumnavigated the globe again, despite being shipwrecked on Ascension Island on the way home.

damp-proof course An impervious layer built into a wall. It usually comprises a thin strip of BITUMEN, felt, slate, or plastic built into the wall just above ground level to prevent ground moisture rising up the wall.

damselfly A predatory insect with two pairs of long, netveined wings. Along with DRAGONFLIES, damselflies form the order Odonata, which includes some 5,000 species. Unlike dragonflies, they are slender, their flight is weak and fluttery, and the eyes are widely separated. They are always found near water, often perched on plants with the wings vertically together. They insert their eggs in the stems of waterplants and the aquatic larvae have three paddle-like external gills at the tip of their abdomen.

damson A small deciduous tree, somewhat spiny, closely related to the cherries. Damsons are sometimes classified as a subspecies of the European PLUM and sometimes as a separate species, *Prunus institia*. Native to western Asia, they bear oval, blue-black fruit about 2 cm (1 inch) long.

Dana (or **Anu, Danu**) In Celtic mythology, the earth-mother and female principle. Her name was given to the legendary Tuatha Dé Danann (People of the goddess Danu), the Irish assembly of gods. In later Irish folklore these survived as the fairy folk.

Danaids In Greek mythology, fifty daughters of Danaus, a king of Argos. He was forced to agree to his daughters marrying their fifty cousins (sons of Danaus' brother, who had driven him out of his native Egypt), but he ordered them to kill their bridegrooms on the wedding night.

Da Nang A port and city (formerly called Tourane, Cua Han, and Thai Pien) in central Vietnam, on the South China Sea; pop. (est. 1992) 382,670. During the Vietnam War it was used as a US military base, the first US marines landing here on 8th March 1965.

Danby, Thomas Osborne, 1st Earl of (1631–1712) English statesman. He entered Parliament in 1665 as a supporter of the restored CHARLES II. He received rapid promotion, becoming Secretary of the Navy in 1671 and Lord Treasurer in 1673. His reluctant negotiations with LOUIS XIV of France to supply Charles II with money led in 1678 to accusations by Parliament of corruption and he was imprisoned until 1684. In 1688 he signed the invitation to William of Orange to come to England, regained royal favour, and became Duke of Leeds in 1694, but following further accusations of corruption he retired from public life after 1695.

dance See BALLET.

dance notation The recording of movement in words, drawings, or symbols. The Benesh system (1956), also called choreology, is used by most ballet companies. The positions of all the parts of the body are indicated on a five-line musical stave, with signs to indicate duration and the missing third dimension. Modern notation systems, usually in combination with video, can provide complete permanent records of dances. A recent innovation that promises to extend the use of notation is the development of computer software to facilitate the writing and learning of notation.

dance of death (French **danse macabre**) A theme in art in which living people are led to their graves by a personification of death, typically a skeleton. The human figures are usually arranged in order of social precedence, the idea being to show, in allegorical form, the inevitability of death and the equality of all men in the face of it.

dandelion A yellow-flowered perennial plant that belongs to the genus *Taraxacum*, part of the SUNFLOWER family, with fleshy thong-like roots and a white latex sap. The common name is said to be derived from the French, *dent de lion*, lion's tooth, in reference to the deeply toothed leaves. The species, though native to Europe and Asia, is now widely spread throughout the temperate regions, partly as a result of its use as a salad plant and because of its wind-borne seed distribution. Dandelions belong to a complex group of species with many intermediate varieties and hybrids. Some are cultivated for their latex, which is made into rubber.

Dandolo, Enrico (*c.*1108–1205) Member of a Venetian family important in the Middle Ages, and DOGE of VENICE. He established military and naval power by personally directing the Fourth CRUSADE to attack Dalmatia and sack CONSTANTINOPLE. Under him, Venice was victorious against Pisa, secured important treaties with Armenia and the HOLY ROMAN EMPIRE, and reformed its laws.

Danegeld The tribute paid in silver by ETHELRED II of England to buy peace from the invading Danes. It was raised by a tax levied on land. The first payment (991) was 10,000 pounds in weight of silver (1 pound equals 0.54 kg); later payments were greater – 16,000 pounds (994), 24,000 pounds (1002), 36,000 pounds (1007), and a massive 158,000 pounds (1012). Later (1012–51) it was levied to maintain a navy and the royal bodyguard (housecarls), when it was known as 'heregeld'; when raised by the NORMAN kings the levy was used for general as well as military purposes.

Danelaw The part of north and east England occupied or administered by Danes from the late 9th century and administered according to their laws until the Norman Conquest.

Daniel A Hebrew prophet, hero of the Book of

Daniel, traditionally active during the Babylonian Captivity of the Jews (*c*.598–538 BC). He is portrayed as an interpreter of the dreams of Nebuchadnezzar and receiver of prophetic visions, cast by King Darius into the lions' den for obeying God rather than him, but saved by divine intervention.

Daniell, John Frederic (1790–1845) British scientist who began his career in a sugar-refining factory. He was an outstanding research worker and at the age of 23 he became a Fellow of the Royal Society. He invented the hygrometer in 1820. Appointed as the first Professor of Chemistry at King's College, London, he shortly afterwards invented an electric cell (now called the **Daniell cell**) having copper and zinc electrodes. This was the first reliable source of electricity, producing a constant voltage over a considerable period of time.

Danish The official language of Denmark (where it is spoken by over 5 million people) and also of Greenland and the Faeroes.

Danish West Indies The former name of the US Virgin Islands which were established as a Danish colony in 1754 and later sold to the USA in 1917 for $25 m.

d'Annunzio, Gabriele (1863–1938) Italian novelist, dramatist, and poet. The publication of his 'Romances of the Rose' trilogy, including *The Child of Pleasure* (1890), established d'Annunzio as a leading Italian literary figure of the *fin de siècle*.

Dante (Alighieri) (1265–1321) Italian poet. His early work consisted mainly of courtly love poetry; his first book, *Vita nuova* (*c*.1290–94), consists of thirty-one poems linked by a prose narrative and tells of his love for Beatrice Portinari (*c*.1265–90). However, Dante's international renown and reputation as the founding figure of Italian literature rests on *The Divine Comedy* (*c*.1309–20), an epic poem telling of his spiritual journey, in the form of an imagined visit to Hell and Purgatory with Virgil as guide and finally to Paradise with Beatrice, now a blessed spirit, as guide. Dante also wrote scholarly treatises on a number of subjects, including philosophy, science, and politics; his political activity led to his spending part of his life in exile from his native Florence. His innovative use of Italian did much to establish a vernacular literature; his Latin treatise *De Vulgari Eloquentia* (*c*.1303) promoted vernacular Italian as a literary language fit to replace Latin.

Danton, Georges (Jacques) (1759–94) French revolutionary. A noted orator, he won great popularity in the early days of the French Revolution. He served as Minister of Justice (1792–94) in the new republic and was a founder member of the governing body, the Committee of Public Safety (1793). Initially an ally of Robespierre and the Jacobins, he later revolted against their radicalism and the severity of the Revolutionary Tribunal, only to be arrested and executed on Robespierre's orders.

Danube A river 2,857 km (1,775 miles) long that rises in the Black Forest in south-west Germany and flows generally south-eastwards to the Black Sea. The Danube, which is Europe's second-longest river, is known as the **Donau** in Germany and Austria, **Dunaj** in Slovakia, **Duna** in Hungary, and **Dunarea** in Romania. The capital cities of Vienna, Budapest, and Belgrade are situated on it. For centuries it has been a vital traffic artery and is now linked to the Rhine by canal. In 1990, regions through which the Danube flows formed a 'working community' to promote cooperation.

Danzig The German name for the port of GDANSK on the Baltic coast of Poland.

Daodejing (or **Tao-te Ching**) '*The Book of the Way and its Power*', a Chinese classic ascribed to Laozi (Lao-tzu; *fl.* 6th century BC), an obscure state official credited as founder of DAOISM. Originally perhaps a handbook for the ruler, the DAODEJING defines the *Dao* ('way') as absolute reality, the source and end of all being. *De* refers to 'virtue', the latent power acquired through understanding the *Dao*. The *Daodejing* advocates 'unmotivated action': letting things take their natural course according to the spontaneous flow of the *Dao*.

Daoism (or **Taoism**) One of the three main Chinese religious and philosophical traditions, the others being CONFUCIANISM and BUDDHISM. Like Confucianism, Daoism has both a philosophical and a religious, or ritualistic, aspect. However, it is markedly different from the practical teachings of Confucianism in its emphasis on inner contemplation, mystical forms of knowledge, and spontaneous, non-active union with the nature of being. Philosophical Daoism developed from the 5th to the 3rd centuries BC; its tenets are found in the DAODEJING, traditionally attributed to Laozi, and in the text known as the ZHUANGZI after its author. The ultimate reality is the *Dao*, in which being and not-being, life and death, are merely aspects of the same reality. Through silence, stillness, and actionless action (*wu wei*) the Daoist aims to achieve unity with the *Dao*. A religious Daoism also developed and was officially recognized in the 3rd century AD; it incorporated certain Buddhist features and developed its own monastic system and cultic practices. Popular Daoism borrowed the concept of reincarnation from the Buddhists, but the final goal was not nirvana but becoming an immortal. Religious Daoism has also tended to be close to certain folk religious practices, and has borrowed elements such as the worship of different local gods. Daoism has been influential in Vietnam, Japan, and Korea, and Daoist religious practice persists in Taiwan. In communist China, Daoist religious practices and monasteries were suppressed, but Daoist thought remains a potent influence in Chinese culture.

Daphne A genus of flowering shrubs containing some 70 species of Old World temperate or subtropical shrubs and small trees, many of them evergreen. They are part of the family Thymelaeaceae, which includes over 500 species, mainly native to Africa. Some species of *Daphne* are grown in gardens for their sweetly scented flowers, notably *D. mezereum* of Europe. The bark of *D. bholua* and other species from the Himalayas is used locally to make paper.

Daphnia (or **water flea**) A small, freshwater CRUSTACEAN found worldwide, forming the suborder Cladocera. They are enclosed in a transparent carapace, with a beaked head, long antennae, prominent eyes, and a terminal spine. The antennae beat to propel the animal jerkily upwards and act as parachutes during descent. The legs filter-feed within the carapace. *Daphnia* brood their eggs, producing only females by parthenogenesis in summer, then in autumn producing male and female offspring which mate to produce eggs which will survive the winter.

Da Ponte, Lorenzo (born Emmanuele Conegliano) (1749–1838) Italian poet and librettist. He became poet to the Court Opera in Vienna in 1784 and wrote the libretti for Mozart's *Marriage of Figaro* (1786), *Don Giovanni* (1787), and *Così fan tutte* (1790).

Darby, Abraham (1678–1717) English ironmaster, the first to smelt IRON with coke. In the 17th century the growing demand for iron was frustrated because the timber for making charcoal (the fuel used for BLAST-FURNACES) was scarce and expensive, and large furnaces were not feasible because charcoal was too soft to support a heavy charge of ore. Raw coal was an obvious alternative, but the presence of SULPHUR in it spoilt the quality of the iron. At his Coalbrookdale works in 1709 Darby solved this problem by using coke, which burnt cleanly. Smelting iron with coke was a key process in the development of the INDUSTRIAL REVOLUTION.

Dardanelles (Turkish **Çanakkale Boğazi**) A narrow strait between Europe and Asiatic Turkey, anciently called the Hellespont. Linking the Sea of Marmara with the Aegean Sea, it is 60 km (38 miles) long. It was the scene of an unsuccessful attack on Turkey by British and French troops in 1915, with Australian and New Zealand contingents playing a major part.

Dar es Salaam The former capital (until 1974) and chief port of Tanzania, founded in 1866 by the Sultan of Zanzibar, who built his summer palace there; pop. (1988) 1,360,850. In Arabic its name means 'haven of peace'. It handles most of Zambia's trade since the building of the Tanzam railway, as well as Tanzania's, and has oil-refining, textile, pharmaceutical, and food industries.

Darío, Rubén (born Félix Rubén García Sarmiento) (1867–1916) Nicaraguan poet, journalist, and diplomat. He published his first major work, *Blue* (1888), in Chile, a collection of verse and prose which broke with the complex literary idiom of the past in favour of a simpler, more direct language. His *Profane Hymns and Other Poems* (1896) was heavily influenced by the French SYMBOLIST poetry, but by the time he was to publish his masterpiece, *Songs of Life and Hope* (1905), he had changed direction and was writing modern, socially committed poetry.

Darius I (known as **Darius the Great**) (*c.*550–486 BC) King of Persia 521–486 BC. His reign divided the empire into provinces governed by satraps, allowing each province its own government while maintaining some centralizing authority. He developed commerce, building a network of roads, exploring the Indus valley, and connecting the Nile with the Red Sea by canal. After suppressing a revolt of the Greek cities in Ionia (499–494 BC), he invaded Greece to punish the mainland Greeks for their interference, but was defeated at Marathon (490 BC).

Darjeeling (or **Darjiling**) A hill station at an altitude of 2,150 m (7,054 ft) in West Bengal, north-east India, near the Sikkim frontier; pop. (1991) 73,090. The surrounding area produces a high-quality tea for export.

Dark Ages The 5th to the 8th centuries in Europe. Following the collapse of the Roman empire, many Germanic tribes crossed through Italy, Germany, France, Spain, and North Africa, often attacking and destroying towns. Rome was sacked on three successive occasions. Many tribes formed their own kingdoms (for example, Vandals in North Africa; Visigoths in Spain; Ostrogoths and Lombards in northern Italy; FRANKS in France and western Germany; ANGLO-SAXONS in England). The Visigoths helped the Romans defeat the Huns of ATTILA at Châlons in 451. The Ostrogoth THEODORIC ruled in Italy (493–526) as the representative of the BYZANTINE EMPIRE, retaining Rome's administrative system.

The period of the Dark Ages saw cultural and economic decline though in the past this has been exaggerated. The period saw the foundation of Christian monasteries which kept scholarship alive. The 7th and 8th centuries saw relative stability and during the 9th century the encouragement of learning at the courts of CHARLEMAGNE and ALFRED the Great.

dark nebula See NEBULA.

Darlan, (Jean Louis Xavier) François (1881–1942) French admiral. He became Minister of Marine in the VICHY GOVERNMENT in 1940 and was regarded by the British as pro-fascist. His secret order to his commanders to scuttle their vessels should the Germans attempt to take them over was not known to the British. When the Allies invaded North Africa in 1942 he was in Algiers, where he began negotiations with the Americans. He ordered the Vichy French forces to cease fire and was proclaimed Head of State in French Africa. A month later he was assassinated.

Darling A river of south-east Australia, whose headstreams rise in the Great Dividing Range and which flows 1,867 km (1,160 miles) in a generally south-westward course to join the Murray River north-west of Mildura. It was named after Sir Ralph Darling (1775–1858), Governor-General of New South Wales from 1825 to 1831.

Darling, Grace (1815–42) British heroine. The daughter of a lighthouse keeper on the Farne Islands off the coast of Northumberland, she became a national heroine when in September 1838 she and her father rowed through a storm to rescue the survivors of the wrecked *Forfarshire*.

Darlington An industrial town in the county of Durham, north-east England, at the junction of the Skerne and Cocker Beck rivers; pop. (1991) 96,700. The world's first passenger railway built by George Stephenson linked Darlington and Stockton in 1825.

Darnley, Henry Stuart, Lord (1545–67) Anglo-Scottish aristocrat, second husband of MARY, QUEEN OF SCOTS. After their union in 1565, Mary produced a son, the future James VI of Scotland and JAMES I of England. Mary's reliance on her secretary David RIZZIO (who may have been her lover) led Darnley to murder him. Darnley was subsequently murdered in a conspiracy involving the Earl of BOTHWELL.

Dart, Raymond Arthur (1893–1988) Australian-born South African anthropologist and anatomist. He obtained the skull of a juvenile hominid from a limestone quarry at Taung near Kimberley in 1924, and a year later coined the genus name *Australopithecus* for it. It was assigned to the species *A. africanus*, and was the first of many specimens of *Australopithecus* obtained in Africa.

darter (bird) Any of four species of water-bird making up the family Anhingidae, found in Africa, India, Australia, and the Americas. They resemble cormorants and are alternatively called anhingas, water turkeys, or snakebirds. They all belong to the genus *Anhinga*. The movement of the narrow head and thin kinked neck, which are often all that is exposed above water, is strongly suggestive of a snake.

darter (fish) A North American freshwater fish belonging to the PERCH family, Percidae. There are some 120 species of darters. They are mostly small, up to 8 cm (3 inches) in length, and rather slender, with two dorsal fins, the first of which is spiny. They have adapted to a wide range of habitats.

Males become brightly coloured in the breeding season.

Dartford A residential and industrial town in Kent, south-east England, to the south of the River Thames and east of London; pop. (1981) 42,000. Built in 1963, Dartford Tunnel the runs under the Thames to Purfleet in Essex. There is also a bridge across the river.

Dartmoor ▶1 A moorland district in Devon, south-west England, which is famous for its wild ponies and was a royal forest in Saxon times, now (since 1951) a national park. **▶2** A major long-term prison near Princetown in this district, originally built to hold French prisoners of war during the Napoleonic Wars.

Dartmouth A fishing port and resort town in Devon, south-west England, on the estuary of the River Dart opposite Kingswear. The *Mayflower* and *Speedwell* sailed from here with the Pilgrim Fathers in August 1620. There is a Tudor castle and the Royal Naval College (opened in 1905).

darts The mainly British indoor target-game of throwing small flighted darts at a circular board. The board has twenty sections, numbered 1–20 in a specified order, with an outer ring which scores double the number, an inner treble ring, and a bull's-eye (the centre of the target). Players throw three darts in turn, standing behind a line about 2.5 m (8–9 feet) from the board. The most popular game is 301: players subtract their totals from 301, and to finish must end with a double that brings their score to zero.

Darwin The capital of the Northern Territory, Australia, on the Beagle Gulf; pop. (1991) 67,950. Originally known as Palmerston or Port Darwin, its name was changed to Darwin in 1911. Development has largely been linked to the exploitation of the territory's mineral wealth. Devastated by a hurricane in 1879, it was again almost completely destroyed by Cyclone Tracy in 1974.

Darwin, Charles (Robert) (1809–82) British natural historian and geologist, proponent of the theory of evolution by natural selection. Grandson of the physician and scientist Erasmus Darwin, he failed to complete his medical training and narrowly achieved a theological degree. Darwin took the post of unpaid naturalist on HMS *Beagle* for her voyage around the Southern Hemisphere (1831–36), during which he collected the material that became the basis for his ideas on natural selection. On his return he made his name as a geologist, in particular with his accounts of the formation of coral reefs and atolls. In 1858, he and A. R. Wallace agreed to publish simultaneously their similar thoughts on evolution, to the consternation of theologians. He went on to write an extensive series of books, monographs, and papers; *On the Origin of Species* (1859) and *The Descent of Man* (1871) changed our concepts of nature and of humanity's place within it.

Darwin, Erasmus (1731–1802) British physician, scientist, inventor, and poet. Darwin is chiefly remembered for his scientific and technical writings, which often appeared in the form of long poems. These include *The Botanic Garden* (1789–91), which was later parodied to Darwin's detriment. Darwin's major work was *Zoonomia* (1794–6), which proposed a Lamarckian view of evolution. His grandsons (by different wives) included Charles Darwin and Francis Galton.

data (in computing) Information that has been prepared, often in a particular format, for a specific purpose. In a more restricted sense, data may be the information input for a particular program, as opposed to the results or output. Data can also be information not in the form of words, sounds, or images: such data is usually information stored in a highly organized and compact form suitable for DATA PROCESSING.

database (in computing) A logically organized collection of related DATA, generally accessed by a set of programs known as a database management system (DBMS), which oversees the creation and use of the database and controls access to the data. The organization of a database obviates the need to duplicate information to meet the various requirements of different groups of users, and ensures that the data always remains consistent.

data processing The use of a COMPUTER to manipulate DATA, particularly the routine tasks undertaken in large organizations. For example, the maintenance, retrieval, and analysis of financial records is faster and easier with the aid of computers. The amount of data which needs to be processed is frequently considerable. Therefore, the data is often organized in the form of a single DATABASE. The database is stored on HARD DISKS, magnetic drums, or magnetic tapes attached to computers of substantial power. Large data-processing facilities are often distributed over NETWORKS in which a user anywhere on the network can access data anywhere else on the network.

data protection Arrangements to ensure that confidential information, and especially computerized information, is available only to people entitled to use it. The twin purposes are to maintain the confidentiality of personal information and business secrets, and to enable the subjects on whom information is stored to ensure its accuracy. Wrongfully obtaining access to material may be a criminal offence.

date-line See INTERNATIONAL DATE-LINE.

date palm A tall tree, *Phoenix dactylifera*, growing up to 30 m (98 feet), with a high crown of large leaves typical of many members of the palm family. The yellowish to reddish-brown fruits of the date palm are either harvested unripe (soft dates) or they are allowed to dry (dried dates). Date palms flourish in the hot, dry regions of Arabia, the Middle East, and North Africa. A vital food plant in these regions, the fruits contain up to 70 per cent sugar. All parts of the tree are useful: the leaves and stems are used in house construction, leaf fibres are used for mats, baskets, saddles, and ropes, and date seeds are fed to livestock.

dating systems Scientific evidence about the prehistory of the human race and of the Earth rests heavily on the accurate dating of recovered artefacts and rocks. Traditional methods of dating depend on stratigraphic succession – for instance, where a layer with one distinctive kind of artefact overlies another with different kinds – or it can be inferred from a sequence of gradual changes in the artefact. Stylistic comparisons with more securely dated objects can sometimes be made in order to establish a rough guide to age. These methods are now reinforced by several much more precise scientific techniques. **Dendrochronology** (or **tree-ring dating**), developed in the 1930s, is based on measurement of growth rings in timber. RADIO-CARBON DATING uses the decay of the radioisotope carbon-14 to date organic material up to 40,000 years old. A similar technique uses the decay of potassium-40 to argon-40 for dating volcanic rocks, and the decay of rubidium-87 to strontium-87 for dating other rocks. Both radio-carbon dating and dendrochronology are absolute dating systems; other methods must be calibrated first. Pottery and burnt flint are dated using thermoluminescence, which measures the light emitted when an object is heated. ELECTRON SPIN RESONANCE is used to date shells, corals, and tooth enamel. In optical dating, a LASER is used to date silt and sediment samples.

datura See THORN APPLE.

Daubigny, Charles François (1817–78) French landscape painter. He was a member of the Barbizon School and is often regarded as a linking figure between this group of painters and the impressionists. His landscapes frequently feature stretches of water, for example *The Banks of the Oise* (1872).

Daudet, Alphonse (1840–97) French novelist and dramatist. He is best known for his sketches of life in his native Provence, particularly the *Lettres de mon moulin* (1869), and as the creator of Tartarin, a caricature of the Frenchman of the south of France, whose comic exploits are first related in *Tartarin de Tarascon* (1872).

Daumier, Honoré (1808–78) French painter and lithographer. From the 1830s he worked as a cartoonist for periodicals such as *Charivari*, in which he produced over 4,000 lithographs sharply satirizing French society and politics. His later oil paintings, such as *Don Quixote* (1868), deal with their subjects in a powerfully realistic and unromanticized manner.

David (died *c.*962 BC) King of Judah and Israel *c.*1000–*c.*962 BC. In the biblical account he was the youngest son of Jesse, and was made a military commander by Saul after slaying the Philistine Goliath. On Saul's death he became king of Judah and later of the whole of Israel, making Jerusalem his capital. He is traditionally regarded as the author of the Psalms, but it is unlikely that more than a fraction of the psalter is his work.

David Two kings of Scotland. **David I** (*c.*1084–1153), sixth son of Malcolm III, reigned 1124–53. Much of his youth was spent at the English court, after his sister Matilda (1080–1118) married King Henry I of England in 1100. After succeeding his brother Alexander (*c.*1080–1124) as king of Scotland, David established a strong administration on the Norman model, bringing many retainers with him from England, encouraging the development of trade, and introducing legal reforms. In 1136, after Henry's death, David invaded England in support of his niece Matilda's claim to the throne, but was decisively defeated at the Battle of the Standard in Yorkshire in 1138. **David II** (1324–71), son of Robert the Bruce, reigned 1329–71. His long reign witnessed a renewal of fighting between England and Scotland, with Edward III taking advantage of the Scottish king's minority to introduce Edward de Baliol (*c.*1283–1364) as an English puppet in his place. After returning from exile in France (1334–41), David was defeated by the English at Neville's Cross (1346) and spent eleven years in prison. His death without issue in 1371 left the throne to the Stuarts.

David, Jacques-Louis (1748–1825) French painter. He is famous for neoclassical paintings such as *The Oath of the Horatii* (1784) and *The Intervention of the Sabine Women* (1799). He became actively involved in the French Revolution, voting for the death of Louis XVI and supporting Robespierre. Famous works of his from the revolutionary era include *The Death of Marat* (1793), which treats contemporary events with a grandeur hitherto reserved for history painting. Imprisoned after the fall of Robespierre, he returned to prominence under Napoleon.

David, St (or **Dewi**) (6th century) Welsh monk. Since the 12th century he has been regarded as the patron saint of Wales. Little is known of his life, but it is generally accepted that he transferred the centre of Welsh ecclesiastical administration from Caerleon to Mynyw, now St David's. He also established a number of monasteries in England and Wales and many churches in South Wales. Feast day, 1 March.

Davies, Sir Peter Maxwell (1934–) British composer and conductor. In 1967, with Harrison Birtwistle, he co-founded the Pierrot Players (later the Fires of London ensemble), for whom he composed many of his works. These include *Taverner* (1970) and *Eight Songs for a Mad King* (1969). Davies's work is influenced particularly by serialism and early English music.

Davies, Robertson (1913–95) Canadian novelist, playwright, and essayist. He is best known as a novelist for his Deptford trilogy: *Fifth Business* (1970), *The Manticore* (1972), and *World of Wonders* (1975). These are first-person narratives that explore the Jungian significance of intertwined events. They were followed by the novels of the Cornish trilogy: *The Rebel Angels* (1981), a work reflecting elements of Davies's life as Master of Massey College, University of Toronto, *What's Bred in the Bone* (1985), and *The Lyre of Orpheus* (1989). His blend of fantasy, sardonic wit, and grotesque elements have earned his style the designation 'Ontario Gothic'.

Davies, W(illiam) H(enry) (1871–1940) British poet. He emigrated to the USA and lived as a vagrant and jobbing labourer there, writing *The Autobiography of a Super-Tramp* (1908) about his experiences. His poems often focus on the natural world; collections include *The Soul's Destroyer and Other Poems* (1905), which earned him the patronage of George Bernard Shaw.

da Vinci, Leonardo See LEONARDO DA VINCI.

Davis, Bette (born Ruth Elizabeth Davis) (1908–89) US actress. She established her Hollywood career playing a number of strong, independent female characters in such films as *Dangerous* (1935), *Jezebel* (1938), and *All About Eve* (1950). Her flair for suggesting the macabre and menacing emerged in later films, such as the melodrama *Whatever Happened to Baby Jane?* (1962) and the thriller *Murder with Mirrors* (1984).

Davis, Jefferson (1808–89) US statesman and president of the Southern CONFEDERACY 1861–65. He served in the Black Hawk War before leaving the army in 1835 to become a Mississippi planter. He commanded the Mississippi Rifles in the MEXICAN-AMERICAN WAR. Davis served two terms in the Senate (1847–51, 1857–61) and was Secretary of War in the administration of President PIERCE (1853–57). He left the Senate when Mississippi seceded from the Union, and in 1861 was named provisional President of the Confederacy. A year later he was elected to a six-year term.

Davis, Joe (1901–78) British billiards and snooker player. Joe Davis was the dominant figure in snooker for many years, holding the world championship from 1927 until his retirement in 1946. He was also world billiards champion (1928–32). His brother **Fred Davis** (1913–) was world snooker champion (1948–49; 1951–56) and world billiards champion (1980).

Davis, John (*c.*1550–1605) English navigator who continued Martin FROBISHER's work in seeking a NORTHWEST PASSAGE through the Canadian Arctic to the Pacific, in 1585 and again in 1586 and 1587. The Davis Strait between Baffin Island and Greenland was named after him.

Davis, Miles (Dewey) (1926–91) US jazz trumpeter, composer, and band-leader. In the 1950s he played and recorded arrangements by Gil Evans in a new style which became known as 'cool' jazz, heard on albums such as *Kind of Blue* (1959). For much of the time between 1955 and 1960 his quintet included John Coltrane.

Davis, Steve (1957–) British snooker player. He won a number of national and international events in the 1980s, becoming UK Professional Champion (1980–81; 1984–87) and World Professional Champion (1981; 1983–84; 1987–89).

Davis Cup (official name **International Lawn Tennis Challenge Trophy**) The trophy awarded to the winner of an annual international team-tennis tournament for men, since 1912 organized under the auspices of the International Lawn Tennis Federation. The trophy was donated in 1900 by US doubles champion and public official Dwight F. Davis (1879–1945) for an amateur contest between the USA and Britain; Davis himself played for the US team in 1900 and 1902. By 1970 the tournament had become international and professional players were allowed to compete. The tournament was reorganized in 1971: preliminary competitions now take place in geographical zones, the champions of each zone competing with each other to proceed to the finals. The format of each round – four singles matches and one doubles match – has remained the same. Recent winners are the USA (1990, 1992, 1995), France (1991, 1996), Germany (1993), and Sweden (1994).

Davisson, Clinton Joseph (1881–1958) US physicist. With Lester Germer in 1927, he demonstrated that electrons possess wave-like properties (see WAVE-PARTICLE DUALITY). in his experiment, electrons bouncing off a nickel surface produced wave patterns similar to those formed by light reflected from a diffraction grating. For his work on electron diffraction he shared the 1937 Nobel Prize for physics.

Davitt, Michael (1846–1906) Irish nationalist and land reformer. The son of an Irish farmer who had been evicted from his holding, he opposed the British-imposed land-holding system in Ireland. In 1865 he joined the IRISH REPUBLICAN BROTHERHOOD, a movement committed to the establishment of an independent republic of Ireland. He was sentenced to 15 years' penal servitude in 1870 for smuggling weapons for the FENIANS. Released in 1877 he helped found the Irish Land League in 1879, an organization formed to achieve land reform. With C. S. PARNELL, he sought to protect Irish peasants against evictions and high rents. He was elected a Member of Parliament in 1882 while in jail, and again in 1892 and 1895. The agitation which he led influenced Gladstone to introduce the 1881 Irish Land Act, guaranteeing fair rents, fixity of tenure, and freedom to sell (the Three Fs) to tenants.

Davy, Sir Humphry (1778–1829) British chemist, a pioneer of electrochemistry. After an apprenticeship with an apothecary-surgeon, he discovered nitrous oxide (laughing gas) and was invited to join the Royal Institution. Using electrolytic decomposition, he discovered the elements sodium, potassium, magnesium, calcium, strontium, and barium. Davy identified and named the element chlorine after he had demonstrated that oxygen was not a necessary constituent of acids, determined the properties of iodine, and demonstrated that diamond was a form of carbon. He appointed Faraday as his assistant.

Dawkins, Richard (1941–) British biologist. Dawkins's books *The Selfish Gene* (1976) and *River Out of Eden* (1995) did much to popularize the theory of sociobiology. In *The Blind Watchmaker* (1986), Dawkins discussed evolution by natural selection and suggested that the theory could answer the fundamental question of why life exists.

day In ancient times, the interval of time between sunrise and sunset, but now the time for one rotation of the Earth counted from one midnight to the next. A **mean solar day** is the time between successive passages of the mean Sun across the observer's meridian and is the same throughout the year. For many astronomical purposes, however, the time between successive passages of the FIRST POINT OF ARIES or the vernal equinox across the observer's meridian is more useful. This is the **sidereal day** and is essentially the time of one apparent revolution of the celestial sphere or stellar background because of the Earth's rotation.

Day, Doris (born Doris Kappelhoff) (1924–) US actress and singer. She became a star in the 1950s with roles in a number of films, at first musicals but later also comedies and light romances. Her films include *Calamity Jane* (1953) and *Pillow Talk* (1959).

Dayan, Moshe (1915–81) Israeli statesman and general. He fought in the British army in World War II, in which he lost an eye. After commanding Israeli forces at the time of the Suez crisis he entered Parliament, originally representing the Labour Party but later forming an independent group with David Ben-Gurion. Dayan became Minister of Defence in 1967 and oversaw Israel's victory in the Six Day War, but resigned in 1974 following criticisms of the country's state of readiness at the start of the Yom Kippur War. As Foreign Minister (1977–79) he played a prominent role in negotiations towards the Israeli–Egyptian peace treaty of 1979, hosted by President Carter at Camp David in the USA.

Day Lewis, C(ecil) (1904–72) British poet and critic. During the 1930s he was associated with a group of left-wing poets which included W. H. Auden and Stephen Spender, and his early volumes of verse, such as *Transitional Poems* (1929), reflect the influence of radical and revolutionary ideas. After 1940, however, he became increasingly a figure of the Establishment; he published several works of criticism, including *The Poetic Image* (1947), and further collections of verse, such as *The Whispering Roots* (1970). He was Poet Laureate 1968–72.

D-Day See NORMANDY CAMPAIGN.

DDT (dichlorodiphenyltrichloroethane) A chlorinated hydrocarbon contact INSECTICIDE. It was first synthesized in 1873, and its insecticidal properties were discovered by the Swiss scientist Paul MÜLLER in 1942. Its most spectacular use was in the eradication of malarial mosquitoes. However, in the 1950s doses of DDT and other insecticides had to be doubled or trebled as resistant insect strains developed, and evidence began to grow that the chemical was concentrated in the food chain. Questions were raised about the chemical's safety, and in over twenty countries (for example, Norway in 1970 and the UK in 1984) DDT was banned. However, it is still widely used for malaria and pest control in Third World countries.

Deacon, Henry (1822–76) British industrial chemist and innovator in the alkali industry. After apprenticeship to an engineering firm, he joined Pilkington's Glassworks in 1848 and so became familiar with the alkali industry. At that time SODIUM CARBONATE was made by the LEBLANC process, involving treatment of common salt with sulphuric acid and releasing hydrochloric acid. Deacon devised a process whereby the gaseous hydrochloric acid could be converted to bleaching powder, a substance in great demand in the textile industry.

dead reckoning See NAVIGATION.

Dead Sea A bitter salt-lake or inland sea in the Jordan valley on the Israel-Jordan border. At 400 m (1,300 ft) below sea-level, it is the lowest point on the surface of the Earth.

Dead Sea Scrolls A collection of Hebrew and Aramaic manuscripts, the first of which were found in 1947 by shepherds in a cave near the north-western shore of the Dead Sea. They belonged to the library of the Jewish (perhaps Essene) community at nearby Qumran, and were probably hidden shortly before the Roman destruction of 68 AD. The scrolls include fragments of nearly every book of the Hebrew BIBLE.

deafness The loss of hearing, which has many causes. Loss of response to high tones is an almost inevitable accompaniment of ageing, and often becomes severe enough to interfere with the understanding of speech. Abnormalities of the inner ear are the usual cause of congenital deafness. Some deaf children need special education in separate units, whereas others may be successfully integrated into normal schools. The deaf are able to communicate by lip-reading or by using a special SIGN LANGUAGE. Total communication usually implies the use of both these methods, as well as speech, finger-spelling, and writing, so that the possibilities of communication are extended and DISABILITY minimized. Those with residual hearing may make use of hearing aids, worn in or behind the ear. The profoundly deaf may benefit from a cochlear implant, an electronic device implanted in the inner ear.

Deakin, Alfred (1856–1919) Australian Liberal statesman, Prime Minister 1903–04, 1905–08, and 1909–10. He accompanied Sir Edmund Barton to London to steer the Commonwealth Bill through Parliament (1900) and as Attorney-General (1901–03) introduced legislation which created the Australian high court. In his second term as Prime Minister he introduced far-reaching legislation, including protectionist tariffs and commercial laws.

Dean, Christopher See TORVILL AND DEAN.

Dean, James (born James Byron) (1931–55) US actor. He starred in only three films, *East of Eden* (1955), *Rebel Without a Cause* (1955; released posthumously), and *Giant* (1956), before dying in a car accident. However, he became a cult figure closely identified with the title role of *Rebel Without a Cause*, symbolizing for many the disaffected youth of the postwar era.

death The cessation of function of the major organs of the body required to sustain life. Failure of the heart, lungs, liver, kidneys, or brain can lead to death of the whole body unless compensatory medical treatment is possible.

The permanent loss of function of the brainstem, which controls respiration and other vital reflexes, is called brain death. This is the modern accepted point at which death can be diagnosed, even if the rest of the body still functions.

death cap One of the many species of deadly poisonous AGARIC fungi that belong to the family Amanitaceae. The death cap, *Amanita phalloides*, has a fruit body with a greenish-white cap, white gills and stalk, a white ring round the stalk, and a membranous cup-like volva at the base. It is found in woods and pasture land. Symptoms of poisoning appear only some hours after it has been eaten, and it is usually fatal. Other deadly poisonous species include the destroying angel, *A. virosa*, the browning amanita of North America, *A. brunnescens*, and fly agaric, *A. muscaria*.

death penalty See CAPITAL PUNISHMENT.

death rate See INFANT MORTALITY; MORTALITY RATE.

death's-head hawkmoth See HAWKMOTH.

Death Valley A desert in eastern California, USA, lying within the Great Basin 85 m (280 feet) below sea-level. It is a long and forbidding desert of alkaline flats and briny pools, with deposits of borax. Summer temperatures reach to above 55°C (130°F), but winter nights can be very cold.

death-watch beetle A beetle whose larvae bore into mature timber, potentially causing immense damage. The adult males strike their heads against the wood as a mating call, making sounds which can be heard on still nights. BOOK LICE can make similar, but fainter, noises. Death-watch beetles belong to the family Anobiidae, which also includes the common woodworm, *Anobium punctatum*. Others of the 1,100 species in this family attack stored foods, tobacco, and even drugs.

de Beauvoir, Simone (1908–86) French existentialist philosopher, novelist, and feminist. While studying philosophy at the Sorbonne in 1929 she began her lifelong association with Jean-Paul Sartre; they became leading exponents of existentialism and founded the review *Les Temps modernes* (1945). De Beauvoir is regarded as an important figure in the 'second wave' of feminism, bringing the ideas of psychology, myth, political theory, and history to bear on the issue in her best-known work, *The Second Sex* (1949).

debenture A fixed INTEREST-yielding SECURITY (in the USA, a BOND) issued by a firm raising a loan. Debentures are normally dated for redemption (repayment) by the holder, but may be irredeemable. They may be secured against a particular asset held by the firm (fixed debentures) or against the whole firm (floating debentures). Debenture holders have higher priority than shareholders when a COMPANY is liquidated, and can force a company's liquidation if their interest is not paid as due.

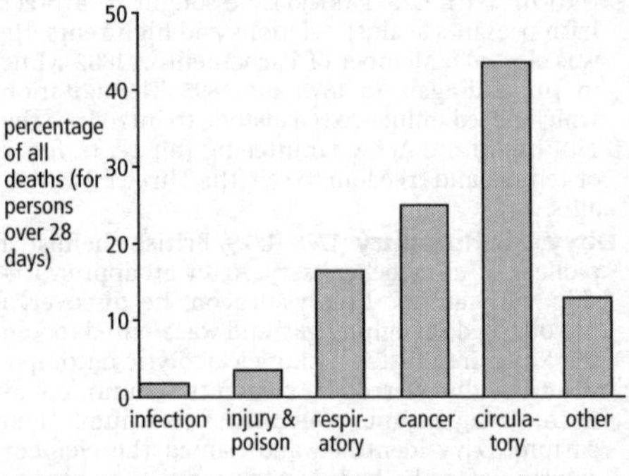

Death The causes of death in the UK in 1996 (excluding perinatal deaths).

Debrett, John (*c.*1750–1822) British publisher. He compiled *The Peerage of England, Scotland and Ireland* (first issued in 1803 and until 1971 issued annually), which is regarded as the authority on the British nobility; it is now published every five years.

de Broglie, Louis-Victor, Prince (1892–1987) French physicist. He was the first to suggest that subatomic particles can also have the properties of waves (known as de Broglie waves). He further developed the study of wave mechanics, which was fundamental to the subsequent development of quantum mechanics. He was awarded the Nobel Prize for physics in 1929.

Debussy, (Achille) Claude (1862–1918) French composer and critic. Debussy carried the ideas of impressionist art and symbolist poetry into music, using melodies based on the whole-tone scale and delicate harmonies exploiting overtones. His orchestral tone-poem *Prélude à l'après-midi d'un faune* (1894) and his books of piano preludes and studies are outstanding examples of the delicate, suggestive character of his music. Debussy was to have a profound influence on later composers such as Berg, Bartók, and Boulez.

Debye, Peter Joseph William (1884–1966) Dutch-born US chemical physicist. He established the existence of permanent electric dipole moments in many molecules, demonstrated the use of these to determine molecular size and shape, modified Einstein's theory of specific heats as applied to solids, pioneered the use of X-ray scattering to determine crystal structure, and solved problems of electrolytic conductance. He received the Nobel Prize for chemistry in 1936.

decathlon See ATHLETICS.

Deccan (Sanskrit *dakshin*, 'south') A triangular plateau covering most of peninsular India south of the River Narbada, bounded by the Satpura Range in the north and by the Western and Eastern Ghats on the other two sides. Tilting eastward, from about 900 m to 450 m (3,000 feet to 1,500 feet), it is drained by the Godavari, Krishna, and Cauvery rivers flowing into the Bay of Bengal. The lava beds in the north-west are characterized by water-retaining black soil, and cotton is grown.

Decca Navigator A short- to medium-range radio aid to navigation, operational in many parts of the world, which allows ships' navigators to find their vessel's position with a high degree of accuracy. Decca is a phase-difference hyperbolic navigation system consisting of a master transmitter and two or three secondary transmitters spread within a radius of 110–220 km (60–120 nautical miles; see KNOT) of the master station. The system gives navigational cover up to 550 km (300 nautical miles) from the master station by day, and is accurate to around 50 m (160 feet) up to 185 km (100 nautical miles) from the master station.

Decembrists Members of a Russian revolutionary society, the Northern Society. A group of Russian army officers, influenced by French liberal ideas, combined to lead a revolt against the accession of NICHOLAS I in 1825. Some of their supporters proclaimed their preference for a republic, others for Nicholas's eldest brother Constantine, in the hope that he would be in favour of constitutional reform and modernization. A few Guards regiments in St Petersburg refused to take an oath of allegiance to Nicholas and marched to the Senate House, where they were met by artillery fire. Betrayed by police spies, five of their leaders were executed, and 120 exiled to Siberia. The Decembrists' revolt profoundly affected Russia, leading to increased police terrorism and to the spread of revolutionary societies among the intellectuals.

decibel (symbol dB) A measure of the relative intensity of a wave, especially a SOUND wave. The intensity is usually compared with the intensity of the smallest sound that can be detected by the human ear. Although the ratio of these two intensities could be used as a measure, it would usually involve a wide range of very large numbers and this would be inconvenient. Instead, ten times the logarithm of the ratio is used to give the value of the relative intensity in decibels. A very loud sound, such as a jet aircraft taking off, may reach 120 dB, conversation in the home is about 60 dB, and a scarcely audible sound, such as the rustle of leaves, is about 10 dB. Decibels are also commonly used to express the strength of electrical signals.

deciduous forest An area consisting mainly of trees which, under normal conditions of growth, regularly shed all their leaves. They are generally found where there is an annual climatic change such as a cold winter or prolonged dry period. At these times, the majority of tree species in deciduous forests will be leafless. They occupy large areas of the tropics, subtropics, and temperate zones, the most familiar being the north temperate forests with their spectacular leaf colours as they synchronously shed them in the autumn (the fall). In the tropics they are known as monsoon forests as compared with the evergreen tropical rain forests.

Decius, Gaius Messius Quintus Trajanus (*c.*201–51) Roman emperor 249–51. He was the first Roman emperor to promote systematic persecution of the Christians in the empire; popular protest eventually forced him to reverse this policy shortly before the end of his reign. He resisted a Gothic invasion of Moesia in 249, but was defeated and killed two years later.

Declaration of Independence The foundation document of the United States of America, which proclaimed American separation from Britain and was adopted by the CONTINENTAL CONGRESS on 4 July 1776. Its principal author was Thomas JEFFERSON, who based its arguments on John LOCKE's ideas of contractual government. Its celebrated preamble declared that all men are created equal and have inalienable rights to life, liberty, and the pursuit of happiness. There followed a detailed list of acts of tyranny committed by George III, his ministers, and Parliament against the American people, similar in tone to those in the English BILL OF RIGHTS (1689). The original document had fifty-six signatories whose names were initially kept secret for fear of British reprisals in the event of American defeat.

Declarations of Indulgence Four proclamations issued by Charles II and James II of England in an attempt to achieve religious toleration. Charles II issued Declarations in 1662 and 1672, stating that the penal laws against Roman Catholics and Protestant dissenters were to be suspended, but protests by Parliament caused both attempts to be abandoned. James II issued similar Declarations in 1687 and 1688, the latter leading to the trial of the Seven Bishops. James II insisted that the Declaration should be read in all churches; a Tory High Churchman, Archbishop Sancroft and six bishops who refused to do so were tried on a charge of seditious libel and were acquitted. The verdict was a popular one and widespread protest and defiance followed during the months leading up to the GLORIOUS REVOLUTION of 1688.

declination See CELESTIAL SPHERE.

decomposition The breakdown of dead plants and animals by organisms, such as bacteria and fungi, a process ensuring that nutrients are continuously recycled in any ECOSYSTEM. The process of decomposition is helped by many invertebrates such as earthworms, snails, and beetles which break down the dead organic material into a form suitable for microorganisms to act upon. Decomposition frees nutrients, which are then available to other organisms, particularly AUTOTROPHIC ORGANISMS, and produces HUMUS. Compost heaps, biogas units (BIOMASS), and sewage works all harness these decomposer organisms under artificial conditions.

decompression chamber See DEEP-SEA AND DIVING TECHNOLOGY.

deconstruction A method of critical analysis of philosophical and literary language, concerned with unravelling the meanings of texts. In *On Grammatology* (1967) the French philosopher Jacques DERRIDA claimed that exposing a text's underlying, but unformulated, ideas revealed meanings which contradicted the apparent meaning or the author's intentions. There was, he argued, no one meaning of a text, but rather a series of often contradictory meanings all elusive and none definitive. Derrida's writings are abstruse, and fierce dispute has erupted over his theory, which some regard as a fearless questioning of the possibility of meaning and others as an adventure playground for intellectual élitism.

Decorated style The second of the three phases into which English GOTHIC ARCHITECTURE is conventionally divided, covering the period *c.*1250–*c.*1375, between Early English and PERPENDICULAR. In Decorated churches the simple Early English lancets were replaced by wider windows with bar TRACERY that developed from simple geometric designs to fanciful flowing patterns. (The terms 'Geometrical' and 'Curvilinear' are often used to characterize this evolution.) Increased ornamentation was seen in other aspects of the Decorated style.

Dedekind, Richard (1831–1916) German mathematician, one of the founders of abstract algebra and modern mathematics. His analysis of the properties of real numbers solved the question of what numbers are, and supplied a satisfactory foundation on which analysis could be based. He is remembered also for his theory of rings of algebraic integers, which cast the theory of algebraic numbers into its general modern form. He introduced collections of numbers as entities of interest in their own right, whose relationships to each other may be studied by means of set theory.

deduction The process or principles by which, in an argument, a conclusion is derived from certain premisses. The term is also used, especially in philosophy, with a narrower sense, in which an argument is said to be deductively valid if it is impossible for all its premisses to be true and its conclusion false. A simple example might be: 'Some Greeks are philosophers. All Greeks are Europeans. So some Europeans are philosophers.'

de Duve, Christian René (1917–) British-born Belgian biochemist. He was a pioneer in the study of cell biology, and his research suggested the existence of organelles that contain and isolate a cell's digestive enzymes. In 1955, with the aid of electron microscopy, he proved the existence of lysosomes. De Duve shared a Nobel Prize in 1974.

Dee, John (1527–1608) English alchemist, mathematician, and geographer. He helped in the first English translation of Euclid's works, and was Elizabeth I's astrologer. In later life he absorbed himself in alchemy, acquired notoriety as a sorcerer, and died in poverty.

deep-freeze An appliance for the long-term storage of food at low temperatures, introduced by BIRDSEYE in 1929. A domestic deep-freeze uses a mechanical HEAT-PUMP similar to that of a refrigerator but maintains its internal temperature below −7°C. This form of REFRIGERATION depends on all the water contained in the food freezing to solid ice, thereby rendering spoilage organisms inactive. Some foodstuffs undergo permanent change on freezing and thawing: the expansion of water as it freezes ruptures cell walls, causing, for example, soft fruits such as strawberries to become flabby.

deep-sea and diving technology Since the late 1960s there have been dramatic advances in diving technology, many arising from the desire of the oil industry to exploit petroleum supplies beneath the sea. For divers working below about 10 m (32 feet) an inflatable dry suit (in which no water penetrates to the skin) is now used, along with a light, plastic helmet containing a gas regulator and communications equipment. For divers working at greater depths, a major problem arises from breathing air at the high pressures encountered there. Nitrogen from the air is absorbed into the bloodstream and if pressure is reduced too rapidly during ascent after a dive, the absorbed nitrogen forms gas bubbles in the blood, causing the condition known as the 'bends' (caisson or decompression disease). The bends can be avoided by stopping for prescribed decompression periods during ascent from a dive. An additional problem at depths greater than 40 m (130 feet) is 'nitrogen narcosis', in which the nitrogen absorbed into the body has adverse effects on the nervous system. Problems of decompression disease and nitrogen narcosis have been largely overcome by using mixtures of oxygen and another, more inert, gas (usually helium) in place of nitrogen. Divers operating with such mixtures can work at depths of 90 m (300 feet) or more, where decompression times are of the order of days. Under such conditions a technique known as 'saturation diving' is necessary to achieve effective work. Divers travel to the underwater work-site in a type of diving-bell known as a submersible decompression chamber (SDC). After working, they return to the ship in the SDC, still at diving pressure. Once on board they transfer to a deck decompression chamber (DDC), a comfortably equipped chamber maintained at the same pressure as the SDC, in which they live for periods of up to 15 days, diving each day in the SDC to the work-site.

Because of the many problems involved in diving to great depths, piloted submersibles equipped with remotely controlled robot arms, or submersibles controlled from the surface (remotely piloted vehicles) are used whenever possible.

deep-sea fish A category that includes a wide range of taxonomic groups. They can be divided into mid-water (bathypelagic) and bottom-living (benthic) forms. The latter range down to the very deepest of ocean trenches. For example, a deep-sea cod of the family Eretmophoridae was caught at 8,000 m (26,500 feet) in the Puerto Rico Trench.

Fishes bearing light-organs, such as LANTERN FISHES, are common in the twilight zone of the deep sea, down to about 1,000 m (3,250 feet). Many species have large eyes to make the most of this living light. Species living below this level often have small eyes which in some cases are covered with skin. Most deep-sea fishes are black or red in colour. The deep sea is relatively poor in sources of food and consequently many of its inhabitants have huge mouths, as in gulper eels, and massive teeth, as in black dragon fish. Some deep-sea anglerfishes, in addition to having luminous fishing lures, large mouths, and huge teeth, have a unique means of ensuring breeding success in that the males are parasites on the much larger females.

deer Any one of some 36 species of large, even-toed, hoofed, land mammals. They make up the family Cervidae and have been common since the Pliocene as browsing animals of the forest and forest edge. They are spread throughout the Northern Hemisphere over Asia, Europe, and North America; in the Southern Hemisphere they are almost entirely limited to South America.

The weight of the body is carried by the third and fourth toes, protected by hoofs, while on either side of the feet are the small second and fifth toes, the dew claws, which do not touch the ground. Deer are characterized by the presence of ANTLERS or tusk-like canine teeth in the males. The muzzle is naked and the ears large. Below the eyes are scent glands, which in the male are odoriferous. The tail, usually short, is held erect at moments of alarm. Deer are RUMINANTS, browsers or grazers, with cud-chewing habits. They come out at dawn and dusk to feed on leaves, grass, berries, shoots, ferns, root crops, and even bark, before settling in a safe, quiet place to chew the cud. All deer are swift and have highly developed senses and social organization, which helps them to avoid danger. They live in herds.

deerfly See HORSEFLY.

deer mouse See WOOD MOUSE.

de Falla, Manuel See FALLA.

defence mechanisms (in psychoanalysis) Unconscious processes that protect the individual from ANXIETY. FREUD argued that anxiety arises from conflict within the individual. It may be due to an ungratified appetite or INSTINCT or to conflict between an appetite and one's moral beliefs. The mechanisms include repression, keeping memories and wishes in the UNCONSCIOUS; denial, simply refusing to accept that something is true; sublimation, finding a socially acceptable outlet for a morally unacceptable impulse (such as sexual desire for one's mother); rationalization, giving a rational but specious account of emotionally driven behaviour; regression, retreating to more immature patterns of behaviour; projection, attributing to other people feelings, such as aggression, which one entertains oneself; and reaction-formation, for example acting and feeling affectionately towards someone one hates.

deficiency disease Any disorder caused by dietary deficiency of essential nutrients. Vitamin deficiency may cause a range of disorders; nicotinic acid deficiency causes pellagra, vitamin D deficiency causes rickets, and vitamin A deficiency causes visual impairment. Deficiency diseases may also be caused by dietary deficiency of protein and minerals. Deficiency diseases are treated with dietary supplements of the lacking nutrient.

deflation (in geomorphology) A type of erosion with the removal of loose particles of rock by wind. It mostly involves the lifting and blowing of sand, silt, and clay. Most common in deserts and in semi-arid areas where the vegetation cover is scanty, deflation also occurs on dry farmland elsewhere: for example, the 'fen blows' of eastern England, or the infamous Dust Bowl of the midwestern USA.

Defoe, Daniel (1660–1731) English novelist and journalist. After a varied career of political journalism and secret service work, Defoe wrote *Robinson Crusoe* (1719) when he was nearly 60. Loosely based on the true story of the sailor Alexander Selkirk, it has a claim to being the first English novel. Its tale of the shipwrecked Crusoe battling for survival in virtual solitude is one of the most familiar and resonant myths of modern literature. Other major works include the novel *Moll Flanders* (1722) and the historical fiction *A Journal of the Plague Year* (1722).

defoliant A chemical agent that causes leaves to fall off trees and bushes, thereby denying cover to the enemy. Some defoliants were under development at the end of World War I, but were never used. At the beginning of US intervention in the civil war in Vietnam, the US Air Force sprayed some jungle areas near Saigon with four pesticides. The most common, Agent Orange, was a defoliant made up of the weed killers 2,4-D and 2,4,5-T.

De Forest, Lee (1873–1961) US pioneer of electronics, especially the THERMIONIC VALVE. In 1896 he graduated in mechanical engineering at Yale University, but then turned his attention to RADIO communication. In 1906 he improved J. A. FLEMING's diode by introducing a third electrode, creating the triode. Originally, the triode served only as an improved device for detecting radio waves, but later its ability to act as a high-frequency oscillator and amplifier made it a key component in the development of radio and other telecommunications.

deforestation The destruction of forest, usually for timber or to clear the land for cultivation or the raising of livestock. Most of western Europe and the Mediterranean lands lost their natural forest centuries ago, and in China wood has been scarce for thousands of years due to deforestation. Huge areas of forest, most of it tropical, are now being cleared – some 12 million hectares or 2 per cent of the remaining forests each year. In South America, the Amazon RAIN FOREST, the world's largest, is particularly under threat and there, as elsewhere, much of the tree-felling is done by multinational companies, which either sell the timber for export or use the cleared land for ranching. As well as decimating the people and the unique wealth of animals and plants in the forests, the burning of trees on a large scale contributes to the GREENHOUSE EFFECT, not only by increasing the amount of carbon dioxide in the atmosphere as a result of the combustion process, but also by eliminating the trees that would have absorbed carbon dioxide in photosynthesis. Tree roots also hold the soil in place, and once they are cut down or burned the soil remains fertile for only a few years, before it is blown or washed away and the land becomes barren.

Degas, (Hilaire Germain) Edgar (1834–1917) French impressionist painter and sculptor. He took part in most of the impressionist exhibitions, including the first in 1874. Unlike other impressionist painters, who often concentrated on landscape, Degas is best known for his paintings of ballet-dancers, such as *Dancer Lacing Her Shoe* (*c*.1878); in his sculpture, to which he turned in later life, he also concentrated on the human form.

de Gasperi, Alcide (1881–1954) Italian statesman. He was elected to the Austro-Hungarian Parliament in 1911, and became Secretary-General of the

Italian People's Party (1919–25). From 1929 to 1943 he was given refuge from MUSSOLINI's regime by the Vatican. He played an important part in creating the Christian Democrat Party as a focus for moderate opinion after the fascist era. De Gasperi was Prime Minister from 1945 to 1953, during which time he adopted a strong stand against communism and in favour of European cooperation.

de Gaulle, Charles (André Joseph Marie) (1890–1970) French general and statesman, head of government 1944–46, President 1959–69. He served in the French army during World War I, and during World War II was a member of the Cabinet at the time of France's surrender in June 1940. He escaped to Britain, where he was an instigator of the resistance and organized the Free French movement. Following the war he became interim President of the new French Republic, but later resigned. Having been asked to form a government, he became President in 1959 and went on to establish the presidency as a democratically elected office (1962). He resigned in 1969 after proposed constitutional changes were rejected by the electorate. In addition to extricating France from the Algerian crisis and strengthening the French economy, he is remembered for his assertive foreign policy (including withdrawing French forces from NATO and blocking Britain's entry to the EEC) and for quelling the student uprisings and strikes of May 1968.

degenerate matter A state of matter that is not gas, liquid, or solid, reached when the central density in a star has become so high (several thousand tonnes per cubic metre) that a state said to be quantum mechanically degenerate is produced. White dwarfs and neutron stars contain degenerate matter and so are often described as degenerate stars.

degrees (of latitude and longitude) Units of circular-arc measurement used to measure distances and specify positions on the Earth's surface, each one degree (1°) comprising sixty minutes (60′), and a minute comprising sixty seconds (60″). A degree of latitude (see LATITUDE AND LONGITUDE) is determined by a length along a MERIDIAN that subtends one degree at the Earth's centre. It averages about 110 km (70 miles), being slightly shorter near the Equator (0°) than at either pole (90° N or S) due to the OBLATENESS of the Earth. A degree of longitude is measured at right angles to latitude, round the AXIS OF THE EARTH. It varies from about 110 km (70 miles) at the Equator to zero at the poles.

de Havilland, Sir Geoffrey (1882–1965) British aircraft designer and manufacturer. Having built the BE series of fighters in World War I, he started his own company in 1920. He designed and built many famous aircraft, including the Moth series, the Mosquito of World War II, and some of the first jet aircraft, and also produced the Gipsy series of aircraft engines.

dehydration The removal of water from a substance, either by heating or by chemical reaction. An excessive loss of water from body tissues can be dangerous. Symptoms include thirst, nausea, and exhaustion. Dehydration is treated by drinking water, but severe cases may require the administration of liquids containing salts, glucose, etc. (oral rehydration therapy) or the intravenous administration of water and salts (which have been lost with the water).

Deighton, Leonard Cyril (known as 'Len') (1929–) British novelist. His reputation is based on his spy thrillers, several of which have been adapted as films and for television. The best known include his first novel *The Ipcress File* (1962) and the trilogy *Berlin Game*, *Mexico Set*, and *London Match* (1983–5).

Deimos The outer satellite of Mars, discovered by the US astronomer Asaph Hall in 1877. It has a nearly circular orbit at 23,460 km from the planet's centre. Markedly irregular in shape, the mean radius of Deimos is about 6 km.

Deirdre The Irish heroine whose renowned beauty brought suffering to her people of Ulster. The intended bride of King Conchobhar, Deirdre fell in love with Naoise, the son of Uisnech, and eloped with him. Eventually allowed to return from their exile in Scotland, Naoise and his brothers were killed and Deirdre died. Their story is the basis of J. M. Synge's play *Deirdre of the Sorrows* (1909).

Dekker, Thomas (*c.*1570–1632) English dramatist and novelist. He is chiefly known for his two-part tragicomedy *The Honest Whore* (1604; 1630), the first part of which he wrote jointly with Thomas Middleton. He is also remembered for the revenge tragedy *The Witch of Edmonton* (1623), in which he collaborated with John Ford and William Rowley (*c.*1585–1626).

de Klerk, F(rederik) W(illem) (1936–) South African statesman, State President 1989–94. Becoming State President only months after assuming leadership of the National Party, he instigated significant political reforms designed to bring about the dismantling of apartheid in South Africa. After freeing Nelson Mandela and other ANC leaders in 1990 he lifted the ban on membership of the ANC and opened the negotiations with black political leaders that led to the country's first true democratic elections in 1994. After the ANC's electoral victory de Klerk was given a Cabinet post as a Deputy State President, but in 1996 he withdrew his party from the ruling coalition. In 1993 he shared the Nobel Peace Prize with Nelson Mandela.

de Kooning, Willem (1904–97) Dutch-born US painter. He and Jackson Pollock are generally regarded as the leading exponents of abstract expressionism. De Kooning's work in this genre from the late 1940s onwards usually retained figurative elements, whether represented or merely hinted at, as in *Painting* (1948). The female form was a central theme in some of his work, notably in the *Women* series (1950–53).

Delacroix, (Ferdinand Victor) Eugène (1798–1863) French painter. The chief painter of the French romantic school, he is known for his use of vivid colour, free drawing, and exotic, violent, or macabre subject-matter. *The Massacre at Chios* (1824) was an early example of his work and attracted much criticism when it was first exhibited. In his later work Delacroix experimented with complementary colours, purifying his palette to exclude black and earth colours and thus anticipating impressionist methods.

de la Mare, Walter (John) (1873–1956) British poet and novelist. Essentially a lyric poet, he had his first major success with 'The Listeners' (1912). His many volumes of verse for children include *Peacock Pie* (1913) and *Tom Tiddler's Ground* (1932).

Delaunay, Robert (1885–1941) French painter. For most of his career he experimented with the abstract qualities of colour, notably in his Eiffel Tower series (1910–12), and he was one of the founder members of Orphism together with his wife, Sonia Delaunay-Terk. He was influenced by early cubism and painted some of the first purely abstract pictures, including his *Formes circulaires cosmiques* series (from 1912).

Delaunay-Terk, Sonia (1885–1979) Russian-born French painter and textile designer. She and her husband Robert Delaunay were among the founders of the movement of Orphism. She created abstract paintings based on harmonies of form and colour, her interest in the use of colour being reflected in her fabric and tapestry designs of the 1920s; her work in this field had a significant impact on international fashion.

Delaware A state of the USA situated on the east coast between New Jersey and Maryland. Though discovered by Henry Hudson, its name derives from Lord de la Warr, governor of Virginia in 1610. It was first settled as New Sweden in 1638, but came under English control in 1664. As the three 'Lower Counties' of Pennsylvania, it enjoyed virtual autonomy under the PENN family but in 1776 it achieved independent statehood. It was the first state to ratify the US constitution in 1787.

Delaware An Algonquian-speaking tribe of North American Indians whose original homelands lay along the Atlantic coast where they cultivated maize. During the 19th century they moved to Kansas and Oklahoma and today others live in Wisconsin and Ontario.

Delcassé, Théophile (1852–1923) French statesman. As Foreign Minister in six successive governments between 1898 and 1905, he was the principal architect of the pre-1914 European alliances. He was the key figure in negotiations which resulted in the *entente cordiale* with Britain (1904) and he paved the way for the Triple Entente with Britain and Russia (1907). In 1911 as Minister of Marine he arranged for cooperation between British and French fleets in the event of war. In 1914 he was again Foreign Minister and helped to negotiate the secret Treaty of London (1915), which persuaded Italy to fight on the side of the Allies in World War I by guaranteeing the retention of the Dodecanese Islands.

de Lenclos, Ninon See LENCLOS.

Delfont, Bernard, Baron Delfont of Stepney (born Boris Winogradsky) (1909–94) British impresario, born in Russia. Having emigrated to Britain with his brother (Lew GRADE) in 1912, he pursued a successful career in theatrical management; from the early 1940s onwards he presented more than 200 shows in London's West End.

Delft A town in the province of South Holland in the Netherlands, 5 km (3 miles) south-east of the Hague; pop. (1991) 89,400. Since the 17th century the town has been noted for its pottery. Delft manufactures spirits, pharmaceuticals, cables, and ceramics.

delftware See MAIOLICA.

Delhi The capital of India comprising **Old Delhi**, a walled city on the River Jumna, and **New Delhi** (pop. 294,150), the present seat of government of India, built 1912–29 to the design of Sir Edwin Lutyens (1869–1944), to replace Calcutta as the capital of British India; pop. (1991) 8,375,200. Delhi was made the capital of the Mogul empire in 1638 by Shah Jahan, who built the Red Fort containing the imperial Mogul palace. The University of Delhi, which has 74 constituent colleges, was founded in 1922 and is located in the southern part of New Delhi as are the airport and the arenas built for the 1982 Asian Games. The place of Gandhi's cremation after his assassination in 1948 is a national shrine. Delhi's industries, mainly of consumer goods of all kinds, are sited in satellite towns. Old Delhi is a centre for skilled crafts.

Delian League A voluntary alliance formed by the Greek city-states in 478–447 BC to seek revenge for losses suffered during the GREEK-PERSIAN WARS. All members paid tribute in the form of ships or money, the latter being stored on the sacred island of Delos, the League's nominal base. At first, under the leadership of Athens, the League actively sought to drive Persian garrisons out of Europe and to liberate the Greek cities of Asia Minor. PERICLES encouraged the conversion of the alliance into the beginnings of the ATHENIAN EMPIRE.

Delibes, (Clément Philibert) Léo (1836–91) French composer and organist. He wrote a number of light operas such as *Lakmé* (1883), but his best-known works are the ballets *Coppélia* (1870) and *Sylvia* (1876).

deliquescence The property of some crystalline substances of dissolving in water that they absorb from the air. Thus they dry the surrounding air, and for this reason they are sometimes used when dry air is required for a process in industrial chemistry.

Delius, Frederick (1862–1934) British composer, of German and Scandinavian descent. He is best known for pastoral works such as *Brigg Fair* (1907) and *On Hearing the First Cuckoo* (1912), but he also wrote songs, concertos, and much choral and theatre music, including operas, often showing his deep interest in German and Scandinavian music and culture. Delius settled in France in the 1890s; blinded and paralysed by illness in 1928 he dictated his last works to an amanuensis, Eric Fenby (1906–97).

della Francesca See PIERO DELLA FRANCESCA.

delocalized electrons Electrons that are not located solely in one atom or in a CHEMICAL BOND between two atoms. Delocalization can extend over more than two atoms: for example, six in benzene and the entire crystal in a metal.

Delorme, Philibert (or **de l'Orme**) (*c*.1510–70) The outstanding French architect of the 16th century. He was an artist of great distinction and originality, but almost all his buildings have been destroyed. The most important of his surviving works are fragments of the château of Anet (*c*.1550), built for Henry II's mistress Diane de Poitiers.

Delphi (Greek **Dhelfoí**) One of the most important sanctuaries of the ancient Greek world, dedicated to Apollo and situated on the lower southern slopes of Mount Parnassus above the Gulf of Corinth. Reputedly the navel of the Earth, it was the seat of the Delphic Oracle, whose often riddling responses to a wide range of religious, political, and moral questions were delivered in a state of ecstasy by the Pythia, the priestess of Apollo.

delphinium An annual, biennial, or perennial plant, belonging to the same family as the buttercup. About 200 species are known and they are chiefly from the temperate zones of the Northern Hemisphere, including Europe and North America. Blue is the predominant colour but there are also red, pink, and white species. *Delphinium hybridum* and *D. grandiflorum* with tall flower spikes are popular garden plants. The larkspur, *Consolida ambigua*, is an annual species with many coloured varieties, and is closely related to the delphiniums.

Delphinus The Dolphin, a CONSTELLATION just north of the celestial equator. It was one of the 48 constellations known to the ancient Greeks, and represents either the messenger of the sea god

Poseidon or the dolphin that carried the musician Arion to safety after he was attacked by robbers on board ship. Its most distinctive feature is a rectangle of stars that form a cluster called Job's Coffin.

del Sarto, Andrea See SARTO.

delta A deposit of silt, sand, and gravel laid down by a river as it enters a body of relatively still water. Deltas range in size from tiny features formed in small lakes by mountain streams, up to the enormous constructions of the Ganges–Brahmaputra and the Yangtze; but all are established in the same way. Coarse material is dropped first, forming horizontal 'top-set' beds; medium-sized debris is carried further out and deposited as sloping 'fore-set' beds, parallel to the shore; and the finest grains settle slowly in deep water in front of the delta, giving horizontal 'bottom-set' beds.

Demachy, Robert (1859–1938) French pictorialist photographer. Influenced by Impressionist painting, he manipulated his prints with gums, oils, and chemicals in order to 'interpret' what was on the negative.

de Maintenon See MAINTENON.

de Maupassant, Guy See MAUPASSANT.

de' Medici, Catherine See CATHERINE DE' MEDICI.

de' Medici, Cosimo See MEDICI,. COSIMO DE'

de' Medici, Giovanni Pope Leo X (see LEO).

de' Medici, Lorenzo See MEDICI,. LORENZO DE'

de Médicis, Marie See MARIE DE MÉDICIS.

dementia A condition characterized by loss of intellectual function, memory, and personality, that is caused by disease of the brain and is commonly associated with old age. Age-related dementia (senile dementia), which is progressive and irreversible, occurs in up to 10 per cent of people over 65 years of age, and up to 20 per cent of those over 80. **Alzheimer's disease** is the commonest form of dementia. Its cause is as yet unknown, although research suggests a genetic component, and there is no known cure. Other irreversible causes of dementia include HUNTINGTON'S DISEASE; HIV-infection and AIDS; CREUTZFELDT-JAKOB DISEASE, which has features in common with BOVINE SPONGIFORM ENCEPHALOPATHY (BSE); ARTERIOSCLEROSIS; head injury such as that sustained during boxing; and chronic excessive alcohol consumption. Reversible causes of dementia include vitamin B_{12} deficiency, hypothyroidism, and normal pressure hydrocephalus. Dementia is characterized by the insidious development of symptoms. Initially, loss of concentration and mild MEMORY impairment occur; progression results in further memory impairment, thought disorders, self-neglect, and behavioural disorders. Mood disturbance and blunted, shallow emotions are common features.

demesne In the Middle Ages, the lands retained by a lord under his direct control. The medieval lord, whether a king or VASSAL, needed land to provide food and all other necessities for himself and his own household. Demesnes were the site of his residences which could be manors, palaces, or castles, and possibly all three.

Demeter In Greek mythology, the goddess of agriculture, fertility, and marriage. She was the sister of Zeus and also the mother of his daughter Persephone.

deMille, Agnes (1909–93) US dancer and choreographer. Her choreographic style incorporated American folk idiom in popular narrative fusions of BALLET and MODERN DANCE as in *Rodeo* (1942) and *Fall River Legend* (1948). In Broadway MUSICALS her choreography was pre-eminent in the integration of dance, song, and action, as in *Oklahoma* (1943), and *Carousel* (1945). She was a niece of Cecil B. deMille.

deMille, Cecil B(lount) (1881–1959) US producer-director, who played a major role in the development of HOLLYWOOD. He was renowned for his pseudo-biblical and historical spectacles, among the most notable of which was *The Ten Commandments* (1923, remade 1956). There followed *The King of Kings* (1927), *The Sign of the Cross* (1932), *Cleopatra* (1934), *The Crusades* (1935), and *Samson and Delilah* (1949). He also made spectacular films with other backgrounds, including such WESTERNS as *The Plainsman* (1937) and *Union Pacific* (1939), and *The Greatest Show on Earth* (1952), about a circus.

democracy A system of government in which sovereignty rests with the whole people, who rule either directly or through representatives. In the contemporary world, democracy is closely associated with the idea of choosing governments by periodic free multiparty elections, but in the past it was understood more literally to mean the people gathering together in an assembly to debate political issues and enact laws. The chief elements of representative democracy are: freedom of speech and expression; periodic free elections to the LEGISLATURE, in which all citizens are entitled to vote and to stand for office; the right to form competing parties to contest these elections; a government which is responsible to the legislature, and thereby to some degree responsive to public opinion. Where one or more of these elements is absent, as in the 'People's Democracies', the one-party states of the communist bloc in the period following World War II, the system is unlikely to be genuinely democratic.

Democratic Party A major political party in the USA. Known in its initial form as the Democratic-Republican Party, it emerged under Thomas Jefferson in the 1790s in opposition to the Federalist Party, drawing its support from Southern planters and Northern yeoman farmers. In 1828, after a split with the National Republicans (soon called WHIGS) led by John Quincy ADAMS and Henry CLAY, a new Democratic Party was formed under the leadership of Andrew JACKSON and John C. CALHOUN. Its strong organization and popular appeal kept it in power for all but two presidential terms between then and 1860, when it divided over slavery. It only returned as a major national party in the last decades of the 19th century. By then, while retaining the loyalty of the deep South, it was gaining support from the ever expanding West and from the immigrant working classes of the industrialized north-east. In the early 20th century it adopted many of the policies of the Progressive Movement and its candidate for President, Woodrow WILSON, was elected for two terms (1913–21). Although in eclipse in the 1920s, it re-emerged in the years of the Great DEPRESSION, capturing Congress and the presidency: its candidate, Franklin D. ROOSEVELT, is the only President to have been re-elected three times. Since then it has tended to dominate the House of Representatives, and has generally held the Senate as well. The Democratic candidate Bill CLINTON won presidential elections in late 1992, but in mid-term elections in 1994 the Democrats suffered devastating losses, the Republicans gaining control of both Houses of Congress for the first time since 1954. Clinton was re-elected in 1997.

Democritus (*c.*460–370 BC) Greek philosopher and scientist who was the first to suggest that all matter consists of atomic particles. He argued that they are in constant movement, that the Earth is composed of heavy aggregations and the heavenly bodies of lighter ones, and that materials differ in quality according to their atomic arrangement.

demography The systematic study of human populations, addressed primarily to their growth, size, and structure. The main sources of data are the CENSUS and vital statistics, which developed in the 19th century. In the 20th century, population studies have developed in two main directions. Formal demography is concerned with abstract population mathematics. It shows how rates of birth, fertility, mortality, marriage, and migration combine to produce different population structures, densities, and distributions. Social demography relates this abstract study to the economics and culture of particular societies in different times and places, in order to determine the causes and influence of changing population trends.

demoiselle crane A species of bird, *Anthropoides virgo*, that is one of the smallest members of the CRANE family, Gruidae. It has a wide breeding range from southeastern Europe to central Asia, wintering in northeastern Africa, India, and China. The head and neck are black with large white ear-tufts while the rest of the body is ashy grey.

de Montespan, Marquise de See MONTESPAN.

de Montfort, Simon See MONTFORT.

De Morgan, Augustus (1806–71) British mathematician and logician who wrote many textbooks on analysis and symbolic logic; among them are *Formal Logic* (1847) and *Trigonometry and Double Algebra* (1849). He became Professor of Mathematics at University College London at the age of 22, and helped to found the London Mathematical Society (1865).

De Morgan, William (1839–1917) British pottery designer and writer, a leading figure of the ARTS AND CRAFTS MOVEMENT. Like his friend William MORRIS, he reacted against the Victorian taste for detailed naturalistic decoration and was a master of bold, flat pattern.

Demosthenes (384–322 BC) Athenian orator and statesman. He is best known for his political speeches on the need to defend Athens against the pretensions of Philip II of Macedon, which are known as the *Philippics*. Demosthenes was at the forefront of the campaign to unite the Greek city-states militarily against Macedon; the Greeks were defeated at the battle of Chaeronea in 338 BC, and Demosthenes committed suicide after the failure of an Athenian revolt against Macedon.

Dempsey, Jack (born William Harrison Dempsey) (1895–1983) US boxer. He was world heavyweight champion 1919–26, and during this time drew extremely large audiences to boxing; his defence of the title in 1921 was the first fight at which a million dollars was taken at the gate.

denaturation The change that occurs in proteins and nucleic acids when they are exposed to temperature and acidity conditions outside their normal range or to some other chemicals. In the case of DNA, it involves the separation of strands in the normally double-stranded structure. In the case of proteins it involves an alteration of the three-dimensional shape of the molecule which is so important to its normal function. In the case of enzyme denaturation, the precise shape of the active site is altered so that the substrate molecules no longer fit and the catalytic action of the enzyme is destroyed.

Denbigh (or **Denbighshire**) A county of north Wales; divided between Clwyd and Gwynedd in 1974, it was reinstated in 1996 with slightly different boundaries; area 884 sq km (327 sq miles); pop. (est. 1996) 91,585; administrative centre, Ruthin.

Dench, Dame Judi(th Olivia) (1934–) British actress. She performed with the Old Vic Company between 1957 and 1961 before joining the Royal Shakespeare Company for a season. Returning to the RSC in 1969, she also appeared in numerous West End and television productions. Her films include *84 Charing Cross Road* (1986) *A Handful of Dust* (1987), *Goldeneye* (1995), and *Mrs. Brown* (1997).

dendrochronology See DATING SYSTEMS.

Deneb A first-magnitude star in the constellation of Cygnus, and also known as Alpha Cygni. It is a very luminous hot SUPERGIANT star at an estimated distance of 500 parsecs, with about 60,000 times the luminosity of the Sun. It is situated at one end of the long arm of Cygnus.

Deneuve, Catherine (born Catherine Dorléac) (1943–) French actress. She is best known for her roles in such films as *Repulsion* (1965) and Luis Buñuel's *Belle de jour* (1967).

dengue A disease that occurs throughout the tropics and subtropics caused by a virus transmitted to man by the mosquito *Aëdes aegypti*. It causes painful joints, headache, fever, and an irritating rash. Dengue is rarely fatal and there is no specific treatment.

Deng Xiaoping (or **Teng Hsiao-p'ing**) (1904–97) Chinese Communist statesman, Vice-Premier 1973–76 and 1977–80; Vice-Chairman of the Central Committee of the Chinese Communist Party 1977–80. Discredited during the Cultural Revolution, he was reinstated in 1977, becoming the most prominent exponent of economic modernization, improving relations with the West, and taking a firm stance in relation to the Soviet Union. Despite the announcement of his retirement in 1989, he was regarded until the end of his life as the effective leader of China. In 1989 his orders led to the massacre of some 2,000 pro-democracy demonstrators in Beijing's Tiananmen Square.

Den Haag See the HAGUE.

De Niro, Robert (1943–) US actor. Since his first major film success, in *Mean Streets* (1972), he has starred in many films, often playing gangsters and other tough characters and frequently working with director Martin Scorsese. He won Oscars for *The Godfather Part II* (1974) and *Raging Bull* (1980). More recently De Niro made his début as a director with *A Bronx Tale* (1994), in which he also acted.

Denis, Maurice (1870–1943) French painter, designer, and art theorist. A founder member and leading theorist of the Nabi Group, he wrote many works on art, including *Théories* (1913) and *Nouvelles Théories* (1921). As a painter he is best known for his group portrait *Hommage à Cézanne* (1900) and his religious paintings.

Denis, St (or **Denys**) (died *c.*250), Italian-born French bishop, patron saint of France. According to tradition he was one of a group of seven missionaries sent from Rome to convert Gaul; he became bishop of Paris, and was martyred in the reign of the emperor Valerian. He was later confused with Dionysius the Areopagite. Feast day, 9 October.

Denmark A Scandinavian country in northern Europe, situated between the North and Baltic Seas and comprising most of the peninsula of Jutland

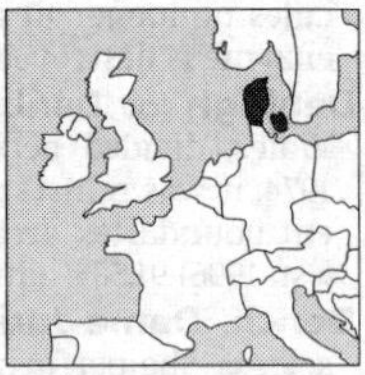

together with many islands, the largest of which are Sjaelland (Zealand), Fyn (Funen), Lolland, and Bornholm. Since the 14th century GREENLAND and the FAEROE ISLANDS have been Danish sovereign territories. The northern end of the peninsula has coasts on the Skagerrak and Kattegat channels, while to the south there is a boundary with Schleswig-Holstein in Germany.

Physical. Denmark is a flat and low-lying country, the sea twisting into it at many points and outwash sand forming much of the subsoil. The climate is temperate with abundant rainfall.

Economy.Both industry and agriculture are important in the Danish economy: agricultural products account for about a quarter of exports, with machinery and chemicals taking another third. Engineering, shipbuilding, petroleum-refining, and furniture manufacture are important industries. In the Faeroe Islands and Greenland fishing is the primary economic activity.

History.There was active Danish participation in the VIKING explorations and conquests after *c.*800. King CANUTE ruled over a great 11th-century empire comprising Denmark, England, Norway, southern Sweden, and parts of Finland. His reign was notable for the spread of Christianity, initially introduced in the 9th century.

After a period of internal disunity, Denmark re-emerged as the leading Scandinavian nation in the 13th century. Civil warfare and constitutional troubles continued, however, until Christopher II (1320–32) made major concessions to the nobles and clergy at the expense of royal authority. His son, Waldemar IV (1340–75), re-established royal power, and his daughter, Margaret I (1387–1412), succeeded in creating the Pan-Scandinavian Union of KALMAR (1397–1523). In 1448 the House of Oldenburg became the ruling dynasty. The 16th-century Protestant Reformation brought a national Lutheran church, and Christian IV (1588–1648) intervened in the THIRTY YEARS WAR as a champion of Protestantism. A sequence of 17th-century wars with Sweden resulted in Denmark's eclipse as the leading Baltic power. ENLIGHTENMENT ideas reached Denmark in the late 18th century, leading to major land reforms in favour of the peasants.

Denmark supported France during the Napoleonic Wars, and in 1814 was forced to cede Norway to Sweden. In 1849 a new constitution ended absolute monarchy and introduced a more representative form of government under a constitutional monarch. In 1863 Denmark incorporated SCHLESWIG-HOLSTEIN, which its king ruled personally as a duke, but this was opposed by Prussia and Austria, whose troops invaded in 1864. Schleswig was then absorbed into the GERMAN SECOND EMPIRE. After World War I north Schleswig voted to return to Denmark, which had remained neutral during the war. Despite another declaration of neutrality at the start of World War II, the Germans occupied the country from 1940 to 1945 when all Schleswig-Holstein passed to the new German Federal Republic. After World War II Denmark joined NATO and in 1960 the newly formed EUROPEAN FREE TRADE ASSOCIATION. Like Britain, it later joined the European Community (1973), its farming community gaining considerably from membership. A close referendum decision in 1992 rejected the draft MAASTRICHT TREATY but in a subsequent referendum in 1993 the Danes voted to ratify the treaty.

Capital: Copenhagen
Area: 43,092 sq km (16,638 sq mi)
Population: 5,223,000 (1995)
Currency: 1 krone = 100 øre
Religions: Evangelical Lutheran 90.6%; Roman Catholic 0.5%; Jewish 0.1%
Ethnic Groups: Danish 97.2%; Turkish 0.5%; other Scandinavian 0.4%; British 0.2%; Yugoslav 0.2%
Languages: Danish (official); Turkish; other minority languages
International Organizations: UN; NATO; OECD; EU; Council of Europe; CSCE

density The ratio of the mass of a body to its volume. The standard units are kilograms per cubic metre, or pounds per cubic foot. Standard measurements for gases are made at 0°C (32°F) and at a pressure of one atmosphere (101 kilopascals or 760 mm of mercury), while liquids and solids are measured at 4°C (40°F), which is the temperature at which water has greatest density. **Relative density** is often a more useful measure than density itself. It is the ratio of the density of a substance to the density of water (at 4°C, 40°F).

dentistry The prevention, diagnosis, and treatment of diseases and conditions that affect any of the tissues of the mouth. It is concerned mainly with the repair and extraction of teeth and the provision of dentures, usually removable artificial replacements for teeth lost through decay, disease, or accident.

Orthodontics is the branch of dentistry involved with changing the position or angle of the teeth to improve their function or appearance. Tooth movements are achieved very slowly, over a period of months, either by the use of removable 'braces' made of wire and plastic, or more reliably and accurately by tiny brackets, glued to individual teeth. SURGERY plays a part in many aspects of dentistry, including extraction of teeth and roots, alteration of bone or gum to aid denture comfort or reduce gum disease, drainage of abscesses, removal of growths and tumours, and placement of implants.

denudation The whole process of lowering of the land surface, by all the agents of **weathering** and EROSION combined. Once rocks or sediments appear above sea-level, because of volcanic or tectonic forces or a drop in the sea-level itself, they become subject to the full force of gravity, to changes in heat and moisture and pressure, which produce chemical and mechanical changes in their composition, and to the disintegrating and eroding actions of wind, rain, frost, ice, running water, waves, plants, animals, and man. These processes combine to alter and sculpt the surface.

Denver The capital and largest city of Colorado, USA, at the junction of the South Platte River and Cherry Creek; pop. (1990) 467,600. Known as the 'Mile High City', Denver is situated at an altitude of 1,608 m (5,280 ft) on the eastern edge of the Rocky Mountains. It first developed as a silver-mining town in the 1870s and later became an important centre for transportation, tourism, commerce, and research. Its manufactures include aircraft, chemicals, and electronics. The national Mint is located here and Denver International Airport is the world's largest airport.

deontology See CONSEQUENTIALISM; ETHICS.

deoxyribonucleic acid See DNA.

Depardieu, Gérard (1948–) French actor. He made his screen début in 1965. His international reputation is based on the many films he has made since the early 1980s; these include *Danton* (1982) *Jean de Florette* (1986), and *Cyrano de Bergerac* (1990).

dependent origination Otherwise known as 'conditioned arising', the central philosophical teaching of BUDDHISM. Buddhists reject the notion of a personal creator GOD, who is the origin of all things. Instead, Buddha formulated the idea of dependent origination to explain how all things come into being and how they cease to be. The doctrine states that all aspects of individual existence or modes of being are conditioned by others; in this world of ours there is nothing permanent, independent, or absolute, not even the individual self.

de Pisan, Christine (or **de Pizan**) (*c.*1364–*c.*1430) Italian writer, resident in France from 1369. After the death of her husband when she was 25, she turned to writing for her living, becoming the first professional woman writer in France. She is best known for her works in defence of women's virtues and achievements.

deportation The removal of an unwanted person from a country. This may be authorized by executive decision in the case of any person who does not have the right of abode under given circumstances. Deportation may be controversial; for example, where immigration authorities deport persons claiming POLITICAL ASYLUM on the grounds that they are in fear for their life, to their country of origin.

deposition (in geology) The laying down by nature of inorganic or organic material. The deposits may be short-lived or endure for hundreds of millions of years, like the swamp vegetation of the CARBONIFEROUS PERIOD which is preserved as coal-seams. Deposition is of three kinds: mechanical, chemical, and organic. Material larger than clay particles transported by wind, water, ice, or mass movements on slopes will be mechanically deposited, or dropped, when the transporting medium loses speed. Dissolved material is chemically deposited, either when the fluid becomes saturated, or because of concentration by organisms such as coral polyps. Finally, organic deposits are laid down by the preservation after death of vast numbers of plant or animal remains, giving peat or lignite, and ultimately coal or oil, and bone or shell beds.

depreciation The reduction in the value of physical assets due to their wearing out or obsolescence. It normally refers to the deterioration of capital goods such as buildings and machinery. When calculating corporation tax, governments usually permit depreciation to be deducted from profits to encourage companies to maintain their capital stocks.

depression (in economics) A long period of significant UNEMPLOYMENT or underemployment of labour, capital, and land (the FACTORS OF PRODUCTION). This contrasts with the short-lived unemployment that characterizes a RECESSION. The causes of depression are debatable, but may include large falls in the MONEY SUPPLY, overproduction, a general lack of demand, and the use of tariff barriers to protect national trade balances. See DEPRESSION, THE GREAT.

depression (in psychiatry) An abnormal and persistent state of very low mood, sufficient to interfere with enjoyment of life or ordinary living. Typical accompanying signs are slowness of speech and movement, loss of interest and appetite, disturbed sleep pattern and feelings of guilt, low self-esteem, and pessimism. Depression is common, more so among women. Contributory factors include genetic predisposition; childhood experience, especially of loss; STRESS and feelings of helplessness; and lack of a supportive social network. In such cases treatment relies particularly on the use of mood-controlling drugs. DRUG treatments may also be used in milder cases, supplemented by attempts to alleviate the stress causing the depression and to modify the way the person copes with it. See also MANIC DEPRESSION.

depression (in meteorology) An area of low pressure in the mid-latitudes which forms, in the lower levels of the troposphere, beneath areas of upper-air DIVERGENCE. The out-flowing air aloft is replaced by rising air from below in the lower levels, and this results in a low centre pressure, into which there is CONVERGENCE. The wind blowing into a depression is deflected by the Earth's rotation and turns anticlockwise in the Northern Hemisphere and clockwise in the Southern. Depressions commonly form along boundaries between cold and warm air. They are sometimes heralded by the appearance of high cirrus cloud (the 'mare's tail' sky of seamen) and sometimes by a halo round the Sun or Moon. Their lifetime is measured in days; but occasionally they travel in families of three or four, with ridges of high pressure between them bringing fair weather.

Depression, the Great (1929–33) A world economic crisis that began in October 1929, when the New York Stock Exchange collapsed, in the so-called stock market crash. As a result US banks began to call in international loans and were unwilling to continue loans to Germany for REPARATIONS and industrial development. Throughout the USA and Germany members of the public began a 'run on the banks', withdrawing their personal savings, and more and more banks had to close. Farmers could not sell crops, factories and industrial concerns could not borrow and had to close, workers were thrown out of work, retail shops went bankrupt, and governments could not afford to continue unemployment benefits even where these had been available. Unemployment in Germany rose to 6 million, in Britain to 3 million, and in the USA to 14 million; in the USA by 1932 nearly every bank was closed. In 1932 Franklin D. ROOSEVELT was elected President of the USA, and gradually financial confidence there was restored, but not before the THIRD REICH in Germany had established itself as a means for the revitalization of the German economy.

Deprez See DES PREZ.

depth-charge A bomb capable of exploding under water, especially for use against submerged SUBMARINES. It was designed during World War I, consisting of a canister filled with explosive and fitted with a pressure-sensitive device designed to detonate the charge at a pre-selected depth. Modern depth-charges include devices carrying a nuclear explosive.

De Quincey, Thomas (1785–1859) British essayist and critic. After first taking opium for toothache at Oxford, he became a lifelong addict. He achieved fame with his *Confessions of an English Opium Eater* (1822), a study of his addiction and its psychological effects, ranging from euphoria to nightmares.

Derain, André (1880–1954) French painter, sculptor, and graphic artist. One of the creators of FAUVISM and an early adherent of CUBISM, he was near the heart of the most exciting developments in art in Paris in the first two decades of the 20th century, but he later adopted a more conservative style.

Derby A city in the Derbyshire Peak District, central England, on the River Derwent; pop. (1991) 214,000. Known to the early Saxons as Northworthy, its name was changed to Deoraby by the Danes in the 9th century. It is the headquarters of Rolls-Royce cars and aero engines.

Derby An annual horse race for three-year-olds that was founded by the 12th Earl of Derby in 1780 and is run over a 2.4 km (1.5 mile) flat course at Epsom in Surrey in June.

Derby, Edward George Geoffrey Smith Stanley, 14th Earl of (1799–1869) British Conservative statesman, Prime Minister 1852, 1858–59, and 1866–68. He led the protectionists in the House of Lords in their opposition to Sir Robert Peel's attempted repeal of the Corn Laws in 1846, and in his last term as Prime Minister he carried the second Reform Act (1867) through Parliament.

Derbyshire A county of central England; area 2,631 sq km (1,016 sq miles); pop. (1991) 915,000; county town, Matlock.

deregulation The reduction or elimination of specific government regulation of commercial enterprises and public bodies. In the 1970s the NEW RIGHT and others argued that excessive regulation was stifling initiative, preventing the emergence of new suppliers and patterns of service, and denying consumers the benefits of choice and competition. In several Western countries, transport, financial services, and TELECOMMUNICATIONS were among the many activities deregulated during the 1980s. By the early 1990s, deregulation was an important concomitant of PRIVATIZATION in formerly socialist countries, allowing existing enterprises more freedom, and permitting new enterprises to be set up. Most governments find it necessary to maintain some degree of regulation of important public services, and of businesses in key sectors of the economy.

derivative (in mathematics) See DIFFERENTIATION.

dermatitis Inflammation of the skin. There are many types, with causes varying from direct skin contact with an irritant substance to being part of an allergic reaction. The irritant may be one to which all skins will react or may be unique to that person. Some allergic types of dermatitis are identical to eczema.

Dermot McMurrough (or **Diarmuid MacMurragh**) (*c.*1110–71), King of Leinster in Ireland 1126–71. In 1166, after feuding with his neighbours, he was defeated and banished by the Irish High King. He sought support from HENRY II of England and obtained the aid of Richard de Clare, Earl of Pembroke ('Strongbow'), offering him his daughter in marriage and the succession of Leinster. Dermot regained his kingdom in 1170 and after his death Leinster became an English fief and Henry II began to establish English dominance in Ireland.

Derrida, Jacques (1930–) French philosopher and critic. His radical critique of traditional Western philosophy and literary analysis led to the emergence of the school of DECONSTRUCTION in Paris in the late 1960s.

Derry See LONDONDERRY.

dervish (from Persian, 'mendicant') Member of an ascetic or mystical order within ISLAM. Emphasizing the emotional, ecstatic, and monastic aspects of religious experience, dervish practices include trance-inducing ecstatic dances (like those of the Mevlevi, or 'whirling dervishes' of Turkey).

Derwent Four English rivers. ▶**1** A river that rises in the Borrowdale Fells in Cumbria, and flows northwards through Derwent Water and Bassenthwaite to the Irish Sea at Workington. ▶**2** A river that rises in the Derbyshire Peak District and flows southwards past Derby to join the River Trent on the Leicestershire border. ▶**3** A river that rises in the Pennines and flows north-eastwards to join the River Tyne near Newcastle. ▶**4** A river that rises in the North Yorkshire Moors and flows south-westwards to join the River Ouse near Selby.

Derwent Water A lake south-west of Keswick in the Lake District of Cumbria, north-west England, formed by the River Derwent. It is 5 km (3 miles) long and up to 2 km wide.

de Sade, Marquis See SADE.

Desai, Anita (1937–) Indian novelist and short-story writer. Her sophisticated novels of urban India include *Voices in the City* (1965), *Fire on the Mountain* (1977), and *Clear Light of Day* (1980). She has also published children's books, and a collection of short stories, *Games at Twilight* (1978).

Desai, Morarji (Ranchhodji) (1896–1995) Indian statesman and nationalist leader. After the death of Jawaharlal Nehru, he was a strong contender for the post of Prime Minister, but his austere and autocratic style made him too many enemies within the Congress Party. In 1977 he was the obvious candidate to lead the Janata opposition to Mrs Gandhi and led his party to victory in the election of that year. As Prime Minister (1977–79) his inflexible style handicapped him in dealing with the economic and factional problems which confronted him and he resigned in 1979.

desalination The removal of salt, usually from sea-water or brackish water. Multi-stage flash distillation (MSF) is commonly used for desalting sea-water (about 3.5 per cent salt), especially in areas in which solar power is available. The water is heated under pressure and fed into a container. The pressure is then reduced, causing the water to boil, and the resulting steam is condensed. Brackish waters (up to 0.5 per cent salt) can be treated by reverse osmosis, in which the water, after filtering, is forced through a semi-permeable membrane that does not allow the passage of salt. In electrodialysis, salts in brackish water are separated by attracting them through membranes to electrodes.

Desani, G(avindas) V(ishnoodas) (1909–) Indian novelist, born in Kenya. He is known for his only novel, *All About H. Hatterr* (1948), in which the protagonist's comical search for wisdom is recounted in a unique style, combining several dialects, jargons, and varieties of wordplay. He also wrote a dramatic prose poem, *Hali* (1950).

Descartes, René (1596–1650) French philosopher, mathematician, and man of science, often called the father of modern philosophy. Aiming to reach totally secure foundations for knowledge, he began by attacking all his beliefs with sceptical doubts. What was left was the certainty of his own conscious experience, and with it of his existence: '*Cogito, ergo sum*' (I think, therefore I am). From this certainty he argued for the existence of God (as the first cause) and the reality of the physical world, and developed a dualistic theory of mind (conscious experience) and matter. His approach was of fundamental importance in the development of modern philosophy, particularly epistemology. In mathematics he developed the use of coordinates to locate a point in two or three dimensions: this enabled the techniques of algebra and calculus to be used to solve geometrical problems.

desert A dry, barren, often sand-covered area of land in hot or mid-latitude areas of the world, characteristically desolate, lacking in water, and with little or no vegetation. About 30 per cent of the world's land surface is arid or semiarid desert.

desert animal An animal that lives in a region in which rainfall is less than 25 cm (10 inches) a year. The dryness is frequently accentuated by high temperatures during the day. Without exception, desert animals show adaptation to the arid conditions. Most important is their impermeable covering, which reduces desiccation. Insects have a waxy cuticle; reptiles, thick horny scales; and mammals, cornified skin impregnated with oily sebum produced from the sweat glands. Water loss is further reduced in many desert mammals, such as the kangaroo rats, by excretion of highly concentrated urine.

Desert cultures Early post-glacial groups of hunter-gatherers in what is now the south-western United States and MEXICO from *c.*8000 BC. They lived mostly on vegetables, and digging sticks and grinders are common among the archaeological finds. Spears were used for hunting. The spread of maize cultivation gave rise to the BASKET-MAKERS. Agriculture started in Mexico soon after 3500 BC, reaching some areas of the south-western USA around the beginning of the Christian era, but in others the Desert cultures continued into the 19th century.

desert dormouse See DORMOUSE.

desertification The process by which land becomes DESERT, usually through a combination of increased drought and the impact of human activity on the land. Desertification came to prominence in the 1970s, when many countries of the semi-arid Sahel zone south of the Sahara in Africa experienced a succession of drought years, soil erosion increased, and sand dunes encroached on formerly productive land, with devastating effects on the people who depend on it. It is estimated that almost a third of the Earth's land is at risk or already suffers from desertification and that hundreds of millions of people live on severely affected land. The UN Environment Programme has estimated, for example, that while just 3.5 per cent of southern Africa is natural desert, almost 25 per cent is at high risk of desertification. Desertification may be seriously exacerbated or even triggered by DEFORESTATION, over-grazing, and over-cultivation of the land, all of which denude the soil and expose it to erosion by wind and occasional rainfall. The enhanced GREENHOUSE EFFECT also accelerates desertification. Land bordering deserts is most susceptible and OVERPOPULATION is a major contributing factor.

desert plant A plant that adapts in one of two main ways to life in dry conditions. Some tolerate them all the year round, and others avoid extreme desert conditions by germinating, growing, flowering, and dying during rainy spells. Plants in the second group are similar in their structure to 'normal' plants, differing only in the speed with which they grow, flower, and set seed. Those in the former group, which includes SUCCULENT PLANTS and CACTI, have a wide pith and cortex layer which acts as an efficient insulator against heat. These plants are thus protected from the full temperature extremes of the desert.

De Sica, Vittorio (1901–74) Italian film director and actor. After acting in more than 150 films, in 1940 he turned to directing, becoming a key figure in Italian neo-realist cinema. His celebrated films in this genre include *Shoeshine* (1946) and the Oscar-winning *Bicycle Thieves* (1948). During the 1960s he made a number of successful films starring Sophia Loren, notably *Two Women* (1960), which won an Oscar.

desk-top publishing (DTP) The production of printed matter with a desk-top computer and printer. The basic items of equipment in a desk-top system are a MICROCOMPUTER with disk drive, a 'monitor' or VISUAL DISPLAY UNIT (VDU), a keyboard with appropriate instructions for operator control of the system, and a print-out device, usually a LASER PRINTER. A DTP system depends on SOFTWARE packages first marketed in the mid-1980s, and it can combine text in a variety of typefaces and formats with line artwork and photographs (if a scanner is included in the equipment) and display it all on the monitor as it will appear when printed. Layouts can be changed on screen, and artwork sized and manipulated as required. Colour reproduction is possible with the appropriate equipment. Using such systems, it is possible to output data to produce film for making printing plates or to produce the plates themselves.

Desmarest, Nicholas (1725–1805) French doctor, geologist, and mineralogist. In 1771 he was among the first to recognize that igneous rocks like basalt are the products of volcanic eruptions and were not formed by sedimentation from primaeval oceans.

Des Moines The capital and largest city of Iowa, USA, at the junction of the Raccoon and Des Moines rivers; pop. (1990) 193,200. Established as a military garrison in 1843, Des Moines later developed as the industrial and retail centre of the Corn Belt, an extensive agricultural region. It replaced Iowa City as state capital in 1857.

Desmoulins, Camille (1760–94) French journalist and Revolutionary. He became an advocate in the Paris *parlement* in 1785, and four years later, after the dismissal of NECKER, he summoned the crowd outside the Palais Royal 'to arms'. On 14 July, the mob stormed the BASTILLE. Soon afterwards he began to publish his famous journal *Les Révolutions de France et de Brabant*, attacking the *ancien régime*. He married Lucile Duplessis in 1790 and began a close association with DANTON. He voted for the execution of LOUIS XVI and campaigned against the GIRONDINS and BRISSOT. His support of Danton's policies of clemency angered ROBESPIERRE and led to his arrest and execution on 5 April 1794. A week later his wife followed him to the guillotine.

De Soto, Hernando (*c.*1500–42) Spanish conquistador and explorer. De Soto took part in the conquest of Central America, before joining Francisco Pizarro's expedition in Peru; he returned to Spain when the Inca King Atahualpa, whom he had befriended, was executed by Pizarro. De Soto was then made governor of Cuba by Emperor Charles V, with the right to conquer the mainland of America. He landed on the Florida coast in 1539 and reached North Carolina before crossing the Appalachian Mountains and returning through Tennessee and Alabama. In 1541 he led another expedition, crossing the Mississippi (which he was probably the first white man to see) and going up the Arkansas River into Oklahoma. They were seeking gold, silver, and other treasure, but returned disappointed. De Soto died on reaching the banks of the Mississippi.

de Spinoza, Baruch See SPINOZA.

des Prez, Josquin (or **des Prés**) (*c.*1440–1521) Flemish composer. Regarded as one of the leading composers of the Renaissance, he wrote eighteen complete masses, 112 motets, and some seventy songs, many of them typical examples of polyphonic song. He is perhaps best known for his Italian song 'El Grillo', with its parody of the chirrup of the cricket.

Dessalines, Jean Jacques (1758–1806) Black emperor of Haiti. A former slave, he served under TOUSSAINT L'OUVERTURE in the wars that liberated Haiti from France. Although illiterate, he had a declaration of independence written in his name in 1804. With the defeat of the French in a war of extermination he became governor-general of Haiti, and in late 1804 had himself crowned Emperor Jacques I. The ferocity of his rule precipitated a revolt of mulattos in 1805. Dessalines was killed while trying to put down this rebellion.

de Staël, Mme (born Anne Louise Germaine Necker) (1766–1817) French novelist and critic. A major precursor of the French romantics, she wrote two semi-autobiographical novels, *Delphine* (1802) and *Corinne* (1807). Her best-known critical work *De l'Allemagne* (1810) introduced late 18th-century German writers and thinkers to France; it was banned on publication by Napoleon.

destroyer A light, fast WARSHIP, smaller than a cruiser, the first being built in the UK in 1893. Destroyers were initially developed to counter the threat of the new TORPEDO-BOATS. Their success was immediate, and the role of the torpedo-boat was taken over by the destroyer. During World War I destroyers were armed with DEPTH-CHARGES and used as anti-submarine vessels, to protect convoys of merchant shipping, and as MINE-LAYERS. The introduction of SONAR in the 1920s improved the destroyer's anti-submarine capability. In World War II, anti-aircraft weaponry became an important part of the destroyer's armament; smaller, slower SLOOPS, CORVETTES, and destroyer escorts took over many of the destroyer's convoy escort duties. Modern destroyers are much larger than their predecessors (up to 8,000 tonnes), with sophisticated electronic equipment to detect and identify targets, and to compute firing data. Their weaponry consists mainly of MISSILES, and many vessels carry helicopters. Modern destroyers are usually optimized for anti-aircraft work, FRIGATES taking over their anti-submarine role.

détente (French, 'relaxation') The easing of strained relations, especially between states. It was first employed in this sense in 1908. The word is particularly associated with the 'thaw' in the COLD WAR in the early 1970s and the policies of Richard NIXON as President and Henry KISSINGER as National Security Adviser (1969–75) and Secretary of State (1973–77).

detergent The active cleaning ingredient in washing powders, SOAPS, and some other cleaning materials. Detergents are substances composed of long-chain molecules: one end of the molecule is hydrophilic (water-soluble), the other is hydrophobic (soluble in organic solvents). Grease, which is insoluble in water, is rendered soluble by the detergent because the hydrophobic parts of detergent molecules bury themselves in the grease particle and thereby cover its surface with hydrophilic groups, which are soluble in water. There are two common types of detergent: SOAPS, which are manufactured from animal fats or vegetable oils; and soapless (synthetic) detergents, which are PETROCHEMICALS. Many synthetic detergents are sodium salts of sulphonic acids, and the principal advantage that they have over soaps is that their cleaning power is not affected by hard water. The first synthetic detergents were not biodegradable; this caused rivers and water-treatment plants to become covered and clogged with an unsightly foam that starved the water of oxygen. Modifications to the hydrophobic part of the molecule have resulted in materials that are biodegradable.

determinant (in mathematics) An array of numbers like MATRICES, but capable of being evaluated by recognized procedures to give a single number. The value of the determinant of a 2×2 matrix which contains the elements a and b in its first row and c and d in its second is given by the expression $ad - bc$.

determinism See FREE WILL.

detonator A small explosive charge that triggers a larger explosion or ignites the propellant charge in a FIREARM; or an electric FUSE that creates a detonation. The use of mercury fulminate as a detonator was pioneered by NOBEL and patented by him in 1864. Lead azide has now largely replaced mercury fulminate. Electric fuses are attached by wire to a small hand-operated generator. The generator makes the current overload the capacity of the fuse, which melts to ignite the explosives.

detritivore An animal that feeds on animal and plant waste or remains, sequentially reducing the particle sizes so that the true decomposers, bacteria and fungi, can break them down to their constituent chemical parts for recycling in the ECOSYSTEM.

Detroit A major industrial city and Great Lakes shipping centre in north-east Michigan, USA, on the Detroit River; pop. (1990) 1,028,000. Founded in 1701 by Antoine de la Motha Cadillac, it was named Le Place du Détroit (French, 'the place of the strait'). It is the centre of the US automobile industry, containing the headquarters of Ford, Chrysler, and General Motors – whence its nickname 'Motown' (short for motor town). It was a famous centre for jazz and later for rock and soul music.

de Troyes, Chrétien See CHRÉTIEN DE TROYES.

Dettingen A village in north-west Bavaria, Germany. In the battle of Dettingen English, Austrian, and Hanoverian troops under George II defeated the French in 1743. It was the last occasion in which a British sovereign took command on a battlefield.

deus ex machina (Latin, 'god from the machinery') Device in GREEK THEATRE in which problems were resolved at the end of a play by the intervention of a god who was apparently brought down from Olympus. In fact he was moved by 'machinery' (a crane). It now refers to any contrived interposition in a novel, play, or film, and in general to any external, unexpected, last-minute resolution of a difficulty.

deuterium (symbol D or ^{2}H) The isotope of hydrogen of mass number 2; its nucleus consists of a proton and a neutron. Deuterium occurs naturally in all hydrogen compounds with an abundance of 0.015 per cent. Its compounds are physically almost identical with the corresponding hydrogen compounds, but their chemical reactions are often slower and their SPECTRA differ. Pure heavy water, D_2O, does not support life. Lithium deuteride is used in hydrogen bombs: neutrons convert the lithium into tritium, ^3H, which then undergoes nuclear FUSION with the deuterium releasing much energy.

de Valera, Eamon (1882–1975) US-born Irish statesman. A fervent Irish nationalist, de Valera was one of the leaders of the Easter Rising in 1916 and was sentenced to death by the British, but was released a year later. He served as leader of Sinn Fein (1917–26) and President of the Irish provisional government (1919–22), and as an opponent of the Anglo-Irish Treaty headed the militant republicans in the ensuing civil war. In 1926 he founded the Fianna Fáil Party, which he led in the Dáil. In 1932 de Valera became President of the Irish Free State, and was largely responsible for the new constitution of 1937, which created the sovereign state of Eire. He served as Taoiseach (Prime Minister) 1937–48, 1951–54, and 1957–59, and President 1959–73.

de Valois, Dame Ninette (1898–) Irish-born dancer, choreographer, and director. With Lilian BAYLIS's support she founded the Vic-Wells Ballet in 1931, later to become the SADLER'S WELLS and then the Royal Ballet in 1956. Although a choreographer of some merit, creating *The Rake's Progress* (1935) and *Checkmate* (1937), she is best known for her tenacity in establishing and nurturing the Royal Ballet companies and schools, remaining artistic director of the Royal Ballet until 1963.

devaluation A reduction in the price of a domestic currency in terms of foreign currencies. A devaluation is usually a result of deliberate change by policy-makers and is equivalent to an appreciation of foreign currencies with respect to the domestic currency. Home-produced output therefore becomes cheaper in terms of foreign currencies; the resulting increase in competitiveness is usually expected to improve the BALANCE OF TRADE by boosting exports and slowing down imports, which become more expensive for domestic residents.

Devanagari The alphabet used for Sanskrit, Hindi, and other Indian languages.

Devas See DIV.

developing and printing See PHOTOGRAPHY.

developing countries (or **less developed countries, underdeveloped countries**) The poorer countries of the world. One definition offered by the World Bank includes all countries in the low or middle income group, that is with GNP per capita of less than $6,000 in 1988. It usually refers to those countries whose economies are not fully modernized (nor centrally planned) and thus includes Latin America, Africa, and some of Asia, as well as a few countries in Europe.

The growing differences between developing countries, in which some, such as the prosperous newly industrializing countries (NICs), have become richer and others, such as Bangladesh or Somalia (sometimes called the 'least developed countries'), have stagnant or even falling incomes, make it an inadequate term.

Devi The great goddess of Hinduism. Devi represents the different aspects of Shiva's wife under various names according to the forms she takes. As Parvati, mother of Ganesha and Karttikeya, she is the beautiful, benevolent goddess of the mountains and opponent of the demons. As Kali, a goddess of fertility and time, she personifies the opposing forces of creation and destruction, and assumes a malevolent aspect: a black, hideous old woman, with a necklace of skulls, a belt of severed heads and a protruding tongue. As Durgā, she is the fierce goddess, often identified with Kali, depicted with eight or ten arms, riding a tiger or lion, and slaying the buffalo demon.

Devil The embodiment of the supreme spirit of evil in Judaism, Christianity, and Islam. Also known as Lucifer and as Satan (the Islamic Shaydban), he is regarded as the enemy of God, contesting God's omnipotence, and tempter of mankind. He is said to be the chief of the fallen angels, and in Islam as Iblis the chief of the djinn, cast out of heaven for disobeying God. Used in the plural, devils, it denotes demons and evil spirits, traditionally important elements in all three religions.

devil ray See MANTA RAY.

Devil's Island (French **Ile du Diable**) A rocky island off the coast of French Guiana in the Iles du Salut group. From 1852 it was part of a penal settlement, originally for prisoners suffering from contagious diseases, especially leprosy; later it was used largely for political prisoners, of whom the most famous was Alfred Dreyfus, and became notorious for its harsh conditions. No prisoners were sent there after 1938, and the last one was released in 1953. The island is now chiefly a tourist attraction.

Devis, Arthur (1711–87) British painter, one of the first artists to specialize in conversation pieces, though he also painted single portraits. His work was virtually forgotten until the 1930s, but since then it has attained popularity because of the charm of his figures and the delicate detail of his settings.

devolution The delegation of legislative or decision-making powers to a regional authority. Within this area, decision-making is shared between the devolved authority and the centre, overall constitutional control remaining with the latter. Devolution of power is often proposed as a device for managing the political tensions created by regional cultural, linguistic, or ethnic divisions, which may otherwise be expressed in separatism.

Devolution, War of An attempt by LOUIS XIV of France to seize the Spanish Netherlands. In 1665, on the death of his father-in-law, Philip IV of Spain, he invoked dubious laws based on local customs by which a child of a first wife (as was his queen Maria Theresa) inherited titles and territory, rather than the son of a second wife. A campaign under the Vicomte de Turenne alarmed Europe, a defensive Triple Alliance was formed by the United Provinces, England, and Sweden to check the French advance, and Louis made peace. He restored most of his conquests, hoping to obtain part of the Spanish empire peacefully on the death of Charles II.

Devon (also **Devonshire**) A county of south-west England; area 6,711 sq km (2,592 sq miles); pop. (1991) 1,008,300; county town, Exeter.

Devonian The fourth period of the Palaeozoic era of geological time, following the Silurian and preceding the Carboniferous, lasting from about 408 to 360 million years ago. During this period fish became abundant, the first amphibians evolved, and the first forests appeared.

Devoy, Susan (1954–) New Zealand squash player. She was ranked first in the world when aged 20, the youngest player to achieve this distinction. She won the British Open Championship seven consecutive times (1984–90) and again in 1992, and was five times world champion between 1985 and 1992.

de Vries, Hugo (1848–1935) Dutch plant physiologist and geneticist. Until about 1890 he worked largely on osmosis and water relations in plants, coining the term *plasmolysis*. He then switched abruptly to work on heredity and variation, carrying out plant-breeding experiments which gave similar results to those of Mendel (of which he was unaware).

dew Water droplets that are deposited on exposed surfaces during calm, clear nights, when the ground loses heat by radiation to the sky and causes the air in contact with it to become saturated. It usually forms on the tops of plants, especially the tips of grass, in places where there is a continuous vegetation cover. The water vapour is derived partly from the air and, for as long as the ground temperature remains above the **dew-point**, partly by evaporation from the soil. The dew-point is the temperature at which the water vapour in the air becomes saturated (the maximum amount of water vapour that the air can hold) and condenses on an available surface to form tiny droplets of dew.

Dewar, Sir James (1842–1923) Scottish chemist and physicist. He is chiefly remembered for his work in cryogenics. He devised the vacuum flask, achieved temperatures close to absolute zero, and was the first to produce liquid oxygen and hydrogen in quantity. Dewar also worked on structural organic chemistry, spectroscopic analysis, high temperature reactions, thin films, and infrared radiation.

Dewey, John (1859–1952) US philosopher and educationist. Working in the pragmatic tradition of William James and C. S. Pierce, he defined knowledge as successful practice, and evolved the educational theory that children would learn best by doing. He published his ideas in *The School and Society* (1899) and convinced many American educationists that it was necessary to create less structured, more pupil-centred, practical schools.

Dewey, Melvil (1851–1931) US librarian. He devised a decimal system of classifying books, using ten main subject categories. The system (which is often known as the Dewey Classification) was first invented for Amherst College Library in 1876.

Dewi See DAVID, ST.

De Wint, Peter (1784–1849) British landscape painter of Dutch extraction. Although he was a fine painter in oils, he is best remembered as one of the outstanding water-colourists of his generation and is particularly associated with views of the countryside around Lincoln.

Dhaka (or **Dacca**) The capital of Bangladesh, on the Ganges delta; pop. (1991) 3,397,200. Formerly a French, Dutch, and British trading post, capital of the Mogul province of East Bengal (1608–1704), capital of the British province of East Bengal and Assam (1905–12), it became capital of East Pakistan in 1947 and Bangladesh in 1971. The city has a striking mixture of architectural styles. Impressive buildings include the 17th-century Lal Bagh Fort and several mosques, the early 20th-century supreme court and university, and the recently constructed Parliament buildings and railway station. Much of the city is low-lying and subject to flooding but this has not deterred the development of shanty towns. Jute-processing, tanning, and the manufacture of chemicals, textiles, and glass are the chief industries in addition to trade in agricultural crops such as rice, oilseed, sugar, and tea.

dharma A central concept within HINDUISM and BUDDHISM. The Indo-European root of the word, *dhar*, literally means 'carrying', but has been variously translated as 'law', 'teaching', 'duty', or 'religion'. In Hinduism the term refers to the material and moral order of the world. Each CASTE has its own particular *dharma*, or religious and ethical rights and duties. In BUDDHISM, where the Pali form *dharma* is frequently used, the term refers primarily to the universal truth, which was discovered by the BUDDHA at the time of his enlightenment and which formed the basis of his teaching. The word also refers to the cosmic laws (karmic rebirth), as well as to morality and righteousness. In philosophy, *dharma* is the characteristic property which determinately or uniquely picks out a thing which is characterized (*dharmin*): for example, light is the *dharma* of a flame. This conception is related to the original idea of appropriateness or 'rightness'. The concept emphasizes the law-like (or 'nomological') way in which the world in its physical, moral, and social senses is ordered. As such it is applied as a regulative idea in all spheres of activity.

Dhivehi (or **Divehi**) The Sinhalese language of the Maldives in the Indian Ocean.

dhole (or **red hunting dog**) A species, *Cuon alpinus*, found in the forests of south-east Asia. It hunts in packs, at first by scent and then by sight. After bringing its prey, often a deer, to bay, the pack encircles it. The lead dog waits for an unguarded moment to leap at the quarry's throat, whereupon the whole pack helps to kill it. The dhole resembles a wolf and has several distinct subspecies, including the east and west Asian dholes.

dhow A trading vessel of the Indian Ocean, Red Sea, and the Gulf, often used to carry merchandise between East Africa and the Arabian countries. There are many different types of dhow. Originally they were lateen rigged, with up to three masts, and required a large crew to handle the yards. Modern dhows are often powered by diesel engines, though the wooden hulls still retain the traditional shape and character, being up to 200 tonnes in displacement, with a high stern and a beaked bow.

diabetes mellitus A pancreatic disorder characterized by persistent, increased blood-glucose concentration (hyperglycaemia) as a result of insulin deficiency or its reduced effectiveness. Glucose in the urine (glycosuria) also commonly occurs. Primary diabetes mellitus is classified as Type I or Type II. Type I diabetes mellitus, also called insulin-dependent and juvenile-onset diabetes mellitus, usually occurs before 30 years of age, although it can occur at any age. Type I diabetes mellitus may be hereditary; other possible causes include virus infection, inadequate diet, and immune-system disorders. Type II diabetes mellitus, also called non-insulin-dependent and maturity-onset diabetes mellitus, is associated with middle or old age. Possible causes include obesity, inadequate diet, and pregnancy.

Symptoms of diabetes mellitus include excessive thirst (polydipsia), excessive urine production (polyuria), dehydration, tiredness, and weight loss. Visual impairment and loss of sensation in the hands and feet, cramps, and constipation may also occur. Persistent severe hyperglycaemia may lead to coma. Treatment of diabetes mellitus aims to restore blood-glucose concentrations to normal with the administration of drugs or insulin, which may reduce susceptibility to the complications associated with diabetes mellitus, such as RETINOPATHY and renal impairment.

diagenesis The processes, mainly chemical, by which changes in sediments are brought about after deposition but before their final conversion into rock. Changes in the water composition or temperature of the sediments usually leads to chemical alteration of the minerals present. An example of diagenesis is the alteration of a FELDSPAR to form a new CLAY mineral.

Diaghilev, **Sergei (Pavlovich)** (1872–1929) Russian ballet impresario. After the closure of his magazine *The World of Art* (1899–1904), he organized opera and ballet productions in Paris and in 1909 formed the Ballets Russes, which he directed until his death. Initially with Nijinsky as his star performer, and later with Massine, he transformed the European ballet scene into a creative centre for a large and varied array of artists, pooling the talents of leading choreographers, painters, and composers of his day.

dialect A variety of a LANGUAGE usually associated with a specific region. Dialects vary in GRAMMAR, vocabulary, and pronunciation or ACCENT, but they are usually mutually intelligible. One language may have more than one standard dialect, for example Standard British English and Standard American English.

dialectic A form of argument or reasoning. In the most informal sense of the term, dialectic is simply discussion in which progress towards the truth is made by critical examination. This method is exemplified in PLATO's dialogues. There are, however, several more technical senses of dialectic. One is associated with KANT, for whom dialectic is the method of showing that any attempt to speculate beyond the limits of possible experience leads to contradictions. Another is associated with HEGEL, for whom dialectic is the interaction of concepts in such a way that one idea (the 'thesis') comes into contradiction with another (the 'antithesis'), out of which a third idea (the 'SYNTHESIS') arises, which is more complete and closer to the truth than either of its predecessors. In this latter sense the term was extended to become the DIALECTICAL MATERIALISM of MARXISM.

dialectical materialism The philosophy of MARXISM as developed by Marx's followers, especially in Germany and the former Soviet Union. It unites two central claims: first, human consciousness is a reflex of processes occurring in the natural world; second, these processes display a dialectical pattern in which each developing force generates its opposite or 'negation', leading to a period of revolutionary change in which a higher synthesis of the two opposing forces is achieved.

dialysis The process in which a semi-permeable membrane (made of cellophane, for example) is used to separate particles of colloidal size (10^{-9} to 10^{-6} m) from a solvent and from smaller molecules and ions dissolved in the solvent. The tiny holes in the membrane are too small to allow passage of the colloidal particles. In HAEMODIALYSIS, dialysis membranes are used to remove impurities from the bloodstream of patients suffering from kidney failure, while retaining proteins and blood cells.

diamond A crystalline form of pure CARBON, the hardest substance known. Formed under intense heat and pressure, often in volcanic conduits at great depth, crystals occur in igneous rocks and in gravels, in regions as far apart as South Africa, Brazil, and Siberia. Colourless diamonds (about 25 per cent of those found) are the hardest and cut cleanest, being highly valued as gemstones. So-called black diamonds are used mainly for industrial purposes as abrasives or drilling bits. Diamonds of industrial quality can also be made synthetically, by subjecting graphite to extremely high temperatures and pressures. In the late 1970s, B. V. Deryaguin and co-workers in the Soviet Union pioneered the growth of thin sheets of polycrystalline diamond using VAPOUR DEPOSITION techniques. Such films have applications as SEMICONDUCTORS and as very hard coatings.

Diana In Roman mythology, the goddess of hunting, chastity, and the Moon, identified with the Greek Artemis.

Diana, **Princess of Wales** (born Lady Diana Frances Spencer) (1961–97) Former wife of Prince CHARLES. The daughter of the 8th Earl Spencer, she married Charles, Prince of Wales, in 1981. The couple publicly announced their separation in 1993 and divorced in 1996. She and her companion Dodi Al Fayed were killed in a car accident in Paris, causing an unprecedented show of grief throughout Britain (thousands of bunches of flowers laid outside royal palaces and a funeral procession witnessed by a crowd estimated at 2 million).

Diana monkey A species of Old World monkey, *Cercopithecus diana*, found in central West Africa. It was so named by the famous naturalist Linnaeus, because of its attractiveness. They have a black head, legs, and tail, a grey body, a red-brown rump, white neck and breast, and a white band on the forehead. Rarely at rest, they move gracefully through the trees, using their long legs and slender body to best advantage. They move generally in troops of up to twelve members and hunt during the day for fruit, birds' eggs, and insects.

dianthus See PINK.

diaphragm (in anatomy) See ABDOMEN; LUNGS.

diaphragm (in photography) See APERTURE.

Dias, **Bartolomeu** (or **Diaz**) (*c.*1450–1500) Portuguese navigator and explorer. He was the first European to round the Cape of Good Hope (1488), thereby establishing a sea route from the Atlantic to Asia via the southernmost point of Africa; he later accompanied Vasco da Gama on the first European expedition to Asia by this route.

diaspora (from Greek, 'dispersion') Jewish communities that have dispersed outside Israel. The process began with Assyrian and Babylonian expulsions in 721 and 597 BC, was continued by voluntary migration, and accelerated by the Roman destruction of the Temple in Jerusalem in 70 AD. By the 1st century AD there were Jewish communities from the Levant to Italy and notably in Babylon and Egypt.

By the early Middle Ages Spain was the main centre of Jewish scholarship, which it remained until the INQUISITION expelled all Jews in 1492. Distinguished Jewish scholars were also found in France and Germany, but from the time of the Crusaders, ANTI-SEMITISM began to develop, many cities confining Jews to ghettos. Poland and Lithuania welcomed Jewish victims of persecution, and by the 17th century Eastern Europe had become the diaspora's centre of gravity until the pogroms of the 1880s drove many westwards, via Germany and Britain, to the USA. The German HOLOCAUST, during World War II, destroyed many Jewish communities that remained in Europe. The main centre of the diaspora is now the USA, with some 6 million Jews.

diathermy The technique of heating parts of the body using high-frequency alternating electric current applied by electrodes. Therapeutic diathermy is used in the treatment of rheumatism and arthritis. In surgical diathermy, one electrode takes the form of a conducting knife or snare, while the current has a coagulating effect and prevents bleeding from small blood vessels.

diatomic molecule A molecule consisting of two atoms bound together by covalent bonds. Particularly important are those in which both atoms are the same, such as oxygen, O_2, nitrogen, N_2, and hydrogen, H_2. There are also many pairs of different atoms which form molecules, as for example carbon monoxide, CO, hydrogen chloride, HCl, and nitrogen monoxide, NO. These molecules usually possess a DIPOLE moment.

diatonic scale See SCALE.

Díaz, Porfirio (1830–1915) Mexican general and statesman, President 1877–80 and 1884–1911. He led a military coup in 1876 and was elected President the following year. During his second term of office he introduced a highly centralized government, backed by loyal mestizos and landowners, which removed powers from rural workers and American Indians. Diaz promoted the development of Mexico's infrastructure and industry, using foreign capital and engineers to build railways, bridges, and mines. Eventually the poor performance of Mexico's economy and the rise of a democratic movement under Francisco Madero (1873–1913) contributed to Díaz's forced resignation and exile in 1911.

diazo printing (or **dye-line printing**) A form of photocopying developed in the 1920s, in which an image is reproduced on a positive printing paper (producing a positive rather than a negative image) impregnated with light-sensitive diazo dye, which dyes the paper fibres. For the process to work, the image must be printed on a transparent or translucent base. Light (often ultraviolet) is shone through the original on to the printing paper. The paper is then passed through an ammonia solution, which develops the dye in the image areas. A major use of diazo printing is for copying architectural drawings and blueprints.

Dickens, Charles (John Huffam) (1812–70) British novelist. His early work consisted mainly of humorous sketches and short pieces for periodical publication; much of his fiction also first appeared in instalments in magazines. Dickens drew on his own childhood experiences of hardship and deprivation in his fiction, and many of his works are set in his native London. His novels are broad in scope and deal with all social classes, but they are particularly notable for their treatment of contemporary social problems, including the plight of the urban poor, corruption and inefficiency within the legal system, and general social injustices. Some of his most famous novels include *Oliver Twist* (1837–38), *Nicholas Nickleby* (1838–39), *Bleak House* (1852–53), and *Great Expectations* (1860–61). His satirical humour and varied characterizations, including such familiar caricatures as Scrooge (*A Christmas Carol*, 1843) and Mr Micawber (*David Copperfield*, 1850), contributed to the great popular appeal of his work.

Dickinson, Emily (Elizabeth) (1830–86) US poet. From the age of 24 she led the life of a recluse in Amherst, Massachussets. Her withdrawal and inner struggle are reflected in her mystical poems, expressed in her own elliptical language, with a greater emphasis on assonance and alliteration than rhyme. Although she wrote nearly 2,000 poems, only seven were published in her lifetime; the first selection appeared in 1890.

dicotyledon A member of the larger of the two classes of ANGIOSPERMS, including the great majority of all trees, shrubs, and plants. Dicotyledons are far more numerous than the other class, the MONOCOTYLEDONS, with around five times as many families. The dicotyledons have two COTYLEDONS, or seed-leaves, and a network of branched veins on the leaves. Their floral parts, such as petals and sepals, occur in fours or fives or multiples thereof. There are individual exceptions to these general characteristics. In temperate regions most food crops, other than cereals, are dicotyledons.

dictatorship A regime in which an individual leader or a small leadership group holds unchallenged power, and in which the leadership is given an exalted status. AUTHORITARIAN STATES can be translated into dictatorships as power is increasingly centralized in the hands of a small group, or as an individual comes to dominate. Frequently, dictatorial leaders dispense with normal legal processes and political institutions, and the regime is sustained by the use of repression and the creation of a POLICE STATE. Prominent 20th-century dictatorships were those of Adolf Hitler (1933–45), Benito Mussolini (1922–45), and Joseph Stalin (1924–53).

Diderot, Denis (1713–84) French philosopher, writer, and critic. He was a leading figure of the Enlightenment in France and principal editor of the *Encyclopédie* (1751–76), through which he disseminated and popularized philosophy and scientific knowledge.

didgeridoo (or **didjeridu**) The only melodic instrument of the Australian ABORIGINES. It is a trumpet, sometimes of bamboo, more often a wooden tube hollowed by termites, and today sometimes metal or plastic piping. Playing techniques can be extremely elaborate, with continuous breathing combined with speech syllabics, spat overtones, and hummed DRONES.

Dido In Greek mythology, the daughter of the king of Tyre, who married her uncle Sychaens. After his murder by Pygmalion, her brother, Dido fled to Africa, where the king of Mauritania offered her as much land as might be covered by an ox-hide. By the device of cutting the hide into narrow strips, she secured space to found the city of Carthage. In Roman mythology, Dido offered refuge to the fleeing Aeneas at Carthage. Their love for each other was doomed, since Aeneas was destined to go on to found the state of Rome. On his departure, Dido took her life on a funeral pyre.

die See DIE CASTING; EXTRUSION; FORGING.

die casting A precision process in which metal objects are formed by injecting molten metal under pressure into a metal mould (die). Products range from tiny parts for sewing-machines to aluminium engine-block castings. Unlike CIRE-PERDUE, the metal mould is designed to be reused many thousands of times. It can be split open, the casting removed, and then reassembled. Injection MOULDING is a similar process for producing plastic components.

Diefenbaker, John George (1895–1979) Canadian statesman. He served as leader of the Progressive Conservative Party 1956–67 and Prime Minister of Canada 1957–63. He introduced some important measures of social reform and sought to encourage economic development, but as Canada experienced increasing economic difficulties in the early 1960s he was forced to devalue the Canadian dollar. In foreign affairs he wished to reduce Canada's dependence on the USA, but his party lost the election of 1963 when he took issue with the USA over the arming with atomic warheads of missiles supplied to Canada.

dielectric See CAPACITANCE AND CAPACITORS.

dielectric constant See PERMITTIVITY.

Dien Bien Phu A village in Lai Chau province, north-west Vietnam, near the Laos frontier, with a military post held by the French until captured by Vietminh forces after a famous 55-day siege in 1954.

Dieppe A resort and channel, commercial, and fishing port of Normandy in the department of Seine-Maritime, northern France, situated at the mouth of the River Arques; pop. (1990) 36,600. There are ferry links with England. The town has been rebuilt after devastation during World War II, particularly during an unsuccessful Allied commando attack in 1942, when it was occupied by the Germans.

Diesel, Rudolf (Christian Karl) (1858–1913) French-born German engineer, inventor of the diesel engine. He studied thermodynamics at Munich before moving to Paris in 1880 to manage a refrigeration plant. In 1892 he patented a design for a new, more efficient internal-combustion engine and developed it, exhibiting the prototype in 1897. It attracted worldwide interest, and a factory to manufacture the engine was built at Augsburg, where Diesel spent most of his life.

diesel engine A type of INTERNAL-COMBUSTION ENGINE in which ignition of the mixture of fuel and air is achieved by compressing the air to a high temperature before adding the fuel. Hence the term 'compression ignition' is used to distinguish it from the spark-ignition engine. Diesel engines run on lower grade DIESEL OIL rather than petrol, and have the highest thermal EFFICIENCY of any form of heat-engine. For this reason they are almost universally used in marine applications, railway locomotives, many stationary purposes, commercial road vehicles, taxis and, increasingly, for private motor cars. A distinction is made between direct-injection engines, in which fuel-oil is sprayed directly into the cylinder, and indirect-injection engines, in which the fuel is injected into a separate combustion chamber, connected to the cylinder by a passage. The former type is gaining ground due to its lower heat loss and hence greater efficiency, despite its greater liability to KNOCK. Because diesel engines use higher pressures than petrol engines they must be made stronger and therefore heavier. To overcome this disadvantage many diesel engines are fitted with a turbocharger, a form of SUPERCHARGER. See also RAILWAYS, HISTORY OF.

diesel oil A fairly heavy PETROLEUM fraction, used as a fuel in DIESEL ENGINES. Diesel oil is predominantly a mixture of straight-chain HYDROCARBONS containing between twelve and sixteen carbon atoms, characterized by its tendency to ignite spontaneously under pressure. It boils at temperatures between 200 and 360°C. Grades of diesel oil are rated by their cetane number, a measure which compares their readiness to ignite with that of cetane (hexadecane), a sixteen-carbon alkane. For use in cars and lorries, diesel oil has a cetane rating of 40–50 per cent cetane.

diet The habitual food consumption of an individual. An animal's diet should contain the several varieties of chemical compounds (nutrients) essential for existence. Special diets are designed to improve physical fitness for sport, or to overcome medical problems such as obesity, diabetes, or genetic defects. In a balanced diet, the fuel CALORIE value should match an individual's energy requirements. A normal diet will include proteins, fats, carbohydrates, water, vitamins, salts, and TRACE ELEMENTS. These must be supplied in the correct relative proportions, or various nutritional disorders may develop. Severe lack of protein causes impaired physical and mental performance and susceptibility to infection. Some intake of fat is necessary to provide essential fatty acids and fat-soluble vitamins, but not more than 30 per cent of calories should be met from fats. Foods of plant origin supply water-soluble vitamins and trace elements. Carbohydrates, consumed in large amounts, provide calories and adequate dietary fibre.

Diet (from medieval Latin, 'a meeting for a single day') A meeting of estates or representatives, or even a legislative assembly. The representatives of the German States in the Holy Roman Empire (and the Emperor) met at the Imperial Diet (Reichstag) until 1806.

Dietrich, Marlene (born Maria Magdelene von Losch) (1901–92) German-born US actress and singer. She became famous for her part as Lola in *Der Blaue Engel* (1930; *The Blue Angel*), directed by Josef von Sternberg. It was her last film before she went to the USA, where she and von Sternberg made a series of films together, such as *Blonde Venus* (1932) and *The Devil is a Woman* (1935). From the 1950s she was also successful as an international cabaret star. She became increasingly reclusive towards the end of her life.

differential equation An equation that involves derivatives (see DIFFERENTIATION). as well as functions. If y is a function of x, then $(dy/dx) + y = 0$ is a differential equation of order 1. The order of the equation is given by the highest order of the derivative. Thus $(d^2y/dx^2) + n^2y = 0$ is a second order equation and describes SIMPLE HARMONIC MOTION. These examples are ordinary differential equations since they involve only one independent variable. Sometimes partial derivatives occur: $\delta^2y/\delta t^2 = a^2\,(\delta^2y/\delta x^2)$ is a partial differential equation of order 2. A differential equation is linear (see LINEARITY) if terms in y, or derivatives of y, are of power 1, and if there are no products of y and its derivatives.

differential gear The mechanism that allows the driven wheels on either side of a vehicle to rotate at different speeds when cornering. The differential is housed within the final drive, which achieves the transmission of power from engine to road wheels. In straight-line driving the small bevels do not rotate on their shaft, but drive both road wheels equally. When cornering, the outer wheel and its bevel rotate more quickly than the inner ones, so the small bevels rotate on their shaft, but each road wheel is still driven with an equal TORQUE. See illustration p. 420.

differentiation (in mathematics) The process of finding the rate of change (derivative) of a function. It is one of the two central operations of infinitesimal CALCULUS. LEIBNIZ introduced the symbol d for differentiation; the rate of change of y with respect to x being written dy/dx. For example, if $y = 3x^2 + 2x + 1$, then the rate of change of y with respect to x is $dy/dx = 6x + 2$. Based on the theory of infinitesimal changes, there are many standard algorithms for differentiation, and DIFFERENTIAL EQUATIONS, involving derivatives, occur in many areas of mathematics.

differentiation (in biology) The process, during the development of a multicellular organism, by which the unspecialized cells formed during the

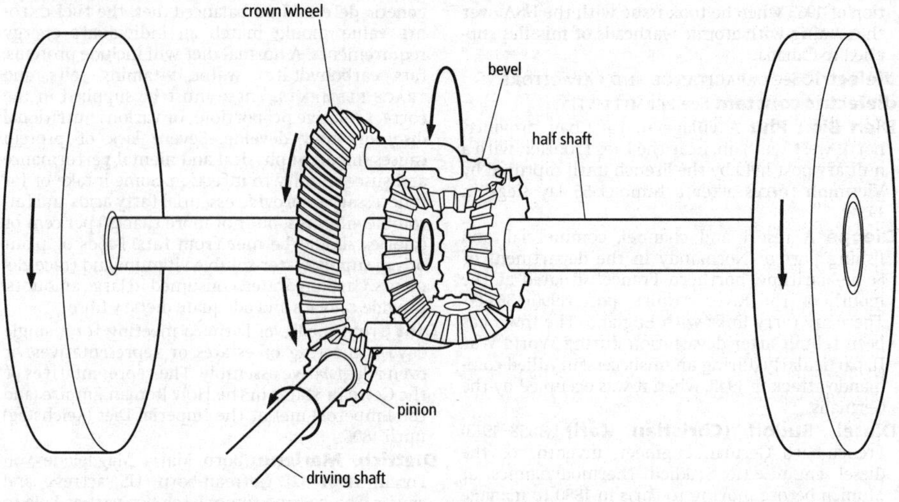

Differential gear A rear-wheel drive differential gear. The driving shaft from the engine and gearbox rotates the crown wheel, which in straight-line driving rotates the half shafts equally. In cornering, the outer wheel and its bevel rotate more rapidly than the inner ones, allowing the wheels to rotate at different speeds.

early stages in the division of the fertilized OVUM become specialized in appearance and function to perform particular activities, for example as nerve cells or muscle cells.

diffraction The spreading or bending of waves as they pass through an aperture or round a barrier. Diffracted waves subsequently interfere with each other producing regions of reinforcement and cancellation (see INTERFERENCE). Diffraction occurs with sound waves, electromagnetic radiation (including light), and with very small moving particles (such as ATOMS, NEUTRONS, and ELECTRONS) which show wave-like properties. In the case of light, alternate bright and dark bands or rings are formed; these are known as diffraction patterns. When a stream of X-rays or fast particles impinges on the atoms of a crystal, their paths are diffracted into a regular pattern (as recorded in X-ray diffraction or electron diffraction). When sound is emitted from a loudspeaker, the loudspeaker itself acts as a barrier and casts a shadow at its rear, allowing only the longer base notes to be diffracted there.

diffraction grating A plate with a large number of closely spaced parallel slits or grooves used to produce and analyse spectra. Gratings are used in SPECTROSCOPY, and can be made for use with ultraviolet and infrared radiation as well as visible light. A typical grating has about 600 lines per mm (15,400 lines per inch).

diffusion (in fluids) The process in which small particles released, or produced, in one part of a fluid spread out to form an even distribution throughout the whole volume of the fluid. For example, a drop of ink added to a bucket of water will disperse and eventually colour all the water in the bucket, even if the water is not stirred. The process is usually slower in liquids, whereas the rate of diffusion of a gas is described by GRAHAM's law: the rate is inversely proportional to the square root of the molecular mass of the gas.

diffusion (in optics) The scattering of beams of radiation. Diffusion occurs when light passes through fog or frosted glass, or is reflected from a rough surface. Then the normal laws of REFLECTION and REFRACTION do not apply.

digestion The process of breaking down food into a form capable of being absorbed into the body of an animal. It usually involves two processes, a mechanical one, and a chemical one. The mechanical part includes tearing, chewing, crushing, and grinding in the mouth, and churning by the STOMACH. Chemical aspects of digestion often begin in the mouth when ENZYMES in the saliva begin to break down the food into simple molecules of sugars, fats, or proteins.

The digestion of food by chemical means may begin outside the body in animals such as spiders. In vertebrates the major part of chemical digestion begins in the ALIMENTARY CANAL. Humans and carnivores rely largely on a supply of special juices from the stomach (gastric juice), PANCREAS (pancreatic juice), and liver (BILE). In RUMINANTS, with additional stomachs, bacterial and protozoan fermentation of vegetation occurs as well. As the food particles are propelled from mouth to stomach, and then, in solution, pass to the elongated, coiled tube of the intestines, they are exposed to a succession of different chemical treatments under the control of hormones and the nervous system.

digital audio tape (DAT) A sound recording system in which audio signals are recorded digitally (see DIGITIZATION) on to a small cassette tape to give recordings of comparable quality to those of a COMPACT DISC. DAT recorders have a rapidly rotating recording head similar to that in a VIDEO RECORDER, which records the audio signal in narrow oblique bands across the tape. DATs were first marketed in Western countries in 1990. Several other digital cassette systems are being developed in competition with DAT.

digital computer See COMPUTER.

digitalis See FOXGLOVE.

digitization The production of information recorded as a succession of discrete units, rather than as continuously varying (analog) parameters. Digital systems most often record information in binary code, using only two states: one and zero. Information such as a message or numerical data can be transmitted from a keyboard by coding the alphabet and other symbols digitally. A sound may also be recorded (MAGNETIC TAPE or COMPACT DISC) or transmitted in digital form. The electrical signal, into which the sound is converted by a MICROPHONE, is analog in form since the voltage is changing continuously with time, but if the signal is sampled at intervals, then each sample voltage can be coded as a binary number. By frequent sampling the whole analog signal can be represented in a digital form. See also TELEPHONY.

Images may also be digitized and held in computer-readable form. In a raster image, the picture is broken up into a rectangular array of pixels, each of which can be represented by a sequence of bits. There are numerous formats for the files holding raster images. In the simplest, a bit-map format, the file essentially contains sequences of bits, one sequence for each pixel. More commonly, some sort of compression is used. Photographs and artwork can be digitized using a scanner.

Another type of image file is a vector file. In this, the file contains instructions for drawing and colouring certain shapes; for instance, "draw a rectangle with sides 2 and 3" or "draw a circle with radius 5". Vector files are not broken into pixels; they are 'digitized' in the sense that the information is held in digital form. They are produced by graphics and computer-aided-design (CAD) programs and are generally smaller files than raster-image files. The digitization of images is particularly important in DESK-TOP PUBLISHING and electronic publishing.

diglossia A linguistic phenomenon that occurs when two standard DIALECTS of one LANGUAGE coexist within one speech community. One, the high dialect, or variety, is used in formal situations like school and church, and in quality literature. The other, the low variety, is used in informal situations. Classical Arabic and standard German (Hochdeutsch) are examples of high dialects. Colloquial Arabic and the various regional dialects of German (for example, Swiss German) are their low counterparts. Some high and low dialects may be considered distinct languages. The phenomenon then is bilingualism, not diglossia.

Dijon An old industrial city in the Côte d'Or department of east-central France; pop. (1990) 151,640. The chief city of the Burgundy region, it is noted for its wine trade and its cuisine.

dikes See COASTAL DEFENCES; DYKES.

dikkop See STONE-CURLEW.

dill A hardy, aromatic, annual herb, *Anethum graveolens*, growing up to 70 cm (2.3 feet). It is a member of the same family as carrot, caraway, and fennel (the Umbelliferae), and is a native of southern Europe and western Asia. The fruits can be used whole or ground. The young feathery leaves, though far less aromatic, can also be used as a flavouring.

DiMaggio, Joseph Paul (known as 'Joe') (1914–) US baseball player. Star of the New York Yankees team 1936–51, he was renowned for his outstanding batting ability and for his outfield play. He was briefly married to Marilyn Monroe in 1954.

Dimbleby, (Frederick) Richard (1913–65) British broadcaster. He was the BBC's first news correspondent (1936) and the first broadcaster to be commemorated in Westminster Abbey. He distinguished himself in his radio and television commentaries on royal, national, and international events and in his reports on current affairs. His sons **David** (1938–) and **Jonathan** (1944–) have both followed their father into careers in news broadcasting.

dimension A measurement of spatial extent in terms of the 'three dimensions' of space: length, breadth, and thickness (or depth, or height). Three COORDINATES are needed to locate a point in space. A flat surface has two dimensions, and two coordinates are enough to define a point on it. A straight line has one dimension, and a point none. In RELATIVITY theory time is treated as a fourth dimension, giving a four-dimensional SPACE-TIME, and in mathematics many results can be generalized to 'spaces' of any number of dimensions. Another meaning in mathematics has to do with equations. A product of two unknown quantities such as xy is said to be of two dimensions; x^2y is of three (two in x plus one in y), and x^3 is also of three dimensions. In physics a quantity can be expressed in terms of other, more fundamental, quantities and these are called its dimensions. For example, speed is distance (length) divided by time, [L]/[T], also written $[L]\,[T]^{-1}$ and is said to be of dimension 1 in length and −1 in time. Density is mass divided by volume: $[M]\,[L]^{-3}$. This concept is useful in relating units of measurement to one another.

diminishing returns, law of The principle in economics that increasing the use of only one FACTOR OF PRODUCTION (capital, labour, or land) in the short run leads eventually to the resulting increases in output becoming smaller and smaller. In other words, the marginal productivity (the extra output per unit employed) of the factor eventually declines as more of it is employed. The principle typifies the concepts used in MARGINAL ANALYSIS.

Dimitrov, Georgi (1882–1949) Bulgarian communist leader. From 1929 he was head of the Bulgarian sector of the COMINTERN in Berlin. When the REICHSTAG was burned (1933) he was accused with other communists of complicity. His powerful defence at his trial forced the Nazis to release him and he settled in Moscow. In 1945 he was appointed head of the communist government in BULGARIA which led to the setting up of the Bulgarian People's Republic (1946) under his premiership, a period marked by ruthless Sovietization.

Dinesen, Isak See BLIXEN.

Dingaan (died 1843) Zulu king 1828–40. He was half-brother to SHAKA, whom he murdered. At first friendly to European settlers, missionaries, and the Voortrekkers, he treacherously killed their leader Piet Retief and his followers. He attacked a white settlement near what is now Durban, but was defeated (1838) at the battle of BLOOD RIVER. He then fled, and was succeeded in 1840 by his brother Mpande. Driven into SWAZILAND, he was assassinated there three years later.

dinghy A small open rowing-boat pulled by one pair of oars, used as a general work-boat; a small sailing boat used for racing; or a small boat carried by larger ships such as YACHTS. Some dinghies are of inflatable rubber. As pleasure-boating spread after World War I, racing dinghies multiplied and in the UK alone there are now more than 300 active classes of dinghy.

Dingiswayo (died 1817) Founder of the ZULU kingdom. In 1807 he became chief of the Mthethwa in the present northern NATAL. By conquering neighbouring Nguni peoples he made himself paramount over all surrounding groups and established a rudimentary military state, developing trade with Mozambique. He had already designated SHAKA as his successor when he was assassinated by Zwide, chief of the Ndurande clan of the Zulu, in a rebellion against his rule.

dingo A wild dog, *Canis familiaris*, the only species of wild dog found in Australia and Australasia. It is not known how or when the dingo arrived in Australia, though its fossil remains are known from the Pleistocene Era, 40,000 years ago, at which time it may have associated with humans. It is found in the open forests and on plains, where it hunts singly or in a pack. The dingo preys upon kangaroos, sheep, and other small animals. It is the size of a large dog with soft fur, usually rusty red or fawn in colour, the toes and tip of the tail being white. Four to eight pups are born in an underground burrow or hollow tree. It does not bark but utters a series of yelps and a plaintive howl.

Dingwall A town in northern Scotland at the head of the Cromarty Firth, the administrative centre of Ross and Cromarty district in Highland Region from 1975 to 1996; pop. (1981) 4,842. Nearby is Foulis Castle, seat of the Chiefs of the Clan Munro.

Dinka A people of the southern Sudan whose language is a Nilotic subgroup of the Eastern Sudanic branch of the Nilo-Saharan language group. Subjected to slavery by Arabs from the north, these people have continued to suffer as a result of Sudan's civil war.

dinosaur An extinct archosaurian REPTILE, one of a group which dominated the Earth during the Mesozoic Era, 245–66 million years ago. There are two separate groups of dinosaurs, the reptile-hipped dinosaurs, such as the BRONTOSAURUS and TYRANNOSAURUS, and the bird-hipped dinosaurs like IGUANODON and TRICERATOPS. These divisions represent skeletal differences, which in turn reflect their origin and evolution. Many dinosaurs reached enormous size although others were quite small. They were very diverse in habits as can be deduced from their dentition, with both herbivores and carnivores. They are believed to have included species which walked on two legs and those which used four. This is once again based upon studies of their fossilized skeletons, and by drawing comparisons with the skeletons of present-day animals. The dinosaurs died out about 66 million years ago, at the end of the Mesozoic Era. The reason for this mass extinction is unclear, but it may be attributed to a sudden cooling of the world's climate caused by massive volcanic activity, and/or the impact of an asteroid. Their nearest living descendants are the BIRDS.

Diocletian (full name Gaius Aurelius Valerius Diocletianus) (245–313) Roman emperor 284–305. Faced with military problems on many frontiers and insurrection in the provinces, in 286 he divided the empire between himself in the east and Maximian (died 310) in the west. In 293 he further divided the empire, giving Galerius (died 311) control of Illyricum and the valley of the River Danube, with Constantius Chlorus (died 306) ruling Gaul, Spain, and Britain. An enthusiast for the old Roman religion, tradition, and discipline, Diocletian insisted on the maintenance of Roman law in the provinces and launched the final harsh persecution of the Christians (303). He abdicated in 305.

diode A two-terminal electronic device that provides simple rectification: it conducts an electric current in one direction but not the other. Diodes were formerly made from THERMIONIC VALVES but are now almost exclusively solid-state SEMICONDUCTOR DEVICES. They are used in rectifier circuits to generate direct-current signals from alternating current, and to protect circuits from power-supply overload or other misconnection. LIGHT-EMITTING DIODES have several applications for visual display. Diodes are also used to demodulate incoming signals in radio and television receivers.

Diogenes (*c.*400–*c.*325 BC) Greek philosopher. He was the most famous of the Cynics and the pupil of Antisthenes (*c.*445–*c.*365 BC). He lived a life of extreme poverty and asceticism in Athens (according to legend, he lived in a tub) and was nicknamed *Kuōn* ('the dog'), from which the Cynics derived their name. He emphasized self-sufficiency and the need for natural, uninhibited behaviour, regardless of social conventions. Among the many stories told of him is that he took a lantern in daylight, saying that he was seeking an honest man.

Dione A satellite of Saturn, discovered by Giovanni Domenico CASSINI in 1684. It has a nearly circular orbit above Saturn's equator at 377,400 km from the planet's centre. Its diameter is 1,120 km. Although many impact craters are visible on Dione, extensive plains of relatively recent origin, as well as troughs and valleys hundreds of kilometres in length, indicate a significant level of activity within the interior of the satellite.

Dionysius Two rulers of Syracuse. **Dionysius I** (known as Dionysius the Elder) (*c.*430–367 BC) ruled 405–367. After establishing himself as a tyrannical ruler in 405, he waged three wars against the Carthaginians for control of Sicily, the third of which (383–*c.*375) resulted in his defeat at Cronium. Nevertheless, his reign made him the principal power in Greek Italy, after the capture of Rhegium (386) and other Greek cities in southern Italy. **Dionysius II** (known as Dionysius the Younger) (*c.*397–*c.*344 BC), son of Dionysius I, ruled 367–357 and 346–344. He lacked his father's military ambitions and signed a peace treaty with Carthage in 367. Despite his patronage of philosophers, he resisted the attempt by Plato to turn him into a philosopher-king, in 366 banishing the wealthy Syracusan Dion (*c.*408–*c.*354), the proponent of the scheme. He was subsequently overthrown by Dion in 357.

Dionysius Exiguus (died *c.*556) Scythian monk and scholar. He is famous for introducing the system of dates BC and AD that is still in use today, accepting 753 AUC (*ab urbe condita* – from the foundation of the city of Rome) as the year of the Incarnation; this has since been shown to be mistaken. He is said to have given himself the nickname *Exiguus* (Latin for 'little'), as a sign of humility.

Dionysos In Greek mythology, the god of wine and ecstasy. He was the son of Zeus and Semele, daughter of a king of Thebes. One of the most popular Greek gods, he was the subject of many legends and his worship, manifesting itself in a frenzied rout of votaries, male and female, Satyrs, Sileni, Maenads, and Bassarids, was often drunken and orgiastic. He was also regarded as a patron of the arts, inspiring music and poetry.

Diophantus (fl. *c.*250 AD) Greek mathematician, of Alexandria. Diophantus was the first to attempt an algebraical notation. In his *Arithmetica* he showed how to solve simple and quadratic equations. His work led Pierre de Fermat to take up the theory of numbers, in which he made his famous discoveries.

Dior, Christian (1905–57) French couturier. In 1947 he showed his first collection, featuring narrow-waisted tightly fitted bodices and full pleated skirts; this became known as the New Look and initially shocked the fashion world by its extravagance. He remained an influential figure in fashion, for example creating the first A-line gar-

Dinosaurs (1) Styracosaurus. (2) Stegosaurus. (3) Parasaurolophus. (4) Stegocerus. (5) Scelidosaurus. (6) Ankylosaurus. All these dinosaurs belong to the order Ornithischia (literally, 'bird hips'), so called because their pelvic girdles resemble those of birds. (7) Segnosaurus. (8) Tyrannosaurus. (9) Diplodocus. These are members of the Saurischia, or 'lizard-hipped' dinosaurs.

ments, and built up a range of quality accessories. He discovered and trained Yves Saint Laurent.

diorite A coarse-grained igneous rock of intermediate composition (that is, with up to 10 per cent of quartz), composed essentially of plagioclase feldspar and ferro-magnesian minerals, typically hornblende. It occurs mainly as minor intrusions.

Dioscorides, Pedanius (*c*.30–80) Cilician botanist and physician in the Roman army. He compiled one of the first pharmaceutical texts, prescribing some 500 herbs for use in medicine.

dioxin (2,3,7,8-tetrachlorodibenzo-*p*-dioxin) A poisonous compound produced as a by-product of the manufacture of certain insecticides and DEFOLIANTS. In 1976 it was the active pollutant in an industrial accident at a chemical plant in Seveso, Italy. An area of 30 km^2 (12 sq mi) had to be evacuated and turned into a no-go area, which still exists today. Dioxin resists washing out by water or organic solvents and is taken up by fatty tissue in the body. It is known to cause chronic skin diseases, muscular dysfunction, cancers, birth defects, genetic mutations, and disorders of the nervous system. Small quantities of dioxin found in bleached paper products have caused public concern, and there has been a move towards the use of paper products made using non-chlorine bleaches.

dip (geological) The angle at which a bed of rock or some other surface (such as a cleavage plane) is inclined to the horizontal plane. The angle measured in the direction where the slope is greatest is the true dip. If this is not known, the angle measured in an exposure is referred to as the apparent dip. The true dip is always at right angles to the strike.

The magnetic dip is the inclination of the Earth's magnetic field to the Earth's surface.

dip-circle An instrument used in physics and for NAVIGATION to measure the inclination of the Earth's magnetic field to the Earth's surface. It consists of a magnetic needle pivoted on a horizontal axis and moving over a graduated scale. It can be used to obtain accurate measurements of magnetic dip and thus complements the MAGNETIC COMPASS, which measures the direction of the horizontal component of the field.

diphtheria A serious, communicable bacterial infection caused by *Corynebacterium diphtheriae*, which colonizes the mouth, throat, and nose. A greyish-white membrane forms in the throat, mouth, and nose and the bacteria release a toxin, which is absorbed. Children under 5 years of age are at increased susceptibility; active IMMUNIZATION is an effective preventive measure. Symptoms of diphtheria are dependent on the site of infection; isolated nasal diphtheria may be asymptomatic. Generally, symptoms include fever, headache, tiredness, nausea, vomiting, non-productive coughing, and difficulty in breathing and swallowing. Damage to heart muscle and the nervous system may also occur. Diphtheria can have life-threatening effects such as circulatory failure and respiratory obstruction.

Diplodocus See DINOSAUR.

diplomatic immunity An important principle of INTERNATIONAL LAW, which involves the granting of reciprocal rights and privileges to a country's official representatives abroad. Diplomatic personnel, their property, and premises are regarded as inviolable, which in practical terms means the exemption of diplomats from the domestic jurisdiction of the country in which they are residing. Violation of diplomatic immunity is regarded as a serious breach of international law.

dipole Two equal and opposite charges that are separated by a distance. Dipoles arise in molecules in which the electric charge is unevenly distributed, for example in the water molecule there is a slight positive charge on the two hydrogen atoms and a slight negative charge on the oxygen. If one element in the molecule is more electronegative than the others, it becomes a centre of negative charge. Since molecules are neutral overall, a concentration of negative charge at one place in the molecule must leave a concentration of positive charge in another place. Thus the molecule has a positive and a negative pole: together these form a dipole. The magnitude of this dipole is given by the **dipole moment**, which is the product of the magnitude of either charge and the effective distance between them. The unit of the dipole moment is the coulomb metre (formerly the debye, equal to 3.3356×10^{-30} cm).

The equivalent in magnetism results from the distinction between north and south poles. If a magnet which has a north and south pole is broken in half, each half has both a north and south pole. This seemingly inseparable pair of poles is called a magnetic dipole.

A dipole is also a simple, non-directional type of ANTENNA (aerial) that is split into two equal halves, each half being the same length as one-quarter of a wavelength of the radiation being used.

dipper A bird which resembles a giant wren, five species of which comprise the family Cinclidae. Dippers are habitually aquatic, and they frequent fast-flowing streams. They plunge or wade in, swim both on and under the water, and even walk on the bottom hunting for food. Like wrens, they build domed nests. Two species are native to Eurasia, two to South America, and one to North and Central America.

diptych A picture consisting of two parts facing one another like the pages of a book and usually hinged. Most popular in the 15th century, the two parts might show two related religious scenes, or, for example, a portrait of the person who commissioned the work on one part facing a picture of the Virgin and Child on the other.

Dirac, Paul Adrian Maurice (1902–84) British theoretical physicist. He applied Einstein's theory of relativity to quantum mechanics in order to describe the behaviour of the electron, including its spin, and later predicted the existence of the positron. He also developed a quantum theory of radiation, and was the co-inventor of Fermi–Dirac statistics, which describe the behaviour of the particles later called fermions. Dirac shared the 1933 Nobel Prize for physics.

Direct Cinema See CINÉMA-VÉRITÉ.

direct current (d.c.) See ELECTRIC CURRENT.

Directoire style Style of decoration and design prevailing in France between the LOUIS XVI and EMPIRE STYLES. It takes its name from the Directoire (French DIRECTORY; 1795–99), but the style flourished roughly between 1793 and 1804. Decoration was simpler and more consciously classical than in the Louis XVI style, the simplicity being partly the result of the havoc that revolution and war had wrought. As a result of Napoleon's campaigns in 1798–99, there was also a fashion for Egyptian-inspired ornament in this period. The latter part of the Directoire period (1799–1804) is sometimes distinguished as the 'Consulat' style, named after the period when Napoleon ruled as Consul (he became emperor in 1804).

Directory, French (1795–99) The government of France in the difficult years between the JACOBIN dictatorship and the Consulate. It was composed of two legislative houses, a Council of Five Hundred and a Council of Ancients, and an executive (elected by the councils) of five Directors. It was dominated by moderates and sought to stabilize the country by overcoming the economic and financial problems at home and ending the war abroad. In 1796 it introduced measures to combat inflation and the monetary crisis, but popular distress increased and opposition grew as the Jacobins reassembled. A conspiracy, led by François BABEUF, was successfully crushed but it persuaded the Directory to seek support from the royalists. In the elections the next year, supported by NAPOLEON, it decided to resort to force.

This second Directory implemented an authoritarian domestic policy ('Directorial Terror'), which for a time established relative stability as financial and fiscal reforms met with some success. By 1798, however, economic difficulties in agriculture and industry led to renewed opposition which, after the defeats abroad in 1799, became a crisis. The Directors, fearing a foreign invasion and a Jacobin coup, turned to Napoleon who took this opportunity to seize power.

disability A physical or mental incapacity. The World Health Organization (WHO) has estimated that 10 per cent of the world's population is disabled in some way, despite the fact that half of all disabilities are preventable. Causes include traffic accidents, war injuries, infectious diseases, malnutrition, psychiatric illness, and degenerative diseases. WHO has developed a conceptual framework for the assessment of individual and population needs. Impairment is defined as a loss or abnormality of an anatomical, physiological, or psychological function, such as the loss of a leg, vision, or mental functioning. Disability is defined as a partial or complete inability, arising from an impairment, to perform an activity in the manner, or within the range, considered normal for a human being. Examples would be inability to walk or to care for oneself. Handicap is defined as a disadvantage, resulting from impairment or disability, which limits or prevents fulfilment of a role that is normal, depending on age and social factors. Thus impairments and disabilities need not necessarily turn into handicaps. This depends on the individual concerned and, critically, on social responses: inability to walk would not prevent a lawyer from working, if his or her colleagues and clients did not discriminate, and if the office were accessible for a wheelchair. Disability prevention can be related to the WHO classification by reducing the occurrence of impairments, limiting or reversing disability, and preventing a disability from becoming a handicap.

disarmament A policy aimed at the banning of armaments, or their reduction to the lowest level possible. It is different from ARMS CONTROL, which seeks to manage the arms race by maintaining a balance between the capabilities of both sides. Disarmament, on the other hand, envisages a dramatic reduction in arms in order to achieve peace. Attempts to achieve disarmament by international agreement began before World War I and in 1932 there was a World Disarmament Conference. In 1952 a permanent United Nations Disarmament Commission was established in Geneva. National disarmament pressure groups have tended to seek unilateral disarmament, for example the CAMPAIGN FOR NUCLEAR DISARMAMENT. Bilateral agreements are negotiated between two governments, while multilateral agreements are sought via international conferences or the UN Commission. Important arms limitation talks include the STRATEGIC ARMS LIMITATION TALKS (SALT) and the STRATEGIC ARMS REDUCTION TALKS (START). In the START II Treaty ratified in 1992, the USA and Russia agreed to reduce their nuclear arsenals by two thirds by 2003. In 1994 the USA and Russia agreed not to aim missiles at each other.

disc (in anatomy) A flat plate of tough, fibrous cartilage that separates the VERTEBRAE in the backbone of vertebrates. The centre of each disc is softer than the rest because of the presence of fluid.

Discs act as fluid-containing cushions which dampen vibrations from the legs or skull that might otherwise pass along the backbone. Because man stands upright, fluid from the disc centres is gradually squeezed into the bloodstream in daytime and re-forms at night. Young people, with healthy, fluid-filled elastic discs, are measurably taller in the morning. With increasing age the amount of fluid decreases as the centres of the discs contract and harden, and old people decrease in stature. Also, the holes through which spinal nerves pass tend to get smaller, nipping the nerves and causing pain and stiffness.

If the spine is suddenly deformed in a fall or accident, the outer edge of the disc may rupture with the result that fluid on one side forms a blister. This causes pain either in the small of the back (lumbago) or from the buttock down the outside of the thigh and lower leg (sciatica), depending on the particular spinal nerve nipped. A so-called 'slipped disc' is a condition in which the disc has burst and fragments press on ligaments and nerves. See also DISK.

disciple Pupil or learner, used specifically to describe an original follower of JESUS CHRIST. In the Jewish society of Jesus' time many religious teachers attracted disciples who came to be taught their master's interpretation of scriptures. Jesus' followers differed from such groups in several respects. For example, he actively sought out disciples and found many of them among people judged socially or morally as outcasts. The Apostles were the twelve chief disciples: PETER (the leader), Andrew, James, John, Philip, Bartholomew, Thomas, Matthew, James (the Less), Thaddeus, Simon, and Judas Iscariot. After the suicide of Judas, who betrayed Jesus, his place was taken by Matthias. PAUL and his original companion Barnabas are also considered as Apostles.

discrimination Unfavourable treatment based on prejudice against certain people or groups. Legislation against discrimination on grounds of RACE, nationality, ethnicity, and gender, is widespread, usually applying to the supply of goods and services, housing, and employment. Discrimination on religious grounds is less often covered (for example, it is not unlawful in the UK except in Northern Ireland). Under EU law, member states have to provide remedies for sex discrimination in relation to employment. See also POSITIVE DISCRIMINATION.

disc-winged bat A bat belonging to the family Thyropteridae, so called because they have a suction disc on each wrist and ankle. These allow the bat to cling to smooth surfaces. The two species occur in Central and northern South America. The Madagascar disc-winged, or sucker-footed, bat,

Myzopoda aurita, belongs to a separate family, not closely related to the true disc-winged bats.

Disestablishment Acts Legislation in Britain to remove the financial and other privileges of the Anglican Church. The Anglican Church had been 'established' in the reign of Elizabeth I as the only church allowed within the state, with large endowments and privileges. These came to be strongly resented by Non-Conformists in Victorian England; but proposals that all financial and other state support should be withdrawn failed. In Ireland, however, it came to be accepted as unjust that the Anglican Church should be the established church in a predominantly Roman Catholic population. It lost its privileges by Gladstone's Irish Church Disestablishment Act (1869). The Welsh also pressed for the disestablishment of the Anglican Church in Wales. Heated arguments over the financial implications of Welsh disestablishment arose in the years just before World War I, the Welsh Church Disestablishment Bill eventually becoming law in 1920.

dish The radiation-collecting curved structure of a RADIO TELESCOPE. It acts as a reflector of radio waves and is usually mounted so that it can be pointed in any desired direction. The dish focuses incoming radio waves on to an aerial (US antenna), often called a feed. A paraboloidal reflector receives radio waves from a small angle along the direction of its axis; the larger the telescope, the smaller is this receiving beam at a given wavelength and the higher the RESOLVING POWER.

disinfectant See ANTISEPSIS.

disk (in computing) See FLOPPY DISK; HARD DISK.

Disney, Walt(er Elias) (1901–66) US animator and film producer. He made his name with the creation of Mortimer (later Mickey) Mouse in 1927; many other familiar cartoon characters, including Minnie Mouse, Goofy, Pluto, and Donald Duck, were invented by Disney. He produced the first full-length cartoon feature film with sound and colour, *Snow White and the Seven Dwarfs* (1937); this was followed by *Pinocchio* (1940), *Bambi* (1942), and many others. Disney also made many animal and adventure films for children; after his death the tradition of animation and film-making was continued under the Disney name. He was also immortalized by the creation of Disneyland, an amusement park in California, which was opened in 1955; the first European Disneyland, called Disneyworld, was established just outside Paris in 1992.

display (in zoology) The presentation of colour, pattern, and movements by an individual as part of its signalling behaviour. Displays are involved in the communication of all sorts of information between animals, both within and between species. Particularly during the breeding season, males may indulge in displays that serve to identify species, initiate COURTSHIP, or maintain pair-bonding through the process of sexual selection. Many birds have highly colourful displays, and it is thought that females prefer the brightest males. In highly polygynous species, such as the ruff (*Philomacus* species), where mating success is often restricted to a few top males, females will visit a large display site or 'lek', where males congregate and compete to display on the small central territories to which females are most attracted. Other birds, such as the blackbird, rely on a sequence of postures and calls.

Displays are also used to defend territories against intruders, or in the assessment of the fighting ability of rivals before risking a potentially damaging fight. Thus, male red deer will indulge in a tiring roaring match before they will consider fighting over access to a group of females. Displays are also used in communication between species to ward off predators, as in the use of bright WARNING COLORATION or the emission of pungent odours by toxic insects. Displays can also communicate false information, as in the frightening eyespots of the peacock butterfly or the feigned injury displays of plovers, which can serve to distract predators away from the nest.

Dispura The temporary capital of Assam, situated 10 km (6 miles) south of the city of Guwahati.

Disraeli, Benjamin, 1st Earl of Beaconsfield (1804–81) British Tory statesman, of Italian Jewish descent; Prime Minister 1868 and 1874–80. He played a dominant role in the reconstruction of the Tory Party after Sir Robert Peel, guiding it away from protectionism and generating enthusiasm for the British Empire. He was largely responsible for the introduction of the second Reform Act (1867), which doubled the electorate. In his second term as Prime Minister he ensured that Britain bought a controlling interest in the Suez Canal (1875) and also made Queen Victoria Empress of India. At home his government passed much useful social legislation, including measures to improve public health and working conditions in factories. He wrote a number of novels, including *Coningsby* (1844) and *Sybil* (1845), which drew on his experience of political life.

dissociation (in chemistry) The reversible splitting of a molecule into two or more smaller molecules or into ions. The extent of dissociation is measured by the dissociation constant, *K*; this is defined as the product of the concentrations of the fragments, divided by the concentration of the parent molecule. Electrolytic dissociation is an important process in chemistry, for nearly all the reactions that take place in solution are between the ions from dissociated molecules. Acids and bases reversibly ionize in solution ($HA \leftrightarrow H^+ + A^-$; $B + H_2O \leftrightarrow BH^+ + OH^-$), and the dissociation constant is then a measure of the acid or base strength respectively. In thermal dissociation, raising the temperature causes a definite fraction of molecules to decompose at a specified temperature; on cooling they recombine.

Dissolution of the Monasteries See MONASTERIES, DISSOLUTION OF THE.

dissolved load The proportion of the sediment being carried in a river which has been reduced to chemical ions and is invisibly mixed with the water. It comes from rainwater falling on the river surface, from solution within the soil and rock of the river basin, and from the breakdown of material in the channel itself, by CORRASION. All rivers have some dissolved load, although it is sparse in tropical areas of hard rocks. The largest quantities occur in areas of soluble limestone, in swampy channels, and where rivers are polluted.

distaff See SPINNING.

distance education Education in which teacher and learner are physically separate. Distance education projects exist in most countries and are directed primarily at adults wishing to obtain qualifications or update occupational skills. They encompass every form of education from basic LITERACY to general secondary, agricultural, and higher education and teacher training. The Toussaint-Langenscheidt school for teaching foreign languages by correspondence, set up in Berlin in 1856, is generally regarded as the first formally organized correspondence school. Thereafter, correspondence schools multiplied, offering both vocational and academic education. Since the 1960s, many projects, such as the UK's Open University, founded in 1969, have successfully linked correspondence with broadcasting and occasional face-to-face tuition. Technological developments such as satellite transmission (which has, for example, made possible the University of the South Pacific) are widening the scope of distance education.

distance modulus The difference between the apparent and absolute MAGNITUDE of a celestial object such as a star or galaxy, used as a way of measuring its distance from the Earth. Distance modulus is particularly used for objects more remote than a few hundred parsecs whose PARALLAX is too small to measure. Often the absolute magnitude as well as the amount of absorption of light by the gas between the star and the Earth can be estimated; the apparent magnitude can be observed directly. For example, there is a well-defined relationship between pulsation period and absolute magnitude of CEPHEID VARIABLE STARS. Hence by observing such stars in a nearby galaxy the distance of the galaxy can be estimated.

Di Stefano, Alfredo (1926–) Argentinian-born Spanish footballer. Considered to be one of the greatest footballers of all time, he made his début in 1944, playing as a forward in his home country and in Colombia before taking Spanish nationality and playing for the national side. With Real Madrid he won the European Cup in each of the first five seasons of the competition (1956–60) scoring in each final.

distemper A contagious disease of dogs, foxes, badgers, etc. Caused by a virus, its symptoms include fever, a discharge from the eyes, and a general malaise. Canine distemper can be prevented by vaccination at 11 weeks with a booster at 2 years.

distillation A purification or separation process of great antiquity, in which a liquid is boiled in a vessel that is connected to a cooled tube. The drop in temperature in the tube causes the liquid vapour to condense into a receptacle at the end of the tube. This is a useful way of purifying a liquid, because solids dissolved in it do not evaporate and are not present in the distillate. Mixtures of liquids of different boiling-points can be separated from each other by FRACTIONAL DISTILLATION. The process can be carried out in the laboratory or on an industrial scale. Other forms of distillation include STEAM DISTILLATION and VACUUM DISTILLATION.

distributor See IGNITION SYSTEM.

district heating A system in which space and water heating are supplied to a number of buildings from a single fuel-burning plant. Often the plant has some other primary function, such as electricity generation or municipal refuse incineration. Heat that would otherwise be wasted is transferred to the points of use by water circulating in well-insulated pipes. At the user end, a central heating system distributes the heat within the building. In Iceland and New Zealand, GEOTHERMAL ENERGY sources (from the Earth) are utilized in such systems.

District of Columbia (DC) A federal district of the USA, co-extensive with the city of WASHINGTON DC, the federal capital. It was established 1790–91 from land ceded by the states of Maryland and Virginia.

diuretic A drug that increases the flow of urine by promoting loss of sodium and water from the kidneys. In heart failure, oedema (the accumulation of fluid under the skin) may occur; diuretics such as frusemide reduce fluid retention so that the oedema disappears. Diuretics can occasionally cause excessive potassium loss and so potassium is often given in conjunction with them.

diurnal libration See LIBRATION.

diurnal motion Motion performed in the course of a day. Because the Earth rotates on its axis once in a sidereal day in an eastward direction, objects such as the Sun, Moon, planets, and stars appear to revolve about the Earth from east to west. The diurnal motion is the basic observed movement of these bodies. However, because all natural celestial bodies have their own intrinsic movement through space, this apparent motion is more complicated, particularly for the Sun and Moon.

Div In Persian mythology, an evil spirit or jinn. Divs are the *daevas* (*devas*) of the Zend-Avesta, malevolent spirits created as counterparts of the good spirits, the *amesha spentas*, by Ahriman, who ruled over them. By contrast, the devas of Vedic Hindu belief are divine, good spirits, the gods as opposed to the demons.

Divali ('Feast of Lights', from Sanskrit *dīpavalī*, 'little row of lights') A five-day Hindu festival celebrated towards the end of October, which marks both a new Moon and a new year. It takes its name from the lamps (*dīpās*) which are lit at this time. The festival is particularly associated with Lakshmi, the consort of VISHNU and goddess of prosperity, giving rise to the tradition of financial stock-taking as well as the exchange of gifts. *Divali* is marked by family entertainment and public celebration. Houses are cleaned and decorated, and spells are cast to ward off financial misfortune. The festival is also celebrated by the Sikhs.

Divehi See DHIVEHI.

diver A grebe-like water bird of the family Gaviidae, with a sharp bill, a long body, and webbed feet. Divers are known as loons in North America. Though clumsy on land, they fly strongly and are expert at swimming and diving. When alarmed they often swim with only their head and neck above the water, like submarines. Their eerie calls resemble a child's shriek of pain. They breed in the northern temperate regions on islands and the shores of lakes, and winter off temperate seacoasts. There are five species, of which the great northern diver, *Gavia immer*, and white-billed diver, *G. adamsii*, are the largest. Both are black and white with boldly chequered upper parts.

divergence A depletion of air in the ATMOSPHERE, and consequent reduction in density resulting from a net outflow of air from a particular region, such as that of a trough in the upper westerly JET STREAM. This is compensated by a vertical motion as air flows up (or down) to the depleted region. A divergence in the upper troposphere results from an upward movement of air, which is limited by the existence of the tropopause and stratosphere. Divergence above is associated with CONVERGENCE below and an increase in cyclonic vorticity. This encourages the development of depressions. In the oceans, divergence of surface water results in deeper water rising to take its place (upwelling).

divergent series A series in which the addition of further terms does not produce a sum which approaches some fixed value: for example $1 + 2 + 3 + 4 + ... + n + ...$ The partial sum to n terms is $n(n + 1)/2$, which gets larger without bound as more terms are added. Less obviously the harmonic series $1 + 1/2 + 1/3 + 1/4 ... + 1/n ...$ is also divergent, even though each individual term $1/n$ gets smaller and even tends to zero.

diversification An increase in the variety of GOODS and services produced by an individual enterprise or CONGLOMERATE, or by an economy. Diversification occurs in many economies as a natural process. In other cases, diversification may be encouraged, either by business owners or by governments, in order to reduce the risk of relying on a narrow range of products, particularly when demand for those products may be subject to large fluctuations.

diverticular disease The presence of diverticula in the gastro-intestinal tract (diverticulosis), which may become inflamed and infected (diverticulitis). Diverticula are small pouches extending outwards into the gastro-intestinal tract. Diverticular disease is commonly asymptomatic (produces no visible symptoms), although inflammation and infection may lead to left-sided abdominal pain, which can be severe, fever, rectal bleeding, and intestinal obstruction. Diarrhoea, constipation, or both may also occur. Inadequate diet is thought to play an important role in the development of diverticular disease, and in its treatment, a high-fibre diet is recommended.

divertimento A suite of movements intended purely to divert, usually written for a small group of players, and often designed for performance out of doors. The word was first used in this sense in the 18th century; in the 19th century it often referred to a selection of 'hit' tunes from an opera. The French word *divertissement* has the same meaning, but it can also mean an entertainment of songs and dances inserted into a larger work, such as an opera or ballet.

divide (in geomorphology) A watershed or 'water-parting'– an area from which rivers or glaciers flow outwards, in different directions and sometimes to different seas. Every DRAINAGE BASIN is surrounded by a divide, separating its sources of surface water from those of its neighbours.

dividend The amount (per SHARE) of a COMPANY's PROFIT that is distributed to shareholders. Dividends are normally distributed yearly, but interim dividends may be paid during the year between annual dividends. A maiden dividend is the first dividend paid to shareholders. Dividends are expressed either as an amount of money per share or as a percentage of the nominal value of the share. The percentage yield of the share is equal to the dividend per share divided by the market price of the share multiplied by 100.

Divine Right of Kings A European doctrine which taught that monarchy was a divinely ordained institution, that hereditary right could not be abolished, that kings were answerable only to God, and that it was therefore sinful for their subjects to resist them actively. It evolved during the Middle Ages, in part as a reaction to papal intrusions into secular affairs. The extension of the principle, to justify absolute rule and illegal taxation, aroused controversy. JAMES I of England upheld the doctrine in his speeches and writings and his son CHARLES I was executed for refusing to accept parliamentary control of his policies. After the GLORIOUS REVOLUTION the doctrine was far less influential, yielding to anti-absolutist arguments like those of John LOCKE. In late 17th-century France LOUIS XIV's monarchy was based on the principle of Divine Right.

diving The pastime and sport of plunging into water. Entering the water from the side of a swimming pool, the object is to enter the water cleanly, the body in a straight line with arms outstretched and fingers pointed. In the sport of diving, competitors take off from a rigid platform 5 m (16 feet) or 10 m (33 feet) above the water or from a flexible springboard. They perform a complicated series of twists and somersaults before striking the water, and judges award marks for each phase of the dive.

diving-bell A container, open at the bottom, used to carry divers and their tools to their work on the bottom of the sea or river. Early bells relied on the air they contained at submersion; later ones were supplied with air pumped into the bell from the surface. See also DEEP-SEA AND DIVING TECHNOLOGY.

diving duck See BAY DUCK.

diving suit See DEEP-SEA AND DIVING TECHNOLOGY.

division of labour The specialization of individuals in particular tasks in the production process. Such specialization promotes more efficient production by exploiting differences between individuals and also economies of scale. The division of labour makes possible mass production of consumer goods such as motor cars and television sets, and becomes pronounced with industrialization.

divorce The formal ending of a marriage, implying, in monogamous societies, entitlement to remarry. In some societies, divorce requires an official act, whereas in others it may be effected by the explicit rejection of the wife by the husband in the presence of witnesses followed by finalization in the courts, as under Islamic law, or by the return of the wife to her kin group. Many societies have allowed divorce by consent between the spouses, but where, as in Japan, a woman may have held inferior social status, she may have little choice. This route was closed to Western Europe after the establishment of Christianity, although after the Council of Trent (1563), there was a divergence in the approach to divorce: Roman Catholic countries disallowed divorce entirely, while Protestant countries allowed it on proof of the commission of a matrimonial offence, usually adultery by the woman. Many Catholic countries mitigated the severity of their law by lenient application of the laws of nullity. Since World War II most Western countries have come to allow divorce to be granted without proof of fault when the parties consent or where it can be shown that the marriage has irretrievably broken down.

Dix, Otto (1891–1969) German painter and printmaker. In the 1920s he was, with George Grosz, the outstanding artist of the *Neue Sachlichkeit* ('New Objectivity') movement. His anti-military stance drew the wrath of the Nazi regime, and his work was branded as 'Degenerate Art'. In 1939 he was gaoled, but was soon released. After the war his work was based on religious mysticism and lost much of its strength.

Dixie (also **Dixieland**) The southern states of the USA; the name is said to be derived from the local Creole pronunciation of the name of Jeremiah Dixon who surveyed the border between the states of Maryland and Pennsylvania (Mason-Dixon Line). The name is used in the song *Dixie* (1859) by Daniel D. Emmett, a popular marching song sung by Confederate soldiers in the American Civil War. The name Dixieland is also given to a kind of jazz with a strong two-beat rhythm and collective improvisation.

Djakarta See JAKARTA.

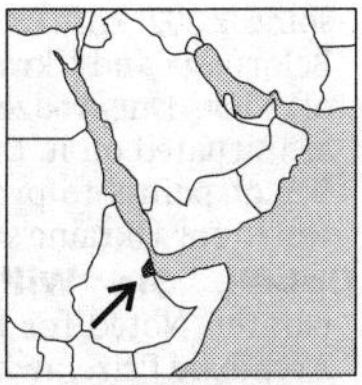

Djibouti A small country of north-east Africa, formerly part of French Somaliland, on the south coast of the Gulf of Aden at the narrow entrance to the Red Sea, opposite Yemen.

Physical. It lies on the Great Rift Valley: Lake Assal lies at 155 m (509 feet) below sea-level. The climate is harsh and much of the country is semi-arid desert.

Economy. Trade is the mainstay of the economy; Djibouti City, the capital, is a free port and through its rail link to Addis Ababa handles trade for Ethiopia and other neighbouring African states. The main exports are livestock and foodstuffs. Agriculture is limited to livestock-rearing by the nomadic population, with market-gardening at the Ambouli oasis and near urban areas.

History. The small enclave of Djibouti was created as a port *c.*1888 by the French and became the capital of French Somaliland (1892). Its importance results from its strategic position on the Gulf of Aden. In 1958 it was declared by France to be the Territory of the Afars and Issas, but in 1977 it was granted total independence as the Republic of Djibouti under President Hassan Gouled Aptidon (re-elected in 1981 and 1987), leading the Popular Rally for Progress (RPP) party. Famine and wars inland have produced many economic problems, with refugees arriving in large numbers from Ethiopia and Somalia. In November 1991 the Front pour la Restauration de la Unité et la Démocratie (FRUD) was formed, mostly of Afar opposition groups opposed to the one-party rule of Gouled Aptidon. There was fighting in the west and south until French mediation in February 1992. Later that year a multi-party constitution was adopted and elections were held. Only one opposition party was allowed to contest the elections; the others called for a boycott of the elections. Less than half the population voted and the RPP won all the seats. Fighting continued until late 1993, when a ceasefire was agreed.

Capital: Djibouti
Area: 23,200 sq km (8,950 sq mi)
Population: 586,000 (1995)
Currency: 1 Djibouti franc = 100 centimes
Religions: Sunni Muslim 94%; Roman Catholic 4%; Protestant 1%; Orthodox 1%
Ethnic Groups: Somali (Issa 33.4%; Gadaboursi 15.0%; Issaq 13.3%;) 61.7%; Afar 20.0%; Arab (mostly Yemeni) 6.0%; European 4.0%; other (refugees) 8.3%
Languages: Arabic, French (both official); Somali; minority languages
International Organizations: UN; OAU; Arab League; Non-Aligned Movement

Djibouti The capital of Djibouti on a peninsula at the mouth of the Gulf of Tadjoura; pop. (1988) 290,000. Built between 1886 and 1900, Djibouti succeeded Obock as capital in 1896 because it had a better natural harbour and ready access to the Ethiopian Highlands. Its economy is based on its role as the transit port for Ethiopia.

Djugurba See ALCHERA.

DNA (deoxyribonucleic acid) A nucleic acid and the hereditary material of all living organisms except for a few viruses that use RNA. It occurs in every cell and determines the characteristics of the organism by controlling the synthesis of PROTEINS.

In plants and animals, the DNA occurs mainly in CHROMOSOMES within the nucleus of the cell. DNA molecules are composed of four nucleotides;

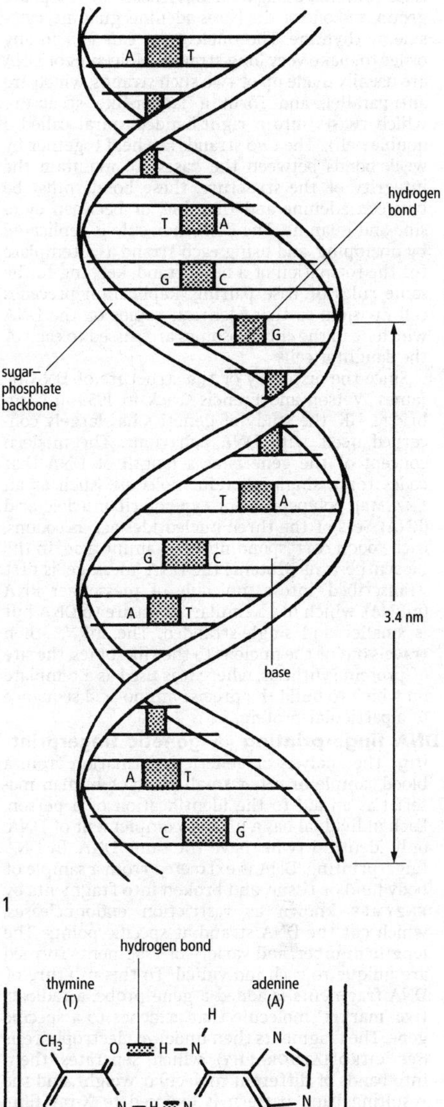

1

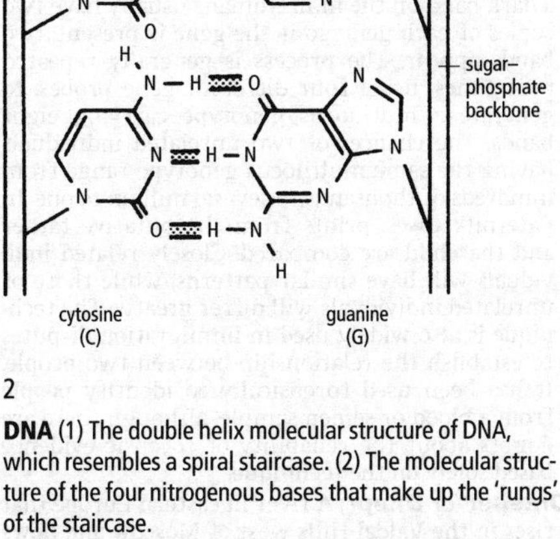

2

DNA (1) The double helix molecular structure of DNA, which resembles a spiral staircase. (2) The molecular structure of the four nitrogenous bases that make up the 'rungs' of the staircase.

each contains a sugar (deoxyribose), a phosphate group, and one of the bases adenine, guanine, cytosine or thymine. The nucleotides can join in any order to make very long strands. Molecules of DNA are usually made up of two such strands, which are anti-parallel, and form a ladder-like structure which twists into a right-handed spiral called a double helix. The two strands are held together by weak bonds between the bases. To maintain the integrity of the structure, these bonds must be between adenine and thymine, or between cytosine and guanine. The DNA molecule is replicated by unzipping, and using each strand as a template for the formation of a new strand, keeping to the same rules of base pairing. Replication precedes cell division, so that identical copies of the DNA which lie in the chromosomes are passed to each of the daughter cells.

Since the discovery of the structure of DNA by James Watson and Francis Crick in 1953 in Cambridge, UK, the study of genetics has largely concerned itself with DNA behaviour. The modern concept of the gene is as a length of DNA that codes for a single protein molecule (such as an ENZYME), polypeptide, or type of ribonucleic acid (RNA). Sets of the three nucleotides act as codons, each codon corresponding to an amino acid. In the biosynthesis of proteins the DNA 'message' is first 'transcribed' into a molecule of messenger RNA (mRNA), which has a similar structure to DNA but is smaller and single-stranded. The mRNA then travels out of the nucleus to the ribosomes, the site of protein synthesis, where it is used as a template on which to build the precise amino-acid sequence of a particular protein.

DNA fingerprinting (or **genetic fingerprinting**) The analysis of genetic information from a blood sample or other small piece of human material as an aid to the identification of a person. Each individual has a unique complement of DNA: only identical twins have the same DNA. In DNA fingerprinting, DNA is extracted from a sample of body fluid or tissue, and broken into fragments by ENZYMES known as restriction endonucleases, which cut the DNA strand at specific points. The length, number, and variety of fragments formed are unique to each individual. To this mixture of DNA fragments is added a gene probe, a radioactive 'marker' molecule that attaches to a specific gene. The fragments then undergo electrophoresis (see CHROMATOGRAPHY) which separates them into bands of different molecular weight, and the resulting band pattern is exposed to X-ray film. Any fragment carrying the gene probe appears as a dark band on the film. Humans usually have two copies of each gene, so if the gene is present, two bands appear. The process is generally repeated four times, using four different gene probes, to generate a multilocus genotype carrying eight bands. The chances of two unrelated individuals having the same multilocus genotype range from hundreds of thousands to several million to one. In paternity cases, prints from the putative father and the child are compared. Closely related individuals will have similar patterns, while those of unrelated individuals will differ greatly. The technique is also widely used in immigration disputes to establish the relationship between two people. It has been used forensically to identify people from a blood or semen sample, although there are doubts about the reliability of forensic evidence based solely on the technique.

Dnieper (or **Dnepr**) A river in eastern Europe that rises in the Valdai Hills west of Moscow and flows some 2,202 km (1,368 miles) southwards through Belorussia and Ukraine to the Black Sea. The cities of Kiev, Dneprodzerzhinsk, and Dnepropetrovsk are situated on it. Dams have been built at a number of points to provide hydroelectric power and water for Ukraine's industries.

Dobell, Sir William (1899–1970) Australian painter. Noted for his portraits, he won the 1943 Archibald Prize, awarded by the Art Gallery of New South Wales, for his portrait of fellow artist Joshua Smith. The award was contested in court by two of the unsuccessful competitors on the grounds that it was not a portrait but a caricature, and created a *cause célèbre* for modernism in Australia.

Döbereiner, Johann Wolfgang (1780–1849) German chemist who invented a lamp in which hydrogen ignited on contact with a platinum sponge. Although the lamp had limited application, the use of finely divided platinum had wider significance in the development of chemical catalysis. Also significant was his observation that certain triads of elements possess a periodicity related to their relative atomic masses. This helped pave the way to the PERIODIC TABLE.

Dobson fly See ALDERFLY.

dock (plant) A perennial plant of the genus *Rumex*, which includes 150 species in north temperate regions. All species are wind-pollinated. They are related to buckwheats and rhubarb, and sorrel. They are troublesome to farmers and gardeners because of the prodigious quantities of seed they produce and their deep taproots. The curled dock, *R. crispus*, is a particularly serious weed on newly turned soils.

documentary film A film dealing with real people and events. The oldest type of documentary is the newsreel, the first regular series of which began in 1907. Documentary was used for a social purpose in Britain in the 1930s in such films as *Coal Face* and *Night Mail* (both 1936), made by the predecessors of the Crown Film Unit, which during World War II produced such documentaries as *Fires Were Started* (1943). In the USA *The March of Time* (1935–51) was a monthly current affairs series. After World War II new techniques such as CINÉMA-VÉRITÉ and FREE CINEMA extended the bounds of the documentary. DISNEY made notable full-length nature films such as *The Living Desert* (1953). Television, however, was increasingly the home of documentary films, and few are now made with the cinema in mind.

dodder A twining plant of the widespread genus *Cuscuta*. Lacking leaves and chlorophyll, dodders are parasitic on other plants and possess suckers (haustoria) which enter the tissues of the host plant, drawing sustenance from them. They belong to the family Convolvulaceae and are related to morning glory and sweet potato. Individual species may grow on a range of hosts within a family or they may be restricted to a single host. Some are troublesome to crops such as clover and flax.

Dodecanese A group of islands in the south-east Aegean, of which the largest is Rhodes, which were occupied by Italy in 1912 during the war with Turkey and ceded to Greece in 1947. Despite its name (Greek = twelve islands) there are, in addition to the 12 main islands, numerous small islands in the group which comprises the greater part of the Southern Sporadhes; area 2,682 sq km (1,036 sq miles); capital, Rhodes.

Dodge City A city in south-west Kansas, USA, pop.

(1990) 21,130. Established in 1872 as a railhead on the Santa Fe Trail, it gained a reputation as a rowdy frontier town and was known as the 'cowboy capital'. The city hall is built on the site of Boot Hill, the famous cowboy burial ground. Once noted for its buffalo hunts and its cattle ranches, the surrounding area now produces large quantities of wheat.

Dodgson, Charles Lutwidge See CARROLL.

dodo An extinct species of large, swan-sized bird (related to the pigeons), which once lived on the island of Mauritius. Its family, Raphidae, which also contained solitaires, is now extinct. It had lost the power of flight, for its wings were very reduced, and it was therefore easy prey to sailors landing on the island for provisions. By the middle of the 17th century it had consequently been rendered extinct. A number of skeletons still exist in museums, and the fragmentary one in the University Museum, Oxford, inspired Lewis Carroll to use the dodo as a character in *Alice in Wonderland*.

Dodoma The capital of Tanzania, situated at an altitude of 1,120 m (3,675 ft) in the centre of the country; pop. (1984) 54,000. It was designated to replace the port of Dar es Salaam as capital in 1974.

dog An animal of the family Canidae, which contains 32 species within the order of CARNIVORES. Dogs appeared very early in the evolution of carnivores and those living today have changed relatively little from their fossil ancestors of 50 million years ago. The dog family, which includes wolves, jackals, foxes, dingo, and dhole, is found worldwide. All dogs have elongated jaws with 42–44 teeth; the canines are especially long and dagger-like to hold on to the prey; the carnassial teeth are for cutting and shearing flesh and sinews. In some species the molars are used for grinding bones. Their claws are not retractile. The female dogs, or bitches, give birth to between two and 16 pups, which, blind at birth, open their eyes at ten days of age. Growth is rapid and they are weaned at six weeks.

Wild species of dog include the bush dog and the Cape hunting dog. Wild dogs can swim, and a few can climb trees, although they are adapted to life on the ground. The muzzle is narrow, the ears large and erect, the limbs slender, and the tail long and bushy. The sense of smell is exceptionally well developed and this, with their good eyesight and keen hearing, allows them to follow a trail through a forest on a dark night. Domestic dogs now include many breeds, which may be classified into groups according to their employment: hounds for hunting, gun dogs, spaniels, non-sporting dogs, sheepdogs, watchdogs, draught animals, and pet dogs. See illustration p. 432.

doge The title of the holder of the highest civil office in Venice, Genoa, and Amalfi from the 7th century until the 18th century. The office originated in Venice; in 1032 hereditary succession was formally banned and election was made increasingly complicated to prevent domination by particular factions, although the Participazio and Candiano families provided most candidates in the 9th and 10th centuries, and the Tiepolo and Dandolo in the 13th and 14th. The system ended with the Napoleonic conquest of 1797. The Genoese introduced a similar system after 1339. Democratic until 1515, it became an aristocratic office thereafter and also succumbed to NAPOLEON. The first doge's palace in Venice was built in 814 and destroyed in 976. The present gothic building was begun in the early 14th century.

dogfish A small SHARK belonging either to the family Scyliorhinidae or to the family Squalidae. The former are known in Europe as dogfish, but in North America as catsharks. Scyliorhinid sharks are rarely more than 1.5 m (5 feet) long; they are bottom-living, usually solitary, heavily patterned in colour, and lay eggs. Squalid sharks, such as *Squalus acanthias*, which are known as spur-dogs in Britain and dogfish sharks in North America, are active mid-water sharks, which feed on fishes and squids. They are mostly grey coloured, with a long spine in front of each dorsal fin, and no anal fin. They give birth to live young.

Dogger Bank A submerged sand-bank in the North Sea, about 115 km (70 miles) off the north-east coast of England.

doggerel Monotonously rhymed, rhythmically awkward, and shallow verse. The unscanned verses of William McGonagall (*c.*1830–1902) are doggerel. Some poets, such as Skelton, have deliberately imitated doggerel for comic effect.

Dogon Inhabitants of Mali, who depend mainly on the cultivation of grain crops such as millet for their livelihood. Traditionally they lived in inaccessible villages on steep hill-sides, and this isolation encouraged the development of their remarkably intricate cosmology and mythology. To the Dogon, MYTHS and symbolism are as real as the material form of things, and every aspect of social life reflects the working of the Universe.

Dog Star See SIRIUS.

dog's-tooth violet A small, spring-flowering, monocotyledonous plant with colourful flowers, the recurved petals of which are said to resemble dogs' teeth. The dog's-tooth violet, *Erythronium dens-canis*, belongs to the lily family, and is totally unrelated to the true violet (*Viola* species). About 20 species are known, all from northern temperate zones. They are popular garden plants.

dogwood (or **cornel**) A deciduous shrub or tree native to the USA, Asia, and Europe. Dogwoods belong to a family of some 100 species, 40 of which belong to the genus *Cornus*. The common European dogwood, *C. sanguinea*, has greenish white flowers and dark purple berries. Its young branches are dark red, and provide attractive winter colour in gardens. The wood of species such as the Cornelian cherry, *C. mas*, and the flowering dogwood, *C. florida*, is sometimes used to make skewers (once known as 'dogs') or shuttles for the textile industry.

Doha (Arabic **Ad Dawhah**) The capital of the State of Qatar in the Persian Gulf, on the east coast of the Qatar peninsula; pop. (est. 1990) 300,000. It developed from a small fishing village into a modern city after the discovery of oil in 1949 and is now a major shipping, engineering, oil-refining, and food-processing centre.

Doisneau, Robert (1912–94) French photographer. He is best known for his photos portraying the city and inhabitants of Paris, which he began taking in the 1930s; one of his most famous images is 'The Kiss at the Hôtel de Ville' (1950). His photojournalism includes pictures taken during the liberation of Paris in 1944.

Dolby system An electronic circuit that reduces the background hissing noise present during replay of MAGNETIC TAPES, developed by Ray Dolby in 1966. The noise arises because of the granular nature of the magnetic coating and is worse at slow tape speeds and with narrow tapes, typical of cassettes. The original recording must have been made with Dolby for the system to be effective in playback.

Dogs (1) English springer spaniel. (2) Golden retriever. (3) Afghan hound. (4) Basenji. (5) Bedlington terrier. (6) Airedale. (7) Pomeranian. (8) Papillon. (9) Affenpinscher. (10) Shih-tzu. (11) Poodle. (12) Bulldog. (13) Boxer. (14) St Bernard.

doldrums An equatorial ocean region of calms, sudden storms, and light unpredictable winds situated between the north-east and south-east trade winds.

Dole, Robert Joseph (known as 'Bob') (1923–) US Republican politician. A senator since 1968, he became leader of the Republican Party in 1992, and was defeated by Bill Clinton in the presidential elections of 1996.

dolerite (US **diabase**) A medium-grained basic igneous rock, dark green in colour, usually with an interlocking texture of plagioclase feldspar and pyroxene crystals, giving the rock a mottled appearance. Common as SILLS and DYKES, dolerites are found throughout the world. They are mainly of scientific interest but are frequently associated with valuable concentrations of copper.

Dolin, Sir Anton (born Sydney Francis Patrick Chippendall Healey-Kay) (1904–83) British ballet-dancer and choreographer. From 1923 until 1926, and again from 1928 to 1929, he was a principal with the Ballets Russes. With Alicia Markova he founded the Markova–Dolin Ballet in 1935; the company lasted until 1938. After a period spent abroad, Dolin returned to Britain in 1948, and in 1950 became artistic director and first soloist of the newly founded London Festival Ballet, a post he held until 1961.

doline A depression in the surface of a limestone region. Dolines are formed by running water which has dissolved the rock and then found its way underground, carrying the calcium carbonate with it in solution and leaving the insoluble material as a clayey deposit in the bottom of the hollow.

D'Oliveira, Basil (Lewis) (1931–) British cricketer and coach, born in South Africa. He made his début for Worcestershire at the age of 33 and for England the following season, going on to win 44 caps and to score five test centuries. South Africa's refusal to allow D'Oliveira into the country led to the cancellation of England's 1968–69 tour and to South Africa's subsequent banishment from test cricket.

Doll, Sir (William) Richard (Shaboe) (1912–) British physician. He investigated the aetiology of lung cancer, leukaemia, and other cancers, and (with Sir A. Bradford Hill, 1897–1991) was the first to provide a statistical link between smoking and lung cancer.

Dollfuss, Engelbert (1892–1934) Austrian statesman, Chancellor of Austria 1932–34. He was elected leader of the Christian Socialist Party and Chancellor in 1932. From 1933 Dollfuss attempted to govern without Parliament in order better to oppose Austrian Nazi moves to force the *Anschluss* (the union of Austria and Germany). Five months after promulgating a new Fascist constitution in 1934, he was assassinated by Austrian Nazis in an abortive coup.

dolmen See MEGALITH.

dolomite (calcium magnesium carbonate) A mineral closely associated with calcite and often found replacing it. It is relatively light in colour and weight. The word 'dolomite' is also used for rock containing more than 50 per cent carbonate, of which more than one-half is the mineral dolomite. To prevent confusion dolomite rock is also known as dolostone. It is used in the building, metallurgical, and chemical industries. The **Dolomite Mountains** are a range of the Alps in northern Italy, so named because the characteristic rock of the region is dolomitic limestone.

dolphin A TOOTHED WHALE of the family Delphinidae, typically beaked. The common dolphin, *Delphinus delphis*, is one of 32 species, and is an inhabitant of the warmer parts of the Atlantic and Mediterranean. Dolphins are schooling animals with a highly developed social organization; schools may include up to 200 individuals, and many will leap some 3 m (9.75 feet), almost synchronously, clear from the water. Some species can maintain a speed of 36 km/hour (23 miles per hour) for several hours. Mating probably occurs in spring and summer, the gestation period lasting eleven months; the single young is 75–90 cm (2.4–3 feet) long at birth. An adult common dolphin may be as long as 2.4 m (8 feet). A vocal mammal, it produces a series of clicks that are audible to man.

Other species include the widely distributed bottle-nosed dolphin, *Tursiops truncatus*, and the killer whale, *Orcinus orca*. The last species hunts in packs, or pods, of 20 or more individuals and will encircle or trap shoals of fishes.

Domagk, Gerhard (1895–1964) German pioneer of CHEMOTHERAPY and discoverer of the SULPHONAMIDE drugs. In 1932 he discovered that Prontosil Red, used to dye leather, controlled streptococcal infections in mice. (Subsequently, J. Trefousel in Paris demonstrated that only part of the molecule, a sulphonamide, was biologically active.) His discovery, unrivalled until the advent of PENICILLIN in the 1940s, made it possible to treat a wide range of dangerous infections. Domagk was awarded the Nobel Prize for Physiology and Medicine in 1939.

dome (in geology) A structure shaped like the dome of a building. In structural geology a dome is an ANTICLINE in which the beds dip outwards in all directions. The word 'dome' is also used to describe bodies of igneous rock: either the curved upper surface of an IGNEOUS INTRUSION or a volcanic dome, a mass of lava pushed up above the crater of a volcano.

dome (in architecture) A curved roof, hemispherical or approximately hemispherical in shape and generally large in scale: usually it is the crowning feature of a major building. The dome evolved from the ARCH and seems to have originated in the ancient Near East where it was a feature of Sassanian architecture. It was first used on a monumental scale by the Romans, most notably in the Pantheon in Rome (120–24 AD), which had an internal diameter of over 40 metres (44 yds). While Michelangelo's dome at St Peter's in Rome and Christopher Wren's dome at St Paul's in London are triumphs of engineering, modern constructional methods have enabled large domes to be built without enormous supports (see, for example, FULLER).

Dome of the Rock An Islamic Byzantine mosque with a rich mosaic exterior capped by a large golden dome in Jerusalem. It surrounds the sacred rock on which, according to tradition, Abraham prepared to sacrifice his son (Genesis 22:9) and from which the prophet Muhammad made his miraculous midnight ascent into heaven. Built in the area of Solomon's Temple and dating from the end of the 7th century, to Muslims it is the third most holy place, after Mecca and Medina, and stands on a sacred site called 'the furthest mosque'.

Domesday Book A survey of property in England conducted in 1086. Conceived by WILLIAM I, but probably to some extent based on pre-Conquest administrative records, it was the most comprehensive assessment of property and land ever undertaken in medieval Europe. Its purpose was to maximize the revenues from the land tax and it caused resentment and even riots. It was given its name on account of its definitive nature; today its volumes are housed in the Public Record Office, London.

Domingo, Placido (1941–) Spanish-born tenor. He moved to Mexico with his family in 1950, and made his operatic début in 1957. He established his reputation as one of the world's leading operatic tenors in the 1970s; his performances in operas by Verdi and Puccini have met with particular acclaim.

Dominic, St (1170–1221) Founder of the DOMINICAN order of friars. He was born in Spain, of noble family, but as a young man adopted an austere life, becoming a priest and canon of Osma Cathedral. In 1215 he attended the Fourth LATERAN Council. In that year he founded his own order known as the **Dominicans** or 'Black Friars' because they wear a white tunic with a black mantle. The order became very popular in the 13th century, being used by several popes for preaching crusades and for the INQUISITION. Feast day, 8 August.

Dominica, Commonwealth of An island country, the second largest of the Windward group of the Caribbean Islands.

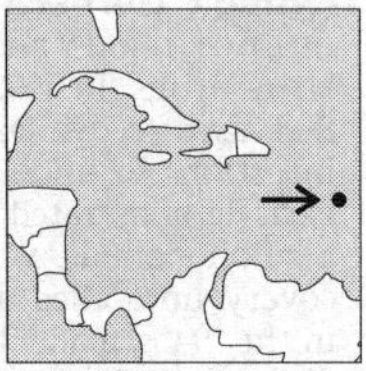

Physical. The loftiest island in the region, it has a mountainous ridge rising to Morne Diablotin, at 1,447 m (4,747 feet). Of volcanic origin, it offers beautiful scenery, with forests, waterfalls, craters, and springs. Only the coastline is cultivable on any scale.

Economy. Dominica's economy is primarily agricultural, with bananas the leading export crop. Other crops include root crops, coconuts, and citrus, but much land is still under forest. Tourism is being developed, while industry is limited to food-processing and soap-making.

History. When Europeans first arrived Dominica was inhabited by Carib Indians, who had driven out the earlier inhabitants, the Arawaks. During the 18th century the French and British fought with each other, and with the Caribs, for control of the island. Britain was in possession of the island in 1805, when the French made their last attempt to capture Dominica but were driven out. In 1958 Dominica joined the West Indian Federation, and it became an autonomous British Associated State in 1967. It gained full independence in 1978.

Dominica was devastated by hurricanes in 1979 and 1980, and there were two attempted coups in 1981. The Dominican Freedom Party (DFP), under Dame Eugenia Charles (1919–), governed the country from 1980 until 1995, when the United Workers' Party (DUWP) won elections.

Capital: Roseau
Area: 750 sq km (290 sq mi)
Population: 72,100 (1995)
Currency: 1 East Caribbean dollar = 100 cents
Religions: Roman Catholic 76.9%; Methodist 5.0%; Seventh-day Adventist 3.2%; Pentecostal 2.9%
Ethnic Groups: Black 91.2%; mixed 6.0%; Amerindian 1.5%; White and other 1.3%
Languages: English (official); French creole
International Organizations: UN; OAS; CARICOM; Commonwealth

Dominican Republic A country in the CARIBBEAN, the eastern part of the island of HISPANIOLA.

Economy. Light industry, expansion of duty-free industrial zones, and tourism are being fostered in the Dominican Republic to diversify a primarily agricultural economy which exports sugar, cocoa, and coffee. Nickel is the chief export, and gold is also important.

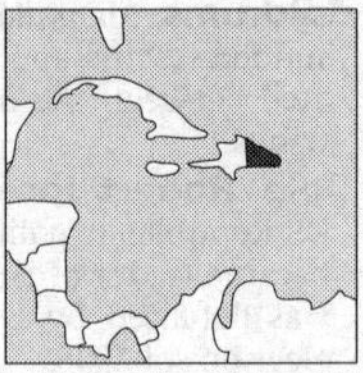

History. The Dominican Republic declared its independence from Spain in 1821, although in the following year it was annexed by Haiti. In 1843 the Dominicans revolted from Haitian domination, winning their second independence in 1844. Between 1861 and 1865 the Dominican Republic was re-annexed to Spain and fought a third war for independence (1865) under Buenaventura Báez. Anarchy, revolutions, and dictatorships followed, and by 1905 the country was bankrupt. The USA assumed fiscal control, but disorder continued and the country was occupied (1916–24) by US marines. A constitutional government was established (1924), but this was overthrown by Rafael TRUJILLO, whose military dictatorship lasted from 1930 to 1961. On his assassination, President Juan Bosch established (1962–63) a democratic government, until he was deposed by a military junta. Civil war and fear of a communist take-over brought renewed US intervention (1965), and a new constitution was introduced in 1966. Since then redemocratization has steadily advanced, the Partido Reformista being returned to power in the 1986 elections. The country occupies a strategic position on major sea routes leading from Europe and the USA to the Panama Canal. The Partido Reformista remained in power after the 1990 elections with Joaquín Balaguer as President. The latter resigned as party leader in 1991, but remained President. An IMF austerity programme in 1991 sharply reduced inflation and there were successful efforts to diversify the economy. In 1994 Balaguer was re-elected, but the result was contested with allegations of corruption and fraud being made. Fresh elections were promised to end the political crisis and these resulted in the election as President of Leonel Fernandez, leader of the centrist Liberation Party (in 1996).

Capital: Santo Domingo
Area: 48,443 sq km (18,704 sq mi)
Population: 7,823,000 (1995)
Currency: 1 Dominican peso = 100 centavos
Religions: Roman Catholic 91.9%; other (mostly evangelical Protestant and followers of voodoo) 8.1%
Ethnic Groups: Mulatto 73.0%; Black 11.0%; White 10.0%
Languages: Spanish (official); Haitian creole
International Organizations: UN; OAS

dominion A country in the BRITISH EMPIRE that, between 1867 and 1947, had achieved a degree of autonomy but still owed allegiance to the British crown. The first country to call itself a dominion was Canada (1867), followed in 1907 by New Zealand. Australia called itself a Commonwealth (1901), South Africa a Union (1910). After World War II the concept became obsolete as the COMMONWEALTH OF NATIONS included countries that were republics and did not owe allegiance to the crown, though accepting the monarch as symbolic head of the Commonwealth.

Domino, Fats (born Antoine Domino) (1928–) US pianist, singer, and songwriter. His music represents the transition from rhythm and blues to rock and roll and shows the influence of jazz, boogie-woogie, and gospel music. He made most of his recordings in the 1950s and early 1960s; his many songs include 'Ain't That a Shame' (1955) and 'Blueberry Hill' (1956).

dominoes A popular table-game played worldwide in many versions. British players use a set of twenty-eight small black rectangular blocks marked on the face with a double set of white spots with values from 6–6 to 0–0. Players draw seven dominoes and lay out one piece in turn, placing it end-on to a piece with a matching number, except in the case of a double-numbered domino which is placed at right angles. The winner is the first to either lay down all his or her pieces or end with the lowest total of spots.

domino theory A political theory based on an analogy with the way a row of dominoes falls until none remains standing. Popular in the cold war, it holds that a political event in one country will lead to its repetition in another, usually neighbouring, country.

Domitian (full name Titus Flavius Domitianus) (51–96 AD) Roman emperor 81–96, son of Vespasian. An energetic but autocratic ruler, on succeeding his brother Titus he embarked on a large building programme, including monumental palaces on the Palatine Hill in Rome. His wife was implicated in his assassination, which ended a period of terror that had lasted a number of years.

Don A river of eastern Europe that rises near Tula in western Russia and flows 1,967 km (1,222 miles) southwards to enter the Sea of Azov beyond Rostov. It is linked by canal to the River Volga.

Donatello (born Donato di Betto Bardi) (1386–1466) Italian sculptor. He was one of the pioneers of scientific perspective, and is especially famous for his lifelike sculptures, including the bronze *David* (probably created between 1430 and 1460), his most classical work. He was in Padua from 1443 to 1453, where he made the equestrian statue *Gattamelata*.

Donatist A member of a Christian sect that arose in North Africa in 311 AD out of a dispute about the election of the bishop of Carthage, and which maintained that it was the only true and pure Church and that the ordinations of others were invalid.

Donatus, Aelius (4th century) Roman grammarian. His treatises on Latin grammar were collected in the *Ars Grammatica* (undated), one of the main textbooks used in schools in the Middle Ages.

Donau See DANUBE.

Doncaster An industrial (railway) town on the River Don, South Yorkshire, England; pop. (1991) 284,300. The St Leger is run annually on the racecourse.

Donegal A county in the province of Ulster in the extreme north-west of the Republic of Ireland; area 4,830 sq km (1,866 sq miles); pop. (1991) 128,000; capital, Lifford.

Dong A minority nationality of southern China, mostly found in Guizhou, Hunan, and Guangxi where the Dong people number *c.*1.4 million.

Donizetti, Gaetano (1797–1848) Italian composer. He is generally regarded as the leading Italian composer of the 1830s, bridging the gap between Verdi and Bellini. He wrote seventy-five operas, including tragedies such as *Anna Bolena* (1830) and *Lucia di Lammermoor* (1835) and the comedies *L'Elisir d'amore* (1832) and *Don Pasquale* (1843).

Don Juan A fictitious character who is a symbol of libertinism. In the earliest, 17th-century Spanish version, as in most subsequent interpretations of the story in opera (Mozart's *Don Giovanni*), on stage (Molière's *Don Juan*), and poems (Byron's *Don Juan*), he is cast as the 14th-century Don Juan Tenorio of Seville.

donkey A relative of the horse, derived from the wild ASS, *Equus asinus*. Its name is thought to originate from the dun colour of its coat. It was probably domesticated during the New Stone Age some 12,000 years ago. The donkey is a placid animal and makes a better pack and draught animal than the horse, to which it is superior when carrying loads and negotiating narrow mountain paths. It has a life expectancy of up to fourteen years. A single foal is usually produced after a gestation period of nine months.

Donkin, Bryan (1768–1855) British engineer. He made pioneering contributions in several fields, including paper-making and printing, patenting (with Richard Mackenzie Bacon, an English writer and printer, 1775–1844) the first rotary press. In the 1830s, he successfully developed a method of food preservation by heat sterilization, sealing the food inside a container made of sheet steel, so producing the first 'tin' can.

Donne, John (1572–1631) English poet and preacher. Generally regarded as the first of the Metaphysical poets, he is most famous for his *Satires* (*c.*1590–99), *Elegies* (*c.*1590–99), and love poems, which appeared in the collection *Songs and Sonnets* (undated). He also wrote religious poems and, as dean of St Paul's from 1621, was one of the most celebrated preachers of his age.

Doolittle, Hilda (1886–1961) US poet. From 1911 she lived in London, where she met Ezra Pound and other imagist poets, whose style and concerns are reflected in her own work. Her many volumes of poetry (published under the pseudonym H.D.) also show the influence of classical mythology; they include *Sea Garden* (1916).

dopamine A derivative of dopa (a physiologically important compound that is required for normal brain function). Dopamine is a catecholamine that functions as a neurotransmitter transmitting nerve impulses within the central nervous system. It is also administered as a drug by injection in heart failure, shock, and septicaemia.

doping See SEMICONDUCTOR DEVICE.

Doppler, Johann Christian (1803–53) Austrian physicist. Doppler qualified in mathematics and held several professorships, mainly in Prague. He is famous for his discovery, in 1842, of what is now known as the **Doppler effect**: that the observed frequency of a wave depends on the relative motions of the source and the observer (heard in the change in the pitch of a train whistle as it passes by). Its effect on light is known as the **Doppler shift**, which causes receding galaxies to appear redder and is evidence of an expanding Universe.

Doppler RADAR and SONAR are used to differentiate between fixed and moving targets by observing the Doppler shift. Measuring this frequency shift accurately determines the velocity of moving targets. Other applications of this effect include use in RADIO aids to navigation.

Dorado The Goldfish, a CONSTELLATION of the south celestial hemisphere. It was introduced by the Dutch navigators Pieter Dirkszoon Keyser and Frederick de Houtman at the end of the 16th century; it is sometimes also known as the Swordfish. Dorado contains most of the Large MAGELLANIC CLOUD, including the Tarantula Nebula.

dor beetle A large, heavily built beetle, with noisy flight. Dor beetles comprise about 300 species in the family Geotrupidae. The males of some species have horns on their heads and many species are metallic blue, purple or green in colour. Their larvae are sedentary and feed on carrion, or dung.

Dung-feeding is the most common life-style for dor beetles.

Dorchester The county and market town of Dorset in southern England, on the River Frome; pop. (1991) 15,037. The town has associations with Judge Jeffreys whose 'Bloody Assizes' were held here in 1685, and in 1834 the Tolpuddle Martyrs were sentenced in the local court house. The Stone Age earthworks of Maiden Castle lie 3 km to the south-west.

Dordogne An inland department of Aquitaine in south-west France containing numerous caves and rock-shelters that have yielded abundant remains of early humans and their artefacts and art; area 9,060 sq km (3,499 sq miles); pop. (1990) 386,365; capital, Périgueux.

Doré, Gustave (1832–83) French book illustrator. He was widely known for his dark, detailed woodcut illustrations of books such as Dante's *Inferno* (1861), Cervantes' *Don Quixote* (1863), and the Bible (1865–66); he produced so many of these that at one time he employed more than forty block-cutters.

Doria, Andrea (1466–1560) DOGE of Venice 1528–60, an outstanding soldier and admiral. He fought for Francis I and Charles V, expelled the French from GENOA in 1528, and took power himself, creating the aristocratic republic. His descendants contributed six doges and numerous officials to the state.

Dorians The tribes speaking the Doric dialect of Greek who probably entered Greece from the north *c.*1100–1000 BC and by the 8th century BC had settled most of the Peloponnese, the southernmost Aegean islands, and the south-west corner of Asia Minor. While culturally distinct in architecture and dialect, the Dorians retained their political system only in Sparta and Crete where the ruling military class subjected the local peoples as serfs and dependants. The Dorians were responsible for the oldest and simplest orders of Greek architecture, known as the Doric order.

dormouse A member of the RODENT families Gliridae or Seleviniidae; the first contains 17 species found throughout Europe, Asia, and Africa, and the second has a single species, the desert dormouse. More like voles than mice in appearance, dormice have long, bushy tails and soft fur. Their common name derives from the deep hibernation undertaken in the northern parts of their range. The common dormouse of Britain, more properly known as the hazel dormouse, *Muscardinus avellanarius*, extends as far east as Russia and Asia Minor. As the name suggests, this dormouse is especially associated with hazel bushes. The edible dormouse, *Glis glis*, was fattened for food by the Romans in *gliraria*, hence the family name. Most species eat a variety of plant products or small animals such as insects and earthworms.

Dorset A county of south-west England; area 2,654 sq km (1,025 sq miles); pop. (1991) 645,200; county town, Dorchester.

Dortmund An industrial city and inland port in North Rhine-Westphalia, north-west Germany, the southern terminus of the Dortmund-Ems Canal which links the Ruhr industrial area with the North Sea; pop. (1991) 601,000. It has a major steel industry and Europe's largest brewery.

dory See JOHN DORY.

dosimeter A device used to measure nuclear radiation for safety purposes. The simplest type consists of a small piece of photographic film worn as a sealed badge. Any nuclear radiation present exposes the film through the sealing, with the amount of exposure being related to the radiation dose. This can be revealed by later photographic development.

Dos Passos, John (Roderigo) (1896–1970) American novelist. He is chiefly remembered for his collage-like portrayal of the energy and diversity of American life in the first decades of the 20th century in such novels as *Manhattan Transfer* (1925) and *U.S.A.* (1938).

Dostoevsky, Fyodor Mikhailovich (or **Dostoyevsky**) (1821–81) Russian novelist. His early socialist activism led to his being sentenced to death, but a last-minute reprieve led instead to exile in Siberia (1849–54). During this time he suffered periods of great mental and physical pain and recurring bouts of epilepsy; his experiences are recounted in *Notes from the House of the Dead* (1860–61). From the 1860s he wrote the novels on which his reputation is based, including *Crime and Punishment* (1866), *The Idiot* (1868), and *The Brothers Karamazov* (1880). These dark works reveal Dostoevsky's keen psychological insight, savage humour, and his concern with profound religious, political, and moral problems, especially that of human suffering.

Douala The chief port and largest city of Cameroon, at the mouth of the Wouri River; pop. (1992) 1,200,000. As capital of German West Africa it was known as Kamerunstadt from 1885 to 1901. Its name was changed to Douala in 1907 and it later became capital of French Cameroon (1940–46). It is a mixture of expensive shops, modern buildings, African markets, and slums.

double bass The largest of the violin family. To make notes easier to reach, basses are tuned in fourths, normally *E′–A′–D′–G′*. Music for the instrument is notated an octave higher than the actual pitch. Three-string basses were used in the 19th century, but four strings are normal today, with sometimes a fifth string tuned to low *B″* or *C′*, or the fourth string extended to that note by mechanism. To avoid carving away so much wood, the backs of basses are often flat, not curved.

double-glazing A system in which two panes of glass separated by an air gap are fixed into a window or door. Single panes of glass have a sufficiently high thermal conductivity to have a low inside surface temperature in winter, causing condensation. Two panes provide improved thermal insulation and a higher surface temperature internally, reducing the likelihood of condensation and conserving energy. The space between the panes is usually sealed at the edges to prevent the entry and condensation of warm moist air. There is also some reduction in sound transmission.

double star See BINARY STAR.

Douglas A resort town on the Irish Sea, capital of the Isle of Man; pop. (1991) 22,210.

Douglas, Lord Alfred (Bruce) (1870–1945) British poet. In 1891 he began his long intimacy with Oscar Wilde, because of which his father, the 8th Marquess of Queensberry, cut off Douglas's allowance and subsequently became involved in a law suit with Wilde, as a result of which Wilde was sent to prison. After Wilde's death Douglas was himself imprisoned in 1923 for libel against Winston Churchill. He published two collections of sonnets, *In Excelsis* (1924) and *Sonnets and Lyrics* (1935), as well as his revealing *Autobiography* (1929).

Douglas fir Any of five species of CONIFER belonging to the pine family. Two occur in North America, and three in the Far East. Their nearest relatives are the hemlocks and they are not true firs. A Douglas fir, *Pseudotsuga menziesii*, felled in British Columbia in 1895 was the tallest living tree known, at 133 m (440 feet).

Douglas-Home, Sir Alec, Baron Home of the Hirsel of Coldstream (born Alexander Frederick Douglas-Home) (1903–95) British Conservative statesman, Prime Minister 1963–64. He served as private secretary to Neville Chamberlain in the negotiations with Hitler from 1937 to 1940. Various ministerial offices followed before his appointment as Foreign Secretary under Harold Macmillan in 1960. When Macmillan resigned in 1963, Douglas-Home became Prime Minister, relinquishing his hereditary peerage as 14th Earl of Home (to which he had succeeded in 1951). His government was defeated by the Labour Party in the 1964 elections. Douglas-Home later served as Foreign Secretary under Edward Heath (1970–74).

Douglass, Frederick (*c.*1817–95) US black ABOLITIONIST. Born in slavery in Maryland, he made his escape to the free states in 1838. In 1841 he became an agent for the Massachusetts Anti-Slavery Society and a prominent advocate of abolition. An adviser of LINCOLN during the AMERICAN CIVIL WAR, he remained throughout his long life an advocate of full civil rights for all.

Dounreay A location on the north coast of Caithness, Scotland, 13 km (8 miles) west of Thurso. It was the site of the UK's only two experimental fast-breeder nuclear reactors. The first, the Dounreay Fast Reactor, operated from 1959 to 1977. The second, the Prototype Fast Reactor, operated from 1974 to 1994. In 1995 the world's first wave-power station in open sea began operating in the Pentland Firth off Dounreay.

douroucouli See NIGHT MONKEY.

dove A bird belonging to any of several groups of the pigeon family, Columbidae. The term 'dove' does not describe any particular taxonomic unit, but most of the species tend to be small ones. The Barbary dove, *Streptopelia risoria*, is kept extensively for its pleasant song; its origin is obscure, but it is thought to be a long-domesticated form of the African collared dove, *S. roseogrisea*. The white dove of peace is a domesticated form of the rock pigeon, *Columba livia*.

Dover A ferry port and resort in Kent, the largest of the Cinque Ports, on the coast of the English Channel; its chalk cliffs are world famous; pop. (1981) 34,300. Dover has been fortified since Roman times and many ancient buildings survive. It is mainland Britain's nearest point to the Continent, being only 35 km (21 miles) across the Strait of Dover (Pas de Calais) from Calais.

Dover The capital of the US state of Delaware; pop. (1990) 27,630. Settled in 1683 and laid out in 1717 by William Penn, it became state capital in 1777. Dover Air Force Base has one of the largest cargo-terminals in the world.

Dover sole See SOLE.

Dowding, Hugh (Caswall Tremenheere), Baron (1882–1970) British Marshal of the RAF. As Commander-in-Chief of Fighter Command (1936–40) Dowding organized the air defence that defeated the Luftwaffe during the Battle of Britain in 1940. He was relieved of his post the same year in controversial circumstances and retired in 1942.

Dow Jones Industrial Average An index of SECURITY prices issued by Dow Jones & Co. (a US firm providing financial information), used on the New York Stock Exchange. It is a narrowly based SHARE INDEX, having 30 constituent companies. Founded in 1884, based then on 11 stocks (mostly in railways), it was reorganized in 1928 when it was given the value of 100. Its lowest point was on 2 July 1932, when it reached 41. In 1987 it exceeded 2,400. There are three other Dow Jones indexes, representing price movements in US home bonds, transportation stocks, and utilities.

Dowland, John (1563–1626) One of the most notable English composers and lutenists of his day. Dowland's music, often imbued with a quality of heavy sadness, consists of solo and PART-SONGS with lute accompaniment, lute dances and FANTASIAS, psalm harmonizations, sacred songs, and several works for lute and viols – including the famous *Lachrimae or Seaven Teares* (1604). He also composed a collection of PAVANS, GALLIARDS (his favourite form), and ALLEMANDES for five-part string CONSORT. His three *Bookes of Songes or Ayres* (1597, 1600, 1603) mark him out as an outstandingly sensitive and imaginative interpreter of the English language.

Down A county of Northern Ireland; area 2,448 sq km (945 sq miles); pop. (1981) 339,200; county town, Downpatrick.

Downing Street A street in Westminster, London, between Whitehall and St James's Park. It was built by the diplomat Sir George Downing (died 1684), described by Pepys as 'a most ungrateful villain'. In 1732 No. 10 was acquired on a Crown lease by Sir Robert Walpole, Britain's first Prime Minister, who accepted it on behalf of all future Lords of the Treasury (still the formal title of the Prime Minister). This house is the official town residence of the Prime Minister, No. 11 that of the Chancellor of the Exchequer, and the Foreign and Commonwealth Office is also situated in this street.

Downing Street Declaration A document, signed on 15 December 1993 by the British Prime Minister, John MAJOR, and the Prime Minister of the Irish Republic, Albert Reynolds, declaring their principles and conditions for the conduct of negotiations to achieve peace in NORTHERN IRELAND. The declaration restated the existing positions of both governments, confirming that they would seek the agreement of the people of both Northern Ireland and the Irish Republic to any change to the status of Northern Ireland and would uphold all existing guarantees to Northern Ireland.

Downpatrick The county town of Down in Northern Ireland, in the valley of the River Quoile; pop. (1981) 7,400. Once the royal seat of the Macdonlevys, it was named Downpatrick in 1177 by the Anglo-Norman John de Courcy. St Patrick, who began his mission to Ireland in 432, is reputed to have been buried in Downpatrick.

Downs A region of chalk hills in southern England forming parallel ranges in Surrey and Kent (**North Downs**) and Sussex (**South Downs**).

Down's syndrome A spectrum of effects of a chromosomal disorder, trisomy-21, in which there are three copies of chromosome 21 instead of the normal two. Features are apparent at birth, and the condition can be diagnosed during pregnancy. Characteristic features of Down's syndrome include wide spaced, slanted eyes; short stature; rounded, short skull; broad, short neck; structural ear abnormalities; and abnormalities of the palms. Learning difficulties are invariably present, although personality remains pleasant and artistic appreciation is substantial. Down's syndrome increases susceptibility to other disorders such as heart disease and leukaemia.

This congenital condition occurs once in every

700 live births, and its frequency is higher among children born to older women (one case in every 46 births to women at 45 years of age, in comparison to one in 26,000 to women aged 19).

downthrow The side of a FAULT that has been thrown down in relation to the rocks on the other side (the upthrow block).

Dowson, Ernest (Christopher) (1867–1900) British poet. Associated with the 'decadent' school of Oscar Wilde and Aubrey Beardsley, he published two books of poems, *Verses* (1896) and *Decorations* (1899), which deal with themes of ennui and world-weariness. He died an alcoholic in France.

Doyle, Sir Arthur Conan (1859–1930) British novelist. He is chiefly remembered for establishing the detective story as a major fictional genre with his creation of the private detective Sherlock Holmes. Holmes and his friend Dr Watson (the narrator of the stories) first appeared in *A Study in Scarlet* (1887) and continued to demonstrate their ingenuity at crime-solving in a long line of stories contained in such collections as *The Adventures of Sherlock Holmes* (1892) as well as in *The Hound of the Baskervilles* (1902). Doyle also wrote historical and other romances.

D'Oyly Carte, Richard (1844–1901) British impresario and producer. He brought together the librettist Sir W. S. Gilbert and the composer Sir Arthur Sullivan, producing many of their operettas in London's Savoy Theatre, which he had established in 1881.

Drabble, Margaret (1939–) British novelist. Her early novels, including *The Millstone* (1963), are mostly realistic examinations of individual dilemmas faced by educated women. *The Ice Age* (1977) is a more ambitious attempt to depict the moral condition of contemporary Britain. Her other novels include *The Middle Ground* (1980). *The Radiant Way* (1987), and *The Gates of Ivory* (1991). She has also edited *The Oxford Companion to English Literature* (1985).

Draco (7th century BC) Athenian legislator. His codification of Athenian law was notorious for its severity in that the death penalty was imposed for both serious and trivial crimes; this gave rise to the adjective *draconian* in English.

Draco The Dragon, a large CONSTELLATION in the north polar region of the sky, one of the 48 constellations known to the ancient Greeks. In mythology it represents the dragon Ladon, who was guardian of the golden apples of the Hesperides, and who was shot by Hercules; in the sky Hercules is depicted with one foot on the dragon's head. The fourth-magnitude star Alpha Draconis is also known as Thuban.

Dracula The chief of the vampires in the novel *Dracula* (1897), written by the Irish-born civil servant Bram Stoker, and partly set in a lonely castle in Transylvania. Vlad Tepes (Vlad the Impaler), also known as Dracula, was a 15th-century Prince of Wallachia, renowned for his cruelty, and the novelist wove this name into a sinister tale of a region with which vampires and werewolves were traditionally associated.

drag-line A machine used for large-scale excavation in OPEN-CAST MINING. A large bucket is positioned by means of a long boom and then dragged across the surface, scooping up earth as it moves. Once the bucket is full, it is raised and the boom traverses to deposit the load at the desired point.

dragon A mythical monster like a reptile, usually with wings and able to breathe out fire. The dragon, which possesses both protective and terror-inspiring qualities, is probably the commonest emblem in oriental art, and the most ancient. It is used as a heraldic emblem, for example in Wales, where it was introduced as a military standard during the Roman occupation in the 1st century AD.

dragonet A spiny fish of the family Callionymidae, which contains about 40 species. The most common European dragonet, *Callionymus lyra*, grows to 30 cm (12 inches) in length. This species is a bottom-living fish which prefers muddy or sandy bottoms at depths of 20–100 m (65–325 feet). The males are brilliantly coloured by comparison with the females and there is an elaborate display of colours during breeding in early spring. Other kinds of dragonet are abundant in the Indo-Pacific region, and also occur on the American coast.

dragonfish A deep-sea fish named for its large mouth and long teeth. Three families are recognized: scaly dragonfishes, the Stomiatidae family, scaleless black dragonfishes, the Melanostomiatidae family, and the family Bathydraconidae. All three families have species with long bodies, luminous organs on the underside, and a barbel on the chin. They are found in deep-water oceans throughout the world.

dragonfly An insect of the order Odonata, and a powerful aerial hunter of other insects, able to hover and fly backwards, with legs, like DAMSELFLIES, placed so as to form a 'basket' beneath the mouth for catching prey. Dragonflies hunt by sight; the enormous compound eyes cover most of the head and can detect movement in a full circle around the insect. Many are brilliantly coloured, and they rest, unlike damselflies, with the wings outspread. They are most often found near still or slow-moving water, although adults may range over several kilometres.

Dragonflies and damselflies have an unusual approach to reproduction. Preliminary to mating, the male grasps the female's neck with claspers at the end of his abdomen, and pairs are often seen flying in tandem. She curves her abdomen forward to receive sperm stored in pockets at the front of his abdomen. Eggs are then dropped into water in flight, or inserted into stems of water plants; in damselflies the male may support the female while she oviposits.

drainage See LAND RECLAMATION; SEWAGE.

drainage basin A catchment area that contributes surface water to a river. They are almost entirely carved by processes involving the movement of water, and their slopes and channels function interdependently.

Drake, Sir Francis (*c.*1540–96) English sailor and explorer. He spent his early career privateering in Spanish seas. He was the first Englishman to circumnavigate the globe; he set off in 1577 with five ships under the sponsorship of Elizabeth I to investigate the Strait of Magellan, tried unsuccessfully to find the North-west Passage, and finally returned to England via the Cape of Good Hope with only his own ship, the *Golden Hind*, in 1580. He was knighted the following year. Drake's raid on Cadiz in 1587 delayed the sailing of the Armada for a year by destroying its supply-ships, and the next year he played an important part in its defeat in the English Channel.

Drakensberg Mountains A range of mountains at the southern edge of the African plateau, stretching in a NE–SW direction for a distance of *c.*1,126 km (700 miles) through Lesotho and the South African regions of KwaZulu-Natal, Free

State, and Mpumalanga. The highest peak is Thabana Ntlenyana (3,482 m, 11,425 ft).

draught and pack animals Domesticated animals used to pull or carry heavy loads. Cattle and equine species are the commonest draught animals, but other animals such as camels, dogs, elephants, and reindeer are also used.

Dravidian ▶**1** A member of an ethnic group of southern India and Sri Lanka (including the Tamils and Kanarese). ▶**2** Any of the group of languages spoken by this people, including Tamil, Telugu, and Kanarese.

drawbridge A bridge that can slide back along a track behind one of the abutments or has a pivoted surface that can be raised at one end. It is usually of low clearance height over a waterway and is moved to allow the passage of a boat. Drawbridges were used over the moat in ancient fortifications to bar entry when raised.

Dreadnoughts A class of BATTLESHIP. They were originally designed by Britain in response to a perceived threat from the German naval development of TIRPITZ (1898), with the first ship – HMS *Dreadnought* – being launched in 1906. They revolutionized naval warfare. Powered by steam turbine engines, their speed of 21 knots and heavy fire power enabled them to fight outside the range of enemy torpedoes.

dream Mental activity during sleep, associated with rapid eye movemts (REM). The dreamer 'sees' images and symbols associated with thoughts and desires; frightening dreams are called nightmares. During about eight hours' sleep, a person dreams for up to two hours on average. The ancients, and some more modern people, regarded dreams as either prophesies of future events or providing insights into mental state. Examining dreams to reveal their hidden meaning is a technique sometimes used in psychoanalysis. See SLEEP.

Dream time See ALCHERA.

dredger A vessel used for deepening harbours and navigable rivers by removing part of the sea-bed or bottom of the river. The commonest form is the bucket dredger, in which a continuous chain of buckets operating through a central well is emptied into barges secured alongside. Where the bottom to be dredged consists of soft mud or silt, a suction dredger is often used; this draws up the dredged material through a suction pipe. Occasionally cutters are needed to scrape the bottom.

Dreiser, Theodore (Herman Albert) (1871–1945) US novelist. His first novel, *Sister Carrie* (1900), an account of a young working girl's rise to success, caused controversy for its frank treatment of the heroine's sexuality and ambition. His later works, such as *America is Worth Saving* (1941), express a growing faith in socialism that replaces the pessimism of his earlier writings.

Dresden A city in east Germany, the capital of the state of Saxony, on the River Elbe; pop. (1991) 485,130. Dresden china, with elaborate decoration and delicate coverings, was originally made at Dresden but from 1710 at nearby Meissen. The city has been rebuilt after being almost totally destroyed by Allied bombing in 1945.

Dreyfus, Alfred (1859–1935) French army officer, of Jewish descent. In 1894 he was falsely accused of providing military secrets to the Germans; his trial, imprisonment, and eventual rehabilitation in 1906 caused a major political crisis in France, polarizing deep-set anti-militarist and anti-Semitic trends in a society still coming to terms with defeat and revolution in 1870–71. Notable among his supporters was the novelist Émile Zola, whose open letter, *J'accuse*, published in 1898, accused the judges at the trial of having convicted Dreyfus at the behest of the War Office.

drift (in geology) See CONTINENTAL DRIFT.

drift-mining A MINING technique in which ore deposits are worked by means of downward-sloping tunnels driven from the surface. As drift-mining requires no vertical shafts, it is much cheaper than deep mining.

drill (vertebrate) See MANDRILL.

drill (invertebrate) A MOLLUSC related to whelks, which uses a special secretion from its foot, together with rasping teeth, to drill holes through oyster shells and so eat the soft inner tissues. The oyster drill, *Urosalpinx cinerea*, is a common pest in America, and was unintentionally introduced to parts of Europe, where it now severely affects oyster fisheries.

drilling rig An apparatus for well-sinking, used in particular in PETROLEUM exploration and recovery for drilling down into the earth or into the sea-bed in search of oil or gas. A modern rig can drill through rock to a depth of up to 8,000 m (26,000 feet). A tower (the derrick) supports hoisting equipment used to raise and lower drill bits and pipes. Most rigs use rotary drilling, in which a rotating drill bit on the end of sections of pipe bears down on the material of the well bottom. Offshore rigs are distinguished by the method of supporting the derrick and drilling equipment. Jack-up rigs actually stand on the sea-bed, whereas semi-submersibles float, and are anchored to the sea-bed by cables.

drinker moth See EGGAR MOTH.

Drogheda A port near the mouth of the River Boyne in Louth County, the Republic of Ireland; pop. (1991) 23,800. The Battle of the Boyne was fought near Drogheda in 1690.

Drogheda, Siege of See CROMWELL, OLIVER.

dromedary See CAMEL.

drone A continuous note of fixed pitch that acts as a permanent bass in some instruments. The best-known example is perhaps the BAGPIPE, which has one or more reed-pipes tuned to the tonic or the tonic and dominant of the KEY of the instrument. Drones are also characteristic of much Indian music and folk music.

drongo A member of a family of birds containing some 20 species that occur in Africa, India, south-east Asia, many of the Pacific islands, and Australia. Predominantly black, they are mostly thrush-sized, though one, the racket-tailed drongo, *Dicrurus paradiseus*, has two greatly elongated tail feathers, making it some 63 cm (25 inches) in overall length. They live chiefly in wooded country and feed mainly on insects.

Drosophila See FRUIT FLY.

drought Lack or insufficiency of rain for an extended period that causes a considerable hydrological inbalance. Drought occurs when evaporation and transpiration exceed precipitation of rain. When prolonged it causes damage to agriculture, depletion of ground and soil water, and limits water available for drinking, sanitation and industry. Streams and lakes dry up, and WATER-TABLES fall. Persistent periods of drought, such as occurred south of the Sahara in the 1970s and in central Australia in the early 1980s, lead to speculations about CLIMATIC CHANGE. Disturbance of global wind patterns is apparently responsible for monsoon failure in Asia and Africa, causing devastating series of droughts such as those which the Bible describes as affecting Egypt.

drug An organic or inorganic substance that alters or influences body function when administered. In medicine, drugs are used in the treatment of disease; they may be used to diagnose, cure, or prevent disease, or for symptom relief. Most drugs elicit a range of actions of which one or more may be therapeutic; the remaining actions are called side-effects. Originally drugs were extracted from plants, but now most are synthesized. The manufacture, preparation, and dispensing of them is called PHARMACEUTICS. The study of drugs is PHARMACOLOGY, which forms an important part of medical training, and includes the study of HORMONES, which may be used in medicines. See also DRUG ABUSE.

drug abuse The excessive or addictive use of drugs for non-medical purposes, usually in order to affect the user's mental state and perceptions. Most societies accept the use of some mild drugs: for example, alcohol, tannin and caffeine (in tea and coffee), and nicotine (in tobacco). However, the use of certain drugs that are considered particularly addictive or powerful is illegal in most countries. These include narcotics or sedatives (opium and its derivatives, such as morphine and heroin); stimulants (cocaine and amphetamines); and hallucinogens (LSD). Cannabis or marijuana is mainly a sedative, but it can be hallucinogenic. Prescription drugs such as tranquillizers, and ordinary household substances such as glues and solvents may also be abused. The major problem of habitual drug abuse is physical or psychological dependence. In the case of some drugs, such as the opiates, tolerance develops, and more and more of the substance must be taken in order to achieve the desired effect. In the worst cases, everything in the drug user's life is subordinated to the craving for the drug and the steps taken to satisfy that craving. The withdrawal symptoms, when the user ceases taking the drug, may be severe. Other dangers involve the use of non-sterile needles or syringes, which may cause infections or transmit viruses such as hepatitis B or AIDS. Drug abuse leads to related crimes, such as robbery, PROSTITUTION, and theft to support the habit, or violence while under the influence of drugs (see DRUG OFFENCES).

drug offences Offences connected with the possession, dealing, or smuggling of proscribed drugs, such as heroin, cocaine, and cannabis. The least serious offences relate to the possession of drugs; there are also crimes which may be drug-related, for instance theft, or violence committed under the influence of drugs, or in order to finance a drug habit. Heavy penalties tend to be reserved for drug-pushers (those who sell drugs and thus profit from the addiction of others) and drug-traffickers, who are usually part of the vast international network of organized crime which controls the cultivation and manufacture of illegal drugs, their importation, and their distribution. Moves to decriminalize cannabis, in order to remove it from the grips of criminal pushers, have not found widespread acceptance. Most addicts of harder drugs, it is recognized, begin their addiction by smoking cannabis. Decriminalization could therefore lead to a greater number of addicts.

Druid A member of the ruling caste of the Gallic CELTS. Knowledge of the Druids is derived chiefly from the hostile accounts of them in the Roman authors Julius CAESAR and TACITUS. Caesar reports that they exercised judicial and priestly functions, worshipped in groves (clearings in forests), and cut mistletoe from the oak tree (sacred to them) with a golden sickle. The religion was stamped out by the Romans, lest it should become a force for resistance to Roman rule.

drum A musical instrument with a membrane, traditionally of animal skin but now frequently plastic, which is struck, or through which passes a stick or cord which is rubbed. Various other instruments, although without membrane, are also called 'drum', for example, slit drum. See also FRAME DRUM; KETTLEDRUM.

drum chime A musical instrument, usually a set of KETTLEDRUMS, each tuned to a different pitch, and usually played as though they formed one instrument. Drum chimes are found in many areas, the best known being Ethiopia and Burma (now Myanmar).

drumlin A small, ice-moulded hill whose shape resembles half a hard-boiled egg, cut lengthways. Drumlins almost always occur in groups in valleys or lowlands, producing what has been called 'basket-of-eggs topography'. Produced by the pressure of moving ice, they are good evidence for the past existence of glaciers or ice-sheets in any area.

drupe A FRUIT with a single seed in a hard case (endocarp), usually enveloped in a juicy edible layer (mesocarp) and coated with a brightly coloured skin, as in the plum (*Prunus domestica*). However, the mesocarp may be fibrous, as in the coconut (*Cocos nucifera*), where it is the coir, or coconut matting, of commerce, or it may be woody, as in the walnut (*Fuglans* species). Aggregates of drupes include such 'berries' as blackberries, raspberries, and loganberries.

Drury Lane, Theatre Royal London's most famous theatre. The first theatre on the site opened in 1663, the second – notable for David Garrick's association with it – in 1674, and the third in 1794. The present theatre, dating from 1812, was not particularly successful until the 1880s, when it became famous for its melodramas and spectacles. Since the 1920s it has staged numerous musicals.

Druse (or **Druze**) A member of a political and religious sect of Muslim origin, concentrated in Lebanon, with smaller groups in Syria and Israel. The sect broke away from Ismaili Shiite Islam in the 11th century over a disagreement about the succession to the imamate (leadership), a position in which spiritual and political leadership were and are indissolubly linked. The Druses followed the seventh caliph of the Fatimid dynasty, al-Hakim b'illah (996–1021), who is claimed to have disappeared and whose return is expected. They regard al-Hakim as a deity, and thus are considered heretics by the Muslim community at large.

Dryads In Greek mythology, nymphs associated with trees or forests.

dry-cleaning A process introduced in Paris in the 1850s in which non-aqueous SOLVENTS are used to remove greasy stains from clothing. These solvents dissolve the grease and, because they boil at low temperatures, they can then be easily reclaimed by evaporation followed by condensation. The solvent most commonly used is perchlorethene, but as this is toxic, it is being replaced by a CHLOROFLUOROCARBON (CFC). However, there is now some concern about this as CFCs are known to cause OZONE depletion.

Dryden, John (1631–1700) English poet, dramatist, and critic. One of the principal exponents of Augustan literature in England, he is remembered for his codification of verse metres and the establishment of the heroic couplet as the favoured verse form. He wrote many plays, including comedies (*Marriage à la mode*; 1673), tragedies such as the blank verse drama *All for Love* (1678), and satires, of which the best known is *Absalom and Achitophel* (1681). His prose writing style is often considered the model for modern English literature. Many of his critical works appear as prefaces to his plays; they include *Of Dramatic Poesie* (1668).

dry dock A watertight basin with one end open to the sea, used for shipbuilding and for the examination, repair, and cleaning of ships' hulls. The open end of the dock can be closed with a gate or caisson. With the caisson open the dock is flooded, and a ship can enter. The caisson is then closed, and the water in the dock is pumped out, exposing the hull for service or repair. Smaller vessels can be hauled up into the dock by means of slips or 'marine railways'.

dry ice CARBON DIOXIDE which has been solidified by cooling it below −78°C (−108°F). At atmospheric pressure it sublimes into carbon dioxide gas on warming, with no intervening liquid state. The liquid state can exist only at pressure above 50 atmospheres. If warm air is blown over dry ice, then a dense white cloud forms, which settles at floor level; this effect is sometimes used in the theatre. Dry ice is also used as a coolant.

drying oil An oil that, when spread into a thin film in the presence of air, dries to form a dry, tough, durable, elastic skin. Naturally occurring drying oils are hempseed oil and linseed oil (from flax), used to preserve wood and to coat canvas to make oilcloth, and to make putty and LINOLEUM. These and similar synthetic oils are used in PAINTS, VARNISHES, and printing INKS.

drypoint A method of ENGRAVING on copper, dating from the 15th century, in which the design is scratched directly into the plate with a sharp tool that is held like a pen. A distinctive feature of drypoint is the 'burr' or rough, upturned edge of the furrow made by the cutting tool. This produces a soft, rich quality in the print, but because it soon wears down only a limited number of good impressions can be taken.

dry rot fungus A fungus that causes dry rot in the timber of buildings. It can spread from infected timber into mortar, so is able to cross walls. Unlike wet rot (a form of chemical decomposition of wet wood), it can attack relatively dry wood if some moisture is present. It can be prevented by keeping structural timber dry and well ventilated.

Drysdale, Sir Russell (1912–81) British-born Australian painter. His subject-matter is the harsh life of the Australian bush, as in *The Rabbiter and Family* (1938); he also deals with the plight of Aboriginals in contact with white settlement, as in *Mullaloonah Tank* (1953).

dry valley A linear depression which does not contain a surface river channel. Although temporary streams may flow after heavy rain or as snow melts, no definite channels are cut. Thus dry valleys differ from WADIS and ARROYOS, whose watercourses are obvious. Most dry valleys occur on highly permeable rocks, especially limestone, chalk, and lava, and were cut by rivers either when the water-table was higher or when PERMAFROST made the surface less permeable.

dualism The general philosophical claim that the world is composed of two ultimate different kinds of substance, typically mind and matter. MONISM, by contrast, holds that the world is composed of but one kind of substance. Dualism in all of its forms leads to the notorious problem of interaction: namely, of understanding how substances of different kinds can affect one another. In theology, dualism refers to the perception of the world as motivated by opposing principles of good and evil, as in, for example, PARSI and some Christian sects' beliefs.

Dual Monarchy See AUSTRIA-HUNGARY.

Dubai ▶**1** One of the seven member-states of the United Arab Emirates; area 3,900 sq km (1,506 sq miles); pop. (1995) 674,100. Since the discovery of oil in 1966 major port facilities have developed at Port Rashid and Mina Jebel Ali. ▶**2** Its capital, a port on the Persian Gulf; pop. (1980) 265,700.

du Barry, Marie Jeanne, Comtesse (1743–93) Favourite of LOUIS XV of France. She was a great beauty who in 1769 became the king's mistress and influenced him until his death in 1774. CHOISEUL criticized her and she may have helped to bring about his dismissal. During the FRENCH REVOLUTION she was arrested by the Revolutionary Tribunal and guillotined.

Dubček, Alexander (1921–92) Czechoslovak statesman, First Secretary of the Czechoslovak Communist Party 1968–69. He is generally regarded as the driving force behind the attempted democratization of Czech political life in 1968 that became known as the Prague Spring. At this time he and other liberal members of the government made plans for a new constitution as well as legislation for civil liberties and began to pursue a foreign policy independent of the Soviet Union. In response, Warsaw Pact forces invaded Czechoslovakia in August 1968 and Dubček was removed from office the following year. After the abandonment of Communism at the end of 1989 he returned to public life and was elected speaker of the Federal Assembly in a new democratic regime.

Dublin (Gaelic **Baile Átha Cliath**) The capital of the Republic of Ireland, situated on the Irish Sea at the mouth of the River Liffey; pop. (1991) 477,700. It is linked by ferry to Holyhead and Liverpool. Built on the site of a Viking settlement, Dublin prospered during the late 18th century when its parliament was temporarily independent of England. The University of Dublin (Trinity College) was founded in 1591 and its library contains the famous *Book of Kells*. The National University (Catholic) was founded in 1909. Dublin has seen much bloodshed in its attempts to secure Irish independence. Today it is the centre of Irish commerce and industry, as well as political and cultural life. It has a major airport and ferry terminal and its industries include textiles, brewing and distilling, electrical products, printing, glass, cigarettes, food processing, and tourism.

Dublin Bay prawn (or **Norway lobster**) A CRUSTACEAN related to true LOBSTERS but with a slender body up to 20 cm (8 inches) long, and coloured pink or red rather than the blue-grey of a real lobster. They live along sandy coastlines, usually in deeper water, staying clear of rock-pools. They are caught for food in Europe, where they are known as **scampi**.

Du Bois, William Edward Burghardt (1868–1963) US black CIVIL RIGHTS leader and author. Seeking a self-sufficient black society, he was a co-founder of the National Association for the Advancement of Colored People (NAACP, 1909). His enrolment in the Communist Party earned him the Lenin Peace Prize (1961); this followed federal indictment (and acquittal) during the years of the MCCARTHY witch-hunts.

Dubrovnik (Italian **Ragusa**) An historic Adriatic resort and seaport on the Dalmatian coast of Croatia; pop. (1991) 49,730. Founded in the 7th century, Dubrovnik became an important trading republic in the Middle Ages, linking the Latin and Slavic worlds. As such, it was a major centre of Serbo-Croatian culture. During the 20th century it developed as a tourist resort but much of its medieval architecture was severely damaged when the city was besieged by Serbs in 1991.

Dubuffet, Jean (1901–85) French artist, one of the chief figures in the modern movement to reject traditional techniques and to place untrained spontaneity above professional skill. His pictures often incorporate materials such as sand and plaster, and he also produced sculptural works made from junk materials. He made a large collection of what he called 'Art Brut' (raw art) – the products of children, illiterates, the insane. He initially caused outrage, but has since been influential as a forerunner of pop art.

Duccio (di Buoninsegna) (*c*.1255–*c*.1319) Italian painter. The founder of the Sienese school of painting, he built on elements of the Byzantine tradition. The only fully documented surviving work by him is the *Maestà* for the high altar of Siena cathedral (completed 1311). His work conveys emotion through facial expression, sequence of colour, and arrangement of scenery, while keeping the composition within Byzantine conventions.

Duchamp, Marcel (1887–1968) French-born US painter, sculptor, and art theorist. His main influence on 20th-century art has been in the area of anti-art movements: the origins of conceptual art can be traced to him, he was a leader of the Dada movement, and in 1913 he originated the ready-made art form, whereby the artist selects a mass-produced article such as a bottle rack and displays it as a work of art.

duck A water bird of the Anatidae family. The family includes swans and geese, but ducks are smaller, with shorter necks, and beat their wings faster in flight. They are much more aquatic than geese and the sexes differ in appearance. Except when moulting (in eclipse), the drakes (males) are generally more brightly coloured than the females. There are over 110 species, distributed worldwide. Some, like the sea-ducks, sawbills (mergansers), and pochards, dive for their food. Others, like the mallard, *Anas platyrhynchos*, the teal, *Anas crecca*, and the widgeon, *Anas penelope*, are surface-feeders that dabble or up-end. Ducks are adapted to an aquatic way of life in having webbed feet and also a water-repellent plumage that gives them added buoyancy.

duck-billed platypus See PLATYPUS.

duckweed One of some 15 species of small floating or submerged perennial plants in the genus *Lemna*, which forms part of the worldwide family Lemnaceae. Most species, such as the common duckweed, *L. minor*, occur in all parts of the world with the exception of the polar regions and parts of the tropics. They often form a green carpet, covering the surface of still or slow-moving water. The closely related genus of *Wolffia* includes the smallest known species of flowering plant. All duckweeds have tiny male and female flowers, which are separate but usually on the same plant.

duct flute A musical instrument, a flute in which the air is guided to the voicing edge by a duct. Most frequently the duct is internal, a block with a narrow windway between the block and the wall of the flute, as with organ pipes, recorders, and flageolets; the duct is sometimes at the back.

Dudley An industrial borough in the West Midlands of England, near Birmingham; pop. (1981) 187,000. Its industries include steel and engineering.

Dudley, Robert, Earl of Leicester (*c*.1532–88) English nobleman. He became a favourite of Elizabeth I soon after her accession in 1558. Following the mysterious death of Dudley's wife, Amy Robsart, in 1560 it was rumoured that he would marry the queen; this did not happen, although Dudley remained in favour with Elizabeth throughout his life and in 1564 was created Earl of Leicester. He was later given the command of the military campaign in the Netherlands (1585–87) and of the forces preparing to resist the Armada (1588).

Dufay, Guillaume (*c*.1400–74) French composer. He was a noted teacher and made a significant contribution to the development of Renaissance polyphony. Of his works, almost 200 are extant; they include much church music (his own Requiem Mass, now lost, was sung at his funeral), motets, and eighty-four songs.

Dufay, Louis (*fl*. 1900–10) French pioneer of colour PHOTOGRAPHY. He and the LUMIÈRE brothers almost simultaneously introduced additive colour-photographic processes – so called because three differently coloured images were added to each other.

Du Fu See TU FU.

Dufy, Raoul (1877–1953) French painter and textile designer. In his early work he was much influenced by fauvism but he later developed his own characteristic style using bright colours, with calligraphic outlines sketched on brilliant background washes. His chief subjects were the racecourse, boating scenes, and society life on the French Riviera and in London.

dugong (or **sea cow**) An entirely aquatic species of mammal of the order Sirenia, *Dugong dugon*, living in warm coastal waters in shallow bays and estuaries from the Red Sea throughout the Indian and Pacific oceans. The dugong is highly adapted for life in water, the streamlined body having a layer of thick blubber; it has poor sight but good hearing. The fore-limbs are large, and the digits joined to form a paddle. There are no hind-limbs and the terminal tail, like that of the whale, is horizontal. It can remain submerged for up to ten minutes, its nostrils closed by valves, while feeding on green seaweed and other vegetation. A single pup is born in the water, and the mother carries it in her flippers.

duiker A small antelope found in the forest and bush country of Africa south of the Sahara Desert. Of the 17 species, 16 are in the genus *Cephalophus*, and one, the common duiker, *Sylvicapra grimmia*, makes up its own genus. All have short legs and stand about 60 cm (2 feet) at the shoulder. In most species, both sexes have horns, which are short and spiked with a tuft of hair between them. In the common duiker only the male has horns. The zebra duiker, *Cephalophus zebra*, has a striking coat of orange-red with tiger-like black stripes on the back. Females give birth to one or two young, generally in May.

Duisburg The largest inland port in Europe, situated at the junction of the Rhine and Ruhr rivers in North Rhine-Westphalia, north-west Germany; pop. (1991) 537,440. Engineering, brewing, oil-refining, and the manufacture of steel, copper, and plastics are all important industries.

Dukas, Paul (1865–1935) French composer. He began composing when he was about 13 and he wrote his first important work, the overture *Polyeucte*, in 1892. There followed, most notably, the piano sonata (1901), his symphony in C (1895–96), a symphonic scherzo *L'Apprenti sorcier* (1897), an opera *Ariane et Barbe-Bleue* (1906), and a ballet *La Péri* (1912).

Dukeries, the A district including part of Sherwood Forest in north-west Nottinghamshire, England, comprising the parks of the former ducal seats of Welbeck, Clumber, Rufford, and Thoresby.

dulcimer A musical instrument with a flat, usually trapezium-shaped, soundbox and numerous wire strings struck with a pair of light hammers. It seems to have derived from the PSALTERY in Europe in the late 15th century, and is still a popular folk instrument, especially in Central Europe.

Dulles, John Foster (1888–1959) US Republican statesman and international lawyer. He was adviser to the US delegation at the conference which set up the United Nations in 1945 and negotiated the Peace Treaty with Japan in 1951. As Secretary of State under President Eisenhower (1953–59) he strove to improve the position of the USA in the Cold War, to which end he strengthened NATO and urged that the USA should stockpile nuclear arms as a deterrent against Soviet aggression.

Dulwich A district of Southwark in south London, England, with a college founded in 1619 by the actor Edward Alleyn. Its famous art gallery was the first to be opened to the public in Britain.

Duma An elective legislative assembly introduced in Russia by NICHOLAS II in 1906 in response to popular unrest. Boycotted by the socialist parties, its efforts to introduce taxation and agrarian reforms were nullified by the reactionary groups at court which persuaded the emperor to dissolve three successive Dumas. The fourth Duma (1912–17) refused an imperial decree in February 1917 ordering its dissolution and established a provisional government. Three days later it accepted the emperor's abdication, but soon began to disintegrate.

Dumas, Alexandre (or **Dumas père**) (1802–70) French novelist and dramatist. A pioneer of the romantic theatre in France, he first achieved fame with his historical dramas, such as *Henry III et sa cour* (1829). His reputation now rests on his historical adventure novels, including *The Three Musketeers* (1844–45) and *The Count of Monte Cristo* (1844–45).

Dumas, Alexandre (or **Dumas fils**) (1824–95), French dramatist. He became one of the most successful dramatists of the Second Empire. His play *La Dame aux camélias* (1852), is the story of a courtesan who voluntarily renounces her love for a respectable young man and then dies of consumption. It was based on Dumas's own novel (1848) and inspired Verdi's opera *La Traviata* (1853).

Dumas, Jean Baptiste André (1800–84) French chemist who established a method for determining vapour density by weighing a known volume of the vapour. He also developed a technique for estimating the nitrogen content of an organic compound and derived a correct composition for chloroform (trichloromethane).

Du Maurier, Dame Daphne (1907–89) British novelist, granddaughter of George du Maurier. Many of her popular novels and period romances are set in the West Country of England, where she spent most of her life. Her works include *Jamaica Inn* (1936) and *Rebecca* (1938).

Du Maurier, George (Louis Palmella Busson) (1834–96) French-born cartoonist, illustrator, and novelist. He is chiefly remembered for his novel *Trilby* (1894), which included the character Svengali and gave rise to the word *Svengali* for a person who has a hypnotic influence.

Dumbarton Oaks Conference (1944) An international conference at Dumbarton Oaks in Washington, DC, when representatives of the USA, Britain, the Soviet Union, and China drew up proposals that served as the basis for the charter of the UNITED NATIONS formulated at the San Francisco Conference the following year. Attention at Dumbarton Oaks was focused on measures to secure 'the maintenance of international peace and security', and one of its main achievements was the planning of a UNITED NATIONS Security Council.

Dumfries A market town in south-west Scotland, on the River Nith, capital of Dumfries and Galloway Region; pop. (1991) 32,130. The poet Robert Burns died here in 1795.

Dumfries and Galloway A local government region in south-west Scotland, which in 1996 became a unitary authority; area 6,396 sq km (2,470 sq miles); pop. (1991) 147,000; capital, Dumfries.

Dumfriesshire A former county (until 1975) in the Scottish Borders, now part of Dumfries and Galloway.

dumping The sale of a good in a foreign MARKET at a price below that which is economically sustainable in the long run. Sellers will thus normally be making a loss on the dumped items. They are prepared to do this in the short term to dispose of surpluses without driving down prices at home, for instance when they have incorrectly forecast the market and have produced too many goods. It may also be used to establish MONOPOLY power in the foreign market and prevent competitors from developing or entering ('predatory dumping').

Dunant, Jean-Henri See RED CROSS.

Dunbar, Battle of (3 September 1650) A battle near the port of Dunbar in Scotland, in which Oliver CROMWELL's force of 14,000 men won a victory over 27,000 Scots, and enormous numbers were taken prisoner together with all the Scottish guns. Cromwell's victory destroyed the STUART cause in Scotland for a decade.

Dunbar, William (*c.*1456–*c.*1513) Scottish poet. His first major poem, 'The Thrissill and the Rois' ('The Thistle and the Rose', 1503), is a political allegory on the marriage of James IV to Margaret Tudor (the daughter of Henry VII) and the first of his many satires. Dunbar is also remembered for his elegies, such as 'Lament for the Makaris' (on Chaucer and other fellow poets).

Dunbartonshire A former county on the Clyde estuary of west-central Scotland. In 1975 it became part of Strathclyde region and in 1996 the unitary authorities East Dunbartonshire and West Dunbartonshire.

Duncan I (*c.*1010–40) King of Scotland 1034–40. He was ruler of Strathclyde which was added to the Scottish kingdom inherited from his grandfather Malcolm II. His accession was unpopular with the northern tribes and twice he was defeated by the Earl of Orkney before being killed in battle by the Earl of Moray, MACBETH.

Duncan II (*c.*1060–94) King of Scotland 1094. He gained the throne through the support of William II of England, who provided the army with which Duncan defeated his uncle and rival Donald Bane.

However, Duncan's English alliance was resented and he was murdered at his uncle's instigation.

Duncan, Isadora (1878–1927) US dancer and teacher. A pioneer of modern dance, she developed a form of 'free' barefoot dancing based on instinctive movements and inspired by classical Greek art. She was much admired in Europe, where she settled and founded several schools of dance; her informal style deeply influenced Diaghilev. She died through being accidentally strangled when her scarf became entangled in the wheels of a car.

Dundalk A port, the county town of Louth in the Republic of Ireland, on Dundalk Bay at the mouth of the Castletown River; pop. (1991) 25,800.

Dundee A city in east-central Scotland on the Tay estuary, the administrative centre of Tayside region from 1975 to 1996; pop. (1991) 165,500. A royal burgh since the 12th century, Dundee developed from a whaling port during the 19th century with the expansion of the textile and jute industries. Its university, which was founded in 1881 as University College, was incorporated with St Andrews until 1967. Dundee's industries include engineering, textiles, electrical products, servicing the North Sea oil industry, and food processing. The Tay road bridge, one of the longest in Europe, was completed in 1966.

dune A heaped accumulation of sand-size particles, shaped by the wind. Although the overwhelming majority of dunes are made of sand, they can also form from dry soil, gypsum, or hard, dry snow; but there must be plenty of dry material of the right dimensions, strong winds, and a fairly flat surface with slight protrusions such as small rocks or plants round which the moving particles can collect. While these conditions obviously occur in many of the world's hot deserts, circumstances are often favourable also in other places, such as along coasts, where small dune fields and isolated dunes frequently form.

Dunedin A city and port of South Island, New Zealand, at the head of Otago Harbour; pop. (1991) 109,500. It was founded in 1848 by Scottish settlers; its name, which reflects the Gaelic word (Duneideann) for Edinburgh, was suggested by the Edinburgh publisher William Chambers. Stimulated by discoveries of gold nearby in the 1860s, Dunedin became the first industrialized city in New Zealand.

Dunfermline An industrial city in Fife, central Scotland, near the Firth of Forth; pop. (1991) 55,000. A number of Scottish monarchs, including Queen Margaret and Robert the Bruce, are buried in its Benedictine abbey. The philanthropist Andrew Carnegie was born in the city in 1835, and it is the headquarters of all the Carnegie trusts. In the 19th century Dunfermline developed as a textile town.

Dungarvan The administrative centre of County Waterford in the Republic of Ireland; pop. (1991) 6,920. Situated on Dungarvan Harbour, it lies to the south of the Comeragh and Monavullagh mountains on the River Colligan. The chief landmarks are a 13th-century Augustinian priory and Dungarvan Castle which was originally built in 1185 by King John.

dung beetle A beetle whose larvae feed on dung, especially that of herbivorous animals. Dung beetles include some 3,200 species of scarab and beetles of the subfamily Aphodiinae, in addition to DOR BEETLES. In many cases they are large and black, the males having horns. The adults dig chambers beneath the dung, in which they lay their eggs, or simply place eggs on the dung. Some species show maternal care for the young, and all serve a useful function in ecosystems by recycling dung.

Dunkirk (French **Dunkerque**) a French channel port, the third-largest in France, situated in the Nord department of Nord-Pas-de-Calais region; pop. (1990) 71,070. It was the scene of the evacuation of the British Expeditionary Force in 1940 after the fall of France. 225,000 British troops, as well as 110,000 of their French allies, were evacuated from Dunkirk between 27 May and 2 June by warships, civilian ships, and a host of small boats, under constant air attack. There are ferry links with English channel ports.

Dun Laoghaire A resort town on the south shore of Dublin Bay in the Republic of Ireland; pop. (1991) 185,400 (Dun Laoghaire-Rathdown). In 1821 its name was changed to Kingstown to commemorate a visit by King George IV, but in 1920 it reverted to Dun Laoghaire. It has a notable yachting harbour and is linked by ferry to Holyhead.

dunlin A small wading bird, *Calidris alpina*, resembling a sandpiper, chestnut and black in summer but grey and white in winter. Dunlins can often be seen on mudflats with other waders, feeding in large flocks. In flight, compact parties twist and wheel in the air with an amazing unity of purpose. Several subspecies occur throughout northern temperate zones.

Dunlop, John Boyd (1840–1921) Scottish inventor. He worked in Edinburgh and Belfast as a veterinary surgeon but is best known for having invented the first successful pneumatic bicycle tyre (1888), which was manufactured by the company named after him. Though his invention was crucial to the development of the motor car, Dunlop himself received little profit from it.

Dunmow A market town in Essex, south-east England. **Great Dunmow** on the River Chelmer near Chelmsford is the scene of the Dunmow Flitch (a side of bacon) awarded to happily married couples since the 13th century. **Little Dunmow** lies to the east of Great Dunmow.

Dunne, John William (1875–1949) British philosopher. His work is especially concerned with time and includes *An Experiment with Time* (1927) and *The Serial Universe* (1934), both of which influenced the plays of J. B. Priestley.

dunnock See HEDGE SPARROW.

Duns Scotus, John (known as 'the Subtle Doctor') (*c.*1265–1308) Scottish theologian and scholar. In opposition to the teaching of St Thomas Aquinas he argued that faith was a matter of will, not dependent on logical proofs. He was also the first major theologian to defend the theory of the Immaculate Conception. His system was accepted by the Franciscans as their doctrinal basis and exercised a profound influence in the Middle Ages. In the Renaissance his followers were ridiculed for their conservatism and abused as enemies of learning, which gave rise to the word *dunce*.

Dunstable A residential and industrial town in Bedfordshire, southern England, at the junction of the ancient routeways of Watling Street and Icknield Way; pop. (1991) 49,666. Dunstable has automobile and printing industries. Nearby to the south is Whipsnade Park Zoo and Dunstable Downs, much used for gliding.

Dunstable, John (*c.*1390–1453) English composer. He was a significant early exponent of counterpoint; his works include secular songs, masses, and motets.

Dunstan, St (*c.*909–88) Anglo-Saxon prelate. During

his tenure as abbot at Glastonbury the monastery became a centre of religious teaching. He was appointed Archbishop of Canterbury by King Edgar in 960, and together they carried through a reform of Church and state. He introduced the strict Benedictine rule into England and succeeded in restoring monastic life; a zealous supporter of education, he also achieved fame as a musician, illuminator, and metalworker. Feast day, 19 May.

duodenal ulcer See ULCER.

duodenum See STOMACH.

du Pré, Jacqueline (1945–87) British cellist, who made her solo début in London at the age of 16. She became famous for her interpretation of the Elgar cello concerto. When her performing career was halted in 1972 by multiple sclerosis, she gave a notable series of master classes. She was married to the pianist and conductor Daniel Barenboim (1942–).

Duralumin See ALLOY.

Duras, Marguerite (pseudonym of Marguerite Donnadieu) (1914–96) French novelist, film director, and dramatist. She established her reputation as a novelist in the 1950s and won the Prix Goncourt with *L'Amant* (1984). As well as directing a number of her own films she wrote screenplays, for example *Hiroshima mon amour* (1959).

Durban A seaport and resort in the Republic of South Africa, on the coast of KwaZulu-Natal province; pop. (1991) 1,137,380. Formerly known as Port Natal, it was renamed in 1835 after Sir Benjamin d'Urban, then governor of Cape Colony. It is South Africa's third-largest city and capital (since 1994) of the province of KwaZulu-Natal. Its heavy industries include ship repairing, oil refining, vehicle assembly, fishing, and chemicals; it also has a wide variety of light industries.

Durbar (Persian and Urdu, 'court') Originally a public audience given by a Mogul emperor of India. Under British rule it was a ceremonial gathering usually connected with some royal event. The most magnificent was George V's Durbar held in Delhi in 1911.

Dürer, Albrecht (1471–1528) German painter and engraver. He is generally regarded as the leading German artist of the Renaissance. He was responsible for developing techniques and raising standards of craftsmanship in his favoured media of woodcut and copper engraving; examples of his work include a series of 92 woodcut blocks in honour of the Emperor Maximilian. He also painted detailed watercolour studies of plants and animals.

Durey, Louis, See SIX, LES.

Durgā See DEVI.

Durham A county of north-east England between the Pennines and the North Sea; area 2,434 sq km (940 sq miles); pop. (1991) 589,800; capital, Durham.

Durham City and county town of Durham, north-east England, on the River Wear; pop. (1991) 85,800. Founded by monks in the 10th century, the Norman cathedral was built at the end of the 11th century and contains the remains of the Venerable Bede (died 735). Durham has a university founded in 1832 and the Gulbenkian Museum of Oriental Art.

Durham, John George Lambton, Earl of (1792–1840) British Whig statesman. A man of strong liberal views, he was Lord Privy Seal in the administration of his father-in-law, Lord Grey, and helped draft the Reform Bill of 1832. In 1838 he was appointed Governor-General of Canada and submitted the influential *Report on the Affairs of British North America*, which advocated the union of Canada.

durian The fruit of a large tree, *Durio zibenthinus*, which is cultivated in Malaysia, Thailand, and Indonesia, and flourishes in the Asian rain forests. It belongs to the same family as the BAOBAB. The large yellowish fruits up to 25 cm (10 inches) in diameter are coarsely spiny with a creamy inner pulp. The smell of the durian has been described as resembling bad drains with a touch of garlic, but some people find the sweet-fleshed fruit delicious. The locals build shelters in the trees in order to collect the ripe fruits the moment they drop. This is partly because the flesh deteriorates rapidly but also because the fruit is peculiarly attractive to wild animals such as monkeys and elephants.

duricrust A very hard layer in the ground which contains high concentrations of iron, aluminium, magnesium, calcium carbonate, or silica. It is formed at the surface in areas where wet and dry seasons alternate, especially in the tropics and subtropics.

Durkheim, Émile (1858–1917) French sociologist. Now regarded as one of the founders of modern sociology, he wrote about the influence of social structures on the behaviour of individuals (*The Division of Labour in Society*, 1893), formalized a methodology for sociological investigation, and examined the social causes of suicide (*Suicide*, 1897).

durmast oak See OAK.

Durrell, Gerald (Malcolm) (1925–95) British zoologist and writer. He acquired an interest in animals as a child in Corfu. From 1947 he organized a number of animal-collecting expeditions, which resulted in a popular series of broadcasts and books, including the autobiographical *My Family and Other Animals* (1956). Durrell became increasingly concerned with conservation and captive breeding, and in 1958 he founded a zoo in Jersey, Channel Islands, which later became the Jersey Wildlife Preservation Trust. He was the younger brother of the novelist Lawrence Durrell.

Durrell, Lawrence (George) (1912–90) British novelist, poet, and travel writer. He spent his childhood in India and his adolescence in Corfu, moving to France in the late 1950s. He first achieved fame with the *Alexandria Quartet* (1957–60), a series of novels set in Alexandria before World War II and written in an ornate, poetic style. He published several collections of poetry and a number of travel books, including *Bitter Lemons* (1957), about Cyprus. He was the elder brother of the zoologist and writer Gerald Durrell.

Dürrenmatt, Friedrich (1921–91) Swiss dramatist and author of detective stories with an ironic twist. Fascinated by the absurd and the grotesque, Dürrenmatt introduces into his black comedies *The Visit* (1956) and *The Physicists* (1962) humorous dialogue and situation before allowing a chilling awareness to dawn that the moral issues raised are no laughing matter.

Duse, Eleonora (1858–1924) Italian actress. She championed the plays of her lover, Gabriele D'Annunzio, acting in his *La città morta* and *La Gioconda* (both 1898). She refused to use stage make-up, preferring not to disguise her mobile, expressive features, and was at her best in strong emotional roles.

Dushanbe The capital of Tajikistan in Central Asia; pop. (1990) 602,000. The city was known as Stalinabad from 1929 to 1961. It is an industrial city with textiles, engineering, and food processing.

Düsseldorf An industrial, commercial, and cultural city, capital of the state of North Rhine-Westphalia in north-west Germany, at the junction of the Rhine and Düssel rivers; pop. (1991) 577,560. It has theatres, museums, art galleries, a university, and an avant-garde film industry. The poet Heinrich Heine was born here in 1797. Its industries include engineering, chemicals, and textiles.

dust bowl An arid or unproductive dry region. The term is applied specifically to an area in the prairie states of the USA that was subject to dust storms and drought in the 1930s when the land was returned to grazing after being cultivated since World War I, and the hooves of animals pulverized the unprotected soil. Increased rainfall, regrassing, and erosion-preventing measures such as contour ploughing have since reduced the area.

Dutch Relating to or associated with the Netherlands, its people, or its language, which belongs to the Germanic language group and is mostly related to German and English. Dutch is spoken by the 13 million inhabitants of the Netherlands and is also the official language of Surinam in South America and the Netherlands Antilles in the Caribbean. The same language is also spoken in parts of Belgium where it is called Flemish. An offshoot of Dutch is Afrikaans which was taken to Africa by Dutch settlers in the 17th century.

Dutch East India Company A CHARTERED COMPANY established (1602) under the aegis of Prince Maurice of Nassau to coordinate the activities of companies competing for trade in the East Indies and to act as an arm of the Dutch state in its struggle against Spain. It was involved in attacks on the Portuguese (then part of the SPANISH EMPIRE), and warfare with native rulers, and created a virtual monopoly in trade in fine spices (for example cloves, nutmeg, and mace) grown under its supervision in the MOLUCCAS and the Banda Islands. In 1619 it made Batavia its headquarters. It ousted the Portuguese from Ceylon, set up trading posts in India, Persia, and Nagasaki, and made the Cape of Good Hope a base for Dutch ships *en route* to and from the East. In 1799 it was liquidated, its debts, possessions, and responsibilities being taken over by the Dutch state.

Dutch East Indies The former name (until 1949) of INDONESIA under Dutch colonial rule.

Dutch empire The overseas territories of the United Provinces of the Netherlands. Dutch wealth rested on the fishing and shipping industries, assisted by Holland's position on the chief European trade routes. Amsterdam became the principal warehouse and trading centre for all Europe. Modern banking methods developed from Amsterdam's exchange bank (1609). Overseas trade with Asia, America, and Africa grew steadily even during war. Spain and Portugal's attempt to exclude the Dutch from the 'New World' prompted them to found the DUTCH EAST INDIA COMPANY (1602). Growing rivalry with Britain led to loss of maritime supremacy and of all Dutch colonies except in south-east Asia.

Dutch Guiana The former name of SURINAM.

Dutchman's pipe A species of woody, deciduous climbing plant, native to the eastern USA. It belongs to the family Aristolochiaceae and, along with some 500 other species, forms the genus *Aristolochia*. Although most species are climbers, some plants in this genus are herbaceous. Relatives of the Dutchman's pipe occur throughout temperate and tropical Eurasia and America. The Dutchman's pipe itself, *A. macrophylla*, has heart-shaped leaves, and grows to a height of 9 m (30 feet). Its yellowish-green, tubular, inflated flowers are bent into a pipe shape (hence the common name), and they are fly-pollinated.

Duvalier, François (known as 'Papa Doc') (1907–71) Haitian statesman, President 1957–71. His regime was noted for being authoritarian and oppressive; many of his opponents were either assassinated or forced into exile by his security force, known as the Tontons Macoutes. He proclaimed himself President for life in 1964 and was succeeded on his death by his son **Jean-Claude Duvalier** (known as 'Baby Doc', 1951–); the Duvalier regime ended in 1986 when a mass uprising forced Jean-Claude to flee the country.

Du Vigneaud, Vincent (1901–78) US biochemist. He specialized in the study of vitamins and hormones that contain sulphur, beginning with insulin. He went on to study the function of methionine, to isolate and determine the structure of biotin, and to contribute to the synthesis of penicillin G. For isolating and synthesizing the pituitary hormones oxytocin and vasopressin, Du Vigneaud was awarded the Nobel Prize for chemistry in 1955.

Dvořák, Antonín (1841–1904) Czech composer. Living at a time of strong national consciousness, he combined ethnic folk elements with the Viennese musical tradition from Haydn to Brahms. He is probably best known for his ninth symphony ('From the New World', 1892–95), which he wrote while working in the USA as director of the New York Conservatoire; it contains motifs from negro spirituals as well as Bohemian melodies. Dvořák also wrote chamber music, operas, and songs.

dwarfism Abnormally short stature. The most common cause is achondroplasia (an inherited disease in which the bones of the arms and legs fail to grow). Achondroplastic dwarfs have normal head, body, and intelligence but very short limbs. Pituitary dwarfs have a deficiency of growth hormone due to a defect in the pituitary gland. Dwarfism is also associated with thyroid deficiency (cretinism), chronic diseases such as rickets, intestinal malabsorption, and shortage of food.

dwarf star A normal star on the main sequence in the HERTZSPRUNG–RUSSELL DIAGRAM. More than 90 per cent of the stars are found in this stage of STELLAR EVOLUTION, in which they obtain their energy by the nuclear FUSION of hydrogen to helium in their cores. The Sun is a fairly typical dwarf star. However, most dwarfs are smaller and cooler than the Sun, and of lower luminosity.

DX coding A system for automatically setting the film speed on a camera. A series of electrically conducting patches on the film cartridge are 'read' by an interface unit in the camera to provide a digital electrical input. This signal is analysed by the camera's microprocessor to select the correct film-speed setting.

Dyak (or **Dayak**) The indigenous non-Muslim peoples of Borneo, subdivided into several named groups including the Land Dyak of south-west Borneo and the Sea Dyak of Sarawak. Reckoned to be early inhabitants of the island, forced inland by subsequent migrations of Malays to the coasts, the people live in long-house communities. Intertribal warfare and head-hunting were formerly characteristic of Dyak society.

Dyck, Sir Anthony Van See VAN DYCK.

dye A substance used to colour textiles, paper, hair, or food. Unlike PAINTS, which remain on the surface, dyes are dispersed into, or chemically bonded to, the material they colour. Dye PIGMENTS contain special chemical groups, known as chromophores, that confer colour on the material. Dyes have been known for many thousands of years. Until recently they were all obtained from natural sources. The first synthetic dye, mauveine, was discovered in 1856 by PERKIN. Many thousands of synthetic dyes have since been made, and the active ingredients of many natural dyes have been chemically synthesized.

Dyfed A former county of south-west Wales, comprising the former counties of Cardiganshire, Carmarthenshire, and Pembrokeshire. Dyfed was abolished in 1996, when these three counties were restored. The capital of Dyfed was Carmarthen.

dyke (in geology) A sheet-like igneous body which cuts across the bedding of the host rock (unlike a SILL, which develops concordantly to the existing rock). Most dykes have been injected under pressure into the surrounding rock while still in a molten state and often occur in large numbers (dyke swarms). They are usually composed of basic IGNEOUS ROCKS.

Dylan, Bob (born Robert Allen Zimmerman) (1941–) US singer and songwriter. The leader of the urban folk-music revival in the 1960s, he became known for his political and protest songs, including 'A Hard Rain's A-Gonna Fall', 'Blowin' in the Wind' (both 1963), and 'The Times They Are A-Changin'', (1964). When on tour in 1966 he caused controversy and aroused severe criticism for using an amplified backing group. His albums include *Highway 61 Revisited* (1965) and *Blood on the Tracks* (1975).

dynamite An EXPLOSIVE used extensively for blasting operations in mines and quarries. It was developed in 1867 by NOBEL, who discovered that certain earths (metallic oxides), such as kieselguhr, will absorb up to three times their weight of NITROGLYCERINE and still remain dry. The absorbed nitroglycerine in this solid form still retains its explosive properties but is much less sensitive. Commercial dynamite is usually moulded into sticks and encased in waxed-paper wrappers. It can be handled and shipped with comparative safety and is exploded with a percussion cap containing a DETONATOR.

dynamo See GENERATOR, ELECTRICAL.

dynamometer A device used in MECHANICAL ENGINEERING to measure the power, or more commonly the TORQUE (turning force), of a rotating shaft. Transmission dynamometers measure the amount of twist imparted to the shaft by rotation, or consist of a special torque meter inserted between sections of the shaft. Absorption dynamometers operate by creating a constant braking force on the shaft: this force may be produced by mechanical friction, fluid friction, or by ELECTROMAGNETIC INDUCTION. The braking mechanism is freely cradled so that it has a tendency to rotate: it is prevented from doing so by a force applied to an arm extending a known distance from the axis of rotation. The value of this restraining force is a measurement of the torque.

dysentery A serious, communicable infective and inflammatory diarrhoeal disease. Amoebic dysentery (amoebiasis) occurs as a result of infection by *Entamoeba histolytica*, and bacillary dysentery (shigellosis) as a result of infection by *Shigella dysenteriae*. Dysentery is transmitted by the ingestion of water or food contaminated with human sewage containing the microorganism. Symptoms of dysentery include watery diarrhoea containing blood or mucus. Vomiting and mild fever may also occur. The persistent, recurring, and distressing desire to defecate but without significant passage of stools is a common feature, and is known as tenesmus. Dehydration is also common, which can be life-threatening in children and the elderly.

dyslexia A difficulty in reading that is disproportionate relative to other intellectual abilities. It is considered to be a congenital disability in organizing, which affects short-term MEMORY, hand skills, and PERCEPTION, leading to difficulties with literary skills. It is typified by erratic spelling, often accompanied by letter reversals or word reversals. This indicates that one of the difficulties lies in imposing a consistent spatial orientation on written material. Other possible causes may lie in relating what words look like to how they sound. Recent research suggests that dyslexia is linked to a neurological abnormality that affects vision. There are about 2.5 million dyslexics in the UK.

dysprosium (symbol Dy, at. no. 66, r.a.m. 162.50) A soft silvery lanthanide metallic element discovered in 1886 by François Lecoq de Boisbaudran. It is extracted by an ion-exchange process from such ores as apatite or gadolinite. It has limited use as a neutron absorber in nuclear technology.

Dzongkha A Tibetan dialect that is the official language of Bhutan.

E

Eads, James Buchanan (1820–87) US engineer, remembered particularly as a bridge builder. As a young man he built up a prosperous business salvaging wrecked steamers on the Mississippi, devising a DIVING-BELL for the purpose. During the American Civil War (1861–65) he built IRONCLADS for use on the western rivers. In 1867 he won a contract to build a railway bridge over the Mississippi at St Louis (completed 1874). The St Louis bridge was the first steel bridge to be built (although it had masonry pillars), and the largest in the world at that time.

Eadwig See EDWY.

eagle Any one of some 56 species of large HAWK of the subfamily Buteoninae, within the hawk family, with worldwide distribution. Most have long, broad wings, spanning up to 1.5 m (5 feet), which are perfectly adapted to flapping, soaring, and gliding flight. The legs are strong, the feet heavily taloned and in some species feathered. The beak is strongly curved, and used for tearing prey. Eagles are generally powerful predators, catching their prey on the ground or snatching it from treetops; a few are carrion-feeders. Live prey includes reptiles, birds, and small mammals. Their plumage is usually brown or black and combined with white. Eagles generally nest high in trees or on cliff faces, sites which give good vantage-points with updraughts to assist take-off. Their nests are untidy heaps of sticks accumulated from year to year and most species lay one or two eggs. Parents hunt over extensive territories, returning to the nest with prey before tearing it up for the chicks. They are diurnal hunters with remarkable eyesight, and can air-lift prey of considerable size. In pastoral areas they occasionally attack lambs and kids.

eagle owl A large, horned OWL of the genus *Bubo*, containing 11 species. They are native to parts of Europe, Asia, and Africa. The European eagle owl, *B. bubo*, is typical with its dark brown barred plumage, feathered legs and feet, and golden-yellow eyes. They are easily recognized by their eartufts, 4–5 cm (about 2 inches) long, and their deep hooting calls. Females weigh up to one and a half times as much as males. They frequent mountains and open woodland, hunting birds, small mammals, and occasionally fish, reptiles, and frogs. They lay two to four eggs in nests on the ground.

Eakins, Thomas (1844–1916) US painter and photographer. He was noted for his portraits and genre pictures of the life of his native city, Philadelphia; boating and bathing were favourite themes. His most famous picture, *The Gross Clinic* (1875), aroused controversy because of its explicit depiction of surgery.

Ealing A residential and commercial outer borough of Greater London; pop. (1991) 263,600. Noted as a centre of British film-making, the first British sound-film studio was built here in 1931.

ear A sense organ that interprets vibrations in water and sound waves in air. In vertebrates the ear is also the organ of balance. Many invertebrates have sense organs which can be called ears; those of crickets and grasshoppers are good examples. The vertebrate ear is a complex structure consisting of three fluid-filled, bony tubes (semicircular canals), and a variety of chambers or additional tubes. Ears always occur in pairs, and usually have some connection with the outside world, via a flexible membrane, called a tympanum, which covers a cavity.

In fishes, the ears are most important as organs of position or motion. The movement of small stones, or otoliths, within hollow chambers, enable fishes to 'feel' acceleration and judge their position relative to gravity. The ears of amphibians and reptiles are a stage more complex than those of fishes, and some species have an opening from the inner ear to the throat. The ears of birds are among the most sensitive of all, especially to different frequencies of sound.

The mammalian ear, which includes that of humans, has three main parts, the outer, middle, and inner ears. The outer ear consists of a fleshy flap, which concentrates directional sounds, and a tube lined with hairs and wax glands, leading to the eardrum (tympanum). The middle ear is an air-filled cavity, connected to the throat, which is crossed by a series of three bones, known commonly as the anvil, hammer, and stirrup bones. They transmit vibrations from the eardrum to a similar membrane closing the fluid-filled tubes of the inner ear. Nerves from the inner ear transmit the information on frequency and volume of the sound to the brain.

Earhart, Amelia (1898–1937) US aviator. In 1932 she became the first woman to fly across the Atlantic solo, completing the journey from Newfoundland to Londonderry in a time of $13\frac{1}{4}$ hours. The aircraft carrying Earhart and her navigator disappeared over the Pacific Ocean during a subsequent round-the-world flight.

earl A British nobleman ranking between marquis and viscount, ranked third in the peerage. From Alfred's time ALDERMEN had charge of shires, but during the 10th century they became more important, with overall control of several shires. King CANUTE's dependence on his Scandinavian jarls (earls) gave them territorial power in England over the regions of Northumbria, East Anglia, and Wessex. They presided over the shire court, commanded its fyrd, and retained one-third of the profits of justice (replaced later by King John with a fixed sum). Under the Norman kings in the 11th century shire administration passed to the sheriffs but the hereditary title of earl survived.

Earl's Court A largely residential district of Greater London between Kensington and Fulham, with a noted exhibition hall. It probably takes its name from the Earls of Warwick who had a mansion house here.

Early English style The first of the three phases into which English Gothic architecture is conventionally divided, covering the period *c.*1175–*c.*1275 and preceding the DECORATED and PERPENDICULAR styles. It is most obviously distinguished from the later styles by the use of simple 'lancet' (tall and narrow) windows, without TRACERY. The choir of Canterbury Cathedral (begun 1174) is generally regarded as the first truly Gothic building in England, and Salisbury Cathedral, begun in 1220, is the archetypal example of the Early English style.

early-warning system A surveillance system that provides early warning of an approaching BALLISTIC MISSILE or high-speed aircraft. Modern systems employ a combination of early-warning satellites and powerful radars. The satellites detect the exhaust heat of ballistic missiles a few seconds after launch, and then radar systems comprising massive arrays of ANTENNAE track the missiles as they rise above the horizon, using initial trajectory data produced by the satellites.

Earp, Wyatt (Berry Stapp) (1848–1929) US gambler and marshal. He went to Tombstone, Arizona, in 1878 and worked as a gambler and guard in the Oriental Saloon. His brother Virgil was marshal and a feud developed between the Earps and the Clantons, leading in 1881 to the gunfight at the OK Corral, which involved Wyatt, Virgil, their brother Morgan, and Doc Holliday, a friend of Wyatt from Dodge City.

Earth The planet third in distance from the Sun and the only one in the Solar System on which life is known to exist. The Earth is 12,756 km (7,926 miles) in diameter at the equator and has a mean density of 5,520 kg/m^3. It rotates in 23 hours 56 minutes about an axis tilted at 23 degrees 26 minutes to a line perpendicular to the Earth's orbit about the Sun. This pronounced axial tilt produces the seasons, governed at each place by the annual variation in the amount of heat received from the Sun. The Earth moves in an almost circular path averaging 149.6 million kilometres (93.5 million miles) from the Sun, taking 365.25 days to complete one orbit. It has one natural satellite, the MOON.

The Earth is composed of three parts: the crust, the mantle, and the core. The crust is a thin layer of rock with an average thickness of about 40 km (25 miles) in the continental areas but only about 6 km (4 miles) under the oceans. Below the crust is the mantle, the boundary between the two being marked by the MOHO DISCONTINUITY or moho. The mantle extends to a depth of about 2,900 km (1,800 miles) and constitutes the bulk of the Earth – about 84 per cent by volume. The oceanic and continental crust, together with the stiffer part of the upper mantle immediately below, constitute the lithosphere, which extends up to a depth of 100 km (62 miles). This is divided into a number of rigid plates that move very slowly in relation to one another and in relation to the Earth's poles, most probably as a result of large-scale convection currents in the mantle. These movements, their cause, and their consequences are the study of PLATE TECTONICS. Below the mantle is the central region of the Earth, the core, with a radius of about 3,471 km (2,156 miles). It is generally agreed that iron constitutes about 90 per cent of the core. Evidence from earthquakes shows that the inner core, with a radius of about 1,171 km (728 miles), is solid, but that the outer core is molten. The bound-

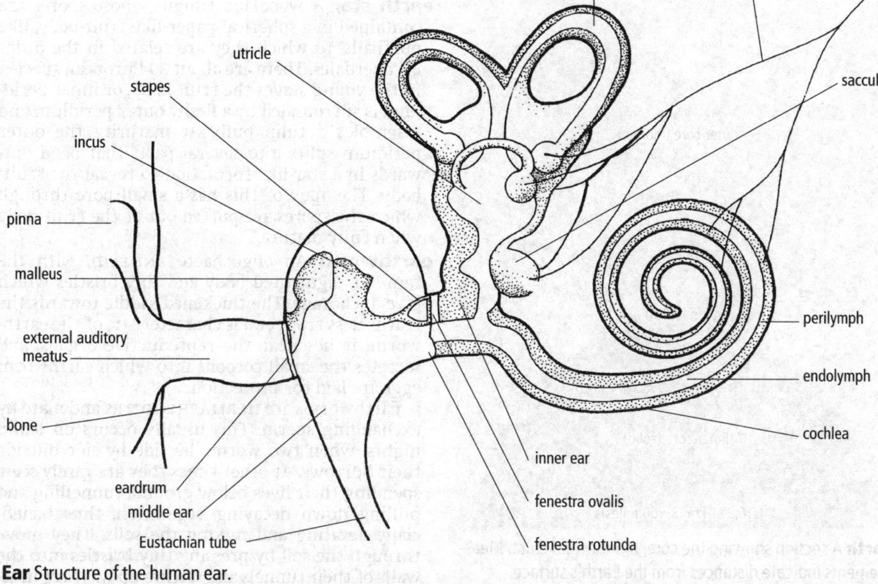

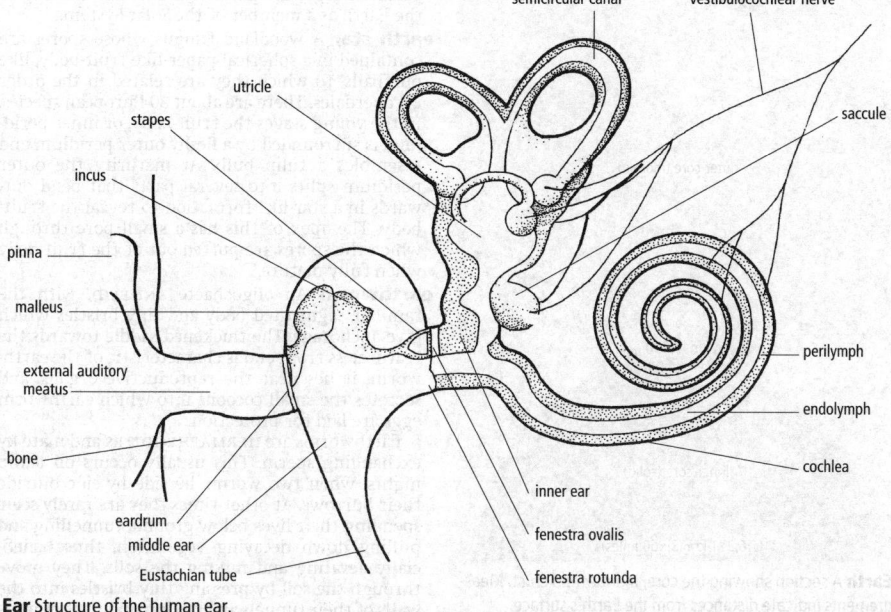

Ear Structure of the human ear.

ary between the mantle and the much denser outer core is marked by the Gutenberg discontinuity.

Seventy per cent of the surface is covered with vast oceans of water, the continental land masses making up the other 30 per cent. The Earth's atmosphere consists of 78 per cent nitrogen, 21 per cent oxygen, and with trace gases making up the other one per cent. This life-supporting atmosphere is quite a recent development. The fluid metallic core of the Earth, carried round by the daily rotation, forms a magnetic field which interacts with the SOLAR WIND to form the Earth's

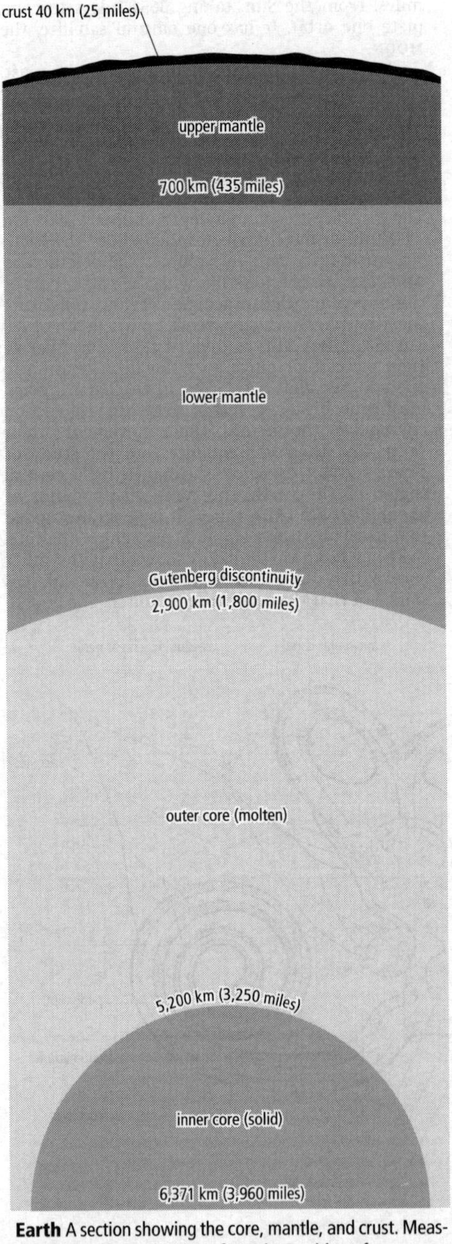

Earth A section showing the core, mantle, and crust. Measurements indicate distances from the Earth's surface.

MAGNETOSPHERE. This envelope round the Earth forms a tail away from the Sun and shields the planet from much harmful cosmic radiation. Atomic particles entering the tail are accelerated and dumped into the Earth's atmosphere near the poles to produce the AURORA. In space around the Earth are the two VAN ALLEN radiation belts.

earthenware Pottery that has been fired at a fairly low temperature, so that the clay has not vitrified (turned glassy); it is therefore slightly more porous and coarser than PORCELAIN or stoneware. To make it suitable for holding liquids, and also for decorative reasons, earthenware is almost always glazed, but it is left unglazed in, for example, flowerpots.

earthquake A violent movement of the surface of the Earth due to the release of accumulated stress as a result of faults in strata or volcanic action. While gentle Earth tremors can occur in any region of the globe, the more severe ones usually occur near the edges of the major 'plates' that make up the Earth's crust. The point at which an earthquake shock originates is called the focus and the point immediately above this on the Earth's surface is the epicentre. The intensity of the earthquake is reported as measured by the Richter scale. Major earthquakes generally measure between about 7 and 9, though in theory there is no upper limit on the scale.

Earth resources satellite An artificial SATELLITE supplying information about land use and about the distribution of natural resources such as water and minerals. Such satellites chiefly measure visible and infrared radiation from the land and sea surface, using optical instruments and radiometers. Earth resources satellites travel in a polar orbit, a north-south orbit that allows information to be collected from almost the whole of the Earth's surface. Information is transmitted to ground stations for processing into visible images.

Earth sciences The sciences that study the Earth, its atmosphere, and its oceans. They include geology, geomorphology, geophysics, geochemistry, glaciology, hydrology, oceanography, meteorology, palaeontology, and parts of astronomy relating to the Earth as a member of the Solar System.

earth star A woodland fungus whose spores are contained in a spherical paper-like fruit-body, like puffballs, to which they are related in the order Lycoperdales. There are about 30 European species. In the young stages the fruit-body, or inner peridium, is surrounded by a fleshy outer peridium and resembles a tulip bulb. At maturity the outer peridium splits into several parts that bend outwards in a star-like formation to reveal the fruit-body. The apex of this has a small pore through which the spores are puffed out of the fruit-body when fully mature.

earthworm An oligochaete ANNELID, with the familiar segmented body and tiny bristles which give anchorage. The thickened saddle towards the featureless front end is characteristic of the earthworm: it lies near the reproductive organs, and secretes the small cocoons into which earthworm eggs are laid for protection.

Earthworms are HERMAPHRODITES and mate by exchanging sperm. This usually occurs on damp nights, when two worms lie side by side outside their burrows. At other times they are rarely seen, spending their lives below ground, tunnelling and pulling down decaying vegetation, thus beneficially aerating and mixing the soils. They move through the soil by pressing tiny bristles into the walls of their tunnels and setting up waves of muscle contraction along their body. In earthworms, as in all annelids, the muscles act antagonistically against the hydrostatic pressure within their COELOM.

earwig An elongate, brownish insect, with a pair of pincers at the tip of the abdomen, which is curved in the males and straight in the females. The front pair of wings is small and thickened, and when at rest the hind pair is folded like a fan beneath them. Earwigs eat both plant and animal material and can be destructive to garden flowers. The females lay their eggs in a batch, often in winter, in soil or under stones, and tend them, constantly 'licking' them to remove destructive fungi, until they hatch as miniature adults. Earwigs make up the order Dermaptera with some 1,200 species found throughout the world.

East Anglia An ancient division of England, now a region of eastern England consisting of the countries of Norfolk, Suffolk, Cambridgeshire, and parts of Essex. Founded in 1963, the University of East Anglia is in Norwich.

Eastbourne A resort town in East Sussex, on the south coast of England; pop. (1981) 78,000. Beachy Head is nearby.

East China Sea See CHINA SEA.

Easter The annual Christian festival celebrating the RESURRECTION of Jesus after the crucifixion, as recounted in the Gospels. Different methods of calculation result in Easter usually being celebrated on different dates in Western and Orthodox churches. Easter is the most important Christian festival. Easter customs include bright illuminations, sunrise services, and the exchange of eggs, symbolizing new life.

Easter Island (Spanish **Isla de Pascua**; Polynesian **Rapa Nui**) An island in the south-east Pacific west of Chile, named by the Dutch navigator Roggeveen who visited it on Easter Day, 1722; area 117 sq km (45 sq miles); pop. (1990) 2,000. Administered by Chile since 1888, it is famous for its many monolithic statues (*moai*) of human heads (up to 10 metres high). Between 1888 and 1952 the greater part of the island was leased to a Chilean-Scottish sheep-ranching company. Nearly 70 per cent of the population lives in the chief town, Hanga Roa.

Eastern Cape A province of South Africa created in 1994 from part of the former Cape Province; pop. (1995) 6,481,300. Its capital is Bisho.

Eastern Island See MIDWAY ISLANDS.

Eastern Orthodox Churches A group of CHRISTIAN CHURCHES, historically centred in Eastern Europe, Greece, Ukraine, Russia, Georgia, and the Middle East. Each Church is independent but they all acknowledge the primacy (not the supremacy) of the Patriarch of Constantinople. There are about 100 million full members worldwide; there is a sizeable Orthodox community in the USA, but most of the Orthodox population live in the countries of the former Soviet Union. The Orthodox Communion is made up of a number of independent autocephalous Churches with their own internal administration which share the same faith and doctrine. These are the four eastern Patriarchates of Constantinople, Alexandria, Antioch (Antakya), and Jerusalem; the Russian, Serbian, Romanian, Bulgarian, and Georgian Patriarchates; and the Orthodox Churches of Cyprus, Greece, Czechoslovakia, Poland, and Albania, with certain other semi-independent Churches. Services have traditionally been held in the vernacular (now archaic in some cases, such as Old Slavonic), leading sometimes to an association with nationalism. In recent years there has been some rapprochement between the Orthodox Churches and the Roman Catholic Church, following the lifting in 1965 of mutual excommunications imposed in 1054. Subject to much persecution during the era of communist ascendancy in Eastern Europe and the former Soviet Union, the Orthodox Churches have recently been permitted to operate freely again.

Eastern Time Standard time used in eastern Canada and the USA or in eastern Australia.

Eastern Transvaal A province of South Africa created in 1994 from part of the former province of Transvaal and now called **Mpumalanga**; pop. (1995) 3,007,100. Its capital is Nelspruit.

Easter Rising (April 1916) An insurrection in Dublin when some 2,000 members of the Irish Volunteers and the Irish Citizen Army took up arms against British rule in Ireland. The IRISH REPUBLICAN BROTHERHOOD had planned the uprising, supported by the SINN FEIN party. A ship carrying a large consignment of arms from Germany was intercepted by the British navy. Roger CASEMENT of the IRB, acting as a link with Germany, was arrested soon after landing from a German U-boat. The military leaders, Pádraic Pearse and James Connolly, decided nevertheless to continue with the rebellion. The General Post Office in Dublin was seized along with other strategic buildings in the city. The Irish Republic was proclaimed on 24 April, Easter Monday, and a provisional government set up with Pearse as president. British forces forced their opponents to surrender by 29 April. The rising had little public support at first. Many Irishmen were serving in British forces during World War I. Sixteen leaders of the rebellion were executed and over 2,000 men and women imprisoned. The executions led to a change of feeling in Ireland and in the 1918 general election the Sinn Fein (Republican) Party won the majority vote.

East Germany The part of Germany that constituted an independent state (official name: German Democratic Republic, GDR; German: Deutsche Demokratische Republik, DDR) in the Soviet-dominated Eastern Bloc after World War II. Created in 1949, it was reunited with West Germany in 1990 after the collapse of communism. Its capital was East Berlin and its area was 108,568 sq km (41,757 sq miles).

East India Company, English A CHARTERED COMPANY of London merchants which gradually transformed trading privileges in Asia into a territorial empire centred on India. Chartered in 1600, the Company soon lost the Spice Islands (MOLUCCAS) to the Dutch, but by 1700 had secured important trading ports in India, notably Madras, Bombay, and Calcutta. In the mid-18th century Anglo-French hostility in Europe was reflected in a struggle for supremacy with the FRENCH EAST INDIA COMPANY. The English commander CLIVE outmanoeuvred the French governor Dupleix in south India, then intervened in the rich north-eastern province of BENGAL. Victory over the Bengal ruler in 1757 initiated a century of expansion, the East India Company emerging as the greatest European trader in India, though with strong French competition. Increasingly the company acted as an instrument of colonial government; having lost its commercial monopolies by 1833, it served as Britain's administrative agent in India. Widespread risings in 1857 during the INDIAN MUTINY determined, through the India Acts, the transfer of India from company to British government control in 1858, and the company was finally dissolved in 1873. See also DUTCH EAST INDIA COMPANY.

East Indies The many islands off the south-east coast of Asia, now sometimes called the Malay Archipelago. The Netherlands East Indies or Dutch East Indies was the former name (until 1949) for Indonesia.

eastings Distances – or angles of longitude – measured eastward from either a defined north–south grid line or a meridian.

East London A port and resort on the south-east coast of South Africa, developed in the 19th century from a military post, in the Eastern Cape province; pop. (1991) 270,130. Its industries include vehicle assembly, furniture, textiles, clothing, and fishing.

East Lothian A local government area and former county of east-central Scotland, which in 1996 became a unitary authority; area 1,716 sq km (663 sq miles); pop. (1993) 85,600. Its chief towns are Haddington and Tranent.

Eastman, George (1854–1932) US inventor and manufacturer of photographic equipment. In 1884 he established a company which in 1892 became the Eastman Kodak Company ('Kodak' was a name Eastman invented). He invented flexible roll-film coated with light-sensitive emulsion, and the Kodak camera (1888) with which to use it. These did much to popularize amateur photography, as did his subsequent development of colour photography.

East Sussex A county of south-east England; area 1,795 sq km (693 sq miles); pop. (1991) 670,600; county town, Lewes.

East Timor See TIMOR.

East-West Schism The schism between the Eastern (or Orthodox) Church and the Western (or Roman) Church, which became definitive in the year 1054. The breach was deepened in 1204 when the Fourth CRUSADE was diverted to Constantinople and sacked the city, and a Latin (Western) Empire was established there for some time. There were various attempts to heal the schism, notably at the ecclesiastical councils of Lyons II (1274) and Florence (1439), but the reunions proved fleeting. These attempts were effectively brought to an end when the OTTOMAN Turks captured Constantinople in 1453 and occupied almost all of the former Byzantine empire for many centuries. It is only in recent years that the dialogue between the two churches to heal the schism has been effectively re-opened.

Eastwood, Clint (1930–) US film actor and director. He became a star with his role in *A Fistful of Dollars* (1964) the first spaghetti western. His performance as the 'dirty cop' in *Dirty Harry* (1971) also proved a box-office success. He started directing in 1971, receiving acclaim for his portrait of the saxophonist Charlie Parker in *Bird* (1988) and for his uncompromising western *Unforgiven* (1992).

eating disorders See ANOREXIA NERVOSA; BULIMIA NERVOSA.

Ebbw Vale An industrial town in Gwent, south-east Wales, 33 km (20 miles) north of Cardiff; pop. (1991) 19,484. Formerly (until the 1970s) a centre of coal, and iron and steel production, the industry of the town is now based around engineering and printing.

EBCDIC See ASCII.

Ebola virus A virus first discovered in 1976 named after the Ebola district of Zaïre (now the Democratic Republic of Congo) in which it was first identified. In humans it causes an infection similar to green monkey disease, which has a mortality rate of up to 80 per cent. No cure is known.

ebony The heartwood of tropical trees of the genus *Diospyros*. Hard, black, and able to take a high polish it is used for black piano keys, in cabinet making, and for knife handles. The most important species are *D. ebenum* from India and *D. reticulata* from Mauritius.

EC See EUROPEAN COMMUNITY.

Eccles An industrial town in Lancashire, England, at the junction of the Bridgewater Canal and Manchester Ship Canal; pop. (1981) 37,800. It is known for its Eccles cakes which are round pastries filled with dried fruit.

Eccles, Sir John Carew (1903–97) Australian physiologist. He demonstrated the means by which nerve impulses are conducted, showing that a chemical neurotransmitter is released to initiate propagation across the synapses, followed by another that inhibits the propagation. Eccles was awarded a Nobel Prize in 1963.

echidna (or **spiny ant-eater**) A monotreme of the family Tachyglossidae, a group of primitive egg-laying mammals from Australia and New Guinea. There are two species, both with a covering of spines which usually project through the fur. When disturbed, the echidna rolls up into a ball like a hedgehog. They are mainly nocturnal and spend the day in crevices or rotten logs. They are powerful diggers, whether tunnelling down into ant nests in search of these insects, or making sleeping burrows. They can run, swim, and climb trees.

echinoderm A member of a phylum of marine invertebrates, Echinodermata, which are familiar as sea urchins and starfish on sea-shores. The 5,300 or so species have many unique features which set them apart from other invertebrate groups, such as their five-rayed symmetry; their internal skeletal plates, often bearing spines; their tiny, hydraulically operated tube-feet, used for feeding and locomotion; and their internal circulatory systems, quite unlike other more conventional blood-systems.

echo A wave reflected from a surface and directed back towards its source. If a short pulse is initiated, such as a cry or a shot, the echo will be heard a certain time later. This time will be that which is taken by the waves to travel to the reflecting surface and back again. Thus, if the time interval is measured and the velocity of the waves is known, the distance of the reflecting surface can be determined. This is the principle used in radar, which sends out and detects short radio waves, and in echosounding, which uses sound waves to reveal sea-floor topography.

Echo In Greek mythology, a nymph who fell in love with the beautiful youth Narcissus and, because her love was unrequited, pined away until nothing but her voice remained.

echo-sounding A type of SONAR used to determine the depth of a body of water. In echo-sounding a pulse of sound is transmitted vertically down towards the sea-bed, and the time elapsed before the return of the reflected echo is accurately measured. Knowing the speed of sound in sea-water (about 1,500 m/s, 5,000 feet per second), this time-value can be converted into a depth measurement.

Eckert, J. Presper See MAUCHLY, JOHN WILLIAM.

eclipse The total or partial disappearance of one celestial object behind another, or within the shadow cast by the other body. Eclipses of the Sun (**solar eclipses**) occur when the Sun is partially or

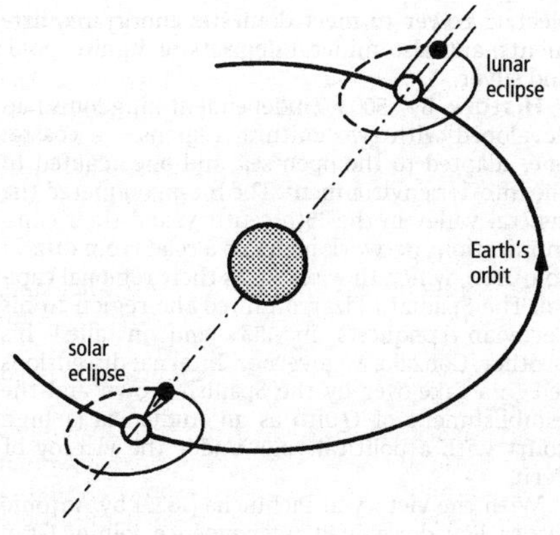

1

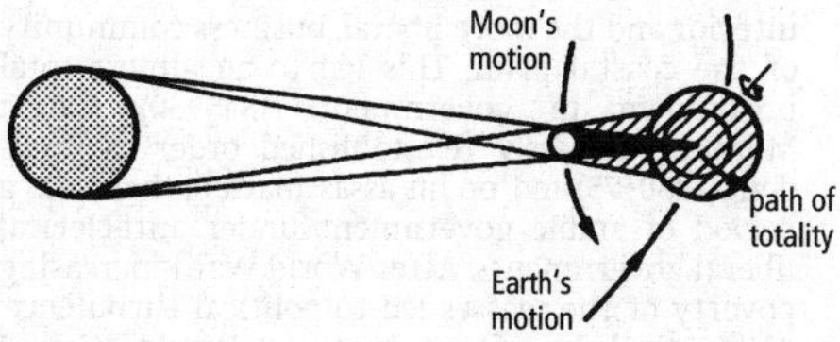

2

Eclipse (1) Solar and lunar eclipses. (2) The Moon's shadow in a solar eclipse.

totally hidden by the new Moon coming between the Earth and the Sun; eclipses of the Moon occur when the full Moon enters the shadow cast by the Earth. The shadow cast by the Moon on the Earth during an eclipse has a dark central area of total shadow, known as the **umbra**, surrounded by a partly shaded region, called the **penumbra**.

It happens that, by chance, the Moon's and the Sun's angular diameter are almost the same so that the new Moon cannot hide the Sun for more than a few minutes. Indeed if the Moon is at APOGEE, the Moon's angular size is slightly smaller than that of the Sun. Such an event is termed an **annular** solar eclipse. If, however, the angular size of the Moon exceeds that of the Sun, and if the line joining their centres intersects the Earth's surface, an observer at or near that point of intersection will see a **total eclipse** of the Sun.

The four large Galilean satellites of JUPITER also exhibit eclipses by Jupiter at regular intervals. In a number of binary star systems, such as Algol, the line of sight from the observer to the system lies so close to the orbital plane of one component star about the other that each star suffers partial or total eclipse at regular intervals. The resulting periodic diminution in the light of the apparently single star reveals its double or binary nature.

eclipsing binary A close BINARY STAR whose orbital plane is nearly in the line of sight, so that one component passes in front of the other, causing the MAGNITUDE to vary in a period equal to that of the orbital motion. Primary minima occur when the component of lower surface brightness passes in front of the one of higher surface brightness. Secondary minima may also be observed, when the brighter component passes in front of the fainter, but the change in magnitude may be too slight to detect. The ECLIPSES, which are more strictly OCCULTATIONS, may be total, annular (transits), or partial. Over 5,000 eclipsing binaries are known.

ecliptic The great circle on the CELESTIAL SPHERE giving the apparent annual path traced out by the Sun against the stellar background. The two intersections of the ecliptic with the celestial equator define the FIRST POINT OF ARIES and the FIRST POINT OF LIBRA. When the Sun reaches the former, spring begins in the Northern Hemisphere and autumn in the Southern Hemisphere; when it reaches the latter, autumn begins in the Northern Hemisphere and spring in the Southern. The ecliptic corresponds to the plane of the Earth's orbit about the Sun.

Eco, Umberto (1932–) Italian novelist and semiotician. Professor of semiotics at the University of Bologna since 1971, he is known both for his extensive writings on his subject, such as *Travels in Hyperreality* (1986) and as a novelist. His best-known fictional work is *The Name of the Rose* (1981), a complex detective novel set in a medieval monastery.

ecology The branch of biology dealing with the relations of organisms to one another and to their physical surroundings. Ecologists consider population dynamics, interaction between species (such as competition, and feeding), the environment (which includes the availability of nutrients), and energy flow through the ecosystem. Patterns of distribution and SUCCESSION and the impact of man are also examined.

Economic Community of West African States (ECOWAS) An economic grouping constituted largely on the initiative of General GOWON at Lagos in 1975 by 15 West African countries, and later (1977) joined by Cape Verde. Its object was to provide a programme of liberalization of trade and to bring about an eventual customs union. A common fund was established to promote development projects, with specialized commissions for trade, industry, transport, and social and cultural affairs. A new treaty was signed in 1993, designating the creation of a free-trade zone and a single currency as specific objectives and planning the establishment of a West African parliament and a new ECOWAS court of justice.

economics, schools of From the mid-16th century to the final quarter of the 20th century, economic thought can be split into five main historical schools: MERCANTILISM; the economics of the French physiocrats; classical economics and neoclassical economics; KEYNESIANISM; and MONETARISM. The mercantilists, between the mid-16th and mid-18th centuries, argued that the WEALTH of nations depended on their BALANCE OF TRADE. With the simple monetary system that existed, proponents of the theory were concerned to maximize the amount of precious metals in the country. PROTECTIONISM was encouraged. The French physiocrats of the 18th century, led by François Quesnay (1694–1774), accorded pre-eminence to the agricultural sector, which they saw as the only source of wealth, and also the source of tax revenue. They believed in the role of government being limited to preserving the natural order. They also believed in free trade. The physiocrats' ideas of *laissez-faire* and free trade were adopted by the classical economists. Much of modern MICROECONOMICS stems from the theories of classical economics, centring on Adam SMITH's *Wealth of Nations* (1776). The marginal analysis of the 19th century led to the development of neoclassical economics as a refinement and progression from classical economics. The central tenet in classical economics is that of competition. The law of SUPPLY AND DEMAND ensures that the price of a good balances supply and demand. Competitive markets ensure that the self-seeking behaviour of individuals results in efficient, socially optimal allocation of RESOURCES and PRODUCTION. The role of government is limited to intervention in cases where a MARKET does not exist or works imperfectly. Those in the classical tradition argued that government should maintain a balanced budget; others argued for government expenditure financed by budget deficits. The issue was resolved by KEYNES in 1936 in *The General Theory of Employment, Interest and Money*. This work laid the foundation of what is now called MACROECONOMICS. Keynesianism favours demand management by government through the use of both fiscal and monetary policy. MONETARISM, prominent in the 1970s and 1980s, represented a resurgence and updating of pre-Keynesian thought on macroeconomic issues. It stressed the importance of the MONEY SUPPLY as the means of controlling aggregate money demand and INFLATION but rejected the notion that either monetary or fiscal policy could exercise any lasting influence on the level of output and employment: the money supply, it was argued, determined only the price level, not the volume of output and employment. See also MARXISM.

ecosphere The region of space including planets where conditions are such that living things can exist.

ecosystem A biological community of interacting organisms and their physical environment. The term was coined by the Oxford ecologist A. G. Tansley in 1934. See ECOLOGY.

ecstasy An illegal hallucinogen with the chemical name MDMA (methylenedioxymethamphetamine). It first became popular in the USA in the 1970s, under its street name, ecstasy, because of the psychedelic effects it causes as a result of depleting the supply of the neurotransmitter serotonin. Its long-term effects are not fully known, but experiments with animals indicate that it can cause brain damage.

Ecuador A country on the north-west coast of South America.

Physical. Ecuador is bounded by Colombia on the north-east and Peru on the east and south. Palms flourish on the sandy, salty parts of the coast, and there are also mangrove swamps. Inland is a rich tropical plain, drained by several meandering rivers, and higher valleys where cocoa and coffee are grown; they extend into the foothills of the ANDES, where there are cinchona and great mahogany trees. The Andes run north to south through the middle of the country. The peaks are lofty, COTOPAXI, at 5,897 m (19,347 feet), being the highest active volcano in the world, and between the peaks are high but fertile valleys where the climate is temperate.

Economy. The oil industry, nationalized since 1988, produces the country's chief export, but otherwise the economy is primarily agricultural with bananas (of which Ecuador is the world's leading exporter), coffee, and, increasingly, fish the other exports of importance. Oil revenues have been invested to develop some manufacturing industry. Ecuador was a member of OPEC until 1992. There are plentiful supplies of natural gas and hydroelectric power to meet domestic energy requirements, and also mineral deposits of lignite, gold, and silver.

History. By *c*.500 AD independent kingdoms had developed with two cultural regions – a coastal one, adapted to the open sea, and one adapted to the interior environment. The Incas conquered the central valley in the 15th century, and their communications network included a road from CUZCO to QUITO, which they set up as their regional capital. The Spaniard Pizarro united the region to his Peruvian conquests in 1535 and installed his brother, Gonzalo, as governor. Internal dissensions led to a take-over by the Spanish crown and the establishment of Quito as an Audiencia (a high court with a political role) under the viceroy of Peru.

With the victory at Pichincha (1822) by Antonio SUCRE Ecuador gained independence, joining Gran COLOMBIA. When this broke up (1830) it became a separate republic, whose politics reflected the tension between the conservative landowners of the interior and the more liberal, business community of the coastal plain. This led to an almost total breakdown in government (1845–60). Garcia Moreno ruthlessly re-established order as President (1860–75) and, on his assassination, there was a period of stable government under anti-clerical liberal governments. After World War I increasing poverty of the masses led to political turbulence. Although US military bases in World War II brought some economic gain, a disastrous war with Peru (1941) forced Ecuador to abandon claims on the Upper Amazon. Between 1944 and 1972 the CAUDILLO José Maria Velasco Ibarra alternated with the military as ruler, being elected President five times. The discovery of oil in the 1970s might have brought new prosperity, but in fact the mass of the population remained poor and illiterate, with the great HACIENDAS surviving intact. Democratic government was restored in 1979 with the election of the social democrat Jaimé Roldos Aquilera as President (1979–81). He had promised reform but died in a mysterious air-crash. His successor, Osvaldo Hurtado Larrea (1981–84), was accused of embezzlement, and President Febres Cordero (1984–88) faced military intervention, a major crisis of external indebtedness, trade union unrest, and a decline in the oil price. The Democratic Left Party under Rodrigo Borja Cevallos came to power in 1988. It took over management of the oil companies, but still faced grave economic problems, with over a third of its 1992 budget allocated to debt servicing. Following elections in 1992 a coalition government was formed under President Sixto Durán Ballén. He introduced several free-market economic reforms and cut public spending, provoking popular unrest, which has continued to be a problem, and was replaced in 1996 by Abdala Bucaram. In 1995 a recurrent border dispute with Peru flared up again, but was settled after several days of fighting. In 1997 Bucaram was ousted on grounds of insanity and Fabián Alarcón became acting President.

Capital: Quito
Area: 269,178 sq km (103,930 sq mi)
Population: 11,460,000 (1995)
Currency: 1 sucre = 100 centavos
Religions: Roman Catholic 93.5%
Ethnic Groups: Quechua 49.9%; Mestizo 40.0%; White 8.5%; other Amerindian 1.6%
International Organizations: UN; OAS; Andean Group; Non-Aligned Movement

eczema See DERMATITIS.

Edberg, Stefan (1966–) Swedish tennis player. He turned professional in 1983 and won his first grand slam title, the Australian Open, two years later. He won Wimbledon twice, in 1990 and 1991, and was ranked first in the world during these years. He excelled on grass but his versatility brought him success on all surfaces. He announced his retirement in 1996.

Edda Two collections of Icelandic literature. The *Elder* or *Poetic Edda* was compiled in the 13th century, and consists of 33 poems in alliterative verse handed down by oral tradition, and dating probably from the 9th to the 12th centuries. The *Prose Edda* or *Younger Edda* (*c.*1223) was written by the Icelandic *skald* or court poet SNORRI STURLUSON. It contains a survey in dialogue form of Nordic mythology; a discussion of Skaldic poetry and versification, giving rules and many examples; and a poem in honour of King Håkon and Earl Skuli of Norway, its 102 STANZAS illustrating different METRES.

Eddington, Sir Arthur Stanley (1882–1944) British astronomer, founder of the science of astrophysics. He established the fundamental principles of stellar structure, discovered the relationship between stellar mass and luminosity, and suggested possible sources of the energy within stars. He wrote one of the finest presentations of Einstein's theory of relativity, and provided some of the best evidence in support of it when his observations of star positions during the solar eclipse of 1919 demonstrated the bending of light by gravity.

Eddy, Mary Baker (1821–1910) US religious leader and founder of the Christian Science movement. Long a sufferer from various ailments, she believed herself cured by a faith-healer, Phineas Quimby (1802–66). After his death she evolved her own system of spiritual healing, set out in her book *Science and Health* (1875), and established the Church of Christ, Scientist, in Boston in 1879. Members believe that God and the mind are the only ultimate reality, and that matter and evil have no existence; illness and sin, they believe, are illusions that can be overcome by prayer and faith. As a consequence they generally refuse medical treatment.

edelweiss A silvery-grey ALPINE PLANT, *Leontopodium alpinum*, belonging to the sunflower family, and native to the mountains of Europe. Great symbolic value is attached to the plant by mountain guides in the European Alps, who traditionally wear a flowering sprig of edelweiss in their hats.

Eden (or **Garden of Eden**) A paradise or place of great happiness. Eden is associated with the abode of Adam and Eve in the biblical account of the Creation.

Eden, (Robert) Anthony, 1st Earl of Avon (1897–1977) British Conservative statesman, Prime Minister 1955–57. He served as War Secretary under Churchill in 1940, in addition to three terms as Foreign Secretary (1935–38; 1940–45; 1951–55). His premiership was dominated by the Suez crisis of 1956. Widespread opposition to Britain's role in this, together with his own failing health, led to his resignation.

Edgar (944–75) King of England 959–75. He became king of Northumbria and Mercia in 957 when these regions renounced their allegiance to his elder brother Edwy, succeeding to the throne of England on Edwy's death. Edgar worked closely with St Dunstan during his reign and was renowned for his support of organized religion.

Edgar the Aetheling (from Anglo-Saxon *aetheline*, 'prince') (*c.*1050–1130) The grandson of Edmund Ironside. His father's death (1057) in exile left Edgar as the heir to EDWARD THE CONFESSOR in 1066, but because of his youth he was rejected in favour of HAROLD II. On Harold's death at the battle of HASTINGS the Witan chose Edgar as king but, despite his involvement in a rebellion against WILLIAM I (1069), he was unable to organize any further resistance and became a member of William's court (1074). He was captured by HENRY I at Tinchebrai (1106) for supporting Henry's older brother Robert of Normandy (Curthose), but was later released.

Edgehill A ridge in Warwickshire, central England, 11 km (7 miles) north-west of Banbury, at which the first pitched battle of the English Civil War was fought in 1642.

Edgeworth, Maria (1767–1849) Irish novelist, born in England. She is best known for *Castle Rackrent* (1800), regarded as the first regional and historical novel in English. Other significant works include *Belinda* (1801), a portrait of contemporary English society, and *The Absentee* (1812), a depiction of the landlord–tenant relationship in rural Ireland.

Edinburgh The capital of Scotland from 1437, lying close to the southern shore of the Firth of Forth; pop. (1991) 421,200. The city grew up round the 11th-century castle built by Malcolm III on a rocky ridge which dominates the landscape. The 'Royal Mile', which links the castle with the Palace of Holyroodhouse at the bottom of the ridge, passes through the old medieval burghs of Edinburgh and the Canongate. Princes Street, to the north, is the main thoroughfare in the 'New Town' which was built in the 18th and 19th centuries. Edinburgh has hosted a famous international festival annually since 1947. It is the headquarters of the Scottish Office, the Forestry Authority, and the British Geological Survey and home of the University of Edinburgh (1583), Heriot-Watt University (1966), and Napier University (1992). Finance, brewing, tourism, and light industry are important.

Edinburgh, Duke of See PHILIP, PRINCE.

Edison, Thomas (Alva) (1847–1931) US inventor. He was employed by the age of 15 as a telegraph operator, from which he developed an interest in electricity and its applications. He took out the first of more than a thousand patents at the age of 21. His chief inventions include automatic telegraph systems, the mimeograph, the carbon microphone for telephones, the phonograph, the carbon filament lamp, and the nickel-iron accumulator. He created the precursor of the thermionic valve, and devised systems for generating and distributing electricity. Edison also established the practice of installing industrial laboratories in commercial organizations.

Edmonton The capital (since 1905) and largest city of Alberta, Canada, 300 km (116 miles) east of the Rockies, on the North Saskatchewan River; pop. (1991) 616,700; 839,920 (metropolitan area). The University of Alberta was founded here in 1907.

Edmund Two kings of England. **Edmund I** (921–46) reigned 939–46. Soon after Edmund succeeded Athelstan, a Norse army took control of York and its dependent territories. From 941 Edmund set about recovering these northern territories, but after his death Northumbria fell again under Norse control. **Edmund II** (known as Edmund Ironside) (*c.*980–1016), son of Ethelred the Unready, reigned 1016. Edmund led the resistance to Canute's forces in 1015 and on his father's death was proclaimed king. After some initial success he was defeated at Ashingdon in Essex (1016) and was forced to divide the kingdom with Canute, retaining only Wessex. On Edmund's death Canute became king of all England.

Edmund, St (born Edmund Rich) (*c*.1175–1240) English churchman and teacher. Archbishop of Canterbury 1234–40, he was the last Primate of all England and the first Oxford University teacher to be canonized. The Oxford college St Edmund Hall takes its name from him. Feast day, 16 November.

Edmund Ironside EDMUND II of England.

Edmund the Martyr, St (*c*.841–70) King of East Anglia 855–70. After the defeat of his army by the invading Danes in 870, tradition holds that he was captured and shot with arrows for refusing to reject the Christian faith or to share power with his pagan conqueror. His body was interred at Bury St Edmunds, Suffolk. Feast day, 20 November.

Edo The former name (until 1868) of Tokyo, capital of Japan. It gave its name to the Edo Period of Japanese history which existed prior to the birth of modern Japan. Under the feudal Tokugawa Shogunate, which lasted from 1603 to 1867, local warlords were kept in check and Japan remained largely isolated from the outside world.

EDSAC See COMPUTER, HISTORY OF.

education The transmission of knowledge and understanding, and the development of the individual personality, by teaching or example. Political theorists as diverse as PLATO and MARX have argued that education gives people power to change their lives. It also enables whole societies to develop. The value of education can be illustrated by its impact in poorer countries. The World Bank has found that where adults have had even a few years of education, their families are often smaller and their children healthier and that their labour may be more productive. For the individual, education means access to better-paid, more varied jobs and higher status. School systems are usually divided chronologically into pre-school, primary, secondary, and higher education. The expansion of universal state provisions in industrialized countries, including COMPREHENSIVE EDUCATION, has been built on the older traditions of INDEPENDENT EDUCATION. Of increasing importance in recent years have been CONTINUING EDUCATION, vocational education, and LITERACY campaigns. The organization of education often reflects the outcome of struggles between the competing interests of, for example, governments, employers, teaching unions, religious bodies, parents, and children. Governments usually wish to hold down the potentially limitless costs of education while ensuring the production of a skilled and law-abiding citizenry, whereas others may have concerns about curriculum, assessment, discipline, and access. In consequence, battles may be fought, but are rarely conclusively won. See also PRIMARY EDUCATION; SECONDARY EDUCATION.

EDVAC See COMPUTER, HISTORY OF.

Edward Six kings of England since the Norman Conquest and also one of Great Britain and Ireland and one of the United Kingdom. **Edward I** (known as 'the Hammer of the Scots') (1239–1307), son of Henry III, reigned 1272–1307. After coming to the throne Edward did much to improve the ineffectual central administration he had inherited; this included summoning the Model Parliament (1295). His campaign against the Welsh Prince Llewelyn ended with the annexation of Wales in 1284. He failed to conquer Scotland, though he had a successful first campaign there in 1296, deposing the Scottish king, John de Baliol (*c*.1250–1313), who had made an alliance with the French against him. From 1297 to 1305 the Scots were in a state of armed insurrection, initially under the leadership of Sir William Wallace. Edward died on his way north to begin a new campaign against the Scots, who were by then led by Robert the Bruce. **Edward II** (1284–1327), son of Edward I, reigned 1307–27. The first English Prince of Wales, he soon proved unequal to the problems left him by his more military father, and early trouble with his barons led to civil war. In 1314 he invaded Scotland, only to be defeated by Robert the Bruce at Bannockburn in the same year. In 1326 Edward's wife, Isabella of France, allied herself with the exiled Roger de Mortimer to invade England. Edward was deposed in favour of his son and was murdered at Berkeley Castle, Gloucestershire. **Edward III** (1312–77), son of Edward II, reigned 1327–77. In 1330 Edward ended the four-year regency of his mother Isabella and her lover Roger de Mortimer by taking control of his kingdom, banishing Isabella, and executing Mortimer. He supported Edward de Baliol (*c*.1283–1364), the pretender to the Scottish throne, and started the Hundred Years War with France by claiming the French throne in right of his mother (1337). Towards the end of his reign effective government fell into the hands of his fourth son, John of Gaunt. **Edward IV** (1442–83), son of Richard, Duke of York, reigned 1461–83. He became king after defeating the Lancastrian king Henry VI in battle in 1461. The early years of his reign were troubled by Lancastrian plots, but the most serious threat arose in 1470–71 as a result of an alliance between his old Lancastrian enemies and his disaffected former lieutenant, the Earl of Warwick. Edward was briefly forced into exile, but returned to crush his opponents at Tewkesbury (1471), thereafter ruling in relative peace until his death. **Edward V** (1470–*c*.1483), son of Edward IV, reigned 1483, but was not crowned. Following his father's death he was illegitimized on debatable evidence of the illegality of Edward IV's marriage; his throne was taken by his uncle, Richard III, who placed young Edward and his brother Richard in the Tower of London. The boys disappeared soon afterwards, and are generally assumed to have been murdered; they have become known as the Princes in the Tower. **Edward VI** (1537–53), son of Henry VIII, reigned 1547–53. During his brief reign as a minor, England was effectively ruled by two protectors, the Duke of Somerset and the Duke of Northumberland. Nevertheless, the king's Protestant beliefs contributed significantly to the establishment of Protestantism as the state religion, especially with the publication of the *Book of Common Prayer* (1549). He was succeeded by his elder sister, Mary I. **Edward VII** (1841–1910), son of Queen Victoria, reigned 1901–10. Edward was kept away from the conduct of royal affairs during the long reign of his mother. Although he played little part in government on finally coming to the throne, his popularity and willingness to make public appearances, both at home and abroad, helped revitalize the monarchy. **Edward VIII** (1894–1972), son of George V, reigned 1936, but was not crowned. A popular Prince of Wales, Edward abdicated eleven months after coming to the throne in order to marry the American divorcee Mrs Wallis Simpson. The **Abdication crisis** arose when the prime minister, Stanley BALDWIN, supported by the Archbishop of Canterbury, Cosmo Lang, informed the King that marriage to Mrs Simpson was unacceptable while he remained on the throne. In a radio broadcast to the nation the ex-King gave a moving account of his reasons for abdication and asked for national support for his brother, the new king, George VI. Created Duke of Windsor, he served as Governor-General of the Bahamas during World War II before spending the rest of his life in France.

Edward, Prince (full name Prince Edward Antony Richard Louis) (1964–) Third son of Elizabeth II. He served in the Royal Marines from 1986 to 1987 after graduating from Cambridge, and has more recently worked in the theatre.

Edwards, Gareth (Owen) (1947–) Welsh Rugby Union player. His international career, during which he played chiefly at scrum half, lasted from 1967 to 1978. He was appointed captain of the Welsh team in 1968, the youngest person ever to hold that position.

Edward the Black Prince (1330–76) Prince of Wales 1343–76, the eldest son of EDWARD III. He was an outstanding example of the chivalric ideal, a military leader who helped restore national pride to the English by a series of victories in the HUNDRED YEARS WAR. He commanded part of his father's army at CRÉCY (1346), and in 1356 won the battle of POITIERS, capturing John II. In 1367 he restored King Pedro to the throne of Castile, but the campaign in Spain ruined his health. By his marriage to Joan, the 'Fair Maid of Kent', he left one son, the future RICHARD II.

Edward the Confessor, St (*c.*1003–66) Son of Ethelred the Unready, king of England 1042–66. Famed for his piety, Edward founded Westminster Abbey, where he was eventually buried. He was dominated through much of his reign by his wife's father, Earl Godwin (died 1053). In later years Edward took less interest in affairs of state, letting effective control fall to Godwin's son, who eventually succeeded him as Harold II. He was canonized in 1161. Feast day, 13 October.

Edward the Elder (*c.*870–924) Son of Alfred the Great, king of Wessex 899–924. During his reign he conquered lands previously held by the Danes, including East Anglia and the Midlands; on the death of his sister, the ruler of Mercia, in 918 he merged the kingdoms of Wessex and Mercia. His conquests made it possible for his son Athelstan to become the first king of all England in 925.

Edward the Martyr, St (*c.*963–79) King of England 975–78. He succeeded his father Edgar as king, but his accession was disputed by supporters of his younger stepbrother ETHELRED II, and while visiting him and his stepmother Alfrida at Corfe Castle in Dorset, Edward was murdered. Miracles were reported at his tomb at Shaftesbury and Ethelred had to pronounce the date of Edward's death (18 March) a solemn festival. He was canonized in 1001 and became the focus of a considerable medieval cult.

Edwy (or **Eadwig**) (died 959) King of England 955–57. He was probably only 15 years old when he became king. Edwy alienated a large part of his kingdom during his short reign; after Mercia and Northumbria had renounced him in favour of his brother Edgar in 957, he ruled only over the lands south of the Thames.

EEC See EUROPEAN ECONOMIC COMMUNITY.

eel A long, slender fish primarily adapted for living in crevices or burrows, although some eels live in the deep sea and are free-swimming. Over 600 different species are known. Most are marine fishes; the freshwater eels all belong to the family Anguillidae, but even they return to the sea to spawn. Because of their burrowing habit their fins are poorly developed, although all have a low dorsal and anal fin which is united around the tail. Eels have no pelvic fins, and the moray eel, in addition, has no pectoral fins. The gill opening is also greatly reduced to a slit, sometimes placed low down on the throat. All eels are predatory, but their diet varies widely from group to group. Moray eels are fish-eaters; most have long, pointed fangs, although some, which eat crustaceans, have blunt teeth. Conger eels have densely packed, triangular teeth, suitable for both soft- and hard-skinned prey, while snipe-eels have minute teeth and feed on planktonic crustaceans.

The European freshwater eel, *Anguilla anguilla*, and its North American counterpart, *A. rostrata*, grow to about 1 m (3.25 feet) in length. Both breed in the general area of the Sargasso Sea, and their leptocephalus larvae (often called glass-fish) migrate across the Atlantic. Although the American eels reach their coastline after one year, it takes three years for the European eels to reach fresh water. They travel far upstream in rivers as ELVERS and can move into lakes (even travelling overland at night).

eelgrass A submerged aquatic plant, *Zostera marina*, with long, dark green, ribbon-like leaves. Male and female flowers may be borne on separate or the same plants. Eelgrasses form a family of 18 species, all found in salt or brackish water in coastal areas of temperate seas. Their pollen has the same relative density as salt water and is distributed by water currents. Submerged freshwater aquatic plants of the genus *Vallisneria* are also sometimes called eelgrasses.

eelworm A featureless ROUNDWORM which lives free in the soil. Eelworms are familiar to farmers and gardeners as the tiny, but incredibly numerous, white, worm-like soil pests which eat plant roots, especially potato tubers and bulbs. They tunnel into any roots they encounter, often causing cysts or galls to form on their food plants.

efficiency (in engineering) A measure of the effectiveness of a machine's operation, defined as the ratio of effective output to effective input. Thus the thermal efficiency of, say, an engine, is its output in joules (see ENERGY) divided by the energy equivalent of its fuel in joules. The efficiency of turbo-machines is defined differently, as the ratio of the actual work output to the ideal output, assuming no energy losses. Practical efficiencies vary from over 99 per cent for electrical generators to about 25 per cent for a petrol engine.

EFTA See EUROPEAN FREE TRADE ASSOCIATION.

Egas Moniz, Antonio Caetano de Abreu Freire (1874–1955) Portuguese neurologist. He developed cerebral angiography as a diagnostic technique, and pioneered the treatment of certain psychotic disorders by the use of prefrontal leucotomy. He shared a Nobel Prize for this in 1949. Egas Moniz was also an active politician and diplomat.

Egbert (died 839) King of Wessex 802–39. In 825 he won a decisive victory near Swindon, bringing Mercian supremacy to an end, and annexed Kent, Essex, Surrey, and Sussex. In 829 Mercia itself fell to Egbert and Northumbria acknowledged his rule. By the time of his death, Mercia had become independent again, but his reign foreshadowed the supremacy that Wessex later secured over all England.

egg A female germ cell or OVUM, or a complex structure which protects and nourishes the true ovum. The eggs of birds and reptiles are examples of what are popularly known as 'eggs'. These are adapted to life on land, as the true germ cell is provided with a food store, in the form of yolk; a protective cushion and water, in the albumen; and an antibacterial barrier in the membranes lying under the shell. Each egg is a self-contained life-support unit for the development of a young bird or reptile. The external shells of reptiles and birds give support to the contents and also provide some degree of mechanical protection.

eggar moth A large, furry-bodied moth, making up 1,000 or so species of the family Lasiocampidae. Eggar moths are mainly tropical, and have caterpillars which are clothed in hairs which can be irritant. Pupation occurs within tough, usually egg-shaped cocoons. Examples include the drinker moth, *Philudoria potatoria*, which is common and widespread over Eurasia, and the oak eggar, *Lasiocampa quercus*, which occurs in Europe and North Africa. The lackey and lappet moths also belong to this family.

egoism Self-interest as the moral basis of behaviour. Egoism thus stands opposed to claims that there are moral demands on individuals which are binding and may require them to abandon their own interests. The egoist (usually in contrast to the amoralist) is thought of as seeking to demonstrate the rationality of his position; most arguments against egoism attempt to show that some inconsistency is involved in the egoist's claim that his self-interest, but not that of other people, provides him with a source of justification.

egret A bird making up 13 species belonging to the genera *Egretta* and *Bubulcus* and related to the heron as a member of the family Ardeidae. Many have all-white plumage, like the little egret, *E. garzetta*. The ubiquitous and familiar cattle egret, *B. ibis*, habitually follows grazing animals to feed on the insects they disturb. Egrets are found throughout the world and are of similar size to herons and bitterns.

Egypt A country in the north-east corner of Africa, bounded by its Mediterranean and Red Sea coasts, Israel in the north-east, Sudan in the south, and Libya in the west.

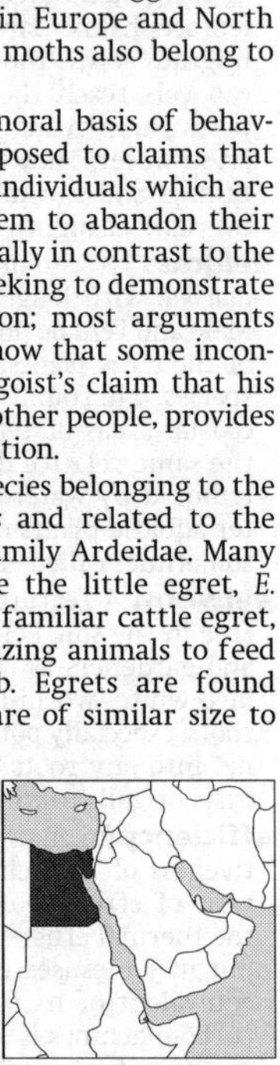

Physical. It is generally hot and arid – the south experiences some years with no rain at all – and civilization depends on the waters of the Nile, which are regulated by the Aswan Dam. To the west of the Nile valley is a desert of rock, sand, and gravel, with a few OASES, and the great Qattara Depression. To the east is a range of hills with limestone and sandstone plateaux dissected by WADIS, and on the east bank of the Gulf of Suez is the Sinai desert. The fan-shaped Nile delta in the north, where the climate is wetter, is very fertile. Egypt's climate has only two seasons: summer, lasting from April to September, and winter, lasting from October to March.

Economy. Egypt's main exports are of crude oil, petroleum products, and cotton. Agriculture is the main economic activity, but Egypt is no longer self-sufficient in food, due partly to swift population growth and partly to the neglect of agriculture. The Aswan High Dam regulates the flow of the Nile essential for most crop irrigation, but has had a deleterious effect on soil fertility; it also produces hydroelectric power. Foreign-exchange earnings from the Suez Canal, from the estimated 3 million Egyptians working abroad, and from tourism, make an important contribution to the economy, which also depends on high levels of US aid and loans.

History. Egypt is the site of one of the first civilizations, together with Mesopotamia, of the Old World. Agriculture and metallurgy were both introduced from western Asia, and the great fertility of the Nile floodplain allowed the growth of a highly distinctive cultural tradition. Two kingdoms, one in the Delta (Lower Egypt) and one centred upstream round Thebes (Upper Egypt), were in existence during the 4th millennium BC These were unified by the conquest of Lower Egypt some time shortly before 3000 BC, initiating the Protodynastic period. The shift of the capital to Memphis, near the head of the Delta, in the Old Kingdom (2700–2200 BC) perhaps indicates the importance of sea-borne trade with the Levant. The major pyramids were constructed here on the desert edge overlooking the river. A period of fragmentation (the first of two 'intermediate' periods) separated the Old from the Middle Kingdom (*c*.2050–1750), when some expansion into Palestine took place and the Nubian frontier was fortified. After a period of domination by foreign rulers (the 'HYKSOS'), the New Kingdom (1550–1050) was a period of imperial expansion when Egypt fought the Asiatic powers for control of Palestine. It was punctuated by the Amarna Period when AKHENATEN founded a new capital and religion. Egypt suffered from attacks of marauding SEA PEOPLES in the 12th century BC, but maintained continuity of tradition into the Late Period (*c*.650–332). However, its independence came to an end with its successive incorporation into Assyrian, Persian, and Hellenistic empires. When the Romans took it, Egypt was virtually self-governing. It was a granary for Rome, and its capital, Alexandria, became the world's chief commercial centre, when, *c*.106 AD, the sea route to India was opened.

Until 451 Alexandria was the intellectual centre of the Christian Church. When the Arab armies reached Egypt in 639, they had little difficulty in taking the country. Under Arab rule taxes were lighter, administration remained in local hands, and there was little pressure for conversion to Islam. The new capital of Misr, now Old Cairo, was the military base for the Arab conquest of North Africa. In the 9th century the caliphate gradually weakened, and Ibn Tulun, a Turk, made it independent for a time. In 969 the FATIMIDS seized the country, and built a new capital named al-Qahira, Cairo. Local administration continued with little change, and the country's prosperity is reflected in Fatimid art and architecture. In 1171 there followed the Fatimid dynasty of Saladin, and then the MAMELUKES, foreign slave rulers under whom Egypt had the most prosperous period in her history (1250–1517). Then, with the rest of North Africa and the Middle East, Egypt fell to OTTOMAN Turkey, although Mamelukes still maintained much local power. In 1798 Napoleon invaded Egypt in an attempt to restrict British trade with the east, but was driven out by the Turkish and British armies in 1801.

Egypt was restored to the Ottoman empire in 1802 but enjoyed almost total independence under the rule of pashas (descendants of Mehemet Ali) in Cairo. The construction of the Suez Canal in the 1860s made Egypt strategically important and in 1882 the British occupied the country in the wake of a nationalist revolt led by Arabi Pasha. They ruled the country in all but name through the Agent and Consul-General Lord Cromer. Egypt became a British protectorate in 1914 and received nominal independence in 1922 when Britain established a constitutional monarchy, with Sultan Ahmed as King Fuad I. Britain retained control of defence and imperial communications. In 1936 an Anglo-Egyptian treaty of alliance was signed, providing for a British garrison for twenty years, but for a gradual British withdrawal. This was interrupted by World War II. In 1948 Egyptian forces failed to defeat the emerging state of Israel, and in 1952 King FAROUK was overthrown by a group of army officers, one of whom, Colonel NASSER, emerged as the head of the new republic. Nasser's nationalization of the SUEZ CANAL in 1956 provoked abortive Anglo-French military intervention, and in the same year he embarked on another unsuccessful war against Israel. Helped by Soviet military and economic aid, Nasser dominated the Arab world, although he suffered another heavy defeat at Israeli hands in the SIX-DAY WAR of 1967. His successor, Anwar SADAT, continued his confrontationalist policies, but after defeat in the YOM KIPPUR WAR of 1973, he turned his back on the Soviet alliance, sought an accommodation with Israel, and strengthened his contacts with the West. This change of policy damaged Egypt's standing in the Arab world and in 1981 Sadat was assassinated by Islamic fundamentalists. His successor, President Mubarak, has followed a policy of moderation and reconciliation. Egypt was formally re-admitted to the Arab League in 1989. In 1991 Egypt sent troops to support the US-led alliance in the GULF WAR and in return had its debts to the USA reduced. Although the Aswan Dam increased productivity of the land, poverty remains a major problem. During the 1990s militant Islamic fundamentalists grew increasingly violent, attacking tourists as well as Egyptians.

Capital: Cairo
Area: 997,739 sq km (385,229 sq mi)
Population: 59,690,000 (1995)
Currency: 1 Egyptian pound = 100 piastres = 1,000 millièmes
Religions: Sunni Muslim 90.0%; Christian (mostly Coptic) 10.0%
Ethnic Groups: Egyptian 99.8%
Languages: Arabic (official)
International Organizations: UN; OAU; Arab League; OAPEC; Non-Aligned Movement

Egyptian language The language spoken in Egypt in antiquity. Its daughter language, Coptic, died out in the 17th century AD. It thus has one of the longest histories of any language. There is a vast literature, both secular (historical and legal texts) and religious (myths, hymns, and rituals). From 650 BC the classicizing tendencies of the scribes gave way to Demotic ('of the people') Egyptian, and Demotic inscriptions are found until the mid-5th century AD. Coptic became dominant in the 4th century AD, but started to decline after the introduction of Arabic in the 7th century (see SEMITIC LANGUAGES). Egyptian inscriptions were written in hieroglyphs (highly stylized pictorial symbols). There were also two cursive scripts based on the hieroglyphs: Hieratic, used for religious documents; and Demotic, for ordinary documents. Coptic was written in the Greek alphabet, with seven extra letters taken from Demotic. Egyptian is part of Afro-Asiatic, a larger group which includes BERBER, CHADIC, CUSHITIC, and Semitic languages.

Ehrenburg, Ilya (Grigorevich) (1891–1967) Soviet novelist and journalist. As a journalist, he became famous during the World War II for his anti-German propaganda in *Pravda* and *Red Star*. His novels include *The Thaw* (1954), a work containing open criticism of Stalinism and dealing with the temporary period of liberalization following Stalin's death.

Ehrlich, Paul (1854–1915) German medical scientist, one of the founders of modern immunology. He developed techniques for staining specific tissues, from which he became convinced that a disease organism could be destroyed by an appropriate magic bullet, thus pioneering the study of chemotherapy. Success in this came in 1911 when a synthetic compound of arsenic proved effective against syphilis. He shared a Nobel Prize in 1908.

Eichmann, (Karl) Adolf (1906–62) German administrator. He was responsible for carrying out Hitler's final solution and for administering the concentration camps, in which 6 million Jews perished. After the war he went into hiding in Argentina, but in 1960 he was traced by Israeli agents, abducted, tried, and subsequently executed.

eider Any one of four species of mainly black and white sea ducks which thrive off the cold northern coasts of America, Europe, and Asia. The common eider, *Somateria mollissima*, is a hefty-looking bird, 60 cm (2 feet) long, with an odd triangular profile to its beak and head. Breeding in colonies, it is well known for the softness of the down which, like other ducks, the female plucks from her breast to line the nest. In Iceland the birds are farmed for this down and its collection does them no harm.

Eiffel Tower A wrought-iron structure designed by the French engineer Alexandre Gustave Eiffel (1832–1923) and erected in Paris for the centenary exhibition of 1889. Still a famous landmark, it was, at 300 m (984 ft), the tallest man-made structure for many years.

Eiger A mountain peak in the Bernese Alps of Central Switzerland, first climbed by C. Barrington in 1858. It is a mountain with three ridges the highest of which rises to 3,970 m (13,101 ft).

Eijkman, Christiaan (1858–1930) Dutch physician. Working in Indonesia, Eijkman discovered the cause of beriberi to be dietary rather than bacteriological. Although he did not correctly recognize the reason for this, his work resulted in a simple cure for the disease. It also led later to the discovery of the vitamin thiamine, a deficiency of which causes beriberi. He shared a Nobel Prize in 1929.

Eilat (or **Elat**) The southernmost town in Israel, a port and resort at the head of the Gulf of Aqaba; pop. (est. 1982) 19,500. Founded in 1949 near the ruins of biblical Elath, it is Israel's only outlet to the Red Sea.

Eindhoven The chief industrial city of the province of North Brabant, in the Netherlands, situated on the River Dommel 88 km (55 miles) southeast of Rotterdam; pop. (1991) 192,900. The city is a major producer of electrical and electronic goods.

Einstein, Albert (1879–1955) German-born US theoretical physicist, founder of the theory of relativity, often regarded as the greatest scientist of the 20th century. In 1905 he published three outstanding papers dealing with the photoelectric effect, Brownian motion, and his special theory of relativity. Relativity abandons the idea of absolute space and time as a reference framework for all bodies; instead a distinction is made between the framework of the observer and that of the object. Among the theory's most important conclusions is that mass and energy are interconvertible, expressed by the equation $e = mc^2$ (c being the speed of light). In 1915 Einstein published the general theory of relativity. This extended his ideas to gravitation, which he treated as a curvature of the space–time continuum. The general theory was vindicated when the predicted deflection of light rays passing through a substantial gravitational field was confirmed by observations during the solar eclipse of 1919. As a Jew, Einstein decided to live in the USA when Hitler came to power in 1933. For the remainder of his life he sought without success a unified field theory embracing electromagnetism, gravitation, and quantum mechanics. In 1939 he wrote to President Roosevelt about the military potential of nuclear energy, greatly influencing the decision to build an atom bomb. After the war he spoke out passionately against nuclear weapons.

Einstein–de Sitter universe See COSMOLOGY.

einsteinium (symbol Es, at. no. 99, r.a.m. 252). An artificial strongly radioactive transuranic element discovered by A. Ghiorso in 1952 from hydrogen bomb fallout. Named after Albert EINSTEIN, it has 11 isotopes.

Einthoven, Willem (1860–1927) Dutch physiologist. He devised the first electrocardiograph, using a string galvanometer with an optical system to amplify the deflection of a fine wire. He was subsequently able to link the resulting electrocardiograms with specific muscular contractions in the heart, and thus begin to diagnose various heart diseases.

Éire (Gaelic, 'Ireland') The former name (from 1937 to 1949) of the Republic of Ireland, still often used in newspapers etc. to distinguish the country from Northern Ireland and from the island as a whole.

Eisenhower, Dwight David (known as 'Ike') (1890–1969) US general and Republican statesman, 34th President of the USA 1953–61. In World War II he was Commander-in-Chief of Allied forces in North Africa and Italy 1942–43 and Supreme Commander of Allied Expeditionary Forces in western Europe 1943–45. As President, he adopted a hard line towards Communism both in his domestic and foreign policy; in the USA an extreme version of this was reflected in McCarthyism.

Eisenstein, Sergei (Mikhailovich) (1898–1948) Soviet film director, born in Latvia. He made his name with *The Battleship Potemkin* (1925), a film commemorating the Russian Revolution of 1905; its innovative use of montage received international acclaim. At odds with the prevailing style of socialist realism, Eisenstein fell into disfavour in 1932 and had to wait for the release of *Alexander Nevsky* (1938) to regain his reputation. His final film was *Ivan the Terrible*; although the first part (1944) was well received, the second (1946) earned Stalin's disapproval and was not released until a decade after Eisenstein's death.

ejection seat A seat fitted with a PARACHUTE, capable of being ejected from an aeroplane in an emergency. It is fired from the aircraft by an explosive charge or rocket, and automatically deploys an auxiliary braking (drogue) parachute. If operated above about 3,000 m (9,800 feet), the main parachute will not automatically deploy until that height is reached. It can be operated at very low altitudes and has saved many lives.

Ekman, Vagn Walfrid (1874–1954) Swedish oceanographer. He recognized the importance of the Coriolis effect on ocean currents, showing that it can be responsible for surface water moving at an angle to the prevailing wind direction. He also explained why water flow at different depths can vary in both velocity and direction, and devised various instruments including a type of current meter that is still in use.

El Aaiún See LA'YOUN.

Elagabalus See HELIOGABALUS.

El Alamein See ALAMEIN, EL.

Elam An ancient kingdom east of the Tigris, established in the 4th millenium BC, with its capital at Susa.

eland Either of two species of antelope with straight, spirally twisted horns. The giant eland, *Taurotragus derbianus*, is the largest of the antelopes, being almost 1.8 m (6 feet) tall at the shoulder; its horns may be up to 99 cm (39 inches) long, though those of the female are more slender. It lives in the open country and forests of East Africa and once ranged as far south as the Cape. The common eland, *T. oryx*, once inhabited much of southern, central, and East Africa, but is now rare.

elasticity (in physics) A solid is elastic if it returns to its original size and shape after it has been deformed. If a small weight suspended from a wire produces an extension of the wire, the wire will recover and return to its original length when the weight has been removed. However, this recovery will not occur if the weight is too great. If a large force is applied to the wire it will acquire a permanent stretch – that is, it will have been plastically deformed. The maximum force which can be applied without plastic deformation occurring is called the elastic limit. The point at which the material begins to 'give' is called the yield point.

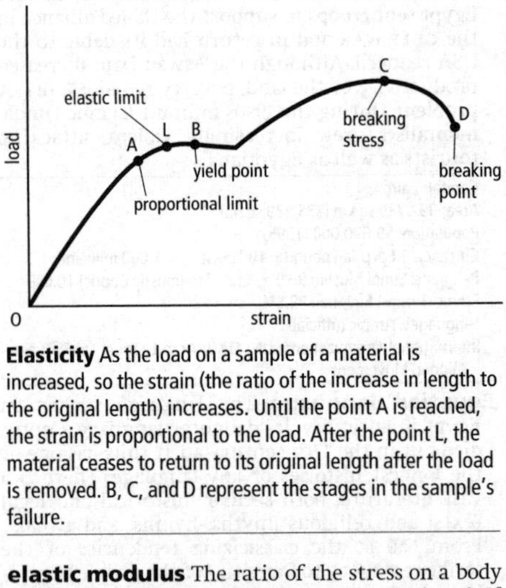

Elasticity As the load on a sample of a material is increased, so the strain (the ratio of the increase in length to the original length) increases. Until the point A is reached, the strain is proportional to the load. After the point L, the material ceases to return to its original length after the load is removed. B, C, and D represent the stages in the sample's failure.

elastic modulus The ratio of the stress on a body obeying HOOKE'S LAW, to the strain produced. If the strain is a change in length, it is known as Young's modulus.

elastomer A plastic material which at room temperature can be stretched under low stress to at least twice its length, but snaps back to its original length on release of stress. This property depends on the fact that the contorted molecular chains making up the POLYMER can be uncoiled by a tensile stress, but return to their original position due to the presence of a small degree of cross-linking between the chains. Natural and synthetic RUBBERS are the commonest elastomers.

Elat See EILAT.

Elba A small island off the west coast of Italy, famous as the place of Napoleon's first exile (1814–15). Its chief town and port is Portoferraio and its highest peak is Mt. Capanne (1,108 m, 3,340 ft).

Elbe (Czech **Labe**) A river of Central Europe which rises in the Czech Republic and flows 1,159 km (720 miles) through Germany to the North Sea. Major cities upon it are Dresden, Magdeburg, and Hamburg. From 1945 until the reunification of Germany in 1990 it formed part of the frontier between East and West Germany.

Elbrus, Mount A peak in the Caucasus Mountains on the frontier between Russia and the Republic of Georgia. Rising to 5,642 m (18,510 ft), it is the highest mountain in Europe.

El Cid See CID, EL.

elder A deciduous shrub or tree found in temperate regions of the Old and New Worlds. Members of the same family as honeysuckle and snowberry, all elders belong to the genus *Sambucus*, with about 20 species. Most have large heads of white flowers followed by blue-black, red, or in some species white or yellow fruits much liked by birds. The flowers and fruits of the common elder, *S. nigra*, are used in wine-making. Other species, especially the American elder, *S. canadensis*, are widely grown for their spectacular flowers.

The plant called GROUND ELDER is an unrelated species of the carrot family.

El Dorado A fictitious country (according to some, a city) abounding in gold, believed by the Spanish and by Sir Walter Raleigh to exist upon the Amazon. The origin of the belief, which led Spanish conquistadors to converge on the area in search of treasure, appears to have been rumours of an Indian ruler, in what is now Colombia, who ritually coated his body with gold dust and then plunged into a sacred lake while his subjects threw in gold and jewels.

Eleanor Cross Any of the stone crosses erected by Edward I to mark the stopping-places of the cortège that brought the body of his queen, Eleanor of Castile, from Nottinghamshire to London in 1290. Three of the 12 crosses survive. See CHARING CROSS.

Eleanor of Aquitaine (*c*.1122–1204) Daughter of the Duke of Aquitaine, queen of France 1137–52 and of England 1154–89. She was married to Louis VII of France from 1137; in 1152, with the annulment of their marriage, she married the future Henry II of England. Her ten children included the monarchs Richard I (Richard the Lionheart) and John, whose accession she strove to secure. She acted as regent (1190–94) while Richard was away on the Crusades.

Eleanor of Castile (*c*.1244–90) Queen of England 1272–90. She was the daughter of Ferdinand III of Castile in Spain and married EDWARD I of England in 1254. Eleanor bore 13 children and accompanied her husband on Crusade (1270–73). After her death at Hadby in Nottinghamshire, her body was embalmed and taken to Westminster Abbey. At each of the ten overnight stopping places Edward ordered a stone cross to be erected to her memory, the 'Eleanor crosses'.

elecampane A sunflower-like plant, *Inula helenium*, with solitary, bright yellow flowers. Though native to Europe and northern Asia, it is now widely distributed in the eastern USA, where it has escaped from gardens. The root may be candied as confectionery.

Elector A prince of the HOLY ROMAN EMPIRE who had the right to elect the emperor. Although the monarchy was elective by the 12th century, it was not until the contested election of 1257 that the number of Electors was fixed at seven. The office of Elector disappeared when Napoleon abolished the empire in 1806.

Electoral College A group of people chosen to elect a candidate to an office. Probably the oldest College is that which meets in Rome to elect a new pope, consisting of the cardinals of the Church. The idea was adapted by the framers of the American Constitution in 1787, each state appointing as many electors as it had members of Congress, these electors then meeting to choose the President of the USA. As states extended their franchise these electors came to be chosen by direct election. With the emergence of organized political parties, the holding of a national party convention to select presidential candidates developed. Candidates in each state are all now chosen beforehand by party associations and their vote is decided by their party's convention. Thus, for each state (except Maine since 1969), following a presidential election, the candidate who has won a majority of the popular vote in that state will gain all that state's electoral votes. In the event of a tied election the President is chosen by a vote in the House of Representatives.

Electra In Greek mythology, the daughter of Agamemnon and Clytemnestra. She supported her brother Orestes when he killed their mother and her lover, Aegisthus, to avenge the murder of their father.

electrical engineering The practical study and exploitation of electricity and magnetism. This applies particularly to the development of electrical machines, such as ELECTRIC MOTORS and GENERATORS, and to power generation, storage, and distribution facilities; also to the conversion of electrical energy to useful work as in lighting, heating, and electric traction. Electrical engineering involves the study of high-power devices. The study of devices that operate at small power levels, using SEMICONDUCTOR DEVICES, is ELECTRONICS.

electric-arc furnace A chamber in which a high temperature is produced by a high-voltage electric arc passing between graphite electrodes. It is used in the IRON AND STEEL INDUSTRY to produce special steels, such as stainless steel, constructional alloys, and tool steels, from a mixture of scrap steel, pig-iron, and alloying additions.

electric bell A bell that is made to sound by closing a switch (bellpush), causing an electric current to pass through an ELECTROMAGNET. This in turn causes a hammer to strike the bell and in doing so to break the circuit. The hammer then springs back to a position that again closes the circuit. The bell thus rings continuously while the switch is closed.

electric car See ELECTRIC VEHICLE.

electric cell See BATTERY.

electric charge A property of certain particles which causes them to attract or repel each other. There are two types, called negative and positive: ELECTRONS carry a negative charge and PROTONS an equal quantity of positive charge. Charges of the same type repel one another, while opposite charges attract. The force between charges obeys COULOMB's law. Atoms are usually electrically neutral because they possess electrons and protons in equal number, and the overall charge is zero. Rubbing materials together can upset this balance, and the materials are then said to be charged with static electricity. Chemical action, as in a BATTERY, can cause a flow of charge, as can the motion of a wire in the magnetic field of a generator. A flow of charge – usually in the form of electrons – is an electric current. Quantities of charge are measured in COULOMBS.

electric constant See PERMITTIVITY.

electric current A flow of electric charge, usually in the form of electrons. In a circuit, it is measured using an ammeter, and the SI UNIT of measurement is the AMPERE (A). It may be direct current (d.c.), in which case the charge flow is one way, as from a battery. Or it may be alternating current (a.c.), as from a mains supply. Here, the charge flows alternately backwards then forwards in a circuit many times every second.

electric field The region around an electric charge in which another charged particle experiences a force. The strength and direction of an electric field can be represented by LINES OF FORCE. The strength (or intensity) for any given point in the field is given by the force per unit charge at that point and is measured in volts per metre.

electric fish A fish that produces an electric current. There are several hundred different species of electric fish from several families. Most produce only a weak current, but several kinds produce one powerful enough to cause a severe shock to man or large animals. In the sea, the only example of the latter are the twenty or so species of electric rays or torpedoes, but all skates and rays can generate weak currents. Torpedoes, especially *Torpedo nobiliana*, use their electric powers to stun the fishes on which they prey, but the skates probably employ theirs for species recognition. Some of the most powerful electric fishes can be found in fresh water, and include the tropical South American electric eel, *Electrophorus electricus*, which can produce currents of 1 amp at 500 volts, and the tropical African catfish, *Malapterurus electricus*.

electricity and magnetism The fundamental phenomena on which electronics and electrical engineering are based. Electrostatics is the study of ELECTRIC CHARGES at rest, and is concerned with charged objects and the forces between them.

If a charged body is connected by a metal wire to one that is neutral, or carries an opposite charge, a charge will be transferred between the two. This flow of charge is known as an ELECTRIC CURRENT, and usually consists of a flow of electrons from the more negatively charged body to the more positively charged one. Metals and other materials that allow the flow of electric charge through them are known as conductors. Materials that resist the passage of an electric current are known as insulators. The difference in electric charge between two bodies that allows a current to flow when they are connected represents a difference in electrical potential, and is known as a potential difference (p.d.). The relation between the potential difference V (in volts) between any two points, the current I (in amperes), and the resistance R between the points (in ohms) is given by OHM's law: $V = IR$. In a battery or GENERATOR, chemical or mechanical work is done to create a p.d. between one pole of the device and the other. When these poles are connected by a conducting path an electrical circuit is formed, through which current flows. This electrical current provides ENERGY to carry out useful work, such as driving an electric motor, or powering a light bulb.

Magnetic phenomena are closely related to electrical phenomena. MAGNETS have positive and negative poles, and as with electric charges, like poles repel while unlike poles attract. A pair of magnetic poles creates a field, a region around the pole in which magnetic forces act. A charged body creates a similar electrical field. More importantly, an electric current flowing through a conductor generates a weak magnetic field around it: if the conductor is wound into a coil, and a core of iron or similar ferromagnetic material is placed in the centre, the magnetic field is greatly increased, and the coil becomes an ELECTROMAGNET. The interaction between electric and magnetic forces is crucial to many of the electrical devices commonly in use. The two most important interactions are ELECTROMAGNETIC INDUCTION, in which an electric current is produced in a conductor if it is moved through a magnetic field (or held in a constantly changing magnetic field), and the related effect whereby a current-carrying conductor placed in a magnetic field experiences a force on it. These phenomena are the basis on which such devices as ELECTRIC MOTORS, GENERATORS, RELAYS, SOLENOIDS, MICROPHONES, and LOUDSPEAKERS operate.

electricity generation and supply Methods of electricity generation vary according to economic resources, but patterns of generation are similar internationally (see ENERGY RESOURCES). Modern electric GENERATORS typically give an a.c. output of around 20,000 V at a FREQUENCY of either 50 or 60 Hz. A three-phase a.c. transmission system is usually used, in which three conductors carry alternating currents that are out of step by one-third of a cycle: this gives a constant flow of power, and hence much smoother and more efficient operation than with a single-phase system. For long-distance transmission, the generated voltage is stepped up using TRANSFORMERS to around 270,000 V, or up to 500,000 V on certain long-distance sections. Very high voltages are used because this substantially cuts power losses in the CABLES. The voltage is then stepped down for domestic supply at local substations, to values of between 110 and 240 V, depending on the supply standards of the country. All common electricity grids are a.c. systems, but recent developments in technology and the development of superconducting cables have led to renewed interest in d.c. distribution systems. Direct-current transmission is competitive over long distances because a cable can carry between two and ten times as much d.c. power as a.c. Long-distance power transmission in most countries is via overhead pylons, while urban distribution is usually by underground cable.

electricity meter A device for measuring the total electric power consumption of households and other premises, for billing purposes. The meter is fitted into the electrical wiring circuit so that when a current flows a small electric motor is actuated. The total movement of this motor is registered on a series of dials, which record the energy consumption in kilowatt hours.

electric lighting See INCANDESCENT LAMP; FLUORESCENT LAMP; ARC LAMP; GAS-DISCHARGE LAMP; LIGHTING.

electric locomotive See RAILWAYS, HISTORY OF.

electric motor A device for converting electrical energy into rotary motion (but see also LINEAR MOTOR). It is the complementary device to the electrical GENERATOR, which converts rotary motion into electric current: most generators can be converted into motors, and vice versa. The key components of an electric motor are a coil mounted on a freely rotating shaft (the rotor or ARMATURE); and a permanent magnet or an electromagnet (the stator) surrounding the rotor. The rotary motion produced by interaction between the rotor and stator relies on ELECTROMAGNETIC INDUCTION.

There are many different types of electric

motor. If the motor uses direct-current (d.c.) electricity, then the stator has a fixed magnetic field, and the current passes through the rotor. Similar motors can operate from an alternating current (a.c.): universal motors, that can use either d.c. or a.c., are of this design and are used in vacuum cleaners, small power tools, and other domestic applications. More important in industrial contexts are induction and synchronous motors. In an induction motor, two or more coils on the stator produce a rotating magnetic field, which induces a current in the rotor. This in turn creates a turning force on the rotor, which continues to act until the rotor is moving at the same speed as the magnetic field. Induction motors are rugged, reliable, and can develop high starting TORQUES. They are suitable for use in haulage or traction. Synchronous motors operate on similar principles, but when full speed is reached, a current is applied to the rotor, which acts to 'lock' it at the same speed as the moving magnetic field. Synchronous motors are used in clocks, record players, tape drives, CD players, navigational equipment, and other applications where accurate maintenance of speed is important.

electric vehicle A vehicle propelled by electric motor. An electric vehicle first became technologically feasible with the development of a suitable storage BATTERY in 1881, and the first electric tricycle ran in the same year. By the end of the 19th century the electric vehicle was competing with steam-powered and internal-combustion vehicles. Electric cars lost ground after the invention of the electric STARTER MOTOR in 1912, but they have continued to be used for short-distances in milk floats and fork-lift trucks. However, the new types of battery currently under development, and recent improvements in FUEL CELLS, may enable electric vehicles to replace those driven by internal-combustion engines, at least for some purposes. As a result of the pollution associated with burning fossil fuels in internal-combustion engines, interest in the polution-free silent electric vehicle has renewed. However, unless the electricity is generated by fuel cells in the vehicles or by non-fossil fuels centrally, there would be no net saving in pollution.

electrocardiograph (ECG) A device used to display the electrical activity of the heart, producing a record called an electrocardiogram. Several recordings are taken using different pairs of electrodes placed on the chest and limbs (and in some cases in the oesophagus or in the heart itself by means of a CATHETER). By testing a patient during exercise, electrocardiography can diagnose acute events, such as myocardial infarction (heart attack), or chronic impairment of function due, for example, to inadequate blood supply. Continuous ECG monitoring is a feature of INTENSIVE-CARE UNITS and in resuscitation, particularly to diagnose potentially fatal abnormal heart rhythms.

electrochemical series A table in which metals are listed in order of their ability to act as reducing agents. The elements at the top of the electrochemical series are stronger reducing agents than those lower down. For example, zinc is higher in the series than copper. Therefore, if zinc is added to a solution of a copper salt, it will displace the copper, which will precipitate as the metal; the zinc will now be present in solution as a salt.

electroconvulsive therapy (ECT) A form of treatment for severe depression or, occasionally, schizophrenia, in which electrodes are placed on the skull and an electrical current is passed through the brain. Introduced in 1938 by the Italians Ugo Cerletti and Lucio Bini, the technique has been modified, notably since 1940, by the use of accompanying muscle relaxants to prevent injury from the convulsions induced. How ECT works is not properly understood, and the technique has been criticized on the grounds that it might cause permanent brain damage. The use of ECT declined during the 1970s, but it is still employed in certain types of severe depression.

electrode A conductive terminal which can be used to apply or extract electrical energy from a circuit or system. Usually made from metals such as copper, zinc, nickel, silver, or gold, electrodes are found in THERMIONIC VALVES, SEMICONDUCTOR DEVICES, electrolytic cells (see BATTERY), and many other devices.

electroencephalograph (EEG) A machine that detects and records electrical activity in the brain by registering potential differences between electrodes placed on the scalp, arising as a result of currents in the brain. Modern EEG machines register as many as 16 'channels' of brain activity on a multi-pen recorder (a polygraph). EEG signals are distinguished by their FREQUENCY and by the region in which they arise. For example, alpha waves (8–13 Hz) arise in the occipital region and are associated with states of relaxation; beta waves (15–30 Hz) arise in the frontal region. The technique can be used in NEUROLOGY to diagnose disordered activity of the brain caused by epilepsy, and sometimes local disorders, such as a tumour.

electrolysis The process of decomposing an electrically conducting compound by the passage of an electric current. For the passage of an electric current two conductors called electrodes are dipped into a solution or melt of the compound. At the negative electrode (the cathode), metal ions and hydrogen gas collect, while at the positive electrode (the anode) negative ions collect. At the cathode metal ions gain electrons to become metal atoms and are deposited on the cathode; this reduction process has important industrial applications in ELECTROPLATING and for reducing the ore of an impure metal to the metal itself.

electrolyte A compound that when molten or in solution conducts electricity and is simultaneously decomposed by it. An electrolyte may be an acid, a base, or a salt. It conducts because it consists of separate positive and negative IONS; these act as charge carriers for the current in a manner similar to electrons in a metal. See also BATTERY.

electromagnet A MAGNET consisting of a coil, carrying electrical current, wound on a core of soft (easily magnetized) iron. When an electric current is passed through the winding, the electromagnet produces a strong magnetic field. Unlike a permanent magnet, the magnetic field of an electromagnet may be switched on and off. The electromagnet is the basis of many electromechanical devices, such as RELAYS, SOLENOIDS, ELECTRIC BELLS, and ELECTRIC MOTORS.

electromagnetic force The FORCE responsible for atomic structure, chemical reactions, and all electromagnetic INTERACTIONS. See also GRAVITATION; STRONG FORCE; WEAK FORCE.

electromagnetic induction The production of an electrical potential difference (p.d.) or voltage across a conductor situated in a changing magnetic field. FARADAY was able to describe this behaviour mathematically: he found that the size of the p.d. produced is proportional to the rate of change of the magnetic flux. This applies whether the flux itself changes in strength or the conductor is moved through it. Electromagnetic induction underlies the operation of GENERATORS, ELECTRIC MOTORS, and most other electrical machines.

electromagnetic radiation Wave-like fluctuations in electric and magnetic fields travelling through free space or a material medium. This radiation is produced by the acceleration of electric charges. The electromagnetic waves travel at a constant speed in a vacuum, called the SPEED OF LIGHT, which is close to 300,000 km/s (186,000 m.p.s.): this may be slower if the waves are travelling in a material medium. They are TRANSVERSE WAVES with a wide spectrum of frequencies. The wavelength of the radiation varies inversely with the frequency of oscillation, which is measured in hertz (Hz). In some situations, such as PHOTOELECTRIC EFFECTS, electromagnetic radiation behaves as if it consisted of a stream of particles, called PHOTONS (see also WAVE-PARTICLE DUALITY). The shortest known electromagnetic waves are GAMMA RAYS, with a wavelength of less than 10^{-11} m. X-RAYS have a wavelength up to 10^{-9} m. Next in the electromagnetic spectrum comes ULTRAVIOLET RADIATION (10^{-9} to 10^{-7} m), then visible LIGHT (10^{-7} to 10^{-6} m), INFRARED RADIATION (10^{-6} to 10^{-3} m), and MICROWAVES (1 mm to 30 cm). The **electromagnetic spectrum** is completed by RADIO waves with wavelengths up to several kilometres.

electromagnetism The study of the interaction between an electric current and a magnetic field. Any conductor that carries a current is surrounded by a magnetic field whose LINES OF FORCE form circles with the conductor at the centre. The strength of the field is proportional to the current. If the conductor is wound into a coil (often called a solenoid) the field is concentrated along the inside, and in many respects the coil behaves like a bar magnet. If the charge moving through the conductor accelerates, then the magnetic field changes along with the associated electric field. By making the fields fluctuate ELECTROMAGNETIC RADIATION can be produced, in which the fluctuations are propagated through space.

electrometer An instrument that uses the mechanical forces existing between electrostatically charged bodies to measure extremely low voltages and currents. Vacuum-tube electrometers (or the more recent semiconductor equivalents that use a pair of field-effect TRANSISTORS) can measure currents as small as 10^{-13} A (about 10,000 electrons per second). Electrometers are an integral part of PH METERS.

electromotive force (e.m.f.) See BATTERY.

electron An elementary particle that possesses one unit of negative charge (-1.602×10^{-19} coulomb). Electrons are one of the three primary constituents of ATOMS, and were discovered by the British physicist Joseph Thomson in 1897. Electrons form ORBITALS which surround the positively charged nucleus and in a free atom the number of electrons is equal to the number of protons in the nucleus, so overall the atom is electrically neutral. When atoms combine to form molecules, some electrons in the VALENCY shell are transferred to or are shared with a neighbouring atom. This is the basis of CHEMICAL BONDING. In METALS and SEMICONDUCTORS the outermost electrons in the valence shell are able to detach themselves and are free to move through the material. These electrons are responsible for the conduction of electricity and heat. A heated wire filament can be made to emit electrons, and if this is done in a vacuum their paths can be controlled by electric or magnetic fields. Such beams of electrons are used to operate television picture tubes and electron microscopes. Electrons are also emitted at high energy from the nuclei of radioactive atoms, and they are then known as beta particles. In some circumstances electrons behave as waves; that is, they exhibit WAVE-PARTICLE DUALITY. Understanding the behaviour of electrons has been crucial to the development of ELECTRICAL ENGINEERING and particularly ELECTRONICS, since electric currents consist of a flow of free electrons. It has also been the basis of chemistry, as chemical interactions take place between the outer electrons of atoms.

electronegativity A measure of the ability of an element to acquire electrons. Different atoms in a stable molecule have different affinities for electrons. In the covalent molecule hydrogen chloride, HCl, for example, the electrons are found to be much closer to the chlorine atom than to the hydrogen atom, and chlorine is said to be the more electronegative atom. The most electronegative element is fluorine and the least is caesium. Compare ELECTROPOSITIVITY.

electronic funds transfer (EFT) The use of computer systems to make financial transactions. Business-to-business EFT is extremely important, but the most visible type of EFT is the automatic teller machine (ATM) serving the general public. ATMs are installed outside banks and other financial institutions to dispense or accept cash when activated with a suitably encoded plastic card. A related development is electronic funds transfer at point of sale (EFTPOS), which enables a purchase transaction to be made electronically with card verification and simultaneous debiting of the purchaser's bank account.

electronic mail (e-mail) The sending of messages via computer systems. Many computer systems are now connected to local or wide-area NETWORKS and users can communicate with other users anywhere on the network. Some services offer facilities that allow users to send and receive messages via a MICROCOMPUTER, a telephone, and a MODEM. The sender and receiver need not be on-line at the time; the message is held in a computer mail-box, which the receiver is able to access.

electronic music Music produced and recorded by electronic means. Strictly speaking, the term applies only to music derived through a SYNTHESIZER, but nowadays it embraces sounds taken from normal musical or everyday sources that have been recorded and perhaps manipulated in some way (formerly referred to as *musique concrète*). Tape recorder, synthesizer, computer, microchip, and other digital recording equipment, have made possible a whole new range of sounds that can be controlled (programmed) in ways that are impossible for conventional instruments and players. See also COMPUTER MUSIC.

electronic publishing The publication of books, magazines, etc., in electronic form rather than on paper, so that the information is accessible with a computer. Electronic publications are typically distributed on CD-ROM and generally contain graphics, photographic images, sound, and video clips as well as text. Publishing on-line is also becoming increasingly important, especially for academic journals.

electronics The study, design, and application of devices that rely on the conduction of electricity through a vacuum, a gas, or a semiconductor. The diode and other THERMIONIC VALVES were responsible for the development of radio and other communications media. The iconoscope, an early device for the production of electronic images, led to the development of TELEVISION, and by the 1930s television broadcasting had begun. After World War II, communications technology continued to develop, but electronics also found applications in a wide range of other industries. A major impetus was the development in 1948 of the first SEMICONDUCTOR DEVICE, the TRANSISTOR. The INTEGRATED CIRCUIT was developed in 1959. The rapid improvement of integrated circuits, and their application in particular to COMPUTERS and INFORMATION TECHNOLOGY, has led to an enormous expansion of the electronics industry.

electronic scanning The use of a computer-controlled laser beam or detector to systematically scan artwork, photographs, or other images in the process of DIGITIZATION to produce a record of that image on computer disk for later use in printing procedures.

electron microscope An instrument that uses an electron beam instead of a light beam to obtain very high magnification of biological and physical samples where optical MICROSCOPES are inadequate. In operation, a stream of ELECTRONS is focused into a very narrow beam and directed on to a specimen. The structure of the specimen causes specific diffraction, or scattering of the beam. The pattern of diffracted electrons is collected and displayed on a CATHODE-RAY TUBE screen or on a photographic plate. The image is representative to some degree of the microstructure of the specimen. Two main types of electron microscope exist: the transmission electron microscope (TEM) and the scanning electron microscope (SEM). In the TEM, the electron beam passes through the specimen, which must be very thin to permit this. The TEM gives a very high magnification, and can examine features typically 2 nm (2×10^{-9} m) wide, but it gives a 'flat' image, devoid of depth. In the SEM, the beam is scattered principally off the surface features of the specimen, and gives information apparently as a 'solid' image. The SEM is therefore used to examine surfaces, although it has lower resolution (ability to distinguish detail) than the TEM.

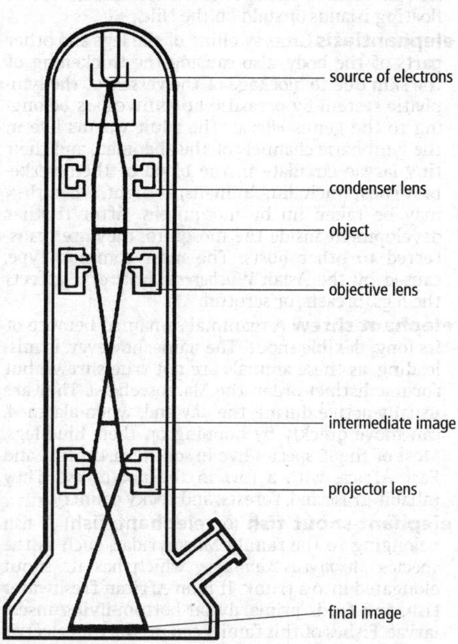

Electron microscope In this transmission electron microscope, the sample is sufficiently thin for the electron beam to pass through it.

electron spin See SPIN.

electron spin resonance (ESR) A technique used to investigate materials containing unpaired electrons. Electrons have a property called SPIN, which can be in one of two states. Most electrons in an atom or molecule are paired, the electrons in these pairs having opposed spin states. If a material containing single unpaired electrons is placed in a magnetic field, the spin of the unpaired electron will line up with the magnetic field. The energy required to cause a single unpaired electron to change from this spin state to one in which it is opposed to the magnetic field is dependent upon the environment of the unpaired electron. Measuring the magnitude of this energy change gives valuable information about the structure of the material.

electron transport chain (or **hydrogen transport system**) One of three stages in the biochemical pathway of RESPIRATION. In this stage, electrons or hydrogen atoms are transferred by coenzymes from the other two stages, namely GLYCOLYSIS and KREBS' CYCLE, and are used (indirectly) to generate molecules of adenosine triphosphate (ATP) from ADP and inorganic phosphate. The electron transport chain consists of a series of carrier molecules, including cytochrome proteins, fixed in the membranes of MITOCHONDRIA or, in bacteria (which lack mitochondria), in the plasma membrane. Within the carrier system, hydrogen atoms are split into their component protons and electrons. The protons are released to the surrounding medium, but the electrons are passed from carrier to carrier along the chain. This transfer is accompanied by the release of energy which is used for making ATP.

electron-volt (symbol eV) A unit of work or energy, being the work done when the charge on one electron moves through a POTENTIAL DIFFERENCE of one volt. It is commonly used in atomic and nuclear physics because energy values are conveniently calculated in this way. 1 eV = 1.602×10^{-19} joule.

electrophoresis See CHROMATOGRAPHY.

electroplating A process in which a thin layer of one metal is deposited from solution on to an article made of another metal by ELECTROLYSIS. The article to be plated is connected to the negative terminal (cathode) of a direct-current power supply and immersed in a solution containing IONS of the plating metal. The positive terminal (anode) is usually connected to an inert conductor. As the current flows through the solution the positive metal ions are attracted to the cathode, where they accept electrons to become uncharged metal atoms, which accumulate as a thin layer. Many metals can be applied by electroplating, including copper, chromium, nickel, zinc, cadmium, tin, gold, silver, and platinum.

electropositivity A measure of the extent to which atoms will part with electrons. It is thus the converse of ELECTRONEGATIVITY. Elements such as the alkali metals, which readily form positive ions, are said to be strongly electropositive.

electrorheological fluid (ER, or 'smart' fluid) A liquid suspension that reversibly solidifies to a jelly-like solid when a high-voltage electric field is applied across it. Most modern ER fluids are zeolites (silicates which absorb other molecules on to their surface) or metals coated with oxides or polymers. Possible applications currently in the research stage include an electrically operated CLUTCH, and a vibration damper whose properties could be varied electrically.

electroscope An electrostatic instrument used to demonstrate the presence of small potential differences and electric charges. The gold-leaf electroscope contains a pair of gold leaves attached to a conductive support inside an electrically insulated chamber. When the support is charged, the charge passes down into the leaves, which visibly separate due to their mutual repulsion.

electrostatic precipitator A device for removing particulate impurities from air or other gases. An electrical discharge is fed into the gas, ionizing the impurity particles (giving them a negative charge). Positively charged electrode plates attract these particles and they are then removed. These devices are now widely used in the chimneys of coal-burning power-stations to remove the fine, pulverized fuel ash.

electrostatics The study of the effects of positive and negative charges. The fundamental charges are the electron, which is negative, and the proton, which is positive. These two charges are the same size. Like charges repel; unlike charges attract. The magnitude of these forces is given by COULOMB's law. Particles with unequal numbers of electrons and protons are said to be charged. Ions are charged atoms or molecules. Larger charged particles are formed when ions or electrons become attached to bits of solid and liquid matter. Atoms or molecules can be charged by putting them in a strong electric field, or by irradiating them with ionizing radiation; certain substances can be charged by rubbing or heating them.

electrum See ALLOY.

elegy An elaborately formal LYRIC poem lamenting the death of a friend or public figure. In Greek and Latin verse, the term referred to the METRE (alternating HEXAMETERS and PENTAMETERS known as elegiacs) of a poem, not to its content: love poems were often included. But since Milton's 'Lycidas' (1637), an elegy in English has usually denoted laments, although Milton called his poem a 'monody'.

element (in chemistry) A substance that cannot be broken down into simpler substances by chemical means. All chemical compounds are made up from different combinations of elements. The smallest particle of an element is an ATOM, which consists of a dense NUCLEUS surrounded by clouds of ELECTRONS. The nucleus consists of protons and neutrons; it is the number of protons, the atomic number, that determines the chemical identity of the atom. There are just over 100 known elements, of which 92 occur naturally. When the elements are arranged in order of their atomic numbers, those with similar properties occur at regular intervals. This is shown in the PERIODIC TABLE. See also ISOTOPE.

elementary particle (in atomic physics) Any subatomic particle that is a constituent of matter. There are two main classes of particle – the HADRONS, which are strongly interacting and are made of various combinations of QUARKS, and the LEPTONS, which are weakly interacting and include the electron, the muon, and the tau, with their neutrinos. All known particles can be accounted for within this classification; and its great success has been the prediction of the existence of other particles, later confirmed by experiment.

elephant The largest and most powerful of the land mammals, once found in tropical jungles and grassy plains over much of Africa and Asia. The African or bush elephant, *Loxodonta africana*, is the largest of the three species living today; the smaller species of the African elephant, the forest elephant (*L. cyclotis*), also lives in Africa. The Asiatic or Indian elephant, *Elephas maximus*, is smaller than the bush elephant and is classified in four subspecies: the Indian, Ceylon, Sumatran, and Malaysian elephants. The trunk, characteristic of these animals, is a flexible, muscular tube. At the tip are two finger-like projections which can pluck leaves and grasses for transfer to its mouth. It can be used to produce loud trumpet-like sounds important in courtship and in communication. The large tusks, the much modified second pair of incisor teeth, grow throughout the life of the animal. These may reach a length of 3.18 m (10.5 feet) and weigh 160 kg (353 pounds). For such a huge creature it can move quite quickly, 9–13 km/hour (6–8 miles per hour), and if enraged at 40 km/hour (25 miles per hour) over a distance of 45 m (150 feet).

Elephants are social animals that live in herds. Each group is usually led by an old cow. Maturity is reached at about fourteen years. There is no fixed breeding season and the gestation period is long, perhaps 21 months. A single calf is born, covered with coarse black hair, and is about 90 cm (3 feet) tall at the shoulder. Suckled by its mother for two years, the calf remains with her for a further two years. A female African or bush elephant can live for 60 years; males for 50 years.

elephant grass Any of several species of tall-growing African grass species, particularly *Pennisetum purpureum*. One species is a constituent of the floating islands of sudd on the Nile.

elephantiasis Gross swelling of the legs and other parts of the body, also causing the thickening of the skin due to blockage of the vessels of the lymphatic system by parasitic ROUNDWORMS belonging to the genus *Filaria*. The adult worms live in the lymphatic channels of the abdomen, and their tiny larvae circulate in the blood of their verbebrate host (including humans) at night, when they may be taken up by mosquitoes. After further development inside the mosquito, they are transferred to other hosts. The most common type, caused by the Asian *Wuchereria bancrofti*, affects the legs, breasts, or scrotum.

elephant shrew A mammal so named because of its long, flexible snout. The name, however, is misleading, as these animals are not true shrews, but form a distinct order, the Macroscelidea. They are usually active during the day and, when alarmed, can move quickly by hopping on their hind-legs. Most of the 15 species live in southern, central, and East Africa, with a few in the northwest. They inhabit grassland, forests, and rocky country.

elephant-snout fish (or **elephant fish**) A fish belonging to the family Mormyridae, such as the species *Mormyrus kannume*, which has its snout elongated into a trunk. It is an African freshwater fish, and feeds primarily on bottom-living insect larvae. Fishes of this family can produce an electric field by means of which they navigate in the rather murky waters of their river homes.

El Escorial A town in the Sierra Guadarrama of central Spain, situated 40 km (25 miles) north-west of Madrid, adjacent to a royal palace and monastery built by King Philip II between 1563 and 1584.

Elgar, Sir Edward (William) (1857–1934) British composer. A self-taught musician from Worcester, he made his mark with the *Enigma Variations* (1899), a set of 14 orchestral variations (on an undisclosed theme), 13 of which are titled by the initials of his friends. He gained an international reputation with the oratorio *The Dream of Gerontius* (1900), the violin concerto (1910), and the cello concerto (1919). In Britain he is perhaps most famous for patriotic pieces such as the five *Pomp and Circumstance* marches (1901–30).

Elgin, Thomas Bruce, 7th Earl of (1766–1841) British diplomat and art connoisseur. When envoy at Constantinople (1799–1803) he feared the destruction of Greek antiquities in the conflict between Turks and Greeks and obtained permission from the Turks to remove them. Between 1803 and 1812 he transported a number of sculptures to England, many from the Parthenon in Athens (which was under Turkish control). The British government vindicated Elgin's actions and purchased the 'Elgin Marbles' from him in 1816 for £35,000 to exhibit them in the British Museum, where they can still be seen, in spite of Greek claims for their return.

El Giza See GIZA.

El Greco (Spanish, 'the Greek'; born Domenikos Theotokopoulos) (1541–1614) Cretan-born Spanish painter. After studying in Venice and working in Rome he settled in Toledo in 1577. His portraits and religious works are characterized by distorted perspective, elongated figures, and strident use of colour. Famous works include the altarpiece *The Assumption of the Virgin* (1577–79) and the painting *The Burial of Count Orgaz* (1586).

Elijah (9th century BC) Hebrew prophet at the time of King AHAB. His mission, as told in the Old Testament of the Bible, was to strengthen the worship of the God of the Israelites, to oppose the worship of all other gods, and to promote moral uprightness and social justice. He rebuked Ahab for his devotion to the fertility god Baal, worshipped by his wife Jezebel. He charged his successor, **Elisha**, with the destruction of the Omri dynasty. Elisha became involved in court affairs, inspiring revolutions in Syria and Israel and, by anointing Jehu as King of Israel, instigated the downfall of the Omri. Elijah was 'translated' into heaven (without dying) in a chariot of fire.

Eliot, George (pseudonym of Mary Ann Evans) (1819–80) British novelist. Deeply influenced by evangelical Christianity in her youth, Eliot renounced her faith in God in 1842, but retained a strong belief in moral duty and human love. In 1854 she published a translation of Feuerbach's heterodox *Essence of Christianity* and at about this time began an unconventional liaison with the writer G. H. Lewes (who was married but separated from his wife). Eliot is best known for her novels *Adam Bede* (1859), *The Mill on the Floss* (1860), *Silas Marner* (1861), and her masterpiece *Middlemarch* (1871–72), a comprehensive and penetrating study of English provincial society.

Eliot, T(homas) S(tearns) (1888–1965) US-born British poet, critic, and dramatist. Associated with the rise of literary modernism, he struck a new note in modern poetry with his verse collection *Prufrock and Other Observations* (1917), which combined satire with allusion and lyricism. In his newly founded literary quarterly *The Criterion*, he published *The Waste Land* (1922), which established him as the voice of a disillusioned generation. In 1927 he became an Anglo-Catholic and subsequent works, such as *Four Quartets* (1943), reveal his increasing involvement with Christianity. His attempt to revive verse plays, with such dramas as *Murder in the Cathedral* (1935) and *The Elder Statesman* (1958), was largely unsuccessful. His book of children's verse, *Old Possum's Book of Practical Cats* (1939), formed the basis of a long-running musical show *Cats* (1981), with music by Andrew Lloyd Webber. He was awarded the Nobel Prize for literature in 1948.

Elisabethville The former name (until 1966) of LUBUMBASHI.

Elisha A biblical figure, the wealthy farmer's son who became the disciple, and then the anointed successor, of ELIJAH in Israel. Portrayed in the Bible as both the helper of all people and the king's counsellor, Elisha became renowned for his miracles far beyond Israel. His sending of a messenger to anoint Jehu, who was leading the rebellion against Ahab, profoundly affected Israel's subsequent history. Alyasa (Elisha) is mentioned in the Koran, and is described by Muslim traditions as the disciple and successor of Ilyas (Elijah).

Elista The capital of the Republic of Kalmykia-Khalmg Tangch (Kalmykia) in southern Russia, situated to the west of Astrakhan; pop. (1990) 85,000. It was known as Stepnoy from 1944 to 1957.

Elizabeth I (1533–1603) Daughter of Henry VIII, queen of England and Ireland 1558–1603. Succeeding her Catholic sister Mary I, Elizabeth re-established a moderate form of Protestantism as the religion of the state. None the less, her reign was dominated by the threat of a Catholic restoration (eventually leading to the execution of Mary, Queen of Scots) and by war with Spain, during which the country was saved from invasion by the defeat of the Armada in 1588. Her reign was characterized by a flowering of national culture, particularly in the field of literature, in which Shakespeare, Marlowe, and Spenser were all active. Although frequently courted, she never married.

Elizabeth II (born Princess Elizabeth Alexandra Mary) (1926–) Daughter of George VI, queen of the United Kingdom since 1952. She has always shown a strong personal commitment to the Commonwealth, and is one of the most travelled 20th-century monarchs, having made extensive overseas tours and many public appearances at home.

Elizabeth, the Queen Mother (born Lady Elizabeth Angela Marguerite Bowes-Lyon) (1900–) Wife of George VI. She married George VI in 1923, when he was Duke of York; they had two daughters, Elizabeth II and Princess Margaret.

Elizabeth Petrovna (1709–62) Empress of Russia 1741–62. She was the unmarried daughter of PETER I (the Great), a beautiful and extravagant woman who seized the throne from the infant Ivan VI. She was more interested in social life and the arts than in affairs of state and government was conducted mainly by her ministers. Russia increased its hold on Poland in the War of the Polish Succession and the SEVEN YEARS WAR. On her death Peter III immediately changed sides, thus making FREDERICK II's ultimate victory possible.

Elizavetgrad See KIROVOHAD.

elk See MOOSE; RED DEER.

Ellesmere Island The northernmost island of North America, lying north-west of Greenland in the Arctic Ocean. Part of Canada's Northwest Territories, it is 800 km (500 miles) long, 40–480 km (25–300 miles) wide, and covers some 196,400 sq km (75,800 sq mi).

Ellice Islands The former name (until 1976) of the TUVALU island group in the Pacific.

Ellington, Duke (born Edward Kennedy Ellington) (1899–1974) US jazz pianist, composer, and bandleader. His band established its fame in the early 1930s and some of its members remained with him for more than thirty years. Ellington wrote over 900 compositions and was one of the first popular musicians to write extended pieces; his first worldwide success was *Mood Indigo* (1930).

ellipse A closed curve, one of the CONIC SECTIONS. It is defined as a locus of points the sum of whose distance from two fixed points (foci) is constant. The major axis is the line joining the foci. The orbit of a planet about the Sun, a satellite about its planets, and the components of a binary star closely resemble ellipses. The shape of an ellipse is defined by its **eccentricity** e, the value of which lies between 0 (when the ellipse is a circle) to very near unity (when it is very elongated). If $e = 1$, the ellipse has turned into a PARABOLA.

ellipsoid A three-dimensional surface obtained by uniformly stretching or compressing a sphere along three perpendicular axes (the principal axes), in general by different amounts. Cutting an ellipsoid with a plane yields an ELLIPSE.

elliptical galaxy See GALAXY.

Ellis, (Henry) Havelock (1859–1939) British psychologist and writer. Ellis qualified as a doctor in 1889 but is remembered as the pioneer of the scientific study of sex. His major technical work was the six-volume *Studies in the Psychology of Sex* (1897–1910, with a seventh volume added in 1928), and he wrote several popular works on the same subject, notably *Man and Woman* (1894).

Ellis Island An island in New York Bay off Manhattan Island. Long used as an arsenal and a fort, from 1892 to 1943 it served as the centre for immigration control. From 1943 until 1954 it acted as a detention centre for aliens and deportees. In 1965 it became part of the Statue of Liberty National Monument, and open to sightseers.

Ellsworth, Lincoln (1880–1951) US explorer. He participated in a number of polar expeditions and was the first person to fly over both the North (1926) and South (1935) Poles. During his Antarctic explorations of 1935 and 1939 he discovered new mountain ranges and named Ellsworth Land after his father.

elm Any one of about 20 species of tree found in the north temperate zone extending southwards to the Himalayas, Malaysia, and Mexico. Elms all have leaves that are asymmetrical at the base and disc-shaped winged fruits with the seed set in the centre. The flowers usually appear before the leaves, though *Ulmus parvifolia* of eastern Asia produces them together. Some are small trees, and dwarf forms are occasionally cultivated, but most are large, providing valuable timber used in construction and for making furniture.

The English elm, *U. procera*, is unusual in that it reproduces itself largely by suckers, rarely producing fertile seed. As a result, the majority of English elms are genetically similar. They have been greatly reduced in number through the depredation caused by Dutch elm disease.

El Niño (Spanish, 'The (Christ) Child') An irregularly occurring and complex series of climatic changes affecting the equatorial Pacific region. The name was originally applied to a warm ocean current which affected the waters of northern Peru and Ecuador annually, beginning usually around Christmas time (hence the reference to Christ). Every few years, this warming is very marked, and the nutrient-poor warmer water has a disastrous effect on fisheries and the breeding success of seabirds. This warm current is now recognized to be one manifestation of a much larger cycle of abnormal phenomena, sometimes lasting for more than a year, in which cause and effect have not been fully distinguished.

El Paso An industrial city in western Texas, USA, on the Rio Grande opposite the Mexican city of Ciudad Juárez; pop. (1990) 515,300. In 1846 Mexico surrendered the town to the USA. A military post was immediately established and a trading post set up six years later in 1852. Fort Bliss is one of the largest air-defence centres in the world. Modern industry includes oil refining and food processing.

El Salvador The smallest Central American country, situated on the Pacific coast. Only some 80 km (50 miles) wide, it is bounded on three sides by Guatemala, Honduras, and Nicaragua and has a 258-km (160-mile) southward-facing coastline.

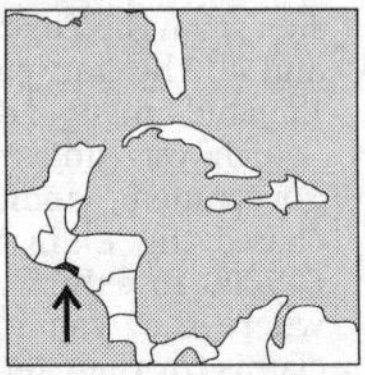

Physical. It comprises a hot, very wet coastal plain with wooded inland slopes, above which rise volcanic mountains with cratered lakes; as the country is at a junction of two crustal plates, earthquakes occasionally occur.

Economy. The economy of El Salvador is primarily agricultural, with coffee and cotton important exports. There is some manufacturing industry, principally textiles, chemicals, food-processing, and paper.

History. After it was conquered by Pedro de Alvarado, a lieutenant of Hernan CORTÉS, El Salvador formed part of the viceroyalty of New Spain, but was subject to the jurisdiction of the captain-general sitting in Guatemala City.

The country gained independence from Spain in 1821, joined (1824) the United Provinces of CENTRAL AMERICA, and with the break-up of that entity in 1838, became an independent republic (1839). Internal struggles between liberals and conservatives and a series of border clashes with neighbours retarded development in the 19th century. By the early 20th century the conservatives had gained ascendancy and the presidency remained within a handful of élite families as if it were their personal patrimony. El Salvador's 20th-century history has been dominated by a series of military presidents. While some of them, such as Oscar Osorio (1950–56) and José M. Lemus (1956–60), appeared mildly sympathetic to badly needed social reform, they were held in check by their more conservative military colleagues in concert with the civilian oligarchy. Fidel CASTRO's Cuban revolution and leftist guerrilla activity in other Central American countries pushed the Salvadoran army steadily to the right. Repressive measures and violations of human rights by the army during the 1970s and 1980s were documented by a number of international agencies, and posed a large refugee problem. Under President Felix Cristiani (elected 1989) negotiations began with the extreme left-wing guerrilla group *Frente Farabundo Marti de Liberación* (FMLN). The UN Secretary-General PÉREZ DE CUÉLLAR sponsored peace-talks throughout 1991 and a peace agreement was reached in 1992. The FMLN was recognized as a political party and took part in the 1994 elections, winning a few seats. The *Alianza Republicana Nacionalista* (ARENA), under President Armando Calderón Sol, won the majority of seats. In 1995 the government announced plans for economic reform.

Capital: San Salvador
Area: 21,041 sq km (8,124 sq mi)
Population: 5,768,000 (1995)
Currency: 1 colón = 100 centavos
Religions: Roman Catholic 92.4%
Ethnic Groups: Mestizo 90.0%; Amerindian (mostly Pipil) 5.0%; White 5.0%
Languages: Spanish (official)
International Organizations: UN; OAS

Elsinore (Danish **Helsingør**) a port on the north-east coast of the island of Zealand, Frederiksborg county, Denmark; pop. (1990) 56,750. The 16th-century Kronborg Castle was the setting for Shakespeare's *Hamlet*.

Elstree A residential suburb of north-west London to the west of Barnet, noted for its film studios, which were established in 1927.

Elton, Charles Sutherland (1900–91) British zoologist. Elton pioneered the study of animal ecology and investigated the relationship between animal populations and their environment. He was a founder of the Bureau of Animal Population at Oxford in 1932 and became the first editor of the *Journal of Animal Ecology* in the same year.

Éluard, Paul (1895–1952) French poet. The poetry of his early years, for example *L'Amour, la poésie* (1929), is primarily lyrical in inspiration. During the 1930s he developed profound communist sympathies, and moved towards a poetry of political involvement. *Cours naturel* (1938) was inspired by the Spanish Civil War and *Poésie et vérité* (1942) by the German occupation of France during World War II.

elver A young freshwater EEL, *Anguilla* species, when migrating up-river following its migration as a leptocephalus larva from its spawning

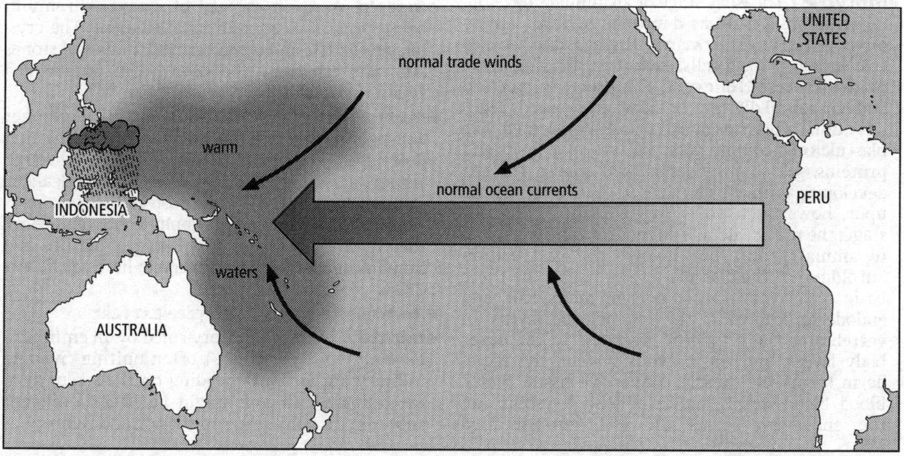

1

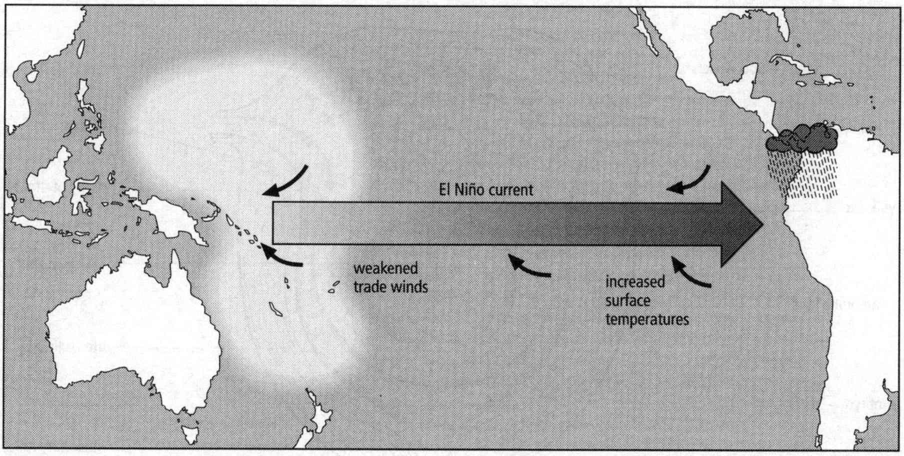

2

El Niño (1) Normal ocean currents usually follow trade winds. Warm waters and rising air in the Eastern Pacific normally bring heavy rainfall to Indonesia, whereas cool waters in the Western Pacific create dry weather in Peru. (2) El Niño reverses the direction of the normal currents, and trade winds are weakened or reversed. This creates torrential rainfall and flooding in Peru and the southern USA, and drought, with the danger of forest fires, in Indonesia and Australia.

grounds in mid-Atlantic. In body form elvers are identical to the adult eel but are no thicker than a matchstick and are about 8 cm (3 inches) long. In Britain elvers run up rivers in huge numbers between February and April, the earliest runs being in western rivers.

Ely A cathedral city in the fenland of Cambridgeshire, eastern England, on the River Ouse; pop. (1981) 9,100. Tradition has it that Hereward the Wake was killed here in what was one of the last Saxon strongholds in Norman England. The cathedral dates from the 11th century and has a unique octagonal lantern tower. The Isle of Ely was a former county of England extending over the northern part of present-day Cambridgeshire.

Elysium (or **Elysian Fields**) In Greek mythology, a place of perfect happiness inhabited by favoured mortals after death. Originally it was thought as being entered only by those whom the gods particularly loved, but later it was conceived of as a home for the righteous dead in general.

embargo See SANCTIONS.

embryo ▶**1** The early stage of an animal's development, before it is released into the environment by birth. After FERTILIZATION, the egg divides into two similarly sized cells, each then dividing again to give a total of four cells. This process of vertical and horizontal division, or cleavage, proceeds regularly until a blastula (a ball of cells) is formed. The blastula cells contain yolk, a mixture of lipids and proteins, which provides a food source for the developing embryo. The sizes of these cells depend upon how much yolk they contain. From this stage, the precise details differ from animal group to animal group, but involve the gastrulation (infolding) of the blastula to give rise to the three basic cell layers: the ectoderm, mesoderm, and endoderm, known as the triploblastic layers. In vertebrates the ectoderm gives rise to the outer body layers, and the nervous system; the mesoderm forms the muscle, connective tissue, bones, blood, blood vessels, and urinogenital system; and the endoderm forms the gut, gut-associated organs, the bladder, and some of the glands. All the nutrient needs of an embryo are met by either yolk stores provided for the egg, or, in mammals, through blood supplied by the mother via the PLACENTA. In humans, the embryo is called a foetus after the first eight weeks of development. ▶**2** The structure in plants that develops from the zygote. In seed plants it lies within the ovule and is protected by integuments that will become the seed coat. At one end are the cells that will develop as the root, those at the other end become the stem, and the embryo contains one or two cotyledons (seed leaves).

embryology The study of the changes in shape, size, and composition of the growing embryo from the fertilized egg stage to birth in animals, or of germination in plants.

Emden A North Sea port in the German state of Lower Saxony, on the estuary of the River Ems; pop. (1991) 51,100. The port developed rapidly after the industrialization of the Ruhr valley and the building of the Dortmund-Ems Canal.

emerald A green variety of BERYL, chromium being present as an additional element. The crystals are brittle and often cracked; unflawed stones are rare, especially the deep green ones which retain their colour in artificial light.

Emerson, **Ralph Waldo** (1803–82) US philosopher and poet. While visiting England in 1832 he met Coleridge, Wordsworth, and Carlyle, through whom he became associated with German idealism. On his return to the USA he evolved the concept of Transcendentalism, a philosophy based on a belief that divinity pervades the whole of nature and humankind; it found expression in his essay *Nature* (1836).

e.m.f. (electromotive force) See BATTERY.

emirate A Muslim territory ruled by an emir (Arabic *amir*, 'lord' or 'prince'), often uniting civil and military authority. Depending on the strength of the caliphate, an emir might be either a diligent subordinate, subject to supervision and removal, as

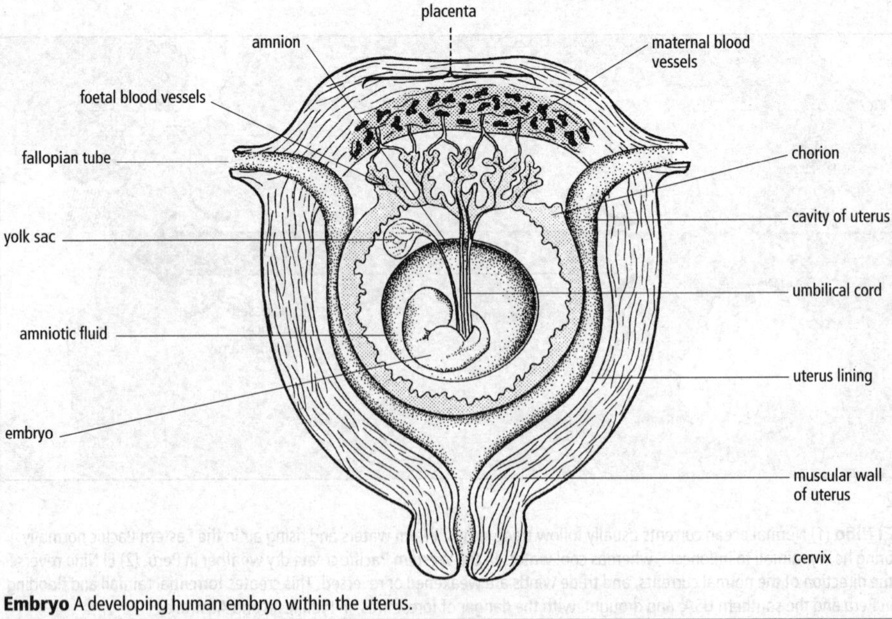

Embryo A developing human embryo within the uterus.

under the early ABBASIDS, or a virtually independent princeling, able to defy his nominal master.

Emirates, Fulani See FULANI EMPIRE OF SOKOTO.

emission spectrum See SPECTRUM.

Empedocles (*c.*493–*c.*433 BC) Greek philosopher, born in Sicily. His hexametric poem *On Nature* taught that the Universe is composed of the four imperishable elements of fire, air, water, and earth, which mingle and separate under the influence of the opposing principles of Love and Strife. According to legend, he leapt into the crater of Mount Etna in order that he might be thought a god.

emperor moth One of the largest moths in the world; the term includes ATLAS MOTHS. Many have an eyespot or transparent window on each wing, and males have conspicuous comb-like antennae. Their caterpillars construct cocoons of silk, which in a few species is used commercially. Most are tropical, but the genus *Saturnia*, which includes some seven species, occurs widely in Europe, Asia, and North America. They include the European peacock moth, *S. pyri*, with a wing-span of 15 cm (6 inches), and the North American *S. mendocino*, with a wing-span of up to 7 cm (3 inches).

emphysema A lung disease in which the air sacs (alveoli) of the lungs are enlarged, reducing the surface area available for the exchange of oxygen and carbon dioxide. This causes breathlessness on exertion and is often accompanied by chronic bronchitis. Associated with cigarette smoking and advancing age, emphysema has no cure but giving up smoking, breathing exercises, and the administration of oxygen can help.

Empire State Building A skyscraper on Fifth Avenue, New York City, USA, which was for long the tallest building in the world. When first erected in 1930–31, it measured 381 m (1,250 ft); the addition of a television mast in 1951 brought its height to 449 m (1,472 ft). It is named after New York, the 'Empire State'.

Empire style A style of furniture and interior decoration in France in the first quarter of the 19th century and associated with the personal taste of Napoleon Bonaparte (emperor 1804–14). It was largely the creation of the architects Charles Percier and Pierre-François Fontaine. Essentially the style was NEOCLASSICAL, with an attempt to copy what was known of ancient furniture and decorative motifs. The term 'Second Empire' is applied to French architecture and decoration under Napoleon III (1852–70) with its tendency to revive various styles of the past in an uninhibitedly ostentatious way. Its most famous work is Garnier's magnificent Paris Opéra (1861–74).

empirical formula See MOLECULAR FORMULA.

empiricism A doctrine in the theory of knowledge (see EPISTEMOLOGY) which stresses the primacy of sense-experience over reason in the acquisition and justification of knowledge. It thus stands opposed to RATIONALISM, and limits A PRIORI knowledge.

Empson, Sir William (1906–84) British poet and literary critic. His intricate, closely reasoned poems, published in the *Collected Poems* (1955), reflect his training as a mathematician. His influential literary criticism includes *Seven Types of Ambiguity* (1930).

Ems See BAD EMS.

emu The only species of bird, *Dromaius novaehollandiae*, in the family Dromaiidae. An adult emu weighs 35–40 kg (80–90 pounds) and is a flightless, long-legged, long-necked bird, the female reaching 2 m (6.5 feet) high. The smaller male incubates the eggs and cares for the chicks.

emulsifier See FOOD ADDITIVE.

emulsion A mixture of two immiscible liquids in which one liquid (the disperse phase) is dispersed in the other liquid (the continuous phase) as fine droplets (10^{-9} to 10^{-7} m in diameter). Many synthetic food products are emulsions: for example, French dressing is an emulsion of vegetable oil in vinegar. Emulsifying agents are used to help form the emulsion, and stabilizing agents are used to help maintain it. Many COSMETICS are also emulsions: some are oil-in-water emulsions (foundation creams); others are water-in-oil emulsions (cold creams). Emulsions can be broken up by heat or mechanical agitation: butter is formed by de-emulsifying milk.

emulsion paint A PAINT in which particles of solid PIGMENT are dispersed in an aqueous liquid (strictly this is known as a sol rather than an emulsion: see COLLOID). The liquid forms a skin on exposure to air, trapping a solid coat on the painted material. Emulsifiers and stabilizers are added to the paint to keep the pigment evenly dispersed, but stirring is usually required before use to ensure consistency. Non-drip emulsion paint is a combination of a foam (a gas dispersed in a liquid) and a sol. Stirring destroys the foam and removes the paint's non-drip properties.

enamel Readily fusible powdered glass that is used to coat metal for protection (as in kitchen utensils) or for decoration (for example, *cloisonné* ornaments). The item to be enamelled is coated with enamel powder and heated until the enamel melts. On cooling, the item has a solid glassy film on its surface. Opaque enamels contain opacifiers such as titanium dioxide. A wide range of colours can be obtained by including metal compounds in the glass – for example, cobalt oxide produces blue enamel and manganese dioxide produces violet. Enamel is also used in a particular form of oil-bound PAINT, giving a hard, glossy finish.

enantiomer Two forms of a compound which have the same molecular structure except that one form is the mirror image of the other, like a pair of gloves. A characteristic property of enantiomers is that they exhibit OPTICAL ACTIVITY, and this is due to the asymmetry of the molecules.

Enceladus A satellite of Saturn, discovered by William HERSCHEL in 1789. It has a nearly circular orbit above Saturn's equator at 238,000 km from the planet's centre. Enceladus is nearly spherical, with a diameter of about 500 km.

enclosure An area of land formed as the result of enclosing (with fences, ditches, and hedges) what had usually been COMMON land so as to make it private property. In Tudor times enclosure was popularly seen as the conversion of the peasants' tilled land to grass on which a landowner's sheep would graze: the sheep were eating men, it was said, because the villagers were losing both their employment and their tillage. Enclosures became a national issue, but although they were denounced by the church (especially by Cardinal WOLSEY and Thomas MORE) and were penalized by statutes and royal proclamations, and even provoked Kett's Rebellion (1549), their financial advantages were so strong that they continued to be carried out.

In the second half of the 18th century enclosure by private Act of Parliament increased dramatically, and the General Enclosure Act of 1801 standardized the procedure. Enclosures were less unpopular in the 18th century, as they enabled farmers to introduce improvements in crops and breeding without reference to their neighbours.

Encyclopédists The '*philosophes*' and others who contributed to and otherwise supported the *Encyclopédie*, published in France in 35 volumes between 1751 and 1780, one of the great literary achievements of the 18th century. It was a complete review of the arts and sciences of the day, explaining the new physics and cosmology and proclaiming a new philosophy of humanism. It was edited by DIDEROT and d'Alembert and articles were contributed by VOLTAIRE, MONTESQUIEU, ROUSSEAU, Buffon, and baron d'Holbach. A decree of 1752 suppressed the first volumes and in 1759 it was placed on the Index (of books forbidden to Roman Catholics), but it continued to circulate. The critical attitudes fostered by the *Encyclopédie* are believed to have contributed to the FRENCH REVOLUTION.

endangered species Animals or plants threatened with extinction, usually because of man's impact on the ecosystem (see ECOLOGY). At present there are probably some 10 million species on the planet, mostly plants and invertebrates, but scientists predict that by the end of the century at least 1 million of these will be extinct. About 500 species and subspecies of mammal (there are 4,000 in all) are listed in the Convention on International Trade in Endangered Species of Wild Flora and Fauna (CITES), including all the whales and their relatives, all big cats, and all primates except man. Another agency for species CONSERVATION, the International Union for Conservation of Nature and Natural Resources (IUCN), lists species at risk in its *Red Data Books*.

Enders, John Franklin (1897–1985) US virologist. He devised a skin test for detecting antibodies to the mumps virus, and, with Frederick C. Robbins (1916–92) and Thomas H. Weller (1915–92), developed a method of growing viruses in tissue cultures. This led eventually to the development of vaccines against mumps, polio, and measles. The three scientists shared a Nobel Prize for this work in 1954.

endive A salad plant, *Cichorum endivia*, of Asian origin, belonging to the sunflower family, and introduced to Britain by the Romans. As its green leaves are bitter, they are blanched for a few weeks before harvesting. The term is sometimes applied to a lettuce with curly, branched leaves. Endives are closely related to CHICORY.

endocrine gland A compact collection of secretory cells that discharges its secretions into the blood, instead of to a free surface through a duct. There are five major ductless glands in mammals, whose only function is the manufacture, storage, and release of one or more specific organic chemical compounds called HORMONES. The five glands are the pituitary, the gonads, the adrenals, the thyroid, and the parathyroids. Other organs, such as the kidney, the stomach, and the pancreas, contain scattered patches of specialist cells with endocrine functions. Endocrine glands coordinate the long-term adjustments of cellular activity required for growth, reproduction, and many other functions. These actions of endocrine glands can be integrated with those of the brain by the hypothalamic control of the PITUITARY GLAND.

endorphin Any one of a group of peptides that occur naturally in certain parts of the body and have pain-relieving activity similar to that of morphine (the word endorphin derives from 'endogenous morphine'). The term is applied particularly to opioid peptides in the pituitary gland, but two endorphins – called **enkephalins** – occur in the brain, spinal cord, and gut. Endorphins are also found in the pancreas, placenta, and adrenal gland. The pain relief experienced by those undergoing ACUPUNCTURE is believed to be produced by endorphins released by this technique.

endoscopy The visual examination of an internal part of a patient's body. Early forms of endoscope, such as the OPHTHALMOSCOPE and laryngoscope (for examining the eyes and vocal cords, respectively), were developed during the 19th century. Since the 1960s, the use of OPTICAL-FIBRE systems, which permit the 'bending' of light rays, has revolutionized endoscope design, resulting in smaller instruments which can be introduced through bodily orifices or, more recently, through tiny incisions. The latter technique is used, for example, to examine joints (arthroscopy), the abdominal cavity (laparoscopy), or the foetus in the womb (foetoscopy). Most endoscopy is for diagnostic purposes (such as to reveal peptic ulcers or stomach cancer), but modern endoscopes can also take a BIOPSY (tissue sample). Therapeutic procedures, such as cutting away an enlarged prostate gland, can also be performed through an endoscope.

endoskeleton A skeleton formed inside the body as a means of maintaining body shape, and which supports the organs in vertebrates. Tendons attach muscles to the bones within the skeleton, and power the system of levers used during locomotory activity. In vertebrates, the endoskeleton consists of an axial skeleton (skull, vertebrae, ribs and sternum) and an appendicular skeleton (fore-limbs, hind-limbs, pectoral girdle and pelvic girdle). The human SKELETON, which represents that of a typical mammal adapted to a bipedal mode of life, possesses a total of 206 bones in the adult, 80 of which are located in the axial skeleton and 126 in the appendicular skeleton. See also EXOSKELETON.

endothermic reaction A chemical reaction in which heat is removed from the surroundings – that is, there is an increase in the ENTHALPY of the reaction mixture. An example of an endothermic process is the dissolving of ammonium nitrate, NH_4NO_3, in water. As the solid dissolves, the temperature of the container decreases as heat is removed from it. An endothermic compound is one that absorbs heat as it is formed. See EXOTHERMIC REACTION.

Endymion In Greek mythology, a handsome youth who was loved by Selene, the Moon goddess. Zeus sent him to sleep for ever so that his youth and beauty might be preserved, and Selene came to embrace him every night.

energy The capacity of objects or systems to do work. The concept of energy emerged during the mid-19th century, when it was realized that moving bodies could be made to move against resisting forces, thus doing work. This ability came to be known as kinetic energy. Raised bodies exhibit a potential for doing work when they fall, a property known as gravitational potential energy. Energy can take many forms, with the important characteristic that the total energy of a system remains constant (i.e. energy is conserved). Other energy forms include chemical energy, thermal energy (heat), electrical energy, and NUCLEAR ENERGY. The standard unit for all forms of energy is the JOULE (J). Power, the rate at which energy is delivered or converted, is measured in joules per second or watts (W). Energy can be transferred from one body to another by work processes (involving movement), by heating (using their temperature differences), by ELECTROMAGNETIC RADI-

ATION (such as light and microwaves) and by electricity (flow of electrical energy). Energy can also be converted from one form to another. For example, the potential energy of water in a highland reservoir is converted into kinetic energy as the water flows down the inlet tube to a TURBINE, where it is converted into electrical energy by a generator driven by the turbine. Although energy is conserved, when it is converted from one form to another, some of the energy is converted into an unwanted form, usually heat. This is especially so when thermal energy is converted into another form, as in internal-combustion engines or power-stations, where the maximum possible conversion efficiency is limited by the temperatures involved. See ENERGY RESOURCES.

energy levels (in physics) The set of permitted energies that a particular system can have according to QUANTUM MECHANICS. For example, the electrons in the orbitals around the nucleus of an atom have a relatively small set of fairly widely spaced energy levels, giving the characteristic electronic configuration of the element. The energy of these levels depends largely on the distance of the electron from the nucleus. In electrical conductors, however, where the electrons are able to move freely throughout the whole material, the energy levels are compressed into bands in which the levels are extremely close together. According to the EXCLUSION PRINCIPLE put forward by Wolfgang PAULI in 1925, two electrons can occupy the same energy level if they have opposite SPIN but otherwise share equal QUANTUM NUMBERS. Molecules can also have vibrational and rotational energy levels.

energy resources Natural sources of useful ENERGY. The world's main energy resources for more than a century have been the FOSSIL FUELS. HYDROELECTRICITY and NUCLEAR ENERGY together contribute some 9% to present world annual energy consumption, and the BIOFUELS, in the form of firewood or other combustible plant or animal materials, are thought to provide about a tenth of the total. Before the INDUSTRIAL REVOLUTION, mechanical power for machines came from flowing water or the wind. The invention of the STEAM-ENGINE brought the new possibility of converting the heat from burning fuels into mechanical energy. The development of the INTERNAL-COMBUSTION ENGINE was followed by a growth in PETROLEUM (oil) consumption. The relative cheapness and convenience of oil and NATURAL GAS meant that by the 1960s they were also the preferred fuels for domestic and industrial heating, further increasing their consumption. The finite nature of the world's fossil-fuel energy resources has caused concern for well over a hundred years. Consumption has continued to rise, but exploration and new methods of extraction have enabled known reserves of coal, oil, and gas to keep pace. There is also concern over the impact on the environment of burning fossil fuels (see GREENHOUSE EFFECT), and serious consideration is being given to alternatives to these fossil fuels. The most developed alternatives to these fuels are nuclear power and hydroelectricity. Hydroelectric power offers potential, but could not satisfy total world demand in the long term because most of the best sites are already used or are too remote to be economical. Nuclear power is controversial because of fears concerning safety and undesirable environmental consequences, especially as a result of the disposal of nuclear waste. Other renewable resources that could in principle meet almost all the world's needs, such as BIOFUELS, SOLAR POWER, WIND POWER, GEOTHERMAL ENERGY, and WAVE POWER, are not yet technologically proven on a world scale, and their economic viability remains to be established. However, not only do these renewable energy sources take the pressure off the reserves of fossil fuels, they are also cheaper and cleaner to use, causing little environmental pollution. Unfortunately, none of them solves the problem of finding a substitute for oil products as an energy source for transport (cars, planes, etc.). See ELECTRIC VEHICLE.

energy storage A system or process for taking up ENERGY and retaining it for use at a later time. The storage of electrical energy and of heat are particularly important for the development of renewable ENERGY RESOURCES, such as SOLAR POWER or WIND POWER, which are intermittent and variable. Useful amounts of electrical energy can be stored economically only by conversion into another form. It can be converted into chemical energy, either in rechargeable BATTERIES or by the electrolysis of water to produce hydrogen and oxygen. In PUMPED STORAGE systems electricity is converted into gravitational potential energy, and in night storage heaters to heat energy. Other systems use motors to convert electrical energy into the kinetic energy of a spinning FLYWHEEL or the mechanical energy of a compressed gas. In terms of the volume of material needed, the capacities of all man-made systems are very low compared with natural ENERGY RESOURCES: to store the energy content of one gallon of oil would require 80 fully charged car batteries, 20 night storage heaters, or 60 tonnes of water raised through 300 m (1,000 feet). At present, the pumped storage of large volumes of water is the only practicable method for storing large amounts of electrical energy.

Engels, Friedrich (1820–95) German socialist and political philosopher, resident chiefly in England from 1842. The founder of modern communism with Karl Marx, he collaborated with him in the writing of the *Communist Manifesto* (1848). Engels also completed the second and third volumes of Marx's *Das Kapital* (1885; 1894). Engels's own writings include *The Condition of the Working Classes in England in 1844* (1845).

engine Any mechanical contrivance of parts working together, but usually referring to a machine producing power from a source of heat (a heat-engine). Examples of engines include STEAM-ENGINES, air-engines (such as the STIRLING engine), INTERNAL-COMBUSTION ENGINES, and GAS-TURBINES.

engineering The application of scientific methods to the design, construction, and maintenance of machines, structures, processes, etc. Traditionally, engineering was divided into two main categories: MECHANICAL ENGINEERING, which dealt with the construction and operation of machinery; and CIVIL ENGINEERING, concerned with the design and construction of large buildings, bridges, and roads. During the course of the 20th century, however, many new categories have had to be defined to take account of increasing specialization. These include electrical, mining, chemical, aeronautical, and systems engineering. See also GENETIC ENGINEERING.

engineering drawing The graphical representation of a solid object. Drawn to scale, using a series of orthogonal projections, side elevation, and plans, engineering drawings convey shape and dimensions in a formal manner to the constructor. Isometric drawings or perspective views – often used when producing designs – may give a clear and accurate representation, but they cannot be dimensionally true to a flat scale.

England A part of Great Britain and the United Kingdom, largely made up of the land area south of the River Tweed (excluding Wales) and containing the capital, London; area 130,478 sq km (50,397 sq miles); pop. (1991) 46,170,300. The north of England is dominated by upland regions such as the Cheviot Hills which rise to 816 m (2,674 ft) at The Cheviot, the Cumbrian Mountains which rise to 977 m (3,210 ft) at Scafell Pike (England's highest peak), and the Pennine Range which stretches south to the Peak District, rising to 636 m (2,088 ft) at Kinder Scout. Extensive areas of upland and moorland also dominate the Welsh border and south-west England, with ranges of low rolling hills such as the Cotswolds, the Chilterns, and the Downs stretching across the south of England. Large areas of flat low-lying land occupy eastern England from the Vale of York to the fenlands of the Wash and East Anglia. The longest river wholly in England is the Thames. England has a mild temperate climate with the highest rainfall in the west. In winter average temperatures are higher in the south and west while in summer the warmest weather is to be found in southern and inland areas. There were settlements in England from at least palaeolithic times, and considerable remains exist of neolithic and Bronze Age cultures. These were followed by the arrival of the Celtic peoples whose civilization spread over the whole country. The Romans under Julius Caesar raided the south of Britain in 55 and 54 BC, but full-scale invasion did not take place until a century later; the country was then administered as a Roman province until the Teutonic conquest of Gaul in the early 5th century and the subsequent withdrawal of the last Roman garrison. In the 3rd to 7th centuries Germanic-speaking tribes, traditionally known as Angles, Saxons, and Jutes, raided and then settled, establishing independent kingdoms, and when that of Wessex became dominant in the 9th century England emerged as a distinct political entity before being conquered by William, Duke of Normandy, in 1066. The neighbouring principality of Wales was gradually conquered during the Middle Ages and politically incorporated in the 16th century. During the period of Tudor rule (1485–1603) England emerged as a Protestant state with a strong stable monarchy and as a naval power. Scotland and England have been ruled by one monarch from 1603, and the two parliaments were formally united in 1707.

English Channel (French **La Manche**) The sea channel separating southern England from northern France. It is 35 km (21 miles) wide at its narrowest point. A tunnel under the English channel linking France and England was opened in 1994.

English Civil War (1642–49) The armed struggle between the supporters of the king (CAVALIERS) and Parliamentarians (ROUNDHEADS), which erupted in 1642 and continued, with an interruption, until 1648. It arose from constitutional, religious, and economic differences between CHARLES I and the Members of the LONG PARLIAMENT. Of these the most decisive factor was religion, since the attempts of LAUD to impose liturgical uniformity had alienated substantial numbers of clergy, gentry, and craftsmen. All sections of society were affected, though many in the localities desired peace not war, and sometimes families were divided by conflicting allegiances.

The king's primary objective in 1642 was the capture of London, a Parliamentary stronghold. After an indecisive engagement at EDGEHILL, he eventually had to take refuge in Oxford, which became his wartime capital. His plan in 1643 to bring together Cavalier armies from Oxford, Newcastle, and the south-west, followed by a march on London, was not realized. Meanwhile the balance was tipping toward the Roundheads, for by the SOLEMN LEAGUE AND COVENANT they secured Scottish assistance, of value in 1644 at MARSTON MOOR. Charles's attempt to march on London (1644) was frustrated at the battle of Newbury. With the formation of the NEW MODEL ARMY, the Roundheads were able to inflict a crushing defeat on the Cavaliers at NASEBY (1645). Charles, having rejected terms previously offered him at the Uxbridge negotiations, eventually surrendered to the Scots near Newark (1646) after Oxford had fallen.

Charles's subsequent attempts to profit from divisions between the Parliamentary factions prevented a settlement from being reached in 1647. His escape to the Isle of Wight and 'Engagement' with the Scots sparked off the second phase of the war (1648). This consisted of unsuccessful Cavalier risings in Wales, Essex, and Kent, and a Scottish invasion which came to grief at PRESTON. PRIDE'S PURGE of Parliament then cleared the way for the trial and execution of the king and the establishment of the English COMMONWEALTH.

English language The language spoken by an estimated 300 million people as a first language in the UK, Ireland, the USA, Canada, Australia, and New Zealand. It has official status in over fifty countries, notably in sub-Saharan Africa and southern Asia, and is the most widely used second language in the world. The Old English period runs from the appearance of the first texts in the late 7th century to the mid-11th century, when the Norman invasion radically changed the nature of English. Over 50 per cent of the vocabulary was replaced by words taken from French and Latin during the subsequent Middle English period (1100–1500). The Modern English period saw the language taken beyond Britain and the establishment of new regional varieties, such as American English. English is a relatively uninflected language, giving it a simple grammar. Spelling, however, is complicated and does not always reflect the spoken language, largely because the spoken language predates the standardization imposed by the advent of printing by many centuries. The language has a remarkable capacity for absorbing foreign words, which has resulted in a large and international vocabulary.

English literature English literature pre-dates the modern form of the English language. Before the first printed books in English (1475), the outstanding literary achievement is the poetry of CHAUCER. With print came the influences of the European RENAISSANCE, especially of PETRARCH, who inspired a succession of courtly English poets from WYATT and SURREY to SIDNEY and SPENSER. The crowning achievements of the English Renaissance, though, are the works of the poet-playwrights working in London between the 1580s and the 1630s, led by MARLOWE, SHAKESPEARE, JONSON, and WEBSTER. After the phase of RESTORATION COMEDY, English drama went into decline until the end of the 19th century. The 17th century saw the flourishing of the METAPHYSICAL POETS, and the composition by MILTON of the greatest epic poem in English, *Paradise Lost*. In the century from 1660, poetry was dominated by elegant satire in the work of DRYDEN, POPE, and JOHNSON, while the prose satires of SWIFT and the more realistic narratives of DEFOE prepared the way for the new tradition of the novel in English – of which the early masters were FIELDING, RICHARDSON, and STERNE. From the end of the 18th century, a major revival of poetry was seen both in the work of the Scottish poet BURNS and in the English exponents of ROMANTICISM: WORDSWORTH, COLERIDGE, BLAKE, SHELLEY, BYRON, and KEATS. Apart from TENNYSON, the later 19th-century poets are relatively minor figures, but the tradition of the 19th-century novel is exceptionally strong, from AUSTEN and SCOTT in the early decades, through DICKENS and the BRONTË sisters to George ELIOT and HARDY in later years. The revival of drama from the 1890s was led by Irish writers (WILDE, SHAW) and continued through the Irish literary renaissance, which also produced the outstanding poet (YEATS) and novelist (JOYCE) of the early 20th century. Apart from WOOLF and LAWRENCE, the literary MODERNISM of this period in Britain was dominated by writers from overseas: CONRAD from Poland, JAMES, POUND, and T. S. ELIOT from the USA. Since the work of the poet AUDEN and the novelist ORWELL in the 1930s and 1940s, literature in Britain has been dominated by such novelists as Angus Wilson, Kingsley AMIS, Graham GREENE, Evelyn WAUGH, POWELL, BURGESS, Lawrence DURRELL, GOLDING, LESSING, and MURDOCH. In the theatre OSBORNE, WESKER, PINTER, BECKETT, STOPPARD, and BENNETT have created a highly respected corpus.

engraving Various processes of cutting a design into a plate or block of metal or wood, and to the prints taken from these plates or blocks. The word usually applies to one of the processes, that of line engraving. The design is cut into a smooth metal (usually copper) plate with a tool called a burin, and prints are taken by inking the plate and pressing it (usually mechanically) against a sheet of paper (an INTAGLIO process). Line engraving produces hard, clear lines, and has been employed chiefly to reproduce works of art.

ENIAC See COMPUTER, HISTORY OF.

Enigma See COMPUTER, HISTORY OF.

Eniwetok An uninhabited island in the North Pacific Ocean forming part of the Ralik Chain in the Marshall Islands. Cleared of its native population, it was used as a testing ground for atomic bombs from 1948 to 1954.

Enlightenment (or **Age of Reason**) The philosophical, scientific, and rational attitudes, the freedom from superstition, and the belief in religious tolerance of much of 18th-century Europe. In Germany the *Aufklärung* ('Enlightenment'), which extended from the middle of the 17th century to the beginning of the 19th century, was a literary and philosophical movement that included LESSING, GOETHE, SCHILLER, and Emanuel Kant. The YIDDISH literature of Eastern Europe experienced a new dynamism, while a similarly invigorating freedom of ideas affected writers as far apart as Sweden, Russia, and Britain. In France the Enlightenment was associated with the *philosophes*, the literary men, scientists, and thinkers who were united in their belief in the supremacy of reason and their desire to see practical change to combat inequality and injustice. The movement against established beliefs and institutions gained momentum throughout the 18th century under VOLTAIRE, ROUSSEAU, Turgot, CONDORCET, and others. Through the publication of the *Encyclopédie* (1751–76) their attacks on the government, the church, and the judiciary provided the intellectual basis for the French Revolution.

The English Enlightenment owed its origin both to the political theories of LOCKE, and to the French example. PAINE, an admirer of the French, advocated American independence, and many writers and poets transmitted Enlightenment ideas. In Scotland an intellectual movement flourished in Edinburgh between 1750 and 1800; its outstanding philosophers were Hume and Adam Smith and important scientific advances were made in chemistry, geology and medicine. The *Encyclopaedia Britannica*, began in 1768–71 as a dictionary of the arts and sciences, was issued by a 'Society of gentlemen in Scotland'. In literature, some have seen a connection between the philosophy of the Enlightenment, the growth of literary REALISM, and the rise of the NOVEL. It influenced the Romantic movement in the arts by releasing the more individualist attitudes in which this movement was based, and as the Romantics themselves reacted against the coldly scientific intellectualism which the Enlightenment represented.

Enniskillen (Gaelic **Inis Ceithleann**) The county town of Fermanagh in Northern Ireland, situated between two channels of the river joining Upper and Lower Lough Erne; pop. (1981) 10,400.

Ennius, Quintus (239–169 BC) Roman poet and dramatist. He was largely responsible for the creation of a native Roman literature based on Greek models. Of his many works (surviving only in fragments) the most important was the *Annals* (undated), a hexametric epic on the history of Rome, which was a major influence on Virgil.

Enoch An early Hebrew patriarch and father of Methuselah. Enoch is said to have lived for 365 years and then, like Elijah, to have been 'translated' into heaven. According to some Jewish legends he invented writing, arithmetic, and astronomy. In Islam Enoch is usually identified with Idris.

enosis See EOKA.

Ensor, James (1860–1949) Belgian painter and printmaker. He was one of the formative influences on EXPRESSIONISM and was claimed by the SURREALISTS as a forerunner, but his work defies classification within any school or group. He made much use of carnival masks, grotesque figures, and skeletons, with a gruesome and ironic humour reminiscent of his great Flemish predecessors BOSCH and BRUEGEL.

Entebbe A town in southern Uganda, on the north shore of Lake Victoria; pop. (1991) 41,640. Founded in 1893, it was capital of Uganda under British rule from 1894 to 1962 when self-government was granted.

entente cordiale (1904) Friendly understanding between Britain and France. It aimed to settle territorial disputes and to encourage cooperation against perceived German pressure. Britain was to be given a free hand in Egyptian affairs and France in Morocco. Germany, concerned over this *entente*, tested its strength by provoking a crisis in Morocco in 1905, leading to the Algeciras Conference (1906). The *entente* was extended in 1907 to include Russia and culminated in the formal alliance of Britain, France, and Russia in World War I against the Central Powers and the Ottoman empire.

enthalpy A measure of the internal energy of a substance; it is a thermodynamic property and is usually measured in kilojoules per mole. It is difficult to measure enthalpy directly; it is considerably easier to measure the enthalpy change accompanying a chemical reaction. In an EXOTHERMIC REACTION, there is a decrease in enthalpy for the reaction mixture; in other words, heat is given out. In an ENDOTHERMIC REACTION, there is an increase in enthalpy; heat is taken in by the reaction mixture.

entisol An immature soil which has had insufficient time for distinct B-HORIZONS to form. Entisols occur on recent deposits, such as loess, till, or alluvium. The upper horizons are distinguished from the weathering parent material largely because they contain humus and are therefore darker in colour. They tend to be relatively shallow.

entomology The study of insects. Like other branches of zoology, it began as a mainly descriptive subject, concerned with collecting and classifying specimens. Well over 1 million species of insect are known to science. The work of FABRE in the nineteenth century did much to arouse interest in the life histories and behaviour of insects, and now entomology deals with all aspects of their biology.

Entre-Deux-Mers An area of south-west France between the Garonne and Dordogne rivers noted for its Bordeaux wines.

entrepôt See FREE PORT.

entropy A thermodynamic property used to determine the way in which a system will change when it is compressed or expanded, heated or cooled. Mathematically, entropy can be calculated from measurements of the heat required to raise the temperature of a body a certain amount, divided by the temperature of the body. Its significance lies in the random manner in which the energy of the particles in the system is distributed. The greater the spread in energies, the greater is the disorder, and hence the entropy is higher. The entropy of a closed system can never become smaller but, if changed at all, must always increase. Applied universally this deduction leads to the idea that all matter is becoming more disordered, i.e., as the inventor of the concept (in 1854), Rudolf CLAUSIUS, said, "the entropy of the Universe tends to a maximum".

E number See FOOD ADDITIVE.

Enver Pasha (1881–1922) Turkish political and military leader. A leader of the Young Turks in the revolution of 1908, he came to power as part of a ruling triumvirate following a coup d'état in 1913. He played a significant role in creating Turkey's alliance with Germany during World War I, and served as Minister of War (1914–18).

environment (in ECOLOGY) The surroundings of organisms, including biological, physical, and chemical factors. In the context of human ecology, it also includes social and cultural surroundings. The environment now encompasses wildlife and ENDANGERED SPECIES and habitats, and the threat to planetary systems posed by POLLUTION, DEFORESTATION, DESERTIFICATION, and other effects of human activity.

enzyme A type of PROTEIN found in all living cells. Enzymes act as biological catalysts, allowing all the chemical reactions of METABOLISM to take place, regulating the speed at which they progress, and providing a means of controlling individual biochemical pathways. Enzymes owe their activity to the precise three-dimensional shape of their molecules. According to the 'lock-and-key' hypothesis, the substance upon which an enzyme acts (which is known as the substrate) fits into a special slot in the enzyme molecule: the active site. A chemical reaction takes place at this site and the products are released, leaving the enzyme unchanged and ready for re-use. This cycle can be repeated as often as 100,000 times per second. Enzymes are very specific in relation to the substrates with which they work, and are normally only effective for one reaction or a group of closely related reactions. They function best in particular conditions of temperature and acidity (pH), and their action can be slowed or stopped by INHIBITORS. Many enzymes need a COENZYME in order to function. The human body contains at least 1,000 different enzymes.

Eocene Epoch The second of the five geological epochs of the TERTIARY era, representing the interval of time from 57.8 to 36.6 million years ago. The temperature was rising at this time. Mammals flourished in great variety: primates, rodents, and other types on land; whales and sea-cows in the seas. Eocene deposits generally show great variation, from continental to marine.

EOKA (National Organization of Cypriot Fighters) The militant wing of the *enosis* (Greek, 'union') movement in Cyprus. Colonel Georgios Grivas (1898–1974), commander of the Greek Cypriot national guard, was its most famous leader. During 1954–59 guerrilla warfare and terrorist attacks were waged against the British forces. In 1956 MAKARIOS was exiled on the charge of being implicated with EOKA. After independence in 1960 the organization was revived as EOKA-B. Renewed demands for *enosis* in 1970, achieved success in 1974. In response Turkey invaded and partitioned the island to protect the Turkish minority.

ephemeris (pl. **ephemerides**) A table giving the positions of a celestial object at various future times. The *Nautical Almanac*, published by the ROYAL GREENWICH OBSERVATORY, is a set of ephemerides of Sun, Moon, planets, and other celestial objects published yearly some years in advance.

Ephesus (Turkish **Efes**) An ancient Greek city and seaport of Asia Minor on the west coast of modern Turkey, site of the temple of Artemis that was one of the Seven Wonders of the World, and an important centre of early Christianity. St Paul visited it several times and St John is said to be buried here.

epic A long narrative poem celebrating the deeds of great heroes, in a grand ceremonious style. The hero, usually protected by or even descended from gods, performs superhuman exploits in battle or in marvellous voyages, often saving or founding a nation, as in Virgil's *Aeneid* (30–20 BC), or the human race itself, as in Milton's *Paradise Lost* (1667). Virgil and Milton wrote what are called 'secondary' epics in imitation of the earlier 'primary' epics of Homer, whose *Iliad and Odyssey* (*c.*8th century BC) evolved from an oral tradition of recitation. The Anglo-Saxon poem *Beowulf* (8th century AD) is a primary epic, as is the oldest surviving epic poem, the Babylonian *Gilgamesh* (*c.*3000 BC). In the Renaissance, epic poetry (also known as 'heroic poetry') was regarded as the highest form of literature.

epicentre See EARTHQUAKE.

Epictetus (*c.*55–*c.*135 AD) Greek philosopher. Originally a slave, he preached the common brotherhood of man and advocated a Stoic philosophy. His teachings were published posthumously in the *Enchiridion*.

epic theatre A form of drama developed in the

1920s by the German dramatists Piscator and BRECHT, who rejected traditional dramatic structure in favour of a detached narrative (hence 'epic') presentation in a succession of loosely related episodes interspersed with songs and commentary by a narrator. Brecht's major plays *Mother Courage* (1941) and *The Good Woman of Setzuan* (1943) are fine examples.

Epicurus (341–270 BC) Greek philosopher. His physics (later expounded by the Roman writer Lucretius) is based on the theory of a materialist Universe, unregulated by divine providence, composed of indestructible atoms moving in a void. From this follows his philosophy of Epicureanism, a restrained type of hedonism: mental pleasure was regarded more highly than physical and the ultimate pleasure was held to be freedom from anxiety and mental pain, especially that arising from needless fear of death and of gods.

epicyclic gear See GEAR.

Epidaurus An ancient Greek city and port on the north-east coast of the Peloponnese, famous for its temple of Asclepius and site of a well-preserved Greek theatre dating from the 4th century BC.

epidemic A rapidly spreading infection or COMMUNICABLE DISEASE, such as influenza, affecting a large proportion of individuals within a population. The widespread outbreak arises as a result of factors or disease not generally present within the affected region, but acquired.

epidemiology The study of the incidence and distribution of diseases, and of their control and prevention. Epidemiology is fundamental to preventive medicine and PUBLIC HEALTH. To reduce the spread of COMMUNICABLE DISEASE the World Health Organization recommends the provision of safe water supplies and sanitation and improved housing and nutrition. IMMUNIZATION against specific childhood diseases is markedly successful, but the control of parasites is less so.

epidermis The outer layer of cells of an animal or plant body. In lower animals and in plants it secretes a protective cuticle. In vertebrates it forms the outermost layer of the SKIN.

epiglottis A flap of tissue attached to the wall of the pharynx in mammals. During swallowing it covers the opening of the trachea (windpipe), preventing food entering the windpipe.

epilepsy A condition characterized by recurrent, paroxysmal, and transitory disturbances of the electrical activity within the brain, which are called seizures, or fits. Epilepsy may be of unknown cause, or can occur as a result of an underlying disorder such as infection, fever, or tumours, or as result of a head injury. The epileptic seizure is a transient episode of lost or altered consciousness, which can be accompanied by loss of control of the muscles. Many varieties of seizures are recognized, most of which only last for a few minutes. Occasionally they are prolonged beyond thirty minutes, or recur so rapidly that full recovery is not achieved between successive attacks. Siezures are most likely to occur in early childhood, during adolescence and in old age.

Epiphany An annual Christian festival on 6 January, originally commemorating the manifestation of Jesus' divinity at his baptism. First mentioned by Clement of Alexandria (217 AD), by the 4th century it was widely celebrated. In the West, Epiphany came to commemorate the revelation of Jesus to the Gentiles, in the visit of the Magi or Wise Men.

epiphyte A plant that lives attached to the outer surface of another plant or a rock, but is not necessarily parasitic. Some epiphytes are climbers which may have some ground roots, while others germinate on the host plant and have no contact with the ground. The latter are best represented in tropical rain forests, where orchids, BROMELIADS, and ferns are the most common types. Some, such as the strangler fig, may grow to envelop the whole host and eventually kill it, the fig being left as a free-standing tree. In temperate regions the bulk of epiphytic organisms are mosses, liverworts, algae, and lichens. In the sea, algae may be epiphytic on other species.

epistemology The philosophical theory of knowledge. It is generally assumed that the difference between a belief which makes a genuine claim to knowledge, and one which is a mere statement of opinion, is that the former can somehow be justified. Epistemology can be regarded as the investigation of what constitutes that justification, and how, or whether, it can be attained. SCEPTICISM is the position that holds that justification, and hence knowledge, is not possible.

Epistle Any of the 21 books of the New Testament written in the form of a letter. 13 are ascribed to St Paul, seven to other authors, and one, the *Epistle to the Hebrews*, is by an unknown author. In many Christian liturgies, the Epistle is the first of the two biblical texts read before the celebration of the Eucharist; although it is usually taken from the Epistles of the New Testament, it may come from other biblical sources.

epochs Units of time used in geology. They are subdivisions of periods. The Pliocene and Pleistocene Epochs are examples. See GEOLOGICAL TIMESCALE.

epoxy resin A thermoset PLASTIC containing epoxy (–O–) linkages. Epoxy resins have outstanding adhesion, toughness, and resistance to attack from chemicals. They form strong bonds and have excellent electrical insulation properties. Large, complex, void-free CASTINGS can be made from them. They are also used as ADHESIVES, and in COMPOSITES.

Epping A residential town at the northern end of Epping Forest in Essex, England, 27 km (17 miles) north of central London. Epping forest, which extends over 2,000 hectares (5,000 acres) was acquired in 1863 by the City of London.

Epsom A residential town in Surrey, south-east England; pop. (1981) 68,500. A noted spa town in the 17th century, it gave its name to Epsom salts, a form of magnesium sulphate used as a purgative and first found occurring naturally here. Its racecourse on Epsom Downs is the venue for the annual DERBY and Oaks horse races.

Epstein, Brian (1934–67) British manager of the Beatles from 1961, who subsequently replaced the drummer Pete Best with Ringo Starr and arranged a contract with Parlophone. Epstein was not successful in financial negotiation, however, failing to capitalize on the US rights to Beatles merchandise. He died suddenly, probably of an accidental drugs overdose.

Epstein, Sir Jacob (1880–1959) US-born British sculptor. His first important commission was a group of eighteen figures for the British Medical Association in the Strand (1907–08); it was the first of many works to arouse violent criticism for the use of distortion and alleged obscenity. He moved towards abstract sculpture and later scored great success in his bronze portraits of the famous, in particular his *Einstein* (1933).

equation An algebraic expression that expresses

equality between quantities or functions. They can be used to describe sets of points or to find solutions for variables under certain prescribed constraints. If a, b, and c are any numbers, then $y = ax + b$ is a linear equation representing the set of points lying on a particular straight line, and $y = ax^2 + bx + c$ is a quadratic equation giving the set of points on a parabola. Solutions, or roots, are those values of the variables for which the equation is true. Thus $5x + 1 = 11$ is true if $x = 2$; and $2x^2 - x - 3 = 0$ has roots $x = -1$ and $x = 3/2$. To solve equations involving many variables at least as many equations are needed as there are variables. Such groups of equations are called simultaneous.

equations of motion The equations in classical physics that completely define the movement of an object with relation to space and time. For a body undergoing constant acceleration a, a series of four equations relate its initial velocity u, its final velocity v, its displacement s, and time t. These equations, $v = u + at$, $s = (u + v)t$, $s = ut + at^2$, and $v^2 = u^2 + 2as$, enable the motion of the body to be described. More generally, the basic equation of motion is derived from the second of NEWTON'S LAWS OF MOTION, which states that the applied force F is equal to the rate of change of momentum, or $F = d(mv)/dt$, where m is the mass of the body and v its velocity. For constant mass this gives $F = ma$, where a is acceleration. A second equation gives the rate of change of angular momentum H about a fixed point as equal to the moment of the resultant force about the same point: $H = r \times mv$ and so $dH/dt = rF$ where r is the displacement. Boundary conditions for position and velocity and knowledge of the FORCES in operation at any instant are necessary to solve completely these equations of motion.

equator The great circle on the surface of a planet, satellite, star, or CELESTIAL SPHERE that is perpendicular to the axis of rotation. A great circle is the line on the surface of a sphere produced by an intersecting plane that passes through the centre of the sphere. The equator divides the sphere into Northern and Southern Hemispheres. All points on the equator are equidistant from the POLES.

Equatorial Guinea A small country in equatorial West Africa on the Gulf of Guinea.

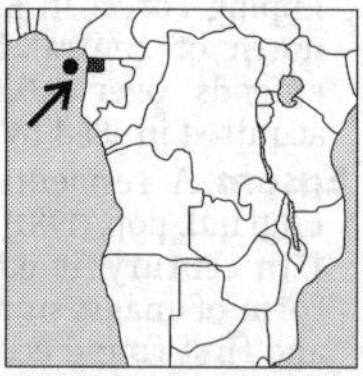

Physical. Equatorial Guinea includes the plateau of Río Muni bounded by Cameroon and Gabon, and the more mountainous and fertile, but smaller, island of Bioko (Fernando Póo).

Economy. Equatorial Guinea has a mainly agricultural economy, the main exports being timber and cocoa. Offshore oil and gold are exploited, and there are deposits of iron ore, copper, manganese, uranium, silica, and titanium. Equatorial Guinea is one of Africa's poorest countries; political upheaval has led to extensive emigration and agricultural neglect, with widespread food shortages. The economy is heavily dependent on foreign aid, largely from Spain.

History. Formerly a Spanish colony, it was a haunt of slave-traders and merchants. The mainland was not effectively occupied by Spain until 1926. Declared independent in 1968, a reign of terror followed until President Macias Nguema was overthrown and executed (1979) by his nephew, Obiang Nguema. The new regime pursued less repressive domestic policies with some degree of success. A referendum in November 1991 appeared to give overwhelming approval for multi-party politics, and in January 1992 an amnesty was granted by President Nguema to returning exiles; but in February a number of opposition leaders were arrested and some later died in prison. The Spanish government announced that promised economic aid was dependent upon implementation of democratization. Multi-party elections were planned, but opposition parties claimed they were not allowed to campaign freely, and called for a boycott of the elections. Few people voted in the elections, which were held in 1993 and were reported as being unfair by international observers. Nguema's ruling party officially won and remained in power. In 1995 the UN reiterated its concern about serious violations of human rights in the country.

Capital: Malabo
Area: 28,051 sq km (10,831 sq mi)
Population: 396,000 (1995)
Currency: 1 CFA franc = 100 centimes
Religions: Christian (mostly Roman Catholic) 88.8%; traditional beliefs 4.6%; atheist 1.4%; Muslim 0.5%
Ethnic Groups: Fang 72.0%; Bubi 14.7%; Duala 2.7%; Ibibio 1.3%; Maka 1.3%
Languages: Spanish (official); Fang, Bubi, and local languages
International Organizations: UN; OAU; Non-Aligned Movement; Franc Zone

equilibrium (in economics) An economic concept describing a situation in which there are no forces at work to bring about a change. For instance, an equilibrium price in a MARKET is one in which there is no excess demand to drive prices up and no excess supply to drive prices down; at equilibrium, demand will equal supply.

equilibrium (in physics and chemistry) The state of a system in which all the forces are balanced. A system is in stable equilibrium if, following a small disturbance, it returns to the equilibrium position. For stable equilibrium to occur, the potential energy P of the system must be at a minimum.

In chemistry, equilibrium is the state of balance in CHEMICAL REACTIONS, when there is no further tendency for the reactants or their products to change their concentrations. The effect of a change in conditions (such as addition to, or removal of, one of the substances; a rise or fall in temperature; or an increase or decrease of pressure) destroys the equilibrium, and the reaction moves in a way indicated by the equilibrium constant. The equilibrium constant provides a measure of whether reactants or products are favoured by the reaction at equilibrium.

equinox One of two instances of time when the centre of the Sun crosses the celestial equator on its annual journey around the ECLIPTIC on the CELESTIAL SPHERE. These crossings occur around 21 March and 23 September each year and are related to the seasons. For inhabitants of the Northern Hemisphere, the point where the Sun crosses from south to north is called the **vernal (spring) equinox** and heralds the official beginning of spring; the other crossing point is called the **autumnal equinox**. The names are reversed for the Southern Hemisphere. In theory, on these days night and day are of equal length; and at each pole the Sun is either rising or setting for the next six months. In practice, however, the Sun's rays are bent by refraction in the atmosphere, so that it appears to rise earlier and set later than theory has it, making day slightly longer than night.

equipartition of energy The way in which energy is shared between a very large number of particles in a system when all parts of the system are at the same temperature. At any particular temperature a system will have a certain total energy and this will be divided so that there is a certain average energy per particle. In essence the equipartition principle states that the total energy is shared on average by all the particles roughly equally, and that it is highly unlikely (if not impossible) that most of the energy will go to a few particles while the remainder have very little.

The energy must not only be shared equally among all the particles; it must also be shared equally between all the different motions of which each particle is capable.

equity (in law) A body of principles developed historically in England by the Court of Chancery to overcome unfairness resulting from the inflexibility and limitations of the law applied in the COMMON LAW courts. These principles, based on conscience, were usually given effect through the creation of new remedies, which could require a litigant who had successfully established legal rights before a common law court to use those rights for the benefit of a person (a 'beneficiary') who had a better claim in equity. In time, such beneficiaries were considered to possess equitable rights. These did not destroy legal rights, but took precedence over them.

equity (in finance) An ordinary SHARE or the ordinary share capital of a COMPANY. An equity market is one in which shares are traded and usually forms the greater part of a STOCK EXCHANGE.

Equuleus The Little Horse, the second-smallest CONSTELLATION in the sky; it lies next to PEGASUS, just north of the celestial equator. Equuleus was among the forty-eight constellations listed by the Greek astronomer Ptolemy in his *almagest*. Its brightest stars are of only fourth magnitude.

era The second largest of the time divisions used in geology. The Earth's Phanerozoic history (that is, the last 570 million years) is divided into three eras: the Palaeozoic, the Mesozoic, and the Cenozoic. Each era is subdivided into a number of periods. See GEOLOGICAL TIMESCALE.

Erasmus, Desiderius (born Gerhard Gerhards) (*c.*1469–1536) Dutch humanist and scholar. During his lifetime he was the most famous scholar in Europe and the first to achieve renown through the printed word. He published his own Greek edition of the New Testament (1516), followed by a Latin translation, and paved the way for the Reformation with his satires on the Church, including the *Colloquia Familiaria* (1518). However, he opposed the violence of the Protestant Reformation and condemned Luther in *De Libero Arbitrio* (1523).

Erastus (born Thomas Lieber, or Liebler, or Lüber) (1524–83) Swiss theologian and physician. He was professor of medicine at Heidelberg University from 1558. A follower of Zwingli, he opposed the imposition of a Calvinistic system of church government in Heidelberg because of the Calvinists' excessive use of excommunication. The doctrine of Erastianism (that the state should have supremacy over the Church in ecclesiastical matters) was later attributed to him, although his views were less extreme.

Eratosthenes (*c.*275–194 BC) Greek scholar, geographer, and astronomer. He was a pupil of Callimachus and head of the library at Alexandria. Active in the fields of literary criticism and chronology, he was also the first systematic geographer of antiquity. He accurately calculated the circumference of the Earth by measuring the angle of the Sun's rays at different places at the same time, and he attempted (less successfully) to determine the magnitude of the Sun and Moon and their distance from the Earth.

erbium (symbol Er, at. no. 68, r.a.m. 167.26) A silvery metal belonging to the lanthanides, used in some alloys and as a neutron absorber.

Erebus, Mount A volcanic peak on Ross Island, Antarctica. Rising to 3,794 m (12,450 ft), it is the southernmost active volcano in the world.

erg (in geography) A sandy desert, especially one in which the climate is hot and the whole land surface is covered by a sand sea.

erg (in physics) The unit of energy in the c.g.s. system, defined as the work done when a force of 1 dyne acts through a distance of 1 cm. 1 erg = 10^{-7} joule.

ergodic theory (in mathematics) The probability of the recurrence of phenomena. This branch of mathematics deals with questions of long-term equilibrium and the stability of a varying system. It has its origin in much of the classical theory of statistical mechanics, exploring such thermodynamic properties as temperature and ENTROPY. Ergodic theory also deals with questions such as whether the Solar System as a whole is stable.

ergonomics (or **human-factors engineering**) The study of the efficient interaction between human beings, their environment, and technological devices and systems, directed specifically towards the problems of the individual at work which impinge on work performance. It examines the effect on work performance of both internal and external factors. Internal factors are such things as the anatomical, physiological, and psychological factors affecting the work. External factors include such things as machine design, layout of equipment, speed of work, and lighting and heating conditions.

ergot A disease that attacks the flowering heads of grasses. It is caused by fungi. The common rye ergot fungus, *Claviceps purpurea*, produces sclerotia, which are commonly referred to as ergots, on the seed heads of rye. These contain a mixture of ALKALOIDS, such as ergotamine and ergotinine, which if eaten can cause convulsions, or gangrene. The latter, which is first experienced as a burning sensation, gave rise to the popular name of St Anthony's fire. This disease was contracted by eating bread made from rye flour infected with ergot and caused thousands of deaths in medieval Europe. In modern medicine, ergot alkaloids have clinical uses, such as in the treatment of migraine.

Ericsson, John (1803–89) Swedish engineer. His inventions included the marine screw propeller (1836). He then moved to the USA, where he built the ironclad *Monitor*, which was the first ship to have a revolving armoured turret and was used in a battle on the Union side in the American Civil War. Ericsson was also a pioneer of solar energy, constructing a steam pump supplied from a boiler heated by a concentrating mirror.

Ericsson, Leif (or **Ericson**) Norse explorer, son of Eric the Red. He sailed westward from Greenland (*c.*1000) and reputedly discovered land (variously identified as Labrador, Newfoundland, or New England), which he named Vinland because of the vines he claimed to have found growing there.

Eric the Red (*c.*940–*c.*1010) Norse explorer. He left Iceland in 982 in search of land to the west, exploring Greenland and establishing a Norse settlement there in 986.

Eridanus The River, a large CONSTELLATION that

meanders from the celestial equator deep into the Southern Hemisphere of the sky. At its southernmost end lies its brightest star, ACHERNAR. Eridanus was one of the 48 constellations known to the ancient Greeks, and was often identified with the River Po in Italy.

Erie, Lake The fourth-largest and shallowest of the five Great Lakes of North America, situated on the frontier between Canada and the USA; area 25,812 sq km (9,966 sq miles); area on the Canadian side of the border, 12,880 sq km (4,973 sq miles); maximum depth 64 m (210 ft). It is linked to Lake Huron by the Detroit River via Lake St Clair and to Lake Ontario by the Welland Canal and the Niagara River which is its only natural outlet.

Eritrea A country in north-eastern Africa, on the Red Sea.

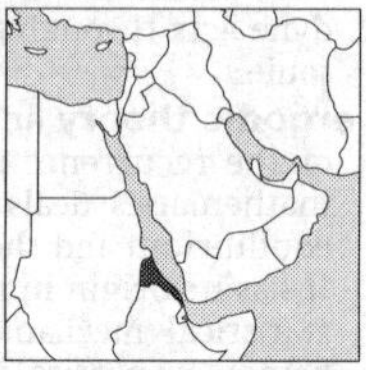

Physical. Eritrea consists of a narrow coastal low-lying area and rises towards the Ethiopian plateau in the south. It is very hot and arid.

Economy. The economy has been badly affected by the war of independence. Agricultural products include sorghum and livestock is raised. There are textile and footwear industries.

History. In 1869 Italy purchased the coastal town of Assab, and in 1885 began the occupation of the rest of Eritrea, which it declared a colony in 1889. It was from here that the Italians launched their disastrous campaign against ETHIOPIA in 1896, ending in their defeat at ADOWA. Under British military administration (1941–52), a plan to join the Muslim west with the Sudan and the Christian centre with Ethiopia failed. Instead, the United Nations voted to make Eritrea a federal area subject to Ethiopia. In 1962 Emperor HAILE SELASSIE declared it a province of Ethiopia and the Eritrean People's Liberation Front (EPLF) then emerged, seeking secession. Fierce fighting between the EPLF and the Ethiopian regime continued through the 1980s, in spite of drought and famine. In February 1990 the EPLF captured Massawa, and in 1991, in an alliance with the Ethiopian People's Revolutionary Democratic Front (EPRDF) and the Tigray People's Liberation Front, the EPLF defeated the Ethiopian government's forces. A transitional Eritrean government was set up by the EPLF and a referendum was held in 1993. Independence was approved by the referendum and was achieved later that year.

Capital: Asmara
Area: 117,400 sq km (45,300 sq mi)
Population: 3,531,000 (1995)
Currency: 1 Ethiopian birr = 100 cents
Religions: Christian (Ethiopian Orthodox) 50.0%; Muslim 50.0%
Languages: Arabic; Tigrinya; Tigré; minority languages
International Organizations: UN;OAU

Erlanger, Joseph (1874–1965) US physiologist. He worked mainly in cardiac physiology, designing a sphygmomanometer to study the components of the pulse wave and examining the conduction of impulses in the heart. Using an oscilloscope with H. Gasser, Erlanger found that the velocity of a nerve impulse is proportional to the diameter of the fibre. Erlanger and Gasser shared a Nobel Prize for this in 1944.

ermine A stoat whose brown winter coat has moulted, leaving a pure white coat, except for the tip of the tail. This occurs in northern latitudes and provides the stoat with excellent camouflage in the snow. Ermine was formerly used as a fashion fur.

Ermine Street ▶**1** The Roman road between London and Lincoln via Huntingdon. ▶**2** The Roman road connecting Silchester with Gloucester.

Ernst, Max (1891–1976) German-born artist who moved to the USA in 1941 and became a US citizen in 1948. He subsequently returned to Europe, taking French citizenship in 1958. Ernst was one of the major figures of SURREALISM. After studying philosophy and psychology and serving in World War I, he became leader of the DADA group in Cologne in 1919. In 1922 he settled in Paris, bringing with him the Dadaist techniques of COLLAGE and photomontage (see MONTAGE), which were adapted to Surrealist uses.

Erode A cotton-processing city in Tamil Nadu, southern India, on the Cauvery River north-east of Coimbatore; pop. (1991) 357,430.

Eros (in astronomy) An ASTEROID discovered by the German astronomer Georg Witt and one of the first of the AMOR GROUP to be found. Eros spends most of the time inside the orbit of Mars, and actually passes close to the Earth.

Eros (in mythology) A Greek god of love, a primeval force, the son of Aphrodite. In Hellenistic times he became associated with romantic love, and was represented as a little winged archer, shooting his arrows at gods and men. The Romans identified him with Cupid.

erosion The wearing away of the Earth's surface by the action of water, wind, etc. Under natural conditions erosion is a slow process but as a result of overgrazing, deforestation, and inappropriate agricultural practices the Earth's topsoil is eroded at a much faster rate.

Erse The Gaelic language of Ireland or the Scottish highlands and islands.

Erté (born Romain de Tirtoff, the initials of which provided his adopted name in French) (1892–1990) Russian-born French fashion designer and illustrator. From 1912 he worked in Paris as a fashion designer, and during World War I his garments became internationally famous through his decorative magazine illustrations. In the 1920s he became a noted art deco designer, moving into the design of household items and fabrics and creating elaborate *tableaux vivants* for Broadway shows such as the *Ziegfeld Follies*.

erythrocyte A red BLOOD cell. In mammals, erythrocytes are biconcave discs that lack a nucleus, and they measure 0.007 mm (0.0003 inch) in diameter; in other vertebrates they are oval and nucleate. The red colour is caused by the high concentration within the cells of the oxygen-transport molecule, HAEMOGLOBIN. There are about five million erythrocytes in one millilitre of human blood; they are produced at the rate of about two million per second by special tissue in the bone marrow, and old cells are destroyed and removed by the spleen.

ESA See EUROPEAN SPACE AGENCY.

Esaki, Leo (1925–) Japanese physicist. He investigated and pioneered the development of quantum-mechanical tunnelling of electrons in semiconductor devices, and designed the tunnel diode. These (also known as **Esaki diodes**), small and fast in operation, are now widespread in electronic devices. Esaki shared the Nobel Prize for physics in 1973.

Esau (Hebrew, 'red') The hunter son of Isaac, older twin brother of Jacob and ancestor of the nation of Edom. Exchanging his birthright (rights due to him as the eldest son) for a 'mess of pottage' (bowl of food), he was then cheated of his dying father's blessing by Jacob impersonating him. The story sets out to explain why Israel, synonymous with Jacob's kingdom, was entitled to dominate the tribes of Edom.

escalator A continuously moving stairway. It carries more passengers than a lift but occupies a greater space. Each step is carried by four wheels on concealed tracks, and is part of a continuous, circular chain. At the top and bottom, the steps level out to form a flat entry or exit section.

escape velocity The minimum velocity that an object, such as a spacecraft or atmospheric molecule, needs to escape from the gravitational field of a massive body. This velocity has a value of $\sqrt{(2GM/R)}$, where G is the constant of gravitation, M is the mass of the body, and R is the distance between the object and the centre of the body. The escape velocities from the surfaces of the Earth and Moon are 11.2 and 2.4 km/s, respectively. The low value for the Moon explains why it has lost all its atmosphere.

eschatology In Christian and Jewish theology the 'last things', including the ultimate fate of the world and the individual soul. However, almost all religions of the world have eschatological features, which may be divided into those based on mythological explanations of the origins and end of the world (see CREATION MYTHS) and those based on historical explanations. The biblical accounts of the history of the Jewish people and the teaching and parables of Jesus are examples of historical eschatology, leading to MILLENARIAN expectations of the coming of the Messiah among Jews, and of the Second Coming among Christians. Contrasting with such views is the expectation of the apocalyptic or cataclysmic intervention of God in history. In both Hinduism and Buddhism.

Escher, M(aurits) C(orneille) (1898–1972) Dutch graphic artist. He is well known for prints making sophisticated use of visual illusion, exploiting, for example, the ambiguity between flat pattern and apparent three-dimensional recession. From the 1940s his work took on a SURREALIST flavour as he made brilliant play with optical illusion to represent, for example, staircases that appear to lead both up and down in the same direction.

eschscholzia A plant of the poppy family that contains about four variable species of annual and perennial herbs, all native to northwest America. The California poppy, *Eschscholzia californica*, is the best known and, as a garden plant, is one of the brightest of annuals.

Escoffier, Georges-Auguste (1846–1935) French chef. He gained an international reputation while working in London at the Savoy Hotel (1890–99) and later at the Carlton (1899–1919). His many culinary inventions include peach Melba, first made in 1893 in honour of the singer Dame Nellie Melba when she was staying at the Savoy.

Esfahan See ISFAHAN.

Eskimo See INUIT.

Eskimo-Aleut languages A group of about ten languages spoken by 90,000 people in Greenland, northern Canada, Alaska, the Aleutian islands, and the Chukchi peninsula of Siberia. Most of the speakers are INUIT (Eskimo); Aleut accounts for just 700 people on the Aleutian islands off Alaska. The two languages are not mutually intelligible.

esparto grass A large tussock grass, *Stipa tenacissima*, found in North Africa, from which a valuable leaf fibre is obtained. Long-leaved varieties yield a product suitable for rope and twine manufacture, while other types are valuable for paper-making. It has been cultivated in Spain for centuries, and in Africa it is harvested by hand.

Esperanto An artificial language devised in 1887 by L. L. Zamenhof, a Polish physician, as a medium of communication for persons of all languages. Its words are based mainly on roots commonly found in Romance and other European languages, and while it has the advantage of grammatical regularity and ease of pronunciation it retains the structure of these languages, which makes Esperanto no easier than any other European language for a speaker whose native tongue falls outside this group.

Essen A city in the state of North Rhine-Westphalia, north-west Germany, the hub of the industrial Ruhr valley; pop. (1991) 626,990. The city was heavily bombed in World War II and has been imaginatively rebuilt.

Essene A member of an ancient Jewish ascetic sect of the 2nd century BC–2nd century AD in Palestine, who lived in highly organized groups and held property in common. Information concerning the Essenes is rudimentary. However, the DEAD SEA SCROLLS may have been created by an Essene community.

essential oil A volatile, naturally occurring oil, often with a characteristic smell, containing as one of its main ingredients a substance belonging to a group of compounds known as terpenes. Essential oils are mostly extracted from plants, and are used mainly as PERFUMES or as flavourings (see FOOD ADDITIVE). They are also used extensively in certain alternative medical therapies.

Essex A county of eastern England to the north of the Thames estuary; area 3,672 sq km (1,418 sq miles); pop. (1991) 1,495,600; county town, Chelmsford.

Essex, Robert Devereux, 2nd Earl of (1567–1601) English courtier, favourite of ELIZABETH I. He distinguished himself as a soldier during the Dutch Revolt (1586), but earned the queen's displeasure by participating in the disastrous Lisbon expedition (1589) and by marrying Sir Philip Sidney's widow (1590). Gradually, his rivalry with the CECIL faction grew. In 1599 Elizabeth sent him as Lord Lieutenant of Ireland to put down the Earl of Tyrone's rebellion. He failed ignominiously and was stripped of his offices. His subsequent attempt to raise the London people in an anti-Cecil coup (1601) led to his trial and execution for treason.

Essex, Robert Devereux, 3rd Earl of (1591–1646) English soldier, commander of the ROUNDHEADS. Although he served Charles I in 1625 he opposed him at the outbreak of the ENGLISH CIVIL WAR and in 1642 was appointed commander of the Roundhead forces, leading them at the battle of Edgehill. After a number of Roundhead defeats, the NEW MODEL ARMY was organized in 1645 and Essex resigned his command.

ester Any of a class of compounds with the general formula RCOOR′, where R and R′ are either ALKYL or ARYL GROUPS. If R and R′ are small groups, the resulting esters are volatile liquids, insoluble in water. They frequently possess characteristic sweet smells. For example, the smell of pear drops is caused by the ester pentyl ethanoate, $CH_3COOC_5H_{11}$. There are many naturally occurring esters. For example, fats are esters of glycerol and carboxylic acids with long carbon chains.

Esther The Jewish heroine who married King Xerxes (Ahasuerus) of Persia after he had banished the Persian Queen Vashti from his court for defying his orders. Esther won legendary favour with her husband by her great beauty and by twice saving his life; she was in time able to anticipate and prevent a massacre of the Jews, who then rounded on their enemies and destroyed them. These events, recorded in the biblical Book of Esther, are still celebrated in the popular Jewish feast of Purim.

Estonia A country of northern Europe, bounded on the north by the Gulf of Finland, on the east by Russia, on the south by Latvia, and on the west by the Baltic Sea.

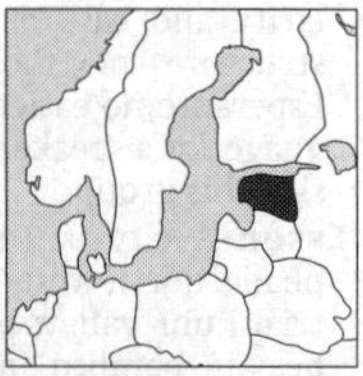

Physical. Two large islands and numerous small ones lie off the coast, which is occasionally icebound in winter although the summers are warm. The mainland comprises a limestone plateau in the north, and a low-lying plain on which are situated forests and lakes of glacial origin.

Economy. The principal mineral resource is bituminous shale, together with peat; industries utilizing oil shale to produce artificial gas and electricity produce much of the power of the northwest region of the former Soviet Union, but at serious environmental cost. Other industries include machinery, chemicals, timber, and textiles. Agriculture concentrates on animal husbandry.

History. Annexed by Russia in 1709, Estonia regained its independence in 1918, at the time of the Bolshevik revolution. Its history during the 1920s was of an agrarian revolution, whereby the great estates of the Baltic barons (mostly German) were broken up, creating a prosperous peasantry. An attempted communist uprising in 1924 was suppressed. Its economy was adversely affected by the Great Depression and from 1934 until 1939 it experienced a highly autocratic, neo-fascist regime led by Konstantin Paets. The latter admired Hitler, but his attempt to make a pact was invalidated by the Nazi-Soviet Pact of August 1939. In September Soviet troops occupied key ports and in 1940 the whole country. It welcomed German troops in 1941, but its anti-Bolshevik Resistance forces could not prevent the Red Army from reoccupying it in 1944. It became a constituent republic of the Soviet Union. In February 1990 there were mass rallies in the capital Tallin demanding independence, and in May its Supreme Soviet reinstated the constitution of the Republic of Estonia of 1920. Talks began with the Soviet Union, which recognized the Republic's independence in September 1991, when it was admitted to the UN General Assembly. The collapse of its markets in Russia during 1991 resulted in an economic crisis, with food and fuel rationing in January 1992, eased by trade agreements with the European Community and by IMF support. In 1992 a new constitution was adopted and Lennart Meri (1929–) was elected President. Russian residents were disturbed by a proposed law that would have denied them Estonian citizenship. The law was amended (1993) before it was passed, making citizenship available to residents who passed Estonian language tests. Two mainly Russian cities voted for autonomy (1993) but the government declared their referendums illegal. In 1994 the last Russian troops withdrew from Estonia.

Capital: Tallin
Area: 45,111 sq km (17,413 sq mi)
Population: 1,487,000 (1995)
Currency: 1 kroon = 100 senti
Religions: Lutheran Church
Ethnic Groups: Estonian 62.0%; Russian 30.0%
Languages: Estonian (official); Russian
International Organizations: UN; CSCE; North Atlantic Co-operation Council

Estoril A fashionable resort town with a mild climate and radioactive hot springs on the Atlantic coast of Portugal, west of Lisbon; pop. (1991) 24,850.

estuary The broad, lowest, tidal section of a river. All rivers flowing into the sea or very large lakes have either estuaries or DELTAS at their mouths. The extent of an estuary depends upon the river's slope, the shape of the valley, and the range of the tidal stream of the water body into which it flows; shallow estuaries of rivers with strong currents often develop TIDAL BORES. Because estuaries are tidal and relatively sheltered, they are often important harbours, although the tendency of rivers to deposit sediments as their currents are checked means that dredging is frequently needed to keep channels open.

etching A method of ENGRAVING in which the design is bitten into the plate with acid. A print produced from such a plate is also called an etching. The design is drawn on a metal (usually copper) plate that has been coated with a waxy, acid-resistant substance. Where the waxy coating is scratched through with the etching needle the bare metal is exposed, and when the plate is placed in a bath of acid the acid bites only the lines so exposed. It is possible to achieve subtle variations of tone by 'stopping out' part of the design (covering it with a protective varnish). Etching was developed in the early 16th century and reached exalted heights in the hands of Rembrandt. It is still a popular technique.

ethane (C_2H_6) A colourless, odourless gas which burns readily in air; it is the second member of the ALKANES. Occurring with methane in natural gas, much of it is burnt directly without separation. It can be separated by liquefaction under pressure and can then be passed through hot tubes, forming hydrogen and ethene, a major petrochemical feedstock.

ethanoic acid (or **acetic acid**, CH_3COOH) The CARBOXYLIC ACID found in vinegar; it is formed when alcoholic drinks go sour, by OXIDATION of the ethanol. It is used as a solvent, as a preservative, and in the manufacture of flavourings and plastics. The pure acid freezes, giving ice-like crystals, and is called glacial ethanoic acid.

ethanol (or **ethyl alcohol**, CH_3CH_2OH) A clear, colourless, low-boiling-point (78.5°C) liquid, the intoxicant in alcoholic drinks. For human consumption it is always produced by FERMENTATION, as in BREWING or WINE-making. For industrial use, it is sometimes produced by fermentation of cheap vegetable matter, such as molasses – as in the production of ethanol for use as a BIOFUEL. Most commonly, however, ethanol is made by reacting ETHENE with water in the presence of a catalyst (usually sulphuric acid or phosphoric acid). Industrial alcohol is treated with additives (often methanol) that are difficult to remove, which make it unpleasant to taste but do not interfere with its chemical properties. Ethanol is used to produce ethanal (acetaldehyde, CH_3CHO), used in the manufacture of vinyl and acrylic plastics. It is also used in the manufacture of vinegar, in the preparation of dyes and perfumes, and as a solvent for lacquers. It burns readily in air; and in some countries where sugar can be grown easily it is employed as a fuel for cars by mixing it with petrol.

Ethelred Two kings of England. **Ethelred I** (died 871), king of Wessex and Kent 865–71, was the elder brother of Alfred the Great. His reign was marked by the continuing struggle against the invading Danes. Alfred joined Ethelred's campaigns and succeeded him on his death. **Ethelred II** (known as Ethelred the Unready) (*c*.969–1016) was king of England 978–1016. Ethelred's inability to confront the Danes after he succeeded his murdered half-brother St Edward the Martyr led to his payment of tribute to prevent their attacks. In 1013 he briefly lost his throne to the Danish king Sweyn I. His nickname came from an Old English word meaning 'lacking good advice; rash'.

ethene (or **ethylene**, $CH_2{=}CH_2$) A colourless, sweet-smelling, flammable gas, which burns readily in air. It occurs in natural gas, and is made by the CRACKING of petroleum. Ethene, the first member of the ALKENES, is the simplest hydrocarbon to contain the reactive carbon-carbon double bond, and is a very important starting material in the PETROCHEMICALS industry. It can be polymerized to form POLYTHENE. It reacts with steam to form ETHANOL, and with oxygen to form epoxyethane, which is used to make antifreeze, synthetic rubber, solvents, herbicides, detergents, and cosmetics. It reacts with chlorine to produce vinyl chloride and with benzene to produce styrene, both of which are precursors of important plastics (PVC and POLYSTYRENE, respectively). Ethene produces ripening in fruit, but also inhibits growth in plants.

ether (in chemistry) Any of a class of organic compounds with the formula ROR′, where R and R′ are either ALKYL or ARYL GROUPS, which need not necessarily be identical. Ethoxyethane (or diethyl ether), $C_2H_5OC_2H_5$ is the most common ether. This is a volatile, highly flammable liquid, insoluble in water. It is used as a solvent, mainly for organic compounds. It also possesses anaesthetic properties.

ether (in physics) A hypothetical substance formerly supposed to pervade the whole of space and be the medium in which light travelled. The Michelson–Morley experiment led to the abandonment of this hypothesis and the acceptance that electromagnetic radiation is a wave motion without a medium.

ethics The philosophical study of the nature and grounds of moral thought and action. Ethical theories in this pure sense are sharply distinguished from moral systems, which are directed towards drawing up particular sets of rules by which to live (such as Christian morality), and from practical or applied ethics, the analysis of arguments advanced for particular moral conclusions (such as the rightness or wrongness of abortion). The most fundamental question in ethics is usually taken to be the justification of morality, that is whether or not it can be demonstrated that moral action is rational.

Ethiopia A country, formerly called Abyssinia, in north-eastern Africa. Sudan is on its eastern border, Eritrea on its northern border, and Kenya on its southern, while Somalia reaches round it on the east.

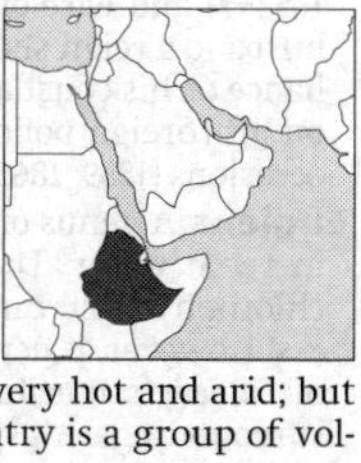

Physical. The low-lying Ogaden region in the east is very hot and arid; but the entire centre of the country is a group of volcanic mountain ranges with high plateaux where the air is mild and there is moderate summer rain. The Great Rift Valley runs through these, and the whole area is cut about with ravines and fertile valleys. In the north-west lies Lake Tana, the source of the Blue Nile, while in the south-west forests rise along the slopes of the mountain ranges.

Economy. The Ethiopian economy has been centrally planned and has been based on collectivized agriculture. Coffee, hides, and skins are the main exports. Ethiopia has an oil refinery, but derives most of its energy from firewood, charcoal, and dung. Industry is limited.

History. By the 2nd century AD the kingdom of AKSUM had a brisk trade with Egypt, Syria, Arabia, and India in gold, ivory, and incense, and minted a gold currency. In the 4th century the court became Christian. Aksum collapsed *c*.1000, and, after a time of confusion, the Zagwe dynasty emerged. In 1270 it was replaced by the Solomonic dynasty claiming lineal descent from SOLOMON and the Queen of Sheba, bringing the Amharas from the mountains of central Ethiopia to prominence. For Europe in the Middle Ages this was possibly the legendary kingdom of PRESTER JOHN. In the 16th century the Muslims of the lowlands attacked the Christian highlands, but were repulsed in 1542 with Portuguese artillery. When Jesuit missionaries came to Ethiopia Emperor Susenyos was converted to Roman Catholicism (1626). His son Fasilidas (1632–67), having forced him to abdicate, made Gondar the capital. Surrounded by Islam, and torn by warring factions, the empire foundered. The only unifying force was the Ethiopian COPTIC CHURCH, and the empire was not reunited until 1855, when Emperor Tewodros II was crowned, and this was continued during the reign of Menelik II.

Ethiopia successfully repelled Italian attempts at colonization by a decisive victory at ADOWA in 1896, but was conquered by MUSSOLINI in 1935–36. The Ethiopian emperor HAILE SELASSIE was restored in 1941 after the Abyssinian campaigns, and in the 1950s and 1960s Ethiopia emerged as a leading African neutralist state. Haile Selassie's failure to deal with severe social and economic problems led to his deposition by a group of radical army officers in 1974. A subsequent coup brought Colonel Mengistu to power in 1977, but his centralized Marxist state was confronted by a Somali-backed guerrilla war in ERITREA. Famine broke out on a massive scale (1984–87), and despite Soviet and Cuban military assistance and an international relief effort to alleviate starvation, neither peace nor plenty returned. In May 1991 Mengistu was forced to flee the country by the Ethiopian People's Revolutionary Democratic Front (EPRDF) and their allies, who included the Eritrean People's Liberation Front (EPLF) and the Tigray People's Liberation Front. Peace talks in London resulted in the recognition of an EPRDF government in Addis Ababa, which largely succeeded in restoring order. In 1991 the country was divided into nine regions, based on ethnic groupings. Eritrea voted to secede and became independent in 1993. A new constitution was adopted in 1994 for the so-called Federal Democratic Republic of Ethiopia, which gave the regions considerable autonomy. The first multi-party elections (1995) were won by the EPRDF, under Meles Zenawi.

Capital: Addis Ababa
Area: 1,223,500 sq km (472,400 sq mi)
Population: 55,053,000 (1995)
Currency: 1 Ethiopian birr = 100 cents

Religions: Ethiopian Orthodox 40.0%; Muslim 40.0%; traditional beliefs 15.0%; other Christian 4.5%
Ethnic Groups: Galla 40.0%; Amhara-Tigre 32.0%; Kafa Sidano 9.0%; Somali 6.0%; Nilotic 6.0%; Afar 5.0%
Languages: Amharic (official); Gallinya; local languages
International Organizations: UN; OAU; Non-Aligned Movement

ethology The study of animal BEHAVIOUR in a natural environment. Ethology is particularly concerned with the animal's interactions with others of the same species and the function of the behaviour, and is directed towards how the evolution of behaviour has been influenced by NATURAL SELECTION. Its theoretical orientation was based on DARWIN's dictum that patterns of behaviour as well as bodily structure are subject to the selective processes of evolution. Its classical formulation is in the works of the Austrian Konrad LORENZ and the Dutchman Niko TINBERGEN, particularly the latter's *The Study of Instinct* (1951). Lorenz demonstrated how experience might direct a fixed action pattern when he discovered IMPRINTING. Ethology spread into systematic observation of human, particularly children's, behaviour, and arguments about innateness of facial expression and other NON-VERBAL COMMUNICATION. Bowlby's theory of attachment is another application of ethological ideas.

ethyl alcohol See ETHANOL.

ethylene See ETHENE.

ethylene glycol See ANTIFREEZE.

ethyne (or **acetylene**, CH≡CH) A colourless gas, the first member of the ALKYNES and the simplest HYDROCARBON to contain the very reactive carbon–carbon triple bond. It is formed from calcium carbide and water, or by oxidation of methane. Ethyne is an important industrial starting material for chemical synthesis and is used to produce ethanal (acetaldehyde, CH_3CHO) and halogenated hydrocarbons, such as the CHLOROFLUOROCARBONS (CFCs). It is also widely used for welding and cutting: the oxy-acetylene flame reaches temperatures of 2,800°C. Ethyne is explosive when pressurized, so for welding it is dissolved under a pressure of 14 bar in acetone (PROPANONE) and contained in cylinders packed with absorbent inert material. Ethyne is also used to make many industrially important materials, such as vinyl chloride, vinyl acetate, and neoprene.

Etna, Mount A snow-capped volcano on the east coast of the island of Sicily in the Italian province of Catania, the highest and most active European volcano (3,323 m, 10,902 ft). Over 135 serious eruptions have been recorded since the 5th century BC.

Eton College A school near Windsor in Berkshire, England, founded in 1440 by Henry VI to prepare scholars for King's College, Cambridge. The Eton wall game, one of the oldest forms of football in existence, is played only on a site at Eton College where scholars (or Collegers) have played non-scholars (Oppidians) on St Andrew's Day (30 November) since *c.*1820.

Etruscans The inhabitants of ancient Etruria (approximating to modern Tuscany, Italy), west of the Apennines and the River Tiber. Twelve independent cities including Vulci, Clusium, and Cortona were formed into a league and came to dominate central Italy in the 7th and 6th centuries BC. Tradition held that they came from Asia Minor in the 10th century BC, though it is now believed that they were native to Italy before that and only culturally influenced by the Greek colonies of south Italy. In the 6th century BC they were driven out of southern central Italy by the Greeks, Latins, and Samnites. In the following century their navy was defeated off Cumae. Traditionally, in 510 BC the last Etruscan king of Rome, TARQUIN, was expelled. In the 4th century they were driven out of Elba and Corsica, defeated by the Gauls in 390, and finally allied themselves with Rome after defeat in 283. From this time they came under Rome's control and began to lose their unique cultural identity.

Etruscan art reveals an aristocratic society in which women enjoyed an emancipated style of life. The Etruscan language has so far proved beyond translation; it was still spoken and written in the 1st century AD but no literature survives.

etymology A branch of historical LINGUISTICS studying the ancestry of the form and meaning of words. It draws on the theory of regular sound change in the development of one LANGUAGE or across languages. For example, 'king' is related to Old English *cyning*; and the Welsh *pedwar* (meaning 'four') is related to the Latin *quattuor*.

EU See EUROPEAN UNION.

eucalyptus A tree or suckering shrub of Australasia, a member of the genus *Eucalyptus* of some 500 species, penetrating northwards into the Lesser Sunda Islands of Indonesia. They are relatives of myrtles and cloves. They all have leathery leaves and an unusual lid, or operculum, over the flower bud, which is lost at flowering. They are typical of the Australian landscape and some, such as the coolabah tree, *Eucalyptus microtheca*, are found in arid country where few other trees will grow. They may be classified in groups according to the form of the bark: gums have smooth bark; bloodwoods have scales; stringy-barks have fibrous bark; iron-barks are black when old, and so on. The suckering species are known as mallee.

The tropical *E. regnans* reaches some 97 m (320 feet) in height and 7.5 m (25 feet) in girth. Many species are of rapid growth, so that they are widely planted for timber. The blue gum, *E. saligna*, and other species, yield oil of eucalyptus, used in medicine, and this and a few other species can be grown in cool, temperate regions.

Euclid (*c.*300 BC) Greek mathematician. He taught at Alexandria, and is famous for his great work *Elements of Geometry*, which covered plane geometry, the theory of numbers, irrationals, and solid geometry. This was the standard work until other kinds of geometry were conceived in the 19th century.

eugenics The study and doctrine of improving a population by controlled breeding for desirable inherited characteristics. The concept was widely discussed in Britain, the USA, and Europe in the late 19th and early 20th centuries, the word having been coined by the British psychologist GALTON in 1883. Because eugenic ideas flourished under Nazism, they became discredited and are not often voiced. However, implicitly eugenic practices continue in many parts of the world.

Eugénie (born Eugénia María de Montijo de Guzmán) (1826–1920) Spanish empress of France 1853–71 and wife of Napoleon III. Throughout her husband's reign she contributed much to the brilliance of his court and was an important influence on his foreign policy. She acted as regent on three occasions (1859; 1865; 1870).

Euglena A genus of single-celled organisms found in fresh water. They contain the green pigment chlorophyll and can make food by PHOTOSYNTHESIS. However, if deprived of sunlight many species of *Euglena* can utilize ready-made foods from their surroundings. All species have two long, whip-like flagella with which they propel themselves through the water. They are now usually classified as a phylum, Euglenophyta, of the kingdom PROTOCTISTA.

eukaryote An organism whose CELLS contain chromosomes within a nucleus, and other distinct organelles. Plants, algae, fungi, protozoa, and animals are all eukaryotes; in contrast, bacteria are PROKARYOTES.

Euler, Leonhard (1707–83) Swiss mathematician. His attempts to elucidate the nature of functions and his successful (though logically dubious) study of infinite series led his successors, notably Abel and Cauchy, to introduce ideas of convergence and rigorous argument into mathematics. One of his best-known theorems defines a connection between two of the most important constants in mathematics, expressed in the equation $e^{i\pi} = -1$, where e is the base of natural logarithms, $i = \sqrt{-1}$, and π is the ratio of the circumference of a circle to its diameter.

Euler, Ulf Svante von (1905–83) Swedish physiologist, the son of Hans Euler-Chelpin. He was the first to discover a prostaglandin, which he isolated from semen. He then searched for the principal chemical neurotransmitter of the sympathetic nervous system, and identified it as noradrenalin. Euler was awarded a Nobel Prize for this in 1970.

Euler-Chelpin, Hans Karl August Simon von (1873–1964) German-born Swedish biochemist. He worked mainly on enzymes and vitamins, and explained the role of enzymes in the alcoholic fermentation of sugar. He shared the Nobel Prize for chemistry in 1929.

eunuch A castrated human male. Eunuchs were used as guardians of harems in ancient China and in the Persian empire of the Achaemenids and also at the courts of the Byzantine emperors and the Ottoman sultans. They became the friends and advisers of the rulers of these powers, as they did of Roman emperors. Castration was also imposed as a form of punishment (ABELARD suffered in this way); was practised voluntarily by some Christian sects (the most notable Christian eunuch being the theologian Origen); and was used to produce male adult sopranos in Italy – castrati – until Pope Leo XIII banned the practice in 1878.

euphausid shrimps (or **krill**) Primitive, filter-feeding relatives of the true SHRIMPS, closely related to the crab, and lobsters. Euphausid shrimps make up the Euphausiacae, one of the most abundant orders of CRUSTACEANS in the plankton of southern oceans, but there are only 90 species. They are the staple diet of whales and large fishes, due to their convenient tendency to swarm.

euphonium A wide-bore, low-pitched, valved BRASS instrument related to the tuba, pitched in 9-foot B♭, a principal melody instrument in the BRASS BAND. In Britain there is a firm distinction between the narrow-bore baritone, the lowest of the cornet family, and the wide-bore euphonium, but elsewhere, especially in the USA, the two terms are almost interchangeable.

euphorbia See SPURGE.

Euphrates A river of south-west Asia that rises in the mountains of eastern Turkey and flows through Syria and Iraq to join the Tigris near Basra, forming the Shatt al-Arab waterway which flows into the Persian Gulf. In Turkey the Euphrates forms a major element of the Grand Anatolian Project to supply irrigation water and hydroelectric power. The Ataturk dam, the largest of Turkey's dams, was completed in 1989. In Syria the Euphrates is the main single source of water for domestic use, irrigation, and industry. The river is about 2,736 km (1,700 miles) long.

Eurasia Europe and Asia combined; they are sometimes considered to be a single continent.

Euratom (in full **European Atomic Energy Community**) An agency set up in 1957 to promote within the European Community the industrial and technical conditions required to utilize discoveries in atomic physics, and particularly the large-scale production of NUCLEAR POWER. Membership was extended to Denmark, Ireland, and the UK in 1973, and to Greece in 1981.

Eureka Stockade The site of Australia's only major civil riot which took place to the east of the gold-mining town of Ballarat, Victoria, in 1854 when aggrieved miners took up arms against police and troops.

Euripides (*c.*480–406 BC) Greek dramatist. He was the last of the trio of important tragedians after Aeschylus and Sophocles. His nineteen surviving plays show important innovations in the handling of the traditional myths, such as their introduction of a low realism into grand subject-matter, their interest in feminine psychology, and their portrayal of abnormal and irrational states of mind. They include *Medea*, *Hippolytus*, *Electra*, *Trojan Women*, and *Bacchae*.

Eurodollar A US dollar deposit held by an individual or an institution in a bank outside the USA (most frequently in Europe). Eurodollars constitute a stock of internationally mobile funds, which act as a source of easily transferable CREDIT and which facilitate trade. Banks benefit by borrowing and lending dollars at different INTEREST rates. The Eurodollar market originated in the late 1950s. Subsequently the market also began to function in other currencies too; thus the term Euro-currency developed.

Europa (in astronomy) A GALILEAN SATELLITE of Jupiter, discovered by Galileo in 1610. It has a nearly circular orbit in the plane of Jupiter's equator at 670,900 km from the planet's centre. Its diameter is 3,138 km and its density of 2,970 kg/m^3 implies that the interior is composed of mainly rocky materials.

Europa (in Greek mythology) A princess with whom Zeus fell in love. He disguised himself as a white bull and when – beguiled by the animal's docile nature – she climbed on his back, he carried her off by sea to Crete, where he resumed his normal shape and ravished her.

Europe A continent of the Northern Hemisphere consisting of the western part of the land mass of which Asia forms the eastern (and greater) part, and including Scandinavia, that part of Russia west of the Urals, and the British Isles; area 9.9 million sq km (3.8 million sq miles); pop. (est. 1988) 496 million. It contains approximately 20 per cent of the world's population and is the second smallest continent after Australia. Falling largely within the northern temperate climatic zone, over two-thirds of Europe is a great plain that stretches E-W between the Scandinavian Highlands in the north and the mountain ranges of the Pyrenees, Alps, and Carpathians in the south. Europe's highest peak is Mt. Elbrus in the Caucasus (5,642 m, 18,510 ft); the most westerly point of the mainland is Cape Roca in Portugal; the northernmost point is the tip of Nordkynn in Norway, and the southernmost point is Tarifa Point in Spain. The largest cities in Europe are Moscow, Paris, London, St Petersburg, Berlin, Madrid, Athens, Rome, Kiev, and Budapest. The

Europe The political boundaries within the continent.

western part of Europe was consolidated within the Roman Empire, but the subsequent barbarian invasions brought political chaos which was only gradually resolved in the medieval and post-medieval periods, the last modern European nation states emerging in the 19th century. Politically and economically pre-eminent in the 18th and 19th centuries, Europe was overshadowed for much of the 20th century as a result of the rise of the superpowers, but it still maintains a high standard of living and political stability.

European Commission (name until 1993 **Commission of the European Communities**) One of the principal institutions of the EUROPEAN UNION, and the one responsible for planning Union policies. Its loyalties are to the EU as a whole, rather than to the individual member states. The present-day European Commission dates from 1967, when a treaty merging the three executive bodies of the three different Communities (the EUROPEAN ECONOMIC COMMUNITY, the European Coal and Steel Community, and the European Atomic Energy Community) came into effect. The Commission heads a large Secretariat in Brussels, which submits proposals for consideration by the Council of Ministers. The Commission is also charged with the implementation of decisions, once they have been made by the Council. It also acts as a mediator between the different EU members. There are seventeen commissioners, appointed by the governments of the member states: two from the UK, Germany, France, Italy, and Spain, and one from other EU member states. Each commissioner has responsibility for a different policy area. The President of the Commission is normally appointed for a four-year term. During the later 1980s criticism, particularly in Britain under Mrs Thatcher, developed against the growing bureaucracy of the Commission under its President, Jacques Delors, who held office from 1985 to 1994. He was succeeded as President by Jacques Santer.

European Community (EC) An organization of Western European countries, which came into being in 1967 through the merger of the European Economic Community (Common Market or EEC), European Atomic Energy Community (Euratom), and European Coal and Steel Community (ECSC), and was committed to economic and political integration as envisaged by the Treaties of Rome. It was superseded in 1993 by the EUROPEAN UNION.

European Convention on Human Rights A convention drawn up in 1950, as the European Convention for the Protection of Human Rights and Fundamental Freedoms by the COUNCIL OF EUROPE, as an attempt to enforce certain of the rights stated in the Universal Declaration of Human Rights. All members of the Council are parties to it. The European Convention emphasizes CIVIL RIGHTS such as the right to life and liberty, the right to a fair trial, and freedom of conscience and association. Any breach of the Convention by a state may be referred (by an individual, a group, or another state) to the European Commission on Human Rights.

European Council of Ministers (name until 1993 **Council of the European Communities**) One of the principal institutions of the EUROPEAN

UNION, and its pivotal decision-making body. The Council, which meets in Brussels, consists of ministers from the governments of each of the member states, and is therefore the institution representing the particular interests of each of these states. Although referred to as the Council, there are in practice a number of different councils, each dealing with different policy areas. Because ministers are only able to be in Brussels for short periods, a Committee of Permanent Representatives (COREPER), consisting of the ambassadors of the member states, aided by a committee of civil servants, prepares the issues awaiting ministerial decision. The office of President of the Council is held for six-month periods by each member state in rotation. The Council acts on proposals submitted to it by the EUROPEAN COMMISSION, after consultation with the EUROPEAN PARLIAMENT and sometimes the Economic and Social Committee. The Council is also responsible for coordinating the general economic policies of its members, and for ensuring that the provisions of the EU treaties are implemented.

European Court of Justice One of the principal institutions of the EUROPEAN UNION, and its main judicial body. The Court, which is based in Luxembourg, was established in 1957 under the Treaties of Rome. It hears cases involving alleged breaches of EU law. It is responsible for interpreting and applying Union treaties, and ensuring that they are fairly observed. It is the final arbiter of EU law, and there is no further appeal. The Court derives its authority from the fact that EU law prevails over national law in cases of conflict. The Court comprises thirteen judges, including at least one from each member state, who are appointed by EU member governments and serve for six-year periods. Because of an increase in the number of cases that have come before the Court, a lower court, or Court of First Instance, has been set up to deal with minor cases.

European Economic Area (EEA) An economic union agreed between the 12 member states of the European Community and the seven EFTA states (Austria, Finland, Iceland, Liechtenstein, Norway, Sweden, and Switzerland) at a meeting in Oporto, Portugal in May 1992 for the purpose of strengthening trade and economic relations by promoting the free movement of goods, services, capital, and people. The EEA extends the EC's Single European Market principles, known collectively as the *acquis*, to over 380 million people.

European Economic Community (EEC or **Common Market**) An economic organization of European states set up by the Treaties of ROME in March 1957. Its member states agreed to coordinate their economic policies, and to establish common policies for agriculture, transport, the movement of capital and labour, the erection of common external tariffs, and the ultimate establishment of political unification. From its inception the EEC provided an extension of the functional cooperation inaugurated by the European Coal and Steel Community (made up of Belgium, France, Federal Republic of Germany, Italy, Luxembourg, and the Netherlands). It owed much to the campaigning initiative of Jean Monnet and to the detailed planning of Paul-Henri SPAAK. Preliminary meetings were held at Messina in 1955, which led to the Treaties of Rome in 1957 and the formal creation of the EEC in January 1958. Cooperation in the EEC was most organized in the area of AGRICULTURE, and the Common Agricultural Policy (CAP) was the largest item in the EC budget. The EEC merged with the European Atomic Energy Community (EURATOM) and the European Coal and Steel Community (ESCA) in 1967 to form the EUROPEAN COMMUNITY (EC).

European Free Trade Association (EFTA) A customs union of Western European countries, established in 1960, created by a British initiative as a trade grouping unencumbered by the political implications of the EC. In 1973 Britain and Denmark entered the EC and left EFTA. Free trade between its original members was achieved by the end of 1966, and all tariffs between EFTA and EC countries were finally abolished in 1984.

European Monetary System (EMS) A system devised by EUROPEAN COMMUNITY members with the aim of promoting monetary stability by limiting exchange-rate fluctuations. The system was set up in 1979 by the then nine members of the EC. The EMS comprised three principal elements: the European Currency Unit (ECU), the monetary unit used in EC transactions; the Exchange Rate Mechanism (ERM), whereby those member states taking part agreed to maintain currency fluctuations within certain agreed limits; and the European Monetary Co-operation Fund, which issues the ECU and oversees the ERM. The 1992 Maastricht Treaty provided for steps towards Economic and Monetary Union (EMU) (proposed in 1989 by the then President of the EUROPEAN COMMISSION, Jacques Delors), including a European Monetary Institute to coordinate the economic and monetary policy of the EU, a European CENTRAL BANK to govern these policies, and the introduction of a single European currency.

European Parliament One of the constituent institutions of the EUROPEAN UNION (formerly the EUROPEAN COMMUNITY), meeting in Strasbourg or Luxembourg. Set up in 1952 under the terms of the treaty which established the European Steel and Coal Community (ECSC), the Parliament was replaced and extended in 1958 to serve two new communities, the EUROPEAN ECONOMIC COMMUNITY and the European Atomic Energy Community (EURATOM). From 1958 to 1979 it was composed of representatives drawn from the Assemblies of the member states. However, quinquennial direct elections have taken place since 1979, and it is now made up of 518 seats, distributed among member states, according to the size of their populations. Its powers have increased, and it is now consulted on all major EU issues, including the annual budget, and it advises on legislation. Although it has the theoretical power to dismiss the EUROPEAN COMMISSION by a vote of censure, its actual powers are restricted, and its role has been advisory rather than legislative. However, under the European Co-operation Procedure formalized under the Single European Act (1987), the Parliament was given a greater say over the proposals for the completion of a single European market in 1992, and under the Maastricht Treaty (1992) the powers of the Parliament were enhanced to include the right of veto on some bills, further budgetary control, and a say in the membership of the Commission.

European Southern Observatory (ESO) A large OBSERVATORY in the Atacama Desert in Chile financed by Belgium, Denmark, France, Germany, Italy, The Netherlands, Sweden, and Switzerland. Located under clear skies, the ESO has more telescopes and a greater variety of instruments than any other observatory.

European Space Agency (ESA) An organization run initially by a group of European nations to provide for and promote collaboration in space research and technology. ESA has enabled Europe to launch its own spacecraft. It has its headquarters in Paris, its technical centre in The Netherlands, its satellite operations centre in Germany, and its data centre in Italy. Though ESA officially began to operate in May 1976, it was formed out of a partial merger of the European Space Research Organization (ESRO), founded in 1964, and the European Launcher Development Organization (ELDO) which was concerned with the construction and launching of large rockets capable of putting European artificial satellites into orbit. The latter has been subsumed into Arianespace, an organization created in 1980 to take responsibility for the Ariane Launcher, the European rocket used to put satellites into orbit. The ESA suffered a major setback in 1996 when its biggest ever rocket, Ariane-5, had to be blown up on its maiden flight following a malfunction.

European Union (EU) An organization of fifteen European countries that replaced the EUROPEAN COMMUNITY in 1993. The EU took over all the EC institutions, such as the EUROPEAN PARLIAMENT, but also extended the scope of the EC according to the terms of the Treaty of MAASTRICHT. The member countries agreed to add a shared foreign policy and commitment to cooperation on security matters, including justice and policing, to their economic and political links under the EC. These constitute the 'three pillars' of the EU, one pillar being the EC, another pillar coordinating foreign and external security policies (designating the WESTERN EUROPEAN UNION as the EU's defence wing), and the third pillar coordinating internal matters and justice (particularly on IMMIGRATION and POLITICAL ASYLUM). Proposals concerning the creation of a single European currency were not acceptable to all members and the issue was complicated further by the withdrawal of the UK and Italy from the Exchange Rate Mechanism (see EUROPEAN MONETARY SYSTEM) in 1992. There have also been disagreements over social policies and the sovereignty of member nations; the UK, which has opposed any suggestion of FEDERALISM, opted out of a common policy on social issues to be adopted by other members.

In 1995 Austria, Finland, and Sweden joined the EU, increasing the total number of members to fifteen. Other countries have applied for membership and the EU has agreed to cooperate with former members of the Communist bloc. With the EUROPEAN FREE TRADE ASSOCIATION (EFTA), the EU established a frontier-free zone in 1994, known as the EUROPEAN ECONOMIC AREA (EEA).

europium (symbol Eu, at. no. 63, r.a.m. 151.96) A soft silvery lanthanide element that occurs in small quantities in bastnaesite and monazite. It was discovered in 1889 by the British scientist Sir William Crookes and is used in the form of its oxide as a phosphor in television screens.

Europoort A major European port facility created since 1958 at the mouth of the New Waterway opposite the Hook of Holland, near Rotterdam in the Netherlands. It can handle the world's largest bulk carriers and container ships and has oil and metal refineries, as well as engineering, ship repair, chemicals, and food-processing plants.

Eurydice In Greek mythology, a Dryad, the wife of Orpheus. She died from a snake bite and Orpheus followed her to the Underworld. There the beauty of his musicianship persuaded Hades, the god of the Underworld, to allow him to bring her back, provided that he did not look round at her before he reached the upper world. He did look round, however, and lost her for ever.

eurypterid See SEA SCORPION.

Eusebius (known as **Eusebius of Caesaria**) (*c.*264–*c.*340 AD) Bishop and Church historian. His *Ecclesiastical History* is the principal source for the history of Christianity (especially in the Eastern Church) from the age of the Apostles until 324.

euthanasia (Greek, 'good death') The practice of ending a human life to relieve a person from physical suffering or prolonged coma, usually due to terminal or degenerative illness. In most JURISDICTIONS, it is illegal, but calls have been made for the legalization of voluntary euthanasia, that is euthanasia with the active consent of the patient, a situation that is accepted in practice in The Netherlands. The withholding of treatment such as respirators and intravenous feeding for the terminally ill ('passive euthanasia') is regarded by some not as euthanasia but as allowing nature to run its course.

eutrophication The accumulation of minerals, particularly phosphates (from sewage and detergents) and nitrates (from agricultural drainage), in a river or lake. This nutrient enrichment accelerates the growth of all the plants but particularly that of aquatic ALGAE and CYANOBACTERIA. Their rapid growth can block waterways and interfere with drinking-water supplies. In summer, vast population increases in the algae (a phenomenon known as algal bloom) may create a dense green mat over the water. This may prevent light reaching other plants, which then die. The rapid growth of algae and the mass of decomposing plant material eventually use up all of the oxygen in the water. This leads to the eventual death of the algae themselves and proliferation of bacteria which do not require oxygen, and produce hydrogen sulphide, a toxic gas. This smells of 'bad eggs' and kills most animal life in the water.

evangelicalism A Protestant Christian movement that emphasizes the authority of the Bible, MISSIONARY WORK, and personal commitment to Christ after being revitalized or 'born again' in him. There are numerous Lutheran and United Protestant churches that include 'evangelical' in their name, such as the Norwegian Evangelical Lutheran Church. However, the word is also used in a more general sense in many Protestant churches. 'Conservative evangelicals' are closely associated with what is known as 'FUNDAMENTALISM', a belief in the verbal inspiration and literal truth of the BIBLE. 'Liberal evangelicals', however, accept liberal theological ideas and a critical approach to the Bible, while still emphasizing the importance of the relationship of the believer to God.

Evangelists Traditionally, the authors of the four Gospels recording the life and teaching of Jesus which are accepted as authentic in Christianity. They are Matthew, Mark, Luke, and John. On the basis of the New Testament Book of Revelation, they are symbolized by a man, a lion, an ox, and an eagle.

Evans, Sir Arthur (John) (1851–1941) British archaeologist. He is best known for his excavations at Knossos (1899–1935), which resulted in the discovery of the Bronze Age civilization of Crete; he called this civilization Minoan after the legendary Cretan king Minos.

Evans, Dame Edith (Mary) (1888–1976) British actress. Her stage repertoire encompassed a wide range of Shakespearian and contemporary roles;

she acted in the first production of George Bernard Shaw's *Heartbreak House* (1921). She is particularly remembered as Lady Bracknell in Oscar Wilde's *The Importance of Being Earnest*, a role which she portrayed for the first time on stage in 1939 and on film in 1952.

Evans, Oliver (1755–1819) US pioneer of high-pressure STEAM-ENGINES. Evans invented an improved CARDING MACHINE and built a fully automated milling plant (1784) before turning to steam-engines. Following work with conventional WATT engines, he experimented with high-pressure steam, which reduced the size of the engine needed for a given power output. By 1804 he had built a successful engine working at a pressure of about 3.5 bar. Concurrently, TREVITHICK was also building high-pressure engines in the UK. Evans constructed some fifty engines, most of them used for pumping.

Evans-Pritchard, Sir Edward (Evan) (1902–73) British anthropologist. He is noted for his studies of African tribal life and cultures, especially those based on his time spent living in Sudan with the Azande and Nuer peoples in the 1920s and 1930s. Among the important works of social anthropology he wrote are *Witchcraft, Oracles and Magic Among the Azande* (1937) and *The Nuer* (1940).

evaporation The conversion of a liquid to a vapour at the free surface of the liquid. It arises because the more energetic particles in the liquid are able to escape when they reach the surface. Once this has occurred there is very little chance of their returning to the liquid again and thus the volume of the liquid is continually reduced. Evaporation increases at high temperatures because the molecules have a higher energy and therefore they can escape from the liquid surface more easily. Because it is the lower-energy particles that are left behind, the liquid tends to become cooler.

Eve According to Jewish, Christian, and Islamic belief, the first woman and consort of Adam. The Book of Genesis recounts how she was created from Adam's rib and tempted by a serpent to eat of the forbidden fruit of the tree of knowledge, encouraging Adam to do likewise. Because of their disobedience, they were expelled from the Garden of Eden. Eve was further punished with the pain of childbirth. The Christian doctrines of the Fall, Original Sin, and redemption through Jesus Christ are based on these accounts.

evection A perturbation of the Moon's motion arising from the variation in its orbital eccentricity caused by the Sun's gravitational attraction. The effect, which has a period of 31.8 days, is one of many perturbations that must be taken into account when developing a lunar theory which seeks to describe the Moon's motion precisely.

Evelyn, John (1620–1706) English diarist and writer. He is remembered chiefly for his *Diary* (published posthumously in 1818), which covers most of his life, describing his travels abroad, his contemporaries, and such important historical events as the Great Plague and the Great Fire of London. He was also a pioneer of English forestry and gardening, and a founder member of the Royal Society.

evening primrose A scented annual, biennial, or perennial plant of the genus *Oenothera*, with large, often yellow flowers. These open at dusk and are pollinated by nocturnal moths. The plants have fleshy roots which are sometimes used as a vegetable. The genus contains over 200 species, including the common *O. biennis*. All are native to North and South America and are part of the same family as clarkia and fuchsias, Onagraceae. Some are widely spread, having escaped from gardens, and as such may be found throughout the Old World. Oil from the seeds is now used medicinally, in the belief that it helps to regulate the body's metabolic and endocrine systems.

evening star See VENUS.

event horizon The boundary surrounding a BLACK HOLE beyond which the black hole is invisible to an external observer. At the event horizon, which is at the SCHWARZSCHILD RADIUS, the ESCAPE VELOCITY from the black hole equals the velocity of light with the consequence that all electromagnetic radiation coming from it is trapped. The presence of the black hole can still be detected by its powerful gravitational influence.

Everest, Mount (Nepali **Sagarmatha**; Chinese **Qomolangma**) The highest mountain in the world (8,848 m, 29,028 ft), in the Himalayas on the border of Nepal and Tibet. It is named after Sir George Everest (1790–1866), surveyor-general of India, and was first climbed in 1953 by the New Zealand mountaineer and explorer (Sir) Edmund Hillary and the Sherpa mountaineer Tenzing Norgay.

Everglades, the A vast area of marshland and coastal mangrove forest in south Florida, USA, extending from Lake Okeechobee southwards to Florida Bay. A national park established in 1947 protects endangered species such as the alligator, bald eagle, and egret.

evergreen A woody plant which keeps a cover of leaves throughout the year, even during adverse periods such as drought or winter. Evergreens include most GYMNOSPERMS and a wide range of ANGIOSPERMS. Familiar examples in cold climates are pines, hollies, and ivy. The majority of tropical rain forest trees are also evergreen. The leaves of all evergreens are usually leathery and more resistant to insect attack than those of deciduous plants. They may have a life-span of several years but eventually fall as new leaves unfold.

evergreen oak See OAK.

Evert, Christine Marie (known as 'Chris') (1954–) US tennis player. Her career began at an early age as a Wightman Cup player (1971) and included winning both the US and French Open championships six times and three Wimbledon titles (1974; 1976; 1981).

Evesham A market town on the River Avon in the Vale of Evesham, Hereford and Worcester, England; pop. (1981) 15,280. Simon de Montfort, founder of the English parliament, was killed in battle here in 1265.

evolution (in astronomy) The change in an object with time. For example, STELLAR EVOLUTION describes the successive forms taken by the structure of a star from its formation out of the interstellar material to its final state. In COSMOLOGY, some models of the Universe are static and non-evolving as in the STEADY STATE THEORY, or are evolving, as in the currently accepted BIG BANG THEORY where the Universe began with an explosion.

evolution (in biology) The theory that all animal and plant SPECIES are related by common ancestry. It provides the unifying basis of all biological science. The history of life is a single process of species-splitting and change. Evidence of evolution is found in the distribution of structures considered to be homologous: structures which share the same developmental (embryonic) origin, and perhaps the same relative position, in different species (for example, the wing of a bird, the foreleg of a dog, a human arm). Homologies can now be identified at the molecular and genetic level of an organism's composition. A hierarchical Linnaean classification can be constructed by studying such similarities and differences. Charles DARWIN recognized the significance of this natural hierarchy (as had earlier naturalists, such as LAMARCK), and argued that it arose from the actual genealogical relationship of organisms. Darwin (and A. R. WALLACE) provided a causal evolutionary mechanism: NATURAL SELECTION.

Many different lines of evidence contribute to current evolutionary theory: GENETICS provides the scientific basis for the study of HEREDITY and MUTATION; BIOGEOGRAPHY supplies evidence of geographical variation within and between species (GALÁPAGOS FINCHES are a good example of this variation); PALAEONTOLOGY and geology have revealed the time-span of the history of life on Earth (over 3,500 million years), and the sequence of origination of the major groups of organisms. Human evolution is based on the theory that humans diverged from ape-like ancestors and took on their present form. The process took at least 5 million years (see HOMINID; AUSTRALOPITHECINE; HOMO HABILIS; HOMO ERECTUS; HOMO SAPIENS; NEANDERTHAL). Many details remain uncertain, particularly of the relationship between the australopithecines and the *Homo* lineage. However, the general outline is becoming clearer with every new discovery and as DATING SYSTEMS become more refined.

Excalibur In Arthurian legend, the name of King Arthur's magic sword. According to one version, the young Arthur alone among many contenders could pull the sword from the stone in which it was fixed, thus confirming his kingship. In a later version, the sword was given to Arthur by the Lady of the Lake. When the king lay mortally wounded after his last battle, he ordered his knights to cast Excalibur back into the lake. The arm of the Lady of the Lake rose from the waters and, brandishing it, sank down into the deep.

excavator A machine that digs soil and soft or loose rock. A back-acter or backhoe is an excavator that has a steel bucket on an articulated arm. The soil is dug by drawing the bucket towards the machine, then deposited clear of the excavated site. A face shovel excavates upwards and away from the machine, but digs only to a limited depth. The DRAG-LINE scrapes up the soil by pulling in a single heavy bucket on a cable. Trenches can be dug with an excavator that pulls a chain of buckets.

excitation (in physics) A process in which a physical system acquires a higher energy level (an excited state) than that of its lowest energy level (its ground state). For an isolated atom in the ground state the electrons fill, in order, the orbitals of lowest energy round the nucleus. Excitation can occur if the atom is irradiated with electromagnetic radiation of suitable frequency or if it is bombarded with electrons. The extra energy enables the atomic electrons to occupy permitted states of higher energy. In a solid, excitation can also be provided by heat energy, which will increase the amplitude of vibration of the atoms, that is, put them in higher vibrational states.

exclusion principle (in physics) A principle stating that the electrons in the same atom must differ in at least one aspect of their quantum properties. It governs the electronic configuration of atoms, which is the way in which the electrons are organized within the atom. The exclusion principle was discovered by Wolfgang PAULI in 1925. He studied the atomic spectra of various atoms to determine the quantum states of the electrons in the atoms. Pauli found that some states in some atoms were missing, and worked out that if these states were present they would have to have the same quantum properties as electron states that were already present. The total absence of these identical states implied that states that were present must be non-identical. Studies made since the exclusion principle was first proposed have confirmed that each electron within an atom is in a state that is unique within that atom. Thus it is possible to construct an accurate picture of the electronic configuration of an atom, which is useful since this is what determines the atom's chemical behaviour.

excommunication The exclusion of an individual from membership and especially the sacraments of the Christian Church. The process was first used against individuals holding unorthodox or heretical religious beliefs, but it was later employed as a disciplinary and political weapon against rulers who opposed the church and especially the papacy; Pope Adrian IV was one of the first to use it in this way. It could include releasing subjects from their duty to obey their lord which could seriously threaten a weak king. King John of England was

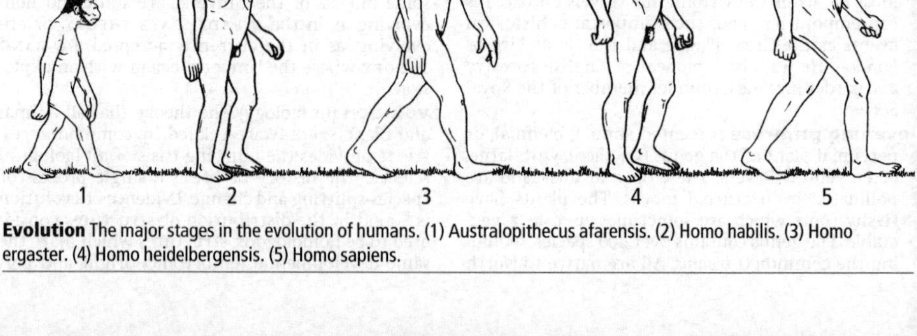

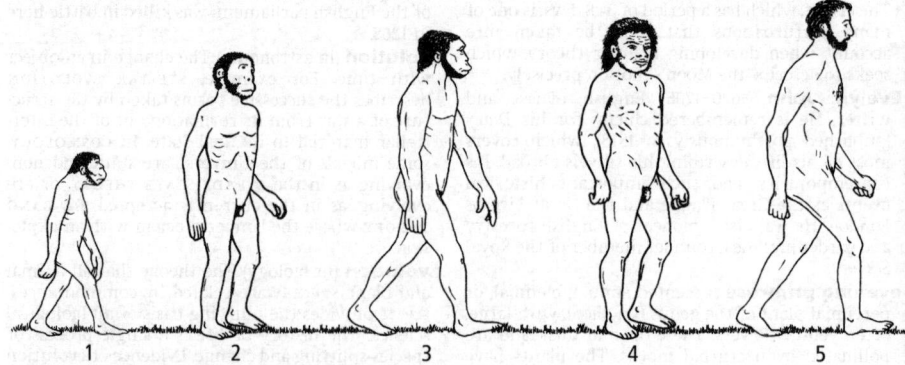

Evolution The major stages in the evolution of humans. (1) Australopithecus afarensis. (2) Homo habilis. (3) Homo ergaster. (4) Homo heidelbergensis. (5) Homo sapiens.

punished in this way, as was the Holy Roman Emperor Henry IV who finally submitted to Pope Gregory VII at CANOSSA. Its effectiveness as a weapon depended on the recipient's willingness to be frightened by it, which is why it was frequently employed in the medieval period when the majority of the populace was greatly concerned with its spiritual welfare. The interdict was a less severe punishment that was also used against the laity.

excretion The disposal of compounds surplus to the requirements of, or harmful to, an organism. Examples of common waste products include carbon dioxide, fatty acids, and nitrogen compounds, such as ammonia and urea. Terrestrial animals, who have a particular need to conserve water, use the KIDNEYS, LUNGS, alimentary tract, and SKIN as organs of excretion, although this is not their sole function. Of these, the lungs and kidneys are the most important. Excess carbon dioxide can be removed rapidly from the lungs if the breathing rate is increased.

Exeter (Latin **Isca Dumnoniorm**; Saxon **Escancestre**) The county town of Devon, south-west England, on the River Exe; pop. (1991) 101,100. Founded by the Romans, it was the western headquarters of Royalist forces during the Civil War. It has a university founded in 1955. The library of the Norman cathedral contains the *Exeter Book*, the largest surviving collection of Anglo-Saxon poems. Exeter is an administrative, marketing, and transport centre with various light industries including tourism.

exfoliation (in geomorphology) The process occurring when curved layers of rock fall from the steep, bare slopes of cliffs or summits; it leaves large hollows or alcoves on the cliff faces, and it rounds summits to form domes. The process occurs in fine-grained rocks with few JOINTS or bedding planes. When steep slopes are cut by rivers or by glaciers, lateral pressure is reduced and the rocks 'bulge' very slightly, creating fine fractures which curve parallel to the surface. The sheer weight of the slabs may cause them to fall; or their spalling may be encouraged by frost and by percolating water.

exhaust system The system by which exhaust gases from a car ENGINE are discharged to the atmosphere. The exhaust gases from each cylinder are led through short pipes to a common exhaust pipe leading to the rear of the vehicle. Often there is an expansion chamber to smooth the pulsating gas flow before passing it to the silencer. Anti-pollution laws increasingly require a CATALYTIC CONVERTER in the exhaust system to limit the emission of pollutant gases.

existentialism A movement in mid-20th-century CONTINENTAL PHILOSOPHY. Existentialist philosophers speculated about the nature of reality, but subordinated traditional metaphysical and epistemological questions to an anthropocentric perspective, in which there takes place a dramatic, often tragic, confrontation between man and the world. Existentialist thought tends to disparage scientific knowledge, particularly PSYCHOLOGY, in so far as it claims to be a science, and to insist on the absence of objective values, stressing instead the reality and significance of human freedom.

Exmoor An area of moorland in north Devon and west Somerset, south-west England, rising to a height of 520 m (1,706 ft) at Dunkery Beacon.

exocrine gland A compact collection of secretory cells that discharges its secretions through tubes or ducts opening on to a body surface or the gut. Exocrine glands are widely distributed in the skin of most terrestrial animals. Frogs, for example, possess a skin gland which forms a mucous secretion to prevent the skin drying out. Some also have poison glands, the secretions of which discourage attacks by predators. Glands within the nostrils and eyes keep delicate surface membranes moist and free from obstruction. Sebaceous glands associated with hair follicles protect the skin of mammals. The sweat glands aid heat loss in mammals. Exocrine glands of the digestive system provide saliva for the mouth, gastric juice for the stomach, pancreatic juice, and bile for the intestines. Mucous glands deliver a sticky coating for the lining membranes of the gut to protect them from the actions of the digestive juices, and to assist the smooth passage of food.

Exodus The departure of the Israelites under MOSES from their captivity in Egypt *c.*1300 BC, recorded in the Old Testament book of Exodus. According to the biblical account, the Israelites were pursued by the pharaoh's army, but were saved by a tidal wave that swept across a region known as the Red Sea (probably near one of the lakes now joined by the Suez Canal). The Israelites then spent over forty years wandering in the wilderness of Sinai, during which time they received through MOSES the Ten Commandments which established their relationship with their God and between one another. After the death of Moses, Joshua became their leader, and his capture of Jericho led to the occupation of CANAAN. The variety of sources make it impossible to regard this narrative as a straightforward historical account, but it is central to Jewish history as evidence of God's favour to his chosen people and is commemorated annually in the Passover feast.

exoskeleton The characteristic tough outer skeleton or covering of some invertebrates, such as arthropods. It does not grow, and so animals with an exoskeleton can increase their size only by shedding or 'moulting' the skeleton at intervals. It is jointed, like armour, to allow movement, particularly by jointed limbs. See also ENDOSKELETON.

exothermic reaction A chemical reaction in which heat is given out to the surroundings – that is, there is a decrease in the ENTHALPY of the reaction mixture. An example of an exothermic reaction is the neutralization of an acid by a base. COMBUSTION reactions are exothermic. For example, energy is released when FOSSIL FUELS are burned. The combustion of carbohydrates by living cells, to form carbon dioxide and water, is a biochemical example of an exothermic reaction and represents a major way in which many cells obtain their energy. An exothermic compound is one whose formation is accompanied by the liberation of heat.

expanding Universe See COSMOLOGY.

expansion (of matter) The increase in size of a body. It can most readily be brought about by heating the body (thermal expansion). This effect is used in many devices, particularly in those which measure or regulate temperature. For example, the expansion of a liquid is used in the mercury thermometer and the expansion of a solid is the basic mechanism in many thermostats. Although such uses can be made of thermal expansion, it can also cause problems; and the effects of expansion must always be considered in the design of any object which is going to operate over a range of temperatures. For example, gaps must be left between railway lines to prevent buckling.

expansion joint A gap that divides a building,

pipeline, bridge, road surface, or other structure into sections to allow for the differential expansion or contraction of members as temperatures vary. (Metals and glass, for example, expand more when heated than do brick and concrete.) The joint provides space into which the sections on either side of the gap can expand without constraint, while maintaining the alignment of their surfaces. Where necessary, a seal to protect the joint from moisture, rain, or wind can be provided by flexible mastic (CEMENT) sealants.

expert system A computer program that attempts to replicate the expertise and decision-making abilities of a human expert. Expert systems are the most widely developed area of ARTIFICIAL INTELLIGENCE, with a variety of applications ranging from medical diagnosis through to financial decision-making and geological prospecting. They often use a heuristic or self-learning approach to the solution of a problem, in which feedback of the results of a particular course of action influences subsequent decisions. Knowledge engineering is the discipline concerned with building expert systems.

explosive A chemical that, when detonated, produces a highly exothermic (heat-producing) chemical reaction with evolution of large volumes of gas (an explosion). There are two main types of explosive: deflagrating, or low explosives, and detonating, or high explosives. Low explosives are used as propellants for bullets and shells and for low-power blasting operations in quarries and mines. Such explosives consist either of intimate mixtures of substances which react with one another to release a considerable amount of energy (such as GUNPOWDER) or of chemical compounds that release energy on decomposition (such as NITROCELLULOSE). In both cases, the explosive reaction has to be started by ignition, but once started, the energy released creates a chain reaction that spreads through the whole quantity of explosive in a small fraction of a second. High explosives decompose more rapidly than low explosives, and generate much higher pressures, resulting in much greater shattering power (brisance). They are used for tunnel-blasting and as military explosives. Some high explosives (for example, DYNAMITE) require detonation rather than ignition before they will explode; this makes them safer to handle.

exponential function A function that varies according to the POWER of another quantity. Exponential functions are written as $y = a^x$ (where a can be any positive number) and their common property is that as x increases by 1, y is multiplied by the value of a. Every such function has the property that a^x is positive for all values of x and its graph passes through the point (0,1). Each function is the inverse of the corresponding LOGARITHM to base a. The function e^x is often called *the* exponential function, where e is an IRRATIONAL NUMBER defined as the limit of $(1 + 1/n)^n$ as n tends to infinity, and is approximately equal to 2.718. The inverse of this function, $\log_e x$, is called the natural logarithm of x.

exports GOODS (visible exports) and services (invisible exports) sold by one country to another. Trade occurs because countries possess resources such as commodities, or are relatively more efficient in the production of some goods and services than of others.

exposure meter (or **light meter**) A device using a light-sensitive cell to measure the light reflected from a scene, or the light falling on it, in order to determine the correct exposure for photographic film. The meter may be a separate item, or it may be built into a CAMERA, perhaps linked to the SHUTTER or APERTURE or to an AUTOMATIC EXPOSURE control. Some meters measure average light from the whole scene, whereas spot meters monitor a small area. Many hand-held meters use selenium cells, which need no batteries. Cadmium sulphide cells are more sensitive and can be used in dim light, but require battery power.

Expressionism The use of distortion and exaggeration for emotional effect, chiefly associated with the visual arts. In its broadest sense it can be used of any art that raises subjective feeling above objective observation, reflecting the state of mind of the artist rather than images that conform to what we see in the external world. The paintings of the 16th-century artists GRÜNEWALD and El GRECO, who conveyed intense religious emotion through distorted, unnaturalistic forms, are outstanding examples of expressionism in this sense (when used in this way the word is usually spelt with a small 'e'). In a narrower sense, the word Expressionism is applied to a broad trend in modern European art that traces its origin to van GOGH, who used colour and line emotionally 'to express...man's terrible passions'. Expressionism represented a rebellion against the naturalism of 19th-century art, and its insistence on the supreme importance of the artist's personal feelings has been one of the foundations of aesthetic attitudes in the 20th century. Representatives of other art-forms in whose work elements of Expressionism are found include the early works of BERG and SCHOENBERG in music, and DOSTOEVSKY and KAFKA in fiction. In drama, Expressionism was a movement that began in Germany in about 1910, and is best typified in the theatre by the plays of Georg KAISER and Ernst Toller. The Expressionist theatre was a theatre of protest, mainly against the contemporary social order.

extinction See CONSERVATION; ENDANGERED SPECIES.

extroversion/introversion Words used by Carl JUNG to distinguish between those who are sociable and outgoing and those who are not. Many personality theorists regard it as a fundamental difference between people. In *Psychological Types* (1921), Jung suggested that introverts are mistrustful and focus on the subjective and private aspects of experience, whereas extroverts direct their energies to the outside world and their relationships with other people. The British psychologist Hans Eysenck held that it is a biological difference: introverts' nervous systems are more aroused than those of extroverts. As too much or too little arousal is unpleasant, introverts avoid stimulation, while extroverts seek it.

extrusion A manufacturing technique for the production of long pieces of material with a common cross-section. The material is forced through a shaped hole, the die, so that it emerges as a continuous length. Extrusion is important in the manufacture of components from metals, ceramics, and plastics. Highly ductile metals such as aluminium are extruded cold (at room temperature) to form hollow bars and tubes for low-strength applications such as window frames. Other metals such as copper and brass are extruded hot to form water pipes and pipe fittings. In the ceramics industry, extrusion is used to form square-section bars which are cut into BRICKS, while viscous alumina slips are extruded into complex, thin-walled honeycombs, used as support media for catalysts. Thermoplastics become viscous on heating and can be extruded in many forms. Extrusion techniques are also used in the manufacture of some foods (see FOOD TECHNOLOGY).

extrusive rock A rock that has been poured out on to the Earth's surface. Some are extruded as molten magma; others as solid fragments. They are also termed 'volcanic' and are most commonly found as BASALTS OR PYROCLASTS.

Eyck, Jan van (died 1441) Flemish painter. He was court painter to Philip the Good, Duke of Burgundy, from 1425 until his death, and travelled on secret diplomatic missions to Spain and Portugal for his master. Van Eyck's technique, in which the pigment is mixed with oil diluted with turpentine and applied in thin glazes, became the accepted model in the Netherlands and rapidly spread elsewhere; within a short time of his death he was famous in Italy as well as in northern Europe. See FLEMISH ART.

Eyde, Samuel See BIRKELAND, KRISTIAN OLAF BERNHARD.

eye An organ of sight or light detection found in animals. In lower animals, eyes consist of light-sensitive cells on the skin surface, usually in the forepart of the body. In the course of evolution such cells have developed into complex organs. These vary from the simple eyes of planarians to the compound eyes of insects, or the eyes of vertebrates. Flies have complex compound eyes, particularly developed to distinguish movement and colour. Birds which hunt prey have eyes which focus in front, like those of humans, while birds which are hunted have eyes on opposite sides of the head to cover a large field of vision. In man, apes, and some other highly-evolved species the eyes permit binocular vision and the ability to recognize and appreciate patterns and shapes. Colour vision is found to some extent in virtually all animals. Some animals are, however, colour-blind, and in some cave-dwelling or deep-sea animals the eyes have become VESTIGIAL ORGANS.

In mammals the eyes are globes lying in fluid-lubricated sockets in the skull. They are moved in all directions by muscles. The eye is protected by a lid lubricated with tears and is enclosed within a thick fibrous capsule modified in front as a transparent disc, the cornea. Beneath this is an adjustable ring of muscle called the iris, which can open in dull light and close in bright light. The lens of the eye lies behind the iris and is controlled by a muscle which can contract to make the lens thin, for looking at distant objects, or relax to make it thicker for close-up work. Inside the back of the eye is a lining called the retina, which contains light-sensitive cells of two types. One type (cones) can detect coloured light, the other (rods) is responsible for black and white images. Between the lens and the retina is a transparent jelly. In man, light from outside passes through the lens and transparent jelly, to be focused on the retina. In twilight, colours cannot be seen because cones need a high light intensity to function correctly. In these conditions rods, which respond to lower levels of light, are used to distinguish shapes and moving objects.

Eyre, Edward John (1815–1901) British-born Australian explorer and colonial statesman. He undertook explorations in the interior deserts of Australia (1840–41) and discovered what came to be known as Lake Eyre. He later served as Lieutenant-Governor of New Zealand (1847–53) and Governor of Jamaica (1864–66).

Eysenck, Hans Jürgen (1916–97) German-born British psychologist. Noted for his strong criticism of conventional psychotherapy, particularly Freudian psychoanalysis, he developed an alternative treatment for mental disorders in the form of behaviour therapy. Eysenck also devised methods for assessing intelligence and personality, and published his controversial ideas in *Race, Intelligence, and Education* (1971).

Ezra (5th or 4th century BC) Jewish priest instrumental in reforming Judaism after the exile in Babylon. Although the Biblical record is unclear, it is thought that he arrived in Jerusalem in 397 BC with authority from the Persian king Artaxerxes II. He reformed the system of worship at the Jerusalem Temple and established a written code of laws and the priestly leadership of Judaism. His work was facilitated by the political successes of NEHEMIAH.

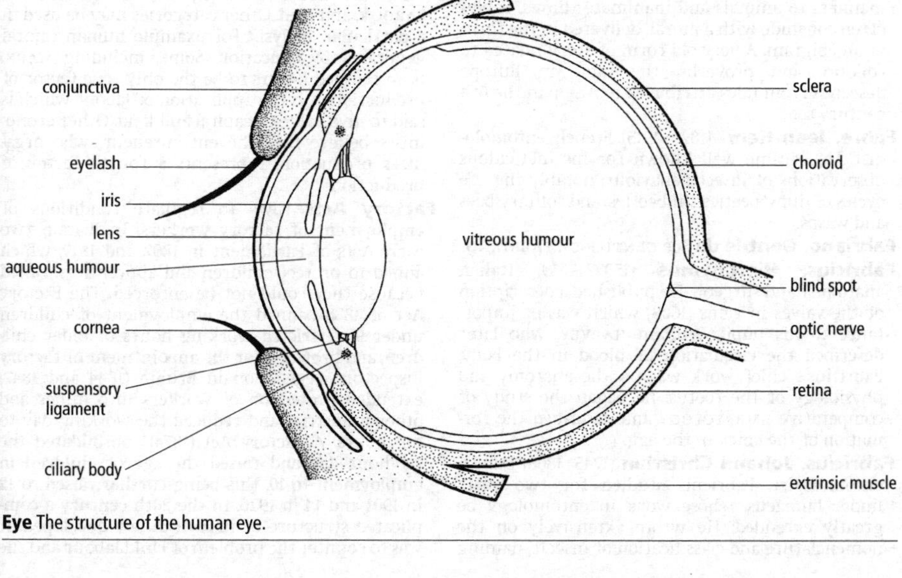

Eye The structure of the human eye.

F

Fabergé, **Peter Carl** (1846–1920) Russian goldsmith and jeweller, of French descent. He is famous for the intricate and imaginative Easter eggs and many other ornaments that he made for the families of tsars Alexander III and Nicholas II and royal households in other countries.

Fabians British socialists aiming at gradual social change through democratic means. The Fabian Society was founded in 1884 by a group of intellectuals who believed that new political pressures were needed to achieve social reforms. It was one of the socialist societies which helped found the Labour Representation Committee, the origin of the LABOUR PARTY, in 1900. Trade Union militancy from 1910 to 1926, and the harshness of unemployment in the 1930s, weakened the appeal of Fabian gradualism but by 1939, with moderate leaders, such as Clement ATTLEE, coming to the forefront, their influence revived.

Fabius (full name Quintus Fabius Maximus Verrucosus, known as 'Fabius Cunctator') (died 203 BC) Roman general and statesman. After Hannibal's defeat of the Roman army at Cannae in 216 BC, Fabius successfully pursued a strategy of caution and delay in order to wear down the Carthaginian invaders. This earned him his nickname, which means 'delayer'.

fable A brief tale in verse or prose which conveys a moral lesson, usually by giving human speech and manners to animals and inanimate things. Fables often conclude with a moral, delivered in the form of an epigram. A very old form of story related to folklore and proverbs, the fable in Europe descends from tales attributed to Aesop in the 6th century BC.

Fabre, **Jean Henri** (1823–1915) French entomologist. He became well known for his meticulous observations of insect behaviour, notably the life cycles of dung beetles, oil beetles, and solitary bees and wasps.

Fabriano, **Gentile da** See GENTILE DA FABRIANO.

Fabricius, **Hieronymus** (1537?–1619) Italian anatomist and surgeon. He published a description of the valves in veins (1603) which was of importance to his pupil, William HARVEY, who later described the circulation of blood in the body. Fabricius's chief work was on the anatomy and physiology of the foetus; he began the study of comparative EMBRYOLOGY and described the formation of the chick in the egg.

Fabricius, **Johann Christian** (1745–1808) Danish entomologist. Fabricius studied for two years under Linnaeus, whose work in entomology he greatly extended. He wrote extensively on the nomenclature and classification of insects, naming and describing some 10,000 new species in the process. Fabricius believed in the evolution of species by hybridization and (ahead of his time) by adaptation to the prevailing environment.

fabrics See TEXTILE.

Fabritius, **Carel** (1622–54) Dutch painter. He was REMBRANDT's most gifted pupil and a painter of outstanding originality and distinction, but he died tragically young and only about a dozen works by him are known. His early works were strongly influenced by Rembrandt, but he created his own style marked by cool colour harmonies, which influenced VERMEER, the greatest of Delft painters. His brother **Barent Fabritius** (1624–73) was also a painter, but of much lesser quality.

Fachang See MUQI (FACHANG).

facsimile transmission See FAX.

factorial The factorial for any whole number, n, is the product of all the whole numbers from 1 up to and including n, and is written $n!$. For example: $10! = 1 \times 2 \times 3 \times 4 \times 5 \times 6 \times 7 \times 8 \times 9 \times 10$. A quick inspection shows that factorials rapidly become very large. Factorials occur in many power series, including that produced by the BINOMIAL EXPANSION, where the coefficient of the term $a^r b^{n-r}$ in the expansion of $(a + b)^n$ is shown to be $n!/[r!\,(n - r!)]$.

factors of production (in economics) The inputs or RESOURCES needed for a productive activity. They are normally categorized into CAPITAL, LABOUR, and land. Other categories may be used in a particular analysis, for example human capital generated by education. Some, including MARX, have claimed labour to be the only true factor of production; it is the application of labour which is said to give value to capital and land. Other economists believe that the entrepreneur, who organizes production, represents a fourth factor of production.

Factory Acts Laws to regulate conditions of employment of factory workers. In Britain two early Acts of Parliament in 1802 and 1819, which aimed to protect children and apprentices, failed because they could not be enforced. The Factory Act of 1833 banned the employment of children under 9, restricted working hours of older children, and provided for the appointment of factory inspectors. Legislation in Britain (1844 and 1847) extended protection of workers into mines and other industries and reduced the working day to ten hours. A Factory Act (1874) consolidated the ten-hour day and raised the age of children in employment to 10, this being further raised to 12 in 1901 and 14 in 1920. In the 20th century a complicated structure of industrial law developed. It was to counter the problem of child labour and the exploitation of factory workers, particularly women, that the INTERNATIONAL LABOUR ORGANIZATION (ILO) was formed by the League of Nations (1919). Despite such initiatives, the exploitation of Third World women and children in such trades as the garment industry remains a matter of serious concern. In Britain workers have been further protected by such legislation as the Employers' Liability (Compulsory Insurance) Act (1969), the Health and Safety at Work Act (1974), and the Employment Act (1989). The 'Social Chapter' of the MAASTRICHT TREATY (1992), harmonizing labour laws throughout the EU, has been adopted by all the member states except the UK.

factory farming Highly intensive animal production. Scientific research into the environmental and nutritional requirements of animals have been applied to all livestock, but particularly to pigs and poultry. Specialist buildings are constructed to minimize heat losses: at optimum stocking rates and with controlled ventilation, animals provide their own heating. Carefully formulated diets fed automatically at regular intervals improve the utilization of animal FEEDSTUFFS. These measures dramatically reduce the costs of raising each animal. ANIMAL BREEDING has helped to increase the yield obtainable from factory farming. In battery farming of poultry, chickens are kept in small groups in cages or 'batteries'. The cages are stacked in buildings in which temperature, humidity, and daylight length are controlled to stimulate maximum production. Battery farming in particular has been criticized for its neglect of the animals' welfare, and for its deleterious effects on meat and egg quality. There is now a growing demand for free-range poultry produce.

faculae Bright regions on the SUN's surface which usually form before sunspots appear. After the spots have disappeared, faculae can persist in the same region for some weeks. Faculae are hotter than their surroundings. In addition, there is a slight strengthening of the MAGNETIC FIELD in those areas.

Faeroe Islands (or **Faeroes**) A group of islands in the North Atlantic between Iceland and the Shetland Isles, belonging to Denmark, but partly antonomous; pop. (1994) 43,700.

Fagatogo The administrative capital of American Samoa, on the south side of Pago Pago Harbor on the east coast of the Pacific Island of Tutuila. Local chiefs ceded the island to the USA here in 1900.

Fahrenheit, Gabriel Daniel (1686–1736) German physicist. He improved the performance of thermometers, found that liquids have their own characteristic boiling-point, developed an instrument to determine atmospheric pressure from the boiling-point of water, and designed a hydrometer. Fahrenheit is best known, however, for his thermometer scale, which he devised in 1715. On this scale the unit of temperature is the degree Fahrenheit (°F), and 0°F was originally the coldest temperature Fahrenheit could achieve using a freezing mixture of salt and ice. On his scale, water freezes at 32°F and boils at 212°F (under set atmospheric conditions). To convert a Fahrenheit temperature to CELSIUS (centigrade), subtract 32, then multiply by 5/9.

faïence See MAIOLICA.

Fairbanks, Douglas (Elton) (born Julius Ullman) (1883–1939) US actor. With Charlie Chaplin, Mary Pickford, and D. W. Griffith, he founded United Artists in 1919 and embarked on the series of swashbuckling films that made him a celebrity, including *The Mark of Zorro* (1920) and *The Thief of Baghdad* (1924). His son, **Douglas Fairbanks Jr.** (1909–), also an actor, played roles similar to those of his father, including that of Rupert of Hentzau in *The Prisoner of Zenda* (1937).

Fairfax, Thomas, 3rd Baron Fairfax of Cameron (1612–71) English Parliamentary general. He was appointed commander of the New Model Army in 1645 and led the Parliamentary forces to victory at the decisive Battle of Naseby. In 1650 he was replaced as commander by Oliver Cromwell for refusing to march against the Scots, who had proclaimed the future Charles II king. Fairfax later helped to secure the restoration of Charles II to the throne in 1660.

Fair Isle A small island about half way between the Orkneys and Shetlands, noted for the characteristic coloured designs in knitting which are named after it.

fairy moss See WATER FERN.

Faisal (or **Feisal**) Two kings of Iraq. **Faisal I** (1885–1933) reigned 1921–33. A British-sponsored ruler, he was also supported by fervent Arab nationalists. Under his rule Iraq achieved full independence in 1932. **Faisal II** (1935–58), grandson of Faisal I, reigned 1939–58. After the Suez crisis he initially pledged Iraq's continuing loyalty to Egypt, but, as relations grew more strained, he united with King Hussein of Jordan against Egypt and Syria. He was assassinated in a military coup, after which a republic was established.

Faisal ibn Abd al-Aziz (1905–75) King of Saudi Arabia 1964–75. Brother of King Saud ibn Abd al-Aziz, he became effective ruler of Saudi Arabia in 1958, dealing with the main consequences for Saudi Arabia of the immense increase of oil revenues. Pro-West, he worked in association with the USA while remaining inflexible in his opposition to Israel's ambitions and unyielding on Arab claims to Jerusalem. Faisal stood against the demands of radical Arab nationalism represented by Egypt under NASSER. He was assassinated by a nephew.

Falange, the (Spanish, 'phalanx') A Spanish political party, the Falange Española. Founded in 1933 by José António Primo de Rivera, the son of General PRIMO DE RIVERA, its members were equally opposed to the reactionary Right and the revolutionary Left. It proposed that Spain should become a syndicalist state on Italian fascist lines. During the SPANISH CIVIL WAR Franco saw the potential value of the Falange and adopted the movement in April 1937. After World War II it ceased to be identified with fascism and its influence waned. It was formally abolished in 1977.

Falasha A member of a group of people in Ethiopia holding the Jewish faith, probably as a result of conversion. They believe in the Old Testament but have no knowledge of postbiblical Judaism. After much persecution, some 7000 were airlifted to Israel in 1984–85. Their name is derived from the Amharic word for an exile or immigrant.

falcon A bird belonging to a large family, Falconidae, of diurnal birds of prey, typically with long, narrow wings, though the name includes broad-winged forest falcons and buzzard-like caracaras. True falcons include the tropical falconets, which are mostly small insect-feeding species, and the larger 'typical' falcons, fast-flying predators which attack other birds in flight. They range in size from the gyrfalcon, *Falco rusticolus*, lanner, *Falco biarmicus*, and peregrine, *Falco peregrinus*, to the much smaller hobbies and kestrels.

Common characteristics are brown, or occasionally barred grey plumage, pointed wings, short tail, a short curved beak, and long clawed talons. Their spectacular hunting methods form the basis of the art of falconry. Falcons usually nest in isolation among crags and on cliffs, laying two to five eggs.

Faldo, Nicholas Alexander (known as 'Nick') (1957–) British golfer. He won the British Open championship in 1987 and 1990 and the US Masters Tournament in 1989, 1990, and 1996.

Falkirk An industrial town in central Scotland, between Edinburgh and Glasgow; pop. (1981) 36,880. Edward I defeated the Scots here in 1298. It has modern business parks with financial and computing business.

Falkland Islands (Spanish **Islas Malvinas**) A crown colony of the UK, consisting of a group of islands in the South Atlantic.

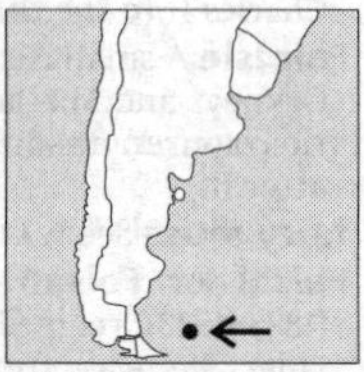

Physical. The group comprises two main islands and nearly a hundred smaller ones, lying some 480 km (300 miles) off the coast of Argentina at latitude 50° S. Inland from the jagged coastlines of East and West Falkland the ground rises to heights of about 690 m (2,260 feet), bare of trees and windswept. The moors are the home of many species of bird and hundreds of thousands of sheep, no cultivation being possible. Winters are long, with much snow, and even summer temperatures seldom rise above 10°C (50°F). South Georgia is an even bleaker island 1,290 km (800 miles) away to the east and further south. The South Sandwich, South Shetland, and South Orkney Islands lie more southward still, only just outside the Antarctic Circle. They are covered with snow and ice all year.

Economy. Wool is the dominant export, though fishing is the largest source of revenue since the declaration of a 241-km (150-mile) fishing zone around the island in 1987. The British government authorized exploration for oil in the 200-mile zone around the islands in 1991 and in 1993 a preliminary report by the British Geological Survey indicated the presence of significant deposits of oil.

History. The Falkland Islands have experienced a complicated history since their discovery in the late 16th century. They were first occupied in 1764 when French settlers began grazing sheep there. Within a year the French were dislodged by the British who claimed the islands on the basis of their discovery in 1592 by Captain John Davis and an expedition a century later under the command of Captain John Strong. When the French were driven out they sold their rights to Spain. In 1806 Spanish rule over Argentina ceased, and in 1820 the Argentinians claimed to succeed Spain in possession of the Falklands. The British objected and reclaimed the islands (1832) as a crown colony. In 1882–83 a British naval squadron occupied the islands for the protection of the seal-fisheries. Since 1833 the Argentinians have exerted their claims and have disputed possession by the British. This rivalry culminated in 1982 with the FALKLANDS WAR in which an Argentine invasion of the islands was defeated by the British. The large British naval and military force in the area was reduced following the completion of Mount Pleasant airport in 1985.

Capital: Stanley
Area: 12,173 sq km (4,699 sq mi)
Population: 3,121 (1991)
Currency: 1 Falkland pound = 100 pence
Languages: English

Falklands War (2 April–14 June 1982) The Argentine–British war in the FALKLAND ISLANDS. Negotiations for the transfer of the islands from British to Argentine rule having failed, an Argentine warship was sent by General Leopoldo Galtieri's military junta to land a party of 'scrap dealers' on South Georgia on 19 March 1982 with the intention of reclaiming the Falkland Islands. This was followed on 2 April by a full-scale military invasion. Attempts by the UN, the USA, and Peru to secure a peaceful resolution to the conflict failed, and Britain dispatched a task force of thirty warships with supporting aircraft to recover the islands. Although all but three Latin American nations supported Argentina, the USA sided with the British. The ten-week conflict, which claimed the lives of nearly 1,000 British and Argentine servicemen and civilians, ceased with the surrender of the Argentine forces on 14 June. The British victory contributed to the downfall of General Galtieri's government. Argentina officially declared a cessation of hostilities in 1989.

Falla, Manuel de (1876–1946) Spanish composer and pianist. While in Paris from 1907 to 1914, he became friends with Ravel and Debussy. Later he composed the ballets *Love, the Magician* (1915) and *The Three-Cornered Hat* (1919); the latter was produced by Diaghilev, with designs by Picasso. After declaring himself a pacifist during the Spanish Civil War, he emigrated to Argentina in 1939.

Fallopian tubes (or **uterine tubes, oviducts**) In mammals, tubes that carry the egg from ovary to uterus. The tube walls contain involuntary muscle and are covered internally by a membrane, lined with cilia, hair-like projections which help to propel the eggs. Fertilization takes place as the ovum passes along the tube.

Falloppio, Gabriello (1523–62) Italian anatomist who studied medicine under VESALIUS. He discovered structures in the human skull, and was also the first to describe FALLOPIAN TUBES.

fall-out Low-altitude atomic bomb explosions (see NUCLEAR WEAPON) throw dust and radioactive material into the lower atmosphere, where most radioactive particles condense on the dust and fall quickly back to Earth. High-altitude hydrogen bomb detonations eject radioactive material into the upper atmosphere, where it remains circling the Earth for several years. Long-lived fall-out products such as STRONTIUM-90 and caesium-137 can enter the food chain, causing serious medical problems.

fallow deer A species of DEER indigenous to southern Europe and Asia Minor, *Dama dama*. The fallow deer has now been introduced to many parts of the world. Its summer coat is reddish-brown with white or yellowish spots. Along its flank is a line of white hairs, while there is a line of black hairs down the spine and tail. In winter the coat becomes a uniform greyish-brown. The male or buck stands 90 cm (3 feet) at the shoulder; the doe is smaller. Only the male carries antlers; these take some six to seven years to develop fully. Usually one fawn is born; twins are rare. The fawn is notable for the large white spots on its coat. The fallow deer inhabits deciduous lowland woods, with thickets for cover and access to pasture land. It feeds on grasses, fruit, herbs, and shrubs, at dusk and dawn.

Falmouth A historic port and sailing centre on the coast of Cornwall, south-west England; pop. (1991)

20,297. The harbour entrance is guarded by Pendennis and St Mawes castles. Falmouth has ship-repairing and engineering industries.

false scorpion See PSEUDOSCORPION.

false vampire bat A bat once erroneously thought to feed on blood, like true VAMPIRE BATS. A better name for members of the family Megadermatidae is yellow-winged bats. Most of the five species are carnivorous, eating small mammals and vertebrates, as well as insects and spiders. They occur in Africa, south-east Asia, and Australia, and are characterized by very large ears. The name is also given to some tropical American bats, such as the American false vampire, *Vampyrum spectrum*, a spear-nosed bat.

famille rose See CHINESE CERAMICS.

family (in sociology) The basic KINSHIP group in all societies. Families usually provide vital support for their members, in the form of security, shelter, and food; they provide for the reproductive needs of the parent members; they are important in caring for, educating, and socializing children; and they traditionally provide sanctuary for older family members. Families vary enormously in structure and size. For instance, the nuclear family usually consists of two adults and their children, biological or adopted. The extended family may include three or four generations, as well as uncles, aunts, and cousins. These may live and work together in common households, or exist simply as an extended kin network, linked by social relationships. In recent years, Western societies have seen an increase in the number of one-parent families, which may consist of an unmarried mother and her child or children, or a father or mother, left without a partner through death or DIVORCE, and his or her children. The problem with one-parent families with small children is that it is often difficult for the parent to both care for the children, without the support of a partner, and to earn a living at the same time. Some governments, therefore, provide financial support for single parents.

family (in biology) A category used in the classification of organisms. Families rank below ORDERS and contain groups of genera (see GENUS). One particular genus, which is considered to be typical of the whole family, gives its Latin name, with an appropriate ending (-idae for animals, -aceae for plants), to the family. See also NOMENCLATURE IN BIOLOGY.

family planning Any measure to control the number of children in a family and the interval between them. These measures include the use of CONTRACEPTION and sterilization of men and women (the most common method in developing countries). ABORTION is promoted as a means of birth control in some government programmes, but most family-planning policy-makers are concerned with preventing conception and regard abortion as a back-up for failed contraception. Concern about spiralling POPULATION growth has led to extensive family-planning programmes in many nations. These programmes are not, however, supported by the Roman Catholic Church, which forbids artificial means of contraception.

The World Health Organization estimates that about 70 per cent of married women of reproductive age in the industrialized world use contraceptive measures and about 45 per cent of women in developing countries. Nevertheless, there are still more than thirty countries (the majority in Africa and the Middle East) in which most people have virtually no access to modern services.

family therapy A form of PSYCHOTHERAPY based on the assumption that some psychological problems arise as a result of unsatisfactory communications and relationships between family members. Several family members are therefore seen together, when possible, by the therapist in order to analyse and, if necessary, modify the way in which they relate together. Various techniques are used in family therapy, but most share the objective of assisting self-understanding, advancing personal development, and helping members of the family to understand the dynamics of their relationships.

famine Widespread acute starvation in a population associated with a sharp increase in mortality. The victims die not only from starvation but also from diseases that are fatal to the debilitated, and which spread rapidly as a result of massive population movements in search of food. Famine should be distinguished from chronic malnutrition. In **famine relief**, the direct supply of FOOD AID to the starving through international relief efforts may be necessary in disasters. However, various approaches to averting incipient famines may be more effective. These include government interventions in local markets to ensure adequate supplies and prevent escalating prices, and measures to increase people's capacity to purchase food themselves, for example by guaranteeing employment during crises. Cash transfers are often more effective than food rations: cash is faster to move and easier to administer, and it does not harm the market for local produce and thus farmers' incentives.

fan, alluvial See ALLUVIAL FAN.

Fangio, Juan Manuel (1911–95) Argentinian motor-racing driver. He first won the world championship in 1951, and then held the title from 1954 until 1957. He retired from racing in 1958.

fantail A small long-tailed bird, 15–20 cm (6–8 inches) long. Fantails are found primarily in south-east Asia, and are members of the subfamily Dicrurinae of the crow family, Corvidae. This subfamily of fantail flycatchers contains some 40 species in the genus *Rhipidura*; they are mainly brown and grey in colour, though many have white tips to the tail feathers. The Australian willie wagtail, *R. leucophrys*, is a glossy blue-black with white underparts and a white eye-stripe. It is found throughout Australia, except Tasmania. All species of *Rhipidura* are arboreal and feed on insects. They build finely woven nests in the forks of horizontal branches.

fantasia In the 16th and 17th centuries the instrumental musical equivalent of the MOTET. In Britain the term 'fancy' was used to describe adaptations of madrigals, popular tunes, and dances to instrumental music. In the 18th century it was a composition using improvisation rather than a rigid form, such as a sonata. In the 19th century it was a short, descriptive mood-piece (as, for example, Schumann's *Fantasy Pieces*), or a selection of operatic tunes. In the early 20th century a 'phantasy', was a loosely structured chamber work, usually in one movement.

Fanti (or **Fante**) A coastal tribe of Ghana belonging to the Akans people, a Kwaspeaking African branch of the Niger-Congo linguistic group. The Fanti played a prominent role in the affairs of Ghana after independence in 1957.

fanworm (or **peacock worm**) A polychaete, ANNELID worm, appearing as protruding tubes at low-tide levels on sandy beaches which are transformed when sea water covers them and the worm's head emerges, bearing fans of tentacles which filter detritus and plankton out of the water. The tentacles are also respiratory, and may bear simple eyes. Fan-worms build their protective tubes out of sand-grains, chalk, or parchment-like mucus. The segmented part of the body remains concealed in the tube.

farad (symbol F) The SI UNIT of capacitance, defined as the capacitance of a capacitor between the plates of which a potential difference of 1 volt appears when it is charged with 1 coulomb. The unit is too large for most applications and the microfarad (10^{-6} F) is more frequently used. The unit is named after Michael FARADAY.

Faraday, Michael (1791–1867) British physicist and chemist. One of the greatest experimentalists, Faraday was largely self-educated. Appointed by Sir Humphry Davy as his assistant at the Royal Institution, he initially concentrated on analytical chemistry, and discovered benzene in 1825. His most important work was in electromagnetism, in which field he demonstrated electromagnetic rotation and discovered electromagnetic induction (the key to the development of the electric dynamo and motor). Faraday's concept of magnetic lines of force formed the basis of the classical field theory of electromagnetic behaviour. He also discovered the laws of electrolysis.

farandole A popular dance of the Middle Ages in which the basic circle of the CAROLE was developed into various floor patterns. The line of linked dancers moved forward, travelling sideways or facing forwards.

farce A kind of COMEDY that inspires hilarity in its audience through an increasingly rapid and improbable series of ludicrous confusions, physical disasters, and sexual innuendoes among its stereotyped characters. The 'bedroom farce', involving bungled adultery in rooms with too many doors, has had prolonged commercial success in London's theatres; Joe ORTON used its conventions to create a disturbing kind of satire in *What the Butler Saw* (1969).

Far East A region of eastern Asia bordering the North Pacific and comprising China, Japan, Mongolia, North Korea, South Korea, and Siberia, but occasionally extended to include other countries in Indo-China and south-east Asia.

farming The combined range of activities carried out in the practice of AGRICULTURE. Nearly half of the world's economically active population engage in farming, either as a means of subsistence or as a profit-making enterprise. In the West farming has attained the status of an industry, in which a small proportion of the population provides the raw materials for food production on a national level. Here, farming involves a high degree of control over the biological processes that underlie agricultural production, for instance in the use of sophisticated methods of tillage, CROP ROTATION, synthetic PESTICIDES, HERBICIDES, and FERTILIZERS, and ANIMAL-BREEDING projects. Although highly productive, these advanced farming systems require large capital investment to maintain and are vulnerable to changes in consumer demand. Arable farming is concerned with growing crops, while livestock farming produces milk, meat, wool, and other animal products. Mixed farming practises both crop and animal husbandry as complementary enterprises. Much ORGANIC FARMING is mixed. Most tropical agriculture takes place in Third World countries, where the scarcity of employment, among other factors, keeps farming labour-intensive. See also FACTORY FARMING.

Farnaby, Giles (*c*.1563–1640) English composer. He published his *Canzonets to Fowre Voyces* in 1598. His vocal music is most attractive, as are his many keyboard pieces – which include FANTASIAS, variations, and several 'character sketches', such as 'Tower Hill' and 'Giles Farnaby's Rest'.

Farnborough A town in Hampshire, southern England, in a military area north of Aldershot; pop. (1990) 48,300. Its Royal Aircraft Establishment is noted as a leading centre of aeronautical research and for its annual air displays.

Farnese An Italian family which ruled the duchy of Parma from 1545 to 1731. Originating in the 11th century, its first outstanding member was **Alessandro** (1468–1549), who became Pope Paul III in 1534 and created the duchy of Parma and Piacenza. His grandson **Alessandro** (1520–89) was named a cardinal at the age of 14, and remained a powerful figure at the papal court for fifty years; he was a noted patron of the arts.

His nephew **Alessandro** (1545–92), Duke of Parma from 1586, was the family's most distinguished scion. After serving against the Ottomans at the battle of LEPANTO (1571), he succeeded Don JOHN OF AUSTRIA as governor-general of the Netherlands and commander-in-chief of the Spanish forces which were dealing with the Dutch Revolts (1578). By subtle diplomacy he detached the southern provinces from the revolt (1579). Then he conducted a sequence of superbly planned military campaigns further north, including the capture of Antwerp (1585). In 1588 PHILIP II diverted him from his campaigns in the north, ordering him to liaise with the SPANISH ARMADA. In 1590 he was diverted again, this time to intervene in the French WARS OF RELIGION, where he managed to relieve Paris (1590) and Rouen (1592), but was wounded and died.

Farouk (1920–65) King of Egypt, reigned 1936–52. On assuming power he dismissed Prime Minister Nahas Pasha, but was forced by the British government to reinstate him. Farouk's defeat in the Arab–Israeli conflict of 1948, together with the general corruption of his reign, led to a military coup in 1952, headed by General Neguib (1901–84) and masterminded by Nasser. Farouk was forced to abdicate in favour of his infant son, Fuad; he was sent into exile and eventually became a citizen of Monaco.

Farquhar, George (1678–1707) Irish dramatist. A principal figure in Restoration comedy, he is remembered for *The Recruiting Officer* (1706) and *The Beaux' Stratagem* (1707), plays marked by realism and genial merriment as well as by pungent satire.

Farrell, J(ames) G(ordon) (1935–79) British novelist. He is best known for his novels *The Siege of Krishnapur* (1973), dealing with events of the Indian Mutiny, and *The Singapore Grip* (1978), describing the fall of Singapore to the Japanese.

Farrell, J(ames) T(homas) (1904–79) US novelist. He achieved fame with his trilogy about Studs Lonigan, a young Chicago Catholic of Irish descent: *Young Lonigan* (1932), *The Young Manhood of Studs Lonigan* (1934), and *Judgement Day* (1935).

Farsi See INDO-IRANIAN LANGUAGES.

fasces Bundles of rods bound with thongs which were the sign of regal or magisterial authority both within and outside ancient Rome. After the expulsion of the ETRUSCAN kings, consuls had twelve fasces (a dictator twenty-four), praetors six, lesser magistrates fewer. Originally axes were included in the bundle; but from the early republic the axe was removed in Rome, in deference to the People's ultimate power in capital cases. In 1919 Musssolini used the symbol for his political party, which derived its name, FASCISM, from this word.

fascism A political ideology of the first half of the 20th century, whose central belief was that the individual should be subjugated to the needs of the state, which in turn should be directed by a strong leader embodying the will of the nation. It arose in opposition to COMMUNISM but adopted communist styles of propaganda, organization, and violence. The word (from the Roman FASCES) was first used by the Fascio di Combattimento in Italy in 1919. MUSSOLINI shaped fascism into a potent political force in Italy and HITLER developed a more racialist brand of it in Germany. Similar movements, which adopted a paramilitary structure, sprang up in Spain (the FALANGE), Portugal, Austria, the Balkan states, France, and South America. In Britain the National Union of Fascists under MOSLEY was founded in 1932, and between 1934 and 1936 adopted a strongly anti-Semitic character.

Once in power (in 1922 in Italy) fascists attempted to impose a military discipline on the whole of society at the expense of individual freedom (though, despite the socialist elements in fascist ideology, there was little interference with private ownership). Democratic institutions were replaced by the cult of the single leader, whose pronouncements were unchallengeable. Fascism was thus a form of TOTALITARIANISM and was finally defeated only by military means in the course of World War II. Since then various extreme right-wing parties based on fascist principles have emerged in Europe and elsewhere, but are generally supported only by a 'lunatic fringe' element in the population.

Fassbinder, Rainer Werner (1946–82) German film director. Fassbinder is remembered for films such as *The Bitter Tears of Petra von Kant* (1972) and the allegorical *The Marriage of Maria Braun* (1979). Influenced by Brecht, Marx, and Freud, Fassbinder's films dealt largely with Germany during World War II and postwar West German society.

Fassi The name given to an inhabitant of Fez in Morocco.

fast breeder reactor A type of NUCLEAR REACTOR that uses no moderator to slow the neutrons produced during nuclear FISSION, and breeds its own fuel in the form of PLUTONIUM. The NUCLEAR FUEL used in the reactor is natural uranium containing additional fissionable material (such as U-235). The advantage of fast breeder reactors using a nuclear fuel enriched in this way is that many neutrons emitted during the fission are absorbed by a 'blanket' of U-238 around the core, leading to the formation of a new type of fissionable material not normally found in nature – plutonium-239. Experimental fast breeder reactors have been built but they have not been used commercially, largely because the higher temperatures, requiring liquid sodium as a coolant, may make the reactor more vulnerable to a catastrophic meltdown than a thermal reactor.

fat See FATS AND OILS.

Fatah, al- (Arabic, 'victory') A militant Palestinian organization. It was founded (1962) in Kuwait to fight for the restoration of PALESTINE to the Arabs. Al-Fatah assumed the leadership of the PALESTINE LIBERATION ORGANIZATION in 1969 and remained the dominant group within the PLO. Its guerrilla units were expelled from Jordan after the civil war in 1970, and it withdrew to southern Lebanon (Fatahland). Subsequently al-Fatah was drawn into the Lebanese imbroglio and became divided; a part was expelled from Lebanon after the Israeli invasion of 1982. Leadership remained in the hands of Yasser ARAFAT, who had led al-Fatah from its foundation. Al-Fatah played a leading role in the achievement of the 1993 peace agreement with Israel. However, divisions within the organization over the progress of PLO–Israeli negotiations became apparent in 1995 with some factions no longer remaining loyal to Arafat.

Fates In Greek mythology, three daughters of Zeus and the Titaness Themis (the personification of justice) who controlled human destiny. Clotho spun the thread of life, Lachesis determined its length, and Atropos cut it off. The Fates are generally depicted as old and ugly.

Fatima (*c.*606–32 AD) Youngest daughter of the prophet Muhammad and wife of the fourth caliph, Ali (died 661). The descendants of Muhammad trace their lineage through her; she is revered especially by Shiite Muslims as the mother of the imams Hasan (624–80) and Husayn (626–80).

Fatimid (or **Fatimite**) A descendant or Arabian dynasty claiming descent from Fatima, the daughter of the Prophet Muhammad. The Fatimids ruled in parts of North Africa from 908 to 1171, and during some of that period in Egypt and Syria.

fats and oils (animal and vegetable) Organic compounds that are major representatives of the LIPIDS. Any organic substance that is insoluble in water but dissolves in organic solvents, such as ether, is classed as a lipid. The molecules of this heterogeneous group of compounds have in common only the fact that they are rich in hydrogen and poor in oxygen, nitrogen, and other groups that would make them water-soluble. Fats and oils are compounds of FATTY ACIDS and glycerol. Each molecule of the most common biological fats consists of one molecule of glycerol (a trihydric alcohol) linked with three molecules of fatty acids. They are an efficient energy store for most organisms, yielding more than twice as much energy per gram as CARBOHYDRATES. Fats are also used for thermal insulation in the subcutaneous fat layer of birds and mammals, and for the mechanical protection of delicate organs, such as kidneys. Fats are also present as energy storage molecules in plants. In general, animals yield saturated fats, which are solid at room temperature, while plants yield unsaturated oils, which are liquid. However, seafood also provides important unsaturated oils.

fatty acid A natural organic compound each molecule of which consists of a carboxylic acid group (–COOH) attached to a chain of carbon atoms with their associated hydrogen atoms. The chain may be 'saturated', containing single bonds only, or 'unsaturated', containing one or more double bonds. Fats normally contain saturated fatty acids; oils contain unsaturated fatty acids. These differences are reflected in the physical state of these compounds at room temperature. The so-called essential fatty acids (EFAs) are polyunsaturated (rich in double bonds): they are essential because they cannot be manufactured in the human body, and small quantities are therefore essential in the diet. Diets in which EFAs form a high proportion of the total fat intake result in lower blood levels of cholesterol. Fatty acids are used as an energy source by the muscles, heart, and other body organs, providing about 40 per cent of the total daily energy requirement in man. In hibernating animals and migrating birds they are the only important energy source.

fatwa See SHARIA.

Faulkner, William (1897–1962) US novelist. His works deal with the history and legends of the American South and have a strong sense of a society in decline; in the first of his major novels, *The Sound and the Fury* (1929), he was also influenced by modernist concerns of form. Other important works include *As I Lay Dying* (1930) and *Absalom! Absalom!* (1936). He was awarded the Nobel Prize for literature in 1949.

Faulkner of Downpatrick, (Arthur) Brian Deane Faulkner, Baron (1921–77) Northern Ireland statesman. A Unionist Member of Parliament at STORMONT (1949–73), he was Minister of Home Affairs 1959–63, 1971–72, and Prime Minister 1971–72. His negotiations with the Westminster government for constitutional changes in NORTHERN IRELAND lost him support in his own party.

fault (in geology) A plane surface fracture caused when stresses within the Earth break and dislocate bodies of rock. The relative movement may be vertical or nearly so (as in normal faults) or horizontal (tear or wrench faults). In areas of extreme compression, rocks may be pushed up and over the fracture (overthrusting). Faults are recognized by the displacement of layers of rock and by the crushing and alteration of material along the fault surface itself. Some fault-lines (such as the SAN ANDREAS FAULT) continue to move jerkily for thousands or millions of years; and although the movement at any one time may be small, the cumulative displacement may be considerable. Major faults can create significant features of the landscape, such as BLOCK MOUNTAINS and RIFT VALLEYS.

Fauré, Gabriel (Urbain) (1845–1924) French composer and organist. He composed songs throughout his career, incorporating some in cycles such as *La Bonne Chanson* (1891–92). His best-known work is the *Requiem* (1887) for solo voices, choir, and orchestra; he also wrote piano pieces, chamber music, and incidental music for the theatre.

Faust (or **Faustus**) (died *c*.1540) German astronomer and necromancer. Reputed to have sold his soul to the Devil in return for knowledge and power, he became the subject of many legends and was the subject of a drama by Goethe, an opera by Gounod, and a novel by Thomas Mann.

Fauvism Style of painting based on the use of intensely vivid non-naturalistic colours, the first of the major avant-garde developments that changed the face of European art between the turn of the century and World War I. The name 'Fauves' (French, 'wild beasts') was given to the artists who painted in the style because of their uninhibited use of colour freed from its traditional descriptive role. Fauvism reached its peak in 1905–06. Although short-lived, it was highly influential, particularly on German EXPRESSIONISM.

Fawcett, Dame Millicent Garrett (1847–1929) British feminist. Sister of Elizabeth Garrett ANDERSON, she was a pioneer of the movement in Britain to secure equality for women in voting, education, and careers. She was strongly supported by her husband, Henry Fawcett, a Liberal politician and academic. In 1897 she became president of the National Union of Women's Suffrage Societies, whose policy was to gain votes for women without the militancy soon to be associated with the SUFFRAGETTES.

Fawkes, Guy (1570–1606) English conspirator. He was hanged for his part in the GUNPOWDER PLOT of 5 November 1605. The occasion is commemorated annually with fireworks, bonfires, and the burning of a guy.

fax (or **facsimile transmission**) A system enabling print and illustrations to be transmitted by the telephone network and reproduced at the specially designed receiver. Modern machines use an array of light-sensitive DIODES to detect light reflected from the subject. Fax is now used widely by businesses and many other organizations, having to a large extent replaced posted letters and Telex.

feather An appendage growing from a bird's skin. Feathers are formed of keratin, the same substance as claws, hair, and nails. They vary from simple down feathers with very few 'hair-like' subdivisions (barbs), to the normal body (contour) feathers, which have barbs laid out in two rows on either side of the shaft (quill). Adjacent barbs are hooked to one another by hooks called barbules. The most elaborate feathers are used for display, such as those of the peacock.

Feathers serve three main functions. First, they provide the basic overcoat that insulates the bird and prevents it from losing heat too rapidly; in water birds the contour feathers, and a thick layer of down feathers provide essential waterproofing. Secondly, they occur in a wide variety of colours, which are used by the bird for camouflage or display; and, thirdly, they form the large surfaces of the wings and tail, which are needed in flight.

feather-star A fragile ECHINODERM, closely related to the SEA LILY, usually living well off shore on rocky outcrops or wrecks. The 550 or so species occur mainly in the Indo-Pacific seas. The feathery arms, commonly ten in number, form a food-catching funnel, and also beat alternately when the animal swims. Feather-stars and their relatives (many of which are stalked and sessile) are the most ancient and primitive of echinoderms.

Fechner, Gustav Theodor (1801–87) German physicist and psychologist. His early work was in electricity, but after a long illness he became interested in psychology. He sought to define the quantitative relationship between degrees of physical stimulation and the resulting sensations, the study

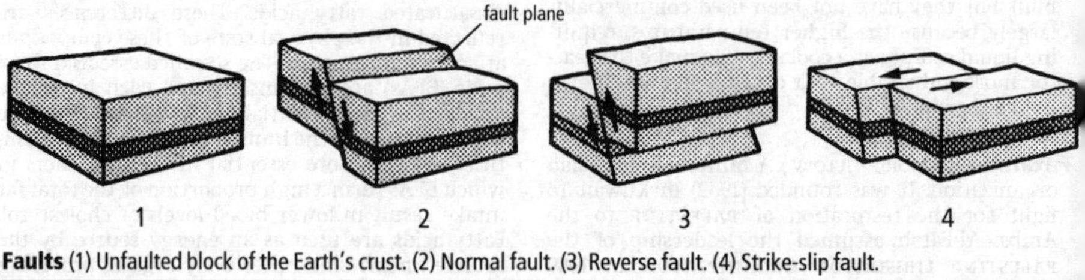

Faults (1) Unfaulted block of the Earth's crust. (2) Normal fault. (3) Reverse fault. (4) Strike-slip fault.

of which he termed *psychophysics*. By associating sensations with numerical values, Fechner hoped to make psychology a truly objective science.

Federal Bureau of Investigation (FBI) The investigative branch of the US Department of Justice. Established by Attorney-General Charles J. Bonaparte (1851–1921) in 1908, it was at first called the Bureau of Investigation. It was reorganized in 1924 when J. Edgar HOOVER was appointed as director, giving it wider powers to investigate violations of federal laws. Hoover successfully led the 1930s drive against gangsters. During World War II the FBI began spying activities against Nazi sympathizers in the USA and Latin America. The later excesses of Hoover, in particular his harassment of political dissidents and radicals such as Martin Luther KING, brought its counter-intelligence activities into disrepute. It was roundly criticized by the Senate in investigations of the WATERGATE scandal in 1975–76.

federalism A form of government in which power is dispersed between one central and several regional legislatures. Federalism contrasts with the unitary system of government, in that SOVEREIGNTY is shared within a national or possibly supra-national framework. A federal constitution allocates powers to different levels of government, some to the central government, and others to the governments of the territories making up the federation. Powers may be allocated either exclusively to one level, or concurrently to both. Unlike a CONFEDERATION, where the confederal government usually lacks its own institutions, each level of government in a federal system maintains institutions, imposes its own laws and taxes, and acts directly on the population.

Federally Administered Tribal Areas An administrative region of north-west Pakistan on the frontier with Afghanistan, comprising the tribal areas of Khyber, Kurram, Malakand, Mohmand, North Waziristan, and South Waziristan; area 27,220 sq km (10,514 sq miles); pop. (1981) 2,199,000. Miram Shah is the chief town.

Federation of Rhodesia and Nyasaland See CENTRAL AFRICAN FEDERATION.

feedback The process by which information about the output of a system is fed back to the input in order to influence the behaviour of the system. Distinction is often made between negative feedback, in which the feedback tends to reduce a system input, and positive feedback, which tends to reinforce it. Negative feedback thus often has a stabilizing effect, while positive feedback can cause system output to grow or oscillate indefinitely. Under dynamic conditions, however (that is, when system input, output and feedback signal are changing with time), the distinction between positive and negative feedback can become less clear. Hence, for example, negative feedback systems can become unstable under certain conditions. Accurate predictions of behaviour require appropriate dynamic modelling of the feedback system as a whole. Feedback occurs widely in biological systems and finds many technological applications, notably in closed-loop CONTROL SYSTEMS, operational AMPLIFIERS, and OSCILLATORS.

feedstuff A food product developed to achieve high yields from domestic animals. Most livestock require a similar diet to humans – a balance of carbohydrate, fat, and protein – but ruminants, such as cattle and sheep, can utilize plant material high in cellulose, and low-quality sources of protein. During the growing season, most livestock are fed on pasture grasses and legumes; outside the growing season, livestock are fed a source of roughage (such as hay, SILAGE, or ROOT-CROPS) supplemented by a high-protein concentrate. Oilcake is a concentrate made from vegetable seeds, such as soya beans or sunflower seeds, after they have been processed to remove the oil. Cereal grains, such as barley and sorghum, may be mixed with oilcake to form a complete feed for pigs and poultry, or a supplement for ruminants and horses. Protein concentrates from animal products include fish, meat, blood, and bone-meal: fish-meal is particularly rich in protein, while bone-meal is high in the minerals calcium and phosphorus. Since the diagnosis of BSE (BOVINE SPONGIFORM ENCEPHALOPATHY) in 1986, tighter controls have been introduced, particularly in the UK, concerning the use of offal as a feedstuff supplement. Other feeds are by-products of other food processing industries, for example sugar-beet pulp, brewers' grains, pineapple bran, and products derived from the milling of wheat.

Feisal See FAISAL.

feldspars (or **felspars**) A highly important group of rock-forming minerals: they constitute about half the rocks seen at the Earth's surface and are essential constituents of IGNEOUS ROCKS of all types. The amount and type of feldspar is an important factor in giving a name to a rock. The various types of feldspar are all aluminosilicates containing varying proportions of sodium, potassium, calcium, and barium. The most common types are orthoclase and PLAGIOCLASE.

Felixstowe A North Sea port on the coast of Suffolk, east England; pop. (1981) 24,460. There are ferry links with Sweden and the Netherlands.

Fellini, Federico (1920–93) Italian film director. He rose to international fame in the 1950s with *La Strada* (1954), which won an Oscar for best foreign film. Other major films include *La Dolce Vita* (1960) – a satire on Rome's high society and winner of the Grand Prix at Cannes – and the semi-autobiographical *8½* (1963).

felsenmeer Or 'block' or 'boulder' field, the jumbled expanse of sharp-edged rocks found on flat surfaces near sea-level in the High Arctic and Antarctic, and on high mountain plateaux and flat areas in lower latitudes.

felt A type of nonwoven fabric, made by rolling and pressing, and shrinking WOOL, hair, or other textile FIBRES. It derives its strength and dimensional stability from mutual entanglement of its fibres. It is used in clothing, upholstery, and draperies, as well as in many industrial processes. A recent development is the making of felts from some SYNTHETIC FIBRES, and these new felts are beginning to be used in large quantities.

feminism A broad-based movement concerning the social, political, and economic rights of women. Its advocates have for the most part demanded equal rights for both sexes, although some have asserted the right of women to separate development. Throughout the ages women had generally been subordinated to men and largely excluded from education, from the ownership of property, from economic independence, and from political representation. A recognizable movement to rectify woman's subordinate position began at the end of the 18th century, finding its British mouthpiece in Mary WOLLSTONECRAFT, whose classic *A Vindication of the Rights of Woman* (1792) has remained a key work.

Contemporary feminism has its roots in such works as Simone de BEAUVOIR's *The Second Sex*

(1949); *The Feminine Mystique* (1963) by the US feminist Betty FRIEDAN; *Sexual Politics* (1969) by the US writer Kate Millett; *The Female Eunuch* (1970) by Germaine GREER; Adrienne Rich's *Of Woman Born* (1977); and *Gyn/Ecology* (1979) by Mary Daly. In particular, the later 1960s saw the advent of women's liberation (popularly known as Women's Lib), arguing that male domination is implicit in all personal and professional relationships. It demanded the improvement of women's status in society and was concerned with changing stereotypes of both sexes. Women's liberation was especially vocal and active as a movement in the USA; in 1966 the National Organization for Women (NOW) was formed in the USA and has remained active since. Practical demands were focused on the right to equal pay and opportunities. In Britain the Sex Discrimination Acts (1975 and 1986) and the creation of the Equal Opportunities Commission in 1975 gave legal effect to some demands, although some employment practices and financial rewards still fail to achieve equality.

During the 1970s women's liberation gave way to a broader feminist movement, which sponsored public campaigns on such issues as ABORTION, childcare provision, PORNOGRAPHY, and domestic violence against women. Other aspects of the movement have aimed to integrate the interests of women who are not of the dominant culture (for example, women of colour, working-class women, and lesbians, who individually have contributed much to the movement) into mainstream feminism, while continuing to strive for gender equality in the workplace and at home.

In developing countries, feminists have been faced with a different order of problem. Women in such countries generally suffer from a greater degree of inequality than their counterparts in Western countries. Their participation in the paid labour force and their LITERACY rates tend to be lower, and their FERTILITY RATES and maternal mortality rates tend to be higher. Less access to education, combined with religious or social traditions, is responsible for women's limited role in economic, public, and political life. The revival of Islamic fundamentalism, with its enforced social isolation of women (see PURDAH), has led to the establishment of segregated systems of banking, commerce, and education in Muslim communities. Nevertheless, in many countries women have tried to improve their status, for example by opposing devisive legal and seclusion codes, and by campaigning against genital mutilation (see CIRCUMCISION). In Africa, development groups are now supporting women agriculturalists (who produce 70 per cent of the continent's food) by giving women greater access to and control of technology.

fen A swampy, low-lying area of freshwater PEAT formed along and between sluggish river channels. The soil is rather alkaline, unlike the acid peat of bogs. When drained, fens make good farmland, as in the fenlands of eastern England.

fencing The sport of duelling with one of three weapons: foil, épée, and sabre. Women compete in foil only. A fencer scores by hitting his or her opponent's target area. To avoid injury, fencers wear a face mask, padded jacket, and glove. The first to score five hits – or lead the scoring when the time (six minutes) expires – wins the bout.

Fender, Leo (1907–91) US guitar-maker. He pioneered the production of electric guitars, designing the Fender Broadcaster of 1948 (later called the Telecaster), which was the first solid-body electric guitar to be widely available, and the Fender Stratocaster, first marketed in 1956.

Fenian Originally a member of a secret revolutionary society, named after the Fianna, the Irish armed force in legendary times. Founded as the Fenian Brotherhood in the USA by John O'Mahony and as the Irish Republican Brotherhood (IRB) by James Stephens in Ireland (1858), the name was later applied to supporters of Irish republicanism. Many of its early members had been actively involved in the YOUNG IRELAND movement. Its military wing was known as the IRISH REPUBLICAN ARMY (IRA). Their exploits drew attention to Irish discontent and helped to convince GLADSTONE of the urgent need to find a solution to Ireland's problems. Several Fenians became Members of Parliament at Westminster during the HOME RULE period. In the latter part of the 1860s the Fenian Brotherhood split into three sections, each in theory supporting the IRB but in practice sharply divided by personalities and policies. The organization was superseded in the USA by Clan-na-Gael, a secret society headed by John Devoy, and by other open Irish-American organizations supporting Irish republicanism.

fennec fox The smallest species of FOX, *Fennecus zerda*, and yet the one with the largest ears. The length of its body from the tip of the nose to the base of the tail is 40 cm (16 inches); the ears are 10 cm (4 inches) long. These enormous ears are associated with the hot, dry climate of the Sahara Desert, the home of this fox, and they help to disperse body heat. The fennec fox has a pale, sandy-coloured coat and feeds at night on rodents, lizards, birds, locusts, and fruit.

fennel *Foeniculum vulgare*, a perennial member of the carrot family, Umbelliferae, native to southern Europe but naturalized in other places, particularly near the coast. It resembles dill in its feathery appearance but has a taste similar to that of anise. The seeds are used as a spice, while the swollen leaf-stems are treated as a vegetable.

fenugreek An annual plant, *Trigonella foenum-graecum*, which belongs to the pea family. Although a native of the Mediterranean region, it is now widely grown in India, where the seeds are an ingredient of curries and the leaves are eaten as salad. Recent investigations suggest the plant may contain substances with contraceptive properties.

Ferdinand (known as **Ferdinand of Aragon** or **Ferdinand the Catholic**) (1452–1516) King of Castile 1474–1516 and of Aragon 1479–1516. His marriage to Isabella of Castile in 1469 ensured his accession (as Ferdinand V) to the throne of Castile with her. During this time, they instituted the Spanish Inquisition (1478). Ferdinand subsequently succeeded to the throne of Aragon (as Ferdinand II) and was joined as monarch by Isabella (as Isabella I). Together they supported Columbus's expedition in 1492. Their capture of Granada from the Moors in the same year effectively united Spain as one country. Their daughter Catherine of Aragon became the first wife of Henry VIII of England.

Ferdinand II (1578–1637) Holy Roman Emperor 1619–37, King of Bohemia 1617–27 and of Hungary 1618–26. He was educated by the Jesuits and developed into a determined spokesman for COUNTER-REFORMATION Catholicism. Before his election to the imperial throne, he used authoritarian measures against the Protestants of Inner Austria, with some success, but in 1619 the largely Protestant Bohemian Diet deposed him in favour of FREDERICK V (the Winter King). This crisis was one of the opening moves in the catastrophic THIRTY YEARS WAR. The first ten years of the conflict did not go badly for Ferdinand. He reached his high point when he issued the Edict of Restitution (1629), which ordered the return of all Roman Catholic property seized since 1552. Subsequently he was seen as a threat to German liberty and opposed by both Catholic and Protestant princes. The interventions of Sweden and France finally turned the tide of the war against him, and he was forced to abandon his more extreme Catholic absolutist ambitions.

Ferdinand VII (1784–1833) King of Spain 1808–33. He succeeded to the throne after the forced abdication of his father, Charles IV, and was in turn forced by the French to abdicate in favour of NAPOLEON's brother, Joseph Bonaparte, spending the years of the PENINSULAR WAR in prison in France. Known as 'The Desired One', he was released in 1814 and restored to the throne. He abolished the liberal constitution of 1812 and instituted his own absolutist rule, relying on the support of the Church and the army. The loss of the colonies in America (SPANISH-SOUTH-AMERICAN WARS OF INDEPENDENCE) deprived the government of a major source of income, and his troops mutinied. The revolutionaries held him practically a prisoner until 1823, when French forces came to his aid. Restored to power, he carried out a bloody revenge on the insurgents.

Ferguson, Alex(ander Chapman) (1941–) Scottish football manager and footballer. After a playing career in Scotland he managed St Mirren (1974–78) and Aberdeen (1978–86), with whom he won the European Cup Winner's Cup in 1983 and a Scottish league and cup double in 1984. He took over as manager of Manchester United in 1986, and in ten years took them to four Premier League championships (1993, 1994, 1996, 1997) and three FA Cup wins (1990, 1994, 1996), including an unprecedented two league and cup doubles.

Ferlinghetti, Lawrence (Monsanto) (born Lawrence Ferling) (1919–) US poet and publisher. From the early 1950s he lived in San Francisco, with whose beat movement he is identified. In 1952 he founded his own bookshop and publishing house, City Lights: the bookshop was the focus for many writers and artists in the late 1950s, while the publishing house produced works such as Allen Ginsberg's *Howl* (1957). His own works include the collection *A Coney Island of the Mind* (1958), the novel *Her* (1960), and a number of experimental plays.

Fermanagh A hilly county of south-west Northern Ireland drained by the River Erne; area 1,676 sq km (647 sq miles); pop. (1981) 51,00; county town, Enniskillen.

Fermat, Pierre de (1601–65) French mathematician and physicist who developed the modern theory of numbers, laid the foundations upon which Isaac NEWTON was to build the CALCULUS, and founded, with Blaise PASCAL, the theory of PROBABILITY. He put forward the principle that light, when reflected or refracted, always takes the path for which its travel time is least. However, his most famous assertion, or 'Fermat's Last Theorem', is that simple relationships of the form $3^2 + 4^2 = 5^2$ are not possible with higher powers than 2.

fermentation An energy-yielding process involving the chemical breakdown of organic compounds (food molecules) by living organisms. Unlike aerobic RESPIRATION, fermentation does not require the presence of an externally supplied oxidizing agent, and it generally occurs only in the absence of oxygen. Energy is generated by the cleavage and rearrangement of food molecules and is harnessed in the form of ATP. Fermentation is generally a much less efficient energy-yielding process than aerobic respiration.

Many different types of fermentation occur in microorganisms. The best-known example is the alcoholic fermentation carried out by some yeasts and moulds, and by a few bacteria; sugars are converted to alcohol (ethanol) and carbon dioxide, and this is exploited commercially in bread-making, BREWING, and WINE-making. Lactic acid fermentation, in which lactic acid is the main product of the fermentation of sugars, occurs in some bacteria, and is exploited in yoghurt and CHEESE MANUFACTURE and in making SILAGE.

In industrial microbiology 'fermentation' is often used rather non-specifically for any metabolic process carried out by microorganisms, even though biologically the process may actually involve respiration rather than fermentation.

Fermi, Enrico (1901–54) Italian-born US atomic physicist. Working at first in Italy, he invented (with Paul Dirac) **Fermi–Dirac statistics**, a mathematical tool of great value in atomic, nuclear, and solid-state physics. He predicted the existence of the neutrino, and produced radioactive isotopes by bombarding atomic nuclei with neutrons. He was awarded the Nobel Prize for physics in 1938. Moving to the US, Fermi directed the first controlled nuclear chain reaction in 1942, and joined the Manhattan Project to work on the atom bomb. The artificial element fermium and a class of subatomic particles, the fermions, are named after him.

fermion (in atomic physics) A particle with half-integral SPIN, such as a proton, neutron, positron, electron or muon.

fermium (symbol Fm, at. no. 100, r.a.m. 257) A strongly radioactive transuranic element first identified by A. Ghiorso in debris from the first hydrogen-bomb explosion in 1952. Ten isotopes are known. It is named after Enrico FERMI.

fern A leafy plant of the phylum Filicinophyta (or, in traditional classifications, the class Filicinae – see PTERIDOPHYTE) spread by SPORES, not seeds. Like mosses and liverworts, clubmosses and horsetails, ferns grow in two physically distinct forms that alternate during their life cycle. For the main part of this cycle, a fern consists of a short stem (rhizome) from which roots grow down into the soil, and leafy fronds grow upwards. This is called the sporophyte generation because it produces spores inside spore cases on the underside or margins of the fronds. These spore cases open and scatter the spores which, when they fall on moist soil, germinate to produce heart-shaped plants 2–3 cm (about an inch) across, called prothalli. These bear the sex organs, which in ferns are cavities containing microscopic egg cells and sperms. The sperms swim to fertilize the egg when the prothallus is wet, so ferns are able to reproduce sexually only in damp habitats. After fertilization the egg cell develops into a new sporophyte plant.

Some ferns reproduce asexually by leaf buds or, in the case of bracken, by rhizomes. Many fossil ferns are known, some of which, unlike modern ferns, had seeds. About 9,000 species of living fern are known. The species *Ophioglossum*, known as adder's tongue, has the highest known chromosome number of any plant (over 1,000). This indicates an ancient lineage. Common temperate species include lady fern, *Anthyrium filix-femina*, male fern, *D. filix-mas*, POLYPODY, and bracken, *Pteridium aquilinum*.

Fernando Póo The former name (until 1973) of the island of Bioko in Equatorial Guinea.

Ferranti, Sebastian Ziani de (1864–1930) British electrical engineer. He was one of the pioneers of electricity generation and distribution in Britain, his chief contribution being the use of high voltages for economical transmission over a distance.

Ferrari, Enzo (1898–1988) Italian car designer and manufacturer. He became a racing driver for Alfa Romeo in 1920 and proceeded to work as one of their designers. In 1929 he founded the company named after him, launching the famous Ferrari marque in 1947 and producing a range of high-quality sports and racing cars. Since the early 1950s Ferraris have won more world championship Grands Prix than any other car.

ferret A domesticated POLECAT of the genus *Mustela*, though the term may also be applied to the highly endangered black-footed ferret, *M. nigripes*, of North America. Ferrets are members of the family Mustelidae. They spread into Europe, possibly with the rabbit, and historical records of them in England date from the 13th century. When hunting rabbits, the ferret is usually muzzled to prevent it killing and eating the rabbit in its burrow. Ferrets have also been used to draw cables through narrow underground pipes. Many are kept purely as pets or for show.

ferric oxide See IRON OXIDE.

Ferrier, Kathleen (1912–53) British contralto, who became a leading concert singer after her London début in Handel's *Messiah* in 1943. She made her operatic début as Lucretia in the first performance of Britten's *The Rape of Lucretia* (1946), and is particularly famous for her performance in 1947 of Mahler's song cycle *Das Lied von der Erde*.

ferrisol An iron-rich soil occurring in tropical climates with high temperature and rainfall. In these conditions soluble minerals are removed from the soil by LEACHING, leaving behind only the iron and aluminium compounds which cause the characteristic red colour of the soil. Ferrisols are found in the Amazon and Congo basins, along the east coast of Brazil, and in Indonesia.

ferrite Any member of a family of electroceramics based on iron oxides, particularly magnetite (Fe_3O_4). Ferrites are capable of holding a permanent magnetic dipole. They are usually very soft magnets (easily magnetized and demagnetized) and are of great importance as transformer cores, especially for high-frequency applications. They are electrical insulators and hence do not undergo losses from eddy currents within a transformer core.

ferromagnesian minerals Rock-forming minerals rich in iron and magnesium: biotite, hornblende, augite, hypersthene, and olivine. They are generally dark in colour. They are primary constituents of basic igneous rocks.

ferromagnetism See MAGNETISM.

ferrous oxide See IRON OXIDE.

Fertile Crescent The fertile land stretching from the Mediterranean coast of Syria, Lebanon, and Israel down the valley of the Tigris and Euphrates rivers to the Persian Gulf. The expression was coined by the archaeologist James H. Breasted to describe that part of the Middle East that formed the cradle of early civilizations such as the Assyrian, Sumerian, Phoenician, Babylonian, Hittite, and Hebrew.

fertility drug A substance used to treat women who experience difficulty in becoming pregnant. One cause of infertility is an inadequate supply of gonadotrophins, HORMONES that control ovulation (the release of an egg from the ovary). Natural gonadotrophins, or drugs, such as clomiphene, which stimulate gonadotrophin production, can bring about ovulation, but often more than one egg is released, resulting in a multiple birth. Another cause of infertility is endometriosis (degeneration of the uterus lining), which can be treated by oral CONTRACEPTIVES. A third type of fertility drug is bromocriptine, used to regularize abnormalities in ovulation and the menstrual cycle.

fertility rate A calculation essential to the prediction of population changes and, in particular, of population growth. The most commonly used rate is the 'total fertility rate' (TFR). The TFR for a country represents the number of children projected to be born, on average, to each woman upon completion of her child-bearing years. Between 1950 and 1955, and 1985 and 1990, TFRs fell in Europe from 2.6 to 1.7 (well below the replacement level of 2.1), from 5.9 to 3.6 in South America, from 6.0 to 3.5 in Asia, and from 6.6 to 6.2 in Africa. Many factors affect fertility rates, not least beliefs, traditions, and the value of the labour children can perform, but where couples believe that their children can expect to survive to become adults and where women are better educated and have easy access to FAMILY PLANNING they marry later and have fewer children.

fertilization The fusion of a male GAMETE (sex cell) with a female gamete to form a **zygote**, which subsequently develops into a new organism. In animals and plants, this occurs during sexual reproduction. Self-fertilization is a process which is confined only to some plants.

Male and female gametes have become adapted to perform their different functions. The male gamete (sperm) moves to fertilize the female and is characteristically smaller, to aid mobility, and more numerous to offset the risk of loss or damage. Female gametes (ova) usually contain food reserves for the developing zygote and are thus larger and less likely to move. Fertilization in animals may be external (fishes, amphibians, and some invertebrates) or internal (reptiles, birds, mammals, and some invertebrates).

fertilizer A natural or artificial AGROCHEMICAL containing nutrients that is added to soil to improve the growth and productivity of plants. Fertilizers are primarily used to provide the three major elements required for plant growth – nitrogen, phosphorus, and potassium – along with other minor and trace elements. Lime, widely applied to combat soil acidity and provide calcium, is also considered a fertilizer. Organic fertilizers, such as manure and composts, have been in use since almost the beginning of agriculture. Sodium nitrate and guano (sea-bird excrement from South America containing phosphates and nitrates) were first used in the UK in the 1830s. Modern chemical fertilizers were first used in the 1840s: one of the earliest was 'superphosphate' (invented by LAWES), made by dissolving bones (later mineral phosphates) in sulphuric acid. A modification of this process forms the basis of today's phosphate fertilizer industry. Nitrogen fertilizers are almost universally derived from synthetic ammonia, produced from atmospheric nitrogen by the HABER–BOSCH PROCESS. Industry has coupled ammonia to a range of other compounds to yield ammonium salt and urea fertilizers. Potassium fertilizers are obtained as various mined salts. Most fertilizers are applied as solids, either powders or granules, but liquid fertilizers are popular in the USA, and ammonia gas can be liquefied under pressure and injected deep into soil. NITRATE fertilizers have given cause for concern because they enter water supplies, with possible harmful consequences.

Fès See FEZ.

Fessenden, Reginald Aubrey (1866–1932) Canadian-born US physicist and radio engineer. He pioneered radio-telephony, devised the amplitude modulation of radio waves for carrying audio signals, and invented the heterodyne receiver. He made the first sound broadcast at Christmas 1906 in the USA. Fessenden was involved in both industrial and academic research, and obtained hundreds of patents for his inventions.

fetus See EMBRYO.

feudal system A medieval European political and economic system based on the holding of lands on condition of homage or military service and labour. Feudalism probably originated in the Frankish kingdom in the 8th century and spread into northern Italy, Spain, and Germany. It was introduced by the NORMANS into England, Ireland, Scotland, southern Italy, and Sicily. The nobility held lands from the crown and provided troops for the king in times of war. The knight was the tenant of the noble and a class of unfree peasants (VILLEIN) lived on the land under the jurisdiction of their lord (MANORIAL SYSTEM). Bishops and abbots were invested by secular lords with their livings in return for services and the church received produce and labour from the peasantry. It became a varied and complex system: lords built up their own military forces and power to the point where they became semi-independent of the king; from the 12th century payments (scutage) could be substituted for military duties. The system broke down in the 12th and 13th centuries as towns (COMMUNE) and individuals achieved independence from their lords, though serfdom survived in some countries for much longer.

Feuerbach, Ludwig (Andreas) (1804–72) German materialist philosopher. He studied theology at Heidelberg and then philosophy under Hegel at Berlin. His best-known work, *The Essence of Christianity*, was published in 1841. He maintained that the dogmas and beliefs of Christianity are figments of human imagination, fulfilling a need inherent in human nature.

Feydeau, Georges (1862–1921) French dramatist. His name has become a byword for French bedroom farce. He wrote some forty plays, including *Hotel Paradiso* (1894) and *Le Dindon* (1896).

Feynman, Richard Phillips (1918–88) US theoretical physicist. He worked in quantum electrodynamics, and introduced important new techniques for studying the electromagnetic interactions between subatomic particles. This approach is expressed in diagrams that describe the exchange of particles (Feynman diagrams). He shared the Nobel Prize for physics in 1965.

Fez (or **Fès**) The oldest of the four imperial cities of Morocco, 160 km (100 miles) east of Rabat; pop. (1993) 564,000. Founded in 808 by Moulay Idriss II, it was a former capital of Morocco and its mosque became the focal point of a famous Muslim university. Fez gives its name to a flat-topped conical red hat with a tassel worn by men in some Muslim countries. Carpets, textiles, and leather goods are produced.

Fíanna Fáil (Gaelic, 'soldiers of destiny') Irish political party. Its main aim is to create a united republican Ireland, politically and economically independent of Britain. Eamon DE VALERA founded the Party in 1926 from opponents of the Anglo-Irish Treaty (1921) which established the IRISH FREE STATE. The Party won control of the government (1932). It dominated Irish politics for the following years, being out of office only for short periods. In 1973 it lost to an alliance of the Fine Gael and the Labour Party, but returned to power for a period in 1977 and again from 1987 to 1994 and from 1997.

Fibonacci, Leonardo (known as **Fibonacci of Pisa**) (*c.*1170–*c.*1250) Italian mathematician. Fibonacci learnt of the 'new' Arabic numerals while in North Africa and the Middle East, and later popularized their use in Europe through such works as *Liber Abaci* (1202, revised 1228). He made many original contributions in complex calculations, algebra, and geometry, and pioneered number theory and indeterminate analysis. He is famous as the discoverer of the Fibonacci series, in which each term is the sum of its two predecessors (1, 1, 2, 3, 5, 8, etc.).

fibre, textile The raw, fibrous material from which fabrics and other TEXTILES are made. Textile fibres may be subdivided into two main groups: those occurring naturally, which may be of animal, vegetable, or mineral origin, and those which are manufactured, mainly from regenerated or synthetic polymers. Fibres are made into YARN by SPINNING.

Three types of fibre occur in plants. The first includes COTTON and KAPOK with the fibres associated with seeds. The second, exemplified by FLAX and JUTE, has fibres derived from stems. The third type of fibre derives from the leaves of plants such as SISAL. Animal fibres provide about 6 per cent of the annual worldwide fibre supply. WOOL is the most important of these fibres. Others include the hair of varieties of goat, which provide MOHAIR and cashmere, and the SILK thread spun by the silkworm. Asbestos is the only significant naturally occurring mineral fibre. With the exception of silk, natural fibres are relatively short (on average, 2–50 cm, 1–20 inches). Such short fibres are generally known as 'staple' fibres.

The remainder of the world's fibre supply is manufactured. Some manufactured fibres are derived from naturally occurring fibre-forming polymers (for example, RAYONS, made from natural cellulose). However, the majority are SYNTHETIC FIBRES, produced from long-chain polymers, usually derived from oil. Manufactured fibres are extruded or 'spun' by pumping the fibre material in solution or in molten form through the fine holes of a spinneret. More than 50 per cent of synthetic filament manufactured is cut or broken to form staple fibre. Most is then used, either alone or in blends with natural fibres, for the manufacture of spun YARNS.

fibreglass See GLASS FIBRE.

fibre optics See OPTICAL FIBRE.

fibre-reinforced plastic Any of a range of COMPOSITE materials comprising comparatively cheap thermosetting or thermoplastic materials reinforced with strong, stiff fibres. Common matrix media are EPOXY RESINS and the thermoplastic polyether etherketone (PEEK). Glass-fibre-reinforced plastics (GFRP) are very important in modern engineering. Mats of glass fibres in thermosetting polyester and epoxy resins are used extensively in the construction of boats, ranging from small yachts and canoes to military ships of about 500 tonnes. GFRP is also important for sports goods, where continuous glass fibres are wound round formers to make hollow, light, stiff shafts for racquets, fishing rods, and golf clubs. It is now being used increasingly in the automobile industry in place of steel body panels: material reinforced with short glass fibres is used, because it can be injection moulded. GFRP is also important as a material for circuit boards. Carbon fibre-reinforced plastics (CFRP) are used extensively in the aerospace industry because of their high elastic stiffness and low weight. They are also used for sports goods and racing-car bodywork. The lightest composites are reinforced with ultra-high-strength polymer fibres, such as aramids (see NYLON).

fibrinogen A soluble protein found in the blood plasma of vertebrates, which is important in the clotting of blood. On injury, the ENZYME thrombin acts upon fibrinogen, which is a substrate, and produces an insoluble protein called fibrin. Fibrin forms a mesh of fibres (a clot) in which BLOOD cells and platelets are caught, thereby preventing the loss of blood.

Fichte, Johann Gottlieb (1762–1814) German philosopher. A pupil of Kant, he postulated that the ego is the only basic reality; the world around it, or the 'non-ego', is posited by the ego in defining and delimiting itself. Fichte preached moral virtues and encouraged patriotic values; his political addresses had some influence on the development of German nationalism and the overthrow of Napoleon.

fief The land held under the FEUDAL SYSTEM by a VASSAL from his lord. Fiefs ranged in size from vast duchies down to the area of land needed to support a single knight, called a knight's 'fee'. Large or small, they provided the agricultural produce which was the source of all wealth. During the early Middle Ages areas which had been forest or barren land came under cultivation and were incorporated into the system.

field (in physics) A region in which a force acts. Thus, for example, a gravitational field is a region in which objects experience a gravitational force and an electric field is a region in which charged bodies experience an electric force. Fields can be imagined as a pattern of LINES OF FORCE. The number of lines in a given space represents the strength of the field. Arrows on the lines represent the direction of the force.

Field, John (1782–1837) Irish composer and pianist. He is noted for the invention of the nocturne and for his twenty compositions in this form. His work inspired several later composers, especially CHOPIN.

fieldfare A bird, *Turdus pilaris*, belonging to the thrush family. This species breeds in wooded areas across much of the central and northern parts of Europe and western Asia, migrating to milder areas for the winter. They are mainly grey in colour, with a paler rump and speckled underparts. Like many thrushes they feed on berries and insects. The untidy, cup-shaped nest is usually made in a tree, and houses three or four eggs. Fieldfares may nest in loose colonies and attack any potential predator.

Fielding, Henry (1707–54) British novelist. After writing several comedies and farces, he provoked the introduction of censorship with his sharp political satire *The Historical Register for 1736*; the resultant Licensing Act of 1737 effectively ended his career as a dramatist. He turned to writing picaresque novels, including *Joseph Andrews* (1742) – which begins as a parody of Samuel Richardson's *Pamela* – and *Tom Jones* (1749). Fielding became Justice of the Peace for Westminster in 1748, and was responsible for the formation of the Bow Street Runners the following year.

field mouse See WOOD MOUSE.

Field of the Cloth of Gold The site near Calais, where HENRY VIII of England met FRANCIS I of France in June 1520, in an attempt to forge a diplomatic alliance. Henry's retinue was made up of more than 5,000 people. He wrestled, danced, jousted, and tilted with Francis for almost a fortnight, amid scenes of great festivity and pageantry. But the two sovereigns retained their initial mutual suspicions, and within days of leaving Francis, Henry met the French king's archrival, Emperor Charles V, at Gravelines.

field of view The range of angles of incoming electromagnetic radiation that an optical instrument can detect simultaneously. For an optical telescope it represents the angular spread in the sky that can be viewed.

Fields, Dame Gracie (born Grace Stansfield) (1898–1979) British singer and comedienne. During the 1930s she enjoyed great success with English music-hall audiences. She went on to star in a series of popular films, including *Sing as We Go* (1934). During World War II she emigrated to the USA with her Italian husband. Although she continued to entertain troops her departure was seen as a betrayal by some of her public.

Fields, W. C. (born William Claude Dukenfield) (1880–1946) US comedian. Having made his name as a comedy juggler he became a vaudeville star, appearing in the *Ziegfeld Follies* revues between 1915 and 1921. His films established him as an internationally famous comic; they include *The Bank Dick* (1940).

field vole (or **short-tailed vole**) A rodent belonging to the genus *Microtus*, whose short tail is its most distinctive feature. Like all VOLES, it has a rounded head and is strictly herbivorous. It prefers long, uncultivated grassland, but it may be found in most parts of northern Europe, provided the habitat contains some grass. It does not hibernate and may continue to breed into winter, but, unlike the BANK VOLE, its breeding is not restricted by the amount of food available.

Fife A local government region in east-central Scotland, between the estuaries of the Forth and Tay; area 1,312 sq km (507 sq miles); pop. (1993) 351,200; capital, Glenrothes. Often referred to as the 'Kingdom of Fife', it has maintained a distinct identity since Pictish times.

Fifteen, the (1715) A JACOBITE rebellion aimed at removing the Hanoverian GEORGE I from the British throne. Queen ANNE's sudden death in August 1714 had caught the Jacobites by surprise. Their lack of preparedness and their inability to win the English Tories to their cause delayed the rebellion until September 1715. A simultaneous rising in Scotland and England was planned, with Thomas Forster to lead the English northern rebels and the indecisive Earl of Mar to command the Scots. Forster was compelled to surrender his small force at Preston and Mar's inconclusive battle at Sheriffmuir virtually ended the rebellion.

Fifth Avenue One of the main thoroughfares of

Manhattan Island, New York City, stretching from Washington Square to the Harlem River. From 59th to 110th Streets it borders Central Park. The Flatiron Building, Empire State Building, New York Public Library, St Patrick's Cathedral, Frick Collection, Guggenheim Museum, and Museum of the City of New York all overlook Fifth Avenue.

fig A large shrub or small tree of the genus *Ficus* (which includes about 600 species) within the family Moraceae. Figs have broad leaves, and bear many-seeded fruits. The most common of several species producing the green, brown, or purple fruits is *F. carica*. Originally native to western Asia, figs were known in Egypt as early as 4000 BC, and today are cultivated in the Mediterranean region and California. They have fleshy, fruit-shaped flowers and, in the widely cultivated Smyrna types, require cross-pollination by tiny fig wasps, which parasitize a proportion of the flowers. When the plants are grown in a new area, the wasps must also be introduced, although the common or Adriatic fig does not require fertilization.

Eaten fresh, dried, or preserved, figs have laxative properties. Many other species are cultivated as ornamental plants, and one, known as the rubber plant, *F. elastica*, has become a common houseplant.

fighter aircraft See MILITARY AIRCRAFT.

fighter-bomber See MILITARY AIRCRAFT.

fighting fish (or **Siamese fighting fish**) A species of Asiatic freshwater cyprinodont fish, *Betta splendens*. Native to Thailand, it has now been distributed throughout the world, and has been kept in semi-domestication for centuries. It occurs commonly in ponds, drainage ditches, and the backwaters of rivers, where it plays an important role in controlling malaria-carrying mosquito larvae. The water in which it lives is frequently deficient in oxygen and it breathes air by means of a respiratory organ above the gills. It lays its eggs in a nest of bubbles produced mainly by the male, and at first the young fishes live in the nest, which keeps them in oxygen-rich water. The males were kept for their fighting qualities and have been bred to develop brightly coloured and aggressive forms.

fig wasp A member of a family of minute black WASPS related to CHALCID wasps, the Agaonidae, essential to the maturation of the fruit of figs. The larvae develop in galls (growths) within figs. When the males, which are wingless, emerge, they eat into galls that contain females, and mate with them. These females enter the compound flowers of young figs and, if it is the right kind of fig, they lay their eggs as well as fertilizing the fig flower. If the fig is the wrong kind, they cannot lay, but nevertheless fertilize it.

Fiji A country comprising a group of islands, in the Melanesian archipelago of the south-west Pacific Ocean.

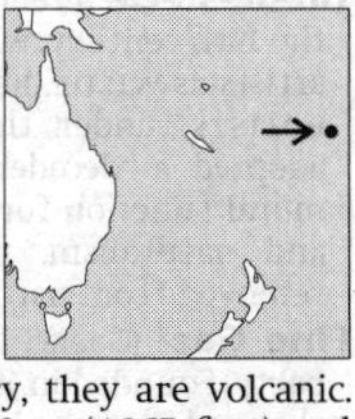

Physical. Fiji consists of two main islands, Viti Levu and Vanua Levu, and over 800 smaller ones. Being situated some 400 km (248.6 miles) from a plate boundary, they are volcanic. Mountains rise to some 1,300 m (4,265 feet) and have thick rain forest on the wetter slopes. The climate is hot, though not unpleasantly so. The islands lie in a hurricane belt, and there is periodic devastation by TORNADOES.

Economy. The economy is agricultural, with sugar the chief crop and export. Other trade is in re-exported petroleum products, coconut oil, fish, and gold. Tourism provides substantial additional revenue. Food-processing is the main industry.

History. The islands first became known to Europeans when Tasman visited them in 1643. Captain Cook landed in 1774. In the 19th century Fuji was notorious for inter-tribal wars and cannibalism, a situation not assisted by an influx of deserting seamen, traders seeking sandalwood, and whalers. The islands became a British crown colony in 1874, the Western Pacific High Commission being set up for the pacification and control of the labour trade. By 1879 Indians began to be imported under the indenture system. By the 1950s Indians outnumbered Fijians and were dominating commercial life, while Fijians owned most of the land. The country became independent in 1970. The election of a government with an Indian majority (1987) brought ethnic tensions to a head, leading to two military coups to restore indigenous Fijian control and to the withdrawal of Fiji from the Commonwealth of Nations. Civilian rule, under a new constitution that guaranteed a Melanesian parliamentary majority, was restored in 1990. There has, since then, been heavy Indian emigration resulting in loss of skills and capital. In 1991 opposition parties attacked the new constitution as racist. There were threats of another military coup, but in 1992 the Fijian Political Party won a majority of seats in the general election and Major General Sitiveni Rabuka, who had led the coups of 1987, became Prime Minister as head of a coalition. The government collapsed in 1994 but was re-elected with Rabuka's party increasing its majority.

Capital: Suva
Area: 18,274 sq km (7,056 sq mi)
Population: 791,000 (1995)
Currency: 1 Fiji dollar = 100 cents
Religions: Christian 52.9%; Hindu 38.1%; Muslim 7.8%; Sikh 0.7%
Ethnic Groups: Indian 48.6%; Fijian 46.3%
Languages: English (official); Fijian; Hindi; local languages
International Organizations: UN; Colombo Plan; South Pacific Commission

filament (in astronomy) A slender thread-like feature on the surface of the Sun. Filaments take different forms depending on their origin. For example, the penumbra of SUNSPOTS shows filaments that radiate away from the central umbra. Filaments may also be prominences that are seen from above and so their loop-like structure is not evident.

filaria A ROUNDWORM mainly found in central Africa, Asia, and the south-west Pacific. The species *Wuchereria bancrofti* and *Brugia malayi* cause the disease **filariasis**. The tiny larval worm (1.4 mm) is transmitted by mosquito or mite bites to humans, in which they grow to 8 cm in length in lymph and blood vessels, causing severe swelling (see ELEPHANTIASIS).

file (computing) A set of information stored in a computer system, usually on a HARD or FLOPPY DISK, or on magnetic tape. Files may contain PROGRAMS, DATA, text, or other suitably coded information. Each file is identified by a name and is normally used to contain logically related information.

filibusters Originally piratical adventurers or freebooters who pillaged the Spanish colonies in the 17th century. Subsequently it was used of anyone who engaged in unauthorized war against foreign states. This meaning led to its use to describe speakers in the US Congress, British parliament, or any other assembly seeking to delay legislation by making long speeches to obstruct business.

filigree Openwork decoration made of very fine wires and tiny balls of metal soldered into a design. The metal is usually gold or silver, but bronze and other metals have also been used. Filigree has been used in jewellery since Greek and Roman times and has also been employed in a wide variety of small decorative objects.

Filipino See AUSTRONESIAN LANGUAGES.

Fillmore, Millard (1800–74) US Whig statesman, 13th President of the USA 1850–53. He succeeded to the presidency on the death of Zachary Taylor. Fillmore was an advocate of compromise on the slavery issue. However, his unpopular enforcement of the 1850 Fugitive Slave Act hastened the end of the Whig Party.

film (in the cinema) A motion picture. As a form of dramatic art, films began as sideshows at fairgrounds or as items in music-hall programmes. They were all short and silent, and included slapstick comedy, trick pictures, short romances, and five-minute dramas. Between 1900 and 1914 the length of a performance increased from a few minutes to two hours, and after World War I HOLLYWOOD in California became the chief centre of production. Sound films evolved in the late 1920s and Technicolor in the 1930s. Among the pioneering geniuses of film-making are EISENSTEIN and the Germans von STERNBERG, LANG, and MURNAU, whose development of EXPRESSIONISM in the cinema paralleled its evolution in art and drama. In France the films of Jean Vigo (1905–34) introduced a form of Surrealist lyricism. In the USA WELLES created new heights of cinematic drama with *Citizen Kane* (1941), while KAZAN directed some of the great classics of the cinema. In France the NOUVELLE VAGUE directors evolved an intimate and influential cinema style in the 1960s, while the technical innovations of the CINÉMA-VÉRITÉ allowed inexpensive but notable film productions to be made. In Britain the FREE CINEMA group were concerned to bring realism to the feature film. Major post-war directors include KUROSAWA, whose works often draw on elements of the Kabuki and samurai traditions, BERGMAN, BUÑUEL, HITCHCOCK, TARKOVSKY, TRUFFAUT, ROSSELLINI, HERZOG, RAY, KUBRICK, COPPOLA, SCORSESE, and SPIELBERG.

film (in photography) Light-sensitive material used for recording images in a CAMERA or CINE-CAMERA. Films for different applications have a variety of formats. Black-and-white film consists of a tough, flexible CELLULOSE ACETATE base carrying a thin layer of a light-sensitive emulsion (silver halide crystals suspended in gelatine) and a protective coating. When a film is exposed, light falling on it causes changes in the structure of the silver halide crystals, recording a latent image of the scene being photographed on the film. In developing, this latent image is converted to a permanent, negative image is converted to a permanent, negative image of light and dark areas. Film for colour PHOTOGRAPHY has three emulsion layers, each sensitive to one of the three primary colours. Films of different speeds have different sensitivities to light: a fast film is very sensitive and so can be used with lower light levels, but it gives a coarser (grainier) picture quality.

filtration The separation of suspended solids from their suspending liquid by passing the suspension through a porous medium. Filtration is a widely used separation and purification procedure in the laboratory and industry: it is used in the manufacture of chemicals and biological substances, in food processing, in PAPER MANUFACTURE, and in water and sewage treatment. Paper, cloth, and fine wire mesh are simple filtration media. Until recently asbestos was used in most types of filter, but its health hazards have led to the development of alternative materials. Filtration apparatus can vary from a simple paper filter in a funnel, to filter beds many square metres in area, or mechanized filtration drums or belts. The suspension or slurry may be forced through the filter under pressure, or a vacuum may be used to draw material through the filter.

Ultrafiltration is the separation of large molecules or particles of colloidal size from a liquid medium, using a thin, semi-permeable cellulose acetate or other filtration membrane supported on a porous substructure. Flow rates are much higher than in conventional filtration, and a cake of solid residue is not formed on the filter surface. Ultrafiltration is widely used to separate proteins from solution: the process can be used in cream-cheese making.

fin A flattened appendage used in swimming, and most highly evolved in fishes. The fins of fishes are essentially double flaps of skin, with a skeletal support of bony elements in bony fishes, and of cartilage in sharks, skates, and rays. In bony fishes, especially, the fins can be erected and depressed and some can be moved by means of muscles attached to the bony rays. These rays are of two types: spines, which are strong and sharp and usually found in the anterior of the dorsal and anal fins; and soft or branched rays, which are segmented and finely divided to their tips.

Fins are named according to their position on the fish's body. The single or multiple dorsal fin runs along the back; the anal fin projects from behind the vent or anus. The tail or caudal fin provides the chief propelling motion in swimming, while the paddle-like pectoral fins (each side behind the head) and pelvic fins (beneath the belly) keep the swimming fish in a level posture.

The fin-like flippers of seals, whales, and dolphins have a very different structure. They are essentially modified limbs of the typical terrestrial mammal and have a bony skeleton.

finch Any of several small, stout-billed birds, but primarily the Fringillidae, a group of about 120 species including canaries, serins, grosbeaks, and crossbills as well as finches. Most species occur in the Old World, but a small number are found in the Americas. Most are sparrow-sized, though many are stockily built and have very stout beaks for opening the seeds upon which they feed. The hawfinch, *Coccothraustes coccothraustes*, can split open olive-stones.

fin-de-siècle (French, 'end-of-century') The end of the 19th century, when European writers and such artists as WILDE, BEARDSLEY, and the French SYMBOLISTS, under the slogan 'art for art's sake', adopted a 'decadent' rejection of any social or moral function for art. Reacting against REALISM and naturalism, they sought a 'pure' beauty removed from nature and contemporary society.

Fine Gael (Gaelic, 'United Ireland') Irish political party. Founded in 1922 as Cumann na nGaedheal, it changed its name in 1933. It originated among supporters of the Anglo-Irish Treaty that created the IRISH FREE STATE. William COSGRAVE was its leader (1922–44). Fine Gael was in power as the dominant element in a coalition from 1948 to 1951, with John Costello as its leader. This government in 1949 declared Ireland to be a republic. Since then, Fine Gael has been intermittently in power (1954–57, 1973–77, 1981–82, 1982–87, 1994–97), but has required coalition support to remain so. It has advocated the concept of a united Ireland achieved by peaceful means.

finfoot A bird of the family Heliornithidae. One species is found in tropical America, *Heliornis fulica*, one in tropical Africa, *Podica senegalensis*, and a third in south-east Asia, *Heliopais personata*. Rather like small brown or black cormorants, they are up to 60 cm (2 feet) long, but with large lobes on each toe, rather than webbed feet. They live on streams and in marshes, often within forests, and eat insects, small fish, and amphibia. They build nests of twigs or reeds in low bushes and lay four or five eggs. The young stay in the nest until quite well grown.

Fingal's Cave A cave on Staffa Island in the Inner Hebrides of Scotland, famous for the clustered basaltic pillars that are its cliffs. It is said to have been the inspiration for Mendelssohn's overture *The Hebrides*, but in fact he noted down the principal theme before his visit to Staffa in 1829.

finger Part of the hand made of the phalangeal bones. Many animals use fingers for grasping, but man is unique among mammals, including apes, because of the ability to oppose thumbs to little fingers. This, among other finger and palm movements, allows humans to hold objects in their palms and to delicately manipulate tools. Fingers and thumbs are moved by numerous small muscles lying in the hands, assisted by the tendons of muscles in the forearm. The skin and muscles of the fingers are well supplied with nerves to permit the recognition of textures and shapes and to allow fine and delicate movement. Each person has a unique set of FINGERPRINT patterns, each finger often having a different pattern.

fingerprint An impression left by the finger tips. Since no two people share the same fingerprints, it is a widespread means of identification, used in particular by the police (since 1901 in the UK) to identify criminals. In most countries a central fingerprint record is kept of those convicted of serious offences so that matches may be made when the police investigate new crimes. See also DNA FINGERPRINTING.

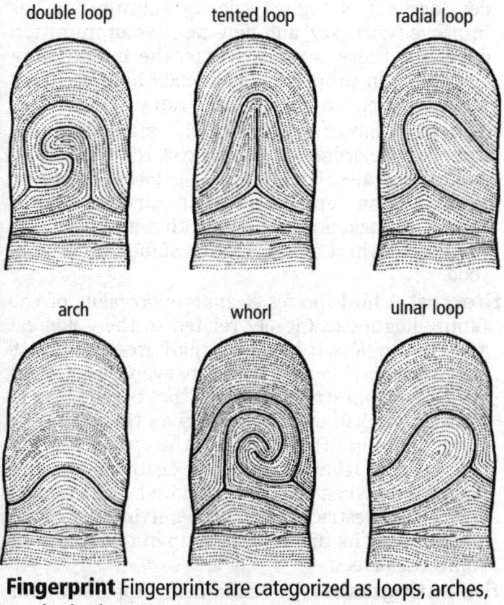

Fingerprint Fingerprints are categorized as loops, arches, or whorls; the most common types are shown here.

Finland (Finnish **Suomi**) A Baltic country, sometimes considered part of SCANDINAVIA. It is bounded by Norway on the north, Sweden and the Gulf of Bothnia on the west, and Russia on the east.

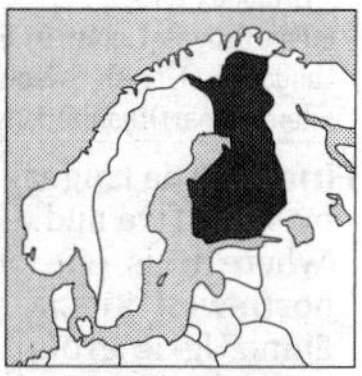

Physical. A long coastline round the west and south, studded with over 6,000 Åland islands, thrusts into the Baltic Sea. Of the rolling, granitic land area, of which the Fennoscandian Shield forms part, only a tenth is cultivable, some 70 per cent being coniferous forest, 11 per cent tundra, and 9 per cent lakes. Its 60,000 lakes are linked by short rivers, sounds, or canals to form busy waterways. A third of the country lies north of the Arctic Circle and is part of LAPLAND.

Economy. Finland is an industrialized country with little agriculture. Owing to its extensive forests paper, timber, and wood-pulp are significant exports. Other industry includes shipbuilding, and the manufacture of machinery, steel, clothing, and chemicals. The only significant mineral resources are chromium and copper.

History. Occupied between 100 and 800 AD by Finno-Ugrian tribes who drove the original Lapp population into its northernmost regions, Finland was conquered and converted to Christianity by Eric IX of Sweden in the late 1150s, and throughout the Middle Ages found itself at the centre of Swedish-Russian rivalry in the Baltic area. In 1556 Gustavus Vasa made Finland into a separate duchy for his second son John, and following the latter's succession to the Swedish throne as John III in 1568 it was elevated to a grand duchy. Although still dominated by Sweden, Finland was allowed its own Diet and granted a degree of autonomy.

However, the Treaty of Tilsit (1807) between Tsar Alexander I and Napoleon led to the annexation of Finland as a grand duchy of Russia until 1917. Attempts to impose the Russian language and military conscription brought discontent and the RUSSIAN REVOLUTION of 1917 offered opportunities for national assertion. Independence was achieved (1919) under Marshal Mannerheim, and a democratic, republican constitution introduced. In 1920 Finland joined the League of Nations, which achieved one of its few successes in resolving the ÅLAND ISLANDS dispute. After the Nazi–Soviet Pact of 1939, Finland was invaded in the FINNISH-RUSSIAN WAR (1939–40). Finnish resistance excited international admiration but no practical help, and surrender entailed a considerable loss of territory (Karelia and Petsamo). When Germany invaded the Soviet Union in 1941 the Finns sought to regain these territories by fighting on the side of the AXIS POWERS, but capitulated to the Soviet Union in 1944 and were burdened with a huge reparations bill. Since World War II Finland has accepted neutrality in international affairs. In January 1992 the Treaty of Friendship, Co-operation, and Mutual Assistance (1948) with the former Soviet Union was replaced by a new treaty with Russia. Finland's economy suffered from the collapse of eastern European markets, and austerity measures were introduced in April 1992. In 1995 Finland became a member of the EUROPEAN UNION.

Capital: Helsinki
Area: 338,145 sq km (130,559 sq mi)
Population: 5,101,000 (1995)

Currency: 1 Markka = 100 pennia
Religions: Evangelical Lutheran 88.9%; Finnish (Greek) Eastern Orthodox 1.1%
Ethnic Groups: Finnish 93.6%; Swedish 6.1%; Lapp (Saami) minority
Languages: Finnish, Swedish (both official); Lapp (Saami)
International Organizations: UN; EU; OECD; Council of Europe; CSCE

Finnish The language of the Finns, which is spoken by some five and a half million people in Finland (where it is one of the two official languages), north-west Russia, and Sweden. It belongs to the Finno-Ugric group, is related to Estonian, and is noted for its complexity; a Finnish noun has 15 different case forms.

Finnish-Russian War (or **Winter War**) (1939–40) A war fought between Finland and the Soviet Union. The Finnish government under General Mannerheim had rejected Soviet demands for bases and for frontier revisions similar to those accepted by the lesser BALTIC STATES. Soviet armies attacked on three fronts, and at first the Finns' superior skill in manoeuvring on skis on the frozen lakes and across the Gulf of Finland, and in the forests of their country, kept the Soviet forces at bay. After fifteen weeks of fierce fighting the Soviets breached the Mannerheim Line and Finland was forced to accept peace on Stalin's terms, ceding its eastern territories and the port of Viipuri (Viborg).

Finno-Ugric (or **Finno-Ugrian**) A group of Ural-Altaic languages, divided into Finnish languages (of which the most important are Finnish and Estonian), and Ugrian (or Ugric) languages of which the most important is Hungarian. The languages are also spoken in scattered areas of central Russia, which is thought to be the original homeland of their speakers.

fin whale (or **common rorqual**) A species, *Balenoptera physalus*, of whalebone whale. It is the fastest of all the whales, swimming at speeds of 48 km/hour (30 miles per hour). The fin whale is greyish in colour and white below, with a long, slender body, and can reach a length of 24 m (80 feet). Mating occurs in warmer seas during winter, before it moves north or south to the polar regions. Ten or twelve months later it returns to calve in tropical waters.

Finzi, Gerald (Raphael) (1901–56) British composer. His *Dies natalis* for tenor and strings (1939) attracted attention, as did the collections of songs that emerged thereafter – particularly the settings of the poetry of Thomas Hardy. His few larger works include a clarinet (1949) and a cello (1956) concerto.

fiord (or **fjord**) A long, narrow inlet of sea between high cliffs, the result of glacial erosion, as in Norway.

fir Any of a number of species of CONIFER, but more properly the 50 or so species of *Abies*, a genus of the north temperate zone and Central America. All are evergreen, with needles borne directly on the stems and not on short side shoots like those of pines and cedars. The silver fir, *A. alba*, of the mountains of southern Europe, provides turpentine as well as good timber. The turpentine of *A. balsamea*, the balsam fir of eastern North America, is known as Canada balsam. Many species are cultivated for ornament as well as for timber.

fire A chemical reaction accompanied by the evolution of gas, heat, and light. The visible manifestation of fire, the flame, occurs when excited atoms or molecules in the hot gas release some of their energy in the form of light (when orbital electrons in these atoms fall from higher to lower energy levels). In most fires the chemical reaction is one in which a combustible material combines with the oxygen in the air. The light produced can be analysed to provide information about the nature of the substances present in the flame. See COMBUSTION.

firearm A hand-weapon from which projectiles are propelled by the combustion of gunpowder or other explosives. The first firearms were smaller versions of CANNON, developed in the 14th century. From around 1425 the firing of such weapons was improved by the invention of the matchlock, a mechanism by which a slow-burning match was brought into precise contact with a small pan of priming powder: burning of the priming powder then ignited the main charge. In about 1515 a new ignition system, the wheel-lock, was developed in Germany. It generated a series of sparks in the priming pan by the movement of a spring-wound serrated wheel against a piece of iron pyrites (like the flint in some cigarette lighters). A simpler ignition method, the flint-lock, used a flint held in a sprung lever, which was struck against a piece of steel to produce sparks. Flintlocks began to be adopted on a large scale in the late 17th century. In the mid-16th century, rifling of the barrels of small weapons was first introduced.

Early in the 19th century the first percussion-ignition systems appeared, using a DETONATOR activated by a sharp blow. CARTRIDGES containing a fixed explosive charge also began to be widely used at about this time. Another major 19th-century advance was the general adoption of breech-loading weapons, as opposed to muzzle-loaders in which charge and shot had to be inserted down the barrel. Centre-fire metal cartridges of the type familiar today were introduced in about 1870. In the last half of the 19th century, the MACHINE-GUN was developed.

In the 20th century firearm design changed little until World War II, when the pistol was superseded by the SUB-MACHINE-GUN, and semi-automatic rifles were introduced. Since World War II there have been many design innovations. Most modern rifles are fully automatic (that is, they continue to fire as long as the trigger is held back) and double as light machine-guns, while sub-machine-guns are now extremely light and compact. The development of higher velocity ammunition has improved accuracy, and new caseless ammunition (in which there is no cartridge, the bullet being embedded in propellant) has made high accuracy possible at extremely rapid fire rates.

firebrat A larger relative of the SILVERFISH, an insect of the order Thysanura, covered with white and black scales. The firebrat, *Thermobia domestica*, needs a high temperature for survival, and is found in bakehouses, large kitchens, and old fireplaces, where it lives on residues of human food.

firecrest A bird species, *Regulus ignicapillus*, of the family Regulidae. Closely related to the goldcrest and the kinglets, it is a very small greenish bird, 9 cm (3.5 inches) long, with a white eye-stripe. On the crown is a bold stripe of colour that is yellowish in females, reddish in males, and gives the species its common name. This stripe on the crown is often concealed by the other crown feathers and displayed only when the bird is excited. The firecrest is virtually restricted to Europe, living in forests and building its tiny nest high up in the canopy of coniferous trees.

fire-extinguisher A hand-held appliance for putting out fires. Different types of extinguisher are available for different kinds of fire. Each extinguisher operates on one or more of three basic principles: the burning material is extinguished by cooling; the fire is blanketed by an inert gas that excludes air; or the air supply is cut off by some solid material such as sand or a fireproof blanket. Water is the most widely used fire-quenching agent. It is applied as a fine spray or fog using carbon dioxide gas, generated within the appliance to expel it from the container. It has a cooling effect and the steam produced helps blanket the fire. Water cannot be used, however, on electrical fires or those involving magnesium alloys, which it aggravates, nor in freezing conditions, unless some antifreeze agent is included. In such cases, a dry chemical extinguisher is needed. This normally contains powdered sodium bicarbonate, which both blankets the fire and generates carbon dioxide, to exclude air. Fire-extinguishers using CHLOROFLUOROCARBONS (CFCs) are used for specific risks, such as computer suites. Replacement extinguishing media are being sought, mainly as a result of the adverse environmental effects of CFCs.

fire-fighting The techniques used to extinguish or control fires. Fire-fighting involves two principal approaches. One is the use of permanently installed equipment, notably sprinkler systems, set to function automatically in response to SMOKE DETECTORS or thermal sensors. The other is based on the mobile fire-engine and ancillary equipment. For a blazing building the fire-engine must provide an extendable, manœuvrable ladder, and a variety of emergency apparatus. This will include hand-held fire hoses supplied from hydrants, and FIRE-EXTINGUISHERS; axes, saws, and other tools for effecting forced entry if necessary; and breathing apparatus to make it possible to enter areas full of smoke or noxious fumes. Structural fires are commonly fought by an over-and-under method, that is, ventilating the fire from below to prevent smoke and heat build-up, while aiming hoses at a level above the fire to prevent its spreading.

Large forest fires cannot usually be extinguished by direct means. Rather, they are contained within a limited area until they burn out, by cutting fire breaks and starting backfires to remove combustible fuel from the path of the fire; by using large teams of volunteers to beat out subsidiary fires; and by dropping water slurries from aircraft on to surrounding vegetation. A fire at an oil or gas well must be 'capped' to exclude oxygen, a job usually requiring a specialist trouble-shooting team.

firefly A soft-bodied, usually brown or black, nocturnal BEETLE of the family Lampyridae. Fireflies are luminous as adults and sometimes as larvae. In some species, such as the glow-worms, *Lampyris* species, the females are wingless and look like larvae. The 1,700 species of fireflies and glow-worms are widely distributed, but particularly numerous in warm climates and damp places. The luminous organs are often borne on the last few segments of the abdomen and the colour, intensity, and intervals of flashing are particular to each species. The light production is often synchronized, and all members of the same species may flash together. Members of several other groups of beetles, such as the cucujos and other CLICK BEETLES, are luminous and sometimes called fireflies.

Fire of London A major fire that devastated London in September 1666. The fire began in a baker's shop and, fanned by an east wind, raged for four days, destroying 87 churches, including St Paul's, and more than 13,000 houses mostly built from wood. It was stopped by blowing up buildings in its path. There are eyewitness accounts in the diaries of PEPYS and EVELYN. Plans for a modern city with wide streets and squares were abandoned, but Sir Christopher Wren rebuilt St Paul's and a number of other churches and public buildings, and designed the Monument (1677) which commemorates the fire.

fireproofing The treatment of flammable materials to reduce the risk of fire. Although many materials are combustible, fireproofing is most commonly identified with wood, plastics, and textiles. Wood in thick sections is surprisingly fire-resistant because it is a poor conductor of heat; however, resistance can be much improved by impregnation with certain chemicals, such as ammonium phosphate or borax. For fireproofing plastics and textiles, organic phosphorus compounds are widely used, but they are subject to certain constraints. They must, for example, be resistant to laundering and, in the case of clothing, be non-irritant.

fireweed See WILLOWHERB.

firework A device that produces coloured flames and explosions in a variety of ways, often used to create a spectacular display against a night sky, but also as distress rockets or flares, or to locate targets in military operations. Fireworks are ignited by lighting a fuse, the heat from which initiates a chemical reaction between components packed in a paper or cardboard tube. The colour of the flame can be varied by including metal salts – for example, strontium produces brick red, and barium gives green. The addition of metal powders produces sparks, and the inclusion of small quantities of explosives results in loud bangs. Components that burn with a sustained and rapid evolution of gas are used in rockets.

firn (Swiss French **névé**) Granular snow which is half-way to becoming glacier ice. Often buried by new falls, it is old snow which has been partly melted and re-frozen. This process joins the particles together into granules, but still leaves air pockets between them.

First Point of Aries The point of intersection of the celestial equator and the ECLIPTIC where the Sun crosses the equator from south to north. The Sun reaches the First Point of Aries about 21 March, the time of the vernal (spring) EQUINOX. Over the past 2,000 years the First Point of Aries has moved westwards along the ecliptic from Aries to its present location in Pisces by PRECESSION at a rate of some 50 arc seconds per year.

First Point of Libra The point of intersection of the celestial equator and the ECLIPTIC where the Sun crosses the equator from north to south. The Sun reaches the First Point of Libra about 21 September, the time of the autumnal EQUINOX. Because of the PRECESSION of the equinoxes the First Point of Libra slips westwards along the ecliptic at a rate of some 50 arc seconds per year.

first quarter See PHASE.

First World War See WORLD WAR I.

Fischer, Bobby (born Robert James Fischer) (1943–) US chess player. He was world champion 1972–75 after defeating Boris Spassky whom he beat again in a 1992 rematch.

Fischer, Emil Hermann (1852–1919) German organic chemist. He studied the structure of sugars, other carbohydrates, and purines, and synthesized many of them. He also worked on peptides and proteins, and confirmed that they consist of chains of amino acids. Fischer's work was to a large extent the basis for the German drug industry, and he was awarded the Nobel Prize for chemistry in 1902.

Fischer, Hans (1881–1945) German organic chemist. His work was largely concerned with the porphyrin group of natural pigments. He determined the complex structure of the red oxygen-carrying part of haemoglobin, the green chlorophyll pigments found in plants, and the orange bile pigment bilirubin. He also synthesized some of these, and was awarded the Nobel Prize for chemistry in 1930.

Fischer-Dieskau, Dietrich (1925–) German baritone. Noted for his interpretations of German lieder, in particular Schubert's song cycles, he made more recordings of songs than any other recording artist and had a very large vocal repertoire.

Fischer-Tropsch process See SYNTHETIC FUEL.

fish An aquatic vertebrate that obtains its oxygen by means of gills. There are three major groups: JAWLESS FISH, CARTILAGINOUS FISH, and BONY FISH.

Most fishes are predatory, and very few subsist wholly on plant material, although some eat both plants and animals. Most lay eggs, usually very numerous, which are typically shed in the water and are unprotected; but parental care of eggs is frequent, either in nests, by mouth brooding, or by brooding by the male. See also FISHING INDUSTRY.

fish curing Processing designed to preserve raw fish from spoilage. The three main fish curing methods are drying, salt curing, and smoking, all of which lower the food's water content and thus greatly inhibit the activity of spoilage bacteria and enzymes. In suitable climates, gutted fish will dry in the open air in about six weeks. In salt curing, the fish are placed in dry salt after removal of the head and backbone. This draws out the moisture and produces brine. The fish are then either pickled by storing in brine or are removed and dried. The first stage in smoking is to cut up the fish and soak them in brine. They are then dried by hanging in the flues of ovens fuelled by smouldering hardwood chips. Fish may artificially be given the appearance and flavour of being smoked by pickling in solutions containing dyes and other chemicals.

Fisher, St John (1469–1535) English churchman. In 1504 he became bishop of Rochester and earned the disfavour of Henry VIII by opposing his divorce from Catherine of Aragon. When he refused to accept the king as supreme head of the Church, he was condemned to death. Feast day, 22 June.

Fisher, Sir Ronald Aylmer (1890–1962) British geneticist and statistician, who wrote *Statistical Methods for Research Workers* (1925), which was extremely influential in biological research. It was followed by *The Genetical Theory of Natural Selection* (1930), putting forward his views on eugenics and contributing greatly to the study of population genetics.

fish-farming A branch of AQUACULTURE involving the rearing of fish under controlled conditions. Ideally, the environment is controlled so that natural predators are eliminated, optimum nutrition is provided, and the fish flourish. Until recently, the main commercial interest was in fresh-water fish-farming of carp, catfish, gourami, milk-fish, salmon, tilapia, and trout. Marine farming, especially of salmon, is now increasing, and crustaceans and molluscs are also farmed in specialist SHELLFISH farming.

fishing The pastime of catching fish, usually with a rod and line, when it is also known as **angling**. Most fishermen specialize in the fish they try to catch – game (salmon, trout), coarse (other freshwater species), or sea fish – and this determines the type and weight of rod they choose, and whether they use edible bait (bait-fishing), natural or artificial flies (fly-fishing), or a fish or metal lure made up to resemble a fish (bait-casting or spinning, and trolling). In colder climates, ice-fishing through a hole bored in the ice is a popular winter pastime.

fishing industry The catching, processing, marketing, and conservation of fish and shellfish. The major fish types caught are demersal fish, living on or near the sea-bed, and pelagic fish, which live in the open sea near the surface. Specialized aspects of the fishing industry deal with molluscs (squid, cuttlefish, octopus, bivalves, and gastropods), crustaceans (crabs, lobsters, crayfish, shrimps, and prawns), mammals (whales, dolphins, seals, and walruses), amphibians, worms, coelenterates, and sponges. Products are sold fresh, frozen, or canned, or are cured by drying, salting, or smoking (see FISH CURING). One-third of the global catch (around 95 million tonnes per year) is used to produce animal feed and other fish products. The main source of fish is the oceans; less than 14 per cent of fish come from freshwater sources. AQUACULTURE, FISH-FARMING, and SHELLFISH farming also make a significant contribution. The majority of the ocean harvest comes from the shallow waters over continental shelves. China is the leading fishing country, followed by Peru, Japan, Chile, the USA, and Russia.

There are many types of fishing vessel, each suited to the type of fish sought, their location, and the duration of fishing voyages. Coastal vessels are between 8 and 40 m (25–130 feet) long with a crew of up to 25. The catch is stored in refrigerated holds and processed on land. Small TRAWLERS fish in shallow waters, such as the North Sea and the English Channel. Long-range fishing fleets stay at sea for months and travel great distances. These factory fleets include processor–catcher vessels with crews of 50–100 people, which can process thousands of tonnes of catch per day. They are supported by refrigerated transporters and supply ships. Fishing gear is suited to the type of fish sought, for example, seine, trawl, and gill nets, longlines, traps, and harpoons. Other fishing methods include fishing with trained animals (for example, otters and cormorants in China); stunning, spearing, or poisoning fish; and the use of harvesting machines such as mechanized dredgers, or gear that separates the catch from the water using pumps.

fission, nuclear The splitting of a heavy atomic nucleus into two approximately equal parts, with the emission of neutrons and large amounts of heat and nuclear RADIATION. Fission can occur spontaneously, or may be induced by the impact of a neutron, an energetic charged particle, or a photon. The only naturally occurring fissionable material is an isotope of URANIUM, U-235. U-235 is most easily split by slow, low-energy neutrons. In natural uranium only about one atom in 140 is U-235; the major isotope is U-238, which is non-fissionable. Natural uranium does not sustain a CHAIN REACTION, in which the splitting of one atom provides at least one neutron for splitting another. This is because U-238 tends to absorb neutrons released by fission before they can split another atom. Two

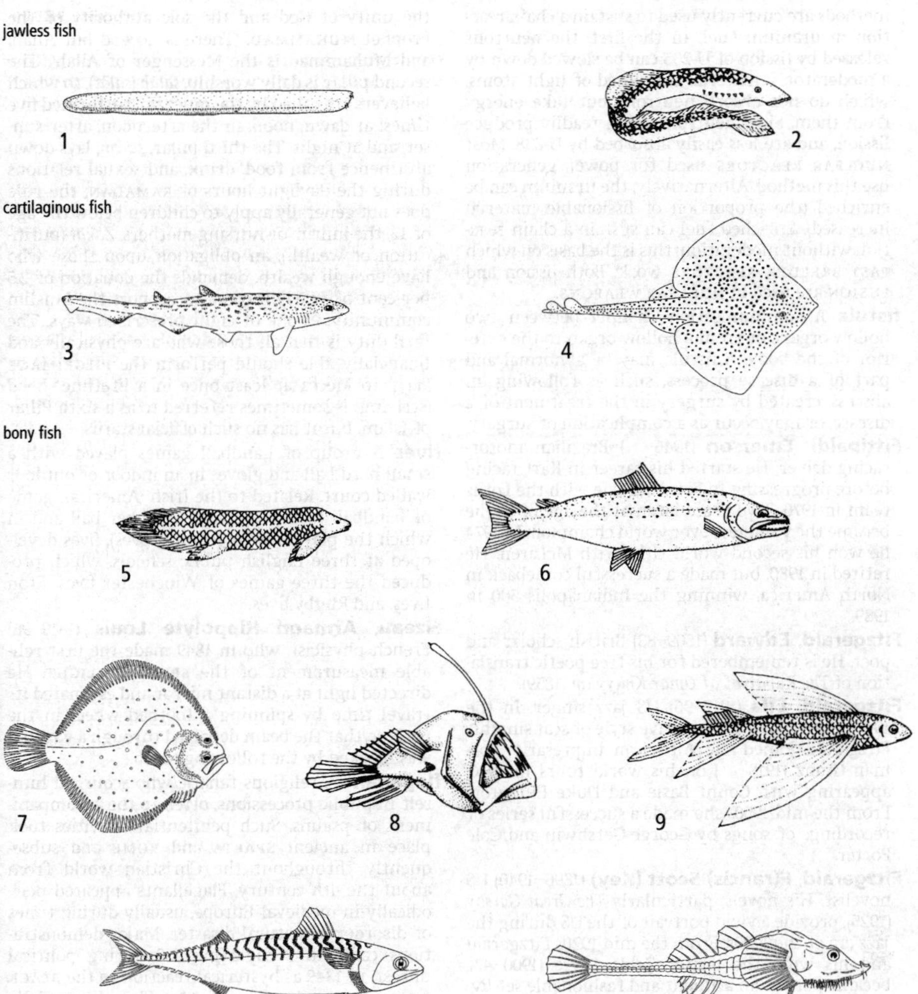

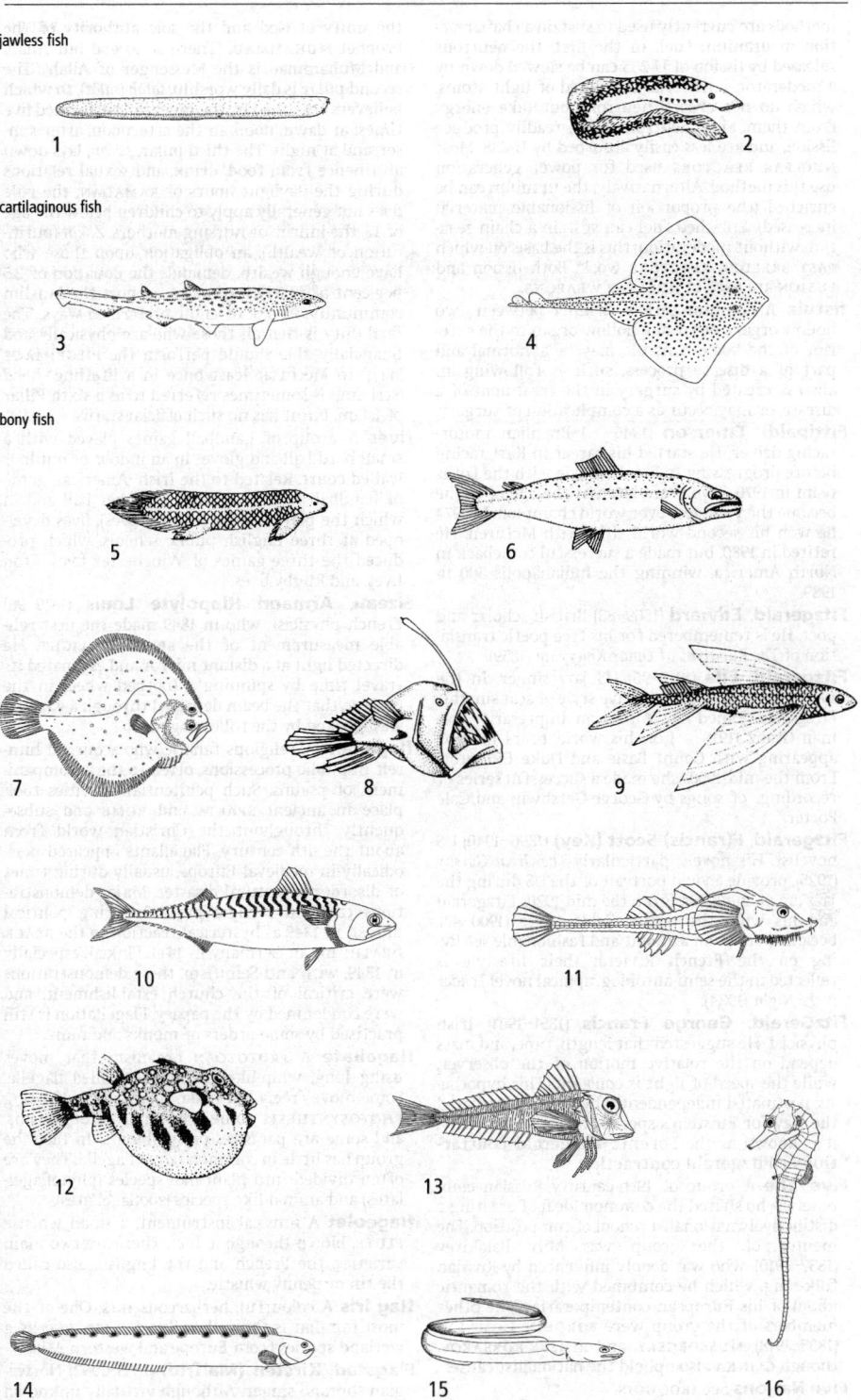

Fish (1) Hagfish. (2) Lamprey. (3) Dogfish. (4) Ray. (5) Lungfish. (6) Salmon. (7) Turbot. (8) Anglerfish. (9) Flying fish. (10) Mackerel. (11) Hook-nose. (12) Pufferfish. (13) Gurnard. (14) Gunnel. (15) Eel. (16) Sea horse.

methods are currently used to sustain a chain reaction in uranium fuel. In the first, the neutrons released by fission of U-235 can be slowed down by a moderator, a material composed of light atoms, which do not absorb neutrons but take energy from them. Slow neutrons more readily produce fission, and are less easily absorbed by U-238. Most NUCLEAR REACTORS used for power generation use this method. Alternatively, the uranium can be enriched (the proportion of fissionable material increased). Enriched fuel can sustain a chain reaction without moderation: this is the basis on which FAST BREEDER REACTORS work. Both fission and FUSION are used in NUCLEAR WEAPONS.

fistula A communication channel between two hollow organs or from a hollow organ to the exterior of the body. A fistula may be abnormal and part of a disease process, such as following an abscess, created by surgery in the treatment of a disease, or may occur as a complication of surgery.

Fittipaldi, Emerson (1946–) Brazilian motor-racing driver. He started his career in Kart racing before progressing to Formula One with the Lotus team in 1970. Two years later, at the age of 25, he became the youngest-ever world champion. In 1974 he won his second world title, with McLaren. He retired in 1980, but made a successful comeback in North America, winning the Indianapolis 500 in 1989.

Fitzgerald, Edward (1809–83) British scholar and poet. He is remembered for his free poetic translation of *The Rubáiyát of Omar Khayyám* (1859).

Fitzgerald, Ella (1917–96) US jazz singer. In the 1940s she evolved a distinctive style of scat singing. Fitzgerald joined the American impresario Norman Granz (1918–) on his world tours in 1946, appearing with Count Basie and Duke Ellington. From the mid-1950s she made a successful series of recordings of songs by George Gershwin and Cole Porter.

Fitzgerald, F(rancis) Scott (Key) (1896–1940) US novelist. His novels, particularly *The Great Gatsby* (1925), provide a vivid portrait of the US during the jazz era of the 1920s. From the mid-1920s Fitzgerald and his wife, the writer Zelda Sayre (1900–47), became part of an affluent and fashionable set living on the French Riviera; their lifestyle is reflected in the semi-autobiographical novel *Tender is the Night* (1934).

FitzGerald, George Francis (1851–1901) Irish physicist. He suggested that length, time, and mass depend on the relative motion of the observer, while the speed of light is constant. This hypothesis, postulated independently by Lorentz, prepared the way for Einstein's special theory of relativity; it is known as the **Lorentz–Fitzgerald contraction** or **Fitzgerald contraction**.

Five, The A group of 19th-century Russian composers, who shared the common ideal of creating a distinctively nationalist school of composition. The mentor of the group was Mily Balakirev (1837–1910), who was deeply influenced by Russian folk-song, which he combined with the romantic idiom of his European contemporaries. The other members of the group were BORODIN, César Cui (1835–1918), MUSSORGSKY, and RIMSKY-KORSAKOV, though GLINKA also upheld the nationalist cause.

Five Nations See IROQUOIS.

Five Pillars of Islam The basic duties and religious observances of ISLAM. The first pillar, *īmān* (faith), prescribes regular recitation of the *shahādah*, a summarized confession of belief, itself often referred to as the first pillar, which affirms the unity of God and the sole authority of the Prophet MUHAMMAD: 'There is no god but Allah; and Muhammad is the Messenger of Allah'. The second pillar is daily worship, *salāh* (*salāt*), to which believers are called by the muezzin, performed five times: at dawn, noon, in the afternoon, after sunset, and at night. The third pillar, *sawm*, lays down abstinence from food, drink, and sexual relations during the daylight hours of RAMADAN; the rule does not generally apply to children below the age of 12, the infirm, or nursing mothers. *Zakāt* (purification of wealth), an obligation upon those who have enough wealth, demands the donation of 2.5 per cent of yearly income to support the Muslim community, in one of eight prescribed ways. The final duty is that all those who are physically and financially able should perform the PILGRIMAGE (*hajj*) to Mecca at least once in a lifetime. *Jihad* (striving) is sometimes referred to as a sixth Pillar of Islam, but it has no such official status.

fives A group of handball games played with a small hard ball and gloves in an indoor or outdoor walled court. Related to the Irish–American game of handball (which employs a rubber ball and in which the players wear softer gloves), fives developed at three English public schools, which produced the three games of Winchester fives, Eton fives, and Rugby fives.

Fizeau, Armand Hippolyte Louis (1819–96) French physicist, who in 1849 made the first reliable measurement of the SPEED OF LIGHT. He directed light at a distant mirror and estimated its travel time by spinning a toothed wheel in the path, so that the beam departed through a gap and was blocked by the following tooth.

flagellant A religious fanatic who scourged himself in public processions, often to the accompaniment of psalms. Such penitential activities took place in ancient SPARTA and ROME and subsequently throughout the Christian world from about the 4th century. Flagellants appeared periodically in medieval Europe, usually during times of disorder or natural disaster. Major demonstrations came in Perugia in 1260 during political unrest; in 1349 as hysterical reaction to the BLACK DEATH; and in Germany in 1414. Linked, especially in 1349, with anti-Semitism, these demonstrations were critical of the church establishment, and were condemned by the papacy. Flagellation is still practised by some orders of monks and nuns.

flagellate A PROTOZOAN organism that moves using long, whip-like appendages called flagella. Some move freely but make their own food using PHOTOSYNTHESIS; some prey on other organisms; and some are parasites or symbionts. In fact the group has little in common *except* flagella. They are often divided into plant-like species (phytoflagellates) and animal-like species (zooflagellates).

flageolet A musical instrument, a small whistle FLUTE, blown through a duct. There are two main varieties, the French and the English, also called the tin or penny whistle.

flag iris A colourful, herbaceous IRIS. One of the most familiar is the yellow flag, *Iris pseudacorus*, a wetland species from Europe and western Asia.

Flagstad, Kirsten (Malfrid) (1895–1962) Norwegian soprano singer. Although virtually unknown outside Scandinavia before 1932, reviews of her Isolde in Wagner's *Tristan and Isolde* in Oslo led to her engagement at Bayreuth (1933). After débuts in New York (1935) as Sieglinde in Wagner's *The Valkyrie*, and London (1936) as Isolde, her standing as an exponent of Wagner's great female roles was unchallenged until her retirement in 1953.

Flamboyant style The final phase of French Gothic architecture, so called because its most distinctive feature is elaborate TRACERY made up of flowing, flame-like shapes (French *flamboyant*, 'flaming'). The style began in about 1370, was almost ubiquitous in France by the mid-15th century, and gradually gave way to the RENAISSANCE style in the early 16th century.

flamboyant tree (or **poinciana**) An evergreen tree of the genus *Delonix*, belonging to the pea family. It is native to Madagascar but very rare there. It is widely cultivated throughout the tropics for its large, bright orange-red flowers. A second species, rarely cultivated, is native to East Africa.

flamenco A dance indigenous to southern Spain. It originates from the classic Moorish dance (itself influenced by dance from northern India) and from the dance and music of Spanish gypsies. These probably combined in the 15th century, when both Moors and gypsies took refuge from the Christians, and produced a dance of forceful rhythmic footwork and sinuous arm movements. During the 19th century it became a recognized art, with the dance inextricably connected to hand-clapping, song, and guitar-playing. Improvisation is stressed and there are two main styles, the serious *jondo*, and the light, sometimes humorous *chico*.

flame-thrower A weapon that shoots a stream of burning oil, petrol, or NAPALM. It was first used by the Germany Army in 1915. The typical layout incorporates one or more tanks of fuel, a cylinder of compressed gas, a flexible hose, and a trigger nozzle. The gas forces the fuel out of the hose, and the nozzle ignites it. Small flame-throwers can be carried on a soldier's back, while larger ones are mounted on tanks or armoured cars. Small flame-throwers can also be used to destroy weeds.

flamingo A water bird of a small family, Phoenicopteridae, of five species, remarkable for their exceptionally long necks and legs and unique crooked bills, which are held upside down to filter algae or small animals from mud and water. They are white or rosy pink in colour, with vivid crimson and black wings, and the largest stand about 150 cm (5 feet) high. They inhabit remote salt-water, brackish, or alkaline lakes and lagoons in flocks which frequently number many thousands. Breeding in dense colonies, they build nests of mud in the shape of truncated cones and nurse their young in creches.

Flamsteed, John (1646–1719) English astronomer. He was appointed the first Astronomer Royal at the Royal Greenwich Observatory, with the task of accurately providing the positions of stars for use in navigation. He eventually produced the first star catalogue, which gave the positions of nearly 3,000 stars. Flamsteed also worked on the motions of the Sun and Moon, tidal tables, and other measurements.

Flanders A medieval principality of Western Europe in the south-western part of the Low Countries, extending along the North Sea coast and lying west of the River Scheldt. Now divided between Belgium, France, and the Netherlands, Flanders developed in medieval times with the expansion of the textile trade. In 862 Baldwin Bras-de-Fer became the first Count of Flanders which was ruled in turn by France, Spain, and Austria. In 1815 that part of Flanders formerly held by the Austrian Habsburgs was granted to the Netherlands, the French having annexed western Flanders between 1668 and 1678. The area was the scene of considerable military activity during World War I when British troops held the sector of the Western Front round the town of Ypres.

flare A sudden disturbance in the Sun's upper CHROMOSPHERE in which a considerable release of energy heats the surrounding material, resulting in a brilliant flame-like cloud of gas. The increase to maximum brightness may be accompanied by the ejection of electrified particles such as protons, ions, and electrons. These particles travel at speeds sufficient to impinge upon the Earth's atmosphere. This heats the atmosphere and in addition causes geomagnetic storms and AURORAE.

flare star A star that exhibits sudden transient increases in its total brightness. Many stars, and particularly cool main-sequence stars of which the Sun is one, are flare stars. The irregularity and short duration of these stellar flares, and the exceedingly strong magnetic fields exhibited by some stars, suggests the phenomenon is akin to a solar FLARE. However, while the Sun's total brightness is enhanced by only 0.01 per cent during a solar flare, some flare stars more than double in brightness. These energetic outbursts last only a few minutes. Flare stars may have wholly convective interiors and this characteristic, together with the complex and strong magnetic fields, is believed to be the cause of the eruptions in these stars.

flash (in photography) An artificial light source giving a brief, very bright illumination, used for photography at night, or indoors, when natural light is insufficient. An electronic flash is produced by a high-voltage discharge between two electrodes, which are enclosed in a glass tube filled with an inert gas. Flash synchronization ensures that the duration of the flash coincides with the maximum opening of the camera shutter: when the shutter is fully open an electrical circuit is completed, and the flash is immediately fired.

flatfish One of some 500 species of mostly marine fishes living in the Atlantic, Indian, and Pacific oceans, in shallow water down to depths of 1,000 m (3,250 feet). Flatfishes include HALIBUT, PLAICE, FLOUNDER, SOLE, and TURBOT. They are not very abundant in deeper water and very few are known from the polar seas of the Arctic. Some soles and tongue-soles live in fresh water, and some, such as the European flounder, do so temporarily.

Flatfishes are distinguished by an asymmetric appearance, with both eyes on one side of the head, the mouth often twisted close to the eyes, and the dorsal and anal fins running along the edges of the body. The eyed side is coloured, the blind side white. Flatfishes are totally adapted to life on the sea-bed. Upon hatching, the larva is bilaterally symmetrical and swims upright, like other fish larvae. Early in its development one eye migrates across the roof of the skull to lie next to the other eye, and the young fish then turns and begins to swim on one side. Whether it is the left or the right eye that migrates varies according to species or groups of species, giving rise to left-eyed and right-eyed categories. The changes which follow this movement of the eye may cause the jaws to become twisted, the pectoral fin on the blind side to atrophy, and the nostrils to be differently developed.

flatworm Any member of the Platyhelminthes, a phylum of soft-bodied invertebrates that includes the free-living PLANARIANS (class Turbellaria) and the parasitic FLUKES (Trematoda) and TAPEWORMS (Cestoda). Flatworms are small, flattened, and very simply constructed to allow oxygen to diffuse into all parts of their body, as they have no COELOM or blood vessels. Most free-living forms have a blind-ending gut, so they are unable to eat large items of food. Some of the parasitic flatworms have no gut, and feed by absorption. These flatworms are adapted for rapid reproduction.

Flaubert, Gustave (1821–80) French novelist and short-story writer. A dominant figure in the French realist school, he achieved fame with his first published novel, *Madame Bovary* (1857). *Trois contes* (1877) demonstrates Flaubert's versatility with different modes of narrative and anticipates Maupassant's experiments with the short story.

flavour (in particle physics) A set of distinguishing properties of QUARKS and LEPTONS. Quarks have any of six flavours: u (up), d (down), c (charm), s (strangeness), b (bottom or beauty), and t (top). (All these names, like flavour itself, are arbitrary choices, and have nothing to do with the ordinary meanings of the words.) By extension the three kinds of leptons and their three neutrinos are regarded as flavours.

flavouring See FOOD ADDITIVE.

flax A fibre plant of the family Linaceae, *Linum usitatissimum*, which has been cultivated for thousands of years in the Mediterranean area and Europe generally. The best fibre is produced in cool, moist, temperate climates and from crops sown densely to induce slender, unbranched stems. To conserve the length of the fibres, the plants are harvested by pulling them out of the ground, complete with roots. The stems are then exposed to weather or water, and to bacteria, in order to disintegrate the woody material and much of the pectin, a process known as 'retting'. The stems are then 'scutched' – they are broken down mechanically to separate the fibres. For the finest YARNS, the separated fibres are drawn through a trough of warm water. They are then spun into yarn for making linen fabrics. Heavier yarns are spun dry and used for CANVASES. Maoris weave fine fabrics from New Zealand flax, *Phormium tenax*.

A faster-growing type, more adapted to the warmer climates of southern Asia and India, was selected for its seeds and is known as linseed. This seed is rich in a drying oil that is valuable as a solvent for paints and varnishes and is also rich in protein. Used in small quantities, after being boiled to remove poisonous compounds, the seed may be fed to cattle.

Flaxman, John (1755–1826) British sculptor, draughtsman, and designer, one of the leading figures of the NEOCLASSICAL movement. His sculpture includes some large groups with standing figures, but his best work is found in simpler and smaller church monuments, sometimes cut in low relief.

flea A small, brown, wingless insect belonging to the order Siphonaptera, which feeds by sucking blood from mammals and birds. There are about 1,400 species, some 60 of which occur in the British Isles. Being laterally compressed and hard, they move easily through fur and feathers; rows of backward-pointing spines and bristles, and strong claws, help them to cling to their host. Their mouthparts are modified for piercing, and injecting saliva containing anticoagulants simultaneously with sucking. All fleas have powerful legs, particularly the hind pair, and can jump more than 30 cm (12 inches) high, two hundred times their body length. Females require a blood meal before laying their eggs in the host's nest, or on the ground in their dwelling. The elongate, pale larvae are scavengers, feeding on detritus, and eventually they pupate in cocoons covered by debris. Vibration, even after years of dormancy, stimulates emergence of the adults, which are attracted by warmth. They can go several weeks before the first meal and between meals.

The cosmopolitan human flea, *Pulex irritans*, became associated with humans when they lived in caves. Modern homes are too clean and dry for larvae, and numbers have declined, though they thrive on pigs. Female jiggers, or chigoes, *Tunga penetrans*, found in many warm countries, burrow under the skin of humans and other animals, and swell into pea-sized egg sacs. Rat fleas, *Xenopsylla cheopis*, transmit the bacterium causing bubonic plague, while rabbit fleas, *Spilopsyllus cuniculi*, are the main VECTORS of myxomatosis.

fleabane A perennial herbaceous plant with showy, daisy-like flowers. This name is used for at least three genera of the sunflower family. The common fleabane of Europe is *Pulicaria dysenterica*, while the garden 'fleabanes' belong to the genus *Erigeron*. Others with this as part of their name include members of the genus *Inula*. The common fleabane was once used to treat skin disorders and dysentery.

Flecker, James (Herman) Elroy (1884–1915) British poet. His best-known works are the verse collection *The Golden Journey to Samarkand* (1913) and the poetic Eastern play *Hassan* (1922), for which Delius wrote incidental music.

Fleet Street A London street between the Strand and the City, in or near which most of the leading national newspapers formerly (until the mid-1980s when many papers moved out of central London) had offices, whence the allusive use of its name to refer to the British press. It is named after the River Fleet, which is now covered in.

Fleming, Sir Alexander (1881–1955) Scottish bacteriologist. He worked mainly at St Mary's Hospital, London, where he investigated the body's defences against bacteriological infection. In 1928 he fortuitously discovered the effect of penicillin on bacteria, and twelve years later Florey and Chain established its therapeutic use as an antibiotic. Fleming was jointly awarded a Nobel Prize in 1945.

Fleming, Ian (Lancaster) (1908–64) British novelist. He is known for the spy novels whose hero is the secret agent James Bond. Many of these stories (of which Fleming completed one a year from 1953 until his death) were successfully turned into feature films, making the character of James Bond world famous.

Fleming, Sir John Ambrose (1849–1945) British electrical engineer. He is chiefly remembered for his invention of the thermionic valve (1900), which was the basis for all electronic devices until the transistor began to supersede it more than fifty years later. He also worked on transformers, radiotelegraphy, and telephony.

Flemish Relating to Flanders, or its people or their language. Spoken by 57 per cent of the people of Belgium (mostly in the north), it is one of the two official languages of that country, the other being French. It is essentially the same language as Dutch; the apparent differences being a matter of spelling convention.

Flemish art The art of FLANDERS, an area of Europe corresponding with present-day Belgium and at times to certain other adjoining regions. In the field of 15th- and 16th-century art the terms Flemish and Netherlandish are often used interchangeably. The founding figure of Flemish painting, Jan van EYCK, combined the delicately detailed technique of the miniaturist with a new, searching naturalism. His successors included Rogier van der WEYDEN, who worked mainly in Brussels, and Hans MEMLINC, who worked mainly in Bruges. Standing somewhat apart from the main tradition was Hieronymus BOSCH, the greatest Flemish painter at the turn of the 16th century. In general the Flemish painters of the 16th century did not match the achievements of their 15th-century predecessors, but the great genius of the period, Pieter BRUEGEL the Elder, influenced his countrymen well into the 17th century with his brilliantly observed scenes of everyday life. The 17th century saw Flemish art invigorated by the genius of Rubens, who had wide influence. After the 17th century Flemish art played a fairly minor role in a European context, but there have been isolated modern artists of importance, for example James ENSOR and René MAGRITTE.

flesh fly A greyish fly of the family Sarcophagidae, with a dark-striped thorax and mottled abdomen. Eggs hatch within the female's body, and larvae are deposited on decaying animal matter. They liquefy this matter with regurgitated ENZYMES, and ingest it while buoyed up by fleshy lobes surrounding the posterior breathing tubes. Pupation takes place in the soil. Flesh flies belong to the same family as BLOW FLIES.

Fletcher, John (1579–1625) English dramatist. A writer of Jacobean tragicomedies, he wrote some fifteen plays with Francis Beaumont, including *The Maid's Tragedy* (1610–11). He is also believed to have collaborated with Shakespeare on such plays as *The Two Noble Kinsmen* and *Henry VIII* (both *c.*1613).

flicker See WOODPECKER.

flight (in animals) The mode of locomotion adopted by birds, bats, and insects. A few other animals have adaptations enabling them to glide (the FLYING FISH, FLYING LIZARD, and COLUGO, for example), but true flight is unique to the above groups. Mechanisms of insect flight differ from those of vertebrates.

Bird wings have an aerofoil cross-section: the top surface of the wing is convex; the lower surface concave. As air moves over them they generate lift. Many gulls, terns, swifts, and albatrosses are able to glide long distances by heading into winds and upcurrents, thus gaining lift. Where there are no air currents, or where extra lift is required, the wings have to be flapped. The secondary FEATHERS connected to the 'forearm' give the wing its aerofoil section. The primary feathers, attached to the 'hand', can be rotated for extra control and on some birds may separate on the upstroke of the wing to save energy. The wings are raised by the elevator muscles situated along the breastbone and connected via long tendons. The powerful depressor muscles, also along the breastbone, then sweep the wings downwards and backwards to give a thrust that provides both lift and propulsion. The tail feathers provide braking, balance, and steering.

flight, history of manned Although such aeronautical devices as the arrow, the KITE, and the BOOMERANG have been known since very early times, human flight was not realized until the 18th century. Research developed along two paths: lighter-than-air BALLOONS and AIRSHIPS, and heavier-than-air GLIDERS and AEROPLANES. Balloon flight was pioneered in France by the MONTGOLFIER brothers and the physicist J. A. C. Charles. After making several models, the Montgolfiers built a hot-air balloon that made the first ever human-carrying flight in 1783. Charles, on hearing of the Montgolfiers' experiments, independently developed a hydrogen-filled balloon, which flew on 1 December of the same year. Heavier-than-air flight was first extensively studied by CAYLEY, who researched many aspects of the theory of flight. The glider flights that he and others, such as LILIENTHAL, carried out in the second half of the 19th century contributed much to the knowledge of heavier-than-air flight.

By the mid-19th century the main stumbling-block to powered flights was the lack of a suitable engine. With the advent of the INTERNAL-COMBUSTION ENGINE in the late 1800s, developments occurred rapidly. By 1900 practical airships were being built in Germany by von ZEPPELIN, while the USA became the crucible for the development of heavier-than-air flight. Extensive experimental work by Samuel Langley (1834–1906) and Octave Chanute (1832–1910) provided the groundwork for the achievements of the WRIGHT brothers, who made the first sustained, powered human flight in an aeroplane in 1903.

World War I was a major period of development for military aviation. At the start of the War aircraft were used mainly for reconnaissance, but by 1918 all the major combatants had large fleets of fighter and bomber MILITARY AIRCRAFT with hugely improved performance. The late 1920s and early 1930s saw a revolution in aeroplane design, the 'stick-and-wire' biplanes being replaced by streamlined monoplanes of all-metal construction. This period also saw the rise of commercial aviation. Airmail services were pioneered in the USA, and by 1936 both Europe and America had extensive airline networks, using fleets of comfortable, purpose-built aircraft.

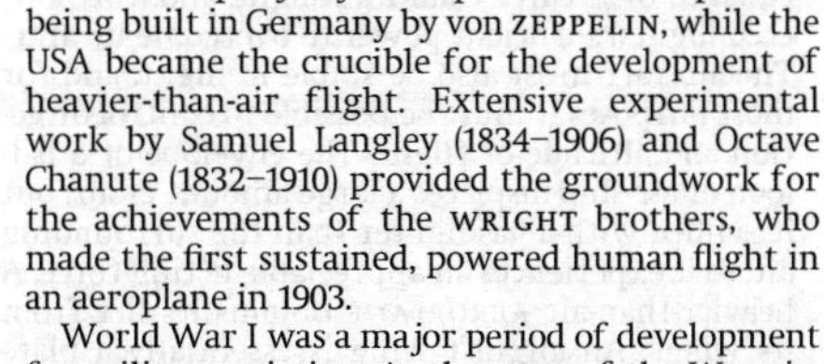

1

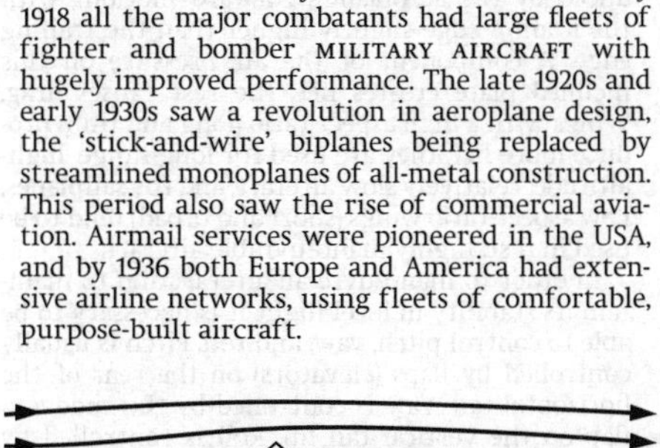

2

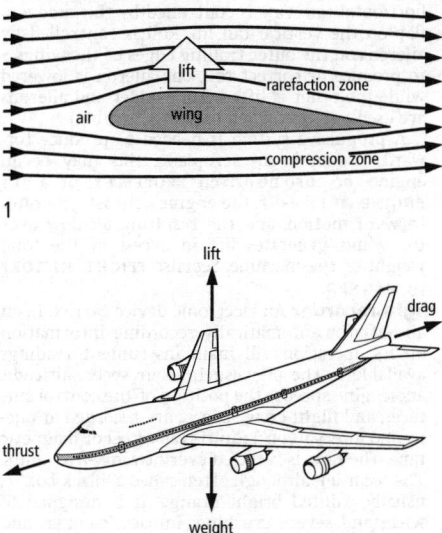

Flight (1) The lift on an aerofoil resulting from the compression zone below it and the rarefaction zone above it. (2) The four forces on a flying object. The thrust must exceed the drag for it to move forward; the lift must exceed the weight for it to stay airborne.

World War II provided another boost to aviation: huge numbers of military aircraft were produced, and there were innovations in design, materials, engines, and in the use of RADAR. Research into JET ENGINES and ROCKET MOTORS accelerated; by 1946 both the UK and Germany were producing jet fighter planes. After World War II jet aircraft gradually replaced propeller-driven aeroplanes in many contexts. SUPERSONIC FLIGHT was achieved in 1947, and produced radical changes in military and commercial aircraft design. In the 1960s the rapidly expanding space programmes and changes in military thinking shifted the emphasis in combat aircraft to low-level flying and electronic countermeasures.

flight, principles of manned For a heavier-than-air aircraft to fly, it must generate a lifting force equal to or greater than its weight, and (for powered flights) sufficient power to overcome its drag. The aircraft must also be stable in flight, and for most purposes it must be possible to control direction and altitude of flight. The envelope of a balloon or air-ship displaces a large amount of air, but it is filled with a gas lighter than the surrounding air, so it experiences an appreciable lifting force. A heavier-than-air AEROPLANE obtains its lift from its wings. An aircraft wing is essentially a plate presented edgewise to a moving air-stream (produced by the aeroplane's forward motion), with the leading edge slightly higher than the trailing edge. A component of the air pressure on this inclined plate creates lift; the rest causes drag. Wings with a high aspect ratio (long and thin) produce more lift: they are used for long-range, high-altitude, relatively slow aircraft, and for sailplanes. Low aspect-ratio wings (short and broad) tend to be used in fast, highly manœuvrable aircraft.

In order to manœuvre an aircraft and to maintain its stability in level flight it is necessary to be able to control pitch, yaw, and roll. Pitch is usually controlled by flaps (elevators) on the rear of the horizontal tail. Yaw is controlled by the rudder, a flap on the vertical tail fin. Roll is controlled by ailerons on the outer trailing edges of the wings – to produce or correct roll, one aileron is lowered while the other is lifted. The rudder and ailerons are used together when banking (turning).

A propulsive system is needed to produce forward motion in an aeroplane; this may be an engine- or turbine-driven PROPELLER, or a JET ENGINE. At take-off, the engine's thrust generates forward motion, and the resulting air-flow over the wings generates lift in excess of the total weight of the machine. See also FLIGHT, HISTORY OF MANNED.

flight recorder An electronic device carried in an aircraft for automatically recording information on its operation. All main instrument readings available to the pilot (such as air speed, altitude, and engine speeds), the position of the control surfaces, and flight-crew speech, are recorded at one-second intervals on a multi-track steel or magnetic tape. The tape is recycled every twenty-five hours. The recorder, although often called a 'black box', is usually painted bright orange; it is designed to withstand severe crushing, impact loadings, and fire. Flight recorders, which are urgently sought after a crash to provide information regarding the cause of the crash, are mandatory by international law on any aircraft certificated after 1969.

flight simulator A piece of electronic equipment that can simulate all the flying characteristics of aircraft. It was originally designed as a completely equipped cockpit in which to train pilots to fly by use of their instruments alone. By mounting the flight simulator on digitally controlled hydraulic support jacks the modern version can give a very real impression of movement. Projections or computer graphics that reproduce the effects experienced visually during take-off, flight, and landing, together with simulated systems, air-flow, and engine noise, can make a simulated flight appear very real, especially with the latest wide-angle displays. The instructor controls all these effects as well as the instruments displayed to the pilot. Simulators are used for initial pilot training, upgrading, training for emergencies, and for simulation of military combat missions.

Flinders, Matthew (1774–1814) British explorer. He explored the coast of New South Wales (1795–1800) before being commissioned by the Royal Navy to circumnavigate Australia (1801–03). During this voyage he charted much of the west coast of the continent for the first time.

Flinders Ranges A range of mountains in South Australia running in a north-south direction to the north of Adelaide and the Mount Lofty Ranges. Copper was discovered here in 1841 and brown coal first mined in 1945.

flint A type of CHERT: a hard material consisting of nearly pure silica (SiO_2) in cryptocrystalline form (the common crystalline form being quartz). It occurs as roundish nodules, usually steely-grey and encrusted with white. As they are not single crystals but amorphous rock, flint stones do not cleave under impact, but instead spall, that is, break into flakes and sharp-edged fragments. Flint tools were among the earliest examples of prehistoric technology: arrowheads could be made from thin flint flakes, while larger stones were shaped into primitive scrapers and choppers.

Flint also has the property of sparking when struck with steel (see FIREARM).

flintlock See FIREARM.

Flintshire A county of north-east Wales; area 411 sq km (158 sq mi); pop. (1996) 144,000; county town Mold. It was part of Clwyd from 1974 to 1996.

flip-flop circuit A fundamental computer component, usually made as an INTEGRATED CIRCUIT. The flip-flop, or bistable, is normally stable in either of two electrical states. On receipt of a suitable signal, it changes state. It is thus usable as a MEMORY DEVICE. Computers typically contain hundreds of thousands of flip-flops.

float glass See PLATE-GLASS.

floating dock See DRY DOCK.

float switch A simple electrical switch operated by a float in a sump, well, or tank. Float switches are used in SEWAGE treatment to control hydraulic loading rates and to prevent pumps running dry. The switch is activated when the depth of the liquid or sludge reaches a certain level, and a pump then begins emptying the tank. When the float falls to a preset level, the switch is turned off.

flocculi Bright patches in the CHROMOSPHERE of the Sun. In early solar studies, flocculi were thought to be regions of incandescent calcium vapour. However, the term has subsequently been applied to a number of different features of the Sun's surface including plages and FILAMENTS.

Flodden The scene of the decisive battle of the Anglo-Scottish war of 1513. A Scottish army under James IV was defeated by a smaller but better-led English force under the Earl of Surrey (sent northwards by Henry VIII, who was on a campaign in France) near the Northumbrian village of Branxton. The Scottish king and most of his nobles were among the heavy Scots losses.

flood control Measures adopted to avoid flooding. The water-carrying capacity of a river depends upon the cross-sectional area of the water and its velocity, either of which can be increased to cope with floods. Greater capacity can be achieved with earth embankments (levées), which increase channel depth, and, if set back from the normal banks, width also. In urban areas, flood walls are used instead of levées, as they require less ground. Water velocity is determined by the channel gradient and its smoothness. Clearing aquatic vegetation often improves smoothness, and gradient can be increased by straightening the channel, particularly at meanders. Rural flood-plains (water meadows) can form temporary reservoirs at times of high rainfall, protecting downstream urban areas from flooding. Flood capacity can further be increased by bypass channels off the main river, controlled by side weirs. Barriers, for example across the River Thames in London, can be constructed to reduce the danger of flooding.

floodplains Flattish areas alongside river channels which are covered by water during floods. Made of alluvium deposited in former floods or as channels shifted their course, they are particularly associated with meandering rivers. Rivers with large loads of fine sediment, like the Mississippi, build their channels above their floodplains and run between LEVEES. When such rivers flood, water flows long distances along the floodplain before re-entering the channel. As the layers of deposited alluvium build up, the land becomes increasingly fertile for farming.

floppy disk A flexible plastic disk with a magnetic coating, used for storing computer DATA or SOFTWARE. Floppy disks are slower in operation, store less information, and are less reliable than HARD DISKS. They can easily be inserted in or removed from a computer. Two types are in use. The 5 1/4-inch disks, which are now falling into disuse, are held in a flexible cardboard envelope. Usually 3 1/2-inch disks are used; these have a rigid plastic jacket with a sliding metal shutter. The surfaces of the disk are divided (formatted) into areas on which information can be stored and the disk is held in a disk drive which rotates it inside its cover. The computer stores information on the disk, or retrieves information from the disk (known as 'writing' and 'reading' operations respectively) by a fixed magnetic head within the disk drive. Floppy disks are sometimes known as "diskettes".

Flora The Roman goddess of fertility, flowers, and spring.

Florence (Italian **Firenze**) The capital city of Tuscany in northern Italy, situated on the River Arno at the foot of the Fiesole Hills; pop. (1990) 408,400. Built near the Etruscan town of Faesulae, Florence ('City of Flowers') stood at the heart of the Roman colony of Florentia from the 1st century BC to the 5th century AD. During early medieval times it became a centre of the Carolingian princedom of Tuscany prior to its emergence as a republic in the 12th century. For most of the period from 1434 to 1737 Florence was ruled by the rich Medici family and under them it became the leading artistic and architectural city of Italy. From the 13th to the 16th century many of the city's fine buildings were created. Many historic buildings were severely damaged by floods in 1966. Florence ceased to be independent and became the capital of the Grand Duchy of Tuscany in 1532. It was the birthplace of opera at the end of the 16th century and home of the literary Accademia della Crusca (1582). Florence is generally regarded as the world's greatest repository of art; it abounds in famous churches, palaces, museums, and monuments.

Florey, Howard Walter, Baron (1898–1968) Australian pathologist. In collaboration with Sir Ernst Chain he isolated and purified penicillin, developed techniques for its large-scale production, and performed the first clinical trials. Florey and Chain shared a Nobel Prize in 1945 with Sir Alexander Fleming.

Florida A state forming a peninsula of the south-eastern USA; area 151,939 sq km (58,664 sq miles); pop. (1990) 12,937,900; capital, Tallahassee. The largest cities are Miami, Tampa, St Petersburg, and Cape Coral. Florida is also known as the 'Sunshine State'. Held by Spain after it was explored in 1513 by Ponce de León, Florida was sold to the United States in 1819. It entered the Union as the 27th state in 1845. Fruit, vegetables, cattle, and forest products are the state's chief produce, but tourism is the most important sector of the economy.

Florida Keys A chain of small coral limestone islands stretching a distance of some 240 km (150 miles) from Virginia Key to Key West around the Florida peninsula, south-eastern USA. Linked to the mainland by a highway, Key Largo is the largest island.

Florio, John (*c*.1553–1625) English lexicographer, of Italian descent. In 1598 he produced an Italian–English dictionary entitled *A Worlde of Wordes*. His most important work was the first translation into English of Montaigne's essays (1603), on which Shakespeare drew in *The Tempest*.

flotation (in economics) The offer for sale of new SHARES in a COMPANY as a means of raising CAPITAL. It is usually the sale of shares by companies not previously quoted on the STOCK EXCHANGE, but may also refer to capital raising by established companies for major investments.

flounder A FLATFISH of the family Pleuronectidae, found in coastal waters from the shoreline to 50 m (162 feet) depth. The European flounder, *Platichthys flesus*, is a right-eyed flatfish which is unique in that the young fish lives in fresh water, mainly in rivers, which it ascends when about 2 cm (1 inch) long, returning to the sea when adult. It lives on soft bottoms of both mud and sand, feeding on bottom-living crustaceans, worms, and molluscs, and is dull brown in colour, with the eyeless side opaque white. Many flatfishes in North America are known as flounders, but only the starry flounder, *P. stellatus*, is a close relative of the European one.

flow chart A design technique depicting the order of logical steps (ALGORITHM) required to solve a problem prior to writing a computer software program, or designing a computer system using SYSTEMS ANALYSIS techniques.

flower The part of a higher plant concerned with sexual reproduction. Each typically consists of an ovary surrounded by other structures. These usually include the male organs, or stamens, which produce pollen. Most flowers have leaf-like petals, which may be brightly coloured, and sepals, which often protect the flower in bud. Flowers may be solitary as in the tulip, or borne in clusters which are called **inflorescences**.

Flowers are unique to the ANGIOSPERMS, which are therefore referred to as 'flowering plants'. In many trees and in some herbaceous plants, the flowers are unisexual, bearing either ovaries or stamens. When the sexual organs occur

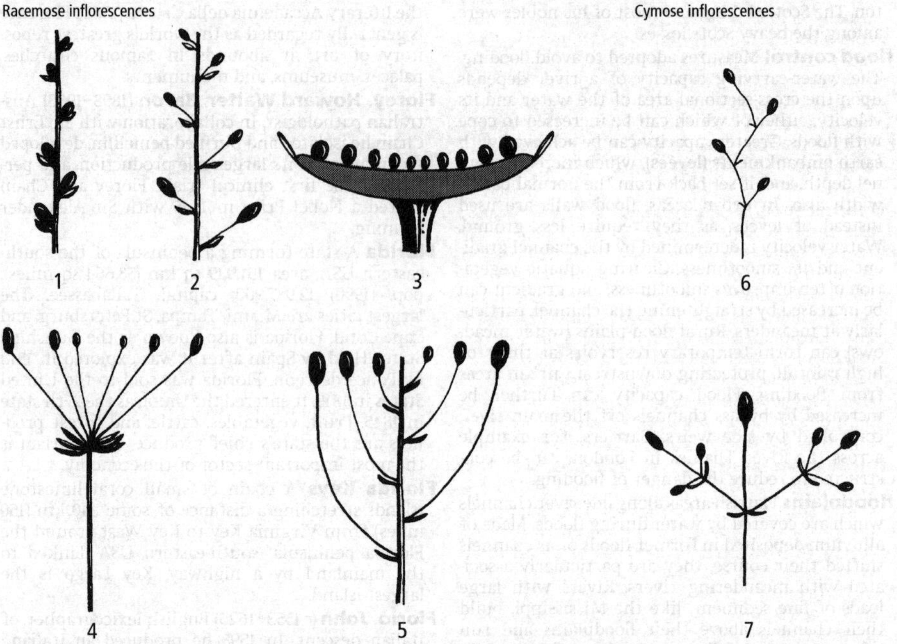

Flower (1) Raceme (e.g. lupin). (2) Spike (e.g. plantain). (3) Capitulum (e.g. daisy). (4) Umbel (e.g. hogweed). (5) Corymb (e.g. candytuft). (6) Monochasial cyme (e.g. forget-me-not). (7) Dichasial cyme (e.g. ragged robin).

on different plants, the plants are said to be dioecious. When together on the same individual, either in the same flower or not, they are said to be monoecious.

Flowers may be less than 1 mm (0.04 inch) across, as in some trees, or up to 1 m (3 feet) across, as in the parasitic *Rafflesia arnoldii*, a rare plant of Sumatra. Inflorescences may be several metres tall in some palms. What is commonly called a 'flower' in plants of the sunflower family and a few other groups is in fact an inflorescence of many flowers.

flowerpecker An agile bird that lives in the tops of trees and bushes from south-east Asia to Australia; the 55 or so species are in the family Dicaeidae. They are warbler- to sparrow-sized, mainly dullish brown birds, but a few species have strong colours. The scarlet-backed flowerpecker, *Dicaeum cruentatum*, has a flaming-red back. They probe into flowers for nectar (hence their name) and also eat many berries, especially those of mistletoe – some species are commonly known as mistletoe birds. Eight Australian species are called pardalotes.

flugelhorn A valved BUGLE used in BRASS BANDS. It is pitched in B♭, like the cornet and trumpet, but has the wide bore of the bugle and thus a broad and rich tone quality.

fluid drive See AUTOMATIC TRANSMISSION.

fluidics The technique of using the flow of jets of gas or liquid as control elements in place of mechanical or electronic controls. Fluidic devices can be used to construct complex circuits to perform a variety of control operations using the interaction of streams of fluids rather than moving parts. Typically, a fluidic element consists of a small block containing shaped passages which function as a supply jet, control jets, interaction region, and one or more output ports. The main advantage of fluidic controls are safety, reliability, ability to work in adverse conditions (for example, extreme heat or cold, vibration, nuclear radiation), and ease of integration with pneumatic or hydraulic systems.

fluidized bed furnace A furnace in which coal is burnt in a hot, turbulent bed of sand or ash, through which air is passed. The bed behaves like a fluid, and the coal is burned very efficiently at lower temperatures, reducing emissions of polluting nitrogen oxides. If limestone is added to the bed along with the coal, the emission of sulphur dioxide to the atmosphere is also greatly reduced.

fluid mechanics The study of systems involving liquids or gases and the forces that act on them. Liquids and gases are considered together as fluids because they behave similarly when flowing. Fluid mechanics can be broken into two subdivisions: statics (fluids at rest) and dynamics (fluids in motion). Statics describes the pressures within stationary volumes of gas or liquid. This is important when designing a dam wall or the skin of a weather balloon. Hydrodynamics and AERODYNAMICS are of far greater importance to modern ENGINEERING, and investigate liquid and gas flow, respectively, around solid and liquid surfaces. There are two main types of flow in fluids: laminar or viscous flow, in which the fluid flows smoothly with low energy losses, and turbulent flow, an irregular and disturbed flow with increased energy losses. The two most important properties in determining flow patterns in a fluid are its density and its viscosity (the amount of internal FRICTION within a fluid between adjacent moving layers). Hydrodynamics is concerned in the design of ships and submarines; it also describes the flow of fluids in pipes ranging in size from oil and petroleum pipelines to blood capillaries.

fluke A parasitic FLATWORM belonging to the class Trematoda of the phylum Platyhelminthes. The monogenetic flukes, which have a single host, are usually ectoparasites on fishes, reptiles, or other cold-blooded animals, while the digenetic flukes have complex endoparasitic life cycles involving two or more hosts. Many of the 6,000 or so species of digenetic flukes are parasites within the gut or internal organs of humans and other vertebrates. They include LIVER FLUKES and BLOOD FLUKES among many medically important species, causing diseases such as BILHARZIA.

fluorescence The emission of light by a substance as a result of its simultaneously absorbing radiation of another wavelength. The electrons of the atoms or molecules of the substance are excited by the radiation and emit the excess energy in returning to their original state. This emission, unlike PHOSPHORESCENCE, ceases as soon as the source of excitation is removed, and so the glow disappears. The light emitted is generally of a lower frequency than the radiation absorbed, which may be visible light of a different colour or ultraviolet light. The effect is used in some dyes and paints.

fluorescent lamp A lamp that generates light by FLUORESCENCE. Such lamps consist of a glass tube containing a vapour (usually mercury), maintained under low pressure. The inside of the tube is coated with a phosphor layer. A current is passed through the gas, which is excited into producing ultraviolet rays. These then bombard the inner walls of the tube, causing the phosphor to fluoresce, and visible light is emitted. Although this is a two-stage process, the efficiency of a fluorescent lamp is much greater than that of comparable INCANDESCENT LAMPS, since little energy is wasted as heat. Fluorescent tubes are widely used for office and industrial lighting. Recently, compact fluorescent bulbs have been introduced, which can be used in place of domestic light bulbs.

fluoridation The treatment of a mains drinking-water supply with fluoride, usually in the form of hydrofluorosilic acid. Fluoridation reduces the incidence of dental caries, particularly in young people. The usual UK dosage is 1.0 mg/l, but the World Health Organization and European Union standards vary according to water temperature. Excessive doses of fluorine can cause brown stains to form on teeth.

fluorine (symbol F, at. no. 9, r.a.m. 19.00) A yellow-green gas and one of the HALOGENS. The most reactive non-metal, it is an extremely powerful oxidizing agent, which forms compounds with all the elements except helium, argon, and neon and reacts explosively with many substances. It occurs widely in the minerals fluorite (fluorspar) and cryolite, but can only be obtained pure by the electrolysis of a molten mixture of hydrogen fluoride, HF, and potassium fluoride, KF. The pure form is used in some rocket fuels. Fluorine compounds are also used in the refining of ALUMINIUM and in separating isotopes of uranium (see NUCLEAR FUEL). Since the 1920s, there has been a growth in the production of organic fluorine compounds. The use of some of these materials (CHLOROFLUOROCARBONS) as refrigerants, propellants, and in expanded foam plastics has declined with concern about pollution, but FLUOROCARBONS and fluorinated polymers still have a wide range of specialist applications. Fluorine is also used for the FLUORIDATION of drinking water.

fluorite (or **fluorspar**) A very common fluoride mineral (calcium fluoride, CaF_2) and the main source of fluorine. Its crystals are hard, fragile, and typically blue or purple in colour. In ultraviolet light it fluoresces. It is found in veins and pockets associated with igneous activity. Fluorite is used in the production of hydrofluoric acid, which is a vital raw material for the plastic and optical industries.

fluorocarbon A HYDROCARBON in which some or all of the hydrogen atoms are replaced by FLUORINE. Fluorocarbons are unreactive, stable, and non-flammable. The most useful is tetrafluoroethene. It can be polymerized to produce PTFE. See also CHLOROFLUOROCARBONS.

flute A musical instrument sounded by blowing across a hole in a tube or vessel. Some are blown across the end of the tube, others into a notch or via a duct (see NOTCH FLUTE; DUCT FLUTE). The Western orchestral flute is the transverse or side-blown flute. They came into Europe through Byzantium in the 10th century. The one-piece flute with six finger-holes was used throughout the Middle Ages and Renaissance, especially by soldiers. A key, for the lowest chromatic note d♯, was added in the late 17th century, and further keys in the late 18th century. Flutes were then made in four pieces or joints and the lowest note was extended from d′ to c′. The flute was brought to its modern form by Theobald Boehm, with two designs in 1832 and 1847: the latter is today's orchestral flute.

flux (in metallurgy) A material that is added to metallic ores during SMELTING to remove impurities in the form of a light, low-melting-point, fluid slag. The term also describes materials that are used to clean the surfaces of metals before joining them by soldering or brazing.

flux (in physics) The rate of flow of energy (or sometimes matter) past a surface at right angles to that surface. Magnetic flux, electric flux and luminous flux are common examples.

fly An insect belonging to the order Diptera, which includes some 85,000 species worldwide. Flies are distinguished from other flying insects by having only one pair of wings, the hind pair, present in other insects, having been modified into drumstick-shaped, gyroscopic organs called halteres. A few parasitic species, such as keds, are wingless. Most have large heads and eyes. Many other sorts of insect are popularly called 'flies', although they do not belong to the order Diptera. It is a diverse group that exploits a range of habitats and lifestyles, and is successful by any criterion. Bot flies and others are pests of man or animals; bloodsuckers such as black flies, and scavengers such as blow flies, are VECTORS of disease; and many, such as carrot flies, are pests of cultivated plants.

Adults have sucking mouthparts variously modified for piercing (mosquitoes) or for lapping (houseflies), although they may be vestigial. Most species eat nectar, but many are blood-sucking or predaceous. Some, such as horseflies, are stout, but the majority, such as midges, are small and soft-bodied.

METAMORPHOSIS is complete, and in many species the last larval skin forms a hard puparium, or 'pupal case'. The legless larvae (or maggots) have mandibles or sharp mouth hooks, and they feed in a variety of ways: some burrow in plant leaves, stems, or roots, or form galls; others are predatory in soil, water, or vegetation; but the majority feed on decaying organic matter. Many species are aquatic, and a few exploit such unlikely habitats as crude petroleum, salt lakes, and formalin-soaked carcasses.

fly agaric See DEATH CAP.

fly-by-wire system An AVIONICS system in which the control surfaces of an aeroplane are activated by electrical signals, or by light pulses transmitted through OPTICAL FIBRES (fly-by-light systems). Such systems reduce weight, provide more control options, and can be closely integrated with flight computers. This has allowed the development of CCVs (control-configured vehicles): aircraft that are inherently unstable in which a computer continually feeds corrections to the control systems to keep the craft in stable flight.

flycatcher A member of one of three distantly related families of birds, the New World (or tyrant) flycatchers, Tyrannidae, which includes about 340 species; the Old World flycatchers, Muscicapidae, with 115 species; and the Australo-Papuan flycatchers, Gopsaltriidae, with 46 species. Tyrant flycatchers take their name from one of the first species described, the kingbird, *Tyrannus tyrannus*, which aggressively attacks birds of any size that come near its nest. Most flycatchers are insectivorous, many hunting by perching on branches and then sallying out after flying insects. Almost all are small, usually less than 23 cm (9 inches) in size, and the large majority are dull brown in colour.

flying boat See SEAPLANE.

Flying Dutchman The spectral ship alleged to appear in the vicinity of the Cape of Good Hope and to lure other vessels to their doom. According to one version of the legend, the ship's captain is condemned to wander until the Last Judgement because he refused to heed the warning of God not to sail round the Cape. The story is the basis of Wagner's opera *The Flying Dutchman* (1843).

flying fish A member of the family Exocoetidae, the 50 species of which all have very large pectoral fins which are spread wide and used as 'wings' to glide once they break through the sea's surface. Propulsion is provided by normal swimming under water and the fishes' 'wings' do not beat. They are adapted for life at the surface, being blue above and silvery-white beneath. Flying fishes inhabit tropical and warm temperate oceans, moving into temperate seas with seasonal warming of the water.

flying fox A tropical, Old World, fruit-eating BAT belonging to the genus *Pteropus* and the suborder Megachiroptera, of which there are 63 species. The common name derives from the fox-like head for, unlike other bats, flying foxes lack the grotesque leaf-like folding on the nostrils necessary for echolocation. They do not need such navigational aids to find fruiting trees even though they are nocturnal and most species rely on their excellent eyesight. The name flying fox may be given to all 173 species of fruit bats, but it is usually restricted to the genus *Pteropus* whose 63 species range from Madagascar to Australia. They are of economic importance as pests of fruit crops and, in some countries, as human food. They include the largest bat, the Samoan flying fox, *Pteropus samoensis*, with a wingspan of 2 m (6.6 feet).

flying frog (or **gliding frog**) A member of one of the two tree frog families, Hylidae and Rhacophoridae. They do not have a true flapping flight, but glide, by spreading the webbing on the fingers and toes, increasing the surface area for gliding, thereby carefully controlling descent from one tree to the next, using limb, finger and toe movements. They also have fringes of skin along the outer surface of the arms and legs and disc-tipped toes to help them grip leaves and tree trunks. Tree frogs of the Hylidae family are found in Central America, and those of the Rhacophoridae in south-east Asia.

flying gurnard A fish of the family Triglidae, which occurs in the tropical and warm temperate oceans. There are about four species, all with blunt, heavily armoured heads and enormously long pectoral-fin rays. These are brightly coloured and are expanded suddenly in order to frighten predators, although they also act as 'wings' in short jumps out of the sea. These bottom-living fishes do not fly but walk along the sea-bed on their short pelvic fins.

flying lemur See COLUGO.

flying lizard A forest-dwelling AGAMID lizard of the genus *Draco*, which occurs in India, south-east Asia, and Indonesia. They have the remarkable capacity of controlled gliding over distances of around 18 m (59 feet) from tree to tree. Their 'wings' are formed by flaps of skin on either side of the body; when the lizard is at rest they remain folded, but when it jumps into the air the flaps are extended by movable elongated ribs.

flying phalanger A tree-dwelling MARSUPIAL, species of which were formerly placed in the family Phalangeridae but are now classified in three different families. The first is the tiny pygmy flying phalanger or feather-tailed glider, *Acrobates pygmaeus*, named after its long, hair-fringed tail and weighing only 15 g (half an ounce). The second group are the gliders, including four species of *Petaurus*, weighing about 130 g (4.5 ounces). Their diet is not restricted to nectar but includes insects and small birds. Lastly, there is the greater flying phalanger, or great glider, *Schoinobates volans*, a herbivore and much the largest at around 1.5 kg (3 pounds) and capable of gliding for over 100 m (330 feet). All species are Australian, except for the sugar glider, *Petaurus breviceps*, of New Guinea.

flying squirrel See SQUIRREL.

Flynn, Errol (born Leslie Thomas Flynn) (1909–59) Australian-born US actor. His usual role was the swashbuckling hero of romantic costume dramas in films such as *Captain Blood* (1935), *The Adventures of Robin Hood* (1938), and *The Master of Ballantrae* (1953).

flywheel A heavy, rotating wheel designed to act as an energy store or to regulate machinery. To maximize the kinetic energy, the mass is often concentrated near the rim, with a thin or open-structured central section. In reciprocating machines, such as PETROL or STEAM-ENGINES, flywheels smooth out power fluctuations by absorbing energy at each power stroke and releasing it between strokes. They are also used more generally for ENERGY STORAGE. Some urban buses have a type of regenerative brake, in which the energy is taken up by the flywheel as the vehicle slows down, and then used later to accelerate the bus.

FM (frequency modulation) See MODULATION.

Fo, Dario (1926–) Italian dramatist. After many years of performing and writing revues and plays for assorted theatre groups, he made his name internationally with the political satire *Accidental Death of an Anarchist* (1970). Subsequent successes include *Trumpets and Raspberries* (1980) and the farcical *Open Couple* (1983), written with his wife, the Italian dramatist Franca Rame (1929–).

foam-nesting frog A frog that makes its nest from a liquid excreted from the female's vent – as does the African species, *Chiromantis xerampelina*, and the south-east Asian species, *Polypedates leucomystax*. The female, and up to three mates, beat the liquid into a foam, using their hind-limbs. Eggs are then laid in the foam, which prevents desiccation. The nests are sited in tree branches over water and when the rains come the developing tadpoles drop into the water, where they complete their metamorphosis.

focal length See FOCUS; LENSES AND LENS SYSTEMS.

Foch, Ferdinand (1851–1929) French general. He strongly supported the use of offensive warfare, which resulted in many of his 20th Corps being killed by German machine-guns in August 1914. He became Supreme Commander of all Allied Forces on the Western Front in early 1918, and served as the senior French representative at the Armistice negotiations.

focus (pl. **foci**) In geometry, one of usually two points such that the sum or difference of their distances from any point of a given curve or solid surface is constant. For example, the ELLIPSE and the parabola, as well as their three-dimensional counterparts, the ELLIPSOID and the paraboloid, all have foci. The shape of a planet's orbit around the Sun is an ellipse with the Sun at one of the foci.

The distance between a lens or mirror and its focus is called its **focal length**. The **focal ratio** of a lens or mirror is found by dividing its focal length by its diameter (aperture). Some radio telescopes use a paraboloidal DISH which reflects incident radio waves on to an aerial (US antenna) at the geometrical focus of the paraboloid.

foetus See EMBRYO.

fog A suspension of minute water droplets in the air at ground level which reduces visibility to less than 1,000 m (3,300 feet). A dense fog will reduce visibility to around 200 m (650 feet). It occurs when the temperature of the air and the DEW-point coincide. Radiation fog forms when the ground and air close to it cool rapidly at night, giving a foggy layer up to about 100 m (330 feet) in depth which is frequently cleared by the heat of the Sun during the day. Advection fog forms when a warm wind blows over a cold sea, steam fog when a cold wind blows over warm water, and frontal fog when rain increases the moisture in the air. Excessive dust or smoke particles in the air will turn fog into a SMOG, while dust without water droplets gives a HAZE. Mist is formed in similar ways to fog, but it is thinner.

föhn (or **foehn**) ▶**1** A hot southerly wind on the northern slopes of the Alps. ▶**2** A warm dry wind on the lee side of mountains.

Fokine, Michel (born Mikhail Mikhailovich Fokin) (1880–1942) Russian-born American dancer and choreographer. He became known as a reformer of modern ballet, striving for a greater dramatic, stylistic, and directional unity. From 1909 he was Diaghilev's chief choreographer and staged the premières of Stravinsky's *The Firebird* (1910) and Ravel's *Daphnis and Chloë* (1912).

Fokker, Anthony Herman Gerard (1890–1939) Dutch-born US pioneer aircraft designer and pilot. He built his first aircraft in 1908, the monoplane Eindecker, a type used by Germany as a fighter aircraft in World War I. He also designed the successful Trimotor F-7 airliners, later versions of which provided the backbone of continental airlines in the 1930s.

fold (in geology) A wavelike form in layered sedimentary rock strata that results from deformational processes in the Earth's crust. Basin-shaped folds in which the beds of rock dip towards each other are known as **synclines**; those in which the beds of rock are folded into an arch shape are known as **anticlines**. More complex folds result where the rock strata are subjected to intense horizontal pressures.

foliation (in geology) The layered appearance of a METAMORPHIC ROCK in which particular groups of minerals are arranged in parallel layers as a result of extreme pressure and temperature. It is typically seen in SCHISTS. The word also describes layers of glacial material formed as a result of shearing processes during ice movement.

Folies-Bergère A variety theatre in Paris, opened in 1869. In an age of decorum its reputation was for lavish productions and pleasurable impropriety.

folk dance Ceremonial, country, and step dances. Among ceremonial dances the sword dance is common in Europe and also appears in India, Borneo, and other areas. Country dances and step dances, such as the Irish and Scots jigs and reels, were performed for social reasons. The intricate patterns woven with swords were adopted by trade guilds, who substituted their own implements for the weapons. Ritual dances, such as the English Morris dance, are widespread throughout Europe and extend to India, parts of Central and South America, and the Middle East. A feature common to all is the animal-man, sometimes bearing deer antlers, masks, and bells fastened to the legs or body. Complex, fast, and rhythmic footwork typifies step forms. Rustic dances developed into formal court variants, such as the MINUET, the quadrille, and the cotillon.

Folkestone A seaport and resort in Kent, on the south-east coast of England; pop. (1981) 44,000. The English terminal of the Channel Tunnel is at Cheriton, near Folkestone. To the east are picturesque cliffs known as the Warren. There is a

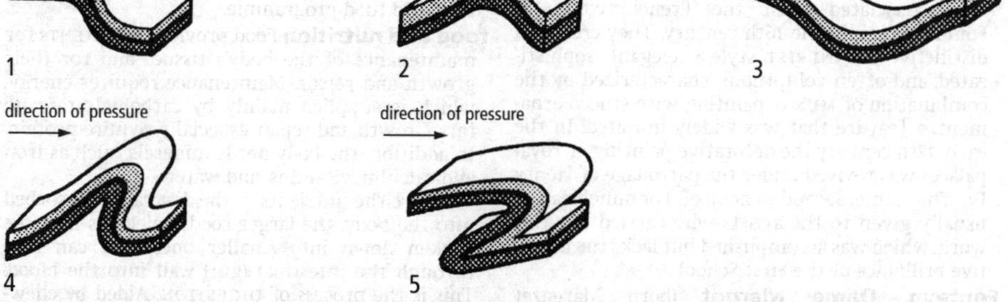

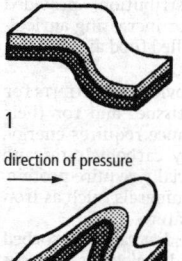

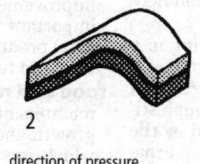

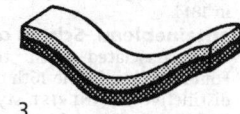

Folds (1) Monoclinal fold. (2) Anticlinal fold. (3) Synclinal fold. (4) Overturned fold. (5) Recumbent fold.

racecourse and a cross-Channel ferry link with France.

folklore The traditional beliefs, knowledge, customs, and orally transmitted culture of a group of people. Many studies of folklore are concerned with oral traditions such as folk-tales and legends, rhymes and proverbs, or folk-music. Folklore is generally seen as co-existing with a dominant, literate culture in the place where it is studied. It is often associated with marginalized minority or ethnic groups, and folklore study is often an important part of nationalist movements.

folk music Music of rural areas or peasant traditions as distinct from art or 'cultivated' (urban) music. While precise definition is difficult, the principal characteristic is that it is transmitted orally, that is, handed down through performance and with no written tradition. As a consequence variations are continually introduced, either through imperfect learning or through the adaptation of material to the changing characteristics of the community, and it is this element of constant reshaping through variation that distinguishes a thriving folk culture.

folly (from French *folie*, 'madness' or 'eccentricity') An ornamental building or structure built purely for decoration, often to provide a focal point for a view. Follies take such forms as towers, temples, and fake medieval ruins and are often deliberately eccentric. During the Renaissance, garden buildings were sometimes conceived as architectural novelties to amuse the beholder, but it was during the 18th century, with the rise of the GOTHIC REVIVAL and the cult of the Picturesque, that the folly became a specific genre. Extravagant, inappropriate, or outrageous buildings are also sometimes called follies.

Fonda A family of US actors. **Henry Fonda** (1905–82) is noted for his roles in such films as *The Grapes of Wrath* (1939) and *Twelve Angry Men* (1957). He won his only Oscar for his role in his final film, *On Golden Pond* (1981). His daughter **Jane** (1937–) was a model and stage actress before becoming a screen star. Her films include *Klute* (1971), for which she won an Oscar, and *The China Syndrome* (1979); she also acted alongside her father in *On Golden Pond*. In the 1980s she became known for her fitness routine. Her brother **Peter** (1939–) is also an actor, as is Peter's daughter **Bridget** (1964–).

Fontainebleau A town in the Seine-et-Marne department of northern France; pop. (1982) 18,750. It was a resort of the French kings who enjoyed hunting in the Forest of Fontainbleau, Francis I eventually building a magnificent French Renaissance palace here. The revocation of the Edict of Nantes was signed in the palace by Louis XIV in 1685 and Napoleon signed his first abdication here in 1814.

Fontainebleau, School of Artists working in a style associated with the French court at Fontainebleau in the 16th century. They created a distinctive MANNERIST style – elegant, sophisticated, and often voluptuous, characterized by the combination of MURAL painting with stucco ornament, a feature that was widely imitated. In the early 17th century the decorative painting of royal palaces was revived under the patronage of Henry IV. The name Second School of Fontainebleau is usually given to the artists who carried out this work, which was accomplished but lacks the inventive brilliance of the First School.

Fonteyn, Dame Margot (born Margaret Hookham) (1919–91) British ballet-dancer. She danced her first major role in Sir Frederick Ashton's *Le Baiser de la fée* (1935), later dancing all the classical ballerina roles and creating many new ones for the Royal Ballet. In 1962 she began a celebrated partnership with Rudolf Nureyev, dancing in *Giselle* and *Romeo and Juliet*. In 1979 she was named *prima ballerina assoluta*, a title given only three times in the history of ballet.

food additive Any of a group of chemicals added to food to alter and improve its qualities. Food colourings may be added to food to restore colour where it has been destroyed or altered by food processing; to ensure that there is no variation in the colour of different batches of food; or to give colour to otherwise colourless foods. More controversially, they can be used to mask the use of inferior ingredients in food, for example, red colouring to hide the use of bone or rusk in sausages. Flavourings may be concentrated natural extracts or ESSENTIAL OILS, or they may be entirely synthetic. CHOCOLATE and vanilla are the most popular flavourings in CONFECTIONERY manufacture. SWEETENERS are an important group of flavourings used particularly in the production of soft drinks and in confectionery. Anti-oxidants inhibit the onset of rancidity and stabilize oxidation. Emulsifiers and stabilizers prevent the coalescence of oil droplets and food preservatives (see FOOD PRESERVATION) are added to inhibit spoilage. In many countries some food additives are under government control, and only approved additives can be used in food. Additives must be of a certain purity, they must not adversely affect the nutritive value of the food, and they must be identified to the consumer. Food additives approved for use in EU countries carry an **E number**; this (or the name of the additive) must be included in the list of ingredients of packaged processed foods.

food aid Food supplied by richer to poorer countries as a form of aid. Food aid constitutes about a fifth of the USA's assistance to other countries, and is a significant proportion of the aid donated by all countries through UN agencies and the EU. Most food aid is known as 'programme food aid' and is given for BALANCE OF PAYMENTS support. The recipient country saves foreign exchange by not having to buy food abroad and, by selling the food aid in its own country, can raise funds for other purposes. 'Project food aid', by contrast, is supplied for disasters, and such specific purposes as food-for-work or supplementary child-feeding projects to combat malnutrition.

Food and Agriculture Organization (FAO) An agency of the UNITED NATIONS, established in 1945. The FAO is one of the largest and most effective of the UN agencies. It has collected and disseminated facts and statistics, given advice on improvements to food distribution, provided important technical advice for increasing agricultural production, and channelled food aid through its world food programme.

food and nutrition Food provides NUTRIENTS for maintenance of the body's tissues and for their growth and repair. Maintenance requires energy, which is supplied mainly by carbohydrates and fats. Growth and repair especially require protein. In addition, the body needs minerals, such as iron and calcium, vitamins, and water.

Before the nutrients in the diet can be absorbed into the body, the larger food molecules must be broken down into smaller ones that can pass through the intestinal (gut) wall into the blood. This is the process of DIGESTION. Aided by chewing and the churning of the gut, ENZYMES in digestive juices break down large carbohydrate molecules into sugars, and proteins into amino acids. Fats are partly chemically digested, partly reduced to minute droplets (emulsified) by the bile salts. Vitamins, minerals, and water need no digestion as their molecules are already sufficiently small. Once inside the body the nutrients become the raw materials for metabolism, the body's chemical processes.

food chain (or **food web**) A way of expressing the feeding relationships between organisms in a COMMUNITY. Food chains describe how energy, locked into food by plants and other AUTOTROPHIC ORGANISMS, passes from organism to organism, a process known to ecologists as energy flow. The most simple food chain, if such a thing existed, would consist of just three organisms: a plant, a herbivore, and a carnivore. The position each occupies in the food chain is called a trophic level and classifies them into producers (such as plants) and consumers (such as animals). The herbivore, which eats the plant, is called the primary consumer; the carnivore, which eats the herbivore, is called the secondary consumer. Energy is lost at each trophic level: only about 10 per cent of the energy of one level is produced from the next, which normally restricts the number of trophic levels to no more than five. Food webs describe situations closer to reality, where each organism may feed at several different trophic levels and produce a complex 'web' of feeding interactions. All food chains begin with a single producer organism, but a food web may involve several producers. The complexity of food webs also acts as a constraint on the number of trophic levels.

food preservation Any method applied to prevent or delay the deterioration of food. Early hunter-gatherers prepared dried meats, such as pemmican, and used caves and other cool places for REFRIGERATION of food. Foods were preserved by FERMENTATION from early times, including milk and preserved DAIRY PRODUCTS such as cheese and yoghurt. Fruits, vegetables, and meat were preserved by pickling, a process in which the food is salted to selectively control microorganisms such as BACTERIA, then fermented to stabilize the treated tissues. Preservation of fruit can also be achieved by concentrating to 56 per cent or more soluble solids, as in jams, marmalades, and jellies. The sugar added to these foods also acts as a preservative. Chemical food preservatives include anti-oxidants, which retard decay due to oxidation, and preservatives such as sodium benzoate, which slow down microbial growth. Other preservation methods include CANNING, FREEZE-DRYING, and IRRADIATION. See also FOOD TECHNOLOGY; FOOD ADDITIVE.

food technology The application of scientific knowledge to the preparation, preservation, and storage of food. Food technology can slow or halt the natural degradation processes of certain foodstuffs and thus make foods available out of season (see FOOD PRESERVATION). The palatability or nutritional qualities of many raw food materials can be enhanced by selective processing. For example, CEREALS may be crushed by milling to produce flour, a process which removes or breaks down the indigestible outer husk of the cereal seeds. The flour can be made more palatable by making it into bread or pasta.

In recent years the market has seen new processing and packaging technologies, allowing an increase in production of, and demand for, 'convenience foods': ready-prepared or easily prepared meals, and foods with an increased shelf life. More recently, advances in technology have led to the extensive use of chemical preservatives, although

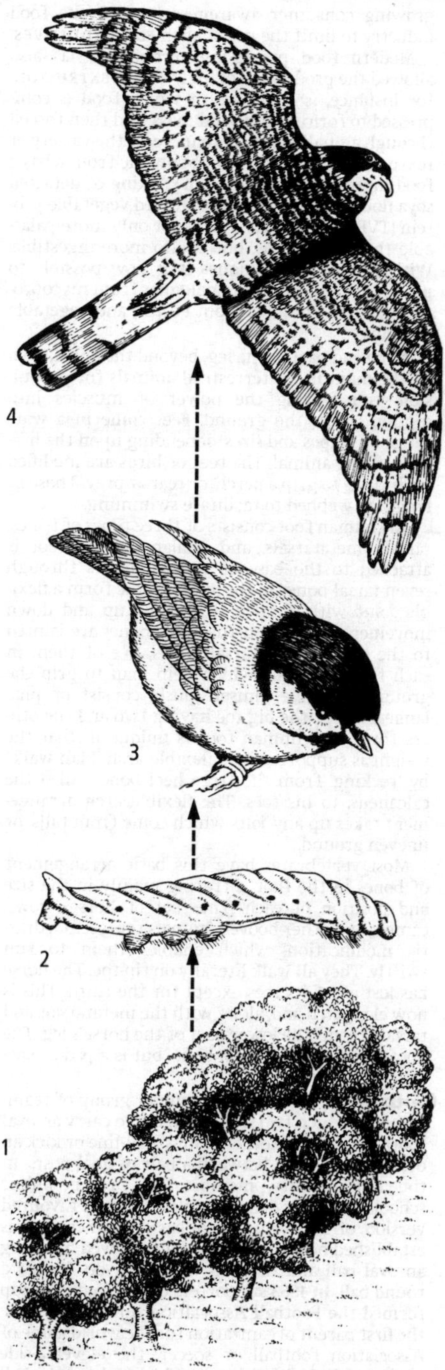

Food chain In this simple food chain, foliage (1) provides food and therefore energy for caterpillars (2), which are eaten by great tits (3), which are preyed on by sparrowhawks (4). The arrows indicate the energy flow in the chain.

growing consumer awareness has led the food industry to limit the use of such FOOD ADDITIVES.

Modern food processing technology has also allowed the production of 'new' foods. EXTRUSION, for instance, is a process in which food is compressed to form a semi-solid mass, and then forced through a small aperture to increase the variety of texture, shape, and colour obtainable from a basic food ingredient. By extrusion cooking of defatted soya flour, a highly fibrous textured vegetable protein (TVP) is produced. TVP is not only more palatable than soya beans, but is also more digestible. With extrusion techniques it is now possible to produce very good meat analogues from mycoprotein (protein obtained from FUNGI) and vegetable proteins.

foot The end part of the leg, beyond the ankle, used by the majority of terrestrial animals for propulsion, transferring the power of muscles into motion across the ground. Feet come in a wide range of shapes and sizes, depending upon the lifestyle of the animal. The feet of birds are modified with claws to grip a perch, or tear at prey. Those of frogs are webbed to facilitate swimming.

The human foot consists of three types of bones: tarsals, metatarsals, and phalanges. The foot is attached to the base of the leg bones through seven tarsal bones in the ankle. These form a flexible joint with the leg, and allow up and down movement of the foot. The tarsal bones are jointed to the slender metatarsal bones, five of them in each foot. The toes, which help man to grip the ground and give himself push, consist of phalangeal bones, the big toe having two and the others three. The human foot is unique in that the weight is supported by a flexible arch. Man walks by 'rocking' from the large heel bone, called the calcaneus, to his toes. The flexible arch arrangement takes up any jolts which come from falls, or uneven ground.

Most vertebrates have this basic arrangement of bones in the foot, differing mainly in the size and position of each. The feet of horses, cows, camels, and other hooved animals represent a drastic modification, which enables them to run swiftly. They all walk literally on tip-toe. The horse has lost all of its toes except for the third. This is now elongated and, along with the metatarsals and tarsals, forms the lower part of the horse's leg. The hoof is not derived from bone, but is a pad of specialized skin.

football The world's most popular group of team-games in which two sides compete to carry an oval football across the other team's goal-line or kick an oval or round ball between a pair of goal-posts. In the 19th century, members of various public schools set about defining rules for their favoured version of football, and a basic distinction was established between games that involved handling an oval ball and those in which players kicked a round ball. In 1863 supporters of the second group formed the Football Association, and this became the first parent organization for the world game of Association football or soccer, the eleven-a-side game in which the object is to kick or head the ball into the opponents' goal. In 1871 English supporters of the handling game formed the Rugby Football Union. In Rugby Union, a fifteen-a-side game, the chief object is to run the oval ball across the opponents' goal-line and ground it to score a try. In 1895 a breakaway group formed the Northern Football Union, ancestor of Rugby League, a thirteen-a-side game similar in many ways to Rugby Union, but in which players were allowed to receive payment. American football, the gridiron game, evolved during the 1880s, is derived from Rugby Union; the chief differences are the line of scrimmage, the introduction of the quarter-back (the chief play-maker), forward passing, blocking players not in possession of the ball, and the division of each team's players into offensive and defensive squads. In Gaelic football, a hybrid game played in Ireland, players score a goal by kicking or punching the ball between the posts and under the crossbar. In Australian Rules football, played on an oval pitch, a goal is scored by kicking the ball between the two central goal-posts. At the top level, both Association football and Rugby football are now professional games.

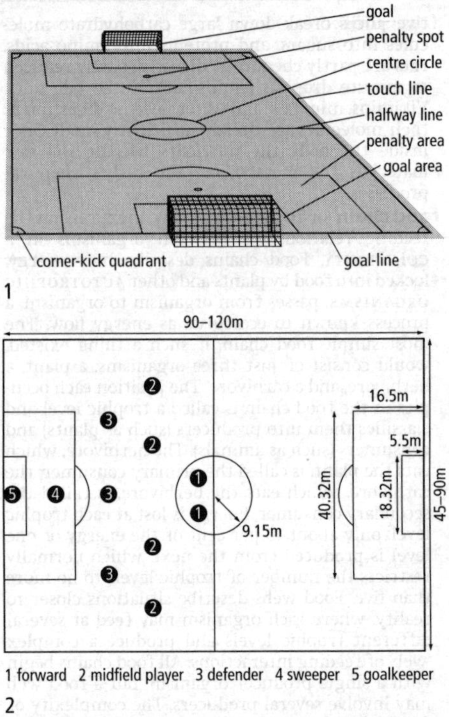

Football (1) The layout of the field in Association football. (2) One of several possible team formations.

footman moth A moth belonging to the same family as the TIGER MOTH, but that is slender and less colourful. The narrow fore-wings are folded tightly around the body at rest, the stiff, elongate appearance giving rise to the popular name. By day the moths are sluggish, and drop from vegetation if disturbed. The caterpillars, which are very hairy, mostly feed on lichens. These moths occur throughout the world but are predominantly tropical or north temperate species.

forage crop A crop grown for animal consumption. The main forage crops are root vegetables – turnip, mangel, swede, and fodder beet – and such crops as kale, which are grown for their green tops. Maize may also be grown to be cut green and converted into SILAGE for winter feeding. All forage crops, whether fed direct or harvested, stored, and fed later, are palatable and either high-yielding or fast-growing. Some, like rape, are used as 'catch' crops, which are sown after harvest and grow quickly to provide autumn feed. See also ARABLE FARMING.

foraminiferan A PROTOZOAN (mainly marine) related to RADIOLARIANS. Unlike radiolarians, their shells are either calcareous or made of foreign particles and often built up of separate chambers added in sequence as the organisms grow. Many species resemble strings of beads, because of their mode of growth, or have spiral shells like tiny snails. Foraminiferan shells always have microscopic holes to allow extensions of the cell (pseudopodia) to protrude and be used for locomotion and feeding, rather like amoebae.

Forbidden City See BEIJING.

force The physical agency (a VECTOR quantity) that changes the VELOCITY of an object. Quite often an object is acted on by several forces simultaneously and a change in velocity occurs only if the net force is not equal to zero. The second of NEWTON'S LAWS OF MOTION defines the net force acting on an object of constant MASS as the product of that mass and the acceleration that is induced in it. It is measured in newtons (N). When a force is exerted over a given distance, work is done; work (or ENERGY) equals force × distance. It is measured in newton metres (Nm) or joules (J). A force continually applied at a certain speed gives rate of working, power, measured in joules per second (J/s) or watts (W). There are two major classes of force. Contact forces act between objects that are touching; for example, the force exerted by a gas on the walls of its container is the result of the collisions between the gas molecules and the walls, and the MOMENTUM they lose during that collision. Action-at-a-distance forces, such as GRAVITY, act through empty space; so does the electromagnetic force between electrically charged particles. The forces between atomic particles also fall into this category but are usually effective only over very short atomic distances. There are four fundamental forces in nature: the gravitational force (see GRAVITATION), the ELECTROMAGNETIC FORCE, the STRONG FORCE, and the WEAK FORCE.

Ford, Ford Madox (born Ford Hermann Hueffer) (1873–1939) British novelist and editor. He was the grandson of the Pre-Raphaelite painter Ford Madox Brown and is chiefly remembered as the author of the novel *The Good Soldier* (1915). As founder of both the *English Review* (1908) and the *Transatlantic Review* (1924), he published works by such writers as Ernest Hemingway, James Joyce, and Ezra Pound.

Ford, Gerald R(udolph) (1913–) US Republican statesman, 38th President of the USA 1974–77. He became President on the resignation of Richard Nixon in the wake of the Watergate affair. The free pardon he granted Nixon two months later aroused controversy.

Ford, Harrison (1942–) US actor. Ford became internationally famous with his leading roles in the science-fiction film *Star Wars* (1977) and its sequels, and in the adventure film *Raiders of the Lost Ark* (1981) and its two sequels (including *Indiana Jones and the Temple of Doom*, 1984). Other films include *The Fugitive* (1993).

Ford, Henry (1863–1947) US motor manufacturer. He was a pioneer of mass production and had a profound influence on the widespread use of motor vehicles. In 1909 Ford produced his famous Model T, of which 15 million were made over the next 19 years at gradually reducing prices due to large-scale manufacture, a succession of simple assembly tasks, and the use of a conveyor belt. He went on to produce a cheap and effective farm tractor, the Fordson, which had a great effect on agricultural mechanization. Control of the Ford Motor Company passed to his grandson, Henry Ford II (1917–87), in 1945 and is now a huge multinational corporation. Among the first Henry Ford's philanthropic legacies is the Ford Foundation (established 1936), a major charitable trust.

Ford, John (1586–c.1639) English dramatist. He often collaborated with other dramatists, notably writing *The Witch of Edmonton* (c.1621) with Thomas Dekker and William Rowley. Robert Burton's *The Anatomy of Melancholy* (1621) exerted a considerable influence on Ford's own plays, which explore human delusion, melancholy, and horror. Among his best-known works are *'Tis Pity She's a Whore* (1633) and *The Broken Heart* (1633).

Ford, John (born Sean Aloysius O'Feeney) (1895–1973) US film director. He is chiefly known for his westerns, which depict the early pioneers and celebrate the frontier spirit. His many films starring John Wayne include *Stagecoach* (1939) and *She Wore a Yellow Ribbon* (1949). Notable films in other genres include *The Grapes of Wrath* (1940), for which he won an Oscar.

Foreman, George (1948–) US boxer. He won the heavyweight gold medal at the 1968 Olympic Games, and became a professional the following year. In 1973 he beat Joe Frazier to take the world heavyweight title, but lost it to Muhammad Ali in 1974. He retired in 1977, but made a comeback in 1991, losing on points to Evander Holyfield in a world title qualifier.

forensic medicine The branch of medicine whose purpose is to provide evidence to be used in civil or criminal law cases. Before 1800 medical advice in legal matters was sought only sporadically. In the present century, forensic medicine, using the pathologist's techniques of post-mortem and laboratory examination, has become firmly established. Additional procedures are designed to maximize information regarding unnatural causes of injury or death, such as assessing the time of death, determining the age and cause of an injury, and identifying bodies, for example from dental evidence. Highly sophisticated laboratory techniques, such as DNA FINGERPRINTING, play an increasing role in forensic medicine.

forest An area of closed vegetation dominated by trees. Forests are the main plant cover over much of the Earth, but have been modified or removed by man from most of the temperate regions and are also rapidly being felled in the tropics. They may be DECIDUOUS FORESTS, coniferous forests, or tropical RAIN FORESTS, depending upon the climate and type of tree that makes up the forest. A forest may be just a few metres (yards) tall, as at the tops of tropical mountains, or may reach heights of 30 m (100 feet) or more. Tropical rain forests are the most species-rich of land vegetation, whereas some coniferous forests consist of a very small number of tree species. Their value lies not only in the production of timber and other materials, such as drugs, fruits, and latex, but also in soil and water conservation.

Forestry is the science and practice of managing forests. The management of trees as a commercial commodity is a branch of forestry termed silviculture. Forests, both coniferous (softwood) and broad-leaved (hardwood) are a source of many valuable products. Apart from timber and fuel, forests provide rubber, dyes, gums, syrups, and pharmaceuticals. Forests worldwide have a buffering effect on local climate and protect soils from erosion. Despite their importance, forests have generally been exploited rather than managed.

The aim of forestry is to reverse this trend and manage forests as renewable resources. See also DEFORESTATION.

Forester, C(ecil) S(cott) (pseudonym of Cecil Lewis Troughton Smith) (1899–1966) British novelist. He is remembered for his seafaring novels set during the Napoleonic Wars, featuring Captain Horatio Hornblower. His other works include *The African Queen* (1935), later made into a celebrated film by John Huston (1951).

forester moth See BURNET MOTH.

Forest of Dean A heavily wooded area in Gloucestershire between the Severn and Wye rivers, formerly a royal hunting-ground and coal-mining area, which had small, private mines.

forgery The offence of creating a false instrument (a document of a formal or informal character) with a view to having it accepted as genuine. Forgery is therefore usually a preparatory step to some other crime involving deception. Such instruments may be any device on which information is stored: typically, share certificates, stamps, credit cards, passports, or birth certificates. The forging of coins or banknotes is known as counterfeiting.

forget-me-not A small, blue-flowered annual or perennial plant. Forget-me-nots are all species of *Myosotis* and belong to the family Boraginaceae. This includes plants such as borage, comfrey, and some 2,000 others. About 40 species have been described, chiefly from Europe and Australia and New Zealand. Several are used as garden plants.

forging A method of shaping metal and increasing its strength by hammering and pressing. Originally practised by the blacksmith, it has become mechanized and developed into a major manufacturing process, particularly in the IRON AND STEEL INDUSTRY. In most forging operations an upper die (a block of hardened material) is forced against a heated workpiece on a stationary lower die. In drop-forging, a hammer is simply raised and then allowed to fall under gravity on to the workpiece. Sometimes the hammering is power assisted, usually at a slow rate with high-force blows. Higher-speed work with lighter blows is also possible, using a mechanical helve-hammer, which is raised by a revolving CAM, and allowed to fall under gravity. In some forging, the blank can be hammered from both sides simultaneously: impact forging uses dies that converge horizontally, while counterblow forging has dies approaching each other vertically. In such machinery the dies absorb each other's energy, and the equipment does not need heavy foundations. Some forging techniques use pressing, with forces ranging from a few hundred to many thousands of tonnes. Roll forging employs matched rotating rolls that have impressions sunk into their surfaces. The metal blank is run between them and emerges with a shape determined by the roll profile.

Forkbeard, Sweyn See SWEYN I.

formaldehyde See METHANAL.

Forman, Milos (1932–) Czech-born US film director. He achieved international success with two films, *The Lives of a Blonde* (1965) and *The Firemen's Ball* (1967). Having taken US citizenship in 1968 he continued to make acclaimed films, including *One Flew Over the Cuckoo's Nest* (1975), which won five Oscars, and his adaptation of Peter Shaffer's stage play *Amadeus* (1983), which won eight Oscars, including that for best director.

Formby, George (born George Booth) (1904–61) British comedian. He became famous for his numerous musical films in the 1930s, in which he projected the image of a Lancashire working lad and accompanied his songs on the ukulele.

formic acid See METHANOIC ACID.

Formosa The former name (from Portuguese *formosa* = the beautiful) of TAIWAN.

Fornax The Furnace, a CONSTELLATION of the southern sky introduced by the 18th-century French astronomer Nicolas Louis de Lacaille.

Forrest, John, 1st Baron (1847–1918) Australian explorer and statesman, Premier of Western Australia 1890–1901. From 1864, as colonial surveyor, he was one of the principal explorers of Western Australia. He did much to secure the colony's self-government and became its first Premier.

Forster, E(dward) M(organ) (1879–1970) British novelist and literary critic. His novels, many of which have been made into successful films, include *A Room with a View* (1908) and *A Passage to India* (1924). Forster's novel *Maurice*, dealing with homosexual themes, was written in 1914, and appeared posthumously in 1971. He is also noted for his critical work *Aspects of the Novel* (1927).

Forsyth, Frederick (1938–) British novelist. He is known for such political thrillers as *The Day of the Jackal* (1971), *The Odessa File* (1972), and *The Fourth Protocol* (1984).

forsythia Any of the seven species of shrub of the genus *Forsythia*, one of which is native to southeast Europe, the rest to the Far East. From the latter have been derived the floriferous spring-flowering shrubs of gardens, notably the hybrid *Forsythia* × *intermedia*. Forsythias belong to the olive family, Oleaceae, along with ash trees and lilacs. They all have yellow flowers and grow rapidly.

Fort-de-France The capital of the French overseas department of Martinique, situated at the head of a bay on the leeward side of the island; pop. (1990) 101,540. Although an administrative centre since 1681, its population and importance only became significant after the eruption of Mont Pelée which destroyed the commercial and cultural town of St Pierre at the north end of the island in 1902.

Fort Knox A US military reservation in Kentucky, famous as the site of the US Depository (built in 1936) which holds the bulk of the nation's gold bullion in its vaults.

Fort Lamy The former name (until 1973) of N'DJAMENA, capital of Chad.

FORTRAN See COMPUTER LANGUAGE.

Fort Sumter Military stronghold in Charleston harbour, USA. The Confederates, having seized Federal funds and property in the South, demanded the evacuation of the Federal Fort Sumter in Charleston Harbor. Major Robert Anderson, in command, refused and General Beauregard bombarded it (12–13 April 1861) just as relief for the Federalists approached. The fall of the fort marked the beginning of the AMERICAN CIVIL WAR.

Forty-Five, the (1745) A JACOBITE rebellion in England and Scotland. Its aim was the removal of the Hanoverian GEORGE II from the throne and his replacement by James Edward STUART, the Old Pretender. Jacobite hopes centred on the facts that Britain was heavily engaged in the War of the AUSTRIAN SUCCESSION, and that the Hanoverians had never been popular. The Pretender sent his 25-year-old son Charles Edward STUART (Bonnie Prince Charlie, the Young Pretender) to represent him. Most of Scotland was soon overrun and the Jacobite victory at Prestonpans was followed by the invasion of England. But the English armies of General Wade and the Duke of CUMBERLAND were closing in and, without any significant numbers of English recruits, Charles was advised by his commanders to return to Scotland. The Jacobites turned back at Derby when barely 160 km (100 miles) from London, where panic at their advance had caused a run on the Bank of England. The decision to retreat meant that the rebellion was doomed. The last Jacobite army was routed at the battle of CULLODEN, which ended any serious Jacobite challenge to the Hanoverian succession.

Fosse Way An ancient road in Britain, so called from the fosse or ditch on each side. It probably ran from Axminster to Lincoln, via Bath and Leicester (about 300 km, 200 miles), and marked the limit of the first stage of the Roman occupation (mid-1st century AD).

fossil The remains of a once-living organism, generally taken to be one that lived prior to the end of the last ICE AGE, that is, fossils are older than 10,000 years. The great majority of fossils consist of such hard parts as the internal skeletons of vertebrate animals and starfish, the shells of molluscs, lamp shells, and crustaceans, and the tough woody parts of plants. Occasionally, however, soft parts are preserved, such as whole insects trapped in amber (fossil resin), and certain large extinct mammals that fell into natural tar pits. Fossils are usually found in consolidated rock, but not always (for example, woolly mammoths living 20,000 years ago were recovered from the frozen TUNDRA of Siberia). When an organism dies its corpse is covered by sediments, such as mud or sand, before it is destroyed by scavengers or the weather. Over millions of years the sediments containing fossils are compressed and converted into rocks of the kind known as sedimentary rocks. Due to subsequent earth movements and erosion, the fossil-bearing rocks may become exposed on the surface of the land. The impression of skeletal remains in surrounding sediments constitutes a 'mould'. Filling of a mould cavity by mineral matter may produce a 'natural cast'. Tracks, trails, burrows, and other evidence of organic activity may also be preserved. These are called TRACE FOSSILS. Fossilizing processes include carbonization, in which chemical action reduces tissues to carbon; permineralization (petrification), in which such tissues as bones and shells are made more dense by deposition of mineral matter; and recrystallization, in which tissues of one composition are recrystallized into more stable composition.

fossil fuel A carbon-based fuel, such as COAL, PETROLEUM, OT NATURAL GAS. All fossil fuels, whether solid, liquid, or gas, are the result of organic material being covered by successive layers of sediment over the course of millions of years. Petroleum and natural gas were formed from the slow decomposition and burying of planktonic marine plants and animals that sank to the muds of the sea floor. Coal is derived from the accumulation of partially decayed land plants. As the sediment solidifies into rock, the organic material decomposes under the influence of great pressure and high temperature. The burning of fossil fuels for energy is a major source of AIR POLLUTION, contributing in particular to ACID RAIN and the GREENHOUSE EFFECT.

fossil hominid A fossil that provides evidence of the evolution of *Homo sapiens*. Fossil hominids are rare, and their relationships to other PRIMATES are the subject of intense debate. The earliest known belong to the genus *Australopithecus* (see AUSTRALOPITHECINES), dating from over 5 to nearly 1 million years ago.

HOMO HABILIS, dated as 2.5 to 1.6 million years old, is the oldest known member of our own genus. It probably evolved into a new species, HOMO ERECTUS, about 1.8 million years ago. Another fossil hominid, *Homo ergaster*, contemporaneous with *H. erectus*, is believed by many anthropologists to

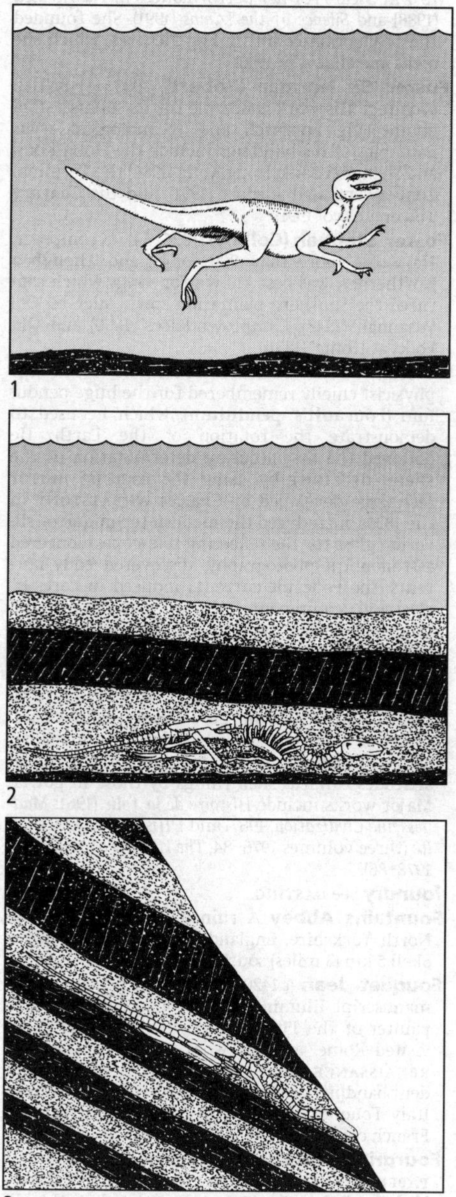

Fossil The formation of a fossil involves the following stages. (1) A dead dinosaur falls into a lake and sinks to the bottom. (2) Its skeleton is covered with layers of sediment, which gradually accumulate and become compressed into rock; the skeleton, too, becomes mineralized. (3) Earth movements have lifted the layers of rock to the surface, where erosion has caused the fossilized dinosaur to be exposed.

have been the ancestor of the NEANDERTHALS and modern humans, HOMO SAPIENS.

Foster, Jodie (1962–) US film actress. She appeared in *Alice Doesn't Live Here Anymore* (1974) before coming to fame with *Taxi Driver* (1976), for which she won an Oscar nomination. She went on to win Oscars for her performances in *The Accused* (1988) and *Silence of the Lambs* (1991). She founded the production company Egg Pictures, which she owns and chairs, in 1990.

Foster, Sir Norman (Robert) (1935–) British architect. His work is notable for its sophisticated engineering approach and technological style. Examples of his buildings include the Hong Kong and Shanghai Bank, Hong Kong (1986) the Terminal Zone at Stansted Airport (1991), and the Century Tower, Tokyo (1991).

Foster, Stephen (Collins) (1826–64) US composer. He wrote more than 200 songs, and, though a Northerner, was best known for songs which captured the Southern plantation spirit, such as 'Oh! Susannah' (1848), 'Camptown Races' (1850), and 'Old Folks at Home' (1851).

Foucault, Jean Bernard Léon (1819–68) French physicist chiefly remembered for the huge pendulum (**Foucault's pendulum**), which he used to demonstrate the rotation of the Earth. He obtained the first accurate determination of the SPEED OF LIGHT by using the rotating mirror technique developed by Charles WHEATSTONE in the 1830s, introduced the modern technique of silvering glass for the reflecting telescope, pioneered astronomical photography, discovered eddy currents (the Foucault currents induced in cores of electrical equipment such as generators), and improved devices such as the arc lamp and the induction coil.

Foucault, Michel (1926–84) French philosopher. A student of Louis Althusser, he was mainly concerned with exploring how society defines categories of abnormality such as insanity, sexuality, and criminality, and the manipulation of social attitudes towards such things by those in power. Major works include *Histoire de la folie* (1961; *Madness and Civilization*, 1967) and *L'Histoire de la sexualité* (three volumes 1976–84; *The History of Sexuality*, 1978–86).

foundry See CASTING.

Fountains Abbey A ruined medieval abbey in North Yorkshire, England, situated by the River Skell 5 km (3 miles) south-west of Ripon.

Fouquet, Jean (*c.*1420–*c.*1481) French painter and manuscript illuminator, the outstanding French painter of the 15th century. In the mid-1440s he visited Rome, and his work shows considerable RENAISSANCE influence, particularly in his confident handling of PERSPECTIVE. On his return from Italy Fouquet became the leading artist at the French court.

Fourdrinier machine A machine for continuous PAPER MANUFACTURE invented by the Frenchman Nicholas Robert in 1799 and patented in the UK during the early 1800s by Henry and Sealy Fourdrinier. Pulped cellulose fibre mixed with water, size, and appropriate filling material is spread as a liquid across a moving wire-mesh screen, under which are rows of suction boxes. The wire screen is agitated sideways to intermingle the cellulose fibres as the water is sucked away. The web of damp paper so produced is then passed through pressing rolls, heated in drying cylinders, and finally calendered to the required finish.

Fourier, Jean Baptiste Joseph (1768–1830) French mathematician. His theory of the diffusion of heat involved him in the solution of partial differential equations by the method of separation of variables and superposition. This led him to study the series and integrals that are now known by his name. His belief that a wide class of periodic phenomena could be described by means of Fourier series was substantially vindicated by later mathematicians, and this theory (Fourier analysis) now provides one of the most important methods for solving many partial differential equations that occur in physics and engineering.

Fourneyron, Benoît (1802–67) French inventor of the outward-flowing WATER TURBINE. After training as a mining engineer, he worked in an ironworks at Le Creusot, where engines were required to drive machinery. He developed a new design for a water turbine in which, unlike a traditional water-wheel, the water flowed outwards through a vertical rotor. His turbines were used at Niagara Falls, Canada, for the world's first major hydroelectric plant.

Four Noble Truths The basic teaching of the BUDDHA in his first sermon in the deer park at Varanasi (Benares), when he explained the cause and nature of suffering, and the goal of enlightenment. The Four Noble Truths follow the structure of a medical diagnosis. The first truth recognizes that there is a disease: suffering (*dukkha*), which is the basis of all existence. The second truth determines the cause of the disease: desire (*tanha*). The third truth acknowledges that there is a cure for the disease, and the fourth truth states what that cure is: the following of the NOBLE EIGHTFOLD PATH.

Fourteen Points (8 January 1918) A US peace programme for a just settlement at the end of World War I contained in President Woodrow WILSON's address to Congress. They comprised freedom of the seas, equality of trade conditions, reduction of armaments, adjustment of colonial claims, evacuation of Russian territory and of Belgium, the return to France of Alsace-Lorraine, recognition of nationalist aspirations in eastern and central Europe, freedom for subject peoples in the Turkish empire, independence for Poland, and the establishment of a 'general association of nations'. Accepted, with some reluctance, by the Allies, they became in large part the basis for the negotiations of the VERSAILLES PEACE SETTLEMENT.

Fowler, H(enry) W(atson) (1858–1933) British lexicographer and grammarian. With his brother **F(rancis) G(eorge) Fowler** (1870–1918) he compiled the first *Concise Oxford Dictionary* (1911). He is most famous for his moderately prescriptive guide to style and idiom, *Modern English Usage*, first published in 1926.

Fowles, John (Robert) (1926–) British novelist. His works include the psychological thriller *The Collector* (1963) the magic-realist novel *The Magus* (1966), and the semi-historical novel *The French Lieutenant's Woman* (1969).

fox A member of the dog family, Canidae. Twenty-one species occur throughout most parts of the world, with the exception of Australasia and south-east Asia. They include such species as the Cape fox, *Vulpes chama*, Arctic fox, *Alopex lagopus*, crab-eating fox, *Dusicyon thous*, and fennec fox, *Fenecus zerda*. All are small dog-like carnivores that also eat fruits in season. The European red, or common, fox, *Vulpes vulpes*, is found from mountains to lowland areas and even around towns. It lives in a den and the surrounding area is often littered with bird, vole, rabbit, sheep, deer, mice, rat, and even insect remains.

The female fox, or vixen, bears four or five cubs which are weaned in thirty to forty days, at which time the vixen begins to teach them to hunt and kill their prey. Initially small animals such as voles are taken, but their diet is gradually widened. The adult male reaches a length of 65 cm (2.5 feet), has a tail 40 cm (16 inches) long, and weighs 9 kg (20 pounds); the vixen is smaller. Their lifespan is up to six years. The adult coat is yellowish or buff-coloured in the forms living in the desert or plains regions, and deep red in the woodland forms.

Fox, Charles James (1749–1806) British Whig statesman. At the age of 19 he entered Parliament advocating American independence, and later welcomed the French Revolution. After Lord North's resignation he became Secretary of State, collaborating with his former opponent North to form a government in 1783. The coalition was brought down the same year and Fox remained in opposition until the death of Pitt the Younger in 1806, when he took office again as Foreign Secretary and passed an anti-slavery bill through Parliament.

Fox, George (1624–91) English preacher and founder of the Society of Friends (Quakers). He began preaching in 1647, teaching that truth is the inner voice of God speaking to the soul, and rejecting priesthood and ritual. Despite repeated imprisonment, he established a society called the 'Friends of the Truth' (*c.*1650), which later became the Society of Friends.

Foxe, John (1516–87) English religious writer. After fleeing to the Continent on the accession of Queen Mary I, he published his *Actes and Monuments* in Strasbourg in 1554; popularly known as *The Book of Martyrs*, it appeared in England in 1563. This passionate account of the persecution of English Protestants fuelled hostility towards Catholicism for generations.

foxglove A biennial and perennial plant with erect spikes of purple, golden, or white flowers. All foxgloves belong to the genus *Digitalis*, with around 100 species known from Europe, Asia, and northern Africa. They give their name to the foxglove family, Scrophulariaceae, which contains about 3,000 species, including antirrhinum, figwort, speedwell, and musk. This family is also known as the figwort or antirrhinum family. The common foxglove, *D. purpurea*, is cultivated for the extraction of compounds with heart-stimulant properties, such as digitoxin and digitalin.

Fox Talbot, William Henry See TALBOT, WILLIAM HENRY FOX.

Fracastoro, Girolamo (1478–1553) Italian physician, the first to put forward the theory that germs spread disease. He also described and gave a name to SYPHILIS. He spent his retirement researching, producing his major work, *On Contagion and Contagious Diseases* (1546), which described how some diseases can be transmitted through INFECTION. His theories about what is now known as COMMUNICABLE DISEASE were not recognized until later work by scientists such as PASTEUR confirmed them.

fractal A geometrical shape or pattern made up of identical parts, which are in turn identical to the overall pattern. The basic unit of the Koch snowflake, first constructed by the mathematician Helge von Koch (1870–1924), is the equilatorial triangle which can be built up into a much larger but still similar pattern. Any part of the snowflake is equally crinkly, whatever scale it is viewed at. Some of the most remarkable fractals are the Julia sets, devised by the French mathematician Gaston Julia (1893–1978).

fractional distillation A distillation process designed to separate mixtures of liquids whose boiling-points are close together. Fractional distillation is the primary method of separating products in PETROLEUM REFINING. An industrial fractionating column typically consists of a series of fractionating trays (as many as 100 in a super-fractionator), each of which is effectively a separate distillation step. Material is introduced part-way up the column: rising vapours become progressively richer in the more volatile components as they gradually cool, while liquids that boil above the entry temperature descend the column, becoming progressively richer in less volatile material. At the top of the column any remaining vapour is condensed, and a proportion of this condensate (the reflux) is passed back down the column. Vapours rising up the column bubble through the reflux liquid on successive trays. When the column reaches equilibrium each tray stays at a constant temperature, and contains mainly liquid boiling at just above that temperature. This counterflow process greatly improves the separation of the liquid mixture into different boiling-point fractions, and is characteristic of fractional distillation.

fracture A complete or partial break in a bone, which occurs as a result of stress above breaking point. Fractures can be simple, which is a complete break with little, if any, damage to surrounding tissues and skin. Compound fractures are a complete break but with substantial damage to surrounding tissues and skin. In childhood, the bones are softer and commonly result in an incomplete break; these are called greenstick fractures. Fractures of bones weakened by disease are described as pathological fractures.

Fragonard, Jean-Honoré (1732–1806) French painter. His paintings, usually landscapes, gardens, and family scenes, embody the Rococo spirit. He is most famous for erotic canvases such as *The Swing* (*c.*1766) and *The Progress of Love* (1771).

Frame, Janet (Paterson) (1924–) New Zealand novelist. Her novels, including *Faces in the Water* (1961) draw on her experiences of psychiatric hospitals after she suffered a severe mental breakdown. Other works include *A State of Siege* (1966), *Intensive Care* (1970), and a three-volume autobiography (1982–85), which was made into the film *An Angel at my Table* (1990).

frame drum A drum with a shell shallower than the diameter of the head and usually a single head. Frame drums are used by many peoples, especially those in the Arctic, where it is often a cult instrument. They often have rattling elements, such as TAMBOURINE jingles or the internal snares of the North African *bendīr*, and the double-headed Portuguese *adufe*, and the suspended rattles of the Siberian shaman's drum.

France A country in western Europe, bounded on the north by the English Channel (la Manche), on the west by the Atlantic Ocean, on the south by the Pyrenees and the Mediterranean, and on the east by Belgium, Germany, Luxembourg, Switzerland, and Italy.

Physical. France is Europe's second largest country after Russia. In the north-west the Brittany peninsula with its low granite hills, Normandy with its fertile uplands, the broad Loire valley, and the Seine Basin, all enjoy a temperate

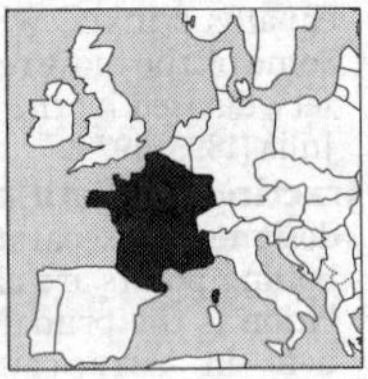

climate. The north-east can be colder; but here there is agricultural land on chalk or limestone well drained by rivers. There are also deposits of coal. Southward the ground rises to the Massif Central, a region of high plateaux and rolling country set on volcanic rock. To the west lie the Bordeaux lowlands and the Gironde Estuary, to the south the plains of Languedoc, and to the east the Rhône valley. Extending from south to north along France's eastern border are the Jura Mountains, the Vosges, and the western Alps, falling away on their northern slopes to Alsace-Lorraine.

French overseas departments and dependencies include **FRENCH GUIANA**, French Polynesia, **GUADE-**

Departments of the Paris Region

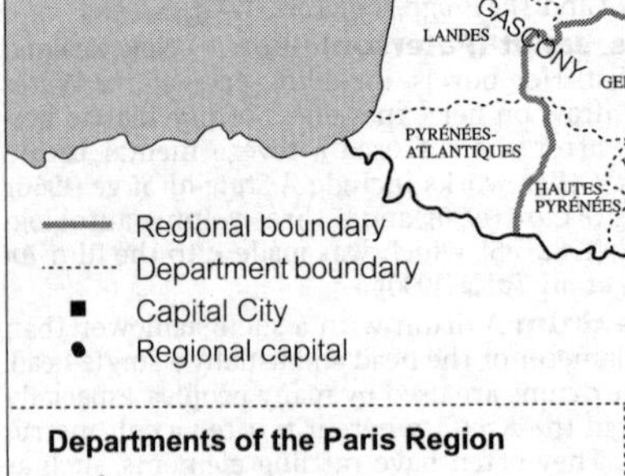

Regions

1	Alsace	12	Midi-Pyrénées
2	Aquitaine	13	Nord-Pas-de-Calais
3	Auvergne	14	Basse Normandie
4	Bourgogne	15	Haute Normandie
5	Bretagne	16	Pays de La Loire
6	Centre	17	Picardie
7	Champagne-Ardenne	18	Poitou-Charentes
8	Franche-Comté	19	Provence-Alpes-Côte d'Azur
9	Languedoc-Roussillon	20	Rhône-Alpes
10	Limousin	21	Ile-de-France
11	Lorraine		

France

LOUPE, MARTINIQUE, Mayotte, New Caledonia, and RÉUNION.

Economy. France has rich mineral deposits of iron, potash, bauxite, zinc, lead, and gold, but also imports raw materials such as oil for processing. The leading agricultural nation of Western Europe, France is also the fourth most industrialized Western country, with a wide range of manufacturing industry. Services account for some three-fifths of GNP, and principal exports are chemicals, machinery, motor vehicles, iron, steel, and textiles, as well as foodstuffs and wines. Major agricultural crops include wheat, barley, maize, sugar-beet, and fruit. Dairy and poultry farming are also substantial. Nuclear power supplies some 70 per cent of electricity, with considerable hydroelectric capacity. The population is concentrated in the north, in the conurbations of Paris and Lyons, and in the south-east.

History. Prehistoric remains, cave paintings, and megalithic monuments attest to a long history of human settlement. The area known as GAUL to the Romans was conquered by the armies of Julius CAESAR, and its native inhabitants thoroughly Romanized by centuries of occupation. After 330 it was invaded by GOTHS, FRANKS, and BURGUNDIANS, and then ruled by Clovis (465–511), a MEROVINGIAN king. It became part of the empire of CHARLEMAGNE and, after repeated assaults from VIKINGS and SARACENS, a CAPETIAN dynasty emerged in 987. Fierce competition with the rival rulers of BRITTANY, BURGUNDY, and, after 1066, with the Norman and Plantagenet kings of England ensued, culminating in the HUNDRED YEARS WAR. France did not emerge as a permanently unified state until the ejection of the English and the Burgundians at the end of the Middle Ages. Under the VALOIS and BOURBON dynasties France rose to contest European hegemony in the 16th to 18th centuries, notably in the wars of LOUIS XIV. In the 18th century, weak government, expensive wars, and colonial rivalry with England wrecked the monarchy's finances, and mounting popular anger culminated in the FRENCH REVOLUTION (1789).

The First Republic (1792–1804), established after the fall of the Bourbon monarchy, lasted until the First Empire (1804–14) under NAPOLEON I, when France became the dominant political power in Europe. After his fall the monarchy was restored (1814) and, with a brief interval in 1815, lasted until the abdication of Louis Philippe (1848). During this period, having lost influence in India and Canada, France began to create an overseas empire in North Africa. The Second Republic, established in 1848, lasted until 1852, when NAPOLEON III proclaimed the Second Empire (1852–70). It saw further expansion of the French empire, particularly in south-east Asia and in the Pacific. The Third Republic (1870–1940) was established after the capture and exile of Napoleon III and France's defeat in the FRANCO-PRUSSIAN WAR (1870). France took part in the Berlin Conference (1884) on Africa, and by 1914 ruled over Morocco, Tunis, Madagascar, and the huge areas of FRENCH WEST AFRICA and FRENCH EQUATORIAL AFRICA. The Third Republic fell in 1940, following defeat by Nazi Germany. Northern France was occupied by the Germans, unoccupied France to the south was under the VICHY GOVERNMENT, and a FREE FRENCH government was proclaimed in London. The Fourth Republic (1946–58) was replaced by the Fifth Republic (1958–), under the strong presidency of Charles DE GAULLE (1959–69). Protracted and costly wars led to the decolonization of Indo-China (1954) and of Algeria (1962), while, from 1956, the rest of the African empire gained increasing independence. After 1945 France regained its position as a major European power and was a founder member of the EUROPEAN ECONOMIC COMMUNITY (1958). As a nuclear power it refused to sign the NUCLEAR TEST-BAN TREATY (1963) and withdrew formally from the military division of NATO in 1966. President de Gaulle's successor, Georges POMPIDOU, supported the extension of the EUROPEAN COMMUNITY (now the EUROPEAN UNION), and President MITTERRAND's referendum in 1992 narrowly endorsed the MAASTRICHT TREATY. Mitterrand did not contest the presidential elections in 1995 and retired from politics; Jacques CHIRAC was elected. French testing of nuclear weapons in the South Pacific in 1995–96 was condemned by many countries.

Capital: Paris
Area: 543,965 sq km (210,026 sq mi)
Population: 58,172,000 (1995)
Currency: 1 franc = 100 centimes
Religions: Roman Catholic 76.4%; other Christian 3.7%; atheist 3.4%; Muslim 3.0%
Ethnic Groups: French 86.8%; Occitan 2.7%; Arab 2.6%; Alsatian 2.3%; Breton 1.0%; Catalan 0.4%
Languages: French (official); minority languages
International Organizations: UN; NATO; EU; OECD; South Pacific Commission; Council of Europe; CSCE

France, Anatole (pseudonym of Anatole-François Thibault) (1844–1924) French novelist and critic. His characteristic mode is elegantly polished social satire, as for example in *La Révolte des anges* (1914). He also wrote several volumes of childhood reminiscences, including *Le Livre de mon ami* (1885), and essays of literary criticism. He won the Nobel Prize for Literature in 1921.

franchise (in economics) A right to use a trade mark, name, or production technique in exchange for payment. A franchise will be granted only if the franchisee meets the quality standards set by the franchising company. The main arguments in favour of a franchise system are that it provides incentives for the franchisee, and that it keeps down the distribution costs of the franchisor.

franchise (suffrage) The right to vote in an election. In most modern DEMOCRACIES, the franchise is an inalienable right, which applies to all adult citizens over a certain minimum age, which ranges from 18 to 25. Categories of individuals not allowed to vote include convicted prisoners in penal institutions, the mentally ill, aliens, and those convicted of corrupt or illegal electoral practices; in some countries, an educational qualification of basic literacy may be required, but in others special allowance is made for illiteracy in voting procedures. In the UK, members of the House of Lords may not vote.

Francis I (1768–1835) Habsburg monarch, last Holy Roman Emperor (as Francis II, 1792–1805), and first Emperor of Austria (as Francis I, 1804–35). Following defeat at AUSTERLITZ he was forced to abdicate the title of Holy Roman Emperor, losing lands to Russia, Bavaria, and France by the Treaty of Schönbrunn (1809). He had little choice but to allow NAPOLEON to marry his daughter, Marie-Louise, in 1810, but he changed sides with decisive effect in 1813 and played a major part in the eventual downfall of Napoleon. In 1815 at the Congress of VIENNA, he regained much of the territories lost in the war, largely as a result of the diplomatic skill of METTERNICH, responsible for foreign affairs. During the last twenty years of his reign he was identified with the HOLY ALLIANCE and its policy of repression.

Francis I (1494–1547) King of France 1515–47. He succeeded his cousin Louis XII in 1515 and soon afterwards took the duchy of Milan. The greater part of his reign (1521–44) was spent at war with the Holy Roman emperor Charles V, with the result that Francis relinquished all claims to Italy. In the early years of his reign Francis generally practised religious toleration towards supporters of the Reformation, although his policies became harsher from the mid-1530s.

Franciscan (or **Grey Friar**) A monk, nun, or sister of a religious order founded in 1209 by St Francis of Assisi. The nuns are known as Poor Clares, after their founder, St Clare (1215).

Francis Ferdinand (1863–1914) Archduke of Austria and heir presumptive to Emperor FRANCIS JOSEPH. He aimed to transform AUSTRIA-HUNGARY into a triple monarchy to include a Slavic kingdom. He was opposed by the Hungarians, who refused to make concessions to Slavs, and by extreme Slav nationalists (including Serbs), who saw no future for the emergent nations within the empire. On 28 June 1914, while on an inspection tour at Sarajevo, he and his wife were assassinated by Gavrilo Princip, a Serbian nationalist. The subsequent ultimatum by Austria to Serbia led directly to the outbreak of World War I.

Francis Joseph (1830–1916) Emperor of Austria 1848–1916, King of Hungary 1867–1916. He succeeded to the throne (aged 18) amid the REVOLUTIONS OF 1848. He suppressed all nationalist hopes until forced to meet Hungarian aspirations in the establishment of AUSTRIA-HUNGARY (1867). His foreign policy lost Habsburg lands to Italy (1859 and 1866) and led to the loss of Austrian influence over German affairs and to the ascendancy of Prussia. Seeking compensation in the BALKAN STATES, he aroused Slav opposition which ultimately resulted in World War I. His wife Elizabeth was assassinated by the Italian anarchist Lucheni. Opposed to social reform, Francis Joseph maintained administrative centralization and opposed the federalist aspirations of the Slavs.

Francis of Assisi, St (born Giovanni di Bernardone) (*c.*1181–1226) Italian monk, founder of the Franciscan order. Born into a wealthy family, he renounced his inheritance in favour of a life of poverty after experiencing a personal call to rebuild the semi-derelict church of San Damiano of Assisi. He soon attracted followers, founding the Franciscan order in 1209 and drawing up its original rule (based on complete poverty). Feast day, 4 October.

Francis of Sales, St (1567–1622) French bishop. One of the leaders of the Counter-Reformation, he was bishop of Geneva (1602–22) and co-founder of the Order of the Visitation, an order of nuns (1610). The Salesian order (founded in 1859) is named after him. Feast day, 24 January.

Francis Xavier, St See XAVIER, ST FRANCIS.

francium (symbol Fr, at. no. 87, r.a.m. 223) The heaviest of the ALKALI METALS. All its isotopes are radioactive, the most stable being francium-223, with a HALF-LIFE of 21 minutes; it is formed by bombardment of thorium with protons. Francium appears to resemble the other alkali metals chemically.

Franck, César (Auguste) (1822–90) Belgian-born French composer. He was a noted organist, becoming organ professor at the Paris Conservatoire in 1872. His reputation rests on a few works composed late in life, particularly the *Symphonic Variations* for piano and orchestra (1885), the D minor Symphony (1886–88), and the String Quartet (1889).

Franck, James (1882–1964) German-born US physicist. He worked on the bombardment of atoms by electrons, and found that the atoms absorb and lose energy in discrete increments or quanta. He then studied the vibration and rotation of dissociated molecules. After moving to the USA in 1935 he eventually joined the Manhattan Project to develop the atom bomb; in the Franck report, completed in 1945, he and other scientists proposed the explosion of the bomb in an uninhabited area to demonstrate its power to Japan, rather than using it directly in war.

Franco, Francisco (1892–1975) Spanish general and statesman, head of state 1939–75. After commanding the Spanish Foreign Legion in Morocco, Franco was among the leaders of the military uprising against the Republican government which led to the Spanish Civil War. In 1937 he became leader of the Falange (Fascist) Party and proclaimed himself 'Caudillo' (leader) of Spain. With the surrender of Madrid and the defeat of the republic in 1939, he took control of the government and established a dictatorship. Despite pressure from Germany and Italy, Franco kept Spain neutral during World War II, although as a dictator his sympathies lay with Hitler and Mussolini. In 1969 he named Prince Juan Carlos as his successor and heir to the reconstituted Spanish throne.

Franco-Prussian War (1870–71) The war between France, under NAPOLEON III, and Prussia. The war itself was provoked by BISMARCK, who had skilfully isolated the French, and altered an uncontroversial message from his king (the Ems telegram). Prussian armies advanced into France; the French forces led by Macmahon were driven out of Alsace whilst a second French army was forced to retire to Metz. MacMahon, marching to relieve Metz, was comprehensively defeated by Moltke at Sedan. Napoleon was captured and, discredited in the eyes of the French, ceased to be emperor. Bismarck refused to make peace, and in September the siege of Paris began. Hopes of a French counterattack were dispelled when Bazaine surrendered at Metz and Paris finally gave way in January 1871. An armistice was granted by Bismarck, and a national assembly elected to ratify the peace, but the population of Paris refused to lay down arms and in March 1871 rose in revolt and set up the Commune of PARIS. The French government signed the Treaty of FRANKFURT in May and French prisoners-of-war were allowed through Prussian lines to suppress the Commune. For Prussia, the proclamation of the GERMAN SECOND EMPIRE at Versailles in January was the climax of Bismarck's ambitions to unite Germany.

frangipani (or **pagoda tree**) The common name of a sappy thick-stemmed shrub, *Plumeria alba*, which, like the other six species in the genus, is native to the warm Americas. As a member of the Apocynaceae family it is related to periwinkles and oleanders. It is much cultivated in the Old World tropics for its flowers, which are used in garlands in Hawaii and offered in Buddhist temples. A scent is prepared from the flowers.

Frank, Anne (1929–45) German Jewish girl. Her diary, first published in 1947, records the experiences of her family living for two years in hiding from the Nazis in occupied Amsterdam. They were eventually betrayed and sent to concentration camps; Anne died in Belsen from typhoid. Her diary has been translated into more than thirty languages, including an English version (*The Diary of a Young Girl*, 1953), and has become a symbol of the suffering of European Jews at the hands of the Germans.

Frankfurt (in full **Frankfurt am Main**) A port and commercial city on the River Main in the state of Hesse, western Germany; pop. (1991) 654,080. It has been a major trading centre since the Roman occupation and for 400 years the Holy Roman Emperors were elected here. It is Germany's financial centre with the headquarters of the Bundesbank and the European Monetary Institute. Since medieval times it has hosted national and international fairs and is a major transportation centre with a large airport. Frankfurt is also a cultural and tourist centre.

Frankfurt School An influential group of thinkers based at the Institute for Social Research founded in 1923 at the University of Frankfurt, Germany. During the Nazi ascendancy, many members fled to the USA and the Institute was affiliated to the University of Columbia, New York, between 1934 and 1949. Its most illustrious members were MARCUSE, ADORNO, and Max Horkheimer. The School emphasized the importance of theory building and of theorists' attempts to transform society. In this it was opposed to positivist social scientists, who favoured investigative research and a detached rather than a partisan approach.

Franklin, Aretha (1942–) US soul and gospel singer. She made her name with the album *I Never Loved a Man (the Way I Love You)* (1967) going on to record more than thirty albums, including the live gospel set *Amazing Grace* (1972). She is known particularly for the song 'I Say a Little Prayer' (1967).

Franklin, Benjamin (1706–90) US statesman, inventor, and scientist. A wealthy printer and publisher, he was one of the signatories to the peace between the USA and Great Britain after the War of American Independence. His main scientific achievements were the formulation of a theory of electricity, based on the concept of an electric fluid, which introduced (and arbitrarily defined) positive and negative electricity, and a demonstration of the electrical nature of lightning, which led to the invention of the lightning conductor. His inventions include the 'Franklin stove' (a kind of free-standing cast-iron heater) and bifocal spectacles.

Franklin, Sir John (1786–1847) British naval officer and Arctic explorer who served under Matthew FLINDERS as a surveyor and at the battle of Trafalgar. In 1819–21 and 1825–27 he commanded explorations of Canada's Northwest Territories by land and sea; the first of these two expeditions suffered appalling hardship. During 1836–43 he was governor of Tasmania; and then, when nearly 60, he set out to discover the NORTHWEST PASSAGE which had eluded everyone from John CABOT onwards. His two ships became ice-bound, and all 134 officers and men perished.

Franklin, (Stella Maria Sarah) Miles (1879–1954) Australian novelist. She is recognized as having written the first true Australian novel, her acclaimed first book *My Brilliant Career* (1901). From 1906 until 1927 she lived in the USA and England.

Franklin, Rosalind Elsie (1920–58) British physical chemist and molecular biologist. Her early work was on the structure of coals, and she went on to investigate the various forms of carbon by means of X-ray crystallography. She then used this technique on DNA, and with Maurice Wilkins contributed to the discovery of its structure. Franklin was using the technique to investigate the structure of viruses at the time of her premature death from cancer.

Franks A group of Germanic tribes who dominated Europe after the collapse of the Western ROMAN EMPIRE. They consisted of Salians from what is now Belgium and Ripuarians from the Lower Rhine. They settled in Gaul by the mid-4th century and ruled it by the following century when the Salians under CLOVIS defeated the Romans at Soissons. Gaul became 'Francia', ruled from the old capital Lutetia Parisiorum (Paris) of the Parisii Gauls. The MEROVINGIAN succession continued until 751. Power then passed from the kings to their palace mayors. In 751 Pepin, son of Charles Martel, became the first CAROLINGIAN ruler of the Franks.

Franz Josef See FRANCIS JOSEPH.

Frasch process An industrial method employed in Louisiana and Texas for obtaining SULPHUR buried beneath layers of quicksand, which prevent conventional mining. It was devised in the 1880s by the German-born US chemist Herman Frasch. Three concentric pipes are sunk to the level of the sulphur deposits. Superheated water, at a temperature of 170°C and a pressure of 7,000 g/cm^3 (100 pounds per square inch), is pumped down the outer pipe and melts the sulphur. Compressed air is pumped down the central pipe and forms an emulsion with the sulphur which, because it is less dense than water, readily flows up the third pipe. The emulsified sulphur solidifies on cooling and is almost completely pure (99.5–99.9 per cent).

Fraser The chief river of British Columbia, Canada. Some 1,370 km (850 miles) long, it rises in the Selwyn Range of the Rocky Mountains, at the Yellowhead Pass. For the last 160 km (100 miles) of its course to the Strait of Georgia it is navigable, and the sediment of its delta provides many thousands of acres of fertile soil.

Fraser, (John) Malcolm (1930–) Australian Liberal statesman, Prime Minister 1975–83. He became the youngest-ever Australian MP in 1955 and was minister for the army, education and science, and defence before becoming leader of the Liberal Party in 1975. He was appointed Prime Minister with the dissolution of the previous administration by the Governor-General and was elected a month later. Unable to curb unemployment, his government was defeated in 1983.

fraud Criminal deception to obtain unjust advantage or to injure the rights or interests of others. Although fraud is not new, it has been described as the archetypal modern crime, opportunities for fraud having multiplied with, for example, the increased use of credit-cards, computers, and the automated transmission of money across the world. Mounting public concern has led in some countries to the setting up of specialist investigative agencies (in the UK, the Serious Fraud Office was established in 1986), closer regulation of businesses and of professionals such as lawyers and accountants whose expertise is crucial for many sophisticated frauds. Attempts to increase international collaboration by tackling money-laundering, improving extradition procedures, and enabling investigative agencies to use evidence obtained in one country in a trial in another, are as yet limited.

Fraunhofer, Joseph von (1787–1826) German optician and pioneer in spectroscopy. He observed and mapped a large number of fine dark lines in the solar spectrum and plotted their wavelengths. These lines (Fraunhofer lines) were later used to determine the chemical elements present in the spectra of the Sun and stars. He became noted for his finely ruled diffraction gratings, used to determine the wavelengths of specific colours of light and of the major spectral lines.

Frazer, Sir James George (1854–1941) Scottish anthropologist. He is often regarded as the founder of British social anthropology and ethnology. In a series of essays, *The Golden Bough* (1890–1915), he proposed an evolutionary theory of the development of human thought, from the magical and religious to the scientific. The first chair in anthropology was created for him at Liverpool University in 1907.

Frazier, Joseph (known as 'Joe') (1944–) US boxer. In 1964 he won the gold medal as a heavyweight at the Tokyo Olympics. He then turned professional, winning the world title in 1968, and in 1971 became the first man to beat Muhammad Ali in a professional fight. He lost his title to George Foreman in 1973 and subsequently lost to Ali twice before his retirement in 1976.

Frederick I (1657–1713) Elector of Brandenburg from 1688, King of Prussia 1701–13. He lacked the ability of his father, FREDERICK WILLIAM, the Great Elector, and dissipated funds in display and extravagance. In 1700 he supported the Holy Roman Emperor Leopold I in the War of the SPANISH SUCCESSION and with his approval was able to proclaim himself king, taking his title from his territory of East PRUSSIA. In 1713 he acquired Upper Gelders. With his second wife Sophia Charlotte he developed Berlin and established the Academy of Science and the University of Halle.

Frederick I (known as **Frederick Barbarossa**, 'Redbeard') (*c.*1123–90) King of Germany and Holy Roman emperor 1152–90. He made a sustained attempt to subdue Italy and the papacy, but was eventually defeated at the battle of Legnano in 1176. He was drowned in Asia Minor while on his way to the Third Crusade.

Frederick II (1194–1250) Holy Roman Emperor 1220–50. The grandson of FREDERICK I (Barbarossa), Frederick II was known as *Stupor Mundi* ('Wonder of the World') because of the breadth of his power and of his administrative, military, and intellectual abilities. He was crowned King of the Germans in 1215 and Holy Roman Emperor in 1220, but his reign was dominated by a long and ultimately unsuccessful struggle for power with the papacy. In 1228 he led a successful crusade to Jerusalem, obtaining, in 1229, Jerusalem, Nazareth, and Bethlehem for Christendom. Twice excommunicated by Pope Gregory IX, and opposed in Italy by the Lombard League, Frederick devolved a great deal of imperial power within Germany on the lay and clerical princes in an effort to maintain their support, and concentrated on building a power base in Sicily, a process completed by the Constitution of Melfi in 1231. He defeated the Lombard League at Cortenuova in 1237 and humiliated Gregory IX prior to the latter's death in 1241, but failed in his efforts to conciliate Innocent IV who appealed to Germany to revolt at the Synod of Lyons in 1245. Frederick's position was crumbling in the face of revolt, papal propaganda, and military defeat when he died in 1250, leaving an impossible situation for his heirs to solve. Many scholars and artists of his court migrated to north Italian cities, becoming precursors of the RENAISSANCE.

Frederick II (known as **Frederick the Great**) (1712–86) King of Prussia 1740–86. On his succession Frederick promptly claimed Silesia, launching Europe into the War of the Austrian Succession (1740–48). During the Seven Years War (1756–63), he joined with Britain and Hanover against a coalition of France, Russia, Austria, Spain, Sweden, and Saxony, and succeeded in considerably strengthening Prussia's position. By the end of his reign he had doubled the area of his country. He was a distinguished patron of the arts.

Frederick III (1415–93) King of Germany 1440–93, Holy Roman Emperor 1452–93. He inherited the HABSBURG domains as Archduke of Austria in 1424. He failed to assert family interest in Hungary, and was troubled by rival claimants to his own lands, and by Turkish attacks, which became more threatening after the fall of CONSTANTINOPLE in 1453. On good terms with the papacy, he was the last Holy Roman Emperor to be crowned by the pope at Rome. He earned unpopularity by his efforts to suppress John HUSS's followers in Bohemia and Hungary. By arranging the marriage of his son Maximilian I to Mary, daughter of CHARLES THE BOLD, he greatly extended the dynastic power of the Habsburgs.

Frederick V (known as 'the Winter King') (1596–1632) Elector Palatine 1610–20 and King of Bohemia 1619–20. In 1613 he married Elizabeth, daughter of JAMES I of England. He then assumed the leadership of the German Protestant Union, and accepted the Bohemian crown when it was offered, following the deposition of FERDINAND II in November 1619. Thenceforth his fortunes merged with the course of the THIRTY YEARS WAR, a struggle in which he took little personal part after his defeat at the battle of the White Mountain (November 1620). He withdrew to The Hague, and forfeited the Palatinate. GEORGE I of Great Britain (1660–1727) was his grandson.

Frederick Louis (1707–51) British prince, the eldest son of GEORGE II, with whom he quarrelled bitterly. As Prince of Wales his home in London, Leicester House, became the meeting place of the opposition leaders who helped to bring down Sir Robert WALPOLE in 1742. His premature death disappointed the hopes of those politicians who had supported him in the expectation of preferment upon his succession. The throne passed to his eldest son, who reigned as GEORGE III.

Frederick William (known as 'the Great Elector') (1620–88) Elector of Brandenburg 1640–88. His programme of reconstruction and reorganization following the Thirty Years War, including the strengthening of the army and the development of the civil service, brought stability to his country and laid the basis for the expansion of Prussian power in the 18th century. In his foreign policy he sought to create a balance of power by the formation of shifting strategic alliances.

Frederick William I (1688–1740) King of Prussia 1713–40. He was the son of FREDERICK I and was known as 'the royal drill-sergeant': he was a strict Calvinist, hardworking, violent tempered, and notorious for his ill-treatment of his son, FREDERICK II. He left a model administration, a large revenue, and an efficient and well-disciplined army. He acquired Stettin in 1720.

Frederick William II (1744–97) King of Prussia 1787–97. He was the nephew of FREDERICK II and a man of little ability, though a patron of the arts. He fought in the early campaigns against the French Revolutionary armies but became more concerned with Poland gaining land, including Warsaw, in the partitions of 1793 and 1795.

Frederick William III (1770–1840) King of Prussia

1797–1840. After his defeat at the Battle of JENA he was forced by the Treaty of Tilsit (1807) to surrender half his dominions by the creation of the kingdom of Westphalia and the grand duchy of Warsaw. In 1811 he joined NAPOLEON in the war against Russia but, following the retreat of Napoleon from Moscow, he signed a military alliance with Russia and Austria. From 1807 onwards he supported the efforts for reform made by Stein and Hardenberg, and at the Congress of VIENNA he won back for Prussia Westphalia and much of the Rhineland and of Saxony. He signed the HOLY ALLIANCE, and became progressively more reactionary during the last years of his reign.

Frederick William IV (1795–1861) King of Prussia 1840–61. A patriarchal monarch by temperament, he was the champion of a united Germany, but could not accept the degree of democracy envisaged by the Frankfurt Parliament of 1848. See REVOLUTIONS OF 1848.) He therefore refused (1849) the offer of a constitutional monarchy for the German Confederation. For Prussia he promulgated a conservative constitution allowing for a parliament, but with a restricted franchise and limited powers. This remained in force until 1918.

Free Cinema A movement founded in Britain in 1956 that aimed to steer the British cinema towards greater social realism. The movement paved the way for feature films, including Reisz's *Saturday Night and Sunday Morning* (1960) and Richardson's *A Taste of Honey* (1961).

freedom of expression (or **free speech**) The right of every individual to free expression of his or her opinions, including the right to receive or impart information through any medium. It is one of the basic HUMAN RIGHTS, included in the Universal Declaration on Human Rights and the European Convention on Human Rights, and enshrined in the First Amendment to the US Constitution. Freedom of expression is regarded as a fundamental part of the democratic process, assisting the emergence of the truth, as well as providing a means of self-fulfilment for the individual. It implies freedom of conscience and religion, the FREEDOM OF THE PRESS, and free participation in political activity, none of which are tolerated in totalitarian societies. However, even in democratic societies, freedom of expression is not an absolute right. It can be curtailed by considerations of national security, or subject to laws relating to privacy, defamation, PORNOGRAPHY, incitement to racial hatred, CONTEMPT OF COURT, protection of confidences, and COPYRIGHT.

freedom of information The principle that information held by state authorities should be available to the public. In most Western democratic countries other than the UK there is legislation which requires state agencies, and sometimes private bodies, to make files available to people with a legitimate interest in seeing them, subject to restrictions necessary to protect competing interests, such as national security, and the privacy and commercial rights of others (see DATA PROTECTION).

freedom of the press The freedom to print information and opinions without previous licence or prior restraint, subject to the laws regarding such matters as defamation or pornography. In democratic countries, press freedom may come into conflict with other rights, such as the individual's right to privacy, or the right of reply to adverse comments made by the press.

Free French, the A World War II organization of Frenchmen and women in exile. Led by General DE GAULLE, it continued the war against the AXIS POWERS after the surrender of VICHY France in 1940. Its headquarters were in London, where, apart from organizing forces that participated in military campaigns and cooperating with the French RESISTANCE MOVEMENT, it constituted a pressure group that strove to represent French interests. In 1941 its French National Committee was formed and this eventually developed into a provisional government for liberated France. The Free French army in French Equatorial Africa, led by General Leclerc (Philippe, Vicomte de Hauteclocque), linked up with the British forces in Tripoli (1943), after completing an epic march of *c.*2,400 km (1,500 miles) from Lake Chad. A provisional Free French government was established in Algiers, moving to Paris in 1944.

free market An economy in which buying, selling, and other transactions can be conducted on whatever terms the parties choose without INTERVENTION by the state. Prices are therefore determined solely by the forces of SUPPLY AND DEMAND. Although it is possible (in theory) to envisage a form of MARKET socialism in which optimum prices are set by the government, the free exchange of goods, services, and labour is likely in practice to lead to a CAPITALIST form of economic organization.

Freemason A member of an international fraternity called 'Free and Accepted Masons', which declares itself to be based on brotherly love, faith, and charity, and is characterized by elaborate rituals and systems of secret signs, passwords, and handshakes. The rituals are based largely on Old Testament anecdotes and moralities and are illustrated by the tools of a mason, the square and compasses. The original 'free masons' were probably skilled itinerant stonemasons who (in and after the 14th century) found work wherever important buildings were being erected, all of whom recognized their fellow craftsmen by secret signs. The 'accepted masons' were honorary members (originally supposed to be eminent for architectural or antiquarian learning) who began to be admitted early in the 17th century. The distinction of being an 'accepted mason' became a fashionable aspiration; before the end of the 17th century the purpose of the fraternities seems to have been chiefly social. In 1717 four of these societies or 'lodges' in London united to form a Grand Lodge, with a new constitution and ritual. The Masonic Order is forbidden to Roman Catholics, as the Church regards certain masonic principles as incompatible with its doctrines.

free port A port that accepts entry and exit of goods and services without the imposition of tariffs or taxes. The purpose of free ports is to encourage entrepôt trade, in which incoming goods can await re-export without going through customs, and to give a competitive advantage to a particular port.

free radicals (in chemistry) Atoms or molecules with one or more unpaired electrons available to form a bond. Free radicals include mainly short-lived species in complex chemical reactions, particularly those initiated by light, namely PHOTOCHEMICAL REACTIONS. A few free radicals, such as nitrogen oxide (NO) and nitrogen dioxide (NO_2) are stable.

Freesia A genus of South African ornamental plants of the family Iridaceae, of which there are 20 species. They grow from corms and have spear-like leaves with highly scented brightly coloured flowers. Most of the widely cultivated varieties grown commercially as cut flowers are hybrids derived from *F. refracta* and *F. armstrongii*.

free speech See FREEDOM OF EXPRESSION.

Free State See ORANGE FREE STATE.

Freetown The capital and chief port of Sierra Leone; pop. (1992) 505,080. It was founded by the British on the Sierra Leone peninsula in 1787 as a settlement for freed slaves. Subsequently it became a naval base. West Africa's oldest university is located on a campus at Fourah Bay in the hills behind the city. It was founded in 1827 and became part of the University of Sierra Leone in 1967. Freetown has an oil refinery and light industries.

free trade An economic policy advocating a free flow of goods between countries to encourage mutual economic development and international harmony by the commercial interdependence of trading nations. A policy of free trade prohibits both tariffs on imports and subsidies on exports designed to protect a country's industry. The doctrine's best early statement was by Adam SMITH in his *Wealth of Nations* (1776). At a conference in Geneva in 1947 a first schedule for freer world trade was drawn up, the GENERAL AGREEMENT ON TARIFFS AND TRADE (GATT). For over a decade after World War II Britain also was a strong supporter of moves to restore freer trade. It was a founder member of the EUROPEAN FREE TRADE ASSOCIATION (EFTA) in 1958, but as adverse economic conditions developed in the 1960s Britain sought entry into the EUROPEAN ECONOMIC COMMUNITY (now the EUROPEAN UNION). In Eastern Europe a similar community, COMECON, was established in 1949; after 1987 COMECON, sought cooperation with EEC countries. The highly successful growth of the Japanese economy after the war led many countries to seek tariffs against Japan. By the 1990s world economic policies were confused, some policies supporting free trade and others supporting trade protection measures. In 1993, at the conclusion of the Uruguay Round, the members of GATT agreed to further cuts in tariffs and export subsidies and to create the WORLD TRADE ORGANIZATION (WTO). The WTO will enforce GATT rules, especially the agricultural measures agreed in the Uruguay Round, which reduced export subsidies and import duties by 20–36 per cent.

free verse Poetry that does not conform to any regular pattern of METRE. The length of its lines is irregular, as is its use of RHYME (if any). Free verse uses flexible patterns of rhythmic repetition, and is now the predominant verse-form in English. It has some precedents in translations of the Psalms and the poems of William BLAKE, but the pioneers of free verse in English were Walt WHITMAN, D. H. LAWRENCE, and the poets of MODERNISM: T. S. ELIOT, Ezra POUND, and William Carlos WILLIAMS.

free will The philosophical problem of understanding how it is possible for people to be held morally responsible for their actions, given that there is reason for thinking that what they do is determined by causes. The problem of free will originates in the context of THEOLOGY: if GOD is omniscient and omnipotent, it appears to follow that everything people do is foreknown by God, and determined by God's will. The same problem, in a secular context, is often seen in terms of a clash between morality and science: whereas moral practices (such as punishment) require our actions to be free, science tells us that everything we do is governed by the inexorable laws of nature – the deterministic view of the world. Two important views of the nature of free will are those of the libertarian and the compatibilist. Libertarians, such as KANT, hold that free will consists in the ability to do otherwise than one in fact does, that is, power of choice, and that this involves a suspension of the laws of nature. Libertarians have difficulty in explaining how this is possible, and Kant thought that for there to be free will, people had to be thought of as being in some sense outside the bounds of nature. Compatibilists, such as HUME, by contrast, deny that this much is needed for free will. They hold instead that a person acts freely so long as he is not constrained by external forces, such as the will of another person. Compatibilists face the problem of explaining why the factors that determine a person's desires or character, such as their genetic make-up or upbringing, over which they have no control, should not be regarded as depriving them of free will.

freeze-drying A method of drying foodstuffs in which the water content is removed by freezing and then heating the material in a high vacuum. Ice crystals that form in the food during freezing are converted straight to vapour without passing through a liquid phase (sublimed). Freeze-drying provides a method of long-term storage without undue effect on flavour. The removal of water inhibits microorganism growth, but the physical structure of the food is retained. Instant coffee is one of a wide range of freeze-dried products. See also FOOD TECHNOLOGY.

freezer See REFRIGERATION.

freezing-point The temperature at which solid and liquid forms of a substance can exist together in equilibrium. It is also known as the MELTING-POINT. The value of the freezing point depends on outside pressure. For water, it is 0°C (32°F) at a pressure of 101 kilopascals (1 atmosphere), and falls by about 0.01°C for each atmosphere increase in pressure.

Frege, Gottlob (1848–1925) German philosopher and mathematician, founder of modern logic. Frege tried to provide a rigorous foundation for mathematics on the basis of purely logical principles, but abandoned the attempt when Bertrand Russell, on whose work he had a profound influence, pointed out that his system was inconsistent.

Frei (Montalva), Edúardo (1911–82) Chilean statesman, President of Chile 1964–70. The programmes he initiated, including agrarian reform and the 'Chileanization' of the copper industry (whose controlling interest had until then been held by US companies), were ambitious, but his failure to check inflation or to redistribute wealth turned many of his supporters against him. His son, Edúardo Frei Ruiz-Tagle, was elected President of Chile in 1993 (inaugurated in 1994).

Frelimo War (1964–75) A war fought between MOZAMBIQUE nationalist groups united into the Mozambique Liberation Front (Frelimo) and Portuguese troops. The Portuguese failed to contain the conflict, and by 1968 Samora Machel claimed one-fifth of the country. Brutal Portuguese counter-terrorism made conciliation even more impossible and Portugal conceded independence in 1974. Frelimo became the dominant political force in the new People's Republic of Mozambique.

Fremantle The principal port of Western Australia, on the Swan River; pop. (1986) 24,000. The city is named after Capt. Charles Fremantle who arrived in 1829 immediately prior to the establishment of Australia's first colony of European free settlers. Superseding Albany as Western Australia's leading port in 1897, its harbour has become an important passenger port and the 'Western Gateway to Australia'.

Frémont, John Charles (known as 'the Pathfinder') (1813–90) US explorer and politician. He was responsible for exploring several viable routes to the Pacific across the Rockies in the 1840s. He made an unsuccessful bid for the presidency in 1856, losing to James Buchanan.

French The native language of some 75 million people in France and its overseas territories as well as in neighbouring countries and in Canada. It is also the official language of a number of African states, having spread as a result of French colonization. It is a Romance language which has developed from the version of the Latin spoken in Gaul after its conquest in 58–51 BC. A number of dialects of French arose, but in recent centuries, since Paris became the French capital, the northern dialects have gained the ascendancy.

French, John Denton Pinkstone, 1st Earl of Ypres (1852–1925) British field-marshal. Having distinguished himself in the Sudan and the Second BOER WAR (1899), he was appointed commander-in-chief of the BRITISH EXPEDITIONARY FORCE in France (1914). Under instructions from Lord KITCHENER he opposed the German advance through Belgium and Flanders. He and his armies were ill-equipped for the kind of trench warfare in which they found themselves involved, and in December 1915 French resigned in favour of Sir Douglas HAIG. At the Irish EASTER RISING in 1916 French dispatched two divisions to suppress the uprising. He served as Lord Lieutenant of Ireland (1918–21) at a time when outrages and reprisals were widespread.

French and Indian wars (1689–1763) Anglo-French conflicts in North America, part of the international rivalry between the two nations. They consisted of King William's War (1689–97), Queen Anne's War (1703–13), King George's War (1744–48), and the French and Indian War (1755–63), the American part of the SEVEN YEARS WAR. As a result of an alliance with Prussia, PITT was able to devote more British resources to America. In 1755 the British commander, General Braddock, led forces into Ohio but was defeated at Fort Duquesne. Other forces defeated the French at the battle of Lake George, but no advantage was taken. The French claimed a number of victories in 1756 and 1757 against the British, already weakened by friction between the new commander, Lord John Loudoun, and the states of Massachusetts and Virginia. In 1759, however, WOLFE defeated the French at the battle of the PLAINS OF ABRAHAM. Quebec surrendered shortly thereafter, followed by Montreal one year later, all Canada then passing into British hands. By the Treaty of PARIS (1763) Britain gained Canada and Louisiana east of the Mississippi.

French Community A political union superseding the French Union, established by France in 1958 and comprising metropolitan France, its overseas departments and territories, and seven former French colonies in Africa, namely, Central African Republic, Chad, Comoros, Congo, Gabon, Madagascar, and Senegal.

French East India Company A commercial organization, founded in 1664 to compete with DUTCH and English EAST INDIA COMPANIES. Until the 1740s it was less successful than its rivals, but led by an ambitious governor, Dupleix, the Company then made a bid to challenge English influence in India, notably by alliances with local rulers in south India. Although a number of trading ports, including PONDICHERRY and Chandernagore, remained in French control until 1949, the Company itself collapsed during the French Revolutionary period.

French empire The colonial empire of France. In the 18th century a long rivalry with Britain ended with the loss of QUEBEC and recognition of British supremacy in India. By 1815 only some West Indian Islands, French Guiana, and Senegal and Gabon were left. The 19th century witnessed a rapid growth of the empire. The conquest of Algeria began (1830), while Far Eastern possessions – Cochin China, Cambodia, and New Caledonia – were added. In the 'Scramble for Africa', Tunisia became a protectorate (1881), and by 1912 MOROCCO, MADAGASCAR, and French Somaliland (DJIBOUTI) had been added to FRENCH EQUATORIAL AFRICA and FRENCH WEST AFRICA to make the African empire twenty times the size of France itself. Britain frustrated French aspirations in Egypt and the Sudan, and rivalry at Fashoda (1898) nearly caused war until the Entente Cordiale brought agreement. After World War I Togoland and the Cameroons, former German colonies, became French Mandates, as did Syria and Lebanon (1923). Defeat in World War II and short-lived post-war governments prevented urgent reforms, causing the loss of both Far Eastern and African empires. In Indo-China the communist leader, HO CHI MINH, established his Vietnamese republic (1945) which France refused to recognize. Open warfare (1946–54) ended with the French capitulation at DIEN BIEN PHU and the consequent independence of Cambodia, Laos, and Vietnam. In Algeria almost the entire French army failed to quell an Arab rising (1954). By 1958 DE GAULLE realized that independence was inevitable, it followed in 1962. In 1946 the empire was formed into the French Union, which was replaced in 1958 by the FRENCH COMMUNITY.

French Equatorial Africa A federation of French colonies created in 1910 to consolidate French territories in west-central Africa. Originally called French Congo, its constituent territories were Gabon, Middle Congo, Chad, and Ubangi-Shari (now the Central African Republic). The federation was dissolved in 1958.

French Foreign Legion A French volunteer armed force consisting chiefly of foreigners. In 1831 LOUIS PHILIPPE reorganized a light infantry legion in Algeria as the *régiment étranger*, the foreign legion. It fought in numerous 19th-century wars and in both World Wars. Following Algeria's independence in 1962 the legion was transferred to France. No questions are asked about the origin or past of the recruits, whose oath binds them absolutely to the regiment whose unofficial motto is *legio patria nostra* ('the legion is our fatherland').

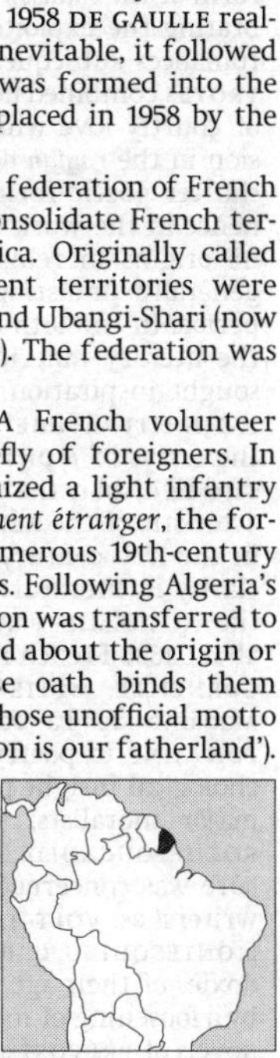

French Guiana (French **Guyane Française**) An overseas department of France in South America, lying to the north of Brazil and east of Surinam; area 90,976 sq km (35,126 sq miles); pop. (est. 1990) 94,700; official language, French; capital, Cayenne. A low-lying territory, French Guiana has a humid tropical climate with a wet season from December to June. Its chief exports are timber, rum, and shrimps. First settled in 1604, it became a territory of France in 1817. It was an official penal colony from 1852 to 1946 when it became an overseas department of France.

French horn A BRASS INSTRUMENT used orchestrally since the mid-17th century as the *corno da caccia* (Italian, 'hunting horn'), played with the bell upwards. Around 1750 players discovered that moving the hand in the bell produced notes other than natural harmonics; this 'hand horn' for which Mozart wrote his horn concertos, was used until the mid-19th century. Valves were invented in 1815.

French Indo-China Former French colonial empire in south-east Asia. Having gained early influence in the area through assisting Gia-Long in establishing the Vietnamese empire in the early 19th century, the French colonized the area between the late 1850s and 1890s, using the term Indo-China to designate the final union of their colonies and dependencies within Annam, Cambodia, Cochin-China, Laos, and Tonkin. Nationalist movements aiming particularly at the formation of an independent and united Vietnam sprang up between the wars, and French influence in the area was fatally undermined in the early 1940s by the collaboration of the VICHY colonial administration with the Japanese. The VIETMINH resistance movement became active during the war; having consolidated a peasant base, it resisted attempts by the French to reassert their control after 1945. A protracted guerrilla war eventually brought France to defeat at DIEN BIEN PHU in 1954. In the same year the Geneva Conference formally ended French control, transferring power to national governments in Cambodia, Laos, and North and South Vietnam.

French literature The earliest literature written in French dates from the 11th century, taking the form of the *chanson de geste*, a narrative poem celebrating the exploits of famous heroes. The verse romances subsequently written by CHRÉTIEN DE TROYES combined heroic inspiration with the ethic of courtly love which found its supreme expression in the *roman de la rose*. In the 15th century a shorter poetic form, the *ballade*, came to prominence in the work of VILLON. French theatre had its origins in religious MYSTERY PLAYS and was generally undistinguished during the medieval period. In the 16th century some writers rejected the literary inheritance of the Middle Ages and sought inspiration in the themes of GREEK and LATIN LITERATURE. The satirical tales of RABELAIS, the essays of MONTAIGNE, and the poems of Ronsard all display the exuberance and erudition characteristic of the RENAISSANCE. This was tempered in the 17th century by an emphasis on order and clarity in literature advocated by MALHERBE and the ACADÉMIE FRANÇAISE among others. After about 1630 French literature reached new heights. CORNEILLE, MOLIÈRE, and RACINE on the stage, Madame de La Fayette in the novel, and LA FONTAINE in poetry displayed a capacity for psychological insight paralleled in the work of three major moralists, PASCAL, LA BRUYÈRE, and LA ROCHEFOUCAULD. By contrast 18th-century literature was concerned primarily with ideas as such writers as VOLTAIRE, ROUSSEAU, DIDEROT, and MONTESQUIEU questioned the ideological orthodoxies of their age. This process was accompanied by a loosening of moral constraints depicted in the novels of PRÉVOST and LACLOS. In the 19th century ROMANTICISM flowered in the 1820s with the publication of poems by LAMARTINE and VIGNY and left its imprint on the novelist STENDHAL. But by the 1830s Théophile Gautier had discovered a more restrained poetic language that anticipated the precision of BAUDELAIRE and the Parnassian poets. This reaction matched the move towards REALISM, seen in the novels of BALZAC and FLAUBERT, which subsequently developed into the more extreme form of naturalism advocated by ZOLA. In the 1880s the SYMBOLISTS rejected slavish depiction of objective reality and developed aesthetic principles that influenced many 20th-century poets including VALÉRY, CLAUDEL, and the SURREALISTS. Since the turn of the century major developments have also taken place in other branches of literature. Alain-Fournier (1886–1914), PROUST, MALRAUX, and the writers of the 'NOUVEAU ROMAN' have brought new vigour to the novel, as GIRAUDOUX, Montherlant, and IONESCO have to the stage. Spanning both genres is SARTRE, the most dominant literary figure since World War II.

French Polynesia (French **Territoire de la Polynésie Française**; formerly **French Oceania**) An overseas territory of France in the South Pacific, comprising five island groups: the Windward Islands (including Tahiti), the Leeward Islands, the Tuamotu Archipelago, the Austral or Tubuai Islands, and the Marquesas Islands; area 3,941 sq km (1,522 sq miles); pop. (est. 1991) 200,000; official language, French; capital, Papeete (on the island of Tahiti). In addition to tourism, the production of copra, vanilla, and mother-ofpearl is important. Under French protection from 1843, the islands were annexed by France in 1880–82 to form the French Settlements in Oceania. Placed under a single administration in 1903, they were accorded the status of overseas territory in 1958. Since 1966 the French have carried out nuclear test explosions on the Mururoa atoll. French Polynesia is administered by a Territorial Assembly which elects a Council of Government.

French Revolution (1789) The political upheaval that ended with the overthrow of the Bourbon monarchy in France and marked a watershed in European history. Various groups in French society opposed the *ancien régime* with its privileged Establishment and discredited monarchy. Its leaders were influenced by the American Revolution of the 1770s and had much popular support in the 1780s and 1790s. Social and economic unrest combined with urgent financial problems persuaded Louis XVI to summon the STATES-GENERAL in 1789, an act which helped to set the Revolution in motion. From the States-General emerged the National Assembly and a new Constitution which abolished the *ancien régime*, nationalized the church's lands, and divided the country into departments to be ruled by elected assemblies. Fear of royal retaliation led to popular unrest, the storming of the BASTILLE, and the capturing of the king by the National Guard. The National Assembly tried to create a monarchical system in which the king would share power with an elected assembly, but after the king's unsuccessful flight to Varennes and the mobilization of exiled royalists, the Revolutionaries faced increasing military threats from Austria and Prussia which led to war abroad and more radical policies at home. In 1792 the monarchy was abolished, a republic established, and the execution of the king was followed by a **Reign of Terror** (September 1793–July 1794). The Revolution failed to produce a stable form of republican government as several different factions (GIRONDINS, JACOBINS, Cordeliers, ROBESPIERRE) fought for power. After several different forms of administration had been tried, the last, the Directory, was overthrown by NAPOLEON in 1799.

French Somaliland The former name (until 1967) of DJIBOUTI.

French Territory of the Afars and Issas The name of DJIBOUTI from 1967 to 1977.

French Union A federation created by France in 1946, comprising France and its overseas departments and territories. The federation was superseded in 1958 by the FRENCH COMMUNITY.

French West Africa A former federation of eight French colonies created in 1895 to consolidate French territory in north and west Africa. Its constituent territories were Dahomey (now Benin), French Guinea, French Sudan, Ivory Coast, Mauritania, Niger, Senegal, and Upper Volta (now Burkina). The federation was dissolved in 1959.

frequency (in physics) The number of cycles occurring within an oscillating system or wave motion in a unit of time. The frequency of a wave motion is in inverse proportion to the WAVELENGTH. Frequency is measured in hertz (symbol Hz), 1 Hz being equivalent to one cycle per second: a string vibrating 440 times a second has a frequency of 440 Hz.

fresco (Italian, 'fresh') A method of wall-painting in which powdered pigments mixed in water are applied to wet plaster freshly laid on the wall. The paint fuses with the plaster, making the picture an integral part of the wall.

Frescobaldi, Girolamo (1583–1643) One of the greatest Italian keyboard composers and organists of his time. In 1608 he became organist at St Peter's in Rome, and in the same year he published his first volume of keyboard music, containing fantasias that show a remarkable grasp of COUNTERPOINT. A volume of toccatas and PARTITAS (1612) demonstrates his gifts as an improviser using unusual harmonies. The CAPRICCIOS of 1624 and the magnificent toccatas of 1627 show a considerable stylistic advance. In 1635 he published his most famous volume, the *Fiori musicali*, a collection of music for use in the Mass, which the young J. S. Bach was to copy and study some sixty years later, and which were to exercise considerable influence on other organ composers such as Buxtehude.

Fresnel, Augustin Jean (1788–1827) French physicist and civil engineer. He took up the study of polarized light and postulated that light moves in a wavelike motion, which had already been suggested by, among others, Christiaan Huygens and Thomas Young. They, however, assumed the waves to be longitudinal, while Fresnel was sure that they vibrated transversely to the direction of propagation, and he used this to explain successfully the phenomenon of double refraction. He invented a converging lens (**Fresnel lens**) made up of a series of concentric rings, each being an element of a simple lens.

Freud, Anna (1895–1982) Austrian-born British psychoanalyst, the youngest child of Sigmund Freud. Anna continued with her father's work and introduced important innovations in method and theory, notably with regard to disturbed children. In 1938 the Freuds narrowly escaped from the Nazis to Britain; after the war Anna set up a child therapy course and clinic in London, and continued to write and lecture extensively. Her major works include *The Ego and Mechanisms of Defence* (1937) and *Normality and Pathology in Childhood* (1966).

Freud, Lucian (1922–) German-born British painter, grandson of Sigmund Freud. He went to Britain in 1931, becoming a British citizen in 1939. Since the 1950s he has established a reputation as a powerful figurative painter. His subjects, especially his portraits and nudes, are painted in a meticulously detailed style based on firm draughtsmanship, often using striking angles.

Freud, Sigmund (1856–1939) Austrian neurologist and psychotherapist. He was the first to draw attention to the significance of unconscious processes in normal and neurotic behaviour, and was the founder of psychoanalysis as both a theory of personality and a therapeutic practice. He proposed the existence of an unconscious element in the mind that influences consciousness, and of conflicts in it between various sets of forces. Freud also emphasized the importance of a child's semi-consciousness of sex as a factor in mental development, and his theory of the sexual origin of neuroses aroused great controversy. His works include *The Interpretation of Dreams* (1899), *Totem and Taboo* (1913), and *The Ego and the Id* (1923).

Frey (or **Yngvi**; Old Norse, 'lord') In Norse mythology, the son of the fertility god Njörd, the most handsome of the gods, ruler of peace who, together with his twin sister FREYJA, brought together the two divine races, the Aesir and the Vanir. He took for his bride, Gerd, a giantess held in the clutches of the frost giants and demons of winter. Himself a god of fertility (his symbol was the boar) as well as the Sun and rain, Frey owned *Skidbladnir*, a magic ship for carrying the gods, a horse named Bloodyhoof, and a victory-winning sword whose lack at the battle of Ragnarök (the doom of the gods) will lead to his defeat by Surt, the sovereign-guardian of Muspelheim, the land of fire.

Freyja (or **Freya**; Old Norse, 'lady') In Norse mythology, a goddess of wealth, fertility, love, battle, and death, from whose name Friday is derived. The sister of FREY and the most beautiful goddess of the Vanir, Freyja was granted the privilege of choosing one-half of the heroes slain in battle for her great hall in Fólk-vangar, the god Odin taking the other half to Valhalla. The trickster god Loki stole her renowned necklace, Brisingamen, forged by dwarfs, and struggled with Heimdall, guardian of the gods' rainbow bridge, for possession of it.

friar (from French *frère*, 'brother') A member of a religious order for men. Friars, together with monks, are known as 'regulars' because they follow a written 'rule' for the conduct of their lives, taking vows of poverty, celibacy, and obedience. Unlike monks, who shut themselves off from the secular world, their duty is to work within the world, preaching and healing. They support themselves largely on the gifts they receive from the laity and are therefore sometimes called mendicants. The four main orders are the Augustinians or Austin friars, who follow the rule of St AUGUSTINE (of Hippo); the FRANCISCANS or Grey Friars; the Dominicans or Black Friars, founded by St DOMINIC; and the CARMELITES or White Friars, the last three being named for the colour of their dress or habit. These orders have survived up to the present day.

friction The force that acts to resist the relative motion of two bodies when one moves over the other. Even if the surfaces are highly polished some friction arises because the atoms on one surface are attracted to those on the other and work has to be done to move one past the other. If the surfaces are rough the friction is greater because the ridges in the surfaces get caught up with one another. The harder the surfaces are forced together the greater is the friction. Frictional forces also operate in liquids and gases, and give rise to VISCOSITY.

Friedan, Betty (1921–) US feminist and writer.

After the birth of her three children she published *The Feminine Mystique* (1963) an instant best seller which presented femininity as an artificial construct and traced the ways in which US women are socialized to become mothers and housewives. In 1966 she founded the National Organization for Women, serving as its president until 1970.

Friedman, Milton (1912–) US economist. A principal exponent of monetarism, he was awarded the Nobel Prize for economics in 1976. He acted as a policy adviser to President Reagan from 1981 to 1989.

Friedrich, Caspar David (1774–1840) German painter. Noted for his romantic landscapes in which he saw a spiritual significance, he caused controversy with his altarpiece *The Cross in the Mountains* (1808), which lacked a specifically religious subject.

Friendly Islands See TONGA.

friendly society A UK institution originally set up in the 19th century as a self-help or cooperative organization, and now a tax-efficient way of saving. The most common form of friendly society is the BUILDING SOCIETY; others are similar to life ASSURANCE companies.

Friends of the Earth See GREEN.

frigate A type of medium-sized warship. The term has been in use since at least the 16th century, but the 'true' frigates were developed by the French in the 1730s and 1740s. Later, frigates grew larger and their armament increased; this trend continued with the introduction of steam. From 1880 the word frigate largely dropped out of use, but towards the end of World War II it was revived for a type of escort ship. After the War frigates became the main medium-sized vessels in most navies. Modern frigates are standard surface warships, very often optimized for anti-submarine work.

frigate bird Any of five species of black tropical seabird of the genus *Fregata*, family Fregatidae; they all have pointed wings, spanning 1.5–2 m (5–7 feet), and forked tails. They are called frigate birds because they attack other birds and force them to disgorge fish; they also catch flying fish as they leap out of the ocean. Frigate birds nest among rocks or low shrubs, raising single chicks. The male frigate birds have a large scarlet sac on their throats which is inflated during courtship displays.

Frigga (or **Frigg**, **Friga**) In Norse and Germanic mythology, a fertility and domestic goddess, the wife of Odin, queen and mother of the gods, often confused with FREYJA. Aware of impending harm to her son Balder, Frigga obtained a promise from all created things except the mistletoe to leave him untouched, and a branch of this plant in time killed him.

frilled lizard A highly spectacular species of mainly tree-dwelling AGAMID lizard from Australia and New Guinea. This species, *Chlamydosaurus kingii*, reaches a total length of about 1 m (3.25 feet). It has a flap of skin (a frill) around its neck, which can be raised and extended to deter enemies. At the same time, the frilled lizard opens its mouth in a wide gape to emphasize its aggressive display. On open ground, if alarmed, it runs quickly upon its hind-legs.

Frink, Dame Elisabeth (1930–93) British sculptor and graphic artist. She made her name with somewhat angular bronzes, often of birds. During the 1960s her figures – typically male nudes, horses, and riders – became smoother, although she retained a feeling for the bizarre.

Frisch, Karl von (1886–1982) Austrian zoologist. He is noted for his work on the behaviour of the honey bee. He studied the vision of bees, showing that they can use polarized light for navigation and see ultraviolet. He also investigated communication between bees, and concluded that they perform an elaborate dance in the hive to show other bees the direction and distance of a source of food. Von Frisch shared a Nobel Prize in 1973 with Konrad Lorenz and Nikolaas Tinbergen.

Frisch, Otto Robert (1904–79) Austrian-born British physicist. With his aunt, Lise MEITNER, he recognized that Otto Hahn's experiments with uranium had produced a new type of nuclear reaction. Frisch named it nuclear fission, and indicated the explosive potential of its chain reaction. During World War II he continued his research in England, and worked on nuclear weapons in the US at Los Alamos.

Frisch, Ragnar (Anton Kittil) (1895–1973) Norwegian economist. A pioneer of econometrics, he shared the first Nobel Prize for economics with Jan Tinbergen (1969).

Frisian The Germanic language of Friesland, most closely related to English and Dutch, with some 300,000 speakers.

Frisian Islands A line of islands in the North Sea off the coast of Denmark, Germany, and the Netherlands, stretching from the Wadden Sea to Jutland. Fishing, cattle-raising, and tourism are important.

Frith, William Powell (1819–1909) British painter. He is remembered for his panoramic paintings of Victorian life, including *Derby Day* (1858) and *The Railway Station* (1862).

fritillary (butterfly) A yellowish- or reddish-brown butterfly chequered with black, a pattern reminiscent of a dice-box (*fritillus* in Latin). The underside of the hind-wing is washed or spotted with silvery or pearly white. Many similarly patterned BRUSH-FOOTED BUTTERFLIES, occurring in Europe, temperate Asia, North Africa, and the Americas, are called fritillaries. Genera such as *Boloria* are largely species of northern temperate regions, some reaching almost to the Arctic Circle. The Duke of Burgundy fritillary, *Hamearis lucina*, of Europe, belongs to the METAL MARK family. Most true fritillaries are fast, powerful fliers. Many caterpillars of the European species feed on violets.

fritillary (plant) An attractive plant of the lily family, with pendent bell-like flowers. About 80 species are known, chiefly from the temperate regions of the Old World and from North America. The snake's head, *Fritillaria meleagris*, grows in wet meadows, and is the best known of the European species. *F. imperialis* is the crown imperial. The bulbs of all species are very poisonous.

Frobisher, Sir Martin (*c.*1535–94) English explorer. In 1576 he led an unsuccessful expedition in search of the North-west Passage, discovering Frobisher Bay (in Baffin Island) and landing in Labrador. He returned to Canada in each of the following two years in a fruitless search for gold, before serving in Sir Francis Drake's West Indies expedition of 1585–86 and playing a prominent part in the defeat of the Spanish Armada (for which he was knighted). He died from wounds received in an attack on a Spanish fort in Brittany.

Froebel, Friedrich (Wilhelm August) (1782–1852) German educationist and founder of the kindergarten system. Believing that play materials, practical occupations, and songs are needed to develop a child's real nature, he opened a school for young children in 1837, later naming it the Kindergarten ('children's garden'). He also established a teacher-training school.

frog An AMPHIBIAN of one of the three major orders. Along with toads, frogs are distinguished in the adult stage by lack of a tail. The popular distinction between frogs and toads applies only in Britain, where frogs have slender bodies, long limbs, and a smooth, moist skin, and toads have stouter bodies, short limbs, and dry, warty skin. In other countries the distinction does not hold, for some families include species with smooth- *and* warty-skinned forms. The pectoral (or shoulder) girdle provides a good structural guide to the difference. Toads have a pair of overlapping cartilage elements in their pectoral girdle, while in frogs the same cartilages meet in the midline but do not overlap.

Members of the genus *Rana* have been called the 'true frogs', and are familiar to most people. Large numbers of the European common frog, *R. temporaria*, and American leopard frog, *R. pipiens*, are used in school and college biology classes, and as experimental animals for research purposes. Larger members of the genus are known as BULLFROGS.

froghopper (or **spittlebug**) A jumping homopteran BUG, occurring worldwide, which sucks sap. The nymphs of most species excrete a substance through which air is forced to form bubbles, often called cuckoo-spit. This is sometimes produced on aerial parts of plants, as in the 800 species of the family Aphrophoridae, or on plant roots, as in the 1,400 species in the family Cercopidae. Some, such as sugar-cane froghoppers, are serious pests.

frogmouth A bird of the family Podargidae, with three species, or Batrachostomidae, with eleven species. They are related to the nightjars, and occur from south-east Asia to Australia. Most species are about the size of crows, but the Papuan frogmouth, *Podargus papuensis*, is larger, being up to 55 cm (22 inches) long. Frogmouths have a mottled brown and grey plumage, which acts as camouflage, a large head with large orange-yellow eyes and an enormous gape. They pounce on frogs and other small animals, mainly hunting at night. They make a loose nest of twigs on a tree branch and raise up to four young.

Froissart, Jean (*c*.1337–*c*.1410) Flemish poet and court historian. His four *Chroniques* provide a detailed, often eye-witness account of European events from 1325 to 1400. His writings were very popular in western Europe in the 15th century.

Fromm, Erich (1900–80) German-born US psychoanalyst and social philosopher. He became a US citizen in 1934, and taught at several universities before being appointed professor of psychiatry at New York in 1962. His works, which include *Escape from Freedom* (1941), *Man for Himself* (1947), and *The Sane Society* (1955), emphasize the role of culture in neurosis and strongly criticize materialist values.

Fronde (from French *fronde*, 'sling') Street fighting in Paris; the word was applied particularly to two revolts against the absolutism of the crown in France between 1648 and 1652 during the minority of LOUIS XIV. The First Fronde began as a protest by the *Parlement* of Paris supported by the Paris mob against war taxation. Disaffected nobles joined in and intrigued with France's enemy, Spain. Peace was restored in March 1649. The Second Fronde began in 1651 with MAZARIN's arrest of the arrogant and overbearing CONDÉ. Throughout France nobles indulged in irresponsible and confused fighting in which certain great ladies played a conspiratorial role. Mazarin fled from France, but Condé and the mutinous nobles who supported him soon lost popularity. Mazarin was able to return, giving the command of the army to the Vicomte de Turenne, who had rejoined the royalist party and quickly recovered Paris for the king. The Fronde ended in Paris in October 1652.

front (in meteorology) An inclined boundary between air masses of different temperatures. The boundary is really a frontal zone, 1 to 2 km (0.6 to 1.2 miles) thick, in which the two types of air are mixed as a result of turbulence. Such a zone may be 100 to 200 km (60 to 120 miles) long at the Earth's surface, which it intersects at an angle of only 0.5 to 2°. At a front the warmer air rises over the denser, colder air. A front is called 'warm' when warmer air is replacing colder at the surface, and 'cold' when the reverse happens. Cold fronts usually travel faster than warm ones and, when they catch them up, the warmer air is lifted above the Earth's surface. The front is now called 'occluded', with cold air both ahead of and behind it. A warm front has layers of cloud up to 800 km (500 miles) wide and 10 km (6 miles) deep associated with it, the cloud thickening towards the surface and often giving a period of continuous precipitation. A cold front has a steeper gradient than a warm one, with a narrower belt of clouds often including cumulonimbus, which give heavier and more intense precipitation.

frost Frozen dew that occurs when the temperature falls to 0°C (32°F) or below. When the water vapour in the atmosphere freezes, which is due usually to radiational cooling of the ground or to the arrival of a cold air mass, the result is an air frost. Hoar-frost, the fluffy deposit of minute ice crystals on grass and brickwork, occurs on calm, clear nights when condensation takes place after freezing.

Frost, Robert (Lee) (1874–1963) US poet. Much of his poetry reflects his affinity with New England, including the verse collections *North of Boston* (1914) and *New Hampshire* (1923). Noted for his ironic tone, conversational manner, and simple language, he won the Pulitzer Prize on three occasions (1924; 1931; 1937).

fruit The ripened ovary of a seed plant and the surrounding tissues. Fruits include many items, such as acorns, pea pods, tomatoes, cucumbers, and wheat grains, which would not be thought of, in common usage, as fruits.

Around the developing seed is a tissue called the pericarp. This may be fleshy, juicy, leathery, oily, fibrous, or hard, and may be subdivided into further layers. Fruits with a fleshy or juicy pericarp, such as DRUPES or BERRIES, are eaten and transported by animals and subsequently deposited in the animal's droppings. Some fruits, such as burs, are adapted to be distributed via the fur of animals – they have their outer pericarp layers formed into hooks. Wind dispersal is exploited by fruits with feathery plumes, such as the dandelion, or membraneous 'wings', such as the sycamore. A few fruits, such as those of the tulip-tree, have fruits with a buoyant pericarp, adapted for water dispersal. The simplest form of dispersal is for the seed to be scattered as the pericarp springs open explosively, such as happens with gorse.

fruit bat See FLYING FOX.

fruit fly A tiny, brownish or yellowish, red-eyed true FLY which is attracted to fermenting fruit and alcoholic drinks. They comprise a large, cosmopolitan family, Drosophilidae, and many species are common; the genus *Drosophila* contains some 1,000 species. They can be a minor pest in orchards or where fruit is stored, particularly in warmer countries. Most feed as larvae on or in decaying fruit and vegetation, and those found in fermenting fruit have been shown to be feeding on yeasts. Other species occur in fungi, on sap runs of trees, as leaf-miners, or in a few species as predators or parasites. Developmental stages of *Drosophila* species are adapted for life in a semi-fluid medium. The adaptations include floats to keep the eggs above the food and breathing 'siphons' in the larvae. *Drosophila* species, particularly the vinegar fly, *D. melanogaster*, have been used extensively in genetics research because they have a short lifespan, are easy to culture, and have large CHROMOSOMES in their salivary glands.

Flies of the family Tephritidae are also known as fruit flies or GALLFLIES, and some species cause great damage to fruit crops. The Mediterranean fruit fly, *Ceratitis capita*, is found wherever fruit is grown.

Frunze The former name (until 1991) of BISHKEK, capital of Kyrgyzstan in Central Asia.

Fry, Christopher (Harris) (1907–) British dramatist. He is chiefly remembered for his comic verse dramas, especially *The Lady's Not for Burning* (1948) and *Venus Observed* (1950). He also wrote several screenplays and translated other dramatists, notably Jean Anouilh.

Fry, Elizabeth (1780–1845) British Quaker prison reformer. In the forefront of the early 19th-century campaign for penal reform, she concerned herself particularly with conditions in Newgate and other prisons, the plight of convicts transported to Australia, and the vagrant population in London and the south-east.

Fry, Roger (Eliot) (1866–1934) British art critic and painter. He was a champion of modern French painting, and of the post-impressionist movement in England. He argued for an aesthetics of pure form, regarding content as incidental. In 1913 he founded the Omega workshops for the benefit of young British artists, and he became Slade Professor of Fine Art at Cambridge in 1933.

Frye, (Herman) Northrop (1912–91) Canadian literary critic. His first major work was *Fearful Symmetry* (1947), a study of William Blake and of the role of myth and symbol in various literary genres. He subsequently analysed the structure and mythology of the Bible in *The Great Code: The Bible and Literature* (1982).

Fuad Two kings of Egypt. **Fuad I** (1868–1936) reigned 1922–36. Formerly sultan of Egypt (1917–22), he became Egypt's first king after independence. **Fuad II** (1952–), grandson of Fuad I, reigned 1952–53. Named king as an infant on the forced abdication of his father, Farouk, he was deposed when Egypt became a republic.

Fuchs, (Emil) Klaus (Julius) (1911–88) German-born British physicist. Fuchs was a Communist who went to England to escape Nazi persecution. During the 1940s he passed to the USSR secret information acquired while working in the US, where he was involved in the development of the atom bomb, and in Britain, where he held a senior post in the Atomic Energy Research Establishment at Harwell. He was imprisoned from 1950 to 1959, and on his release he returned to East Germany.

Fuchs, Sir Vivian (Ernest) (1908–) British geologist and explorer. He led the Commonwealth Trans-Antarctic Expedition (1955–58). His party met Sir Edmund Hillary's New Zealand contingent, approaching from the opposite direction, at the South Pole, and went on to complete the first overland crossing of the continent.

fuchsia A shrub, sometimes with short-lived shoots, native to the Pacific region, especially tropical America. Fuchsias belong to a family of worldwide distribution, Onagraceae, which also includes the willow-herbs and evening primroses. The genus *Fuchsia* has some 100 species, although many familiar garden fuchsias are hybrids with double flowers. Forms of *F. magellanica* are widely used as hedging plants, notably in Ireland. The flowers of most fuchsias are visited by bees or honeybirds and the fruits are edible. In Australia, the term fuchsia is used for species of the unrelated genus *Correa*.

Fucus A genus of brown ALGAE, which includes those commonly called wracks, such as bladder and knotted wrack. They usually grow, often abundantly, in the inter-tidal zone on the sea-shore, attached to rocks by a disc-shaped 'hold-fast' and making a slippery mat at low tide.

fuel additive See LEAD TETRAETHYL.

fuel cell An electrochemical cell that produces an electric current from chemical reactants continuously supplied to its ELECTRODES from an external source. This arrangement differs from ordinary battery or accumulator cells, which cease to function when their original reactants are exhausted. Two reactants are consumed in a fuel cell: one must be oxidizing and take in electrons, and the other must be reducing and liberate electrons (see OXIDATION AND REDUCTION). The usual oxidant is oxygen, and the reductant fuels have, to date, included hydrogen, hydrocarbons, and alcohols. Fuel cells still have only specialist applications because they are expensive to manufacture and use rare materials. For optimum efficiency and size, high internal pressures and temperatures are required. Fuel cells offer a possible future source of power for electric vehicles.

fuel injection See CARBURETTOR.

fuel-oil A heavy oil burnt in BOILERS to provide heat for homes, factories, ships, or power generation. The main components of fuel-oil are high-molecular-weight, involatile residues from various PETROLEUM REFINING processes, mixed with lighter refining products to produce the correct physical characteristics for the type of burner. Low viscosity is important for small domestic boilers. The melting-point, or pouring-point of the oil may also be important. Many fuel-oils solidify in the range 2–20°C, and may need warming before use.

Fuentes, Carlos (1928–) Mexican novelist and writer. His first novel, *Where the Air is Clear* (1958) took Mexico City as its theme and was an immediate success. Other novels include *Terra nostra* (1975), which explores the Spanish heritage in Mexico, and *The Old Gringo* (1984).

Fugard, Athol (1932–) South African dramatist. Many of his plays, including *Blood Knot* (1963) and *The Road to Mecca* (1985), deal with social deprivation and other aspects of life in South Africa during the apartheid era.

fugue A type of contrapuntal, musical composition (see COUNTERPOINT) in which the voices (parts) enter one by one with the same short theme, referred to as the subject. Fugues can be for any number of voices, four being the most frequent. When all the voices have entered, the exposition (statement of material) is complete and the composition proceeds through an exploratory middle section (the middle entries) to a final statement of the thematic material (the final entries). In the exposition, as soon as one voice has stated the subject and the second voice takes over, the first voice continues with a counter-subject, which then passes to the second voice as the third takes over the subject.

Fujairah One of the seven member-states of the United Arab Emirates whose people are largely of the Sharqiyin tribe; area 1,300 sq km (502 sq miles); pop. (1995) 76,250. Recognized as a separate emirate in 1952, it is the only emirate with no coastline on the Persian Gulf.

Fuji, Mount (Japanese **Fujisan**, **Fujiyama**) An active volcano in Chubu Region on the island of Honshu, Japan, 88 km (52 miles) west of Tokyo. It is the highest peak in Japan (3,776 m, 12,385 ft), forming a snowcapped cone of exceptional beauty. A sacred mountain which has inspired Japanese poets and artists for centuries. Its last eruption was in 1707.

Fujian (formerly **Fukien**) A mountainous province of south-east China facing the China Sea; area 123,100 sq km (47,547 sq miles); pop. (est. 1986) 27,490,000; capital, Fuzhou. Timber, rubber, oils and resins, rice, sugarcane, tobacco, fruit, and fish are its chief products.

Fujiyama See FUJI, MOUNT.

Fukuoka (formerly **Hakata**) A commercial and industrial city on the north coast of Kyushu Island, southern Japan; pop. (1990) 1,237,100. It is a port and capital of a prefecture of the same name with ferry links to other Japanese islands and to Pusan in Korea.

Fulani A nomadic cattle-herding people of the Sahel region of West Africa, especially in Senegal, Guinea, Niger, Mali, Chad, and Nigeria, whose language belongs to the Niger-Kordofanian language group.

Fulani empire of Sokoto West African Islamic empire. In the late 18th century the Fulani came into contact with the nominally Muslim Hausa states. One of their clerics, Uthman dan Fodio (1754–1817), had built up a community of scholars at Degel in the Hausa state of Gobir, whose new sultan in 1802 enslaved Uthman's followers. A quarrel developed, Uthman was proclaimed 'commander of the faithful', and in the ensuing *jihad* (holy war) all the Hausa states collapsed. By 1810 Uthman had created a vast empire, to be administered by emirs in accordance with Koranic law. High standards of public morality replaced the corruption of the Hausa states and widespread education was achieved. In 1815 he retired, appointing his son Muhammed Bello his successor and suzerain over all the emirates. Bello had built the city of Sokoto, of which he became the sultan, and he considerably extended the empire, establishing control of west Bornu and pushing down into the YORUBA empire of Oyo. Although losing some of its high ideals, the Fulani empire of Sokoto continued under Bello's successors. In the late 19th century British penetration of the empire increased. Kano and Sokoto were sacked in 1903, when the empire ended, although the emirates survived under the system of indirect rule instituted by the first High Commissioner, Frederick Lugard.

Fulbright, (James) William (1905–95) US senator. His name designates grants awarded under the Fulbright Act of 1946, which authorized funds from the sale of surplus war materials overseas to be used to finance exchange programmes of students and teachers between the US and other countries. The scheme was later supported by grants from the US government.

Fuller, R(ichard) Buckminster (1895–1983) American designer and architect. An advocate of the use of technology to produce efficiency in many aspects of life, he is best known for his post-war invention of the geodesic dome. These domes enable large spaces to be enclosed with great efficiency – in line with Fuller's ideals of using the world's resources with maximum purpose and least waste.

Fuller, Roy (Broadbent) (1912–91) British solicitor, poet, and novelist; professor of poetry at Oxford University 1968–73. His later poetry, including *New Poems* (1968), *The Reign of Sparrows* (1980), and *Available for Dreams* (1989), earned him a considerable reputation. His several novels include *The Image of a Society* (1956) and *The Carnal Island* (1970). His collected memoirs, *The Strange and the Good*, was published in 1989.

Fuller, Thomas (1608–61) English cleric and historian. He is chiefly remembered for *The History of the Worthies of England* (1662), a description of the counties with short biographies of local personages.

fullerene See BUCKMINSTERFULLERENE.

fuller's earth See MONTMORILLONITE.

fulmar A large, heavily built bird of the same family as PETRELS, Procellariidae. The two species of the genus *Fulmarus*, the common fulmar, *F. glacialis*, and northern fulmar or silver-grey petrel, *F. glacialoides*, have narrow wings and gliding flight, and pick their food off the sea surface. They are native to Arctic and sub-Arctic regions.

Fulton, Robert (1765–1815) US pioneer of the steamship. During the Napoleonic Wars he spent some time in France and proposed both torpedoes and submarines, constructing a steam-propelled 'diving-boat' called *Nautilus* in 1800 which submerged to a depth of 7.6 m (25 ft). He returned to America in 1806 and built the first successful paddle-steamer, the *Clermont*.

fumarole A volcanic vent from which steam and other hot gases emerge. Fumaroles are characteristic of a late stage of volcanic activity when violent eruptions have ceased. The Valley of Ten Thousand Smokes in Alaska is well known for its fumaroles.

fumitory A member of a group of slender annual plants from the temperate regions of the Old World. They give their name to the family Fumariaceae, which contains 400 species of annual or perennial plants including bleeding heart, *Dicentra spectabilis*. The European fumitory, *Fumaria officinalis*, a weed of cultivation and waste places (and naturalized in the USA), was held in high esteem by DIOSCORIDES for its purifying powers.

Funan A former kingdom of south-east Asia extending over much of present-day Cambodia and southern Vietnam from the 1st to the 6th centuries. It owed its prosperity to its position on the great trade route between India and China and subsequent Khmer dynasties viewed Funan as the state from which they were descended. The name is a transliteration of the ancient Khmer form of the word *phnom* (= hill).

Funchal The capital and chief port of the Portuguese island of Madeira in the Atlantic; pop. (1991) 109,960. Situated on the south coast of the island, the city was founded in 1421. It is a year-round tourist resort and port of call for cruise ships.

functional groups (in chemistry) Atoms or groups of atoms in an organic molecule that cause it to react in a particular way. All the members of a HOMOLOGOUS SERIES possess the same functional group, and differ only in the number of atoms in the carbon chain. For example, the carboxylic acids all have the general formula RCOOH, where R is either hydrogen or an ALKYL or an ARYL GROUP, and the functional group is the carboxyl group, –COOH. If a molecule contains more than one functional group, its chemical properties are generally the sum of the separate properties associated with each group. However, when the two groups are very close, they modify each other.

functionalism (in architecture and design) A doctrine that the design of a building or object should be determined solely by its function, rather than by decorative considerations, and that anything perfectly designed for its purpose will be inherently beautiful. Although aspects of the idea can be traced back to Greek antiquity, it was not until the 20th century that it became an aesthetic creed, expressed, for example, in LE CORBUSIER's dictum that 'a house is a machine for living in'.

functionalism (in philosophy) A doctrine in the philosophy of mind formulated as a response to the failure of BEHAVIOURISM to give an intuitively satisfying account of the mind. Functionalism claims that we can give a full account of a mental state only if we appeal to all its causes and all its effects, rather than just its behavioural effects. So functionalism, unlike behaviourism, can see mental states as causally interacting with other mental states and so can solve many of the difficulties inherent in the behaviourist approach.

fundamentalism In CHRISTIANITY, a Protestant religious movement that stresses traditional Christian doctrines, especially the literal truth of the Bible. Fundamentalism developed in the 1920s in opposition to modern techniques of biblical criticism; its adherents have been particularly powerful in the USA, especially among the various Baptist groups. Fundamentalists were and are particularly noted for their hostility to DARWIN's theory of evolution, as shown by the prosecution of J. T. Scopes in Tennessee. Fundamentalism is associated with EVANGELICALISM, and has re-emerged in recent years as an influential movement, particularly in the USA, where fundamentalist views reach a wide audience through religious broadcasting. Fundamentalists promote the teaching of creationism (that is, the biblical account of the creation) rather than evolutionary theories in schools. Fundamentalism also occurs in other religions. Fundamental JUDAISM, like Christianity, rejects scientific theories of cosmology that conflict with the account given in the Old Testament. See also ISLAMIC FUNDAMENTALISM.

Fundy, Bay of An inlet of the Atlantic Ocean between the Canadian provinces of New Brunswick and Nova Scotia. It is subject to fast-running tides, the highest in the world, reaching 21 m (70 ft) and now used to generate electricity.

fungicide Any PESTICIDE that kills fungi. Fungicides based on the broadly toxic elements copper, mercury, and sulphur were among the earliest AGROCHEMICALS: copper sulphate and mercury chloride were used in the 18th century, and lime sulphur was used to treat mildew from 1802 onwards. These compounds have now been largely superseded by synthetic systemic compounds that enter the plant via the roots or shoots and are then transported to all other tissues. Diseases such as rusts, mildews, and blights spread rapidly once established. Fungicides are thus routinely applied to growing and stored crops as a preventive measure, generally as foliar sprays or seed dressings. Disease forecasting aids the farmer in determining when to spray for early protection.

fungus A member of a KINGDOM of eukaryotic organisms, the Fungi, which differ from plants in having no chlorophyll and in being incapable of photosynthesis, but which resemble plants in that they generally have a cell wall and absorb food molecules in soluble form. Many fungi grow in the form of microscopic threads called hyphae, which typically branch extensively to form a weft called a mycelium. All fungi reproduce and spread mainly by means of SPORES, each microscopic spore being capable of germinating to produce a new hypha.

Fungi are subdivided into four phyla. Members of the Zygomycota (such as the common pin-mould) form non-flagellated asexual spores and thick-walled, sexually-derived resting spores (called zygospores). The Deuteromycota (Fungi Imperfecti) includes fungi with no known sexual stage, although they typically produce asexual spores in abundance; they include 'moulds' such as *Penicillium*. The Ascomycota includes fungi which produce sexually-derived spores (called ascospores) in microscopic sac-like structures called asci; examples in this group include brewers' and bakers' YEASTS, the cup fungi and the MORELS. The Basidiomycota includes fungi which produce sexually-derived spores (called basidiospores) at the surface of microscopic structures called basidia; the basidia are usually borne on or in relatively large fruiting structures such as the familiar mushrooms, toadstools, puffballs and bracket fungi. Organisms traditionally regarded as fungi, such as the SLIME MOULDS and oomycetes (water moulds, downy mildews, etc.), are now usually classified as PROTOCTISTA, although some authorities continue to classify them as fungi.

Some fungi are parasitic and can cause diseases such as rusts, smuts, and mildews in plants, and, less often, diseases in animals such as ringworm and athlete's foot. Some can form mutually beneficial associations with animals or plants: AMBROSIA BEETLES, LICHENS, MYCORRHIZAS and TERMITES are all examples of such associations. Certain fungi are useful commercially as sources of antibiotics, while some species of mould are used in the making of blue cheeses. Mould is also an important ingredient of tempeh, a food based on soya beans. Such fungi as mushrooms, truffles, and black fungus are grown or collected for food. Mushrooms are a good source of fibre, are low in fat, and contain more protein per unit weight than almost any other vegetable. However, many fungi are capable of detrimental effects such as food spoilage and timber decay.

funicular railway A railway in which a cable is used to move a vehicle running on rails up and down a steep slope. In most systems two vehicles, running on separate lines, are joined by the haulage cable and as one descends the other ascends, so minimizing the power required. Early funiculars used water balance, steam, or hydraulic power, but most have now been rebuilt to use electrical power.

Funk, Casimir (1884–1967) Polish-born US biochemist. He showed that a number of diseases, including scurvy, rickets, beriberi, and pellagra, were each caused by the deficiency of a particular dietary component. He coined the term *vitamins* (originally *vitamines*) for the chemicals concerned, from his belief (later shown to be inaccurate) that they were all amines. His work formed the basis of modern dietary studies.

Furies In Greek and Roman mythology, three terrifying goddesses – Alecto, Megaesa, and Tisiphone – who pursued and punished the perpetrators of certain crimes, particularly murder of kin. They were generally represented as old women with snakes for hair.

furnace See BLAST-FURNACE; BOILER; FLUIDIZED BED FURNACE; SOLAR FURNACE.

furniture Furniture has been made of a wide variety of materials (wood, metal, textiles, glass, plastics) and decorated in many ways, including painting, gilding, carving, and inlay with semi-precious materials. The most common material for furniture, however, has been wood, and because this material is easily subject to decay, little furniture survives from early times. It is only from about 1400 that furniture survives in sufficient quantity to be able to trace a continuous history. The Industrial Revolution brought with it the general commercial production of furniture. With the foundation of the Century Guild in Britain in 1882 there began a revival of craftsmanship through the ARTS AND CRAFTS MOVEMENT. In the 20th century the leaders in modern design have been Scandinavia and Germany, while the BAUHAUS furniture, based on mechanized production and the use of new materials, set a standard of creative design in Europe and the USA. Modern furniture ranges from bent tubular steel to moulded plywood, soft and hard plastics, and refined sculptural forms in wood.

furniture beetle A small, brown BEETLE of the family Anobiidae, related to the death watch beetle. Its larvae, commonly called woodworms, are the most important beetle pest of hardwood, even of wickerwork, and naturally occur in dead wood in the wild. The head of the adult beetle is under the thorax and is not visible from above. It lays its eggs in cracks in unpainted wood, and the larvae bore tunnels in the wood, filling them with excreta as they feed. When nearly mature, they move to just below the surface, where they pupate. The adult leaves a circular hole when it eats its way out. There are some 1,100 species of beetles in the Anobiidae, which occur worldwide.

further education See CONTINUING EDUCATION.

Furtwängler, Wilhelm (1886–1954) German conductor. He was chief conductor of the Berlin Philharmonic Orchestra from 1922, and often worked at Bayreuth. He is noted particularly for his interpretations of Beethoven and Wagner.

fuse A simple safety device for preventing excessive or damaging electric current flow. The fuse consists of a short piece of bare wire with a low melting-point, suspended between two contacts by which it is connected into an electrical circuit. On overload, the current rapidly heats the wire; the wire quickly melts, breaking the circuit and cutting off the current. Fuses are specified according to the maximum current that they will carry before melting. Unlike a CIRCUIT-BREAKER, fuses are not reusable and must be replaced after being overloaded. In modern domestic practice, cartridge fuses are used in which the fuse wire is enclosed in a glass or ceramic cartridge.

Fuseli, Henry (born Johann Heinrich Füssli) (1741–1825) Swiss-born British painter and art critic. In 1763 he went to England, where he became a prominent figure of the romantic movement. His work is often derived from literary themes (notably those of Shakespeare and Milton) and is inspired by a vivid imagination, tending towards the horrifying and the fantastic, as in *The Nightmare* (1781). In 1799 he was appointed professor of painting at the Royal Academy.

fusion, nuclear A **thermonuclear reaction** in which two or more light atomic nuclei combine to form a heavier atomic nucleus, with the release of very large amounts of energy. In the fusion of, for example, two hydrogen nuclei to form a helium nucleus, there is some loss of mass, and this mass is completely converted to energy (see NUCLEAR ENERGY). The loss of mass resulting from the fusion of light elements tends to be greater than that resulting from the nuclear FISSION of heavy elements, and therefore fusion generates more energy than fission. Most of the world's energy comes ultimately from fusion reactions taking place in the Sun, in which hydrogen nuclei are fused at extremely high temperatures (10 million °C) to form helium. An enormous amount of money and effort has been invested worldwide in fusion research, because of its potential as a limitless source of energy. The first result of this research was the manufacture of the hydrogen bomb (see NUCLEAR WEAPON) in 1952. Since then research has been directed at producing a **thermonuclear reactor** to provide a source of energy. Research has been along two main lines. In the first, a plasma (a totally ionized gas) of deuterium and tritium is raised to a temperature of about 100 million degrees in a toroidal (ring-shaped) reactor called a **tokamak**. The plasma is prevented from melting the reactor vessel by containment, i.e. constricting the plasma by means of powerful magnetic fields to prevent it from contacting the containing vessel. A second line of research is laser fusion, in which a small pellet of deuterium and tritium is imploded by concentration of the energy of several powerful lasers on it. By the mid 1990s, neither method had yielded more energy from fusion than had been put into the system. Estimates for the arrival of successful energy production vary from the year 2010 to 2200.

futures markets Markets in which contracts to buy and sell at future dates are traded. Futures markets exist for foreign currencies, some goods (chiefly COMMODITIES), and SECURITIES. Dealers contract to buy or sell a specified amount for a specified price on a specified future date. In some cases the contract itself may be subsequently traded. Futures markets exist to diminish risk by removing price uncertainty from particular transactions. With agricultural commodities crops may be sold before harvest (the amount specified in the deal being whatever a certain acreage yields), thus insuring the farmer against harvest failure. See also ARBITRAGE.

Futurism Italian art movement founded in 1909 by the poet Filippo Tommaso Marinetti. It was originally a literary movement, but the dominant figures were painters and it also embraced sculpture, architecture, music, the cinema, and photography. The aim of the movement, which was outlined in various manifestos, was to break with the past and to celebrate modern technology, dynamism, and power. The rendering of movement was one of the key concerns of Futurist painters, and their work at times approached abstraction. As an organized movement Futurism did not last much beyond the death of BOCCIONI and the end of World War I, but it had wide influence, notably in Russia, where there was a Russian Futurist movement, and also in Britain, on VORTICISM. The DADAISTS also owed something to it, particularly in their noisy publicity techniques.

G

gabbro A coarse-grained IGNEOUS ROCK composed of light-grey or greenish minerals: pyroxene, plagioclase feldspar, and occasionally olivine. There are many varieties, but gabbro is the coarse-grained or plutonic equivalent of BASALT, so all gabbros have crystallized at depth and are basic rocks (low in silica). The rock is too fragile for use as a construction material, but it often contains valuable quantities of chromium, nickel, cobalt, platinum, and copper.

Gable, (William) Clark (1901–60) US actor. He became famous through his numerous roles in Hollywood films of the 1930s: they include *It Happened One Night* (1934), for which he won an Oscar, and *Gone with the Wind* (1939), in which he starred as Rhett Butler. His last film was *The Misfits* (1961), in which he played opposite Marilyn Monroe.

Gabo, Naum (born Naum Neemia Pevsner) (1890–1977) Russian-born US sculptor. With his brother, Antoine Pevsner, he was a founder of Russian constructivism, and was one of the first sculptors to use transparent materials. The brothers' *Realistic Manifesto* of 1920 set down their artistic principles, including the idea of introducing time and movement into sculpture; Gabo made his first kinetic sculpture, a vibrating metal rod powered by an electric motor, in 1920.

Gabon An equatorial country on Africa's Atlantic coast, bounded inland by Equatorial Guinea, Cameroon, and Congo.

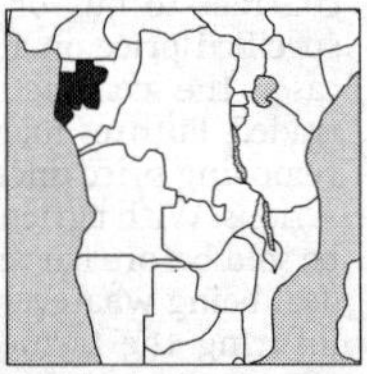

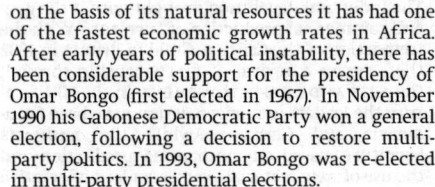

Physical. Along the coast of Gabon are lagoons, mangrove swamps, and large deposits of oil and natural gas. A broad plain covered by thick rain forest rises gradually to a plateau which surrounds a central river valley, and near the head this vegetation gives way to SAVANNAH.

Economy. Gabon is the wealthiest mainland African country, with one of the continent's fastest economic growth rates, based on substantial, albeit now falling, revenues from offshore oilfields. Gabon was a member of OPEC from 1975 until 1996. Mineral deposits also include gold and diamonds, manganese, and uranium. The country is also rich in a soft timber, *okoumé*, used for making plywood. Sugar-cane, cassava, and plantains are the chief agricultural crops.

History. In 1839 the French made it a naval base to suppress slave trade. Thus a French colony developed, exploiting the rare woods, gold, diamonds, other minerals, and oil. The country became autonomous within the French Community in 1958 and fully independent in 1960. Almost entirely on the basis of its natural resources it has had one of the fastest economic growth rates in Africa. After early years of political instability, there has been considerable support for the presidency of Omar Bongo (first elected in 1967). In November 1990 his Gabonese Democratic Party won a general election, following a decision to restore multi-party politics. In 1993, Omar Bongo was re-elected in multi-party presidential elections.

Capital: Libreville
Area: 267,667 sq km (103,347 sq mi)
Population: 1,156,000 (1995)
Currency: 1 CFA franc = 100 centimes
Religions: Roman Catholic 65.2%; Protestant 18.8%; African indigenous Christian 12.1%; traditional religions 2.9%; Muslim 0.8%
Ethnic Groups: Fang 30.0%; Eshura 20.0%; Mbete 15.0%; Kota 13.0%; Omyene 15.0%
Languages: French (official); Fang; Eshura; local languages
International Organizations: UN; OAU; Non-Aligned Movement; Franc Zone

gaboon viper A very thick-bodied snake, *Bitis gabonica*, sometimes growing to just over 2 m (6.75 feet) in length, and found in the rain forests of equatorial Africa and south as far as Natal. The fangs are notably long, over 5 cm (2 inches) in large individuals, and a bite can be very dangerous. When not seeking ground-living animals as prey, this colourful but beautifully camouflaged snake is often sluggish. It is a true viper and belongs to the same family as the PUFF ADDER.

Gabor, Dennis (1900–79) Hungarian-born British scientist who invented HOLOGRAPHY (1947), a means of creating an image in three-dimensional space. Early holograms were poor in quality, but the possibilities of holography were enormously increased with the advent of the LASER in 1960. Gabor was awarded the Nobel Prize for Physics in 1971.

Gaborone A city in southern Africa, capital of Botswana, situated near the Ngotwane River on the main railway line linking South Africa with the Frontline States; pop. (1991) 133,470. Established in the 1890s and named after the chief of the Batlokwa tribe, Gaborone was chosen in 1962 as the site of the new capital of Botswana in preparation for independence in 1966. For a year prior to independence it was capital of the Bechuanaland Protectorate. It is one of the fastest growing cities in Africa and contains the University College of Botswana (1976), the National Museum, and Art Gallery.

Gabriel The archangel and traditional messenger of God in the Bible whose name in Hebrew means 'mighty one of God'. He appeared to Daniel to interpret his visions, to Zacharias to foretell the birth of John the Baptist, and to Mary to announce that she would have a son called Jesus. In Islamic tradition the whole Koran was revealed to Muhammad by the archangel Jibrīl (Gabriel), who is sometimes called the Faithful Spirit. In later legends he is alleged to have shown Adam the site of Mecca, to have helped the prophets, and to have announced the birth of Yahya (John) to Zachariya (Zacharias).

Gabrieli, Giovanni (*c.*1553–1612) Italian composer and organist. He was the nephew of the composer and organist **Andrea Gabrieli** (*c.*1533–86), and like him became organist of St Mark's, Venice (1585). His music consists mainly of MOTETS, a handful of MADRIGALS, and much instrumental music. He developed the idiomatic use of instruments, made the contrasts of sound and texture more acute, and increased the use of dissonance. Many of his works (vocal and instrumental) exploit the idea of groups of performers arranged antiphonally, the spatial effect of sounds coming from different directions. The contrasts that his compositions created between loud and soft, voice and instrument, contributed significantly to the evolution of the CONCERTO GROSSO.

Gaddafi, Mu'ammer Muhammad al (or **Qaddafi**) (1942–) Libyan colonel, head of state since 1970. After leading the coup which overthrew King Idris (1890–1983) in 1969, he gained power as chairman of the revolutionary council and established the Libyan Arab Republic. As self-appointed head of state Gaddafi has pursued an anti-colonial policy at home, expelling foreigners from Libya and seeking to establish an Islamic Socialist regime. He has been accused of supporting international terrorism and has been involved in a number of conflicts with the West, as also with neighbouring Arab countries. Since 1979 he has held no formal post, although he has the ceremonial title 'leader of the revolution'.

gadfly See BOT FLY; HORSEFLY.

gadolinium (symbol Gd, at. no. 64, r.a.m. 157.25) A soft silvery metal belonging to the lanthanide group. Because it is a strong neutron absorber it has been used in nuclear technology. It is also used in some ferromagnetic alloys.

Gael A Scottish or Gaelic-speaking Celt.

Gaelic A language spoken in Ireland and Scotland in two distinct varieties, referred to also as Irish (or Erse) and Scots Gaelic respectively, forming, together with Manx, the Goidelic group of the Celtic language group. From about the 5th century AD the language was carried to Scotland by settlers from Ireland (see DALRIADA), and became the language of most of the highlands and islands; in time the Scottish variety diverged to the point where it was clearly a different dialect. Scots Gaelic is spoken by only about 75,000 people in the far west of Scotland; there is a small flourishing literary movement. A number of English words are taken from it, e.g. *bog, cairn, slogan, whisky*.

Gaelic literature See SCOTTISH-GAELIC LITERATURE; IRISH LITERATURE.

Gagarin, Yuri (Alekseevich) (1934–68) Soviet cosmonaut. In 1961 he made the first manned space flight, completing a single orbit of the Earth in 108 minutes. He was killed in a crash while testing an aeroplane.

Gage, Thomas (1721–87) British general, appointed British commander in America in 1763, after service in Flanders, at CULLODEN, and in the FRENCH AND INDIAN WAR. His responsibilities shifted from frontier defence to quelling unrest in such towns as New York and Boston. He was appointed governor of Massachusetts in 1774 to enforce the Coercive Acts, but he bungled Lexington and Concord, and resigned after BUNKER HILL.

Gaia (or **Gaea**, **Ge**) In Greek mythology, the Earth, personified as a goddess, daughter of Chaos (the goddess representing primeval emptiness). She was the mother and wife of Uranus (Heaven); their offspring included the Titans and the Cyclopes.

Gaia hypothesis The theory, put forward by the British scientist James Lovelock in 1969, that the entire range of living matter on Earth defines the material conditions needed for its survival, functioning as a vast organism (which he named after the goddess Gaia) capable of modifying the biosphere, atmosphere, oceans, and soil to produce the physical and chemical environment that suits its needs.

Gainsborough, Thomas (1727–88) British painter. From 1760 he worked in Bath and from 1774 in London, where he became a society portrait painter. Although he was famous for his portraits, such as *Mr and Mrs Andrews* (1748) and *The Blue Boy* (*c.*1770), landscape was his preferred subject; his works reflect the influence of the naturalistic approach to landscape of 17th-century Dutch painting and include *The Watering Place* (1777). He was a founder member of the Royal Academy of Arts (1768).

Gaitskell, Hugh (Todd Naylor) (1906–63) British Labour politician. Having served in the Attlee government in several ministerial posts, including Chancellor of the Exchequer (1950–51), he became leader of the Labour Party in opposition from 1955 until his death. Although his leadership covered a period of upheaval and reassessment within his party following successive election defeats, he eventually succeeded in restoring party unity. He was particularly vigorous in his opposition to the government over the Suez crisis and in resisting calls for unilateral disarmament within his own party.

galactic equator The intersection of the plane containing the disc of the GALAXY with the CELESTIAL SPHERE. It is inclined at about 63 degrees to the celestial equator and is used as a reference plane in a system of COORDINATES to locate objects within the Galaxy. Such objects are referred to by their galactic longitude and galactic latitude.

galactic halo The large spherical volume of the GALAXY enclosing the more luminous disc. It contains old, faint Population II stars and globular CLUSTERS, as well as the outer regions of the galactic magnetic field, electromagnetic radiation, cosmic rays, and tenuous, highly ionized gas at a temperature of about 10^6 K. The stars and clusters in the galactic halo do not have any general systematic motion, but travel in randomly orientated orbits, and from the vantage point of the Earth often have large RADIAL VELOCITIES.

galactic rotation The rotation of a GALAXY about an axis within it. The PROPER MOTIONS of stars in our own galaxy and stellar dynamics and kinematics, show that stars, clusters, and molecular clouds all orbit about the galactic centre under NEWTON'S LAW OF GRAVITATION. Spectroscopic studies of nearby galaxies like the Andromeda Galaxy reveal that they too are in rotation.

galago See BUSHBABY.

Galahad In Celtic and medieval Christian mythology, the son of Lancelot and Elaine, daughter of the Grail King Pelles. In Malory's *Le Morte D'Arthur* (1470), Galahad alone among ARTHUR's knights could occupy the Siege Perilous (that seat at the

Round Table reserved for the knight who should find the Holy Grail). He died in ecstasy after his vision of Christ with the Grail.

Galápagos finches Fourteen (or in some classifications thirteen) species of bird belonging to the finch family, Fringillidae, also known collectively as Darwin's finches and often separated as the subfamily Geospinizae. They are confined to the Galápagos Islands, except for one, the Cocos Island finch, *Pinaroloxias inomata*. Most are sparrow-sized birds, the males tending to be black, the females greyish. The main variations are in bill shapes, which vary from very heavy, finch-like beaks, through smaller bunting-like ones, to a fine warbler type. They are famous for their description in Charles Darwin's theory of evolution. Darwin realized that all the species were so similar that they must have descended from a common ancestor. The present-day range of species of Galápagos finches is a result of the adaptation of different varieties to particular ways of life. Some are seed-eaters, others insect-eaters, and both types have bill shapes to match their way of life.

Galápagos Islands A group of 13 large islands and many small ones spread across the Equator in the Pacific Ocean, belonging to Ecuador. The Galápagos Islands are situated about 1,000 km (600 miles) west of Ecuador, in whose sovereign territory they lie. They consist mainly of volcanoes that have developed on an east–west-trending fracture zone and which rise up to 3,000 m (10,000 feet) from the sea floor. They then stand a further 1,800 m (6,000 feet) above sea-level. The resulting scenery is striking: large summit craters, fresh lava flows, and impressive sea cliffs diversify a generally rugged topography. There is a rich wildlife with many endemic species including birds (some flightless), iguanas, and giant tortoises.

Galatia An ancient region in central Asia Minor, settled by invading Gauls (the Galatians) in the 3rd century BC. In 64 BC it became a protectorate of Rome and, in 25 BC, with the addition of some further territories, was made a province of the Roman empire.

galaxy An association of stars, dust, and gas, with a total mass ranging from 10^6 to 10^{13} times the mass of the Sun. The Milky Way, known as the GALAXY, is our own galaxy, and the Sun is only one star of the 100 billion stars in it.

There are many types of galaxy, the principal ones being spiral and elliptical galaxies, and there have been several attempts to classify them using strict lettering and numbering schemes, such as the HUBBLE CLASSIFICATION. However, many types fall outside the scope of these schemes and are named after the astronomer who first listed them as a distinct type (such as Seyfert and Markarian galaxies) or letters from classification schemes (for example, N- and cD-type galaxies). Galaxies with no obvious form are classified as irregular. All galaxies contain stars, gas, and dust, but in very different proportions, and even within one galaxy the distribution of these constituents may vary enormously. Many have a distinct nucleus or central concentration of material which may be active, that is, emitting large amounts of energy, and even exploding. Some emit jets of material at speeds close to the velocity of light. Although galaxies contain enormous amounts of matter by terrestrial standards, they usually occur in even larger groupings or **clusters**, with the smaller clusters having only a few members but larger clusters may contain several thousand galaxies. However, the origin and evolution of galaxies is still not fully understood.

SPIRAL GALAXIES are probably the best-known type of galaxy. The term is used to describe galaxies which have an obvious spiral structure, such as the Andromeda Galaxy. Our own galaxy is believed to be a spiral. Their appearance is similar to that of a Catherine wheel with the majority of the stars and luminous material forming the spiral arms. The spiral arms also contain an interstellar medium of dust and neutral hydrogen gas; the latter is now extensively studied using its twenty-one centimetre line, which is only accessible to radio astronomers. The masses of almost all spiral galaxies fall in the range 10^9 to 3×10^{11} times the mass of the Sun. **Elliptical galaxies** are also a common type of galaxy. They appear as ellipses on astronomical photographs, with no evidence of spiral structure. The classification covers a wide range of sizes, from small dwarf ellipticals with masses of only a few million times that of the Sun to giant ellipticals and **cD-type galaxies** with masses of 10^{13} times that of the Sun. Most of the matter in an elliptical galaxy is in the form of stars and hot gas. The largest known galaxies are cD-type galaxies. These are massive elliptical galaxies, and occur at the centre of a few of the largest clusters of galaxies. They are distinguished by having a large nucleus, or they may have several nuclei in rapid motion with respect to each other, but all within an extensive envelope. Often they are fairly strong radio sources. Markarian galaxies were first classified by the Soviet astronomer Beniamin Markarian in 1967. They have very strong emission in the ultraviolet part of the spectrum. Their spectrum is similar to that of HII regions within our own galaxy. An **N-type galaxy** has a star-like nucleus and a very faint haze around it. These galaxies are usually strong radio sources, and it has been suggested that they evolve into QUASARS. On an astronomical photograph, a SEYFERT GALAXY looks like a spiral galaxy except for its nucleus, which is very much brighter than in a normal spiral. Seyfert galaxies are also distinguished by their spectra which show broad bright emission lines, implying the presence of a large amount of a rapidly moving hot gas in the nucleus. This type was discovered by the US astronomer Carl Seyfert in 1943.

Galaxies that can be observed optically and which are also strong radio sources are called RADIO GALAXIES. They include Seyfert, cD- and N-type galaxies, as well as quasars.

Galaxy The GALAXY to which the Solar System belongs. A star system containing at least 100 billion stars, it has three main regions: the central bulge, the disc, and the GALACTIC HALO. The bulge consists of old Population II stars and may even have a BLACK HOLE at its centre (the nucleus), responsible for the energetic processes seen there. With interstellar matter, the bulge is some 6,000 parsecs (20,000 light-years) in diameter in the plane of the disc and 3,000 parsecs (10,000 light-years) in diameter at right angles to the disc. The disc, containing young Population I stars, interstellar material, open (or galactic) CLUSTERS, and spiral arms, is of diameter 30,000 parsecs (100,000 light-years) but only 1,000 parsecs (3,000 light-years) in thickness. The halo, roughly spherical and concentric with the disc and the bulge, consists of stars, most of which are members of globular clusters. These stars are old Population II stars.

The Sun is about two-thirds of the way from the disc centre to the edge; its position in the plane of the disc (the galactic equator) ensures that the disc stars seen from the Earth are concentrated into a narrow band, the **Milky Way**, seen right round the celestial sphere and inclined at about 63 degrees to the equator. The Milky Way is uneven in brightness, being brightest in the constellations of Cygnus and Aquila in the Northern Hemisphere and in Scorpius and Sagittarius in the Southern Hemisphere. The galactic centre lies in Sagittarius but is impossible to observe in visible light because of the dark NEBULAE obscuring the light from the many stars beyond them. Since most of these dark nebulae lie near to or in the Galaxy's equatorial plane, they form conspicuous gaps in the Milky Way. Radio and infrared radiation can penetrate this galactic 'smog' enabling astronmers to map out not only the galactic centre but also the structure of the disc.

Galba (full name Servius Sulpicius Galba) (*c*.3 BC–69 AD) Roman emperor 68–69 AD. He was a governor in Spain when invited to succeed Nero as emperor in 68 AD. Once in power, he aroused hostility by his severity and parsimony, as well as alienating the legions in Germany by removing their commander. In 69 AD he was murdered in a conspiracy organized by Otho.

Galbraith, **John Kenneth** (1908–) Canadian-born US economist. He is well known for his criticism of consumerism, the power of large multinational corporations, and a perceived preoccupation in Western society with economic growth for its own sake. His books have a broad appeal and include *The Affluent Society* (1958) and *The New Industrial State* (1967).

gale A wind blowing at speed of 34–47 knots (63–87 km/h, 39–54 m.p.h.) on the BEAUFORT SCALE, anything faster being a storm or a hurricane. Gales arise in DEPRESSIONS and are usually accompanied by rain. At sea, waves reach 7 m (23 feet) in height during a strong gale; there are white streaks of foam, and the crests topple and roll over.

Galen, **Claudius** (129–199) Graeco-Roman physician, a surgeon to gladiators. He became physician to the emperor Marcus Aurelius. From experiments, including the dissection of monkeys and other animals, he added greatly to medical knowledge by describing functions of the brain, spinal cord, ureter, and arteries (until then believed to be full of air, not blood). He regarded the body as the vehicle of the soul, and his works dominated medicine throughout the Middle Ages.

galena (lead sulphide, PbS) An ore mineral and an important source of lead. The crystals are shiny lead-grey cubes which blacken with time. It is very dense but rather soft. Deposits are widespread, the most extensive being in Missouri, Oklahoma, and Kansas (USA).

Galicia The name of two separate areas settled by GAULS, is a region in north-western Spain. In the 6th century AD it was a kingdom of the GOTHS. It became a centre of resistance against the MOORS in the 8th century and in the 13th century passed to Castile.

The other region extends west of the Ukraine and east of Hungary, Romania, and Bohemia. In the Middle Ages this second region was an independent kingdom based on Kiev. It extended as far west as Cracow in modern Poland. Under Polish rule from 1349 it passed to Austria in the 18th century.

Galilean satellites The four satellites of Jupiter named IO, EUROPA, GANYMEDE, and CALLISTO, first observed by Galileo in 1610.

Galilee (Hebrew **Galil**) A northern region of ancient Palestine, west of the Jordan River, associated with the ministry of Jesus.

Galilee, **Sea of** (or **Lake Tiberias**) A salt lake in northern Israel, north of the plain of Esdraelon. The River Jordan flows through it from north to south; area 166 sq km (64 sq miles). Its surface is 215 m (705 ft) below sea-level.

Galileo Galilei (1564–1642) Italian astronomer and physicist, one of the founders of modern science. His discoveries include the constancy of a pendulum's swing, later applied to the regulation of clocks. He formulated the law of uniform acceleration of falling bodies, and described the parabolic trajectory of projectiles. Galileo applied the telescope to astronomy and observed craters on the Moon, sunspots, the stars of the Milky Way, Jupiter's satellites, and the phases of Venus. His acceptance of the Copernican system was rejected by the Catholic Church, and under threat of torture from the Inquisition he publicly recanted what the Church held to be heretical views. He is, however, said to have added under his breath "eppur si muove" (still it moves – a reference to the Earth, which the Catholic Church insisted was stationary at the centre of the Universe). The Vatican graciously absolved Galileo of heresy – in 1992.

galingale An ornamental perennial SEDGE, *Cyperus longus*, from lakes and stream-sides in Europe and North America. The roots were at one time highly regarded as a tonic or a cure for stomach disorders.

Galla language See CUSHITIC LANGUAGES.

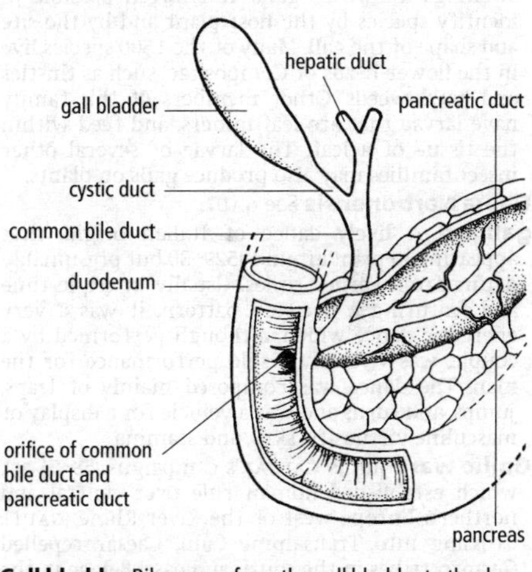

Gall bladder Bile passes from the gall bladder to the duodenum via the common bile duct.

gall bladder A muscle-walled sac attached closely to the liver. BILE is manufactured in the liver and passed to the gall bladder for storage and concentration. It passes its contents into the small intestine, where the salts it contains lower surface tension and aid digestion and absorption. The green pigments in bile are waste products derived from the breakdown of red blood cells; they cause the faeces to be coloured brown. Only animals with a liver have a gall bladder.

galleon A sailing WARSHIP of the late 16th century. Galleons eventually replaced the less manoeuvrable carracks as the principal type of European trading ship (see SAILING SHIPS AND BOATS). From the designs of Sir John HAWKINS, English galleons were the first to develop the characteristic beaked prow and modestly sized forecastle. These features were later incorporated in the great Spanish and Portuguese galleons which were used for overseas trade. In particular, 'plate fleets' of Spanish and Portuguese galleons brought large quantities of gold and silver from the Americas to Europe during the 16th and early 17th centuries. Spain continued to use galleons until the late 17th century.

galley A WARSHIP used principally in the Mediterranean from the 2nd millennium BC. The galley's major weapon was originally a ram on the waterline, used to hole enemy ships or to smash their oars. It was propelled by oars in battle, and carried sails for use in favourable winds. The success of the galley as a warship was due to its great speed and manoeuvrability. This type of galley reached its furthest development in ancient Greece. The best-known type of Greek galley was the TRIREME, with three banks (rows) of oars; a famous trireme battle took place between the Greek and Persian fleets at SALAMIS in 480 BC. The Viking LONGSHIP was a small but durable type of galley. Galleys continued to be of military importance until the 16th century; LEPANTO (1571) was the last great naval battle involving large numbers of galleys. Galleys continued to be used as convict ships until the 18th century.

gallfly A small fly with banded or spotted wings. Gallflies belong to the family Tephritidae, and are often called FRUIT FLIES. Their larvae live and feed in plant tissues, inducing abnormal growth and swellings known as galls. It is often possible to identify species by the host plant and by the site and shape of the gall. Many of the 1,500 species live in the flower-heads of Compositae, such as thistles and hawk-weeds. Other members of this family have larvae that are leaf-miners, and feed within the tissue of a leaf. The larvae of several other insect families may also produce galls on plants.

Gallia Narbonensis See GAUL.

galliard A lively dance of Italian origin, first appearing in print around 1529–30 but presumably dating from earlier times. Usually in triple time and featuring a five-step pattern, it was a very energetic dance which, although performed by a couple, was virtually a solo performance for the man. The dance was composed mainly of leaps, jumps, and turns and was a vehicle for a display of masculine virtuosity, skill, and stamina.

Gallic wars Julius CAESAR's campaigns (58–51 BC), which established Roman rule over central and northern Europe west of the River Rhine (GAUL). Crossing into Transalpine Gaul, Caesar repelled German tribes in the south and east, Belgae in the north, and Veneti in the west. He even crossed the Rhine to demonstrate Roman control of that crucial natural frontier. With speed and ruthlessness and helped by inter-tribal disunity he subdued the northern and western coasts. He twice (55 and 54 BC) invaded Britain, which was regarded as a Belgic refuge and threat to Rome. In the winter of 53–52 BC, VERCINGETORIX rallied the central Gallic tribes in unusual unity. In a long and bitter war, Caesar defeated him and his successors, and he was executed. Caesar's war dispatches, *De Bello Gallico*, supply most of the information about these events.

gallinule Any of several species of RAIL belonging to the genus *Gallinula*, which means 'little hen' in Latin and alludes to the birds' appearance and calls. Best known are the common moorhen or gallinule, *G. chloropus*, and the richly coloured purple gallinule, *G. martinica*, which breeds in the south-eastern USA and has deep purple and bronze-green plumage, a red and yellow bill, pale blue forehead, and yellow legs. The latter name is sometimes used of the large purple moorhen or swamphen, *Porphyrio porphyrio*, a rail widespread in the Old World.

Gallipoli (Turkish **Gelibolu**) A peninsula on the European side of the Dardanelles, the scene of heavy fighting during World War I. In an attempt to force a passage through the Dardanelles to open a sea route to Russia and remove Turkey from the war, in 1915–16 both the Turks and the Allies, notably Australian and New Zealand troops, suffered a quarter of a million casualties.

gallium (symbol Ga, at. no. 31, r.a.m. 69.72) A silvery-white metallic element that melts in the hand. Gallium is in Group 13 (formerly IIIB) of the periodic table; it is rather unreactive, but forms ionic compounds in which it shows a valency of 3. Its major commercial application is in combination with ARSENIC or PHOSPHORUS as a dopant in SEMICONDUCTOR DEVICES. It is also used in light-emitting diodes and phosphors.

gall midge A minute fly of the family Cecidomyidae, which has antennae resembling strings of beads, often covered with whorls of hairs. The habits of the larvae are varied, but many cause abnormal growths of tissue called galls on flowering plants and are consequently pests. The hessian fly, *Mayetiola destructor*, originally from Asia, is now a pest of cereals in Europe and North America. Among this large family of flies are species whose larvae feed on decaying vegetable matter, in addition to gall-forming types.

Galloway An area of south-west Scotland consisting of the two former counties of Kirkcudbrightshire and Wigtownshire, and now part of Dumfries and Galloway region. The area is noted for its western peninsula, called the Rhinns, of which the southern tip, the Mull of Galloway, is the most southerly point of Scotland. Galloway gives its name to a breed of hornless black cattle.

gallstone One of several stones which can form in the gall bladder (a condition known as cholelithiasis), which may be composed of cholesterol, bile pigment, or may be mixed; stones may also contain variable quantities of calcium salts. Cholesterol gallstones are the most commonly encountered. Bile pigment stones are brittle, black or brown, and hard, although if they contain calcium, they may be soft. Mixed stones are commonly small and multiple. The majority of gallstones are asymptomatic, although obstruction of the neck of the gall bladder causes pain. If the bile duct is obstructed, cholestatic JAUNDICE may develop. Surgical removal of gallstones may be necessary.

gall wasp A member of a family (Cynipidae) of small, black WASPS which lay their eggs on selected parts of flowering plants, especially oaks and roses. The plants react to secretions of the larvae by producing characteristic growths called galls. Most species produce two generations, one all-female, the other with both sexes. The plants produce different galls for the two generations. Oak-apple galls are an example of the galls caused by these wasps.

Galois, Évariste (1811–32) French mathematician. His memoir on the conditions for solubility of polynomial equations was highly innovative but was only published posthumously in 1846. He was imprisoned for his republican activities aged 19, and died aged 20 after a duel.

Galsworthy, John (1867–1933) British novelist and dramatist. He wrote several plays on social and moral themes, but is remembered chiefly for his sequence of novels known collectively as *The Forsyte Saga* (1906–28), tracing the changing fortunes of an affluent middle-class family in the years leading up to World War I. These novels gained a wider audience through their adaptation for television in 1967. Galsworthy was awarded the Nobel Prize for literature in 1932.

Galtieri, Leopoldo Fortunato (1926–) Argentinian general and statesman, President 1981–82. He was one of the leaders of the right-wing junta that ordered the invasion of the Falkland Islands in 1982, precipitating the Falklands War. After the British victory in the war, Galtieri was court-martialled and, in 1986, sentenced to twelve years in prison.

Galton, Sir Francis (1822–1911) British scientist. A man of wide interests and a cousin of Charles Darwin, he is remembered chiefly for his founding and advocacy of eugenics. He introduced methods of measuring human mental and physical abilities, and developed statistical techniques to analyse his data. Galton also carried out important work in meteorology, especially on the theory of anticyclones, and pioneered the use of fingerprints as a means of identification.

Galvani, Luigi (1737–98) Italian anatomist. He studied the structure of organs and the physiology of tissues, but he is best known for his discovery of the twitching of frogs' legs in an electric field. He concluded that these convulsions were caused by 'animal electricity' found in the body. This was disputed by Alessandro Volta who, in the course of this argument, invented his electrochemical cell. The current produced by this device was for many years called *galvanic electricity*.

galvanizing The process of covering a metal, usually iron, with a layer of ZINC to protect it from corrosion. Grease is removed from the surface with hot sodium hydroxide solution; any oxide layer is removed by 'pickling' in dilute sulphuric acid. The coating may be applied by dipping the iron into molten zinc. A layer of zinc–iron alloy forms on the surface; a further layer of zinc adheres to this and solidifies to produce a protective layer. Alternatively, the zinc may be applied by ELECTROPLATING, giving a layer of uniform thickness. Compare SHERARDIZING.

galvanometer A type of AMMETER used to measure extremely small electric currents. The commonest type consists of a fine coil of wire wound on a cylinder and suspended between the poles of a permanent magnet by a phosphorbronze wire. When current passes through the coil, it interacts with the magnetic field of the magnet (see ELECTROMAGNETIC INDUCTION), producing a twisting force (torque) on the coil. The coil rotates an amount proportional to the amount of current passing through it: the angle of rotation is measured either by a pointer mounted on the coil, or by the angle through which a mirror attached to the coil deflects a beam of light.

Galveston A city and port in Texas, USA, south-east of Houston at the entrance to Galveston Bay, an inlet of the Gulf of Mexico; pop. (1990) 59,100.

Galway ▶**1** A county of the Republic of Ireland, on the west coast of the province of Connacht; area 5,939 sq km (2,294 sq miles); pop. (1991) 180,300. ▶**2** Its county town, a sea-port and resort town on the River Corrib at the head of Galway Bay; pop. (1991) 50,800. Developed as an Anglo-Norman colony by Richard de Burgh in the 13th century and settled by the '14 Tribes of Galway', it became a noted centre of education in the 16th century. Renowned in medieval times as a centre of learning, its University College was founded in 1845.

Galway Bay A bay on the west coast of Ireland, an inlet of the Atlantic Ocean from which it is separated by the Aran Islands. Bounded by the counties of Galway and Clare, its chief port is Galway.

Gama, Vasco da See DA GAMA.

Gambia, The A country on the West African coast.

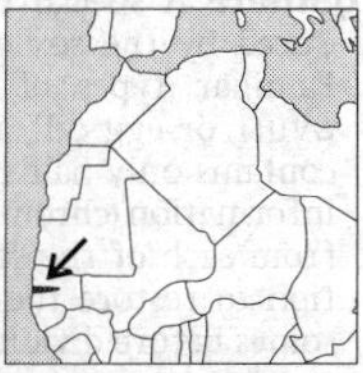

Physical. The Gambia runs west to east along the lower 320 km (nearly 200 miles) of the River Gambia, entirely surrounded inland by Senegal. Its territory on either bank is no more than about 24 km (15 miles) in width. The River Gambia is broad and navigable, though its banks are marshy; and its valley is fertile. Climatically the country is warm and arid between November and April, when the Harmattan blows from the interior. Summers are hot and very wet.

Economy. The Gambian economy is heavily dependent on groundnuts, with fish, the re-exporting of imports, mainly to Senegal, and tourism providing additional revenue. Gambia imports about a third of its food requirements.

History. The beginning of the colony was the building of a fort by the British at Banjul in 1816, as a base against the slave trade. Renamed Bathurst, the new town was placed under SIERRA LEONE in 1821. Gambia became a British colony in 1843. The Soninki-Marabout Wars in neighbouring Senegal caused serious disturbances and were ended by Anglo-French intervention in 1889. A British Protectorate over the interior was proclaimed in 1893. Gambia became an independent member of the Commonwealth in 1965, and a republic in 1970, with Sir Dawda Kairaba Jawara as the country's first president. In 1982 The Gambia and Senegal formed a limited confederation, Senegambia, for defence, economic, and foreign policy purposes, but this had lapsed by 1989. In April 1992 Jawara was re-elected President, his fifth term of office. In 1994 Jawara was ousted in a military coup by Lieutenant Yahya Jammeh, who was elected President in 1996.

Capital: Banjul
Area: 10,689 sq km (4,127 sq mi)
Population: 1,115,000 (1995)
Currency: 1 dalasi = 100 butut
Religions: Muslim 95.4%; Christian 3.7%; traditional beliefs 0.9%
Ethnic Groups: Mandingo 40.4%; Fulani 18.7%; Wolof 14.6%; Dyola 10.3%; Serahuli 6.5%
Languages: English (official); Mandingo; Fulani; local languages
International Organizations: UN; OAU; Commonwealth; ECOWAS; Non-Aligned Movement

gamelan A Javanese orchestra, the best-known being an ensemble of bronze percussion instruments: sets of bronze bars on stands, *sarons* which play the nuclear melody, and *genders* which decorate it; there are also kettle-gongs resting on stands (*bonangs*), elaborating the melody, and *kenongs*, which punctuate it; hanging GONGS and *kempuls*, both punctuating instruments; XYLOPHONES (*gambangs*), which elaborate further; fiddle (REBAB); DUCT FLUTE (*suling*); drums (*kendang*), which direct the ensemble, and singers. Most instruments are duplicated, one set being tuned to each of the Javanese scales, *pelog* and *slendro*.

game-shooting The sport of shooting birds and mammals. To protect the game, seasonal limits and codes of conduct are usually imposed: in the UK, 12 August to 10 December for grouse shooting, 1 October to 1 February for pheasant shooting, and 1 September to 1 February for partridge shooting. Shooting may be of big game, such as deer, antelopes, bears, and wild boars, or of small game, such as grouse, partridges, pheasants, ducks, geese, and rabbits.

gamete A special type of reproductive cell produced by the sex organs of plants and animals. Familiar types of gamete include the female OVUM, or egg cell, and the male SPERM cell. Each contains only half the normal amount of genetic information (chromosomes) of a body cell. Gametes from each of the sexes fuse together at fertilization to restore the full complement of chromosomes before dividing to begin a new organism.

game theory A branch of mathematics concerned with the analysis of conflict in war, economics, games of skill, etc. It represents conflicts as mathematical problems (often modelled on real games like chess and bridge), so as to decide optimal strategies. An early difficulty in the theory was how to quantify desirable results. At first personal gain was used as an index of desirability. Later, moral factors were acknowledged to affect judgements of desirability. The theory was first developed by John von NEUMANN in 1928. In 1944, with Oskar Morgenstern, he applied it to economics. It is also widely used in evolutionary studies.

gamma-ray astronomy The observation of gamma rays produced by a variety of extraterrestrial events, such as matter–antimatter collisions, radioactive decay, SYNCHROTRON RADIATION, BREMSSTRAHLUNG, collisions of high-energy particles, and PLASMAS at high temperatures. Gamma rays have wavelengths shorter than X-rays and it is customary to place the boundary between gamma rays and X-rays at PHOTON energies of one million electron volts. Celestial sources producing gamma rays of low energy have to be observed by scintillation counters or spark chambers in satellites, but high-energy gamma rays penetrate to the Earth's surface and can be measured by ground-based detectors of CERENKOV RADIATION.

gamma rays One type of emission from the decaying nuclei of radioactive atoms. They are high energy electromagnetic waves, with wavelengths of less than 10^{-11} m. Their high energy enables them to pass deep into matter before being absorbed.

Gamow, George (1904–68) Russian-born US physicist. He explained (with Ralph Asher Alpher (1921–) and Hans Albrecht Bethe (1906–) the abundances of chemical elements in the Universe, and was a proponent of the big bang theory. He also suggested the triplet code of bases in DNA, which governs the synthesis of amino acids.

Gance, Abel (1889–1991) French film director. He was a notable early pioneer of technical experimentation in film; *Napoléon* (1926), for example, was significant for its use of the split-screen, hand-held camera, and wide-angle photography. His other films include *J'accuse* (1918) and *La Roue* (1921).

Gandhi, Indira (1917–84) Indian stateswoman, Prime Minister 1966–77 and 1980–84. The daughter of Jawaharlal NEHRU, she had already served as president of the Indian National Congress (1959–60) and Minister of Information (1964) when she succeeded Lal Bahadur Shastri (1904–66) as Prime Minister. In her first term of office she sought to establish a secular state and to lead India out of poverty. However, in 1975 she introduced an unpopular state of emergency to deal with growing political unrest, and the Congress Party lost the 1977 election. Mrs Gandhi lost her seat and was unsuccessfully tried for corruption. Having formed a breakaway group from the Congress Party – known as the Indian National Congress (I) – in 1978, she was elected Prime Minister again in 1980. Her second period of office was marked by prolonged religious disturbance, during which she alienated many Sikhs by allowing troops to storm the Golden Temple at Amritsar; she was assassinated by her own Sikh bodyguards.

Gandhi, Mahatma (born Mohandas Karamchand Gandhi) (1869–1948) Indian nationalist and spiritual leader. After early civil-rights activities as a lawyer in South Africa, in 1914 Gandhi returned to India, where he became prominent in the opposition to British rule and was frequently imprisoned. The president of the Indian National Congress (1925–34), he never held government office, but was regarded as the country's supreme political and spiritual leader and the principal force in achieving India's independence. The Salt March to Dandi (1930) was followed by a campaign of civil disobedience until 1934, individual *satyagraha*, 1940–41, and the 'Quit India' campaign of 1942. As independence for India drew near, he cooperated with the British despite his opposition to the partition of the sub-continent. In political terms Gandhi's main achievement was to turn the small, upper-middle-class Indian National Congress movement into a mass movement. In intellectual terms his emphasis was upon the force of truth and non-violence (*ahimsa*) in the struggle against evil. His acceptance of partition and concern over the treatment of Muslims in India made him enemies among extremist Hindus. One such, Nathuram Godse, assassinated him in Delhi. Widely revered before and after his death, he was known as the Mahatma (Sanskrit, 'Great Soul').

Gandhi, Rajiv (1944–91) Indian statesman, Prime Minister 1984–89. The eldest son of Indira GANDHI, he entered politics following the accidental death of his brother Sanjay (1946–80), becoming Prime Minister after his mother's assassination. His premiership, at the head of the Indian National Congress (I) party, was marked by continuing unrest and he resigned in 1989; he was assassinated during the election campaign of 1991.

Ganesha (or **Ganesa**) In Hinduism, the elephant-headed son of Shiva and Parvati. He is the patron deity of prosperity and learning, invoked at the beginning of literary works, rituals, and new undertakings as a remover of obstacles. Ganesha is usually depicted as a jolly, pot-bellied figure with four arms, a broken tusk, and riding a rat.

Ganges (Hindi **Ganga**) A river in the north of India, held sacred by the Hindus who seek to wash away their sins in its waters. It flows 2,494 km (1,550 miles) from the Gangotri Glacier in the Himalayas south-east to Bangladesh, where it reaches the Bay of Bengal in the world's largest delta. Many of India's largest cities lie in the valley of the Ganges. Thousands of pilgrims visit the 18th-century temple near the source of the Ganges at **Gangotri** where Hindu legend claims the daughter of heaven came down to Earth.

Gang of Four Four radical Chinese leaders. Jiang Qing, MAO ZEDONG's fourth wife, Wang Hongwen, Yao Wenyuan, and Zhang Chungqiao all rose to prominence during the CULTURAL REVOLUTION, with a power base in Shanghai. They occupied powerful positions in the Politburo after the Tenth Party Congress of 1973. After the death of Mao in

1976 they are alleged to have planned to seize power, and in 1980 were found guilty of plotting against the state. They have been blamed for the excesses of the Cultural Revolution.

Gangtok The capital of the Himalayan state of Sikkim in northern India, in the foothills of the Kanchenjunga Range on the Ranipool River; pop. (1991) 24,970. The Namgyalk Institute of Tibetology established in 1958 has one of the world's largest collections of books and rare manuscripts on the subject of Mahayana Buddhism.

gangue The valueless minerals or earthy matter associated with the valuable minerals in ORES.

gannet A large sea-bird of the genus *Sula*. The three species, which are white and black, with pale yellow heads in adult birds, are native to temperate latitudes. Their family, Sulidae, also includes six pied or brown tropical species of BOOBIES. Gannets are long-winged, with webbed feet, a long conical beak, and a wedge-shaped tail. They fly in groups low over the sea, catching fish by plunge-diving, after which their buoyancy allows a quick take-off. Their foods include shoaling fish and squid. They nest colonially on islands and isolated mainland coasts, in trees, on cliffs, or on flat ground. Nests are rudimentary collections of sticks or seaweed and, although they lay up to three eggs, they seldom raise more than one chick successfully.

Ganymede (in astronomy) A GALILEAN SATELLITE of Jupiter, discovered by Galileo in 1610. It has a nearly circular orbit in the plane of Jupiter's equator at 1,070 million km from the planet's centre. With a diameter of 5,262 km it is the largest satellite in the whole Solar System and is in fact larger than Mercury. Its density of 1,940 kg/m^3 implies that the interior contains both water ice and rocky materials, probably in different regions.

Gao See SONGHAI.

gaper See CLAM.

Garbo, Greta (born Greta Gustafsson) (1905–90) Swedish-born US actress. In 1924 her first important Swedish film led to a Hollywood contract; she gained instant recognition for her compelling screen presence and enigmatic beauty in *The Torrent* (1925). She made the transition from silent pictures to sound in *Anna Christie* (1930), later starring in *Mata Hari* (1931), *Anna Karenina* (1935). and *Camille* (1936). *Ninotchka* (1939), unlike her previous films, was a highly successful comedy. In 1941 she retired and lived as a recluse for the rest of her life.

García Lorca See LORCA.

García Márquez, Gabriel (1928–) Colombian novelist. His left-wing sympathies brought him into conflict with the Colombian government and he spent the 1960s and 1970s in voluntary exile in Mexico and Spain. During this time he wrote *One Hundred Years of Solitude* (1967) which has come to be regarded as a classic example of magic realism. More recent novels include *The General in His Labyrinth* (1990). He was awarded the Nobel Prize for literature in 1982 and was formally invited back to Colombia, where he has since lived.

Garcia y Iñigues, Calixto (1836–98) Cuban nationalist. He led his country's preliminary struggles for independence from Spain. A leader during the Ten Years' War (1868–78), and the Little War (1879–80), his military efforts enjoyed scant success and resulted in his prolonged imprisonment. Cuban troops under his command supported US forces during the Spanish-American War, but Garcia, shortly before his death, rejected his erstwhile allies, fearing that Cuba had simply exchanged one master for another.

Garda, Lake (Italian **Lago di Garda**) The largest lake in Italy, situated on the frontier between the northern regions of Lombardy and Venetia; area 370 sq km (143 sq miles). It is fed by the River Sarca and its outlet is the River Mincio, a tributary of the Po.

gardenia An Old World shrub that gives its name to a genus, and is related to coffee. The species with evergreen leaves are widely cultivated for their heavily scented flowers, particularly in the semi-double white forms.

Gardner, Ava (Lavinia) (1922–90) US actress. Her beauty won her her first screen roles, and she came to prominence in *The Killers* (1946). She received critical praise for her performances in films such as *Bhowani Junction* (1956) and *The Night of the Iguana* (1964). She was married to Mickey Rooney, Frank Sinatra, and the jazz musician Artie Shaw.

Gardner, Erle Stanley (1899–1970) US novelist and short-story writer. He practised as a defence lawyer (1922–38) and went on to become famous for his series of novels featuring the lawyer-detective Perry Mason, many of which end with a dramatic courtroom scene.

Garfield, James A(bram) (1831–81) US Republican statesman, 20th President of the US March–September 1881. A major-general who had fought for the Union side in the American Civil War, he resigned his command to enter Congress, where he served as leader of the Republican Party (1863–80). He was assassinated within months of taking presidential office.

garfish (or **needlefish**) A fish of which there are nearly 30 species in the family Belonidae. They are primarily marine, surface-living fishes of tropical and temperate seas, although several species live in fresh water, principally in South America. All are slender-bodied, with very long beak-shaped jaws. Both mandibles of the jaw are lined with needle-like teeth, which they use when capturing a wide range of smaller fishes. Most species grow to about 1 m (3.25 feet) in length, but some are larger. They leap out of the water very freely. They lay large eggs in the surface waters, each egg having long filaments which tangle with floating weed.

garganey A small, mottled, brown and white dabbling DUCK, *Anas querquedula*. The drake has a conspicuous curved white stripe from eye to nape. The single species is confined to the Palearctic region.

gargoyle A spout in the form of a grotesque figure either human, animal, or monstrous, projecting from a cornice or parapet and allowing water from the roof gutters to escape clear of the walls. There are many examples on Gothic cathedrals and churches throughout Europe, bearing witness to the lively imagination of medieval craftsmen. With the introduction of lead drainpipes in the 16th century gargoyles were no longer necessary, but examples were occasionally made in lead.

Garibaldi, Giuseppe (1807–82) Italian patriot and military leader. He was a hero of the Risorgimento (the movement for the unification and independence of Italy), who began his political activity as a member of the Young Italy Movement. After involvement in the early struggles against Austrian rule in the 1830s and 1840s he commanded a volunteer force on the Sardinian side in 1859, and successfully led his 'Red Shirts' to victory in Sicily and southern Italy in 1860–61, thus playing a vital part in the establishment of a united kingdom of Italy. He was less successful in his attempts to conquer the papal territories around French-held Rome in 1862 and 1867.

Garland, Judy (born Frances Gumm) (1922–69) US singer and actress. The daughter of vaudeville entertainers, she became a child star and was under contract to MGM at the age of 13. Her most famous early film role was as Dorothy in *The Wizard of Oz* (1939), in which she sang 'Over the Rainbow'. Later successful films included *Meet Me in St Louis* (1944) and *A Star is Born* (1954). She apparently died of a drug overdose after suffering many personal problems. Among her children is the actress Liza Minelli (1946–) her daughter from her marriage to the film director Vincente Minelli (1910–86).

garlic A bulbous plant, *Allium sativum*, related to the onion, growing up to 1 m (3.25 feet) in height, with flat leaves sheathing the lower stem, which ends in a cluster of small bulbs called cloves. Cultivated on a large scale in southern and eastern Europe, it has been popular at least since ancient Egyptian times. Used excessively it makes the breath obnoxious, which perhaps explains why it was valued in the Middle Ages for its alleged ability to keep vampires at a distance.

garnet Any one of a group of silicate minerals (orthosilicates) occurring principally in metamorphic rocks, although found also in sediments as rounded grains. The deep red varieties are known as Bohemian garnets, Cape rubies, or Arizona rubies, according to their place of origin. Purplish red ones are called carbuncles and come from Brazil or Sri Lanka, as do the golden or cinnamon hessonites. Bright green ones are demantoids, from the Urals.

Garonne A river of south-west France, which rises in the Pyrenees and flows 645 km (400 miles) northwestwards through Toulouse and Bordeaux to join the Dordogne at the Gironde estuary.

Garrick, David (1717–79) British actor, manager, and dramatist. His style of acting was characterized by an easy, natural manner of speech, and he was equally successful in tragic and comic roles in both Shakespearian and contemporary plays. In 1747 he became involved in the management of the Drury Lane Theatre and later became its sole manager.

garrigue A type of evergreen scrub vegetation characterized by aromatic herbaceous plants that grow on limestone soils around the Mediterranean, especially in southern France, Corsica, Sardinia, and Malta.

Garvey, Marcus (Mosiah) (1887–1940) Jamaican political activist and black nationalist leader. He was the leader of the Back to Africa Movement, which advocated the establishment of an African homeland for black Americans, and founder of the Universal Negro Improvement Association (1914). He was chiefly active in the USA, attracting a large following in support of his calls for black civil rights and economic independence. He died in obscurity, however, after his movement lost support during the Depression, but his thinking was later an important influence in the growth of Rastafarianism.

gas One of the three PHASES OF MATTER commonly encountered, the other two being solid or liquid. Like liquids, gases have no fixed shape, but in addition they have no fixed volume: they fill whatever space they occupy. In gases, the atoms or molecules have sufficient thermal energy to break away from their neighbours and move around freely. Most gases can be turned into liquids and then solids by cooling them sufficiently; similarly many solids and liquids can be turned into gases by heating, though in some cases they decompose or burn before changing their state. Gases can also be liquefied by pressure alone, but their temperature must be less than the critical temperature for this to be possible. The gaseous form of substances that are solid or liquid at room temperature is often called a vapour at temperatures up to the critical temperature, and a gas only at higher temperatures.

The **gas laws** describe the behaviour of IDEAL GASES under different conditions of temperature and pressure. CHARLES' LAW states that the volume (V) of a fixed mass of gas is directly proportional to its thermodynamic temperature (T, in KELVIN) if the pressure (P) is constant. BOYLE's law states that the volume of a fixed mass of gas is inversely proportional to its pressure if the temperature is constant. The pressure law states that the pressure of a fixed mass of gas is directly proportional to its temperature (in kelvin) if the volume is constant. These laws are combined into the universal gas law: $PV = nRT$, where n is the amount of gas present (in moles) and R is the GAS CONSTANT. The gas laws only apply accurately to ideal gases, but real gases obey them to a limited extent. Real gases obey the gas laws best at high temperatures and low pressures, i.e. when the influence of intermolecular forces is at its lowest.

gas, natural See NATURAL GAS.

Gascoigne, Paul (known as 'Gazza') (1967–) British footballer. Gascoigne established himself as a gifted attacking midfielder and irrepressible personality after joining Tottenham Hotspur from Newcastle United in 1988, and he quickly became a member of the England team. During the 1991 FA Cup Final Gascoigne sustained a career-threatening knee injury, but after a long recovery period moved to the Italian club Lazio and then to Glasgow Rangers in 1995. At both clubs he continued to attract controversy both on and off the field.

gas constant The constant (R) that appears in the IDEAL GAS law, i.e. $PV/nT = R$ (see GAS). It is usually known as the universal gas constant and has the value of 8.314 joule per kelvin.

Gascony (French **Gascogne**) A former province of south-west France, in the northern foothills of the Pyrenees. Having united with Aquitaine in the 11th century, it was held by England between 1154 and 1453.

gas-cooled reactor See MAGNOX REACTOR; NUCLEAR REACTOR.

gas-discharge lamp A lamp in which light is produced by the application of a high voltage across a tube containing gas at low pressure. Normally gases are poor conductors, but at a sufficiently high voltage, gas molecules are ionized, splitting into ions and electrons, and current is carried through the tube by these charged particles. Light is produced by decay of excited ions and molecules. The collisions of electrons with molecules cause further ionizations, which help to maintain the current even when the voltage across the tube is reduced. Gas-discharge lamps are used for luminous signs, the colour of the light emitted being dependent on the gas in the discharge pulse. The best-known example is neon, which gives an orange light. In a fluorescent tube the light does not come directly from the gas in the tube but from a coating on the inside. This fluoresces because of irradiation by ultraviolet radiation produced in the gas discharge.

gas-engine An INTERNAL-COMBUSTION ENGINE using a gaseous fuel. This was the first successful form of internal-combustion engine, dating from about 1860, when LENOIR's first engines appeared. Although now replaced for transport purposes by PETROL and DIESEL ENGINES, gas-engines are still used in many stationary applications. They can burn almost any type of flammable gas; most engines now use NATURAL GAS (methane), but LIQUID PETROLEUM GASES are used in some vehicles. The low cost of gas-engines makes them suitable for COMBINED HEAT AND POWER GENERATION.

gas grid A system of pipes carrying gas and linking storage points with user pipe networks. A grid prevents local shortages through surges in demand, by removing dependence on a single source of supply. It also allows flexibility in locating sources of supply or storage facilities. Gas grids are generally constructed of pipelines of about 1 m (3 feet) diameter, set underground. Most countries with a gas grid developed the grid to take advantage of a regular supply of NATURAL GAS For example, the UK has a gas grid that was set up in the 1970s and 1980s to take advantage of natural gas from beneath the North Sea.

Gaskell, Elizabeth (Cleghorn) (1810–65) British novelist. An active humanitarian from a Unitarian background, she is famous for *Mary Barton* (1848), *Cranford* (1853), and *North and South* (1855); all of these display her interest in social concerns. She also wrote a biography (1857) of her friend Charlotte Brontë.

gas laws See GAS.

gas lighting A method of LIGHTING based on the combustion of a gas, typically COAL-GAS or NATURAL GAS. The first street-lighting using coal-gas was installed in Westminster, London, in 1814. The original burners – in which the gas burned as a simple non-aerated jet – were smoky and had low luminosity. Aerated burners, introduced from about 1840, were a considerable improvement, but the situation was transformed by the advent of AUER's gas-mantle in 1885. Gas lamps are now mainly used where portable lighting is required. They commonly use a burner and are fuelled with PROPANE gas from an attached cylinder.

gasoline See PETROL.

Gassendi, Pierre (1592–1655) French astronomer and philosopher. He is best known for his atomic theory of matter, which was based on his interpretation of the works of Epicurus, and he was an outspoken critic of Aristotle. He observed a new comet, a lunar eclipse, and a transit of Mercury (confirming Kepler's theories), and he coined the term *aurora borealis*.

Gasser, Herbert Spencer (1888–1963) US physiologist. Collaborating with Joseph Erlanger, he used an oscilloscope to show that the velocity of a nerve impulse is proportional to the diameter of the fibre. He also demonstrated the differences between sensory and motor nerves. Gasser and Erlanger shared a Nobel Prize in 1944.

gastraphetes See CROSSBOW.

gastric ulcer See ULCER.

gastropod See MOLLUSC.

gastroscope See ENDOSCOPY.

gas-turbine A form of ENGINE in which a continuous stream of hot gases is directed against the blades of a TURBINE, causing it to turn. In most cases the gas, usually air, is first compressed in a COMPRESSOR before passing into combustion chambers, where a portion of the gas is mixed with fuel and burned. The rest of the gas bypasses the combustion chamber and mixes with the hot gases emerging after combustion. This is then forced through nozzles to drive a turbine. Part of the power from this turbine is used to drive the compressor; the remaining power can be used in various ways, depending on the function of the engine: it may drive the propeller shaft of a turboprop aircraft or ship, the drive-shaft of a locomotive, or an electric generator. Alternatively, a turbine just big enough to drive the compressor can be used, and the remaining energy of the hot exhaust gases used to give a high-speed exhaust jet and hence a forward thrust; this is the JET ENGINE. Gas-turbines are used in electricity generation for standby and peak-load service, in portable power plants, and in combined-cycle power generation. The high power-to-weight ratio of gas-turbines has led to their use in AEROPLANES, and also in railway locomotives and naval vessels.

Gates, William (Henry) (known as 'Bill') (1955–) US computer entrepreneur. In 1975 he co-founded Micro-Soft (later Microsoft), a private company for the manufacture and sale of computers. As its chairman and chief executive, Gates expanded the firm overseas in the early 1980s; by the end of the decade Microsoft was a leading multinational computer company and had made Gates the youngest multi-billionaire in American history. The company's success continued with the introduction of Windows 95 (1995), a successor to the original Windows system of 1985.

Gateshead An old industrial town in the Tyne and Wear metropolitan region, north-east England, on the south side of the River Tyne opposite Newcastle upon Tyne; pop. (1991) 196,500. Its heavy industries have given way to light industries. In 1997, on the outskirts of the town, the largest sculpture in the UK – Antony Gormley's 'Angel of the North' with a wingspan of 53 m (175 ft) – was erected.

Gatling, Richard Jordan (1818–1903) US inventor. Gatling was a prolific inventor, first designing sowing machines, ploughs, and other agricultural machines and later turning to armaments. He is best known for the Gatling gun, invented in 1862, which was the first successful rapid-fire gun. It consisted of ten parallel barrels which were rotated by a hand crank and fired in turn, and was first put to use in the American Civil War.

GATT See GENERAL AGREEMENT ON TARIFFS AND TRADE.

Gatwick An international airport in West Sussex, south-east England, to the south of London. It was constructed in 1956–58 as a second London airport.

gaucho A horseman of South America, often Indian or mestizo. Early in the 19th century the gauchos took part in the SPANISH–SOUTH AMERICAN WARS OF INDEPENDENCE, and later were prominent on the Argentine pampas in the development of the cattle industry. By the late 19th century the pastoral economy had given way to more intensive land cultivation in fenced-off estancias (estates), forcing many gauchos to become farmhands or peons.

Gaudí (y Cornet), Antonio (1853–1926) Spanish architect. A leading but idiosyncratic exponent of art nouveau, he worked chiefly in Barcelona, designing distinctive buildings such as the Parc Güell (begun 1900) and the Casa Batlló (begun 1905), notable for their use of ceramics, wrought-iron work, flowing lines, and organic forms. He began work on his most ambitious project, the church of the Sagrada Familia, in 1884; unfinished at his death, it is still under construction.

Gaudier-Brzeska, Henri (1891–1915) French sculptor and draughtsman, who worked in England from 1911 to 1914 before being killed during World War I. As a sculptor he first imitated RODIN before developing a highly personal manner of carving in which shapes are radically simplified. In England, EPSTEIN alone was producing sculpture as stylistically advanced at this time.

Gauguin, (Eugène Henri) Paul (1848–1903) French painter. He left Paris in search of an environment that would bring him closer to nature, going first to Brittany, where he painted works such as *The Vision After the Sermon* (1888), and later briefly to stay with Van Gogh at Arles. In 1891 he left France for Tahiti; he spent most of the rest of his life there, painting enigmatic works, such as *Faa Iheihe* (1898). He was a post-impressionist whose painting was influenced by primitive art, freeing colour from its representational function to use it in flat contrasting areas to achieve decorative or emotional effects. His work had an enormous influence on 20th-century art.

Gauhati See GUWAHATI.

Gaul An ancient region of Europe, corresponding to modern France, Belgium, the south Netherlands, south-west Germany, and northern Italy. The area was settled by groups of Celts, who had begun migration across the Rhine in 900 BC, spreading further south beyond the Alps from 400 BC onwards and ousting the Etruscans. The area south of the Alps was conquered in 222 BC by the Romans, who called it **Cisalpine Gaul**. The area north of the Alps, known to the Romans as **Transalpine Gaul**, was taken by Julius Caesar between 58 and 51 BC, remaining under Roman rule until the 5th century AD. Within Transalpine Gaul the southern province, parts of which had fallen to the Romans in the previous century, became known as *Gallia Narbonensis*.

Gaulle, Charles de See DE GAULLE.

Gaunt, John of See JOHN OF GAUNT.

gaur A large species of Asian wild CATTLE, sometimes called the Indian bison. The bull can attain a height of over 1.8 m (6 feet) at the shoulder, and is dark brown to black, like the yak, but with shorter hair; it has broad upturned horns tipped with black. The cow is smaller and reddish-brown in colour. The gaur, *Bos gaurus*, feeds on grasses and bamboo shoots and is vulnerable to the loss of its tropical forest habitats in south-east Asia.

Gauss, Karl Friedrich (1777–1855) German mathematician, astronomer, and physicist. Regarded as the 'prince of mathematics', he laid the foundations of number theory, and in 1801 he rediscovered the lost asteroid Ceres using advanced computational techniques. He contributed to many areas of mathematics, and applied rigorous mathematical analysis to such subjects as geometry, geodesy, electrostatics, and electromagnetism. He was involved in the first worldwide survey of the Earth's magnetic field. Two of Gauss's most interesting discoveries, which he did not pursue, were non-Euclidean geometry and quaternions.

Gautama Siddhartha See BUDDHA.

Gauteng A province of South Africa created in 1994 as Pretoria-Witwatersrand-Vereeniging from part of the former province of Transvaal and renamed Gauteng in 1995; pop. (1995) 7,048,300. Its capital is Johannesburg.

Gavaskar, Sunil Manohar (1949–) Indian cricketer. He made his test début in the West Indies at the age of 20, making his mark by scoring an aggregate of 774 runs. He later captained India and achieved several world batting records, in 1987 becoming the first batsman to score 10,000 runs in test cricket.

Gaveston, Piers (*c*.1284–1312) Earl of Cornwall. He was a Gascon who was brought up in the English royal household as the foster-brother of the future EDWARD II, and he exploited his infatuation for him. Edward gave him the earldom of Cornwall in 1307, and appointed him Regent of England (1307–08). The enraged English barons called for his banishment; Edward twice complied (1308, 1311), but Gaveston returned and in 1312 was killed by the Earl of Warwick.

gavial See GHARIAL.

gavotte A French dance in duple TIME, beginning on the third beat. Originally a folk dance, it was absorbed into the repertory of *ballet de cours* in the 16th century, and became one of the optional movements in the Baroque dance SUITE. Its steady, lively rhythm allowed the development of intricate steps and gestures of the arms.

Gawain In Celtic mythology, the son of King Lot of Orkney and Morgan le Fay, ARTHUR's half-sister. An exemplary Knight of the Round Table, Gawain went in search of the Holy Grail. In his encounter with the Green Knight, however, his reputation was tested and found wanting. He died supporting Arthur in the rebellion led by Modred. He is linked with Gwalchmei, the Sun-god of Welsh mythology.

Gay, John (1685–1732) English poet and dramatist. He is now chiefly known for *The Beggar's Opera* (1728), a ballad opera combining burlesque and political satire and dealing with life in low society. A major success in its day, it has been revived several times this century, and was adapted by Brecht in *The Threepenny Opera* (1928).

Gaye, Marvin (1939–84) US soul singer and songwriter. Gaye moved to Detroit with the vocal group the Rainbows, and signed a contract with Motown in 1961. He later began recording as a solo singer and had a succession of hits, including his best-known song 'I Heard It Through the Grapevine' (1968). His albums include *Let's Get It On* (1973) and *Midnight Love* (1982). He was shot dead by his father during a quarrel.

Gay-Lussac, Joseph Louis (1778–1850) French chemist and physicist. He is best known for his work on gases, and in 1808 he formulated the law usually known by his name, that gases which combine chemically do so in volumes that are in a simple ratio to each other. He developed techniques of quantitative chemical analysis, confirmed that iodine was an element, discovered cyanogen, improved the process for manufacturing sulphuric acid, prepared potassium and boron, and made two balloon ascents to study the atmosphere and terrestrial magnetism.

Gaza Strip A strip of coastal territory in the south-east Mediterranean, including the town of Gaza; area 363 sq km (140 sq miles); pop. (1993) 748,400. Administered by Egypt from 1949, it was occupied by Israel in 1967. Over 50 per cent of the Palestinian Arabs of Gaza live in refugee camps which were created after the 1948–49 Arab-Israeli war. Used as a base for Arab fedayeen guerrilla attacks on Israel during the 1950s, Gaza was the focal point of the anti-Israeli *intifada* or Palestinian uprising which began in 1987. In 1991 Israeli troops were withdrawn from Gaza as part of an agreement transferring power from Israel to the Palestinians.

gazelle An antelope of the family Bovidae found in the hottest, driest parts of the stony plains or deserts of southern Asia and Africa. There are some eighteen species of gazelles, including the gerenuk, blackbuck, springbok, and Thomson's gazelle. Most are 90 cm (3 feet) or less in height at the shoulder. They usually have lyre-shaped, ringed horns that curve backwards and upwards, but these are generally smaller or absent in the female. Sandy-brown in colour, they may have black and white bands on the face and flanks. Gazelles are amongst the most graceful and fast-moving of animals, with an average speed of 48 km/hour (30 miles per hour) and can easily pull ahead of a vehicle travelling at 64 km/hour (40 miles per hour).

Gdańsk (German **Danzig**) An industrial port and shipbuilding centre in northern Poland, on an inlet of the Baltic Sea; pop. (1990) 465,100. Originally a member of the Hanseatic League, it was disputed between Prussia and Poland during the 19th century. It was a free city under a League of Nations mandate from 1919 until 1939, when it was annexed by Nazi Germany, precipitating hostilities with Poland and the outbreak of World War II. It passed to Poland in 1945. In the 1980s the Gdańsk shipyards were the site of the activities of the Solidarity movement, which eventually led to the collapse of the Communist regime in Poland in 1989.

GDP (gross domestic product) A measure of the total flow of GOODS and services produced by an economy in a specified time period (normally a year). GDP is calculated by summing the output of all firms and the government. A firm's output is its value added, which is the total sales revenue minus the cost of any intermediate goods purchased from other producers. Government output is measured by summing the wages and salaries of public servants. GDP is initially measured 'at market prices'. Then the indirect taxes, which raise prices above production cost, are subtracted and SUBSIDIES are added. The result is GDP 'at factor cost', which measures the costs of producing the goods and services. Net domestic product is GDP minus DEPRECIATION of fixed capital goods. See also GNP.

GDR (German Democratic Republic) See EAST GERMANY.

gean See CHERRY.

gear A toothed or grooved wheel or other shape that can be used to transmit mechanical power. The earliest gearwheels were made of wood, with wooden teeth; by the 1st century AD all the simple gear types were well known. By the 6th century AD they were used in WINDMILLS, WATER WHEELS, and other mechanical devices. For more precise machines, smaller metal gears were evolved; a calendrical device from 87 BC used small bronze wheels, and miniature gears were later developed for CLOCKS and navigational instruments. In the early 19th century machine-tools made it possible to stamp out gearwheels automatically: the clock trade was among the first to adopt this system. Today gears are most commonly cut by a gear-hobbing machine, using a type of milling machine. Although gears are mostly in rolling contact there is a degree of sliding, and lubrication is needed to reduce friction and wear. As well as transmitting rotary power, gears can be used to obtain a MECHANICAL ADVANTAGE: if one gearwheel has twice as many teeth as the gear that drives it, it will travel half a turn for every full turn of the smaller wheel, but will exert twice the TORQUE (turning force). Conversely, gears can be used to obtain a speed increase: if a large wheel is used to drive a smaller one, the smaller wheel will turn faster (but with less torque). The wide range of applications in which gears are used has led to the development of many gear types. See also GEARBOX.

gearbox Strictly the casing of a gear train, an arrangement of GEARS designed to transmit motion between two shafts, but in some applications, in particular in the MOTOR CAR, the gearbox includes the gear train as well as the casing. A car needs a gear-box because INTERNAL-COMBUSTION ENGINES work efficiently and give high power only at high engine speeds, whereas the car needs to be able to travel at a wide range of road speeds. The gearbox solves this problem by keeping the engine speed fairly high and varying the road speed through the use of different gears. With a manual gearbox, the engine is disengaged from the drive during gear changing, and then progressively re-engaged, by means of the CLUTCH. (In vehicles with AUTOMATIC TRANSMISSION this disengagement does not occur.) Synchromesh on all gears except reverse aids smooth changing from gear to gear.

Geber (Latinized name of Jabir ibn Hayyan) (*c.*721–*c.*815) Arab chemist. He was a member of the court of Harun ar-Rashid, the caliph of Baghdad. Although many works are attributed to him there is doubt about the authenticity of some of them, and his name was used by later writers. He was familiar with many chemicals and laboratory techniques, including distillation and sublimation.

gecko A LIZARD belonging to a family of about 670 species, Gekkonidae, distributed in warm countries worldwide. Many species have rather flat bodies covered with granular scales. The majority are at least partly nocturnal and lack movable eyelids, the eye being protected by a transparent membrane. One small group, the genus *Ptenopus*, or barking geckos, differ from many other lizards in being vocal, the sounds produced being a series of chirping cheeps and clucks. Some house geckos can walk up vertical surfaces and even upside-down across ceilings; this is achieved by the action of specialized toe-pads that can cling to very small surface irregularities.

Geelong A port and oil-refining centre on Corio Bay on the south coast of Australia, the largest city in the state of Victoria; pop. (1991) 126,300. First settled in the 1830s, it is also a major wool-selling centre.

Ge'ez The classical literary language of Ethiopia, a Semitic language thought to have been introduced from Arabia in the 1st century BC. It is the ancestor of all the modern Ethiopian languages such as Amharic, and survives in the liturgical language of the Coptic Church in Ethiopia.

gegenschein That part of the zodiacal light seen in the region of the sky opposite to the Sun. The gegenschein (German for **counterglow**) is a faint oval patch of light about 6 degrees by 10 degrees in extent, the long axis being in the ECLIPTIC. Although it is seen in the opposite direction to the Sun, that is, looking out of the Solar System, it is not (as was once suggested) due to the Earth having a comet-like dust tail.

Geiger, Hans (Johann) Wilhelm (1882–1945) German nuclear physicist. He worked with Sir Ernest Rutherford at Manchester on radioactivity, and in 1908 developed his prototype radiation counter for detecting alpha particles. In 1925 he was appointed professor of physics at Kiel, where he improved the sensitivity of his device with Walther Müller.

Geiger–Müller counter An instrument for detecting and measuring nuclear RADIATION, one of the first electrical devices to be used in radiation

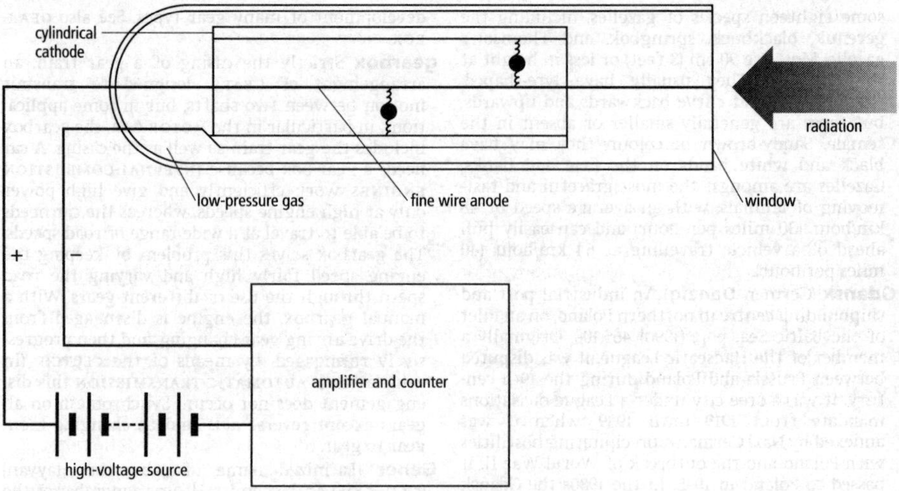

Geiger–Müller counter Incoming radiation enters the tube through the window, causing an electric discharge between the anode and cathode. The electrical pulse produced passes to the counter.

research, perfected by Hans GEIGER and W. Müller at Kiel University, Germany, in 1925. It consists of an aluminium tube containing argon gas at low pressure, through which passes a wire ELECTRODE. A potential difference of about 400 V is applied between the electrode and the tube wall. The end of the tube is sealed with a mica window thin enough to allow alpha-, beta-, and gamma-radiation to pass through. When a charged radiation particle enters the tube, the argon becomes ionized (charged), triggering an avalanche of IONS between the electrodes, and a pulse of current flows. Each pulse is recorded, and can be displayed as radioactive counts per second. The frequency of pulses is proportional to the radiation intensity.

Geikie, Sir Archibald (1835–1924) British geologist of Scottish extraction who pioneered the study of Britain's volcanic past, publishing seminal works in 1888 and 1897. He was also famous for his insistence that EROSION by glaciers and rivers has been the main influence on the Scottish landscape as it appears today.

gel A dispersion of a finely divided solid in a liquid; particles of the solid link up to form a network in which droplets of the liquid become trapped. Gelatine forms gels in this manner; droplets of water are trapped in the protein network that forms as the gel solidifies. Photographic FILM consists of a layer of gelatine gel containing silver bromide particles, supported on a film of CELLULOSE ACETATE. Gelatine is an elastic gel, but other gels (for example, silica gel) may be rigid. See COLLOID.

Geldof, Bob (1954–) Irish rock singer and charity promoter. Joint founder of the Boomtown Rats (rock band) in 1975, he organized Band Aid in 1984, which raised £8 million for famine relief in Ethiopia. For this, and subsequent charitable work, he received an honorary KBE from the UK, an Irish Peace Prize, and a UN World Hunger Award.

gelignite A stable explosive jelly that is both plastic and water-repellant, composed of 8 per cent gun-cotton (a form of NITROCELLULOSE) and 92 per cent NITROGLYCERINE. Invented and produced by NOBEL in 1875, it is one of the most powerful explosives known. It is used for blasting rocks. Reducing the proportion of nitroglycerine to gun-cotton produces a slower-burning explosive.

Gell-Mann, Murray (1929–) US theoretical physicist. He coined the word *quark*, proposed the concept of strangeness in quarks, and made major contributions on the classification and interactions of subatomic particles. He was awarded the Nobel Prize for physics in 1969.

Gemayel, Pierre (1905–84) Lebanese political leader. A Maronite Christian, he founded the right-wing Phalange Party (1936) and served as a member of parliament 1960–84; during this time he held several government posts and led the Phalange militia forces during the civil war (1975–76). His youngest son, **Bashir** (1947–82), was assassinated while President-elect; his eldest son, **Amin** (1942–), served as President 1982–88.

Gemini The Twins, a CONSTELLATION of the zodiac. In mythology it represents the twins CASTOR AND POLLUX, sons of the god Zeus and Queen Leda of Sparta. The two brightest stars in the constellation are named Castor and Pollux.

Geminiani, Francesco (Xaverio) (1687–1762) Italian composer and violinist. After studying in Milan, and in Rome with CORELLI, he worked in theatre orchestras in Lucca and Naples, becoming accepted as a virtuoso of exceptional ability before settling in London (1714–47). His last years were spent mainly in Dublin. Geminiani's music (violin sonatas and concerti grossi) is notable for the expressive qualities of its melodies and the brilliance of its virtuoso figuration. His example helped to establish the Baroque violin as a legitimate solo instrument.

Geminids An active METEOR SHOWER that reaches its peak on 14 December each year, when about 60 meteors per hour can be seen. Meteors from this RADIANT (right ascension 7 hours 28 minutes, declination +32 degrees) appear from 7–16 December.

gemstones Precious or semi-precious stones or crystals of flawless quality that are cut and polished to accentuate either their colour, clarity, or lustre. Diamonds, sapphires, emeralds, and rubies are typical gemstones.

gene A unit of inheritance. Genes are passed from parents to offspring as part of a CHROMOSOME. The word appeared early in the science of genetics, and as the science has progressed, its original meaning has been modified. The generally accepted meaning is that a gene is a length of DNA, comprising a sequence of nucleotides, that encodes a specific function; for example, the synthesis of a single polypeptide chain (length of amino acids). See GENETICS; GENE THERAPY; GENETIC ENGINEERING.

General Agreement on Tariffs and Trade (GATT) An international trade agreement. Established by the UNITED NATIONS in 1948, and with a secretariat in Geneva, Switzerland, it had 125 member countries at the end of 1994. The aim of its members (who together account for some 90 per cent of all world trade) has been to promote international trade by removing obstacles and trade barriers, to lay down maximum tariff rates, and to provide a forum for the discussion of trading policies. By the 1980s there were demands for modification of the GATT agreements. In 1986 the 'Uruguay Round' of talks (so called because they were held in the Uruguayan capital, Montevideo) undertook to resolve outstanding agricultural issues. The discussions, frequently deadlocked, continued into 1993 seeking a compromise agreement on farm subsidies, prior to talks in Geneva in 1994 for global trade deals. In April 1994 the Final Act of the Uruguay round was formally signed, concluding negotiations for broad cuts in tariffs and export subsidies and for the creation of the WORLD TRADE ORGANIZATION (WTO) as successor to GATT.

General Strike (UK) (1926) A British trade union strike. It was in support of the National Union of Mineworkers whose members were under threat from mine owners of longer hours and lower wages because of trading difficulties. The owners had locked out the miners from the pits to try to compel acceptance. The General Council of the Trades Union Congress responded by calling workers out on strike in certain key industries such as the railways, the docks, and electricity and gas supply. This began on 4 May 1926 and ended nine days later. Irresolute trade union leadership, skilful government handling of information to the public, and help by troops and volunteers to keep vital services running, all led to the collapse of the strike. It was followed in 1927 by a Trade Union Act, restricting trade union privileges.

generator, electrical A device for the conversion of mechanical, chemical, or other form of energy into electrical energy. The most common type of generator, for example a bicycle dynamo, relies on ELECTROMAGNETIC INDUCTION to convert mechanical energy into electrical energy. Such a generator is essentially a reversed ELECTRIC MOTOR, with a rotor carrying one or more coils surrounded by a magnetic field, typically supplied by a permanent magnet or ELECTROMAGNET. Mechanical energy (often from a STEAM-TURBINE) is used to rotate the rotor, which induces an electric current in the rotor coil. In the case of a generator providing direct current, a mechanical switch or commutator switches the current every half-rotation so that it remains unidirectional. Large modern generators (**alternators**) in POWER-STATIONS provide alternating-current output for general distribution (see ELECTRICITY GENERATION AND SUPPLY). There are many other types of electric generator. Electrostatic generators like WIMSHURST MACHINES, and on a larger scale VAN DE GRAAFF generators, are principally used for specialist applications that require very high voltages but only a low current, such as providing power for PARTICLE ACCELERATORS. Other types of generator include BATTERIES, FUEL CELLS, and SOLAR CELLS.

genet A small CARNIVORE of the civet family, Viverridae. Genets are closely related to civets and linsangs. There are ten species in the genus *Genetta*, mainly African, although some extend into the Middle East and one, the common genet, *Genetta genetta*, occurs in southern Europe, where it is probably native. Genets feed on a variety of small birds, rodents, and insects. They also take fruit and the West African forest genet, *G. maculata*, has been found to sip nectar, pollinating the flowers in the process. Genets are spotted and cat-like in appearance, but have elongated snouts with sharp, blade-like incisor teeth. The aquatic genet, *Osbornictis piscivora*, is known from only 16 specimens from the Democratic Republic of Congo.

Genet, Jean (1910–86) French dramatist and novelist. His life of crime led him to prison where, in 1942, he began to write novels exalting his own immoral values and subsequently dramas on more positive, existentialist themes. It was his plays, *Les Bonnes* (1947), *Le Balcon* (1956), *Les Nègres* (1959), and *Les Paravents* (1961) that brought him to prominence. These reject the western tradition of realism and imitate the stylized conventions of eastern drama.

gene therapy Treatment that is currently under investigation for diseases caused by defective genes; it involves the introduction of new genes, using the techniques of GENETIC ENGINEERING, to either replace the defective ones or counteract their effects. The most feasible approach – somatic cell gene therapy – involves introducing the new genes into somatic cells (nonreproductive body cells); the genetic manipulation of germ cells, so that the new gene would be inheritable, is regarded as dangerously unpredictable and unethical. Gene therapy offers the possibility of treating such diseases as cystic fibrosis and muscular dystrophy, in which the faulty gene fails to produce a vital protein: the replacement gene restores production of the protein. It is also being explored for the treatment of certain cancers, with the aim of introducing genes whose products specifically target and destroy the cancerous cells.

genetic code The 'language' of the genetic molecules DNA and RNA. These molecules comprise sequences of nucleotides, each consisting of a sugar (deoxyribose or ribose), phosphate, and one of four bases: adenine (A), cytosine (C), guanine (G), and thymine (T) or uracil (U). DNA influences the PHENOTYPE of an organism by directing the production of PROTEINS which are made of AMINO ACIDS. The DNA is first transcribed into messenger RNA (mRNA). This is translated into protein, which is 'written' in a different language: amino acids. The properties of a protein are determined in part by the sequence of amino acids, which in turn is determined by the sequence of bases in the DNA molecule.

The genetic code is a triplet code; that is, three bases (a codon) act as a code for one amino acid. There are 64 possible triplets of the four bases and 61 of these code for a particular amino acid: GGA, for example, codes for glycine. The remaining three triplets act as punctuation signals ('stop' codons), which tell the translation process where to stop translating the mRNA.

genetic engineering The deliberate modification of the genetic make-up (genome) of an organism by manipulation of its DNA. Genetic engineering techniques include cell fusion and the use of recombinant DNA (rDNA). Since the late 1960s these techniques have held out the most exciting promise for BIOTECHNOLOGY and – more recently – for GENE THERAPY.

Whereas cell fusion is a somewhat imprecise 'shotgun' approach to creating genetic novelty, recombinant DNA (rDNA) techniques are capable of transferring specific genetic activity from one organism to another. If, for example, a gene for a property such as production of the hormone insulin is isolated from a human or animal cell and transferred to a swiftly replicating bacterium like *Escherichia coli*, insulin can be produced in large enough quantities to be commercially profitable (see BIOTECHNOLOGY). The success of such techniques relies on 'tools' supplied by microorganisms: bacterial plasmids and ENZYMES. Plasmids are small, circular pieces of DNA lying outside the main bacterial chromosome. The most important enzymes are restriction endonucleases, which cut DNA strands at specific points; reverse transcriptase, which makes a DNA strand from a strand of RNA; DNA ligase, which can be used to join strands of DNA together; and Taq polymerase, which can make a double-stranded DNA molecule from a single-stranded 'primer' molecule.

In such a new field controversy inevitably abounds. Worries concerning release of genetically novel bacteria into the environment, or the possible manipulation of human embryos, have led to the setting up in the USA of the Genetic Manipulation Advisory Group (GMAG). Legislation governing genetic research has also been passed in several other countries.

genetic fingerprinting See DNA FINGERPRINTING.

genetics The study of the passing of biological characters from parent to offspring and of the structure, function and evolution of hereditary factors, called GENES, which control these characters. It was first formalized by MENDEL, who found that genetic factors are independent, in the sense that they do not 'blend'. He crossed different strains of peas, which varied according to the height of the plants, texture of the seeds, or colour of the flowers. When he crossed tall and short strains, the progeny were always either all tall, or short and tall; they were never of medium height. He also inferred from the pattern of inheritance that each character, such as height, must be controlled by two copies of each factor, one from the female parent the other from the male. Mendel's factors came to be called genes and were associated with CHROMOSOMES, which also exist in two copies in body cells. Each gene can exist in two or more different forms called ALLELES.

Geneva A city of south-west Switzerland, on Lake Geneva; pop. (1990) 167,200. For long a cultural centre of French-speaking Switzerland (la Suisse romande), it was in the 16th century a stronghold of the reformer John Calvin, who rewrote its laws and constitution and founded an Academy (1559), which later became a university. More recently it has become the head-quarters of international bodies, such as the Red Cross, the League of Nations (1922–46), and the World Health Organization. A series of international agreements, known as the GENEVA CONVENTIONS, were concluded at Geneva between 1864 and 1977 with the object of mitigating the harm done by war to both service personnel and civilians by governing the status of hospitals, ambulances, the wounded, etc. Its light industries include the manufacture of watches, jewellery, precision instruments, machinery, clothing, and confectionery.

Geneva, Lake (French **Lac Léman**) A lake in south-west Switzerland and eastern France, surrounded by the Alpine ranges of the Savoy Alps, Vaud Alps, and Jura Mts.; area 581 sq km (224 sq miles). The River Rhône flows into the lake and leaves it at Geneva. Its southern shore forms part of the border between France and Switzerland.

Geneva Conventions A series of international agreements on the treatment of victims of war, ratified in whole or partially by the majority of states and certain non-state organizations, such as the PLO (the Palestine Liberation Organization) and SWAPO (the South West Africa People's Organization). The first Geneva Convention was established by the Swiss founder of the RED CROSS, Henri Dunant, in 1864, and concerned the treatment of the wounded in war and the protection of medical personnel. Subsequent Conventions in 1907, 1929, 1949, and 1977 covered the treatment of prisoners of war and the protection of civilians, forbidding such acts as DEPORTATION, torture, hostage-taking, collective punishment or reprisals, and the use of chemical and biological weapons. The 1977 Convention dealt with more extensive non-combatant protection, and covered problems arising from internal wars.

Genghis Khan (1162–1227) The founder of the Mongol empire. Originally named Temujin, he took the name Genghis Khan ('ruler of all') in 1206 after uniting the nomadic Mongol tribes under his command and becoming master of both eastern and western Mongolia. He then attacked China, capturing Beijing in 1215. When he died his empire extended from the shores of the Pacific to the northern shores of the Black Sea. His grandson Kublai Khan completed the conquest of China.

Genoa (Italian **Genova**) A commercial and industrial city and seaport on the Ligurian coast of north-west Italy, capital of Liguria region; pop. (1990) 701,030. It has oil-refining, chemical, vehicle, and textile industries. The heavy industries of shipbuilding and steel are in decline. Genoa gave its name to the twilled cotton cloth now used to make jeans and was the birthplace of Christopher Columbus in *c.*1451.

genocide The systematic policy of destruction of a group or nation on grounds of race or ethnic origin. Following the Nazi policy of genocide of the Jews and of ethnic groups such as gypsies, the Convention on the Prevention and Punishment of the Crime of Genocide was adopted by the UN in 1948. Since the signing of the Convention, many conflicts in the world have split groups along ethnic or tribal lines, and claims of genocide have been made. Examples include the Nigeria–Biafra conflict in 1969; Uganda in the 1970s; the Pol Pot regime in Kampuchea (Cambodia) (1976–79); Iraq's treatment of the Kurds (1986–); the ethnic cleansing of Bosnian Muslims by Christian Serbs (1992–95); and the attempts by Hutus and Tutsis to annihilate each other in Burundi and Rwanda (1993–). The international community has failed in most cases to respond effectively to claims of genocide: firm evidence is hard to obtain and states are reluctant to intervene in the domestic affairs of another state on the grounds that this is a violation of national SOVEREIGNTY.

genome All the chromosomal DNA in a cell. It is frequently qualified: for example, haploid genome refers to the DNA in one set of CHROMOSOMES, diploid genome in two sets of chromosomes. The bacterial and mitochondrial genomes refer to the DNA in the bacterial and mitochondrial chromosomes.

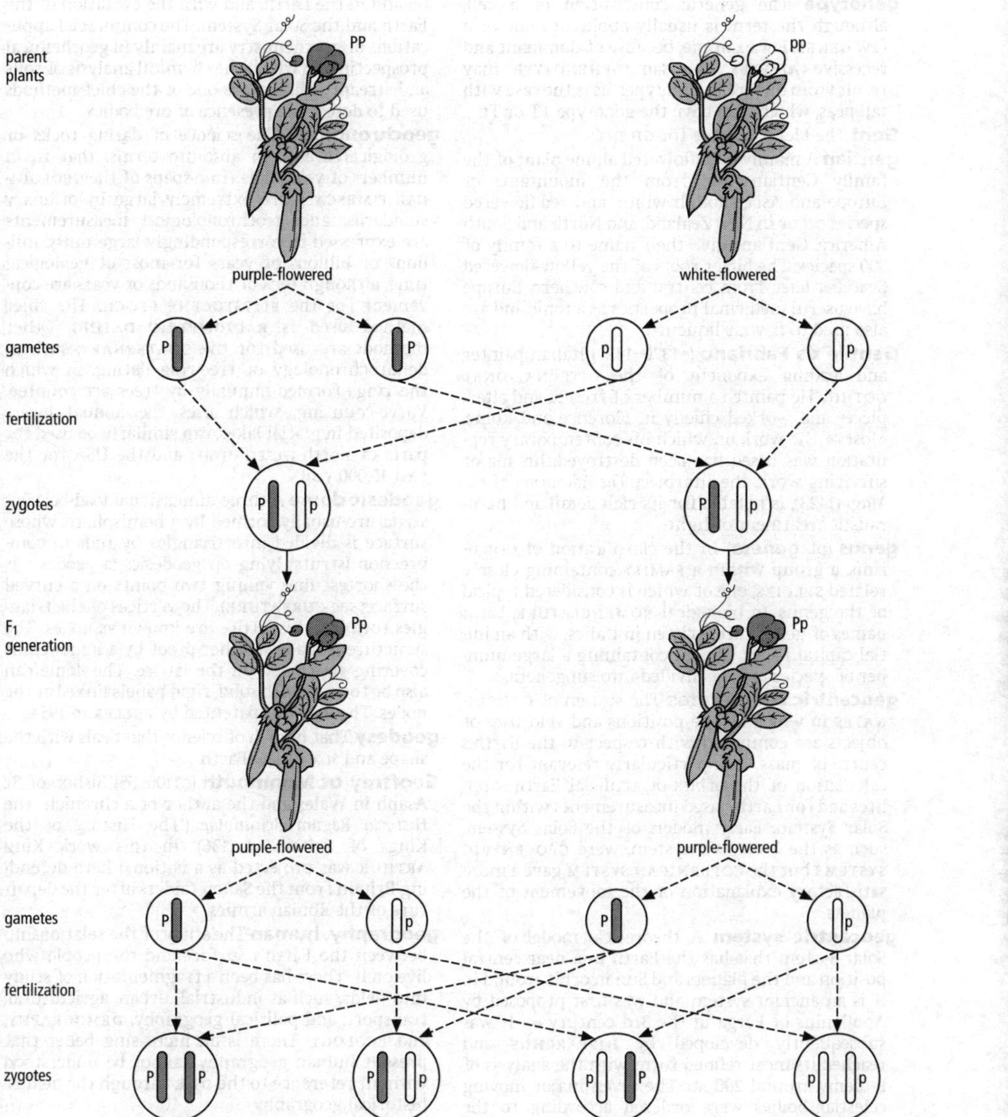

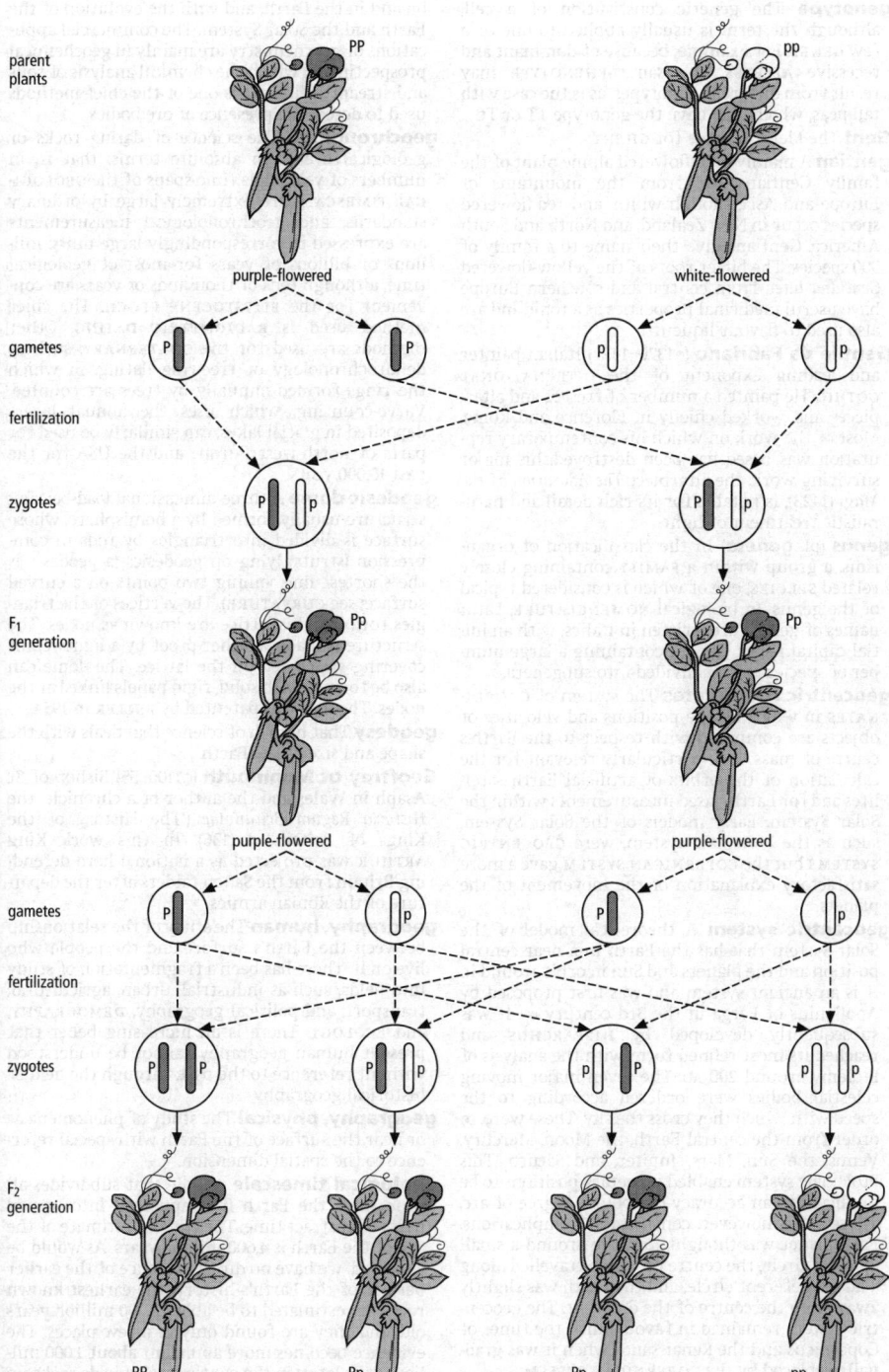

Genetics In his classic experiments with pea plants, Gregor Mendel crossed pure-bred purple-flowered plants with pure-bred white ones. All the first-generation (F_1) plants had purple flowers. Self-pollination of this generation resulted in a second (F_2) generation of about 75% purple-flowered and 25% white-flowered plants. The character of flower colour is determined by a pair of alleles (alternative forms of a gene); the allele for purple flowers (P) is dominant to that for white flowers (p). The pairs separate independently into different gametes, so that all combinations of alleles are found in the subsequent generation.

genotype The genetic constitution of a cell, although the term is usually applied to one or a few GENES. For example, because of dominant and recessive ALLELES, the same PHENOTYPE may result from different genotypes, as is the case with tall peas, which may have the genotype TT or Tt.

Gent The Flemish name for GHENT.

gentian A mainly blue-flowered alpine plant of the family Gentianaceae, from the mountains of Europe and Asia, though white- and red-flowered species occur in New Zealand, and North and South America. Gentians give their name to a family of 900 species. The bitter roots of the yellow-flowered *Gentiana lutea* from central and southern Europe have useful medicinal properties as a tonic and are also used to flavour liqueurs.

Gentile da Fabriano (*c.*1370–1427) Italian painter and leading exponent of the INTERNATIONAL GOTHIC. He painted a number of frescos and altarpieces and worked chiefly in Florence and Rome. Most of the work on which his contemporary reputation was based has been destroyed; his major surviving work, the altarpiece *The Adoration of the Magi* (1423), is notable for its rich detail and naturalistic treatment of light.

genus (pl. **genera**) In the classification of organisms, a group within a FAMILY containing closely related SPECIES, one of which is considered typical of the genus. In biological NOMENCLATURE, Latin names of genera are written in italics, with an initial capital letter. Genera containing a large number of species may be divided into subgenera.

geocentric coordinates The system of COORDINATES in which all the positions and velocities of objects are computed with respect to the Earth's centre of mass. It is particularly relevant for the calculation of the orbits of artificial Earth satellites and for Earth-based measurements within the Solar System. Early models of the Solar System, such as the Ptolemaic system, were GEOCENTRIC SYSTEMS but the COPERNICAN SYSTEM gave a more satisfactory explanation of the movement of the planets.

geocentric system A theoretical model of the Solar System that has the Earth in a near central position and the planets and Sun in orbit around it. It is an ancient system and was first proposed by Apollonius of Perga in the 3rd century BC. It was subsequently developed by HIPPARCHUS and reached its most refined form with the analysis of Ptolemy around 200 AD. The seven major moving celestial bodies were ordered according to the speed with which they cross the sky. These were, in order from the central Earth, the Moon, Mercury, Venus, the Sun, Mars, Jupiter, and Saturn. This Ptolemaic system enabled planetary positions to be predicted to an accuracy of about 1 degree of arc. There were, however, considerable complications. Each planet was thought to move around a small epicycle circle, the centre of which travelled along a larger deferent circle; and the Earth was slightly away from the centre of the deferent. The geocentric system remained in favour until the times of Copernicus and the Renaissance when it was gradually replaced by the COPERNICAN SYSTEM.

geochemistry The study of the chemistry of the EARTH. It is concerned with the distribution of elements and their ISOTOPES in the Earth, in the mantle and core as well as the crust, and including those elements (trace elements) that are present only in very low concentrations. It is also concerned with the relationships between these elements; with the chemical processes that take place on and in the Earth; and with the evolution of the Earth and the Solar System. The commercial applications of geochemistry are mainly in geochemical prospecting, in which the chemical analysis of soils and stream sediments is one of the chief methods used to detect the presence of ore bodies.

geochronology The science of dating rocks or geological events in absolute terms, that is, in numbers of years. The time-spans of the GEOLOGICAL TIMESCALE are extremely large by ordinary standards, and geochronological measurements are expressed in correspondingly large units: millions or billions of years for most of geological time, although tens of thousands of years are convenient for the PLEISTOCENE EPOCH. The chief method used is RADIOMETRIC DATING. Other methods are used for the QUATERNARY, such as dendrochronology or tree-ring dating, in which the rings formed annually by trees are counted. Varve-counting, which uses the annual layers deposited in glacial lakes, can similarly be used for parts of north-west Europe and the USA for the past 10,000 years.

geodesic dome A three-dimensional load-bearing structure usually formed by a hemisphere, whose surface is divided into triangles by rods in compression (struts) lying on geodesics (a geodesic is the shortest line joining two points on a curved surface; see CURVATURE). The vertices of the triangles forming this lattice are known as nodes. The structure is made weather-proof by a lightweight covering supported on the lattice. The dome can also be formed with solid, rigid panels linked at the nodes. The idea was patented by FULLER in 1954.

geodesy That branch of science that deals with the shape and size of the Earth.

Geoffrey of Monmouth (*c.*1100–55) Bishop of St Asaph in Wales and the author of a chronicle, the *Historia Regum Britanniae* ('The History of the Kings of Britain') (*c.*1136). In this work King ARTHUR was projected as a national hero defending Britain from the Saxon raiders after the departure of the Roman armies.

geography, human The study of the relationship between the Earth's surface and the people who live on it. There has been a fragmentation of study into fields, such as industrial, urban, agricultural, transport, and political geography, DEMOGRAPHY, and ECOLOGY. There is an increasing belief that present human geography cannot be understood without reference to the past, through the field of historical geography.

geography, physical The study of phenomena at or near the surface of the Earth with special reference to the spatial dimension.

geological timescale A scale that subdivides all time since the Earth first appeared into named units of abstract time. The current estimate of the age of the Earth is 4,600 million years. As would be expected, we have no direct evidence of the earlier periods of the Earth's history; the earliest known rocks are estimated to be about 3,700 million years old, and they are found only in a few places. The evidence becomes more abundant about 1,000 million years later: in the continental shields rocks up to 2,800 million years old are not uncommon. The two great divisions of geological time are the PRECAMBRIAN and the PHANEROZOIC; the dividing-line between them is dated at about 570 million years ago. The Precambrian thus represents the great bulk of geological time, though our knowledge of the Phanerozoic is much more detailed. The Phanerozoic is divided into three **eras**: the

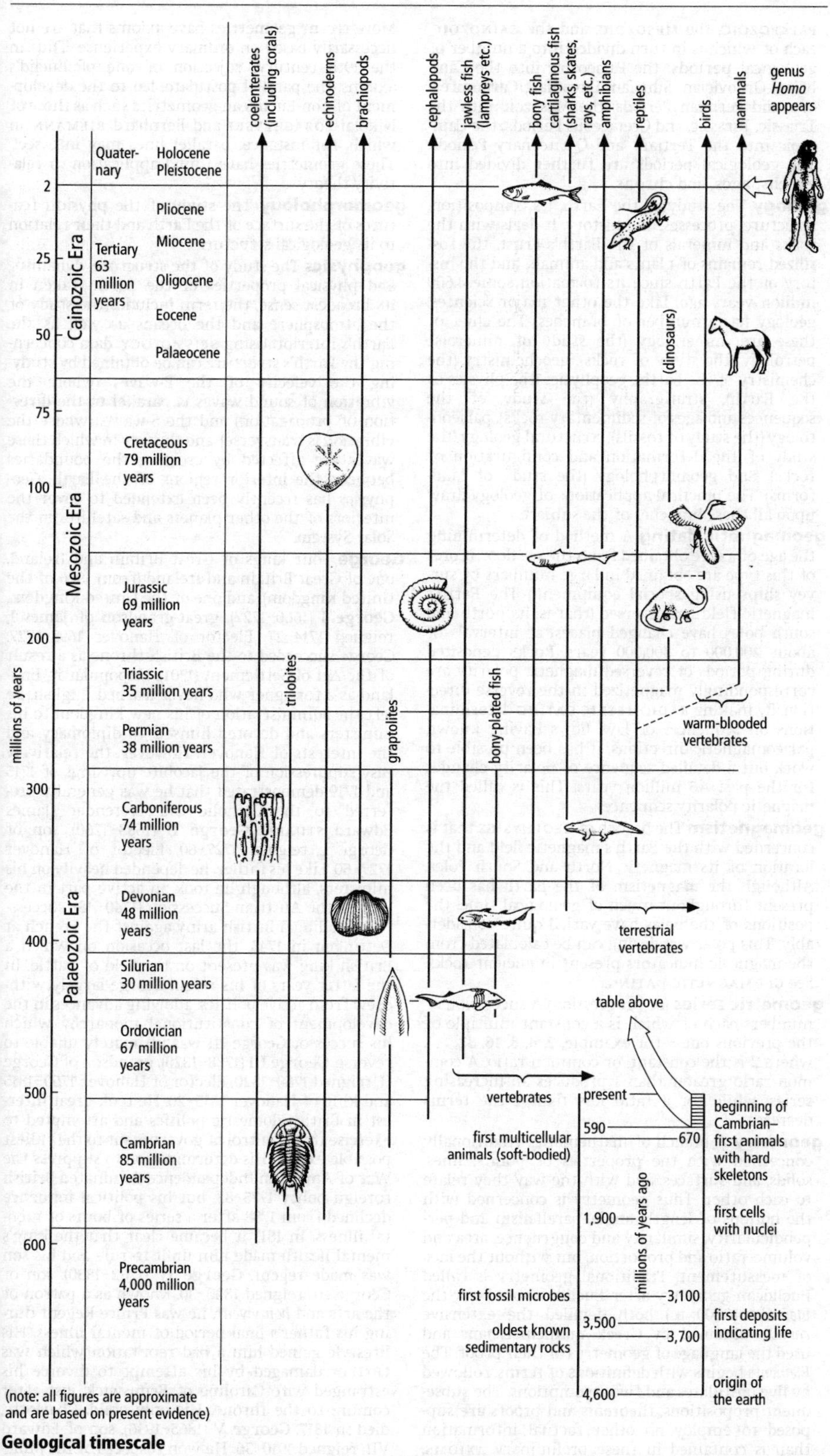

Geological timescale

PALAEOZOIC, the MESOZOIC, and the CAINOZOIC, each of which is in turn divided into a number of geological **periods**: the Palaeozoic into the Cambrian, Ordovician, Silurian, Devonian, Carboniferous, and Permian Periods; the Mesozoic into the Triassic, Jurassic, and Cretaceous Periods; the Cainozoic into the Tertiary and Quaternary Periods. The geological periods are further divided into **epochs**, **ages**, and **chrons**.

geology The study of the Earth, its composition, structure, processes, and history. It deals with the rocks and minerals of the Earth's crust, the fossilized remains of plants and animals, and the history of the Earth since its formation some 4,600 million years ago. Like the other major sciences, geology has a number of branches. The chief of these are: mineralogy (the study of minerals), petrology (the study of rocks), geochemistry (the chemistry of the Earth), geophysics (the physics of the Earth), stratigraphy (the study of the sequences and ages of sedimentary rocks), palaeontology (the study of fossils), structural geology (the study of the deformation and configuration of rocks), and geomorphology (the study of landforms). The practical applications of geology draw upon all these branches of the subject.

geomagnetic dating A method of determining the age of a core obtained from the sea floor. (Cores of this type are obtained in large numbers by survey ships using special equipment.) The Earth's magnetic field has reversed (that is, its north and south poles have changed places) at intervals of about 200,000 to 300,000 years. Rocks deposited during periods of reversed magnetic polarity are correspondingly magnetized in the reverse direction. By making RADIOMETRIC DATING determinations on sequences of lava flows having known palaeomagnetic directions, it has been possible to work out a detailed sequence of polarity changes for the past 4.5 million years. This is called the magnetic polarity sequence.

geomagnetism The branch of GEOPHYSICS that is concerned with the Earth's magnetic field and the location of its magnetic North and South Poles. Although the magnetism of the Earth has been present throughout much of geological time, the positions of the poles have varied quite considerably. This polar wandering can be calculated from the magnetic indicators present in ancient rocks. See GEOMAGNETIC DATING.

geometric series (or progression) A succession of numbers each of which is a constant multiple of the previous one – for example, 2, 4, 8, 16, 32, . . ., where 2 is the constant, or common ratio. A common ratio greater than 1 produces an increasing series, while for a ratio less than 1 the terms decrease.

geometry A branch of mathematics traditionally concerned with the properties of points, lines, solids, and surfaces, and with the way they relate to each other. Thus geometry is concerned with the notions of length, angle, parallelism and perpendicularity, similarity and congruence, area and volume, ratio and proportion, but without the idea of measurement. Traditional geometry is called Euclidean geometry after Euclid, whose book the *Elements* (*c.*300 BC) both detailed the extensive results obtained by Greek mathematicians and used the language of geometry for their proof. The *Elements* begins with definitions of terms, followed by five postulates and five assumptions. The subsequent propositions, theorems and proofs are supposed to employ no other factual information than is contained in these preliminary AXIOMS. More recent geometries have axioms that are not necessarily based on ordinary experience. Thus in the 19th century, rejection of one of Euclid's axioms, the parallel postulate, led to the development of non-Euclidean geometries such as those of Nikolai LOBACHEVSKI and Bernhard RIEMANN in which, for instance, parallel lines may intersect. These geometries have found application in relativity theory.

geomorphology The study of the physical features of the surface of the Earth and their relation to its geological structures.

geophysics The study of the structure, dynamics, and physical properties of the Earth. Taken in its broadest sense, the term includes the study of the atmosphere and the oceans as well as the Earth's interior. Using SEISMOLOGY, data concerning the Earth's structure can be obtained by studying the velocity of the P-waves (where the vibration of sound waves is parallel to the direction of propagation) and the S-waves (where the vibration is transverse), and the way in which these waves are affected by crossing the boundaries between the interior regions of the Earth. Geophysics has recently been extended to cover the interiors of the other planets and satellites in the Solar System.

George Four kings of Great Britain and Ireland, one of Great Britain and Ireland (from 1920 of the United Kingdom), and one of the United Kingdom. **George I** (1660–1727), great-grandson of James I, reigned 1714–27, Elector of Hanover 1698–1727. George succeeded to the British throne as a result of the Act of Settlement (1701). Unpopular in England as a foreigner who never learned English, he left the administration of his new kingdom to his ministers and devoted himself to diplomacy and the interests of Hanover. However, the relatively easy suppression of the Jacobite uprisings of 1715 and 1719 demonstrated that he was generally preferred to the Catholic Old Pretender (James Edward STUART). **George II** (1683–1760), son of George I, reigned 1727–60, Elector of Hanover 1727–60. Like his father, he depended heavily on his ministers, although he took an active part in the War of the Austrian Succession (1740–48), successfully leading a British army against the French at Dettingen in 1743, the last occasion on which a British king was present on the field of battle. In the latter years of his reign, George largely withdrew from active politics, allowing advances in the development of constitutional monarchy which his successor George III was ultimately unable to reverse. **George III** (1738–1820), grandson of George II, reigned 1760–1820, Elector of Hanover 1760–1815 and king of Hanover 1815–20. He took great interest in British domestic politics and attempted to exercise royal control of government to the fullest possible extent. His determination to suppress the War of American Independence dominated British foreign policy 1775–83, but his political influence declined from 1788 after a series of bouts of mental illness. In 1811 it became clear that the king's mental health made him unfit to rule and his son was made regent. **George IV** (1762–1830), son of George III, reigned 1820–30. Known as a patron of the arts and *bon viveur*, he was Prince Regent during his father's final period of mental illness. His lifestyle gained him a bad reputation which was further damaged by his attempt to divorce his estranged wife Caroline of Brunswick just after coming to the throne. His only child, Charlotte, died in 1817. **George V** (1865–1936), son of Edward VII, reigned 1910–36. He won respect for his punctilious attitude towards royal duties and responsibilities, especially during World War I. He exercised restrained but none the less important influence over British politics, playing an especially significant role in the formation of the government in 1931. **George VI** (1894–1952), son of George V, reigned 1936–52. He was created Duke of York in 1920 and came to the throne on the abdication of his elder brother Edward VIII. Despite a retiring disposition he became a popular monarch, gaining respect for the staunch example he and his family set during the London Blitz.

George, St Patron saint of England. Little is known of his life, but his historical existence is now generally accepted. He may have been martyred near Lydda in Palestine some time before the reign of Constantine (d. 337), but his cult did not become popular until the 6th century, and the slaying of the dragon who threatened both a princess and the inhabitants of her city (possibly derived from the legend of Perseus) was not attributed to him until the 12th century. His rank as patron saint of England (in place of Edward the Confessor) probably dates from the reign of Edward III, who founded the Order of the Garter (*c*.1344) under the patronage of St George, who by that time was honoured as the ideal of chivalry.

Georgetown The capital of Guyana, a port at the mouth of the Demerara River; pop. (est. 1990) 185,000. Fishing and food processing are the chief industries.

Georgia (Asia) A mountainous country in west Asia. It is separated from Russia in the north by the Caucasus Mountains. It has a coast on the Black Sea, shares a border with Turkey to the west, and is bounded by Azerbaijan and Armenia to the east and south.

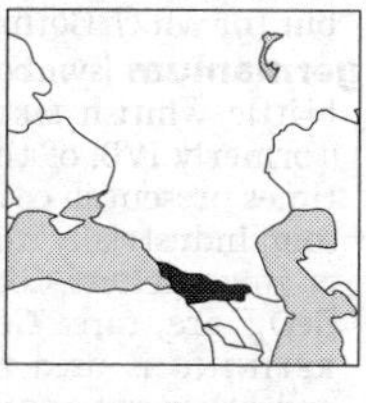

Physical. About one-third of the land is forest. The climate is subtropical, with cool winters and hot summers, very wet in the west and arid in the east. On the coastal plain and in the central valley fruit trees, palms, and eucalyptus flourish. By contrast, the east is treeless grassland, but rich in minerals.

Economy. Georgia's mineral resources include coal, petroleum, and manganese. Industry is based on the exploitation of these resources; there is also some machinery production and other light industry. Agriculture includes viticulture; tea, tobacco, and citrus are the main crops.

History. Georgia has been a distinctive state since the 4th century BC. In the 3rd century AD it became part of the Sassanian empire (see SASSANID) but the Persians were expelled *c*.400. The 12th and 13th centuries saw territorial expansion and cultural achievement cut short by Mongol destruction. Revival was likewise curtailed by the ravages of TAMERLANE (1386–1403) and national decline was confirmed by the decision of Alexander I to split the kingdom between his three sons. After some two and a half centuries of partition, the western half being under OTTOMAN rule, the eastern under Persian, the area was reunited by the Russian conquest of 1821–29.

Throughout the 19th century, Tzarist Russia continued to suppress Georgian nationalism. A strong Social Democrat Party of Mensheviks emerged in Georgia in the early 20th century, which formed a brief republic (1918–21), under British protection. In 1921 Georgia was conquered by the Red Army from Russia, and became part of the Transcaucasian Soviet Federal Socialist Republic with Azerbaijan and Armenia. A large-scale anti-communist uprising was suppressed in 1924 and in 1936 the Georgian Soviet Socialist Republic became a full member of the Soviet Union. Another uprising in the capital Tbilisi in 1956 was suppressed, and in April 1989 there were extensive riots, again brutally suppressed. In April 1991, however, it gained independence under President Zviad Gamsakhurdia. Opposition to Gamsakhurdia's 'dictatorial methods' led to his deposition, following the outbreak of civil conflict in December 1991. In March 1992 Eduard Shevardnadze (Soviet Foreign Minister 1985–91) returned to his native Georgia to become Chairman of the State Council. In September he was elected President. The civil conflict continued throughout 1992 and 1993 as forces loyal to Gamsakhurdia attempted to gain control. In November, however, with the aid of Russian troops, government forces routed the rebels from Georgia. The country was also beset by other armed conflicts within its borders. In 1989 a rebellion erupted in South Ossetia when the region demanded greater autonomy and secession from Georgia. A cease-fire was eventually agreed in mid-1992 and South Ossetia confirmed its intention to secede. In August 1992 a period of violent armed conflict began, following periodic unrest since 1989, over the region of Abkhazia's demands for independence. By September 1993, after intensive fighting, Georgian forces were defeated and expelled from the region. Following UN-sponsored peace talks, a provisional cease-fire was negotiated in April 1994, when Shevardnadze agreed to cede considerable autonomy to Abkhazia. Meanwhile, in December 1993, Georgia finally agreed to join the COMMONWEALTH OF INDEPENDENT STATES (CIS) and, in February 1994, signed a ten-year treaty of friendship and cooperation with Russia. In March 1995 Shevardnadze signed a military agreement with Russia. He was re-elected in presidential elections later that year.

Capital: Tbilisi
Area: 69,700 sq km (26,900 sq mi)
Population: 5,514,000 (1995)
Currency: 1 lari = 100 tetri
Religions: Georgian Eastern Orthodox Church
Ethnic Groups: Georgian 80.0%; Armenian 8.0%; Russian 6.0%; Azeri 6.0%; Abkhazian and Ossete minorities
Languages: Georgian (official); Russian; minority languages
International Organizations: CSCE

Georgia (USA) A state of the south-eastern USA, on the southern Atlantic coast; area 152,576 sq km (58,910 sq mi); pop. (1990) 6,478,220; capital, Atlanta. It was founded in 1732 as an English colony with English parliamentary support both as a bulwark against the Spanish in FLORIDA and as a new start for English debtors. The trustees under James Oglethorpe established tightly controlled settlements at Savannah (1733) and elsewhere, prohibiting slavery, rum, and land sales, and encouraging silk and wine production. With the relaxation of this regime in the 1750s and immigration from Europe and other colonies, it slowly prospered. Georgia was a strong centre of loyalism during the War of INDEPENDENCE, and did not join the Union until 1782. A member state of the CONFEDERACY during the AMERICAN CIVIL WAR, Georgia suffered heavily, with Atlanta falling to General SHERMAN's army in September 1864. Decline in the state's original source of wealth, cotton growing, in the 20th century has been offset by investment in manufacturing industries. In 1977, Democratic former state governor of Georgia, Jimmy CARTER, was elected President of the USA.

geostationary orbit (or **geosynchronous orbit**) The orbit of an artificial SATELLITE about the Earth such that the point on the Earth's surface directly below the satellite (the subsatellite point) is almost stationary. This greatly simplifies spacecraft-to-Earth communications, a requirement for most telecommunication and many meteorological satellites. To be geostationary, the orbit must be geosynchronous, with low eccentricity and inclination so these orbits are confined to a narrow belt, and traffic problems arise there. Over time the subsatellite point gradually drifts away in the east–west direction because of the perturbations produced by the non-spherical shape of the Earth, and manoeuvres with rockets are required to keep the satellite on station.

geosyncline An elongated basin in the Earth's crust in which great quantities of sediment accumulate. Geosynclines were considered to be downwarped areas which formed parallel to the continental masses and, as a result of receiving vast amounts of land-derived sediments, developed under the sheer weight of sediment accumulation. This terminology has now fallen into disuse since their mechanism of formation is now best explained with reference to the more unifying theory of PLATE TECTONICS.

geothermal energy Energy originating from, or produced by the internal heat of the Earth. Installations for obtaining heat from dry rock or from hot water deep below the Earth's surface exist in many parts of the world as alternative energy sources. An industrial plant at Larderello in Italy, already using geothermal energy, was the site of the first commercial geothermal power-station, in 1913. This is still in operation, and similar stations have been built in the Yellowstone National Park, USA, Wairakei in New Zealand, and in Iceland, raising the total world generating capacity to about 4,000 MW.

geranium Any hardy species of the plant genus *Geranium*, which includes CRANESBILLS. The name is also used by amateur gardeners for varieties of the South African plant genus *Pelargonium*, of which there are several groups, including zonal, regal, and the scented- and ivy-leaved kinds. Most of them have bright, showy flowers and are often grown as pot plants. Oil is extracted from the scented-leaved kinds and may be used as a base for perfumes.

gerbil (or **jerbil**) A member of the rodent genus *Gerbillus* with 34 species; the name is also used for the family Gerbillinae, with a total of 81 species (including the genus *Gerbillus*). All species are small, long-legged animals inhabiting desert regions of Africa and Asia Minor. They spend the day in sandy burrows, emerging at night to forage for seeds, roots, and insects. They often hop on their elongated hind-legs like miniature kangaroos. They have many physiological adaptations to desert life, including a very efficient water-retrieval system in their hind gut.

Géricault, (Jean Louis André) Théodore (1791–1824) French painter. His rejection of the prevailing classicism of his day and use of bright colours in a bold, romantic style brought him criticism from the art world. His most famous work, *The Raft of the Medusa* (1819), depicts the survivors of a famous shipwreck of 1816, with realistic treatment of the macabre. He also painted landscapes and scenes of horse-races.

German A Germanic language spoken by some 100 million people. It is the official language of Germany and of Austria, and one of the official languages of Switzerland. **High German** is the variety of Teutonic speech, originally confined to 'High' or southern Germany, now accepted as the literary language of the whole country. Its chief distinctive characteristic is that certain consonants have been altered from their original Teutonic sounds which the other dialects in the main preserve. The spread of this form of the language owes much to the Biblical translations of Martin Luther in the 16th century. **Low German** is the collective name for the dialects of Germany which are not High German. It is spoken in the lowland areas of northern Germany, and is most closely related to Dutch and Friesian.

German Democratic Republic See EAST GERMANY.

German East Africa A former German protectorate in East Africa (1891–1918), corresponding to present-day Tanzania, Rwanda, and Burundi. Conquered by Britain during World War I, it was administered thereafter under League of Nations mandates by Britain and Belgium.

Germanic The branch of Indo-European languages including English, German, Dutch, and the Scandinavian languages. These different languages reflect a dialectal split into West Germanic (English and German), North Germanic (the Scandinavian languages for which the oldest evidence is that of Old Norse), and East Germanic, which has died out but for which Gothic provided the oldest evidence.

germanium (symbol Ge, at. no. 32, r.a.m. 72.59) A brittle whitish METALLOID element in Group 14 (formerly IVB) of the PERIODIC TABLE. It is sometimes present in coal and can be found in chimney soot. Industrially it is extracted from the flue dust of zinc smelters. Compounds, except for the oxide, GeO_2, are rare. Germanium purified by ZONE REFINING is used to make transistors, rectifiers, and other SEMICONDUCTOR devices. Germanium dioxide is used in the manufacture of specialized optical glasses.

German literature Literary work written by the German-speaking peoples of Europe. Despite a substantial amount of religious writing in the 8th and 9th centuries, a continuous literary tradition in the German language began only in the 11th century, when a lay audience emerged for secular works reflecting the courtly ethos to which they aspired. Their desire for romances and for courtly love lyrics (*Minnesang*) was satisfied at the high point of medieval German literature between 1150 and 1250 notably by Gottfried von Strassburg, Hartmann von Aue (*c*.1165–1210), Wolfram von Eschenbach, and the lyric poet Walther von der Vogelweide. Although Germany produced a number of Renaissance and humanist authors, their influence remained limited: the literature of the Middle Ages in all its variety remained popular up to the 16th century, until the controversies of the Reformation and the influence of Martin LUTHER, whose idiomatic prose style marks the beginning of a new age in the history of the German language and its literature. The 17th and 18th centuries are characterized by critical attempts to improve and refine German literature. This resulted initially in a literature influenced by French practice and combined with Baroque rhetoric. The most readable author of the period is Hans von Grimmelshausen (*c*.1625–76). Through the work of LESSING, KLOPSTOCK, and Christoph Wieland, German literature finally found its own voice, culminating in the plays of the STURM UND DRANG movement and then in the mature classicism of GOETHE and SCHILLER, whose genius influenced many authors both within and beyond Germany throughout the 19th century. Reaction to these models came firstly from the Romantics, who built partly on impulses from *Sturm und Drang*, concentrating on the irrational, fantastic, and even subconscious: the SCHLEGEL brothers, Ludwig Tieck (1773–1853), Wilhelm Heinrich Wackenroder (1773–98), Novalis (1772–1801), and HOFFMANN; and secondly from *Junges Deutschland*, a disparate group of writers including Heinrich HEINE, with more radical political interests. The 19th century produced notable prose-writers, including the Swiss German Gottfried KELLER, Wilhelm Raabe (1831–1910), Adalbert Stifter (1805–68), and Theodor Storm (1817–88), whose realism was developed further and given a sharp critical edge in the naturalistic idiom adopted by Gerhart HAUPTMANN and Hermann Sudermann (1857–1928). The novels of the Berlin writer Theodore Fontane (1819–98) give a critical account of Prussian society. The lyric poet Stefan George was chiefly responsible for the revival of German poetry at the close of the 19th century, while in Rainer Maria RILKE Austria produced one of the great poets of the 20th century. Of the literary groups critical of the moral emptiness and hypocrisy of bourgeois society in the early 20th century, most significant were the Expressionists, Georg Heym (1887–1912), Georg KAISER, August Stramm (1874–1915), Georg Trakl (1887–1914), and WEDEKIND. Reaching its height during World War I, the movement declined in the 1920s. The German-speaking Czech Franz KAFKA offered complex and enigmatic visions of alienation in modern society in his novels and short stories. From their accession to power in 1933 onwards, the Nazis drove into exile or silenced within Germany almost every author of significance, most notably the highly innovative and influential Marxist playwright and poet Bertolt BRECHT.

The post-World War II development of German literature was complicated by the addition of ideology to the political divisions that existed in the German-speaking world. In the German Federal Republic (West Germany) the initial post-war restorative tendencies gave way to criticism of German complacency of the 'economic miracle' and the reluctance to face the Nazi past. This was led by the dramatists Wolfgang Borchert (1921–47), Rolf Hochhuth (1931–), and the novelists Alfred Andersch (1914–), Siegfried Lenz (1926–), Günter GRASS, and Heinrich BÖLL. In the 1960s the sense of crisis, which dominated the literary scene, encouraging a political social and artistic radicalization of literature, was expressed in the documentary literature of Günter Wallraff (1947–), the novels of Nicolas Born (1937–79), Max von der Grün (1926–), and in the plays of Tancred Dorst (1925–) and the Austrian Peter Handke (1942–). The literary scene in the German Democratic Republic (East Germany) was, until reunification in 1990, affected by phases of cultural repression and relaxation. A dominant theme of East German literature, whether critical of the regime or not, has been the position of the individual in a socialist society and his or her attitudes to the capitalist society beyond the Berlin Wall. This manifested itself in the writings of Christa Wolf (1929–), Hermann Kant (1926–), and Ulrich Plenzdorf (1934–). A number of writers were banished or sought exile in the West: Sarah Kirsch (1935–), Botho Strauss (1944–), and Erich Loest (1926–), though not all survived, artistically speaking, the transplantation.

German Second Empire (or **Second Reich**) (1871–1918) A continental and overseas empire ruled by Prussia. (The First Reich was the Holy Roman Empire, which ended in 1806.) It replaced the German Confederation and the short-lived North German Confederation (1866–70). It was created by BISMARCK following the FRANCO-PRUSSIAN WAR, by the union of 25 German states under the Hohenzollern King of Prussia, now Emperor William I. During WORLD WAR I most German African territories were conquered and at the VERSAILLES PEACE SETTLEMENT Germany was stripped of its overseas empire, which became mandated territories, administered by the victorious powers on behalf of the LEAGUE OF NATIONS. At the end of the war the emperor abdicated and the WEIMAR REPUBLIC was created.

German South West Africa A former German protectorate in south-west Africa (1884–1918), corresponding to present-day Namibia. Administered by South Africa under a League of Nations mandate until 1968.

Germany A former country in central Europe. Germany was originally occupied by Teutonic tribes who were driven back across the Rhine by Julius CAESAR in 58 BC. When the Roman empire collapsed eight Germanic kingdoms were created, but in the 8th century CHARLEMAGNE consolidated these kingdoms under the FRANKS. The region became part of the HOLY ROMAN EMPIRE in 962, and almost 200 years later was invaded by the Mongols. A period of unrest followed until 1438 when the long rule of the HABSBURGS began. The kingdom, now made up of hundreds of states, was torn apart during the THIRTY YEARS WAR; when this ended with the Peace of Westphalia in 1648, the Elector of Brandenburg-Prussia emerged as a force ready to challenge Austrian supremacy. By the end of the NAPOLEONIC WARS, the alliance of 400 separate German states that had existed within the Holy Roman Empire (962–1806) had been reduced to 38. At the Congress of VIENNA these were formed into a loose grouping, the German Confederation, under Austrian leadership. The German Confederation was dissolved as a result of the AUSTRO-PRUSSIAN WAR (1866), and in 1867 all northern Germany formed a new North German Confederation under Prussian leadership. This was in turn dissolved in 1871, and the new GERMAN SECOND EMPIRE proclaimed. After Germany's defeat in World War I, the WEIMAR REPUBLIC was instituted, to be replaced in 1933 by the THIRD REICH under Adolf HITLER. After the end of World War II the country divided into the Federal Republic of GERMANY (West Germany) and the German Democratic Republic (EAST GERMANY), which reunited in October 1990.

Germany, Federal Republic of A country in central Europe. In the west it extends across the Rhine valley, in the south it includes the central Alps, and in the east it is partially bounded by the River Oder. Germany has borders with Denmark, Poland, the Czech Republic, Austria, Switzerland, France, Luxembourg, Belgium, and the Netherlands.

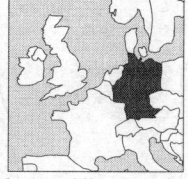

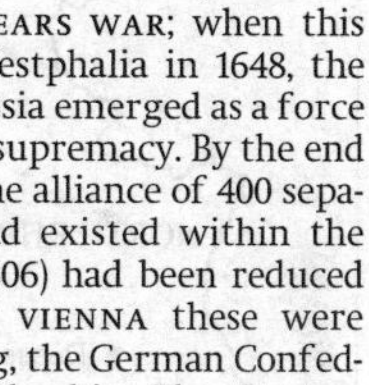

Physical. The whole of northern Germany, through which run the Weser, the Elbe, and smaller rivers, is set in the North European Plain. The Rhine Basin encompasses some of the most beautiful landscape and best wine-growing regions in Europe. Towards the east, this consists of morainic hills containing fertile LOESS soil. More than a quarter of the whole of Germany is covered with forest. Among the major ranges of the mid-German highlands are the Teutoburger Wald, the Harz Mountains, the Sauerland, Westerwald, and Taunusgebirge. In the west are the Ruhr coalfields, while in the east there are large lignite deposits. Southward the ground gradually rises to the Black Forest (Schwarzwald), and the Swabian Jura, with dense pine forests and moorland, and potash, salt, and other minerals. In Bavaria, further south, the land becomes rugged. Here are patches of mountain pasture and lakes; to the east is the deep Danube valley.

Economy. Despite the huge cost of restructuring the industy of the former GDR, Germany has a highly successful industrial economy, which continues to be the dominant economic force in Europe. It also enjoys excellent labour relations, and a high degree of worker participation in management. Industry includes mechanical and electrical engineering, electronics, vehicles, chemicals, and food-processing, with machinery, electronic goods, optical and scientific instruments, transport equipment, and chemical and pharmaceutical products the principal exports. Mineral resources include coal, lignite, salt, and some natural gas. Nuclear power generates around one-quarter of Germany's electricity. The main agricultural crops are potatoes, sugar-beet, wheat, and barley. Viticulture is most extensive in the Rhine and Mosel valleys in West Germany and is an important export industry.

History. The Federal Republic of Germany was

Germany

created in 1949 from the British, French, and US zones of occupation of GERMANY. It became a sovereign state in 1955, when ambassadors were exchanged with world powers, including the Soviet Union. Konrad ADENAUER, as Chancellor (1949–63), was determined to see eventual reunification of Germany and refused to recognize the legal existence of the German Democratic Republic. A crisis developed over Berlin in 1958, when the Soviet Union demanded the withdrawal of Western troops and, in 1961, when it authorized the erection of the BERLIN WALL. The Berlin situation began to ease in 1971, during the chancellorship of the social democrat Willy BRANDT (1969–74) with his policy of OSTPOLITIK. This resulted in treaties with the Soviet Union (1970), Poland (1970), Czechoslovakia (1973), and one of mutual recognition and cooperation with the German Democratic Republic (1972), with membership of the UN following in 1973. Economic recovery was assisted after the war by the MARSHALL PLAN. The challenge of rebuilding shattered cities and of absorbing many millions of refugees from eastern Europe was successfully met, as was that of re-creating systems of social welfare and health provision. The Federal Republic joined NATO in 1955, when both army and airforce were reconstituted; large numbers of US and British troops remained stationed there. In 1957 it signed the Treaty of ROME, becoming a founder-member of the EUROPEAN ECONOMIC COMMUNITY in 1958. Although the pace of economic growth slackened, the economy remained one of the strongest in the world, under a stable democratic regime. Following economic and monetary union with the Democratic Republic in June 1990, a Treaty of Unification was signed in August and unification took place in October. Since then, the country has consisted of sixteen *Länder* or states, each of which has wide powers over its domestic affairs. Chancellor Helmut KOHL's Christian Democratic Union won control of four out of the five new *Länder*; but their economic problems were soon to produce a sense of disillusion, with unemployment rising to 17 per cent and a resurgence of support for the former communists. The cost of restructuring the economy of the former GDR proved far higher than expected, obliging the Bundesbank to maintain very high interest rates. This in turn caused tensions with the ERM (the Exchange Rate Mechanism, whereby those member states taking part agree to maintain currency fluctuations within certain limits), and turmoil in the money markets. Germany's liberal policies on asylum resulted in a large influx of migrants, legal and illegal, with accompanying social problems. A resurgence of right-wing extremism in the form of attacks on Jews and foreign citizens led the government to ban four far-right organizations in late 1992. Following unification, the economies of eastern and western Germany remained divergent as the costs of the process continued to affect German industrial and economic health. A number of trials opened in 1992 involving senior politicians and other members of the former communist regime in East Germany, the most prominent of whom was Erich Honecker, the former East German head of state. Against a background of recession and political disillusionment in western Germany, further measures were taken in 1993 to fund the restructuring of the eastern German economy. In the presidential elections of May 1994 Roman Herzog was elected to replace Richard von Weizsäcker. In October the federal coalition, led by Helmut Kohl since 1982, was re-elected with a greatly reduced majority. The transfer of the seat of government and administrative departments from Bonn to the capital-designate Berlin is estimated to be complete by the year 2000.

Capital: Bonn (capital-designate is Berlin)
Area: 356,954 sq km (137,820 sq mi)
Population: 81,912,000 (1995)
Currency: 1 Deutschmark = 100 Pfennige
Religions: FRG (1987): Roman Catholic 42.9%; Lutheran 41.6%; Muslim 2.7%; former GDR (1987): Protestant 47.0%; unaffiliated 46.0%; Roman Catholic 7.0%
Ethnic Groups: (nationality) German 93.2%; Turkish 2.3%; Yugoslav 0.9%; Italian 0.8%
Languages: German (official); minority languages
International Organizations: UN; EU; OECD; NATO; Council of Europe; CSCE

germination The restarting of growth of an embryo after dormancy in plant seeds. It begins with the emergence of a root or shoot from the seed, once conditions of moisture, light, and temperature are suitable. Dormancy may be almost non-existent in some tropical trees, in which germination takes place before dispersal of the fruit. In other species, there is a period of 'after ripening' which can be broken only by exposure to certain wavelengths of light and plentiful water. Some seeds can remain dormant in the soil for up to a century.

Geronimo (*c.*1829–1909) Apache chief. He led his people in resistance to white encroachment on tribal reservations in Arizona, waging war against settlers and US troops in a series of raids, before surrendering in 1886.

Gershwin, George (born Jacob Gershovitz) (1898–1937) US composer and pianist, of Russian Jewish descent. He had no formal musical training, but gained early experience of popular music from working in New York's Tin Pan Alley. He made his name in 1919 with the song 'Swanee' and went on to compose many successful songs and musicals. The lyrics for many of these were written by his brother Ira (Israel, 1896–1983), who was also the librettist for the opera *Porgy and Bess* (1935). In 1924 George Gershwin successfully turned to orchestral music with his jazz-influenced *Rhapsody in Blue*.

gesso (Italian, 'chalk') A brilliant white preparation of CHALK (or a similar substance) mixed with glue, much used in the Middle Ages and Renaissance to coat panels or CANVAS and prepare them for painting upon.

Gestalt psychology (German *Gestalt*, 'form') An approach, particularly to PERCEPTION and cognitive problems, developed from 1912 onwards by Max Wertheimer (1880–1943), Kurt Koffka (1886–1941), and Wolfgang Köhler (1887–1967), all of whom emigrated from Europe to the USA. Their principal claim was that the structural laws of wholes determine what occurs in their parts rather than vice versa. They used examples, such as squares or melodies, in which we can perceive the same form (*Gestalt*) even when its constituent parts such as size or key are different. Their empirical work, which centred on problem-solving and visual illusions, showed that the mind imposes on its surroundings interpretations that it is constantly trying to simplify – an idea at odds with those of reductionism and BEHAVIOURISM. The Gestalt psychologists anticipated modern COGNITIVE PSYCHOLOGY and were a dominant influence on the development of SOCIAL PSYCHOLOGY after World War II.

Gestalt therapy A psychotherapy that emphasizes awareness, immediate experience, and personal responsibility. It is not an offshoot of GESTALT PSYCHOLOGY, but was developed largely under the influence of the German-born psychoanalyst Fritz Perls (1893–1970), drawing on ideas from many sources. Popular in the USA since the late 1960s, Gestalt therapy adopts a holistic approach, giving equal weight to mind and body. Conflicts within the individual's personality are explored, sometimes by acting them out, and in a group session, with the object of removing obstacles to personal growth.

Gestapo The Nazi secret police or *Geheime Staatspolizei*. In 1933 Hermann GOERING reorganized the Prussian plain-clothes political police as the Gestapo. In 1934 control of the force passed to HIMMLER, who had restructured the police in the other German states, and headed the SS or *Schutzstaffel*. The Gestapo was effectively absorbed into the SS and in 1939 was merged with the SD or *Sicherheitsdienst* (Security Service), the intelligence branch of the SS, in a Reich Security Central Office under Reinhard HEYDRICH. The powers of these organizations were vast: any person suspected of disloyalty to the regime could be summarily executed. The SS and the Gestapo controlled the CONCENTRATION CAMPS and set up similar agencies in every occupied country.

gesture See NON-VERBAL COMMUNICATION.

Gethsemane, Garden of The garden to which Christ went with his disciples after the Last Supper, and which was the scene of his agony and betrayal. It lies in the valley between Jerusalem and the Mount of Olives.

Getty, Jean Paul (1892–1976) US industrialist. He made a large fortune in the oil industry and was also a noted art collector. He founded the museum, which bears his name at Malibu in California.

Gettysburg A small town in Pennsylvania, USA, scene of a decisive battle of the American Civil War, fought in the first three days of July 1863. The Confederate Army of Northern Virginia, commanded by General Lee, was repulsed in a bloody engagement by the Union Army of the Potomac, commanded by General Meade, forcing Lee to abandon his invasion of the north. The famous Gettysburg address was a speech delivered on 18 November 1863 by President Abraham Lincoln at the dedication of the National Cemetery on the battlefield.

Getz, Stan (born Stanley Gayetsky) (1927–91) US jazz saxophonist. He played with other prominent jazz musicians such as Stan Kenton, Benny Goodman, and Woody Herman. He was a leader of the 'cool' school of jazz and developed a distinctive style that was both emotive and attacking. His recordings include 'Early Autumn' (1948) and the highly popular 'The Girl from Ipanema' (1963).

geum A perennial herb with basal rosettes of leaves, and yellow, red, or white flowers. Geums are part of the rose family. The clove-scented roots of the herb bennet, *Geum urbanum*, were formerly used to flavour beer and as a medicament. Other species are popular, herbaceous garden plants.

geyser (Icelandic, 'to rush forth') A natural spring that intermittently spouts hot water and steam out of the ground. Where volcanic action has cracked the crust, and water in the depths has boiled, it erupts like a fountain, squirting violently to heights of over 60 m (200 feet). The regularity of eruption depends on the time it takes for the underground gusher system to fill. Mineral salts blown out with the water deposit mounds of lime and silica round the vents, in time forming fantastic rock formations which may contain pools, terraces, and waterfalls.

Ghali, Boutros Boutros- See BOUTROS-GHALI.

Ghana A West African country with a south-facing coast, bounded by the Côte d'Ivoire on the west, Burkina Faso on the north, and Togo on the east.

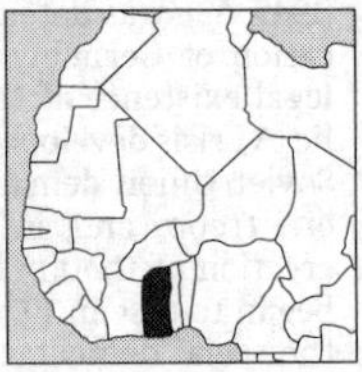

Physical. Ghana's flat and sandy coast is backed by a rolling plain of scrub and grass, except in the west, where moderate rains produce thick forest. The forest extends northward to the Ashanti plateau, which produces cocoa and tropical hardwoods, as well as manganese, bauxite, and gold. Further north, up-country of the valley of the Volta, it is very hot even in winter, though the HARMATTAN brings relatively cool (and dusty) conditions from the interior of West Africa.

Economy. The Ghanaian economy is mainly agricultural. Exports are cocoa, gold, and timber. Off-shore oil deposits await development; other mineral extraction includes gold, manganese, diamonds and bauxite. There is some light industry and manufacturing of aluminium. Hydraulic power accounts for much of the country's electricity production.

History. The area now covered by Ghana was composed of several kingdoms in the middle ages. From the late 15th century, the Portuguese and other Europeans began trading with the area, which they called the Gold Coast. It became a centre of the slave trade from the 16th century onwards. British influence gradually predominated. In 1850 the British Colonial Office purchased residual Danish interests in the region and gave some protection to the FANTI Confederation. Inland the area was dominated throughout the 19th century by the ASHANTI Confederation. Britain occupied the capital Kumasi after wars with the Ashanti in 1824 and 1874, when the colony of the Gold Coast was established. Further wars against the Ashanti followed in 1896 and 1900. After 1920 economic growth based on mining and the cocoa industry, combined with high standards of mission schooling, produced a sophisticated people demanding home rule. Following World War II, in which many Ghanaians served, there were serious riots in Accra (1948) leading to constitutional discussions. In 1957 the Gold Coast and British Togoland to the east were combined to become the independent Republic of Ghana, under the leadership of Kwame NKRUMAH, the first British African colony to be granted independence. Nkrumah transformed the country into a one-party state. Economic problems and resentment over political repression and mismanagement led to his overthrow by the army in 1966. Since his fall continuing economic and political problems have unbalanced Ghana. After a succession of coups, a group of junior officers under Flight-Lieutenant Jerry Rawlings (1942–) took power in 1979, executed three former heads of state, and installed a civilian government. When this failed, Rawlings again seized power (December 1981), suspending the constitution and establishing a Provisional National Defence Council, with himself as Chairman. During the 1980s with IMF support it regained some economic and political stability, but western aid donors demanded a move to restore democracy. A Movement for Freedom and Justice developed, and a new Constitution was adopted in April 1992, legalizing political parties. In November 1992 Rawlings was victorious in multi-party presidential elections, but opposition parties contested the result. In 1993 Rawlings was sworn in as President; he was re-elected in 1996.

Capital: Accra
Area: 238,533 sq km (92,098 sq mi)
Population: 16,472,000 (1995)
Currency: 1 cedi = 100 pesewas
Religions: Protestant 27.9%; traditional beliefs 21.4%; Roman Catholic 18.7%; African indigenous churches 16.0%; Muslim 15.7% (of which Ahmad*yah 7.9%)
Ethnic Groups: Akan 52.4%; Mossi 15.8%; Ewe 11.9%; Ga-Adangme 7.8%
Languages: English (official); Akan; Mole Dagbani; local languages
International Organizations: Commonwealth; ECOWAS; Non-Aligned Movement; OAU; UN

Ghana, kingdom of An ancient kingdom in what is now east Senegal, south-west Mali, northern Guinea, and southern Mauritania. As early as *c.*800 al-Fazari called Ghana 'the land of gold'. The name was adopted by the former British colony of the Gold Coast when it became independent in 1957.

gharial (or **gavial**) A large CROCODILE of the family Gavialidae, exceeding 6 m (20 feet) in length, and found in deep, fast-flowing rivers in parts of the northern Indian subcontinent. It has a very narrow snout, well adapted for seizing swimming fish. Adult males develop a tough, fleshy lump on the snout close to the nostrils; this bulbous structure probably aids recognition between sexes. The false gharial, *Tomistoma schlegeli*, occurs in rivers of other parts of south-east Asia. This belongs to the family Crocodylidae and not to that of the true gharial, *Gavialis gangeticus*.

Ghassanid A dynasty ruling the Arab kingdom of Ghassan which flourished during the 6th–7th century in what is now Syria, Jordan, and part of Israel. The Ghassanids, who supported the Byzantines against the Persians, were eventually overthrown by the Muslims in the 7th century.

Ghats Two mountain ranges in central and southern India that run parallel to the coast on either side of the Deccan Plateau. The **Eastern Ghats** stretch southwards from Orissa to the Nilgiri Hills in the states of Kerala and Tamil Nadu. The **Western Ghats** extend southwards from Maharashtra state to the southern tip of India. At Anai Mudi Peak in the Cardamon Hills the Ghats reach a height of 2,695 m (8,842 ft).

Ghent (Flemish **Gent**; French **Gand**) A city and port in west Belgium at the junction of the Leie and Scheldt Rivers; pop. (1991) 230,200. Connected to the North Sea by canals, Ghent is the historic capital of Flanders and capital of the modern Belgian province of East Flanders. It was founded in the 10th century around a fortress built by the first count of Flanders and became a major centre of wool production in the Middle Ages. In English it was sometimes called Gaunt. With the development of river port facilities and canals in the 19th century Ghent's trade and industry expanded to include the manufacture of steel, chemicals, vehicles, paper, and food products.

Ghent, Treaty of (1814) A treaty ending the WAR OF 1812 between Britain and the USA. It did not address the issues that had caused the war, but provided for the release of all prisoners, restoration of all conquered territory, and the appointment of a commission to settle the north-eastern boundary dispute. Other questions, including naval forces on the Great Lakes and fishing rights, were left to future settlement.

ghetto A part of a city, especially a slum area, occupied by a minority group or groups. Ghetto (Italian, 'foundry') was first applied to a site in Venice in 1516 to which Jews were restricted. The concept of a Jewish ghetto was revived by the Germans in Warsaw in World War II. Some 100,000 Jews staged an uprising in the ghetto in 1943 and were subsequently murdered by the Germans.

Ghiberti, Lorenzo (1378–1455) Italian sculptor and goldsmith. His career was dominated by his work on two successive pairs of bronze doors for the baptistery in Florence. The second, more famous, pair (1425–52) depicts episodes from the Bible laid out on carefully constructed perspective stages.

Ghirlandaio (born Domenico di Tommaso Bigordi) (*c.*1448–94) Italian painter. He worked mainly in Florence and is noted for his religious frescos, painted in a naturalistic style and including detailed portraits of leading contemporary citizens. His major works include the fresco *Christ Calling Peter and Andrew* (1482–84) in the Sistine Chapel, Rome.

ghost moth See SWIFT MOTH.

ghost pipefish Any one of five species of fish in the family Solenostomidae, which are relatives of the PIPEFISHES. They have a long snout but the body is thickset, with large, bony plates and well-developed pelvic fins and two dorsal fins. They live in shallow water in the tropical Indo-Pacific. The females carry the eggs in a pouch formed by the pelvic fins.

ghoul (from Arabic *ghūl* (male), *ghūlah* (female)) In Islamic mythology, an evil spirit, sometimes classified as a jinn. Ghouls are believed to frequent graveyards, inhabit desert places, and lead travellers astray. In Islamic tradition Muhammad is usually said to have denied their existence or ability to change shape.

Giacometti, Alberto (1901–66) Swiss sculptor and painter. He experimented with both naturalistic sculpture and surrealism, but his most characteristic style, which he adopted after World War II, features human figures that are notable for their emaciated and extremely elongated forms, exemplified in such works as *Pointing Man* (1947).

giant horsetail See CALAMITE.

giant planet One of the PLANETS Jupiter, Saturn, Uranus, or Neptune. They are described as giants because they have radii that are 11.18, 9.42, 3.84, and 3.93 times that of the Earth. They are also 317.8, 95.1, 14.5, and 17.2 times more massive; in fact Jupiter and Saturn together account for around 92 per cent of the total mass of the planetary system.

giants Legendary beings of great size and brutish strength, shaped like humans. In Greek mythology, the giants were a race of huge creatures who attacked Olympus and were defeated by Zeus and the other gods. Giants figure in almost all mythologies and were often portrayed, as in Norse and American Indian legends, as the first race of people to inhabit the Earth.

giant salamander The largest of the living AMPHIBIANS, sometimes attaining a length of 1.8 m (6 feet). Giant salamanders have squat, heavy bodies and broad, flattened heads. They are sluggish animals, living in cold, deep mountain streams. They undergo only partial metamorphosis for, although the adult lacks the larval gills, it never leaves the water. There are two species, *Megalobatrachus japonicus* from Japan and *M. davidianus* from China.

Giant's Causeway A formation of basalt columns dating from the Tertiary Period on the coast of

Antrim, Northern Ireland. It was once believed to be the end of a road made by a legendary giant to Staffa in the Inner Hebrides, where there is a similar formation.

giant sloth An extinct mammal that lived in South America during the Pleistocene Epoch, about 1.5 million years ago. Giant sloths reached a length of about 6 m (19.5 feet) and, unlike the living sloths to which they are closely related, they were ground-dwelling and could rear up on their hind feet to browse among the tree-tops.

giant star A star located to the upper right of the main sequence in the HERTZSPRUNG–RUSSELL DIAGRAM. When a DWARF STAR has exhausted the hydrogen available in its core for nuclear fusion to helium, it continues to consume the hydrogen in a shell around the core, and begins to evolve to the giant stage of STELLAR EVOLUTION, expanding to conserve energy. The masses of typical giant stars in our own galaxy range from two to ten times that of the Sun. Stars with a mass much less than that of the Sun evolve much more slowly, so few of them have yet had time to evolve to the giant stage. The diameters of giant stars are mostly in the range from five to a hundred or more times that of the Sun, and their luminosities range from about twenty-five to a thousand or more times that of the Sun.

giant water bug Any one of some 100 species of aquatic BUGS of the family Belastomatidae. Brownish, oval, and flattened, they are rapacious predators, and include fish and frogs in their diet. Some, such as *Lethocerus grandis*, are 11 cm (4.5 inches) long, and are among the largest insects. The hindlegs are flattened and hair-fringed for swimming. They sometimes fly far from water and are attracted to lights at night.

Giap, Vo Nguyen (1912–) Vietnamese military and political leader. As North Vietnamese Vice-Premier and Defence Minister, he was responsible for the strategy leading to the withdrawal of American forces from South Vietnam in 1973 and the subsequent reunification of the country in 1975. His book *People's War, People's Army* (1961) was an influential text for revolutionaries.

gibbon The smallest of the APES. They are lithe and slender, with such long fore-limbs that when they stand their fingers touch the ground; no other ape or monkey can travel through the trees with the same speed. The nine species of gibbon, all in the genus *Hylobates*, live in the canopy of the forest in south-east Asia, swinging from branch to branch, or walking erect along horizontal limbs of trees, feeding on fruits, leaves, and young shoots, and occasionally on insects. A social animal, it travels in small groups, usually four individuals to a family, communicating with loud shrieks and cries that can be heard over considerable distances. A single young is born, after a gestation period of seven months, and is carried by the mother for 18 months while it slowly develops. Each species of gibbon occurs in a particular part of south-east Asia.

Gibbon, Edward (1737–94) British historian. While on a visit to Rome in 1764 he conceived the plan for what has become the most celebrated historical work in English literature, *The History of the Decline and Fall of the Roman Empire* (1776–88), a six-volume study that traces the connection of the ancient world with the modern, encompassing such subjects as the establishment of Christianity, the Teutonic tribes, the conquests of Islam, and the Crusades. The work is distinguished by the author's great erudition and elegant and lucid prose style, and is enlivened by ironic wit.

Gibbon, Lewis Grassic (pseudonym of James Leslie Mitchell) (1901–35) Scottish writer. Encouraged by H. G. Wells he began writing short stories, which from 1927 were regularly published in the *Cornhill Magazine*. In 1930 he published his first novel, *Stained Radiance*. His greatest achievement was probably the trilogy *A Scots Quair* (1932–34).

Gibbons, Grinling (1648–1721) Dutch-born English sculptor. From 1671 he worked in England, where he was introduced to Charles II by the writer John Evelyn, and became Master Carver in Wood to the Crown. He is famous for his decorative carvings (chiefly in wood) of fruit and flowers, small animals, and cherubs' heads; examples of his work can be seen in the choir stalls of St Paul's Cathedral, London.

Gibbons, Orlando (1583–1625) English composer and musician. Gibbons is regarded as one of the greatest of the early English composers. He became a chamber musician to King James I in 1619 and the organist of Westminster Abbey in 1623. He composed mainly sacred music, including anthems, motets, and madrigals, notably *The Silver Swan* (1612). His oeuvre also includes forty keyboard pieces and thirty fantasies for viols.

gibbous Moon See PHASE.

Gibbs, James (1682–1754) British architect. An admirer of Sir Christopher Wren, he developed Wren's ideas for London's city churches, especially in his masterpiece, St Martin's-in-the-Fields (1722–26). The latter's combination of steeple and portico was influential in subsequent church design. He also designed the Radcliffe Camera (1737–49) in Oxford.

Gibbs, Josiah Willard (1839–1903) US physical chemist. He was the founder of the study of chemical thermodynamics and statistical mechanics, though the importance of his theoretical work was not generally appreciated until after his death.

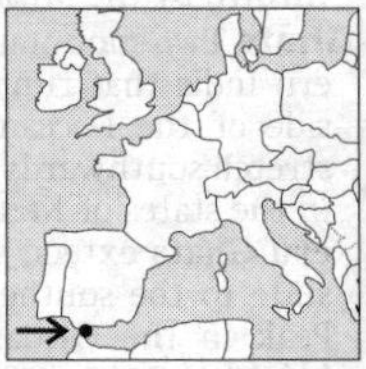

Gibraltar A British dependency near the southern tip of the Iberian peninsula, at the eastern end of the Strait of Gibraltar; area 5.86 sq km (2.26 sq miles); pop. (1991) 28,075; official languages English and Spanish. Occupying a site of great strategic importance, Gibraltar consists of a fortified town and military base at the foot of a rocky headland (the **Rock of Gibraltar**) 426 m (1,398 ft) high. In Arabic the territory is known as Gebel-al-Tarik ('hill of Tarik'), taking its name from a Saracen commander of the 8th century. The site has been in British hands since it was captured during the War of the Spanish Succession in 1704 and formally ceded to Britain by the Treaty of Utrecht (1713); Britain is responsible for defence, external affairs, and internal security. Since World War II Spain has pressed her claim to the territory. Remains of what was later called Neanderthal man were first discovered in Gibraltar in 1848 but were not recognized to be this species until the discovery of other remains in the Neander Valley in 1857. Gibraltar is a popular tourist and cruise ship destination.

Gibraltar, Strait of (Arabic **Bab al Zakak**) A channel between the southern tip of the Iberian peninsula and North Africa, forming the only outlet of the Mediterranean Sea to the Atlantic. Varying in width from 24 km (15 miles) to 40 km (25 miles) at its western extremity, it stretches east-west for some 60 km (38 miles).

Gibran, Khalil (or **Jubran**) (1883–1931) Lebanese-born US writer and artist. He emigrated to Boston in 1895, but in 1898 returned to his native Beirut to study. He published his first literary essays on his return to Boston in 1903, and devoted himself to writing and painting. His writings, in both Arabic and English, are deeply romantic, displaying his religious and mystical nature.

Gibson, Mel (Columcille Gerard) (1956–) US-born Australian actor and director. Gibson lived in Australia from the age of 12 and had his first film success there, starring in *Mad Max* (1979). Gibson won worldwide recognition with the film's sequel *Mad Max II: The Road Warrior* (1986), and his unsmiling, brooding screen presence led to a series of energetic, masculine roles in films that included the police thriller *Lethal Weapon* (1987) and its two sequels (1989, 1992). In 1993 he made his directorial début with *The Man Without a Face*; in 1995 he directed and starred in *Braveheart*, which won five Oscars, including those for best director and best film, the following year.

Gibson Desert A desert region in Western Australia, situated between the Nullarbor Plain and the Great Sandy Desert.

Gide, André (Paul Guillaume) (1869–1951) French novelist, essayist, and critic. He was a prolific writer, completing more than fifty books in his lifetime and coming to be regarded as the father of modern French literature. His works include *The Immoralist* (1902), *La Porte étroite* (1909, *Strait is the Gate*), *Si le grain ne meurt* (1926, *If I die . . .*), *The Counterfeiters* (1927), and his *Journal* (1939–50). He was awarded the Nobel Prize for literature in 1947.

Gideon The Hebrew hero divinely appointed to help the Israelites regain Canaan after God had punished them with the Midianite invasion. Gideon, guided by an angel, first cleansed his father's house of Baal worship and then, by night, he attacked the Midianites, driving them beyond the Jordan. He refused the Israelite offer of kingship.

Gielgud, Sir (Arthur) John (1904–) British actor and director. A notable Shakespearian actor, he is particularly remembered for his interpretation of the role of Hamlet, which he performed for the first time in 1929; he also appeared in contemporary plays, such as those by Harold Pinter. Gielgud has also appeared on television and in numerous films, taking on many roles late in his life; he won an Oscar for his role as a butler in *Arthur* (1980).

Giffard, Henri (1825–82) French aeronautical engineer. Initially a railway engineer, he became attracted to the design and construction of AIRSHIPS. He built a propulsion unit, comprising a 2.25-kW (3-horsepower) STEAM-ENGINE driving a 3-m (10-foot) screw PROPELLER. In 1852, he propelled a semi-rigid airship with rudder steering at 8 km/h (5 m.p.h.) for a distance of 27 km (17 miles). He later built huge captive balloons for various international exhibitions.

Giffen goods (in economics) Goods that do not obey the 'law of demand', in that the amount demanded of a Giffen good becomes greater if the price increases, rather than less. The name is that of Sir Robert Giffen (1837–1910), who observed that when the price of bread rose, the demand for it by the poor also rose. This is because the income effect of the price change was both negative and larger than the substitution effect. A negative income effect occurs when the amount of bread demanded falls as real income rises, because when people are better off they prefer higher-grade food.

Gigli, Beniamino (1890–1957) Italian operatic tenor. He made his Milan début with the conductor Toscanini in 1918, and retained his singing talents to a considerable age, touring the USA in 1955. Notable roles included Rodolfo in *La Bohème*, the Duke of Mantua in *Rigoletto*, and Cavaradossi in *Tosca*.

gigue A dance or tune, a courtly version of the English jig, imported into France in the mid-17th century. It was played in lively triple or duple TIME, with rhythms that were predominantly dotted. The Italian version (*giga*) tended to be much quicker. The gigue was the customary closing movement of the Baroque dance SUITE.

Gila monster A species of large lizard, *Heloderma suspectum*, found in the south-western USA in desert areas, especially near the Gila River. Along with the beaded lizard, *H. horridum*, it forms the family Helodermatidae. Among a total of 3,000 species of lizards, these two are the only poisonous ones. The Gila monster has a short, thick tail which contains a fat-store, enabling it to survive considerable fasting periods. Its venom glands are situated in the lower jaw, the teeth are grooved, and venom flow is enhanced by chewing motions. The venom is remarkably toxic, comparable to that of the cobra, although few human fatalities have been recorded. It hunts by 'smelling' out prey such as birds' eggs in nests, or other reptiles in burrows.

Gilbert, Sir Humphrey (*c*.1539–83) English explorer. After a distinguished career as a soldier, Gilbert led an unsuccessful attempt to colonize the New World (1578–79). On a second voyage in 1583 he claimed Newfoundland for Elizabeth I and established a colony at St John's, but was lost on the trip homewards when his ship foundered in a storm off Nova Scotia.

Gilbert, William (1544–1603) English physician and physicist. He worked on terrestrial magnetism, discovered how to make magnets, and was the first to use the term *magnetic pole*. His book *De Magnete* (1600) is one of the most important early works on physics published in England.

Gilbert, Sir W(illiam) S(chwenck) (1836–1911) British dramatist. His early writing career was chiefly devoted to humorous verse, such as his *Bab Ballads* (1866–73). However, he is best known for his collaboration with the composer Sir Arthur Sullivan; between 1871 and 1896 he wrote the libretti for fourteen light operas, including *Trial by Jury* (1875), *HMS Pinafore* (1878), *The Pirates of Penzance* (1879), *Iolanthe* (1882), *The Mikado* (1885), and *The Gondoliers* (1889).

Gilbert and Ellice Islands A former British colony (1915–75) in the central Pacific, consisting of two groups of islands straddling the equator: the **Gilbert Islands**, now a part of Kiribati, and the **Ellice Islands**, now Tuvalu.

gilding The technique of decorating a surface with a very fine layer of gold. The metal can be beaten into extremely fine sheets (known as gold foil or gold leaf) and this can be applied to various surfaces by means of an adhesive. Silver-gilt is silver that has been covered with a thin layer of gold.

Gilgamesh A legendary king of the Sumerian city-state of URUK in southern Mesopotamia. The *Epic of Gilgamesh*, one of the best-known works of ancient literature, was written in cuneiform on twelve clay tablets in *c*.2000 BC, and discovered among the ruins of Nineveh. The epic contains an account of a great flood that has close parallels with the Biblical story of NOAH.

gill A structure by which aquatic animals obtain oxygen from the surrounding water. Gills are extensions of the circulatory system which increase the area over which oxygen may be absorbed. In many invertebrates, gills are simply tuft-like projections, whereas in larger invertebrates, such as bivalve molluscs, they are elaborate structures. In vertebrates, such as fishes, they are hidden and protected within a body cavity called a gill chamber. To successfully function as a respiratory organ a gill must have a flow of water constantly passing over its surfaces. In fishes this is achieved by drawing water into the body through the mouth, and passing it out of the body across the gills. In fishes, gills are the feathery, blood-red structures beneath the gill-cover, arranged on the outer edge of a cartilaginous gill arch. The large, whitish projections on the throat side of the arch are gill rakers, which retain food. The gills are composed of slender filaments, each of which contains many small plates called gill lamellae, which are semicircular or leaf-like in form. Blood flows in fine capillaries through these very thin lamellae, and in this way the blood takes up oxygen from the water passing through the lamellae, as well as surrendering wastes, such as carbon dioxide, from the fish's body.

Gill, (Arthur) Eric (Rowton) (1882–1940) British sculptor, engraver, and typographer. His best-known sculptures are the relief carvings *Stations of the Cross* (1914–18) at Westminster cathedral and the *Prospero and Ariel* (1931) on Broadcasting House in London. He illustrated many books for the Golden Cockerell Press, and designed printing types for the Monotype Corporation.

Gillespie, Dizzy (born John Birks Gillespie) (1917–93) US jazz trumpet player and band-leader. He was a virtuoso trumpet player and a leading exponent of the bebop style. After working with various other groups he formed his own in New York in 1944, and thereafter toured the world almost annually.

gilt-edged securities (or **gilts**) UK government BONDS (marketable SECURITIES with an original maturity of not less than twelve months, which pay fixed annual interest). They are called gilt-edged because there is no significant danger of the government failing to pay interest or redeem the bonds when they mature. Most gilts are issued in units of £100 and may be purchased through a bank or stockbroker (on the Bank of England Register) or by post (through the National Savings Register).

ginger A tropical, perennial species of monocotyledonous plant, *Zingiber officinale*. It gives its name to the ginger family, Zingiberaceae, also including cardamom and turmeric. From swollen rhizomes, or roots, a spice is obtained, and appears on the market as the root, as powdered, dried ginger (particularly from West Africa, Jamaica, and India), or as preserved ginger (chiefly from China). The latter is produced when the young rhizomes are boiled with sugar before being packed in syrup. The aromatic, highly pungent spice is used in cooking throughout the world and is one of the more important constituents of curry powder. Ginger is a native of tropical Asia, although the family as a whole occurs throughout the tropics. All species have branched, fleshy underground rhizomes, and have broad leaves growing from a central stem. The ginger family has some 1,300 species worldwide.

ginkgo A GYMNOSPERM of the genus of the same name, comprising one living species, *Ginkgo biloba* (the maidenhair tree), and a number of species known only as fossils. The living tree is native to China, where it is grown around houses, probably for its edible seeds. It is also used as a street tree in other parts of the world. It provides a useful timber and an oil. The tree is deciduous with leaves shaped like the pinnules of a maidenhair fern. It is dioecious (bearing either male or female flowers) and the male gamete (sperm) is unusual in using hair-like cilia for locomotion.

Ginsberg, Allen (1926–97) US poet. A leading poet of the beat generation, and later influential in the hippy movement of the 1960s, he was notable for his *Howl and Other Poems* (1956) in which he attacked American society for its materialism and complacency. He later campaigned for civil rights, gay liberation, and the peace movement.

Giolitti, Giovanni (1842–1928) Italian statesman, Prime Minister five times between 1892 and 1921. A former lawyer, he was responsible for the introduction of a wide range of social reforms, including national insurance (1911) and universal male suffrage (1912).

Giorgione (born Giorgio Barbarelli; also called Giorgio da Castelfranco) (*c*.1478–1510) Italian painter. He was an influential figure in Renaissance art, especially for his introduction of the small easel picture in oils intended for private collectors. Although the attribution of many of his works is doubtful, paintings such as *The Tempest* typically feature enigmatic figures in pastoral settings and gave a new prominence to landscape. He worked with Titian, who is said to have completed some of his works, such as *Sleeping Venus* (*c*.1510), after his death.

Giotto (full name Giotto di Bondone) (*c*.1267–1337) Italian painter. He is an important figure in the development of painting for his rejection of the flat, formulaic, and static images of Italo-Byzantine art in favour of a more naturalistic style showing human expression. Notable works include the frescos in the Arena Chapel, Padua (1305–08), and those in the church of Santa Croce in Florence (*c*.1320).

giraffe The tallest species of animal in the world, *Giraffa camelopardalis*, which is quite unmistakable with its extremely long neck. The male is larger than the female and has a shoulder height of 3.5 m (12 feet), and a total height of 5.5 m (18 feet). There are nine subspecies, including the blotched giraffe, found over most of Africa south of the Sahara, and the larger, reticulated giraffe, found in East Africa.

The head bears short, straight horns, which are bony outgrowths covered by skin. The large, brown eyes are protected by long eyelashes, and the tongue is prehensile and can be extended some 50 cm (20 inches). A short mane runs along the neck and back. The long neck and tongue allow it to browse high in the trees. Special mechanisms prevent changes of blood flow when it raises its head from near the ground to its full height. The weight of the neck is balanced on the fore-limbs. In spite of its long neck, the giraffe is a graceful animal able to gallop at speeds of up to 50 km/hour (32 miles per hour), the legs on the same side of the body moving in unison.

A single young is born after a gestation period of fourteen to fifteen months.

Giraudoux, Jean (1882–1944) French dramatist and novelist. Some of his plays, for example *Amphitryon 38* (1929) or *Intermezzo* (1933), are built around plots of little substance, which are sustained by his stylistic virtuosity. Others, like *Siegfried* (1928), adapted from Giraudoux's own novel, or *La Guerre de Troie n'aura pas lieu* (1935), are serious discussions of ethical issues.

Gironde A river estuary in Aquitaine, south-west France, formed at the junction of the Garonne and Dordogne rivers north of Bordeaux. It flows northwestwards for 72 km (45 miles) into the Bay of Biscay between the Médoc and Côtes vineyards.

Girondin A member of a French political party whose main exponents came from the Gironde region. The Girondins were closely associated with the JACOBINS in the early days of the FRENCH REVOLUTION. They held power at a critical time and were responsible for provoking the wars with France's enemies. The eventual failure of these wars led not only to the king's execution but also to the downfall of the party and the introduction of the Reign of Terror.

Giscard d'Estaing, Valéry (1926–) French statesman, President 1974–81. As Secretary of State for Finance (1959–62) and Finance Minister (1962–66) under President de Gaulle, he was responsible for the policies which formed the basis of France's economic growth. Dismissed following mounting opposition to his policies, he regained the finance portfolio under President Pompidou, whose death in 1974 paved the way for Giscard d'Estaing's own election to the presidency. However, French economic conditions worsened during his term of office and he was defeated by François Mitterrand. He was a member of the European Parliament 1989–93, and has been leader of the centre-right Union pour la démocratie française since 1988.

Gish, Lillian (1896–1993) US actress. She and her sister **Dorothy** (1898–1968) appeared in a number of D. W. Griffith's films, including *Hearts of the World* (1918) and *Orphans of the Storm* (1922).

Gislebertus (early 12th century) French ROMANESQUE sculptor. One of the great geniuses of medieval art, his name has survived only because he carved his signature on his sculpture of *The Last Judgement* (*c*.1125–35) above the west doorway of Autun Cathedral. On stylistic grounds most of the rest of the carved decoration of the cathedral is attributed to him.

Gissing, George (Robert) (1857–1903) British novelist. His own experiences of poverty and failure provided material for much of his fiction. His many novels include *New Grub Street* (1891), *Born in Exile* (1892), and *The Private Papers of Henry Ryecroft* (1903). He also wrote a notable biography of Charles Dickens (1898).

Giulio Romano (*c*.1499–1546) Italian painter and architect. He was RAPHAEL's chief pupil and assistant in Rome and one of the major figures of MANNERISM. The great monument to his genius is the Palazzo del Tè, begun in 1526 for Federigo Gonzaga. This was one of the first Mannerist buildings, deliberately flouting the canons of classical architecture as exemplified by BRAMANTE in order to shock and surprise the spectator. His style owed much to MICHELANGELO as well as to Raphael, and proved widely influential.

Giza (or **El Giza**; Arabic **Al Jizah**) A suburban city south-west of Cairo in northern Egypt, on the west bank of the Nile, site of the Pyramids of Khufu, Khephren, and Menkaure and of the Great Sphinx; pop. (est. 1990) 2,156,000. The pyramid area has been designated a world heritage site by UNESCO.

gizzard shad A species of North American freshwater fish, *Dorosoma cepedianum*, of wide distribution in eastern Canada and the USA. It is a member of the herring family, Clupeidae, but is very deep-bodied with a bluntly rounded head. As an adult it feeds on minute algae, and is adapted to digest this food by having a thick-walled, gizzard-like stomach and an extremely long gut. The gizzard shad grows to a length of 30 cm (1 foot).

glacial period A period in the Earth's history characterized by an unusual extension of polar and mountain ice sheets over the Earth's surface. The Pleistocene and the preceding Pliocene epoch included a number of such periods, interrupted by warmer phases called interglacials, and it may be that the climate of the present day represents such a warm phase and that another ice age is to follow. During the coldest time, about 18,000 years ago, extensive ice sheets covered much of Europe, North America, and Asia, and sea-levels were as much as 200 m lower than they are today. In the Southern Hemisphere glaciation was less extensive owing to the isolation of the Antarctic ice sheet from the other southern continents.

glaciation The action of moving ice on the land surface, and the state of being covered by ice. Ice-caps, ice-sheets, and glaciers each produce characteristic landforms, both while the ice remains (sometimes called glacierization) and after it melts. The impact of glaciation depends upon the kind of ice, the nature of the landscape being covered, how long the cover lasts, how the ice moves, and the number of episodes which occur within a particular geological period. It also depends on the length of time which has elapsed since the ice melted and how active other, subsequent processes have been. Upland glaciation is largely erosional. It leaves steep, shattered peaks and arêtes (ridges), CIRQUES, flat-floored, steep-sided valleys, some of them hanging, rock basins and finger lakes, striations and lines of MORAINE. Lowland glaciation varies in impact, according to whether the rocks are more or less resistant. On hard rocks, as in the Canadian Shield, it smoothes, polishes, and flutes the bedrock, leaving millions of small, irregular basins. In other areas, the surface is blanketed by till and outwash deposits, producing irregular but rather flat surfaces, pitted by KETTLE-HOLES, or ridged by eskers and DRUMLINS.

glacier A mass of moving land ice formed by the accumulation of snow on high ground and in polar regions. Glacier ice can be a powerful agent of erosion, cutting deep valleys, plucking blocks of rock from the ground, and smoothing rock surfaces by abrading or breaking off small fragments. Glacial deposits formed when ice melts create distinct landforms that range from sediments of glacial till covering extensive areas of land to ridge and hill features such as moraines, drumlins, and eskers.

gladiator Literally 'swordsman', a slave or prisoner trained to fight other gladiators, wild beasts, or condemned criminals for the entertainment of the people in ancient Rome. Gladiators belonged to four categories: the Mirmillo, with a fish on his helmet, and the Sammite, both heavily armed with oblong shield, visored helmet, and short sword; the Retiarius, lightly clad, fighting with net and trident; and the Thracian, with round shield and curved scimitar. Thumbs up or down from the crowd spelt life or death for the loser. Formal combat degenerated into butchery watched by huge crowds. Women and even the physically handicapped sometimes fought.

gladiolus A plant of the genus *Gladiolus*, which takes its name from the Latin *gladius*, sword, describing the shape of the leaves. Gladioli are members of the IRIS family, which includes the crocus. Their underground corms annually send up two or three leaves, followed by spikes of large, attractive flowers. Hybridization of the species, which occurs mainly in East and South Africa, has resulted in many colourful garden varieties, bearing spikes of trumpet-shaped flowers.

Gladstone, William Ewart (1809–98) British Liberal statesman, Prime Minister 1868–74, 1880–85, 1886, and 1892–94. After an early career as a Conservative minister, he joined the Liberal Party, becoming its leader in 1867. His ministries were notable for the introduction of a series of social and political reforms (including the introduction of elementary education, and the passing of the Irish Land Acts and the third Reform Act) and for his campaign in favour of Home Rule for Ireland, which led to the defection of the Unionists from the Liberal Party.

Glamis A village in the Strathmore valley, Angus, north-east Scotland adjacent to which is Glamis Castle, home of the family of the earls of Strathmore since 1372. Glamis Castle was the childhood home of Queen Elizabeth the Queen Mother and the birthplace of Princess Margaret.

gland A secreting organ of varying structure and size. In animals, the preparation, storage, and expulsion of secretory material by glandular cells involves intricate, energy-using processes, controlled by the nervous and endocrine systems, and glands are generally divided into two categories (see ENDOCRINE GLAND; EXOCRINE GLAND). Plants often have external glands that secrete such substances as resins or nectar.

Glasgow The largest city in Scotland; pop. (1992) 681,470. Situated on the River Clyde, the city owes its growth successively to the tobacco, cotton, iron and steel, and shipbuilding industries. Although these industries are no longer of major significance, Glasgow has remained an important commercial and cultural centre with attractions that include the Glasgow School of Art, product of Charles Rennie Mackintosh the art nouveau designer and architect, the Burrell Collection, Kelvingrove Art Gallery and Museum, the Hunterian Museum, Provands Lordship (the oldest house in Glasgow), and Glasgow Cathedral (12th century). It is the site of the University of Glasgow (1451), the University of Strathclyde (1964), and the Queen's University, and the headquarters of the Royal Scottish Geographical Society. The city has undergone a massive programme of slum clearance and road building. It has numerous light industries including electronics, carpets, textiles, printing, chemicals, and tourism

Glasgow School Either of two quite distinct groups of Scottish artists working mainly in Glasgow in the late 19th and early 20th centuries respectively. The earlier group (also known as the 'Glasgow Boys') was a loose association of painters who were in revolt against the conservatism of the Royal Scottish Academy and were advocates of open-air painting. The later group created a distinctive version of ART NOUVEAU. Its most important member was MACKINTOSH.

Glashow, Sheldon Lee (1932–) US theoretical physicist. In 1967 Glashow began work at Harvard University on the interactions between subatomic particles. He independently developed a unified theory to explain electromagnetic interactions and the weak nuclear force, and extended the quark theory of Murray Gell-Mann. Glashow shared the Nobel Prize for physics in 1979.

glasnost and perestroika The concepts of 'openness' and 'restructuring' whose effects led to major changes in Soviet society as well as profoundly influencing the world BALANCE OF POWER and East–West relations. Introduced into Soviet domestic politics by Mikhail GORBACHEV, who became Soviet leader in 1985. The concepts are described in his book *Perestroika* (1987). The twin processes aimed to reduce inefficiency and corruption in the former Soviet Union, and to encourage political liberalization. Internally the results of the 'Gorbachev doctrine' were mixed and contributed to growing unrest, provoked by nationalist demands and economic discontent, which in 1991 brought about the disintegration of the structure of the Soviet Union, the secession of the Baltic republics, the displacement of the Communist Party from its formerly dominant position, and the formation of a new COMMONWEALTH OF INDEPENDENT STATES.

glass A hard, brittle, amorphous (non-crystalline) CERAMIC, usually comprising inorganic polymers of mixed oxides based around the silicon dioxide (SiO_2) unit. Glass is transparent to light, generally inert to chemical attack, and a very good electrical insulator. Other materials can also form glasses if cooled sufficiently rapidly from the liquid or gaseous phase to prevent the formation of an ordered crystalline structure. Glasses such as obsidian (see FLINT) occur naturally. Commercial glasses are manufactured by fusing together sand (silica, SiO_2), LIMESTONE, and soda (SODIUM CARBONATE) at temperatures around 1,400–1,500°C. On cooling, the melt becomes very viscous: at about 500°C (known as the glass transition temperature) the melt solidifies to form soda glass. The early history of glass is obscure, but it was probably invented in western Asia or Egypt in the third millennium BC. Glassware was brought to a high degree of sophistication by the Romans, notably in the Portland Vase (British Museum) made in the reign of Augustus (27 BC to 14 AD). The art of glass-making declined after the break-up of the Roman Empire, until it was revived within the world of Islam from the middle of the 8th century. The art of making clear, colourless glass (crystal glass) was discovered in Venice in the 15th century. With this material the Venetian craftsmen of the first half of the 16th century produced forms of great beauty, which were to make it famous as the greatest of all glass-making centres. Subsequently, many other places have become noted for glass-making. Bohemia, for example, had a large number of factories that took up Venetian innovations in the 16th century.

Silica-based glasses are of enormous importance in the modern world. Windows and light bulbs are their most obvious uses, while **optical glass** is manufactured for lenses for spectacles, cameras, telescopes, and microscopes. Glass is also used for drinking vessels, containers, and cooking utensils. The brittleness of glass can be reduced by thermally treating the surface (safety glass), or by making a LAMINATE of glass layered with plastic sheets. Glass can be drawn when molten into very thin GLASS FIBRES, used in insulation, COMPOSITES, and in optical applications. See also PLATE-GLASS.

Glass, Philip (1937–) US composer. An interest in Indian music led him to develop a type of MINIMAL MUSIC in which small rhythmic figures are repeated and made to evolve over a long period with powerful hypnotic effect. The melodic figures are themselves simple, as are the harmonic structures through which they move. His work is at its most effective in such operas as *Einstein on the Beach* (1976) and *Satyagraha* (1980).

glass-blowing The art of shaping molten GLASS by blowing air into it. The technique was invented in about 100 BC, probably in Syria. A mass of molten glass is gathered on to a narrow iron tube about 1 m (3 feet) long, and air is blown down the tube, forming a bubble of air within the glass. During the gradual hardening of the glass as it cools, it is possible to shape the bubble into a wide variety of forms. A balloon of glass can also be blown inside a mould, to make a predetermined shape.

glass fibre (or **fibreglass**, **spun glass**) Thin filaments of glass used to make yarns and textiles, for insulation, in FIBRE-REINFORCED PLASTICS, in other COMPOSITES, and for OPTICAL FIBRES. Mats of glass fibre were first produced in the 1930s from molten glass in both the USA and the UK. This form of glass fibre is mainly used for thermal insulation, and for air filters. Later, continuous glass fibres were melt-spun through spinnerets (see SPINNING), in a similar way to SYNTHETIC FIBRES. Glass-fibre yarns are used to make fire-resistant fabrics, electrical insulation materials, and glass-fibre-reinforced plastics. For optical-fibre use the glass must be very pure and of constant diameter. This is achieved by VAPOUR DEPOSITION of filaments using silica-containing gases. Extremely long fibres may be manufactured by this method.

glass-fibre-reinforced concrete See CONCRETE.

glass harmonica (or **armonica**) An elaboration of the musical glasses, invented by Benjamin Franklin in 1761. A series of glass bowls, of gradually diminishing size and fine-tuned by grinding, are nested within each other and mounted on a spindle, which is turned by a pedal-operated crank, with just enough of each bowl projecting from the last to be accessible to the player's fingers. Water in a trough keeps the rims of the bowls moist so that they will sound when rubbed.

glass snake Not a snake but a legless LIZARD belonging to the genus *Ophisaurus*. There are several species related to the slow-worm, found in North America, south-eastern Europe, and parts of Asia. Their name refers to their fragility; when roughly handled or if struck by a stick, they may shed their long tails, a phenomenon that may lead an untutored observer to believe that the whole animal has broken to pieces.

glasswort A plant of the genus *Salicornia*, with fleshy jointed stems and no leaves. Glassworts are adapted to live in the desiccating environment of salt marshes and sea-shores throughout the world. They belong to the same family, Chenopodiaceae, as beetroot and spinach. The ash glassworts have a high soda (sodium carbonate) content and were formerly used in the manufacture of glass and soap.

Glastonbury A town in Somerset, England; pop. (1991) 7,747. It is the legendary burial place of King Arthur and Queen Guinevere and the site of a ruined abbey held by legend to have been founded by Joseph of Arimathea. It was also identified in medieval times with the mythical Avalon. It has a leather industry making sheepskin products. **Glastonbury tor** is the nearby site to which Joseph of Arimathea reputedly brought the Holy Grail of the Last Supper; planting his staff into the ground, it grew into the Glastonbury thorn that flowers on Christmas Day. In the early Middle Ages it was claimed that the graves of King Arthur and Queen Guinevere had been discovered at Glastonbury, and that St Patrick had been laid to rest here.

glaucoma An eye disorder in which the pressure within the eye (intraocular pressure) is abnormally high. Intraocular pressure is raised because of an imbalance between the production of the fluid within the eye (aqueous humour) and its normal drainage mechanisms. Closed-angle glaucoma, also called acute congestive and narrow-angle glaucoma, is caused by structural abnormality within the eye, which inhibits effective drainage of aqueous humour; it commonly affects only one eye. Acute closed-angle glaucoma results in sudden, severe eye pain, headache, blurred vision, nausea, and vomiting; blindness may occur if prompt treatment is not available. Chronic closed-angle glaucoma causes less severe, recurrent attacks.

Open-angle glaucoma, also called simple, chronic simple, and wide-angle glaucoma, occurs in the absence of any structural abnormality within the eye; the cause is unknown and it commonly affects both eyes. The onset of open-angle glaucoma is slow and insidious; initially, there is gradual loss of peripheral vision. Progressive visual impairment affects the entire field and blindness may occur. Secondary glaucoma occurs as a result of other eye disorders, such as cataract. Treatment of glaucoma is aimed at reducing intraocular pressure and preventing further visual impairment and blindness.

glaze A glass-like coating applied to pottery to make it watertight and to give it a smooth, glossy finish. The essential ingredient of glazes is sand, technically silica, which is combined with a fluxing agent, the purpose of which is to cause the glaze to melt and adhere to the pottery at a manageable temperature. The glaze is usually applied after the pot has been 'biscuit-fired' to harden it: the glazed pot is then fired a second time to a higher temperature, to harden the glaze. Generally, the type of fluxing agent used gives the glaze its name, for example lead glaze and tin glaze. Salt glazing is a cheap finish for earthenware products: salt reacts with the constituents of the fired clay to produce a sodium-containing, low-melting-point glass.

Glazunov, Aleksandr (Konstantinovich) (1865–1936) Russian composer. He was a pupil of Rimsky-Korsakov (1880–81) and his work was influenced by Liszt and Wagner. His output includes orchestral and chamber music, songs, and the ballet *The Seasons* (1901).

glebe Land belonging to a parish church used to support its priest. The size of glebes varied enormously from 1 ha. (2 acres) to a few hundred hectares; priests might afford to engage labourers or be obliged to work the land themselves, and they could sub-lease part or all of the land. Since the glebe was a freeholding, the lord of the manor could not demand labour duties of the priest, although this immunity was not always observed.

glee See PART-SONG.

Glencoe A glen in the Scottish Highlands to the south-east of Fort William, scene of the massacre in 1692 of Jacobite Macdonald clansmen by Campbell soldiers acting for the government of William III. While this massacre has often been considered a particularly foul violation of the rules of Highland hospitality in continuation of the long-standing feud between the Campbells and the Macdonalds, it was in fact a deliberate government attempt to make an example of one of the most notorious Jacobite clans, badly botched by the men on the spot (who killed less than a third of about 140 intended victims).

Glendower, Owen (or **Glyndwr**) (*c*.1354–*c*.1417) Welsh chief. A legendary symbol of Welsh nationalism, he was leader first of armed resistance to English overlordship and then of a national uprising against Henry IV. He proclaimed himself Prince of Wales and allied himself with Henry's English opponents, including Henry Percy ('Hotspur'); by 1404 this policy had proved sufficiently successful for Glendower to hold his own Parliament. Though suffering subsequent defeats, he continued fighting against the English until his death.

Glen More See GREAT GLEN.

gleying A process that occurs when soils become waterlogged, causing some substances, particularly iron compounds, to become reduced or depleted of oxygen by soil bacteria. The reduction of iron gives a characteristic blue-grey colour to the soil. Gleying is a common feature of meadow and tundra soils and of some PODZOLS.

glider A fixed-wing AEROPLANE that is unpowered while in flight. Gliders are launched either by being towed into the air behind an aircraft or motor vehicle, or from a winch or catapult, or using a small engine in the glider itself. Originally made of wood and fabric, modern gliders use FIBRE-REINFORCED PLASTICS and high-technology designs to produce a very efficient, lightweight aeroplane. By using thermals (rising currents of hot air) and warm fronts often found on the windward side of hills and mountain ridges, a glider can stay airborne for long periods and travel great distances. See also HANG-GLIDER.

gliding frog See FLYING FROG.

Glinka, Mikhail (Ivanovich) (1804–57) Russian composer. Regarded as the father of the Russian national school of music, he is best known for his operas *A Life for the Tsar* (1836), inspired by Russian folk music, and *Russlan and Ludmilla* (1842), based on a poem by Pushkin.

global warming See GREENHOUSE EFFECT.

globe A MAP of the world in the form of a sphere on which all its continents and features are shown at the same scale and with their correct shapes and areas. A globe presents information in a form which no map PROJECTION on to a plane can achieve, except for small areas. The form is used mainly, however, to show the relationship between different countries and continents rather than to give their details.

globe flower A member of the plant genus *Trollius*. About 20 species are known, mainly from Europe, Asia, and North America. They are close relatives of buttercups, but with larger, globe-shaped flowers, usually yellow or orange. All prefer moist habitats.

globular cluster See CLUSTER, STAR.

glockenspiel A musical instrument with steel bars laid out like a XYLOPHONE, played with mallets of wood, ceramic, hard plastic, or brass. Keyboard glockenspiels have been used but are inefficient and poor in tone quality; works written for them such as Paul Dukas's *L'Apprenti sorcier* are now played on normal instruments. Marching glockenspiels for military bands are fitted to a lyre-shaped frame on a pole.

Glorious Revolution The bloodless English revolution of 1688–89 in which JAMES II was removed from the throne and was replaced by his daughter Mary and her husband WILLIAM of Orange. It marked the end of Stuart attempts at despotism, and the establishment of a constitutional form of government.

From his accession in 1685, James II's actions aroused both Whig and Tory concern. In defiance of the law he appointed Roman Catholics to important positions in the army, the church, the universities, and the government. He claimed the right to suspend or dispense with the laws as he pleased, and his two DECLARATIONS OF INDULGENCE suspended penal laws against Roman Catholics and dissenters. The birth of a son to the king in 1688 appeared to ensure the Roman Catholic succession and provoked leading politicians of both the main parties to invite the king's son-in-law William of Orange to England. William landed with a Dutch army in Devonshire in November. James's army refused to obey its Catholic officers, his daughters deserted him, and he was allowed to escape abroad. Parliament asked William and Mary to take over the vacant throne. James II landed in Ireland with French troops (March 1690), besieged LONDONDERRY, and was defeated at the battle of the BOYNE (July 1690). He returned to exile in France. The Act of SETTLEMENT of 1701 provided for the Protestant succession.

glossopteris A fossil tree that dominated the flora of the Southern Hemisphere during Permian times (286–245 million years ago). The leaves were shaped like long tongues and had a prominent midrib and net-like veining. Seed-bearing reproductive organs were attached to the base of the leaves. The trunk grew to 4–6 m (13–19 feet) in height and reached up to 40 cm (15 inches) in diameter. Because the fossils are found in sedimentary rocks of the same age in India, South Africa, South America, Australia, and Antarctica, they provide good evidence that these continents formed a single land mass (known as Gondwanaland) in the Mesozoic Period.

Gloucester An ancient city in south-west England, the country town of Gloucestershire, situated on the River Severn north-east of Bristol; pop. (1991) 91,800. It has a major aircraft industry. Gloucester was founded by the Romans, who called it Glevum, in 96 AD. Its cathedral, noted for its Perpendicular style, contains the tomb of King Edward II and a cross commemorates Bishop Hooper, martyred in 1555. The Three Choirs Music Festival takes place every three years at Gloucester.

Gloucestershire A county of south-west England; area 2,643 sq km (1,021 sq miles); pop. (1991) 520,600; county town, Gloucester. It gives its name to a kind of hard cheese originally made in Gloucestershire.

glow-worm See FIREFLY.

gloxinia A tuberous-rooted plant with rounded or heart-shaped leaves and colourful (often velvety) bell-like flowers. Members of the same family as African violets (Gesneriaceae), gloxinias are a mainly tropical group and are popular greenhouse plants in temperate climates. Most of the florists' varieties are derived from the Brazilian species *Sinningia speciosa*.

Gluck, Christoph Willibald von (1714–87) German composer. From early operas in the Italian style he went on to seek a balance of music and drama in his 'reform' operas, reducing the emphasis on the star singer and attempting a continuous musical unfolding of the narrative. He spent much of his working life in Paris as a protégé of Marie Antoinette. His most notable works include *Orfeo ed Euridice* (1762) and *Iphigénie en Aulide* (1774).

glucose A simple sugar with the molecular formula $C_6H_{12}O_6$, belonging to the monosaccharide group of CARBOHYDRATES. It is the most important fuel used for RESPIRATION in most animals and plants. In plants, it is generated by PHOTOSYNTHESIS. In the human diet, other carbohydrates are converted into glucose, which circulates dissolved in the blood plasma until used by the body tissues. Once glucose has been consumed, it is stored as GLYCOGEN in the liver and muscles, or may be converted into fat, being released later by the breakdown of these substances. Its concentration in the blood plasma is kept constant by the hormones insulin and glucagon.

glue See ADHESIVE.

gluon (in nuclear physics) A particle that functions as a carrier of the STRONG FORCE, which binds together QUARKS to form hadrons, such as protons and neutrons, and holds hadrons together to form nuclei. There are eight different types of gluon: they have no mass, travel at the speed of light and have COLOUR and anti-colour. Their behaviour is described by the theory of quantum chromodynamics (see QUANTUM MECHANICS).

glutton See WOLVERINE.

glycerol (propan-1,2,3-triol, glycerine, $CH_2OH.CHOH.CH_2OH$) A clear, colourless, viscous, sweet-tasting liquid belonging to the ALCOHOL group. It is obtained as a by-product of SOAP and is synthesized industrially from propene and sugar. It is used domestically as an ingredient of soft icing, and industrially as a sweetener and in the manufacture of paints, cosmetics, and explosives.

glycogen A natural organic compound belonging to the polysaccharide group of CARBOHYDRATES. Each molecule comprises a branching network containing hundreds of GLUCOSE molecules joined together. It can be very rapidly built up or degraded by enzyme action and is used as an energy storage material in many bacteria, fungi, protozoa, and in most animals. In vertebrates, the hormone insulin promotes glycogen formation in the liver and the muscles, and other hormones, such as glucagon and adrenaline (epinephrine), cause its breakdown, which releases glucose.

glycol (ethane-1,2-diol, ethylene glycol, $CH_2OH.CH_2OH$) A colourless viscous liquid which is miscible with water. It is manufactured from ethene, and is widely used as an ANTIFREEZE, and in the production of solvents.

glycolysis The first stage in the biochemical pathway of RESPIRATION, carried out by most living organisms. GLUCOSE ($C_6H_{12}O_6$) is progressively broken down to yield two molecules of pyruvic acid ($C_3H_4O_3$). Initially, ATP is used up in making the glucose molecule more reactive, but later steps release energy so that there is a net gain of two molecules of ATP for the process as a whole. Hydrogen atoms from the breakdown of glucose are taken up by COENZYMES and can be transferred to the ELECTRON TRANSPORT CHAIN, resulting in the production of more ATP. In FERMENTATION, the hydrogen atoms removed from glucose are transferred to pyruvate via coenzymes, to generate products such as ethanol or lactic acid (depending upon the type of fermentation).

Glyndebourne An estate near Lewes in East Sussex, England, at which an annual festival of opera is held. The original opera house was built by the owner of the estate, John Christie (died 1962), who founded the festival in 1934 to stage ideal performances in a beautiful setting. The inspiration for the enterprise was his wife, the soprano Audrey Mildmay. The opera house was rebuilt in 1992–94. Nearby is the village of Glynde.

Glyndwr See GLENDOWER.

glyptodont An extinct armadillo-like animal of the genus *Glyptodon* that lived in South America during the Pleistocene Epoch 1.5 million years ago. It was up to 3 m (10 feet) in length, and the almost spherical body was covered by a shell of small, thick bones. Some species had a spiky armoured tip to their tail. They became extinct about 100,000 years ago.

GMT See GREENWICH MEAN TIME.

gnat See MOSQUITO.

gneiss A coarse-grained banded rock formed as a result of recrystallization under intense heat and pressure. Gneisses are high-grade METAMORPHIC ROCKS. The banding is caused by the segregation of light- and dark-coloured minerals during metamorphism.

GNP (gross national product) The most widely used measure of national prosperity. It is based on GDP, to which is added property income (interest, profits, and dividends arising from the ownership of assets) accruing to domestic residents from abroad minus similar income paid from the domestic economy to foreigners. The GDP is the gross product produced within the geographical boundary of a country, whereas the GNP is the gross product accruing to the residents of the country. Net national product is GNP minus DEPRECIATION.

gnu (or **wildebeest**) A grazing antelope belonging to the same tribe (a taxonomic group below the subfamily) as the HARTEBEEST. The two species of gnu are found on the African veld, where they are perhaps the fastest of the animals. The brindled gnu, *Connochaetes taurinus*, travels in herds of a dozen to several hundred individuals, frequenting the open plains in search of grass and a regular supply of water. Brindled in colour, it has brown stripes on the neck and shoulders, and a black tail; the horns are smooth and spread outwards. A single calf is born after a gestation period of eight and a half months. The white-tailed gnu, *C. gnou*, once common over much of the South African veld, is now restricted to reserves.

Goa A state on the west coast of India; area 3,702 sq km (1,430 sq miles); pop. (1991) 1,168,600; capital, Panaji. Formerly a Portuguese territory, it was seized by India in 1961, and together with two other Portuguese territories, Daman and Diu, formed a Union Territory of India until it achieved separate statehood in 1987. Goa's population is racially mixed and predominantly Catholic. St Francis Xavier is buried in its Baroque cathedral which, together with colonial churches and convents, are world heritage monuments. The state's main industrial products are pharmaceuticals, clothing, footwear, pesticides, and fishing nets. Tourism is of major importance.

goanna See MONITOR LIZARD.

goat A RUMINANT mammal of the subfamily Caprinae. The 26 species of this subfamily also include the chamois, musk ox, and sheep. Three species are actually called goats: the mountain goat, *Oreamnos americanus*, the wild goat, *Capra aegagrus*, and the Spanish goat, *C. pyrenaica*. The wild goat is native to Asia Minor and parts of India, but has now been spread worldwide as a domestic breed. The horns are directed backwards and upwards, and are transversely ridged; males have a distinct beard and a gland beneath the short tail which gives off a pungent odour. The Spanish goat is similar in habits and appearance to the true wild goat, differing only in the shape of its horns. It is restricted to the Pyrenees. The mountain goat does not belong to the same genus as the wild and Spanish goats, but is more closely related to the chamois. It is found in mountainous and northern areas of North America. Other species in the genus *Capra*, or true goats, include the ibex, *C. ibex*, markhor, *C. falconeri*, east Caucasian tur, *C. cylindricornis*, and west Caucasian tur, *C. caucasia*. These and other species have many, locally named, subspecies.

goat moth A large moth that has large, wood-boring caterpillars which smell of goats. Some have a wing-span of up to 18 cm (7 inches). These caterpillars, sometimes known as carpenter worms, take three or four years to reach maturity, and can inflict considerable damage on trees. Their family, Cossidae, is worldwide in distribution and in Australia includes the witchetty grubs, considered a delicacy by the Aborigines.

goatsucker See NIGHTJAR.

Gobbi, Tito (1915–84) Italian operatic baritone. Particularly renowned for his interpretations of Verdi's roles, he also gained notable successes with his performances in the title role of Berg's *Wozzeck* and as Scarpia in Puccini's *Tosca*.

Gobelins A French state-owned TAPESTRY factory named after Jean and Philibert Gobelin, 15th-century scarlet-dyers, whose works were situated on the outskirts of Paris. In or near these buildings some tapestry looms were set up in the first decade of the 17th century, and in 1662 the buildings were bought by LOUIS XIV and reorganized as a factory producing furnishings for the royal palaces. The factory closed in 1694 and although it reopened in 1699, thereafter it made only tapestries. It was temporarily closed during the Revolutionary period, but reopened again by Napoleon. Carpets as well as tapestries continue to be produced there.

Gobi Desert A barren plateau of southern Mongolia and northern China, extending over an area of *c*.1,295,000 sq km (500,200 sq miles). Its name means 'Stony desert'.

Gobind Singh (1666–1708) The tenth and last of the Sikh GURUS. Gobind Singh encouraged the militarization of the Sikhs against the Mogul empire. During *Baisakhi* (the new year festival) in 1699, he called upon five Sikhs to give up their lives, but instead of killing the volunteers he rewarded their courage and loyalty by initiating them into the *khalsa*, a newly formed army of soldier-saints.

Gobineau, Joseph Arthur, Comte de (1816–82) French diplomat and scholar, the intellectual founder of 'racism'. His most famous book, *Essay on the Inequality of Human Races* (1853–55), put forward the thesis that the races are innately unequal and that the white Aryan race is not only the purest but also superior to all others. His writings were to have a sinister influence on the German NAZI theorists, for whom they became a justification for ANTI-SEMITISM.

goblin A mischievous, ugly demon of European folklore. The name is probably derived from the Latin *gobelinus*, a spirit, which is also related to *kobold*, the German demon of mines.

goby A member of the largest family of marine fishes, Gobiidae, containing more than 1,000 species. Mostly, they live in shallow, inshore waters, from high-tide mark on the shore down to 200 m (650 feet), but a substantial number have invaded fresh water. They are small, possibly averaging only 5 cm (2 inches) in length, the largest being about 35 cm (14 inches). The smallest, a species from the Philippine Islands growing to only 12 mm (half an inch) long, is one of the smallest known vertebrates. Gobies are blunt-headed fishes, with two dorsal fins, fully scaled bodies, and pelvic fins joined to form a weak, disc-like sucker. The family includes the MUDSKIPPERS, which are abundant on tropical shores.

God The transcendent being postulated as the creator and ruler of the Universe. Various forms of worship, from sacrifice to public acts of honour, to private prayer, are typically linked with concepts of God. Emotions such as awe, fear, and gratitude are often experienced in such religious activities with God as their object. In the various world RELIGIONS gods vary in the degree to which they are personal or impersonal, mythical or abstract. Religions also vary in the number of gods acknowledged. Some are polytheistic, with complex pantheons as, for example, in ancient Greece and some forms of HINDUISM. Others, like JUDAISM and ISLAM, insist on a strict monotheism. In CHRISTIANITY God is perceived as a trinity. It is also possible to combine polytheistic and monotheistic conceptions of god in a metaphysical or epistemological hierarchy. In many African religions, a supreme being is worshipped over and above lesser deities.

Godalming A residential town in Surrey, south-east England, on the River Wey 7 km (4 miles) south-west of Guildford; pop. (1981) 18,900. The town is noted for its old almshouses, its town hall (1814), and its Norman church.

Godard, Jean-Luc (1930–) French film director. He was one of the leading figures of the NOUVELLE VAGUE; his films frequently deal with existentialist themes and are notable for their use of improvised dialogue, disjointed narratives, and unconventional shooting and cutting techniques. In addition to his more commercial works, such as *Breathless* (1960) *Alphaville* (1965), and *Slow Motion* (1980), he has also explored the use of film for more overtly political purposes, for example in *Wind from the East* (1969).

Goddard, Robert Hutchings (1882–1945) US physicist. He carried out pioneering work in rocketry, and designed and built the first successful liquid-fuelled rocket (1926). NASA's Goddard Space Flight Center is named after him.

Gödel, Kurt (1906–78) Austrian-born US mathematician. He made several important contributions to mathematical logic, especially the **incompleteness theorem** (**Gödel's proof**): that in any sufficiently powerful, logically consistent formulation of logic or mathematics there must be true formulas which are neither provable nor disprovable. This makes such formulations essentially incomplete, and entails the corollary that the consistency of such a system cannot be proved within that system.

godetia An annual plant native to western North America. Godetias are closely related to the evening primroses, but differ in having rose-purple or reddish flowers. *Godetia amoena* and *G. grandiflora* are the parents of many colourful garden varieties.

Godiva, Lady (died 1080) English noblewoman, wife of Leofric, Earl of Mercia (died 1057). According to a 13th-century legend, she agreed to her husband's proposition that he would reduce some particularly unpopular taxes only if she rode naked on horseback through the market-place of Coventry. Later versions of the story describe how all the townspeople stayed indoors at Lady Godiva's request, except for peeping Tom, who as a result was struck blind.

Godthåb (or **Godthaab**) the former Danish name, until 1979, of NUUK, capital of Greenland.

Godunov, Boris See BORIS GODUNOV.

Godwin, William (1756–1836) British social philosopher and novelist. At first a dissenting minister, he subsequently became an atheist and expounded theories of anarchic social organization based on a belief in the goodness of human reason and on his doctrine of extreme individualism. His ideological novel *Caleb Williams* (1794), which exposes the tyranny exercised by the ruling classes, was an early example of the crime and detection novel. In 1797 he married Mary WOLLSTONECRAFT, who died after giving birth to their daughter who became Mary Shelley.

Godwin Austen See K2.

godwit Any one of four species of large WADING BIRD of the species *Limosa*, which belong to the Scolopacidae family, distributed worldwide. Godwits resemble curlews, but their long beaks are straight or slightly upturned. Like many waders they have two plumages: in winter they are dull grey-brown, but in summer their neck and underparts turn a bright chestnut colour.

Goebbels, (Paul) Joseph (or **Göbbels**) (1897–1945) German Nazi leader and politician. In 1933 he became Hitler's Minister of Propaganda, with control of the press, radio, and all aspects of culture. With a total disregard for the truth, he manipulated the media in order to further Nazi aims. A supporter of Hitler to the last, he committed suicide rather than surrender to the Allies.

Goering, Hermann Wilhelm (or **Göring**) (1893–1946) German Nazi leader and politician. In 1934 he became commander of the German air force, and was responsible for the German rearmament programme. Until 1936 Goering headed the Gestapo, which he had founded; from then until 1943 he directed the German economy. In that year he fell from favour, was deprived of all authority, and was finally dismissed in 1945 after unauthorized attempts to make peace with the Allies. Sentenced to death at the Nuremberg war trials, he committed suicide in his cell.

Goes, Hugo van der (*fl.* *c.*1467–82) Flemish painter, born in Ghent. He worked chiefly in his birthplace, though his best-known work is the large-scale *Portinari Altarpiece* (1475), commissioned for a church in Florence.

Goethe, Johann Wolfgang von (1749–1832) German poet, dramatist, and scholar. In his early career he was involved with the *Sturm und Drang* movement, an early aspect of romanticism. In 1775 he moved to Weimar (later becoming a close friend of Friedrich von Schiller) and held a number of government posts 1776–86, after which he spent two years in Italy. His writing began to move away from the energy and romanticism of *Sturm und Drang* and became more measured and classical in style, as in the 'Wilhelm Meister' novels (1796–1829), which are also the prototype of the *Bildungsroman*. His works include the epic drama *Götz von Berlichingen* (1773), the epistolary novel *The Sorrows of Young Werther* (1774), and the two-part poetic drama *Faust* (1808–32), as well as the classical dramas *Iphigenia in Tauris* (1787) and *Tasso* (1790).

Gog and Magog Mythical symbols of evil. In the Old Testament Ezekiel referred to Gog as the leader of a people and to Magog as their land. In the New Testament Book of Revelation they are the nations under the dominion of Satan. In an independent British legend, Gog and Magog are survivors of a race of giants destroyed by Brutus the Trojan, legendary founder of London. A pair of statues in London's Guildhall depicts them. Originating in the reign of Henry V, they were destroyed by the Fire of London (1666) and again in the Blitz (1940). The present statues were created in 1953.

Gogh, Vincent van (1853–90) Dutch painter and draughtsman, with CÉZANNE and GAUGUIN the greatest of POST-IMPRESSIONIST artists. During his lifetime he sold only one picture and waged a grim battle against poverty, alcoholism, and insanity. Although his career lasted only ten years, his output was prodigious (about 800 paintings). His early works deal mainly with the life of peasants and are sombre in colour and mood. After he moved to Paris in 1886, however, he was influenced by IMPRESSIONISM and Japanese woodcuts (see *ukiyo-e*). As a result, his work became lighter and featured a broader range of subjects, including landscapes, portraits, and still lifes. In 1888 he settled at Arles in the south of France, where he produced an enormous amount of work but suffered recurrent nervous crises, with bouts of hallucination and depression. He was joined by Gauguin, but they quarrelled, precipitating the episode in which van Gogh cut off part of his own ear. In the last seventy days of his life he painted seventy pictures before shooting himself.

Gogol, Nikolai (Vasilevich) (1809–52) Russian novelist, dramatist, and short-story writer, born in Ukraine. He first became famous for his play *The Inspector General* (1836), a savagely satirical picture of life in a provincial Russian town. His St Petersburg stories (including *Notes of a Madman*, 1835, and *The Greatcoat*, 1842) also display a trenchant satirical wit. Living mainly abroad from 1836 to 1848, he wrote the comic epic novel *Dead Souls* (1842), widely regarded as the foundation of the modern Russian novel, but after a spiritual crisis he burned the manuscript of the second part.

goitre An enlargement of the thyroid gland, which is seen as a swelling in the neck. Goitre is a feature of a wide range of thyroid disease, and its structure and characteristics depend on the disease involved. Overactivity (hyperthyroidism), underactivity (hypothyroidism), and inflammation of the thyroid gland (thyroiditis) are all associated with goitre. Dietary iodine deficiency, now rare, may also cause goitre. Treatment is directed towards the underlying cause.

Gokhale, Gopal Krishna (1866–1915) Indian nationalist politician. The leader of the moderate faction in the Indian National CONGRESS, he became prominent in the Indian legislative Council established under the Morley–Minto Reforms in 1910, specializing in finance. He also founded in 1905 the Servants of India Society, an austere organization dedicated to the service of India.

Golan Heights A range of hills on the border between Syria and Israel, north-east of the Sea of Galilee. Formerly under Syrian control, the area was occupied by Israel in 1967 and annexed in 1981. Many KIBBUTZIM have been set up in the area, which Israel maintains is of strategic importance in its defence (before 1967 Syria used the Heights as an artillery base from which to bombard part of Isreal). Pop. (1983) 19,700.

gold (symbol Au, at. no. 79, r.a.m. 196.97) A soft, yellow, metallic element, one of the TRANSITION METALS. It is very unreactive, though attacked by halogens and AQUA REGIA. Occurring in nature as small particles of the free metal, in quartz or in ALLUVIUM, it caused the 19th-century GOLD RUSHES in America and Australia; today it is produced mainly in Russia and South Africa. Panning for gold in rivers has been superseded by HYDRAULIC MINING and deep MINING. Gold is extracted from the deposit by treatment with cyanide and displacement with zinc. It is further purified by ELECTROLYSIS or treatment with nitric and sulphuric acids. Its rarity, appearance, and lack of reactivity have led to gold being highly valued throughout history. Its value is thought to be more stable than that of many currencies, and it is widely held as an investment. Another major use is as jewellery; gold is the most ductile and malleable of metals. A good conductor of heat and electricity, it is used widely in electronics. Pure gold is too soft for most applications and is generally hardened by alloying it with copper or silver. The gold content of alloys is measured in carats, with 24 carats corresponding to pure gold.

Gold Coast The former name (until 1957) of GHANA.

goldcrest A species of bird, *Regulus regulus*, in the family Regulidae, which also contains the firecrest and kinglets. It is a small greenish bird with a partially concealed black-edged crown stripe, yellowish in the female, golden in the male. At about 6 g (less than a quarter of an ounce) in weight, it is the smallest British bird. Widespread in Europe and Asia, it builds its nest high up in trees, often in conifers or on the ivy-covered trunks of hardwoods.

Golden Calf In the Old Testament, an idol that the Hebrews asked Aaron to construct while his brother Moses was absent on Mount Sinai. Moses had the Calf melted down, pulverized, and mixed with water. The people were then made to drink the mixture. Those who had not worshipped the Golden Calf survived the ordeal, while the idol-worshippers died of a plague.

golden eagle A large, reddish-brown EAGLE, *Aquila chrysaetos*, which is thinly but widely distributed over northern Europe, Asia, and throughout North America. Five sub-species are recognized. Northern populations tend to migrate south in winter. They feed mainly on small mammals and ground birds, which they catch in extensive home ranges, but are often scavengers in their mountain and moorland haunts. They nest among high crags, rearing one or two young.

Golden Fleece In Greek mythology, the fleece of a winged ram that JASON and the ARGONAUTS sought to recover from Colchis to enable Jason to claim his inheritance. Overcoming many hazards, they eventually recovered the fleece with the help of Medea, who married Jason.

Golden Gate A deep channel connecting San Francisco Bay with the Pacific, spanned by a suspension bridge completed in 1937. It was named during the gold-rush of 1849.

Golden Horde, the See KIPCHAK EMPIRE.

Golden Horn, the (Turkish **Haliç**) A curved inlet of the Bosporus, separating the northern and southern districts of of Istanbul, Turkey. It is crossed by the Galata, Ataturk, and Haliç bridges and forms a natural harbour 8 km (5 miles) in length.

golden mole An insectivore of the family Chrysochloridae, only distantly related to true moles but of similar appearance and habits except that some of the 18 species hunt on the surface. They have a flexible snout terminating in a stout nose-pad, which is used extensively in digging. Golden moles are found in southern Africa and on isolated mountains in East Africa in suitable soils. They range in size from Grant's desert golden mole, *Eremitalpa granti*, which is 8 cm (3 inches), to the giant golden mole, *Chrysospalax trevelyani*, which is 20 cm (8 inches).

golden orfe The golden variety of the fish known as the ide, a member of the carp family which is widespread in central and eastern Europe. Because of its golden coloration it is kept as an ornamental fish in lakes and occasionally escapes from these into rivers. It has been found in several English rivers. Superficially like a CHUB, it has small scales. It spawns in late spring over water-plants in shallow water.

golden section The division of a line or figure in such a way that the ratio of the smaller section to the larger is the same as the ratio of the larger to the whole; this common ratio (the **golden ratio** or **golden mean**) is $(\sqrt{5}-1)/2$, or about 0.618. The proportion has been discussed since classical times and is supposed to possess inherent aesthetic value because it corresponds with the laws of nature or the Universe.

goldfinch Any one of a number of bird species in the finch family, Fringillidae, especially the American and the Eurasian goldfinches. The former, *Carduelis tristis*, is a small species in which the male is bright yellow, with black wings, and a black tail and cap. The female is dull olive-green without a black cap. It breeds over a wide area of northeastern North America. The Eurasian goldfinch, *C. carduelis*, is widespread over Europe and western Asia; both sexes have a brownish back and white belly with a striking red and white face. The wings are black, with a broad golden-yellow wing bar, which is conspicuous in flight and thus gives the species its name. Both these species live in open country close to woodland, and feed primarily on small weed seeds. The genus *Carduelis* has twenty-four species, some known as siskins or greenfinches.

goldfish A golden-coloured pond or aquarium fish, often with elaborate fins. The tail fin may be double in some of these varieties. The variation is due to the selection of stock by fish-breeders to emphasize various colours, body forms, and fin shapes. Many goldfish are liberated into the wild and in warm temperate areas may form breeding populations, but generally they are seen and eaten by predators.

A native of Siberia, northern China, and Korea, the wild goldfish, *Carassius auratus*, lives in weed-filled lakes and backwaters of rivers. It spawns among vegetation in midsummer, the eggs adhering to the leaves. It is very resistant to extremes of temperature and low oxygen levels, two qualities that have made it a successful ornamental fish. In eastern Europe it is represented by a subspecies, called the giebel carp or Prussian carp.

Golding, Sir William (Gerald) (1911–93) British novelist. He achieved literary success with his first novel, *Lord of the Flies* (1954), about a group of boys who revert to savagery when stranded on a desert island. The human capacity for evil and guilt is a predominant theme in Golding's work, including *The Inheritors* (1955), which describes the extermination of Neanderthal man by modern *Homo sapiens*. Later works include *The Spire* (1964) and *Fire Down Below* (1989). He was awarded the Nobel Prize for literature in 1983.

Goldman, Emma (known as 'Red Emma') (1869–1940) Lithuanian-born US political activist. She emigrated to the USA in 1885, where she later became involved in New York's anarchist movement. With Alexander Berkman (1870–1936) she founded and co-edited the anarchist monthly *Mother Earth* (1906–17). She was imprisoned in 1917 with Berkman for opposing US conscription; they were released after two years and deported to Russia. She eventually settled in France. Her disenchantment with and opposition to the Soviet system are related in *My Disillusionment in Russia* (1923).

Goldmark, Peter Carl (1906–77) Hungarian-born US inventor and engineer. He made the first colour television broadcast in 1940, invented the long-playing record in 1948, and pioneered video cassette recording.

gold moth (or **pollen-feeding moth**) A tiny, metallic, day-flying moth of the family Micropterigidae, less than 12 mm (0.5 inch) in wing-span. Gold moths comprise a unique suborder of Lepidoptera (moths and butterflies) which occurs worldwide, for, unlike other moths, they lack a proboscis but have jaws with which they feed on pollen. Their caterpillars probably feed on mosses, and pupae have movable legs and jaws.

gold rushes Sudden influxes of people to newly discovered gold fields. The most famous gold rush was to California, where in 1848 gold was found by a Swiss settler, J. A. Sutter. As news spread, adventurers from all over the world made for California. Hard-drinkers and gamblers, the 'forty-niners' created an archetypal saloon society, where more fortunes were made from speculation in land and goods than from gold. The second great rush was to Australia, where gold was first found near Bathurst in New South Wales in 1851 and later in Victoria at Bendigo and Ballarat, the richest alluvial gold field ever known. A ten-year boom brought diggers back across the Pacific from the declining California field, as well as from Britain, where Cornish tin-mining was declining. The population of Victoria rose from 97,000 to 540,000 in the years 1851–60. Later rushes were to New Zealand (1860), to North Australia, Alaska, Siberia, and South Africa (1880s), and to Klondike in Canada and Kalgoorlie in West Australia (1890s). The most important was probably to Witwatersrand, South Africa, in 1886, where the influx of loose-living miners (*uitlanders* or outlanders) precipitated political tensions which led to the Second BOER WAR.

Goldschmidt, Victor Moritz (1888–1947) Swiss-born Norwegian chemist, the founder of modern geochemistry. He carried out fundamental work on crystal structure, suggesting a law relating it to chemical composition, and used X-ray crystallography to determine the structure of many compounds.

Goldsmith, Oliver (1728–74) Irish novelist, poet, essayist, and dramatist. After studying medicine and travelling in Europe, in 1756 he settled in London, where he practised as a physician and began his literary career as a journalist and essayist. He is now best known for his novel *The Vicar of Wakefield* (1766), the poem *The Deserted Village* (1770), and the comic plays *The Good-Natur'd Man* (1768) and *She Stoops to Conquer* (1773).

gold standard A monetary system under which a country's monetary authority is prepared to exchange its currency for gold on demand at the price declared. Exchange rates between the currencies of member countries are then necessarily fixed. Each monetary authority has to maintain a certain reserve of gold to honour its obligation. In 1821 Britain became the first country to introduce an official gold standard. It was followed some 50 years later by France, Germany, and the USA, and by 1900 the major countries had adopted the gold standard. It was suspended in World War I owing to the difficulty of transporting gold in wartime and resumed in 1925. It was finally abandoned in 1931; the gold standard is not currently in effect anywhere in the world.

gold-tail moth See TUSSOCK MOTH.

Goldwyn, Samuel (born Schmuel Gelbfisz; changed to Goldfish then Goldwyn) (1882–1974) Polish-born US film producer. He produced his first film in 1913; his film company, Metro-Goldwyn-Mayer (MGM), which he formed with Louis B. Mayer in 1924, soon became world famous. His successful films include an adaptation of Emily Brontë's novel *Wuthering Heights* (1939), *The Little Foxes* (1941), and the musical *Guys and Dolls* (1955). Goldwyn is also famous for introducing a number of catch-phrases (such as 'Include me out') to the English language.

golem (Hebrew, 'embryo or anything incompletely developed') In Jewish folklore, an effigy made of clay and brought to life by means of a charm. In the Middle Ages, the golem was portrayed as an automaton who carried out his master's commands. He later assumed a more powerful form as general protector of persecuted Jews. The most famous legend about a golem centres around Rabbi Juda Löw (*c*.1525–1609) of Prague, who was forced to destroy the creature that he had created after it had run amok. This legend forms the basis for Gustav Meyrink's novel *Der Golem* (1916).

golf A popular game that probably originated in Scotland but is now played worldwide by amateurs and professionals, using a selection of wood- and metal-faced clubs to hit a small white ball across uneven terrain and hole it in a circular cup with the least number of strokes. A full-length golf course, usually 4,600–6,400 m (5,000–7,000 yards) in length, consists of 18 holes of varied character, laid out with a long, narrow fairway of mown grass terminating in a roughly circular green where a flag marks the hole. Along the way are numerous hazards: long grass, bushes, and trees next to the fairway, perhaps a stream or lake, and almost always a series of sand bunkers. A handicap system allows for even competition among players of differing abilities.

Golgi, Camillo (1844–1926) Italian histologist and anatomist. He devised a method of staining nerve tissue with silver salts to reveal details of the cells and nerve fibres, classified types of nerve cell, and described a complex structure in the cytoplasm of most cells (the **Golgi body** or **apparatus**) that is now known to be involved in secretion. Golgi shared a Nobel Prize with Ramón y Cajal in 1906.

Golgotha The Hebrew name of Calvary near Jerusalem, where the crucifixion of Jesus took place (Hebrew *Gulgoleth* = skull).

Goliath The Philistine warrior giant from Gath who challenged the Israelites in the time of Saul. He was slain by the boy David with a stone from his sling.

Goliath beetle See HERCULES BEETLE.

Gollancz, Sir Victor (1893–1967) British publisher and philanthropist. In 1928 he founded his own publishing company. A committed socialist, he was active in campaigning against the rise of Fascism, founded the Left Book Club (1936), and also contributed to the growing influence of the Labour Party in British politics. After World War II he organized aid for refugees and founded the charity War on Want.

Gómez, Juan Vicente (1864–1935) Venezuelan statesman. During his twenty-seven-year rule as President (1908–35) he established an absolute dictatorship. The foreign investment that he attracted to Venezuela enabled him to build extensive railways, highways, and other public works. Rich petroleum discoveries (1918) in the Lake Maracaibo basin provided a budgetary surplus which not only enabled Gómez to pay off the foreign debt but also assured him a favourable reputation abroad. Because of the brutal nature of the dictatorship, this reputation was not shared at home. When he died in office the city of Caracas marched in celebration.

Gomorrah A town of ancient Palestine, probably south of the Dead Sea, destroyed by fire from heaven (according to Genesis 19:24), along with Sodom, for the wickedness of its inhabitants.

Gomułka, Władysław (1905–82) Polish politician. He was Secretary-General during the crucial period 1943–49 when the Polish United People's Party was being formed. Gomułka's attempted defiance of Stalinism led to his dismissal and imprisonment (1951). He was restored to power (1956) on the intervention of Khrushchev, after Polish and Soviet frontier troops had exchanged fire in the wake of serious rioting in Poznań. He helped to sustain a degree of post-Stalinist liberalism, but resigned in 1970 following popular disturbances against increases in food prices.

gonad A male or female reproductive organ. Gonads occur in pairs in most vertebrates but are reduced to a single organ in some birds, fishes, and reptiles. The male glands (testes) are found in the scrotum of warm-blooded vertebrates; the female glands (ovaries) lie inside the abdomen. The gonads have two functions: the production of reproductive cells called sperm (male) or ova (female); and the secretion of the sex hormones testosterone (male), and oestrogen and progesterone (female). The gonads are present at birth but are non-functional until puberty.

Goncharov, Ivan (Aleksandrovich) (1812–91) Russian novelist. The hero of his masterpiece *Oblomov* (1859) embodies one of the great myths of the Russian man, presenting him as lazy, impractical, and fatalistic; this created a literary archetype recognized the world over.

Goncourt, Edmond de (1822–96) French novelist and critic. He collaborated closely with his brother, **Jules de Goncourt** (1830–70), in his writing, originally producing art criticism and social history. They regarded their highly detailed realist novels, such as *Germinie Lacerteux* (1864) and *Madame Gervaisais* (1869), as a form of contemporary social history. They also wrote the *Journal des Goncourt*, a detailed record of cultural life in Paris between 1851 and 1896.

Gondwana (or **Gondwanaland**) The postulated supercontinental mass that once included Australia, Antarctica, India, Africa, and South America, separated as a result of CONTINENTAL DRIFT, before the Carboniferous Period. It was named Gondwanaland by the German meteorologist Alfred Wegener in 1912, who named the northern supercontinent LAURASIA.

gong A bronze disc with turned-back rim, with either a flat face, usually then of indefinite pitch like the orchestral tam-tam, or with a central boss. Tam-tams seem to have originated in Central Asia and were perhaps known in ancient Greece and Rome. They travelled also to China and came thence into 19th-century Europe. Bossed gongs, always tuned to definite pitches, reached their peak of development in Java, where the great gong *ageng* and many smaller gongs make up the classical GAMELAN.

goniometer Any instrument for measuring angles. This includes the protractor, a transparent plastic semicircle or circle marked in degrees and used for measuring or setting out angles. More specifically, a goniometer is an instrument that measures the angle between the reflecting surfaces of a crystal or prism. Two rays of light from a collimator (a system of lenses and slits designed to create parallel light beams) are directed on to two adjacent surfaces of the crystal: the beams are reflected from the two faces, and the angle between the two reflected beams (twice the angle between the prism or crystal surfaces) is measured.

A goniometer is also a device sometimes used with radio or radar transmitters. It allows a signal to be transmitted in any direction, or the direction of an incoming signal to be determined, without the use of a physically rotating antenna.

gonorrhoea A SEXUALLY-TRANSMITTED DISEASE resulting from bacterial infection caused by *Neisseria gonorrhoeae*, which is characterized in men by pain on urination together with increased frequency and a feeling of urgency to pass urine; there may also be a discharge. In women, there may be no symptoms, or vaginal discharge and pain on urination may occur. Treatment is successful but must be early to avoid complications, such as sterility and pain and erosion of the joints.

Goodall, Jane (1934–) British zoologist. Goodall obtained employment in Tanzania with Louis Leakey in 1957, and has been based at the Gombe Stream Reserve by Lake Tanganyika since 1970. She has made prolonged and intimate studies of the chimpanzees of Gombe, which has become a respected centre of primate research. Her first popular work, *In the Shadow of Man* (1971) depicted a rather idealized view of chimpanzee behaviour, but her later book *Through a Window* (1990) showed that hunting, murder, war, and cannibalism are integral parts of their life.

Good Friday The annual Christian commemoration of the crucifixion of JESUS CHRIST, directly preceding Easter Sunday. It is a time of fasting and penance, often with a three-hour service from noon until 3 pm in which the Passion or suffering of Jesus on the cross is narrated. Good Friday is known as 'Great Friday' in the Orthodox Church.

Goodman, Benjamin David (known as 'Benny') (1909–86) US jazz clarinettist and band-leader. He formed his own big band in 1934, and soon gained a mass following through radio and live performances. Goodman chose players for their musicianship regardless of their colour, and his bands were the first to feature black and white musicians together. The advent of his distinctive style marked the start of a new era in the history of jazz; he soon became known as the 'King of Swing'. He also performed a wide variety of classical clarinet music; Bartók, Hindemith, and Copland all composed works for him.

Goodricke, John (1764–86) British amateur astronomer who founded the study of VARIABLE STARS. A severe illness in infancy left him a deaf-mute. His astronomical work, in which he collaborated with his neighbour Edward Piggott in York, was confined to the last five years of his short life, and was largely devoted to the study of variable stars visible to the naked eye. He investigated ALGOL, and in 1782 discovered its period of 2.87 days, correctly speculating that its variation in magnitude is due to eclipses by a darker object orbiting the star. In 1784 he discovered the variation of BETA LYRAE and of Delta Cephei (the first of the class of CEPHEID VARIABLE STARS), and measured their periods. He was awarded the Copley Medal of the Royal Society in 1784 and became a Fellow in 1786 but died two weeks later, aged 21, apparently from pneumonia contracted while observing Delta Cephei.

goods (in economics) Physical commodities which either directly or indirectly provide for the satisfaction of human wants. Consumer goods (or final-demand goods) are those used for CONSUMPTION purposes. They can be classified into non-durable goods (such as food) and durable goods (such as refrigerators). Producer goods are those used to produce other goods and services. These comprise intermediate goods (raw materials and semi-finished items) and fixed capital goods (buildings and equipment). Services are normally distinguished from goods by their intangible nature. 'Bads' also exist; they have a negative value and an adverse effect on human satisfaction (for example, pollution). Public goods are those which, when consumed by one individual, are not depleted (for example, street lighting and national defence).

Goodwin Sands An area of sandbanks in the Strait of Dover, off the coast of south-east England. Often exposed at low tide, the sandbanks are a hazard to shipping.

Goodwood A racecourse near Chichester in West Sussex, south-east England, at the north end of Goodwood Park. It is the scene of an annual summer race-meeting. Nearby Goodwood House was built in 1739 by the Earl of Richmond.

Goodyear, Charles (1800–60) US inventor of the VULCANIZATION process for rubber. As a young man in his father's hardware business, he became aware of the tendency of rubber goods to become tacky when warm, and brittle when cold. After some years of experimenting with additives to overcome the defect, he eventually achieved success in 1839, when he accidentally dropped some rubber blended with sulphur and white lead on to a hot stove. He was granted a patent in 1844, a year after MACINTOSH and Hancock in the UK had patented similar vulcanization processes.

Goonhilly Downs An area of barren uplands on the Lizard Peninsula in Cornwall, south-west England. The area is noted for its many ancient earthworks and modern satellite tracking station with its prominent communications transmitter-receiver.

goose A large, web-footed waterfowl belonging to the family Anatidae, closely related to swans and ducks, with stout bodies and long necks. True geese belong to the subfamily Anserinae, but the term is used in such a way that 'geese' and 'ducks' cannot be taxonomically separated. Although good swimmers, geese are mainly terrestrial, spending much time grazing. They breed in high northern latitudes and migrate south in winter, when they form noisy flocks or gaggles on marshes, grassland, and arable land. They fly in skeins, sometimes in neat V-formation. The sexes are similar in colour in all fourteen species. There are nine so-called grey geese, such as the whitefront and the greylag, and five predominantly black species, which include the barnacle, brent, and Canada geese.

gooseberry A heavily thorned, hardy, deciduous shrub, grown in cool temperate areas, belonging to the genus *Ribes* and the family Grossulariaceae. Like their relatives, the currants, they produce edible fruits which vary widely in colour and size. Most are yellowish-green, some are distinctly yellow, and others reddish or purplish. Certain varieties produce berries sweet enough for eating raw, whereas others, containing more acid, are more suitable for cooking.

An unrelated species, *Physalis peruviana*, which belongs to the potato family, is known as the Cape gooseberry.

Goossens, Sir (Aynsley) Eugene (1893–1962) British conductor, violinist, and composer, of Belgian descent. After conducting in the USA (1923–45), in 1947 Goossens was appointed the director of the New South Wales Conservatorium and conductor of the Sydney Symphony Orchestra. His compositions include opera, ballet, and symphonies. His brother **Leon** (1897–1988) was a virtuoso oboist, and his sister **Marie** (1894–1991) a distinguished harpist.

gopher In North America, a GROUND SQUIRREL of the genus *Spermophilus*, or a member of a quite distinct family of RODENTS, Geomyidae. These are more accurately called **pocket gophers** because of their huge fur-lined external cheek pouches.

There are 32 species of *Spermophilus*, with the greatest number of species in North America. These ground squirrels are diurnal and mainly herbivorous, feeding on seeds, nuts, and roots, but they will also eat small birds and rodents if they can catch them. They usually live in burrows, hibernating in winter.

Pocket gophers are mole-like and live underground in extensive burrow systems, which they excavate with their huge, chisel-like, front teeth and powerful, clawed front feet. The 34 species, which are found only in North America, feed underground on roots and bulbs.

goral Either of two species of goat-antelope of the genus *Nemorhaedus*, intermediate in appearance between goats and antelopes and part of the same subfamily as goats. They are found in mountains from the Himalayas to Korea at altitudes of 900–2,700 m (3,000–9,000 feet). When among tall grass, gorals are difficult to see, as they stand only 70 cm (28 inches) at the shoulder. It has a coarse coat of grey or brown. Both sexes have short horns that curve slightly to the rear. If alarmed it utters a penetrating hiss.

Gorazde A predominantly Muslim town in eastern Bosnia-Hercegovina, on the River Drina south-east of Sarajevo. Despite being declared a safe haven by the UN, it was the subject of a prolonged siege by Bosnian Serbs during 1993–94.

Gorbachev, Mikhail (Sergeevich) (1931–) Soviet statesman, General Secretary of the Communist Party of the USSR 1985–91 and President 1988–91. He was born in Russia. His foreign policy was notable for bringing about an end to the cold war, largely through arms control negotiations with the West that culminated in the signing of treaties with the US in 1987 (the INF treaty) and 1991 (the START treaty). Within the USSR he introduced major political, economic, and cultural reforms, including the eventual removal of the Communist Party's monopoly of power, moves towards a market economy, and more open government (policies known as glasnost and perestroika). Opposition to his policies led to an attempted coup in 1991, and eventually his wish to retain a centrally controlled union of Soviet states conflicted with the Soviet republics' desire for autonomy. Losing his battle with his chief political opponent, Boris YELTSIN, he resigned in December 1991. He was awarded the Nobel Peace Prize in 1990.

Gordimer, Nadine (1923–) South African novelist and short-story writer. Her first collection of stories, *The Soft Voice of the Serpent* (1953), showed a precise psychological observation. Her later work is increasingly concerned with racial politics, notably *A Guest of Honour* (1970), set in a newly independent African nation, and *July's People* (1981), which envisages a future civil war. Gordimer won the Booker Prize for *The Conservationist* (1974) and in 1991 she was awarded the Nobel Prize for literature.

Gordium An ancient city of Asia Minor, the capital of Phrygia in the 8th and 9th centuries BC. According to Greek legend the city was founded by King Gordius, who tied the knot cut by Alexander the Great during his expedition of 334 BC. The city, now in ruins, lies beside the River Sakarya in north-west Turkey 80 km (50 miles) west of Ankara.

Gordon, Charles George (1833–85) British general and colonial administrator. He went to China in 1860 while serving with the Royal Engineers, and became known as 'Chinese Gordon' after crushing the Taiping Rebellion (1863–64). In 1884 he was sent to rescue the Egyptian garrisons in Sudan from forces led by the Mahdi (Muhammad Ahmad of Dongola, 1843–85), but was trapped at Khartoum and killed before a relieving force could reach him.

Gordon riots Anti-Catholic riots in London in 1780. They were led by Lord George Gordon (1751–93), who objected to parliamentary moves towards CATHOLIC EMANCIPATION. His followers terrorized London for a fortnight. Prisons were broken open, property damaged, and people killed before order was restored. Gordon was acquitted of high treason, but was later convicted of libel and died in Newgate Prison.

Gordonstoun A public school 6 km (4 miles) west of Lossiemouth in north-east Scotland. It was founded in 1935 by Kurt Hahn (1886–1974), a German educationalist who fled from Germany in 1933. The Duke of Edinburgh and Prince Charles were educated here.

Gore, Al(bert) (1948–) US Democratic politician, Vice-President of the USA since 1993. An editorial writer and land developer, he was senator for Tennessee from 1985 to 1993. His publications include *Earth in the Balance* (1992).

Górecki, Henryk (Mikołaj) (1933–) Polish composer. He studied at Katowice Conservatory and with Olivier Messiaen in Paris. His works are chiefly for orchestra and chamber ensemble; they include three symphonies and a chamber trilogy, *Genesis* (1963). In *Old Polish Music* (1969) he draws on medieval Polish religious music as his source of inspiration, while his Third Symphony (1976), also called the *Symphony of Sorrowful Songs*, is heavily influenced by church music.

Gorgio The Romany name for a nongypsy.

gorgonian (or **horny coral**) A common octocorallian CORAL of reef communities. Gorgonians have a central skeletal axis, with POLYPS arranged around this, often giving a branched, tree-like appearance. They are usually brightly coloured, the precious red coral, for example, being brilliantly coloured. The flexible branching skeleton is an ideal shape for trapping suspended food; the large surface area collects countless tiny animals as the coral sways with the current.

Gorgons In Greek mythology, three female monsters who were sisters; they had wings, claws, and human heads with snakes for hair. Their names were Euryale, Medusa, and Sthenno. Medusa, loved by Poseidon, was the only one who was mortal. Her gaze was so terrifying that it turned anyone who beheld her to stone, but she was killed by Perseus, who looked at her reflection in a polished shield. Chrysaor and the winged horse Pegasus sprang from her blood when she died.

Gorgonzola A village in Lombardy, northern Italy, 18 km (11 miles) north-east of Milan, famous for its rich Strachino or Gorgonzola cheese with bluish-green veins: pop. (1990) 16,190.

gorilla The largest of the great APES, *Gorilla gorilla*. The male is heavily built and may stand 1.7 m (5.5 feet) in height, with an arm-spread of 2.4 m (8 feet). It has a large head with a short neck, prominent mouth, thin lips, and small ears. The female is smaller than the male. This huge animal has formidable canine teeth, yet it feeds on fruit and vegetables and has no natural enemies. A group consists of about six individuals of the immediate members of the family – the adult male, one or two females, their babies and adolescent young. Most of the day is spent on the ground; they usually walk on all fours leaning on the knuckles of their hands, but occasionally upright. At night the group makes camp and each animal prepares a nest, the females and young in the trees, the adult males on the ground.

Three subspecies of gorillas are known: the huge western and eastern lowland gorillas, which live, respectively, in the rain forests along the west and east coasts of equatorial Africa, and the mountain gorilla of the montane forests around Lake Kivu and in the ranges that extend from the Congo east to the border of Uganda.

Gorky, Arshile (1904–48) Turkish-born US painter. At first influenced by Picasso, he later gained inspiration from the surrealist techniques of artists such as Miró to develop a distinctive style of abstract expressionism. He is best known for his work of the early 1940s, which uses ambiguous biomorphic forms characterized by bright colours, fluid handling of the paint, and black sinuous outlines, and is represented by paintings such as *Waterfall* (1943).

Gorky, Maxim (pseudonym of Aleksei Maksimovich Peshkov) (1868–1936) Russian writer and revolutionary. He became famous for the short stories that he published between 1895 and 1900; he later turned to writing novels and plays. Among his best-known works are the play *The Lower Depths* (1901) and his autobiographical trilogy (1915–23). He was imprisoned for his involvement in the Russian Revolution of 1905 and exiled for his revolutionary activity. On his final return to the Soviet Union in 1931 after periods spent abroad, he was honoured as the founder of the new, officially sanctioned socialist realism.

Gorno-Altai (or **Gornyy-Altay**) A republic of the Russian Federation in Siberia on the frontier with Mongolia; area 92,600 sq km (35,740 sq miles); pop. (1989) 192,000; capital, Gorno-Altaisk. Established as the Oirot Autonomous Region in 1922, its name was changed in 1948. After the breakup of the Soviet Union it was declared a republic of the Russian Federation in 1992. Cattle-farming, timber production, and the mining of gold, mercury, and coal are the chief industries.

Gorno-Altaisk The capital of the Republic of Gorno-Altai in Siberian Russia, on the Katun River; pop. (1990) 39,000. It was known as Ulala until 1932 and Oirot-Tura 1932–48.

gorse (or **furze**, **whin**) The common name for plants of the genus *Ulex*. They are spiny shrubs of the pea family, common along the Atlantic coasts of Europe on heathland. The spines are reduced shoots with minute leaves, though seedlings have more typical leaves. They all have yellow flowers with an unusual method of pollination. When a bee alights on the keel of the flower, its weight causes an 'explosion' within the flower which leads to the release of the stamens and forces pollen on to the bee's body. The seeds have two means of dispersal. Firstly, the pods split violently and scatter the seeds. Secondly, the seeds have a juicy area, attractive to insects, notably ants, which carry the seed away.

Gospels See BIBLE.

Gosport A residential town and former naval base in Hampshire, southern England, at the entrance to Portsmouth Harbour; pop. (1991) 72,800.

Gothenburg (Swedish **Göteburg**) A seaport in south-west Sweden, on the Kattegat at the mouth of the River Göta; pop. (1990) 433,000. It is the second-largest city in Sweden and capital of Göteborg och Bohus county. Shipbuilding, engineering, and the manufacture of chemicals and vehicles are its chief industries.

Gothic art and architecture The style of art and architecture that succeeded ROMANESQUE. It originated in France in the mid-12th century, spread rapidly to other countries, and lasted into the 16th century in many areas, particularly in northern Europe. The Gothic style of architecture is characterized by three features: the pointed ARCH (as opposed to the round arch of Romanesque architecture); the rib VAULT, in which transverse arches springing from the wall of the building support (or appear to support) the ceiling; and the flying BUTTRESS, a type of external support that is not placed solidly against a wall, but is instead connected to it by an arch. Another highly characteristic feature of Gothic architecture that developed slightly later was the use of TRACERY, decorative stonework in window openings or applied as ornament to wall surfaces. Window tracery, in fact, evolved in such distinctive and elaborate ways that its variations (or absence) have often been used as the most convenient method of classifying the different stages of the development of Gothic architecture. Conventionally English Gothic is divided into three stages: EARLY ENGLISH STYLE, which began in about 1180; DECORATED, which began to take over in the late 13th century; and PERPENDICULAR, which began in about 1330 and lasted well into the 16th century. The Perpendicular style, so called because of the predominating vertical lines and rectilinearity of its tracery and decorative panelling, was unique to England. Its greatest monument is the Chapel of King's College, Cambridge. The word 'Gothic' has a much less precise meaning when applied to painting or sculpture than it has in an architectural context, although a swaying elegance is often considered typical of Gothic figures, which are generally much more naturalistic and less remote than those of the Romanesque period. In late Gothic Germany woodcarving reached great heights of beauty and elaboration. Gothic painting is seen at its best in manuscript illumination, and in stained glass, which reached its peak as an adjunct to Gothic architecture. Panel painting came more into its own with the development of the late branch of the style known as INTERNATIONAL GOTHIC, which flourished from the turn of the 14th century. Among the other arts in which the Gothic period excelled were embroidery and tapestry. See also GOTHIC REVIVAL.

Gothic novel A story of terror and suspense, usually set in a gloomy castle or monastery (hence 'Gothic'). The heyday of the Gothic novel in Britain lasted from the publication of Horace WALPOLE's *The Castle of Otranto* (1765) to the 1820s. The leading Gothic novelist was Ann RADCLIFFE, whose *Mysteries of Udolpho* (1794) had many imitators. She was careful to explain away the apparently supernatural occurrences in her stories, but other writers, like M. G. Lewis in *The Monk* (1796), made free use of ghosts and demons. The fashion for such novels, ridiculed by Jane AUSTEN in *Northanger Abbey* (1818), gave way to a vogue for HISTORICAL NOVELS, but it contributed to the new emotional climate of ROMANTICISM. The claustrophobic, sinister atmosphere of later 19th-century fiction is often based on Gothic novels, which can also claim to have inspired modern SCIENCE FICTION through Mary SHELLEY's partly Gothic *Frankenstein* (1818).

Gothic Revival (or **neogothic**) A movement in architecture and associated arts in which the Gothic style of the Middle Ages was revived. Beginning in the mid-18th century, it was partly of literary origin and partly a breakaway from the rigid Palladian rules of architectural design then prevailing. Initially, Gothic forms were used in a ROCOCO spirit for their picturesque qualities, with

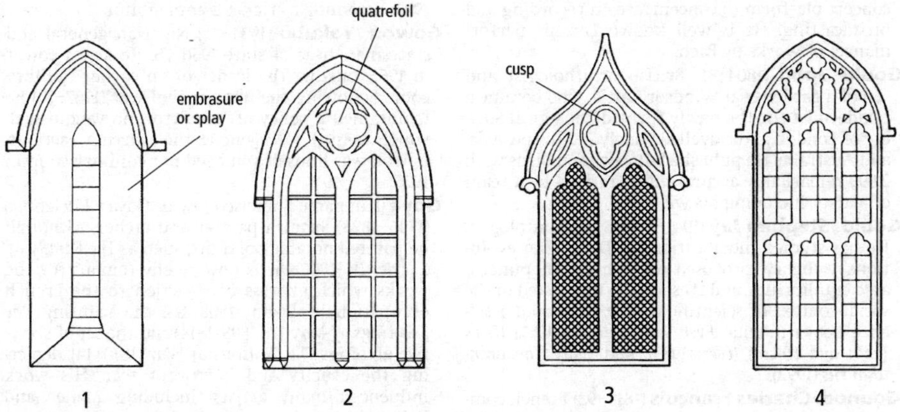

Gothic architecture (windows) (1) Lancet (13th century). (2) Geometic bar tracery (13th century). (3) Decorated curvilinear tracery with ogee arch (14th century). (4) Perpendicular tracery (15th century).

no regard for archaeological accuracy. One of the earliest and most influential examples was Fonthill Abbey, near Bath, built by James WYATT, even though its 85-metre (278-ft) tower collapsed. In the early 19th century, however, the Romantic interest in medieval forms and fancies gave way to a more serious approach, as the Gothic style became closely identified with a religious revival; it was advocated by such architects as PUGIN as the only one suitable for churches. The culmination of Gothic Revival in Britain was the rebuilt Houses of Parliament (1834–45) by BARRY and Pugin. Other leading Gothic Revivalists were BURGES, BUTTERFIELD, George Gilbert SCOTT, and WATERHOUSE.

Goths Germanic tribes that overran the Western Roman empire. Originally from the Baltic area, by the 3rd century AD they had migrated to the northern Black Sea and the Lower Danube. The eastern group on the Black Sea were known as OSTROGOTHS, the western settlers on the Danube in Dacia were known as VISIGOTHS.

Göttingen A historic university town in Lower Saxony, north-central Germany, on the River Leine; pop. (1991) 124,000. It has many unspoilt old buildings and a university founded in 1734 by the Elector George Augustus (later King George II of Britain). Its light industries include optical and precision instruments.

gouache Opaque WATER-COLOUR. The degree of opacity varies with the amount of white pigment added to the colour, but in general it is sufficient to prevent the reflection of the paper through the paint, and it therefore lacks the luminosity of transparent water-colour wash. Gouache was used for manuscript illumination, on fans, and for preparatory sketches.

Gouda A market town in the Dutch province of South Holland, 15 km (9 miles) north-east of Rotterdam, noted for its cheese and its stained-glass windows; pop. (1991) 65,900.

Goudsmidt, Samuel Abraham (1902–78) Dutch-born US physicist who, with George Uhlenbeck in 1925, first suggested that the electron possesses SPIN. The concept proved to be of fundamental importance in the development of QUANTUM MECHANICS.

Gould, Glenn (Herbert) (1932–82) Canadian pianist and composer. He made his début as a soloist with the Toronto Symphony Orchestra at the age of 14 and gave many performances both in Canada and abroad until 1964, when he retired from the concert platform to concentrate on recording and broadcasting. He is well known for his performances of works by Bach.

Gould, John (1804–81) British ornithologist and son of a gardener at Windsor Castle, who became a taxidermist for the newly formed Zoological Society of London and travelled widely in Europe, Asia, and Australia. He published 41 works on birds with 2,999 remarkably accurate illustrations by a team of artists, including his wife.

Gould, Stephen Jay (1941–) US palaeontologist. He has studied modifications of Darwinian evolutionary theory, proposed the concept of punctuated equilibrium, and is especially interested in the social context of scientific theory. His popular science books include *Ever Since Darwin* (1977) *Hen's Teeth and Horses' Toes* (1983), and *Bully for Brontosaurus* (1992).

Gounod, Charles François (1818–93) French composer, conductor, and organist. He achieved his first operatic success in 1859 with *Faust*, a grand opera in the French tradition, but with a grace and naturalism new to the genre. Gounod's later operas have not maintained their popularity to the same extent as *Faust*, but *Roméo et Juliette* (1867) and several of his songs are still performed.

gourami An Asiatic fish belonging to either of two families, the Belontiidae or the Osphronemidae. The former contains many small, brightly coloured, tropical freshwater fishes, including the FIGHTING FISH. The Osphronemidae family includes the gourami, *Osphronemus goramy*, a 60 cm (25 inches) long food-fish. Gouramis are found throughout Asia in ditches draining paddy-fields, swamps, streams, and ponds, and have a special breathing organ in the gills which permits them to breathe air. They make bubble nests at the water surface for their eggs.

gourd A climbing, often perennial, plant belonging to the pumpkin family, Cucurbitaceae. This includes cucumbers, melons, and marrows. Several different species are given the name of gourd, although the name is used when referring mainly to *Cucurbita* species. Other species include the bottle gourd, *Lagenaria siceraria*, the bitter gourd, *Momordica charantia*, and the snake gourd, *Trichosanthes cucumerina*. Although some *Cucurbita* species have fruits that can be used as a vegetable, most are grown for their hard-skinned fruits which, although inedible, have a multitude of uses.

gout See ARTHRITIS.

governor A mechanism to control the speed of a machine or engine. The centrifugal governor has weights attached to the engine shaft, which tend to move outwards as rotation speed increases; this movement raises a grooved collar, which in STEAM-TURBINES and engines moves a lever controlling the steam supply. GAS-ENGINES use a hit-and-miss governor, which cuts off the gas supply for one or more strokes of the engine if its speed rises too greatly. In PETROL ENGINES, DIESEL ENGINES, and GAS-TURBINES the governor controls the rate of fuel supply. For large installations the power of the governor has to be augmented by a SERVO-MECHANISM.

Gower A limestone peninsula on the coast of south Wales, projecting into the Bristol Channel between Swansea Bay and Carmarthen Bay, and a popular holiday resort.

Gower, David Ivon (1957–) British cricketer. A left-handed batsman, he captained England from 1984 to 1986 and in 1989, having previously played for Leicestershire and Hampshire. He retired in 1993, becoming a cricket commentator.

Gowon, Yakubu (1934–) Nigerian general and statesman, head of state 1966–75. He seized power in 1966, ousting the leader of an earlier military coup. Following the Biafran civil war (1967–70) he maintained a policy of 'no victor, no vanquished' which helped to reconcile the warring factions. Gowon was himself removed in a military coup in 1975.

Goya (full name Francisco José de Goya y Lucientes) (1746–1828) Spanish painter and etcher. Although he painted notable portraits, such as *The Family of Charles IV* (1800), he is now chiefly famous for the works which express his reaction to the French occupation of Spain (1808–14): the painting *The Shootings of May 3rd 1808* (1814) and the set of sixty-five etchings *The Disasters of War* (1810–14), depicting the cruelty and horror of war. His work influenced many artists, including Manet and Delacroix.

Graaf, Regnier de (1641–73) Dutch physician and anatomist, author of works on the nature and function of pancreatic juice and the ovaries. He gave his name to **Graafian follicles**, small sacs in the ovary of a mammal in which the ova are matured prior to release and fertilization.

Gracchus, Tiberius Sempronius (*c*.163–133 BC) Roman tribune. He and his brother, **Gaius Sempronius Gracchus** (*c*.153–121 BC), were responsible for radical social and economic legislation, passed against the wishes of the senatorial class. Tiberius was killed by his opponents after the passing of his agrarian bill (133 BC), which aimed at a redistribution of land to the poor. Gaius continued his brother's programme and instituted other reforms to relieve poverty, but was killed in a riot.

Grace, W(illiam) G(ilbert) (1848–1915) British cricketer. He began playing first-class cricket for Gloucestershire in 1864 and played in his last test match at the age of 50. During his career he made 126 centuries, scored 54,896 runs, and took 2,864 wickets. He twice captained England in test matches against Australia (1880 and 1882).

Graces In Greek mythology, daughters of Zeus and of Hera, usually three in number – Aglaia (brightness), Euphrosyne (joyfulness), and Thalia (bloom).

grackle A New World ORIOLE of the subfamily Emberizinae making up six species in the genus *Quiscalus*. The males are mostly shiny black, with a bronze, blue, or green sheen, and have long tails which may reach 42 cm (17 inches). The females are often browner and smaller. Grackles live in open, bushy country and out of the breeding season often gather in large flocks. They eat a wide range of foods, mainly insects in summer and seeds in winter and can be a serious pest to farmers.

grade (in geology) The concentration of a metal or other useful element in an ORE. The cut-off grade is the lowest grade at which the ore can be extracted at a profit.

Grade, Lew, Baron Grade of Elstree (born Louis Winogradsky) (1906–) British television producer and executive, born in Russia. Having emigrated to Britain with his brother (See DELFONT) in 1912, he established a reputation as one of the pioneers of British commercial television in the 1950s; he was long associated with the television company ATV (Associated Television), later serving as its president from 1977 to 1982. His nephew Michael Grade (born 1943) became chief executive of Channel Four in 1988.

grader A six-wheeled machine that accurately shapes surfaces (particularly for roads) after bulk excavation by an excavator, scraper, or bulldozer. It is also used to maintain unsurfaced roads. The grader is steered by the two front wheels, which are linked by a beam to the four-wheeled tractor unit. A steel blade (the mould board) is suspended from the beam and can be raised, lowered, and precisely angled. As the grader advances, the mould board shaves the ground surface or smoothes out loose material until the required camber is formed.

Graf, Steffi (full name Stephanie Graf) (1969–) German tennis player. She was ranked top women's player at the age of 16; in 1988 she won the Australian, French, and US Open championships, as well as the Wimbledon trophy and an Olympic gold medal. She won her seventh Wimbledon singles title in 1996.

grafting In surgery, the removal of tissue and its transplantation to a new site. Autografting (using the patient's own tissue) is generally successful provided that infection is avoided and adequate replacement tissue is found. Skin grafting, which was first achieved in 1817, is the major example of autografting and a mainstay of modern plastic surgery. Large skin grafts are used to treat extensive burns. Recently, small samples of patients' skin have successfully been grown in laboratory conditions to produce larger areas for grafting. Tissues used as autografts need not necessarily replace identical tissues: vein grafts, for example, may replace blocked sections of coronary arteries. Homografting (using donor tissue) can give rise to problems of incompatibility: that is, the body may reject the 'foreign' tissue. Since the late 1960s, tissue typing and immunosuppressant drugs have reduced these difficulties (see TRANSPLANT SURGERY). Certain blood disorders can be treated by bone-marrow transplantation from matched donors. Some homografting, notably of corneas, does not encounter rejection problems.

In horticulture, grafting is the practice of cutting a shoot from one plant and inserting it into a cut in another (the stock), from which it receives sap. It is undertaken to propagate plants quickly, or because a cutting on its own is not as vigorous as one grafted into existing root stock.

Graham, Martha (1893–1991) US dancer, teacher, and choreographer. She established her own studio in 1927, and during the 1930s produced works on the theme of American roots and values, such as *Appalachian Spring* (1931). Her later works include *Care of the Heart* (1946).

Graham, Thomas (1805–69) British physical chemist. He studied the diffusion of gases, and suggested a law (**Graham's Law of Diffusion**), which states that the rate of diffusion of a gas is inversely proportional to the square root of its density. He also investigated the passage of dissolved substances through porous membranes, and coined the word *osmose* (an earlier form of *osmosis*); he was also the first (in 1861) to use the word *colloid* in its modern (chemical) sense.

Graham, William Franklin (known as 'Billy') (1918–) US evangelical preacher. A minister of the Southern Baptist Church, he became world famous as a mass evangelist; he has conducted large, theatrically staged religious meetings throughout the world, including several in Britain, as well as others in South Korea and the former Soviet Union.

Grahame, Kenneth (1859–1932) Scottish-born writer of children's stories, resident in England from 1864. He is most famous for *The Wind in the Willows* (1908), a collection of stories about animals of the river-bank, now regarded as a children's classic. The main characters (Rat, Mole, Badger, and Toad) became even more familiar to British children through A. A. Milne's musical version of the story (*Toad of Toad Hall*, 1930) and various television adaptations of Grahame's work.

Grail, the Holy In Arthurian legend the Holy Grail is identified as the chalice used by Christ at the Last Supper. The Grail was later used by Joseph of Arimathea to catch the blood of the crucified Christ; in some versions, he brought it to north Wales at the end of his lengthy wanderings. The Grail appeared uniquely to Galahad, a Knight of King Arthur distinguished by his great purity, who, overwhelmed by its beauty, died in ecstasy.

Grainger, (George) Percy (Aldridge) (1882–1961) Australian-born US composer and pianist. From 1901 he lived in London, where he gained fame as a concert pianist; in 1914 he settled in the USA. He joined the English Folk Song Society in 1905 and collected, edited, and arranged English folk-songs. As a composer he is best known for his light music incorporating traditional melodies, such as *Shepherd's Hey* (1911), *Handel in the Strand* (1912), and *Country Gardens* (1919).

Gram, Hans Christian Joachim (1853–1938) Danish bacteriologist. He devised a method of staining some bacteria with iodine and crystal violet, or similar dye, for microscopical examination. Those which retain the stain ('Gram-positive') are generally attacked successfully by penicillin, while 'Gram-negative' bacteria have to be treated with streptomycin.

grammar The study of the formal properties of the words and sentences of a language. Traditionally, it includes morphology, which describes the ways in which words are formed from smaller units or other words, and syntax, which describes how words combine into sentences. It sometimes also includes PHONOLOGY and SEMANTICS. A central branch of modern LINGUISTICS is generative grammar, which seeks to provide precise formal descriptions of the grammatical systems of languages and to develop a theory of universal grammar: a set of general statements about the structure of human languages. Transformational grammar is a form of generative grammar which makes use of operations known as 'transformations', which systematically indicate the links between various types of sentence and derive one type from the other.

Gramme, Zénobe-Théophile (1826–1901) Belgian electrical engineer who designed and built the first practical electric GENERATOR. In 1870 he invented a continuous-current dynamo with a ring ARMATURE, which produced much higher voltages than other dynamos of the time. Designed to be driven by STEAM-ENGINES, these dynamos were immediately successful and were used for a variety of purposes, including factory lighting, ELECTROPLATING, and LIGHTHOUSES.

gramophone (or **phonograph**, **record player**) A machine that records or replays sounds using the vibration of a stylus in the groove of a cylinder or disc. Thomas Edison's phonograph of 1877 could both record and replay. The sound was recorded by the varying amount of indentation a needle made in a tin-foil cylinder, and was reproduced by another needle following the inscribed pattern. Gramophone was the trademark of Emil Berliner's instrument of 1894, which was the first to use a flat disc instead of a cylinder; by 1915 the shellac-based RECORD had virtually replaced the cylinder. The advent of electrical SOUND RECORDING AND REPRODUCTION in the 1920s led to development of the electric gramophone, in which a pick-up passed electrical signals to an amplifier, and the amplified signal drove electrical loudspeakers. About this time competition from radio broadcasts led to a demand for longer playing times. Automatic record changers were introduced on many gramophones (by then combined with radios and known as radiograms). However, the problem was not effectively solved until the introduction of the long-playing vinyl record after World War II. STEREOPHONIC records became commercially available in 1958, and the improved sound quality led to the production of HIGH-FIDELITY SYSTEMS. The gramophone has now been superseded by the hi-fi system, which in addition to being a radio and record player, is also able to play magnetic tapes and COMPACT DISCS.

Grampian A former local government region in north-east Scotland. Formed from ABERDEENSHIRE, Banff, Kincardine, and MORAY in 1975, it was abolished in 1996 when Aberdeenshire and Moray were reformed with adjusted boundaries and the city of Aberdeen became a unitary authority.

Grampian Mountains (or **Grampians**) A mountain range in north-central Scotland. Its southern edge forms a natural boundary between the Highlands and the Lowlands.

Gramsci, Antonio (1891–1937) Italian political theorist and activist. A founder of the Italian Communist Party, he became its leader and was elected to the Chamber of Deputies in 1924. He was imprisoned when the Communist Party was banned by the Fascists in 1926, and died shortly after his release. Gramsci's most notable writings date from his imprisonment, and include *Letters from Prison* (1947).

Granada An ancient city at the foot of the Sierra Nevada in Andalusia, southern Spain; pop. (1991) 286,700. Founded in the 8th century, it became the capital of the Moorish kingdom of Granada in 1238. The Palace of the Alhambra, residence of the Moorish rulers of Granada, is one of Spain's major tourist attractions. The city's 16th-century cathedral contains the tombs of Ferdinand and Isabella. The poet Federico Garcia de Lorca was born in Granada in 1898.

granadilla (or **passion fruit**) A species of PASSION VINE, or *Passiflora*. The large granadilla, *P. quadrangularis*, has large yellowish fruits with white, juicy flesh; the young green fruits may be boiled and eaten as a vegetable. Granadilla is best suited to the hot, moist, tropical lowlands. Another tropical South American species, the sweet granadilla, *P. edulis*, is a popular crop in the mountains of Mexico and Central America, and has been naturalized in Hawaii. Its smaller, brownish fruits have more aromatic flesh than the large granadilla.

Granby, John Manners, Marquis of (1721–70) British army officer. He became a hero during the SEVEN YEARS WAR. He was made commander-in-chief of the British army in 1766, but was subjected to bitter political attacks. Unnerved by such savage criticism, and in declining health, he resigned most of his public offices in 1770, and died in debt.

Gran Chaco (Spanish, 'great hunting-ground or riches') A vast, sparsely populated lowland plain in central South America, extending from southern Bolivia through Paraguay to northern Argentina. The discovery of oil in the Chaco Boreal to the north of the Pilcomayo River precipitated the Chaco War (1932–35) between Paraguay and Bolivia in a dispute about the interstate boundary.

Gran Colombia A country formed in north-west South America following the wars of independence against Spain. Created in 1819 and initially known as the Republic of Colombia, it comprised what is now Colombia, Ecuador, Panama, and Venezuela. Gran Colombia was dissolved following the secession of Venezuela in 1829 and Ecuador in 1830. Its capital was the city of Bogota.

Grand Alliance, War of the See NINE YEARS WAR.

Grand Banks The upper part of a submerged plateau lying south-east of Newfoundland, with an area of about 93,000 sq km (36,000 sq mi). It is part of the submerged continental shelf of eastern North America. The warm water of the Gulf Stream meets the cold water of the Labrador Current in the vicinity of the Banks, and the favourable conditions that result have made it one of the world's greatest fishing grounds. However, the convergence of contrasting air masses has also made it one of the world's foggiest areas.

Grand Canal ▶**1** A series of waterways in eastern China, extending from Beijing southwards to Hangzhou, a distance of 1,747 km (1,092 miles). First constructed in 486 BC as a link between the Yangtze and Yellow rivers, it was extended over the centuries until its present length was reached in 1327 AD. Its original purpose was to transport rice from the river valleys to the cities. It is the longest artificial waterway in the world. ▶**2** The main waterway of Venice in Italy. It is lined on each side by fine palaces and is spanned by the Rialto Bridge. A gondola race is held on the Grand Canal every September.

Grand Canyon A deep gorge about 440 km (277 miles) long formed by the Colorado River in Arizona, USA. It is 8–24 km (5–15 miles) wide and, in places, 1,800 m (6,000 ft) deep. The oldest sedimentary rocks in the canyon date back almost 2,000 million years. It was designated a national monument in 1908 and a national park in 1919. It is visited by 3 million people each year.

Grand Remonstrance (1641) A document drawn up by opposition members of the English LONG PARLIAMENT, indicting the rule of Charles I since 1625 and containing drastic proposals for reform of church and state. Although it passed the HOUSE OF COMMONS by just eleven votes, and swords were first drawn in the Commons over the question of its printing, many saw it as a vote of no confidence in the king. It drove Charles into his disastrous attempt to arrest its prime movers, including John Pym, an act of force that further alienated opposition Members of Parliament.

Grand Siècle The age of LOUIS XIV (1643–1715), the period of France's greatest magnificence, when it replaced Spain as the dominant power in Europe and established its cultural pre-eminence. The genius of RICHELIEU as chief minister (1624–42) had established the authority of the monarchy and achieved a far greater degree of internal unity for France than was possessed by its rivals. Europe was impressed by the splendours of the court of VERSAILLES. French military predominance was won by the brilliant victories of CONDÉ and Turenne and the creation of the first modern standing army. The splendour of the *Grand Siècle*, based as it was on heavy taxation of the poorest classes, and a commitment to expensive military campaigns, gave way after the king's death to the more turbulent climate of the 18th century.

grand unified theory (GUT) An attempt to describe, using a single theory, all the interactions governed by the four fundamental forces. Grand unified theories are also called unified field theories or theories of everything, and have occupied physicists for some time. The theory of electromagnetism was a first step: MAXWELL's equations unified the electric and magnetic forces into a single electromagnetic force. Current attempts at unification are motivated by the belief that there is a unity in nature – a single principle governing all natural phenomena. So far, theories have been proposed which provide unifications of WEAK and STRONG FORCES and the electromagnetic force. The inclusion of the gravitational force is proving extremely difficult, although proponents of STRING THEORY hope to make some progress.

granite A coarse-grained intrusive igneous rock that commonly contains orthoclase feldspar, quartz, and mica. Hornblende may be present in addition to, or in place of, mica. The general colour is light: grey, pink, yellow, or green. Granites are of all geological periods and are the most widespread rocks on the continents. They are particularly common in the ancient Precambrian shields of Russia, Africa, Canada, and South America; and well-known examples occur in the western Coastal Range of North America (from California to Alaska). They are widely used as building stones and for road surfacing. Only rarely are they a source of valuable minerals.

Grant, Cary (born Alexander Archibald Leach) (1904–86) British-born US actor. He made his Hollywood screen début in *This is the Night* (1932) after appearing in Broadway musicals. He acted in more than seventy films, including *Holiday* (1938) and *The Philadelphia Story* (1940).

Grant, Duncan (James Corrow) (1885–1978) Scottish painter and designer. He was a cousin of Lytton Strachey and a member of the Bloomsbury Group. He exhibited in the second post-impressionist exhibition (1912), and became a pioneer of abstract art in Britain. He was a gifted designer, working for Roger Fry's Omega workshops and producing a variety of work that included textiles, pottery, and murals. He also worked in collaboration with Vanessa Bell, with whom he lived from 1914.

Grant, Ulysses S(impson) (born Hiram Ulysses Grant) (1822–85) US general and 18th President of the USA 1869–77. Having made his reputation through a series of victories on the Union side in the American Civil War (most notably the capture of Vicksburg in 1863), Grant was made supreme commander of the Unionist armies. His policy of attrition against the Confederate army eventually proved successful in ending the war. He became President in 1869, but was unable to check widespread political corruption and inefficiency.

Grantham A market and engineering town in Lincolnshire, east-central England; pop. (1991) 33,243. It was the birthplace in 1925 of Margaret THATCHER.

granulation Fine markings on the surface of the Sun as if the surface is made up of grains or granules 700 to 1,000 km across. Granulation results from the turbulent and violent convective activity in the Sun's surface material. Each granule is short-lived; after a few minutes the granule has cooled, darkened, and sunk back towards the solar interior.

granulites See METAMORPHIC ROCKS.

Granville-Barker, Harley (1877–1946) British dramatist, critic, theatre director, and actor. As co-manager of the Royal Court Theatre, London (1904–07), he presented plays incorporating social comment and realism, including works by Ibsen and Shaw. His own plays, such as *The Voysey Inheritance* (1905), also dealt naturalistically with social and moral issues. His Shakespearian productions and his *Prefaces to Shakespeare* (1927–46) were influential for subsequent interpretation and staging of Shakespeare's work.

grape The fruit of the grape vine, a perennial, climbing plant of the genus *Vitis* (family Vitaceae). Many varieties of the species *V. vinifera* are cultivated for their grapes, used for eating or for making wine. They are successfully grown in areas of the world with the dry, hot summers and cool, wet winters characteristic of Mediterranean areas. Grapes used for wine production are juicy, seedy, and acidic. Dessert grapes tend to be less seedy or seedless, with up to 25 per cent sugar content. Some varieties of dessert grapes are dried to produce raisins, sultanas, and currants.

grapefruit A species of *Citrus* tree, *Citrus × paradisi*, grown in tropical and warm temperate regions of the world for its large yellow fruits, up to 12 cm (5 inches) in diameter. It is probably so-named because these fruits are produced in clusters. About 70 per cent of the world's crop comes from the USA, but the grapefruit probably originated in Barbados as a hybrid. Varieties exist which differ in their flesh colour (from pale yellow to pink) or are relatively seedless. Its West Indian name is pomelo, not to be confused with the pummelo or shaddock.

grape hyacinth A plant of the genus *Muscari*, with approximately 50 species grown from bulbs, native to the Mediterranean region and Asia Minor. They belong to the lily family and produce leaves and spikes of blue, or occasionally yellow or green flowers in spring and early summer. The bulbs are dormant during the rest of the year.

graph A way of representing statistical, experimental, or mathematical information diagrammatically, usually to make the information easier to interpret. Because graphs show how one quantity varies in relation to another, they are used to display functions – mathematical statements of how two variables are related – and to solve equations. A straight-line graph has an equation of the form $y = mx + c$, where x and y are two variables, m is the slope (gradient) of the line produced when x is plotted against y, and c is the point at which the line crosses the y-axis (see CARTESIAN COORDINATES). The steps on graph axes do not always represent equal increments. In science they often represent logarithmic increments. Such axes enable wide-ranging data to be compressed on to a reasonably sized graph. They also transform EXPONENTIAL FUNCTIONS (often encountered in science) into straight-line graphs, which are easier to interpret.

Graph theory, despite its name, has little to do with the graphs described above, but is concerned with the study of networks involving points, lines, and paths. It arose from the investigation of puzzles, properties of electrical circuits, and representations of chemical structures.

graphics (computer) The use of computers to process and display visual information. Computer graphics are used for a wide range of tasks, from the presentation of numerical information as simple graphs to the generation of complex images of near-photographic quality. Early digital computers were used to produce graphics, but they were initially severely limited by the available OUTPUT DEVICES and the amount of computer power needed to process pictorial information. Advances in technology throughout the 1970s and 1980s reduced the cost and improved the performance of graphics hardware. Most computers now have visual display units and printers that can produce graphics as well as text. The rapid advances in hardware have been accompanied by the development of software to support many new applications, such as DESK-TOP PUBLISHING, COMPUTER-AIDED DESIGN, IMAGE PROCESSING, computer animation, and molecular modelling. The availability of graphic visual displays for personal computers and workstations has led to the development of graphic user interfaces. See also COMPACT DISC.

graphite An ALLOTROPE of the element CARBON. It occurs naturally in metamorphic rocks, but can also be synthesized from petroleum or coke. Graphite has a laminar crystal structure, consisting of layers or sheets of strongly bonded carbon atoms. The sheets are held together by weaker forces and slide very easily over one another. The softness of graphite led to its first application; the manufacture of pencil 'leads' in the 17th century, but it now has many other applications. Graphite is a good solid lubricant. It also conducts electricity like a metal, and is used in sliding electrical contacts in motors. It is also used as a moderator in some NUCLEAR REACTORS.

Grappelli, Stephane (1908–97) French jazz violinist. After early classical training, he turned to jazz in the late 1920s; in 1934, together with the guitarist Django Reinhardt, he formed the Quintette du Hot Club de France, becoming famous for his improvisational style of swing, and making many recordings with the group until it split up in 1939. Grappelli went on to pursue a successful international career, both as a soloist and with groups.

graptolite A small, colonial marine animal, known only from fossils of the lower Palaeozoic Era (245–570 million years ago). Graptolites first appear near the end of the Cambrian Period (505 million years ago) and are among the most common Ordovician and Silurian fossils. They finally became extinct at the end of the Silurian Period, some 408 million years ago. They formed branching colonies with stems bearing numerous little skeletal cups which protected the individuals. Graptolites are believed to be relatives of the living ACORN WORMS.

grass A member of one of the largest families of flowering plants, the Gramineae, which contains over 9,000 species, many of which are of major economic importance. They are MONOCOTYLEDONS with fibrous roots and upright stems, and are distributed throughout the world, occurring in most kinds of habitat, from tropical rain forests and swamps to the hot, arid desert areas of the subtropics. They dominate such areas as the steppes of Asia, the prairies of North America, and the savannahs of Africa. This domination is largely a result of the grazing pressure of animals, which encourages grass at the expense of other herbaceous plants.

In an exceedingly diverse family, the only woody species are the BAMBOOS. Grasses differ from other plants in that the vegetative growth is made up mostly of leaf tissue. Tubular leaf sheaths support the parallel-veined leaf blades. The growing points, or buds, of grasses are near ground-level and consequently are not damaged by grazing; grasses form the main food of many grazing animals. The characteristic branching pattern of grasses, known as tillering, occurs as a result of the buds developing into new side-shoots, and some species can spread by means of stolon or rhizome development. The flowers (florets) of grasses are insignificant; being wind-pollinated they have no need for showy petals. They are often clustered together in compact, elongated spikes, as in wheat. The 'seeds' (really FRUITS) can be quite large and contain a large proportion of carbohydrate. The higher-yielding, easily collected, and cultivated species have been exploited as CEREALS by man since agriculture began.

Grass, Günter (Wilhelm) (1927–) German novelist, poet, and dramatist. He won international acclaim with his first novel, *The Tin Drum* (1959) a picaresque tale drawing on Grass's own experiences as a youth in Nazi Germany. He is known for his outspoken socialist views, which are reflected in the play *The Plebeians Rehearse the Uprising* (1966). His other well-known novels include *Dog Years* (1965), *The Flounder* (1978), *The Rat* (1986), and *Toad Croaks* (1992).

grasshopper A large insect belonging to one of two distinct groups: the LONGHORN GRASSHOPPERS or the SHORTHORN GRASSHOPPERS, which include locusts. Grasshoppers, along with crickets, comprise the order Orthoptera, with some 17,000 species. They all have strong, biting mouthparts and most species have leathery fore-wings; the hind ones, being broad and delicate, are folded fanwise under the fore-wings when the insect is at rest. Some species have reduced wings or no wings at all. Almost all male grasshoppers produce sounds characteristic of the species, and are plant-feeders, although a few are carnivorous.

grass moth A small moth with a wing-span of up to 3 cm (approximately 1 inch) that belongs to the subfamily Crambinae. Grass moths are abundant in grassy places, where they rest by day on stems, often head-down, with their straw-coloured wings tightly wrapped around their body and the prominent mouth-parts projecting forward like a horn. Their caterpillars, known as webworms, spin silken galleries low down among the grasses on which they feed.

grass snake Any of various species of non-venomous snake that can be found over most of the world. Up to 2 m (6.6 feet) in length, they are often found in moist habitats. Their diet includes frogs, newts, and occasionally fishes. Coloration is variable, but the body is usually a greenish-grey and the neck often has a black-bordered, yellow, white, or orange collar, as does the European grass snake, *Natrix natrix*. Grass snakes usually deposit clutches of 30–40 eggs in warm sites, such as piles of decaying vegetation.

Grattan, Henry (1746–1820) Irish statesman, a champion of Irish independence. He was born and educated in Dublin, where he trained as a barrister and entered the Irish Parliament in 1775. A brilliant orator, he led the movement to repeal Poynings' law, which made all Irish legislation subject to the approval of the British Parliament. After considerable agitation the British government yielded and repealed the Act (1782). He also strongly opposed the Act of UNION (1801), which merged the British and Irish parliaments. In 1806 he became member for Dublin in the British House of Commons and devoted the rest of his life to the cause of CATHOLIC EMANCIPATION.

gravel An unconsolidated deposit in the form of pebbles laid down by melting ice, rivers, or the sea. The pebbles in ice-laid gravels are generally angular; those of river-laid ones smoother and sometimes flat; and those of wave-beaten ones (shingle) rounder. The pebbles in glacial gravels typically show the greatest variety; those of river gravels the least. Some gravels contain gemstones or gold; others, metals such as tin, washed from neighbouring regions.

Graves, Robert (Ranke) (1895–1985) British poet, novelist, and critic. His early poetry was written during World War I, but he is better known for his later work, which is individualistic and cannot be associated with any school or movement. He was professor of poetry at Oxford University 1961–66. His prose includes autobiography (*Good-bye to All That*, 1929; *Occupation Writer*, 1950), historical fiction (*I, Claudius*, 1934; *Claudius the God*, 1934), and non-fiction (*The White Goddess*, 1948). All of his writing reflects his keen interest in classics and mythology. His self-imposed exile in Egypt, France, and Majorca distanced him from literary developments in Britain.

Gravesend An industrial town in Kent, south-east England, on the River Thames to the east of London; pop. (1981) 53,640. It has engineering, papermaking, and cement industries.

gravitation The attraction exercised by every particle of matter on every other by virtue of its mass. The **gravitational field** is the region within which one massive body exerts a gravitational force on other massive bodies. The gravitational force is one of the four fundamental forces that occur in nature. More than 300 years ago NEWTON proved three things: that this gravitational force is directly proportional to the masses of the interacting bodies, it decreases as the inverse square of their distance apart, and it is directed along the line joining the centres of mass.

Gravitation has a peculiar property known as **non-saturation**, as a result of which it becomes bigger and bigger as the masses of the interacting objects increase. Thus, although gravitation is a relatively weak force, the combined effects of the gravitational pull exerted by all the bodies in the Universe is the dominating force in COSMOLOGY. The gravitational attraction exerted by a mass is **spherically symmetric**; that is, it depends only on the distance from its centre of mass but not on direction.

The motion of the planets around the Sun as well as the satellites around the planets, can be predicted to an extremely high degree of accuracy on the basis of gravitation alone. The centripetal acceleration, which is a consequence of a body's orbital velocity, arises through this gravitational attraction and prevents the bodies from falling towards each other, as non-orbiting unsupported masses would do.

Newton's Law of Gravitation breaks down in regions where the gravitational force is very strong. Under these circumstances the general theory of RELATIVITY has to be introduced. This was first expounded by EINSTEIN in 1915. According to this theory the force of gravitation changes the geometry of space so that it becomes curved. Ripples in the surface of the space–time continuum are known as GRAVITATIONAL WAVES.

gravitational waves Tiny wave-like disturbances in the curvature of SPACE–TIME. Einstein's general theory of RELATIVITY predicts the existence of gravitational waves travelling from a source at the speed of light. They interact with matter in a manner somewhat similar to that of travelling tidal forces oscillating at right angles to the direction of propagation. Because GRAVITATION is a much weaker force than the electromagnetic force, the task of building gravitational wave detectors sensitive enough to measure such waves is very difficult. The achievement of sufficient sensitivity is the goal of a number of laboratories at the present time using laser INTERFEROMETRY between freely suspended masses separated by at least 1 km (0.6 miles) and much progress has been made since the pioneering work of the US physicist Joseph WEBER in the 1970s.

graviton (in atomic physics) The carrier of the gravitational force. Theories of fundamental interactions require that the fundamental forces have associated with them a particle to carry the force. The graviton has no mass, is stable, has a spin of 2, has no electrical charge and travels at the speed of light. The graviton interacts only very slightly with matter and so it is extremely hard to detect; the experimental evidence for its existence is inconclusive.

gravity The FORCE of attraction between the Earth and any other massive body within its gravitational field (see GRAVITATION). The gravitational force was first expressed mathematically by NEWTON in his *Principia* (published in 1687). He found that the force F between two bodies of masses m_1 and m_2, these bodies being a distance d apart, was given by $F = Gm_1m_2/d^2$. The constant of proportionality, G, is known as the **gravitational constant**. Newton also proved that a uniformly dense spherical body behaves gravitationally as if its mass were concentrated at a point, known as the **centre of mass** of the body. Thus the centre of the Earth is the point to which the force of gravity attracts all bodies on or near the Earth. All bodies fall towards the Earth with the acceleration of free fall (also called the acceleration due to gravity).

gravure printing An INTAGLIO printing process, in which the printing image is made up of a series of very small cells etched into the surface of a metal cylinder. When printing, the cylinder is flooded with liquid ink, and the surface is then scraped clean with a 'doctor blade'. This leaves ink only in the image areas, which are recessed into the cylinder. To transfer the image, paper is rolled against the cylinder under heavy pressure, and absorbs ink from the recessed cells. Gravure cylinders are expensive to produce, but the gravure process gives a high-quality product and can accommodate very long print runs. It is now used mainly for popular illustrated magazines.

Gray, Asa (1810–88) US botanist. He was the author of many textbooks which greatly popularized botany. Finding no conflict between evolution and his view of divine design in nature, he supported Darwin's theories at a time when they were anathema to many.

Gray, Thomas (1716–71) British poet. He first gained recognition with the poem 'Elegy Written in a Country Church-Yard' (1751), which remains his best-known work. It was written in Stoke Poges, Buckinghamshire, where he is buried. His other poems include two Pindaric odes, 'The Bard' (1757) and 'The Progress of Poesy' (1757); these mark a clear transition from neoclassical lucidity towards the obscure and the sublime and are regarded as precursors of romanticism.

grayling A species of fish, *Thymallus thymallus*, related to the salmon and trout in the family Salmonidae. It is distinguished by the adipose fin (a small dorsal fin near the tail) and high, many-rayed dorsal fin. It also has moderately large scales and is said to smell of thyme. Essentially a fish of fast-flowing, well-oxygenated, cool rivers, it is widely distributed throughout western Europe, although rare in some areas due to pollution. It is replaced in North America by the Arctic grayling, *T. arcticus*. Both species feed on bottom-living insect larvae, crustaceans, and molluscs, and also take flies at the surface.

graywacke See GREYWACKE.

Graz A city in southern Austria, capital of the state of Styria; pop. (1991) 232,155. Situated on the River Mur, it is the second-largest city in Austria. Its old buildings include a 15th-century Gothic cathedral and several medieval churches. Its industries include iron and steel, machinery, and chemicals.

Great Australian Bight A wide bay on the south coast of Australia, part of the Southern Ocean. Underlain by the continental shelf, its coast is lined with the cliffs of the Nullarbor Plain.

Great Barrier Reef A coral reef in the western Pacific, off the coast of Queensland, Australia. It extends for about 2,000 km (1,250 miles), roughly parallel to the coast and is the largest coral reef in the world. It is studded with some 700 small islands or 'cays' formed by the deposition of detritus on the reef exposed at low tide and anchored by vegetation. Island groups from north to south include the Tropical North Islands, Whitsunday Islands, Southern Reef Islands, and Fraser and Moreton Bay Islands. There are only 10 navigable passages penetrating the reef, often found opposite river mouths where fresh water and silt inhibit coral growth. The Great Barrier Reef was declared a marine park in 1979 and a world heritage site by UNESCO.

Great Bear See URSA MAJOR.

Great Bear Lake A large lake in the North-west Territories, Canada, the largest lake wholly in Canada and fourth-largest in North America; area 31,328 sq km (12,095 sq miles). It drains into the Mackenzie River via the Great Bear River.

Great Britain See UNITED KINGDOM.

Great Britain, SS The most important of I. K. BRUNEL's three ship designs. The *Great Britain* was a large iron STEAMSHIP driven by a screw PROPELLER, designed as a transatlantic liner. It was the first large, screw-driven iron ship to be built, and it embodied many other constructional innovations, such as a double bottom to the hull, and bulk-heads dividing the ship into watertight compartments.

great circles The circles that can be described on the surface of a sphere with their planes passing through its centre: they are the largest circles it is possible to draw on a sphere. Round the Earth, opposite meridians meet at the poles and thus form great circles; and the Equator is one, although other parallels of latitude are not. When a great circle passes through two particular points it represents the shortest distance between them and is generally followed by ships and aircraft when unimpeded by bad weather, mountains, or other obstacles.

Great Dividing Range (or **Great Divide**) the crest of the Eastern Highlands of Australia, curving roughly parallel to the coast for almost its entire north-south length from Cape York in Queensland to the Grampians of Victoria.

Greater Antilles See ANTILLES.

Greater London A metropolitan area comprising central LONDON and the surrounding regions; area 1,579 sq km (610 sq miles); pop. (1991) 6,378,600. From 1965 to 1986 the whole metropolitan area was administered by the Greater London Council. After the abolition of the GLC by a Conservative government, its functions were transferred to the City of London, 12 Inner London Boroughs, and 20 Outer London Boroughs. In 1998 a referendum accepted the government's proposal for a Mayor of London to take office in 2000.

Greater Manchester A metropolitan county of north-west England; area 1,287 sq km (497 sq miles); pop. (1991) 2,445,200. It is divided into 10 administrative metropolitan districts.

Great Exhibition A major international trade exhibition held in London in 1851 under the sponsorship of Prince Albert. It was housed in the vast Crystal Palace, designed by Joseph Paxton (1801–65), built in London's Hyde Park entirely of glass and iron, except for the flooring and joists. The exhibition, which lasted 23 weeks, attracted 17,000 exhibitors and more than 6 million visitors. The profits were invested, and are still being used, to promote education and science. The Crystal Palace was dismantled and moved to the London suburb of Sydenham, where it burnt down in 1936.

Great Glen (or **Glen More**) A glen or valley in the Highlands of Scotland extending from the Moray Firth south-west for 96 km (60 miles) to Loch Linnhe. It is traversed by the Caledonian Canal and contains the 37 km-(23 miles-)long Loch Ness. The glen has been excavated along a zone of weakness caused by the Great Glen Fault.

Great Indian Desert See THAR DESERT.

Great Lakes A group of five large inter-connected lakes in central North America, consisting of Lakes Superior, Michigan, Huron, Erie, and Ontario. With the exception of Lake Michigan, which is wholly within the USA, they lie on the Canada–US border. They constitute the largest area of fresh water in the world. Connected to the Atlantic Ocean by the St Lawrence Seaway, they form an important commercial waterway. The total surface area of the lakes is *c.*245,300 sq km (94,747 sq miles). Lake Superior, the largest and deepest of the lakes, is the largest lake in North America and second-largest lake in the world. The Great Lakes were formed at the end of the last Ice Age when glacially eroded basins were filled with meltwater. The first Europeans to explore the Great Lakes in the 17th century were French fur traders, notably Etienne Brulé, Samuel de Champlain, and Robert LaSalle.

Great Leap Forward (1958) Chinese drive for industrial and agricultural expansion through 'backyard' industries in the countryside and increased production quotas to be reached by the people's devotion to patriotic and socialist ideals. Massive increases in the quantity of production were announced, but quality and distribution posed serious problems. In agriculture, COMMUNES became almost universal, but disastrous harvests resulting in famine with an estimated 13 million victims, together with poor products discredited the Leap. Its most important advocate, MAO ZEDONG, took a back seat until the late 1960s. The CULTURAL REVOLUTION can be seen partly as his attempt to reintroduce radical policies.

Great Ouse See OUSE.

Great Plague (1664–65) A disastrous epidemic, mainly confined to London and south-east England. Bubonic plague had recurred at intervals since the Middle Ages, but there had been no serious outbreak for thirty years and its violent reappearance was not expected. About a fifth of London's population of almost half a million died. Business in the city came to a standstill. The court and all those able to move into the countryside prudently did so, as the disease was less virulent there. At the height of the epidemic plague pits were dug to receive the dead, and hand-carts were taken from house to house, collecting the bodies. The FIRE OF LONDON in the following year destroyed many of the close-packed slums in which the plague flourished, and after 1665 the disease disappeared from London.

Great Plains A vast area of plains to the east of the Rocky Mountains in North America, extending from the valley of the Mackenzie River in Canada to southern Texas.

Great Red Spot A huge oval hurricane system in the outer atmosphere of Jupiter's Southern Hemisphere at a latitude of 20 degrees south. 14,000 km wide and 24,000–40,000 km long, it has persisted for at least three centuries, being first recorded by the British scientist Robert Hooke in 1664. It is not a fixed feature but drifts westwards at the rate of about 0.5 degrees per day and oscillates relative to the north–south axis by about 1,800 km every 90 days. Infrared observations indicate that the spot is an anticyclonic high-pressure region that is much colder than its surroundings and elevated about 8 km above the adjacent clouds.

Great Rift Valley The most extensive system of rift valleys in the world, a geological fault system running some 6,400 km (4,000 miles) from the Jordan valley in Israel, along the Red Sea into Ethiopia, and through Kenya, Tanzania, and Malawi into Mozambique. It is marked by a series of steep-sided lakes such as Lakes Turkana, Tanganyika, and

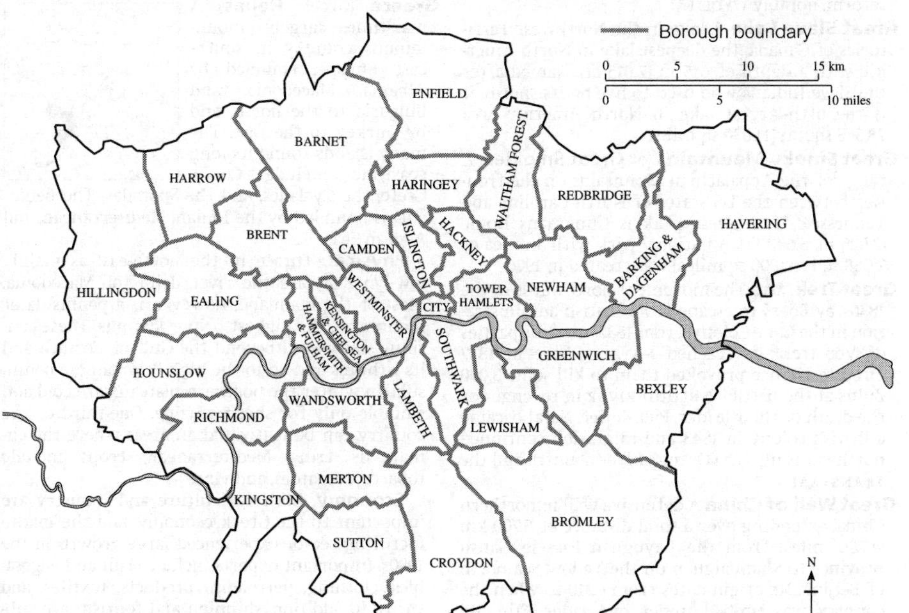

Greater London The 32 boroughs.

Nyasa, and a series of volcanoes including Mt. Kilimanjaro.

Great Salt Lake A salt lake in northern Utah, USA, near Salt Lake City, bounded by the Great Salt Lake Desert to the west and the Wasatch Mountain Range to the east. It is the largest salt lake in north America; area *c.*2,590 sq km (1,000 sq miles). The lake is a remnant of the prehistoric Lake Bonneville which once covered an extensive area of the Great Basin.

Great Sandy Desert (or **Empty Quarter**; Arabic **Rub' al Khali**) A vast sandy desert on the Arabian peninsula stretching from the Nejd of central Saudi Arabia to the Hadhramaut of Yemen and frequented by Bedouin of the Murra and Rashidi tribes. The first European crossing was made by Bertram Thomas in 1930–31, with later explorations by Harry St John Philby and William Thesiger.

Great Schism Two breaches in the Christian Church. The Great or EAST-WEST SCHISM (1054) marked the separation of the Eastern (Orthodox) and Western Christian churches. The Great Schism of 1378–1417 resulted from the removal of the papacy from Italy to France in 1309. Feuds among the Italian cardinals and their allies among the Italian nobility led to Pope Clement V (1305–14) moving the papal residence from Rome to Avignon in southern France. French interests came to dominate papal policy and the popes, notorious for their luxurious way of life, commanded scant respect. An attempt to return the papacy to Rome was followed by schism as two rival popes were elected by the cardinals, Urban VI by the Roman faction and Clement VI by the French faction. The period of popes and rival ANTIPOPES lasted until the Council of CONSTANCE (1417) elected Pope Martin V of the Roman party and deposed his French rival. The division of the papacy discredited the Church and was criticized by those demanding reform, notably WYCLIF.

Great Slave Lake A lake in the Northwest Territories of Canada, the deepest lake in North America, with a depth of 615 m (2,015 ft). Named after the Slave Indians who used to live on its shores, it is the fifth-largest lake in North America; area 28,568 sq km (11,030 sq miles).

Great Smoky Mountains (or **Great Smokies**) A range of the Appalachian Mountains on the frontier between the US states of North Carolina and Tennessee. Its highest peak is Clingmans Dome (2,025 m, 6,643 ft). A national park with an area of 2,068 sq km (800 sq miles) was created in 1926.

Great Trek, the The movement northwards in the 1830s by Boers to escape from British administration in the Cape Colony. From 1835 onwards parties of Voortrekkers reached NATAL, where in 1837 ZULU resistance provoked them to kill some 3,000 Zulus at the battle of BLOOD RIVER in revenge for the death of their leader, Piet Retief. Natal became a British colony in 1843 and migration continued northwards into the Orange River country and the TRANSVAAL.

Great Wall of China A defensive wall in northern China, extending over a total distance of 6,700 km (4,200 miles) from the Jiayuguan Pass in Gansu province to Shanhaiguan on the Yellow Sea north of Beijing. Its origin dates from *c.*210 BC when the country was unified under one ruler (Qin Shi Huang), and the northern walls of existing rival states were linked to form a continuous protection against nomad invaders. It was rebuilt in medieval times largely against the Mongols, and the present wall dates from the Ming Dynasty (1368–1544). Although principally a defensive wall it served also as a means of communication, and is said to be the only man-made feature that would be visible from a space orbit.

Great Yarmouth A port and resort town on the coast of Norfolk, eastern England; pop. (1991) 89,000. Once an important fishing port, it now services the North Sea oil industry.

Great Zimbabwe The massive ruins of a city in Zimbabwe, 28 km (17 miles) south-east of Masvingo, dating from the 13th–15th centuries when it prospered in connection with the Arab gold trade.

greaved turtle (or **Arrau turtle**) The largest of the side-necked turtles, which has a shell-length of up to 90 cm (35 inches) and a weight of up to 90 kg (200 pounds). It is a member of the family Pelomedusidae, and is found mainly in tributaries of the Amazon and Orinoco rivers of South America. Local people take adult turtles and eggs for food and oil, and the greaved turtle has become an endangered species.

Greaves, James (known as 'Jimmy') (1940–) British footballer. He made his début as a striker for Chelsea in 1957, going on to join AC Milan, Tottenham Hotspur, and West Ham United and scoring 357 goals in 517 league matches. He also won 57 international caps (from 1959), scoring 44 goals. After his retirement he became a television football presenter.

grebe Any one of some 21 species of duck in the family Podicipedidae. They differ from other ducks in having lobed toes, pointed bills, slender erectly held necks, and practically no tails. They rarely come to land, even building their nests on water. The grebes have a worldwide distribution. The little grebe, *Tachybaptus ruficollis*, and a few other small grebes are known as DABCHICKS.

Greco, El See EL GRECO.

Greece (Greek **Hellas**) A maritime, largely mountainous country in south-east Europe, bounded by Albania, Macedonia, and Bulgaria to the north, and by Turkey to the east. The many islands round its long coastline include Corfu, Crete, the Cyclades, and the Sporades. The peninsula is bounded by the Ionian, Mediterranean, and Aegean Seas.

Physical. Thrace in the north-east is mainly low-lying, as are the river deltas of Macedonia. Most of the mainland, however, is a peninsula of mountains, the highest being Olympus. These continue southward beyond the Gulf of Corinth and its isthmus and on to the high Peloponnese peninsula. In winter the northern plateaux are cold and suitable only for sheep grazing. One-third of the country can be cultivated; in areas where the climate is truly Mediterranean, crops include tobacco, tomatoes, and vines.

Economy. Both agriculture and industry are important to the Greek economy, and the manufacturing sector experienced large growth in the 1980s. Important exports include fruit and vegetables, clothing, petroleum products, textiles, and yarns. In addition, shipping and tourism are substantial earners of foreign exchange.

History. Greek history begins *c.*2000–1700 BC with the arrival in the mainland of Greek-speaking peoples from the north. There followed the MYCE-

NAEAN CIVILIZATION which flourished until overthrown by the DORIANS at the end of the 12th century BC. After an obscure period of history (the Greek 'Dark Ages') the city-state (polis) emerged.

In the early 5th century the Greeks repulsed Persian attempts to annex their land. ATHENS and SPARTA were now the major sea and land powers respectively, and after a prolonged struggle it was Sparta who by 404 had crushed Athens and destroyed the Athenian empire in the PELOPONNESIAN WAR. In the 4th century THEBES toppled Sparta, but Greece as a whole was soon forced to bow before an outside conqueror – PHILIP II of Macedonia. After the death of his son, ALEXANDER III (the Great), the Greek world was dominated by the Hellenistic kingdoms with the cities of Greece playing comparatively minor parts in the power struggle. Then Rome intervened in the MACEDONIAN WARS, until the year 146 BC saw the defeat of the Achaean League (see ACHAEA), the sacking of Corinth, and the final incorporation of Greece into the Roman empire. Later it was part of the BYZANTINE EMPIRE, but fell under the control of the Ottoman Turks in 1460. It remained under Turkish jurisdiction, apart from a brief period in the late 17th and early 18th centuries when Venice controlled parts of the country, until independence in the early 19th century.

The GREEK WAR OF INDEPENDENCE (1821–33) resulted in the establishment of an independent Greece, with Duke Otto of Bavaria as king. Otto was deposed in 1862 and a Danish prince, William, installed, taking the title George I of the Hellenes (1863–1913). A military coup established a republic (1924–35). GEORGE II was restored in 1935 but fled into exile in 1941. After repulsing an attempted invasion by Italian forces in 1940, Greece was occupied by the Germans in World War II, and the country suffered bitter fighting between rival factions of communists and royalists. The monarchy was restored by the British in 1946, and civil war broke out, lasting until 1949, when the communists were defeated. With the help of aid from the USA, recovery and reconstruction began. Field-Marshal Alexandros Papagos became civilian Prime Minister (1952–55). In 1967 a military coup took place. King Constantine II fled to Rome and government by a military junta (the 'Colonels') lasted for seven years, the monarchy being abolished in 1973. A civilian republic was established in 1974 and in the 1981 general election Andreas Papandreou became the first socialist Prime Minister, remaining in office until 1989. Greece had joined the European Community in 1981, whose agricultural policies boosted its economy; but as tariff barriers were reduced, a balance-of-payments crisis developed. During 1992 strong opposition emerged against the name of the proposed republic of Macedonia, since Greece regards its own northern province as having sole right to the name. This issue and that of the ailing economy led ultimately to the fall of the right-wing government of Constantine Mitsotakis in June 1993. Andreas Papandreou was subsequently returned to power; his government officially opposed the recognition of Macedonia by other EUROPEAN UNION countries. A dispute over territorial waters in the Aegean threatened war with Turkey in late 1994, while Greece rejected a Serbian proposal for a confederation between Greece, Macedonia, and Serbia. Relations between Greece and Turkey further deteriorated in June 1995. In 1996, Costas Simitis became Prime Minister, replacing Papandreou, who had resigned due to ill-health; shortly afterwards, Papandreou died.

Capital: Athens
Area: 131,957 sq km (50,949 sq mi)
Population: 10,493,000 (1995)
Currency: 1 drachma = 100 lepta
Religions: Greek Orthodox 97.6%; Roman Catholic 0.4%; Protestant 0.1%; Muslim 1.5%
Ethnic Groups: Greek 95.5%; Macedonian 1.5%; Turkish 0.9%; Albanian 0.6%
Languages: Greek (official); minority languages
International Organizations: UN; EU; NATO; OECD; Council of Europe; CSCE

Greek The Indo-European language of Greece, in its ancient form spoken in the Balkan peninsula from the 2nd millennium BC; the earliest evidence is to be found in the Linear B tablets dating from 1500 BC. Like Latin, it was a highly inflected language with strict rules and rather complicated grammar. The alphabet normally used as adapted from the Phoenician *c.*1000 BC; the capitals have remained unaltered, and the lower case letters have developed from them. There were four main dialects, but with the rise of Athens the dialect of the city (Attic) predominated and formed the basis of the Koine, which became the standard dialect from the 3rd century BC onwards. It was the official language of the Byzantine empire, but in the four centuries when Greece was under Turkish rule oral speech and dialects developed unchallenged. Today Greek is spoken by some 10 million people in mainland Greece and the Aegean archipelago, and is the official language of Greece. Modern Greek has changed from ancient Greek in various ways; some vowels, dipthongs, and consonants have changed or modified their sounds, there are fewer grammatical forms, and the structure is simpler. Two forms of the language are in use: demotic, the common language, and *katharevousa*, an imitation of classical Greek, which has been revived for literary purposes. Demotic is gaining ground not only for conversation but also in literature.

Greek art and architecture The art and architecture of Greek-speaking societies from the beginning of the IRON AGE (11th century BC) to the late 1st century BC. Earlier (BRONZE AGE) art of the Greek mainland and islands (with the exception of Crete, where there was a distinct tradition called MINOAN art) is known as Mycenaean art, and later Greek art, known as HELLENISTIC ART, is considered part of the culture of the Roman Empire. Solid bronze statuettes of men, and particularly horses, are the earliest Greek sculpture. The first nearly life-sized statues were made about 650 BC in stone. In the beginning of this, the 'Archaic Period', the sculptor, to avoid cutting the stone deeply, rendered features and muscles as markings on the surface. Sculptors of the 6th and early 5th centuries studied the forms of the body, gradually working out its proportions. Statues were painted throughout the Greek period. Many, buried in the debris after the Persians had sacked the Athenian Acropolis (citadel) in 480 BC, were excavated with their colour still preserved. The victories over the Persians in the early 5th century BC found characteristic expression in grander sculpture, as at Olympia. Myron's Discobolos, an athlete hurling the discus, made in about 450 BC, was originally in bronze, but survives only in Roman marble copies. Indeed most sculptors of this period worked in bronze. Few life-size bronzes survive, except in copies, but we have one, by an unknown sculptor, which must be among the greatest – the bronze statue of Zeus hurling a thunderbolt, found in the sea off Cape Artemisium, and dated about 470–460 BC. In the 5th century emotion was shown in the whole figure rather than in the face, which was generally shown with calm features. Fourth-century sculptors such as Scopas concentrated on representing intellect and emotion through the face, and this led to the development of PORTRAITURE. as demonstrated by the works of PRAXITELES (mid-4th century BC), who worked mainly in marble.

Greek architecture has an equally long and distinguished history. Early Greek temples were small hut-like buildings of rubble or mudbrick, sometimes thatched. Colonnaded temples of stone were rare before the 6th century. The design was simple – a rectangular building on a foundation of usually three steps, with columns (see ORDERS OF ARCHITECTURE) at the porch, at either end, or all round. The Greeks did not use the ARCH. Figure sculpture in the round filled the triangular gable (pediment) at each end of the building, and reliefs were carved on the horizontal beams supported by the columns. Pediment figures with elaborate scenes of movement have been preserved from temples at Aegina (early 5th century), Olympia, and the Parthenon (mid-5th century BC). (See ELGIN). Little is left of large-scale Greek wall-painting, except for some remarkable tomb paintings of the 4th and 3rd centuries BC, notably the royal tombs at Vergina, Macedonia. The Greeks were adept at other arts: superb bronzeworks have been found at Vix in central France (*c*.500 BC), for example. Greek art did not end with the Roman conquest of Greece, or even with the transition from the ancient to the medieval world; it developed as Hellenistic art and later as BYZANTINE ART, and has been at the foundation of the art of western Europe.

Greek astronomy The Greeks were, so far as we know, the first people to make planned observations in order to determine the size and structure of the Universe. Thales of Miletus is said to have improved the art of navigation by the stars, borrowing ideas from the Phoenicians, and to have used Babylonian tables to forecast an eclipse of the Sun in 585 BC. His pupil Anaximander thought the heavenly bodies were holes in tubes of mist containing wheels of fire circling the Earth. Pythagoras of Samos and his followers thought that the Earth and other heavenly bodies (including the Sun) were spherical, moving in perfect circles about an invisible central fire. A second phase in Greek astronomy was the more systematic teaching at Plato's Academy and Aristotle's Lyceum in Athens. Plato (*c*.429–347 BC) adopted the Pythagorean ideal of circular motion but preferred a GEOCENTRIC SYSTEM; he encouraged astronomical speculation as an exercise to improve the mind, but discouraged observation. Aristotle (384–322 BC), originally a follower of Plato, gradually moved away from this position, but retained a geocentric model. The flowering of Greek observational astronomy came in the third phase, the Hellenistic Age (3rd century BC to 2nd century AD), when the main centre of learning was Alexandria. Outstanding astronomers of this period were ARISTARCHUS, the first known proponent of a HELIOCENTRIC SYSTEM; ERATOSTHENES, who determined the size of the Earth; HIPPARCHUS, probably the greatest astronomer of antiquity; and Ptolemy, whose Ptolemaic system, described in the *Almagest*, was accepted as essentially correct for well over a thousand years.

Greek fire A combustible composition set alight on contact with water. It was invented around 673 AD by Kallinikos, a Syrian architect in Byzantine service. Its main ingredients were probably naphtha and quicklime, which started burning on contact with water. It was first used against Arab ships besieging Constantinople in 674–76 AD.

Greek literature, classical The earliest European literary works are the epic masterpieces the *Iliad* and the *Odyssey*, attributed to HOMER. Lyric poetry, for choral performance, together with the song and dance in the ceremonies honouring Dionysus in Athens, laid the foundations for the GREEK THEATRE, both TRAGEDY and COMEDY. IAMBIC VERSE was employed especially for invective by poets like Archilochus (7th century BC); the METRE, well suited to more colloquial speech, went on to be the vehicle for the non-choral parts of drama. Elegiac verse was widely employed, for epitaphs and even, as by Solon (*c*.630–*c*.560 BC), for political exhortation. The great age of oratory, however, is the 4th century, the most notable name being that of the Athenian Demosthenes (384–322 BC). At this time, too, literature and philosophy were married to wonderful effect in the dialogues of PLATO, whose pupil Aristotle (384–322 BC) was to create for Western civilization a whole vocabulary of literary, philosophic, and scientific thinking. By this time 'Old Comedy', with its free criticism, gave place in a less libertarian world to the stereotypes of 'New Comedy'. This marked the end of the classical age of Greek literature *c*.320 BC, though what followed was interesting in itself and important for its effect on LATIN LITERATURE, which was developing at the same time. The next period of Greek literature reached its peak in Hellenistic Alexandria, where a number of major writers were employed. CALLIMACHUS' poetry is noted for its brevity, sophistication, and inventiveness in form. Apollonius of Rhodes (3rd century BC), in his long poem on the voyage of the Argonauts, adapted the language of Homer to a romantic epic, while Theocritus (*c*.270 BC) broke altogether new ground with his *idylls*, which do not restrict themselves to the pastoral. He was followed by the biographer and philosopher PLUTARCH (*c*.46–126 AD), whose *Parallel Lives* was later to supply, for example, the material for some of Shakespeare's plays. Most Greek poetry which survives from the period after the Alexandrian Age is in the form of epigram. An attractive product of later Greek literature was the witty and satirical œuvre of the prose-writer Lucian (*c*.120–after 180 AD) whose *True History* influenced such writers as Rabelais and Swift. A reaction against the extravagance of some Asian Greek oratory initiated a period of 'Atticism', when the restraint and even the vocabulary of the earlier Athenian orators became the norm. Such antiquarianism set its mark on literature for many centuries, affecting both the great Christian writers of the 4th century and their Byzantine successors until the fall of Constantinople in 1453.

Greek-Persian wars Conflicts that dominated the history of the eastern Mediterranean in the first half of the 5th century BC. In 499 BC the Greek cities of Ionia in Asia Minor revolted from the Persian empire. With some short-lived support from Athens and Eretria, they captured and burnt the important city of Sardis, but gradually the Persians regained control, the Greek fleet being finally crushed at Lade in 494. In 490 a Persian expeditionary force sailed across the Aegean. The capture of Eretria – the first goal – was achieved after a week-long siege and with help from Eretrian traitors. The Persians then landed in Attica but after a defeat at MARATHON they were forced to withdraw to Persia.

In 480 a much larger invasion force threatened Greece, advancing along the northern and western shores of the Aegean. A small Greek army and a large Greek fleet were positioned respectively at THERMOPYLAE and Artemisium, but despite vigorous fighting on land and sea the Greeks were forced to withdraw to the Isthmus of Corinth. With central Greece lost, the Athenians evacuated their city, while the Greek fleet, at THEMISTOCLES' urging, lured the Persians into battle off SALAMIS. In these narrow waters the Greek warships had the advantage and won a decisive victory which caused the Persian king XERXES to withdraw to Asia. Mardonius, his second-in-command, remained to continue the campaign with the army. In 479 Greeks and Persians met at Plataea. The Greeks were eventually successful, the Spartans and their Tegean allies ensuring victory when they overcame the élite Immortals (the Persian royal bodyguards) and killed Mardonius. Meanwhile a Greek fleet was winning another great victory off Mycale in Asia Minor. Soon afterwards some of the Greeks formed the DELIAN LEAGUE to be the instrument by which they would continue the war against the Persians.

Greek religion The religion of the ancient Greek world. It was polytheistic, involving the worship of several gods and goddesses. The most important deities were the sky-god Zeus (ruler of Olympus), his wife Hera (goddess of marriage), Poseidon (god of sea and earthquakes), the virgin goddess Athene (learning and the arts), Apollo and his sister Artemis (Sun and Moon, the one patron of music and poetry, the other of chastity and hunting), Hephaestus (fire and metalwork), Aphrodite (love and beauty), Ares (war), Demeter (crops), Hestia (hearth and home), and Hermes, the messenger of the gods. Although all were revered, different cities had different individual gods as their special patrons.

Greek theatre The drama of the ancient and classical eras of Greece. It was characteristically performed on a flat, circular space containing the altar of Dionysus, called the *orchestra*, where the CHORUS sang and danced and the actors spoke. The *skene* or stage-buildings were at first very simple, and the audience sat on wood or stone seats, rising around the orchestra. Plays were performed in the open air and in daylight. A notable tradition of drama grew up in Athens, where both COMEDY and TRAGEDY were regularly performed at the festival of Dionysus, a god of the fertility of nature associated with religious rites. Poets presented three tragedies (often not connected in theme) and a satyr play (lighter in tone). Prizes were given for the best poet, and the victor was wreathed in ivy. Early developments are obscure, but the Attic poet Thespis (*c*.534 BC) is said to have made the decisive step of introducing an actor whose role it was to conduct a dialogue with the chorus. The Athenian AESCHYLUS is said to have brought in a second actor, SOPHOCLES a third. Though the choral element remained important, its changing character can be traced in the surviving plays of the three great exponents of tragedy, Aeschylus, Sophocles, and EURIPIDES. The subject-matter of Greek tragedy is almost always mythological, though occasionally contemporary events could be presented, as in Aeschylus' *Persians*. ARISTOTLE's precepts for the best kind of tragedy, given in his *Poetics*, do not fit many of the surviving plays. In 'Old Comedy' (*c*.5th century BC), which we can properly judge only from ARISTOPHANES, and which presented political, literary and philosophical parodies interspersed with personal lampooning, the chorus again plays an important part. Its address to the audience in the poet's name, and unconnected with the action of the drama, is known as the *parabasis*, and its grotesque costume, with the phallus *de rigueur* for male roles, symbolizes the irreverence that governed the whole occasion. After a transitional 'Middle Comedy' (*c*.400–*c*.320 BC), we come to 'New Comedy', starting in the last part of the 4th century BC and now easier to recapture in the newly discovered *Ill-Tempered Man* of MENANDER. It contains little contemporary reference, and its domestic plots and characters are largely stereotyped. There is a regular division into five acts, and the dramatic chorus, once the representative of forces larger than life, has either completely disappeared or become a small band of musicians and dancers who provide light entertainment. Both Greek tragedy and 'New Comedy' had their imitators in Latin (see LATIN LITERATURE). See also THEATRE.

Greek War of Independence (1821–32) The revolt by Greek subjects of the OTTOMAN EMPIRE against Turkish domination. It had its origins in the nationalistic ideas of the Hetairia Philike ('Society of Friends'), who chose Alexander Ypsilanti, a Russian general, and son of the ruler of Wallachia, to lead the revolt. Links were established with Romanian peasants, Serb rebels, and Ali Pasha, the warlord of western Greece. Ypsilanti crossed into Turkish territory in March 1821, but only after his defeat in June did the Greeks rebel. Although atrocities took place on both sides, the revolt gained the popular support of the Christian world and many foreign volunteers (of whom Lord Byron, who went out in 1823, was the most celebrated) joined the Greek forces. By the end of 1821 the Greeks had achieved striking successes on land and sea and in January 1822 an assembly met to declare Greece independent. Four years later, however, Mehemet Ali of Egypt reconquered the Peloponnese and threatened to restore Turkish control. At the Treaty of London in 1827, Britain and Russia offered to mediate and secure an autonomous Greek state. When the Turks refused, Britain, Russia, and France sent a combined fleet which destroyed the Egyptian fleet at Navarino (1827). The following year the Russian army seized Adrianople and threatened Constantinople. The Turks agreed to make peace (1829), and the Conference of London (1832) confirmed Greek independence. The following year a Bavarian prince, Otto I, was crowned King of GREECE.

Green (in politics) An advocate of a political system promoting policies that safeguard the environment. The Green movement is made up of numerous pressure groups, national and international, as well as Green political parties in many countries. Pressure groups include **Friends of the Earth**, **Greenpeace** (known for direct actions to defend species, such as whales, and environments), and the **World Wide Fund for Nature**. Green parties have enjoyed limited political success since their emergence in the early 1970s. The German Green Party won sufficient support in the 1987 federal elections to secure it 42 seats in the national parliament (*Bundestag*). The world's first was the Values Party founded in New Zealand in 1972, closely followed by the British Ecology Party (now known as the Green Party) in 1973.

Greenaway, Kate (full name Catherine Greenaway) (1846–1901) British artist. She is known especially for her illustrations of children's books such as *Under the Windows* (1879) and *Mother Goose* (1881). An annual award for the best children's book illustration in Britain is named after her.

Greenaway, Peter (1942–) British film director. Greenaway first won substantial critical recognition with *The Draughtsman's Contract* (1982). His often contrived and controversial works are concerned with sex, human mutability, and gamesmanship; among his later films are *The Cook, The Thief, His Wife, and Her Lover* (1989), *Prospero's Books* (1991), and *The Baby of Mâcon* (1993).

Greene, (Henry) Graham (1904–91) British novelist. He became a Roman Catholic in 1926; the moral paradoxes of his faith underlie much of his work. Well-known works that explore religious themes include *Brighton Rock* (1938), *The Power and the Glory* (1940), and *Travels with My Aunt* (1969). Among his other novels are thrillers, which Greene classed as 'entertainments', such as his first successful novel, *Stamboul Train* (1932), and *The Third Man* (1950); the latter was originally written as a screenplay and filmed in 1949.

greenfinch A sparrow-sized, greenish-yellow Eurasian bird, *Carduelis chloris*, with bright yellow patches in the wings and tail and a powerful beak. It is common in mixed woodland and open country over wide areas of Europe and western Asia. As a seed-eating species, it often comes to bird-tables in winter. In eastern Asia there is also a similar species, the oriental greenfinch.

greenfly See APHID.

greengage Any one of several varieties of a tree of the genus *Prunus*, regarded by some authorities as a subspecies of the European PLUM, and by others as a separate species. Their small, round fruits differ from plums in having green or greenish-yellow skin, greenish-brown flesh, and a stone that does not separate easily from the flesh.

Greenham Common The site of a former US airbase near Newbury in Berkshire, southern England, the scene of a women's protest against the deployment of US cruise missiles that lasted from 1981 until the withdrawal of missiles in 1990 following the end of the Cold War.

greenhouse A building of glass or clear plastic supported by a light framework of wood or metal, used to grow plants more quickly than would be possible out of doors, or to grow plants that would not normally flourish in the local climate. Greenhouses provide the maximum possible light to an enclosed area, and tend to trap and retain heat. In most cases the temperature and humidity levels are artificially controlled. See also HYDROPONICS.

greenhouse effect The retention of heat by the lower layer of the Earth's atmosphere. Just as the glass of a greenhouse is transparent to sunlight but opaque to the infrared radiation emitted by the warmed surfaces within, so certain atmos-

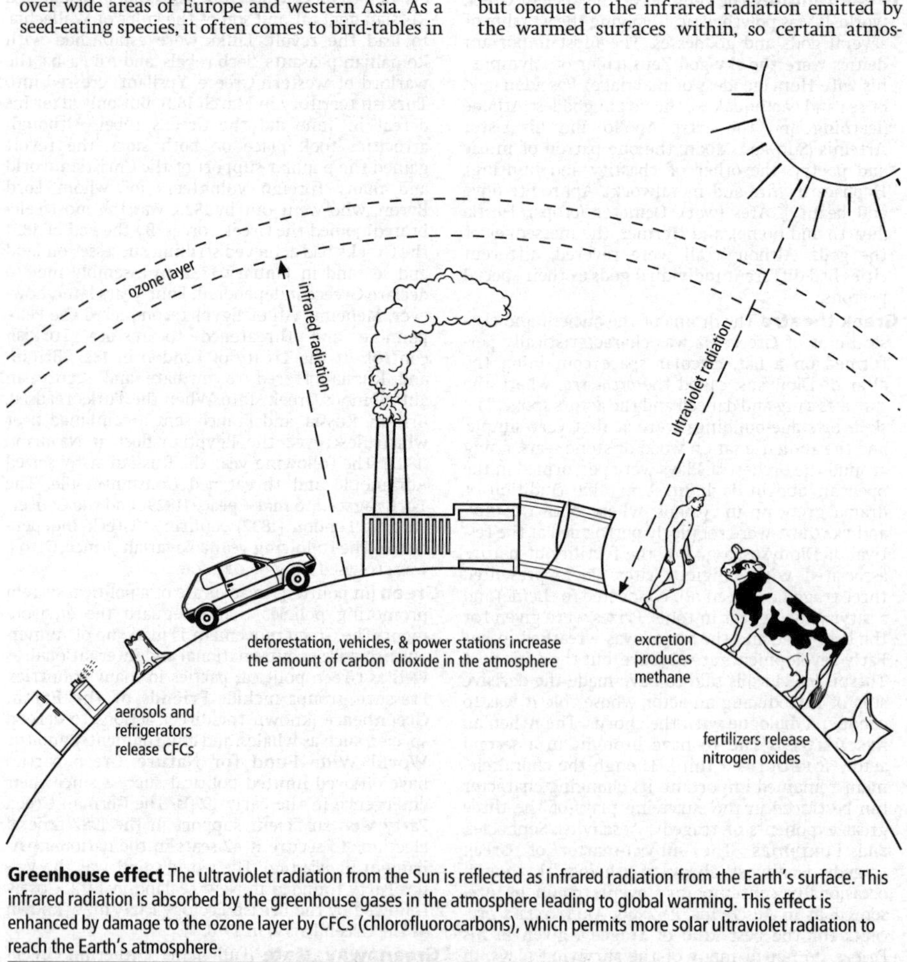

Greenhouse effect The ultraviolet radiation from the Sun is reflected as infrared radiation from the Earth's surface. This infrared radiation is absorbed by the greenhouse gases in the atmosphere leading to global warming. This effect is enhanced by damage to the ozone layer by CFCs (chlorofluorocarbons), which permits more solar ultraviolet radiation to reach the Earth's atmosphere.

pheric gases (including water vapour, CARBON DIOXIDE, METHANE, and CHLOROFLUOROCARBONS, known collectively as greenhouse gases) allow sunlight (especially its ultraviolet component) to pass unimpeded but absorb infrared radiation from the Earth's surface. The atmospheric concentration of carbon dioxide has increased by an average of more than 15 per cent in the last hundred years or so, due mainly to the burning of such FOSSIL FUELS as coal, gas, and oil. This, combined with DEFORESTATION, is leading to a continuing increase in the amount of carbon dioxide in the atmosphere. Many scientists believe that such an increase in greenhouse gases may lead to global warming as a result of this greenhouse effect. There are many uncertainties over the rate at which greenhouse gases accumulate and the resulting consequences, but scientists of the Intergovernmental Panel on Climate Change (IPCC) have estimated that a doubling of the present carbon dioxide concentration (or its equivalent in other gases) could cause a rise in the average surface temperature of 1 to 3.5°C and that such a doubling may occur by late in the 21st century unless steps are taken to reduce the emission of greenhouse-gases. Under the Kyoto Protocol agreed at a Conference of the Parties to the UN Framework Convention on Climate Change held in Kyoto in December 1997, nations agreed to reduce emissions at the global level by about 65.2 per cent by 2012. The agreement allowed nations to trade emission permits, by sponsoring emission-reducing projects in other countries as an alternative to curtailing their own emissions by an equivalent amount. Most approaches to emission reduction involved increasing the efficiency with which ENERGY is used, encouraging this reduction by 'green taxes' on fuels, while also encouraging nuclear energy and renewable energy sources as alternatives to fossil fuels.

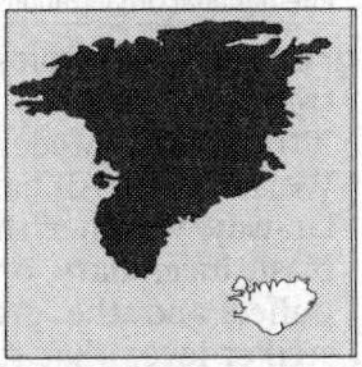

Greenland (Danish **Grønland**; Inuit **Kalaallit Nunaat**) An island, the largest in the world, lying to the north-east of North America and mostly within the Arctic Circle; area *c.*2,175,600 sq km (840,325 sq miles), of which 16 per cent is ice-free; pop. (1993) 55,100, mostly Inuit; capital, Nuuk (Godthåb). It was discovered and named by the Norse explorer Eric the Red in 986 and settled in coastal pockets by Norse colonists. Although only five per cent of Greenland is habitable, it was from 1721 resettled by the Danes, and became part of Denmark in 1953, with internal autonomy from 1979; it withdrew from the EC in 1985. The economy of Greenland is largely based on inshore and deep-water fishing.

Green Paper See BILL.

green revolution An agricultural programme of the 1960s and 1970s, funded by private charities and governments of the industrialized nations, that attempted to solve the problems of Third World hunger by a package of measures to improve crop yields. The package comprised high-yielding varieties of cereal crops combined with mechanization, increased use of FERTILIZERS to increase yields, PESTICIDES to combat disease, and water for irrigation. Large increases in crop yields were achieved in many Asian countries, for example India and the Philippines. However, since the mid-1980s yields have levelled off, and there has been criticism of the programme, as in some places it has tended to benefit the large landowner at the expense of smaller farmers.

greensand A marine SANDSTONE containing the green mineral glauconite, of which it is the main source. Common in CRETACEOUS and Eocene sediments, it is found especially in New Jersey and Delaware on the coastal plains of the eastern USA. Modern greensands are forming off the coasts of Africa, Australia, and northern America, among other places.

In Europe the term Greensand is used as the name of a stratigraphical division of the Cretaceous Period.

greenshank A grey and white SANDPIPER, *Tringa nebularia*, resembling a redshank, *Tringa totanus*, but distinguished from them by having no wing-bar, green legs, and a longer and slightly upcurved beak. They breed as far apart as Sunderland, UK, and the former Soviet Union, and winter as far south as southern Africa and Australia.

Greenwich A borough of east-central London, England, to the south of the River Thames; pop. (1991) 200,800. It was the site of the Royal Observatory, founded in 1675 by Charles II, in a building designed by Christopher Wren. Soon after World War II the observatory was moved to Herstmonceux in East Sussex. The buildings at Greenwich itself, together with many of the old instruments, now form part of the National Maritime Museum. The Royal Naval College (Christopher Wren) and Queen's House (Inigo Jones) stand on the site of a Tudor royal palace. The *Cutty Sark* tea clipper and *Gipsy Moth IV* are popular tourist attractions.

Greenwich Mean Time (GMT) The mean solar time on the Greenwich Meridian of longitude, which was defined to pass through the Airy Transit Circle at Greenwich in England and was adopted internationally as the zero of longitude at a conference in Washington in 1884. Its acceptance was facilitated by the overwhelming use of the Greenwich Meridian in navigation and the adoption, in the USA and Canada, of time zones based on Greenwich. Originally different towns in Great Britain kept their own local time, varying according to longitude. In the mid-19th century Greenwich time was adopted by railways throughout Britain for the sake of uniformity. However, it was only in 1880 that Greenwich Mean Time became the legal time throughout Great Britain. The international reference time-scale for civil use is now based on atomic clocks but is subject to step adjustments (leap seconds) to keep it close to mean solar time on the Greenwich Meridian. The formal name of the time-scale is UTC (a language-independent abbreviation of coordinated universal time) but it is still widely known as Greenwich Mean Time.

Greenwich Village A district of New York City, USA, on the lower west side of Manhattan, to the south of 14th Street and west of Washington Square. Once a separate village, it became an exclusive residential area associated with writers and musicians. Some of the few surviving wooden houses built in Manhattan (built in the 1840s) are located in Greenwich Village.

Greer, Germaine (1939–) Australian feminist and writer. She first achieved recognition with her influential book *The Female Eunuch* (1970) an analysis of women's subordination in a male-dominated society. She has since become a high-profile figure in the women's movement; other books include *The Change* (1991), about social attitudes to female ageing.

Gregorian calendar The modified CALENDAR,

also known as the 'New Style', introduced by Pope Gregory XIII in 1582. It is a modification of the JULIAN CALENDAR and is now in use throughout most of the Christian world. The Julian year of 365.25 days was 11 minutes 10 seconds too long. Ten days were suppressed in 1582 and, to prevent further displacement, Gregory provided that of the centenary years (1600, 1700, etc.) only those exactly divisible by 400 should be counted as leap years.

Gregory, St (known as **St Gregory the Great**) (*c.*540–604) Pope (as Gregory I) 590–604 and Doctor of the Church. He made peace with the Lombards after their invasions of Italy and appointed governors to the Italian cities, thus establishing the temporal power of the papacy. He sent St Augustine to England to lead the country's conversion to Christianity. He is also credited with the introduction of Gregorian chant. Feast day, 12 March.

Gregory VII, St (monastic name Hildebrand) (*c.*1021–85) Pope (1073–85). He argued for the moral reform of the Church and that the Christian West should be united under the overall leadership of the papacy. His most formidable opponent was the Holy Roman Emperor Henry IV. When in 1077 he submitted to the pope at CANOSSA papal supremacy seemed nearer. However, Henry's submission was merely a tactical one and he later attacked Rome itself, forcing the pope to retreat to Salerno in southern Italy, where he died.

Gregory of Nazianzus, St (329–89) Doctor of the Church, bishop of Constantinople. With St Basil and St Gregory of Nyssa he was an upholder of Orthodoxy against the Arian and Apollinarian heresies, and influential in restoring adherence to the Nicene Creed. Feast day, (in the Eastern Church) 25 and 30 January; (in the Western Church) 2 January (formerly 9 May).

Gregory of Nyssa, St (*c.*330–*c.*395) Doctor of the Eastern Church, bishop of Nyssa in Cappadocia. The brother of St Basil, he was an Orthodox follower of Origen and joined with St Basil and St Gregory of Nazianzus in opposing the heresy of Arianism. Feast day, 9 March.

Gregory of Tours, St (*c.*540–94) Frankish bishop and historian. He was elected bishop of Tours in 573; his writings provide the chief authority for the early Merovingian period of French history. Feast day, 17 November.

Grenada A state comprising the southernmost of the Windward Islands in the CARIBBEAN and several small islands, part of the Grenadines archipelago.

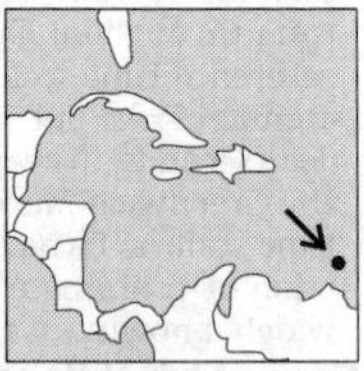

Physical. The island of Grenada contains rugged, forested mountains, rising to Mount Saint Catherine at 838 m (2,749 feet), with crater lakes and springs. The mountains are of volcanic origin and enclose valleys where bananas, spices, and sugar cane are grown.

Economy. Grenada's economy is primarily agricultural, although there is limited manufacturing industry, mostly food-processing, and tourism is a growing source of revenue. The principal exports are nutmeg, bananas, cocoa, and mace. Other crops include coconuts, sugar-cane, and citrus. There is a high level of foreign debt.

History. Grenada was discovered by Columbus in 1498. Colonized by the French governor of Martinique in 1650, it passed to the control of the French crown in 1674. The island was conquered by the British during the SEVEN YEARS WAR and ceded to them by the Treaty of Paris (1763). An uprising in 1795 against British rule, supported by many slaves, was put down the following year, and Grenada remained a British colony for almost two centuries. Universal adult suffrage was granted in 1950 when the United Labour Party, led by Matthew Gairy, emerged. The Windward Islands were granted self-government in 1956 and became a member of the West Indies Federation (1958–62). Following the break-up of the federation, the various Windward Islands sought separate independence. This was gained by Grenada in 1974, when Gairy became Prime Minister. He was deposed in a bloodless coup (1979) by Maurice Bishop (1944–83), leader of a left-wing group, the New Jewel Movement, who proclaimed the People's Revolutionary Government (PRG). He encouraged closer relations with Cuba and the Soviet Union but, following a quarrel within the PRG, he was overthrown and killed by army troops led by General Austin in 1983. Military intervention by the USA prevented a Marxist revolutionary council from taking power. US troops left the island in December 1983, after the re-establishment of democratic government. Under Prime Minister Herbert Blaise (1984–89) political stability was restored, with some economic success which continued through the 1980s. By the end of the decade, however, difficulties with the economy resulted in an IMF austerity programme. In June 1995 a general election brought the New National Party (NNP) to power under Prime Minister Keith Mitchell.

Capital: St George's
Area: 345 sq km (133 sq mi)
Population: 92,000 (1995)
Currency: East Caribbean dollar
Religions: Roman Catholic 64.4%; Anglican 20.7%; Seventh-day Adventist 3.1%; Methodist 2.1%
Ethnic Groups: Black 84.0%; mixed 12.0%; East Indian 3.0%; White 1.0%
Languages: English (official)
International Organizations: UN; OAS; CARICOM; Commonwealth

grenade An explosive weapon, used by special troops (grenadiers), from the 17th century to the 19th century. Modern grenades date from early in World War I. All hand grenades operate in a similar way, whether they are fragmentation, smoke, blast, incendiary, or gas grenades. A safety pin is pulled and the grenade is thrown, releasing a striker-lever that sets off a timed fuse. The fuse ignites, detonating the explosive filler; the grenade explodes, breaking up the case. Rifle grenades use the energy of a bullet leaving the muzzle of a rifle to propel an explosive grenade.

Grenadine Islands (or **Grenadines**) A chain of small islands, reefs, and sand bars in the West Indies, part of the Windward Islands. They are divided between St Vincent and Grenada. The principal islands are Bequia, Mustique, Canouan, Mayreau, Union Island, Carriacou, Little Martinique, and Ronde Island.

Grendel The man-eating water monster of BEOWULF, an Old English epic poem. Grendel plagued the mead hall of the Danish king Hrothgar. Beowulf, who later became king of the Geats in Scandinavia, grappled with him, tearing off the monster's arm and mortally wounding him. The following night Grendel's mother killed Hrothgar's trusted friend, Aschere, in revenge, but she in turn was killed by Beowulf.

Grenfell, Joyce (Irene Phipps) (1910–79) British entertainer and writer. She specialized in portraying gauche and toothy females, often spinsters or schoolteachers, and appeared in revues and several one-woman shows, such as *Joyce Grenfell Requests* *the Pleasure* (1954). She also appeared in many films, notably Ealing comedies and the St Trinian's series, and was often seen on television.

Grenoble A resort and industrial city and capital of the department of Isère in the Dauphiné Alps of south-east France, at the junction of the Drac and Isère rivers; pop. (1991) 153,970. Grenoble developed in the 19th century in association with its soap factories and oil mills, and pioneered the use of hydroelectric power. It is now an important winter-sports and tourist centre with industries based around nuclear research, engineering, chemistry, and computer technology.

Grenville, Sir Richard (1542–91) English naval commander. He became Member of Parliament for Cornwall (1571), led the unsuccessful expedition to colonize Roanoake planned by his cousin Sir Walter RALEIGH, and supplied three ships to the force assembled against the Spanish Armada. He died after an epic battle off the Azores, during which his ship *Revenge* held out for fifteen hours against a powerful Spanish fleet.

Gresham, Sir Thomas (*c.*1519–79) English financier. He founded the Royal Exchange in 1566 and served as the chief financial adviser to the Elizabethan government. He founded Gresham College in 1579 as a venue for public lectures and the ROYAL SOCIETY grew from these meetings at Gresham's house. His fame rests on **Gresham's Law**, wrongly attributed to him in the 19th century, which states that 'bad money drives out good'. According to this law, if there are two coins in circulation with different ratios of face value to intrinsic value (in terms of the precious metal content of the coins), the coin with the higher intrinsic value will tend to be taken out of circulation for hoarding or melting down.

Gresley, Sir (Herbert) Nigel (1876–1941) British railway engineer. He became locomotive engineer of the Great Northern Railway in 1911, continuing as chief mechanical engineer on the newly formed London and North Eastern Railway from 1923. He is most famous for designing express steam locomotives, such as the A3 class exemplified by *Flying Scotsman*. His A4 pacifics hauled the first British streamlined train service in 1935, and in 1938 one of these engines, *Mallard*, achieved a world speed record of 126 m.p.h., never surpassed by a steam locomotive.

Gretna Green A village just north of the Scottish–English border near Carlisle, formerly a popular place for runaway couples from England to be married according to Scots Law without the parental consent required in England for those who had not attained their majority. A valid marriage could be contracted in Scotland merely by a declaration of consent by the two parties before a witness (traditionally the village blacksmith, who also read the marriage service to couples for sentiment's sake). The practice lapsed after 1857 when Scots Law prescribed certain conditions for 'irregular' marriages, though it recognized such marriages until 1939.

Gretzky, Wayne (1961–) Canadian ice-hockey player. He made his professional début in 1978 with the Indianapolis Racers, soon moving to the Edmonton Oilers. A prolific scorer, from 1980 to 1987 he was voted Most Valuable Player (MVP) in the National Hockey League.

Greuze, Jean-Baptiste (1725–1805) French painter. He first gained recognition with his narrative genre painting *A Father Reading the Bible to his Children* (1755). Much of his later work, such as *The Broken Pitcher* (*c.*1773), consisted of pictures of young women, often in *décolleté* dress.

Grey, Charles, 2nd Earl (1764–1845) British statesman, Prime Minister 1830–34. He was an advocate of electoral reform and his government passed the first Reform Act (1832) as well as important factory legislation and the Act abolishing slavery throughout the British Empire.

Grey, Sir George (1812–98) British statesman and colonial administrator, Prime Minister of New Zealand 1877–79. He was appointed as governor in South Australia (1840), New Zealand (1845; 1861), and Cape Colony (1854), in each case at a time of conflict between the native peoples and European settlers. As Prime Minister of New Zealand he brought peace to the country and established good relations with the Maoris, learning their language and studying their mythology and culture.

Grey, Lady Jane (1537–54) The 'Nine Days' Queen' of England in July 1553. As a descendant of HENRY VII's younger daughter Mary, she had some claim to the English throne, and her father-in-law, the Duke of NORTHUMBERLAND, persuaded EDWARD VI to name her as his successor. MARY I ousted her easily, and she was beheaded after her father had incriminated her further by participating in WYATT'S REBELLION.

Grey, Zane (born Pearl Grey) (1872–1939) US writer. He wrote 54 westerns, which sold more than 13 million copies during his lifetime. His stories, the best known of which is *Riders of the Purple Sage* (1912), deal with cowboy life in a somewhat romanticized and formulaic style.

greyhound racing An international sport that is primarily a vehicle for betting. Up to eight (usually six) trained greyhounds race each other round an oval circuit approximately 370–490 m (400–550 yards) long in pursuit of a mechanical hare. At the beginning of the race, the dogs wait in traps lined across the course. The hare moves past the traps on an electric rail, triggering the trap doors when it is some 11 m (12 yards) ahead of the dogs.

greylag goose A typical Old World 'grey' GOOSE, *Anser anser*, looking like its farmyard descendants, with greyish-brown plumage barred with white, and a white stern. The western race has an orange beak and pink legs. In Britain greylag now breed naturally in northern Scotland and have been successfully reintroduced elsewhere.

greywacke (US **graywacke**) A type of impure SANDSTONE formed in regions in which sediments are being deposited while mountain-building is in progress. These sediments, called turbidites, are transported by strong currents of water. Greywackes are dark in colour, consisting of angular and subangular fragments of various sizes in a matrix of clay. They occur extensively; examples can be seen in the Lower Palaeozoic rocks of Wales and the Lake District in Britain.

grey whale A species of unique, bottom-feeding WHALEBONE WHALE, *Eschrichtius robustus*. It was almost exterminated by whaling but is now protected; the two remaining populations are reaching reasonable numbers, although it is still threatened by hunting and pollution throughout its entire range. It migrates enormous distances each year, further than any other mammal on Earth, with a round trip of 16,000 km (10,000 miles) from the Arctic feeding grounds to the breeding lagoons of Baja, California. The female, which is slightly larger than the male, can reach 15 m (50 feet) in length.

grid, electricity See ELECTRICITY GENERATION AND SUPPLY.

Grieg, Edvard (1843–1907) Norwegian composer, conductor, and violinist. He took much of his inspiration from Norwegian folk music, as in many of his songs and the incidental music to Ibsen's play *Peer Gynt* (1876). He avoided the larger forms of opera in favour of songs, orchestral suites, and violin sonatas. Other famous works include the Piano Concerto in A minor (1869).

Grierson, John (1898–1972) Scottish film director and producer. His pioneering work in British documentary film-making is represented by films for the Empire Marketing Board (1928–33) and the GPO Film Unit (1933–36); his work for the latter includes *Night Mail* (1936), with a verse commentary by W. H. Auden. Grierson is also notable for establishing the National Film Board of Canada (1937) and for his television series *This Wonderful World* (1957–68).

griffin In European and Near Eastern mythology, a fabulous creature with an eagle's head and wings, a lion's body, and sometimes a serpent's tail. The Old Testament cherubim are often depicted as griffin-like creatures. The chariots of the Greek gods were said to be drawn by griffins. In medieval times griffin-claws were thought to have magical properties.

Griffith, Arthur (1872–1922) Irish nationalist leader and statesman, President of the IRISH FREE STATE 1922. In 1905 he founded and became president of SINN FEIN. Griffith was among those who established the unofficial Irish Parliament, the Dáil Éireann, in 1919, becoming Vice-President of the republic it declared in the same year. With Michael COLLINS, he negotiated the Anglo-Irish Treaty (1921) establishing the Irish Free State, of which he was elected President in 1922. He died in office several months later.

Griffith, D(avid) W(ark) (1875–1948) US film director. A significant figure in the history of film, he began to discover the elements of cinematic expression in his early one-reel films, and is responsible for introducing the techniques of flashback and fade-out. Notable films include his epic of the American Civil War *The Birth of a Nation* (1915), *Intolerance* (1916), and *Broken Blossoms* (1919). He made only two sound films, in 1930 and 1931, before retiring.

griffon vulture A large carrion-feeding VULTURE in the family Accipitridae (species *Gyps*), with wings spanning almost 3 m (10 feet). There are four species widespread in Africa, southern Europe, and Asia. Birds of grassland and semi-desert, they soar high on thermals to spot fallen game, descending to feed in flocks. Griffons nest on crags and cliffs and rear a single chick which is fed by both parents on meat regurgitated from the crop.

Grignard, François Auguste Victor (1871–1935) French chemist who discovered the alkyl magnesium halides, which are prepared by reacting magnesium with a halocarbon in dry ether. These **Grignard reagents** facilitate a number of chemical reactions and are extremely important in organic syntheses. Grignard spent much of his life working on them and for his discovery he shared the 1912 Nobel Prize for Chemistry with Paul Sabatier (1854–1941).

Grimaldi, Francesco Maria (1618–63) Italian Jesuit physicist and astronomer, discoverer of the diffraction of light. He verified Galileo's law of the uniform acceleration of falling bodies, drew a detailed map of the Moon, and began the practice of naming lunar features after astronomers and physicists.

Grimaldi, Joseph (1779–1837) English circus entertainer. He created the role of the clown in the circus; it was in his honour that later clowns were nicknamed Joey. From 1806 until his retirement in 1823 he performed at Covent Garden, where he became famous for his acrobatic skills.

Grimm, Jacob (Ludwig Carl) (1785–1863) and **Wilhelm (Carl)** (1786–1859) German philologists and folklorists, who were brothers. Jacob produced a historical German grammar (1819, 1822) and in 1852 the brothers jointly inaugurated a dictionary of German on historical principles; it was continued by other scholars and completed in 1960. The brothers are also remembered for the anthology of German fairy tales which they compiled; this appeared in three volumes between 1812 and 1822.

Grimond, Jo(seph), Baron (1913–93) British Liberal politician. As leader of the Liberal Party (1956–67), he advocated British membership of the European Economic Community and sought unsuccessfully to make the Liberal Party the only radical alternative to Conservatism.

Grimsby (official name **Great Grimsby**) A port on the south shore of the Humber estuary, in the East Riding of Yorkshire, east England; pop. (1991) 88,900. A fishing port, it trades in fish, grain, coal, and timber.

Gris, Juan (1887–1927) Spanish painter, sculptor, graphic artist, and designer, active mainly in Paris, where he settled in 1906. Almost all his serious painting belongs to the Cubist movement, though his work was generally more calculated than that of PICASSO or BRAQUE, and he is regarded as the chief originator of the 'synthetic' type of Cubism. In the 1920s his style became more fluid. His output included a number of book illustrations and numerous designs for stage sets and costumes, notably for the great Russian ballet impresario DIAGHILEV.

grisaille (from French *gris*, 'grey') A painting done entirely in shades of grey or another neutral greyish colour. Grisaille is sometimes used for underpainting or for sketches (Rubens often painted sketches in grisaille), and in the Renaissance it was used for finished works imitating the effects of sculpture. The earliest known use of grisaille is in Giotto's series of *Virtues* and *Vices* (*c*.1305) in the Arena Chapel in Padua.

Grivas, George (Theodorou) (1898–1974) Greek-Cypriot patriot and soldier. A lifelong supporter of the union of Cyprus with Greece, he led the guerrilla campaign against British rule in Cyprus during the 1950s, which culminated in the country's independence in 1959. Grivas was rewarded for his role in this by promotion to general in the Greek army. He returned to Cyprus in 1971 to organize guerrilla opposition to President Makarios and died a fugitive.

Gromyko, Andrei (Andreevich) (1909–89) Soviet statesman, President of the USSR 1985–88. Born in Russia, he pursued a career in the Soviet diplomatic service. He was appointed Foreign Minister in 1957, a post which he held until becoming President in 1985. As Foreign Minister he represented the Soviet Union abroad throughout most of the Cold War. His appointment to the presidency (at that time largely a formal position) by Mikhail GORBACHEV was widely interpreted as a manoeuvre to reduce Gromyko's influence and make possible an ending of the Cold War.

Gropius, Walter (1883–1969) German-born US architect. He was the first director of the Bauhaus School of Design (1919–28) and a pioneer of the international style; his intention was to relate architecture more closely to social needs and to the industrial techniques and modern construction materials on which it increasingly relied. He left Germany in 1934 and eventually settled in the USA in 1938; he was professor of architecture at Harvard University until 1952 and designed the Harvard Graduate Center (1949).

grosbeak One of several heavily beaked birds, especially some Northern Hemisphere members of the finch family, Fringillidae, including relatives of the hawfinch, *Coccothraustes coccothraustes*. The pine grosbeak, *Pinicola enucleator*, is a relative of the crossbills and rosefinches. New World grosbeaks comprise six species in the bunting subfamily, related to the cardinals. All species feed primarily on seeds, using their large beaks to crush nuts in order to reach them.

gross domestic product See GDP.

Grosseteste, Robert (*c.*1175–1253) English churchman, philosopher, and scholar. He taught theology at Oxford before becoming bishop of Lincoln in 1235. His interests were wide-ranging and his experimental approach to science, especially in optics and mathematics, inspired his pupil Roger Bacon. His writings include translations of Aristotle, philosophical treatises, and devotional works.

Grossmith, George (1847–1912) British singer and writer. He took many roles in the operettas of Gilbert and Sullivan before collaborating with his brother, **Weedon Grossmith** (1854–1915), in writing *The Diary of a Nobody* (1892), a successful novel mocking lower-middle-class aspirations.

gross national product See GNP.

Grosz, Georg (1893–1959) German-born US painter and draughtsman. From 1917 to 1920 he was prominent among the DADA group in Berlin and during the 1920s he became a leading exponent of *Neue Sachlichkeit* ('New Objectivity'). He denounced a decaying society in which gluttony and depraved sensuality exist alongside poverty and disease; prostitutes and profiteers are frequently depicted in his work. In 1933, despairing of the political situation in Germany, he moved to the USA, where his work declined in quality.

grotesque Originally a type of mural decoration – painted, carved, or moulded in stucco – incorporating floral motifs, animal and human figures, and masks, combined into fanciful and playful schemes. This type of ornamentation was used in Roman buildings and was revived during the Renaissance; the buried ruins in which examples were discovered were called *grotte* ('caves' or 'grottoes'), hence the name. Any bizarre, distorted, or incongruous representation is often called a grotesque.

Grotius, Hugo (born Huig de Groot) (1583–1645) Dutch jurist and diplomat. His fame rests on the legal treatise *De Jure Belli et Pacis*, written in exile in Paris and published in 1625, which established the basis of modern international law.

ground beetle Any of the beetles making up the family Carabidae with some 25,000 species. Their main feature is a set of strong jaws pointing forward and a hard, black cuticle. They are often metal-coloured, and almost all are ferocious predators, and thus help control pests. Most species live on the ground, although some live on trees. Several species have their wing-cases fused together and so cannot fly. Their larvae have long legs and are also carnivorous.

ground cuckoo See COUCAL.

ground elder A pernicious, perennial plant of the carrot family, *Aegopodium podagraria*, native to Eurasia but naturalized in many parts of the world. It spreads by means of underground rhizomes, and is a particularly troublesome garden weed. In the past, it was often found in the vicinity of monasteries and, because of this and its reputation for curing gout, it is also called bishop's weed or goutweed.

ground-guidance system Any transport system developed as an alternative to the concept of a coned and flanged steel wheel running on steel rails. Following experiments in the 1930s, the Paris Métro adopted pneumatic-tyred rolling stock for running on concrete track outside the normal track. Similar systems have been adopted at Lille (France), Montreal (Canada), Mexico City, and elsewhere. More recent experiments have involved lifting the vehicle clear of the track, either with a cushion of air (as in the hover-train) or by use of magnetic fields (magnetic levitation or maglev). With a magnetic levitation system the principles of the LINEAR MOTOR are used in conjunction with a special track to provide a lifting force as well as traction. At present a small, low-speed system operates in the UK at Birmingham Airport, and in Germany and Japan, where experiments continue, test vehicles have reached speeds of about 500 km/h (310 m.p.h.).

groundnut See PEANUT.

groundsel The common name for several species of the plant genus *Senecio*. The north temperate common groundsel, *S. vulgaris*, is a rapid-maturing annual plant of waste places and cultivated ground. It belongs, along with other *Senecio* species such as ragworts and fleaworts, to the sunflower family. The seeds, which have long silky hairs, are easily distributed by wind.

ground squirrel Any of various burrowing SQUIRRELS, especially those of the genus *Spermophilus*. They are most common in the tropics, but there are numerous species – including some commonly called GOPHERS and PRAIRIE DOGS – in North America, where they spend the winter hibernating. African and Eurasian ground squirrels belong respectively to the genera *Xerus* and *Citellus*. All are predominantly herbivorous, but some will eat insects and other animal matter. Many species have prominent stripes down their sides and their common names often refer to these stripes, or to their absence.

groundwater Subsurface water lying in a zone of rock that is completely saturated with water. Most of it comes from rain or other precipitation, or by infiltration from streams and rivers: this is called meteoric water. A small proportion (called connate water) is water that was present in sedimentary rocks when they were deposited. Some groundwater also comes from igneous intrusions: this is juvenile water. Where groundwater levels reach the surface, springs develop, as on the lower edges of chalk escarpments. Groundwater levels fluctuate according to rainfall. In areas near the sea, groundwater can often be polluted by seawater. Porous sedimentary rocks provide the best reservoirs for groundwater storage.

grouper A fish belonging to the family Serranidae, or sea basses, which comprises some 370 species. In general, the name grouper is applied to the larger members, such as the Queensland grouper, *Epi-*

nephelus lanceolatus, which in Australian seas is known to grow to 270 kg (680 pounds) in weight and 12 m (37 feet) in length. They are rather heavy-bodied, thickset fishes with big heads and wide mouths, with two dorsal fins, the first of which is spiny. All groupers are carnivorous, eating fishes, octopuses, and crustaceans. Many are hermaphrodites, but most are female when first mature and male later in life. They are mostly tropical marine fishes, but some are found in warm temperate seas.

Group of Seven (G7) The seven leading industrial nations of the world, namely, the USA, Japan, Germany, France, the UK, Italy, and Canada.

group theory The study of the properties of mathematical groups. A group consists of a set of elements (for example, real numbers) and an operation (for example, addition) which together satisfy the conditions of (i) CLOSURE, (ii) association, (iii) existence of an identity, and (iv) existence of an inverse for every element. Finite groups are those with a finite number of elements; the number of elements in a group is called its order. A subgroup is a subset of the elements which themselves form a group under the same operation. Of particular interest are cyclic groups, in which all the elements are generated by repetition of the operation on one element. Groups capture the notion of symmetry algebraically and have been used widely in all branches of mathematics and in particle physics, crystallography, and spectroscopy.

group therapy The psychotherapeutic treatment of several persons at once. Groups, usually composed of six to twelve, meet regularly with one or two therapists. The shared experience and interaction of group members may prove mutually beneficial by allowing individuals to recognize patterns of behaviour and feeling in themselves and in each other. Group therapy is sometimes used in therapeutic communities, for example for victims of CHILD SEXUAL ABUSE, for depressives, and for the rehabilitation of alcoholics and drug abusers. With the help of skilled therapists group members can gain insight into neurotic mechanisms in themselves and others that block their development. Extensions of group activities include psycho-drama, in which members act out roles relevant to their problems, one object of which is to make individuals aware of the differences between their self-images and the way in which they are perceived by others.

grouse Any of the 17 members of the family Tetraonidae, of northern temperate regions, including the capercaillie, black grouse or blackcock, prairie chicken, and ptarmigan. The name is more specifically applied to certain species of the family, such as the ruffed grouse, *Bonasa umbellus*, a common forest species in North America, and the red grouse, *Lagopus lagopus*, which is the British race of the Eurasian willow grouse, a moorland bird. Many species of this family, including ruffed and red grouse, are highly valued as gamebirds. All grouse nest on the ground, and lay 5–12 eggs with very little nest material.

Grove, Sir George (1820–1900) British musicologist. He is chiefly remembered as the founder and first editor of the multi-volume *Dictionary of Music and Musicians* (1879–89), the modern editor of which is Dr Stanley Sadie. He was also instrumental in establishing the Royal College of Music (1883–95) and served as its first director (1883–94).

growth substance (in biology) See PLANT HORMONE.

Groznyy A city in south-west Russia, on the River Terek near the border with Georgia, capital of the Chechen Republic; pop. (1990) 401,000. Founded as a frontier fortress town, it has (since 1893) grown into a major oil centre with petrochemical industries. The city was badly damaged during the confrontation between Chechen nationalists and Russian forces in 1994–95.

Grünewald, Mathias (born Mathis Nithardt; also called Mathis Gothardt) (*c*.1460–1528) German painter. His most famous work, the nine-panel *Isenheim Altar* (completed 1516), exemplifies his style: figures with twisted limbs, contorted postures, and expressive faces, painted in glowing colour against a dark background.

Grus The Crane, a CONSTELLATION of the southern half of the sky. It was introduced by the Dutch navigators Pieter Dirks-zoon Keyser and Frederick de Houtman at the end of the 16th century, and represents the long-necked water bird, the crane. Its brightest star is Alpha Gruis, known as Alnair, of magnitude 1.7.

Gruyère (or **Gruyères**) A village in western Switzerland, 23 km (15 miles) south-west of Fribourg, that gives its name to a firm pale cheese originally made in the surrounding area.

guacharo See OILBIRD.

Guadalajara The capital of the state of Jalisco in west-central Mexico; pop. (1990) 2,846,720. Situated at an altitude of 1,567 m (5,141 ft), it is the second-largest city in Mexico. It is the commercial and industrial centre of the western highland area and is a spacious city with many Spanish colonial buildings, parks, and squares. It has a 16th-c. cathedral and an 18th-c. university. Guadalajara's industries include vehicle assembly, photographic equipment, textiles, and clothing. It is also famous for its glassware, pottery, and other handicrafts. The warm, dry climate makes it a popular health resort.

Guadalcanal An island in the western Pacific, the largest of the Solomon Islands; area 5,302 sq km (2,048 sq miles); pop. (est. 1987) 71,300. Its chief town is Honiara. During World War II it was the scene of the first major US offensive against the Japanese (August 1942).

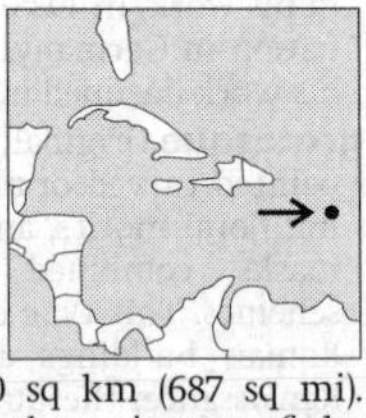

Guadeloupe A French overseas region (*département*) in the eastern CARIBBEAN, comprising two main islands, Grande Terre and Basse-Terre, together with a number of smaller island dependencies; pop. (1991) 387,030. Guadeloupe's territory covers a total of 1,780 sq km (687 sq mi). Tourism and agriculture are the mainstays of the economy, with sugar cane, rum, and bananas the chief exports. French aid sustains a relatively high standard of living, but some political groupings favour independence.

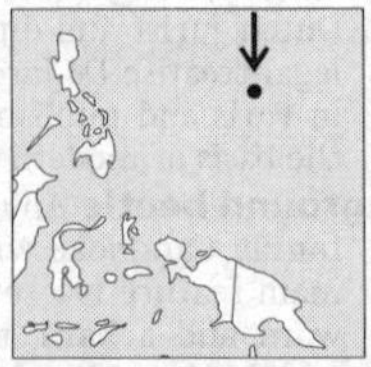

Guam The largest and southern-most of the Mariana Islands in the western Pacific Ocean, administered as an unincorporated territory of the USA and serving as a general trans-shipment centre for goods crossing the Pacific; area 541 sq km (209 sq miles); pop. (1990) 132,000; official language, English; native language, Chamorro; capital, Agaña. Discovered by Magellan in 1521, Guam was ceded to the USA by Spain in 1898. Its economy is based on financial services, petroleum refining, and the servicing of a military installation. Agricultural exports include copra, palm oil, and fish.

guan See CURASSOW.

guanaco A species of llama, *Lama guanicoe*, and a New World relative of the camel. It is found in South America, where herds of about a hundred individuals range through the pampas and mountains. It stands about 1 m (3.25 feet) at the shoulder and has a coat of soft woolly hair, which is pale yellowish-brown in colour on the body and ash-grey on the head. A single young is born after a gestation period of ten to eleven months. The guanaco is now raised on farms for its wool.

Guangxi (formerly **Kwangsi**) A mountainous region in southern China, on the border with Vietnam; area 220,400 sq km (85,129 sq miles); pop. (est. 1986) 39,460,000; capital, Nanning. In 1958 it was made an autonomous region for the Zhuang people, China's largest region for the Zhuang people, China's largest minority nationality. Its chief products are timber, pine resin, wood oils, tin, coal, rice, sugar-cane, and fruit.

Guangzhou (or **Canton**; formerly **Kwangchow**) A city in southern China, the capital of Guangdong province, situated on the Pearl River (Zhu Jiang) delta; pop. (est. 1991) 3,580,000. It is the leading industrial and commercial centre of southern China. The Chinese revolutionary SUN YAT-SEN was born at Tsuiheng near the city. The Huaisheng mosque, built in 670 AD, is said to be the oldest in China. It has shipyards, a steel complex, paper and textile mills, chemicals, and diverse light industries.

guano The nitrogen-rich droppings of fish-eating seabirds. It is valued as a fertilizer and was once commercially exploited in Peru.

Guardi, Francesco (1712–93) Italian painter. He came from a family of artists working in Venice and was a pupil of Canaletto. His paintings of Venice are notable for their free handling of light and atmosphere. His works include *View of S. Giorgio Maggiore* (1775–80).

guardian One who looks after the interests of a child (the ward), and is entitled to exercise parental rights and duties over him or her. A guardian may be appointed by a WILL or by a court, either after the death of a child's parents or if the parents are unable or unwilling to fulfil their parental role. Guardianship is a legal status that gives the guardian broadly the same rights and duties as those of a natural parent: for example, financial maintenance, care and custody, and responsibility for education.

Guarini, Guarino (1624–83) Italian architect. The spiritual heir of the great BORROMINI, Guarini was a priest, a philosopher, and a mathematician, facts relevant to his architecture, for his buildings combine geometrical complexity with a sense of spiritual exaltation. He built churches in places as far apart as Lisbon, Messina, Paris, and Prague, but almost all his surviving work is in Turin. His most famous buildings are the Chapel of the Holy Shroud (1667–90) in Turin Cathedral and the church of S. Lorenzo (1668–87), celebrated for their breathtaking openwork domes of interwoven arches. Guarini also designed secular buildings, notably the Palazzo Carignano in Turin (1679–83), which has a spectacular curved façade.

Guarneri, Giuseppe (known as 'del Gesù') (1687–1744) Italian violin-maker. The most famous of a family of three generations of violin-makers based in Cremona, he is noted for the attention he gave to the tone quality of his instruments. The first violin maker of the family was his grandfather **Andrea Guarneri** (died 1698).

Guatemala A Central American country, bounded by Mexico on its north and west and by Honduras and El Salvador on its south-east. It has a southern coast on the Pacific Ocean and access to the Caribbean Sea on the east, where it is also bounded by Belize.

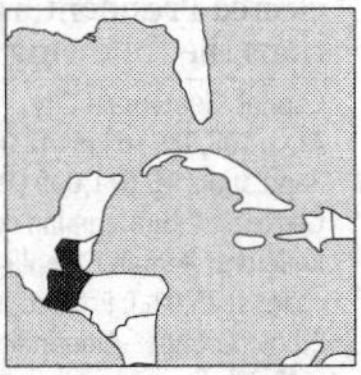

Physical. A very high range of volcanic mountains crosses Guatemala from east to west and rivers water the lower slopes, which support crops of coffee. The plateaux have a mild climate, the lowlands a hot one. Earthquakes are frequent, the country lying near a junction of crustal plates.

Economy. Guatemala has a primarily agricultural economy, the largest in Central America, with coffee, cotton, sugar, and bananas accounting for half of exports. Crude oil was discovered in the 1970s, and the revenues from oil production have been used to develop manufacturing industry.

History. In prehistory Guatemala was culturally linked to the YUCATÁN peninsula and witnessed the rise of pre-Maya and MAYA civilizations. (The modern Guatemalan population is largely descended from Maya ancestors.) In the northern and central lowlands arose the great, classic Maya cities such as Tikal, Uaxactún, Altar de Sacrificios, Piedras Negras, Yaxhá, and Seibal; in the southern highlands were the cities of Zacualpa, Kaminaljuyú, Cotzumalhuapa, and others. They had political and economic connections with each other, and with prehistoric cities in southern and central Mexico, such as TEOTIHUACÁN and Monte Albán (in Oaxaca). Spanish CONQUISTADORES arrived in 1523, seeking new American conquests, and the region soon became the Audiencia (a high court with a political role) of Guatemala, under the viceroyalty of New Spain. For almost three hundred years, Guatemala remained under Spanish rule. In 1821 it declared itself independent from Spain and became part of the short-lived Mexican empire of Iturbide. When that collapsed (1823), Guatemala helped to found the United Provinces of Central America (1823–38). Strong opposition to federation, led by Rafael Carrera, resulted in its collapse, Guatemala declaring itself an independent republic with Carrera its first President (1839–65). His successors as President became increasingly despotic. A left-wing government under Jacobo Arbenz (1951–54) instituted social reforms, before being forced to resign, following US intervention through the CENTRAL INTELLIGENCE AGENCY. Ten years of disorder were followed by the peaceful election of Julio César Méndez Montenegro as President (1966) on a moderate platform. But military intervention recurred, and during the 1970s and early 1980s violent suppression through the violation of human rights occurred. In 1985 civilian elections were restored. Vinico Cerezo was elected President (1986–91). His successor, Jorge Serrano Elias, opened negotiations with the left-wing guerrilla movement URNG, and began a purge against the military for its corruption and repressive measures. In September 1991 he ended the long dispute over BELIZE, recognizing that country's existence. In May 1993 Serrano was ousted following attempts to acquire dictatorial powers. Ramiro de Léon Carpio was elected President in June. Peace talks between the government and URNG guerrillas were resumed in an attempt to end the thirty-three-year civil war. In 1995 Alvaro Arzu was elected President, retaining power in further elections the following year.

Capital: Guatemala City
Area: 108,889 sq km (42,042 sq mi)
Population: 10,621,000 (1995)
Currency: 1 Guatemalan quetzal = 100 centavos
Religions: Roman Catholic 75.0% (of which Catholic/traditional syncretist 25.0%); Protestant (mostly fundamentalist) 25.0%
Ethnic Groups: Amerindian 55.0%; Ladino (Hispanic/Amerindian) 42.0%
Languages: Spanish (official); Mayan languages
International Organizations: UN; OAS

Guatemala City The capital city of Guatemala, in the Guatemalan Highlands at an altitude of 1,500 m (4,920 ft); pop. (est. 1995) 1,167,495. It is the largest city in Central America and has an equable climate. It was founded in 1776 to replace the former capital, Antigua Guatemala, destroyed by an earthquake in 1773. The city was severely damaged by earthquakes in 1917–18 and again in 1976. To the west of the city lie the Mayan ruins of Kaminal Juyú. Guatemala city is a commercial and industrial centre. Its industries account for half the country's output and include textiles, silverware, and food processing.

guava A small tropical fruit tree of the genus *Psidium*, up to 10 m (33 feet) tall, with scaly reddish-brown bark and green to yellow berries. Guavas belong to the myrtle family, Myrtaceae, which also includes cloves and eucalyptus. One species in particular, *P. guajava*, originating in Central America, is also widely grown for its fruit in Africa, Asia, the Philippines, and the Pacific islands. The main commercial plantations are in India, Guyana, Brazil, and Florida.

Guayaquil A city in Ecuador, the country's principal Pacific seaport and second-largest city, situated at the mouth of the Guayas River; pop. (est. 1995) 1,877,030. Named after the legendary Indian prince and princess Guayas and Quil, the city was founded in 1537 by Francisco de Orellana, a Spaniard who made one of the earliest European descents of the Amazon. In addition to trading in fruit and oil refining, Guayaquil has many industries producing plastics, textiles, pharmaceuticals, food products, vehicles, and electrical equipment.

Guderian, Heinz (1888–1954) German general and tank expert. A proponent of the BLITZKRIEG tactics, he used tanks in large formations in the conquest of Poland (1939) and of France (1940). As commander-in-chief of the Panzer (tank) forces, he played a leading role in the German victories of 1940–41, but was dismissed when he disagreed with Hitler's order to stand fast in the 1941–42 Soviet counter-offensive outside Moscow. In 1944 he became chief-of-staff to the German Army High Command, but in March 1945 was again dismissed, this time for advocating peace with the Western Allies.

gudgeon Either a species of fish, *Gobio gobio*, in the carp family, which is native to Europe, or a fish of the family Eleotridae, of which there are 150 species worldwide. The European species lives close to the muddy or stony river- or lake-beds, and has a flattened belly and a pair of barbels at the corners of the mouth. It feeds on bottom-living insect larvae, crustaceans, and molluscs. It rarely grows longer than 20 cm (8 inches).

guelder rose A deciduous European shrub related to elder and honeysuckle in the family Caprifoliaceae. It belongs to the genus *Viburnum*, which includes about 120 species spread over much of Europe, Asia, and the Americas. The common guelder rose, *V. opulus*, has flattened heads of creamy-white flowers and bright red fruits. The outer flowers of the head have large petals but no sexual organs and act as visual attractants to insects. A variety with only the large, sterile flowers is the snowball tree, *V. opulus* 'Roseum', of gardens.

Guelph A member of a faction originating in the German Welf family, who were dukes of Saxony and Bavaria. The Welfs were the traditional opponents of the HOHENSTAUFENS in Germany and Italy (where they were known as Guelphs and the latter were known as the Ghibellines). In the 12th century the Guelph leader was HENRY THE LION and he tended to support the papacy against the aspirations of the Holy Roman Emperors. Guelph support was in the major Italian towns and cities. Their rivals were the imperial party and their strength came mainly from the great aristocratic families. In local feuds, no matter what the cause, the antagonists came to associate themselves with one or other of the opposing families whose names continued to be used for many years after the original disputes were forgotten.

Guericke, Otto von (1602–86) German engineer and physicist. He invented an air pump, using it to produce a partial vacuum. He was the first to investigate the properties of a vacuum, and devised the Magdeburg hemispheres to demonstrate atmospheric pressure. Guericke also built the first known electrostatic machine.

Guernica (or **Guernica y Luno**) A town in the Basque Provinces of northern Spain, 25 km (16 miles) east of Bilbao; pop. (1981) 17,840. Formerly the seat of a Basque parliament, it was bombed in 1937, during the Spanish Civil War, by German planes in support of Franco, an event depicted in a famous painting by Picasso.

Guernsey An island in the English Channel, to the north-west of Jersey; area 63 sq km (24 sq miles); pop. (1991) 58,870. Its chief town is St Peter Port. The island, which is the second-largest of the Channel Islands and a popular holiday resort, gives its name to a breed of dairy cattle.

guerrilla (Spanish, 'little war') A person taking part in irregular fighting by small groups acting independently. The word was coined during the PENINSULAR WAR (1807–14) to describe the Spanish partisans fighting the armies of Napoleon. From Spain the use of the word spread to South America and thence to the USA.

Guerrilla warfare avoids full-scale military confrontation while keeping the enemy under pressure with many small-scale skirmishes. The technique is suited to harsh terrain, particularly jungle and mountainous areas, and has been used effectively by materially weak forces against militarily strong opponents, where there are few opportunities for conventional military forces to use superior firepower. During WORLD WAR II guerrillas formed the basis of the RESISTANCE MOVEMENTS that harassed the Japanese and German occupying forces. In post-war years they have become associated with such revolutionary movements as those in South America under GUEVARA. See also TERRORISM.

Guettard, Jean Étienne (1715–86) French geologist who publicly proposed that the Earth is older than contemporary Christian belief held, a view which he was compelled at the time to recant. He pioneered the study of the distribution of different kinds of rocks, minerals, and fossils, and showed that strata in Brittany are similar to those in south-west Britain. His correct suggestion that some fossil forms are those of extinct marine species, and his view of mountains in the Massif Central as ancient volcanoes, were received with derision.

Guevara, Che (full name Ernesto Guevara de la Serna) (1928–67) Argentinian revolutionary and guerrilla leader. He played a significant part in the Cuban revolution (1956–59) and as a government minister under Fidel Castro was instrumental in the transfer of Cuba's traditional economic ties from the USA to the Communist bloc. In 1967 he was captured and executed while training GUERRILLAS for a planned uprising against the Bolivian government. He became a hero figure among radical students in the West during the 1960s and early 1970s.

Guggenheim, Meyer (1828–1905) Swiss-born US industrialist. With his seven sons he established large mining and metal-processing companies. His children established several foundations providing support for the arts, including the Guggenheim Foundation, established in 1925 to provide financial support for scholars, artists, and writers. In 1937 Guggenheim's son Solomon (1861–1949) established a foundation for the advancement of art; it now operates the Guggenheim Museum in New York and directs the Guggenheim Collection in Venice.

Guiana (Amerindian, 'land of waters') A region in northern South America, bounded by the Orinoco, Negro, and Amazon rivers, and the Atlantic Ocean. It now comprises SURINAM, GUYANA, FRENCH GUIANA, and the **Guiana Highlands** of south-east Venezuela and northern Brazil.

guided missile A MISSILE, though not usually a TORPEDO, that is powered for part or all of its flight and is guided to its target. It has a control mechanism, which changes the flight path when instructed by the weapon's guidance system. Most missiles change direction using aerodynamic forces, others have small thrusters or a swivelling rocket nozzle. Long-range BALLISTIC MISSILES and CRUISE MISSILES launched against fixed targets are guided by INERTIAL NAVIGATION systems. Shorter-range missiles directed against moving targets may be steered by an operator, sending signals by radio or along wires (command line-of-sight guidance); for targets that are outside the operator's line of sight the missile may incorporate a television camera. Some missiles carry detectors that lock on to radiation emitted from the target, so that, after launching, they require no intervention by an operator. These are known as 'fire-and-forget' missiles. Those using infrared guidance home in on heat sources, such as engines, whereas radar-homing missiles lock on to the target's RADAR or electromagnetic radiation signals. Guidance systems may be active, semi-active, or passive. A missile with semi-active radar guidance is equipped with a radar receiver, but needs the target to be continuously 'illuminated' by radar transmissions from an external source, such as an aircraft or a ship, so that it can home in on the reflections of these signals from the target. The system will work within a range of about 100 km (60 miles), but the transmitted signal may expose the source to detection and enemy counter-attack. With active radar homing, the missile itself contains both a radar receiver and a transmitter for illuminating the target. Passive homing entails no preliminary illumination of the target; an infrared (heat-seeking) missile, for example, simply identifies the heat source and homes in on it. Generally, passive homing is used for short-range missiles, semi-active radar homing for medium-range missiles, and active radar homing for long-range missiles. There are many variants of homing systems, some using laser beams or ELECTROMAGNETIC RADIATION of higher frequency than radio waves.

guild An association of townspeople formed to provide mutual protection of trading practices. Religious guilds, mainly devoted to devotional, charitable, and social activities, were important in English towns and parishes throughout the Middle Ages. From the early 11th century merchants and traders combined to regulate trade. The merchant guilds they formed controlled markets, weights and measures, and tolls, and negotiated charters granting their towns borough status. They maintained the charitable work of the earlier religious guilds. However, their monopolistic character forced the small crafts and trades to form their own associations, craft guilds, before the end of the 12th century. Each craft had its own guild which set quality standards and evolved a hierarchy consisting of master, journeymen, and apprentices (serving for up to twelve years). Guilds declined from the 16th century, being unable to adapt to the emergence of new markets.

Guildford A residential town in Surrey, south-east England, on the River Wey, 45 km (28 miles) south-west of London; pop. (1991) 65,998. It has a modern brick-built cathedral (1964) and the Royal King Edward Grammar School (1557). The University of Surrey was founded in 1966 and the Yvonne Arnaud Theatre opened in 1965.

guillemot A small, fast-flying seabird of two northern genera. The common and thick-billed Brünnich's guillemots, *Uria aalge* and *U. lomvia*, are widespread on breeding cliffs of the northern Atlantic and Pacific and the Arctic Ocean. Black guillemots (tysties), *Cepphus grylle*, breed in the Arctic and North Atlantic areas only, and pigeon guillemots, *C. columba*, are North Pacific breeders. All are strongly gregarious, nesting in huge cliff or island colonies and feeding in groups at sea. Little nesting material is used as the normally solitary eggs and chicks are brooded on the feet of the adults. Guillemots feed mainly on plankton and small fishes, using their narrow wings to swim underwater.

guillotine The instrument used to inflict capital punishment by decapitation during the FRENCH REVOLUTION. A similar device had been used in Europe since the Middle Ages and had fallen into disuse when Dr Guillotin (1738–1814) suggested its reintroduction. After satisfactory tests on dead bodies it was erected on the Place de Grève in Paris in 1792. 'La Guillotine' was used extensively during the Reign of Terror, accounting for 1,376 victims between 10 June and 27 July 1794.

Guimard, Hector (1867–1942) French architect and designer, France's leading exponent of ART NOUVEAU. His finest building is the Castel Bérenger (a block of flats) in Paris (1894–98). Guimard is most widely known not for buildings, however, but for his entrances to Paris Métro stations (mostly *c.*1899–1900), in which he used cast iron in imaginative plant-like forms.

Guinea A West African country with an Atlantic coast, bounded on the north by Senegal and Mali, on the east by Côte d'Ivoire, and on the south by Liberia and Sierra Leone.

Physical. Inland from the marshy coast is a plain with large bauxite deposits. This rises to a sandstone plateau, the Fouta Djallon. Southward is

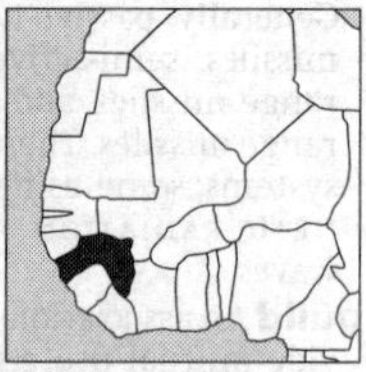

the source of the Niger River; and further south still (the country bends like a hook) are large reserves of iron ore. The climate is hot; the southernmost part is drier than the coast.

Economy. Guinea has a broadly based agricultural economy: the chief crops include cassava, rice, pineapples, coffee, and palm oil. The major exports are bauxite, alumina, gold, and diamonds. Iron-ore mining is being developed.

History. From the 5th to the 8th centuries AD, the far north of modern Guinea formed part of the kingdom of GHANA. This area of the country was incorporated in the Mali Empire in the 16th century. From 1849 onwards, French encroachment upon the region increased, leading to conflict with the empire of Samori Touré in eastern Guinea *c.*1879–91, when Guinea became a French colony. In 1895 Guinea was made part of the huge territory of French West Africa, and remained a French colony until 1958, when a popular vote rejected membership of the French Community, and Ahmed Sékou TOURÉ became first President. His presidency was characterized by severe unrest and repression, and almost complete isolation from the outside world, although before his death in 1984 a degree of liberalization was introduced. This trend has continued under the military regime of President Lansana Conté whose regime boosted the mining of bauxite. In 1990 Conté established a Transitional Committee for National Recovery, following a referendum for a new constitution. The slow pace of democratization, however, together with an IMF-imposed austerity programme, led to a general strike in 1991, after which the government introduced a multi-party system. In 1993, in the country's first multi-party elections, Conté was re-elected. Opposition candidates, however, refused to recognize the results and called for the election to be annulled.

Capital: Conakry
Area: 245,857 sq km (94,926 sq mi)
Population: 6,700,000 (1995)
Currency: 1 Guinean franc = 100 centimes
Religions: Muslim 85.0%; traditional beliefs 5.0%; Christian 1.5%
Ethnic Groups: Mande 48.0%; Peul 28.0%; Mande-fu 11.0%
Languages: French (official); Malinke; Poulor; local languages
International Organizations: UN; OAU; ECOWAS; Non-Aligned Movement

Guinea-Bissau A small tropical country on the coast of West Africa, bounded by Senegal on the north and Guinea on the south. Off-shore is the Bijagós archipelago with a score of inhabitable marshy islands.

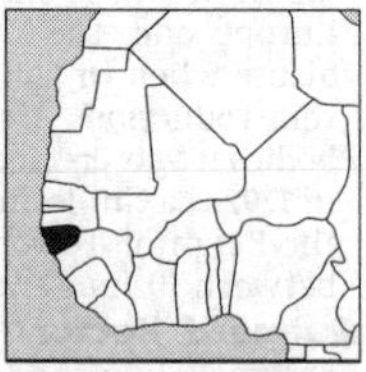

Physical. The deeply indented coast of Guinea-Bissau, stretching for some 240 km (150 miles) from north to south, is marshy and contains the mouths of three major rivers. The interior, which extends eastward for some 300 km (185 miles), consists mainly of river valleys filled with rain forest; it rises to above 200 m (650 feet) only in the south.

Economy. Guinea-Bissau has a mainly agricultural economy, whose significant exports are cashews, fish, groundnuts, and palm kernels. Further cash crops are being developed. Bauxite and phosphate reserves are yet to be exploited. Off-shore oil deposits have not been developed because of boundary disputes with Guinea and Senegal.

History. Portuguese explorers and traders were active around the coast from the mid-15th century, developing the area into a centre of the slave trade. First incorporated as part of the Portuguese Cape Verde Islands, it became the separate colony of Portuguese Guinea in 1879. Its boundaries were fixed by the 1886 convention with France. In the 1960s a movement for liberation from colonial rule emerged and grew under the leadership of Amilcar CABRAL, and in 1974 Portugal formally recognized its independence. In 1977 an unsuccessful attempt was made to unite with Cape Verde (a newly formed republic of islands to the west). In 1980 a military coup established a revolutionary council with João Vieira as President and a National Assembly elected from the ruling Marxist party, the PAIGC. In 1989 Vieira was re-elected and in 1991 the National Assembly agreed to the introduction of multi-party democracy. The country's first multi-party elections, in 1994, were won by the ruling party and Vieira was re-elected President.

Capital: Bissau
Area: 36,125 sq km (13,948 sq mi)
Population: 1,073,000 (1995)
Currency: 1 Guinea-Bissau peso = 100 centavos
Religions: Traditional beliefs 65.0%; Muslim 30.0%; Christian 5.0%
Ethnic Groups: Senegambian 60.0%; Peul 20.0%; Manding 13.0%
Languages: Portuguese (official); Balante; Fulani; local languages
International Organizations: UN; OAU; Non-Aligned Movement; ECOWAS

guineafowl Any one of six species of bird belonging to the family Numididae and related to other gamebirds. Most are the size of large domestic hens, usually greyish in colour, and speckled with paler markings. The vulturine guineafowl, *Acryllium vulturinum*, is unusual in having a bright blue neck and upper breast and long black and white hackles on the lower neck. All species are native to Africa south of the Sahara, but the helmeted guineafowl, *Numida meleagris*, has been widely introduced as a semi-domesticated bird and now breeds in a feral state in many parts of the world. The nest is a scrape on the ground, usually with eight to twelve eggs. The downy young leave the nest soon after hatching.

guinea-pig A species of CAVY, *Cavia porcellus*, related to the Patagonian hare, desert cavy, and rock cavy. It is known as a domestic animal and attempts to identify the ancestral species among wild cavies have been unsuccessful. The guinea-pig became known in Europe during the 16th century, following the Spanish conquest of South America, the home of present-day cavies. They had already been domesticated by the Incas, who kept them for food, allowing them the run of the house and surrounds to scavenge their food. The name guinea-pig is curious, for they do not come from Guinea and are certainly not pigs. It is likely that ships bringing guinea-pigs to Europe called at ports in Guinea and the animal was mistakenly associated with that country. There are many breeds of guinea-pig, which are now kept mainly as pets, although they continue to be used as food in South America.

Guinevere See ARTHUR.

Guinness, Sir Alec (1914–) British actor. His stage career ranges from Shakespeare to contemporary drama and includes a notable interpretation of Hamlet. His films include *Great Expectations* (1946), *Kind Hearts and Coronets* (1949), *Bridge on the River Kwai* (1957), and *Star Wars* (1977). He is also known for his portrayal of the espionage chief George Smiley in television versions of John Le

Carré's *Tinker, Tailor, Soldier, Spy* (1979) and *Smiley's People* (1981–82).

Guise A branch of the ducal house of Lorraine that rose to prominence in 16th-century France. **Claude de Lorraine** (1496–1550) was created duke in 1528; he had distinguished himself in a number of French military victories, including Marignano (1515). **Francis** (1519–63), his son and heir, became the most effective commander in the armies of Henry II. He was active throughout the 1550s, capturing Calais from the English (1558) and helping to bring about the Peace of Cateau-Cambrésis in 1559. His brother **Charles** (1524–74) became Cardinal of Lorraine in 1550, and his sister **Mary** (1515–60) married James V of Scotland and was the mother of MARY, Queen of Scots.

In 1559, on the accession of Francis II, the Catholic Guise family was the most influential in France. Its dealings with the HUGUENOTS and BOURBONS (1559–62) led directly to the outbreak of the French WARS OF RELIGION. Francis was assassinated in 1563. His son **Henry** (1550–88), the third duke, fought in the third and fourth wars, and was one of the instigators of the ST BARTHOLOMEW'S DAY MASSACRE. In 1576 he took the lead in organizing the Holy League, but Henry III had him assassinated in 1588, when he was being put forward as a possible heir to the throne. His brother, **Charles** (1554–1611), kept the Guise and extremist Catholic causes alive until 1595, when he submitted to HENRY IV. The Guise ducal line died out in 1688.

guitar A plucked musical instrument, usually with six strings. Early guitars had four courses or pairs of strings. The 19th-century guitar was radically redesigned, with six single strings, and the modern body-shape was created by Antonio de Torres Jurado (1817–92). There is a wide diversity of types, some played with a plectrum, from the steel-string and the twelve-string folk guitars to electric and now electronic instruments. Electric guitars can, through a variety of accessories, produce a wide range of sounds, all recognizably those of a plucked string. Electronic instruments, with a mini-computer, can imitate any other instrument. In addition, there is a considerable range of local guitar types around the world. The Spanish guitar is used for Spanish flamenco music and for classical music. It has a flat back, round sound hole, and six strings tuned in fourths.

guitarfish A CARTILAGINOUS FISH in the family Rhinobatidae, related to rays, which lives in shallow water in tropical and warm temperate seas. Guitarfishes are flattened from above but the tail is well developed, as are the dorsal and tail fins. They tend to be more active swimmers than rays or skates. Bottom-living, they feed mainly on crustaceans and molluscs and their small, closely packed teeth are well suited for eating hard-shelled invertebrates.

Gujarat A highly industrialized state in western India, with an extensive coastline on the Arabian Sea; area 196,024 sq km (75,714 sq miles); pop. (1991) 41,174,060; capital, Gandhinagar. Its principal port is Kandla. It was formed in 1960 from the northern and western parts of the former state of Bombay. One of the leading industrial states of India, Gujarat, which has large reserves of coal, oil, gas, fluorite, bauxite, and china clay, is a major producer of salt and soda-ash.

Gujarati A language descended from Sanskrit and so belonging to the Indo-Iranian language group, spoken by over 25 million people mainly in the Indian state of Gujarat. It is written in a form of the Devanagari script.

Gulbenkian, Calouste Sarkis (1869–1955) Turkish-born British oil magnate and philanthropist, of Armenian descent. He was a pioneer in the development of the oil industry in the Middle East and his company (established in 1911) was the first to exploit the Iraqi oilfields. He bequeathed his large fortune and valuable art collection to the Calouste Gulbenkian Foundation (based in Lisbon); this disburses funds for the advancement of social and cultural projects in Portugal and elsewhere.

Gulf States The states with a coastline on the Persian Gulf (Bahrain, Kuwait, Oman, Qatar, Saudi Arabia, and the United Arab Emirates; sometimes also including Iran and Iraq).

Gulf Stream A warm ocean current that flows from the Gulf of Mexico parallel with the North American coast towards Newfoundland, continuing (as the North Atlantic Drift) across the Atlantic Ocean and along the coast of north-west Europe, where it has a significant effect upon the climate.

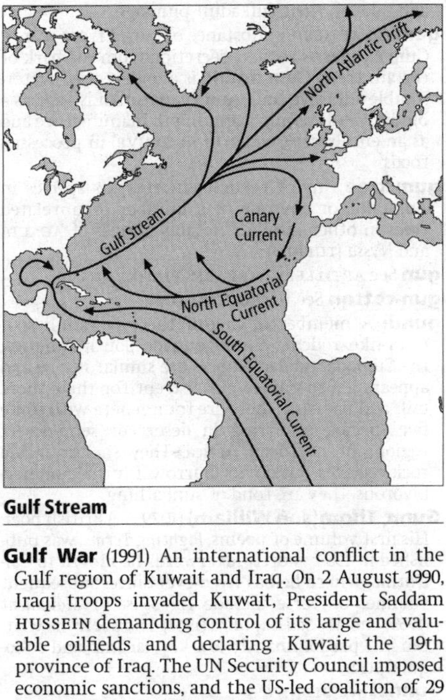

Gulf Stream

Gulf War (1991) An international conflict in the Gulf region of Kuwait and Iraq. On 2 August 1990, Iraqi troops invaded Kuwait, President Saddam HUSSEIN demanding control of its large and valuable oilfields and declaring Kuwait the 19th province of Iraq. The UN Security Council imposed economic sanctions, and the US-led coalition of 29 countries was mobilized. Intense diplomatic activity failed, and on 17 January 1991 a massive air attack was launched. Strategic targets, some placed by Hussein in densely populated areas, were immobilized by electronically guided bombs. By 24 January Allied forces had established air supremacy, 'carpet bombing' Iraqi forces, which could not shelter in the deserts of southern Iraq. The land war, named by Hussein as 'the mother of all battles', and by the UN forces under their Commander-in-Chief, General Norman Schwarzkopf, as 'Operation Desert Sabre' lasted from 24 to 28 February, during which time the Iraqi forces were routed by a massive Allied tank advance. The Allied offensive by air was called 'Operation Desert Storm'. On the Allied side the war was fought with sophisticated electronic equipment and weapons systems, notably the F-117 Stealth Fighter, laser-guided bombs, and depleted uranium shells for penetrating armour. Iraq's defence system, which included chemical and biological warheads intended for delivery by Soviet SCUD ballistic missiles, had been rendered ineffective by Allied bombing. By the end of February 1991, Hussein, having set fire to over 700 Kuwaiti oil wells, accepted the UN cease-fire terms, but had openly flouted these by early 1993. Final casualties of the war numbered some 33,000 Kuwaitis killed or captured, 234 Allied dead, and between 85,000 and 100,000 Iraqi soldiers killed.

gull A bird belonging to the widespread subfamily Larinae, including 46 species. Predominantly seabirds, generally white with fawn (juvenile), grey, or black backs, they are gregarious surface-feeders or scavengers, roosting in flocks and often nesting in large colonies. Most species live in the Northern Hemisphere. Gulls lay two or three cryptically coloured eggs in untidy grass nests; the chicks leave soon after hatching, but depend on parental feeding for several weeks. Many species take three to four years to reach sexual maturity and take on their full adult plumage.

gum An ADHESIVE substance obtained from plants. Gum exudes as a sticky secretion from the bark of certain trees. **Gum arabic** is a widely used water-soluble adhesive, and **gum tragacanth** is used as a binding and coating agent in pill manufacture and as an emulsifier (see FOOD ADDITIVE) in processed foods.

gum tree Any of certain EUCALYPTUS species in Australia, or any one of a number of unrelated trees in other families, notably species of ACACIA and *Nyssa* (TUPELO).

gun See ARTILLERY, FIREARM, PISTOL, RIFLE.

gun-cotton See NITROCELLULOSE.

gundi A member of one of the few families of CAVY-like rodents found outside South America, the Ctenodactylidae. Gundis are similar in size and appearance to guinea-pigs, except for their short tails and flat ears. There are four genera with some five species, occurring in desert or semi-desert regions of northern Africa. They shelter inside rock crevices but do not burrow. Diurnal and herbivorous, they are fond of sunbathing.

Gunn, Thom(son William) (1929–) British poet. His first volume of poems, *Fighting Terms*, was published in 1954; shortly afterwards he moved to California, where he has lived ever since. Subsequent volumes of verse include *The Sense of Movement* (1959) and *My Sad Captains* (1961). His poetry is written in a predominantly low-key, laconic, and colloquial style.

gunnel See BLENNY.

Gunnell, Sally (Jane Janet) (1966–) British athlete. Gunnell made her British début as a sprinter in 1984 but quickly became a hurdles specialist, concentrating especially on the 400-metres hurdles. After winning a silver medal at the world championships in this event in 1991, Gunnell went on to take the Olympic title in 1992 and the world championship title the following year. She announced her retirement in 1997.

gunnera A perennial herbaceous plant chiefly from South America and New Zealand, which grows in moist habitats. The best known is the South American species *Gunnera manicata*, with giant leaves, 2 m (6.5 feet) wide, on stalks up to 3 m (9.75 feet) high. It is also known as hairy or giant rhubarb, although not in the same family as true rhubarb. It belongs to a small family of some 180 species, which includes water milfoil and other aquatic plants.

gunpowder An EXPLOSIVE consisting of a mixture of potassium nitrate, CHARCOAL, and SULPHUR. The constituents are first ground separately, then mixed, moistened with water, and ground together. The mass is then pressed into grains of the desired size and dried. The potassium nitrate provides the OXYGEN for the rapid combustion of the sulphur and charcoal and the almost instantaneous production of a large volume of hot gas. In addition to gas, several solid substances are produced, and these, together with any unburned sulphur and charcoal, constitute the smoke that results from the explosion. Gunpowder was known to the Chinese, and possibly to the Arabs, by the 10th century; its use in European warfare dated from the 14th century until about 1904. It has now been replaced by other explosives and is rarely used.

Gunpowder Plot A Catholic scheme to murder JAMES I of England and his Parliament at the state opening on 5 November 1605, to be followed by a national Catholic uprising and seizure of power. The plotters, recusants led by Robert Catesby, saw violent action as the only way to gain toleration for English Catholics. They were subsequently disowned by the majority of their fellow religionists, who had little sympathy for the conspiratorial tradition established by Roberto Ridolfi, Francis Throckmorton, and Anthony Babington. It has been suggested that Robert CECIL manufactured the plot, in order to discredit the Catholic cause. Cecil learned of the plot through Lord Mounteagle, a Catholic peer. On the eve of the opening, Guy FAWKES was discovered in the cellar under the House of Lords on guard over barrels of gunpowder. The other plotters were overcome in the Midlands after brief resistance. Fawkes and seven others, including Sir Everard Digby were tried before COKE and executed in January 1606. Immediately afterwards, the penal laws against Catholics were stiffened, and an Oath of Allegiance imposed, but to the chagrin of many Puritans and Anglicans, enforcement of the new legislation soon became sporadic. Bonfires, fireworks, and the burning of 'guys' still mark 5 November in Britain.

gun-sight A device to help aim when using a FIREARM. Foresights and backsights for RIFLES became common in the 19th century. The foresight is usually a vertical blade, while the backsight is V-shaped with a sliding scale to adjust its height according to the estimated distance of the target. To aim, the tip of the foresight and the V of the backsight are aligned with the target. An aperture backsight has a circular hole. Artillery uses a telescopic or stereoscopic sight on the gun-carriage and marked with a reticle. Tank gun-sights often have infrared devices for night use.

guppy A species of fish, *Poecilia reticulata*, native to north-eastern South America and Trinidad, but which has been widely introduced to warm temperate and tropical regions around the world. It is a member of the order Cyprinodontiformes. A popular aquarium fish, it has also been employed as a destroyer of mosquito larvae. It grows to 6 cm (2.5 inches) in length, the males being smaller. It bears live young and inhabits ditches, streams, and pools of fresh or brackish water.

Gupta A Hindu dynasty established in 320 by Chandra Gupta I in Bihar. The Gupta empire eventually stretched across most of northern India, but began to disintegrate towards the end of the 5th century, only north Bengal being left by the end of the 6th century.

Gurdjieff, George (Ivanovich) (1877–1949) Russian spiritual leader and occultist. After travels in

India, Tibet, and the Middle East, he founded the Institute for the Harmonious Development of Man in Paris (1922). Those who attended the Institute were taught to attain a higher level of consciousness through a programme of lectures, dance, and physical labour. His ideas were published posthumously in *All and Everything* (1950) and *Meetings with Remarkable Men* (1963).

Gurdwara (Punjabi, 'door of the guru') The Sikh place of worship. A Gurdwara is any place in which the sacred book of the Sikhs, the *adi granth*, is kept, as well as a temple. The centre-piece of the temple is a throne or dais holding the *Adi Granth*. The book, usually covered by a canopy, is brought out to be read early in the morning and returned to its resting place in the evening. It is fanned with a sceptre set with peacock feathers or animal hairs as a sign of its authority. The Sikh temple is a community centre, visited by many people throughout the day, as well as a place of worship; it also contains a *langar*, or communal kitchen, where food is distributed. The holiest Sikh temple is the *Harimandir*, or Golden Temple, built in 1604 at Amritsar in the Punjab, India. The temple, which stands on a lake, has four doors, indicating that it is open to all CASTES.

Gurkha A military people of Hindi descent and Sanskritic speech, who settled in the province of Gurkha, Nepal, in the 18th century and made themselves supreme. A regiment of Nepalese soldiers in the British Army are known as Gurkhas.

gurnard Any one of about 70 species of bottom-living fish belonging to the family Triglidae, found in tropical and temperate seas. Known in America as sea-robins, possibly on account of their predominantly red coloration, they are well known for their ability to make noises by means of muscles attached to their very large swimbladders. They have hard, bony heads, frequently with long spines on the gill cover. The first of their two dorsal fins is composed of strong spines, and the lower rays of the pectoral fins are separate and mobile. Gurnards creep over the sea-bed searching for food with the sensitive finger-like rays of their pectoral fins.

The FLYING GURNARDS are not closely related, and belong to the family Dactylopteridae.

Gurney, Ivor (Bertie) (1890–1937) British poet and composer. He fought on the Western Front during World War I, and wrote the verse collections *Severn and Somme* (1917) and *War's Embers* (1919). Gurney also wrote nearly 300 songs, many of which were influenced by Elizabethan music. He suffered a breakdown and spent the last 15 years of his life in a mental hospital.

guru (Hindi, 'teacher', from Sanskrit, 'heavy') In HINDUISM, a spiritual teacher who assists people in their search for God, leading them from darkness to enlightenment. Hindus are encouraged to seek a guru to help them attain *moksha*, or spiritual liberation. In SIKHISM, the term applies to any of the first ten leaders of the Sikh religion. Sikhism was founded in the 15th century by Guru NANAK, whose authority and personality were transferred to nine further Gurus in succession. They include the third, Amar Das (1479–1574), who introduced the *langar*, or communal kitchen; the fifth, Arjan Dev (1563–1606), who founded the *Harimandir* or Golden Temple at Amritsar, compiled the *adi granth*, the Sikh holy book, and was martyred by the Mogul emperor Jahangir; and the tenth, GOBIND SINGH, who founded the *khalsa*, or army of soldier-saints. Before his death, he declared that the religious authority of the Guru was considered to be vested in the *Adi Granth* from that time on. The ten Sikh Gurus are seen as perfect men who have achieved spiritual union with God and have escaped from the cycle of REINCARNATION.

gusher See GEYSER.

Gustavus Adolphus (1594–1632) King of Sweden 1611–32. He raised Sweden to the status of a European power by his victories against Denmark, Poland, and Russia in the first part of his reign. In 1630 he intervened on the Protestant side in the Thirty Years War, revitalizing the anti-imperialist cause with several victories and earning himself the title of 'Lion of the North'. At home he instituted reforms in administration, economic development, and education, laying the foundation of the modern state.

Gutenberg, Johannes (*c.*1400–68) German printer. He is remembered as the first in the West to print using movable type; he introduced type-casting using a matrix, and was the first to use a press. By *c.*1455 he had produced what later became known as the Gutenberg Bible, the first book to be printed from movable type and the oldest book still extant in the West.

Guthrie, Woody (born Woodrow Wilson Guthrie) (1912–67) US folk-singer and songwriter. His radical political stance and commitment to causes such as the hardships of the rural poor during the Depression inspired many of his best-known songs, such as 'This Land is Your Land' (1944). His work was responsible for a revival of interest in folk music and influenced later singers and songwriters such as Bob Dylan.

Gutiérrez, Gustavo (1928–) Peruvian theologian. He was an important figure in the emergence of liberation theology in Latin America, outlining its principles in *A Theology of Liberation* (1971). Gutiérrez argued that the theologian should be concerned with liberating the poor and oppressed, and that this entailed responding to local needs rather than applying alien ideas and solutions.

Guwahati (or **Gauhati**) The largest city of the state of Assam, north-east India, on the Brahmaputra River; pop. (1991) 578,000. It is a centre for oil refining, the grain trade, and the production of textiles. Its Kamakshya Temple is a centre for Tantric Hinduism, attracting many pilgrims, and the Navagrah Temple was an ancient seat of astronomy and astrology.

Guyana A country on the north-east coast of South America, extending for 800 km (500 miles) from north to south and for 460 km (285 miles) from east to west.

Physical. Guyana is bordered by the Atlantic Ocean to the north, Surinam to the east, Brazil to the south and south-west, and Venezuela to the west. Much of the country is covered with dense rain forest.

Economy. The economy is based on agriculture and mining. Major exports are bauxite and alumina, sugar (the province of Demerara gave its name to a type of sugar that originated there), and rice. There are rich mineral deposits and huge timber reserves, but these are largely unexploited, and lack of foreign exchange has led to food shortages. There is potential for hydroelectricity which would reduce its dependence on imported oil.

History. The country was first settled by the Dutch in the 17th century. British rule was formally secured in 1831 when three colonies, Essequibo, Demerara, and Berbice (named from the three rivers) were consolidated to form the crown colony of British Guiana. Boundary problems with neighbours dominated the 19th century. During World War II the lease of military and naval bases to the USA proved useful to the Allied war effort. Britain granted independence to the colony in 1966 and Guyana became a nominally cooperative republic in 1970. Its Prime Minister, Forbes Burnham, became executive President (1980–86) with supreme authority under an authoritarian constitution. He was succeeded by Desmond Hoyte, who embarked on a policy of restoring good relations with the USA by a 'rolling back of cooperative socialism'. Hoyte survived an IMF-imposed austerity programme, but in December 1991 proclaimed a state of emergency, postponing a general election. To boost the economy, his government leased over 5 million acres of rain forest to foreign companies for exploitation. In the general election of October 1992 a victory by the People's Progressive Party, under Cheddi Jagan, ended 28 years of rule by the People's National Congress. The new government pledged to follow the free market policies of the previous administration, while the country continued to experience protracted economic crisis. Jagan died in 1997 and was succeeded as President by the former Prime Minister, Samuel Hinds.

Capital: Georgetown
Area: 215,083 sq km (88,044 sq mi)
Population: 770,000 (1995)
Currency: 1 Guyana dollar = 100 cents
Religions: Protestant 30.5%; Hindu 37.1%; Roman Catholic 11.4%; Muslim 8.7%; non-religious 3.7%
Ethnic Groups: East Indian 51.4%; Black (African Negro and Bush Negro) 30.5%; Mixed 11.0%; Amerindian 5.3%; Chinese 0.2%
Languages: English (official); English creole; also Caribbean, Hindi, and Amerindian languages
International Organizations: UN; Commonwealth; CARICOM; Non-Aligned Movement; OAS

guyot A flat-topped mountain of volcanic origin rising from the ocean floor, particularly in the Pacific. It is named after the Swiss-American scientist, Arnold Guyot (1807–89).

Gwent A former county of south-east Wales, formed in 1974 from most of Monmouthshire, part of Breconshire, and Newport. In 1996 it was abolished; Monmouthshire was re-established with changed boundaries and four new county boroughs, including Blaenau Gwent, were created.

Gweru (formerly **Gwelo**) The third-largest city in Zimbabwe and administrative capital of the Midlands province; pop. (1992) 124,735. Established in the 1890s as a coaching station on the Harare–Bulawayo route, Gweru developed in association with the nearby gold mines. The Dabuka rail marshalling yard is the biggest container-handling facility in the country. It changed its name from Gwelo to Gweru in 1982.

Gwynedd A county of north-west Wales; area 1,027 sq km (397 sq mi); pop. (est. 1996) 80,000; administrative centre Caernarvon. Originally formed in 1974 from Anglesey, Caernarvonshire, part of Denbighshire, and most of Merionethshire, in 1996 it was reorganized, losing Anglesey, which was reinstated as a county, and part of the north-east.

Gwynn, Nell (full name Eleanor Gwynn) (1650–87) English actress. Originally an orange-seller, she became famous as a comedienne at the Theatre Royal, Drury Lane, London. She was a mistress of Charles II; one of her sons was later created Duke of St Albans.

gymnastics A competitive sport demanding strength, agility, and artistic execution, practised at the highest level at the OLYMPIC GAMES. In national and international events, men compete in six set exercises: floor exercises, vault, pommel horse, parallel bars, horizontal bars, and rings. Women compete in four: floor exercises, vault, beam, and asymmetrical bars. Competitors are required to perform two routines on each apparatus, one a compulsory set and the other of the athlete's own devising. Marks are awarded by judges out of ten. At a more everyday level, the term gymnastics also covers a broader range of fitness exercises, using apparatus such as that mentioned above and carried out in a gymnasium, which, in English-speaking countries, means a room or hall set aside for physical activities.

gymnosperm A member of one of the two major subdivisions of the seed-bearing plants. Gymnosperms are characterized by producing their ovules and seeds on the surface of a modified leaf, and having no petals. Formerly more dominant, they have been ousted from much of the world's vegetation by ANGIOSPERMS, though the conifers, which are gymnosperms, dominate much of the cool, temperate forest in the Northern Hemisphere. The other groups of gymnosperms are probably not closely related, but merely represent a level of sophistication in the seed-bearing plants. They include the GINKGO and the CYCADS. The gymnosperms comprise some 600 or so species.

gynaecology See OBSTETRICS AND GYNAECOLOGY.

gypsies (from 'Egypt', supposed to be their place of origin) Also known as Romany (from Romany *Rom*, man), a nomadic people originating in northern India and now found mostly in Europe and parts of North Africa, and also in North and South America. It is estimated that there are some 6 million gypsies worldwide, speaking a distinct INDO-IRANIAN LANGUAGE, Romany. Traditionally, gypsies were nomads who travelled in groups of households of varying sizes, under the authority of a chief, who is elected for life. They worked as horse-traders, metal- or basket-workers, wood-carvers, and fortune-tellers. Gypsy music, performed in public exclusively by men, remains highly popular in Central Europe. The gypsy code demands that women be subservient to men and that married women always wear a headscarf. Gypsies have often been persecuted, most notably under the Nazis when some 500,000 perished between 1933 and 1945. Post-war communist regimes throughout Eastern Europe forced gypsies to settle in high-rise housing blocks in industrial towns, breaking up extended families and forcing them to work in factories. Post-communist governments have allowed gypsies to form political parties and to campaign for recognition as an ethnic minority. Associations and pressure groups such as the Hungarian 'Phralipe' (Romany, 'brotherhood') have been formed to campaign for special schools and for books in the Romany language. However, the majority still face racial discrimination (particularly in Romania), are poorly housed, often unemployed, and have a lower life expectancy than their compatriots.

gypsophila See PINK.

gypsum A light-coloured, soft evaporite mineral composed of calcium sulphate ($CaSO_4.2H_2O$). It is found as crystals, scattered nodules, and as vein deposits. Transparent crystals (selenite), granular masses (ALABASTER), and rosette-shaped nodules ('desert roses') are well-known varieties. It occurs in large quantities in sedimentary rocks formed by evaporation of seawater or salt-rich lakes, together with calcite and clays. It is a common deposit in the USA in rocks dating from the ORDOVICIAN to the present. On heating, gypsum gives the hemihydrate $(CaSO_4)_2.H_2O$, which can be ground to a fine powder to form plaster of Paris. Plaster of Paris sets solid when mixed with water, and the setting results in a slight increase in volume, so the plaster fits into any mould. It is the main constituent of plaster for the interiors of buildings. Gypsum is also used in the manufacture of PORTLAND CEMENT, blackboard chalk, PLATE-GLASS, terra-cotta, POTTERY, and orthopaedic and dental plasters.

gypsy See GYPSIES.

gypsy moth A species of TUSSOCK MOTH, *Lymantria dispar*, notorious for its accidental introduction to North America in 1869, which led to one of the worst insect plagues known. The caterpillars attack many species of deciduous and evergreen trees, often completely defoliating them. It is probably extinct in the British Isles, though common in the rest of Europe. Gypsy moths are members of the family Lymantriidae.

gyre A circular or spiral motion of water, usually in a current system. Gyres are generated mainly by surface winds and move clockwise in the Northern Hemisphere and anticlockwise in the Southern Hemisphere. See also OCEAN CURRENT, CIRCULATION.

gyrfalcon The largest species of FALCON, *Falco rusticolus*, with pointed wings and distinctive grey-brown, or even white plumage. In summer they range throughout the Arctic, feeding on ptarmigan, lemmings, and other small live prey. In winter they fly south to the sub-Arctic and warmer latitudes.

gyrocompass (or **gyroscopic compass**) A compass that relies on the properties of a GYROSCOPE for its action. It was invented independently (*c.*1908) by two men, Hermann Anschutz-Kaempfe in Germany and Sperry in the USA, after a principle first demonstrated by the French physicist J.-B.-L. Foucault in 1852. In a gyrocompass, a gyroscope is aligned on a north–south axis, and maintains this alignment as the ship or aircraft carrying it changes direction through gyroscopic inertia. The gyrocompass is unaffected by the metal components of a vehicle, and points to true rather than magnetic north. A 'master' compass can be used to operate several repeater compasses, and can provide information to an AUTOMATIC PILOT or helmsman. The gyrocompass has replaced the MAGNETIC COMPASS for NAVIGATION in most ships, and is standard equipment in virtually all aircraft.

gyromagnetic compass See MAGNETIC COMPASS.

gyroscope A small, accurately made FLYWHEEL mounted in gimbals. If the flywheel is spun at high speed, it will maintain its spin axis in space no matter how the frame is tilted. A second property of gyroscopes is known as precession. If a force is applied to the axis of the spinning gyroscope, the rotor axle moves, not directly away from the force, but at right angles to it. The gyroscope was named and first accurately described by the French physicist J.-B.-L Foucault in 1852. Its ability to maintain a fixed direction (gyroscopic inertia) has led to its widespread use as a direction indicator in the GYROCOMPASS. Gyroscopes are also used in INERTIAL NAVIGATION, automatic pilots and helmsmen, ship STABILIZERS, rate-of-turn indicators, ARTIFICIAL HORIZONS in aircraft and other vehicles, stabilized bomb and GUN-SIGHTS, and stabilized platforms for guns and radar.

H

Haakon IV Haakonsson (the Old) (1204–63) King of Norway *c.*1220–63. His reign was troubled by internal dissensions and he had Earl Skule executed in 1239. Iceland and Greenland were added to the Norwegian crown but control of the HEBRIDES was lost. This followed his defeat by ALEXANDER III of Scotland in the decisive battle at Largs in 1263.

Haakon VII (1872–1957) King of Norway 1905–57. Formerly Prince Charles of Denmark, he was elected by the Norwegian Storting (parliament) to the throne in 1905. In April 1940 he was driven out by the German invasion. Refusing the suggestion of the government of Vidkun QUISLING to abdicate, he continued the struggle from London. He returned to Norway in 1945. He dispensed with much of the regal pomp attached to the monarchy, and became known as the 'people's king'.

Haarlem A commercial and industrial city in the Netherlands, capital of the province of North Holland and commercial centre of the Dutch bulb industry, 20 km (12 miles) west of Amsterdam; pop. (1991) 149,470. Haarlem has shipyards and machinery industries.

habeas corpus (Latin, 'you must have the body') An ancient COMMON-LAW right that in the form developed in England since the 15th century, requires an official to provide legal justification before the courts for the imprisonment of a detained person. A habeas corpus writ is a means of testing whether a person has been accorded full legal rights; it does not establish his or her guilt or innocence.

Haber, Fritz (1868–1934) German chemist. In the early 1900s, he was Professor of Chemistry at Karlsruhe and subsequently (in 1911) became Director of the Kaiser-Wilhelm Institute in Berlin. His fame rests largely on his development of the HABER–BOSCH PROCESS. Haber was also responsible for introducing poison gases for chemical warfare in World War I. Haber was awarded the Nobel Prize for chemistry in 1918.

Haber–Bosch process A method for producing AMMONIA from the elements NITROGEN and HYDROGEN. Hydrogen is produced by the reaction of NATURAL GAS with steam in the presence of a nickel CATALYST. (Carbon monoxide is also formed, but it is converted to carbon dioxide and then removed by absorption.) Air is introduced, and the oxygen in the air is removed by reaction with some of the hydrogen to form water. The remaining mixture of hydrogen and nitrogen is then passed over an iron catalyst at a high pressure (150–300 bar) and moderately high temperature (350–450°C) to form ammonia. Any unreacted nitrogen and hydrogen are recycled. The ammonia is liquefied and removed for storage. The process represents the most viable way of 'fixing' atmospheric nitrogen and is therefore essential for nitrogenous fertilizer production.

Habermas, Jürgen (1929–) German social philosopher. He was a principal figure of the Frankfurt School, and was heavily involved in its reappraisal of Marxism in terms of the cultural and aesthetic dimensions of modern industrial society. His publications include *Theory of Communicative Action* (1981).

habitat The place in which an organism lives defined by the food, space, microclimate, other organisms, and physical and chemical conditions that it provides. An organism fitted to a particular set of conditions is said to show adaptation to that habitat. Most natural habitats are classified according to the physical features of their vegetation and include woodland, grassland, freshwater, or coastal habitats. Each broad category can be further subdivided; thus grassland comprises chalk grassland, hay meadow, pasture, and many other habitats.

Habsburg The most prominent European royal dynasty from the 15th to the 20th century. Their name derives from Habichtsburg (Hawk's Castle) in Switzerland, built in 1020. The founder of the family power was Rudolf I, who was King of the Romans 1273–91 and conqueror of AUSTRIA and Styria, beginning the family's rule over Austria. Habsburg domination of Europe resulted from the shrewd marriage policy of Maximilian I (1459–1519), whose own marriage gained The Netherlands, Luxembourg, and Burgundy and that of his son, Philip, which brought Castile, Aragon, and the Spanish New World possessions as well as Naples, Sicily, and Sardinia. Habsburgs also ruled Hungary and Bohemia from 1526 to 1918. Thus the zenith of Habsburg power came under Charles I, King of Spain and emperor (as Charles V, 1519–56) in the 16th century. In 1700 the Spanish line became extinct and in the subsequent War of the SPANISH SUCCESSION (1703–13) the Spanish inheritance passed to the Bourbons. The Austrian Habsburgs (after 1740 the House of Habsburg-Lorraine) flourished again under MARIA THERESA (1717–80) and her son Joseph II (1741–90). The Habsburgs ended the Napoleonic wars with the loss of the Austrian Netherlands and the title Holy Roman Emperor, but continued to rule over Austria. Following the AUSTRO-PRUSSIAN WAR of 1866 they had to make concessions to Hungarian nationalism with the formation of AUSTRIA-HUNGARY. The emperor FRANCIS JOSEPH came increasingly to clash with Russian ambitions in the BALKANS. Nationalist aspirations led eventually to the disintegration of his empire during World War I. The last Habsburg monarch, Emperor Charles I of Austria (Charles IV of Hungary), renounced his title in November 1918 and was later deposed.

hacienda A large estate with a dwelling-house, originally given by monarchs in Latin America as a reward for services done. Such estates are known as *estancias* in Argentina and *fazendas* in Brazil. The first major eruption of violence, calling for the break-up of the haciendas, occurred in Mexico in 1910. Most Latin American countries have experienced similar demands during the 20th century, and they have remained a major political issue.

hacking (in computing) The gaining of unauthorized access to a computer system from a remote point via the telephone network, especially by guessing or deducing a password. The challenge of breaching the system's security may be undertaken for personal satisfaction, but it can also be a means to a more sinister end, such as gaining access to confidential information, diverting funds, or modifying, corrupting, or destroying information or programs. Hacking was made illegal in the UK by the Computer Misuse Act 1990.

Hackney A borough of north-east London, England, said to have given its name to the hackney coach, which began to ply in London in 1625.

haddock A fish, *Melanogrammus aeglefinus*, of the cod family, which occurs in depths of 40–300 m (130–980 feet) on both the European and American coasts of the North Atlantic. It lives close to the sea-bed and feeds mainly on bottom-living animals. It is a valuable food-fish.

Hades (Greek **Aïdes**) In Greek mythology, the kingdom of one of the sons of Cronus, lord of the lower world (which is known as the House of Hades).

hadith (Arabic, 'traditions') The teachings and acts of MUHAMMAD and his followers, constituting the *sunna*, or 'rules of life', the basis of the *sharia*. Although disputed, the *hadith* are highly revered sources of historical, moral, religious, and ritual authority, second only to the authority of the KORAN. Six *hadith* collections, chiefly the one compiled by Bukhari (810–70 AD), are accepted as authoritative by orthodox SUNNIS, whereas five, based upon the authority of the Caliph Ali and the other *imams*, are accepted by Shiites.

hadj See HAJJ.

Hadlee, Sir Richard (John) (1951–) New Zealand cricketer. An all-rounder, he made his test début in 1973; in 1989 he became the first bowler to take more than 400 test wickets, finishing his career with a total of 431. He was knighted in 1990 and was the first cricketer to receive this honour while still playing in test matches.

Hadley, George (1685–1768) British lawyer and climatologist who first formulated the theory describing the trade winds and the associated meridional circulation pattern now known as the Hadley cell. He realized that the additional heat from the Sun received by equatorial regions explains the global pattern of surface and high-level winds. Warm air which rises near the Equator becomes colder and denser as it flows aloft towards the poles. This air then sinks to the surface, causing the TRADE WINDS which blow back towards the Equator, thus completing the cell circulation.

Hadrian (full name Publius Aelius Hadrianus) (76–138 AD) Roman emperor 117–38. He became emperor as the adopted successor of Trajan, and spent much of his reign touring the provinces of the Empire, promoting good government and loyalty to Rome, and securing the frontiers. The building of **Hadrian's Wall** was begun after his visit to Britain in 122. This defensive fortification in northern Britain is 117 km (73 miles) long, a stone barricade with a turf section in the west. The wall was damaged several times by the Picts, and was finally abandoned in 383 but long stretches of the wall still stand.

hadron An elementary particle subject to the STRONG FORCE. Hadrons are formed of a combination of QUARKS. There are two main groups: the BARYONS, which have half-integral spin, and the MESONS, which have zero or integral spin. Particles not subject to the strong interaction are called LEPTONS.

Haeckel, Ernst Heinrich (1834–1919) German biologist and enthusiastic supporter of the theories of Darwin. He applied these ideas in his zoological work and many popular books, most of which were translated into English. His work on embryology and the descent and relationship of various members of the animal kingdom, from protozoa to man, was influential in its time. Among the new words which he introduced to biology is ECOLOGY.

haematite (Fe_2O_3) The most important ore mineral of iron; the iron content is over 70 per cent. Commonly found as dark-brown kidney-shaped nodules, it is very dense and moderately hard. The largest deposits are found round Lake Superior, Quebec, and in Brazil. Crushed haematite (red ochre) is used as a pigment and as a fine abrasive powder.

haematology The study of the BLOOD and its disorders.

haemodialysis The removal of waste products that accumulate in the blood in cases of kidney failure. In the artificial kidney (dialyser), blood diverted from the patient's circulation flows over one side of a selectively permeable membrane (one that allows the passage of some particles but not others) before being returned to the body. On the other side of the membrane, a specially prepared fluid (the dialysate) circulates, into which waste products pass by diffusion (the movement of particles from a region of high concentration to one of low concentration). Since its introduction in the 1940s, haemodialysis has become widespread for patients waiting for donor kidneys. Smaller, portable dialysis units can be used in the home.

haemoglobin A red-coloured protein containing iron, which is the respiratory pigment of vertebrates. It is packed into red blood cells, thereby giving blood its characteristic colour. Its efficient oxygen-carrying ability enables about 200 ml of oxygen to be transported in each litre of blood. The haemoglobin molecule can carry oxygen or carbon dioxide, exchanging one for the other when passing through tissues with high concentrations of carbon dioxide. On its passage through the lungs, haemoglobin traps oxygen from the inhaled air, simultaneously releasing the carbon dioxide it carried to the lungs.

haemophilia An inherited disease characterized by a deficiency of blood clotting factors. Haemophilia A is the most common form, in which there is a deficiency of Factor VIII. This form almost exclusively affects men, although women may be carriers, and can pass the disease on to male offspring. Haemophilia B (known as Christmas disease), in which there is a deficiency of Factor IX, is less common. The clinical features of both forms are identical.

Haemophilia causes excessive haemorrhage in

response to minor injury because the blood clotting mechanism is inhibited. Life-threatening haemorrhage can occur following major surgery or injury. Treatment includes the administration of Factor VIII and Factor IX, derived from pooled plasma from blood donors.

haemorrhage Internal or external loss of blood from damaged blood vessels. Arterial haemorrhage can result in loss of a large volume of blood because of the high arterial blood pressure; it can be life-threatening and cause SHOCK. In veins, the blood pressure is relatively low, and haemorrhage does not normally result in the loss of large volumes of blood. Minor haemorrhage in the very small veins results in bruises. Haemorrhage is stopped by the process of blood clotting

hafnium (symbol Hf, at. no. 72, r.a.m. 178.49) One of the TRANSITION METALS; it closely resembles ZIRCONIUM and is usually found in zirconium minerals. It is rather unreactive, and shows valency 4 in most of its compounds. A strong neutron absorber, it is used for control rods in nuclear reactors.

Haganah A Jewish defence force in Palestine. It was established in 1920 first as an independent, armed organization and then under the control of the Histadrut to defend Jewish settlements. During the 1936–39 Arab rebellion it was considerably expanded. It gained a general staff and was put under control of the Jewish Agency, acquiring new duties of organizing illegal Jewish immigration and preparing for the fight against Britain, who held the mandate over Palestine. In 1941 the Palmah (assault platoons) were formed. In 1948 Haganah provided the nucleus of the Israeli Defence Force, formed to protect the newly created state of Israel.

hagfish A primitive, fish-like vertebrate, a member of one of the two families of JAWLESS FISHES (the other one consists of the lampreys). In addition to lacking jaws they have no pelvic or pectoral fins and no true rays in the other fins. The mouth is a slit, with fleshy barbels, and they have one to sixteen gill openings along their sides. They live in all the major oceans, burrowing in the sea-bed and scavenging for food or catching worms and crustaceans. They have a rasp-like tongue which can be used to bore into dead or disabled fishes. There are 19 species in the family Myxinidae.

Haggard, (Sir Henry) Rider (1856–1925) British writer. Southern Africa provided the setting for his most celebrated novels, *King Solomon's Mines* (1885), *Allan Quatermain* (1887), and *She* (1887). In all he wrote 34 adventure novels variously set in Mexico, Iceland, Egypt, and Turkey.

Hague, The (Dutch **Den Haag, 's-Gravenhage**) The seat of government and administrative centre of the Netherlands, on the North Sea coast in the province of South Holland; pop. (1991) 444,240. It is the third-largest city in the Netherlands and seat of the International Court of Justice which is housed in the Palace of Peace (1913). The Hague Convention of 1907 formulated much of the law governing the conduct of international warfare.

Hague School Group of Dutch painters including the brothers Jacob, Matthijs, and Willem Maris and Anton Mauve who worked in The Hague between about 1860 and 1900. The group is particularly associated with landscapes and beach scenes, but its members also painted street scenes, views of everyday life, and church interiors.

Hahn, Otto (1879–1968) German chemist, co-discoverer of nuclear fission. He pioneered the study of radiochemistry in England, first with Sir William Ramsay in London and then with Sir Ernest Rutherford in Manchester, identifying various radioactive isotopes of thorium. His fruitful partnership with Lise Meitner began shortly after his return to Germany and ended when she fled from the Nazis in 1938. They discovered the new element protactinium in 1917, but the culmination of their collaboration occurred in 1938 when, with Fritz Strassmann (1902–80), they discovered nuclear fission. Hahn was awarded the Nobel Prize for chemistry in 1944.

hahnium (symbol Ha, at. no. 105, r.a.m. 260) An artificial transuranic element synthesized in the USA in 1970. It is named after Otto HAHN.

Haidarabad See HYDERABAD.

Haifa The chief port of Israel, in the north-west of the country on a peninsula jutting into the Mediterranean Sea; pop. (est. 1993) 248,200. It is the third-largest city in Israel and site of the Baha'i Shrine. Its industries include chemicals, textiles, and electrical equipment.

Haig, Douglas, 1st Earl Haig of Bemersyde (1861–1928) British Field Marshal. During World War I he served as Commander-in-Chief of British forces in France (1915–18). He believed that the war could be won only by defeating the German army on the Western Front and maintained a strategy of attrition throughout his period of command. The strength of the main German army was eventually broken by this means, albeit with a very high cost in lives. In 1921 Haig helped to establish the Royal British Legion to improve the welfare of ex-servicemen.

haiku A form of Japanese LYRIC verse that encapsulates a single impression of a natural object or scene, within a particular season, in 17 syllables arranged in lines of five, seven, and five syllables. Arising in the 16th century, it flourished in the hands of BASHŌ and Buson (1715–83). During the Tokugawa or Edo period (1603–1867) it was known as a *hokku*, but it became a separate form under the influence of Masaoka Shiki (1867–1902). The haiku convention, in which feelings are suggested by natural images, has appealed to many modern Western imitators, especially POUND.

hail See PRECIPITATION.

Haile Selassie (born Tafari Makonnen) (1892–1975) Emperor of Ethiopia 1930–74. He lived in exile in Britain during the Italian occupation of Ethiopia (1936–41), but was restored to the throne by the Allies and ruled until deposed in a Communist military coup. As a statesman, he made his country a prominent force in Africa and helped establish the Organization of African Unity in the early 1960s. He was deposed by left-wing army officers in 1974 and assassinated the following year. He is revered by the Rastafarian religious sect, which is named after him.

Hailwood, Mike (full name Stanley Michael Bailey Hailwood) (1940–81) British racing motorcyclist. He achieved a record fourteen wins in the Isle of Man TT races between 1961 and 1979, and was world champion nine times in three different classes between 1961 and 1967.

Hainan An island in the South China Sea forming an autonomous region of China; area 34,000 sq km (13,132 sq miles); pop. (1990) 6,420,000; capital, Haikou. Produce includes rubber, sugar, fruit, coffee, cocoa, and minerals such as iron ore, limestone, marble, and china clay.

Hainaut (Flemish **Henegouw**) A province in southern Belgium to the north of the Ardennes;

area 3,788 sq km (1,463 sq miles); pop. (1991) 76,785; capital, Mons.

Haiphong A port in northern Vietnam on the Cam River which forms part of the delta of the Red River (Bac Bo); pop. (est. 1992) 783,100. Developed by the French, who took possession of a small market town here in 1874, it is the third-largest city in the country and the leading industrial centre of north Vietnam. The city was badly damaged during air raids in 1946 and from 1965 to 1972, during the Vietnam War.

hair Any long, threadlike structure, as found on plant stems and leaves or forming the outer covering of mammals. Mammalian hairs are produced from groups of skin cells that form hair follicles. The hair strand is continually produced from its expanded base within the follicle. This is the hair 'root' and comprises a mass of dividing cells. The main body of the hair strand is composed of a fibrous protein called keratin, also found in feathers, hooves, and horns. The core of the hair strand contains a pigment, giving the hair its colour. The centre may or may not be hollow. The strand is capable of being moved by small muscles attached to the hair follicle.

hair-streak A butterfly that, together with BLUES and COPPERS, comprises the family Lycaenidae. The name derives from distinct transverse lines on the otherwise uniformly coloured underside of the wings. As with many lycaenid butterflies, there is often an eye-spot on the underside of the hindwings and one or more delicate 'tails'. These help the butterfly to confuse predators into thinking the eye-spot and 'tail' are the head, thus deflecting attacks away from the vulnerable body. The deception is most elaborate in tropical species, which include the majority of the 1,500 species.

Haiti A Caribbean country that occupies the western third of the island of HISPANIOLA.

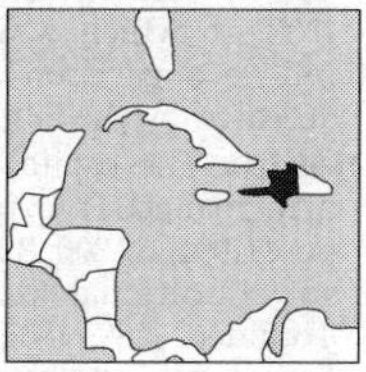

Physical. Haiti is mainly mountainous with three main mountain ranges. Much of it is forested but the valleys support agriculture.

Economy. Haiti has a predominantly agricultural economy, with coffee the most important agricultural export; bauxite is also an important export. Tourism has been a major source of foreign exchange. There is some light industry, especially textiles and the assembly or finishing of imported goods.

History. Hispaniola was discovered by Columbus during his first voyage to the New World, and became a Spanish colony in the 16th century. French corsairs settled on the western part of the island in the 17th century and Spain recognized the French claims to the area in 1697 in the Treaty of Ryswick. Known as Saint Domingue in the 18th century, it became a rich source of sugar and coffee for the European market. African slaves replaced a decimated Indian population and by the end of the 18th century the population of Haiti was predominantly black. French rule was challenged in 1791 by a slave insurrection led by TOUSSAINT L'OUVERTURE.

The country declared its independence (1804) and DESSALINES was proclaimed emperor. After his assassination (1806) a separate kingdom was set up in the north, while the south and west became republican. The country was re-united in 1820 as an independent republic. Haiti and the eastern part of the island (later the DOMINICAN REPUBLIC) were united from 1822 to 1844. In 1859 it became a republic on its own again, whose anarchic history has been exacerbated by the mulatto–black hostility. The USA, fearing that its investments were jeopardized and that Germany might seize Haiti, landed its marines (1915) and did not withdraw them until 1934. The country was dominated by President François DUVALIER (1957–71), and by his son and successor, Jean Claude (1971–86). When the latter was exiled to France, a council assumed power. A new constitution and elections followed, but they in turn were followed by a series of military coups and violence under General Prosper Avril. Strikes and yet more violence ended his regime, and elections in December brought a dissident Roman Catholic priest, Jean-Bertrand Aristide, into office. In September 1991 rebel troops seized the President and civil violence flared up against a new military regime. Aristide fled to Venezuela and appealed to the ORGANIZATION OF AMERICAN STATES (OAS) for help. International aid was suspended and trade sanctions imposed, but negotiations failed. An army-backed government led by Prime Minister Marc Bazin came to power in June 1992. Renewed OAS and US diplomatic efforts at restoring President Aristide to office led to the appointment by Aristide of a new Prime Minister, Robert Malval, in August 1993. An upsurge in army- and police-sponsored violence, however, prevented Aristide's return, while increased sanctions held the economy in a state of crisis. In September 1994 US troops landed on Haiti to oversee the transfer of power to Aristide, following an agreement with military leaders negotiated by former US President Jimmy Carter. Aristide returned in October and, in March 1995, military authority was transferred from the US-led multinational force to the UN Mission in Haiti (UNMIH). In mid-1995 the Lavalas Political Organization, endorsed by Aristide, won legislative elections, but results were contested by opposition parties and the elections were marred by irregularities and violence. Presidential elections in 1995 were won by René Préval, an associate of Aristide.

Capital: Port-au-Prince
Area: 27,400 sq km (10,579 sq mi)
Population: 6,589,000 (1995)
Currency: 1 gourde = 100 centimes
Religions: Roman Catholic 80.3%; (of whom about 90% also practise voodoo); Protestant 15.8% (of which Baptist 9.7%); Pentecostal 3.6%; non-religious 1.2%
Ethnic Groups: Black 95.0%; Mulatto 4.9%; White 0.1%
Languages: Haitian (French) creole, French (both official)
International Organizations: UN; OAS

Haitink, Bernard (1929–) Dutch conductor. He was artistic director and principal conductor with the Amsterdam Concertgebouw, with whom he made notable recordings of all of Mahler's and Bruckner's symphonies, between 1964 and 1987. Haitink fulfilled a similar role with the London Philharmonic Orchestra (1967–79) and was musical director of Glyndebourne (1977–87) before becoming musical director at Covent Garden in 1987.

hajj (or **hadj**) An Islamic pilgrimage to Mecca required of Muslims once in a lifetime.

hake A relative of the cod living near the continental shelf mainly in temperate areas of the Atlantic and Pacific oceans. They are long-bodied fishes with long-based dorsal and anal fins, large heads, and heavily toothed jaws. They feed on fishes, squids, and crustaceans, and usually live in moderate depths, down to 1,000 m (3,280 feet). They are valuable food-fishes; several of the ten or so species, including the European species, *Merluccius merluccius*, have been heavily over-fished. In North America the hakes are known as whitings, and the word hake is applied to distantly related *Urophycis* species.

Hakluyt, Richard (1552/3–1616) English geographer and chronicler whose *Principall Navigations* (1589) contains accounts from manuscript sources and from personal interviews with mariners, of famous voyages of discovery up to his time of writing and gave great impetus to discovery and colonization.

Haldane, J(ohn) B(urdon) S(anderson) (1892–1964) British mathematical biologist. Haldane helped to lay the foundations of population genetics. He also worked in biochemistry, and on the effects of diving on human physiology. Haldane became well known as a popularizer of science and for his outspoken Marxist views.

Haldane, Richard Burdon, Viscount Haldane of Cloan (1856–1928) British politician. As Secretary for War (1905–12) he showed great organizational skill in the reforms of the British army. A small expeditionary force ready for instant action was formed with a Territorial Army as a reserve, and an Imperial General Staff to organize military planning on an improved basis. Haldane was sent on a mission to Berlin in 1912 to secure a reduction in naval armaments, but failed.

Hale, George Ellery (1868–1938) US astronomer. He discovered that sunspots are associated with strong magnetic fields, and invented the spectroheliograph. He initiated the construction of several large telescopes, culminating in the 5-metre (200-inch) reflector at Mount Palomar in California, named the **Hale reflector** in his honour.

Hales, Stephen (1677–1761) English chemist and physiologist, who studied blood circulation in humans and the physiology of plants. His first discoveries were that plants used the air to nourish them and light to grow. He noticed that plant sap didn't circulate like blood. Hales' measurements of the human pulse, blood pressure and the rate of blood flow resulted in much greater understanding of the circulation.

Haley, Bill (full name William John Clifton Haley) (1925–81) US rock and roll singer. He was the first to popularize rock and roll with the release of his song 'Rock Around the Clock' (1954), recorded with his group The Comets.

half-life The time it takes for half of the radioactive atoms in a sample to decay. This can range from small fractions of a second to billions of years: for example, the half-life of the most abundant uranium ISOTOPE (uranium-238) is 4.5×10^9 years, that of radium (radium-226) is 1,600 years, and that for radioactive iodine (iodine-128) is 25 minutes. Any other phenomenon in which numbers or intensity diminish in accordance with an EXPONENTIAL FUNCTION can be said to have a half-life. For example, a drug injected into the body has a certain half-life; after this time its concentration in the body's tissues is halved.

half-tone process A process in which tonal variations in photographs and other continuous-tone originals are converted into patterns of dots, in order to allow reproduction by printing. Traditionally done in a camera or contact frame, the process interposes a finely ruled screen between the original and the reproduction, dividing the image into dots that differ in size according to the density of the tones in the original. The screen gradation – normally 12–21 dots per cm^2 (80–133 dots per square inch) – is varied to suit the quality of paper on which the image will be printed. Screening is now more often achieved by ELECTRONIC SCANNING. In colour printing, the first stage is colour separation, in which an electronic scanner or a camera using blue, green, and red filters, separates out the primary COLOUR elements of yellow, magenta, and cyan present in the original, plus a black element. These separations are then screened to produce dotted images for each colour. The resultant film images are transferred to separate printing plates, and the original is recreated by printing the four colour elements on top of each other. The dotted images are aligned so that the colours do not coincide but are very close together. The eye combines the colours in each area to re-create the original shades.

halibut A species of FLATFISH with a large head, wide mouth, and powerful teeth. It lives in the deep waters of the cool North Atlantic. Its diet consists of fishes, squids, and crustaceans, and unlike most flatfishes it actively hunts its prey in mid-water as well as on the sea-bed. A valuable food-fish, it is captured by long-lining as well as trawling.

halide A chemical compound of a HALOGEN with another element or group. The halides are typically ionic, for example, sodium fluoride (Na^+F^-), but there are examples that exhibit covalent bonding, such as aluminium chloride ($AlCl_3$). There are many naturally occurring mineral forms including HALITE and FLUORITE, which frequently occur as precipitates resulting from the evaporation of saline waters.

Halidon Hill A hill in Northumberland, north-east England, 3 km (2 miles) north-west of Berwick-upon-Tweed. It was the scene of a battle on 19 July 1333 at which a Scottish army attempting to relieve a garrison at Berwick-upon-Tweed were defeated by the English under Edward III.

Halifax The capital of Nova Scotia, and Canada's principal ice-free port on the eastern seaboard; pop. (1991) 67,800; 320,500 (metropolitan area). It is an educational centre with four universities (founded 1789, 1802, 1818, and 1925). Originally a French fishing station, it was settled in 1749 by the English, who named it after the 2nd Earl of HALIFAX, President of the Board of Trade. The port handles bulk cargoes and container traffic and has oil refineries, iron foundries, and numerous light industries. Fishing is also important.

Halifax A town in West Yorkshire, England, on the River Calder near Bradford; pop. (1981) 77,350. It developed in the Middle Ages as a cloth-making town.

Halifax, George Montagu Dunk, 2nd Earl of (1716–71) British Tory statesman. In 1748 he became president of the Board of Trade and was active in colonial development, founding and giving his name to HALIFAX, Nova Scotia. He held other positions of state, including Lord Lieutenant of Ireland (1761–63), Lord Privy Seal (1770), and Secretary of State for the Northern Department (1762–63, 1771).

halite (or **rock salt**) An evaporite mineral formed by the evaporation of BRINE. It is the chief source of table salt. It is sodium chloride (NaCl) occurring as crystals, which are soft, light, and fragile and usually colourless or white. It is found worldwide, notably in Stassfurt (Germany) and Louisiana and Texas (USA); and although soluble it occurs also beneath the sea, notably the Mediterranean and Red Seas, where it is protected by overlying impervious sediments.

Hall, Charles Martin (1863–1914) US industrial chemist. He investigated different processes for producing aluminium from bauxite, and settled on electrolysis, obtaining the best results with alumina dissolved in molten cryolite. This remains the usual commercial method.

Hall, Sir Peter (Reginald Frederick) (1930–) British theatre and opera manager and director. Among his most memorable productions was the first English-language staging of Beckett's *Waiting for Godot* (1955). He was founder and managing director of the Royal Shakespeare Company (1960–68) and director of the NATIONAL THEATRE (1973–88).

Hall, (Marguerite) Radclyffe (1883–1943) British novelist and poet. Her novels attracted both acclaim and outrage; while *Adam's Breed* (1926) was awarded the James Tait Black Memorial Prize, *The Well of Loneliness* (1928), with its exploration of a lesbian relationship, was banned for obscenity (in Britain though not in the USA), despite the support of writers, such as Virginia Woolf and Arnold Bennett. The ban was overturned after Hall's death.

Hallé, Sir Charles (born Karl Halle) (1819–95) German-born pianist and conductor. He went to Manchester from Paris in 1848 to escape the revolution and remained there for the rest of his life. He founded his own orchestra (still known as the Hallé Orchestra and based in Manchester) and inaugurated a series of orchestral concerts (the Hallé Concerts) in 1858.

Haller, Albrecht von (1708–77) Swiss anatomist and physiologist. He pioneered the study of neurology and experimental physiology, and wrote the first textbook of physiology.

Halley, Edmond (1656–1742) English astronomer and mathematician. Halley became an influential Fellow of the Royal Society and friend of Newton, the publication of whose *Principia* was due largely to him. He became professor of geometry at Oxford and was later appointed Astronomer Royal. He realized that nebulae were clouds of luminous gas among the stars, and that the aurora was a phenomenon connected with the Earth's magnetism. Halley is best known for recognizing that a bright comet (see HALLEY'S COMET) had appeared several times, and for successfully predicting its return.

Halley's Comet A bright intermediate-period COMET that returns to the inner Solar System about every 76 years. It orbits the Sun in the opposite direction to the planets and has a perihelion distance of 0.59 astronomical units; at aphelion it is beyond the orbit of Neptune. It was the first comet to be recognized as being periodic, a discovery made by HALLEY in 1696. The comet was first recorded in 240 BC and has been visible to the naked eye on all of its thirty recorded appearances. It was captured by Jupiter into its present orbit some 200,000 years ago, at a time when its nucleus was around 19 km in diameter. This nucleus is now about 11 km across and in 300,000 years' time will have decayed away completely. The 1986 reappearance of the comet was photographed by the European spacecraft GIOTTO, which flew past it.

hallmarks A set of up to five marks stamped on articles of silver, gold, and (since 1975) platinum made in Britain, as a guarantee of purity. The marks consist of an assay office mark, a quality mark, a date mark, and (between 1784 and 1890) a duty mark indicating that the appropriate excise had been paid. A maker's mark is also usually included. Hallmarks may be abolished to make the marking of precious metals consistent within the EU.

Hallowe'en A shortening of All Hallows Eve, the evening before All Saints' Day. Hallowe'en falls on 31 October, which in pre-Christian Britain was New Year's Eve, when the souls of the departed were believed to revisit their homes. It later became associated with the Christian festival of All Saints' Day, but has gradually become secularized as an occasion for games played by children, especially in the USA. A jack-o'-lantern, a pumkin carved to look like a demonic face with a lighted candle within it, is carried by children from door to door with a demand for a "treat". If the demand is not conceded the children are entitled to play a "trick" on the householder.

Hallowes, Odette (born Odette Marie Céline Brailly) (1912–95) French heroine of World War II. She entered occupied France in 1942 and worked secretly as a British agent until captured by the Gestapo in 1943. Imprisoned until 1945, she refused to betray her associates despite being tortured. For her work and her courage she was awarded the George Cross (1946).

hallucination A sensation or perception experienced as real but without any external stimulus. An hallucination can occur in any of the five senses. Drugs, exhaustion, and sensory deprivation can produce hallucinations in normal people. Different kinds of hallucination are associated with different pathological conditions. For example, 'organic' PSYCHOSES (caused by degenerative changes in the brain) may produce fragmentary visual hallucinations, while hallucinations in the form of voices which speak about the patient are a primary symptom of SCHIZOPHRENIA, one of the 'functional' psychoses. Drugs that cause hallucinations are called **hallucinogens**; they include cannabis, ECSTASY, and LSD, all of which can cause addiction (see DRUG ABUSE).

halo (in astronomy) A short-lived, incomplete ring of bright light, with the Sun or Moon at its centre, caused by the random refraction of light by ice crystals in high cloud. More complete rings and other complex features such as mock Suns and Sun pillars may be formed if the ice crystals have a preferred orientation and concentrate the light. The shape and appearance of haloes vary with the Sun's elevation and the orientation of the ice crystals.

halocarbon An organic compound derived from a HYDROCARBON, in which one or more hydrogen atoms are replaced by HALOGEN atoms. Examples are the CHLOROFLUOROCARBONS, and the fluorocarbons. The latter are chemically unreactive and tetrafluoroethene, C_2F_4, forms a POLYMER, polytetrafluoroethene, known as teflon or PTFE. In contrast, halocarbons containing the other halogens are more reactive and toxic. The main reaction they undergo is nucleophilic substitution, in which the nucleophile displaces the halogen as the halide ion. For example, chloromethane, CH_3Cl, reacts with hydroxide ions, OH^-, to form methanol, CH_3OH, and chloride ions, Cl^-.

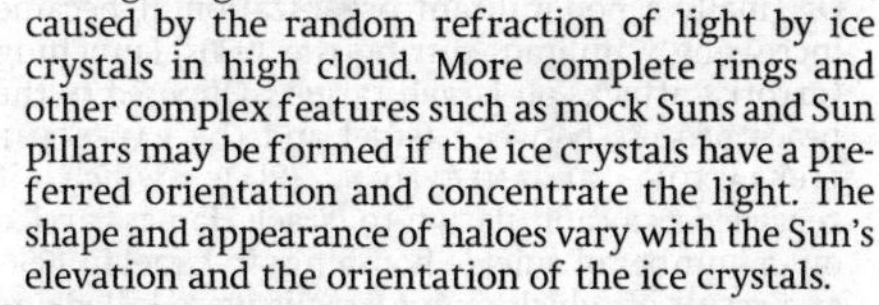

1 2 3 4

Hallmarks (1) The maker's initials. (2) The sterling silver quality mark. (3) The London assay office mark. (4) The date mark for 1957.

halogen An element of Group 17 (formerly VII) in the PERIODIC TABLE, namely fluorine, chlorine, bromine, iodine, and astatine. The halogens are all non-metals, fluorine and chlorine being gases, bromine a volatile liquid, and iodine a solid, at room temperature; astatine is a radioactive element, with a HALF-LIFE too short to permit detailed study of its chemistry. Halogens are reactive elements. They do not occur free in nature, but in compounds such as sodium chloride (common salt). They react with most elements, forming the corresponding HALIDE, their reactivity decreasing down the periodic group.

Hals, Frans (*c*.1582–1666) Dutch portrait and genre painter. His use of bold brushwork to capture the character, mood, and facial expressions of his subjects gave a vitality to his portraits and represented a departure from conventional portraiture. His best-known portraits include groups, such as *The Banquet of the Officers of the St George Militia Company* (1616), and single figures, such as *The Laughing Cavalier* (1624). His genre pictures, painted during the 1620s, reflect the influence of the Dutch followers of Caravaggio.

Ham The second son of the Hebrew figure Noah, father of Cush, Mizraim, Phut, and Canaan and supposed ancestor of the southern peoples, such as the Ethiopians, Egyptians, and Babylonians. Egypt was referred to as the 'Land of Ham'.

Hamada, Shoji (1894–1978) Japanese potter. He visited England in 1920 and collaborated with his friend Bernard Leach before returning to Japan in 1923 to set up his own kiln at Mashiko. He worked mainly in stoneware, producing utilitarian items of unpretentious simplicity; he was a firm believer in the beauty and individuality of the handmade object.

hamadryad See KING COBRA.

Hamas The Islamic Resistance Movement founded in 1976 by Sheikh Yassin Ahmed, with the aim of creating an Islamic state in the former Palestine. Originally a non-militant organization, it became increasingly militant during the 1990s, launching terrorist attacks on Israeli targets. Opposed to the peace process between Israel and the PALESTINE LIBERATION ORGANIZATION (PLO), which it regarded as a capitulation to Israel, Hamas carried out a number of suicide bombings in Israel in 1996, as a result of which many Israelis were killed and hawkish elements in Israeli politics were encouraged to vote out the peace-seeking Shimon Peres in favour of the right-wing Binyamin Netanyahu.

Hamburg A city-state and industrial port of northern Germany, on the River Elbe; area 755 sq km (292 sq miles); pop. (1991) 1,668,760. Founded by Charlemagne in the 9th century, it was a founder member of the Hanseatic League, and became a state of the German Empire in 1871. It was the birthplace of Brahms and Mendelssohn; its university was founded in 1919. At least half of the city was devastated by gigantic fires set off by air raids during World War II. It has been completely reconstructed as the largest port in Germany, with extensive shipyards, petrochemical, electronics, and food-processing industries.

Hamelin (German **Hameln**) A carpet-making and tourist town in Lower Saxony, north-west Germany, on the River Weser; pop. (1983) 57,000. It was a medieval market town, the setting of the legend of the *Pied Piper of Hamelin*, which may be based on actual events which occurred in 1284.

Hamilcar Barca (*c*.270–229 BC) Carthaginian general and father of Hannibal. He fought Rome in the first Punic War and negotiated terms of peace after the Carthaginian defeat of 241, which led to the loss of Sicily to the Romans. From 237 he and Hannibal were engaged in the conquest of Spain.

Hamilton A major industrial city and port in central Canada, in south Ontario, at the western end of Lake Ontario; pop. (1991) 599,760 (metropolitan area). It has been the home of McMaster University since 1930.

Hamilton A manufacturing town in west central Scotland, in South Lanarkshire, near Glasgow; pop. (1991) 50,000.

Hamilton The capital of the Bermuda Islands in the North Atlantic and chief port of Great Bermuda; pop. (1991) 1,100. Established in 1612, it became capital in 1815.

Hamilton, Alexander (*c*.1757–1804) US Federalist politician. As First Secretary of the Treasury under George Washington (1789–95), he established the US central banking system. Hamilton was a prime mover behind the Federalist Party's commitment to strong central government in the aftermath of American independence. He died from a gunshot wound after a duel with Aaron Burr.

Hamilton, Sir Charles (1900–78) New Zealand inventor and motor-racing driver. He is best known for his development of the jet boat, being knighted in 1974 for his services to manufacturing. Hamilton was also a successful motor-racing driver and was the first New Zealander to exceed 100 m.p.h.

Hamilton, Emma, Lady (born Amy Lyon) (*c*.1765–1815) British beauty and mistress of Lord Nelson. In 1791 she married Sir William Hamilton (1730–1803), the British ambassador to Naples, after living with him there for five years. She first met Lord Nelson in Naples in 1793; they became lovers after his second visit in 1799. She had a daughter by him in 1801 and lived with him after her husband's death.

Hamilton, Sir William Rowan (1806–65) Irish mathematician and theoretical physicist. Hamilton made influential contributions to optics and in the foundations of algebra. He invented quaternions while investigating the subject of complex numbers. Hamilton's formulation of mechanics was incorporated into the equations of quantum mechanics.

Hamitic A group of African languages including ancient Egyptian, Berber, and Cushitic, probably related in the past to the Semitic languages.

Hamito-Semitic (or **Afro-Asiatic**) A family of languages spoken in the Middle East and in northern Africa, divided into Semitic, Hamitic, and Chadic subgroups.

Hammarskjöld, Dag (Hjalmar Agne Carl) (1905–61) Swedish diplomat and politician. He was chairman of the Bank of Sweden (1941–48) before becoming Swedish foreign affairs minister (1951–53). As Secretary-General of the United Nations (1953–61) he was influential in the establishment of the UN emergency force in Sinai and Gaza (1956), and also initiated peace moves in the Middle East (1957–58). He was posthumously awarded the 1961 Nobel Peace Prize after his death in an air crash in Zambia.

hammerhead A member of a family of SHARKS, Sphyrnidae, containing nine species, distinguished by the remarkable head, which is flattened and expanded in the shape of a hammer or spade. The eyes are placed at the extremity of these hammer-lobes and the nostrils are widely spaced on the front edge. The structure of the head may result in enhanced ability to trace scents in the water, but its function is not entirely certain.

Living in all the tropical oceans, they are mainly coastal sharks, but they do migrate far out to sea. They feed on a wide range of fishes and some of the larger species have been known to attack man. The great hammerhead, *Sphyrna mokarran*, of world-wide distribution, grows to 6 m (19 feet) in length.

hammerkop (or **hammerhead stork**) A bird, *Scopus umbretta*, related to the storks and herons, but usually put in a family of its own, Scopidae. It lives in the warmer parts of Africa, stands about 60 cm (2 feet) high and is brown in colour, with a large crest spreading behind the head. It catches fish and amphibians with its powerful, heron-like beak. Its most unusual characteristic is that it builds an enormous, domed nest of sticks and mud among the branches of large trees. The entrance, or entrances, are in the side and the nest may be used for many seasons.

Hammersmith A district of London, England, that (since 1965) has formed with Fulham an inner borough to the north of the Thames; pop. (1991) 136,500. The Olympia exhibition centre and the BBC Television centre are located here.

Hammerstein II, Oscar (1895–1960) US librettist. He collaborated with the composers Jerome Kern (for example in *Showboat*, 1927), Sigmund Romberg, and most notably with Richard RODGERS. He also wrote the libretto for the musical *Carmen Jones* (1943), an adaptation of Bizet's opera *Carmen*.

Hammett, (Samuel) Dashiell (1894–1961) US novelist. His detective fiction, based in part on his own experiences as a detective, is characterized by a hard-boiled style and influenced Raymond Chandler and other writers in the genre. Many of Hammett's stories, including *The Maltese Falcon* (1930) and *The Thin Man* (1932), were made into successful films. He lived for many years with the dramatist Lillian HELLMAN; they were both persecuted for their left-wing views during the McCarthy era.

Hammond, Dame Joan (1912–96) Australian operatic soprano, born in New Zealand. She made her operatic début in Sydney in 1929 and went on to an international career with a wide repertoire. Her operatic successes included Puccini's *Madame Butterfly* and *Turandot*; she also performed in choral works and oratorios, such as Handel's *Messiah*.

Hammurabi (died 1750 BC) The sixth king of the first dynasty of Babylonia, reigned 1792–1750 BC. He made Babylon the capital of Babylonia and extended the Babylonian empire. He instituted one of the earliest known legal codes, which took the form of 282 case laws dealing with the economy and with family, criminal, and civil law.

Hamnett, Katharine (1952–) British fashion designer. After working as a freelance designer she established her own company in 1979. Her designs are characterized by their loose, simple lines and use of utilitarian fabrics. She also made a name for herself as a feminist and supporter of CND.

Hampshire A county on the coast of southern England; area 3,780 sq km (1,460 sq miles); pop. (1991) 1,511,900; county town, Winchester.

Hampstead A residential suburb of north-west London. It contains Hampstead Heath, a large tract of open common land within the city, popular for recreation.

Hampton Court A palace on the north bank of the River Thames in the London borough of Richmond, England. It was built by Cardinal Wolsey as his private residence but later presented by him to Henry VIII, and was a favourite royal residence until the reign of George II. William III had part rebuilt by Sir Christopher Wren and the gardens laid out in formal Dutch style. Its collections, gardens, and maze are a major tourist attraction.

Hampton Court Conference (1604) A meeting in which the new king of England, JAMES I, presided over an assembly of bishops and Puritans. The 'Millenary Petition' presented by the Puritans in 1602 had listed church practices offensive to them and had asked for reform in the Anglican Church. Most of their demands were refused, although it was agreed to produce a new translation of the BIBLE, the Authorized Version of 1611.

Hampton Roads A deep-water estuary 6.4 km (4 miles) long, formed by the James River where it joins Chesapeake Bay, on the Atlantic coast of south-east Virginia, USA. It has been used as a natural anchorage since colonial times. The comprises the harbours at Newport News, Norfolk, and Portsmouth.

hamster A rodent of the subfamily Cricetinae: a relative of rats, mice, voles, and gerbils, with which it shares the family Muridae. Hamsters, of which there are 24 species, typically have soft fur, rounded faces, and large eyes. These features make them attractive as pets, of which the golden hamster, *Mesocricetus auratus*, is the most popular. All the captive stock of the golden hamster is descended from one female and twelve young which were collected in Syria in 1930. Its range includes much of the Middle East but the animal is little known in the wild. Another Middle Eastern species, the long-tailed hamster, *Cricetulus longicaudatus*, is rather rat-like in appearance. The common or European hamster, *Cricetus cricetus*, occurs in central Europe, the Caucasus, and western Siberia. In eastern Siberia, Manchuria, and northern China, there are three species known as dwarf hamsters, *Phodopus* species. All hamsters have huge cheek pouches in which they store food. They eat mainly seeds and grasses, and occasionally insects. They live communally in extensive burrow systems.

Hamsun, Knut (pseudonym of Knut Pedersen) (1859–1952) Norwegian novelist. He worked in a variety of manual jobs before the publication of his first novel, *Hunger* (1890), a semi-autobiographical account of the mental and physical hardships he experienced during this period. This successful novel was followed by further works exploring the human psyche and written in a similar fragmentary, vivid style, including *Growth of the Soil* (1917). He was awarded the Nobel Prize for literature in 1920.

Han The Chinese dynasty that ruled from 206 BC until 200 AD with only a brief interruption. During this period the territory was expanded, administration was in the hands of an organized civil service, Confucianism was recognized as the state philosophy, and detailed historical records were kept. The arts flourished, and technological advances included the invention of paper.

Hancock, Tony (full name Anthony John Hancock) (1924–68) British comedian. He made his name in 1954 with the radio series *Hancock's Half Hour*, in which he played a materialistic, lonely misfit and was noted for his sardonic wit. The series readily adapted to television (1956–61); Hancock later turned to writing his own material and starred in other comedy shows, as well as appearing in several films, but failed to repeat his earlier success. He committed suicide in 1968.

hand An appendage at the end of the arm, which

has a very similar bone structure to that of feet, differing mainly in the names of the bones. The tarsals and metatarsals of the foot become carpals and metacarpals in the hand. They are best recognized in primates, including humans, where the forelimbs are used to collect and manipulate food and tools. The FINGERS are the main agents of manipulation, although the wrist bones (carpals) are more flexible than their equivalents in the foot. Human hands are distinguished from those of other primates by having wide tips, or balls, to the thumb. The ability to press each finger tip against the thumb ball, allows man to grip and manipulate objects with a much finer degree of control than other primates.

Handel, George Frederick (born Georg Friedrich Händel) (1685–1759) German-born composer, resident in England from 1712. He was a major Baroque musician whose prolific output included choral works, chamber music, operas, concerti grossi, and orchestral pieces. He is now chiefly remembered for his oratorios, the most famous of which is *Messiah* (1742); other choral works include *Samson* (1743) and *Judas Maccabaeus* (1747). Of his many other works, perhaps the best known is the *Water Music* suite for orchestra (*c*.1717), written for George I's procession down the River Thames. Handel was also a noted organist and invented the organ concerto, which he intended to be performed between the acts of his own oratorios.

Handley Page, Frederick See PAGE.

Handy, W(illiam) C(hristopher) (1873–1958) US blues musician. As a cornettist he became leader of the band the Mahara Minstrels (1896–1903). He then began to write pieces for his own band and set up a music publishing house in 1914. His transcriptions of traditional blues, such as the 'St Louis Blues' (1914), were influential in establishing the accepted pattern of the modern twelve-bar blues.

hang-glider A lightweight type of GLIDER, usually manœuvred by shifting of the pilot's body weight. Often the pilot is suspended beneath the flexible or rigid wing. Hang-gliders can have a monoplane or biplane configuration. Hang-gliding as a sport began in California in the late 1960s, and went to Europe in around 1973. It has since grown in popularity with the introduction of lightweight materials.

hanging valley A (usually tributary) valley that has not had its floor cut down to the level of the valley or plain it joins. In glaciated mountains hanging valleys represent the former channels of small glaciers, which could not dig their beds as deeply as the main glacier they merged with. They also occur along fault lines where blocks of land have been suddenly uplifted, disrupting river channels. The step below a hanging valley is often the site of a waterfall.

Hangzhou (formerly **Hangchow**) The capital city of Zhejiang province in eastern China, situated on Hangzhou Bay, an inlet of the Yellow Sea, at the southern end of the Grand Canal; pop. (1990) 2,589,500. Its chief industries include oil refining and the manufacture of silk, satins, brocades, iron, steel, electronics, and machinery.

Hanks, Tom (full name Thomas J. Hanks) (1956–) US actor. Hanks built a reputation as a deft comedian in light-hearted films such as *Splash!* (1984), and won major international success with *Big* (1988). He went on to win Oscars for his performances in *Philadelphia* (1993) and *Forrest Gump* (1994).

Hannibal (247–182 BC) Carthaginian general. He precipitated the second Punic War by attacking

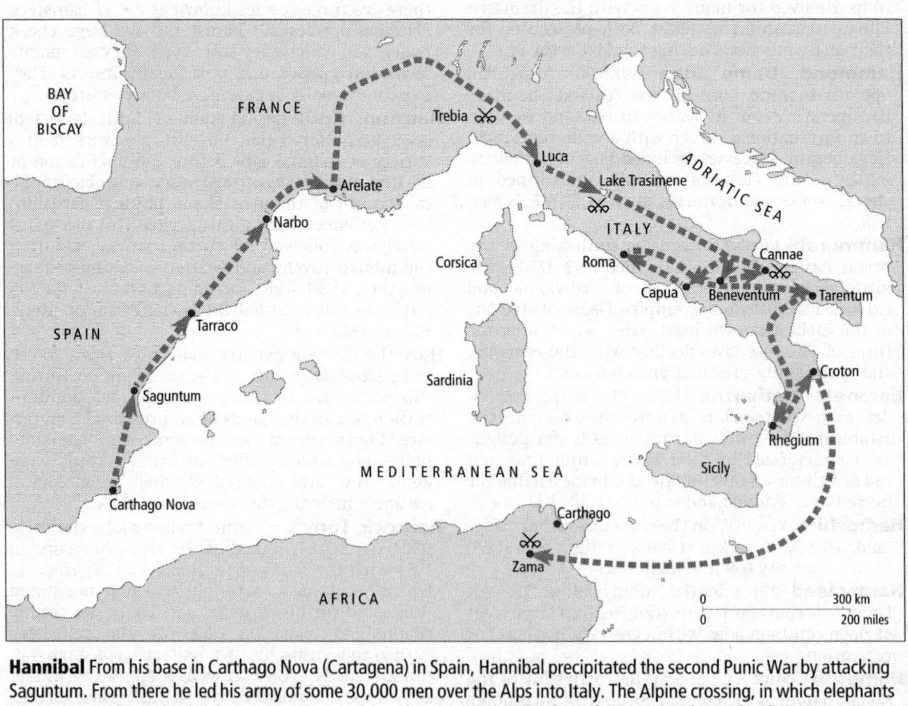

Hannibal From his base in Carthago Nova (Cartagena) in Spain, Hannibal precipitated the second Punic War by attacking Saguntum. From there he led his army of some 30,000 men over the Alps into Italy. The Alpine crossing, in which elephants were extensively used to haul equipment, was achieved in only 15 days – a feat of ancient warfare. After failing to capture Rome, he was recalled to Carthage; his defeat at Zama brought the second Punic War to an end.

the town of Saguntum in Spain, an ally of Rome. In 218, in a pre-emptive move, he led an army of about 30,000 over the Alps into Italy. There he inflicted a series of defeats on the Romans (see CANNAE), campaigning for 16 years undefeated but failing to take Rome itself. After being recalled to Africa he was defeated at Zama by Scipio Africanus in 202.

Hanoi The capital and second-largest city of Vietnam, on the Red River; pop. (est. 1984) 925,000, Greater Hanoi pop. (1989) 1,089,700. It was the capital of French Indo-China from 1887 to 1946 and of North Vietnam before reunification of North and South Vietnam in 1975. It manufactures vehicles, machine tools, chemicals, and textiles.

Hanover (German **Hannover**) ▶**1** An industrial and cultural city and capital of Lower Saxony, northern Germany, on the River Leine; pop. (1991) 517,480. George I of Britain is buried here. It has a trade fair in the spring and its industries manufacture steel, chemicals, rubber, and textiles. ▶**2** A former state and province in northern Germany. It was an electorate of the Empire from 1692 until 1806, ruled by the Guelph dynasty, and from 1866 until 1945 was a province of Prussia. In 1714 the Elector of Hanover succeeded to the British throne as George I, and from then until 1837 the same monarch ruled both Britain and Hanover. With the succession of Victoria to the British throne, however, Hanover passed to her uncle, Ernest, Duke of Cumberland, the Hanoverian succession being denied to a woman as long as a male member of the Guelph family survived.

Hanseatic League An association of north German cities (Hanse Towns), formed in 1241 as a trading alliance. Cologne, which had enjoyed special trading privileges with England, was joined by other traders following an agreement between Hamburg and Lübeck (1241) and a Diet of 1260. The towns of the League dealt mainly in wool, cloth, linen, and silver. In the later Middle Ages the League, with about 100 member towns, was an independent political power with its own army and navy. It began to collapse in the early 17th century and only three major cities (Hamburg, Bremen, and Lübeck) remained in the League until it was finally broken up in the 19th century.

Hanukkah (Feast of Lights or Dedication) Jewish festival that lasts eight days during November or December. The festival commemorates the cleansing of the Temple in Jerusalem by Judas Maccabeus in 165 BC, after it had been given over to idolatry by Antiochus Epiphanes, who denied the Jews access. A seven-branched receptacle for oil or candles (*menorah*) is lit, signifying, among other things, the seven days of creation. On each day of Hanukkah, one more candle is lit, and the ceremony culminates in games and the exchange of presents.

Hanuman In Hindu and Buddhist mythology, the agile monkey-chief son of the wind-god Vayu, whose semi-divine nature enabled him to fly and change his shape and size. As general of the army of the monkey-king Sugriva, Hanuman helped Rāma defeat Rāvaŋdb.a's forces and save Sītā. Chinese Buddhist legend recounts how, as Sun Houzu, Hanuman helped the great Chinese pilgrim, Xuanzang, on his pilgrimage to India.

Hapsburg See HABSBURG.

hara-kiri (Japanese, 'belly-cutting') The ritual suicide, more properly called *seppuku*, practised by Japanese samurai warriors. In ZEN Buddhism the belly is the spiritual centre of the body, thus hara-kiri may be understood as a spiritual act. The samurai preferred death to dishonour, and *seppuku*, a legal and ceremonial process, was performed to avoid disgrace, to atone for a failure of duty, or to demonstrate loyalty and resolve. See also *bushido*.

Harare (formerly **Salisbury**) The capital, largest city, and marketing centre of Zimbabwe, at an altitude of 1,470 m (4,825 ft) in the province of Mashonaland East; pop. (1992) 1,184,170. Originally named Fort Salisbury in honour of the British prime minister Lord Salisbury, the city was first settled by Europeans in 1890. It was designated capital of Southern Rhodesia in 1902. It is a modern city with the world's largest tobacco market and produces a wide range of food-stuffs, building materials, and consumer goods.

Harbin (or **Ha-er-bin**) A port and industrial centre on the Songhua River in north-east China; pop. (1990) 3,597,400. It is the capital of Heilongjiang province.

hard disk (or **Winchester disk**) A device capable of storing large quantities of information (usually more than ten million BYTES) for long periods in a computer system. Unlike a FLOPPY DISK, a hard disk is made of rigid aluminium covered by a magnetic layer. The disk spins continuously and is sealed within the disk drive. Data is read from or written to the disk by the magnetic heads of the disk drive.

hard-edge painting A type of painting (predominantly abstract) in which forms, although not necessarily geometrical, have sharp contours and are executed in flat colours. The term was first used in 1958 and it is applied mainly to the type of painting that emerged in the USA as a reaction to the spontaneity of ABSTRACT EXPRESSIONISM.

Hardie, (James) Keir (1856–1915) Scottish Labour politician. He worked as a miner before entering Parliament in 1892, becoming the first leader of the Independent Labour Party the next year. In 1906 he became a co-founder and first leader of the Labour Party. His pacifist views prompted his withdrawal from Labour politics when the majority of his party's MPs declared their support for British participation in World War I, although he remained an MP until his death.

Harding, Warren (Gamaliel) (1865–1923) US Republican statesman, 29th President of the USA 1921–23. He died suddenly in office, before the worst revelations of his administration's incompetence and corruption had been made.

hardness of water The presence of calcium or magnesium compounds in water. When soap is added to hard water, an insoluble scum is formed instead of a lather; this is because soap contains sodium stearate, which reacts with calcium and magnesium ions, forming the insoluble calcium or magnesium stearate. This leaves less stearate available for combining with the dirt it is meant to remove. Hard water is often found in areas containing chalk or limestone. If hard water contains calcium or magnesium hydrogencarbonate, it can be softened by boiling, because the soluble hydrogencarbonate decomposes to the insoluble carbonate, which is precipitated out, as it is in the fur found in kettles. Hardness that can be removed by boiling is called temporary hardness. Water containing calcium or magnesium chlorides or sulphates cannot be softened by boiling, because these compounds do not decompose; such water is called permanently hard. Permanent hardness can be removed by the addition of sodium carbonate or washing-soda, or by the use of ZEOLITES. Hardness does not affect the cleansing action of DETERGENTS.

hardpan (or **duricrust**) A hardened or cemented layer that occurs in or below the soil PROFILE. Hardpans are formed when material is washed out of the upper part of the soil by eluviation and redeposited as a distinct horizon lower down. Nodules of cemented material, or CONCRETIONS, formed by the same process may represent the beginning of hardpan formation. Hardpans vary in thickness from a few millimetres to a metre or more, depending on how long they have been forming. Many different substances can act as cementing agents. The most common are iron, silica, calcium carbonate, clay, and humus. Thick ironpans are formed by iron and aluminium oxide accumulation in latosols, producing a material known as laterite. Laterite is used in Indo-China as a building material, because cut blocks become very hard when dried. Calcium carbonate hardpans are known by many names, such as calcrete, caliche, kunkar, and travertine. They are common in desert soils and sierozems. Humus-cemented hardpans, which are also called orstein and coffee rock, are found in PODZOLS, where they occur above thin pans of iron and clay. Most hardpans are impermeable and so they profoundly affect the drainage of water through the soil profile.

hardware (in computers) The physical parts of a computer system, including the CENTRAL PROCESSING UNIT, MEMORY, BUS, and clock, as well as PERIPHERALS such as PRINTERS, disk and tape drives, keyboards, and VISUAL DISPLAY UNITS. Hardware cannot function usefully without SOFTWARE.

Hardy, Thomas (1752–1832) Scottish radical leader, a champion of parliamentary reform. He moved to London in 1774, where he became a shoemaker. In 1792 he founded the London Corresponding Society, whose aim was to achieve universal manhood suffrage. The country was at war with Revolutionary France and the government became alarmed at the Society's growing influence. In 1794 Hardy was arrested on a charge of high treason but at the subsequent trial he was acquitted.

Hardy, Thomas (1840–1928) British novelist and poet. He spent most of his life in his native Dorset (the 'Wessex' of his novels). A recurrent theme in Hardy's work is the struggle of human beings against the indifferent force that inflicts the sufferings and ironies of life. Major novels include *The Mayor of Casterbridge* (1886), *Tess of the D'Urbervilles* (1891), and *Jude the Obscure* (1896). He turned to writing poetry in the late 1890s and published eight volumes of poems, as well as a drama in blank verse, *The Dynasts* (1904–08).

hare A mammal of the order Lagomorpha, which also includes the RABBITS and PIKAS. Hares are distinguished from rabbits, with which they share the family Leporidae, by the production of young in an advanced stage, fully furred and with open eyes. Also, they never burrow like rabbits but rest during the day in 'forms', which are shallow depressions in the ground. There are some 27 species of hare, including the American JACKRABBITS, the African bushman hare, *Bunolagus monticularis*, and red rockhares, *Pronolagus* species. The common or European brown hare, *Lepus europaeus*, has a huge range from southern Finland to Iran. Hares have also been introduced into Australia, New Zealand, and South America. Some, including the blue or Arctic hare, *L. timidus*, change colour from brown to white in winter.

Hare, Robert (1781–1858) US chemist who is mainly remembered for the apparatus he devised for comparing the densities of two liquids. The liquids are drawn up separate vertical tubes by sucking on a mouthpiece connected to both. The densities of the liquids are in inverse proportion to the heights raised.

Hare, William See BURKE.

harebell See CAMPANULA.

Harefoot, Harold Harold I of England. See HAROLD.

Hare Krishna (International Society for Krishna Consciousness) A modern Hindu sect brought to the West in the 1960s by A. C. Bhaktivedanta Swami, and based on the teachings of Guru Chaitanya (1486–1534). Members attend temple services or dedicate themselves fully to an austere, monastic life of service and devotion to Krishna. The way of Krishna Consciousness forbids alcohol and demands a vegetarian diet. Followers stress the spiritual benefits of music, ecstatic trance, and chanting, particularly the MANTRA 'Hare Krishna, Hare Rama', as a way of concentrating the mind in devotion on Krishna's various manifestations in the AVATARS of VISHNU. Full members often assume Hindu dress and customs, and are encouraged to chant and proselytize in the streets.

harelip (or **cleft lip**) A facial defect, present at birth, in which there is a cleft in the upper lip. There is often also a cleft in the roof of the mouth (CLEFT PALATE). These defects make speech indistinct, but can be repaired by surgery.

Hargreaves, James (*c*.1720–78) British engineer who played a major role in mechanizing the cotton industry. While a hand-loom weaver in Blackburn, Lancashire, he invented (*c*.1760) a CARDING MACHINE that doubled the speed of the carding process, but his major invention was the spinning-jenny (1764), a hand-driven SPINNING-machine that could spin a number of threads at once.

Haringey A northern inner borough of Greater London, containing the districts of Hornsey, Wood Green, and Tottenham; pop. (1991) 187,300.

Harlech A village in Gwynedd, west Wales, on Tremadoc Bay; pop. (1991) 1,223. It was the ancient capital of Merionethshire and has the remains of a famous castle built in the 13th century by Edward I.

Harlem A district of New York City, USA, synonymous with a mostly black commercial and residential area, which in 1964 saw major race riots.

harlequinade A theatrical performance in which Harlequin plays the leading role. As a theatre form it originated in the fusion of the Italian *commedia dell'arte* with the dumbshows of the actors at the Paris fairgrounds, where dialogue was forbidden. Harlequinade was an important element in the development of the English PANTOMIME. Harlequin was later transformed into the persecuted lover, fantastically dressed in a silken suit of brightly coloured diamond patches, and retaining from his origins his black mask and his magic wand, or bat. The harlequinade eventually dwindled into a short epilogue to what became the present English pantomime. It was finally abandoned completely.

harlequin bug See SHIELDBUG.

Harley Street A street in London, England, associated with the premises of eminent physicians and surgeons since about 1845. It was named after the ground landlord, Edward Harley, 2nd Earl of Oxford.

Harlow A town in west Essex, south-east England, 33 km (21 miles) north of London; pop. (1991) 73,500.

It was designated a New Town in 1947 and has numerous light industries.

Harlow, Jean (born Harlean Carpenter) (1911–37) US film actress. A platinum blonde with considerable sex appeal, she led a tempestuous life, becoming a film extra in Hollywood after eloping from Kansas when she was 16. Her first success came with Howard Hughes's *Hell's Angels* (1930). She made six films with Clark Gable, including *Red Dust* (1932) and *Saratoga* (1937), before her death from uraemic poisoning.

harmattan A parching, dusty land-wind blowing off the Sahara to the coast of west Africa from December to March.

harmonica A mouth-blown free-reed musical instrument, also called a MOUTH-ORGAN or blues harp by folk musicians, invented by Christian Buschmann about 1821 and developed by later makers. Simple harmonicas are diatonic; chromatic instruments have a slide which, when pressed in, blocks off the basic row of reeds and opens access to a second row a semitone higher. Both models have reeds for the common chord sounding on blow, and the other notes of the scale sounding on draw; players block the unwanted reed chambers with the tongue to sound notes one by one or in particular chords.

harmonics The lesser vibrations produced by voices or instruments that add colour to the main note. Voices and instruments produce their sound when something is made to vibrate – the vocal cords, a column of air, a stretched string. Each main vibration contains a series of lesser vibrations. Thus a string vibrates alongs its whole length, and also in halves, thirds, quarters, fifths, and so on. The main note that we hear is that of the whole vibrating string, the first harmonic or fundamental. The lesser vibrations (harmonics, overtones, or partials) produce their own sounds, though these are largely overshadowed by the first harmonic. The harmonics enable us to distinguish between the sound of different voices or instruments. Each emphasizes different harmonies and therefore has a characteristic timbre. Harmonics follow a mathematical progression, and as the series rises the intervals between them grow smaller.

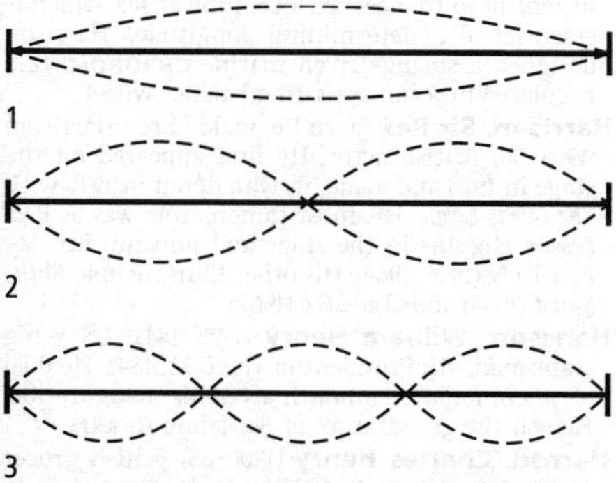

Harmonics (1) When a string vibrates along its whole length the note heard is the first harmonic (or fundamental). (2) When the vibration takes place over only half the string's length the second harmonic (or first overtone) is heard. This has a frequency double that of the fundamental. (3) When the vibration takes place over a third of the string's length the third harmonic (second overtone) is heard. This has a frequency three times that of the fundamental.

harmonium A musical instrument, a reed-organ blown by pedal-operated bellows. It is often used as a substitute for a church organ, with free-reeds instead of pipes, especially in chapels and small churches. The harmonium was also popular for domestic use. Strictly the harmonium blows air past the reeds, as opposed to an American organ, which sucks air past them.

harmony (in music) The art of using chords, involving not only the way in which individual chords are constructed, but also their relationship. This aspect of music only began to be codified into a specific 'grammar' with the establishment of a system of TONALITY during the 17th century; harmonies began to be thought of as entities in themselves, as distinct from being the vertical outcome of horizontal lines in combination: POLYPHONY giving way to homophony. Such vertical combinations of notes as seemed pleasant to the ear were known as concords. Those that seemed less pleasant were discords. Both were linked by accepted methods of progression that stemmed, ultimately, from the harmonic series. Discords always needed to be 'resolved' on to concords, and concords moved in stately progression from one to the other. Fundamental to this practice was the idea of diatonic harmony – chords built from the notes of the major or minor SCALE. Chords involving notes outside the scales were said to be chromatic. It was only when chromatic harmonies began to be accepted as the norm, at the end of the 19th century, that the tonal system was undermined and new ways of explaining music (such as SERIALISM) had to be found.

Harmsworth, Alfred Charles William See NORTHCLIFFE.

Harold Two kings of England. **Harold I** (known as Harold Harefoot) (died 1040) reigned 1035–40. Harold was an illegitimate son of Canute and first came to the throne when his half-brother Hardecanute (Canute's legitimate heir) was king of Denmark and thus absent at the time of his father's death. When a third royal claimant was murdered a year later, Harold was formally recognized as king, although Hardecanute returned to the kingdom when Harold himself died. **Harold II** (*c.*1019–66) reigned 1066, the last Anglo-Saxon king of England. He succeeded Edward the Confessor, having dominated the latter's court in the last years of his reign, but was faced with two invasions within months of his accession. He overcame his half-brother Tostig and the Norse king Harald Hardrada at Stamford Bridge, but was killed and his army defeated at the Battle of Hastings; the victor, William of Normandy, took the throne as William I.

Harold I (*c.*850–933) First King of all Norway (872–933). A series of battles with minor kings culminated in his decisive victory at Hafrsfjord. He then succeeded in bringing the Orkney and Shetland islands, together with much of northern Scotland, into his kingdom and forced out many Vikings who went on to conquer Iceland and land in western Europe.

Haroun-al-Raschid See HARUN AR-RASHID.

harp A plucked musical instrument with strings rising vertically from the resonator to an arm or neck. A forepillar may hold the arm from the resonator, but many regional harps are open, with either a curved or an acutely angled arm. Harps were perhaps the earliest stringed instruments of civilization, possibly even older than LYRES. In the 18th century various pedal mechanisms were invented, each controlling all the strings of one note name. In 1810 Sébastien Érard patented his double-action harp in which each pedal has three positions: this became the basis of the modern concert harp. The present Celtic harp derives its size and shape – with the column out-curved in older Irish and medieval style – from the 'portable Irish harp', produced in Dublin about 1819 by the maker John Egan as a drawing-room successor to the old professional Irish harp. 'Bardic' or 'knee harps' (Gaelic *clàrsach*) are based on the medieval Irish and Scottish models. The Welsh triple harp was known in Italy around 1600 and adopted by the Welsh harpists in the 17th century, replacing an older single-strung harp and becoming their normal instrument, until almost wholly replaced by the pedal harp after the mid-19th century.

Harpers Ferry A small town in Jefferson County, West Virginia, USA, at the junction of the Potomac and Shenandoah rivers. It is famous for a raid in October 1859 in which John Brown and a group of Abolitionists captured a federal arsenal.

harpsichord A keyboard musical instrument. A wooden jack resting on each key jumps up so that a quill, set in a tongue, plucks the string. As the jack falls back, the tongue tips, preventing the quill plucking again. During the 16th century two distinctive types of harpsichord developed, the bright-sounding Italian and the rather richer Flemish. By the 18th century, French, German, and English harpsichords were also established, each with a characteristic tone quality; thus Bach, Couperin, Scarlatti, and Handel each wrote for different sonorities.

harpy In Greek mythology, a type of loathsome monster with an insatiable hunger, conceived of as a repulsive bird of prey with a woman's head and trunk.

harpy eagle One of the largest species of EAGLE, *Harpia harpyja*, with wings spanning 2 m (6.5 feet). Harpy eagles live in the canopy of South American rain forests, seldom appearing above or below it. Their prey includes monkeys, sloths, and birds.

harquebus See FIREARM.

harrier A member of a cosmopolitan subfamily of ten species of HAWK of the genus *Circus* with long, square-cut wings, and long legs. In flight they swoop low over the ground when hunting. They spot their prey from trees or posts, or by quartering systematically over likely ground. Small mammals, frogs, insects, and ground birds are typical prey. Many species of harrier are migratory, avoiding extreme cold. Harriers nest on the ground but courtship involves a spectacular aerial dance, during which the male passes food to the female.

Harris The southern part of the largest and northernmost island (Lewis and Harris) of the Outer Hebrides, off the north-west coast of Scotland. The chief settlements are Tarbert and Leverburgh. It is famous for its hand-woven tweed (Harris tweed).

Harris, Sir Arthur (Travers), 1st Baronet (known as 'Bomber Harris') (1892–1984) British Marshal of the RAF. After joining the Royal Flying Corps in World War I, Harris served as Commander-in-Chief of Bomber Command in World War II from 1942 to 1945. He organized mass bombing raids against German towns and cities which, as well as inflicting major economic damage, resulted in large-scale civilian casualties. This strategy aroused some controversy but had Churchill's full support.

Harris, Frank (born James Thomas Harris) (1856–1931) Irish writer. He spent much of his life in England, where he gained a reputation as a fearless journalist, editing several journals including the *Saturday Review* (1894–98). His autobiography, the three-volume *My Life and Loves* (1923–27), became notorious for its unreliability and sexual frankness. He also wrote biographies of Oscar Wilde and Bernard Shaw.

Harris, Joel Chandler (1848–1908) US author of children's fiction and short stories. He published the first of his Uncle Remus stories in 1879. These verses and tales were based on the folklore of former plantation slaves, told in dialect by the storyteller Uncle Remus. The central animal characters, led by Br'er Rabbit and Br'er Fox, are noted for their humorous dialogue and homely wisdom. Harris also wrote stories set in Georgia for adults.

Harris, Roy (1898–1979) US composer. His large output includes 16 symphonies, written between 1933 and 1979, of which the Third (1937) made a particularly strong impression. His music is stark and forceful, highly contrapuntal (see COUNTERPOINT), and often based on American folk idioms and Protestant hymn tunes.

Harrisburg The state capital of Pennsylvania, USA, on the Susquehanna River; pop. (1990) 52,370. A trading post was set up here by John Harris in 1718 and a town established by his son in 1785. A nuclear reactor at nearby Three Mile Island was, in 1979, the scene of a near catastrophic accident that led to a reassessment of US nuclear-safety standards.

Harrison, Benjamin (1833–1901) US Republican statesman, 23rd President of the USA 1889–93. He was the grandson of William Henry HARRISON.

Harrison, George (1943–) British rock and pop guitarist. Harrison was the lead guitarist of the Beatles, to whom he contributed occasional songs (one of the best known being 'Something', 1969). His fascination with India (he sometimes played sitar on Beatles records) was reflected in the solo career that he pursued after the group's breakup in 1970; latterly he has concentrated on running a film production company.

Harrison, John (1693–1776) British horologist. In 1726, he invented the grid-iron pendulum, which increased the accuracy of clocks by automatically compensating for changes in pendulum length caused by temperature variations. To meet the urgent need to measure local time at sea, which is essential for determining longitude, Harrison designed a spring-driven marine CHRONOMETER, regulated by a compensating balance wheel.

Harrison, Sir Rex (born Reginald Carey Harrison) (1908–90) British actor. He first appeared on the stage in 1924 and made his film début in 1930 with *The Great Game*. His most famous role was as Professor Higgins in the stage and film musical *My Fair Lady* (1956, 1964). His other films include *Blithe Spirit* (1944) and *Cleopatra* (1962).

Harrison, William Henry (1773–1841) US Whig statesman, 9th President of the USA, 1841. He died of pneumonia one month after his inauguration. He was the grandfather of Benjamin HARRISON.

Harrod, Charles Henry (1800–85) British grocer and tea merchant. In 1853 he took over a shop in Knightsbridge, London, which, after expansion by his son Charles Digby Harrod (1841–1905), became a prestigious department store.

harrow A type of CULTIVATOR used to break up soil clods to produce a suitable seed-bed, or to break up the root systems of weeds such as couch grass. Some harrows have solid spikes, known as tines. These may be fixed or sprung, and more recently power-operated machines have been designed that perform several operations at one pass. Chainlink harrows are used to tear out the matt of dead grass, allowing air into the soil and encouraging the regrowth of fresh shoots.

Harrow A borough of north-west London, England. Harrow-on-the-Hill, around which most of the borough lies, is dominated by the public school (**Harrow School**), founded by John Lyon in 1572.

Hart, Lorenz See RODGERS, RICHARD.

Harte, (Francis) Bret (1836–1902) US short-story writer and poet. He is chiefly remembered for his stories about life in a gold-mining settlement, which were inspired by his own brief experience of mining and collected in works such as *The Luck of Roaring Camp* (1870).

hartebeest A species of grazing antelope, *Alcelaphus buselaphus*, found in large herds on the open plains and desert areas of Africa. It feeds during the day on grass and seems to need very little water. When herds are grazing, a sentinel is posted on an ant-hill; this timid animal rarely attempts to defend itself even when wounded and is preyed upon by lions and other predators. It is amongst the fastest of the larger antelopes. There are many subspecies of hartebeest, including the korrigum, topi, senegal, western hartebeest, kongoni, and the bubal hartebeest. The coat is reddish or yellowish-brown, varying in the different subspecies. The face is long and thin, while the horns, present in both sexes, are short and stout.

Hartford The state capital of Connecticut, north-east USA, on the Connecticut River; pop. (1992) 131,995. Founded by Dutch settlers in 1623, the city has developed into a major centre for insurance companies. It manufactures aircraft engines, office and domestic equipment, and firearms.

Hartlepool An industrial town, port, and unitary authority on the North Sea coast of Durham, north-east England; pop. (1991) 87,310. It has engineering and brewing industries.

Hartley, L(eslie) P(oles) (1895–1972) British novelist. Much of his work deals with memory and the effects of childhood experience on adult life and character, as in his trilogy *The Shrimp and the Anemone* (1944), *The Sixth Heaven* (1946), and *Eustace and Hilda* (1947), as well as the novel *The Go-Between* (1953).

Hartnell, Sir Norman (1901–79) British couturier. He is remembered as the dressmaker to Queen Elizabeth II (whose coronation gown he designed) and to the Queen Mother.

hart's tongue A fern, *Asplenium scolopendrium*, with undivided, strap-shaped fronds of a bright, shiny green. The spore-cases are in regular lines running from the central vein to the margin of the frond. It belongs to a group of relatively small ferns, many with fronds divided into tiny leaflets. Other species in this genus include wall rue, *A. ruta-muraria*, rusty-back fern, *A. ceterach*, several species of spleenworts, and BIRD's nest fern.

Harun ar-Rashid (or **Haroun-al-Raschid**) (763–809) Fifth Abbasid caliph of Baghdad 786–809. He was the most powerful and vigorous of the Abbasid caliphs; he and his court were made famous by their portrayal in the *Arabian Nights*.

Harut and Marut In Islam, the two fallen angels, featured in the Koran, who taught sorcery and magic and sowed discord between husband and wife among the citizens of Babel. According to Islamic legend Harut and Marut chose suffering in this world as their punishment for succumbing to the sexual charms of a woman and for killing the man who had witnessed their crime. In a similar Jewish legend the fallen angels are 'Uzza and 'Azael.

Harvard The oldest American university, founded in 1636 at Cambridge, Massachusetts. It is named after John Harvard (died 1638), an English settler, who bequeathed to it his library and half his estate.

Harvard classification See SPECTRAL CLASSES.

harvestman (or **daddy-long-legs**) A familiar spindly-legged ARACHNID of the order Opiliones, abundant in humus and on tree trunks. Harvestmen resemble spiders, but lack a narrow waist. The legs of some species may be forty times the body length. A distinctive feature of many of the 3,200 worldwide species is that their eyes are often placed on a tubercule in the centre of the thorax, or carapace. Some harvestmen produce noxious secretions, and a few actually spray these at attackers. Defence can also involve deliberately shedding legs, if gripped by a predator, or feigning death for minutes at a time.

harvest-mite (or **bracken bug**) The bright red parasitic larval stage of a very common subfamily of MITE, the Trombiculinae, which has free-living adults. The larvae bite any warm-blooded animals, especially rabbits, and can cause severe irritation to humans when the knife-like mouthparts penetrate, especially around ankles and armpits. A salivary secretion is injected before tissue fluids are sucked out; fortunately these particular mites are not carriers of disease.

harvest mouse One of the smallest species of RODENT, *Micromys minutus*, with a body length of some 65 mm (2.6 inches). They have a wide distribution from south-east Asia through Eurasia to the Arctic Circle. Contrary to popular legend, numbers of harvest mice have not declined drastically as a result of the introduction of combine harvesters since they breed commonly in hedges. The name harvest mouse is also given to 19 species of very different mice of the genus *Reithodontomys*, from Central and South America.

Harvey, William (1578–1657) English discoverer of the mechanism of blood circulation and physician to James I and Charles I. Harvey set out to provide a satisfactory account of the motion of the heart, and in *De Motu Cordis* (1628) concluded that it forcibly expelled blood in contraction. He drew attention to the quantity of blood emerging from the heart into the arteries, and deduced that it must pass through the flesh and enter the veins, returning once more to the heart. Harvey also studied embryology and animal locomotion.

Harwich A port in Essex, on the North Sea coast of south-east England; pop. (1988) 15,543. It has an extensive freight terminal and ferry links with northern Europe.

Harz Mountains A range of mountains in central Germany, between the Leine and Saale rivers, the highest of which is the Brocken (1,142 m, 3,747 ft). The region is the source of many legends about witchcraft and sorcery.

Hasan, Muhammad Abdille Sayyid (1864–1920) Somali nationalist leader, known to the British as the 'Mad Mullah'. He believed that Christian colonization was destructive of Islamic faith in Somaliland and in 1899 he proclaimed a *jihad* (holy war) on all colonial powers. Between 1900 and 1904 four major expeditions by the British, Italians, and Ethiopians failed to defeat him. After a truce (1904–20) he resumed war again and was routed and killed by a British attack in 1920.

Hasdrubal (died 207 BC) Carthaginian general. He was the son of Hamilcar and younger brother of

Hannibal. At the start of the second Punic War in 218 he was left in command of Carthaginian forces in Spain after Hannibal had departed for Italy. After a defeat, Hasdrubal campaigned with only moderate success before crossing the Alps with the aim of joining Hannibal, but was intercepted and killed in battle.

Hašek, Jaroslav (1883–1923) Czech novelist and short-story writer. He is chiefly known as the author of an unfinished four-volume work published in Czechoslovakia between 1921 and 1923; it first appeared in Britain in a bowdlerized form as *The Good Soldier Schweik* (1930). The book is a comic novel satirizing military life and bureaucracy; its central character is the archetypal 'little man' fighting against the system.

Hashemite An Arab princely family descended from the Prophet Muhammad. Hashim was the great-grandfather of Muhammad. Jordan, ruled by the Hashemite King Hussein, is known officially as the Hashemite Kingdom of Jordan.

hashish See CANNABIS.

Hasidism ▶1 A strictly orthodox Jewish sect in Palestine in the 3rd–2nd centuries BC which opposed Hellenizing influences on their faith and supported the Maccabean revolt. **▶2** A mystical Jewish movement founded in Poland in the 18th century in reaction to the rigid academic formation of rabbinical Judaism. Its founder was Israel ben Eliezer (died 1760), called Bad-Shem-Tov (Hebrew, 'master of the good name') because of his reputation as a miraculous healer. The movement was denounced as heretical in 1781 and declined sharply in the 19th century with the spread of modernism. However, fundamentalist Hasidic communities are currently a force in Jewish life, particularly in Israel and New York, where they oppose non-Orthodox Jews, who they regard as violating the moral and religious principles of their faith. Hasidic men wear black suits and 18th-century black hats; they do not shave and have curled side-locks.

Hastings A resort town on the coast of East Sussex, England, north of which William the Conqueror defeated the Anglo-Saxon king Harold II at a famous battle (**Battle of Hastings**) in 1066; pop. (1991) 78,100. It is one of the CINQUE PORTS on the Channel coast and former base of the Royal Fleet.

Hastings, Warren (1732–1818) British colonial administrator. In 1774 he became India's first Governor-General and during his term of office introduced many of the administrative reforms vital to the successful maintenance of British rule in India. On his return to England in 1785 he was impeached for corruption; he was eventually acquitted in 1795 after a seven-year trial before the House of Lords.

Hatfield A town in Hertfordshire, south-east England, to the north of London; pop. (1981) 33,300. It was designated a New Town in 1948 and is a centre of engineering industries. The University of Hertfordshire (formerly Hatfield Polytechnic) was established here in 1992. The 17th-century Hatfield House is the home of the politically influential Cecil family.

Hathaway, Anne (*c.*1557–1623) The wife of Shakespeare, whom she married in 1582. They had three children, a daughter (Susannah) and a twin daughter and son (Judith and Hamnet). Her cottage near Stratford-upon-Avon can still be seen.

Hatshepsut (*c.*1540–*c.*1481 BC) The daughter of Thutmose I of Egypt. After the death of her half-brother and husband, Thutmose II, the young Thutmose III succeeded, but she soon replaced him as the effective ruler and reigned until her death twenty years later. As well as furthering her father's building programme at KARNAK, she had a magnificent temple constructed at Deir al-Bahri.

Haughey, Charles (1925–) Irish politician, Prime Minister of the Republic of Ireland 1979–81, 1982, and 1987–92. He was president of Fianna Fáil from 1979 to 1992. He resigned as a result of a number of scandals.

Hauptmann, Gerhart (1862–1946) German dramatist. He was an early pioneer of naturalism in the German theatre; his plays, such as *Before Sunrise* (1889) and *The Weavers* (1892), treat social and moral issues with directness and realism. He also wrote plays which combined naturalism with symbolism, such as *The Ascension of Joan* (1893). He was awarded the Nobel Prize for literature in 1912.

Hausa The people of north-western Nigeria and southern Niger. The original Hausa states, which include KANO and Zaria, were for many years the vassals of Bornu (see KANEM-BORNU). Muslim missionaries seem to have come in the 14th century, but during the reign of Muhammad Rumfa of Kano (1463–99) the celebrated divine al-Maghili is said to have introduced the *shariah* (the Muslim code of law), SUFISM, and a body of constitutional theory. The Hausa states were conquered by the SONGHAI in 1513 and by the FULANI in the early 19th century.

Their traditional trading activities contributed to the spread of the Hausa language as a LINGUA FRANCA throughout most of West Africa (see CHADIC LANGUAGES). Their society is hierarchical, consisting of several hereditary classes. In the wet season, the land is cultivated collectively by members of a patrilineage; millet, sorghum, and maize are grown for subsistence, while cotton, tobacco, and groundnuts are important cash crops. In the dry season, the Hausa take time off to travel or to trade.

havan (from Sanskrit, 'homa', 'fire offering') One of the elements of Hindu worship, or *puja*. It originates from the sacrificial fire of the Vedic rites. The priest lights a sacred fire on a portable altar and throws melted butter (ghee) on it. In wedding ceremonies, the bride and groom take seven steps around the sacrificial fire.

Havana The capital of Cuba and chief port of the West Indies, on the north coast of the island of Cuba; pop. (1994) 2,241,000. Originally located on the south coast, the city was founded in its present location by Diego Velásquez in 1519. It was the principal Spanish port in the West Indies and the blowing up of the US battleship *Maine* in 1898 led to the Spanish–American War. Since 1898 it has been capital of independent Cuba. Chief exports are cigars, coffee, and sugar. Its industries include oil refining, textiles, rum distilling, and the making of the famous Havana cigars.

Havel, Václav (1936–) Czech dramatist and statesman, President of Czechoslovakia 1989–92 and of the Czech Republic since 1993. Having written plays, such as *The Garden Party* (1963) which were critical of totalitarianism, in the 1970s he became the leading spokesman for Charter 77 and other human rights groups and was twice imprisoned as a dissident. Shortly after his release in 1989 he founded the opposition group Civic Forum and led a renewed campaign for political change; in December of that year he was elected President following the peaceful overthrow of Communism (the velvet revolution). He remained as President of the Czech Republic after the partition of Czechoslovakia on 1 January 1993.

Havering A residential outer borough at the eastern extremity of Greater London, containing the districts of Hornchurch, Romford, Rainham, and Upminster; pop. (1991) 224,400.

Hawaii A state of the USA comprising a chain of islands in the North Pacific stretching from the island of Hawaii to Kure Island (but excluding the Midway Islands); area 16,641 sq km (6,425 sq miles); pop. (1990) 1,108,230; capital, Honolulu (on Oahu). Its largest cities are Honolulu and Hilo. The eight principal islands of the group are Oahu, Hawaii, Maui, Kauai, Molokai, Lanai, Kahoolawe, and Niihau. Hawaii is also known as the Aloha State. First settled by Polynesians, Hawaii was visited in 1778 by Captain Cook who named them the Sandwich Islands. Its indigenous kingdom was abolished in 1894 and the islands were annexed by the USA in 1898, becoming the 50th state in 1959. In addition to tourism, the islands depend on the export of agricultural produce such as pineapples, sugar, coffee, bananas, and nuts. In 1996 Hawaiians voted in favour of self-government in a referendum.

Hawaiian goose A relation of the Canada goose, also called ne-ne from its call. With their habitat confined to Hawaii, the numbers of this goose, *Branta sandvicensis*, had fallen to about 40 before a remarkable rescue operation saved them from almost certain extinction. In 1950 three individuals were imported to a wildfowl reserve in Britain. They bred successfully and hundreds have since been raised there; some have been returned to their native Hawaii.

hawfinch Any one of three species of bird belonging to the genus *Coccothraustes*, within the finch family. The common hawfinch, *C. coccothraustes*, breeds over wide areas of Europe and Asia; the other two species, the masked hawfinch, *C. personatus*, and black-tailed hawfinch, *C. migratorius*, live in eastern Asia. All three species are greyish-brown with glossy blue-black wings and white-marked tails. They have very large beaks and break open large seeds to extract the kernels.

hawk A bird of the family Accipitridae, which includes the true hawks, buzzards, eagles, harrier-eagles, harriers, kites, fish eagles, bathawks, ospreys, and vultures. Hawks are a large, highly successful family of diurnal birds of prey, ranging in size from tiny insect-feeding sparrowhawks to eagles with a 2 m (6.5 feet) wing-span. Common characteristics include dull, barred, brown or grey plumage, a powerful, strongly curved beak with nostrils mounted on a cere, long legs, and strongly taloned feet. Beak and feet are used jointly to tear open prey. Females are often larger than males. Flight patterns range from soaring and gliding (eagles, vultures) to high-speed precision swooping.

Many hawks migrate away from extreme winter conditions, some following migrating prey species. As 'top' predators in the FOOD CHAINS, hawks are especially vulnerable to insecticides and other agricultural poisons. They are also destroyed as vermin, and the eggs and young of some species are in demand for falconry.

Hawke, Edward, 1st Baron (1705–81) British admiral. He won fame by his great victory over the French at Finisterre in 1747. During the SEVEN YEARS WAR he blockaded the French Atlantic fleet at Brest, and when it broke out in 1759 he destroyed it at the battle of QUIBERON BAY, thus effectively cutting France's communications with its Canadian colonies. Hawke then retired from active service.

Hawke, Robert James Lee (known as 'Bob') (1929–) Australian Labor statesman, Prime Minister 1983–91. He was elected leader of the Australian Labor Party in 1983, becoming Prime Minister a month later following his party's election victory over the Liberal government. During his premiership he pursued an economic programme based on free-market policies and tax reform. In 1990 he won a record fourth election victory but lost a leadership challenge the following year to Paul Keating.

Hawking, Stephen William (1942–) British mathematical physicist famous for his work on BLACK HOLES and COSMOLOGY. His theories are based on a combination of quantum mechanics and RELATIVITY. Although suffering from a progressive neurological illness and confined to a motorized wheelchair, he travels widely and produces outstanding theoretical research on these topics. He was one of the youngest persons ever to be elected to the Royal Society at the age of 32. His book *A Brief History of Time* was an immediate bestseller when it was published in 1988.

Hawkins, Coleman Randolph (1904–69) US jazz saxophonist. During the 1920s and 1930s he was influential in making the tenor saxophone popular as a jazz instrument; playing with the Fletcher Henderson band (1923–34), he used a stiff reed which enabled him to be heard as a soloist over the band. His playing was characterized by its deep and rich expressive tone.

Hawkins, Sir John (or **Hawkyns**) (1532–95) English sailor. In the 1560s and early 1570s he became involved in the slave trade and participated in early privateering raids in the Spanish West Indies. He was appointed treasurer of the Elizabethan navy in 1573 and played an important part in building up the fleet which defeated the Spanish Armada in 1588. He died at sea during an unsuccessful expedition to the West Indies.

Hawkins, Sir Richard (or **Hawkyns**) (1560–1622) English sailor, son of Sir John HAWKINS. Commander in the Elizabethan navy serving against the SPANISH ARMADA (1588). In 1593 he left England with the intention of surveying eastern Asia, where he hoped to establish an English trading empire. On the way, he plundered Valparaiso in Spanish America, and was held by the Spaniards until a ransom was paid in 1602.

hawkmoth (or **sphinx moth**) A powerful, fast-flying moth with long, narrow fore-wings and a stout body, occurring in most parts of the world, especially the tropics. Hawkmoths comprise the family Sphingidae, with some 1,000 species. Many species hover whilst feeding from flowers, using the proboscis to reach deep into the flower. The proboscis of the convolvulus hawk, *Agrius convolvuli*, is 15 cm (6 inches) long, that is to say greater than its wing-span; and that of a Madagascan species exceeds 30 cm (1 foot). Most feed by dusk or night on pale flowers, which they pollinate, but the hummingbird hawk, *Macroglossum stellatarum*, and bee hawks, *Hemaris* species, are diurnal. The caterpillars of many hawkmoths have a horn at the rear, and in America are called hornworms; some, such as the tobacco hornworm, are pests. The adult death's-head hawkmoth, *Manduca atropos*, will enter beehives to feed on honey.

Hawks, Howard (1896–1977) US film director, producer, and screenwriter. He entered the film industry in 1922, directing and writing the screenplay for his first film in 1926. Over the next 40 years he directed some of the most famous stars in comedies, westerns, musicals, and gangster films. His best-known films include *Scarface* (1931), *The Big Sleep* (1946), *Gentlemen Prefer Blondes* (1953), and *Rio Bravo* (1959).

Hawksmoor, Nicholas (1661–1736) English architect. He began his career at the age of 18 as a clerk to Sir Christopher Wren, and from 1690 worked with Vanbrugh at Castle Howard and Blenheim Palace. In 1711 he was commissioned to design six London churches; notable examples include St Mary Woolnoth (1716–24) and St George's, Bloomsbury (1716–30).

Hawkyns See HAWKINS.

Haworth, Sir Walter Norman (1883–1950) British organic chemist. He was a pioneer in carbohydrate chemistry, making major contributions to understanding the structure and classification of sugars and polysaccharides. His book *The Constitution of the Sugars* (1929) became a standard work. Haworth also determined the structure of vitamin C and later synthesized it, the first person to make a vitamin artificially. He shared the Nobel Prize for chemistry in 1937.

hawthorn A species of the plant genus *Crataegus*, of which there are about 200 species in the north temperate zone. They are deciduous small trees and shrubs closely related to *Cotoneaster*. They hybridize readily with one another, especially in North America, which makes classification difficult; as many as 1,000 different 'species' have been named. Many are armed with spines which are really dwarf branches. Some American species are known as cockspur thorns. Hawthorn is widely used for hedging and the white or pink flowers are followed by red fruits (haws). The wood is used in the same way as BOX. Hawthorns belong to the rose family and are thus related to apple.

Hawthorne, Nathaniel (1804–64) US novelist and short-story writer. Hawthorne's New England Puritan background is evident in much of his fiction, which uses allegory and symbolism to explore themes of hereditary guilt, sin, and morality. His works include collections of short stories, such as *Twice-Told Tales* (1837), and the novels *The Scarlet Letter* (1850) and *The House of Seven Gables* (1851). He also wrote a number of books for children, including *Tanglewood Tales* (1853).

Hay, Will(iam Thomson) (1888–1949) British actor and comedian. Regarded as a master of comic timing, he is remembered for his screen characterizations of incompetent authority, especially of an ineffectual schoolmaster. His 17 films include *Oh, Mr Porter!* (1937), *The Goose Steps Out* (1942), and his last, *My Learned Friend* (1944).

Haydn, (Franz) Joseph (1732–1809) Austrian composer. He was a major exponent of the classical style and a teacher of Mozart and Beethoven. In 1761 he joined the household of the Hungarian Prince Esterházy as musical director, a post that he held for nearly 30 years and which was conducive to his prolific output and his development of musical forms. His work comprises more than 100 symphonies and many string quartets and keyboard sonatas, and he played a significant role in the development of the symphony and the string quartet in their classical four-movement forms. His choral music includes twelve masses and the oratorios *The Creation* (1796–98) and *The Seasons* (1799–1801).

Hayek, Friedrich August von (1899–1992) Austrian-born economist and political scientist. A prolific writer, Hayek was a LIBERTARIAN, famous for his strong defence of *laissez-faire* liberalism and FREE MARKET economics. His tract, *The Road to Serfdom* (1944), condemned social democracy and the WELFARE STATE as harbingers of TOTALITARIANISM. In economic theory he emphasized the importance of market prices as disseminators of information to market participants, both about each others' behaviour and about technological possibilities. He also made contributions to capital theory and TRADE-CYCLE theory.

Hayes, Rutherford B(irchard) (1822–93) US Republican statesman, 19th President of the USA 1877–81. His administration brought the Reconstruction era in the South to an end; power returned from Federal government to white southern leaders, who then introduced a policy of racial segregation.

hay fever An allergic response of eye and nose membranes to pollen, causing profuse watery discharges and common COLD symptoms. It often occurs in several members of a family, and in association with asthma and eczema. Desensitization by injections of pollen extract will often prevent the attacks, but it needs to be started well in advance of the pollen season. Antihistamine drugs are moderately effective.

haymaking The process by which fresh grass, or a grass–legume mixture, is made into a high-volume feed with a low moisture content, suitable for storage. Grass for hay is cut later than for SILAGE, after the seed has set. Traditionally it was turned using forks, exposing it to drying by the wind and Sun. Modern agricultural machinery lightly crushes the stem to speed water loss. When dry, the hay used to be tightly compressed into stacks or carried to barns for storage. Modern BALERS make high-density bales, reducing labour requirements at harvest time. Hay quality is judged by its colour, smell, and the absence of dust or fungus.

Hayworth, Rita (born Margarita Carmen Cansino) (1918–87) US actress and dancer. She began her career as a dancer at the age of 12 and made her screen début in 1935. Hayworth achieved stardom with a succession of film musicals including *Cover Girl* (1944). She also played leading roles in several films of the *film noir* genre, notably *Gilda* (1946) and *The Lady from Shanghai* (1948), in which she co-starred with her second husband Orson Welles.

haze A suspension of solid particles, such as smoke and dust, in the atmosphere. Normally it does not reduce visibility to less than 1 km (0.6 mile), but when encountered in deserts or in industrial areas the density of the dust may obscure objects closer at hand. It differs from mist in appearing bluish or yellowish.

hazel A deciduous shrub or more rarely a small tree of the genus *Corylus*. There are about 15 species native to temperate regions of North America, Europe, and China. They belong to the same family as the BIRCHES, alders, and hornbeams. The common hazel, *Corylus avellana*, is a deciduous hedgerow shrub of Europe valued for its nuts. In spring, the male flowers form conspicuous long catkins, in contrast to the unremarkable females. They are wind-pollinated. Formerly, hazel was an important constituent of woodlands where coppicing was practised. The slender, flexible shoots produced by coppicing were used for the hoops of barrels, thatching, fencing, and many other constructional uses.

Hazlitt, William (1778–1830) British essayist and critic. From about 1812 he wrote many articles on diverse subjects for several periodicals, including the *Edinburgh Review* and the *Morning Chronicle*; his essays were collected in *Table Talk* (1821–22) and *The Plain Speaker* (1826). Among his critical works are *Lectures on the English Poets* (1818) and *The Spirit of the Age* (1825). His style, marked by clarity and conviction, brought a new vigour to English prose writing.

head (in anatomy) The front end of the body in all vertebrates, except in humans and some apes, who have adopted an upright posture. It contains the brain, and the organs of special sense: the eyes, ears, nose, and tongue. The whole body is directed and coordinated by the head. Attached to the front of the head are the face, jaws, and mouth. In the course of evolution the head has assumed greater importance because of the enlargement of the brain. The reason for the development of the head is that it is the part of the body which first meets new stimuli in the environment, on the assumption that most animals move in one direction.

Head, Edith (1907–81) US costume designer. She joined Paramount studios in 1923, and worked on films ranging from westerns to musicals and comedies. She was awarded Oscars for costume design in several films, including *All About Eve* (1950). Head later worked for Universal, where she won a further Oscar for the costumes in *The Sting* (1973).

health screening A way of detecting disease by examining people before they show symptoms. In developed countries, pregnant women are often screened for diseases that may affect the health of the foetus, such as syphilis or diabetes, and the foetus may be screened for a range of abnormalities, such as spina bifida or Down's Syndrome. Infants and children are routinely screened for defects in hearing or vision, and adults may be screened for breast and cervical CANCER, HEART DISEASE, or AIDS. Screening programmes have had some notable successes in detecting and thereby reducing certain diseases (tuberculosis and glaucoma are examples).

health services Provision of hospital, medical, and dental services. During the 19th century there was startling progress in medical science, but also an increased awareness of health hazards and the need for improved urban public health. In the mid-20th century the development of public health-service hospitals and clinics became one of the main provisions of the WELFARE STATE, the British **National Health Service** being introduced in 1946. It provides a comprehensive, largely free, medical and surgical service for the whole UK population. Funded from national taxation, it is the largest employer in Europe. Although the founders expected costs to fall or remain constant as the health of the nation improved, in fact they have escalated as a result of medical advances making more therapeutic procedures available and a marked increase in longevity (largely as a result of the service), resulting in increased demands by the elderly. Successive governments have grappled with the problem of maintaining the standard of service within acceptable budgets, largely by reorganizing the way in which the service is managed and financed.

During the communist regimes of the former Soviet Union and east European republics, state health services alone were officially available, which is still the case in communist Cuba, while in Britain and many western countries health services through privately financed insurance schemes are an alternative to state services. In the USA most health facilities are so funded, apart from Medicare and Medicaid.

Heaney, Seamus (Justin) (1939–) Irish poet. He was born in Northern Ireland and his early poetry, such as *Death of a Naturalist* (1966), reflects the rural life of his youth. In 1972 he took Irish citizenship; the same year saw a marked change in his poetry, which began to deal with wider social and cultural themes. Later collections include *North* (1975), which deals with the conflict in Northern Ireland, *The Haw Lantern* (1987), *Seeing Things* (1991), and *The Spirit Level* (1996). He was awarded the Nobel Prize for literature in 1995.

hearing The ability to detect and interpret sound. Many animals have evolved this ability. It is usually based upon hair-like structures being directly or indirectly stimulated by mechanical vibration. These then send electrical messages along the auditory nerves to the brain. In vertebrates the sound receptor is frequently the EAR, but fish are sensitive to vibration along the length of their LATERAL LINE.

Hearing has a number of functions. The most important are those of communication and location. Male mosquitoes locate females by sound. Grasshoppers and related species can transmit sounds that call mates, display aggression, and warn of danger. Many vertebrates, notably birds and frogs, use sound in a similar way. In man hearing is used mainly for complex auditory communication. Cetaceans, including dolphins, also communicate by sounds. In addition, the dolphin uses echolocation for navigation. Insectivorous bats use ultrasound echolocation to hunt insects. Some moths have evolved an ability to detect the high frequencies emitted by bats and thus avoid capture.

hearing aid An electrical or electronic device designed to make sounds audible to those with hearing problems. It comprises three elements: a microphone, an amplifier, and an earphone or vibrator. Its predecessors were the acoustic ear-trumpet and the speaking-tube. The earliest electrical hearing aids (*c.*1898) used batteries and carbon transducers similar to those then found in telephone receivers. The development of the miniaturized THERMIONIC VALVE made portable electronic hearing aids possible. Modern hearing aids use integrated circuits and miniaturized batteries: they can be worn behind the ear, or even fit inside it.

Hearst, William Randolph (1863–1951) US newspaper publisher and tycoon. He is noted for his introduction of large headlines, sensational crime reporting, and other features designed to increase circulation; his innovations revolutionized US journalism. At the peak of his fortunes in the mid-1930s he had acquired a number of newspapers and magazines, radio stations, and two film companies. He was the model for the central character of Orson Welles's film *Citizen Kane* (1941).

heart A muscular organ that pumps blood around the body. In invertebrates the heart is a simple contractile tube that receives blood from one end and then pumps it to the other, creating an open flow along the body.

The evolution of the vertebrate heart shows a progressive division into two, three, and four chambers through which the blood is separated into the left and right sides. In fishes, the blood passes through a simple heart comprising a single atrium and ventricle, from which it is pumped to the gills via the conus arteriosus. In amphibians, two ventricles have developed, with a single atrium, although the atrial blood is partly separated by a spiral valve in the conus. The terrestrial

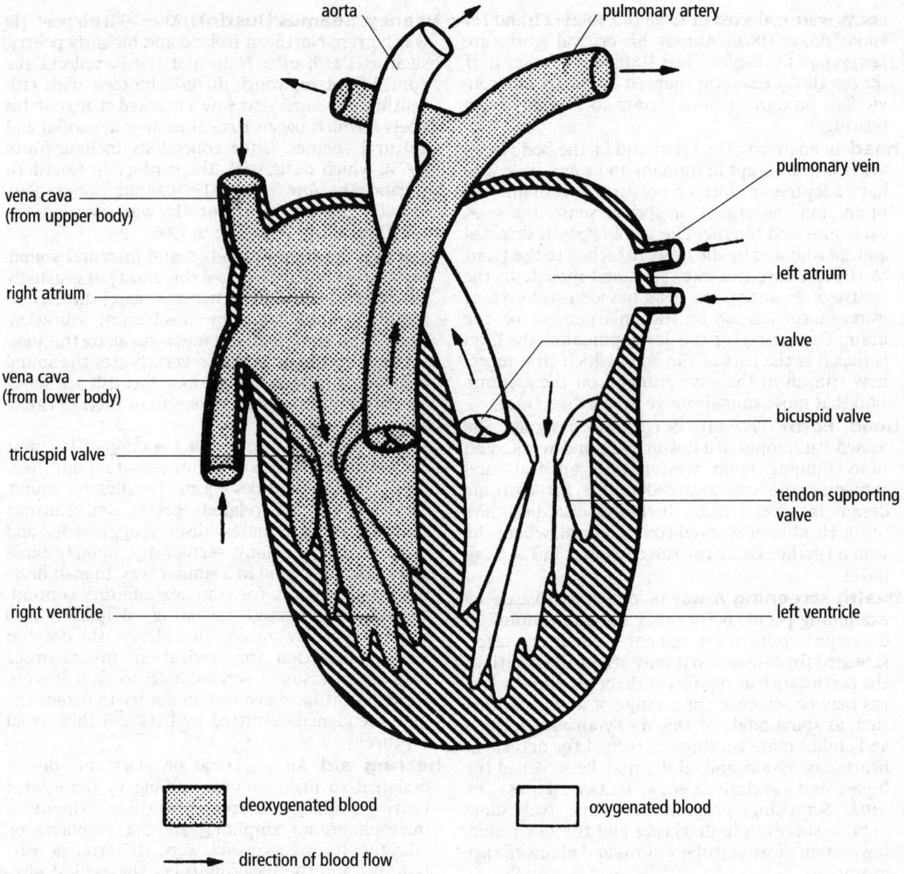

Heart The right and left sides of the mammalian heart are completely separate from each other, so there is no mixing of oxygenated and deoxygenated blood.

reptiles and birds show progressive division of the atrium into left and right sides, culminating in the mammals, which possess two ventricles and two atria. This complete separation in mammals leads to a much more efficient circulatory system, which avoids mixing oxygen-rich and deoxygenated blood. The right ventricle contracts to force blood, which it has received from the right atrium, through the lungs, where it is oxygenated before returning to the heart via the left atrium. This oxygenated blood is passed into the left ventricle, which pumps it out of the heart through the body's largest artery, the aorta. From this, it flows around the body along arteries, then capillaries, before returning to the heart via veins.

The movement of blood through the heart is controlled by valves, allowing it to flow in one direction only. The heart muscle is of a special type, called cardiac muscle, and beats rhythmically throughout life, under the control of the AUTONOMIC NERVOUS SYSTEM. In humans the heart is cone-shaped, about the size of a clenched fist, and set in a cavity between the lungs. It lies within a double set of membranes, which give it the freedom to beat without being squashed.

heart disease (or **cardio-vascular disease**) A congenital or acquired abnormality in the structure or function of the heart. It is estimated that about half the deaths in the developed world are caused by cardio-vascular disease. Some aspects of the modern Western way of life have been identified as risk factors for the disease, particularly SMOKING, excessive consumption of animal fats, STRESS, and lack of exercise. There is evidence to suggest that heart attacks can be prevented (or at least postponed) if people change their behaviour. However, there are other factors, such as family predisposition, sex (men are more prone to the disease than premenopausal women, who are conferred a degree of protection by female hormones), and high blood-pressure. In developing countries, cardio-vascular disease accounts for an increasing proportion of deaths, following changes in the way people live, particularly in urban areas. In Brazil, for instance, it is already the most common cause of death. See also CARDIOLOGY AND CARDIAC SURGERY; CORONARY THROMBOSIS.

heart–lung machine The apparatus that replaces the functions of the heart and lungs during major cardiac surgery. Its use allows the heart to be stopped, making intricate heart surgery possible. It was first used by Gibbon in 1953. To replace heart action, the patient's blood circulation is diverted through tubing to a peristaltic PUMP, specially designed to avoid damaging the blood. Lung function is usually replaced by passing blood and oxygen over opposite sides of a selectively permeable membrane to remove carbon dioxide from the blood and to absorb oxygen.

heart urchin See SEA URCHIN.

heat and temperature Heat is the process of energy transfer from one body to another as a result of a temperature difference. Formerly, the energy contained by a body was also regarded as the amount of heat it contained. This is, however, confusing. A body contains the kinetic and potential energy of its atoms and molecules: this is now known as its internal energy (U). If this body changes its temperature, there is a corresponding change (ΔU) in its internal energy. According to the first law of THERMODYNAMICS, $\Delta U = Q - W$, where Q is the heat absorbed from or lost to the surroundings and W is the work done on or by the surroundings at the same time. Thus, to call both U and Q heat leads to confusion. It is for this reason that Q should be called heat and U internal energy.

On this basis, temperature is the property of a body that determines whether heat will flow into it or out of it from its surroundings. If there is no such heat flow the body and its surroundings are said to be in thermal equilibrium. Temperature is a measure of the mean kinetic energy of its constituent particles, whereas the internal energy is a measure of their total energy. Temperature is measured in terms of degrees and fixed points on an arbitrary scale. The Celsius scale of temperature uses two fixed points. The melting-point of pure water under normal Earth-surface conditions is taken to be 0°C, and the boiling-point of water is taken to be 100°C. Temperature can also be expressed in terms of the **thermodynamic temperature**, measured in kelvin (K). See also THERMOMETER.

The SI unit of heat and energy is the joule (J). Other units of energy applied to heat are the calorie (cal: 1 cal = 4 J) and the British Thermal Unit (BTU: 1 BTU = 1,055 J).

heat capacity The quantity of heat energy required to raise the temperature of a body by one degree Celsius. It depends on the material of which the body is made and on its mass. The heat capacity for unit mass (1 kg), the **specific heat capacity**, is tabulated for most materials.

heat engine See ENGINE.

heat exchanger A system for transferring heat energy between two fluids. The aim is to achieve good thermal contact while maintaining physical separation. A common system allows one fluid to pass over pipes through which the other flows, for example in a motor-car radiator. An alternative is a slowly rotating drum of honeycombed metal. Each section absorbs heat as hot gas passes through it, and transfers this to a cool gas half a revolution later. Such 'heat wheels' are increasingly being employed for regenerative warming of the air entering a building, using heat from the departing stale air.

Heath, Sir Edward (Richard George) (1916–) British Conservative statesman, Prime Minister 1970–74. In 1973 his long-standing commitment to European unity was realized when Britain joined the European Economic Community. His premiership was marked by problems of inflation and balance of payments (exacerbated by a marked increase in oil prices in 1973); attempts to restrain wage rises led to widespread strikes. After a second national coal strike Heath called an election to strengthen his position, but was defeated.

heath butterfly A yellowish-orange butterfly, a BROWN, which frequents heathland and grassland. There are some 20 species in Europe and temperate Asia, including a few in North America. The large heath, *Coenonympha tullia*, has conspicuous white-centred black spots on the undersides of the wings, and is known as the ringlet in North America.

heather Originally the Scottish name for ling, *Calluna vulgaris*, though it is widely used nowadays for species of the closely related *Erica*. The heather, or heath, family (Ericaceae) contains some 3,000 species, which occur worldwide. The relatives of *Calluna* and *Erica* include rhododendron and bilberry. Virtually all species depend upon fungal MYCORRHIZA for successful growth. Heathers are evergreen shrubs of acidic soil, especially moors and heaths.

Heathrow An international airport, which began operation in 1946, it now has four terminals. It is situated in the outer London borough of Hounslow 25 km (15 miles) west of the centre of London. It is also known as London Airport.

heat-pump A machine that transfers heat from a cooler to a warmer environment. The cooling units of refrigerators and AIR-CONDITIONING units are heat-pumps in the technical sense, but in common usage the term is usually restricted to systems whose purpose is to provide space heating. To heat a building, the pump extracts low temperature energy from the surroundings and delivers it at a higher temperature to the interior. Another type of heat-pump is the Peltier pump, in which an electric current through the junction of two dissimilar metals causes cooling at one junction and heating at the other. Peltier pumps are used commercially to cool sensitive electronic components such as solid-state lasers. See also THERMOELECTRIC DEVICE.

heatstroke A rise in the body temperature, absence of sweating, and eventual loss of consciousness caused by overexposure to high temperatures (especially from the Sun). It is potentially fatal unless treated immediately by cooling the body with damp cloths and giving drinks or intravenous injections of salted water.

heat transfer See HEAT AND TEMPERATURE; HEAT EXCHANGER.

heat treatment See ANNEALING; TEMPERING.

heat waves Prolonged spells of unusually hot, dry weather. They are usually associated with stable, anticyclonic conditions. In mid-latitudes in the Northern Hemisphere they are normally caused by ANTICYCLONES blocking the eastward movement of depressions, while on the western side of such anticyclones tropical continental or tropical maritime air is transported polewards from low latitudes. It is a phenomenon of summer. When temperatures reach 30°C (86°F) people suffer the risk of HEATSTROKE or sunstroke, given lengthy exposure with physical activity.

heat wheel See HEAT EXCHANGER.

heaven A place believed to be the dwelling place of God, and of the righteous after death. In Judaeo-Christian belief, heaven is a state in which, after judgement, the saved soul sees God face to face. In traditional Christian belief, the human body, in a glorified form, will be reunited with the soul in heaven after the Last Judgement. In Islamic belief, heaven is depicted as a blissful paradise of material delights, a description generally supposed to be more allegorical than literal. See also NIRVANA.

Heaviside, Oliver (1850–1925) British physicist and electrical engineer. His theoretical contributions improved long-distance telephone communication and had significance to both cable and wireless telegraphy. He studied inductance, introduced the concept of impedance, and pioneered the use of calculus for dealing with the properties of electrical networks. In 1902 he suggested (independently of A. E. Kennelly) the existence of a layer in the atmosphere responsible for reflecting radio waves back to Earth. It is now known as the Heaviside or Kennelly–Heaviside layer, or the E region of the IONOSPHERE.

heavy chemical See CHEMICAL INDUSTRY.

heavy industry A broad grouping of large-scale industries, usually operating with heavy machinery or plant, which require extensive capital investment. Heavy industry includes metal-processing, such as steel and iron manufacturing, petroleum-refining, hydroelectric plants, motor-vehicle production, etc. Heavy industry has been held responsible for much environmental damage and POLLUTION.

heavy water See WATER.

hebe See SPEEDWELL.

Hebe In Greek mythology, the goddess of youth. She was the daughter of Zeus and Hera and the handmaiden of the gods.

Hebrew A member of the Hamito-Semitic language family spoken by people who were originally centred in ancient Palestine, traditionally from the middle Bronze Age. Spoken and written for more than 1,000 years, it is written from right to left in an alphabet consisting of 22 letters, all consonants; not until the 6th century AD were vowel signs added to the Hebrew text of the Old Testament to facilitate reading. By *c.*500 BC it had come greatly under the influence of Aramaic, which largely replaced it as a spoken language by *c.*200 AD, but it continued as the religious language of the Jewish people. It was revived as a spoken language in the 19th century, with the modern form having its roots in the ancient language but drawing words from the vocabularies of European languages, and is now the official language of the State of Israel. See SEMITIC LANGUAGES.

Hebrew literature Literature written in the Hebrew language and produced uninterruptedly since at least the 12th century BC. From *c.*1200 BC to *c.*200 AD, historical, legal, ethical, and liturgical works were compiled to create the Old Testament of the Bible. Later the main juridical and religious laws were committed to writing in the *Mishnah* (*c.*200 AD), itself expanded into the *Gemarah* and ultimately the *Talmud*, which was written down in the 4th and 5th centuries AD. After *c.*220 AD Hebrew became a literary language only. The centre of Jewish culture moved first to North Africa, then to Muslim Spain (7th to 15th centuries), where both the liturgy and secular poetry in Hebrew were raised to a level of excellence by poets including Solomon IBN GABIROL and Yehuda Halevi (*c.*1080–1140). The Judeo-Arabic school reached its zenith with Maimonides (1135–1204), who formulated a code of rabbinic law, the *Mishneh Torah*. In the 16th and 17th centuries Poland emerged as a major centre of Jewish learning. The period from the mid-18th century saw the renaissance of secular Hebrew literature during the *Haskalah* (Hebrew Enlightenment) in Germany, Galicia, and Russia, where BIALIK was the dominant figure, the flowering of Hebrew poetry and journalism and, in the late 19th century, the revival of Hebrew as a spoken language. From the 1880s the centre of Hebrew literature shifted from Europe to Palestine (after 1948 Israel), where new literary styles based on the living language steadily developed in modern Hebrew.

Hebrides Two groups of islands (Inner and Outer) off the north-west coast of Scotland.

Physical. The Inner Hebrides include Skye, Mull, Jura, and Islay (the four largest), and Rhum, Eigg, and the island of Iona among many others. The Outer Hebrides or Western Isles, which lie in an arc beyond the Little Minch channel and the Sea of the Hebrides, include Lewis and Harris (the name of a single island), North and South Uist (two islands), Benbecula, and Barra in the south. Formed of Lewisian GNEISS, they are one of the oldest rock formations in the world. Over a hundred out of the total of some 500 are habitable. All have been fashioned and scoured by glaciation. There are few trees anywhere. The climate is mild, the scenery is beautiful, and there are rare geological structures.

History. The largest few dozen islands have been inhabited since *c.*3800 BC, settled by PICTS and then, from the 3rd century AD, by Scots. Except in the VIKING era, their way of life changed little until the 19th century, when large-scale sheep farming and subsequent clearances of crofters caused depopulation and widespread deprivation.

Hebron (Hebrew **Hevron**; Arabic **El Khalhil** or **El Khalil**) A city lying in the Judaean Hills between Jerusalem and Beersheba, in the Israeli-occupied West Bank area of Jordan. It is one of the most ancient cities in the Middle East, probably founded in the 18th century BC and is sacred to both Jews and Arabs who regard themselves as being descended from Abraham who made his home here. Its chief landmark is the Tomb of the Patriarchs which (as the cave of Machpelah) was the family vault created by Abraham and the site of a synagogue built by Herod in 20 BC. It came under Jordanian control in 1948, but was reoccupied by Israel in 1967. During the 20th century it was the scene of massacres of the Jews by militant Palestinian Arabs in 1929 and 1994. Its chief industries are glass-making and food processing.

Hecate In Greek mythology, a goddess with many functions but mainly associated with black magic – the patron of witches and sorcerers. At night she wandered with the ghosts of the dead, haunting graveyards and crossroads, where offerings were put out for her.

Hector In Greek mythology, the greatest hero on the Trojan side in the Trojan War. He was the son of Priam and Hecuba and was killed in combat by Achilles.

Hecuba In Greek mythology, queen of Troy, the wife of Priam and the mother of Cassandra, Hector, and Paris. After the fall of Troy she was given as a captive to Odysseus.

hedgehog An insectivore of the family Erinaceidae, which they share with moon rats, a subfamily of Asia which lacks the spines of true hedgehogs. The western European hedgehog, *Erinaceus europaeus*, has been introduced into New Zealand, where it has become very common. It is replaced by a very similar species, *E. concolor*, in eastern Europe and Asia. Of the twelve species, four occur in Africa, and most resemble the European hedgehog, though three species of desert hedgehogs have distinctly larger ears and longer legs. They do not occur in the New World.

Hedgehogs feed on a variety of invertebrates, as well as amphibians and the eggs or young of ground-nesting birds. They curl up when threatened so that the spines, which are present only on the back, protect the soft underparts.

hedge sparrow (or **dunnock**) A member of the ACCENTOR family of birds, not closely related to the true sparrows. It breeds over much of Europe and western Asia. The hedge sparrow, *Prunella modularis*, gets its name from its sparrow-like plumage, though it is a dull blue-grey below. It has a fine, sharply pointed beak with which it eats insects and small seeds. It lays three to five bright blue eggs in a nest concealed in thick vegetation.

hedonism Both an ethical view and a psychological theory. As an ethical view, hedonism (from the Greek *hēdonē*, 'pleasure') states that the only things regarded as having value in themselves are states of pleasure or happiness. As a psychological theory, hedonism suggests that all behaviour is determined and explained by the desire for pleasure or happiness. Hedonism in this second sense seems to conflict with the view that people are, at least sometimes, motivated by moral requirements and that they may prefer to sacrifice their own prospects altruistically for the sake of others, making hedonism akin to EGOISM. The Cyrenaics, a minor school of philosophers who flourished in the 4th century BC, saw the satisfaction of immediate, sensual pleasures as the single dominating factor in life. A more subtle and complex theory of hedonism was professed by the Epicureans, though their philosophy has often been misunderstood. It came under great pressure from the rise of Christianity, and doctrines of asceticism. MILL defended hedonism in both senses as part of his argument for UTILITARIANISM.

Hegel, Georg Wilhelm Friedrich (1770–1831) German philosopher. He is especially known for his three-stage process of dialectical reasoning (set out in his *Science of Logic*, 1812–16), which underlies his idealist concepts of historical development and the evolution of ideas; Marx based his theory of dialectical materialism on this aspect of Hegel's work. Other major works include *The Phenomenology of Mind* (1807), which describes the progression of the human mind from consciousness through self-consciousness, reason, spirit, and religion to absolute knowledge.

hegira (Arabic *hijra*, 'exodus', 'migration', or 'breaking of ties') MUHAMMAD's secret departure from MECCA in 622, accompanied by ABU BAKR, to live among the people of Yathrib, later MEDINA, thus founding the first Muslim community. Under the second caliph, umar, this key event in the history of Islam was chosen as the starting-point for the Muslim calendar.

Heidegger, Martin (1889–1976) German philosopher. In *Being and Time* (1927) he examines the setting of human existence in the world. He regards *Angst* (dread) as a fundamental part of human consciousness, a symptom of the gravity of the human situation with its radical freedom of choice and awareness of death. Consequently human beings are continually attempting to escape their destiny, either by disguising it or by distracting their attention from its inevitability. Although he did not consider himself an existentialist, his work had a significant influence on existentialist philosophers, such as Jean-Paul Sartre.

Heidelberg An industrial city in Baden-Württemberg, south-west Germany, on the River Neckar; pop. (1991) 139,390. It is noted for its university, which received its charter in 1386 and is the oldest in Germany, and for its medieval castle. It is also noted for the manufacture of printing machinery and precision instruments.

Heifetz, Jascha (1901–87) Russian-born violinist, assuming US citizenship in 1925. Taught by his father, Heifetz made his public début aged five. While still a student he played Tchaikovsky's concerto with the Berlin Philharmonic Orchestra (1912). After his US début in 1917, his position among the greatest violinists was secured. He commissioned a concerto from Walton in 1939.

Heilbronn An industrial city and river port in Baden-Württemberg, Germany, on the River Neckar north of Stuttgart; pop. (1991) 117,430. Its industries produce wine, paper, chemicals, and metal goods.

Heimlich manoeuvre (or **abdominal thrust**) A technique in first aid, named after the US physician H. J. Heimlich (1920–), for dislodging food or other foreign matter from the windpipe of a person who is choking. It involves wrapping one's arms around the victim from behind and giving one or more sudden upward thrusts to the victim's upper abdomen with a clenched fist (which is grasped with the other hand).

Heine, (Christian Johann) Heinrich (born Harry Heine) (1797–1856) German poet. His reputation rests on his lyric poetry, particularly that in *Das Buch der Lieder* (1827), much of which was set to music by Schumann and Schubert. In 1830 Heine emigrated to Paris, where his works became more political; they include *Zur Geschichte der Religion und Philosophie in Deutschland* (1834), a witty and savage attack on German thought and literature, and his two verse satires *Atta Troll* (1843) and *Deutschland* (1844).

Heinz, Henry John (1844–1919) US food manufacturer. In 1869 he established a family firm for the manufacture and sale of processed foods. Heinz devised the marketing slogan '57 Varieties' in 1896 and erected New York's first electric sign to promote his company's pickles in 1900. By the turn of the century, his firm was one of the largest in the USA; since his death, it has become a major multinational company.

Heisenberg, Werner Karl (1901–76) German mathematical physicist and philosopher, who developed a system of quantum mechanics based on matrix algebra. For this and his discovery of the allotropic forms of hydrogen he was awarded the 1932 Nobel Prize for physics. He stated his famous UNCERTAINTY PRINCIPLE (that the momentum and position of a particle cannot both be precisely determined at the same time) in 1927.

Hejaz (or **Hijaz**) A coastal region of western Saudi Arabia, extending along the Red Sea and containing the holy cities of Mecca and Medina.

Helen In Greek mythology, the most beautiful of mortal women. She married King Menelaus of Sparta, but was abducted by Paris and carried off to Troy, thus causing the Trojan War. When Troy fell ten years later, she returned to Menelaus.

Helena, St (*c*.255–*c*.330 AD) Roman empress and mother of Constantine the Great. She was a convert to Christianity and in 326 visited the Holy Land, where she founded basilicas on the Mount of Olives and at Bethlehem. Later tradition ascribes to her the finding of the cross on which Christ was crucified. Feast day (in the Eastern Church) 21 May; (in the Western Church) 18 August.

Helgoland (or **Heligoland**) A small island in the North Sea. Originally the home of Frisian seamen, it was Danish from 1714 until seized by the British navy (1807). It was ceded to Britain (1815) and held until exchanged with Germany for ZANZIBAR and Pemba (1890). Germany developed it into a naval base of great strategic importance. Under the terms of the VERSAILLES PEACE SETTLEMENT its naval installations were demolished (1920–22). They were rebuilt by the Nazis and again demolished (1947). It was returned to the Federal Republic of Germany (1952).

helicopter An aircraft that derives both lift and control from one or more sets of rotors (rotating AEROFOILS), driven by piston or gas-turbine engines about a vertical or near-vertical axis. In a helicopter the rotor blades act as a series of wings, which generate lift through circular rather than forward motion. Each rotor blade is also hinged (an arrangement first developed for the AUTOGYRO) so that it can move up and down independently of the others; without such hinging, small movements of the blades as they rotate would tend to destabilize the aircraft and make control difficult. The pitch of each rotor blade (the angle at which it meets the air-stream) can also be varied. At take-off all the blades are pitched steeply, to give maximum lift. For forward flight the pitch control is adjusted so that the pitch of each blade increases as it moves to the rear of its sweep. This has the effect of lifting the whole aircraft forwards, giving a forward component to the rotor's thrust in addition to the lift. The circular motion of the helicopter rotor generates an opposite, reactive force on the rest of the vehicle, tending to spin it in the opposite direction. This tendency is overcome either by using two opposite-rotating rotors, or by the use of a small tail rotor or jet generating a thrust in the opposite direction (this tail rotor can also be used to steer the aircraft). Paul Cornu flew the first free-flight, piloted helicopter in 1907 to a height of 30 cm (1 foot) but the craft was not really practicable. The first really practical helicopter was the single-rotor SIKORSKY VS-300 (1940). The Vietnam War (1962) saw the development of the helicopter as a heavily armed, ground-attack gunship. Helicopters also played a major role in the Gulf War (1991). Despite their slow speed and very high fuel consumption, helicopters are invaluable to the military, ambulance, and rescue services, and also to the police, due to their manœvrability. They are especially useful over difficult terrain, where no landing strip may be available.

Heligoland See HELGOLAND.

heliocentric system The system of COORDINATES in which all the positions and velocities of objects in the Solar System are computed with respect to the Sun's centre of mass. It is the most physically meaningful reference system, but NEWTON'S LAWS OF MOTION do not directly apply. Therefore computations of perturbations in the orbits of the planets are somewhat more difficult in this system.

The heliocentric system is a model of the Solar System in which the Sun is at the centre and all the planets orbit around it. Early models of the Solar System were GEOCENTRIC SYSTEMS but the COPERNICAN SYSTEM gave a more satisfactory explanation of the movement of the planets.

Heliogabalus (or **Elagabalus**) (born Varius Avitus Bassianus) (204–22 AD) Roman emperor 218–22. He took his name from the Syro-Phoenician Sun-god Elah-Gabal, whose hereditary priest he was. During his reign he became notorious for his dissipated lifestyle and neglect of state affairs; he and his mother were both murdered.

Heliopolis The Greek name for an ancient Egyptian city, situated near the apex of the Nile delta, at what is now Cairo. It was an important religious centre and the centre of Sun worship; its name means 'city of the Sun'. It was the original site of the obelisks known as Cleopatra's Needles.

Helios In Greek mythology, the Sun personified as a god.

heliostat An optical device that keeps an image of the Sun in a fixed position as the Sun crosses the sky. Like the COELOSTAT, it continuously directs the image into the aperture of a telescope. Though the image produced by the heliostat rotates slowly, this is not normally a disadvantage.

helium (symbol He, at. no. 2, r.a.m. 4.0) A colourless, odourless gas; it is one of the NOBLE GASES, and forms no true chemical compounds. Although it occurs to a small extent on Earth, it was first discovered in the Sun from the analysis of the solar spectrum. The element makes up about one-third of the mass of the Universe. Although it is thought that most helium in the Universe was created in the first few minutes of the life of the Universe after the BIG BANG, it is also the end-product of the CARBON–NITROGEN CYCLE and the PROTON–PROTON REACTION within main sequence stars, in which hydrogen is converted into helium with the production of energy which the stars radiate. Helium liquefies at −268°C (−514°F), and remains a liquid down to absolute zero; it can only be solidified under pressure. At −271°C (−520°F) it becomes a superfluid; its viscosity disappears, and its thermal conductivity becomes very high. Helium is found in ores of uranium and thorium but the main source of the element is natural gas, from which it is obtained by liquefaction of all the other components; it is used to provide an inert atmosphere in welding and as a safe alternative to hydrogen in balloons. Mixed with oxygen, it forms a breathing mixture that reduces the danger of 'the bends' in deep-sea diving. Liquid helium is an important coolant for SUPERCONDUCTING systems and other low-temperature applications.

hell The hypothetical abode of evil spirits, and the place in which the wicked are believed to be condemned to eternal punishment after death. In JUDAISM, the notion of *Sheol*, the shadowy underworld of departed souls, gave way to that of *Gehenna*, a place for punishing the wicked. Christian theologians define hell as the eternal deprivation of God's presence, the logical outcome of the soul's adherence to its own will and rejection of the will of God. It is traditionally described as a fiery subterranean abyss in which the souls of the wicked are condemned to everlasting torment, populated by demons and ruled over by Satan or Lucifer, a fallen angel who rebelled against God and was cast out of HEAVEN. ISLAM also depicts hell (*Jahannam*, a name derived from *Gehenna*) as full of fire and torment, but punishment is not necessarily eternal. In Hindu and Buddhist belief there are multiple hells (as there are multiple heavens) through which beings may pass as part of the cycle of REINCARNATION.

Hellas The Greek name for GREECE.

hellebore A plant of the genus *Helleborus*, of which there are about 20 species native to Europe and Asia Minor. Hellebores are herbaceous perennials, belonging to the buttercup family, with deeply divided, evergreen leaves and large white, green, or purplish flowers. The botanical name, from the Greek *elein*, injure, and *bora*, food, indicates the very poisonous nature of some species.

Hellenistic art Greek and Greek-inspired art and architecture from the late 4th to the late 1st century BC. In the Hellenistic period, when Greek civilization spread over the Mediterranean and Near

East, some works, such as the Venus de Milo (*c.*150 BC) continued earlier traditions. The Victory of Samothrace (*c.*200 BC) is full of life and grand in conception. A lively feeling for movement and emotion is shown in the Great Frieze of battling gods and giants on the Great Altar of Zeus at Pergamum (3rd century BC), now in Berlin, and in the Laocoon group, which is probably considerably later, in the Vatican. The painting of the Hellenistic period is well known from tombs in southern Russia, Macedonia, and Alexandria, as well as from copies found at Pompeii and Herculaneum. Interest in perspective and elaborate colour schemes continued, and a new interest developed in still life and landscape. Pictures were also executed in lively and decorative mosaic. Portraiture was introduced into art at this time. The features of rulers appeared on coins.

Hellenistic civilization The result of the adoption of the Greek language and culture by non-Greeks. (Hellas, an area of southern Thessaly, was synonymous with Greece from the 7th century BC.) It has come to refer specifically to the civilization that arose in the wake of the conquests of Alexander the Great. The many cities founded by him and his successors were the centres for a fusion of Greek and 'barbarian' ways of life, with ALEXANDRIA in Egypt becoming the literary focus of the Mediterranean world.

Heller, Joseph (1923–) US novelist. His experiences in the US air force during World War II inspired his best-known novel *Catch-22* (1961) an absurdist black comedy satirizing war. The book's hero tries to avoid combat duty by pleading insanity, only to be told that anyone wishing to avoid combat must be sane and therefore fit to fight; the novel's title has passed into the language as a name for a dilemma that is inescapable because of two mutually incompatible but necessary conditions.

Hellespont The ancient name for the Dardanelles, the narrow strait in modern Turkey linking the Sea of Marmara with the Aegean, named after the legendary Helle who fell into the strait and was drowned while escaping with her brother Phrixus from their stepmother, Ino, on a golden-fleeced ram. The scene of the legend of HERO and Leander.

Hellfire Club (1745–63) A notorious English society that met in the ruins of Medmenham Abbey in Buckinghamshire. It was founded by Sir Francis Dashwood in 1745, and its members reputedly indulged in debauchery and in the mocking of organized religion by the performance of blasphemous 'black masses'. Its membership included many politicians, the most famous of whom were John Wilkes, the Earl of BUTE, and the Earl of Sandwich.

Hellman, Lillian (Florence) (1907–84) US dramatist. She gained her first success with *The Children's Hour* (1934), which was followed by plays such as *The Little Foxes* (1939) and the anti-Fascist *Watch on the Rhine* (1941). Hellman was a socialist and a feminist, and her plays frequently reflect her political concerns. For more than thirty years she lived with the detective-story writer Dashiell HAMMETT; both were blacklisted during the McCarthy era.

Helmholtz, Hermann Ludwig Ferdinand von (1821–94) German scientist who, during a distinguished and varied career in both physics and physiology, invented the ophthalmoscope used by opticians, did much to advance the study of THERMODYNAMICS and the law of CONSERVATION OF ENERGY, and developed a theory of SOUND. He devised a two-coil system for producing a uniform magnetic field, and carried out research into the properties of oscillating electric currents. This research was continued by his assistant, Heinrich HERTZ, who discovered radio waves as a result.

Helmont, Joannes Baptista van (1577–1644) Belgian chemist and physician. He made early studies on the conservation of matter, was the first to distinguish gases, and coined the word *gas*. Having failed to realize that green plants take in carbon dioxide, he concluded that they are composed entirely of water.

Héloïse (1098–1164) French abbess. She is chiefly remembered for her passionate but tragic love affair with ABELARD, which began after she became his pupil (at the instigation of her uncle, Fulbert) *c.*1118. She gave birth to a son, after which the two were secretly married; when the affair came to light relatives of Héloïse castrated Abelard, while Héloïse was forced to enter a convent. She later became abbess of Paraclete.

helot An inhabitant of ancient Greece forced into serfdom by conquering invaders. Helots were used as agricultural labourers and in domestic service. The Messenians, subjected by SPARTA, greatly outnumbered the Spartan citizens, and fear of their rebellion caused the city to keep them under ruthlessly tight military control.

Helpmann, Sir Robert (1909–86) Australian dancer, actor, and choreographer. He studied with Pavlova and de Valois, and was one of the first dancers of the Vic-Wells Ballet, known for his comic and dramatic roles. His own choreography includes *Hamlet* (1942), *Miracle in the Gorbals* (1944), and *Elektra* (1963). He returned to direct the Australian Ballet in 1965.

Helsingfors See HELSINKI.

Helsingør See ELSINORE.

Helsinki (Swedish **Helsingfors**) The capital of Finland, a seaport on the Gulf of Finland; pop. (1990) 492,400. Founded by Gustavus Vasa of Sweden in 1550, Helsinki was rebuilt by Alexander I of Russia after being destroyed by fire in 1808. It replaced Turku as capital of Finland in 1812. It is Finland's largest port and manufacturing centre with shipbuilding, chemical, textile, sugar-refining, printing, and ceramic industries. It has a neoclassical cathedral (1852) and an impressive railway station designed by Eero Saarinen. It has Finland's largest and oldest university (1849), a technical university (1908), and many museums, galleries, halls, and stadiums.

Helsinki Conference (1973–75) Meetings at Helsinki and later Geneva, attended by leaders of thirty-five nations representing the entire membership of NATO, the WARSAW PACT, and the non-aligned countries, at which the Conference on Security and Co-operation in Europe (CSCE) was launched (1975). The conference produced the Helsinki Final Act containing a list of agreements concerning political freedom, mutual cooperation, and human rights; it can be considered the major achievement of DÉTENTE. The 34 heads of state also adopted the Charter of Paris for a New Europe. In 1992 the CSCE decided to create its own armed peacekeeping force; it now has 53 member states.

Helvetia An archaic name used in poetic reference to Switzerland, derived from the Latin name (HELVETII) given by the Romans to the Celtic tribe. The name Helvetia is still used on Swiss postage stamps.

Helvetii Celts who migrated from southern Germany to south and west of the Rhine in the 2nd century BC. In 102 BC they joined the Cimbri and Teutones in invading Italy and were defeated by

Emperor MARIUS. Under pressure of Germanic migrations they attempted a mass migration into Roman GAUL in 58 BC. Julius CAESAR drove them back. AUGUSTUS incorporated their territory into Belgic GAUL. Overrun in the 5th century by a succession of Alemanni, FRANKS, Swabians, and Burgundians their name is preserved in the formal name for SWITZERLAND – the Helvetic Confederacy (or Helvetia).

Hemel Hempstead A residential and light industrial town in Hertfordshire, south-east England, on the River Gade; pop. (1986) 81,000. It was designated a New Town in 1947.

hemichordate A member of the phylum Hemichordata, which contains three classes of marine invertebrates, the extinct Graptolithina (see GRAPTOLITE), the Pterobranchia, and the largest and best known, Enteropneusta, containing about 70 species all known as ACORN WORMS.

Hemingway, **Ernest (Miller)** (1899–1961) US writer. After World War I he lived in Paris, where he came into contact with such writers as Ezra Pound and worked as a journalist before publishing short stories and then novels. His early novels reflect the disillusionment of the postwar 'lost generation'; they include *The Sun Also Rises* (1926) and *A Farewell to Arms* (1929). During World War II he joined in the D-Day landings as a war correspondent. In Hemingway's later works there is a developing theme of the strength and dignity of the human spirit; the most famous are *For Whom the Bell Tolls* (1940) and *The Old Man and the Sea* (1952). He was awarded the Nobel Prize for literature in 1954. A depressive, he committed suicide.

hemlock A tall perennial plant, *Conium maculatum*, with fern-like leaves, related to the carrot or parsley and widely distributed in Europe, Asia, and North Africa. It is one of the most poisonous plants known to man and was used in ancient Greece for the execution of criminals. The poison extracted from the plant contains coniine and other alkaloids. It was this poison that many believe was taken by Socrates.

hemlock spruce A coniferous tree with some 11 species in the genus *Tsuga*, spread over North America and the Far East. The name derives from the fact that the crushed foliage of some species smells like hemlock. The Western hemlock, *T. heterophylla*, from western North America, produces useful timber and bark for tanning.

hemp The FIBRE extracted from the stems of the CANNABIS plant, a tall, dock-like annual with a strong smell. Cultivated in Asia for thousands of years, it is now grown for its fibre wherever the climate is humid but temperate; the former Soviet Union, China, Japan, Italy, Yugoslavia, and the USA are the major producers. The cultivation of hemp is similar to that of the other temperate fibre crop, FLAX, although the fibre itself is tougher and is used for coarse fabrics and ropes.

Several other plants are also known as 'hemp', but should not be confused with true hemp. Manila hemp is obtained from the banana-like *Musa textilis*, and sunn hemp is obtained from the leaves of the legume *Crotalaria juncea*, in India. Strong elastic white fibres taken from leaves of the bowstring hemp, a *Sansevieria* species, were used in African bows.

Hendrix, **Jimi** (born James Marshall Hendrix) (1942–70) US rock guitarist and singer. Remembered for the flamboyance and originality of his improvisations, he greatly widened the scope of the electric guitar. He gave notable live performances with his groups, playing with the Jimi Hendrix Experience at the Monterey pop festival (1967) and with the Band of Gypsies at the Woodstock festival (1969). His best-known singles include 'Purple Haze' (1967) and 'All Along the Watchtower' (1968). He died of a drugs overdose.

Hendry, **Stephen (Gordon)** (1969–) Scottish snooker player. He made his professional début in 1985, becoming the youngest world snooker champion in 1990. He regained the title in 1992 and held it until 1996, when he won his sixth championship. He was the first player to win all nine world-ranking tournaments and in 1996 held the record for the most breaks over 100.

Hengist (died 488) Semi-mythological Jutish leader. He and his brother **Horsa** (died 455) are said by Bede to have been invited to Britain by the British king Vortigern in 449 to assist in defeating the Picts, and later to have established an independent Anglo-Saxon kingdom in Kent. The historicity of the brothers has been questioned, and they may have been mythological figures (their names mean 'gelding' and 'horse').

Henley (full name **Henley-on-Thames**) A town in south Oxfordshire, England, on the River Thames; pop. (1991) 10,558. It is associated with rowing and especially the Royal Henley Regatta, which has been a fashionable annual event since 1839.

henna (or **Egyptian privet**) A shrub of the family Lythraceae, *Lawsonia inermis*, that has been cultivated as a dye plant for centuries in Egypt, Arabia, and India. The orange dye that can be extracted from its leaves was used by the women of ancient Egypt, and is still used by modern Muslims to colour their hands a reddish-brown. The dye is also used as a colouring in hair rinses, and also for dyeing leather.

Henri, **Robert** (1865–1929) US painter. He was an advocate of realism and believed that the artist must be a social force; as a teacher at various schools of art in New York (1902–28), he encouraged his students to turn away from academicism and towards a realistic depiction of everyday life. The Ashcan School of painters was formed largely as a result of his influence.

Henrietta Maria (1609–69) Daughter of Henry IV of France, queen consort of Charles I of England 1625–49. Her Roman Catholicism heightened public anxieties about the court's religious sympathies and was a contributory cause of the English Civil War. From 1644 she lived mainly in France.

henry (symbol H) The SI UNIT of inductance, defined as that which gives an electromotive force of one volt in a closed circuit with a rate of change of one ampere per second. It is named after the US physicist Joseph HENRY.

Henry Eight kings of England. **Henry I** (1068–1135), youngest son of William I, reigned 1100–35. On the death of his brother, William II, Henry seized the throne in the absence of his other brother, Robert of Normandy; Henry conquered Normandy in 1105. After his only son was drowned in 1120 there were problems with the succession, and although Henry extracted an oath of loyalty to his daughter Matilda from the barons in 1127, his death was followed almost immediately by the outbreak of civil war. **Henry II** (1133–89), son of Matilda, reigned 1154–89. The first Plantagenet king, Henry restored order after the reigns of Stephen and Matilda, added Anjou and Aquitaine to the English possessions in France, established his rule in Ireland, and forced the king of Scotland to acknowledge him as overlord of that kingdom. Henry was less successful in reducing the power of the Church; opposition to his policies was led by Thomas à Becket, who was eventually murdered by four of Henry's knights. **Henry III** (1207–72), son of John, reigned 1216–72. Until Henry declared himself of age to rule personally in 1227, his regent the Earl of Pembroke kept the rebellious barons in check, but afterwards the king's ineffectual government caused widespread discontent, ending in Simon de Montfort's defeat and capture of the king in 1264 in the second Baron's War. Although Henry was restored after the defeat of the rebels a year later, real power resided with his son, who eventually succeeded him as Edward I. **Henry IV** (known as Henry Bolingbroke) (1367–1413), son of John of Gaunt, reigned 1399–1413. He returned from exile in 1399 to overthrow Richard II and establish the Lancastrian dynasty. His reign was scarred by rebellion, both in Wales and in the north, where the Percy family raised several uprisings. Although Henry defeated Sir Henry Percy ('Hotspur') in 1403, the Percy threat did not abate until the head of the family was killed in 1408. **Henry V** (1387–1422), son of Henry IV, reigned 1413–22. He renewed the Hundred Years War soon after coming to the throne and defeated the French at Agincourt in 1415. By the Treaty of Troyes (1420) Henry was named successor to Charles VI of France and betrothed to his daughter Catherine of Valois. When the Dauphin repudiated the treaty, Henry returned to France but fell ill and died, leaving his infant son to inherit the throne. **Henry VI** (1421–71), son of Henry V, reigned 1422–61 and 1470–71. Succeeding his father while still an infant, Henry VI proved to have a recurrent mental illness which made him unfit to rule effectively on his own. During his reign the Hundred Years War with France was finally lost, and government by the monarchy, in the hands of a series of regents and noble favourites, became increasingly unpopular. In the 1450s opposition coalesced round the House of York, and, after intermittent civil war between the followers of that House and those of the House of Lancaster (the Wars of the Roses), Henry was deposed in 1461 by Edward IV. In 1470 Henry briefly regained his throne following a Lancastrian uprising, but was deposed again and murdered soon after. **Henry VII** (known as Henry Tudor) (1457–1509), the first Tudor king, son of Edmund Tudor, Earl of Richmond, reigned 1485–1509. Although he was the grandson of Owen Tudor, it was through his mother, a great-granddaughter of John of Gaunt, that he inherited the Lancastrian claim to the throne. Having grown up in exile in France, Henry returned to England in 1485 and ascended the throne after defeating Richard III at Bosworth Field. Threatened in the early years of his reign by a series of Yorkist plots, Henry eventually established an unchallenged Tudor dynasty, dealing ruthlessly with other claimants to the throne. As king he continued the strengthening of royal government commenced by his Yorkist predecessors. **Henry VIII** (1491–1547), son of Henry VII, reigned 1509–47. Henry had six wives (Catherine of Aragon, Anne Boleyn, Jane Seymour, Anne of Cleves, Catherine Howard, Katherine Parr), two of whom he had executed and two of whom he divorced. His efforts to divorce his first wife, Catherine of Aragon, which were opposed by the pope, led to England's break with the Roman Catholic Church and indirectly to the establishment of Protestantism. Henry's ensuing dissolution of the monasteries not only destroyed most of the remaining vestiges of the old religious Establishment but also changed the pattern of land ownership. The final years of Henry's reign were marked by wars and rebellion.

Henry Seven kings of the Germans, six of whom were also Holy Roman emperors. **Henry I** (known as Henry the Fowler) (*c.*876–936) reigned 919–36. As duke of Saxony, he was elected king by the nobles of Saxony and Franconia following the death of Conrad I (903–18). He waged war successfully against the Slavs in Brandenburg, the Magyars, and the Danes, from whom he gained the territory of Schleswig in 934. **Henry II** (known as Saint Henry) (973–1024) reigned 1002–24, Holy Roman emperor 1014–24. **Henry III** (1017–56) reigned 1039–56, Holy Roman emperor 1046–56. He brought stability and prosperity to the empire, defeating the Czechs in 1041 and fixing the frontier between Austria and Hungary in 1043. A devout Christian, he introduced religious reforms, attacked corruption in the Church, and strengthened the papacy, securing the appointment of four successive German popes. **Henry IV** (1050–1106), son of Henry III, reigned 1056–1105, Holy Roman emperor 1084–1105. Following the end of his regency in 1065 he came into increasing conflict with Pope Gregory VII (*c.*1020–85), which culminated in 1076 when Henry called a council to depose the Pope. Gregory retaliated by excommunicating Henry and absolving his subjects from their oaths of loyalty to him. In 1077 Henry obtained absolution by doing penance before Gregory at Canossa in Italy, and spent the next three years waging war on his rebellious subjects. He finally managed to depose Gregory in 1084, being crowned emperor by his successor in the same year. **Henry V** (1086–1125) reigned 1099–1125, Holy Roman emperor 1111–25. **Henry VI** (1165–97) reigned 1169–97, Holy Roman emperor 1191–97. **Henry VII** (*c.*1269/74–1313) reigned 1308–13, Holy Roman emperor 1312–13.

Henry (known as **Henry the Navigator**) (1394–1460) Portuguese prince. The third son of John I of Portugal, he was a leading patron of voyages of exploration, from which he earned his title. He established a school of navigation at Cape St Vincent and organized and funded many voyages of discovery, most notably south along the African coast. The efforts of his captains, who reached as far south as Cape Verde and the Azores, laid the groundwork for later Portuguese imperial expansion south-east round Africa to the Far East.

Henry I (the Fowler) Henry I of the Germans. See HENRY (kings of the Germans).

Henry IV (known as **Henry of Navarre**) (1553–1610) King of France 1589–1610. As king of Navarre, Henry was the leader of Huguenot forces in the latter stages of the French Wars of Religion, but on succeeding the Catholic Henry III he became Catholic himself in order to guarantee peace. He founded the Bourbon dynasty, established religious freedom with the Edict of Nantes (1598), and restored order after prolonged civil war. He was assassinated by a Catholic fanatic.

Henry, Joseph (1797–1878) US physicist. He made important discoveries concerning electromagnetism, including electromagnetic induction (independently of FARADAY). He also devised an electromagnetic relay. The unit of inductance is named after him.

Henry, O. (pseudonym of William Sydney Porter) (1862–1910) US short-story writer. He became a prolific and popular author after a period in jail for embezzlement, turning out tales of great technical skill which were often based on the lives of ordinary New Yorkers, notably in his collection *The Four Million* (1906).

Henry Bolingbroke Henry IV of England. See HENRY (kings of England).

Henry's law (in chemistry) A gas law stating that at a constant temperature the mass of gas dissolved by a given volume of liquid is proportional to the pressure of the gas in equilibrium with the solution, if there is no chemical reaction between the gas and the liquid. It is named after the British chemist, **William Henry** (1774–1836), who formulated it in 1801.

Henry the Lion (1129–95) Duke of Saxony and Bavaria. He was the son of Henry the Proud of the German Welf family. He obtained his duchies with the help of Emperor FREDERICK I Barbarossa, expanding his territories and influence as far as the Baltic, and encouraging trade. Ambitious and powerful, he lost the emperor's favour and was banished in 1180. He was welcomed in England, as his second wife was the daughter of HENRY II and he became a power in ANGEVIN political life. By 1190 he had regained much of his former territory. His son, Otto IV, continued the challenge to the HOHENSTAUFEN.

Henry Tudor Henry VII of England. See HENRY (kings of England).

Henze, Hans Werner (1926–) German composer and conductor. His musical style is diverse, displaying a respect for classical forms such as the sonata and influenced by both Italian opera and serialism. His many works include *The Raft of the Medusa* (1968, a requiem for Che Guevara) the operas *We Come to the River* (1974–76) and *The English Cat* (1982), seven symphonies, and ballet and chamber music.

hepatitis Acute or chronic inflammation of the liver. Acute viral hepatitis is a COMMUNICABLE DISEASE caused by hepatitis viruses. Hepatitis A is caused by hepatitis A virus, which is transmitted by ingestion of water or food contaminated with human sewage containing the virus. Hepatitis B is caused by hepatitis B virus, which is transmitted by sexual intercourse, contact with infected secretions, infected blood transfusion or blood products, and injecting drug misuse by using contaminated needles (needle sharing). Hepatitis C and the recently identified hepatitis G have the same mode of transmission as hepatitis B, and hepatitis D may occur with or after infection with hepatitis B. Hepatitis E may cause epidemics in countries with poor sanitation. Acute alcoholic hepatitis is caused by excessive alcohol consumption. Symptoms of different acute viral and alcoholic hepatitis are similar and may include jaundice, impairment of taste, abdominal distention and pain, nausea, vomiting, skin rashes, and joint pain. Complications associated with acute hepatitis include liver failure from fulminating disease.

Chronic hepatitis can last six to twelve months or longer; it commonly follows acute viral or alcoholic hepatitis. Chronic persistent hepatitis may be asymptomatic, or may cause only mild symptoms. Chronic active hepatitis is often associated with excessive alcohol consumption; it is more common in women.

Hepburn, Audrey (1929–93) US actress, born in Belgium. After pursuing a career as a stage and film actress in England, she moved to Hollywood, where she starred in such films as *Roman Holiday* (1953), for which she won an Oscar, and *War and Peace* (1956). She is perhaps best known for her performance as Eliza Doolittle in the film musical *My Fair Lady* (1964).

Hepburn, Katharine (1909–) US actress. After her screen début in 1932 she went on to star in a wide range of films, including many in which she formed a partnership with Spencer Tracy. Her films include *The Philadelphia Story* (1940) *Woman of the Year* (1942), *The African Queen* (1951), and *On Golden Pond* (1981), for which she won her fourth Oscar.

Hepplewhite, George (1726–86) British cabinet-maker and furniture designer. None of his furniture has been identified, and his fame depends on the posthumously published book of his designs, *The Cabinet-Maker and Upholsterer's Guide* (1788). This contains almost 300 designs, which sum up the neoclassical taste of the period in pieces that are characterized by their light and elegant lines.

Hepworth, Dame (Jocelyn) Barbara (1903–75) British sculptor. A pioneer of abstraction in British sculpture, in the 1930s she worked chiefly in wood and stone, using forms suggested by the inherent qualities of these materials and assimilating them to organic forms or to the human figure. From the 1950s onwards she also worked in bronze, producing simple monumental works for landscape and architectural settings. Her works include the nine-piece group *The Family of Man* (1972).

Hera In Greek mythology, the supreme goddess, the sister and wife of Zeus. She was constantly at odds with Zeus because of his infidelities and she often plotted against his lovers and his offspring.

Heracles See HERCULES.

Heraclitus (*c*.500 BC) Greek philosopher. He regarded the Universe as a ceaselessly changing conflict of opposites, all things being in a harmonious process of constant change, and held that fire, the basic constituent of the Universe, is their origin. He believed that the mind derives a false idea of the permanence of the external world from the passing impressions of experience.

Heraklion (Greek **Iráklion**) A seaport and administrative centre of the Greek island of Crete, on the north coast of the island; pop. (1991) 117,000. Known as Candia in medieval times, it has been the island's capital since 1971. Its harbour has an impressive Venetian fortress and arsenals. It exports wine, olive oil, raisins, and almonds.

heraldry The study of coats of arms worn for individual identification, and of the accessories of crests, badges, mottoes, and flags that accompanied them. Its origins are military. Soldiers in armour and helmets could not easily be identified in battle and so the practice evolved of displaying a sign or device on the shield and on the linen surcoat worn over the armour (from which the terms 'coat-of-arms' and 'court armoury' derive). The first heraldic designs may have been worn by the Crusaders, but their use became widespread in Europe in the 12th century. A similar system also emerged in Japan during the 12th century.

By the 13th century heraldry had so developed that it had its own terminology, based on Old French. Its colours are called 'tinctures' of which there are two metals – gold (*or*) and silver (*argent*) – and five colours – blue (*azure*), black (*sable*), green (*vert*), purple (*purpure*), and red (*gules*). In England heralds were formed into the College of Arms (1484), which still controls the grant of arms. Scotland has its Court of the Lord Lyon (1592).

Herat (or **Harat**) A city in western Afghanistan; pop. (est. 1988) 177,300. Near the site of several ancient cities, Herat was a scientific and cultural centre in the 15th century. It is now a focus for commerce.

herb A plant of use in medicine or cooking. In a botanical sense, however, it refers to non-woody seed-bearing plants, the aerial parts of which are ephemeral, hence the term herbaceous. Medicinal herbs are the source of a number of drugs still used in modern medicine. Culinary herbs are of value in flavouring foods, formerly often foods which would otherwise have been unpalatable. Certain herbs have so-called essential oils in their stems and leaves. For example, the leaves of mint, sage, thyme, and parsley, the stems of angelica and fennel, and the fruits of anise and caraway are rich in such oils. Often the last two are referred to as SPICES.

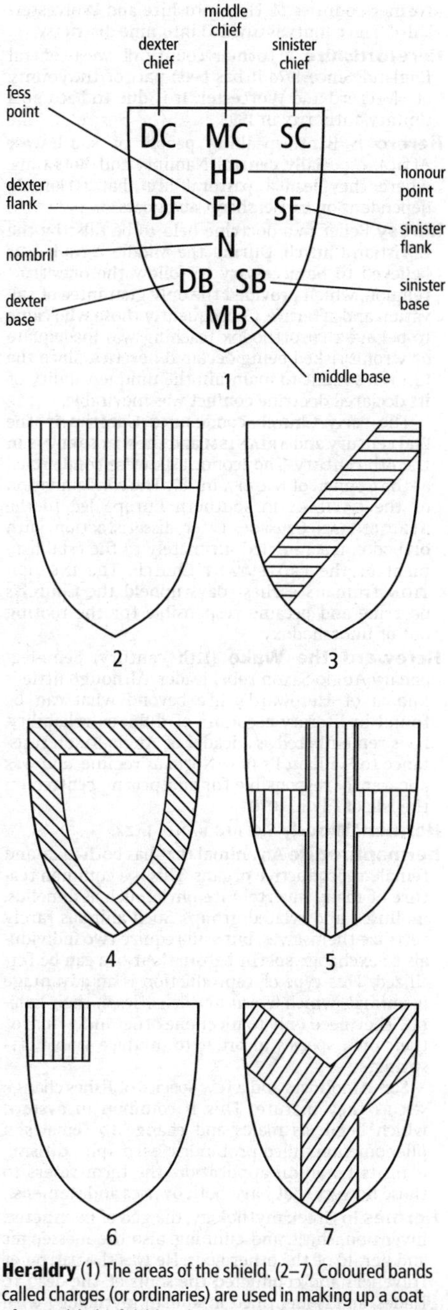

Heraldry (1) The areas of the shield. (2–7) Coloured bands called charges (or ordinaries) are used in making up a coat of arms: (2) chief; (3) bend sinister; (4) bordure; (5) cross; (6) canton; and (7) pall.

herbal medicine A system of COMPLEMENTARY MEDICINE using plants and plant extracts to prevent and cure disease by stimulating the body's own powers of healing. Until quite recently, many drugs were based on plant extracts (with some animal and mineral products), but the pharmaceutical industry has isolated the active components of some plant extracts and now synthesizes them by industrial chemical techniques. Herbal medicine is a reversion to the use of pure plant extracts, on the principle that humans should exist in harmony with their environment, and that local plants are likely to be able to cure many ailments: for example, asthma is said to be responsive to local honeys on the grounds that they will lead to desensitization to local pollens that can cause asthma.

Herbert, Sir A(lan) P(atrick) (1890–1970) British writer and politician. He was a writer of versatility and humour, who contributed to the magazine *Punch* for many years, wrote libretti for a number of comic operas, and published a number of novels. He also campaigned for several causes, most notably the reform of the divorce laws; as Independent MP for Oxford University (1935–50) he was responsible for introducing the Matrimonial Causes Act (1937), which radically amended the legislation.

Herbert, George (1593–1633) English Metaphysical poet. In 1630 he became the vicar of Bemerton, near Salisbury, after a brief time spent as MP for Montgomery (1624–25). His devout religious verse is pervaded by simple piety and reflects the spiritual conflicts he experienced before submitting his will to God. His poems are marked by metrical versatility and homely imagery; most were published just after his death in *The Temple: Sacred Poems and Private Ejaculations*.

herbicide A PESTICIDE toxic to plants, used to kill weeds or other unwanted vegetation. Herbicides may be non-specific AGROCHEMICALS, killing all plants: examples of such 'total' herbicides are sodium chlorate and paraquat. Alternatively they may be more selective, for example killing only broad-leaved plants. These herbicides are effective when growing cereals or other thin-leaved crops. Herbicides are usually used in a liquid form, and sprayed on to the crops. Although designed to be selectively toxic to plants, some herbicides also have limited toxicity in humans, and must be used with great care. Concern about the harmful effects of persistent chemicals has led to the development of products that break down when they enter the soil. In contrast, pre-emergent herbicides are designed to persist in the soil, and kill weeds at their most vulnerable stage, as they germinate.

herbivore An animal that depends entirely upon plants for its food. Such a diet has a profound influence upon the teeth and digestive system. The cheek teeth are usually much developed, the premolars and molars having large and complex surfaces that function to divide the plant material into fine shreds as an aid to digestion. The front teeth have become variously modified and a gap (diastema) has developed between these and the cheek teeth. The diastema allows the passage of food backwards and forwards into the cheek pouches. The incisors of rodents, which are mostly herbivores, grow continuously and, having enamel on one side only, provide a sharp cutting edge.

The cell walls of plants are made of cellulose, a substance that is not readily broken down. Mammals lack the necessary enzymes for its digestion and so their alimentary canal contains microorganisms adapted for this task. In the horse, microorganisms aid fermentation in the enlarged colon and large intestine. Food takes 30–45 hours to pass through the gut of a horse. Ruminants regurgitate the cud and chew it again. They have a complex stomach consisting of four compartments; the passage of food takes 70–100 hours in a cow. Rodents and rabbits pass food twice through the digestive tract in order to obtain essential vitamins not released on the initial passage of the plant material. Termites also harbour microbial populations, allowing them to feed on wood.

Hercegovina See BOSNIA-HERCEGOVINA.

Herculaneum An ancient Roman town, near Naples, on the lower slopes of Mt. Vesuvius. The eruption in 79 AD buried it deeply under volcanic ash and thus largely preserved it. Excavations have continued since 1709.

Hercules (or **Heracles**) (in Greek mythology) The greatest of all heroes, famed for his strength and courage. He was the son of Zeus (from whom he inherited an insatiable sexual appetite) and Alcmene, a mortal. He performed a great variety of stupendous feats, triumphing over evil against all odds, but he is most famous for his Twelve Labours, undertaken as a penance for killing his wife and children in a fit of madness induced by Hera. The Labours were: killing the Nemean Lion; killing the Hydra, a seven- (or nine-) headed water serpent; capturing the Erymanthian Boar; capturing the Hind of Ceryneia; driving away the man-eating Stymphalian Birds; cleaning the Augean Stables; capturing the Cretan Bull; taming the horses of Diomedes; carrying off the girdle of Hippolyta, queen of the Amazons; capturing the Oxen of Geryon; carrying off the golden apples of the Hesperides; capturing Cerberus. After his death (brought about by treachery) he ascended to the heavens and became the only mortal to be raised to the same level as the Olympian gods. Hebe was given to him as his bride.

Hercules (in astronomy) A large CONSTELLATION of the Northern Hemisphere of the sky, one of the 48 figures known to the ancient Greeks. It represents the mythical character who carried out 12 labours, and it is the fifth-largest constellation. In the sky, Hercules is seen kneeling with one foot on the head of Draco, the dragon.

Hercules beetle *Dynastes hercules*, among the largest of all BEETLES, reaching up to 16 cm (6.5 inches) in length, typically with horns on the head and the front of the thorax. It occurs in tropical America.

heredity The transfer of properties of organisms from one generation to the next. There are two main kinds of heredity: genetic and exogenetic. Exogenetic heredity is not caused by genes and involves the transfer of property and cultural information by learning.

Only factors inherited from the parental generation are handed on by their progeny. Any acquired character, such as learned behaviour, cannot be genetically inherited. Genetic heredity is particulate and is carried by molecules of DNA, on structures called CHROMOSOMES (see GENETICS).

Hereford A market city in the county of Hereford and Worcester, west-central England, on the River Wye; pop. (1991) 49,800. Its Norman cathedral has a library of chained books and a famous 14th-century *Mappa Mundi*. It shares the Three Choirs Festival with Worcester and Gloucester. The actor David Garrick was born here in 1717.

Hereford and Worcester A county of west-central England, on the border with Wales; area 3,926 sq km (1,516 sq miles); pop. (1993) 694,800, county town, Worcester. It was formed in 1974 from the former counties of Herefordshire and Worcestershire. The county is divided into nine districts.

Herefordshire A former county of west-central England. Since 1974 it has been part of the county of Hereford and Worcester. It is due to become a unitary authority in 1998.

Herero A Bantu-speaking people of south-west Africa, especially central Namibia and Botswana, where they lead a pastoral life that is largely dependent on cattle, sheep, and goats.

heresy Belief in a doctrine held to be false by the Christian Church. During the Middle Ages it was believed to be necessary to follow the one 'true' religion, which provided the only guarantee of salvation and afterlife. Consequently those who came to believe that orthodox teaching was inadequate or wrong risked being declared heretics. Since the Church sought to maintain the unique validity of its declared doctrine conflict was inevitable.

The early Church condemned Gnostics in the 2nd century and ARIANISM and the NESTORIANS in the 4th century. The Iconoclasts were condemned at the Council of NICAEA in 787. The condemnation of the CATHARS in southern Europe led to the ALBIGENSIAN Crusade. Later dissatisfaction with orthodox teaching led ultimately to the establishment of the PROTESTANT Church. The INQUISITION from its earliest days upheld the Church's doctrine and became responsible for the rooting out of unorthodoxy.

Hereward the Wake (11th century) Semi-legendary Anglo-Saxon rebel leader. Although little is known of Hereward's life beyond what can be found in literary accounts of dubious reliability, he is remembered as a leader of Anglo-Saxon resistance to William I's new Norman regime, and was apparently responsible for an uprising centred on the Isle of Ely in 1070.

Herman, Woody See BIG BAND; JAZZ.

hermaphrodite An animal that has both male and female reproductive organs. This is a common feature of many invertebrate phyla, such as annelids, molluscs, and related groups. Such animals rarely fertilize themselves, but still require two individuals to exchange sperm before their ova can be fertilized. This type of reproduction is an advantage in animals which live at low densities in their habitat. They need only to meet one other individual of their own species in order to produce viable offspring.

Some molluscs and a few species of fishes change sex as they mature. This is common in oysters, which begin as males and change to females, a phenomenon called protandric hermaphroditism.

In its botanical application, the term refers to those flowers that have both ovaries and stamens.

Hermes In Greek mythology, the god of commerce, invention, theft, and cunning, also the messenger and herald of the other gods. He was the patron of travellers and conducted the souls of the dead to Hades, and is identified in Roman mythology with Mercury.

hermit (from the Greek word for 'desert') Someone

who for religious reasons takes up a solitary life. The first Christian hermits, from the late 3rd century onwards, were most numerous in and around Egypt; some of them were highly influential and were visited by pilgrims. St Basil the Great (*c.*330–79) prepared a monastic rule that is still followed in the Eastern Church. The eremitic way of life influenced European monastic orders such as the CARTHUSIANS and CARMELITES.

hermit crab A crab with a soft, unprotected abdomen, unlike most other CRABS. Hermit crabs must seek security in abandoned mollusc shells, carefully choosing one to fit. The abdomen of these crabs is asymmetrically twisted, so it can be inserted snugly into snail shells, leaving only head and pincers protruding. Hermits may fight over a new shell when they have outgrown their present lodgings. Many carry 'passengers' on the shell, especially sea anemones, which can assist their defence, and they will carefully transfer their anemone on to the new shell. Some tropical hermits are land-dwelling, though they always require water nearby to dampen the body and for drinking; they have reduced gills, and breathe through modified lungs. Hermit crabs belong to two superfamilies of crustacean. Some species use bamboo or hollow mangrove roots as homes.

hernia (or **rupture**) Protrusion of part of an organ through an opening in the surrounding structures. Protrusion of part of the intestine through the abdominal wall is called an inguinal hernia, which commonly occurs in the groin, although it may also occur at other sites such as the scrotum and top of the thigh. A hiatus hernia is the protrusion of part of the stomach through the diaphragm at the opening that allows the oesophagus to enter the abdominal cavity. An umbilical hernia is protrusion of part of the intestine through the abdominal wall at the umbilicus; it is usually present at birth and surgical repair is necessary. Hernias may become fixed (incarcerated) or strangulated; loss of blood supply to that portion of the organ may result in gangrene.

Hero (in Greek mythology) A beautiful priestess of Aphrodite at Sestos on the European shore of the Hellespont (the strait – now called the Dardanelles – separating Europe from Asia Minor). She was loved by Leander, a youth who lived on the opposite shore and swam across every night to see her. One stormy night he was drowned, and Hero in despair threw herself into the sea.

Hero (known as **Hero of Alexandria**) (1st century) Greek mathematician and inventor. His surviving works are important as a source for ancient practical mathematics and mechanics. He described a number of hydraulic, pneumatic, and other mechanical devices designed both for utility and amusement, including elementary applications of the power of steam.

Herod Four rulers of ancient Palestine. **Herod the Great** (*c.*74–4 BC) ruled 37–4 BC. He built the palace of Masada and rebuilt the Temple in Jerusalem. Jesus is thought to have been born during his reign; according to the New Testament (Matt. 2:16), he ordered the massacre of the innocents. **Herod Antipas** (22 BC–*c.*40 AD), son of Herod the Great, was tetrarch of Galilee and Peraea 4 BC–40 AD. He married Herodias and was responsible for the beheading of John the Baptist. According to the New Testament (Luke 23:7), Pilate sent Jesus to be questioned by him before the Crucifixion. **Herod Agrippa I** (10 BC–44 AD), grandson of Herod the Great, was king of Judaea 41–44 AD. He imprisoned St Peter and put St James the Great to death. **Herod Agrippa II** (27–*c.*93 AD), son of Herod Agrippa I, was king of various territories in northern Palestine 50–*c.*93. He presided over the trial of St Paul (Acts 25:13 ff.).

Herodotus (known as 'the Father of History') (*c.*490–*c.*425 BC) Greek historian. His *History* tells of the Persian Wars of the early 5th century BC, with an account of the earlier history of the Persian empire and its relations with the Greeks to explain the origins of the conflict. He was the first historian to collect his materials systematically, test their accuracy to a certain extent, and arrange them in a well-constructed and vivid narrative.

heroic couplet A rhymed pair of iambic PENTAMETER lines in poetry, called 'heroic' from their use by Dryden in heroic (EPIC) verse and drama. An important English verse-form first used by Chaucer, the heroic couplet was perfected by Dryden and Pope into a balanced, polished medium sharing the qualities of epigram.

heroin A powerful narcotic analgesic derived from morphine. Chemically it consists of diamorphine, which has fewer side effects than morphine. Because it leads to physical dependence, its use in medicine is restricted, mainly to the terminally ill. Heroin is extensively abused (see DRUG ABUSE) with a number of street names, 'smack' being the most common.

heron A stork-like bird that, together with bitterns and egrets, belongs to the family Ardeidae. They are typically slender, with long necks and legs. Some species of egret herons (*Egretta*) develop long plumes on their head, neck, and back. In flight the neck of most herons is retracted, the broad wings flap slowly, and the feet project beyond the tail. When hunting, a solitary heron will stand motionless in the shallows and snap up a fish, eel, or frog with a sudden lunge of its bill. Most of the 49 widely distributed species breed in colonies called heronries, building stick nests in trees.

Herophilus (4th–3rd centuries BC) Greek anatomist, regarded as the father of human anatomy. Based in Alexandria, he made fundamental discoveries concerning the anatomy of the brain, eye, and reproductive organs, and some of his terms are still in use. Herophilus distinguished nerves from tendons, recognizing that nerves are connected to the brain and that they can be either sensory or motor in function. He also distinguished between veins and arteries, showing that they contain blood, and carried out the first systematic study of the pulse. None of his works survive.

Héroult, Paul-Louis-Toussaint (1863–1914) French chemist who invented the ELECTRIC-ARC FURNACE and (independently of HALL) an electrolytic process for manufacturing aluminium. After a year at the Paris School of Mines, he began experimenting with the production of aluminium by ELECTROLYSIS of alumina (aluminium oxide) dissolved in fused salts. He patented his process in 1886, but was involved in some fifteen years of litigation with Hall, whose process was basically very similar. Héroult's process was first worked in 1887 at Neuhausen, using HYDROELECTRICITY from the famous falls on the Rhine.

herpes simplex virus infection A communicable infection caused by herpes simplex viruses. Herpes simplex virus type 1 (HSV-1) causes cold sores (herpes labialis), which is reactivation of the virus acquired during a previous primary infection. A characteristic crop of vesicles occur around the lips; the condition resolves in about two weeks without treatment.

Anogenital herpes simplex infection is caused mainly by herpes simplex virus type 2 (HSV-2) but may be caused by HSV-1; it is a SEXUALLY-TRANSMITTED DISEASE. Initial symptoms include a large number of painful vesicles on the genitals and anogenital region; associated symptoms include malaise, fever, and loss of appetite. The initial phase resolves in two to four weeks, which is followed by recurrent attacks. Transmission may take place in the absence of active vesicles. It is treated with antiviral drugs.

herpes zoster See SHINGLES.

Herrick, Robert (1591–1674) English poet. He is best known for *Hesperides*, a collection of poems published in 1648, which contained a section of religious poems, *Noble Numbers*. His secular poems, which deal chiefly with country rituals, folklore, and love, show a clear debt to the classical poets, particularly Horace and Catullus; notable examples include 'To the Virgins, To Make Much of Time' and 'Cherry Ripe'.

herring An abundant surface-living fish, *Clupea harenga*, found in the waters of the continental shelf on both sides of the North Atlantic. A related species, *C. pallasi*, occurs in the North Pacific. Both species are moderately slender, their bodies fully scaled and with a single dorsal fin. Their bodies are brilliantly blue on the back, silvery-white on the belly, with brassy tinges on the sides. Herring feed on planktonic animals, the major food item being copepod crustaceans of the genus *Calanus*, but any other planktonic creatures will also be eaten. They are themselves eaten by larger fishes such as cod, salmon, and tuna, by mammals such as dolphins and seals, and by seabirds, especially gannets. Young herring in the WHITEBAIT stage are preyed upon by terns and puffins. Spawning occurs in spring and summer and each local population has a specific spawning ground, sometimes on shallow, stony banks in 15–40 m (49–130 feet) of water, or offshore as deep as 200 m (650 feet). The eggs are laid on the sea-bed, sometimes in thick layers.

The herring is an extremely important food fish, being caught in surface trawls, although for many centuries it was caught in drift nets. It is eaten fresh, and cured in various ways to be sold as kippers, bloaters, red herring, and rollmops. In many areas it has been over-fished.

herring gull The commonest northern GULL species, *Larus argentatus*, with a grey mantle and black primary feathers. There are five or six subspecies. They breed throughout northern Europe, the northern former Soviet Union, North America, and the Arctic. Herring gulls integrate with the lesser black-backed gulls, *Larus fuscus*, in parts of their range.

Herriot, James (pseudonym of James Alfred Wight) (1916–95) British short-story writer and veterinary surgeon. His experiences at work as a vet in North Yorkshire inspired a series of stories, collected in *If Only They Could Talk* (1970), *All Creatures Great and Small* (1972), and *The Lord God Made Them All* (1981), which were made into a British television series as well as a number of films.

Herschel, Sir John (Frederick William) (1792–1871) British astronomer and physicist, son of William HERSCHEL. He extended the sky survey to the Southern Hemisphere, cataloguing many new clusters and nebulae. He carried out pioneering work in photography, to which he introduced the words *positive* and *negative*, and also made contributions to meteorology and geophysics.

Herschel, Sir (Frederick) William (1738–1822) German-born British astronomer, the father of stellar astronomy. He was a skilful telescope maker whose painstaking cataloguing of the skies resulted in the discovery of the planet Uranus. His unsuccessful attempts to measure the distances of the stars from the Earth convinced him of their remoteness, while his mapping of stellar distributions suggested to him that the Sun was a member of a great star system forming the disc of the Milky Way. He was elected first president of the Royal Astronomical Society in 1820.

Hertfordshire One of the Home Counties of south-east England; area 1,636 sq km (632 sq miles); pop. (1991) 951,500; county town, Hertford. The county is divided into 10 districts.

hertz (symbol Hz) The SI unit of FREQUENCY: one hertz is one cycle every SECOND. The unit is named after Heinrich HERTZ, who in 1888 first demonstrated the existence of radio waves, theoretically predicted several years earlier by James Clerk MAXWELL.

Hertz, Heinrich Rudolf (1857–94) German physicist and pioneer of radio communication. He worked for a time as Hermann Helmholtz's assistant in Berlin, and in 1886 began studying the electromagnetic waves that James Maxwell had predicted. He demonstrated them experimentally, and also showed that they behaved like light and radiant heat, thus proving that these phenomena, too, were electromagnetic. In 1889 he was appointed professor of physics at Bonn; he died of blood-poisoning at the early age of 37.

Hertzsprung, Ejnar (1873–1967) Danish observational astronomer who initiated several important developments in astronomical photography. In 1905 he investigated the relationship between the surface temperature (or colour) and absolute brightness of stars. A few years later RUSSELL illustrated this relationship graphically in what is now known as the HERTZSPRUNG–RUSSELL DIAGRAM, which has become fundamental to the study of stellar evolution. Hertzsprung also applied photography to PHOTOMETRY and the study of binary stars and variable stars.

Hertzsprung–Russell diagram (H–R diagram) A chart on which stars are plotted according to their temperature (or COLOUR INDEX or SPECTRAL CLASS) and brightness (LUMINOSITY or absolute MAGNITUDE). Also known as a **colour–luminosity diagram**, it is named after the Danish astronomer HERTZSPRUNG and the US astronomer RUSSELL, who published the first such diagram in 1914. The hottest stars are towards the left of the H–R diagram, and the most luminous stars are towards the top. When a representative sample of stars is plotted, most are found to form a band running from upper left to lower right, called the **main sequence**, or DWARF STARS. The Sun is a main sequence star. The most luminous main sequence stars also have the largest stellar mass. Above the main sequence are found, successively, the subgiants, GIANT STARS, and SUPERGIANTS; below it are the subdwarfs and WHITE DWARFS. These groups are called **luminosity classes**.

Herzegovina See BOSNIA-HERCEGOVINA.

Herzl, Theodor (1860–1904) Hungarian-born journalist, dramatist, and Zionist leader. He worked for most of his life as a writer and journalist in Vienna, advocating the establishment of a Jewish state in Palestine; in 1897 he founded the Zionist movement, of which he was the most influential statesman.

Herzog, Werner (born Werner Stipetic) (1942–) German film director. He occupied a leading position in German cinema in the 1970s. His first feature, *Signs of Life* (1967) displays themes of remoteness in time and space that remained dominant elements throughout his films. Among his other films are *Aguirre, Wrath of God* (1973), *The Enigma of Kaspar Hauser* (1974), and *Fitzcarraldo* (1982).

Hesiod (*c*.700 BC) One of the earliest Greek poets. Only two surviving poems are likely to be his, both in HEXAMETERS. The *Theogony* deals with the mythology of the gods and Zeus' rise to supremacy. The *Works and Days* describes peasant life, with a strong moralizing element and some personal detail.

Hesperides In Greek mythology, a group of nymphs, sisters (their number varies from three to seven in different accounts), who guarded the golden apples given to Hera when she married Zeus. The apples grew in a remote garden (the Garden of the Hesperides) and were guarded by a fearsome dragon. One of Hercules' Labours was to carry off the apples.

Hess, Germain Henri (1802–50) Swiss-born Russian chemist, who applied the first law of THERMODYNAMICS to the heat changes accompanying a chemical reaction and formulated Hess's law of constant heat summation. This states that the net heat evolved or absorbed during a chemical reaction is independent of the path taken and depends only on the initial and final stages.

Hess, Dame Myra (1890–1965) British pianist. She was noted for her performances of the music of Schumann, Beethoven, Mozart, and Bach. Her many piano transcriptions of Baroque music include 'Jesu, Joy of Man's Desiring' from Bach's Cantata No. 147. During World War II her daily lunch-time recitals in London's National Gallery were highly acclaimed morale boosters.

Hess, (Walther Richard) Rudolf (1894–1987) German politician. He was deputy leader of the Nazi Party (1934–41) and a close friend of Hitler. In 1941, secretly and on his own initiative, he parachuted into Scotland to negotiate peace with Britain. He was imprisoned for the duration of the war, and after his conviction at the Nuremberg war trials was sentenced to life imprisonment in Spandau prison, where he died.

Hess, Victor Franz (Francis) (1883–1964) Austrian-born US physicist who divided his academic career between Austria and the USA. His research interests in atmospheric electricity and RADIOACTIVITY culminated in the discovery of COSMIC RAYS, which led to the discovery of the positively-charged electron or positron by the US physicist Carl Anderson (1905–91). They shared the 1936 Nobel Prize for physics.

Hesse, Hermann (1877–1962) German-born Swiss novelist and poet. In 1911 he visited India, where he became interested in Indian mysticism; this experience, together with his involvement with Jungian analysis in 1916–17, had a marked effect on his work, which emphasizes spiritual values as expressed in Eastern religion. His novels – titles include *Siddhartha* (1922), *Der Steppenwolf* (1927), and *The Glass Bead Game* (1943) – met with renewed interest in the 1960s and 1970s. Hesse was awarded the Nobel Prize for literature in 1946.

heterotroph An organism that obtains organic food molecules, such as carbohydrates and proteins, ready-made from other organisms. All animals and fungi are heterotrophs, as are many bacteria. Many heterotrophs are herbivores, feeding directly on plants (AUTOTROPHIC ORGANISMS), which first manufacture the food by photosynthesis. In turn, carnivorous heterotrophs may feed on the herbivores. PARASITES are heterotrophs which

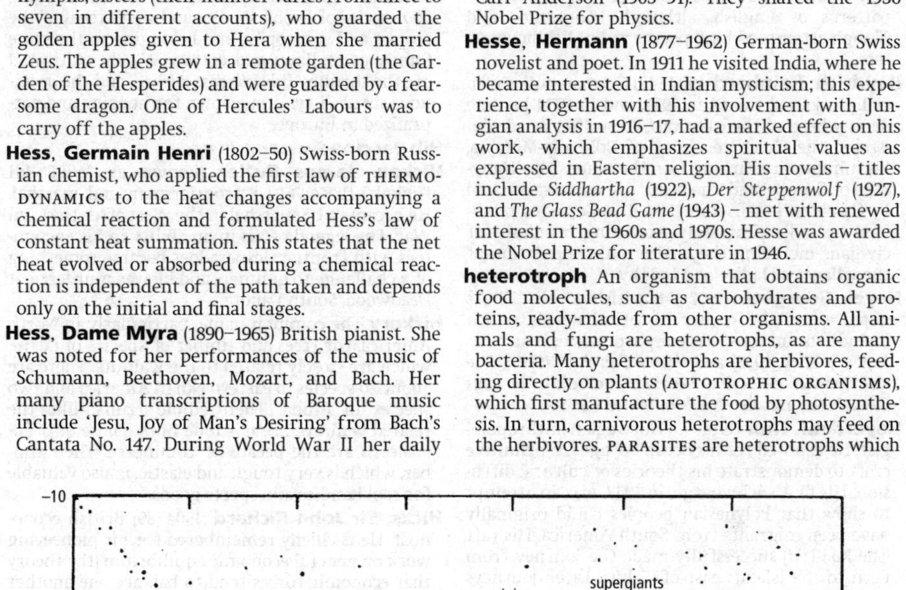

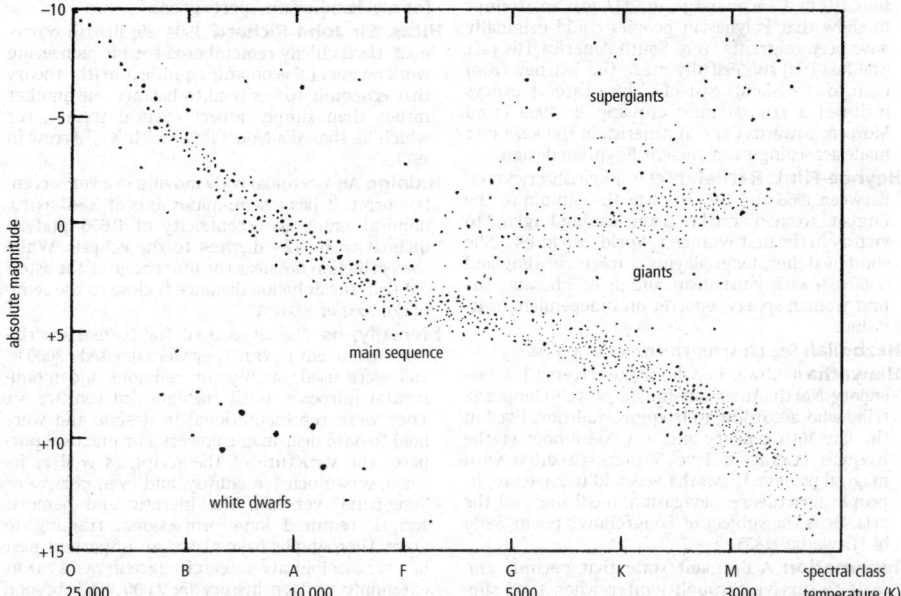

Hertzsprung–Russell diagram The spectral class of a star is plotted against its absolute magnitude. The hottest stars are towards the left and the most luminous towards the top. Most stars fall on the diagonal band called the main sequence. Other luminosity classes (e.g. white dwarfs, giants) fall in other parts of the diagram.

derive their food from other organisms while they are still alive. SAPROPHYTES are heterotrophs that feed on the dead remains and waste products of plants and animals.

Hevesy, George Charles de (1885–1966) Hungarian-born radiochemist. He worked in seven different European countries, and made fundamental contributions to the study of radioisotopes, an interest he acquired while working with Sir Ernest Rutherford in Manchester. He invented the technique of labelling with isotopic tracers, for which he was awarded the Nobel Prize for chemistry in 1943. Hevesy was also co-discoverer of the element hafnium (1923).

hexameter A verse line consisting of six metrical units ('feet'). Greek and Roman poets used dactylic hexameters in epic poetry, and for ELEGIES and satires. This METRE was later imitated by Goethe and Pushkin, but does not easily fit the stress-patterns of English, although Longfellow and Clough attempted long poems in English hexameters.

Heydrich, Reinhard (1904–42) German police official. He joined the SS in 1931, and in 1934 became deputy head of the GESTAPO. From 1941 he administered the Czech territory of Bohemia-Moravia, his inhumanity earning him the names the 'Hangman of Europe' and 'the beast'. He was assassinated by Czech nationalists in 1942. The Germans retaliated by indiscriminately executing hundreds of civilians including the entire male population of the villages of Lidice and Ležáky.

Heyer, Georgette (1902–74) British novelist. She is noted especially for her historical novels, which include numerous Regency romances, such as *Regency Buck* (1935) and *Faro's Daughter* (1941). She also wrote detective stories, including *Envious Casca* (1941) and *Detection Unlimited* (1953).

Heyerdahl, Thor (1914–) Norwegian anthropologist. He is noted for his ocean voyages in primitive craft to demonstrate his theories of cultural diffusion. His first such voyage, in 1947, was an attempt to show that Polynesian peoples could originally have been migrants from South America. His raft (the *Kon-Tiki*) successfully made the journey from Peru to the islands east of Tahiti. Later journeys included a transatlantic crossing in 1969 from Morocco towards Central America in the *Ra*, a raft made according to an ancient Egyptian design.

Heyhoe-Flint, Rachel (1939–) British cricketer. Between 1966 and 1977 she was the captain of the England women's cricket team, leading England to victory in the first Women's World Cup in 1972. She combined her long playing career for England (1960–83) with journalism, and in 1972 became the first woman sports reporter on Independent Television.

Hezbollah See ISLAMIC FUNDAMENTALISM.

Hiawatha (Ojibwa, 'he who makes rivers') The legendary North American Indian of the Onondaga tribe who, according to Iroquois tradition, lived in the late 16th century and was co-founder of the Iroquois League of Five Nations. Credited with magical powers, Hiawatha was said to have taught people agriculture, navigation, medicine, and the arts. He is the subject of Longfellow's poem 'Song of Hiawatha' (1855).

hibernation A dormant state that permits animals to survive through winter when food supplies would otherwise be inadequate. Most hibernating animals allow their body temperature to fall. This saves energy by reducing the metabolic rate of the organism, so that the body fat reserves last until food becomes available the following spring. There are two main strategies for hibernation: uncontrolled body temperature fall, or an overall lowering of body temperature to a pre-set level. Some species of bats use the first of these and allow their temperature to fall to that of their surroundings.

The other strategy is to control the hibernation body temperature. The dormouse maintains its temperature a few degrees above that of its surroundings. Bears often sleep through the winter, allowing their body temperature to fall to as little as 3–4°C (37–39°F). Most hibernators can restore their body temperature in minutes rather than hours and they may emerge during mild days in winter.

Hibernia An archaic poetic and literary name for Ireland.

hibiscus A member of the genus *Hibiscus* of some 300 species of herbs, shrubs, and small trees of the tropics and subtropics, and belonging to the same family as mallows and cotton. Widely cultivated are the shrubby *Hibiscus rosasinensis*, and the deciduous shrub *H. syriacus*, grown for hedging and naturalized in Europe.

Hib vaccine See MENINGITIS.

Hickok, James Butler (known as 'Wild Bill Hickok') (1837–76) US frontiersman and marshal. He became a US marshal in the West after the Civil War. The legend of his invincibility in his encounters with frontier desperadoes became something of a challenge to gunmen, and he was murdered at Deadwood, South Dakota.

hickory The common name, particularly in North America, for trees and timber of species of *Carya*, which are closely related to the walnuts. There are about 20 species in eastern North America and two species in China. Their edible fruits, like the related walnuts, are not true nuts. Those of *C. illinoinensis* are the pecans of commerce. Their timber, which is very tough and elastic, is also valuable for tool handles and sports goods.

Hicks, Sir John Richard (1904–89) British economist. He is chiefly remembered for his pioneering work on general economic equilibrium (the theory that economic forces tend to balance one another rather than simply reflect cyclical trends), for which he shared a Nobel Prize with K. J. Arrow in 1972.

Hidalgo An asteroidal body moving in a very eccentric orbit. It has a semi-major axis of 5.861 astronomical units, an eccentricity of 0.656, and an inclination of 42.4 degrees to the ecliptic. While the perihelion lies near the inner edge of the asteroid belt, the aphelion distance is close to the semi-major axis of Saturn.

hieroglyphs The signs used for formal inscriptions in ancient EGYPT. They were devised *c.*3000 BC and were used, mainly for religious and monumental purposes, until the late 3rd century AD. They were representational in design, and were held to have near-magic powers. For practical purposes the structure of the script, as well as its form, was much too clumsy, and even cursive or 'long-hand' versions, the hieratic and demotic scripts, required long professional training to learn. Hieroglyphs have played an important part of archaeological research (ROSETTA STONE), extending written history by 2,000 years beyond classical times. The term has been applied more loosely to other complicated but ornamental scripts used by the MINOAN civilization, the HITTITES, and the MAYA. See also WRITING.

high-fidelity system An electronic device capable of producing sound, particularly music, virtually indistinguishable from the original recording. Good hi-fi systems aim to reproduce sound with the minimum of distortion over a wide range of frequencies, and with a broad dynamic range and low levels of background noise. Human hearing has a frequency range of about 20–20,000 Hz, and the maximum range of sound intensity required is around 90 DECIBELS (dB). Most GRAMOPHONE, tape, and RADIO reproduction falls short of these ranges, with a frequency range of around 14,000 Hz and a dynamic range of about 70 dB. However, the digital sound recording and reproduction of COMPACT DISCS produces virtually distortion-free sound reproduction between 4 and 20,000 Hz, with a dynamic range of around 90 dB.

Highgate A district of north London, north-east of Hampstead Heath, that takes its name from a tollgate that once operated.

Highland A local government area of northern Scotland; area 25,398 sq km (9,810 sq miles); pop. (1993) 206,900; administrative centre, Inverness. From 1975 to 1996 it was called Highland Region and was divided into eight districts.

Highsmith, Patricia (born Patricia Plangman) (1921–95) US writer of detective fiction. Many of her novels have been made into films, most famously her first novel *Strangers on a Train* (1949), filmed by Alfred Hitchcock in 1951. Her works featuring her psychotic hero Tom Ripley are considered her best. Examples include *The Talented Mr Ripley* (1956) and *Ripley Under Water* (1991).

high-speed train A train developed to travel at speeds in excess of 200 km/h (125 m.p.h.). Such trains fall into two main categories. First, there are those trains designed to operate on completely new railways at speeds of 260 km/h (160 m.p.h.) or more, such as the Japanese *shinkansen* ('bullet') trains and the French *train à grande vitesse* (TGV). Secondly, are new trains for operation on existing railways. These include the British high-speed train (HST or InterCity 125) and the French and Canadian turbo-trains, powered by GAS-TURBINES. Higher speeds may be attained with acceptable passenger comfort by tilting the train by up to 9 degrees on curves.

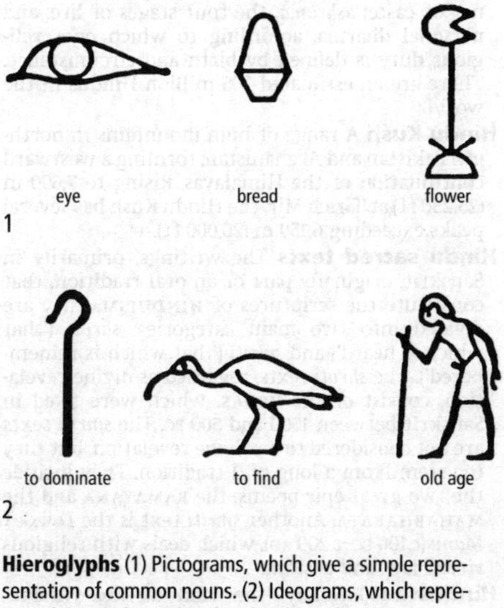

Hieroglyphs (1) Pictograms, which give a simple representation of common nouns. (2) Ideograms, which represent abstract ideas related to the object drawn.

High Wycombe A town in Buckinghamshire, England, on the River Wye north-west of London; pop. (1981) 70,200. It has a long tradition of furniture-making and has a Chair and Local History Museum.

Hijaz See HEJAZ.

hijra (Arabic, 'emigration') The departure of MUHAMMAD and following him of about one hundred followers separately from Mecca, where they faced opposition and persecution, to Medina in 622 AD, from where Muhammad's teaching spread. The significance of this event was realized during the reign of the caliph Umar, who made 622 the first year of the ISLAMIC CALENDAR, in recognition that the community phase of Islam dates from then.

Hilary, St (*c.*315–*c.*367) French bishop. In *c.*350 he was appointed bishop of Poitiers, in which position he became a leading opponent of the heresy of Arianism. Feast day, 13 January (in the Roman Catholic Church, 14 January).

Hilbert, David (1862–1943) German mathematician. He proved fundamental theorems about rings, collected, systematized, and extended all that was then known about algebraic numbers, and reorganized the axiomatic foundations of geometry. He set potential theory and the theory of integral equations on its modern course with his invention of **Hilbert space** (an infinite-dimensional analogue of Euclidean space), and formulated the formalist philosophy of mathematics and mathematical logic. In 1900 Hilbert proposed 23 problems which crystallized mathematical thinking for the next few decades.

Hilda, St (614–80) English abbess. Related to the Saxon kings of Northumbria, around 658 she founded a monastery for both men and women at Whitby. She was one of the leaders of the Celtic Church delegation at the Synod of Whitby, but accepted the eventual decision in favour of Roman rather than Celtic customs. Feast day, 17 November.

Hildegard of Bingen, St (1098–1179) German abbess, scholar, composer, and mystic. A nun of the Benedictine order, she became Abbess of Diessem in 1136, later moving her community to Bingen. She described and illustrated her mystical experiences in *Scivias*, and also wrote poetry and composed sacred music. Her scientific writings covered a range of subjects, including the circulation of the blood and aspects of natural history.

Hill, Benny (born Alfred Hawthorne) (1925–92) British comedian. After working in clubs and seaside shows he made an early and successful transition to television in 1949, being named TV Personality of the Year in 1954. His risqué humour, as seen in the series of programmes *The Benny Hill Show*, had an international appeal; television rights for the show were sold worldwide.

Hill, Damon (1960–) British motor-racing driver, son of Graham HILL. He was Formula One world champion in 1996, having been runner-up in 1994.

Hill, (Norman) Graham (1929–75) British motor-racing driver. He won the Formula One world championship in 1962 with the BRM team before returning to his original team, Lotus, and becoming world champion again in 1975. He was killed when his plane crashed in north London.

Hill, Octavia (1838–1912) British housing reformer. An active campaigner for the improvement of housing for the poor, she met John Ruskin while working for a Christian Socialist association. In 1864 Ruskin provided financial assistance for Hill to fund the first of several housing projects, the purchase and refurbishment of three London slum houses. She was also a co-founder of the National Trust.

Hill, Sir Rowland (1795–1879) British educationist, administrator, and inventor. He was initially a teacher who introduced a system of self-government at his school in Birmingham and wrote on the challenges of mass education. In the 1830s he invented a rotary printing-press. Hill is chiefly remembered for his introduction of the penny postage-stamp system in 1840; he later became Secretary to the Post Office (1854–64).

Hillary, Sir Edmund (Percival) (1919–) New Zealand mountaineer and explorer. In 1953 Hillary and Tenzing Norgay were the first people to reach the summit of Mount Everest, as members of a British expedition. Hillary later led the New Zealand contingent of the Commonwealth Trans-Antarctic Expedition (1955–58) organized by Sir Vivian Fuchs.

Hilversum A residential town in the Netherlands, in the province of North Holland, 20 km (12 miles) south-east of Amsterdam; pop. (1991) 84,600. It is the centre of the Dutch radio and television network.

Himalayas A vast mountain system in southern Asia, extending over 2,400 km (1,500 miles) from Kashmir eastwards to Assam. It covers most of Nepal, Sikkim, and Bhutan and forms part of the northern boundary of the Indian subcontinent. It is a series of parallel ridges rising up from the Ganges basin to the Tibetan plateau, at over 3,000 m (9,840 ft) above sea-level, and includes the Karakoram, Zaskar, and Ladakh ranges. The backbone is the Great Himalayan Range, the highest range in the world, with several peaks rising to over 7,700 m (25,000 ft), the highest being Mount Everest (8,848 m, 29,028 ft), which rises on the frontier between Nepal and Tibet and K2 (8,611 m, 28,250 ft) in the Karakoram Range of the north-west Himalayas.

Himmler, Heinrich (1900–45) German leader, chief of the SS (1929–45) and of the Gestapo (1936–45). He established and oversaw the programme of systematic genocide of more than 6 million Jews and other disfavoured groups between 1941 and 1945. He was captured by British forces in 1945, and committed suicide by swallowing a cyanide capsule.

Hims See HOMS.

Hinault, Bernard (1954–) French racing cyclist. During his professional career he won the Tour de France five times between 1978 and 1985; he also achieved three wins in the Tour of Italy between 1980 and 1985.

Hindemith, Paul (1895–1963) German composer. His music forms part of the neoclassical trend, which began in the 1920s. Hindemith believed that music should have a social purpose and that audiences should participate as well as listen; his *Gebrauchsmusik* ('utility music') compositions are intended for performance by amateurs. A prolific composer, he wrote operas (such as *Mathis der Maler*, 1938), concertos, and orchestral and chamber music. He left Germany in the 1930s after Nazi hostility to his work, eventually settling in the USA.

Hindenburg, Paul Ludwig von Beneckendorff und von (1847–1934) German Field Marshal and statesman, President of the Weimar Republic 1925–34. He was recalled from retirement at the outbreak of World War I and appointed Commander-in-Chief of German forces from 1916, directing the war effort in partnership with Erich Ludendorff. He was elected President in 1925 and re-elected in 1932, and was reluctantly persuaded to appoint Hitler as Chancellor in 1933.

Hindi ►**1** A literary form of Hindustani with vocabulary based on Sanskrit, written in the Devanagari script, an official language of India. Hindi is the most widely spoken language in India, with some 180 million speakers. ►**2** A group of spoken dialects of northern India, belonging to the Indo-European family of languages and related to Urdu.

Hindu festivals Hindus celebrate hundreds of different festivals, which vary from place to place. The following are some of the main ones: DIVALI ('Festival of Lights') in October or November celebrates the new year. HOLI is a joyful spring festival in February or March. The birth of Rama is celebrated in April or May with the nine-day festival of *Rama-navami*, during which stories from the RAMAYANA are narrated. *Rāksha Bandan* (July or August), celebrated mainly in northern and western India, marks the middle of the monsoon. In August or September, *Janmashtami* commemorates the birth of Krishna, while September or October sees the major festival of *Navarātri* (another nine-day festival), connected with the autumnal equinox. During this time *Durga-puja*, commemorating the Great Goddess Durga, is celebrated, and the nine-day festival ends with *Dussehra*, commemorating the death of Ravana, as recounted in the *Ramayana*.

Hinduism A system of religious beliefs and social customs, especially influential in India. As both a way of life and a rigorous system of religious law, Hinduism developed over a period of about 50 centuries. Unlike most religions, it requires no one belief regarding the nature of God: it embraces polytheism, monotheism, and monism. More important are the beliefs concerning the nature of the Universe and the structure of society. The former is described by the key concepts of DHARMA, the eternal law underlying the whole of existence; KARMA, the law of action by which each cause has its effect in an endless chain reaching from one life to the next; and *moshka*, liberation from this chain of birth, death, and rebirth. The latter is prescribed by the ideals of *varna*, the division of mankind into four classes or types, the fore-runner of caste; *ashrama*, the four stages of life; and personal dharma, according to which ones religious duty is defined by birth and circumstance. There are an estimated 705 million Hindus in the world.

Hindu Kush A range of high mountains in northern Pakistan and Afghanistan, forming a westward continuation of the Himalayas. Rising to 7,690 m (25,230 ft) at Tirich Mir, the Hindu Kush has several peaks exceeding 6,150 m (20,000 ft).

Hindu sacred texts The writings, primarily in Sanskrit, originally part of an oral tradition, that constitute the scriptures of HINDUISM. They are divided into two main categories: *shruti* ('that which is heard') and *smriti* ('that which is remembered'). The *shruti* texts, regarded as divine revelation, consist of the VEDAS, which were fixed in Sanskrit between 1500 and 500 BC. The *smriti* texts are not considered to be divine revelation, but they too stem from a long oral tradition. They include the two great epic poems, the RAMAYANA and the MAHABHARATA. Another *smriti* text is the *Laws of Manu* (*c*.100 BC–*c*.200 AD), which deals with religious ritual, law, and custom.

Hindustan Literally 'the land of the Hindus', loosely the whole of the Indian subcontinent but more specifically India north of the Deccan plateau, especially the plains of the Ganges and Jumna rivers.

Hindustani A language based on the Western Hindi dialect of the Delhi region with an admixture of Arabic, Persian, etc., current as the standard language and lingua franca in much of northern India and (as colloquial Urdu) Pakistan.

Hinshelwood, Sir Cyril Norman (1897–1967) British physical chemist. He made fundamental contributions to reaction kinetics in gases and liquids. He later applied the laws of kinetics to bacterial growth, and suggested the role of nucleic acids in protein synthesis. Hinshelwood was simultaneously president of both the Royal Society and the Classical Association. He shared the Nobel Prize for chemistry in 1956.

Hipparchus (*c.*170–after 126 BC) Greek astronomer and geographer, working in Rhodes. His major works are lost, but his astronomical observations were developed by Ptolemy. He constructed the celestial coordinates of 800 stars, indicating their relative brightness, but rejected Aristarchus' hypothesis that the Sun is the centre of the planetary system. Hipparchus is best known for his discovery of the precession of the equinoxes. He suggested improved methods of determining latitude and longitude, and is credited with the invention of trigonometry.

Hippocrates (*c.*460–*c.*370 BC) The most celebrated physician of Greek antiquity, known as 'the Father of Medicine', who was the first to separate medicine from philosophy and superstition. He taught that disease has natural causes, and his treatment was founded on the healing power of nature. The Hippocratic Oath, taken in some countries by newly qualified doctors as a pledge of ethical behaviour towards patients, cannot be ascribed to Hippocrates, although it does reflect his medical outlook.

hippopotamus One of the largest living terrestrial mammals, weighing up to 3,200 kg (7,050 pounds). Hippos have an enormous head with a bulbous snout, and a large, barrel-like body, up to 3.5 m (11.3 feet) long, set on short, stout legs. In spite of their size and weight, they are surprisingly agile and well able to overtake a running man. Most of their life is spent in water, in which they can float, or sink, and walk along the bottom. The sense organs, the nose, eyes, and ears, are all set on the upper surface of the head, and the nostrils can be closed.

Only two species are now found. The common hippopotamus, *Hippopotamus amphibius*, is 1.4 m (4.5 feet) tall at the shoulders. Once it frequented most of the large lakes and rivers and even brackish waters of Africa, but it is now much less widespread. It feeds mainly on reeds and grasses in and around the water. At night a herd of 20–30 individuals will travel some 40 km (25 miles) along a river gathering food. The hippo has the largest mouth of any mammal, with an awesome gape which exposes the long incisor and canine teeth, used in DISPLAY. The lower canines may reach a length of 60 cm (2 feet). A single calf is produced. It suckles while in water, can swim before it can walk, and will ride on its mother's back when she is in the water. The pygmy hippo, *Choeropsis liberiensis*, is about 90 cm (3 feet) tall at the shoulders. It is found in rivers in the forests of West Africa or in swamps. Its habits are similar to those of the common hippo.

hip replacement The surgical removal of the upper end of the femur (thigh bone) and its replacement by a PROSTHESIS of steel, plastic, or other material. The operation is performed either because the joint surfaces have worn out (in osteoarthritis) or eroded (in rheumatoid arthritis) or because the bone has fractured. Fractures are more common in older women who suffer from weakened bones (osteoporosis). If the fracture tears the blood vessels to the bone, it will not heal normally and a replacement operation is necessary. If the blood vessels are not damaged, then instead of replacement, the bone may be 'pinned' with steel wires or screws to hold it steady during the healing period.

Hirohito (born Michinomiya Hirohito) (1901–89) Emperor of Japan 1926–89. Regarded as the 124th direct descendant of Jimmu, he ruled as a divinity and generally refrained from involvement in politics. In 1945, however, he was instrumental in obtaining his government's agreement to the unconditional surrender which ended World War II. He was obliged to renounce his divinity and become a constitutional monarch by the terms of the constitution established in 1946.

Hiroshima Japanese city in southern Honshu. Hitherto largely undamaged by the US bombing campaign, Hiroshima became the target of the first atomic bomb attack on 6 August 1945, which resulted in the virtual obliteration of the city centre and the deaths of about one-third of the population of 300,000. The attack on Hiroshima, together with that on NAGASAKI three days later, led directly to Japan's unconditional surrender and the end of World War II.

Hirst, Damien (1965–) British artist and sculptor. His dead animals preserved in formalin created a considerable stir and he was awarded the Turner Prize (1995).

Hispaniola An island of the Greater Antilles in the West Indies, divided into the states of Haiti and the Dominican Republic. It was originally named La Isla Española ('the Spanish Island') by Columbus who discovered it in 1492. The western part of the island was frequented by French pirates who successfully established plantations and in 1697 that part of the island was ceded to France. In 1804, after a slave rebellion, the western third of the island declared itself independent of France as the Republic of Haiti and in 1844 the eastern two-thirds gained its independence from Spain. Pico Duarte in the Cordillera Central is the highest peak in the West Indies (3,175 m, 10,417 ft); area 76,192 sq km (29,430 sq miles); pop. (est. 1990) 13,700,000. The principal cities are Santo Domingo and Port-au-Prince.

hispid bat (or **slit-faced bat**) A bat belonging to the family Nycteridae, with 11 species confined to Africa and the Middle East. The description 'slit-faced' refers to the longitudinal groove on the muzzle. There is a saucer-like depression between the eyes, which gives the group yet another name: hollow-faced bats. The name hispid is used in reference to the shaggy coat of these bats. They are insect-eaters and have a distinctive T-shaped tip to their tail.

Hiss, Alger (1904–96) US public servant. In 1948 he was accused of copying and passing on State Department documents to a Communist. Having protested his innocence before the House Committee on Un-American Activities, Hiss was charged with perjury, and controversial trials followed. The first resulted in a hung jury, but he was then convicted, and the case led to an upsurge of anti-Communist feeling and the rise of Senator Joseph McCarthy. Hiss was released in 1954.

histamine A compound derived from the AMINO ACID histidine. It is found in nearly all tissues of the body. Histamine has pronounced pharmacological activity, causing dilation of blood vessels and contraction of smooth muscle (for example, in the lungs). It is an important mediator of inflammation and is released in large amounts after skin damage (such as that due to animal venoms and toxins), producing a characteristic skin reaction (consisting of flushing and a weal). Histamine is also released in allergic conditions, including asthma, and gives rise to some of the symptoms of these conditions. Its effects are countered using ANTIHISTAMINES.

histogram A type of graph in which the frequency of values of a quantity are represented by vertical rectangles. The width of the rectangles is proportional to the class interval being considered and the areas of the rectangles are proportional to the relative frequency of the occurrence. For example, in a sample of 100 people, one-tenth (0.1) of the sample may have heights in the range 180–190 cm (the class interval). Thus the relative frequency of heights in this range is 0.1, and this would be represented by a column of height 0.1. The column would be centred on the mid-point of the range (185 cm) on a horizontal axis. A histogram consists of the complete set of such columns for a particular sample.

histology The microscopic study of tissues, either living or after they have been 'fixed' to preserve their structure. Stains or dyes are used to pick out specific structures within them. Thin, living tissues can be examined either under the phase-contrast microscope, or, after treatment with dyes, under an ordinary light microscope. Organs are examined after being cut into thin slices. Small samples can be harmlessly removed from living subjects to aid the diagnosis of disease. The electron microscope permits higher magnification, but requires pieces of tissue to be cut into ultrathin slices and suitably stained. Tissue surfaces can also be examined at high magnification by using a scanning electron microscope, after coating the tissue with metals such as gold. See also CYTOLOGY.

historical geography The study of past geographies and of past landscapes involving the analysis of changing patterns and processes over a period of time.

historical novel A NOVEL in which the action takes place a generation or more before the time of writing, and in which some attempt is made to depict accurately the customs and mentality of the period. The central character, real or imagined, is usually entangled in divided loyalties within a larger historic conflict.

histosol A highly organic soil that forms on poorly drained sites. Peaty histosols occur in cold climates where the soil is saturated with water for most of the year and the decomposition of plant remains is therefore extremely slow. They tend to be very thick, acidic, and low in plant nutrients. Such soils commonly occur in the Canadian muskeg and in central Siberia. Histosols are also found in mid-latitudes, typically on former glacial lake-floors. Commonly called mucks, these are relatively thick accumulations of fine-grained, sticky black material. Muck soils tend to be nutrient-rich and are often used intensively for agriculture.

Hitchcock, Sir Alfred (Joseph) (1899–1980) British film director. Having established his reputation in Britain in the 1930s with films, such as *The Thirty-Nine Steps* (1935) and *The Lady Vanishes* (1938), in 1939 he moved to Hollywood, where his first film was *Rebecca* (1940). Outstanding among his numerous later works are the thrillers *Strangers on a Train* (1951), *Psycho* (1960), with its famous shower murder, and *The Birds* (1963). His films are notable for their ability to generate suspense and for their technical ingenuity.

Hitchens, Ivon (1893–1979) British painter. His main interest was in landscape, which he represented in an almost abstract style using broad fluid areas of vibrant colour, usually on a long rectangular canvas, as in *Winter Stage* (1936).

Hite, Shere (1942–) US feminist. She published her research into sex, gender definition, and private life in the groundbreaking work *The Hite Report on Female Sexuality* (1976), which she followed with *The Hite Report on Male Sexuality* (1981), *Women and Love* (1987), and *Hite on the Family* (1994), all based on the anonymous responses of thousands of people to questionnaires.

Hitler, Adolf (1889–1945) German dictator. He was born in Austria, the son of Alois Hitler and his wife Klara Poelzl. He volunteered for the Bavarian army at the start of World War I, becoming a corporal. After demobilization he joined a small nationalist group, the German Workers' Party, which later became the National Socialist German Workers (or NAZI) Party. In Vienna, he had imbibed the prevailing ANTI-SEMITISM and this, with tirades against the VERSAILLES PEACE SETTLEMENT and against Marxism, he used as a basis for his oratory in winning over a Germany humiliated by defeat. In 1921 he became leader of the Nazis and in 1923 staged an abortive uprising, the Munich 'beer-hall putsch'. During the months shared in prison with Rudolph HESS he dictated *Mein Kampf*, a political manifesto in which he spelt out Germany's need to rearm, strive for economic self-sufficiency, suppress trade unionism and communism, and exterminate its Jewish minority. The Great DEPRESSION beginning in 1929 brought him a flood of adherents. After the failure of three successive Chancellors, President HINDENBURG reluctantly appointed Hitler head of the government (1933). As a result of the REICHSTAG fire, Hitler established his one-party dictatorship, and the following year eliminated his rivals in the 'Night of the Long Knives'. On the death of Hindenburg he assumed the title of President and 'Führer of the German Reich'. He began rearmament in contravention of the Versailles Treaty, reoccupied the RHINELAND in 1936, and took the first steps in his intended expansion of his THIRD REICH: the ANSCHLUSS with Austria in 1938 and the piecemeal acquisition of Czechoslovakia, beginning with the SUDETENLAND. He concluded the Nazi–Soviet non-aggression pact with Stalin in order to invade Poland, but broke this when he attacked the Soviet Union in June 1941. His invasion of Poland had precipitated WORLD WAR II. Against the advice of his military experts he pursued 'intuitive' tactics and at first won massive victories; in 1941 he took direct military control of the armed forces. As the tide of war turned against him, he intensified the mass assassination that culminated in the Jewish HOLOCAUST. He escaped the JULY PLOT to kill him (see STAUFFENBERG, CLAUS GRAF VON), and undertook a vicious purge of all involved. In 1945, as the Soviet army entered Berlin, he went through a marriage ceremony with his mistress, Eva Braun, with whom he committed suicide.

Hitler Youth A NAZI agency to train young Germans. In 1931 Baldur von Schirach was appointed

Youth Leader of the Nazi Party. In 1936 HITLER outlawed all other youth organizations and announced that all young Germans should join the Jungvolk (Young Folk) at the age of 10, when they would be trained in out-of-school activities, including sports and camping, and receive Nazi indoctrination. At 14 the boys were to enter the Hitler Youth proper, where they would be subject to semi-military discipline, out-door activities, and Nazi propaganda, and girls the League of German Maidens, where they would learn motherhood and domestic duties. At 18 they would join the armed forces or the labour service. By 1936 3.6 million members had been recruited, and by 1938 7.7 million, but efforts to enrol young people were failing, so that in March 1939 a conscription order was issued.

Hittite A member of an ancient people of Asia Minor who gained control of central Anatolia *c.*1800–1200 BC. The Hittite empire reached its zenith under the totalitarian rule of Suppiluliuma I (*c.*1380 BC), whose political influence extended from the capital, Hattusas, situated at Boğazköy (about 35 km (22 miles) east of Ankara in modern Turkey) west to the Mediterranean coast and south-east into northern Syria. In their struggle for power over Syria and Palestine the Hittites clashed with the troops of Rameses II of Egypt in a battle (1285 BC) at Kadesh on the River Orontes which seems to have ended indecisively. The subsequent decline and demise of Hittite power by 700 BC resulted from internal and external dissension, probably following an outbreak of famine.

Hizbullah See ISLAMIC FUNDAMENTALISM.

hoar-frost See FROST.

hoatzin An extraordinary bird, *Opisthocomus hoatzin*, placed in a family of its own, Opisthocomidae. It was once thought to be a distant relative of the gamebirds, but is now considered to be related to the cuckoos. About 60 cm (2 feet) in length, including a long tail, it is a dark brown bird, streaked with pale markings and with a loose, untidy crest. It lives in bushy vegetation along river banks in northern South America, eating leaves and fruit. It lays two to three eggs in a simple nest of twigs built in bushes. If disturbed, the young can jump from the nest into the water and, when danger has passed, clamber back into the nest using hooked claws on their still rudimentary wings.

Hobart The capital and chief port of Tasmania, Australia, at the mouth of the Derwent River; pop. (1991) 127,130. A penal colony named after Lord Hobart (1760–1816), Secretary of State for the Colonies, was moved to the city's present site on Sullivan Cove in 1804; it became the island's capital in 1812. From a whaling centre it developed into a major yachting, fishing, and trading port exporting fruit, textiles, and processed food. There is an annual Sydney to Hobart Yacht Race.

Hobbema, Meindert (1638–1709) Dutch landscape painter. He was a pupil of Jacob van Ruisdael and was one of the last 17th-century Dutch landscape painters, since demand for such work was diminishing in the late 1660s. His work features a narrow range of favourite subject-matter, often including a water-mill and trees round a pool. Among his best-known paintings is *Avenue at Middelharnis* (1689).

Hobbes, Thomas (1588–1679) English philosopher. There were two key components in Hobbes's conception of humankind: he was a materialist, claiming that there was no more to the mind than the physical motions discovered by science, and a cynic, holding that human action was motivated entirely by selfish concerns, notably fear of death. His view of society was expressed in his most famous work, *Leviathan* (1651), in which he argued, by means of a version of a social contract theory, that simple rationality made social institutions and even absolute monarchy inevitable.

Hobbs, Sir John Berry (known as 'Jack') (1882–1963) British cricketer. His career as a batsman in first-class cricket extended from 1905 to 1934, during which time he scored a total of 61,237 runs and 197 centuries. He first played for England in 1907 and went on to make 61 test appearances.

hobby A bird belonging to a cosmopolitan group of three species of small, long-winged FALCON that hunt birds and insects on the wing. The European hobby, *Falco subbuteo*, grey-barred with white underparts, takes a higher proportion of birds than most. Widely distributed across Europe and Asia, it breeds in temperate latitudes and winters as far south as North Africa, Myanmar, and India. The others are the African hobby, *F. cuvierii*, and the Oriental hobby, *F. severus*.

hobgoblin A mischievous imp or terrifying apparition of English folk belief. Also called Puck and Robin Goodfellow, the name hobgoblin is formed from Hob, the diminutive form of Robin, and goblin.

Hochhuth, Rolf (1933–) Swiss dramatist whose controversial plays include *The Representative* (1962), in which he exposes Pope Pius XII to criticism for his acceptance of German persecution of the Jews, and *The Soldiers* (1966), in which he suggests that Churchill was responsible for the air crash that killed the Polish general, Vladislaw SIKORSKI. His novel *German Love Story* (1980) blames the whole German nation for Nazi atrocities.

Ho Chi Minh (born Nguyen That Thanh) (1890–1969) Vietnamese Communist statesman, President of North Vietnam 1954–69. He was a committed nationalist who was instrumental in gaining his country's independence from French rule. He founded the Indo-Chinese Communist Party in 1930, and led the Vietminh in guerrilla warfare against the Japanese during World War II. He then fought the French for eight years until their defeat in 1954, when Vietnam was divided into North Vietnam, of which he became President, and South Vietnam. Committed to the creation of a united Communist country, Ho Chi Minh then deployed his forces in the guerrilla struggle that became the Vietnam War.

Ho Chi Minh City A city in southern Vietnam, on the Saigon River; pop. (1992) 3,015,700. Made capital of the French colony of Cochin China in 1859, it was known as Saigon until 1975 when it was named after the Vietnamese Communist statesman who led his country in its struggle for independence from French rule. It is now the largest city and one of the chief industrial centres of Vietnam centred on the adjacent town of Cholon. Industries include ship-building, textiles, machinery, pharmaceuticals, and the manufacture of diverse consumer goods. The deep-water port on Kanh Ho Island handles almost all the trade of southern Vietnam.

hockey, field An amateur game most keenly pursued in the UK and Commonwealth countries and in Europe. Eleven players on each side use a hooked stick to hit or push a hard ball into their opponents' goal. The pitch, 91.44 m (100 yards) long by 54.86 m (60 yards) wide, is similar in dimensions to various types of FOOTBALL pitch but the goal is smaller, the posts being 3.6 m (4 yards) apart and the crossbar 2.1 m (7 feet) high. Scoring shots must be struck inside the shooting circle, a semi-circular line of 14.63 m (16 yards) radius drawn around the goal. Increasingly goalkeepers wear thick body-padding to protect themselves, together with leg-guards, gloves, and a barred helmet. Hockey is a difficult game to keep flowing, especially on bumpy pitches, and clubs are turning increasingly to plastic, all-weather surfaces.

hockey, ice A six-a-side skating version of field hockey played on ice with a puck or rubber disc. Originating in Canada in the 1870s, it is the fastest team game in the world. The rink should be 56–61 m (184–200 feet) long and 26–30 m (85–98 feet) wide, surrounded by barrier boards up to 1.2 m (4 feet) high. All players wear specialized protective padding, the goalminders most of all. A team consists of some 20 players who (usually with the exception of the goalminder) periodically replace each other on the ice. There are three periods of 20 minutes each. The world's top professionals play in the National Hockey League of North America. At the OLYMPIC GAMES the most prominent nations have been the USA, Russia, Canada, the Czech Republic, Sweden, and Finland.

Hockney, David (1937–) British painter and draughtsman. His work of the early 1960s was associated with the pop art movement; deliberately naive and characterized by an ironic humour, it reflected the influence of graffiti and children's art. While in California in the mid-1960s he produced perhaps his best-known work: a series of paintings, such as *A Bigger Splash* (1967) which depict flat, almost shadowless architecture, lawns, and swimming-pools.

Hoddle, Glen (1957–) British footballer and manager. After a distinguished career, which included playing for England, a successful period at Tottenham Hotspur (1975–87), and a year as player-manager of Chelsea (1995–96), he became coach of the English team in 1996, taking the side to the 1998 World Cup Finals in France.

Hodeida (or **Al Hudaydah**) The principal port of Yemen, on the Red Sea; pop. (est. 1993) 246,000.

Hodgkin, Sir Alan Lloyd (1914–) British physiologist. Hodgkin worked mainly at Cambridge University, where he was a research professor from 1952 to 1970. He collaborated with Andrew Huxley on the physiology of nerve transmission, studying chiefly the giant nerve fibres of squid. Hodgkin and Huxley demonstrated that the passage of a nerve impulse involves a movement of sodium and potassium ions associated with a change in the electrical potential of the cell membrane. They were awarded a Nobel Prize in 1963.

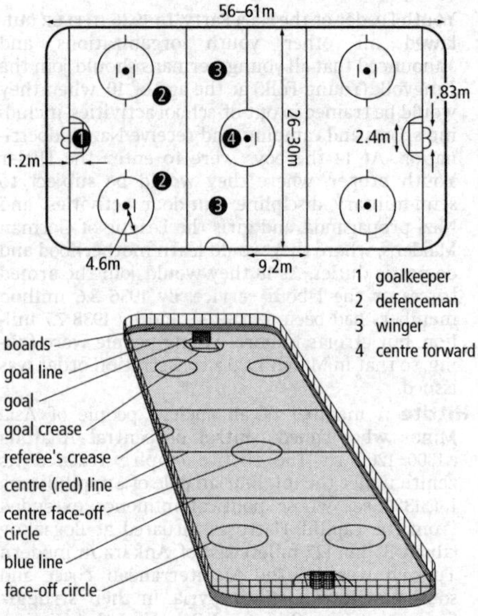

Ice hockey The dimensions of the rink and the positions of the players.

Hodgkin, Dorothy (Crowfoot) (1910–94) British chemist. She worked mainly at Oxford, where she developed Sir Lawrence Bragg's X-ray diffraction technique for investigating the structure of crystals and applied it to complex organic compounds. Using this method Hodgkin determined the structures of penicillin (1945), vitamin B_{12} (1956), and (after many years work) the large insulin molecule (1969). She was awarded the Nobel Prize for chemistry in 1964.

Hodgkin, Thomas (1798–1866) British Quaker

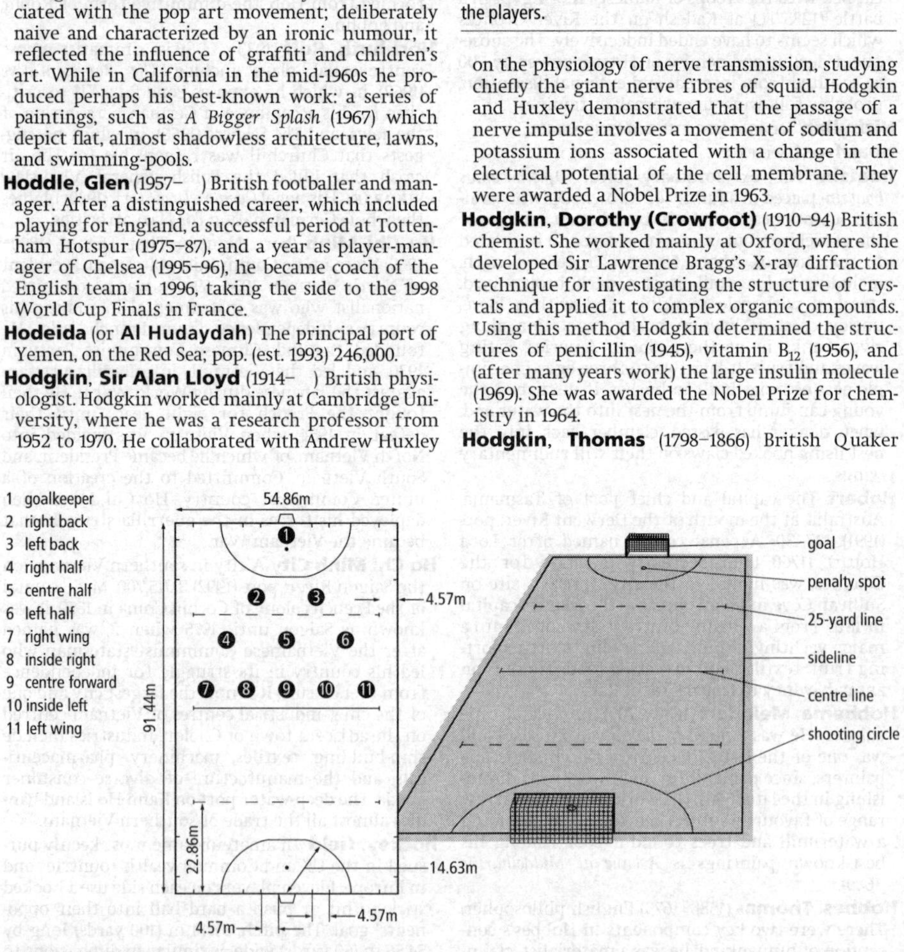

Field hockey The field and the positions of the players.

physician and pathologist, the first to describe **Hodgkin's disease**: a malignant disease of the lymphatic glands which causes weight loss, fever, and itching, but is now usually curable.

Hoe, Richard March (1812–86) US inventor and industrialist. In 1846 he became the first printer to develop a successful rotary press. This greatly increased the speed of printing compared with the use of a flat plate; by 1857 *The Times* had a Hoe press printing 20,000 impressions an hour. This machine had still to be fed with individual cut sheets, but by 1871 Hoe had developed a machine fed from a continuous roll.

Hofer, Andreas See TYROL.

Hoffa, James Riddle (known as 'Jimmy') (1913–*c*.1975) US trade union leader. He joined the Teamsters union in 1931 and became president in 1957. After investigations for corruption he was imprisoned in 1967 for attempted bribery of a federal court judge, fraud, and looting pension funds. His sentence was commuted by President Nixon and he was given parole in 1971 on condition that he resigned as president of the union. He disappeared in 1975, and is thought to have been murdered.

Hoffman, Dustin (Lee) (1937–) US actor. His first major film was *The Graduate* (1967); he has since appeared in a wide variety of roles, including that of a man pretending to be a woman in the comedy *Tootsie* (1983). Other films include *Midnight Cowboy* (1969) and *Rain Man* (1989), for which he received his second Oscar.

Hoffmann, E(rnst) T(heodor) A(madeus) (1776–1822) German novelist, short-story writer, and music critic. He is best known for his extravagantly fantastic stories; his shorter tales appear in collections such as *Phantasiestücke* (1814–15), while longer works include *Elixire des Teufels* (1815–16). His stories provided the inspiration for Offenbach's opera *Tales of Hoffmann* (1881).

Hofmann, August Wilhelm von (1818–92) German chemist who discovered several organic compounds, isolated benzene from coal-tar, and gave his name to a number of reactions, including the conversion of amides to primary amines. When the Royal College of Chemistry was established in London in 1845 he was appointed superintendent, and was later chemist at the Royal Mint. After 20 years of invaluable work in England, he became Professor of Chemistry at Berlin.

Hofmannsthal, Hugo von (1874–1929) Austrian poet and dramatist. He wrote the libretti for Richard Strauss's operas *Elektra* (1909), *Der Rosenkavalier* (1911), *Ariadne auf Naxos* (1912), and *Arabella* (1933). With Strauss and Max Reinhardt he helped found the Salzburg Festival. His *Jedermann* (1912), a modernized form of a morality play, was first performed at the opening of the festival in 1920.

Hogarth, William (1697–1764) British painter and engraver. He contributed to the development of an English school of painting, both by his criticism of the contemporary taste for foreign artists and by encouraging the establishment of art institutions in England, a process which later culminated in the foundation of the Royal Academy (1768). Notable works include his series of engravings on 'modern moral subjects', such as *A Rake's Progress* (1735) and *Marriage à la Mode* (1743–45), which satirized the vices of both high and low life in 18th-century England.

Hogg, James (1770–1835) Scottish poet. He was a shepherd in the Ettrick Forest whose poetic talent was discovered by Sir Walter Scott; he gained the nickname 'the Ettrick Shepherd'. He made his reputation as a poet with *The Queen's Wake* (1813), but is better known today for his prose work *The Confessions of a Justified Sinner* (1824).

Hohenstaufen A German royal house, members of which held the throne of the Holy Roman Empire (1138–1254), the rivals of the HOHENZOLLERNS. The emperor Henry IV (1084–1106) gave them the duchy of Swabia and in 1138 Duke Conrad became emperor as Conrad III. The family provided many emperors, including FREDERICK I (Barbarossa) who attempted to build up German power in Italy. The relationship between the papacy and the Hohenstaufen was frequently acrimonious, resulting from their respective claims to land and personal powers. The empire grew to include Germany, northern Italy, and Sicily but proved too large to be managed in the face of papal and Lombard opposition, and the dynasty's last ruling member, Manfred of Sicily, was killed in battle in 1266.

Hohenzollern Formerly a Prussian province, now part of the state of Baden-Württemberg in Germany, that gave its name to a powerful German princely family whose roots can be traced back to the 11th century. From 1415 they ruled the electorate of BRANDENBURG and the following century saw great expansion, Margrave Albert becoming grand master of the TEUTONIC KNIGHTS in 1511. In 1614 the duchy of Cleves was acquired and in 1701 the Elector Frederick III of Brandenburg took the title of Frederick I of PRUSSIA. In 1871 William I of Prussia took the title Emperor William I of the German Empire. His grandson WILLIAM II abdicated in 1918. A member of a second branch, Prince Charles Hohenzollern-Sigmaringen, was elected Prince of ROMANIA in 1866, becoming King Carol in 1881. His brother Leopold was offered the throne of Spain in 1870 and turned it down, an incident that Bismarck used to provoke war with France by altering the Ems telegram.

Hohhot (formerly **Huhehot** or **Kwesui**) The capital of Inner Mongolia autonomous region in northeastern China, at the junction of former caravan routes to Mongolia and Xinjiang; pop. (1990) 1,206,000. It is a trading centre with industries that include sugar refining and the manufacture of textiles, and chemicals. The original Mongol city, named Kukukhoto, was founded in the 16th century and was an important religious centre for Tibetan Buddhism. It was renamed Kwesui by the Chinese in the 18th century and Hohhot in 1954, when it became a provincial capital. A Stone Age village was discovered near here in 1973.

Hojo A branch of a powerful Japanese family, the Taira. After Minamoto Yoritomo's death they provided regents for puppet Shoguns, nominated by themselves. From 1219 the regency was hereditary, and the country prospered under them until *c*.1300. They refused tribute to KUBLAI KHAN and executed his envoys. His two invasions, though failures, weakened Hojo power. Vassals the Hojo were unable to reward for their victories turned against them. From 1331 there was war between the regent's forces and those attempting to restore imperial rule under Go-Daigo. Their power ended (1333) when ASHIKAGA TAKANJI, a Hojo vassal, defected to the emperor and another vassal took KAMAKURA. The last regent and his family committed *seppuku* (ritual suicide).

Hokkaido The most northerly and second-largest of the four main islands of Japan, constituting an administrative region; area 83,519 sq km (32,259 sq miles); pop. (1990) 5,644,000. Separated from Honshu Island by the Tsugaru Strait but linked by the Seikan Tunnel, its chief cities are Sapporo (regional capital) and Hakodate.

Hokusai, Katsushika (1760–1849) Japanese painter and wood-engraver. He was a leading artist of the ukiyo-e school who vividly represented many aspects of Japanese everyday life in his woodcuts. His best-known pictures are contained in the ten-volume *Mangwa* (1814–19) and the *Hundred Views of Mount Fuji* (1835). His prints were a significant stylistic influence on the work of impressionist and post-impressionist artists such as Van Gogh.

Holbein, Hans (known as **Holbein the Younger**) (*c*.1497–1543) German painter. He worked in Basle, where he produced the series of woodcuts the *Dance of Death* (*c*.1523–26), and in England, which he first visited in 1526. In England he became a well-known portraitist, depicting Sir Thomas Cromwell and other prominent courtiers, and painting group portraits such as *The Ambassadors* (1533). In 1536 he was appointed painter to Henry VIII; his commissions included portraits of the king's prospective brides, such as *Christina, Duchess of Milan* (1538) and *Anne of Cleves* (1539).

Hölderlin, (Johann Christian) Friedrich (1770–1843) German poet. His early poetry contained some political idealism fostered by the French Revolution, but most of his poems express a romantic yearning for ancient Greek harmony with nature and beauty. While working as a tutor he fell in love with his employer's wife, who is portrayed in his novel *Hyperion* (1797–99). Her death in 1802 exacerbated his already advanced schizophrenic condition.

Holi Major Hindu spring festival celebrated in northern India, occurring over the full Moon in February or March, and originating from an ancient fertility festival. According to mythical tradition, the young prince Prahlāda, a worshipper of VISHNU, survived an ordeal by fire despite the evil demoness Holikā. Bonfires are lit to symbolize the triumph of good over evil. The festival is also associated with the merry pranks of the young KRISHNA, and it is celebrated in boisterous and sometimes licentious ways. The usual restrictions of CASTE and gender are disregarded, and participants enjoy throwing coloured water and powdered dyes at each other.

Holiday, Billie (born Eleanora Fagan) (1915–59) US jazz singer. Following an early life of poverty and work in a brothel, she became a singer in the clubs of Harlem; in 1933 she began her recording career with Benny Goodman's band and went on to perform with many small jazz groups. Her style was characterized by dramatic intensity and vocal agility, as of a jazz musician playing a solo. Her autobiography *Lady Sings the Blues* (1956) was made into a film in 1972.

Holinshed, Raphael (died *c*.1580) English chronicler. Although the named compiler of *The Chronicles of England, Scotland and Ireland* (1577) Holinshed in fact wrote only the *Historie of England* and had help with the remainder. In 1587 the work was revised and reissued, and this edition was widely used by Shakespeare and other dramatists.

holism See ATOMISM.

Holland A former province of the Netherlands now divided into North Holland and South Holland. When the Kingdom of the Netherlands was established in 1814, Holland was used interchangeably with the Netherlands as the name of the country.

Holland, Parts of One of the three former administrative divisions or 'ridings' of the county of Lincoln, East England, prior to the local government reorganization of 1974 that created the districts of Boston and South Holland. Its chief town was Boston.

Hollerith, Herman (1860–1929) US engineer. He invented a tabulating machine using punched cards for computation, an important precursor of the electronic computer. He founded a company in 1896 that later expanded to become the IBM Corporation.

holly An evergreen tree, *Ilex aquifolium*, of southern and western Europe and a member of the family Aquifoliaceae. Holly is valued for its attractive red berries borne through winter, and its white wood. Its most familiar use is in Christmas decorations, but it is also a plant surrounded with ancient superstition. The trees are dioecious, with male and female flowers on different trees. Hedgehog holly has prickles on the surface as well as the margins of the leaf. There are some 400 other species of *Ilex* throughout the world, not all evergreen. Other unrelated prickly plants are sometimes called holly, such as *Olearia* species in New Zealand and *Eryngium maritimum* (sea holly) in Europe.

Holly, Buddy (born Charles Hardin Holley) (1936–59) US rock and roll singer, guitarist, and songwriter. Initially a hillbilly singer, Holly went on to become an important figure in early rock and roll, helping to shape rock guitar styling and being among the first to use a line-up of two guitars, bass, and drums. In 1955 Holly and some friends formed the band known as the Crickets, recording such hits as 'That'll be the Day' and 'Oh Boy' in 1957. The group toured Britain in 1958 (inspiring the name of the Beatles), before Holly left to go solo later the same year. He was killed in a plane crash.

hollyhock A tall, showy perennial related to mallows and cotton. The familiar garden varieties of hollyhock are derived from the species *Alcea rosea*. The flowers, which have medicinal uses, have also been used in dyeing.

Hollywood A district of Los Angeles, California, USA. US film-making was originally based on New York, but southern California, with its sunshine and scenic variety, appealed to film-makers from as early as 1907. In 1911 the first studio was established in Hollywood and 15 others followed in the same year. The Hollywood studio system reached its peak in the 1930s, but by 1950 television had become a serious competitor, and many films are now made for that medium.

Holman Hunt, William See HUNT, WILLIAM HOLMAN.

Holmes, Arthur (1890–1965) British geologist and geophysicist. He pioneered the dating of rocks using isotopic decay, and he was the first to use it to provide absolute dates for the geological timescale. He was one of the first supporters of the theory of continental drift. His book *Principles of Physical Geology* (1944) became a standard text.

Holmes, Oliver Wendell (1809–94) US physician and writer. He was professor of anatomy and physiology at Dartmouth College, New Hampshire, where he discovered that puerperal fever was contagious, and then professor of anatomy at Harvard University 1847–82. His humorous writings, both verse and prose, include 'Old Ironsides' (1830) and his 'Breakfast Table' essays. These witty conversational pieces appeared in the *Atlantic Monthly* from 1857 onwards and were collected in four volumes.

holmium (symbol Ho, at. no. 67, r.a.m. 164.9304) A soft silvery metal belonging to the lanthanides. It was discovered in 1879 by P. T. Cleve, who named it in honour of his native city, Stockholm. It has only one natural isotope, Ho-165, and few uses.

holm oak See OAK.

Holocaust, the The ordeal suffered by the Jews in Nazi Europe from 1933 to 1945. Conventionally it is divided into two periods, before and after 1941. In the first period various ANTI-SEMITIC measures were taken in Germany, and later Austria. In Germany, after the Nuremberg Laws (1935) Jews lost citizenship rights, the right to hold public office, practise professions, inter-marry with Germans, or use public education. Their property and businesses were registered and sometimes sequestrated. Continual acts of violence were perpetrated against them, and official propaganda encouraged Germans to hate and fear them. As intended, the result was mass emigration, halving the half-million German and Austrian Jewish population by the start of World War II. The second phase, which occurred during World War II from 1941, spread to Nazi-occupied Europe, and involved forced labour, massed shootings, and CONCENTRATION CAMPS, the latter being the basis of the Nazi 'final solution' (*Entlösung*) of the so-called Jewish problem through mass extermination in gas chambers. The last stages of the final solution were decided upon at the Nazi conference held at Wannsee in 1942. At this conference the grotesque plan and schedules were laid down, to be carried out by Adolf EICHMANN. During the Holocaust an estimated six million Jews died. Out of a population of three million Jews in Poland, less than half a million remained in 1945, while Romania, Hungary, and Lithuania also suffered grievously. The Holocaust has raised many problems concerning the nature of European civilization and the influence of Christianity (the Roman Catholic Church knew what was happening but failed to raise its voice in protest).

Holocene Epoch (or **Recent Epoch**) The later of the two geological epochs into which the QUATERNARY PERIOD is divided: the period of geological time from 10,000 years ago to the present. During this period, human intervention has considerably modified the landscape.

holography The production and recording of holograms, three-dimensional images formed by the interference of (usually LASER) light beams from a coherent light source. Holography was first proposed by GABOR in 1947, but only became practicable when the laser was invented in 1960. For recording, laser light is split into two beams, one being reflected from an object, and the other being used as a reference beam. The two beams are then recombined. The light from a laser is coherent, which means that the light WAVES are all in step. After the light has been reflected from an object, this is no longer the case. As a result, some of the reflected waves tend to cancel the waves in the unaltered reference beam, while others reinforce each other. This produces an interference pattern of dark and bright areas which, when recorded on a photographic plate, is called a hologram. The reflected beam can be reconstructed from the hologram by illuminating it with a laser beam. This produces a three-dimensional image of the original object. A different view is seen when the hologram is looked at from different angles, just as if it were a real object. Some holograms, like those placed on credit cards to prevent fraud, can be seen with ordinary white light. Holograms can also be made with other coherent electromagnetic radiation, for example sound or radio waves.

Holst, Gustav (Theodore) (1874–1934) British composer, of Swedish and Russian descent. He made his reputation with the orchestral suite *The Planets* (1914–16), which was an instant success when first publicly performed in 1919. He took inspiration for his music from a range of sources: the *St Paul's Suite* for strings (1913) written for the string orchestra of St Paul's Girls' School, where he was a teacher, reflects his interest in English folk-song, while his enthusiasm for Sanskrit literature resulted in works such as the four sets of *Choral Hymns from the Rig Veda* (1908–12).

Holt, Harold Edward (1908–67) Australian statesman. He represented the United Australia Party and then the Liberal Party, holding a series of portfolios from 1939. After MENZIES retired in 1966, Holt became Prime Minister. His term of office coincided with Australia's increasing and controversial involvement in the VIETNAM WAR.

Holy Alliance (1815) A loose alliance of European powers pledged to uphold the principles of the Christian religion. It was proclaimed at the Congress of VIENNA (1815) by the emperors of Austria and Russia, and the king of Prussia. All other European leaders were invited to join, except the pope and the Ottoman sultan. The restored French king Louis XVIII did so, as did most others; Britain did not. As a diplomatic instrument it was short-lived and never effective and it became associated with repressive and autocratic regimes.

Holyhead (Welsh **Caer Gybi**) A port on Holy Island, in Anglesey, north Wales; pop. (1991) 11,696. There is a ferry link with Dun Laoghaire in the Republic of Ireland and a container terminal.

Holy Land A region on the eastern shores of the Mediterranean in what is now Israel and Palestine. It has religious significance for Judaism, Christianity, and Islam. In the Christian religion, the name has been applied by Christians since the Middle

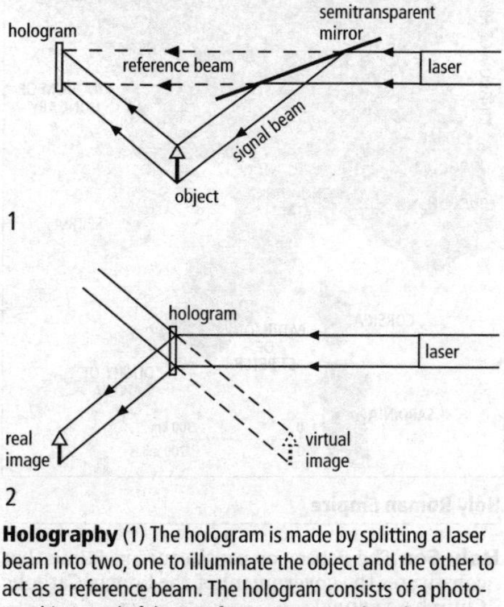

Holography (1) The hologram is made by splitting a laser beam into two, one to illuminate the object and the other to act as a reference beam. The hologram consists of a photographic record of the interference pattern when the two beams are recombined. (2) Two three-dimensional images of the original object are recreated by illuminating the hologram with laser light; one image is real, the other virtual.

Ages with reference both to its having been the scene of the Incarnation and to the existing sacred sites there, especially the Church of the Holy Sepulchre at Jerusalem.

Holyoake, Sir Keith (Jacka) (1904–83) New Zealand National Party statesman, Prime Minister 1957 and 1960–72. One of New Zealand's longest-serving statesmen, Holyoake first entered politics in 1932 as the youngest member in the House of Representatives; after two terms as Prime Minister he went on to serve as Governor-General 1977–80.

Holy Roman Empire The empire set up in western Europe following the coronation of Charlemagne as emperor, in the year 800. Of the emperors, after 1250 only five were crowned as such; the dignity was abolished by Napoleon in 1806. In true apocalyptic style the empire lasted about 1,000 years. The creation of the medieval popes, it has been called their greatest mistake; for whereas their intention was to appoint a powerful secular deputy to rule Christendom, in fact they generated a rival. The emperor never ruled the whole of Christendom, nor was there any substantial machinery of imperial government. From Otto I's coronation (962) the Empire was always associated with the German Crown, even after it became a Habsburg/Austrian preserve in the 15th century. Its somewhat mystical ideal was formal unity of government, based on coronation in Rome, memories of the old Roman Empire as well as Charlemagne, and devotion to the Roman Catholic Church.

Holy Roman Empire

Holy See The papacy or papal court in Rome that constitutes the government of the Roman Catholic Church (see POPE).

Home Counties The counties surrounding London, England, into which London has extended, comprising chiefly Kent, Surrey, Essex, Buckinghamshire, and Hertfordshire.

Home Guard A World War II military force raised in Britain. In 1908 the Territorial Force, a home defence organization, had been created, which became the Territorial Army in 1921. The Home Guard, known originally as the Local Defence Volunteers, existed from 1940 to 1944. In 1942 enrolment in the force became compulsory for sections of the civilian population. About a million men served in their spare time, and in its first vital year it possessed considerably more men than firearms. It never went into battle, but it did relieve the army of some duties and it boosted morale in 1940–42.

Home of the Hirsel of Coldstream, Baron See DOUGLAS-HOME.

Homer (8th century BC) Greek epic poet. He is traditionally held to be the author of the *Iliad* and the *Odyssey*. Various cities in Ionia claim to be his birthplace, and he is said to have been blind. Modern scholarship has revealed the place of the Homeric poems in a pre-literate oral tradition, in which a succession of bards elaborated the traditional stories of the heroic age; questions of authorship are thus very difficult to answer. In later antiquity Homer was regarded as the greatest and unsurpassable poet, and his poems were constantly used as a model and source by others.

Homer, Winslow (1836–1910) US painter. He illustrated magazines such as *Harper's Weekly* (1859–67) before recording scenes from life at the front in the Civil War (for example *Prisoners from the Front*, 1866). He is now best known for his seascapes, such as *Cannon Rock* (1895). His naturalistic style combines imagination and strength, and is considered to express the American pioneering spirit.

Home Rule, Irish A movement for the re-establishment of an Irish parliament responsible for internal affairs. An association, founded in 1870 by Isaac Butt, sought to repeal the Act of UNION (1800) between Britain and Ireland. This became a serious possibility when Charles PARNELL persuaded the Liberals under GLADSTONE to introduce Home Rule Bills. The first (1886) was defeated in the House of Commons. Gladstone's second Bill (1893) was also defeated. The third Bill (1912), introduced by Asquith, was passed by Parliament but its operation was postponed when war broke out in Europe in 1914. It left unresolved the question of how much of Ulster was to be excluded from the Act. When World War I ended the political situation in Ireland was greatly changed. The EASTER RISING in 1916 and the sweeping majority for SINN FEIN in the 1918 general election were followed by unrest and guerrilla warfare. Lloyd George was Prime Minister when the fourth Home Rule Bill (1920) was introduced in the Westminster Parliament. The Bill provided for parliaments in Dublin and Belfast linked by a Federal Council of Ireland. The Northern Ireland Parliament, to govern the six north-eastern counties of Ulster, was set up in 1920. Following the Anglo-Irish treaty (1921) the IRISH FREE STATE was set up and NORTHERN IRELAND became a self-governing province within the UK. The 26-county Irish Free State had a vague DOMINION status at odds with the independence claimed by Dáil Éireann in 1919. The Anglo-Irish treaty was approved by 64 votes to 57 in the Dáil. The majority group wanted peace and partial independence, the minority group, headed by Eamon DE VALERA, desired the immediate independence of all Ireland and the setting up of a republic. The Irish Free State (called Éire from 1937 to 1949) left the Commonwealth in 1949 and became the Republic of IRELAND.

homicide The killing of a human being by another. Some homicide may be considered lawful, as when a convicted offender is executed by the state, or excusable, as in self-defence. Unlawful homicide is treated by almost all legal systems as a crime of extreme gravity. Homicide is often categorized into different types, which attract different punishments. Within the UK legal system and many that are related to it (see COMMON LAW SYSTEMS), two major categories are recognized: murder and manslaughter. In both murder and manslaughter, the *actus reus* ('guilty act') is identical: the unlawful killing of the victim, but the categorization of the act depends on the offender's CRIMINAL RESPONSIBILITY. Murder requires the offender to have killed the victim with 'malice aforethought' (that is intending to kill or to cause grievous injury), while manslaughter does not. In CIVIL LAW systems, all unlawful killings are usually classified as homicide, but there may be different penalties, according to the circumstances of the crime.

hominids Members of the family Hominidae, including our own species, HOMO SAPIENS; various FOSSIL HOMINIDS, such as HOMO ERECTUS and HOMO HABILIS; and forms believed to be closely related, called collectively the AUSTRALOPITHECINES. Many scientists now also include the African great apes – the two chimpanzees and gorilla – in the human family too, rather than grouping them with the more distantly related Asian apes, the orang-utan, gibbon, and siamang. The traditional way of grouping the large apes (chimpanzees, gorilla, and orang-utan) is in their own family, Pongidae. Estimates of the date of divergence of the ape and human lineages vary. The Asian apes probably branched off 8–12 million years ago and the African apes 10–5 million years ago.

homoeopathy A system of COMPLEMENTARY MEDICINE, first described by the German physician Samuel Hahnemann (1755–1843). Hahnemann observed that quinine (an anti-malarial drug) taken by healthy patients produced symptoms similar to those of malaria, and proposed that any compound that produced symptoms similar to those of an illness could cure the illness. This is now known as 'proving', and is the basis of modern homoeopathic practice; compounds are taken in very small doses and the symptoms they produce are noted. A medicine (the simillimum) whose symptomatology in the proving stage is exactly similar to that of the patient will be curative. Homoeopathy requires the practitioner to treat the patient as a whole, rather than treating a specific symptom. It also advocates the 'minimum dose', the aim being simply to stimulate the body's own power of healing. Remedies are therefore often given in very dilute solutions, having the great virtue of never harming the patient: the most potent remedies are so dilute that there is a negligible probability of even one molecule of active constituent being present.

Homo erectus ('upright man') A FOSSIL HOMINID who lived in Africa and Asia and possibly in Europe. This HOMINID was larger than the AUSTRALOPITHECINES and HOMO HABILIS and its brain approached the size of a modern human's. However, the facial bones remained relatively massive and the skull was long and low. One of the hallmarks of this species was a teardrop-shaped stone tool flaked on both sides, the ACHEULIAN handaxe, which was more specialized than the OLDOWAN tools of *Homo habilis*. *Homo erectus* was the first member of the human lineage to control and use fire and this, and perhaps clothing, may have contributed to its spreading so widely from its place of origin in tropical East Africa. It had evolved presumably from *Homo habilis*, by 1.6 million years ago. By around 1 million years ago or not long before these hominids are presumed to have begun their travels that took them as far as China (PEKING MAN) and Indonesia (JAVA MAN). The last representatives disappeared 400,000–200,000 years ago.

Homo habilis ('handy man') A FOSSIL HOMINID found at OLDUVAI GORGE in Tanzania in the early 1960s, and now known from other eastern African sites, especially KOOBI FORA in Kenya and perhaps also from southern Africa. They date from about 2.5 million to 1.6 million years ago. Although similar in size to the contemporary AUSTRALOPITHECINES, their brains were larger, their faces more human-like, and it is thought that they evolved into HOMO ERECTUS. They were probably the first makers of stone tools – simple pebble and flake artefacts collectively called the OLDOWAN industry.

homologous series (in chemistry) A group of organic compounds with the same general molecular formula. Each member of a series has one more carbon atom than the previous one. An example is provided by the ALKANES, for which the general molecular formula is C_nH_{2n+2}, where *n* is a whole number. Successive members of the series differ in formula by a CH_2 unit.

homophony See POLYPHONY.

Homo sapiens ('wise man') Our own species, which is thought to have evolved some 500,000 years ago from an early species of hominid called *Homo heidelbergensis*, remains of which have been found in Europe (Heidelberg man, Boxgrove man) and in Africa. The evolution of *H. heidelbergensis* itself remains a matter of debate. It was thought to have evolved from HOMO ERECTUS, but recent discoveries have suggested that another species, *Homo ergaster*, may have been its ancestor. The subsequent evolution of *H. sapiens* is also somewhat obscure as the *Homo heidelbergensis* lineage apparently split into two main lines, one leading to the NEANDERTHALS (*Homo neanderthalensis*), the other to fully modern people (*Homo sapiens*). The latter development took place gradually during the past 125,000 years. Anatomical and genetic evidence support the idea that this happened in Africa, but it is possible that there was at least one parallel development in the Far East. In the Middle East, anatomically modern humans had appeared by around 50,000 years ago; in Europe, they came slightly later, and more abruptly around 35,000 years ago. The earliest modern Europeans are often called CRO-MAGNONS. It is not known what part, if any, the Neanderthals played in these Middle Eastern and European developments. Although they were not our ancestors, they may have interbred with modern people entering Europe from Africa via the Middle East.

homosexuality A sexual preference for members of one's own sex, distinguished from heterosexuality (preference for members of the opposite sex) and bisexuality (attraction towards either sex). Homosexual women are usually known as lesbians (from the Greek island of Lesbos, home of the 7th-century BC homosexual poet Sappho). At different times and in different cultures, homosexual behaviour has been approved of, tolerated, or banned. There is a conflict between theories of nature and those of nurture. Early psychologists, such as Richard von KRAFT-EBING and Havelock ELLIS, regarded homosexuality as a congenital condition. There is some evidence, from the study of identical and non-identical twins, that genetic factors may enter into homosexuality, but other theorists suggest that it is determined by critical childhood experiences, or by social learning. Lack of available contact with the opposite sex (as in prisons or boarding schools) may be a cause of homosexual behaviour in otherwise heterosexual individuals. In addition, the acceptability of homosexual behaviour in different societies, also suggests that it is in part socially determined. For many years in Western societies homosexuality was subject to legal punishment. Now, however, it is argued that homosexuality is a variant of sexual behaviour, and not a pathological condition. Homosexual behaviour between consenting adults in private is generally legal in most states of the USA and in Europe; in the UK, it was made legal in 1967, although it is still illegal to commit homosexual acts with a young person under 18 or with anyone in public places. In recent years, following the civil rights movements of the 1960s, many homosexuals have publicly acknowledged their sexual preferences (a process known as 'coming out'), and have chosen to describe themselves as 'gay'. They have demanded equal rights in such matters as housing or employment, and the right for their partnerships to be treated on an equal footing with heterosexual marriages. However, the spread of AIDS among male homosexuals has led, in some instances, to a resurgence of DISCRIMINATION.

Homs (or **Hims**) An industrial city in western Syria, on the River Orontes close to the Lebanese border; pop. (1993) 537,000. Site of ancient Emesa and of a major Crusader fortress, it has long been an important trading centre.

Honan See LUOYANG.

Honda, Soichiro (1906–92) Japanese motor manufacturer. In 1928 he opened his own garage; his first factory, producing piston-rings, was established in 1934. He began motorcycle manufacture in 1948, becoming the world's largest producer. During the 1960s he successfully expanded his operations into car production; the Honda Corporation has since become involved in joint ventures with such firms as the British car manufacturer Rover.

Honduras A Central American country bounded on the north and west by Guatemala and El Salvador and on the south by Nicaragua.

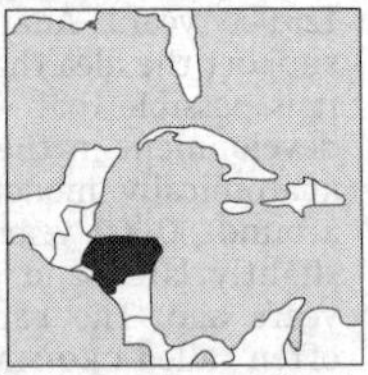

Physical. Honduras has a long, north-east coast on the Caribbean Sea and a short, south-west coast on the Pacific Ocean. Most of it is mountainous and heavily forested, and the soil is generally poor and acid. The climate varies with altitude but is predominantly tropical.

Economy. Honduras has an agricultural economy with bananas and coffee the principal exports; there are extensive forests (45 per cent of land area) and timber is also exported. Zinc, lead, and silver are mined, and there is limited light industry.

History. The native inhabitants of Honduras are mestizo Indians. One of the lieutenants of Hernan CORTÉS, Francisco de las Casas, founded the first settlement, the port of Trujillo, in 1523. Honduras was attached administratively to the captaincy-general of GUATEMALA throughout the Spanish colonial period.

When independence came in 1821 it briefly became part of the empire of Agustin de Iturbide before joining the United Provinces of Central America (1825–38). Separate independent status dates from 1838, when the union broke up. An uninterrupted succession of CAUDILLOS dominated the remainder of the 19th century. Improvement in the political process came slowly in the 20th century. Military dictators continued to be more prominent than civilian presidents, but the election in 1957 of Ramón Villeda Morales gave hope for the future. This optimism proved premature as the Honduran army overthrew him before he could implement the reform programme he had pushed through the congress. Military entrenchment was further solidified as Honduras fought a border war with El Salvador in 1969. In 1982 a new, US-backed constitution aimed to increase democratic activity. As a condition for US support, however, the country provided a base for 'Contra' rebels from NICARAGUA. In 1985 a new President, José Azcona (1985–90) threatened to stop 'Contra' activity, as well as to reduce the power of the military. Honduras, however, remained economically dependent upon the USA, and in 1989 Rafael Callejas was elected President with US support. He faced economic turbulence, left-wing guerrilla activity, and security forces almost totally out of control, with forty assassinations and over 4,000 known violations of human rights in one year. Despite assistance loans from the IMF and the World Bank, the government's economic structural adjustment plan, launched in 1990, provoked sustained hostility from unions, peasant groups, and private business, causing social unrest and political instability in 1992. In September the long-standing border dispute with El Salvador was resolved by an INTERNATIONAL COURT OF JUSTICE ruling. In the presidential elections of November 1993 Carlos Roberto Reina, who opposed Callejas, was elected. The declared priorities of the new government were the economy and the reduction of the military's role in politics. Honduras remained the focus of international human rights concern.

Capital: Tegucigalpa
Area: 112,088 sq km (43,277 sq mi)
Population: 5,512,000 (1995)
Currency: 1 Honduran lempira = 100 centavos
Religions: Roman Catholic 94.6%; other (mostly Protestant) 5.4%
Ethnic Groups: Mestizo 89.9%; Amerindian 6.7%; Black (including Black Carib) 2.1%; White 1.3%
Languages: Spanish (official); Black Carib (Garifuna); minority languages
International Organizations: UN; OAS

Honecker, Erich (1912–94) East German Communist statesman, head of state 1976–89. He was appointed First Secretary of the Socialist Unity Party in 1971, becoming effective leader of East Germany in 1973, and head of state (Chairman of the Council of State) three years later. His repressive regime was marked by a close allegiance to the Soviet Union. Honecker was ousted in 1989 after a series of pro-democracy demonstrations. In 1992 he was arrested but proceedings against him for manslaughter and embezzlement were later dropped because of his ill health.

Honegger, Arthur (1892–1955) French composer, of Swiss descent. He lived and worked chiefly in Paris, where he became a member of the anti-romantic group Les Six. His orchestral work *Pacific 231* (1924), a musical representation of a steam locomotive, brought him his first major success; his work also includes five symphonies (1930–51) and the dramatic oratorio *Joan of Arc at the Stake* (1935).

honey badger See RATEL.

honeybee A social bee of the genus *Apis*, which normally occurs only in domestication. Honeybees may set up colonies in hollow trees but they do not usually survive long in the wild, having been bred for centuries in hives. Hives are kept throughout the world and there are a number of races which differ in productivity and temperament. A colony passes the winter with a single queen and a large number of workers, which keep close together to conserve heat. In the spring, the workers start to forage, bringing in pollen, called bee bread, and nectar, which mature into honey. They collect water to cool the hive and help to build and clean it. Wax is secreted from glands between their abdominal segments, and this is used to build the vertical combs.

The queen bee controls the production of workers, drones (which are males) or new queens by laying two types of egg. Fertilized eggs develop into workers, which are technically non-reproductive females. Queens are produced by feeding some of these grubs with high-protein foods. In late summer the queen lays unfertilized eggs which develop as drones. The new queens and drones leave the nest to mate. After a mating flight, the drones die, while the queens return to their hive, collect workers, and swarm to set up new colonies. Honeybees have complex methods of communication, particularly between the workers with their famous bee dances, which tell where nectar may be found. The queen produces substances which control the working of the hive, almost in the manner of some form of chemical slavery.

honey buzzard A small KITE, *Perius apivorus*, widespread in Europe and Asia throughout the summer. Its plumage is dark reddish-brown, and its wing-span over 1.2 m (4 feet). Honey buzzards feed on insects, notably wild bees and wasps, hunting both in the air and in trees, often destroying bee and wasp nests for the grubs inside. European populations move south after breeding to winter in Africa.

honeyeater A bird making up the family Meliphagidae, with some 182 species inhabiting the forests of the Australasian region and some Pacific islands. Ranging from the size of a sparrow to that of a small crow, honeyeaters are mostly brown and green in colour, but many also have conspicuous patches of bright yellow, white, or black. The beak is usually thin and sharply pointed, but is strongly curved in some species. The tongue is long and protrusible, and is brush-shaped at the end to facilitate lapping nectar. They feed on a wide range of insects, fruit, and nectar (hence their name), and build open-cup nests in which they lay one to four eggs. In some species, several birds (in addition to the parents) may defend and raise the young. Some ornithologists consider the SUGARBIRDS to belong to this family.

honeyfungus An AGARIC fungus, parasitic on a wide range of trees, shrubs, and herbaceous plants, which it kills and then lives on. A mass of fungal threads invades the wood and produces brown toadstools clustered at the base of the tree. It can spread to other parts of the tree, or neighbouring trees, by means of boot-lace-like structures called rhizomorphs, hence its other name, boot-lace fungus. It is faintly luminescent. Several other species of fungi of the genus *Armillaria* resemble tree honeyfungus, *A. mellea*.

honeyguide A bird native to Africa, except for two species in India and south-east Asia. The 17 species make up a distinct family, Indicatoridae, and are thrush-sized, with brownish or olive-green plumage. All of them appear to be parasitic, and to lay their eggs in the nests of other birds, who then raise the young. They are insectivorous, in particular seeking out the nests of bees. Some species of honeyguide have bacteria in their digestive tract that enables them to digest the wax of bees' nests. They were given their name because the greater or black-throated honeyguide, *Indicator indicator*, attracts the attention of people (and some animals, including the honey badger or ratel) by calling and leading them to bees' nests. Once the person, or animal, has broken open the nest to get at the honey the honeyguide can eat its share.

honeysuckle Any one of various trees, shrubs, and climbers which produce large amounts of nectar. In Europe and North America, these are generally species of *Lonicera*, which are members of the same family as snowberry, elder, and guelder rose. They are usually climbers (LIANAS) with strongly scented flowers, visited by moths in the evening and known in Shakespeare's time as woodbine. In other countries, unrelated plants are called honeysuckle: in South Africa, for example, the name is used for *Tecomaria capensis* and species of *Halleria*, which have red, bird-pollinated flowers.

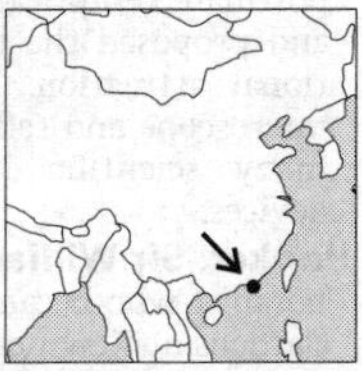

Hong Kong (Chinese **Xiangjiang**) A former British dependency on the south-east coast of China, adjoining the Chinese province of Guangdong; area 1,071 sq km (414 sq miles); pop. (est. 1990) 5,900,000; languages, English and Chinese (official). Including over 200 islands and a portion of the mainland east of the Pearl River, it comprises Hong Kong Island, ceded by China under the Treaty of Nanking in 1842, the Kowloon peninsula, acquired by the Convention of Peking in 1860, and the New Territories, leased from China in 1898 for 99 years. The climate is tropical, with a dry sunny season from September to March. Hong Kong is a free port, and a major financial and manufacturing centre, exporting textiles, electronics, toys and re-exported goods. By an agreement between the Chinese and British governments (signed in 1984), China resumed sovereignty over Hong Kong in 1997, which then became a Special Administrative Region whose basic law guarantees the present systems and lifestyles for a period of 50 years.

Honiara A port and the capital of the Solomon Islands, on the north-west coast of Guadalcanal; pop. (1990) 35,290.

Honolulu The capital and principal port of Hawaii, situated on the south-east coast of the island of Oahu; pop. (1990) 836,230. It became capital of the Kingdom of Hawaii in 1845 and capital of the 50th US state in 1959. The Japanese attack on the US naval base at Pearl Harbor on 7 December 1941 brought the USA into World War II. It is the headquarters of the US Pacific Fleet and its landmarks include Diamond Head volcanic crater, Waikiki Beach, the royal palace of Iolani, and the USS *Arizona* Memorial at Pearl Harbor. Tourism is a major industry together with sugar processing and pineapple canning.

Honshu The largest of the four main islands of Japan, comprising the regions of Kanto, Chubu, Kinki, Chugoku, and Tohoku; area 230,897 sq km

(89,184 sq miles); pop. (1990) 99,254,000. Its chief cities are Tokyo, Yokohama, Osaka, and Nagoya, and landmarks include Mt. Fuji (3,776 m, 12,385 ft), the largest mountain in Japan and Lake Biwa, the largest lake in Japan.

Hood, Thomas (1799–1845) British poet and humorist. He was the editor of a number of literary magazines and a friend of Charles Lamb, William Hazlitt, and Thomas De Quincey. He wrote much humorous verse but is now chiefly remembered for serious poems such as 'The Song of the Shirt' (1843) and 'The Bridge of Sighs' (1844).

hooded crow See CARRION CROW.

hoof See CLAW.

Hooghly (or **Hugli**) The most westerly of the rivers of the Ganges delta, in West Bengal, India. It flows 192 km (120 miles) into the Bay of Bengal and was navigable to Calcutta before silting made it necessary to develop the outport of Hadeida.

Hooke, Robert (1635–1703) English scientist. He began as Boyle's assistant, and soon became curator of experiments for the new Royal Society. After the Fire of London (1666) he was made a surveyor to the City, and designed several of London's prominent buildings. His scientific achievements were many and varied: he proposed an undulating theory of light, formulated the law of elasticity (HOOKE'S LAW), introduced the term *cell* to biology, postulated elliptical orbits for the Earth and Moon, and proposed the inverse square law of gravitational attraction. He improved the compound microscope and reflecting telescope, and invented many scientific instruments and mechanical devices.

Hooker, Sir William Jackson (1785–1865) British botanist who became first director of the Botanic Gardens at Kew near London. He revived the gardens and founded a museum there. His son **Sir Joseph Dalton Hooker** (1817–1911) succeeded his father as director of Kew Gardens. He joined a voyage of exploration to the Antarctic and returned with an immense collection of plants from the Southern Hemisphere. Their distribution, he remarked, indicated an ancient linkage between the landmasses of Australia and South America, an idea later supported by the theory of continental drift. Later he spent three years in the northeast of India and sent home large numbers of rhododendrons, starting a fashion for them.

Hooke's law The law of elasticity, formulated by Robert HOOKE, stating that when a material is stretched, the change in length of the material is directly proportional to the stretching force. If an object can be deformed under pressure and then regains its original shape when the pressure is removed, the object is said to be elastic. Hooke's law describes this elastic behaviour: it was first used to describe the deformation of a spring. The limit beyond which the law does not apply is called the elastic limit.

Hook of Holland (Dutch **Hoek van Holland**) A cape and port of the Netherlands, 15 km (9 miles) south-east of The Hague, linked by ferry to Harwich, Hull, and Dublin. Its Dutch name means 'corner of Holland'.

hookworm A common parasite of humans in tropical and subtropical regions. The parasites, two species of ROUNDWORM about 1 cm (0.5 inch) long, live in the upper gut, often in large numbers. One species, *Necator americanus*, occurs in the tropical regions of America, while the other, *Ancylostoma duodenale*, is an important parasite of the Old World regions. Each worm consumes a few drops of blood daily, and a heavy infestation will cause a severe anaemia. The eggs, passed in the faeces, develop in the soil into larvae which can penetrate the skin. They then travel by the bloodstream to the gut to complete their development. Modern treatment can eliminate the worms with little upset to the patient.

hoopoe A bird, *Upupa epops*, classified in a family by itself, Upupidae, but related to bee-eaters and rollers. A separate species, *U. africana*, is sometimes recognized. It occurs over wide areas of Africa, Europe, and south-east Asia. The hoopoe is the size of a small crow, and has a salmon-pink body and large, erectile crest. Its wings and tail are strikingly patterned in black and white and its beak is long and curved. It lives mostly on the ground, catching large insects and lizards, and nests in a hole in a tree or on a cliff face, laying four to six white eggs.

Hoover, Herbert C(lark) (1874–1964) US Republican statesman, 31st President of the USA 1929–33. He first gained prominence for his work in organizing food production and distribution in the USA and Europe during and after World War I. As President he was faced with the long-term problems of the Depression which followed the stock market crash of 1929. He returned to relief work after World War II as coordinator of food supplies to avert the threat of postwar famine.

Hoover, J(ohn) Edgar (1895–1972) US lawyer and director of the FBI 1924–72. Beginning his term of office with the fight against organized crime in the 1920s and 1930s, he went on to be instrumental in reorganizing the FBI into an efficient, scientific law-enforcement agency. However, he came under criticism for the organization's role during the McCarthy era and for its reactionary political stance in the 1960s.

Hoover, William (Henry) (1849–1932) US industrialist. In 1908 he bought the patent of a lightweight electric cleaning machine from James Murray Spangler, a janitor, and formed the Electric Suction Sweeper Company to manufacture it. The machine proved an international success and in 1910 the company was renamed Hoover.

Hoover Dam A hydroelectric dam on the Colorado River at Boulder Canyon on the border between the US states of Arizona and Nevada. Completed in 1936, its reservoir (Lake Mead) was then the largest man-made lake in the world. It was known as the Boulder Dam (1937–47), being renamed in honour of President Hoover. The dam is 221 m (726 ft) high.

hop A climbing plant, *Humulus lupulus*, belonging to the same family as HEMP. The stems wind clockwise around other plants. The hop is cultivated as a flavouring for beer. A number of bitter herbs have been used to flavour beer but hops have been used more than any other since the Middle Ages. The greenish, cone-like female flower-buds of this perennial are the only parts used in brewing. Hops are grown throughout the temperate areas of Europe, America, and Australasia.

Hope, Bob (born Leslie Townes Hope) (1903–) British-born US comedian. His dry allusive style gave him the character of a humorously cowardly incompetent, always cheerfully failing in his attempts to become a romantic hero, particularly in *Road to Singapore* (1940) and the rest of the series of *Road* films (1940–62), in which he starred with Bing CROSBY and Dorothy Lamour (1914–96).

Hopi A Uto-Aztecan Indian tribe of North America associated with the pueblos of Arizona, Colorado, and New Mexico. Known as 'the peaceful ones', the

Hopi are descended from people who migrated into the south-west before 1,000 BC. They number *c.*9,000 in Arizona.

Hopkins, Sir Anthony (Philip) (1937–) British actor. His acting career began on the stage in 1961, with his screen début following in 1967. His films include *The Elephant Man* (1980) *The Bounty* (1984), and *The Remains of the Day* (1993). He won an Oscar for his performance in *The Silence of the Lambs* (1991).

Hopkins, Sir Frederick Gowland (1861–1947) Pioneer British biochemist, remembered particularly for work leading to the discovery of VITAMINS. After research on natural pigments and proteins and the physiology of muscle contraction, he directed his attention to the relationship between growth and diet, and by 1906 he had identified 'accessory food factors' (vitamins) as being essential for health. He was unable, however, to isolate any of these substances. In 1929 he shared the Nobel Prize for physiology and medicine with Christiaan Eijkman.

Hopkins, Gerard Manley (1844–89) British poet. Influenced at Oxford by John Henry Newman, Hopkins converted to Roman Catholicism in 1866 and became a Jesuit two years later. He wrote little poetry until 1876, when the shipwreck of a vessel carrying nuns and other emigrants to America the previous year inspired him to write 'The Wreck of the Deutschland'. The poem makes bold use of Hopkins's 'sprung rhythm' technique (in which each foot has one stressed syllable followed by a varying number of unstressed), as do his best-known poems 'Windhover' and 'Pied Beauty', both written in 1877. His work, collected in *Poems* (1918), was published posthumously by his friend Robert Bridges.

Hopper, Edward (1882–1967) US realist painter. He supported himself as a commercial illustrator before gaining recognition for his paintings in the 1920s. He is best known for his mature works, such as *Early Sunday Morning* (1930) and *Nighthawks* (1942), depicting scenes from everyday US urban life in which still figures appear in introspective isolation, often in bleak or shabby settings.

Hor See HORUS.

Horace (full name Quintus Horatius Flaccus) (65–8 BC) Roman poet of the Augustan period. His two books of *Satires* departed from earlier convention with their realism and irony directed at both the satirist and his targets. His *Odes*, displaying a mastery of poetic form in the style of earlier Greek lyric poets, celebrate friendship, love, good wine, and the contentment of a peaceful rural life in contrast to the turmoil of politics and civil war. (Horace had fought with Brutus and Cassius at Philippi in 42.) They were much imitated by later ages, especially by 17th-century and 18th-century English poets. Horace was also a notable literary critic; his *Ars Poetica* influenced John Dryden and his fellow Augustans in their critical writing.

Hordern, Sir Michael (Murray) (1911–95) British actor. He built a strong reputation in the classical theatre, playing King Lear (1960) and Prospero in the 1978 Stratford production of *The Tempest*. He displayed versatility with acclaimed performances in modern plays such as Tom Stoppard's *Jumpers* (1972) and made a succession of film and television appearances.

horizon, soil A distinct layer, roughly parallel to the surface of the land, within the soil PROFILE. Horizons can normally be distinguished one from another by characteristic differences in physical or chemical composition, organic content, texture, or structure. The formation of horizons results from the action of soil-forming processes on weathered rock material through time. There are three major horizons. The near-surface mineral layer, in which organic matter tends to accumulate, is known as the A-horizon of the soil; but because clay and minerals such as iron and aluminium are often washed out of it by eluviation, it is sometimes also called the E-horizon. Beneath this is the B-horizon; here the minerals washed out from above accumulate. Lastly, the partially weathered rock material at the base of the soil is termed the C-horizon.

Horkheimer, Max (1895–1973) German philosopher and sociologist. He was director of the Frankfurt Institute for Social Research from 1930 to 1958 and a principal figure in the Frankfurt School of philosophy. His reputation is based on a series of articles written in the 1930s expounding the school's Marxist analysis of modern industrial society and culture; these were collected into the two-volume *Critical Theory* (1968). Other works include *Dialectic of the Enlightenment* (1947), written with his colleague Theodor ADORNO.

hormone A chemical messenger, usually a protein or a steroid, formed in animals by ENDOCRINE GLANDS. Hormones are discharged into the blood and circulated in low concentrations to all tissues. Individual hormones recognize their respective 'target' organs or cell systems by binding to specific chemical groups (receptors) on cell surface membranes. Once bound, they induce complicated, often quite slow, changes that lead to such processes as growth of the body, to sexual development, or to digestion. 'Target' organs are often some distance from their controlling glands. For example, gonadotrophins (pituitary hormones), released from the pituitary gland at the base of the skull, cause growth of the gonads in the pelvis, while insulin, produced in the pancreas, causes liver and muscle cells to take up excess glucose from the blood. In general, hormones control body functions over longer periods than the nervous system and also direct growth and development.

hormone replacement therapy (HRT) The administration of female sex hormones (usually a combination of an OESTROGEN and a progestogen) for the relief of menopausal symptoms or following surgical removal of the ovaries. HRT has proved to be effective in preventing post-menopausal osteoporosis, and it is also claimed to have preventive action against coronary heart disease. The drugs may be taken as tablets, applied to the skin in the form of skin patches or a gel, or inserted as an implant beneath the skin.

Hormuz (or **Hormoz**, **Ormoz**) A strait separating Iran from the Arabian peninsula and linking the Persian Gulf with the Gulf of Oman which leads to the Arabian Sea. It is of strategic importance as a waterway through which sea traffic to and from the oil-rich states of the Persian Gulf must pass.

horn (in zoology) A hard permanent outgrowth on the head of cattle, sheep, and other (especially ungulate (hoofed)) mammals. A true horn is seen in members of the cattle family, and consists of a core of bone, which is fused with the skull, encased within a hollow cone composed of keratin. This horny sheath grows throughout the animal's life and gradually thickens. Neither the core of bone nor the sheath of horn are shed except in the PRONGHORN. Perhaps the most primitive type of horn, from which both horns and antlers may have developed, is that of the giraffe. Its horns are unbranched and covered with skin and hair; the bony core is separable in the young giraffe, becoming fused to the skull later. The horns of the rhinoceros consist of a mass of coarse, keratinized strands which are a modified form of hair. They are not true horns, as they lack a bony core.

horn (in music) Any wind instrument sounded by applying buzzing lips to a hole in a tube. Some are made of horn, but ivory, shell, wood, bamboo, gourd, pottery, or metal are used as often. The earliest horns were probably animal horns and CONCHES. Most are end-blown, but in Africa, Oceania, parts of tribal India, South America, and Bronze Age Ireland, horns have also been blown from the side of the tube. Ivory horns were often status symbols in Africa, but they and horns of other materials are also widely used for music and signalling. Ivory horns, called olifants, were also used in Europe in the early Middle Ages, sometimes replacing a written charter as a symbol of land ownership or rights of usage, but usually, and also in the Renaissance, as status symbols. In ancient Egypt, Israel, Greece, and Rome, horns of bronze and other metals were used. The only other horns of similar antiquity that have survived are the Scandinavian bronze *lurs* and the slightly later Irish bronze horns. In medieval European iconography, short horns, presumably cow horns, can be seen in the BAYEUX TAPESTRY, and longer horns, of wood or metal, in Anglo-Saxon and Mozarabic manuscripts. Coiled horns, ancestors of our FRENCH HORN, appear from the 16th century onwards.

Horn, Cape The southernmost point of South America. It is a headland in the archipelago of TIERRA DEL FUEGO, south of the Strait of Magellan. Standing 424 m (1,391 feet) high, it is part of the ancient volcanic chain which extends from the Andes to South Georgia. It is infamous for the violence of the sea, 'rounding the Horn' at any time of the year meaning having to face the bitterly cold winds – the ROARING FORTIES – and strong currents which sweep from the Pacific Ocean into the Atlantic. The name is taken from Cape Hoorn, the home in Holland of the chief financial backer of a trading expedition which used the route in 1616.

hornbeam See BIRCH.

hornbill A bird of the family Bucerotidae, with 54 species native to Africa, Asia, and Australasia. They are medium to large birds 37.5–150 cm (15–60 inches) long, and mostly brown, black, and white. Their most striking feature is the large, red or yellow, slightly curved beak, usually with a bony structure (casque) on top of the upper mandible. Many live on a diet of fruit, but some, such as the largest species, the great hornbill, *Buceros bicornis*, eat a wide range of animals, which they kill with their powerful beaks. Most species nest in large holes in trees: the female often enters the hole before laying and walls herself in with faeces and mud brought by the male; only a small crack is left through which the male can pass food. The female stays in the nest during egg-laying and incubation, until halfway through the nestling period, when she breaks out and helps the male collect food for the large young.

hornblende A common dark green or black mineral, one of the AMPHIBOLES: a silicate containing calcium, sodium, iron and aluminium. It occurs as hard, lustrous crystals in igneous rocks and in metamorphosed calcareous rocks. It is found notably in Edenville, New York (USA), and Kotaki (Japan), but is of no commercial interest.

horned toad An amphibian that gets its name from the triangular, horn-like projections of skin that extend from their upper eyelids. Horned toads include species of the genus *Bufo*, the South American horned toads, *Ceratophrys*, and the Asiatic horned toads, *Megophrys*, which are not closely related, but belong to different families of toads.

A group of squat-bodied American iguanid lizards are also sometimes called horned toads or **horned lizards**. These spiny, scaled lizards are able to survive arid, even desert conditions by drinking the night dew, which collects around the scales surrounding their mouths.

hornet Any large species of social WASP. They occur throughout north temperate regions and the Old World tropics and the queens in some species may have a wing-span of as much as 8 cm (3 inches). The term is particularly applied to the European species, *Vespa crabro*, which has a brown and yellow striped body, as opposed to the black and yellow of smaller wasps. They almost always nest in hollow trees and their sting is more unpleasant than that of wasps; that of some tropical species can be fatal.

Horn of Africa (or **Somali Peninsula**) A peninsula of north-east Africa separating the Gulf of Aden from the main part of the Indian Ocean. It comprises Somalia and parts of Ethiopia.

hornpipe A single-reed musical instrument with a horn bell and often also a horn fixed over the reed to keep it dry. The reed is a cane tube with a vibrating tongue cut from its surface, like the DRONE reeds of a Highland BAGPIPE; hornpipes are also often bagless chanters blown by mouth. Two British examples are the Welsh pibcorn and Scots stock-and-horn. Some hornpipes, such as the Basque *alboka* and Tunisian *zukra*, have two pipes, fixed side by side, often with different numbers of finger-holes in each.

The hornpipe is also an energetic dance popular in the late 17th and 18th centuries. It was originally performed in triple TIME; later, when associated with the Navy, a simple duple time was used.

horntail See SAWFLY.

Hornung, Ernest William (1866–1921) British novelist. He is remembered as the creator of the gentleman burglar Raffles, who first featured in *The Amateur Cracksman* (1899). Hornung was the brother-in-law of Sir Arthur Conan Doyle.

Horologium The Pendulum Clock, a faint CONSTELLATION of the southern sky, introduced by the 18th-century French astronomer Nicolas Louis de Lacaille. It is a barren area of sky, consisting of no stars brighter than fourth magnitude.

Horowitz, Vladimir (1904–89) Russian-born US pianist. He first toured the USA in 1928, and settled there soon afterwards. He was a leading international virtuoso and was best known for his performances of Scarlatti, Liszt, Scriabin, and Prokofiev. His concert career was interrupted by periodic bouts of illness.

Horsa See HENGIST.

horse A member of the same family, Equidae, as asses and zebras. All seven members of this family are in the same genus, *Equus*, and can interbreed to produce sterile hybrids, such as MULES. All have only a single functional digit, the middle one, which terminates at its very tip in a hoof, on which the horse walks. The teeth are typical of HERBIVORES. The horse's ancestors include *Hyracotherium* (eohippus) and *Mesohippus*.

The wild horse is now represented by only one race, **Przewalski's horse** or the Mongolian wild horse, *Equus przewalskii*. It is found in the steppes and semi-deserts of southern Siberia, Mongolia, and western China, and is a sturdy animal with a

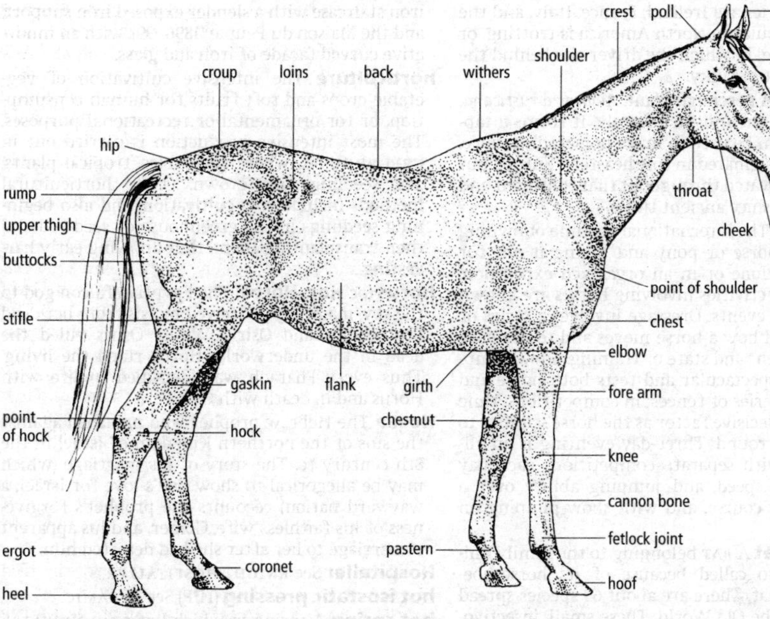

Horse Anatomical parts of a horse.

rather large head, small ears, and heavy jaws. The mane is short and erect, black or brown in colour, edged with lighter hairs, and the tail is long-haired, black or brown in colour. In summer the body colour is reddish-brown with some white on the muzzle; in winter the hair is longer and paler. Przewalski's horses are now being bred in zoos and on a new semi-wild reserve with the result that numbers continue to increase.

Domesticated horses, *E. caballus*, can be divided into light and heavy types. The light horses are used for HORSE-RIDING and for drawing traps. Among the riding horses, the Arab is considered to be one of the most beautiful and has been crossed with other breeds to produce swift horses for racing. The heavy or draught horses are used for pulling carts and farm work.

horsefly (or **gadfly**) A robust, blood-sucking true FLY which has colourful, iridescent eyes. Horseflies are members of the family Tabanidae (2,000 species), which also includes species known as deerflies and clegs. Only female horseflies feed on blood, by first making a puncture with the strong, blade-shaped, sucking mouthparts, and then continuing to lap up blood, which may flow for some time. The males are nectar-feeders. The usual victims of blood-feeding are cattle and horses, but humans are often bitten, these bites leading to painful swellings at the site of the incision. Eggs are laid as compacted masses on plants growing in damp places, and, upon hatching, the larvae drop to the ground and feed on worms and other small invertebrates. In some countries, horse flies are VECTORS of diseases, especially of a parasitic roundworm which causes the disease lòa-lòa or loiasis.

horsehair worm A worm-like animal with some 230 species, comprising a small phylum, the Nematomorpha. They may be up to 1 m (3 feet) long but are rarely even 1 mm (0.04 inch) thick. Larval stages parasitize arthropods, especially aquatic insects, absorbing food across their body wall. The adults live freely in fresh water, or in soils, or in the sea, and do not feed.

Horsehead Nebula A dark NEBULA in the constellation of Orion. It resembles a horse's head and neck in shape, and is conspicuous because of its much brighter background. The nebula is near the bright star Zeta Orionis, the eastern-most of the three stars forming ORION's belt.

horse latitudes A belt of calms in each hemisphere at 30–35° north and south of the equator, between the trade winds and the westerlies. The origin of the name is uncertain; some hold that it arose from the alleged practice of throwing overboard horses, which were being transported to the Americas or West Indies, when the ship's voyage was unduly prolonged by lack of a favourable wind.

horse mackerel (or **scad**) A species of fish of the family Carangidae, which contains a number of species known as jacks in North America. Widely distributed in European seas, the horse mackerel, *Trachurus trachurus*, is distinguished by the series of broad scales along the sides, which become heavy and sharply pointed towards the tail. A schooling fish, it lives near the surface down to a depth of 100 m (325 feet) both inshore and in the open sea. Young horse mackerel shelter beneath the trailing tentacles of jellyfishes. Adults feed on small fishes, crustaceans, and squids.

horse-racing The sport in which specially bred and trained horses race against each other before spectators, many of whom bet on the outcome of each race. In the UK, the chief categories are flat-racing – a summer sport organized by the Jockey Club – and jump-racing, a winter sport subdivided into hurdle-racing and steeplechasing and organized according to National Hunt rules. Most jockeys taking part in these programmes are professional; for amateur riders, there are point-to-point races held over cross-country courses and organized by local hunts. Top horses and jockeys now travel the world to race. Other major horse-racing countries are Ireland, France, Italy, and the USA. Also popular in North America is trotting, or harness-racing, in which the driver sits behind the horse in a cart or sulky.

horseradish A perennial plant, *Amoracia rusticana*, a member of the mustard family. It forms a taproot which can be used to make horseradish sauce. It probably originated in southeastern Europe but has been cultivated throughout that continent and western Asia since ancient times.

horse-riding The international pastime of owning or hiring a horse or pony and taking it out for rides either alone or in an organized expedition. Competitive activities involving horses are known as equestrian events. Dressage involves a series of tests to reveal how a horse moves and to measure its development and state of training. Show-jumping is more spectacular and tests both horse and rider over a series of fences; in competitions, time is as much a decisive factor as the horse's ability to jump a clear round. Three-day eventing is an all-round test with separate competitions each day for dressage, speed, and jumping ability over a cross-country course, and with show-jumping on the final day.

horseshoe bat A BAT belonging to the family Rhinolophidae, so called because of its horseshoe-shaped noseleaf. There are about 69 species spread throughout the Old World. These small, insectivorous animals are mainly tropical, but five species occur in Europe and two in Britain, including the endangered greater horseshoe bat, *Rhinolophus ferrumequinum*. Those species that occur in colder parts of the group's range hibernate in caves during the winter.

horseshoe crab (or **king crab**) A large primitive marine ARTHROPOD (but not a crab) of the subclass Xiphosura (class Merostomata), about 60 cm (2 feet) long, distantly linked to the arachnids. Only five species survive, in America and Asia; all their closest relatives are extinct, although they are known back to the Cambrian Period, *c*.550 million years ago. The horseshoe-shaped shell covers jaws, walking legs, and respiratory book-gills, while a long mobile tail-spine projects behind. Small invertebrates are gathered from the sea-bed by touch and smell; the tiny lateral eyes probably detect danger only from above. Horseshoe crabs come inshore in vast numbers for nocturnal mating. Males mount females, fertilizing 200–1,000 eggs as they are laid in a shallow sandy depression. Hatchlings are tailless, and resemble fossil TRILOBITES.

horsetail A primitive spore-bearing plant (CRYPTOGAM), related to ferns, which comprises the phylum Sphenophyta (or in traditional classifications the class Sphenopsida). Horsetails have whorls of green branches at regular intervals along the upright stem, and minute scale-like leaves. Like CLUBMOSSES, they were much larger in size and more diverse in the Carboniferous Period *c*.320 million years ago, when, as we know from fossils, forests of horsetails called CALAMITES existed. Today there are only 25 species and some, such as common horsetail, *Equisetum arvense*, are troublesome weeds on cultivated clay ground, and are poisonous to livestock.

horst A long plateau with a geological fault on each side. Horsts can form BLOCK MOUNTAINS and are the geological opposites of grabens.

Horta, Victor (1861–1947) Belgian architect. He was a leading figure in art nouveau architecture and worked chiefly in Brussels. His buildings include the Hôtel Tassel (1892), notable for its decorative iron staircase with a slender exposed iron support, and the Maison du Peuple (1896–99), with an innovative curved façade of iron and glass.

horticulture The intensive cultivation of vegetable crops and soft fruits for human consumption, or for ornamental or recreational purposes. The most intensive production is carried out in GREENHOUSES, where vegetables, tropical plants, and seedlings are grown. Other horticultural methods include row cultivation, and also beginning seedlings in the greenhouse or seed-bed and then transplanting them, thus allowing early harvesting.

Horus (or **Hor**, **Horos**) The Egyptian falcon god to the sky, magically conceived by Isis from her dead brother-husband Osiris. Whilst Osiris ruled the dead in the underworld, Horus ruled the living. Thus every Pharaoh was identified in life with Horus and in death with Osiris.

Hosea The Hebrew prophet who preached against the sins of the northern Kingdom of Israel in the 8th century BC. The story of his marriage (which may be allegorical to show God's love for Israel, a wayward nation) recounts the prophet's forgiveness of his faithless wife, Gomer, and his apparent remarriage to her after she had deserted him.

Hospitaller See KNIGHT HOSPITALLER.

hot isostatic pressing (HIP) See CERAMIC.

hot spring A spring in which hot GROUNDWATER emerges from the land surface, either as a steady trickle into a pool or more spectacularly as a GEYSER, shooting into the air. Hot, or thermal, springs are caused through the penetration by underground water deep into the Earth, where it is heated to the temperature of the rocks or volcanic magma (molten rock) that it encounters. Hot springs are rich in dissolved minerals and may be classified as sulphate-, chloride-, carbonate-, or acid-bearing water depending on the dissolved mineral. Their healing properties have been recognized since earliest times.

Hotspur The nickname of Sir Henry Percy (see PERCY).

Hottentot A people related to the Bushmen now found chiefly in south-west Africa. They formerly occupied the region near the Cape but were largely dispossessed by Dutch settlers. Their language (also known as *Nama*) which is spoken in Namibia by about 50,000 people has a number of 'click' consonants made by drawing air into the mouth and clicking the tongue.

Houdini, Harry (born Erik Weisz) (1874–1926) Hungarian-born US magician and escape artist. In the early 1900s he became famous for his ability to escape from all kinds of bonds and containers, from prison cells to aerially suspended straitjackets.

houri (from Arabic *ḥawira*, 'black-eyed') In Islam, one of the permanent virgins who await good Muslims in Paradise, referred to as 'purified wives', and 'spotless virgins' in the Koran. Later tradition states that the number of houris allotted to each man for co-habitation will be proportionate to his fasting and good works on Earth. For some Muslims the houri is a symbol of a spiritual state rather than of a physical being.

housefly A true FLY of the family Muscidae that commonly enters houses. In particular, the name is used for the common housefly, *Musca domestica*, which has spread worldwide in association with humans and is not only a nuisance but a threat to health. It breeds in decaying organic matter, including excrement, and adult flies feed indiscriminately on this and on sweet substances. Contamination of food occurs through pathogens carried on the fly's feet, and also because, while feeding, they regurgitate saliva and partially digested food to liquefy sugar and other materials. This regurgitated liquid contains many microorganisms harmful to humans, which have been picked up from contaminated food by the fly. The liquid food is mopped up with the spongy proboscis or tongue. Fly-spots consist of regurgitated food or faeces. The lesser housefly, *Fannia canicularis*, has similar habits.

house martin A species of bird, *Delichon urbica*, in the swallow family, Hirundinidae, which breeds across most of Europe and Asia and spends the winter in Africa, India, or south-east Asia. It is glossy blue-black above with a white rump and underparts. The house martin's nest of mud is usually built under the eaves of houses, hence the bird's name. Like others in the swallow family, it feeds on flying insects.

house mouse A small rodent of the family Muridae which has long lived in close proximity to man, but is perfectly capable of surviving in the wild in hedgerows and on arable land. Indeed, some mice alternate between houses in winter and the countryside in summer. The true house mouse is *Mus musculus*, but other species of *Mus* enter houses in various parts of the world. The original range of *M. musculus* was probably southern Eurasia, including the Mediterranean region, but its distribution is now worldwide due to human introductions. It has been present in Britain since at least the Iron Age. It is a pest of stored foodstuffs, which it contaminates with its droppings as well as eats. It is potentially a health hazard in the spread of disease. The domesticated form is widely used as a laboratory animal as well as being popular as a pet.

House of Commons The lower chamber of the British PARLIAMENT. It began as an element of the Parliaments summoned by the king in the later 13th century: both knights of the shire and burgesses of BOROUGHS were summoned to Simon de MONTFORT's Parliament in 1265. It took over 500 years for the Commons to become supreme in the tripartite division of power between it, the HOUSE OF LORDS, and the monarchy. Following a series of REFORM ACTS and other legislation (1832, 1867, 1884, 1918, 1928, 1945, 1969) members of the House of Commons are today elected by universal adult suffrage. By the Parliament Act of 1911, the maximum duration of a Parliament became five years. Members of the House of Commons (MPs) are elected by 650 single-member constituencies in first-past-the-post elections.

The life of a Parliament is divided into sessions, usually of one year in length. As a rule, Bills likely to raise political controversy are introduced in the Commons before going to the Lords, and the Commons claim exclusive control in respect of national taxation and expenditure. Since 1911 Members have received payment. The House of Commons is presided over by an elected Speaker, who has power to maintain order in the House.

House of Lords The upper chamber of the British PARLIAMENT. It began as a form of the medieval kings' Great Council. In the 13th and 14th centuries, as the councils gave way to parliaments, the Lords evolved into a separate body, which, together with the HOUSE OF COMMONS, presented bills to the crown for enactment as statutes. Following the 1832 REFORM ACT, its influence gradually declined as that of the House of Commons increased. The Parliament Act of 1911 reduced the Lords' powers to a 'suspensory veto' of two years (further reduced to one year in 1949). By it bills can be delayed, but if passed again by the Commons, become law. The House of Lords has no power to revise or delay money bills.

Members of the House of Lords include the Lords Spiritual (26 archbishops and bishops in order of seniority), the Lords Temporal (approximately 1,000 hereditary and life peers), and the Lords of Appeal in Ordinary (Law Lords), the most senior members of the JUDICIARY. Non-hereditary peers have been created since the Life Peerage Act of 1958; they tend to be more active members of the Lords than many hereditary peers.

House of Representatives The lower chamber of the two chambers of the US Congress, the other being the SENATE. The House of Representatives comprises 435 members, the number for each state being determined by population, though every state is entitled to at least one Representative. The size of the House increased with the USA's population until 1929 when the number of representatives was fixed. Seats are apportioned every ten years.

The House and the Senate have an equal voice in legislation; however, the right to originate finance bills is given to the House by the Constitution. The House also has the power to begin IMPEACHMENT proceedings, through which the President, a judge, or other official can be removed from office for misbehaviour, if the resolution of the House to impeach is adopted by the Senate.

Housman, A(lfred) E(dward) (1859–1936) British poet and scholar. His best-known work, *A Shropshire Lad* (1896), was a series of 63 nostalgic LYRICS largely in BALLAD form and often addressed to a farm-boy or soldier. Many of his earlier poems, preserved in notebooks, appeared in later volumes; his *Collected Poems* were published posthumously in 1939. *Praefanda* (1931) is a collection of bawdy and obscene passages from Latin authors. His lecture 'The Name and Nature of Poetry' (1933) illuminates the process of poetic creation.

Houston An inland deep-water port of Texas, USA, linked to the Gulf of Mexico by the Houston Ship Canal and a great financial, commercial, and industrial centre; pop. (1990) 1,630,550. It is the fourth-largest city in the USA, and has since 1961 been an important centre for space research and manned space flight. The city is named after Samuel Houston (1793–1863), US politician and military leader. It is one of the world's major oil centres with refineries and petrochemical works; it has steel mills, shipyards, breweries, and meat-packing plants, as well as many electronics and avionics research firms and consumer goods industries. Houston is also a major cultural and tourist centre.

Hove A resort town and residential suburb on the south coast of England, adjacent to Brighton in East Sussex; pop. (1981) 67,140.

hovercraft A vessel designed to float on a cushion of compressed air between the hovercraft itself and the surface over which it is travelling. The problems of designing and building such a vehicle were not solved until the 1950s, when COCKERELL designed the first practical hovercraft, the SRN-1, launched in 1959. Like later vessels of the same type, it used a GAS-TURBINE engine to power a large aircraft PROPELLER, which drew air into a space under the craft. The air-cushion was contained by a rubber skirt, and forward motion was achieved by a second propeller. The hovercraft's amphibious ability has led to its successful use as a ferry, assault craft, and survey vessel.

hoverfly A medium-sized true FLY of the family Syrphidae. Many hoverflies have pronounced black and yellow markings. The adults are often to be seen hovering with shimmering wings above flowers, only to dart off and reappear a short distance away. Adults eat nectar and pollen, but their larvae feed on plants, aphids, tree sap, decomposing organic matter, or debris in bee, wasp, or ant nests. Among the most useful are those which consume huge quantities of aphids which would otherwise eat crop-plants. The larvae of some hoverfly species are known as rat-tailed maggots, since they possess a telescopic breathing snorkel which enables them to live in stagnant mud.

hover-train See GROUND-GUIDANCE SYSTEM.

Howard, Catherine (*c*.1521–42) Fifth wife of Henry VIII. She married Henry soon after his divorce from Anne of Cleves in 1540, probably at the instigation of her ambitious Howard relatives. She was accused of infidelity, confessed, and was beheaded in 1542.

Howard, John (1726–90) British philanthropist and prison reformer. In 1773 his sense of horror at conditions in Bedford jail led him to undertake a tour of British prisons; this culminated the following year in two Acts of Parliament setting down sanitary standards. His work *The State of Prisons in England and Wales* (1777) gave further impetus to the movement for improvements in the design and management of prisons.

Howard, John (Winston) (1939–) Australian Liberal statesman, Prime Minister from 1996. He was elected an MP in 1974 and held several posts in the Cabinet, including Federal Treasurer (1977–83). He was leader of the Liberal Party in opposition 1985–89 and from 1995 before becoming Prime Minister of a coalition government.

Howard, Leslie (born Leslie Howard Stainer) (1893–1943) British actor. After making his film début in *Outward Bound* (1930) he played the archetypal English gentleman (although he was of Hungarian descent) in a series of films such as *The Scarlet Pimpernel* (1935) and *Pygmalion* (1938), which he also directed. Other films include *Gone with the Wind* (1939) and the patriotic *The First of the Few* (1942), which he also directed and produced. He died returning from Lisbon to London when his plane was shot down by German aircraft.

Howard, Trevor (Wallace) (1916–88) British actor. Howard was a versatile film actor who starred in the highly successful *Brief Encounter* (1945) and *The Third Man* (1949) and had a distinguished career in film and television. In the 1970s and 1980s he made many appearances in character roles, often eccentric ones, in films such as *Gandhi* (1982) and *White Mischief* (1987).

Howe, Elias (1819–67) US inventor. In 1846 he patented a sewing machine with an eyed needle to carry the upper thread and a holder resembling a shuttle for the lower thread. The machine's principles were adapted by Isaac Merrit Singer and others, in violation of Howe's patent rights, and it took a seven-year litigation battle to secure the royalties.

Howells, Herbert (Norman) (1892–1983) British composer. His early work includes songs and orchestral and chamber music, written in a rhapsodic, pastoral style that owed much to VAUGHAN WILLIAMS and DELIUS. The success of his highly personal requiem *Hymnus Paradisi* (1950) renewed his interest in liturgical music, of which he became the foremost English practitioner. He is a master of complex contrapuntal textures, soft dissonance, and a quality of sensuous spirituality.

howitzer See ARTILLERY.

howler monkey A thick-set, heavy-bodied animal, up to 75 cm (2.5 feet) in body length and with a prehensile tail, also up to 75 cm (2.5 feet) long in some species. Howler monkeys include the largest species of the New World monkeys, and are found from Mexico through Central to South America in forests and more open woodland. All six species share the genus *Alouatta*. Their fur is usually black in colour, but one species, the red howler, *Alouatta seniculus*, is bright golden red. The face is naked but a heavy beard hangs from the chin. A family group of five to 20 individuals, led by an old male, will occupy a territory. Most active in early morning and evening, the group will travel some 700 m (0.5 mile) in a day through the tallest trees, choosing fruit to eat. Breeding takes place throughout the year.

Hoxha, Enver (1908–85) Albanian statesman, Prime Minister 1944–54 and First Secretary of the Albanian Communist Party 1954–85. In 1941 he founded the Albanian Communist Party and led the fight for national independence. As Prime Minister and thereafter First Secretary of the Communist Party's Central Committee, he rigorously isolated Albania from Western influences and implemented a Stalinist programme of nationalization and collectivization.

Hoyle, Sir Fred (1915–) British astrophysicist, one of the proponents of the steady-state theory of cosmology. He also formulated theories about the origins of stars, and of the processes by which atoms of the heavier chemical elements are built up within the stars, writing a seminal paper on the subject in 1956 with the US physicist William A. Fowler (1911–95). His later theories have been controversial, including the suggestions that life on Earth has an extraterrestrial origin, and that viruses arrived from space. His publications include works of popular science and science fiction.

Hoysala An Indian dynasty, first Jain and later Hindu, which ruled the south Deccan *c*.1006–1346, from a capital at Dwarasamudra (near Mysore). Beginning as marauding hill chieftains, they finally established sway over a region corresponding to the later MYSORE state.

Hsiung-nu See XIONGNU.

Hua Guofeng (or **Hua Kuo-feng**) (1920–) Chinese statesman. Hua won a succession of key posts between 1968 and 1975, becoming acting Premier after the death of ZHOU ENLAI in 1976. He succeeded MAO ZEDONG as chairman of the Central Committee, having defeated a challenge from the GANG OF FOUR. Hua resigned as Premier in 1980 and as chairman in 1981. He was re-elected to the CCP Central Committee in 1987, and again in 1992.

Huainan An industrial and mining city in east central China, in the province of Anhui; pop. (1990) 1,228,000.

Huambo A city in western Angola, founded in 1912; pop. (est. 1995) 400,000. It was called Nova Lisboa until 1978.

Huang He (or **Hwang Ho**) (Chinese, 'Yellow River') The great river of north China, flowing for some 4,700 km (2,900 miles) from its source in the Kunlun Mountains of the Tibetan autonomous region to a northern gulf of the Yellow Sea. It runs turbulently at first, through a series of gorges, and once off the plateau turns north to skirt the Ordos desert in a great bend. Forced south again by the

Lang Shan highlands it enters LOESS country, picking up huge quantities of yellow silt. After receiving its two main tributaries, the Fen He and the Wei He, it turns east through the Sanmen Gorge and so emerges on to the North China Plain. Here it broadens out to become fan-shaped, the yellow silt forming a vast delta which has become one of China's most fertile regions.

Hubble, Edwin Powell (1889–1953) US astronomer. In 1929 he demonstrated that the distance of a galaxy from the Earth is directly proportional to its observed velocity of recession from us (**Hubble's law**), a natural consequence of a uniformly expanding Universe. It implies that the age of the Universe is inversely proportional to a constant of proportionality (**Hubble's constant**) in the mathematical expression of the law. Current estimates of this constant are still uncertain to a factor of at least two, but suggest an age for the Universe of between ten and twenty thousand million years.

Hubble classification A scheme suggested by HUBBLE for the classification of galaxies. It was originally thought that it gave some insight into the evolution of galaxies with time. Hubble thought that almost spherical elliptical galaxies (designated Eo) gradually flattened until they resembled thin lenses (E7), then took one of two paths, becoming normal SPIRAL GALAXIES (So to SC) or BARRED SPIRAL GALAXIES (SBa to SBc). The So galaxies, known as LENTICULAR GALAXIES, have a central bulge and disc but no spiral arms. A normal spiral galaxy was thought to develop spiral arms at the expense of the massive central nucleus, the arms becoming more loosely coiled from Sa to Sc. In the case of barred spiral galaxies it was thought that a brightly luminous bar developed across the nucleus, with a spiral arm springing from each end of the bar. More recent study of galaxies and the stars within them has cast doubt on this evolutionary scheme but as a handy classification of the different kinds of galaxy it is still useful.

Hubble space telescope (HST) A 2.4 m (94-inch) REFLECTING TELESCOPE, named after Edwin Powell HUBBLE, put into Earth orbit on 25 April 1990 by the space shuttle *Discovery*. The telescope, which is controlled from Earth, is designed to make observations in the ultraviolet, optical, and infrared regions of the spectrum and has a wide variety of auxiliary equipment including two spectrographs, a photometer and two cameras. The data are transmitted to Earth stations for analysis. From its position above the Earth's atmosphere, the HST enables a volume of the Universe some 350 times as large as the present observable Universe to be examined, and detects light from objects which are seven times further from the Earth than has been possible using Earth-based telescopes. Unfortunately, a built-in error in shaping the secondary mirror prevented the telescope from operating to its full potential. The error was corrected in space by astronauts from the space shuttle *Endeavour* in 1993.

huckleberry The fruit of two *Gaylussacia* species native to North America. The dwarf huckleberry or dangleberry has a large, round, bluish fruit. The black huckleberry has shining, black berries, and grows in woodlands and swamps of northeast America. Blueberries are sometimes wrongly called huckleberries.

Hud In Islamic belief, one of the four prophets sent specifically to the Arabs. Numerous legends surround Hud, who, in the Koran, preached monotheism unsuccessfully to his people, 'Ad, a tribe 'who built monuments in high places' and who are associated with Iram of the Columns, a legendary terrestrial paradise.

Huddersfield A town that developed as a textile-manufacturing centre in West Yorkshire, England, on the River Colne; pop. (1981) 148,540. The University of Huddersfield (formerly Polytechnic of Huddersfield) was established here in 1992. It has developed light industries.

Hudson A river rising in the Adirondacks in north-east USA, and flowing south for over 500 km (300 miles) to enter New York Bay. The scenic grandeur of its upper reaches, with their falls and rapids, gives way to wider vistas south of Lake Champlain where it is joined by the Mohawk. From here on it is navigable. The final stretch, called the North River, is linked by the Harlem River to the East River and Long Island Sound.

Hudson, Henry (*c.*1565–1611) English explorer. He discovered the North American bay, river, and strait which bear his name. In 1607 and 1608 he conducted two voyages in search of the North-east Passage to Asia, reaching Greenland and Spitzbergen on the first and Novaya Zemlya on the second. In 1609 he explored the NE coast of America, sailing up the Hudson River to Albany. During his final voyage in 1610 he attempted to winter in Hudson Bay, but his crew mutinied and set Hudson and a few companions adrift, never to be seen again.

Hudson, William Henry (1841–1922) British naturalist and writer, born in Argentina. Hudson was brought up by his US parents in Argentina, moving to England in 1869. After he had spent some thirty years in London he received a pension which enabled him to spend periods elsewhere, and he became a prolific author. Hudson was an astute observer and lover of nature, his works ranging from the exotic (*The Naturalist in La Plata*, 1892) to the familiar (*Nature in Downland*, 1900).

Hudson Bay A penetration of the Arctic Ocean, well over 1,000 km (600 miles) into the north-east of the North American continent. Its depression was created when that part of the CANADIAN SHIELD was crushed by Pleistocene ice-sheets. Only the coasts and islands of the southern half are forested. The western shores tend to be low and marshy, the eastern ones rocky and more barren. Many rivers run into the Bay, which is generally navigable from July to October. It connects with the Atlantic Ocean through the Hudson Strait and with the Arctic Ocean through the Foxe Channel.

Hudson's Bay Company A company chartered in 1670 to Prince RUPERT and 17 others by Charles II to govern and trade in the huge area of the Canadian north-west, called Rupert's Land, which drained into Hudson Bay. Although huge profits accrued from the fur trade, the company was, until 1763, threatened by competition and military attack from the French. From 1787 there was occasionally murderous conflict with the North-West Company over control of the fur trade until the two companies amalgamated in 1821.

Hué A port and industrial city in central Vietnam, near the mouth of the Hué River in the province of Binh Tri Thien; pop. (est. 1992) 219,150. A former capital of Vietnam (1802–1945), it was the ancient capital of the Nguyen dynasty. In addition to the imperial city there are many pagodas and royal tombs. It is a market centre of a rich farming area.

Huggins, Sir William (1824–1910) British astronomer. He pioneered spectroscopic analysis in astronomy, showing that nebulae are composed of luminous gas, and that some comets contain hydrocarbon molecules. He discovered the red shift in stellar spectra, correctly interpreting it as being due to the Doppler effect and using it to measure recessional velocities.

Hughes, Howard (Robard) (1905–76) US industrialist, film producer, and aviator. When his father died in 1924 he took control of the Hughes Tool Company; this formed the basis of his large fortune. He made his début as a film director in 1926; notable titles include *Hell's Angels* (1930) and *The Outlaw* (1941). From 1935 to 1938 he broke many world aviation records, sometimes while flying an aircraft of his own design. For the last 25 years of his life he lived as a recluse.

Hughes, (James Mercer) Langston (1902–67) US writer. He began a prolific literary career with *The Weary Blues* (1926), a series of poems on black themes using blues and jazz rhythms. He is best known for his poetry, which includes the collections *The Negro Mother* (1931) and *Shakespeare in Harlem* (1941). Among his other writings are two novels, collections of stories, and a number of plays.

Hughes, Ted (full name Edward James Hughes) (1930–) British poet. His work is pervaded by his vision of the natural world as a place of violence, terror, and beauty, as can be seen in his first volume of poetry, *The Hawk in the Rain* (1957). This vision is continued in later works; *Crow* (1970) explores the legends surrounding creation and birth through the character of the sinister and mocking crow. Hughes was appointed Poet Laureate in 1984. From 1956 to 1963 he was married to the US poet Sylvia PLATH; the poems in his *Birthday Letters* (1998) commemorate their life together.

Hughes, Thomas (1822–96) British novelist. He is remembered as the author of *Tom Brown's Schooldays* (1857), evoking Rugby School which he attended when Dr Thomas Arnold was headmaster. Other works include *Tom Brown at Oxford* (1861), biographies, memoirs, and sermons.

Hugli See HOOGHLY.

Hugo, Victor(-Marie) (1802–85) French poet, novelist, and dramatist. He was a leading figure of French romanticism, and brought a new freedom of diction, subject, and versification to French poetry; his many collections include *Les Feuilles d'automne* (1831). He set out his ideas on drama in the preface to his play *Cromwell* (1827); this included the view that the theatre should express both the grotesque and the sublime of human existence and became a manifesto of the romantic movement. The success of his drama *Hernani* (1830) signalled the triumph of romanticism over the conventions which had prevailed in French theatre since the time of Racine and Corneille. *Notre Dame de Paris* (1831) and *Les Misérables* (1862) are among his best-known novels and demonstrate Hugo's concern for social and political issues. Between 1851 and 1870 he lived in exile in Guernsey, where he wrote his satire against Napoleon III (*Les Châtiments*, 1853).

Huguenot In the 16th and 17th centuries, a French Protestant who followed the beliefs of CALVIN. By 1561 there were 2,000 Calvinist churches in France and the Huguenots had become a political faction that seemed to threaten the state. Persecution followed and during the French WARS OF RELIGION the Huguenots fought eight civil wars against the Catholic establishment and triumphed when, by the Edict of NANTES in 1598, HENRY IV gave them liberty of worship and a 'state within a state'. Their numbers grew, especially among merchants and skilled artisans, until they were again persecuted. The centre of their resistance in 1627 was LA ROCHELLE, which the RICHELIEU government had to besiege for over a year before capturing it. In 1685 the Edict was revoked; many thousands of Huguenots fled to England, the Netherlands, Switzerland, and Brandenburg, some settling as far away as North America and the Cape of Good Hope. All these places were to benefit from their skill in craftmanship and trade, particularly as silk-weavers and silversmiths.

Huhehot See HOHHOT.

Huitzilopochtli (from Aztec, 'humming bird' and 'left') The Aztec war-god, god of the Sun, lightning, and storms, and protector of travellers. Conceived when some hummingbird feathers, associated in Aztec belief with the soul of a dead warrior, fell from heaven, Huitzilopochtli emerged from the womb of the Earth-goddess Coatlicue fully armed. He saved her from the anger of her 400 other offspring, the stars of the southern sky, and the Moon goddess. His animal disguise was the eagle. Often portrayed with hummingbird feathers and snakes, Huitzilopochtli's primary weapon was a turquoise snake. He was the pre-eminent god to whom large numbers of human sacrifices were made at the time of the Spanish conquest.

Hukbalahap Filipino peasant resistance movement with roots in the pre-war *barangay* (village) and tenant organizations in central Luzon. Led by Luis Taruc, the movement developed during World War II into the Anti-Japanese People's Army, a left-wing guerrilla organization which was as much opposed to the Filipino landlord élite and their US backers as to the Japanese. Active against the latter from 1943, the 'Huks' controlled most of central Luzon by the end of the war, but were denied parliamentary representation and went into open rebellion against the Manila government until all but destroyed by government forces between 1950 and 1954.

Hull (officially **Kingston upon Hull**) A city, port, and unitary authority in north-east England, situated at the junction of the Hull and Humber rivers; pop. (1991) 252,200. It is linked to the south bank of the estuary by a bridge completed in 1981. The University of Hull was founded in 1954 and the University of Humberside (formerly Humberside Polytechnic) was established in 1992. Formerly a fishing port its trade is now with northern Europe. It has engineering and chemical industries.

hull-and-core structure See SKYSCRAPER.

Human Genome Project A coordinated international project, begun in 1988, to map the entire sequence of genes on all 23 pairs of chromosomes making up the human genome. The total number of genes has been estimated at about 100,000, although some scientists have suggested that a figure of around 2 million may be more realistic. Completion of the project is expected within the first ten years of the 21st century. The project has already resulted in the identification of the genes associated with specific hereditary diseases, and in the discovery of a genetic component in many other diseases. It is hoped that this will lead to the development of drugs for treating such diseases and to screening tests for people known to be susceptible to them.

human immunodeficiency virus (HIV) See AIDS.

humanism An intellectual movement in which man is regarded the centre of the Universe. There is no systematic theory of humanism, but any world-view claiming that the only source of value in the world is man, or more loosely that man supplies the true measure of value, may be described as humanist. The relations between humanism and religious thought are complex, but humanism, by virtue of its belief in human perfectibility, contradicts the doctrine of ORIGINAL SIN. In this way humanism also has connections with individualism, the notion that the goal for man includes the fulfilment of each person by the cultivation of his or her own individual nature, and with a belief in the possibility of social progress.

Historically, humanism was fully articulated for the first time in the 15th-century RENAISSANCE. Humanists were originally Christian scholars who studied and taught the humanities (grammar, rhetoric, history, poetry, and moral philosophy) by rediscovering classical Latin texts, and later also Greek and Hebrew texts. They came to reject medieval SCHOLASTICISM, and made classical antiquity the basis of western Europe's educational system and cultural outlook. Among their ranks can be numbered PETRARCH, Guicciardini, and MACHIAVELLI. They had no coherent philosophy, but shared an enthusiasm for the dignity of human values in place of religious dogma or abstract reasoning.

The invention of PRINTING enabled the movement's ideas to spread from its birthplace in Italy to most of western Europe. Thomas MORE, ERASMUS, and John Colet all contributed to the humanist tradition. Its spirit of sceptical enquiry prepared the way for both the REFORMATION and some aspects of the COUNTER-REFORMATION.

MARX may be described as a humanist, and in this century humanism has been given expression, in both secular and religious forms, in EXISTENTIALISM.

human rights The rights to which all humans are held to be entitled. The human rights guaranteed by international codes fall into three broad classes: first, individual civil and political liberties (freedom from arbitrary arrest, detention without trial, and torture or other maltreatment; freedom of movement, association, and expression; religious, conscientious, and philosophical liberty); secondly, social and economic rights and freedoms (rights to EDUCATION, health care, work, fair conditions of employment, and maintenance of at least a minimum standard of living); thirdly, the 'third-generation' collective rights (the rights of peoples), designed to advance the position of minorities and bolster self-determination and equality, as well as to control the capacity of richer nations to use their resources to exploit poor ones. The international codes that set out these rights include the Universal Declaration of Human Rights (1948); the EUROPEAN CONVENTION ON HUMAN RIGHTS (1950); the INTERNATIONAL COVENANT ON CIVIL AND POLITICAL RIGHTS (1966); the International Convention on Economic, Social, and Cultural Rights (1969); the AFRICAN CHARTER ON HUMAN AND PEOPLE'S RIGHTS (1981); and the International Convention on the Rights of the Child (1989). These treaties bind states that are parties to them in INTERNATIONAL LAW, but do not automatically form part of the municipal law of any state. However, they require states to ensure that citizens have adequate legal redress for breaches of the guaranteed rights. See also BILL OF RIGHTS; CIVIL RIGHTS.

Humayun (1508–56) The second MOGUL emperor of India (1530–40, 1554–55). His name means 'fortunate', yet after ten years of precarious rule he was driven into exile in Persia, recovering his empire only shortly before his death in an accident.

Humber A river estuary in Humberside, north-east England, formed at the junction of the Ouse and Trent rivers near Goole. The Humber flows 60 km (38 miles) eastwards to enter the North Sea at Spurn Head.

Humberside A former county of north-east England. It was formed in 1974 from parts of the East and West Ridings of Yorkshire and the northern part of Lincolnshire. In 1996 it was abolished and administrative powers were devolved to the unitary authorities of Kingston upon Hull, East Riding, North Lincolnshire, and North East Lincolnshire.

Humboldt, Friedrich Heinrich Alexander, Baron von (1769–1859) German explorer and scientist. Humboldt travelled in Central and South America (1799–1804) and wrote extensively on natural history, meteorology, and physical geography. He proved that the Amazon and Orinoco river systems are connected, and ascended to 5,877 m (19,280 ft) in the Andes, the highest ascent ever made at that time, researching the relation of temperature and altitude. He spent the next 20 years in Paris writing up his results, returning later to Berlin, where he served at the Prussian court. He wrote a popular work in several volumes, *Kosmos* (1845–62), describing the structure of the Universe as it was then known.

Humboldt Current See PERU CURRENT.

Hume, David (1711–76) Scottish philosopher, economist, and historian. His philosophy rejected the possibility of certainty in knowledge, and he agreed with John Locke that there are no innate ideas, only a series of subjective sensations, and that all the data of reason stem from experience. His philosophical legacy is particularly evident in the work of 20th-century empiricist philosophers. In economics, he attacked mercantilism and anticipated the views of such economists as Adam Smith. Among his chief works are *A Treatise of Human Nature* (1739–40) and a five-volume *History of England* (1754–62).

humerus See ARM.

humidity The degree to which air is moist or damp; it can be measured as absolute humidity, specific humidity, or relative humidity. Absolute humidity is the actual mass of WATER VAPOUR in a given volume of air and is expressed in kilograms per cubic metre. Specific humidity is the mass of water vapour in a given total mass of air (including the water vapour). Relative humidity is the proportion of this quantity to the mass that would be present if the air were saturated (containing the maximum amount of water vapour) at the same temperature. It is usually expressed as a percentage, completely dry air having a relative humidity of 0 per cent, and fully saturated air 100 per cent. In terms of the Earth's atmosphere, relative humidity is the more significant quantity, especially with regard to meteorological processes, biological response, and human comfort. This is because the body's perspiration does not evaporate as readily when the relative humidity is high, so to keep cool in humid heat humans perspire more profusely. In hot weather a fall in humidity can bring as much relief as a fall in temperature. The amount of water vapour the air is capable of holding before condensation occurs depends on temperature: warm air can contain more water vapour than cold air.

hummingbird A member of a large family,

Trochilidae, containing about 320 species, which are confined to the New World, mostly to South and Central America. They include the vervain humming bird, *Mellisuga minima*, the smallest of all birds at 6 cm (2.25 inches) long, and weighing 2 g (0.08 ounce). The largest, the giant humming bird, *Patagona gigas*, is only just over 20 cm (8 inches) long. Most are dark green with a bright sheen, but they may have bright iridescent patches of other colours, especially reds and blues. Many species are crested or have distinctively shaped tails. All have long, thin beaks and long tongues with which they can gather nectar from flowers as they hover in flight. Some also take insects and small spiders. They build neat, tiny nests and lay two pure white eggs; those of the vervain hummingbird weigh only 0.2 g (0.008 ounce). Most stay in the same area all the year round, but the ruby-throated hummingbird, *Archilochus colubris*, which breeds as far north as Canada, migrates to Central and South America for the winter.

humpbacked whale A species of WHALEBONE WHALE, *Megaptera novaeangliae*, so named by whalers because it arches its back when rolling over to dive. These whales congregate every spring in Hawaiian waters, remaining there for several months, to give birth and to mate. One calf is born about a year after mating. Solitary males sing day and night for months on end, and a song can last for 35 minutes before being repeated. While following its regular migration routes, the humpbacked whale visits every ocean, spending the winter in the tropics, travelling in schools or alone. A large individual can reach a length of 15 m (50 feet) and weigh up to 50,000 kg (110,000 pounds).

Humperdinck, Engelbert (1854–1921) German composer. He was influenced by Wagner, whose opera *Parsifal* he helped to prepare for performance. He is chiefly remembered as the composer of the opera *Hänsel und Gretel* (1893).

humus A mixture of organic matter in various states of decay and the organisms that have caused its decomposition (largely bacteria and fungi). It is formed by the decomposition of dead plants and animals in natural ECOSYSTEMS. A modified form may be produced naturally as COMPOST. Humus is essential to the structure and drainage properties of soil. It helps to retain nutrients and water in sandy soils, and assists aeration of heavy, fine-particle, clay soils.

Hunan A province of east-central China, to the south of the Yangtze River; area 210,000 sq km (81,112 sq miles); pop. (1990) 60,660,000; capital, Changsha. Its chief products are coal, lead, zinc, antimony, rice, tobacco, sugarcane, and oil-bearing crops, such as rape and sesame.

hundred An administrative subdivision of an English SHIRE between the 10th century and the Local Government Act (1894), which established District Councils. Hundreds were probably based upon units of 100 hides. (A hide was a measure of land, calculated to be enough to support a family and its dependants, ranging from 25 to 50 ha. (60–120 acres) according to locality.) They did not exist in every shire. Their equivalents in the DANELAW were wapentakes, in Kent lathes, in Yorkshire ridings, and in Sussex rapes. The hundred court of freeholders met once a month to deal with military defence, private pleas, tax levies, and to prepare indictments for the royal justices. The hundred bailiff served the sheriff's writs and the constable maintained law and order.

Hundred Days (20 March–28 June 1815) The period between NAPOLEON's return from the island of Elba and the date of the second restoration of LOUIS XVIII. Napoleon landed at Cannes on 1 March while the European powers were meeting at the Congress of VIENNA. He won great popular acclaim as he moved north through Grenoble and Lyons. He arrived in Paris on 20 March, less than 24 hours after Louis had fled. Napoleon's attempt to win over moderate royalist opinion to a more liberal conception of his empire failed. Moreover, he failed to persuade the Allies of his peaceful intentions, and had to prepare to defend France against a hastily reconstituted 'Grand Alliance'. By the end of April he had only raised a total strength of 105,000 troops, the Allies having a force of almost 130,000 men. Nevertheless, Napoleon took the offensive and forced the Prussians to retreat at Ligny. Two days later, on 18 June, Napoleon was defeated at WATERLOO. He returned to Paris and on 22 June abdicated for the second time. Six days later Louis XVIII was restored to power.

Hundred Flowers Movement (1956–57) Chinese political and intellectual debate. The campaign was initiated by MAO ZEDONG and others in the wake of Khrushchev's denunciation of Stalin. Mao argued that self-criticism would benefit China's development. After some hesitation, denunciation of the Communist Party and its institutions appeared in the press and there was social unrest. The party reacted by attacking its critics and exiling many to distant areas of the country in the Anti-Rightist Campaign.

Hundred Years War A war between France and England that lasted for more than a century between the 1340s and 1450s, not as one continuous conflict but rather a series of attempts by English kings to dominate France. The two key issues were the sovereignty of Gascony (the English king was Duke of Gascony and resented paying homage for it to the kings of France), and Edward III's claim, through his mother, to the French throne, following the death of the last CAPETIAN king. Rivalry over the lucrative Flanders wool trade and provocative French support for the Scots against England also contributed.

In 1328 Philip of Valois was crowned King of France and his subsequent confiscation of AQUITAINE (1337) provoked Edward's invasion of France (1338). The English won a naval battle at Sluys (1340) and major military victories at CRÉCY (1346), Calais (1347), and POITIERS (1356), where EDWARD THE BLACK PRINCE captured and later ransomed Philip's successor, John II. In 1360 the Treaty of Brétigny gave Edward considerable territories in France in return for abandoning his claims to the French throne. The French gradually improved their position and in the reign of Edward's successor, his grandson, RICHARD II, hostilities ceased almost completely.

The English retention of Calais and Bordeaux, however, prevented permanent peace, and English claims to France were revived by HENRY V (invoking SALIC LAW). He invaded Harfleur and won a crushing victory at AGINCOURT (1415), followed by occupation of Normandy (1419) and much of northern France. The treaty of Troyes (1420) forced Charles VI of France to disinherit his son, the dauphin, in favour of the English kings. However, following Henry V's early death (1422) the regents of his ineffectual son HENRY VI gradually lost control of conquered territory to French forces under the leadership of JOAN OF ARC. The English were defeated at Orleans (1429) and by 1450 France had conquered Normandy and much of Gascony; Bordeaux, the last English stronghold, was captured in

1453. This effectively ended the war and thereafter the English retained only Calais (until 1558). The English were forced to turn attention to internal affairs, notably the Wars of the ROSES and gave up all claims to France. In France the virtual destruction of the nobility saw the VALOIS monarchy emerge in a strong position.

Hungarian The official language of Hungary, one of the Finno-Ugric languages, spoken by some 11 million people in Hungary and Romania, the only major language of the Ugric branch.

Hungarian Revolution (23 October–4 November 1956) A revolt in Hungary. It was provoked by the presence in the country of Soviet troops, the repressive nature of the government led by Erno Gerö, and the general atmosphere of de-Stalinization created in February at the Twentieth Congress of the CPSU. Initial demonstrations in Budapest led to the arrival of Soviet tanks in the city, which served only to exacerbate discontent, Hungarian soldiers joining the uprising. Soviet forces were then withdrawn. Imre NAGY became Prime Minister, appointed non-communists to his coalition, announced Hungary's withdrawal from the WARSAW PACT, and sought a neutral status for the country. This was unacceptable to the Soviet Union. Powerful, mainly Soviet but some Hungarian, forces attacked Budapest. Resistance in the capital was soon overcome. Nagy was replaced by János KÁDÁR, while 190,000 Hungarians fled into exile. The Soviet Union reneged on its pledge of safe conduct, handing Nagy and other prominent figures over to the new Hungarian regime, which executed them in secret.

Hungary A central European country, bounded by Czech Lands on the north, Romania on the east, Croatia and Serbia on the south, and Austria on the west; it is also conterminous with Ukraine in the north-east.

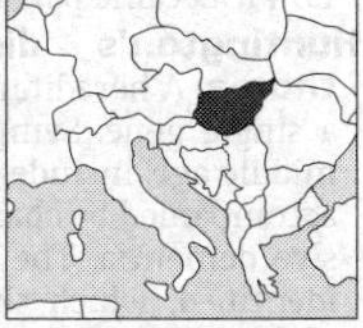

Physical. From north to south through the centre flows the Danube, in a broad plain (the puszta) which extends eastwards to the river Tisza across pastureland and areas suited to agriculture. West of the river is the Bakony Forest of mainly deciduous trees, Lake Balaton (the largest and shallowest lake in central Europe), and a fertile plateau with granite hills. The climate, with cold winters and hot summers, is continental.

Economy. The principal crops are wheat, maize, barley, sugar-beet, potatoes, and grapes, while mineral resources include bauxite, brown coal, lignite, and copper. Increases in Western joint ventures, new management techniques, and the replacement of outdated machinery are measures which aim to revive industrial profitability. Hungary's main exports are machinery and transport equipment, agricultural produce, and computer software. Tourism is an expanding source of revenue.

History. The region comprising the Roman provinces of Pannonia and Dacia was overrun by Germanic tribes in the DARK AGES and then conquered by CHARLEMAGNE. By 896 elected MAGYAR Arpad leaders ruled and Hungary emerged as the centre of a strong Magyar kingdom in the late Middle Ages. A Mongol invasion devastated the population in 1241 and the Arpad line ended in 1301. Thereafter, the crown was usually passed to a foreigner. The advance of the OTTOMAN EMPIRE threatened, especially after the battle of Nicopolis in 1396, when Sigismund, King of Hungary, was defeated by the Turks. John Hunyadi (died 1456) and his son Matthias Corvinus brought revival, but in 1490 the Jagiellons gained the throne, and, in 1515, a HABSBURG claim arose. The disastrous defeat of the Hungarian king, Louis II, at Mohács (1526), led to the partition of Hungary between the Habsburgs and the Ottomans although TRANSYLVANIA retained its independence. By 1711 all of Hungary had come under Habsburg rule and remained part of the Habsburg empire until 1919.

In the 19th century Magyar nationalism was antagonized by the repressive policies of METTERNICH, leading to rebellion under KOSSUTH in 1848. The Austrians, with Russian help, reasserted control. After defeat by PRUSSIA the Austrians compromised with the Magyars in 1867, setting up AUSTRIA-HUNGARY, or the Dual Monarchy, which was first and foremost an alliance of Magyars and Austrian Germans against the Slav nationalities. Defeat in World War I led to revolution and independence, first under Károlyi's democratic republic, then briefly under Béla KUN's communist regime. Dictatorship followed in 1920 under Horthy, and lasted until 1944. Allied to the AXIS POWERS in World War II, defeat brought Soviet domination and a communist one-party system. This was resented and, briefly, in 1956, the HUNGARIAN REVOLUTION saw resistance to the Soviet Union. Hungary experienced some degree of liberalization during the latter years of János KÁDÁR's regime (1956–88). Demonstrations in Budapest in 1988 resulted in multi-party politics being restored. Elections brought to power the Hungarian Democratic Forum (MDF) early in 1990; but after the collapse of COMECON, trade fell and there was rising unemployment and popular discontent. Refugees from Romanian Transylvania and from disintegrating Yugoslavia caused additional problems. A programme of ambitious reforms to revive the economy and introduce a free-market system were launched in 1990. These reforms progressed steadily with the privatization of many companies in 1991, accompanied by increasing foreign investment. However, continued economic recession and domestic political problems resulted, in the general election of May 1994, in the heavy defeat of the MDP. A new coalition, led by the Hungarian Socialist Party under Gyula Horn, took office. A small degree of economic growth was recorded in 1995, despite a sense of economic crisis in the country, which led to the introduction of economic austerity measures.

Capital: Budapest
Area: 93,033 sq km (35,920 sq mi)
Population: 10,231,000 (1995)
Currency: 1 forint = 100 filler
Religions: Roman Catholic 62.4%; Protestant 23.4%; atheist and non-religious 12.9%; Orthodox 0.5%; Jewish 0.8%
Ethnic Groups: Magyar 96.6%; German 1.6%; Slovak 1.1%; Romanian and gypsy 0.7%
Languages: Hungarian (official); minority languages
International Organizations: UN; CSCE; Council of Europe; North Atlantic Co-operation Council

Huns Pastoral nomads famed for their horsemanship, who in *c.*370 AD invaded south-eastern Europe and conquered the OSTROGOTHS. In 376 they drove the VISIGOTHS into Roman territory and early in the 4th century themselves advanced west, driving the VANDALS and others west into Gaul, Italy, and finally Spain. Under ATTILA (434–53) they ravaged the Balkans and Greece, but a defeat was finally inflicted on them in 451 at the CATALAUNIAN FIELDS by the Romans and Visigoths under the command of Aetius. However that did not prevent them penetrating and plundering Italy the following year. Two years after the death of Attila they were decisively defeated near the unidentified River Nedao, and thereafter ceased to be of historical significance. The White Huns occupied Bactria and territory west towards the Caspian Sea. They vigorously attacked the power of the SASSANIDS, defeating and killing Peroz in 484, but then moved south to establish an empire in northern India at the expense of the GUPTAS.

Hunt, (William) Holman (1827–1910) British painter. In 1848 he co-founded the Pre-Raphaelite Brotherhood and was the only member of the group to remain true to its aims. He made several visits to Egypt and the Holy Land to ensure that his biblical scenes accurately reflected local settings, as in *The Scapegoat* (1855). Much of his painting has a didactic or moral purpose which is reinforced by his extensive use of symbolism, as in *The Light of the World* (1854).

Hunter, John (1728–93) Scottish anatomist and pioneer of modern surgery. He studied anatomy under his elder brother **William Hunter** (1718–83), London's foremost obstetrician, going on to become a founder of scientific surgery and making valuable investigations in pathology, physiology, and biology. He selected specimens to illustrate his ideas and exhibited them in a house he had built in London. Some of his exhibits were bought from the notorious 'resurrection men', who stole from graveyards to supply anatomists; he once paid £500 for the cadaver of an Irishman 2.5 m (8 feet) tall.

hunter-gatherers People who subsist from the natural environment, without involvement in agriculture or animal husbandry. They survive by gathering wild fruit and vegetables, and by hunting. Theirs is the earliest and simplest form of human organization, and has been found all over the world: Australian ABORIGINES, the Arctic INUIT, and the !KUNG-SAN in southern Africa are all examples of hunter-gatherers. They have a nomadic way of life, following seasonal food supplies. They are organized in bands consisting of close kin, but these bands fluctuate in size as members move in and out, according to food availability. MARRIAGE is a very loose institution, and lineage is not considered of great importance. Hunter-gatherer society is egalitarian: leadership is usually based on individual ability and is not hereditary. Relations between men and women are also more egalitarian than in many sedentary societies, though there is a basic division of labour, the men hunting game while the women do most of the gathering. Many hunter-gatherers are now threatened by economic development, which is destroying the natural environment upon which their survival depends. See also PALAEOLITHIC; STONE AGE.

hunting The pursuit of game or other wild animals for profit or for sport. In the UK, the most popular legitimate form of hunting is the cross-country pursuit of foxes by their scent by mounted members of a hunt and hounds, the latter being controlled by the notes blown on the huntsman's horn. In beagling, hares are the quarry, and the hunters run with or behind their dogs. Some ANIMAL RIGHTS activists oppose hunting as cruel; supporters maintain it is necessary (for purposes of culling or controlling overpopulation) and that as part of the culture of the countryside it should not be interfered with by townspeople. In 1997 the House of Commons voted to ban hunting with hounds.

hunting dog (or **African wild dog**) A species of wild dog, *Lycaon pictus*, found in bush, plains, and semi-desert south of the Sahara Desert. It is found in packs of 4–60 individuals and preys mostly on antelopes. As sick and aged animals lag behind they are caught and rapidly devoured by the dogs. The pack moves continually in search of food, communicating with a soft, clear, musical 'who-who'. At breeding time the dominant female produces a litter which is reared by the entire pack. Four to 16 young may be born and they may live for nine or ten years.

Huntingdon A town in Cambridgeshire, England, on the River Ouse 24 km (15 miles) north-west of Cambridge; pop. (1981) 17,600. It was the birthplace of Oliver Cromwell in 1599.

Huntingdon, Selina Hastings, Countess of (born Selina Shirley) (1707–91) British religious leader. On her husband's death in 1746 she devoted herself to religious and social work and was instrumental in introducing Methodism to the upper classes. Following the expulsion of six theological students from Oxford University on allegations of Methodism, she established Trevecca House in mid Wales as a college for the training of evangelical clergymen in 1768. She was a follower of the English evangelical preacher George Whitefield (1714–70) and made him her chaplain. The Calvinistic Methodist chapels which she helped to establish are still known as 'Countess of Huntingdon chapels'.

Huntingdonshire and Peterborough A former county of eastern England, formed in 1965 from Huntingdonshire and the Soke of Peterborough (an administrative county from 1888 to 1965). In 1974 it became part of Cambridgeshire.

Huntington's disease (or **Huntington's chorea**) A hereditary disease caused by a defect in a single gene. Symptoms, which appear in early middle age, include jerky involuntary movements accompanied by changes in behaviour and progressive dementia. The defective gene has now been identified, which should enable those at risk to make use of genetic screening. The disease is named after the US physician James Huntington (1850–1916), who first described it.

hunting wasp A solitary WASP, the females of which hunt, catching live prey to supply the nest cells in which their young develop. They sting the prey so that it is either killed or paralysed. If it is killed, they inject a chemical to prevent it from decomposing. The spider-hunting wasps (Pompilidae) catch only spiders, but others, including the sand wasps, prey on various insects, especially caterpillars.

Nest cells are usually made in the earth, although in some cases they are constructed with shaped mud pellets. After each cell is filled with food, one egg is laid and the cell sealed. Many families of wasps contain species which can be described as hunting wasps.

Huntsman, Benjamin (1704–76) British inventor of the crucible process for making steel (see IRON AND STEEL INDUSTRY). After apprenticeship to a clock-maker, in about 1740 he set up his own business in Doncaster to make clocks, locks, roasting-jacks, and other small mechanisms. Dissatisfied with the steel available, he set out to improve it, moving to the steel-making area of Sheffield. There, he designed a coke-fired furnace (*c.*1745) that could melt steel in small crucibles, separating out impurities to leave a high-quality steel. Huntsman initially had to sell his steel in France, as the Sheffield cutlers rejected it as being too hard. However, the superiority of imported French cutlery forced them to accept Huntsman's steel.

hurdy-gurdy A musical instrument with strings rubbed by a wheel, instead of a bow. One or two strings are stopped by pressing wooden blades against them with the fingers; others are DRONES. The instrument is thus a stringed equivalent of the BAGPIPE. It derived from the earlier forms, such as the 11th-century organistrum and the 13th-century symphony. It was one of the aristocratic 'folk' instruments of Marie Antoinette's court, but after the Revolution of 1789 it reverted to folk use, and is still found over much of Europe.

Huron (or **Wyandot**) A confederation of five Iroquoian Indian groups living north-east of Lake Huron. Known to themselves as Wyandot or Wendat ('people of the peninsula') and surviving today in Quebec and Oklahoma, they were named Huron ('bristly-headed ruffian') by the French explorer Samuel de Champlain when he first encountered them in 1615.

Huron, Lake The second-largest of the five Great Lakes of North America, divided between Canada and the USA; area 63,096 sq km (24,361 sq miles); area on the Canadian side of the border, 39,473 sq km (15,240 sq miles); maximum depth 229 m. It is linked to Lake Michigan in the west by the Straits of Mackinac, to Lake Superior in the north by St Mary's River, and to Lake Erie in the south via Lake St Clair and the St Clair River.

hurricane A severe tropical revolving storm, in particular one in which the wind reaches a speed of 65 knots or more (120 km/h, 75 m.p.h.). A hurricane is also the name sometimes given to a wind of hurricane force on the BEAUFORT SCALE, with a minimum speed as above. Such a wind is not necessarily associated with a tropical revolving storm.

Hurston, Zora Neale (1901–60) US novelist. In 1928 she graduated in cultural anthropology and continued her studies into the folklore of the Deep South until 1932. Her novels, which include *Jonah's Gourd Vine* (1934), *Moses, Man of the Mountain* (1938), and *Seraph on the Suwanee* (1948), reflect her continuing interest in folklore. Her work was largely ignored after her death until the novelist Alice Walker instigated a revival of interest in her writings, many of which, including her autobiography *Dust Tracks on a Road* (1942), have since been reprinted.

Husain The second son of Ali and of the Prophet Muhammad's daughter Fatima, and martyred third Imam of *Ithnā 'Asharī* in Shiite Islam. Refusing to swear allegiance to the Umaiyad caliph Yazid, Husain and his small force of warriors were massacred. Under the Buyids, and later even more so under the Iranian Safavids, the martyrdom of Husain and his companions became a central event in Shiite history. Husain's tomb in Kerbala is the most important Shiite shrine. According to one legend, Husain married Shahrbanu, a daughter of Yazdagird, the last Sassanian king of Persia. The Safavids, who transformed Shiism into the state religion of Iran, claimed descent from this union.

Husain, ibn Talal See HUSSEIN, IBN TALAL.

Husain, Saddam See HUSSEIN, SADDAM.

Husák, Gustáv (1913–91) Czechoslovak statesman, leader of the Communist Party of Czechoslovakia 1969–87 and President 1975–89. He succeeded Alexander Dubček as leader of the Communist Party; the latter had been removed in the wake of the Soviet military invasion which suppressed the Prague Spring, the attempted democratization of Czech politics in 1968. Husák's objectives were to re-establish order, to purge the party of its reformist element, and to implement a new federalist constitution. He was ousted during the velvet revolution of 1989.

Huss, John (or **Jan Hus**) (*c*.1372–1415) Bohemian religious reformer. A preacher in Prague and an enthusiastic supporter of WYCLIF's views, he aroused the hostility of the Church, was excommunicated (1411), tried (1414), and burnt at the stake. By his death he was acclaimed a martyr and his followers (HUSSITES) took up arms against the HOLY ROMAN EMPIRE and inflicted a series of dramatic defeats on the imperial army.

hussar A soldier of a light cavalry regiment. Hussars were originally mounted troops raised in 1485 by Matthias Corvinus, King of Hungary, to fight the Turks. As good light cavalry was scarce, other countries soon developed their own hussars: FREDERICK II (the Great) proved the superiority of Prussian hussars over those of Austria during the War of the AUSTRIAN SUCCESSION. Britain hired hussars from several German states in the 18th century, sending them to America where they were hated by the patriots.

Hussein, Abdullah ibn See ABDULLAH IBN HUSSEIN.

Hussein, ibn Ali (1856–1931) Arab political leader. A member of the Hashemite family, he was sharif of Mecca and leader of the 1916 Arab revolt. In 1916 he assumed the title of King of the Arab Countries, but the Allies only recognized him as King of the HEJAZ. As ruler of the Hejaz (1916–24) he came into conflict in 1919 with Ibn SAUD, the Emir of Najd. He abdicated in favour of his son Ali in October 1924. His son Abdullah became ruler of TransJordan, and another son, FAISAL I, founded the royal line of Iraq.

Hussein, ibn Talal (or **Husain**) (1935–) King of Jordan since 1953. Throughout his reign Hussein has steered a middle course in his policies, seeking to maintain good relations both with the West and with other Arab nations. However, in 1967 he attacked Israel in the Six Day War, was defeated, and lost the West Bank and half the city of Jerusalem. After this defeat the Palestine Liberation Organization based itself in Jordan but after a short civil war in 1970 the Palestinians were expelled. In 1990 he acted as a mediator between the opposing sides following the Iraqi invasion of Kuwait, but in the subsequent Gulf War Jordan was the only Middle Eastern country to give open support to Iraq. More recently he has advocated peaceful relationships in the Middle East, gaining the support of President Clinton with whom he had talks in 1993. In 1994 he signed a treaty normalizing relations with Israel, and in the same year had talks with Itzhak RABIN, at whose funeral in 1995 he spoke of continuing the peace process.

Hussein, Saddam (or **Husain**) (full name Saddam bin Hussein at-Takriti) (1937–) Iraqi President, Prime Minister, and head of the armed forces since 1979. In 1968 he played a leading role in the coup that returned the Baath Socialist Party to power. As President he suppressed opposing parties, built up the army and its weaponry, and made himself the object of an extensive personality cult. During his presidency Iraq fought a war with Iran (1980–88) and invaded Kuwait (1990), from which Iraqi forces were expelled in the Gulf War of 1991. Forced to accept the UN terms for a ceasefire, he failed to cooperate with UN inspectors. He also ordered punitive attacks on Kurdish rebels in the north of Iraq and on the Marsh Arabs in the south.

Husserl, Edmund (Gustav Albrecht) (1859–1938) German philosopher. His work forms the basis of the school of phenomenology; having originally trained as a mathematician he turned to philosophy, seeking in his work the clarity and certainty he found in mathematics and science. He rejected metaphysical assumptions about what actually exists, and explanations of why it exists, in favour of pure subjective consciousness as the condition for all experience, with the world as the object of this consciousness. He taught at the University of Freiberg, where Martin Heidegger was among his pupils.

Hussey, Obed (1792–1860) US inventor of a mechanical reaper, which he patented in 1833. It embodied a saw-toothed cutter working with two guard bars. He began manufacture in Cincinnati, but encountered a rival in MCCORMICK, who had patented his own reaper in 1834. Bitter competition developed between them, but Hussey's refusal to adapt his machine in light of other new inventions resulted in McCormick's firm emerging as leader of the US market.

Hussites Followers of John HUSS, the Bohemian religious reformer who was put to death by the Council of CONSTANCE in 1415. Even before his death Huss had a large following in various parts of his native country BOHEMIA and his execution at the stake sparked a nationwide protest, notably in the signing of a solemn protest by 452 nobles on 2 September 1415. Later the Hussite movement split into two main parties: the moderate Utraquists and the Taborites (named after Mount Tabor, their fortified stronghold), who held more extreme theological and social views. The Taborites were eventually defeated by an alliance of Utraquists and Roman Catholic forces at the battle of Lipany in 1434. Most of the Utraquist demands were granted by the Church at the Compactata of Prague in 1436. Some groups of Hussites survived until today, under various names, but the movement was largely overtaken by the Reformation in the 16th century.

Huston, John (1906–87) US-born film director. After a varied background as a boxer, cavalryman, journalist, and actor, he made his début as a film director in 1941 with *The Maltese Falcon*. A number of successful adventure films followed, including *The Asphalt Jungle* (1950), *The African Queen* (1951), and *Moby Dick* (1956); more recent successes include *Prizzi's Honour* (1985). He became an Irish citizen in 1964.

hutia A cavy-like RODENT that, with the coypu, forms the family Capromyidae. Hutias differ from coypus in possessing harsh coats rather than soft fur and in being terrestrial and not aquatic. They are confined to the Caribbean, where 12 living species (nine restricted to Cuba) and four recently extinct species are known. The populations of those hutias that survive are generally in decline.

Hutton, James (1726–97) Scottish geologist. Hutton's views, controversial at the time, became accepted tenets of modern geology. In opposition to Abraham Werner's Neptunian theory, he emphasized heat as the principal agent in the formation of land masses, and held that rocks such as granite were igneous in origin. He described the processes of deposition and denudation and proposed that such phenomena, operating over millions of years, would account for the present configuration of the Earth's surface; it therefore followed that the Earth was very much older than was believed. Hutton's views were not widely known until a concise account was published in 1802.

Hutton, Sir Leonard (known as 'Len') (1916–90) British cricketer. In his long career he played for Yorkshire (1934–55) and for England (1937–55). He scored a record 364 in the 1938 test against Australia and became the first professional captain of the England team in 1953.

Hutu A Bantu farming people of East Africa, who comprise the majority of the people of Rwanda and Burundi.

Huxley, Aldous (Leonard) (1894–1963) British novelist and essayist. During the 1920s and 1930s he lived in Italy and France; his fiction during this period included *Antic Hay* (1923), *Point Counter Point* (1928), and the futuristic *Brave New World* (1932), probably his best-known work. In 1937 he left for California, where he remained for the rest of his life and pursued his interests in Eastern mysticism and parapsychology. In 1953 he experimented with psychedelic drugs, writing of his experiences with mescalin in *The Doors of Perception* (1954).

Huxley, Andrew Fielding (1917–) British physiologist and grandson of Thomas Henry HUXLEY. He worked with Sir Alan HODGKIN on the physiology of nerve transmission.

Huxley, Sir Julian (1887–1975) British biologist. He contributed to the early development of the study of animal behaviour, was a notable interpreter of science to the public through writing and broadcasting, and became the first director-general of UNESCO (1946–48). He was the grandson of Thomas Henry HUXLEY.

Huxley, Thomas Henry (1825–95) British biologist. A qualified surgeon, Huxley made his reputation as a marine biologist during service as a ship's surgeon off the coast of northern Australia. Later he turned to the study of fossils, especially of fishes and reptiles, and became a leading supporter of Darwinism in opposition to Richard Owen. On the basis of a detailed study in anthropology he wrote *Man's Place in Nature* (1863), and coined the word *agnostic* to describe his own beliefs. Huxley was a supporter of education for the less privileged and argued for the inclusion of science in the school curriculum. He was the grandfather of Sir Julian HUXLEY and Aldous HUXLEY.

Huygens, Christiaan (1629–95) Dutch physicist, mathematician, and astronomer, best known for his pendulum-regulated clock invented in 1656. He improved the lenses of his telescope, discovered a satellite of Saturn, and also Saturn's rings, which had eluded GALILEO. In dynamics he studied such topics as centrifugal force and the problem of colliding bodies, but his greatest contribution was his wave theory of light, made public in 1678. He formulated what has become known as 'Huygen's principle', that every point on a wave front is the centre of a new wave, which enabled him to explain the REFLECTION and REFRACTION of light.

Hwang Ho See HUANG HE.

hyacinth A perennial bulb-bearing plant of the genus *Hyacinthus*, of which about 30 species are known, chiefly from the Mediterranean region. Hyacinths are members of the lily family. The popular florists' varieties, with their densely packed spikes of scented flowers, are descended from *Hyacinthus orientalis* and its variety *provincialis*. The variation in flower colour, which occurs naturally in this species, has been exploited by plant breeders and a multitude of red, blue, creamy yellow, and white varieties are now available for indoor or outdoor garden cultivation. A well known closely related plant is the common English bluebell, *Hyacinthoides nonscripta*, which has deep blue or occasionally pink or white tubular flowers.

Hyatt, John Wesley (1837–1920) US inventor and pioneer of the plastics industry. His inventions included a water-purification system, a sugar-cane mill, a machine for straightening steel rods, a multi-stitch sewing-machine, and a widely used roller bearing. In the 1860s he became interested in finding a substitute for the ivory used to make billiard balls. With his brother Isaac he developed CELLULOID, a blend of NITROCELLULOSE and camphor, for which he took out a patent in 1870.

hybrid An organism resulting from interbreeding between different species, varieties, strains, races, or populations. In nature, hybridization between SPECIES is usually prevented by differences in courtship behaviour, physical incompatibility, or abortion of the hybrid embryo. This is important since, although any particular species is well adapted to its way of life, hybrids may not be so. When hybrids between species do arise, as in the case of the mule (offspring of a mare and a male ass) and the zebroid (from a horse or ass and a zebra), they are infertile.

In contrast, hybridization between individuals of races, subspecies, strains or varieties of the same species often occurs. For example, all breeds of dog belong to the same species, and hybrids between breeds are easily produced. The same is true of many plants. The offspring of such mixed parentage frequently show hybrid vigour, growing much faster and to a greater size than either parent and often with the beneficial characteristics of both parents. This phenomenon has been used to advantage in the breeding of new varieties of crops such as maize and rice. The rice strain IR8, developed in the 1960s, shows high yield, low tendency to lodge (collapse), pest and disease resistance, and a favourable response to fertilizers. The superiority of hybrids has encouraged plant breeders in particular to attempt to overcome the barriers to interbreeding between species, and many of the superior seeds on sale today are 'F_1 hybrids'.

hydatid A stage in the life cycle of the TAPEWORM genus *Echinococcus*. Adult worms inhabit the gut of a variety of carnivores, including dogs, and larvae are found as cysts in the tissues of sheep. If ingested by humans, the eggs develop into cysts, several centimetres in diameter, which contain many daughter cysts. Surgical removal is difficult as rupture may lead to multiple recurrence.

Hyde, Edward See CLARENDON, EDWARD HYDE, EARL OF.

Hyde Park The largest of the royal parks in west-central London, between Bayswater Road to the north and Kensington Road to the south. Once owned by the Church as part of the Manor of Hyde, it was taken by the Crown in 1536. At the instance of Queen Caroline the park was improved in the 1830s with the creation of the Serpentine and the building of walkways, lodges, ponds, and arches to a plan by Decimus Burton. The south-east corner of the park is known as **Hyde Park Corner** and the north-east corner near Marble Arch, with its soap-box orators, is known as Speakers' Corner.

Hyderabad A city, capital of the state of Andhra Pradesh in central India, on the River Musi; pop. (1991) 3,005,000. Founded in 1589 as a Muslim stronghold, it was capital of the kingdom of Golconda and of the former state of Hyderabad, and has many ancient buildings including tombs and mosques. It has four universities (founded 1918, 1964, 1972, and 1974) and research institutions. Hyderabad is a commercial centre and a centre of craft industries.

Hyderabad (or **Haidarabad**) A city in south-east Pakistan, on the Indus; pop. (1991) 1,000,000. Founded by Ghulam Shah Kalhora in 1768, it was until the arrival of the British in 1843 the capital of the province of Sind. Its university was founded in 1947 and its industries produce clothing, leather shoes, lacquered-wood furniture, and handicrafts.

hydra A cylindrical POLYP belonging to the phylum Cnidaria, and part of the class Hydrozoa along with colonial hydroids such as the Portuguese man-of-war. Hydras may be found amongst almost any pondweed; each polyp will extend to about 1 cm (0.4 inch) if undisturbed. The tentacles sway gently, until contacted by *Daphnia* or other aquatic organisms, whereupon stinging cells discharge and the prey is drawn into the mouth, its empty skin being ejected hours later. Hydras can move by cartwheeling on their tentacles to reattach their base to another plant or rock. They can reproduce by budding from their own stalk, releasing the new hydras once they are large enough. Most species exist as separate males or females; males release sperm into the water around females to fertilize the egg. The egg is produced as a resistant shell which overwinters.

Hydra (in Greek mythology) A many-headed monster slain by Hercules as one of his Labours. When Hercules cut off one head, two more grew in its place. He solved this problem by instructing a companion to hold a burning brand to the wound as each head fell.

Hydra (in astronomy) The Water Snake, the largest CONSTELLATION, winding more than one-quarter of the way around the sky. It straddles the celestial equator, and in Greek mythology represents the multi-headed serpent slain by Hercules as one of his labours. Its brightest star is Alpha Hydrae of second magnitude and known as Alphard, an Arabic name meaning 'the solitary one'.

hydrangea A shrub of the genus *Hydrangea*, which belongs to the saxifrage family. This genus includes 80 species of deciduous shrubs, a few trees, and some climbers, native to an area stretching from the Himalayas to Japan and south-east Asia, and to the temperate New World. Many are cultivated for their showy heads of flowers. In many species there are sterile, usually marginal flowers, which act as visual attractants to insect pollinators. There are also forms with globular heads of entirely sterile flowers, known as hortensias. The flowers may be white, pink, or blue; some of the blue forms produce pink flowers if grown on lime-rich soils.

hydrate A compound that contains WATER OF CRYSTALLIZATION. Hydrates are crystalline solids containing a definite proportion of water molecules. The water may be held in the crystal in various ways but is loosely bonded, and on warming is driven off, leaving an anhydrous salt. Some common examples include copper(II) SULPHATE ($CuSO_4.5H_2O$) and washing soda ($Na_2CO_3.10H_2O$). If the salt contains a TRANSITION METAL, there is often a colour change when the water of crystallization is removed: copper(II) sulphate changes from blue to white.

hydraulic mining A surface MINING technique in which mineral deposits are removed by a large jet of water under high pressure. It requires an enormous supply of water together with a means of recovering the ore from the rock–water slurry produced. In the hydraulic mining of GOLD, the gold settles behind baffles, while the lighter waste matter is washed away. In hydraulic COAL-MINING, the water simply breaks coal fragments from the seam and washes them to a collecting point. Debris disposal is a problem, and hydraulic mining has been criticized for its effect on the environment. It is used only where less drastic techniques cannot be employed. Hydraulic mining coupled with suction removal is also used for the mining of mineral deposits on the sea-bed.

hydraulic ram The piston–cylinder combination used to operate a press, a jack, or part of a machine, such as the jib of a CRANE or an agricultural implement using hydraulic power transmission. A simple water pump used in rural areas and in Third World countries for domestic or farm water supply from a stream is also called a hydraulic ram.

hydraulics The study of the flow of fluids for engineering purposes. Hydraulic power is power transmitted by means of a fluid, usually water or oil. Since liquids are almost incompressible, large pressures can be used to exert very great force by means of a HYDRAULIC RAM. In 1795 BRAMAH invented the hydraulic press using this principle, and in 1802 went on to propose hydraulic power transmission, using a pump and motor. During the 19th century hydraulic power was widely adopted in ports and cities, using water in an extensive pipe distribution system, with central steam-driven pumping stations and hydraulic accumulators. The latter were tall, vertical rams carrying a large dead weight, which could move up and down to accommodate fluctuating loads. The chief uses of hydraulic power were for cranes, dock gates, swing-bridges, and lifts: Tower Bridge in London is hydraulically operated. Oil later replaced water as the working fluid, being a better lubricant for pumps, motors, and rams, and avoiding CORROSION and freezing. A range of hydraulic pumps is available, which can achieve pressures of more than 300 bar (30×10^6 N/m^2). Hydraulic motors are generally similar to pumps. A typical hydraulic circuit consists of supply tank, filter, pump and relief valve, control-valve, motor or ram, and oil cooler – the last is needed because energy losses in any component appear as heat, which must be removed. A major application is in farm TRACTORS for controlling the plough or other implement. Hydraulic power is also used in earth-moving equipment. Many machine-tools, especially presses, are hydraulically operated, as are winches, steering gear, and other items aboard ships. Many large aircraft rely on hydraulic operation of main control surfaces, landing gear, and brakes. Motor-car BRAKING SYSTEMS are usually hydraulic.

hydrocarbon A member of a large group of organic chemicals, containing only the elements HYDROGEN and CARBON. They are major constituents of crude petroleum and NATURAL GAS, from which certain fractions are extracted for use as fuel and as raw materials for the CHEMICAL INDUSTRY. In hydrocarbon molecules, carbon atoms form chains, which may be straight, branched, or joined to form rings. Hydrocarbon molecules containing only single bonds between carbon atoms (alkanes) are said to be saturated; those with double (alkenes) or triple bonds (alkynes) are unsaturated. Hydrocarbons that contain the BENZENE RING in their structure are called aromatic; those without such a ring are called aliphatic. The wide range of structural features in hydrocarbon molecules gives rise to a vast number of different compounds, many of which are important in manufacturing plastics, textiles, and drugs. See also HOMOLOGOUS SERIES.

hydrochloric acid (HCl) An aqueous solution of the strong corrosive acid, hydrogen chloride. Hydrogen chloride gas was made originally from the reaction of SULPHURIC ACID with sodium chloride (SALT), but it is now obtained as a by-product of reactions between CHLORINE and HYDROCARBONS. Hydrochloric acid is used widely in the chemical industry to manufacture metal chlorides, dyes, adhesives, and glucose. Large quantities are used to remove oxide coatings from iron or steel that is to be galvanized, tin-plated, or enamelled.

hydrodynamics The study of the motion of bodies in any fluid, not necessarily water. The fluid is usually an incompressible liquid, motion in gases usually being regarded as AERODYNAMICS. It is customary to treat the liquid as a continuous medium for the purpose of modelling real situations: for example, the flow of oil in a pipeline, or the performance of submarines. ARCHIMEDES formulated his famous law of flotation while studying the properties of solid bodies immersed in fluids, giving rise to the notion of fluid pressure. Other phenomena that are studied include fluid density, viscosity, and turbulence.

hydroelectricity The generation of electric power using the energy of flowing water. Hydroelectric systems range from small local generators producing a few hundred watts to major POWER-STATIONS producing more than 1,000 MW (1GW). The

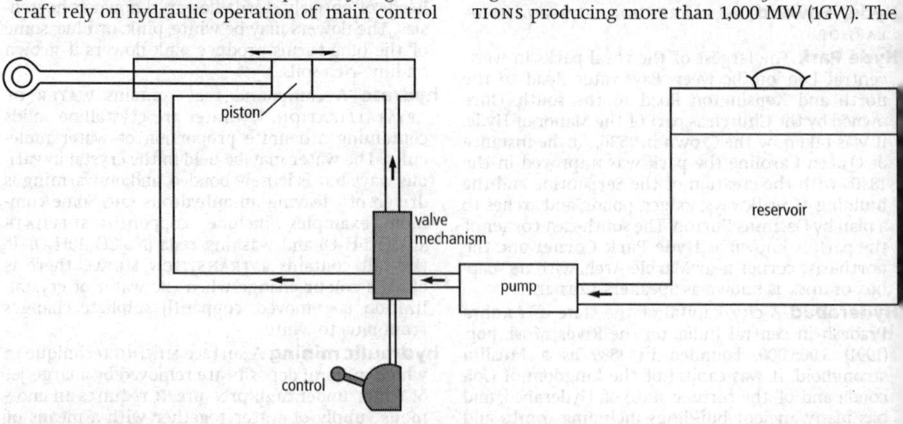

Hydraulic ram The pump creates a hydraulic pressure and the valve mechanism controls the direction in which this pressure forces the piston to move.

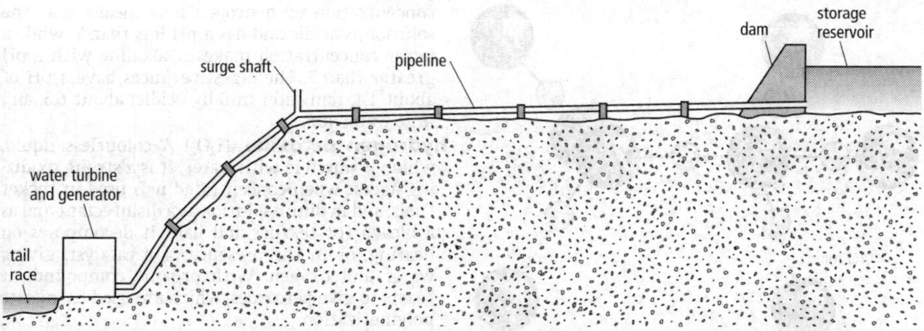

Hydroelectricity Water stored in a reservoir behind a dam is allowed to fall through a pipeline to the water turbine below it. The turbine drives a generator. The amount of electric power generated depends on the distance through which the water falls (the head) and the volume of water delivered to the turbine in unit time.

earliest hydroelectric plant was commissioned in 1880 on a private estate (Cragside) in Northumberland, UK, and the first installation in the USA followed within two years. In the late 1980s hydroelectricity accounted for nearly a fifth of the world's electric power. The main features of any hydroelectric installation have remained essentially the same for 100 years. They are the GENERATORS and the TURBINES that drive them, and a DAM, or barrage, to store water to allow a degree of independence from fluctuations in the natural supply. The head (the vertical distance through which the water falls) determines the speed and pressure of the water at the turbines, and the power output depends upon this and on the volume of water delivered per second. These two factors also largely govern the design of the installation. A power-station on a slowly flowing river or a tidal estuary requires a water control system and turbines suitable for large volumes of water at a relatively low head. In mountainous regions, where the head is much greater, the water is usually fed through tunnels, shafts, and pipes (the penstocks) and reaches the turbines as a fast-flowing stream, often at high pressure. See also PUMPED STORAGE.

hydrofluoric acid (HF) An extremely corrosive acid, a solution of hydrogen fluoride in water. It reacts with glass (it is used for etching glass) and is stored in either wax or plastic bottles. Anhydrous liquid hydrofluoric acid is widely used as a CATALYST in the PETROCHEMICALS industry and as a reagent for producing fluorine-containing compounds.

hydrofoil A light craft designed to travel largely above rather than along the water surface. Below the hull are foils (specially shaped surfaces akin to AEROFOILS) mounted on struts. Sails or engines provide power, and as the craft gains speed the foils rise, lifting the hull out of the water. In 1956 the first commercial hydrofoil went into operation. There are two basic types of hydrofoil. In the first, surface-piercing foils support the vessel completely out of the water, with the foils travelling along the surface. In the second type the foils remain partially submerged, improving stability and control but reducing speeds.

hydrogen (symbol H, at. no. 1, r.a.m. 1.01) A colourless, odourless gas that burns readily in air; in its free state it consists of diatomic molecules, H_2, and has the lowest density of all gases. Hydrogen is by far the most abundant element in the Universe. It accounts for two-thirds of the mass of the Universe and it is thought that it was created in the earliest moments after the BIG BANG, when the temperature fell to such a level that protons and electrons could combine to form hydrogen atoms. Hydrogen is present in stellar interiors, where some of it is converted to helium by nuclear fusion reactions; it also exists in interstellar space, where it radiates at the twenty-one centimetre line. On Earth it is less abundant, although it occurs in water, petroleum, coal, and all living matter. Except in negligible quantities, it does not occur naturally as a free element. It reacts with metals to form compounds containing the H^- ion, and with non-metals to give covalent compounds; in this respect it is similar to the HALOGENS. However, some of its compounds when dissolved in water give H^+ ions; and here hydrogen resembles the ALKALI METAL elements. In consequence it is not placed in a group in the periodic table. H^+ ions cause acidity; the pH of a solution is related to the HYDROGEN ION CONCENTRATION. Hydrogen is formed industrially from steam or oxygen and methane, or from steam and coke. It is also a by-product of the CASTNER-KELLNER CELL. It is used in the manufacture of ammonia by the HABER–BOSCH PROCESS, in hydrotreatment, in making methanol and petrochemicals, and in the hydrogenation of foodstuffs, such as the manufacture of margarine. Liquid hydrogen is used as a fuel for ROCKET MOTORS. It is no longer used for filling large balloons; it has been replaced by helium, which has less lifting power, but is not flammable. Hydrogen is in many ways the ideal fuel, providing large amounts of energy when burned, with water vapour as the only combustion product. There has been much interest in the idea of a hydrogen energy 'economy', in which hydrogen produced from water (most probably by ELECTROLYSIS) could be used for heating, powering vehicles, etc.

hydrogen bomb See NUCLEAR WEAPON.

hydrogen bond A weak bond between a hydrogen atom in one molecule and an atom in a second molecule (or a different part of the same molecule). Hydrogen bonds only form in certain circumstances: both the atom to which the hydrogen atom is linked in its own molecule, and the atom in the second molecule, must be strongly electronegative (fluorine, oxygen, or nitrogen). The resulting attraction is a hydrogen bond, the strongest of the INTERMOLECULAR FORCES. A result of hydrogen bonding is a high melting-point and boiling-point. A compound is likely to dissolve in a solvent with which it can form hydrogen bonds. Ethanol can form a hydrogen bond with water, so it mixes

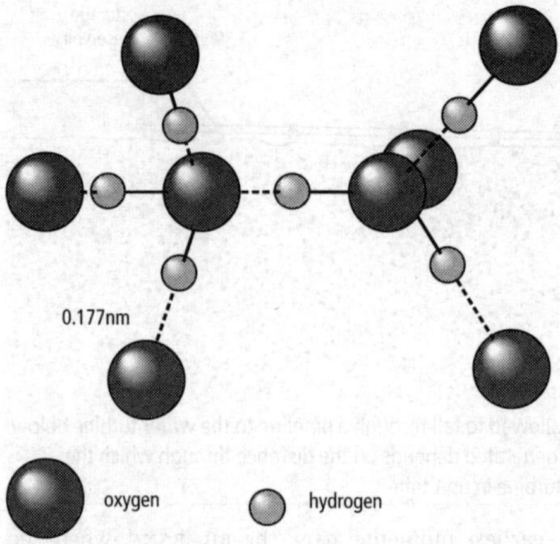

Hydrogen bond Hydrogen bonds (shown as dotted lines) between water molecules.

readily with water. In contrast, ethane cannot, so it is insoluble. The complex structure of many biological molecules is a result of hydrogen bonding. For example, the helical structure of many proteins results, to a large extent, from hydrogen bonding between different parts of the helix.

hydrogen ion concentration A measure of the number of hydrogen ions present in a solution. Although these ions are produced by the DISSOCIATION of acids, the concentrations are still small. They are therefore expressed as the logarithm of the reciprocal of the actual hydrogen ion concentration $[H^+]$. This measure is called the pH (an abbreviation for 'potential of Hydrogen'), and is expressed mathematically as $pH = -\log [H^+]$. It can be determined absolutely using a glass electrode, or less accurately by using coloured indicators and a calibrated scale. In alkali solutions the concentration is so small that very sensitive equipment is needed to obtain a meaningful measurement. The rate of many chemical reactions in solution, particularly those in the body, depends critically on the hydrogen ion concentration; it is carefully controlled and stabilized in BUFFER SOLUTIONS. In neutral solutions the pH works out at 7; a greater concentration of hydrogen ions means that the solution is acidic and has a pH less than 7, while a lesser concentration makes it alkaline with a pH greater than 7. The digestive juices have a pH of about 1.4, rainwater (mildly acidic) about 6.5, and lime water 10.5.

hydrogen peroxide (H_2O_2) A colourless liquid, which is miscible with water. It is a strong oxidizing agent; when concentrated it is used in rocket fuels, and in dilute solution as a disinfectant and as a bleach for textiles and hair. It decomposes on heating, or in the presence of a catalyst, giving water and oxygen. With organic compounds it reacts to give peroxides, which are used to initiate polymerization.

hydrogen sulphide (H_2S) A colourless, poisonous gas. Natural gas and volcanic emissions contain hydrogen sulphide, and it is produced by putrefying organic matter, such as bad eggs. Its foul smell is characteristic of stink bombs.

hydrological cycle (or **water cycle**) The continuous, cyclic movement of water molecules between oceans, atmosphere, and land, little water being gained from volcanic eruptions or lost to the upper atmosphere. The transfers involve changes of state between vapour, liquid, and solid, and the energy producing these changes comes from heat derived from solar radiation. Water itself is a major heat store, so its cycling involves transfers of heat. The oceans store 97 per cent of all the water in the system. This moves slowly between the Equator and the poles, and between the surface and abyssal depths, as currents driven both by winds and by differences in temperature and salinity. Of the remaining 3 per cent of global water stores, 2.25 per cent is locked in glaciers and icecaps, perhaps for thousands of years. A further 0.75 per cent is stored in rivers, lakes, and as groundwater, while only 0.001 per cent is stored in the atmosphere. Movement of water between these stores ensures a worldwide annual average of 86 cm (34 inches) of precipitation. Water evaporates from the sea and is carried by winds until it falls as rain, hail, or snow. If it falls into the ocean, the cycle is completed; but if it falls on land, more complex processes occur. Snow must melt into water. Some of the rain is intercepted by plants or buildings and may evaporate. Of that which reaches the surface, some is stored for short peri-

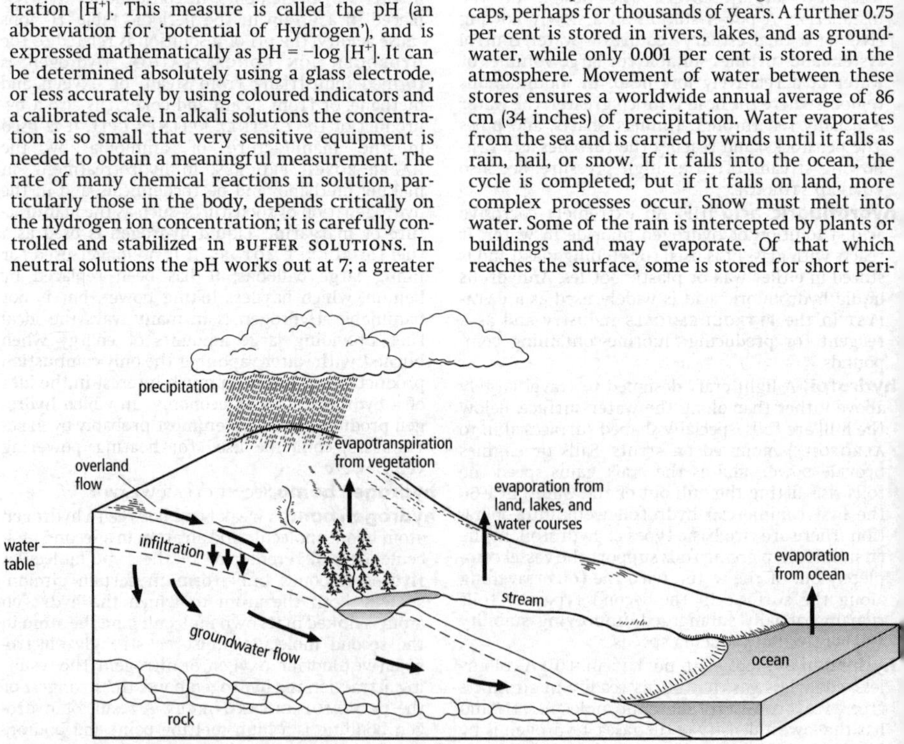

Hydrological cycle Water flows between the oceans, clouds, and land in a continuous cycle. Some 97 per cent of the Earth's water is stored in the oceans.

ods in hollows and may either evaporate or undergo infiltration. Some will infiltrate immediately and be stored in the soil. It may subsequently be lost by evapotranspiration, or it may either travel through the soil as 'throughflow' to rivers or sink to the WATER-TABLE and become 'groundwater'. Heavy rain or melting snow may pass as surface runoff into rivers and lakes. River channels transfer runoff, throughflow, and groundwater from springs, to lakes or the sea, thereby completing the cycle.

hydrology The study of water and its effects on land areas. Estimating the relative proportions of precipitation, evaporation, transpiration, infiltration, and surface runoff of the HYDROLOGICAL CYCLE in a particular locality is fundamental to water resources management. In planning dams, irrigation schemes, methods of flood control, hydroelectric power projects, or indeed any use of lakes and rivers, understanding is required of variations in the supply and flow of water in a particular place, and of the sediment it carries. Measurements of the changing volume and chemical composition of surface water are related to variations in climatic and ground conditions. Predictions are made of the occurrence of floods and low flows in rivers. The changing yields of AQUIFERS and springs are monitored.

hydrolysis A chemical reaction in which a molecule is broken down by water, and the water itself is also decomposed. For example, an ester, such as ethyl ethanoate, $CH_3COOC_2H_5$, reacts with water in the presence of an acid catalyst to form ethanoic acid, CH_3COOH, and ethanol, C_2H_5OH. One of the hydrogen atoms in the water is incorporated into the ethanol, and the oxygen and the other hydrogen into the ethanoic acid.

hydrometer An instrument used to measure the relative density of a liquid. It consists of a large glass float with a long calibrated stem. The hydrometer is weighted so that it floats vertically with the stem partially immersed. The depth of immersion depends on the relative density of the liquid: the greater the relative density, the less liquid is displaced by the hydrometer, and the less it is immersed. To avoid an unduly long stem, hydrometers usually cover only a limited range. Optical and electrical systems can be linked with a hydrometer if continuous recordings are required.

hydroponics The process of growing plants on a sterile inert material such as sand, gravel, or liquid, without soil but continuously provided with nutrients in solution. In this way it is possible to control the balance of inorganic nutrients such as potassium, sulphur, magnesium, and nitrogen, supplied to the plant, and to provide the correct mixture for a particular stage of plant growth. Crops are planted in 1-m (3-foot) wide beds with movable shades to control sunlight. Hydroponics has a particular application for the production of crops, such as green peppers and aubergines in GREENHOUSES, but has also been applied on a larger scale, particularly in desert regions, where water supply and soil are very poor.

hydrosphere The whole body of water that exists on or close to the surface of the Earth. This includes the oceans, seas, lakes, and the water in the atmosphere.

hydroxide ion (OH^-) An ion found in metal hydroxides. In solution hydroxide ions give rise to alkalinity, and when they are added to the H^+ ions present in acidic solutions they form water molecules, and neutralize the acid.

hydroxyl group An oxygen atom covalently bonded to a hydrogen atom. Hydroxyl groups are characteristic of alcohols, phenols, and carboxylic acids. Oxygen has a higher ELECTRONEGATIVITY than hydrogen, so a hydroxyl group has a DIPOLE moment, the hydrogen being the positive end of the dipole. This polarity determines much of the chemistry of the hydroxyl group. For example, under certain circumstances, the hydrogen dissociates as an H^+ ion and the molecule acts as an acid. Because of the high concentration of negative charge on the oxygen, it can act as a NUCLEOPHILE, as in the formation of esters.

Hydrus The Little Water Snake, a CONSTELLATION of the southern sky introduced by Pieter Dirkszoon Keyser and Frederick de Houtman at the end of the 16th century, snaking between the Large and Small MAGELLANIC CLOUDS. Its brightest star, Beta Hydri, is of third magnitude.

hyena A mammal of the family Hyaenidae, containing four Old World species including the aardwolf, found on the plains of Africa, Arabia, and India. The coat of coarse fur is tawny grey or black with either irregular blotches of black or brown, or black stripes on the body and legs. The head is broad with large, rounded ears. They may be 80 cm (2.6 feet) tall at the shoulders and, as the fore-limbs are longer than the hind, the body slopes down to the long, 30 cm (1 foot) tail of coarse hair. Their gait is rolling since the fore- and hind-limb on each side move forward simultaneously.

Although usually considered scavengers, with powerful jaws and teeth, all species will kill animals for food. The spotted hyena, *Crocuta crocuta*, will hunt in packs to kill prey as large as a zebra.

hygrometer See METEOROLOGICAL INSTRUMENTS.

Hyksos (from Egyptian, 'rulers of foreign lands') Invaders, probably from Palestine, who ruled Lower Egypt and part of Upper Egypt from *c.*1674 BC. Their power lasted until *c.*1550 BC, when they were overthrown by a rebellion started by the Egyptians of Thebes. The introduction of the horse and chariot was attributed to them. Egyptian remained the official language.

Hylas See ARGONAUTS.

Hymen In Greek and Roman mythology, the god of marriage, represented as a young man carrying a torch and a veil.

hymn A song or poem set to music in praise of a divine or venerated being. Hymns from India, the Sanskrit *Rigveda*, survive from *c.*1200 BC, and Greek hymns from about the 7th century BC. Christian hymns in the West (in Latin, until the Reformation) date from St Ambrose in the 4th century, the major English writers being Watts and WESLEY in the 18th century. In the 19th century the Hymn Book produced in 1873 by D. L. Moody (1837–99) and I. D. Sankey (1840–1908) contains many popular hymns.

Hypatia (*c.*370–415) Greek philosopher, astronomer, and mathematician. She taught geometry, algebra, and astronomy at Alexandria, and was head of the Neoplatonist school there. Hypatia wrote several learned treatises as well as devising instruments such as an astrolabe. She was murdered by a Christian mob opposed to the scientific rationalism advocated by her Neoplatonist philosophy.

hyperbola A curve with two distinct but identical sections, called branches, each bounded by asymptotes. It is obtained by slicing a cone at a steep angle, so is one of the three kinds of CONIC SECTION. Alternatively it can be regarded as the locus of points in a plane such that the difference

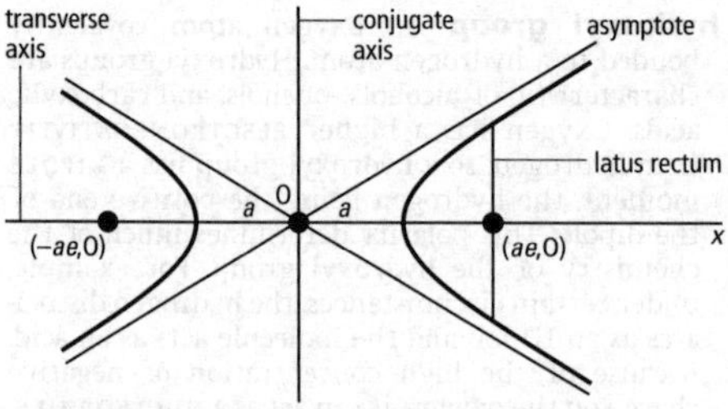

Hyperbola Each branch of a hyperbola is bounded by asymptotes. The points (ae,0) and (–ae,0) are the foci; e is called the eccentricity.

between their distances from two fixed points, the foci, is constant. The simplest algebraic equation for a hyperbola is $x^2/a^2 - y^2/b^2 = 1$; and the asymptotic lines are solutions of $x^2/a^2 - y^2/b^2 = 0$, that is, $y/x = \pm b/a$. If $a = b$ then the asymptotes are at right angles to each other and the curve is called a rectangular hyperbola.

Hyperion A satellite of Saturn discovered independently by the British amateur astronomer William Lassell and the US astronomer George Bond in 1848. Its orbit has a semi-major axis of 1.48 million km and a sizeable eccentricity of 0.104. Hyperion and TITAN are at similar distances from Saturn but their orbital motions are locked together and Hyperion is prevented from approaching Titan too closely because for every three orbits of Hyperion, Titan completes four and the conjunction always occurs when Hyperion is farthest from Saturn. Hyperion is probably the remnant of a catastrophic collision in the early Solar System.

hypermetropia (or **long-sightedness**) The condition that occurs when parallel rays of light come to a focus behind the retina of the eye. This has the effect of making near vision blurred. It is for this reason that most people require reading glasses in middle-age (45–55). These glasses consist of convex lenses, which restore the image to its correct place on the retina.

hypersonic flight Flight at speeds in excess of Mach 5, at which speeds a thin layer of highly turbulent, extremely hot air is formed around the forward portion of the vehicle. Fully hypersonic flow can usually be said to occur at MACH NUMBERS greater than about 8.

hypertension See BLOOD PRESSURE.

Hyphasis The ancient name for the BEAS.

hypnosis A trance-like condition involving apparent alteration in consciousness and MEMORY, during which the subject becomes susceptible to the hypnotist's suggestions. These may produce anaesthesia (absence of sensation), analgesia (insensitivity to pain), paralysis, or apparent regression to childhood. Suggestions made during hypnosis influence the subject after the trance has ended and may induce the subject to forget what has occurred (post-hypnotic amnesia). Hypnosis is a contentious issue. Some believe that it is a special state of consciousness, pointing out that similar trance-like states have been reported since ancient times and in all cultures. Hypnosis has been used in DENTISTRY, obstetrics, and PSYCHOTHERAPY. In all cases the patient's belief in its efficacy seems crucial.

hypnotic See PSYCHOTROPIC DRUG.

hypocaust A Roman heating system in which hot air from a furnace circulates inside a hollow floor. Off a sloped base, 60-cm (2-feet) high brick pillars support large tiles on which the decorative floor is laid. Hollow tiles often line the walls above, forming flues with outlets at high level and increasing the area emitting heat.

hypothalamus The region of the brain in vertebrates that regulates a variety of physiological processes. The main function of the hypothalamus is in coordinating nerve systems that control the viscera, or internal organs. In reptiles, birds, and mammals it is the site of the 'thermostat' that regulates body temperature. In mammals, it controls heartbeat, respiration rate, and blood pressure. It also integrates the NERVOUS SYSTEM and ENDOCRINE GLANDS.

hypothermia A reduction of the body temperature below the normal range. It is liable to occur in babies and the elderly if they are inadequately clothed or live in inadequately heated accommodation. If the body temperature falls very low dangerous internal changes can occur, but above this limit gentle warming will restore the temperature to normal. Hypothermia is also induced deliberately during surgery, especially heart surgery, to reduce the patient's oxygen requirements.

hyrax A primitive ungulate (hoofed mammal), distantly related to elephants and sea-cows. They are about the size of large domestic rabbits, and look like guinea-pigs. The eleven species in the family Procaviidae (order Hyracoidea) occur in Africa and the Middle East. Their resemblance to elephants is seen in the skeleton, the tusk-like incisors, and in the reproductive system, particularly the testes, which do not descend into a scrotum but remain within the abdomen. There are three main groups: rock hyraxes, bush hyraxes, and tree hyraxes. All species are herbivorous.

hyssop A bushy herb of the Mediterranean, *Hyssopus officinalis*, sometimes evergreen and formerly much used in medicine. It was also used in cooking, like its relative, mint. There are about 14 other species within its genus, extending from the Mediterranean to central Asia; the hyssop of the Bible was probably capers, an unrelated plant.

hysterectomy The surgical removal of the womb in cases of cancer of the womb or in non-malignant conditions, such as fibroids, in which there is excessive menstrual bleeding. In an **abdominal hysterectomy** the womb is removed through an incision in the abdominal wall, whereas in a **vaginal hysterectomy** it is removed through the vagina. Although childbearing is no longer possible after a hysterectomy, sexual activity is unaffected.

hysteresis A physical phenomenon in which an induced effect lags behind the cause inducing it. It occurs in several forms, the most common being in induced magnetism, in which the magnetic induction of a ferromagnetic material lags behind the magnetic field. This can be clearly seen in the closed S-shaped graph obtained by plotting the magnetic induction against the inducing field.

hysteria A NEUROSIS often featuring emotional outbursts or sensory abnormalities. There is no evidence of an organic cause. It was while treating hysteria that FREUD formulated his basic psychoanalytic ideas. He suggested that the symptoms were a 'conversion' of repressed sexual conflicts. More recent writers have considered the role of ANXIETY, STRESS, and DEPRESSION in the genesis of hysterical symptoms. The condition causes much distress to sufferers, but is difficult to treat.

I

iambic verse The commonest type of English verse, consisting of metrical units ('feet') known as iambs: these have one unstressed syllable followed by one stressed syllable, as in the word 'beyond'. The most important English form is the ten-syllable iambic PENTAMETER, which is unrhymed in BLANK VERSE and rhymed in HEROIC COUPLETS; the eight-syllable iambic tetrameter is also a common English verse line. In Greek and Latin verse, iambs consist of one short syllable followed by one long syllable, and are found mainly in dramatic dialogue.

Iapetus A satellite of Saturn discovered by Giovanni Domenico CASSINI in 1671. Its orbit has a semi-major axis of 3.56 million km and is inclined to Saturn's orbital plane at 7.5 degrees though the inclination is variable due to perturbations from the Sun. The diameter of Iapetus is 1,460 km and its density is 1,200 kg/m^3.

Ibadan The second-largest city of Nigeria, situated north-east of Lagos; pop. (est. 1991) 1,295,000. It is an industrial and commercial city, capital of the state of Oyo, and intellectual and cultural centre of Yorubaland. Its world-famous university was established in 1948.

Ibarra, Francisco de (1539–75) Spanish explorer credited with the exploration and colonization of Nueva Vizcaya, the huge area of Mexico which today encompasses most of the states of Durango, Chihuahua, and part of Sonora. With funds provided by his uncle, who had made a fortune in the Zacatecas silver mines, Ibarra, as governor of Nueva Vizcaya, opened up much of the northern frontier of New Spain in the 1560s before returning to Mexico City.

Ibarruri Gomez, Dolores (known as 'La Pasionaria') (1895–1989) Spanish Communist politician. A founder of the Spanish Communist Party (1920), she was elected to Parliament in 1936. During the Spanish Civil War (1936–39) she became famous as an inspirational leader of the Republicans. She left Spain after the Nationalist victory and did not return until 1977, when she won re-election to the National Assembly at the age of 81.

Iberia The ancient Roman name for what is now Spain and Portugal. It takes its name from *Iberus*, the Roman name for the River Ebro.

Iberian Peninsula The extreme south-west peninsula of Europe, containing present-day Spain and Portugal. In ancient times it was a centre of Carthaginian colonization until the Third Punic War (149–146 BC), after which it came increasingly under Roman influence. It was invaded by the Visigoths in the 4th–5th century AD and by the Moors in the 8th century.

Ibert, Jacques (François Antoine) (1890–1962) French composer. The Impressionistic orchestral suite *Escales* (1922) reflects his travels in the Mediterranean area. He later worked in Rome as director of the Académie de France (1937–60). Of his seven operas, the witty *Angélique* (1926) has proved the most popular. Though his style is eclectic it is basically NEOCLASSICAL in conception: elegant, humorous, and designed to please.

ibex A species of wild GOAT, *Capra ibex*, found in Asia and Europe. It lives in the vicinity of precipitous cliffs and mountain crags at high altitudes, often above the snowline. It is a typical bearded goat with enormous horns, up to 1.2 m (4 feet) long, which rise close together and sweep back in a wide arc. The coat is usually yellowish-brown in colour. One or two young are born in May or June.

ibis A medium-sized, long-legged bird of the same family as the spoonbill, Threskiornithidae, with a long down-curved bill. The glossy ibis, *Plegadis falcinellus*, is widely distributed throughout the world, but most other species are tropical or subtropical. The sacred ibis, *Threskiornis aethiopicus*, was treated as holy by the ancient Egyptians and often mummified.

Ibiza (or **Iviza**) ▶**1** The third-largest and westernmost of the Spanish Balearic Islands in the Mediterranean Sea; area 572 sq km (220 sq miles). ▶**2** (or **Eivissa**) Its capital, a port and major tourist resort on the south-east coast of the island; pop. (1981) 25,490.

Iblīs In Islam, a fallen angel also called Shayṭan, the personification of evil and the Muslim counterpart of Lucifer (see SATAN). In the Koran it is said that Iblīs refused God's command to bow down before Adam through pride. Instead of immediately being cast into exterior darkness for his sin, God agreed to allow him to tempt mankind until the Day of Judgement. In Islamic belief Iblīs is often considered a jinn, and chief of various demons who afflict the world.

Ibn Batuta (*c.*1304–68) Arab explorer. From 1325 to 1354 he journeyed through North and West Africa, India, and China, writing a vivid account of his travels in the *Rihlah* (undated).

Ibn Gabirol, Solomon Ben-Judah (*c.*1020–*c.*1070) Spanish-Jewish philosopher and poet. Born probably in Malaga, he was the most outstanding of Hebrew secular and religious poets during the Jewish Golden Age in Moorish Spain. He fused the heritage of Hebrew literature with that of the dominant Arab culture of Andalusia, drawing in the KORAN, Arab poetry, philosophy, and ethics. His major philosophical work, *The Fountain of Life*, originally written in Arabic, was in the 12th century translated into Latin under the name of Avicebron. In his *The Royal Crown*, a long meditative poem, he describes the splendours of the Universe, the smallness of man, and the divine grace that infuses both.

ibn Hussein, Abdullah See ABDULLAH IBN HUSSEIN.

Ibo (or **Igbo**) A people of south-east Nigeria whose language, spoken by eight million people, belongs to the Niger–Congo language group. See also BIAFRA.

Ibsen, Henrik (1828–1906) Norwegian dramatist. After the success of his verse drama *Peer Gynt* (1867), he turned to writing prose plays on social issues, including *A Doll's House* (1879) and *Ghosts* (1881). He is credited with being the first major dramatist to write tragedy about ordinary people in prose, and was an important influence on George Bernard Shaw. Ibsen's later works, such as *The Master Builder* (1892), deal increasingly with the forces of the unconscious and were admired by Sigmund Freud.

Icarus (in Greek mythology) The son of Daedalus. Imprisoned by King Minos in Crete, his father built wings of wax and feathers for their escape. Icarus flew too close to the Sun and fell to his death when the wax melted.

Icarus (in astronomy) An ASTEROID discovered by BAADE in 1949. Its orbital perihelion distance of 0.1867 astronomical units ensures that it crosses the orbit of Mercury.

ice ages Periods when the Earth, or part of it, experienced repeated GLACIATION and mean temperatures were about 6°C (13°F) lower than at present. There is geological evidence for several distinct periods when one or more continents were permanently covered in ice; the most recent began about 70,000 years ago and is often called 'the Ice Age'. Ice ages may be initiated as a result of fluctuations in solar radiation and associated variations in meteorological parameters and circulation patterns, in combination with tectonic processes and CONTINENTAL DRIFT.

iceberg A floating mass of ice, usually a detached portion of a polar ice-sheet (see ICE-CAP) or glacier. Icebergs may drift for hundreds of kilometres on ocean currents and last for two years or so before melting. Only a ninth of each mass projects above the surface and the coldness of the surrounding sea encourages fog, so they are a great hazard to shipping.

ice-breaker Any ship built or adapted to break ice. Typically, an ice-breaker is a large ship with extremely powerful engines and a specially strengthened and shaped hull, used to open a passage through pack-ice in high northern or southern latitudes. Where ice is particularly thick, the engines force the bows to ride up over the ice face, and the weight of the ship breaks the ice. HOVERCRAFT have also proved effective in breaking ice by this method. Very large nuclear-powered ships were built as ice-breakers in the former Soviet Union, capable of clearing a channel 30.5 m (100 feet) wide through pack-ice 2.5 m (8 feet) thick.

ice-cap A vast, thick dome of land ice that builds up when low temperatures and heavy snowfalls encourage the transformation of snow into ice. The major examples today are in Antarctica and Greenland, now more properly called **ice-sheets** because of their great size, but more existed in cold periods of the Pleistocene Epoch and they do not necessarily form over high ground: the Greenland cap – more than 3,000 m (10,000 feet) thick at the centre – is located largely over lowland, with mountains at its eastern edge. The sheer weight of the ice depresses the surface beneath, and the ice moves very slowly except where outlet GLACIERS spill over mountain rims.

ice fish A mainly Antarctic fish of the family Channichthyidae, with a large, rather spiny head, and long body without scales. Their most notable feature is their pale, almost colourless appearance, even the gills being pallid, due to the lack of the red blood pigment haemoglobin, which normally transports oxygen within the body. In ice fishes sufficient oxygen to meet their needs is carried in solution in the blood plasma, for they have a sedentary, inactive lifestyle. In recent years they have been caught in numbers by trawling.

ice hockey See HOCKEY, ICE.

Iceland An island country just south of the Arctic Circle in the north-east Atlantic Ocean.

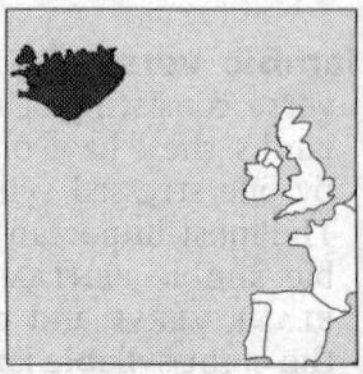

Physical. It is approximately 460 km (285 miles) long by 280 km (174 miles) wide; but only its coastal areas can be used for settlement and agriculture because the rest is a wasteland of ice, ash, and lava flows. It lies at the edge of the Eurasian plate, on the MID-ATLANTIC RIDGE. A hundred volcanoes rise from it – several to over 1,500 m (5,000 feet) – and there are GEYSERS and HOT SPRINGS. The climate is ameliorated by the NORTH ATLANTIC DRIFT.

Economy. Hydroelectric power stations provide over three-quarters of the country's electricity needs and geothermal energy is abundant. Six-sevenths of the land area is agriculturally unproductive. The fishing industry is of vital importance to the economy, accounting for three-quarters of exports; other exports are aluminium (produced from imported alumina) and ferro-silicon. Sheep are grazed in the coastal areas. Iceland has had high rates of inflation, ranging from 40 to 100 per cent in recent years.

History. Iceland was conquered by the VIKINGS between 874 and 930. Its capital, Reykjavik, was founded, and the country was governed by some 36 chieftains, who met periodically in the Althing, an official assembly. A lawspeaker was appointed, and, in 1005, a Supreme Court. Authority, once derived from the pagan priests and temples, changed with conversion to Christianity in *c.*1000 to a partnership of Church and Althing. In 1262 Iceland passed to Norway and, in 1380, with Norway to the Danish crown. Under the rule of Denmark since 1380, a nationalist movement achieved the restoration of the Althing or parliament in 1845. Iceland acquired limited autonomy in 1874 and independence in 1918, although it shared its king with Denmark till 1943. It became an independent republic in 1944. An Allied base during WORLD WAR II, it joined the UNITED NATIONS and NATO (1949). It engaged in sometimes violent disputes with Britain over fishing limits, resulting in the 'Cod War' of 1972–76. In the late 1970s strong opposition to the presence of US bases developed, and Iceland became a nuclear-free zone in 1985. In 1990–91 Iceland attempted to restrict fishing within its territorial waters during negotiations between the EUROPEAN FREE TRADE ASSOCIATION (EFTA) and the EUROPEAN COMMUNITY (EC) over a common European Economic Area (EEA), which it boycotted. However, following the election of a new centre-right coalition government in April 1991,

Iceland managed to secure a restriction on fishing in its waters and introduced measures of economic liberalization, leading to the privatization of many state-owned industries. It also favoured closer relations with the USA, which maintained NATO naval bases in Iceland. The country's worsening economic situation in 1992, caused by losses in the fishing industry (its economic mainstay), led the government to introduce emergency measures and to devalue the króna in 1993. Having finally approved the EEA agreement Iceland made moves towards applying for membership of the EUROPEAN UNION (EU), following the example of Sweden and Finland. In April 1995 a new coalition government was formed, led by David Oddsson, following a general election, and in 1996 Olafur Ragnar Grimsson was elected President.

Capital: Reykjavik
Area: 103,000 sq km (39,769 sq mi)
Population: 269,000 (1995)
Currency: 1 króna = 100 aurar
Religions: Evangelical Lutheran 92.9%; other Lutheran 3.4%; non-religious 1.3%; Roman Catholic 0.9%
Ethnic Groups: (Place of birth, 1988): Iceland 96.3%; Denmark 0.9%; USA 0.5%; Sweden 0.4%; Germany 0.3%
Languages: Icelandic (official)
International Organizations: UN; EFTA; OECD; NATO; Council of Europe; CSCE

Iceni A pre-Roman tribe of eastern England. By the time of the Roman invasion of 43 AD they were part-Romanized and had come under the rule of the dynasty of CYMBELINE. Their ruler Prasutagus was a treaty ally of Rome until his death in 60 AD. The treaty was broken by Rome and his widow BOUDICCA led the tribe in a revolt, which was brutally suppressed.

ice-sheet See ICE-CAP.

ice-skating A popular pastime carried out on outdoor rinks, frozen ponds, lakes, and rivers as well as in purpose-built indoor rinks equipped with an artificial surface. Beginners progress through basic movements to learn elementary turns and spins; they may then go on to ice-dancing and figure-skating, both of which are competitive sports practised to Olympic level. Another activity is long-distance or speed-skating, especially popular in countries with large expanses of outdoor ice, such as the USA, Canada, The Netherlands, Scandinavian countries, Russia, and elsewhere in north-eastern Europe.

ichneumon fly A small, parasitic WASP (not a fly), comprising the largest suborder within the Hymenoptera (bees, ants, wasps, and sawflies) with an estimated 30,000 species. Females search out characteristic microhabitats, such as rotting vegetation, and lay eggs in, on, or near to any suitable host they find. Each species of ichneumon may have a specific host which it parasitizes, or may attack a broad range of insects. Their larvae feed on the larvae or pupae of other insects and spiders, and on spider eggs. Since the host is gradually consumed and eventually dies, they are more like predators than parasites and are now termed parasitoids. Adults are wide-ranging, some feeding on nectar or honeydew, but many do not feed at all. The female characteristically has a long thread-like ovipositor with which she places her eggs into hosts. Some species do not have wings and can reproduce by parthenogenesis.

ichthyology The study of FISHES, including all aspects of their biology.

ichthyosaur A member of a group of extinct marine reptiles, the Ichthyosauria, which lived throughout the Mesozoic Era (245–66 million years ago). They evolved very DOLPHIN-like bodies: no neck, a streamlined form, fish-like tail, large eyes, and limbs transformed into specialized paddles. Ichthyosaurs were permanently aquatic, and certain forms produced live young, rather than laying eggs on land. Their relationship to other reptiles remains uncertain.

Icknield Way An ancient pre-Roman track that crosses England in a wide curve from Wiltshire to Norfolk through the Berkshire Downs and the Chilterns.

icon (Greek *eikon*, 'likeness') An image of a saint or other holy personage particularly of the Byzantine Church and the Orthodox Churches. Icons are generally images that are regarded as sacred in themselves and capable of aiding contact between the worshipper and the person portrayed. They vary considerably in size and appearance, but most typically they are fairly small panels featuring the head of Christ or another holy figure.

Iconoclastic controversy (from the Greek, 'breaking of images') A movement within the Eastern Christian Church in the 8th and 9th centuries that opposed the veneration of icons, both religious paintings and statues. Emperor Leo III banned such veneration in 726 and despite popular antagonism the decision was confirmed by Constantine V in 753. In the seventh ecumenical council of 787 at NICAEA Empress Irene overturned the decrees but they were again enforced under the emperors Leo V, Michael II, and Theophilus. Veneration of icons was finally restored in 843 and the practice still survives in the Eastern Orthodox Church.

iconography The branch of art history dealing with the identification, description, classification, and interpretation of the subject-matter of painting, sculpture, and the graphic arts.

Ictinus (5th century BC) Greek architect. His most famous building was the Parthenon in Athens, which he is said to have designed with the architect Callicrates and the sculptor Phidias between 448 and 437 BC.

id In psychoanalytical theory, the part of unconscious mind governed by instinctive forces, such as the libido and aggression. These forces seek immediate relief in action or in symbolic form. The id is therefore said to be governed by the pleasure principle rather than by reality or logic.

Idaho A state of the north-western USA, bordering on British Columbia to the north and containing part of the Rocky Mountains; area 216,432 sq km (83,564 sq miles); pop. (1990) 1,007,750; capital, Boise. The largest cities are Boise, Pocatello, and Idaho Falls. It is also known as the Gem State, Spud State, or Panhandle State. Idaho was acquired by the USA as part of the Louisiana Purchase in 1803 and became the 43rd state of the Union in 1890. Explored by Lewis and Clark in 1805–06, the first permanent US settlement was eventually established by Mormons at Franklin in 1860. In addition to extensive timber resources the state is rich in minerals such as silver, antimony, cobalt, lead, mercury, vanadium, and zinc. Since World War II irrigated farming (producing one-fourth of the US potato crop) and tourism have become important, the state's chief attractions being the Craters of the Moon National Monument, Nez Percé National Historic Park, Hagerman Fossil Beds National Monument, City of Rocks National Reserve, and the Sun Valley winter-sports resort.

ideal gas (in physics) A hypothetical gas in which the atoms or molecules are assumed to be so small as to be negligible in volume, and there are no forces between them. They travel at high speed and occasionally collide with one another, but these collisions are elastic collisions – that is the total energy of motion of two particles before they collide is exactly the same as it is after the collision. Using these ideas it is possible to derive a very simple relationship between the pressure of a gas, its volume, and its thermodynamic temperature (see GAS).

idealism (in philosophy) A set of views according to which the physical world is dependent upon the mind; we somehow create the world. These doctrines are not as counter-intuitive as they seem because idealists are not saying that our experience of the world is other than it is, but that the explanation of our experience is other than we take it to be. So an idealist will not deny that tables and chairs are physical objects but he or she will give an account of what it is to be a physical object that makes the physical dependent upon the mental.

identikit A composite picture of a person's face, often someone wanted by the police, made up from eye-witness descriptions. Descriptions from different sources often emphasize different features, such as shape of ears and nose, level of hairline, regularity of teeth, and so on. The police identikit uses all these separate features to reconstruct a likeness. Identikit features may be drawn by an artist, or photographs of facial features (photofit pictures) may be used.

ideology A political belief-system that both explains the world as it currently is and suggests how it should be changed. The term was given currency by MARX, who used it to describe the belief-systems of SOCIAL CLASSES, and especially that of the capitalist class or bourgeoisie. Some have sought to reserve the term for political outlooks that are seen as rigid and extreme in contrast to those that are more pragmatic and moderate. It seems better, however, to recognize the pervasiveness of ideology as the means by which people order their perceptions of the social world, whether or not they consciously subscribe to a political creed.

Id ul-Adha (Arabic, 'festival of sacrifice') One of the two major annual Muslim festivals, which occurs on the tenth day of the twelfth month (*Dhu al-Hijja*). It marks the completion of the PILGRIMAGE (*hajj*) to Mecca, and commemorates Abraham's willingness to sacrifice his son Ishmael. The substitution of a ram for Ishmael is symbolized by the sacrifice of animals, performed by both pilgrims and believers throughout the world, and is followed by prayer and celebration. The flesh of the animal is cooked and shared by the donors or given to the poor. The second major festival, *Id ul-Fitr*, marks the end of the month of RAMADAN.

Ieper The Flemish name for YPRES.

Ignatius Loyola, St (1491–1556) Spanish theologian and founder of the Jesuits. After sustaining a leg wound as a soldier, he renounced military life and turned to prayer and mortification. In 1534 he founded the Society of Jesus and became its first general. His *Spiritual Exercises* (1548), an ordered scheme of meditations on the life of Christ and the truths of the Christian faith, is still used in the training of Jesuits. Feast day, 31 July.

igneous intrusion A body of IGNEOUS ROCK that has made its way into pre-existing rock (country rock). Igneous intrusions are emplaced as MAGMA, which is less dense than solid rock and therefore tends to move upwards. It can then force its way through cracks in the rocks and can wedge them apart or, if it is hot enough, it can melt and replace them.

igneous rock Rock that has originated from molten or semi-molten MAGMA. Igneous rocks are composed almost entirely of silicate minerals. Of many different types, they can be classified in various ways: by composition, crystal size, or mode of occurrence. One method is to divide them according to their silica (SiO_2) content into three main groups: acid rocks, basic rocks, and intermediate rocks. Those igneous rocks that crystallize below the Earth's surface are called intrusive if they were formed at shallow depths, such as dolerite. Those that were formed deeper down, such as granite, are said to be plutonic. All these rocks have relatively large crystals produced by slow cooling of the molten magma. Igneous rocks that are extruded at the Earth's surface are called extrusive or volcanic: basalt is an example. The rapid cooling that occurs at the surface does not allow large crystals to form, and these rocks are glassy or contain only small crystals.

ignition system A means of initiating combustion, either for a steady flame, as in an oil or gas burner, or of the fuel–air mixture in a PETROL ENGINE. A common method of gas ignition is by means of a PIEZOELECTRIC CRYSTAL; when subjected to pressure a voltage is produced in the crystal, which can be used to make a spark. In oil burners a continuous spark is produced by an induction COIL, a form of high-voltage transformer. An induction coil is also at the heart of a petrol-engine ignition system. The primary winding of the coil is supplied with a current from the battery through a contact in the distributor. This circuit is broken at exactly the right time by a CAM-operated contact-breaker. The sudden stoppage of current causes a very high voltage, about 25,000 V, to be induced in the secondary winding of the induction coil. This voltage is passed to a spark-plug by the rotating arm of the distributor, which connects each cylinder in turn to the supply. More recent ignition systems use an electronic switch instead of the mechanical contact-breaker. In diesel engines ignition of oil-air mixture is by pressure alone – no spark being required.

Iguaçu Falls One of the great sights of Brazil, on the Iguaçu River just east of its junction with the Paraná, in south-central South America. Hundreds of waterfalls, interspersed among rocky islands along an escarpment of approximately 5 km (3 miles) long, each drop 60 m (200 feet) and more. They provide tremendous potential for hydroelectric power.

iguana A LIZARD making up a family, Iguanidae, comprising over 630 species, which occur mainly in the New World, but also have representatives in Madagascar and Polynesia. Like their Old World counterparts, the AGAMID lizards, iguanas are a diverse family. They are active during the day, and terrestrial, tree-dwelling, and partly aquatic species occur. Most species eat insects but some larger species have a short, fleshy tongue and serrated teeth, and are principally herbivorous. The common, or green, iguana, *Iguana iguana*, may attain a total length of about 2 m (6.5 feet), the tail being much longer than the body. It lives mainly in trees but it is also an excellent swimmer. Other species include the ANOLES, BASILISKS, and SEA LIZARDS.

Iguanodon A genus of bird-hipped DINOSAURS that existed 120–65 million years ago. They were up to 11 m (36 feet) long, were capable of walking bipedally, and had numerous small blade-like teeth suitable for a diet of vegetation. When worn down, the teeth could be replaced by new ones growing from below. The 'thumb' terminated in a sharp, horny spine which may have been used for defence. Their fossil remains have been found in western and central Europe.

IJssel, Lake (Dutch **IJsselmeer**) a shallow lake in the north-west Netherlands forming part of the Zuyder Zee land-reclamation works. A broad barrier dam stretching 30 km (19 miles) from the coast of North Holland to the coast of Friesland was completed in 1932, turning the former inland sea (Zuyder Zee) into a lake (Lake IJssel) on the edge of which five great polders were created, increasing the land area of The Netherlands by six per cent; area 1,200 sq km (463 sq miles).

Ikhnaton See AKHENATEN.

Ile-de-France A region of north-central France, incorporating the city of Paris and comprising the departments of Ville de Paris, Seine-et-Marne, Essonne, Yvelines, Hauts-de-Seine, Seine-Saint-Denis, Val-de-Marne, and Val d'Oise; pop. (1990) 10,660,550.

ilex See HOLLY.

Iliad See HOMER.

Ilium See TROY.

Illich, Ivan (1926–) Austrian-born US educationist and writer. He is chiefly known as a critic of the centralized nature of Western industrial society and as an advocate of the deinstitutionalization of education, religion, and medicine. His books include *Deschooling Society* (1971) and *Limits to Medicine* (1978).

Illinois A state in the Middle West of the USA, to the south and west of Lake Michigan; area 145,934 sq km (56,345 sq miles); pop. (1990) 11,430,600; capital, Springfield. The largest cities are Chicago, Rockford, Peoria, and Springfield. It is also known as the Prairie State. Ceded by France to Britain in 1763 and acquired by the USA in 1783, Illinois became the 21st state of the Union in 1818. The state has associations with Abraham Lincoln whose home (1844–61) in Springfield is a national historic site. Illinois is a leading centre of manufacturing, coal-mining, and agricultural exports.

illumination The decoration of manuscripts with paintings and ornaments, an art that can be traced back as far as the ancient Egyptians and which flourished particularly in the Middle Ages. The decorations can be classified into three main types: miniatures, or small pictures, which sometimes occupy a whole page; initial letters; and borders. The initials and borders sometimes contained devotional and domestic scenes, but were often composed of purely decorative, floral motifs. The art of illumination declined with the invention of the printed book in the 15th century, although early printed books sometimes have illumination added by hand.

illuviation The accumulation or deposition in the lower soil HORIZONS of soluble salts, organic matter, or clay particles (either from suspension or solution) which have been washed down from the upper part of the profile in the process known as LEACHING.

Illyria An ancient region along the east coast of the Adriatic Sea, including Dalmatia and what is now Montenegro and northern Albania. It was subsequently the Roman province of Illyricum.

ilmenite A black mineral consisting of a mixed iron oxide and TITANIUM oxide; an important ore of titanium.

Ilyushin, Sergey Vladimirovich (1894–1977) Soviet aircraft designer. He designed the series of military and civilian aircraft that bear his name, including the DB-3 twin-engined BOMBERS deployed against Finland in 1939–40. He designed jet bombers with I. Yakovlev, and after 1950 also designed jet airliners. His main Soviet rival was TUPOLEV.

image intensifier An electronic instrument that increases the brightness of an image too dim to be seen with the naked eye. The original image is focused on to the screen of a photo-cathode. This device emits electrons in proportion to the light falling on the screen, thus forming an image with electrons. The image is focused on to one or more amplifying elements, each increasing the electron intensity typically 50 times. Finally, a fluorescent screen converts the electrons back to visible light, reproducing the original image, which is now bright enough to see. Image intensifiers are used for night vision with cameras or military equipment, and in astronomy.

image processing Techniques used by computer systems to extract useful information from an image, or two-dimensional representation of a real-world scene. Image processing is related to pattern recognition and ARTIFICIAL INTELLIGENCE and is often used, in some form, in ROBOTICS. It is also widely used on images from, for example, EARTH RESOURCES SATELLITES. In most real-world scenes or other images there is an enormous amount of information, much of it extraneous. The task of the image processing system is to select only those features which are important for interpretation of the image. Such features include boundaries, contours, points, and regions of high contrast or specific texture.

imaginary numbers A subset of the COMPLEX NUMBERS $a + ib$ in which $a = 0$. All numbers of the form ib, where $i = \sqrt{(-1)}$, are imaginary because $i^2 = -1$ does not have a real-number solution. In terms of the ARGAND diagram, they are located on the vertical axis through the origin. The term 'imaginary' is one of several that have been used since the 16th century to describe these numbers; other terms, indicating greater doubt about their acceptability within mathematics, have been 'impossible' or 'absurd' numbers. Imaginary numbers are widely used in science, electronics, and engineering.

imago The sexually mature form of an insect. It is formed after metamorphosis in the life cycle of the insect.

imam (Arabic, 'leader') Among Sunni Muslims, a title conferred upon the person chosen by the community to lead congregational prayer in a MOSQUE. Although the *imam* is usually a person who possesses a theological education, no special qualification is necessary, and any respectable Muslim may fulfil the duty of leading the prayer. The term is also applied by Sunni Muslims to the orthodox caliphs, and to any important teacher or religious leader. In Shiite belief, the title has a complex range of meaning. It indicates the highest rank of authority, spiritual and legitimately temporal, bestowed by the Prophet on a direct descendant of Muhammad and Ali; or the *imam* of the time under Divine guidance.

IMF See INTERNATIONAL MONETARY FUND.

Imhotep (fl. *c.*2700 BC) Egyptian architect and scholar. He is usually credited with designing the step pyramid built at Saqqara for the 3rd-dynasty pharaoh Djoser (*c.*2686–*c.*2613 BC) and, through this, with pioneering the use of hewn stone in building. He was later deified; in Egypt, he was worshipped as the patron of architects, scribes, and doctors, while in Greece he was identified with the god Asclepius.

immigration The movement of people as permanent settlers into a country not their own. The principal motives for immigration are usually the search for better wages and for secure employment, but some immigrants are REFUGEES fleeing political or natural disasters. In recent years, the main flows of immigrants have been from less developed to more developed economies, Germany, the USA, the UK, Canada, Australia, and Italy being the principal destinations. Immigration policies differ, but most countries restrict by law the number of immigrants they will accept, and impose educational, financial, or other requirements on applicants for temporary or permanent residence, or CITIZENSHIP. Discrimination (for or against) immigrants from particular countries is not uncommon. Illegal immigrants may be expelled, and migrant workers may be offered financial and technical assistance as an incentive to return to their country of origin.

Immingham A major container port on the east coast of England, on the Humber estuary northwest of Grimsby; pop. (1981) 11,500.

immobilized cell technology The technique of immobilizing cells by absorbing them on to glass or plastic beads or some other solid support. (ENZYMES can also be immobilized in this way.) Large tonnages of high-fructose syrups and of aspartic and malic acids are produced by FERMENTATION of immobilized bacteria in a bioreactor. Immobilized mammalian cells are used to produce vaccines (see IMMUNIZATION), enzymes, HORMONES, and other substances. Immobilized cells remain productive for longer than cells in a conventional culture, and they are easier to separate from the fermentation products.

immunity The ability of an organism to resist infection by means of the immune system. The immune system has two main parts: white blood cells, and antibodies circulating in the bloodstream. Antibodies are proteins produced by B-lymphocytes (a type of white blood cell) in response to exposure to antigens (*anti*body *gen*erators). Antigens can be microorganisms, blood from transfusions, cells in transplanted tissues, and any other material not recognized as belonging to the body, such as those that cause ALLERGY. Antibodies are dormant until they attach to the specific antigens against which they are effective. They then become activated, and may directly destroy the antigen or 'label' it so that a white blood cell can engulf and destroy it. After the body has been exposed to an antigen, 'memory' ensures that a later exposure causes antibodies to be produced more quickly and in larger amounts than on the first occasion. This can produce immunity to a harmful antigen, such as a virus, since it is eliminated before it has time to act. In addition, immunity also detects and eliminates the body's own abnormal cells and denatured proteins, which is a self-monitoring function called immunosurveillance.

Cell-mediated immunity, leading to the production of specific white blood cells (T-cells) in response to antigens, is the most reactive part of the immune system. Humoral immunity is responsible for the production of specific antibodies to the antigens. The components may act alone or in combination depending on the situation.

Immunity may be induced by artificial means (see IMMUNIZATION). See also IMMUNOLOGY.

immunization The practice of inducing IMMUNITY (especially to infection) in a person or animal. This is usually achieved by VACCINATION, in which a vaccine (a preparation containing antigens) is used to stimulate the production of antibodies and therefore induce active immunity. The vaccine is usually administered by injection, and generally contains either live but attenuated organisms (reduced in virulence), or dead organisms which retain their ability to stimulate antibody production. Active immunity lasts many years. Passive immunity is induced by the administration of antibodies against a particular infection (passive immunization). Antibodies collected from humans are called immunoglobulins, and those from animals, antisera. Passive immunity lasts for only a few weeks.

immunodeficiency A disorder of the immune system characterized by the inability to establish effective IMMUNITY and response to challenge by antigens. Any part of the immune system may be affected. Immunodeficiency results in increased susceptibility to opportunistic INFECTION and certain types of CANCER. It may arise as a result of disease, such as HIV-infection leading to AIDS, or may be induced by drug administration (immunosuppression) such as in the treatment of auto-immune diseases or prevention of transplant rejection. Individuals with immunodeficiency are said to be immunocompromised.

immunoglobin See IMMUNIZATION.

immunology The study of IMMUNITY and the immune system, its components, actions, and mechanisms. The role of the immunologist is being increasingly recognized in the treatment of disease. The immune system is involved in a diverse range of diseases such as ALLERGY, INFECTION, and CANCER. Immune system disorders may also cause auto-immune diseases, such as rheumatoid arthritis, in which the immune response is directed towards the body's own tissues.

Immunology is also concerned with diagnosis. It is possible to diagnose certain diseases by mixing known antibodies with serum from a suspected case and observing the reaction: an example is the Wasserman test for syphilis. By combining molecules of dye with antibodies, microscope slides of tissues containing certain antigens (for example, liver infected with a virus) can be selectively stained with colour.

impasto Thickly applied paint that retains the marks of the brush, knife, or other instrument of application. The textural qualities it creates can be one of the most personal aspects of OIL PAINTING, and impasto is also a feature of certain types of ACRYLIC PAINT; it is not possible, however, with WATER-COLOUR or TEMPERA. Rembrandt is one of the great artists particularly associated with rich impasto.

impeachment A judicial procedure by which a public official may be tried by the LEGISLATURE for treason or other serious crime. In the UK, the impeachment procedure has passed into disuse since the 18th century, but has never been abolished. In the USA, the House of Representatives institutes the impeachment proceedings and the Senate acts as judge. In 1974 the House of Representatives was preparing articles of impeachment against President Richard NIXON on the grounds of obstruction of justice and misuse of power after he refused to cooperate with inquiries into the illegal electronic SURVEILLANCE of his political opponents at the Watergate Hotel in Washington, DC. He preempted proceedings by resigning.

impedance The total opposition to current flow in an electrical circuit, measured in ohms (Ω). In a direct-current circuit the impedance (symbol *Z*) is equivalent to the resistance (*R*), but in an alternating-current circuit it is the ratio of the alternating voltage to alternating current, and is composed of the combined resistance, inductive REACTANCE (inductance), and capacitive reactance (capacitance), according to the equation:

$$I^2 = R^2 + X^2,$$

where X is the reactance.

Imperial College of Science, Technology and Medicine A school of London University, founded in 1907 to give specialized instruction in science. It is a federation of three earlier institutions, the Royal College of Science (founded 1845), the Royal School of Mines (1851), and the City and Guilds College (1884), which have preserved their respective identities within the College framework. In 1953 Imperial College was chosen as the leading UK institution to provide more university-trained scientists and engineers. In 1988 St Mary's Hospital Medical School (1854) joined the college; in 1997 the Royal Post-Graduate Medical School and the Charing Cross and Westminister Medical Schools merged with the College.

imperialism The policy of extending a country's influence over less powerful states. Historically imperialism has existed in all periods: Greece, Rome, Ottoman Turkey, Spain, and Britain have all extended their respective domains by imperial rule. The INDUSTRIAL REVOLUTION introduced a new form of imperialism as European countries competed throughout the world both for raw materials and for markets. In the late 19th century imperial ambitions were motivated in part by the need for commercial expansion, the desire for military glory, and diplomatic advantage. Imperialism generally assumed a racial, intellectual, and spiritual superiority on the part of the newcomers. The effects of imperialism, while in some measure beneficial to the subjected population, often meant the breakdown of traditional forms of life, the disruption of indigenous civilization, and the imposition of new religious beliefs and social values. The dreams of imperialism faded in the 1920s as anti-imperialist movements developed, and from the 1940s many colonies gained their independence.

impetigo A bacterial infection of the skin caused by staphylococci, streptococci, or both. Children are most commonly affected, especially on the hands and face. It is highly contagious but usually responds to topical applications of antibiotics.

impotence An inability for a man to have penetrative sexual intercourse, as a result of a failure to achieve an erection or to ejaculate. The cause may be a physical disease, such as diabetes, taking certain drugs, such as diuretics, or to psychological or emotional problems, which can often be satisfactorily treated by counselling or psychotherapy.

Impressionism A movement in painting originating in the 1860s in France and regarded as perhaps the most momentous development in 19th-century art. The Impressionists were not a formal group with clearly defined principles and aims but an association of artists, linked by a community of outlook. The central figures involved were CÉZANNE, DEGAS, MANET, MONET, Camille PISSARRO, RENOIR, and SISLEY, and their commitment to Impressionism varied considerably. Manet was much respected as a senior figure, although he never exhibited with the group. The Impressionists reacted against academic teaching and conventions and were also opposed to the basic principle of ROMANTICISM, that art should convey intense personal emotion. They were interested in the objective recording of contemporary life, trying to capture an 'impression' of what the eye sees at one particular moment. Landscape is considered the theme most typical of the Impressionists, but they painted many other subjects. Degas depicted such subjects as horse-races, ballet-dancers, and laundresses, while Renoir is famous for his pictures of pretty women and children. The Impressionists' desire to look at the world with freshness and immediacy was encouraged by photography and by scientific research into colour and light. In trying to capture the effects of light on varied surfaces, particularly in open-air settings, they transformed painting, using bright colours and sketchy brushwork that seemed bewildering or shocking to traditionalists. The name 'Impressionism' was coined derisively, when it was applied after the first Impressionist exhibition, held in Paris in 1874, to a picture by Monet, *Impression: Sunrise* (1872, stolen from the Musée Marmottan in Paris in 1985 and now listed by Interpol as one of the ten 'most wanted artworks missing'). Although Impressionism was at first greeted with hostility and many of its practitioners had to endure financial hardship early in their careers, it began to win critical acceptance in the 1880s and its influence was enormous – much of the history of late 19th-century and early 20th-century painting is the story of developments from it or reactions against it.

imprinting A process of early learning by which the new-born forms attachment to the object it sees first after birth. It was made famous by the Austrian pioneer in ETHOLOGY, Konrad LORENZ, who described it in *Studies on Animal and Human Behaviour* (1935). Recently hatched swimming and walking birds, such as ducklings, follow almost any noticeable moving object, normally their mother, thereby improving their chances of survival. Such 'filial imprinting' is attachment to an individual care-giver. 'Sexual imprinting' is preference for the species of that same individual in later mate selection. Imprinting is a form of learning which requires no reward. Indeed, the more effort the young has to exert to follow, the stronger the imprinting is. It shows how INSTINCT interacts with circumstance in the development of behaviour and how important early experience may be. See also LEARNING.

Inca The pre-Columbian Indian people of western South America. They comprised Quechua-speaking tribes around CUZCO (their capital), who formed a state contemporary to, and eventually superseding that of CHIMÚ. Sixteenth-century records indicate that the ruling dynasty was founded *c.*1200 AD by Manco Capac, but real expansion did not take place until 1438, forming an empire stretching from northern Ecuador, across Peru, to Bolivia and parts of northern Argentina and Chile by 1525 (some 3,500 km, 2,175 miles, north to south). Three important rulers carried out these conquests and the development of the imperial administration: Pachacuti (1438–71), Topa Inca (1471–93), and Huayna Capac (1493–1525). After Huayna Capac civil wars broke up the empire of his son ATAHUALPA just before Spanish troops led by Francisco PIZARRO landed on the coast in 1532. Atahualpa was captured in 1533 and killed shortly thereafter. In the same year Pizarro captured Cuzco, and by 1537, after the defeat of Manco Capac, most of the empire had been subdued by Spain.

Inca technology was of a high standard and included specialized factories and workshops producing ceramics, textiles, and metal artefacts, with fine decoration, incorporating many regional styles. Architecture included accurately fitted stone masonry. Agriculture was based on systems of hillside terracing and included the potato, quinoa, and maize, and the guinea pig (for food), domestic dog, llama, and alpaca. Religion was centralized, local gods being respected but secondary to the Sun cult as the divine ancestor of the ruling dynasty and Viracocha, the creator god.

Inca art See SOUTH AMERICAN INDIAN ART.

incandescent lamp A source of illumination consisting of a glass bulb filled with an inert gas at low pressure, and containing a finely wound metal filament (usually tungsten, but osmium and TANTALUM are also used). When current is passed through the filament, it heats up, attaining temperatures of up to 2,500°C, and emits intense visible light. The incandescent lamp is a convenient source of light, but has relatively poor efficiency: only about 10 per cent of the energy supplied is converted into visible light. More efficient fluorescent light bulbs are now available as replacements for domestic incandescent bulbs.

incense An aromatic mixture of gums, especially benzoin, burnt to provide an odour that is believed to encourage religious activities. It was used in pagan rituals in ancient Egypt, Greece, and Rome as well as in early Jewish rituals. It has been used by Christians since the 6th century AD, but is now largely restricted to Orthodox and Roman Catholic liturgies.

incest Sexual relations between certain categories of close kin. These categories vary between societies, but some measure of prohibition of incest is generally found in all societies. Prohibited categories can range from specified individuals, such as, for example, parents, brothers, sisters, or cousins, to much larger groups of kin who may be only distantly related. Although it is often thought that incest prohibitions are designed to avert the incidence of genetic in-breeding, there is little evidence for this; the variety of prohibitions that exist in different societies suggests that this explanation cannot account for them all. The incest TABOO is sometimes seen as maintaining certain forms of MARRIAGE by encouraging people to look outside their own social group for partners.

Inchon A port on the west coast of South Korea, on the Yellow Sea west of Seoul; pop. (1990) 1,818,300. Fishing and the manufacture of steel and textiles are important industries. US forces landed here at the outset of the Korean War in 1950.

inch worm See LOOPER.

incomes policy See PRICES AND INCOMES POLICY.

income tax A tax levied on the income of an individual. In Britain it was imposed on the incomes of the propertied classes for the first time in December 1798 by William PITT the Younger, to help finance the war with France. It was temporarily abolished by Parliament against the government's wishes in 1816. It was revived in 1842 by PEEL in exchange for a reduction in customs and excise duties. In the 1850s GLADSTONE planned to abolish it gradually, but was in fact obliged to raise it to finance the Crimean War, and by the 1860s it had become accepted as a permanent necessity on higher incomes. In the 20th century tax liability tended to reach further down the social scale so that by World War II most full-time employees were taxed. Income taxes were introduced in some European countries during the 19th century and in the British dominions from 1891. In the USA federal income tax was imposed in 1862 to help finance the American Civil War. An attempt by the federal government to reintroduce it in 1894 was declared unconstitutional by the Supreme Court, and a federal tax did not become effective until 1913. By then most individual US states had their own income tax.

incubator A transparent container, the internal environment of which is controlled to keep temperature and humidity at constant and pre-set levels, used to maintain premature babies in a controlled environment, protected from infection. Incubators are also used for hatching eggs, and to grow bacteria.

incubus A male demon in medieval European folklore, believed to be capable of having sexual intercourse with sleeping women, making them pregnant with offspring that would turn into witches or demons. The female equivalent, a **succubus**, was believed to inhabit the dreams of men.

incunabula (from Latin *cunae*, 'cradles') A collective term for printed books published during the earliest period of TYPOGRAPHY, from the invention of printing in Europe in the 1450s to the end of the 15th century. Incunabula tend to be rare, and the number a library possesses is often used as a rough guide to its importance. The British Library in London has about 10,000, estimated to be about a quarter of all those published.

independence See SOVEREIGNTY.

Independence, American War of (or **American Revolution**) (1776–83) The American revolution against British rule. It was triggered by colonial resentment at the commercial policies of Britain and by the lack of American participation in political decisions that affected their interests. Disturbances, such as the Boston Tea Party (1773), developed into armed resistance in 1775 (for example at Lexington and Concord and BUNKER HILL), and full-scale war, with the DECLARATION OF INDEPENDENCE in 1776. Britain, fighting 3,000 miles from home, faced problems of supply, divided command, slow communications, a hostile population, and lack of experience in combating guerrilla tactics. America's disadvantages included few trained generals or troops, a weak central authority unable to provide finance, intercolonial rivalries, and lack of sea power. The French Alliance (1778) changed the nature of the war. Though France gave only modest aid to America, Britain was thereafter distracted by European and West and East Indian challenges.

The course of the war can be divided at 1778. The first, northern, phase saw the British capture of New York (1776), their campaign in the Hudson valley to isolate New England culminating in defeat at SARATOGA SPRINGS (1777), and the capture of Philadelphia (1777) after the victory of Brandywine. The second phase switched British attentions to the south, where large numbers of Loyalists could be recruited. Philadelphia was relinquished (1778) and WASHINGTON camped at West Point to threaten the British headquarters at New York. After Clinton's capture of Charleston (1780), CORN-

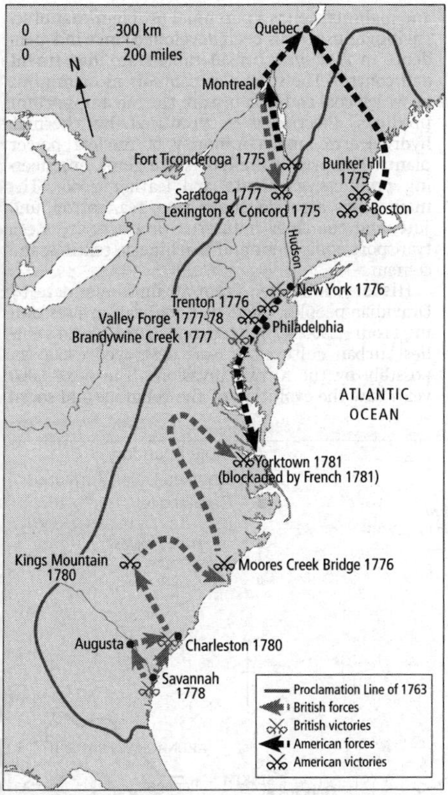

American War of Independence In the first stage of the war, the British strategy of breaking up the union of the colonies succeeded with the capture of New York and Washington's retreat to Pennsylvania. However, their campaign in the Hudson valley culminated in defeat at Saratoga. In the second phase the British began a campaign in the south leading to an American surrender at Charleston. Subsequently the British were trapped at Yorktown and as a result of the French blockade were unable to be reinforced. This defeat effectively ended the war.

WALLIS vainly chased the Southern Army under Greene before his own exhausted army surrendered at Yorktown, Virginia (October 1781), effectively ending hostilities. Peace was concluded at PARIS (1783).

Despite frequent victories, the British did not destroy Washington's or Greene's armies and could not break the American will. America's success has been depicted as influencing the French Revolution (1789) and subsequent revolutions in Europe and South America.

independent education Education offered in schools and other educational institutions for which the state is not responsible. The proportion of primary school children in independent education ranges from, for example, none in the People's Republic of China (where it is banned) to more than a quarter in some sub-Saharan African countries, Belgium, and Spain. In most countries religious bodies are the principal providers. Some independent schools charge fees, while others are free. Independent schools complement state schools, either by offering programmes parents and children find preferable or, as in many developing countries (where their numbers are increasing rapidly), by offering facilities that governments cannot afford. They are sometimes supported by state subsidy and in the UK are awarded charitable status, which exempts them from income tax. In the UK, the independent secondary schools formerly known as **public schools**, some of which date back to the 16th century, are often boarding schools providing opportunities for children to learn in classes considerably smaller than those in comprehensive state schools. They charge high fees, which enables them to provide teacher–pupil ratios of about 10 (compared to 15 in state secondary schools). Some 7 per cent of UK schoolchildren attend independent schools. Although the arguments for state and for COMPREHENSIVE EDUCATION are strong, on the grounds that they are less socially divisive than independent schools, many independent schools are centres of excellence to which talented children whose parents cannot afford the full fees can have access through the government's Assisted Places Scheme.

Independent Labour Party (ILP) British socialist organization. It was founded at Bradford in 1893 under the leadership of Keir HARDIE. Its aim was to achieve equality in society by the application of socialist doctrines. The ILP was one of the constituent groups of the Labour Representation Committee (1900), which in 1906 became the LABOUR PARTY. A split developed between the ILP and the Labour Party between the two World Wars. The sympathy of the ILP for communism, its pacifism, and its theoretical approach to politics were regarded as electoral liabilities by leading Labour politicians; from 1939 its influence declined.

index, financial A series of numbers starting from a base period (when the index is set at 100) and representing the average percentage change in prices since the base period. A financial index may show how share prices (or other financial assets) have changed (see SHARE INDEX) or it may be an index of INFLATION, showing how retail prices have changed. The most common index used as a measure of general inflation is the RETAIL PRICE INDEX (RPI). This index is used for **indexation**, i.e. raising wages and salaries in proportion to increases in the RPI over the same period, so that they keep pace with inflation. Indexed bonds are those with interest and capital repayments that change in line with an index; for example, in the UK some gilt-edged securities are linked to the RPI.

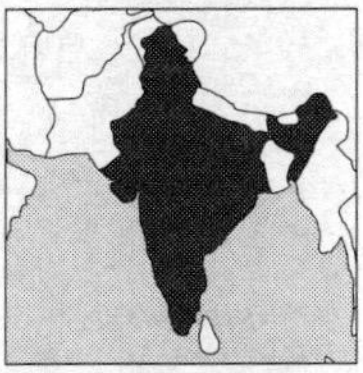

India A South Asian country occupying most of the southward-pointing peninsula of the Indian subcontinent. It is bounded by Pakistan on the north-west, China, Nepal, and Bhutan on the north, and Myanmar (Burma) on the east.

Physical. India is roughly triangular in shape, most of the northern frontier following the Himalayas, the world's highest mountains. The two southern sides are formed by a coastline on the Arabian Sea and another on the Bay of Bengal: they are backed by the ranges of the Western and Eastern Ghats. In its north-east corner are the BRAHMAPUTRA valley and the wet, tea-bearing hills of Assam, bounding Bangladesh. In the extreme north is Kashmir, embraced by the

Karakoram range. Then, across a northern belt of the Himalayas, are the Thar (or Great Indian) Desert, the central Punjab watershed with its fields of wheat, the Ganges FLOODPLAIN, and Bengal which produces jute. In the west are the cotton-growing areas of Gujarat. From here the land rises to the middle of the country, Madhya Pradesh, and the forested hills of Orissa. Extending southward is the Deccan plateau, terminating in the Nilgiri Hills where tea and coffee are grown. The southern coasts, Malabar and Coromandel, are famous for their paddy fields and citrus fruit. India has two MONSOONS: the south-west, which brings moderate-heavy rain to most of the country from June to September; and the north-east, which blows from October to February.

Economy. India's economy is largely agrarian, and India has become self-sufficient in food, although agricultural yields are comparatively low and malnutrition is a perennial problem. Manufacturing industry has been developed since independence in 1947, with considerable state investment and control. The state also controls most mining, of which coal and iron ore are the most important products. Electricity is produced by thermal, hydroelectric, and a minority of nuclear power plants. The principal exports are gems, engineering products, garments, and leather goods. The main crops are rice, sugar-cane, tea, cotton, and jute, and the chief industrial products are steel, transport equipment and machinery, textiles, and cement.

History. Inhabited from an unknown date by Dravidian peoples, the INDUS civilization sites, dating from *c.*2500 BC, indicate one of the world's earliest urban cultures. It was destroyed *c.*1500 BC, possibly by the ARYAN invasions. The next 1,000 years saw the evolution of the religious and social

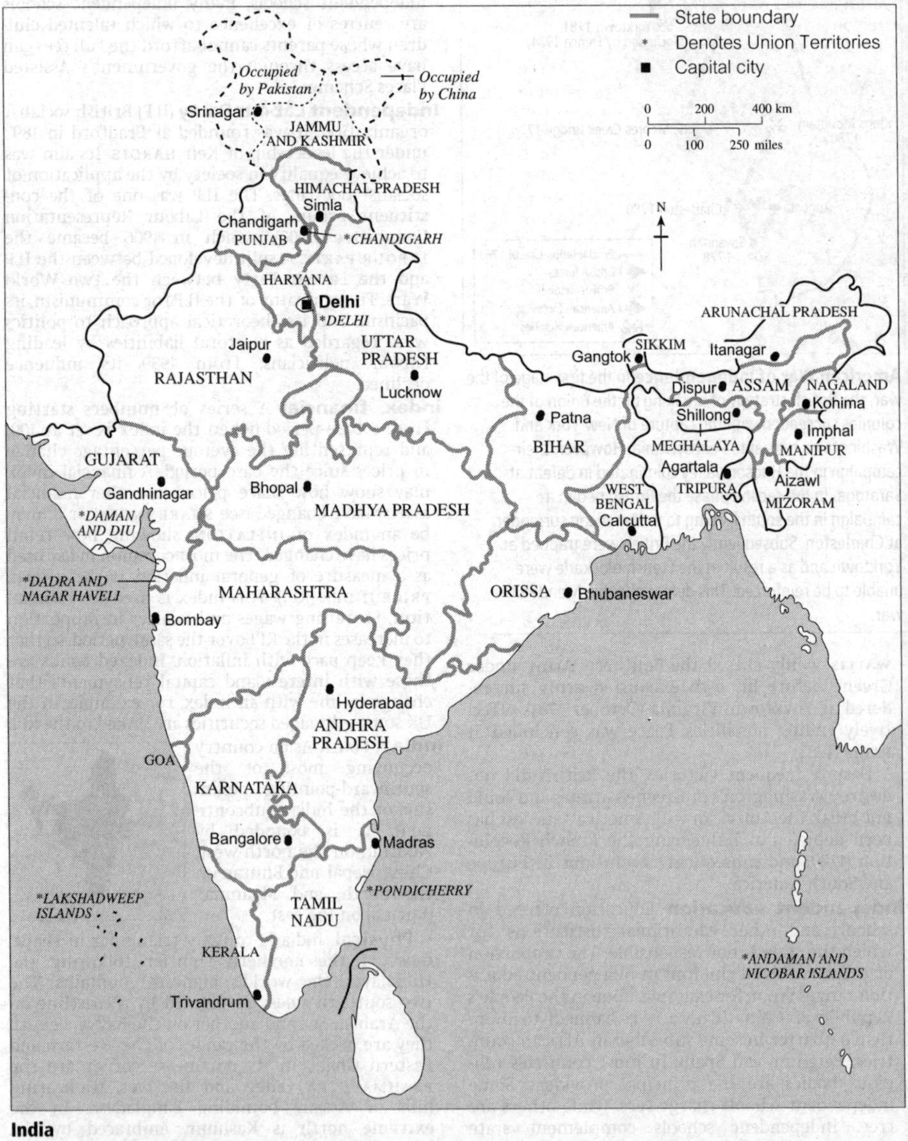

India

systems which remain characteristic of HINDUISM. Regional kingdoms rose and fell under Hindu, and later Buddhist, dynasties, but mastery over the entire subcontinent was rarely achieved. The MAURYAN EMPIRE (*c.*325–185 BC), was the first all-India empire, only the southern tip remaining outside its influence. After its disintegration, internecine struggles between local powers remained the characteristic pattern.

Waves of invasion from from Central Asia from the 11th to the 16th century resulted in Muslim control over the north and the Deccan, and the evolution, through immigration and conversion, of India's largest minority. Only in a few areas, notably the RAJPUT states and Vijayanagar, was Hindu political power maintained. Rule by the MOGULS (1526–1857), who claimed most of the subcontinent, marked the height of Indo-Muslim civilization. On their decline European trading powers were poised to take advantage of the power vacuum and the renewal of internecine struggle. Victorious over its French rival, the English EAST INDIA COMPANY laid the basis in the 18th century for the subsequent hegemony of the BRITISH RAJ. Following the INDIAN MUTINY control of India passed, via The Act for the Better Government of India (1858) from the English East India Company to the British Crown. The India Acts of the late 19th and early 20th century granted greater Indian involvement in government. The Indian National CONGRESS, founded in 1885, conducted, under the leadership of M. K. GANDHI, major campaigns for self-rule and independence. During 1945–47 Congress negotiated with Britain for independence, which was achieved in 1947 when Britain transferred power to the new states of India and PAKISTAN.

The Republic (or Union) of India opted to remain within the COMMONWEALTH even though it adopted a republican constitution. The princely states within the boundaries of the Indian Union plus KASHMIR all acceded to the Union, though pressure had to be used in some instances, especially Travancore-Cochin and HYDERABAD. Eventually the Princely States were integrated or set up as separate states. The French voluntarily surrendered their few possessions in India, while the Portuguese territories agitating for accession were integrated through military action. The semi-autonomous state of Sikkim was absorbed into India through political pressure but without bloodshed. PAKISTAN's claims over Kashmir, the bulk of which is formally integrated with India, remain a source of dispute. India is a federation of 25 states and 6 Union territories organized primarily on a linguistic basis. Since independence it has had three wars with Pakistan and one with China, and the relationship with SRI LANKA is strained by the Indian Tamils' support for the Sri Lankan Tamils' movement for autonomy. The Sikh demand for autonomy and their terrorist action remain intractable problems in the Punjab. India's first Prime Minister was Jawaharlal NEHRU (1947–64), who initiated a policy of planned economic growth and non-alignment. Indira GANDHI, his daughter, became Prime Minister in 1966. After splitting the Congress party and experimenting with autocratic rule (1975–77) she suffered electoral defeat. She returned to power (1980) and adopted a firm approach to separatists in 1984 when she suppressed a militant Sikh movement that demanded autonomy for the Punjab. She was assassinated by a Sikh in the same year. Her son, Rajiv Gandhi (1944–91), succeeded her as Prime Minister (1984–89). In 1987–89 India undertook large-scale military intervention in Sri Lanka to subdue Tamil rebels. Rajiv failed to win the 1989 election but, after his assassination by Tamil militants the Congress (I) Party under Narasimha Rao regained political control with a minority government. In December 1992 Hindu extremists demolished the ancient Babri mosque at Ayodhya, Uttar Pradesh, which led to severe sectarian clashes in 1993. Almost 10,000 people perished in an earthquake in east-central India in the same year. Following the poor performance of the ruling Congress (I) Party in the 1994 state elections, the authority of Narasimha Rao was further undermined the following year by a leadership crisis and split in the party. In 1996 Rao's party was defeated in general elections by the Hindu nationalist Bharatiya Janata Party (BJP), which formed a short-lived government that was replaced by a coalition led by Deve Gowda. This itself was replaced in 1997 by a new coalition led by Inder Kumar Gujral. General elections in 1998 were won by the BJP; Atal Behari Vajpayee became Prime Minister at the head of a multi-party coalition.

Capital: New Delhi
Area: 3,166,414 sq km (1,222,559 sq mi)
Population: 935,744,000 (1995)
Currency: 1 Indian rupee = 100 paisa
Religions: Hindu 82.64%; Muslim 11.35%; Christian 2.43%; Sikh 1.97%; Buddhist 0.71%; Jain 0.48%; Parsee 0.01%
Ethnic Groups: (based on language) Hindi 28.1%; Telugu 8.2%; Bengali 8.1%; Marathi 7.6%; Tamil 6.9%; Urdu 5.2%; Gujarati 4.7%; Malayalam 4.0%; Kannada 3.9%; Oriya 3.6%; Bhojpuri 2.6%; Punjabi 2.5%; Assamese 1.6%; Chhattisgarhi 1.2%; Magadhi 1.2%; Maithili 1.1%
Languages: Hindi, English (both official); Gujarati, Bengali, Marathi, Telugu, Tamil, Urdu, Oriya, Malayalam, Kannada, Punjabi and Bhojpuri are each spoken by over 20 million people
International Organizations: UN; Commonwealth; Colombo Plan; Non-Aligned Movement

Indiana A state in the Middle West of the USA, to the south of Lake Michigan; area 93,720 sq km (36,185 sq miles); pop. (1990) 5,544,160; capital, Indianapolis. The largest cities are Indianapolis, Fort Wayne, Evansville, Gary, and South Bend. Indiana is also known as the Hoosier State. Ceded to Britain by the French in 1763 and acquired by the USA in 1783, it became the 19th state of the Union in 1816. Indiana, with its industrial waterfront on Lake Michigan, is a major producer of iron and steel, limestone for building, and agricultural products. Major landmarks include the Indiana Dunes National Lakeshore, Lincoln Boyhood National Memorial in Lincoln City, and George Rogers Clark National Historical Park commemorating a hero of the War of Independence.

Indianapolis The capital of the US state of Indiana, on the White River at the geographical centre of the state; pop. (1990) 741,950. It is one of the leading US grain markets, with an important livestock trade and meat-processing industry. Pharmaceuticals, vehicle parts, electronic goods, and medical equipment are also produced. The city hosts and annual 500-mile (804.5-km) motor-race (the Indianapolis 500).

Indian art The art and architecture of the INDIAN SUBCONTINENT. The earliest Indian art belonged to the Indus Valley civilization of about 2500–1500 BC, but after that there was a long gap before Mauryan art, which flourished mainly in the 3rd century BC. Ashoka, the greatest of the Mauryan rulers, was a convert to Buddhism, consequently Buddhism and Hinduism provided the inspiration for most Indian art until the coming of Islam. Two early traditions are represented by Gandhára art and Mathura art, but early Indian art reached its peak slightly later in the Gupta era, the finest flowering of which was in the 5th century AD. Painting (notably at the AJANTA CAVES) and sculpture attained new heights and the great age of temple building was firmly established. Elephanta, Ellora, and KHAJURAHO are among the most illustrious of India's temples. Traditional values in Indian art, however, were eventually overthrown by the Muslims, who conquered virtually all of the vast subcontinent between the 11th and 15th centuries, bringing India into the sphere of Islamic art. The highpoint of Islamic art in India came with the MOGUL dynasty, which in the period from about 1550 to about 1650 included among its rulers three celebrated patrons of the arts. One of them, Shah Jahan, was responsible for the most famous of all Indian buildings, the Taj Mahal at Agra (built from 1632 to 1649). Exchanging gifts was important in Mogul court life and this encouraged the decorative arts to flourish in luxury articles, such as carpets, jewellery, and inlaid weapons. With the decline of the Mogul empire, the British emerged as the dominant power among the European nations with a presence in India. By the mid-18th century much of the country was under British control; government was initially in the hands of the East India Company, but after the Indian Mutiny of 1857 the control of the whole country passed to the British crown (1858). Indian painting produced for European patrons, known as company painting, is often attractive, but the finest artistic expressions of the period of European rule were in architecture. Many major cities have Victorian public buildings that are as impressive as anything of the same type in Britain; usually they are in GOTHIC REVIVAL styles, but sometimes with features inspired by Indian tradition. The culmination of the taste for the grandiose came with Sir Edwin LUTYENS's designs for the new capital at New Delhi (1913 onwards). The most famous artistic monument created since India became independent in 1947 is LE CORBUSIER's new town of Chandigarh (1950 onwards). Among modern Indian artists the best known is the painter Jamini Roy (1887–1974) who successfully combined influences from European modernism with ancient traditions. See also BUDDHIST ART.

Indian bean tree See CATALPA.

Indian fig See PRICKLY PEAR.

Indian Mutiny (1857–58) An uprising against British rule in India. It began as a mutiny of Indian sepoys in the army of the English EAST INDIA COMPANY, commencing at Meerut on 10 May 1857, and spreading rapidly to Delhi and including most regiments of the Bengal army as well as a large section of the civil population in Uttar Pradesh and Madhya Pradesh. The immediate cause was the soldiers' refusal to handle new cartridges apparently greased with pig and cow fat (an outrage to Muslims and Hindus respectively). The mutineers seized Delhi. The rebels restored the former Mogul Emperor Bahadur Shah II to his throne, whereupon the movement spread to LUCKNOW, which was besieged, and to Cawnpore (now Kanpur), where the massacre of the British garrison is believed to have been instigated by Tantia Topi, a Maratha Brahman who became the military leader of the rebels. The recapture of Delhi by forces from the Punjab on 14 September 1857 broke the back of the mutiny. Following the restoration of British control, the East India Company's rule was replaced by that of the British Crown.

Indian National Congress See CONGRESS, INDIAN NATIONAL.

Indian Ocean The ocean to the south of India, extending from the east coast of Africa to the East Indies and Australia. It is the third-largest of the world's oceans and was known in ancient times as the Erythræan Sea. Straddling the equator, the Indian Ocean reaches its maximum depth of 7,725 m (25,345 ft) in the Java Trench, Indonesia. Its principal islands and island groups are Sri Lanka, Madagascar, La Réunion, Mauritius, the Seychelles, the Maldives, the Andaman and Nicobar Islands, the Laccadive Islands (Lakshadweep), the Cocos Islands, and the Chagos Archipelago.

Indian subcontinent The part of Asia south of the Himalayas that forms a peninsula extending into the Indian Ocean, between the Arabian Sea and the Bay of Bengal. Historically forming the whole territory of greater India, the region is now divided between India, Pakistan, and Bangladesh. Geologically, the Indian subcontinent is a distinct unit, formerly part of the ancient super-continent of Gondwana. As a result of continental drift it became joined to the rest of Asia, perhaps as recently as 40 million years ago, in a collision that created the Himalayas.

Indic The group of Indo-European languages comprising Sanskrit and the modern Indian languages, which are its descendants.

indium (symbol In, at. no. 49, r.a.m. 114.82) A soft, silver, metallic element in Group 13 (formerly IIIB) of the PERIODIC TABLE. It was named after the bright indigo line of its spectrum. It reacts readily with acids, the halogens, and sulphur with a principal valency of 3. It is used in the manufacture of semiconductor devices, and to monitor neutron fluxes near nuclear reactors.

Indo-Arayan Any of the Arayan peoples of India or the Indic languages.

Indo-China ▶**1** The peninsula of south-east Asia containing Myanmar (Burma), Thailand, Malaya, Laos, Cambodia, and Vietnam. ▶**2** A region of south-east Asia that now consists of Laos, Cambodia, and Vietnam and was a French dependency from 1862 to 1954.

Indo-European languages A family of languages spoken originally throughout Europe, Asia Minor (present-day Asian Turkey), Iran, northern and central India, and as far east as Chinese Turkistan. Following the period of European colonial expansion, which began in the late 15th century, modern Indo-European languages (notably English, and the ROMANCE LANGUAGES of Spanish, Portuguese, and French) spread to much of the rest of the world, including the Americas, Australasia, and the continent of Africa. Virtually all the modern languages of Europe belong to this group, the only exceptions being Basque, Finnish, Hungarian, and Turkish.

Indo-Greek dynasties Rulers of parts of north-west India from the 3rd to the 1st century BC. In 326 BC Alexander the Great's army had invaded India and explored the Indus valley. His direct impact was slight, but in the next century Greek commanders, who already held BACTRIA in Central Asia again crossed the Indus, this time to establish power in the Punjab. Their successors were driven out of India after 200 years, but the 'Yavana' (Greek) rulers had an important impact on art and architecture, astrology and medicine. Evidence for Greek activity in India comes mainly from their inscribed coins.

Indo-Iranian languages The largest sub-group within INDO-EUROPEAN LANGUAGES. Modern Indo-Iranian languages have official status in Afghanistan, Bangladesh and India (Bengali, or Bangla), Iran, Nepal, Pakistan, and Tajikistan, and are also spoken elsewhere. Speakers number approximately 700 million. The group falls into two distinct branches: Indic (or Indo-Aryan) and Iranian, both of which have very long histories.

Indonesia (formerly **Dutch East Indies**) A country composed of hundreds of tropical islands in south-east Asia, in the region where the Pacific and the Indian Oceans meet.

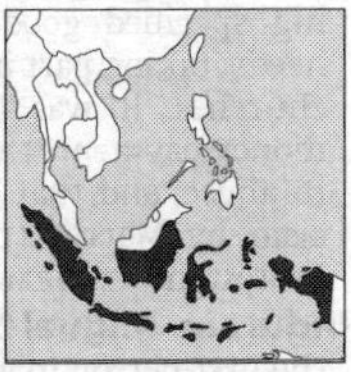

Physical. Its east-west length is greater than the width of Australia or the USA, for among its larger islands are included parts of New Guinea (Irian Jaya) and Borneo (Kalimantan) and all of Sumatra, Java, and Sulawesi (once Celebes). Among its smaller islands are Bali, Timor, Flores, and the Moluccas. This vast area lies at the edge of the Eurasian plate. It contains over 70 volcanoes, some periodically active like Krakatoa; and it is subject to severe earthquakes. While many of the beaches are black with volcanic mud, others are coral, with very clear water. With both a north-west MONSOON (December to March) and a south-east one (April to October), the natural vegetation inland is dense rain forest and the main crop is rice.

Economy. Agriculture is important, principal exports being timber, coffee, rubber, shrimps, pepper, and palm oil, and Indonesia is the most important oil producer of the region. Other mining products include nickel, bauxite, copper, iron, and tin. There is some light industry, and manufacturing is increasing in importance.

History. The Hindu Srivijaya Empire, based on Palembang, flourished between the 7th and 13th centuries AD. Towards the end of the 12th century the Majapahit kingdom, which was based on JAVA began to dominate the area of present-day Indonesia. During the 16th century the area was occupied by the Portuguese, the British, and the Dutch. The Dutch East India Company had acquired control of most of the islands of Indonesia by the end of the 17th century, with headquarters in present-day Jakarta (then Batavia).

The islands were formed into the Netherlands-Indies in 1914. By the 1920s, indigenous political movements were demanding complete independence. Prominent here was SUKARNO's Indonesian Nationalist Party (*Partai Nasionalis Indonesia*), banned by the Dutch in the 1930s. The Japanese occupation of 1942–45 strengthened nationalist sentiments, and, taking advantage of the Japanese defeat in 1945, Sukarno proclaimed Indonesian independence and set up a republican government. Dutch attempts to reassert control were met with popular opposition (the INDONESIAN REVOLUTION), which resulted in the transfer of power in 1949. By 1957 parliamentary democracy had given way to the semi-dictatorship or 'Guided Democracy' of President Sukarno, a regime based on the original 1945 constitution, with a strong executive and special powers reserved for the army and bureaucracy. Sukarno's popularity began to wane after 1963, with the army and right-wing Muslim landlords becoming increasingly concerned about the influence of communists in government. Rampant inflation and peasant unrest brought the country to the brink of collapse in 1965–66 when the army under General Suharto (1921–) took advantage of a bungled coup by leftist officers to carry out a bloody purge of the Communist Party (PKI) and depose Sukarno (1967). Despite his initial success in rebuilding the economy and restoring credit with its Western capitalist backers, Suharto's regime remained authoritarian and repressive, moving ruthlessly against domestic political opponents. His regime achieved a high growth rate in the economy, but there was growing international concern over the pace of deforestation, as well as over abuse of human rights. In 1976 Indonesia annexed the former Portuguese colony of East TIMOR, causing thousands of civilian deaths. The United Nations (UN) disputed the action and conflict between the independence movement and government forces in East Timor continued in the early 1980s. In the early 1990s UN-sponsored talks over East Timor took place between Indonesia and Portugal and in 1994 Indonesia agreed to allow access to East Timor for human rights and UN organizations. Conflict also erupted in the province of Irian Jaya, part of the island of New Guinea, where a rebellion was staged in support of unification with PAPUA NEW GUINEA. New border arrangements agreed between the two countries put a stop to fighting in 1979, but conflict broke out again in 1984, causing many refugees to flee from Irian Jaya to Papua New Guinea. Accords were signed by Indonesia and Papua New Guinea over security and trade issues in 1992, but further clashes between government troops and separatist rebels occurred in 1993. Although in 1988 legislation had affirmed the dual military and socio-economic role of the Indonesian Armed Forces (ABRI) in the government of Indonesia, there was growing demand for greater democracy in the country in the early 1990s. While Suharto did appear to accept these demands, the activities of new pro-democracy organizations were met with government repression. In 1990–91 a separatist rebellion in the province of Aceh (Sumatra) was crushed by government forces. In 1993 Suharto was re-elected to serve his sixth term as President, while Try Sustrino, an ABRI candidate, was elected Vice-President. In 1994 there was a government crack-down on the press, and the arrest of pro-democracy campaigners in 1996 resulted in demonstrations and civil unrest. In 1997 the country faced an economic crisis with the collapse of the rupiah, which led to food riots and civil disorder. The International Monetary Fund provided a financial rescue package on condition that Suharto implemented policies aimed at reversing the economic collapse. He was elected for a seventh term of office in 1998.

Capital: Jakarta
Area: 1,919,443 sq km (741,101 sq mi)
Population: 195,283,000 (1995)
Currency: 1 Indonesian rupiah = 100 sen
Religions: Muslim 86.9%; Christian 9.6% (of which Roman Catholic 3.1%); Hindu 1.9%; Buddhist 1.0%
Ethnic Groups: Javanese 40.1%; Sundanese 15.3%; Bahasa Indonesian 12.0%; Madurese 4.8%; Chinese minority
Languages: Bahasa Indonesian (official); also Javanese, Sundanese, and many others
International Organizations: UN; OPEC; ASEAN; Non-Aligned Movement; Colombo Plan

Indonesian Revolution (1945–49) Nationalist struggle for independence from Dutch rule in INDONESIA. In 1945, SUKARNO proclaimed Indonesia's independence. Attempts by the Dutch to re-establish their colonial administration led to fighting which was temporarily brought to an end by a compromise agreement (1946). This provided for the establishment of a United States of Indonesia tied to the Netherlands under a federal constitution. But the nationalists refused to accept this, forcing the Dutch to launch a new offensive which recaptured most of the estate areas and ended in a cease-fire in 1947. A second Dutch 'police action' a year later increased international pressure and forced the Dutch to convene a conference at The Hague in 1949. As a result, all of the Dutch East Indies, with the exception of western New Guinea, were transferred to the new state of Indonesia in 1949. Western New Guinea (now Irian Jaya) came under Indonesian administration in 1963.

Indo-Pakistan War (September 1965) A border conflict between India and Pakistan following an attempt by Pakistan to assist Muslim opponents of Indian rule in Kashmir. Fighting spread to the Punjab, but a UN cease-fire was accepted and by the Tashkent Declaration of 11 January 1966, a troop withdrawal was agreed. A renewal of frontier fighting occurred in 1971, at a time when BANGLADESH was seeking independence from Pakistan.

Indra In Persian mythology a minor, evil god, but in Hinduism the chief of the Vedic gods with Agni and Surya. Lord of the thunderbolt and rain, Indra is the divine patron of the warrior caste who slew Vṛtra (Ahi), the serpent of drought, and rescued the sacred cows of the gods from the *asuras* (demons).

Indre A river in central France that rises in the Massif Central and flows 265 km (166 miles) northwestwards to meet the Loire near Tours.

indri The largest species of LEMUR, *Indri indri*, which is up to 70 cm (2 feet 3 in) long. It is found only in the northern part of the east-coast rain forests of Madagascar. Grey and black in colour, it has very long back legs with which it can make enormous vertical leaps from one tree to another. It lives in small social groups of two to four adults and communicates with eerie howls which carry over great distances. A single young is born and is carried by its mother. It is a much-threatened species because of the destruction of its habitat.

induction (in logic) A process in which previously observed regularities are taken as the ground for predicting future regularities. For example, from the basis that all swans observed up to the present have been white, we could infer that all future swans will be white. As this example shows, however, inductive inferences are fallible: they can lead from true premisses to false conclusions (there are black swans in Australia). This has led to doubts whether inductive inferences can be the basis of scientific reasoning (see POPPER) and even whether they are processes of reasoning at all (see HUME). See also PROBABILITY.

induction (in mathematics) A technique for proving generalized results, such as $1 + 4 + 9 + \ldots + n^2 = 1/6n(n + 1)(2n + 1)$, in which the nth term is a function of n. The technique involves three stages: (i) assume that the formula is true for some value of n, say k; (ii) show that, if this assumption is true, the formula also holds for $n = k + 1$; (iii) show that the assumption is true for a particular value of n, usually $n = 1$, and thus that it is true for all subsequent values of n. Different arguments, generalizing from particular results, are often required to derive the formula to be proved. De Moivre's theorem can be proved by induction.

induction (in physics) See ELECTROMAGNETIC INDUCTION.

induction motor See ELECTRIC MOTOR.

indulgence The cancelling by the Christian Church of the temporal punishment still owed for sins after they have been forgiven. The idea was found in various forms in the early Church, but as a widespread doctrine it dated from the 11th century, especially with the granting of indulgences to those who went on CRUSADES. They could be obtained by saying certain prayers or by performing specified good works, such as helping the needy, taking part in a Crusade, or giving money to churches. It was through the connection with money payments that indulgences were most open to abuse, and that they became a focus for criticism by Martin LUTHER and others during the Protestant REFORMATION.

Indurain, Miguel (1964–) Spanish cyclist. He was the first person to win the Tour de France five consecutive times, from 1991 onwards, setting the record for the fastest average speed in 1992.

Indus (in astronomy) The Indian, a CONSTELLATION of the southern sky, introduced by Pieter Dirkszoon Keyser and Frederick de Houtman at the end of the 16th century. It represents a North American Indian. Its brightest stars are of third magnitude.

Indus A river of southern Asia, about 2,900 km (1,800 miles) in length, flowing from Tibet through Kashmir and Pakistan to the Arabian Sea. Along its valley an early culture flourished from *c.*2600 to 1760 BC, with important centres at Mohenjo-Daro and Harappa, characterized by towns built to a grid-like plan with granaries, drainage systems, and public buildings, copper-bronze technology, a standard system of weights and measures, and steatite seals with (undeciphered) hieroglyphic inscriptions. Its economic wealth was derived from well-attested sea and land trade with the Indian subcontinent, Afghanistan, the Gulf, Iran, and Mesopotamia. In the early 2nd millennium its power declined, probably because of incursions by Aryans.

industrial action Action taken to apply pressure to the other party involved in INDUSTRIAL RELATIONS between employers and employees. Industrial action by employees is intended to disrupt production and may include overtime bans (refusal to work beyond normal hours); the go-slow or work-to-rule (strict adherence to employment contracts); and strikes and PICKETING. Sit-ins (US sit-downs), occupations, and boycotts or 'blacking' also occur. Industrial action may also be taken by employers in the form of lock-outs (refusal to admit employees to their workplaces), punitive dismissals, or the operation of blacklists of potential employees. The right to strike is recognized in most countries, but subject to restrictions, which may include a ban on strikes in essential services or the public sector, obligatory cooling-off periods or ballots before strike action, compulsory conciliation or arbitration, and limits to picketing, all of which have been incorporated at times in industrial law.

industrial archaeology The systematic study of industrial artefacts. It is concerned with archaeological remains of all ages – such as the copper mines of Tharsis in Spain and the water-mill at Barbegal, in France, both dating from Roman times – but particularly with commercial enterprises since the INDUSTRIAL REVOLUTION of the 18th and 19th centuries. Although machinery and transport systems are its major areas of interest, it also draws on information from archival material, such as account and order books.

industrial relations The relationship between managers (often referred to as 'the employers') and workers (usually represented by TRADE UNIONS) in the workplace. It is accepted that the objectives of managers may differ from those of their subordinates, leading to industrial conflict. Differing objectives are most commonly expressed by disagreements over rates of pay but can also involve working practices (hours of work, working conditions, and conditions of employment). Industrial disagreements sometimes have a political dimension, which may, or may not, involve government intervention. **Arbitration** and **conciliation** are methods of settling an industrial conflict or dispute by using an independent third party. Conciliation is a process in which an independent party assists the two parties to a dispute to reach agreement. In the UK the major independent party used in industrial disputes is ACAS (the Advisory Conciliation and Arbitration Service). The results of arbitration are not legally binding in the UK (unlike the USA), but normally are accepted as the basis for settlement.

Industrial Revolution The change in the organization of manufacturing industry that transformed Britain from a rural to an urban economy. The process began in England in the 18th century as a result of improved agricultural techniques, which freed workers from the land and made it possible to provide food for a large non-agricultural population. A combination of economic, political, and social factors, including internal peace, the availability of coal and iron ore, the availability of capital, and the development of steam power – and later the INTERNAL-COMBUSTION ENGINE and electricity – led to the construction of factories, which were built for the mass production of manufactured goods. A new organization of work known as the factory system increased the division and specialization of labour. The textile industry was the prime example of industrialization and created a demand for machines, and for tools for their manufacture, which stimulated further mechanization. Improved transport became necessary and was provided by the expansion of the CANAL system and the subsequent development of RAILWAYS and roads. The skills acquired during this period were exported to other countries and this helped to make Britain the richest and most powerful nation in the world by the middle of the 19th century. Simultaneously the process of industrialization radically changed the face of British society, leading to the growth of large industrial cities, particularly in the Midlands, the North, Scotland, and South Wales. As the population shifted from the countryside to the cities a series of social and economic problems arose, the result of such factors as low wages, slum housing, and the use of child labour. Similar changes followed in other European countries, in the USA, and in Japan during the 19th century, while in the 20th century Eastern Europe, China, India, and south-east Asia have undergone a similar industrialization process.

inert gases See NOBLE GASES.

inertia A property of all objects that makes them resist any change to their state of rest or uniform motion in a straight line. Any force applied to a body will be resisted by the inertia of that body. The principle of inertia is fundamental to the first of NEWTON'S LAWS OF MOTION, laws that only apply in systems in which inertia is maintained (inertial frames of reference). In a rotating system inertia is not maintained, as a force has to be applied to keep a body rotating at a constant angular velocity. Mach's principle explains inertia as a result of the presence of the rest of the Universe.

inertial navigation A system of GYROSCOPES and ACCELEROMETERS, mounted on an extremely stable platform and linked to a COMPUTER that continuously monitors a vehicle's position and heading. The gyroscopes maintain the alignment of the platform horizontally, vertically, and in a north–south direction. Changes in the relationship of the vehicle to this stable platform are monitored to provide precise information about the vehicle's orientation, while velocity data is obtained from the accelerometers, which measure the vehicle's acceleration in the horizontal and (if necessary) vertical planes. The orientation and speed information is used by the computer to calculate the vehicle's position. Inertial navigation was first developed in 1942 by von BRAUN for the V2 rocket: it is now used in submarines, ships, aircraft, spacecraft, and GUIDED MISSILES.

infant mortality The number of deaths of infants before their first birthday for every thousand live births. In the UK the rate has fallen from about 140 in 1901 to 7.4 in 1991. Between the 1950s and 1990s rates have fallen all over the world, for example, from 181 to 73 in Asia, from 187 to 106 in Africa, and from 126 to 58 in South America. Infant mortality is often regarded as the best indicator of the general health and social conditions of a population. Improved nutrition, sanitation, living conditions, and health services, as well as reduced FERTILITY RATES (which lessen the ill-health of mothers), have all contributed to improvements in infant mortality rates.

infection The invasion of body tissues by microorganisms that produce disease (PATHOGENS), the subsequent multiplication of these microorganisms, and the resulting disease state. Multiplication is essential to establish progressive infection; bacterial infection generally requires large numbers to result in infection, whereas only small numbers are necessary for viral infection. Most bacterial infection can now be cured with ANTIBIOTICS, and some viral infections can be prevented by IMMUNIZATION.

infertility The inability to conceive a child. In much of the world an estimated 6 per cent of couples are involuntarily childless, excepting Africa, where the proportion is about 10 per cent, and the Middle East and Latin America, where the proportion is about 3 per cent. Investigating and treating infertility is complex and costly and is largely confined to wealthy industrialized countries. Childless couples may decide on ADOPTION, but some couples decide on ARTIFICIAL INSEMINATION by a donor to enable the woman to bear a child although her partner is infertile. Women may be treated for infertility by drugs or surgery. If this is unsuccessful IN VITRO FERTILIZATION (IVF), by which eggs are fertilized outside the body by sperm and then replaced in the womb, may be tried. IVF has opened the way to the use of sperm on eggs donated (or illegally sold) to the couple by strangers or relatives. Embryos created by IVF may also be frozen for later implantation. In surrogate motherhood, another woman may volunteer or be paid to bear a child fertilized by sperm from the husband of the childless couple.

inflammation The body's response to injury. Acute inflammation is the immediate defensive reaction of tissues to injury resulting from infection, chemicals, or physical agents. It involves pain, redness, swelling, and heat. Blood vessels dilate, the blood flow increases, and white blood cells engulf bacteria and other foreign particles. Macrophages (large scavenger cells) from the tissues remove and consume dead cells, sometimes producing pus. This enables the healing process to proceed. In certain circumstances healing does not occur and chronic inflammation results.

inflation A persistent upward movement of the general price level (or a decline in the purchasing power of MONEY), usually measured as a percentage rate per annum (see RETAIL PRICE INDEX). Keeping inflation low is a major economic objective for most governments since, although there is no conclusive proof that inflation adversely affects economic growth, it tends to generate a number of unwelcome effects. First, it penalizes holders of cash and those on fixed incomes. Secondly, it may distort the allocation of resources by altering relative prices, including 'real' INTEREST rates (the 'real' rates being nominal rates minus the expected inflation rate) and exchange rates. This may also be associated with a redistribution of income and wealth between creditors and debtors because the interest repaid after inflation will be lower than previously expected in real terms. Levels at which taxation is paid may also be distorted. Thirdly, price confusion may arise: consumers may not know the market price for a rarely bought commodity. Fourthly, inflation magnifies uncertainty about the future, which discourages investment. Lastly, inflation may make exports and import-competing goods more expensive and thus adversely affect the BALANCE OF TRADE unless the exchange rate is devalued. Monetarists prescribe tight control of the money supply, with the possible consequence of high and prolonged unemployment, in order to reduce inflation. A second 'demand pull' theory postulates that inflation arises when aggregate demand for goods and services exceeds supply, usually as a result of incorrect monetary or fiscal policies. A further model to explain inflation is the 'cost-push' theory, in which costs are increased by a rise in import prices or in one of the components of domestic income (most commonly wages), leading to a price-wage spiral.

in-flight refuelling The refuelling of an aircraft in flight to extend its range. A cone-shaped device (drogue) fitted to the end of a delivery hose is lowered from a tanker aircraft. The aircraft requiring fuel is fitted with an extended refuelling intake pipe (probe). Its pilot flies the aircraft up to the tanker aircraft until its probe engages into the drogue. Fuel is then transferred into his tanks and, when full, the drogue is released. In-flight refuelling is much used for MILITARY AIRCRAFT, particularly fighters and HELICOPTERS.

inflorescence See FLOWER.

influenza A highly contagious viral infection affecting the respiratory system, which is transmitted by coughs and sneezes. Symptoms include headache, fever, aching joints, weakness, etc. Bed rest, with aspirin or paracetamol, enable most cases to recover within several days but a few may develop pneumonia or secondary bacterial infections requiring antibiotics. 'Flu' epidemics can occur when new strains of the virus appear, to which the body's immune system and existing vaccines are ineffective. However, elderly people and vulnerable groups (e.g. those with heart disease) are recommended to have injections of influenza vaccines in the autumn. The worst epidemic of infuenza in the 20th century occurred in the aftermath of World War I (in 1918–19), when some 20 million lives were lost worldwide.

information retrieval The use of COMPUTERS to access information stored electronically. For many applications there are significant advantages over traditional paper-based storage. A computer, running suitable retrieval SOFTWARE, can search vast quantities of data and recover information very rapidly. For example, many DATABASES containing medical, financial, or legal information are available on-line (directly under the control of the central processor) via computer NETWORKS or MODEMS over telephone lines. With the continuing reduction in the cost of storage, and particularly the development of COMPACT DISCS, information retrieval is an increasingly important use for computers.

Information Superhighway See INTERNET.

information technology (IT) Practical applications of COMPUTER systems. Key factors in the recent rapid spread of microelectronics and information technology (often known simply as 'new technology') have been the drastic reduction in electronic hardware costs during the 1970s and 1980s; the so-called 'convergence' of computing and TELECOMMUNICATIONS; and the emergence of various formal standards and informal agreements within the IT industry.

The combination of computing with private and public telecommunication networks has been particularly significant in retailing and banking. BAR CODES on products can be read automatically at check-outs, and the information used both to print a customer's receipt and to reorder necessary stocks. ELECTRONIC FUNDS TRANSFER using an 'intelligent' cash register or point-of-sale terminal can then complete the cycle of electronic information flow by automatically debiting the customer's bank or credit-card account by the appropriate amount. Sales records held by the store's central computer can be used to develop overall retailing strategies; records of the purchasing patterns of particular customers can be exploited for direct marketing of goods or services.

The IT revolution has been just as great in the manufacturing and processing industries. An early application was the NUMERICAL CONTROL of machine-tools, in which digital electronics were used to control lathes and other equipment. Now it has become common for a wide range of industrial equipment (sensors, control systems, robots, and so on) to incorporate microelectronics and to be interconnected (networked) so that information can be gathered, communicated, and processed in order to optimize the activity. ARTIFICIAL INTELLIGENCE, in which computer programs mimic certain aspects of human behaviour, is beginning to play a role in areas such as process control, as well as in mechatronic products combining aspects of electronic, mechanical, and software engineering. Again, the convergence of telecommunications and computing has been a vital factor, allowing the computer to become fully integrated into the manufacturing or other processes (see COMPUTER-INTEGRATED MANUFACTURE), thus transcending individual applications such as COMPUTER-AIDED DESIGN.

information theory (in mathematics) A theory of communication that concerns the transmission of information by signals. It covers the capacity of communication channels, the corruption of messages (by 'noise' or interference), and the detection and correction of errors. It is much used in COMPUTER and TELECOMMUNICATIONS systems, but the theory is not specifically electronic. Much pioneering work on information theory was done by Claude Shannon in the USA during the 1940s. Practical applications range from the International Standard Book Number (ISBN) on all books, which incorporates a check digit, to the reception of messages from satellites.

infrared astronomy The observation of the extraterrestrial Universe by detecting ELECTROMAGNETIC RADIATION at infrared wavelengths. The Earth's atmosphere is transparent to several wavebands of infrared radiation, particularly in the shorter wavelengths, and observations in selected wavebands can be made by ground-based telescopes at specially chosen sites. The United Kingdom infrared telescope (UKIRT) stationed at MAUNA KEA, Hawaii, at a height of 4,200 m (13,800 feet) is well above the atmospheric water vapour which is the prime cause of opacity to the cosmic infrared radiation. Infrared observations are also made from rocket flights and balloon platforms. However, the most successful enterprise has been the Dutch–UK–US satellite carrying a telescope-photometer system. This Infrared Astronomical Satellite (IRAS) was launched in January 1983 and surveyed more than 96 per cent of the total sky area in four wavebands at 12, 25, 60, and 100 μm. Over its ten months of operation it catalogued some 250,000 point sources and some 20,000 small extended sources.

infrared radiation ELECTROMAGNETIC RADIATION with a wavelength of 10^{-6} to 10^{-3} m, which is slightly longer than that of visible light. It lies in the spectrum between red light and microwaves, is emitted by hot bodies (most intensely if they are red or white hot), and is sometimes called thermal RADIATION. Its energy is in the same range as that of atomic and molecular vibrations in solids; when it enters a material it is therefore able to impart its energy to the vibrating atoms so that their AMPLITUDE of oscillation is increased. Hence it is often used as a means of heating. Indeed, it is by infrared radiation from the Sun that the Earth is heated, the rays having the power to penetrate the atmosphere, haze, and fog.

Ingenhousz, Jan (1730–99) Dutch scientist. His early work was in medicine, and he popularized the inoculation of live smallpox vaccine as a protection against the disease. He is best known, however, for his work on photosynthesis, discovering that sunlit green plants take in carbon dioxide, fix the carbon, and 'restore' the air (oxygen) required by animals for respiration. Ingenhousz investigated Brownian motion, and introduced the use of cover slips for microscopy. He also worked in physics.

Ingres, Jean Auguste Dominique (1780–1867) French painter. He was a pupil of David and a vigorous opponent of romanticism, upholding neoclassicism in paintings such as *Ambassadors of Agamemnon* (1801). Ingres's many nudes, including the *Bather* (1808), reflect his skills as a draughtsman. In his feeling for pure form, he was admired by Degas.

Ingushetia (or **The Ingush Republic**) An autonomous republic of Russia, to the north of Georgia, largely populated by Ingush people of the northern Caucasus. It was constituted as an autonomous area of the Terek Autonomous Republic of the USSR in 1924 but was united with Chechenya from 1934 until the breakup of the Soviet Union in 1991. Its capital is Nazran. See also CHECHENYA.

inhibitor A substance that slows down or prevents chemical or biochemical reactions, such as the catalytic action of ENZYMES. Competitive inhibitors resemble the normal substances upon which enzymes work and fit into the active site. Non-competitive inhibitors, including poisons, such as cyanide, bind elsewhere on the enzyme molecule, changing its properties so that its activity is destroyed. Naturally occurring inhibitors control the METABOLISM of living cells by switching off enzymes that are no longer needed.

injunction A court order that either restrains a person from performing a particular action, or compels a person to do something. In COMMON LAW SYSTEMS it is granted at the court's discretion, especially where DAMAGES would be inadequate or inappropriate; for example, an injunction may restrain a person from playing loud music in a residential area at night or prevent the publication of defamatory material. Failure to comply with an injunction constitutes CONTEMPT OF COURT, which may result in imprisonment. The injunction is a remedy little used in CIVIL LAW systems, with the exception of Germany, where it is used to protect against interference with property, and to supplement the slander laws.

ink A PIGMENT mixed with a liquid or semiliquid vehicle, used for writing or printing. Inks were first used in China *c.*2000 BC. Most early inks were a mixture of carbon, oil, and gum. Writing inks are now formulated for the pens they serve – free-flowing water-based inks for fountain pens, and thicker, more concentrated mixtures for ballpoints. In the 15th century varnish was introduced into printing ink, heralding the development of the many inks used for LETTERPRESS, LITHOGRAPHY, GRAVURE PRINTING, and other processes. Apart from the differing pigments, vehicles, resins, and varnishes that they use, printing inks are now largely distinguished by their drying methods. Lithography and letterpress inks dry by penetration and oxidation; flexographic and gravure inks by evaporation; and newspaper inks mostly by absorption. Many of the web (continuous-paper) and some of the sheet-fed printing processes use hot air, infrared, or ultraviolet radiation to force-dry the ink.

Inkatha A South African organization founded by Chief BUTHELEZI to promote the independence of the ZULUS. Inkatha supported the development of South Africa into a nonracial democracy, although some Blacks accused it of collaboration with Whites in achieving it. In the 1990s clashes occurred between Inkatha and the African National Congress, but have largely died down since three Inkatha supporters joined the government after the elections in 1994.

ink-jet printing A form of computer-controlled printing developed during the 1970s. Ink is ejected under pressure from a fine nozzle as a series of tiny droplets. These droplets cross a small gap between the nozzle and the printing medium, and are precisely steered in flight to form the desired image on the printing surface. The positioning of the droplets on the print surface is controlled by a computer, which works from an electronic record of the image to be printed. Various methods of controlling the ink droplets in the air are used, and printers may have one ink-jet to scan the whole image, or an array of ink-jets, making much greater print speeds possible.

Inland Sea (Japanese **Seto Naikai**) An almost landlocked arm of the Pacific Ocean surrounded by the Japanese islands of Honshu, Shikoku, and Kyushu. Its chief port is Hiroshima.

Inner Mongolia (Chinese **Nei Monggol**) An autonomous region of northern China, comprising grassland and desert on the frontier with Mongolia; area 1,183,000 sq km (456,933 sq miles); pop. (1990) 21,457,000; capital, Hohhot.

inner planet A planet that is closer to the Sun than the asteroid belt, which has a mean radius of 2.8 times that of the orbit of the Earth. The inner planets are therefore Mercury, Venus, the Earth, and Mars (and some would argue to the Moon as well because of its size). These planets, also known as **terrestrial planets**, have much smaller masses than the OUTER PLANETS but have much larger densities, being composed largely of rock and iron with very little hydrogen and helium, and very little volatile molecules, such as carbon dioxide, methane, and ammonia.

Innocent III (1160–1216) Pope 1198–1216. As pope he was an active and vigorous reformer of the Church. He reasserted control over the PAPAL STATES and was acknowledged as the overlord of SICILY. In Germany he asserted the pope's right to choose between two rival candidates for the imperial crown; he eventually supported FREDERICK II's claims provided that he did homage for Sicily. He intervened in English affairs, excommunicating King JOHN for refusing to recognize Stephen LANGTON as Archbishop of Canterbury and declaring MAGNA CARTA void; he also attempted to curb the independence of PHILIP II of France.

Innsbruck A resort and industrial city of western Austria, on the River Inn; pop. (1991) 115,000. A winter-sports centre and capital of the state of Tyrol, situated on a historic routeway between Germany and Italy and between Vienna and Switzerland. It was founded as a market town in 1180 and was a ducal residence from 1420 to 1665. Innsbruck's industries include metal products, textiles, and printing.

Inns of Court Four sets of buildings in London (Inner Temple, Middle Temple, Lincoln's Inn, and Gray's Inn) belonging to the legal societies of England and Wales with the exclusive right of 'calling persons to the bar' (the partition, real or imaginary, across a law court, separating the judge, jury, and certain lawyers from the public), and thereby enabling them to practise as BARRISTERS. Each Inn is governed by officers called benchers (Masters of the Bench), who mainly comprise judges and Queen's Counsels (QCs). Most London barristers have 'chambers' (offices) in the Inns of Court. In 1926 an Inn of Court was established in Belfast.

inoculation See VACCINATION.

inorganic chemistry See CHEMISTRY.

input device (computing) A PERIPHERAL that allows information from an external source to be fed into a computer system. The standard input device for most modern computer systems is a keyboard, similar to a typewriter's but with additional keys to provide a larger range of characters and control functions. Many computers are also equipped with a MOUSE. Scanners, digitizers, or even video cameras are used for GRAPHICS systems. Point-of-sale terminals may have BAR-CODE readers. OPTICAL CHARACTER RECOGNITION systems are used in banking, to read codes printed on cheques, or in DESK-TOP PUBLISHING systems to convert printed documents into ASCII codes so that they can be stored and processed digitally. Scanners are used to digitize illustrations, so that they can be stored electronically and fed into page-make-up programs.

inquest A legal or judicial inquiry to determine matters of fact. In COMMON LAW SYSTEMS, a coroner's inquest is a legal inquiry that has to take place in the event of a sudden, violent, or suspicious death, in order to determine the cause. Coroners' inquests are sometimes held before a JURY, but are not criminal proceedings. The coroner may make recommendations (for example, about a dangerous product) to prevent similar deaths in future. Coroners also hold inquests on treasure trove (money, gold, or silver found and the ownership of which is unknown).

Inquisition (or **Holy Office**) An ecclesiastical court established *c.*1232 for the detection and punishment of heretics, at a time when sectarian groups were threatening not only the orthodoxy of the Catholic religion but the stability of contemporary society. The Inquisition came into being when FREDERICK II issued an edict entrusting the hunting-out of heretics to state inquisitors; Pope Gregory IX claimed it as a papal responsiblity and appointed inquisitors, mostly drawn from the Franciscan and Dominican orders. He had previously ordered the Dominicans to crush the ALBIGENSIANS (1223). Those accused of heresy who refused to confess were tried before an inquisitor and jury and punishments were harsh, including confiscation of goods, torture, and death. The Index (a list of books condemned by the Church) was issued by the Congregation of the Inquisition in 1557. The SPANISH INQUISITION was a separate organization established in 1479 by the Spanish monarchy with papal approval. In 1965 the Holy Office was renamed the Sacred Congregation for the Doctrine of the Faith.

insect An ARTHROPOD of the class Insecta, the body of which is divided into three parts: head, thorax and abdomen. The head bears many structures, including one pair of antennae, two compound eyes, and the mandibles. The thorax consists of three segments, each of which bears a pair of legs, although these may be modified as grasping or swimming organs in some species. In most insects the thorax also bears two pairs of wings on the second and third segments. The wings are strengthened with veins and are usually transparent, although they may be covered with scales or hairs. The front pair of wings may be thickened for protecting the hind ones, as in beetles and earwigs. Some insects, such as silverfish and springtails, are wingless.

The insect abdomen has 6–13 segments and may bear various appendages, especially those for mating and egg-laying. The insect body receives oxygen through fine tubes, the tracheae, ramifying through the body and opening into spiracles on the sides of the body. They have a simple digestive system, and waste products are removed from the open circulatory system by organs called Malpighian tubules. These extract nitrogenous wastes and excrete them into the hind gut as crystals of uric acid.

Insects are divided into some 30 orders. Of these, nine have a life history involving complete METAMORPHOSIS, and the rest have incomplete metamorphosis. See also INSECT PESTS.

insecticide A PESTICIDE designed to kill INSECT PESTS. It includes both natural and chemical agents directed against insects, mites, nematodes, and molluscs. The earliest insecticides, pyrethrum, derris, and nicotine, were extracted from plants. A major advance was the introduction of chlorinated HYDROCARBON (organochlorine) insecticides, such as DDT. Persistent, and active against most pests,

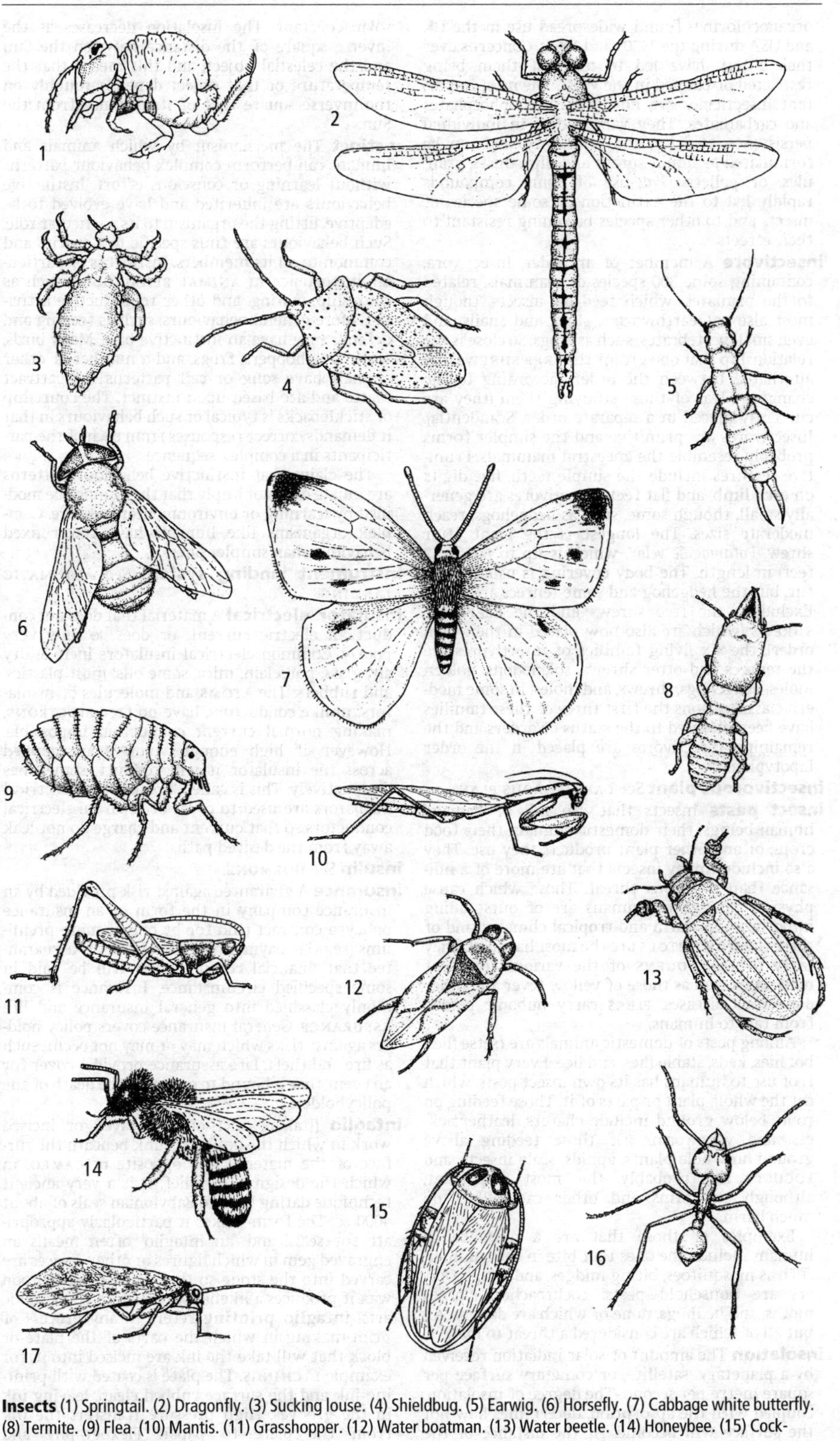

Insects (1) Springtail. (2) Dragonfly. (3) Sucking louse. (4) Shieldbug. (5) Earwig. (6) Horsefly. (7) Cabbage white butterfly. (8) Termite. (9) Flea. (10) Mantis. (11) Grasshopper. (12) Water boatman. (13) Water beetle. (14) Honeybee. (15) Cockroach. (16) Ant. (17) Caddis fly.

organochlorines found widespread use in the UK and USA during the 1950s and 1960s. Concerns over their safety have led to most of them being restricted or banned in the West. The most important insecticides are now the organophosphates and carbamates. They vary widely in individual persistence, toxicity, and selectivity, and can be formulated as liquid sprays and dips, dusts, granules, or pellets. Over-use of some compounds rapidly led to the extinction of some species of insects and to other species becoming resistant to their effects.

insectivore A member of an order, Insectivora, containing some 300 species of mammals, related to the primates, which feed on insects, though most also eat earthworms, slugs and snails, and even small vertebrates, such as frogs. So close is the relationship that one group, the TREE SHREWS, has alternated between the orders according to the changing ideas of those studying them (they are currently placed in a separate order, Scandentia). Insectivores are primitive and the simpler forms probably resemble the ancestral mammals. Primitive features include the simple teeth, five digits on each limb, and flat feet. Insectivores are generally small, though some, such as hedgehogs, reach moderate sizes. The longest is the giant otter shrew, *Potamogale velox*, which is up to 60 cm (2 feet) in length. The body covering is usually soft fur, but the hedgehog and some tenrecs are spiny. Excluding the tree shrews and the ELEPHANT SHREWS (which are also now placed in their own order), the six living families of insectivores are the tenrecs and otter shrews, solenodons, golden moles, hedgehogs, shrews, and moles. In some modern classifications the first three of these families have been elevated to the status of orders and the remaining insectivores are placed in the order Lipotyphla.

insectivorous plant See CARNIVOROUS PLANT.

insect pests Insects that can kill or damage human beings, their domestic animals, their food crops, or any other plant products they use. They also includes many insects that are more of a nuisance than a serious threat. Those which cause physical damage to humans are of outstanding importance in warm and tropical climates, and of these the MOSQUITOES are the most harmful. They carry the PATHOGENS of the various forms of malaria, as well as those of yellow fever and other dangerous diseases. FLEAS carry bubonic plague from rats to humans.

Among pests of domestic animals are tsetse flies, bot flies, keds, stable flies, and lice. Every plant that is of use to humans has its own insect pests, which eat the whole plant or parts of it. Those feeding on roots below ground include chafers, leatherjackets, and wireworms. Of those feeding above ground on whole plants, aphids, scale insects, and LOCUSTS are probably the most important, although cutworms and other caterpillars do much harm.

Examples of those that are a nuisance to humans include the ones that bite in the summer, such as mosquitoes, biting midges, and wasps. Others are household pests: cockroaches, clothes moths, and bedbugs, none of which are dangerous, but all of which are considered a threat to man.

insolation The amount of solar radiation received by a planetary, satellite, or cometary surface per square metre per second. The degree of insolation, coupled with the absorption, determines how hot the surface will become. At the distance of the Earth from the Sun, the insolation is called the solar constant. The insolation decreases as the inverse square of the distance between the Sun and the celestial object, and this means that the temperature of that object depends roughly on the inverse square root of its distance from the Sun.

instinct The mechanism by which animals and humans can perform complex behaviour patterns without learning or conscious effort. Instinctive behaviours are inherited and have evolved to be adaptive, fitting the organism to its particular role. Such behaviours are thus specific to a species and common to all its members. Instinct is of particular importance in ANIMAL BEHAVIOURS, such as courtship, mating, and other reproductive activities. More general behaviours, such as feeding and defence may have an instinctive base. Many birds, some grasshoppers, frogs, and a number of other animals have song or call patterns that attract mates and are based upon instinct. The courtship of sticklebacks is typical of such behaviours in that it demands correct responses from each of the participants in a complex sequence.

The claim that instinctive behaviour patterns are innate does not imply that they cannot be modified by learning or environmental pressure. Complex organisms like humans have fewer fixed behaviour than simpler ones.

instrument landing system See AUTOMATIC LANDING.

insulator, electrical A material that does not conduct an electric current, or does so only very poorly. Common electrical insulators include dry air, glass, porcelain, mica, some oils, most plastics, and rubbers. The ATOMS and molecules of insulators, unlike conductors, have no free ELECTRONS, making normal current conduction impossible. However, if high enough voltages are applied across the insulator it will conduct, sometimes destructively. This is called 'breakdown'. Electrical insulators are used to cover or separate electrical conductors so that current and charge do not leak away from the desired path.

insulin See HORMONE.

insurance A guarantee against risk provided by an insurance company in the form of an insurance policy, a contract paid for by one or more premiums (regular payments). The contract is a guarantee that financial compensation will be paid in some specified circumstance. Insurance is commonly classified into general insurance and life ASSURANCE. General insurance covers policy holders against risks which may or may not occur, such as fire and theft. Life assurance provides cover for an event that is bound to occur, i.e. the death of the policyholder.

intaglio (Italian, 'incision') Engraved or incised work in which the design is sunk beneath the surface of the material, the opposite of CAMEO, in which the design is in relief. It is a very ancient technique dating back to Babylonian seals of about 4000 BC. The form makes it particularly appropriate for seals, and 'an intaglio' often means an engraved gem in which figures or other devices are carved into the stone so that when pressed upon wax it produces a likeness in relief. In the graphic arts, **intaglio printing** refers to any process of print-making in which the parts of the plate or block that will take the ink are incised into it, for example ETCHINGS. The plate is coated with printing ink and the surface rubbed clean, leaving ink in the grooves. High pressure transfers the ink from the plate to paper. Flexography and GRAVURE PRINTING are also intaglio processes.

integrated circuit (IC) A single chip (sometimes called a **microchip**) of silicon or other suitable semiconductor carrying a complete electronic circuit, manufactured as one unit. Each chip contains TRANSISTORS, DIODES, RESISTORS, and CAPACITORS as the main building blocks of the electronic circuit. The integrated circuit underpins all microelectronics technology. The manufacture of an integrated circuit is a complex process, which may embody 50 or more separate stages. Silicon chips are made from specially grown, extremely pure, tubular silicon crystals up to 1 m (3.3 feet) long and 15 cm (6 inches) in diameter. The crystals are first sliced into wafers or circular discs. Individual, identical chips are made simultaneously on each wafer in a series of optical and chemical processes. These processes introduce specific impurities into defined areas of the chip, forming SEMICONDUCTOR DEVICES. The devices are connected electrically by deposits of aluminium, and the wafer is then broken into separate chips, which are individually encapsulated. Integrated circuits can serve many functions. MICROPROCESSOR chips carry out arithmetical operations and can control other circuits. Dynamic random-access MEMORY chips (DRAMs) can store up to 4 million BITS of data. Other chips may carry computer programs, and applications-specific circuits are tailored to the requirements of a particular device.

integration (in mathematics) The reverse of DIFFERENTIATION. That is, given a function (say the squared function, $y = x^2$), the object is to find another function, the integral, which when differentiated yields the original (x^2). The integral of x^2 is $(x^3/3) + K$ where K is an arbitrary constant number, called the **constant of integration**. This is written $\int x^2\,dx = (x^3/3) + K$. There are several techniques for integrating functions, such as integration by substitution, and integration by parts. The type of integration described above is indefinite integration. It is distinguished from definite integration, where the answer is always a number rather than a function. Definite integration developed separately from indefinite integration as a method for calculating irregular areas and volumes. The notation for a definite integral is $\int_1^3 x^2 dx$. The integral sign $\int$ is an elongated 's', standing for summation. The term $x^2\,dx$ represents the area of an infinitesimally wide rectangular strip. Thus the notation symbolizes the summation of infinitesimal strips. The numbers at the top and bottom of the integral sign (that is 1 and 3) are the **limits of integration**.

intellectual property A type of property that includes COPYRIGHTS, PATENTS, TRADEMARKS and certain information. Most countries have intellectual property laws, and international agreements exist. The World Intellectual Property Organization (WIPO), an agency of the UN, is responsible for promoting the protection of intellectual property throughout the world and attempting to harmonize different intellectual property laws. In some parts of the world, particularly in south-east Asia, the piracy of Western books, records, videos, computer programs, and brand-name products has been a growing problem.

intelligence The mental faculties involved in understanding and solving problems. Animals other than humans show BEHAVIOUR that appears to indicate the presence of intelligent faculties. Although it is difficult to demonstrate reasoning in animals, it is often unclear whether this is because animals do not have the faculties for solving complex problems, or because the problems are being asked in an inappropriate way. Monkeys show intelligence when presented with a wide variety of visual problems, whereas rats, which have poor eyesight, respond intelligently to problems with smells as cues.

In humans, as measured by INTELLIGENCE TESTS, there is some correlation between intelligence, educational achievement, and occupational status. However, there are many forms of intelligence. Mentally handicapped 'idiots savants' occasionally show prodigious memory or exceptional drawing skills. Child psychologists emphasize qualitatively distinct stages in intelligence, as COGNITIVE DEVELOPMENT progresses from infancy to adulthood. Intelligence in technological societies may also be defined in relation to verbal and spatial skills, which make for success in school. Heredity, the environment, and the interplay between the two probably all play a role in the development of intelligence, but their relative importance is disputed.

intelligence services Government organizations dedicated to the collection and evaluation of information, primarily about the intentions of other countries that are seen as adversaries. Such information can be economic, political, or military, and can relate either to general trends or to specific groups such as terrorists, individuals, and institutions. Much intelligence is gathered from public sources, but intelligence services have also developed extensive covert activities, designed to protect and enhance national security. They have also acquired functions in COUNTER-INTELLIGENCE, in order to safeguard their own operations and to manipulate those of adversaries.

intelligence test A measure of individual differences in INTELLIGENCE, the first being devised by BINET in 1908. The most widely known is the Wechsler test, which measures verbal and non-verbal abilities such as vocabulary, reasoning by analogy, memory, and spatial abilities to yield an Intelligence Quotient (IQ). For any population the average IQ score is 100. An IQ test score higher than 130 is obtained by no more than 5 per cent of the population and this may define intellectual giftedness. In the UK a score below 70 legally defines mental handicap.

intensive-care unit (ICU) A specialist hospital ward dedicated to the (usually short-term) monitoring, treatment, and nursing of life-threatening conditions. A unit may be devoted to the care of patients with respiratory failure (see RESPIRATOR) or renal failure (see HAEMODIALYSIS). Other specialist ICUs deal with people having severe burns, or premature babies, or patients who have had cardiac surgery or a heart attack. Some patients admitted to ICUs require immediate support of the function of one or more vital organs, using drugs or machines; for other patients, constant monitoring may be sufficient. ICUs are expensive to run because of the equipment and staffing levels needed, and their availability is limited.

interactions (in physics) The ways in which one particle has an effect on another. They result from the four fundamental forces. On the human scale the most obvious is GRAVITATION, which makes objects fall to the ground under the gravitational attraction of the Earth. On the atomic and subatomic scale, however, gravitation is so weak that it is much less important than the other three kinds of interaction that are known: the strong, the electromagnetic, and the weak. All three, unlike gravitation, act only on certain classes of particle. Strong interactions result from the

STRONG FORCE. They occur over a very short distance and in a very short time – typically of the order of 10^{-23} second – the time it takes for light to cross an atomic nucleus. In these interactions the FLAVOUR of the particles remains unchanged (is 'conserved'). It is thought that the gluons that bind QUARKS together are the agents of strong interactions. Electromagnetic interactions result from the ELECTROMAGNETIC FORCE. They occur in times of 10^{-15} to 10^{-20} second between charged particles, such as when an electron and a positron collide to form photons. The photon is the agent of electromagnetic interactions, and it operates over all distances. The weak interaction results from the WEAK FORCE. It has been the subject of intense interest, and was first noted as the agency responsible for the beta decay of radioactive nuclei. It can occur over a very wide range of times – from 10^{-13} second to 10^{10} years. The process occurs by the exchange of very heavy BOSONS, and flavour is not conserved. Although it is called weak, at sufficiently high energies it can be as strong as an electromagnetic interaction. Its range is the shortest of all the interactions. It is the goal of some physicists to combine the theories for each of these interactions into one single GRAND UNIFIED THEORY. So far, a joint theory of electromagnetic and weak interactions has been developed; it appears satisfactory, but a full unified theory has yet to come.

intercontinental ballistic missile (ICBM) See BALLISTIC MISSILE.

intercropping The practice of growing one crop between rows of another. The technique is used both by conventional and by ORGANIC FARMERS: the by-products of one crop can provide nutrients, shade, or support to the other and can encourage insects that eat the pests of the neighbouring crop. Intercropping also ensures that the earth is never left totally bare and exposed to erosion by wind or rainfall.

interest (in economics) Payments made by a borrower to a lender during specified time periods in return for the use of a capital sum. To the borrower these payments represent the cost of borrowing. To the lender they are a reward for postponing CONSUMPTION (by saving rather than spending) and for the risk involved in making the loan. Interest may be calculated as **simple interest**, i.e. $I = PRt/100$, where I is the interest, P is the capital sum borrowed, R is the rate of interest (i.e. the annual rate of return expressed as a percentage), and t is the period of the loan in years. Alternatively interest may be calculated as **compound interest**, in which case $I = P(1 + R/100)t$. In this case the interest is not paid annually to the lender but is added to the capital sum borrowed. In the UK, if an interest rate is quoted for a period of less than one year, the equivalent annual percentage rate (APR) must be stated.

interference (in physics) A phenomenon that occurs when two or more wave motions with the same WAVELENGTH overlap one another. When this happens the waves reinforce each other at some points, where their crests coincide, and cancel at others, where a crest coincides with a trough. Light of a single wavelength can be used to demonstrate interference. If the light is made to pass through two slits that are close together, a pattern of light and dark bands called interference fringes is produced when the light strikes a screen; the fringes represent points of reinforcement and cancellation. Interference phenomena occur throughout the electromagnetic spectrum. See INTERFEROMETRY.

interferometry The analysis of INTERFERENCE patterns formed by ELECTROMAGNETIC RADIATION. An instrument that combines two or more waves to create an interference pattern is called an **interferometer**. Interferometry is widely used in astronomy to give data on the size and structure of astronomical objects. Although interferometry can be applied to most parts of the electromagnetic spectrum, it is most commonly used in RADIO ASTRONOMY. A radio interferometer gives an interference pattern obtained by adding together two signals from a star or other source of radiation with a clearly defined phase difference between them. This phase difference depends on the separation (baseline) between two aerials (US antennas). The longer the baseline, the higher the RESOLVING POWER that can be achieved.

interferon A soluble protein discovered by Alick Isaacs in 1957, produced by animal cells when they are attacked by viruses. Interferons inhibit the growth of the virus and are an important first stage in the development of IMMUNITY, before the appearance of antibodies. Because they are present only in minute amounts, it is difficult to obtain them pure and in quantities sufficient for clinical purposes. However, human interferon can now be obtained by techniques of GENETIC ENGINEERING and is being evaluated in the treatment of certain forms of hepatitis and of multiple sclerosis. Interferons may protect patients having undergone immunosuppression from dangerous viral infections. They inhibit the growth of some tumours and have been investigated as a treatment for cancer.

interglacial The comparatively warm periods that separated periods of glaciation during the PLEISTOCENE EPOCH. Characterized by similar flora and fauna to those of the present day, although maximum temperatures may have been 2–3°C (4–5°F) higher, they varied between about 20,000 and 70,000 years in length.

Interlaken The chief resort town of the Bernese Alps in central Switzerland, situated on the River Aare between Lake Brienz and Lake Thun; pop. (1980) 4,850. It has a clock and watch industry.

intermezzo In the 18th century, a short comic opera performed between the acts of a serious opera. In the 19th century, an orchestral interlude separating the scenes or acts of an opera. Since then an intermezzo may be a short movement in a symphony, concerto, or sonata, or a short piano piece.

intermolecular forces Forces that act between molecules. In gases, intermolecular forces, which are often known as van der Waals' forces, prevent real gases from behaving as an IDEAL GAS. Intermolecular forces also hold the molecules together in liquids and in some solids. They are many times weaker than the covalent bonds within the molecules. They are caused by dipole interactions between the molecules; the force is inversely proportional to the seventh power of the distance. In a compound that has a permanent DIPOLE moment, such as hydrogen chloride, the attraction is a dipole-dipole interaction. It is also possible for a dipole in one molecule to induce a dipole in a neighbouring molecule to give a dipole-induced dipole interaction. Even if there is no permanent dipole moment, as in the case of nitrogen, instantaneous dipoles can occur because of changes in the electron distribution within the molecule. This can also happen in atoms of gases, such as the rare gases. Forces resulting from such instantaneous dipoles are known as dispersion forces. The HYDROGEN BOND is a particularly strong form of intermolecular force, intermediate in strength between normal van der Waals' forces and classical chemical bonds.

internal-combustion engine A heat-engine in which the fuel is burnt within the ENGINE itself so that the working fluid is a hot gas, produced by combustion of air and fuel. Thus it is distinguished from an external-combustion system, such as a STEAM-ENGINE, in which fuel is burnt in a BOILER to provide steam as the working fluid. The flow of hot gas may be continuous, as in a GAS-TURBINE, or intermittent, as in a RECIPROCATING ENGINE or a ROTARY ENGINE. See also DIESEL ENGINE; PETROL ENGINE.

internal energy The total energy possessed by the atoms or molecules in a system by virtue of their motion and their interactions with one another. In a gas the molecules are in continuous rapid motion. They are constantly colliding with one another; and although in these collisions energy is transferred from one molecule to another it can never be lost. The hotter a gas is, the more rapidly the molecules move and the greater its internal energy. Thus temperature is a measure of internal energy. (See also HEAT AND TEMPERATURE.) Internal energy is an important concept in THERMODYNAMICS. Although the total internal energy (U) of a system can rarely be measured, the change in internal energy (ΔU) can. For a closed system, this is equal to the heat absorbed by the system from its surroundings (Q) less the work done (W) by the system on its surroundings, i.e. $\Delta U = Q - W$. This statement is known as the first law of thermodynamics.

International Atomic Energy Agency (IAEA) An international organization based in Vienna, Austria, which was established in 1957, under the auspices of the UN. The Agency, of which 113 states are members, encourages the peaceful uses of atomic power in such fields as agriculture, medicine, industry, and energy supply. It offers technical assistance and guidance on safety standards. It seeks to ensure that nuclear materials and equipment intended for peaceful use are not diverted to military purposes. In accordance with the Nuclear Non-Proliferation Treaty (1968), it inspects nuclear installations in those states that have acceded to it.

International Brigades International groups of volunteers in the SPANISH CIVIL WAR. They were largely communist, on the side of the republic against FRANCO. At no time were there more than 20,000 in the Brigades. They fought mainly in the defence of Madrid (1936) and in the battle of the River Ebro (1938).

International Court of Justice A judicial court of the UNITED NATIONS that replaced the Cour Permanente de Justice in 1946 and meets at The Hague in The Netherlands. It is one of the six principal organs of the United Nations, and its main judicial body. It has 15 judges elected for renewable nine-year terms by the General Assembly and the Security Council. It is concerned with disputes between states.

International Covenant on Civil and Political Rights A covenant adopted by the UNITED NATIONS in 1966, with 88 countries as signatories. The covenant promulgates the civil and political rights enumerated in the Universal Declaration of Human Rights of 1948. Whereas the Declaration is not legally binding, the covenant has the legal force of a treaty for the parties to it.

international date-line Nominally the meridian of longitude 180°, which runs through the Pacific Ocean over very little land. At this line the date is deemed to change when a ship or aircraft crosses it. For convenience to the inhabitants of Fiji, Tonga, and some of New Zealand's islands, the line is made to deviate eastwards by 7° between latitudes 10° and 50° S.

International Gothic A style in painting, sculpture, and the decorative arts that spread over Europe between *c*.1375 and *c*.1425. The style was characterized by aristocratic elegance and delicate naturalistic detail and was formed by a mingling of elements from Italian and northern European art, encouraged by the cultural rivalry of major courts and the increasing freedom with which major artists travelled. Lombardy, Burgundy, and Bohemia were among the areas in which the style flourished, and major exponents included GENTILE DA FABRIANO, PISANELLO, and the Limburg Brothers. Elements of the style are present in the work of several of the leading artists of the early Italian RENAISSANCE, such as Fra ANGELICO, GHIBERTI, and UCCELLO.

International Labour Organization (ILO) An agency founded in 1919 to improve labour and living standards throughout the world. At first affiliated to the League of Nations, in 1946 the ILO became the first specialized agency of the UNITED NATIONS. The ILO sets international guidelines for improving working conditions, TRADE-UNION rights, the rights of women and children, MINIMUM WAGE levels, hours, and health and safety at work. It provides technical assistance to developing countries, promotes employment, and researches and reports on trends in employment and industrial-relations practice and law. The ILO received the Nobel Peace Prize in 1967. The USA withdrew in 1977, claiming that the ILO had become dominated by politics, but rejoined in 1980. By 1993 162 countries were members of the ILO.

international law The body of rules and principles that states consider legally binding on them in their international relations. The three major sources of international law according to Article 38 of the Statute of the INTERNATIONAL COURT OF JUSTICE are: international CONVENTIONS or TREATIES; international customs; and the general principles of law as recognized by civilized nations. Modern international law has evolved over the last 400 years. It grew, in part, out of the usages and practices of modern European states in their relations with each other. The 19th century saw a great interest in international law with the rise of powerful new states, the expansion of European colonialism, new industrial innovations, and the increased destructiveness of war. The 20th century has also seen major advances. The Permanent Court of Arbitration was established by the Hague Conferences of 1899 and 1907, and the Permanent Court of International Justice was set up in 1921 and succeeded in 1946 by the INTERNATIONAL COURT OF JUSTICE. Since World War II international organizations such as the UNITED NATIONS and its related bodies have also contributed to the expansion and increased scope of international law. While there is a tendency to focus on the failures of international law in the realm of peace and war, these are the exception rather than the rule. By the early 1990s international law had not only shown its flexibility by expanding to cover new areas of international relations, but also its efficacy when, through the machinery of the UN,

Iraq's aggression against Kuwait in 1990 was effectively repudiated.

International Monetary Fund (IMF) An international economic institution, and specialized agency of the UN. Proposed at the BRETTON WOODS CONFERENCE in 1944, the IMF was established in 1945 and is based in Washington, DC. In 1991 it had 151 members. Unlike the WORLD BANK, to which it is closely allied, the IMF is not a development agency. Its principal aims are to encourage international monetary cooperation and the expansion of international trade, to stabilize exchange rates, and to eliminate foreign-exchange restrictions. Member states subscribe funds in accordance with their wealth. The Fund offers its members an orderly system for settling financial transactions among themselves. It also makes loans to countries with BALANCE-OF-PAYMENTS difficulties.

Internationals Associations formed to unite socialist and communist organizations throughout the world. There were four Internationals. The First (1864), at which MARX was a leading figure, met in London but was riven by disputes between Marxists and anarchists. By 1872 it had become clear that divisions were irreconcilable and it was disbanded (1876). The Second, or Socialist, International (1889) aimed at uniting the numerous new socialist parties that had sprung up in Europe. With headquarters in Brussels, it was better organized and by 1912 it contained representatives from all European countries and also from the USA, Canada, and Japan. It did not survive the outbreak of World War I, when its plan to prevent war by general strike and revolution was swamped by a wave of nationalism in all countries. The Third, usually known as the Communist International or COMINTERN (1919), was founded by LENIN and the BOLSHEVIKS to promote world revolution and a world communist state. It drew up the Twenty-One Points of pure communist doctrine to be accepted by all seeking membership. This resulted in splits between communist parties, which accepted the Points, and socialist parties, which did not. The Comintern increasingly became an instrument of the Soviet Union's foreign policy. In 1943 Stalin disbanded it. The Fourth International (1938), of comparatively little importance, was founded by TROTSKY and his followers in opposition to STALIN. After Trotsky's assassination (1940) it was controlled by two Belgian communists, Pablo and Germain, whose bitter disagreements had by 1953 ended any effective action.

International Telecommunication Union (ITU) An organization founded in Paris in 1865 as the International Telegraph Union; it became a specialized agency of the United Nations in 1947. Its role is to promote and coordinate telegraph, telephone, and RADIO services worldwide, including space telecommunications. It is responsible for allocating and registering radio-frequency WAVEBANDS.

Internet A global NETWORK that connects other computer networks, together with software and protocols for controlling the movement of data. The Internet, often referred to as 'the Net', stems from a network called ARAPNET (Advanced Research Project Agency Network), which was initiated in 1969 by a group of universities and private research groups funded by the US Department of Defense. Often referred to as the **Information Superhighway**, it now covers almost every country in the world. Its organization is informal and deliberately nonpolitical – its controllers tend to concentrate on technical aspects rather than on administrative control.

The Internet offers users a number of basic services including data transfer, ELECTRONIC MAIL, and the ability to access information in remote databases. A notable feature is the existence of user groups, which allow people to exchange information and debate specific subjects of interest. In addition, there are a number of high-level services. For example, MBONE (multicast backbone service) allows the transmission of messages to more than one destination. It is used in videoconferencing. The **World Wide Web**, known as 'the Web', is another high-level Internet service, developed in the 1990s at CERN in Geneva. It is a service for distributing multimedia information, including graphics, pictures, sounds, and video as well as text. A feature of the World Wide Web is that it allows links to other related documents elsewhere on the Internet. Documents for publication on the Web are presented in a form known as HTML (hypertext mark-up language). This allows a specification of the page layout and typography as it will appear on the screen. It also allows the inclusion of active links to other documents. Generally, these appear on the screen display as highlighted text or as additional icons. Many commercial and public organizations now have their own Web site (specified by an address code) and publish a 'home page', giving information about the organization.

Up to the mid-1990s, the major users of the Internet were academic and research organizations. This has begun to change rapidly with individual home users linking in through commercial access providers and with a growing interest by companies in using the Internet for publicity, sales, and as a medium for electronic publishing.

interplanetary medium The dust and PLASMA that occupies the space between the planets. The plasma is known as the SOLAR WIND and consists of protons and electrons that are being blown away from the solar corona. Normally the plasma at the Earth's orbit contains around five protons and electrons per cubic centimetre and these are moving past at a velocity of 400 km/s. The medium also contains dust particles and these are found in a symmetrical flattened cloud surrounding the Sun. Sunlight scattered from this cloud creates the zodiacal light. Dust is also found in a series of METEOR STREAMS containing meteoroids which can have masses ranging from thousands of kilograms to less than a million millionth of a gram. The small particles are being blown away from the Sun by radiation pressure, whereas the larger bodies are slowly spiralling into the Sun as they lose momentum.

Interpol (International Criminal Police Organization) An international organization of police forces, aimed at promoting exchange of information and more effective law enforcement. Interpol was established in 1923, in Vienna, and since the end of World War II its headquarters has been in Paris. Its operations are based on cooperation between its members, the national police forces of 138 countries, and on a central clearing-house for information, which maintains records on international criminals. The growing internationalization of crime has created an increasing need for Interpol's services, particularly in dealing with arms smuggling, drugs networks, money-laundering, and those who take refuge in other countries after committing offences.

interstellar medium The dust and gas that make up about 10 per cent of the mass of the Galaxy. In some regions the material is relatively cool (100 K) and is detectable by infrared telescopes. Such clouds contain neutral hydrogen (**HI regions**), molecular hydrogen, and other molecular radicals that can be identified by radio telescopes. In other regions, closer to luminous stars, the gas may be hot (1,000–10,000 K) with the hydrogen being ionized (**HII regions**). From measurements of the effects of the dust on the light of the background stars, the particles are thought to be about 0.1 μm in size, comprising carbon and silicates, and having icy surfaces. They originate from the atmospheric winds of cool stars and from SUPERNOVA explosions. This dust goes into the mixture which will eventually provide the material for the birth of new stars.

interstitial compounds Crystalline solids that contain additional atoms between the regular sites of the crystal lattice. They form between the TRANSITION METALS and elements with small atoms, especially hydrogen, carbon, and nitrogen. They resemble metals in that they are shiny and are good conductors of electricity. They do not have definite chemical formulae, as not all the gaps in the metal are always filled; but they are stable over quite wide composition ranges. Graphite also forms interstitial compounds between its layers.

intervention (in economics) Any action by government designed to alter or limit the market forces of supply and demand. Examples are the regulation of industry by price control or quantity restrictions, trade PROTECTIONISM, and official financing to support the BALANCE OF PAYMENTS or the exchange rate. In practice, nearly all governments are interventionist to some extent, but there is much debate among both economists and politicians over the degree of intervention that is desirable.

intestine The part of the ALIMENTARY CANAL that connects the stomach to the anus. It ranges from a single tube in invertebrates to a complex system of segments devoted to different tasks in mammals. Its purpose, in all animals, is to aid the breakdown of food into such substances as sugars, amino acids, or fats, which can then be absorbed by the intestinal cells. This is achieved through the secretion of ENZYMES by the intestinal cells, and by keeping the food in the body long enough for them to act.

The intestine of humans is divided into two main regions, the small intestine, and the large intestine. Most of the breakdown and absorption of food occurs in the former, while the latter, which includes the COLON and RECTUM, is largely involved in extracting water from the food remains. The intestinal contents are moved along by wave-like contractions of the muscular intestinal wall, called peristalsis. Absorption of substances is helped by small finger-like extensions of the intestine wall, called villi, which greatly increase the surface area of the intestine.

intifada (Arabic, 'uprising') A sustained campaign of violence, which began late in 1987, by Palestinian rsidents against the Israeli occupation of the West Bank and the Gaza Strip, after the Six Day War in 1967. Although a peace agreement between the Palestinians and Israelis was signed in 1993, a number of terrorist acts by Arabs has perpetuated the violence and disrupted the peace process.

intra-uterine device (IUD) See CONTRACEPTION.

intrazonal soil A soil whose main characteristics are determined by local conditions, related to topography, drainage, or the nature of the bedrock, rather than to regional factors, such as climate and vegetation. Rendzinas and ANDOSOLS, which form on limestone and basic volcanic deposits respectively, are examples of intrazonal soil; with them the character of the parent material is the most important influence on the formation of the soil. Intrazonal soils also form under conditions of poor drainage, such as in bogs, on river floodplains, or in the playa lake basins of deserts.

Inuit (or **Innuit**) A member of a North American people inhabiting Alaska, northern Canada, Greenland, and eastern Siberia. A semi-nomadic hunting and gathering people, they were noted for their adaptation to a harsh environment and were sometimes called Eskimos. Their languages belong to the Inuit-Aleut family and are divided into two main branches: the Inupik or Inuk (spoken in Greenland, Labrador, the Arctic coast of Canada, and northern Alaska) and the Yupik or Yuk (spoken in southern Alaska and Siberia). There are approximately 40,000 Inuit-speakers in Greenland, 25,000 in Alaska, 15,000 in Canada, and several hundred in Siberia.

invar An alloy of iron containing 36 per cent nickel with small amounts of carbon, manganese, and silicon. It has a negligible coefficient of thermal expansion: that is, it does not expand or contract on heating or cooling. It is used for measuring tapes and pendulum rods, and in precision instruments and THERMOSTATS.

Invercargill A city of New Zealand, on the Waihopai River at the southern tip of South Island; pop. (1991) 51,980. Founded in 1857 and named after William Cargill (1784–1860), Superintendent of Otago, it is the southernmost city of New Zealand and a market centre for the surrounding Southland Plain.

Inverness A city in northern Scotland, on the River Ness at the mouth of the Beauly Firth; pop. (1991) 41,230. It has diverse light industries and is the administrative centre of Highland, lying at the north-eastern end of the Caledonian Canal.

inverse square law A law describing the behaviour of physical phenomena that spread out equally in all directions from a single source. For example, objects exert a gravitational force, which acts outwards equally in all directions. The strength of the gravitational force decreases with distance, so at a distance r away from the object, the strength of the force is inversely proportional to r. As the intensity of the force is spread out over the surface of a sphere radius r, this surface area is proportional to r^2, therefore the intensity of the force at any point is inversely proportional to r^2. Thus the intensity of the field is related to distance by an inverse square law.

inversions (in meteorology) The reversal of the usual decrease of temperature with height within the troposphere, temperature increasing with height within limited zones. They commonly develop at night near the Earth's surface, as the ground cools due to conduction and long-wave radiation. The result is the creation of an inversion, with the greatest fall in air temperature nearest to the ground, and the rate and amount of cooling decreasing with height. Because of the inverse temperature gradient of such inversions, atmospheric pollutants are unable to escape beyond the inversion layer, causing the concentration of pollutants to increase close to the surface of the Earth and helping in the formation of SMOG. Inversions also develop when warm air flows over a cold land or sea surface. The warm air rises over the cold. A further instance is when air, sinking from higher in the troposphere, is warmed by compression.

invertebrate An animal with no backbone, which includes about 97 per cent of all species of living animals. They are much more diverse than the vertebrates, and much less well studied, despite their enormous diversity. They range from simple jellyfish and sea anemones to such complex animals as the octopus, lobster, or bumblebee. Some are built with a circular plan of radial symmetry, like jellyfish and sea urchins; others have long, thin bodies, which are bilaterally symmetrical, either soft and sinuous like the worms, or with a stiff outer covering and jointed legs, like the arthropods. All the features familiar in vertebrates are foreshadowed in the invertebrates, from which the former are thought to have evolved.

investment casting See CIRE-PERDUE.

in vitro fertilization (IVF) A technique for helping infertile couples to conceive, popularly known as the 'test-tube baby' technique. The woman is induced to produce eggs (ovulate) by HORMONE treatment. The eggs are then removed and fertilized in the laboratory (*in vitro*) by her partner's sperm. The resulting early embryos are checked for normal development before being placed in the woman's uterus to continue growing until birth. The technique is also used in animals to produce a large number of offspring from the eggs of one female. The embryos are placed in the uteri of other, surrogate mothers, suitably treated with hormones to maintain the pregnancy. Unless the patients are chosen very carefully, the success rate of *in vitro* fertilization in humans is very low. IVF in animals, however, is widely used with success.

Io In Greek mythology, a beautiful princess beloved by Zeus. He changed her into a heifer to escape the jealousy of Hera, but she discovered the ruse and sent a gadfly to torment the unfortunate animal, which was forced to wander over the face of the Earth. Eventually Io recovered her human shape and bore Zeus a son.

Io (in astronomy) A GALILEAN SATELLITE of Jupiter discovered by Galileo in 1610. Its almost circular orbit is nearly in Jupiter's equatorial plane with a semi-major axis of 421,600 km. The orbital motions of Io, EUROPA, and GANYMEDE are locked together which causes strong tidal effects resulting in the heating and melting of Io's interior. Io's diameter of 3,630 km and its density of 3,570 kg/m^3 are close to the values for the Earth's Moon.

iodine (symbol I, at. no. 53, r.a.m. 126.90) A black shiny solid in Group 17 (formerly VIIB), the HALOGENS, of the periodic table. On gentle warming it sublimes to a violet vapour; both the solid and the vapour contain I_2 molecules. It dissolves in many organic solvents and in potassium iodide solution, but it is not very soluble in water. Less reactive than the other halogens, it forms compounds with most metals and non-metals; and it also forms compounds in which it has the valencies 1, 3, 5, and 7. Sodium iodide is a minor constituent of sea water and is concentrated in seaweed, which has been used as a source of iodine. The main source is a mineral found in Chile called caliche. It is used in quartz-halogen lamps, to make photographic materials, and as an antiseptic (tincture of iodine). Iodine is an essential element in the body, occurring mainly in the thyroid gland: a radioactive isotope of iodine, iodine-131, is used in medicine to check for abnormal activity of the thyroid (see NUCLEAR MEDICINE).

ion An atom or group of atoms that are electrically charged as a result of losing or gaining electrons. Ionization can be produced if atoms are passed through a high electric field, as in an electrical discharge tube, or if they are bombarded by energetic particles; and those which are accelerated to high speeds can be stripped of electrons when they pass through thin sheets of material. Gaseous ions are produced by high-energy electromagnetic radiation such as X-rays. Many compounds when in solution separate into groups of ions. For example, copper(II) sulphate, ($CuSO_4$), when dissolved in water dissociates into Cu^{2+} ions, which are positively charged, and $SO_4{}^{2-}$ ions, which are negatively charged. In solids, electrons are often transferred to a neighbouring atom, thereby forming a negative–positive pair of ions, which attract one another. This is one of the mechanisms of CHEMICAL BONDING in solids. If ions are mobile, as in a gas, a solution, or a liquid, they can act as charge carriers and the material becomes an electrical conductor; this process is called ionic conductivity. The activity and mobility of an ion can influence chemical reactions in solution.

Iona An island in the Inner Hebrides, site of a monastery founded by St Columba *c.*563 which became a centre for Celtic Christian missions to Scotland and a place of pilgrimage. There are many Celtic crosses and 60 Scottish, Norse, and Irish kings are said to be buried near the restored cathedral. Iona is now a major tourist destination.

Ionesco, Eugène (1912–94) Romanian-born French dramatist. A leading exponent of the Theatre of the Absurd, he achieved fame with his first play *The Bald Prima Donna* (1950), which blended a dialogue of platitudes with absurd logic and surrealist effects. In *Rhinoceros* (1960), he depicted a totalitarian society whose members eventually conform by turning into rhinoceroses.

ion-exchange resin An insoluble polymer in the form of small granules used to remove IONS from solutions. In water softeners, the resin contains active sites that exchange their sodium ions (which do not cause hardness) for magnesium and calcium ions (ions in the water that cause hardness). When the active sites become spent, the resin can be regenerated by treatment with sodium chloride (SALT) solution. Ion-exchange resins are also used in desalination and in some forms of CHROMATOGRAPHY.

Ionia In classical times, the central part of the west coast of Asia Minor. In the 11th century BC tribes speaking the Ionic dialect of Greek settled in the Aegean Islands and in the coastal area of Asia Minor, later known as Ionia, which was also colonized by the Greeks from the mainland from about the 8th century BC. They retained their distinctive dialect (Ionic), which was also spoken in Athens, and are noted for their contributions in science, poetry, and architecture. Throughout the eastern Mediterranean 'Yawani' (Ionians) became the generic word for Greek.

Ionian Islands A chain of about 40 islands off the western coast of Greece, of which the largest are Corfu and Cephalonia. The islands constitute a region of modern Greece and are a major tourist attraction; area 2,307 sq km (891 sq miles); pop. (1991) 191,000.

Ionian Sea The part of the Mediterranean Sea between western Greece and southern Italy, at the mouth of the Adriatic. According to one ancient Greek tradition it is named after Io, priestess of

Hera, who crossed it in her wanderings, rather than after the Ionians.

ionic bond See CHEMICAL BOND; IONIC COMPOUND.

ionic compound A compound formed when a metal reacts with a non-metal; the metal atoms give away one or more electrons, forming positively charged IONS, and the non-metal atoms accept the electrons, becoming negatively charged ions. The product is a solid consisting of a regular arrangement or lattice of positive and negative ions, and it is held together by the forces of attraction between them. These are called ionic bonds. Ionic compounds have high melting-points because of the high attractive forces in the bond. When the solid is melted or dissolved, the ions are no longer arranged in a regular pattern, but move about independently of each other. Cations are formed most easily by metals, and anions by either single non-metal atoms or groups of them. For example, sodium chloride is ionic and has the ionic formula Na^+Cl^-. However, cations containing only non-metals do exist, for instance the ammonium ion, NH_4^+. Thus, the ionic formula of ammonium chloride is $NH_4^+Cl^-$. Whereas ionic compounds are electrical insulators when solid, they conduct electricity when molten, or in solution. This conduction is accompanied by chemical decomposition, and is called ELECTROLYSIS.

ionization The process by which an electrically neutral atom or molecule becomes either positively or negatively charged due to the removal or addition of one or more electrons. Once an atom or molecule has been ionized, it is called an ION. The amount of energy needed to remove an electron from an atom or molecule is called the ionization potential. Ionization can be caused by the passage of electric currents, in chemical reactions, during collisions between atoms and by electromagnetic radiation (which is then known as ionizing radiation). Ionization can also occur as a result of heating, in which case it is called thermal ionization.

ionosphere Electrically charged zone of the Earth's ATMOSPHERE, extending from a height of about 50–80 km (30–50 miles) for some 400–600 km (250–370 miles) into space. X-rays and ultraviolet radiation from the Sun cause nitrogen and oxygen molecules in the air there to ionize, producing free electrons. The resulting layer of charged particles enables radio waves to be reflected round the Earth.

Iowa A state in the Middle West of the USA, to the north of Missouri; area 145,753 sq km (56,275 sq miles); pop. (1990) 2,776,770; capital, Des Moines. The largest cities are Des Moines, Cedar Rapids, Davenport, and Sioux City. It is also known as the Hawkeye State. The USA gained control of Iowa in 1803 as part of the Louisiana Purchase, and it became the 29th state in the Union in 1846. Food processing and manufacturing are the chief industries of Iowa which is a leading grain, soybean, livestock, and hog-marketing state. Timber and minerals such as cement, coal, gypsum, limestone, sand, and gravel are also produced. The state's principal landmarks are the Fort Dodge Historical Museum, the seven Amana Colonies, the birthplace of President Herbert Hoover, and the Effigy Mounds National Monument.

Ipatieff, Vladimir Nikolaievich (1867–1952) Russian-born US chemist. He worked mainly on the catalysis of hydrocarbons, particularly the use of high-pressure catalysis and of metallic oxides as catalysts. These techniques became vitally important to the petrochemical industry, which he helped to establish in both pre- and post-revolutionary Russia. Ipatieff continued his research on catalysis after moving to the USA in 1930.

Iphigenia In Greek mythology, a daughter of King Agamemnon and his queen Clytemnestra. To appease the wrath of Artemis, whose stag he had killed, Agamemnon offered Iphigenia as a sacrifice to obtain fair winds so that the Greek fleet could sail against Troy. Artemis was moved by Iphigenia's innocence, however, and saved her by substituting a deer for the sacrifice. Iphigenia was then entrusted with the care of Artemis' temple at Tauris.

Ipswich The county town of Suffolk in east England, a port and industrial town on the estuary of the River Orwell; pop. (1991) 115,500. It was a major wool port in the 16th century. Its trade links are with nearby European ports and its light industries include malting, brewing, flour-milling, and printing.

Iqbal, Muhammad (1876–1938) Indian philosopher, poet, and political leader. He took an active part in politics in the Punjab and was President of the MUSLIM LEAGUE in 1930 when he advanced the idea of a separate Muslim state in north-west India, the beginning of the concept of Pakistan.

Iran (formerly **Persia**) A country of the Middle East in central-west Asia. Bordering on Turkey and Iraq on the west, Turkmenistan on the north, and Afghanistan and Pakistan on the east, it has a northern coast on the Caspian Sea and a southern coast on the Gulf and Arabian Sea.

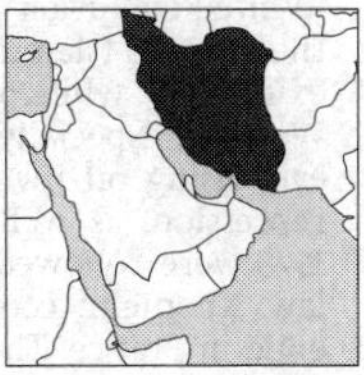

Physical. Iran consists mostly of arid tableland surrounded by mountains (the Elburz in the north and the Zagros in the south-west) and containing extensive salt deserts: the Great Salt Desert or Dasht-e-Kavir in the north and the Dasht-e-Lut in the south-east. The climate varies from hot to cool according to season and altitude.

Economy. Iran's economy is based on its huge reserves of oil, which accounts for some 95 per cent of exports; however, oil and gas production are restricted due to war damage. Substantial mineral deposits of coal, copper, and iron ore are relatively undeveloped, and ambitious industrial and infrastructural projects embarked on under the Shah have been curtailed. Banks, insurance, and most industries have been nationalized since the revolution. The chief industries are mining, machinery production, and textiles. The neglect of agriculture, which focuses on producing grains and rice, and rearing sheep and cattle, has not yet been successfully reversed, and there is food rationing.

History. Early Persian dynasties included the ACHAEMENIDS, whose rule ended with Alexander the Great's defeat of Darius III, and the SASSANIDS who were overthrown by the Arabs. Since the fall of the Sassanian empire in 642, it has been under the rule of Islam. Persians were prominent in the empires of their Arab, Seljuk, and Mongol overlords for nine centuries, until Ismail I established a strong Persian state and converted the population to Shiite Islam. After ABBAS I Safavid power declined until the Qajar dynasty, founded by Agha Mohammad Khan and ruling from Tehran, took power in 1796.

Trade between Muslim countries and European powers had developed throughout the 19th century and both Russia and Britain were anxious to increase their influence over the Qajar dynasty in Iran. In 1906 Muzaffar al-Din granted a constitution; his successor sought to suppress the *Majlis* (Parliament) which had been granted, but was himself deposed. In 1901 oil concessions were granted to foreign companies to exploit what is estimated as one-tenth of the world's oil reserves. In 1909 the Anglo-Persian Oil Company (later BP) was founded and southern Iran came within Britain's sphere of influence, while Russia dominated northern Iran. Following the RUSSIAN REVOLUTION of 1917 British troops invaded Russia from Iran; at the end of this 'war of intervention' an Iranian officer, Reza Khan, emerged and seized power (1921), backed by the British. In 1925 he deposed the Qajar dynasty and proclaimed himself as REZA SHAH PAHLAVI. In World War II Iran was occupied by British and Soviet forces and was used as a route for sending supplies to the Soviet Union. The Shah abdicated (1941) and was replaced by his son Muhammad Reza Shah PAHLAVI. It took him 20 years to establish political supremacy, during which time one of his Prime Ministers, Mussadegh, nationalized the Anglo-Iranian Oil Company (1951). In 1961 the Shah initiated a land-reform scheme and a programme of modernization, the so-called 'White Revolution' (1963–71). The secularization of the state led Islamic leaders such as KHOMEINI into exile (1964), while popular discontent with secular Western, especially US, influence was masked by ever-rising oil revenues, which financed military repression, as well as industrialization. Riots in 1978 were followed by the imposition of martial law. Khomeini coordinated a rebellion from his exile in France. The fall and exile of the Shah in 1979 was followed by the return of Khomeini and the establishment of an Islamic Republic which proved strong enough to sustain the Iran hostage crisis of 1979–81 and to fight the long and costly IRAN–IRAQ WAR (1980–88), which claimed the lives of perhaps a million young Iranians. Following the death of Khomeini in 1989 and a confused power-struggle, Hashemi Rafsanjani was elected President. A skilful negotiator and moderate pragmatist, he achieved restoration of good relations with Western states without unduly alienating the Islamic fundamentalists. His government played a key role in achieving the release of Western hostages during 1991, and gave shelter to some 1.5 million Shia and Kurdish refugees from Iraq, following the GULF WAR, during which Iran remained neutral. Rafsanjani's programme of social and economic reforms, however, caused discontent in Iran and serious rioting occurred in several major cities in mid-1992. Despite a loss of popular support for his policies, Rafsanjani secured a majority for his supporters in the *Majlis* following the 1992 general election; in 1993 he was re-elected President. During the early 1990s alleged abuses of human rights in Iran, including attacks against the Kurds, and the implications of the procurement of arms for the stability of the Gulf region were causes of international concern. Iran's relations with the USA were strained by Iran's hostility to American interference in the region following the Gulf War and to the Israeli–PLO peace accord, signed in September 1993. The question of Iran's military expansion also caused friction. Since the break-up of the USSR in 1991, Iran has strengthened its links with the newly independent states of Central Asia; this has caused some concern in the West over Iran's growing political and religious influence in the region. In 1995 the USA announced complete trade and investment sanctions against Iran in an attempt to halt the country's alleged involvement in international terrorism and its rumoured nuclear weapons programme. The Iranian leadership defiantly condemned the sanctions, while the country's economy continued to be beset with crises. In 1997 presidential elections were won by the moderate Mohammed Khatemi.

Capital: Tehran
Area: 1,648,196 sq km (636,372 sq mi)
Population: 61,271,000 (1995)
Currency: 1 toman = 100 rials
Religions: Shia Muslim 91.0%; Sunni Muslim 7.8%; Christian 0.7%; Jewish 0.3%; Baha'i minority
Ethnic Groups: Persian 45.6%; Azeri 16.8%; Kurdish 9.1%; Gilani 5.3%; Luri 4.3%; Mazandarani 3.6%; Baluch 2.3%; Arab 2.2%; Bakhtiari 1.7%
Languages: Farsi (Persian) (official); Azeri Turkish; Kurdish; Arabic and other minority languages
International Organizations: UN; OPEC; Colombo Plan; Non-Aligned Movement

Iranian An Indo-European group of languages including Persian (Farsi), Pashto, Avestan, and Kurdish.

Iran–Iraq War (1980–88) A border dispute between IRAN and IRAQ, which developed into a major war. In 1980 President Saddam HUSSEIN of Iraq abrogated the 1975 agreement granting Iran some 518 sq km (200 sq miles) of border area to the north of the Shatt-al-Arab waterway in return for assurances by Iran to cease military assistance to the Kurdish minority in Iraq, which was fighting for independence. Calling for a revision of the agreement to the demarcation of the border along Shatt-al-Arab, a return to Arab ownership of the three islands in the Strait of Hormuz (seized by Iran in 1971), and for the granting of autonomy to minorities inside Iran, the Iraqi army engaged in a border skirmish in a disputed but relatively unimportant area, and followed this by an armoured assault into Iran's vital oil-producing region. The Iraqi offensive met strong Iranian resistance, and Iran recaptured territory from the Iraqis. In 1985 Iraqi planes destroyed a partially constructed nuclear power plant in Bushehr, followed by bombing of civilian targets which in turn led to Iranian shelling of Basra and Baghdad. The war entered a new phase in 1987 when Iran increased hostilities against commercial shipping in and around the Gulf, resulting in naval escorts being sent to the area by the USA and other nations. Senior officers of the Iranian army began to lose confidence as their troops suffered from shortages of arms and equipment, while Iraq continued to be supplied by the West. Early in 1988 the UN Security Council called for a cease-fire. Iraq agreed, but not Iran. Skilful negotiations by the UN Secretary-General, PÉREZ DE CUÉLLAR, however, achieved an armistice in July and a peace settlement in August. Nothing had been gained, but an estimated 1.5 million lives were lost.

Iraq A West Asian country bordering on Turkey on the north, Iran on the east, Syria and Jordan on the west, and Saudi Arabia and Kuwait on the south.

Physical. A waterway, Shatt al-Arab, at the delta of the Euphrates, gives Iraq access to the Gulf in the south-east. The Euphrates and its tributary the Tigris traverse the whole country from north-west to south-east, bringing silt to a vast depression which would be

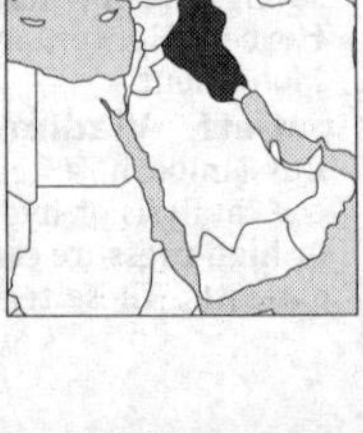

widely cultivable were it not for salinity and EROSION. This land, once known as Mesopotamia, was the site of early civilizations. To the north are mountains and desert plateaux, to the west all is desert; and the climate is one of extremes.

Economy. The economy is based on exports of oil. The main industries are petroleum products and chemicals. Iraq relies on imports of foodstuffs, its main agricultural products being grains, livestock, and dates. The economy has suffered as a result of recent wars, the US-led trade embargo, and the UN ban on exports of oil.

History. As MESOPOTAMIA, the area of present-day Iraq is known as 'the cradle of civilization'. It became a Muslim state in the 7th century AD following conquest by Arabia. It became a part of the Ottoman Empire in 1534, remaining such until the outbreak of World War I when the Turks were driven out by British forces. Following the British Mesopotamian Campaign in World War I, the country was occupied by Britain, who was then granted responsibility under a League of Nations mandate (1920–32). In 1921 Britain offered to recognize amir Ahd Allah Faisal, son of HUSSEIN, sharif of Mecca, as King Faisal. British influence remained strong until the fall of the monarchy in 1958. Further political rivalries ended with the 1968 coup, which led to rapid economic and social modernization paid for by oil revenues and guided by the general principles of the Ba'ath Socialist Party. A heterogeneous society, of many ethnic and religious groupings, Iraq has long been troubled by periodic struggles for independence for its KURDS. It has often been isolated in Arab affairs by its assertiveness in foreign policy, though the long and bloody IRAN–IRAQ WAR launched against Khomeini's Iran by President Saddam HUSSEIN in 1980 received financial support from formerly critical monarchist Arab states. During 1990 a frontier dispute with Kuwait was followed by the Iraqi invasion and an international crisis, leading to UN sanctions and to the GULF WAR. Following the end of the war, widespread uprisings among both Shia and Kurdish peoples were brutally suppressed. UN-imposed peace terms, a pre-requisite to the lifting of sanctions, included the destruction of chemical and other weapons, acceptance of UN inspectors, and disclosure of Iraq's nuclear capability, and the release of all prisoners-of-war. Some progress was made, but in 1992 Iraq refused to accept a UN proposal that oil sales be resumed for humanitarian purposes, pending resolution of outstanding differences, such as Iraq's refusal to accept a UN resolution on the longer-term monitoring of its weapons programme. In mid-1992 Iraqi Kurds, who controlled an area of northern Iraq, elected their own national assembly, following a deadlock in negotiations over a Kurdish Autonomous Region and an economic blockade on the area by the Iraqi government. Renewed attacks by government forces on the Shia communities in southern Iraq in 1992–93 led to the establishment by Western powers of an exclusion zone over the area. Violation of the zone by Iraqi forces resulted in air attacks by Western forces in 1993. President Saddam Hussein assumed the additional title of Prime Minister in 1994 and formally recognized the sovereignty of Kuwait. Fighting between rival Kurdish groups also broke out in northern Iraq and continued in 1995–96. The United Nations continued to renew the period of economic sanctions on Iraq, in place since the Gulf crisis of 1991, while Iraq continued to reject the UN resolution to sell its oil to fund humanitarian efforts as a violation of its sovereignty. There was widespread speculation in 1995 over the stability of Saddam Hussein's regime as there were reports of attempted coups to overthrow him and as a senior minister and key members of the ruling clique defected from the country. However, in a national referendum 99 per cent of Iraqi voters favoured the continuation of Saddam's leadership for a further seven years. In 1996 government forces attacked Kurdish towns in the north of the country. In response, the USA bombed strategic targets in southern Iraq. In 1997 Iraq's failure to cooperate with UN weapons inspectors led the USA to threaten airstrikes against strategic sites. The crisis was averted in 1998 when Saddam permitted weapons inspections to resume and the UN Secretary-General, Kofi Annan, admitted the possibility of an early end to sanctions against Iraq.

Capital: Baghdad
Area: 435,052 sq km (167,975 sq mi)
Population: 20,413,000 (1995)
Currency: 1 Iraqi dinar = 20 dirhams = 1,000 fils
Religions: Shia Muslim 53.5%; Sunni Muslim 42.3%; Christian 3.5%
Ethnic Groups: Arab 77.1%; Kurdish 19.0%; Turkmen 1.4%; Persian 0.8%; Assyrian 0.8%
Languages: Arabic (official); Kurdish and minority languages
International Organizations: UN; Arab League; Non-Aligned Movement; OAPEC; OPEC

Irbil See ARBIL.

Ireland An island of the British Isles, lying west of Great Britain; area 83,694 sq km (32,327 sq miles); pop. (1991) 5,093,370. Four-fifths of it is occupied by the Irish Republic (see IRELAND, REPUBLIC OF) and the remainder by NORTHERN IRELAND, which is part of the United Kingdom. The soil is fertile and the pasturage lush, swept by warm damp winds from the Atlantic; the economy relies heavily on agriculture, especially beef production and dairy farming. Settled by the Celts, the country became divided into independent tribal territories over which the lords of Tara exercised nominal suzerainty. Christianity reached Ireland, probably in the 4th century, to be consolidated by the work of St Patrick, and after the breakup of the Roman Empire the country became for a time a leading cultural centre, with the monasteries fostering learning and missionary work. English invasions began in the 12th century under Henry II, but the authority that he established was never secure and by the 16th century was confined to an area around Dublin (the English Pale) until the Tudors succeeded in extending it over the whole of the island. Revolts against English rule, and against the imposition of Protestantism (which met with unexpectedly stubborn resistance), resulted in the **plantation** of Ireland by English (and later Scottish) families on confiscated land in an attempt to anglicize the country and secure its allegiance. In Ulster in particular the descendants of such settlers retained a distinctive identity. After an unsuccessful rebellion in 1798, political union of Britain and Ireland followed in 1801. In spite of genuine efforts towards its success Ireland sank deeper into destitution. A share of Britain's industrial prosperity reached Protestant Ulster, but the rest of the island found its agricultural assets dropping in value, and at the failure of the potato crop (Ireland's staple) in the 1840s thousands died in the famine, thousands more fled abroad. The Home Rule movement, led by Parnell, failed to achieve its aims in the 19th century and implementation of a bill passed in 1910 was delayed by the outbreak of World War I. An armed uprising at Easter, 1916, was suppressed. Ireland was parti-

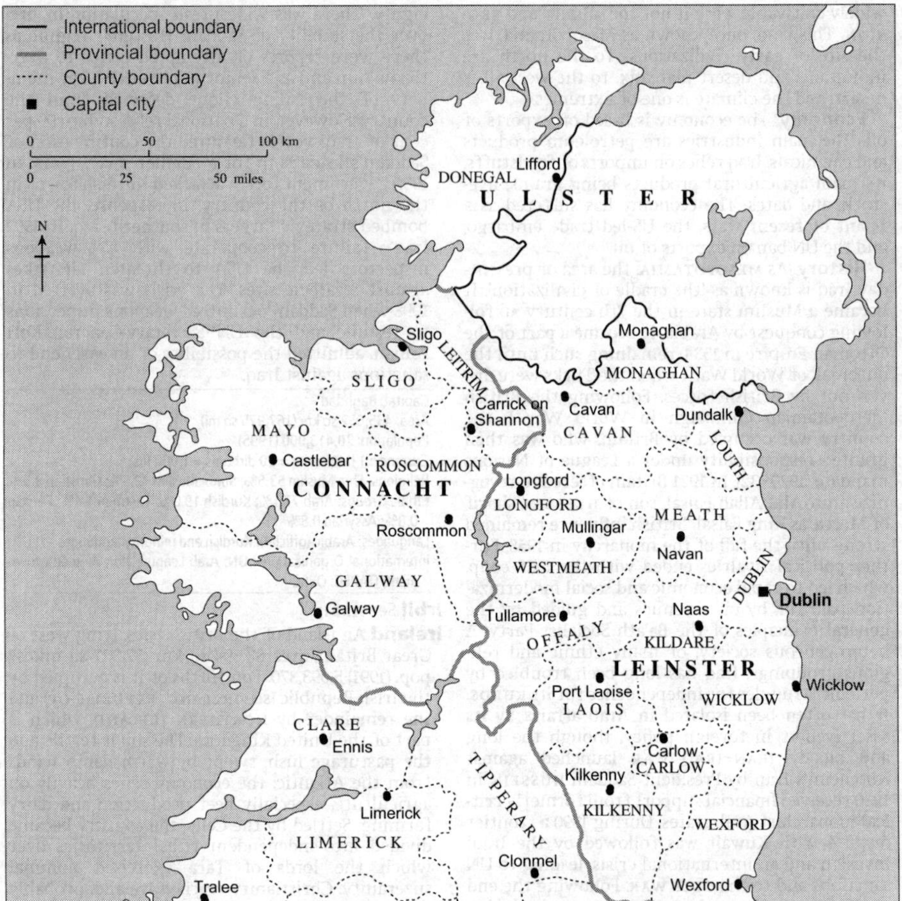

Ireland

tioned by the Anglo-Irish Treaty of 1921, which gave dominion status to Ireland with the exception of six of the counties of Ulster (Northern Ireland), whose Protestant majority wished to preserve the Union and which remained part of the United Kingdom.

Ireland, **John (Nicholson)** (1879–1962) British composer and pianist. His music reflects the influence of Debussy and Ravel and found its most persuasive outlet in songs and piano pieces. His second Violin Sonata (1917) made a considerable impact, as did his Piano Concerto (1930) and two Impressionistic programme works: *The Forgotten Rite* (1913) and *Mai-Dun* (1921). The light-hearted overture *Satyricon* (1946) revealed a less introspective side of his nature.

Ireland, **Republic of** A country in western Europe comprising four-fifths of the island of IRELAND, to the west of Great Britain.

Physical. A flat and fertile plain surrounds a central lake, Lough Ree, and the basin of the River Shannon. It is surrounded by coastal areas of great beauty: the Wicklow Mountains in the south-east reach to nearly 1,000 m (3,300 feet); the Connemara Mountains in the west stand up above great lakes, while those of Kerry in the south-west reach to over 1,000 m (3,282 feet) and point like rugged fingers to the sea. Many islands, among them

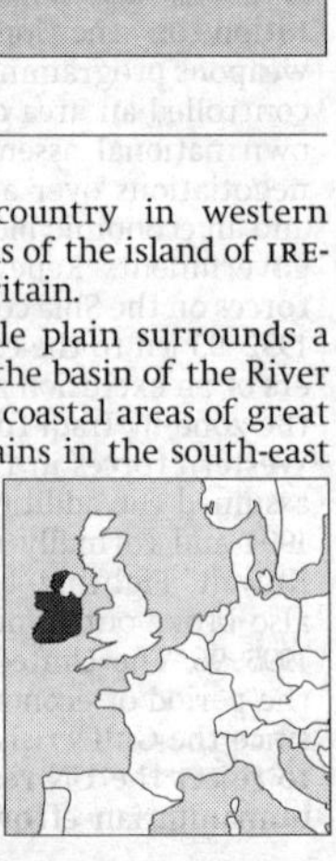

Aran, lie in the deep bays of the western coast, where there are sandy beaches among the rocks. Warm, damp winds from the Atlantic keep the country largely free of frost, while rainfall is moderate to heavy.

Economy. Ireland has a diversified economy in which agriculture predominates, although industry has become increasingly important; the chief exports are foodstuffs (especially beef), electrical machinery, and chemicals. Other industries include textiles, and tourism is also important. The country generates 15 per cent of its electricity by burning peat, of which there are extensive reserves. Ireland has a higher rate of emigration than any other member of the EU. However, in recent years the economy has grown rapidly, with inflation remaining low. Irish citizens have had the right to reside, work, and vote in the UK since independence.

History. After years of intermittent fighting, the Anglo-Irish Treaty of December 1921, concluded by Lloyd George with the SINN FEIN leaders, gave separate DOMINION status to Ireland (as the Irish Free State) with the exception of six of the counties of Ulster, which formed the state of NORTHERN IRELAND. Irish republicans led by DE VALERA rejected the agreement and fought a civil war against the Irish Free State forces, but were defeated in 1923. After the FÍANNA FÁIL victory in the election of 1932, de Valera began to sever the Irish Free State's remaining connections with Great Britain. In 1937 a new constitution established it as a sovereign state with an elected president; the power of the British Crown was ended and the office of governor-general abolished. The title of Irish Free State was replaced by Ireland; in Irish, Eire. An agreement in 1938 ended the British occupation of certain naval bases in Ireland. Having remained neutral in World War II, Ireland left the COMMONWEALTH OF NATIONS and was recognized as an independent republic in 1949. De Valera was elected president in 1959. He was succeeded as Taoiseach (prime minister) by Sean Lemass (1959–66) and Jack Lynch (1966–73). In 1973 Ireland joined the European Community and a FINE GAEL–Labour coalition led by Liam Cosgrave came to power. Subsequent governments have been controlled alternately by the Fíanna Fáil under Charles Haughey (1979–81; 1982; 1987–92) and the Fine Gael–Labour coalition under Dr Garret Fitzgerald (1981–82; 1982–87). In November 1985 Ireland signed the Anglo-Irish Accord (the Hillsborough Agreement) giving the republic a consultative role in the government of Northern Ireland. The agreement thus ensured a role for the republic on behalf of the nationalist minority in the north. The election as President, in December 1990, of Mary Robinson, of the Irish Labour Party, represented a move towards greater liberalism within Irish society; but opposition to abortion remained strong. Economically the republic has gained from its membership of the European Community (now the EUROPEAN UNION), which it continues strongly to support. In 1992 Haughey was replaced by Albert Reynolds, who resigned in 1994 following the collapse of his coalition. The Fine Gael leader, John Bruton, became Prime Minister at the head of a new coalition with Labour and the Democratic Left. In December 1993 Albert Reynolds had joined the UK Prime Minister John Major in issuing the DOWNING STREET DECLARATION, which set out general principles for the holding of future peace talks on NORTHERN IRELAND and represented a significant step towards peace in the province. In August 1994 the IRISH REPUBLICAN ARMY (IRA) announced a complete cease-fire, and the Irish government agreed to the early release of IRA prisoners as a move to consolidate the peace process. Despite the presentation by John Major and John Bruton of a joint framework document for all-party talks on a durable settlement for Northern Ireland in early 1995, a deadlock in progress towards talks developed over the British government's insistence on the IRA decommissioning of weapons before any talks began. The IRA's cease-fire was broken in early 1996 and there were bomb attacks on mainland Britain. Peace talks began in June 1996, from which Sinn Fein (the political wing of the IRA) was excluded, but in 1997, following a further IRA cease-fire, talks resumed with Sinn Fein included. In January 1998 the Irish and British governments issued, as a basis for negotiation, a joint document containing proposals for the future government of Northern Ireland, which would include a north–south ministerial council to promote cooperation between the Republic and Northern Ireland. In April 1998 a peace agreement based on these proposals was signed by the Irish and British prime ministers (Bertie Ahern and Tony Blair) and by the negotiating parties.

Capital: Dublin
Area: 70,285 sq km (27,137 sq mi)
Population: 3,590,000 (1995)
Currency: 1 Irish pound = 100 new pence
Religions: Roman Catholic 93.1%; Church of Ireland (Anglican) 2.8%; Presbyterian 0.4%
Ethnic Groups: Over 94.0% Irish nationality
Languages: English, Irish (both official)
International Organizations: EU; OECD; UN; Council of Europe; CSCE

Irenaeus, St (*c.*130–*c.*200 AD) Greek theologian. He became bishop of Lyons in Gaul in 177, and was the author of *Against Heresies* (*c.*180), a detailed attack on Gnosticism. Feast day (in the Eastern Church) 23 Aug.; (in the Western Church) 28 June.

Irgun (Hebrew, in full *Irgun Zvai Leumi*, 'National Military Organization'; byname ETZEL) An underground ZIONIST terrorist group dedicated to the foundation of a Jewish state, active (1937–48) in Palestine against Arabs and later Britons. Under the leadership of Menachem BEGIN from 1944, it blew up the King David Hotel in Jerusalem (22 July 1946), with the loss of 91 lives. It was disbanded when its objectives were achieved with the creation of Israel.

Irian Jaya (or **West Irian**) A province of eastern Indonesia comprising the western half of the island of New Guinea together with the adjacent small islands; area 421,981 sq km (162,990 sq miles); pop. (est. 1993) 1,828,700; capital, Jayapura. Prior to its incorporation into Indonesia it was known as Dutch New Guinea. A 1962 agreement between Holland and Indonesia made provision for the Irianese to vote on their joining the Indonesian republic, but the referendum was waived and in 1969 Irian Jaya was fully incorporated into Indonesia. Since then an Irianese separatist movement has been engaged in guerrilla activities and thousands of refugees have fled across the border into Papua New Guinea.

iridium (symbol Ir, at. no. 77, r.a.m. 192.22) A hard, unreactive element, one of the PLATINUM metals. It is found free in nature, usually associated with other platinum metals and mixed with gold, silver, copper, nickel, or iron. Alloyed with platinum, it produces very hard metals used for the tips of fountain-pen nibs, surgical tools, electrical contacts, and chemical equipment. The standard kilogram mass is a platinum–iridium alloy.

iris Any one of approximately 200 species of plant of the genus *Iris*, found in temperate regions of the Northern Hemisphere. Most have flattened or, less often, rounded leaves, which arise from a basal rootstock called a RHIZOME or from a CORM below the ground. The flowers, which are often large and showy, have equal numbers of upright and pendulous petals, termed standards and falls. The bearded irises (with hairy filaments on the falls) are a group of irises which have been extensively hybridized by man as garden plants. *Iris* × *germanica* 'Florentina' is the source of orris root, used as a base for perfumed powders.

Irish (or **Erse**) The Celtic language of Ireland, forming a distinct variety of Gaelic. It was brought to Ireland by Celtic invaders *c*.1000 BC, and down to the end of the 18th century was spoken by the great majority of the people, especially in areas other than the cities. Its earliest attestation is in inscriptions from the 4th century AD, written in the Ogham script, and there has been a tradition of literature since the 6th century, with a mass of material from the 9th to 19th century. English gained ground rapidly and Irish is now spoken regularly only in certain areas in the west of Ireland. Since 1922 the Irish government has organized its revival, and it is now taught in all the schools, but despite this active support and the establishment of Irish as an official language there are probably fewer than 60,000 speakers. It is the first official language of the Irish Republic (the second is English).

Irish elk A giant deer, *Megaloceros giganteus*, that lived in the Pleistocene Epoch, 1.5 million years ago, in Europe and Asia. Their antlers were enormous, having a span of up to 4 m (13 feet). It probably died out only a few thousand years ago and its partially fossilized remains have been found in peat bogs.

Irish Famine (1845–51) A period of famine and unrest in Ireland. In 1845 blight affected the potato in Ireland and the crop failed, thus depriving the Irish of their staple food. Farmers could not pay their rents; often they were evicted and their cottages destroyed. Committees to organize relief works for such unemployed persons, together with soup kitchens, were set up, and, especially in the western counties, large numbers sought refuge in workhouses. Deaths from starvation were aggravated by an epidemic of typhus, from which some 350,000 died in the year 1846–47. The corn harvest in 1847 was good and, although the blight recurred, the worst of the famine was over. It is estimated that one million people died in Ireland of starvation in the five years 1846–51 and another million emigrated to the USA or elsewhere.

Irish Free State The name for southern Ireland from 1921, when it gained dominion status on the partition of Ireland, until 1937, when it became the sovereign state of Eire, before becoming the Republic of IRELAND in 1949.

Irish literature Irish-language literature was written in the Celtic language of Erse Gaelic. It was first recorded in the Roman alphabet in the 8th century, but earlier verse has been preserved in manuscripts. The earliest datable Irish poem is Amra Choluim Chille, a eulogy in praise of Saint Colum Cille (died 597). The Ulaid cycle, a group of legends and tales dealing with the heroic age of the Ulaids, a people who gave their name to Ulster, was recorded from oral tradition between the 8th and 11th centuries. Outstanding in Irish literature, they are preserved in the 12th-century manuscript, the *Book of the Dun Cow*. Tales and BALLADS centring on the deeds of the legendary Finn MacCumhaill (MacCool) were recorded in manuscript in *The Interrogation of the Old Man* (*c*.1200), and have remained a vital part of Irish folklore. The gradual infiltration of a Norman and English aristocracy and the intense hardships suffered under British rule undermined the old literature, which was preserved only as a folk tradition. Satire flourished, and the old poetic metres were abandoned in favour of the vernacular. By the middle of the 19th century literary activity in Gaelic had all but ceased. In the 20th century works in Gaelic have been published, and novels such as Flann O'BRIEN's *At Swim-Two-Birds*, published in English (1939), translated into Gaelic (1956).

A renaissance of Irish literary culture and nationalism, which began in the last quarter of the 19th century and continued to flourish until the 1920s. The movement drew on the heritage of the earlier Celtic works. The leading figure of the movement was W. B. YEATS, whose poems such as *The Wanderings of Oisin and other poems* (1889), were inspired by traditional and nationalist themes. He expressed the mysticism of the Irish in *The Celtic Twilight* (1893), a collection of stories, which gave a name to the Irish Revival movement. In 1899 Yeats, Augusta, Lady Gregory (1852–1932), and Edward Martyn (1859–1923) founded the Irish Literary Theatre to encourage Irish drama. This subsequently became the Irish National Theatre Society, which in 1904 acquired the Abbey Theatre, Dublin, where J. M. SYNGE's play *The Playboy of the Western World* caused outrage and riots in 1907. The Abbey Theatre also staged plays by Yeats and SHAW, while O'CASEY's controversial play *The Plough and the Stars* (1926) provoked a nationalist riot. George Russell ('A.E.') edited *The Irish Homestead* from 1905 to 1923, which encouraged interest in Irish literature and culture, as did the *Dublin University Review*. Other poets, including JOYCE, Padraic Colum (1881–1972), James Stephens (1882–1950), and Oliver St John Gogarty (1878–1957), contributed to the new literary stature of Irish writing.

Irish Republican Army (IRA) Terrorist organization fighting for a unified republican Ireland. Originally created by the FENIAN Brotherhood in the USA, it was revived by SINN FEIN in 1919 as a nationalist armed force. Its first commander in Ireland was Michael COLLINS and at one time Sean McBride was chief of staff. Since its establishment the IRA has been able to rely on support from sympathizers in the Irish-American community. Bomb explosions for which the IRA was held responsible occurred in England in 1939 and hundreds of its members were imprisoned. During World War II many more members were interned without trial in Ireland. In 1956 violence erupted in NORTHERN IRELAND and the IRA performed a series of border raids. Following violence against civil rights demonstrators and nationalists by both the IRA and ULSTER UNIONISTS, the IRA split into Provisional and Official wings (1969). The Provisional IRA (PIRA) and the Irish National Liberation Army (INLA) have in recent years staged demonstrations, assassinations, and bombings in both Northern Ireland and Britain. These include the murder of Lord Mountbatten and the British MP Airey Neave in 1979, a bomb attack on the entire British cabinet in Brighton in 1984, a bombing in Enniskillen on Remembrance Day 1987, attacks on British military bases in England and Germany in 1989, the murder of Ian Gow MP in 1990, mortar attacks on Downing Street (1991) and on Heathrow Airport (1994), a bomb in the City of London (1992), and another in Warrington in 1993. In August 1994 the IRA announced a complete cessation of its military operations, following peace initiatives by the British and Irish governments and by Northern Ireland politicians. The issue of decommissioning IRA weapons became a stumbling block in 1995 in the progress towards all-party talks on a lasting peace settlement for Northern Ireland. The cease-fire broke down in 1995, with the resumption of IRA bombing campaigns in mainland Britain, notably in London Docklands and Manchester. The absence of cease-fire agreements resulted in the exclusion of Sinn Fein from peace talks in mid-1996. After a further cease-fire, Sinn Fein joined resumed peace talks in 1997.

Irish Republican Brotherhood (IRB) A secret organization founded in Dublin in 1858 by James Stephens (1824–1901) to secure the creation of an independent Irish republic. It was closely linked with the FENIAN Brotherhood in the USA and its members came to be called Fenians. The primary object of the IRB was to organize an uprising in Ireland; the Fenian Brotherhood worked to support the IRB with men, funds, and a secure base. The British government acted swiftly; IRB leaders including Stephens were arrested. The 1867 Fenian Rising, led by Thomas Kelly, was a failure. The HOME RULE League, the LAND LEAGUE, the Irish Volunteers, and SINN FEIN often appeared to supersede the IRB as political forces; but Fenians were active in all these organizations. The Home Rule Bills failed to satisfy them and in World War I the IRB, led by Pádraic Pearse, sought German help for the abortive EASTER RISING. The IRB was subsequently superseded by the IRISH REPUBLICAN ARMY.

Irish Sea The sea separating Ireland from England and Wales.

iron (symbol Fe, at. no. 26, r.a.m. 55.85) A silvery-grey ferromagnetic TRANSITION METAL. Iron is a strong, malleable, ductile metal, which is a good conductor of heat and electricity, but its properties are affected by the presence of other elements. Its melting-point is 1,535°C (2,795°F), and it is believed to be the main component of the Earth's core. Iron ores are found in many kinds of rock throughout the world, the chief among them being haematite, magnetite (loadstone), and siderite (ironstone). The yellow iron pyrites (FeS_2) is known as fool's gold. Iron is obtained by heating iron oxide, the ore's main constituent, with carbon (from COKE). The carbon reacts with oxygen to form carbon dioxide, releasing the iron. In the BLAST-FURNACE carbon is provided in the form of COKE. The resulting pig-iron is brittle and contains 3–4 per cent carbon and other impurities. Cast iron is made from pig-iron by re-melting and cooling. It is especially useful in CASTING. Wrought iron is produced from pig-iron by puddling. It has less than 0.2 per cent carbon, is malleable and ductile, and was used for making chains, anchors, bolts, and ornamental frameworks until it was superseded by mild STEEL. The element reacts with acids and non-metals, and forms RUST in moist air. It forms two sets of compounds: iron(II) compounds (ferrous compounds), which contain the Fe^{2+} ion, and iron(III) compounds (ferric compounds), which contain the Fe^{3+} ion. Iron(II) compounds are often pale green, and iron(III) compounds yellow-brown; the colours of many rocks are caused by the presence of iron. Iron oxide (Fe_2O_3) is a red powder used as a paint pigment. Iron sulphate ($FeSO_4.7H_2O$) is employed as a weed-killer and wood preservative and in the manufacture of inks, dyes, and pigments. See also IRON AND STEEL INDUSTRY.

Iron is an essential element in diet and in the human body. It is present in enzymes, which control oxidation reactions, and in haemoglobin, which transports oxygen in the blood. Haemoglobin also binds other inorganic molecules, including carbon monoxide, which prevents uptake of oxygen. Pharmaceuticals containing iron are important for treating anaemia.

Iron Age The period of prehistory distinguished technologically by the use of iron. This was first mastered on a large scale by the HITTITES in Anatolia between 1500 and 1200 BC, and spread to the Aegean, and thence to south-east and central Europe and Italy. The spread was slow across Europe, as it only gradually replaced bronze. In Africa the Iron Age immediately followed the STONE AGE, bronze entering much later. In America, iron was not discovered before being introduced from Europe.

iron and steel industry The industry that extracts IRON from its ore and produces iron and STEEL. Iron and its derivative steel are the most widely used metals: most tools and machinery are made from one or the other. Iron was originally made from its ore in small-scale smelting operations, using charcoal as the source of carbon. The introduction of the BLAST-FURNACE to England at the beginning of the 16th century enabled pig-iron to be produced continuously.

To convert pig-iron into STEEL, it is necessary to reduce its carbon content to between about 0.1 and 1 per cent, depending on the type of steel being made. In the 1850s BESSEMER in the UK and KELLY in the USA developed furnaces for the conversion of large tonnages of pig-iron into structural steel. At about the same time, Charles SIEMENS in association with the brothers Émile and Pierre Martin developed the OPEN-HEARTH FURNACE for the conversion of pig-iron to steel. With the increasing availability of electricity in the 20th century, the ELECTRIC-ARC FURNACE was developed for the production of high-grade alloy steels. In the 1950s the Linz–Donawitz (LD) process was developed in Austria. Sometimes called the basic oxygen process or oxygen-lance process, it is used to convert pig-iron from the blast-furnace into usable steel. A jet of pure oxygen is blown into a molten mixture of pig-iron and scrap steel, converting the non-metallic impurities to oxides, which either escape as gases or form a slag floating on the surface. Four hundred tonnes of molten iron can be converted to steel in about 12 minutes. The process thus combines the low capital cost of the Bessemer process with the high-quality product of the open-hearth process, and is now the major means of steel production in many countries.

Steel is particularly useful as a structural material because it is strong and stiff, is easy to obtain from ores that are widely available, and is readily shaped through FORGING, rolling, and EXTRUSION. However, it has the major disadvantage that it corrodes easily; although there are special (and expensive) stainless steels that resist corrosion, these are not used for general structural purposes. Steel can be protected by painting, ELECTROPLATING, GALVANIZING, or by cathodic protection (see CORROSION). A large range of steels with widely differing properties can be made by alloying steel with different metals. Exceptional degrees of strength, stiffness, toughness, hardness, and magnetism can be obtained.

ironclads The first wooden battleships protected

by armour-plating. As a result of the loss of French and British wooden battleships during the CRIMEAN WAR, the French government ordered the construction of five armour-plated vessels for service in the Black Sea, the first, the frigate *Gloire*, entering service in 1859. The second ironclad to enter service, built entirely of iron with an internal wooden backing, was the British BATTLESHIP *Warrior*, launched in 1860. In 1862, during the AMERICAN CIVIL WAR, the first ironclad battle, between the *Monitor* and *Merrimack* took place. The design was quickly adopted by most nations until succeeded by steel-framed, DREADNOUGHT-type battleships at the beginning of the 20th century.

Iron Curtain The colloquial name for the former frontier between East European countries dependent on the former Soviet Union and Western non-communist countries. Its application to countries within the Soviet sphere of influence originated in a leading article by GOEBBELS in *Das Reich*, February 1945. This was reported in British newspapers, and the phrase was first used by Churchill: 'I view with profound misgivings the descent of an iron curtain between us and everything to the eastward.' It was generally agreed to have gone by 1990, with the disintegration of Soviet influence in eastern Europe and the collapse of the Union itself in 1991.

iron lung See RESPIRATOR.

iron oxide Any of three different compounds. Iron(II) oxide (or ferrous oxide, FeO) is a black powder; it forms iron(II) salts when treated with acids, but gives iron(III) oxide on heating in air. It is used as a pigment in glass. Iron(III) oxide (or ferric oxide, Fe_2O_3) in the form of HAEMATITE is the commonest ORE mineral of iron. When ground to powder it is used as a red pigment and for polishing diamonds. It forms a number of hydrates of varying compositions; one is RUST, produced by the action of water, oxygen, and carbon dioxide on iron. Iron(II) di-iron(III) oxide (ferroso-ferric oxide, Fe_3O_4) occurs as the mineral MAGNETITE, the second most important ore mineral of iron; it is also formed when steam is passed over hot iron. It is used as a black pigment.

Ironsides See NEW MODEL ARMY.

Iroquoian A language family of eastern North America, including Cherokee and Mohawk.

Iroquois The League of Five (later Six) Nations of North American Indian tribes (i.e. Huron, Mohawk, Oneida, Seneca, Onondaga, and Cayuga), speaking the Iroquoian languages, which joined in confederacy *c.*1570 by the efforts of the Huron prophet Deganawida and his disciple Hiawatha. A powerful force in early colonial history, the divisions in the confederacy occasioned by conflicting support of the various contestants in the War of American Independence saw the rapid decline of the Six Nations in the late 18th century, with half the League (i.e. the Cayugas, Mohawks, and Seneca) migrating north to Canada, where they accepted grants of land as allies of the defeated Loyalists and where they still continue to live. Traditional Iroquois society revolved around matrilineal residential and social organization.

irradiation (of food) A method of FOOD PRESERVATION in which harmful microorganisms are destroyed by controlled doses of radiation. High doses of radiation kill all organisms in food, but also produce an unpleasant taste. Lower doses kill most microorganisms, but do not markedly affect food flavour. At present few countries allow food to be irradiated, and those that do impose very strict controls.

irrational number A number that cannot be written as a fraction, p/q, where p and q are integers. That such numbers exist was known to the Greeks at least 2,200 years ago, when it was shown that the side of a square cannot be expressed as a fraction of the diagonal (they are incommensurable). For a square with sides of unit length, the diagonal is $\sqrt{2}$, which is irrational. Irrational numbers have infinite, non-repeating decimal expansions. Examples include $\sqrt{7}$, $\sqrt{2}$, π, and e.

Irrawaddy (Burmese **Ayeyarwady**) The principal river of Myanmar (Burma), 2,090 km (1,300 miles) long. Formed at the junction of two headwaters in Kachin State, it flows southwards and eventually forms a large delta that empties into the eastern Bay of Bengal.

irrigation Supply of water to land to grow crops or to increase crop yields. The amount of water used or lost to the atmosphere by crops, minus the annual rainfall, determines the quantity of irrigation water needed. In traditional irrigation systems, water is spread over the ground surface. Efficiency is between 40 and 75 per cent, and such systems are relatively inexpensive to build and maintain. Sprinkler and trickle-feed systems are generally between 60 and 80 per cent efficient, but have high capital and maintenance costs; they are suited to high-value crops. In 'basin' irrigation – commonly used in paddy-fields for growing rice – the ground is levelled and a low bund (embankment) retains the irrigation water. 'Furrow' and 'border' methods, with sloping ground for drainage, suit crops that cannot tolerate waterlogging.

Irving, Sir Henry (born Henry Brodribb) (1838–1905) British actor-manager. In 1874 he first played Hamlet at the Lyceum Theatre, and proceeded to manage the theatre from 1878 to 1902. During this period he entered into a celebrated acting partnership with Ellen Terry; they were particularly noted for their performances in Irving's productions of Shakespeare.

Irving, Washington (1783–1859) US writer. His first publication was a series of satirical essays (1807–08) entitled *Salmagundi*. He travelled extensively in Europe and also served as US ambassador to Spain 1842–46; he is best known for *The Sketch Book of Geoffrey Crayon, Gent* (1819–20), which contains such tales as 'Rip Van Winkle' and 'The Legend of Sleepy Hollow'. He also wrote the burlesque *History of New York* (1809), under the name Diedrich Knickerbocker.

Isaac The Hebrew patriarch, son of Abraham and Sarah, husband of Rebecca, and father of Jacob and Esau. According to the Old Testament, the 90-year-old Sarah, gave birth to Isaac as part of Abraham's covenant with God. Isaac's willingness to be sacrificed to God by Abraham has linked Isaac symbolically to Jesus in Christianity. Ishaq (Isaac) is mentioned in the Koran as a gift from God to Ibrahim (Abraham). Muslims generally consider that Ibrahim intended to sacrifice Ishmael, not Ishaq.

Isabella I (known as 'Isabella the Catholic') (1451–1504) Queen of Castile 1474–1504. She united her kingdom with that of Aragon by her marriage with its king, FERDINAND, in 1469, retaining sole authority in Castilian affairs. She was noted for her Catholic piety, encouragement of the SPANISH INQUISITION, and her intolerance towards Jews and Muslims. She patronized Spanish and Flemish artists, and supported the exploration of AMERICA.

Isabella II (1830–1904) Queen of Spain 1833–70. The daughter of FERDINAND VII, her accession was contended by her uncle, Don Carlos, and this led to the Carlist Wars that raged until 1839. Her reign, after two unpopular regencies, was a succession of personal scandals, governmental changes, and conflicts between political factions. Isabella finally fled to France after an insurrection (1868), and was deposed. The crown, offered by the new constitutional Cortes to five successive candidates, was accepted by the sixth, the Duke of Aosta (1845–90), the second son of Victor Emanuel I of Italy. As Amadeus I he ruled from 1871 to 1873, when he abdicated and the first Spanish republic was declared.

Isabella of France (1292–1358) Daughter of Philip IV of France. She was queen consort of Edward II of England from 1308, but returned to France in 1325. She and her lover Roger de Mortimer organized an invasion of England in 1326, forcing Edward to abdicate in favour of his son, who was crowned Edward III after his father's murder in 1327. Isabella and Mortimer acted as regents for Edward III until 1330, after which Edward took control of the kingdom and Isabella was banished.

Isaiah (8th century BC) Hebrew prophet, who preached during the reigns of Jotham, Ahaz, and Hezekiah. Isaiah's message was that the safety of Judah was in God's hands and the king should trust him and not rely on foreign allies. He advised Hezekiah to acknowledge Assyrian power and not ally with Egypt; when Judah was invaded by Israelites and Syrians in 735 BC, and by the Assyrians in 710 BC, and again in 703–701 BC, Isaiah promised that faith in God would guarantee the people's deliverance. According to one tradition Isaiah was martyred in the reign of Manasseh by being sawn in two. The biblical Book of Isaiah incorporates many prophecies from a later age, concerning the Babylonian Exile, the victories of Cyrus, and the deliverance of the Jews. The fulfilment of these prophecies increased Isaiah's fame posthumously. In Christianity his prophecies concerning the Messiah are seen as fulfilled in the person of Jesus.

Ischia A volcanic island in the Tyrrhenian Sea off the west coast of Italy, about 26 km (16 miles) south-west of Naples. Known as the Emerald Isle, it has been noted for centuries for its warm mineral springs, which are a major tourist attraction.

Isfahan (or **Esfahan**, **Ispahan**) An industrial city in west-central Iran, the country's third-largest city; pop. (1991) 1,127,000. Abbas I made it his capital city from 1598, and it became one of the largest and most beautiful cities of this period until captured and destroyed by the Afghans in 1722. It has a Great Bazaar and a large number of mosques, tombs, palaces, and schools. It has traditional industries of carpets and rugs, textiles, and metalwork.

Isherwood, Christopher (William Bradshaw) (1904–86) British-born US novelist. His novels *Mr Norris Changes Trains* (1935) and *Goodbye to Berlin* (1939; filmed as *Cabaret*, 1972) vividly portray Germany on the eve of Hitler's rise to power and reflect Isherwood's experiences in Berlin from 1929 to 1933. He collaborated with W. H. Auden on three verse plays and emigrated with him to the USA in 1939.

Ishiguro, Kazuo (1954–) Japanese-born British novelist. In 1960 he moved with his family to Great Britain. He gained recognition with his novel *An Artist of the Floating World* (1986); his next novel, *The Remains of the Day* (1989), won the Booker Prize and was made into a film (1993).

Ishizuchino, Mount The highest peak on the Japanese island of Shikoku; height 1,981 m (6,500 ft).

Ishmael The son of the Hebrew patriarch Abraham and Hajar (Hagar), the Egyptian serving maid of Abraham's wife Sarah. Cast out with his mother into the desert because of Sarah's jealousy, Ishmael in turn had twelve sons from whom twelve northern Arabian tribes are supposed to descend. In Islam Ishmael is considered a Prophet Messenger (*nabī rasūl*), and patriarch. In the Koran, the son whom Ibrahim (Abraham) was prepared to sacrifice is not named; he is thought by Muslims to be Ishmael, and the site to be near Mecca at Mina.

Ishtar In Babylonian mythology, a fertility and mother-goddess, the personification of Venus, sister-wife of Tammuz, and scorned lover of Gilgamesh. As daughter of the Akkadian sky-god An, Ishtar was worshipped as a goddess of love and desire. As the Moon-god Sin's daughter, she was the warrior goddess, worshipped in Assyria, who sent the vanquished to the underworld.

Isidore of Seville, St (Latinized name Isidorus Hispalensis) (*c.*560–636) Spanish archbishop and Doctor of the Church. He is noted for his *Etymologies*, an encyclopedic work used by many medieval authors. Feast day, 4 April.

Isis Ancient Egyptian goddess of magical power and divine mother, sister-wife to Osiris and mother of Horus. In human form she is depicted wearing either the throne-sign of her name or the cow's horns and Sun disc on her head. Hathor, goddess of love and childbirth, is often assimilated with Isis. Isis was worshipped throughout the Western world, most notably at Rome in the first century BC, and she was identified with the goddesses Astarte, Minerva, Venus, and Diana of other cultures.

Islam The religion of the Muslims, a monotheistic faith founded by the Prophet Muhammad in the Arabian Peninsula in the 7th century AD and is now the professed religion of nearly 1,000 million people worldwide. To become a Muslim means both to accept and affirm an individual surrender to God, and to live as a member of a social community. The Muslim performs prescribed acts of worship and strives to fulfil good works within the group; the FIVE PILLARS OF ISLAM include profession of the faith in a prescribed form, observance of ritual prayer (five obligatory prayer sequences each day as well as non-obligatory prayers), giving alms to the poor, fasting during the month of Ramadan, and performing the pilgrimage to Mecca. These ritual observances, as well as a code governing social behaviour, were given to Muhammad as a series of revelations, codified in the Koran and supplemented by the deeds and discourse of the Prophet. Islam is regarded by its adherents as the last of the revealed religions (following Judaism and Christianity), and Muhammad is seen as the last of the Prophets, building upon and perfecting the examples and teachings of Abraham, Moses, and Jesus. Islam carries three interrelated significations: the personal individual submission to Allah; the 'world of Islam' as a concrete historical reality comprising a variety of communities sharing not only a common religious outlook but also a common fund of cultural legacies; and finally, the concept of an 'ideal Muslim community', as set forth in the Koran and supporting sources.

Islamabad The capital of Pakistan, a modern planned city in the north of the country, which replaced Karachi as capital in 1967; pop. (1981) 201,000.

Islamic art and architecture The artistic expression of nations and peoples professing the faith of ISLAM. The focal point of Islamic religious life is the congregational mosque. The pattern for early mosque architecture was set by Muhammad's house in Medina, built after his migration from Mecca in 622 AD as a place of meeting and worship. It was a fortified courtyard house, looking inwards for protection, with a veranda for shade on the north and south sides and living rooms on the east. As the congregation increased, the veranda was enlarged by adding more columns, and this type was developed into the many-columned mosque with arcades on three sides of an open courtyard. As prayers are said facing Mecca, an important component of the mosque is the indication of the direction of prayer by an ornate niche in the appropriate wall. Other components include the minaret, first introduced in 673 for the call to prayer, and areas for ritual washing (*ziyāda*). The dome or *qubba*, which had special significance as a symbol of the heavens and divinity, especially in the Dome of the Rock in Jerusalem (685–91). This was built by the UMAYYADS at the place from which Muhammad undertook his journey to heaven. In OTTOMAN mosques of 16th-century Istanbul, the DOME became highly prominent, inspired by the 6th-century Byzantine church of Hagia Sophia. Although generally discouraged by Islam, the building of funerary monuments became widespread. One of the earliest known is the hexagonal Qubba al-Sulaybiya (862), built in Samarra for an Abbasid Caliph. In Central Asia square, brick, domed mausolea, such as that of the Samanid dynasty in Bukhara (before 942), are ethnically Turkish in origin. In Seljuk Iran, a fashion for round, fluted and polygonal, often isolated, tomb towers developed, culminating in the massive, domed tomb of Sultan Oljaitu in Sultaniyeh (1305–13) and influencing the mausolea of the Timurids and Moguls. Perhaps the most famous Islamic mausoleum is the Taj Mahal, built by the Mogul emperor Shah Jajan in 1632–49 for his wife. Built of white marble, its symmetrical design reflects a Persian influence. Although there is no special Koranic proscription against representing human figures, tradition prohibits their depiction and so these are never found in religious buildings. In mosques, decoration was restricted to floral, geometric, and calligraphic designs from an early date. This proscription against figurative decoration was largely maintained on coins, until the secular movements of the 19th and 20th centuries.

Three major periods of development can be distinguished in traditional Islamic art. Firstly the period of the classical inheritance which saw borrowings from the Sassanids and from the classical and Byzantine worlds in Syria, Mesopotamia, and Spain. The second phase is marked by the eastern influence of the Turkish peoples of Central Asia and Iran, up to and including the Seljuk period. Turkish traditions had already influenced some aspects of ABBASID art, such as the use of seated figures on monochrome lustrewares, and carving styles. In architecture, decorative brickwork and the use of the *muqarnas* or stalactite vault also probably spread from the east. The third phase introduces colour into the external decoration of buildings. In Spain, North Africa, Egypt, and Syria coloured stone *ablaq* was used architecturally, and in Persia and Central Asia coloured tile and tile mosaic emerged in the Seljuk period. Strong Chinese influence was felt particularly in miniature painting and CERAMICS throughout the Islamic world after the Mongol conquests of the 13th century, especially in Egypt and Iran. European influence became a factor from the 16th century, particularly in painting. Traditional styles and techniques continued in the decorative arts, but by the 19th century the quality of Islamic art as a whole had declined greatly. In architecture Western styles were imported and became dominant in the 20th century, but, particularly since the 1970s, there has been a reaction against such 'aesthetic imperialism' in favour of buildings that express national traditions. This movement has been stimulated by the Aga Khan Awards for Architecture, presented every three years since 1980.

Islamic calendar A calendar based upon lunar months. Unlike the Gregorian solar calendar, it avoids the use of leap years, and therefore each Muslim year begins eleven to twelve days earlier than the previous one. The Muslim era begins with the *hijra*, the year in which Muhammad left Mecca for Medina, 622 AD. Although it is impossible to match the Muslim months exactly with the Gregorian months, a formula exists for calculating corresponding Gregorian years with Muslim years: AH (After Hijra) = 33/32 (AD–622), or AD = 32/33 (AH + 622).

Islamic fundamentalism The belief that the revitalization of Islamic society can only come about through a return to the fundamental principles and practices of early Islam. Fundamentalist movements have often been a response to political and economic decline, which is ascribed to spiritual and moral decay. In the 20th century, activist organizations, such as the Muslim Brotherhood, which was founded in Egypt in 1928 and has or had national independent organizations in Jordan, Kuwait, Palestine, Sudan, and Syria, and is influential in Afghanistan, India, and Pakistan, and other more radical groups, such as **Hizbullah** (or **Hezbollah**) (Party of God), have become prominent. Such groups are characterized by emphasis on the literal interpretation of the Koran and SHARIA. Fundamentalists tend to stress the penal code and restrictions on women contained in the *sharia*, at least in part because such provisions have become symbols of cultural identity and antagonism to Westernization. Some Western observers have regarded the recent resurgence in Islamic religious practice and the Iranian Revolution of 1979 as examples of fundamentalism.

Islamic law See SHARIA.

Isla Mujeres A limestone island in the Gulf of Mexico, situated 7 km (5 miles) off the east coast of the Mexican state of Quintana Roo. A popular resort island, it was named the 'Island of Women' by Spanish explorers who found the island adorned with terracotta images of women in 1517.

Islay An island in the Inner Hebrides of Scotland, to the south of Jura in Strathclyde Region; area 608 sq km (235 sq miles). Its chief ports of entry are Port Ellen and Port Askaig, and its principal industry is the distillation of whisky. Finlaggan was the former administrative centre of the Lords of the Isles.

Isle of Man An island in the Irish Sea, which is a British Crown possession enjoying home rule, with its own legislature (the *Tynwald*) and judicial system; area 572 sq km (221 sq miles); pop. (1991) 69,790; capital, Douglas. Its highest point is Snaefell (621 m, 2,036 ft) and its longest river is the Sulby (117 km, 10.5 miles). The island was part of the Norse kingdom of the Hebrides in the Middle Ages, passing into Scottish hands in 1266 for a time, until the English gained control in the early 15th century. Its ancient language, Manx, is still used for ceremonial purposes. The island hosts an annual series of Tourist Trophy motorcycle races, and is popular with both holiday-makers and tax-exiles.

Isle of Wight An island off the south coast of England, a county since 1974; area 381 sq km (147 sq miles); pop. (1991) 126,600; county town, Newport. It lies at the entrance to Southampton Water and is separated from the mainland by the Solent.

Isles of Scilly (or **Scillies**) A group of about 40 small islands, situated 28 miles west of the mainland of south-west England off Land's End; area 16 sq km (6 sq miles); pop. (1991) 2,900. Its chief settlement is Hugh Town (on St Mary's). Five of the islands are inhabited and because they lie in the path of the Gulf Stream they enjoy a mild climate. Numerous prehistoric remains are evidence of their settlement since the Bronze Age and since 1337 the islands have largely belonged to the Duchy of Cornwall.

Islington An inner borough of Greater London, both residential and industrialized, lying to the north of the City of London; pop. (1990) 155,200. The Sadler's Wells Theatre is to be found in Finsbury in the south of the borough.

Ismaili A member of a Shiite Muslim sect that seceded from the main group in the 8th century over the question of succession to the position of imam. They regarded Ismail, eldest son of the sixth imam, as the seventh and final imam, while the rest of the Shiites supported the second son, Musa al-Kazim. It eventually split into many sub-sects, of which the best-known is that headed by the Aga Khan. Ismailis are now found especially in India, Pakistan, and East Africa, with smaller groups in Syria, Iran, and some other countries.

isobar A line or contour drawn on a weather map to link places with the same barometric PRESSURE. Isobars usually represent the sea-level pressure distribution. Before they can be drawn the pressures measured at weather stations must be adjusted to sea-level by allowing for the decrease of pressure with altitude. Moreover, the pressure at the various places must be that at a given time or the average value over a given period.

Isocrates (436–338 BC) Athenian orator. His written speeches are amongst the earliest political pamphlets; they advocate the union of Greeks under Philip II of Macedon and a pan-Hellenic crusade against Persia.

isomerism (in chemistry) The existence of two or more molecules, isomers, with the same molecular formula but different three-dimensional structures. There are two main types of isomerism, structural isomerism and stereo-isomerism. In structural isomerism, the isomers differ in the arrangement in which the atoms are joined. For example, there are two structural isomers of C_2H_6O. Ethanol is an alcohol, and has the structure CH_3CH_2OH, whereas its isomer, dimethyl ether, has the structure CH_3OCH_3. They have different physical and chemical properties. There are two kinds of stereoisomerism. Geometrical isomerism occurs in structurally rigid molecules such as alkenes, in which rotation about a particular bond is restricted. The alkene but-2-ene, $CH_3CH{=}CHCH_3$, forms two geometrical isomers. In the cis-isomer, the two hydrogen atoms are both on one side of the carbon–carbon double bond, while the two methyl groups ($-CH_3$) are both on the other side. In the trans-isomer, the two hydrogen atoms are on opposite sides, as are the two methyl groups. The cis- and trans-isomers differ in all their physical and many of their chemical properties. The other form of stereoisomerism is optical isomerism. If an organic molecule contains a carbon atom to which four different groups are joined, the compound can exist in two isomeric forms differing in the sequence in which the groups are joined. These two isomers are called ENANTIOMERS. They have identical physical properties, and most chemical properties are identical. The most important way in which they differ is that they rotate the plane of plane-polarized light in opposite directions. See OPTICAL ACTIVITY.

isomorphism (from Greek *isos*, 'equal', and *morphē*, 'form') The existence of two or more systems that have the same structure. In crystallography two minerals of similar chemical composition, which have the same crystal structure are called isomorphs. In mathematics isomorphism means that results obtained from working in one system can be applied to the other system. Thus there must be a one-to-one correspondence between the elements which preserves the results of the operations.

isotherm A line on a map connecting places having the same temperature at a given time or on average over a given period.

isothermal change A change in which the temperature of a body or a system is maintained constant throughout the change. This very often means that for an isothermal process to occur heat must be allowed to enter or leave the system. For example, if a gas is compressed under normal conditions, it will heat up; if this is to be achieved isothermally, the gas must be compressed sufficiently slowly for the heat produced to have time to leak away, so that the temperature remains constant. This is in contrast to an ADIABATIC CHANGE, in which no heat is allowed to enter or leave a system.

isotope One of two or more forms of an ELEMENT that differ in relative atomic mass (atomic weight) and nuclear properties, but are chemically identical. Atomic nuclei are composed of protons and neutrons. It is the number of protons (the atomic number) that determines to which element a particular atom belongs, but the number of neutrons can vary; the isotopes of an element have the same number of protons in their nuclei but different numbers of neutrons. For example, uranium-238, the common isotope of uranium, has a nucleus containing 92 protons and 146 neutrons ($92 + 146 = 238$); uranium-235 has 92 protons and 143 neutrons. Isotopes have the same chemical properties (because they have the same number of extranuclear electrons) but slightly different physical properties (owing to their different relative atomic masses). Some isotopes exhibit radioactivity, and over a period decay into an isotope of a different element. Knowing the rate of decay one can sometimes calculate the age of an object from the proportion of isotopes present in it. This is the basis of the RADIOMETRIC DATING. Radioactive isotopes are important technologically, and many are produced by artificial means for use in medicine, weaponry, and the nuclear power industry.

isotopic dating See RADIOMETRIC DATING.

Ispahan See ISFAHAN.

Israel A country of south-west Asia at the eastern end of the Mediterranean Sea. It is bounded on the north by Lebanon, on the east by Syria and Jordan, and on the south by Egypt.

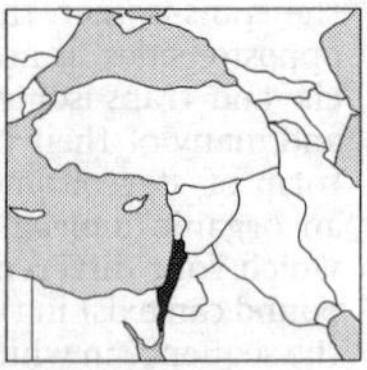

Physical. The coastal plain is very warm in summer and suited particularly to the growth of citrus fruits. The north includes the Sea of Galilee and part of the River Jordan, while the east extends to the Dead Sea with its deposits of potash and reserves of natural gas. Southward is a hot and arid RIFT VALLEY (part of the Great Rift Valley system) running down the eastern side of the rocky Negev Desert. Massive irrigation programmes have brought large areas of former desert under cultivation.

Economy. The Israeli economy has a well-developed manufacturing base, the main products being chemicals and small metal manufactures. However, high military expenditure and reliance on imported fuels and minerals have resulted in a high rate of inflation and dependence on foreign, mostly US, aid. Agriculture, largely carried out by communes (kibbutzim) and cooperatives (moshavim), has been successfully developed by irrigation, and Israel is self-sufficient in food. Exports include diamonds, chemicals, small metal manufactures, and fruit.

History. The modern state of Israel has developed from the Zionist campaign for a Jewish state in PALESTINE and the BALFOUR Declaration (1917) in which the Jewish demand for a national home was supported by Britain. Under the British mandate (from 1922) in Palestine the Jewish community increased from about 10 per cent of the population in 1918 to about 30 per cent in 1936. In 1937 the Peel Commission recommended the partition of Palestine and the formation of Jewish and Arab states. Subsequently Britain abandoned the partition solution, but, after its referral of the Palestine problem to the United Nations in 1947, a United Nations Special Commission recommended partition and a resolution to that effect passed the General Assembly. The British mandate ended on 14 May 1948 and the independent Jewish state of Israel in Palestine was established. The creation of the state was opposed by the Palestinian Arabs supported by Syria, Lebanon, Jordan, and Egypt, but after a violent conflict Israel survived and considerably enlarged its territory at the expense of the proposed Arab state. A substantial Palestinian refugee problem was created as many Arabs fled from Israel-controlled territory. Further Israeli-Arab wars took place in 1956 (SUEZ WAR), 1967 (SIX-DAY WAR), 1973 (YOM KIPPUR WAR), and 1982 (Lebanon War). As a result of these wars Israel extended its occupation to include all the territory of the former British mandate. After 1948 immigration into Israel took place from over 100 different nations, especially Jews from former communist and Arab countries, as well as from Europe, raising the population from about 700,000 in 1948 to 5.3 million by 1994. Despite a high inflation rate, the development of the economy has made Israel the most industrialized country in the region, greatly aided by funding from the USA and European powers. The right-wing leader of the Likud Party, Yitzhak SHAMIR, led a government (1986–92) firmly opposed to any concessions over the Palestine problem. Under his successor as Prime Minister, the Labour leader Yitzhak RABIN, progress towards an eventual settlement began. Intense diplomatic efforts, led by the USA, during 1991–92 resulted in several sessions of Middle East peace talks. Israel also indicated the possibility of a future peace agreement with Syria by making territorial concessions in the Golan Heights. Arab–Israeli peace talks were disrupted in late 1992 by violent clashes between Palestinians and Israeli security forces in the occupied territories and by the deportation of over 400 Palestinians, causing the PLO to halt negotiations. Despite the escalating violence in the occupied territories in 1993, Middle East peace talks resumed but remained deadlocked. An unexpected breakthrough in negotiations between Israel and the PLO, led by Yasser ARAFAT, resulted in a declaration of principles on Palestinian self-rule in the occupied territories. The declaration was welcomed internationally as a significant step forward in the peace process, while there was widespread opposition from right-wing Israeli political groups. Israel signed a peace treaty with Jordan in 1994 and had withdrawn its forces from all Jordanian territories by early 1995. The issue of Jewish settlement in the occupied West Bank, a long-standing source of dispute, sparked a crisis in the peace process in 1995; the assassination of Prime Minister Yitzhak Rabin in November by a Jewish extremist cast doubt over the future and once again threw the Middle East peace process into confusion. Shimon Peres succeeded Rabin and in 1996 HAMAS launched a number of suicide bomb attacks on Israeli cities. In the elections of 1996 (May) Peres, a supporter of the peace process, lost to the hawkish Binyamin Netanyahu, furthering the fundamentalist causes on both sides, for whom the peace process was unacceptable. Since then, little progress has been made in the peace process.

Capital: Jerusalem
Area: 20,700 sq km (7,992 sq mi)
Population: 5,386,000 (1995)
Currency: 1 New (Israeli) sheqel = 100 agorot
Religions: Jewish 82.0%; Muslim (mostly Sunni) 13.9%; Christian 2.3%; Druze and other 1.8%
Ethnic Groups: Jewish 83.0%; Arab 16.8%
Languages: Hebrew, Arabic (both official); Yiddish; Russian; Romanian; English
International Organizations: UN

Israel ▶**1** (or **Children of Israel**) The Hebrew nation of people traditionally descended from the patriarch Jacob (his alternative name was 'Israel'), whose 12 sons became founders of the 12 tribes. ▶**2** The northern kingdom of the Hebrews (*c.*930–721 BC, in contrast to Judah), whose inhabitants were carried away to captivity in Assyria. The name Israel is first found on the Moabite Stone (*c.*850 BC) commemorating the successes of the king Moab against Israel.

Israfil In Islamic tradition, the counterpart of Raphael, and the archangel of awe-inspiring aspect whose trumpet clarion will announce the Day of Resurrection and Last Judgement from a holy rock in Jerusalem. Although not mentioned by name in the Koran, in Islamic tradition Israfil appears in several legends and is credited with having trained Muhammad for prophethood for three years before Jibril (Gabriel) revealed the Koran to him.

Issigonis, Sir Alec (Arnold Constantine) (1906–88) Turkish-born British car designer. His most famous designs were the Morris Minor (1948), produced until 1971, and the Mini (1959).

Istanbul A great historic city, port, and the former capital (until 1923) of Turkey, situated on the Bosporus and partly in Europe, partly in Asia, to which it is linked by two suspension bridges; pop. (1990) 6,620,240. The largest city in Turkey, Istanbul was founded *c.*660 BC by Dorian Greeks. It was known as Byzantium until it became the second capital of the Roman Empire and was renamed Constantinople in 330 AD by Constantine I. Declared capital of the Eastern Roman Empire in 395, the city was largely rebuilt by Justinian (527–65). Captured by the Turks in 1453, most of its characteristic buildings, such as the Topkapi Palace, the Blue Mosque, and the Mosque of Suleiman the Magnificent, date from the Ottoman period (1453–1923). Istanbul has the world's largest covered bazaar. It is Turkey's commercial, religious, and cultural centre, and as a cosmopolitan city it has many foreign communities. Its port handles two-thirds of Turkey's trade and it has both heavy and light industries, including ship-building, cement, textiles, consumer goods of all kinds, and tourism.

Italian The official language of Italy, a Romance language, which in many ways has remained closer to Latin than have the others of this group. It is spoken by some 60 million people in Italy and Switzerland, and by large numbers of speakers in the US and South America.

Italian Lakes Glacial lakes in north Italy, including Maggiore and Lugano (both shared with Switzerland), Como, Garda, and other smaller ones. They are long glacial lakes blocked largely by MORAINES and famed for their beauty. Maggiore, Como, and Garda (the largest) are each 50 km (30 miles) or more long and surrounded by mountains of the Alps in the north and foothills in the south. The climate of the lakes is cool to mild.

Italic languages The early INDO-EUROPEAN LANGUAGES of Italy, of which Latin was by far the most important. They fall into two main groups: Oscan-Umbrian, which is named after its two major languages, but includes minor dialects of central Italy; and Latin-Faliscan. Oscan and Umbrian share broadly the same patterns of grammar and inflection as Latin, but diverge widely in PHONOLOGY and vocabulary. Faliscan is attested in a small number of inscriptions from Falerii, north of Rome.

Italy A country bounded on the north by France, Switzerland, Austria, and Slovenia, the mainland forming a peninsula in the Mediterranean Sea, and including the islands of Sardinia, Sicily, Ischia, and Capri.

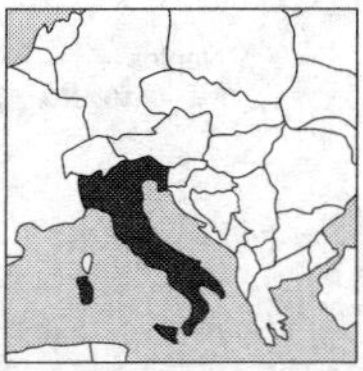

Physical. Among the southern foothills of the Alps in the north of the mainland are the Italian Lakes. Below them the River Po runs west–east across the fertile Lombardy Plain to the Adriatic Sea. The Apennines are the backbone of the peninsula itself. To their west are the hills and plains of Tuscany; further south the Tiber flows across the Pontine Marshes to the Tyrrhenian Sea. Further south still the coastal plain is enriched by the debris of Vesuvius and the climate becomes warmer. To the south is Calabria, where the mountains fall steeply to the sea and in summer the land bakes brown. Eastward, stretches a wide and arid limestone plain.

Economy. With a developed industrial economy, Italy's main exports incude electrical machinery (especially office equipment), chemicals, clothing, motor vehicles, textiles, and footwear. The public sector is significant, and industry is concentrated in north and central Italy with the south remaining predominantly agricultural and relatively poor. There are few large mineral deposits, excepting sulphur, mercury, and some oil in Sicily; crude oil accounts for some 15 per cent of imports. The tourist industry is significant. There are over 3 million agricultural holdings, with only a small degree of mechanization compared with other European countries. The chief agricultural products are sugar-beet, grains, tomatoes, citrus, and olives.

History. Italy had come under ETRUSCAN, Greek, and Celtic influence before it was united in *c.*262 BC under Roman rule. In the 5th century it was overrun by the barbarian GOTHS and Lombard tribes. In 775 CHARLEMAGNE conquered the north and it became part of the Carolingian empire, while the south was disputed between the Byzantine empire and the Arab conquerors of Sicily. By the 12th century city-states had emerged in northern and central Italy and the south united under first Norman and then, in 1176, Spanish control. The 14th century was a time of great commercial activity, followed by the RENAISSANCE period. The country, now divided between five major rival states, came under first Spanish (1559–1700) and then, after the Treaty of UTRECHT in 1713, Austrian domination. In 1796–97 Italy, having been used to maintain the balance of power in Europe, was invaded by NAPOLEON and hopes of independence and unification re-emerged. However, in 1815, the country reverted to a grouping consisting of Lombardy and Venetia, ruled by the HABSBURGS from Vienna; the kingdom of Piedmont Sardinia, which then consisted of most of Savoy, Piedmont, and the island of Sardinia; the Papal States, ruled by the popes in Rome; the duchies of Tuscany, Parma, and Modena, also ruled by the Habsburgs; and the Kingdom of the Two Sicilies, now ruled by restored Bourbons from Naples. France ruled part of Savoy and Corsica, but had lost Genoa to Piedmont. Revolutionary societies, such as the CARBONARI and YOUNG ITALY, were formed. The new forces of the RISORGIMENTO created hopes of independence from Austrian and French rule. Under such leaders as CAVOUR, MAZZINI, and GARIBALDI, unification of Italy was finally achieved, and in 1861 VICTOR EMANUEL II was crowned king of Italy. In an effort to join the 'scramble for Africa' the Italian Premier and Minister of Foreign Affairs, Francesco Crispi, claimed (1889) the colony of ERITREA, but the abortive bid for ETHIOPIA led to a decisive defeat (1896) at the battle of ADOWA. During the Turko-Italian War (1911–12), Italy conquered north Tripoli and by 1914 had occupied much of Libya, declaring it an integral part of the country in 1939. In World War I Italy supported the Allies, regaining Trieste and part of the Tyrol. The fascist dictator MUSSOLINI, determined to establish an Italian empire, successfully invaded (1935) Ethiopia, combining it with Eritrea and Italian Somaliland to form Italian East Africa. In World War II Mussolini at first allied himself with Hitler, but by 1943 the country had lost its North African empire and in the same year declared war on Germany. In 1946 the king abdicated in favour of a republic. The immediate post-war period brought remarkable and sustained economic growth but also political instability, characterized by frequent changes of government. The Italian Communist Party successfully adjusted to democracy, but during the 1970s there were Red Brigade terrorist kidnappings and outrages. Governments of the republic have mostly been formed by elaborate coalitions, dominated by the Christian Democrats, but Italian politics became increasingly incompetent, with accusations of corruption. As a result, there were calls in 1991 by President Francesco Cossiga

(1985–92) for constitutional reform. Continued attempts to eliminate the MAFIA largely failed. In 1992 President Cossiga resigned and was succeeded by Oscar Luigi Scalfaro, while the government's economic reform policies led to large-scale anti-government protests. Allegations of corruption against politicians and government ministers in 1993 further seriously undermined the authority of the government. The country's electoral process was changed from a proportional representation system to a first-past-the-post system, after overwhelming approval by the populace in nationwide referendums. Former ministers, meanwhile, were the subject of investigations into corrupt activities. The general election of 1994 brought to power, under the new electoral system, a right-wing coalition government led by *Forza Italia*, a party recently formed by media magnate, Silvio Berlusconi, who became Prime Minister. Following conflicts of interest between Berlusconi's political

Italy

and commercial interests, he was forced to resign when the Northern League party withdrew from the coalition. Lamberto Dini replaced Berlusconi as Prime Minister in 1995 and, despite surviving a vote of no confidence, announced his intention to step down at the end of the year. A general election held in 1996 was won by a left-wing coalition headed by Romano Prodi. The early 1990s saw Mafia violence escalate, provoking public outrage at the authorities' inability to curb it. The government responded by increasing police and judiciary powers and key arrests were made. By 1994 official reports indicated a significant reduction in Mafia-related crimes.

Capital: Rome
Area: 301,277 sq km (116,324 sq mi)
Population: 57,386,000 (1995)
Currency: 1 lira = 100 centesimi
Religions: Roman Catholic 83.2%; non-religious 13.6%; atheist 2.6%
Ethnic Groups: Italian 94.1%; Sardinian 2.7%; Rhaetian 1.3%
Languages: Italian (official); Sardinian; minority languages
International Organizations: EU; NATO; OECD; UN; Council of Europe; CSCE

Ithaca (or **Ithaka**; Greek **Itháki**) An Ionian island off the west coast of Greece, separated from Cephalonia by the Ithaca Channel; area 114 sq km (44 sq miles). Its chief port is Vathy. The island was the legendary home of Odysseus who was associated with the Grotto of the Nymphs and the Fountain of Arethusa.

Ito, Prince Hirobumi (1841–1909) Japanese statesman, Premier four times between 1884 and 1901. In 1889 he was prominent in drafting the Japanese constitution, and the following year helped to establish a bicameral national diet. He was assassinated by a member of the Korean independence movement.

Ivan Six rulers of Russia. **Ivan I** (*c*.1304–41) was grand duke of Muscovy 1328–40. He strengthened and enlarged the duchy, making Moscow the ecclesiastical capital in 1326. **Ivan II** (known as Ivan the Red) (1326–59) was grand duke of Muscovy 1353–59. **Ivan III** (known as Ivan the Great) (1440–1505) was grand duke of Muscovy 1462–1505. He consolidated and enlarged his territory, defending it against a Tartar invasion in 1480, and adopting the title of 'Ruler of all Russia' in 1472. **Ivan IV** (known as Ivan the Terrible) (1530–84) was grand duke of Muscovy 1533–47 and first tsar of Russia 1547–84. His expansionist foreign policy resulted in the capture of Kazan (1552), Astrakhan (1556), and Siberia (1581). However, the Tartar siege of Moscow (1572) and Ivan's defeat by the Poles in the Livonian War (1558–82) left Russia weak and divided. He grew increasingly unpredictable and tyrannical; in 1581 he killed his eldest son Ivan in a fit of rage, the succession passing to his retarded second son Fyodor. **Ivan V** (1666–96) was nominal tsar of Russia 1682–96. **Ivan VI** (1740–64) was infant tsar of Russia 1740–41.

Ives, Charles (Edward) (1874–1954) US composer. Influenced by popular music and the sounds of everyday life, he developed the use of polyrhythms, polytonality, quarter-tones, note-clusters, and aleatoric techniques. He is noted for his second piano sonata *Concord* (1915), and his chamber work *The Unanswered Question* (1906), scored for two unsynchronized orchestras.

IVF See IN VITRO FERTILIZATION.

Iviza See IBIZA.

Ivory, James (1928–) US film director. He has made a number of films in partnership with the producer Ismail MERCHANT, including *Heat and Dust* (1983) *A Room with a View* (1986), *Maurice* (1987), *Howard's End* (1992), and *The Remains of the Day* (1993).

Ivory Coast See CÔTE D'IVOIRE.

ivy A climbing shrub of the genus *Hedera*, belonging to the Araliaceae family. One of the few LIANAS of temperate Europe, it is an evergreen climber, which attaches itself by means of its roots. Ivy leaves have three to five triangular lobes in juvenile foliage but are unlobed and narrowly pointed in mature, sexual shoots. These shoots produce no roots and bear green flowers in the autumn, when they are visited by many insects, including moths and wasps. The black fruits survive the winter and are a valuable source of food for birds at this time. Ivy has a bad reputation as a strangler of trees, although in healthy trees this is unfounded. Other plants of the family Araliaceae are also known as ivy.

Ivy League A group of eight old-established US colleges and universities with prestigious standing, both academically and socially. Originally members of a 19th-century conference for intercollegiate sports, called the Ivy League, they now include Brown, Columbia, Cornell, Dartmouth, and Pennsylvania, as well as the three top names – Yale, Harvard, and Princeton.

Iwo Jima A small volcanic island, the largest of the Volcano Islands in the western Pacific, 1,222 km (760 miles) south of Tokyo. During World War II it was the heavily fortified site of a Japanese airbase, and its attack and capture in 1944–45 was one of the severest US campaigns. It was returned to Japan in 1968.

Izmir (formerly **Smyrna**) A seaport and naval base in western Turkey, on an inlet of the Aegean Sea; pop. (1990) 1,757,410. It is the third-largest city in Turkey. Founded by the Greeks in *c*.1000 BC, it was captured by the Ottoman Turks in 1424, occupied by the Greeks in 1919 but retaken by the Turks in 1922, when it was devastated by fire. It produces a wide range of goods including carpets and foodstuffs for export. The province of the same name is rich in minerals; area 12,825 sq km (4,952 sq miles).

J

jabiru A large stork, *Jabiru mycteria*, with a white body and blue head and neck, often with a red patch at the base of the neck. It is found in Central and South America.

jacamar A bird that lives in the tropical forests of Central and South America, making up the 18 species of the family Galbudidae. They are sparrow- to thrush-sized birds, with long tails and long, straight beaks. They are iridescent green or greenish-black above and most have chestnut underparts and white throats. They perch on branches and dart out after passing insects. They nest in holes in banks and lay one to four white eggs.

jacana (or **lily-trotter**) Any one of eight species of tropical and subtropical long-legged WADING BIRD of the family Jacanidae. They have elongated toes and hind-claws which spread their weight and enable them to walk on floating vegetation. They frequent sheltered inland waters, including rivers.

jacaranda A tree of the genus *Jacaranda*, comprising some 50 species of trees of the tropical Americas. Members of the family Bignoniaceae and related to catalpas, they are often grown as a street tree. The species most widely seen is *J. acutifolia*, a fast-growing tree from Brazil, with feathery leaves and large heads of pale violet flowers.

jackal The common wild canid of the warmer parts of the Old World. The four species are usually found in open or lightly wooded parts of Africa and Asia, sometimes even in outlying districts of towns and villages, where they search for food amongst garbage. They are scavengers who serve a useful purpose in removing carrion, and are also excellent mouse and rat catchers. Stealthy and secretive, they spend most nights hunting in family groups or packs of three to six individuals. The four species of jackals are the golden, *Canis aureus*, silver or black-backed, *C. mesomelas*, Simien or Ethiopian, *C. simensis*, and side-striped, *C. adustus*.

jackdaw A species of bird, *Corvus monedula*, belonging to the crow family, which occurs over much of Europe and western Asia. It is a smallish bird, 32 cm (13 inches) long, black above except for the nape and the area over the ears, and underparts, all of which are greyish-black. It has a striking greyish-white eye. In eastern Asia there is a form which has a white collar and white underparts; this is called the Daurian jackdaw, *Corvus dauuricus*. The jackdaw lives in open, wooded country, in city parks, or on cliffs, nesting in holes in trees or among rocks. It also commonly nests in holes in tall buildings such as church towers. It has a reputation for stealing money and other shiny objects.

Jacklin, Antony (known as 'Tony') (1944–) British golfer. In 1969 he won the British Open and the following year won the US Open, the first British player to do so for 50 years. He played in the Ryder Cup (1967–80) and was non-playing captain of the European team from 1983 to 1989.

jackrabbit A hare of the same genus (*Lepus*) as European hares. Jackrabbits have larger legs and ears than other hares but otherwise they are similar in appearance and behaviour, and are particularly noted for their leaping habits. Jackrabbits are confined to western North America, where they inhabit arid rangeland. Six species are recognized, including the white-tailed jackrabbit, *L. townsendi*, which inhabits the slopes of the northwestern Rocky Mountains, and the black-tailed jackrabbit, *L. californicus*. The latter is called the varying hare because it often turns white in winter.

Jackson The state capital of Mississippi, USA, on the Pearl River; pop. (1990) 196,640. Founded as a trading post by the French Canadian trader Louis LeFleur and later named after President Andrew Jackson, the city became state capital in 1822. It developed as a railway junction and administrative centre during the 19th century and further expanded after the discovery of natural gas nearby in the 1930s.

Jackson, Andrew (1767–1845) US general and Democratic statesman, 7th President of the USA 1829–37. After waging several campaigns against American Indians, he defeated a British army at New Orleans (1815) and successfully invaded Florida (1818). As President, he replaced an estimated 20 per cent of those in public office with Democrat supporters, a practice that became known as the spoils system.

Jackson, Glenda (1936–) British actress and politician. Throughout her acting career she appeared on stage and television, but is best known for her film work. She won Oscars for her performances in *Women in Love* (1969) and *A Touch of Class* (1973); other films include *Sunday Bloody Sunday* (1971) and *Turtle Diary* (1985). In 1992 she became Labour MP for the London constituency of Hampstead and Highgate and was appointed to a junior post in the government after the 1997 election.

Jackson, Jesse (Louis) (1941–) US politician and clergyman. After working with Martin Luther King in the civil-rights struggle, he competed for but failed to win the Democratic Party's 1984 and 1988 presidential nominations.

Jackson, Michael (Joe) (1958–) US singer and songwriter. In the 1970s he performed with his four older brothers in the pop group the Jackson Five. His career suffered a setback in 1993 after allegations of child molestation concerning young boys. In 1994 he married Lisa Marie Presley

(1968–), the daughter of Elvis Presley; the couple separated in 1996.

Jackson, Thomas Jonathan (known as 'Stonewall Jackson') (1824–63) US general. During the American Civil War he made his mark as a commander at the first Battle of Bull Run in 1861; a successful defensive stand there earned him his nickname. As the deputy of Robert E. Lee, he played an important part in the Confederate victories in Virginia in the first two years of the war.

Jacksonville A major transport centre, and industrial, commercial, and financial city and port in north-east Florida, USA, on the St Johns River 19 km (12 miles) inland from its mouth; pop. (1990) 672,970. Formerly known as Cowford, it was renamed in honour of President Andrew JACKSON. A very extensive city with shipyards and naval installations, and many light industries including tourism and sports facilities.

Jack the Ripper (19th century) Unidentified British murderer. From August to November 1888 some five prostitutes were brutally killed in the East End of London, the bodies being mutilated in a way that indicated a knowledge of anatomy. The authorities received taunting notes from a person calling himself Jack the Ripper and claiming to be the murderer, but the cases remain unsolved.

Jacob (Hebrew, 'trickster', or 'supplanter') Hebrew patriarch, the younger twin son of Isaac and Rebecca, whose favourite he was, and the shepherd ancestor of the 12 tribes of Israel. By trickery Jacob won the birthright and the father's blessing due to his older brother, Esau. Esau's anger caused Jacob to flee to their ancestral land of Haran, where he had a vision at Bethel of a ladder from heaven to Earth and of his own promised blessing and prosperity. While in Haran he married his uncle Laban's two daughters, Leah and Rachel. Crossing a river on his way back to Canaan he wrestled until dawn with a mysterious, unseen presence at Peniel and for his perseverance received from it the name of 'Israel' ('he that strives with God'). Ya'qub (Jacob), in early Meccan *shūras* of the Koran, appears as the brother of Ishaq (Isaac), and the son of Ibrahim (Abraham). He is regarded as a prophet, and was temporarily blinded by the grief he experienced at the loss of Yusuf (Joseph). In post-Koranic legend, Ya'qub and Esau are said to have fought in their mother's womb over who should be born first. Ya'qub allowed his brother preference to spare his mother pain.

Jacobi, Karl Gustav Jacob (1804–51) German mathematician. He worked on the theory of elliptic functions, in competition with Niels Abel. Jacobi also investigated number theory, mathematical analysis, geometry, and differential equations, and his work on determinants is important in dynamics and quantum mechanics.

Jacobin The most famous of the political clubs of the FRENCH REVOLUTION. It had its origins in the Club Breton, which was established after the opening of the STATES-GENERAL in 1789, and acquired its new name from its headquarters in an old Jacobin (Dominican) monastery in Paris. Its membership grew steadily and its carefully prepared policies had great influence in the National Assembly. By August 1791 it had numerous affiliated clubs and branches throughout the country. Its high subscription confined its membership to professional men who, at first, were not distinguished by extreme views. By 1792, however, ROBESPIERRE had seized control and the moderates were expelled. The club became the focus of the Reign of Terror the following year, and in June was instrumental in the overthrow of the GIRONDINS. Its success was based on sound organization and the support of the SANS-CULOTTES. It was closed after the fall of Robespierre and several attempts to reopen it were finally suppressed in 1799.

Jacobite A Scottish or English supporter of the exiled royal house of STUART. The Jacobites took their name from Jacobus, the Latin name for JAMES II, who had been deprived of his throne in 1688. Their strength lay among the Highland CLANS of Scotland, whose loyalty was personal; the weakness of Jacobitism was that it failed to win over the Tories in England, who might have made it a more powerful and dangerous movement. The Jacobites were politically important between 1688 and 1745. The FIFTEEN and the FORTY-FIVE were their major rebellions, but neither succeeded and after 1745, with the government's suppression of the clans, Jacobitism ceased to have a firm political base.

Jacobs, W(illiam) W(ymark) (1863–1943) British short-story writer. He is noted for his tales of the macabre, such as 'The Monkey's Paw' (1902).

Jacopo della Quercia See QUERCIA, JACOPO DELLA.

Jacquard A mechanism, invented in 1801 by Joseph-Marie Jacquard (1754–1834), for automating the weaving of patterned fabrics. The lifting of the WARP threads, carried out by assistants on earlier draw LOOMS, was placed under the control of the weaver. A system of perforated cards controlled the rise and fall of the warp threads to produce the desired pattern; the system was operated with a treadle. In modern weaving machines, punched-card Jacquards have largely been replaced by Jacquard mechanisms controlled by MICROPROCESSORS.

jade Either of two mineral semi-precious stones, jadeite and nephrite, which are usually whitish to dark green. Jadeite or Chinese jade, the rarer, is a silicate of sodium and aluminium found not only in the East but also in Guatemala. Nephrite, a calcium, magnesium, iron silicate, comes mainly from New Zealand, America, and Russia. So-called Indian jade, aventurine, is a form of quartz. All types of jade have been used for making vessels and ornaments since prehistoric times in various parts of the world, China having the richest tradition in the medium. The Aztecs and Maoris used nephrite to make tools and weapons.

jaeger A SKUA of the genus *Stercorarius*, which is sometimes separated from the genus *Catharacta*. This genus of gull-like birds includes three slender, fast-flying hunters of the northern tundra: the Arctic, pomarine, and long-tailed jaegers, all of which feed on small mammals and birds. They nest on the ground or on cliffs, laying two or three eggs. In autumn they fly south and feed mainly at sea, penetrating far into the Southern Hemisphere.

Jael Hebrew heroine, the wife of Heber the Kenite (believed to be descendants of Cain), who, when the Israelites were being attacked by the Canaanites, gave refuge and hospitality in her tent to an enemy of her people, the Canaanite commander, Sisera. Lulling him to sleep, she killed him by driving a tent peg through his skull.

Jaffa (Hebrew **Yafo**; ancient name **Joppa**) A city and port on the Mediterranean coast of Israel, forming a southern suburb of the Tel Aviv conurbation, and since 1949 united with Tel Aviv; pop. (1994) 355,200. Occupied since prehistoric times, Jaffa was the seat of a bishop of the Byzantine empire until captured by the Arabs in 636 and was a stronghold of the Crusaders. It has associations with Noah's son Japheth who is said to have founded the town after the Flood, and with the legendary Perseus, who rescued Andromeda here.

Jagannath Temple A temple to the Hindu God Jagannath, 'Lord of the Universe', in the city of Puri, Orissa, India. Every June/July a chariot carrying a massive wooden image of Jagannath is pulled through the streets by 4,000 men, a vehicle that has given the English language the word *juggernaut*.

Jagger, Mick (full name Michael Philip Jagger) (1943–) British rock singer and songwriter. He formed the Rolling Stones *c.*1962 with guitarist Keith Richards (1943–), a childhood friend. Originally a rhythm and blues band, the Rolling Stones became successful with a much-imitated rebel image and Jagger–Richards songs such as 'Satisfaction' (1965) and 'Jumping Jack Flash' (1968). In the 1970s they evolved a simple, derivative, yet distinctive style, heard on albums such as *Exile on Main Street* (1972) and *Some Girls* (1978), which they retained almost unchanged into the 1990s.

jaguar The biggest CAT species, *Panthera onca*, found in the New World, from Patagonia through South and Central America as far north as Texas, New Mexico, and Arizona in the USA. One of the most handsome of the cats, it may be as much as 2.43 m (8 feet) long. It has a rich yellow or tawny coat marked with a chain of black spots down the back, bordered by five rows of black rosettes running lengthwise along each side. The tail, limbs, and head are heavily spotted and lined with black. Black jaguars may be found in the valley of the River Amazon. Among its prey are capybara, alligators, turtles, peccaries, and even man.

Jahangir (1569–1627) Emperor of India 1605–27, whose contribution to MOGUL greatness was artistic rather than military. His name means 'holder of the world', but control over the huge empire he inherited was threatened by court quarrels and by the dominance of his Persian wife, Nur Jahan. He was criticized for addiction to alcohol and opium, but his own artistic interests encouraged a new naturalism in the work of his court painters.

Jainism A non-theistic religion founded in India in the 6th century BC by Vardhamana Mahavira as a reaction against the teachings of orthodox Brahminism. Its central doctrine is non-injury to living creatures. Salvation is attained by perfection of the soul through successive lives. Numbering some 3.6 million adherents, its followers in India are mostly found in Gujarat and Maharashtra states. There are two major sects: the white-robed *Svetambaras* and the naked *Digambaras*.

Jaipur (formerly **Jeypore**) A city of western India, the capital of Rajasthan; pop. (1991) 1,455,000. Founded in 1725 by Sawai Jai Singh II, maharaja of the Kacchwaha Rajputs, who laid it out according to Hindu rules of town planning with a grid pattern and wide avenues. Notable buildings include the Palace of the Winds (Hawa Mahal), the 18th-century observatory (Jantar Mantar), and the city palace. It is noted for its carpets and handicrafts including jewellery and miniature paintings.

Jakarta (or **Djakarta**) The capital of Indonesia, situated in north-west Java on an inlet of the Java Sea; pop. (1990) 8,222,500. Founded by the Dutch in the early 17th century, it was the headquarters of the Dutch East India Company. It was known as Batavia until 1949, when it became capital of the newly independent state of Indonesia. The old city centre with its Dutch colonial architecture is surrounded by residential suburbs and shanty towns. It is the administrative, commercial, and cultural centre of Indonesia with eleven universities founded between 1950 and 1960. Its industries include textiles, metals, and timber. It exports tea and rubber.

Jakobson, Roman (Osipovich) (1896–1982) Russian-born US linguist. In 1941 he emigrated to the USA and from 1949 to 1967 was professor of Slavic languages and literature and general linguistics at Harvard University. In *Child Language, Aphasia, and Phonological Universals* (1941) he developed the hypothesis that there may be a universal sequence according to which speech sounds are learned. His *Fundamentals of Language* (1956) postulates a phonological system of 12 binary oppositions to cover all the permutations of sounds in the world's languages.

Jalal ad-Din ar-Rumi (or **Mawlana**) (1207–73) Persian poet and Sufi mystic. He was born in Balkh (in modern Afghanistan), but lived for most of his life at Konya in Anatolia, where he founded the order of whirling dervishes, a sect noted for their ecstatic rituals and use of hypnotic trance-states. He wrote much lyrical poetry and an influential epic on Sufi mystical doctrine.

Jamaica A Caribbean island country lying south of Cuba.

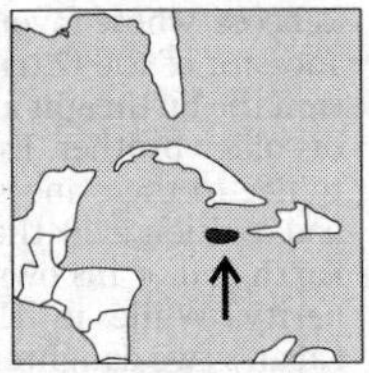

Physical. Jamaica is about 235 km (146 miles) from west to east and 80 km (50 miles) from north to south at its widest point, the third largest island in the Caribbean. Along its spine is a range of limestone hills which rises to 2,256 m (7,400 feet) in the Blue Mountains in the east. Streams flow both north and south, the northern rivers reaching a coast which is very beautiful, with palm-fringed beaches and long, sandy bays. Temperatures are hot, and rainfall exceeds 1,000 mm (40 inches) a year.

Economy. Jamaica is the world's fourth largest producer of bauxite; bauxite and alumina dominate exports. Both agriculture and industry are important, with sugar, bananas, and coffee the principal agricultural exports, and there is also a developing manufacturing industry. Tourism is an important source of foreign exchange. A high level of debt, sporadic outbreaks of criminal violence, and hurricane damage in 1988 have damaged the economy.

History. Originally inhabited by Arawak Indians, Jamaica was discovered by Columbus in 1494 and settled by the Spanish in 1509. In 1655 it was captured by the British and prospered as a BUCCANEER base. The importation of slaves to work on sugar-cane plantations made Jamaica the leading sugar producer of the 18th century. When slavery was abolished (1834) its economy suffered. A Negro rebellion in 1865 was ruthlessly suppressed by Governor Eyre. In 1866 it became a crown colony, and representative government gradually developed from 1884.

In the 1930s there was widespread rioting, caused by racial tension and economic depression, and in 1944 self-government, based on universal adult suffrage, was granted. Economic recovery followed World War II. In 1958 Jamaica became a founding member of the Federation of the West Indies. When this collapsed, the Jamaican Labour

Party (JLP) under William A. BUSTAMANTE negotiated independence as a dominion in the COMMONWEALTH OF NATIONS. Administrations have alternated between the JLP and PNP (People's National Party), whose leader Michael Manley introduced many social reforms in the 1970s. In 1980 the JLP returned to office under Edward Seaga, whose conservative economic policies failed to reverse economic decline. The PNP returned to power in 1989 under Michael Manley, an enthusiast for CARICOM. Inheriting both high inflation and rising unemployment, his policy was to deregulate the economy. This resulted in protests that the PNP had betrayed its social democratic principles. Ill-health obliged Manley to retire in March 1992. He was replaced as Prime Minister and as leader of the PNP by Percival J. Patterson, who despite his continuation of economic austerity policies, boosted the government's popularity. The general election called in 1993 was preceded by violent clashes between rival party supporters; a landslide victory for the PNP was disputed by the JLP, amid allegations of fraud and thuggery involving police members. The JLP boycotted the new parliament, demanding electoral and police reforms, and in 1994 the two parties agreed to suspend all general and municipal elections pending electoral reform.

Capital: Kingston
Area: 10,991 sq km (4,244 sq mi)
Population: 2,520,000 (1995)
Currency: 1 Jamaican dollar = 100 cents
Religions: Church of God 18.4%; non-religious or atheist 17.7%; Baptist 10.0%; Anglican 7.1%; Seventh-day Adventist 6.9%; Pentecostal 5.2%; Roman Catholic 5.0%; Rastafarian 5.0%
Ethnic Groups: Black 76.3%; Afro-European 15.1%; East Indian and Afro-East Indian 3.4%; White 3.2%; Chinese and Lebanese minorities
Languages: English (official); English creole; Hindi; Chinese
International Organizations: CARICOM; Commonwealth; Non-Aligned Movement; OAS; UN

James Seven Stuart kings of Scotland. **James I** (1394–1437), son of Robert III, reigned 1406–37. Captured by the English while a child, James remained a captive until 1424. He returned to a country divided by baronial feuds, but managed to restore some measure of royal authority. He was murdered in Perth by rebel nobles. **James II** (1430–60), son of James I, reigned 1437–60. After ascending the throne as a minor, he eventually overthrew his regents and considerably strengthened the position of the Crown by crushing the powerful Douglas family (1452–55). He was killed during the siege of Roxburgh Castle. **James III** (1451–88), son of James II, reigned 1460–88. He proved increasingly unable to control his nobles, who eventually raised an army against him in 1488, using his son, the future James IV, as a figurehead. The king was defeated and killed in battle at Sauchieburn, near Stirling. **James IV** (1473–1513), son of James III, reigned 1488–1513. He re-established royal power throughout the realm, notably in the Highlands. He took an active part in European alliance politics, forging a dynastic link with England through his marriage to Margaret Tudor, the daughter of Henry VII, and revitalizing the traditional pact with France. When England and France went to war in 1513, he supported the latter and invaded England at the head of a large army. He died along with many of his nobles when his army was defeated at Flodden. **James V** (1512–42), son of James IV, reigned 1513–42. Both during his long minority and after his marriage to the French noblewoman Mary of Guise, Scotland was dominated by French interests. Relations with England deteriorated in the later years of his reign, culminating in an invasion by Henry VIII's army and the defeat of James's troops near the border at Solway Moss in 1542. **James VI** The Scottish title of James I of England. See JAMES (kings of England). **James VII** The Scottish title of James II of England. See JAMES (kings of England).

James Two kings of England, Ireland, and Scotland. **James I** (1566–1625), son of Mary, Queen of Scots, was king of Scotland (as James VI) 1567–1625, and of England and Ireland 1603–25. After his minority ended in 1583, he was largely successful in restoring royal authority in Scotland. He inherited the throne of England on the death of Elizabeth I, as great-grandson of Margaret Tudor, daughter of Henry VII. His declaration of the divine right of kings, his favouritism towards the Duke of Buckingham, and his intended alliance with Spain made him unpopular with Parliament. He was succeeded by his second son, Charles I. **James II** (1633–1701), son of Charles I, was king of England, Ireland, and (as James VII) Scotland 1685–88. His Catholic beliefs led to the rebellion of the Duke of Monmouth in 1685 and to his deposition in favour of William of Orange and Mary II three years later. Attempts to regain the throne resulted in James's defeat at the Battle of the Boyne in 1690. He died in exile in France, leaving the Jacobite claim to the throne in the hands of his son, James Stuart.

James, C(yril) L(ionel) R(obert) (1901–89) Trinidadian historian, journalist, political theorist, and novelist. After working as a cricket columnist, he established a reputation as a historian with his study of the Haitian revolution, *Black Jacobins* (1938). A Trotskyist from 1934, he wrote a number of political works, including *World Revolution: 1917–1936* (published in 1937).

James, Henry (1843–1916) US-born British novelist and critic. He settled in England in 1876, and in his early novels dealt with the relationship between European civilization and American life, notably in *The Portrait of a Lady* (1881). In *The Bostonians* (1886) he portrayed American society in its own right, before producing many novels of English life. He is also remembered for his ghost story *The Turn of the Screw* (1898), the subject of Benjamin Britten's opera by the same name (1954). He was the brother of William JAMES.

James, Jesse (Woodson) (1847–82) US outlaw. He joined with his brother Frank (1843–1915) and others to form a notorious band of outlaws, which specialized in bank and train robberies and inspired many westerns.

James, P(hyllis) D(orothy), Baroness (1920–) British writer of detective fiction. She is noted for her novels featuring the poet-detective Adam Dalgleish, including *Death of an Expert Witness* (1977) and *A Taste for Death* (1986). Her books have been used as a basis for many TV films.

James, St Christian saint, referred to as 'the Lord's brother' in the Gospels, and regarded as the Apostle James the Less by Roman Catholics (although others see them as separate figures). James, with Peter, became leader of the Christian Church in Jerusalem. He was reputedly put to death by the Sanhedrin. The Epistle of St James is ascribed to him.

James, St (known as 'the Great') One of the Twelve Apostles, the fisherman son of Zebedee and Salome, and brother of John. Put to the sword by Herod Agrippa in 44 AD, he was the first Apostle to be martyred. Later Christian documents allege James preached and was buried in Spain, where he is greatly venerated.

James, William (1842–1910) US philosopher and psychologist. Influenced by C. S. Peirce, James was a leading exponent of pragmatism, who sought a functional definition of truth rather than a depiction of a structural relation between ideas and reality. Major works include *The Will to Believe* (1897) and *Essays in Radical Empiricism* (1912). In psychology he published the definitive and innovative *The Principles of Psychology* (1890), and he is credited with introducing the concept of the stream of consciousness. He was the brother of Henry JAMES.

Jamestown The site of an English colony established on the Virginia Peninsula in 1607 during the reign of James I, the first permament English settlement in the New World. Built on a marshy and unhealthy site, the town suffered badly at the hands of fire, disease, and Indians, and was finally abandoned when the colony's capital was moved to Williamsburg at the end of the 17th century.

Jamestown The capital and chief port of the island of St Helena; pop. (1981) 1,500.

Jammu The railhead and winter capital of the state of Jammu and Kashmir in north-west India, on the Tawi River, a tributary of the Chenab; pop. (1991) 206,000. The Old Fort and the maharaja's palace dominate the city.

Jammu and Kashmir A state in north-west India; area 100,569 sq km (38,845 sq miles); pop. (est. 1991) 7,718,700; capital, Srinagar (summer), Jammu (winter). Over 60 per cent of the predominantly Urdu-speaking population are Muslims. See KASHMIR.

Jamshid The legendary Persian king whose pride in his own power caused God to plunge his empire into chaos. In the epic poem by Firdausi, *Shāhnāmah* (*c.*1000), Jamshid is credited with the invention of iron weaponry, the art of medicine, the making of clothing, jewellery, and perfume. He was eventually sawn in two by the evil king Zahhak.

Janáček, Leoš (1854–1928) Czech composer. Influenced at first by Dvořák, from 1885 he began to collect the Moravian folk-songs whose pitch inflections and rhythmic speech patterns pervade his music. His works include nine operas, notably *Jenufa* (1904) and *The Cunning Little Vixen* (1924), the *Sinfonietta* (1926), and the *Glagolitic Mass* (1927).

Janissaries (from Turkish *yeni cheri*, 'new troops') An élite corps of slave soldiers, bound to the service of the OTTOMAN sultans. They were originally raised from prisoners of war, but from the time of BAYEZID I (1389–1403) they were largely recruited by means of the *devshirme* ('gathering'), a levy of the fittest youths among the sultan's non-Muslim subjects. Having been converted to Islam, most, after intensive training, served as foot soldiers, while the ablest passed into civil administration. Decimation in the great wars against Persia and Austria (1578–1606) lowered the traditionally high quality of the intake and opened the corps to Muslims. They exercised a powerful role in political life until their abolition in 1826.

Jansen, Cornelius Otto (1585–1638) Flemish Roman Catholic theologian and founder of JANSENISM. A strong opponent of the Jesuits, he proposed a reform of Christianity through a return to St Augustine. To this end he produced his major work, *Augustinus* (1640), which was published by his followers after his death. The four-volume study followed St Augustine's teachings and formed the basis of Jansenism.

Jansenism A religious movement of the 17th and 18th centuries, based on the writings of the theologian Cornelius JANSEN and characterized by general harshness and moral rigour. Its most famous exponent was Pascal. The movement received papal condemnation and its adherents were persecuted in France (though tolerated in the Netherlands) during most of the 18th century.

Jansens, Cornelius See JOHNSON, CORNELIUS.

Jansky, Karl Guthe (1905–50) US engineer who discovered radio waves from the centre of the Galaxy. This discovery eventually led to the development of RADIO ASTRONOMY. With a steerable aerial, Jansky, in 1931, discovered an unusual source of radio 'noise' which appeared only when the centre of the Milky Way in Sagittarius passed through the beam of his aerial. Jansky published his results in 1932 but did not pursue his discovery. His name is given to an ASTRONOMICAL UNIT that measures the amount of power received at the Earth's surface from a radio source.

Janus (in mythology) The Roman god of gates, doorways, and bridges. He was represented with two heads facing opposite ways, suggesting vigilance – looking both fore and aft. He was regarded as the guardian of the Roman state during war, when the doors of his temple were left open; in times of peace they were closed.

Janus (in astronomy) A satellite of Saturn discovered in 1966 by the French astronomer Audouin Dollfus. Subsequently lost, it is now accepted to be satellite 1980S1 orbiting Saturn in an almost circular orbit of radius 151,472 km in a period of 0.69433 days. It is a small satellite of diameter no more than 220 km. Janus is a CO-ORBITAL SATELLITE with Epimetheus.

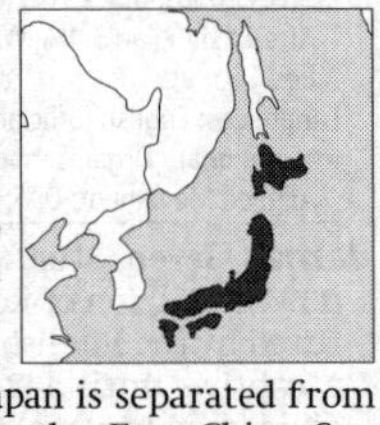

Japan (Japanese **Nihon** or **Nippon**) A country occupying an archipelago off the coast of east Asia. It stretches about 2,400 km (1,500 miles) from Hokkaido in the north-east through Honshu, Shikoku, and Kyushu to the Ryukyu Islands in the south-west. Japan is separated from China to the south-west by the East China Sea, from Siberia and Korea to the west by the Sea of Japan, and from the islands of Sakhalin and the Kuriles to the north and north-east by the Sea of Okhotsk and the Nemuro Strait.

Physical. The deeply indented coastlines are surrounded by many smaller islands, with the Inland Sea forming an important constituent of the country. The islands curve along the edge of the Eurasian plate, one of the Earth's geologically most active zones, creating almost perpetual earthquake and much volcanic activity. Mountains cover two-thirds of Japan's surface, and the rivers are generally unsuited for navigation. Generally the climate varies from the long Hokkaido winter of deep snow to subtropical conditions of the south, influenced by the Kuroshio and the Tsushima Currents. During the seasonal periods of heavy rainfall and typhoons, flooding becomes a major problem.

Economy. The Japanese economy is the second largest in the world and is still growing rapidly. Economic growth has been built on a huge level of exports, and Japan has export surpluses with all its major trading partners, which include developed economies such as the USA and Germany, as well as the developing economies of its neighbours such as China and the ASEAN states of south-east Asia. Japan leads the world in the manufacture of electrical appliances and electronic equipment, which, along with motor vehicles, iron, and steel, make up most of the country's exports. The shipping and chemicals industries are also important. Japan is under pressure to facilitate access to its domestic markets for imports of foreign manufactured goods. Japan is a leading financial market, and the Tokyo stock market is one of the world's foremost financial centres. There are gas fields around the main island of Honshu, but Japan is short of mineral and energy resources, being the world's largest importer of oil. It has a substantial nuclear energy capacity, which with hydroelectric plants provide much of the country's energy. Only one-sixth of Japan's land can be farmed or is habitable; agriculture is dominated by rice cultivation, and a quarter of food needs must be met by imports. With the rise in the value of the yen since the mid-1980s, Japan has invested heavily overseas, and contributed increasing amounts of aid, often in the form of Japanese goods and services, to developing countries.

History. Originally inhabited by native Ainu, the Japanese themselves are thought to be descendants of people who migrated from various areas of mainland Asia. By the 5th century AD the YAMATO clan loosely controlled much of Japan and began to establish imperial rule. The developing state was much influenced by Chinese culture. BUDDHISM was introduced in the 6th century and, after a brief conflict, coexisted with the Japanese religion, SHINTO. In the 7th century Prince Shotoku was partially successful in establishing an administrative system based on that of SUI China. However, by the 9th century the FUJIWARA family had gained control over the imperial court and its power was undermined.

The growing strength of feudal lords and of Buddhist monasteries resulted in civil war for most of the 12th century, the ultimate victor being Minamoto Yoritomo, who in 1192 became the first shogun and established a military administration (see SHOGUNATE). From then effective power lay with the shogun rather than the emperor. Yoritomo's KAMAKURA shogunate was replaced in 1333 by the Ashikaga shogunate, but its rule was one of prolonged civil strife. In the late 16th century three warriors, Oda Nobunaga, Hideyoshi, and TOKUGAWA IEYASU, broke the power of the feudal lords (daimyo), and Ieyasu's TOKUGAWA shogunate provided stable but repressive rule until the restoration of the emperor in 1868.

Europeans had begun to trade with Japan in 1542 and Catholic missionaries, including Matteo Ricci, made numerous converts. The Tokugawa shogunate excluded all foreigners in 1639, except for a few Dutch and Chinese at Nagasaki, and proscribed Christianity. During the 18th and 19th centuries the wealth and power of merchants began to increase and Japan extended its influence over the northern island of Hokkaido.

In the first half of the 19th century Tokugawa power was gradually undermined by economic problems, insurrection, and the arrival of Western trading and naval expeditions, most notably those of the US Commodore Perry (1853–54). The shogunate's failure to resist foreign penetration served as the catalyst for armed opposition, which in 1868 finally succeeded in replacing the shogunate with a new regime led formally by the emperor MEIJI TENNO (the Meiji Restoration). In the succeeding decades feudalism was dismantled and a centralized state created which was dedicated to the rapid modernization of society and industrialization. Japan's new strength brought victory in the SINO-JAPANESE WAR (1894–95) and the RUSSO-JAPANESE WAR (1904–05), and established it as the dominant power in north-east Asia. Japan fought on the Allied side in World War I, but thereafter its expansionist tendencies led to a deterioration in its diplomatic position, most notably *vis-à-vis* the USA. In the inter-war period, expansionist-militarist interests gradually gained power within the country, and, after the occupation of Manchuria (1931) and the creation of MANCHUKUO (1932), full-scale war with China was only a matter of time. The Sino-Japanese War finally broke out in 1937, and, having already allied itself with Germany and Italy in the ANTI-COMINTERN PACT, Japan finally entered World War II with a surprise attack on the US fleet at PEARL HARBOR in December 1941. Initially overrunning the colonial empires of south-east Asia at great speed, Japanese forces were eventually held and gradually driven back (the Pacific Campaigns). In September 1945, after the dropping of two atomic bombs, Japan was forced to surrender and accept occupation. A new Japanese constitution was introduced, and full independence was formally returned in 1952. Japan embarked on another period of rapid industrial development, to become one of the major economic powers in the world. Its relations with China and south-east Asian countries improved, but the large imbalance in its favour in its trade with Western nations (particularly the USA), resulted in economic instability. The Liberal Democratic Party (LDP) held office continually throughout these years, surviving numerous financial scandals. In 1992 a further series of scandals threatened the stability of the government, led by Kiichi Miyazawa, and the future of the LDP, while Japan's economy continued to be affected by the global recession. In 1993 the government was defeated in a vote of no confidence and a general election was called in which the LDP split and lost its overall majority. The opposition formed a seven-party coalition and ejected the LDP from office for the first time since its formation in 1955. The new government, led by Morihiro Hosokawa, introduced a political reform bill proposing a system of single-seat constituencies and legislators elected by proportional representation; the measures were passed and implemented by the end of 1994. Hosokawa's resignation in the same year brought a short-lived coalition government, led by Tsutomu Hata, to power; it was replaced with a coalition of the LDP, the Social Democratic Party of Japan (SDPJ) and Sakigake, under Tomiichi Murayama. In January 1995 a large earthquake caused extensive damage to the city of Kobe, killing more than 5,000 and leaving 310,000 homeless. The instability of the coalition government became apparent as deep ideological divisions between the participating parties and divisions within the SDPJ manifested themselves. In 1995 the SPDJ announced that it was disbanding and in 1996 Ryutaro Hashimoto became Prime Minister. There was widespread public concern in response to a series of gas attacks on public transport believed to have been carried out by a religious sect, Aum Shinrikyo, whose leader was arrested and charged in May. To mark the 50th anniversary of the end of the Pacific War, the government agreed to issue an official apology for Japan's actions during the conflict. A large economic stimulation package was also unveiled by the government in an attempt to bring the Japanese economy out of its longest recession since 1945. Friction between the USA and Japan over trade issues – particularly Japan's trade surplus with the USA – which had long dominated US-Japanese relations, eased slightly in the early 1990s as a series of trade agreements were reached improving access to Japan's markets. However, talks to end the dispute over the valuable sector of cars and components failed and a trade war was narrowly avoided in 1995.

Capital: Tokyo
Area: 377,835 sq km (145,883 sq mi)
Population: 125,362,000 (1995)
Currency: yen
Religions: Joint adherents of Shinto and Buddhism 80.0%; Christian 1.2%
Ethnic Groups: Japanese 99.4%; Korean 0.5%; Chinese and other 0.1%
Languages: Japanese (official)
International Organizations: OECD; UN; Colombo Plan

Japan, Sea of A sea of the western Pacific Ocean separating the islands of Japan and of Sukhalin from Korea, China, and Siberia. It covers about 1,048,950 sq km (405,000 sq mi) and at its deepest is 3,742 m (12,276 feet).

Japan Current See KUROSHIO.

Japanese The official language of Japan, spoken by virtually the whole population of that country. Japanese is an agglutinative language. It contains many Chinese loan-words and has no genders, no article, and no number in nouns or verbs. It is written vertically or horizontally, in a system that is partly ideographic and partly syllabic. The ideographs (known as *kanji*) were adopted from the Chinese in the early centuries of the Christian era and designate the chief meaningful elements of the language. They are supplemented by two groups of syllabic characters (*kana*), known as *hiragana* and *katakana*, for the agglutinative and inflexional endings.

Japanese architecture The architecture of Japan from ancient times to the present day. Evidence of buildings from Neolithic times survives in the form of models of houses buried in tombs, but it is not until after the introduction of Buddhism in the 6th century AD that a continuous tradition can be traced. As with the Buddhist religion, architecture in Japan has been strongly affected by the influence of China (see CHINESE ART AND ARCHITECTURE), using wood as its main building material and the column as the main structural element. Japanese architecture, however, tends to be less grandiose than Chinese and to pay greater attention to the integration of a building with its surroundings, particularly in the siting of Shinto shrines. In essentials, Japanese traditional architecture has changed little over the centuries, and continuity has been preserved by the fact that some religious structures have been periodically rebuilt in exactly the same form for ritual purposes. Buddhist temples were often built as monastic colleges and had numerous types of building within a compound; the *to* or pagoda housing a holy relic; the *kondō*, housing images of the deities worshipped at the temple; the *korō* or drum- or bell-tower; the *kyōzō* or *sutra* (scriptural narratives) or storage hall; the *kōdō* or lecture hall; the *sōbō*, or dormitories; and the *jikidō* or dining hall. The beauty of many Japanese buildings depends as much on the subtle curvature of the roofs as on any decorative treatment, which included the painting of pillars and beams and the use of gilding. The high point of Buddhist architecture in Japan was reached in the Todaiji monastery in Nara, which was founded in 745 and marks the adoption of Buddhism as a state religion. The Hall of the Great Buddha, dedicated by the Emperor Shomu in 752 (reconstructed in 1709), is still the largest wooden building in the world.

Japanese domestic architecture is noted for its simplicity and refinement. Sliding panels of wood or rice-paper flexibly sub-divide the living area into a series of airy spaces. A space is sometimes set aside within the house for the tea ceremony, associated with contemplation and the cultivation of the arts, but tea-houses are often separate pavilions in the garden. Palaces were modest by Western or Chinese standards but, following the introduction of European firearms in the 16th century, a number of imposing castles were built. They were constructed on massive stone bases and had multi-storey central towers. Himeji Castle is the most impressive. From the mid-17th to the mid-19th century Japan pursued an isolationist policy, with virtually no contact with the West, but from the 1860s it began to industrialize along Western lines and adopt the European architectural tradition. Frank Lloyd WRIGHT designed the Imperial Hotel in Tokyo (1916–20, destroyed) and the International Style of the MODERN MOVEMENT was adopted in the 1930s. It was not until the 1950s that Japan began to make a distinctive contribution to modern world architecture. TANGE is the outstanding figure in modern Japanese architecture, his pupils include Arata Isozaki (1931–).

Japanese drama The classical Japanese theatre dates from the late 14th century. It consists of three elements – No, Kabuki, and the puppet theatre, *jōruri*. **No** (meaning 'accomplishment') is a form of lyric drama with dancing, noble in tone and sonorous in language. Each programme consists of five plays (including a god play and a warrior play). The subject-matter is mainly taken from JAPANESE LITERATURE. The No actors (all male) are accompanied by a chorus and an orchestra of drums and flute. **Kabuki** and the *jōruri* puppet theatre evolved in the 17th century. Livelier and more popular in their appeal, they provided entertainment for the expanding merchant class. Kabuki actors – once again all male – are trained from childhood, and their art lies in their ability to express emotions through stylized movements of their whole body. As well as the shamisen, two types of clappers are used to orchestrate the performance and highlight the climaxes. The rise of the puppet theatre was encouraged by the increased complexity of puppets and their manipulation. The action of the puppets is accompanied by musical recitative, and by the playing of the shamisen. The most notable Japanese playwright, Chikamatsu Monzaemon (1653–1725), wrote both puppet and Kabuki plays. No and Kabuki are still regularly performed, together with new types of theatre, such as *shimpa*, which combines elements of Kabuki with less exaggerated acting and the use of actresses.

Japanese literature Although Japanese was not written till the 6th century, there was a considerable oral tradition before that. Writing began when Chinese characters were introduced, but although the influence of CHINESE LITERATURE on Japanese culture was very great, the Chinese writing system was far from ideally suited to the Japanese language. In 712 the *Kojiki* (Record of Ancient Matters) was finished. In 720 the *Nihon Shoki* (Chronicles of Japan) appeared, and the *Man'yōshū* collection of poetry, which included both short poems (*tanka*) and long poems (*chōka*), was compiled some time after 760. The Heian period (794–1185), named after the then capital (now known as Kyoto), produced the *Kokinshū* ('Poems Old and New'; 905), using the newly developed *kana* script in which it was easier to write the native language. The two classic works of Heian literature are *The Tale of Genji* and *The Pillow Book of Sei Shōnagon*. Medieval Japan was plagued by civil wars and out of this came *The Tale of the Heike*, the saga of the rise and fall of the Taira (Heike) clan. In the 14th and 15th centuries, No drama (see JAPANESE DRAMA), underpinned by Zen Buddhism became popular.

In the Tokugawa period (1603–1867), Japan entered a period of isolation, and the city of Edo (later Tokyo) grew in economic and cultural importance. The art and literature of the Floating World became popular, as witnessed by the stories of Saikaku, while the pre-eminent poet was BASHŌ, and the dramatist Chikamatsu Monzaemon (1653–1725) wrote historical and domestic tragedies for the puppet theatre.

Modern Japanese literature can be dated from the Meiji Restoration (1868), and the first modern Japanese novel, Futabatei Shimei's *Ukigumo* ('Floating Cloud'), the story of a clerk, appeared in 1887–89. Akutagawa Ryūnosuke (1892–1927) gave a modern psychological edge to traditional Japanese stories, such as *Rashōmon*, which Kurosawa later adopted in his famous film. Two other important late Meiji novelists were Natsume Sōseki (1867–1916) and Mori Ōgai (1862–1922), whose *Dancing Girl* (1890) was the first of the influential autobiographical novel genre. Kawabata Yasunari (1899–1972) won the Nobel Prize for literature in 1968, and his *Snow Country* (1935–47), *Thousand Cranes* (1949–51), and *House of the Sleeping Beauties* (1939) all deal with guilt and the psychology of the erotic. Major writers of modern Japan include Tanizaki Jun'ichirō (1886–1965), Mishima Yukio (1925–70), and Kenzaburō Oē (1935–), who was awarded the Nobel Prize for literature in 1994.

japonica A deciduous Chinese shrub, *Chaenomeles speciosa*, known in North America as the Japanese quince. Related to the quince, it produces red or pink flowers early in spring before the leaves expand. The quince-like fruit can be used to make jelly.

Jaques-Dalcroze, **Emile** (1865–1950) Swiss music teacher and theoretician who developed a system termed 'eurhythmics' for translating rhythm into movement. He taught many of the dancers of the period, such as RAMBERT and Wigman.

Jarman, **Derek** (1942–94) British film director. Jarman worked in costume and set design for the Royal Ballet and was a production designer for Ken Russell's *The Devils* (1970). His controversial first feature film, *Sebastiane* (1976), heralded a succession of rich, extravagant films informed by gay sensibilities, such as *Jubilee* (1977), *Caravaggio* (1985), and *The Last of England* (1987). He published a number of books, including the autobiographical *Dancing Ledge* (1984).

Jarrow A town and port in Tyne and Wear, north-east England, on the Tyne estuary east of Newcastle; pop. (1981) 31,310. From the 7th century until the Viking invasions its monastery was a centre of Northumbrian Christian culture.

Jarry, **Alfred** (1873–1907) French dramatist. His satirical farce *Ubu Roi* (1896) is widely claimed to have anticipated surrealism and the Theatre of the Absurd.

Jaruzelski, **Wojciech** (1923–) Polish general and Communist statesman, Prime Minister 1981–85, head of state 1985–89, and President 1989–90. After becoming Premier in 1981 he responded to Poland's economic crisis and the rise of the independent trade-union movement Solidarity by imposing martial law and banning union operation. Following the victory of Solidarity in the 1989 free elections, Jaruzelski supervised Poland's transition to a novel 'socialist pluralist' democracy.

jasmine The common name of a number of species of *Jasminum*, a genus of some 300 species, related to the forsythias. They are mostly climbers of the tropics and subtropics except in North America and belong to the family Oleaceae. The most frequently seen are the white-flowered *J. officinale* of southern Europe, the oil of which is used in perfumery, and winter jasmine, *J. nudiflorum*, a Chinese species with yellow petals.

Jason In Greek mythology, one of the most famous of heroes. In order to recover his father's kingdom, usurped by his uncle Pelias, Jason undertook to capture the Golden Fleece (the magic fleece of a winged ram) owned by King Aetes of Colchis. Accompanied by the ARGONAUTS and helped by **Medea** (Aetes' daughter) he accomplished this. He recovered his kingdom and married Medea, but later deserted her for Creon's daughter. In revenge, the passionately jealous Medea killed her own children and Jason's new wife.

jasper See CHALCEDONY.

Jasperware See WEDGWOOD, JOSIAH.

Jatakas ('Birth-stories') Stories of the previous lives of the Buddha in various animal and human forms. Although contained in the Canon of the *Theravāda*, the Jataka are found throughout the Buddhist world and provide the themes for many Buddhist works of art. They have been absorbed into the folklore of many countries. Some show similarities with the *pañchatantra* and even with AESOP's *Fables*.

jaundice Accumulation of bilirubin, the by-product of haemoglobin breakdown, in the blood, resulting in yellow discoloration of the mucous membranes, skin, and the sclera of the eyes; some forms of jaundice may also result in yellow discoloration of the urine. Jaundice is a symptom of other disorders, such as disorders of the liver or biliary tract, which must be treated to relieve jaundice.

Obstruction of the bile duct and the resultant failure of bile to reach the gall bladder (cholestasis) causes cholestatic jaundice. Haemolytic jaundice is caused by the excessive destruction of red blood cells, which releases haemoglobin, and consequently bilirubin accumulation occurs. Hepatocellular jaundice is caused by damage to liver cells (hepatocytes), as in HEPATITIS, in which liver cells are unable to remove bilirubin. Physiological jaundice, also called neonatal jaundice, appears 24 hours following birth, and is caused by immature liver function that is unable in the early days of life to remove bilirubin effectively; it is more common in premature babies, and disappears within a few days.

Jaurès, **Jean** (1859–1914) French socialist leader. Entering parliament (1885), his campaign on behalf of DREYFUS and against ANTI-SEMITISM strengthened socialist support in France. In 1905 he formed the United Socialist Party, which put pressure on the radical governments in order to achieve reforms for the working class. He opposed militarism, but tried to reconcile socialist internationalism and French patriotism. He was assassinated by a French nationalist in 1914.

Java (Indonesian **Jawa**) A large island in the Malay Archipelago, forming part of Indonesia; area

132,187 sq km (51,057 sq miles); pop. (1993) 112,158,200 (with Madura). Java contains almost 60 per cent of the population of Indonesia. Over 100 volcanoes, many of them active, traverse the island from east to west; most are densely forested and there are millions of acres of teak plantations. Rubber, tea, coffee, cacao are also grown in the highlands; rice and sugar-cane on fertile lowland soils. Java has been the cultural and economic centre of the region for centuries. The island was chiefly under Dutch rule from the 17th century and was occupied by Japanese troops during World War II. Its chief city is Jakarta.

Java (in computing) A computer language used for programming on the INTERNET, especially applicable to the World Wide Web; it was developed from 1990 at Sun Microsystems. The output produced by a Java compiler, known as **bytecode**, can be interpreted on any computer on which the Java system is installed. This avoids the need to generate unique versions for different types of machine.

Java man The human fossilized bones found at Trinil on the Solo River in Java. Originally classified as *Pithecanthropus erectus* ('erect ape-man'), these remains are now included within the species HOMO ERECTUS. Their date is uncertain but is probably 750,000–500,000 years ago. Subsequent finds of hominids, probably also *Homo erectus*, in Java were made at Sangiran and Modjokerto. Some of these may be rather older (up to 1.3 million years ago) than the Trinil remains.

Javanese The language of Java, which belongs to the Malayo-Polynesian group of languages.

jaw The opposing set of bones that form the framework of the mouth and masticating apparatus in vertebrates. The upper jaw is fixed to the skull. The lower jaw is freely movable, being slung by strong muscles and fibrous cords from joints at the base of the skull just in front of the ear. It can be moved upwards and from side to side in mammals. In contrast to the powerful closing muscles, the muscles that open it are few and weak, opening helped by gravity in man and many other animals. The lower jaw of some snakes can be dislocated downwards to allow large prey to be swallowed whole.

jawless fish (or **agnathan**) A very primitive fish that has not evolved the paired jaws of other fish. These fish form the class or subphylum Agnatha, one of the three major groups of fishes, and include the very earliest fossil vertebrates from the Palaeozoic Era, approximately 465 million years ago. The living jawless fishes are subdivided into two orders: LAMPREYS and HAGFISHES. These are rather specialized, indirect descendants of the extinct forms and are considered to be the most primitive living vertebrates.

jay A large bird belonging to the crow family, Corvidae; its 37 species are found in many countries. About 35 cm (14 inches) in length, jays are sturdily built birds with powerful bills. Many are quite brightly coloured, often having blue in their plumage; and a number of species are crested, including the Eurasian species *Garrulus glandarius*. They live in woodland and eat insects, small birds, fruits, and seeds. Several species, for example the Florida scrub jay, *Aphelocoma corrulescens*, live all the year round in tight-knit family groups, which together may even care for the offspring of a single nest.

jazz A type of popular music that developed in the Southern states of the USA around the end of the 19th and beginning of the 20th century, principally in New Orleans and largely in the hands of black musicians. Although certain outstanding practitioners, such as Ferdinand 'Jelly Roll' MORTON, claimed to have invented it, hundreds of musicians contributed to its evolution. Common characteristics of this music are an emphasis on improvisation, a rhythmic 'swing' resulting from small departures from the regular pulse, and an emphasis on individuality of instrumental or vocal sound. Musical elements that went into the evolution of jazz include the hymn tunes of 19th-century revivalist meetings; white imitations of slave music, as in the black-face minstrel shows popular from the 1830s; the BLUES and work songs of the black slaves; and the syncopated rhythms of RAGTIME. Because it arose out of a black oral tradition the early history of jazz is obscure. Most New Orleans musicians name Buddy Bolden as the earliest jazz player, though there were two musicians of that name in New Orleans at the time. Although it began as a black music, jazz was initially brought to a wider public by white musicians. The Original Dixieland Jazz Band were a white New Orleans group who became immensely popular in New York playing Dixieland music (see DIXIE). In 1917 they made the first jazz recordings, and by the end of that year jazz was becoming a nationwide phenomenon. Of great importance were the early recordings (1923) of Joseph 'King' Oliver, who numbered among his players the trumpeter Louis ARMSTRONG. Armstrong's imaginative playing marked the emergence of the soloist as a shaping influence on the way jazz developed. As jazz spread to Chicago and New York, and thence to London, Paris, and the rest of Europe, it became more ambitious and sophisticated. The 'arranger' came into existence, scoring the music so that improvisation (the life-blood of the style) was still possible. The typical seven-piece ensemble now began to develop into the big band, and with it came the first of the great jazz composers: Edward 'Duke' ELLINGTON. The big band style led to the development of a much smoother style of playing known as swing. Typical swing bands were led by virtuoso players, such as the clarinetists Benny GOODMAN, Artie Shaw, and Woodrow 'Woody' Herman, and the pianist William 'Count' BASIE. In its turn, swing was overtaken in the 1940s by a more rhythmic style of jazz known as bebop, so called after the practice of imitating its sound by scat singing. Among the leading exponents of the new style were the saxophonist Charlie 'Bird' PARKER, the trumpet-player John 'Dizzie' GILLESPIE. In the 1950s the rise of RHYTHM AND BLUES and ROCK MUSIC led to a decline in jazz audiences. Jazz continued to develop, but along several pathways. Some musicians moved towards a blending of jazz and classical styles; this cool or West Coast jazz involved such musicians as Miles DAVIS and Gerry Mulligan; it was further developed by John Lewis's Modern Jazz Quartet. Miles Davis and saxophonist John COLTRANE later introduced modal playing, which was used as the basis for improvisation. In the late 1950s such players as Ornette Coleman and Cecil Taylor abandoned scales altogether and began to play 'free' jazz, which has continued as a minority form. In the late 1960s Miles Davis was once again at the forefront of a new development in jazz, fusing jazz idioms with elements of rock music. In the 1970s and 1980s there has been an increasing use of electric and electronic instrumentation in jazz.

Jean Paul (pseudonym of Johann Paul Friedrich Richter) (1763–1825) German novelist. He is noted for his romantic novels, including *Hesperus* (1795), and for comic works such as *Titan* (1800–03).

Jeans, Sir James Hopwood (1877–1946) British physicist and astronomer. He began as a mathematician, but his major contributions were in molecular physics and astrophysics. Jeans proposed a theory for the formation of the Solar System, according to which the planets were formed from natural material pulled out of the Sun by the gravity of a passing star. He was the first to propose that matter is continuously created throughout the Universe, one of the tenets of the steady-state theory. He also became a popularizer of science, especially as a radio lecturer.

Jeddah (or **Jiddah**) A large deep-water seaport on the Red Sea coast of Saudi Arabia, west of Mecca; pop. (est. 1986) 1,400,000. It is the administrative capital of Saudi Arabia, commercial capital of Makkah province, and Saudi Arabia's largest port. It is also a port of entry on the pilgrimage route to Mecca, often through the ultra-modern airport.

Jefferies, (John) Richard (1848–87) British writer and naturalist. He is renowned for his observation of English rural life. Important works include *Bevis* (1882), an evocation of his country childhood in Wiltshire, and his autobiography *The Story of My Heart* (1883).

Jefferson, Thomas (1743–1826) US Democratic Republican statesman, 3rd President of the USA 1801–09. Jefferson was the principal drafter of the Declaration of Independence (1776) and played a key role in the American leadership during the War of Independence. He advocated decentralization and the restrained use of presidential power, in defiance of Alexander Hamilton. While President, Jefferson secured the Louisiana Purchase (1803), by which the western part of the Mississippi valley was sold to the USA by France.

Jefferson City The state capital of Missouri, USA, on the Missouri River; pop. (1990) 35,480. Selected to be state capital in 1821, it was named after President Thomas Jefferson. It is the home of Lincoln University of Missouri (1866).

Jeffreys of Wem, George Jeffreys, 1st Baron (1645–89) English judge and Lord Chief Justice. He presided at the trials of the Rye House conspirators, of Titus Oates after the POPISH PLOT, and of Richard BAXTER, but he is chiefly associated with the BLOODY ASSIZES (1685). Contemporary reports of his brutality may have been prejudiced, but he certainly browbeat witnesses and his sentencing of the 80-year-old Alice Lisle to be burnt for treason caused widespread revulsion. At the accession of William III he was imprisoned and died before proceedings were taken against him.

Jehangir See JAHANGIR.

Jehovah See YAHWEH.

Jehovah's Witness A member of a Christian sect believing in the imminent end of time and the elevation of 144,000 'elect of Jehovah' to be with God in a Messianic kingdom. They deny most of the fundamental Christian doctrines and refuse to acknowledge the claims of the state when these conflict with the sect's principles. It was founded by Charles Russell in 1878 in Pittsburgh, USA, together with his magazine *The Watchtower*, which is still published and acts as the sect's focal point. There are about 2 million members, mainly in English-speaking countries.

Jehu The army commander and then king of Israel who was called upon by the prophet Elisha to destroy the house of Ahab and the Baal-worship it had encouraged. Famous for his swift action and for driving his chariot at great speed, Jehu has become a synonym for a fast driver.

Jekyll, Gertrude (1843–1932) British horticulturalist and garden designer. Forced to abandon painting because of her failing eyesight, Jekyll turned to garden design. She met the architect Edwin Lutyens in 1889 and had a long association with him, designing more than 300 gardens for his buildings.

Jellicoe, John Rushworth, 1st Earl (1859–1935) British admiral. He commanded the Grand Fleet at the inconclusive battle of JUTLAND (1916) and then became First Sea Lord with an influence on strategic planning. He implemented the CONVOY SYSTEM introduced by LLOYD GEORGE, but was dismissed from office in December 1917. After the war he was appointed governor-general of New Zealand (1920–24).

jellyfish A marine invertebrate of the phylum Cnidaria. Like the related corals and sea anemones, jellyfish subdue prey with special stinging-cells on their tentacles, which hang below their floating body. Occasionally these stings can harm humans.

They have only a thin layer of cells on their inner and outer surfaces, most of the body being non-living, jelly-like material forming the familiar 'bell'. Simple muscles pull this bell in and out, expelling water from the mouth, so the animal jets into the upper water and parachutes gently down again, trapping prey as it descends. They have a complex life-cycle involving a tiny larval (planula) stage and a POLYP stage, which buds off small immature jellyfish, which may develop directly into an adult jellyfish or medusa.

Jena A university town in Thuringia, central Germany, on the River Saale; pop. (1991) 100,970. It was the scene of a battle (1806) in which Napoleon defeated the Prussians. It produces chemicals and optical instruments.

Jencks, Charles See POST-MODERNISM.

Jenkins, Roy (Harris), Baron Jenkins of Hillhead (1920–) British Labour and Social Democrat MP and scholar. He was a Labour MP between 1948 and 1976, rising to deputy leader of the Labour Party (1970–72). He was president of the European Commission 1977–81 and co-founded the Social Democratic Party in 1981, representing Glasgow Hillhead between 1982 and 1987. He then became Chancellor of Oxford University. Among his works are numerous biographies of political figures, including *Mr Attlee* (1948), *Asquith* (1964), *Truman* (1986), and *Gladstone* (1995).

Jenkins's Ear, War of (1739–41) A war between Britain and Spain that broke out as a result of Britain's trade with South America. The Peace of UTRECHT, which gave the British South Sea Company a limited trade monopoly with the Spanish American colonies, caused general friction, but the main trouble-makers were illicit traders who defied both the Company and the Spanish government. In 1737 British merchants were protesting at a tightening-up of Spanish control. The Spanish government and WALPOLE both wanted peace but Walpole's enemies made it an excuse to attack him: a merchant captain named Jenkins was produced to tell a story of torture and the loss of an ear. Popular clamour was such that Walpole consented reluctantly to declare war. Admiral Vernon captured Porto Bello and France sent two squadrons to the West Indies. In 1740 the war merged into that of the AUSTRIAN SUCCESSION.

Jenner, Edward (1749–1823) British physician, the pioneer of vaccination. A local belief that dairymaids who had had cowpox did not catch smallpox led Jenner to the idea of deliberately infecting people with cowpox in order to protect them from the more serious disease. The practice was eventually accepted throughout the world, leading to the widespread use of vaccination for other diseases and eventually to the eradication of smallpox in the late 20th century. In intervals between medical practice he indulged his keen interest in natural history, and wrote a paper on the habits of the cuckoo.

jerbil See GERBIL.

jerboa A desert RODENT of the family Dipodidae, distinguished by its extremely long hind-legs. The range of the 29 species extends from North Africa across central Asia to northern China. Although only mouse-sized, they are capable of leaps of up to 3 m (10 feet) when fleeing from predators. While foraging, they either hop on all fours like rabbits or walk on their hind-legs. Their food consists of plants and insects.

Jeremiah (born *c.*640 BC) Hebrew prophet. He was called to prophesy during the reign of King JOSIAH. As Babylonian power increased, he maintained that resistance was useless and that the fall of Jerusalem was inevitable, views popular neither with the king nor with the people. After the fall of Jerusalem in 586 BC, he remained in the city until taken to Egypt by Jewish dissidents. His messages, always intensely personal, were preserved and edited by his scribe-secretary Baruch.

Jerez (in full **Jerez de la Frontera**) A town in the Andalusian province of Cadiz, southern Spain; pop. (1991) 184,020. It is the centre of the sherry-making industry and gives its name to the wine.

Jericho (Arabic **El Riha**) An ancient oasis town of Palestine, in the West Bank north of the Dead Sea. It has been occupied from at least *c.*9000 BC and is reckoned to be one of the oldest continuously inhabited cities in the world. According to the Old Testament, Jericho was destroyed by the Israelites after they crossed the Jordan into the Promised Land, its walls having been flattened by the shout of the army at the blast of the trumpets (Joshua 2–6). In the surrounding area irrigated agriculture produces dates, bananas, and oranges. It was designated the administrative centre for Palestinian self-rule in Gaza and the West Bank in 1993.

Jerome, Jerome K(lapka) (1859–1927) British novelist and dramatist. He is chiefly remembered for his humorous novel *Three Men in a Boat* (1889).

Jerome, St (*c.*342–420) Doctor of the Church. Born in Dalmatia, he acted as secretary to Pope Damasus in Rome (382–85) before settling in Bethlehem, where he ruled a newly founded monastery and devoted his life to study. He is chiefly known for his compilation of the Latin version of the Bible, the Vulgate. Feast day, 30 September.

Jersey The largest of the Channel Islands; area 116 sq km (45 sq miles); pop. (1990) 82,810; capital, St Helier. It gives its name to a type of woollen pullover and to a breed of light-brown dairy cattle that originated in Jersey, producing milk with a high fat content. Market gardening is important and the island is a popular holiday resort and tax-haven.

Jerusalem A holy city to Jews, Christians, and Muslims, lying in the Judaean hills about 30 km (20 miles) from the River Jordan; pop. (est. 1993) 561,900. It was originally a Jebusite settlement, captured by DAVID *c.*1000 BC. Solomon's Temple, the central shrine of Judaism, destroyed by Nebuchadnezzar in 586 BC, was rebuilt in 516 BC and even more magnificently by HEROD the Great. Jerusalem was razed by the Romans in 70 AD and the Temple destroyed. All that now remains is the Western (or Wailing) Wall of the Temple Mount, on which both Temples were built. In 135 the Romans built the city of Aelia Capitolina on the site of the remains of Jerusalem. St PAUL regarded it as the home of the original Christian congregation, headed until his death in 62 by St JAMES, the apostle of JESUS CHRIST. Constantine marked its significance by building the Church of the Holy Sepulchre (*c.*335) over the supposed tomb of Christ. Muslim rule from 637 was symbolized by the Dome of the Rock, the city's holiest Muslim mosque, built in 691. The Christian knights of the CRUSADES controlled the city from 1099 to 1187 as the chief city of the Latin Kingdom of Jerusalem, when it fell to SALADIN. The Ottoman Turks conquered the city in 1516; Suleiman the Magnificent rebuilt the walls of the city in 1538, which are the walls still enclosing the old city. During World War I the British took over Jerusalem (1917) and held it under the Palestine mandate from 1922 to 1948. When the State of Israel was declared in 1948, Jerusalem was divided between Israel and Jordan. Jerusalem became the capital of Israel in 1950 and, during the Six Day War in 1967, the Arab sector of Jerusalem was taken over by Israel, who has retained the entire city as its capital ever since. The city's unique historical importance to three religions has made it a focus of religious and ethnic unrest.

Jervis, John, Earl St Vincent (1735–1823) British admiral. In 1795 he was put in command of the British fleet, and in 1797, with Nelson as his commodore, led his forces to victory over a Spanish fleet off Cape St Vincent; Jervis was created Earl St Vincent in recognition of this achievement.

Jespersen, (Jens) Otto (Harry) (1860–1943) Danish philologist, grammarian, and educationist. He promoted the use of the 'direct method' in language teaching with the publication of his theoretical work *How to Teach a Foreign Language* (1904). Other books include his seven-volume *Modern English Grammar* (1909–49).

Jesuit A member of the Society of Jesus, an order of priests founded in 1534 in Paris by IGNATIUS LOYOLA, Francis XAVIER, and others. The Society became the spearhead of the Counter-Reformation, though originally intended as a missionary order. Its genius is found in Ignatius' *Spiritual Exercises*. The success of Jesuits as missionaries, teachers, scholars, and spiritual directors – as well as the fear they have inspired – manifests how close they have been to their ideal of a disciplined force, effective in the cause of the Roman Church.

Jesus Christ (*c.*6 BC–*c.*30 AD) The central figure of CHRISTIANITY, believed by his followers to be the Son of God, of one essence with God the Father and God the Holy Spirit (the doctrine of the TRINITY). The Gospels of the New Testament are the main sources of information about Jesus. According to them, Jesus was born at Bethlehem to Mary, by tradition a virgin, in the reign of Augustus Caesar. He was brought up at Nazareth in Galilee and received a traditional Jewish education. He may have been a carpenter, the trade of Mary's husband, Joseph. About 27 AD he was baptized in the River Jordan by JOHN the Baptist and shortly thereafter started his public ministry of preaching and healing (with reported MIRACLES). Through his popular style of preaching, with the use of parables and proverbs, he proclaimed the imminent approach of the Kingdom of God and the ethical and religious qualities demanded of those who were to enjoy it (summarized in the Sermon on the Mount). His interpretation of Jewish law did not reject ceremonial observances but regarded them as less important than the fundamental principles of charity, sincerity, and humility. From among his followers in Galilee he selected 12 DISCIPLES to be his personal companions and to teach his message. His preaching brought him into conflict with the Jewish authorities. Aware of this, he travelled to Jerusalem, where he was betrayed by Judas Iscariot, one of his disciples, and condemned to death by the Sanhedrin, the highest Jewish court. He then appeared before the Roman governor, Pontius PILATE, who sentenced Jesus to death by crucifixion. His followers claimed that three days after the sentence had been carried out the tomb in which his body had been placed was empty and that he had been seen alive. Belief in his resurrection from the dead spread among his followers, who saw in this proof that he was the Messiah or Christ. His followers started to form Christian communities around Jerusalem from which developed the CHRISTIAN CHURCH.

jet A hard, black variety of LIGNITE or brown coal, light in weight and capable of being carved and highly polished. There are deposits in the USA, Spain, France, and Germany, but the chief source is Yorkshire, UK, where it can be found on the shore, having been dislodged by waves from the seaside cliffs. Small decorative objects, particularly jewellery, can be made of jet.

jet engine A form of GAS-TURBINE engine used in aircraft, in which the thrust is generated by a jet of exhaust gas discharged from a nozzle at the rear of the engine. Jet engines were developed concurrently in the UK and in Germany. WHITTLE's centrifugal flow turbojet was patented in 1930 and first tested later in the same year. The first jet aeroplane to fly was the German Heinkel He. 178 in 1939, powered by an engine designed by von OHAIN. In a turbojet, air is taken into the engine and compressed, then mixed with fuel and burnt. The combustion gases then pass through a turbine, the power from which drives the COMPRESSOR, after which the remaining energy in the gas is converted to kinetic energy in the exhaust cone and ejected as a high-velocity jet. Turbojets are most efficient at high speeds: for speeds below 800 km/h (500 m.p.h.) a more efficient engine is the turboprop. This works on the same principle as the turbojet, but most of the energy of the combustion gases drives the turbine, which is used to power a propeller as well as the compressor. A small amount of forward thrust is also obtained from the exhaust gases. In the bypass jet engine two air compressors, one low-pressure and one high-pressure, are used. After passage through the first, low-pressure compressor, part of the air intake bypasses the combustion chamber and turbine. The combination of cold air jet and the hot exhaust jet gives a much larger mass of air and therefore increased thrust, without an increase in fuel consumption. This principle is taken even further in the turbofan engine, which incorporates a large fan to accelerate still more air outside the engine proper, as well as using the bypass principle.

jet stream A narrow meandering band of very strong wind, which generally exceed 100 knots (187 km/h, 116 m.p.h.) and encircles the globe in the upper and middle troposphere. Jet streams are caused by the extremely large temperature contrasts between adjacent air masses, such as those which occur along the polar front. Jet streams have an important effect on air travel across the Atlantic and Pacific oceans. Rapid west–east travel times can be achieved by riding the easterly flowing jet; conversely, east–west journey times may be retarded by the strong headwinds.

Jewish calendar A lunar calendar, normally consisting of 12 months, which alternate between 29 and 30 days, as each lunar month is actually 29.5 days. Tradition calculates the day of creation as occurring in 3760 BC; the present Jewish year is therefore calculated by adding 3,760 to the present Gregorian year.

Jewish people A people claiming descent from the ancient Israelites of the Old Testament or who practise JUDAISM. During the exile from the land of Israel (597–538 BC) following the Babylonian conquest, their religion developed from a sacrificial temple cult into an elaborate code for daily living, which became the basis for communal identity. The revolt of the MACCABEES in 167 BC showed their determination to preserve that identity, which survived the Roman destruction of the Temple in 70 AD and of JERUSALEM in 135 AD.

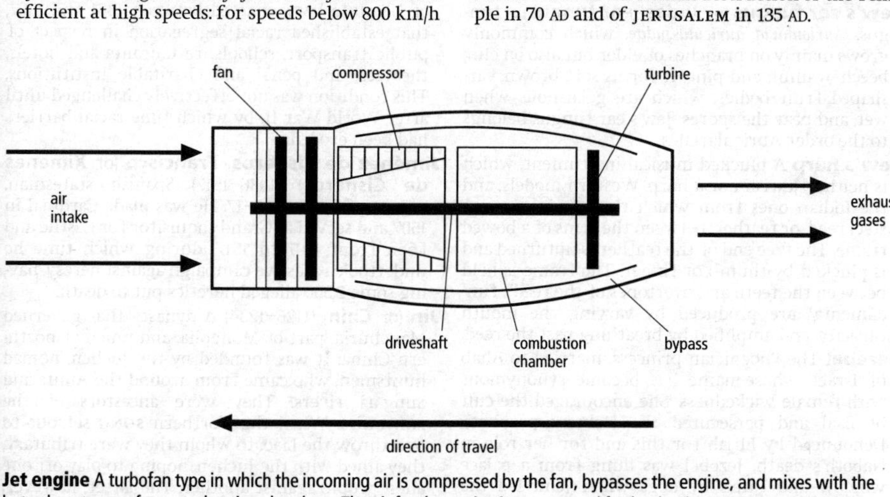

Jet engine A turbofan type in which the incoming air is compressed by the fan, bypasses the engine, and mixes with the hot exhaust gases from combustion chambers. The air for the engine is compressed further by the compressor, which is driven by the turbine.

Dispersed (see DIASPORA) throughout the Roman empire, they suffered much discrimination at the hands of its Christian successors and often welcomed ARAB conquests, which brought greater toleration. In Christendom, they were free to engage in usury, a sin for Christians, and were herded into ghettos. Though they were tolerated for their usefulness, they suffered periodic persecution. The Jews who went to Spain and Portugal in the Diaspora are known as the Sephardim (from *Sepharad*, Hebrew for a region in the Bible thought to be modern Spain). Having been expelled from Spain in 1492, the Sephardim, speaking Ladino, a Spanish dialect, found refuge in north Africa, the Levant, the Ottoman Empire, the Netherlands, and Italy. Jews who went to France and Germany in the early Middle Ages are known as Ashkenazim (from the biblical Ascanians of Phrygia, taken to be inhabitants of modern Germany). They spoke Yiddish, a variant of German, and established themselves in north-west and eastern Europe.

It is estimated there are 17.5 million Jews worldwide, with about 40 per cent in the USA, 20 per cent in ISRAEL, 12 per cent in the republics of the former Soviet Union, and significant numbers in Argentina, Brazil, Canada, France, South Africa, and the UK, where some 110,000 Jews live.

Mainly city-dwellers in their recent history, many Jews are immigrants following massive population movements as a result of anti-Semitism, which found its most violent expression in the HOLOCAUST of World War II, when an estimated 6 million Jews were murdered by the Germans. More recently, large numbers of Soviet Jews have emigrated to Israel, following the relaxation of Soviet emigration laws. However, in most societies Jews are now more assimilated than ever before, while retaining a Jewish ethnic identity, although many have rejected the religion. (See also FALASHAS). They retain prominence far beyond their numerical significance in world political, cultural, and economic affairs.

Jewison, Norman (1926–) Canadian film director and producer. Jewison achieved recognition with the dramas *The Cincinnati Kid* (1965) and *In the Heat of the Night* (1967), which won five Oscars. Later films include the musical *Fiddler on the Roof* (1971) and the romantic comedy *Moonstruck* (1987).

Jew's ear fungus (or **Judas' ear fungus**) A fungus, *Auricularia auricula-judae*, which commonly grows mainly on branches of elder but also on elm, beech, walnut, and pine. It forms soft brown, ear-shaped fruit bodies, which are gelatinous when wet, and bear the spores. Jew's ear fungus belongs to the order Auriculariales.

Jew's harp A plucked musical instrument, which is neither Jewish nor a harp. Western models, and the Indian ones from which they derive, have a steel reed, or feather, between the arms of a bowed frame. The free end of the feather is upturned and is plucked by thumb or finger. The frame is held between the teeth and overtones of the reed's fundamental are produced by varying the mouth capacity, and amplified by breathing past the reed.

Jezebel The Phoenician princess, married to Ahab of Israel, whose name has become synonymous with female wickedness. She encouraged the cult of Baal and persecuted the Hebrew prophets. Denounced by Elijah for this and for her role in Naboth's death, Jezebel was flung from a palace window and eaten by dogs when Jehu led the rebellion that terminated Ahab's dynasty.

Jiang Jie Shi See CHIANG KAI-SHEK.

Jiangsu (formerly **Kiangsu**) A province of eastern China; area 103,000 sq km (39,784 sq miles); pop. (1990) 67,057,000; capital, Nanjing (Nanking). It includes the lower reaches of the River Yangtze and is the most densely populated of the provinces of China. It is a major producer of agricultural and industrial goods including rice, wheat, maize, oil seed, silkworm cocoons, textiles, paper, and cigarettes.

Jiangxi (formerly **Kiangsi**) A province of south-east China to the south of the River Yangtze; area 169,000 sq km (65,276 sq miles); pop. (1990) 37,710,000; capital, Nanchang. It includes Poyang, China's largest freshwater lake. Coal, porcelain, rice, timber, livestock, and fruit are its chief products.

Jibril See GABRIEL.

Jibuti See DJIBOUTI.

jigger See FLEA.

jihad (Arabic, literally 'struggle') In Islam, a holy war. One of the basic duties of a Muslim, prescribed as a religious duty by the KORAN and by tradition, is to struggle against external threats to the Islamic community and also against personal resistance to the rules of divine law within oneself. Jihad in theory is controlled by the strict laws of war in Islam, which prescribe conditions under which war may be declared, usually against an enemy who inhibits the observance of the faith. In practice it has often been used by ambitious Muslim rulers to cloak political aims with religious respectability. In recent years, the concept of jihad has played a significant role in some ISLAMIC FUNDAMENTALIST and revivalist movements, justifying political violence or TERRORISM.

Jilin (formerly **Kirin**) **▶1** A province of north-east China; area 187,000 sq km (72,229 sq miles); pop. (1990) 24,659,000; capital, Changchun. Occupying part of the north-east plain, its chief resources include coal, iron ore, gold, copper, and timber. Agricultural crops include maize, soy beans, sugar beet, rice, millet, and ginseng. **▶2** An industrial city in Jilin province; pop. (1990) 2,251,800.

Jim Crow laws US discriminatory statutes against blacks. 'Jim Crow', as a synonym for blacks, derives from the minstrel show of that name in about 1828. Applied to legislation, it distinguishes a body of US state laws, enacted between 1881 and 1907, that established racial segregation in respect of public transport, schools, restaurants and hotels, theatres, and penal and charitable institutions. This condition was not effectively challenged until after World War II, by which time racial barriers had been eroded.

Jiménez de Cisneros, Francisco (or **Ximenes de Cisneros**) (1436–1517) Spanish statesman, regent of Spain 1516–17. He was made Cardinal in 1507 and served as Grand Inquisitor for Castile and Léon from 1507 to 1517, during which time he undertook a massive campaign against heresy, having some 2,500 alleged heretics put to death.

Jin (or **Chin**) (1126–1234) A dynasty that governed Manchuria, part of Mongolia, and much of northern China. It was founded by the Juchen, nomad huntsmen, who came from around the Amur and Sungari rivers. They were ancestors of the MANCHUS. When the Northern SONG set out to overthrow the Liao, to whom they were tributary, they allied with the Juchen, hoping to play off one alien people against another. The latter, however, once having conquered the Liao, sacked the Song capital, Kaifeng, in 1126. The Song retreated south, establishing their new capital at Xingsai (Hangzhou).

The Juchen were in time tamed by their Chinese subjects, who far outnumbered them. Their frontier with Southern Song was stabilized. Jin emperors studied the Chinese classics and wrote poetry in Chinese. Their nomad vigour was sapped by a sedentary life. By 1214 much of their territory, including Beijing, their central capital, was in GENGHIS KHAN's hands. The dynasty survived, ruling from Kaifeng, until a final Mongol onslaught 20 years later.

jinn (or **djinn**, **genie**) In Islam, an order of spirits, lower than angels, sometimes referred to as *jann*, who, being of flame or air, are believed to have the power of assuming human or animal form and exercising supernatural influence over men and women. Said in the Koran to have been created from smokeless fire, jinn are given legal status in Islam. Muhammad is alleged to have converted some, and the Mosque of the Jinn in Mecca commemorates the place where he came to an agreement (*bay'ah*) with them. In Islamic belief there are various orders of jinn, some beneficent, others malevolent.

Jinnah, Muhammad Ali (1876–1948) Indian statesman and founder of Pakistan. He headed the Muslim League in its struggle with the Hindu-oriented Indian National Congress, and from 1928 onwards championed the rights of the Muslim minority at conferences on Indian independence. After 1937, when self-governing Hindu provinces began to be formed, his fear that Muslims would be excluded from office led him to campaign for a separate Muslim state. With the establishment of Pakistan in 1947 he became its first Governor-General.

Jivaro An American Indian people of South America living a subsistence life of hunting, fishing, and farming in the tropical forests of eastern Ecuador and Peru. Their language belongs to the Andean-Equatorial group of languages.

Jizo The Japanese name for the Mahāyāna Buddhist *bodhisattva* ('Buddha-to-be'), Kshitigarbha, known as Dìzàng in China. Numbered among the eight great bodhisattvas, Jizo is believed to be concerned with the welfare of children, travellers, and lost souls, and to be the guardian of highways and of mountain passes. He is sometimes shown in a series of six images.

Joachim, Joseph (1831–1907) Hungarian violinist and composer. After studying in Vienna (1841–43), Joachim went to Leipzig where he was taught by MENDELSSOHN. In 1849 he became leader of the Weimar court orchestra, under LISZT. A superb interpreter of the classical concerto, Joachim was the first player of Brahms's concerto.

Joan of Arc, St (known as 'the Maid of Orleans') (*c*.1412–31) French national heroine. Inspired by 'voices' of St Catherine and St Margaret, she led the French armies against the English in the Hundred Years War, relieving besieged Orleans (1429) and ensuring that Charles VII could be crowned in previously occupied Reims. Captured by the Burgundians in 1430, she was handed over to the English, convicted of heresy, and burnt at the stake in Rouen. She was canonized in 1920. Feast day, 30 May.

Job The Hebrew hero of the biblical Book of Job, which deals with the fundamental problem of undeserved suffering. Afflicted through Satan with the loss of family and possessions, and then with disease, the upright Job accepted all as the will of God. Only after friends had argued with him that suffering was the result of sin, did Job, sure of his faithfulness, lose patience and question God's omnipotence. In the epilogue, probably a later addition, he is restored to his former fortunes when he submits again to the will of God, which, however, remains mysterious and inscrutable. Ayyub (Job) and his sufferings are mentioned in the Koran.

Jobs, Steven (Paul) (1955–) US computer entrepreneur. Jobs produced the first Apple computer in 1976, setting up the Apple computer company later that year with Steve Wozniak (1950–). He was chairman of the company until 1985, when he resigned at the age of 30 following internal disagreements.

Jodhpur A city in the state of Rajasthan, western India, on the southern edge of the Thar Desert; pop. (1991) 648,620. Founded in 1459 by Rao Jodha, chief of the Rathore Tajput clan, it is the second-largest city in Rajasthan and has light industries. The city gives its name to close-fitting riding breeches.

Jodl, Alfred (1890–1946) German Nazi general. Throughout World War II he was chief of the Armed Forces' Operations Staff, and was Hitler's closest adviser on strategic questions. His diaries reveal his complicity in many of Hitler's war crimes and he was condemned to death at the NUREMBERG TRIALS.

Jodrell Bank The site in Cheshire, England, of the Nuffield Radio Astronomy Laboratory of Manchester University. It has one of the world's largest radio telescopes, with a giant reflector, 76 m (250 ft) in diameter, that can be tilted in any direction. The telescope was named the Lovell Telescope in 1987, after its sponsor Sir Bernard LOVELL.

Joffre, Joseph Jacques Césaire (1852–1931) French Marshal. During World War I he was Commander-in-Chief of the French army on the Western Front (1914–16). Joffre was chiefly responsible for the Allied victory in the first Battle of the Marne, but resigned after the costly Battle of Verdun (1916).

Jogjakarta See YOGYAKARTA.

Johannesburg The largest city in South Africa, the centre of its gold-mining industry, and the financial and commercial capital of the prosperous Witwatersrand; pop. (1991) 1,916,000. Founded in 1886 and probably named after Johannes Meyer, the first mining commissioner, it lies at the centre of a large conurbation of municipalities and townships including the township of Soweto, at an altitude of 1,754 m (5,750 ft). It was made capital of the region of Gauteng in 1994. It has chemical, pharmaceutical, metal, machinery, and textile industries. It is also a diamond-cutting centre.

John (known as John 'Lackland') (1165–1216) King of England 1199–1216, son of Henry II. He lost Normandy and most of his French possessions to Philip II of France by 1205. His refusal to accept Stephen Langton as Archbishop of Canterbury caused an interdict to be placed on England in 1208, and led to his own excommunication the following year. In 1215 John was forced to sign Magna Carta by his barons. When he ignored its provisions, civil war broke out (the first Barons' War) and he died on campaign.

John Six kings of Portugal. **John I** (known as John the Great) (1357–1433) reigned 1385–1433. Reinforced by an English army, he won independence for Portugal with his victory over the Castilians at Aljubarrota (1385). He established an Anglo-Portuguese alliance (1386), married a daughter of John of Gaunt (1387), and presided over a long period of peace and prosperity which was notable for his encouragement of voyages of discovery. **John II** (1455–95) reigned 1481–95. **John III** (1502–57) reigned 1521–57. **John IV** (known as John the Fortunate) (1604–56) reigned 1640–56. The founder of the Braganza dynasty, he expelled a Spanish usurper and proclaimed himself king. He defeated the Spanish at Montijo (1644) and drove the Dutch out of Brazil (1654). **John V** (1689–1750) reigned 1706–50. **John VI** (1767–1826) reigned 1816–26.

John III (known as **John Sobieski**) (1624–96) King of Poland 1674–96. He was elected king of Poland after a distinguished early career as a soldier. In 1683 he relieved Vienna when it was besieged by the Turks, becoming the hero of the Christian world.

John XXIII (born Angelo Giuseppe Roncalli) (1881–1963) Pope 1958–63. During his pontificate he made energetic efforts to liberalize Roman Catholic policy, especially on social questions. Particularly notable were his encyclicals, *Mater et Magistra*, on the need to help the poor, and *Pacem in Terris*, on the need for international peace. He also summoned the Second Ecumenical Vatican Council (1962–65) to revitalize the life of the Church by bringing up to date its teaching, discipline, and organization, with the unity of all Christians as its ultimate goal. He was succeeded by Paul VI.

John, Augustus (Edwin) (1878–1961) British painter. He is perhaps best known for *The Smiling Woman* (1908), a portrait of his second wife Dorelia, which portrayed a robust gypsy type of beauty; the gypsies of his native Wales were frequent subjects of his work. He was subsequently noted for his portraits of the wealthy and famous, particularly prominent writers such as Thomas Hardy, George Bernard Shaw, W. B. Yeats, James Joyce, and Dylan Thomas. He was the brother of Gwen JOHN.

John, Barry (1945–) Welsh Rugby Union player. His international career, during which he played at half-back and scored a record 90 points for his country, lasted from 1966 until his retirement in 1972. He played a prominent part in the British Lions' victorious tour of New Zealand in 1971.

John, Sir Elton (Hercules) (born Reginald Kenneth Dwight) (1947–) British pop and rock singer, pianist, and songwriter. He has written many hit songs, the majority of them with lyricist Bernie Taupin (1950–); they include 'Your Song' (1970) and 'Nikita' (1985). In 1979 he became the first Western rock star to tour the Soviet Union. In 1997 he sang a revised version of his earlier song 'Candle in the Wind' at the funeral of Diana, Princess of Wales.

John, Gwen (1876–1939) British painter. After studying with Whistler in Paris (1898), she settled in France and worked as Rodin's model (1904), becoming his devoted friend and mistress. She converted to Catholicism in 1913; her paintings, mainly watercolours, often depict nuns or girls in interior settings and are noted for their grey tonality. She was the sister of Augustus JOHN.

John, St (known as **St John the Evangelist** or **St John the Divine**) An Apostle, son of Zebedee and brother of James. He has traditionally been credited with the authorship of the fourth Gospel, Revelation, and three epistles of the New Testament. Feast day, 27 December.

John Bull A character invented by John Arbuthnot in *The History of John Bull* (1712), which was soon regarded as representative of the typical patriotic Englishman, and even of England itself. He was much used by caricaturists in the late 18th century in various (not always flattering) situations. He gained a new lease of life from the cartoonists of *Punch* magazine who made him so universally known that he was often used as a label for anything British.

John Chrysostom, St See CHRYSOSTOM, ST JOHN.

John Dory A deep-bodied, flattened fish, *Zeus faber*, with a large head and expansible mouth. It has a very distinct black blotch with an encircling yellow ring on each side of its body. Living in shallow coastal waters of Europe, the John Dory has a close relative which lives in North American Atlantic coastal waters, called the American John Dory, *Zenopsis acellata*. They swim slowly, either singly or in a small school, often sheltering among algae or under moored boats, and feed on fishes, which are captured by stealth. Dories comprise several species within the family Zeidae and are regarded as a food-fish.

John of Austria, Don (1545–78) Spanish general and admiral. He was an illegitimate son of Emperor CHARLES V, educated in Spain, and recognized as his half-brother by PHILIP II. He was appointed commander-in-chief of the Spanish navy in 1568, and organized the suppression of the Revolt of the Moriscos (1569–70). He commanded the Holy League fleet which defeated the Turks at LEPANTO (1571), and went on to conquer Tunis (1573). His career began to founder after his posting to the Netherlands as governor-general (1576), at a critical point in the Dutch Revolts. His impatience with negotiation led to the resumption of hostilities in 1577–78; and meanwhile he entertained schemes of marrying MARY, QUEEN OF SCOTS and replacing ELIZABETH I on the English throne. He died of typhus before he could effect these plans.

John of Damascus, St (*c.*675–*c.*749) Syrian theologian and Doctor of the Church. After championing image worship against the iconoclasts, he wrote his encyclopedic work on Christian theology, *The Fount of Wisdom*. Its last section summarized the teachings of the Greek Fathers of the Church on the principal mysteries of the Christian faith and was influential for centuries in both Eastern and Western Churches. Feast day, 4 December.

John of Gaunt (1340–99) Son of Edward III of England. Born in Ghent, he was created Duke of Lancaster in 1362. John of Gaunt headed the government during the final years of his father's reign and the minority of Richard II, and was effective ruler of England in this period. His son Henry Bolingbroke later became King Henry IV.

John of the Cross, St (born Juan de Yepis y Alvarez) (1542–91) Spanish mystic and poet. A Carmelite monk and priest, he joined with St Teresa of Ávila in trying to reassert the original Carmelite observance of austerity, and in 1568 founded the 'discalced' or barefoot Carmelite order for monks. He also wrote mystical poems including 'The Dark Night of the Soul', describing the soul's purgation. Feast day, 14 December.

John o' Groats A village at the extreme north-east point of the Scottish mainland in the district of Caithness. It is said to be named from a house built there in the 16th century by a Dutchman, John Groot.

John Paul II (born Karol Jozef Wojtyla) (1920–) Polish cleric, pope since 1978. The first non-Italian pope since 1522, he has travelled abroad extensively during his papacy, especially in Central and South America. He has upheld the Church's traditional opposition to contraception and abortion, as well as condemning homosexuality, the ordination of women, and the relaxation of the rule of celibacy for priests.

Johns, Jasper (1930–) US painter, sculptor, and printmaker. A key figure in the development of pop art, he rebelled against abstract expressionism and depicted commonplace and universally recognized images such as the US flag. He is best known for his *Flags, Targets*, and *Numbers* series produced in the mid-1950s; in these, he was noted for his use of encaustic (wax-based) paint. In the late 1950s he produced sculptures of such objects as beer cans and light bulbs cast in bronze.

John Sobieski See JOHN III.

Johnson, Amy (1903–41) British aviator. In 1930 she became the first woman to fly solo to Australia, although her time of $19^1/_2$ days was three days short of the record. She later set a record with her solo flight to Tokyo (1931) and broke the solo-flight record to Cape Town (1932). She joined the Auxiliary Air Force in 1939, but was lost when her plane disappeared in a flight over the Thames estuary.

Johnson, Andrew (1808–75) US Democratic statesman, 17th President of the USA 1865–69. His lenient policy towards the southern states after the American Civil War brought him into bitter conflict with the Republican majority in Congress, who impeached him (1868); he was acquitted by a single vote.

Johnson, Cornelius (or **Jansens**) (1593–*c*.1661) English-born Dutch portrait painter. He painted for the court of Charles I, where he was influenced by Van Dyck and became noted for his individual portrait heads. After the outbreak of the English Civil War he emigrated to Holland (1643).

Johnson, Jack (1878–1946) US boxer. In 1908 he took the world heavyweight title, becoming the first black holder of the title; he retained it until 1915.

Johnson, Lyndon Baines (known as 'LBJ') (1908–73) US Democratic statesman, 36th President of the USA 1963–69. His administration continued the programme of social and economic reform initiated by John F. Kennedy, passing the 1964 and 1965 Civil Rights Acts and legislating to reduce taxation. However, the increasing involvement of the USA in the Vietnam War undermined his popularity and he refused to seek re-election.

Johnson, Magic (born Earvin Johnson) (1959–) US basketball player. He had a highly successful playing career (1979–91) with the Los Angeles Lakers in the National Basketball League (NBA), being named several times the NBA's Most Valuable Player and selected for the All-Star Team (1980, 1982–89). He retired as a player in 1991, following his highly publicized diagnosis as being HIV-positive, but resumed his career in 1992 and again in 1996.

Johnson, Michael (Duane) (1967–) US athlete who became world (1995) and Olympic (1996) champion in both the 200- and 400-metre sprints. He was the first man to be ranked world number one in the 200-metre and 400-metre events simultaneously (1990, 1991, 1994, 1995), and holds the world record for the 200 metres (19.32 seconds).

Johnson, Robert (1911–38) US blues singer and guitarist. Despite his mysterious early death and small recording output, he was very influential on the 1960s blues movement. His intense, haunting singing and piercing guitar style are displayed in songs such as 'I Was Standing at the Crossroads', 'Love In Vain', and 'I Believe I'll Dust My Broom'.

Johnson, Samuel (known as 'Dr Johnson') (1709–84) British lexicographer, writer, critic, and conversationalist. His principal works include his *Dictionary of the English Language* (1755), one of the first to use illustrative quotations, his edition of Shakespeare (1765), and *The Lives of the English Poets* (1777). A leading figure in the literary London of his day, he formed the Literary Club (1764), which numbered Edmund Burke, Oliver Goldsmith, Sir Joshua Reynolds, David Garrick, and Johnson's biographer James Boswell among its members.

John the Baptist, St Jewish preacher and prophet, a contemporary of Jesus. In *c*.27 AD he preached on the banks of the River Jordan, demanding repentance and baptism from his hearers in view of the approach of God's judgement. Among those whom he baptized was Christ. He was imprisoned by Herod Antipas after denouncing the latter's marriage to Herodias, the wife of Herod's brother Philip; Herodias' daughter Salome, offered a reward by Herod for her dancing, asked for the head of John the Baptist and thus caused him to be beheaded (Matt. 14:1–12). Feast day, 24 June.

John the Evangelist, St See JOHN, ST.

John the Fortunate John IV of Portugal. See JOHN (kings of Portugal).

John the Great John I of Portugal. See JOHN (kings of Portugal).

Johore A Malay sultanate founded by Sultan Mahmud, the last sultan of MALACCA before it was captured by the Portuguese in 1511. He tried unsuccessfully to retake Malacca a number of times but was finally defeated in 1526. Thereafter Johore was in frequent conflict with ACHEH, an emerging north Sumatran state. After Johore assisted the Dutch capture of Malacca in 1641, it established its rule over much of the southern Malay peninsular. However, an argument over a royal marriage led to its defeat by the Sumatran state of Jambi in 1673. Its capital moved to Rhio (on the island of Bintang) and a much weakened state only continued with support of BUGIS mercenaries.

joint (in anatomy) A part of a skeleton or rigid tissues that enables movement to occur between two or more bones. In vertebrates there are three main types of joint: the freely movable or synovial joints, which include ball-and-socket joints of the hip; pivot joints, as at the base of the neck; and hinge joints, as in the elbow or knee. Slightly movable joints, in which bones have the potential to move over one another to a small extent, occur along the spine. Immovable joints include the interdigitating sutures of the skull bones, mobile only in babies.

joint (in geology) A fracture in rock that has not undergone any movement – if it had it would then be a FAULT. Joints may be formed by shrinkage (on cooling) of an igneous rock, by sheeting (pressure-release), or by tectonic forces (the brittle fracture of rocks during flexure).

joint-stock company A company whose capital ownership is split into small equal parts known as SHARES (or common stock in the USA). Numerous investors can own different proportions of the company, all protected by LIMITED LIABILITY for the company's debts. Thus any company with shares is a joint-stock company, including all public limited companies (PLCs). See also CHARTERED COMPANY.

Joliot, Jean-Frédéric (1900–58) French nuclear physicist. He gave up engineering to study radioactivity and became Madame Curie's assistant at the Radium Institute. There he worked with her daughter **Irène Curie** (1897–1956), whom he married; subsequently they both adopted the name Joliot-Curie. Their joint discovery of artificial radioactivity earned them the 1935 Nobel Prize for chemistry. Shortly before the war Joliot-Curie demonstrated that a nuclear chain reaction was possible, and later he and his wife became involved with the establishment of the French atomic energy commission, only to be removed because of their Communism.

Jolson, Al (born Asa Yoelson) (1886–1950) Russian-born US singer, film actor, and comedian. He made the Gershwin song 'Swanee' his trademark, and appeared in the first full-length talking film *The Jazz Singer* (1927).

Jonah The recalcitrant Hebrew prophet who sought to avoid God's call for him to prophesy disaster to the Assyrian city of Nineveh, notorious for its wickedness. Taking a ship that would carry him away from Nineveh, he was caught in a storm and swallowed by a fish, to be regurgitated alive three days later on land. Jonah then went to Nineveh, where his prophecies caused its inhabitants to repent. He pitied a plant that perished, but abhorred the idea that God's compassion should extend to Gentiles. God chastised him, affirming that his mercy encompassed Jews and Gentiles alike. As Yunus, Jonah is mentioned in the Koran as a prophet, and is frequently depicted in Islamic painting with a fish.

Jonathan The warrior son of the Hebrew king Saul and beloved friend of the future King David. After defeating the Philistines many times, Jonathan was killed at the battle of Mount Gilboa. David lamented the deaths of Saul and Jonathan in a moving elegy.

Jones, Daniel (1881–1967) British linguist and phonetician. From 1907 he developed the recently invented International Phonetic Alphabet at the first British department of phonetics, at University College, London. He went on to invent a system of cardinal vowels, used as reference points for transcribing all vowel sounds. In his *English Pronouncing Dictionary* (1917), he described the influential system of received pronunciation, the English spoken by BBC newsreaders.

Jones, Inigo (1573–1652) English architect and stage designer. He introduced the Palladian style to England and is best known as the architect of the Queen's House at Greenwich (1616) and the Banqueting Hall at Whitehall (1619) with its ceiling painted by RUBENS. He also pioneered the use of the proscenium arch and movable stage scenery in England, and was for many years involved with costume design for court masques.

Jones, John Paul (born John Paul) (1747–92) Scottish-born American naval officer. In 1775 he joined the American Continental Navy and carried out a daring series of attacks on shipping in British waters, his best-known exploit being his engagement and sinking of the naval frigate *Serapis* while in command of the *Bonhomme Richard* (1779). In 1788 he joined the Russian navy as a rear-admiral.

Jones, Tom (born Thomas Jones Woodward) (1940–) British pop singer. He was heard in 1963 by the songwriter Gordon Mills, who advised him to change his name to Tom Jones and promoted his powerful voice and masculine image. The song 'It's Not Unusual' (1965) sold 3 million copies. Jones's other hits include 'The Green, Green Grass of Home' (1966) and 'Delilah' (1968).

Jong, Erica (Mann) (1942–) US poet and novelist. She made her name with the award-winning poetry collection *Fruits and Vegetables* (1971). Her international reputation is based on the picaresque novels *Fear of Flying* (1973), recounting the sexual exploits of its heroine Isadora Wing, and *Fanny* (1980), written in a pseudo-18th-century style.

jongleur A medieval travelling entertainer, a combination of MINSTREL, conjuror, clown, and acrobat. Descendants of the MIME of Roman times, *jongleurs* formed a link during the theatreless Middle Ages between the earlier pagan drama and the emergent liturgical drama. They were vagabonds working sometimes in groups and sometimes independently, and included both sexes. They are not to be confused with the *trouvères*, who were attached to particular households and whose material was more uplifting and sometimes used by the *jongleurs*.

Jonson, Ben(jamin) (1572–1637) English dramatist and poet. With his play *Every Man in His Humour* (1598) he established his 'comedy of humours', whereby each character is dominated by a particular obsession. His vigorous and often savage wit is evident in his comedies *Volpone* (1606), *The Alchemist* (1610), and *Bartholomew Fair* (1614). During the reign of James I his prestige and influence were unrivalled, and he became the first Poet Laureate in the modern sense.

Joplin, Janis (1943–70) US singer. At the age of 17 Joplin left Port Arthur, Texas, to hitchhike across America. She drifted into the hippy subculture of San Francisco, where she became vocalist with Big Brother and the Holding Company, and gave a powerful performance with them at the Monterey pop festival in 1967. Joplin's most successful album, *Pearl*, and her number-one single 'Me and Bobby McGee' were released shortly after her death from a heroin overdose.

Joplin, Scott (1868–1917) US pianist and composer. One of the creators of ragtime, he was the first to write down his compositions. Two of Joplin's best-known rags, 'Original Rags' and 'Maple Leaf Rag', were written in 1899. The latter was so successful that a million copies of the sheet music were sold. Joplin's music, including the rag 'The Entertainer', was featured in the film *The Sting* (1973), causing a revival of his work and the first successful performance of his ragtime opera *Treemonisha*.

Jordaens, Jacob (1593–1678) Flemish painter. Influenced by Rubens, he painted in warm colours and is noted for his boisterous peasant scenes. His major works include *The King Drinks* (1638).

Jordan A mainly inland Middle Eastern country, correctly the Hashemite Kingdom of Jordan, a part of historical Palestine. It borders on Syria in the north, Iraq in the east, Saudi Arabia in the south-east, and Israel in the west.

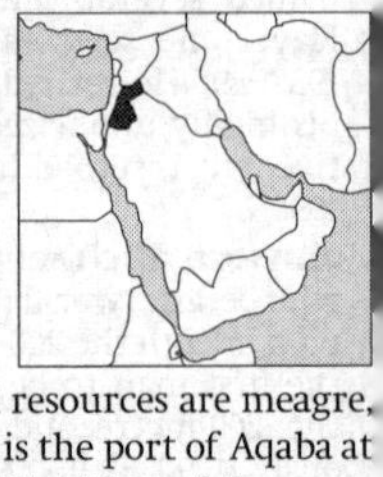

Physical. Jordan's natural resources are meagre, and its only outlet to the sea is the port of Aqaba at the north-east end of the Red Sea. Most of the country is on a desert plateau which has only about 250 mm (10 inches) of rain a year; but in the west is the Jordan River valley (whose West Bank is occupied by Israel) where some crops can be grown.

Economy. Jordan's economy is dependent on

foreign aid and remittances from Jordanian workers abroad, particularly those working in the Gulf states; the loss of income caused by the 1991 Gulf War was disastrous and was compounded by the fact that Iraq had been the major trading partner. Phosphates, potash, and agricultural produce are the mainstay of the economy. In 1996 the doubling of food prices led to riots.

History. The region was part of the OTTOMAN EMPIRE until 1918, when it came under the government of King Faisal in Damascus. In 1920 Transjordan, as it was then called, was made part of the British mandate of Palestine. In 1921 Britain recognized Abdullah ibn Hussein as ruler of the territory and gave him British advisers, a subsidy, and assistance in creating a security force. In 1946 the country was given full independence as the Hashemite Kingdom of Jordan, with Abdullah ibn Hussein as king. In 1948–49 the state was considerably enlarged when Palestinian territories on the West Bank, including the Old City of Jerusalem, were added. As a result of the SIX-DAY WAR in 1967, these West Bank territories passed under Israeli occupation. The king was assassinated in 1951, his son Talal was deposed in 1952 as mentally unstable, and since 1953 Jordan has been ruled by Talal's son, Talal ibn HUSSEIN. Palestinian refugees from territory under Israeli occupation established a commando force (*fedayeen*) in Jordan to raid Israel. Hostility from Palestinian refugees from the West Bank to the moderate policies of Hussein erupted in 1970 between the guerrillas and the government. The mainly Bedouin regiments loyal to the king broke up the military bases of al-FATAH, and the PALESTINE LIBERATION ORGANIZATION moved its forces (1971) to Lebanon and Syria. During the YOM KIPPUR war Jordan sent tanks to aid Syria, but there was no fighting along the Jordan frontier. In 1974 Jordan's relations with other Arab countries improved when it accepted that 'the PLO is the sole and legitimate representative of the Palestinian people'. It supported Iraq in the IRAN–IRAQ WAR and suffered severely during the Gulf crisis and GULF WAR from the effects of UN sanctions against Iraq, and from the arrival of many thousands of expatriates from the Gulf. In June 1991 the 34-year ban on political parties was lifted; among those who formed an opposition was the Muslim Brotherhood, which opposed the important role that Jordan was playing in the Middle East peace process. Jordan gradually distanced itself from Iraq as it continued to participate in Middle East peace talks. In 1993 the first multi-party election since 1956 was held in which independent candidates loyal to the king were victorious. Despite the signing of the Israeli-PLO peace accord (1993), Jordan continued its own negotiations with Israel. In 1994 the two countries signed a declaration formally ending the state of conflict between them and agreed a peace treaty. Opposition parties continued to oppose any agreement with Israel, while relations with Saudi Arabia, strained during the Gulf crisis, improved.

Capital: Amman
Area: 88,947 sq km (34,342 sq mi)
Population: 4,187,000 (1995)
Currency: 1 Jordanian dinar = 1,000 fils
Religions: Sunni Muslim 93.0%; Christian 4.9%
Ethnic Groups: Arab (including Palestinian and Bedouin) 99.2%; Circassian 0.5%; Armenian 0.1%; Turkish 0.1%; Kurdish 0.1%
Languages: Arabic (official); minority languages
International Organizations: UN; Arab League; Non-Aligned Movement

Jordan A river flowing from the Anti-Lebanon mountains on the Lebanon–Syria frontier southward for 320 km (200 miles) through the Sea of Galilee and into the Dead Sea. It has many biblical associations, especially with the life of Jesus.

Jordan, Michael (Jeffrey) (1963–) US basketball player. Playing for the Chicago Bulls from 1984, he was the National Basketball Association's Most Valuable Player four times (1988, 1991, 1992, 1996) and the leading points scorer between 1987 and 1992. A member of the US Olympic gold-medal-winning teams in 1984 and 1992, he retired in 1993, but returned in 1995.

Joseph In the Old Testament, the favoured son of the Hebrew patriarch Jacob and his wife Rachel. Sold into slavery by his half-brothers, who were jealous of their father's gift to Joseph (a 'coat of many colours'), Joseph eventually attained high office in Egypt because of his power to interpret the Pharaoh's dreams. His foresight saved Egypt from a famine, during which his brothers came from Israel for food. Joseph, forgiving them, sent for Jacob and for their families to settle in Egypt under his care. His name eventually became equated with all the tribes that made up the northern Kingdom. As Yusuf, Joseph is a favourite figure in Islam, renowned for his beauty and regarded as a prophet.

Joseph, St Carpenter of Nazareth, husband of the Virgin Mary. At the time of the Annunciation, he was betrothed to Mary. A devout Jew, descended from the House of David, he settled in Nazareth, where he probably died, before the crucifixion. Feast day, 19 March.

Josephine (born Marie Joséphine Rose Tascher de la Pagerie) (1763–1814) Empress of France 1796–1809. Born in the West Indies, she was married to the Viscount de Beauharnais before marrying Napoleon in 1796. Their marriage proved childless and Josephine was divorced by Napoleon in 1809.

Joseph of Arimathaea In the New Testament, a wealthy member of the Jewish Sanhedrin who was a secret disciple of Jesus. With Nicodemus, Joseph obtained the body of Jesus and laid it in his own tomb. According to the apocryphal Gospel of Nicodemus, Joseph helped found one of the first Christian communities at Lydda. A medieval legend associates him with Glastonbury in England, where he is alleged to have come with the Holy Grail, the cup used by Jesus in the Last Supper, and to have planted a thorn tree that flowers on Christmas Day.

Josephus, Flavius (born Joseph ben Matthias) (*c*.37–*c*.100) Jewish historian, general, and Pharisee. A leader of the Jewish revolt against the Romans from 66, he was captured in 67; his life was spared when he prophesied that Vespasian would become emperor. He subsequently received Roman citizenship and a pension, and is remembered as the author of the *Jewish War*, an eyewitness account of the events leading up to the revolt, and of *Antiquities of the Jews*, a history running from the Creation to 66.

Joshua The Hebrew leader who succeeded Moses. After the Exodus from Egypt, Joshua led the Israelites across the miraculously dried-up River Jordan into the Promised Land of Canaan. An inspired fighter, his campaigns, including the razing of the walled city of Jericho, helped to consolidate Israel's hold on Canaan.

Josiah (649–609 BC) King of JUDAH (640–609 BC) in succession to his father Amon. At the age of 17 he undertook a major reform of worship in and around Jerusalem, suppressing the worship of local gods, closing down outlying shrines, and making the Jerusalem Temple the sole centre of worship. Because of his concern for the Jewish faith, he is described in the Bible as a model king, the last good king of Judah. He died at the Battle of Megiddo, defeated by the Egyptians.

Josquin des Prez See DES PREZ.

joule (symbol J) The SI UNIT of ENERGY or work. It is defined as the work done when a force of 1 newton moves a distance of 1 metre in the direction of the force. A joule per second is a WATT. The joule is named after the British physicist, James Prescott JOULE.

Joule, James Prescott (1818–89) British physicist. Experimenting in his private laboratory and at the family's brewery, he established that all forms of energy were basically the same and interchangeable – the basic principle of what is now called the first law of THERMODYNAMICS. Among other things, he measured the thermal effects of an electric current due to the resistance of the wire, establishing the law governing this. In 1852 he and William Thomson, later Lord Kelvin, discovered the fall in temperature when gases expand (the Joule–Thomson effect), which led to the development of the refrigerator and to the science of cryogenics.

journalism The collection and dissemination of news and other information for NEWSPAPERS, periodicals, BROADCASTING, and TELEVISION. Print journalism falls broadly into three divisions: news, features, and comment. News and features are usually submitted by staff reporters, correspondents, freelances (or stringers), and news agencies. News concentrates on factual reporting of current events, while features examine a subject in detail, and also cater for general interest topics, such as the arts. A newspaper's editorial stance is most evident in its 'leader' column, in which views on one or more of the main news stories are given. Broadsheet newspaper journalism often allows reporters the space for an in-depth news account. Broadcast journalism's strength is its immediacy. In tabloid journalism writing tends to concentrate on the sensational. In recent years pictures published in tabloid papers, often bought from freelance photographers (paparazzi), have ignored the calls to respect the individual privacy of celebrities.

Joyce, James (Augustine Aloysius) (1882–1941) Irish writer. He left Ireland in 1904 and thereafter lived in Trieste, Zurich, and Paris, becoming one of the most important writers of the modernist movement. His first major publication was *Dubliners* (1914), a collection of short stories depicting his native Dublin, which was followed by the semi-autobiographical novel *A Portrait of the Artist as a Young Man* (1914–15). His novel *Ulysses* (published in Paris in 1922 but banned in the UK and the US until 1936) revolutionized the form and structure of the modern novel and influenced the development of the stream of consciousness technique. *Finnegans Wake* (1939) pushed linguistic experimentation to the extreme.

Juan Carlos (full name Juan Carlos Victor María de Borbón y Borbón) (1938–) Grandson of Alfonso XIII, king of Spain since 1975. He was nominated by Franco as his successor and became king when Franco died. His reign has seen Spain's increasing liberalization and its entry into NATO and the European Community.

Juárez, Benito Pablo (1806–72) Mexican statesman, President 1861–64 and 1867–72. His refusal to repay Mexico's foreign debts led to the occupation of Mexico by Napoleon III and the establishment of Maximilian as emperor of Mexico in 1864. The withdrawal of the occupying French forces in 1867 prompted the execution of Maximilian and the rehabilitation of Juárez in the same year.

Juba The capital of the southern region of Sudan, on the White Nile; pop. (est. 1990) 100,000. Since 1983 the city has been virtually isolated by the civil war in Sudan.

Judaea The southernmost region of ancient Palestine whose chief city was Jerusalem. At the end of the second millennium BC it was established by the Israelite tribe of Judah as an independent kingdom, which lasted until it was overrun by the Babylonians in 587 BC. The Jews returned to Judaea in 537 BC after the Babylonian captivity, and in 165 BC the Maccabees again established it as an independent kingdom. It became a province of the Roman Empire in 63 BC, and was subsequently amalgamated with Palestine.

Judah The most powerful of the 12 tribes of Israel. After the reign of Solomon it formed a separate kingdom, with Benjamin, which outlasted that of the northern tribes.

Judaism The religion of the JEWISH PEOPLE, with a belief in one God and a basis in Mosaic and rabbinical teachings. The Jews were called to reject polytheism and worship the one God, the Creator, whose will is revealed in the TORAH, which comprises the first five books of the Bible (also known as the Pentateuch) and which contains the Ten Commandments. This monotheism, inherited by both Christianity and Islam, is the heart of Judaism. Jews believe that as a result of the COVENANT made by God with Abraham, they have a unique relationship with God (that they are the Chosen People). They also believe that an annointed person (the Messiah) will be sent by God to gather all of the peoples of Israel into the promised land and bring everlasting peace to Earth. Christians, but not Jews, believe that Jesus was the Messiah. See also KOSHER; MISHNAH; SYNAGOGUE; TALMUD.

Judas See JUDE, ST.

Judas Iscariot The Apostle destined to betray Christ to the Jewish authorities. After the Last Supper he led an armed band to the Garden of Gethsemane, where he identified Christ to the soldiers by kissing him. For this he was given 30 pieces of silver, the price commonly paid for a slave. He bought a potter's field, and there hanged himself.

Judas Maccabaeus (died *c.*161 BC) Jewish leader. He led a Jewish revolt in Judaea against the Seleucid king Antiochus IV Epiphanes from around 167, and succeeded in recovering Jerusalem, dedicating the Temple anew, and protecting Judaism from Hellenization. He also features in the Apocrypha as the hero of the Maccabees.

Jude, St (or **Judas**) An Apostle, supposed brother of James. Thaddaeus (mentioned in St Matthew's Gospel) is traditionally identified with him. According to tradition he was martyred in Persia with St Simon. Feast day (with St Simon), 28 October.

judge A public officer appointed to hear and try cases in a COURT OF LAW. A judge may sit alone, or with lay assessors, with a JURY, or, as is common in appeal courts, with other judges. Where a judge sits with a jury, it is usually the jurors who decide questions of fact, such as guilt or innocence, while the judge decides on questions of law (such as whether evidence is admissible), and passes sentence. In COMMON LAW SYSTEMS, it is an accepted part of the judge's task not only to apply the law, but also to interpret it. In certain circumstances, decisions by judges can set PRECEDENTS which may, or even must, be followed. In CIVIL LAW systems, there is traditionally little scope for judges to make law by setting precedents, but as new problems arise that are not covered by existing legal provisions, judges are increasingly having to play a part in the interpretation and development of the law. Judges attain their positions in a variety of ways. In England, judges are appointed by or on the advice of the Lord Chancellor (the highest judicial officer of the Crown) from practising lawyers of many years' standing. On the other hand, judges in France, Italy, Germany, and most civil law systems are career judges: young people, having qualified by examination, enter the judicial service direct, and are promoted to higher courts on the basis of age, ability, and experience. In the USA, judges of the Supreme Court, known as Justices, are appointed for life by the President, subject to confirmation by the Senate.

judicial review A legal procedure in which the judiciary reviews the legality or constitutionality of the behaviour or decisions of another public body. There are broadly two types of judicial review: judicial review of administrative action (see ADMINISTRATIVE LAW) and judicial review of legislation. The latter allows judges to strike down legislation held to be inconsistent with the constitution and is most common in jurisdictions with an entrenched CONSTITUTION, such as the USA, Australia, Canada, France, and Germany, and particularly in those countries with a BILL OF RIGHTS.

judiciary The body of JUDGES within a legal system making up the third branch of government, the other two being the LEGISLATURE and the executive. An independent judiciary is a bulwark of constitutional government and essential for the rule of law, but the relationship between politics and the judiciary is complex. Political influences are often present in the appointment of judges. In the USA, for instance, the PRESIDENT nominates and the SENATE must confirm appointments to the federal judiciary.

Judith The Jewish heroine of the apocryphal Book of Judith, who saved her city of Bathulia when it was besieged by Nebuchadnezzar's general, Holofernes. Judith, a widow of great beauty, went to the enemy's camp, beguiled Holofernes into a drunken stupor with her charms, and then beheaded him with a sword.

judo See MARTIAL ARTS.

Jugurtha (died 104 BC) Joint king of Numidia *c.*118–104. His attacks on his royal partners prompted intervention by Rome and led to the outbreak of the Jugurthine War (112–105). He was eventually captured by the Roman general Marius and executed in Rome.

jujube The common name of a number of plants of the genus *Zizyphus*, which are relatives of the BUCKTHORNS. The Chinese jujube, *Z. jujuba*, is one of the five major fruits of China, where some 300 varieties of it are grown. It is a deciduous tree or shrub bearing oblong DRUPES. The name is also used for lozenges or rubbery sweets originally prepared from jujubes but today usually made with synthetic materials.

Julian (known as **Julian the Apostate**; full name Flavius Claudius Julianus) (*c.*331–63 AD) Roman emperor 360–63, nephew of Constantine. He restored paganism as the state cult in place of Christianity, but this move was reversed after his death on campaign against the Persians.

Julian Alps An Alpine range in north-east Italy and western Slovenia, rising to a height of 2,864 m (9,395 ft) at Triglav.

Julian calendar A calendar introduced by Julius Caesar in 46 BC and slightly modified under Augustus, in which the ordinary year has 365 days, and every fourth year (with the exception of the century year) is a leap year of 366 days.It has largely been superceded by the GREGORIAN CALENDAR.

Julian of Norwich (*c.*1342–*c.*1413) English mystic. Her name probably derives from St Julian's Church, Norwich, outside which she is said to have lived as a religious recluse. She is chiefly associated with the *Revelations of Divine Love* (*c.*1393), which describe a series of visions she had at the end of a serious illness in 1373. In her account, she affirms the love of God and depicts the Holy Trinity as Father, Mother, and Lord.

Julius II (born Guiliano della Rovere) (1443–1513) Pope 1503–13 He strove to restore and extend the PAPAL STATES and to establish a strong independent papacy. He crushed Cesare BORGIA and sponsored the League of CAMBRAI and the Holy League against France in 1510. Before the end of 1512 the French were forced to leave Italy and several new territories were added to the papacy's holdings.

July Plot See STAUFFENBERG, VON.

July Revolution (1830) A revolt in France. It began when CHARLES X issued his ordinances of 25 July, which suspended the liberty of the press, dissolved the new chamber, reduced the electorate, and allowed him to rule by decree. His opponents erected barricades in Paris and after five days of bitter street fighting Charles was forced to abdicate. The Duc d'Orléans, LOUIS PHILIPPE, was invited to become 'King of the French', a title which replaced the more traditional 'King of France'. His accession marked the victory of constitutional liberal forces over arbitrary and absolutist rule.

jumbo jet See WIDE-BODIED AIRCRAFT.

jumping plant louse A small BUG with transparent wings and strong hind-legs for jumping, belonging to the family Psyllidae, which contains some 1,300 species. In temperate regions most species overwinter as eggs; the young hatch in the spring, and become adult in the summer, so that there is only one generation a year. The adults are about the same size as aphids, and resemble tiny cicadas. The larvae can do considerable damage to fruit trees, and also produce copious amounts of sweet-tasting honeydew, which spreads over leaves.

Juneau The state capital of Alaska, a seaport on the Gastineau Channel with an ice-free harbour, an inlet of the Pacific Ocean; pop. (1990) 26,750. It developed after the discovery of gold by Joseph Juneau in 1880. It was designated capital of the Territory of Alaska in 1900 and became state capital in 1959. Fishing, lumbering, and tourism are important industries.

Jung, Carl (Gustav) (1875–1961) Swiss psychologist. He collaborated with Sigmund Freud in the development of the psychoanalytic theory of personality, though he later divorced himself from Freud's viewpoint because of its preoccupation with sexuality as the determinant of personality. Jung originated the concept of introvert and extrovert personality, and of the four psychological functions of sensation, intuition, thinking, and feeling. In his major work, *The Psychology of the Unconscious* (1912), he proposed the existence of a collective unconscious, which he combined with a theory of archetypes for studying the history and psychology of religion.

Jungfrau A mountain in the Bernese Alps of south-central Switzerland, 5,158 m (13,642 ft) high. Ascended by J. R. and H. Meyer in 1811, it was one of the first major mountains of the Alps to be climbed.

junglefowl Any one of four species of the genus *Gallus* which is part of the pheasant family, Phasianidae. All live in south-east Asia in wooded country. The males are shiny greenish-black on the wings and tail, and many of the tail feathers are elongated and curved; the feathers of the neck and back are orange-chestnut and the underparts are black. The females are brown. All species have a distinctive red comb and wattles. The red junglefowl, *G. gallus*, is the ancestor of the domestic chicken.

juniper An evergreen tree or shrub of the conifer genus *Juniperus*, which comprises some 60 species of the northern temperate zone, extending to the tropics in the Kenya highlands. The common juniper, *J. communis*, is the only tree species native to the northern temperate regions of both the Old and New Worlds. This and other species have needle-like leaves throughout life, while some other species of *Juniperus* have small ones pressed close to the stems, as in *J. sabina*, the savin of Eurasia. The cone is modified to form a fleshy mass surrounding the seeds and is eaten by birds. The 'berries' of the common juniper are used in the production of gin, to which it has given its name. The timber of some species is valuable, that of the American red pencil cedar, *J. virginiana*, being used in pencil manufacture.

junk A flat-bottomed, high-sterned sailing vessel, common to seas in the Far East and used especially by the Chinese. Junks developed in China from about 1500 BC. Over 70 different types are now found, though all junks have essentially similar characteristics. The hull is strong and rigid, with a wide, flat stern, a square, sloping bow, and a deep rudder that can be raised or lowered to act also as a centreboard. The sails consist of a series of narrow panels of cloth or matting, stiffened with horizontal battens, each panel having its own sheets (ropes). They can be hauled round to allow the boat to sail somewhat into the wind, and are easily adjusted.

Juno (in mythology) The greatest of the Roman goddesses, sister and wife of Jupiter, identified with Hera in Greek mythology. She was particularly concerned with marriage and the well-being of women.

Juno (in astronomy) An ASTEROID discovered by the German astronomer Carl Harding in 1804. Its orbital semi-major axis, eccentricity, and inclination to the ecliptic are 2.671 astronomical units, 0.255, and 13 degrees, respectively. Juno's diameter is 244 km, and its albedo is 0.22.

junta (Spanish, 'council', 'meeting') A group of political or military leaders forming an administrative council or committee, particularly in the aftermath of a *coup d'état* or REVOLUTION when there is no legal government. If a single dominant leader or small group emerges from a junta, it can be transformed into a DICTATORSHIP.

Jupiter (in mythology) The supreme Roman god, identified with the Greek god Zeus.

Jupiter (in astronomy) The fifth PLANET from the Sun and the largest planet of the Solar System, easily visible with the unaided eye. Its mass is about twice as large as the sum of the masses of all the other planets, and is about one thousandth of that of the Sun. Like all the other giant outer planets, it emits more energy than it receives from the Sun, thus implying the existence of an internal energy source. Although Jupiter is essentially a gaseous body, it has an inner core composed of rocky material, with a mass of perhaps ten to 20 times that of the Earth, surrounded by a liquid envelope of lighter elements, and a massive atmosphere. The satellite system comprises four large satellites, discovered by Galileo at the beginning of the 17th century; they orbit about the planet in nearly circular, equatorial orbits. There are also a number of smaller satellites, divided into three groups. The first is composed of small satellites in orbits very close to the planet; the second and the third are on larger and more eccentric and inclined orbits; those in the case of the outermost group are retrograde, that is, move in the opposite direction to Jupiter's motion in its orbit. The abundance of light elements, such as hydrogen and helium, in Jupiter, compared with their relative deficiency in the inner planets, suggests that when the planet was formed the core was able to attract and trap the gas that fell on the forming planet and now constitutes most of its mass. The atmosphere is characterized by parallel bands that move with respect to each other, driven by Jupiter's internal energy source; darker bands are called **belts**, and lighter ones **zones**. At the boundaries between belts and zones, vortices are present. One of these is the long-known GREAT RED SPOT, a gigantic storm system larger than the Earth, in which clouds rise several kilometres above the clouds of surrounding regions. Jupiter is a strong emitter of radio signals. The magnetic field is much stronger than that of the Earth, with a correspondingly much larger MAGNETOSPHERE. Observations from the VOYAGER spacecraft led to the discovery of a tenuous ring system about the planet, much less spectacular and massive than that of Saturn. It is mostly composed of particles about 10^{-6} m in size.

Jura A system of mountain ranges, on the border of France and Switzerland, which has given its name to the JURASSIC period when most of its rocks were laid down. The highest peak in the Jura Mts. is Crête de la Neige (1,718 m, 5,636 ft).

Jura An island of the Inner Hebrides, separated from the west coast of Scotland by the Sound of Jura. Area 381 sq km (147 sq miles), pop. (1981) 239; principal settlement Craighouse.

Jurassic The second period of the Mesozoic era, following the Triassic and preceding the Cretaceous, lasting from about 213 to 144 million years ago. During this period dinosaurs and other reptiles attained their maximum size and were found on land, in the sea, and in the air. The first birds appeared towards the end of the period, which takes its name from the JURA mountains.

jurisprudence The philosophy or science of law. It entails philosophical and practical enquiry into law and legal systems and encompasses at least four broad types of study. First, there are studies of legal systems to identify their constituent elements, such as rules, rights, and duties, and the bonds between them. There are different theories about the relationship between legal rules and morality (see JUSTICE). Legal positivists have regarded legal systems as distinct from systems of morality, while exponents of NATURAL LAW have disagreed. Secondly, there are studies of the growth and social impact of law in such fields as medicine, business, and the environment. Thirdly, there are studies of the behaviour and beliefs of legal officers and institutions (POLICE, LEGISLATURES, and JURIES, for example). This field was pioneered by US 'legal realists', who argued that legal rules were often not the decisive factor in the outcome of cases. Finally, there are studies of all the social mechanisms associated with the law, in particular those maintaining order and resolving disputes.

jury A group of lay persons (usually 12) summoned to a COURT OF LAW or an INQUEST in order to decide the facts of a case and give a verdict. The jury system's development was exclusive to England. Initially, jurors were regarded as sworn (Latin, *jurati*) witnesses to the accuracy of a claim. In the Anglo-Saxon 'compurgation' an accused person could be cleared simply on the sworn word of 12 neighbours to his good character. The Assize of Clarendon (1166) instructed jurors to present their evidence and suspects before the king's justices. Trial by jury was adopted in civil cases when the Lateran Council (1215) forbade the trial by ordeal, and it became compulsory for certain criminal cases under the Statute of Westminster (1275).

Trial by jury is currently found almost only in the UK and in countries influenced by the English legal system. In the UK, juries are mainly used in criminal trials, or in a few civil cases such as libel. In the USA there are two types of jury: the grand jury, which investigates possible criminal wrongdoing, hears the state's evidence, and if satisfied that a trial should take place, hands down a formal accusation or indictment; and the petit or trial jury, which is used in both criminal and civil trials. The members of a jury are randomly selected, but the defendant has the right to challenge the composition of the jury and to object to jurors on the grounds of prejudice or unsuitability. In the UK jurors may not be challenged with no reason being given. The role of the jury is to decide on questions of fact and to issue a verdict, while the JUDGE directs them on matters of law and sums up the evidence for them. The verdict of the jury is traditionally expected to be unanimous, but where this is impossible, a majority verdict may be sufficient. The use of a jury is intended to ensure that the defendant is given a fair trial by ordinary people chosen at random, who bring to the proceedings impartiality and common sense.

Jussieu, Antoine Laurent de (1748–1836) One of a family of French botanists whose home was a centre for plant collection and research. In *Genera Plantarum* (1789) he developed the system on which modern plant classification is based. From extensive observation, he grouped plants into families on the basis of common features.

justice The principle of fairness, especially in relation to the administration of the law. Theories of justice have been elaborated by philosophers, political scientists, legal theorists, economists, and others. Both PLATO and ARISTOTLE regarded justice as the essential virtue enabling humans to live together in harmony. In this wider sense justice is closely linked with morality and ETHICS. In recent times, many theorists have also been concerned with theories of social justice, which examine the question of poverty and the distribution of resources in a society. Ideas of equality pervade most theories of justice and it is usually accepted that departures from equality are unjust. However, the nature of equality and the grounds for justifying inequality are highly controversial. Despite the popular expectation that the law exists to achieve just results and will operate in procedurally just ways, there is ample potential for conflict between legal systems, NATURAL LAW, and morality, which gives rise to difficult questions about the nature and application of justice. See also JURISPRUDENCE.

Justinian (full name Flavius Petrus Sabbatius Justinianus) (483–565) Byzantine emperor 527–65. He set out to recover the lost provinces of the Western Empire, and through his general Belisarius (*c.*505–65) succeeded in reclaiming North Africa from the Vandals, Italy from the Ostrogoths, and Spain from the Visigoths. Justinian's codification of Roman law in 529 had a significant impact on the development of law in European countries. He carried out an active building programme throughout the Empire and commissioned the construction of St Sophia at Constantinople in 532.

Justin, St (known as **St Justin the Martyr**) (*c.*100–165) Christian philosopher. Born in Samaria, he became a Christian convert at Ephesus (*c.*130). He is remembered for his *Apologia* (*c.*150), a defence of Christianity. Tradition holds that he was martyred in Rome together with some of his followers. Feast day, 1 June.

jute A FIBRE crop that became important as a replacement for hemp when a method of spinning the new material was developed in Scotland in the mid-19th century. There are two species of plant of the genus *Corchorus* from which jute fibre is extracted. They belong to the lime-tree family, Tiliaceae. *C. capsularis* is grown in India and Bangladesh, while *C. olitorius* is cultivated for jute fibre in part of Africa.

The plant stems are cut by hand and, after drying, are immersed in water for up to five weeks (a process known as 'retting'). The extracted fibres can be up to 3 m (10 feet) long but are weaker than flax or hemp. The spun yarn is woven to produce hessian (called 'gunny' in the USA), usually used for sacking and bag manufacture.

Jute A Low-German tribe that invaded southern England (according to legend under Horsa and Hengist) in the 5th century and set up a kingdom in Kent.

Jutland (Danish **Jylland**) A peninsula of northwest Europe stretching northwards into the North Sea from Germany to form the mainland of Denmark together with the north German state of Schleswig-Holstein.

Jutland, Battle of (31 May 1916) A battle fought off the coast of Jutland in the North Sea between Britain and Germany. It was the only major battle fought at sea in World War I and began between two forces of battle cruisers, the British under BEATTY and the German under von Hipper. Suffering heavy losses, Beatty sailed to join the main British North Sea Fleet under JELLICOE, which now engaged the German High Seas Fleet under Scheer. Battle began at 6 p.m. at long range, but as the Germans headed for home in the night, they collided with the British fleet, several ships sinking in the ensuing chaos. Both sides claimed victory. The British lost 14 ships, including 3 battle cruisers; the Germans lost 11 ships, including 1 battleship and 1 battle cruiser; but the British retained control of the North Sea, the German fleet staying inside the Baltic for the rest of the war.

Juvenal (full name Decimus Junius Juvenalis) (*c.*60–*c.*140) Roman satirist. His 16 verse satires present a savage attack on the vice and folly of Roman society, chiefly in the reign of the emperor Domitian. They deal variously with the hardship of poverty, the profligacy of the rich, and the futility of ambition.

juvenile court A special COURT OF LAW dealing with legal problems connected with children and young people. These may be either criminal matters, such as offences committed by children (see JUVENILE DELINQUENCY), or civil matters, such as the problems of abandoned or neglected children. Juvenile courts originated in the USA in 1889. It was believed that children who offended should be treated differently from adult offenders, and that they were in need more of reform than of punishment. Juvenile courts are now found in Europe, Latin America, Japan, and elsewhere (in the UK they are called youth courts). Sometimes matters normally dealt with in a juvenile court come before a family court. There are wide variations in procedure and structure in juvenile courts, but in general they tend to be less formal and intimidating than ordinary courts.

juvenile delinquency Criminal or anti-social activities by children and young people. Statistics tend to show that a high proportion of crime is committed by young people. (In England and Wales almost half known offenders are under 20.) Commonly committed crimes include theft (often shoplifting), vandalism, and car-stealing. Juvenile delinquency is also used to refer to behaviour not prohibited to adults, for example in many societies it is illegal for children and young people below a specified age to drink alcohol, run away from home, and take part in sexual activities. Juvenile delinquents are treated differently from adult offenders, in many countries being dealt with in JUVENILE COURTS. The emphasis is often on rehabilitation rather than punishment, with the young person being placed on PROBATION or working for the benefit of the community.

Jylland See JUTLAND.

K

K2 (or **Dapsang**) The highest mountain in the Karakoram range, on the border between Pakistan and China. It is the second-highest peak in the world, rising to 8,611 m (28,250 ft). Discovered in 1856, it was named K2 because it was the second peak measured in the Karakoram range. It has also been known as Mt. Godwin-Austen, after Col. H. H. Godwin-Austen, who first surveyed it.

Kaaba The sacred shrine in Mecca, Saudi Arabia, to which Muslims turn daily in prayer, and the focal point for Muslim pilgrimage. It is a cube-shaped building covered with a black cloth, embroidered in gold with Koranic quotations. In a wall of the Kaaba is embedded a sacred black stone. A tradition says that the black stone was given to Abraham by the Angel Gabriel, and it is believed to symbolize God's covenant with the worshipper. The authentic Muslim tradition, according to the Koran, is that the Kaaba was originally built by Abraham and Ishmael. See also FIVE PILLARS OF ISLAM.

Kabardino-Balkaria (official name **The Kabarda-Balkar Republic**) A republic of the Russian Federation in the northern Caucasus on the border with Georgia; area 12,500 sq km (4,825 sq miles); pop. (1990) 768,000; capital, Nalchik. Absorbed into the Russian empire in the 16th century, it was designated an Autonomous Soviet Republic in 1936 and became a federal republic of Russia in 1991.

Kabbalah (Hebrew, 'tradition') The main tradition of Jewish MYSTICISM. Kabbalistic belief maintains the possibility of a direct 'vision' of divine attributes, based upon ASTROLOGY and the study of occult interpretations of the Old Testament and other texts, which define the spiritual and symbolic value of numbers and letters. The main Kabbalistic work, the *Zohar* ('Splendour'), a 13th-century mystical interpretation of the TORAH, was influential in modern HASIDISM. It taught ten ways of understanding God, while maintaining that God himself is beyond comprehension.

Kabuki See JAPANESE DRAMA.

Kabul The capital of Afghanistan, a historic city situated on the River Kabul in a narrow mountain valley, commanding the mountain passes through the Hindu Kush, especially the Khyber Pass; pop. (est. 1993) 700,000. It has existed for more than 3,000 years and has been destroyed and rebuilt several times in its history. It was capital of the Mogul empire, 1504–1738, and in 1773 replaced Kandahar as capital of an independent Afghanistan. It was the scene of bitter fighting during the 19th-century Afghan Wars and again during the civil war that began in 1979. It is Afghanistan's cultural and commercial centre with textile, footwear, and vehicle component industries.

Kabwe The capital of Central province and the oldest lead- and zinc-mining town in Zambia; pop. (1990) 167,000. It was known as Broken Hill from 1904 to 1965.

Kabylia The region of the Algerian Atlas Mountains occupied by the Berber Kabyle people.

Kachin A mountain people of northern Myanmar (Burma) and adjacent areas of China and India speaking a variety of Tibeto-Burman languages. They number *c.*245,000.

Kádár, János (1912–89) Hungarian statesman, First Secretary of the Hungarian Socialist Workers' Party 1956–88 and Prime Minister 1956–58 and 1961–65. He replaced Imre Nagy as Premier after crushing the Hungarian uprising of 1956. Kádár consistently supported the Soviet Union, involving Hungarian troops in the 1968 invasion of Czechoslovakia, while retaining a degree of decentralization for the economy. His policy of 'consumer socialism' made Hungary the most affluent state in eastern Europe. He was removed as First Secretary following his resistance to the political reforms of the 1980s.

Kaduna An industrial city and capital of Kaduna state in northern Nigeria, on the Kaduna River; pop. (est. 1986) 280,000. Founded under British rule in 1913, it was formerly capital of Nigeria's Northern Region. In addition to brewing and oil refining, its industries produce textiles, cement, vehicles, and metal goods.

Kaffir A member of the Xhosa-speaking peoples of South Africa, many of whom were settled on a Cape Colony reserve known as Kaffraria established by the British in 1847 on land lying between the Keiskamma and Kei rivers.

Kafir A native of the Hindu Kush mountains of north-east Afghanistan.

Kafka, Franz (1883–1924) Czech novelist, who wrote in German. A sense of guilt haunts Kafka's stories, which are characterized by his portrayal of an enigmatic and nightmarish reality, in which the individual is perceived as lonely, perplexed, and threatened. *Metamorphosis* (1917) was one of the few works published in Kafka's lifetime: his novels *The Trial* (1925) and *The Castle* (1926) were published posthumously by his friend the writer Max Brod (1884–1968), against the directions of his will.

Kagoshima A city and port in Japan; pop. (1990) 537,000. It is situated on the southern coast of Kyushu Island, on the Satsuma Peninsula, beside an active volcano, Sakurajima. It has a navy yard and rocket base, and industries producing porcelain, clothing, and tinware.

kagu A bird, *Rhynochetus jubata*, making up the family Rhynochetidae, found only in the forests of the Pacific island New Caledonia. It is related to the cranes and rails, and resembles a squat heron, standing about 60 cm (2 feet) high with long legs and beak. It is pale grey, speckled with brown, and has a loose crest.

Kahn, Louis (1901–74) Estonian-born US architect, based mainly in Philadelphia, where he studied and taught at the University of Pennsylvania (he was appointed professor of architecture in 1955). From the 1950s he came to prominence with a series of buildings, many for universities and educational institutions, in which he moved beyond the smooth elegance of the MODERN MOVEMENT to a style that, while still strongly geometrical, was more bold and rugged. The Yale University Art Gallery (1951–53) and the Kimbell Art Musuem, Fort Worth, Texas (1966–72), are among his best-known works. He had wide influence through his writing and teaching as well as his buildings.

Kaifeng An ancient city in Henan province, eastern China, to the east of Zhengzhou and south of the Yellow River; pop. (1990) 693,100. Established in the 4th century BC, it is one of the oldest cities in China and, from 907 to 960, as Pien Ling, its capital under the Sung dynasty. It has developed into an industrial city producing agricultural machinery, chemicals, electrical goods, and silk.

Kaiser, Georg (1878–1945) German Expressionist dramatist. Author of some 60 plays, he is best known for his expressionist plays *The Burghers of Calais* (1914), and *Gas I* (1918) and *Gas II* (1920); the last two provide a gruesome interpretation of futuristic science ending with the extinction of all life by poisonous gas.

Kaiser Wilhelm See WILHELM II.

Kalahari An arid plateau, largely desert, some 900–1,200 m (3,000–4,000 feet) high between the Zambezi and Orange rivers in southern Africa; it forms the western part of Botswana. With annual rainfall varying between 130 mm (5 inches) in the south-west and 500 mm (20 inches) in the north-east, the only perennial river is the Okavango, which flows from the north into the swampy Okavango Basin north of Lake Ngami. The plateau is covered mainly by reddish sand and the vegetation comprises dry grass, scattered acacias, and thin thorn-scrub. In the south is the Kalahari Game Reserve.

kale See CABBAGE.

Kalgoorlie A gold-mining town at the western end of the Nullarbor Plain in Western Australia; pop. (1991) 25,010 (with Boulder). Gold was first discovered here in 1887 and it was a centre of the Coolgardie gold-rush in the 1890s.

Kali (Hindi, 'the Black One') Another name for the Great Goddess SHAKTI or DEVI, the consort of SHIVA, who is worshipped independently of him. Kali represents destructive, primal energy, and is associated with disease and death. She is often depicted as a fearsome and bloody figure bearing weapons.

Kalidasa Indian poet and dramatist. He is best known for his drama *Sakuntala*, the love story of King Dushyanta and the maiden Sakuntala. Kalidasa probably lived in the 5th century AD, although there is some diversity of opinion on this point.

kalimba See SANSA.

Kalinin, Mikhail Ivanovich (1875–1946) Soviet statesman, head of state of the USSR 1919–46. Born in Russia, he was a founder of the newspaper *Pravda* in 1912.

Kaliningrad Capital of the Russian region of Kaliningrad, an industrial seaport on the Baltic coast; pop. (1990) 406,000. It was founded in the 13th century and in the 15th century became the capital of East Prussia. It was known by its German name of Königsberg until 1945, when it was ceded to the Soviet Union under the Potsdam Agreement and renamed in honour of President Kalinin. Its port is ice-free all the year and is a significant base for the Russian fleet. It is also a major fishing port with shipbuilding and machinery industries.

Kalmar, Union of (1397) The joining together of the crowns of Denmark, Sweden, and Norway. Margaret I (1353–1412), daughter of the King of Denmark and wife of Haakon VI of Norway (died 1387), defeated (1389) the King of Sweden and persuaded the Diets of Denmark, Norway, and Sweden to accept Eric of Pomerania, her grandnephew, as king. He was crowned (1397), the beginning of the Union of Kalmar, though Margaret herself ruled the three kingdoms until her death. The union was dissolved by Gustavus I of Sweden in 1523.

Kalmykia (official name **The Republic of Kalmykia-Khalmg Tangch**) A republic in the Russian Federation, on the Caspian Sea south of the Volga; area 75,900 sq km (29,300 sq miles); pop. (1990) 325,000; capital, Elista. Declared an independent republic on the breakup of the Soviet Union in 1991, over 45 per cent of its people are Kalmyks, who migrated from western China to the Russian steppe in the 17th century.

Kaluga An industrial city and river port in western Russia, on the River Oka south-west of Moscow; pop. (1990) 314,000. It produces iron and steel and railway equipment.

Kamakura A resort and residential town on the coast of Honshu Island, Japan, at the head of the Miura-hanto peninsula to the south of Tokyo; pop. (1990) 174,300. Capital of Japan from 1192 to 1333, its most famous landmark is the great bronze figure of Buddha, the Kamakura Daibutsu, which was cast in 1252. The city gives its name to a period of Japanese history characterized by the establishment of the first feudal military shogunate based at Kamakura.

Kamchatka A vast mountainous peninsula of the north-east coast of East Siberia in the Russian Federation, separating the Sea of Okhotsk from the Bering Sea; chief port Petropavlovsk-Kamchatskiy. It is a volcanically active zone containing 22 active volcanoes and many hot springs.

Kamchatka Current A continuation of the Aleutian or Subarctic Current, flowing south-westward along the shores of the Kamchatka Peninsula and eventually bringing cold water into the North Pacific Ocean. Much of its water is derived from melting of the polar ice; icebergs that have broken off the Arctic ice mass are often carried south by this current.

kame A short ridge or mound of stratified sands and gravels that have been deposited by glacial meltwater. **Kame terraces** are formed by meltwater deposits laid down between the side of a decaying glacier and a valley wall.

Kamerlingh Onnes, Heike (1853–1926) Dutch physicist, who studied cryogenic phenomena. Using the Joule–Thomson effect he succeeded in liquefying helium in 1908, and achieved a temperature of less than one degree above absolute zero. Onnes discovered the phenomenon of superconductivity in 1911, and was awarded the Nobel Prize for physics in 1913.

kami In Shinto, the sacred being(s) who are worshipped as gods. These include the Sun goddess Amaterasu and other spirits, illustrious ancestors, and forces of nature, both good and evil. Animate and inanimate phenomena, such as rocks, plants, birds, animals, and fish, may all be treated as kami. There are believed to be an infinite number of kami. Humans, especially those with special talents, may be considered to be kami in their own right. Kami are a source of power and benefit that enrich human life.

kamikaze (Japanese, 'Divine Wind') Originally the fierce storms that twice saved Japan from Mongol invasion (in 1274 and 1281). In World War II a kamikaze was an aircraft laden with explosives and suicidally crashed by the pilot into an enemy ship. The Japanese naval command resorted to these desperate measures in 1944 in an attempt to halt the Allied advance across the Pacific. At first volunteers were used, but the practice soon became compulsory. Off OKINAWA in 1945 over 300 kamikaze pilots died in one action.

Kampala The capital of Uganda; pop. (1991) 773,460. It is situated on the northern shores of Lake Victoria (Victoria Nyanza), and replaced Entebbe as capital when the country became independent in 1963. It was originally the site of a royal palace and is built on a number of hills.

Kampuchea See CAMBODIA.

Kanagawa, Treaty of (or **Perry Convention**) (31 March 1854) A treaty between Japan and the USA. After three years of negotiation, the US Commodore Perry came to an agreement with the Tokugawa SHOGUNATE, opening two ports to US vessels, allowing the appointment of a consul, and guaranteeing better treatment for shipwrecked sailors. The Treaty of Kanagawa was followed within two years by similar agreements with Britain, Russia, and the Netherlands, and in 1858 by the more wide-ranging Treaty of EDO with the USA, and marked the beginning of regular political and economic intercourse between Japan and the Western nations.

Kanaka A native Hawaiian, or more generally any Pacific Islander. Kanakas, mainly from the New Hebrides and the Solomon Islands, were brought to Australia between 1863 and 1904 as cheap labour. Theoretically, they voluntarily entered contracts for fixed terms. In practice, they were subjected to kidnap, slavery, and murder. Their entry to Australia was banned in 1904. Most of those in Australia were deported back to the islands from 1906 onwards, as part of the White Australia Policy.

Kanchenjunga (or **Kangchenjunga**, **Kinchinjunga**) A mountain in the Himalayas on the border between Nepal and Sikkim. Rising to 8,598 m (28,209 ft), it is the world's third-highest mountain. Its summit is split into five separate peaks, whence its name, which in Tibetan means 'the five treasures of the snows'. It was first climbed in 1955 by a British expedition led by Charles Evans.

Kandahar (or **Qandahar**) A city in southern Afghanistan, capital of the province of Kandahar; pop. (est. 1988) 225,500. It was the first capital of Afghanistan after it became independent, from 1748 until replaced by Kabul in 1773. It is a wool, grain, and tobacco trading centre of the Pashtun people.

Kandinsky, Wassily (1866–1944) Russian painter and theorist. He was a pioneer of abstract art, producing non-representational works as early as 1910. His treatise *On the Spiritual in Art* (1912) urged the expression of inner and essential feelings in art rather than the representation of the natural world. In 1911 he co-founded the Munich-based *Blaue Reiter* group of artists; he later taught at the Bauhaus (1922–33).

Kandy ▶**1** A resort and sacred city in the highlands of central Sri Lanka; pop. (1990) 104,000. Originally known as Senkadagala, it became an important centre of Buddhist political power in the 15th century. Since 1542 it has been the home of the Buddha's Tooth which is paraded through the streets each July–August during the 15-day festival of Esala Perahera, Sri Lanka's greatest festival. ▶**2** A former independent kingdom in Ceylon. The city of Kandy was its capital from 1480 to 1815.

Kanem-Bornu Two successive major African states in the Lake Chad region between the 11th and the 19th centuries. Ethnically and linguistically the peoples were mixed. They include Arab, Berber, and other African elements, and were mostly Muslims. An Islamic sultanate of Kanem, ruled by the Seyfawa family, existed by the 11th century, which, under Dunama (1221–59), came to extend from Fezzan and Wadai to the Niger, and included Bornu. Following civil wars this empire collapsed in 1398, but a member of it created a new state of Bornu with N'gazargamu as capital, and Kanem as a province. Idris Aloma (ruled 1571–1603) was the most powerful of the Bornu rulers; he introduced firearms into the army and Bornu reached the peak of its power under his rule. A long period of stability followed until 1808, when the FULANI sacked N'gazargamu. Muhammad al-Kanemi, a leading chief, restored the titular kings, retaining effective power himself. The last Mai, or titular king, was executed in 1846.

kangaroo A member of a family of 50 species of big-footed MARSUPIALS, Macropodidae, which also include WALLABIES. The red kangaroo, *Macropus rufus*, and the grey kangaroo, *M. giganteus*, may reach a weight of 90 kg (200 pounds) and a height of 1.8 m (6 feet) or more. The large, heavily built, muscular hindquarters and tail balance the small, lightly built, mobile forequarters. The fore-limbs are held clear of the ground during bipedal locomotion, and while collecting and eating food. For such large animals they move easily, with leaps of 8 m (26 feet) in length. The teeth and digestive system are adapted for a herbivorous diet. It does not chew the cud but the food is regurgitated and swallowed again.

Like all marsupials, the kangaroo has a pouch into which the minute young, or joey, crawls immediately after it is born. The joey remains in the pouch for some 190 days before it leaves for short periods. A second offspring may be born while the larger young is still suckling; and the mother produces two milks vastly different in composition to satisfy their different needs.

kangaroo rat A desert RODENT of North America; the 22 species fill a niche occupied by the jerboas in the Old World. Like them, they live in burrows during the day and emerge at night to feed on plant material and insects. They hop on their very long hind-legs after the manner of kangaroos. They are part of the POCKET MICE family, Heteromyidae.

KaNgwane A former self-governing state of the Swazi people established in eastern Transvaal in 1971. Its capital was Nyamasane. It is now part of Mpumalanga.

Kangxi (or **K'ang-hsi**) (1654–1722) The second QING emperor of China (1662–1722). He extended the Qing empire by a series of military campaigns, subduing opposition to Manchu rule in southern

China (1673–81), incorporating TAIWAN into China for the first time in 1683, and personally leading a campaign into Outer MONGOLIA (1693). He opened certain ports to overseas traders and the Treaty of Nerchinsk (1689), established diplomatic contact with Russia. In 1692 he permitted Catholic missionaries to make converts and he employed JESUITS to teach astronomy and mathematics. He was renowned for his history of the Ming dynasty and an encyclopedia of literature.

Kang Youwei (or **K'ang Yu-wei**) (1858–1927) Chinese philosopher and political reformer. A scholar, whose utopian work *Da Tong Shu* (*One World Philosophy*, 1900) portrayed Confucius as a reformer, he believed that China's crisis could only be solved through the modernization of institutions along modified western lines. In 1898 he persuaded the emperor Guangxu to adopt his policies. The resulting Hundred Days Reform was brought to a premature end by the empress dowager CIXI's conservative coup, and Kang spent the next 15 years in exile. He remained a monarchist and spent his last years trying unsuccessfully to engineer an imperial restoration.

kanji Japanese writing using Chinese characters.

Kannon In Buddhism, the Japanese name for the *bodhisattva* (Buddha-to-be') Avalokitesvara, a manifestation of Amitabha. In Japan, Kannon, usually represented as female, is the most popular Buddhist figure, widely venerated for her mercy and compassion. She is believed to assume diverse forms, one of which is a four-handed figure with 11 heads.

Kano The chief city of northern Nigeria, capital of Kano state, and Nigeria's third city; pop. (est. 1986) 553,100. Originally a Hausa settlement, it was captured by the Fulani in the 19th century and developed as the terminus of a trans-Saharan trade route. It is a major commercial and industrial city, particularly famous for its leather work and its great market, and is in addition a Muslim educational and religious centre. Tourism is also important.

Kanpur (formerly **Cawnpore**) A city in Uttar Pradesh, northern India, on the River Ganges; pop. (1991) 2,111,280. An important garrison town under British rule, it was the site of a massacre of British soldiers and European families in July 1857, during the Indian Mutiny. Kanpur is now a major industrial city with sugar, vegetable oil, textile, leather, aviation, and chemical industries.

Kansas A state in the Middle West of the USA, between the Missouri River and the Rocky Mountains; area 213,098 sq km (82,277 sq miles); pop. (1990) 2,477,570; capital, Topeka. The largest cities are Wichita, Kansas City, Topeka, and Overland Park. Kansas is also known as the Sunflower State or the Jayhawk State. Ceded to Spain by France in 1763, the territory reverted back to France in 1800 before being sold to the USA as part of the Louisiana Purchase in 1803. It was organized as a territory in 1854 and became the 34th state of the Union in 1861. Early settlements such as Fort Larned, Fort Scott, and Dodge City were designed to protect westbound travellers on the Oregon and Santa Fe trails. Grain, cattle, and vegetables are important products of the state which also produces oil, coal, zinc, lead, salt, and the country's largest quantities of helium. Its chief landmarks are the 'cowboy capital' Dodge City and the historic frontier posts at Fort Scott and Fort Larned.

Kansas City Either of two adjacent cities with the same name situated at the junction of the Missouri and Kansas rivers, one in north-east Kansas (1990 pop. 149,770) and the other in north-west Missouri (1990 pop. 435,150). Kansas City (Kansas) is an amalgamation of eight separate towns, the oldest of which, Wyandot City, was settled in 1843 by the Wyandot Indians. Now an industrial railway centre, it produces steel, vehicles, grain, and soap. Kansas City (Missouri) is a major industrial and distribution centre, trading in grain and livestock and producing refined petroleum, steel, vehicles, and processed food. It was laid out in 1838 as the easternmost outfitting post on the Santa Fe Trail.

Kant, Immanuel (1724–1804) German Idealist philosopher. In the *Critique of Pure Reason* (1781) he countered Hume's empiricism by arguing that the human mind can neither confirm, deny, nor scientifically demonstrate the ultimate nature of reality. He claimed, however, that it can know the objects of experience, which it interprets with notions of space and time and orders according to 12 categories of thought, grouped under the classes of quantity, quality, reason, and modality. Kant's *Critique of Practical Reason* (1788) deals with ethics and affirms the existence of an absolute moral law – the categorical imperative – whose motivation is reason.

kantele A musical instrument, a Finnish ZITHER, originally carved from solid wood but now usually built up from slats. In the 19th century and earlier the kantele had only five strings, but more have been added recently. It is played with a plectrum or the fingers. Similar instruments are called *kannel* in Estonia, *kokle* in Latvia, *kanklės* in Lithuania, and *gusli* in Russia; early examples have been found in Gdańsk and Novgorod.

Kanto A region of Japan on the island of Honshu; area 32,309 sq km (12,479 sq miles); pop. (1990) 38,541,000; chief city, Tokyo.

Kaohsiung The chief port of Taiwan, situated on the south-west coast of the island; pop. (1990) 1,390,000. It has dry-dock, container-handling, and shipbreaking facilities.

kaolin See CHINA CLAY.

kaolinite See CHINA CLAY.

Kapachira Falls A series of rapids on the Shire River in the Majete Game Reserve to the west of Blantyre in southern Malawi, formerly known as the Murchison Falls or Murchison Rapids.

Kapil Dev (Nikhanj) (1959–) Indian cricketer. He made his début for India in 1978 as a medium-pace bowler, soon developing into an all-rounder. He had two spells as captain, in one of which he led India to victory in the 1983 World Cup. In 1994 he passed Richard Hadlee's world record of 431 test match wickets.

kapok A fine fluffy material that surrounds the seeds of various tropical trees. The main commercial sources are the trees *Ceiba pentandra* and *Bombax ceiba*, both members of the tropical rain forest family, Bombacaceae, including balsa, baobab, and durian trees. The main centres for commercial plantation are Asian countries such as Thailand. The fruit capsules of these trees enclose wax-coated fibres up to 3 cm (1.25 inches) long, which are believed to aid seed or fruit dispersal by water. This floss is very buoyant and light (eight times as light as cotton) and is used to fill lifejackets and cushions, and for insulation.

Kapoor, (Prithvi) Raj (1924–88) Indian actor and director. In 1944 he founded the Prithvi Theatres in Bombay, a company notable for the realism it brought to Hindi drama. Kapoor went on to direct a large number of films for the Indian market. Productions, in which Kapoor often played the lead, include *Pathan* (1946).

Kapteyn, Jacobus Cornelius (1851–1922) Dutch astronomer who founded the Groningen Astronomical Laboratory. At this laboratory he undertook the analysis of photographic plates of the southern sky and produced the *Cape Photographic Durchmusterung*, a catalogue of 450,000 stars. By using statistical sampling he was able to describe the structure of the Galaxy by measuring the PARALLAX, MAGNITUDE, and proper motion of stars in small selected areas of the sky. Although Kapteyn's methods were sound, he made two erroneous assumptions. He neglected interstellar absorption and therefore underestimated the size of the Galaxy; also he assumed incorrectly that the Sun was near the centre of the Galaxy.

karaburan A strong, warm, north-easterly wind that blows over central Asia often carrying large amounts of fine-grained soil which is deposited as loess.

Karachay-Cherkessia (official name **The Karachay-Cherkess Republic**) A republic of the Russian Federation in the northern Caucasus; area 14,100 sq km (5,442 sq miles); pop. (1995) 436,000; capital, Cherkessk. An autonomous Karachai republic existed until 1943 after which Stalin deported many of its ethnic Muslim Karachai population. After the breakup of the Soviet Union it was declared a republic of the Russian Federation in 1992.

Karachi A major industrial, commercial, and financial city and port in Pakistan, capital of Sind province; pop. (est. 1991) 6,700,000. Situated on the Arabian Sea near the mouth of the Indus River, it was capital of Pakistan 1947–59, before being replaced by Islamabad. Karachi has heavy industries including automobile assembly, oil refining, steel, shipbuilding, as well as textile, printing, food-processing, chemical, and engineering industries.

Karadžić, Radovan (1945–) Serbian political leader. He practised psychiatry in Sarajevo until 1990, when he helped found the Serbian Democratic Party. In 1992, when the Bosnian Serbs declared an independent state, the Republika Srpska, within BOSNIA-HERCEGOVINA, Karadžić became its president. With the support of Serbian president Slobodan Milošević, he instituted a ruthless campaign (1992–95) to drive non-Serb Bosnians from the republic. In 1995, when Milošević withdrew support, Karadžić reluctantly signed the US-brokered Dayton peace accord. Twice that year he was indicted by the UN for war crimes, including 'ethnic cleansing'. He resigned as president of both the Republika Srpska and the Serbian Democratic Party in 1996, but remains influential.

Karadžić, Vuk Stefanović (1787–1864) Serbian writer, grammarian, lexicographer, and folklorist. He modified the Cyrillic alphabet for Serbian written usage and compiled a Serbian dictionary in 1818. Widely claimed to be the father of modern Serbian literature, he undertook the task of collecting and publishing national folk stories and poems (1821–33).

Karaite A Jewish sect chiefly in the Crimea, founded in the 8th century, rejecting rabbinical tradition and basing its tenets on a literal interpretation of the Scriptures.

Karajan, Herbert von (1908–89) Austrian conductor. He is chiefly remembered as the principal conductor of the Berlin Philharmonic Orchestra (1955–89), although he was also associated with the Vienna State Opera (1957–64). Karajan was artistic director of the Salzburg Festival (1956–60; 1964) and founded the Salzburg Easter Festival of operas in 1967.

Karakalpakstan An autonomous region of western Uzbekistan, Central Asia, on the lower Amu Darya (Oxus River); area 164,900 sq km (63,920 sq miles); pop. (1990) 1,244,700; capital, Nukus. Absorbed into the Russian empire in the late 19th century, it became an autonomous region of Kazakhstan in 1925, and an Autonomous Soviet Republic within Uzbekistan in 1936. It is a largely agricultural region producing cattle, sheep, goats, and wine.

Karakoram A great chain of mountains in central Asia, stretching for about 480 km (300 miles) between the Pamirs and the Himalayas and standing mainly in Kashmir. In the centre is K2; some 60 other peaks rise to over 6,700 m (22,000 feet), and the only passes are in regions of perpetual snow. The Karakoram Pass at 5,800 m (19,000 feet) is the old route between Kashmir and Xinjiang, while the slightly lower Khunjerab Pass now carries the **Karakoram Highway**, opened in 1978 to connect China and Pakistan.

Karakorum The ruins of a city in central Mongolia, which was the ancient capital of the Mongol empire, established by Genghis Khan in 1220. The capital was later moved by Kublai Khan to Khanbaliq (modern Beijing) in 1267, and Karakorum was destroyed by Chinese forces in 1388.

Kara Kul A lake in north-eastern Tajikistan, lying at an altitude of 3,960 m (13,000 ft) on a plateau between the Pamirs and the Altai Mts.; area 310 sq km (120 sq miles). It gives its name to Karakul sheep, which are bred in the low-lying regions of central Asia for their astrakhan wool.

karate See MARTIAL ARTS.

Karelia A region on the frontier of Finland and Russia, which formed an independent Finnish state in medieval times and whose folk-tales were the source of the Finnish epic, the *Kalevala*. In the 16th century Karelia came under Swedish rule and in 1721 it was annexed by Russia. Following Finland's declaration of independence in 1917, part of Karelia became a region of Finland and part was subsequently designated an autonomous republic of the Soviet Union. After the Russian–Finnish War of 1939–40 the greater part of Finnish Karelia was ceded to the Soviet Union.

Karelia, Republic of A republic of the Russian Federation; area 172,400 sq km (66,589 sq miles); pop. (1989) 792,000; capital, Petrozavodsk. Formerly known as Olonets Province, it was designated an autonomous republic of the Russian Soviet Federal Socialist Republic in 1923. With the addition of Finnish territory after World War II, it became the Karelo-Finnish Soviet Socialist Republic, but in 1956 it reverted to autonomous republic status. With the breakup of the Soviet Union in 1991, it declared itself the Republic of Karelia.

Karen A group of non-Burmese Mongoloid tribes, most of whom live in the Karen or Kawthoolay State in east Myanmar (Burma) on the frontier with Thailand, where they have declared themselves independent of the government of Myanmar. Their language is of the Sino-Tibetan family and their name is derived from the Burmese word *kareng* ('dirty, low-caste man').

Kariba A man-made lake, created by the damming of the Zambezi River between 1955 and 1959. Before flooding took place the settlements of the Tonga people were relocated and wild animals were moved to higher ground, rescued from drowning by Operation Noah. Drawing water from a catchment area of 663,000 sq km (256,083 sq miles), it forms a reservoir with a capacity of 180,600 million cubic metres at maximum operating level. It also forms the Lake Kariba Recreational Park with an area of 5,200 sq km (2,008 sq miles).

Karloff, Boris (born William Henry Pratt) (1887–1969) British-born US actor. His name is chiefly linked with horror films, such as *Frankenstein* (1931) and *The Body Snatcher* (1945).

Karlovy Vary (German **Carlsbad** or **Karlsbad**) A spa town in the West Bohemia region of the Czech Republic, at the junction of the Tepla and Ohre rivers; pop. (1991) 56,290. Famous for its alkaline thermal springs, it was founded in the 14th century by the Bohemian king and Holy Roman emperor Charles IV. It is also known for its ceramic and glass industries.

Karlskrona A Baltic seaport and capital of the province of Belkinge, southern Sweden, at the entrance to the Kalmar Sound; pop. (1990) 59,050. Founded in 1680 by Charles XI as a headquarters for the Swedish fleet, it became Sweden's second-largest town in the 18th century. After years of decline it developed industries that include fish processing, shipbuilding, and the manufacture of electrical goods.

Karlsruhe An industrial town and port on the Rhine in the state of Baden-Württemberg, western Germany; pop. (1991) 278,580. Capital of the former German state of Baden, it is now a centre for oil refining, engineering, and the production of chemicals, textiles, and rubber goods.

Karlstad An industrial town in central Sweden, on the north shore of Lake Vänern; pop. (1990) 76,470. Named after Charles IX who granted its municipal charter in 1584, it manufactures wooden products, chemicals, and textiles.

Karl XII See CHARLES XII.

karma (Sanskrit, 'deed') Central moral concept within Indian religion, denoting the underlying moral law of cause and effect, which generates the process of birth, death, and rebirth (SAMSARA) until liberation. In HINDUISM, karma binds the soul to rebirth; it refers to single thoughts or deeds, their consequences, and the sum of all consequences, which determine one's condition and disposition in a future life. Karmic release is achieved by surrender to the will of God, acting righteously, and thus building up good karma. BUDDHISM rejects the continuity of the 'soul' through various lives, but it admits a causal connection between them. The intention behind a deed, whether good or bad, is the factor that determines individual spiritual destiny. Release from rebirth depends on knowledge of the Real. This knowledge, in turn, permits action that is without hate, desire, or delusion, and which is therefore karmically neutral. Karma dictates the situation into which one is born, it does not affect the manner in which one may choose to act.

Karnak The religious centre of ancient THEBES, situated on the east bank of the Nile, where the great temple of Amun was constructed. This complex of buildings, the work of some 2,000 years, includes the Hypostyle Hall with 134 columns each *c.*24 m (79 ft) high. It was begun by Ramesses I and completed by Seti I and RAMSES II. A road lined with statues of sphinxes linked the site to nearby Luxor.

Karnataka A state in south-west India that was known as Mysore until 1973; area 191,791 sq km (74,079 sq miles); pop. (1991) 44,817,400; capital, Bangalore. It is a largely agricultural state producing coffee, ragi, groundnuts, cotton, and rice.

Karoo (or **Karroo**) An elevated semi-desert plateau in Cape Province, South Africa, between the Orange River and the Cape of Good Hope, which provides grazing land for sheep and, when irrigated, fertile farm land. It is divided into the **Upper Karoo**, the **Great Karoo**, and the **Little Karoo**. The Karoo National Park, in the Great Karoo near Beaufort West, was established in 1979.

Karpov, Anatoli (1951–) Russian chess player. He was world champion from 1975 until defeated by Gary Kasparov in 1985.

karren (or **lapiés**) A small, often intricate channel on the bare surface of hard limestone. Different names are given to different shapes and sizes of karren. Those that are quite shallow, but have very sharp ridges between the channels, are called rillenkarren. These are formed by the action of rainwater, seawater or melting snow dissolving the calcium carbonate in the limestone when it is exposed on the surface, especially if there is a steep slope that allows the water to run off rapidly. Larger, more rounded flutings are called rinnenkarren. These often form under a layer of soil, where the limestone is attacked more slowly and deeply by percolating water carrying dissolved acids from the soil. When rinnenkarren are exposed to the atmosphere, rillenkarren can develop on their slopes.

Karsh, Yousef (1908–) Canadian portrait photographer. Born in Armenia, Karsh learned photography in Boston, Massachusetts, from John Garo. His magnificent portrait of Winston Churchill appeared on a *Life* magazine cover in December 1941. It was the beginning of Karsh's international reputation as the greatest modern photographer of masculine heroes.

Karst (Slovenian **Kras**) An arid limestone region near Trieste in Slovenia noted for its caves, geological formations, and erosional features. It lends its name to similar limestone regions in other parts of the world.

Kasavubu, Joseph (1910–69) Congolese statesman. He became the first President (1960–65) of the Democratic Republic of Congo (called Zaïre from 1971 to 1997). He was a member of undercover nationalist associations to free the Congo of the Belgians. In 1955 he became President of Abako (Alliance des Bakongo), a cultural association of the Bakongo tribe, and turned it into a powerful political organization. On independence in 1960 he became Head of State. His Abako party formed a coalition with LUMUMBA's party, and then ousted him as premier. In 1965 he himself was deposed from the Presidency by MOBUTU in a bloodless military coup.

Kashgar (or **Kaxgar**, **Kashi**) The chief commercial centre of western Xinjiang autonomous region, China, and chief city of Chinese Turkestan, on the Kashgar River; pop. (1986) 202,000.

Kashgaria An alternative name for Chinese Turkestan, a region of western Xinjiang autonomous region in north-west China.

Kashmir A former state on the border of India, since 1947 disputed between India and Pakistan. The state, exposed successively to Hindu and Muslim rule, was annexed (1819) to the expanding Sikh kingdom. After the first SIKH WAR the territory was acquired by Gulab Singh, then Hindu raja of the Jammu region. It was a Princely State for the rest of the British period. The Maharaja, a Hindu ruling over a predominantly Muslim population, initially hoped to remain independent in 1947, but eventually acceded to the Indian Union. War between India and Pakistan (1948–49) over Kashmir ended when a United Nations peace-keeping force imposed a temporary cease-fire line which divided the Indian Union state of Jammu and Kashmir from Pakistan-backed Azad Kashmir. Kashmir remains divided by this line. Conflicts between India and Pakistan over Kashmir flared up again in 1965 and 1971, together with demands for a UN-supervised plebiscite. In 1989 militant supporters of either Kashmiri independence or union with Pakistan intensified their campaign of violent civil unrest and Indian government troops were sent into the state. Direct rule by the President was imposed in 1990 and fighting has continued.

Kasparov, Gary (born Gary Weinstein) (1963–) Azerbaijani chess player, of Armenian Jewish descent. At the age of 22 he became the youngest-ever world champion, defeating Anatoli KARPOV in 1985. He has retained the title ever since, defending it against challenges from Karpov in 1986, 1987, and 1990. In 1996 he took on IBM's Deep Blue computer, and defeated it 4–2.

Kassel An industrial city in the state of Hesse, central Germany, on the River Fulda; pop. (1991) 196,830. Founded *c.*913, it was the capital of the kingdom of Westphalia (1807–13) and of the Prussian province of Hesse-Nassau (1866–1944). It produces textiles, vehicles, machinery, and optical equipment.

Kassites See BABYLON.

katabatic wind A light, local wind generated when a sloping ground surface cools during the night. The air in contact with the ground is cooled by radiation, increases in density, and flows downhill and along the valley bottom. See also ANABATIC WIND.

Katanga The former name (until 1972) of the south-eastern mining region of the former Belgian Congo that now constitutes the southern province of Shaba in the Democratic Republic of Congo.

kathak A major classical dance form from northern India, performed by men and women for entertainment or religious functions. It developed from the 15th to the 18th centuries and was elaborated by connection with north Indian classical music and dance-dramas expressing moods of love and devotion to Krishna. The feet, which have about 100 tiny bells attached to them, execute intricate rhythmic patterns at high speed, the rest of the body remaining motionless, and sequences of rapid pirouettes are assisted by the flowing skirts of the costume. Musical accompaniment is provided by drums, sarangi (a bowed string instrument), and a singer.

kathakali A form of Indian classical dance originating in the 17th century in Kerala, in the extreme south. Kathakali relates stories from the RAMAYANA and other religious texts through dance-drama, accompanied by singing and by instrumental music with an emphasis on percussion. Most characters wear towering headgear, billowing skirts, and elaborate make-up in which different characters are represented by different facial colours. Performances generally take place at night and in the open air. Traditionally the roles are played by men.

Kathmandu The capital of Nepal, situated at the confluence of the Bagmati and Bishnumati rivers in the Himalayas at *c.*1,370 m (4,500 ft); pop. (1991) 419,000. Founded in 723 AD by the Licchavi king Gunakamadeva, it once stood at the junction of important trade routes. The Singha Durbar palace (built in 1901) was once the largest building in Asia. The first surfaced road reached Kathmandu in 1956 and subsequently the city developed as the centre of the country's tourist industry.

Katowice A city in south-west Poland, the industrial centre of the Upper Silesian coal-mining region; pop. (1990) 349,360. It is capital of a province of the same name.

Kattegat A strait, 225 km (140 miles) in length, between Sweden and Denmark. It is linked to the North Sea by the Skagerrak and to the Baltic Sea by the Øresund, and was once of considerable strategic importance. Its name means 'cat's throat'.

katydid See LONGHORN GRASSHOPPER.

Katyn massacre A massacre in Katyn forest in the western USSR. In 1943 the German army claimed to have discovered a mass grave of some 4,500 Polish officers, part of a group of 15,000 Poles who had disappeared from Soviet captivity in 1940 and whose fate remained unknown. Each victim had a bullet in the base of his skull. The Soviet Union denied involvement in the massacre until April 1990, when it was confirmed that the officers had been killed in the early days of close Nazi-Soviet collaboration, by order of Stalin. The incident resulted in a breach between the exiled Polish government of General SIKORSKI in London and the Soviet Union and led to the agreement at Teheran (1943) that the post-war Polish-Soviet border should revert to the so-called Curzon Line (1920).

Katz, Sir Bernard (1911–) British biophysicist, born in Germany, whose work on the mechanism by which signals are transmitted in the nervous system won him a share in the Nobel Prize for physiology and medicine in 1970.

Kauffmann, Angelica (1741–1807) Swiss painter. Having formed her style in Rome, she lived from 1766 to 1781 in London, where she enjoyed great professional and personal success. In 1768 she became a founder member of the Royal Academy, and was a close friend of its President, Sir Joshua REYNOLDS. She worked initially as a portraitist, but then devoted herself more to historical scenes and to decorative work for Robert ADAM and other architects. She married the decorative painter Antonio Zucchi in 1781 and returned to Rome, where she continued her successful career.

Kaunda, Kenneth (David) (1924–) Zambian statesman, President 1964–91. He led the United National Independence Party to electoral victory in 1964, becoming Prime Minister and the first President of independent Zambia. As chairman of the Organization of African Unity (1970–71; 1987–88) he played a key role in the negotiations leading to Namibian independence in 1990.

kauri pine A broad-leaved conifer of the genus *Agathis*, found in south-east Asia and Australasia. About 17 species are known. The New Zealand kauri pine, *A. australis*, reaches 46 m (150 feet) in height and yields valuable timber, while the klinki pine, *A. husteinii*, is a source of plywood. All species yield a resin, and copal or dammar from the Malaysian *A. alba* is a commercial product.

Kaválla A port on the Aegean coast of north-east Greece, the second-largest city of Macedonia; pop. (1991) 56,520. Originally a Byzantine city and fortress controlling Macedonia, it was Turkish until 1912, when it was ceded to Greece. Now a centre of the tobacco and cotton trade, it occupies the site of Neapolis, the port of ancient Philippi. It was a port of arrival and departure on the journey between Europe and the Levant, and was the birthplace in 1769 of Mehmet Ali who later became pasha of Egypt.

Kawabata, Yasunari (1899–1972) Japanese novelist. Known as an experimental writer in the 1920s, he reverted to traditional Japanese novel forms in the mid-1930s. His novels include *The Izu Dancer* (1925), *Snow Country* (1935–47), and *The Sound of the Mountain* (1949–54). He won the Nobel Prize for literature in 1968, the first Japanese writer to do so.

Kawasaki A major industrial city on the south-east coast of Honshu Island, Japan, situated north-west of Tokyo; pop. (1990) 1,174,000. It is the capital of Kanagawa prefecture in Kanto Region and has steel mills, oil refineries, electrical, and engineering works.

Kay, John (1704–*c*.1764) British inventor of textile-weaving machinery. As a young man, he set up as a clock-maker in Lancashire, the centre of the cotton-weaving industry, and assisted ARKWRIGHT. His interest in mechanical devices led him to invent the flying shuttle (1733), which greatly increased the speed of weaving and the width of the woven cloth. His machinery was attacked by angry weavers who feared unemployment, and he retired to France in 1741, introducing his shuttle there.

Kaye, Danny (born David Daniel Kominski) (1913–87) US actor and comedian. After a successful Broadway career he made his first feature film in 1944, and went on to take a number of roles in which he became known for his mimicry, comic songs, and slapstick humour. His films include *The Secret Life of Walter Mitty* (1947), *Hans Christian Andersen* (1952), and *The Court Jester* (1956).

Kazakh A people of central Asia known as Kirgiz until 1925 and comprising an ethnic mixture of Turkish and Mongol tribes who speak a Turkic language. Traditionally clan-based nomadic herders, they practise a religion that combines Islam and shamanistic beliefs.

Kazakhstan A country of western central Asia, stretching for some 3,200 km (2,000 miles) from the Caspian Sea to Xinjiang. It is bounded by China on the east, Kyrgyzstan and Uzbekistan on the south, the Caspian Sea and Turkmenistan on the west, and Russia on the north.

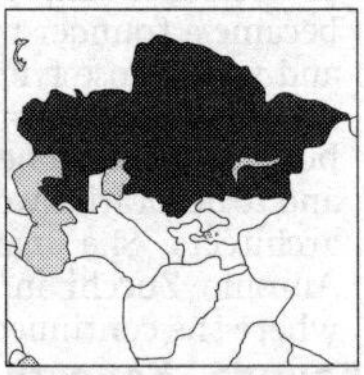

Physical. In the north a belt of fertile steppe with rich, black earth (chernozem) provides scope for cultivation. Southward, however, it becomes more arid, degenerating into the Kara-Kum desert. On the east Caspian coast, oil and natural gas are found. Further east, towards the Aral Sea, is a clay desert plateau; east and south-east of it, sand desert. To the east of this are the stony Kazakh uplands with huge coal deposits in their northern slopes and copper in their southern ones. Here is the extensive and partly saline Lake Balkhash, which is slowly evaporating.

Economy. Kazakhstan has rich and varied mineral deposits, including tungsten, copper, lead, uranium, diamonds, coal, iron ore, natural gas, and petroleum. Industry is largely based on the exploitation of these reserves. There is also some light and manufacturing industry. Grain production and sheep-rearing dominate agriculture.

History. For centuries, the steppelands of Kazakhstan were the home of nomadic Kazakh herdsmen, ruled by Mongol khans, whose territories were steadily annexed by Tsarist Russia during the 19th century, the KHANATE being abolished in 1848. A nationalist movement developed in the early 20th century and there was a bloody anti-Tsarist revolt in 1916. In 1917 a national government was proclaimed in the capital Alma Ata; but this was suppressed by the Red Army, which occupied the country (1919–20), and large numbers of Russians and Ukrainians moved in. It became the Kazakh Autonomous Soviet Socialist Republic, which in 1936 became a full republic within the Soviet Union. Vast areas (some ten million acres) were developed for agriculture as state farms, while there was also heavy industrialization during the 1930s and 1940s. Large mineral deposits, including uranium, were discovered and exploited, particularly around Lake Balkhash. After 1941 Stalin's regime forcibly moved German, Greek, and Armenian deportees into the republic. In October 1990 it proclaimed its sovereignty, and in December 1991 its independence was recognized. The Communist-derived ruling party has remained in power, under President Nursultan Nazarbayev. In December 1997 the capital started to transfer from Almaty to Aqmola.

Capital: Aqmola
Area: 2,717,300 sq km (1,048,887 sq mi)
Population: 16,669,000 (1995)
Currency: 1 tenge = 100 tiyn
Religions: Sunni Muslim; Eastern Orthodox
Ethnic Groups: Kazakh 40.0%; Russian 38.0%; Ukrainian 5.0%; Tatar, Armenian, Azeri, German, Greek, and Korean minorities
Languages: Kazakh (official); Russian; minority languages
International Organizations: UN; CSCE; Commonwealth of Independent States; North Atlantic Co-operation Council

Kazan A city and port on the River Volga, capital of the Tatar Republic in western Russia; pop. (1990) 1,103,000. Founded in 1401, it became capital of the powerful Tatar khanate in 1445 and later a frontier capital of the Russian Volga region. Its university was founded in 1804 and its students have included Tolstoy and Lenin. Kazan has chemical, electrical, shipbuilding, oil refining, and machine tools industries as well as traditional handicrafts.

Kazan, Elia (born Elia Kazanjoglous) (1909–) Turkish-born US film and theatre director. In 1947 he co-founded the Actors' Studio, one of the leading centres of method acting. Kazan's stage productions include *A Streetcar Named Desire* (1947), which he made into a film four years later; both starred Marlon Brando. Other films include *On the Waterfront* (1954), again with Marlon Brando, and *East of Eden* (1955), starring James Dean.

Kazantzakis, Nikos (1883–1957) Greek poet and novelist. He was born on Crete, and the island is a recurrent focus in his writing. His work reveals a complex and ever-evolving set of intellectual influences (including Bergson, Nietzsche, Lenin, and Buddha). He himself saw the core of his work as the short metaphysical volume 'The Ascetic' and his modern epic poem 'The Odyssey', which embodies a doctrine of heroic but nihilistic liberty. However, he is best known for his novels, notably *The Life and Manners of Alexis Zorba* (1946), *Christ Recrucified* (1948), and *The Last Temptation of Christ* (1955), and for his autobiography *Report to Greco* (1961), where his ethical and metaphysical preoccupations found their most convincing literary expression.

kea A species of bird, *Nestor notabilis*, in the parrot family, Psittacidae, confined to the mountains of the South Island of New Zealand. It is the size of a large crow, bronze-green all over with blue and red in the wing and a red rump. It has a powerful beak, more curved in the male than in the female. Keas eat a wide range of fruits and insects and will also feed on dead sheep, an action that has led to the erroneous belief that they are sheep-killers. They nest in holes among rocks or in hollow trees.

Kean, Edmund (1787–1833) British actor. He achieved fame with his performance as Shylock at London's Drury Lane theatre in 1814, and became particularly renowned for his interpretations of Shakespearian tragic roles, notably those of Macbeth and Iago.

Keating, Paul (John) (1944–) Australian Labor statesman, Prime Minister 1991–96. He entered politics in 1969 when he became a member of the House of Representatives. He served as federal treasurer (1983–91) and deputy Prime Minister (1990–91) under Bob Hawke, whom he replaced as Premier in 1991. His term of office was notable for a vociferous republican campaign as well as for measures to combat high unemployment.

Keaton, Buster (born Joseph Francis Keaton) (1895–1966) US actor and director. His deadpan face and acrobatic skills made him one of the biggest comedy stars of the silent-film era. Major films include *Our Hospitality* (1923), *The Navigator* (1924), and *The General* (1926).

Keats, John (1795–1821) British poet. In 1816 he qualified as an apothecary, but gave up medical practice in favour of his literary pursuits. His long narrative poem *Endymion* (1818) was attacked by the critics as the writing of an ignorant apothecary's apprentice. During 1818–19 he reached his creative heights and wrote some of his greatest poems in spite of the death of his brother and his inconclusive relationship with Fanny Brawne. These include 'The Eve of St Agnes', with its rich and vivid imagery; 'Isabella'; 'La Belle Dame sans Merci', much admired by the Pre-Raphaelites; 'Ode to a Nightingale'; 'Ode on a Grecian Urn'; 'To Autumn'; 'Lamia', inspired by BURTON's *Anatomy of Melancholy*, which reflected Keats's recurring preoccupation with the relationship between the real and the ideal; and the unfinished epic poem *Hyperion*. Suffering from tuberculosis, he left for Rome in 1820, where he died. Keats is regarded as one of the principal figures of ROMANTICISM.

Keble, John (1792–1866) British churchman. His sermon on national apostasy (1833) is generally held to mark the beginning of the Oxford Movement. Politically, it failed to win support for its idea that the law of the land need not coincide with the Church's teaching; theologically, however, the work of Keble's followers did much to revive traditional Catholic teaching, as well as to define and mould the Church of England.

ked See LOUSE FLY.

Keegan, (Joseph) Kevin (1951–) British footballer and manager. He played as an attacker for clubs which included Liverpool (1971–77) Hamburg (1977–80), and Newcastle United (1982–84), and won 63 caps for England (1972–82). He was voted European Footballer of the Year in 1978 and 1979. He became manager of Newcastle United in 1992, leading them into the Premier League the following season as First Division champions. In 1997 he moved to Fulham.

keel In a wooden ship, the principal timber running the length of the base of the hull, and serving as its spine; in a steel ship the keel is the lowest continuous line of plates, extending the whole length, to which are attached the stem, stern-post, and frames. The keel may extend downwards into the water, to reduce sideways drift: this kind of keel probably appeared first in the 6th century AD. Wooden ships often have a 'false keel', for protecting the true keel or further reducing sideways movement. In large steel ships two additional keels, known as bilge or docking keels, are fitted along each side of the hull where it narrows and turns underneath: these support the ship in DRY DOCK. Some small modern yachts are fitted with twin bilge keels instead of a single central keel. To increase speed under sail, designers shorten and deepen keels, leaving a central fin rather than a full-length keel. To make such fin keels as efficient as possible, wings may be fitted to the base of the fin, or the keel itself may be curved outwards so that it is thicker towards its base.

Keeler, Christine (1942–) British model and showgirl. She achieved notoriety in 1963 through her affair with the Conservative Cabinet minister John Profumo at a time when she was also mistress of a Soviet attaché. Profumo resigned and Keeler's patron, Stephen Ward, committed suicide after being charged with living off the immoral earnings of Keeler and her friend Mandy Rice-Davies. Keeler was imprisoned on related charges, but her trial was called into question after the publication of her autobiography and the release of the film *Scandal* (1989).

Keeling Islands An alternative name for the COCOS ISLANDS.

Keelung A major seaport and industrial centre at the northern tip of Taiwan; pop. (1982) 351,700. It is the second-largest port on the island and when held by the Spanish (1626–41) was known as Santissima Trinidad. Shipbuilding, chemicals, and machinery are important industries.

Keene, Charles Samuel (1823–91) British illustrator and caricaturist. He is remembered for his work in the weekly journal *Punch* from 1851.

Keflavik A fishing port in south-west Iceland, 40 km (25 miles) west of Reykjavik; pop. (1990) 7,525. Iceland's international airport is located nearby.

Keitel, Wilhelm Bodewin Johann Gustav (1882–1946) German field-marshal. As chief-of-staff of the High Command of the German armed forces (1938–45), he handled the armistice negotiations with France in 1940 and ratified the unconditional surrender of Germany in 1945. He was a close adviser of HITLER, and bore some of the responsibility for repressive measures taken by the army in occupied territory. He was hanged after trial at Nuremberg.

Kekulé von Stradonitz, (Friedrich) August (1829–96) German chemist who is regarded as one of the founders of structural organic chemistry. His training as an architect may have prompted his interest in the structure of molecules and in 1857 he proposed that the carbon atom can form four bonds with other atoms, furthermore, they could combine with other carbon atoms and form complex chains. In 1865 he suggested a structure for the BENZENE ring in which the six carbon atoms are arranged in the form of a regular hexagon, and thus established a basis for the study of AROMATIC COMPOUNDS.

Keller, Gottfried (1819–90) Swiss poet, writer of short stories and novels. He is best known for his collections of stories *The People of Seldwyla* (1856 and 1874). Each story is based upon an obsession, but the moralizing is tempered by irony and humour. The collection is remarkable for its range of comic technique and moods. *Green Henry* (1854–80), a partly autobiographical novel which exists in two distinct versions, is optimistic in its view of human development, whereas *Martin*

Salander (1886) is pessimistic about the effects of social and political complacency in a society that is beginning to disintegrate.

Keller, Helen (Adams) (1880–1968) US writer, social reformer, and academic. Blind and deaf from the age of 19 months, she learned how to read, type, and speak and went on to champion the cause of blind, deaf, and dumb people throughout the world. She is particularly remembered for her campaigning in aid of the American Foundation for the Blind.

Kellogg, Will Keith (1860–1951) US food manufacturer. He collaborated with his brother, a doctor, to develop a process of manufacturing a breakfast cereal for sanatorium patients that consisted of crisp flakes of rolled and toasted wheat and corn. The product's success led to the establishment of the W. K. Kellogg company in 1906 and a subsequent revolution in Western eating habits.

Kellogg-Briand Pact (or **Pact of Paris**) (1928) A multilateral agreement condemning war. It grew out of a proposal by the French Premier, Aristide BRIAND, to the US government for a treaty outlawing war between the two countries. The US Secretary of State, Frank B. Kellogg, proposed a multilateral treaty of the same character. In August 1928 15 nations signed an agreement committing themselves to peace; the USA ratified it in 1929, followed by a further 46 nations. The failure of the Pact to provide measures of enforcement nullified its contribution to international order.

Kells (Gaelic **Ceannanus Mór**) A town in County Meath, north-east Ireland, in the valley of the River Blackwater; pop. (1991) 2,187. A monastic settlement was founded here in the 6th century by St Columba. About the beginning of the 9th century an illuminated Latin manuscript of the four gospels, the famous *Book of Kells*, was produced here (it is now in Trinity College Library, Dublin). There are remains of St Columba's House, a round tower, and several Celtic Crosses.

Kelly, Gene (1912–96) US dancer, choreographer, and film director. He appeared in musicals in the 1940s and achieved success with *An American in Paris* (1952). He is best known for his appearance in the musical *Singing in the Rain* (1953). He choreographed extensively for both stage and film in the popular MUSICAL genre.

Kelly, Grace (Patricia) (1928–82) US film actress. Her first starring role came in the classic western *High Noon* (1952). She won an Oscar for her performance in *The Country Girl* (1954) and also made three Hitchcock films, including *Rear Window* (1954). Kelly retired from films on her marriage to Prince Rainier III of Monaco (1923–) in 1956, when she became Princess Grace of Monaco. She died in a car accident.

Kelly, Ned (1855–80) Australian outlaw. He was the leader of a band of horse and cattle thieves and bank raiders operating in Victoria. A bushranger from 1878, Kelly was eventually hanged in Melbourne.

Kelly, Petra (Karin) (1947–92) German political leader. Formerly a member of the German Social Democratic Party, she became disillusioned with their policies and in 1979 co-founded the Green Party, a broad alliance of environmentalists, feminists, and anti-nuclear activists. She became the Party's leading spokesperson and in 1983 was one of 17 Green Party members elected to the West German Parliament. The cause of her death remains a subject of controversy.

Kelly, William (1811–88) US pioneer of the IRON AND STEEL INDUSTRY. He began experiments at his ironworks in Kentucky in 1847, and discovered that an air blast could be used to burn the carbon out of molten iron, reducing fuel costs and converting iron into steel. Between 1851 and 1856 he secretly built converters that used this technique, and in 1856 applied for a patent. Although BESSEMER had already acquired a US patent for a similar 'air-boiling' process for steel, Kelly succeeded in gaining his patent in 1857, on the grounds of prior discovery. He was bankrupted, and the first steel made in the USA under his patent (1864) used a Bessemer converter.

kelp An exclusively marine brown ALGA. Kelps include the largest known alga, *Macrocystis*, which may be 60 m (197 feet) long. Oarweed (*Laminaria*) and FUCUS are common off European coasts and grow below the high-water mark. They have long, strap-like fronds attached to rocks by a root-like holdfast. Kelps are used in manures and as a source of alginic acid, and iodine.

kelvin (symbol K) The SI UNIT of thermodynamic temperature, equal in magnitude to the degree Celsius. It is formally defined as the fraction 1/273.16 of the thermodynamic temperature of the triple point of water, i.e. the triple point of water contains exactly 273.16 kelvins. The **kelvin scale** is a temperature scale based on the idea that temperature is a measure of internal energy. Thus the zero point on the kelvin scale is the point at which a substance has only the zero-point energy. This point is called ABSOLUTE ZERO, and is equivalent to −273.15°C on the Celsius scale. Since the degrees on the kelvin scale are the same size as degrees Celsius, 0°C = 273.15 K. The kelvin scale is based on energy considerations, and therefore measures **thermodynamic temperature**. It is named after William THOMSON, Lord Kelvin.

Kelvin See THOMSON, WILLIAM, LORD KELVIN.

Kemal Pasha See ATATÜRK.

Kemble, Frances Anne (known as 'Fanny') (1809–93) British actress. The daughter of Charles Kemble and the niece of Sarah Siddons, she was a success in both Shakespearian comedy and tragedy, playing such parts as Portia, Beatrice, Juliet, and Lady Macbeth.

Kemble, John Philip (1757–1823) British actor-manager, brother of Sarah Siddons. He was noted for his performances in Shakespearian tragedy, notably as Hamlet and Coriolanus, and for his interpretations of historical roles such as Brutus in *Julius Caesar*. He was manager of the Drury Lane (1788–1803) and Covent Garden (1803–17) theatres. His younger brother **Charles Kemble** (1775–1854) was also a successful actor-manager.

Kempe, Margery (*c.*1373–*c.*1440) English mystic. From about 1432 to 1436 she dictated one of the first autobiographies in English, *The Book of Margery Kempe*. This account of her spiritual life describes in a vernacular style her series of pilgrimages to Jerusalem, Rome, Germany, and Spain, as well as details of her ecstatic visions.

Kempis, Thomas à (1379–1471) German Augustinian canon and religious writer. He was the author of the *Imitatio Christi*, an influential work which emphasized the need for asceticism, and reacted against the worldliness of the 15th-century Catholic establishment.

kenaf A tropical, annual plant, related to cotton and mallow, with tall, slightly prickly straight stems up to 4 m (13 feet) tall. The species *Hibiscus cannabinus* is cultivated in Africa and Asia for the fibre obtained from its stem. Similar to jute but somewhat coarser, it is used mainly in the manufacture of sacking. Its seeds contain about 20 per cent oil, similar to cotton-seed oil.

Kendal A town in the Lake District of Cumbria, north-west England, on the River Kent; pop. (1991) 25,461. There are remains of a Norman castle which was the birthplace in 1512 of Catherine Parr, sixth wife of Henry VIII.

Kendall, Edward Calvin (1886–1972) US biochemist. He was the first to isolate crystalline thyroxine from the thyroid gland. From the adrenal cortex he obtained a number of steroid hormones, one of which was later named cortisone, and several of which are now of great value in the treatment of rheumatic, allergic, and inflammatory diseases. He shared a Nobel Prize in 1950.

Keneally, Thomas (Michael) (1935–) Australian novelist. He first gained notice for *The Chant of Jimmy Blacksmith* (1972). Later works include war novels such as *Confederates* (1979), and the Booker Prize-winning *Schindler's Ark* (1982), the true story of the German industrialist Oskar Schindler, who helped more than 1,200 Jews to escape death in Nazi concentration camps; the book was filmed by Steven Spielberg in 1993 as *Schindler's List*. His later novels include *The Playmaker* (1987) and *Jacko: the Great Intruder* (1994).

Kenilworth A market town in Warwickshire, central England, 8 km (5 miles) south-west of Coventry; pop. (1991) 21,623. Its ruined 12th-century castle, in which Edward II was forced to abdicate, featured in Sir Walter Scott's novel *Kenilworth*.

Kenilworth, Siege of (June–December 1266) An episode during the second Barons' War when HENRY III attacked Kenilworth Castle, refuge of the Montforts and their supporters. The Dictum of Kenilworth (31 October 1266) asserted the king's powers over the barons and offered inducements to peace by allowing them to recover their confiscated lands: the beseiged earls finally surrendered in December.

Kennedy, Cape See CAPE CANAVERAL.

Kennedy, Edward Moore (known as 'Teddy') (1932–) US Democratic politician. The brother of John F. KENNEDY and Robert F. KENNEDY, he was elected to the Senate in 1962. His subsequent political career was overshadowed by his involvement in a mysterious fatal car accident at Chappaquiddick Island (1969), although he remains a prominent Democratic spokesman.

Kennedy, John F(itzgerald) (known as 'JFK') (1917–63) US Democratic statesman, 35th President of the USA 1961–63. A national war hero during World War II, Kennedy became, at 43, the youngest man ever to be elected President, as well as the first Catholic. He gained a popular reputation as an advocate of civil rights, although reforms were delayed by Congress until 1964. In foreign affairs he recovered from the fiasco of the Bay of Pigs invasion of Cuba to demand successfully the withdrawal of Soviet missiles from the country, and negotiated the Test-Ban Treaty of 1963 with the USSR and the UK. Kennedy was assassinated while riding in a motorcade through Dallas, Texas, in November 1963; Lee Harvey Oswald was charged with his murder, but was himself shot before he could stand trial. Oswald was said to be the sole gunman by the Warren Commission (1964), but the House of Representatives Assassinations Committee (1979) concluded that more than one gunman had been involved; the affair remains the focus for a number of conspiracy theories.

Kennedy, Robert F(rancis) (1925–68) US Democratic statesman. The brother of John F. KENNEDY and Edward KENNEDY, he closely assisted his brother John in domestic policy, serving as Attorney-General (1961–64), and was a champion of the civil-rights movement. Robert Kennedy stood as a prospective presidential candidate in 1968, but was assassinated during his campaign.

Kennelly, Arthur Edwin (1861–1939) US electrical engineer. His principal work was on the theory of alternating currents, and he also worked on the practical problems of electrical transmission. Kennelly independently discovered the layer in the atmosphere responsible for reflecting radio waves back to Earth (see HEAVISIDE). He helped to develop electrical units and standards, and promoted the adoption of the metric system.

Kennelly layer See HEAVISIDE, OLIVER.

Kenneth Three kings of Scotland. **Kenneth I** (MacAlpin) (died *c*.859) reigned *c*.843–58. He united the Scots and Picts to form the kingdom of Scotia (*c*.843), having succeeded in *c*.841 as King of Dalriada in the Highlands. In *c*.848 he moved the relics of St COLUMBA to Scone, where the kings of Scotland were crowned. **Kenneth II** (died 995) reigned 971–95. In return for recognizing the lordship of King EDGAR of England, he received Lothian two years after his accession in 971. He was murdered by Constantine III who, in turn, was killed by **Kenneth III** (died 1005), whose brief reign of civil wars (997–1005) ended with the accession of MALCOLM II.

Kensington A fashionable residential district in central London. Part of the Royal borough of Kensington and Chelsea, it lies to the west and south of Hyde Park. At the west end of Kensington Gardens is Kensington Palace, originally known as Nottingham House, the seat of a 17th-century Lord Chancellor; it was the birthplace of Queen Victoria and the home of Diana, Princess of Wales. The Natural History Museum, the Victoria and Albert Museum, the Science Museum, the Royal Albert Hall, and the Imperial College are all in South Kensington.

Kent A county on the south-east coast of England; area 3,731 sq km (1,441 sq miles); pop. (1991) 1,485,600; county town, Maidstone. Kent is divided into 14 districts.

Kent, William (*c*.1685–1748) English architect and landscape gardener. He promoted the Palladian style of architecture in England and is renowned for such works as the Treasury (1733–37) and Whitehall (1734–36). Holkham Hall, begun in 1734, was one of the first English buildings to feature interiors and furniture designed by the architect. Kent is chiefly remembered, however, for his landscape gardens at Stowe House in Buckinghamshire (*c*.1730). His design principles overturned the formal taste of the time and anticipated the innovations of Capability Brown.

Kenton, Stan (born Stanley Newcomb) (1912–79) US band-leader, composer, and arranger. Kenton began his professional career in 1934 as a pianist and arranger and formed his own orchestra in 1940. He had early hits with 'Artistry in Rhythm' (1941) and 'Eager Beaver' (1943), but is particularly associated with the big-band jazz style of the 1950s.

Kentucky A state in the south-eastern USA; area 104,660 sq km (40,409 sq miles); pop. (1990) 3,685,300; capital, Frankfort. The largest cities are Louisville and Lexington. Kentucky is also known as the Bluegrass State. Ceded by the French in 1763 and first settled in the 1770s, Kentucky entered the Union as the 15th state in 1792. Coal-mining and agriculture are important and the Bluegrass country around Lexington is a noted centre of race-horse breeding.

The state's principal landmarks are the Mammoth Cave National Park, the Big South Fork National River and Recreation Area, Cumberland Gap National Historic Park, and the Abraham Lincoln Birthplace National Historic Site.

Kenya An equatorial country in east Africa, bounded inland by Somalia on the east, Ethiopia and Sudan on the north, Uganda on the west, and Tanzania on the south.

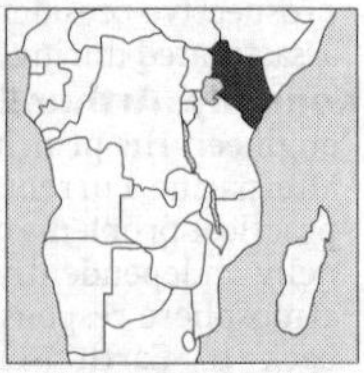

Physical. In the south-east of Kenya is a hot, damp coast on the Indian Ocean, into which run two long rivers, the Tana and the Galana. They rise in the central highlands, a region containing Mount Kenya and cool slopes and plateaux suitable for farming of various kinds, particularly the cultivation of tea and coffee. The highlands are split by part of the Great Rift Valley, a region of lakes, and to the west fall away to the eastern shore of Lake Victoria. Northward is a rift-valley lake, Turkana (once called Rudolf), and to its east is a vast, hot, dry region with thorny scrub. In the south there is a smaller lake, Magadi, with major deposits of soda.

Economy. Kenya has an agricultural economy with a developing industrial sector. Main exports are coffee, tea, and petroleum products (from imported crude oil) from the oil refinery at MOMBASA. Tourism is an important sector of the economy, while the textiles, chemical, and vehicle-assembly industries are also significant. There is a developed financial services sector, and a flourishing informal sector. Kenya obtains some two-thirds of its electricity from hydroelectric dams. There are mineral deposits of soda ash, fluorspar, salt, and gold. Agriculture is diverse: the highlands produce maize, coffee, tea, and sisal, while lowland crops include coconuts, cashew nuts, and cotton.

History. In areas of the Great Rift Valley, such as Lake Turkana, palaeontologists have discovered some of the earliest fossil HOMINID remains. Arabs settled on the coast during the 7th century. During the 16th and 17th centuries, Portuguese traders operated in the region. The MAASAI pastoral people came into the area in the 18th century from the north, but during the 19th century they were largely displaced by the agricultural KIKUYU, who steadily advanced from the south. British coastal trade began in the 1840s, and in 1887 the British East African Association (a trading company) secured a lease of coastal strip from the Sultan of Zanzibar. The British East Africa Protectorate was established in 1896, when thousands of Indians were brought in to build railways. The British crown colony of Kenya was created in 1920. By then a great area of the 'White Highlands' had been reserved for white settlement, while 'Native Reserves' were established to separate the two communities. During the 1920s there was considerable immigration from Britain, and a development of African political movements, demanding a greater share in the government of the country. Kikuyu nationalism developed steadily, led by Jomo KENYATTA. From this tension grew the Kenya Africa Union, and the militant MAU MAU movement (1952–57). An election in 1961 led to the two African political parties, the Kenya African National Union (KANU) and the Kenya African Democratic Union (KADU), joining the government. Independence was achieved in 1963, and in the following year Kenya became a republic with Kenyatta as President. Under him, Kenya remained generally stable, but after his death in 1978 opposition to his successor, Daniel arap Moi, mounted, culminating in a bloody attempted coup in 1982. Elections in 1983 saw the return of comparative stability with Moi still President, but of an increasingly corrupt and autocratic regime. In December 1991 Moi reluctantly agreed to end single-party politics, as a result of pressure from the Forum for the Restoration of Democracy (FORD), supported by Western aid-donor nations. Multi-party elections, held in 1992 and 1997, were won by Moi amid allegations of electoral fraud. Sporadic outbreaks of ethnic and political violence have continued.

Capital: Nairobi
Area: 582,646 sq km (224,961 sq mi)
Population: 28,626,000 (1995)
Currency: 1 Kenya shilling = 100 cents
Religions: Protestant 26.5%; Roman Catholic 26.4%; traditional beliefs 18.9%; African Indigenous 17.6%; Muslim 6.0%; Orthodox 2.5%
Ethnic Groups: Kikuyu 20.9%; Luhya 13.8%; Luo 12.8%; Kamba 11.3%; Kalenjin 10.8%; other African 29.2%; other including Asian 1.2%
Languages: Swahili (official); English; local languages
International Organizations: Non-Aligned Movement; OAU; UN; Commonwealth

Kenya, Mount (or **Kirinyaga**) A mountain in central Kenya of volcanic origin, just south of the equator, rising to a height of 5,200 m (17,058 ft). The second-highest mountain in Africa, it gave its name to the country, Kenya. Its first sighting by European explorers was in 1849 and in 1899 it was climbed by an expedition led by Sir Halford McKinder.

Kenyatta, Jomo (*c.*1891–1978) Kenyan statesman, Prime Minister of Kenya 1963 and President 1964–78. He was imprisoned from 1952 to 1961 for alleged complicity in the Mau Mau uprising. On his release he was elected president of the Kenya African National Union and led his country to independence in 1963, subsequently serving as independent Kenya's first President.

Kepler, Johannes (1571–1630) German astronomer who was the first to describe accurately the elliptical orbits of the Earth and the planets around the Sun. Kepler worked with Tycho BRAHE at Tycho's observatory outside Prague and took over the observatory when Tycho died in 1601. Tycho left Kepler his tables of stellar and planetary positions. From these, after a great deal of analysis trying one mathematical model after another, Kepler deduced what are now known as KEPLER'S LAWS, but the physical explanation of these laws had to await NEWTON'S LAW OF GRAVITATION. Kepler also made discoveries in optics, general physics, and geometry.

Kepler's Laws Three laws of planetary motion formulated by KEPLER from a study of the long series of naked-eye observations by the Danish astronomer Tycho BRAHE. They are:

The orbit of a planet about the Sun is an ELLIPSE with the Sun at one focus of the ellipse.

The **radius vector** (an imaginary line) joining a planet to the Sun sweeps out equal areas in equal times.

The squares of the PERIODS of revolution of the planets in their orbits are proportional to the cubes of their orbital semi-major axes.

Although subsequent more accurate observations have shown that celestial objects, such as planets orbiting the Sun or satellites orbiting planets, do not obey Kepler's Laws exactly, they are still a close enough approximation to the truth to remain useful.

Kerala A region in India that occupies the narrow Malabar coastal plain between the Western Ghats and the Arabian Sea. Its name evokes an ancient kingdom, Keralaputra, to which there are references in ASOKA's inscriptions (3rd century BC). From early times trade developed with distant parts of the world. The dominant rulers up to the 5th century AD were the Cheras, but the region subsequently fragmented into separate kingdoms and was never again united. However the evolution of the Malayalam language maintained some cultural unity.

The arrival of Vasco DA GAMA at Calicut (1498) began an era of European dominance of the spice trade. Cochin, which developed as a Portuguese port, was conquered by the Dutch in 1663. By the late 18th century British influence predominated, signalled by the annexation of Malabar District (1792). In 1795 the southern princely state of Travancore accepted British protection.

Kerala A state on the coast of south-west India; area 38,863 sq km (15,010 sq miles); pop. (1991) 29,011,230; capital, Thiruvananthapuram (Trivandrum). It was created in 1956 from the former state of Travancore-Cochin and part of Madras.

keratin A group of fibrous proteins occurring in hair, feathers, hooves, and horns. Their strong elastic structure results from their coiled polypeptide chains, which combine to form supercoils of linked polypeptide. Aggregates of these supercoils are embedded in a protein matrix.

Kerch The chief port and industrial centre of the Crimea, at the eastern end of the Kerch Peninsula; pop. (1990) 176,000. Founded in the 6th century BC by Greek colonists, it was capital of the European part of the Kingdom of Bosporus in the 5th–4th centuries BC. It was developed as a Genoese trading centre (renamed Korchev) in the Middle Ages before being captured by the Crimean Tatars in 1475 and then absorbed into the Russian empire in 1772. Its industries include iron, shipbuilding, chemicals, and fishing.

Kerensky, Alexander Feodorovich (1881–1970) Russian revolutionary. He was a representative of the moderate Labour Party in the Fourth Duma (1912) and joined the Socialist Revolutionary Party during the RUSSIAN REVOLUTION. After the emperor's abdication in March (February, old style), he was made Minister of War in the Provisional Government of Prince Lvov, succeeding him as Premier four months later. Determined to continue the war against Germany, he failed to implement agrarian and economic reforms, and his government was overthrown by the BOLSHEVIKS in the October Revolution. He escaped to Paris, where he continued as an active propagandist against the Soviet regime.

Kerinci A volcanic peak in the Barisan Mountains of west-central Sumatra, Indonesia. Rising to a height of 3,806 m (12,487 ft) it is the highest mountain on Sumatra and the highest active volcano in Indonesia.

Kermanshah (or **Bakhtaran**) A city in western Iran, in the Zagros Mountains; pop. (1991) 624,000. Now one of the largest cities of western Iran, it lay on an ancient trading route to Baghdad. Known throughout its long history as Kermanshah ('city of the king'), its alternative provincial name was used for nearly a decade after the 1979 Islamic revolution. It is the centre of a rich agricultural region and also manufactures carpets, shoes, and textiles.

Kern, Jerome (David) (1885–1945) US composer. He wrote several musical comedies, including *Showboat* (1927), which proved a major influence in the development of the musical. It also featured the song 'Ol' Man River'. Kern's many other songs include 'Smoke Gets in Your Eyes'.

kerosene See PARAFFIN.

Kerouac, Jack (born Jean-Louis Lebris de Kérouac) (1922–69) US novelist and poet, of French-Canadian descent. A leading figure of the beat generation, he is best known for his semi-autobiographical novel *On the Road* (1957). Other works include *Big Sur* (1962).

Kerry A county of south-west Ireland, in the province of Munster; area 4,701 sq km (1,816 sq miles); pop. (1991) 121,720; county town, Tralee. It gives its name to a breed of small black dairy cattle and to the Kerry blue, a terrier of a breed with a silky blue-grey coat.

Kesey, Ken (Elton) (1935–) US novelist. His best-known novel, *One Flew Over the Cuckoo's Nest* (1962) is based on his experiences as a ward attendant in a mental hospital. Kesey's adventures with the Merry Pranksters, a group who pioneered the use of psychedelic drugs, are described in *The Electric Kool-Aid Acid Test* (1967) by Tom Wolfe.

Kesselring, Albrecht (1885–1960) German field-marshal. He commanded the BOMBING OFFENSIVE over Poland, the Netherlands, and France before commencing the Battle of BRITAIN, when he was hampered by interference from GOERING and HITLER. Posted to the Mediterranean soon after, from 1943 to 1945 he commanded all German forces in Italy, and in 1945 in the West. Condemned to death as a war criminal in 1947, he had his sentence commuted to life imprisonment and was freed in 1952.

Kesteven, Parts of One of the three former administrative divisions or 'ridings' of the county of Lincoln, east England, prior to the local government reorganization of 1974 that created the districts of North and South Kesteven. Its chief town was Sleaford.

kestrel A small FALCON of the genus *Falco*, with broad, pointed wings and a long square-cut tail, characteristically seen hovering 5–6 m (16–19 feet) above ground while searching for prey. The European kestrel or windhover, *F. tinnunculus*, is heavily barred in pale and dark brown, and is widespread over Europe, Africa, and Asia. Its counterpart in the USA is the sparrow hawk, *F. sparverius*, and about a dozen other closely related species occur more locally in Africa, Australia, and on oceanic islands. Their prey is insects, small rodents, reptiles, and occasionally small ground-living birds.

Keswick A market town and tourist centre near the north end of Derwent Water in Cumbria, north-west England, on the River Greta; pop. (1981) 5,645.

ketch A two-masted SAILING SHIP with a mizen (rear) mast and sail considerably smaller than the mainmast and sail. The original 'catches' were small coastal traders (though the name may imply a type of fishing boat) in the 17th century. These early ketches may not have been ketch-rigged, the name possibly referring to a type of hull or the vessel's use.

ketone An organic compound in which the carbon atom of a CARBONYL GROUP is bonded to two other carbon-containing groups, such as ALKYL or ARYL GROUPS. These need not necessarily be identical. If these two groups are denoted by R and R′, the general formula for a ketone is RCOR′. Like the ALDEHYDES, the principal reactions of ketones are addition and condensation reactions (see CHEMICAL REACTION). However, unlike the aldehydes, they are not easily oxidized to carboxylic acids. Thus, they fail to produce a positive reaction with chemical tests for detecting reducing compounds.

Kettering, Charles Franklin (1876–1958) US automobile engineer. His first significant development was the electric starter (1912). He was leader of research at General Motors until 1947, discovering with his team tetraethyl lead as an antiknock agent and defining the octane rating of fuels. He did important work on two-stroke diesel engines, which came into widespread use for railway locomotives and road coaches, and was also responsible for the development of synchromesh gearboxes, automatic transmissions, and power steering.

kettledrum (or **timpani**) A drum with a closed, often hemispherical, shell as a body. The term derives from the cauldron, or cooking pot, with a skin over the opening. Kettledrums are used worldwide, often in pairs and made of pottery, metal, or wood, the latter in Africa sometimes carved as a human trunk and legs. Small Middle Eastern kettledrums, *naqqāra*, were imported into Europe by returning Crusaders, and were known as nakers; they were common throughout medieval Europe. Larger kettledrums, played on camel-back in the Turkish armies, were taken up by late 15th-century European potentates and became TIMPANI.

kettle-hole A small, enclosed depression found in areas of glacial deposits and which may contain ponds or marshes. If a large number occur close together, they give the surface an irregular, pockmarked appearance. They are thought to be formed by large blocks of ice which became detached from a glacier or ice-sheet and were covered and surrounded by rock debris, which insulated them. As the blocks slowly melted, the covering subsided to fill the depression, creating a kettle-hole.

Kett's Rebellion (July–August 1549) An orderly English peasant protest against the profiteering and ENCLOSURES of local Norfolk landlords. Led by Robert Kett, a well-to-do tradesman, 16,000 small farmers encamped outside Norwich, and eventually gained control of the city. By their disciplined self-government, the rebels aimed to impress the authorities and shame the local magnates. The rebellion was suppressed by forces under John Dudley (later Duke of NORTHUMBERLAND) who routed the rebels at Dussindale on 27 August. Kett and his brother William were among those executed.

Keuper The uppermost division of the TRIASSIC system. It is represented by marine deposits in central Europe, but in Britain by continental deposits: barren red mudstones (Keuper Marl) and sandstones, and salt.

Kew Gardens The Royal Botanic Gardens at Kew, in Richmond upon Thames, London, England. Originally the garden of Kew House, it was established in 1759 as a botanic garden by the mother of George III, with the aid of Sir Joseph Banks. It was presented to the nation in 1841 and continued to develop into a major institution with important reference collections, archives, library, and research laboratories.

key In musical composition, a general adherence to the notes of the major and minor scales. There are 12 major keys: one for each of the semitones available in the chromatic SCALE of Western music. Each has a relative minor key that shares the same general pitch area, but whose scale starts on a different note. Thus the scale represented by the 'white notes' of the piano, which has C as its tonic (starting note), is the key of C major. A white-note scale starting on A is the key of A minor. The tonic note of the minor key is always three semitones below that of its relative major key. Each major key contains seven steps. Two are semitones and five are tones. These are arranged as two identical four-note sequences, linked by a tone. These tone-tone-semitone sequences are known as tetrachords.

A similar, but slightly more complex, principle

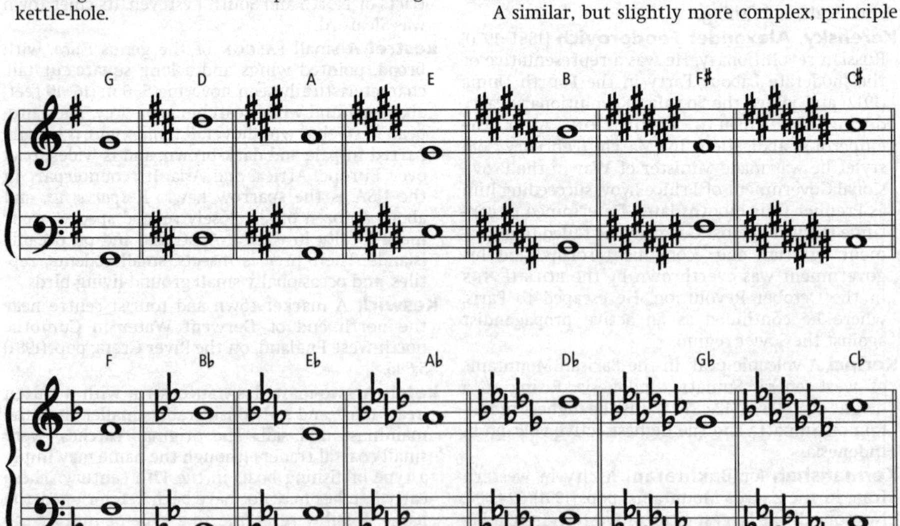

Keys There are 12 major keys: C, G, D, E, B, F, B♭, E♭, C♭ = B, G♭ = F♯, and C♯ = D♭. The key of C is not shown as it has neither sharps nor flats. Each major key has a relative minor key with the same key signature. The keynote of the minor key is three semitones below that of the major key (e.g. A minor is the relative of C major).

governs the construction of minor scales. This invariable scale-structure explains the system of key relationships that underlies the idea of TONALITY. Keys are in their nearest relationship one with the other when their scales share every note but one. The new note is introduced in order to preserve the tone-tone-semitone structure of the tetrachords. This relationship exists between keys whose scales start on tonics that are five notes apart. Thus the keys immediately related to the C major example are G above and F below. In the key of G major the scale requires an F sharp in order to preserve its hexachord pattern, while F major requires a B flat. Keys are thus related to each other in a continuous cycle of fifths, and each key is identified by the number of sharps or flats required for the maintenance of the tetrachords. These are usually grouped at the beginning of each line of music in the form of a key signature. The key signature may be changed during the course of a composition, when the tonality changes. It may also be contradicted, briefly, by the use of accidentals (new sharps, flats, or naturals applied to individual notes). The process of passing from the note-area of one scale into the note-area of another is known as modulation. Reference to the piano keyboard will show that the keys of C sharp major and D flat major involve the same notes, as do C flat major and B major. These keys are said to be enharmonic versions of each other – they sound the same but have different notation.

keyboard (in music) A set of levers ('keys') which, when struck by the player's fingers, set in motion the mechanism of such instruments as the organ, harpsichord, and piano. The keys correspond to the 12 notes of the chromatic scale and are grouped in two rows: a lower row of seven 'white' keys for the diatonic scale of C major, and an upper row of five 'black' keys, grouped in sets of two and three, for chromatic notes necessary to complete the other scales. Early keyboards often employed a 'short octave' arrangement for the lowest registers, in which certain rarely used chromatic notes were omitted from the tuning and their corresponding 'black' keys made to operate diatonic notes. The complete diatonic octave was thus compressed into a shorter span that enabled the left hand to tackle larger intervals. The colour of the keys, though now universally black and white, has been a matter of fashion. In the 17th and 18th centuries the present-day black and white arrangement was often reversed.

Key Largo A resort island off the south coast of Florida, USA, the northernmost and the longest of the Florida Keys; pop. (1990) 11,330. John Pennekamp Coral Reef State Park, the first underwater marine park designated in the USA, lies just off the east coast.

Keynes, John Maynard, 1st Baron (1883–1946) British economist. Keynes served as an adviser to the Treasury during both world wars and was its representative at the Versailles peace conference (1919), subsequently becoming one of the most influential critics of the Treaty of Versailles. He laid the foundations of modern macroeconomics with *The General Theory of Employment, Interest and Money* (1936). In this he argued that full employment is not a natural condition but is determined by effective demand, requiring government spending on public works to stimulate this. His theories, known as **Keynesianism**, influenced Roosevelt's decision to introduce the American New Deal. Keynesianism is opposed by MONETARISM.

Keystone Kops See SENNETT, MACK.

Key West A fishing port and tourist city in southern Florida, USA, at the southern tip of the Florida Keys; pop. (1990) 24,800. Originally known as Cayo Hueso (Spanish, 'bone island'), it is the southernmost city in continental USA, linked to the southern tip of Florida by the Overseas Highway, which was completed in 1938.

KGB (Russian abbreviation, Committee of State Security) Formed in 1953, it was responsible for external espionage, internal counter-intelligence, and internal 'crimes against the state'. The most famous chairman of the KGB was Yuri Andropov (1967–82) who was Soviet leader 1982–84. He made KGB operations more sophisticated, especially against internal dissidents. In 1992 the KGB was dissolved, to be replaced by the Central Intelligence Service of the Russian Republic. This pledged itself to work with Western Intelligence in the prevention of nuclear proliferation and the development of chemical and biological weapons, and to fight terrorism and drug trafficking.

Khachaturian, Aram (Ilyich) (1903–78) Soviet composer. Of Armenian descent, Khachaturian attracted international interest with his Piano Concerto (1936). His ballets *Gayane* (1942, containing the popular 'Sabre Dance') and *Spartacus* (1954) have come to be performed all over the world. His finest music is richly romantic and reflects the influence of Armenian folk-song.

Khadija (*c*.555–619) The Prophet MUHAMMAD's first wife, some 15 years his senior, and a wealthy widow with her own caravan trade. Revered by Muslims as one of the four 'perfect women' of Islam, Khadija's proposal and marriage to Muhammad are surrounded by legendary features. Tradition always depicts her favourably for her support of Muhammad and for his revelations, and attests to his deep grief at her death.

Khajuraho The site of a vast group of temples in the Madhya Pradesh province of central India. Khajuraho was a capital of the Chandella dynasty and the temples were built in the 10th and 11th centuries; originally there were about eighty of which about a quarter are still standing. The most famous is the Kandarya Mahadera temple, dedicated to the Hindu god Shiva, which has one of the world's greatest groupings of architectural sculpture, including many beautiful erotic scenes.

Khakassia, Republic of A republic of the Russian Federation, to the west of the upper Yenesei River in East Siberia; area 61,900 sq km (23,855 sq miles); pop. (1990) 569,000; capital, Abakan. It became an autonomous region of the Soviet Union in 1930 and following the breakup of the USSR in 1991 it became a republic of the Russian Federation.

Khalsa (Punjabi, 'pure ones') A group within SIKHISM consisting of those who have accepted full initiation into the faith. The *Khalsa* was instituted by the tenth Sikh GURU, GOBIND SINGH, in 1699, when he formed an army of soldier-saints, prepared to fight for their faith. Nowadays, both men and women can be initiated into the *Khalsa* by drinking *amrit* ('nectar'; a mixture of sugar and water) in the presence of five Sikhs, and promising to wear the 'five Ks': uncut hair (*kesh*); a comb (*kangha*); a bracelet (*kara*); shorts (*kaccha*); and a sword or dagger (*kirpan*). To these male members added the turban, giving the Sikhs a distinctive appearance. In addition, smoking, alcohol, and sexual incontinence are forbidden. Members of the *Khalsa* must accept the teachings of the GURUS, and be prepared to sacrifice all for the faith. Men who are initiated are given the additional name of

Singh ('lion'), while women adopt the additional name of *Kaur* ('princess').

Khama, Sir Seretse (1921–80) Botswanan statesman, Prime Minister of Bechuanaland 1965 and President of Botswana 1966–80. An heir to the chieftainship of the ruling tribe in Bechuanaland, he was banished because of opposition to his marriage to an Englishwoman in 1948. He returned with his wife in 1956 and formed the Democratic Party in 1962, leading the party to a landslide victory in the elections of 1965; he became Botswana's first President the following year. A strong believer in multiracial democracy, he achieved nationwide free education.

khamsin An oppressive, hot, south or south-east wind occurring in North Africa and the Arabian Peninsula intermittently in late winter and early spring. The name is derived from the Arabic, *khamsun*, meaning fifty, for the approximate period of days during which it blows.

Khan, Ayub See AYUB KHAN.

Khan, Imran (full name Imran Ahmad Khan Niazi) (1952–) Pakistani cricketer. He made his test début in 1970 and served as captain of his country in four periods between 1982 and 1992. A batsman and fast bowler, he also played county cricket for Worcestershire (1971–76) and Sussex (1977–88). After retiring from cricket in 1992, he entered politics in Pakistan.

Khan, Jahangir (1963–) Pakistani squash player. In 1979 he became world amateur champion at the age of 15; after turning professional he was world squash champion five consecutive times (1981–85) and again in 1988.

khanate The region ruled by a **khan** (a Mongol or Turkic supreme tribal leader elevated by the support of his warriors). On GENGHIS KHAN's death in 1227 his empire was divided into four parts, each ruled by one of his descendants. By the mid-13th century the MONGOL empire consisted of four khanates; the khanate of the Western Kipchaks (the GOLDEN HORDE); the khanate of Persia, whose ruler was called the Il-khan; the khanate of Turkistan (the White Horde of the Eastern Kipchaks), and the khanate of the Khakhan in East Asia. The three khans were subject to the Khakhan (the Great Khan), but were generally resentful in their relations with him. After the death of KUBLAI KHAN (1294) the Khakhan's authority was nominal. In 1368 the Mongols were driven out of China and by *c.*1500 all four khanates had disappeared. A number of lesser khanates emerged; the khanates of Kazan, Astrakhan, the Crimea, Khiva, Bukhara, Tashkent, Samarkand, and Kokand. These long presented a threat to the communities surrounding them. One by one all were absorbed by Russia. The last to fall was Kokand (1876).

Khardangla Pass A high-altitude pass in the western Himalayas of Kashmir to the north of the Indus. Reaching a height of 5,662 m (18,576 ft), it is reckoned to be one of the highest passes in the world. It is used by the Indian Army as a supply route linking the town of Leh with outposts on the Siachen Glacier near Mt. K2.

Kharkiv (formerly **Kharkov**) An industrial and market city, and railway junction in north-east Ukraine, situated to the east of Kiev in the Donets coal basin at the confluence of the Kharkov, Lopan, and Udy rivers; pop. (1990) 1,618,000. Founded in 1665 as a Cossack frontier headquarters, its coal and metal industries developed in the mid-19th century. It was the first capital of the Ukrainian Soviet Socialist Republic from its establishment in 1919 until replaced by Kiev in 1934. It produces agricultural and mining machinery, machine tools, railway wagons, electrical equipment, and foodstuffs.

Khartoum The capital of Sudan, situated at the junction of the Blue Nile and the White Nile; pop. (1993) 924,500. Originally established in 1821 as an Egyptian army camp, it developed into a garrison town. In 1885 a British and Egyptian force under the command of General Charles Gordon (1833–85) was besieged here for ten months by the Mahdists, who eventually stormed the garrison, killing most of the defenders, including Gordon. It remained under the control of the Mahdists until they were defeated by the British in 1898 and the city was recaptured by General Kitchener. It was the capital of the Anglo-Egyptian government of Sudan until 1956, when it became capital of the independent Republic of Sudan. The city centre lies on a curved strip of land like an elephant's trunk which gives its name to the city (Arabic *Ras-al-hartum*, 'end of the elephant's trunk'). Across the Blue Nile is a modern industrial zone with pharmaceutical, textile, leather, and food-processing industries.

Khayyam, Omar (died 1132) Persian poet. Originally he was most famous in the Iranian world as an astronomer and mathematician. But he was also known as the master of the minor poetical form of *rubaiyat* or QUATRAINS. His wider fame is due to the inspired English translation, or interpretation, of his poems by Edward FITZGERALD.

Khilafat Movement An Indian Muslim movement. It aimed to rouse public opinion against the harsh treatment accorded to the Ottoman empire after World War I and specifically against the treatment of the Ottoman sultan and caliph (khalifa). The movement began in 1919 and, under the leadership of the Ali brothers, Muhammad Ali (1878–1931) and Shaukat Ali (1873–1938), assumed a mainly political character in alliance with the Indian National CONGRESS, adopting the non-cooperation programme in May 1920. The Khilafat movement had considerable support from Muslims but was extinguished in 1924 after the abolition of the caliphate by ATATÜRK.

Khitai See CATHAY.

Khmer ▶**1** An ancient kingdom in south-east Asia, which reached the peak of its power in the 11th century, ruling over the entire Mekong valley from the capital at Angkor, and was destroyed by Siamese conquests in the 12th and 14th centuries. ▶**2** The indigenous people of Cambodia and parts of Vietnam whose monosyllabic language belongs to the Mon-Khmer group of the Austro-Asiatic family. The (centre Khmer) are people of the ricelands of west and central Cambodia; the (lower Khmer) are people of Vietnam's Mekong delta; and the (upper Khmer) are the hill people of north-east Cambodia.

Khmer Republic The former official name (1970–75) for CAMBODIA.

Khmer Rouge Cambodian communist movement. Formed to resist the right-wing, US-backed regime of Lon Nol after the latter's military coup in 1970, the Khmer Rouge, with Vietnamese assistance, first dominated the countryside and then captured the capital Phnom Penh (1975). Under POL POT it began a bloody purge, liquidating nearly the entire professional élite as well as most of the government officials and Buddhist monks. The majority of the urban population were relocated on worksites in the countryside where large numbers perished. The regime was responsible for an estimated 2 million deaths in CAMBODIA (Kampuchea), and for the dislocation of the country's infrastructure. Frontier disputes with Vietnam provoked an invasion by the latter in 1978 which led to the overthrow of the Khmer Rouge regime, although its forces have continued a guerrilla war against the Vietnamese-backed Heng Samrin regime from bases in Thailand. As the Party of Democratic Kampuchea, with its former leader Pol Pot still influential, it agreed to join the UN-backed Supreme National Council, following the peace agreement of October 1991. However, the Khmer Rouge refused to participate in multi-party elections in 1993 and has continued to wage a guerrilla war against the elected government.

Khoisan languages A group of 'click' languages spoken in southern and eastern Africa, chiefly by Bushmen and Hottentots.

Khomeini, **Ruhollah** (known as **Ayatollah Khomeini**) (1900–89) Iranian Shiite Muslim leader. After 16 years in exile he returned to Iran in 1979 to lead an Islamic revolution which overthrew the shah. He established a fundamentalist Islamic republic, supported the seizure of the US embassy (1979) by Iranian students, and relentlessly pursued the Iran–Iraq War 1980–88. In 1989 he issued a *fatwa* condemning Salman Rushdie, author of *The Satanic Verses* and offering a reward for his murder, provoking criticism from the West.

Khrushchev, **Nikita (Sergeevich)** (1894–1971) Soviet statesman, Premier of the USSR 1958–64. Born in Ukraine, Khrushchev became First Secretary of the Communist Party of the USSR (1953–64) after the death of Stalin. He played a prominent part in the 'de-Stalinization' programme that began in 1956, denouncing the former leader in a historic speech, and went on to succeed Bulganin as Premier (Chairman of the Council of Ministers) in 1958. He came close to war with the USA over the Cuban Missile Crisis in 1962 and clashed with China over economic aid and borders. He was ousted two years later by Brezhnev and Kosygin, largely because of his antagonism to China.

Khufu See CHEOPS.

Khuzestan An oil-producing province of south-west Iran, on the frontier with Iraq from which it is separated by the Shatt al-Arab Waterway; area 67,236 sq km (25,970 sq miles); pop. (1982) 2,197,000; capital, Ahvaz. Between 1890 and 1925 the predominantly Arab Khuzestanis maintained their autonomy under a tribal sheik. Subsequently absorbed into Iran, their claim to autonomy has been supported by Iraqis who have named the region Arabistan.

Khyber Pass A mountain pass in the Hindu Kush, on the border between Pakistan and Afghanistan at a height of 1,067 m (3,520 ft). The pass was for long of great commercial and strategic importance, the route by which successive invaders entered India, and was garrisoned by the British intermittently between 1839 and 1947.

kiang The largest and most handsome subspecies of the Asiatic wild ASS, *Equus hemionus kiang*. It inhabits the high mountain plateau of Tibet up to 5,000 m (16,000 feet). The dung of this ass is gathered for fuel.

Kiangsu See JIANGSU.

kibbutz (Hebrew, 'gathering', 'collective') An Israeli collective settlement, usually agricultural but sometimes also industrial. The land was originally held in the name of the Jewish people by the Jewish National Fund, and is now owned or leased at nominal fees by its members, who also manage it. The first kibbutz, Deganya, was founded in 1910 by Professor Franz Oppenheimer; they now number around 300 in Israel.

Kibo The highest peak of Mt. Kilimanjaro in Tanzania, East Africa (5,895 m, 19,340 ft). Once an active volcano, its summit is permanently snow-covered although only just south of the equator.

Kidd, **William** (known as **Captain Kidd**) (1645–1701) Scottish pirate. Sent to the Indian Ocean in 1695 in command of an anti-pirate expedition, Kidd became a pirate himself. In 1699 he went to Boston in the hope of obtaining a pardon, but was arrested in the same year and hanged in London.

Kidderminster A town of west-central England, in Hereford and Worcester, on the River Stour; pop. (1981) 50,750. It gives its name to a type of reversible carpet made of two cloths of different colours woven together.

kidney One of a pair of organs normally present in the abdomen of vertebrates. They function mainly as organs of excretion, but also play a part in the control of blood salt concentration.

The general pattern for all vertebrates is that blood passes continually through the kidney, where it is 'cleaned' of all waste compounds, or excesses of useful salts and substances. Inside the kidney are special tubes, called nephrons, which filter out water and soluble substances. They also absorb small molecules from the blood. The useful

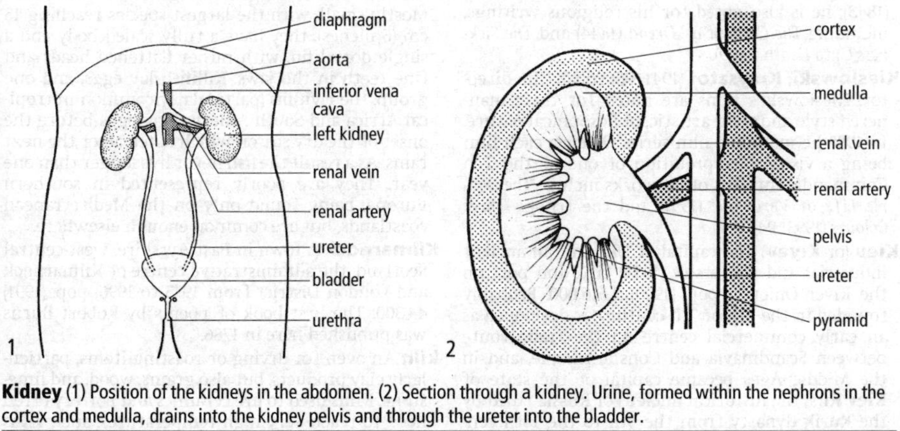

Kidney (1) Position of the kidneys in the abdomen. (2) Section through a kidney. Urine, formed within the nephrons in the cortex and medulla, drains into the kidney pelvis and through the ureter into the bladder.

compounds, and some water, are then actively reabsorbed back into the blood from the nephrons, which thereby carefully control their level in the blood. The waste products and water are passed out of the kidney as urine, and collect in the BLADDER.

During the breakdown of proteins the body discards large amounts of nitrogen, usually in the form of the toxic but soluble gas, ammonia. This is carried away from cells by the bloodstream. In aquatic freshwater animals, water loss is not a problem and they rid themselves of ammonia by producing a large quantity of dilute urine. Terrestrial animals cannot afford to do so; instead they convert the toxic ammonia into the less toxic form, UREA. This is then filtered out by the kidneys and excreted in a more concentrated form. In birds and reptiles most of the ammonia is converted into an insoluble compound called uric acid. This packs more nitrogen into a smaller space and is excreted as a white paste, equivalent to urine.

kidney machine See HAEMODIALYSIS.

Kiel A naval port with large shipyards in northern Germany, capital of the state of Schleswig-Holstein; pop. (1991) 247,100. Situated on the Baltic Sea coast at the eastern end of the Kiel Canal, it was Germany's chief naval base from 1871 to 1945 and is now an international yachting centre.

Kiel Canal A man-made waterway 98 km (61 miles) in length in Schleswig-Holstein, north-west Germany, running westwards from Kiel to Brunsbüttel at the mouth of the Elbe. It connects the North Sea with the Baltic and was constructed in 1887–95 to provide the German navy with a shorter route between these two seas.

Kielder Water A reservoir in Northumberland, north-east England, created by the damming of the River Tyne and constructed between 1974 and 1982 to supply water to the industrial towns of the north-east. It is one of the largest man-made lakes in Europe and the nearby Kielder Forest, which stretches to the Scottish border, is with neighbouring planted areas one of the largest forest plantations in Europe.

Kierkegaard, Søren (Aabye) (1813–55) Danish philosopher. Viewed as one of the founders of existentialism, he opposed the prevailing Hegelian philosophy of the time by affirming the importance of individual experience and choice. Accordingly, he refused to subscribe to the possibility of an objective system of Christian doctrinal truths, and held that one could know God only through a 'leap of faith'. His philosophical works include *Either-Or* (1843); he is also noted for his religious writings, including *The Concept of Dread* (1844) and *The Sickness Unto Death* (1849).

Kieslowski, Krzysztof (1941–96) Polish film director. Kieslowski's films are noted for their mannered style and their artistic, philosophical nature. In 1988 he made the film series *Dekalog*, each film being a visual interpretation of one of the Ten Commandments. His other works include *The Double Life of Véronique* (1991) and the trilogy *Three Colours* (1993–94).

Kiev (or **Kiyev**) The capital of Ukraine, an ancient industrial and university (1834) city, and port on the River Dnieper; pop. (1990) 2,616,000. Probably founded in the 6th or 7th century, it developed as an early commercial centre on the trade route between Scandinavia and Constantinople, and in the Middle Ages became capital of the state of **Kiev Rus**, the historical nucleus of Russia ruled by the Rurik dynasty from the 9th to the 13th centuries. Destroyed by the Mongols in 1240, the city was successively held by Lithuania and Poland until the Cossack revolt of 1648 when it briefly became the capital of a Ukrainian state. Under Russian control in 1654, it eventually became the capital of the Ukrainian Soviet Socialist Republic in 1934. In 1991 it became capital of an independent Ukraine. Its important industries include engineering, food processing, chemicals, and electrical engineering.

Kigali The capital and chief commercial centre of Rwanda in central Africa; pop. (1993) 234,500. It is situated to the east of Lake Kivu.

Kikuyu An agricultural people of East Africa, the largest Bantu-speaking group in Kenya.

Kilbrennan Sound (or **Kilbrannan Sound**) An arm of the Firth of Clyde forming a channel between the island of Arran and the Kintyre peninsula, west-central Scotland.

Kildare A county of the Republic of Ireland, in the east, in the province of Leinster; area 1,694 sq km (654 sq miles); pop. (1991) 122,520; county town, Naas.

Kilimanjaro, Mount An extinct volcano in northern Tanzania. It has twin peaks, the higher of which, Kibo (5,895 m, 19,340 ft), is the highest mountain in Africa. Its lower southern slopes are intensively cultivated, coffee and plantains being the chief crops.

Kilkenny ▶1 A county of the Republic of Ireland, in the south-east, in the province of Leinster; area 2,062 sq km (796 sq miles); pop. (1991) 73,610. **▶2** Its county town, on the River Nore; pop. (1991) 8,510. Capital of the pre-Norman kingdom of Ossary, Kilkenny is named after the 6th-century church founded by St Canice. In 1366 the Statute of Kilkenny made it high treason for an Anglo-Norman to marry an Irishwoman and for an Irishman to live in a walled town.

Killarney A resort town and market centre on Lough Leane in County Kerry, in the south-west of the Republic of Ireland; pop. (1991) 7,250. Set amidst scenic lakes and hills, the Killarney area has long been popular with poets, writers, and artists.

Killiecrankie, Pass of A wooded gorge south-east of Blair Atholl in Perth and Kinross, Scotland; the site of a battle in 1689 in which the forces of William III were defeated by the Jacobites under Graham of Claverhouse, who was killed during the battle. The River Garry flows through the pass.

killifish (or **tooth carp, top-minnow**) A member of a family, Cyprinodontidae, of at least 300 species of fresh- and brackish-water fishes, found in tropical and warm temperate regions of the world. Mostly small, with the largest species reaching 15 cm (6 inches), they have a fully scaled body and a single dorsal fin, with rather flattened heads and fine teeth in the jaws. Killifish lay eggs, and one group, the rivulins (particularly common in tropical Africa and South America) lay eggs before the onset of the dry season which hatch after the next rains. As a result the fish never live longer than one year. They are poorly represented in southern Europe, being found only on the Mediterranean coastlands, but are common enough elsewhere.

Kilmarnock A town in East Ayrshire, west-central Scotland, the administrative centre of Kilmarnock and Loudon District from 1975 to 1996; pop. (1991) 44,300. The first book of poems by Robert Burns was published here in 1786.

kiln An oven for drying or roasting items, particularly clay products, but also grains, wood, and limestone. Kilns used to fire ceramics and pottery often need to reach very high temperatures: such kilns are lined with special bricks or other REFRACTORY materials. Kilns can be of two types: those in which the materials in the kiln come in contact with the furnace flames (as, for example, in LIME KILNS), and those in which the kiln chamber is heated indirectly (for example, pottery kilns). In the ceramics industry, batch kilns are being replaced by tunnel and other continuous kilns. In tunnel-kilns, the objects to be fired travel through a long kiln which is cool near the entrance and exit, but becomes hotter towards the centre.

kilogram (symbol kg) The SI base unit of MASS. It is defined as the mass of a particular cylinder of platinum–iridium alloy held by the International Bureau of Weights and Measures at Sèvres, France. One kilogram is equal to 2.205 pounds.

Kimberley (or **The Kimberleys**) A mining and cattle-rearing region in the far north of Western Australia, situated to the north of the Great Sandy Desert between the Fitzroy and Ord rivers. Its chief settlements are the port of Wyndham (which is the terminus of the Great Northern Highway), the old pearling town of Broome, the cattle town of Derby, and Halls Creek, scene of the first gold-rush in Western Australia in 1885. The meteorite crater at Wolf Creek is the second-largest in the world.

Kimberley A city in South Africa, capital (since 1994) of the Northern Cape province; pop. (1991) 167,060. Named after the 1st Earl of Kimberley (British Colonial Secretary), it has been a diamond-mining centre since the early 1870s and gave its name to kimberlite, a rare blue-tinged igneous rock that sometimes contains diamonds.

kimberlite A type of PERIDOTITE containing mica in addition to olivine. The name of the rock comes from the Kimberley district of South Africa, where volcanic necks filled with kimberlite are mined for diamonds.

Kim Il Sung (born Kim Song Ju) (1912–94) Korean Communist statesman, first Premier of North Korea 1948–72 and President 1972–94. In the 1930s and 1940s he led the armed resistance to the Japanese domination of Korea; following the country's partition at the end of World War II he became Premier of the Democratic People's Republic of Korea (1948). He ordered his forces to invade South Korea in 1950, precipitating the Korean War (1950–53), and remained committed to the reunification of the country. He maintained a one-party state and created a personality cult around himself and his family; on his death he was quickly replaced in power by his son **Kim Jong Il** (1942–).

Kinabalu, Mount A mountain in the state of Sabah in eastern Malaysia, the highest peak of Borneo and of south-east Asia, rising to a height of 4,094 m (13,431 ft). First climbed in 1888 by a zoologist, John Whitehead, it was designated part of the 754-sq km (290-sq mile) Mt. Kinabalu National Park in 1964.

Kinchinjunga See KANCHENJUNGA.

kinetic art Art that incorporates real or apparent movement. In its broadest sense kinetic art encompasses a diverse range of phenomena, including cinematic motion pictures, but most usually it is applied to sculpture incorporating motors or driven by air currents, such as Alexander CALDER's mobiles.

kinetic energy The ability of a body to do work as a result of its motion, i.e. it is the work the body could do on coming to rest. For a body of mass m and velocity v, its kinetic energy is equal to $mv^2/2$, and in SI UNITS is measured in joules. For a rotating body the kinetic energy is given by $I\omega^2/2$, where I is the MOMENT OF INERTIA and ω the angular velocity. Many energy changes involve the interconversion of kinetic energy and POTENTIAL ENERGY, the energy resulting from the position of a body. For example a child's swing has its greatest kinetic energy as it moves through the lowest point on its path; here it is moving fastest. As the swing rises it loses kinetic energy (it slows down) but gains potential energy as it rises from the ground. The swing has its greatest potential energy where it has its least kinetic energy: at its highest point above the ground.

kinetic theory A theory developed in order to calculate the properties of gases when their pressure, temperature, or volume is changed. It assumes that all the molecules in a gas are tiny, elastic spheres in rapid motion and that they collide with one another in a random manner. From such a simple description it is possible to account convincingly for many properties, such as the HEAT CAPACITY and CONDUCTION of gases. The theory was largely the work of Benjamin THOMPSON, Count Rumford, James JOULE, and James Clerk MAXWELL.

King, B. B. (born Riley B. King) (1925–) US blues singer and guitarist. He became an established blues performer in the 1950s and early 1960s, but only came to the notice of a wider audience in the late 1960s, when his style of guitar playing was imitated by rock musicians.

King, Billie Jean (1943–) US tennis player. She won a record 20 Wimbledon titles, including six singles titles (1966–68; 1972–73; 1975) ten doubles titles, and four mixed doubles titles. King retired in 1983.

King, Martin Luther (1929–68) US Baptist minister and civil-rights leader. King opposed discrimination against blacks by organizing non-violent resistance and peaceful mass demonstrations, notably the year-long black boycott of the local bus company in Montgomery, Alabama, in 1955 and the march on Washington involving 200,000 demonstrators in 1963. At the latter, King delivered his celebrated speech beginning 'I have a dream ...'. He was awarded the Nobel Peace Prize in 1964. King was assassinated in Memphis in 1968.

King, William Lyon Mackenzie (1874–1950) Canadian Liberal statesman, Prime Minister 1921–26, 1926–30, and 1935–48. The grandson of William Lyon Mackenzie, he represented Canada at the imperial conferences in London (1923; 1926; 1927), where he played an important role in establishing the status of the self-governing nations of the Commonwealth. He went on to strengthen ties with the UK and the USA and introduced a number of social reforms, including unemployment insurance (1940).

kingbird A member of the tyrant FLYCATCHER group, Tyrannidae, restricted to the New World, where they live in open, wooded country. There are 12 species in the genus *Tyrannus*. They are the size of a small thrush, blackish or greenish with paler underparts. They get their name from their aggressive domination of any other species of bird which comes close to their nests.

king cobra (or **hamadryad**) The world's largest species of venomous snake, *Ophiophagus hannah*, from south-east Asia, with reliably recorded lengths of up to 5.72 m (18.75 feet). The female builds a nest out of vegetation, into which she deposits her eggs, and remains coiled above them or patrols the nest until they hatch. The king cobra feeds mainly on other snakes.

king crab A large relative of the stone crab, found in the northern Pacific. King crabs have long, slender legs, with a span over 1 m (3 feet), and both the legs and body have a heavily sculptured EXOSKELETON. These crabs are trapped in large numbers off Alaska, as food. Confusingly, the HORSESHOE CRABS, which are not crustaceans at all, are also sometimes known as king crabs.

kingcup (or **marsh marigold**) A species of plant, *Caltha palustris*, with large yellow flowers. It is a member of the buttercup family and is widely distributed over much of Europe and Asia, being found chiefly in water meadows and by the sides of streams.

kingdom In biology, the highest category used in the classification of organisms. Traditionally only two kingdoms were recognized: Animalia (ANIMALS) and Plantae (PLANTS). With the development of the microscope in the 17th century, the existence of microorganisms was revealed, and in the 19th century the German biologist HAEKEL proposed a third kingdom, Protista, to include them. In the 20th century further work on BACTERIA revealed that they were fundamentally different from other microbes, and they were assigned to a new kingdom, Monera. More recently, the fungi and algae (traditionally classified as plants) and protozoa (traditionally classified as animals) have been placed in other kingdoms.

Most modern classifications now recognize five kingdoms: Animalia, Plantae, Fungi (see FUNGUS), PROTOCTISTA (including protozoa and algae), and Prokaryotae (or Monera; bacteria). However, some biologists have suggested an alternative classification in which the highest category is the **domain**. Organisms are classified into three domains: Archaea (containing between two and 40 kingdoms of primitive bacteria living in extreme environments, such as hot springs and the ocean depths); Bacteria (containing a single kingdom, Eubacteria, the so-called 'true' bacteria); and Eukarya (containing the established kingdoms of animals, plants, and fungi as well as the single-celled organisms of the old kingdom Protista).

kingfisher A small to medium-sized bird of a group that comprises three families, Alcedinidae, Dacelonidae, and Cerylidae, and includes the kookaburras of Australasia. There are 91 species of kingfisher, with short legs, rounded wings, and brilliant plumage. Many species plunge into water to catch fish, but the majority live on insects and other small animals. They nest in holes in banks or tree trunks. The common kingfisher, *Alcedo atthis*, has subspecies which span much of the Eurasian landmass as well as many Pacific islands down to New Guinea.

Kingitanga A MAORI movement in New Zealand intended to unify the Maori under an hereditary kingship and restrain individual chiefs from selling land. In 1858, under the guidance of Wiremu Tamihana (the king-maker), Potatau, the first king, was recognized by tribes of central North Island. The Kingitanga sought to establish and enforce its own laws, but its more moderate leaders, including Tamihana, were willing to contemplate a defined authority under the British crown. Governor George GREY was disinclined to recognize a movement which would hinder British authority and settlement. Independent-minded members of the Kingitanga such as Rewi Maniapoto became involved in the Taranaki war and gave Grey grounds for invading the Waikato in 1863. Even so, for many years, government authority did not run in 'the King Country'. In 1883, the King Country chiefs admitted settlement and King Tawhiao returned to his traditional land in lower Waikato. In the 20th century, largely under the influence of Te Puea, Tawhiao's niece, the Kingitanga came to terms with government and became a focus for economic and cultural revival.

Kingsley, Charles (1819–75) British novelist and clergyman. He is remembered for his historical novel *Westward Ho!* (1855) and for his classic children's story *The Water-Babies* (1863).

King's Lynn A market town and port in Norfolk, eastern England, on the River Ouse just south of the Wash; pop. (1981) 37,970. Nearby is the royal palace of Sandringham.

Kingston The capital and chief port of Jamaica; pop. (1991) 538,140. Situated on the south-east coast of the island and capital since 1870, it was founded in 1693 after the destruction of Port Royal during an earthquake. It is the home of the University of the West Indies (1948) and is the largest English-speaking city in the Americas south of Miami. Its industries include oil refining, food and tobacco processing, shoes and clothing. It is the commercial centre for the coffee trade.

Kingston upon Hull The official name of HULL.

Kingston upon Thames An outer borough of London, England, on the south bank of the Thames opposite Hampton Court; pop. (1991) 130,300. It was the coronation place of at least six Anglo-Saxon kings. Kingston University (formerly Kingston Polytechnic) was established in 1992.

Kingstown The capital and chief port of St Vincent in the Windward Islands of the Caribbean; pop. (1991) 26,220. Situated on Kingstown Bay at the south-west corner of the island, the town is surrounded by a ring of steep hills. Its Botanical Gardens, founded in 1763, are the oldest in the Americas.

kinkajou A carnivore, *Potos flavus*, belonging to the racoon family, Procyonidae. Although mainly a fruit-eater, it also takes insects, small mammals, and birds' eggs. In appearance it is rather like a monkey, with its flat face, round head, and prehensile tail. It is a stocky animal, sometimes reaching 57 cm (23 inches) in length, without the 55 cm (22 inches) tail, and weighing from 1.5 to 3 kg (3–7 pounds). It lives in tropical forests of Central and northern South America and spends its time entirely in trees. It is nocturnal and usually solitary. Its soft, dense fur is used locally.

Kinnock, Neil Gordon (1942–) British politician and Leader of the Opposition 1983–92. Elected to Parliament in 1970, in 1978 he became a member of the National Executive Committee of the Labour Party, and after his party lost office in 1979, he was an effective opposition spokesman for Education. In 1983 he was elected Leader of his Party and thus led the Opposition to Thatcher's second administration. Following Labour's electoral defeats in 1987 and 1992 Kinnock resigned. In 1994 he became a European Commissioner.

Kinross A town in Perth and Kinross District, east-central Scotland, on the north-west shore of Loch Leven; pop. (1981) 3,500. Kinross House was built by Sir William Bruce, architect royal to King Charles II. It is an agricultural centre with a cashmere spinning mill.

Kinross-shire A former county of east-central Scotland, since 1975 part of Perth and Kinross District. Its county town was Kinross.

Kinsey, Alfred Charles (1894–1956) US zoologist and sex researcher. He co-founded and directed the Institute for Sex Research at Indiana University, carrying out pioneering studies by interviewing large numbers of people. His best-known work, *Sexual Behaviour in the Human Male* (1948) (often referred to as the *Kinsey Report*), was controversial but highly influential. It was followed five years later by a companion volume, *Sexual Behaviour in the Human Female*.

Kinshasa The capital of the Democratic Republic of Congo, a port on the Congo River; pop. (1991) 3,804,000. Founded in 1881 by the explorer H. M. Stanley, it was known until 1966 as Leopoldville and became the capital in 1960. It is a communications focus and a major industrial and cultural centre.

kinship A system of relationships between people either through biological links, such as parentage and descent, or through social links such as MARRIAGE. Kinship is important in all societies, although kinship systems vary from society to society. The organization of economic life, access to political power, the conduct of religious ritual: all of these areas of life may be organized and explained in terms of kinship. Kinship systems may involve rules concerning descent, inheritance, succession, INCEST and MARRIAGE, as well as structuring the more intimate world of friendship and FAMILY. The comparative study of kinship has been one of the central concerns of social ANTHROPOLOGY. Anthropologists have divided in analysing kinship either in terms of alliances, such as marriage, following LÉVI-STRAUSS, or in terms of descent. Recently emphasis has been placed on the relationship between kinship and economic life.

Kintyre A peninsula on the west coast of Scotland, to the west of Arran, extending southwards for 64 km (40 miles) from West Loch Tarbert to the Mull of Kintyre and separating the Firth of Clyde from the Atlantic Ocean. Its chief town is Campbeltown. There are ferry links to the islands of Arran, Gigha, Islay, and Jura.

Kipchak Empire, the (or **the Golden Horde**) A Turkish khanate established over central and southern European Russia in the 13th century by Batu, one of the sons of Genghis Khan. Uniting with the Kingdom of the White Horde (East Kipchak) a century later, it eventually fell to the Tatar conqueror Tamerlane. Its capital was Sarai on the lower Volga.

Kipling, (Joseph) Rudyard (1865–1936) British novelist, short-story writer, and poet. He was born in India, where he worked as a journalist 1882–89, and set many of his writings in the India of the Raj. His best-known poems, such as 'The White Man's Burden', 'If', and 'Gunga Din', came to be regarded as epitomizing the British colonial spirit. Of his vast and varied output, Kipling is perhaps now primarily known for his tales for children, notably *The Jungle Book* (1894), *Kim* (1901), the *Just So Stories* (1902), and *Puck of Pook's Hill* (1906). In 1907 he became the first British writer to be awarded the Nobel Prize for literature.

Kipping, Frederic Stanley (1863–1949) British pioneer of the chemistry of silicon. In 1897 he was appointed Professor of Chemistry at University College, Nottingham. His research ranged widely, and his work laid the foundation for the development of SILICONE polymers, with applications ranging from heavy greases to mobile fluids and synthetic rubber.

Kirchhoff, Gustav Robert (1824–87) German physicist who worked with the German chemist Robert Bunsen (1811–99) and made major advances in the study of light spectra (he was a co-founder of spectroscopy), thermal radiation, and electric circuit theory. His name is given to a law linking the radiating and absorbing powers of a surface. He also established two laws used in analysing electrical circuits, and discovered the elements caesium and rubidium (1850–51).

Kirchner, Ernst Ludwig (1880–1938) German expressionist painter. In 1905 he was a founder of the first group of German expressionists, Die BRÜCKE, who sought inspiration from medieval German and primitive art and were influenced by Van Gogh and Gauguin. His paintings, such as *Five Women in the Street* (1913), are characterized by the use of bright contrasting colours and angular outlines, and often depict claustrophobic street scenes. He committed suicide in 1938 after condemnation of his work by the Nazis.

Kirghiz A Mongol people living in central Asia between the Volga and the Irtysh rivers. Closely related to the Kazakhs and making up 52 per cent of the population of Kyrgyzstan, they speak a Turkic language. Until the 20th century they were a nomadic herding people.

Kirghizia A former name for KYRGYZSTAN in Central Asia while it was part of the Soviet Union.

Kiribati A country comprising a widely scattered archipelago of 33 islands in the Pacific Ocean, lying either side of the Equator and between longitudes 169° W and 147° E.

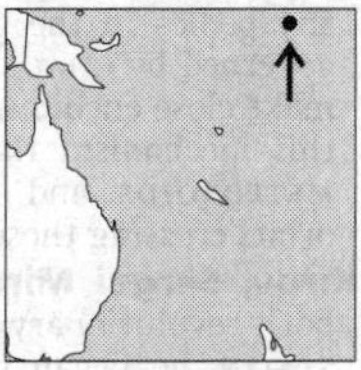

Physical. Many of the islands are mere coral atolls not more than 1 km (0.5 mile) across. Kiribati comprises the 16 former Gilbert Islands, eight of the Line Islands, the eight Phoenix Islands, and Ocean Island (Banaba).

Economy. The economy of Kiribati is based on fishing and subsistence farming. The main resource is the coconut palm, from which copra is produced for export. The phosphate deposits on Ocean Island, once a major source of revenue, are now exhausted.

History. Inhabited by Micronesians when sighted by the Spanish in the 16th century, the largest island group was named the Gilbert Islands in the 1820s by the Russian hydrographer Krusenstern. From 1837 European sperm whale hunters and traders began to inhabit the group, over which Britain declared a protectorate in 1892. In 1916 the group was named a crown colony, as the Gilbert and Ellice Islands. In 1942 Japanese naval forces occupied the islands, and in 1943 US marines landed and crushed Japanese resistance after fierce fighting. In 1974 the Ellice Islanders voted to secede from the colony, and the Ellice Islands became independent as TUVALU in 1978. The Gilbert Islands became the independent nation of Kiribati in 1979. Falling exports in copra and fish resulted in a trade deficit in 1990 of $24 million, with which the government of Teatao Teannaki (elected May 1991) had to contend. In 1994 Teannaki's government lost a vote of confidence and Teburoro Tito was elected President.

Capital: Bairiki (on Tarawa Atoll)
Area: 811 sq km (313 sq mi)
Population: 80,400 (1995)
Currency: 1 Australian dollar = 100 cents
Religions: Roman Catholic; Protestant
Ethnic Groups: I-Kiribati (over 97%)
Languages: English (official); I-Kiribati
International Organizations: Commonwealth; South Pacific Forum

Kirin See JILIN.

Kiritimati See CHRISTMAS ISLAND.

Kirkcaldy An industrial town in Fife, eastern Scotland, a port on the north shore of the Firth of Forth; pop. (1991) 47,150. It is often called 'the Lang Toun' from its 4-mile-long main street. Developed as a textile-manufacturing town in the 19th century, its industries now produce linoleum, clothing, and plastics.

Kirkcudbrightshire A former county of south-west Scotland, since 1975 part of Dumfries and Galloway.

Kirkwall The chief town and port of the Orkneys, situated on the mainland of Orkney, on a narrow neck of land between the Bay of Kirkwall and Scapa Flow; pop. (1981) 6,000. Its principal landmarks are the 12th-century St Magnus Cathedral and the 17th-century Earl Patrick's palace.

Kirkwood gap Any of several narrow regions in the belt of ASTEROIDS in which very few bodies are found. These gaps, named after the US astronomer Daniel Kirkwood, who pointed them out in 1867, correspond to orbits characterized by resonances with Jupiter, that is, having PERIODS nearly equal to simple fractions (3/1, 5/2, 7/3, 2/1) of Jupiter's orbital period. This causes the orbits of any bodies in the gaps to become unstable and, governed by CHAOS THEORY, they may eventually make close encounters with planets. It is probably this mechanism that is responsible for putting METEOROIDS and APOLLO–AMOR OBJECTS into orbits crossing those of the inner planets.

Kirov, Sergei Mironovich (1886–1934) Russian-born revolutionary leader. A strong supporter of STALIN, he began his revolutionary activities in Caucasia but moved to Leningrad (1928) and became a member of the POLITBURO (1930). In 1934 he was assassinated by a young party member, Leonid Nikolayev, possibly at Stalin's instigation. Stalin used Kirov's murder to launch the show trials and party purges of the late 1930s.

Kirov Ballet Russian ballet company based at the Kirov Theatre, St Petersburg. The principal company in Russia, it was called the Maryinsky until 1935, when it was renamed in honour of S. M. KIROV. PETIPA and FOKINE choreographed for it, and dancers Tamara Karsavina, Anna Pavlova, and NIJINKSY were trained at its school. After the revolution Agrippina Vagonava became ballet director; she maintained the classical purity and elegance which are still the Kirov's hallmarks. NUREYEV, Natalia Makarova, and BARYSHNIKOV were all members of the company and its current stars include Attynai Assylmouratova and Faroukh Rusimatov. Its current director, Oleg Vinogradov, is looking to Western choreographers to expand the repertoire.

Kirovograd See KIROVOHAD.

Kirovohad A city in central Ukraine, on the River Ingul; pop. (1990) 274,000. Founded in 1761 as Elizavetgrad, it was known as Zinoviesk (1924–36), Kirovo (1936–39), and Kirovograd (1939–92). It is a major producer of farm machinery.

Kirundi A Bantu language, the official language of Burundi.

Kisangani A city in the Democratic Republic of Congo on the Congo River; pop. (1991) 373,400. Founded in 1882 by the explorer H. M. Stanley, it was known as Stanleyville until 1966. Now a manufacturing, commercial, and communications centre.

Kishibojin (or **Kishimojin**) In Buddhism, the Japanese name for Hariti, a child-eating ogress, converted by the Buddha into a protectress of children and of women in childbirth. Sometimes regarded as a feminine form of Kannon, Hariti is usually depicted either surrounded by children or carrying a child, and holding a pomegranate or cornucopia.

Kishinev See CHISINAU.

Kissinger, Henry (Alfred) (1923–) German-born US statesman and diplomat, Secretary of State 1973–77. As presidential assistant to Richard Nixon for national security affairs (1968–73) he helped to improve relations with both China and the Soviet Union. His role in negotiating the withdrawal of US troops from South Vietnam in 1973 was recognized when he was jointly awarded the Nobel Peace Prize that year. Later in 1973 he restored US diplomatic relations with Egypt in the wake of the Yom Kippur War and became known for his 'shuttle diplomacy', while subsequently mediating between Israel and Syria.

Kiswahili A Bantu language of the Niger-Congo group of languages spoken in East Africa. It is one of the six languages preferred for use in Africa by the Organization of African Unity.

Kitasato Shibasaburo (1852–1931) Japanese physician and bacteriologist. From 1885 to 1891 he worked in the bacteriologist Robert Koch's laboratory in Germany, and, together with Emil von Behring, developed an anti-toxin for IMMUNIZATION against diphtheria. On returning to Japan, he founded an institute for the study of infectious diseases, and in 1894 discovered the infectious agent of bubonic plague.

Kitchener, (Horatio) Herbert, 1st Earl Kitchener of Khartoum (1850–1916) British soldier and statesman. After defeating the Mahdist forces at Omdurman and reconquering Sudan in 1898, he served as Chief of Staff (1900–02) in the Second Boer War and Commander-in-Chief (1902–09) in India. At the outbreak of World War I he was made Secretary of State for War, in which capacity he was responsible for organizing the large volunteer army that eventually fought the war on the Western Front. His commanding image appeared on recruiting posters urging 'Your country needs you!' He died when the ship taking him to Russia was sunk by a mine.

kitchen-sink drama A theatrical genre that included John OSBORNE's *Look Back in Anger* (1956) and the plays by Arnold WESKER using working-class settings rather than the drawing-rooms of polite comedy. As modern dramatists enlarged their settings to cover many different environments the description no longer seemed appropriate. See also ANGRY YOUNG MEN.

kite (in the animal kingdom) A member of a subfamily of HAWKS, Pandioninae, with slender bodies and wings and long tails. True kites live in open country, partly as hunters but mostly as scavengers. Red kites, *Milvus milvus*, once scavenged London streets but are now rural over most of Europe. Black kites, *M. migrans*, still scavenge widely in Africa, Australia, and Eurasia. The name applies also to fork-tailed kites (honey-buzzard) and white-tailed kites, a subfamily of small kites that hover like kestrels and feed on insects and small mammals.

kite (in technology) A non-powered, heavier-than-air aircraft anchored to or towed from the ground and sustained in flight by the wind. Kites depend on a moderate wind speed of 13–32 km/h (8–20 m.p.h.) to stay aloft. They come in a variety of forms and materials, such as paper, nylon, or cotton, and often have a tail for stability. More than one control line can be fitted to manœuvre a kite in flight. The Chinese have used kites since 1000 BC, and kites had reached Europe by the 13th century. An early function of the kite was to ward off evil spirits when flown above a house at night. Since then, they have been used for many purposes, including military observation, signalling, fishing, and sport.

kitsch (German, 'trash') Art that is considered vulgar, tawdry, or pretentious, especially work designed to have a popular, sentimental appeal. It has been most often applied to mass-produced items, such as cheap tourist souvenirs, but it can also refer to intentionally vulgar images used by artists, for example Andy Warhol's silk-screen prints of Campbell's soup cans.

kitten moth See PUSS MOTH.

kittiwake Either of two species of cliff-nesting GULL, *Rissa tridactyla*, common on most Arctic and cool temperate coasts, and *R. brevirostris*, confined to the Bering Sea area. They breed on sea cliffs, raising one to three chicks on narrow, unprotected ledge nests. They feed communally at sea on fish and large plankton, and are seldom seen inland.

Kitt Peak National Observatory An OBSERVATORY in Arizona, USA, with a wide variety of telescopes. These include the McMath solar telescope of 1.5 m (59 inches) aperture, the Mayall REFLECTING TELESCOPE with an aperture of 4 m (157 inches), and two radio DISH telescopes of 11 m (36 feet) and 12 m (39 feet) diameter. The observatory's high altitude of 2,060 m (6,750 feet) and its range of facilities make it one of the most active and important observing stations in the world. Organizations operating its facilities include the Association of Universities for Research in Astronomy (a group of 17 US university astronomy departments), the National Radio Astronomy Observatory, and the Steward Observatory. The Mayall reflector has a twin at the Cerro Tololo Inter-American Observatory in Chile.

Kitty Hawk A small town on a narrow sand peninsula on the Atlantic coast of North Carolina, USA. It was here that, in 1903, the Wright Brothers made their first powered aeroplane flight in the USA, which is commemorated by the Wright Brothers National Memorial.

Kitwe A city in the Copperbelt province of northern Zambia, 50 km (31 miles) north of Ndola; pop. (1987) 449,440. The second-largest city in Zambia, it is a centre of copper-mining and industry.

Kitzbühel A winter sports resort in the state of Tyrol, western Austria; pop. (1981) 7,840. Founded in the 12th century, it was a prosperous town, with copper and silver mining.

Kitzinger, Sheila (Helena Elizabeth) (1929–) British childbirth educator. As a member of the advisory board of the National Childbirth Trust, and as one of the Trust's teachers, she has been a pioneer of natural childbirth and a leading advocate of breastfeeding. Her many books include *The Experience of Childbirth* (1962).

Kivu, Lake A lake in central Africa, on the border between the Democratic Republic of Congo and Rwanda: area 2,699 sq km (1,042 sq miles). Drained by the Ruzzi River, it is the highest lake in Africa at 1,460 m (4,788 ft).

kiwi Any one of three species of mainly nocturnal, flightless birds of the family Apterygidae, living in New Zealand. Kiwis are about the size of a large chicken, with a large head and a long, curved beak. They have powerful legs and brownish or greyish feathers which look like hair. The females are larger than the males. Kiwis eat a variety of food, including berries and worms, some of which they trace by smell. They nest in a hole in the ground, the male doing most of the incubating of the usually single egg.

kiwi fruit The fruit of a climbing plant native to southern China, *Actinidia chinensis*. The name comes from the national bird of New Zealand, since that country exports the fruit to Europe and the USA. They are also known as Chinese gooseberries, as they resemble large brown, hairy gooseberries. Their pale green flesh is extremely rich in vitamin C.

Klagenfurt The capital city of the state of Carinthia (Kärnten) in southern Austria, on the Glan River; pop. (1991) 89,500.

Klaproth, Martin Heinrich (1743–1817) German chemist, one of the founders of analytical chemistry. He discovered three new elements (zirconium, uranium, and titanium) in certain minerals, and contributed to the identification of others. A follower of Lavoisier, he helped to introduce the latter's new system of chemistry into Germany.

Klee, Paul (1879–1940) Swiss painter, resident in Germany from 1906. He began as a graphic artist and exhibited with Kandinsky, whose *Blaue Reiter* group he joined in 1912. He later concentrated on painting and developed an art of free fantasy, describing his drawing method as 'taking a line for a walk'. His paintings often have a childlike quality, as in *A Tiny Tale of a Tiny Dwarf* (1925). He taught at the Bauhaus (1920–33), after which he returned to Switzerland. Many of his works appeared in the 'degenerate art' exhibition mounted by the Nazi regime in Munich in 1937.

Klein, Calvin (Richard) (1942–) US fashion designer. In 1968 he formed his own company, since when he has gained a reputation for his understated fashions for both men and women, including designer jeans. He is also known for his ranges of cosmetics and household linen.

Klein, (Christian) Felix (1849–1925) German mathematician and educator who disapproved of the increasing tendency towards abstraction in mathematics. An important mathematician in his own right, he used the concepts of GROUP THEORY to unify and classify the disparate geometries which were being studied at the time. He claimed that every geometry was nothing more than the study of those properties of figures which remained invariant under a particular group of transformations.

Klein, Melanie (1882–1960) Austrian-born psychoanalyst. Klein was the first psychologist to specialize in the psychoanalysis of small children: she discovered surprising levels of aggression and sadism in young infants, and made an important contribution to the understanding of the more severe mental disorders found in children. She moved to London in 1926, becoming an influential member of the British Psychoanalytical Society.

Klein bottle See TOPOLOGY.

Kleist, Bernd Heinrich von (1777–1811) German dramatist and writer of short stories. The theme of the conflict of reason and emotion lies at the heart of all Kleist's work; it disturbs the comic resolution of *The Broken Pitcher* (1808) and is a source of tragic error in *The Schroffenstein Family* (1803), a reworking of the Romeo and Juliet tragedy, and *Penthesilea* (1808), a work which contains some of Kleist's most powerful dramatic verse. Kleist's personal relationships were highly disturbed, and he took his own life in a suicide pact.

Klemperer, Otto (1885–1973) German-born conductor and composer. While conductor at the Kroll Theatre in Berlin (1927–31), he was noted as a champion of new work and opera; his premières included Janáček's opera *From the House of the Dead*. He left Germany in 1933 and became a US citizen in 1937. Klemperer subsequently established a reputation as a conductor of symphonies by Beethoven, Brahms, and Mahler, and received particular acclaim for his Beethoven recordings in London during the 1950s. He adopted Israeli citizenship in 1970.

Klerk, F. W. de See DE KLERK.

Klimt, Gustav (1862–1918) Austrian painter and designer. In 1897 he co-founded and became the first president of the avant-garde group the Vienna Secession. His work combines stylized human forms with decorative and ornate clothing or backgrounds in elaborate mosaic patterns, often using gold leaf. He depicted mythological and allegorical subjects, and painted a number of portraits, chiefly of women; his works include *Judith I* (1901) and *The Kiss* (1908).

klipspringer An antelope, *Oreotragus oreotragus*, found on rocky slopes in Africa from the Cape of Good Hope to Ethiopia. It is only 50 cm (20 inches) high at the shoulder. The bucks have horns that rise almost straight from the head, bending only slightly forwards. Its coat is a yellowish-brown in colour, speckled with yellow, the hair being long and brittle. It is an agile creature that can obtain a foothold on a rocky projection 2–3 cm (1 inch) in diameter. Family groups feed together on leaves, shrub roots, and grass. If alarmed the klipspringer can utter a shrill whistle.

Klondike An eastern tributary of the Yukon River, flowing 150 km (93 miles) from its source in the Tintina to the Yukon at Dawson City. It gives its name to a region of Yukon Territory, north-west Canada, noted as the focal point of a celebrated gold-rush in 1897–98, which was known as the Klondike stampede.

Klopstock, Friedrich Gottlieb (1724–1803) German poet. His reputation was established by the first three cantos of *The Messiah* (1748, completed 1773), an epic poem on the passion of Jesus Christ and salvation of Man modelled on Milton's *Paradise Lost* (1667).

Klosters An Alpine winter sports resort near Davos in Graubünden canton, eastern Switzerland, on the River Lanquart.

klystron See THERMIONIC VALVE.

Klyuchevskaya Sopka A volcanic peak on the Kamchatka Peninsula, far-eastern Russia. Rising to a height of 4,750 m (15,584 ft), it is the highest active volcano in Russia and the continent of Asia.

Kneller, Sir Godfrey (1646–1723) German-born painter who settled in England in the mid-1670s and became the leading portraitist there in the late 17th and early 18th centuries. The finest portraits from his own hand are highly regarded, but his studio turned out much inferior work. He is best known for portraits of the members of the fashionable Kitcat Club.

Knesset The parliament of the state of Israel. Its name is derived from a Hebrew word meaning a 'gathering'.

knighthood The special honour bestowed upon a man by dubbing (when he is invested with the right to bear arms) or by admission to one of the orders of chivalry. In England the emergence of knighthood was slow (the Anglo-Saxon word *cniht* means 'servant'). In the late 11th and early 12th centuries, knights were the lowest tier of those who held land in return for military service. During the 12th century their economic and social status improved, as society became more complex, and the market in free land developed. They became involved in local administration, and the new orders of knights, which emerged in Europe in the aftermath of the CRUSADES, helped to give them a distinct identity. First to appear were the military orders of the KNIGHTS HOSPITALLERS (*c.*1070), the Knights of the Sepulchre (1113), and the KNIGHTS TEMPLARS (1118). Their potential for military colonization was best realized by the German Order of the TEUTONIC KNIGHTS (1190), which pushed eastwards on the frontiers with Poland and acquired Prussia for itself. The Order of the Livonian Knights gained similar successes along the Baltic. The Order of the Garter (1348) was England's first and most important order of knighthood, followed by the Order of the Bath (1399). France created the Order of the Star (1352), and BURGUNDY the Order of the Golden Fleece (1429).

Knight Hospitaller A member of a military religious order, formally the Knights Hospitallers of St John of Jerusalem, so called after the dedication of their headquarters in Jerusalem to St John the Baptist. From 1310 they were known as the Knights of Rhodes, from 1530 the Knights of Malta. They began in *c.*1070 with Muslim permission to run a hospital for sick pilgrims in Jerusalem, and were made a formal order when the city fell in 1099 to the First CRUSADE. They adopted a black habit bearing a white eight-pointed (Maltese) cross. Under the first Master their function became primarily military and spread to Western Europe. They followed the Augustinian rule and were divided into three classes: knights, chaplains, and serving brothers. When they were driven out by SALADIN they went to Acre, only to be expelled a century later when Cyprus became their headquarters. In 1310 they captured the island of Rhodes and retained it till 1522. Given the island of Malta by Emperor Charles V they held it, having fought off the assaults of the Turks, until it finally fell to NAPOLEON I. By this time the order had lost its former influence. Some members moved to Russia where Paul I was made Grand Master. His death in 1801 led to a period of confusion. The English branch of the order was revived in the 1830s and today cares for the sick.

Knightsbridge A district in London, England, to the south of Hyde Park and west of Piccadilly. It is noted for its fashionable shops and stores including Harrods, which was founded by Charles Harrod in 1849 and is the largest department store in Britain.

Knight Templar A member of a military religious order properly called the Poor Knights of Christ and of the Temple of Solomon, founded in 1118 by Hugh de Payens, a knight of Champagne in France. He and eight companions vowed to protect pilgrims travelling on the public roads of the Holy Land (PALESTINE). At the Council of Troyes (1128) approval was given to their version of the BENEDICTINE rule. They quickly became very influential, attracting many noble members and growing in wealth, acquiring property throughout Christendom. When Jerusalem fell in 1187 they moved to Acre together with the KNIGHTS HOSPITALLERS and great rivalry and hatred developed between the orders. In 1291 when Acre also fell, they retreated to Cyprus. In Cyprus their great wealth enabled them to act as bankers to the nobility of most of Europe and this affluence attracted much hostility, in particular that of PHILIP IV of France. In 1307 they were charged with heresy and immorality. Though some of the charges may have been true, envy of their wealth seems to have been the reason for their persecution. They were condemned, their wealth confiscated, and the order suppressed. The Grand Master and many others were burned at the stake.

knitting A method of making fabric by forming interlocking YARN (especially WOOL) loops. The advantage it has over weaving is that it can be done by working directly from one simple ball or bobbin of yarn. Knitting by forming loops around pins mounted on a board was practised in the Middle East in biblical times; the method using two hand-held needles came much later. Simple knitted fabrics have high flexibility and conformability, and a cellular construction which, by trapping air in the fabric, gives thermal insulation. These attributes have led to the widespread use of knitting for the manufacture of stockings and cold-weather clothing. Hand knitting involves laying a single thread of yarn to and fro across the width of the fabric (weft knitting). Knitting machines may also form stitches in this way, or they may form loops simultaneously on threads running along the length of the fabric (warp knitting). Warp knitting is more productive, but weft knitting is more versatile. Both types of machine are widely used commercially.

A knitting machine has one or two closely packed rows of needles (similar to crochet hooks), one needle for each stitch in the width of the fabric. Yarn is laid in the needle hooks as they are sequentially withdrawn, forming new stitches and shedding the old. For hosiery manufacture the needles are mounted not in a straight line, but in a closed circle, to produce fabrics which are tubular.

knock (or **pinking**) The characteristic noise in INTERNAL-COMBUSTION ENGINES when uncontrolled combustion occurs. In petrol engines this may happen when the 'end gas', the last part of the mixture to burn, becomes over-heated and undergoes spontaneous combustion ahead of the flame front: shock waves strike the cylinder head and walls wasting energy. In DIESEL ENGINES knock occurs because of delay in the onset of ignition. The COMPRESSION RATIO and OCTANE NUMBER of the PETROL or other fuel are the chief factors in determining the onset of knock. Fuel additives such as LEAD TETRAETHYL are used to prevent knock from occurring, although the use of lead pollutants is now discouraged.

Knock A locality in County Mayo, Ireland, a holy shrine since 1879 when an apparition of the Virgin Mary was sighted at the parish church. In 1979 it was visited by Pope John Paul II, who was the first pope to set foot on Irish soil. Since then the shrine has been known as the Basilica of Our Lady, Queen of Ireland. It is one of Ireland's leading centres of pilgrimage and has an international airport.

Knossos The principal city of Minoan Crete, near the port of Heraklion. It was occupied from neolithic times until *c.*1200 BC. Excavations by Sir Arthur Evans from 1900 onwards revealed remains of a luxurious and spectacular decorated complex of buildings which he named the Palace of Minos, with frescoes of landscapes, animal life, and the sport of bull-leaping. In *c.*1450 BC Crete was overrun by the Mycenaeans, but the palace was not finally destroyed until the 14th century or early 13th century BC, possibly by an earthquake.

knot The unit of speed measurement at sea and sometimes in the air. One knot is one international nautical mile (1,852 m; 6,076 feet) per hour. The word originated from the early methods of speed measurement in ships, in which a LOG tied to a knotted rope was thrown over the stern, and the number of knots paid out within a fixed time period gave an estimate of the ship's speed.

knotweed (or **knotgrass**) Many species of the plant genus *Polygonum*, related to rhubarb and sorrels. This genus includes 150 species of annual and perennial plants with pink or white flowers, which are found throughout Eurasia. The creeping stems of the common knotweed, *P. aviculare*, have distinctive swollen joints, narrow leaves, and very small flowers; it is a plant of cultivated land and wasteland. Other species of *Polygonum* include the tall, perennial Himalayan knotweed, *P. polystachyum*. The closely related Japanese knotweed, *Reynoutria japonica*, is now a common naturalized plant in Europe.

Knox, John (*c.*1505–72) Scottish Protestant reformer. After early involvement in the Scottish Reformation he spent more than a decade preaching in Europe, during which time he stayed in Geneva and was influenced by Calvin. In 1559 he returned to Scotland and played a central part in the establishment of the Church of Scotland within a Scottish Protestant state. A fiery orator, he became the spokesman of the religious interests opposed to the Catholic Mary, Queen of Scots when she returned to rule in her own right in 1561.

Knox, Ronald Arbuthnott (1888–1957) British theologian and writer. In 1917 he converted to Roman Catholicism and later served as Catholic chaplain at Oxford University (1926–39). His translation of the Bible from the Vulgate (1945–49) was accepted for use in the Roman Catholic Church. His literary output was varied and included detective fiction and humour.

Knut See CANUTE.

koala A herbivorous MARSUPIAL, *Phascolarctos cinereus*, found from Queensland to Victoria, Australia. It lives in eucalyptus and other trees, and feeds on their foliage. Superficially it resembles a small bear, having a wide head and a thickset body, and weighs about 9 kg (20 pounds). Like all marsupials, it has a brood-pouch with a pair of teats; a single young is born about 35 days after mating, and it makes its way into the pouch immediately after birth. Not until it is four to five months of age will it venture out of the pouch to travel on its mother's back, returning to the pouch at intervals until it is six months old. It may live for up to 20 years. Considered an endangered species, it is today increasing in numbers, saved by an active programme of conservation. The koala is a member of the family Phascolarctidae.

Kobe A seaport in Hyogo prefecture, central Honshu Island, Japan, on Osaka Bay; pop. (1990) 1,477,420. Since it was built in 1868 its harbour has become one of the leading ports of Japan. It has steel and shipbuilding industries. It was devastated by a major earthquake in 1995.

Koblenz See COBLENZ.

Koch, Robert (1843–1910) German bacteriologist. He successfully identified and cultured the bacillus causing anthrax in cattle, devised better methods for obtaining pure cultures, and identified the organisms causing tuberculosis and cholera. He also studied typhoid fever, malaria, and other tropical diseases, and formulated the conditions to be satisfied before a disease can be ascribed to a specific microorganism. The techniques that Koch devised are the basis of modern bacteriological methods. He was awarded a Nobel Prize in 1905.

Kochi A port and market city at the head of an inlet on the south coast of the island of Shikoku, Japan; pop. (1990) 317,090. It is capital of a prefecture of the same name. It exports dried fish, coral, cement, and paper.

Kodály, Zoltán (1882–1967) Hungarian composer. He was influenced by Debussy's music while studying in Paris (1910), but his main source of inspiration was his native land; he was much involved in the collection and publication of Hungarian folk-songs. His best-known compositions include the choral work *Psalmus Hungaricus* (1923), the opera *Háry János* (1925–27), and the *Marosszék Dances* (1930).

Kodiak Island An island of Alaska, USA, home of the Kodiak bear, which is the largest living carnivorous animal; area 13,921 sq km (5,375 sq miles). Its chief settlement is Kodiak.

Koestler, Arthur (1905–83) Hungarian-born British novelist and essayist. In 1940 he settled in Britain and published his best-known novel, *Darkness at Noon*, which exposed the Stalinist purges of the 1930s. In later works such as *The Sleepwalkers* (1959), a study of the Copernican revolution in astronomy, he questioned some of the common assumptions of science. He became increasingly interested in parapsychology and left money in his will for a university chair in the subject, subsequently founded at Edinburgh. He and his wife committed suicide together when he became terminally ill.

Kohl, Helmut (1930–) German statesman, Chancellor of the Federal Republic of Germany 1982–90, and of Germany since 1990. He became chairman of the Christian Democratic Party in 1973, and was leader of the opposition until 1982, becoming Chancellor of the Federal Republic of Germany when the ruling coalition collapsed. As Chancellor he showed a strong commitment to NATO and to closer European union within the European Community. In 1990 he presided over the reunification of East and West Germany and was elected Chancellor of the united country later the same year. The longest-serving postwar German leader, he won a fourth term in 1996.

kohlrabi A plant derived from the same species as CABBAGE, but with a very different shape. The edible base of the single stem is swollen, and can develop to a large size, resembling a knobbly green turnip. Its value as a vegetable has been known since Roman times.

Kohoutek's Comet A long-period COMET discovered in 1973. It was found by the Czech astronomer Lubos Kohoutek who was looking for the long-lost fragments of BIELA'S COMET. Kohoutek's Comet was at the remarkably large distance of 4.75 astronomical units from the Sun when it was discovered. If it had brightened in the way that most comets do, it would have been spectacular when it reached its perihelion of 0.14 astronomical units. This failed to happen, but nevertheless the comet was comprehensively observed.

Koil See ALIGARH.

Kokchetav see KÖKSHETAU.

Kokkola (Swedish **Gamla Karleby**) A town in western Finland, at the head of an inlet of the Gulf of Bothnia; pop. (1990) 34,635. It exports timber and has chemical and metal goods industries.

Kokoschka, Oskar (1886–1980) Austrian painter, graphic artist, and writer who became a British subject in 1947. Throughout his long life he was unaffected by modern developments and pursued his own highly personal and imaginative version of pre-1914 EXPRESSIONISM. His varied output included portraits, large allegorical decorative paintings, and a particular kind of town view seen from a high viewpoint. His writings include an autobiography (1971) and several plays.

Kökshetau (Russian **Kokchetav**) A city in northern Kazakhstan, at the centre of a mining and dairy-farming region; pop. (1990) 139,400.

Kola Peninsula A peninsula on the north coast of Russia, separating the White Sea from the Barents Sea. The port of Murmansk lies on its northern coast.

Kolle, Wilhelm (1868–1935) German bacteriologist. He worked under the pioneer German bacteriologist Robert KOCH in the Institute for Infectious Diseases, Berlin. He had a lifelong interest in the treatment of bacterial diseases by vaccines and chemotherapy. With August Pfeifer, in 1896 he used killed cultures against typhoid, and he introduced Asiatic cholera vaccine. He also did research on rinderpest in cattle. With the German bacteriologist August von Wassermann, noted for his diagnosis of syphilis (1906), he edited the multi-volume *Manual of Pathogenic Micro-organisms*.

Koller, Carl (1857–1944) Austrian-born US ophthalmologist and pioneer of local ANAESTHESIA. He became a close friend of Sigmund FREUD, who in 1884 became intensely interested in the possibility of using cocaine to cure morphine addiction. Koller noticed that cocaine had a numbing effect on the tongue and, after experimenting with animals, introduced it as a local anaesthetic in ophthalmology. It was also quickly adopted for nose and throat surgery and for dentistry.

Kollwitz, Käthe (1867–1945) German Expressionist graphic artist and sculptor. She concentrated on tragic themes, much of her work being intended as social protest – against, for example, the working conditions of the urban poor. Many of her best works were devoted to the mother and child theme, and most of the later ones were pacifist in intention (her son was killed in World War I and her grandson in World War II). Her work conveys both power and poignancy and represents one of the high points of Expressionist art.

Komi A republic of the Russian Federation in the northern Urals; area 415,900 sq km (160,641 sq miles); pop. (1990) 1,265,000; capital, Syktyvkar. Annexed to Moscow in the 14th century, it became an autonomous region of the USSR in 1921 and an autonomous republic in 1936. Following the breakup of the Soviet Union in 1991 it declared itself a republic of Russia. It has a wide range of natural resources including coal, gas, oil, asphalt, and timber, and dairy farming is important. About 23 per cent of the population are Finno-Ugrian Komi people.

Komodo dragon (or **ora**) The largest living species of lizard, *Varanus komodoensis*, attaining lengths in excess of 3 m (10 feet). These MONITOR LIZARDS are restricted to a few of the Lesser Sunda Islands, Indonesia. An adult Komodo dragon is a formidable predator, quite capable of killing and eating small deer, which it brings down by grasping a leg or the throat with its sharp, curved teeth.

Konfrontasi Diplomatic and military confrontation between INDONESIA and MALAYSIA (1963–66). It centred on the formation of the Federation of Malaysia (1963), which President SUKARNO saw as a Western-inspired ploy to oppose anti-colonist forces in south-east Asia. Asserting that the Federation was part of a British plot against Indonesia, Sukarno launched a guerrilla war in Malaysia's Bornean territories, Sarawak and Sabah, in April 1963, hoping for support from local Chinese communist elements. His 'confrontation' policy, however, only served to increase support for the new federal arrangements within the Malaysian states (only BRUNEI, with its massive oil reserves, remaining aloof). It led to increased disaffection in the Indonesian army which ultimately contributed to his downfall. With the guerrilla forces defeated by Malaysians with British, Australian, and New Zealand help, Sukarno's successor General Suharto ended Konfrontasi in 1966.

Kongo A kingdom in Central Africa, established south of the River Congo by 1300 which became one of the most powerful kingdoms in the region. The Kongo people traded over long distances, exploiting iron and salt mines. On Loanda Island they had a monopoly of *nzimbu* shells, which provided a local currency. It was the first African kingdom after Ethiopia to be converted to Christianity, by Portuguese missionaries in the 16th century. The Portuguese also brought the slave trade, which encouraged civil wars and weakened the Kongo kingdom by the mid-17th century.

Königsberg The former German name (until 1946) of KALININGRAD in Russia.

Konya A city on the south-west edge of the central plateau of Turkey; pop. (1990) 513,350. Originally settled by Phrygians in the 8th century BC and known in Roman times as Iconium, it became the capital of the Seljuk sultans of Rum towards the end of the 11th century and was renamed Konya. In the 13th century It was the home of the Islamic poet and mystic Jalal al-Din Rumi, founder of the sect of whirling dervishes. Besides being a market for agricultural produce, Konya is an important carpet-making centre.

Koobi Fora A large area in northern Kenya where early HOMINID remains (from over 160 individuals), have been found, including the remarkably complete '1470 skull' found in 1972. The dating of the hominids and tools was once controversial but it now seems clear that most of the finds date to between 2 and 1.4 million years ago. The '1470 skull' is evidence of a large-brained hominid in East Africa at an early date in human evolution. Scientists still question its affinity but most now agree that it is an early representative of *Homo*, possibly HOMO HABILIS, and was the maker of the OLDOWAN tools of the same age (about 2 million years). By 1.6 million years ago, HOMO ERECTUS with advanced Oldowan tools called the Karari Industry appeared; ACHEULIAN tools came a little later.

kookaburra (or **laughing jackass**) A very large bird, growing up to 45 cm (18 inches) long, and a member of the kingfisher family which lives in Australia, New Guinea, and adjacent islands in open, wooded country, feeding on large insects and lizards and nesting in holes in trees. The most familiar species is the laughing kookaburra, *Dacelo novaeguineae*, which is common in many parts of Australia, especially down the eastern side of the continent. Its very loud, almost hysterical, peals of laughter are one of the most conspicuous features of the Australian dawn.

Kooning, Willem de See DE KOONING.

Köppen, Wladimir (1846–1940) German climatologist and biologist who in 1900 classified CLIMATIC TYPES by relating them to the Earth's natural vegetation zones and defining them in terms of mean annual temperature and precipitation. His system of classification remains one of the most easily understood and widely used.

kora A musical instrument, the bridge-harp or harp-lute, used by the professional bards of the Manding peoples of West Africa. There are 21 strings, 11 on the left and 10 on the right side of the bridge, which stands upright, on the skin belly of the large hemispherical gourd body.

Koran (or **Qur'an**) The Holy Scripture of ISLAM. Muslims believe the Koran to be the word and will of God, as revealed to his messenger Muhammad (570–632) through the angel Jibril or Gabriel over the period 610–32. Written in classical Arabic, it consists of 114 *sūras* (chapters) of varying length, each *sūra* being composed of a number of *āyas* (normally translated as verses because assonance is involved, although the Koran is a prose work). The first revelation on *Lailat al-Qadr*, the Night of Power, is commemorated during RAMADAN. The early revelations are highly charged and rhetorical, but the style becomes more relaxed with the passing of time. The contents are diverse, particularly prominent themes being the omnipotence of Allah, the duty to believe in Allah alone, descriptions of the Day of Judgement, heaven, and hell, stories of the Prophets, and, in the latest phase, social legislation. Since the Koran is regarded by Muslims as a literal transcription of God's revelations, for many years translations of the text were not permitted, and although today translations do exist, Muslims are taught to memorize and chant the original Arabic text. Calligraphic renditions of the text are a distinctive aid to worship in Islam.

Korbut, Olga (1955–) Soviet gymnast, born in Belarus. Her performances (especially at the 1972 Olympic Games, where she won two individual gold medals) greatly increased the popularity of the sport.

Korchnoi, Viktor (Lvovich) (1931–) Russian chess player. From about 1960 he was one of the world's leading players for about 30 years, ranking third (*c.*1967–75) and second (*c.*1975–80). In 1976 he left the USSR feeling that his career was in jeopardy, and moved first to the Netherlands, then Switzerland, for whom he played in the 1978 Olympics.

Korda, Sir Alexander (born Sándor Kellner) (1893–1956) Hungarian-born British film producer and director. He settled in Britain in 1930 and founded London Film Productions two years later. His productions included *The Private Life of Henry VIII* (1933), which he also directed, *Sanders of the River* (1935), *Things to Come* (1936), and *The Third Man* (1949).

Korea A region of eastern Asia forming a peninsula between the Sea of Japan and the Yellow Sea, now divided along the 38th parallel into South KOREA and North KOREA. Possessed of a distinct national and cultural identity and ruled from the 14th century by the Korean Yi dynasty, Korea has suffered from its position between Chinese and Japanese spheres of influence. Chinese domination was ended by the Sino-Japanese War (1894–95) and after the Russo-Japanese War a decade later the country was finally annexed by Japan in 1910. After the Japanese surrender at the end of World War II, the northern half of the country was occupied by the Soviets and the southern half by the Americans. Separate countries were created in 1948 and two years later the Northern invasion of the South resulted in the Korean War (1950–53). A 250 km-long demilitarized zone was established between the two countries at the end of hostilities but both

North Korea and South Korea were some time in recovering from the devastation caused by military operations. While North Korea remains under Communist rule, South Korea is now one of the most rapidly growing industrial nations in the world.

Korea, North (official name **Democratic People's Republic of Korea**) A north-east Asian country. Consisting of the northern half of the Korean peninsula, mostly above the 38th parallel, North Korea was formed from the zone occupied by the Soviet Union at the end of World War II. It borders to the south with South Korea and to the north with the People's Republic of China.

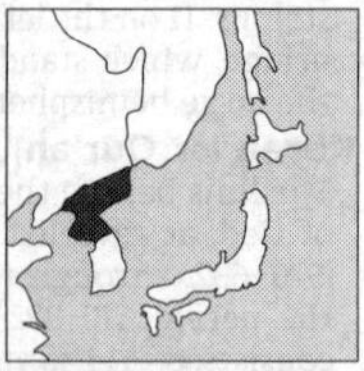

Physical. North Korea is largely mountainous with narrow valleys, extensive forests, and rivers which freeze in winter.

Economy. North Korea is rich in metal deposits such as iron ore, magnesite, phosphate, sulphur, zinc, and copper, which are major exports. Ninety per cent of cultivated land is owned by cooperatives producing the principal crops of rice, maize, and potatoes. The main trading partners have been the former Soviet Union and China; North Korea received substantial aid from the former. It is believed that over a quarter of GNP is spent on the armed forces, which are thought to be amongst the world's largest.

History. The Democratic People's Republic was proclaimed an independent state on 1 May 1948. Intent on reuniting Korea, North Korea launched a surprise attack on South KOREA in June 1950, suffering considerable damage and loss of life in the following three years of the indecisive KOREAN WAR. After the war, the ruling communist party of KIM IL SUNG (first President of North Korea) undertook a programme of reconstruction, using the country's mineral and power resources to finance economic development. From the early 1980s, however, the economy was stagnant and then in decline. This was a factor in the decision in 1985 to hold a series of economic talks with South Korea, after the many years of tension. The result was a marked upturn in trade between the two countries ($25 million in 1990 to $192 million in 1991). Kim Il Sung was re-elected in 1990; he supported a policy of seeking 'normalization' with South Korea, but not of reunification. Talks between respective premiers began in September 1990 and continued into 1992, when an economic agreement was signed. Tensions flared again in 1994 when North Korea refused to allow international inspectors to examine its nuclear reactors, amid allegations that it was building nuclear weapons. Following US intervention, North Korea agreed to inspections of its nuclear sites, but disputes between the two Koreas continued. Kim Jong Il (1942–) succeeded his father as President in 1995. From 1995 to 1997 the country was hit by floods and famine.

Capital: Pyongyang
Area: 122,400 sq km (47,300 sq mi)
Population: 23,487,000 (1995)
Currency: 1 won = 100 chon
Religions: Atheist or non-religious 67.9%; traditional beliefs 15.6%; Ch'ondogyo 13.9%; Buddhist 1.7%; Christian 0.9%
Ethnic Groups: Korean 99.8%; Chinese 0.2%
Languages: Korean (official); Chinese
International Organizations: UN

Korea, South (official name **Republic of Korea**) A north-east Asian country. Consisting of the southern half of the Korean peninsula, mostly beneath the 38th parallel, South Korea was formed from the zone occupied by US forces after World War II.

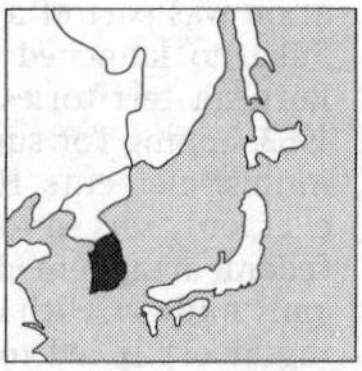

Physical. The terrain of South Korea is made up of low hills and wide valleys. Numerous small islands in the sovereign territory of South Korea lie off its western coast, in the Yellow Sea. The climate is milder than in the north of the peninsula.

Economy. South Korea has a mixed economy with a rapidly expanding and successful export-based industrial sector, and an agricultural sector which provides self-sufficiency in food and high yields in rice production. The principal manufacturing industries are petrochemicals, shipbuilding, textiles, and electronics. The chief exports are transport equipment, electrical machinery, footwear, and textiles. South Korea has few minerals except for large tungsten deposits. South Korea is regarded as a successful example of a newly industrializing country, and it plays an increasingly important role in worldwide investment.

History. The independent Republic of Korea was proclaimed on 15 August 1948. Badly damaged by the KOREAN WAR (1950–53), the South Korean economy was initially restricted by its lack of industrial and power resources and by a severe post-war refugee problem. Unemployment and inflation damaged the reputation of the government of President Rhee, and its increasing brutality and corruption finally led to its overthrow in 1960. After a second civilian government had failed to restore the situation, the army, led by General Park Chung Hee, seized power in 1961. Park, who assumed the powers of a civilian president (1963–79) organized an extremely successful reconstruction campaign which saw South Korea emerge as a strong industrial power, but his repressive policies soon engendered serious unrest. Tension with North Korea remained high during this period, until an agreement between the two governments, signed in July 1972, laid foundations for possible future reunification. Park Chung Hee was assassinated by the head of the South Korean Central Intelligence Agency in a coup in 1979. His successor, General Chun Doo Hwan, continued his policies until forced partially to liberalize the political system after student unrest in 1987. A referendum was held and a new constitution proclaimed. President Roh Tae Woo was elected, and in 1990 his party, the Democratic Justice Party, amalgamated with others to form the Democratic Liberal Party (DLP), which advocated reunion with the north and normalization of relations with the Soviet Union and, later, Russia. There were student demonstrations in 1991, and feuding within the DLP, which lost the general election of 1992. Kim Young-sam was elected President in 1992. Relations with North Korea again worsened in 1994, with the latter's refusal to submit its nuclear energy programme to inspection by the International Atomic Energy Agency; large-scale civil defence exercises were held in Seoul. In 1996 the DLP (renamed the New Korea Party) formed a new government. Kim Dae Jung was elected President in 1998.

Capital: Seoul
Area: 99,237 sq km (38,316 sq mi)
Population: 44,834,000 (1995)

Currency: 1 South Korean won = 100 jeon
Religions: Atheist or non-religious 57.4%; Buddhist 19.9%; Protestant 16.1%; Roman Catholic 4.6%; Confucian 1.2%
Ethnic Groups: Korean 99.9%
Languages: Korean (official)
International Organizations: UN; Colombo Plan

Korean The language of North and South Korea spoken by some 65 million people. Its linguistic affiliations are uncertain although it seems most similar to Japanese. Its vocabulary and orthography have been heavily influenced by Chinese. The Korean Alphabet is the only true alphabetical script native to the Far East and the two systems of romanization employed are the Ministry of Education system and the internationally accepted McCune-Reischauer system.

Korean War (1950–53) War fought between North Korea and China on one side, and South Korea, the USA, and United Nations forces on the other. From the time of their foundation in 1948, relations between North and South Korea were soured by rival plans for unification, and on 25 June 1950 war finally broke out with a surprise North Korean attack that pushed US and South Korean forces far south towards Pusan by September. In the temporary absence of the Soviet representative, the Security Council asked members of the UN to furnish assistance to South Korea. On 15 September US and South Korean forces, under command of General MACARTHUR, launched a counter-offensive at Inchon, and by the end of October UN forces had pushed the North Koreans all the way back to the Yalu River, the frontier with the People's Republic of China. Chinese troops then entered the war on the northern side, driving south to recapture the South Korean capital of Seoul by January 1951. After months of fighting, the conflict stabilized in near-deadlock close to the original boundary line (the 38th parallel). Peace negotiations, undertaken in July 1951 by General M. B. Ridgway (who had succeeded MacArthur in April of that year), proved difficult, and it was not until 27 July 1953 that an armistice was signed at Panmunjom and the battle line was accepted as the boundary between North and South Korea.

Korngold, Erich Wolfgang (1897–1957) Austrian-born US composer. His ballet *The Snowman* (1910) was followed in 1916 by a remarkable first opera *Violanta*. His masterpiece, *The Dead City* (1920), conquered the world's operatic stages. In 1934 he settled in Hollywood, becoming one of the most imaginative and fluent composers of film music; the scores for *Robin Hood* and *Anthony Adverse* received Oscars. Korngold's music is highly chromatic (see HARMONY), sumptuously scored, and romantic to the point of decadence.

Koror The capital of the Republic of Belau, on Koror Island in the Caroline Islands of the western Pacific.

Koryo A Korean kingdom that gave its name to the whole country. From 986 its kings ruled a united Korea from their Chinese-style capital, Kaesong. Chinese influence was strong in the administration of the kingdom and Buddhism flourished. A period of disorder in the 12th century was checked after 1196 by military families with powers similar to those of the Japanese SHOGUNATE. Tributary to the SONG, Koryo also had to pay tribute to the Liao and JIN. After 1231 the Mongols repeatedly invaded and despoiled Koryo, which later depended entirely on YUAN support. After the overthrow of the Yuan, a Koryo general, Yi Song-gye, seized Kaesong and in 1392 established the Yi dynasty.

Kosciusko, Mount The highest peak in Australia, in south-east New South Wales, rising to 2,228 m (7,310 feet). It is a crystal block or HORST lying on a lofty plateau in the Muniong Range of the Australian Alps, here known as the Snowy Mountains, and is the centrepiece of a national park. The mountain was named, in 1840, after the Polish statesman, Tadeusz KOSCIUSZKO.

Kosciuszko, Tadeusz (or **Thaddeus**) (1746–1817) Polish soldier and patriot. A trained soldier, he fought for the American colonists during the War of American Independence, returning to Poland in 1784. Ten years later he led a nationalist uprising, defeating a large Russian force at Racławice. Captured and imprisoned by the Russians (1794–96), he eventually moved to France, where he devoted the rest of his life to the cause of Polish independence.

kosher (Hebrew, 'proper') Food and wine that are suitable for Jews, based upon prohibitions found in the TORAH. Animals that have divided hooves and do not chew the cud (pigs), as well as shellfish, certain birds, and most insects, are forbidden, as is any mixing of meat and milk, or any meat that still contains its 'life' blood. These rules also apply to utensils used in the preparation of food to the extent of having separate dishes, refrigerators, or even kitchens. Strict kosher observance (*glatt kosher*) is maintained in ORTHODOX JUDAISM, but not as rigorously in REFORM JUDAISM and other traditions of Judaism.

Kosovo A province of southern Serbia; area 10,887 sq km (4,205 sq miles); pop. (1991) 1,956,200; capital, Pristina. Kosovo was granted a degree of autonomy by the former Yugoslav government in 1974, but following ethnic conflict between Albanians (who make up over 75 per cent of the population) and Serbs the Serbian government dissolved the Kosovo Assembly in 1990 and imposed direct rule. Demands for independence by ethnic Albanians continued, culminating in 1998 in massive demonstrations, which were violently suppressed by Serbian police.

Kossuth, Lajos (1802–94) Hungarian statesman and patriot. Long an opponent of Habsburg domination of Hungary, he led the 1848 insurrection and was appointed governor of the country during the brief period of independence which followed. In 1849 he began a lifelong period of exile when the uprising was crushed, although he continued to strive for Hungarian independence.

Kosygin, Alexei Nikolayevich (1904–81) Soviet politician. He joined the Communist Party in 1927 and became an expert in economics and industry. He was Chairman of the Council of Ministers from 1964 to 1981. During his period in office he shared power with BREZHNEV, who came to overshadow him. Kosygin achieved a notable diplomatic success in bringing the 1965–66 INDO-PAKISTAN WAR to an end.

Kota Kinabalu A seaport of Malaysia on the north coast of Borneo, capital of the state of Sabah; pop. (1980) 56,000. Its name means 'fort of (Mount) Kinabalu'. Originally established as a trading post on Pulau Gaya island in 1881, it was rebuilt on the mainland by the North Borneo Chartered Company and named Jesselton after one of the company directors, Sir Charles Jessel. It was renamed Kota Kinabalu in 1967.

koto, zheng, and **kayagüm** Musical instruments, the long ZITHERS of Japan, China, and Korea. A bridge under each string allows scales to be set by moving bridges rather than retuning strings. Pitches are varied by depressing the strings behind the bridges. The *kayagüm* is plucked with the flesh of the fingers, the *zheng* with fingernails, and the *koto* with artificial nails. The Chinese *qin* differs by not having bridges and by making more use of harmonics, whose positions are indicated by spots set into the sound-board; its use and repertoire are very ancient.

Kotzebue, August von (1761–1819) German dramatist. His many plays were popular in both Germany and England; the tragedy *Menschenhass und Reue* (1789) was produced by Richard Sheridan as *The Stranger*, and *Das Kind der Liebe* (1790) was adapted in England as *Lovers' Vows*. He was a political informant to Tsar Alexander I and was assassinated by the Germans. His son, Otto von Kotzebue (1787–1846), was a navigator and explorer; he discovered an inlet of NW Alaska (Kotzebue Sound) now named after him.

Kourou A town on the north coast of French Guiana, at the mouth of the River Kourou; pop. (1990) 11,200. Nearby is a satellite-launching station of the European Space Agency established in 1967. The site was chosen because of its nearness to the equator where the Earth is moving fastest.

Kowloon A densely populated peninsula on the south-east coast of China, forming part of Hong Kong. It is separated from Hong Kong island by Victoria Harbour which is crossed by ferries and a road tunnel. Kowloon has a population density of 28,500 people per sq km. Asia's largest container port is located at Kwai Chung; Kai Tak, Hong Kong's international airport, is to the east of Kowloon, partly built over the sea. There is a rail link to Guangzhou on the Chinese mainland.

Kozhikode See CALICUT.

Krafft-Ebing, Richard von (1840–1902) German physician and psychologist. He is best known for establishing the relationship between syphilis and general paralysis, and for his *Psychopathia Sexualis* (1886), which pioneered the systematic study of aberrant sexual behaviour.

Krafla An active volcano in north-east Iceland rising to a height of 654 m (2,145 ft). After being dormant for over two centuries it erupted in 1975 and again in 1984. During the 1970s a geothermal power-station was established nearby.

krait Any one of a dozen species of mainly nocturnal venomous snakes of the genus *Bungarus*, related to the cobra, which occur in south-east Asia and western Indonesia. Kraits often have a colour pattern of black and white or black and yellow bands. They are docile, coiling up loosely and making jerky body movements when threatened. The banded krait, *B. fasciatus*, grows to 1.2 m (4 feet) in length. Their venom is very toxic and bites are dangerous. Most species feed on other snakes, though some are fish-eaters.

Krajina A region of Croatia with predominantly Serbian population which designated itself the Republic of Serbian Krajina following Croatia's declaration of independence from Yugoslavia in 1991.

Krakatoa A small volcanic island in Indonesia, lying between Java and Sumatra, scene of a great eruption in 1883 (the world's greatest recorded explosion) which destroyed most of it. The tsunamis generated by the explosion are calculated to have killed 36,000 people.

Krasnodar ▶**1** A kray (territory) of southern Russia in the north Caucasus; area 88,578 sq km (34,200 sq miles); pop. (1990) 5,135,000. ▶**2** Its capital city, a port on the lower Kuban River; pop. (1990) 627,000. Founded in 1794 as a military outpost on Russia's southern frontier, it was known as Yekaterinodar until 1920. Its industries include oil refining, chemical production, railway engineering, and food processing, and it is an important centre of a wheat-growing region.

Krasnoyarsk ▶**1** A kray (territory) of the Russian Federation in west Siberia; area 2,404,000 sq km (928,000 sq miles); pop. (1990) 3,612,000. There are extensive mineral and timber resources. ▶**2** Its capital city, a port and rail centre on the Yenisei River; pop. (1990) 922,000. Founded in 1628, it expanded with the discovery of gold and the development of the Trans-Siberian Railway. It builds heavy railway equipment.

kray A first-order administrative division of Russia equivalent to a territory. In addition to autonomous republics and oblasts Russia's first order administrative divisions include the six krays of Altay, Khabarovsk, Krasnodar, Krasnoyarsk, Primorye, and Stavropol.

Krebs, Hans Adolf (1900–81) German-born British biochemist, best known for his work on the citric acid or KREBS' CYCLE, a series of chemical reactions which help to break down carbohydrates to release energy. He was also responsible for discovering the urea cycle, the process by which organisms break down waste amino acids to form urea. Krebs fled from Germany to Britain after the Nazis came to power. He worked at Sheffield University between 1935 and 1954, receiving the Nobel Prize for physiology and medicine in 1953.

Krebs' cycle (or **citric acid cycle**, **tricarboxylic acid cycle**) A cyclic sequence of reactions, catalysed by enzymes, which plays a central role in the metabolism of nearly all aerobic organisms. It comprises the second stage of RESPIRATION. Pyruvate formed from glucose by GLYCOLYSIS is converted to acetylcoenzyme A with release of a molecule of carbon dioxide. Acetylcoenzyme A then reacts with oxaloacetate (a 4-carbon compound) to form citrate (a 6-carbon compound, a tricarboxylic acid); in the series of reactions that follows, oxaloacetate is regenerated (ready to react with another molecule of acetylcoenzyme A), two molecules of carbon dioxide are produced, and one molecule of ATP and eight atoms of hydrogen (carried by coenzymes) are generated. The hydrogen atoms are then oxidized to water via the ELECTRON TRANSPORT CHAIN. Thus pyruvate is effectively completely oxidized to carbon dioxide and water.

Intermediates in the Krebs' cycle are also used by the cell for making other cell components.

Kreisler, Fritz (1875–1962) Austrian-born US violinist and composer. He made his first public appearances in the USA in 1889 and became a US citizen in 1943. A noted interpreter of the standard classics, in 1910 he gave the first performance of Elgar's violin concerto, which was dedicated to him.

Kremlin, the The citadel in Moscow, centre of administration of the Russian government and formerly of the Soviet Communist government. Covering an area of 28 hectares, its palaces, churches, and monuments are surrounded by a wall 2,235 m (7,333 ft) in length. The building of the Kremlin began in 1156 when Prince Yuri Dolgoruky ordered a wooden fort to be built on Borovitsky Hill. This later became the residence of the Grand Dukes of Moscow and the site where Russian emperors and empresses came to be crowned.

krill See EUPHAUSID SHRIMP.

Kripke, Saul (1940–) US philosopher. Kripke believes that many philosophical claims have been based on a failure to distinguish between the metaphysical notion of necessity, the epistemological notion of A PRIORI reasoning, and the linguistic notion of analyticity. In *Naming and Necessity* (1972), Kripke asserts that there is no reason to believe that something is necessarily true (that is, it could not have been otherwise) if it is only knowable a priori (independently of experience). Kripke's work has prompted philosophers to reconsider many traditional views.

Krishna (Sanskrit, 'black') The eighth incarnation or AVATAR of the Hindu god Vishnu. In Hinduism, Krishna the Dark One is the preserver and Almighty Prince of Wisdom. He features most notably as the hero of the MAHABHARATA. A mass of legends and fables have collected about Krishna, relating to three phases of his life: as a mischievous child-god, which includes his slaying of Kaṃsa of Mathura, his wicked uncle; as the cowherd in love with the milkmaid, Rādhā, herself a reincarnation of Lakshmi, in which role he embodies the perfect deification of life; and finally as Arjuna, Pāṇḍava's divine charioteer. Krishna was killed by an arrow fired by the hunter Jara ('old age').

Krishnamurti, Jiddu (1895–1986) Indian spiritual leader. He was originally associated with the Theosophical Society and was declared a World Teacher by Annie Besant. In 1929 he broke away from the society, advocating his own spiritual philosophy based on a rejection of organized religion and the attainment of self-realization by introspection. His teachings enjoyed a revival of interest in the 1960s and he settled in California in 1969.

Kropotkin, Prince Peter (1842–1921) Russian anarchist. He was a geographer who carried out explorations of Siberia, Finland, and Manchuria before devoting his life to political activities. He became an influential exponent of anarchism and was imprisoned in 1874. He escaped abroad two years later and only returned to Russia after the Russian Revolution in 1917. His works include *Modern Science and Anarchism* (1903).

Kruger, Stephanus Johannes Paulus (known as 'Oom (uncle) Paul') (1825–1904) South African soldier and statesman. He led the Afrikaners to victory in the First Boer War in 1881 and afterwards served as President of Transvaal from 1883 to 1899. His refusal to allow equal rights to non-Boer immigrants was one of the causes of the Second Boer War, during which Kruger was forced to flee the country. He died in exile in Switzerland.

Krupp, Alfred (1812–87) German arms manufacturer. In the 1840s he began to manufacture ordnance at the ironworks founded in Essen by his father, and built up the company to become the largest such manufacturer in Europe. Under the management of successive members of the family the Krupp Works played a pre-eminent part in German arms production through to the end of World War II. Alfried Krupp (1907–67) was a Nazi supporter, who made use of slave labour, for which he was imprisoned as a war criminal.

krypton (symbol Kr, at. no. 36, r.a.m. 83.80) A colourless unreactive gas used together with other NOBLE GASES in discharge lamps. It forms a few unstable compounds such as krypton difluoride, KrF_2.

Kshitigarbha See JIZO.

Kuala Lumpur The capital city of Malaysia, at the junction of the Klang and Gombak rivers in the south-west of the Malay Peninsula; pop. (1991) 145,000. Founded in 1857 by Chinese tin miners, it became capital of the Federated Malay States in 1896. It is a major transportation and commercial city at the centre of a rubber-growing and tin-mining region.

Kublai Khan (1216–94) Mongol emperor of China, grandson of Genghis Khan. Between 1252 and 1259 he conquered southern China with his brother Mangu (then Mongol Khan). On Mangu's death in 1259 he was elected Khan himself, completing the conquest of China and founding the Yuan dynasty; he established his capital on the site of the modern Beijing. He successfully invaded Korea and Burma, but failed in attacks on Java and Japan.

Kubrick, Stanley (1928–) US film director, producer, and writer. He first gained acclaim as a director with the thriller *The Killing* (1956). The coldly enigmatic science-fiction epic *2001: A Space Odyssey* (1968) set new standards for special effects. Other notable films include *Lolita* (1962), *Dr Strangelove* (1964), *A Clockwork Orange* (1971), *Barry Lyndon* (1975), *The Shining* (1980), and *Full Metal Jacket* (1987).

kudu A large, lightly striped African antelope. The greater kudu, *Tragelaphus strepsiceros*, may reach a height of 1.3 m (4.4 feet) at the shoulders, with horns 1 m (3.25 feet) long with an open spiral of at least two and a half turns. The female is smaller and lacks horns, and is fawn in colour with a few thin stripes of white on the back. The kudu is found in East, central, and southern Africa, mostly in hilly or broken country with thorn bushes or tall grass. It lives in small groups and feeds at dawn and dusk. There is an elaborate courtship and a single calf is born. The lesser kudu, *T. imberbis*, is similar in appearance and habitats, but occurs in East and parts of northeast Africa.

Kufic (or **Cufic**) An early angular form of the Arabic alphabet found chiefly in decorative inscriptions. It takes its name from Kufa, an ancient city to the south of Baghdad in Iraq.

Ku Klux Klan (KKK) A secret society founded (1866) in the southern USA after the AMERICAN CIVIL WAR to oppose reconstruction and to maintain white supremacy. Famous for its white robes and hoods, it spread fear among blacks to prevent them voting. Its use as a cover for petty persecution alienated public opinion and led to laws in 1870 and 1871 attempting to suppress it. The Klan reappeared in Georgia in 1915 and during the 1920s spread into the north and mid-west. It was responsible for some 1,500 murders by lynching. At its height it boasted four million members and elected high federal and state officials, but it also aroused intense opposition. A series of scandals and internecine rivalries sent it into rapid decline. Klan activity increased during the 1950s and 1960s, as it violently opposed the civil rights movement. It survives at the local level in the southern states and during the early 1990s there was concern that support for the Klan was increasing.

Kun, Béla (1886–1937) Hungarian communist leader. In World War I he was captured on the Russian front and joined the BOLSHEVIKS. He was sent back to Hungary to form a communist party and in March 1919 persuaded the Hungarian communists and Social Democrats to form a coalition government and to set up a communist state under his dictatorship. His Red Army overran Slovakia, but promised Soviet help was not forthcoming. In May 1919 he was defeated by a Romanian army of intervention. Kun fled the country and is assumed to have been liquidated in one of Stalin's purges.

Kundera, Milan (1929–) Czech novelist. His books were proscribed in Czechoslovakia following the Soviet military invasion of 1968. He emigrated to France (1975), was stripped of his Czech citizenship in 1979, and became a French citizen two years later. Major novels include *Life is Elsewhere* (1973), *The Book of Laughter and Forgetting* (1979), *The Unbearable Lightness of Being* (1984), and *Immortality* (1990).

Kung Fu An ancient Chinese form of combat, related to karate (see MARTIAL ARTS).

!Kung-San (Kalahari bushmen) A dwindling group of nomadic HUNTER-GATHERERS, living in the southern African Kalahari desert and speaking one of the KHOISAN LANGUAGES. Their traditional social unit is the camp, consisting of a group of siblings and cousins, who move around in territory surrounding water holes, often sheltering in caves. Many rock surfaces still bear witness to the !Kung-San's rich mythology and skill in drawing. The groups do not regard their territories as property in the strict sense, nor are there any organized political structures: a camp leader may be a man or a woman whose skills and judgement are respected, but decisions are made by consensus. The !Kung-San depend for their livelihood on fruits, berries, and nuts gathered by the women and on animals hunted by the men. This traditional way of life is rapidly disappearing, however; recent settlement by migrating farmers has introduced property relations and wage labour to !Kung society.

Kunming A city on Lake Dianchi in south-west China, capital of Yunnan province; pop. (1990) 1,976,000. First settled in the 3rd century BC and situated at an altitude of 1,890 m (6,200 ft), it is known as the 'city of eternal spring' because of its pleasant climate. Its industries produce textiles, chemicals, machinery, and optical instruments and air links with other cities have encouraged its development since the 1970s.

Kuomintang (or **Guomindang**; Chinese, 'National People's Party') Chinese political party. Originally a revolutionary league, it was organized in 1912 by Song Jiaoren and SUN YAT-SEN as a republican party along democratic lines to replace the Revolutionary Alliance which had emerged from the overthrow of the QING dynasty. Suppressed in 1913 by Yuan Shikai, it was reformed in 1920 by Sun and reorganized with COMINTERN assistance in 1923 in an arrangement that allowed individual communists to become members. At the party congress in 1924 it formally adopted the 'Three Principles of the People': nationalism, democracy, and 'people's livelihood'. In 1926 its rise to power began in earnest with the commencement of CHIANG KAI-SHEK's Northern Campaign. The communists were purged in 1927 and the capture of Beijing in 1928 brought international recognition for its Nanjing-based Nationalist Government. It fought the CHINESE CIVIL WAR with the communists and retreated to Chongqing after the Japanese invasion of 1937. After World War II, the civil war recommenced, and by 1949 the Kuomintang's forces had been decisively defeated and forced to retreat to TAIWAN, where it still continues to form the government of Taiwan (the Republic of China), having won the country's first multiparty elections in 1991. Further elections, in 1995, saw the Kuomintang narrowly retain its majority, yet with its lowest vote (46 per cent) since 1945.

Kurchatov, Igor Vasilevitch (1903–60) Soviet physicist. Appointed director of nuclear physics at the Leningrad Institute in 1938, he was in charge of Soviet research into nuclear fission during World War II. He built the first nuclear reactor in the Soviet Union in 1946 and was responsible for the team that constructed the Soviet atom bomb (1949) and the hydrogen bomb (1953).

Kurdistan An extensive plateau and mountainous region of the Middle East, south of the Caucasus, including large parts of Turkey, northern Iraq, western Iran, eastern Syria, Armenia, and Azerbaijan. For centuries it has been the traditional home of the Kurdish people. The creation of a separate state of Kurdistan was proposed by the Allies after World War I, but this was abandoned in 1923 when Turkey reasserted its territorial authority in the region. Although not officially recognized as a state, this region is called Kurdistan by its inhabitants.

Kurds A mainly pastoral Aryan Islamic people speaking a dialect of Persian and inhabiting the region known as KURDISTAN. Claiming descent from Noah and numbering nearly 20 million, they have maintained their own cultural tradition and language for some 3,000 years but have never been united under one ruler. During the 19th century Kurdish nationalist movements generally operated independently of each other in each of the countries encompassed by Kurdistan. The first major Kurdish revolt took place in Turkey in 1925, but it was not until the illegal establishment of a Kurdish Democratic Party in Turkey in 1967 that militant nationalism gripped the five south-eastern provinces of Turkey. During the 1960s and early 1970s there were risings against the Iraqi government, and after the Iranian revolution of 1979 there was an increase in Kurdish dissidence in Iran. International attention focused on the Kurds in 1988–89, when Iraq initiated a policy of depopulating Kurdish areas on the frontier with Turkey, and in 1991 when, after the Gulf War, the Iraqi government relaunched its campaign against the Kurds in northern Iraq. Subsequently, 'safe havens' were established for the Kurds of northern Iraq.

Kurile Islands (Japanese **Chishma-Retto**) An archipelago of 56 islands extending for 1,200 km (750 miles) from the Kamachtka Peninsula in Siberia to Hokkaido Island in Japan. The islands lie within the geologically unstable circle of the Pacific Ocean, and contain 35 active volcanoes and many hot springs. Parallel to the islands on the ocean floor runs the Kurile Trench 2,900 km (1,800 miles) long, which itself marks the beginning of a chain of oceanic trenches extending from the Bering Sea to the Philippine Trench. Thickly forested and rich in gold, silver, and other precious metals, the southern Kuriles are washed by some of the richest fishing grounds in the world.

Kurma In Hinduism, the second incarnation or AVATAR of Vishnu, in which he assumed the form of a giant tortoise in response to the gods' weakened strength because of a curse laid on Indra. By supporting Mount Mandara, which served as a churning stick, Kurma enabled the gods and demons to churn the ocean and retrieve the treasures of the Vedic tribes, lost in the Deluge. The gods were eventually restored to their former strength and authority.

Kurosawa, Akira (1910–) Japanese film director. He first gained international acclaim with *Rashomon* (1950) and later became known for his samurai films, such as *The Seven Samurai* (1954) and *Ran* (1985), a Japanese version of Shakespeare's *King Lear*. He also treats modern themes, mainly of social injustice, in films such as *Living* (1952), and has made adaptations of Dostoevsky (*The Idiot*, 1951) and Maxim Gorky (*The Lower Depths*, 1957).

Kuroshio (or **Japan Current**; Japanese, 'black stream') A strong fast-moving current flowing north-eastward from the northern Philippines up the east coast of Japan. As a continuation of the North Equatorial Current, it carries warm waters into the North Pacific Ocean, much as the Gulf Stream does in the Atlantic. It is about 80 km (50 miles) wide but only 400 m (1,300 ft) deep.

Kursk An industrial city and commercial centre in western Russia, situated on the Siem River between Moscow and Kharkhov; pop. (1990) 430,000. Kursk is the centre of a major iron-ore field (Kursk Magnetic Anomaly) and steel industries.

Kutch A part of Gujarat in west-central India. In the north is the Rann (marsh) of Kutch, an area of saline mudflats that was formerly an extension of the Arabian Sea but which has been filled by sediment. The Great Rann has an area of 18,000 sq km (7,000 sq mi).

Kutuzov, Mikhail Ilarionovich, Prince of Smolensk (1745–1813) Russian field-marshal. He distinguished himself in the Russo-Turkish War (1806–12), bringing Bessarabia into Russia. He commanded the Russian armies in the wars against Napoleon and was forced to retreat after the defeat of BORODINO (7 September 1812). Kutuzov's decision to disperse in the face of the advancing *grande armée* undermined Napoleon's plans for a swift victory, and forced him to retreat from Moscow before the severe Russian winter.

Kuwait A small country in the north-west corner of the Gulf, flanked by Iraq and Saudi Arabia.

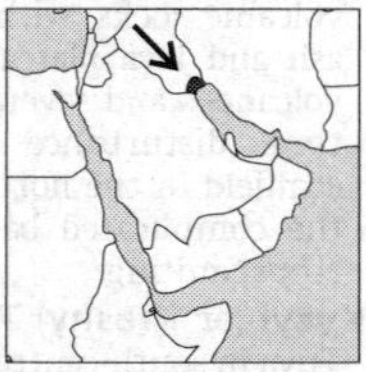

Physical. Kuwait is mainly low desert, very hot in summer but cool in winter, and extremely arid.

Economy. With an estimated 10 per cent of the world's petroleum reserves, Kuwait's economy is based on oil extraction, refining, and petrochemical industries; there is also an entrepôt trade, and income from overseas investments is believed to equal that from oil production before the Iraqi occupation.

History. Kuwait was founded in the early 18th century by members of the Utub section of the Anaiza tribe, and has been ruled since 1756 by the al-Sabah family. In 1899 the ruler, Muvarak, signed a treaty with Britain which established a *de facto* British protectorate over Kuwait, although it remained under nominal Ottoman suzerainty until 1914, when the protectorate was formalized. Kuwait became independent in 1961, when an Iraqi claim was warded off with British military assistance. Oil had been discovered in 1938; after World War II, Kuwait became one of the world's largest oil producers. The country's defensive pact with Britain lapsed in 1971, after which it tried to pursue a policy of neutrality. Its massive wealth was in part channelled into modernization programmes. But in 1990 Iraq revived the frontier dispute of 1961, and on 2 August 1990 began its seven-month occupation of Kuwait. In the period before liberation in the GULF WAR, thousands of Kuwaitis were killed, kidnapped, or taken hostage. After the war, reconstruction costs were estimated at up to $100 billion, with serious environmental damage caused by Iraqi sabotage of 732 oil wells. In 1992 the first parliamentary elections in the country's history were held, in which only 13 per cent of the population was eligible to vote; the franchise only extended to male Kuwaiti nationals over the age of 21, whose families had lived in Kuwait since before 1921. Even so, many opposition candidates were elected. Further minor raids by Iraqi troops in 1993 led to the UN moving the border a few metres northwards, into Iraq.

Capital: Kuwait City
Area: 17,818 sq km (6,880 sq mi)
Population: 1,691,000 (1995)
Currency: 1 Kuwaiti dinar = 1,000 fils
Religions: Sunni Muslim 63.0%; Shiite Muslim 27.0%; Christian 8.0%; Hindu 2.0%
Ethnic Groups: Kuwaiti Arab 40.1%; non-Kuwaiti Arab 37.9%; Asian 21.0%; European 0.7%
Languages: Arabic (official); minority languages
International Organizations: UN; Arab League; Gulf Co-operation Council; OPEC; OAPEC

Kuwait City The capital of the Gulf state of Kuwait, on the south side of Kuwait Bay, an inlet of the Arabian Gulf; pop. (1985) 44,335. Its deep-water port lies in the industrial suburb of Shuwaikh and its international airport is 16 km (10 miles) from the city centre.

Kuybyshev See KUIBISHEV.

Kvasir In Norse and Germanic mythology, the god whose death brought poetry into the world. Famed for his wisdom, Kvasir was murdered by dwarfs, but Odin caught the blood and transformed it into a sacred mead which, in the form of poetry, he brought to the dwelling place of the gods. A giant stole the mead, but Odin, disguised as an eagle, rescued it and carried the liquid back in his crop.

Kwa A language group of the Niger-Congo family of languages spoken in west Africa. It includes Akan, Ashanti, Bini, Ewe, Ibo, Ijo, Nupe, and Yoruba. See NIGER-CONGO LANGUAGES.

KwaNdebele A former self-governing state of the Southern Ndebele people created in north-east Transvaal in 1981, now part of the region of Mpumalanga. Its capital was Moutjana.

Kwangchow See GUANGZHOU.

Kwangsi See GUANGXI.

kwashiorkor (or **protein-energy malnutrition**) A serious nutritional disease of children fed solely on a diet of maize, prevalent in early infancy in tropical regions. A lack of calories and protein causes delayed growth, severe loss of weight, and retention of tissue fluids. Affected children develop distended bellies and swollen legs as well as other symptoms. The disease can be fatal if not treated promptly.

KwaZulu-Natal An eastern province of South Africa between the Indian Ocean and the Drakensberg Mountains created in 1994 from the former province of Natal and the former Zulu homeland of KwaZulu; pop. (1995) 8,713,100. Its capital is Durban. Annexed to the Cape Colony in 1844, Natal became a separate colony in 1856 and a province of the Union of South Africa in 1910, its capital (until 1994) being Pietermaritzburg. The self-governing national state of KwaZulu, formerly known as Zululand, was created in 1971 but was reunited with Natal in 1994.

Kwesui See HOHHOT.

Kyd, Thomas (1558–94) English dramatist. His anonymously published *The Spanish Tragedy* (1592), an early example of revenge tragedy, was very popular on the Elizabethan stage. The only work published under his name was a translation of Robert Garnier's *Cornelia* (1594; reissued as *Pompey the Great*, 1595). Other works attributed to Kyd are *The Tragedy of Solyman and Perseda* (1592) and a lost pre-Shakespearian play on Hamlet.

Kyoto An industrial city in the Kinki region of central Honshu Island, Japan; pop. (1990) 1,461,140.

Founded in the 6th century, it was capital of Japan from 794 until 1868. There are many historic landmarks including the 14th-century Golden Pavilion, 15th-century Ryoanji temple of the Zen sect, and the 17th-century Nijo Castle. Kyoto Imperial University was founded in 1897. Uniquely undamaged during World War II, its many industries include manufacture of electrical equipment, precision tools, and cameras, as well as food processing, chemicals, and textile machinery.

Kyrenia A port on the central part of the north coast of the island of Cyprus, in the Turkish Republic of Northern Cyprus; pop. (1985) 6,900. In July 1974 Turkish forces invading the island landed here. Its many old buildings and picturesque ruins made it a popular tourist destination.

Kyrgyzstan (formerly **Kirghizia**) A country in central Asia bounded by Kazakhstan on the north and north-west, Uzbekistan on the south-west, and Tajikistan on the south.

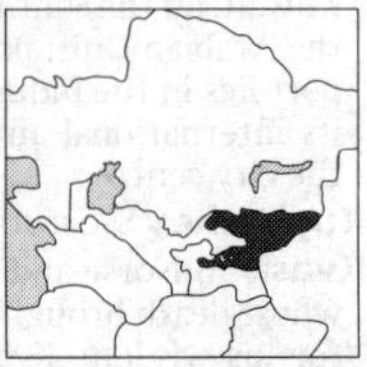

Physical. On the south-east the TIAN SHAN range of mountains, which rise to 7,439 m (24,406 feet), shares a border with China. Kyrgyzstan is a mountainous country with many snowfields, glaciers, and deep lakes. Its lower plains are exposed to hot desert winds. Its middle reaches are forested, while the lower slopes provide pasture for millions of sheep.

Economy. Kyrgyzstan has substantial mineral reserves, including coal, petroleum, and natural gas, but other than coal-mining these have not been fully prospected or exploited. Industry is based on mineral extraction and processing, and there is also some light industry such as food-processing and textile manufacture. Agriculture is based on livestock-raising and crops such as fruit, cereals, cotton, sugar-beet, tobacco, and opium poppies.

History. Absorbed into the Russian empire during the 19th century, Kyrgyzstan became an autonomous province of the Soviet Union in 1924 and the Kirghiz Soviet Socialist Republic in 1936. In 1990 Askar Akayev, a supporter of reforms and of independence for Kyrgyzstan, was elected President. He survived an attempted coup in 1991 and resigned from the Communist Party of the Soviet Union. The Kirghiz Communist Party then dissolved itself and the country became independent as Kyrgyzstan. New constitutions were adopted in 1993 and 1994 and the first multi-party elections were held in 1995. Akayev remained President and continued to introduce economic reforms.

Capital: Bishkek
Area: 198,500 sq km (76,460 sq mi)
Population: 4,483,000 (1995)
Currency: 1 som = 100 tyiya
Religions: Sunni Muslim; Eastern Orthodox
Ethnic Groups: Kirghiz 52.0%; Russian 22.0%; Uzbek 12.0%; Ukrainian and Tatar minorities
Languages: Kirghiz (official); Russian; minority languages
International Organizations: CSCE; UN; Commonwealth of Independent States; North Atlantic Co-operation Council

Kyushu The most southerly of the four main islands of Japan. It occupies a junction between two volcanic arcs, one from SHIKOKU to the east and the other from the Ryukyu Islands to the south-west. As a consequence it is dominated by volcanic rocks, with a rugged relief of dissected ash and lava plateaux; there are fine individual volcanoes and several small alluvial plains. Structural disturbance is common: the important coalfield in the north lies in a tectonic basin, and the complicated bays of the west partly result from faulting.

Kyzyl (or **Krasny**) The capital of the Republic of Tuva in south-central Russia, at the junction of the Bei and Khua rivers; pop. (1989) 80,000. Its industries include brick making, timber, and food processing.

L

Laayoune See LA'YOUN.

Laban, Rudolf von (1879–1958) Hungarian choreographer and dancer. He was a pioneer of the central European school of modern dance and is especially significant for his contribution to the theory of dance. In 1920 he published the first of several volumes outlining his system of dance notation (known as *Labanotation*). In 1938 he moved to England, where he concentrated on modern educational dance.

la Barca, Pedro Calderón de See CALDERÓN DE LA BARCA.

Labe See ELBE.

Labor Party (Australia) The oldest surviving political party in Australia. Founded in the 1880s and 1890s, the title of the Labor groups varied from state to state until 1918, when all adopted the name Australian Labor Party. It was replaced in 1916 by a Nationalist-Country Alliance, until the general election of 1929 returned it to power under J. H. Scullin (1929–31). Labor split again over policy differences during the Great DEPRESSION. Some Labor followers combined with the Nationalist Party to form the United Australia Party under J. A. Lyons. Together with the Country Party it dominated federal and state politics until 1937, usually in coalition governments. The Labor Party was again in power 1941–49. A breakaway Labor group emerged in 1955 over the attitude of the Party to communism, a group of federal Labor members forming the new Anti-Communist Labor Party, which later became the Democratic Labor Party.

labour (in economics) The FACTOR OF PRODUCTION that helps to produce GOODS and services through the application of human physical and intellectual effort. The other main factors are CAPITAL and land. (In a wider sense, all work, unpaid as well as paid, is labour.) Labour finds many different types of employment, both manual and non-manual, with different levels of skill, PRODUCTIVITY, and COST, in the various sectors of industry. DIVISION OF LABOUR underlies the creation of the modern economy, especially the process of industrialization.

Labour Party (Britain) A major political party in Britain. Following the third REFORM ACT (1884), a movement developed for direct representation of labour interests in Parliament. In 1889 a Scottish Labour Party was formed, winning three seats in 1892, including one by Keir HARDIE, who in 1893 helped to form the INDEPENDENT LABOUR PARTY, advocating pacifism and SOCIALISM. In 1900 a Labour Representative Committee was formed which in 1906 succeeded in winning 29 seats and changed its name to the Labour Party. In 1918 the Party adopted a constitution drawn up by the Fabian Sidney WEBB. Its main aims were a national minimum wage, democratic control of industry, a revolution in national finance, and surplus wealth for the common good. By 1920 Party membership was over four million. The Party now became a major force in British municipal politics, as well as gaining office with the Liberals in national elections in 1923 and 1929. The Party strongly supported war in 1939 and through such leaders as ATTLEE, BEVIN, and MORRISON played a major role in Winston CHURCHILL's government (1940–45). In 1945 it gained office with an overall majority and continued the programme of WELFARE STATE legislation begun during the war. It was in power 1964–70, when much social legislation was enacted, and 1974–79, when it faced grave financial and economic problems. During the 1970s and early 1980s left-wing activists pressed for a number of procedural changes, for example in the election of Party leader. From the right wing a group of senior party members split from the party in the 1980s to form the Social Democratic Party (see LIBERAL DEMOCRATS). After its defeat in 1987 it embarked, under its leader Neil KINNOCK (1983–92), on a major policy review which recommended more democratic processes and a less ideological approach to foreign affairs and economic problems. However, the party received only 34 per cent of the vote in the general election of 1992. Tony BLAIR, who became leader in 1994, supported private enterprise and promoted many reforms in the party, finally abandoning the ideological union-led principles of 'Old Labour' under a more popular and pragmatic manifesto, which gave Labour a landslide victory in the 1997 election. Once in power 'New Labour', with an overwhelming majority, set about renewing the country's failing educational system and providing a more positive approach to the country's participation in the European Union.

Labour Party (New Zealand) A major political party in New Zealand. It was formed in 1910 out of the trade union movement but was rivalled by the militant 'RED FEDS'. Re-formed in 1916, the Party supported compulsory industrial arbitration and constitutional change. Its policies favoured nationalization of much industry and state leasehold of land, and these were further modified before it won office in 1935 under Michael SAVAGE. The first Labour government (1935–49) effected radical change, stimulating economic recovery through public works, state support for primary produce marketing, and minimum wages. It introduced SOCIAL SECURITY, including free medical care. In World War II the Labour government declared war on Germany, introduced conscription for military service, and entered strongly into collective security arrangements. The Labour Party held office again (1957–60, 1972–75, 1984–90). Under its Prime Minister David Lange (1984–90) it carried its non-nuclear policy to the point of banning all nuclear-powered or nuclear-armed ships. The party was decisively defeated in the general election of October 1990, at a time of severe economic difficulty.

Labrador The north-eastern peninsula of Canada, from Hudson Bay to the mouth of the St Lawrence, forming the mainland section of the province of Newfoundland. It has a deeply indented Atlantic coastline some 1,125 km (703 miles) in length and comprises a granite plateau rising 300 m above sea-level. Forming part of the Canadian shield, it is mostly barren rock and tundra although its river valleys are forested. The Torngat Mountains include the highest peaks east of the Rockies. Labrador was the subject of a territorial dispute between Newfoundland and Quebec which arose in 1902 and was settled in Newfoundland's favour in 1927. Cod, salmon, and trout fishing are important.

Labrador Current A cold ocean current that flows southwards from the Arctic Ocean along the north-east coast of North America during December to May. It meets the warm Gulf Stream in an area off the coast of Newfoundland which is noted for its dense fog.

La Bruyère, Jean de (1645–96) French satiric moralist. His single book, *Les Caractères* (1688), is a study of the social types and institutions of late 17th-century France. It consists of separate remarks varying in length from maxims to extended portraits through which there emerges a pessimistic and conservative view of man. His moralistic stance as an observer of society's vices parallels the satirical intent of MOLIÈRE in his comedies of manners.

laburnum A poisonous deciduous tree of the pea family, with pendent inflorescences of yellow flowers. Of the three species in the genus *Laburnum*, the most familiar is *L. anagyroides* of southern Europe.

labyrinth fish One of a group of distantly related fishes that can breathe air through a convoluted organ in the upper part of the gill chamber. Air is taken in through the mouth and passed over the labyrinth, where oxygen is absorbed by blood in the capillaries. As a result these fishes, which include gouramis, fighting fish, and snakeheads, can live in stagnant water, which is deficient in dissolved oxygen. Several families are represented in fresh waters of southern Asia and Africa.

Lacan, Jacques (1901–81) French psychoanalyst and writer. He founded the Freudian School in Paris (1964) and carried out influential work in reinterpreting Freudian psychoanalysis in the light of developments in structural linguistics and anthropology. His most significant contributions to the field concern his theory of the unconscious, which he saw as being structured like, and developing simultaneously with, language. His theories formed an element in the development of post-structuralism. A number of Lacan's articles and lectures are collected in *Écrits* (1966).

laccolith An intrusive body of IGNEOUS ROCK, more or less circular in plan, with a flat floor and a domed roof. Laccoliths have been injected as molten rock (MAGMA) into the surrounding rock, mostly along bedding planes. First described by Grove GILBERT, a US geologist, from the Henry Mountains of Utah, they can be many miles across. Some are mined as a source of economically important minerals.

lace A delicate decorative openwork fabric. Lace may be made from many kinds of thread, including COTTON and SILK, but the most usual is fine white linen. Lace is almost exclusively ornamental, and much is still made by hand, by weaving thread in patterns. There are two distinct types of lace: bobbin lace, in which threads are twisted or knotted together to form a solid pattern standing out against a net-like background; and needle lace, the oldest type, which is created by drawing the threads in a piece of linen fabric to create the pattern of the lines. In addition, net can be embroidered to make lace. Most modern lace is made on machines of the type developed by John Levers (*c*.1820), based on an earlier machine by John Heathcoat. Many lace-like fabrics are made on a large scale, using warp KNITTING machines.

lacebug A plant-feeding BUG of the family Tingidae with a network of fine sculpturing on the whitish wings and thorax. There are 800 species, found mainly in Mediterranean regions. Their eggs are frequently inserted into plant tissues, and covered with a brown secretion that hardens to a scab. Nymphs are often spiny and lack the adult patterning.

Lacerta The Lizard, a CONSTELLATION of the northern sky, introduced by the Polish astronomer Johannes Hevelius (1611–87). It lies on the edge of the Milky Way and has been the site of three novae during the 20th century.

lacewing A delicate green or brown insect, with two pairs of large, net-veined transparent wings and, often, bright golden eyes. Lacewings belong to the order Neuroptera, with around 5,000 known species, including the ANT LIONS and some species with mantis-like forelegs. Lacewings attach their eggs to plants by means of silk stalks, and both adults and larvae are active predators of plant-eating insects and important destroyers of aphids.

lackey moth See TENT CATERPILLAR.

Laclos, Pierre(-Ambroise-François) Choderlos de (1741–1803) French novelist. He is remembered for his epistolary novel *Les Liaisons dangereuses* (1782), which caused a scandal with its depiction of the corrupt, erotic schemes of an aristocratic couple.

Laconia (or **Lakonia**) A modern department and ancient region of Greece, in the south-east Peloponnese; area 3,636 sq km (1,414 sq miles); pop. (1991) 94,910. Throughout the classical period the region was dominated by its capital, Sparta, which remains the administrative centre of the modern department.

La Coruña The Spanish name for CORUNNA.

lacquer See VARNISHES AND LACQUERS.

lacrosse A ball-and-goal game for teams of ten a side, popular in Australia, Canada, the UK, and the USA, and deriving from an ancient game played by North American Indians. Players carry a stick with a triangular net at one end in which they catch the hard rubber ball, pass it, and shoot at goal. The pitch is a rectangle some 100 m (110 yards) long by 64 m (70 yards) wide.

lactation The secretion of milk by the MAMMARY GLANDS, which usually begins at the end of a pregnancy and is controlled by the hormones PROLACTIN and OXYTOCIN.

lactic acid (or **2-hydroxypropanoic acid**, $CH_3CH(OH)COOH$) A sour syrupy liquid manufactured by the fermentation of lactose from milk.

During strenuous exercise pyruvic acid is reduced to lactic acid, which may accumulate in the muscles and cause cramp.

lactose A sugar consisting of one glucose molecule linked to a galactose molecule. It occurs in the milk of all mammals; cows' milk contains 4.7 per cent lactose.

Ladislaus I (canonized as **St Ladislaus**) (*c*.1040–95) King of Hungary 1077–95. He conquered Croatia and Bosnia and extended Hungarian power into Transylvania, as well as establishing order in his kingdom and advancing the spread of Christianity. He was canonized in 1192. Feast day, 27 June.

Ladislaus II (Polish name Władysław) (*c*.1351–1434) King of Poland 1386–1434. He was grand duke of Lithuania from 1377 to 1401, during which time he was known as Jogaila, and acceded to the Polish throne on his marriage to the Polish monarch, Queen Jadwiga (1374–99), thus uniting Lithuania and Poland. He converted Lithuania to Christianity and was the founder of the Jagiellon dynasty, which ruled the two states until 1572.

Ladoga (Russian **Ozero Ladozhskoye**) A large lake in north-west Russia, north-east of St Petersburg, near the border with Finland. It is the largest lake in Europe, with an area of 17,703 sq km (6,835 sq miles).

ladybird A red, yellow or black BEETLE of the family Coccinellidae, often marked with spots or blotches, with a roundish outline and strongly convex wing-covers. Both adults and larvae are active predators of plant-eating insects and important destroyers of aphids.

lady fern See FERN.

Ladysmith A town in eastern South Africa, in KwaZulu-Natal. It was founded in the early 19th century and named after the wife of the governor of Natal, Sir Harry Smith. It was subjected to a four-month siege by Boer forces during the Second Boer War and was finally relieved on 28 February 1900 by Lord Roberts, who replaced General Sir Redvers Buller as commander of the British forces.

Laënnec, René-Théophile-Hyacinthe (1781–1826) French inventor of the STETHOSCOPE. A professor at the Charité hospital and the Collège de France, in Paris, he observed in 1816 two children with their ears close to the ends of a long stick, listening to the transmitted sound when they tapped it. This inspired his invention of the stethoscope, initially a wooden tube 30 cm (1 foot) long, for listening to sounds within the body, especially the heart and lungs.

Lafayette, Marie Joseph Paul Yves Roch Gilbert du Motier, Marquis de (or **La Fayette**) (1757–1834) French soldier and statesman. In 1777 he went to America and became one of the leaders of the French Expeditionary Force, which fought alongside the American colonists in the War of Independence. On his return he played a crucial part in the early phase of the French Revolution, commanding the National Guard (1789–91) and advocating moderate policies. He became an opposition leader in the Chamber of Deputies (1825–30) and participated in the Revolution of 1830.

La Fontaine, Jean de (1621–95) French poet. He is chiefly remembered for his *Fables* (1668–94), drawn from oriental, classical, and contemporary sources; they include such tales as 'The Cicada and the Ant' and 'The Crow and the Fox'. He also wrote *Contes et nouvelles* (1664–74), a collection of bawdy verse tales drawn from Ariosto, Boccaccio, and others.

Lagerkvist, Pär (Fabian) (1891–1974) Swedish novelist, poet, and dramatist. *The Dwarf* (1944), set in Renaissance Italy, deals with man's destructiveness; *Barabbas* (1950) heralded a series of novels whose central concern is man's search for God. Lagerkvist's poetry collection *Angest* (1916) is startling in its emotional intensity and forceful language and he developed into one of Sweden's greatest LYRIC poets. He was awarded the Nobel Prize for literature in 1951.

Lagerlöf, Selma (Ottiliana Lovisa) (1858–1940) Swedish novelist. She made her name with *Gösta Berlings Saga* (1891), a book inspired by local legends and traditions, as were many of her later novels. She was awarded the Nobel Prize for literature in 1909, the first woman to be the sole winner of a Nobel Prize (Marie Curie shared one in 1903).

lagoon ▶**1** A stretch of salt water separated from the sea by a low sandbank, coral reef, etc. ▶**2** The enclosed water of an atoll. ▶**3** An artificial pool for the treatment of effluent or to accommodate an overspill from surface drains during heavy rain.

Lagos The chief city of Nigeria, a port on the Gulf of Guinea, situated on islands interconnected by causeways; pop. (1992) 1,347,000. A former Yoruba town and centre of the slave-trade between the 16th and 19th centuries, it was held by Britain from 1851 until 1960. It was capital of Nigeria from 1960 till the designation of a new federal capital at Abuja in 1982. It has many light industries and craft products.

Lagrange, Joseph Louis, Comte de (1736–1813) Italian-born French mathematician. He is remembered for his proof that every positive integer can be expressed as a sum of at most four squares, and for his study of the solution of algebraic equations, which later provided the inspiration for the founding of the theory of groups and Galois theory. His most influential work, however, was the *Traité de mécanique analytique* (1788), which was the culmination of his extensive work on mechanics and its application to the description of planetary and lunar motion. See LAGRANGIAN POINTS.

Lagrangian points Places in the vicinity of two orbiting masses at which the total acceleration due to gravitational and centrifugal forces is zero. There are five Lagrangian equilibrium points. Three are located along the line joining the centres of mass of the bodies: one in between the two masses and two outside, one on each side. They are therefore **collinear** points. The remaining two are located at the vertices of the equilateral triangles having the two orbiting masses at the other vertices. In the case of the Sun and Jupiter, these locations are occupied by the Trojan group of asteroids.

Lahore The capital of Punjab province and second-largest city of Pakistan, situated on the Ravi River near the border with India; pop. (est. 1991) 3,200,000. In Hindu legend it was founded by Loh, son of Rama, and in the 16th century it became a capital of the Moghul empire. In 1767 it was taken by the Sikhs and in 1849 it came under British control. Following independence in 1947 Lahore was capital of West Punjab and from 1955 to 1970 it was capital of West Pakistan. Lahore is a commercial, banking, and marketing centre with a diverse range of industries.

Laing, R(onald) D(avid) (1927–89) Scottish psychiatrist. He became known for his controversial views on madness and in particular on schizophrenia, in which he proposed that what society calls insanity is in fact a defensive façade in response to the tensions of the close-knit nuclear family. Major works include *The Divided Self* (1960) and *Sanity, Madness, and the Family* (1965).

laissez-faire (French, 'let do') A concept that was introduced by the French physiocrats in the 18th century, denoting government abstention from interference with individual action. Subsequently taken up by such classical economists as Adam SMITH, it signifies minimum government INTERVENTION in the economic system, and maximum scope for MARKET forces. See also ECONOMICS.

lake A body of water surrounded by land formed either when hollows fill with water or when natural drainage is obstructed so that water piles up behind the barriers. Some freshwater lakes are the result of earth movement, as in RIFT VALLEYS. Others, long and narrow, such as the Scottish lochs, or broad, such as some in the USA and Canada, are caused by GLACIATION. Yet others are the water-filled craters of extinct volcanoes or the result of water seeping into limestone rocks and forming caves, the roofs of which then collapsed. Sometimes the lava from a volcano or the moraine of a glacier blocks a valley, and a river then fills the land behind the barrier. Many lakes are fed by melting snow and become larger in the spring. Saltwater lakes may be parts of oceans or seas cut off by earth movement, or their salinity may have resulted from evaporation. Lakes are useful in many ways – checking the flow of rapid rivers, absorbing floodwater, providing routes for travel, serving as reservoirs, and supplying headwater for irrigation and the generation of electricity.

Lake District A scenic region of mountains and lakes in the north-west of England, UK. It includes 15 lakes, several falls, and some of England's highest peaks. Composed of rocks of the Palaeozoic Age, the region was the centre of intense volcanic activity over 350 million years ago. It is a domed structure with a radial drainage pattern; streams have cut deep gorges and ancient ice-sheets are responsible for the development of broad U-shaped valleys. Crags, bare fells, and ravines add to its rugged beauty. See also LAKE POETS.

Lake poets The English poets who lived in the LAKE DISTRICT at the beginning of the 19th century. The principal Lake poets are William WORDSWORTH and Samuel Taylor COLERIDGE. Robert SOUTHEY is sometimes grouped with them although he did not support their theories of poetry.

Lakshmi The Hindu goddess of fortune and prosperity, renowned for her beauty, wife of Vishnu. Born from the churning of the ocean by the gods and demons, Lakshmi assumed various forms to accompany her husband in his incarnations, becoming Sītā when he was Rama and Rādhā when he was Krishna. Lakshmi is usually depicted seated or standing on a lotus, and holding a lotus and a pot of ambrosia (the nectar of immortality).

Lalique, René (1860–1945) French jeweller. He achieved fame with his display of art nouveau brooches and combs at the International Exhibition in Paris in 1900. He became interested in glass and, stimulated by demand for perfume bottles, developed a personal style of moulded glass with iced surfaces and patterns in relief. His display at the Paris Exhibition of 1925 further enhanced his reputation.

Lallan (or **Lallans**) A form of Lowland Scots dialect, developed especially as a literary language by modern Scottish writers.

Lalo, Edouard (Victoire-Antoine) (1823–92) French composer. He remained in relative obscurity working as a teacher and violinist until the 1870s, when his *Symphonie espagnole* (1875) for violin and orchestra made a favourable impression. His third opera, *Le roi d'Ys*, was begun during this period; it reached the stage in 1888 and was an overwhelming success.

Lamaism A form of BUDDHISM practised in TIBET and MONGOLIA. (Lama, 'Superior One', is the name given to its higher clergy.) It is a fusion of Bon, the native animist religion of Tibet, with Mahayana Buddhism introduced from north-west India in the 8th century by the scholar Padmasambhava. In times of disorder monks built fortress monasteries and by the 13th century spiritual and temporal power had fused. In the 14th century the Red Sect, whose lamas wore red robes, was discredited though not entirely displaced by the new Yellow Sect. Red Sect lamas were not celibate, sons succeeding fathers as abbots of monasteries. The Yellow Sect, by contrast, demanded of its lamas a life of celibacy and poverty. The head of the Yellow Sect, the Dalai ('All-Embracing') Lama, based in Lhasa, became Tibet's priest-ruler. Below him was the Panchen Lama, based in Shigatse. When either of these lamas died a child believed to be his reincarnation succeeded him.

Lamarck, Jean-Baptiste Pierre Antoine de Monet, Chevalier de (1744–1829) French biologist who, among others, anticipated DARWIN in conceiving the idea of organic evolution, but accounted for it by the theory that all living organisms are continually trying to improve themselves. Like Darwin, he wrongly believed that characteristics acquired in an individual's lifetime are passed on to its offspring. This was central to Lamarck's theory, but played only a minor part in Darwin's ideas.

Lamartine, Alphonse Marie Louis de (1790–1869) French poet, statesman, and historian. His first volume of poems, *Méditations poétiques* (1820), brought a fresh lyricism to French poetry and established him as a leading figure of French romanticism. During the 1830s he devoted more time to politics and spoke out on behalf of the working classes. He served as Minister of Foreign Affairs in the provisional government following the Revolution of February 1848, but was deposed in June. His writings include *Histoire des Girondins* (1847).

Lamb, Charles (1775–1834) British essayist and critic. He devoted much of his life to caring for his sister Mary, who suffered from a recurrent mental illness; together they wrote *Tales from Shakespeare* (1807). He also compiled *Specimens of English Dramatic Poets* (1808), an anthology of scenes and speeches from Elizabethan and Jacobean dramatists, with accompanying critical comments. His essays were published in leading periodicals; the best known are the semi-autobiographical *Essays of Elia* (published in a collected edition in 1823).

Lambert, (Leonard) Constant (1905–51) British composer, conductor, and critic. While still a student he was commissioned by Diaghilev to write the music for the ballet *Romeo and Juliet* (1926). Thereafter he took a leading part in the establishment of British ballet as musical director of Sadler's Wells (1930–47). His other works include *The Rio Grande* (1929), a work in a jazz idiom for orchestra, piano, and voices.

Lambeth A borough of inner London, England, on the south bank of the Thames between Wandsworth and Southwark; pop. (1991) 220,100. Landmarks include LAMBETH PALACE, St Thomas's Hospital, The Oval, the Old Vic Theatre, the Royal Festival Hall, and the Imperial War Museum.

Lambeth Palace A palace in the London borough of Lambeth, that since 1197 has been the London residence of the Archbishop of Canterbury.

laminate A COMPOSITE in which thin layers of one or more materials are bonded together. Laminates of more than one material have properties intermediate between those of the materials they are made from. Materials that are anisotropic (whose physical properties vary with direction) can be laminated to produce a more homogeneous material. Plywood is an example of this type of laminate: it is made from thin sheets (veneers) of wood, each oriented differently from those either side, bonded together with resins. Laminated wood is similar to plywood, but the grains of the different veneers all run in the same direction. Laminates can also be made from sheets of asbestos, cloth, and paper impregnated with thermosetting resins. They are much stronger than the resins themselves, and are used when insulation and strength are required together. Such materials are, however, increasingly being replaced by improved plastics, which are cheaper to manufacture. Laminated glass uses metal wires or plastic sheet in conjunction with glass to make a transparent material that cracks but does not fragment on impact. A further important laminate is used in power transformer cores, where the iron in the core is laminated to minimize eddy currents.

Lammas A medieval church harvest festival formerly celebrated on 1 August. Once a quarter day in England, it still is in Scotland. The word derives from Old English, meaning 'loaf-mass', because the festival used to involve consecration of loaves made from the new season's wheat.

lammergeier (or **bearded vulture**) A species of large Old World VULTURE, *Gypaetus barbatus*, with an eagle-like appearance and a wing-span of 3 m (10 feet), fully feathered neck, and dark 'beard' on either side of the beak. Soaring birds of remote mountain regions of Africa, Asia, and southern Europe, they are rare everywhere and persecuted by man. They breed on high crags, and are mainly carrion feeders, though suspected of attacking farm stock as well.

Lammermuir Hills A range of hills in East Lothian and the Borders, south-east Scotland, rising to 533 m (1,749 ft) at Meikle Says Law.

Lampedusa, Giuseppe Tomasi de (1896–1957) Italian novelist. After a nervous breakdown he devoted himself to a life of intellectual activity. In 1955 he began writing his only novel, *Il Gattopardo* (*The Leopard*), which was originally rejected by publishers but won worldwide acclaim on its posthumous publication in 1958.

lamprey A member of the family Petromyzonidae, one of the two families of JAWLESS FISHES (the others are hagfishes). They are primitive eel-like vertebrates that have seven separate gill-openings each side of their body, and lack pectoral and paired fins. Lampreys are mainly freshwater fishes. Some species migrate to the sea to feed but return to breed in fresh water. They occur in the temperate zones of both Northern and Southern Hemispheres. Many lampreys are parasitic when adult, sucking blood from fishes. The sea lamprey, *Petromyzon marinus*, greatly affected the fish populations of the American Great Lakes once it had become established there, but others do not feed as adults. All have a larval life of several years when they lie buried in river mud. During this time the larvae are called ammocetes.

lamp shell (or **brachiopod**) A marine invertebrate resembling BIVALVE molluscs, yet actually related to BRYOZOANS. Lamp shells form the phylum Brachiopoda, with 280 living species. Their two-valved, chalky shell is not symmetrical, having a large ventral valve and smaller dorsal valve rather than matching left and right halves as in bivalves. Within this shell is a complex, ciliated, filter-feeding organ, quite unlike the flat, sheet-like gills of a bivalve. Most species live attached to rock or to other organisms in the sea, and a few burrow in sand. They are very common as fossils, with 30,000 named fossil 'species', and have considerably declined in number since the Mesozoic Era.

LAN (local area network) See NETWORK.

Lanarkshire A former county of south-central Scotland, incorporated into Strathclyde Region in 1975 and divided into the local government areas of North and South Lanarkshire in 1996.

Lanby buoy A large automatic navigational BUOY introduced in the latter part of the 20th century, as a cheaper substitute for a LIGHTSHIP. The buoy is circular, and fitted with a lattice mast carrying a characteristic light with a visibility of about 25 km (15 miles) in clear weather, a fog signal, and a RADAR beacon. The buoy is designed to operate for six months without attention, and its performance and position are monitored from a shore station.

Lancashire A county of north-west England, on the Irish Sea; area 3,070 sq km (1,186 sq miles); pop. (1991) 1,365,100; county town, Preston. The county was noted for the production of textiles, especially cotton goods, between the 16th and 19th centuries. Both cotton manufactures and coal-mining have virtually ceased. Tourism is important on the coast and Pennine hills. Lancashire is divided into 14 districts.

Lancaster A city in Lancashire, north-west England, on the estuary of the River Lune; pop. (1981) 44,450. The town developed around a castle and a Benedictine priory built in the 11th century on the site of a former Roman fortification. It was the county town and administrative centre of Lancashire until 1974. It has a university founded in 1964, and numerous light industries.

Lancaster, Burt(on Stephen) (1913–94) US film actor. He made his film début in *The Killers* (1946) and was often cast in 'tough guy' roles. He took more dramatic parts in such films as *From Here to Eternity* (1953), *Elmer Gantry* (1960), for which he won an Oscar, and *Birdman of Alcatraz* (1962). Later films include *Atlantic City* (1980) and *Field of Dreams* (1989).

Lancaster, Sir Osbert (1908–86) British cartoonist and writer. After studying art at the Slade School he produced several books on architecture, including *Homes, Sweet Homes* (1939), in which he coined the phrase 'stockbroker Tudor'. From 1939, for many years he produced cartoons for the *Daily Express*, using his character Maudie Littlehampton to satirize upper-class preoccupations.

Lancastrian A descendant or supporter of John of GAUNT, Duke of Lancaster. The Lancastrians held the throne of England as HENRY IV, V, and VI (their badge was a red rose). In the Wars of the ROSES, a series of battles for the throne fought with the YORKISTS from 1455 onwards, the Lancastrians suffered a major reverse in the displacement of Henry by Edward IV in 1461; they took refuge in France, and under the leadership of MARGARET OF ANJOU invaded England and succeeded in restoring Henry to his kingdom in October 1470. Henry's rule was ended after a few months by the Yorkist victories at BARNET and TEWKESBURY; most of the remaining Lancastrian leaders died in the latter battle. Yet the Lancastrian party was ultimately successful, for it then supported Henry Tudor, who in 1485, by his victory at BOSWORTH FIELD, became king as HENRY VII.

lancelet (or **amphioxus**) A small, slender, fish-like animal growing up to 9 cm (4 inches) in length. There are about 25 species known, of worldwide distribution in shallow seas. They burrow in clean sand where the tidal current is moderate and lie with the head end exposed to catch floating food particles in the fine tentacles around the mouth. Lancelets have features of both vertebrates and invertebrates and have been claimed to be a link between them. They are classified as a subphylum, Cephalocordata, of the phylum Chordata.

Lanchow See LANZHOU.

Landau, Lev (Davidovich) (1908–68) Soviet theoretical physicist, born in Russia. He created an influential school of theoretical physics at Moscow State University, studying a wide range of problems. He contributed to thermodynamics, particle physics, quantum mechanics and electrodynamics, astrophysics, condensed matter physics, and several other areas. Landau was awarded the Nobel Prize for physics in 1962 for his work on the superfluidity and thermal conductivity of liquid helium.

landing craft A flat-bottomed vessel, usually of box-section, designed to lift assault troops and vehicles from ships at sea and land them ashore. There is an opening ramp at the bow, propellers usually set into the stern for protection when taking the ground, and efficient arrangements for streaming and retrieving anchors when approaching the beach. Since the Suez War (1956), helicopters have also been used in a landing craft role, and more recently HOVERCRAFT and HYDROFOILS.

Land League An agrarian organization in Ireland. It was founded in 1879 by an ex-FENIAN, Michael DAVITT, to secure reforms in the land-holding system. With Charles PARNELL as president, it initiated the boycotting of anyone replacing a tenant evicted because of non-payment of rent (see BOYCOTT, CHARLES CUNNINGHAM). The campaign for land reform was linked with parliamentary activity by the Irish HOME RULE Members of Parliament. The British government declared the Land League illegal and imprisoned Davitt and Parnell. Branches of the League were formed in Australia, the USA, and elsewhere. Between 1881 and 1903 British governments passed Land Acts to remove the worst features of the landlord system in Ireland.

Landor, Walter Savage (1775–1864) British poet and prose writer. A sense of control and formality characterizes much of his verse, which is in sharp contrast to that of other ROMANTIC poets. His skill as a lyricist is demonstrated in his EPIC poem *Gebir* (1798), an oriental tale. He is remembered for his *Imaginary Conversations of Literary Men and Statesmen* (1824–29), a prose work with dialogues concerning political, social, and literary questions, which range from classical antiquity to the 19th century.

land reclamation The improvement of land for agriculture, building, or other purposes. Arid land requires IRRIGATION. COASTAL DEFENCES protect land reclaimed from the sea. Bogs and swamps are usually drained by a network of open ditches and channels sloping towards a river. The river banks may need to be raised to prevent flooding of the reclaimed area. Land derelict from mining or industry may need stabilizing; for example, loose ground can be compacted, holes filled in, and any noxious residues treated. Poisonous substances can either be removed (though their transport may be hazardous) or left in place and isolated by an impenetrable casing. Methane and other gases generated in landfill sites can be vented to prevent their migration or build-up in the ground.

Landsat See EARTH RESOURCES SATELLITE.

landscape painting The art of depicting natural scenery in painting. Although Western examples of landscape painting by the Romans survive from Pompeii, it was not until the 16th century that landscape began to emerge as a distinctive subject in European art. The German Altdorfer is generally credited with being the first western artist to paint a pure landscape and it was in northern Europe that interest in the subject chiefly developed. From being a highly stylized art, using conventional arrangements of trees, rock-forms and so on, it became one of naturalistic depiction – 17th-century Dutch painting marks one of the high points of naturalistic landscape, particularly in the works of RUISDAEL, HOBBEMA, SEGHERS, and REMBRANDT. At the beginning of the 17th century Annibale Carracci invented the ideal landscape, a grand and highly formalized arrangement suitable as a setting for small figures from serious religious, historical, or mythological subjects, a tradition carried on by Claude and Poussin. Other approaches also emerged, however, notably in the work of Romantic artists, such as Friedrich and Turner, who explored the poetic aspects of nature. In the late 19th century the Impressionists established landscape as probably the single most popular category of painting. In modern painting landscape has also been the basis for Surrealist fantasy or abstract compositions. See also CHINESE ART AND ARCHITECTURE.

Landseer, Sir Edwin (1802–73) British painter, sculptor, and engraver of animal subjects. Though his work delighted the Victorian public, his reputation has since declined, for although he had great skill in depicting animals, his sentimental and moralizing compositions do not appeal to modern taste. However, the bronze lions modelled (in 1867) for the base of Nelson's Column in London's Trafalgar Square are still widely admired. In his last years he suffered from bouts of madness aggravated by alcohol.

Land's End A rocky promontory in south-west Cornwall, which forms the westernmost point of England. The approximate distance by road from Land's End to John o' Groats, at the north-east tip of Scotland, is 1,400 km (876 miles). Its natural beauty has been destroyed by a theme park.

landslide (or **landslip**) A sudden movement of rock and soil that occurs when the ground surface is shaken, overloaded, or inadequately supported. Shaking occurs during earthquakes, blasting operations, and the passage of heavy vehicles. Overloading is caused by heavy snow or rain or by building roads, reservoirs, or houses at the top of slopes. Poor support occurs where rivers, glaciers, the sea, or building operations have cut away the lower sections of hillsides. Water is a major and particular factor in the incidence of landslides. It adds to the weight on the slope when it soaks into the surface and it also acts as a lubricant. As a result, material saturated by heavy rain can slip a long way down even gentle slopes. The most dramatic and devastating landslides occur in mountainous areas and can involve the collapse of entire hillsides. Sometimes a cushion of air is trapped under the falling mass. Then it will travel a very long way, even uphill, like a hovercraft. More often a semicircular chunk of the slope rotates backwards as it gives way, leaving a cliff or scar above a lobe of debris. The area of debris remains dangerous as further slipping and sliding may easily be triggered.

Landsteiner, Karl (1868–1943) Austrian-born US physician. His main interest was immunology, and he devised the system of classifying blood into four main immunological groups (A, B, AB, and O), which made it possible for blood transfusions to be carried out successfully. Landsteiner was awarded a Nobel Prize for this in 1930, and in 1940 he was the first to describe the rhesus factor in blood.

Lanfranc (*c.*1010–89) Scholar, teacher, and Archbishop of Canterbury (1070–89). He was born in Italy, and set up a school at Avranches, Normandy (1039). He studied as a monk at the abbey of Bec, Normandy (1042), becoming its prior (1046) and making it into one of the finest schools in Europe, whose pupils included ANSELM and Theobald, both future archbishops of Canterbury. Lanfranc's association with WILLIAM I began with his negotiation of papal approval for William's marriage while he was Duke of Normandy (1053) and continued after the conquest of England. Lanfranc sought to reform the English Church and to unite it under Canterbury, but he also recognized the king's right to intervene in Church affairs. He supported WILLIAM II in the rebellion of 1088.

Lang, Fritz (1890–1976) Austrian-born film director. A pioneer of German cinema, during the 1920s he directed such notable silent films as *Metropolis* (1927), making the transition to sound in 1931 with the thriller *M*. When *The Testament of Dr Mabuse* (1933) was banned by the Nazis, Lang left Germany. He eventually settled in the USA and made a range of films, including westerns (such as *Rancho Notorious*, 1952) and *films noirs* (such as *The Big Heat*, 1953).

Langland, William (*c.*1330–*c.*1400) English poet. A minor friar, he devoted much of his life to writing and rewriting *Piers Plowman* (*c.*1367–70), a long allegorical poem in alliterative verse; it takes the form of a spiritual pilgrimage, through which the narrator is guided by the Plowman and experiences a series of visions, with vivid vignettes of contemporary life, on his journey in search of Truth.

Langley, Samuel Pierpoint (1834–1906) US astronomer and aviation pioneer. He invented the bolometer (1879–81) and used it to study the radiant energy of the Sun. His work on aerodynamics contributed to the design of early aeroplanes.

Langmuir, Irving (1881–1957) US chemist and physicist. His principal work was in surface chemistry, especially the phenomenon of adsorption and the application of this to catalysis. He worked on high-temperature electrical discharges in gases, introducing the use of inert gas in the tungsten lamp, developing an atomic-hydrogen welding torch capable of reaching temperatures up to 3,000°C, and first using the term *plasma*. While studying atomic structure he introduced the terms *covalence* and *electrovalence*.

Langton, Stephen (*c.*1150–1228) English prelate. His reputation rests mainly on his promotion of the interests of the English Church in the face of conflicting pressures from the papacy and the English throne. As Archbishop of Canterbury he defended the Church's interests against King John, was intermediary during the negotiations leading to the signing of Magna Carta, and protected the young Henry III against baronial domination.

Langtry, Lillie (born Emilie Charlotte le Breton) (1853–1929) British actress. Born in Jersey and the daughter of the dean of the island, she was noted for her beauty and became known as 'the Jersey Lily' from the title of a portrait of her painted by Sir John Millais. She made her stage début in 1881 and was one of the first actresses from an aristocratic background. She became the mistress of the Prince of Wales, later Edward VII.

language The method of human communication, either spoken or written, consisting of the use of words in an agreed way. Scholars of LINGUISTICS conceive of language in various ways. For example, SAUSSURE viewed language as an arbitrary and conventional system of signs used for communication, while for CHOMSKY it is a set of rules and principles in the mind of a speaker. Language is central to the transmission of culture. For example, the study of verbal TABOO – that which is so sacred or important that it cannot be talked about unless using ritual speech or euphemisms – reveals society's values and beliefs. The use of language also has important political implications. It may be an indicator of identity for ethnic minorities whose identity or existence is threatened, and it expresses group or class membership, as in the use of DIALECT or jargon. Distinguishing between languages is often more a matter of social, historical, and administrative than of linguistic criteria. If the languages have no standard forms, or if the local dialects are not affected by the standard forms, it may be impossible to find a boundary between them. For example, the dialects of Spain, France, and Italy form a continuum and it used to be hard to say where the linguistic borders were. Standard languages themselves do not always differ more than dialects; for instance, Danish, Swedish, and Norwegian are easily mutually intelligible. The ability of humans to acquire and use language is the primary feature distinguishing them from animals, although animals are capable of using signalling systems. Bees' communication by dancing is an example. Such systems, however, are inborn rather than acquired and lack the complexity of human language.

languages, classification of A major task in LINGUISTICS. Linguists commonly distinguish between natural languages, those which human beings speak, and artificial languages, such as computer languages and logical systems. They classify natural languages in two different ways: genetic and formal. Genetic classifications group together languages which have a common ancestor. For example, most of the languages of Europe and northern India, including English, French, German, Hindi, Italian, Russian, and Welsh, are classified as INDO-EUROPEAN LANGUAGES because it can be shown that they are descended from a common source. Likewise, Arabic, Hebrew, and Maltese are classified as SEMITIC LANGUAGES. Formal classifications group together languages which have grammatical properties in common, whether or not they are related. It was once common to classify languages on the basis of the nature and extent of their word-formation processes. More recently, it has been common to classify languages on the basis of the order of the main constituents of a sentence: subject, verb and object. English has the order subject-verb-object. In the sentence *John loves Mary*, *John* is the subject, *loves* the verb, and *Mary* the object. Other languages, for example Turkish, have the order subject-object-verb (*Murat*

Yasemin'i seviyor, 'Murat loves Yasemin') and others, for example Welsh, have the order verb-subject-object. It is also common to classify languages on the basis of how fixed or free word order is in a sentence.

Languedoc A former province of southern France that extended from the Rhône valley to the northern foothills of the eastern Pyrenees and formed a broad coastal plain lying between the Cévennes Mountains and the Mediterranean. It derives its name from the *langue d'oc*, a form of medieval French spoken south of the Loire, the basis of modern Provençal. Lower Languedoc has united with the former province of Roussillon to form the modern French region of Languedoc-Roussillon which comprises the departments of Aude, Gard, Herault, Lozère, and Pyrénées-Orientales; area 27,376 sq km (10,574 sq miles); pop. (1990) 2,114,985. Its chief town is Montpellier.

lanner One of the largest of the true FALCONS, *Falco biarmicus*, widespread throughout the Mediterranean area, Africa, and Arabia. Narrow-winged and speedy, it is a desert predator, feeding on spiny lizards and other ground prey, and also on birds, especially migrants on passage.

Lansing The state capital of Michigan, USA, on the Grand River; pop. (1990) 127,320. First settled in 1847, the city developed after 1887 when R. E. Olds began to build and sell one of the USA's earliest automobiles, the Oldsmobile. Its heavy industries produce vehicles, metal goods, and machinery. East Lansing is the home of Michigan State University (1855).

lantern fish A small marine fish of the family Myctophidae, that lives in the open ocean in all areas including polar seas; some 220 species are known. They are distinguished by their blunt snout, large eyes, usually a small dorsal fin near the tail (adipose fin), and the presence of small light organs on the head and body. The arrangement of these light organs is unique for each species, and there is no doubt that they play an important role in species recognition. Fishes of the deep sea, they ascend towards the surface at night although in daylight they will be caught at depths of 700–1,000 m (2,000–3,250 feet).

lantern fly A BUG, often brightly coloured, of the family Fulgoridae. In many of the 600 or so species the front of the head is enormously enlarged and inflated (hence the popular name 'alligator bug') but, despite the insect's name, does not glow in the dark. They feed by sucking the sap from trees.

lanthanide (or **lanthanoid**, **rare-earth element**) Any of a series of silvery-white metallic elements with atomic numbers from 57 (lanthanum) to 71 (lutetium), although some authorities exclude lanthanum itself from the series. The series is also called the rare-earth elements because their oxides (earths) were formerly thought to be rare; in fact even the rarest, thulium, is more common than silver. All the lanthanides have very similar chemical properties, because they all have the same number of electrons in their outer shell; the additional electron added to each element across the series goes to fill an incomplete inner shell and is not greatly involved in CHEMICAL BONDING. The lanthanides are predominantly very electropositive elements, which give ions with a charge of +3. They occur together in monazite and certain other minerals, mainly in the USA, Russia, India, and Scandinavia, and are separated from other elements by PRECIPITATION and from each other by ion exchange. Cerium is used in cigarette lighter flints and the europium ion as the red phosphor in colour television tubes.

lanthanum (symbol La, at. no. 57, r.a.m. 138.9055) The first of the series of LANTHANIDE (rare-earth) elements. The silvery metal is used in misch metal with other rare earths in making lighter flints. Its compounds include an oxide (La_2O_3) and a chloride ($LaCl_3$).

Lanzarote One of the Canary Islands, the most easterly island of the group, part of the Spanish province of Las Palmas; area 795 sq km (307 sq miles); chief town, Arrecife. It is a popular tourist resort. The island's landscape was dramatically altered after a series of volcanic eruptions in about 1730. It is noted for the black sand of its beaches and for the 'Mountains of Fire' in the south-west, an area of several hundred volcanoes which still emit heat.

Lanzhou (formerly **Lanchow**) A city of northern China, on the upper Yellow River, capital of Gansu province; pop. (1990) 1,480,000. Its chief industries are engineering, oil refining, and atomic energy.

Laois (or **Laoighis**, **Leix**) A county of the Republic of Ireland, in the province of Leinster; area 1,720 sq km (664 sq miles); pop. (1991) 52,325; county town, Portlaoise. It was formerly (until 1920) called Queen's County.

Laos A long, thin, landlocked country in south-east Asia, bordering China and Myanmar (Burma) on the north, Thailand on the west, Cambodia on the south, and Vietnam on the east.

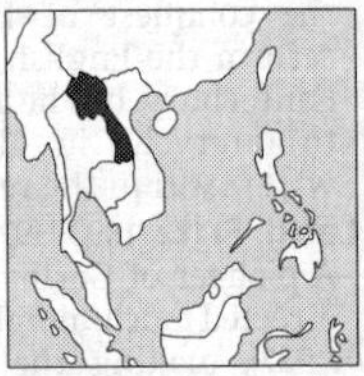

Physical. Laos is mostly high and hilly, with evergreen forest, this terrain also supporting maize. The Mekong River runs through the north of the country, down the western boundary, and through it again in the south; and its wide valley, swept by a summer monsoon, is ideal for rice growing.

Economy. The Lao economy is mainly agricultural, rice being the chief crop and coffee an export crop. The forests are rich in teak wood, a major export to Thailand at the cost of the destruction of much forest land. High-grade tin is mined. The development of hydroelectric power has made exports of electrity to Thailand the largest export. Limited industry includes food-processing and textiles.

History. The Lao, originating in southern China, were driven south by MONGOL pressure. In 1354, following a period of Khmer rule, they set up the Buddhist kingdom of Lanxang ('Million Elephants'), which for a time was very powerful. Laos broke up into rival kingdoms in the 18th century and gradually fell under Siamese (Thai) domination before Siam was forced to yield its claim to France in 1893. Occupied by the Japanese during World War II, it emerged briefly as an independent constitutional monarchy (1947–53), but was undermined by guerrilla war as a result of the increasing influence of the communist PATHET LAO as a political force in the mid-1950s. A coalition government was established under Prince SOUVANNA PHOUMA in 1962, but fighting broke out again soon after, continuing into the 1970s, with Laos suffering badly as a result of involvement in the VIETNAM WAR. A ceasefire was signed in 1973 and a year later Souvanna Phouma agreed to share power in a new coalition with the Pathet Lao leader, his half-brother Prince Souphanouvong (1902–95); but by 1975 the Pathet Lao were in almost complete control of the country and on 3 December the monarchy was finally abolished and the People's Democratic Republic of Laos established, which, under Kaysone Phomvihane (Prime Minister 1975–92), maintained close links with Vietnam. In 1989 there began some relaxation of his regime and moves to restructure the economy. A new constitution was promulgated in 1991, which envisaged a strong presidency, but no relaxation of control by the Lao People's Revolutionary Party. In 1992 Kaysone was elected President, but died later that year; he was succeeded by Nouhak Phousavanh. The USA restored full diplomatic relations and in May 1992 an IMF loan was negotiated. In 1995 the USA lifted its embargo on aid donations to Laos.

Capital: Vientiane
Area: 236,800 sq km (91,400 sq mi)
Population: 4,882,000 (1995)
Currency: 1 kip = 100 at
Religions: Buddhist 57.8%; tribal religions 33.6%; Christian 1.8%; Muslim 1.0%; atheist 1.0%
Ethnic Groups: Lao 67.1%; Palaung-wa 11.9%; Tai 7.9%; Miao (Hmong) and Man (Yao) 5.2%; Mon-Khmer 4.6%
Languages: Lao (official); minority languages
International Organizations: UN; ASEAN

Laozi (or **Lao-tzu**; known as 'Master Lao') A probably mythical Chinese philosopher, long honoured in China as the founder of DAOISM. He is said to have worsted CONFUCIUS, reputedly his junior, in debate. The *Daodejing* (*Dao Te Ching*), which dates from about the 3rd century BC (about 300 years after Confucius), was attributed to him. Daoists later claimed he was an immortal who left China for India, where he converted the BUDDHA to Daoism.

La Paz The capital of Bolivia, in the north-west of the country near the border with Peru; pop. (1992) 711,040. Situated in the Andes at an altitude of 3,660 m (12,000 ft), La Paz is the highest capital city in the world. It was founded by the Spanish in 1548 on the site of an Inca settlement. Its industries include textiles, electrical appliances, and chemicals.

lapis lazuli A deep blue or bluish gemstone consisting of a sodium aluminium silicate with other minerals. It is found in metamorphosed limestones. The main deposits are in Afghanistan and Chile, although the USA, Russia, and Myanmar (Burma) also have workings.

Laplace, Pierre-Simon, Marquis de (1749–1827) French mathematician and astronomer who demonstrated the stability of the Solar System from NEWTON'S LAW OF GRAVITATION. He incorporated his mechanics of the Solar System in his *Mécanique Céleste* (1799–1825) which included the proposal of what is now known as the LAPLACE NEBULAR HYPOTHESIS of the birth of the Solar System. He also conceived the idea that a star might be so massive that particles of light could not escape from it, similar to the modern BLACK HOLE theory.

Laplace nebular hypothesis A theory of the origin of the Solar System proposed by the French scientist Pierre-Simon de LAPLACE in 1796. He suggested that a rotating cloud of gas, contracting under its gravitational field, would rotate faster to conserve angular momentum and so be forced to take the shape of a spinning disc. A ring of gas would be left behind by the contracting disc whenever the growing centrifugal force equalled the gravitational force. The material in each ring would collect to form a proto-planet. This process would continue, and it was thought possible that the system of satellites of a planet would form in a similar way from the planet as it contracted. The Sun would form at the centre of the whole system. Versions of the nebular hypothesis, such as Weizsacker's theory utilizing modern ideas, still form the most plausible theories of the creation of the Solar System.

Lapland The region of northern Europe that extends from the Norwegian Sea to the White Sea and lies mainly within the Arctic Circle. It consists of the northern parts of Norway, Sweden, and Finland, and the Kola Peninsula of Russia.

La Plata A port in Argentina, on the River Plate, south-east of Buenos Aires; pop. (1991) 640,000. Founded in 1882, it was known as Eva Perón from 1946 to 1955. It is one of the chief outlets for produce from the pampas of Argentina such as grain and refrigerated meat; it is a major oil-refining centre. It is also a cultural centre, with a national university (1897), colleges, and museums.

Lapp A member of an Arctic society of semi-nomadic PASTORALISTS, sometimes known as the Sameh, found also in Norway, Sweden, Finland, and the Russian Federation (see LAPLAND). Their seasonal migration with the reindeer herds begins in the spring, when small groups of between ten and a hundred people move from their winter encampments to pastures for the calving season. In early summer, there is a second move to highland pasture, followed by a move back to the lowland pasture in the autumn, before the final move to winter quarters. In common with other pastoralists, the basic unit of social organization is the family, and there is no overall form of authority. Kinship and trading links provide the basis for creating bonds that extend beyond the immediate family group. Although SHAMANISM was the traditional form of religious belief, many Lapps are now Christians, and have settled in permanent villages.

lappet moth See EGGAR MOTH.

lapwing A bird of the genus *Vanellus*, and a member of the PLOVER family, Charadriidae. Many of the 23 species have crests, like the one popularly known in Britain as the peewit, or green plover, *V. vanellus*. Others have wattles on the face, and sharp spurs on the wings, as in the African spur-winged plover, *V. spinosus*. Lapwings are fierce defenders of their breeding territories.

L'Aquila See AQUILA.

Lara, Brian (Charles) (1969–) West Indian cricketer. Born in Trinidad, he first played for the West Indies in 1990. Two years later Lara made his mark on international cricket with an innings of 277 against Australia in Sydney. In 1994 he scored 375 against England in Antigua, breaking the record test score previously set by Gary Sobers in 1957. A few weeks later, playing for Warwickshire against Durham, he scored 501 not out, a world record in first-class cricket.

larch A deciduous conifer of the genus *Larix*, which comprises 10–12 species native to the north temperate zone. Belonging to the pine family, and closely allied to cedars, they are unusual among temperate region conifers in being deciduous. The European larch, *L. decidua*, produces valuable timber, used for stakes, telegraph poles, and planking. The North American tamarack larch, *L. laricina*, is also grown widely for its timber.

Lardner, Ring(gold) (1885–1933) US sports columnist and writer. While working as a reporter on baseball, he wrote a number of short stories about baseball players in his first collection, *You Know Me, Al* (1916). His stories were collected in *Ring Lardner's Best Short Stories* (1938). He also wrote novels, poetry, plays, and an autobiography, but only his short stories have survived.

Lares and Penates In Roman mythology, household gods. The Lares were regarded as protectors of particular localities or houses. The Penates were guardians of the store-cupboard. Eventually they became barely distinguishable. Lares and penates has come to refer to treasured household possessions.

Large Magellanic Cloud See MAGELLANIC CLOUDS.

lark A bird of the family Alaudidae, which includes some 91 species. Most are greyish-brown and buff above, usually streaked with black, and pale below with little streaking. The tail is often edged with white. The beak, used for feeding on insects or small seeds, is usually longish and sharply pointed. Most species of lark are less than 22 cm (8 inches) long. They are found in many parts of the world, but are poorly represented in South America. They live in open country, from grassland to desert. Many, such as the skylark, *Alauda arvensis*, have beautiful songs given in flight. They nest on the ground, usually under cover of the edge of a tuft of grass or a stone.

Larkin, Philip (Arthur) (1922–85) British poet. His distinctive poetic voice first became apparent in *The Less Deceived* (1955), and was further developed in *The Whitsun Weddings* (1964) and *High Windows* (1974). His style is notable for its adaptation of contemporary speech rhythms and colloquial vocabulary to poetic metre; many poems are set in urban and suburban landscapes and are pervaded by an air of melancholy, bitterness, and stoic wit.

larkspur See DELPHINIUM.

Larnaca A port, industrial town, and resort on the south coast of Cyprus, on Larnaca Bay; pop. (1990) 62,600. It was the birthplace of Zeno the Stoic in 335 BC, and of Apollonius the Alexandrian physician *c.*50 BC. Since the partition of Cyprus Greek Cypriots have developed Larnaca as the principal international tourist airport.

La Rochefoucauld, François, Duc de (1613–80) French classical author. His *Maximes* (1665, fifth enlarged edition 1678) are terse, highly polished observations on human nature, which undermine the concept of disinterested virtue and the power of the will depicted by CORNEILLE in his plays. La Rochefoucauld substitutes a pessimistic picture of man in which subconscious self-love lies behind every action. His views reflect the changing moral climate of the later 17th century, also seen in the work of Mme de La Fayette.

La Rochelle A seaport on the Bay of Biscay, capital of the department of Charente-Maritime, western France; pop. (1990) 73,740. A former Huguenot stronghold, it was besieged and devastated by Richlieu in 1627–28. Nearby La Palice is the departure point for the Ile de Ré. La Rochelle has shipbuilding, fish-canning, and saw-milling industries.

Larousse, Pierre (1817–75) French lexicographer and encyclopedist. He edited the 15-volume *Grand dictionnaire universel du XIX*[e] *siècle* (1866–76), which aimed to treat every area of human knowledge. In 1852 he co-founded the publishing house of Larousse, which continues to issue the dictionaries and reference works that bear its name.

larva The immature stage of any animal, which differs from the adult in appearance and often in habits as well. In land animals, the larva is usually a stage of growth, like a caterpillar, and the transition to the adult form may occur through a resting stage, the pupa. In marine animals, the larva is more often a stage by which the organism is distributed and the adult form is reached before much growth in size has taken place. In some animals, particularly insects, there may be several larval stages, each differing in appearance, before the adult form appears.

Larwood, Harold (1904–95) British cricketer. He built a reputation as a fearsome fast bowler with Nottinghamshire. In the 1932–33 MCC tour of Australia he bowled fast short-pitched 'bodyline' deliveries, and was involved in controversy when several of the home batsmen were injured. He retired from test cricket after that tour, and his cricketing career was cut short by an injury to his left foot.

laryngoscope See ENDOSCOPY.

larynx (or **voice box**) A cavity which occurs in the throat of most amphibians and other four-limbed vertebrates. The thyroid and cricoid cartilages are jointed and can move in relation to one another. Two very small cartilages are jointed to the back of the cricoid and from each an elastic membrane, the vocal cord, passes forward to join on to the thyroid cartilage. A complex series of tiny muscles allows the cords to be voluntarily opened, closed, shortened, and lengthened. In humans the larynx is capable of adjustment to form a greater range of sounds than any other animal. In **laryngitis**, the larynx is infected by bacteria or viruses, causing the cords to swell, and making the voice sound hoarse.

La Salle, René-Robert Cavelier, Sieur de (1643–87) French explorer. A settler in French Canada, he sailed down the Ohio and Mississippi rivers to the sea in 1682, naming the Mississippi basin Louisiana in honour of Louis XIV. In 1684 he led an expedition to establish a French colony on the Gulf of Mexico; over two years were wasted in fruitless searches for the Mississippi delta. La Salle eventually landed in Texas by mistake and was murdered when his followers mutinied.

La Scala See MILAN.

Lascaux A cave with palaeolithic drawings and paintings generally held to be the finest examples of prehistoric art; discovered in 1940 in the Dordogne region of south-west-central France. Now closed for reasons of preservation, its artwork is reproduced in caves nearby (Lascaux II).

laser (light *a*mplification by stimulated *e*mission of *r*adiation) A device producing an intense monochromatic (a single wavelength), coherent (the waves are in phase), and parallel beam of light, or ultraviolet or infrared radiation. (A related instrument is the MASER.) Before a laser can operate, it must be 'pumped': an energy source is used to excite the ATOMS in the emitting material, so that most of them are in a high-energy state. Spontaneous emission of light from one atom in the excited material then produces a chain reaction in which the light emitted from one atom stimulates emission of light of the same wavelength and phase from others. The ends of the lasing material are mirrored, one mirror being half-silvered: light is reflected between these mirrors, stimulating more emission, until the beam becomes bright enough to pass through the half-silvered mirror. The first laser, built by Theodore MAIMAN in 1960, produced pulses of red light from a ruby rod using light from a flash tube as the energy source. By 1963 lasers had been made from liquids, gases, and SEMICONDUCTORS, giving continuous or pulsed beams of many different wavelengths. Liquid dye lasers can be tuned to give a range of wavelengths.

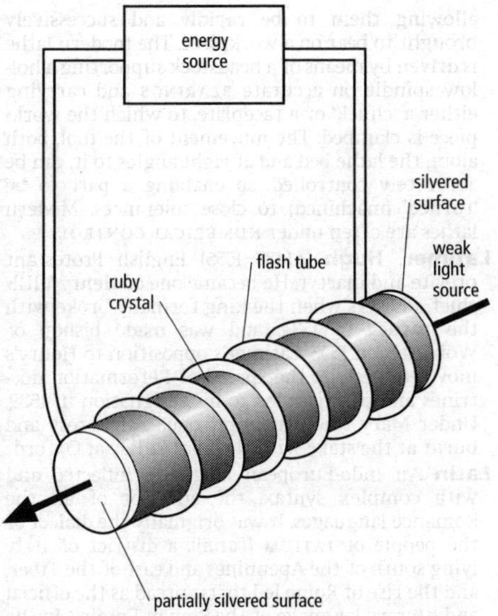

Laser In the ruby laser, chromium ions in the ruby crystal are excited by an intense flash from the flash tube. A weak beam of monochromatic light causes stimulated emission to occur from these excited ions. The resulting beam is amplified by reflections back and forth along the ruby rod before being sufficiently bright to pass through the partially silvered end as a pulsed laser beam.

Gas lasers (such as the low-power, red helium–neon laser and the high-power, infrared carbon dioxide laser) use electrical discharge for energy. The tiny but durable and efficient semiconductor or diode lasers also use electrical energy, producing red or infrared beams. They are used in OPTICAL-FIBRE communication systems, and for recording and playing compact discs. Laser light can be focused to a very tiny spot, concentrating its energy so that it can be used for cutting and welding in industry and in medical surgery. Other uses include alignment and length measurement, weapons-guidance systems (see LASER WEAPON), reading supermarket BAR CODES, and HOLOGRAPHY. Lasers are also used in printing (see LASER PRINTING), and in nuclear FUSION research.

laser printing Printing the output of a computer using a minute, digitally controlled beam of LASER light directed by an optical system towards a rotating drum. The drum is coated with a photoconductive material, which becomes electrically charged on exposure to light. Areas of the photoconductive layer exposed to the laser become selectively attractive to tiny particles of powder, supplied from a toner cartridge. As the drum turns, the powder image is electrostatically transferred to the paper stock and fused to the paper by heat (see PHOTOCOPIER). Resolution is usually at least 120 dots/cm (300 per inch), sufficient for most DESKTOP PUBLISHING work.

laser weapon A targeting, ranging, or attacking device that employs high-energy LASER beams. Laser weapons normally consist of a power source and a projector. In range-finders, with which all modern tanks are equipped, a laser is used to calculate the distance to the target. The beam from the targeting device is detected by sensors in a missile or artillery SHELL, which then homes in on the target designated. Similar devices are used by aircraft to drop laser-guided bombs. Laser beams can also be used to 'blind' enemy tanks by directing them at the delicate range-finding optical equipment or even into the crew's eyes. High-energy laser beams of the order of hundreds or thousands of kW could melt through the armour of enemy tanks, or easily puncture any thinner metal. However, the large power requirements at present preclude such weapons from effective use. See also STRATEGIC DEFENSE INITIATIVE.

Las Palmas (in full **Las Palmas de Gran Canaria**) A port and resort on the north-east coast of the island of Gran Canaria, capital and largest city of the Canary Islands; pop. (1991) 347,670. Exports sugar, bananas, and tomatoes.

La Spezia An industrial port at the head of the Gulf of La Spezia in Liguria, north-western Italy; pop. (1990) 103,000. Since 1861 it has been Italy's chief naval station. There is a ferry link with Corsica.

Lassa fever A serious virus disease that occurs in Central West Africa and was first described in 1969 in the Nigerian village of Lassa. Death from kidney or heart failure occurs in 50 per cent of cases. Treatment with plasma from recovered patients is the best therapy.

Lassus, Orlande de (Italian name Orlando di Lasso) (*c.*1532–94) Flemish composer. He was a notable composer of polyphonic music and wrote more than 2,000 secular and sacred works, including masses, motets, madrigals, and settings of psalms.

Las Vegas A desert city in southern Nevada, USA, noted for its casinos and night-clubs; pop. (1990) 258,295. An early camping site on the westward-bound trail across the continent, Las Vegas was settled in 1855–57 by Mormons. It later became a centre of mining and ranching and was purchased by a railway company in 1903.

lateen rig A form of fore-and-aft rig, used mainly in Arabian and Mediterranean waters. A triangular sail is set on a long yard attached to a short forward-raked mast, the upper corner or peak of the sail being checked by braces. The lateen rig was used on the mizen (rear) mast in early three-masted sailing ships.

La Tène The second phase of the European Iron Age, named after the type-site at the east end of Lake Neuchâtel, Switzerland, and dating from the mid-5th century BC until the Roman conquest. The culture of this period (which follows the Hallstatt) represents the height of early Celtic achievement. It is characterized by hill-forts, developments in agriculture, rich and elaborate burials, and artefacts of excellent craftsmanship and artistic design.

latent heat The energy absorbed or released by a substance when it changes its physical state (e.g. from liquid to solid) at the same temperature. The energy released as latent heat when a liquid changes to a solid is equal to the energy absorbed when such a change of state occurs in the reverse direction. Values can be large. For example, ice at 0°C absorbs almost as much energy in changing to liquid water as is needed to heat this water from 0°C to 100°C; and it takes over six times as much energy again to change water at 100°C into steam at the same temperature. Thus the latent heat of vaporization is thé energy a substance absorbs from its surroundings in order to overcome the attractive forces between its molecules as it changes from a liquid to a gas and in order to do work against the external atmosphere as it expands. The **specific latent heat** is the heat absorbed or released by unit mass of a substance in the course of an isothermal change of state.

lateral line A conspicuous line visible along the sides of a fish. This marks the position of a series of sensory organs that act as vibration receptors, and are used by the fish to detect other individuals from the vibrations they set up in water.

Lateran The site in Rome containing the basilica of St John the Baptist (St John Lateran), which is the cathedral church of Rome, and the Lateran Palace in which the popes resided until the 14th century. Five general ecclesiastical councils of the Western Church were held in the basilica (1123, 1139, 1179, 1215, 1512–17). The **Lateran Treaty**, signed in the Lateran Palace in 1929, was a concordat between the kingdom of Italy and the Holy See, recognizing as fully sovereign and independent a new (papal) state called Vatican City.

laterite The upper layer of soil in which large quantities of iron and aluminium oxides are concentrated by seasonal fluctuations of the WATER-TABLE. Laterites form in tropical areas, particularly on plains and plateaux. When fresh, they are mottled in red, yellow, and grey, but after exposure to the atmosphere, the sand and clays they contain are washed out by LEACHING and the reddish material which remains hardens to form a very tough crust. Iron-rich laterites contain up to 30 per cent iron oxide, while those enriched with aluminium – bauxites – may have over 40 per cent concentration and are mined commercially.

latex A fluid produced by some flowering plants, often confined to a system of long, branched tubes in the phloem. It is a milky liquid containing substances in suspension which, if separated out, have a rubbery quality. Their function is unknown, but in some plants, such as SPURGES, the latex is poisonous. Several plant species produce latex which can be used to produce rubber. Opium is obtained from the latex of the poppy *Papaver somniferum*, and most natural rubber from that of *Hevea brasiliensis*.

lathe The earliest and still the most important machine-tool. Its major function is to produce items of circular cross-section by spinning the workpiece on its axis and cutting its surface with a sharp stationary tool: the tool may be moved sideways to produce a cylindrical object and moved towards the workpiece to control the depth of cut. The earliest lathes had fixed conical 'centres' between which the workpiece was supported. A cord was wrapped round the workpiece and held taut by a bow: by reciprocating this bow the workpiece rotated to and fro. A chisel supported by a tool rest was used for cutting. Lathes had spread from the Middle East to the Mediterranean and India by the second millennium BC. A development was the pole lathe, in which the cord was attached at its upper end to a springy pole and at its lower end to a foot treadle, so freeing both hands to hold the tool. In the INDUSTRIAL REVOLUTION, lathes were power-driven (an electric motor is now commonly used), which allowed continuous rotation of the workpiece at a variety of speeds. In the early 19th century, all-metal lathes were developed in which the cutting tool was held in a slide rest, the movement of which could be accurately controlled by two screws at right angles to each other. Lathes of this kind could be used to machine-cut screw-threads. A further development in the later 19th century was the turret lathe, in which several cutting tools could be clamped in a rotatable turret, allowing them to be rapidly and successively brought to bear on a workpiece. The modern lathe is driven by means of a headstock supporting a hollow spindle on accurate BEARINGS and carrying either a 'chuck' or a faceplate, to which the workpiece is clamped. The movement of the tool, both along the lathe bed and at right angles to it, can be accurately controlled, so enabling a part to be 'turned' (machined) to close tolerances. Modern lathes are often under NUMERICAL CONTROL.

Latimer, Hugh (*c.*1485–1555) English Protestant prelate and martyr. He became one of Henry VIII's chief advisers when the king formally broke with the papacy in 1534, and was made bishop of Worcester in 1535. Latimer's opposition to Henry's moves to restrict the spread of Reformation doctrines and practices led to his resignation in 1539. Under Mary I he was imprisoned for heresy and burnt at the stake with Nicholas Ridley at Oxford.

Latin An Indo-European language, inflected and with complex syntax, the ancestor of all the Romance languages. It was originally the dialect of the people of LATIUM (*Latini*), a district of Italy lying south of the Apennines and east of the Tiber, and the rise of Rome led to its spread as the official and literary language of the Roman Empire. In the Middle Ages it remained the international medium of communication in western Europe, the language of law, the sciences, and in particular of liturgy; it was the official language of the Roman Catholic Church until the mid-20th century. Latin of the post-classical period is distinguished chronologically as late Latin (*c.*200–600 AD) and medieval Latin (*c.*600–1500); silver Latin is the literary language and style of the century following the death of Augustus in 14 AD; the term Low or Vulgar Latin is applied to popular and provincial forms of Latin used in the Middle Ages, especially those from which the Romance languages developed.

Latin America The parts of Central and South America where Spanish or Portuguese is the main language.

Latin literature The literature of the Roman republic (*c.*500–*c.*44 BC), imperial Rome (*c.*30 BC–*c.*400 AD), and medieval Europe. Little or no Latin writing untouched by GREEK LITERATURE has been preserved. The first work of note was the adaptation of HOMER's *Odyssey* (3rd century BC) by the slave Livius Andronicus. Drama, firmly based on GREEK THEATRE and epic poetry, developed during the 2nd century BC. ENNIUS introduced the HEXAMETER into Latin with the *Annals*, a poem on the history of Rome. The greatest of Roman dramatists was PLAUTUS, who adapted his plays from the 'New Comedy' of the Greek theatre. As in Greece, prose developed later than poetry. Annalistic history grew gradually from the records of the priests, but Greek influence was also crucial. The first Roman histories were in Greek, and the first known history in Latin, Cato the Elder's *Origins* (*c.*149 BC), was influenced by Greek writers. TERENCE adapted Greek themes for his own polished and urbane comedies. Oratory, an important weapon in Roman republican politics, took on Greek sophistication and rhythms from the time that the tribune Gaius Gracchus (died 121 BC) delivered his speeches, reaching its peak in the work of CICERO in the next century. This period produced some of the greatest figures in Latin literature: CATULLUS wrote some of the finest lyric poetry, employing the hexameter for mythological subjects, as well as experimenting in the elegiac couplet, while LUCRETIUS showed how poetry could accommodate philosophy, and Sallust brought a new style and dignity to the writing of history. The fall of the republic did much to stifle the art of oratory and of historical writing, and the classic Augustan period is marked mainly by the poetry of OVID, the later work of VIRGIL, the lyrics of HORACE, and the maturity of Roman ELEGY. It was followed by the writers of the Silver Age, notably Statius (*c*.45–96 AD), whose epic *Thebaid* influenced Dante and Chaucer. The literature of this period is preoccupied with wit, epigram, and melodrama. In the 1st century AD this manner put its mark on epic poetry, most notably in LUCAN, but it also affected the tragedy and prose of SENECA. Classical Latin is rounded off at the start of the second century by two mordant writers, JUVENAL, who perfected Roman satire, and by the sceptical historian TACITUS. Apart from the extraordinary writings of Apuleius (2nd century AD), there is little of note until Christianity brought new inspiration. Latin literature survived in Africa and Europe through the so-called Dark Ages of the 5th and 6th centuries in hymns and other religious verse, notably the influential allegory *Psychomachia* (*c*.405) by the Spanish poet Prudentius; in the philosophical reflections of Boethius, whose *Consolatio* (*c*.524) was later translated by Chaucer; and in the historical writings of the English monk BEDE. From the end of the 11th century a reawakening of Latin poetry began in France, stimulating the production of secular verses by wandering scholars, notably in the CARMINA BURANA. Important Latin prose works of the late Middle Ages include the letters of the philosopher and scholar Peter ABELARD, the theological writings of Thomas AQUINAS, and the very popular mystical work *De Imitatione Christi* (*The Imitation of Christ*) by Thomas à KEMPIS. The learned humanists of the 16th century, led by ERASMUS, wrote significant Latin works, including *Utopia* (1516) by the statesman and scholar Sir Thomas MORE. In the next century the English poets MILTON and MARVELL wrote some of their poems in Latin.

latitude and longitude (mapping) A conceptual grid of lines covering the Earth's surface and used on MAPS to enable positions to be accurately specified. Latitude lines (parallels) run east to west with their centres on the Earth's axis and their planes at right angles to it. The latitude of any of these circles, in degrees, is the angle that a line from it to the centre of the Earth makes with a similar line from the Equator, which has latitude 0°. The greatest possible latitude is 90°, that of the poles. Due to the OBLATENESS of the Earth the length of a DEGREE of latitude increases slightly towards the poles. Lines of latitude are generally shown according to scale; on world maps at intervals of 5°, with the Arctic and Antarctic Circles and the tropics of Cancer and Capricorn intervening. Together with lines of longitude they form a grid on which the position of any place can be specified. Longitude lines (meridians) run from north to south meeting at the Poles: a longitude is expressed as the angle made at the Earth's centre by the plane of the meridian with that of the PRIME MERIDIAN (or Greenwich meridian) at 0°. Lines of longitude thus range from 0° to 180° east or west of the prime meridian (180° E and 180° W being the same: the INTERNATIONAL DATE-LINE).

Latium (Italian **Lazio**) A region of west-central Italy, west of the Apennines and south of the River Tiber, comprising the provinces of Frosinone, Latina, Rieti, Roma, and Vitebor; area 17,203 sq km (6,645 sq miles); pop. (1990) 5,191,480; capital, Rome. The ancient region of Latium was settled during the early part of the first millennium BC by a branch of the Indo-European people known as the Latini. By the end of the 4th century BC the region had become dominated by Rome.

La Tour, Georges de (1593–1652) French painter. He was largely forgotten until his rediscovery in the 20th century, when he was hailed as the most inspired of the painters in the style of Caravaggio. He is best known for his nocturnal religious scenes, with their subtle portrayal of candlelight and sombre mood. His works include *St Joseph the Carpenter* (1645) and *The Denial of St Peter* (1650).

Latvia A country lying on the shores of the Baltic Sea and the Gulf of Riga. It borders on Estonia to the north, Russia to the east, and Lithuania to the south.

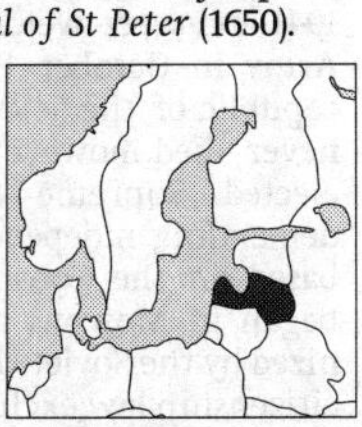

Physical. Latvia is generally flat, though hilly in the lakelands of the east and well forested with fir, pine, birch, and oak. It has a modified continental climate.

Economy. Mineral resources are limited, although there are unexplored reserves of oil. Latvia produces about half its energy requirements (the Dvina and its tributaries are the source of hydroelectric power) and is dependent for the rest on imports and the unified grid of the former Soviet Union's north-west region. Manufacturing

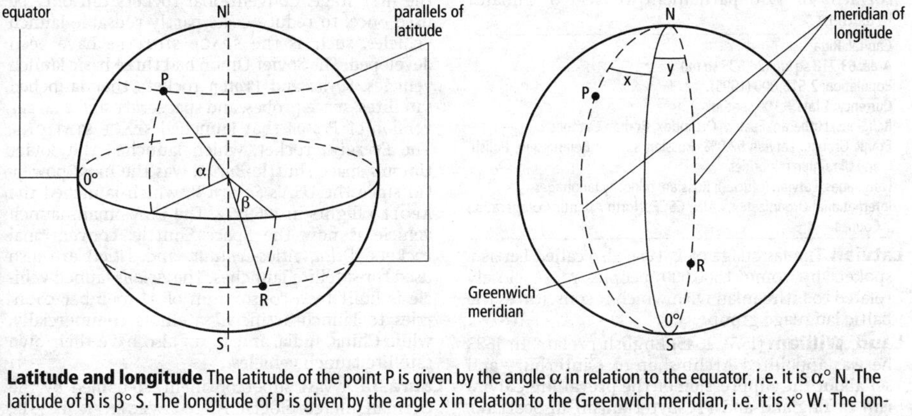

Latitude and longitude The latitude of the point P is given by the angle α in relation to the equator, i.e. it is α° N. The latitude of R is β° S. The longitude of P is given by the angle x in relation to the Greenwich meridian, i.e. it is x° W. The longitude of R is y° E.

industry concentrates on machinery, metal engineering, and durable consumer goods; light industry is also well developed. Agriculture specializes in dairy and meat production, and grains.

History. Originally inhabited by Lettish peoples, it was overrun by the Russians and Swedes during the 10th and 11th centuries, and settled by German merchants and Christian missionaries from 1158. In the 13th century the HANSEATIC LEAGUE forged commercial links, while the TEUTONIC KNIGHTS and German bishops imposed feudal overlordship. With Estonia it became part of Livonia in 1346, was partitioned under IVAN IV of Russia, and came under Lutheran influence in the REFORMATION. It then fell to the Poles, and in the 17th century to the Swedes. Their rule lasted until 1721, when parts again reverted to Russia, the remainder succumbing in the partitions of POLAND. From the 1880s Tsarist governments imposed a policy of Russification to counteract growing demands for independence, which was proclaimed in April 1918. After a confused period of war between Latvians, Germans, and Bolshevik Russians, international recognition was gained in 1921 and the Constitution of the Republic agreed in 1922. During the years 1922–40 sea-ports and industry declined with the loss of Russian markets, but agriculture flourished, many of the great estates being broken up. In 1934 a neo-fascist regime was formed by Karlis Ulmanis, who vainly tried to win Hitler's support, but was sacrificed in the Nazi-Soviet Pact of 1939. The Red Army occupied it in June 1940, but German troops took Riga on 1 July 1941 and were welcomed. Re-occupied by the Red Army in October 1944, it became a constituent republic of the Soviet Union. Latvian nationalism never died however, and in May 1990 a newly elected Supreme Soviet passed a resolution demanding independence from the Soviet Union, based on the Constitution of 1922. Negotiations began in Moscow, and independence was recognized by the Soviet Union in September 1991. A new citizenship law excluded from political activity all who were not citizens of pre-war Latvia or their descendants, thus excluding 48.2 per cent of the population, most of whom were Russians. A new government was elected in 1993 under President Guntis Ulmanis. In 1994 the citizenship law was modified slightly but tensions between the Russian and Latvian communities have continued. The last Russian troops were withdrawn from Latvia in August 1994. General elections in 1995 produced no clear winner and a coalition government was formed. In 1996 parliament re-elected Ulmanis President.

Capital: Riga
Area: 63,718 sq km (24,595 sq mi)
Population: 2,515,000 (1995)
Currency: 1 lats = 100 santimi
Religions: Lutheran; Eastern Orthodox, Roman Catholic
Ethnic Groups: Latvian 52.0%; Russian 35.0%; Belarussian, Polish, and Ukrainian minorities
Languages: Latvian (official); Russian; minority languages
International Organizations: UN; CSCE; North Atlantic Co-operation Council

Latvian The language of Latvia, also called Lettish, spoken by some 1,500,000 people, most closely related to Lithuanian with which it constitutes the Baltic language group.

Laud, William (1573–1645) English prelate. In 1633 he was appointed Archbishop of Canterbury and set about the suppression of the prevailing Calvinism in England and Presbyterianism in Scotland. His moves to impose liturgical uniformity by restoring pre-Reformation practices aroused great hostility; they led to war in Scotland and were a contributory cause of the English Civil War. In 1640 Laud was impeached and imprisoned; he was later executed for treason.

Lauda, Niki (full name Nikolaus Andreas Lauder) (1949–) Austrian motor-racing driver. He was world champion in 1975 and went on to win two more championships (1977 and 1984), despite suffering severe injuries in a crash in the 1976 German Grand Prix. He retired in 1985.

Lauder, Sir Harry (born Hugh MacLennan Lauder) (1870–1950) Scottish music-hall performer. In 1900 he made his London début and became highly popular there singing songs such as his compositions 'I Love a Lassie' and 'Roamin' in the Gloamin''. He entertained troops at home and abroad in both world wars and made many successful tours of the USA and the Commonwealth countries.

Laue, Max Theodore Felix von (1879–1960) German physicist, who devised the first practical method of analysing the wavelengths present in an X-RAY beam. The experiment was performed in 1913 by his assistants who directed a narrow beam of X-rays at a crystal and measured the pattern formed on a photographic plate by waves scattered from the regularly arranged atoms (see INTERFERENCE). This technique, called X-ray diffraction, was further developed by William and Lawrence BRAGG and is now used extensively to study crystal structures. Von Laue won the Nobel Prize for physics in 1914.

laughing gas See ANAESTHESIA.

Laughton, Charles (1899–1962) British-born US actor. He began his acting career on the English stage, turning to film in 1932. His appearance suited him for character roles such as Henry VIII (*The Private Life of Henry VIII*, 1933), Captain Bligh (*Mutiny on the Bounty*, 1935), and *Rembrandt* (1936); he also played Quasimodo in *The Hunchback of Notre Dame* (1939). He became a US citizen in 1950.

launch vehicle A vehicle used to send an artificial SATELLITE or spacecraft into space. Enormous power is needed to accelerate a spacecraft sufficiently to reach Earth orbit or to escape Earth's gravity completely. Such power requires large ROCKET MOTORS, whose fuel constitutes most of the weight of the vehicle at launch. Therefore vehicles have several 'stages', which separate and fall away when their fuel is used up. Extra power is often supplied by booster rockets strapped to the first stage. Conventional rockets can only be used once; to reduce costs partly reusable launch vehicles, such as the SPACE SHUTTLE have been developed. The Soviet Union had three basic launch vehicles: *Soyuz* and *Proton* rockets that launched satellites, space probes, and spacecraft, and a larger version of *Proton* that launched SPACE STATIONS. The *Energiya* rocket, which launched the Soviet Union's space shuttle *Buran*, was the most powerful since the USA's *Saturn V*, which launched the APOLLO flights in 1969–72. The USA's main launch vehicle is now the Space Shuttle; conventional rockets (*Delta*, *Atlas-Centaur*, and *Titan*) are also used for satellite launches. The *Ariane* launch vehicle is built by a consortium of 11 member countries to launch artificial satellites commercially, while China, India, and Japan also have their own satellite launch vehicles.

Laurasia A vast supercontinent, so-named by the German meteorologist Alfred WEGENER in 1912, who presented the theory of CONTINENTAL DRIFT.

He deduced that late in the Palaeozoic Era, which ended 225 million years ago, all the continents were united into a vast supercontinent which he called Pangaea. Later, this broke into two supercontinental masses: Laurasia, which existed in the Northern Hemisphere and contained North America (formerly Laurentia) and Eurasia, and GONDWANA.

laurel Any one of several quite distinct but superficially similar shrubs, though strictly the name should be applied only to the BAY LAUREL, *Laurus nobilis*. The laurels in northern Europe are usually species of the cherry genus, *Prunus*, notably cherry laurel, *P. laurocerasus*, and Portugal laurel, *P. lusitanica*.

Laurel and Hardy US comedy duo. British-born **Stan Laurel** (born Arthur Stanley Jefferson) (1890–1965) played the scatterbrained and often tearful innocent, **Oliver Hardy** (1892–1957) his pompous, overbearing, and frequently exasperated friend. They brought their distinctive slapstick comedy to many films from 1927 onwards.

Laurence, (Jean) Margaret (1926–87) Canadian novelist. She lived in Somalia and Ghana 1950–57, a period that influenced her early work, including her first novel, *This Side Jordan* (1960). In 1962 she moved to England, where she wrote her *Manawaka* series. This draws on the harsh Scots Presbyterianism of her small home town in Manitoba, and includes *The Stone Angel* (1964) and *The Diviners* (1974).

Laurentian Shield See CANADIAN SHIELD.

Laurier, Sir Wilfrid (1841–1919) Canadian Liberal statesman, Prime Minister 1896–1911. He became the leader of the Liberal Party in 1891 and five years later was elected Canada's first French-Canadian and Roman Catholic Prime Minister. While in office he worked to achieve national unity in the face of cultural conflict; he also oversaw the building of a second transcontinental railway and the creation of the provinces of Alberta and Saskatchewan.

Lausanne A resort town on the north shore of Lake Geneva, south-west Switzerland, capital of the Vaud canton; pop. (1990) 122,600. It is the seat of the International Olympic Committee.

lava A very hot, molten rock emitted from a volcanic vent or from a fissure (before it is emitted it is MAGMA). The rock that is formed when this material has cooled and solidified is also called lava. Its chemical composition affects the way it moves and the type of scenery it produces. Acidic lava rich in silica moves slowly as a thick mass and cools quickly, producing upstanding peaks like Etna or Mount Saint Helens. Lavas containing less silica are more fluid and can flow appreciable distances before cooling. Basic, silica-poor lavas, such as BASALTS, tend to form broad shield volcanoes with gentle slopes – as in the Hawaiian Islands – or to 'flood' wide areas, producing vast plateaux, such as the Deccan, India, or the Columbia Plateau in north-west USA. The tendency of acid lavas to cool rapidly often causes a plug to form in the vent of the volcano. Pressure builds up under it and a violently explosive eruption can result, as at KRAKATOA. The emission of basic lava is much less dramatic. Lava is frequently emitted at places on the Earth's surface as a result of the movements of tectonic plates.

Laval, Carl Gustaf Patrik de (1845–1913) Swedish inventor. An engineer by profession, his interests ranged from aerodynamics to metallurgy and his diaries record several thousand inventions. Laval is probably best known for his high-speed centrifugal cream-separator (1878), adopted by large dairies throughout the world. He also experimented with STEAM-TURBINE designs (1882–93).

Laval, Pierre (1883–1945) French politician. He trained as a lawyer before entering politics as a socialist. Gradually moving to the right, in 1931–32 and 1935–36 he was Prime Minister but was best known as Foreign Minister (1934, 1935–36), when he was the co-author of the Hoare–Laval pact for the partition of Ethiopia between Italy and Ethiopia. He fell from power soon after, but after France's defeat in 1940 he became chief minister in the VICHY GOVERNMENT. He advocated active support for Hitler, drafting labour for Germany, authorizing a French fascist militia, and instituting a rule of terror. In 1945 he was tried and executed in France.

lavender One of about 28 species of *Lavandula*, a genus of shrubs belonging to the mint family. They are found from the Atlantic islands through the Mediterranean to India. *L. vera* is widely cultivated for its flowers and for its oil, which is used in scent and soap.

laver An edible, pinkish-purple seaweed of the genus *Porphyra*, common worldwide on rocks near the edge of the sea. Its thin, wavy fronds are used as food in Wales, parts of southwestern England, and Japan.

Laver, Rod(ney George) (1938–) Australian tennis player. In 1962 he became the second man (after Don Budge in 1938) to win the four major singles championships (British, US, French, and Australian) in one year; in 1969 he was the first to repeat this.

Lavoisier, Antoine Laurent (1743–94) French scientist, regarded as the father of modern chemistry. He caused a revolution in chemistry by his description of the true nature of combustion, his rigorous methods of analysis, and his development of a new rational chemical nomenclature. He realized that it was Joseph Priestley's 'dephlogisticated air' that combined with substances during burning, and (believing it to be a constituent of acids) he renamed the gas *oxygen*. He held a number of important public offices, and his involvement in the collection of indirect taxes led to his death by guillotine in the French Revolution.

law A collection of precepts creating obligations within the community to which they apply. Secular legal systems may be differentiated from moral and religious laws by the derivation of their constituent elements from identifiable political sources. Although often associated with the infliction of punishment in case of violation, it is clear that laws perform many functions other than penal, such as conferring powers on individuals to enter CONTRACTS, form companies, transfer property, and make wills (typical subjects of private law), as well as defining social and power relationships (see JURISPRUDENCE; PUBLIC LAW). Law may have originated from expectations about how disputes between individuals should be resolved, generating custom and eventually CASE LAW. The Roman legal theorists reduced these practices into systematic expositions which acquired their own authority. The 6th-century codification of ROMAN LAW, *Corpus Juris Civilis* ('Body of Civil Law'), forms the basis of the systems of most continental European countries, which are therefore called CIVIL LAW systems. Many of these countries codified their laws during or after the Napoleonic era (1799–1815), but these codes retained many of the concepts of the civil law. The law in England developed relatively independently from civil law influence, and it formed the basis of the COMMON LAW SYSTEMS which evolved in countries colonized by Britain. In many countries, the precepts of religious communities or of tribal custom govern various aspects of the lives of their members (particularly in family law), alongside the law of the state, resulting in legal pluralism (see SHARIA (Islamic law); TALMUD (Jewish law); CUSTOMARY LAW). Besides the national law identified with particular states, a body of principles has developed over the years governing relationships between states. This includes the laws governing diplomatic relations and the observance of treaties. This customary INTERNATIONAL LAW has been supplemented in the 20th century by institutional mechanisms such as the INTERNATIONAL COURT OF JUSTICE and the UNITED NATIONS. International law binds states, but still lacks effective means of collective enforcement. In recent years, a new body of supra-national law, which can bind states as well as individuals within states, has arisen within the EU under the Treaty of Rome and subsequent agreements.

Law, (Andrew) Bonar (1858–1923) British politician. He became leader of the Conservative Party in 1911, and supported Ulster's resistance to HOME RULE. A tariff reformer, in 1915 he joined ASQUITH's coalition as Colonial Secretary and continued under LLOYD GEORGE, serving as Chancellor of the Exchequer (1916–19) and Lord Privy Seal (1919–21). In 1922 the Conservatives rejected the coalition government of Lloyd George and he was appointed Prime Minister. He resigned the following May for reasons of ill health.

Law, Denis (1940–) Scottish footballer. At the age of 18 he made his international début and went on to win 55 caps as a striker for Scotland. He signed for Manchester City in 1960 and spent most of his playing career in England, apart from a short period with the Italian club Turin. In 1962 he joined Manchester United, with whom he had great success, although he missed their 1968 European Cup victory through injury.

Lawes, Sir John Bennet (1814–99) British agricultural scientist. After early academic failure, from 1834 he devoted himself to the management of his family estate at Rothamsted, Hertfordshire, UK. There, with the help of J. H. Gilbert, he established the principles of scientific agriculture, showing a particular interest in the use of synthetic FERTILIZERS: he patented a mineral superphosphate fertilizer in 1842. In 1889 he established a trust to ensure that Rothamsted continued as an internationally famous agricultural research station.

Lawrence, D(avid) H(erbert) (1885–1930) British novelist, poet, and critic. He was born near Nottingham, the son of a miner and an ex-teacher. He qualified as a teacher, and in 1912 met Frieda Weekley (*née* von Richthofen) with whom he eloped to Germany. Together they travelled widely for the remainder of his life, and their relationship was to form the underlying theme of much of his later fiction. His first major novel *Sons and Lovers* (1913), set in a Nottinghamshire coal-mining village, reflects his early life and strong attachment to his mother. *The Rainbow* (1915) is a study of the 'recurrence of love and conflict' within a rural family, but it was officially banned as obscene. His next novel, *Women in Love* (1921), diagnoses the self-destructive mood of his time and is usually regarded as his most important work. His other novels include *The Lost Girl* (1920), *Kangaroo* (1923), based on his visit to Australia, and *The Plumed Serpent* (1926), set in Mexico, concerning a girl's search for a mystical rebirth. His last novel, *Lady Chatterley's Lover*, completed in Italy when Lawrence was already dying of tuberculosis, was printed privately in Florence in 1928 and finally published in an unexpurgated edition in 1960, after its publishers were acquitted in a celebrated obscenity trial.

Lawrence, Ernest Orlando (1901–58) US physicist. He developed the first circular particle accelerator, later called a cyclotron, capable of achieving very high electron voltages. This opened the way for the new science of high-energy physics, with the production of many new isotopes and elements, and Lawrence and his team investigated some of the subatomic particles generated. He also worked on providing fissionable material for the atom bomb. He received the Nobel Prize for physics in 1939.

Lawrence, St (Latin name Laurentius) (died 258) Roman martyr and deacon of Rome. According to tradition Lawrence was ordered by the prefect of Rome to deliver up the treasure of the Church; when in response to this order he presented the poor people of Rome to the prefect, he was roasted to death on a gridiron. Feast day, 10 August.

Lawrence, Sir Thomas (1769–1830) British painter. He first achieved success with his full-length portrait (1789) of Queen Charlotte, the wife of King George III. Many portrait commissions followed and by 1810 he was recognized as the leading portrait painter of his time. In 1818 he was sent by the Prince Regent (later George IV) to paint the portraits of heads of state and military leaders after the allied victory over Napoleon.

Lawrence, T(homas) E(dward) (known as **Lawrence of Arabia**) (1888–1935) British soldier and writer. From 1916 onwards he helped to organize and lead the Arab revolt against the Turks in the Middle East. His campaign of guerrilla raids contributed to General Allenby's eventual victory in Palestine in 1918; Lawrence described this period in *The Seven Pillars of Wisdom* (1926). In 1922 he enlisted in the RAF under an assumed name to avoid attention and remained in the ranks of that service for most of the rest of his life. He was killed in a motorcycle accident.

lawrencium (symbol Lr, at. no. 103, r.a.m. 257) A synthetic transuranic element discovered in 1961 and named after E. O. LAWRENCE. All known isotopes have very short half lives and the element has no uses.

Lawson, Nigel, Baron (1932–) British politician, Conservative Chancellor of the Exchequer 1983–89. He resigned from Mrs Thatcher's government as a result of unauthorized comments by her economic advisor and her unwillingness to allow the UK to take part in the EUROPEAN MONETARY SYSTEM.

laxative (or **purgative**) A substance, such as castor oil, magnesium sulphate, cascara, or methylcellulose, used to relieve constipation. However, a high fibre diet combined with regular exercise may be preferable to the regular use of laxatives.

Laxness, Halldór (Gudjónsson Kiljan) (1902–98) Icelandic novelist. Influenced by Catholic, communist, and socialist ideas, he later developed a more individualistic approach. *Salka Valka* (1931–32), *Independent People* (1934–35), and *World Light* (1937–40), all set in Iceland, feature individuals in search of independence, struggling against a hostile world. *The Atom Station* (1948) criticizes US bases in peacetime Iceland, and *The Happy Warriors* (1952), a travesty in saga style, attacks modern power politics. Laxness was awarded the Nobel Prize for literature in 1955.

Layamon (late 12th century) English poet and priest. He wrote the verse chronicle known as the *Brut*, a history of England from the period of the legendary Brutus to that of the 7th-century king Cadwalader. One of the earliest major works in Middle English, the poem introduces for the first time in English the story of King Arthur and other figures prominent in later English literature.

lay (from Old French *lai*) A short LYRIC or narrative poem; a medieval song-form. The *Contes* (*c*.1175) of Marie de France were narrative *lais* of Arthurian legend and other subjects from Breton folklore. Cultivated by the troubadours and *trouvères* (see MINSTREL), they had several STANZAS, each with a different poetic structure and each therefore set to different music. They provided the model for the so-called 'Breton lays' in English in the 14th century, which include Chaucer's 'Franklin's Tale' and the anonymous *Sir Orfeo*. Since the 16th century, a lay has been a short narrative poem, as in Macaulay's *Lays of Ancient Rome* (1842).

La'youn (or **Laayoune**; Arabic **El Aaiún**) The capital of Western Sahara, on the Atlantic coast of north-west Africa; pop. (1982) 96,800.

Lazarus (from Hebrew, 'God has helped') A friend of Jesus, the brother of Mary and Martha in Bethany, who, after four days in his tomb, was brought back to life by Jesus. Another Lazarus, in a parable told by Jesus, is cast as the beggar who lay suffering at the gates of a rich man, traditionally referred to as Dives. In life, Dives ignored the plight of Lazarus, but after death the rich man, parching in hell, pleaded in vain for water from Lazarus, now in heaven.

Lazio The Italian name for LATIUM.

LD process See IRON AND STEEL INDUSTRY.

Leach, Bernard (Howell) (1887–1979) British potter, born in Hong Kong. After studying in Japan he settled in Britain in 1920 and, with the Japanese potter Shoji Hamada, founded his pottery at St Ives in Cornwall. He practised and taught for more than 50 years, becoming a key figure in British 20th-century ceramics. His work amalgamated the ideas, methods, and traditions of Japanese and English pottery and his products were designed to combine beauty with functionality.

leaching A process that occurs when weakly acidic solutions from rainwater or plant acids are washed downward through the soil. This causes elements, such as sodium, potassium, magnesium, and calcium, to be released from the soil. These substances form alkaline compounds, which are then carried down through the soil PROFILE in solution, a process known as eluviation. As a result of the removal of these elements the upper horizons of the soil become increasingly acidic. The effects of leaching can be seen in the formation of the white salty deposits that often appear on the outside of earthenware flowerpots.

Leacock, Stephen Butler (1869–1944) Canadian humorist. The author of over 60 books, he is best known for many collections of humorous sketches, parodies, and essays, beginning with *Literary Lapses* (1910), and including *Sunshine Sketches of a Little Town* (1912), *Arcadian Adventures of the Idle Rich* (1914), and *My Discovery of England* (1922). He also wrote biographies of his masters, Twain and Dickens.

lead (symbol Pb, at. no. 82, r.a.m. 207.2) A soft, dense, grey metal that occurs in Group 14 (formerly IVB) of the PERIODIC TABLE. The principal ore is lead sulphide (PbS), commonly called galena, which is mined extensively in the USA. Lead oxide is obtained by roasting the ore, which is then reduced to lead by heating in a BLAST-FURNACE with coke and scrap iron. It can be further refined by ELECTROLYSIS. Chemically, lead is an unreactive element; it dissolves slowly in nitric acid but resists other acids, water, and oxygen. In its compounds it shows the VALENCIES 2 and 4. Because it is cheap and corrosion-resistant, it has been employed widely for roofing and for protecting cables and pipes underground; and as it absorbs radiation, it is used to shield X-ray equipment and nuclear reactors. It is also made use of in storage batteries, as ammunition, and in low-melting alloys such as solder and pewter – but not in pencils, the 'lead' in which is a mixture of graphite and clay. Lead tetraethyl, $Pb(C_2H_5)_4$, is extensively used as an ANTIKNOCK additive in petrol, although like all other lead compounds it is toxic; the use of lead-free petrol is therefore encouraged. Lead carbonate and lead chromate are used as paint pigments, and paints containing red lead (see LEAD OXIDE) are effective rust inhibitors. Four lead isotopes occur naturally: ^{204}Pb, ^{206}Pb, ^{207}Pb, and ^{208}Pb. Each is the end-product of a radioactive decay chain. The isotopic composition of lead therefore varies from place to place, and the relative atomic mass of lead is not constant.

lead chamber process The first industrial method for the manufacture of SULPHURIC ACID, developed originally by the British physician and inventor John Roebuck in 1746 but refined and improved over the next hundred years. Sulphur dioxide, obtained by burning SULPHUR or roasting sulphide ores, was converted to sulphuric acid by reaction with gaseous NITRIC ACID and oxides of nitrogen in a lead-lined reaction vessel (hence the name). This method of production has been largely superseded by the CONTACT PROCESS.

lead oxide Any of three different compounds. Lead(II) oxide (PbO) is a red solid used in making lead storage batteries, and in glass-making. Lead(IV) oxide (PbO_2) is a strong oxidizing agent, and on heating gives off oxygen. It is used in the manufacture of safety matches. Dilead(II) lead(IV) oxide (red lead (Pb_3O_4) is formed by oxidation of PbO; it is used in corrosion-resistant paints, especially to prevent rust.

lead sulphide (PbS) A blackish compound, occurring naturally in cubic crystals as galena, from which lead is extracted commercially. It is used in rectifiers and in detectors of infrared radiation.

lead tetraethyl (or **tetraethyl lead**) A liquid compound added to petrol to increase its OCTANE NUMBER and thus reduce engine KNOCK, caused by premature combustion of the fuel. The anti-knock properties of lead tetraethyl were discovered in 1921 through empirical investigations made by Thomas MIDGLEY. However, lead compounds from car exhausts cause AIR POLLUTION, which constitute a health hazard; during the last decades of the 20th century lead-free petrol has been widely marketed and is the only form of petrol permitted in some countries.

leaf An outgrowth from the stem of a plant which is usually green and flattened. Leaves form the foliage of a plant and act to trap sunlight to be used in PHOTOSYNTHESIS. A leaf consists typically of a petiole (stalk) and a lamina (blade) strengthened and served by veins. Its surface, particularly that away from the light, is covered with openings, called stomata, which regulate the movement of gases such as carbon dioxide, oxygen, and water

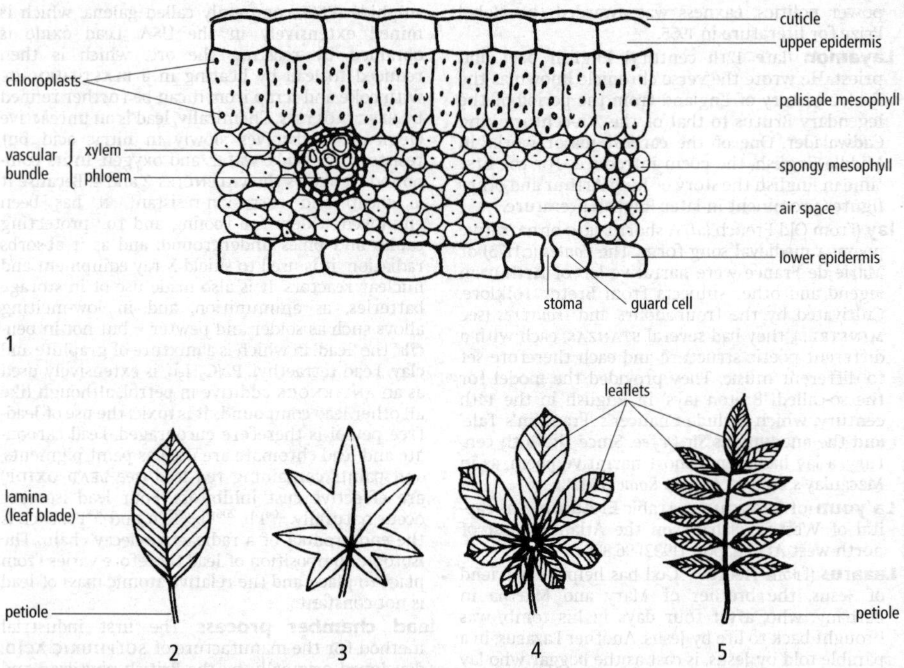

Leaf (1) Transverse section through a leaf. The vascular bundle, or vein, consists of two types of tissue. Xylem conducts water from the roots; phloem carries food materials made in the mesophyll to other parts of the plant. Opening and closing of the stomata is controlled by guard cells. (2–3) Types of simple leaf, in which there is a single blade that may be indented. (4–5) Compound leaves, in which the blade is divided into separate leaflets.

gases such as carbon dioxide, oxygen, and water vapour, in or out of the plant.

Leaves can be simple, with a single leaf blade, or compound, with several leaflets. Their surface can be naked, hairy, or waxy depending upon the habitat in which a plant is adapted to grow. Leaves can be modified to form protective scale leaves, or may be lost. Many desert cacti lack leaves, but have green stems through which they photosynthesize.

leaf beetle (or **chrysomelid**) A member of a large family of BEETLES, with over 20,000 species. The adult beetles are often convex, metallic-coloured species with large 'feet' (tarsi) and bead-like antennae. Their larvae, and often the adults themselves, feed on plants, and the family includes many pest species such as the COLORADO BEETLES. Among their number are the flea beetles, tortoise beetles, and bloody-nosed beetles.

leaf-chinned bat Any one of eight species of bat making up the family Mormoopidae. All have a plate-like extension of the lower lip, which presumably functions like a nose-leaf in echo-location, since the latter is absent. They occur in Central and tropical South America, as well as in the West Indies. Their preferred habitat is forest or riverine forest, where they feed on insects.

leaf-cutter bee A small, solitary BEE belonging to the genus *Megachile*, which is found worldwide. It builds its nest cells out of pieces cut from plant leaves, often in rotten wood. The shapes of the pieces of leaves that are cut vary, as they are tailored to the part of the cell for which they are to be used.

leafhopper A BUG of the family Cicadellidae, with almost 8,500 species distributed worldwide. Both the adults, which can reach 1 cm (0.5 inch) in length, and nymphs suck the sap of plants. They are one of the commonest groups of bugs and are very agile jumpers.

leaf insect A large, green relative of the STICK INSECTS, with which they make up 2,500 or so species of the order Phasmida. The body is flattened and bears leaf-like extensions that closely mimic the plants on which they feed. They are confined to the Old World tropics and include *Phyllium crucifollium*.

leaf-nosed bat A bat belonging to the family Hipposideridae, which has a well-developed nose-leaf forming part of its echo-location system. Of the 59 species, the nose-leaf is most elaborately developed in the flower-faced bat, *Anthops ornatus*. Leaf-nosed bats are confined to the tropics and warmer parts of the Old World. They are typical insect-eating bats and often very common. They roost in caves and houses in groups of several hundreds. The name leaf-nosed bat is also given to some species of New World tropical fruit bats and the false vampires.

League of Nations An organization for international cooperation established in 1919 by the VERSAILLES PEACE SETTLEMENT. A League covenant embodying the principles of collective security, arbitration of international disputes, reduction of armaments, and open diplomacy was formulated. Germany was admitted in 1926, but the US Congress failed to ratify the Treaty of Versailles, containing the covenant. Although the League, with its headquarters in Geneva, accomplished much of value in post-war economic reconstruction, it failed in its prime purpose as a result of the refusal of member nations to put international interests before national interests. The League was powerless in the face of Italian, German, and Japanese expansionism. In 1946 it was replaced by the UNITED NATIONS.

Leakey, Louis (Seymour Bazett) (1903–72) British-born Kenyan archaeologist and anthropologist. Leakey is noted for his work on human origins in East Africa, where after World War II his excavations brought to light the remains of early hominids and their implements at Olduvai Gorge. His wife, **Mary (Douglas) Leakey** (1913–96), was also an anthropologist, discovering *Australopithecus* (or *Zinjanthropus*) *boisei* at Olduvai in 1959 and initiating work at the nearby Laetoli site in the mid-1970s. Their son, **Richard (Erskine) Leakey** (1944–), continued his parents' work on early hominids; he was appointed director of the new Kenya Wildlife Service in 1989, but resigned in 1994 following a controversial political campaign to remove him. He subsequently founded a new political party in opposition to the ruling party in Kenya.

Leamington Spa (or **Royal Leamington Spa**) A residential town in Warwickshire, central England, on the River Leam south-east of Birmingham; pop. (1981) 57,350. Noted for its saline springs, it was granted the status of royal spa after a visit by Queen Victoria in 1838.

Lean, Sir David (1908–91) British film director. He made his début as a director in 1942 and went on to make many notable films, including *Brief Encounter* (1945), *Great Expectations* (1946), *The Bridge on the River Kwai* (1957), *Lawrence of Arabia* (1962), *Dr Zhivago* (1965), and *A Passage to India* (1984).

Leander See HERO.

Lear, Edward (1812–88) British humorist and illustrator. He worked as a zoological draughtsman, and was especially noted as a bird artist; his *Illustrations of the Family of the Psittacidae* was published in 1832. He later came under the patronage of the 13th Earl of Derby, for whose grandchildren he wrote *A Book of Nonsense* (1845), incorporating his own limericks and illustrations; subsequent collections of nonsense verses include *Laughable Lyrics* (1877). He also published illustrated accounts of his travels in Italy, Greece, and the Holy Land.

learning The process by which animals acquire knowledge about their environment and their relationship to it during their own lifetime. Learning is thought to occur when, as a result of experience, connections in the brain are made which allow an animal to form an association between events in the world around it: either between an event and a consequence of it which affects the animal, or between an action and an event. Learning is therefore inferred to have taken place when an animal changes its behaviour in response to previous experience. Learning, which has been demonstrated in the simplest animals, may involve anything from very simple learned responses, such as aversion to noxious stimuli, to the very complex learning of speech in humans.

Leary, Timothy (Francis) (1920–96) US psychologist and advocate of drug use. In 1963 Leary was dismissed from his teaching post at Harvard University after he began to experiment with consciousness-altering drugs. He became a figurehead for the hippy drug culture in the mid-1960s when he continually praised the qualities of LSD. Leary was imprisoned for possession of marijuana in 1970, but resumed his lecturing and writing on his release in 1976.

least squares method A means of ascertaining the line or curve of 'best' fit for a set of data points. If the data points are plotted on a graph and a smooth line is drawn through the midst of them, the distance of the points from the line gives the difference between the observed and predicted results. The average of the squares of these distances gives a measure of 'goodness of fit' for the line. The line of best fit is that for which this mean square deviation is least. It can be shown that this line must pass through the arithmetic MEAN $(\bar{x}, \bar{y})$ of the array, and its equation can be expressed as $y = \bar{y} + r(s_y/s_x)(x - \bar{x})$, where r is the CORRELATION coefficient and s_x and s_y are the sample STANDARD DEVIATIONS of the x- and y-values respectively. This technique for curve-fitting was developed by Adrien LEGENDRE in the context of geodesy and by Karl GAUSS in that of computing approximate orbits for planets from only a few observations of varying accuracy.

leather The skin of an animal preserved and made flexible by chemical and physical processes known as TANNING. It is water-repellent, strong, flexible, and very long-lasting if kept well. Leather can be used for a wide range of applications, depending on the animal from which it comes, and the way in which it is cured. Examples include footwear, clothing, upholstery, harness and saddlery, musical instruments, such as drums, and industrial equipment, such as buffing wheels and machine belts. In the past, leather was even more widely used: examples of such applications include shields and armour, buckets, bottles and other containers, boats, vellum as a writing material, and leather panelling. Leather remains an important by-product of domestic LIVESTOCK FARMING with many uses, although synthetic leather made from plastic materials has replaced it for some cheaper applications.

Leavis, F(rank) R(aymond) (1895–1978) British literary critic. As a teacher of English at Cambridge from the 1920s and founder and editor of the quarterly *Scrutiny* (1932–53), he exerted a considerable influence on literary criticism. He regarded the rigorous critical study of English literature as central to preserving cultural continuity, which he considered to be under threat from technology and the mass media. He was a champion of D. H. Lawrence and led the way for a more serious appreciation of Charles Dickens. His books include *The Great Tradition* (1948) and *The Common Pursuit* (1952).

Lebanon A country of the Middle East at the eastern end of the Mediterranean Sea, bounded by Syria on the north and east and Israel on the south.

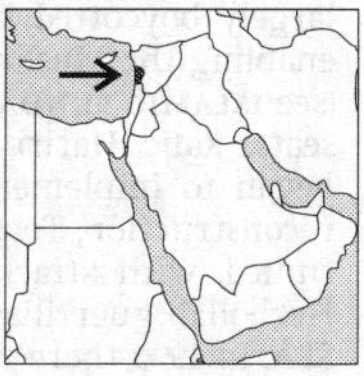

Physical. Lebanon is some 200 km (125 miles) from north to south and 50–80 km (30–50 miles) from east to west. On the narrow coastal plain summers are sunny and warm; fruits of all kinds grow well. Inland the ground rises quickly, to two ranges of high mountains, where there is much winter frost and snow. Between them is the fertile Bekaa Valley, well suited to agriculture, while much of the eastern boundary resembles steppe.

Economy. Agriculture, industry, and commerce have been devastated by the civil war; however, food and drink, machinery, and textiles are among the major exports. Fuels have to be imported. Beirut, formerly the Middle East's leading centre of finance, trade, and tourism, faces a period of reconstruction: the stock market was reopened in 1995.

History. Much of present-day Lebanon formed part of Phoenicia, including the important trading towns of Tyre, Sidon, Byblos, and Arvad, which retained their importance under Roman rule. Mount Lebanon was a refuge for persecuted minorities such as the Christian Maronites, who settled there from the 7th century AD, and the Muslim Druze, who occupied the southern part of the mountain from the 11th century. After the Arab conquest during the 7th century Arab tribesmen settled in Lebanon. Successive governments in the region usually left the people of the mountain to manage their own affairs and contented themselves with exercising authority on the coastal plain. Part of the Ottoman empire from the 16th century, it became a French mandate after World War I. A Lebanese republic was set up in 1926. The country was occupied (1941–45) by FREE FRENCH forces, supported by Britain.

Independence was achieved in 1945. Growing disputes between Christians and Muslims, exacerbated by the presence of Palestinian refugees, undermined the stability of the republic. Hostility between the differing Christian and Muslim groups led to protracted civil war and to the armed intervention (1976) by Syria. The activities of the PALESTINE LIBERATION ORGANIZATION brought large-scale Israeli military invasion and led to Israeli occupation (1978) of a part of southern Lebanon. A UN peace-keeping force attempted unsuccessfully to set up a buffer zone. A full military invasion (1982) by Israel led to the evacuation of the Palestinians. A massacre by the Phalangist Christian militia in Israeli-occupied West Beirut of Muslim civilians in the Chabra and Chatila refugee camps brought a redeployment of UN peace-keeping forces. Syria again intervened in 1987, but many problems remained unresolved. Israel established a South Lebanon Army (SLA), and there were 20 Israeli air-raids during 1988. In March 1989 the MARONITE Christian General Aoun launched an all-out war against Syrian troops. In October 1989 the Arab League successfully negotiated an Accord in Taif, Saudi Arabia, whereby the Maronite dominance in government would be reduced. This Taif Accord was reluctantly accepted, and a frail peace established under continued Syrian protection, which was formalized by a treaty in May 1991. In 1992 the first general elections since 1972 were largely boycotted by Maronite Christian parties, enabling the Muslim parties, Amal and Hezbollah (see ISLAMIC FUNDAMENTALISM), to gain the most seats. Rafic Hariri became Prime Minister and began to implement a programme of economic reconstruction. Tension in southern Lebanon continued, with attacks by the radical, Iran-backed Hezbollah guerrillas against the Israeli-supported SLA. In 1996 there were further violent clashes in southern Lebanon between Hezbollah and Israeli troops. Thousands of civilians fled following Israeli air attacks.

Capital: Beirut
Area: 10,230 sq km (3,950 sq mi)
Population: 13,009,000 (1995)
Currency: 1 Lebanese pound = 100 piastres
Religions: Shia Muslim 32.0–41.0%; Sunni Muslim 21.0–27.0%; Maronite Christian 16.0–24.5%; Druze 7.0%; Armenian Christian 4.0%; Greek Catholic 3.0–4.0%; Greek Orthodox 5.0–6.5%
Ethnic Groups: Lebanese Arab 82.6%; Palestinian Arab 9.6%; Armenian 4.9%; Syrian, Kurdish, and other 2.9%
Languages: Arabic (official); Armenian; French; Kurdish
International Organizations: UN; Arab League

Lebensraum (German, 'living-space') NAZI political doctrine claiming a need to acquire more territory in order to accommodate the expanding German nation. First introduced as a political concept in the 1870s, the concept was given patriotic significance by HITLER and GOEBBELS. The corollary to '*Lebensraum*' was the '*Drang nach Osten*' (German, 'drive to the East'), which claimed large areas of eastern Europe for the THIRD REICH to enable the so-called Nazi master race to subjugate and colonize the Slavic peoples.

Lebesgue, Henri Léon (1875–1941) French mathematician whose primary achievement was to extend the notion of definite integrals. By generalizing the ideas of length and area to a general concept of the measure of a set, he allowed an integral to be assigned to a much broader class of functions. A superb teacher and popularizer of mathematics, he also wrote on its history.

Leblanc, Nicolas (1742–1806) French surgeon and chemist. Leblanc became interested in the large-scale manufacture of soda because of the offer of a prize. He developed a process for making soda ash (sodium carbonate) from common salt, making possible the large-scale manufacture of glass, soap, paper, and other chemicals. The factory he set up with others was confiscated during the French Revolution, and he later committed suicide.

Lebrun, Charles (1619–90) French painter, designer, and decorator. He was prominent in the development and institutionalization of French art. In 1648 he helped to found the Royal Academy of Painting and Sculpture, becoming its director in 1663; from this position he sought to impose orthodoxy in artistic matters, laying the basis of academicism. His work for Louis XIV at Versailles (1661–83), which included painting, furniture, and tapestry design, established him as a leading exponent of 17th-century French classicism.

Le Carré, John (pseudonym of David John Moore Cornwell) (1931–) British novelist. His spy novels are characterized by their unromanticized view of espionage and frequently explore the moral dilemmas inherent in such work; they often feature the British agent George Smiley and include *The Spy Who Came in from the Cold* (1963) and *Tinker, Tailor, Soldier, Spy* (1974).

Le Châtelier, Henri-Louis (1850–1936) French chemist who formulated the principle (**Le Châtelier's Principle**) that if a system is subjected to a change in conditions, the system will respond in a way that tends to counteract the change. Thus, if a reversible reaction gives out heat, increasing the temperature will tend to reverse the reaction.

Leclanché, Georges (1839–82) French chemist and a pioneer of the electric BATTERY. While working as a railway engineer, he spent much time in developing the electric cell that bears his name. It consisted of a zinc ANODE and a carbon CATHODE immersed in a solution of ammonium chloride, with a mixture of powdered manganese dioxide and carbon surrounding the cathode. In 1867 Leclanché resigned from his post to devote himself to improving the cell. It was soon widely adopted wherever small intermittent currents were required (for example in telegraphy), and was later developed into the universally familiar dry battery, consisting of one or more such cells using a paste of ammonium chloride and a zinc casing.

Leconte de Lisle, Charles Marie René (1818–94) French poet. He was leader of the Parnassians, a group that emphasized strictness of form. He published a number of collections of poetry, including *Poèmes antiques* (1852) and *Poèmes barbares* (1862); his work often draws inspiration from mythology, biblical history, and exotic Eastern landscape.

Le Corbusier (born Charles Édouard Jeanneret) (1887–1965) French architect and town planner, born in Switzerland. Influential both as an architect and as a theorist, he was a pioneer of the international style, a style characterized by new building materials (especially steel and reinforced concrete), wide windows, uninterrupted interior spaces, simple lines, and strict geometric forms. He later developed his theories on functionalism, the use of industrial techniques in architecture, and the Modulor, a modular system of standard-sized units, in books such as *Towards a New Architecture* (1923) and *Le Modulor I* (1948). His buildings include the block of flats in Marseilles known as the *Unité d'habitation* ('living unit', 1945–50); he also planned the city of Chandigarh in India.

Leda In Greek mythology, a queen of Sparta who was beloved by Zeus. He took the form of a swan to seduce her, and the children he fathered by her – Castor and Pollux – were hatched from an egg. Her other children were Clytemnestra and Helen, but accounts vary as to whether they were fathered by Zeus.

Lee, Bruce (born Lee Yuen Kam) (1941–73) US actor. He was an expert in kung fu and starred in a number of martial arts films featuring elaborately staged fight scenes, such as *Fists of Fury* (1972) and *Enter the Dragon* (1973).

Lee, Christopher (Frank Carandini) (1922–) British actor. Since the late 1940s he has made a variety of films, including thrillers and adventure films, but his reputation is chiefly based on the horror films that he made for the British film company Hammer. These include *Dracula* (1958) and seven sequels (the last in 1973), and *The Mummy* (1959).

Lee, Gypsy Rose (born Rose Louise Hovick) (1914–70) US striptease artist. In the 1930s she became famous on Broadway for her sophisticated striptease act, imbuing what was previously considered vulgar entertainment with a new artistic content and style.

Lee, (Nelle) Harper (1926–) US novelist. She won a Pulitzer Prize with her only novel, *To Kill a Mockingbird* (1960). The plot turns on the sensational trial of a black man falsely charged with raping a white woman, as seen through the eyes of the daughter of the white defence lawyer.

Lee, Jennie, Baroness (1904–88) British politician. She was a Labour MP (1929–31; 1945–70) and minister for the arts (1967–70), when she had responsibility for setting up the Open University (see DISTANCE EDUCATION). She married Aneurin BEVAN in 1934 and entered the House of Lords in 1970.

Lee, Laurie (1914–97) British writer. He is best known for his autobiographical novels *Cider With Rosie* (1959) and *As I Walked Out One Midsummer Morning* (1969), evocative accounts of his rural childhood in Gloucestershire and his travelling experiences in pre-war Europe. Lee's volumes of poetry include *The Sun My Monument* (1944) and *My Many-Coated Man* (1955).

Lee, Robert E(dward) (1807–70) US general. He was the commander of the Confederate army of Northern Virginia, leading it for most of the American Civil War. Although he did much to prolong Confederate resistance against the Union's greater manpower and resources, his invasion of the North was repulsed by General Meade at the Battle of Gettysburg (1863) and he eventually surrendered to General Grant in 1865.

Lee, Spike (born Shelton Jackson Lee) (1957–) US film director. Lee's declared intention is to express the richness of African-American culture: he first won recognition for the comedy *She's Gotta Have It* (1986) while later films, such as *School Daze* (1988), *Do the Right Thing* (1989), and *Malcolm X* (1992), sparked controversy with their treatment of racism. Lee aided Jesse Jackson in his presidential campaign of 1988.

leech An ANNELID of one of the three main classes, the Hirudinea. Leeches lack clear segmentation and have a sucker at either end. They are found mostly in fresh water, where they seek other animals from which they extract a meal of blood. They are usually flattened rather than cylindrical, though this may not be true when they are bloated after a large meal. Most leeches prefer invertebrates or cold-blooded hosts, such as cshes. Relatively few will take blood from mammals, but the famous medicinal leech, *Hirudo medicinalis*, does so, and has a powerful anticoagulant to keep the blood flowing freely. It was used extensively in the past for bleeding patients. The anticoagulant, hirudin, is now collected in 'leech farms' in Wales. Leeches have razor-like jaws inside the front sucker and are believed to anaesthetize the host's skin before biting.

Leeds An industrial city and local government district in West Yorkshire, northern England, on the River Aire; pop. (1991) 674,400. Founded in Roman times, Leeds developed as a wool town in the Middle Ages, becoming a centre of the clothing trade in the Industrial Revolution. Every three years Leeds hosts an international piano competition. The University of Leeds was founded in 1904 and the Leeds Metropolitan University (formerly Leeds Polytechnic) was established in 1992. Until recently Leeds was Britain's major producer of ready-made clothing and textile machinery. It now has diverse light industries and is a cultural centre and commercial city.

leek A vegetable, *Allium ampeloprasum*, belonging to the same family as the ONION and originating in Near Eastern and Mediterranean regions. Onions have been cultivated since ancient times for their solid, white leaf-bases, which form elongated, cylindrical bulbs.

Leeuwenhoek, Antoni van (1632–1723) Dutch naturalist. Apprenticed to a Delft cloth-merchant, he developed a lens for scientific purposes from those used to inspect cloth, and was the first to observe bacteria, protozoa, and yeast. He accurately described red blood cells, capillaries, striated muscle fibres, spermatozoa, and the crystalline lens of the eye. Being without Latin he was out of touch with the scientific community, and his original work on microorganisms only became known through the Royal Society's translation and publication of his letters (1673–1723).

Leeward Islands A group of islands in the West Indies, constituting the northern part of the Lesser Antilles. The group includes Guadeloupe, Antigua, St Kitts, and Montserrat. The name refers to the fact that the islands are further from the direction of prevailing winds, which are easterly, than the Windward Islands.

Le Fanu, Joseph Sheridan (1814–73) Irish novelist. He is best known for his stories of mystery, suspense, and the supernatural; notable works include *The House by the Churchyard* (1861), *Uncle*

Silas (1864), and the collection of ghost stories *In a Glass Darkly* (1872).

Lefkosia The Greek name for the city of NICOSIA.

leg A limb modified for walking. Any slender appendages, usually jointed, used by animals in locomotion are loosely referred to as legs. The simplest form of leg occurs in the ARTHROPODS, whose name literally means 'jointed legs'. Those of insects, for example, are made of five sections which, starting with the basal section, are called the coxa, trochanter, femur, tibia, and tarsus.

The legs of vertebrates follow the basic pattern of having two main sections to the leg, jointed in the middle at the knee. The larger section is formed of the femur, or thighbone, which is jointed to the hips. The lower section is composed of two bones, a thick tibia, or shin-bone, and a thinner bone of the outside part of the leg, called the fibula. The bases of the lower leg bones are jointed to the foot. In mammals, including man, there is a small bone called the patella, or kneecap, in the tendon at the joint between the upper and lower halves of the leg. The kneecap protects and articulates the lower end of the thighbone. The leg is pulled forward by powerful thigh muscles, and back by the hamstring muscles. The 'hamstrings' are tendons from the upper muscles, which pass beneath the knee to the lower leg. The Achilles tendon extends from the calf muscles in the lower leg to the foot.

legal aid Professional legal advice and assistance, including representation in COURTS OF LAW and TRIBUNALS, given either free or for a reduced sum to people on low incomes. For many people, one of the basic CIVIL RIGHTS, the right of access to the courts, is meaningless because they cannot afford the cost of litigation. In criminal cases, too, a person accused of a crime may not be able to afford an effective defence. In the UK, France, and Germany, the state pays the fees of lawyers in private practice to enable them to undertake legal aid work in both criminal and civil cases. Many countries also provide legal services through publicly funded law centres.

Legendre, Adrien Marie (1752–1833) French mathematician noted for his work on the theory of numbers and the publication *Theorie des nombres* (1830). He devised, independently of Karl GAUSS, the LEAST SQUARES METHOD, which he applied to the elliptical movement of planets. He taught in Paris and also published a geometry textbook.

Léger, Fernand (1881–1955) French painter. From about 1909 he was associated with the cubist movement, but then began to develop a distinctive style inspired by the beauty of machinery and celebrating modern technology; works include the *Contrast of Forms* series (1913). He was also involved with theatre decor and cinema, and made the experimental film *Ballet mécanique* (1924).

Leghorn (Italian **Livorno**) A port and industrial town in north-west Italy, on the Ligurian coast of Tuscany; pop. (1990) 171,265. It was laid out as an 'ideal' city for the Medici family by Buontalenti in the 16th century and subsequently developed as a trading centre between Europe and the East. It is the site of the Italian Naval Academy and has heavy industries associated with its port functions.

legionnaires' disease An acute bacterial infection of the respiratory tract by *Legionella pneumophilia*, which occurs naturally in ponds, stagnant water, and soil at temperatures exceeding 25°C; the optimum temperature being 30°C to 38°C. The microorganism has been found in stagnant cisterns and shower heads, although the principal sources of outbreaks commonly are humidifier systems in air-conditioning units; the organism is transmitted by inhalation of water droplets derived from these sources. Legionnaires' disease of unknown cause may also occur.

Legionnaires' disease, which was first described in 1976 after an outbreak among US legionnaires in Philadelphia, can cause serious, life-threatening PNEUMONIA, although in more severe cases, other organs, such as liver and kidneys, may also be involved. Treatment is the administration of antibacterial drugs and is usually successful.

legislation See LAW.

legislature A national assembly with the function of making or changing LAW. Legislatures are often, but need not be, elected bodies, and go by different names such as Chamber of Deputies, Congress, Diet, Legislative Assembly, Parliament, or Supreme Soviet. They may be bicameral, as in the USA or UK, or unicameral, as in New Zealand or Israel. A freely elected assembly is regarded as an important component of DEMOCRACY. There are many different types of legislature, but they may be categorized according to the relative effectiveness and independence of the legislature in relation to the executive. Two main types emerge: first, presidential government, in which the legislature is separate from the executive, although in the USA, for example, the PRESIDENT (the chief executive) has the right to veto legislation as well as to propose it; secondly, parliamentary government, as in the UK, in which members of the executive are drawn from the legislature. Mixed or transitional relationships between the legislature and the executive are also common, as in France.

legume Any plant of the PEA family (Leguminosae), many of which are used as food crops. Legumes are rich in protein; the pods, seeds, or leaves of many species have always been an essential part of man's diet in virtually every part of the world. Those which have edible seeds, such as beans, chick-peas, and soya beans, are called grain legumes, or pulses. The proteins of these pulses contain a different range of amino acids to those contained in cereal proteins, and to a large extent complement such true grains. The staple diet of many different peoples consists of a mixture of cereal and pulses. Other legumes, such as alfalfa and clover, are economically important fodder crops, or are used to improve pasture quality.

All legumes have the ability to convert nitrogen from air into compounds suitable for uptake by the plant, and ultimately protein synthesis. This ability is conferred by their possession of the bacterium *Rhizobium* in root nodules, a microorganism that is able to 'fix' nitrogen from a gaseous form into nutrients suitable for uptake into the plant.

Lehár, Franz (Ferencz) (1870–1948) Hungarian composer. He is chiefly known for his operettas, of which the most famous is *The Merry Widow* (1905).

Le Havre France's second-largest port in the Seine-Maritime department of north-west France, on the English Channel at the mouth of the Seine; pop. (1990) 197,220. Founded in the 16th century by François I, the city was largely rebuilt after destruction in World War II. It has banking, oil refining and chemical industries, and ferry links with the UK.

Lehmann, Lotte (1888–1976) US soprano, born in Germany. After studying in Berlin, she made her debut in Hamburg in 1910. She became a US citizen in 1938, appearing frequently at the New York

Metropolitan Opera and London Covent Garden, frequently in the operas of Richard Strauss.

Leibniz, Gottfried Wilhelm (1646–1716) German rationalist philosopher, mathematician, and logician. He spent his life in the diplomatic and political service and in 1700 was appointed first president of the Academy of Sciences in Berlin. Leibniz is chiefly known as an exponent of optimism; he believed that the world is fundamentally harmonious and good, being composed of single units (monads), each of which is self-contained but acts in harmony with every other; these form an ascending hierarchy culminating in God. Their harmony is ordained by God, who never acts except for a reason that requires it, and so this world is the best of all possible worlds (a view satirized in Voltaire's *Candide*). Leibniz made the important distinction between necessary (logical) truths and contingent (factual) truths, and proposed a universal logical language that would eliminate ambiguity. He also devised a method of calculus independently of Newton.

Leibovitz, Annie (1950–) US photographer. She was chief photographer of *Rolling Stone* magazine from 1973 until 1983, when she moved to *Vanity Fair*. She has had numerous exhibitions, including those at the Smithsonian National Portrait Gallery, Washington, DC (1991) and produced portraits of celebrities, such as John Lennon, Ella Fitzgerald, and Arnold Schwarzenegger.

Leicester A city in central England on the River Soar, the county town of Leicestershire; pop. (1991) 270,600. It was founded as a Roman settlement where Fosse Way crosses the Soar (50–100 AD), and has a 14th-century cathedral. The University of Leicester was founded in 1957 and the De Montfort University (formerly Leicester Polytechnic) was established in 1992. It is noted as a hosiery, textile, and engineering city.

Leicester, Earl of See DUDLEY.

Leicestershire A county of central England; area 2,553 sq km (986 sq miles); pop. (1991) 860,500; county town, Leicester.

Leichhardt, (Friedrich Wilhelm) Ludwig (1813–48) Australian explorer, born in Prussia. After emigrating to Australia in 1841, he began a series of geological surveys, crossing from Moreton Bay near Brisbane to Port Essington on the coast of Arnhem Land (1843–45); he disappeared without trace during another attempt at a transcontinental crossing in 1848.

Leiden (or **Leyden**) A city in the west Netherlands, in the province of South Holland 15 km (9 miles) north-east of The Hague; pop. (1991) 111,950. It is the site of the country's oldest university, founded in 1575. The painter Rembrandt was born in the city in 1606, and the Pilgrim Fathers spent 11 years in the city before sailing to America. The electrical condenser known as the 'Leyden jar' was invented here in 1745.

Leif Ericsson See ERIC THE RED.

Leigh, Vivien (born Vivian Mary Hartley) (1913–67) British actress, born in India. She made her screen début in 1934; major film roles include her Oscar-winning performances as Scarlett O'Hara in *Gone with the Wind* (1939) and Blanche du Bois in *A Streetcar Named Desire* (1951). From 1935 Leigh also pursued a successful career on stage, often playing opposite Laurence Olivier, to whom she was married from 1940 to 1961.

Leighton, Frederic, Baron Leighton of Stretton (1830–96) British painter and sculptor, one of the dominant figures of Victorian art. He was President of the Royal Academy from 1878 and shortly before his death he was raised to the peerage, the first English artist to be so honoured. His varied output included portraits and book illustrations, but he is best known for his beautifully drawn and opulently coloured paintings of classical Greek subjects.

Leinster A province of the Republic of Ireland, comprising the counties of Carlow, Dublin, Kildare, Kilkenny, Laois, Longford, Louth, Meath, Offaly, Westmeath, Wexford, and Wicklow; area 19,633 sq km (7,583 sq miles); pop. (1991) 1,860,040; its capital is Dublin.

Leipzig An industrial city in the state of Saxony, east-central Germany, a centre of the publishing and the music trade; pop. (1991) 503,190. An annual trade fair has been held here since the 12th century. J. S. Bach is buried in St Thomas' Church.

Leipzig, Battle of (or **Battle of the Nations**, 16–19 October 1813) A decisive battle in the NAPOLEONIC WARS. It was fought just outside the city of Leipzig in Saxony, by an army under Napoleon of some 185,000 French, Saxon, and other allied German troops, which were beaten by a force of some 350,000 troops from Austria, Prussia, Russia, and Sweden, under the overall command of Schwarzenberg. Following the battle French power east of the Rhine collapsed as more and more German princes deserted Napoleon, who abdicated in 1814.

leitmotif (German, 'leading motive') A musical theme associated with a person, object, or emotion in OPERA and PROGRAMME MUSIC. An invention of the 19th century, it is used to great advantage in WAGNER'S music-dramas, where a network of such themes enables him to weave a coherent symphonic commentary on the action, spread out over many hours.

Leitrim A county in the Republic of Ireland, in the province of Connaught; area 1,526 sq km (589 sq miles); pop. (1991) 25,300; county town, Carrick-on-Shannon.

Leix See LAOIS.

Lely, Sir Peter (born Pieter van der Faes) (1618–80) Dutch portrait painter, resident in England from 1641. He became principal court painter to Charles II and consolidated the tradition of society portrait painting. By 1650 he had a large studio and produced hundreds of portraits of court figures in a Baroque style. Notable works include his series of *Windsor Beauties*, painted during the 1660s.

Lemaitre model See COSMOLOGY.

Léman, Lac See GENEVA, LAKE.

Le Mans An industrial town in north-west France, capital of the department of Sarthe; pop. (1990) 148,465. There are remains of a 3rd–4th century Gallo-Roman fortress and a Romanesque cathedral. It is the site of a motor-racing circuit, on which a 24-hour endurance race (established in 1923) for GT and sports cars is held each summer.

lemma (in mathematics) An auxiliary result often required in the course of proving a more important theorem, but is proved separately in order not to break the thread of ideas in the development of the main argument. Lemmas tend to be unimportant mathematically in their own right and frequently are of a technical nature. If it were not for their role in helping to establish the main theorem, they would probably not be worth noting.

lemming A rodent making up part of a large family of 110 species, which includes 99 species of VOLE and mole-vole. Of the 11 species of lemming the Norway lemming, *Lemmus lemmus*, is the best known. Other species occur throughout the Arctic in both the New and Old Worlds. They are about the size of a stocky rat, with dense fur and small ears. They live in steppe regions, where they construct deep burrows, foraging for vegetable matter in the winter along tunnels in the snow. Lemmings are most famous for their so-called migrations, which are, in fact, mass movements following build-ups of population. The lemmings peak in numbers about every three or four years, probably in relation to over-exploitation of the food resources. Migrating lemmings sometimes meet the sea, and attempt to swim across what, for all they know, is a narrow channel. Mass drownings may occur, giving rise to the myth of deliberate suicide.

Lemmon, Jack (born John Uhler) (1925–) US actor. He made his name in comedy films such as *Some Like It Hot* (1959); he later played serious dramatic parts in such films as *Save the Tiger* (1973), for which he won an Oscar, *The China Syndrome* (1979), and *Missing* (1981).

Lemnos (Greek **Límnos**) A Greek island in the northern Aegean Sea off the north-west coast of Turkey; area 476 sq km (184 sq miles). Its chief settlement is Kástron or Mírina (ancient Myrina).

lemon One of 60 species of *Citrus* tree, *Citrus limon*, a member of the family Rutaceae, which produces distinctively shaped fruit with nipple-shaped ends. The juice of this fruit contains about four times the level of citric acid found in the sweet orange, making it unsuitable to be eaten raw. As a crop, it is intolerant of temperature extremes and is grown mainly in regions with a Mediterranean-type climate. It is commercially exploited as a major source of citric acid.

lemon sole A species of FLATFISH, *Microstomus kitt*, which is not a sole but is related to the plaice and flounder. It lives on the Atlantic coast of northern Europe and in the North Sea, on mud, sand, and gravel bottoms, at depths of 40–200 m (130–650 feet). It has a small head and mouth which limits the size of its prey; mostly it feeds on worms and small crustaceans. It is a moderately valuable commercial fish, usually caught in trawls.

lemur A primate found only in the forests of Madagascar. The destruction of these forests threatens many species with extinction. Lemurs vary in size from small, mouse-like members of the family Cheirogaleidae to animals the size of a domestic dog. Some of the 22 species can stand erect and walk or hop when they descend to the ground; others walk quadrupedally. They have large, dark eyes that look forward over the small, slightly pointed nose. All are timid creatures that feed on insects and fruit. Some species feed at night, while others are active during the day. They breed once a year and produce a single offspring; the mother carries it spreadeagled on her breast or on her back. They are the living representatives of an ancient group of primates called prosimians, and have found a niche in Madagascar due to the absence of monkeys.

Typical lemurs include the ruffed lemur, *Varecia variegata*, the lesser mouse lemur, *Microcebus murinus*, and the fat-tailed lemur, *Cheirogaleus medius*. All of the lemurs are tree-dwellers except the ring-tailed lemur, *Lemur catta*, which lives in a dry, rocky habitat almost destitute of trees. The AYE-AYE and INDRI are also lemurs.

Lena A river in Siberia that rises in the mountains on the western shore of Lake Baikal, and flows generally north-east and north for 4,400 km (2,734 miles) via a vast delta into the Laptev Sea, a part of the Arctic Ocean. It is one of the three great Siberian rivers flowing to the Arctic Ocean, famous for the gold-fields in its basin. The river is frozen over for eight months of the year.

Lenclos, Ninon de (born Anne de Lenclos) (1620–1705) French courtesan. She was a famous wit and beauty and numbered many prominent writers and nobles among her lovers. She advocated a form of Epicureanism and defended her philosophy and lifestyle in her book *La Coquette vengée* (1659). In later life she presided over one of the most distinguished literary salons of the age.

Lendl, Ivan (1960–) Czech-born tennis player. He won many singles titles in the 1980s and early 1990s, including the US, Australian, and the French Open championships. He became a US citizen in 1992.

Lend-Lease Act An arrangement (1941–45) according to which the USA supplied equipment to Britain and its Allies in World War II. It was formalized by an Act passed by the US Congress allowing President F. D. ROOSEVELT to lend or lease equipment and supplies to any state whose defence was considered vital to the security of the USA. About 60 per cent of the shipments went to Britain as a loan in return for British-owned military bases. About 20 per cent went to the Soviet Union.

Lenin, Vladimir Ilich (born Vladimir Ilich Ulyanov) (1870–1924) The principal figure in the Russian Revolution and first Premier (Chairman of the Council of People's Commissars) of the Soviet Union 1918–24. Lenin was the first political leader to attempt to put Marxist principles into practice, though, like Marx, he saw the need for a transitional period to full communism, during which there would be a 'dictatorship of the proletariat'. The policies that he pursued led ultimately to the establishment of Marxism-Leninism in the Soviet Union and, later, in China. Born in Russia, he lived in Switzerland from 1900, but was instrumental in the split between the Bolsheviks and Mensheviks in 1903, when he became leader of the more radical Bolsheviks. He returned to Russia in 1917, established Bolshevik control after the overthrow of the tsar, and in 1918 became head of state; he founded the Third International (or Comintern) the following year to further the cause of world revolution. With Trotsky's help he defeated counter-revolutionary forces in the Russian Civil War, but was forced to moderate his socio-economic policies to allow the country to recover from the effects of war and revolution. During the last years of his life he denounced, but was unable to prevent, the concentration of power in the hands of Stalin.

Leningrad A former name (1924–91) of ST PETERSBURG.

Leningrad, Siege of (September 1941–January 1944) The defence of Leningrad (now St Petersburg) by the Soviet army in World War II. The German army had intended to capture Leningrad in the 1941 campaign but as a result of slow progress in the Baltic area and the reluctance of Germany's Finnish ally to assist, the city held out in a siege that lasted nearly 900 days.

Leninism See COMMUNISM.

Lennon, John (1940–80) British pop and rock singer, guitarist, and songwriter. He was a founder member of the Beatles, and with Paul McCartney wrote most of their songs. Their first single, 'Love Me Do' (1962), was followed by many more, including 'She Loves You' (1963) and 'Help' (1965). In 1969 Lennon announced his intention of leaving the group, and the Beatles split up acrimoniously the following year. A more controversial and acerbic figure than McCartney, Lennon frequently collaborated with his second wife Yoko Ono in his subsequent recording career. He took up residence in the USA and was assassinated outside his home in New York.

Lenoir, Jean-Joseph Étienne (1822–1900) Belgian pioneer of GAS-ENGINES. A self-taught engineer, with wide-ranging interests, he built his first gas-engine in 1860. Over a period of five years, he made several hundred engines of around 1.5 kW (2 horsepower), which were popular within small-scale industry. Later, however, the superior four-stroke engine introduced by OTTO in 1876 offered severe competition to Lenoir's gas-engine.

Le Nôtre, André (1613–1700) French landscape gardener. He designed many formal gardens, including the parks of Vaux-le-Vicomte and Versailles, begun in 1655 and 1662, respectively. These incorporated his ideas on architecturally conceived garden schemes: geometric formality and perfect equilibrium of all the individual elements – sculpture, fountains, parterres, and open spaces.

lenses, photographic The standard camera lens gives an image that resembles the eye's normal vision as closely as possible. Wide-angle lenses have a relatively short focal length, and record a wide angle of view. Extremely wide-angle (fish-eye) lenses give a field of view of over 100 degrees, but they produce a distorted image. Telephoto lenses have a relatively long focal length: they act like a telescope to enlarge distant objects, the degree of magnification being directly related to the focal length of the lens. In zoom lenses, the focal length can be continuously altered to produce differing degrees of magnification, allowing the photographer to 'zoom' in on the subject. A wide variety of zoom lenses is available, covering a range of focal lengths.

lenses and lens systems Pieces of glass or other transparent material with one or both sides curved to refract (bend) rays of light, used singly or in combination, especially in optical instruments. Devices for focusing other types of ELECTROMAGNETIC RADIATION may also be called lenses. Single lenses are used in magnifying glasses and in SPECTACLES. Lens systems contain more than one lens: they are used in instruments, such as cameras (see LENSES, PHOTOGRAPHIC), MICROSCOPES, and TELESCOPES. A lens always has at least one regular, curved surface, usually a section of the surface of a large sphere. Various lens shapes are possible, but they can be broadly classified as either converging or diverging, according to how they bend light. In the case of beams of light parallel to the lens's principal axis, a converging lens focuses the light approximately to a single point, the principal focus or focal point of the lens. In a diverging lens parallel light rays are spread, so that they appear to come from a focal point on the other side of the lens. The thickness and curvature of a lens determine its focal length, while the diameter of the lens determines its light-gathering power. When a lens refracts diverging light rays from an object or light source, a real or apparent focus is produced at a different location, at which a visual image is formed. This image may be real (detectable on a screen or on photographic paper) or virtual (visible upon looking through the lens). Converging lenses may form real or virtual images, whereas diverging lenses always form virtual images. A single lens with spherical surfaces will not produce a sharp image of a large object or

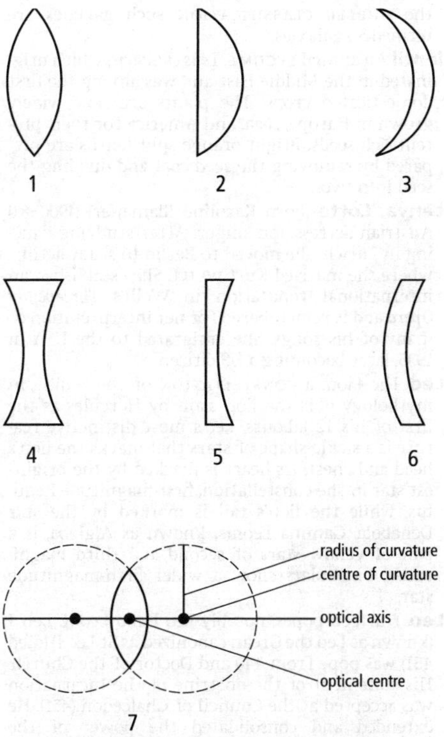

Lenses Converging lenses include: (1) biconvex lenses, (2) planoconvex lenses, and (3) converging meniscus lenses. Diverging lenses include: (4) biconcave lenses, (5) planoconcave lenses, and (6) diverging meniscus lenses. (7) The main parts of a lens.

scene unless the diameter of the lens is made very small. Blurring and distortion effects, called aberrations, are present even in a lens with perfectly shaped spherical surfaces. Chromatic aberrations may also occur, due to light of different colours being differently refracted (see ACHROMATIC LENS). Aberrations can be reduced by combining several lenses together along a common axis according to a pre-calculated design; also precisely calculated non-spherical surfaces can be used to minimize aberrations.

Lent A 40-day period in the Christian year of fasting and penance in preparation for EASTER, traditionally commemorating Jesus' temptations and crucifixion. Fixed by the date of Easter, Lent is measured differently in East and West, as the East excludes weekends from its 40-day fast while the West excludes only Sunday. Beginning in the West on what is known as Ash Wednesday, Lent includes Holy Week (the week preceding Easter) and concludes at dawn on Easter Sunday. The traditional rules of abstinence in Lent have been largely abandoned in the West. However, the custom of voluntary abstinence from some food or pleasure is still widely observed by Christians, and extra commitment to Christian study or attendance at worship is encouraged.

lenticular galaxy A type of GALAXY that appears lens-shaped. It shows no sign of spiral structure but does possess a central nucleus and traces of a disc. Those stars that are visible appear to be old. In the HUBBLE CLASSIFICATION such galaxies are termed So galaxies.

lentil An annual LEGUME, *Lens culinaris*, which originated in the Middle East and was among the first domesticated crops. The plants are now widely grown in Europe, Asia, and America for their protein-rich seeds. Bright orange split lentils are prepared by removing the seed coat and dividing the seed into two.

Lenya, Lotte (born Karoline Blamauer) (1900–81) Austrian actress and singer. After studying dancing in Zurich, she moved to Berlin to study acting, where she married Kurt WEILL. She established an international reputation in Weill's *Threepenny Opera* and is remembered for her interpretation of many of his songs. She emigrated to the USA in 1935, later becoming a US citizen.

Leo The Lion, a CONSTELLATION of the zodiac. In mythology it is the lion slain by Hercules as the first of his 12 labours. Leo's most distinctive feature is a sickle-shape of stars that marks the lion's head and chest. Its heart is marked by the brightest star in the constellation, first-magnitude Regulus, while the lion's tail is marked by the star Denebola. Gamma Leonis, known as Algieba, is a pair of yellow stars of second and third magnitudes; binoculars show a wider fifth-magnitude star.

Leo Thirteen popes, notably Leo I and Leo X. **Leo I** (known as Leo the Great; canonized as St Leo I) (died 461) was pope from 440 and Doctor of the Church. His statement of the doctrine of the Incarnation was accepted at the Council of Chalcedon (451). He extended and consolidated the power of the Roman see, claiming jurisdiction in Africa, Spain, and Gaul. He persuaded the Huns to retire beyond the Danube and secured concessions from the Vandals when they captured Rome. Feast day (in the Eastern Church) 18 February; (in the Western Church) 11 April. **Leo X** (born Giovanni de' Medici) (1475–1521) was pope from 1513. He excommunicated Martin Luther and bestowed on Henry VIII of England the title of Defender of the Faith. He was a noted patron of learning and the arts.

Leo III (*c*.680–741) Byzantine emperor 717–41. He repulsed several Muslim invasions and carried out an extensive series of financial, legal, administrative, and military reforms. In 726 he forbade the use of images in public worship; this policy, enforced by teams of iconoclasts, met with much popular opposition and a split with Rome.

Leo Minor The Little Lion, a CONSTELLATION of the northern sky, introduced by the Polish astronomer Johannes Hevelius (1611–87). Its brightest stars are of only fourth magnitude and there are no objects of special interest though it does contain a number of small and faint galaxies within its borders.

León A province in northern Spain, once an independent kingdom. It was captured from the Iberians by the Carthaginian general HANNIBAL in 217 BC and later became the Roman province of Lusitania. It was conquered by the VISIGOTHS in the 5th century and fell to the MOORS in the 8th century. It was freed from Muslim control by the Asturians and united with ASTURIAS and Galicia in the 10th century. Ferdinand I of Castile seized it and it was finally united with Castile in 1230. The armies of the kingdom were important in the reconquest of Spain from the Moors.

León A city in north-west Nicaragua, near the Pacific coast; pop. (1985) 100,980. Founded in 1524, the original settlement was destroyed by an earthquake in 1609. Rebuilt on another site, it was capital until 1858 and has become the second-largest city of Nicaragua. Its university was founded in 1804 and its cathedral is the largest in Central America. Its industries include timber, chemicals, and food processing.

Leonard, Elmore (John) (1925–) US writer of thrillers. He worked as an advertising copywriter in the 1950s and 1960s before concentrating on writing and becoming acknowledged as one of the leading crime writers in the USA. His books, notable for their pace and understated, credible style, include *Unknown Man No. 89* (1977) *Freaky Deaky* (1988), and *Get Shorty* (1990).

Leonardo da Vinci (1452–1519) Italian painter, scientist, and engineer. He spent his early life in Florence; thereafter he worked also in Milan, Rome, and France. Although Leonardo's paintings are relatively few in number, they are notable for their use of the technique of *sfumato* and reflect his studies of nature; they include *The Virgin of the Rocks* (1483–85), *The Last Supper* (*c*.1498), a tempera painting on the wall of the refectory at Santa Maria delle Grazie in Milan, and *Mona Lisa* (*c*.1504–05), his most famous easel painting, showing a woman with an enigmatic smile. In addition to painting, he devoted his mental energy to a wide range of subjects, from anatomy and biology to mechanics and hydraulics. His 19 notebooks contain meticulously observed drawings of plants, clouds, skeletons, etc., studies of the human circulatory system, and plans for a helicopter-like flying machine, an armoured tank, and a submarine.

Leoncavallo, Ruggiero (1858–1919) Italian operatic composer. Of his 15 operas, only *I Pagliacci* (1892) remains a firm member of the international repertoire. His version of *La Bohème* (1897) appeared a year after Puccini's opera of the same name and is rarely performed.

Leonidas (died 480 BC) King of Sparta. He won immortal fame when he commanded a Greek force against the invading Persian army at the pass of THERMOPYLAE. He held the pass long enough to make possible the naval operation at Artemisium (GREEK-PERSIAN WARS). When counter-attacked he remained behind with 300 Spartans and 700 Thespians, and died fighting – an action which allowed his allies to escape.

Leonids A meteor storm that occurs approximately every 33 years on about 13 November. Leonid observations in 1799 led to the concept of the RADIANT. On the night of 12 November 1833 some 240,000 meteors were seen during a period of seven hours. The Leonids were correctly predicted to return in 1866, and were well observed. The calculation of the orbit of the METEOR STREAM showed that it was very similar to the orbit of comet 1866 I. This led to the realization that meteor streams were the product of cometary decay.

leopard One of the smaller and most widespread of the big CATS, *Panthera pardus*, found throughout Africa, Asia Minor, India, China, Korea, and Siberia. It can reach a length of 2 m (6.5 feet), 90 cm (3 feet) of this being tail. The coat is a dark shade of yellow marked on the back and flanks with black rosettes, the centres of which are dark yellow. The texture of the fur varies from thick and rich to short and coarse, depending upon the climate in which the animal lives and the subspecies. It preys upon deer, monkeys, dogs, pigs, porcupines, and other such animals.

Leopards are solitary animals, except in the breeding season. After a gestation period of about three months, two to five cubs are born. The family remains together for about two years until the cubs are nearly mature. One individual has lived in captivity for 23 years, but the lifespan of the leopard is shorter in the wild.

leopard moth A moth that occurs worldwide, and belongs to the same family as the goat moth, the Cossidae. Adults are stout-bodied, fluffy moths, with coal-black spots on the white wings and thorax. The leopard moth caterpillar has a wedge-shaped head and burrows through the wood of various trees. It takes two or three years to mature. The caterpillar is occasionally a pest of fruit trees in Europe and North America.

leopard snake A species of harmless COLUBRID SNAKE, *Elaphe situla*, growing up to about 1 m (3.25 feet) in length, found in parts of southern Europe and Asia Minor. It has a distinctive pattern of reddish-brown blotches or stripes and is widely regarded as the most beautiful of the European snake species. It feeds mainly on rodents and is usually encountered in rocky habitats.

Leopold Two kings of Belgium. **Leopold I** (1790–1865) was first king of Belgium 1831–65. The fourth son of the Duke of Saxe-Coburg-Saalfield, Leopold was an uncle of Queen Victoria, whom he advised during the early part of her reign. In 1830 he refused the throne of Greece, but a year later accepted that of the newly independent Belgium, reigning peacefully thereafter. **Leopold II** (1835–1909) was king of the Belgians 1865–1909. His reign saw considerable industrial and colonial expansion, due in large part to the wealth gleaned from the CONGO. The Berlin Colonial Conference (1884–85) had recognized Leopold as independent head of the newly created Congo Free State and he proceeded to amass great personal wealth from its rubber and ivory trade. Thanks to the report of an Englishman, Edmund Morel, his maltreatment of the Congo native population became an international scandal (1904) and he was forced (1908) to hand over the territory to his parliament.

Leopold I (1640–1705) Holy Roman Emperor (1658–1705). His long reign saw a major revival of Habsburg power, particularly after the OTTOMAN attack on Vienna in 1683 was repulsed by an army led by King JOHN III (Sobieski) of Poland. The subsequent eastern campaigns brought the reconquest of Hungary, confirmed by the Peace of Carlowitz (1699). Increasing resentment at LOUIS XIV's intervention in German affairs also allowed him to re-establish imperial leadership in Germany, an important contributory factor to the coalitions which inflicted heavy defeats on France between 1689 and 1713. After the removal of the Ottoman threat Vienna became a major European capital.

Léopoldville The former name (until 1966) of Kinshasa, capital of the Democratic Republic of Congo.

Leo the Great Pope Leo I. See LEO (popes).

Lepanto A strait at the western entrance to the Gulf of Corinth, scene of a naval battle (1751) in which the fleet of the Holy League (the papacy, Venice, and Spain) under the command of Don John of Austria defeated a large Turkish fleet, ending for the time being the Turkish naval threat in the Mediterranean.

Lepidoptera See BUTTERFLY; MOTH.

Lepidus, Marcus Aemilius (died *c.*13 BC) Roman statesman and triumvir. After supporting Julius Caesar in the civil war against Pompey, Lepidus was elected consul in 46. He was appointed one of the Second Triumvirate with Octavian and Antony in 43 as well as consul again in 42. Lepidus was given control over Africa after losing the provinces of Gaul and Spain to his two more powerful partners. He retired from public life following a failed revolt in Sicily against Octavian in 36.

leprosy (or **Hansen's disease**) An infection by *Mycobacterium leprae*, which infects skin and peripheral nerves, resulting in nerve damage and loss of sensation. The mode of transmission is not clear, although the organism may infect the skin or nasal passages. Initial infection is called indeterminate leprosy, and is characterized by lesions, which may have loss of sensation within them. This is commonly self-limiting and the lesions resolve; however, some cases may progress to tuberculoid, lepromatous, or borderline leprosy, which are types of determinate leprosy.

Tuberculoid leprosy is characterized by localized infection of skin and peripheral nerves with well-defined lesions; it occurs in patients with a degree of resistance. Loss of sensation and reduced sweating may occur, and necrosis of nerves can lead to paralysis of the extremities. Lepromatous leprosy is a widespread infection caused by deficient host resistance; it is the communicable form of leprosy, until treatment is commenced. In lepromatous leprosy, there are numerous lesions affecting the peripheral nerves, eyes, nasal mucous membrane, upper respiratory tract, kidneys, testes, and muscles and bones of the hands, feet, and face. Destruction of nerves results in damage of organs and tissues affected; in the skin, loss of sensation may lead to injury and secondary infection. Borderline leprosy is between tuberculoid and lepromatous leprosy. Lepra reactions are acute exacerbations and reactions that occur with all types of determinate leprosy; they are commonly severe and can result in substantial damage in a short time.

Leprosy is best treated with a combination of antibacterial drugs, called 'multidrug therapy'.

lepton Originally, a light particle such as the electron, as opposed to a heavy particle (a BARYON). However, a lepton is now defined as any particle that participates in the electromagnetic INTERACTION and weak interaction but not the strong interaction. Leptons known to exist are the electron, the muon, and the tau, their respective NEUTRINOS, and the antiparticles (see ANTIMATTER) of each of these, giving a total of 12. All leptons have a SPIN of ½, the antileptons having the same spin but in an opposite direction.

Lepus The Hare, a CONSTELLATION of the southern celestial hemisphere, one of the 48 constellations known to the ancient Greeks. It represents a hare crouched beneath the feet of Orion, the hunter. Its brightest star is the third-magnitude Alpha Leporis, known as Arneb from the Arabic meaning 'hare'. R Leporis is a red giant variable star of the Mira Ceti type that varies between about sixth and 12th magnitudes every 430 days.

Lêr (or **Lir**) In Gaelic mythology, the sea-god, one of the Tuatha Dé Danann (Gaelic, 'People of the Goddess Danu'), perhaps to be identified with the British sea-god Lyr. The three children of Lêr were changed into swans by their jealous stepmother Aoife, and condemned to spend 900 years on the seas and lakes of Ireland.

Lermontov, Mikhail (Yuryevich) (1814–41) Russian poet and novelist. Steeped in European ROMANTICISM, especially the works of BYRON, and exposed to the atmosphere and legends of the Caucasus, he wrote obsessively redrafted long poems, which include *The Demon* and *The Novice*. Lermontov also turned to prose and in *A Hero of our Time*

(1840) produced a pioneering psychological novel. Moody and petulant, he was killed in a duel.

Lerner, Alan J(ay) (1918–86) US lyricist and dramatist. His collaboration with composer Frederick Loewe (1904–88) produced a series of musicals, which were also filmed, including *Paint Your Wagon* (1951; filmed 1969) and *My Fair Lady* (1956; filmed 1964). He won Oscars for the films *An American in Paris* (1951) and *Gigi* (1958).

Lerwick The capital of the Shetland Islands Area of northern Scotland, situated on the Mainland; pop. (1981) 7,560. The most northerly town in the British Isles, it is a fishing centre and a service port for the oil industry. The annual mid-winter Up-Helly-Aa festival takes place here every January.

Lesage, Alain-René (1668–1747) French novelist and dramatist. He is best known for the picaresque novel *Gil Blas* (1715–35).

Lesbos (Greek **Lésvos**) A Greek island in the east-ern Aegean, off the coast of north-west Turkey, the third-largest of the Greek islands; area 1,630 sq km (630 sq miles); chief town, Mytilene. Its artistic golden age of the late 7th and early 6th centuries. BC produced the poets Alcaeus and Sappho.

Lesotho A small landlocked country entirely surrounded by the Republic of South Africa.

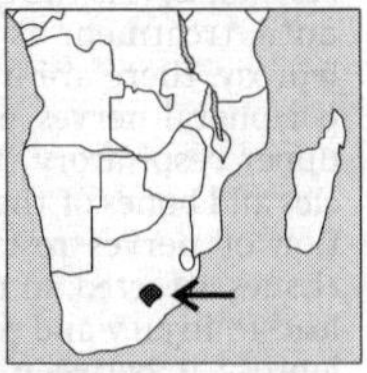

Physical. Lesotho lies in the central and highest part of the Drakensberg Mountains, where summer rains cause severe soil erosion and in winter the temperature can be as low as −16°C (2°F). The Orange River rises here, in a terrain most suitable for grazing sheep and mountain goats, and only in its lower valley and to the west is there much scope for cultivation.

Economy. South Africa dominates the economy of Lesotho, being the principal trading partner. Almost half Lesotho's adult male population work as migrant workers in South Africa, and their remittances are an important source of revenue. The major exports are manufactures, wool and mohair, food, and livestock. Erosion caused by over-grazing makes soil conservation an urgent priority; droughts are also recurrent. Diamonds are the chief mineral resource; the South African firm de Beers owns 75 per cent of the currently non-operative diamond mines; the Highlands water and power project will supply water to South Africa and hydroelectricity to Lesotho. Tourism is an expanding source of income. Limited industry includes food-processing, textiles, and metal-processing. Lesotho is a member of the Southern African Customs Union.

History. Lesotho was founded as Basutoland in 1832 by Moshoeshoe I, who built a stronghold on Thaba Bosigo and unified the Sotho (Basuto). After fighting both Boers and British, Moshoeshoe put himself under British protection in 1868, and until 1880 Basutoland was administered from Cape Colony. In 1884 it was restored to the direct control of the British government with the Paramount Chief as titular head. When the Union of South Africa was formed in 1910, Basutoland came under the jurisdiction of the British High Commissioner in South Africa. It was re-named Lesotho and became independent in 1966 as a constitutional monarchy, with a National Assembly (1974) to work with hereditary chiefs. The National Assembly was disbanded in 1986 after a South African-backed military coup, by which the King was to rule through a Military Council. In November 1990 King Constantine Moshoeshoe II was deposed and replaced by his son, Letsie III. As chairman of the Military Council, Colonel Elias Ramaena held all effective power. He was ousted in a bloodless coup in 1991 by Major-General Justin Lekhanya, who established a democratic constitution. Multi-party elections were held in 1993 but tensions between the government and opposition parties led to a political crisis. Letsie III suspended the government and the constitution in 1994. After a negotiated settlement the government was restored and Letsie III abdicated in favour of his father, who returned to the throne in 1995. King Moshoeshoe II was killed in a car accident in 1996 and Letsie III returned to the throne.

Capital: Maseru
Area: 30,355 sq km (11,720 sq mi)
Population: 2,057,000 (1995)
Currency: 1 loti = 100 lisente
Religions: Roman Catholic 43.5%; Protestant (mainly Lesotho Evangelical 29.8%; Anglican 11.5%; other Christian 8.0%; tribal 6.2%
Ethnic Groups: Sotho 99.7%
Languages: Sotho, English (both official)
International Organizations: UN; OAU; SADC; Commonwealth

Lesseps, Ferdinand Marie, Vicomte de (1805–94) French diplomat. While in the consular service in Egypt he became aware of plans to link the Mediterranean and the Red Sea by means of a canal, and from 1854 onwards devoted himself to the project. Work began in 1859 and the Suez Canal was opened ten years later. In 1881 he embarked on the building of the Panama Canal, but had not anticipated the difficulties of this very different enterprise; the project was abandoned in 1889. The canal was not opened until 1914, after completion by US engineers.

Lessing, Doris (May) (1919–) British novelist and short-story writer, brought up in Rhodesia. An active Communist in her youth, she frequently deals with social and political conflicts in her fiction, especially as they affect women; *The Golden Notebook* (1962) was hailed as a landmark by the women's movement. Other works include *The Grass is Singing* (1950), about interracial relationships in Africa, a quintet of science-fiction novels collectively entitled *Canopus in Argus: Archives* (1979–83), the autobiography *Under My Skin* (1994), and *Love Again* (1996).

Lessing, Gotthold Ephraim (1729–81) German dramatist and critic. He wrote tragedies, such as *Miss Sara Sampson* (1755) and *Emilia Galotti* (1772), the former considered to be the first significant domestic tragedy in German; a comedy, *Minna von Barnhelm* (1767); and the dramatic poem *Nathan der Weise* (1779), a plea for religious toleration. In his critical works, such as *Laokoon* (1766), he criticized the reliance of German literature on the conventions of the French classical school and suggested that German writers should look to Shakespeare and English literature instead.

Letchworth A town in Hertfordshire, south-east England; pop. (1991) 31,418. Built in 1903, it was the first English 'garden city'. It has printing industries.

Lethe In Greek mythology, one of the rivers of the underworld, whose water when drunk made the souls of the dead forget their life on Earth.

letterpress printing The original method of relief PRINTING, in which paper is pressed into contact with previously inked raised metal type and illustration blocks. The Chinese were printing from wooden type by the 11th century, while GUTENBERG was the first to use metal type, in

1448. This method progressed from hand-operated presses, through specialized flat-bed printing presses, in which the type passes mechanically under inking rollers and paper carried on an impression cylinder, to rotary presses using curved printing plates. Speeds have increased dramatically during the last two centuries, and with better paper and machine controls, quality has also improved. Recently, however, letterpress printing has been largely superseded by OFFSET LITHOGRAPHY.

Lettish See LATVIAN.

lettuce Probably the best-known of all green salad vegetables. Lettuce has been cultivated for so long that its origin is uncertain. It belongs to the sunflower family and varieties have been derived from the species *Lactuca sativa*. These can be divided into two major groups. Cabbage lettuces have roundish heads, and their leaves vary in texture from soft to crisp. Cos lettuces have more elongated, upright heads.

leucocyte A white blood cell, in contrast to a red blood cell or ERYTHROCYTE. Leucocytes are found in large numbers in the tissues and at sites of wounding or invasion by foreign organisms, such as bacteria and parasites, and include a diverse range of cell types. **Lymphocytes**, found in blood, tissues, and lymph, are involved in cellular IMMUNITY and the production of ANTIBODIES; a particular subset of lymphocytes, the T-cells (or T-lymphocytes), is invaded and killed by the human immunodeficiency virus (HIV) in AIDS patients. Leucocytes that engulf and digest foreign material are collectively known as **phagocytes** (literally, 'eating cells'). Blood monocytes differentiate in the tissues into phagocytic macrophages, which kill and destroy foreign organisms and help to stimulate lymphocytes in the immune response. **Granulocytes** (granular leucocytes) are so called because their cytoplasm contains 'packages' of enzymes and toxic substances, which look like granules when subjected to certain cytological techniques. The contents of these packages kill or digest foreign material. Eosinophil granulocytes, which are involved in allergic responses, increase in number in the blood of people suffering from hay fever or infection with parasitic worms. Neurophil granulocytes are always present in very high numbers (approximately 5 million per millilitre of human blood) because they destroy not only invading organisms but the body's own dead or damaged cells.

leukaemias A group of progressive malignant diseases (CANCER) of tissues that are responsible for forming blood cells in the bone marrow. Leukaemias are characterized by increased production of white blood cells. Normal bone marrow is progressively replaced by malignant forms, and the production of other normal blood elements, such as red blood cells and platelets, is reduced. However, leukaemias are not exclusively related to increased numbers of white blood cells; the cells may be normal in number but structurally defective or may even be normal in both number and structure.

Acute leukaemias are characterized by failure of white blood cells to mature, which proliferate in the bone marrow and accumulate in the blood. Symptoms of a 'flu-like' nature are common initially; haemorrhage may also occur in areas, such as the gums and the nose. Chronic leukaemias are characterized by the failure of removal of mature white blood cells from the blood circulation, which accumulate. Symptoms include tiredness, weight loss, difficulty in breathing, loss of appetite, and bruising. There are a range of both acute and chronic leukaemias, which are classified according to origin, cell abnormalities, and course of the disease. Generally, in acute leukaemias, life-expectancy is short without treatment; in chronic leukaemias, life-expectancy may be many years.

Levant ▶**1** The eastern part of the Mediterranean with its islands and neighbouring countries. ▶**2** A region of eastern Spain forming an alluvial plain between the Iberian cordillera and the coast of the Gulfs of Valencia, Alicante, and Murcia.

levanter (or **solano**) The mild and humid east wind that affects the western Mediterranean, especially the south-east coast of Spain and the Balearic Islands.

leveche A hot, dry, southerly wind that blows northwards into Spain from Morocco.

levée An artificial river embankment or a broad low ridge of alluvium laid down naturally by a river in flood.

Levellers English radicals of the mid-17th century. The Levellers were led by John Lilburne, William Walwyn, and John Wildman, and their early strength lay with the London poor. By 1647 they had won considerable support among the lower ranks of the NEW MODEL ARMY. In that year Leveller 'Agitators' were elected from each regiment to participate in the Putney debates, with CROMWELL and the Army Grandees, in an attempt to resolve disagreements. Their political programme, embodied in such documents as the *Agreement of the People*, was less radical than that of the True Levellers or Diggers. It demanded the abolition of the monarchy and House of Lords, sovereignty for the people, manhood suffrage, social reform, liberty of conscience, and equality before the law. Exasperated by the conservatism of the Grandees and Parliament, they mutinied in 1647 and 1649. By May 1649 both the civilian and military wings of the movement had been broken.

Leven, Loch A loch in Kinrossshire, central Scotland, the largest freshwater loch in lowland Scotland. Mary Queen of Scots was imprisoned in Loch Leven Castle (1567–68). The Loch, which is a noted European centre for wildfowl and wintering geese, has been a national nature reserve since 1964. Its only outlet is the **River Leven**, which flows 26 km (16 miles) eastwards to the Firth of Forth at **Leven**, a summer resort famous for its golf links.

lever A simple device used to move a large load by means of a small FORCE, or to move a small load through a large distance. It is of very ancient origin; the mathematical basis of the lever was understood by the 4th century BC. There are three possible arrangements of load, pivot (or fulcrum), and operating effort in a lever. In the first-order levers the fulcrum is between load and effort; if the distance from fulcrum to force is five times that from fulcrum to load there is a MECHANICAL ADVANTAGE of 5:1 – five times as much force is exerted at the load. However, the total work (force × distance) done by the effort is the same as that done by the load, since the load moves only one-fifth the distance of the effort. In second-order levers the load is between fulcrum and effort; the same principle of mechanical advantage applies. In third-order levers the operating force is between fulcrum and load. Here the mechanical advantage is less than one, but the load moves a greater distance than the operating force. See illustration p. 812.

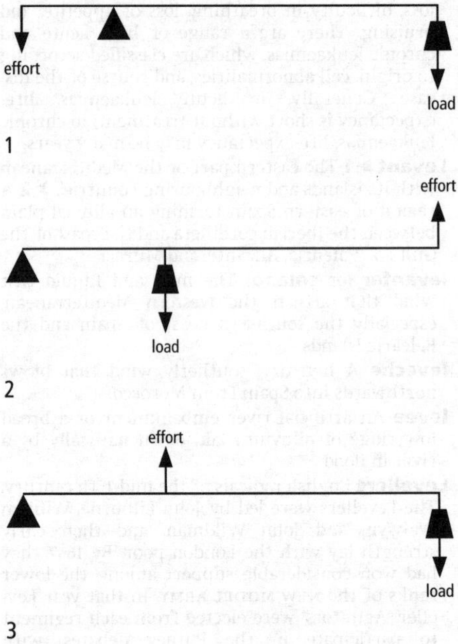

Lever (1) In the first-order lever the fulcrum is between the load and the effort. (2) In second-order levers the load is placed between the fulcrum and the effort. (3) In third-order levers the effort operates between the fulcrum and the load.

Leverhulme, **William Hesketh Lever**, **1st Viscount** (1851–1925) British industrialist and philanthropist. He and his brother started the manufacture of soap from vegetable oil (instead of tallow) under the trade name Sunlight. In the 1880s they founded and built the industrial new town and factory complex of Port Sunlight in Cheshire (now in Merseyside); workers were accommodated in model housing and were entitled to medical care, pensions, and a form of profit-sharing. In the 20th century Leverhulme's company, Lever Bros., formed the basis of the international corporation Unilever.

Le Verrier, **Urbain** (1811–77) French mathematician. His analysis of the motions of the planets suggested that an unknown body was disrupting the orbit of Uranus, the same conclusion being reached almost simultaneously by John Couch Adams. Under the prompting of Le Verrier, the German astronomer Johann Galle (1812–1910) searched the region of the sky in which the mysterious object was predicted to lie, and discovered the planet Neptune on 23 September 1846.

Levi The third son of Leah and of the Hebrew patriarch Jacob, whose descendants, the Levites, were given by God the sole right to the Jewish priesthood in the time of Aaron. Referred to as priests before the Exile in Babylon, they were not assigned a specific territory. Many of them became dispersed along with the other northern tribes of Israel, and in time became Temple servants with subordinate duties.

Levi, **Carlo** (1902–75) Italian doctor and writer. A Jew and a vociferous antifascist, he was banished to southern Italy in 1935. His *Christ Stopped at Eboli* (1947), based on his experiences in the region, was an international bestseller. Other books include *Words and Stones* (1958).

Levi, **Primo** (1919–87) Italian chemist, novelist, and poet, of Jewish descent. His experiences as a survivor of Auschwitz are recounted in his first book *If This is a Man* (1947); other books include *The Periodic Table* (1985), a collection of memoirs. His *The Drowned and the Saved* (1988) was published after he had committed suicide.

Leviathan The animal, mentioned in the Old Testament, variously identified as a crocodile, whale, or dolphin. Possibly related to the Phoenician snake-god Lotan, in the Book of Isaiah, the name Leviathan also symbolizes the mighty Assyrian and Babylonian empires, hence its use to denote anything very large or powerful.

Lévi-Strauss, **Claude** (1908–) French social anthropologist. He was an influential pioneer in the use of a structuralist analysis to study cultural systems; he regarded language as an essential common denominator underlying cultural phenomena, a view that forms the basis for his theories concerning the relationships of such societal elements as religion, myth, and kinship. His books include the two-volume *Structural Anthropology* (1958; 1973).

Lewes A town in southern England, north-east of Brighton, the administrative centre of East Sussex; pop. (1991) 15,376. Simon de Montfort, founder of the English Parliament, defeated Henry III at the Battle of Lewes in 1264.

Lewis The northern part of the island of Lewis with Harris, in the Outer Hebrides in Scotland. Its chief town is Stornoway.

Lewis, **Carl** (full name Frederick Carleton Lewis) (1961–) US athlete. In 1984 he won four Olympic gold medals (in the 100 and 200 metres, long jump, and 4 × 100 metre relay); he won golds for the 100 metres and long jump in the Olympics of 1988, for the long jump and 4 × 100 metre relay in 1992, and for the long jump in 1996. He has broken the world record for the 100 metres on several occasions.

Lewis, **C(ecil) Day** See DAY LEWIS.

Lewis, **C(live) S(taples)** (1898–1963) British literary scholar, critic, and novelist. His critical works include his early publication *The Allegory of Love* (1936). Among Lewis's popular religious and moral writings is *The Screwtape Letters* (1940), which purports to be advice from one devil to another on the art of temptation. He also wrote 'space fiction' with a strong Christian flavour (*Voyage to Venus*, 1943, reworks the story of the Garden of Eden), and the *Narnia* series of novels, including *The Lion, the Witch, and the Wardrobe* (1950), for children. *Surprised by Joy* (1955) is his spiritual autobiography. The death of his Jewish American wife, Joy Davidman (1915–60), was the subject of the 1993 film *Shadowlands*.

Lewis, **Gilbert Newton** (1875–1946) US chemist who proposed that a bond between two atoms could be formed not only through the complete transfer of electrons but also through the sharing of electrons to form a COVALENT COMPOUND. He extended the definition of an ACID to include all substances capable of accepting a pair of electrons from another compound; similarly he defined a BASE as a substance capable of donating a pair of electrons – the so called Lewis acid-base theory. In 1943 he became the first person to prepare heavy water (D_2O), formed from oxygen and DEUTERIUM, an isotope of hydrogen. See also WATER.

Lewis, **Jerry Lee** (1935–) US rock and roll singer and pianist. In 1957 he joined Sun Records in Memphis, and with his second release, 'Whole Lotta

Shakin' Going On' (1957) earned a gold disc. This was followed by a succession of hits, including 'Great Balls of Fire' (1957), but his career was interrupted when his marriage to his 14-year-old cousin caused a public outcry. He made a comeback in 1961, and despite a series of scandals and health problems continued to perform into the 1990s.

Lewis, (Harry) Sinclair (1885–1951) US novelist. He gained recognition with *Main Street* (1920), a social satire on small-town life in the Midwest. His later novels, such as *Babbitt* (1922), *Elmer Gantry* (1927), and *Dodsworth* (1929), continued in a similar vein, using satire and caricature to attack targets such as the urban middle class and the Church. He was awarded the Nobel Prize for literature in 1930, the first US writer to achieve this.

Lewis, (Percy) Wyndham (1882–1957) British novelist, critic, and painter, born in Canada. He was a leader of the vorticist movement, and with Ezra Pound edited the magazine *Blast* (1914–15). His satirical novels and polemical works include *The Apes of God* (1930) and the trilogy *The Human Age* (1928–55); he expounds his philosophical ideas in *Time and Western Man* (1927). He later aroused hostility for his fascist sympathies and his satirical attacks on his contemporaries (especially the Bloomsbury Group).

Lewisham A borough of Greater London, England, between Southwark and Greenwich; pop. (1991) 215,300. It has light engineering industries but is mainly residential. It includes the districts of Lewisham and Deptford.

Lewis with Harris (or **Lewis and Harris**) The largest and northernmost island of the Outer Hebrides in Scotland; area 2,134 sq km (824 sq miles); chief town, Stornoway (on Lewis). The island, which is separated from the mainland by the Minch, consists of a northern part, Lewis, and a southern part, Harris.

Lexington A city in north-central Kentucky, USA, south-east of Frankfort; pop. (1990) 255,370 (with Fayette). Founded in 1779 and named after the Battle of Lexington and Concord (1775) in the American War of INDEPENDENCE, it became a major producer of the hemp used by New England clipper ships. It is now a centre of thoroughbred horse-breeding and has the world's largest tobacco market. Lexington is the home of the University of Kentucky (1865) and of the first jockey club which was founded here in 1797.

Leyden See LEIDEN.

Leyte Gulf, Battle of (October 1944) A naval battle off the Philippines. In the campaign to recover the Philippines, US forces landed on the island of Leyte. Four Japanese naval forces converged to attack US transports, but in a series of scattered engagements 40 Japanese ships were sunk, 46 were damaged, and 405 planes destroyed. The Japanese fleet, having failed to halt the invasion, withdrew from Philippine waters.

Lhasa The capital of Tibet, which since 1959 has constituted an autonomous region of south-west China; pop. (1990) 139,800. It is situated in the Himalayas at *c.*3,600 m (11,800 ft), on a tributary of the Brahmaputra. Enforced immigration of Chinese has greatly increased the population since 1982. Inaccessibility and the hostility of the Tibetan Buddhist priests to foreign visitors – to whom it was closed until the 20th century – earned Lhasa the title of the Forbidden City. The spiritual centre of Tibetan Buddhism, it was the seat of the Dalai Lama until 1959, when direct Chinese administration was imposed on the city. Its chief landmark is the 17th-century Potala Palace.

liana Any woody climbing or scrambling plant that supports itself on bushes or trees. Lianas are most conspicuous in tropical rain forests. They include RATTANS, which scramble upwards using hooks. Others may have twisting stems or leaf-stalks, sucker-pads, or spines. Of the small number of temperate lianas, clematis, ivy, and honeysuckle are best known.

Liaodong Peninsula A peninsula in north-east China that extends southwards into the Yellow Sea between the Gulf of Chihli (Bo Hai) and Korea Bay; area 53,000 sq km (21,600 sq miles). Forming part of Liaoning province, its cities include Dalian, the largest trading port and shipbuilding centre in China; Anshan, China's steel capital; Fushun, China's leading coal-mining city; and the Liaohe oilfield. Noted for fruit-growing, sea-salt production, and textile manufactures, the peninsula was declared an open economic zone in 1988.

Liaoning A province of north-east China, separated from North Korea to the east by the Yalu River; area 146,000 sq km (56,392 sq miles); pop. (1990) 39,460,000; capital, Shenyang. It has become one of China's most important industrial regions and is a leading producer of iron, steel, coke, and chemicals.

Libby, Willard Frank (1908–80) US chemist who developed the RADIOCARBON DATING technique for determining the age of organic matter. A graduate of the University of California, he taught there until 1945, when he moved to the University of Chicago. From 1941 to 1945 he also worked on the MANHATTAN PROJECT, helping to develop a method of separating uranium isotopes for the building of an atomic bomb. In 1947 he and a group of his students developed the technique of radiocarbon dating. He was awarded the Nobel Prize for chemistry in 1960.

Liberace (full name Wladziu Valentino Liberace) (1919–87) US pianist and entertainer. He was known for his romantic arrangements of popular piano classics and for his flamboyant costumes. His television show ran for five years (1952–57) and he gave a great many spectacular live performances.

Liberal Democrats A British political party that adopted this name in 1989. The party, which was formed in 1988, was formerly known as the Social and Liberal Democrats. The Social and Liberal Democrats were a merger of the **Social Democratic Party** (SDP) and the LIBERAL PARTY. The SDP itself was established by four dissident members of the Labour Party (Roy Jenkins, David Owen, Shirley Williams, and William Rogers), known as the 'gang of four'. As a new centre party, the SDP under David Owen's leadership, formed an alliance with the Liberal Party. However, after a poor showing in the 1987 election, the SDP voted to merge with the Liberal Party, forming the Social and Liberal Democrats under the leadership of Robert Maclennan. David Owen attempted to revive a reduced SDP in 1988 but wound it up in 1990.

The present leader of the Liberal Democrats, Paddy ASHDOWN, managed to substantially increase the number of Liberal Democrat MPs in the 1997 election.

liberalism A political outlook attaching supreme importance to safeguarding the freedom of the individual within society. Liberal ideas first took shape in the struggle for religious toleration in the 16th and 17th centuries. The liberal view was that religion was a private matter; it was not the business of the state to enforce a particular creed. This later developed into a more general doctrine of the limited and constitutional state, whose boundaries were set by the natural rights of the individual (for instance in the political thought of LOCKE). Around 1800 liberalism became associated with the doctrines of the FREE MARKET and LAISSEZ-FAIRE, and reducing the role of the state in the economic sphere. This tendency was reversed later in the 19th century with the arrival of 'New Liberalism', committed to social reform and welfare legislation. In contemporary debate both schools of thought are represented, some liberals harking back to the classical economic ideas of the late 18th century (for instance, HAYEK), others embracing the MIXED ECONOMY and the WELFARE STATE (for instance, RAWLS). Despite their economic disagreements, liberals unite in upholding the importance of personal liberty in the face of encroachment by the state, leading to demands for constitutional government, CIVIL RIGHTS, and the protection of privacy.

Liberal Judaism A Jewish movement that began in about 1780 in Germany, in response to the need to redefine the meaning and practical observance of the TORAH in a changing society. Liberals saw the Torah's revelations as progressive rather than static, expressing God's teaching rather than God's law. This allowed for evolution in religious law and practice and resulted in dramatic changes in both diet and custom, including the use of the vernacular in services and the relaxation of Sabbath laws. In Europe the movement is also known as Progressive, and is roughly equivalent to US REFORM JUDAISM.

Liberal Party (Australia) A major political party in Australia. The original party emerged in 1910 as an alliance of various groups opposed to the Australian LABOR PARTY, led by FORREST. They were known for a while as the Fusion Party, adopting the title Liberal in 1913. The new Liberal Party was created in 1944 by Robert MENZIES, and a Liberal-Country coalition has alternated with Labor since then, being in office under Malcolm Fraser (1975–83). After five successive Labor governments, the Liberal Party returned to power in 1996 under John Howard.

Liberal Party (Britain) Formerly, a major political party in Britain. It emerged in the mid-19th century as the successor to the Whig Party and was the major alternative party to the CONSERVATIVES until 1918, after which the LABOUR PARTY supplanted it. Lord Palmerston's administration of 1854 is regarded as the first Liberal government. After World War II it was an opposition party of varying fortune, forming a Lib–Lab pact with the Labour government (1977–78), and then the Alliance (1983–87) with the Social Democratic Party, with which it merged in 1988 to form the Social and Liberal Democrats (later renamed the LIBERAL DEMOCRATS).

Liberal Party (Canada) A major political party in Canada. Following the Confederation of Canada in 1867, a Liberal Party took shape as a major political force and remained so, forming a government (1873–78) under Alexander Mackenzie. The Liberal Party has had a strong appeal for French Canadians. With its power base in Quebec, the Party suffered from the *Québecois* secessionist demands, and failed to win federal office after 1984. It endorsed the all-party constitutional proposals of 1992 designed to prevent the break-up of the Canadian federation, although this in fact was rejected in a referendum in 1992. In 1993 the Liberal Party was re-elected and Jean CHRÉTIEN, its leader since 1990, became Prime Minister.

liberation theology (in Christianity) A theological movement developed in the 1960s principally by the Latin American ROMAN CATHOLIC CHURCH. Liberation theology is a response to the widespread poverty and social injustice found in much of Latin America. Drawing on MARXISM and the ideas of dependency theory, which viewed the inequalities of the Third World as springing from dependence on the exploitative capitalism of the developed world, liberation theology attempts to address the problems of political and social inequality in addition to the spiritual matters often regarded as the only legitimate concern of the Church.

Liberia A tropical country on the Atlantic coast of West Africa, flanked by Sierra Leone, Guinea, and Côte d'Ivoire.

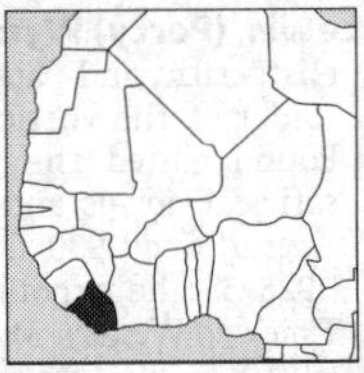

Physical. The climate is hot and very wet. Rain forest and swamp cover the coastal plain, which is traversed by several rivers flowing down from savannah-covered uplands.

Economy. There are links with Guinea and Sierra Leone through the Mano River Union. Iron ore is Liberia's chief export. Rubber, diamonds, timber, and coffee are the other main exports. Bauxite and manganese are mined. Cassava, rice, and sugar cane are important crops. Industry is limited to food-processing. Shipping registration fees contribute substantial revenues; ships are registered in Liberia because of its low taxation and lenient inspection policies. Monrovia is a free port. The civil war and low world commodity prices have contributed to economic decline.

History. Liberia is the oldest independent republic in Africa (1847). It owes its origin to the philanthropic American Colonization Society. US negotiations with local rulers for a settlement for the repatriation of freed slaves began in 1816. The first settlements were made in 1822, and the name Liberia was adopted in 1824. Independence was proclaimed by Joseph Jenkins Roberts, first President, in 1847. The real beginning of prosperity was in the 1920s, when the Firestone Rubber Company provided a permanent and stable market for rubber. W. V. S. TUBMAN was President from 1944 until his death in 1971. With a decline in world rubber prices, the economy suffered in the 1970s and a bloody revolution in 1980 brought in the People's Redemption Council, a military government, under Master-Sergeant Samuel Doe. The latter was named President and Commander-in-Chief, and his ten-year autocratic rule was one of deep corruption, ending in 1990 with civil war. Two rebel groups, one led by Charles Taylor and a second by Prince Yormie Johnson, assailed the capital Monrovia, and some 150,000 refugees fled the country. A peace-keeping force from ECOWAS intervened, Doe was murdered, and a cease-fire arranged in 1990. Fighting between rival factions continued, while ECOWAS negotiators tried to restore peace. A peace agreement made in 1991 was not upheld, but in 1993 a further agreement was signed, which included provisions for the implementation of multi-party democracy. A transitional legislature was set up in 1994 but the peace process has remained fragile and violence has continued. A peace accord was formulated in 1995. Factional fighting broke out again in April 1996, but a cease-fire was agreed in July 1996. Charles Taylor was elected President in 1997.

Capital: Monrovia
Area: 111,400 sq km (43,000 sq mi)
Population: 2,380,000 (1995)
Currency: 1 Liberian dollar = 100 cents
Religions: Christian 67.7%; Muslim 13.8%; traditional beliefs and other 18.5%
Ethnic Groups: Kpelle 19.4%; Bassa 13.8%; Grebo 9.0%; Gio 7.8%; Kru 7.3%; Mano 7.1%
Languages: English (official); Mande; Kru-Bassa
International Organizations: UN; OAU; ECOWAS

libertarianism A radical form of LIBERALISM holding that the role of the state should be reduced to an absolute minimum and looks to private property and market exchange as the basis of the good society. According to libertarians, the role of the state should be confined to police protection, the enforcement of contracts, and national defence. Some would go further still, and claim that personal protection could be provided by private associations on a market basis; here libertarianism becomes a form of ANARCHISM.

Liberty, Statue of A statue on an island at the entrance to New York Harbour, a symbol of welcome to immigrants, representing a draped female figure carrying a book of laws in her left hand and holding aloft a torch in her right. Dedicated in 1886, it was the work of the French sculptor F. A. Bartholdi (who used his mother as a model) and was the gift of the French to the American people, commemorating the alliance of France and the USA during the War of American Independence and marking its centenary.

Liberty Bell A large bell that is the traditional symbol of US freedom, bearing the legend 'Proclaim liberty throughout all the land unto all the inhabitants thereof' (Leviticus 25: 10). Hung in the State House Steeple, Philadelphia, in 1753, it was first rung on 8 July 1776 to celebrate the first public reading of the Declaration of Independence, and cracked irreparably when rung to commemorate George Washington's birthday in 1846. It is now housed near Independence Hall, Philadelphia.

libido In the theory of PSYCHOANALYSIS, the libido was regarded by FREUD as an individual's sexual drive. Like the death instinct, it was said to be one of the fundamental sources of energy for all mental life. According to Freud psychiatric illness could often be caused by misdirection or inadequate fulfilment of the libido.

Li Bo See LI PO.

Libra The Scales, a CONSTELLATION of the zodiac. The ancient Greeks knew this area of sky as the claws of the neighbouring scorpion, Scorpius, but about 2,000 years ago the Romans made it into a separate constellation, representing a pair of scales. Sometimes it is visualized as the scales of justice held by neighbouring Virgo. The stars Alpha and Beta Librae are known as Zubenelgenubi and Zubeneschamali, Arabic names that mean 'southern claw' and 'northern claw', a reminder of the constellation's origin.

libration The rocking motion of an orbiting body. For example, while the Moon generally keeps the same face towards the Earth, over a period of time 59 per cent of its face can be seen from the Earth, the parts near the edge of the Moon's disc becoming alternately visible and hidden. This apparent rocking motion has three main causes. The Moon rotates on its axis at a constant rate, but its orbital velocity about the Earth varies because its orbit is elliptical. This results in **libration in longitude**. The Moon's equator is inclined to the plane of its orbit. This causes the Moon to appear to nod up and down each month and is known as **libration in latitude**.

The Earth rotates faster than the Moon revolves in its orbit about the Earth so that when the Moon rises we can see slightly over the western edge of the Moon's disc and at moonset slightly over the eastern edge. This is due to differences in line of sight and is called **diurnal libration**.

Mercury exhibits librational behaviour with respect to the Sun, and HYPERION and TITAN with respect to Saturn. Physically, libration occurs when two motions are locked in resonance.

Libreville The capital of Gabon in west-central Africa, a major port on the Atlantic coast at the mouth of the Gabon River; pop. (1992) 352,000. Founded in 1849 on the site of a Roman Catholic mission and trading post, it was originally a refuge for slaves. It has expanded rapidly in recent years with the exploitation of Gabon's mineral resources.

Libya A country on the north coast of Africa, bounded by Tunisia and Algeria on the west, Niger and Chad on the south, and Sudan and Egypt on the east.

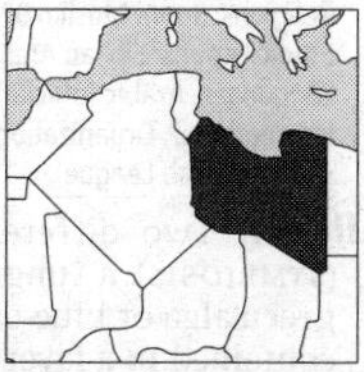

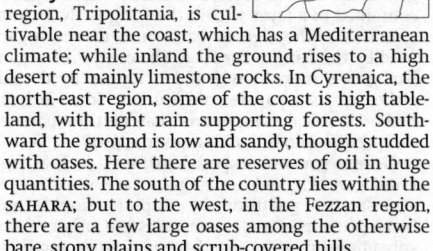

Physical. The north-west region, Tripolitania, is cultivable near the coast, which has a Mediterranean climate; while inland the ground rises to a high desert of mainly limestone rocks. In Cyrenaica, the north-east region, some of the coast is high tableland, with light rain supporting forests. Southward the ground is low and sandy, though studded with oases. Here there are reserves of oil in huge quantities. The south of the country lies within the SAHARA; but to the west, in the Fezzan region, there are a few large oases among the otherwise bare, stony plains and scrub-covered hills.

Economy. The economy and exports are dominated by crude oil. Attempts at diversification and infrastructural development, such as the ambitious project (Great Man-Made River) to bring water from the Mediterranean to the south, have been slowed by declining oil revenues. Industry is limited mainly to petroleum by-products and agriculture is limited by the arid nature of most of the country.

History. During most of its history Libya has been inhabited by Arab and BERBER nomads, only the coastlands and oases being settled. Greek colonies existed in ancient times, and later under the Romans; under the Arabs the cultivated area lapsed into desert. Administered by the Turks from the 16th century, Libya was annexed by Italy after a brief war in 1911–12. The Italians, however, like the Turks before them, never succeeded in asserting their full authority over the Sanussi tribesmen of the interior desert.

Heavily fought over during World War II, Libya was placed under a military government by the Allies before becoming an independent monarchy in 1951 under Emir Sayyid Idris al-Sanussi, who in 1954 granted the USA military and air bases. Idris was overthrown by radical Islamic army officers in 1969, and Libya emerged as a radical socialist state under the charismatic leadership of Colonel Muammar GADDAFI. It has used the wealth generated by exploitation of the country's rich oil resources to build up its military might and to interfere in the affairs of neighbouring states.

Libyan involvement in Arab terrorist operations has blighted its relations with western states and produced armed confrontations with US forces in the Mediterranean. In April 1986, there were US air strikes against Tripoli and Benghazi. In 1989 it joined the Maghreb Union, a trading agreement of north-west African states. President Gaddafi condemned the Iraqi occupation of Kuwait in 1990, taking a neutral stance. But Libya again clashed with the USA during 1992 over its refusal to extradite two Libyans accused of organizing the bombing of a PanAm aircraft over LOCKERBIE in Scotland in 1988. In April 1992 the UN Security Council imposed sanctions on this issue. The sanctions were tightened in 1993 and began to affect the economy. In 1994 a peace settlement with Chad was agreed concerning the Aouzou Strip, in Northern Chad, which Libya had seized in 1973.

Capital: Tripoli
Area: 1,757,000 sq km (678,400 sq mi)
Population: 15,407,000 (1995)
Currency: 1 Libyan dinar = 1,000 dirhams
Religions: Sunni Muslim 97.0%
Ethnic Groups: Libyan Arab and Berber 89.0%
Languages: Arabic (official)
International Organizations: UN; OAU; OAPEC; OPEC; Maghreb Union; Arab League

lichen Two different organisms in partnership (SYMBIOSIS): a fungus that provides shelter, and a green alga or blue-green bacterium whose cells are contained in a layer within the fungus. By PHOTOSYNTHESIS, the alga or bacterium makes sugars used by the fungus for food. The combined organism grows more slowly and is longer lived than either of its separate constituents. Some lichens make chemical compounds that neither partner can produce alone, including some used as dyes.

Lichens grow on exposed surfaces, such as tree trunks, rocks, and walls; most are sensitive to atmospheric pollution by sulphur dioxide gas. Some grow as crusts on surfaces but others form spreading branches. The fungal partner produces spores, and the lichen partnership is reproduced and spread by algal (or bacterial) and fungal cells in small dry clumps which blow away from the parent lichen. About 35,000 species are known. They are one of the few organisms to have colonized Antarctica.

Lichtenstein, Roy (1923–97) US painter and sculptor. A leading exponent of pop art, he chiefly based his work on images from commercial art or made parodies of the work of other painters. He became known in the 1960s for paintings inspired by comic strips; these paintings are made up of thick black outlines enclosing areas of dots in imitation of the half-tones used to print blocks of colour in comics. One of the best-known examples of this style is *Whaam!* (1963).

Liddell, Eric (1902–45) British athlete and missionary, born in China. In the 1924 Olympic Games the heats of his own event (the 100 metres) were held on a Sunday and he withdrew on religious grounds; he ran in the 400 metres instead, winning the race in a world record time. His exploits were celebrated in the film *Chariots of Fire* (1981). Liddell went on to serve as a missionary in China and died there in a Japanese prisoner-of-war camp.

Liddell Hart, Sir Basil Henry (1895–1970) British military historian and theorist. Appalled at the slaughter produced by trench warfare in World War I, he formulated a strategy using an indirect approach, in which attacks would be made with tanks and aircraft to destroy enemy command centres, communications, and supply lines. His theories were particularly influential in Germany, where the idea of strategic penetration by tank divisions was successfully adopted in World War II.

Lie, Trygve Halvdan (1896–1968) Norwegian Labour politician, first Secretary-General of the United Nations 1946–53.

Liebig, Justus von, Baron (1803–73) German chemist and teacher. With Friedrich Wöhler he discovered the benzoyl radical, and demonstrated that such radicals were groups of atoms that remained unchanged in many chemical reactions. He applied chemistry to physiology and to agriculture, stressed the importance of artificial fertilizers, and developed techniques for quantitative organic analysis. The Liebig condenser is a widely used piece of laboratory equipment.

Liechtenstein In central Europe, one of the smallest countries in the world. It lies on the border between Austria and Switzerland, to the south of Lake Constance.

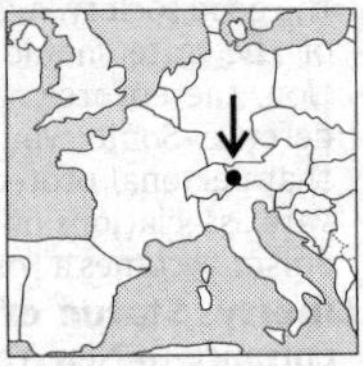

Physical. The western section of Liechtenstein occupies part of the floodplain of the upper Rhine, while to the east it extends up the forested and then snow-covered slopes of the Rätikon Massif, part of the central Alps. Its mild climate is significantly affected by the warm FÖHN wind from the south.

Economy. The economy is based on manufacturing industry; tourism and agriculture play a role, and the registration of foreign holding companies provides a source of tax income and stimulus to financial activity. The main exports are machinery and metal and chemical products. There is a customs and monetary union with Switzerland.

History. The principality of Liechtenstein was founded in 1719 when the two independent lordships of Schellenberg and Vaduz were united within the Holy Roman Empire. Liechtenstein remained part of the Empire until 1806, when it became part of the Rhine Federation. It joined the German Confederation in 1815 and became independent in 1866. A unicameral parliament was established by the 1921 constitution but the country has remained a monarchy, headed by the Prince. Any 900 persons or three communes may initiate legislation in the Diet (parliament). In 1989 Prince Hans-Adam II (1945–) succeeded his father, Prince Franz Joseph II (1906–89). Liechtenstein became industralized after World War II. Women were given the right to vote on national, but not local, issues in 1984. A constitutional row began to develop in 1996 following the stated intention of the government to remove certain powers from Prince Hans-Adam II, who announced that he would abandon the country unless he retained his full rights. In 1992 a referendum approved Liechtenstein's entry into the European Economic Area.

Capital: Vaduz
Area: 160 sq km (61.6 sq mi)
Population: 30,900 (1995)
Currency: 1 Swiss franc = 100 rappen (or centimes)
Religions: Roman Catholic 87.0%; Protestant 9.0%
Ethnic Groups: Liechtensteiner 63.9%; Swiss 15.7%; Austrian 7.7%; German 3.7%
Languages: German (official); Italian; French
International Organizations: CSCE; EFTA; Council of Europe

Lied A song in the German language, usually with a piano accompaniment that is as important as the vocal line. Though intimate in scale, *Lieder* are likely to be thought-provoking. The musical setting may repeat for each verse, or change according to the demands of the poem (through-composed). The *Lied* is essentially a product of ROMANTICISM and was popular with such composers as Schubert, Schumann, Brahms, Wolf, Mahler, and Richard Strauss.

lie detector See POLYGRAPH.

Liège (Flemish **Luik**) ▶**1** A province of eastern Belgium, comprising the districts of Huy, Liège, Verviers, and Waremme; area 3,863 sq km (1,492 sq miles); pop. (1991) 999,650. Formerly ruled by independent prince-bishops, it became a part of the Netherlands in 1815 and of Belgium in 1830. ▶**2** Its capital city, a major river port and industrial centre at the junction of the Ourthe and Meuse rivers; pop. (1991) 194,600. An early centre of coal-mining, its industries produce chemicals, electronics, textiles, tobacco, and glassware.

life The physical state perpetuated by functional systems through which an organism obtains energy, grows and reproduces itself. Life as we know it probably first arose on Earth about three to four thousand million years ago. Many explanations of how this occurred have been proposed, although the following sequence of events is most widely accepted at present.

At that time, the Earth's atmosphere was composed largely of a mixture of ammonia, methane, hydrogen, and water vapour. It has been shown that simple organic molecules can be synthesized if mixtures of these gases are exposed to gamma radiation, electrical discharges, or ultraviolet light under various physical conditions. All of these sources of energy are likely to have occurred in the atmosphere. Having been formed, these molecules could have fallen to the ground in rain to accumulate in the rivers and seas.

The organization of these molecules into cells capable of obtaining energy and reproducing themselves is the most difficult step to explain. In some way, suitable combinations of molecules came together, became surrounded by a type of membrane, and acquired integration. These early organisms must have required energy to grow and multiply. They probably took in organic molecules from their watery surroundings and then broke them down by anaerobic RESPIRATION (since the atmosphere probably lacked free oxygen) to release energy. The first REPRODUCTION was presumably simple asexual division.

The subsequent development of a huge variety of life forms from these beginnings is explained by EVOLUTION.

lifeboat Any water craft specially built for rescue purposes. Relatively simple lifeboats are carried by ships for use in case of accident: many vessels now also carry inflatable life-rafts for this purpose. Shore-based lifeboats are generally larger, and are designed to stay afloat in extreme conditions. In 1824 the UK became the first country to organize a national lifeboat service, shortly followed by Denmark and other countries. Modern lifeboats are sturdy, self-righting craft, manœuvrable in severe seas. They vary in size from 5-m (15-foot) inflatables to vessels of 17 m (55 feet) or more, capable of taking on board as many as 150 people.

life cycle The phases of an organism's life, and the manner in which it produces the next generation. This includes the production of GAMETES and their fusing during FERTILIZATION and the transition from an EMBRYO stage to the final mature adult stage.

Most organisms have a life cycle involving a single adult stage preceded by egg and juvenile, or larval, stages. The stages within each life cycle are adaptations for optimal survival of offspring. Most vertebrates have young which resemble their parents in most respects except sexual maturity. Many invertebrates have highly specialized immature stages, such as the caterpillar stage of some insects, or the floating planktonic larvae of crabs and marine molluscs.

In plants, including mosses and ferns, and in some algae, **alternation of generations** may be observed – they have two types of 'adult'. In mosses, these consist of a leafy gamete-producing plant called a gametophyte, and a spore-producing plant called a sporophyte. In ferns, the dominant plant is the sporophyte, while the other type, the gametophyte, is a small fleshy plant.

Aphids also show alternation of life cycle with regard to their mode of reproduction and the structure of the adult.

life expectancy The average number of further years that a person of a specified age in a given population may expect to live. The most common calculation is life expectancy at birth, often used as an indicator of the PUBLIC HEALTH and social development of a country. Between 1950 and 1955 and 1985 and 1990, life expectancy at birth rose from 65 to 74 years in Europe, from 51 to 65 years in South America, from 41 to 61 years in Asia, and from 38 to 52 years in Africa. The UN predicts that this convergence will continue. One consequence of increased life expectancy is an ageing population (especially of women, whose life expectancy is longer than that of men). See also MORTALITY RATE.

life-support machine See HEART–LUNG MACHINE; RESPIRATOR; INTENSIVE-CARE UNIT.

Liffey A river of eastern Ireland, which flows for 80 km (50 miles) from the Wicklow mountains to Dublin Bay. The city of Dublin is situated at its mouth.

Lifford The county town of Donegal in the Republic of Ireland, separated from Strabane in Tyrone, Northern Ireland, by the River Finn; pop. (1986) 1,460. It was a seat of the O'Donnells.

lift (US **elevator**) An enclosed platform (car) that transports goods or passengers in a vertical passage (shaft). In the electric lift, wire ropes run over a pulley support the car at one end and a counterweight at the other. The mechanism is driven by an electric motor at the shaft top. The load to be raised is thus the difference in weight between the car and the counterweight. A hydraulic lift is supported from below by a vertical ram extending beneath the lift shaft, and the car is raised by pumping oil into the ram. In 1990, the first lifts driven by LINEAR MOTORS were installed in Japan. The motor is incorporated into the lift counterweight. Modern automatic lifts are directed by microprocessors to answer calls in physical rather than chronological sequence. Doors will open only when the car is properly aligned with the floor. Door-edge sensors detect obstructions, stopping the lift until they are cleared. In skyscrapers, a combination of local and express lifts is used.

ligand (in chemistry) A molecule or negative ion that can bond to a metal forming a complex ion. Ligands all possess a LONE PAIR of electrons; H_2O, NH_3, and CN^- are common examples. Ligands that have several atoms each of which can bond to a metal are called polydentate or chelating; EDTA (ethylene-diaminetetraacetic acid) is the most important polydentate ligand.

Ligeti, György (Sándor) (1923–) Hungarian composer. His early studies were interrupted by World War II, and later his most advanced music, influenced by SCHOENBERG and WEBERN, was banned in Hungary. When the 1956 Soviet invasion made the political situation even worse, he emigrated to the West. In such works as *Atmosphères* (1961) he removed melody, harmony, and rhythm as distinct features, replacing them with an overall cluster of sound. The *Requiem* (1965) elaborates this idea in terms of a highly complex evanescent counterpoint, though later works, such as the *Double Concerto* (1972), go some way towards rediscovering melody.

light ELECTROMAGNETIC RADIATION to which the human eye is sensitive. It can be regarded either as a wave motion or as a stream of particles: the photon is the 'particle' of wave energy. The wave nature of light is demonstrated by DIFFRACTION and INTERFERENCE; the particle nature is evident from the PHOTOELECTRIC EFFECT. This visible radiation region lies between about 380 and 750 nm WAVELENGTH, the actual boundaries varying slightly from person to person. The eye is not equally sensitive to all the wavelengths in this region, the sensitivity being low at the boundaries and maximizing in the green-yellow part between around 500 and 550 nm. Light occupies only a narrow portion of the total electromagnetic spectrum, a portion sandwiched between the ultraviolet and the infrared. The colour of the light changes with the wavelength and white light can be broken into a spectrum of colours using a prism, diffraction grating, or a rainbow-producing raindrop. NEWTON categorized this spectrum in terms of seven colours: red, orange, yellow, green, blue, indigo, and violet. White light is a mixture of all the colours, consisting of a continuous range of wavelengths.

Light is produced when electrons in solids and gases that have been excited to higher energies by heat or an electrical discharge return to their original ground state; the excess energy is then released as radiation, although not all of it needs be in the visible range. For true white light to appear, the temperature of the body emitting it must be about 6,000°C. The SPEED OF LIGHT in a vacuum is approximately 3×10^8 m/s (9.85×10^8 feet per second) and is the maximum speed that can be obtained in the Universe. The radiation travels in a straight line for as long as the medium through which it passes is homogeneous. If, however, it passes into another medium, part of it may be subject to REFLECTION at the boundary and the remainder subject to REFRACTION as it enters the new medium – that is, the direction of its path is altered. The action of light on the chlorophyll in plants (photosynthesis) supplies energy for reactions that convert carbon dioxide from the air and water from the ground into starches and sugars; its action in initiating various other PHOTOCHEMICAL REACTIONS (such as those that occur on photographic film) is studied in photochemistry.

light bulb See INCANDESCENT LAMP.

light-emitting diode (LED) A solid-state source of illumination, essentially a semiconductor DIODE that emits light when it conducts. LEDs are used in electronics principally as indicators, since they do not generally provide enough power for usable illumination; they are also used in optical transmitters in OPTICAL FIBRE systems. Common applications include displays for calculators and digital watches, and numerical read-outs of all kinds. In these instances, they are usually arranged as groups of seven-segment displays. However, for much battery-powered portable equipment, LEDs consume too much power, and have been superseded in these instances by LIQUID CRYSTAL DISPLAYS.

lighter See BARGE.

lighthouse A tower or other structure containing a beacon light to warn or guide ships at sea. Until the 19th century lighthouses were lit by wood, oil, or coal. The light signal was dramatically improved by the use of LENSES (especially the FRESNEL lens) and reflectors to concentrate the beam. Later, beacons were rotated using motors. In the early 20th century acetylene gas lamps, and later electricity, were used instead of oil lamps. Individual lighthouses display characteristic patterns of light – fixed, flashing, fixed and flashing, or occulting (with short dark intervals) – that allow them to be identified. Light signals are often supplemented by sound produced by horns, sirens or radio and radar beacons that are detectable by navigators. Until recently, lighthouses were crewed, but increasingly they are changing to automatic operation. In conditions in which lighthouses cannot operate, LIGHTSHIPS OF LANBY BUOYS are used.

lighting The production of illumination by artificial means. All forms of lighting used up to 100 years ago depended on the combustion of either solid or liquid fuels. Oil lamps were improved steadily until the beginning of the 20th century. The paraffin lamp was extensively used in rural districts. GAS LIGHTING was in common use in urban areas by the mid-19th century in houses, factories, and for street-lighting. Around 1870 the INCANDESCENT LAMP was invented independently by SWAN and EDISON, heralding the beginning of the modern lighting era. The ELECTRICITY GENERATION AND SUPPLY industry initially arose to supply power for electric lighting. The development of tungsten filaments in the early 1900s was an important advance, allowing lamps to run at a higher temperature and therefore emit more and whiter light for the same electrical input. The neon light was developed during the late 19th century, and was used for decoration and advertising. Other GAS-DISCHARGE LAMPS using mercury and sodium were used for street-lighting; xenon discharge tubes are used in lighthouses. In the 1930s the FLUORESCENT LAMP was developed; this is very efficient for lighting interiors. More recent developments include microscopic filament lamps, enabling surgeons to examine the internal cavities of a patient's body (ENDOSCOPY).

light meter See EXPOSURE METER.

lightning An enormous spark generated by the discharge of static electricity within a cloud, between two clouds, or between a cloud and the ground. If the flash takes a zigzag or branching path through the atmosphere it is known as forked lightning, while if the flash is diffused by clouds it is known as sheet lightning. The presence of ice in the upper portions of a CUMULONIMBUS cloud is particularly associated with the generation and separation of ELECTRIC CHARGES. A flash occurs when a large enough charge has built up within the cloud, and it heats the air so rapidly that the air along it suddenly expands, producing thunder.

lightning conductor A pointed metal rod projecting above a building to provide an easy path for a lightning strike to discharge to Earth, without causing structural damage. The point of the rod ionizes the surrounding air, making it more conductive so that it attracts lightning. Several lightning conductors may be fixed to the highest parts of a structure and connected to a thick metal tape running down the structure and into the ground. The principle was discovered by FRANKLIN in the late 18th century.

lightship A dumb vessel (one without motive power) moored over a shoal or bank, serving the same purpose as a LIGHTHOUSE. The warning light is mounted on a mast amidships, and the ship carries special markings for recognition by day. The lightship is also fitted with acoustic fog and submarine signalling equipment, and with a RADAR beacon. Lightships were first used in the late 18th century. Normally each ship carries a crew of three or four men, but increasingly they are changing to automatic operation. See also LANBY BUOY.

light-year The distance covered in one year by light or other electromagnetic radiation travelling in a vacuum. One light-year is equal to 9.46×10^{15} m, 63,000 ASTRONOMICAL UNITS, or 0.31 PARSECS. Although astronomers more usually use the parsec for stellar and larger distances, the light-year more easily indicates light travel times. For example, a radio message would take 2 million years to travel the 2 million light-years to the Andromeda Galaxy.

lignite An organic brown sedimentary rock that tends to crumble on exposure to the air. It is a low-grade COAL made up of accumulated plant material and wood. It contains about 60 to 70 per cent carbon and burns with a smoky flame. Extensive deposits occur in the CRETACEOUS and TERTIARY coalfields of North America and Europe.

lignum vitae The wood of six species of the tree genus *Guaiacum*, native to tropical America. All are evergreen trees and the common name of lignum vitae is often applied to *G. officinale*. This has a greenish-brown, hard, heavy wood, from which medicinal guaiacum is obtained.

lilac A small tree of the genus *Syringa*. There are some 30 species of lilac, all with scented flowers. They are members of the olive family. Common lilac, *Syringa vulgaris*, has white or purple flowers in conical, drooping bunches. Persian lilac, *Syringa × persica*, is a hybrid with common lilac as one parent. The Indian tree, *Melia azedarach*, belonging to the mahogany family, is known by several other names, including lilac, China tree, pride of India, and bead tree.

Lilienthal, Otto (1848–96) German pioneer of aeronautics. In about 1880, after a close study of bird flight, he began to experiment with gliders. This stimulated popular interest in gliding as a sport, and he himself made more than 2,000 flights. In 1895 he built a biplane incorporating a small motor to flap the wings, but a mechanical defect led to a fatal crash the following year.

Lilith In Hebrew folklore, the female demon who attempts to kill new-born children. In the Talmud, Lilith is said to be Adam's first wife, dispossessed by Eve. In another version of the legend, Lilith deserts Adam to become a fiend.

Lille An industrial city of north-west France, near the border with Belgium, capital of the department of Nord in the Nord-Pas-de-Calais region; pop. (1990) 178,300. It is the home of the Pasteur Institute and was the first place in the world to introduce an automatic metro system (1982). It is a commercial, cultural, and manufacturing centre renowned for its textiles.

Lillee, Dennis (Keith) (1949–) Australian cricketer. He was a notable fast bowler who took 355 wickets in 70 matches during his career in test cricket (1971–84).

Lilongwe The capital of Malawi, a modern town built after its designation in 1975; pop. (1987) 233,970. It is an agricultural trading centre.

lily The common name for many members of the family Liliaceae, whose 3,500 worldwide species make it one of the largest families of monocotyledonous flowering plants. This family includes many popular garden plants, such as tulips, *Tulipa* species, hyacinths, *Hyacinthus* species, and the true lilies, *Lilium* species. It also includes vegetables such as onions, *Allium* species, leeks, *A. porrum*, and garlic, *A. sativum*. Most members of the family arise from bulbs, corms, or fleshy roots.

The true lilies, with some 80 species and many hybrids, include the Madonna lily, *L. candidum*, the martagon or Turk's cap lily, *L. martagon*, and the tiger lily, *L. tigrinum*. Other species within the lily family, which are given the common name of lily, include the African lily, *Agapanthus* species, the glory lily, *Gloriosa simplex*, and the day-lilies, *Hemerocallis* species. WATERLILIES and the Guernsey lily, *Nerine sarniensis*, are unrelated plants.

Lima The capital and largest city of Peru, situated on the River Rímac at the foot of the Cerro San Cristóbal; pop. (1993) 5,706,130. It was founded in 1535 by Francisco Pizarro who named it the 'city of the kings' and was capital of the Spanish colonies in South America until the 19th century. Its port on the Pacific coast is Callao. One of the largest cities of South America, its university (founded 1551) is the oldest in the western hemisphere. Lima is the site of most of Peru's manufacturing industries.

Limassol A port and resort town on the south coast of Cyprus, on Akrotiri Bay; pop. (est. 1993) 143,400. Its economy has expanded considerably since the partition of Cyprus. There is a British military base nearby.

Limbe A resort town in the south-west province of Cameroon, situated on the Atlantic coast west of Douala; pop. (1981) 32,920. Formerly known as Victoria, it was for a time the capital of British Cameroon.

limbo In medieval Christian theology, a region on the border of hell, the supposed abode of pre-Christian righteous persons, such as the patriarchs and prophets of the Old Testament, and of unbaptized infants and adults, who merit neither the torments of hell nor the bliss of heaven in their afterlives.

Limburg (French **Limbourg**) A province in north-east Belgium, comprising the districts of Hasselt, Maaseik, and Tongeren; area 2,422 sq km (935 sq miles); pop. (1991) 750,435; capital, Hasselt. The province gives its name to the soft white and strong-smelling Limburger cheese which was originally made here.

lime ▶**1** A thick-skinned greenish fruit of the tree *Citrus aurantifolia*. The juice of limes is very sour, containing up to 8 per cent citric acid, which may be extracted commercially. All citrus fruit juices are rich in vitamin C, and lime juice was once drunk by sailors in the British navy to prevent scurvy – hence their nickname of 'Limeys'. ▶**2** See LIME TREE.

lime (or **quicklime**, **calcium oxide**, CaO) A white, caustic, alkaline solid, obtained by roasting limestone (calcium carbonate) to drive off carbon as carbon dioxide. Lime reacts vigorously with water to form slaked lime (calcium hydroxide). Lime and slaked lime are used in building for MORTARS, PLASTERS, and CEMENT, and in agriculture to neutralize acid soils. Lime is a major raw material for the chemical industry, and in the IRON AND STEEL INDUSTRY it is used to form slag. It is also used as a refactory, and as a dehydrating agent. In agriculture, calcium carbonate and other alkaline substances used to treat acid soils are referred to as 'lime'.

Limerick ▶**1** A county of south-west Ireland, in the province of Munster; pop. (1991) 161,856; area 2,686 sq km (1,026 sq miles). ▶**2** Its county town, on the River Shannon; pop. (1991) 52,040. A commercial and food-processing centre, noted for its ham and bacon.

limestone A sedimentary rock consisting mainly of calcium carbonate ($CaCO_3$) in the form of calcite but also of magnesium carbonate. It can be of organic or inorganic origin, or it may be detrital (derived from an earlier limestone). Most limestones are organic: CHALK and OOLITE are examples. Pure limestones are usually white or whitish, and consist of the calcium carbonate remaining from the secretions, shells, or skeletons of plants and animals (such as corals, molluscs, and crustaceans). Chemically formed limestones are precipitated from water containing dissolved calcium carbonate. They are generally less soluble and more resistant to weathering. Travertine is a type of limestone deposited by springs, and is used as an ornamental material. All limestones may be coloured by impurities, such as sulphur, carbon, and iron.

Limestones for commercial use are obtained by quarrying and used extensively for a wide range of purposes. In the construction industry, it is used as a structural material in building and sculpture, and as road ballast. It is subject to attack by acid, and high levels of industrial pollution cause rapid and obvious corrosion. It is one of the raw materials used to make CEMENT. On heating, it decomposes to produce LIME and carbon dioxide gas. It is used to remove sulphur from coal and sulphur dioxide from industrial waste gases. It is also used to remove silicon-based impurities in the BLAST-FURNACE production of iron.

lime tree A tree belonging to the genus *Tilia*, of which there are 50 or so species, mostly confined to the north temperate zone. Lime trees have heart-shaped leaves and sweetly scented flowers which produce large amounts of nectar to attract insect pollinators. Their soft, pale wood is used for plywood and brush handles, that of *T. americana* being the basswood of commerce. Limes form part of the family Tiliaceae, which also includes many species whose bark is a source of fibre or jute, for rope making and matting.

The LIME fruit is produced by unrelated trees of the citrus family.

lime water A solution of calcium hydroxide, $Ca(OH)_2$, in water used as an antacid or more commonly to detect the presence of carbon dioxide, CO_2. When carbon dioxide is passed through lime water, the solution will turn milky as calcium carbonate, $CaCO_3$, is precipitated.

limited liability A limitation on the financial liability of the shareholders in a COMPANY for the debts of that company; they can lose only the value of their share-holdings. A limited company may be a private limited company or a public limited company (PLC); the latter is one whose shares are traded on the STOCK EXCHANGE. Owners of businesses with unlimited liability may have to use their personal property to pay the debts of the business.

Limoges A city of west-central France, capital of the department of Haute-Vienne and principal city of the Limousin Region; pop. (1990) 136,400. It was famous in the 16th–17th centuries for enamel work and later for porcelain. Hydroelectric power, the mining of uranium, and the manufacture of shoes are important industries.

limonite Any rock rich in iron oxides that cannot be identified without complex laboratory tests. It is always of secondary origin and is often the product of tropical weathering of iron ore. It is rarely found in old rocks but is common in bogs and LATERITE.

limpet A conical gastropod MOLLUSC common on rocky shores. Limpets cling tightly to the rock using a broad, muscular foot, resisting wave action and predators. When the tide covers them, they move over the rocks to browse on algae and always return to the same precise home-site. The trail left by their rasping 'tongue' is a familiar sight on otherwise algae-coated rocks. There are many species around the world.

limpkin An American water-bird, *Aramus guarauna*, with a single species in the family Aramidae. Glossy olive-brown flecked with white, it inhabits wooded marshes, feeds on snails leaving the shells undamaged, and utters loud wailing cries, mainly at night.

Limpopo A river of south-east Africa that rises as the Crocodile River near Johannesburg, South Africa, and flows 1,770 km (1,100 miles) in a great curve north and east to meet the Indian Ocean north-east of Maputo in Mozambique. For much of its course it forms the boundary between north-east South Africa and the neighbouring countries of Botswana and Zimbabwe.

linac See LINEAR ACCELERATOR.

Linacre, Thomas (*c.*1460–1524) English physician and classical scholar. In 1518 he founded the College of Physicians in London, and became its first president. He wrote textbooks on Latin grammar, and his students of Greek included Thomas More and probably Erasmus. Linacre's translations of Galen's Greek works on medicine and philosophy into Latin brought about a revival of studies in anatomy, botany, and clinical medicine in Britain.

Lin Biao (or **Lin Piao**) (1908–71) Chinese Communist statesman and general. After joining the Communists (1927) he became a commander of Mao Zedong's Red Army in the fight against the Kuomintang. He was appointed Minister of Defence (1959) and then Vice-Chairman under Mao (1966), later being nominated to become Mao's successor (1969). Having staged an unsuccessful coup in 1971, Lin Biao was reported to have been killed in an aeroplane crash while fleeing to the Soviet Union.

Lincoln A city in eastern England, on the River Witham, county town of Lincolnshire; pop. (1991) 81,900. Known to the Romans as Lindum Colonia, it lay at the junction of Fosse Way and Ermine Street. Its cathedral, begun in the 11th century, has one of the four original copies of the Magna Carta. The city specializes in the manufacture of farm machinery.

Lincoln The capital and second-largest city of the US state of Nebraska; pop. (1990) 191,970. Founded in 1856 and originally known as Lancaster, it was renamed in honour of Abraham Lincoln and made state capital in 1867. It is the home of the University of Nebraska (1869). A marketing and financial centre.

Lincoln, Abraham (1809–65) US Republican statesman, 16th President of the USA 1861–65. His election as President on an anti-slavery platform antipathetic to the interests of the southern states helped precipitate the American Civil War. He eventually managed to unite the Union side behind the anti-slavery cause and emancipation was formally proclaimed on New Year's Day, 1864. Lincoln won re-election in 1864, but was assassinated shortly after the surrender of the main Confederate army had ended the war. During his lifetime Lincoln was noted for his succinct, eloquent speeches, including the Gettysburg address of 1863.

Lincolnshire An eastern county of England; pop. (1990) 573,900; area 5,918 sq km (2,286 sq miles); county town, Lincoln.

Lincoln's Inn One of the Inns of Court in London where legal societies traditionally admit people to the English bar. Thomas de Lincoln, king's sergeant in the 14th century, may have been an early landlord.

Lind, James (1716–94) Scottish physician. After a period as a naval surgeon he performed some famous experiments which demonstrated that sailors could be cured of scurvy by supplementing their diet with citrus fruit. It was not until just after his death that the Royal Navy officially adopted the practice of giving lime juice to sailors. His work was a major step towards the discovery of vitamins.

Lind, Jenny (born Johanna Maria Lind Goldschmidt) (1820–87) Swedish soprano. Known as 'the Swedish nightingale' for the purity and agility of her voice, she achieved international success with her performances in opera, oratorio, and concerts. She funded musical scholarships and other charitable causes in England and Sweden.

Lindbergh, Charles (Augustus) (1902–74) US aviator. In 1927 he made the first solo transatlantic flight, taking 33½ hours to fly from New York to Paris, in a single-engined monoplane, *Spirit of St Louis*. Lindbergh moved to Europe with his wife to escape the publicity surrounding the kidnap and murder of his two-year-old son in 1932.

Linde, Carl Paul Gottfried von (1842–1934) German engineer, an early innovator of REFRIGERATION. In 1879 he designed the first domestic refrigerator, which he manufactured until 1892. In 1895 he designed a plant for the large-scale liquefaction of air, some seven years before CLAUDE. He later (1901) developed a process for obtaining oxygen from liquid air, which led to the development of many industrial processes utilizing oxygen.

Lindemann, Frederick Alexander See CHERWELL.

Lindisfarne (or **Holy Island**) A small island off the coast of Northumberland, north-east England, north of the Farne Islands. It is linked to the mainland by a causeway exposed only at low tide. Lindisfarne is the site of a church and monastery founded by St Aidan (635), a missionary centre of the Celtic Church. Driven from the island by Vikings in 875, the monks returned to rebuild the priory in 1082 renaming the island Holy Island. In 1903 Lindisfarne Castle was restored to a design by Edwin Lutyens for Edward Hudson, the owner and founder of the magazine *Country Life*.

Lindsey A region of eastern England, in Lincolnshire. An area of early settlement by the Angles, it became an Anglo-Saxon kingdom ruled by its own kings until the 8th century. Known also as the Parts of Lindsey, the region was one of three administrative divisions or 'ridings' of Lincolnshire (the others were Holland and Kesteven) until 1974, when it was divided between Humberside and Lincolnshire.

linear accelerator (or **linac**) A PARTICLE ACCELERATOR in which charged particles are repeatedly accelerated through a long straight tube by an electric field of radio frequency produced by a klystron or magnetron. The accelerated high-energy particles are used in high-energy research. Some linear accelerators up to 3.5 km long can accelerate electrons to 50 GeV. The engineering problems associated with such a device are clearly formidable, however, and proton synchrotrons have therefore largely replaced them for high-energy research.

linearity (in mathematics) A relationship between two variables (x and y, say) which if plotted as a GRAPH is a straight line. Direct proportionalities, such as that between speed and distance travelled in a certain time, are examples. All linear relationships are described by equations like $y = mx + c$, where m and c are arbitrary constants.

Linearity has another meaning in the context of DIFFERENTIAL EQUATIONS. For linear differential equations, if functions $F(x)$ and $G(x)$ are each solutions, then $aF(x) + bG(x)$ is also a solution. (Here a and b are arbitrary constants, and this way of combining functions is called a linear combination.) An exact analogy is with a tuned string on an instrument. It can vibrate at several frequencies, all related to a fundamental (or lowest) frequency. Equally, its mode of vibration can be any combination of those frequencies. (This partly accounts for the richness of musical sounds.) Non-linear equations lack this property. They are often insoluble without a computer, and are intimately connected with CHAOS. The concept of linearity (in its second sense) is widely used in mathematics, physics, and engineering.

linear motor A type of induction ELECTRIC MOTOR, providing straight-line movement rather than rotation, principally designed for high-speed railway systems and other traction applications (see GROUND-GUIDANCE SYSTEMS). In high-speed railway systems, one conductor is attached to the track and the other mounted on the vehicle base. Electric power for energizing the conductors is provided on board the train, or from a track-based supply. Coils on the vehicle generate a magnetic field in which the poles move along the length of the vehicle. The field induces electric currents in the track, which itself generates a magnetic field. The two fields interact, moving the vehicle along the track. The vehicle and track do not make significant contact, ensuring high speeds and comfort. However, because the technology is radically different from established traction systems, linear motors have not yet found widespread use in transportation. Other proven applications include high-speed conveyor systems, and electrostatic PUMPS. The linear motor was developed by E. R. Laithwaite (1921–89).

linear script A script used to write the language of the Minoan civilization in Crete. Linear A was used between 1700 and 1450 BC. Some 400 inscriptions on clay tablets are known, but the language is undeciphered. Linear B, adapted from Linear A by the invading Mycenaeans to write their own language, is seen on several thousand clay tablets dating from 1400 to 1100 BC. Linear B was deciphered by Michael Ventris (1922–56) in 1952, who found it to be an early form of Greek.

Lineker, Gary (Winston) (1960–) British footballer. A fast, alert striker, Lineker started his career with Leicester City (1976–85) before going on to play for Everton (1985–86), Barcelona (1986–89), and Tottenham Hotspur (1989–92). He played for England 80 times (1984–92), scoring 48 goals, one short of Bobby Charlton's England record. After a spell in Japan he retired in 1994 and became a television sports broadcaster.

linen See FLAX.

liner A ship employed on a scheduled ocean route carrying passengers, although some liners also carry cargo. Most of the STEAMSHIP companies operating such services began as mail-carriers, the government subsidies providing the economic base for future expansion. The extensive emigrations of Europeans to the USA during the 19th century led to a rapid expansion of liner services. By World War I liners of over 30,000 tonnes and capable of carrying more than 2,000 passengers were in operation to accommodate the demand for travel. In the years between the two World Wars demand doubled, with liners of up to 83,000 tonnes carrying passengers in luxury at speeds of about 30 KNOTS. During World War II liners were extensively used as troopships. After World War II air travel began to compete seriously with the ocean liner. By 1957 more passengers were travelling by air than by sea. Most of the large liners became obsolete, but a few continue to operate as cruise ships.

lines of force The imaginary patterns in space that represent the strength and the direction of a magnetic or electric field at any point. They are usually represented in diagrams as sets of lines, which are close together in some places and further apart in others. The direction of the lines indicates the direction of the field and the density of lines in a particular area is a measure of the strength of the field.

ling (animal) An elongate fish, *Ophiodon elongatus*, of the cod family, with two dorsal fins, a single anal fin, and the typical chin barbel. It is a moderately deep-water fish living on rocky grounds and especially on wrecks, and growing to a length of 2 m (6.5 feet). It feeds almost exclusively on fishes, ranging from northern Norway and Iceland, southwards to the Bay of Biscay.

ling (plant) See HEATHER.

lingua franca A LANGUAGE used among people with no common native language. English and French are the most widespread lingua francas. Other examples include Swahili in East Africa and Latin in medieval Europe. Originally lingua franca, meaning 'French language' referred to a variety of Provençal used during the Crusades (11th–14th centuries) by Crusaders of different native languages.

linguistic philosophy A school of PHILOSOPHY that emphasizes the analysis of concepts as they are used in everyday natural (as opposed to artificial) languages, such as English. Suggested by the work of WITTGENSTEIN, it is part of the tradition of ANALYTIC PHILOSOPHY and prominent in British philosophy in the 1950s and 1960s, when its leading figures were Gilbert RYLE and J(ohn) L(angshaw) AUSTIN. Linguistic philosophers believe that many philosophical problems arise because of the lack of clarity that results from the way in which we use language; in particular, from our lack of attention to the differences between words and phrases that are used in superficially similar ways. For example, Austin approached the problem of FREE WILL by contrasting the use of 'if' in 'he could have done so if he had chosen' with the uses of 'if' in straightforward indicative conditionals such as 'if it is raining you will get wet'.

linguistics The science of LANGUAGE. As a science, it is concerned to develop theories and evaluate them on the basis of objective data. Measurement and experiment are also features of some branches of linguistics. Central to modern linguistics is the study of languages as formal systems through GRAMMAR, PHONOLOGY, and SEMANTICS. Also important is the study in PSYCHOLINGUISTICS of the way language is used by speakers, and the study in sociolinguistics of the way language functions in society. Modern linguistics is mainly synchronic (concerned with languages at a single point in time), but some work is diachronic (concerned with language change over time). A further important distinction is between theoretical or descriptive linguistics, which is concerned to increase our understanding of language, and applied linguistics, which seeks to use this understanding in various ways, especially in connection with language teaching. Historical and comparative linguistics studies the development of particular languages and their relationship to each other. See also CLINICAL LINGUISTICS.

Linklater, Eric (1899–1974) Scottish writer. He taught English at Aberdeen University before moving to the USA (1928–30). In America he wrote *Poet's Pub* (1929) and *Juan in America* (1931). His later books include *Private Angelo* (1946) and *The House of Gair* (1953).

Linnaeus, Carolus (born Carl von Linné) (1707–78) Swedish botanist, founder of modern systematic botany and zoology. He devised a classification system for flowering plants based on stamen type and number of pistils, and became the authority to whom collectors all over the world sent specimens. He described over 7,000 plants, introducing binomial Latin names, although his classification was later superseded by that of Antoine Jussieu. His classification of animals was less satisfactory, as he paid little attention to internal anatomy. He set out his system in *Systema Naturae* (1735) and other works. The tenth edition of this (1758) and *Species Plantarum* (1753) are internationally recognized as the starting-points for zoological and botanical nomenclature respectively.

linnet A common FINCH found in much of Europe and western Asia, where it occurs in open, bushy country. The female is rather sparrow-like, but the male has a brown back, a greyish head with a red crown and a red breast. The species *Carduelis cannabina* is commonly kept as a cage-bird because of its pleasing, melodious song.

linoleum A durable floor-covering material. First made *c*.1860, linoleum consists of a layer of a cork-like material, typically about 3 mm (0.12 inch) thick, backed by a textile fabric. The cork-like material (consisting of finely ground cork bound together by natural resins and oxidized linseed oil) is extruded as a uniform sheet and is pressed into ADHESIVE contact with the base fabric (usually woven jute). Linoleum was almost completely displaced by cheaper synthetic materials until the advent of its modern equivalent, marmoleum, in the 1990s.

Linotype See TYPESETTING.

Lin Piao See LIN BIAO.

linseed oil See FLAX; DRYING OIL.

Linz The chief industrial city of northern Austria, on the River Danube; pop. (1991) 202,855. It is capital of the state of Upper Austria. For several years the composer Anton Bruckner was the organist at Linz cathedral. It has iron and steel, chemical, and textile industries.

lion The second largest of the big CATS (after the tiger), *Panthera leo*, now restricted to Africa, except for a few Asiatic lions surviving in a reserve. The African lions live in prides of three to 30 individuals on the veld and in scrub country, each pride with its own territory. Prides can cover 48 km (30 miles) in a night. When chasing, lions can reach a speed of 48 km/hour (30 miles per hour) over a short distance. Their prey includes zebra, waterbuck, and antelope, but they will eat anything from carrion to fish.

The male lion stands about 90 cm (3 feet) at the shoulders; the lioness is a little smaller. The mane on the shoulders and head of the male makes him seem even larger than he is. After a gestation of about 105 days, two or three cubs are born, each about 30 cm (1 foot) long.

Lipari Islands (formerly **Aeolian Islands**) A group of seven Italian islands and ten islets in the Tyrrhenian Sea off the north coast of Sicily. They are the summits of a submerged chain of volcanoes, reaching a maximum height of 962 m (3,156 feet) above sea-level on Salina. Only the eastern volcanoes are still active; Stromboli's last major eruption was in 1921, and Vulcano erupted in 1890. There are hot springs on Lipari, largest of the islands.

Lipchitz, Jacques (born Chaim Jacob Lipchitz) (1891–1973) Lithuanian-born French sculptor. In 1909 he moved to Paris, where he produced cubist works, such as *Sailor with a Guitar* (1914). During the 1920s he produced his influential series of 'transparent' sculptures, which explore the interpenetration of solids and voids, and by the time he moved to the USA in 1941 he had become internationally recognized. His later works include the massive *Prometheus Strangling the Vulture II* (1944–53).

lipid An organic compound, part of a major group comprising FATS AND OILS, waxes, phospholipids, and steroids. The molecules of all these substances contain a high proportion of CH_2 groups and therefore are generally not soluble in water, but are readily soluble in organic solvents, such as ethanol and chloroform. Fats and oils are built up from FATTY ACIDS and glycerol and are commonly used for energy storage. Waxes are formed from fatty acids and complex alcohols and provide a waterproof surface layer on the leaves of plants and the exoskeletons of insects; bees use wax for building their honeycombs. Phospholipids have a similar structure to fats, but one of the fatty acids is replaced by a phosphate group, which links the molecule to a complex alcohol. This creates a molecule one end of which dissolves easily in water (hydrophilic), while the other end is insoluble in water (hydrophobic).

Lipizza (Slovenian **Lipica**) A village in Slovenia, formerly the home of the Austrian Imperial Stud where the white **Lipizzaner** horse was originally bred. Noted since Roman times as a centre of horse breeding, the stud was established in 1580 by Archduke Charles of Austria. The horses have long been trained to give spectacular displays at the Spanish Riding School in Vienna.

Li Po (or **Li Bo**, **Li T'ai Po**) (701–62 AD) Chinese poet. He had a bohemian lifestyle at the emperor's court, alternating with long periods of wandering. Typical themes in his poetry are wine, women, and the beauties of nature.

Lippi, Filippino (*c*.1457–1504) Italian painter, son of Fra Filippo LIPPI. Having trained with his father and Botticelli he completed the fresco cycle on the life of St Peter in the Brancacci Chapel, Florence (*c*.1481–83), a project begun by Masaccio. His other works include the series of frescos in the Carafa Chapel in Rome (1488–93) and the painting *The Vision of St Bernard* (*c*.1486).

Lippi, Fra Filippo (*c*.1406–69) Italian painter. He joined a Carmelite order, but later renounced his vows in order to marry; he was the father of the painter Filippino LIPPI. He was inspired by Masaccio, whose influence can be seen in the fresco *The Relaxation of the Carmelite Rule* (*c*.1432). His characteristic later style is more decorative and less monumental than his early work; typical works depict the Madonna as the central feature, stressing the human aspect of the theme. His paintings influenced the Pre-Raphaelites.

lip-reading A way of understanding spoken LANGUAGE by watching the position of the lips of the speaker, used by the deaf as an alternative to a SIGN LANGUAGE. Because the position of the lips is the same for several sounds, for example, 'm', 'b', and 'p', a special signing system distinguishing between the sounds often accompanies the speaker's performance.

liquefied natural gas NATURAL GAS that has had its LIQUID PETROLEUM GAS fraction removed, and has then been cooled and pressurized to make it liquefy. At normal pressure, natural gas (largely METHANE) liquefies at about −160°C. Until the 1960s, this low temperature made it impractical to transport large quantities of liquefied natural gas, although liquefaction reduces the volume by a factor of 600. Since then, specialist tankers have been developed to carry liquefied gas cargoes. Liquefied gas is also used as an underground storage medium.

liquid One of the three most common PHASES OF MATTER, the others being solids and gases. Like gases, liquids have no fixed shape, but they do have a fixed volume (as long as the temperature does not vary): they do not expand to fill the space available, and they are very difficult to compress into a smaller volume. The molecules or atoms in a liquid have sufficient thermal energy to move around freely, but there is also considerable intermolecular attraction between them. Liquids may be turned into solids by cooling them, and into gases or vapours by heating.

liquid crystal A PHASE OF MATTER, in addition to the more common solid, liquid, and gas. A small proportion of organic compounds, of which the ESTERS of cholesterol are the best known, can be obtained in the liquid crystal state. Their solids melt to form a turbid fluid, the liquid crystal; this fluid changes into a clear liquid, the true liquid state, at a higher temperature. The characteristic of liquid crystals is that although they are fluid, like ordinary liquids, they possess a far greater degree of ordering of their molecules than liquids, somewhat similar to that in a crystal. They contain long molecules which lie parallel to one another but which can move over each other. They have unusual optical properties, and these have given rise to important applications. A thin clear layer of liquid crystal placed between two glass surfaces becomes opaque when a voltage is applied across it, and this is used in electronic displays (see LIQUID CRYSTAL DISPLAY), such as in digital watches. Some liquid crystals have colours that are highly temperature-sensitive, and these have been used in medicine, electronics, and the production of simple thermometers.

liquid crystal display (LCD) A type of display that has replaced the LIGHT-EMITTING DIODE in

WATCHES, CALCULATORS, and other portable, battery-operated applications. It consists of two polarizing filters, each of which allows passage of light waves in one plane. Below the filters is a mirror, and between them is a LIQUID CRYSTAL, a complex chemical whose molecules rearrange their crystal structure when an electric voltage is applied. When no voltage is present, the crystal rotates the light through 90 degrees. This allows the light to pass through both polarizing filters, and reflect back from the mirror, giving the display a light appearance. When a voltage is applied to any portion of the display, the liquid crystal in that portion rearranges, and light passes through it unrotated. The light cannot now pass through the second polarizing filter and the display appears black. Digits thus appear in black on a light background. LCDs are most commonly in the form of seven-segment displays, but also appear in many other forms, including complete screens and laptop and smaller portable computers. The power consumption of an LCD is negligible.

liquidity (in economics) The ease with which an asset can be exchanged for MONEY promptly and at little or no loss. For example, most deposits in banks and building societies are highly liquid, since they can be easily turned into cash. Shares and bonds may also be fairly liquid, if there is a well-organized and accessible market in these assets. Fixed CAPITAL, including housing, is typically an illiquid asset; even if a buyer can be found, selling takes time and transaction costs are significant.

liquid petroleum gas (LPG) A mixture of gases obtained from petroleum or NATURAL GAS, and stored as a liquid. The gases are kept in liquid form either by dissolving them in solvent oils or by storage in pressurized containers. The two main LPG gases are PROPANE (C_3H_8) and BUTANE (C_4H_{10}), which are either extracted from natural gas or produced in petroleum refining. LPG will stay liquid at much lower pressures than unprocessed natural gas, and is therefore easier and safer to store and transport. It is used in pressurized bottles as a fuel in caravans, boats, and homes without piped gas supply. LPG is also a viable alternative to petrol for powering vehicles. See also LIQUEFIED NATURAL GAS.

liquorice A perennial herbaceous plant, *Glycyrrhiza glaba*, which is unusual among legumes in that it is cultivated for the strongly flavoured extract from its roots, as opposed to using the seed or pods. Since ancient times it has been used to mask unpleasant tastes in foods. More recently, its flavour has been used in sweets, and also in various drinks and cough mixtures. It is grown mainly in the Mediterranean region, where the dried roots are often chewed.

lira A number of bowed, stringed musical instruments, among them the Greek and Turkish fiddles, but pre-eminently for the *lira da braccio*, the 15th- to 16th-century precursor of the VIOLIN. This was the size of a large viola, with five fingered strings and two DRONES. A larger instrument, the *lira da gamba* or *lirone*, resembled a bass VIOL but with many more strings. It was designed for playing chords as a CONTINUO instrument and remained in use into the 17th century.

Lisbon (Portuguese **Lisboa**) The capital of Portugal, built on seven hills at the mouth of the River Tagus; pop. (1991) 677,790. Occupied by the Romans in 205 and by the Moors in 714. Lisbon became capital of Portugal in the 13th century when Alfonso III transferred his court from Coimbra. It prospered during the Age of Discovery but was devastated by an earthquake in 1755. Much of the city was subsequently rebuilt by the Marqués de Pombal. Landmarks include St George's Castle, a 14th-century cathedral, the elevator built by Eiffel, the Monument of the Discoveries (1960), the 16th-century Tower of Belém, and the Convento dos Jerónimos de Belém which was built to commemorate Vasco da Gama's voyage to India in 1497. The city's industries include steel, oil refining, and shipbuilding and repair.

Lister, Joseph, 1st Baron (1827–1912) British surgeon, inventor of antiseptic techniques in surgery. In 1865 he became acquainted with Louis Pasteur's theory that putrefaction is due to microorganisms, and realized its significance in connection with sepsis in wounds, a major cause of deaths in patients who had undergone surgery. In the same year Lister first used carbolic acid dressings, and later he used a carbolic spray in the operating theatre. After about 1883 aseptic rather than antiseptic techniques became popular, though Lister believed in the use of both.

Listeria A genus of aerobic rodlike bacteria. The single species, *L. monocytogenes*, can infect warm-blooded animals. Infected animals or animal products, if consumed, can cause **listeriosis** in humans. This produces symptoms resembling influenza but can also cause meningoencephalitis (inflammation of the brain) and damage to the foetus in pregnant women. It can be treated with antibiotics.

Liston, Sonny (born Charles Liston) (1932–70) US boxer. He was encouraged to box at Missouri State penitentiary while serving a sentence for robbery, and launched a professional career in 1953. In 1962 he became world heavyweight champion by defeating Floyd Patterson, but in 1964 lost his title to Muhammad Ali (then Cassius Clay).

Liszt, Franz (1811–86) Hungarian composer and pianist. He was a key figure in the romantic movement and a virtuoso pianist; many of his piano compositions combine lyricism with great technical complexity. His orchestral works include the Faust and Dante Symphonies (1854–57; 1855–56); his 12 symphonic poems (1848–58) created a new musical form. He also composed masses, and oratorios, such as *Christus* (1862–67). Apart from his own influence as a composer and teacher, Liszt was also significant as a champion of the works of Wagner, who married Liszt's daughter, Cosima.

Li T'ai Po See LI PO.

litchi (or **lychee**) An evergreen tree, *Litchi chinensis*, belonging to a family (Sapindaceae) of 2,000 species of tropical and subtropical trees, shrubs, and lianas. The litchi, about 10 m (33 feet) tall, is a native of southern China and produces a round, thin-skinned, spiny fruit about 3 cm (1.25 inches) in diameter. The fruits may also be dried, when they are known as litchi nuts. Cultivation throughout the tropics has been only partially successful as the tree requires a cool, dry season to fruit well and does not prosper in moist, lowland regions. The rambutan has a very similar fruit with a prickly red skin. This is sometimes known as the hairy litchi.

literacy The ability to read and write. According to UNESCO, a person is literate 'who can with understanding both read and write a short simple statement on his everyday life', while a functionally literate person can 'engage in all those activities in which literacy is required for the effective functioning of his group and community'. Even taking the first definition, it is estimated that only three in four of the world's adults are literate. Levels of illiteracy are highest among women because, historically, women have had less access to EDUCATION than men. In 1985 two-thirds of the world's illiterates were women. The size of this gender gap is accounted for chiefly by the extremely large numbers of illiterate women in countries in South Asia, such as Bangladesh and Pakistan. Although illiteracy worldwide has been significantly reduced since World War II, recent figures suggest a slackening of pace. The task is complex. For example, a literacy student can achieve fluency more rapidly in his or her mother tongue than in a second language. But the multiplicity of languages and dialects within many developing nations, for example NIGER-CONGO LANGUAGES in Africa, and the fact that some are spoken but not written can present formidable obstacles to literacy teaching in the mother-tongue. In China, a nation with almost a fifth of the world's population, a command of at least 2,000 characters is necessary. Although Japanese experience shows that ideographic writing is not a bar to universal literacy, in China it imposes a heavy educational burden. None the less, much can be achieved by energetic national action.

lithium (symbol Li, at. no. 3, r.a.m. 6.94) A soft, metallic element in Group 1 (formerly IA) of the periodic table, the ALKALI METALS. It is obtained by the ELECTROLYSIS of a fused mixture of potassium and lithium chlorides. Lithium is reactive, and is stored under oil; it combines with non-metals, water, and acids, forming ionic compounds in which it has the charge +1, and a few covalent compounds. Lithium carbonate is used in glasses and ceramics, and as a tranquillizer in manic depression; lithium hydride is used as a source of hydrogen, and lithium hydroxide is used to absorb carbon dioxide in submarines. Lithium salts of fatty acids are widely used in LUBRICATING OILS as thickeners. The isotope lithium-6 forms TRITIUM when bombarded with neutrons.

lithography A method of printing from a design drawn directly on to a slab of stone or other suitable material, invented in 1798. The process is based on the antipathy of grease and water, the design being drawn with a greasy crayon on the stone. After it has been chemically fixed, the stone is wetted and then rolled with oily ink, which adheres only to the greasy drawing, the rest of the surface, being damp, repelling the ink. Prints can then be taken in a press. Many distinguished artists of the 19th century worked in the lithographic technique, notably Daumier. Once widely used for reproducing illustrations, the original process (direct lithography) has now been superseded by OFFSET LITHOGRAPHY.

lithosol A soil that forms in mountainous regions on steep slopes where erosion removes loose, weathered material very rapidly. Lithosols tend to be thin, generally less than 10–15 cm (6–12 inches). They are stony and lack distinct HORIZONS. They contain little organic matter because vegetation is sparse in rocky, upland areas.

lithosphere The crust and upper mantle of the Earth. It varies in thickness from 32 km (20 miles) to 64 km (40 miles).

lithotripsy The crushing of abnormal stone-like deposits within the bladder, using an instrument (a lithotrite) introduced into the urethra. The invention of the lithotripter in 1973 has made it possible to fragment some stones of the renal system, and of the gall bladder, using high-powered ULTRASOUND.

Lithuania A Baltic country, lying between Latvia to the north, Belarus to the east, and Poland to the south.

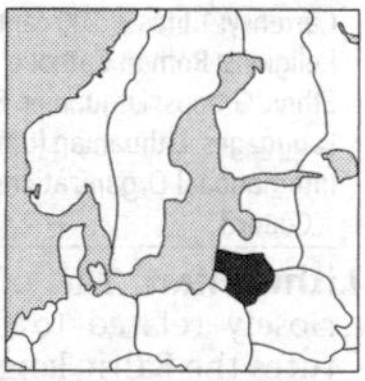

Physical. Lithuania has just some 25 km (15 miles) of Baltic Sea coast, and is predominantly flat, though hilly in the east, where there are many lakes. The lowland plain is forested and fertile; it is drained by the Nemen and its tributaries.

Economy. Lithuania is agriculturally self-sufficient, specializing in meat and milk production, but it depends on imports for supplies of energy and raw materials. There is some electricity production, but Lithuania relies on the unified grid of the north-west former Soviet Union for much of its electricity supply. Mineral resources are varied, including various chemicals, iron ore, and unexploited offshore oil deposits. Lithuania's main industries are machinery, shipbuilding, electronics, chemicals, and oil-refining, together with light industries such as food-processing.

History. Lithuania was a vast grand-duchy during the Middle Ages, stretching at one time from the Baltic to the Black Sea and almost to Moscow. By 1569 it had united with Poland and was absorbed into Russia in 1795 in the Third Partition. After an uprising in 1863 the Lithuanian language was forbidden, but nationalist and strong Social Democrat movements developed from the 1880s. It was occupied by German troops (1915–18), and in March 1918 a German king was elected. He was deposed in November and a republic proclaimed. Bolshevik troops now invaded from Russia and a short Russo-Lithuanian War ended in March 1920 with the Treaty of Moscow. This gave Lithuania German-speaking Memel, but it failed to gain Vilna (the present capital Vilnius), which went to Poland. At first a democratic republic, its politics polarized and a neo-Fascist dictatorship under Antanas Smetona was established in 1926. In October 1939 a Soviet-Lithuanian Pact allowed Lithuania to claim Vilna, Memel having been lost to the Germans. In July 1940 the Assembly voted for incorporation into the Soviet Union; but the country was occupied by the Germans (1941–44), when its large Jewish population was almost wiped out. Re-occupied by the Red Army in 1944, it became again a constituent Republic of the Soviet Union. In 1956 there were serious anti-Soviet riots, ruthlessly suppressed. In March 1990 a unilateral declaration of independence was made. The Soviet Union at first responded by an economic blockade, cutting off oil and gas supplies, but in May it agreed to negotiate, and in September 1991 recognized independence. In December citizenship was restricted to those with ten years residence, a knowledge of the language and constitution, and a source of income. During 1992 Lithuania negotiated a treaty of friendship with Poland and was granted IMF membership. A new constitution gave increased executive powers to the President. The Democratic Labour Party (the renamed Lithuanian Communist Party) won elections in 1992. In 1996 Prime Minister Adolfus Slezevicius was forced out of office for his part in a financial scandal. In June 1996 parliament ratified a treaty of association with the EU. With the other Baltic states of Estonia and Latvia, Lithuania is a member of the Baltic Council.

Capital: Vilnius
Area: 65,207 sq km (25,170 sq mi)
Population: 3,700,000 (1995)

Currency: 1 litas = 100 centai
Religions: Roman Catholic; Eastern Orthodox; Lutheran
Ethnic Groups: Lithuanian 80.0%; Russian 9.0%; Polish 7.0%
Languages: Lithuanian (official); Russian; minority languages
International Organizations: UN; CSCE; North Atlantic Co-operation Council

Lithuanian The official language of Lithuania, closely related to Latvian, with which it constitutes the Baltic language group.

litmus One of the oldest acid-base indicators: when added to acidic solutions it turns red, but in alkaline solutions it is blue. It is a mixture of dyes extracted from lichens, and is commonly absorbed on to filter paper to make litmus papers. Blue litmus papers are used to test for acidity, while red papers test for alkalinity.

Little Big Horn, Battle of (25 June 1876) Scene of General CUSTER's last stand in South Dakota when he and 266 men of the 7th Cavalry met their deaths at the hands of larger forces of Sioux. The battle was the final move in a well-planned strategy by the Sioux leader CRAZY HORSE, following the invasion of the Sioux Black Hills by white GOLD RUSH prospectors in violation of a treaty of 1868.

Little Dipper See URSA MINOR.

little owl A small grey-brown OWL, *Athene noctua*, that is widely distributed over Europe, Asia, and Africa and has been successfully introduced into New Zealand. The other species of the genus *Athene* are the spotted owlet, *A. brama*, and the forest owlet, *A. blewitti*. Evening and early-morning hunters of open woodlands and plains, all three species have taken readily to parkland, towns, and farms, where they hunt small rodents and insects. Their calls are shrill whistles and shrieks and they nest in trees, buildings or on cliffs, laying four or five eggs.

Little Rock An industrial centre and the capital of the state of Arkansas, USA, on the Arkansas River opposite North Little Rock; pop. (1990) 175,800. Named by French explorers to differentiate it from larger rock outcroppings further up river, Little Rock became state capital in 1821 when the seat of government was moved from Arkansas Post.

Littlewood, (Maud) Joan (1914–) British theatre director. She is best known for co-founding the Theatre Workshop (1945), which set out to present established plays in radical productions and to stage plays with contemporary working-class themes in the Theatre Royal, Stratford in east London. Memorable productions included Brendan Behan's *The Quare Fellow* (1956). Littlewood's name is most closely associated with the direction of the musical *Oh, What a Lovely War* (1963).

Littré, Émile (1801–81) French lexicographer and philosopher. He was the author of the major *Dictionnaire de la langue française* (1863–77) and also wrote a history of the French language (1862). He was a follower of Auguste Comte, and became the leading exponent of positivism after Comte's death.

liturgy (in Christianity) An act of worship, specifically the ordered services of the Church. CHRISTIAN CHURCHES have different liturgies with varying emphases. The principal form of liturgy is called the 'Mass' in the ROMAN CATHOLIC CHURCH, but in EASTERN ORTHODOX CHURCHES 'the Divine Liturgy', and sometimes (in all Churches) 'the Eucharist'. The Roman Catholic Mass has been held in the vernacular or spoken language of a country since 1970 following the Second Vatican Council (1962–65). In PROTESTANT Churches the liturgy is usually less formal, with the emphasis on the sermon and readings from the BIBLE, and the Eucharist is celebrated less often. In most Churches there has been increased emphasis on lay participation in recent years, though in the Catholic, Orthodox, and Anglican Churches a priest is needed for the consecration and celebration of the Eucharist.

Litvinov, Maxim Maximovich (1876–1951) Soviet revolutionary politician. He joined the BOLSHEVIKS (1903), and from 1917 to 1918 was Soviet envoy in London, having married an Engishwoman, Ivy Low in 1916. He headed delegations to the disarmament conference of the League of Nations (1927–29), signed the KELLOGG–BRIAND PACT (1928), and negotiated diplomatic relations with the USA (1933). An advocate of collective security against Germany, Italy, and Japan, he was Soviet foreign minister from 1930 until he was dismissed (1939), before STALIN signed the Nazi–Soviet Pact.

Liu Shaoqi (or **Liu Shao-ch'i**) (1898–*c*.1974) Chinese statesman. He served as a communist trade union organizer in Guangzhou (Canton) and Shanghai before becoming a member of the Central Committee of the CHINESE COMMUNIST PARTY in 1927, and its chief theoretician. On the establishment of the People's Republic in 1949 he was appointed chief vice-chairman of the party. In 1959 he became chairman of the Republic, second only to MAO ZEDONG in official standing, but during the CULTURAL REVOLUTION he was fiercely criticized by RED GUARDS as a 'renegade, traitor, and scab', and in 1968 he was stripped of office; his death was announced in 1974. In 1980 he was posthumously rehabilitated.

liver The main organ of METABOLISM in vertebrates. It lies in the abdominal cavity, near the stomach, and receives blood from the intestines via the hepatic portal vein. This blood carries the products of digestion, to be either stored or broken down into products readily available to tissues. Excess amino acids are converted in the liver to urea, which is excreted. The liver also receives blood from the SPLEEN with broken-down products from the digestion of red blood cells. These, together with similar products formed locally, are discharged into the intestine as BILE pigments. Bile salts formed in the liver are also discharged into the intestine with the pigments, and aid digestion. In humans, excess alcohol may indirectly lead to irreversible liver destruction and early death (see CIRRHOSIS).

liver fluke A FLUKE that is parasitic within the bodies of vertebrates. The Chinese liver fluke, *Opisthorchis sinensis*, and the sheep liver fluke, *Fasciola hepatica* are both leaf-like as adults, with an anterior mouth and two suckers. They live within liver tissues of vertebrates, hanging on with the suckers. The Chinese fluke has two intermediate hosts before it reaches humans. Eggs released from the gut of a human hatch to infect a secondary carrier, usually a snail. The larvae multiply, then a free-swimming stage leaves the snail to seek a new vertebrate host, such as a fish. Humans can therefore pick up liver flukes by eating undercooked fish. The sheep liver fluke uses a snail as a single intermediate host for the primary host, the sheep, which is infected by eating grass with liver fluke larvae encysted on it.

Liverpool A city and seaport in Merseyside, northwest England; pop. (1991) 448,300. Its port trade developed in the 17th century; it became an important centre of the slave traffic from Africa to the West Indies and later of the textile industry, importing cotton from the USA and exporting the textiles produced in Lancashire and Yorkshire. Liverpool's traditional industries of shipbuilding and engineering have declined, but it remains one of the chief Atlantic ports of Europe. The University of Liverpool was founded in 1903 and Liverpool John Moores University (formerly Liverpool Polytechnic) was established in 1992. It has two cathedrals including a Roman Catholic cathedral of modern design.

Liverpool, Robert Banks Jenkinson, 2nd Earl of (1770–1828) British Tory statesman, Prime Minister 1812–27. His government opposed both parliamentary reform and Catholic Emancipation, and took repressive measures to deal with popular discontent at the time of the Peterloo massacre. Lord Liverpool was later influenced by more liberal figures such as Sir Robert Peel to introduce some important reforms.

liverwort Any one of some 10,000 species of BRYOPHYTE that occur in moist terrestrial, or aquatic habitats. They are CRYPTOGAMS in which the gametophyte (sex-organ-bearing stage) is predominant and may be either leafy, or simply flat and spreading. Most grow on the surfaces of soil, trees, or rocks. The spore-bearing stage (sporophyte) is shorter-lived than that of mosses, lasting only a day or two. Its capsule releases the spores by splitting open into four segments, and not by scattering them from one end as most mosses do.

livery company One of the London city companies that replaced the medieval craft GUILDS, so called on account of the distinctive dress worn by their members. The liverymen constituted the freemen of the City of London, indirectly responsible for electing the mayor as well as the aldermen, while several of their companies, such as the Goldsmiths and Merchant Taylors, played an important role in the regulation of their trade and had monopoly powers within London. Since the 17th century there have been nearly 100 London livery companies but few have retained any importance other than as social and charitable institutions.

livestock farming The raising of animals on a farm. Dairy and beef CATTLE, SHEEP, POULTRY, and PIGS are raised for meat, milk, eggs, and wool. Horses are bred for recreation or sport, and animals, such as mink and ermine, are bred in fur-farms. Bovine and equine species are also raised as draught animals. Ruminant (cud-chewing) animals such as sheep, cattle, and goats are important for their ability to convert pasture, roughage, and non-protein nitrogen sources such as urea into meat, milk, and wool. Over 60 per cent of farmland worldwide is used for pasture. With the exception of ORGANIC FARMING, modern livestock farming practices are highly intensive. ANIMAL BREEDING is controlled to select animals for a particular function. Pigs and poultry are often raised by FACTORY FARMING, in which food intake, temperature, light, and other conditions are tailored to maximize conversion of food into the desired product. A more scientific understanding of the nutritional requirements of animals has made it possible to develop FEEDSTUFFS that provide a balanced and palatable diet throughout the year. However, the feeding of sheep offal to ruminants, such as bovines, has been said to be the cause of the outbreak of BOVINE SPONGIFORM ENCEPHALOPATHY (BSE). The offal is thought to have contained the agent responsible for scrapie, a disease endemic in sheep, which possibly mutated into the causative agent of BSE.

Livingstone, David (1813–73) Scottish missionary and explorer. He first went to Bechuanaland as a missionary in 1841; on his extensive travels in the interior he discovered Lake Ngami (1849), the Zambezi River (1851), and the Victoria Falls (1855). In 1866 he led an expedition into central Africa in search of the source of the Nile; after many hardships he was eventually found in poor health by the explorer Sir Henry Morton Stanley on the eastern shore of Lake Tanganyika in 1871.

Livingstone daisy See MESEMBRYANTHEMUM.

Livonia (German **Livland**) A former region on the east coast of the Baltic Sea, north of Lithuania, comprising most of modern Latvia and Estonia. It was named after the Livs, a Finno-Ugrian people living in part of the coastal region, ancestors of the modern Estonians. It was converted to Christianity in the early 13th century by the Livonian Brothers of the Sword, a crusading order of knights who united with the Teutonic Knights and ruled Livonia until the late 16th century. Between 1558 and 1582 the region was disputed by Poland, Sweden, and Russia in the Livonian War. It was taken by Poland, passing to Sweden in 1692, and was finally ceded to Peter the Great of Russia in 1721. It was divided between Estonia and Latvia in 1918.

Livorno The Italian name for LEGHORN.

Livy (Latin name Titus Livius) (59 BC–17 AD) Roman historian. His history of Rome from its foundation to his own time contained 142 books, of which 35 survive (including the earliest history of the war with Hannibal). Livy is notable for his power of vivid historical reconstruction as he sought to give Rome a history that in conception and style might be worthy of her imperial rise and greatness.

lizard A REPTILE comprising about 3,000 living species, which include a highly diverse array distributed throughout the world except for some cold regions. They have a wide range of life-styles: many are terrestrial, whereas others are adapted for tree-dwelling, aquatic, or burrowing existences. Most have well-developed limbs, although these are reduced or lost in some snake-like species, such as glass snakes, the slow worm, some species of skinks, and pygopodids. Their tails are usually quite long and many species, if caught, are able to shed their tails, a mechanism called autotomy. This act often distracts the predator for long enough to allow the lizard to escape.

Some of the main lizard families are: AGAMIDS, CHAMELEONS, MONITOR LIZARDS, PYGOPODIDS, IGUANAS, SKINKS, GECKOS, and SLOW WORMS.

Lizard, the A promontory near the western tip of Cornwall, south-west England, the southernmost point of the British mainland. There is a space-satellite communications station at Goonhilly Downs nearby.

Ljubljana (German **Laibach**) The capital of the Republic of Slovenia in south-east-central Europe, situated on the Sava and Ljubljanica rivers; pop. (1991) 267,000. It was founded (as Emona) by the Roman emperor Augustus in 34 BC. Under the rule of the Habsburgs from the 13th century, it became capital in 1809 of the Illyrian Provinces and between 1816 and 1849 of the Austrian kingdom of Illyria. It became a part of Yugoslavia in 1918. Its industries produce textiles, electronics, paper, and chemicals.

llama A New World species of the camel family, *Lama glama*, domesticated like the alpaca and related to the guanaco and vicuna. Found at altitudes of 2,300–4,000 m (7,600–13,000 feet), it is the principal beast of burden in the Andes of Peru, Bolivia, Argentina, and Chile though only stallions are used to carry loads, of up to 80 kg (176 pounds) for up to 30 km (19 miles) per day. The llama provides meat, wool, fat for candles, and valuable hide. It is about 1.2 m (4 feet) tall at the shoulders and has a thick fleece, which varies in colour from white to black. The neck and head are long, and the eyes and ears quite large. A foal is born after a gestation period of 11 months, and is suckled for four months.

Llandudno A resort town in Conwy county borough, northern Wales, situated on the Irish Sea at the mouth of the River Conwy; pop. (1991) 14,578.

Llanelli A town in the county of Carmarthenshire, south-west Wales, on Carmarthen Bay at the mouth of the River Burry; pop. (1991) 44,953. The town grew with steel and tin-plate industries, now in decline.

Llanfairpwllgwyngyll (also **Llanfair P. G.**) A village on the island of Anglesey, north-west Wales, famous for its unabbreviated name, Llanfairpwllgwyngyllgogerychwyrndrobwllllantysiliogogogoch, which is the longest name in the UK. The first Women's Institute in Britain was founded here in 1915.

Llangollen A resort town in Denbighshire, north-east Wales, on the River Dee; pop. (1991) 3,267. International *eisteddfods* have been held here since 1947.

llano A treeless grassy plain or savanna in tropical South America, notably in the Orinoco basin. It is frequently burnt by graziers to stimulate the growth of new grass during the following wet season. An inhabitant of the llanos is known as a llanero.

Llewelyn I See LLYWELYN AP IORWERTH.

Llewelyn II See LLYWELYN AP GRUFFYDD.

Llosa, Mario Vargas See VARGAS LLOSA.

Lloyd, Harold (Clayton) (1893–1971) US film comedian who became one of the most popular cinema personalities of the 1920s. He performed his own hair-raising stunts, using physical danger as a source of comedy in silent movies, such as *High and Dizzy* (1920), *Safety Last* (1923), and *The Freshman* (1925). He was presented with an honorary Academy Award in 1952.

Lloyd, Marie (born Matilda Alice Victoria Wood) (1870–1922) British music-hall entertainer. She made her first stage appearance in 1885 and soon achieved fame for her risqué songs and extravagant costumes; she later took her act to the USA, South Africa, and Australia.

Lloyd George, David, 1st Earl Lloyd George of Dwyfor (1863–1945) British Liberal statesman, Prime Minister 1916–22. As Chancellor of the Exchequer (1908–15) he introduced old-age pensions (1908) and national insurance (1911). His 'People's Budget' (1909), intended to finance reform by raised death duties and other taxes, was rejected by the Lords and led to a constitutional crisis which was eventually resolved by the Parliament Act of 1911. Supported by the Conservatives, he took over from Asquith as Prime Minister at the end of 1916 and led the coalition government for the remainder of World War I. In the postwar period his administration was threatened by increasing economic problems and trouble in Ireland; he resigned in 1922 after the Conservatives withdrew their support.

Lloyd's of London (or **Corporation of Lloyds**) An institution that acts as an international MARKET for INSURANCE (particularly marine insurance). Founded in the 17th century in a coffee shop owned by Edward Lloyd, there are now some 20,000 members (the underwriters), who pay out if a successful claim is made. These underwriters, called names, each deposit a substantial sum with Lloyd's and accept unlimited liability. They are grouped into some 279 syndicates to deal with Lloyd's insurance brokers, who act as intermediaries between underwriters and clients seeking insurance cover. In the period 1988–94 some syndicates made substantial losses, causing extreme financial hardship to many names. As a result changes were made to its institution, including allowing limited companies to become names. The Lloyd's Register of Shipping is the world's largest ship-classification society.

Lloyd Webber, Andrew, Baron (1948–) British composer. He has written many successful musicals, several of them in collaboration with the lyricist Sir Tim Rice; they include *Jesus Christ Superstar* (1970) *Evita* (1976), *Cats* (1981), *The Phantom of the Opera* (1986), *Aspects of Love* (1989), and *Sunset Boulevard* (1993).

Llywelyn ap Gruffydd (or **Llewelyn II**) (died 1282) Prince of Gwynedd in North Wales. In 1258 he proclaimed himself prince of all Wales and four years later formed an alliance with Simon de Montfort, leader of the baronial opposition to Henry III. He later signed a treaty with Henry, which made him chief of the other Welsh princes but recognized Henry as his overlord (1265). His refusal to pay homage to Edward I led the latter to invade and subjugate Wales (1277–84); Llywelyn died in battle after raising a rebellion against Edward's rule.

Llywelyn ap Iorwerth (or **Llewelyn II**; known as **Llywelyn the Great**) (died 1240) Prince of Gwynedd (north Wales), the most powerful ruler in medieval Wales, his authority over other Welsh leaders being confirmed by the Treaty of Worcester (1218). Although married (1205) to Joan, the illegitimate daughter of King JOHN, Llywelyn took advantage of the political confusion in England to extend his influence over South Wales. He also had close ties with the marcher lords.

loach A small, eel-like freshwater fish of the family Homalopteridae, related to the carp family. Loaches are most abundant in tropical Asia, but their range extends across Europe and temperate Asia and part of northeast Africa. They are adapted for life on the river-bed, either hidden under stones or burrowing in mud, and having numerous barbels around their mouth. There are about 150 species.

Loach, Ken(neth) (1936–) British film director. He started in television, highlighting social problems with such films as *Cathy Come Home* (1966), which dealt with homelessness. He continued to explore social and political issues, for example in his first feature film *Poor Cow* (1967), in his best-known work *Kes* (1969), and in his TV documentary *Questions of Leadership* (1983), which was banned on political grounds. Other films include *Land and Freedom* (1995).

loadstone (or **lodestone**) See MAGNETITE.

loam A spongy or crumbly soil formed from mixtures of sand, silt, and clay in roughly equal proportions. They can hold water without becoming waterlogged, are rich in organic matter, and are thus good for growing plants.

Lobachevski, Nikolai Ivanovich (1792–1856) Russian mathematician. At about the same time as Gauss in Germany and János Bolyai (1802–60) in Hungary, he independently discovered non-Euclidean geometry. His work was not widely recognized until the non-Euclidean nature of space–time was revealed by the general theory of relativity.

lobelia A species of annual or perennial plant of the genus *Lobelia*. Lobelias are both herbs and shrubs, which have a worldwide distribution. The flowers may be red, yellow, or white, though the predominant colour is blue. In the mountains of central Africa and South America are species which grow to 2 m (6.5 feet) or more in height. In contrast, *Lobelia erinus*, the South African parent of numerous garden varieties, is a dwarf species only 10 cm (4 inches) in height. Lobelias, together with other genera showing a wide range of small growth forms, form a family of some 1,200 species. Some are epiphytes, others resemble palms, and yet others have developed needle-like leaves.

loblolly pine (or **frankincense pine**) One of the yellow pines, *Pinus taeda*, of North America, native to the southeast USA, though widely planted elsewhere, especially in Australia. It may reach some 30 m (110 feet) in height and its needles are arranged in bunches of three. The wood is used for many purposes in the USA, but the tree does not grow well in Britain.

lobster The most massive of all living ARTHROPODS, weighing up to 23 kg (50 pounds). They belong to the CRUSTACEAN order Decapoda (crabs, prawns, crayfish), and have eight walking legs and two large pincers. Unlike crabs, lobsters and CRAYFISH have an elongate body; lobsters also have unequal pincers, the larger one being used to crush shellfish.

Lobsters usually lead a scavenging or carnivorous existence and they can retreat rapidly using an emergency flicking action of the abdomen when threatened. They live in crevices in rocky sea-beds and corals, which explains their willingness to enter lobster-pots, probably explored as potential homes. A lobster moults its CUTICLE many times over several years before reaching maturity, and the females then breed at two-year intervals. They can produce at least 100,000 eggs, which they carry around with them beneath the abdomen for many months before releasing them as tiny larvae.

lobster moth A species of large moth, *Stauropus fasi*, belonging to the same family as the puss moth. It has a bizarre, reddish-brown, lobster-like caterpillar, with pointed humps on its back. When alarmed, the caterpillar throws back the head, raising the unusually long, red, thoracic legs, and throws forward the swollen hind-end, which bears a pair of stiff filaments.

local area network (LAN) (computing) See NETWORK.

local government Administration by local or regional authorities. In unitary states, local government is the conferment of limited legislative and executive powers by central government upon local authorities. These generally consist of councils of locally elected representatives, who appoint paid officials to provide a range of services or to act as agents of the central government in a specified locality. Under FEDERALISM, local government is responsible to and under the legal control of the territories making up the federal union, rather than the federal government. The concerns of local government may include EDUCATION, local highways, municipal services, some areas of social welfare, and recreation. The degree to which local government is locally representative varies in different countries.

Local Group of galaxies The cluster of 20 or so galaxies to which the GALAXY belongs. The Group is dominated by three SPIRAL GALAXIES: our own galaxy (2×10^{11} times the mass of the Sun), the Andromeda Galaxy (3×10^{11} times the mass of the Sun), and M33 which, at 10^{10} solar masses, is less than a tenth of the mass of the other two galaxies. Other members of the Group are the MAGELLANIC CLOUDS and small elliptical and irregular galaxies, most of which cluster around the two large spiral galaxies. The diameter of the Local Group is approximately 1 million parsecs (3 million light-years). In comparison to other clusters of galaxies, such as the VIRGO cluster, the Local Group contains relatively few galaxies, of relatively small mass.

Local Supercluster A large group of some 50,000 galaxies containing the LOCAL GROUP OF GALAXIES to which our galaxy belongs. Also known as the VIRGO Supercluster because it contains the large Virgo Cluster, it includes several nearby clusters. The Supercluster is roughly lens-shaped with a diameter of at least 20 megaparsecs.

Locarno, Treaties of (1 December 1925) A series of international agreements drawn up in Locarno, a health resort in Switzerland at the north end of Lake Maggiore. Their object was to ease tension by guaranteeing the common boundaries of Germany, Belgium, and France as specified in the VERSAILLES PEACE SETTLEMENT in 1919. Gustav Stresemann, as German Foreign Minister, refused to accept Germany's eastern frontier with Poland and Czechoslovakia as unalterable, but agreed that alteration must come peacefully. In the 'spirit of Locarno' Germany was invited to join the LEAGUE OF NATIONS. In 1936, denouncing the principal Locarno treaty, HITLER sent his troops into the demilitarized Rhineland; in 1938 he annexed the SUDETENLAND in Czechoslovakia, and in 1939 invaded Poland.

Loch Leven See LEVEN, LOCH.

Loch Lomond See LOMOND, LOCH.

Loch Ness A deep loch in the Highlands of Scotland to the south-west of Inverness, forming part of the Caledonian Canal. With a length of 39 km (24.2 miles) and a maximum depth of 230 m (755 ft), it is the longest and largest (by volume of water) lake in Great Britain. There have been reported appearances of an aquatic 'monster' since the time of St Columba (6th century), but no evidence has been produced.

lock, canal An enclosed part of a CANAL in which the water level can be changed by opening and closing gates. It allows boats to transfer between sections (reaches) of the canal with different water levels. In navigating upstream, for example, a boat enters the lock from the lower reach. A gate closes behind it and water is allowed to flow into the lock from the upper reach until the level in the lock is raised to that in the upper reach. The gate to the upper reach can then be opened to enable the boat to continue its journey upstream.

Locke, John (1632–1704) English philosopher, a founder of empiricism and political liberalism. Both his major works were published in 1690. In *Two Treatises of Government* he justified the Revolution of 1688 by arguing that, contrary to the theory of the divine right of kings, the authority of rulers has a human origin and is limited. In *An Essay Concerning Human Understanding* he denied that any ideas are innate, and argued instead for a central empiricist tenet that all knowledge is derived from sense-experience. He concluded that it is not possible to know everything of the world and that our limited knowledge must be reinforced by faith.

Lockerbie A town in south-west Scotland, in Dumfries and Galloway. It was the scene in 1988 of the explosion of a US jumbo jet, caused by a terrorist bomb, in which 276 people died. In 1991 a US court indicted two Libyans for the crime, but Libya refused to release them for trial.

Lockyer, Sir (Joseph) Norman (1836–1920) British astronomer. Following the first observation of solar prominences (streams of incandescent gas issuing from the Sun) during an eclipse, Lockyer demonstrated that they could be seen at other times with suitable equipment. His spectroscopic analysis of the Sun led to his discovery of a new element, which he named *helium*. Lockyer also studied possible astronomical alignments in ancient monuments such as Stonehenge. He is perhaps best known for founding both the Science Museum in London and the scientific journal *Nature*, which he edited for 50 years.

locomotive See RAILWAYS, HISTORY OF; STEAM LOCOMOTIVE.

locust A SHORTHORN GRASSHOPPER that exists in two phases, the solitary and the migratory, each differing in appearance and behaviour. In the solitary phase, the adults and the young tend to be green and fat and individuals lead almost solitary lives. The migratory-phase individuals are darker and gather in groups when quite young. These hopper bands eventually mature and swarms are formed. Migratory swarms left uncontrolled will totally destroy all vegetation, but eventually, after bad breeding seasons, they revert to the solitary phase. The best-known locusts, all members of the family Acrididae, are the migratory locust, *Locusta migratoria*, which occurs from the Mediterranean region to New Zealand, usually in areas of good rainfall, and the desert locust, *Schistocerca gregaria*, which occurs in dry areas, especially of North Africa and the Near East; this is the locust of biblical plagues. The red locust, *Nomadacris septemfasciata*, of South Africa, can also be destructive, as can species in North and South America.

locust tree See ROBINIA.

lodestone (or **loadstone**) See MAGNETITE.

Lodge, David (John) (1935–) British novelist and academic. He became honorary professor of Modern English Literature at the University of Birmingham in 1976. His novels are generally satires on academia and literary criticism, and include *Changing Places* (1975) and *Small World* (1984); *Nice Work* (1989) contrasted industry and academic life. He has done much to introduce and explain continental literary theory in Britain; his critical works include *The Language of Fiction* (1966) and *Write On* (1986).

Lodge, Sir Oliver (Joseph) (1851–1940) British physicist. He made important contributions to the study of electromagnetic radiation, and was a pioneer of radiotelegraphy. He also devised an ingenious experiment to demonstrate that the hypothetical ether did not exist, and he carried out intensive studies of psychic phenomena.

loess A deposit of fine light-coloured wind-blown dust found especially in the basins of large rivers and very fertile when irrigated.

Loewi, Otto (1873–1961) US pharmacologist and physiologist, born in Germany. He is chiefly remembered today for his contributions in the field of chemical transmission of nerve impulses. By means of experiments using a pair of isolated frog hearts he was the first to show that a chemical neurotransmitter is produced at the junction between a parasympathetic nerve and a muscle; he later identified it as the substance acetylcholine. Loewi shared a Nobel Prize with Sir Henry Dale in 1936.

log An instrument used to measure the speed of a vessel through water. The name derives from the early practice of throwing a log tied to a knotted line over the ship's stern, and measuring the distance (in KNOTS) travelled away from the log in a fixed time period. This was recorded in the log-book. Modern measurement methods include recording the speed of rotation of an impeller attached to the keel of a vessel; measuring the current generated by the flow of seawater over an electromagnetic probe; and the use of Doppler SONAR.

Logan, Mount A mountain in Kluane National Park, south-west Yukon Territory, Canada. It is the highest peak in Canada and second-highest in North America (5,951 m, 19,524 ft). Its first ascent in 1925 was achieved after a 44-day trek up the Chitina valley and over glacier ice.

loganberry A natural hybrid, *Rubus loganobaccus*, probably between the raspberry and the dewberry, believed to have originated in about 1881 in California in the garden of Judge J. H. Logan.

logarithm The inverse of an EXPONENTIAL FUNCTION. If $y = a^x$, then x is said to be the logarithm of y to base a (written $y = \log_a x$). Thus 2 is the logarithm of 100 to base 10, because $100 = 10^2$. Logarithms are not always positive, nor always whole numbers; in which case the decimal part is called the mantissa and the whole number part is called the characteristic. The logarithm of 3 to base 10 is about 0.477; the logarithm of 30 is about 1.477; and for 300 it is about 2.477. This sequence of numbers shows that adding numbers to logarithms corresponds to multiplication of the number whose logarithm is being added to. (In the sequence above, adding 1 to the logarithm corresponds to multiplication by 10.) Before cheap electronic calculators existed, complicated multiplications and divisions were carried out by consulting tables of logarithms and adding or subtracting logarithms, and converting the answer back from logarithms. (John NAPIER devised this technique.) Slide rules do the same job mechanically. Logarithms are widely used in science and mathematics, not now for computation but for representing phenomena, which often obey logarithmic laws (the response of the human ear to sound intensity is approximately logarithmic). In these fields, base e rather than 10 is often used (e is an IRRATIONAL NUMBER, approximately equal to 2.7183). This is because DIFFERENTIATION and INTEGRATION of logarithmic functions to base e is tidier than to any other base. Logarithms to base e are called natural logarithms. Axes of GRAPHS are often divided logarithmically to allow wide-ranging data to be plotted. For instance, an axis marked in steps from 0 to 6 could, using logarithms to base 10, represent numbers in the range 1 to 1,000,000.

logic The science of reasoning and proof. In the 19th century there was an increasing distrust of intuition and experience in mathematics. It led to greater reliance on formal mathematical logic, starting from stated and accepted AXIOMS, or logical propositions, and providing rules for determining the accuracy of arguments and truth of conclusions. Apart from this use of logic to put mathematics on a more secure foundation, there developed in the 19th century the new branch of mathematical logic. This was instigated mainly by

George BOOLE. His Boolean algebra uses algebraic symbols and operations to represent propositions and the relationships between them. His ideas became the basis of symbolic logic, which has found application in some branches of computing and electronics. Logic is not concerned with the subject of an argument but with its form schematically represented. For example, the arguments; *all men are mortal, Socrates is a man, Socrates is mortal*, and *all lying is wicked, that is a lie, that is wicked*, share a form despite the difference in their subject, and that form can be represented by the schema; All As are B, C is an A, C is a B. Logic describes and explains the validity of arguments by describing and explaining the validity of argument schema; a particular argument is valid only if it is an instance of a valid argument schema. No universal logic characterizes all valid arguments because there are so many different types. Instead different logical systems have been developed and classified by appeal to their logical constants, the words around whose meanings the validity of the arguments revolve. For example, propositional logic deals with arguments whose validity revolves around the meaning of the words (or phrases) *if*, *and*, *or*, *not*, and *if-and-only-if*, whilst the constants of predicate logic (whose precursors were the SYLLOGISMS of ARISTOTLE) are these plus the words *all* and *some*. There are formal logics under construction that characterize arguments of many kinds, including those involving time (tense logic), morality (deontic logic), belief (epistemic logic), and possibility (modal logic). The question of which words can play the role of logical constants is important in philosophical logic. See also DEDUCTION; INDUCTION.

logical positivism A set of doctrines put forward by a group of philosophers calling themselves the Vienna Circle, who met in Vienna during the 1920s and 1930s. In the tradition of ANALYTIC PHILOSOPHY and influenced strongly by EMPIRICISM and especially by HUME, logical positivism was an attempt to develop empiricist views with the help of LOGIC and mathematics, in particular, in the work of RUSSELL and the young WITTGENSTEIN. According to logical positivists, sense experience is all we can appeal to in justifying our beliefs or in explaining the meaning of our words. These views give rise to the verificationist principle on which the meaning of a sentence is the procedure by which it can be verified. The logical positivists believed that adoption of their ideas would dissolve all the problems of philosophy because any question to which the answer could not be provided by some experience would be meaningless. Logical positivism was spread in the UK by AYER's work and in the USA by the forced emigration of CARNAP.

logic gate (computing) One of the fundamental electronic circuits from which a digital COMPUTER is built. Originally constructed from individual components (first THERMIONIC VALVES then TRANSISTORS), they are now made as INTEGRATED CIRCUITS (ICs). A very complex IC, such as a MICROPROCESSOR, may contain many thousands of logic gates. Each gate has one or more inputs and a single output, the value of which is determined by the states (voltage levels) of the inputs. As they are digital devices, both inputs and outputs can assume only one of two states, representing 0 or 1.

The three basic logic gates are the AND gate (two or more inputs and one output when both inputs are on), the OR gate (two or more inputs and one output when either or both inputs are on), and the NOT gate (one input and one output; an off output when the input is on and an on output when the input is off). NAND, NOR, XOR, and XNOR gates are also important in digital electronics. In a NAND gate, the output is 0 only when all inputs are 1; otherwise the output is 1. NAND gates alone can realize any other logic operation and are easy to implement with transistors. In a NOR gate, the output is 1 only if all the inputs are 0; otherwise the output is 0. XOR (exclusive-OR) gates have their output as 1 only when any one of the inputs is 1 and all others are 0. XNOR is 0 when one input is 1 and the others are 0. Boolean algebra, invented by the British mathematician George Boole in 1857, allows calculations to be made about systems that have only two allowed states. It can be used to prove that combinations of logic gates, known as logic circuits, will perform their intended function.

Lohengrin The Knight of the Swan, a hero of the German version of a widely spread legend. Lohengrin is summoned from the temple of the Grail to help a lady in distress, Elsa of Brabant. He is borne on a swan-boat to Antwerp and saves Elsa from an unwanted suitor. Lohengrin will marry Elsa if she does not ask his origin; but she does, and the swan-boat carries him back to the castle of the Holy Grail. The story is the subject of Wagner's opera *Lohengrin* (1850).

Loire A river of west-central France, which rises in the Massif Central and flows 1,015 km (630 miles) north and west to the Atlantic at St Nazaire. Principal cities on its route are Orléans, Tours, and Nantes. The longest river in France, it is noted for the châteaux and vineyards that lie along its course.

Lollard Originally a follower of John WYCLIF, a Lollard was later anyone seriously critical of the Church. Lollards probably owed their name to the Dutch word *lollaerd*, meaning a mumbler (of prayers). Lollardy began in the 1370s as a set of beliefs held by Oxford-trained clerks who were keenly interested in Wyclif's teachings on papal and ecclesiastical authority; in an age unsettled by war and threatened by disease (especially the BLACK DEATH), it also appealed to other educated sectors of society. They attacked clerical celibacy, INDULGENCES, and pilgrimages. RICHARD II, who was himself an opponent of calls for ecclesiastical egalitarianism, none the less retained in his household some knights known to favour Lollardy. The nobility abandoned it only when HENRY IV came to the throne and backed Archbishop Arundel in a vigorous persecution of Lollards; further reaction against it, among the gentry, also resulted from the abortive Lollard uprising attempted by Sir John Oldcastle in January 1414. Thereafter, Lollardy's appeal seems to have been limited to craftsmen, artisans, and a few priests in the larger towns.

Lombardy (Italian **Lombardia**) A region of central northern Italy, between the Alps and the River Po, which became part of the kingdom of Italy in 1859; area 23,833 sq km (9,205 sq miles); pop. (1990) 8,939,430; capital, Milan. Founded in the 6th century by the Germanic Lombards (also known as *Langobards* 'long beards'), it was taken by Spain in the 16th century, was ceded to Austria in 1713, and finally became a part of the kingdom of Italy in 1859.

Lombok A volcanic island of the Lesser Sunda group in Indonesia, situated between Bali and Sumbawa; area 4,727 sq km (1,826 sq miles); pop.

(1991) 2,500,000. The majority of the population are Muslim Sasaks who converted to Islam in the 16th century. Its principal town in Mataram and its highest point is Mt. Rinjani (3,726 m, 12,224 ft), the second-highest peak in Indonesia. Chief among its exports are rice, pumice stone, tobacco, cotton, seaweed, and a variety of spices including the chilli peppers that give the island its Javanese name.

Lomé The capital and chief port of Togo in West Africa, on the Gulf of Guinea; pop. (1990) 450,000. In 1975 a trade agreement, subsequently known as the **Lomé Convention**, was reached here between the EEC and 46 African, Caribbean, and Pacific Ocean States (ACP States), for technical cooperation and development aid. A second agreement was signed in 1979 by a larger group. The modern deep-water port handles primary products from the landlocked states of Mali, Niger, and Burkina.

Lomond, **Loch** A loch in west-central Scotland. It is the largest freshwater lake in Great Britain, with an area of 70 sq km (27.5 sq miles) and a length from north to south of 36.4 km (22.6 miles).

Lomonosov, **Mikhail (Vasilyevich)** (1711–65) Russian scientist, poet, political reformer, and polymath. Of humble northern origin, he came to Moscow and then St Petersburg, where he was taken up by the German founders of the Academy of Sciences and sent abroad to study. He returned in 1740 to lay the foundations of achievement in poetry, verse theory, grammar, and many other fields of scholarly and scientific endeavour. He proposed a theory of gases, similar to KINETIC THEORY, and did much to further the study of science in Russia. At his death his notes, outlining his humanitarian ideas, were suppressed by Catherine the Great, and his complete *Works* were published only in 1950–57.

London The capital and largest city of the United Kingdom, situated on the River Thames, it is a leading world commercial, business, cultural, and tourist centre; pop. (1991) 6,378,600. Greater London, which is divided into the City of London and 32 Boroughs (see GREATER LONDON), was administered by a single Greater London Council from 1965 to 1986. The GLC was then abolished by the Conservative government and its functions were transferred to the borough councils. Settled by the Romans at the lowest crossing of the Thames as a port and trading centre (*Londinium*), London has flourished since the Middle Ages. After the plague of 1665 and the fire of 1666 much of it was rebuilt under the direction of Sir Christopher Wren. Air raids in World War II obliterated whole areas of streets and damaged most public buildings; postwar reconstruction has added tower blocks of geometric aspect to the landscape. It is the home of the University of London (1836), the Royal College of Art (1837), the City University (1966), the University of East London (1992), the University of Greenwich (1992), Middlesex University (1992), Southbank University (1992), Thames Valley University (1992), and the University of Westminster (1992). It is the centre of British government and political power; its many major buildings include Buckingham Palace, Houses of Parliament, British Museum, Westminster Abbey, St Paul's Cathedral, and the Tower.

London, **Jack** (pseudonym of John Griffith Chaney) (1876–1916) US novelist. He grew up in poverty, scratching a living in various ways and taking part in the Klondike gold rush of 1897–98; his experiences provided the material for his works and also made him a socialist. His most famous novels are *The Call of the Wild* (1903) and *White Fang* (1906).

Londonderry ▶**1** A county of Northern Ireland, between Lough Neagh and the Atlantic northern coast of Ireland, formerly an administrative area; area 2,067 sq km (798 sq miles); pop. (1981) 186,750; ▶**2** Its chief town, a city and port on the River Foyle near its outlet on the north coast; pop. (1981) 62,700. Built on the site of an abbey founded by St Columba in 546 AD, it was formerly called Derry, a name still used by many. In 1613 it was granted to the City of London for colonization and became known as Londonderry. In 1689 it resisted a siege by James II for 105 days before being relieved.

lone pair A pair of electrons in a molecule that are not part of a CHEMICAL BOND – that is, not shared between two atoms. There are eight electrons round the oxygen atom in a water molecule; two pairs of electrons form the bonds to the hydrogen atoms, and the other four electrons form two lone pairs. Lone pairs are important in determining the shapes of molecules and are used for forming new bonds in many reactions.

Long Beach A port, industrial, and resort city in southern California, situated on the Pacific coast to the south of Los Angeles; pop. (1990) 429,430. In 1967 the ocean liner *Queen Mary* was brought to Long Beach and converted into a hotel and tourist attraction. Its industries include oil refining, aircraft, automobile, and missile manufacturing.

Longchamps A world-famous race-course in the Bois de Boulogne, Paris, France, created in 1857. Flat-racing takes place during May, September, and October.

Longfellow, **Henry Wadsworth** (1807–82) US poet. His *Ballads and Other Poems* (1841) contains such well-known pieces as 'The Wreck of the Hesperus' and 'The Village Blacksmith'. Longfellow's popularity increased with subsequent volumes, especially his narrative poems. His best-known work is *The Song of Hiawatha* (1855), which tells in romantic style of the life and legendary exploits of the American Indian chieftain Hiawatha. The poem's repetitive metre, derived from the Finnish *Kalevala*, attracted both imitators and parodists.

Longford ▶**1** A county of the Republic of Ireland, in the province of Leinster; area 1,044 sq km (403 sq miles); pop. (1991) 30,290. ▶**2** Its county town, on the River Camlin; pop. (1991) 6,390.

Longhi, **Pietro** (1702–85) Italian painter, best known for small genre scenes of life in Venice. These charming and often gently satirical scenes were very popular and much duplicated by pupils. His son **Alessandro** (1733–1813) was a successful portraitist.

longhorn beetle A BEETLE of the family Cerambycidae, characterized by the length of its antennae, which are as long as, or longer than, the rest of the animal, and generally longer in the males than in the females. The body is elongate, often colourful, and varies in size. Indeed, they include the longest known beetles such as the South American species *Titanus giganteus*, which can reach 20 cm (8 inches) in body length. The adults, if they feed at all, eat leaves or pollen, but the larvae feed internally on plants, often in wood, and their lifespan may be three or more years. They occur throughout the world and many of the 20,000 species are injurious to timber.

longhorn grasshopper (or **bush cricket**, **katydid**) A grasshopper with antennae longer than its body. The front wings of the males are modified for sound production, while the females have prominent scimitar-like ovipositors. Their stridulation (song) is loud and frequent, more so than that of SHORTHORN GRASSHOPPERS. They are almost all plant-feeders, often on trees or shrubs, but also in marshy country and in caves. They insert their eggs into slits cut into plants. They comprise some 5,000 species in the family Tettigonidae and are found worldwide.

longhorn moth A moth belonging to the family Incurvariidae, with long, thread-like antennae often many times the length of the body. They are small moths, often brilliantly metallic coloured, and fly by day. Their tiny caterpillars feed by mining within leaves or flower heads; older ones make cases of leaf fragments.

Longinus (fl. 1st century AD) Greek scholar. He is the supposed author of a Greek literary treatise *On the Sublime*, a critical analysis of literary greatness showing concern with the moral function of literature and impatience with pedantry. After its translation into French in 1674 it became a very influential work with Augustan writers such as Dryden and Pope.

Long Island The USA's fourth-largest island, extending for 190 km (118 miles) along the coast eastward from the mouth of the Hudson River, separated from Connecticut to the north by **Long Island Sound**. Its western tip comprises the New York districts of Brooklyn and Queens. It is separated from Manhattan by the East River but linked to it by the Brooklyn Bridge and road tunnels. At its eastern end are two tail-like peninsulas, parts of MORAINES left by the ice age. Low, wooded hills lie to the north of the moraines, a flat plain to the south. Wide bays, long beaches, and lagoons form the south coast. The land is fertile enough for farming, and there are glacial deposits of gravel and sand.

longitude See LATITUDE AND LONGITUDE; PRIME MERIDIAN.

Long March (1934–35) The epic withdrawal of the Chinese communists from south-eastern to north-western China. By 1934 the Jiangxi Soviet was close to collapse after repeated attacks by the KUOMINTANG army. In October a force of 100,000 evacuated the area. MAO ZEDONG took over the leadership of the march in January 1935. For nine months it travelled through mountainous terrain cut by several major rivers. In October Mao and 6,000 survivors reached Yan'an, having marched 9,600 km (6,000 miles). Other groups arrived later, in all about 20,000 surviving the journey. The march established Mao as the effective leader of the Chinese Communist Party, a position he consolidated in his ten years in Yan'an.

Long Parliament (1640–60) The English Parliament called by Charles I after the BISHOPS' WARS had bankrupted him. Led by the Parliamentarian John Pym, by August 1641 it had made a series of enactments depriving him of the powers that had aroused so much opposition since his accession. These reforms were intended to rule out absolutism for the future, and were eventually incorporated in the Restoration settlement, and again during the GLORIOUS REVOLUTION. The Parliament was also responsible for the execution of the king's advisers LAUD and Thomas Wentworth, Earl of Strafford. Without its Cavalier members, the Long Parliament sat on throughout the ENGLISH CIVIL WAR, since it could be dissolved only with its own consent. Serious divisions emerged between the Presbyterian and Independent members, culminating in PRIDE'S PURGE (1648). The remnant, the Rump Parliament, arranged the trial and execution of Charles I, and the establishment of the COMMONWEALTH (1649). CROMWELL ejected the Rump by force in 1653, but it was recalled after his son's failure as Lord Protector in 1659. In the next year General MONCK secured the reinstatement of those members 'secluded' by Pride. Arrangements for the Convention Parliament were made, and the Long Parliament dissolved itself in March 1660.

longship A VIKING ship, especially a warship. They were built usually of fir planks, and differed from the vessels of the Angles, Saxons, and Frisians in having a massive vertical keel of oak instead of a shallow horizontal one; this enabled them to carry a mast and sail. The clinker-built construction of overlapping planks secured by clench nails conferred great strength with flexibility, and the hulls were waterproofed with tar, seams between the planks being caulked with wool and hair. Later examples were over 46 m (150 ft) long and could carry hundreds of warriors who were also rowers. Longships were of extremely seaworthy design, and the addition of sails made very long voyages feasible, while the shallow draught meant that raiders could penetrate far inland by river. The violent expansion of the Norse peoples was dependent on the skilful use of such vessels.

long-tailed duck A species of small black and white sea duck, *Clangula hyemalis*, known as an 'old squaw' in North America, which is abundant throughout the Arctic. They dive to remarkable depths and fly very fast. The drake has long needle-like tail feathers. Both sexes have different seasonal plumages.

long wave See WAVEBAND.

loofah An Asian climbing plant, *Luffa cylindrica*, that is a member of the pumpkin family, together with cucumbers and marrows. The young fruits of the loofah are eaten fresh or cooked. The ripe fruit has a complex network of fibres, which are exploited in the familiar sponge-like bathroom loofah. It is also used in industrial filters. The loofah material also has shock- and sound-absorbing properties, useful, for example, in military helmet linings.

loom An apparatus for weaving YARN or thread into fabric. Most woven cloth consists of lengthways threads (WARP) and crossways threads (WEFT). A loom interweaves these threads by passing the weft thread to and fro across the width of the cloth, under and over the warp threads. The pattern of the interweaving of warp and weft threads determines the weave of the finished fabric. A simple loom has two light heddle shafts – bars carrying fine wire loops through which the warp threads pass. When one heddle shaft is raised and the other lowered, alternate warp threads are separated to form a clear passage or 'shed' through the width of the fabric, through which the weft passes (see figure). The traditional way of passing weft through the shed is with a shuttle, which unwinds the yarn as it crosses the loom.

From the mid-18th century most hand-looms had flying shuttles, which substantially speeded their operation. In the UK, the power-loom largely replaced the handloom in the mid- to late 19th century. In Europe and elsewhere, mechanization of weaving came somewhat later. Modern industrial looms are generally shuttleless, using a method of weft insertion other than a shuttle. The first commercially successful shuttleless loom was the Sulzer weaving machine, introduced in about 1950. In it the weft was inserted in measured lengths from one side of the loom only.

looper (or **inch worm**, **measuring worm**, **span-**

worm) A caterpillar belonging to the moth family Geometridae, which includes the carpet moths. The name geometer means ground-measurer, and describes how these caterpillars move, by arching or looping the body, bringing the hind claspers or prolegs up to the thoracic (or true) legs, and then moving these forward. Many geometer caterpillars rest with the body attached to a twig by the claspers and held erect, in imitation of a twig.

Loos, Adolf (1870–1933) Austrian architect, a pioneer of MODERNISM. Although he worked mainly in Vienna, from 1893 to 1896 he was in the USA, where he was influenced by SULLIVAN and the CHICAGO SCHOOL. His best-known work is the Steiner House in Vienna (1910–11), austerely geometrical and one of the first private houses built of concrete. Loos was in charge of municipal housing in Vienna in 1920–22, and in 1923–28 lived in Paris, where he associated with the Dadaists.

loquat A small evergreen tree from China, *Eriobotrya japonica*. The genus is included within the rose family, Rosaceae, like their close relatives the apples. They are cultivated in the Mediterranean region, Japan, and India, in addition to their native country. They produce smallish, yellow, pear-shaped fruits.

Loran (*lo*ng *ra*nge *n*avigation) A long-range RADIO aid to navigation, developed in the USA from the British World War II navigation aid, GEE. The original system (Loran-A) was used extensively in Europe and North Africa in 1944 for night-bombing operations, but it has been largely replaced by Loran-C, developed in the 1950s. A Loran-C 'chain' consists of a master radio-transmitting station with two, three, or four secondary stations disposed around it at a distance of 1,100–1,800 km (600–1,000 nautical miles; see KNOT). A ship or aircraft finds its position using this system by measuring differences in the phase and time of arrival of radio-wave pulses from master and secondary transmitters. Loran-C has an accuracy of about 500 m (1,640 feet) up to 2,000 km (1,080 nautical miles) from the master station. Loran-C covers the North Atlantic and North Pacific oceans, including the South China Sea, the Gulf of Mexico, the Norwegian Sea, the Mediterranean, and the waters around Saudi Arabia.

Lorca, Federico García (1898–1936) Spanish poet and dramatist. His volumes of verse include *Gypsy Ballads* (1928), strongly influenced by the folk poetry of his native Andalusia. However, he is particularly known for intense, poetic tragedies evoking the passionate emotions of Spanish life; they include *Blood Wedding* (1933), *Yerma* (1934), and *The House of Bernarda Alba* (published posthumously in 1945). He was murdered by Nationalist partisans after the outbreak of the Spanish Civil War.

Lord Lieutenant An English magnate, originally commissioned to muster, administer, and command the militia of a specified district in times of emergency. HENRY VIII was the first to appoint them, and in 1551 during Edward VI's reign there were attempts to establish them on a permanent basis. From 1585 it became usual for every shire to have a lieutenant, and deputy lieutenants, and by the end of the 16th century they assumed additional roles, exercised on behalf of the sovereign, including the appointment of magistrates. They lost their military responsibilities in the army reforms of 1870–71, but still represent the crown in the counties.

Lord's A cricket ground in St John's Wood, north-west London, England, headquarters since 1814 of the MCC. It is named after the cricketer Thomas Lord (1755–1832).

Lorelei A rock or cliff on the right bank of the Rhine near Sankt Goarshausen. It has a remarkable echo and is held in German legend to be the home of a siren of the same name whose song lures boatmen to destruction.

Loren, Sophia (born Sophia Scicolone) (1934–) Italian actress. She has starred in many Italian and US films, ranging from the romantic melodrama *The Black Orchid* (1959) and the slapstick comedy *The Millionairess* (1960) to the wartime drama *La Ciociara* (1961), for which she won an Oscar. She received an honorary Academy Award in 1991.

Lorentz, Hendrik Antoon (1853–1928) Dutch theoretical physicist. He worked on the forces affecting electrons, making substantial advances on the work of Maxwell and realizing that electrons and cathode rays were the same thing. Lorentz's name is applied to various concepts and phenomena which he described. For their work on electromagnetic theory, he and his pupil Pieter Zeeman (1865–1943) shared the 1902 Nobel Prize for physics.

Lorentz–Fitzgerald contraction See FITZGERALD, GEORGE FRANCIS.

Lorenz, Konrad Zacharias (1903–89) Austrian zoologist, founder of the science of ethology – the study of animal behaviour in a natural environment. He believed that it is important to learn about animals in nature, rather than in a laboratory. Lorenz realized how vital BEHAVIOUR was in influencing natural selection. His belief that much behaviour was genetically fixed (innate) led to controversy when he applied the same theories to the behaviour of humans. He shared the Nobel Prize with TINBERGEN and von FRISCH in 1973.

Lorenzetti Two Italian brothers who were both painters. **Pietro** (fl. 1320–48) and **Ambrogio** (fl. 1319–48) were among the outstanding Italian artists of their time, but their lives are poorly documented – both are assumed to have died in the Black Death. They worked independently, but shared a certain affinity of style, the weightiness of their figures (showing the influence of GIOTTO) setting them apart from the graceful tradition of Sienese art exemplified by DUCCIO and Simone MARTINI. Ambrogio was the more innovative of the brothers, and his greatest work, the fresco series representing *Good and Bad Government* (1338–39) in the Town Hall at Siena, is one of the most remarkable achievements of the 14th century. Pietro's work is noted for its emotional expressiveness.

Lorenzo de' Medici (known as **Lorenzo the Magnificent**) (1449–92) Italian statesman and scholar. The grandson of Cosimo de' Medici, he came to power in Florence in 1469 following his father's death. He was a patron of the arts, promoted humanist learning and Neoplatonic philosophy, and was a noted poet and scholar in his own right; Botticelli, Leonardo da Vinci, and Michelangelo were among the artists who enjoyed his patronage.

loris Either of two species of small, nocturnal primate, which have enormous, forward-facing eyes and well-developed, grasping hands. They are omnivorous, eating insects, fruit, leaves, birds' eggs, small lizards, and mammals. The adults sleep in the hollow of a tree or clasped to the fork of a branch. They are solitary or live in pairs. A single offspring is born after a gestation period of three to five months. The baby is carried by the mother until it becomes independent. The slender loris,

Loris tardigradus, found in southern India and Sri Lanka, is 23 cm (9 inches) long. The slow or grey loris, *Nycticelous coucang*, dwells in the forests of southern Asia and the East Indies region. It moves more slowly than the slender loris. Dark brown in colour, it is 33 cm (13 inches) long. BUSHBABIES are also part of the loris family.

Lorrain, Claude See CLAUDE GELLÉE.

Lorraine ▶**1** A medieval kingdom on the west bank of the Rhine, extending from the North Sea to Italy, and divided in the 10th century into two duchies, Upper and Lower Lorraine. Upper Lorraine (south of the Ardennes), as a province of France passed to the French Crown in 1766; part of Lorraine was acquired (with Alsace) by Germany in 1871 but was restored to France after World War I. ▶**2** A region of north-east France between the Plain of Champagne and the Vosges Mountains, comprising the departments of Meurthe-et-Moselle, Meuse, Moselle, and Vosges; area 23,547 sq km (9,095 sq miles); pop. (1990) 2,305,725. Its iron deposits are some of the richest in Europe. Its chief towns are Metz and Nancy.

Lorre, Peter (born Laszlo Lowenstein) (1904–64) Hungarian-born US actor. He achieved international recognition as the child murderer in the German film *M* (1931), and went on to play the Japanese detective Mr Moto in eight Hollywood films (1937–39). He was cast in other sinister roles in *The Maltese Falcon* (1941), *Casablanca* (1942), and *The Raven* (1963).

Los Alamos A town in northern New Mexico, USA; pop. (1990) 11,450. It has been a centre for nuclear research since the 1940s, when it was the site of the development of the first atomic and hydrogen bombs.

Los Angeles A city on the Pacific coast of southern California, the second-largest in the USA, and one of the largest built-up areas in the world; pop. (1990) 3,485,400. Founded in 1781, it developed after the arrival of the Southern Pacific Railroad and the discovery of oil in 1894. It has become a major commercial, industrial and urban complex in the 20th century, its metropolitan area having expanded to include towns such as Beverly Hills, Hollywood, Santa Monica, and Redondo Beach. Its high motor-vehicle density has created a serious problem of 'smog' pollution. Major industries include aircraft, oil refining, and entertainment (film and TV). It is also a cultural and tourist centre.

lost-wax process See CIRE-PERDUE.

Lot The nephew of the Hebrew patriarch Abraham, who accompanied him to Canaan. When their flocks became too large, Lot settled on the outskirts of Sodom near the southern end of the Dead Sea in Israel. A messenger from God came to warn the God-fearing Lot of the imminent destruction of the city because of the wickedness of its inhabitants, and urged him and his family to flee. Lot's wife was turned to a pillar of salt for disobeying God's order not to look back. In Islam, Lut (Lot) is mentioned several times in the Koran for having warned his people of God's impending punishment for their indecency and perverse sexual acts. In Islamic legend, Lut's wife is said to have been turned into a pillar of salt because she used ostentatiously to borrow salt from neighbours to show that her husband was entertaining forbidden guests.

Lothian A former local government region in east-central Scotland, on the Firth of Forth, divided in 1996 into the local government districts (unitary authorities) of Midlothian, East Lothian, West Lothian, and Edinburgh.

Loti, Pierre (pseudonym of Louis Marie Julien Viaud) (1850–1923) French novelist. His novels were written while he served as a naval officer and his voyages provided the background for his work. His fame chiefly rests on three novels: *Mon frère Yves* (1883), *Pêcheur d'Islande* (1886), and *Matelot* (1893). These tell of the struggles of sailors who leave Brittany to fish in the waters around Iceland and the heartbreak of those left behind.

Lotto, Lorenzo (*c*.1480–*c*.1556) Italian painter. He is said to have trained with GIORGIONE and TITIAN in the studio of Giovanni BELLINI, but he had a highly personal style, and stands somewhat apart from the central Venetian tradition. His work draws on a wide variety of sources and is extremely uneven, but at the same time shows acute freshness of observation. He is now perhaps best known for his portraits, in which he often conveys a mood of psychological unrest, but he worked mainly as a religious painter.

lotus Either of two species of waterlily of the genus *Nelumbo*. The pink-flowered sacred lotus, *N. nucifera*, is native to eastern Asia, though it has been introduced into other parts of the tropics; the yellow-flowered American lotus, *N. lutea*, is native to the southern USA. The flowers and leaves of both species are held well above the water and their fruits are carried in a swollen receptacle which, after ripening, breaks away from the stem and floats; when this decays, the fruits are released and sink to the bottom. The fruits and rhizomes are used as food in some parts of the world.

Lotus Sūtra (Sanskrit *Saddharma Pundarīka Sūtra*, 'Lotus of the True Law') A collection of Buddhist teachings dating from around the 1st century AD. It is recognized by MAHAYANA Buddhists as containing the essential teachings of the BUDDHA, and thus the most complete discourse of their doctrine. It contains a speech given by the transcendent, rather than earthly, Buddha to all sentient creatures. In it he explains the many ways to enlightenment: the role of the Buddha; the benefits of appealing to Bodhisattvas, particularly Avalokiteshvara (see DALAI LAMA); the meaning of Buddha-nature; and the importance of faith.

loudspeaker A device for converting electrical audio signals into sound; loudspeakers perform the reverse function to MICROPHONES. Common applications of loudspeakers are in SOUND RECORDING AND REPRODUCTION equipment, in telephone receivers, and in RADIO and TELEVISION RECEIVERS. Most loudspeakers are of the moving-coil type. This comprises a coil, which is free to move backwards and forwards short distances within the field of a permanent magnet. Attached to one end of the coil is a stiff paper or plastic cone. When an electrical signal is applied to the coil, the coil is pushed backwards and forwards due to the interaction between the magnetic field and the signal (see ELECTROMAGNETIC INDUCTION). The rapid oscillations of the coil are reproduced in the cone, producing sound waves.

Loughborough A town in Leicestershire, central England, on the River Soar; pop. (1991) 46,867. Once noted for lace-making and bell-founding, the bell of St Paul's Cathedral in London was cast here in 1881. Loughborough University of Technology was founded in 1966. It is now a market town with light industries.

Louis Eighteen kings of France. **Louis I** (778–840), son of Charlemagne, was king of the West Franks and Holy Roman emperor 814–40. **Louis II** (846–79) reigned 877–79. **Louis III** (863–82), son of Louis II, reigned 879–82. **Louis IV** (921–54) reigned 936–54. **Louis V** (967–87) reigned 979–87. **Louis VI** (1081–1137) reigned 1108–37. **Louis VII** (1120–80) reigned 1137–80. **Louis VIII** (1187–1226) reigned 1223–26. **Louis IX** (canonized as St Louis) (1214–70), son of Louis VIII, reigned 1226–70. His reign was dominated by his two crusades to the Holy Land, neither of which proved successful: the first (1248–54) ended in disaster with his capture by the Egyptians, the second (1270–71) in his own death from plague in Tunis. Feast day, 25 August. **Louis X** (1289–1316) reigned 1314–16. **Louis XI** (1423–83), son of Charles VII, reigned 1461–83. He continued his father's work in laying the foundations of a united France ruled by an absolute monarchy. His reign was dominated by his struggle with Charles the Rash, Duke of Burgundy. This ended with Charles's death in battle in 1477 and France's absorption of much of Burgundy's former territory along her border. **Louis XII** (1462–1515) reigned 1498–1515. **Louis XIII** (1601–43), son of Henry IV of France, reigned 1610–43. During his minority, the country was ruled by his mother Marie de Médicis. Louis asserted his right to rule in 1617, but from 1624 he was heavily influenced in policy-making by his chief minister Cardinal Richelieu. **Louis XIV** (1638–1715), son of Louis XIII, reigned 1643–1715. He is known as the 'Sun King' from the magnificence of his reign, which represented the high point of the Bourbon dynasty and of French power in Europe, and during which French art and literature flourished. However, his almost constant wars of expansion united Europe against him, and, despite the reforms of Colbert, gravely weakened France's financial position. The Peace of Utrecht (1713–14), which ended the War of the Spanish Succession, represented the ultimate failure of Louis's attempt at European hegemony, preventing as it did the union of the French and Spanish crowns. **Louis XV** (1710–74), great-grandson and successor of Louis XIV, reigned 1715–74. He led France into the Seven Years War (1756–63). **Louis XVI** (1754–93), grandson and successor of Louis XV, reigned 1774–92. He inherited a situation of growing political discontent and severe problems of debt in the state finances. When the French Revolution broke out, he took refuge in a series of half measures, such as constitutional reforms and concessions to the republicans, which proved disastrous to his cause. After Louis's unsuccessful attempt to flee the country (1791), the Revolution became progressively more extreme and, with foreign invaders massing on the borders, the monarchy was abolished and Louis and his wife Marie Antoinette were executed. **Louis XVII** (1785–95), son of Louis XVI, was a titular king who died in prison during the Revolution. **Louis XVIII** (1755–1824), brother of Louis XVI, reigned 1814–24. Following the outbreak of the French Revolution he went into exile in 1791; two years later he pronounced himself regent for his nephew Louis XVII. After his nephew's death Louis XVIII became titular king until the fall of Napoleon in 1814, when he returned to Paris on the summons of Talleyrand and was officially restored to the throne. Louis introduced a constitutional monarchy in the same year, but was forced to flee the capital when Napoleon regained power briefly in 1815. After the latter's defeat at Waterloo, Louis returned to Paris and inaugurated parliamentary government.

Louis I (known as **Louis the Great**) (1326–82) King of Hungary 1342–82 and of Poland 1370–82. He fought two successful wars against Venice (1357–58; 1378–81), and the rulers of Serbia, Wallachia, Moldavia, and Bulgaria became his vassals. Under his rule Hungary became a powerful state, though Poland was troubled by revolts.

Louis, Joe (born Joseph Louis Barrow) (1914–81) US boxer. Known as 'the Brown Bomber', he was heavyweight champion of the world 1937–49, defending his title 25 times during that period.

Louis, St Louis IX of France. See LOUIS.

Louisiana A state in the southern USA, bordering on the Gulf of Mexico; area 123,677 sq km (47,752 sq miles); pop. (1990) 4,219,970; capital, Baton Rouge. The largest cities are New Orleans, Baton Rouge, and Shreveport. It is also known as the Pelican State, Creole State, or Sugar State. The territory was claimed by France in 1682 and named in honour of Louis XIV. It was sold by the French republic to the USA in 1803 (see LOUISIANA PURCHASE), becoming the 18th state in 1812. Louisiana is a major producer of natural gas, petroleum, salt, and sulphur, and a leading supplier of furs from muskrat, opossum, raccoon, and otter. Its principal tourist attractions are the French Quarter of New Orleans, the coastal bayous, the Jean Lafitte National Historic Park, and the Poverty Point National Monument.

Louisiana Purchase (1803) US acquisition from France of over two million sq km (828,000 sq miles) of territory stretching north from the mouth of the Mississippi to its source and west to the Rockies. France had ceded Louisiana to Spain in 1762 but regained it by treaty in 1801. Concerned at the possible closure of the Mississippi to commerce and the related threat to US security, President JEFFERSON sent James MONROE to France in 1803 to help negotiate free navigation and the purchase of New Orleans and west Florida. At war again with Britain, Napoleon was anxious not to have extensive overseas territories to defend and sold the whole of Louisiana to the USA for $15 million. Although the Constitution gave no authority to purchase new territory or promise it statehood, the Senate confirmed the agreement, increasing US territory by some 140 per cent, and transforming the USA into a continental nation.

Louis-Napoleon Napoleon III of France. See NAPOLEON.

Louis Philippe (1773–1850) King of France 1830–48. As the Duc d'Orléans, Louis Philippe participated in the early, liberal phase of the French Revolution, but later went into exile abroad. Returning to France after the restoration of the Bourbons that followed Napoleon's fall, he became the focus for liberal discontent, and after the overthrow of Charles X in 1830 was made king. His bourgeois-style regime was popular at first but it was gradually undermined by radical discontent and overthrown in a brief uprising in 1848, with Louis once more going into exile.

Louisville An industrial city in north-west Kentucky, USA, on the Ohio River; pop. (1990) 269,060. Named after Louis XVI of France, it developed as an important portage point around the falls on the Ohio River. The annual Kentucky Derby, the oldest race in the USA, takes place on the Churchill Downs race-track. Its university was founded in 1798 and its industries produce bourbon, paint and varnish, home appliances, and synthetic rubber.

Louis Quinze style Style of interior decoration and design in early 18th-century France, more or less equivalent to the ROCOCO style in painting. It coincided only very roughly with LOUIS XV's reign

(1715–74), emerging around 1700, reaching its peak from about 1720 to about 1750, and being long outmoded by the time of his death.

Louis Seize style Style of interior decoration and design prevailing in France from about 1760 to the Revolution of 1789. Its development thus antedates the reign of LOUIS XVI (1774–92), after which it is named. The style marked a reaction against the frivolity of the LOUIS XV style and a return to greater solidity and sobriety.

Lourdes A town in the department of Hautes-Pyrénées, south-west France, at the foot of the Pyrenees; pop. (1990) 16,580. In 1858 a peasant girl, Bernadette Soubirous, claimed to have had visions of the Virgin Mary here. At the same time a spring appeared, and miraculous healings were reported. It is now a major centre of pilgimage.

Lourenço Marques The former name (until 1976) of MAPUTO, capital of Mozambique.

louse A small, flattened, generally wingless insect which is an external parasite of birds and mammals. There are three distinct orders of lice. They are the BOOK LICE, BITING LICE, and SUCKING LICE. The name is usually associated with the sucking lice species, *Pediculus humanus*, which infest humans.

louse fly A highly modified true FLY of the family Hippoboscidae. Louse flies are external blood-sucking parasites of birds and large mammals. They are flattened and leathery, with long, curved claws on the feet. Some species are winged; others, such as the sheep-ked, *Melophagus ovinus*, are wingless and tick-like. Females produce only one fully developed larva at a time, and this immediately pupates.

lousewort A small semi-parasitic plant usually found on grasses growing in wet meadows. The generic name *Pedicularis* is from the Latin *pediculus*, a louse, because it was assumed louseworts were responsible for lice in sheep. The 350 or so species are widely distributed, chiefly in the northern temperate regions of the world. Together with figworts, antirrhinums, and others, they belong to the foxglove family, Scrophularicaceae.

Louth A county of the Republic of Ireland, in the province of Leinster on the frontier with Northern Ireland; area 821 sq km (317 sq miles); pop. (1991) 90,700; county town, Dundalk.

Louvre The national museum and art gallery of France, in Paris, housed in the former royal palace, on the site of an earlier fortress and arsenal, built by Francis I (died 1547) and later extended. When the court moved to Versailles in 1678 its conversion into a museum was begun. It was Francis I who set the pattern for royal collecting and patronage which persisted until the French Revolution, and the royal collections, greatly increased by Louis XIV, formed the nucleus of the national collection which is an epitome of French history and culture. A controversial glass pyramid, designed by I. M. Pei, was erected in the forecourt in 1989.

love-bird A bird of the genus *Agapornis*, which comprises nine species within the parrot family, Psittacidae. All are African mainland species, except one, which lives in Madagascar. All are small, up to 16 cm (6 inches) long, and mainly green, though many have white, red, or dark brown on their heads. The females of several species carry grass and other materials for nesting by tucking it in among their feathers rather than carrying it in their beaks. They were given their name because they live in pairs and spend a great deal of time preening each other.

Lovelace, Augusta Ada King, Countess of (1815–52) British mathematician and active collaborator with BABBAGE, the pioneer of mechanical computing. Lovelace, the legitimate daughter of Lord Byron, met Babbage in 1833; she began to assist in the development of the analytical engine and published notes on the work. She was one of the first to recognize the potential of computers and has been called the first computer programmer. The programming language Ada is named after her.

Lovelace, Richard (1618–57) English poet. A Royalist, in 1642 he was committed to prison, where he probably wrote the poem 'To Althea from Prison'. He rejoined Charles I in 1645 and was again imprisoned in 1648; during this time he prepared his collection of poetry *Lucasta*, which includes the lyric 'On going to the wars'.

love-lies-bleeding A plant, *Amaranthus caudatus*, typical of the family Amaranthaceae, which also includes cocks-combs (*Celosia* species). This family of over 900 species has a mainly tropical distribution, but provides many popular garden species for temperate regions. Love-lies-bleeding, which is native to India, may reach a height of 1.5 m (5 feet) or more. The red flowers are borne in long pendent chains; hence the common name.

Lovell, Sir (Alfred Charles) Bernard (1913–) British astronomer and physicist, and pioneer of radio astronomy. He became professor of radio astronomy at Manchester University in 1951, and founded the university's radio observatory at Jodrell Bank. He directed the construction of the large radio telescope there, now named after him.

Lovelock, James (Ephraim) (1919–) British scientist. Lovelock was the first (in 1966) to detect CFCs, released from aerosols and coolants and now known to damage the ozone layer, in the atmosphere. He is best known for the GAIA HYPOTHESIS – first presented by him in 1972 – in which he likens the Earth to a vast self-regulating organism, modifying the biosphere to suit its needs. Lovelock discussed the hypothesis in the popular book *Gaia* (1979) and in several sequels.

low A region of low atmospheric pressure (below 1,000 millibars) usually associated with rain and high winds. See DEPRESSION.

Low, Sir David (Alexander Cecil) (1891–1963) British cartoonist, born in New Zealand. He came to England in 1919 and worked for newspapers, joining the *Evening Standard* in 1927. Here he earned a worldwide reputation for his political cartoons, inventing the character Colonel Blimp and producing a series of anti-Nazi cartoons during World War II. In 1953 he joined the *Manchester Guardian*. He published more than 30 collections of cartoons, including *Low's Company* (1952).

Low Countries The three adjacent north-west European countries of the NETHERLANDS, BELGIUM, and LUXEMBOURG. Much of the Netherlands and small parts of Belgium are in fact below sea-level. Southern Belgium and Luxembourg are higher, rising to over 600 m (2,000 feet) in the Ardennes.

Lowell, Amy (Lawrence) (1874–1925) US poet and literary critic. A member of a distinguished Massachusetts family, she joined in 1913, and later led, the group of poets known as Imagists, editing several anthologies with the title *Some Imagist Poets*. Her own work is marked by technical experiments, notably the FREE VERSE form 'polyphonic prose'. She wrote three critical studies, *Six French Poets* (1915), *Tendencies in Modern American Poetry* (1917), and *John Keats* (1925).

Lowell, James Russell (1819–91) US poet and critic. His works include volumes of verse, the satirical *Biglow Papers* (1848 and 1867; prose and verse), memorial odes after the Civil War, and various volumes of essays, including *Among My Books* (1870) and *My Study Window* (1871).

Lowell, Percival (1855–1916) US astronomer. Lowell founded an observatory in Flagstaff, Arizona, which now bears his name. He inferred the existence of a ninth planet beyond Neptune, and when it was eventually discovered in 1930 it was given the name Pluto, with a symbol that also included Lowell's initials. He claimed to have seen the supposed canals on Mars, and was a devout believer in the existence of intelligent life on the planet. He was the brother of poet Amy LOWELL.

Lowell, Robert (Traill Spence) (1917–77) US poet. In 1940 he married and was converted to Roman Catholicism. His first volume, *Land of Unlikeness* (1944), reflects his conflicts with Catholicism and his Boston ancestry. His personal life was marked by recurring bouts of manic illness, alcoholism, and marital discord; his poetry is notable for its intense confessional nature and for its ambiguous complex imagery, as in the volumes *Life Studies* (1959), *For the Union Dead* (1964), and *The Dolphin* (1973).

Lower California See BAJA CALIFORNIA.

Lower Canada See QUEBEC.

Lowestoft A fishing port and resort town on the North Sea coast of Suffolk, east England; pop. (1991) 62,907. It is the most easterly English town.

low-ground-pressure vehicle An all-terrain vehicle (ATV) designed to be able to move on all surfaces. Such vehicles originated in Canada around 1960. Typically they consist of sturdy watertight hulls with as many as eight driven wheels fitted with wide, soft, low-pressure tyres that obviate the need for conventional springing and suspension. The large-volume tyres also make these vehicles amphibious, the spinning tyres providing 'paddle-wheel' propulsion when used on water.

Lowry, L(aurence) S(tephen) (1887–1976) British painter. He spent most of his life in Salford, near Manchester, which provided the characteristic industrial setting of his pictures. Deliberately adopting a childlike manner of visualization, he painted small matchstick figures set against the iron and brick expanse of urban and industrial landscapes, providing a wry perspective on life in the industrial North.

Loyola, St Ignatius See IGNATIUS LOYOLA, ST.

LSD (lysergic acid diethylamide) A hallucinogen drug that has unpredictable effects and is illegal in most countries. In the 1960s the US psychologist Timothy LEARY and the British writer Aldous HUXLEY claimed that it enhanced perception and increased awareness. The perceptions produced are now regarded as distorted rather than enhanced and the drug can cause schizophrenia-like symptoms. Taken by pregnant women, it can cause deformed foetuses.

Luanda The capital city of Angola, a seaport and naval base on the Atlantic coast of West Africa at the mouth of the Cuanza River; pop. (est. 1995) 2,250,000. Founded by the Portuguese in 1575, it became a major centre for the trans-shipment of slaves to Brazil during the 17th and 18th centuries.

Luba A Bantu kingdom founded *c*.1500, lying north of Lake Kisale in the Republic of Congo. The founders, the Balopwe clan, came from further north, and imposed their sovereignty over existing chiefdoms. Some of the Luba moved eastwards *c*.1600, and founded a kingdom among the Lunda; from there a large number of small chiefdoms proliferated stretching from eastern Angola to north-eastern Zambia, and making previously existing chiefdoms their vassals. The largest was the kingdom of Mwata Yamvo; others were the Bemba in north-eastern Zambia, Kazembe in the Luapula valley, and Kasanje in central Angola. They all paid tribute to the central kingdoms, but the organization was decentralized, and the kings served as settlers of disputes between communities. These were occupied not only by agriculture, but also in mining and trade in copper and salt against European goods obtained from the Portuguese. Kazembe was the richest and most important.

Lübeck A port on the Baltic coast of northern Germany, in the state of Schleswig-Holstein north-east of Hamburg; pop. (1991) 211,000. Formerly a Slavonic principality, it became a part of Holstein in 1143. Between the 14th and 19th centuries it was an important city within the Hanseatic League. Its trade is mostly with Scandinavia.

Lubitsch, Ernst (1892–1947) German-born US film director. He had become famous through his German films when, in 1922, he moved to the USA, where his polished, witty, often amoral comedies were said to have the 'Lubitsch touch'. His first sound film, *The Love Parade* (1930), was a musical, as were *Monte Carlo* (also 1930) and *The Merry Widow* (1934). Of his best comedies, *Trouble in Paradise* (1932), *Bluebeard's Eighth Wife* (1938), and *Ninotchka* (1939), with Greta GARBO, are his best known. *To Be or Not to Be* (1942) satirized the Nazis through the tribulations of a troupe of actors in occupied Poland.

Lublin A manufacturing city in eastern Poland, capital of Lublin county; pop. (1990) 351,350. It has a 16th-century cathedral and a university founded in 1944. The **Union of Lublin** (1569) between Poland and Lithuania was signed here.

lubricating oil Any of a group of oils used to reduce friction in engines and machinery, and to protect metal against wear and corrosion. Originally, tallow and castor oil were used. Modern lubricating oils are produced in PETROLEUM REFINING by VACUUM DISTILLATION of the involatile residue (the atmospheric residue) from the FRACTIONAL DISTILLATION of petroleum. The most important group of lubricating oils are those for internal-combustion engines, which are graded according to their viscosity at −18°C, by the Society of Automotive Engineers (SAE) in the USA. SAE numbers generally range from about 5 to 50. Multigrade car oils have a second grading indicating the relative viscosity at 99°C. Gear oils have sulphur additives, developed to prevent actual contact between metal surfaces, and to reduce corrosion, promote stability at high temperatures, and control viscosity. Greases are lubricating oils thickened by substances such as soaps, lithium, carbon, or polyethylene.

Lubumbashi A city in the south-east of the Democratic Republic of Congo, near the border with Zambia; capital of the Shaba cobalt- and copper-mining region; pop. (1991) 739,100. Founded by Belgian colonists in 1910, it was called Elizabethville until 1966.

Lucan (full name Marcus Annaeus Lucanus) (39–65 AD) Roman poet. Nephew of the younger Seneca, he wrote an unfinished EPIC, the *Pharsalia* or *Bellum Civile*, describing the civil war between Caesar and Pompey, is melodramatic and brilliantly phrased, with rhetorical speeches and unflagging appeal to the emotions of the reader.

Lucas, George (1944–) US film director, producer, and screenwriter. He is chiefly known as the director and writer of the science-fiction adventure film *Star Wars* (1977). He produced and wrote the screenplays for two further episodes in the saga, namely *The Empire Strikes Back* (1980) and *Return of the Jedi* (1983), as well as for Steven Spielberg's *Raiders of the Lost Ark* (1981) and its two sequels.

Lucas van Leyden (*c.*1494–1533) Dutch painter and engraver. He produced his most significant work as an engraver and was active in this field from an early age; his *Muhammad and the Murdered Monk* dates from 1508 and *Ecce Homo* from 1510. His later work was influenced by that of Dürer, whom he met in 1521. His paintings include portraits, genre scenes, and religious subjects, such as the triptych *The Last Judgement* (1526–27).

Lucca A town in Tuscany, northern Italy, capital of Lucca province; pop. (1990) 86,440. It was the capital of an independent republic during the 11th–13th centuries and was famous for its silk. It is the centre of a noted olive oil producing region.

lucerne See ALFALFA.

Lucerne, Lake (or **Lake of Lucerne**; German **Vierwaldstätter See**) A lake in central Switzerland, surrounded by the four cantons of Lucerne, Nidwalden, Uri, and Schwyz and sometimes also known as the Lake of the Four Forest Cantons; area 114 sq km (44 sq miles).

Lucifer In early Christian belief, the angel who rebelled against God and was cast out of heaven with his followers to become the devil (Satan), who tempts people to evil. He is also conceived of as the personification of evil in Judaism and Islam.

Lucknow A city in northern India, on the Gomti River, capital of the state of Uttar Pradesh; pop. (1991) 1,642,130. In 1775 it became the capital of the province of Oudh and in 1857, during the Indian mutiny, its British residency was twice besieged by Indian insurgents (the **Siege of Lucknow**). It is a centre for handicrafts such as silversmithing.

Lucretius (full name Titus Lucretius Carus) (*c.*94–*c.*55 BC) Roman poet and philosopher. His didactic hexametric poem *On the Nature of Things* is an exposition of the atomist physics of Epicurus; it is based on a firmly materialistic view of the Universe, which is directed to the goal of giving humans peace of mind by showing that fear of the gods and of death is without foundation.

Lucullus, Lucius Licinius (died *c.*57 BC) Roman general who served with SULLA. He successfully conducted the third war against Mithridates, but after his troops mutinied Pompey took over and Lucullus retired to a life of food, wine, and extravagant banquets (known as **Lucullan feasts**).

Luddite A member of a 19th-century protest group of British workers, who destroyed machinery, which they believed was depriving them of their livelihood. The movement began in Nottinghamshire in 1811, when framework knitters began wrecking the special type of 'wide frames' used to make poor-quality stockings, which were undercutting the wages of skilled craftsmen. The men involved claimed to be acting under the leadership of a certain 'Ned Ludd' or 'King Ludd', although it is doubtful whether such a person ever existed. The outbreaks of violence spread rapidly and by the early part of 1812 were affecting Yorkshire and Lancashire. Large groups of men stormed the cotton and woollen mills in order to attack the power looms. The government responded harshly by making machine-breaking an offence punishable by death. There were further sporadic outbreaks in 1816, but the movement subsequently died out.

Ludendorff, Erich (1865–1937) German general. Shortly after the outbreak of World War I he was appointed Chief of Staff to General von Hindenburg and they jointly directed the war effort until the final offensive failed (September 1918). Ludendorff later joined the Nazi Party and served as a member of the Reichstag (1924–28).

Ludwig Three kings of Bavaria. **Ludwig I** (1786–1868) reigned 1825–48. His reactionary policies and lavish expenditure were the cause of radical protests in 1830; his domination by the dancer Lola Montez led to further unrest and he was forced to abdicate in favour of his son. **Ludwig II** (1845–86) reigned 1864–86. He came increasingly under Prussian influence and his country eventually joined the new German Empire in 1871. A patron of the arts, in particular of Wagner, he later became a recluse and concentrated on building a series of elaborate castles. He was declared insane and deposed in 1886. **Ludwig III** (1845–1921) reigned 1913–18.

Lugano A resort town and financial centre in Ticino canton, southern Switzerland, on the north shore of Lake Lugano (which extends into Italy); pop. (1990) 26,010.

Lugh In early Irish Celtic mythology, the Sun god and chieftain who killed the leader of the Fomors, the giant predecessors of the Tuatha Dé Danann in Ireland. Lugh had a spear of deadly accuracy and was skilled in the arts of war and peace. The name of Lugh was assumed by the heroes of much of Irish mythology.

Lugosi, Bela (born Béla Ferenc Blasko) (1884–1956) Hungarian-born US actor. From 1904 he pursued a successful career as a classical actor in the Hungarian theatre, before emigrating to the USA in 1921. Lugosi became famous with his performance in the title role of *Dracula* (1927) on Broadway; in 1931 he recreated the role for Hollywood in the first Dracula film. He subsequently appeared in a succession of horror films, including *Mark of the Vampire* (1935) and *The Wolf Man* (1940).

lugworm A polychaete worm of the genus *Arenicola*. Lugworms are dug by fishermen as bait from sandy beaches and marine estuaries, where their worm-casts betray them. They live in U-shaped burrows and feed by swallowing sand and detritus. They void the sand, as the cast at the tail-end of the burrow, roughly once every 40 minutes. Lugworms are related to bristle worms, but lack the lateral paddles; instead they bear frilly, red gills, to facilitate breathing in stagnant mud or sand.

Lukács, György (1885–1971) Hungarian philosopher, literary critic, and politician. A major figure in Western Marxism, he is best known for his philosophical work *History and Class Consciousness* (1923), in which he stresses the central role of alienation in Marxist thought. His literary criticism is noted for its realist standpoint, notably in *The Theory of the Novel* (1916) and *The Historical Novel* (1955).

Luke, St An evangelist, closely associated with St Paul and traditionally the author of the third Gospel and the Acts of the Apostles. A physician, he was possibly the son of a Greek freedman of Rome. Feast day, 18 October.

Lully, Jean-Baptiste (born Giovanni Battista Lulli) (1632–87) French composer, born in Italy. He lived in France from the age of 14 and entered the service of Louis XIV in 1653. From 1664 he collaborated with Molière, writing incidental music for a series of comedies, including *Le Bourgeois Gentilhomme* (1670). In 1673 he turned to composing operas; his works, which include *Alceste* (1674) and *Armide* (1686), mark the beginning of the French operatic tradition.

lumbago A low backache of any cause. It is often a result of a 'slipped disc' (a prolapsed intervertebral disc) or of a strained muscle or ligament. It is sometimes associated with SCIATICA.

lumbar puncture The introduction into the spinal canal, normally between the third and fourth lumbar vertebrae, of a hollow needle, either for removal of cerebrospinal fluid (CSF), or for administration of a drug or a radio-opaque contrast medium for RADIOLOGY. Measurement of CSF pressure and analysis of CSF composition are techniques used in the diagnosis of several different conditions. Drugs may be administered via lumbar puncture for ANAESTHESIA, or to access the central nervous system directly, rather than via the bloodstream.

lumen (symbol lm) The SI unit of luminous flux equal to the light emitted in one second by a point source of one candela in a cone of one steradian solid angle.

Lumière French brothers, who were inventors and pioneers of cinema. In 1895 **Auguste Marie Louis Nicholas** (1862–1954) and **Louis Jean** (1864–1948), patented their 'Cinématographe', a cine-camera and projector in one; it had its first public demonstration later the same year. They also invented an improved process of colour photography.

luminosity The radiation output per unit time from a star or other celestial object, usually expressed as a multiple of the Sun's output. It is a measure of **brightness** and is given by the formula

$$\log (L/L_\odot) = 0.4\,(M_\odot - M),$$

where L and M are the luminosity and absolute MAGNITUDE of the object, and $L_\odot$ and $M_\odot$ are the corresponding quantities for the Sun. The comparison is usually made in visible light, but can be made in other ranges of wavelength. For total radiation output the luminosity is either determined with a BOLOMETER or is calculated from multi-wavelength PHOTOMETRY.

Luminosity classes are groups of stars which do not lie on the main sequence of the HERTZSPRUNG–RUSSELL DIAGRAM.

luminous paint Paint that glows in the dark. It contains phosphor, a material that absorbs short-wavelength light and re-emits it as transient light of a longer wavelength after the energy source has been withdrawn (examples are zinc sulphide and calcium sulphide). Luminous paints that glowed indefinitely, containing small amounts of RADIUM salts, were used extensively for the hands and numbers on watch faces, but the dangers of the radioactive radium salts led to their withdrawal (see OCCUPATIONAL DISEASE).

lumpsucker A fish of the family Cyclopteridae, of which there are 140 species. The Atlantic lumpsucker, *Exclopterus lumpus*, is a species of almost spherical fish with rows of large, coarsely spined plates on the sides and back. It has a round sucker-disc on the belly, by means of which it attaches itself to rocks, especially in late winter, when it lays its eggs in clumps which are guarded by the male. It is known as lumpfish in North America, and its roe is used as a substitute for caviar.

Lumumba, Patrice (Emergy) (1925–61) Congolese nationalist and politician. He founded the influential MNC (Mouvement National Congolais) in 1958 to bring together radical nationalists. He was accused of instigating public violence and was jailed by the Belgians, but was released to participate in the Brussels Conference (January 1960) on the Congo. He became Prime Minister and Minister of Defence when the Congo became independent in June 1960. Sections of the army mutinied, the Belgian troops returned, and Katanga province declared its independence. Lumumba appealed to the UNITED NATIONS, which sent a peace-keeping force. President Kasavubu, his rival in power, dismissed him and shortly afterwards he was put under arrest by Colonel Mobutu. He escaped, but was recaptured and killed.

lunar calendar A CALENDAR based on the variations of the phases of the Moon as seen from Earth. The lunar year contains 12 synodic months, these consisting of 29.5305882 days, the synodic month being defined as the time interval (SYNODIC PERIOD) between new moons. Therefore, the lunar year of 354.3672 days is about 11 days shorter than the solar year of 365.24219 days. A true lunar calendar quickly gets out of step with the seasons and is often replaced by a luni-solar calendar in which every third or fourth year contains 13 as opposed to 12 lunar months, a leap month being intercalated (added) as required. Islamic, Jewish, Hindu, Buddhist, and all Christian festivals except Christmas itself are timed according to the lunar calendar. The synodic month was probably the first exact interval of time to be calculated by ancient civilizations.

lunar module See APOLLO PROGRAMME.

Lundy An uninhabited granite island in the Bristol Channel, south-west England, off the coast of north Devon. Its name is derived from Norse ('Puffin Island'). Lundy has one of the most important seabird colonies in southern England and the surrounding waters are a marine nature reserve.

lung An organ that is used to draw in air and bring it into contact with the blood in all tetrapod (four-legged) vertebrates and the lungfishes. The lungs lie in cavities in the chest, on either side of the heart. In adult amphibians they are simple sac-like structures, which are inflated by forcing air into them using the tongue and the mouth cavity. In virtually all other vertebrates, the lungs have an elastic tissue framework containing numerous thin-walled air-containing sacs, richly supplied with blood by capillaries (small blood vessels).

Air entering the lungs passes down rigid-walled tubes (trachea and bronchi), which lead to muscular-walled tubes (bronchioles), then to the air sacs (alveoli). In mammals, air is sucked into the lungs when a muscular membrane, called the diaphragm, descends and the rib-cage elevates. Air is expelled due to the elastic recoil of the lungs when the muscles relax.

Some snails and scorpions have lungs, but have no regular ventilated system of air movement, relying on diffusion of oxygen across their walls.

lungfish A member of one of the two extant groups of sarcopterygian BONY FISHES (the other containing the COELACANTH). The living lungfishes comprise two families: the Australian lungfishes, and the South American and African lungfishes. The first family contains a single species, *Neoceratodus forsteri*, which has a single lung and functional gills. The South American lungfish, *Lepidosiren paradoxica*, and the four African species of the genus *Protopterus* have reduced internal gills, paired lungs, and are obligate air breathers.

The African and South American lungfishes live inside a burrow in the bed of the lake during the dry season, and can survive drought. The African species form a 'cocoon' in the mud and can survive up to two years of drought. The Australian lungfish lives in waters which do not annually dry out and uses its lung when the water becomes stagnant. Lung-fishes are relatively large freshwater fishes, some attaining 1.5 m (5 feet) in length.

lungless salamander A member of the largest family of SALAMANDERS, Plethodontidae, containing approximately 215 species. A few species fail to metamorphose and remain as permanent, gilled larvae, breeding in the larval state, but the majority undergo complete METAMORPHOSIS. However, unlike other salamanders, they do not develop lungs to replace the larval gills, depending instead upon respiration through the thin, moist skin of the body and pharynx (throat). They vary widely in size, from 4 to 30 cm (1.5 to 12 inches), and may occupy a variety of aquatic, terrestrial, and arboreal habitats.

lungworm A parasite of many large mammals, including cattle, deer, pigs, and sheep, as well as amphibians such as frogs. Lungworms are ROUNDWORMS, especially of the family Metastrongylidae, living within the lung; the host coughs up eggs and swallows them. The young larvae are released in faeces, up to five million per day. New hosts then pick them up when grazing. Lungworms are white and thread-like, about 5 cm (2 inches) long, and severe infestations cause coughing, fever, and even death in livestock.

Luoyang (formerly **Honan**) An industrial city in Henan province, north-central China, in the valley of the Luo River; pop. (1990) 1,190,000. It was founded in the 12th century BC as the imperial capital of the Chou dynasty and was the capital of several subsequent dynasties. Between the 4th and 6th centuries AD the construction of cave temples to the south of the city made it an important Buddhist centre.

lupin (US **lupine**) An annual or perennial species of the genus *Lupinus*, some of which are popular herbaceous garden plants. The long spikes of pea-like flowers, in a wide variety of colour combinations, are a classic example of selective breeding. They are members of the pea family and related to clovers, beans, and many other familiar plants.

Lupus The Wolf, a CONSTELLATION of the Southern Hemisphere of the sky, one of the 48 constellations known to the ancient Greeks. It represents a wild animal impaled on a pole by neighbouring Centaurus, the Centaur. Lupus lies in a rich area of the Milky Way and contains numerous interesting double stars for small telescopes, among them Epsilon Lupi, Kappa Lupi, Mu Lupi, and Xi Lupi.

Lusaka The capital city of Zambia; pop. (1990) 982,000. Founded in 1905, it was developed as a railway town, becoming capital of Northern Rhodesia in 1935. It is the centre of a fertile agricultural region and also has car-assembly and textile plants.

Lusitania A British transatlantic liner (named after the ancient Roman province in the Iberian peninsula), torpedoed (7 May 1915) off the Irish coast without warning by a German submarine, with the loss of 1,195 lives. The sinking, which took 128 US lives, created intense indignation throughout the USA, which until then had accepted Woodrow WILSON's policy of neutrality. Germany refused to accept responsibility for the act, and no reparations settlement was reached. Two years later (1917), following Germany's resumption of unrestricted submarine warfare, the USA severed diplomatic relations and entered the war on the side of the Allies.

lute A plucked stringed musical instrument. Generically it is any instrument with integral neck and resonator and strings running parallel with the resonator, but in Western music a lute is specifically an instrument with a resonator resembling a halved pear, which was, in the Renaissance, hailed as 'Queen of Instruments All'. The lute, in this latter sense, derived in the 13th century from the Arab *'ūd*, which is still widely used, plucked with a plectrum, in North Africa, the Middle East, and the Balkans. By the 15th century the lute had four double courses (pairs of gut strings). A fifth was added before the end of the century, and players changed to finger-plucking, which made polyphonic play-

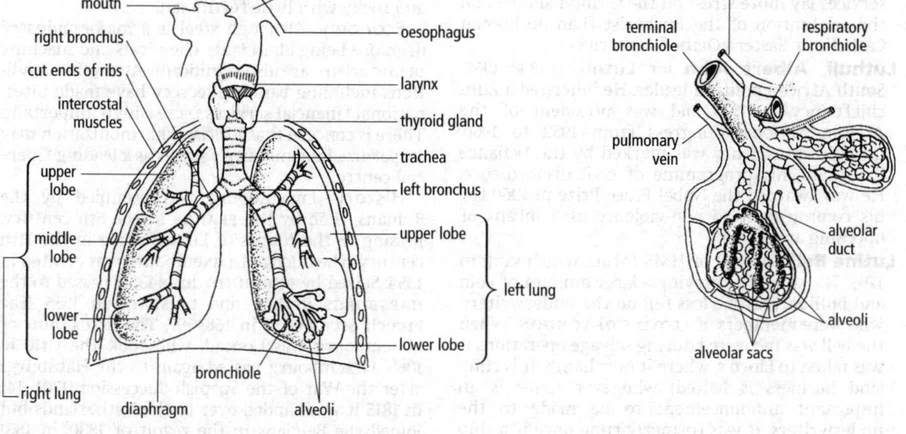

1 2

Lung (1) The lungs and the main air passages supplying them. (2) Detailed structure of the alveoli.

ing much easier. From about 1500 a sixth course was added, establishing a tuning of 4th, 4th, 3rd, 4th, and 4th, covering two octaves, with a single uppermost course tuned to g′ or a′. This remained the standard size, but by the 17th century there was a range of sizes, from a small instrument with a top string tuned to c″, to basses with extended necks carrying unstopped strings. The latter had various names – archlute, chitarrone, and theorbo – and were mainly CONTINUO instruments. The mean, or standard, lute was both a solo instrument and an accompanist to singers and other instrumentalists. It was a favourite instrument throughout the 16th and 17th centuries, surviving well into the 18th.

lutetium (symbol Lu, at. no. 71, r.a.m. 174.967) The heaviest of the LANTHANIDE elements, named after Paris (Latin name *Lutetia*) the native city of G. Urbain who first isolated it in 1907. It is separated from other lanthanides by ion-exchange techniques. It is sometimes used as a catalyst.

Luther, **Martin** (1483–1546) German Protestant theologian, the principal figure of the German Reformation. From 1508 he taught at the University of Wittenberg, latterly as professor of scripture (1512–46). He began to preach the doctrine of justification by faith rather than by works; his attack on the sale of indulgences with his 95 theses (1517) was followed by further attacks on papal authority, and in 1521 Luther was condemned and excommunicated at the Diet of Worms. At a meeting with Swiss theologians at Marburg (1529) he opposed Zwingli and gave a defence of the doctrine of consubstantiation (the presence in the Eucharist of the real substances of the body and blood of Christ); the next year he gave his approval to Melanchthon's Augsburg Confession, which laid down the Lutheran position. His translation of the Bible into High German (1522–34) contributed significantly to the spread of this form of the language and to the development of German literature in the vernacular.

Lutheran Church A PROTESTANT Church widespread in Germany, Scandinavia, and the USA, and also found in Canada and Australasia, with about 25 million full members. Traditional Lutheran teaching, based on that of Martin LUTHER, emphasizes that faith alone is necessary for salvation. Many Lutheran Churches are established, with the head of state as the head of the Church. Lutheran services lay more stress on the sermon and less on the celebration of the Eucharist than do Roman Catholic or Eastern Orthodox services.

Luthuli, **Albert John** (or **Lutuli**) (*c.*1898–1967) South African political leader. He inherited a Zulu chieftaincy in 1935 and was president of the African National Congress from 1952 to 1960. Luthuli's presidency was marked by the Defiance Campaign, his programme of civil disobedience. He was awarded the Nobel Peace Prize in 1960 for his commitment to non-violence as a means of opposing apartheid.

Lutine Bell The bell of HMS *Lutine*, which sank in 1799. The ship was carrying a large amount of coin and bullion, and the loss fell on the underwriters, who were members of LLOYD'S OF LONDON. When the bell was recovered during salvage operations it was taken to Lloyd's, where it now hangs. It is rung (and business is halted) whenever there is an important announcement to be made to the underwriters. It was formerly rung once if a ship had sunk and twice for good news.

Luton An industrial town and unitary authority in Bedfordshire, southern England, north-west of London; pop. (1991) 167,300. At one time noted for millinery, its principal industry now is the building of cars and trucks. It is the site of a major airport.

Lutosławski, **Witold** (1913–94) Polish composer. He is noted for his orchestral music, including three symphonies (1947; 1967; 1983), *Mi-parti* (1976), and *Chain 3* (1986). From the early 1960s, his works have been characterized by a blend of notational composition and aleatoric sections.

Lutyens, **Sir Edwin (Landseer)** (1869–1944) British architect. He established his reputation designing country houses, moving from a romantic red-brick style to Palladian-influenced formal designs. Lutyens is perhaps best known for his plans for New Delhi (1912), where he introduced an open garden-city layout; his Viceroy's House (1915–30) combined classical features with decoration in the Indian idiom. He is also remembered for the Cenotaph in London (1919–21) and his unfulfilled design for the Roman Catholic cathedral in Liverpool (1929).

Lutyens, **(Agnes) Elizabeth** (1906–83) British composer. She was one of the first English composers to use the serialist 12-note system (in which the notes are used on an equal basis without dependence on a key system); the Chamber Concerto No. 1 (1939) is an example of her interpretation of this technique. Her works include operas, orchestral and choral works, and chamber music; she also wrote many scores for films and radio, as well as incidental music for plays. She was the daughter of Sir Edwin Lutyens.

Luxembourg The capital of the Grand Duchy of Luxembourg, on the Alzette and Petrusse rivers; pop. (1991) 75,620. It is the seat of the European Court of Justice and the Secretariat of the Parliament of the EU. It is a commercial, cultural, and industrial centre with iron and steel and many light industries.

Luxembourg, **Grand Duchy of** A small country in north-west Europe surrounded by Belgium to the west and north, Germany to the east, and France to the south.

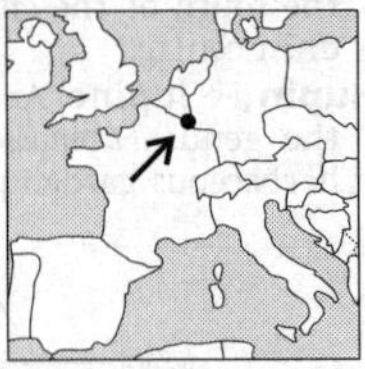

Physical. The climate is temperate continental and there are sizeable forests, but the ground is hilly and rocky with little fertile soil.

Economy. Although steel is a major industry (iron ore being abundant), chemicals and machine manufacture are also significant. Attractive conditions including banking secrecy have made international financial services increasingly important. There is concern that EU fiscal harmonization may jeopardize Luxembourg's status as a leading financial centre.

History. Luxembourg was occupied by the Romans, then by the FRANKS in the 5th century, passing to the counts of Luxembourg in the 11th century. The duchy of Luxembourg was created in 1354. Seized by BURGUNDY in 1443, it passed to the HABSBURGS in 1477 and to SPAIN in 1555. The French occupied it in 1684–97. The first Count of Luxembourg was Conrad, who took the title in 1060. Luxembourg passed again to the Habsburgs after the War of the Spanish Succession (1701–14). In 1815 it was handed over to the Netherlands but joined the Belgians in the revolt of 1830; in 1831 Luxembourg was divided, the Walloon-speaking region becoming part of Belgium. The rest of Luxembourg remained within the Netherlands and became the Grand Duchy of Luxembourg in 1839, with its own government. In 1890 the King of the Netherlands died without a male heir and from then on the two countries were headed by different royal families. Grand Duke Jean (1921–) succeeded in 1964 when his mother, Grand Duchess Charlotte (1896–1985), abdicated in his favour. Luxembourg entered into an economic union with Belgium in 1921. The Netherlands joined this union in 1948, forming the Benelux Economic Union, which was the first free-trade area in Europe. Luxembourg was a founder member of the EUROPEAN ECONOMIC COMMUNITY (now the EUROPEAN UNION). The socialist coalition, which has held power since 1984, was re-elected in 1994.

Capital: Luxembourg
Area: 2,586 sq km (999 sq mi)
Population: 409,000 (1995)
Currency: 1 Luxembourg franc = 100 centimes (Belgian currency also legal tender)
Religions: Roman Catholic 93.0%; Protestant 1.3%
Ethnic Groups: Luxembourger 73.8%; Portuguese 8.1%; Italian 5.4%; French 3.3%; German 2.3%; Belgian 2.3%
Languages: French, German (both official); Letzeburgesch; minority languages
International Organizations: UN; EU; OECD; NATO; Council of Europe; CSCE

Luxemburg, Rosa (1871–1919) Polish-born German revolutionary leader. She cofounded what became the Polish Communist Party (1893), before obtaining German citizenship in 1898. Imprisoned in 1915 for opposing World War I, she cofounded the revolutionary and pacifist group known as the Spartacus League (the Spartacists) in 1916 with the German socialist Karl Liebknecht (1871–1919). After her release from prison in 1918 she cofounded the German Communist Party; the following year she and Liebknecht were assassinated after organizing an abortive Communist uprising in Berlin.

Luxor (Arabic **El Uqsur**) A city in eastern Egypt on the east bank of the Nile; pop. (1991) 142,000. It is the site of the southern part of ancient Thebes and contains the ruins of the temple built by Amenhotep III between 1411 and 1375 BC and of monuments erected by Rameses II in the 13th century BC. It was the site of a massacre of 58 tourists by Muslim fundamentalists in 1997.

Luzon An island in the Philippines; area 104,688 sq km (40,420 sq miles). It is the most northerly and largest of the Philippine islands. Its chief towns are Quezon City and Manila, the country's capital.

lychee See LITCHI.

Lycurgus (9th century BC) Spartan lawgiver. He is traditionally held to have been the founder of the constitution and military regime of ancient Sparta.

lyddite See EXPLOSIVE.

Lydgate, John (*c*.1370–*c*.1450) English poet and monk. He is noted for his copious output of verse, often in Chaucerian style, and for translations. Of the latter the best known are the *Troy Book* (1412–20), written at the request of Prince Henry (later Henry V), and *The Fall of Princes* (1431–38), based on a French version of a book on tragedy by Boccaccio.

Lydia An ancient region of western Asia Minor, south of Mysia and north of Caria. It became a powerful kingdom in the 7th century BC but in 546 BC its final king, Croesus, was defeated by Cyrus and it was absorbed into the Persian empire. Lydia was probably the first realm to use coined money. The region gives its name to the Lydian mode, a musical term for the mode represented by the natural diatonic scale.

Lyell, Sir Charles (1797–1875) Scottish geologist. His textbook *Principles of Geology* (1830–33) influenced a generation of geologists. He held that the Earth's features were shaped over a long period of time by natural processes, and not during short periodic upheavals as proposed by the catastrophist school of thought. In this he revived the theories of James Hutton, but his influence on geological opinion was much greater. Lyell's views cleared the way for Darwin's theory of evolution, which he accepted after some hesitation.

Lyly, John (*c*.1554–1606) English prose writer and dramatist. He is remembered for his prose romance in two parts: *Euphues, The Anatomy of Wit* (1578) and *Euphues and his England* (1580). Both were written in an elaborate style that became known as *euphuism*.

lymph node A compact structure, often the size and shape of a small bean, distributed in groups throughout the body along vessels of the **lymphatic system**. (They are also known as **lymph glands**, but this is incorrect as they contain no glandular tissue.) Like blood vessels, lymphatic vessels are placed so that fluid (**lymph**) draining from tissues passes into them. Valves in the vessels direct the lymph towards collecting ducts which convey it back to the blood. Nodes, which receive a rich blood supply, consist of dense collections of

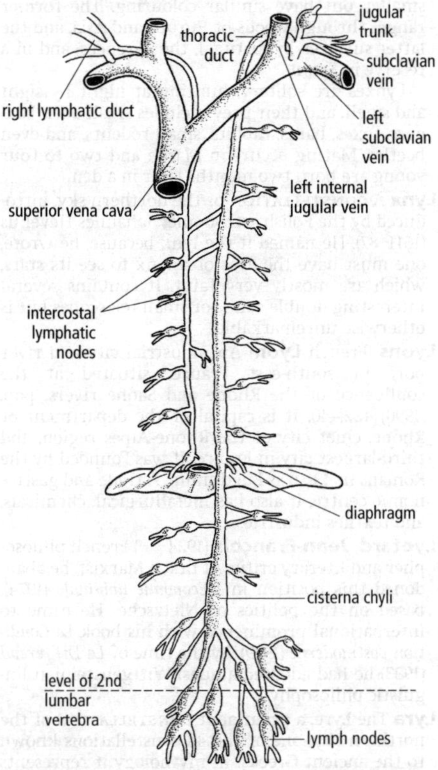

Lymph nodes Lymph nodes occur at intervals along the lymphatic system. This system carries lymph from the body's tissues and drains it into the bloodstream at the right lymphatic and thoracic ducts. Foreign particles are filtered from the lymph by the lymph nodes.

white blood cells called lymphocytes, and a series of channels, organized as a fine mesh, which filter out all large particles before they can enter the blood system. Scavenger cells, or macrophages, process the trapped matter and stimulate nearby lymphocytes to produce antibodies specific to any foreign protein molecules (antigens) released. Lymphocytes recirculate from the blood to the nodes and back every few hours, ensuring that the body's immunity to foreign molecules is kept up to date. Infected nodes enlarge and can become painful.

lymphocyte See LEUCOCYTE; LYMPH NODE.

Lynn, Dame Vera (born Vera Margaret Lewis) (1917–) British singer. During World War II she sang to the troops and became known as 'the Forces' Sweetheart'. She is remembered for such songs as 'We'll Meet Again' and 'White Cliffs of Dover'. She had a number of postwar successes, including 'Auf Wiederseh'n, Sweetheart' (1952).

lynx A species of the CAT family, *Felix lynx*, that occurs in the north of the Northern Hemisphere from Siberia through Europe and North America. There are several subspecies including the Canadian lynx, which is found from Alaska to the northern part of the USA. It is some 120 cm (4 feet) long and 60 cm (2 feet) high at the shoulder. The coat is a mixture of black, dark brown, and tawny yellow, and the underparts are cinnamon, the cheek ruffs black and white, and the tail has a black tip. The European and Spanish lynxes are smaller but have similar colouring. The former ranges through woods of Europe and Asia, and the latter survives in Portugal, the Pyrenees, and in a reserve in Spain.

Lynxes are solitary, hunting at night by sight and smell, and their prey includes small deer, badgers, foxes, hares, rabbits, small rodents, and even beetles. Mating occurs in March and two to four young are born two months later in a den.

Lynx A CONSTELLATION of the northern sky, introduced by the Polish astronomer Johannes Hevelius (1611–87). He named it the lynx because, he wrote, one must have the eyes of a lynx to see its stars, which are mostly very faint. It contains several interesting double stars for small telescopes but is otherwise unremarkable.

Lyons (French **Lyon**) An industrial city and river port in south-east France, situated at the confluence of the Rhône and Saône rivers; pop. (1990) 422,440. It is capital of the department of Rhône, chief city of the Rhône-Alpes region, and third-largest city in France. It was founded by the Romans in 43 AD as Lugdunum. A trade and gastronomic centre, it also has metallurgical, chemicals, and textiles industries.

Lyotard, Jean-François (1924–) French philosopher and literary critic. At first a Marxist, he abandoned this position in *L'Economie libidinale* (1974), based on the politics of Nietzsche. He came to international prominence with his book *La Condition postmoderne* (1979). By the time of *La Différend* (1983) he had adopted a quasi-Wittgensteinian linguistic philosophy.

Lyra The Lyre, a prominent CONSTELLATION of the northern sky, one of the 48 constellations known to the ancient Greeks. In mythology it represents the instrument played by Orpheus, although it has also been seen as an eagle or vulture. Its brightest star is VEGA. Near Vega is Epsilon Lyrae, a star popularly known as the 'Double Double'. Through binoculars it appears as a double star, but telescopes show that each star is a twin, making this a quadruple star. Every April the Lyrid meteors radiate from the constellation.

lyre A stringed musical instrument with two arms and a cross-bar forming a yoke. The plane of the strings is parallel to the belly of the resonator. It was of high antiquity in Mesopotamia and the Near East and was the instrument of King David in the Bible and the bards of ancient Greece and the early Middle Ages. Homeric epics, and those such as Beowulf, were chanted to the lyre, not spoken. With the adoption of HARPS as principal instruments before 1200, the lyre fell into disuse, but reappeared around 1400, when it was often bowed instead of plucked, with a fingerboard running up the centre of the yoke. This form developed into the CRWTH.

lyrebird Either of two birds, *Menura alberti* or *M. novaehollandiae*, that resemble long-legged brown chickens, except for the striking, long tail-feathers of the male, the outer two of which are white, banded with brown and curved outwards at the end. When the tail of lyrebirds is raised, the shape resembles a lyre. The displaying male is very noisy and mimics a wide range of other birds and even dogs and cats. The female builds a large, domed nest of twigs and leaves, often on the ground, in which she lays a single egg. The family, Menuridae, has very restricted ranges in eastern Australia.

lyric Any fairly short poem expressing the personal mood, feeling, or meditation of a single speaker (who may sometimes be an invented character, not the poet). Lyric poetry is the most extensive category of verse, especially since the decline (since the 19th century in the West) of the other principal kinds: narrative and dramatic verse. In ancient Greece, a lyric was a song for accompaniment on the lyre, but the current sense has prevailed since the Renaissance. Lyrics may be composed in almost any METRE and on almost every subject, although the most usual emotions presented are those of love and grief. Among the common lyric forms are the SONNET, ode, ELEGY, HAIKU, and some HYMNS.

Lysander (died 395 BC) Spartan general. He commanded the Spartan fleet that defeated the Athenian navy in 405. Lysander captured Athens in 404, so bringing the Peloponnesian War to an end.

Lysenko, Trofim Denisovich (1898–1976) Soviet biologist and geneticist. He was an adherent of Lamarck's theory of evolution by the inheritance of acquired characteristics. Since his ideas harmonized with Marxist ideology he was favoured by Stalin and dominated Soviet genetics for many years. Among other false claims, he stated that the process of vernalization – growing a plant, especially a food crop, in a cold climate – will adapt the plant genetically to resist low temperatures.

Lysippus (4th century BC) Greek sculptor. His name is associated with a series of bronze athletes, notably the Apoxyomenos (*c*.320–315), which represents a young male athlete scraping and cleaning his oil-covered skin. With such works Lysippus introduced a naturalistic scheme of proportions for the human body into Greek sculpture.

Lytton, Edward George Earle Bulwer-Lytton, 1st Baron (1803–73) British novelist, dramatist, and statesman. His prolific literary output includes *Pelham* (1828), a novel of fashionable society with which he had his first success, many historical romances (such as *The Last Days of Pompeii*, 1834), and plays. He entered Parliament as an MP in 1831 and later served as Colonial Secretary in Lord Derby's government (1858–59).

M

Maasai (or **Masai**) PASTORALISTS living in Kenya and Tanzania. In the past they dominated the grasslands of the Rift Valley, raiding their neighbours for cattle. Traditionally, the Maasai live off the blood and milk of their cattle, although they also keep sheep and goats. Maasai men belong to age-sets; following CIRCUMCISION, a group of young men become *moran* (warriors), and for ten years are responsible for herding the cattle and killing predators. Once the *moran* become junior elders they are allowed to marry. The Maasai are under pressure to give up pastoralism and settle in villages.

Maastricht A multilingual industrial city in the Netherlands, capital of the province of Limburg, situated on the River Maas (Meuse) near the Belgian and German frontiers; pop. (1991) 117,420. Its cathedral, one of the oldest in the Netherlands, dates from the 6th century. An agreement on political, economic, and monetary union in the EU, known as the MAASTRICHT TREATY, was signed here in February 1992.

Maastricht Treaty A treaty, agreed in February 1992, to come into effect on 1 November 1993, by the 12 member states of the EUROPEAN UNION following ratification at national level. The treaty – officially known as the 'Treaty on European Union' – envisaged political union, with the concept of 'union citizenship'; eventual monetary union under a European Central Bank; common policies on foreign affairs and security, with the WESTERN EUROPEAN UNION becoming the military arm of the Community; greater cooperation on domestic and environmental matters; some strengthening of the European Parliament; and 'subsidiarity', that is, an effective level of demarcation between the powers and responsibilities of the EU institutions and individual member states. The ratification was complicated by disagreements over certain clauses of the treaty. Britain refused to accept the Social Charter, a section of the treaty that protects the rights of employees, which was eventually omitted from the treaty and signed by the other member countries as a separate protocol. Britain secured the right to refuse to adopt the single European currency. Denmark at first rejected the treaty in a referendum, but agreed to ratify it in a second referendum, having negotiated the right to 'opt out' of various provisions regarding monetary union, citizenship, and defence.

Ma'at The Egyptian goddess of cosmic order, truth, and harmony. Daughter of Re, she is depicted as wearing an ostrich feather on her head. It was the duty of every Pharaoh to uphold *ma'at* (cosmic order) during his reign; failure to do so would wreak chaos and disorder. The feather of Ma'at was used as a counter-balance against the hearts of the dead during the Weighing of the Heart in front of Osiris.

Mabinogion, the A collection of Celtic stories of which the Four Branches of the Mabinogi are the most outstanding. The title, derived from the Welsh word *mab*, 'youth', and subsequently applied to 'tales of youth', was given by Lady Charlotte Guest to her translation (1838–49) of the stories. They are taken from *The Red Book of Hergest* (1375–1425) and form part of a cycle of legends of ancient Irish and Welsh mythology and later myths, including the Arthurian legend, in Roman and Christian Britain.

Mabuse, Jan (Flemish name Jan Gossaert) (*c.*1478–1532) Flemish painter. In 1508 he visited Italy, where the art of the High Renaissance made a lasting impression on him; he subsequently became one of the first artists to disseminate the Italian style in the Netherlands. He painted religeous pictures and portraits, including nudes (in mythological subjects).

McAdam, John Loudon (1756–1836) British road engineer, of Scottish extraction. After making a fortune in commerce in the USA, he returned to Scotland in 1783 to finance experiments designed to improve the construction of roads. In 1798 he moved to Cornwall, UK, to continue his experiments under government auspices. Unlike his contemporary TELFORD, who believed in massive construction, he established that relatively light roads could bear heavy traffic provided that they were well drained, impervious to water, and laid on a well-compacted subsoil. The McAdam road surface consisted of rocks and small chips bound together with gravel or slag.

MacAlpin, Kenneth See KENNETH I.

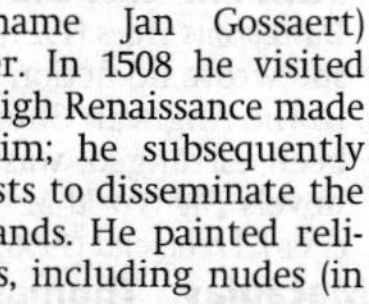

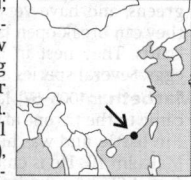

Macao (Portuguese **Macáu**; Chinese **Aomen**) A Portuguese territory on a narrow peninsula on the Zhu Jiang (Pearl River) estuary, near Guangzhou (Canton), China. The territory covers a total area of 16 sq km (6 sq mi), with the city of Macao occupying almost the entire peninsula. Portuguese traders and missionaries established themselves there in 1557 with permission of the local authorities and called their settlement City of the Name of God in China. From its foundation until the late 17th century it had a flourishing trade with Japan. After the Shimabara rebellion in 1637 Japanese Christians sheltered there. It became the staging-post and refuge for Europeans trading with or trying to enter China. Sovereignty will revert to China in 1999.

macaque An Old World monkey that forms a genus, *Macaca*, containing some 15 species. Macaques possess cheek pouches in which they temporarily store leaves and fruit. The hardiest of all the monkeys, they can live in quite cold climates as well as in the hottest parts of India and Myanmar. The majority are found in Asia and the East Indies region. The head is large with a naked face, pointed ears, prominent eyebrows, and large eyes; the buttocks are bare and often a bright colour; the tail is usually long. They congregate in troops of anything from a few up to a hundred or so individuals, spending their time almost equally between the ground and the trees. The macaques include the rhesus monkey, *M. fuscata*, well known because of the human blood factor named after it. Other species include the BARBARY APE and the pig-tailed, lion-tailed, long-tailed, and toque macaques.

MacArthur, Douglas (1880–1964) US general. He was in command of US (later Allied) forces in the SW Pacific during World War II. He formally accepted Japan's surrender in 1945, and administered that country during the Allied occupation that followed. In 1950 he was put in charge of UN forces in Korea, but was relieved of his command the following year.

Macassar (or **Makasar**, **Makassar**) The former name (until 1970) of UJUNG PANDANG.

Macaulay, Dame (Emilie) Rose (1881–1958) British novelist and essayist. After works such as *Dangerous Ages* (1921) and *They Were Defeated* (1932) she wrote no fiction for over a decade. Her return to the Anglican Church, from which she had long been estranged, was followed by her best-known novels *The World My Wilderness* (1950) and *The Towers of Trebizond* (1956).

Macaulay, Thomas Babington, 1st Baron (1800–59) British historian, essayist, and philanthropist. As a civil servant in India (1834–38) he established an English system of education and devised a new criminal code, before returning to Britain and devoting himself to literature and politics. Among his best-known works are *The Lays of Ancient Rome* (1842) and his *History of England* (1849–61), which covers the period from the accession of James II to the death of William III from a Whig standpoint.

macaw A large bird belonging to the parrot family, Psittacidae. Macaws live in South or Central America or the Caribbean islands. Although some are smaller, the best-known ones are about the size of large crows with long tails. They are brilliantly coloured, mostly with blues, reds, yellows, and greens, and have very powerful bills with which they can break open large nuts; they also eat many fruits. They nest in holes in trees and lay white eggs. Several species are in danger of extinction.

Macbeth (*c*.1005–57) King of Scotland 1040–57. He came to the throne after killing his cousin Duncan I in battle, and was himself defeated and killed by Malcolm III. He is chiefly remembered as the subject of Shakespeare's tragedy *Macbeth*, in which the historical events are considerably embroidered.

Maccabees A Jewish dynasty founded by JUDAS MACCABEUS (the Hammerer). In 167 BC the Syrian king Antiochus IV plundered the Temple in Jerusalem, set up an altar to the Greek god Zeus, and proscribed Jewish religious practices. A Jewish revolt began, led by Mattathias, an elderly priest, and guerrilla tactics were used against the Syrians. When Mattathias died in 166, his second son, Judas, assumed leadership. After a series of successful encounters with Syrian forces Judas retook the Temple area in 164 and cleansed the Temple in a ceremony that has from that time been commemorated annually as the feast of Hanukkah. Judas died in 160 and his brothers continued the struggle until independence from the Syrians was achieved, the third brother, Simon, becoming high priest, governor, and commander. The conquests and forced conversions of later rulers caused much discontent, and the dynasty ended with the arrival of the Romans in 63 BC.

McCarthy, Joseph R(aymond) (1909–57) US Republican politician. Between 1950 and 1954, latterly as chairman of a government committee, he was the instigator of widespread investigations into alleged Communist infiltration in US public life. Although most of those accused during the period of 'McCarthyism' were not in fact members of the Communist Party, many of them were blacklisted, lost their jobs, or were otherwise discriminated against in a mood of hysteria, which abated only after the public censure of McCarthy in December 1954.

McCarthy, Mary (Therese) (1912–89) US novelist and critic. Her novels are satirical social commentaries that draw on her experience of intellectual circles and academic life; they include *The Groves of Academe* (1952), which describes political persecution under McCarthyism, and *The Group* (1963), tracing the lives and careers of eight college girls.

McCartney, Sir (James) Paul (1942–) British pop and rock singer, songwriter, and bass guitarist. He was a founder member of the Beatles, and with John LENNON wrote most of their songs; McCartney is known particularly for such songs as 'Yesterday' (1965) and 'Penny Lane' (1967). After the group broke up in 1970 he formed the band Wings, with whom he recorded hit singles such as 'Mull of Kintyre' (1977). Thereafter his musical career has included solo albums, film scores, and a classical composition, the *Liverpool Oratorio* (1991), written with the US composer Carl Davis (1936–).

Macclesfield An industrial town in Cheshire, England, on the River Bollin to the south of Stockport, once famous for silk manufacturing; pop. (1991) 50,270. Its industries produce textiles, paper, plastics, and pharmaceuticals.

McClintock, Barbara (1902–92) US plant geneticist, who discovered the phenomenon of 'jumping genes' (also called transposable elements or transposons). Whilst working on maize (corn) she noticed that genetic information could leap from one chromosome to another. Though the importance of her work was not realized for a long time, she was the first woman to be the sole recipient of the Nobel Prize for physiology and medicine, in 1983.

McCormick, Cyrus Hall (1809–84) US agricultural engineer. His father was a manufacturer of agricultural implements, but failed in his attempt to construct a mechanical reaper. McCormick took up the challenge and had a prototype model at work in 1831. Hearing of the rival machine of HUSSEY in 1834, he patented his design, involving a knife and cutter-bar. This led to serious rivalry with Hussey and competition from at least 30 US manufacturers, but McCormick eventually emerged as market leader.

McCullers, (Lula) Carson (1917–67) US writer. Born in Georgia, McCullers spent most of her adult life in New York. Paralysis of one side confined her permanently to a wheelchair at the age of 29. Her work deals sensitively with loneliness and the plight of the eccentric; her first book, *The Heart is a Lonely Hunter* (1940), won instant acclaim. Other works include the novella *The Ballad of the Sad Café* (1951), which was dramatized by Edward Albee in 1963.

MacDiarmid, Hugh (pseudonym of Christopher Murray Grieve) (1892–1978) Scottish poet and nationalist. As a poet, he is chiefly remembered for his lyrics in a synthetic Scots that drew on the language of various regions and historical periods, such as the poems in the volume *A Drunk Man Looks at the Thistle* (1926). In the 1930s he wrote political poetry, including *First Hymn to Lenin and Other Poems* (1931). He was a founder member (1928) of the National Party of Scotland (later the Scottish National Party).

Macdonald, Sir John Alexander (1815–91) Scottish-born Canadian statesman, Prime Minister 1867–73 and 1878–91. Entering politics in the 1840s, he became leader of the Conservatives and joint Premier (with George-Étienne Cartier) in 1856. Thereafter he played a leading role in the confederation of the Canadian provinces, and was appointed first Prime Minister of the Dominion of Canada in 1867.

MacDonald, Flora (1722–90) Scottish Jacobite heroine. She aided Charles Edward STUART's escape from Scotland, after his defeat at Culloden in 1746, by smuggling him over to the Isle of Skye in a small boat under the eyes of government forces.

MacDonald, (James) Ramsay (1866–1937) British Labour statesman, Prime Minister 1924, 1929–31, and 1931–35. In 1922 he became leader of the Labour Party, and served as Britain's first Labour Prime Minister in the short-lived Labour government of 1924; he was elected Prime Minister again in 1929, but without an overall majority. Faced with economic crisis, and weakened by splits in his own party, he formed a national government with some Conservatives and Liberals; this led to his being expelled from the Labour Party.

mace See NUTMEG.

Macedonia ▶1 (or **Macedon**) An ancient country in south-east Europe, at the northern end of the Greek peninsula, including the coastal plain around Salonica and the mountain ranges behind. In classical times it was a kingdom, which under Philip II and Alexander the Great became a world power. The region is now divided between Greece, Bulgaria, and the Former Yugoslav Republic of MACEDONIA. **▶2** (Greek **Makedhonia**) A region in the north-east of modern Greece, between the Aegean Sea and the country's north-west frontier; area 34,177 sq km (13,200 sq miles); pop. (1991) 2,263,000; capital, Salonica (Thessaloníki).

Macedonia, Former Yugoslav Republic of (FYROM) A landlocked country in the Balkan peninsula bordering Serbia in the north, Albania in the west, Greece in the south, and Bulgaria in the east; formerly a constituent republic of Yugoslavia.

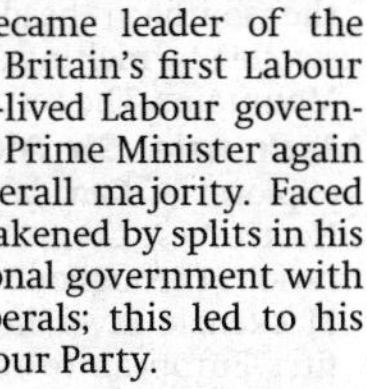

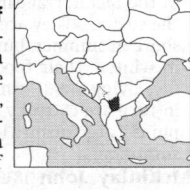

Physical. Most of the republic's territory is a plateau, from which rise forested mountain peaks.

Economy. Mineral resources include iron ore, lead, zinc, and nickel. Macedonia is almost agriculturally self-sufficient, the chief crops being cereals, rice, and tobacco. Sheep and cattle are also reared. Industry comprises steel, chemicals, and textile production. An estimated 100,000 Macedonians are migrant workers in Germany and Switzerland.

History. The country comprises part of the area of MACEDONIA, which was divided in 1913 between Greece and Serbia. The Serbian part of Macedonia was known as southern Serbia from 1918 until 1947, when it became the Republic of Macedonia within the Federal Republic of Yugoslavia, with its own regional Parliament. Following elections in 1990 the anti-Communist Democratic Party was the largest in a hung Parliament. In January 1991 it declared the Republic of Macedonia 'sovereign and independent', while not at this stage rejecting membership of a Yugoslav Union of States. The declaration was overwhelmingly supported by a referendum and Parliament adopted a new constitution. The country's independence was recognized by Bulgaria and Turkey, but, although it had rejected 'all territorial claims on other countries', Greece persuaded the EC to delay recognition, on the grounds that Greek Macedonia was the only region entitled to the name Macedonia. In 1993 Greece agreed to recognize the country on condition that it be known as the Former Yugoslav Republic of Macedonia (FYROM). Negotiations over the name and the use of symbols and emblems considered by Greece to be Greek property continued. FYROM agreed in 1995 to change its national flag. Kiro Gligorov was elected President in 1991 and was re-elected in 1994. He was seriously injured in an assassination attempt in 1995.

Capital: Skopje
Area: 25,713 sq km (9,928 sq mi)
Population: 2,104,000 (1995)
Currency: 1 denar = 100 paras
Religions: Eastern Orthodox
Ethnic Groups: Macedonian 65.0%; Albanian 21.0%; Turkish, Serb, gypsy, and Vlach minorities
Languages: Macedonian; Serbo-Croat; minority languages
International Organizations: UN

Macedonian wars Conflicts fought between Rome and Macedonia in the 3rd and 2nd centuries BC. In the first war (211–205) Philip V was opposed by an alliance of Rome, Aetolia, and Pergamum, but with Rome also deeply involved in the second of the PUNIC WARS he was able to force Aetolia to accept terms, and then to agree favourable ones with Rome itself. But war broke out again (200) and this time Philip was defeated decisively at Cynoscephalae (197). Philip's son Perseus came to the throne in 179, and set about winning influence and friends in Greece. This caused Roman suspicion, the outbreak of a third war, and another Roman victory, this time at Pydna in 168. Macedonia was divided into four republics. In 149–148 Andriscus, claiming to be a son of Perseus, attempted to set himself up as king but was defeated and Macedonia became a Roman province.

McEnroe, John (Patrick) (1959–) US tennis player. A temperamental player, he dominated the game in the early 1980s; among his many titles are seven Wimbledon titles, three for the singles (1981, 1983–84) and five for the doubles (1979, 1981, 1983–84, 1992), three victories in the US Open doubles (1979, 1981, 1983), and four US Open singles championships (1979–81, 1984).

McGonagall, William (1830–1902) Scottish poet. He became a popular figure when travelling around Scotland, giving public readings of his own poetry and selling it in broadsheets. His verse, including 'The Tay Bridge Disaster' (1880), is naive yet entertaining doggerel, which has won him a reputation as one of the worst poets in the world.

Mach, Ernst (1838–1916) Austrian physicist and philosopher of science. His belief that all knowledge of the physical world comes from sensations, and that science should be solely concerned with observables, inspired the logical positivist philosophers of the Vienna Circle in the 1920s. Mach also influenced scientists, such as Einstein, in the formulation of his theory of relativity, and Niels Bohr in quantum mechanics. In commemoration of his work on aerodynamics, his name has been preserved in the MACH NUMBER.

Machaut, Guillaume de (*c*.1300–77) French composer and poet, associated with Rheims for most of his life. Although a cleric, Machaut wrote relatively little church music and it is for his secular songs that he was admired. He greatly expanded their length in comparison with earlier examples by ADAM DE LA HALLE and L'Escurel, and introduced much more complex textures.

Machiavelli, Niccolò di Bernardo dei (1469–1527) Italian statesman and political philosopher. After holding high office in Florence he was exiled by the Medicis on suspicion of conspiracy, but was subsequently restored to some degree of favour. His best-known work is *The Prince* (1532), a treatise on statecraft advising rulers that the acquisition and effective use of power may necessitate unethical methods that are not in themselves desirable. He is thus often regarded as the originator of a political pragmatism in which 'the end justifies the means'.

machine code The BINARY code used to represent the instructions that a COMPUTER executes. It represents the lowest possible level at which a computer can be programmed. Any PROGRAM written in a high-level COMPUTER LANGUAGE or ASSEMBLY LANGUAGE must be translated into machine code before it can be executed.

machine-gun A FIREARM that shoots a number of rounds of ammunition in rapid succession. Experimental multiple-fire weapons were made from as early as 1350, but the earliest practical weapons were the US Gatling gun (1862) and the French mitrailleuse (1870), both multi-barrelled guns fired by means of a hand crank. The first successful automatic machine-gun was developed by MAXIM in 1884. It used the energy of the recoil as a bullet was fired to push back the bolt, eject the spent cartridge, and load the next round of ammunition. Other machine-guns were gas-operated, utilizing the pressure of gas from the barrel to reload. The calibre of machine-guns was originally that of rifle ammunition, but heavier-calibre weapons were later developed. Light gas-operated machine-guns have become the most common kind in modern armies. See also SUB-MACHINE-GUN.

machine translation A branch of ARTIFICIAL INTELLIGENCE concerned with the use of computers to translate between natural human languages, such as English and French. An all-purpose translation machine that can retain the subtleties and nuances of meaning between languages is far beyond current computing capabilities. However, there are simpler machines that provide limited translation facilities. Examples are METEO, an English–French translation system used in Montreal, Canada, since 1977 to translate public weather forecasts; and SYSTRAN, a system developed in the USA, initially for Russian-English translation, and now used by the US Air Force, NASA, and (since 1976) the European Commission.

Mach number The speed of an object passing through a fluid relative to the speed of sound in that fluid. It is named after the Austrian physicist Ernst MACH. The speed of sound varies with density and temperature. Thus Mach 1 is 1,240 km/h (770 m.p.h.) in air at sea-level and 20°C, but decreases at higher altitudes and lower temperatures.

Machu Picchu The ruins of a fortified, abandoned Inca town dramatically perched on a steep-sided ridge in the Andes of central Peru. It contains a palace, a temple to the Sun, and extensive cultivation terraces. Never found by the Spanish conquistadores, it was discovered by Hiram Bingham in 1911 and named after the mountain that rises above it.

Macintosh, Charles (1766–1843) British industrial chemist, of Scottish extraction, best known for his method of waterproofing clothing. In 1785 he set up as a dyer and manufacturer of sal ammoniac (ammonium chloride); 12 years later he founded the first Scottish ALUM works. In 1823 he patented a process for waterproofing fabric by treating it with RUBBER dissolved in naphtha. Later, he went into partnership in Manchester, UK, with Hancock, inventor of a rubber VULCANIZATION process. Waterproof coats were soon so popular that they became universally known as 'mackintoshes' (*sic*).

Mackenzie A river, some 1,800 km (1,100 miles) long, in north-west Canada between the Great Slave Lake and the Arctic Ocean. With its head-rivers, the Athabasca, the Peace, and the Slave, it forms the second largest river system in North America. For most of the long winter months, the whole system is ice-covered. When spring arrives, the southern head-streams thaw first and are swollen by melting snow from the Canadian Rocky Mountains. The result is widespread flooding.

Mackenzie, Sir Alexander (1764–1820) Scottish explorer of Canada. He entered the service of the North-West Company in 1779, undertaking explorations throughout NW Canada. He discovered the Mackenzie River in 1789 and in 1793 became the first European to reach the Pacific Ocean by land along a northern route.

Mackenzie, Sir (Edward Montague) Compton (1883–1972) British novelist, essayist, and poet. He produced essays, memoirs, poems, and biographies, but is best known as a novelist. His works include the semi-autobiographical *Sinister Street* (1913–14) and the comic novel *Whisky Galore* (1947).

mackerel A fish making up part of a family (Scombridae) of torpedo-shaped fishes, often with a blue-green back, irregular black curving lines, and silvery sides. A series of finlets above and beneath the tail shows their relationship with the tunas in this family. The common mackerel, *Scomber scombrus*, occurs on both sides of the North Atlantic and in the Mediterranean, living in huge schools near the surface. They are found both inshore and offshore in summer, but lie inactive near the sea-bed in winter. Their food comprises all kinds of surface-living small fishes and crustaceans; and they in turn are eaten by larger fishes, sharks, and dolphins. Large quantities are caught for human consumption.

McKinlay, John (1819–72) British explorer. Having emigrated to New South Wales in 1836, McKinlay was appointed by the South Australia government in 1861 to lead an expedition to search for the missing explorers Burke and Wills. Although he found only traces of part of the Burke and Wills party, he carried out valuable exploratory work in the interior.

McKinley, Mount (Aleut **Denali**) A peak in Alaska to the north of Anchorage, the highest in North America, rising to a height of 6,194 m (20,320 ft). Situated at the centre of a national park established in 1917, it is named after President William McKinley and was first climbed in 1913.

McKinley, William (1843–1901) US Republican statesman, 25th President of the USA 1897–1901. He supported US expansion into the Pacific, fighting the Spanish–American War of 1898 which resulted in the acquisition of Puerto Rico, Cuba, and the Philippines as well as the annexation of Hawaii. He was assassinated by an anarchist.

Mackintosh, Charles Rennie (1868–1928) Scottish architect and designer. He was a leading exponent of art nouveau and a precursor of several trends in 20th-century architecture. In particular, he pioneered the new concept of functionalism in architecture and interior design. His influence was very great abroad, especially in Austria and Germany, but less so in Britain. His fame chiefly rests on his Glasgow School of Art (1898–1909) and four Glasgow tearooms (1897–1912), designed with all their furniture and equipment.

Maclaurin, Colin (1698–1746) Scottish mathematician who developed Isaac NEWTON's work in calculus, geometry (mostly of curves), and gravitation. The Maclaurin series, a power series expansion for a function was named in his honour but the series was well known before Maclaurin published it. He also wrote papers on astronomy and did actuarial work.

Maclean, Alistair (1922–87) Scottish novelist. His numerous thrillers and adventure stories, many of which were made into films, include *The Guns of Navarone* (1957), *Where Eagles Dare* (1967), and *Bear Island* (1971).

Maclean, Donald Duart (1913–83) British Foreign Office official and Soviet spy. After acting as a Soviet agent from the late 1930s he fled to the USSR with Guy Burgess in 1951, following a warning from Kim Philby of impending proceedings against him.

Macleod, John James Rickard (1876–1935) Scottish physiologist. He specialized in carbohydrate metabolism and held various chairs in physiology, notably at the University of Toronto. He provided facilities there for the research on pancreatic extracts by F. G. Banting and C. H. Best, much of which was directed by Macleod personally, and which led to the discovery and isolation of insulin. Macleod shared the Nobel Prize for physiology and medicine with Banting in 1923.

McLuhan, (Herbert) Marshall (1911–80) Canadian writer and thinker. He became famous in the 1960s for his theories on the role of the media and technology in society. He is particularly known for claiming that the world had become 'a global village' in its electronic interdependence, and that 'the medium is the message', because it is the characteristics of a particular medium rather than the information it disseminates that influence and control society. His books include *Understanding Media: The Extensions of Man* (1964).

McMahon Line A boundary line dividing Tibet and India. It was marked out by the British representatives led by Sir Henry McMahon at the Simla Conference (1914) between Britain, Tibet, and China. The Chinese government refused to ratify the agreement, and after the reassertion of control by China over Tibet in 1951 boundary disputes arose between India and China culminating in the Indo-Chinese War of 1962.

Macmillan, (Maurice) Harold, 1st Earl of Stockton (1894–1986) British Conservative statesman, Prime Minister 1957–63. His term of office saw the signing of the Test-Ban Treaty (1963) with the USA and the USSR. He advocated the granting of independence to British colonies but his attempt to take Britain into the European Economic Community was blocked by the French President de Gaulle (1963). Macmillan resigned on grounds of ill health shortly after the scandal surrounding the Secretary of State for War, John Profumo.

MacMillan, Sir Kenneth (1929–92) British dancer, choreographer, and director. He worked for both Sadler's Wells companies in the 1940s and 1950s, and was appointed resident choreographer (1965), and director of the ROYAL BALLET (1970–77). He worked also for American Ballet Theater. He represented the expressionist direction of modernism in ballet.

MacNeice, (Frederick) Louis (1907–63) Northern Irish poet. He was part of W. H. Auden's circle at Oxford, where he published his first volume of poetry in 1929; later volumes include *Autumn Journal* (1938), and *Collected Poems* (1966). His work is characterized by the use of assonance, internal rhythms, and ballad-like repetitions absorbed from the Irish background of his youth. He also wrote documentaries and plays for radio, notably the fantasy *The Dark Tower* (1947), with music by Benjamin Britten.

Mâcon The capital of Saône-et-Loire department in southern Burgundy, east-central France, on the River Saône; pop. (1990) 38,500. It is the centre of the Mâconnais wine-producing region.

Macquarie, Lachlan (1762–1824) Scottish-born Australian colonial administrator. He served as governor of New South Wales 1809–21; the colony was chiefly populated by convicts, but during his term of office he improved its prosperity, expanded opportunities for former convicts, and promoted public works, further settlement, and exploration.

McQueen, Steve (1930–80) US film actor. His initial success was in *The Magnificent Seven* (1960). His later films, in which he played laid-back heroes, included *The Great Escape* (1963) and *Bullitt* (1968). He died prematurely of lung cancer.

macroeconomics The areas of economics that view the economy as a single unit, rather than as a large collection of individual economic agents and markets. It is thus concerned with the behaviour of broad economic aggregates, notably aggregate demand (and its components CONSUMPTION, investment, and government spending), national income, the BALANCE OF PAYMENTS, the level of employment, and the price level. A central focus of macroeconomics is the role of government, especially the impact of monetary and fiscal policy on economic performance.

macromolecule A very large molecule consisting of a chain of between 10^2 to 10^6 atoms. For example, the synthetic POLYMERS that have been developed in this century are all macromolecules; they are formed from monomers, which are capable of reacting with themselves, building up long chains in which a small unit is repeated many times. Polyalkenes, polyamides, and polyesters are of this type. Many naturally occurring substances are also formed of macromolecules, for example rubber, cellulose, starch, proteins, and nucleic acids. If the chains are cross-linked by chemical bonds, as in vulcanized rubber or synthetic resins, they form hard, insoluble materials.

Madagascar A large island country lying 450–900 km (280–560 miles) distant from the south-east African coast, to which it runs parallel.

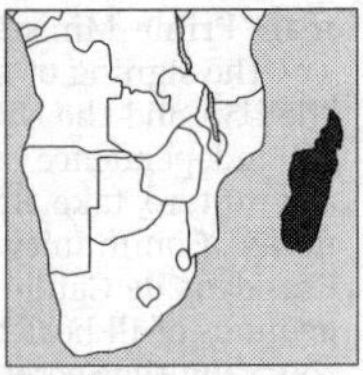

Physical. A broad plain in the west rises to the Ankaratra Mountains, which slope steeply eastward to the Indian Ocean. The eastern coast is hot, very wet, subject to cyclones, and densely clad with rain forest. The south and west are drier, and the centre mild. Here, on upland plateaux, there is fine grazing. As a result of the island becoming separated from Africa during the period of CONTINENTAL DRIFT, many of its plant and animal species, for example lemurs (prosimians), are unique.

Economy. Economic activity in Madagascar is mainly agricultural: coffee, vanilla, and cloves are major exports. Rice, cassava, and sweet potatoes are the chief food crops; cattle-breeding is extensive. Mining of chrome ore is significant, and there are bauxite deposits. An oil refinery produces petroleum-based products. Industry is limited mostly to food-processing.

History. The Madagascan people are of Indo-Melanesian and Malay descent, mixed with some Bantu, Arabs, Indians, and Chinese. The time of arrival of different groups is controversial. Arab traders were probably visiting by the 10th century. In 1500 a Portuguese sea captain, Diego Dias, chanced on the island, calling it São Lourenço. However, Marco Polo had already named it Madagascar from hearsay knowledge, and this name endured. In the following centuries Dutch, English, and Portuguese vessels made frequent visits, and the French set up trading centres. Many of these were used as pirate bases. By the beginning of the 17th century a number of small Malagasy kingdoms emerged, and later the Sakalawa, from the west of the island, conquered northern and western Madagascar, but their kingdom disintegrated in the 18th century. The Merina people of the interior were later united under King Andrianampoinimerina (ruled 1787–1810), and became the dominant group on the island by the early 19th century.

In 1860 King Radama II gave concessions to a French trading company. This led in 1890 to a French Protectorate, although resistance lasted until 1895. After 1945 Madagascar became an Overseas Territory of the French Republic, sending Deputies to Paris. It became a republic in 1958, and regained its independence (1960) as the Malagasy Republic, changing its name back to Madagascar in 1975. Severe social and economic problems caused recurrent unrest and frequent changes of government. Admiral Didier Ratsiraka was elected President in 1982 and again in 1989, working closely with a Supreme Revolutionary Council. Although he ended one-party rule in 1990, there were anti-government riots in April 1991. In October 1991 the Revolutionary Council and National Assembly were both dissolved, pending agreement on a new constitution. The new multi-party constitution was adopted in 1992 and Albert Zafy became President following elections in 1993. In 1996 he was impeached, and later defeated in presidential elections by Ratsiraka.

Capital: Antananarivo
Area: 587,041 sq km (226,658 sq mi)
Population: 14,763,000 (1995)
Currency: 1 Malagasy franc = 100 centimes
Religions: Roman Catholic 26.0%; Protestant 22.8%; traditional beliefs 47.0%; Muslim 1.7%
Ethnic Groups: Malagasy 98.9% (Merina 26.6%; Betsimisaraka 14.9%; Betsileo 11.7%; Tsimihety 7.4%; Sakalava 6.4%); Antandroy 5.3%; Comorian 0.3%; Indian and Pakistani 0.2%; French 0.2%; Chinese 0.1%
Languages: Malagasy, French (both official)
International Organizations: UN; OAU

Madeira (Portuguese **Ilha da Madeira**) The largest of a group of islands in the Atlantic Ocean off north-west Africa; area 739 sq km (285 sq miles); pop. (1991) 257,690. Its chief port and city is Funchal and its highest mountain is the Pico Ruivo (1,861 m, 6,106 ft).

Madhya Pradesh A state in central India; area 443,446 sq km (171,261 sq miles); pop. (1991) 66,135,860; capital, Bhopal. Formed in 1956, it is the largest of the states of India. Although its economy is dominated by the production of agricultural crops including rice, wheat, pulses, and cotton, Madhya Pradesh is rich in minerals including bauxite, iron ore, manganese, coal, and limestone.

Madison The state capital of Wisconsin, USA, on an isthmus between Lake Mendota and Lake Monona; pop. (1990) 191,260. Founded as state capital in 1837 and named after President James Madison, it is a cultural and manufacturing centre associated with the architect Frank Lloyd Wright and the Prairie School movement. Madison is the home of the University of Wisconsin-Madison (1845).

Madison, James (1751–1836) US Democratic Republican statesman, 4th President of the USA 1809–17. Before taking office, he played a leading part in drawing up the US Constitution (1787) and proposed the Bill of Rights (1791). His presidency saw the US emerge successfully from the War of 1812 against Britain.

Madison Square Gardens An arena for sporting events built in 1968 on the site of the former Pennsylvania Station in New York City, USA. It replaced an earlier structure on Eighth Avenue at 50th Street, a popular venue for circuses and boxing matches.

Madonna (born Madonna Louise Ciccone) (1958–) US pop singer and actress. She rose to international stardom in the mid-1980s through her records and accompanying videos, cultivating her image as a sex symbol. Among her singles are 'Holiday' (1983), while her albums include *Like a Virgin* (1984) and *Erotica* (1992). Her best-known films include *Desperately Seeking Susan* (1985) and *Evita* (1996).

Madras (official name (since 1995) **Chenai**) A seaport on the east coast of India, capital of the state of Tamil Nadu; pop. (1991) 5,361,470. Established in 1639 by a British merchant named Francis Day and expanded in the 17th century as a fortified settlement called Fort St George, Madras developed as a leading centre of the East India Company to become India's third-largest city. It has textile mills, tanneries, chemical plants, and engineering and car works.

Madrid The capital and largest city of Spain, situated on a high plateau almost exactly in the centre of the country; pop. (1991) 2,984,580. It replaced Valladolid as capital of Spain in 1561. Its most noted buildings include the 18th-century Royal Palace and the Prado art gallery. It is Spain's second-largest industrial centre (after Barcelona) and has aircraft, electrical, and agricultural machinery industries.

madrigal A musical composition for several unaccompanied voices. The words are usually secular and light-heartedly amorous. Pastoral, allegorical, and satirical subjects are also to be found. The madrigal, which is mainly contrapuntal, took shape in 16th-century Italy, achieving its finest flowering in the work of Marenzio, Gesualdo, and Monteverdi. It also took root in England, following the publication in 1588 of an Italian collection, *Musica transalpina*. Byrd, Morley, Gibbons, Wilbye, and Weelkes are among the many British composers who made outstanding contributions to this genre.

Maeander (Turkish **Menderes**) The ancient name of a river in western Turkey that rises near Afyon and flows west for *c*.384 km (240 miles) to the Aegean. Its legendary wanderings gave rise to the English word 'meander'.

Maecenas, Gaius (*c*.70–8 BC) Roman statesman. He was a trusted adviser of Augustus but shunned official position. Himself a writer, he was a notable patron of such poets as Virgil and Horace (a role for which his name became a byword).

maelstrom A great whirlpool or a state of confusion. It takes its name from a powerful current in the Arctic Ocean with a dangerous and legendary tidal race that is funnelled through a channel in the Lofoten Islands off the north-west coast of Norway. Mariners used to tell tall tales of ships from miles around being drawn into its violent whirlpool.

Maeterlinck, Maurice (1862–1949) Belgian poet, dramatist, and essayist. He lived much of his life in Paris and was associated with the SYMBOLISTS. He is chiefly remembered for his plays, most of which were produced at the Théâtre de l'œuvre, the home of symbolist drama. The most famous of these, *Pélleas et Mélisande* (1892), which was set to music by DEBUSSY in 1902, displays a simplicity and suggestive power shared by his principal collection of poetry, *Serres chaudes* (1889), and such essays as *La Vie des abeilles* (1901) and *La Mort* (1913).

Mafeking (or **Mafikeng**) A town in the former South African homeland of Bophuthatswana, made famous when a small British force under the command of BADEN-POWELL was besieged by the Boers for 215 days in 1899–1900. Although the town was of little strategic importance, its successful defence, at a time when the Boer War was going very badly for the British, excited great interest, while its relief was hailed almost with a national sense of jubilation. In 1980 its name reverted to its original form, Mafikeng (Tswana, 'place of stones'), when it was ceded to the newly independent homeland of Bophuthatswana and in 1994 it became capital of the newly created North West province.

Mafia An international secret society originating in Sicily. In its modern form the Mafia (Italian 'boldness') can be said to date from the period 1806–15, when, under British pressure, attempts were being made to break up the huge estates of the Sicilian feudal aristocracy. In the 1880s many Sicilians emigrated to the USA and the Mafia, as Cosa Nostra (Our Business), became established in New York and Chicago. In the 1920s the fascist government in Italy brought Mafia leaders to trial, but some escaped to the USA, where they were active during the PROHIBITION ERA. After World War II, notably after the opening-up of the former Soviet bloc, Mafia activities spread worldwide, increasingly centred on the drug trade. The Mafia is also involved in organized PROSTITUTION, FRAUD, theft, and kidnapping. In the USA, the Mafia is notable also for its infiltration of legitimate business; for example, in transport, construction, gambling, and fast-food, and its use of these businesses for money-laundering. Mafia members are required to live by a code of silence and eschew all cooperation with legitimate authorities: any violation of this code is severely punished.

Magdalenian Denoting the latest palaeolithic industry of Europe, named after the type-site at La Madeleine in the Dordogne region of France and dated to *c*.15,000–11,000 BC. It is characterized by a range of bone and horn tools, including elaborate bone harpoons; cave art reached a zenith during this period.

Magdeburg An industrial city and river port of Germany, the capital of Saxony-Anhalt, situated on the River Elbe and linked to the Rhine and Ruhr by the Mittelland Canal; pop. (1991) 275,240. It produces machinery, chemicals, and scientific instruments. It was the site in 1657 of the famous experiment which demonstrated the pressure of air.

Magellan, Ferdinand (Portuguese name Fernão Magalhães) (*c*.1480–1521) Portuguese explorer. In 1519, while in the service of Spain, he commanded five vessels on a voyage from Spain to the East Indies by the western route. He reached South America later that year, rounding the continent through the strait which now bears his name and emerging to become the first European to navigate the Pacific. He reached the Philippines in 1521, but soon after was killed in a skirmish on Cebu. The survivors, in the one remaining ship, sailed back to Spain round Africa, thereby completing the first circumnavigation of the globe (1522).

Magellan, Strait of A passage through the islands of Tierra del Fuego at the southern tip of South America, connecting the Atlantic and Pacific Oceans. It is named after Ferdinand Magellan who discovered it in October 1520. It was a dangerous passage for sailing ships and safer for steamships. Its importance declined with the opening of the Panama Canal.

Magellanic Clouds Two small GALAXIES in orbit around our own galaxy, and of great importance because they are sufficiently close for detailed study. The first Europeans to see the Clouds were Portuguese navigators in the 16th century who named them in honour of Ferdinand MAGELLAN. Part of the LOCAL GROUP OF GALAXIES, to the naked eye they appear as hazy, cloud-like patches close to each other and to the south celestial pole. The **Large Magellanic Cloud**, also known as **Nubecula Major**, is at a distance of 50,000 parsecs (160,000 light-years) and its mass is believed to be some 10 billion times that of the Sun. Long-exposure photographs reveal an almost circular disc of stars, while shorter exposures are dominated by a densely starred 'bar', resembling a BARRED SPIRAL GALAXY. The Cloud contains many star CLUSTERS, stellar associations, and diffuse NEBULAE including the Tarantula Nebula which is the largest diffuse nebula known anywhere in the Universe. The **Small Magellanic Cloud** (**Nubecula Minor**) is less massive (about one billion times the mass of the Sun) and more distant (57,000 parsecs, or 185,000 light-years). Its structure is less clear with fewer clusters, associations, and nebulae. Part of the Small Cloud extends towards the Large Cloud possibly due to its gravitational attraction. The important PERIOD-LUMINOSITY LAW for CEPHEID variable stars was discovered in the Small Magellanic Cloud.

Magenta A town in Lombardy, northern Italy, to the west of Milan; pop. (1990) 23,780. It was the site of a battle in 1859 at which the Austrians were defeated by a combined French and Sardinian army. In honour of the victory, the textile town's name was given to a brilliant mauvish-crimson aniline dye.

Maggiore, Lake (Italian **Lago Maggiore**) The second-largest of the lakes of northern Italy, extending into the canton of Ticino in southern Switzerland; area 212 sq km (82 sq miles). Resorts on its shores include Arona, Ispra, Stresa, and Locarno.

maggot (or **gentle**) The larva of species of true FLIES, in which the head and the mouthparts are replaced by hardened structures developed in the thorax. The best known are the white maggots of blow flies, flesh flies, and houseflies. When fully grown, maggots form PUPAE within the last larval skin, which hardens and darkens. Their feeding habits are varied: those of blowflies feed on rotting flesh, and it is these that are most often used for fishing bait.

Maghreb (or **Maghrib**; Arabic, 'west') A region of north and north-west Africa between the Atlantic Ocean and Egypt, which has both a cultural and geographical unity. It comprises the coastal plain and Atlas Mountains of Morocco, together with Algeria, Tunisia, and sometimes parts of Mauretania, Chad, Mali, and Libya, forming a well-defined zone bounded by sea or desert. It formerly included Moorish Spain. In 1989 Algeria, Morocco, Tunisia, Libya, and Mauretania formed an economic union called the Grand Maghreb, designed to promote a regional common market in an area with a population of *c.*62 million people.

Magi, the In Christian tradition, the men from the East who, possessing astronomical and astrological wisdom, followed a star that led them to the birthplace of the infant Jesus, in Bethlehem. There they paid homage to him with gold, the gift bestowed on kings, frankincense, used to worship at the altar of God, and myrrh, an embalming agent for the dead. In later tradition the magi became three kings (Caspar, Melchior, and Balthasar).

magic A belief that specific ends can be achieved through RITUAL actions, often involving spells and incantations, which invoke supernatural forces. Studies of magic have often been linked to studies of RELIGION. Early anthropologists, such as FRAZER, saw magic as a stage in social EVOLUTION, and regarded it as a kind of primitive science, but this was challenged by MALINOWSKI, whose own interpretation of magic, in keeping with his FUNCTIONALISM, treated it as a means to allow emotional expression. Contrary to the predictions of such sociologists as WEBER, magic has not disappeared, despite the advances of scientific rationalism.

Maginot Line The line of defensive fortifications built along France's north-eastern frontier from Switzerland to Luxembourg, completed in 1936, in which the French placed excessive confidence. Partly because of objections from the Belgians, who were afraid they would be left in an exposed position, the line was not extended along the Franco-Belgian frontier to the coast. Consequently, although the defences proved impregnable to frontal assault, the line was easily outflanked when the Germans invaded France in the spring of 1940. It is named after the French Minister of War André Maginot (1877–1932).

magistrate Any person exercising judicial authority. In England and Wales, a magistrate is usually a lay person appointed by the Lord Chancellor as a Justice of the Peace (JP) and advised in court on matters of law by a SOLICITOR known as a clerk of the justices. A stipendiary magistrate is a full-time salaried magistrate, who must be a BARRISTER or a SOLICITOR. Magistrates' courts are mainly concerned with criminal law. It is their job to decide whether those charged with a serious offence should be tried before a JUDGE and JURY, while they themselves both try and sentence those charged with less serious offences. They also adjudicate on certain claims under CIVIL LAW.

maglev See GROUND-GUIDANCE SYSTEM.

magma Molten rock, a molten silicate liquid with water and other gases dissolved in it. It originates within the EARTH's mantle, probably at depths of 70 km (45 miles) or more, but it forms only a very small proportion of the mantle. If conditions allow, as at plate margins, magma may move towards the surface, injecting and melting its way into the rocks of the crust. If it fails to reach the surface it forms an IGNEOUS INTRUSION, such as a batholith, sill, or dyke. If it reaches the surface it is ejected from volcanoes or fissures as lava and solidifies. The temperature of magma reaching the surface ranges from 850 to 1,200°C (1,550 to 2,200°F).

Magna Carta (Latin, 'Great Charter') The document that the English barons, aided by Stephen LANGTON, forced King JOHN to seal at Runnymede on 15 June 1215. It was a charter of 61 or 63 clauses (the final clause is sometimes subdivided into three) covering a wide range of issues, mainly limiting the power of the king. John sought and obtained papal condemnation of the charter on 18 June 1215, which led to the first Barons' War four months later. Although the charter was often violated by medieval kings, it came to be seen as an important document defining the English Constitution.

magnesia The common name for magnesium oxide, MgO, which occurs in the mineral periclase. A white, tasteless substance, it is used in heat insulation and as an antacid. It can be made by burning magnesium in oxygen or from the ignition of the metal hydroxide, carbonate, or nitrate. Milk of magnesia, used to neutralize stomach acidity, is a suspension of magnesium hydroxide, $Mg(OH)_2$.

magnesite An important ore of magnesium. It forms as hard, yellow-grey masses of magnesium carbonate ($MgCO_3$) produced by the alteration of magnesium-rich rock by water containing carbon dioxide. Large deposits exist in Styria (Austria), Manchuria (China), and along the coastal range of California (USA).

magnesium (symbol Mg, at. no. 12, r.a.m. 24.31) A grey metallic element of low density in Group 2 (formerly IIB) of the periodic table, the ALKALINE EARTH METALS. Reacting readily with acids and non-metals, it forms ionic compounds in which it has charge +2. It is an abundant element: magnesium chloride is present in seawater, from which magnesium is obtained by ELECTROLYSIS, and magnesium ores such as dolomite, magnesite, talc, and asbestos are widespread. Magnesium is also used in flash-bulbs and flares, as it gives an intense white light when it reacts with oxygen. Because of its low density it is also widely used as a component of lightweight, strong alloys in the DIE CASTING or EXTRUSION of articles. The pure metal is soft, and has to be strengthened by alloying with aluminium, zinc, zirconium, and thorium. Important compounds of magnesium include magnesium hydroxide ($Mg(OH)_2$), used as an antacid and laxative, magnesium sulphate (Epsom salts, $MgSO_4$), and Grignard reagents, used in synthetic organic chemistry.

magnet A device that produces a MAGNETIC FIELD external to itself. Natural magnets (lodestones) of magnetic iron oxide have been known for many centuries. A simple bar magnet has two poles, north and south, around each of which there is a magnetic field. Magnets can be permanent magnets, or ELECTROMAGNETS (temporary magnets), and the materials used for each type of magnet differ. A ferromagnetic material (one that can be magnetized) can be made into a magnet by placing it in the centre of an electric coil or solenoid and passing a large current through the coil. If the material is magnetically 'hard', it will retain its magnetism once the current has been switched off. Permanent magnets are made from such hard materials as steel, nickel, and cobalt. Such magnetic alloys are used in electrical equipment and electronic devices. Magnetically 'soft' materials retain little or no magnetism once the current has been removed: they are used in electromagnets, TRANSFORMERS, and other applications. See also ELECTRICITY AND MAGNETISM.

magnetic compass An instrument comprising a magnetized needle pivoted so that it can always point to magnetic north, used, often in conjunction with a MAP or chart, for direction-finding. The origins of the compass are obscure: it is thought that it may have been in use in China as early as the 5th century AD. However, there is no evidence of a compass being used at sea until the 11th century in China, and the 12th century in Europe. The earliest compasses consisted of a magnetized needle floating on a bowl of water. Later, the needle was attached to a card marked with the cardinal directions and balanced on a pivot. By the 16th century the compass was mounted on gimbals (self-aligning bearings) that kept it level at sea. The use of iron in ship-building caused compasses to deviate from true reading because of the magnetic effects of the ship's ironwork. This problem was overcome by mounting the compass on a stand or binnacle containing pieces of unmagnetized iron and small magnets to neutralize the ship's magnetic influence. In the 19th century, liquid compasses were introduced, in which the compass card and needle are immersed in fluid to reduce friction and damp down oscillations due to the ship's motion. With the development of aviation in the 20th century, compasses that could be used in aircraft became necessary. One answer to the problem was the gyro-magnetic compass, in which the inertia of a GYROSCOPE was used to keep the compass card level as the aircraft banked or dived. However, it was not until the introduction of the GYROCOMPASS that the problems of direction-finding in aircraft were satisfactorily solved.

magnetic constant See PERMEABILITY.

magnetic field A region in which magnetic substances, such as iron, and charged particles experience a force produced by a magnet, or by a conductor carrying an electric current, or by a flow of charged particles. The most common examples of this phenomenon are the orientation of a compass needle in the Earth's magnetic field, or the alignment of iron filings along the LINES OF FORCE of a magnet, easily demonstrated if the filings are scattered on top of a horizontally held card under which the magnet is placed. Magnetic fields occur in a wide scale of intensity throughout the Universe in planets and stars, and the interplanetary, interstellar, and intergalactic environments. The strength of a particular magnetic field operating through a given area is given by its MAGNETIC FLUX.

magnetic flux A measure of quantity of magnetism, usually defined in terms of the electromotive force generated when a MAGNETIC FIELD is cut by a moving conductor. If 1 volt is generated between the ends of the conductor, it is cutting through 1 weber of flux per second; the weber (Wb) is the SI UNIT of magnetic flux. The **magnetic flux density** is the magnetic flux per unit area of a magnetic field at right angles to the magnetic force. See also PERMEABILITY.

magnetic pole Each of the points near the extremities of the axis of rotation of the Earth, at which a magnetic needle dips vertically. The position of these poles varies over time, and sometimes the positions of the north and south magnetic poles are reversed. The Earth's core contains a high concentration of molten ferromagnetic material, which is thought to be responsible for the terrestrial magnetic field with its own magnetic poles. The resulting dynamo effect produces a magnetic field that appears to enter and leave the Earth at a north and south pole. The Earth's magnetic poles are not coincident with the geographic poles, and the study of their locations and movements forms part of GEOMAGNETISM.

magnetic resonance imaging (MRI) The application of nuclear magnetic resonance (NMR) techniques to obtain images of cross-sections through the human body. The technique involves passing low-frequency radiation through the soft tissues of the body in the presence of a strong magnetic field, and scanning the temporary magnetic realignment this produces in the nuclei of certain elements (for example, hydrogen, fluorine, and phosphorus). This gives valuable information about the structure of the substance. MRI can produce cross-sectional images in all three planes, like COMPUTERIZED TOMOGRAPHY (CT); unlike a CT scanner, however, an MRI scanner produces a clear image of soft tissue even if it is obscured by bone, and it produces images with greater contrast.

magnetic tape A plastic strip coated or impregnated with magnetic particles, which can record and play back audio or video signals or store information. The earliest TAPE RECORDERS used steel wire or ribbon; plastic tape coated with iron oxide particles was first used in the German magnetophon tape recorder of 1935. Modern magnetic tape is coated with iron oxide, chromium dioxide, or pure iron particles: the latter gives the highest-quality sound. Professional recording studios use multi-track tapes on open reels, and sound recordings are now usually digitized. Compact cassettes, introduced by Philips in 1964, dominate the domestic market. Open reels of magnetic tape are used as a storage medium on larger computers and VIDEO RECORDERS, while some microcomputers use tape cartridges for back-up storage. Domestic video recorders use videotape cassettes. See also SOUND RECORDING AND REPRODUCTION.

magnetism A set of phenomena associated with MAGNETS and with moving electric charges, both of which produce MAGNETIC FIELDS in the space surrounding them. The magnetic properties of MATTER are largely determined by the behaviour of the negatively charged electrons that orbit the nuclei of atoms. The magnetic field of a single electron has two components, one resulting from the spin of the electron about its own axis, and the other from its orbital motion about the nucleus. Both kinds of motion may be considered as tiny circular currents – moving charges – thus linking electronic and magnetic effects at a fundamental level.

Charged particles are surrounded by electric fields, and when they move, or spin, magnetic fields are created. An electric current will produce a magnetic field encircling the current, the strength of the field being proportional to the current. Conversely, if a conductor moves through a magnetic field, an electric current will flow in it. These effects are studied in ELECTROMAGNETISM. The unification of electric and magnetic principles in a complete mathematical theory was achieved by James Clerk MAXWELL in 1864. The quality of some metals, which enables them to become magnetized when placed in a magnetic field, developing their own internal fields, is known as **ferromagnetism**.

magnetite Naturally magnetized iron oxide (Fe_3O_4), a dark dense mineral, which is also the second most important ore of iron, after HAEMATITE. It is the only strongly magnetic natural substance known, and was called **lodestone** (or **loadstone**) by the ancients, who used it to make the first compasses.

magnetohydrodynamic generator A system for the generation of electric power using the effect of a MAGNETIC FIELD acting on a stream of electrically charged particles. Magnetohydrodynamic effects are related to the fact that a beam of charged particles experiences a sideways force if it travels through a magnetic field. The observation that this will cause a voltage to develop across the beam is known as the Hall effect (discovered 1879). Its practical application as a power source is more recent, however. A magnetohydrodynamic generator uses hot combustion gases, which contain free electrons as a result of thermal ionization (enhanced by adding substances of low ionization potential to the flame). The hot gases are passed through a strong magnetic field. Several decades of research in the Soviet Union and the USA led to output powers of 50,000 kW. These generators can increase the efficiency of power generation using a gas turbine, by making use of the exhaust gases in this way.

magnetohydrodynamics (MHD) A branch of physics in which properties of a PLASMA or an electrically conducting fluid under the action of electric and magnetic fields is studied. Since plasmas occur in stars, especially in the processes creating a NOVA OR SUPERNOVA, the study of magnetohydrodynamics is an important aid in understanding such processes. ALFVÉN's theory describes how magnetohydrodynamic waves can propagate in a highly conducting fluid in the presence of a magnetic field.

magnetometer An instrument for measuring the strength and direction of a MAGNETIC FIELD. Apart from those designed for terrestrial use, various kinds of magnetometers have been flown in rockets, satellites, and planetary space missions, and some of them have been taken to the surfaces of the Moon, Mars, and Venus.

magnetopause See MAGNETOSPHERE.

magnetosheath See MAGNETOSPHERE.

magnetosphere A cylindrical region surrounding the Earth in which the SOLAR WIND is accelerated by the Earth's magnetic field. In the early 1960s it was found from satellite measurements that the Earth's magnetic field does not extend indefinitely but is constrained to exist in a cavity within the Solar System, which is called the magnetosphere or **magnetosheath**. The cavity has the shape of a blunt-nosed cylinder and is produced by the interaction of the hot plasma escaping from the Sun (the solar wind) with the weak outer regions of the Earth's magnetic field. The nose of the cylinder is in the direction of the Sun with the boundary, known as the **magnetopause**, at about ten Earth radii. On the night side the magnetosphere is stretched out into a large tail well beyond the orbit of the Moon. Other planets with magnetic fields, such as Mercury and Jupiter also have magnetospheres. In the magnetosphere, charged particles are accelerated by changing magnetic fields, and form the VAN ALLEN radiation belts and the AURORA. The magnetosphere protects the Earth from harmful cosmic rays.

magnetron See THERMIONIC VALVE.

magnitude A measure of the brightness of a star. A star's magnitude may be illusory: a faint star near the Earth may appear to be brighter than a bright star further away because the intensity of light received from a star decreases in proportion to the square of its distance from the Earth. The **apparent magnitude** of a star describes how bright the star appears to be as observed from the

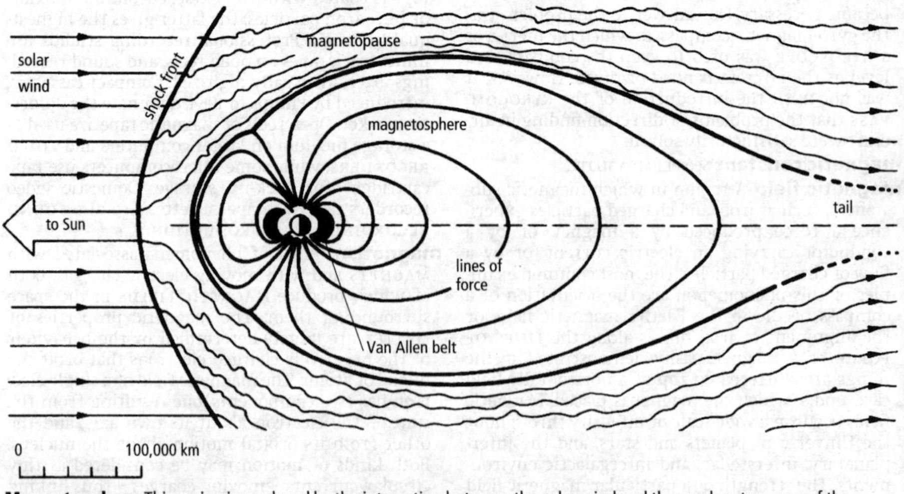

Magnetosphere This region is produced by the interaction between the solar wind and the weak outer areas of the Earth's magnetic field. The Van Allen radiation belts are shown.

Earth. In contrast, **absolute magnitude** is a measure of the actual brightness (LUMINOSITY) of a star: it is the apparent magnitude that the star would have if it were at a distance of 10 PARSECS. The present magnitude scale was established by assigning numbers to a representative group of stars near the north celestial pole. Then magnitudes could be assigned to all the other stars in the sky. This is a logarithmic scale on which a first-magnitude star is one hundred times brighter than a sixth-magnitude star.

magnolia Any one of some 80 species of tree or shrub of the genus *Magnolia*, native to North and Central America, eastern Asia, and the Himalayas. Members of the family Magnoliaceae, they have rather large leaves and conspicuous flowers, often with large, conspicuous sepals which are indistinguishable from the petals. The seeds are red and dangle on threads from the fruits when they split open. Some are evergreen, such as *Magnolia grandiflora* of the southeastern USA, which is also found in Britain, often growing up walls; others are deciduous.

Magnox reactor (*mag*nesium *ox*ide) A type of thermal NUCLEAR REACTOR developed in the UK, which uses pressurized carbon dioxide gas as a coolant, and graphite as a moderator (see FISSION, NUCLEAR). Magnox reactors were the first to be used for commercial nuclear power generation, the first, the CALDER HALL REACTOR, being opened in 1956. The fuel used in Magnox reactors is uranium metal, encased in a cladding of magnesium alloy. In the mid-1960s the advanced gas-cooled reactor was designed as an improvement on the Magnox.

magpie Any one of about 19 species (genus *Pica*) of the CROW family with a wide distribution in both Old and New Worlds, with the exception of Africa. They have smallish thrush-sized bodies, but long tails. Most are strikingly coloured, often blue and white or green and white. The European or American common magpie, *P. pica*, is shiny blue-black and white and one of the few birds to be common in both regions. They build domed nests of sticks in bushes or trees, and have a reputation for stealing almost anything that shines, thus collecting a wide range of objects, hence the metaphorical use of their name.

magpie lark An Australian bird, *Grallina cyanoleuca*, that lives in open woodlands and is common in gardens. It is a striking black and white thrush-sized bird with staring white eyes; it eats mainly insects. The magpie lark builds a nest of plant fibres which are held together with mud, and usually placed on the horizontal branch of a tree.

magpie moth A mottled or spotted moth, usually black on white; most belong to the family Geometridae. The magpie, or currant moth, *Abraxas grossulariata*, is strikingly black-spotted on white with touches of orange, and is abundant and widespread throughout Eurasia. Their similarly patterned LOOPER caterpillars are often a pest on currant and gooseberry bushes.

Magritte, René (François Ghislain) (1898–1967) Belgian painter. His paintings are typical examples of surrealism; they display startling or amusing juxtapositions of the ordinary, the strange, and the erotic, all depicted in a realist manner. He had a repertory of images that appear in incongruous settings, for example in *Threatening Weather* (1928), a chair, a table, and a torso hover like clouds over the sea.

Magyar A member of the race speaking a Finno-Ugric language, whose ancestors came from an area round the River Volga in Russia. Under Prince Arpád, they entered what became HUNGARY in the 9th century. They harassed the German kingdom but were finally defeated and repulsed by Otto I at the Battle of Lechfeld. Pope Sylvester crowned Stephen as the first king of their country in 1000 and he established unity and introduced Christianity. He was canonized after his death.

Mahabharata ('The Great Story of the Bharatas') One of the two great EPICS of SANSKRIT literature in India and regarded as one of the HINDU SACRED TEXTS. Comprising 110,000 COUPLETS, it is probably the longest single poem in world literature. Its central theme is the struggle between two families of cousins, the Kauravas and the ultimately successful Pandavas, for control of Kurukshetra, the region north of Delhi. The *Mahabharata* is not the work of a single poet but representative of the whole range of ancient Indian bardic poetry, probably compiled between 400 BC and 200 AD.

Maharashtra A large state in western India, bordering on the Arabian Sea, formed in 1960 from the south-eastern part of the former Bombay state; area 307,690 sq km (118,845 sq miles); pop. (1991) 78,748,215; capital, Bombay.

Mahayana The more general form of Buddhism. It survived in India until the Muslim era and also spread to Central Asia, China, Japan, Java, and Sumatra. The stress of the ancient schools (e.g. Theravada) on personal enlightenment is superseded by the ideal of the bodhisattva who postpones his own salvation for the love of others.

Mahdi In popular Muslim belief, a spiritual and temporal leader who will rule before the end of the world and restore religion and justice. The title has been claimed by various leaders; the most widely known of these was Muhammad Ahmad of Dongola in Sudan (1843–85), who proclaimed himself Mahdi in 1881 and launched a political and revolutionary movement which captured Khartoum and overthrew the Egyptian regime. For Shiite Muslims the title *Mahdi* refers to the twelfth imam.

Mahfouz, Naguib (1911–) Egyptian novelist and short-story writer. His novels include the Cairo Trilogy (1956–57), which monitors the stages of Egyptian nationalism up to the revolution of 1952, and *Miramar* (1967), an attack on President Nasser's subsequent policies; his short stories of the late 1960s examine the aftermath of the 1967 war with Israel. In 1988 he became the first writer in Arabic to be awarded the Nobel Prize for literature.

mahjong A game for four played with tiles, originally from China and brought to the West after World War I. In its modified English-language version, a complete set of tiles (once made of ivory, wood, or bone, now of plastic) consists of a suit of 36 bamboo tiles (four sets, numbered 1–9), 36 circles, and 36 characters similarly subdivided, 12 dragons (red, green, and white) and 16 winds (East, North, West, and South), with the optional addition of 16 flowers and seasons. Players draw 13 tiles by a complicated process from four 'walls' (the Great Wall of China) and play anti-clockwise in turn, discarding one tile and picking up another. The winner is the first to collect four 'pungs' (three like tiles of the same suit and rank) and a pair, or another scoring set, such as combinations of a quong (a pung plus the first matching tile) and a chow (a run of three tiles of the same suit). There are also other special winning combinations, such as seven pairs (seven sisters).

Mahler, Gustav (1860–1911) Austrian composer, conductor, and pianist. He was director (1897–1907) of the Vienna State Opera. His large-scale works include nine complete symphonies (1888–1910) and the symphonic song-cycle *Das Lied von der Erde* (1908). His music forms a link between the romantic tradition of the 19th century and the experimentalism of 20th-century composers, such as Schoenberg; there has been a significant revival of interest in his work in the second half of the 20th century.

mahogany A tree of tropical and subtropical regions. Mahoganies belong to the family Meliaceae. This contains about 550 species, among which the genera *Swietenia* and *Khaya*, each with eight species, produce the highly decorative reddish timber called mahogany. The *Swietenia* species are native to the Americas, while *Khaya* is restricted to Africa. The original mahogany, brought to Europe by 16th-century Spanish explorers, came from *S. mahagoni* from the Caribbean area. Most of the wild trees of this species are now poor specimens, the best having been removed long ago. The impoverishment of the stock is a classic example of genetic erosion. Most American mahogany now comes from *S. macrophylla*, native to South and Central American rain forests. The paler timber of American mahogany comes from three different species of *Khaya* native to West African rain forests.

Mahón (or **Port Mahon**) The seaport capital of the island of Minorca in the Balearic Islands; pop. (1991) 21,800. Thought to have been founded by the Carthaginians, the town was held by the Moors between the 8th and 13th centuries and by the British from 1708 to 1783.

Mahore (French **Mayotte**) A small island group in the Indian Ocean east of the Comoro Islands, administered by France. It comprises the main island of La Grande Terre with an area of 362 sq km (140 sq miles) and pop. (1991) 94,410, and the smaller island of La Petite Terre (or Pamanzi) with an area of 11 sq km (4 sq miles) and pop. (1985) 9,775. Its capital is Mamoutzou (on La Grande Terre); its official language is French and its chief spoken language is Mahorian, an Arabized dialect of Swahili. Mahore became a French colony in 1843 and was attached to the Comoros until that island group became independent in 1974, at which time the people of Mahore voted to remain a French dependency. In 1976 the island became an overseas collectivity of France. Its chief products are coffee, cinnamon, copra, vanilla, cloves, and essence of ylang-ylang.

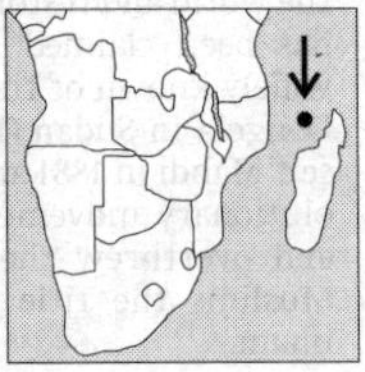

Maiden Castle A prehistoric fort on a chalk hill in Dorset, southern England, occupied from Neolithic to Iron Age times.

maidenhair fern A fern, *Adiantum capillus-veneris*, of western Europe, including Britain and western Ireland. Maidenhair ferns belong to the family Adiantaceae, and are popular greenhouse plants. All are deciduous, with spores on the end of their unmistakable fronds which are in the form of wedge-shaped leaflets along branching, wiry, blackish-brown stalks.

maidenhair tree See GINKGO.

Maidenhead A town in Berkshire, southern England, on the River Thames to the west of London; pop. (1991) 59,605. Printing, boat building, engineering, and the production of chemicals are important industries.

Maidstone The county town of Kent in south-east England, on the River Medway; pop. (1991) 133,200. A market town with brewing, paper-making, and agricultural industries.

Mailer, Norman (1923–) US novelist and essayist. He gained recognition with his first novel, *The Naked and the Dead* (1948), which drew on his experiences in World War II. The effect of war and violence on human relationships is a recurrent theme in his work, which frequently also includes an element of social criticism. Such novels as *The Presidential Papers* (1963) and *The Armies of the Night* (1968) combine journalism, autobiography, political commentary, and fictional passages in a wide range of styles. His more recent works include *Pieces and Pontifications* (1982), *Tough Guys Don't Dance* (1984), and *Harlot's Ghost* (1991).

Maiman, Theodore Harold (1927–) US engineer who in 1960 built the first working laser, which produced pulses of very intense monochromatic light. This was a major achievement, although a number of earlier workers had explored the theoretical background to the amplification of microwaves.

Maimonides (born Moses ben Maimon) (1135–1204) Jewish philosopher and Rabbinic scholar, born in Córdoba in Spain. He eventually settled in Cairo, where he became head of the Jewish community. His writings include the *Guide for the Perplexed* (1190), which endeavoured to reconcile Talmudic scripture with the philosophy of Aristotle. His work had a great influence on medieval Christian thought.

Main A river in western Germany that rises in the Fichtelgebirge in northern Bavaria and flows 500 km (310 miles) westwards through Frankfurt to meet the Rhine at Mainz.

Maine A north-eastern state of the USA, on the Atlantic coast; area 86,156 sq km (33,265 sq miles); pop. (1990) 1,227,930; capital, Augusta. Its largest city is Portland. Maine is also known as the Pine Tree State. Visited by John Cabot in 1498 and colonized from England in the 17th–18th centuries, it became the 23rd state of the USA in 1820. Maine is a major producer of pulp and paper products, sardines, lobsters, and shoes; potatoes, blueberries, apples, dairy products, poultry, and eggs are the chief agricultural products. A popular summer vacation area for hunters, anglers, canoeists, and campers, its major tourist attractions include Acadia National Park, St Croix Island International Historic Site, and the northernmost section of the Appalachian National Scenic Trail.

main sequence stars See HERTZSPRUNG–RUSSELL DIAGRAM.

Maintenon, Marquise de (title of Françoise d'Aubigné) (1635–1719) Mistress and later second wife of the French king Louis XIV. Already a widow, in 1669 she became the governess of Louis's children by his previous mistress, Madame de Montespan. In 1674, with the king's assistance, she bought the marquisate of Maintenon. She was married to Louis after his first wife's death in 1683.

Mainz A city in west Germany at the confluence of the Rhine and the Main, capital of the Rhineland-Palatinate state; pop. (1991) 182,870. An ancient market town, it holds Germany's biggest wine market each year. It has a university founded in 1477. Printing was developed here *c.*1448 by Johannes Gutenberg. The museum of printing holds a Gutenberg Bible printed in 1452–55.

maiolica (or **majolica**, from its reputed place of origin, Majorca) A type of tin-GLAZED EARTHENWARE decorated with bright colours over a white ground, popular during the Renaissance. Maiolica decoration often featured figurative scenes, many of them more or less freely adapted from engravings. There were factories in several Italian cities, and the fame of Italian maiolica led to the establishment of centres of production in northern Europe during the 16th century. The tin-glazed earthenware of northern Europe was known as faïence, after the Italian city of Faenza. Towards the middle of the 17th century the Dutch faïence industry became concentrated in Delft, hence the name 'delftware' to describe Dutch blue and white maiolica. Tin-glazed earthenware was also made in Bristol in the 17th and 18th centuries.

Maitreya (Sanskrit, 'friendly one') The future BUDDHA, now residing in heaven, awaiting his rebirth on Earth. His appearance is keenly anticipated by all Buddhists. In eastern Asia he is often depicted as a fat, laughing figure, holding a bag of good fortune and a rosary, representing good deeds, ready to restore truth on Earth.

maize An annual grass, *Zea mays*, popularly known in North America as CORN. It grows up to 4.5 m (15 feet) tall and is the only cereal of American origin. It was first cultivated over 5,000 years ago in Central America and is now grown throughout the tropical, subtropical, and warm temperate regions of the world. The plant is unusual among the grasses in that its male and female flowers are separate and occur on the same plant. Most of the maize varieties cultivated today are hybrid forms. These give high yields but may be susceptible to disease.

There are several types of maize. 'Flourcorn' has grains with soft starch that can be stirred into a paste, whereas 'flintcorn' cannot, as the starch is quite hard. The grain of another type, known as SWEET CORN, contains mostly sugars rather than starch and is eaten as a vegetable. Yet another kind of maize has a high water content causing it to explode on heating to produce the familiar popcorn.

Major, John (1943–) British Conservative statesman, Prime Minister 1990–97. He became Prime Minister following the resignation of Margaret Thatcher, and in 1992 he was returned for a further term. His premiership saw the joint DOWNING STREET DECLARATION of the UK and Irish governments, intended as the basis of a peace initiative in Northern Ireland, and the negotiations leading to the signing of the MAASTRICHT TREATY. Major survived a leadership challenge in 1995, and was faced with divisions within the Conservative Party over the degree to which Britain should integrate with Europe. He led the Conservatives to a dramatic defeat in the 1997 election. He was subsequently appointed a guardian of Princes William and Harry, after the death of their mother.

Majorca (Spanish **Mallorca**) The largest of the Balearic Islands in the western Mediterranean; area 3,640 sq km (1,406 sq miles); pop. (1990) 614,000; capital, Palma. Taken by James I of Aragon in 1229, it is administered by Spain as part of the Baleares autonomous region. Its main industry is tourism.

Makarios III (Mihail Christodoulou Mouskos) (1913–77) Greek Cypriot archbishop and statesman. Primate and archbishop of the Greek Orthodox Church in CYPRUS (1950–77), he reorganized the movement for *enosis* (the union of Cyprus with Greece). He was exiled (1956–59) by the British for allegedly supporting the EOKA terrorist campaign of Colonel Grivas against the British and Turks. Makarios was elected President of Cyprus (1960–76). A coup by Greek officers in 1974 forced his brief exile to London, but he was reinstated in 1975 and continued in office until his death.

Makassar (or **Makasar** or **Macassar**) The former name (until 1970) of UJUNG PANDANG.

Malabar Coast The southern part of the west coast of India, including the coastal region of Karnataka and most of the state of Kerala. It is named from the Malabars, an ancient Dravidian people.

Malabo The seaport capital of Equatorial Guinea, situated on the island of Bioko (formerly Fernando Póo) in the Gulf of Guinea; pop. (1988) 37,000. Until 1973 it was known as Santa Isabel and while under British rule in the 1820s was named Port Clarence or Clarencetown. It exports cocoa and timber.

Malacca A former Muslim sultanate on the west coast of Malaya, which flourished from about 1403 to 1511, when it was conquered by the Portuguese. It played an important role in the development of trade between Europe and the East, especially China. See also MELAKA.

Málaga A seaport at the mouth of the Guadalmedina River on the Andalusian coast of southern Spain, capital of the province of Málaga; pop. (1991) 524,750. It gives its name to a sweet wine produced locally. It has light industries and is a popular resort.

Malagasy The people of Madagascar or their Malayo-Polynesian language, which is related to Malay.

Malamud, Bernard (1914–86) US novelist and short-story writer. The son of Russian Jewish immigrants, he is perhaps best known for his novel *The Fixer* (1967), the story of a Jewish handyman or 'fixer' in tsarist Russia. Other works include *The Assistant* (1957), *A New Life* (1961), *The Tenants* (1971), and *God's Grace* (1982).

malaria A protozoal infection by *Plasmodium* species, *P. falciparum*, *P. ovale*, *P. vivax*, and *P. malariae*, which occurs in tropical regions of Africa, Asia, and South America. Transmission is by the female *Anopheles* mosquito. Initially, 'flu-like' symptoms are apparent with tiredness, loss of appetite, headache, and muscle pain. This is followed by episodic attacks every 48 hours of high fever, nausea, vomiting, and diarrhoea may also occur. The attacks progress to hot flushes, palpitations, headache, difficulty in breathing, and fainting. In between attacks, patients are generally well with only mild symptoms. Complications may occur, especially with *P. falciparum* malaria, which include coma, kidney failure, jaundice, excessive destruction of red blood cells (haemolysis), and anaemia.

Treatment of *P. falciparum* malaria is an emergency because it is life-threatening. Prevention of malaria is essential where malaria is prevalent. However, preventive measures using drugs (chemoprophylaxis) are not 100 per cent effective; other measures such as nets and insect repellents are also required.

Malawi A long, narrow, landlocked country running north to south in south-eastern Africa. Its eastern boundary includes much of Lake Malawi; Tanzania is to the north and Zambia to the west, while Mozambique almost encloses its southern half.

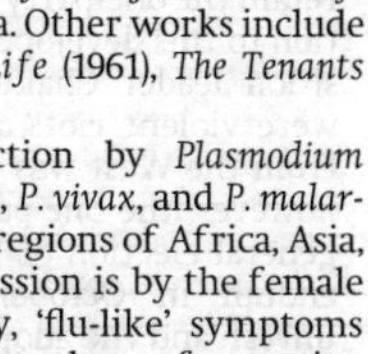

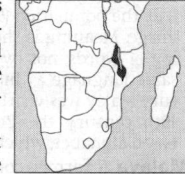

Physical. Malawi lies at the southern end of the

Great Rift Valley. The Shire River falling from Lake Malawi is flanked by high ground until it enters swampland, with three smaller lakes. A very warm, wet summer permits the growth of rice and sugar. To the north the ground rises westward from the lake to plateaux which are cooler and wetter for most of the year.

Economy. The economy is mainly agricultural, exports being dominated by tobacco, sugar, and tea. Groundnuts, cotton, and maize are also grown. The only mineral resource is BAUXITE. Industrial development is being financed through foreign aid. Light industries include beer, cement, and cigarette manufacture. Electricity is generated mainly from hydroelectric sources.

History. The area has been inhabited since at least 8000 BC, and several kingdoms had risen and fallen before Malawi was first explored by the Portuguese in the 17th century. Slave-traders from ZANZIBAR raided the area frequently in the 1840s, and its desolation is described by LIVINGSTONE in 1859. In 1875 Scottish missionaries settled, and for a while governed parts of the country. Colonial administration was instituted when Sir H. H. Johnston proclaimed the Shire Highlands a British Protectorate in 1889. This became British Central Africa in 1891, then Nyasaland from 1907 until 1964. Unwillingly a member of the CENTRAL AFRICAN FEDERATION (1953–63), it gained independence (1964) as Malawi, with Dr Hastings BANDA as first Prime Minister. When the country became a republic in 1966, he became President and was proclaimed Life President in 1971. Regular elections were held to the National Assembly, but all candidates had to be members of the Malawi Congress Party. At its Convention in 1991 the party voted to retain the one-party system; but increasing opposition to this developed early in 1992, with the opposition leader Chakufwa Chilana arrested. There were violent riots, and all non-humanitarian aid from the West was suspended. In spite of protest, however, the one-party system continued for the general election of June 1992. Banda held a referendum in October 1992, following continued unrest, and the adoption of a multi-party political system was approved. A new constitution was adopted in 1993 and elections in 1994 were won by the United Democratic Front (UDF), with Bakili Muluzi becoming President.

Capital: Lilongwe
Area: 118,484 sq km (45,747 sq mi)
Population: 9,939,000 (1995)
Currency: 1 kwacha = 100 tambala
Religions: Protestant 33.7%; Roman Catholic 27.6%; traditional beliefs 19.0%; Muslim 16.2%
Ethnic Groups: Chewa 46.0%; Lomwe 19.0%; Yao 14.0%; Ngoni 9.0%; Tumbuka 6.0%
Languages: English, Chichewa (both official); Lomwe; local languages
International Organizations: UN; Commonwealth; Non-Aligned Movement; OAU; SADC

Malawi, Lake Another name for Lake NYASA.

Malay The language of the Malay people of Malaysia and Indonesia. It belongs to the Malayo-Polynesian language group and is spoken mainly in Malaysia where it is the mother tongue of about half the population (9 million) and the official language. Meaning is shown by the order and grouping of words, not by inflexions. It is virtually the same language as Indonesian. From the 14th century Malay was written in Arabic script but in the 19th century the British constructed a Roman-based alphabet, which is in general use today.

Malaya A former country in south-east Asia, consisting of the southern part of the Malay peninsula and some adjacent islands (originally including Singapore), now forming the western part of the Federation of MALAYSIA, and known as West Malaysia. Malaya was dominated by the Buddhist kingdom of Srivijaya from the 9th to the 14th centuries and by the Hindu kingdom of Majaphit in the 14th century. Islam was introduced with the rise of the princely states, especially Malacca, in the 15th century. The area was opened up by the Dutch and Portuguese, and eventually Britain became dominant, investing heavily in rubber plantations using much immigrant labour from China and India. The several Malay states federated under British control in 1896. Malaya was occupied by the Japanese from 1941 to 1945. After the war, Britain fought a successful 12-year campaign against Communist guerrillas, mainly Chinese. The country became independent in 1957, the federation expanding into Malaysia in 1963.

Malayalam The Dravidian language of the state of Kerala in south-west India.

Malay Archipelago A very large group of islands, including Sumatra, Java, Borneo, the Philippines, and New Guinea, lying south-east of Asia and north and north-east of Australia. It is the largest island group in the world and constitutes the bulk of the area formerly known as the East Indies.

Malay language See AUSTRONESIAN LANGUAGES.

Malay peninsula A peninsula in south-east Asia separating the Indian Ocean from the South China Sea. It extends approximately 1,100 km (700 miles) southwards from the Isthmus of Kra and comprises the southern part of Thailand and the whole of Malaya (West Malaysia).

Malaysia A country in south-east Asia, having two parts, West and East, separated by the South China Sea.

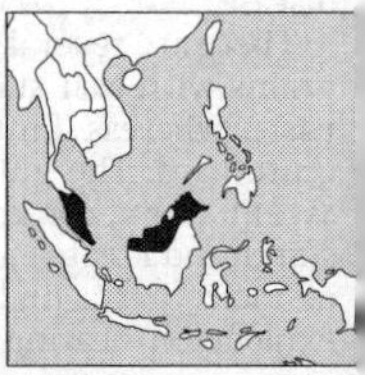

Physical. East Malaysia comprises SARAWAK and SABAH in the north and north-west of the island of Borneo. West, or Peninsular, Malaysia comprises the former Federation of MALAYA and occupies the southern end of the Malay Peninsula, extending south from the south-east Asian mainland and

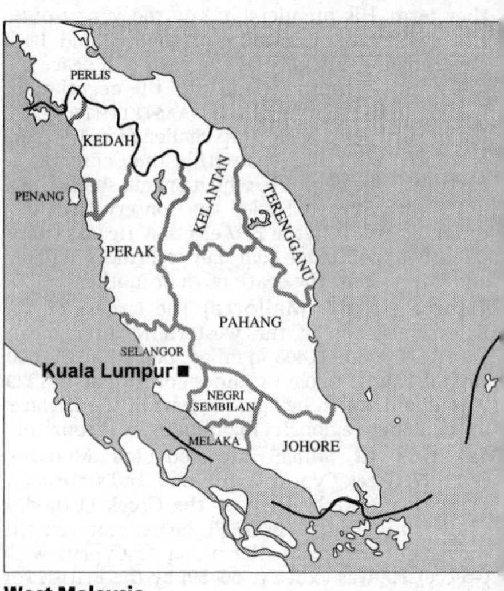

West Malaysia

bounded on the north by Thailand and on the south by Singapore; it has a south-western coast on the Strait of Malacca. The climate of Malaysia is very warm and affected by the monsoons, which bring about 2,300 mm (90 inches) of rain in a year. The red soil provides for paddy-fields in the lowland areas, where rice is cultivated, and high-yield rubber, oil palm, and cocoa plantations in the west of the peninsula, tin is also dredged. Inland, the Malayan highlands are forested and provide tropical hardwoods. East Malaysia and off-shore waters are rich in mineral oil.

Economy. Manufacturing industry produces automobiles, electronics, cigarettes, tyres, sawn logs, and cement. Crude oil is an important export. Agriculture, with rice the principal subsistence crop, remains the mainstay of the economy, despite high industrial growth in recent years. Malaysia is the world's largest producer of rubber, palm oil, and tin; timber is also an important export. Other mineral resources include bauxite, iron ore, and copper. The New Economic Policy (NEP), initiated after ethnic riots in 1970, introduced ethnic quotas in an attempt to promote economic growth and eradicate the association of race with occupation.

History. Established in 1963, the Federation of Malaysia originally included SINGAPORE but it was forced to secede in 1965 because of fears that its largely Chinese population would challenge Malay political dominance. BRUNEI refused to join the Federation. The establishment of Malaysia was first suggested (1961) by Tunku ABDUL RAHMAN, who became its first Prime Minister (1963–70). The Federation aroused deep suspicion in Indonesia, and provoked President SUKARNO's policy of confrontation (KONFRONTASI), resulting in intermittent guerrilla war in Malaysia's Borneo territories, which was only defeated with Commonwealth military assistance (1963–66). In 1969, inequalities between the politically dominant Malays and economically dominant Chinese resulted in riots in Kuala Lumpur, and parliamentary government was suspended until 1971. As a result, there was a major restructuring of political and social institutions designed to ensure Malay predominance, the New Economic Policy being launched to increase the Malay (*bumiputra*) stake in the economy. The largest single political party remained the United Malays National Organization, which had been created by Tunku Rahman. Since 1971 this has ruled in uneasy alliance with the Malaysian Chinese Association and some other ten parties in a coalition, the National Front. Mahathir bin Mohamed became its leader and Prime Minister in 1981. A leading member of the ASSOCIATION OF SOUTH-EAST ASIAN NATIONS, Malaysia replaced the New Economic Policy in 1991 by a New Development Policy, whose aim was to diversify the economy. At the same time it has incurred international criticism for its exploitation of its rain-forests. During 1994 a scandal over Britain's lending Malaysia £234 million to build the Pergau dam in an aid-for-trade agreement caused controversy in Britain and strained relations between the two countries. The ruling coalition was re-elected in 1995.

Capital: Kuala Lumpur
Area: 330,442 sq km (127,584 sq mi)
Population: 19,948,000 (1995)
Currency: 1 ringgit = 100 sen
Religions: Muslim 52.9%; Buddhist 17.3%; Chinese popular religions 11.6%; Hindu 7.0%; Christian 6.4%
Ethnic Groups: Malay, Orang Asli, Iban, Land Dayak, Bajan, and Kadazan 60.0% Chinese 31.0%; Indian, Pakistani, and Bangladeshi 8.0%
Languages: Malay (official); English; Chinese; Tamil; minority languages
International Organizations: UN; Commonwealth; Non-Aligned Movement; Colombo Plan; ASEAN

Malcolm Four kings of Scotland. **Malcolm I** (died 954) reigned 943–54. **Malcolm II** (*c.*954–1034) reigned 1005–34. **Malcolm III** (known as Malcolm Canmore, from Gaelic *Ceann-mor* 'great head') (*c.*1031–93), son of Duncan I, reigned 1058–93. He came to the throne after killing Macbeth in battle (1057). One of the monarchs most responsible for welding Scotland into an organized kingdom, Malcolm spent a large part of his reign involved in intermittent border warfare with the new Norman regime in England, eventually being killed in battle near Alnwick. **Malcolm IV** (known as Malcolm the Maiden) (1141–65), grandson of David I, reigned 1153–65. His reign witnessed a progressive loss of power to Henry II of England; he died young and without an heir.

Malcolm X (born Malcolm Little) (1925–65) US

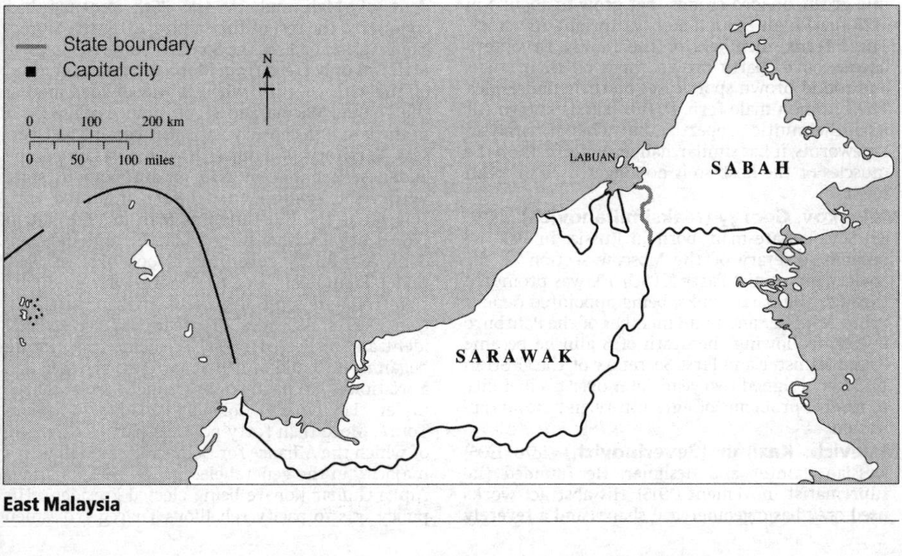

East Malaysia

political activist. He joined the Black Muslims (Nation of Islam) in 1946 and during the 1950s and early 1960s became a vigorous campaigner against the exploitation of blacks. He advocated the use of violence for self-protection and was opposed to the cooperative approach that characterized the rest of the civil-rights movement. In 1964, after converting to orthodox Islam, he broke away from the Black Muslims and moderated his views on black separatism; he was assassinated the following year.

Maldives A country consisting of a chain of coral islands in the Indian Ocean some 650 km (400 miles) south-west of Sri Lanka.

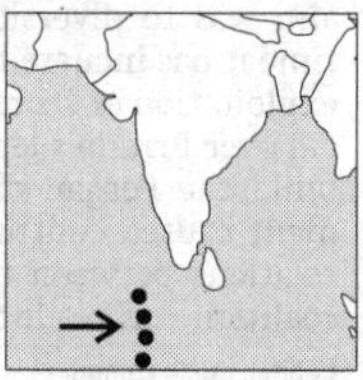

Physical. The islands comprise some 1,800 small atolls and sandbanks built on the summits of old, submerged volcanoes.

Economy. The economy of Maldives is based on fishing, clothing, shipping, and tourism. Ecological change threatens the future of the country, since many of its islands are a mere 1.8 m (6 feet) above sea level.

History. From 1887 to 1952 the islands were a sultanate under British protection. Maldivian demands for constitutional reform began in the 1930s; internal self-government was achieved in 1948 and full independence in 1965. In 1968 the sultanate was abolished, and a republic declared. The Maldives became a full member of the COMMONWEALTH OF NATIONS in 1985. In 1988, with Indian help, President Maumoun Abdul Gayoom (first elected 1978) suppressed an attempted coup. He was re-elected the following year, and again in 1993.

Capital: Malé
Area: 298 sq km (115 sq mi)
Population: 253,000 (1995)
Currency: 1 Maldivian rufiyaa = 100 laaris
Religions: Virtually 100% Sunni Muslim
Ethnic Groups: Majority Sinhalese and Dravidian; Arab, African, and Negrito minorities
Languages: Divehi (official)
International Organizations: UN; Commonwealth; Colombo Plan

Malé The capital and largest atoll of the Maldives, in the Indian Ocean; pop. (est. 1991) 55,130.

male fern A FERN of the genus *Dryopteris*, with mid-green, divided fronds that grow to about 1 m (3.25 feet) high from a stocky, upright rootstock. These ferns, members of the family Dryopteridaceae, have chaffy brown scales on their stalks and round brown spore-cases on their undersides. The common male fern, *D. filix-mas*, is known for its anthelmintic properties, but while it paralyses tapeworms, it has similar, dangerous effects on the muscles of the host, so is no longer used in treatment.

Malenkov, Georgy (Maksimilianovich) (1902–88) Soviet statesman, born in Russia. In 1930 he became secretary of the Moscow section of the Soviet Communist Party (CPSU). He was promoted through the party ranks, being appointed deputy Prime Minister and a full member of the Politburo in 1946. Following the death of Stalin he became Prime Minister and First Secretary of the CPSU in 1953 but resigned two years later over his inability to resolve problems of agriculture and industrialization.

Malevich, Kazimir (Severinovich) (1878–1935) Russian painter and designer. He founded the suprematist movement (1915). His abstract works used only basic geometrical shapes and a severely restricted range of colour, culminating in the *White on White* series (*c.*1918). The Soviet government suppressed modern art, but Malevich later had immense influence on western European art.

Malherbe François de (1555–1628) French poet. An architect of classicism in poetic form and grammar, he sternly criticized excess of emotion and ornamentation and the use of Latin and dialectal forms.

Mali A landlocked country in north-west Africa, sharing common boundaries with Mauritania, Algeria, Niger, Burkina Faso, Côte d'Ivoire, Guinea, and Senegal.

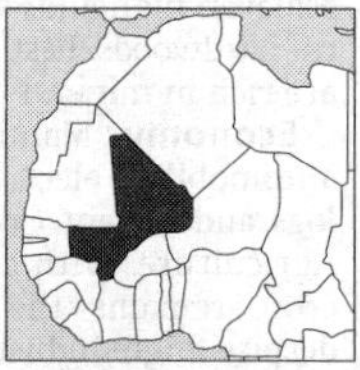

Physical. The northern part of Mali is in the dry Sahara and its south is in the tropics where there is about 1,200 mm (nearly 50 inches) of rainfall each year. From the south-west, and through its centre flows the Niger, which provides fish. The Niger here has an inland delta which permits the seasonal growing of rice, while other areas contain sufficient pasture for cattle, sheep, and goats.

Economy. Mali is amongst the world's poorest countries. The economy is agricultural, with livestock-rearing predominant in the drought-ridden north, and cotton cultivation in the southern savannah. Cotton, livestock, and gold are the chief exports. Millet, sorghum, and rice are also important subsistence crops. Light industry is based on clothing and food-processing. Hydroelectric power contributes substantially to electricity supplies. There are deposits of gold, marble, limestone, salt, and phosphates.

History. The Mali empire in the upper Niger region of West Africa was established in the 13th century. The founder, Sundjata, conquered the remains of the empire of GHANA *c.*1235–40 with his army of Malinke soldiers. Mali soon controlled the rich trade across the Sahara and became a major supplier of gold. The empire reached its peak in the early 14th century under Mansa Musa, who established an efficient administration. The Muslim traveller Ibn Battuta (1304–78) visited Mali in 1351–52 and gave a detailed account of the court and trade. However, by then the empire was beginning to decline. In 1335 SONGHAI became independent of Mali and by the 15th century had conquered the rest of the empire. After the Moroccan invasion of 1591, the Songhai empire collapsed. Mali was only freed from Moroccan rule at the end of the 18th century, when it was divided among the Tuareg, Macina, and Ségou. France colonized it in the late 19th century. In 1946 it became an Overseas Territory of France. It was proclaimed the Sudanese Republic in 1958, an autonomous state within the FRENCH COMMUNITY. It united with Senegal as the Federation of Mali in 1959, but in 1960 Senegal withdrew and Mali became independent. A military government took over in 1968, under Lieutenant Moussa Traoré, who gradually re-introduced some degree of civilian participation. In 1974, as General Traoré he was elected President, and re-elected in 1985. Pro-democracy rioting began in 1990, and in 1991 Traoré was arrested and a National Reconciliation Council took charge under Lieutenant Colonel Amadou Toumani Touré. More than forty political parties emerged, of which the Alliance for Democracy in Mali won a majority in the general election of 1992, its leader Alpha Oumar Konare being elected President. His policy was to pacify rebellious Tuareg tribesmen in the north (a peace agreement was reached in 1992) and to try to win UN support to rebuild an economy which had suffered severely from drought. He was re-elected President in 1997.

Capital: Bamako
Area: 1,240,192 sq km (478,841 sq mi)
Population: 9,008,000 (1995)
Currency: 1 CFA franc = 100 centimes
Religions: Muslim 90.0%; traditional beliefs 9.0%; Christian 1.0%
Ethnic Groups: Bambara 31.9%; Fulani 13.9%; Senufo 12.0%; Soninke 8.8%; Tuareg 7.3%; Songhai 7.2%; Malinke 6.6%; Dogon 4.0%; Dyula 2.9%; Bobo 2.4%; Arab 1.2%
Languages: French (official); Bambara; Fulani; local languages
International Organizations: UN; OAU; Franc Zone

Malibu A fashionable resort to the west of Los Angeles on the Pacific coast of California, USA; pop. (est. 1990) 7,000. It is noted for its surf and secluded beaches and its private Malibu Beach Colony is home to some of the film industry's biggest stars. The J. Paul Getty Museum, one of the world's greatest private art collections, is in Malibu.

Malin Head A point on the coast of County Donegal, the northernmost point of Ireland. The shipping forecast area **Malin** covers the Atlantic north of Ireland and west of the southern-half of Scotland.

Malinowski, Bronisław Kaspar (1884–1942) Polish anthropologist. An influential teacher, from 1916 onwards he was chiefly based in England and the USA. He initiated the technique of 'participant observation', in which the anthropologist spends a period living with a community; he first applied this in his study of the people of the Trobriand Islands, conducted from 1915 to 1918. He also developed the functionalist approach to anthropology, especially in his studies of the Pueblo Indians in Mexico and Bantu-speaking peoples in Africa.

mallard A widely distributed, familiar species of dabbling DUCK, *Anas platyrhyncos*, from which most farmyard breeds are descended. The drake's iridescent green head, white collar, and purple-brown breast are distinctive. Females are mottled brown. Mallards inhabit all types of inland water, even ornamental ponds in towns, and usually spend the winter on estuaries and coasts.

Mallarmé, Stéphane (1842–98) French poet. His best-known poems include 'Hérodiade' (*c.*1871) and 'L'Après-midi d'un faune' (1876). He was a symbolist, who made use of elaborate symbols and metaphors in his work and experimented with rhythm and syntax by transposing words and omitting grammatical elements. These tendencies culminated in the poem 'Un Coup de dés jamais n'abolira le hasard' (1897), which makes revolutionary use of typographical possibilities to suggest a musical score.

Malle, Louis (1932–95) French film director. He won recognition with *Ascenseur pour l'échafaud* (1958) and the erotic *Les Amants* (1959), which are examples of the French *nouvelle vague*. He gained international acclaim with a series of successful films, such as *Pretty Baby* (1978), *Au Revoir les enfants* (1987), and *Damage* (1992).

mallee fowl A bird, *Leipoa ocellata*, of central and southern Australia. It is one of ten species of bird making up a family, Megapodiidae (megapodes), related to other gamebirds. They are mostly dullish brown or greyish birds and pheasant-like in size and appearance. They occur in south-east Asia, Australia, New Guinea, and some Pacific islands. Their most extraordinary feature is that they bury their eggs in sand warmed by the Sun, warm volcanic ash, or rotting vegetation; the heat of these substances hatches the eggs. The family name of these birds refers to their large feet, which are adapted to digging 'incubation' holes for the eggs. The mallee fowl itself builds a special mound, which it keeps opening and adjusting to keep the temperature constant. On hatching, the young fight their way to the surface and can fly within a few hours; they receive no parental care.

mallow An annual, biennial or perennial plant of the genus *Malva*, from Europe, Asia, and North Africa. The mallow family, Malvaceae, also includes cotton, hibiscus, and hollyhock. They have lobed leaves and purple, rose, or, occasionally, white flowers. Most species are in the genus *Malva*, though the name is also applied to the perennial marsh mallow, *Althaea officinalis*, a plant much valued since early times as a vegetable and for its medicinal properties.

Malmö A port and fortified city in south-west Sweden, situated on the Øresund (The Sound) opposite Copenhagen, with which it is connected by ferry; pop. (1990) 233,900. It is the third-largest city in Sweden, capital of Malmöhus county, and an industrial centre with shipyards, chemicals, food processing, and textiles.

Malory, Sir Thomas (died 1471) English writer. Although his exact identity is uncertain, it is probable that he was Sir Thomas Malory of Newbold Revel, Warwickshire. His major work, *Le Morte d'Arthur* (printed 1483), is a prose translation of a collection of the legends of King Arthur, selected from French and other sources. It was one of the earliest works to be printed by Caxton, and is the standard source for later versions in English of the Arthurian romances.

Malpighi, Marcello (1628–94) Italian microscopist. He investigated the structures of the kidney, skin, and blood vessels, confirming Harvey's views on blood circulation. He also traced the development of the chick embryo, studied the anatomy of the silkworm, discovered the breathing system of insects, and examined plant cells. The **Malpighian body**, part of the nephron, the **Malpighian layer** of the skin, and **Malpighian tubules** in insects were named after him.

Malplaquet A village in the department of Nord in northern France, on the border with Belgium about 16 km (10 miles) south of Mons, scene of the victory in 1709 of allied British and Austrian troops over the French.

Malraux, André (1901–76) French novelist, politician, and art critic. Malraux was involved in the Chinese communist uprising of 1927 and fought in the Spanish Civil War and World War II. He then became a Gaullist, and was appointed the first Minister of Cultural Affairs (1959–69). He is best known for such novels as *La Condition humaine* (1933) and *L'Espoir* (1937), which in several respects anticipate the existentialism of Jean-Paul Sartre.

Malta The largest of a group of three islands constituting a country of the same name in the central Mediterranean Sea between Tunisia and Sicily, the others being Gozo and the tiny Comino.

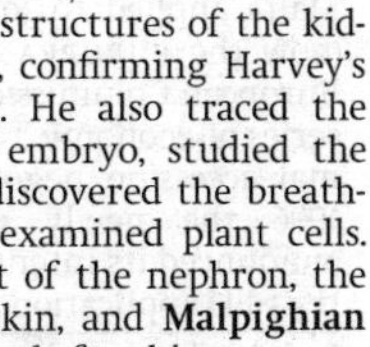

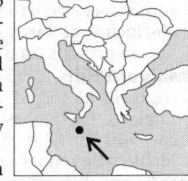

Physical. The main island is some 27 km (17 miles) long by 14 km (9 miles) wide and rises to hills in the south-west. The climate is very warm and rather dry, with fierce winds, and the land is barren in appearance, with few trees and no rivers or streams.

Economy. Malta's major exports incude clothing, machinery, and instruments; ship repair is significant and an offshore financial sector is being developed. Offshore oil exploration is being undertaken, and tourism is an important economic activity intended to replace loss of income from UK defence expenditure after the UK naval base was removed in 1979. Malta is the most densely populated country in Europe, with two-thirds of the population under 40.

History. Malta was settled, possibly as long as six thousand years ago, during the NEOLITHIC era. In historic times it was a Carthaginian centre, falling to the Romans in 218 BC who named it Melita. The Byzantine empire controlled it until 870 when it was conquered by the Arabs. The NORMANS annexed it to their kingdom of SICILY, but, after having been retaken by Muslim forces, it finally fell to the Spanish kingdoms of Aragon and Castile and thence to Spain itself. Under Emperor Charles V it was given to the KNIGHTS HOSPITALLERS (1530), who defended it against Turkish attacks and fortified and enriched it. They were eventually expelled by Napoleon I of France (1798) and the island was taken by the British in 1800. The Treaty of Amiens (1802) returned Malta to the Knights Hospitallers but the Maltese people protested and requested British sovereignty, provided that Malta remained Roman Catholic and that the Maltese Declaration of Rights was honoured. Britain accepted these terms and the country was formally ceded to Britain by France in 1814. Malta developed as a strategic air and naval base and was awarded the George Cross for its resistance to German attack (1940–42). It gained full independence within the COMMONWEALTH OF NATIONS in 1964 and in 1974 became a republic. Malta applied to join the European Community (now the EUROPEAN UNION) in 1990; in 1993 the European Commission instructed it to carry out a series of economic reforms before the start of formal accession negotiations in 1997. However, in 1996 the newly elected Labour government announced its intention of withdrawing the country's EU application.

Capital: Valletta
Area: 316 sq km (122 sq mi)
Population: 370,000 (1995)
Currency: 1 Maltese lira = 100 cents = 1,000 mils
Religions: Roman Catholic 97.0%; Anglican 1.0%
Ethnic Groups: Maltese (of Italian, British, and Phoenician origin) 96.0%; British 2.0%
Languages: Maltese, English (both official)
International Organizations: UN; Commonwealth; Council of Europe; CSCE

Malthus, Thomas Robert (1766–1834) English economist and clergyman. He was a pioneer of the science of political economy and is known for his theory, as expressed in *Essay on Population* (1798), that the rate of increase of the population tends to be out of proportion to the increase of its means of subsistence; controls on population (by sexual abstinence or birth control) are therefore necessary to prevent catastrophe.

Malvern Hills A range of hills of ancient volcanic rocks in Hereford and Worcester, west-central England. The highest point is Worcestershire Beacon (425 m, 1,394 ft). The resort town of Great Malvern lies on its eastern edge.

Malvinas, Islas The name by which the FALKLAND ISLANDS are known in Argentina. It is derived from the French *Malouines* which reflects early connections with fishermen from Saint-Malo, France.

mamba One of the world's most venomous SNAKES. Mambas are related to cobras and range through tropical Africa south to Natal and South West Africa. There are four species: three arboreal green mambas, *Dendroaspis* species, and the black mamba, *D. polylepis*, which is essentially terrestrial. The black mamba is a large, fast-moving snake, which preys on squirrels and rock hyraxes. Its bite is very dangerous; the venom contains a powerful nerve toxin which inhibits breathing. The green mambas, *D. angusticeps*, *D. viridis*, and *D. jamesoni*, although venomous, are much less aggressive and feed on small birds and mammals.

Mameluke (from Arabic *mamluk*, 'possessed' or 'slave') Name of two Egyptian dynasties. Mamelukes or slave soldiers were a distinctive feature of Islamic armies from the 9th century. Captured in childhood, they were trained in every branch of warfare and had an exacting academic education. Turkish and Mongol slaves were bodyguards of the Ayyubid sultan al-Salih (1240–49). On his death a popular power struggle developed and the Bahri mameluke generals elected one of their number as sultan al-Malik al Muizz. After some confusion, succession became hereditary and in 1291 the last Franks were driven from Egypt. The Turkish Bahri sultans recruited Burji slaves as bodyguards, stationing them in Cairo's citadel. These were chiefly Circassian (from the Caucasus). In 1390 they too usurped the sultanate under al-Malik an-Nasir. The Burji ruled until 1517. Mameluke rule extended over Egypt and Syria (including the present Israel, Jordan, Lebanon, and western Arabia). There was an elaborate court, and a highly organized civil service and judiciary. Active encouragement of trade and commerce brought great prosperity throughout their dominions, as is witnessed by the splendid monuments which they built in Cairo and elsewhere. Their external trade reached across Africa as far as Mali and Guinea, and throughout the Indian Ocean as far as Java. In 1517 the Ottoman Turks captured Cairo and overthrew the Mamelukes. As Turkish power waned they re-established themselves as rulers. NAPOLEON defeated them in 1798 and they were brought down by Muhammad Ali in 1811.

Mamet, David (1947–) US dramatist, director, and screenwriter. In 1974 he co-founded the Chicago-based St Nicholas Theater Company, for which he wrote and directed a succession of plays noted for their approach to social issues, including *Glengarry Glen Ross* (1984), which won the Pulitzer Prize. Other works include the film *House of Games* (1986), which he wrote and directed, and the play *Oleanna* (1992), whose portrayal of a case involving false accusations of sexual harassment caused much controversy.

mammal A vertebrate animal that bears its young alive and feeds them with milk, secreted by specialized skin glands called MAMMARY GLANDS. They are also warm-blooded animals with large brains, sweat glands in their skin, and body hair. The toes and fingers terminate in claws, nails, or hoofs. The dentition includes incisor, canine, premolar, and molar teeth, the number and shape varying greatly with the mode of feeding. There is only one replacement of teeth and the dentition and digestive system ensure efficient food utilization.

There are three subclasses of mammals: the egg-laying or monotreme mammals, the MARSUPIALS, and the placental or eutherian mammals. There are around 4,250 species of mammals, which have a wide distribution on land, in water, and in the air. In size they range from the pygmy white-toothed or Etruscan shrew, *Suncus etruscus*, only 80 mm

Mammals (1) Black bear. (2) Porcupine. (3) Fruit bat. (4) Soay sheep. (5) Rabbit. (6) Giant armadillo. (7) Genet. (8) Killer whale. (9) Baboon. (10) Walrus.

(3.25 inches) in length including its tail, to the largest animal that has ever lived, the blue whale, 33.3 m (109.3 feet) long.

The majority of mammals are quadrupeds; only a few have given up this gait. The exceptions include humans, which are bipedal, jumping mammals, such as kangaroos and jumping mice, and species which have adapted to an aquatic life. A few groups of mammals have modified their body plan for flight, as in bats, or gliding, as in phalangers. The diversity of forms and their ability to occupy all available habitats is a measure of their success in adaptation.

mammary gland A gland characteristic of female mammals, which produces milk for suckling their young. The supply of milk after birth depends on its regular removal by suckling or milking. The glands lie beneath the skin of the abdominal wall and open into separate teats, whose number depends, in general, upon the size of the litter. Pigs and dogs have numerous pairs whereas there is usually only a single pair in humans, although supernumerary glands and nipples are sometimes found in line along the chest and abdominal wall.

In primates, including humans, both sexes have mammary glands and teats or nipples, but the breasts enlarge only in females, on reaching sexual maturity, due to fat deposits around the gland. The gland becomes active and greatly enlarged during pregnancy and after birth due to hormonal stimulation.

mammography An imaging technique for the diagnosis and screening of breast CANCER. It involves X-ray examination of the breast using low-energy X-rays. See HEALTH SCREENING; RADIOLOGY.

mammoth A large extinct elephant in the genus *Mammuthus*, which occurred in Africa and the Northern Hemisphere from the Pliocene Epoch onwards. Mammoths reached a height of 4.5 m (15 feet) at the shoulder and had a pair of long, curved tusks up to 5 m (16 feet) long. A number of frozen carcasses have been found in Siberia, from which it is known that they had long, dense hair and also a thick layer of blubber. They disappeared about 12,000 years ago, probably because of the warming of the climate. Cave paintings of mammoths by Stone Age man suggest that they constituted an important source of food, clothing, and ivory for tools.

man The sole living member of the family Hominidae (see HOMINIDS), HOMO SAPIENS, and as such part of the order Primates. The chief specializations of humans, which distinguish them from other primates, include elaboration of the brain and behaviour, communication by speech, erect posture, and long postnatal development. The brain of adult man is at least twice as large as that of any adult living ape.

The difference in behaviour between humans and apes is considerable, but perhaps the most striking is related to communication by speech, together with the power of abstract thought. Humans are also able to store information in written records, and more recently by electronic means, and to pass it on from one generation to another. The gait of humans is totally bipedal, the body being fully and continuously balanced on the two hind-limbs.

After a gestation period of nine months one baby (but occasionally larger numbers of non-identical or identical offspring) is born, which suckles for periods ranging up to several years before weaning, depending upon cultural practices. The rate of development is slow and the period of childhood prolonged, which has a great influence on the family and social organization of humans.

Man, Isle of See ISLE OF MAN.

Managua The capital of Nicaragua, on the southern shore of Lake Managua; pop. (1985) 682,110. The city was severely damaged by earthquakes in 1931 and 1972 and also during the civil war in the late 1970s. Besides its administrative functions it is Nicaragua's chief commercial and industrial city.

manakin A bird that makes up a subfamily, Piprinae, of 52 species in the flycatcher family, Tyrannidae, which occur only in rain forests in South and Central America, feeding mainly on small fruits. They are cousins of the cotingas but are only sparrow-sized. The males of many species are brightly coloured, often with black bodies and white, yellow, or red heads. Some have blue bodies, and one or two have elongated tail feathers, though most have short tails. The males of most species display in leks, each bird having a separate court, though some have communal displays. The females look after the young by themselves.

Manama (Arabic **Al Manamah**) The seaport capital of the state of Bahrain, on Bahrain Island in the Persian Gulf; pop. (est. 1991) 140,400. It is a centre of banking, commerce, and oil refining.

manatee A large, aquatic, herbivorous mammal of the order Sirenia, belonging to a genus of SEA-COWS, *Trichechus*. The three species are found on tropical and subtropical Atlantic coasts, estuaries, and great rivers, where they feed upon marine or freshwater plants. The West Indian manatee, *T. manatus*, can reach a length of 4.6 m (15 feet) and is torpedo-shaped, with the digits of the fore-limbs modified as paddles; the hind-limbs are absent. The tail is powerful, flattened horizontally, and provides the main propulsive force. The flattened, rather pig-like, bristly snout has a large, muscular upper lip, the corners of which pluck the vegetation. A single calf is born after a gestation period of about five months; the mother takes great care of it and suckles it lying on her back. Exploitation of these animals has occurred for their meat. The other species are the West African manatee, *T. senegalensis*, and the Amazonian manatee, *T. inunguis*. The name of the order, Sirenia, which includes manatees and DUGONGS, alludes to the myth of sirens, or MERMAIDS, which is thought to be based on distant sightings of sea-cows.

Manchester (Latin **Mancunium**) An industrial city in the metropolitan county of Greater Manchester, north-west England, on the River Irwell; pop. (1991) 397,400. Founded in Roman times, it developed in the 17th century as a textile town that eventually became the centre of the English cotton industry. Manchester's built-up area merges with surrounding towns, such as Salford and Stockport. It is a banking centre second in Britain only to London and also has printing and publishing industries. During the 19th century it gave its name to the Manchester School of Economics and was the headquarters of the Anti-Corn Law League led by Richard Cobden and John Bright. Manchester is the site of the University of Manchester (1880), the University of Manchester Institute of Science and Technology (1824), and Manchester Metropolitan University (formerly Manchester Polytechnic). Its magnificent Victorian public buildings include the Town Hall and Free Trade Hall.

Manchester Ship Canal A waterway in north-west England, linking the city of Manchester to the Irish Sea. Opened in 1894, it is 57 km (36 miles) long.

Manchu ▶**1** A member of a Tartar people who conquered China and founded the Ch'ing dynasty (1644–1912). ▶**2** Their language, which belongs to the Tungusic group in the Altaic family of languages. At one time it was an official language of China, but it is now only spoken in parts of northern Manchuria.

Manchukuo Japanese puppet state in Manchuria (1932–45). Using the Mukden Incident as a pretext, the Japanese seized the city of Mukden in September 1931 and within five months had extended their power over all Manchuria. Japanese expansion to the west was halted by the Soviet army in 1939, but the Japanese remained in control of Manchukuo until the Chinese communists (with support from the Soviet Union, who removed large quantities of industrial equipment) took over at the end of World War II.

Manchuria A mountainous region of north-east China, now comprising the provinces of Jilin, Liaoning, and Heilongjiang. In 1932 it was declared an independent state by Japan and renamed MANCHUKUO; it was restored to China in 1945.

Mandalay (Burmese **Mandale**) A port on the Irrawaddy River in central Myanmar (Burma); pop. (1983) 533,000. Founded in 1857, it was the capital of the Burmese kingdom 1857–85. It is an important Buddhist religious centre with a pagoda (Kuthodaw Pagoda) within which the entire Buddhist canons are inscribed on marble slabs.

mandarin (in botany) A variety of the CITRUS tree *C. reticulata*, together with tangerines and satsumas. They all produce fruit that is smaller than an orange and is sometimes slightly flattened in shape. A range of types exists varying particularly in skin colour, but all easily peeled. Cultivated in Japan and China for centuries, they are now grown in southern Europe as well as the southern USA. The mandarin is a parent of several hybrid citrus fruits, including the clementine and tanget.

mandarin (in history) (Portuguese *mandarim*, from the Sanskrit *mantrin*, 'counsellor') A senior official in imperial China. From the Song dynasty (960 AD), officials were recruited predominantly by examination in the Confucian classics. (Since the HAN dynasty (206 BC) examinations had been used within the civil service.) There were nine grades of mandarin.

Mandarin The most widely spoken form of Chinese and the official language of China.

Mandela, Nelson (Rolihlahla) (1918–) South African statesman, President since 1994. From his twenties he was an activist for the African National Congress (ANC); he was first jailed in 1962 and was sentenced to life imprisonment in 1964. His authority as a moderate leader of black South Africans did not diminish while he was in detention, and he became a symbol of the struggle against apartheid. On his release in 1990 Mandela resumed his leadership of the ANC, and engaged in talks with President F. W. de Klerk on the introduction of majority rule. He shared the Nobel Peace Prize with President de Klerk in 1993, and in the country's first democratic elections was elected President the following year.

Mandelbrot, Benoit (1924–) Polish-born French mathematician who coined the term FRACTAL: a mathematical model for natural shapes that are irregular and do not form perfect squares, pyramids, spheres, and so on. He invented a basis for the theoretical investigation of complex dynamics. One application of this method, the so-called Mandelbrot Set, is that used to explain the length of a coastline. See also CHAOS THEORY.

Mandelstam, Osip (Emilevich) (or **Mandelshtam**) (1891–1938) Russian poet. As one of the Acmeist group of poets (with Anna Akhmatova), Mandelstam favoured concrete detail, clarity, and precision of language as a reaction against the mysticism of contemporary Russian symbolist poetry. During the 1920s his poetry met with increasing official criticism; Mandelstam was sent into internal exile (1934–37) and eventually died in a prison camp. Major works include *Stone* (1913) and *Tristia* (1922). His widow, Nadezhda, immortalized him in her memoirs, *Hope Against Hope* (1970) and *Hope Abandoned* (1974).

Mandeville, Sir John (14th century) English nobleman. He is remembered as the reputed author of a book of travels and travellers' tales that takes the reader to Turkey, Tartary, Persia, Egypt, and India. Written in French and much translated, it was actually compiled by an unknown hand from the works of several writers.

mandolin An Italian stringed musical instrument. There are numerous varieties: Vivaldi and other early composers wrote for the Milanese mandolin, which has six pairs of gut strings plucked with the fingers; the best known mandolin now is the Neapolitan, which has four pairs of wire strings, is tuned like a violin, and plucked with a plectrum. Both have rounded backs, the Neapolitan being the deeper. A Sicilian variant of the Neapolitan has a flat back, and was the origin of the American mandolin, which also has a flat back and usually an arched belly.

mandora A variety of small treble LUTES, most with rounded backs (though the Spanish *bandurria* usually has a flat back), from the 16th century onwards. Some were ancestral to the MANDOLIN.

mandrake (or **devil's apple**) A plant known to botanists as *Mandragora officinarum*, a small perennial of the potato family. This strange plant is native to southern Europe and the Mediterranean region, and since ancient times has been a source of mystery and superstition. The fleshy root is said to shriek when pulled from the ground. This root was used in ancient Greece to alleviate pain and as an aphrodisiac. The white or purple flowers are produced at ground level. They are followed by poisonous golf-ball-sized fruits. The American mandrake, or may apple, *Podophyllum peltatum*, is a quite unrelated plant of damp woodlands and flood-meadows. Other species in the genus *Podophyllum* may be referred to as mandrake, but are more closely related to barberry.

mandrill The largest and perhaps the most colourful species of BABOON, a member of the genus *Papio*. The mandrill, *P. sphinx*, is dark brown with white cheek fringes, a yellow beard, and a tuft of hair on the crown. The face of the adult male is brilliantly coloured, unlike that of its close relative the drill, *P. leucophaeus*, which is black. The colours are present but much duller in the female. The buttocks are also brightly coloured, blue and white.

It is found mainly near the coast of West Africa, where it lives on the forest floor but will also climb. It eats fruit, berries, bark, and roots. Troops of up to 60 individuals may travel together.

Manet, Édouard (1832–83) French painter. He adopted a realist approach that greatly influenced the impressionists, and abandoned half-tones and shadings in favour of pure colour to give a direct unsentimental effect. Several of his paintings aroused outrage because of the frank and unidealized treatment of their subject-matter; *Olympia* (1865) depicted a nude woman with clear indications that she was a prostitute. Among other notable works are *Déjeuner sur l'herbe* (1863) and *A Bar at the Folies-Bergère* (1882).

Manetho (3rd century BC) Egyptian priest. He wrote a history of Egypt (*c.*280) from mythical times to 323. He arbitrarily divided the succession of rulers known to him into 30 dynasties, an arrangement which is still followed.

manganese (symbol Mn, at. no. 25, r.a.m. 54.94) A reddish-white, hard, brittle TRANSITION METAL. It is quite reactive, and its compounds show VALENCIES from 2 to 7. It is extracted mainly from the ore pyrolusite, (MnO_2), although also occurring naturally on the sea-bed. Manganese is widely added to metals to improve their hardness and wear resistance. Manganese steels contain about 12 per cent manganese, and are very tough, being used in railway lines and rock-crushers.

mangel-wurzel (or **mangold**) See BEETROOT.

mango A large, spreading evergreen tree, *Mangifera indica*, widely distributed throughout the tropics but native to India. Mangoes belong to a family of some 600 species of trees, shrubs, and climbers, Anacardiaceae, which includes cashew and poison ivy. A well-defined dry season is vital for successful fruit development but, even then, good crops usually occur only in alternate years. The yellow, green, or red fruits have an unpalatable skin, but some varieties are widely cultivated for their edible flesh.

mangosteen A small conical tree, *Garcinia mangostana*, native to the humid equatorial countries of Malaysia and Indonesia. It belongs to the Guttiferae, a family of around 1,000 species of tree and shrub found all over the world, but particularly common in the tropics. Its close relatives include the mammey apple and St John's wort. It has globular berries which are reddish-purple, the size of a small orange, with a thick skin surrounding several ivory-white segments.

mangrove A tropical tree of several genera that grows on muddy coastlines and in estuaries. These trees, especially species of *Rhizophora*, develop extensive roots that trap mud and silt. At high tide, the roots are inundated with salt water, a physiological stress that would kill any other tree. Though mangroves are adapted to this, it is not a requirement for their successful growth as they are easily raised in botanic gardens away from the coast. They cope with salt in a variety of ways. Some species have 'filters' on their roots to exclude it; others allow the salt in but excrete it from the twigs, or let it accumulate in leaves that are then dropped. Many species have seeds that germinate in the fruit and produce a long, sharp-pointed root, which embeds into the mud when the fruit is dropped. Others have salt-resistant floating seeds.

Manhattan An island near the mouth of the Hudson River, forming part of the city of New York, USA. The site of the original Dutch settlement of New Amsterdam, it is now a borough containing the cultural and commercial centre of New York City and is famous for its skyscrapers. Among its most notable buildings are the World Trade Center, the Empire State Building, and the UN Headquarters. It takes its name from the Algonquian tribe from whom the Dutch settlers claimed to have bought the island in 1626 for $24 of merchandise.

Manhattan Project The code name for the secret project to develop the atomic bomb (see NUCLEAR WEAPON) in the USA during World War II. When it became apparent in the late 1930s that it was feasible to build such a bomb and that German scientists were working on the technology, the project received high priority. The task of designing and assembling the bomb at Los Alamos, New Mexico, was directed by OPPENHEIMER, who had the collaboration of the University of Chicago, where FERMI built the first ATOMIC PILE. Also involved were Columbia University, New York; the Berkeley Radiation Laboratory, University of California; and scientists from the UK. URANIUM-235 was produced at Oak Ridge, Tennessee, and PLUTONIUM-239 at an atomic plant at Hanford, Washington state. The project culminated in the successful explosion of the first atomic bomb at Alamogordo, New Mexico, on 16 July 1945.

manic depression A cyclical mood disorder in which periods of hyperactivity, elation, self-importance, and (often unwarranted) optimism alternate with the despair of DEPRESSION. Although in extreme form it has the disorganizing quality of PSYCHOSIS, lesser degrees of manic-depressive behaviour can be seen in some moody people who, in the 'up' phase, can often manage feats of great creativity or achievement: the British World War II leader Winston Churchill was a notable example. Manic depression, the tendency to which is inherited, is due to spontaneous fluctuations in the levels of chemicals in the BRAIN that control mood. Accordingly, the most successful treatment is with mood-stabilizing PSYCHOTROPIC DRUGS, which act to redress this imbalance of brain chemistry.

Manichaeism The teaching of Manes (*c.*216–76), a Persian influenced by Mithraism (see MITHRAS), Christianity, and Gnosticism. He taught a dual principle of Good and Evil in conflict, symbolized as Light against Darkness, God against Satan. He counselled asceticism for an elect group following the teaching of the Jewish prophets, JESUS CHRIST, BUDDHA, and himself. Zoroastrians drove him into exile in India, flayed him alive, and crucified him. His followers were condemned by DIOCLETIAN, though this did not prevent their influence spreading to Rome and Africa by the 4th century. The sect survived in Chinese Turkistan until the 10th century and influenced various heresies in medieval Christianity.

Manila The capital and chief port, financial, and industrial centre of the Philippines, on the south-west coast of the island of Luzon at the mouth of the Pasig River; pop. (1990) 1,599,000. Founded in 1571, it was an important trade centre of the Spanish until taken by the USA in 1898. **Metro Manila**, with a population of *c.*6 million, extends over 17 communities and towns including Quezon City and Caloocan. Its many industries include automobile assembly, metallurgical, chemical, and textile manufactures, as well as light industries such as food processing and pharmaceuticals.

Manitoba A province of central Canada, with a coastline on Hudson Bay; area 649,950 sq km (250,947 sq miles); pop. (1991) 1,091,940; capital, Winnipeg. Its largest settlements are Winnipeg, Brandon, Thompson, Portage La Prairie, and Flin Flon and its highest point is Baldy Mountain (832 m, 2,730 ft). Ceded to Canada by the Hudson's Bay Company in 1869 and created a province of Canada in 1870, its boundaries were extended in 1881, 1884, and 1912 from the original Red River Settlement. Its economy is dependent on food processing, distilling, the manufacture of agricultural machinery, the generation of hydroelectric power and the production of wheat, sunflowers, sugar-beets, nickel, and copper.

Manjusri (Chinese, **Wénshū**; Japanese, **Monju**) In Mahayana Buddhist belief, the *bodhisattva* ('Buddha-to-be'), personifying supreme wisdom. Although usually considered a celestial bodhisattva, Manjusri is alleged to have taken various human, historical forms, including that of the monk Vairocana. He is usually depicted with princely ornaments, holding a palm-leaf manuscript and sword, and seated on a lion or lotus.

Manley, Michael (Norman) (1923–97) Jamaican statesman, Prime Minister 1972–80 and 1989–92. He became the island's first Vice-President in 1955 and leader of the People's National Party in 1969. Elected Prime Minister on a socialist platform, he introduced policies to strengthen Jamaica's economy through the expansion of public works and the encouragement of local industry; he also introduced a system of free education.

Mann, Thomas (1875–1955) German novelist and essayist. He achieved recognition with his first novel *Buddenbrooks* (1901), which describes the decline of a merchant family and has strongly autobiographical features. The role and character of the artist in relation to society is a constant theme in his works, and is linked with the rise of Nazism in *Dr Faustus* (1947). Other notable works include the novella *Death in Venice* (1912). When Hitler came to power Mann was forced into exile; he became a US citizen in 1944 but later settled in Switzerland. He was awarded the Nobel Prize for literature in 1929.

Mannar ▶**1** An island off the north-west coast of Sri Lanka, linked to India by the chain of coral islands known as Adam's Bridge. ▶**2** A town on this island; pop. (1981) 14,000.

Mannar, Gulf of An inlet of the Indian Ocean lying between north-west Sri Lanka and the southern tip of India. It lies to the south of Adam's Bridge, which separates it from the Palk Strait.

Mannerism (Italian *maniera*, 'style' or 'stylishness') A movement in Italian art from about 1520 to 1600. It was popularized by the writings of the 16th-century artist and biographer VASARI, who used it to signify grace, poise, and sophistication. From the 17th century, however, most critics thought that the Italian art of the mid- to late 16th century marked a decline from the peaks reached during the High RENAISSANCE. Mannerism then came to describe an art characterized by artificiality and distortion. The origins of Mannerism are generally traced back to the late works of Raphael, when he was moving away from the clear and balanced idiom of the High Renaissance to a more complex and emotional style. In sculpture, the archetypal Mannerist was Giambologna, whose elaborate twisting poses and smoothly flowing and polished forms were immensely influential. Benvenuto CELLINI is among the leading Mannerist sculptors, as well as a supreme goldsmith. Although some critics characterize MICHELANGELO as Mannerist, others consider him so original that he lies outside categorization.

Michelangelo, who was also an extremely inventive architect, is often cited as the fountainhead of Mannerist architecture. However, the first great Mannerist building is generally agreed to be GIULIO ROMANO's Palazzo del Tè in Mantua (begun 1526). Outside Italy, Mannerism is most often applied to the School of FONTAINEBLEAU in France. Other non-Italian art that has been called Mannerist includes much work by 16th-century Netherlandish artists and the ecstatic paintings of El GRECO in Spain.

In literature, Mannerism is even more loosely defined. Writing characterized by ornateness, involved syntax, and the use of far-fetched images has sometimes been called Mannerist. The prose romance *Euphues* (two parts, 1578 and 1580) by John Lyly is perhaps the best-known example. In music Mannerism has been applied, for example, to the Italian madrigal composer Carlo Gesualdo, whose work is characterized by unusual harmonies, sudden changes of tempo, and vivid expression.

Mannheim An industrial port at the confluence of the Rhine and the Neckar in the state of Baden-Württemberg, south-west Germany; pop. (1991) 314,685. Industries include engineering, oil refining, and the production of chemicals, motor cars, and machinery.

Manning, Olivia (Mary) (1908–80) British novelist. Manning published her first novel, *The Wind Changes*, in 1937, before marrying and going abroad with her husband in 1939. Returning to London in 1946, she became an acclaimed and prolific novelist, publishing 11 novels between 1949 and 1980. Her experiences in Bucharest, Athens, and Egypt formed the basis for her Balkan trilogy (1960–65) and her Levant trilogy (1977–80), the two together forming a single narrative, *Fortunes of War*.

manometer A U-shaped tube, generally containing mercury, used as a pressure gauge for gases and liquids. One end is connected to the fluid under pressure and the other end is left open to the atmosphere. The level of the mercury rises or falls in relation to the pressure difference between the fluid and the atmosphere. A Pitot tube can also be used as a manometer. It is an open-ended, right-angled tube used to measure the speed or flow of a fluid by measuring the pressure of the fluid flow.

manorial system The social, economic, and administrative system that emerged in Europe in the 5th century from the chaos and instability following the collapse of the Roman empire. Farmers sought the protection of powerful lords and in return surrendered certain rights and control over their lands. Gradually a system of obligations and service emerged, especially relating to manorial agrarian management, and set down in records called custumals.

The manor consisted of demesne land (private land of the lord) and tenants' holdings. Tenants were free or unfree (villeins), rank being determined by personal status or the status of their land. Not all manors had this balance of demesne, free land, and unfree land. In addition, meadow land for grazing livestock was available to all, and thus known as common land. Access to woodland for timber and grazing of pigs might be a further facility. The lord presided over the manorial court and received money or labour services from his tenants regularly (week work) or seasonally (boon work). A tendency in the 12th century for labour services to be commuted to cash rents was reversed after *c.*1200, when inflation encouraged landlords again to exact services in kind. Labour shortages following the BLACK DEATH (1348), when Europe's population fell from 80 million to 55 million, enclosures, tenant unrest, and rebellions such as the PEASANTS' REVOLT (1381), effectively ended the manorial system in England by *c.*1500.

Mansart, François (1598–1666) French architect. His first major work was the rebuilding of part of the château of Blois, which incorporated the type of roof now named after him, the mansard: this has four sloping sides, each of which becomes steeper halfway down. Other buildings include a number of town houses in Paris, the château of Maisons (1642–46), and the church of the Val-de-Grâce, Paris (1645).

Mansell, Nigel (1954–) British motor-racing driver. He won the Formula One world championship in 1992 and the Indy car championship in 1993, the only driver to win both titles.

Mansfield, Katherine (pseudonym of Kathleen Mansfield Beauchamp) (1888–1923) New Zealand short-story writer. Her stories show the influence of Chekhov and range from extended impressionistic evocations of family life to short sketches. Collections include *In a German Pension* (1911) and *Bliss* (1920). She married the British writer and critic John Middleton Murry (1889–1957) in 1918 and spent much of the remainder of her short life travelling in Europe in search of a cure for the tuberculosis from which she eventually died.

manslaughter See HOMICIDE.

Manson, Charles (1934–) US cult leader. In 1967 he founded a commune based on free love and complete subordination to him. Two years later its members carried out a series of murders, including that of the US actress Sharon Tate (1943–69), for which he and a number of his followers received the death sentence. They later escaped this owing to a Supreme Court ruling against capital punishment.

Manson, Sir Patrick (1844–1922) Scottish physician, pioneer of tropical medicine. Working for many years in China, he discovered the organism responsible for elephantiasis and established that it was spread by the bite of a mosquito. After returning to London he suggested a similar role for the mosquito in spreading malaria, and studied a number of tropical parasites and infections. He was the chief founder of the London School of Tropical Medicine.

manta ray A giant, cartilaginous ray fish of the family Mobulidae, which lives in tropical seas. About ten species are known of which the largest, the Atlantic manta, *Manta birostris*, may be 6 m (19.5 feet) wide. They swim near the surface, feeding on small fishes and planktonic animals which are funnelled into the large mouth between the fleshy flaps ('horns') on the head and are then filtered from the water by the gill rakers. These horns are responsible for the alternative name of these fish, devil ray.

Mantegna, Andrea (1431–1506) Italian painter and engraver. He is noted especially for his frescos, which include those painted for the bridal chamber of the ducal family in Mantua, with both the ceiling and walls painted in an illusionistic style which extends the interior space and gives the impression that the room is open to the sky. His work reveals his knowledge of the artefacts and architecture of classical antiquity, as can be seen in his nine paintings depicting the *Triumph of Caesar* (*c.*1480–95).

Mantell, Gideon Algernon (1790–1852) British geologist. Mantell worked mainly as a surgeon in Sussex, though fossil-hunting was his major interest. He is best known as the first person to recognize dinosaur remains as reptilian, and in 1825 he published a description of the teeth of a 'giant fossil lizard' which he named *Iguanodon*. Mantell accumulated a large collection of fossils, which he eventually sold to the British Museum.

mantissa See LOGARITHM.

mantis shrimp A flattened, shrimp-like crustacean, with one pair of legs enormously expanded and so resembling those of the praying mantis. Mantis shrimps make up the order Stomatopoda. They wait in burrows, shooting out these barbed limbs to grasp and spear passing shrimps or fish. When mantis shrimps are in captivity, blows from these powerful limbs can crack aquarium glass. They are mainly tropical, up to 36 cm (14 inches) long, and brightly coloured. Temperate species such as *Squilla empusa*, though smaller and less colourful, show the same remarkable habits.

mantle That region of a planetary interior that lies between the thin surface crust and the core. In the case of the Earth the mantle extends from a depth of 10–80 km (6–50 miles) to a depth of about 2,900 km (1,800 miles); the region below 1,000 km (625 miles) is known as the lower mantle. The divisions of the mantle are defined in terms of the velocities of the seismic waves that travel through them. The mantle consists of hot rock undergoing a very slow convective turnover. The temperature varies from 1,000°C to 3,000°C as the depth increases. Even at the higher of these temperatures the rock remains solid because of the high pressures to which it is subjected. The mantle is heated by radioactive decay.

mantra (from Sanskrit, 'spell' or 'charm') A mystic formula or verse, used in Hinduism and Buddhism, which by repeated chanting forms an aid to MEDITATION. Mantras are believed to have magical qualities, such as the ability to protect the user from evil powers. Hindu mantras are based either on Sanskrit verses taken from the VEDAS, or on sacred syllables, such as Om (Aum), which represents supreme reality. See also TANTRA.

Mantua (Italian **Mantova**) A town in Lombardy, northern Italy, on the River Mincio; pop. (1990) 54,230. The Roman poet Virgil was born nearby in the village of Andes (Pietole Virgilio). Mantua became an important political and artistic centre of Europe during the 14th–17th centuries.

Manx ►**1** Of or relating to the Isle of Man or its people. ►**2** The Celtic language of the Isle of Man, a dialect of Gaelic. There are no native speakers alive now but it is still in use for ceremonial purposes.

Manzoni, Alessandro (1785–1873) Italian novelist, dramatist, and poet. He is remembered chiefly as the author of the historical novel *I Promessi sposi* (1825–42). The novel is a powerfully characterized historical reconstruction of 17th-century Lombardy during the period of Spanish administration.

Maori A member of the aboriginal people of New Zealand. Having arrived there first as part of a wave of migration from Tahiti, probably in the 9th century, by 1200 they had established settlements in various parts of the islands. The Maoris ceded all their rights and powers of sovereignty to the British Crown in 1840 with the signing of the Treaty of Waitangi. Maori Wars were fought intermittently in 1845–48 and 1860–72 between Maoris and the colonial government of New Zealand over the enforced sale of Maori lands to Europeans. In 1986 the Maoris numbered 404,775. In 1994 and 1995 the New Zealand government agreed to pay compensation to two tribal groups whose land had been seized illegally by settlers and to return traditional Maori lands in the government's possession. Many more Maori claims to land are under consideration.

Mao Zedong (or **Mao Tse-tung**) (1893–1976) Chinese statesman, chairman of the Communist Party of the Chinese People's Republic 1949–76 and head of state 1949–59. After studying Marxism as a student he was among the founders of the Chinese Communist Party in 1921, becoming its effective leader following the Long March (the withdrawal of the Communists from SE to NW China, 1934–35). He eventually defeated both the occupying Japanese and rival Kuomintang nationalist forces to form the People's Republic of China, becoming its first head of state (1949). Although he initially adopted the Soviet Communist model, following Khrushchev's denunciation of Stalin (1956) Mao began to introduce his own measures, central to which were the concepts of permanent revolution, the importance of the peasantry, and agricultural collectivization. A brief period of freedom of expression (the Hundred Flowers) ended with the introduction of the economically disastrous Great Leap Forward (1958–60). Mao resigned as head of state in 1959 but retained his position as chairman of the Communist Party, and as such remained China's most powerful politician. He was the instigator of the Cultural Revolution (1966–68), which was intended to effect a return to revolutionary Maoist beliefs; during this time he became the focus of a powerful personality cult, which lasted until his death.

maple A tree of the genus *Acer*, comprising some 200 species of the north temperate zone, a member of the family Aceraceae. They are deciduous and have winged fruits. Some of the North American species, such as the sugar maple, *A. saccharum*, have sap which is the source of maple syrup. A number of Japanese species are widely grown for the spectacular red or yellow colour of their leaves. Timber and charcoal are obtained from many species. One of the most widespread maples in Europe is the sycamore, *A. pseudoplatanus*.

maps and charts Diagrammatic representations of all or part of the Earth on a plane surface. A map is usually confined to land areas, whereas a representation of a sea area is called a chart.

Modern maps can be classified as either topographical, showing the physical and natural features of an area, or thematic, being based on topographical maps but showing some sort of statistical data (for example, population) in map form. Navigational charts for air or sea use show selected topological features, but also such information as the location of radio navigation beacons, lights and buoys, and water depths and prevailing currents. Until the advent of aerial photography, land surveying provided most of the basic topological information for maps. However, modern map-making relies much more on aerial surveying techniques using stereo photography, and information obtained from Earth resources satellites using remote sensing techniques such as infrared photography. Topographical information from from photographs and land surveys is now digitized and fed into a computer. This provides a flexible database from which maps of various sizes and in various projections can be drawn. In the UK the Ordnance Survey began to convert its larger maps into a digital form in 1973.

Maputo The capital and chief port of Mozambique; pop. (1991) 1,098,000. Founded as a Portuguese fortress in the late 18th century, it became the capital of Portuguese East Africa in 1907. It was known as Lourenço Marques until 1976. Maputo stands on a large natural harbour and its development was based on its transit trade with the Johannesburg area of South Africa. It is Mozambique's leading manufacturing centre.

Maquis (from Corsican Italian *macchia*, 'thicket') French RESISTANCE MOVEMENT in World War II. After the fall of France in 1940, it carried on resistance to the Nazi occupation. Supported by the French Communist Party, but not centrally controlled, its membership rose in 1943–44, and constituted a considerable hindrance to the German rear when the Allies landed in France. Its various groups, often operating independently, were co-ordinated into the Forces Françaises de l'Interieur in 1944.

Mara In Buddhist belief, the demon 'Lord of the Senses' who tempted the Buddha on several occasions. In the Buddha's bodhisattva form of Gautama, Mara attempted unsuccessfully to distract him as he meditated under the Bo tree. After his Enlightenment, Mara tried to persuade him not to preach the law. In Hindu mythology, Mara is sometimes an aspect of Kama, god of desire and love.

marabou A large species of STORK, *Leptoptilos crumeniferus*, reaching 1.5 m (5 feet) in height, and found throughout most of the warmer areas of Africa. It is mainly greyish above with paler underparts, and has a whitish ruff at the base of the neck and a long pink pouch. It is best known as a scavenger and is commonly seen gathering with vultures at kills. These storks will also take small frogs and other small animals such as locusts.

Maracaibo A commercial and industrial city and port in north-west Venezuela, situated on the channel linking the Gulf of Venezuela with Lake Maracaibo; pop. (1991) 1,400,640. It is capital of the state of Zulia, the second-largest city in the country, and the 'oil capital' of South America.

Maracaibo, Lake (Spanish **Lago de Maracaibo**) A large lake in north-west Venezuela, linked by a narrow channel to the Gulf of Venezuela and the Caribbean; area 13,261 sq km (5,120 sq miles). It is the largest lake in South America. Discovered in 1917, over 70 per cent of Venezuela's oil output comes from the lake area.

maracas A pair of rattles used in Latin American music. They are made from gourds, with a stick as the handle, with the seeds left inside to rattle or with pellets, such as small stones, inserted. Coconut shells are sometimes used instead, and nowadays plastic is common. Proper maracas are always made so that one is lower pitched than the other.

Maradona, Diego (Armando) (1960–) Argentinian footballer. He was captain of the victorious Argentinian team in the 1986 World Cup, but aroused controversy with his handball when scoring a goal in Argentina's quarter-final match against England. In 1984 he joined the Italian club Napoli, and subsequently contributed to that team's victories in the Italian championship (1987) and the UEFA Cup (1989). However, clashes with authority culminated in Maradona being suspended from football for 15 months in 1991 for cocaine use, and then sent home from the 1994 World Cup after failing a drugs test. He received a further ban after failing a drugs test in 1997.

Marat, Jean Paul (1743–93) French revolutionary and journalist. The founder of a radical newspaper, he became prominent during the French Revolution as a virulent critic of the moderate Girondists and was instrumental (with Danton and Robespierre) in their fall from power in 1793. Suffering from a skin disease, he spent much of his time in later life in his bath, where he was murdered by the Girondist Charlotte Corday. This was used as a pretext by Robespierre and the Jacobins to purge their Girondist rivals.

Maratha A Hindu warrior people of western India who in the 17th and 18th centuries led a military revival against Muslim expansion. They rose to prominence under the inspired leadership of SHIVAJI, who, after victories against the MOGULS, established a Maratha kingdom in 1674. Their great age was the early 18th century when, after a temporary collapse, they benefited from Mogul decline to sweep over the north and central Deccan. They seemed poised for all-India mastery, but failure in 1761 of their bid to take Delhi (in the Battle of Panipat) was followed by increasing internal disunity and a failure to make a united stand against expanding British power.

marathon A long-distance running-race, standardized in 1908 at 42,195 m (26 miles 385 yards). It commemorates the heroic run in 490 BC by a Greek soldier from MARATHON to Athens to bring news of the Greek victory against the Persians. The race was introduced in 1896 at the first modern OLYMPIC GAMES (held in Athens) and is now recognized as the ultimate test for distance-runners of either sex.

Marathon A plain in eastern Attica, Greece, scene of a battle in 490 BC in which the Greeks under Miltiades defeated a much larger Persian army. The non-stop run of a courier named Pheidippides bringing the news to Athens has given the name to the race (see MARATHON).

marble A hard, crystalline rock formed when limestone has been subjected to great heat and pressure; it can take a high polish and has been much used in sculpture and architecture. It is a metamorphic rock formed by the recrystallization of limestone and DOLOMITE; it therefore consists mainly of the mineral calcite ($CaCO_3$) or dolomite (calcium magnesium carbonate) in the form of a fine- to coarse-grained mosaic. White when pure, it is often red-grey or mottled grey as a result of mineral inclusions. Certain types of marble have been particularly prized by sculptors. Marble is also a common facing stone in the building industry.

Marble Arch An arch with three gateways designed by John NASH as part of his reconstruction of Buckingham Palace, in front of which it was erected in 1827. It was moved in 1851 to its present site at the north-east corner of Hyde Park.

marcasite A common, pale yellow, lustrous mineral with the same chemical composition (FeS_2) as PYRITE but formed at lower temperatures. It oxidizes in air to a white powder and forms in ore veins, as a replacement deposit in limestone, and as CONCRETIONS in sedimentary rocks. Mined in large quantities at Galena, Illinois, USA, it is used for the extraction of sulphuric acid.

Marceau, Marcel (1923–) French actor, the finest modern exponent of MIME. In 1945 he joined the company of BARRAULT, but a year later abandoned conventional acting to study mime, basing his work on the character of the 19th-century French PIERROT and evolving his own character, Bip, a white-faced clown with sailor trousers and striped jacket.

Marches, the The parts of England along the borders with Wales and Scotland.

Marciano, Rocky (born Rocco Francis Marchegiano) (1923–69) US boxer. In 1952 he became world heavyweight champion and successfully defended his title six times until he retired, undefeated, in 1956.

Marconi, Guglielmo (1874–1937) Italian pioneer of RADIO communication. In 1894 he began to experiment with techniques for wireless communication after reading about the experiment on electric waves carried out by HERTZ. Within a year, he had transmitted and received signals over a distance of more than 2 km (1.2 miles). Unable to gain support in Italy, he came to London, and in 1896 took out a UK patent and demonstrated his invention to the British Post Office. By 1899 he had sent messages to France, and in 1901 he bridged the Atlantic. He patented a magnetic detector of electrical signals in 1902, and a horizontal directional ANTENNA in 1905. From 1916 Marconi devoted his attention to exploring the possibilities of short-wave radio transmission and to the considerable business interests that had grown up around his invention. He shared the Nobel Prize for physics in 1909 with BRAUN, who invented a coupled wireless transmitter and receiver.

Marco Polo (*c.*1254–*c.*1324) Italian traveller. Between 1271 and 1275 he accompanied his father and uncle on a journey east from Acre into central Asia, eventually reaching China and the court of Kublai Khan. After service with the emperor and travelling widely in the empire for a decade and a half, Polo returned home (1292–95) via Sumatra, India, and Persia. His book recounting his travels gave considerable impetus to the European quest for the riches of the East.

Marcos, Ferdinand Edralin (1917–89) Filipino statesman, President (1965–86). A ruthless and corrupt politician, he initially achieved some success as a reformer and identified closely with the USA, but after his election to a second term he became increasingly involved in campaigns against nationalist and communist guerrilla groups, and in 1972–73 he first declared martial law and then assumed near dictatorial powers. Hostility to Marcos intensified after the murder of the opposition leader Benigno Aquino Jr in 1983. US support for his regime waned as a result of his failure to achieve consensus, and in February 1986 he was forced to leave the country.

Marcus Aurelius See AURELIUS, MARCUS.

Marcuse, Herbert (1898–1979) German-born US philosopher. He was an associate at the Frankfurt Institute of Social Research and a leading figure in the Frankfurt School (the school of philosophy involved in reappraising Marx) until 1933, when he left Germany and eventually settled in the USA. His works include *Eros and Civilization* (1955), *Soviet Marxism* (1958), a rejection of bureaucratic Communism, which argues that revolutionary change can come only from alienated élites, such as students, and *One-Dimensional Man* (1964).

mare (pl. **maria**) A vast expanse of very dark, iron-rich basaltic lava that has flooded out from cracks in the lunar crust to fill large impact CRATERS on the Moon. Most of this flooding took place 3–4 billion years ago. The maria, also known as ring plains, are, in the main, confined to the Earth-facing side of the Moon because the lunar crust is at its thinnest on this side.

Marengo A village near Turin, scene of a decisive French victory of Napoleon's campaign in Italy in 1800. After military reverses had all but destroyed French power in Italy, Napoleon crossed the Alps to defeat and capture an Austrian army, returning Italy to French possession.

Margaret (Rose), Princess (1930–) Only sister of Elizabeth II. In 1960 she married Antony Armstrong-Jones (1930–), who was later created Earl of Snowdon; the marriage was dissolved in 1978.

Their two children are David, Viscount Linley (1961–) and Lady Sarah Chatto (1964–).

Margaret, St (*c*.1046–93) Scottish queen, wife of Malcolm III. She exerted a strong influence over royal policy during her husband's reign, and was instrumental in the reform of the Scottish Church. Feast day, 16 November.

Margaret of Anjou (1430–82) Queen of England. Her marriage to HENRY VI in 1445 ensured a truce in the war between England and France. Henry's weakness caused the LANCASTRIAN party to centre on his indomitable wife; in February 1461 she won the second Battle of ST ALBANS but by her hesitation lost the chance to keep Henry on the throne, and she had to flee to Scotland and thence to France. Except for the few months that Henry regained the throne in 1470–71, she spent most of the rest of her life in her native Anjou.

margarine A butter-like spread made from a mixture of animal and/or vegetable FATS AND OILS with aqueous milk products, plus such additives as salt, emulsifiers, and flavouring. Margarine was first developed in the late 1860s by the Frenchman H. Mège-Mouriès; the manufacturing process was later simplified in the USA. Animal fats were originally most commonly used in margarines, but there has been a trend towards the use of vegetable oils, often hardened by hydrogenation with a CATALYST. In recent years, high-cholesterol foods such as BUTTER have come to be seen as something of a health risk, and this has led manufacturers to develop margarines high in polyunsaturated fatty acids.

Mariana Islands (or **Marianas**) See GUAM.

Mariana Trench An ocean trench in the Pacific to the south-east of the Mariana Islands, with the greatest known ocean depth (11,034 m, 36,200 ft); its bottom was reached in 1960 by the US bathyscape *Trieste*.

Maria Theresa (1717–80) Archduchess of Austria, queen of Hungary and Bohemia 1740–80. The daughter of the Emperor Charles VI, Maria Theresa married the future Emperor Francis I in 1736 and succeeded to the Habsburg dominions in 1740 by virtue of the Pragmatic Sanction (by which her father made provision for her to succeed him). Her accession triggered the War of the Austrian Succession (1740–48), during which Silesia was lost to Prussia. She attempted but failed to regain Silesia from the Prussians in the Seven Years War (1756–63). After the death of Francis I in 1765 she ruled in conjunction with her son, the Emperor Joseph II.

Marie Antoinette (1755–93) French queen, wife of Louis XVI. A daughter of Maria Theresa and the Emperor Francis I, she married the future Louis XVI of France in 1770, becoming queen four years later. She became a focus for opposition to reform and won widespread unpopularity through her extravagant lifestyle. Like her husband she was imprisoned during the French Revolution and eventually executed.

Marie de Médicis (born Maria de' Medici) (1573–1642) Queen of France. The second wife of Henry IV of France, she ruled as regent during the minority of her son Louis XIII (1610–17). She continued to exert a significant influence after her son came to power, and plotted against Cardinal Richelieu, her former protégé, but was eventually exiled in 1631.

marigold A member of the sunflower family, related to the daisy. There are three kinds of marigold: French, African, and pot. Strangely, the names do not indicate the countries of origin, for both the French and African marigolds are derived from Mexican species *Tagetes patula* and *T. erecta* respectively. The pot marigold, *Calendula officinalis*, is an annual plant native to southern Europe. It has long been cultivated for its attractive orange flowers and as a kitchen and medicinal herb.

marimba See XYLOPHONE.

marine iguana See SEA LIZARD.

Mariner A highly successful series of US spacecraft launched to explore the planets Mercury, Venus, and Mars. In December 1962 Mariner 2 made the first successful fly-past of Venus and in July 1965 Mariner 4 made the first successful fly-past of Mars. Mariner 9 was put into orbit around Mars in November 1971. Its 7,329 pictures enabled the entire Martian surface to be mapped. Close-up views were also taken of the two small moons of Mars. The VIKING spacecraft later landed on the surface of Mars. In February 1974, Mariner 10, used the gravitational field of Venus to change its trajectory, enabling it to rendezvous with Mercury. It made three close fly-pasts of Mercury and provided more than 10,000 pictures of its surface.

Marinetti, Filippo Tommaso (1876–1944) Italian poet and dramatist. He launched the futurist movement with a manifesto published in the newspaper *Le Figaro* (1909), which exalted technology, glorified war, and demanded revolution and innovation in the arts. In his poems he abandoned syntax and grammar; in the theatre he renounced verisimilitude and traditional methods of plot development and characterization and introduced the simultaneous staging of unrelated actions.

Marius, Gaius (*c*.157–86 BC) Roman general and politician. Consul for the first time in 107, he established his dominance by victories over Jugurtha and invading Germanic tribes. He was subsequently involved in a struggle for power with Sulla and was expelled from Italy, only to return and take Rome by force in 87. He was again elected consul in 86 but died soon afterwards.

marjoram Any one of several species of plant of the genus *Origanum*. They belong to the mint family, and like mint are used as herbs. Wild marjoram, *O. vulgare*, is an erect perennial, growing up to 70 cm (2.3 feet) tall; it is widely distributed over Europe. Sweet marjoram, *O. majorana*, is more popular as a culinary herb. Like the smaller pot marjoram, *O. onites*, it comes from the Mediterranean region. Wild marjoram from warmer countries, which has a stronger flavour, is dried and sold as the herb oregano.

Mark, St An Apostle, companion of St Peter and St Paul, traditional author of the second Gospel. Feast day, 25 April.

Mark Antony (Latin name Marcus Antonius) (83–30 BC) Roman general. He had served with CAESAR at the end of the GALLIC WARS. As tribune in 49 he defended Caesar's interest in the Senate as civil war loomed. He was present at Pharsalus, and represented Caesar in Italy. His offer of a crown to Caesar was refused. After Caesar's murder he took the political initiative against the assassins, and delivered the funeral speech. Octavian, however, was Caesar's designated heir and hostility arose between the two. During Antony's struggle for ascendancy over the Senate led by CICERO, he was denounced in the 'Phillippic' orations and defeated at Mutina by the forces of the consuls and Octavian. He was then reconciled with Octavian, and together with Lepidus they formed the Second Triumvirate, disposed of enemies including Cicero and defeated the 'Liberators', Brutus and Cassius, at PHILIPPI in 42.

Antony received the government of the eastern Mediterranean and began (42) his liaison with Cleopatra. Although a powerful ally she cost him much support at Rome. Their marriage, Antony's fifth, was illegal in Roman law. In 34 he declared Caesarion (Cleopatra's son allegedly by Caesar) as Caesar's heir in Octavian's place and divided the east among his family. War followed. After ACTIUM he committed suicide in Egypt.

market (in economics) The arrangements to permit or facilitate exchange between buyers and sellers. In any market, buyers demand goods or services, and sellers supply them. In a well-functioning **market economy**, price will respond to the market forces of SUPPLY AND DEMAND. If would-be purchases exceed would-be sales, price will rise, thus reducing demand and stimulating further supply. The reverse will happen if planned sales exceed planned purchases. Markets are, therefore, of crucial importance to the allocation of resources. If markets do not exist or have undesirable features, such as MONOPOLY power, government intervention may be appropriate. In a **planned** (or **command**) **economy** supplies are controlled by a central government planning agency in response to anticipated demand and sold at a price determined by the government. The failure of command economies in Eastern Europe and their return to market economies in the 1990s is an indication of the comparative merits of the two systems.

marketing The creation or enlargement of demand for a good or service by a company. It may involve the use of MARKET RESEARCH, mass media ADVERTISING, and other forms of promotion, including sponsorship, special offers, and free gifts; packaging at point of sale (see MERCHANDIZING); pricing; product policy, including the creation of brands and new product development; personal selling; and distribution. Successful marketing involves defining and satisfying customers' needs. Although marketing was developed in relation to consumer goods, the principles of marketing are being applied increasingly to industrial goods, to services, and for non-profit-making activities, such as charities and local and national government activities.

market research The study of consumers' needs and preferences, and of the acceptability of goods and services offered for sale; in economics, the study of the requirements of MARKETS. Generally the aim is to obtain information that will help design a product or service and its presentation (packaging and MARKETING) so that sales and profits can be maximized. Techniques may be relatively simple: testing the expectations of sales staff, for example, or looking at previous sales of the same or a similar product, or at competing products. More sophisticated surveys of consumer attitudes may be conducted, by mail, telephone, or personal interview, with a population sample selected with due attention to age, sex, socioeconomic grouping, or geographical location (see SOCIAL CLASS). A new product may be test-launched in a limited area. Market research achieved recognition as an occupation in the 1920s and 1930s; after World War II, US and Japanese companies took the lead in its use and development.

markhor A species of wild goat, *Capra falconeri*, found from Kashmir through Afghanistan to the former Soviet Union, living in the open or in forests on steep barren slopes and precipitous crags. It rarely goes above the snowline. Males may reach a shoulder height of 1.04 m (3.4 feet); females are smaller. The compressed, spiral horns vary in size and shape, the longest being 1.65 m (5.4 feet). The hair is long and silky and, in the male, grey-brown in colour, becoming white in old age; the females are dark fawn. One or two kids are born after a gestation period of six months.

Markova, Dame Alicia (born Lilian Alicia Marks) (1910–) British ballet-dancer. In 1931 she joined the Vic-Wells Ballet, where she was the first English dancer to take the lead in *Giselle* and *Swan Lake*; she also created roles in new ballets such as Sir Frederick Ashton's *Façade* (1931). She founded the Markova–Dolin Ballet with Anton Dolin in 1935; they later both joined the emergent London Festival Ballet (1950), with which Markova was prima ballerina until 1952.

Marks, Simon, 1st Baron Marks of Broughton (1888–1964) British businessman. In 1907 he inherited the Marks and Spencer Penny Bazaars established by his father and Thomas Spencer (1851–1905). These became the nucleus of the successful company created in 1926 as Marks & Spencer, a chain of retail stores selling clothes, food, and household goods under the brand name 'St Michael'.

Marlborough, John Churchill, 1st Duke of (1650–1722) British general. He was appointed commander of British and Dutch troops in the War of the Spanish Succession and won a series of victories over the French armies of Louis XIV, most notably Blenheim (1704), Ramillies (1706), Oudenarde (1708), and Malplaquet (1709), which effectively ended Louis's attempts to dominate Europe. The building of Blenheim Palace, Marlborough's seat at Woodstock in Oxfordshire, was funded by Queen Anne as a token of the nation's gratitude for his victory.

Marley, Robert Nesta (known as 'Bob') (1945–81) Jamaican reggae singer, guitarist, and songwriter. In 1965 he formed the trio the Wailers, with whom he went on to become the first internationally acclaimed reggae musician. Bob Marley was a devout Rastafarian and supporter of black power whose lyrics frequently reflect his religious and political beliefs. Among his albums are *Burnin'* (1973) and *Exodus* (1977).

marlin (or **spearfish**) A fish of the family Istiophoridae, which has a spear-like bill that is round in cross-section. The dozen or so species are all streamlined fishes with a powerful body, a long dorsal fin, and high lobes to the tail fin. They are probably the fastest-swimming fishes in the world, and live near the surface of the sea in all tropical and warm temperate oceans. The larger species include the blue marlin, *Makaira nigricans*, which grows to 4.6 m (14.6 feet) in length and around 450 kg (992 pounds) in weight. They are popular sporting fishes in certain tropical areas, and also commercially important as a food-fish. Members of the genus *Tetrapturus* are rather smaller, but include the white marlin, *T. albidus*, which occurs as far north as Nova Scotia.

Marlowe, Christopher (1564–93) English dramatist and poet. As a dramatist he brought a new strength and vitality to blank verse; major works include *Tamburlaine the Great* (1587–88), *Doctor Faustus* (c.1590), *Edward II* (1592), and *The Jew of Malta* (1592). His poems include 'Come live with me and be my love' (published in *The Passionate Pilgrim*, 1599) and the unfinished *Hero and Leander* (1598; completed by George Chapman). His work had a significant influence on Shakespeare's early historical plays. Marlowe was killed during a brawl in a tavern.

marmoset A PRIMATE making up a curious group found in South America, which, with the tamarins, form the family Callitrichidae. The eight species are all less than 30 cm (1 foot) in length, and have extremely long tails which are not prehensile. The digits on their hands and feet have hooked claws, except for the big toe which has a nail. They are tree-dwellers in equatorial forests, a life to which they are well adapted. They show a range of coloration from drab to quite vivid reds, browns, and greys. Many species have distinctive crests, whiskers, and beards.

marmot An animal closely related to the GROUND SQUIRREL but rather stockier in build, weighing up to 7.6 kg (16.5 pounds) and having a relatively shorter tail. In North America, much of temperate Asia, and in parts of Europe, 11 species occur. They construct large burrows; some species, such as the European alpine marmot, *Marmota marmota*, form colonies, but others are more solitary. They are herbivorous, and can become pests of crops. Marmots, such as the hoary marmot, *M. caligata*, are famous for their prolonged hibernation, which usually occupies six months of the year.

Marne A river of east-central France, that rises in the Langres Plateau north of Dijon and flows 525 km (328 miles) north and west to join the Seine near Paris. Its valley was the scene of two important battles in World War I. The first battle (September 1914) halted and repelled the German advance on Paris; the second (July 1918) ended the final German offensive.

Maronite A member of a Christian sect of Syrian origin, living chiefly in Lebanon. They claim to have been founded by St Maro, a friend of Chrysostom (died 407), but it seems certain that their origin does not go back beyond the 7th century. Since 1181 they have been in communion with the Roman Catholic Church.

Marquesas Islands A group of volcanic islands in the South Pacific, forming part of the overseas territory of French Polynesia; area 1,049 sq km (405 sq miles); pop. (1988) 7,540; its chief settlement is Taiohae on the island of Nuku Hiva. The islands were annexed by France in 1842. They are described by the US writer Herman Melville in his novel *Typee*, written after he visited them in 1842. The largest island is Hiva Oa, on which the French painter Paul Gaugin spent the last two years of his life (1901–03).

marquetry In furniture-making, a VENEER made of pieces of wood or other suitable materials (ivory, for example) shaped and fitted together to form a design. If the design forms a regular geometric pattern it is called parquetry. Marquetry originated in Germany and the Low Countries in the 16th century and spread to France and Britain in the 17th century.

Marquette, Jacques (1637–75) French Jesuit missionary and explorer. He travelled to North America in 1666 and played a prominent part in the attempt to Christianize the American Indians there, especially during his mission among the Ottawa tribe. In 1673 he was a member of an expedition which explored the Wisconsin and Mississippi rivers as far as the mouth of the Arkansas.

Márquez See GARCÍA MÁRQUEZ.

Marrakesh (or **Marrakech**) A town in western Morocco, in the northern foothills of the High Atlas Mountains, one of the four imperial cities of Morocco; pop. (1993) 602,000. It was founded in 1062 by Yusuf ibn Tashfin as capital of the Almoravides, a Moorish people whose dynasty spread from North Africa to Spain in the 11th and 12th centuries. It is a centre of tourism and winter sports and has leather and textile industries.

marram A species of grass, *Ammophila arenaria*, found in arid habitats, such as the sandy coasts and dunes of western Europe. It is a perennial with tightly rolled leaves, very resistant to wind and salt spray, and has a creeping rhizome which effectively binds otherwise loose sands. It has been usefully employed for stabilizing sands subject to erosion by wind and tides.

marriage A socially recognized relationship between a man and a woman, which accords status to their offspring. In many cultures, marriage is theoretically regarded as a permanent bond, dissoluble only through DIVORCE, but marriage may also be a temporary arrangement, as in Iran and other Muslim countries. Most Western legal systems have, since World War II, attempted to provide equal legal rights for both parties, but in other systems, such as Islamic law, women do not have equal rights. A person may have only one partner (monogamy) or many partners (polygamy: in polygyny, a man has more than one wife, and in polyandry, a woman has more than one husband). Most societies have rules prohibiting marriage amongst certain categories of kin (see INCEST), but people may be forced to marry within a circumscribed category (endogamy), as in the CASTE SYSTEMS of India. Although Western societies place great emphasis on individual choice of marriage partner, in most other societies the wider kin group plays an important part in the choice of marriage partner. Arranged marriages are therefore the norm in many Hindu and Muslim communities, even when these communities exist in Western societies. In Christianity matrimony is regarded as a SACRAMENT. However, unmarried cohabitation is an increasing phenomenon, especially in countries in which a diminishing number of people are influenced by the concept of a Christian sacrament.

marrow (or **vegetable marrow**) The plant species *Cucurbita pepo*, which produces long, cylindrical fruits. These are usually green but may also be yellow, white, or striped. Like their relatives melons and cucumbers, they are climbing or trailing annuals, with large, prickly leaves and stems. In North America these fruits are known as summer SQUASHES, and include the American pumpkin. They originated in tropical America and are now grown all over the world as a vegetable. Other varieties of *C. pepo* include ornamental gourds, and those with fruit used when young as courgettes, which are also known as zucchini.

Marryat, Frederick (known as **Captain Marryat**) (1792–1848) British novelist. In 1830 he resigned his commission in the navy to concentrate on writing. He produced a number of novels dealing with life at sea, such as *Peter Simple* (1833) and *Mr Midshipman Easy* (1836), while his books for children include the historical story *The Children of the New Forest* (1847).

Mars (in mythology) The Roman god of war. He was identified with the Greek Ares, but was a much more important figure in Roman mythology than Ares in Greek mythology, ranking second only to Jupiter among the gods.

Mars (in astronomy) The fourth PLANET from the Sun. Mars moves in a markedly elliptic orbit, its mean distance from the Sun being 1.52 times that of the Earth's. Its diameter is approximately 6,800 km, a little more than half that of the Earth. Its period of revolution is 1.88 years, giving it a SYNODIC PERIOD of 2.14 years. At opposition its distance from the Earth can vary from 100 million km at aphelion to about 50 million km at perihelion, very close oppositions occurring every 15 or 17 years on average. At such times Mars is a bright, reddish, star-like object and the subject of extensive telescopic study. By study of the orbits of its two moons, PHOBOS and DEIMOS, discovered by the US astronomer Asaph Hall in 1877, the mass of Mars can be measured to be one-tenth that of the Earth. The pictures from various spacecraft show a solid surface with a wide variety of features: thousands of impact craters; many huge volcanic craters, none of which are now active; a great equatorial valley running eastwards for 3,000 km before turning northwards; and many smaller valleys and chasms. Two white polar caps change size as the Martian seasons come and go. However, it has no canals; the network of waterways thought by LOWELL and others in the late 19th century to cover the surface does not exist.

The planet's thin atmosphere (at the surface it is only 1 per cent of the density of Earth's atmosphere) is mainly composed of carbon dioxide. The polar caps are made of snow, ice, and carbon dioxide. Clouds and sandstorms are often seen. At the equator the temperature can vary from 10°C to below −75°C. The automatic laboratories of the Viking landers detected no definite signs of life. However, in 1996 it was claimed that fossil remains of primitive microbes had been found in a meteorite originating on Mars.

Marsala A fishing port and wine-making town at the western tip of Sicily that gives its name to a dark, sweet fortified dessert wine that was originally made here; pop. (1990) 80,760. Founded by the Carthaginians in 397 BC, the town was originally known as Lilybeum before its name was changed to Marsa Allah by Arabs in the Middle Ages.

Marseilles (French **Marseille**) A major industrial city and port on the Mediterranean coast of southern France, to the east of the Rhône estuary; pop. (1990) 807,725. It was settled as a Greek colony, called Massilia, in about 600 BC and became an ally of the Romans in their campaigns in Gaul in the first century BC. It was an important embarkation point during the Crusades of the 11th to the 14th centuries AD and in the 19th century served as a major port for French Algeria. It is capital of the department of Bouches-du-Rhône, the largest port and the second-largest city in France. Its industries include the processing of primary products, chemicals, and shipbuilding.

marsh A poorly drained, low-lying area alongside a pond, lake, river, or coastline which is flooded fairly regularly and supports specialized water-tolerant (and often salt-tolerant) vegetation. Geomorphologists sometimes make a distinction between marshes and fens or bogs, using the former name when their soils are largely made up of mineral particles, especially silts and clays, rather than organic, peat deposits.

Marsh, Dame Ngaio (Edith) (1899–1982) New Zealand writer of detective fiction. Her works include *Vintage Murder* (1937), *Surfeit of Lampreys* (1941), and *Final Curtain* (1947); many of the novels feature Chief Detective Inspector Roderick Alleyn.

Marshall, George C(atlett) (1880–1959) US general and statesman. As US Secretary of State (1947–49) he initiated the programme of economic aid to European countries known as the MARSHALL PLAN. He was awarded the Nobel Peace Prize in 1953.

Marshall Islands A country consisting of a cluster of 29 low-lying atolls and five islands in the central Pacific.

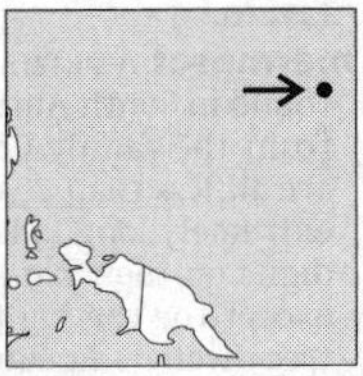

Physical. The archipelago comprises two parallel chains of islands, the Ratak (sunrise) chain to the east and the Ralik (sunset) chain to the west. The islands are coral caps over dome volcanoes and have a tropical climate.

Economy. Farming and fishing are the main economic activities. Coconut oil and copra are exported.

History. The islands were originally inhabited by Micronesians. They were sighted by European sailors in 1529 but were not exploited. The islands were named after a British captain who visited them in 1788. In 1886 the Marshall Islands became a German protectorate. After World War I the islands were administered by Japan, and after World War II they became a UN Trust Territory under US administration. From 1946 the US used BIKINI and other atolls in the group for atomic bomb tests. In 1986 they were given semi-independence in a 'compact of free association' in which the USA maintained control over military activities. The Trusteeship was terminated in 1990 and the country joined the United Nations the following year. Amata Kabua became President in 1980; he was re-elected in 1984, 1988, and 1992. The islands, which have the highest reported rates of certain cancers in the world, were used by the USA as sites for the testing of nuclear weapons (1946–58). In 1992 the US government made the first payments of compensation for personal injury to islanders. In 1993 the Australian government commissioned the building in the islands of a research station to monitor changes in sea-level; even a comparatively small rise in sea-level could submerge the entire country.

Capital: Majuro
Area: 181.48 sq km (70.07 sq mi)
Population: 56,200 (1995)
Currency: 1 US dollar = 100 cents
Religions: Protestant 90%; Catholic 8.5%; other 1.4%
Ethnic Groups: Marshallese 96.9%
Languages: Marshallese (Kajin-Majol); English
International Organizations: UN

Marshall Plan (or **European Recovery Program**) US aid programme. Passed by Congress in 1948 as the Foreign Assistance Act to aid European recovery after World War II it was named after the Secretary of State, George MARSHALL. It invited the European nations to outline their requirements for economic recovery in order that material and financial aid could be used most effectively. The Soviet Union refused to participate and put pressure on its East European satellites to do likewise. To administer the plan, the Organization for European Economic Co-operation was set up, and between 1948 and 1951 some $13.5 billion was distributed.

marsh deer A swamp-loving animal, *Blastocerus dichotomus*, the largest species of the South American DEER. It stands 1.10 m (3.7 feet) at the shoulders. The coat is of a rich, deep, chestnut-red colour in summer, becoming browner in winter. The males usually have eight points to their antlers. It occurs in marshes across central South America.

marsh harrier A slender HAWK with a long tail and wings, widely distributed in Britain, Sweden, northern Asia, and eastern Mediterranean countries, though nowhere numerous. The three species are the Eurasian marsh harrier, *Circus aeruginosis*, the African marsh harrier, *C. ranivorus*, and the eastern marsh harrier, *C. spilonotus*. Characteristically, they fly low over moorland and marshes, hunting for the small mammals and insects.

marsh marigold See KINGCUP.

Marston Moor A moor about 11 km (7 miles) west of York, site of the largest battle (1644) of the English Civil War, in which the combined Royalist armies of Prince Rupert and the Duke of Newcastle were defeated by the English and Scottish Parliamentary armies. The defeat destroyed Royalist power in the north of England and fatally weakened Charles's cause.

marsupial A mammal belonging to an infraclass (Metatheria) now mainly confined to Australasia, but represented in the New World by the OPOSSUMS. Marsupials differ from other mammals primarily in their reproductive processes, in that the young are not nourished in the womb through a placenta but are born in a very undeveloped state. Most growth takes place in the pouch (marsupium), which is a fold of skin, usually facing forwards, enclosing the nipples. The pouch is absent from most American opossums. The abundance of marsupials in Australia is due to its separation from other landmasses before the biologically more successful placental mammals could become established there. A feature of marsupial evolution is that it shows a parallel with the evolution of mammals elsewhere. Thus there are equivalents to wolves, bears, badgers, cats, ant-eaters, rats, mice, and moles. Marsupial 'cats' are comparable to genets. BANDICOOTS are rabbit-like in appearance but insectivorous, while others look like true insectivores. The FLYING PHALANGERS parallel flying squirrels and there are even otter-like water opossums. Australian 'opossums' (PHALANGERS) resemble monkeys. KANGAROOS can be considered as equivalent to antelopes as they occupy similar ecological niches.

marsupial mole An animal, *Notoryctes typhlops*, similar in appearance and size to true moles but rather different in habits. Marsupial moles do not construct permanent burrows; those they dig collapse behind them. Notable features include a nose-shield, powerful front claws for digging, and silky white to golden fur. The eyes are vestigial and the pouch, unusually for a marsupial, opens to the rear. They are members of the family, Notoryctidae, and are the only Australian mammal to have adapted to a burrowing life.

Martel, Charles See CHARLES MARTEL.

marten A carnivore of the family Mustelidae, which also includes the weasels, stoats, otters, and badgers. Martens look like large versions of the related stoats, except that the tail is bushier. There are eight species, which occur throughout temperate regions of the Northern Hemisphere. All are carnivorous, hunting in trees, with squirrels as their favourite prey, although they will take any other small mammal or bird including chickens. There are two species in America: the fisher, *Martes pennanti*, and the American marten, *M. americana*. The former belies its name in being more of a terrestrial carnivore than a fisherman. The Old World martens are sometimes named after their preferred habitat, such as pine marten, *M. martes*, and beech, or stone marten, *M. foina*. These two species extend south to the Mediter-

Marsupials (1) Flying phalanger. (2) Opossum. (3) Wombat. (4) Koala. (5) Red kangaroo. (6) Tasmanian devil.

ranean region, but the SABLE, *M. zibellina*, is confined to the coniferous forests of Siberia.

Martha A friend of Jesus Christ, the sister of Mary and Lazarus of Bethany, who chose to express her devotion to Jesus by preparing a meal for him while her sister Mary sat in his presence. In Christian allegory she symbolizes the active life united to God, and her sister the contemplative.

Martha's Vineyard A resort island off the southeast coast of Massachusetts, USA, to the south of Cape Cod; area 280 sq km (108 sq miles). Its chief settlement is Edgartown. Settled in 1642 by the English, who are said to have found wild grapes here, it was an important fishing and whaling centre during the 18th–19th centuries.

Martial (Latin name Marcus Valerius Martialis) (*c.*40–*c.*104 AD) Roman epigrammatist, born in Spain. His 15 books of epigrams, in a variety of metres, reflect all facets of Roman life; they are witty, mostly satirical, and often coarse.

martial arts A group of fighting techniques developed in Oriental countries and now practised worldwide. They offer a valued means of self-defence and are also practised as competitive sports. **Jujitsu** is a Japanese method of self-defence involving throws, arm- and wrist-locks, kicks, chopping movements, and punches. It gave birth to the modern combat sport of **judo**, a form of wrestling from a standing position. **Karate** students learn deep mental control as a prelude to unleashing latent forces, which enable them to deliver lethal blows with the hands and feet. **Kung-fu** is the Chinese form of kick-fighting; variations are practised also in Taiwan and Thailand. **Aikido** is a Japanese form of wrestling that uses circular moves, wrist-locks, and throws. **Kendo**, also from Japan, is Samurai fencing, carried out with long staffs; contestants wear padded gloves, a breastplate, and face-mask. Another version, **tai kwan do**, originated in Korea.

martial law Government by military authorities in times of emergency, such as war or civil unrest. Martial law may also be imposed over long periods to stifle opposition to a particular regime. It imposes a more restrictive regime than is normal, and often CIVIL RIGHTS, such as free speech are suspended.

martin A bird of which there are 20 different species within the SWALLOW family, Hirundinidae. They vary from about 10–20 cm (4–9 inches) in length and most have glossy black plumage with a purple or green sheen. Very agile on the wing, they feed on flying insects. Martins occur in most areas of the world, those that breed at high latitudes migrating long distances to warmer climates for the winter.

Martin, Dean (born Dino Paul Crocetti) (1917–95) US singer and actor. He became known originally for his comedy and singing act with Jerry Lewis (1925–). In 1948 they first appeared on television, going on to make a series of comedy films that began with *My Friend Irma* (1949). They parted in 1956 and Martin joined with Frank Sinatra and Sammy Davis Jr (1925–90) – forming the 'Rat Pack' – in a number of films, including *Bells are Ringing* (1960). Martin also had his own television show from 1965 until the 1970s.

Martin, St (died 397) French bishop, a patron saint of France. While serving in the Roman army he gave half his cloak to a beggar and received a vision of Christ, after which he was baptized. He joined St Hilary at Poitiers and founded the first monastery in Gaul. On becoming bishop of Tours (371) he pioneered the evangelization of the rural areas. Feast day, 11 November.

Martin, Steve (1945–) US actor and comedian. He successfully moved from zany stand-up comedy to farcical film comedies with *The Jerk* (1979), which he co-wrote. He went on to star in films such as *Parenthood* (1989) and *Sgt Bilko* (1996) and wrote, produced, and starred in *Roxanne* (1987) and *LA Story* (1991).

Martineau, Harriet (1802–76) British writer. She overcame deafness and heart disease to become one of the foremost English intellectuals of her day. She wrote mainly on social, economic, and historical subjects, achieving recognition with works such as her 25-volume series *Illustrations of Political Economy* (1832–34). Her other works include her acclaimed two-volume translation of Auguste Comte's *Philosophie positive* (1853). Her candid *Autobiography* was published posthumously in 1877.

Martini, Simone (*c.*1284–1344) Italian painter. His work is characterized by strong outlines and the use of rich colour. He worked in Siena and Assisi in Italy, and for the papal court at Avignon in France (*c.*1339–44). Notable works include *The Annunciation* (1333).

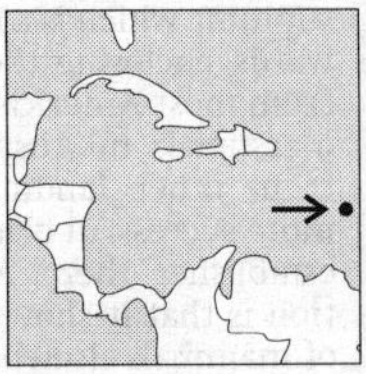

Martinique A volcanic Caribbean island in the Lesser Antilles between Dominica and St Lucia, administered by France as an overseas department; area 1,079 sq km (417 sq miles); pop. (1990) 359,570; capital, Fort-de-France. Colonized by France in 1635, its former capital St Pierre was completely destroyed by an eruption of Mount Pelée in 1902. Tourism, oil refining, and the production of fruit and rum are the chief economic activities.

martyr Originally meaning a legal 'witness', a martyr became anyone who died for his or her Christian beliefs after St Stephen, the first Christian martyr, was stoned to death in Jerusalem (*c.*35). Martyrs ranked before all other SAINTS, were venerated for their courage and faith, and were considered powerful intercessors between man and God. Martyrs' graves became shrines.

In Islam, the *shahīd* ('witness') is a similar concept: those who die in a *jihad* or holy war are considered martyrs, and are guaranteed a place in heaven. Sikhs commemorate the martyrdoms of two of their GURUS, Arjan and Tegh Bahadur. In Judaism, the six million Jews murdered by the Germans during World War II are remembered as martyrs.

Marvell, Andrew (1621–78) English poet. He served as an MP (1659–78) and was best known during his lifetime for his verse satires and pamphlets attacking Charles II and his ministers, particularly for corruption at court and in Parliament. Most of his poetry was published posthumously (1681) and did not achieve recognition until the early 20th century, when it was reappraised along with the work of other METAPHYSICAL POETS, such as John Donne. His best-known poems include 'To His Coy Mistress', 'Bermudas', and 'An Horatian Ode upon Cromwell's Return from Ireland'.

Marx, Karl (Heinrich) (1818–83) German political philosopher and economist, resident in England from 1849. The founder of modern communism, he collaborated with ENGELS in the writing of the *Communist Manifesto* (1848). Thereafter Marx spent much of his time enlarging the theory of this pamphlet into a series of books, the most important being the three-volume *Das Kapital*. The first volume of this appeared in 1867 and the remainder was completed by Engels and published after Marx's death (1885; 1894). See MARXISM.

Marx Brothers A family of US comedians, consisting of the brothers **Chico** (Leonard, 1886–1961), **Harpo** (Adolph Arthur, 1888–1964), **Groucho** (Julius Henry, 1890–1977), and **Zeppo** (Herbert, 1901–79). Their films, which are characterized by their anarchic humour, include *Horse Feathers* (1932) *Duck Soup* (1933), and *A Night at the Opera* (1935).

Marxism The system of economic and political ideas first developed by Karl MARX and Friedrich ENGELS and later developed by their followers together with DIALECTICAL MATERIALISM to form the basis for the theory and practice of COMMUNISM. At the heart of Marxism lies the materialist conception of history, according to which the development of all human societies is ultimately determined by the methods of production that people adopt to meet their needs. A particular technique of production determines a set of property relations to organize production (for instance slavery, feudalism, CAPITALISM), as well as the politics, religion, philosophy, and so on of a given society. The conflict between the particular social classes that emerged led to the next stage of social EVOLUTION. Feudalism had been followed by capitalism, which was destined to make way for SOCIALISM/COMMUNISM. In this way Marx and Engels sought to establish the importance of the CLASS STRUGGLE. Their attention was focused on capitalist societies, which they viewed as increasingly polarized between an exploiting capitalist class and an impoverished working class. Crucial to Marx's economic analysis of capitalism was his elaboration of the labour theory of value held by the classical economists SMITH and RICARDO. Marx saw capitalists as expropriating the surplus value created by workers, and accumulating ever-increasing amounts of capital, as the workers (the proletariat) grew ever poorer. The development of industry would render capitalism obsolete, at which point the working class would be ready to overthrow the system by revolutionary means and establish a socialist society. Marx and Engels said little about the economics and politics of socialism; after their death, Lenin and his followers in the former Soviet Union and elsewhere used Marxist ideas to underpin COMMUNISM, the ideology later being dubbed 'Marxism-Leninism', while other Marxists were critical of communist methods and regarded the Russian revolution (1917) as premature. Since then Marxists have had to grapple with the failure of the socialist societies to live up to the humanistic beliefs of Marx himself, and also with political developments, such as the rise of fascism, that appeared to contradict historical materialism. Marxism-Leninism as practised in the USSR, and in other countries of the Soviet bloc, collapsed in the 1990s, when the command economy on which it was based was replaced by a market economy. In spite of this practical failure of Marxism, Marx's injunction that to understand a society we should first investigate its mode of production continues to influence many social scientists.

Mary (known as the **(Blessed) Virgin Mary**, **St Mary**, or **Our Lady**) Mother of Jesus. According to the Gospels she was a virgin, betrothed to Joseph at the time of the Annunciation, who conceived Jesus by the power of the Holy Spirit. She has been venerated by Catholic and Orthodox Churches from the earliest Christian times. The doctrines of her Immaculate Conception and Assumption are taught by some Churches. Feast days, 1 January (Roman Catholic Church), 25 March (Annunciation), 15 August (Assumption), 8 September (Immaculate Conception).

Mary Two queens of England. **Mary I** (born Mary Tudor) (1516–58), daughter of Henry VIII, reigned 1553–58. Having regained the throne after the brief attempt to install Lady Jane Grey in her place, Mary attempted to reverse the country's turn towards Protestantism, which had begun to gain momentum during the reign of her brother, Edward VI. She married Philip II of Spain, and after putting down several revolts began the series of religious persecutions which earned her the name of 'Bloody Mary'. She died childless and the throne passed to her Protestant sister, Elizabeth I. **Mary II** (1662–94), daughter of James II, reigned 1689–94. Although her father was converted to Catholicism, Mary remained a Protestant, and was invited to replace him on the throne after his deposition in 1689. She insisted that her husband, William of Orange (WILLIAM III), be crowned along with her and afterwards left most of the business of the kingdom to him, although she frequently had to act as sole head of state because of her husband's absence on campaigns abroad.

Mary, Queen of Scots (born Mary Stuart) (1542–87) Daughter of James V, queen of Scotland 1542–67. Mary was sent to France as an infant and was married briefly to Francis II, but after his death returned to Scotland in 1561 to resume personal rule. A devout Catholic, she was unable to control her Protestant lords; her position was made more difficult by her marriages to Lord Darnley and the Earl of Bothwell, and after the defeat of her supporters she fled to England in 1567. There she was imprisoned and became the focus of several Catholic plots against Elizabeth I; she was eventually beheaded.

Mary, St See MARY.

Maryland A state of the eastern USA on the Atlantic coast, surrounding Chesapeake Bay; area 27,092 sq km (10,460 sq miles); pop. (1990) 4,781,470; capital, Annapolis. It was founded as a proprietary colony by the Roman Catholic Lord Baltimore in 1632 and named after Queen HENRIETTA MARIA. It became a major tobacco producer. Despite its Toleration Act (1649) it suffered religious uprisings from Puritan settlers in the 1650s and a revolution in 1689, after which it became a royal colony, though in 1715 it reverted to being a proprietary colony. In the American War of INDEPENDENCE, Maryland was responsible for forcing other states to cede their western lands to the national government. It was one of the original 13 states of the USA (1788). Vegetable canning and the manufacture of aircraft, clothing, and chemicals are important industries. Landmarks include Harpers Ferry National Historical Park, Chesapeake and Ohio Canal National Historical Park, Catoctin Mountain Park, Greenbelt Park, Fort Washington Park, Piscataway Park, and the Goddard Space Flight Center.

Mary Magdalene, St (in the New Testament) A woman of Magdala in Galilee. She was a follower of Jesus, who cured her of evil spirits (Luke 8:2); she is also traditionally identified with the 'sinner' of Luke 7:37. Feast day, 22 July. Mary Magdalene witnessed the crucifixion and was the first to see Jesus after his resurrection.

Masaccio (born Tommaso Giovanni di Simone Guidi) (1401–28) Italian painter. He was based chiefly in Florence and is remembered particularly for his frescos in the Brancacci Chapel in Santa Maria del Carmine (*c*.1424–28). He was the first artist to develop the laws of perspective (which he learned from Brunelleschi) and apply them to painting.

Masada The site, on a steep rocky hill on the south-west shore of the Dead Sea, of the ruins of a palace and fortification built by Herod the Great in the 1st century BC. It was a Jewish stronghold in the Zealots' revolt against the Romans (66–73 AD) and was the scene in 73 AD of a mass suicide by the Jewish defenders, when the Romans breached the citadel after a siege of nearly two years. The site is an Israeli national monument and tourist attraction.

Masai See MAASAI.

Masaryk, Jan (1886–1948) Czechoslovak diplomat and statesman. The son of Tomáš MASARYK, he helped in establishing the Czech republic and thereafter was mainly involved in foreign affairs. As ambassador to Britain (1925–38), he resigned in protest at his country's betrayal at MUNICH (1938). On the liberation of Czechoslovakia by the Allies (1945) he became Foreign Minister, and was dismayed at the Soviet veto of Czechoslovak acceptance of US aid under the MARSHALL PLAN. At the request of President BENEŠ, he remained in his post after the communist coup of February 1948, but he either committed suicide or was murdered three weeks later.

Masaryk, Tomáš (Garrigue) (1850–1937) Czechoslovak statesman, President (1918–35). A founder of modern Czechoslovakia, during World War I he was in London, where he founded the Czechoslovakian National Council with Edvard BENEŠ and promoted the cause of his country's independence. When this was achieved in 1918 he became Czechoslovakia's first President. In 1935 he retired in favour of Beneš.

Mascagni, Pietro (1863–1945) Italian composer and conductor. His compositions include operas and choral works; he is especially remembered for the opera *Cavalleria Rusticana* (1890).

mascon A region of the Moon's surface in which the rock has a higher density than the other material below or around it. A mascon, which is short for 'mass concentration', is produced by layers of basalt lava rising up through the Moon's surface crust and solidifying on top of the low-density crust. Mascons were first detected by spacecraft orbiting the Moon when they measured the slight changes in the Moon's gravity over the mascons. The Imbrium Basin is a mascon.

Masefield, John (Edward) (1878–1967) British poet and novelist. His fascination with the sea is reflected in his first published book of poetry, *Salt-Water Ballads* (which contained 'I must go down to the sea again', 1902). His other works include several narrative poems and novels, and the children's story *The Midnight Folk* (1927). He was appointed Poet Laureate in 1930.

maser (*m*icrowave *a*mplification by *s*timulated *e*mission of *r*adiation) A source of intense, coherent (the waves are in phase) radiation of a single frequency in the microwave area of the electromagnetic spectrum. Masers are used as OSCILLATORS, and as microwave AMPLIFIERS. They operate by 'pumping' or exciting the ELECTRONS of a solid or gas to higher energy levels, by means of an input of energy. The electrons are then allowed to fall to their ground state, and in doing so they emit energy in the form of electromagnetic radiation of a single frequency. A LASER works on similar principles to a maser, but emits energy in the form of visible light.

Maseru The capital of Lesotho, a transportation centre on the Caledon River near the country's western frontier with South Africa; pop. (est. 1992) 367,000. It was the capital of Basutoland from 1869 to 1871 and from 1884 to 1966.

Masolino da Panicale (*c*.1383–*c*.1447) Italian painter. His career is closely linked with that of MASACCIO, but the nature of the association remains ill-defined. They worked together on the decoration of the Brancacci Chapel in Santa Maria del Carmine in Florence (*c*.1425–28). After Masaccio's death Masolino reverted to the more decorative style he had practised early in his career.

Mason, A(lfred) E(dward) W(oodley) (1865–1948) British novelist. His work includes adventure stories (*The Four Feathers*, 1902), historical novels (*Musk and Amber*, 1942), detective novels featuring Inspector Hanaud, and several plays.

Mason, James (Neville) (1909–84) British actor. He became an established stage actor after making his début in 1931. He made his first film appearance in 1935 and went on to act in more than 100 films. Notable examples include *Odd Man Out* (1947) and *Lolita* (1962); he received Oscar nominations for his performances in *A Star is Born* (1954), *Georgy Girl* (1966), and *The Verdict* (1982).

mason bee A relation of the LEAF-CUTTER BEE, which shows similar behaviour in making its cells in rotten wood or in holes in masonry. Instead of using leaves, mason bees use small blobs of clay, moulded together.

Mason-Dixon Line (or **Mason and Dixon Line**) The boundary line between Pennsylvania and Maryland, which was laid out in 1763–67 by the English surveyors Charles Mason and Jeremiah Dixon. The name was later applied to the entire southern boundary of Pennsylvania, and in the years before the American Civil War it represented the division between the Northern states and the slave-owning states of the South.

mason wasp (or **potter wasp**) A solitary WASP of the family Eumenidae. The females build piles of mud cells, placed one on top of another, to form cup-shaped nest cells. Each cell is provisioned with insect prey before an egg is laid and one cell is capped before the next is started. Similar species also use mud to build nest cells in the cracks of walls.

masque A spectacular indoor performance combining poetic drama, music, dance, song, lavish costume, and costly stage effects, which was favoured in England in the first half of the 17th century. Members of the court would enter disguised, taking the parts of mythological characters, and enact a simple allegorical plot, concluding with a dance joined by members of the audience.

mass (in physics; symbol m) The quantitative measure of inertia, a fundamental property of all matter. Although mass is defined in terms of inertia, as the ratio of the FORCE acting on a body to the acceleration produced, in accordance with NEWTON'S LAWS OF MOTION, it is conventionally expressed as WEIGHT (W): the weight of a body is proportional to its gravitational mass, as defined by Newton's law of gravitation, i.e. $W = mg$, where g is the ACCELERATION of free fall. On the Earth, weight is the force exerted on matter by the gravitational attraction of the Earth. The equivalence principle of Lorand Eotvos states that the inertial mass is exactly proportional to the passive gravitational mass, which is related to the quantity of material contained in the body. The equivalence principle has been verified to an extremely high degree of accuracy. Mass is a scalar quantity, unlike weight. Two masses are equal if they have identical weight when measured in the same place in a gravitational field. The SI UNIT of mass is the kilogram (kg). At speeds close to the speed of light, inertial mass varies with speed. One of the startling discoveries of modern physics was the equivalence of mass and energy, a fact predicted by RELATIVITY theory in the equation $E = mc^2$, where E is energy and c is the SPEED OF LIGHT. They are often defined as a single quantity known as mass-energy. The conversion of mass to energy occurs during nuclear FISSION and FUSION.

mass (in religion) The principal service of the Roman Catholic Church, in which bread and wine are consecrated and consumed (see TRANSUBSTANTIATION). There are two types of mass: the High Mass, which is sung, and the Low Mass, which is spoken. The most important parts of the High Mass are the five sections that never vary, and are said to constitute the Ordinary of the mass. They are: *Kyrie eleison* ('Lord have mercy'); *Gloria in excelsis Deo* ('Glory be to God on high'); *Credo in unum Deum* ('I believe in one God, the Father Almighty'); *Sanctus* and *Benedictus* ('Holy, holy, holy, Lord God Almighty' and 'Blessed is He that cometh in the name of the Lord'); and *Agnus Dei* ('Lamb of God, that takest away the sins of the world, have mercy on us'). Unlike the remaining sections of the mass (known as the Proper), these texts are always the same whatever the occasion (although the *Gloria* is usually omitted in Advent and Lent). The texts of the Ordinary, and their traditional PLAINSONG, were established during the 7th to 11th centuries and have been set to music by composers ever since. The Protestant equivalent of the mass is the Office of Holy Communion.

Massachusetts A state of New England in the north-eastern USA, on the Atlantic coast; area 21,456 sq km (8,284 sq miles); pop. (1990) 6,016,425; capital, Boston. It was founded as a colony in 1630 by the Puritan Massachussetts Bay Company. Persecution and economic depression in England drove some 20,000 people to emigrate in the 1630s, including leading Puritan ministers and gentry. They were granted a charter authorizing trade and colonization. The first governor, John Winthrop, chose Boston as capital and seat of the General Court, the legislature, and established a strict congregational regime. Massachusetts fought a delaying battle against royal interference, but its charter was revoked in 1684 and direct government substituted. After 1689 it became a royal colony in which Plymouth Colony was incorporated. It played a leading role in the American War of INDEPENDENCE. After Shays's Rebellion (1786), in which state troops had to defend a federal arsenal, its élite clamoured for a new federal constitution to strengthen central government. The Massachusetts constitution became a pattern for later American states. Massachusetts was one of the original 13 states of the USA (1788). The state produces vegetables, fruit, garden produce, and the largest crop of cranberries in the USA but it is an overwhelmingly industrial state with a predominantly urban population. Landmarks include the Boston, Lowell, and Minute Man National Historical Parks.

Massachusetts Institute of Technology (MIT) A privately controlled US university with an emphasis on science and technology. It was founded in 1861 as part of a move to meet a growing demand for engineers in US industry. Its priorities are basic research in computing, engineering, the social and physical sciences, and management. It offers state-of-the-art research facilities to students from undergraduate level upwards.

mass defect In nuclear physics, the difference between the mass of a particular nucleus and the sum of the masses of its constituent particles. It represents the reduction in energy of the particles when they are bound together in the nucleus as predicted by the equivalence between mass and energy in RELATIVITY theory.

Massenet, Jules (Émile Frédéric) (1842–1912) French composer. His first performed opera was heard in 1867 and success came in 1872 with his sixth opera, *Don César de Bazan*. Of his 34 operas, the most successful were *Hérodiade* (1881), *Manon* (1884), *Werther* (1892), *Thaïs* (1894), and *Le Jongleur de Notre-Dame* (1902). He also composed many fine songs and several effective orchestral works.

Massif Central A mountainous plateau in south-central France. Covering almost one-sixth of the country, it rises to a height of 1,887 m (6,188 ft) at Puy de Nancy in the Auvergne. It is bounded to the south-east by the Cévennes.

Massine, Léonide Fëdorovich (born Leonid Fëdorovich Myassin) (1895–1979) Russian-born choreographer and ballet-dancer. In 1914 he joined Diaghilev's Ballets Russes as a dancer; he took up choreography the following year and went on to create ballets, such as *Le Tricorne* (1919). He was the originator of the symphonic ballet, including *Les Présages* (1933), based on Tchaikovsky's Fifth Symphony. He also danced in and choreographed the film *The Red Shoes* (1948). He settled in Europe and became a French citizen in 1944.

Massinger, Philip (1583–1640) English dramatist. He wrote many of his works in collaboration with other dramatists, most notably John Fletcher. His plays include tragedies (for example *The Duke of Milan*, 1621–22) and the social comedies *A New Way to Pay Old Debts* (1625–26) and *The City Madam* (1632).

mass media The means of producing and disseminating news, information, and entertainment to a universal audience, including NEWSPAPERS, magazines, RADIO, and TELEVISION. The mass media are industrial operations of considerable size and influence in political, economic, and cultural life. They fashion a mass society characterized by greater consensus, public participation, and awareness of the 'global village' in which we live, but also, more negatively, by increasing conformity, passivity, and ALIENATION. Mergers and acquisitions, as well as the integration of production, distribution, and equipment supply, have produced media empires operating on a multi-national or indeed worldwide basis. In non-industrialized countries and those with authoritarian or totalitarian governments, government ownership or control more directly affect the mass media. The degree of control exercised by the mass media, their power to influence public opinion, their allegiance to political IDEOLOGIES, and what is seen as a tendency to pander to the lowest common denominator of public taste, have been hotly debated.

Masson, André (1896–1987) French painter and graphic artist. He joined the surrealists in the mid-1920s; his early works pioneered the use of 'automatic' drawing, a form of fluid, spontaneous composition intended to express images emerging from the unconscious. His later works are characterized by themes of psychic pain, violence, and eroticism; they include the painting *Iroquois Landscape* (1942).

mass production A system of industrial production involving the manufacture of a product or part in large quantities at comparatively low unit cost. It was in the automobile industry, initially in the US Ford Company in 1913, that the age of mass production was fully inaugurated. Standardized parts were brought together on a moving ASSEMBLY LINE to turn out standardized cars at low cost, but with high wages and profits. At the same time, time-and-motion studies were undertaken to analyse and improve efficiency. Mass production methods thereafter were steadily introduced into other areas of manufacturing, for example in World War II in shipbuilding and aircraft manufacture.

Until recently, the high degree of mechanization and AUTOMATION involved in mass production required the standardization of both the product and the raw materials used in its manufacture. However, the development of flexible manufacturing systems for product monitoring and control has led to improved flexibility. The development of mass-production methods for high-quality items, in particular electronic devices, has led to a shift in emphasis from quality control, in which sub-standard or damaged products are rejected at the end of the production process to quality assurance, in which the whole production process is designed to ensure that the products are of a high standard.

mass spectrometer An analytical instrument for determining the structure of complex molecules or the isotopic content (see ISOTOPE) of elements. A small sample of the material under investigation is introduced into an evacuated area, where it is vaporized and ionized. The positively charged ions are then accelerated by an electrical field, and separated by mass, most commonly by means of a magnetic field, which causes each ion to follow a curved path. The amount each ion is deflected by the magnetic field depends upon its mass. The separated ions are then detected either by a collector (which converts the ion impacts into electrical currents that are either recorded or stored in a computer) or on a photographic plate. Complex molecules are fragmented by the ionization process, and the pattern of ion fragments produced gives information about their structure.

Master of the Queen's (or **King's**) **Music** The only surviving music post in the British royal household. It was established in the reign of Charles I, when the holder was the head of the king's private band of strings. Since 1893 the post has been given to some eminent musician who may do as much, or as little, as he chooses in return for the recognition, which carries virtually no pay. The present holder (since 1975) is Malcolm Williamson (1931–).

mastectomy The surgical removal of a breast, usually as a treatment for breast cancer. In a **partial mastectomy** (also known as a lumpectomy) only the tumour is removed. In a **simple mastectomy** the skin of the breast, and possibly the nipple, are not removed to enable a normal appearance to be retained by means of implanting a prosthesis (breast implant). In a classical **radical mastectomy**, the breast, underlying pectoral muscles, and lymphatic tissue are all removed. In the modern modified radical mastectomy the pectoral muscles are preserved. The mastectomy may be combined with chemotherapy and/or radiotherapy.

mastitis Inflammation of the breast. Acute mastitis may occur during the first month of commencing breast feeding; the commonly encountered bacterium is *Staphylococcus aureus*. Chronic mastitis is a misnomer because it is not an infection, but the formation of cysts in the breast; it is the commonest cause of 'breast lumps'. Acute mastitis is treated with antibacterial drugs. Chronic mastitis does not require treatment, although the possibility of breast cancer must be excluded.

mastodon An extinct elephant-like animal, very abundant during the Tertiary Era (66 to 1.6 million years ago) throughout the world; they were shorter and heavier in build than elephants. In addition to the curved upper pair of tusks, in the male mastodon there was a shorter pair of lower tusks which protruded forwards in some later species. Like the mammoths, mastodons had long, hairy coats.

Matabele A people of Zulu stock living in Zimbabwe. See NDEBELE.

Matabeleland A former province of Southern Rhodesia, lying between the Limpopo and Zambezi rivers and occupied by the Matabele people. The area is now divided into the two provinces of Matabeleland North and South, in southern Zimbabwe.

Mata Hari (born Margaretha Geertruida Zelle) (1876–1917) Dutch dancer and secret agent. She became a professional dancer in Paris in 1905 and probably worked for both French and German intelligence services before being executed by the French in 1917. Her name derives from Malay *mata* eye and *hari* day.

matamata A species of large SNAKE-NECKED TURTLE, *Chelus fimbriata*, with a shell-length up to 40 cm (16 inches), from northern South America and Trinidad. It has a very bizarre appearance with its flattened head being characterized by fringes of skin, tiny eyes, elongate snout, wide mouth, and rough shell. It feeds by suddenly opening its jaws and expanding its neck, creating an inrush of water to carry a fish into its mouth.

matchlock See FIREARM.

materialism The philosophical view that reality is material or physical. Materialism is therefore a form of MONISM. Materialism is rarely argued for directly, and is usually taken to be borne out by the success of the physical sciences. HOBBES may be cited as a modern proponent of materialism. For materialism to be true, minds or mental states must in some sense be identical with physical phenomena (presumably states of the brain or nervous system), a proposition which raises complex philosophical questions. A different sense of materialism is associated with MARX (see DIALECTICAL MATERIALISM).

mathematics The abstract science of space, number, and quantity. It was practised by the ancient Egyptians, Sumerians, Indians, and Chinese in a rudimentary form, notably for surveying and commercial purposes. Pure mathematics was developed by the Greeks and later by the Arabs, who introduced the old Hindu numerals to Europe in the 10th century. The Renaissance gave it great impetus: and in the 17th century there were advances in many fields, with the invention of LOGARITHMS, algebraic geometry, and CALCULUS. The new mathematics arose in the 20th century after investigation into the logical foundations of the subject. The theory of sets was introduced, and the arrival of the computer imposed disciplines of its own, as well as freeing mathematicians from the drudgery of lengthy computation. Recent developments in CHAOS suggest a view of mathematics as an empirical science, alongside physics, chemistry and biology.

Matilda (or **Maud**; known as the **Empress Matilda** or **Maud**) (1102–67) English princess, daughter of Henry I. She was Henry's only legitimate child and was named his heir in 1127. In 1135 her father died and Matilda was forced to flee when his nephew Stephen seized the throne. Her claim was supported by King David I of Scotland, and she and her half-brother Robert, Earl of Gloucester (died 1147) invaded England in 1139. She waged an unsuccessful civil war against Stephen and eventually left England in 1148. Her son became Henry II.

Matisse, **Henri (Émile Benoît)** (1869–1954) French painter and sculptor. He was influenced by the impressionists, Gauguin, and oriental art. His use of non-naturalistic colour in works such as *Open Window Collioure* (1905) led him to be regarded as a leader of the fauvists. Large figure compositions, such as *The Dance* (1909), heralded a new style based on simple reductive line, giving a rhythmic decorative pattern on a flat ground of rich colour. Later works include abstracts made of cut-out coloured paper, such as *The Snail* (1953). His sculpture displays a similar trend towards formal simplification and abstraction.

Mato Grosso A high plateau region of south-west Brazil forming a watershed between the Amazon and Plate river systems. Its Portuguese name means 'dense forest'. The region is divided into the two states of Mato Grosso and Mato Grosso do Sul.

matriarchy The authority of women over men, the converse of PATRIARCHY. Some 19th-century thinkers, including the German social theorist Friedrich ENGELS, believed that matriarchy was the characteristic form of the earliest human societies. In *The Origin of the Family, Private Property and the State* (1884) he argued that evidence could be found in myths, in the early history of religions, and in the tendency for agricultural societies to worship the fertility principle in the form of a goddess. Matrilineality, in which power (often that of men) is inherited through the female line of descent, found in certain peoples in non-industrial societies, was interpreted as a vestige of bygone matriarchy.

matrices In mathematics, a rectangular array of elements. Matrices can be added to or multiplied by suitable similar matrices. The arrays are usually enclosed by a pair of round brackets. An *n*-by-*m* matrix has *n* rows and *m* columns; an *n*-by-*n* matrix is called square. Although possessing many of the properties of numbers, they do not in general show COMMUTATIVITY with respect to multiplication.

Matsya In Hinduism, the first incarnation of Vishnu as a horned fish to save the world from destruction. When Matsya was a very small fish, Manu saved its life by taking it from the ocean and placing it in ever larger bowls as it grew. In return for this Matsya saved Manu from the Deluge by acting as moorage for his ship.

matter That which has mass and occupies space. Sometimes matter refers to everything, apart from radiation, present in the Universe; and it is sometimes defined as a specialized form of energy. Often, however, it is applied only to atoms and molecules in bulk that are close enough together to form gases, liquids, solids, or plasmas. All forms of matter share certain fundamental properties. Every physical entity has both gravitational MASS and inertial mass. According to Albert EINSTEIN's special relativity, matter's inertial mass and its energy are equivalent. Therefore, matter can be converted into energy and energy into matter.

Matterhorn (French **Mont Cervin**; Italian **Monte Cervino**) A spectacular mountain in the Alps, on the border between Switzerland and Italy with a distinctive pyramidal peak. Rising to 4,477 m (14,690 ft), it was first climbed in 1865 by the British climber Edward Whymper.

Matthew, **St** An Apostle, a tax-gatherer from Capernaum in Galilee, traditional author of the first Gospel. Feast day, 21 September.

Matthew Paris (*c*.1199–1259) English chronicler and Benedictine monk. His *Chronica Majora*, a history of the world from the Creation to the mid-13th century, is a valuable source for events in the years 1235–59.

Matthews, **Sir Stanley** (1915–) British footballer. He played on the right wing for Stoke City and Blackpool, and was famous for his dribbling skill. His career in professional football lasted until he was 50, during which time he played for England 54 times.

Matthias, **St** An Apostle, chosen by lot after the Ascension to take the place left by Judas. Feast day (in the Western Church) 14 May; (in the Eastern Church) 9 August.

Mauchly, **John William** (1907–80) US research engineer and computing pioneer. While on the staff of the University of Pennsylvania, he and J. Presper Eckert (1919–95) developed (1946) for the US Army Ordnance Department what was probably the first general-purpose electronic computer (see COMPUTER, history of). Called ENIAC (Electronic Numerical Integrator And Calculator), it was a vast machine, consuming 100 kW of electric power and containing 18,000 electronic valves. Their successful UNIVAC computer (1951) was the first commercial computer, and introduced MAGNETIC TAPE for programming.

Maud See MATILDA.

Maugham, **(William) Somerset** (1874–1965) British novelist, short-story writer, and dramatist. He was born in France, where he spent his childhood, returning to live on the Riviera in 1926. His life and wide travels often provide the background to his writing; his work for British intelligence during World War I is reflected in the *Ashenden* short stories (1928), while a visit to Tahiti gave the setting for the novel *The Moon and Sixpence* (1919). Other works include the novels *Of Human Bondage* (1915) and *Cakes and Ale* (1930), and the play *East of Suez* (1922).

Mau Mau A militant nationalist movement in Kenya. Its origins can be traced back to the Kikuyu Central Association, founded in 1920, and it was initially confined to the area of the White Highlands which Kikuyu people regarded as having been stolen from them. It imposed fierce oaths on its followers. It was anti-Christian as well as anti-European. From 1952 it became more nationalist in aim and indulged in a campaign of violence, killing some 11,000 black Africans who were opposed to its brutalities and some 30 Europeans. Jomo KENYATTA was jailed as an alleged Mau Mau leader in 1953. In a well-organized counter-insurgency campaign the British placed more than 20,000 Kikuyu in detention camps. Widespread political and social reforms followed, leading to Kenyan independence in 1963.

Mauna Kea A massive 'shield' volcano on the island of Hawaii, in the central Pacific. It is situated in the centre of the island, to the north of Mauna Loa. Rising to 4,205 m (13,796 ft), it is the highest peak in the Hawaiian islands and the highest island mountain in the world. It is the site of Mauna Kea Observatory, the world's largest.

Mauna Loa An active volcano on the Pacific island of Hawaii, situated to the south of Mauna Kea. Rising to 4,169 m (13,678 ft), it is the second-highest active volcano in the world. Major eruptions took place in 1881, 1942, 1949, and 1984.

Maupassant, (Henri René Albert) Guy de (1850–93) French novelist and short-story writer. He embarked on a literary career after encouragement from Flaubert, joining Zola's circle of naturalist writers. He contributed the story 'Boule de Suif' to their collection *Les Soirées de Médan* (1880) and became an immediate celebrity. He wrote about 300 short stories and six novels, portraying a broad spectrum of society and embracing themes of war, mystery, hallucination, and horror; these are written in a simple direct narrative style. His best-known novels include *Une Vie* (1883) and *Bel-Ami* (1885).

Mauriac, François (1885–1970) French novelist, dramatist, and critic. His works include the novels *Thérèse Desqueyroux* (1927) and *Le Noeud de vipères* (1932), and the play *Asmodée* (1938). His stories, usually set in the country round Bordeaux, explore the conflicts suffered by prosperous bourgeois people pulled in different directions by convention, religion, and passions. He was awarded the Nobel Prize for literature in 1952.

Mauritania A coastal country in north-west Africa, bounded by Morocco and Algeria on the north and by Mali and Senegal on the east and south.

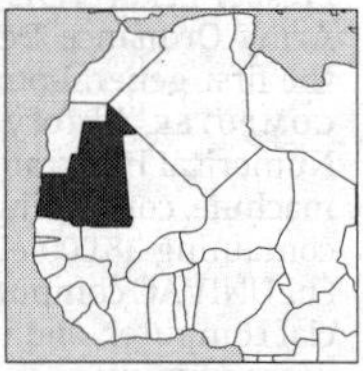

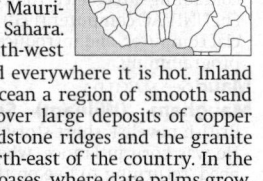

Physical. Most of Mauritania lies in the Sahara. Except in the south-west corner it is arid, and everywhere it is hot. Inland from the Atlantic Ocean a region of smooth sand dunes slowly rises, over large deposits of copper and iron ore, to sandstone ridges and the granite highlands of the north-east of the country. In the east there are a few oases, where date palms grow, and in the south groundnuts and some cereals are cultivated.

Economy. Mauritania's exports are dominated by iron ore and fish. Agriculture, confined mainly to the Senegal River valley in the south, despite attempts to extend irrigation by constructing dams, includes the growing of millet, dates, and rice. Nomadic livestock-rearing has declined with periodic droughts and the expansion of mining. Apart from mining, industrial activity involves a small amount of light manufacturing. There are deposits of copper, gypsum, phosphates, sulphur, gold, and uranium.

History. Dominated from *c.*100 AD by nomadic Berber trines (who still form one-quarter of its population), Mauritania was first sighted by Europeans in the 15th century. French penetration of the interior began in 1858, and in 1903 the country became a French protectorate. In 1920 Mauritania was made a territory of French West Africa. It became an autonomous republic within the FRENCH COMMUNITY in 1958, and fully independent in 1960. Following the Spanish withdrawal from WESTERN SAHARA in 1976 MOROCCO and Mauritania divided between them the southern part of this territory, known as Tiris-el-Gherbia. Bitter war with the Polisario Front (who demanded Western Saharan independence) ensued, but in 1979 Mauritania relinquished all claims and withdrew, leaving Morocco to annex the formerly Mauritanian region. The country's first president, Moktar Ould Daddah, was replaced in 1978 by a military government, the Military Committee for National Salvation (CMSN), which would appoint a President and civilian Council of Ministers. In 1991 a referendum voted overwhelmingly in support of a new constitution for what was to be an 'Islamic, African, and Arab republic' operating multi-party politics, with an elected executive president. In January 1992 Colonel Moaouia Ould Sidi Taya was duly elected, having been first appointed President by the CMSN in 1984. In 1989 some 40,000 black Mauritanians were expelled to Senegal, following ethnic violence in both countries. A border war with Senegal lasted from 1989 until April 1992. Ethnic tensions within Mauritania have continued.

Capital: Nouakchott
Area: 1,030,700 sq km (398,000 sq mi)
Population: 2,274,000 (1995)
Currency: 1 ouguiya = 5 khoums
Religions: Muslim 99.0%; Christian 0.5%
Ethnic Groups: Moor (mixed Arab-Berber and African-Sudanic) 81.5%; Tukulor 8.0%; Fulani 5.0%
Languages: French, Arabic (both official); ethnic languages
International Organizations: UN; OAU; Arab League; Maghreb Union

Mauritius An island country in the southern Indian Ocean, about 800 km (500 miles) east of Madagascar; it is also the name of the chief island (the others are Rodriguez and the Agalega Islands).

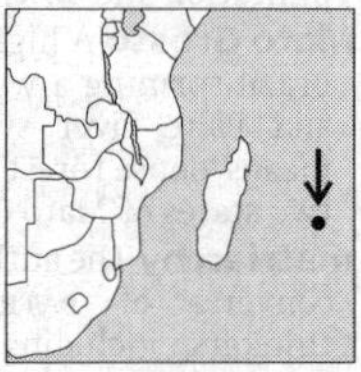

Physical. The main island, Mauritius itself, is volcanic in origin and nearly 2,000 sq km (770 sq mi) in area, having steep hills and plains of lava, which have weathered into fertile soil. The slopes are forested, and the plains are green throughout the year with natural vegetation.

Economy. The main exports of Mauritius are textiles and sugar. Tourism is an important source of revenue. Tea, fruit, and vegetables are important agricultural crops. There are no significant minerals.

History. Visited by the Arabs in the 10th century and discovered by the Portuguese in 1511, the island was held by the Dutch (1598–1710), and the French (1710–1810). The British took it in 1810, and under their rule massive Indian immigration took place. Mauritius became an independent state within the COMMONWEALTH OF NATIONS in 1968. Sugar has always been the principal crop, and the fall of world prices in the 1980s resulted in a vigorous programme of agricultural diversification. Politically it has maintained stability as a multicultural state, with the Mauritian Socialist Party, led by Sir Aneerood Jugnauth, in power from 1982. Following an election victory in 1991, the Party carried through a constitutional change, whereby Mauritius became a republic in 1992 but remained within the Commonwealth. Caseem Uteem was elected to the largely ceremonial role of President in 1992. General elections were held in 1995 following the collapse of the government and the opposition alliance, led by Navin Ramgoolam, was elected.

Capital: Port Louis
Area: 2.040 sq km (788 sq mi)
Population: 1,128,000 (1995)
Currency: 1 Mauritian rupee = 100 cents
Religions: Hindu 52.5%; Roman Catholic 25.7%; Muslim 12.9%; Protestant 4.4%; Buddhist 0.4%

Ethnic Groups: Creole 55.5%; Indian 39.6%; European 3.8%; Chinese 0.6%
Languages: English (official); French creole; Bhojpuri; Hindi; other Indian languages
International Organizations: UN; Non-Aligned Movement; Commonwealth; OAU; SADC

Maury, Matthew Fontaine (1806–73) US oceanographer. He conducted the first systematic survey of oceanic winds and currents, publishing charts which were of great value to merchant shipping. Maury also produced the first bathymetric charts, including a transatlantic profile, and pilot charts which enabled voyages to be considerably shortened. His work on physical oceanography was flawed in the eyes of many scientists by the religious tone of his writing.

Mauryan empire (*c*.325–185 BC) The first empire in India to extend over most of the subcontinent. The dynasty was founded by Chandragupta Maurya (*c*.325–297 BC), who overthrew the Magadha kingdom in north-eastern India. He established his capital at Pataliputra, then expanded westwards across the River Indus, annexing some trans-Indus provinces deep into Afghanistan from ALEXANDER's Greek successors. His son, Bindusara (*c*.297–272 BC), moved south, annexing the Deccan as far as Mysore. Although the third emperor, ASOKA (*c*.265–238 BC) soon renounced militarism, his reign marked the high peak of Mauryan power, for his humane rule permitted the consolidation of his father's huge empire. On his death decline quickly set in, and the dynasty finally ended with the assassination of Birhadratha (185 BC) by the founder of the subsequent Sunga dynasty.

mausoleum A large and stately tomb, particularly one in the form of a building. The first such building was planned by Mausolus (died 353 BC), Persian satrap (provincial governor) in Caria in Asia Minor, as a splendid tomb for himself, which was erected at Halicarnassus (now in Turkey) by his wife after his death. Built of white marble and richly decorated by some of the leading sculptors of the day, it was regarded as one of the Seven Wonders of the World. It was destroyed by an earthquake in the Middle Ages, but some of the sculpture survives in the British Museum. Other famous mausoleums include the TAJ MAHAL and Lenin's tomb in Moscow (1935).

Mawlid an-Nabi (Arabic, 'time of the prophet') A festival celebrating the birthday of the Prophet MUHAMMAD, believed to be 20 August 570. Celebrations are spread throughout the month of *Rabī ul-Awwal* (culminating on the twelfth day), and include the re-telling of stories about Muhammad's life, to expound his personality and spiritual greatness.

Maxim, Sir Hiram Stevens (1840–1916) Versatile US-born British engineer and inventor of the Maxim MACHINE-GUN. A keen inventor from early days, he obtained his first patent in 1866. In London in 1889, he produced the first fully automatic, water-cooled gun, firing ten shots per second from a 250-round cartridge belt. This was adopted as a standard weapon by the British Army (1889) and Navy (1892) and subsequently by many countries throughout the world. He also developed a type of smokeless powder (see NITROCELLULOSE) to improve the gun's efficiency.

Maximilian (full name Ferdinand Maximilian Joseph) (1832–67) Emperor of Mexico 1864–67. Brother of the Austro-Hungarian emperor Franz Josef and Archduke of Austria, Maximilian was established as emperor of Mexico under French auspices in 1864. In 1867, however, Napoleon III was forced to withdraw his support as a result of US pressure, and Maximilian was confronted by a popular uprising led by Benito Juárez. His forces proved unable to resist the rebels and he was captured and executed.

Maxwell, James Clerk (1831–79) British physicist and first director of the Cavendish Laboratory at Cambridge. He developed the theory of electromagnetism, and was the first to predict the existence of ELECTROMAGNETIC RADIATION and to describe light as an electromagnetic wave. Underlying his theory were four equations that contained the laws of magnetic and electric attraction, the laws linking magnetic fields and electric currents, and a new concept – a 'displacement current' caused by an electrical strain which could exist even in a vacuum. He also made major contributions to the KINETIC THEORY of matter and discovered the law governing the distribution of velocities among gas molecules (the MAXWELL-BOLTZMANN DISTRIBUTION).

Maxwell, (Ian) Robert (born Jan Ludvik Hoch) (1923–91) Czech-born British publisher and media entrepreneur. In 1940 he went to Britain, served as a captain in the British army, and founded Pergamon Press, the basis of his publishing empire, in 1951. A Labour MP 1964–70, he became the proprietor of Mirror Group Newspapers in 1984. He died in obscure circumstances while on his yacht off Tenerife; it subsequently emerged that he had misappropriated company pension funds.

Maxwell-Boltzmann distribution A statistical equation giving the distribution of energy among the molecules of a gas in thermal equilibrium. As the temperature changes there is a shift in this energy distribution. At low temperatures, most molecules have low energies, whereas there will be more with high energies as the temperature is increased. The distribution shows how many molecules have any given energy, and how this varies with temperature. It is named after James MAXWELL and Ludwig BOLTZMANN, who developed it independently of one another.

Maxwell Davies, Sir Peter See DAVIES, SIR PETER MAXWELL.

Maya An American Indian people of Yucatán and Central America who still maintain aspects of their ancient culture, which developed over an extensive area and reached its peak in the 4th–8th centuries, a period distinguished by a spectacular flowering of art and learning. Remains include stone temples built on pyramids and ornamented with sculptures. Among the most striking of the Maya achievements are a system of pictorial writing and a calendar system, more accurate than the Julian, that was still in use at the time of the Spanish conquest in the 16th century. The unexplained collapse of the early Mayan civilization with a population of as many as 16 million took place *c*.900–1500 but at least four million descendants still speak the Mayan language.

Mayakovsky, Vladimir (Vladimirovich) (1893–1930) Soviet poet and dramatist, born in Georgia. From 1910 he aligned himself with the Russian futurists, signing the futurist manifesto 'A Slap in the Face for Public Taste' in 1912. His early poems are declamatory in tone and employ an aggressive avant-garde style. After 1917, Mayakovsky saw a clear political role for futurism in the Bolshevik revolution and the new society, altering his style to have a comic mass appeal. He fell from official favour by the end of the 1920s, and committed suicide in 1930; five years later his reputation was restored by Stalin.

Mayer, Louis B(urt) (born Eliezer Mayer) (1885–1957) Russian-born US film executive. In 1907 he acquired a chain of cinemas, moving into production with Metro Films in 1915. He joined with Samuel Goldwyn to form Metro-Goldwyn-Mayer (MGM) in 1924; he was head of MGM until 1951 and the company was responsible for many successful films. He also helped establish the Academy of Motion Picture Arts and Sciences (1927), and received an honorary award from the Academy in 1950.

Mayflower See PILGRIM FATHERS.

mayfly A delicate, weak-flying insect belonging to the order Ephemeroptera, with two or three filamentous 'tails', found near fresh water. The 1,500 worldwide species have short antennae but large eyes, and at rest the wings are closed vertically. They have two pairs of gauze-like wings, the front pair much larger than the hind pair. They are well known to fishermen, because the aquatic, herbivorous, three-tailed nymphs are a major fish food. The flying, hair-covered, sub-adult, or dun, which moults into the adult proper (spinner), is used as a fishing fly.

Mayo A county in the Republic of Ireland, in the province of Connacht; area 5,398 sq km (2,085 sq miles); pop. (1991) 110,700; capital, Castlebar.

Mayotte The French name for MAHORE.

Mayr, Ernst Walter (1904–) German-born US zoologist best known for his attempt at assembling a neo-Darwinian theory of evolution to take account of the recent discoveries.

Mazarin, Jules (born Giulio Mazzarino) (1602–61) Italian-born French statesman. In 1634 he was sent to Paris as the Italian papal legate; he became a naturalized Frenchman and entered the service of Louis XIII in 1639. He was made a cardinal in 1641 and the following year succeeded Cardinal Richelieu as chief minister of France, which he governed during the minority of Louis XIV. His administration aroused such opposition as to provoke the civil wars of the Fronde (1648–53).

mazurka A traditional Polish dance in triple time with a dotted rhythm on the first beat and a strong accent on the second. In performance it requires a proud bearing and it is characterized by stamping, clicking heels, and the 'holubiec', a unique turning step. It has been used on many occasions in ballet to convey national character. It was introduced into the concert hall by Chopin as one aspect of his nationalism.

Mazzini, Giuseppe (1805–72) Italian nationalist leader. While in exile in Marseilles he founded the patriotic movement Young Italy (1831) and thereafter worked for the independence and unification of Italy, becoming one of the Risorgimento's most committed leaders and planning attempted insurrections in a number of Italian cities during the 1850s. He continued to campaign for a republican Italy following the country's unification as a monarchy in 1861.

Mbabane The capital of Swaziland in the highveld of southern Africa; pop. (1986) 38,290. Noted for its gaming casinos, it replaced Manzini as capital in 1902.

Mboya, Tom (1926–69) Kenyan political leader. In 1960, as leader of the Kenya Independence Movement, he attended a conference in London on the future of Kenya, and was instrumental in securing a constitution which would give Africans political supremacy. In 1960 he became Secretary-General of the newly formed Kenya African National Union. After Kenya gained its independence (1963) he served in various senior ministerial posts. He was assassinated in 1969.

Mdina A town at the centre of the island of Malta, formerly the capital of Malta; pop. (1983) 930. It is the site of the National Museum of Natural History and a cathedral built to replace an 11th-century cathedral destroyed in an earthquake in 1693.

ME (myalgic encephalomyelitis) See CHRONIC FATIGUE SYNDROME.

Mead, Margaret (1901–78) US anthropologist and social psychologist. She worked in Samoa and the New Guinea area and wrote a number of specialized studies of primitive cultures, but was also concerned to relate her findings to current American life. Her writings made anthropology accessible to a wide readership and demonstrated its relevance to Western society. Her books include *Coming of Age in Samoa* (1928) and *Male and Female* (1949).

meadow pipit A species of WAGTAIL or pipit, *Anthus pratensis*, that is a streaky, olive-green bird with white outer tail feathers. It is the size of a small sparrow with a thin, sharply pointed beak, and breeds in all but the southernmost areas of Europe and western Asia. This species lives on rough, open, grassy ground and nests on the ground near the side of a clump of grass.

meadow saffron See AUTUMN CROCUS.

meadowsweet A perennial plant, *Filipendula ulmaria*, belonging to the rose family. Its normal habitats are flood-meadows, marshes, and the margins of wet woodlands distributed throughout Europe, the Mediterranean, and Asia Minor. It also occurs as a garden escape in the eastern USA. The creamy-white scented flower-heads were made into a popular herbal drink in medieval times.

mean An AVERAGE value of a set of numbers found by computation. There are three principal types: arithmetic mean, geometric mean and harmonic mean.

The **arithmetic mean** is the one usually meant by the word 'average'. It is calculated by adding up all the members of the set and dividing by the number of members. For the set ½, 3, 2½, 7, −3 it is 2, which does not appear in the set. (A mean may coincidentally be identical to a member of the set.)

The **geometric mean** of *n* numbers is the *n*th root of their product. For example, the geometric mean of 16, 8 and 0.5 is $\sqrt[3]{64} = 4$. (A cube of side 4 units would have the same volume as a rectangular block with dimensions 16, 8 and 0.5 units.)

The **harmonic mean** is, for two numbers *a* and *b*, defined by $(1/H = \frac{1}{2}(1/a + 1/b)$ where H represents the harmonic mean. If a boat sails downstream at speed v_1 and the same distance upstream at speed v_2, the average speed for the journey is the harmonic mean of v_1 and v_2. See also MEDIAN.

meandering The development of series of bends and loops in river channels, which change over the centuries. Their amplitude and wavelength depend on river width, the wider the stretch of river the bigger being its meanders. Most meanders form in fine-grained material on flattish flood-plains, although incised meanders cut deeply into the bedrock, probably as a result of rejuvenation. All flowing fluids tend to develop meanders – the Gulf Stream and jet streams show them – but those of rivers produce asymmetric channels. There is a tendency for a river to cut off a loop, where two curves bend towards one another, leaving an OX-BOW LAKE.

mean solar day See DAY.

mean solar time See TIME.

measles A highly communicable infection by the

measles virus, which is transmitted from an individual with measles by inhalation of infected droplets derived from coughing or sneezing. Initially, 'cold-like' symptoms and muscle pain, are common. In the mouth, characteristic white spots surrounded by a red ring (Koplick's spots) may appear. This catarrhal stage, which lasts three or four days is followed by the exanthematous stage; the Koplick's spots disappear and a dark red rash appears on the face and neck, and spreads quickly to the rest of the body. The rash fades in two or three days as the fever subsides. Complications associated with measles include mouth ulceration, PNEUMONIA, and, rarely, inflammation of the brain (postviral encephalitis). Active IMMUNIZATION is an effective measure. Passive immunization is afforded to breast-fed babies, by the antibodies contained in breast milk.

measuring worm See LOOPER.

Meath A county of the Republic of Ireland, in the province of Leinster; area 2,339 sq km (903 sq miles); pop. (1991) 105,540; capital, Navan.

Mecca A city in western Saudi Arabia, an oasis town located in the Red Sea region of Hejaz, east of Jiddah; pop. (est. 1986) 618,000. The birthplace of the Prophet MUHAMMAD, it is the holiest city of Islam. Lying in a narrow valley in an arid region, it nevertheless prospered from trade and from the cult associated with its central shrine, the Kaaba. Muhammad's life was crowned by the incorporation of pilgrimage to the Kaaba into Islam. The city soon lost its commercial significance, its prosperity resting henceforth on the PILGRIMAGE. It was sacked in 930 by the Qarmatians, a radical Ismaili sect, and fell under OTTOMAN suzerainty in 1517.

mechanical advantage (or **force ratio**) The ratio of the force exerted by a mechanism to the force put in. The simplest example is the LEVER. Another example is a rope-and-pulley arrangement; if the rope passes up and down twice between upper and lower pulleys, then the mechanical advantage is four to one. According to the law of conservation of energy for a mechanical advantage of 4:1 the input force has to move through a distance at least four times that moved by the load.

mechanical engineering That branch of engineering that deals with machines and mechanized processes. In particular, mechanical engineering is concerned with power production, transmission, and utilization. Thus it includes machine-tools, ENGINES, transport of all kinds, CRANES, LIFTS, LOCKS, PUMPS, SERVO-MECHANISMS, and ROBOTICS. Originally mechanical engineering was regarded as a branch of civil engineering, that is, non-military engineering. With the development of locomotives for RAILWAYS and STEAM-ENGINES for industrial and marine uses, mechanical engineering came to be recognized as a separate discipline.

mechanics In mathematics, the interaction between matter and the forces acting on it. Statics is the study of systems at rest and dynamics is the study of systems in motion under the influence of forces. Much of the theory of mechanics is built upon NEWTON'S LAWS OF MOTION and the EQUATIONS OF MOTION, which involve the relationships between masses and forces in terms of time, lengths, and angles. Dynamics is concerned with the velocities and accelerations resulting from the action of forces. The process of modelling required by the mathematics relies on the idealization of certain physical phenomena, to give mathematical entities, which can then be described geometrically and analytically. Frictionless impacts, perfectly inelastic bodies, and point particles are all such idealizations. QUANTUM MECHANICS is mechanics of systems which do not follow Newton's laws.

mechanization See AUTOMATION.

Mecklenburg A former state of north-east Germany on the Baltic coast, now part of Mecklenburg-West Pomerania. Inhabited originally by Germanic tribes, it was occupied in about 600 AD by Slavonic peoples but was reclaimed by Henry the Lion, Duke of Saxony, in 1160. It was divided in the 16th and 17th centuries into two duchies, Mecklenburg-Schwerin and Mecklenburg-Strelitz, which were reunited as the state of Mecklenburg in 1934. The region was part of the German Democratic Republic between 1949 and 1990.

Mecklenburg-West Pomerania A state of north-east Germany, on the coast of the Baltic Sea; area 23,838 sq km (9,207 sq miles); pop. (est. 1990) 2,100,000; capital, Schwerin. The modern state consists of the former state of Mecklenburg and the western part of Pomerania.

Medan A city in Indonesia, on the Deli River in north-east Sumatra, capital of North Sumatra province; pop. (1990) 1,730,000. Established as a trading centre in 1682, it became the Dutch capital of the region and leading commercial centre of Sumatra. It trades in oil, rubber, and palm oil.

Medawar, Sir Peter (Brian) (1915–87) British immunologist and author. He studied the biology of tissue transplantation, and his early work showed that the rejection of grafts was the result of an immune mechanism. His subsequent discovery of the acquired tolerance of grafts encouraged the early attempts at human organ transplantation. In later life he wrote a number of popular books on the philosophy of science, notably *The Limits of Science* (1985). Medawar shared a Nobel Prize in 1960.

Medbh (or **Maeve**) (Gaelic, 'drunken woman') The legendary queen of Connacht in Ireland. A fierce goddess, she led her people in battle against the forces of Ulster. Among her many lovers were king Ailil and the hero Fergus. A bird and a squirrel, sitting on her shoulder, are associated with her.

Mede A member of an ancient Indo-European people whose homeland, MEDIA, lay south-west of the Caspian Sea. In the 7th–6th centuries BC they were masters of an empire that included most of modern Iran and extended to Cappadocia and Syria; it passed into Persian control after the defeat of King Astyages by Cyrus in 549 BC.

Medea See JASON.

Medellín A city in eastern Colombia, the second-largest city in the country; pop. (1992) 1,581,300. A major centre of coffee production, it has in recent years gained a reputation as a centre for cocaine production and the hub of the Colombian drug trade.

Media An ancient region of Asia to the south-west of the Caspian Sea, corresponding approximately to present-day Azerbaijan, north-west Iran, and north-east Iraq. The region is roughly the same as that inhabited today by the Kurds. Originally inhabited by the MEDES, the region was conquered in 549 BC by Cyrus the Great of Persia.

median (in statistics) The middle value (or average of two middle values) of a group of numbers arranged in size order. As a representative 'average' or measure of central tendency it is unaffected by irregular or freak values, unlike the mean. The median of 1, 1, 2, 2, 3, 4, and 99 is 2, whereas the arithmetic MEAN is 16.

medical ethics The moral issues arising in health care. Attention has focused, for example, on the proper limits of confidentiality, how far doctors are morally obliged to involve patients in decisions about treatment, EUTHANASIA, the allocation of scarce medical resources, the moral status of the human embryo and foetus (see ABORTION), genetic engineering, medical participation in torture, and the principles that should govern clinical trials on human subjects. Philosophers, lawyers, and theologians, as well as health-care professionals, are to be found working on medical ethics, often within hospital-based ethical committees. Legislation on these issues rarely keeps pace with scientific developments and is invariably contentious.

Medici, Catherine de See CATHERINE DE MEDICI.

Medici, Cosimo de (1389–1464) Florentine banker, the first member of the Medici family to rule Florence. In Florence the struggle for power between rival patrician families was intense and Cosimo was expelled from the city in 1433 before triumphing over his rivals in 1434. The basis of his wealth was the highly successful Medici bank. He was a keen patron of the arts.

Medici, Lorenzo de (known as **Lorenzo the Magnificent**) (1449–92) Aged 20 he became joint ruler of Florence with his brother Giuliano. In 1478 the brothers were the targets of a plot organized by the rival Pazzi family and the pope: Giuliano was killed but Lorenzo survived. His main concern was the promotion of his family, and he was rewarded by seeing his second son become Pope Leo X. He was a collector of antiquities and was Michelangelo's first patron.

medicine The study and practice of disease diagnosis, treatment with DRUGS, and its prevention. Medicine involves studying the structure and functions of the body systems, and abnormality caused by disease processes. This facilitates the study of drug actions and mechanisms that can be used in the treatment of diseases. In addition, study of the causes of diseases enables effective preventive measures such as IMMUNIZATION to be instituted. The diverse range of body systems has resulted in the development of specialities in medicine such as NEUROLOGY and IMMUNOLOGY. General practice medicine is the role of family doctors who are responsible for primary care; they can refer patients to doctors of a particular speciality, who are usually hospital-based.

Médicis, Marie de See MARIE DE MÉDICIS.

medieval music (*c*.700–*c*.1500) The music that survives from the European Middle Ages falls primarily into three categories. First, church chant or PLAINSONG: the main 'Gregorian' repertory perhaps dates back to the 6th century but is not clearly documented before the 9th. It is entirely monophonic (that is, a single vocal line without accompaniment) and covers a wide variety of styles, many of which continued to be used until the present century. Secondly, early church POLYPHONY (or part-music): the earliest substantial polyphonic repertory is in the 'Winchester Troper', copied shortly before the Norman conquest in 1066; but the finest music is in the great Parisian repertory of Notre Dame from the years around 1200. Much of this music has one voice singing chant, with up to three added voices; the composers Leoninus (documented 1179–1201) and Perotinus (fl. *c*.1190–1210) appear to have been the leaders here. From the 13th century the first evidence of the MOTET occurs. The third main repertory is in the songs of the Provençal troubadours, the northern French *trouvères*, the German Minnesinger, and related poets in other languages, *c*.1100–1300. Here the texts are well preserved, but the music – again monophonic – survives in a form that raises considerable questions about how it was performed.

Medina (Arabic **Al Madinah**) A city in western Saudi Arabia, an oasis some 320 km (200 miles) north of MECCA; pop. (est. 1981) 500,000. Formerly known as Yathrib and controlled by Jewish settlers, in 622 AD it became the refuge of the Prophet Muhammad's infant Muslim community after its expulsion from Mecca. It was renamed Medina, meaning 'the city', by Muhammad and made the capital of the new Islamic state until it was superseded by Damascus in 661. It was Muhammad's burial place and the site of the first Islamic mosque, constructed around his tomb. It is considered by Muslims to be the second most holy city after Mecca and a visit to the prophet's tomb at Medina forms a frequent sequel to the formal pilgrimage to Mecca. The Islamic University was established in 1962.

meditation A means believed to develop spiritual awareness or devotion through contemplation. In Christianity, meditation consists of reflection on themes from the BIBLE or from the lives of SAINTS. In Eastern religions, meditation is claimed to be a method of achieving enlightenment, as the individual spirit is integrated into a greater cosmic reality. YOGA, for example, employs discipline over physical and mental processes in order to aspire to purity of thought. In many religions, meditation is assisted through the repetition of sacred syllables, names, or texts, such as Hindu and Buddhist MANTRAS or Islamic *dhikr*, or through focusing the mind on images and symbols, known as mandalas. Other practices include the use of rhythmic movement and dance, or such devices as prayer beads, rosaries, or prayer wheels. Eastern methods of meditation have been popularized in the West in recent years by such organizations as the Transcendental Meditation movement.

Mediterranean Sea An almost landlocked sea between southern Europe, the north coast of Africa, and south-west Asia. It is connected with the Atlantic by the Strait of Gibraltar, with the Red Sea by the Suez Canal, and with the Black Sea by the Dardanelles, the Sea of Marmara, and the Bosporus; area *c*.2,589,000 sq km (1,000,000 sq miles); length *c*.3,200 km (2,000 miles).

medium wave (or **medium frequency**) See WAVEBAND.

medlar A species of deciduous tree of the genus *Mespilus*, related to the apple in the rose family. Native to southeastern Europe and Asia Minor, it is grown throughout Europe as much for its ornamental appearance as for the edible fruits, which are small, orange-brown, and plum-shaped. The fruits are unusual in that they have a large opening in the bottom through which the seed vessels are visible.

Medoc A district of Aquitaine in south-west France, between the Bay of Biscay and the estuary of the Gironde River, noted for its fine red claret. Its chief towns are Pauillac and Lesparre.

Medusa See GORGONS.

meerkat Any one of several species of southern African mammal. Most commonly, it refers to the grey or sticktailed meerkat or suricate, *Suricata suricatta*, a mongoose of the family Herpestidae.

Meerkats also include the yellow meerkat or mongoose, *Cynictis penicillata*, a species that lives in small, family-based groups, and the fan-tailed meerkat, *Xerus inauris*, which is a ground squirrel of the family Sciuridae. Meerkats are highly sociable and forage by day for insects and small vertebrates.

meerschaum A hydrated magnesium silicate, occurring in river deposits and in veins in the Earth. It appears as a soft pale mass, similar to white clay, and is easily carved before drying. Used for pipe bowls, it rapidly absorbs the smoke and becomes brown. Asia Minor is the main source, but Greece, Morocco, and Spain also have supplies.

megalith Literally a large stone. The practice of building with large stones occurred in such diverse places as Inca Peru, ancient Egypt, and Easter Island. Megaliths usually consist of blocks built into tombs and other monuments in western Europe in the NEOLITHIC to BRONZE AGE, *c*.4000–1500 BC. They were once thought to have been derived from a single source, but further study and close dating suggest that that is too simple a view, and that many areas were involved.

While many monuments consist of separate stones raised on end as MENHIRS, stone circles (as at STONEHENGE), and avenues (as seen at CARNAC, in France), the same technique was often used in walling chambers. Roofs could be of horizontal capstones to make the so-called **dolmens**, or of oversailing courses of slabs, which are known as corbelled vaults. The largest block recorded is the capstone of the tomb at Browneshill, County Carlow, Ireland, estimated to weigh 100 tonnes. The movement, handling and dressing of such large stones, and, in some cases, their precise orientation, indicate that those responsible had considerable skill in mechanics, mathematics, and the organization of labour.

megapode See MALLEE FOWL.

Megiddo (modern name **Tel Megiddo**) An ancient city of north-west Palestine, situated 32 km (20 miles) south-east of Haifa in present-day Israel. Founded in the 4th millennium BC, the city controlled an important route linking Syria and Mesopotamia with the Jordan valley, Jerusalem, and Egypt. Its commanding location on the southern edge of the plain of Esdraelon made the city the scene of many early battles, and from its name the word **Armageddon** ('hill of Megiddo') is derived. It was the scene in 1918 of the defeat of Turkish forces by the British under General Allenby.

Meiji Tenno (born Mutsuhito) (1852–1912) Emperor of Japan 1868–1912. He took the name Meiji Tenno when he became emperor. His accession saw the restoration of imperial power after centuries of control by the shoguns. During his reign he encouraged Japan's rapid process of modernization and political reform and laid the foundations for the country's emergence as a major world power; the feudal system was abolished, cabinet government introduced, and a new army and navy were established.

meiosis A special type of cell division (compare with MITOSIS) that produces GAMETES for sexual reproduction. A cell normally contains two copies of every chromosome but a gamete contains only one of each different chromosome. Meiosis involves halving the number of chromosomes. The process of gamete formation involves two division stages. In the first, the chromosomes come together as pairs and exchange genetic material; this is called recombination or crossing over. Each chromosome of a pair migrates to opposite ends of the cell. In the second division stage, the chromosomes undergo a mitotic type of division to pro-

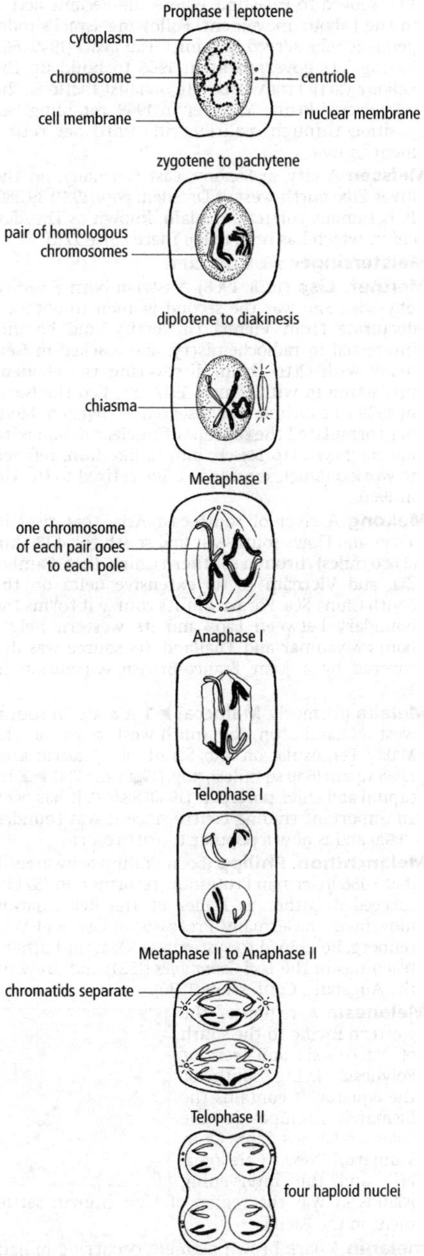

Meiosis The stages prophase I to telophase I involve the exchange of genetic material between pairs of homologous chromosomes (represented by the chiasma) and their subsequent separation to opposite poles of the cell. In the stages metaphase II to telophase II each chromosome of a pair, consisting of two chromatids, divides. This produces four genetically non-identical nuclei, each containing half the number of chromosomes in the original cell.

duce four gamete cells, each with only one copy of each chromosome from the parent cell.

Meir, Golda (born Goldie Mabovich) (1898–1978) Israeli stateswoman, Prime Minister 1969–74. Born in Ukraine, she emigrated to the USA in 1907 and in 1921 moved to Palestine, where she became active in the Labour movement. Following Israel's independence she served in ministerial posts (1949–66); having left government in 1966 to build up the Labour Party from disparate socialist factions, she was elected Prime Minister in 1969, retaining her position through coalition rule until her retirement in 1974.

Meissen A city in Saxony, east Germany, on the River Elbe north-west of Dresden; pop. (1981) 39,280. It is famous for its porcelain, known as Dresden china, which has been made there since 1710.

Meistersinger See MINSTREL.

Meitner, Lise (1878–1968) Austrian-born Swedish physicist. She was the second woman to obtain a doctorate from Vienna University, and became interested in radiochemistry. She worked in Germany with Otto Hahn, discovering the element protactinium with him in 1917, but fled the Nazis in 1938 to continue her research in Sweden. Meitner formulated the concept of nuclear fission with her nephew Otto Frisch, but, unlike him, refused to work on nuclear weapons. She retired to the UK in 1960.

Mekong A river of south-east Asia, that rises in Tibet and flows south-east and south for 4,180 km (2,600 miles) through southern China, Laos, Cambodia, and Vietnam to its extensive delta on the South China Sea. For part of its course it forms the boundary between Laos and its western neighbours Myanmar and Thailand. Its source was discovered by a joint Franco-British expedition in 1994.

Melaka (formerly **Malacca**) ▶**1** A state in south-west Malaysia, on the south-west coast of the Malay Peninsula, on the Strait of Malacca; area 1,658 sq km (640 sq miles); pop. (1980) 464,750. ▶**2** Its capital and chief port; pop. (1980) 88,070. It has been an important trading centre since it was founded *c.*1400 and is now a popular tourist resort.

Melanchthon, Philipp (born Philipp Schwarzerd) (1497–1560) German Protestant reformer. In 1521 he succeeded Luther as leader of the Reformation movement in Germany. Professor of Greek at Wittenberg, he helped to systematize Martin Luther's teachings in the *Loci Communes* (1521) and drew up the Augsburg Confession (1530).

Melanesia A region of the western Pacific to the south of Micronesia and west of Polynesia. Lying south of the equator, it contains the Bismarck Archipelago, the Solomon Islands, Santa Cruz, Vanuatu, New Caledonia, Fiji, and the intervening islands. It was the region of first human settlement in the Pacific.

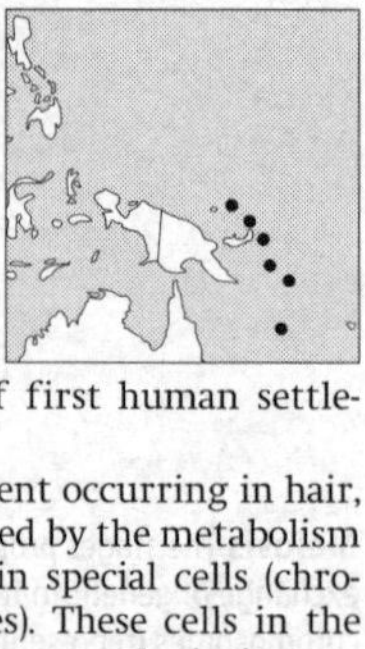

melanin A dark-brown pigment occurring in hair, skin, and the eye. It is produced by the metabolism of the amino acid tyrosine in special cells (chromatophores or melanophores). These cells in the epidermis of skin produce more melanin in sunlight (causing tanning), which protects the underlying skin layers from solar radiation.

melanoma A form of cancer that mainly occurs in the skin in melanin-forming cells. Excessive exposure to sunlight is a contributory factor. The cancer can spread to other parts of the body, especially the lymph nodes and liver. Surgical excision of tumours can effect a complete cure in many cases.

Melba, Dame Nellie (born Helen Porter Mitchell) (1861–1931) Australian operatic soprano. She was born near Melbourne, from which city she took her professional name. Melba gained worldwide fame with her coloratura singing.

Melbourne The capital of Victoria, south-east Australia, on the Bass Strait opposite Tasmania; pop. (1991) 2,762,000. Founded in 1835 and named after the British Prime Minister Lord Melbourne, it became state capital in 1851 and was capital of Australia from 1901 until 1927. Situated on Port Philip Bay, it is a major port, financial, commercial, and industrial centre, and the second-largest city in Australia. The Melbourne Cup horse-racing event is held annually in November. Melbourne has two universities: Monash (1958) and La Trobe (1964) and a famous Botanical Gardens (1845).

Melbourne, William Lamb, 2nd Viscount (1779–1848) British Whig statesman, Prime Minister (1834 and 1835–41). He was appointed Home Secretary under Lord Grey in 1830, before becoming Premier in 1834. Out of office briefly that year, he subsequently became chief political adviser to Queen Victoria after her accession in 1837. His term was marked by Chartist and anti-Corn Laws agitation. His wife, **Lady Caroline Lamb** (1785–1828), whom he married in 1805, had a notorious affair with Lord Byron, but the Lambs separated in 1825, before Lord Melbourne's premiership.

Meleager (fl. 1st century BC) Greek poet. He is best known as the compiler of *Stephanos*, one of the first large anthologies of epigrams. Meleager was also the author of many epigrams of his own and of short poems on love and death.

Mellon, Andrew W(illiam) (1855–1937) US financier and philanthropist. He donated his considerable art collection, together with funds, to establish the National Gallery of Art in Washington, DC, which opened in 1941.

melodeon See ACCORDION.

melodrama A popular form of sensational drama that flourished in the 19th-century theatre, surviving in different forms in modern cinema and television. A melodrama, meaning 'song-drama' in Greek, originally referred to plays or scenes accompanied by music, as in opera. In early 19th-century London, many theatres were only permitted to produce musical entertainments, and from their simplified plays the modern sense of melodrama derives: emotionally exaggerated conflicts of pure maidenhood and scheming villainy in a violent plot of suspense.

melody Any succession of musical notes, varying in pitch, with a recognizable and organized shape. Melody is the horizontal aspect of music, as opposed to its vertical aspect, HARMONY. Rhythm is an important element of melody: a change of rhythm can completely disguise a well-known tune. The music of many cultures has concentrated on melodic development, while harmony is a relatively modern invention and by no means universally adopted. Being closely associated with words (as in folk-song), melody reflects the characteristics of language and thus often conveys a sense of national identity.

melon A member of the very variable species of annual, sprawling plant, *Cucumis melo*. Originating in tropical Africa, melons are closely related to the cucumber and members of the pumpkin family.

The various types are distinguished mainly by characteristics of their fruit.

Melos (Greek **Mílos**) A Greek island in the Aegean Sea, in the south-west of the Cyclades group, midway between Athens and Crete; area 153 sq km (59 sq miles). It was the centre of a flourishing civilization in the Bronze Age and is the site of the discovery in 1820 of a Hellenistic marble statue of Aphrodite (the Venus de Milo), now in the Louvre in Paris. Minerals including sulphur, alum, kaolin, and barium are mined on the island, which was an important source of obsidian in ancient times.

melting-point The temperature at which solid and liquid forms of a substance can exist together in equilibrium. It is the same as the FREEZING-POINT, but melting-point usually refers to substances that are solid at room temperature. The melting-point of a pure material is usually lowered by the presence of impurities. It is generally measured at atmospheric pressure.

Melton Mowbray A town in Leicestershire, central England, on the River Wreake, whose name is associated with pork pies and Stilton cheeses; pop. (1991) 24,348.

Melville, Herman (1819–91) US novelist and short-story writer. After first going to sea in 1839, Melville made a voyage on a whaler to the South Seas in 1841; this experience formed the basis of several novels, including *Moby Dick* (1851). He is also remembered for his novella *Billy Budd* (first published in 1924), a symbolic tale of a mutiny, which inspired Benjamin Britten's opera of the same name (1951).

membrane (in biology) Any thin layer of tissue that encloses or covers part of a living organism. This includes multicellular membranes, such as the peritoneum, which encloses the organs of the mammalian abdomen, and the mucous membrane, which lines the intestine, genital, and respiratory tracts. Membrane that forms the boundary of a CELL is called plasma membrane. It is present in both plant and animal cells. Each cell membrane consists of a double layer of phospholipid and protein, and it serves to maintain the cell's integrity and to control the import and export of molecules.

Memlinc, Hans (or **Memling**) (*c.*1430–94) Netherlandish painter, active in Bruges. His softened and sweetened version of the style of Rogier van der WEYDEN (who is said to have been his teacher) made him the most popular Netherlandish painter of his day. Memlinc's paintings are quiet, restrained, and pious, his style changing very little during his career. There is a museum devoted to him in Bruges.

memory (in biology and psychology) The capacity of animals, including humans, to store information in the brain as a result of LEARNING. When an animal learns to associate two events, such as a stimulus followed by food, connections are made in the brain, which form a representation of these two events and their relationship to each other. This is what constitutes memory. It is an essential process enabling animals to suit their behaviour to the environment surrounding them, making use of the information learned by retrieving it at a later stage and applying it to a similar situation.

Psychologists have distinguished between two main types of memory. Short-term memory is used for the temporary holding of information that is of current concern. It has been associated with attention and the contents of consciousness, although now it is described as a 'working memory', by contrast with the long-term memory that contains inactive stored information, which can be retrieved and placed into short-term holding if required for current thought processes. Psychologists also distinguish different parts of memory in the long-term store, those for visual images, personal life-events, knowledge of word meanings, and skilled physical behaviour, for example. It is thought that some long-term change in the brain's physiology must act as a mechanism for memory, possibly through changes in the connections between nerve fibres. The mechanism of short-term memory is thought possibly to be electrical in nature, involving the temporary activation of information being currently processed or 'thought about' by the brain. The study of MEMORY DISORDERS may throw light on some of these questions.

memory (in computing) The part of a COMPUTER system used to store DATA temporarily or permanently. There are many types, each with a specific application. Most types of computer memory are made from SEMICONDUCTORS. For very high-speed operations associated with the CENTRAL PROCESSING UNIT (CPU), real (primary) memory is used. This includes read-only memory (ROM) and random access memory (RAM). Information is stored permanently in a ROM and cannot normally be altered once programmed, but various types of erasable programmable ROM (EPROM) are now quite common. Computers use ROM-based information for some essential tasks, such as BOOTSTRAPPING. The OPERATING SYSTEM and some small programs may also be stored in ROM. RAMs are used for short-term storage of information and programs, including instructions, data, and partial results, and are intimately associated with the high-speed operation of the CPU. Virtual (secondary) memory is not directly addressable by the CPU, but is used to store much larger amounts of data, although this is only accessible at relatively low speeds compared with the operation of the computer. It usually resides on disk units, such as HARD and FLOPPY DISKS. Cache memory is a small but very fast memory interposed between a computer and its main memory. The computer first checks whether data is in the cache before going to the (relatively slow) main memory. A new erasable computer memory chip made partly from a CERAMIC, and known as a ferroelectric random-access memory (FRAM), is under development. It retains data when its power source is switched off, and could eventually replace ROM and RAM.

memory disorder An inability either to recall previously learned knowledge or to retain new knowledge after brain damage. **Retrograde amnesia** results in not being able to recall events prior to the onset of the amnesia (memory loss), though how far back in time this period extends varies, typically shrinking with time. A common cause of brain damage resulting in amnesia is head injury in road accidents. APHASIA, the loss of learned speech skills, may result from such a blow. Deficiency of thiamine (vitamin B_1), which can result from excessive alcohol drinking, can cause amnesia, which is also associated with DEMENTIA. There is no agreement about how normal memory functions, and no accepted treatment for memory loss; eventual spontaneous recovery is common in amnesia from head injury.

Memphis An ancient city of Egypt, whose ruins are situated on the Nile about 15 km (10 miles) south of Cairo. It is thought to have been founded as the capital of the Old Kingdom of Egypt in *c.*3100 BC by King Menes, the ruler of the Egyptian dynasty, who united the former kingdoms of Upper and Lower Egypt. Associated with the god Ptah, it remained one of Egypt's principal cities even after Thebes was made capital of the New Kingdom in *c.*1570 BC. It is the site of the pyramids of Saqqara and Giza and the great sphinx.

Memphis A river port and railway junction on the Mississippi in the extreme south-west of Tennessee, USA; pop. (1990) 610,340. Founded in 1819, it is named after the ancient Egyptian city because of its river location. Memphis is a leading commercial centre trading in cotton and agricultural produce.

Menai Strait A channel separating Anglesey from the mainland of north-west Wales. It is spanned by two bridges, the first built by Thomas Telford between 1819 and 1826, the second (a railway bridge) built on the foundations of the Britannia Tubular Bridge constructed by Robert Stephenson between 1846 and 1850, and burnt down in 1970.

Menander (*c.*342–*c.*290 BC) The leading writer of COMEDY in the Hellenistic period of GREEK THEATRE. An Athenian, he wrote 100 plays, of which one complete play (*The Ill-Tempered Man*) has come to light, together with substantial fragments of several others. His plays deal with domestic situations and his verse stays close to colloquial speech.

menarche See MENSTRUATION.

Mencius (Chinese name Meng-tzu or Mengzi, 'Meng the Master') (*c.*371–*c.*289 BC) Chinese philosopher. He is noted for developing Confucianism; two of his central doctrines were that rulers should provide for the welfare of the people and that human nature is intrinsically good. His teachings, contained in one of the Four Books of Confucianism, formed the basis of primary and secondary education in imperial China from the 14th century.

Mencken, H(enry) L(ouis) (1880–1956) US journalist and literary critic. From 1908 he boldly attacked the political and literary Establishment, championing such diverse writers as George Bernard Shaw, Nietzsche, and Mark Twain. He strongly opposed the dominance of European culture in the USA, and in his book *The American Language* (1919) defended the vigour and versatility of colloquial American usage.

Mendel, Gregor Johann (1822–84) Moravian monk, the father of genetics. From his experiments with peas, he demonstrated that parent plants showing different characters produced hybrids exhibiting the dominant parental character, and that the hybrids themselves produced offspring in which the parental characters re-emerged unchanged and in precise ratios. After the rediscovery of Mendel's work in 1900, Mendelism was often thought, wrongly, to be the antithesis of the Darwinian theory of natural selection; in fact, Mendel had demonstrated the primary source of variability in plants and animals, on which natural selection could then operate.

Mendeleev, Dmitri (Ivanovich) (1834–1907) Russian chemist. He developed the periodic table, in which the chemical elements are classified according to their relatively atomic masses (atomic weights) in groups with similar properties. This allowed him to systematize much chemical knowledge, pinpoint elements with incorrectly assigned atomic weights, and successfully predict the discovery of several new elements. His study of gases and liquids led him to the concept of critical temperature, independently of Thomas Andrews.

mendelevium (symbol Md, at. no. 101, r.a.m. 256) A radioactive transuranic element belonging to the ACTINIDE group. The element was first identified in 1955 and all isotopes have very short half-lives.

Mendelssohn, Felix (full name Jakob Ludwig Felix Mendelssohn-Bartholdy) (1809–47) German composer and pianist. As a child prodigy, Mendelssohn first performed in public at the age of nine, proceeding to compose a String Octet at 16 and the overture to *A Midsummer Night's Dream* at 17. His romantic music is known for its elegance and lightness, as well as its melodic inventiveness. Other works include the overture *Fingal's Cave* (also called *The Hebrides*; 1830–32, writen on a visit to Britain), his violin concerto (1844), and the oratorio *Elijah* (1846).

Mendès-France, Pierre (1907–82) French statesman. Elected as a Radical-Socialist Deputy in 1932, he was an economics minister in the government of Leon BLUM in 1938. He was imprisoned by the VICHY GOVERNMENT, escaped to London (1941), and joined the exiled Free French government of General DE GAULLE. He became Premier in May 1954, after the disaster of DIEN BIEN PHU, promising that France would pull out of Indo-China. He resigned from the Radical Party in 1959, after which he never had an effective power-base, becoming increasingly opposed to the autocratic use of presidential power by de Gaulle.

Mendips, the (or **Mendip Hills**) A range of limestone hills in Somerset, south-west England, rising to 325 m (1,068 ft) at Black Down. The Cheddar Gorge cuts through the hills and there are many underground caverns such as Wookey Hole.

Mendoza, Antonio de (*c.*1490–1552) Spanish colonial administrator. He served as the first viceroy of New Spain (which centred on present-day Mexico City) from 1535 to 1550, and did much to improve relations between Spaniards and American Indians, fostering economic development (especially in mining) and educational opportunities for both groups. From 1551 he was viceroy of Peru.

Menelaus In Greek mythology, a king of Sparta, the brother of Agamemnon and the husband of Helen. When Helen was abducted by Paris, Menelaus appealed to the other Greek kings to join him in waging war on Troy. After Troy's defeat, Helen returned with him to Sparta.

Menes Egyptian pharaoh, reigned *c.*3100 BC. He founded the first dynasty that ruled ancient Egypt and is traditionally held to have united Upper and Lower Egypt with Memphis as its capital.

Ménière's disease A disease of the inner ear that causes episodes of deafness, ringing in the ears (**tinnitus**), and dizziness. It is thought to be caused by the build-up of fluid in the inner ear. It can be helped by the insertion of grommets and the use of various drugs. It was first described by the French physician P. Ménière (1799–1862).

menhir A standing stone. See MEGALITH.

meningitis Inflammation of the membranes (meninges) covering the brain and spinal cord, which are the dura mater, pia mater, and arachnoid membranes. Bacterial meningitis is most commonly caused by *Streptococcus pneumoniae*, *Haemophilus influenzae* type B, and *Neisseria meningitidis* (meningococcal meningitis). The **Hib vaccine**, which provides protection against *H. influenzae* type B, is now routinely administered to infants in the UK. Meningococcal meningitis is transmitted by inhalation of droplets derived from an infected patient. Tuberculous meningitis is caused by *Mycobacterium tuberculosis* derived as a result of TUBERCULOSIS. *Listeria monocytogenes*, found in contaminated food, may also cause bacterial meningitis, especially in patients with IMMUNODEFICIENCY, diabetics, and pregnant women. Bacterial meningitis usually arises from respiratory or ear infection from which the organisms gain entry into the meninges. Symptoms of meningitis include fever, headache, vomiting, neck stiffness, excessive shivering, and delirium; other symptoms may include convulsions, deafness, facial paralysis, and impaired consciousness. Meningococcal meningitis may also cause a skin rash. Viral meningitis may be caused by a range of viruses including mumps virus, influenza virus, and human immunodeficiency virus; it is much less serious than bacterial meningitis and complete recovery is usually attained.

Mennonite A member of a Protestant sect originating in Friesland in the 16th century, maintaining principles similar to those of the Anabaptists, being opposed to infant baptism, the taking of oaths, military service, and the holding of civic offices. In the following centuries many emigrated, first to other European countries and to Russia, later to North, Central, and South America, in search of political freedom.

menopause The time in a woman's life when MENSTRUATION becomes irregular and finally ceases. It happens normally between the ages of 45 and 55. A decline in activity of the ovaries, which fail to respond to the pituitary gland's gonadotrophic hormones, leads to reduction in the output of oestrogen, a female sex hormone.

During this period physical symptoms, such as hot flushes (sensations of warmth spreading up to the face), sweating, obesity, and some wasting away of breasts, uterus, and vagina may occur. Emotional problems and depressions can trouble some women. Severe menopausal symptoms due to oestrogen deficiency may be helped by HORMONE REPLACEMENT THERAPY.

Menorca The Spanish name for MINORCA.

Menotti, Gian Carlo (1911–) Italian-born US composer. *Amelia goes to the Ball* (1935) established him as a successful opera composer, and his importance in this field was consolidated by such works as *The Medium* (1945), *The Telephone* (1946), *Amahl and the Night Visitors* (1951), and most particularly *The Consul* (1949). His style is basically tonal and depends upon unabashed melody, piquant harmony, and a flair for theatrical effect.

Mensa The Table Mountain, a CONSTELLATION near the south celestial pole. It was introduced by the 18th-century French astronomer Nicolas Louis de Lacaille in honour of Table Mountain in southern Africa, from where he observed the southern stars in 1751–52. The Large MAGELLANIC CLOUD, part of which lies in the constellation, represents the cloud that caps the real Table Mountain. Mensa is a faint constellation, with no stars brighter than fifth magnitude.

Menshevik See BOLSHEVIK.

menstruation A phase of the menstrual cycle of sexually mature women. A flow of blood, cell debris, and mucus from the inner lining of the uterus escapes from the vagina for about five days. It occurs once a month on average from the first menstrual cycle, or **menarche**, until the MENOPAUSE.

The menstrual cycle is under hormonal control. Gonadotrophins from the pituitary, acting on the ovary, induce an output of oestrogen, the shedding of an ovum about two weeks after menstruation begins, and release of progesterone. Oestrogen and progesterone cause renewal of the linings of the uterus cast away during menstruation. Should the ovum, on its passage to the uterus, become fertilized, it implants there. Implantation induces hormonal adjustments, which prevent the appearance of menstruation, an early indication of pregnancy.

mental handicap Imperfect mental development, characterized by limited intelligence and a restricted capacity to learn the social and intellectual skills for independent living. Mental handicap, which is usually present at birth and is a permanent DISABILITY, should be distinguished from MENTAL ILLNESS, which usually affects adults and is often successfully treated. Among its many causes are genetic and chromosomal abnormalities; damage to the foetus through the mother's heavy drinking or drug use, or through an infection, such as rubella; and injury at birth. Levels of mental handicap, which are measured by INTELLIGENCE TESTS, range from mild (indicating slow development), to profound (indicating the need for constant care). The most severely affected often have multiple disabilities of sight, hearing, speech, and movement. In industrialized countries, about 2 per cent of the population are mentally handicapped, of whom one-fifth are severely affected.

mental illness A disorder of the mind. Mental illnesses include PSYCHOSES (severe conditions, such as SCHIZOPHRENIA and MANIC DEPRESSION), NEUROSES (less severe but none the less distressing conditions, such as PHOBIAS and OBSESSIONS), DEPRESSION, DEMENTIA, and PERSONALITY DISORDERS. Mental illness is widespread, those at special risk including victims of disaster, communal conflict, and war; refugees and migrants; older people and ethnic minorities. Bereavement, marriage breakdown, and unemployment also place people at risk. The World Health Organization estimates that at any time at least 350 million people are affected by it worldwide. Many forms of treatment are available (see PSYCHIATRY), and in the UK, as elsewhere, the vast majority of people are treated through the primary health care services or as out-patients. Of the small minority requiring hospital admission most enter voluntarily, only a few being subject to compulsion.

Menuhin, Yehudi, Baron (1916–) US-born violinist of Russian parentage, who became a British subject in 1985. A child prodigy, Menuhin studied with the Romanian composer and violinist George Enescu (1881–1955) before his 1927 New York début. In 1932, at the age of 16, he recorded Elgar's violin concerto, the composer conducting. Bartók wrote his solo violin sonata for him (1942). Among the most notable modern violin virtuosi, he has directed the Bath Festival and founded a school for young musicians.

Menzies, Sir Robert Gordon (1894–1978) Australian Liberal statesman, Prime Minister 1939–41 and 1949–66. Australia's longest-serving Prime Minister, he implemented policies resulting in fast industrial growth in the 1950s and gave impetus to the development of Australian universities. Menzies was noted for his anti-Communism, making an abortive attempt to abolish the Australian Communist Party in 1951 and actively supporting the USA in the Vietnam War.

mercantilism The 17th-century economic belief that aimed to exploit natural resources fully to promote exports and limit imports. Mercantilists believed that the possession of gold or 'bullion' was all-important and countries without a source of precious metal must obtain it by commerce; a nation's WEALTH was seen as chiefly dependent on its BALANCE OF TRADE. Trading was controlled by government-backed companies, tariffs were imposed, and trade wars, such as the ANGLO-DUTCH WARS were fought. Later supporters of free trade (*laissez-faire*) opposed the mercantilist theory that the volume of trade is fixed and that to increase one's share one must lessen that of others. In a celebrated essay of 1752, HUME contradicted the mercantilist view, arguing that a country's bullion reserves were essentially determined by the size of its economy and its consequential need for MONEY as a circulating medium, and would not be permanently influenced either way by government interference with trade.

Mercator, Gerardus (born Gerhard Kremer) (1512–94) Flemish geographer and cartographer, resident in Germany from 1552. He is best known for inventing the system of map projection that is named after him. In the **Mercator Projection** lines of longitude are parallel. Principally used by navigators because compass courses appear as straight lines, this projection tends to distort land areas in the higher latitudes, making them appear too large. His world map of 1569 showed a navigable North-west Passage between Asia and America, and a large southern continent. Mercator is also credited with introducing the word *atlas* to refer to a book of maps, following the publication of his *Atlas* of part of Europe (1585).

mercenary A soldier who joins an army (usually a foreign army) for payment, rather than from political obligation or affiliation. Most mercenaries serve in the ranks, not as officers. Before the rise of nationalism in Europe, many armies were composed of mercenaries; poor conditions or disaffection often caused them to desert to seek a better living in another army. In the modern era, mercenaries from Europe have frequently been engaged to fight in other countries, particularly in Africa. They often take part in CIVIL WARS, being hired either by government forces or by rebel forces.

merchandizing The promotion of GOODS and services for sale to consumers, particularly through advertising, packaging, and display. Merchandizing at the point of sale in retail trading outlets can take the form of packaging, window displays, labelling, devising a special layout, offering discounts or free samples and gifts, and promotion of sales by staff. In the USA merchandizing includes the wider functions of MARKETING.

Merchant, Ismail (1936–) Indian film producer. In 1961 he became a partner with James IVORY in Merchant Ivory Productions and is noted for a number of films made in collaboration with Ivory, including *Shakespeare Wallah* (1965), *The Europeans* (1979), *The Bostonians* (1984), *Howard's End* (1992), and *The Remains of the Day* (1993).

Mercia A former kingdom of central England. It was established by invading Angles in the 6th century AD in the border areas between the new Anglo-Saxon settlements in the east and the Celtic regions in the west. Becoming dominant in the 8th century under Offa, it expanded to cover an area stretching from the Humber to the south coast. Its decline began after Offa's death in 796 and in 926, when Athelstan became king of all England, it finally lost its separate identity. In modern times the name has been revived, for example, in the 'West Mercia Authority', an area of police administration covering the counties of Hereford and Worcester, and Shropshire.

Merckx, Eddy (1945–) Belgian racing cyclist. During his professional career he won the Tour de France five times (1969–72 and 1974). He also gained five victories in the Tour of Italy between 1968 and 1974.

Mercosur (Portuguese **Mercosul**) A regional trade organization in South America, whose full title is the Southern Cone or South American Common Market. Founded in March 1991, with the aim of creating a common market in the area, Mercosur's member states are Argentina, Brazil, Paraguay, and Uruguay. Following protracted negotiations on tariffs, the final presidential accord to create the customs union was signed on 17 December 1994 and Mercosur was inaugurated on 1 January 1995. Chile joined as an associate member in 1996. Mercosur and the European Union signed a cooperation agreement in 1995 and pledged to open negotiations on the eventual creation of a Mercosur–EU free trade zone.

Mercouri, Melina (born Anna Amalia Mercouri) (1925–94) Greek actress and politician. She came to international prominence with her roles in films, such as *Never on Sunday* (1960) and *Phaedra* (1962). She was exiled and deprived of her nationality owing to her active opposition to the military junta which took power in Greece in 1967, but was elected to Parliament in the socialist government of 1978, becoming Minister of Culture in 1985.

mercury (symbol Hg, at. no. 80, r.a.m. 200.59) A silver-coloured metallic element belonging to Group 12 (formerly IIB) of the periodic table. Mercury is the only pure metal that is a liquid at room temperature. It is rather unreactive but forms complexes and organomercury compounds; it forms compounds in which it shows VALENCY 2 and a few less stable compounds where its valency is 1. The main ore, cinnabar (MgS), is reduced to mercury by roasting in air, and purified by distillation. Most metals dissolve in mercury; the solutions are called AMALGAMS. Having a very high surface tension, it does not wet glass, and it is therefore widely used in THERMOMETERS and BAROMETERS. As an electrical conductor it is employed in switches and relays. When an electric discharge is passed through mercury vapour, it gives off a blue light, and mercury discharge lamps are widely used. Important compounds include mercury(II) chloride ($HgCl_2$), which is an antiseptic and fungicide, and mercury(II) oxide (HgO) and sulphide (HgS), which are pigments. Their use is limited, because mercury and its compounds are highly toxic.

Mercury (in Roman mythology) The god of commerce, travel, and theft, and the winged messenger of the other gods – associated with Hermes in Greek mythology.

Mercury (in astronomy) The innermost PLANET of the Solar System. It is visible as a MAGNITUDE 0 star at approximately two-monthly intervals alternating between the evening and morning twilight. The planet follows a remarkably elliptical orbit moving from 46 to 70 million kilometres from the Sun and completes one orbit every 88 days. In a small telescope it shows PHASES like those of the Moon, due to its varying position relative to the Earth and Sun. Very occasionally, the Earth, Mercury, and the Sun line up precisely and the planet is then seen to TRANSIT the Sun as a small dark spot crossing the solar disc. This last occurred on 12 November 1986 and will occur again on 14 November 1999. Observations of faint dusky markings seen on Mercury through large telescopes around 1900 led astronomers to conclude that the planet rotated on its axis and revolved round the Sun at the same 88-day rate, keeping the same face pointing sunwards. After being accepted for 80 years, the 88-day rotation period was finally replaced by the correct 58.5-day period deduced from radar observations. Mercury is 4,878 km in diameter, midway in size between Mars and the Moon.

Mercury, Freddie (born Frederick Bulsara) (1946–91) British rock singer, born in Zanzibar. He was the camp, outrageous vocalist of the band Queen, which formed in 1971. Queen initially played heavy rock but soon added extravagant, almost operatic elements to their sound, as exemplified by the hugely successful 'Bohemian Rhapsody' (1975). Their appearance at the international event Live Aid (1985) brought them still further acclaim. Mercury died of Aids in November 1991, and the group disbanded.

Meredith, George (1828–1909) British novelist and poet. His semi-autobiographical verse collection *Modern Love* (1862) describes the disillusionment of married love. Meredith's reputation rests chiefly on his novels, particularly *The Egoist* (1879).

merganser (or **sawbill**) A largely coastal duck that chases fish under water. Unlike other ducks, mergansers have slender, tapering beaks, each mandible of which is edged with saw-like teeth for grasping slippery prey. The seven species include the red-breasted merganser, *Mergus serrator*, the goosander, *Mergus merganser*, and the smew, *Falco columbarius*. Most of them have crests.

meridian An imaginary circle of constant longitude, passing through a given place and the north and south poles. It is described by the angle it forms east or west of the which has a value of 0° and runs through Greenwich in England.

Merionethshire A former county of north-west Wales, which became part of the county of Gwynedd in 1974. Its county town was Dolgellau.

merlin (or **pigeon hawk**) A small, swift FALCON, *Falco columbarius*, widespread in northern Europe, Asia, and North America as eight or nine subspecies. Their swift, erratic flight enables them to strike at birds and insects on the wing. In winter they fly south to warm temperate and tropical areas such as North Africa.

Merlin In Celtic mythology, the enchanter and wise man associated with the Arthurian legends, whose alleged prophecies were a potent influence in medieval Europe. Linked with personages in earlier Celtic mythology, in particular with Myrddin in Wales, Merlin used his magic arts to bring about the birth of Arthur and acted as counsellor for his future kingship. In some versions, his love for Nineve, the Lady of the Lake, led to his death.

mermaid In world mythology, a sea-creature with the head and body of a woman, and a fish's tail in place of legs. Thought of as beautiful but treacherous, mermaids are said to lure sailors to their death. Mermaids and their male counterparts, mermen, have been a part of maritime mythology since ancient Babylonian, Semitic, and Greek civilizations. It is suggested that the manatee (sea-cow), related to the dugong, seen from a distance, may have added credence in such creatures.

Merovingians A dynasty of kings of the FRANKS, named after Mérovée (died 458), the grandfather of CLOVIS. The Merovingians were warriors rather than administrators, few of them showing any interest in government. After the death of Dagobert I in 638, power passed from the kings to the 'mayors of the palace'. The mayor of the palace was originally the head of the royal household and came to represent royal authority in the country, administer the royal domains, and command the army in the king's absence. The most notable mayors of the palace were Pepin (ruled 687–714), CHARLES MARTEL (ruled 714–41), famous for his victories over SARACEN invaders from Spain, and PEPIN, the father of CHARLEMAGNE, who in 751 deposed the last of the Merovingian kings and usurped the throne.

Mersey A river in north-west England, which rises in the Peak District and flows 112 km (70 miles) to the Irish Sea near Liverpool.

Merseyside A metropolitan county of north-west England; area 652 sq km (252 sq miles); pop. (1991) 1,376,800. Administered by a separate council until 1986, it is divided into five districts.

Merthyr Tydfil An industrial town and county borough in South Wales; pop. (1991) 44,767 (town).

mesembryanthemum (or **Livingstone daisy**) A member of a large family of succulent plants, Aizoaceae, containing 1,500 species, found mainly in South Africa. The leaves are swollen and fleshy, and most species are adapted to grow under arid, desert-like conditions. In some, only two leaves are produced on a very short stem and the relatively large flower is produced from a slit between the leaves. The flowers are, for the most part, large and colourful, as in the popular garden annual *Mesembryanthemum criniflorum*.

Meseta See IBERIAN PENINSULA.

mesite Any one of three little-known species of bird, *Mesites unicolor*, *M. variegata* and *Monias benschi*, belonging to the family Mesithornithidae, confined to Madagascar. They belong to the same order as rails, bustards and cranes, but their relationships are uncertain. These unusual birds are about 25 cm (10 inches) long, and greyish, greenish, or brownish in colour. They feed on a wide range of snails and insects and build nests of twigs low down in bushes.

Mesmer, Franz Anton (1734–1815) Austrian physician. He had a successful practice in Vienna, where he used a number of novel treatments. Mesmer is chiefly remembered for introducing hypnotism – formerly known as **animal magnetism** or **mesmerism** – as a therapeutic technique. However, it was much steeped in archaic ideas, mysticism, and sensationalism, and Mesmer effectively retired following the critical report of a royal commission in 1784.

Meso-America The central region of America, from northern Mexico to Nicaragua, especially as a region of ancient civilizations and Native American cultures before the arrival of the Spanish settlers.

Mesolithic The Middle Stone Age, a transitional period between the PALAEOLITHIC and NEOLITHIC ages. Its people were the hunting and gathering groups that existed about 10,000 years ago as the climate became warmer at the end of the last Ice Age. In western Europe, Mesolithic hunting societies continued to exist at the same time as Neolithic farming groups further east.

meson A strongly interacting elementary particle composed of a QUARK and an antiquark. Mesons form one of the two main groups of HADRONS (the others being the BARYONS) and have either zero or integral SPIN.

mesopause The upper boundary of the MESOSPHERE at a height of around 75 km (47 miles). This is the coldest part of the atmosphere and the temperature is about −90°C. The mesopause is above the OZONE layer and below the IONOSPHERE, both of which are relatively warm. The atmospheric pressure in this region is about one millionth of that at sea-level and the molecules move about a centimetre before striking other molecules.

Mesopotamia An ancient region of south-west Asia in present-day Iraq, lying between the rivers Tigris and Euphrates. Its alluvial plains were the site of the ancient civilizations of Akkad, Sumer, Babylonia, and Assyria, now lying within Iraq.

mesosphere The region of the atmosphere extending from the top of the stratosphere to an altitude of about 80 km (50 miles).

Mesozoic The geological era between the Palaeozoic and Cenozoic, comprising the Triassic, Jurassic, and Cretaceous periods, and lasting from about 248 to 65 million years ago. It was a time of abundant vegetation and saw the dominance of dinosaurs and other reptiles, although by its close they were being rapidly replaced by mammals.

mesquite A deciduous tree of the genus *Prosopis* of tropical America, with a taproot that reaches down 15 m (50 feet) or more. This characteristic makes it valuable in reafforestation of devastated dry country. It is a member of the pea family, and produces protein-rich 'beans', which are used as fodder. There are some 40 species of *Prosopis*, and all those in cultivation are also called algaroba.

Messalina, Valeria (or **Messallina**) (*c*.22–48 AD) Roman empress, third wife of Claudius. She married her second cousin Claudius in about 39, and became notorious in Rome for the murders she instigated in court and for her extramarital affairs. She was executed on Claudius' orders, after the disclosure of her secret marriage to one of his political opponents.

Messerschmidt, Wilhelm Emil (known as 'Willy') (1898–1978) German aircraft designer and industrialist. Messerschmidt designed and constructed his first glider in 1915 and set up a company in 1923, while still a student. The Nazi authorities encouraged the development of aircraft in the 1930s, resulting in the Messerschmidt 109, which became the standard fighter of the Luftwaffe during World War II. Messerschmidt continued to be active in aerospace companies until his death.

Messiaen, Olivier (Eugène Prosper Charles) (1908–92) French composer. Messiaen was organist of the church of La Trinité in Paris for more than 40 years. His music shows many influences, including Greek and Indian rhythms, birdsong, the music of Stravinsky and Debussy, and the composer's Roman Catholic faith. His *Quartet for the End of Time* for violin, clarinet, cello, and piano (1941) was written and first performed in a prison camp in Silesia during World War II. Other major works include *La Nativité du Seigneur* for organ (1935), the *Turangalîla Symphony* for large orchestra (1946–48), *Catalogues d'oiseaux* for piano (1956–58), and *La Transfiguration de Notre Seigneur Jésus-Christ* (1969) for chorus and orchestra.

Messiah The Old Testament concept of an annointed one (Hebrew *mashiah*) sent by God to bring eternal peace to mankind in general and the Jews in particular. In the Old Testament the Messiah is usually envisaged as a wise and resourceful king; in some Jewish traditions the proclamation of a king called David is a necessary condition for the coming of the Messiah.

In the New Testament the concept is interpreted differently. Jesus, the son of God, was regarded by his followers as the Messiah and was therefore called the Christ (from Greek *kristos*, the annointed one, a translation of the Hebrew *mashiah*). Although it is not entirely clear whether or not Jesus regarded himself as the Messiah, the question of Jesus' Messiahship remains one of the most intractable differences between Jews and Christians. Most Jews would regard the continual strife and warfare of the last 2,000 years, much of it inspired by Christianity itself, as an indication that the messianic event, if there is to be one, has yet to happen.

Messier, Charles (1730–1817) French astronomer. Without any technical training, Messier became a clerical assistant at the Paris Observatory and soon began a search for new comets that was to be his lifelong obsession. While doing so he came across a number of nebulae, galaxies, and star clusters, which he designated by M numbers and made into a list that had reached a total of 103 items by 1784. Almost all of these designations, such as M1 (the Crab Nebula), are still in use, though the list of such objects has been greatly extended.

Messina A busy seaport and commercial and industrial centre in north-east Sicily, Italy; pop. (1990) 274,850. Founded in 730 BC by the Greeks, it is situated on the Strait of Messina. In December 1908 the city was very badly damaged by an earthquake and tidal wave that killed 60,000 people.

Messina, Strait of A channel separating the island of Sicily from the 'toe' of Italy. It forms a link between the Tyrrenhian and Ionian seas. The strait, which is 32 km (20 miles) in length, is noted for the strength of its currents. It is traditionally identified as the location of the legendary sea monster Scylla and the whirlpool Charybdis.

mestizo (feminine **mestiza**) A Spaniard or Portuguese of mixed race, especially the offspring of a Spaniard and a Native American.

metabolism The chemical reactions taking place in an organism. Metabolism is subdivided into catabolism, in which complex substances are broken down into simpler ones, and anabolism, in which new compounds are built up.

The most important catabolic reactions are those of RESPIRATION and FERMENTATION, which release energy. A high proportion of the energy released in catabolism is in the form of heat. The overall rate of all these chemical reactions is called the metabolic rate; metabolic rate is usually expressed in terms of the amount of heat (in kilojoules) released per square metre of body surface per hour. The rate increases during times of growth, muscular activity, or illness, and decreases during inactivity. **Basal metabolic rate** (BMR) is the minimum rate of energy release needed to keep the organism alive. For an adult man, the BMR is about 165 kJ m^{-2} hr^{-1}, while for a woman about 150 kJ m^{-2} hr^{-1} is normal; children have a much higher BMR.

Anabolism uses basic organic compounds (originally produced by PHOTOSYNTHESIS) to make proteins, lipids, and other complex molecules. Anabolic processes use energy in the form of ATP, which has been produced by catabolic processes. The body of an organism normally maintains a delicate balance between catabolic and anabolic processes.

metal An element with characteristic properties which are a consequence of its electronic structure. Metals constitute the largest set of elements and are generally shiny, malleable and ductile, and good conductors of heat and electricity. These properties result from their structure; this consists of a regular arrangement of positively charged ions, surrounded by ELECTRONS, which are free to move throughout the metal. This structure is held together by the **metallic bonds** deriving from the electrostatic attraction between the positive ions and the delocalized electrons. When metals are bombarded by ultraviolet or X-radiation, they emit electrons. Metals occur mainly on the left-hand side of the periodic table. Group 1 contains the ALKALI METALS, and Group 2 the ALKALINE EARTH METALS. The TRANSITION METALS, LANTHANIDES, and ACTINIDES are all metallic elements. Although a few metals are found uncombined, most occur naturally as their oxides or sulphides. Many of these can be reduced to the metals by carbon, but for reactive metals ELECTROLYSIS is needed. Metals react with non-metals to form ionic compounds in which the metal becomes positively charged. Many metals react with dilute acids, forming salts and giving off hydrogen. Metal oxides and hydroxides are usually basic – that is, they neutralize acids; some, such as aluminium oxide, Al_2O_3, are amphoteric – that is, they can also neutralize alkalis. Metals can be mixed with other metals, and with some non-metals, to form alloys. These are not true chemical compounds and do not have fixed compositions; they often have properties that differ from the pure metal, however, and alloying is often used to increase the strength or some other property of the metal.

metal detector An instrument for detecting hidden metal objects, developed during World War II to detect landmines. One type of metal detector has two tuned circuits, one carried in the head of the device. The presence of metal near the tuned circuit in the head changes its oscillating frequency. The difference between this frequency and the frequency in the other, reference, circuit creates a signal that can be heard through headphones or registered on a meter. Metal detectors have many applications: in the food industry, they are routinely used to test for metal contamination; archaeologists use them to survey their digs; and builders use them to detect hidden pipes or wiring.

metal fatigue The weakening and eventual failure of metals, resulting from the repeated application of loads far smaller than those required to cause failure in a single loading (stress cycle). In most metals the larger the number of stress cycles, the lower the stress level needed to cause failure. For such metals an endurance limit is quoted. However, for other metals, such as steel and titanium alloys, there is a definite stress level (the fatigue limit) below which fatigue failure will never occur. It has been estimated that 90 per cent of all mechanical failures are caused by fatigue. Parts of machines and engines that are subject to vibration are particularly susceptible. Fatigue failures often occur in a catastrophic manner, with no gross distortion preceding collapse. The size and location of the cracks formed in a structure by the fatigue process often make their detection during routine inspection almost impossible.

metalloid An element that cannot be classified as either a METAL or a NON-METAL; some common examples are boron, silicon, germanium, arsenic, and antimony. Metalloids lie in a diagonal band in the middle of the PERIODIC TABLE, between the metals on the left and the non-metals on the right. They are all SEMICONDUCTORS; unlike the non-metals, they do conduct electricity, although much less so than metals. Unlike metals, their conductivity increases with temperature. Because of their electrical properties, metalloids have been widely used in transistors and, more recently, in microelectronic circuitry.

metallurgy and metalworking The regular arrangement of atoms in metals gives them a crystalline structure not easily seen on the surfaces of polished metals, comprising a patchwork of irregular crystals called grains. The size, shape, orientation, and composition of these grains have a significant effect on the properties of the metal. In general, a metal with fine grains will be harder and stronger than one with coarse grains. The early workers of metal developed, by trial and error, techniques that modified the grain structure to produce desirable properties. Heat treatment, such as quenching, TEMPERING, or ANNEALING, controls the nature of the grains in the metal. Adding even small amounts of other metals (less than 1 per cent in some cases) to a pure metal can have a significant effect on its grain structure and hence its properties (see ALLOY). The variety of properties that can now be obtained is quite remarkable, with combinations of lightness, strength, and stiffness unimaginable 100 years ago.

The ways of working a metal are dependent on its properties. Many metals can be melted and cast in moulds, but special conditions are required for metals that react with air. POWDER METALLURGY allows complex shapes to be formed without melting. All metals can be formed by drawing, rolling, hammering, and EXTRUSION, but some require hot-working. Metals are subject to METAL FATIGUE, and to creep, the slow increase in length under stress causing deformation and eventually failure. Both effects are taken into account by engineers when designing, for example, aeroplanes, gas-turbines, and pressure vessels for high-temperature chemical processes. Metals can be shaped and finished by removing waste material, using machine-tools such as the lathe, milling machine, shaper, and grinder. See also CERMET; COMPOSITE.

metal mark (or **judy**) A butterfly found almost exclusively in the New World. The 1,000 or so species of small, colourful butterflies comprise the family Riodinidae, which also includes the snouts (Libythinae). Most species range from 2 cm (0.75 inch) to 6.5 cm (2.5 inches) in wing-span. In many ways they resemble the blue butterflies, some species having metallic colours. The sole European representative, the Duke of Burgundy fritillary, *Hamearis lucina*, is not a true fritillary, but resembles one in colour and pattern.

metamorphic rock Rock that has been altered by intense heat or pressure, or both. It may originally have been SEDIMENTARY ROCK or IGNEOUS ROCK, or even different metamorphic rock. The changes that take place during metamorphism can affect both the structure of the rock and its composition. Very often the rock is recrystallized. Contact metamorphism is a localized form of metamorphism that is produced by the heat of an IGNEOUS INTRUSION. Limestone may then be altered into marble, and clay into a hard, tough rock (a hornfels). The zone affected in this way is called a metamorphic aureole. Hydrothermal metamorphism, or metasomatism, is produced by hot aqueous fluids emanating from igneous intrusions. China clay is produced in this way from granite. In dynamic metamorphism, or cataclasis, rocks are broken down mechanically by shearing and crushing; mylonite, a fine-grained banded rock, is a typical product. Regional metamorphism takes place on a large scale. The rocks are subjected to heat, deformation, and the action of hot fluids that may affect their chemical composition. In the lowest grades of regional metamorphism, slates and phyllites (the latter with better-developed crystals than

SLATE) are formed. More intense regional metamorphism results in the development of SCHISTS, rocks with a characteristic wavy foliation. At the highest grades, GNEISSES are formed: coarsely crystalline rocks with alternate light and dark bands. The normal sequence, from lower to higher metamorphic grade, is known as prograde metamorphism. The process can be reversed if, for example, rocks of a high grade are subsequently maintained for a long time at a lower temperature than was reached during the first metamorphism. Alteration from a higher to a lower grade is retrograde metamorphism.

metamorphosis A change of form, and often of physiology, during the life cycle of an animal. Such changes are distinct from changes in size and those associated with sexual maturity. Metamorphosis is described as either complete or incomplete and it may be abrupt or gradual. In a complete metamorphosis, as between a caterpillar and a butterfly, an intermediate stage called the PUPA is found. In incomplete metamorphosis, as in a grasshopper, the young resemble the adults except that they have wing-buds in place of wings, and the feeding habits are the same. The most abrupt changes are also found in insects: a legless crawling maggot may turn into a housefly in the course of a few days. The transformation from tadpole to frog is an example of gradual metamorphosis, with the development of legs, and loss of gills and tail, taking place over a considerable period. Metamorphosis does not imply an increase in complexity; many parasitic adult animals are much less structurally complex than the free-living larvae from which they derive.

metaphor A figure of speech in which one thing, idea, or action is referred to by the name of another, suggesting some common quality shared by the two. In metaphor, this resemblance is assumed as an imaginary identity rather than directly stated as a comparison: referring to a person as 'that pig' is metaphorical, whereas 'he is like a pig' is a SIMILE. The use of metaphor to create new combinations of ideas is a major feature of POETRY, but much of our everyday language is also made up of metaphorical words and phrases.

Metaphysical poets A group of 17th-century British poets who share certain characteristics of expression, notably DONNE, HERBERT, CRASHAW, COWLEY, VAUGHAN, TRAHERNE, and MARVELL. They are distinguished by their habitual use of elaborate and surprising metaphors: these are frequently taken from science or technology, rather than from nature or conventional mythology; a famous example is Donne's comparison of parted lovers to a pair of geometrical compasses. The poems often use an intimate or argumentative tone, and the natural language of a 'speaking voice'. The Metaphysicals were largely ignored until the revival of their reputation in the 20th century, notably by T. S. ELIOT.

metaphysics (from Greek, 'the things after the physics', from the ordering of ARISTOTLE's works) That branch of philosophy that studies the most general categories and concepts presupposed in descriptions of ourselves and the world. Examples are causality, substance, ONTOLOGY, TIME, and reality. Metaphysical questions have a very broad scope. Whereas the physical scientist might ask 'How does *x* cause *y*?', the metaphysician asks 'What does it mean for anything to cause anything else?' Whereas the chemist might investigate particular substances, the metaphysician asks what it means to be a substance, and whether there is one basic substance, or many. Metaphysical questions can become the subject of more specialized philosophical inquiry. We can ask whether our actions are subject to causality, which gives rise to the problem of FREE WILL. And the question of whether our mental experiences involve a separate substance from body is a major issue in the philosophy of mind. Although metaphysics dates back to the ancient Greeks, there have been occasions on which its status as a legitimate inquiry have been questioned. The rise of science in the 17th century led to attempts by some philosophers, such as HUME and LOCKE, to limit the claims of metaphysics, and earlier this century scientifically minded philosophers, such as the LOGICAL POSITIVISTS, claimed that metaphysical assertions were meaningless.

metasequoia A deciduous conifer of the genus *Metasequoia*, a primitive group of trees that flourished many millions of years ago and is related to the REDWOODS. The dawn redwood, *Metasequoia glyptostroboides*, was discovered in China in 1941 and is really a 'living fossil' as all other members of the genus are known only from fossils. It is readily recognized by the soft, pale green leaves arranged as flat 'fronds' in opposite pairs. It was confined to a single valley and in danger of extinction, but is now widely planted as an ornamental tree throughout temperate regions.

meteor The streak of light seen in a clear night sky when a METEOROID burns itself out in the Earth's upper atmosphere. The meteoroid has a velocity of between 74 km/s, if it hits the Earth head-on, and 11 km/s, if it is catching the Earth up. At these speeds the friction between the meteoroid and the atmosphere usually creates enough heat to vaporize it entirely and it burns up in the region between 75 and 115 km (50 to 70 miles) above the Earth's surface. The friction also causes the evaporating meteoroid to leave behind a thin stream of glowing atmospheric gas and a trail of ionized atoms and molecules, which can reflect radar pulses. Meteoroids that are visible or that can be detected by radar have masses of between a microgram and 1,000 kilograms. Meteoroids smaller than this are not visible and, after losing speed in the atmosphere, merely float down to the Earth's surface. Very large meteoroids that survive their journey through the atmosphere and reach the ground are called METEORITES. A typical visual meteor, also known as a **shooting star**, is produced by a meteoroid about a centimetre in size with a mass of about a tenth of a gram and a density of only about one-third that of water.

meteorite The remnant of a METEOROID that has survived its passage through the Earth's atmosphere as a METEOR. For a meteoroid to reach the Earth's surface its mass must be at least several grams and it must enter the upper atmosphere with a low velocity. Even then, only 25 per cent of the meteoroid remains to reach the ground. Meteorites are named after the geographical localities in which they are seen to fall or are found. Immediate recovery of meteorites that have been observed to fall gives a reasonably unbiased indication of the abundance of the different types. The vast majority (84 per cent) are CHONDRITE stones; 8 per cent are achondrites, that is, stones that have no chondrules; 1 per cent are stony-iron meteorites known as **siderolites**; and 7 per cent have an exceptionally high iron content. Meteorites that are recovered some time after they have fallen are frequently of the iron type, simply because they are easier to recognize in the ground; other types of meteorites tend to go unnoticed. About six new fallen meteorites are recovered each year. Stone meteorites have masses between about 100 grams and 1,500 kg and iron meteorites between a few grams and 20,000 kg. Meteorites smaller than a few grams are hard to find, even if they reach the Earth's surface, and those much larger than the largest recovered meteorites produce craters in the Earth's surface and are blown apart on impact.

meteoroid A small body that, if it enters and burns out in the Earth's atmosphere, produces a METEOR. Meteoroids are fragments of COMETS or are dust particles in the INTERPLANETARY MEDIUM, and have masses ranging from thousands of kilograms to less than a million millionth of a gram. The larger ones are porous, friable aggregates of stony or metallic dust. Meteoroids are often grouped into a METEOR STREAM, the debris of a decaying comet. If the Earth passes through such a stream a METEOR SHOWER is observed.

meteorological instrument An instrument for studying the Earth's atmosphere, especially weather-forming processes, and used in weather forecasting. In modern meteorology, three parameters are of particular significance: pressure, temperature, and wind-speed. These are measured by the BAROMETER, the THERMOMETER, and the ANEMOMETER, respectively. An important variation of the simple thermometer is the maximum-minimum thermometer, which records both maximum and minimum temperatures over a given period. Auxiliary instruments include hygrometers to measure humidity; precipitation gauges to measure falls of rain and snow; and gauges to measure the daily hours of sunshine. Weather is determined not only by conditions on the surface of the Earth but also by those high in the atmosphere. In the 18th century kites were used for upper-air measurements. They were replaced by manned and free balloons in the 19th century, but systematic recording has only been possible during the second half of the 20th century. This has involved high-altitude sounding balloons, aircraft, rockets, and METEOROLOGICAL SATELLITES, using telemetry to relay observations quickly to ground stations. Perhaps the most significant new meteorological tool is the COMPUTER. Extremely fast computers with large amounts of memory are needed to digest the vast amounts of observational data collected and formulate it into a forecast sufficiently quickly to be of use. Computer 'models' of the atmosphere can also be used to make longer-term, more speculative predictions of climate change.

meteorological satellite An artificial SATELLITE that orbits the Earth collecting information on the atmosphere and weather. The satellites carry radiometers, which measure light and infrared radiation from the clouds and from land and sea surfaces. These data, processed to produce visual images, give information on cloud heights and temperatures, land and sea surface temperatures, wind-speeds, and humidity. The satellites also collect information from remote automatic weather stations, such as buoys at sea, weather balloons, and aircraft, and relay it to ground stations.

meteorology The scientific study of the atmosphere on a global scale, within regions, and at particular localities, and the formation of conclusions as to forthcoming weather. It is especially concerned with the energy budget, water balance, and CIRCULATION, and involves the measurement of elements, such as pressure and temperature, instrumentally. Of other elements, such as cloud types and amounts of cloud, visual estimates are made. The interpretation of data and understanding atmospheric processes require a knowledge of mathematics and physics, together with an appreciation of the influence on atmospheric conditions of natural features, such as oceans and mountain ranges, and of unnatural environments such as large urban areas. Dynamical meteorology is concerned with atmospheric motion of all kinds, from small-scale cloud formation to the large-scale migrations of pressure areas that form part of the pattern of global circulation; and equations in HYDRODYNAMICS and THERMODYNAMICS are formulated to give mathematical precision to the descriptions and explanations. Synoptic meteorology is the branch of the science that forms the basis of weather forecasting. It involves study, on a day-to-day or hour-to-hour basis, of the changing patterns of elements, such as air temperature and pressure, wind speed and direction, and cloud cover.

meteor shower A group of METEORS that appear to come from the same point, known as the RADIANT, on the celestial sphere. A meteor shower occurs whenever the Earth passes through a METEOR STREAM, and the number of meteors per hour, known as the rate, reaches its peak when the Earth crosses the centre of the stream. The showers last for as long as the Earth is in the stream and this can vary from a day to a few weeks. Showers are named after the constellation in which the radiant lies.

meteor stream An elliptical ring of debris, principally dust and rubble, occupying the orbit of a COMET. As a comet approaches the Sun, radiation pressure and the SOLAR WIND cause dust and gas to be ejected. This debris has a velocity of a few kilometres per second with respect to the comet. Depending on the angle of emission some of the material gains on and some falls behind the cometary nucleus. Gradually the dust and gas spreads out right around the comet's orbit. The resulting ring gets broader as it ages but is thinner near perihelion than at aphelion. When the Earth's orbit intersects the meteor stream there is a chance of seeing a METEOR SHOWER. A meteor stream is also known as a **meteoroid stream**.

methanal (or **formaldehyde**, HCHO) A pungent flammable gas, the first member of the ALDEHYDES. Formed by the oxidation of methanol, it is usually stored either as its polymer, paraformaldehyde, from which it is re-formed on heating, or as its aqueous solution, formalin. It forms a variety of resins with phenol, for example the first synthetic plastic, Bakelite, and urea; and it is also used as a disinfectant and for embalming.

methane (CH_4) A colourless, odourless gas, and the simplest HYDROCARBON, being the first member of the ALKANE series. It is formed by the decomposition of organic matter in the absence of oxygen, as in swampy environments (hence the name marsh gas), and is the main constituent of the biogas produced at refuse dumps. Methane occurs widely as the main component of NATURAL GAS, being formed during the conversion of marine organic matter to OIL and of terrestrial organic matter to COAL. It is therefore common in coal-mines, where it is a constituent of firedamp. It is unreactive towards many chemical reagents but burns readily in air with a hot flame; it is widely used as a fuel for cooking and heating. Industrially it is reacted with steam at high temperatures to produce hydrogen. Methane is an important starting material for the manufacture of organic solvents, ammonia, methanol, and other chemicals.

methanoic acid (or **formic acid**, HCOOH) A colourless liquid with a pungent aroma, made by the action of sulphuric acid on sodium methanoate (NaCOOH), which is itself made from carbon monoxide and sodium hydroxide. Methanoic acid is used as a reducing agent (see OXIDATION AND REDUCTION) in the textile and leather industries, and has miscellaneous uses, including as a coagulant in making latex rubber, and as a food preservative.

methanol (or **methyl alcohol**, CH_3OH) The simplest ALCOHOL, a clear colourless liquid, sometimes known as wood spirit because it was first produced by destructive distillation of wood. It is now produced by the reaction of carbon oxides with hydrogen. Methanol is very toxic, causing blindness and death. It is used for ANTIFREEZE, as a solvent, and for the manufacture of methanal (formaldehyde) and other important industrial chemicals.

method acting See STANISLAVSKY.

Methodist A member of any of several Protestant religious bodies (now united) originating in an 18th-century evangelistic movement. This movement grew out of a religious society (nicknamed the 'Holy Club') established within the Church of England (from which it formally separated in 1791) by John and Charles Wesley at Oxford. Its theology is Arminian, and its ordained ministry usually presbyterian; its governing body is the Conference, composed of ministers and laymen. The United Methodist Church is the largest single Methodist Church; it had almost nine million members in 1989. The World Methodist Council, founded in 1881, provides a link between the 40 million Methodists in the world.

Methodius, St The brother of St CYRIL.

Methuselah The Hebrew patriarch who was the son of Enoch and grandfather of Noah. According to the Bible he fathered Lamech at 187 and died at the age of 969 years.

methylated spirits A mixture of distilled ETHANOL to which up to 10 per cent METHANOL has been added, making it unfit to drink. Traces of pyridine, to give an unpleasant taste, and a purple dye are often also added. Methylated spirits are used commercially as a fuel and as a solvent.

metre (in measurement; symbol m) The SI UNIT of length originally defined as one ten-millionth of the distance from the Equator to the North Pole, but since redefined a number of times to give a more accurate definition. The latest definition, agreed in 1983, is that a metre is the length of the path travelled by light in a vacuum in 1/299,792,458 of a second, the SPEED OF LIGHT being a universal constant. One metre is equal to 39.37 inches.

metre (in poetry) The regular but variable rhythmic pattern in verse lines. In English and other Germanic languages this pattern is based on combinations of stressed and unstressed syllables, but in some other languages it is the length ('quantity') of syllables (as in Greek and Latin or Arabic and Persian) or the number of syllables in a line (French, Japanese) that counts. Different metres are distinguished by the kind of metrical unit ('foot') that predominates in the poem: in English, iambic metres, such as the iambic PENTAMETER, are commonest, although trochees (reversed iambs), DACTYLS, and anapaests (reversed dactyls) are sometimes used instead.

metric system A system of measurement based on the decimal system. It has been widely used in Europe since the 1830s. It was formally introduced in France in 1791, when the METRE was first defined. This unit, together with the gram, litre, and are, were made legal standards in France in 1799. British affection for Imperial units prevented the adoption of metric units until the 1960s. The Metrication Board, set up in 1969 with the task of completing the metrication of British industry within six years, was disbanded in 1980 having failed to meet its target. In science and engineering the metric-based SI UNITS are now used throughout Europe and the UK, but not entirely in the USA. The UK retains Imperial units for beer and milk and signposts still give distances in miles. Some groceries are now sold by the kilo, but some are still sold by the pound. The protracted transition period, due to end in the year 2000, is likely to extend well into the next millennium.

metronome A device for setting the tempo of a musical composition by reference to the number of beats per minute. This can be as simple as a pendulum, whose swing varies with its length, or more sophisticated, like the 19th-century clockwork Maelzel Metronome or the present-day battery-operated electronic version, which can tick or flash as required. The composer sometimes places a 'metronome mark' at the head of the score as a guide to the preferred speed.

Metropolitan Museum of Art A museum of art and archaeology on 5th Avenue in New York City, USA. Opened in 1880, it is the largest repository of art and antiquities in the Western Hemisphere. There are 18 departments and 248 galleries.

Metternich, Klemens Wenzel Nepomuk Lothar, Prince of Metternich-Winneburg-Beilstein (1773–1859) Austrian statesman. As Foreign Minister (1809–48), he was one of the organizers of the Congress of Vienna (1814–15), which devised the settlement of Europe after the Napoleonic Wars. He pursued policies that reflected his reactionary conservatism at home and abroad until forced to resign during the revolutions of 1848.

Metz An industrial city in Lorraine, north-east France on the River Moselle near the German border; pop. (1990) 123,920. Formerly the capital of the medieval Frankish kingdom of Austrasia, the city grew to prosperity in the 13th century when it was a free town within the Holy Roman Empire, ruled by a virtually independent bishop. Annexed in 1552 by Henry II of France, who defended it against a siege by the Emperor Charles V in the same year, it was formally ceded to France in 1648. It fell to a siege by the Prussians in 1870 and was annexed to the German Empire in 1871. It was restored to France in 1918, after World War I, and is now capital of the department of Moselle. Metz lies at the centre of a fertile agricultural area and the iron and steel region of Lorraine.

Meuse (Flemish and Dutch **Maas**) A river of western Europe, which rises in north-east France and flows 950 km (594 miles) through Belgium and the Netherlands to the North Sea south of Dordrecht.

Mexican-American War (1846–48) A conflict between the USA and Mexico. Hostilities between the two countries began shortly after the USA annexed (1845) the Mexican state of TEXAS and sought to expand the boundaries of the state to include still more territory. In the ensuing war General Stephen Kearny took over the New Mexico territory and Captain John FRÉMONT annexed the California territory almost without a fight. In northern Mexico stiffer opposition was encountered as General Zachary Taylor invaded Mexico across the Rio Grande and defeated General Antonio López de Santa Anna in the bloody Battle of Buena Vista (22–23 February 1847). The fiercest fighting occurred in central Mexico. General Winfield Scott's order of a mortar bombardment of Vera Cruz resulted in the deaths of hundreds of civilians. The US army then moved inland to Mexico City, where hotly contested engagements were fought at Molino del Rey, and Chapultepec Hill (12–13 September 1847). The US capture of the capital city (1847) occasioned the Mexican surrender. The Treaty of Guadalupe Hidalgo (1848) ended hostilities. By the terms of the treaty the USA confirmed its claim to Texas and gained control of the area, which would later become the states of New Mexico, Arizona, and California (where gold had recently been discovered). The USA agreed to pay Mexico 15 million dollars in return.

Mexican and Central American Indian languages Languages spoken by the indigenous peoples of Central America before the Spanish invasion of 1519. Most are still spoken, in spite of a dramatic fall in the number of speakers, but linguistic boundaries do not correspond with modern political borders. The region is a meeting-place for the language groups of North and South America (it is generally believed that the indigenous peoples of South America travelled there from the North via this narrow area), which is an argument in favour of the theory that most American Indian languages are related, however distantly. Central American languages may be classified into three groups: Northern Amerind, Central Amerind, and a southern group called Chibchan-Paezan. Mexico has speakers of languages belonging to all three groups. Hokan is spoken in the north-east of the country and in the south Californian peninsula, while Penutian is spoken in eastern and southern Mexico, and includes the important Mayan languages Yucatec, Quiché, Cakchiquel, Kekchi, and Mam. Two families belonging to Central Amerind are spoken throughout Mexico: Uto-Aztecan and Oto-Manguean. Uto-Aztecan, which includes the Comanche, Hopi, and Aztec languages, stretches from Mexico up into the western USA; Aztec, the most important Mexican language, has about a million speakers. Oto-Manguean is spoken by over 1.5 million people in southern Mexico; there are 17 languages, of which the most important are Otomi, Mixtec, and Zapotec. The Chibchan-Paezan languages are spoken in a small area in south-west Mexico, and throughout Central America from Guatemala to Panama. The Pre-Columbian civilizations of the region had an oral rather than written literature, although Mayan had a writing system which has not yet been properly deciphered. Spanish-based scripts have been devised for some languages.

Mexican burrowing toad A toad, *Rhinophrynus dorsalis*, with a small head, small eyes, a round distended body, and short limbs, which are partially hidden in the body skin. They are well adapted to burrowing, using large spade-like prominences on the feet. They feed almost exclusively on ants and termites, which they lick up using a rod-like tongue, apparently a unique method of feeding in frogs and toads.

Mexico A country lying partly on the North American continent, bordering on the USA in the north, and partly in Central America, bordering on Guatemala and Belize in the south, with extensive coastlines on the Atlantic and Pacific Oceans.

Physical. Geographically, Mexico divides into several distinct areas. The Isthmus of Tehuantepec, together with the curving eastern coastal plain and the north-eastward-thrusting Yucatán Peninsula, constitutes the main lowland area. In the far north-west, the splinter-like peninsula of Lower California, with its high sierras, is a southward extension of the Sierra Nevada. So also is the mountainous western Sierra Madre on the mainland, while the eastern Sierra Madre is an extension of the Rocky Mountains. The narrow coastal plain facing the Pacific Ocean in the west is largely covered by forests, yielding mahogany in southern areas, where rain is abundant. In clearings, sisal and sugar can be grown; on the mountain slopes, cotton, coffee, and tobacco. Between the mountains lie high plateaux where, in the more temperate climate, cacti grow. There are several large lakes, saline in the north but fresh in the south, from which streams run in torrents through deeply cut canyons. Most of the country is subject to humid trade winds from the east between May and August and tropical hurricanes from August to October.

Economy. Crude oil accounts for a majority of Mexico's foreign earnings, and oil revenues have been used to develop an industrial base. However, the economy has suffered from a massive external debt, with high unemployment. There is considerable mineral wealth, particularly oil reserves, silver, and zinc, as well as uranium and copper, not all of which has been fully exploited. Mexico supplies a quarter of the world's requirements in fluorspar. Mexico's main exports are chemicals, non-ferrous ores, motor vehicles, and petroleum products. Agriculture relies on irrigation. The main food crop is maize, and export crops include fruit, vegetables, and coffee. In 1993, Mexico concluded the NORTH AMERICAN FREE TRADE AGREEMENT with the USA and Canada. However, despite this and the establishment of *maquiladoras* – assembly plants set up in Mexico by mainly North American companies – large numbers of illegal emigrants enter the USA annually across the northern border in search of work. Mexico City is the world's largest urban centre, with severe problems of pollution, infrastructure, and overcrowding.

History. In prehistory Mexico formed the greater part of ancient Mesoamerica, within which arose a succession of related civilizations which shared many cultural traits: socio-political organization based on cities; ceremonial plazas of pyramids, platforms, and temples; similar deities; calendrical systems; long-distance trading; and the ritual ball game. Some of these were the OLMEC (Gulf Coast), MAYA (Yucatán), TEOTIHUACÁN (Central Valley), Zapotec and Mixtec (Oaxaca), TOLTEC (North Central), western cultures, and AZTECS.

The conquest of the Aztec empire by CORTÉS was complete by 1521, and New Spain became the first Spanish-American viceroyalty, eventually including all of ancient Mesoamerica, northern Mexico, the Caribbean, and most of the south-western USA. A rigid colonial administration, including repression and exploitation of the native population, lasted for the next 300 years. As many as 90 per cent of the indigenous population had died of European-introduced diseases by the early 17th century, and thereafter their numbers only slowly increased.

In the early 19th century, inspired by French revolutionary ideas, an independence movement developed, led by two priests, Miguel Hidalgo y Costilla and José Maria Morelos y Pavón, both of whom were captured and shot by the Spanish authorities (1810 and 1814). In 1821 Augustín de Iturbide briefly created an independent Mexican empire, which included the captaincy-general of GUATEMALA. Following his exile (1823), the first Mexican constitution was proclaimed (1824), based on the US constitution. Two parties, the Federalist and the Centralists, quickly appeared, and in 1833 the liberal federalist Antonio López de Santa Anna emerged as President. He was not able to prevent the declaration of independence of TEXAS (1836) nor the MEXICAN–AMERICAN WAR (1846–48), which resulted in the loss of huge territories, added to by the Gadsden Purchase of Arizona in 1853. A period of reform followed, and a new constitution (1857) was promulgated. But economic difficulties and French imperialist dreams resulted in the imposition by troops of NAPOLEON III of the Habsburg prince MAXIMILIAN as emperor (1864–67). When French troops were withdrawn, Maximilian was defeated, captured, and shot. There followed the long dictatorship of Porfirio DÍAZ (1876–1910) and then the prolonged Mexican Revolution (1910–40). Under President Miguel Alemán (1946–52), the process of reconciliation begun by his predecessor, Avilo Camacho, continued. Since then democratic governments have continued to follow moderate policies, while seeking further to modernize the economy, bolstered by oil revenues. The presidency of Miguel de la Madrid Hurtado (1982–88) was faced by a fall in oil prices, a massive national debt, and one of the fastest growing birth-rates in the world. The 1988 elections were again won by the PRI (Partido Revolucionario Institucional) with Carlos Salinas de Gortari as President, who played a central role in the pacification programme for Central America. He continued the austerity programme initiated by his predecessor, but at the same time entered into discussions with Canada and the USA, leading to the North American Free Trade Agreement, which was ratified in 1993. In spite of massive foreign debt, Mexico continued to enjoy the advantages of a strong manufacturing base, self-sufficiency in oil and natural gas, and large capitalist investment in a modernized agricultural system. In early 1995 there was an armed uprising in the poverty-stricken state of Chiapas, led by an Indian guerrilla group, the Zapatista National Liberation Army (EZLN), who demanded social and economic reforms. After negotiations with the government a peace agreement was reached in 1995. The PRI candidate, Ernesto Zedillo, was elected President in August 1994 amid allegations by the opposition of electoral fraud.

Capital: Mexico City
Area: 1,958,201 sq km (756,066 sq mi)
Population: 91,145,000 (1995)
Currency: 1 peso = 100 centavos
Religions: Roman Catholic 92.6%; Protestant (incl. Evangelical) 3.3%; Jewish 0.1%
Ethnic Groups: Mestizo 55.0%; Amerindian 30.0%; European 15.0%
Languages: Spanish (official); Amerindian languages
International Organizations: UN; OAS; NAFTA

Mexico, Gulf of A vast embayment of the western Atlantic, bounded by the USA on the north and east and by Mexico on the west and south-west. With a west-east length of over 1,800 km (1,100 miles) and a width of 1300 km (800 miles), it is the largest gulf in the world. The mainland coastline (5,000 km or 3,100 miles long) is generally low and sandy, with many lagoons, and contains the great deltas of the Mississippi. Formed as a result of the

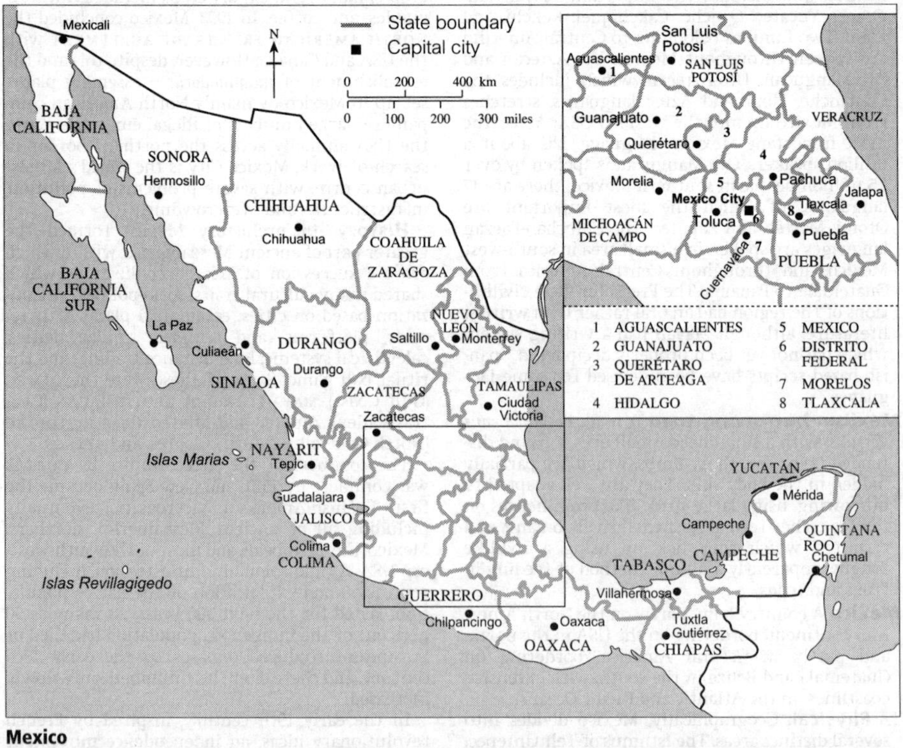

Mexico

plate activity that gave rise to the Atlantic Ocean, the Gulf is a subsiding continental margin. Under great thicknesses of sediment lie some of the world's largest reserves of oil and natural gas. A branch of the Equatorial Current enters through the Yucatán Channel; the water is warmed by the constant Sun and flows out as the Gulf Stream through the Straits of Florida. The tide in the Gulf is almost unique, being diurnal: it has high and low water only once every twenty-four hours.

Mexico City (Spanish **Ciudad de México**) The capital of Mexico; pop. (1990) 13,636,130. Founded in about 1300 as the Aztec capital Tenochtitlán, it was taken by the Spanish conquistador Cortez, who destroyed the old city in 1521 and rebuilt it as the capital of the Viceroyalty of New Spain. Situated at an altitude of 2,240 m (7,350 ft), it is one of the most populous cities in the world. Its many light and heavy industries employ more than half of all Mexico's industrial workers. Mexico City is also the financial, commercial, political, and cultural centre of the nation, as well as a great tourist attraction. It was the scene of an earthquake in 1985 that killed some 2,000 people. Landmarks include the cathedral, national palace, Castle of Chapultepec, and Anthropological Museum.

Meyerbeer, **Giacomo** (born Jakob Liebmann Beer) (1791–1864) German composer. He made his mark as a pianist before achieving success as an opera composer during a stay in Italy (1816–24). He then settled in Paris, establishing himself as a leading exponent of French grand opera with a series of works including *Robert le diable* (1831), *Les Huguenots* (1836), and *L'Africaine* (1865).

Meyerhof, **Otto Fritz** (1884–1951) German-born US biochemist. He worked in Germany on the biochemical processes involved in muscle action, including the production of lactic acid and heat as by-products, and provided the basis for understanding the process by which glucose is broken down to provide energy. He shared a Nobel Prize in 1922, and fled the Nazis in 1938 to continue his work in the USA.

mezzotint A method of ENGRAVING that produces tonal areas rather than lines; a mezzotint is also the name for a print made by this method. A copper plate is roughened with a tool called a rocker, which raises a 'burr' on the surface. The design is formed by scraping away the burr where the light tones are required and by polishing the metal quite smooth in the highlights. When the plate has been inked and then wiped, the ink is retained where the plate is rough and will print an intense black, but where it has been smoothed less ink is held and a lighter tone occurs. Mezzotint was invented in the Netherlands in the mid-17th century and soon spread to England, where it became an extremely popular method for reproducing portraits. The technique became virtually extinct in the later 19th century with the development of photography.

MHD See MAGNETOHYDRODYNAMICS.

MI5 and MI6 (Military Intelligence) The popular names for the Security Service and the Secret Intelligence Service in Britain. The sphere of MI5, founded in 1909, covers internal security and counterintelligence on British territory while MI6, formed in 1912, covers all areas outside the UK. Since the disintegration of the Soviet Union MI5 and MI6 have sought a new role, to include the fight against organized crime.

Miami A city and port on the coast of south-east Florida, USA; pop. (1990) 358,550. It is an important financial, trading, and industrial centre, and its subtropical climate and miles of beaches make it a year-round holiday resort. Miami is also the prime gateway to Latin America and its port is the largest embarkation point for cruise ships in the world, and the landing-place for immigrants from the Caribbean.

mica A group of common rock-forming minerals. Important members are BIOTITE and MUSCOVITE. All micas have a good basal cleavage that makes their crystals platy in form. Chemically they are silicates of the layer type (phyllosilicates), containing aluminium and also potassium, sodium, magnesium, iron, or lithium; and they give rocks a shiny appearance. Block mica (sheet mica) is used commercially in furnace windows and mica splittings are bonded with synthetic resins to make Micanite and other inculating sheets.

Michael In Judaism, Christianity, and Islam (as Mikāl), the archangel, and guardian of mankind against the devil. Mentioned in Christian apocryphal writings as fighting the serpent Satan, Michael is depicted in armour standing over the devil in the shape of a dragon. In Islamic legend Mikāl and Jibrīl (Gabriel) were the first to obey God's command to bow down before Adam.

Michaelmas daisy See DAISY.

Michelangelo (Buonarroti) (1475–1564) Italian sculptor, painter, architect, and poet. A leading figure during the High Renaissance, Michelangelo established his reputation in Rome with statues, such as the *Pietà* (1498–99) and then in Florence with his marble *David* (1501–04). Under papal patronage Michelangelo decorated the ceiling of the Sistine Chapel in Rome (1508–12) and painted the fresco *The Last Judgement* (1536–41), both important works in the development of the mannerist style. His architectural achievements include the design of the Laurentian Library in Florence (1524–34), as well as the completion of St Peter's in Rome, including the design of its great dome (1546–64).

Michelin, **André** (1853–1931) French industrialist. In 1888, with his brother **Édouard** (1859–1940), he founded the Michelin Tyre Company, and the brothers pioneered the use of pneumatic tyres on motor vehicles in the 1890s. The company also introduced steel-belted radial tyres in 1948.

Michelozzo (di Bartolommeo) (1396–1472) Italian architect and sculptor. In partnership with Ghiberti and Donatello he led a revival of interest in classical Roman architecture. His most famous building is the Palazzo Medici-Riccardi in Florence (1444–59), one of the most influential palace designs of the early Renaissance.

Michelson, **Albert Abraham** (1852–1931) US physicist who, with Edward MORLEY, performed a celebrated experiment to measure the effect of the motion of the Earth through the 'ETHER' – a medium that was believed to fill the Universe – on the SPEED OF LIGHT. No effect was detected, however, and this unexpected result led to the proposal of the Fitzgerald contraction and ultimately to the development of relativity theory. Michelson continued to work in optics and in 1907 became the first American to win the Nobel Prize for physics.

Michelson-Morley experiment See ETHER.

Michigan A state in northern USA, bordered in the west, north, and east by Lakes Michigan, Superior, Huron, and Erie; area 151,586 sq km (58,527 sq miles); pop. (1990) 9,295,300; capital, Lansing. The largest cities are Detroit, Grand Rapids, Warren, Flint, Lansing, Sterling, Ann Arbor, and Livonia.

Michigan is also known as the Wolverine State. Explored by the French in the 17th century, it was ceded to Britain in 1763 and acquired by the USA in 1783, becoming the 26th state in 1837. Rich in minerals such as iron, copper, iodine, gypsum, and bromine, its cities are major centres of industry, producing motor vehicles, hardware, and processed cereals. In addition to water sports, its chief tourist attractions are Mackinac Island, Isle Royale National Park, and Pictured Rocks National Lakeshore.

Michigan, Lake The third-largest of the five Great Lakes of North America and the only one to lie wholly within the USA; area 57,757 sq km (22,300 sq miles); maximum depth 281 m (922 ft). The cities of Chicago and Milwaukee are on its shores. It is linked to Lake Huron by the Strait of Mackinac.

microbiology The study of microorganisms, such as bacteria, viruses, algae, yeasts, and moulds. This field of science started in the 17th century with the invention of the microscope, and since then the techniques have improved so that now microorganisms are being studied at a molecular level. The advances made possible by the invention of the electron microscope have led to new scientific disciplines, such as genetic engineering and virology. The techniques of microbiology have had great impact on the medical sciences, enabling pathogenic organisms to be identified and isolated, and cures discovered. Applications in BIOTECHNOLOGY help to produce antibiotics, vitamins, metals, and proteins industrially.

microchip See INTEGRATED CIRCUIT.

microclimate The climate of a small or very small geographical area. They are often distinct from those of neighbouring areas because of slight differences between the amounts of INSOLATION they receive and the temperature and precipitation characteristics of the neighbouring areas. Almost infinitely numerous, they are especially important because most of the living world is concentrated within them.

microcomputer A complete computer based around a MICROPROCESSOR. Primary MEMORY, input and output interfaces, and a CLOCK are added to the microprocessor to make a microcomputer. Personal computers (PCs), WORD PROCESSORS, video games, and most workstations are microcomputers. For relatively simple computing needs, such as in domestic products and toys, the complete microcomputer can often be implemented on a single INTEGRATED CIRCUIT.

microeconomics The parts of economics concerned with the behaviour of individual decision-making units (economic agents), as opposed to MACROECONOMICS, which studies broad aggregates such as national income and the price level. Economic agents comprise households (consumers) and firms. Agents interact in markets, buying and selling goods and services. Consumer demand theory studies the quantities purchased by consumers, as derived from consumer preferences, income, and output prices.

microelectronics See ELECTRONICS; INFORMATION TECHNOLOGY.

microfiche A sheet of photographic film on which a large number of pages of text or other material are stored by photographically reducing an image of the text. Low-density microfilming was first used in the 1920s for copying bank cheques, but the popularity of the process accelerated in the 1960s as a means of storage in libraries and for business records. High-density microfiche can now store 3,000 pages on one 105 × 148 mm (4 × 6 inch) sheet of high-resolution, fine-grain film. The reader must have a viewing device with high magnification and resolution, and in addition a rapid-scan facility.

microlight (US **ultralight aircraft**) In its most basic form a HANG-GLIDER powered by an engine. The official definition of this very lightweight, simple type of aeroplane is a one- or two-seat aeroplane whose empty weight does not exceed 150 kg (330 pounds), with a wing area in square metres of not less than $W/10$, where W is the weight in kilograms (for example, a wing area of at least 10 m^2 for a weight of 100 kg). Many variants of this type of aeroplane, first seen in the pioneer designs before World War I, have been built since about 1970, when microlight flying became a popular sport.

micrometer An instrument for accurately measuring very small distances or objects. The commonest type is that in which the distance is measured by the rotation of a fine-pitched screw. The outer casing of the instrument is graduated so that fractions of a single rotation can be easily determined. This type of micrometer consists of a G-shaped clamp with a fixed anvil, against which the object is held by a graduated screw. The screw is tightened until the gap between it and the object is just closed. With fine adjustment, such a gauge is accurate to around 2.5 μm (10^{-4} inches). In MICROSCOPES and TELESCOPES, a rack-and-pinion or micrometer screw mechanism can be used in conjunction with a graduated scale to measure the size of objects seen through the instrument.

micron (symbol μ) A distance of one-millionth of a metre (10^{-6} m). In SI UNITS, the micron is called the micrometre (μm).

Micronesia A division of Oceania in the west Pacific Ocean (South Seas). Micronesia includes KIRIBATI, GUAM, the MARSHALL ISLANDS, NAURU, TUVALU, and the Federated States of MICRONESIA.

Micronesia, Federated States of A country in the west Pacific Ocean, comprising a group of islands divided into four states: Yap, Chuuk (formerly Truk), Pohnpei (formerly Ponape), and Kosrae.

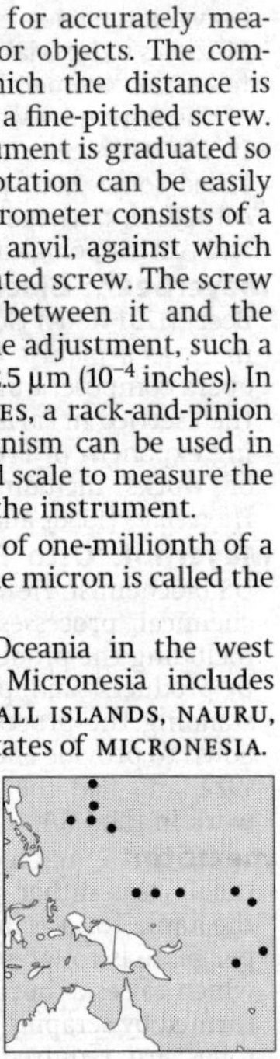

Physical. The Federated States of Micronesia forms part of the Caroline Islands group, one of the archipelagos east of the Philippines. The islands are low coral caps surmounting submerged extinct volcanoes. The climate is tropical, and the area is prone to typhoons.

Economy. Micronesia's principal crops are coconuts (providing the main export, copra), cassava, breadfruit, and sweet potatoes. Industry is confined to garment production.

History. The first settlers on the islands were probably Melanesians who arrived in about 1500 BC. Micronesia was colonized by Spain in the 17th century and was sold to Germany in 1898. The islands were occupied by Japan from 1914 until their capture by American forces in 1944. In 1947 Micronesia became part of the UN Trust Territory of the Pacific Islands, administered by the USA. From 1965 there were increasing demands for autonomy and Micronesia became independent in 1979. The US administration was not formally ended until 1986 and was not ratified by the UN until 1990. A compact of free association was signed with the USA in 1982, giving the USA responsibility for Micronesia's defence. Micronesia's economy is weak and the country depends on financial assistance from the USA. Bailey Olter, first elected in 1991, was re-elected in 1995.

Capital: Palikir (on Pohnpei)
Area: 701 sq km (270 sq mi)
Population: 105,000 (1995)
Currency: 1 US dollar = 100 cents
Religions: Christianity
Ethnic Groups: Trukese 41.1%; Pohnpeian 25.9%; Mortlockese 8.3%; Kosraean 7.4%; Yapese 6.0%
Languages: English (official); Micronesian languages
International Organizations: UN

microphone A device that converts sound energy into electrical energy. Microphones have many uses, for example, in telephones, TAPE RECORDERS, HEARING AIDS and in RADIO and TELEVISION broadcasting. In all microphones, sound waves are translated into mechanical vibrations in a thin, flexible diaphragm. These vibrations are then converted by various methods into an electrical signal. In a capacitor microphone the diaphragm acts as one plate of a capacitor, and vibrations produce changes in a voltage maintained across the capacitor plates. Capacitor microphones are expensive and require an external power supply, but give a high-quality sound signal and are used in laboratory and studio recording applications. In the dynamic microphone a small movable COIL, in the field of a permanent magnet, is attached to the diaphragm. When the diaphragm vibrates, the coil moves in the magnetic field, producing a varying electrical signal in the coil (see ELECTROMAGNETIC INDUCTION). Dynamic microphones are robust and relatively inexpensive, and are used in a wide variety of applications. In ribbon microphones a thin, corrugated metal ribbon is suspended in a magnetic field: vibration of the ribbon in the magnetic field generates a changing voltage. Ribbon microphones detect sound in a bidirectional pattern: this characteristic is useful in such applications as radio and television interviews, where it cuts out much extraneous sound.

microprocessor One of a small number of INTEGRATED CIRCUITS that implements all the functions of the CENTRAL PROCESSING UNIT of a computer. When combined with memory, a clock, and interfaces, a microprocessor functions as a MICROCOMPUTER. Microprocessors are small and cheap enough to have been incorporated into a very wide range of products. Small, very powerful desk-top computers use 32-bit processors, but the largest market is in 4-bit microprocessors, which are extensively used in such domestic products as washing-machines, video recorders, and televisions.

microscope An optical microscope is an instrument that uses a LENS or combination of lenses to magnify very small structures illuminated by light. Other microscopes are analogous in function but employ radiation other than visible light. A magnifying glass is a simple microscope, but the compound microscope gives higher magnification. It was probably invented in about 1590 by a Dutch spectacle-maker, Zacharias Janssen, although others working at the same time have also been cited as the inventor. The object to be magnified is placed on the 'stage' and the objective lens forms an inverted image inside the microscope tube. The eyepiece lens gives an enlarged, inverted image of the first image, thus reproducing the original object. Generally light passes through the specimen into the microscope. Specimens thin enough to transmit light, usually mounted on glass slides and protected by thin glass cover slips, are often colourless, so stains are used to reveal structures. Polarized light is used to study crystals, and ultramicroscopy, in which liquid suspensions are illuminated from the side, shows particle movement as flashes against a dark background. Stereoscopic microscopes, often used in surgery, have one microscope for each eye, arranged so that the specimen is viewed from slightly different angles, giving a three-dimensional picture. Oil-immersion objective lenses increase resolving power (ability to distinguish detail) at high magnifications by using a drop of special oil between the objective lens and the cover slip. Light microscopes have an inherent upper magnification limit of about ×2,000.

ELECTRON MICROSCOPES can magnify over 1 million times. Other types of microscope have more recently been developed for specialist and research applications. Proton microscopes use a tightly focused beam of high-energy protons to scan a specimen. They can be used on thicker specimens than electron microscopes, and can provide information on the chemical composition of the sample. In X-ray microscopy, concentrated X-RAY sources scan a sample to produce images of the crystalline structure of materials. In emission microscopy, electrical fields or high temperatures are used to stimulate the sample to emit sub-atomic particles: such microscopes can show reactions at solid surfaces, such as CORROSION and VAPOUR DEPOSITION. Acoustic microscopy uses high-frequency ULTRASOUND in place of visible light: sound waves reflected from the sample vary in intensity depending on how much acoustic

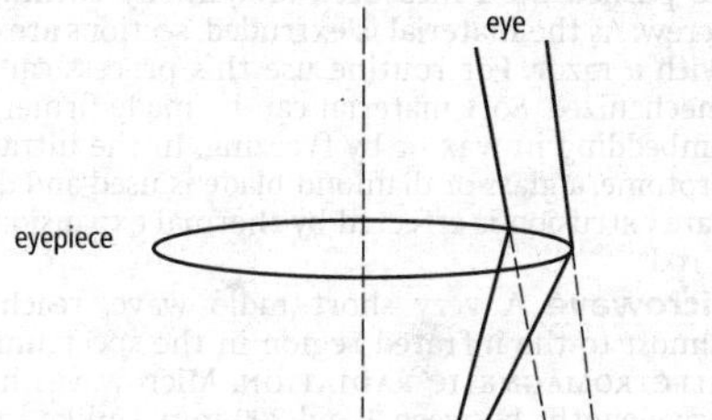

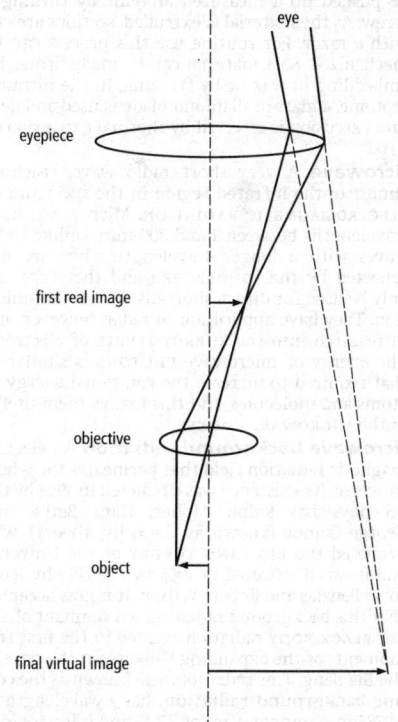

Microscope In a compound microscope the objective forms a real inverted image within the microscope tube. The eyepiece produces an enlarged virtual image of the first image.

energy has been absorbed by that portion of the sample. Acoustic microscopy is used in biological research, and for detecting faults in INTEGRATED CIRCUITS. A very recent development for studying surfaces is the scanning tunnelling microscope (STM). This measures the separation distance between a fine-point detector and the surface of the sample, using a phenomenon known as tunnelling, by which electrons transfer between the sample surface and the detector, causing a minute current flow. The STM can resolve images down to below atomic dimensions.

Microscopium The Microscope, a small CONSTELLATION of the southern sky, introduced by the French astronomer Nicolas Louis de Lacaille in 1752 as one of a series of modern instruments of science and the arts. It is a faint and barren constellation with brightest stars of only fifth magnitude.

microsurgery Intricate surgery performed using MICROSCOPES, enabling the tissue to be operated on with miniaturized surgical instruments. Microsurgery has only become possible in recent years. It relies on the surgeon's ability to connect together the ends of very small arteries, veins, nerves, or muscles in order to preserve nutrition to tissues, which may otherwise die. It is used in a variety of surgical specialities, for example to reattach severed limbs, in brain surgery, and in ear and eye surgery.

microtome An instrument for cutting very thin sections of material for examination under a MICROSCOPE. In its simplest form, it consists of a hollow metal cylinder, in which the material for examination is placed, containing a piston that can be pushed up a measured amount by turning a screw. As the material is extruded, sections are cut with a razor. For routine use this process can be mechanized. Soft material can be made firmer by embedding in wax or by freezing. In the ultramicrotome, a glass or diamond blade is used and delicate extrusion is effected by thermal expansion of a rod.

microwave A very short radio wave, reaching almost to the infrared region in the spectrum of ELECTROMAGNETIC RADIATION. Microwaves have wavelengths between 1 and 300 mm. Unlike radio waves with a longer wavelength, they are not reflected by the IONOSPHERE and therefore can only be used for direct, short-distance communication. They have application in radar, however, and in research into the ENERGY LEVELS of electrons. The energy of microwave PHOTONS is similar to that required to increase the rotational energy of atoms and molecules, and this makes them useful in the MICROWAVE COOKER.

microwave background radiation An electromagnetic radiation field that permeates the whole Universe. Its existence was predicted in 1948 by the US physicists Ralph Alpher, Hans Bethe, and George Gamov (known as the α-β-γ theory), who proposed the BIG BANG THEORY of the Universe, and it was discovered in 1965 by the US physicists Arno Penzias and Robert Wilson. It is now accepted that this background radiation is a remnant of the hot BLACK BODY radiation created in the first few moments of the expanding Universe at the time of the Big Bang. This radiation, also known as the **cosmic background radiation**, has a wavelength of 0.0735 m, a temperature of 2.7 K, and is isotropic to within one part in 100,000. However, it may contain tiny irregularities that are the echoes of the galactic formation process in the early Universe.

microwave cooker An appliance that cooks food by ELECTROMAGNETIC RADIATION in the MICROWAVE region. Microwave cookers for the catering trade were first sold in the USA around 1953, but domestic microwaves did not achieve widespread popularity until about 1980. Microwaves are generated by a magnetron, a type of THERMIONIC VALVE first developed for use in RADAR. A rotating blade scatters the microwaves into the small box-shaped oven. Loosely bound liquid molecules (mostly water) in the food become excited by the radiation, generating heat throughout the food. Food cooks much more quickly in a microwave than in a conventional oven. However, microwave heating alone does not brown or crisp food on the outside, and microwaves cook some foods unevenly.

Midas In Greek mythology, a king who was granted a wish by Dionysus and asked that everything he touched be turned to gold. When even his food turned to gold and became inedible, he realized how foolish he had been and he was relieved of his unwanted power by bathing in the River Pactolus. In another story, Midas offended Apollo by declaring that Pan was a better musician, and was punished by the god by having his ears turned into those of an ass.

Mid-Atlantic Ridge The set of submarine ridges and islands extending north-south down the middle of the North and South Atlantic Ocean, as part of a larger system of MID-OCEANIC RIDGES. In the centre of the ridge new crust is being formed by the upwelling of MAGMA. This is then dragged to the east or west of the central ridge, probably by very slow convection currents in the mantle, at the rate of a few centimetres a year. Where the ridge reaches the surface – as in Iceland – volcanic activity is forming new crust. Some 1,500 km (900 miles) wide in total, the ridge is a zigzag feature, which rises rather gently from the deep abyssal plains on either side and has a depression running along the centre, the axial valley. This is a RIFT VALLEY, formed as the two sides move apart. The zigzags correspond roughly to the zigzag shapes of the continents on either side and are marked by FAULTS, which run across the line of the ridge.

Middle Ages The period in Europe from *c.*700 to *c.*1500. The decline of the Roman empire in the West and the period of barbarian invasions in the 5th and 6th centuries (DARK AGES) was followed by the emergence of separate kingdoms and the development of forms of government. The coronation of CHARLEMAGNE in 800 AD is held to mark the end of anarchy and the revival of civilization and learning. England, under ALFRED, similarly saw the encouragement of learning and the establishment of monastic houses. Territorial expansion by VIKINGS and NORMANS throughout Europe in the 9th and 10th centuries, initially violent and disruptive, led to their assimilation into local populations. Trade and urban life revived.

The High Middle Ages (12th and 13th centuries) saw a growth in the power of the papacy, which led to clashes between the pope and secular rulers over their respective spheres of jurisdiction. The creation of new monastic orders encouraged scholarship and architecture. The obsession with PILGRIMAGE to holy shrines was the impetus behind the CRUSADES, in which thousands of Christian knights went to Palestine to fight the Muslims and convert them to Christianity. Society was organized on a military basis, the FEUDAL SYSTEM, in which land was held in return for military service. But although war dominated this period, it also saw the growth of trade (notably the English wool trade), the foundation of UNIVERSITIES, and the flowering of scholarship, notably in philosophy and theology (SCHOLASTICISM). Gothic art and architecture had its finest expression in the cathedrals built from the 12th century for the following 300–400 years.

During the 13th and 14th centuries various factors combined to cause social and economic unrest. The BLACK DEATH, and the HUNDRED YEARS WAR between France and England, resulted in a falling population and the beginnings of anticlericalism. In the 15th and 16th centuries the RENAISSANCE in Italy marked a new spirit of sceptical enquiry and the end of the medieval period.

Middle East An extensive area of south-west Asia and northern Africa, stretching from the Mediterranean to Pakistan, including the Arabian Peninsula, and having a predominantly Muslim population.

Middle English literature English literature during the period between about 1100 and 1500. During this time the language lost its inflections and incorporated Norman French vocabulary and structure. Middle English literature is varied and international in character. From the French influence of the troubadours or aristocratic poet-musicians came the code of courtly love and rhyme, which co-existed with a freer style of alliterative verse. Many long romances come from both French and Anglo-Saxon sources, among them 'King Horn', 'Havelok the Dane', and 'Amadis of Gaul'. Layamon's *Brut* (*c.*1200) is a nationalist EPIC. The first of many continental-style debate poems, 'The Owl and the Nightingale', in which the two birds debate the virtues of the monastic and the secular ways of life, dates from before 1250, and is the ancestor of CHAUCER's 'Parliament of Fowls'. The 'alliterative revival' includes a debate poem 'Winner and Waster' (*c.*1353) and LANGLAND's moral allegory, *Piers Plowman*. 'Pearl', a richly-patterned poem using rhyme and alliteration and meaningful on several symbolic levels, is probably by the same hand as 'Gawain and the Green Knight'. These poems are in the north-west Midlands dialect, which is less close to modern English than the London English of Chaucer. The code of chivalry of King Edward III (1327–77) may have created the interest in the Celtic legends of Arthur and Gawain that gave rise to many romances, which MALORY was to collect in prose. The religious works of the hermit Richard Rolle (*c.*1300–49) influenced the evolution of prose style. The *Travels* of Sir John Mandeville (*c.*1356) was a popular series of unlikely traveller's tales. Chaucer's contemporary John Gower (*c.*1330–1408) wrote the *Confessio Amantis*, a collection of *exempla* or moral stories told in lucid style. After Chaucer came the autobiographical poems of Thomas Hoccleve (*c.*1368–1426), the enormous output of John Lydgate (*c.*1370–1449), and the Scots Robert Henryson, DUNBAR, Gavin Douglas (1475–1522), and James I (1394–1437). The MORALITY PLAYS and MYSTERY PLAYS of the early 16th century are of a high literary value, particularly those of Yorkshire, as are very many lyrics and carols, including 'Alysoun' and 'Sumer is icumen in' (*c.*1250).

Middlesborough A town in North Yorkshire in north-east England, a port on the estuary of the River Tees; pop. (1991) 141,100. The University of Teesside (formerly Teesside Polytechnic) was established in 1992.

Middlesex A former county of south-east England, situated to the north of London. In 1965 it was divided between Hertfordshire, Surrey and Greater London. It is still used as a postal address. The name of the county arose from its location between the lands of the east and west Saxons.

Middleton, Thomas (*c.*1570–1627) English dramatist. After collaborating with Thomas Dekker on the first part of *The Honest Whore* (1604), Middleton wrote the two tragedies for which he is best known, namely *The Changeling* (1622), written with William Rowley (*c.*1585–1626), and *Women Beware Women* (1620–27).

midge A small fly, groups of which swarm, particularly at dusk and near water, in large numbers. The biting midges, of the family Ceratopogonidae, are known in North America as punkies or no-see-ums. They are tiny flies whose females suck blood from insects, birds, or mammals, including humans. Their bites are out of all proportion to their size. Their scavenging larvae are aquatic or live in damp places.

Non-biting midges, of the family Chironomidae, resemble mosquitoes, and the males have feathery antennae. The larvae of most are aquatic, feeding on decaying plant material, and include the bloodworms of stagnant water and sewage works. These are red in colour because they contain the respiratory pigment HAEMOGLOBIN, which helps them to obtain oxygen in stagnant water.

Mid Glamorgan A former county of south Wales. It was formed in 1974 from parts of Breconshire, Glamorgan, and Monmouthshire. In 1996 it was abolished and administration powers were handed over to four county boroughs.

Midgley, Thomas, Jr. (1889–1944) US engineer and chemist. While at Dayton Engineering Laboratories Company in Ohio, he studied the problem of KNOCK in PETROL ENGINES, and discovered that LEAD TETRAETHYL is an effective anti-knock additive (1921). He also introduced the concept of the OCTANE NUMBER for petrol. In the 1930s, while working for the Du Pont Company, he developed Freons (CHLOROFLUOROCARBONS) as refrigerants and fire-extinguishing agents. By the 1980s both lead tetraethyl and Freons had been condemned as dangerous atmospheric pollutants.

Midi, le The hinterland of southern France to the north of the Mediterranean coast. Its name, which means 'midday', refers to the intensity of the Sun in the middle of the day.

Midlands, the The inland counties of central England, including Derbyshire, Leicestershire, Northamptonshire, and Nottinghamshire (East Midlands); Warwickshire, West Midlands, and Staffordshire (West Midlands); and Bedfordshire, Buckinghamshire, and Oxfordshire (South Midlands). For economic planning in a European context the Midlands are divided into East Midlands (Nottinghamshire, Derbyshire, Northamptonshire, Leicestershire, and Lincolnshire) and West Midlands (Hereford and Worcester, West Midlands, Shropshire, Staffordshire, and Warwickshire).

Midlothian A local government area (unitary authority) and former county in central Scotland. It was a part of Lothian region from 1975 to 1996. Centred on Edinburgh, it was formerly known as Edinburghshire.

mid-oceanic ridges (or **mid-oceanic rises**) Elongated mountain ranges that extend along the approximate centre-lines of oceans. They are found in the North and South Atlantic, the Pacific, the Indian, and the Southern Oceans. The ridges rise from the sea floor to heights of 3,000 m (10,000 feet) and more. For the most part they are submerged, but their peaks and crests appear above the surface in a few places, such as Iceland and

Tristan da Cunha. Oceanic ridges are sites of SEA-FLOOR SPREADING. In the Atlantic, Indian, and Southern Oceans, basaltic rocks are erupted along the ridge. Creation of new crustal material thus accompanies the separation of the crustal plates; the old material is moved away from the ridges, ultimately to slowly disappear beneath the bordering continents.

Midrash (Hebrew, 'exposition') In Judaism, the interpretation of the Hebrew scriptures using the oral traditions codified in the MISHNAH. The Halakhic *Midrashim* (from *halakhah*, 'law') are legal collections of interpretations based on Exodus, Leviticus, Numbers, and Deuteronomy. The Haggadic *Midrashim* (from *haggadah*, 'narrative') are the non-legal collections, which examine biblical lore; some of these are homilies on the special readings for festivals, for example the *Haggadah* read at PASSOVER.

Midway Islands Two small islands (Sand Island and Eastern Island), and a surrounding coral atoll, at the western end of the Hawaiian chain in the central Pacific Ocean; area 5 sq km (2 sq miles). The islands, which lie outside the state of Hawaii, were annexed by the USA in 1867 and remain a US territory and naval base administered by the US Navy. The Midway Islands have been used as a submarine cable station, aircraft stop-over, and military base, and were the scene in 1942 of a decisive naval battle, which marked the end of Japanese expansion in the Pacific during World War II.

midwifery The practice and profession of a person, usually a woman, who attends a mother during pregnancy, childbirth, and in the first days of a child's life. In developed countries, midwives usually undergo a nursing training followed by specialist courses in obstetrics and gynaecology. In the industrialized world midwives work as part of a broad team of health professionals and most births take place in hospital. In developing countries, half of all births are attended by untrained traditional midwives, but an increasing number of countries have established training courses in essential obstetric care and safe motherhood.

midwife toad A European toad belonging to the genus *Alytes*, so called because of the unique mode of parental care exhibited by the male. He carries a rosary-like string of eggs entwined around the hind-limbs. Initially the eggs are yellowish but, as development proceeds, they darken and are taken to, or deposited near, the water by the male. The tadpoles reach maturity in two to three months in the summer; late brood tadpoles usually overwinter. Three species of midwife toads are known; they are found in western Europe, Majorca, and Morocco. All are nocturnal and have a whistling call likened to the sound of chiming bells – hence the alternative name of bell toads. In the daytime they may dig burrows or hide away in the spaces in drystone walls. The name is also used for the African midwife toad of the genus *Xenopus*.

Mies van der Rohe, Ludwig (1886–1969) German-born architect and designer. In the 1920s he produced unexecuted designs for glass skyscrapers and designed the German pavilion at the 1929 International Exhibition at Barcelona; the latter is regarded as a classic example of pure geometrical architecture. He is also noted for his design of tubular steel furniture, notably the 'Barcelona Chair'. He became director of the Bauhaus in 1930 but emigrated to the USA in 1937; his most celebrated American design is probably the Seagram Building in New York (1954–58).

migraine A common type of irregularly recurrent, severe headache. An attack usually starts with a flickering or blurring of vision and this may progress to coloured zigzag lines and partial loss of vision. At the same time, the headache begins, usually on one side of the head, and the sufferer may be sick. Attacks last 2–72 hours. The condition results from a spasm and subsequent overdilation of certain arteries in the brain. Effective preventive therapies now exist and such drugs as sumatripan may be used to treat acute attacks.

migration (in the animal kingdom) The movement by animals from one place to another to find suitable breeding conditions or food. The distance travelled may be large or small. The arctic tern travels up to 40,000 km (25,000 miles) each year. The daily vertical migration of zooplankton in the ocean is measured in metres. Not all migrations are return journeys. Mass migrations of locusts occur when they have stripped one site of all vegetation. Reindeer move on when food supplies are depleted, as do wildebeest in Africa and the red kangaroo of Australia. The period between migrations may be from a few hours to several years.

Mihailovich, Draza (1893–1946) Serbian army officer who, after the fall of Yugoslavia in World War II, organized royalist partisans against German forces. He structured his forces into bands (četa, prounced cheta), and these became known as chetniks. Their relations with the communist partisans of TITO was uneasy. After Tito gained power, Mihailovich was tried and shot for collaboration with Germans and war crimes.

Milan (Italian **Milano**) A city in north-west Italy, capital of Lombardy region; pop. (1990) 1,432,180. Settled by the Gauls in about 600 BC, it was taken by the Romans in 222 BC, becoming the second city, after Rome, of the Western Empire. Although devastated by Attila the Hun in 452 AD, it regained its powerful status, particularly from the 13th to the 15th centuries as a duchy under the Visconti and Sforza families. From the 16th century it was contested by the Habsburgs and the French, finally becoming a part of Italy in 1860. The city is now Italy's leading industrial, financial, and commercial centre. Its industries include motor cars, machinery, chemicals, textiles, clothing, and printing. It has an immense Gothic cathedral and its opera house, La Scala, which was built in 1776–78, is one of the largest in the world.

mildew Any mouldy fungal growth, for example on damp stored materials. However, there are also two kinds of plant disease known as downy and powdery mildews, caused by fungi of the family Peronosporaceae and of the order Erysiphales, respectively. Powdery mildew of cereals, caused by *Erysiphe graminis*, is economically serious, and is controlled by breeding resistant crops or by the application of fungicide.

Miletus One of the leading Ionian cities of Asia Minor. It established a number of colonies on the Hellespont and Black Sea coasts in the 7th and 6th centuries BC, and traded widely. It continued to thrive even after coming within CROESUS' sphere of influence, and in 499 led the revolt of the Ionians against Persia. After its final defeat in 494 it was razed, and never thereafter recovered its former power. It revolted from the Athenian empire in 412, but then came under Persian control. The city's economic decline was hastened by the silting up of the harbour while it was part of the Roman empire.

Milford Haven (Welsh **Aberdaugleddau**) A port and oil-refining centre in the county of Pembrokeshire, south-west Wales, on the northern shore of the tidal estuary of the River Cleddau; pop. (1991) 13,494.

Milhaud, Darius (1892–1974) French composer. He became famous as one of Les SIX, with such ballets as *Le Boeuf sur le toit* (1919) and the jazz-inspired *La Création du monde* (1923). His energetic, eclectic style gave rise to a vast quantity of music, including 15 operas, 17 ballets, 18 string quartets, 12 full-scale symphonies, and six chamber symphonies.

military aircraft Aeroplanes (or dirigibles) designed for military use. Aircraft have been used for military purposes since very early in their history. The French formed the first balloon corps in history in 1793, and first used free balloons for military reconnaissance at the Battle of Fleurus, in Flanders, in 1794. With the development of the navigable AIRSHIP from the balloon, true military aviation began. Airships were used extensively in World War I, when the German Zeppelins were employed on long-range reconnaissance flights and night-time bombing raids. Experiments with the use of guns and bombs in aeroplanes were made from 1910 onwards, and by the end of World War I purpose-built BOMBER and fighter aircraft had been developed, with performance capabilities far beyond those of aircraft flying in 1914. Twin-engined flying boats were being used for long reconnaissance flights over water, and the first flights had already been made from the deck of a moving ship.

By the start of World War II most European and US aircraft were all-metal monoplanes (see FLIGHT, HISTORY OF MANNED). Supercharged engines, closed cockpits, and oxygen masks meant that fighter aircraft could operate effectively at heights of 4,500–6,300 m (15,000–20,000 feet), while bombers reached heights of 9,000 m (30,000 feet). Fighter armament improved as the war progressed, and bomb weights rose from 225–550 kg (500–1,000 pounds) to around 10,000 kg (22,000 pounds). The widespread adoption of RADAR, for detection and guidance of aircraft from the ground and for use on board aircraft, led to improvements in air defence, night flying, and bombing accuracy. The first jet aircraft flew towards the end of World War II. Soon afterwards the intercontinental BALLISTIC MISSILE was developed, and by the mid-1960s had largely replaced the long-range bomber as the major nuclear deterrent. At around the same time, MILITARY SATELLITES took over many of the aeroplane's roles in reconnaissance and information-gathering. In the 1950s and early 1960s ever-faster military jets were tested, but by the mid-1960s military aviation had begun to change. Strategies were evolved to avoid radar detection, such as low, terrain-following flights and electronic or other means of jamming or confusing enemy radar. More recently the USA has put much research effort into 'stealth' aircraft, designed to have low radar visibility and made of radar-absorbing materials. Developments in AVIONICS in the 1970s and 1980s provided aircraft that could automatically fly at very low altitudes, and weapons and navigation systems that would automatically locate and attack targets. Fighters and bombers have been replaced by strike aircraft, which attack targets deep in enemy territory, interceptors designed to shoot down enemy aircraft, and close air-support aircraft with the role of supporting ground troops. Aircraft are designed to carry a variety of different weapons so as to be able to fulfil multiple roles, while further flexibility is found in VTOL or STOL AIRCRAFT, which can operate from sites other than conventional airstrips. HELICOPTERS have become increasingly important as manœuvrability and flexibility take precedence over speed.

military government A form of rule in which the major institutions of government are controlled, either directly or indirectly, by the military. Military government usually arises as a result of a military *coup d'état*. Military leadership may be by a small group (often called a JUNTA) or by an individual 'strong man'. In the contemporary world, military governments are common in states in which political institutions and democratic traditions are weak. This has been particularly the case in Latin America and in the former colonial territories of Africa and the Middle East, but they have also been found in countries, such as Greece, Portugal, Spain, and Turkey. Many military governments are repressive by nature, and ignore the civil and HUMAN RIGHTS of their citizens, justifying such action by the imposition of MARTIAL LAW to maintain stability.

military satellite Any artificial SATELLITE orbiting the Earth that is used for military purposes. More than 2,000 have been launched to date, mainly by the USA and the Soviet Union. They include COMMUNICATIONS SATELLITES, METEOROLOGICAL SATELLITES, and NAVIGATION SATELLITES, some of these being shared by civilian users. Spy satellites (called 'ferrets') listen in to enemy radio communications and track military movements by radio signals or RADAR. Surveillance satellites photograph military installations or battle areas: originally photographic film was used for this purpose, as it gave great detail, but it had to be returned to Earth for processing. Modern surveillance satellites transmit to Earth images detailed enough to distinguish between military and civilian personnel and between real vegetation and camouflage. Early-warning satellites can detect missile launches and nuclear explosions, and progress has been made towards developing 'killer' satellites, which will be able to destroy enemy military satellites, either by exploding near them or by using LASER WEAPONS to destroy them or disable their instruments.

militia A military force composed of citizens, enlisted or conscripted in times of emergency, usually for local defence. In England, it developed during the Middle Ages from the Anglo-Saxon fyrd. Its forces were usually raised by impressment (forcible recruiting), and until the 16th century it was supervised by the local sheriff. Then the Lord Lieutenants were given the responsibility until the later 19th century.

Modern militias fulfil a variety of roles. Although generally restricted to infantry or light-armoured roles on land, in certain cases (for example, the US National Guard), they are deployed play in air and coastal defence. Such countries as Israel, Switzerland, the former Yugoslavia, and Sweden have based much of their defence planning on the use of militia units, and people's militias were a feature of former communist states, such as East Germany and Czechoslovakia. Militia forces can also play an important role in internal conflicts, where they may be raised and controlled by factions; in such cases, the dividing line between militia and GUERRILLA forces can be blurred.

milk A fluid that has high nutritional value and is manufactured by female mammals to nourish their young. The principal constituents of milk are water, milk sugar (lactose), fat, and protein. It is rich in calcium, poor in iron, and contains vitamins. Most substances dissolved in the maternal blood appear in the milk, including drugs, alcohol, and antibiotics.

Milk is produced by a complicated sequence of chemical and physical reactions by mammary glands. The glands of mammals enlarge during pregnancy under the influence of hormones. At the same time the secreting tissues and ducts are prepared for the production and ejection of milk after the birth of the young.

Human milk contains less protein than other milks, and babies take about six months to double their birthweight. About two days after birth, milk flows from the ducts of the mammary glands in response to suckling of the teats or nipples. The 'first milk' secreted, a yellowish fluid called colostrum, gives the young some protection against infections. See also DAIRY PRODUCT.

milkfish A species of large, silvery fish, *Chanos chanos*, which grows to 1.8 m (6 feet) in length, and looks superficially like a herring. An Indo-Pacific fish, it has transparent, needle-like fry which are collected from estuaries and tidal pools when about 1 cm (0.5 inch) long, and reared in freshwater pools until they reach a marketable size.

milkweed A perennial plant belonging to the genus *Asclepias*, which consists of 200 species native to America and Africa. The brightly coloured flowers of milkweeds, often reds and yellows, have reflexed petals and are carried in umbels. The milky sap of many species contains poisonous ALKALOIDS and this property is used by insects such as the MONARCH BUTTERFLY, whose caterpillars feed on milkweeds and obtain their toxins from them.

milkweed butterfly See MONARCH BUTTERFLY.

Milky Way See GALAXY.

Mill, John Stuart (1806–73) Scottish philosopher and economist. He won recognition as a philosopher with his defence of empiricism in *System of Logic* (1843). Mill is best known, however, for his political and moral works, especially *On Liberty* (1859), which argued for the importance of individuality, and *Utilitarianism* (1861), which developed Jeremy Bentham's theory, considering explicitly the relation between utilitarianism and justice. In other works he advocated representative democracy, criticized the contemporary treatment of married women, and claimed that an end to economic growth was desirable as well as inevitable.

Millais, Sir John Everett (1829–96) British painter. A founder member of the Pre-Raphaelite Brotherhood, he initially adhered to a pure vision of nature with unidealized figures in such paintings as *Christ in the House of his Parents* (1850). However, with the success of *The Blind Girl* (1856) and other paintings, he gradually departed from the moral and aesthetic rigour of the early Pre-Raphaelites, going on to produce lavishly painted portraits, landscapes, and sentimental genre pictures, notably *Bubbles* (1886).

millenarianism (or **millennialism**) The belief in the imminent end of the present world order and the establishment of a new and radically different one. Millenarian movements, which are found all over the world in many different societies, usually occur at times of change and upheaval. The millenarian idea that divine intervention will bring about a reversal of worldly expectations resulting in an earthly paradise, tends to appeal to those who are dispossessed both culturally and economically. Much millenarianism has its roots in the Jewish expectation of the coming of the MESSIAH. It takes its name from the early Christians' anticipation of Christ's Second Coming, to be followed by a millennium, or thousand-year reign of peace and tranquillity. In Christianity, the early expectation of Christ's imminent return to this world was replaced by the theologian St AUGUSTINE's allegorical model of an other-worldly City of God. Millenarian Christian beliefs thereafter became associated with dissident sects, and are expressed today in the beliefs of sects such as the JEHOVAH'S WITNESSES, Seventh Day ADVENTISTS, CHRISTADELPHIANS, and MORMONS. In Islam, Shiite Muslims and sects such as the DRUSE await the return of the hidden *imam* or *mahdi*; in the Islamic Republic of Iran, the spiritual leader, the *Walī Faqīh*, is stated to be the leader in the absence of the *mahdi*. The BAHA'I religion originates from a millenarian proclamation in 1844, the 1,000th anniversary of the hidden *imam*'s disappearance. For many Jews, the establishment of the state of Israel was the fulfilment of millenarian beliefs (see ZIONISM), and the Afro-Caribbean RASTAFARIAN cult envisages the black people's repatriation to Africa. Millenarian beliefs are less prominent in Buddhism, but in Hinduism, Kalki, the last AVATAR of VISHNU, is expected to destroy the degeneration of this age and instigate a new cosmic era.

millennium A period of 1,000 years. In the context of the system of dates based on the birth of Jesus Christ (nominally taken as year 0), the second millennium is the end of 1999 or the beginning of 2000. Some Christian sects believe Jesus will return to Earth, at this millennium, to bring peace and security to its inhabitants (see MILLENARIANISM). In the UK, a more secular celebration of the arrival of the 21st century will be the **Millennium Dome**, erected at Greenwich on the River Thames, east of London. Less of a celebration, and more of a costly burden, is the **millennium bug**, a problem that arises in vast numbers of computer programs that are unable to cope with the change of year from 1999 to 2000. Banks and governments, with enormous computer installations, have had to pay for large numbers of programmer hours to rectify this lack of foresight.

Miller, Arthur (1915–) US dramatist. After first attracting attention with *All My Sons* (1947), he produced a sequence of powerful plays: the classic study of American failure *Death of a Salesman* (1949); the re-creation of the 17th-century Salem witch-hunt in *The Crucible* (1953); and the Brooklyn family melodrama *A View From the Bridge* (1955). *After the Fall* (1964), to some extent based on his second wife, the actress Marilyn Monroe, was less successful. *The Ride down Mount Morgan* (1991), *The Last Yankee* (1992), and *Broken Glass* (1994) are among his latest plays. Miller also wrote a novel, short stories, theatre essays, and *The Misfits* (1960), a filmscript for Marilyn Monroe. *Timebends* (1987) is his autobiography.

Miller, (Alton) Glenn (1904–44) US jazz trombonist and band-leader. From 1938 he led his celebrated swing big band, with whom he recorded his signature tune 'Moonlight Serenade'. He joined the US army in 1942 and died when his aircraft disappeared on a routine flight across the English Channel.

Miller, Henry (Valentine) (1891–1980) US novelist. From 1930 to 1940 he lived in France, where he published the autobiographical novels *Tropic of Cancer* (1934), about his life in Paris, and *Tropic of Capricorn* (1939), dealing with his youth in New York. Their frank depiction of sex and use of obscenities caused them to be banned in the USA until the 1960s. Other works include *The Air-Condi-*

tioned Nightmare (1945), reflections on a return to the USA.

millet Any of various grasses characterized by their very small seeds and used as a cereal since ancient times. With the exception of bulrush millet, they are smaller plants than sorghum or maize. They are important cereals of the tropics and warm, temperate regions, tolerating drought and intense heat, and growing rapidly and maturing, even on poor soil. They keep well, the finger millet, *Eleusine coracana*, of the semi-arid areas of southern India and Africa being particularly useful as a famine reserve, since heads of it can be stored for five years.

Tef, *Eragrostis tef*, is the staple millet of Ethiopia, where it was first cultivated thousands of years ago. Common millet, *Panicum miliaceum*, is widespread as a food crop for both man and livestock in the former Soviet Union, China, Japan, India, and southern Europe. In North America, common millet is known as hog millet. Foxtail millet, *Setaria italica*, is used in Britain and North America only as bird-seed, but elsewhere in the warm temperate regions, it is grown for human food.

Millet, Jean-François (1814–75) French painter. He studied art in Cherbourg, and then in 1837 travelled to Paris to work with Paul Delaroche (1797–1859), the professor of painting at the École Nationale Supérieure des Beaux-Arts. From 1850 he concentrated on the peasant subjects, such as *Sower* (1850) and *The Gleaners* (1857). He achieved considerable recognition after the Great Exhibition in Paris (1867).

Millett, Kate (full name Katharine Murray Millett) (1934–) US feminist. She became involved in the civil-rights movement of the 1960s, and in 1970 she published her influential book *Sexual Politics*, in which she advocated a radical feminism. *Going to Iran* (1981) tells of her experiences in and expulsion from that country in 1979 while campaigning for women's rights.

Milligan, Spike (born Terence Alan Milligan) (1918–) British comedian and writer, born in India. His work is characterized by his sense of the absurd. He came to prominence in the cult radio programme *The Goon Show* (1951–59) and thereafter appeared regularly on stage and television, and in minor film roles. He also wrote children's books, poetry, and autobiographical novels, such as *Adolf Hitler, My Part in His Downfall* (1971).

Millikan, Robert Andrews (1868–1953) US physicist. He was the first to give an accurate figure for the electric charge on an electron. Progressing from this to study the photoelectric effect, he confirmed the validity of Einstein's equation and gave an accurate figure for Planck's constant. Millikan also worked on the spectrometry of the lighter elements, and investigated cosmic rays. He was awarded the 1923 Nobel Prize for physics, and did much to establish the scientific reputation of the California Institute of Technology.

millipede A many-legged, herbivorous ARTHROPOD that lives in thick humus, burrows, or even caves. Millipedes considerably outnumber their relatives, the carnivorous centipedes, especially in the tropics, with over 7,500 species making up the class Diplopoda. They can be distinguished by shorter legs, arranged with two pairs per segment; and the body is usually more cylindrical than in the flatter, more agile centipedes. They protect themselves with unpleasant secretions, such as phenols or hydrogen cyanide, or by rolling into a ball when threatened.

Mills, Sir John (Lewis Ernest Watts) (1908–) British actor. He is well known for his appearances in war films, such as *This Happy Breed* (1944), in classics, such as *Great Expectations* (1946), and in adventure films, such as *Scott of the Antarctic* (1948) and *Ice Cold in Alex* (1958). Mills won an Oscar for his portrayal of a village idiot in *Ryan's Daughter* (1971). His daughters Juliet Mills (1941–) and Hayley Mills (1946–) have also had acting careers.

Milne, A(lan) A(lexander) (1882–1956) British writer of stories and poems for children. He is remembered for his series of nursery stories written for his son Christopher Robin (1920–96), namely *Winnie-the-Pooh* (1926) and *The House at Pooh Corner* (1928). He also wrote two collections of verse for children: *When We Were Very Young* (1924) and *Now We Are Six* (1927).

Milstein, César (1927–) Argentinian-British biochemist, discoverer of monoclonal antibodies. Cells in the spleen called lymphocytes are responsible for producing antibodies to defend the body against infection. Milstein found antibodies could be produced artificially by removing lymphocytes from the spleen and fusing them with cancerous cells. Such cells can be grown very easily in the laboratory and produce large amounts of 'monoclonal antibodies'. These antibodies can be used to identify blood groups and attack malignant tumours. Milstein shared the Nobel Prize for physiology and medicine with his co-workers in 1984.

Milton, John (1608–74) English poet. Milton's prolific early writings include the masque *Comus* (1637) and the elegy 'Lycidas' (1638). He became politically active during the Civil War, publishing the *Areopagitica* (1644), which demanded a free press, and writing a defence of republicanism on the eve of the Restoration (1660). His three major poems, all completed after he had become blind (1652), have biblical subjects and show his skilful use of blank verse: they are *Paradise Lost* (1667, revised 1674), an epic on the fall of man, *Paradise Regained* (1671), on Christ's temptations, and *Samson Agonistes* (1671), on Samson's final hours.

Milton Keynes A town in Buckinghamshire, south-central England, headquarters of the Open University; pop. (1991) 172,300. It was built as a New Town around the village of Milford to a design by Richard Llewelyn-Davies in 1967, and has become a byword as an archetypical modern shopping centre.

Milwaukee An industrial port and city in southeast Wisconsin, USA, on the west shore of Lake Michigan; pop. (1990) 628,090. First settled in 1822, the city developed from the 1830s, attracting large numbers of settlers from Germany in the 1840s and from Poland and Italy later in the century. It is noted for its brewing industry and is an important port on the St Lawrence Seaway.

mime To play a part with mimic gestures, usually without words. Even at its highest level the mime differs from more conventional forms of drama by its preoccupation with character-drawing rather than plot, a necessary consequence of its more or less improvised nature. Modern mime has nothing in common with the original Roman mime, and approximates far more closely to the art of the Roman *pantomimus*, being entirely dependent on gesture and movement, usually accompanied by music, but wordless. An outstanding exponent of mime in the 20th century has been Marcel MARCEAU. In recent years a new form of mime has developed, particularly in the work of Philippe Gaulier and Monica Pagneaux at the Le

Coq School in Paris, in which dialogue is not prohibited but arises out of improvisation and is subservient to the physical component.

mimicry A form of PROTECTIVE COLORATION in nature that uses colours or shapes to confuse potential predators. There are two main types of mimicry, Batesian and Müllerian, named after the scientists who first described them. In Batesian mimicry a harmless species, known as the mimic, resembles a poisonous or dangerous species, known as the model. A predator that has had the unpleasant experience of trying to eat the model, will learn to avoid not only the model in future, but also the mimic. Hornets, for example, have a dangerous sting and a distinctive black and yellow colour pattern. The harmless hornet clear-wing moth has evolved not only the black and yellow stripes, but also transparent wings, so that it looks remarkably like its model.

In Müllerian mimicry, a group of distasteful or well-defended species have evolved a common colour pattern. Many wasps and bees have the same barred black and yellow coloration. The advantage to individuals of these species is that a predator will sample a few unpleasant individuals of any one species, learn to associate their colour pattern with the experience, and then avoid all species with similar colour patterns.

Some organisms also use mimicry for other purposes, such as evading detection by their prey, as with the flower-mimicking mantids, or even in order to pretend to be members of the opposite sex, as in reef fish. Some plants also employ mimicry: bee orchids have evolved flowers that look so like bees that they deceive the real insects into copulating with them, in the process picking up or delivering their pollen.

mimosa See ACACIA.

Minch, the (or **the Minches**) A channel of the Atlantic between the mainland of Scotland and the Outer Hebrides. The northern stretch is called the **North Minch**, the southern stretch, north-west of Skye, is called the **Little Minch**.

MIND (National Association for Mental Health) A British voluntary organization that runs advice centres for the mentally ill and campaigns for better services for and understanding of mental illness. It was founded in 1946.

Mindanao The second-largest island of the Philippines; area 102,000 sq km (39,400 sq miles); pop. (1990) 14,297,000. Its chief cities are Davao, Zamboanga, Cagayan de Oro, Butuan, Iligan, and General Santos. Mindanao is the centre of a long-standing secessionist movement.

Minden An industrial city in North Rhine-Westphalia, north-west Germany, on the River Weser; pop. (1985) 80,000. Founded by Charlemagne *c.*800, it was the scene of a battle in 1759 during which the French were defeated by a British and Hanoverian army.

Mindszenty, József (born József Pehm) (1892–1975) Hungarian prelate. He was imprisoned by the Hungarian puppet government (1944–45) and was sentenced to penal servitude for life, commuted to house detention. Freed at the time of the HUNGARIAN REVOLUTION, on the return of Soviet forces, he sought refuge in the US Legation in Budapest, staying there until 1971.

mine (in warfare) An explosive device placed in water or buried underground, which is designed to destroy ships, vehicles, and personnel. Naval mines are triggered by an electric current transmitted from shore through a cable. More recent naval mines are triggered by the magnetic field of a passing ship, the effect of a ship on the local water pressure, or the sound waves from a ship's engines or propellers. Some mines combine two of these mechanisms. Limpet mines are fixed by divers on to the hulls of ships and detonated by a timed fuse. Land-mines were developed between the two World Wars. At first they had metal cases, but the use of mine-detectors led to alternative casings of plastic or wood. Land-mines are fitted with a fuse that is triggered by pressure. These antipersonnel mines remain in the ground long after the conflict that made use of them has ended. In the mid-1990s it has been estimated that 100 million antipersonnel mines remain buried in some 50 countries, where they cause devastating mutilations to civilians, especially children. The crusade to ban their use, led by Diana, Princess of Wales shortly before her death, has earned the backing of many countries, including the UK, but not the USA.

mine-layer A ship purpose-built or adapted to lay MINES. The mines are stowed on or below deck on rails, and are laid through stern doors, usually at precisely calculated positions. Some submarines have been adapted to lay mines, and other ship types can also temporarily be fitted as mine-layers. Ground mines, laid on the sea-bed in shallow water, are usually laid by aircraft.

mineral A naturally occurring substance of inorganic origin that is homogeneous and has a definite chemical composition. Nearly all the 2,500 or so minerals so far identified are crystalline; their molecular structures are regular and their chemical composition varies only within specific limits. If a mineral has no crystal form it is said to be amorphous. Minerals are generally classified by their chemical composition. The principal groups are: native elements (such as gold and silver); halides (evaporite minerals found in salt lakes and arid environments); sulphides (such as galena – a common lead mineral); oxides (usually hard, dense minerals, such as the iron ore haematite); carbonates (soft, light-coloured minerals, such as calcite and dolomite); sulphates (common minerals, such as gypsum); phosphates (such as apatite); and silicates (the largest mineral group, containing most rock-forming minerals: quartz, feldspar, and mica). Their uses vary: some are sources of rare or essential metals; some are used as catalysts or fluxes in chemical reactions; some are of aesthetic value as collectors' items or jewellery stones.

mineralogy The science of the chemical composition, physical properties, and occurrence of MINERALS; and the classification of individual minerals into an overall system and their specific identification are important aspects of the subject. The earliest known book on minerals is by Theophrastus (327–287 BC); systematic study was first begun by Georgius Agricola in 1527 in Bohemia as an aid to research in the mining industry. The scientific study of minerals is still of great importance to both mining and chemical industries.

miner's cat See RING-TAILED CAT.

Minerva In Roman mythology, the goddess of wisdom and the arts, identified with Athena in Greek mythology.

minesweeper (or **mine-hunter, mine countermeasures vessel**) A vessel designed or modified to sweep or explode MINES laid at sea. Wooden or glass-reinforced plastic hulls are necessary to avoid detection by magnetic mines, which can be detonated by an LL sweep. This consists of two electric cables that generate an electric charge in the water between them, exploding any magnetic mines present. Acoustic mines are destroyed by simulated propeller noise, while pressure mines can be located by SONAR and detonated by a remote-controlled SUBMERSIBLE.

Ming The Chinese dynasty founded in 1368 by Chu Yuan-chang after the collapse of Mongol authority in China, and ruling until succeeded by the Manchus in 1644. It was a period of expansion and exploration, with lasting contact made in the 16th century between China and Europe, and a culturally productive period in which the arts flourished. The capital was established at Peking (Beijing) in 1421.

Mingus, Charles (known as 'Charlie') (1922–79) US jazz bassist and composer. After studying the double bass in Los Angeles with Louis Armstrong, he became part of the 1940s jazz scene alongside Dizzy Gillespie, Thelonious Monk, and Charlie Parker. Well-known compositions of that time included 'Goodbye Porkpie Hat' and 'The Black Saint and the Sinner Lady'.

miniature A very small painting, particularly a portrait that can be held in the hand or worn as a piece of jewellery. The word is also applied to manuscript ILLUMINATIONS. The small portraits that we now call miniatures were known as 'limnings' or 'pictures in little' during the Elizabethan period, when the art – in the hands of Nicholas Hilliard – had its finest flowering. They were usually painted on vellum, occasionally on ivory or card. Miniature portraiture continued to flourish until the mid-19th century, when photography virtually killed the art.

minicomputer A COMPUTER that is intermediate in performance between a mainframe computer and a MICROCOMPUTER. The minicomputer first appeared in the mid-1960s to meet a demand from scientists and engineers who wanted computing power for specific applications but did not require a mainframe. The machines generally incorporated 16-BIT and then, later, 32-bit data BUS architecture. In the 1970s minicomputers spread into business applications, but the development of sophisticated microcomputers has eroded the traditional minicomputer market.

minimal art A trend in painting and more especially sculpture, arising during the 1950s, in which only the most basic geometric forms were used. Minimal art is associated particularly with the USA, and its impersonality is seen as a reaction against the emotiveness of ABSTRACT EXPRESSIONISM. Carl Andre is a leading exponent and his works have been controversial.

minimal music (or **minimalism**) A type of music that emerged in the 1960s and involves the repetition of brief musical figures in a simple harmonic field. The US composers Steve REICH, Terry Riley (1935–), and Philip GLASS are particularly associated with this kind of music, which is in part a reaction against the intellectual aridity of the work of some of their contemporaries. The hypnotic effect of incessant repetition, in which figures gradually evolve over a long timespan, suggests the influence of oriental music.

minimum wage A state-sanctioned and legally enforceable minimum rate of pay. The practice of minimum wage regulation, first developed in New Zealand and Australia around 1900, is widespread in both developing and industrialized countries. In some countries, regulations affect workers in only a few low-paid occupations, whereas in most countries in Africa, Latin America, and the Middle East, employees in almost all occupations are covered although those working in the informal sector may not benefit. Although minimum wage rates tend to be low, infrequently updated, and difficult to enforce, they have, according to the INTERNATIONAL LABOUR ORGANIZATION, contributed to an improvement in wage levels in many places. In the UK no minimum wage exists although the Labour government intends to introduce one. It is a statutory condition of the social chapter of the Maastricht Treaty for members of the EU. It is sometimes argued that a minimum wage can increase unemployment because employers may be unwilling to take on staff to perform low-paid menial tasks. Not all economists agree with this view.

mining Excavation for the removal of ORES and minerals from the Earth's crust. PROSPECTING for mineral deposits is now a highly technical operation requiring extensive knowledge of Earth sciences and the use of a wide range of techniques. Such surveys must take into account the nature of the rocks surrounding the ore deposit, as they will affect the overall economics of the operation. If the located deposit lies near the surface, OPEN-CAST MINING or HYDRAULIC MINING might be appropriate. For deeper deposits a vertical shaft may be sunk, with horizontal TUNNELS running off into the mineral (deep mining); a horizontal tunnel running into the deposit may be dug into the side of a hill or mountain (adit mining or DRIFT-MINING); or an inclined shaft may be sunk parallel to the deposit, with horizontal tunnels connected to the mineral vein at intervals. Large rotary drills plus blasting are used for tunnelling, in conjunction with systems for hauling and hoisting the debris to the surface. Some excavated sections will need no reinforcement, but sometimes both ceilings and walls need support. In BORD-AND-PILLAR MINING the mine is constructed so that unmined material supports the roof. In LONG-WALL MINING the seam is excavated along a face up to 350 m (1,150 feet) in length. See also COAL-MINING.

mink A carnivore related to the weasel and the otter. There are two species, the North American mink, *Mustela vison*, and the much rarer European mink, *M. lutreola*, which is now confined to the former Soviet Union east of the Urals and western France. Mink are prized for their fur and many are bred on fur farms. Escapes have led to the American mink becoming established as a wild species in Scandinavia, Iceland, Germany, the former Soviet Union, and most of mainland Britain. Mink are generalized carnivores and feral mink occasionally become pests.

Minkowski, Hermann (1864–1909) Russian-born German mathematician. He studied the theory of quadratic forms, and contributed to the understanding of the geometrical properties of sets in multidimensional space. Minkowski was the first to suggest the concept of four-dimensional space–time, which was the basis for Einstein's later work on the general theory of relativity.

Minneapolis An industrial city and port at the head of navigation on the Mississippi River in south-east Minnesota; pop. (1990) 368,380. Settled in 1847, it is a major processing and distribution centre for the grain and cattle farms of the upper Midwest agricultural region.

Minnesota A state in the north-central USA, on the Canadian border; area 218,601 sq km (84,402 sq miles); pop. (1990) 4,375,100; capital, St Paul. The largest cities are Minneapolis and St Paul. Minnesota is also known as the North Star or Gopher

State. Part of it was ceded to Britain by the French in 1763 and acquired by the USA in 1783, the remainder forming part of the Louisiana Purchase in 1803. Minnesota was organized as a territory in 1849 and became the 32nd US state in 1858. In addition to producing 75 per cent of the country's iron ore, which is mined from the world's largest opencast iron mine, it produce large quantities of grain, vegetables, and livestock. Its principal landmarks include Voyageurs National Park, Mississippi National River and Recreation Area, and the Pipestone and Grand Portage national monuments.

Minoan An ancient civilization centred on Crete (*c.*3000–1100 BC). It was the earliest on European soil, and was first revealed by the excavations of Sir Arthur Evans, who gave it its name, based on the legendary King Minos. It had reached its zenith by the beginning of the late Bronze Age, extending over the islands of the south Aegean while its wares were exported to Cyprus, Syria, and Egypt. Urban centres were dominated by palaces such as those at Knossos, Mallia, Phaistos, and Zakro. Divided into two periods by a devastating earthquake that occurred *c.*1700 BC, the Minoan civilization was noted particularly for its Linear A script and distinctive palatial art and architecture. It greatly influenced the later Mycenacans, whose presence in Crete is attested from the 16th century BC and who succeeded the Minoans in control of the Aegean *c.*1400 BC.

Minorca (Spanish **Menorca**) The most easterly and second-largest of the BALEARIC ISLANDS; area 689 sq km (266 sq miles); pop. (1981) 58,700; capital, Mahón.

minor planet See ASTEROID.

Minos See MINOTAUR.

Minotaur In Greek mythology, a monster with a man's body and a bull's head. It was kept by **Minos**, king of Crete, in a labyrinth built by Daedalus. The citizens of Athens had to send a yearly tribute of seven youths and seven maidens to be eaten by the Minotaur, until Theseus – with Ariadne's help – killed it.

Minsk An industrial and commercial city in eastern Europe, capital of the Republic of Belarus (Belorussia); pop. (1990) 1,612,800. Formerly held by Lithuania and Poland, it passed to Russia in 1793. Its large Jewish population was annihilated in concentration camps during World War II. In 1991 it became capital of the newly independent state of Belorussia. Its factories make motor vehicles, machinery, electronic goods, and textiles.

minstrel A professional entertainer of the 11th to 17th centuries, as opposed to the church musicians. The French minstrels were called **jongleurs**, while in Germany they were **Gaukler** and in Britain **gleemen**. *Jongleurs* were entertainers, including musicians, who travelled throughout Europe, from the 11th to the 13th centuries. **Troubadours** were poet-musicians of the South of France (Provence) and adjoining areas of Italy and Spain in the 11th to 13th centuries. Their songs are commonly on the theme of courtly love, and their language was Old Provençal or *Langue d'Oc*. Many were of noble birth. **Trouvères** were poet-musicians of northern France, writing in the *Langue d'Oïl* dialect. They were similar to the troubadours, but existed at a slightly later date. **Minnesinger** were the German equivalent of the troubadours in the 12th to 14th centuries. The word *minne* means 'courtly love'. Later came the **Meistersinger** guilds of amateur musicians that flourished during the 15th, 16th, and 17th centuries in Germany as a middle- and lower-class continuation of the aristocratic *Minnesinger*. Waits were street musicians in medieval England who acted as town watchmen, marking the hours of day by sounding instruments. By the 16th century they had formed themselves into town bands. Some also sang – hence Christmas carollers are also called 'waits'.

mint An aromatic plant belonging to the genus *Mentha*. The most familiar of several species is the common or spear mint (*M. spicata*), a perennial, lilac-flowered plant growing up to 90 cm (3 feet) tall. Indigenous to southern Europe, this species is now widely grown as a garden herb. Other mints, including water mint, *M. aquatica*, and corn mint, *M. arvensis*, are true species, but some, such as peppermint and French mint, are hybrids. The leaves of mints are covered with glandular hairs and are used as culinary herbs.

Minton, Thomas (1765–1836) British pottery and china manufacturer. He was an engraver with Josiah Spode before founding his own business in Stoke-on-Trent (1789). Four years later he built a pottery works in Stoke, where he popularized the willow pattern, and in 1820 started producing bone china. During the 19th century the Minton factory became the best-known source of made-to-order tableware in the UK.

minuet A stately dance in triple time, which originated as a popular dance but was taken up and refined by the French court in the 17th century. In a minuet the couple moved through set figures performing circling movements around each other, presenting right and then left hands. It became one of the optional movements of the Baroque dance SUITE, and thus gained entry into the symphony as a standard third movement.

minute ▶**1** A unit of time equal to 60 SECONDS or one sixtieth of an hour. ▶**2** A unit of angle equal to 60 seconds, or one sixtieth of a degree.

Miocene Epoch The fourth of the five geological epochs of the TERTIARY era, spanning the time-interval from 23.7 to 5.3 million years ago. The Miocene was a period of great Earth-movements during which the Alps, the Himalayas, and the western CORDILLERA of America were being formed. Sediments of Miocene age are found in southern Europe.

Mir A SPACE STATION put into Earth orbit by the Soviet Union on 20 February 1986 and manned by successive crews of cosmonauts. Each crew is able to spend some months in orbit carrying out programmes of scientific and technological research before being returned to Earth. Mir has a habitable volume of 100 cubic metres. Since its launch it has been increased in size by attaching new segments, such as the Kvant astrophysics module, making it the largest continuously manned space station. Astronauts from a number of nations including Austria, Britain, France, Germany, and the USA have been included in the crews. It is regularly supplied by unmanned Progress vehicles. A series of mishaps in 1997 raised questions about the future of the space station.

Mirabeau, Honoré Gabriel Riqueti, Comte de (1749–91) French revolutionary politician. Mirabeau rose to prominence in the early days of the French Revolution, when he became deputy of the Third Estate in the States General. His moderate political stance led him to press for a form of constitutional monarchy; he was made President of the National Assembly in 1791, but died shortly afterwards.

miracle (from Latin *mirari*, 'to wonder at') An event

for which no logical explanation can be given; it is therefore attributed to a supernatural agency. Belief in miracles is common to practically all religions, particularly in their popular forms. The biographies of great religious leaders, such as Buddha, Moses, Jesus, or Muhammad, commonly include stories of miraculous events. Muhammad, however, denied that he possessed miraculous powers, choosing to regard the KORAN as the great miracle. In Christianity the issue of the literal truth of a miracle is of greater importance than in other religions because of the function of miracles in the accounts of Jesus' life in the Gospels: the virgin birth, the miracles of healing, and the resurrection are all believed to attest Jesus' divinity.

miracle play See MYSTERY PLAY.

mirage An optical illusion that occurs when sharp differences in temperature and therefore in density develop between thin layers of air at and immediately above the ground. This causes light to be bent, or refracted, as it travels through one layer to the next. As a result, the relationship between objects and the horizon becomes distorted. During the day, when a warm layer occurs next to the ground, objects near the horizon often appear to be reflected in flat surfaces, such as beaches, deserts, roads, and water. This produces the shimmering, floating images which are commonly observed on very hot days.

Miranda A satellite of Uranus, discovered by the Dutch-American astronomer Gerard Kuiper in 1948. It has a nearly circular orbit at 129,390 km from the planet's centre with an inclination of 4.2 degrees to the equator of Uranus; its diameter is about 480 km.

mirid bug (or **capsid**) A heteropteran bug of the family Miridae, occurring on vegetation almost everywhere, from sea-shore to mountaintop. Most species suck plant juices, but a few are carnivorous, and they vary widely in appearance and habits, constituting the largest family of BUGS with over 6,000 species. Few mirid bugs exceed 1 cm (0.5 inch) in length, most are elongate and soft-bodied, and many are green or brown. The tarnished plant bug, *Lygus pabulinus*, and apple capsid, *Plesiocoris rugicollis*, are pests wherever fruit trees are grown. They feed on buds, young shoots, and developing fruit. Some species are good mimics of ants, and probably feed on their larvae.

Miró, Joan (1893–1983) Spanish painter, sculptor, and designer. From 1919 he spent much of his time in Paris, returning to live in Spain in 1940. One of the most prominent figures of surrealism, he painted a brightly coloured fantasy world of variously spiky and amoebic calligraphic forms against plain backgrounds. Major works include *Harlequinade* (1924–25).

mirror A smooth surface that reflects light, forming images. A plane (flat) mirror forms a full-sized, reversed image that appears to be as far behind the mirror as the object is in front. Concave curved mirrors give upright enlarged images of close objects or inverted images of far objects. They are used as reflectors for searchlights and headlights (condensing the beam), and to collect light in astronomical telescopes (see REFLECTING TELESCOPE). Convex curved mirrors produce smaller upright images with a wide field of view and are used as rear-view driving mirrors.

MIRV See MULTIPLE INDEPENDENTLY TARGETABLE RE-ENTRY VEHICLE.

miscarriage See ABORTION.

Mishima, Yukio (pseudonym of Hiraoka Kimitake) (1925–70) Japanese writer. He won acclaim for his first novel, *Confessions of a Mask* (1949), in which he describes coming to terms with his homosexuality. His best-known work, the four-volume *The Sea of Fertility* (1965–70), deals with themes of reincarnation and the sterility of modern life. He was an avowed imperialist, who committed suicide by disembowelling himself in public after a failed attempt to incite soldiers against the postwar regime.

Mishnah (Hebrew, 'teaching by repetition') The earliest and most authoritative collection of Jewish oral laws or traditions, the final compilation of which was under the direction of Rabbi Judah (135–217 AD). The Mishnah is composed of six major sections: religious laws concerning agriculture; ritual and religious observance; women, marriage, and family life; civil and criminal law; the Temple and rules pertaining to sacrifice; and laws on ritual purity. The Gemara (Aramaic, 'completion') are the commentaries on the Mishnah, which together constitute the TALMUD.

missel-thrush (or **mistle-thrush**) A largish, greyish THRUSH, *Turdus miscivorus*, 25 cm (10 inches) long, with a rather upright stance and a harsh chattering call. It is a species found across most of Europe, and on the higher ground of eastern Asia. It lives in open country with scattered clumps of trees, and feeds on many small animals, fruits, and berries. The name, mistle-thrush, is derived from its habit of eating mistletoe berries.

missile An object, normally a weapon, that is thrown or projected at a target. In modern usage, missiles are self-propelled, explosive weapons, usu-

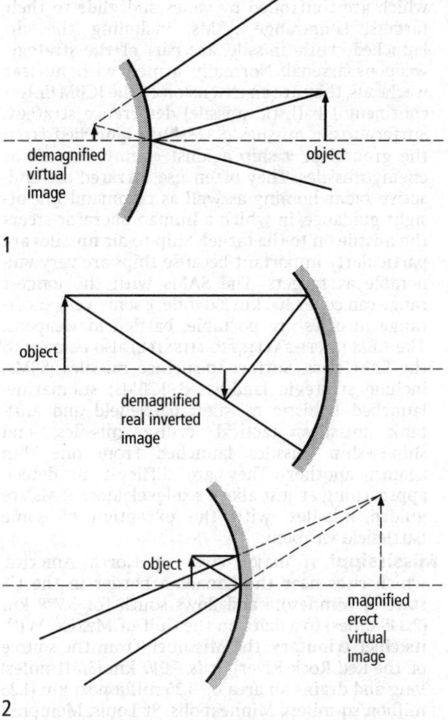

Mirrors (1) A convex curved mirror forms an upright virtual image. (2) A concave curved mirror can form an inverted real image or an upright virtual image.

ally powered by a ROCKET MOTOR. Many missiles are simply aimed at the target and fired; others, GUIDED MISSILES, are steered on to the target during flight, either automatically or under remote control by an operator. Some guided missiles can pursue a target even when it is taking evasive action.

The first truly guided missiles were used operationally during World War II, when Germany bombarded London and other Allied cities with the V2 rocket, a BALLISTIC MISSILE, and the V1 pulse jet, a primitive CRUISE MISSILE. Other types, including air-to-surface and surface-to-air missiles, were also being developed in Germany before the war ended. Subsequently, the USA, the Soviet Union, France, the UK, and many other countries began research on this type of weapon.

Modern-day missiles are classified according to their use. Air-to-air missiles (AAMs) are fired from an aeroplane or a helicopter at an airborne target. They are usually guided missiles employing active or semi-active radar homing. Infrared (heat-seeking) missiles of the 'fire-and-forget' type – that is, once launched, they receive no further guidance – are effective in good conditions at ranges of up to 20 km (12 miles). A missile launched from an aircraft to attack a target on the ground or at sea is called an air-to-surface missile (ASM). Some unguided ASMs are employed in mass bombardment of a local target. Many others, however, use sophisticated guidance technologies, including television, infrared radiation, laser-illumination, and active or semi-active radar homing. Some ASMs are tactical (short-range) weapons, directed against targets such as ships, tanks, and bridges; they include unpowered, so-called 'smart' bombs, which are controlled by vanes and glide to their targets. Long-range ASMs, including the air-launched cruise missile, are part of the strategic weapons arsenal. Normally armed with nuclear warheads, they are an extension of the ICBM (intercontinental ballistic missile) deterrence strategy. Surface-to-air missiles (SAMs) are launched from the ground or a ship against enemy aircraft or enemy missiles. They often use infrared or semi-active radar homing as well as command line-of-sight guidance, in which a human operator steers the missile on to the target. Ship-to-air missiles are particularly important because ships are very vulnerable as targets. The SAMs with the longest range can cover 100 km (60 miles); some very short-range missiles are portable, battlefield weapons. The ABM (ANTI-BALLISTIC MISSILE) also belongs to the SAM class. Surface-to-surface missiles (SSMs) include strategic land-based ICBMs; submarine-launched ballistic missiles; battlefield and anti-tank missiles; tactical cruise missiles; and ship-to-ship missiles launched from one ship against another. They are difficult to detect, approaching at just above sea-level. Most SSMs are guided missiles, with the exception of some battlefield weapons.

Mississippi A major river of North America, which rises near the Canadian border in the US state of Minnesota and flows south for 3,778 km (2,348 miles) to a delta on the Gulf of Mexico. With its chief tributary, the Missouri (from the source of the Red Rock River), it is 6,019 km (3,741 miles) long and drains an area of 3.25 million sq km (1.25 million sq miles); Minneapolis, St Louis, Memphis, and New Orleans lie on the Mississippi. Known to the Indians as the 'Great Water', it provided a route into North America for early explorers, such as de Soto (1539), Joliet (1672), and La Salle (1681). From the 1830s onwards it was famous for the stern-wheeler steamboats that plied between New Orleans, St Louis, and other northern cities. The river, its traffic, and its people were celebrated in the writings of Mark Twain.

Mississippi A state of the southern USA, on the Gulf of Mexico, bounded to the west by the lower Mississippi River; area 123,515 sq km (47,689 sq miles); pop. (1990) 2,573,210; the capital and largest city is Jackson. Mississippi is also known as the Magnolia State. A French colony in the 18th century, it was ceded to Britain in 1763 and to the USA in 1783, becoming the 29th state in 1817. Formerly dependent on cotton, its agriculture now produces large quantities of soyabeans, corn, peanuts, pecan, rice, and sugar cane. Landmarks include Vicksburg National Military Park, Tupelo National Battlefield, and the 712-km (445-mile) long Natchez Trace Parkway.

Mississippian Period The earlier of the two epochs or subsystems into which the CARBONIFEROUS PERIOD is subdivided in North America (the other being the PENNSYLVANIAN PERIOD). It covers the span from 360 to 320 million years ago.

Missolonghi (Greek **Mesolóngion**) A city in western Greece, on the north shore of the Gulf of Patras, capital of the department of Aetolia and Acarnania; pop. (1991) 10,900. It resisted the Turkish forces in the War of Greek Independence (1821–29) and is noted as the place where the poet Byron, who had joined the fight, died in 1824.

Missouri A major river of North America, one of the main tributaries of the Mississippi. It rises in the Rocky Mountains in Montana and flows 3,725 km (2,315 miles) to meet the Mississippi just north of St Louis. Its total length to the head of the Red Rock is 4,125 km (2,564 miles).

Missouri A state of central USA, bounded on the east by the Mississippi River; area 180,516 sq km (69,697 sq miles); pop. (1990) 5,117,070; capital, Jefferson City. The largest cities are Kansas City, St Louis, Springfield, and Independence. Missouri is also known as the Show-Me State. Acquired from the French as part of the Louisiana Purchase (1803), it became the 24th state in 1821. Grain, cotton, vegetables, and tobacco are produced and important industrial goods include aerospace and transportation equipment. Lead, zinc, coal, and limestone are the principal mineral resources. Notable landmarks include the Ozark National Scenic Riverway, Wilson's Creek National Battlefield, George Washington Carver National Monument, Harry S. Truman National Historic Site, and Ulysses S. Grant National Historic Site.

mistletoe A parasitic plant with green leaves and roots that penetrate the host plant. Mistletoes comprise some 1,300 species of the family Vixcaceae, with a mainly tropical distribution, but extending into temperate regions. Most species absorb nutrients from their host and some tropical species are a problem in citrus plantations. They produce small flowers that develop into small fruits with sticky flesh, which adheres to the beaks of birds. The mistletoe seeds are distributed by birds, which feed on their berries, often being placed on new host plants as the birds clean their beaks.

Mistletoe is used as a Christmas decoration in Europe and North America. The common Eurasian mistletoe, *Viscum album*, is a parasite of trees such as oak, hawthorn, and apple. The equivalent species in North America is *Phoradendron flavescens*.

mistral A cold, northerly wind that blows down the

Rhône valley of southern France into the Mediterranean; in summer it increases the danger of forest fires.

Mistral, Frédéric (1830–1914) French Provençal poet. He was the leader of a movement called *le Félibrige*, whose object was the revival of PROVENÇAL language and literature. His own masterpiece, *Mirèio* (1859), a poem about rural life, inspired Gounod's opera *Mireille* (1864). His example encouraged the revival of Catalan and stimulated interest in regional literature elsewhere.

Mitchell, Joni (born Roberta Joan Anderson) (1943–) Canadian singer and songwriter. After making her name as a singer and guitarist in Toronto clubs, she became known as a songwriter in the late 1960s. Mitchell's career as a recording artist began in 1968; her many albums include *Blue* (1971) *Mingus* (1979), and *Dog Eat Dog* (1986).

Mitchell, Margaret (1900–49) US novelist. She is known for the best-selling novel *Gone with the Wind* (1936), set during the American Civil War. It was awarded the Pulitzer Prize, as well as being made into a successful film (1939).

Mitchell, R(eginald) J(oseph) (1895–1937) British aeronautical engineer. He is best known for designing the Spitfire fighter aircraft; 19,000 aeroplanes based on his 1936 prototype were used by the RAF during World War II, although he did not live to see the success of his plane.

Mitchum, Robert (1917–97) US actor. He was a workman and professional boxer before going to Hollywood in 1943 and becoming a film extra. He later starred in such films as *Out of the Past* (1947) *Night of the Hunter* (1955), and *Farewell My Lovely* (1975).

mite A tiny, often beautifully coloured ARACHNID. Most mites are less than 1 mm (0.04 inch) long and so able to live in minute habitats unavailable to other arthropods, usually on land but sometimes underwater. They belong to the order Acarina, which also includes TICKS among the 35,000 species, some of them a threat to human health or to commercial products. In mites the front and back parts of the typical arachnid body are fused to give a simple ovoid shape with eight short legs. Males and females are similar, although the female may be larger, and mating involves the transfer of sperm packages by the male, using his jaws. The young stages have only six legs.

Mites are very diverse in their habits. Some eat green plants, and the spider mites are pests of cotton and fruit trees. Many scavenge on dry products, like the house-dust mite, *Dermatophagoides*, which is notorious for causing human allergies. 'Chiggers', *Trombicula*, are attracted by warm carbon dioxide in mammals' breath. Their larvae are parasites, feeding off skin and producing severe itching in humans. Mites can transmit disease in the tropics, above all mange and scabies.

Mitford, Nancy (Freeman) (1904–73) British writer. Nancy and her sister **Jessica (Lucy)** (1917–96), also a writer, were born into an aristocratic family; their other sisters included **Unity** (1914–48), who was an admirer of Hitler, and **Diana** (1910–), who married Sir Oswald Mosley in 1936. Nancy achieved fame with her comic novels, including *The Pursuit of Love* (1945) and *Love in a Cold Climate* (1949). She was also the editor of *Noblesse Oblige* (1956), which popularized the terms 'U' and 'Non-U', used by the British linguist Alan Ross to categorize the speech and behaviour of the upper class. Jessica became a US citizen in 1944 and was a member of the American Communist Party in the 1940s and 1950s. She is best known for her works on American culture, notably *The American Way of Death* (1963) and *The American Way of Birth* (1992).

Mithras The central figure of **mithraism**, a cult popular among Roman soldiers of the later empire. Scholars are divided as to whether there is real continuity between this cult and the reverence for 'Mithra', an Indo-Iranian creator Sun-god, shown in much earlier scriptures of HINDUISM and ZOROASTRIANISM. The Roman cult focused on secret rituals in cave sanctuaries devoted to sculptures of Mithras killing a cosmic bull. Initiates underwent severe tests, which demonstrated the cult's concern with the soldierly virtues of courage and fortitude. Women were excluded. Mithraism flourished along the empire's frontiers – the rivers Danube, and Rhine, and in Britain – but finally succumbed to the challenge of Christianity.

Mithridates VI (or **Mithradates VI**) (*c*.132–63 BC) King of Pontus 120–63. His expansionist policies led to a war with Rome (88–85), during which he occupied most of Asia Minor and much of Greece, until driven back by Sulla. Two further wars followed (83–82, 74–66); he was defeated by the Roman general Lucullus (*c*.110–*c*.57) and finally by Pompey.

mitochondrion A minute, cigar-shaped or branching structure found in the cytoplasm of all CELLS except those of BACTERIA. Mitochondria are about 0.003 mm (0.0001 inch) long, and are the site of a vital process called RESPIRATION, in which energy is released for the cell's needs. The series of chemical reactions that occurs in respiration comprise KREBS' CYCLE, in the fluid centre of the mitochondrion, and those of the ELECTRON TRANSPORT CHAIN, producing ATP, positioned on the folded inner membrane. The outer membrane forms a simple barrier between the mitochondrion and the rest of the cell. Mitochondria, like plant chloroplasts, also contain ribosomes and small amounts of DNA, and this observation has given rise to a theory, known as the 'endosymbiont hypothesis', that these organelles were originally symbiotic bacteria that became adapted to live within cells.

mitosis The process by which one CELL divides to produce two genetically identical cells, each known as a daughter cell. In plants and animals, all growth occurs through mitotic divisions. Mitosis first involves the division of the nucleus and CHROMOSOMES, then the division of the cytoplasm to form two discrete cells.

There are four phases recognized in mitosis (prophase, metaphase, anaphase, and telophase) and these are preceded by the chromosomes becoming apparent as thread-like strands in the nucleus. These strands shorten and become more prominent during prophase. There are normally two copies of every chromosome in each cell, and during prophase each chromosome reproduces itself. This gives each chromosome a double appearance as each now consists of two halves or chromatids. During metaphase and anaphase, these 'double' chromosomes are pulled apart, each chromatid (now called a true chromosome) migrates to opposite ends of the cell where it is surrounded by a new nuclear membrane; the cell then separates to form two new cells. See illustration p. 916.

Mitterrand, François (Maurice Marie) (1916–96) French statesman, President 1981–95. After working to strengthen the Left alliance, Mitterrand became First Secretary of the new Socialist Party in 1971. As President he initially moved to raise basic wages, increase social benefits, nationalize key industries, and decentralize government.

After the Socialist Party lost its majority vote in the 1986 general election, Mitterrand asked the right-wing politician Jacques Chirac to serve as Prime Minister. Mitterrand was re-elected as President in 1988 and served until his retirement due to ill-health in 1995. He died the following year.

mixed economy An economy that has both a predominant PRIVATE SECTOR and a sizeable PUBLIC SECTOR, so that resources are allocated both by the MARKET and by the state. In the private sector, the market or price system will determine what quantities of goods and services are produced, and to whom they are distributed. In the public sector, such decisions will be made by government. The economies of all modern states except the communist PLANNED ECONOMIES are mixed. The relative importance of the two sectors varies, however, and in the 1980s many countries favoured PRIVATIZATION and DEREGULATION of public-sector enterprises. In a mixed economy, there may also be some government INTERVENTION in private-sector economic activity.

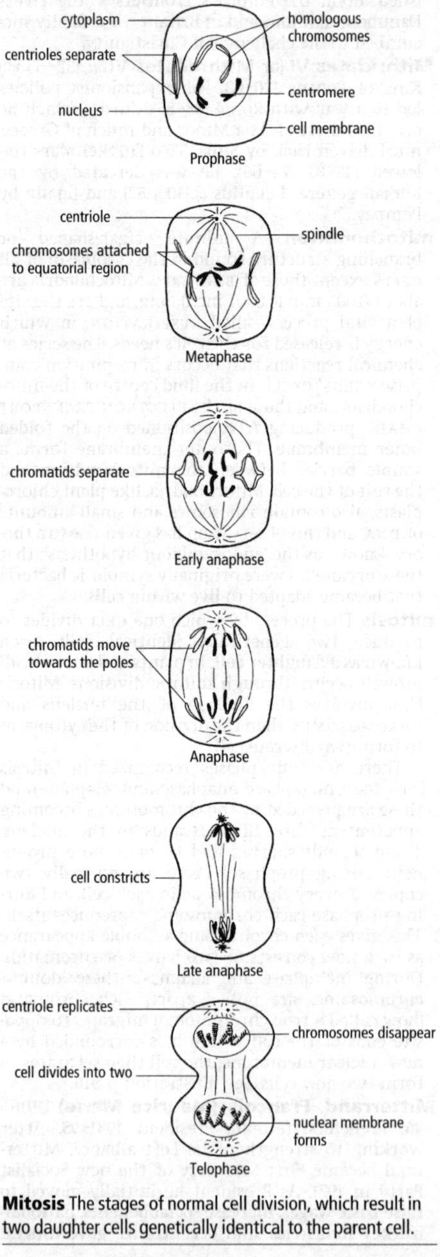

Mitosis The stages of normal cell division, which result in two daughter cells genetically identical to the parent cell.

mixture (in chemistry) Any quantity of one substance randomly distributed through another substance without any chemical reaction taking place between the components. Mixtures differ from compounds in that the latter contain two or more elements joined together in fixed proportions by chemical bonds. Mixtures retain the chemical properties of their components and can be separated by physical means into their components, whereas compounds have distinct chemical properties and can only be separated into their components by chemical means.

Mizar A second-magnitude MULTIPLE STAR in the constellation of Ursa Major, and also known as Zeta Ursae Majoris. Two components are hot DWARF STARS moving in an orbit of very long period, and forming the first double star to be discovered, by Giambattista Riccioli in 1650. The brighter star was also the first spectroscopic BINARY STAR to be found, by the US astronomer Edward Pickering in 1889, and the fainter star is another spectroscopic binary.

moa An extinct member of the ratite group of flightless birds, which includes the RHEA of South America, the CASSOWARY, EMU and KIWI of Australasia, and the OSTRICH of Africa. Ratites presumably evolved from ancestors that could fly, but have reduced wings, and a sternum lacking a keel for the insertion of flight muscles. The moas were one of the most spectacular ratites, and grew to around 3 m (10 feet) in height. They lived on both the North and South Islands of New Zealand, diversifying into at least 12 species between the Pleistocene Era and their extinction, perhaps as recently as 1,000–250 years ago.

Moabite A member of a Semitic people traditionally descended from Lot, living in Moab, an ancient region east of the Dead Sea and now part of Jordan.

Mobile An industrial city and port in south-west Alabama, USA, at the head of Mobile Bay, an arm of the Gulf of Mexico; pop. (1990) 196,280. Shipbuilding, food processing, and the manufacture of paper, textiles, and petroleum products are its chief industries.

Möbius strip A one-sided surface named after the German mathematician August Ferdinand Möbius (1790–1868). It may be formed from a long, rectangular band of paper. The band is twisted in the middle through 180°, and then the two ends are glued together. Such a strip has remarkable topological properties, including the fact that, unlike the original band, which is two-sided, it has only one side and one edge. Another unexpected property of a Möbius strip is that it is non-orientable, i.e. the distinction between left- and right-handedness cannot be preserved consistently over the whole surface. When it is pierced through the middle and cut all the way round, parallel to the edge, other interesting phenomena appear; and cutting one-third of the distance from the edge produces quite a different result.

Mobutu, **Sese Seko** (full name Mobutu Sese Seko Kuku Ngbendu Wa Za Banga) (1930–97) Zaïrean statesman, President 1970–97. After seizing power in a military coup (1965), he changed his original name (Joseph-Désiré Mobutu) as part of his policy of Africanizing names; in 1971 he changed the name of his country (until then and since 1997 known as the Democratic Republic of Congo) to Zaïre. He remained in power despite opposition from tribal groups and small farmers until he was deposed by rebels led by Laurent Kabila in 1997.

mockingbird A member of the family Mimidae, confined to the New World and including catbirds. In appearance a little like long-tailed thrushes, several of the 34 species are greyish or brownish above with dark-spotted, pale underparts. The Galapagos mockingbird, *Nesomimus trifasciatus*, is striking for having developed several different forms on different islands, though these have not diverged as far as the Galapagos finches. They were so named because of the remarkable ability of the eastern mockingbird, *Mimus polyglottos*, to mimic the songs of a wide range of other birds.

mock orange A deciduous shrub of the genus *Philadelphus*, native to the northern temperate zone, particularly the Far East. They are members of the family Saxifragaceae, and are widely cultivated for their white flowers, which have a heavy scent, similar to that of orange blossom. Sometimes they are known as syringa, causing confusion with the unrelated plants of the genus *Syringa* – the lilacs.

mode (in statistics) A form of AVERAGE. It is the value that occurs most frequently in a set, and so represents the most popular one. It is less often used than the arithmetic MEAN and the MEDIAN, but is valuable, for instance, in stock control.

mode (in music) A way of ordering the notes of a SCALE. A system of church modes dominated European music up to about 1600. The earliest description of these modes, from the 8th century, lists only eight modes, but with the evolution of POLYPHONY in the 15th century the number grew to 12. The modes were said to be based on scales used by the ancient Greeks, but scholars now believe that the church modes were evolved independently. The Ionian and Aeolian modes have survived as the major and minor scales.

Model Parliament The English Parliament summoned by EDWARD I (November 1295) and subsequently idealized as the model for all parliaments since it was supposed to be truly representative of the people. In addition to earls (seven attended), barons (41), archbishops, bishops, abbots (70), heads of religious houses, two knights from each shire, two representatives from every city or borough, Edward called representatives of the lower clergy (one from each cathedral chapter, two from each diocese). The 'model' was hardly effective. Knights and burgesses did not attend regularly until the mid-14th century. Representatives of religious houses disappeared at the Reformation. The lower clergy preferred their own parliament, Convocation.

modem (*mo*dulator–*dem*odulator) A computer PERIPHERAL used to provide TELECOMMUNICATIONS links for computer data. The modem generally converts digital electrical signals into tones, which can be transmitted along a telephone line. At the other end of the line, a similar modem operating in reverse converts the frequencies back into digital electrical signals. Modems work to internationally agreed standards, the most important characteristic being the rate at which the data is transmitted, measured in bits per second. See also BAUD.

Modena A city in northern Italy, on the Panaro River north-west of Bologna; pop. (1990) 177,500. An ancient settlement on the Via Emilia, Modena became an independent city-state *c.*1135 and was the seat of the dukedom of Ferrara. The city was absorbed into Italy in 1860 and is now capital of the province of Modena in the Emilia-Romagna region. It is also a noted centre for the production of balsamic vinegar, agricultural machinery, and machine tools.

modern art and architecture Avant-garde art and architecture of the late 19th and 20th centuries. Various dates have been suggested as convenient points to mark the beginning of modern art. Among them are 1855, when COURBET expressed his unconventionality and hatred of authority by organizing a pavilion of his own work at the Paris Universal Exhibition, and 1863, the year of the Salon des Refusés. This was an exhibition held in Paris to show work that had been refused by the selection committee of the official Salon, many artists having protested at being rejected. It drew huge crowds, who came mainly to ridicule, and MANET'S *Déjeuner sur l'herbe* in particular was subjected to furious abuse. Artists now began to organize their own exhibitions (notably the Impressionists in 1874) and art dealers became of increasing importance. For most people the phrase 'modern art', however, suggests the 20th century, and its beginnings may be plausibly located in the fertile period between the turn of the century and World War I. In the late 19th century the notion that painting and sculpture were concerned with recognizably representing natural appearances was seriously undermined by such artists as GAUGUIN and MUNCH, and in the early 20th century was completely overthrown by a series of revolutionary movements, notably FAUVISM, EXPRESSIONISM, and CUBISM. Cubism was the most radical and influential of these movements, for it stimulated many other developments and was one of the main sources of ABSTRACT ART. A movement that, in its very different way, proved equally far-reaching in its implications, was DADA, which was founded during World War I and began questioning the nature and validity of art.

Despite the apparent confusion of modern art, the traditional easel painting continues to hold its place, and the human figure still remains the central concern for many artists. In the field of architecture, modernism is generally thought to reside in the development of a functional style, largely or entirely stripped of historical ornament (see FUNCTIONALISM). Late 19th-century US architects, such as RICHARDSON and SULLIVAN, are placed in the vanguard of this movement. However, the Modern Movement (or 'International Style' or 'International Modern') refers to a style developed in the 1920s by LE CORBUSIER, MIES VAN DER ROHE, GROPIUS, and other architects, characterized by cubic shapes (with white usually the dominant colour), large windows, often arranged in horizontal bands, and a spartan absence of detailing. 'POST-MODERNISM' refers to recent architecture that rejects such functionalism and borrows from historical styles, sometimes ironically.

modern dance A theatre dance sharing the revolutionary assumptions of MODERNISM across the arts. It rejected BALLET, flowered between 1910 and 1945, but continues to the present. Early signs are found in the work of the US dancer-choreographers DUNCAN and St Denis. The first European Expressionist dances were seen in the *ausdrucktanz* of LABAN, Jooss, and Wigman in Germany in the 1920s. *Ausdrucktanz* differed from US modern dance in two respects. First, it attracted both sexes, resulting in a wider dynamic range than in the female-dominated American modern dance. Secondly, prevailing artistic and cultural influences were highly relevant. The German Expressionists' radical innovations and Laban's links with the BAUHAUS exemplify this. *Ausdrucktanz* was an intense, emotional style. Academic classicism was replaced by dance based on everyday actions, individual psychological states, and a liberated technique. By the mid-20th century the Americans GRAHAM and Humphrey emerged as the major figures in modern dance. Their distinctive ways of moving were tempered by abstraction. Greek myths, psychological states, political comment, and reflections on the mechanization of modern society were common themes, but the most important was the emotional statement. Ballet was regarded as inadequately expressive, and modern dance took 'natural' actions of walking, running, and breathing, exemplified in Graham's 'contraction and release' and Humphrey's 'fall and recovery'. The later trend towards abstraction, seen in the work of CUNNINGHAM, introduced compositional principles of chance derived from the composer CAGE. Cunningham's compositional work provided the starting-point for the postmodern dance movement of the early 1960s. Latterly, the European tradition has been revived in the dramatic works of Germany's Pina BAUSCH. Alienation of the individual from the group and within male–female relationships provide her expressionistic subject-matter.

modernism A wide range of experimental trends in the arts of the early 20th century. At its broadest, the term embraces CUBISM and SURREALISM in visual arts, the music of STRAVINSKY, and the Modern Movement in architecture, as well as the innovations in literature to which it is more frequently applied. Modernist literature is characterized by a rejection of the 19th-century consensus between author and reader; the conventions of REALISM, for instance, were abandoned by KAFKA and the writers of the *noueau roman*. Many writers saw themselves as an avant-garde disengaged from bourgeois values, and disturbed their readers by adopting complex and obscure forms and styles. In fiction, the accepted continuity of chronological development was upset by CONRAD, PROUST, and FAULKNER, while JOYCE and WOOLF attempted new ways of tracing the flow of characters' thoughts in their STREAM OF CONSCIOUSNESS styles. In poetry POUND and T. S. ELIOT, using FREE VERSE instead of traditional METRES, replaced logical thoughts with fragmentary images. PIRANDELLO, BRECHT, and IONESCO opened up the theatre to new forms of abstraction. Modernist writing often expresses a sense of cultural disintegration following World War I. In English, its landmarks are Joyce's *Ulysses* and Eliot's *The Waste Land* (both 1922).

Modigliani, Amedeo (1884–1920) Italian painter and sculptor, resident in France from 1906. Influenced by Botticelli and other 14th-century artists, his portraits and nudes are noted for their elongated forms, linear qualities, and earthy colours. Modigliani's works include the sculpture *Head of a Woman* (1910–13) and the portrait *Jeanne Hébuterne* (1919).

modulation (in music) See KEY.

modulation (in physics) The superimposition of an electrical information signal on to a RADIO or other carrier wave, allowing the information to be transmitted over long distances. The signal is modulated before transmission, then at the receiver the carrier wave is removed to regain the information signal (demodulation). The simplest form of modulation is turning the carrier wave on and off in accordance with some sort of code, as in TELEGRAPHY. For transmission of audio and visual signals, other forms of modulation are needed. In **amplitude modulation** (AM), the information signal is used to modify the amplitude of the carrier wave. **Frequency modulation** (FM) works on a similar principle, but the frequency of the carrier wave is modified rather than its amplitude (see RADIO). FM transmission is less susceptible to noise than AM, but it requires a greater BANDWIDTH, available only in the VHF or UHF wavebands. Pulse-code modulated, digital signals are used in telegraphy, TELEPHONY, and increasingly in other applications. They are amenable to MULTIPLEXING and are less affected by interference.

modulus The magnitude of a real or complex number without regard to its sign. The modulus of any number Z is denoted $|Z|$: thus $|-3| = |+3| = 3$. For a complex number, $Z = a + ib$, $|Z| = \sqrt{(a^2 + b^2)}$. A completely different meaning of modulus comes from number theory. Here arithmetic modulo n refers to a system in which the results of addition and multiplication are given as the remainders after all the multiples of n have been removed from the numbers. Here n is called the modulus of the system. For example, in arithmetic modulo 7, $4 + 5 = 2$, since $4 + 5 = 9$ has remainder 2 when divided by 7, and $4 \times 5 = 6 \pmod 7$.

Mogadishu (or **Muqdisho**; Italian **Mogadiscio**) The capital of Somalia, a port on the Indian Ocean; pop. (1982) 377,000. Founded by the Arabs in the 10th century, it was leased to the Italians in 1892

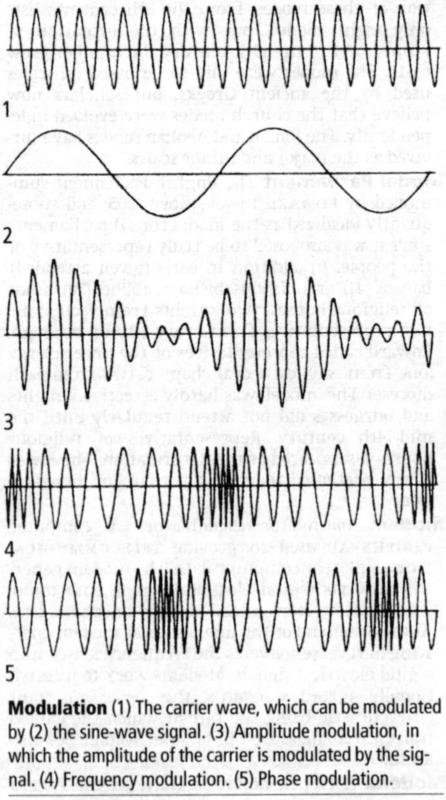

Modulation (1) The carrier wave, which can be modulated by (2) the sine-wave signal. (3) Amplitude modulation, in which the amplitude of the carrier is modulated by the signal. (4) Frequency modulation. (5) Phase modulation.

and sold to them in 1905. It was the capital of Italian Somaliland from 1892 to 1960. Following 12 years of civil war in Somalia the city was badly devastated by fighting during 1990–94.

Mogul (or **Mughal**) A Muslim dynasty of mixed Mongol and Turkish descent, which invaded India in 1526, expanded over most of the subcontinent except the extreme south, and ruled in strength until the early 18th century. The first emperor was BABUR (1483–1530). He was succeeded by a line of remarkable emperors: HUMAYUN, AKBAR, JAHANGIR, SHAH JAHAN, and AURANGZEB. They created a strong administration for the rapidly growing empire, and the official attitude of conciliation towards the majority Hindu population encouraged religious harmony. Culturally, the introduction of the Persian language and Persian artistic styles led to a distinctive Indo-Muslim style in miniature painting and architecture, the legacy remaining today in the tombs and palaces of Delhi, and Agra (see TAJ MAHAL), and several other cities of India and Pakistan.

Internal and external pressure accelerated the weakening of central power during the 18th century. Rival court factions undermined the position of less capable rulers, allowing provincial governors to seize local power. The abandonment of conciliatory religious policies encouraged a resurgence of Hindu power, notably among the MARATHAS. Hostile invasions from central Asia revealed the hollowness of the dynasty's claim to all-India hegemony, so that by 1803, when Delhi fell to the EAST INDIA COMPANY, all real power had already been lost. For another half-century they enjoyed a 'twilight era' as nominal 'kings of Delhi', dependent on British goodwill, but in 1857 the last Mogul king was exiled and the title abolished.

Mogul art See ISLAMIC ART AND ARCHITECTURE.

mohair A textile fibre obtained from the angora goat. The fineness and lustre of the fibre combines the richness of SILK with the warmth of WOOL, making mohair a luxury material in great demand. Since the early 19th century, the supply from Turkey has been insufficient to meet demand, leading to cross-breeding and the introduction of the angora goat in Australia, South America, and other parts of the world.

Mohammed See MUHAMMAD.

Mohave Desert See MOJAVE DESERT.

Mohawk A subgroup of the North American Iroquois tribe originally found in New York state and Canada.

Mohenjo-Daro An ancient city of the civilization of the Indus Valley (*c.*2600–1700 BC), now a major archaeological site in Pakistan, south-west of Sukkur. It was first excavated by the Indian Archaeological Survey under Sir John Marshall in 1922 and 1931.

Mohican (or **Mahican**, **Mohegan**) An Algonquian-speaking North American Indian tribe formerly occupying the western parts of Connecticut and Massachusetts (not to be confused with the Mahicans of the Hudson River valley in upper New York state). They were made famous in James Fenimore Cooper's book *Last of the Mohicans*.

Moho discontinuity (or **Mohorovičić discontinuity**) The boundary in the Earth's interior between the crust and the upper mantle, occurring at about 35 km (22 miles) below the continents and at *c.*10 km (6 miles) below the oceans. It is named after its discoverer, Andrija Mohorovičić (1857–1936), a Croatian seismologist, who first identified it in 1909 by studying the speeds of shock waves from earthquakes.

Moholy-Nagy, **László** (1895–1946) Hungarian-born US painter, sculptor, and photographer. Based in Berlin from 1920, he became identified with the constructivist school, pioneering the experimental use of plastic materials, light, photography, and film. Moholy-Nagy taught with Walter Gropius at the Bauhaus (1923–29), later heading the new Bauhaus school in Chicago (1937–38).

Moissan, **Ferdinand Frédéric Henri** (1852–1907) French chemist. In 1886 he succeeded in isolating the very reactive element fluorine. In 1892 he invented the electric arc furnace that bears his name, in which he claimed to have synthesized diamonds. This is now in doubt, but the very high temperatures achieved in the furnace made it possible to reduce some uncommon metals from their ores. An influential teacher, he was appointed professor of inorganic chemistry at the Sorbonne in 1900. Moissan was awarded the Nobel Prize for chemistry in 1906.

Mojave Desert (or **Mohave**) A desert in southern California, USA, to the south-east of the Sierra Nevada and north-east of Los Angeles. Edwards Air Force Base, in the Antelope Valley, is a centre of aerospace technology and the small town of Mojave was once a centre of the trade in borax.

moksha (Sanskrit, 'release' or 'liberation') The release of the soul (ATMAN) from the bonds of SAMSARA, the cycle of birth, death, and rebirth. It is the highest spiritual goal within most schools of HINDUISM.

molarity See MOLE.

molasses See SUGAR PROCESSING.

Moldau The German name for the VLTAVA in the Czech Republic.

Moldavia A former principality of south-east Europe. Formerly part of the Roman province of Dacia, the region became a principality in the 14th century, coming under Turkish rule in the 16th century. The province of Bukovina in the north-west was ceded to Austria in 1777 and Bessarabia, in the north-east, was ceded to Russia in 1812. In 1859 Moldavia united with Wallachia to form the independent kingdom of Romania. Its capital was Iasi (Jassy) and its chief port on the Danube was Galatz (Galaţi).

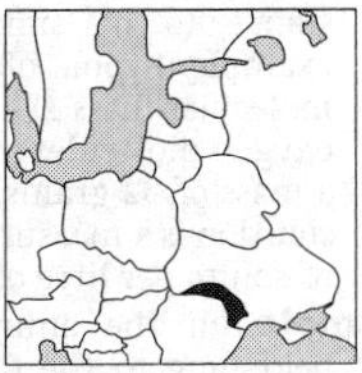

Moldova A country in eastern Europe bounded on the north, east, and south by Ukraine, and on the west by Romania. Wider Moldova comprises lands between the Carpathian Mountains in the west and the Dneister River in the east, including the north-east of modern Romania.

Physical. The Prut River waters the western part of Moldova, Bessarabia. Although landlocked, its proximity to the Black Sea gives it a mild climate. From the north into the centre runs a belt of hills with deep valleys in which vines and fruit trees flourish. Further south are low-lying steppes supporting grain, sugar beet, and tobacco.

Economy. Moldova's mineral resources are meagre, but the soil is fertile and agriculture prospers, with viticulture, fruits and vegetables, tobacco, grains, and industrial crops, such as sunflower seeds, of importance. Industry concentrates on food-processing, machinery, and other light industry.

History. Moldova at one time formed part of

Bessarabia, control over which was long disputed between Russians and Ottoman Turks, Russian occupation being confirmed in 1812. Although at first granted autonomy 1818–28, this was succeeded by a policy of Russification. A nationalist movement developed from 1905 and in November 1917 Bessarabia declared independence, voting in December 1918 for alliance with Romania. In June 1940 the Soviet Union demanded the return of Bessarabia and of northern Bukovina, and the Moldavian Soviet Socialist Republic was created. The northern region of Bukovina and the coastal plain from the Danube to the Dniester went to the Ukraine. Romania briefly re-occupied the area in 1941, but the 1940 situation was restored in 1947. In August 1991 the country declared its independence from the Soviet Union as the Republic of Moldova. The regions of Dnestr and Gagauz also declared themselves to be separate republics, but their declarations were annulled by the Moldovan government. Ethnic violence broke out in the Dnestr region and Russian troops were sent in to protect Russian residents. A strong movement for unification with Romania increased inter-ethnic tensions. However, Moldova's first multi-party elections, held in 1994, were won by supporters of Moldovan independence. A new constitution granted autonomous status to the Dnestr and Gagauz regions but, despite the withdrawal of Russian troops from the Dnestr region in 1995, the situation remains tense. Moldova ratified its membership of the COMMONWEALTH OF INDEPENDENT STATES in 1994.

Capital: Chisinau
Area: 33,700 sq km (13,000 sq mi)
Population: 4,350,000 (1995)
Currency: 1 leu = 100 bani
Religions: Eastern Orthodox
Ethnic Groups: Moldovan (Romanian) 65.0%; Ukrainian 14.0%; Russian 13.0%; Gagauz, Jewish, and Bulgarian minorities
Languages: Romanian (official); Russian; minority languages
International Organizations: UN; CSCE; Commonwealth of Independent States; North Atlantic Co-operation Council

mole (in scientific measurement; symbol mol) The SI UNIT of an amount of substance. This amount of substance is a set number of atoms, molecules, or ions and is defined as the number of atoms in 0.012 kg of the isotope carbon-12; it is equal to 6.022×10^{23}, and is called the **Avogadro constant** or **number**. This definition enables one mole of a substance to be simply identified by mass. For example, 1 mole of hydrogen molecules (relative molecular mass 2) has a mass of 2 grams, 1 mole of oxygen molecules (relative molecular mass 32) has a mass of 32 grams, and so on. The **molarity** of a solution is a measure of its concentration in moles of solute per litre of solvent.

mole (in the animal kingdom) An insectivore belonging to the family Talpidae. In addition to the European mole, *Talpa europaea*, the family includes 28 other species, such as the very similar American moles, mole-like shrew moles, and desmans. Most moles construct a system of underground burrows in grassland, throwing up the excavated soil at intervals to form molehills. The mole uses its burrows as a trap to catch earthworms that fall through into the tunnels. Surplus earthworms are immobilized by chewing their anterior ends and the still-living worms are stored in underground chambers for later consumption.

The desmans, of which there are two species, the Russian, *Desmana moschata*, and Pyrenean, *Galemys pyrenaicus*, are well adapted to an aquatic life. Their fur is two-layered, with a dense, waterproof underlayer, and their toes are partly webbed. The star-nosed mole, *Condylura cristata*, of North America has a sensitive snout which extends into pinkish, fleshy tentacles; these are used to 'feel' for food.

mole cricket A large CRICKET that burrows in soil, with its front pair of legs modified for digging. They are unable to jump. The males trill loudly underground. They fly freely at night and may damage root crops. The common mole cricket, *Gryllotalpa gryllotalpa*, one of 50 species, has been introduced to North America from continental Europe.

molecular biology The scientific study of living processes at a molecular level. It involves both BIOCHEMISTRY and BIOPHYSICS. It has been important in the study of genetics, genetic engineering, and the processes occurring in cells. Important molecules identified by the techniques of molecular biology include DNA, RNA, and many enzymes.

molecular distillation A special form of DISTILLATION, conducted under extremely high vacuum, in which the condensing apparatus is located so close to the boiling liquid that the molecules condense without colliding with each other. This makes the process extremely efficient. Industrial applications include the separation of vitamins; the separation of mono-, di-, and triglyceride fats, and the distillation of paraffin wax for coating milk cartons.

molecular formula The number of atoms of each element in a molecule. Ethane has the formula C_2H_6, i.e. an ethane molecule consists of two carbon atoms and six hydrogen atoms, covalently bonded together. Only molecular compounds have molecular formulae; IONIC COMPOUNDS, such as sodium chloride, NaCl, and giant lattices, such as silica, SiO_2, do not contain molecules, and their formulae, called **empirical formulae**, give only the ratios of numbers of atoms present.

molecular weight See RELATIVE MOLECULAR MASS.

molecule Two or more ATOMS chemically bonded together. The atoms can be the same, as in oxygen, O_2, or different, as in water, H_2O. Molecules are electrically neutral, and the atoms are held together by covalent bonds, in which the atoms share pairs of electrons. Not all substances consist of molecules: some, such as the noble gas helium, consist of free atoms, and many consist of electrically charged ions. Gases usually consist of molecules, as do many liquids and some solids. In gases the molecules are widely separated from each other and are in constant rapid motion. In liquids the molecules are in contact with each other but can still move about. In solids the molecules are tightly packed in a regular arrangement, and can only vibrate.

mole rat A RODENT that makes up two distinct families, whose similarity is due to convergent evolution. The family Bathyergidae, or African mole rats, includes some nine species, while the Muridae, or rat and mouse family, includes 16 species such as the blind mole rats, East African mole or root rats, and Central Asiatic mole rats or zokors. All dig extensive burrows and feed mainly on roots. Unlike moles, they burrow, not with their feet, but with their huge front teeth. The most unusual is the African naked mole rat, *Heterocephalus glaber*, which is the nearest mammalian equivalent to social insects, with reproductive and worker 'castes'.

mole salamander An amphibian belonging to a small family, Ambystomatidae, of approximately

33 species of small to moderately large salamanders, up to 40 cm (16 inches) long. The majority are stoutly built, terrestrial animals with broad heads and sturdy limbs, and have deep, vertical grooves along the body (marking the positions of the ribs). An aquatic stage is always present and persists in some, including the well-known AXOLOTLS. Typically, adult male salamanders are terrestrial and capable burrowers.

Molière (pseudonym of Jean-Baptiste Poquelin) (1622–73) French dramatist. In 1658 he established himself in Paris as an actor, dramatist, and manager of his own troupe. His high reputation as a writer of French comedy is based on more than 20 plays, which took the vices and follies of contemporary France as their subject, simultaneously adopting and developing stock characters from Italian *commedia dell'arte*. Major works include *Tartuffe* (1664), *Don Juan* (1665), *Le Misanthrope* (1666), and *Le Malade imaginaire* (1673). Molière also collaborated with the composer Lully for *Le Bourgeois Gentilhomme* (1670).

mollusc A member of the second largest of animal phyla, Mollusca, containing 120,000 species; far smaller than the arthropods but at least twice as numerous as vertebrates. Molluscs perhaps rank highest of all in terms of diversity of appearance: snails, oysters, sea slugs, and octopuses are all molluscs. They live in every possible ecological NICHE, from deep sea to deserts, and have evolved forms as diverse as mobile carnivores, sessile filterers of planktonic food, or rapacious consumers of garden vegetables.

The basic molluscan body-plan is fairly constant. There is a soft body, often with a creeping, slug-like foot and a covering of hard chalky shell, made of crystals of calcium carbonate embedded in a special protein, giving great strength. The head and foot can be withdrawn into the shell for safety in species with a one-piece coiled shell, the **gastropods**, such as snails and winkles. In those species with a two-piece shell, the BIVALVES, all the soft parts are enclosed and even the foot rarely protrudes. In the third main class, the CEPHALOPODS, the shell is often vestigial and the soft body is adapted for high-speed jet propulsion instead.

Molluscs are abundant animals, especially in shallow seas and on rocky shores, where their protective body-plan is especially appropriate. They form a vital food source for fish, birds, and man. They are one of very few invertebrate groups successful on land; a special ribbon of teeth, the radula, enables them to eat tough green vegetation, and the shell or thick mucus secretions give considerable protection against desiccation.

Molotov, Vyacheslav (Mikhailovich) (born Vyacheslav Mikhailovich Skryabin) (1890–1986) Soviet statesman. Born in Russia, he was an early member of the Bolsheviks and a staunch supporter of Stalin after Lenin's death. As Commissar (later Minister) for Foreign Affairs (1939–49; 1953–56), he negotiated the non-aggression pact with Nazi Germany (1939) and after 1945 represented the Soviet Union at meetings of the United Nations, where his frequent exercise of the veto helped to prolong the cold war. He was expelled from his party posts in 1956 after quarrelling with Khrushchev.

Moluccas (or **Moluccas Islands, Maluku**) An island group in Indonesia, between Sulawesi (Celebes) and New Guinea; area 74,505 sq km (28,777 sq miles); pop. (est. 1993) 2,001,200; capital, Amboina. Settled by the Portuguese in the early 16th century, the islands were taken a century later by the Dutch, who controlled the lucrative trade in the spices produced on the islands. The islands were formerly known as the Spice Islands.

molybdenum (symbol Mo, at. no. 42, r.a.m. 95.94) A hard grey TRANSITION METAL of high melting-point obtained from its main ORE, molybdenite (MoS_2), by roasting and reducing the oxide with hydrogen. It is alloyed with other metals to increase their high-temperature strength: it is used in electric lamps as a support for tungsten filaments, while molybdenum steels are used for high-speed LATHE tools. Molybdenum disulphide is a lubricant, and is used as an additive in oils.

Mombasa A seaport and industrial city in south-east Kenya, on the Indian Ocean; pop. (est. 1989) 465,000. Established by the Portuguese as a fortified trading post in 1593, it is the leading port, with a major oil refinery, and second-largest city of Kenya. There are many tourist hotels. It was the capital of the British East Africa Protectorate from 1888 until 1907.

moment (in physics) The turning effect produced by a FORCE acting at a distance on an object. It is found by multiplying the force applied by the perpendicular distance between the point of application of the force and the object on which it has an effect. In a mechanical system – for example, in the use of a spanner to tighten a nut – the moment of force is called the TORQUE.

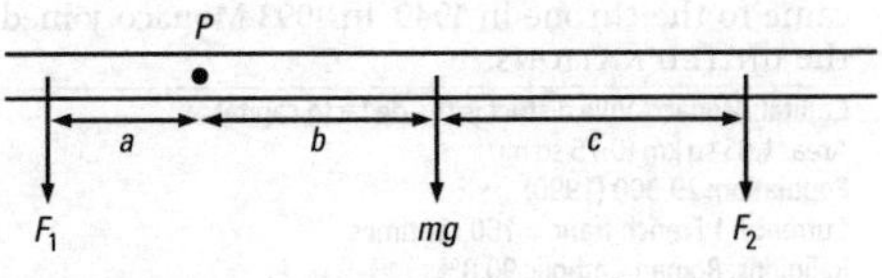

Moment The bar is suspended about a fulcrum at P. For equilibrium the moment of force F_1 about P, i.e. F_1a, must equal the moment of the bar's weight, mgb, plus the moment of the force F_2, $F_2(b + c)$.

moment of inertia The equivalent, in a rotating system, of MASS. Symbol *I*, the moment of INERTIA of a particle about any line is $I = mr^2$, where *m* is its mass and *r* its perpendicular distance from the line. For a system of particles, it is the sum of their separate moments of inertia.

momentum (or **linear momentum**) The quantity that measures the tendency of a moving body to continue in motion. It is calculated by multiplying the mass of the body by its velocity, and is a VECTOR quantity. A stationary body has no momentum. Momentum is conserved as long as no outside force is acting, so the fragments of a stationary object immediately after exploding still have zero total momentum: the momentum of fragments in one direction is balanced by that of others in the opposite direction. Angular momentum is the tendency of a rotating body to continue to turn.

Mommsen, Theodor (1817–1903) German historian. He is noted for his three-volume *History of Rome* (1854–56; 1885) and his treatises on Roman constitutional law (1871–88). Mommsen was also editor of the *Corpus Inscriptionum Latinarum* (1863) for the Berlin Academy. He was awarded the Nobel Prize for literature in 1902.

Monaco A small principality located in the south of France in the hills above the Mediterranean Sea.

Physical. The ancient town and fortress perch on a rocky outcrop that projects into the Mediterranean Sea. On this part of the Riviera, steep, white limestone cliffs, representing the incipient Alps,

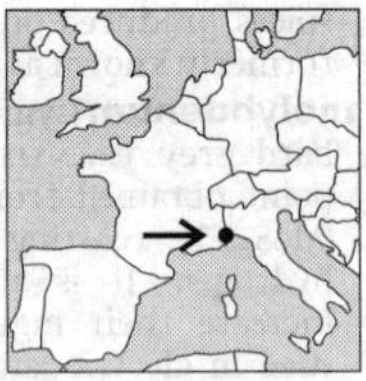

stand out along the coastline with sheltered intervening bays. The numerous caves and grottoes were long occupied by Palaeolithic peoples.

Economy. Tourism is Monaco's major industry, with gambling the chief attraction; the casino (built in 1861) has been state-run since 1967. Postage stamps also provide an important source of government revenue. Light industry includes electronics and pharmaceuticals. Financial and trading interests are a growing sector. Mineral resources are lacking, and agriculture is very limited.

History. Monaco was held by the Genoese from 1191 until 1297, when it passed to the Grimaldi family. The Grimaldis were allies of France, except for a period of allegiance to Spain (1524–1641), but Monaco was annexed by France in 1793 under the French Revolutionary Regime. The Congress of VIENNA returned the principality to the Grimaldis but placed it under the protection of Sardinia. In 1861 France restored Monaco's independence. Monaco adopted its first constitution in 1911, formalizing its status as a hereditary principality. A more democratic constitution was adopted in 1962, but the monarchy was retained. Prince Rainier III came to the throne in 1949. In 1993 Monaco joined the UNITED NATIONS.

Capital: Monaco-Ville district is the de facto capital
Area: 1.95 sq km (0.75 sq mi)
Population: 29,300 (1990)
Currency: 1 French franc = 100 centimes
Religions: Roman Catholic 90.0%
Ethnic Groups: French 46.8%; Monégasque 16.6%; Italian 16.5%
Languages: French (official); Italian; Monégasque
International Organizations: UN; CSCE

Monaghan ▶**1** A county of the Republic of Ireland in the province of Ulster; area 1,290 sq km (498 sq miles); pop. (1991) 51,260. ▶**2** Its county town, a market centre on the Ulster Canal; pop. (1991) 5,750.

monarch butterfly (or **milkweed butterfly**) A large, tough, toxic (when eaten) butterfly, strikingly patterned with some combination of orange, black, and white. There are some 200 species in the family Danaidae, with a mainly tropical distribution; they are sometimes known as tiger butterflies. Most species incorporate poisons from their larval food plants and serve as models for palatable mimics. Males have scent patches on the hind-wings, and clustered hairs at the tip of the abdomen for disseminating the scent. Most are found in the Asian tropics, but they also occur in Africa, Australia, and America. The North American monarch, *Danaus plexippus*, migrates south in winter to enormous communal roosts in southern California, Florida, and Mexico. Successive summer broods move as far north as Canada, and occasional vagrants reach Britain. This same species is also common over most of the Pacific region, including Australia.

monarchy Rule, commonly hereditary, by or in the name of a single individual. Absolute monarchs wielding unlimited authority were once the norm throughout Europe, but are now rare. Most contemporary monarchs are constitutional rulers, with severely limited or even purely ceremonial powers. Succession to the position of monarch is usually hereditary, though other methods, including election, have been known. The association of monarchy with ARISTOCRACY and privilege can be politically divisive, but constitutional monarchs can often provide a head of state as a symbol of national unity without the need to involve party politics in the election of a president.

Monash, Sir John (1865–1931) Australian general. After commanding the 4th Australian Brigade at Gallipoli (1915), he served with distinction as commander of the 3rd Australian Division in France (1916).

Monasteries, Dissolution of the (1536–40) The systematic abolition of English monasticism and transfer of monastic property to the Tudor monarchy, as part of the English REFORMATION. Thomas CROMWELL, HENRY VIII's vicar-general, pointed the way ahead by commissioning the *Valor Ecclesiasticus* (1535), a great survey of Church wealth, and by sending agents to investigate standards within the religious houses. An Act of Parliament (1536) dissolved monasteries with annual revenues of under £200. This provoked an uprising, the PILGRIMAGE OF GRACE. In its aftermath, Cromwell forced certain abbots to surrender larger houses to the king. Another Act (1539) confirmed all surrenders that had been, and still were to be, made and monastic lands passed to the Court of Augmentations of the King's Revenue, a state department. Resistance was minimal. By 1540 all 800 or more English houses were closed. Eleven thousand monks, nuns, and their dependants were ejected from their communities, most with little or no compensation.

The Dissolution had a number of consequences apart from the immediate wholesale destruction of monastic buildings and the despoliation of their libraries and treasures. The nobility and gentry benefited financially from the distribution of former monastic lands, which were used to form the basis of new private estates, and the laity gained a monopoly of ecclesiastical patronage which survived for the next three centuries. The termination of monastic charity and the closure of monastery schools stimulated the introduction of the POOR LAW system and the foundation of grammar schools.

monastery A community of monks living by prayer and labour in secluded, often remote, locations. Such communities, which are meant to further the communal and individual practice of ASCETICISM, are common to most religions. BUDDHA founded a monastic order (sangha) and a code of discipline, which is still used and was spread by missionaries throughout Asia. The *sangha*, remains an important element in Theravada Buddhism, with well over 250,000 members despite the hostility of communist governments in China and elsewhere. In HINDUISM monasticism takes the form of ASHRAMS, or retreats, where the influence of a guru or holy man and practices, such as YOGA, are important. In the Hindu concept of the four ideal stages of life, *āshrama*, the last two stages, following parenthood, are devoted to contemplation and asceticism. ISLAM did not fully develop a monastic organization until the Sufis formed the Rifaite and Mawlawite brotherhoods in the 12th century. Although monasticism is not part of mainstream JUDAISM, the Essenes, a messianic sect (2nd century BC) founded a remote community by the Dead Sea.

Christian monasticism evolved from the hermit communities founded in the 3rd century by men fleeing from Roman persecution to the Egyptian and Syrian deserts, where they sought union with God. Although St Antony (*c.*251–*c.*356) is usually regarded as the founder of Christian monasticism, it was St Pachomius (*c.*292–*c.*346) who founded the first organized community at Tabennisi in Egypt. Monasticism then spread rapidly in Eastern Europe through the Rule of St Basil (*c.*330–79), the first known Christian monastic rule, and in Western Europe with through the Rule of Benedict of Nursia (*c.*480–*c.*550). In the ROMAN CATHOLIC CHURCH, however, there are numerous orders whose members are often bound by vows of poverty, prayer, and meditation. Communities have both spiritual and practical functions, such as EDUCATION and social work. Among these, the Benedictine order, based on the original Rule of Benedict, emphasizes a balance of prayer, Bible reading, rest, and physical work. From the 10th century the reformed Benedictine Order at CLUNY in France (founded 909) built a series of 'daughter houses' which extended throughout Europe, all under the direct control of the powerful abbot of Cluny. The CISTERCIANS (founded 1098) also built monasteries in Europe and England, though these foundations enjoyed a semi-autonomous position and were only subject to the direct influence of the abbot of Citeaux at an annual council. The Cistercian Order follows the reformed Benedictine Rule; Cistercians of the Strict Observance (Trappist) form the largest contemplative order. Other orders were the Carthusians (1098), the Premonstratensians (1120), and the Gilbertines (1131). The Dominican Order, founded by St Dominic in 1220, and the Franciscan Order, founded by St FRANCIS OF ASSISI in 1209, were originally mendicant orders of friars, living from charity, although now most of their members are based in community houses.

Monasticism in the ANGLICAN COMMUNION has become more prominent since the 19th-century Anglo-Catholic movement, with the re-foundation of some ancient orders and the establishment of new orders, such as the Community of the Resurrection, founded in 1892. The ecumenical Taizé community in France, founded in 1940, is the best-known Protestant order. Although Christian monasticism is declining in Europe, it is expanding in the developing world, where it plays an important role in providing educational and other welfare services.

Monck, George, 1st Duke of Albemarle (1608–70) English general, admiral, and statesman. He began his career as a Royalist and was taken prisoner during the ENGLISH CIVIL WAR; but he was given a command by Parliament and later completed the suppression of the Royalists in Scotland. In the first ANGLO-DUTCH WAR he fought three naval battles before returning to Scotland in 1654. He was trusted by CROMWELL, but after Cromwell's death he acted to secure the restoration of Charles II in 1660, and he received many honours. Monck was placed in charge of London during the GREAT PLAGUE (1665) and FIRE OF LONDON (1666).

Mond, Ludwig (1839–1909) German-born British industrial chemist. He moved to the UK in 1862, and patented a process for recovering SULPHUR from the waste produced in the LEBLANC sodium carbonate process. In 1873, he went into partnership with J. T. Brunner (UK) to work on the much improved soda-manufacturing process perfected by SOLVAY in Belgium. He also developed a new process for refining NICKEL and devised a gas battery.

Mondrian, Piet (born Pieter Cornelis Mondriaan) (1872–1944) Dutch painter. He was a co-founder of the De Stijl movement and the originator of neoplasticism, one of the earliest and strictest forms of geometrical abstract painting. His use of vertical and horizontal lines, rectangular shapes, and primary colours is typified by such paintings as *Composition with Red, Yellow, and Blue* (1921).

Monel metal See ALLOY.

Monet, Claude (1840–1926) French painter. He was a founder member of the impressionists; his early painting *Impression: soleil levant* (1872) gave the movement its name. Of all the group, Monet remained the most faithful to the impressionist principles of painting directly from the subject (often out of doors) and giving primacy to transient visual perception. His fascination with the play of light on objects led to a series of paintings of single subjects painted at different times of day and under different weather conditions, notably the *Haystacks* series (1890–91), *Rouen Cathedral* (1892–95), and the *Water-lilies* sequence (1899–1906 onwards).

monetarism A school of economics that emerged mainly in the 1960s and 1970s, with FRIEDMAN as its leading exponent. It is a revival of the classical (pre-Keynesian) approach to MACROECONOMICS. Monetarist models assume that money, prices, and wages are flexible but that aggregate output and employment will automatically tend towards an optimal equilibrium. Therefore government policy should concentrate on achieving and maintaining the stability of the price level, which monetarists believe depends on proper management of the MONEY SUPPLY mainly through monetary rather than fiscal policy.

money A medium of exchange allowing goods and services to be valued in terms of a legal tender consisting of objects with a high intrinsic value (gold) or a token value (banknotes), rather than traded directly as would occur in a barter economy. Coins of fixed values issued by a government first appeared in the 8th century BC both in Lydia, in Asia Minor, and in China. Britain's first coins, of silver and copper, appeared in the 1st century BC. Thereafter until recently most coins have been made of gold and silver, with copper and bronze used for coins of low value. Token money (such as banknotes) has an intrinsic value less than its face value. Banknotes were first issued by banks who undertook to pay the sum of money that appeared on the note from their deposits of gold. The BANK OF ENGLAND issued notes from its foundation in 1694 and banknotes are now the principal form of money in circulation.

money supply (in economics) The amount of MONEY circulating in an economy at a particular time. The definition of what comprises money varies because various different assets can be used as a medium of exchange. One major definition includes notes and coins in circulation (that is, not in bank vaults) and bank sight (or current) accounts on which cheques can be drawn. Elements of near-money (for example, money-market deposits) may also be included in money-supply measures. See also MONETARISM.

Mongol empire An empire founded by GENGHIS KHAN early in the 13th century. Loosely related nomadic tribesmen who lived in felt huts (yurts) and subsisted on meat and milk – and fermented mares' milk (*koumiss*) – were united for the first time under his leadership. From Mongolia they swept out to Asia and eastern Europe. Splendid horsemen and archers, their onslaught was difficult to resist. Khakhans (Great Khans) elected from among Genghis's descendants continued his conquests. Central Russia, Poland, Hungary, Bulgaria, and Romania were overrun, but following the death of the Khakhan Ogodei in 1241 the Mongols withdrew to attend an election in their capital, Karakorum, in Mongolia. However, the GOLDEN HORDE remained in control of Russia. In 1245 an advance towards MESOPOTAMIA began. In 1258 Hulagu, Genghis's grandson, sacked Baghdad, but was defeated by the MAMELUKES at Ain Jalut (1260). The conquest of China, begun under Genghis, was completed 65 years later under KUBLAI KHAN.

After Kublai shifted the capital to Khanbaligh (now Beijing), it became increasingly difficult to maintain the Khakhan's authority over remote parts of the empire. Quarrels over succession, corrupt and incompetent administration, and revolts accelerated disintegration. After 1300 the KHANATES were fully independent. By 1368 the Mongols were driven out of China and in 1372 a Chinese army burned Karakorum.

Mongolia A country in central Asia, bordered by Siberia, Russia on the north and China on the south. It was formerly known as Outer Mongolia (Inner Mongolia is now an autonomous region of China).

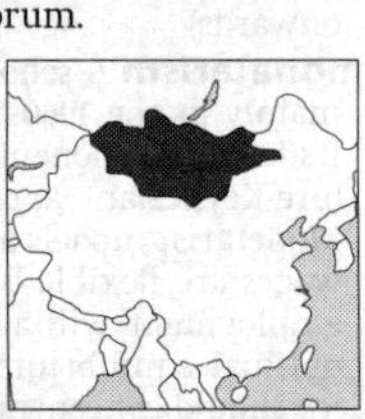

Physical. Mainly a high, barren plateau, Mongolia has mountains and saline lakes in the north-west and the Gobi Desert in the south-east. In winter it is very cold, and rainfall is light. Even so, there are areas of steppe on which livestock can be supported, and some grain is grown.

Economy. Mongolia is making the transition from a planned economy to a free-market economy. Aid from the former Soviet Union enabled infrastructural and limited industrial development, but has left Mongolia with a large foreign debt, and dependent on trade with the former Soviet Union, including imports of fuel, equipment, and spare parts. The predominantly nomadic pastoral economy is based on animal-breeding, with meat, livestock, and wool the main exports. However, agriculture, particularly cereal production, is being extended. Mineral resources such as fluorite and copper are exploited.

History. Although Mongolia is named after the Mongols, up to the 12th century they only controlled a small area near the sources of the Orkhon River, and other nomadic tribes, such as the Merkit and Naiman, held greater power in the Eastern steppes. In the 13th century, however, the Mongols swept out to create the MONGOL EMPIRE. In the 16th century they were converted to LAMAISM. During the 17th century the MANCHUS won control of Inner and then of Outer Mongolia.

Outer Mongolia remained part of the Chinese empire until the fall of the QING dynasty in 1911, although Russia mounted an increasingly strong challenge for the area in later years. While the neighbouring region of Inner Mongolia remained in Chinese hands, Outer Mongolia seized independence in 1911 and reasserted it after brief Chinese and White Russian occupations in 1919–21. Outer Mongolia became communist in 1924 as the Mongolian People's Republic and remained so, following a policy of alliance with the Soviet Union. In July 1990 it became a multi-party democracy, but the Communist Party, now the Mongolian People's Revolutionary Party (MPRP), retained power under Dashiyn Byambasuren. Trade with the former Soviet Union fell and, with price deregulation, an economic crisis developed, with rationing of basic foodstuffs in January 1991. In 1992 the Prime Minister successfully negotiated commercial cooperation with Russia. The country, now called the State of Mongolia, adopted a new democratic constitution, which legalized private ownership. A general election, held in 1992, was again won by the MPRP. Punsalmaagiyn Ochirbat, first elected President in 1990, was re-elected in 1993, in the first direct presidential elections. However, in subsequent elections in 1996, the opposition Democratic Union coalition won a landslide victory and formed the first non-Communist administration for over 70 years. In 1997 Natsagiin Bagabandi was elected President.

Capital: Ulan Bator
Area: 1,566,500 sq km (604,800 sq mi)
Population: 2,307,000 (1995)
Currency: 1 tugrik = 100 mongo
Religions: Buddhism; Shamanism; Islam
Ethnic Groups: Khalkha 77.5%; Kazakh 5.3%; Dorbed 2.8%; Bayad 2.0%; Buryat Mongol 1.9%; Draiganga Mongol 1.5%
Languages: Khalkha Mongolian (official); minority languages and dialects
International Organizations: UN

Mongolian A racial division occupying regions of east Asia, south-east Asia, and arctic North America, speaking a number of related languages and dialects (including Buryat, Kalmuck, and Khalkha Mongol) which together form the Mongolian group in the Altaic family. During the 13th century the Mongols under Genghis Khan established a large empire that stretched across northern China and Russia to eastern Europe.

Mongolian language See ALTAIC LANGUAGES.

mongolism See DOWN'S SYNDROME.

Mongoloids One of the major human racial groups, distributed widely through Asia from the Caspian Sea eastwards. They are also found on many islands off the Asian mainland and, as Inuits and Aleuts, in northern Canada and in Greenland. The AMERICAN INDIANS, the other indigenous peoples of America, are also sometimes grouped with the Mongoloids.

mongoose A carnivore belonging to a family, Herpestidae, that also includes the MEERKATS. The subfamily Galidiinae includes four species of Madagascan mongooses, some of which are striped. The African and Asian mongooses (subfamily Herpestinae) include 27 unpatterned species. They feed on a variety of prey (including snakes), some being purely insectivorous, but most take rodents, eggs, and any other small vertebrate they can catch. Most mongooses are solitary but some, such as the banded mongoose, *Mungos mungo*, and meerkats, are social and forage in bands. Mongooses are roughly the size of an otter but the smallest, the dwarf mongoose, *Helogale parvula*, weighs only about 0.7 kg (1.5 pounds). Some Indian species have been introduced to the Caribbean to control rats in sugar plantations, but usually they become very destructive to native mammals and birds.

Monica, St (332–*c*.387) Mother of St Augustine of Hippo. Born in North Africa, she is often seen as the model of Christian mothers for her patience with her son's spiritual crises, ending with his conversion in 386. She became the object of a cult in the late Middle Ages and is frequently chosen as the patron of associations of Christian mothers. Feast day, 27 August (formerly 4 May).

monism The philosophical belief that the world consists entirely of a single substance or kind of substance. Opposed to the DUALISM of mind and body, the most obvious forms of monism claim either that the world is entirely material (MATERIALISM) or that it is entirely mental (IDEALISM). Monist doctrines will frequently explain the *apparent* differences between kinds of things as subjective, resulting from our different ways of understanding a single thing. The most extreme monism, held, for example, by SPINOZA, claims that the world is a single thing, and that all seeming diversity is a product of partial understanding.

monitor lizard A member of a family, Varanidae, which includes the Komodo dragon, the largest living lizard. Roughly half of the 30 known species are found in Australia, where they are commonly referred to as goannas; the remainder occur in Africa through Asia to the East Indies. Most are strikingly elongate and of alert appearance. They flick out their long, forked tongue to examine their environment, rather in the manner of snakes. They can defend themselves with their strong jaws or heavy claws and by thrashing around their powerful tails. Monitor lizards are all very similar in form, being long and slender, with a long neck, head, and tail. Most are heat-loving, terrestrial or arboreal species, but at least one species, the Nile monitor, *Varanus niloticus*, is at home in water.

monk See MONASTERY.

Monk, Thelonious (Sphere) (1917–82) US jazz pianist and composer. In the early 1940s he played alongside Dizzy Gillespie and Charlie Parker in Harlem, becoming one of the founders of the bebop style. He achieved popularity in the late 1950s, as the new style of 'cool' jazz reached a wider audience. Memorable compositions include 'Round Midnight', 'Straight, No Chaser', and 'Well, You Needn't'.

monkey An arboreal PRIMATE with a relatively large brain, acute vision, and hands developed as useful grasping organs. Two distinct groups have arisen, apparently independently, from prosimian ancestors. One group, the New World monkeys, is found in South America. These are called platyrrhines (flat-noses) and some have prehensile (grasping) tails. This group is represented by a variety of forms, including capuchins and marmosets. The second group is the Old World monkeys, called catarrhines (drop-noses), of Africa and Asia. They include the colobus monkeys, mangabeys, and baboons. The Old World monkeys are not markedly different in general habits and organization from those of the New World and it would appear that the two groups have made many changes in parallel.

monkey puzzle tree (or **Chilean pine**) A native of Chile belonging to the family Araucariaceae, and an example of a subtropical conifer. It is one of 18 species of the genus *Araucaria* found in New Guinea, eastern Australia, the islands of the Pacific, and parts of South America. The monkey puzzle has a regular dome-shaped crown of downward-pointing branches with close-set, leathery, pointed leaves. These stay on the tree for up to 20 years, so that even the old branches are clothed in leaves. It is the nearest living example to the trees of the Carboniferous Period around 365–290 years ago, which gave rise to our main coal deposits. The seeds of the monkey puzzle are edible. Other species of *Araucaria* include the Norfolk Island pine, *A. heterophylla*, and Paraná pine, *A. angustifolia*. All produce useful timber.

monkfish (or **angelshark**) A CARTILAGINOUS FISH of the family Squatinidae. The body is flattened from above and the pectoral and pelvic fins are expanded, though the former are not joined to the head as in the rays. It is an ugly fish, with gill-openings on the side of the head and a terminal mouth, both of which are shark features. It is found in shallow water in the warm temperate parts of the Atlantic and Pacific, and one species is a summer visitor to southern Britain. Its food comprises mostly bottom-living fishes, especially flatfishes and rays. It gives birth to litters of 9–16 young in summer. It is a food-fish with very firm flesh.

Mon-Khmer languages See AUSTRO-ASIATIC LANGUAGES.

monkshood See ACONITE.

Monmouth, James Scott, Duke of (1649–85) English claimant to the throne of England. The illegitimate son of Charles II, he became the focus for Whig supporters of a Protestant succession. In 1685 he led a rebellion against the Catholic James II; he proclaimed himself king at Taunton in Somerset, but his force was defeated at the Battle of Sedgemoor and he was executed. See MONMOUTH'S REBELLION.

Monmouthshire A county of south-east Wales, on the border with England; pop. (1996) 81,000. The major part of it was incorporated into Gwent in 1974. When Gwent was abolished in 1996 administration was passed to a reduced Monmouthshire. Its administrative centre is Cwmbran.

Monmouth's Rebellion (1685) An insurrection in south-west England against JAMES II, led by the Duke of Monmouth, illegitimate son of Charles II. The Duke of Argyll led a revolt in Scotland against James and persuaded Monmouth to launch a rebellion in the south-west. He landed at Lyme Regis in Dorset, and was proclaimed king at Taunton, but could muster only limited support. He failed to take Bristol and, with forces inferior in training, experience, and equipment to the king's army, was routed at SEDGEMOOR. Monmouth was captured a few days later and executed; his followers were harshly punished by the BLOODY ASSIZES.

Monoceros The Unicorn, a CONSTELLATION straddling the celestial equator, introduced by the Dutchman Petrus Plancius (1552–1622) and representing the mythical one-horned beast. Despite its faintness (the brightest stars are of fourth magnitude) it lies in the Milky Way and contains several fascinating objects including the Rosette Nebula.

monocline A set of strata that dips more or less uniformly in one direction. It can be thought of as one half of a syncline or anticline without the other half.

monoclonal antibodies Antibodies (see IMMUNITY) derived from a single antibody-producing cell, or produced artificially by a single CLONE and consisting of identical antibody molecules. Antibodies resulting from IMMUNIZATION are a complex mixture, impossible to separate. Monoclonal antibodies are produced by injecting a mouse or rabbit with a specific antigen. After some weeks, antibody-producing cells from its spleen are extracted and fused with myeloma (cancer) cells, producing hybrid cells that can thrive in culture and will produce antibodies indefinitely. From the many different hybrid cells formed, a cell producing the required antibody is identified; it is then cultured separately, providing a source of identical antibody molecules. Monoclonal antibodies are used to detect and measure particular antigens in screening blood and they can act as specific antigens.

monocotyledon A member of the smaller of the

two classes of ANGIOSPERMS, characterized by having a single COTYLEDON in the seed, leaves with parallel veins, and flowers with parts arranged in threes or multiples thereof. Those, such as palms and bamboos, that have woody stems, develop in a different way from DICOTYLEDONS. There are many exceptions to these general features, for example yams have a network of leaf veins like dicotyledons. Monocotyledons include palms, grasses, and bamboos, orchids, irises, and lilies. Although there are fewer families and species than in the dicotyledons, they dominate the grasslands of the world and are economically important as food crops. CEREALS are the most important monocotyledons to humans, but others include onions, pineapples, bananas, and many fibre or spice plants.

Monod, Jacques Lucien (1910–76) French biochemist. Monod joined the Pasteur Institute after World War II and became its director in 1971. He worked on bacterial genetics in collaboration with his fellow French biochemist François Jacob (1920–) and they formulated a theory to explain how genes are activated. In 1960 they coined the term **operon** for a gene that regulates others, and a year later proposed the existence of messenger RNA, which transmits the information from genes to the site of protein synthesis. Monod and Jacob were awarded a Nobel Prize in 1965, and in 1971 Monod published his wide-ranging popular work *Chance and Necessity*.

monody A particular kind of vocal style developed around 1600 as a reaction against elaborate POLYPHONY. Monody sought to convey the rhythmic values and meaning of words with the greatest clarity and accuracy. The vocal line therefore avoided the regular patterns of 'tunefulness' and aimed to become melodic speech. It was accompanied in the simplest possible way with a few supporting chords. The monodic style became the basis of early OPERA.

monomer A molecule that can react with other molecules of the same or other compound to form a new product with a higher RELATIVE MOLECULAR MASS. A simple example is ethene, which reacts with itself to form polyethene:

$n\mathrm{CH_2{=}CH_2} \rightarrow (\mathrm{-CH_2-})_{2n}$.

monopoly (in economics) A situation in which there is a single supplier (a monopolist) in the MARKET for a good or service. Monopoly power is the ability of a single producing firm to affect price to make profits above those necessary to cover costs, including a normal return on capital. Such profits are known as monopoly profits. Monopoly power may also accrue to oligopolistic firms (see OLIGOPOLY). Governments may try to restrict the emergence of monopolies since a monopoly's power to influence prices and supplies of a good is commonly considered detrimental.

monopsony (in economics) A situation in which there is a single buyer (a monopsonist) in the market for a particular good or service. This may be compared with MONOPOLY, where there is a single seller. Monopsony power is the ability to affect price through buying power. An example of a monopsonistic market is that of defence equipment, where most sales are to one buyer, the national government.

monosaccharide A carbohydrate consisting of a single sugar molecule possessing either a keto group (C=O) or an aldehyde group (CHO). The most widely occurring monosaccharides are either pentoses (with five carbon atoms) or hexoses (with six carbon atoms), both of which can exist as either ring structures or straight chains.

Monotype The trade name of an automated TYPESETTING system for metal type, invented in the USA by Tolbert Lanston in 1887 and developed during the 1890s by the Lanston Monotype Corporation (USA). Keyboards produce coded paper tape to control casting machines, which cast each letter and space sequentially in type metal from individual matrices (moulds). The system was universally adopted for quality typesetting. Hot-metal typesetting has now been superseded, and the Monotype Corporation today makes filmsetting equipment.

Monroe, James (1758–1831) US Democratic Republican statesman, 5th President of the USA 1817–25. In 1803, while minister to France under President Jefferson, he negotiated and ratified the Louisiana Purchase, by which territory formerly owned by France was sold to the USA. He is chiefly remembered, however, as the originator of the **Monroe Doctrine**, a principle of US foreign policy that any intervention by external powers in the politics of the Americas is a potentially hostile act against the USA. It was first expressed in Monroe's address to Congress in 1823 against a background of continued involvement and threat of expansion from European colonial powers in South America.

Monroe, Marilyn (born Norma Jean Mortenson, later Baker) (1926–62) US actress. After a career as a photographer's model, she starred in a series of comedy films, including *Gentlemen Prefer Blondes* (1953) and *Some Like it Hot* (1959), emerging as the definitive Hollywood sex symbol. Her last film was *The Misfits* (1961), written for her by her third husband, the dramatist Arthur MILLER. She is thought to have died of an overdose of sleeping-pills, although there is continuing controversy over the cause of her death.

Monrovia The capital and chief port of the West African state of Liberia; pop. (1985) 500,000. Originally known as Christopolis, but later renamed after US President James Monroe, it was founded in 1822 by the American Colonization Society as a settlement for slaves repatriated from North America.

Mons (Flemish **Bergen**) A town in the province of Hainaut, southern Belgium, at the centre of a major coal-mining and industrial region; pop. (1991) 91,730. It was the site of the first British battle on the Continent in World War I, in August 1914.

monsoon A wind in southern and other parts of Asia, especially in the Indian Ocean, blowing from the south-west in summer (**wet monsoon**) and the north-east in winter (**dry monsoon**). Monsoons also describe the heavy rainfall in Ethiopia and West Africa.

montage A pictorial technique in which cut-out illustrations, or fragments of them, are arranged together and mounted; the term is also applied to the picture so made. Montage differs from COLLAGE in that it uses only ready-made images.

Montaigne, Michel (Eyquem) de (1533–92) French essayist. Often regarded as the originator of the modern essay, he wrote about prominent personalities and ideas of his age in his sceptical *Essays* (1580; 1588). Translated by John Florio in 1603, they were an influence on Shakespeare, Francis Bacon, and others.

Montale, Eugenio (1896–1981) The greatest Italian poet of the 20th century, recipient of the Nobel Prize for literature in 1971. Among his main books of poems are: *Cuttle-fish Bones* (1925), *Occasions* (1932), *The Storm and Others* (1943–54), and *Diary of 1971 and 1972* (1973).

Montana A state in the western USA on the Canadian border east of the Rocky Mountains; area 380,848 sq km (147,046 sq miles); pop. (1990) 799,065; capital, Helena. The largest cities are Billings, Great Falls, and Missoula. Montana is also known as the Treasure State. It formed part of the Louisiana Purchase in 1803 and was enlarged in 1846 with land obtained from Britain under the Oregon Treaty. In 1889 it became the 41st state of the Union. Once a leading centre of copper mining, Montana produces grain, vegetables, sheep, and cattle. Major landmarks include Glacier National Park, Yellowstone National Park, and Custer Battlefield National Monument.

Montana, Joe (known as 'Cool Joe') (1956–) US football player. He joined the San Francisco 49ers as quarterback in 1980 and played in four winning Super Bowls (1982; 1985; 1989; 1990). He retired in 1995 after two seasons with the Kansas City Chiefs.

Mont Blanc A peak in the Alps on the border between France and Italy, rising to 4,807 m (15,771 ft). It forms part of a massif of 25 peaks over 4,000 m (13,120 ft) and is the highest mountain in western Europe. It was first climbed in 1786 by J. Balmat and M. G. Paccard.

montbretia A hybrid species of plant derived from South African plants with swollen rootstocks (corms) and belonging to the iris family. The leaves are sword-shaped and the spikes of trumpet-shaped flowers may be yellow, orange, or red. The popular garden montbretia is a cross between *Crocosmia* species, *Crocosmia* × *crocosmiflora*. Other true species of *Crocosmia* are sometimes also called montbretias.

Montcalm, Louis Joseph de Montcalm-Gozon, Marquis de (1712–59) French general. He defended Quebec against British troops under General Wolfe, but was defeated and mortally wounded in the battle on the Plains of Abraham.

Monte Carlo A resort in Monaco, forming one of the four communes of the principality; pop. (1985) 12,000. It is famous as a gambling resort and as the terminus of the annual Monte Carlo Rally. Its casino was built in 1879–85 by Charles Garnier.

Monte Carlo method A way of analysing stochastic processes that are so difficult that a purely mathematical treatment is not practical. The procedure is to construct an artificial model of the real-world problem and then perform sampling experiments on it. The random devices that were first used in such a simulation included roulette wheels, dice, and spinning pointers, and gave the method its name. It is now possible to perform simulations on a large scale with computers, and it is a very widely used process.

Monte Cassino A hill in west-central Italy near the town of Cassino, midway between Rome and Naples. It is the site of the principal monastery of the Benedictines, founded by St Benedict *c*.529. The monastery, demolished and rebuilt several times in its history, was almost totally destroyed during World War II, but has since been restored. In 1944 Allied forces advancing towards Rome were halted by German defensive positions in which Monte Cassino played a major part. The Allies succeeded in capturing the site only after four months of bitter fighting and the destruction of the town and the monastery. See also CASSINO.

Montenegro (Serbo-Croat **Crna Gora**) A mountainous landlocked republic in the Balkans; area 13,812 sq km (5,335 sq miles); pop. (1988) 632,000; official language, Serbo-Croat; capital, Podgorica (formerly Titograd). Joined with Serbia before the Turkish conquest of 1355, Montenegro became independent in 1851. In 1918 it became part of the federation of Yugoslavia, of which it remained, with Serbia, a nominal constituent. When Yugoslavia disintegrated during 1991 it remained in alliance with Serbia, confirmed by a referendum in 1992. Serbia and Montenegro declared themselves to be an independent country, the Federal Republic of Yugoslavia, but this country has not been internationally recognized because of its involvement in the civil war in Bosnia-Hercegovina.

Montespan, Françoise-Athénaïs de Rochechouart, Marquise de (1641–1707) French noblewoman. She was mistress of Louis XIV from 1667 to 1679, and had seven illegitimate children by him. She subsequently fell from favour when the king became attracted to their governess, Madame de Maintenon.

Montesquieu, Charles Louis de Secondat, Baron de La Brède et de (1689–1755) French political philosopher. A former advocate, he became known with the publication of his *Lettres Persanes* (1721), a satire of French society from the perspective of two Persian travellers visiting Paris. Montesquieu's reputation rests chiefly on *L'Esprit des lois* (1748), a comparative study of political systems in which he championed the separation of judicial, legislative, and executive powers as being most conducive to individual liberty, holding up the English state as a model. His theories were highly influential in Europe in the late 18th century, as they were in the drafting of the American Constitution.

Montessori, Maria (1870–1952) Italian educationist. Her success with mentally retarded children led her, in 1907, to apply similar methods to younger children of normal intelligence. Montessori's system, set out in her book *The Montessori Method* (1909), advocates a child-centred approach, in which the pace is largely set by the child and play is free but guided, using a variety of sensory materials. Her ideas have since become an integral part of modern nursery and infant-school education.

Monteverdi, Claudio (1567–1643) Italian composer. From the 1580s he published many books of madrigals, noted for their use of harmonic dissonance. Monteverdi is also remembered for his opera *Orfeo* (1607), which introduced a sustained dramatic focus and more fully defined characters, interweaving the instrumental accompaniment and the singing with the drama. His other Baroque operas include *The Return of Ulysses* (1641) and *The Coronation of Poppea* (1642). As a composer of sacred music, he is particularly associated with the *Vespers* (1610).

Montevideo The capital and chief port of Uruguay, on the River Plate; pop. (est. 1991) 1,360,250. Founded in 1726, it has been capital of Uruguay since 1830. It is the commercial and financial centre of Uruguay, the base of a large fishing fleet, and has various light industries.

Montez, Lola (born Marie Dolores Eliza Rosanna Gilbert) (1818–61) Irish dancer. While performing in Munich in 1846 she came to the notice of Ludwig I of Bavaria; she became his mistress and exercised great influence on his ruling of the country until banished the following year.

Montezuma II (1466–1520) Aztec emperor 1502–20. The last ruler of the Aztec empire in Mexico, he was defeated and imprisoned by the Spanish conquistadors under Cortés in 1519. Montezuma was killed while trying to pacify some of his former subjects during the Aztec uprising against his captors.

Montfort, Simon de, Earl of Leicester (*c.*1208–65) English soldier, born in Normandy. He was the son of the French soldier Simon de Montfort. As leader of the baronial opposition to Henry III, he campaigned against royal encroachment on the privileges gained through Magna Carta, and defeated the king at Lewes, Sussex, in 1264. The following year he summoned a Parliament, which included not only barons, knights, and clergymen, but also two citizens from every borough in England. He was defeated and killed by reorganized royal forces under Henry's son (later Edward I) at Evesham.

Montgolfier brothers French inventors. Sons of a paper manufacturer, **Joseph Michel** (1740–1810) and **Jacques Étienne** (1745–99) pioneered experiments in hot-air ballooning. In 1782 they built a large balloon from linen and paper, lit a fire on the ground, and with the rising hot air successfully lifted a number of animals; the first human ascents followed in 1783.

Montgomery The capital of the US state of Alabama, on the Alabama River; pop. (1990) 187,100. Settled in 1819, it was the first capital of the Confederate States of America until its capture by Union troops in July 1861. The capital was subsequently moved to Richmond, Virginia. Martin Luther King, who was a pastor here from 1954 to 1960, directed the bus boycott that initiated the US civil rights movement in the 1960s.

Montgomery, Bernard Law, 1st Viscount Montgomery of Alamein (known as 'Monty') (1887–1976) British Field Marshal. In 1942 he commanded the 8th Army in the Western Desert, where his victory at El Alamein proved the first significant Allied success in World War II. He was later given command of the Allied ground forces in the invasion of Normandy in 1944 and accepted the German surrender on 7 May 1945.

Montgomery, Lucy Maud (1874–1942) Canadian novelist. She is chiefly remembered for her first novel *Anne of Green Gables* (1908), the story of a spirited orphan girl brought up by an elderly couple. It became an instant bestseller and was followed by seven sequels.

Montgomeryshire A former county of central Wales. It became a part of Powys in 1974.

month In astronomy, a period of time related to the Moon's orbit about the Earth. Five months of different lengths can be defined:

synodic month or **lunation**, the time between successive similar geometric positions of Sun, Moon, and Earth; for example, the time between successive new moons;

sidereal month, the time it takes the Moon to rotate once round the Earth with respect to the stellar background;

anomalistic month, the time between successive passages of the Moon through perigee;

tropical month, the time between successive passages of the Moon through the vernal EQUINOX;

nodical or **draconitic month**, the time between successive passages of the Moon through the same node.

In civil usage the month is any of usually 12 periods of time into which the year is divided, or any period between the same dates in successive such portions.

Montmartre A district in northern Paris, on a hill above the Seine, much frequented by artists in the late 19th and early 20th centuries, when it was a village separated from Paris. Many of its buildings have artistic associations, e.g. the Moulin de la Galette, which was painted by Renoir, the Bateau-Lavoir occupied successively by Renoir, van Dongen, and Picasso, and various houses associated with Utrillo.

montmorillonite A clay mineral of complex composition but essentially aluminium silicates. It is opaque, soft, and feels greasy to the touch. The minute crystals can take up or lose water or positive ions such as sodium, Na^+, or calcium, Ca^{2+}. Montmorillonite is found very extensively and is an important industrial mineral, being used as a base for paper and cosmetics and for purifying liquids. It is sometimes referred to as **fuller's earth**.

Montparnasse A district of Paris, on the left bank of the River Seine. Noted for its cafés, it was frequented in the late 19th century by writers and artists and is traditionally associated with Parisian cultural life. The Pasteur Institute and the catacombs are situated in Montparnasse.

Mont Pelée A volcano on the island of MARTINIQUE, in the volcanic arc of the CARIBBEAN. It is famed for the appalling catastrophe of 1902, when, heralded by a great explosion, a NUÉE ARDENTE swept down the flanks of the volcano and devastated St Pierre, the port and capital of the island, killing 30,000 people.

Montpelier The capital of the US state of Vermont, situated on the Winooksi River at the centre of a popular vacation area; pop. (1990) 8,250.

Montpellier An industrial city in the Languedoc-Roussillon region of southern France, capital of the department of Hérault; pop. (1990) 210,870. It developed in the 10th century as a trading centre on the spice route from the Near East, and was a stopover on the pilgrimage to Santiago de Compostela in Spain. A distinguished medical school, world-famous in medieval times, was founded here in 1221 and was confirmed as a university by Pope Nicolas IV in 1289.

Montreal (French **Montréal**) A port on the St Lawrence in southern Quebec, Canada; pop. (1991) 1,017,700; (3,127,240 metropolitan area). It is the second-largest city in Canada and nearly two-thirds of its population are French-speaking. Founded as a missionary outpost in 1642 and named Ville Marie de Montréal, it developed as a trading post under French rule until 1763. Montreal hosted Expo '67, celebrating Canada's centennial in 1967. In addition to being a commercial and financial centre, its industries produce chemicals, textiles, tobacco, steel, iron, and petroleum. Montreal is the home of the University of Montreal and McGill University.

Montreux A resort town in Vaud canton, south-west Switzerland, at the east end of Lake Geneva; pop. (1990) 19,850. It is the site of an international jazz festival, which has been held here annually every July since 1967, and an annual television festival, which has been held here every spring since 1961.

Montrose, James Graham, 1st Marquess of (1612–50) Scottish general. Montrose supported Charles I when Scotland entered the English Civil War and, commanding a small army of Irish and Scottish irregulars, inflicted a dramatic series of defeats on the stronger Covenanter forces in the north (1644–45) before being defeated at Philiphaugh. After several years in exile, he returned to Scotland in 1650 in a bid to restore the new king Charles II, but was betrayed to the Covenanters and hanged.

Mont-Saint-Michel A rocky islet off the coast of Normandy, north-west France, in the Gulf of St-Malo. An island only at high tide, it is surrounded by sandbanks and linked to the mainland, since 1875, by a causeway. It is crowned by a magnificent medieval Benedictine abbey-fortress founded in 708.

Montserrat An island in the West Indies, one of the Leeward Islands; area 102 sq km (39 sq miles); pop. (est. 1997) 4,000; official language, English; capital, Plymouth. Visited by Columbus in 1493 and named after a Benedictine monastery on the mountain of Montserrat in Spain, it was colonized by Irish settlers in 1632. It was part of the British federal colony of the Leeward Islands from 1871 to 1956 when it became a separate UK Dependent Territory. In addition to offshore finance, it is a base for the production of light consumer goods, electronic components, and goods made from locally grown cotton. It is governed by a Governor who presides over an Executive Council and a Legislative Council. Many of the islanders were evacuated in 1997 following a major volcanic eruption.

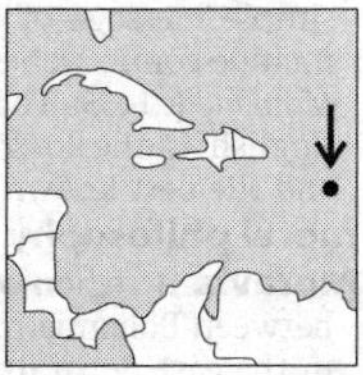

Monza An industrial city in Lombardy, northern Italy, forming part of the Milan conurbation; pop. (1990) 123,190. The cathedral, founded by Queen Theodolinda in the 6th century, contains a 9th-century iron crown of the kings of Italy, said to have been forged from a nail used in Christ's Crucifixion. Monza was the scene of the assassination of King Umberto I in 1900. The city is noted for its motor-racing events. Textiles and carpets are local industries.

Moog, Robert (1934–) US inventor. Qualified in physics and engineering, Moog set up a company to develop a keyboard instrument capable of producing electronically synthesized music. The first Moog synthesizer was unveiled in 1964 and quickly became standard equipment in popular music.

Moon The Earth's only natural satellite. The Moon's surface is highly irregular, the main large-scale features being the MARIA, the mountains, the CRATERS, and bright rays which may be ejecta. The maria, conspicuous dark almost level plains, are depressions filled with solidified lava. The largest of them are over a thousand kilometres wide. The other three features are almost certainly the results of a colossal bombardment of the Moon's surface in the early period of the Solar System, a bombardment lasting some hundreds of millions of years, while debris was being swept up by the Moon and the planets. This debris, formed of objects ranging in size from asteroids of up to a hundred kilometres across down to dust particles, created the Moon's main features, as well as producing a surface layer of rock that has been shattered, melted, vaporized, ejected, and cooled. The period of bombardment was followed by a flooding of the maria regions by basaltic lavas as a consequence of radioactive heating in the Moon's interior. Seismic activity, also known as **moonquakes**, has been recorded by the APOLLO PROGRAMME instruments and the lunar samples brought back to Earth by astronauts show that the Moon must be at least 4.3 billion years old, probably the same age as the Earth. The types of rock found are made of the same chemical elements that make up the Earth, in much the same proportions. The Moon has no atmosphere and probably never had one to any marked extent, and life does not seem to have ever been present before men landed there. However, in 1998 US probes detected the presence of water on the Moon. A recent theory suggests that the Moon's origin may have been a collision between a Mars-like planetesimal and the very young Earth. The temperature of the surface of the Moon reaches 100°C in the lunar daytime and falls to below −200°C during the lunar night. There is no erosion except for the slow crumbling of rock under repeated expansion and contraction and the occasional sudden localized disturbance due to the impact of a meteorite.

The Moon's mass, 1/81.38 that of the Earth, is accurately measured by tracking artificial lunar satellites, and its diameter of 3,476 km is 1/3.67 that of the Earth. The Moon rotates such that the longest axis always points in the general direction of the Earth, the Moon's period of rotation being equal to its period of revolution about the Earth so that, apart from LIBRATION effects, it always keeps the same side to the Earth. The mean density of the Moon is 3,330 kg/m^3, very close to that of the basic rocks under the Earth's crust, and the surface gravity is only about one-sixth that at the Earth's surface. See also TIDE; ECLIPSE; PHASE.

Moon, Sun Myung (1920–) Korean industrialist and religious leader. In 1954 he founded the Holy Spirit Association for the Unification of World Christianity, which became known as the Unification Church; his followers are popularly known as 'Moonies'.

moonfish See OPAH.

Moonies See MOON, SUN MYUNG; UNIFICATION CHURCH.

moonquake See MOON.

moonstone A semiprecious fine-grained feldspar of various colours, with transparent or opalescent appearance. It is described by ancient writers as a stone that changes appearance with the waxing and waning of the Moon.

Moor A member of a Muslim people of mixed Berber and Arab descent, inhabiting north-west Africa and southern Spain from the 8th to the 15th centuries. Their name is derived from a Greek word (*Mauros*) for the inhabitants of ancient Mauretania.

Moore, Bobby (full name Robert Frederick Moore) (1941–93) British footballer. He is chiefly remembered as the captain of the English team that won the World Cup in 1966.

Moore, Brian (1921–) Irish-born Canadian novelist, who left his native Belfast for Canada in 1948 and moved to the USA in 1959. His books, which often show a preoccupation with Roman Catholicism and the world of dreams, include *The Lonely Passion of Judith Hearne* (1956), *Fergus* (1971), *Catholics* (1972), *The Colour of Blood* (1987), and *The Statement* (1995).

Moore, Dudley (Stuart John) (1935–) British actor, comedian, and musician. Moore appeared in the highly successful television show *Beyond the Fringe* (1959–64) for which he also wrote the music. He then joined Peter Cook in what was to become a noted partnership for the TV series *Not Only . . . But Also* (1964–70). Moore starred in several films, including *Arthur* (1981) and *Crazy People* (1990), and regularly performed and recorded with the Dudley Moore Trio as an accomplished jazz pianist.

Moore, Francis (1657–*c.*1715) English physician, astrologer, and schoolmaster. In 1699 he published an almanac containing weather predictions in order to promote the sale of his pills, and in 1700 one with astrological observations. There are now several almanacs called 'Old Moore', and predictions range far beyond the weather.

Moore, George (Augustus) (1852–1933) Irish novelist. From about 1870 he lived in Paris, where he studied painting and gained a knowledge of the works of writers such as Balzac and Zola. On his return to London (1880) Moore embarked on a career as a novelist; influenced by Zola, he experimented with naturalistic techniques in works such as *A Mummer's Wife* (1885), set in the Potteries in North Staffordshire, and *Esther Waters* (1894). He became involved in the Irish literary revival and collaborated in the planning of the Irish National Theatre, established in 1899.

Moore, G(eorge) E(dward) (1873–1958) British philosopher. He led the revolt against the Hegelianism prevalent at the turn of the century, objecting that it was inapplicable to the familiar world of 'tables and chairs'. In his best-known work, *Principia Ethica* (1903), he argued that good was a simple, indefinable, unanalysable, and non-natural property, but that it was still possible to identify certain things as pre-eminently good. These he declared to be 'personal affection and aesthetic enjoyments', values seized upon by several of his associates in the Bloomsbury Group.

Moore, Henry (Spencer) (1898–1986) British sculptor and draughtsman. In the 1920s he rejected modelling in favour of direct carving in stone and wood, and allowed natural qualities, such as texture and grain, to influence form. Moore subsequently received major commissions for architectural sculpture, including large reclining figures for the UNESCO building in Paris (1957–58). Prominent themes for the postwar period were upright figures, family groups, and two and three-piece semi-abstract reclining forms; Moore was keen that these sculptures should be viewed in the open air. As an official War Artist (1940–42) he produced a series of poignant drawings of people sheltering from air-raids in London underground stations.

Moore, Sir John (1761–1809) British general. From 1808 he commanded the British army during the Peninsular War, conducting a successful 250-mile retreat to Corunna in mid-winter before being mortally wounded by his French pursuers. His burial was the subject of a famous poem by the Irish poet Charles Wolfe (1791–1823).

Moore, Thomas (1779–1852) Irish poet and musician. He wrote patriotic and nostalgic songs, which he set to Irish tunes, and collected in *Irish Melodies* (1807–34). His most famous songs include 'The Harp that once through Tara's Halls' and 'The Minstrel Boy'. He is also noted for his oriental romance *Lalla Rookh* (1817).

moorhen See GALLINULE.

moose The largest living member of the DEER family known in Europe as the elk, *Alces alces*. A bull stands up to 1.8 m (6 feet) at the shoulder and has huge antlers 1.8 m (6 feet) across with numerous points. The head is long, the ears large, and the nose bulbous. A growth of skin and long hair hanging from the throat is known as the bell. The moose can reach high into willow trees to browse on leaves and twigs. In the rutting season in autumn, the bulls fight for possession of the cows. One or two young, or on rare occasions three, are born. The calf is like its mother in colour, unlike the young of other deer, which have stripes or spots.

moraine An area covered by rocks and debris carried down and deposited at the margin of a glacier.

morality play A religious drama popular in England, Scotland, France, and the Netherlands in the 15th and early 16th centuries. Morality plays are allegories, in which personified virtues, vices, diseases, and temptations struggle for the soul of Man as he travels from birth to death. They instil a simple message of Christian salvation, but often include comic scenes, as in the lively obscenities of *Mankind* (*c.*1465). The earliest surviving example in English is the long *Castle of Perseverance* (*c.*1420), and the best known is *Everyman* (*c.*1510).

moral philosophy See ETHICS.

Moravia A region of the Czech Republic, situated between Bohemia in the west and the Carpathians in the east. Separated from Silesia in the north by the Sudeten Mountains and drained by the River Morava, it is a fertile agricultural region, rich in mineral resources. Its chief town is Brno. Formerly the western part of the medieval Slavonic kingdom of Greater Moravia, it became a province of Bohemia in the 11th century. It was made an Austrian crownland in 1848, becoming a part of Czechoslovakia in 1918.

Moravia, Alberto (born Alberto Pincherle) (1907–90) Italian novelist. He played a major part in shaping neorealism in Italian fiction after World War II. His first novel, *The Time of Indifference* (1929), portrays a middle-class society sick with a moral inertia, which favoured the rise of fascism. *Two Women* (1957), the most lyrical and complex of his novels, deals with the close of the war, when Italy was occupied by both Germans and Allies. *The Woman of Rome* (1947) and *Roman Tales* (1957) draw on the language and culture of the Roman working classes in order to criticize middle-class values. Other full-length novels, notably *The Conformist* (1951) and *1934* (1983), explore the psycho-sexual basis of politics.

Moravian A member of a Protestant sect founded in Saxony in 1722 by emigrants from Moravia, holding views derived from the Hussites and a simple unworldly form of Christianity with the Bible as the only source of faith.

Moray A local government area and former county (Morayshire) of northern Scotland, bordered on the north by the Moray Firth. It was a district of Grampian Region from 1975 to 1996; area 2,224 sq km (859 sq miles); pop. (1993) 86,250; its administrative centre is Elgin.

moray eel An eel belonging to a family, Muraenidae, of some 80 species mainly found in tropical and subtropical waters. These eels, which reach 1.5 m (5 feet) in length, are voracious predators with sharp teeth, normally eating other fish but also striking at divers who approach too closely.

Moray Firth A deep inlet of the North Sea on the north-east coast of Scotland. The city of Inverness is near its head.

mordant A substance used to improve the fastness of natural DYES. The material is treated with the mordant before dyeing, and the resultant colour is much less likely to fade or be washed out. The word 'mordant' is based on an old French word meaning 'to bite', so called because the mordant 'bit' into the dye and prevented its escape. The most commonly used mordant is ALUM. The colour of some dyes (for example, madder) can be changed by the use of different mordants.

Mordvinia (official name **Mordvinian Republic**) An autonomous republic in western Russia; area 26,200 sq km (20,220 sq miles); pop. (1990) 964,000; capital, Saransk. Absorbed into the Russian empire in the 13th century, the region was constituted as a Mordovian Area in the Middle-Volga Territory of the Soviet Union in 1928. It was an autonomous republic of the USSR from 1934 until 1991. Over 30 per cent of its population are Finno-Ugric Mordvinians.

More, Sir Thomas (canonized as **St Thomas More**) (1478–1535) English scholar and statesman, Lord Chancellor 1529–32. From the time of the accession of Henry VIII (1509), More held a series of public offices, but was forced to resign as Lord Chancellor when he opposed the king's divorce from Catherine of Aragon. He was imprisoned in 1534 after refusing to take the oath on the Act of Succession, sanctioning Henry's marriage to Anne Boleyn. After opposing the Act of Supremacy in the same year, More was beheaded. Regarded as one of the leading humanists of the Renaissance, he owed his reputation largely to his *Utopia* (1516), describing an ideal city-state. Feast day, 22 June.

Moreau, Jeanne (1928–) French actress. She was acclaimed for her portrayals of isolated and autonomous women in such films as *Ascenseur pour l'échafaud* (1958) *Les Liaisons dangereuses* (1959), and *Jules et Jim* (1961). Later she had some success as a director, especially with *L'Adolescente* (1978), and she also continued to act, her more recent films including *Nikita* (1990).

Morecambe, Eric (born John Eric Bartholomew) (1926–84) British comedian. In 1941 he formed a double act with comedian Ernie Wise (1925–) that led to the immensely popular *The Morecambe and Wise Show*, which ran on television from 1961. In 1968 Morecambe suffered a heart attack but recovered to continue his TV work, appear in three films, and write a number of books, including the children's book *The Reluctant Vampire* (1982). He carried on performing until his death from another heart attack.

Morecambe Bay An inlet of the Irish Sea, on the north-west coast of England, between Lancashire and the Furness peninsula of Cumbria. The name was derived in the 18th century from a reference in a work of the 2nd-century Greek geographer Ptolemy to *mori kambe*, from the old Celtic name for the Lune estuary, *mori cambo* 'curved bay'. The resort town of **Morecambe**, pop. (1991) 46,657, is situated on the bay. It was known as Poulton-le-Sands until 1870.

morel A fungus of the genus *Morchella*, one of the cup fungi (order Pezizales). The common morel, *Morchella esculenta*, has a fruiting body which is club-shaped with a pale stalk and darker head covered with a network of ridges; in all it is about 15 cm (6 inches) high. It is edible and appears in spring. The similar-looking 'false morel', *Gyromitra esculenta*, is poisonous.

Morgan, Sir Henry (*c*.1635–88) Welsh BUCCANEER, the scourge of Spanish settlements and shipping in the Caribbean between the 1660s and 1680s. Although he had semi-official employment as a privateer, he was little more than a pirate. Although knighted and appointed lieutenant-governor of Jamaica in 1674, he continued to encourage piracy and lawlessness. He was disgraced in 1683 but restored just before his death.

Morgan, John Pierpont (1837–1913) US financier and philanthropist. A member of a distinguished family of financiers, he came to New York from Boston in 1857. He established his own company there in 1860, becoming increasingly interested in railways. Morgan believed in the merits of centralization, working to eliminate wasteful competition, but his banking opponents saw him as a monopolist. In 1893 and 1907 his personal weight was sufficient to stabilize critically unbalanced financial markets. He was perhaps the leading private art collector of his day.

Morgan, Thomas Hunt (1866–1945) US zoologist. He is best known for demonstrating the mechanism in the animal cell responsible for inheritance. His studies with the rapidly reproducing fruit fly *Drosophila* showed that the genetic information was carried by genes arranged along the length of the chromosomes. Though this work was not widely accepted initially, Morgan was awarded a Nobel Prize in 1933.

morganatic marriage A legal marriage of medieval German origin in which a royal or noble man marries a commoner on the understanding that neither she nor her children will succeed to inherited dignities or property. The word comes from the Latin *matrimonium ad morganaticum*, a marriage based on a morning gift, a present given after the consummation, representing the husband's only commitment. Such a marriage was suggested for Edward VIII and Mrs Simpson but was unacceptable to the Church. A morganatic marriage between Prince Charles and Mrs Parker-Bowles has also been suggested.

Morisco (or **Moresco**; from Spanish, 'Little Moor') The Moors in Spain (or their descendants) who accepted Christian baptism. When the Christians reconquered Muslim Spain in the 11th–15th centuries the Islamic religion and customs were at first tolerated, but after the fall of Granada in 1492 Islam was officially prohibited and Muslims were forced to become Christians or go into exile. Many who remained practised their own religion in private, in spite of persecution, but their political loyalty was suspect and in 1609 they were expelled, mainly to Africa.

Morisot, Berthe (Marie Pauline) (1841–95) French painter. A pupil of Corot, she was the first woman to join the impressionists, exhibiting with them from 1874. Her works typically depicted women and children, as in *The Cradle* (1872), and waterside scenes, notably *A Summer's Day* (1879).

Morland, George (1763–1804) British painter. Although indebted to Dutch and Flemish genre painters such as David Teniers the Younger, he drew his inspiration for his pictures of taverns, cottages, and farmyards from local scenes, as with *Inside a Stable* (1791). His art achieved widespread popularity through the engravings of William Ward (1766–1826).

Morley, Edward Williams (1838–1923) US chemist. He specialized in accurate quantitative measurements, such as those of the combining weights of hydrogen and oxygen. He is best known, however, for his collaboration with Albert Michelson in their 1887 experiment to investigate the ETHER. See MICHELSON.

Morley, Thomas (*c*.1558–1602) English composer, writer, and publisher. In 1592 he was sworn in as a Gentleman of the CHAPEL ROYAL, and thereafter published both his own compositions and Italian works, so that the vogue for MADRIGALS, *balletts* (a 16th-century type of Italian dance song) and *can-*

zonets became firmly established. He also wrote anthems, motets, and other sacred music in English and Latin, as well as solo songs, keyboard, lute, and CONSORT music. From 1598 until his death he had a monopoly of music publishing in England.

Mormon A member of the Church of Jesus Christ of Latter-Day Saints, which was founded in New York in 1830 by Joseph Smith (1805–44). He claimed to have discovered, through divine revelation, the 'Book of Mormon', relating the history of a group of Hebrews who migrated to America *c.*600 BC. This work is accepted by Mormons as Scripture along with the Bible. A further revelation led him to institute polygamy, a practice that brought the Mormons into conflict with the Federal Government and was abandoned in 1890. Smith was succeeded as leader by Brigham Young (1801–77), who moved the Mormon headquarters to Salt Lake City, Utah, in 1847. Mormon teaching is strongly adventist; the movement has no professional clergy, self-help is emphasized, and tithing and missionary work are required of its members.

Morocco A country in the north-west corner of Africa bounded inland by Algeria and Western Sahara and with coasts on both the Mediterranean Sea and the Atlantic Ocean.

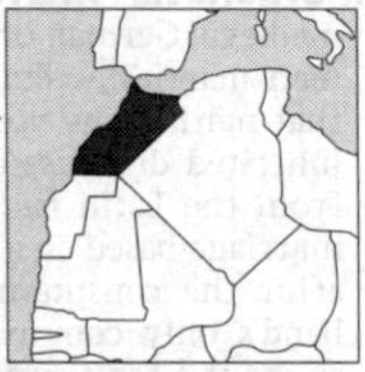

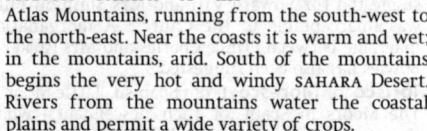

Physical. Much of Morocco consists of the Atlas Mountains, running from the south-west to the north-east. Near the coasts it is warm and wet; in the mountains, arid. South of the mountains begins the very hot and windy SAHARA Desert. Rivers from the mountains water the coastal plains and permit a wide variety of crops.

Economy. Morocco's main export is phosphates, of which it has the world's largest reserves; other minerals extracted include anthracite, iron, lead, and manganese. Morocco is dependent on imported fuel for most of its energy needs, and also relies on imports to meet food requirements. Other than phosphate production, industry concentrates on textiles and motor vehicles. Tourism is regarded as an expanding source of revenue. Traditional methods of farming keep exports of crops such as grains, citrus fruit, vegetables, and grapes low. However, vineyards, olive-gardens, and date-palm groves thrive, especially on the inland Fez–Meknès plain.

History. By the 5th century BC PHOENICIANS had stations on the Moroccan coast, when the Carthaginian admiral, Hanno, passed the Straits of Gibraltar, and perhaps reached the Gulf of Guinea. A kingdom of Mauritania was formed in northern Morocco in the 4th century BC; the Romans made it the province of Mauritania Tingitana, based on Tangier. Vandals from Spain occupied the region from 428, but the Berbers controlled the interior even after the Byzantines had recovered the coast in 533. It did not come under Arab control until Musa ibn Nusayr's conquest in *c.*705. Under Byzantium the puritanism of the Berber character had been manifested in the DONATIST heresy; under Islam a similarly austere movement, Kharijism, arose. True Arab domination was brief, and Berber dynasties emerged, Idrisids (788–974), FATIMIDS (909–73), ALMORAVIDS (1056–1147), ALMOHADS (1145–1257), Merinids (1248–1548), and finally the Sharifian dynasties from 1524 until the present. Having defeated the Portuguese at Alcazarquivir (1578), Morocco itself attempted colonial expansion, defeating the SONGHAI empire with the help of firearms in 1591, but ruling it inefficiently.

By the 19th century, Morocco had lapsed into endemic disorder and became the target for French and Spanish imperial ambitions. In the early 20th century, German opposition to French expansionism produced serious international crises in 1905 and 1911 which almost resulted in war. In 1912 it was divided between a French protectorate, a Spanish protectorate, and the international Zone of Tangier. Rif rebels under ABD EL-KRIM fought the Spanish and French occupying powers in the 1920s, and Morocco became an independent monarchy under Muhammad V in 1956 when it absorbed Tangier. Muhammad was succeeded by his son Hassan II in 1961, but opposition sparked the suspension of parliamentary government in 1965, and royal authority has been maintained in the face of abortive military coups in the early 1970s and intermittent republican opposition. In 1980 a new constitution proclaimed the kingdom of Morocco to be a constitutional monarchy. From the mid-1970s Morocco has been involved in an inconclusive desert war in the former Spanish Sahara (see WESTERN SAHARA). A convention was signed in 1976 dividing this mineral-rich area between Morocco and Mauritania; but the latter renounced its claims in 1979 in favour of a nationalist group, the Polisario Front. Morocco annexed the land from which Mauritania had withdrawn, despite violent resistance from the Polisario Front. Major battles were fought in 1979 and 1980, and Moroccan troops built a series of desert walls; but increasing international support was given to the Polisario Front, who in 1976 had proclaimed the Saharan Arab Democratic Republic. A cease-fire was negotiated in 1991, pending a UN-conducted referendum, but little progress has been made in negotiations to secure a permanent peace accord. Morocco was the only Maghreb country to send troops in support of the UN in the GULF WAR. A new constitution, adopted in 1992, increased the powers of the government while retaining the hereditary monarch as head of state. A programme of privatization was launched by the government in 1993. The first general election since 1984 was held in 1993.

Capital: Rabat
Area: 458,730 sq km (177,117 sq mi)
Population: 26,980,000 (1995)
Currency: 1 dirham = 100 francs
Religions: Muslim (mostly Sunni) 98.7%; Christian 1.1%
Ethnic Groups: Arab-Berber 99.5%
Languages: Arabic (official); Berber; Spanish; French
International Organizations: UN; Non-Aligned Movement; Arab League; Maghreb Union

Moroni The capital of the Comoros Islands, on the island of Grand Comore; pop. (1980) 20,110.

morphine See ANALGESIC; PSYCHOTROPIC DRUG.

morpho A large, South American forest butterfly of the subfamily Morphinae. In most of the 200 or so species, the male is a vivid metallic blue on the upper side. The iridescent blue colour is a result of fine structures on the wing scales splitting up white light, rather than a pigment in the scale. Their wings have been used abundantly in decorative work, particularly jewellery. In some countries they are now protected by law. Females and males of some species are brown with yellow, white, or blue markings, and one species is silvery-white. Some fly slowly over the ground, others soar around tree-tops. The gregarious caterpillars are usually vividly coloured, often bristly, with yellow and red stripes; they feed on forest trees or bamboos.

morphology (in biology) The study of the form and structural arrangements exhibited by living things. Humans and other mammalian embryos are morphologically indistinguishable until they reach the foetal stage. By contrast morphological differences do exist between races, and between individuals of the same race. These differences have a genetic origin, but some morphological changes can be brought about by environmental influence. For example, in humans, teeth can be straightened in the jaw by use of metal bands. The study of morphology strongly supports the theory of evolution and is the foundation of PALAEONTOLOGY.

morphology (in linguistics) See GRAMMAR.

Morris, William (1834–96) British designer, craftsman, poet, and socialist writer. He was a leading figure in the Arts and Crafts Movement, and in 1861 he established Morris & Company, an association of craftsmen whose members included Edward Burne-Jones and Dante Gabriel Rossetti, to produce hand-crafted goods for the home. Morris's Kelmscott Press, founded in 1890, printed limited editions of fine books using his own type designs and ornamental borders, and was an important influence on English book design. He is also noted for his poetry and many prose romances, especially *News from Nowhere* (1891), which portrays a socialist Utopia.

Morris, William Richard See NUFFIELD, VISCOUNT.

Morris dance See FOLK DANCE.

Morrison, James Douglas (known as 'Jim') (1943–71) US rock singer. Morrison was the flamboyant lead singer of the Doors, a group formed in 1965. Associated with the psychedelia of the late 1960s, the group is remembered for dramatic songs such as 'Light My Fire' (1967) and 'Riders on the Storm' (1971). Morrison died in Paris, of a heart attack in his bath. His poetry was published in two volumes, *The Lords* and *The New Creatures* (first printed privately, 1969).

Morrison, Toni (full name Chloe Anthony Morrison) (1931–) US novelist. She is noted for her novels depicting the black American experience and heritage, often focusing on rural life in the South, as in *The Bluest Eye* (1970). Other works include *Song of Solomon* (1976), *Tar Baby* (1979), and the Pulitzer Prize-winning *Beloved* (1987), a tale of a runaway slave who commits infanticide in mid-19th-century Kentucky. Morrison was awarded the Nobel Prize for literature in 1993, becoming the first black woman writer to receive the prize.

Morrison, Van (full name George Ivan Morrison) (1945–) Northern Irish singer, songwriter, and musician. Van Morrison has developed a distinctive personal style from a background of blues, soul, folk music, and rock. Among his albums are *Astral Weeks* (1968) *Moondance* (1970), and *Irish Heartbeat* (1989). He started his career as lead singer of the 1960s band Them.

Morrison of Lambeth, Herbert Stanley Morrison, Baron (1888–1965) British politician. As leader of the London County Council (1934–40), he unified the transport system under public ownership and created a 'green belt' around the metropolis. Morrison was Minister of Supply and then Home Secretary in CHURCHILL's coalition government during World War II. He drafted the programme of nationalization and social services in the 1945 election. In 1945 he was deputy prime minister, but was defeated by GAITSKELL in the election for leadership of the Labour Party in 1955.

Morse, Samuel Finley Breese (1791–1872) US pioneer of TELEGRAPHY. In 1832, while on a return journey from Europe, he was prompted by a conversation to consider the possibility of an electric telegraph. By 1837, he had developed a practicable system, but found he had been anticipated by WHEATSTONE and COOKE in the UK. Eventually the US Government commissioned him to build an experimental telegraphic line from Washington to Baltimore, completed in 1844. He simplified the telegraph receiver to a pen that made dots and dashes on paper, a system that became known as the MORSE CODE.

Morse code The representation of letters and numbers by different combinations of dots and dashes. Devised by MORSE in the late 1830s, it was used for electric TELEGRAPHY. The code can be transmitted audibly, the dots and dashes being represented by short and long bursts of sound respectively; visually, by short and long flashes of light; or by printed dots and dashes on a paper tape.

mortality rate The ratio of deaths to a given population over a specified period. The most common measure, called 'the crude death rate', is usually calculated as the annual number of deaths per thousand population.

mortar (in building) A mixture of binder, AGGREGATE, and water which forms a cohesive paste for bedding BRICKS and stone and for finishing walls and ceilings. Normally, lime and cement are used as binders, with fine sand as the aggregate; sometimes chemicals are added to improve specific properties. In primitive technology, mud, dung, and straw mixtures are widely used.

mortar (in armaments) An artillery piece that fires projectiles in a high, arching trajectory. The earliest mortars were very heavy guns and were used mainly in sieges. The modern mortar can be carried by two people. It consists of a smooth-bore barrel with a base plate; a bipod stand is attached about halfway up the barrel. A bomb is dropped into the barrel and slides down until it strikes a fixed firing pin, which ignites propellant CARTRIDGES on the bomb. The subsequent explosion hurls the bomb out towards the target. Because of their lightness, mobility, and ease of camouflage, mortars have taken over the role of light artillery in much of modern warfare. Their high angle of fire also enables mortars to reach targets inaccessible to other supporting weapons.

mortgage A legal contract between a borrower (mortgagor) and a lender (mortgagee) secured by assets (commonly land or buildings) owned by the borrower. The ownership of the assets is transferred to the lender only if certain conditions of the loan agreement are broken. A mortgage is unlike a hire-purchase agreement in that the mortgaged property belongs to the borrower. Mortgages of various kinds are typically extended by BUILDING SOCIETIES, BANKS, and insurance companies to businesses and individual house-buyers. In case of default, a mortgagee has a number of remedies, but normally seeks possession and sells the property.

Mortimer, Roger de, 8th Baron of Wigmore and 1st Earl of March (*c.*1287–1330) English noble. In 1326 he invaded England with his lover Isabella of France, forcing her husband Edward II to abdicate in favour of her son, the future Edward III. Mortimer and Isabella acted as regents for the young Edward until 1330, when the monarch assumed royal power and had Mortimer executed.

Morton, Jelly Roll (born Ferdinand Joseph La Menthe Morton) (1885–1941) US jazz pianist, composer, and band-leader. He was one of the principal links between ragtime and New Orleans jazz, and formed his own band, the Red Hot Peppers, in 1926. For the next four years he and his band made a series of notable jazz recordings, but Morton's popularity waned during the 1930s.

Morton, John (*c.*1420–1500) English prelate and statesman. He rose to become Henry VII's chief adviser, being appointed Archbishop of Canterbury in 1486 and Chancellor a year later. He is traditionally associated with the Crown's stringent taxation policies, which made the regime in general and Morton in particular widely unpopular.

Morton, William Thomas Green (1819–68) US pioneer of ANAESTHESIA. In 1844 he set up in practice in Boston as a dentist in partnership with Horace Wells, who was interested in the anaesthetic properties of nitrous oxide. He was also in touch with Charles Jackson, who was using ether as a local anaesthetic for pain relief when filling teeth. This led Morton to use ether as a general anaesthetic in dental surgery (1846). The same year, ether anaesthesia was used for general surgery, and it was soon widely adopted. Morton became involved in protracted controversy and litigation with Wells, Jackson, and others over claims of priority.

mosaic The art of making patterns and pictures by arranging coloured fragments of glass, marble, or other suitable materials and fixing them into a bed of cement or plaster. The Romans used mosaic particularly for pavements, and examples survive throughout the empire. The early Christian period (4th–9th centuries AD) was a time of rapid development in the art, which also flourished during the Renaissance. More recently the expense of carrying out mosaic has limited its use, though some excellent modern examples exist, such as the library of the National University in Mexico City (1951–53).

Mosander, Carl Gustaf (1797–1858) Swedish chemist. He succeeded Berzelius in Stockholm and continued his work on the rare-earth elements, isolating new elements successively from preparations that turned out to be mixtures. In 1839 Mosander discovered and named the element lanthanum, which was present as the oxide in a mineral that had also yielded cerium. Four years later he announced the discovery of the new elements erbium and terbium, and the supposed element of didymium (in fact a mixture of two elements, praseodymium and neodymium).

Moscow (Russian **Moskva**) The capital and largest city of Russia, situated at the centre of the vast plain of European Russia, on the Moskva River; pop. (1990) 8,801,000. First mentioned in medieval chronicles in 1147, it soon became the chief city of the increasingly powerful Muscovite princes. In the 16th century, when Ivan the Terrible proclaimed himself Tsar of all the Russias, Moscow became the capital of the new empire, its central position giving it supreme military and economic value. Though Peter the Great moved his capital to St Petersburg in 1712, Moscow remained the heart of Russia and centre of the Russian Orthodox Church. In 1812 it was attacked and occupied by Napoleon and three-quarters of the city was destroyed by fire. By the mid-19th century Moscow had become a large and growing industrial city. After the Bolshevik Revolution of 1917 it was made the capital of the USSR and seat of the new Soviet government, with its centre in the Kremlin, the ancient citadel of the 15th-century city. It is a major industrial and cultural centre, with world-famous theatres and museums, and is the home of the Bolshoi Ballet. There are heavy steel, machinery, and vehicle industries, as well as diverse light industries in suburban areas.

Mosel (French **Moselle**) A river of western Europe that rises on the slopes of the Ballon d'Alsace in the Vosges Mountains of north-east France and flows 550 km (346 miles) north through Lorraine, Luxembourg, and Germany to meet the Rhine at Coblenz. The Mosel valley in Germany is a noted wine-producing region.

Moseley, Henry Gwyn Jeffreys (1887–1915) British physicist who, while working with Ernest Rutherford, bombarded different elements with electrons and analysed the X-rays emitted. He established a precise link between the wavelengths of the X-rays and the positions of the elements in the PERIODIC TABLE, and deduced that each element could be identified according to the charge on the nucleus, which he called the ATOMIC NUMBER. In 1913 he stated his findings mathematically in a law which now bears his name. He was killed in action in World War I.

Moses (13th century BC) Hebrew patriarch and prophet, who delivered his people from slavery and founded the religious community called ISRAEL. According to biblical accounts, he was a Hebrew foundling adopted and reared at the Egyptian court. In Midian in north-west Arabia he saw a burning yet unconsumed bush and experienced the voice of God (YAHWEH) commanding him to lead his people from Egypt. In the EXODUS that followed, the pursuing Egyptians were engulfed by the Red Sea, which had parted to allow the Israelites to cross. On Mount Sinai (Horeb) Jehovah revealed the Covenant, including the Ten Commandments, between himself and the people of Moses. Moses died within sight of CANAAN, the Promised Land allegedly at Moab.

Moses, Anna Mary (known as **Grandma Moses**) (1860–1961) US painter. She lived as a farmer's wife until widowed in 1927, when she took up painting, after arthritis made farm work impossible. Her work began to appear in exhibitions from the late 1930s. Grandma Moses produced more than 1,000 naive paintings, principally colourful scenes of American rural life.

Moses, Ed(win Corley) (1955–) US athlete. The outstanding 400-metres hurdler of his generation, he won gold medals in the 1976 and 1984 Olympics. He finished first in 122 consecutive races between 1977 and 1987 and set four successive world records. He combined this with his profession as an engineer, having received a degree in physics in 1978.

Mosley, Sir Oswald Ernald (1896–1980) British political leader. Mosley was a Member of Parliament successively as Conservative (1918–22), Independent (1922–24), and Labour (1925–31). Calling for a dictatorial system of government, he formed the National Union of Fascists in 1932. ANTI-SEMITIC and FASCIST in character, the Union staged violent rallies in the East End of London. Mosley was interned during 1940–43. In 1948 he founded the 'Union Movement', whose theme was European unity.

mosque (from Arabic *masjid*, 'place of prostration') A holy building used as a meeting place, for public prayer and worship, and for study within ISLAM. The building of a mosque was one of the first actions performed by MUHAMMAD upon arrival at Medina. Traditionally built of brick or stone, mosques are square or rectangular, surrounding a courtyard, which usually contains washing facilities. Minarets, towers from which an official (the **muezzin**) calls followers to prayer, mark the corners or front. Shoes are removed on entry, and women must cover their heads. The *qibla* wall marks the direction of Mecca with a niche (*mihrab*), to the right of which stands a pulpit (*minbar*), from which the Friday sermon is preached. There is usually a partitioned area for female worshippers, whose attendance at mosque prayer is not compulsory. All images of human or animal forms are forbidden, but mosques are often decorated with calligraphic extracts from the Koran, and geometric designs derived from calligraphy representing eternity. See also ISLAMIC ART AND ARCHITECTURE.

mosquito A delicately built true FLY of the suborder Nematocera, with long legs and narrow wings bearing scales and hairs. The wing-span of a mosquito ranges from less than 3 mm up to 15 mm (0.125–0.5 inch). Their antennae are long, with whorls of hairs which are more developed in the males. The mouthparts are adapted for piercing and sucking and most females feed on the blood of mammals or birds; males are usually nectar feeders. Their larvae are always aquatic, in fresh, brackish, or sometimes fully salt water. The buoyant eggs are laid either in floating rafts, or singly. The larvae (wrigglers) have brush-like mouthparts and feed by filtering microscopic plankton or detritus from water. They breathe through modified organs on the tail. Some gain air by piercing plant stems. The pupae are active, having well-developed muscles in the tail, and they breathe through trumpet-shaped organs on the thorax. Mosquitoes are by far the most important insect VECTORS of human disease, the various forms of MALARIA being foremost, although yellow fever and filariasis are also frequently spread by mosquitoes. Less harmful mosquitoes are known as gnats. More than 1,600 mosquito species are known throughout the world.

Mosquito Coast A sparsely populated strip of swamp, lagoon, and tropical forest along the Caribbean coast of Nicaragua and Honduras, occupied by the Miskito Indians (the name of the coast is a corruption of 'Miskito'). The British maintained a protectorate over the area intermittently from the 17th century until the mid-19th century, granting authority to a series of kings. In 1894 Nicaragua appropriated the territory and in 1960 the northern part was awarded to Honduras.

moss A BRYOPHYTE plant of the class Musci, which contains about 15,000 species. Like liverworts, ferns, horsetails, and clubmosses, they exist in two morphologically distinct forms during their LIFE-CYCLE. The first form, the gametophyte, is the leafy plant, popularly called 'moss', which is the larger and lasts longer. This carries the male and female organs and, after fertilization, produces the second form of moss 'plant', the sporophyte. This is the spore-bearing capsule, which is raised on a leafless stalk above the leafy plant. The spores released from the capsule blow away and germinate in damp places to produce new leafy plants.

Mosses have no vascular (conductive) tissue and are therefore unable to keep their internal tissues supplied with water from the soil. They can only grow in habitats that are permanently or frequently wet, forming either transverse wefts or cushions of vertically growing shoots. They grow on soil, rocks, and tree trunks, and a few species can grow underwater. SPHAGNUM moss can cover large areas of wet, acid uplands. Large species of *Polytrichum* can grow up to 80 cm (2.6 feet) in height; *Polytrichum commune* is used to make brushes.

Moss, Stirling (1929–) British motor-racing driver. He was especially successful in the 1950s, winning various Grands Prix and other competitions, though the world championship always eluded him.

moss animal A member of a phylum, Bryozoa, of very common creatures (about 4,000 marine and freshwater species), so tiny that they are rarely seen by the layman. Each animal, living in its own box-like skeletal casing made of CHITIN, protein, and calcium carbonate, measures less than 1 mm (0.04 inch), but being colonial they form encrusting masses on rocks, pilings, and ship-hulls. Many form flat, mossy sheets, known as sea mats, often covering seaweeds. Others form branching colonies like tiny trees or fans, and their papery remains washed up on beaches are regularly dismissed as 'dead seaweed'. When these colonies are living, countless crowns of ciliated tentacles emerge, as each animal feeds on passing plankton.

Mostar A largely Muslim city in Bosnia-Hercegovina, on the River Neretva south-west of Sarajevo; pop. (1991) 126,000. It is the chief town of Hercegovina. For many years its chief landmark was the old Turkish bridge over the Neretva, destroyed during a siege in 1993.

motet A short, unaccompanied polyphonic setting of sacred words. It came into existence in the 13th century when new words (*mots*) were added to the lively upper parts in certain cadences (*clausula*) in which the main lower part moved in the slow notes of PLAINSONG. The motet reached its greatest development in the music of Palestrina, Victoria, Byrd, Tallis, and their contemporaries, being in effect the sacred counterpart of the MADRIGAL. In BAROQUE MUSIC the motet sometimes acquired an instrumental accompaniment. In the Anglican service the motet was replaced by the ANTHEM.

moth An insect characterized by two pairs of wings covered with microscopic, overlapping scales. The scales are coloured, and some are specialized as scent-gland outlets. Moths, together with butterflies, constitute the order Lepidoptera, containing more than 1,000 species. Moths tend to be stouter-bodied and duller in colour than butterflies and comprise 80 per cent of the total number of species of Lepidoptera. Most species fly at night; some, however, such as burnet moths, are brightly coloured and day-flying. Unlike butterflies, most moths rest with the wings overlapping the body, and fore- and hind-wings are held together with a hook-and-eye arrangement.

They range in size from large atlas moths to tiny microlepidoptera, many of which have a wing-span of only 2 mm (0.08 inch) or so. Characteristically, moths use their proboscis to feed on nectar; but gold moths have jaws and eat pollen, and some adults, such as emperor moths, never feed. The antennae of many males are feathery or comb-like, and are covered with microscopic scent receptors to detect the female PHEROMONES.

The caterpillars of most species of moths feed on plants, many, like the owlet moths, being catholic in their choice of plant. Moth caterpillars also include species which bore into timber, eat hair, wax, or even drugs. The variety of life-styles is enormous, ranging from tiny, concealed leaf-miners to the gaudy black and yellow caterpillars of the cinnabar moth, *Tyria jacobaeae*. As in butterflies, METAMORPHOSIS is complete, and a pupa, often enclosed in a cocoon spun of silk, is formed in protected crevices, or in the soil.

Motherwell A district in Strathclyde Region, central Scotland from 1975 to 1996; in 1996 it became part of North Lanarkshire.

motmot A bird belonging to a small family, Momotidae, of nine species allied to the kingfisher, all restricted to warm areas of the New World. They vary in size from that of a small thrush to that of a crow and are mainly green, though the head is often marked with blue and black. The tail is long, especially the two central tail feathers, which are bare of vanes for a short distance before the end, so giving a racquet-like appearance to the tip. They hunt by flying out from perches to catch flying insects and nest in burrows which they dig in banks.

motor, electric See ELECTRIC MOTOR.

motor car As with the aeroplane, the idea of self-propelled road TRANSPORT was current for many years before the technology for a practicable vehicle became available. The vehicle generally recognized as the first motor car was a steam-powered vehicle, built by CUGNOT in 1769. Over the next 100 years this idea was developed, particularly in the UK, but steam-powered vehicles never achieved widespread acceptance. The mainstream development of the motor car had to await the invention of the INTERNAL-COMBUSTION ENGINE (1876) by the German engineer Nikolaus OTTO and its subsequent commercial application by his two compatriots, Karl BENZ and Gottlieb DAIMLER. Benz began to sell his car in 1887, and Daimler in 1889. In France in 1891, Panhard-Levassor built the first vehicle to adopt what was to become the most common layout: four WHEELS, a front ENGINE, GEARBOX, foot-operated CLUTCH, and rear-wheel drive. Early improvements to the motor car included the float-type CARBURETTOR, designed by Daimler's partner Wilhelm Maybach in 1892; the steering wheel (1894); the propeller-shaft transmission (1895); and the universal joint (1899). Developments were rapid in most of Europe and in the USA, but in the UK until 1896 progress was stifled by restrictive laws requiring that cars on the highway had to be preceded by a person on foot carrying a red flag. In the early days of the car both steam and ELECTRIC VEHICLES provided competition to the petrol engine, and electric vehicles remained popular until 1912, particularly in the USA, when the electric ignition tipped the balance in favour of the petrol engine.

MASS-PRODUCTION techniques were largely developed by Henry FORD for his hugely successful Model T, introduced in 1908. Ford used MASS PRODUCTION and standardization to achieve economies of scale, and thus brought the car within the price range of ordinary people. Similar economy cars, such as the Fiat 500 (Italy) and the 'Baby' Austin (UK), appeared in Europe after World War I, and by the early 1920s the car had become a practical means of transport.

The 1930s was the era of the 'classic car': Rolls-Royce, Hispano-Suiza, and Bugatti exploited the luxury car market, while firms such as Citroën, Volkswagen, Fiat, Austin, Morris, and Vauxhall mass-produced small cars. After World War II much technical progress made in the aircraft industry was applied to motor-car manufacture. Lightweight, chassis-less car bodies, and curved wind-screens were adopted.

From the 1950s onwards, car manufacturers increasingly thought in terms of an international market. In the 1960s the Japanese car industry began its rise to its present position as the world's largest car manufacturer. Car safety became an increasingly important aspect of design, with the introduction of seat belts, anti-burst door locks, collapsible steering wheel, head restraints, and automatically inflating air bags. The worldwide fuel crisis in the 1970s saw a shift in emphasis towards fuel economy, and public concern about the environmental pollution caused by cars has led to the introduction of CATALYTIC CONVERTERS and unleaded petrol in many countries. The major change in the car industry in the 1980s and 1990s was the increasing use of MICROPROCESSORS to control ignition and fuel supply.

motor cycle A two-wheeled, motor-driven vehicle, although some may have three wheels. A Michaux velocipede (see BICYCLE) was fitted with a steam-engine in 1868; this was perhaps the first motor cycle. Early motor cycles were adaptations of bicycles or tricycles: tricycles and even quadricycles were initially popular, but in 1901 several practical two-wheeled designs with PETROL ENGINES appeared, which established the classic layout of the motor cycle. During World War I motor cycles were used for dispatch-carrying and, when fitted to sidecars, as mobile machine-gun platforms. Many technical improvements were made during this war and in the postwar period motor cycles enjoyed a boom, with the USA and the UK producing many classic designs. After World War II new developments included the smaller moped and motor scooter, and the motor-cycle industry continued to grow. British and European models predominated until the 1960s, when Japan began to dominate world production, which has continued into the 1990s. Modern motor cycles incorporate many features of the MOTOR CAR, such as electric starters, electronic ignition, shaft drive, water-cooled engines, and disc brakes. The traditional spoked wheels have been largely replaced by ones of cast MAGNESIUM alloy, which are stronger, cheaper to make, and require less maintenance.

motor-racing The various forms of racing in specially built or adapted cars. Long-distance road-racing is known as rallying; the Monte Carlo Rally, first held in 1911, is the most famous and the Paris-Dakar is currently the most dangerous. Track-racing is divided into categories, such as Formula Three, Formula Two, and Formula One. The last named is the most prestigious, and Grand Prix cars are built by such famous designers as Ferrari, McLaren, and Williams, whose drivers battle for the world championship over a nine-month season at celebrated venues all over the world, such as Silverstone in England and Monza in Italy. In the USA, motor-racing is particularly varied, with categories for club-racing (sports cars), off-road racing (four-wheel-drive vehicles), stock-cars, drag-racers, which compete in ferocious sprints over a short straight course, and such races as the Indianapolis 500 for high-powered racing cars.

mouflon The smallest of the wild SHEEP, *Ovis musimon*, native to Corsica and Sardinia and related to the argalis. Mouflons inhabit mountains, living in small flocks, in rough and often precipitous terrain. The coat of the mature male is reddish-brown with a whitish saddle. Both sexes usually have horns, although those of the female are often very small. After a gestation period of about six months, one to three lambs are born.

mould (in mycology) A saprophytic or parasitic FUNGUS that grows as a mass of microscopic threads (mycelium) with small lollipop-like, spore-producing bodies. Mould spores are abundant in the air, so they can easily infect and decay damp organic materials, or cause plant or animal diseases in the case of parasitic fungi. Moulds produce both useful and poisonous chemicals, for example the antibiotic penicillin and the poison aflatoxin. Blue mould is caused by saprophytic species, such as *Penicillium roquefortii*, and gives certain cheeses their flavour. Grey mould on fruit is caused by the parasite *Botrytis cinerea* and causes serious damage to crops, but is welcomed as '*pourriture noble*' by wine-growers as it aids the production of sweet wines. Fungal moulds are not to be confused with the SLIME MOULDS.

moulding A technique used to obtain complex three-dimensional forms from a malleable material by the application of pressure or heat. Moulding processes are used for many PLASTICS, GLASS, BRICKS, and other materials. In vacuum forming, a thin sheet of heated, softened material is sucked down over a shaped mould and takes on the surface contours of that mould. On cooling, the plastic sets into this shape and can then be removed. This process is used extensively to produce shell-shaped objects. Blow moulding uses a heated tube of material, sealed at one end, which is surrounded by a shaped mould of cylindrical cross-section. The tube is inflated so that it fits the contours of the mould. Large numbers of glass and plastic objects are produced in this way. Injection moulding requires softened material to be injected into a cavity that is exactly the shape of the desired object. It is used to produce a variety of articles, from nylon gear-wheels to polypropylene washing-up bowls.

mound-builders American Indian tribes in Ohio and Illinois who, from *c.*1000 BC, erected richly furnished circular burial mounds, resembling the European BARROWS in shape and function. In the Mississippi basin some centuries later (*c.*700 AD), larger and more complex mounds, presumably for ceremonial gatherings, were raised to support temples. Though most were rectangular, and frequently built in large groups as at Cahokia in Illinois, there are more bizarre ones, such as the 400 m (1,300 ft) long snake mound in Adams County, Ohio. These may have been influenced from Mexico.

mountain A large upland mass that generally rises to distinct peaks. Although there is no absolute definition, the summits usually stand at least 700 m (2,200 feet) above surrounding valleys or plains, uplands with less elevation being accounted hills or plateaux. Mountains can be single, isolated peaks (as is Shasta, USA; Egmont, New Zealand; or Ararat, Turkey) resulting from large volcanic eruptions, block faulting, or simply very long periods of DENUDATION. More often, however, they stand in lines of peaks, forming ranges or chains (as in the southern Andes or the Appalachians); these may contain extinct or active volcanoes as well as complicated sequences of folded and faulted rocks, for ranges appear to mark places where two plates of the Earth's crust have collided during the process of CONTINENTAL DRIFT (see also MOUNTAIN BUILDING). Most impressively, mountains may occur in huge and complex masses (as in the great system running from Turkey through to eastern China); these seem to be caused by major collisions between crustal plates, such as the northward drift of the Indian subcontinent against Asia. The younger the mountains are, the higher they stand above surrounding lowlands; for sooner or later mountain building gives way to DENUDATION.

mountain ash See ROWAN.

mountain beaver The most primitive RODENT alive today, *Aplodontia rufa*, occurring in western North America. A more appropriate name of this species is sewellel, which comes from a Chinook word for the cloak made from the animal's skin. It does not look much like a beaver as it has only a short tail, and is up to 1.5 kg (3 pounds 5 ounces) in weight and 40 cm (16 inches) in body length. The animal spends much of its time in its extensive burrow. It is a herbivore and is usually found near water.

mountain building (or **orogenesis**) The processes within the Earth's crust that produce the uplift of mountain ranges. These processes are tectonic and appear to be linked to the movement of great chunks of crust over the Earth's surface, as described in the modern theory of PLATE TECTONICS. Where plates collide, deep movements of molten rock, earthquakes, and volcanoes result. Strata are thrust upwards, and folding, faulting, and metamorphism occur. Over millions of years these processes build mountains. OROGENIES (periods of mountain building) seem to be rather spasmodic in geological history: the continents of Europe and North America show traces of three or four separate episodes. Owing to erosion, the oldest mountains are much lower than the youngest ones.

mountaineering The sport of climbing mountains. It was first taken up in the mid-19th century, when groups of English climbers began tackling the European Alps, helped by Swiss, Italian, and French guides. Edward Whymper was one of the first great mountaineers, present at the first ascent, in 1865, of the Matterhorn (4,478 m, 16,690 feet). After the Alps, interest moved to other great ranges, such as the Andes, the Rockies, the high peaks of Africa, and the Himalayas. Mount Everest, at 8,848 m (29,028 feet), became the ultimate goal, conquered in 1953 by Edmund Hillary and Tenzing Norgay.

Mount Athos (Greek **Agion Oros**) A semi-autonomous district that forms a peninsula on the Aegean coast of Macedonia in northern Greece; area 336 sq km (130 sq miles); pop. (1991) 1,557. Its chief port is Daphne and its administrative centre is Karyes. Mount Athos, which rises to 1,956 m (6,417 ft), is the Holy Mountain of the Greek Orthodox Church and around it are 20 monasteries. Since 1060 women and all female animals have been excluded from the district.

Mountbatten, Louis (Francis Albert Victor Nicholas), 1st Earl Mountbatten of Burma (1900–79) British admiral and administrator. A great-grandson of Queen Victoria, Mountbatten served in the Royal Navy before rising to become supreme Allied commander in SE Asia (1943–45). As the last viceroy (1947) and first Governor-General of India (1947–48), he oversaw the independence of India and Pakistan. He was killed by an IRA bomb while on his yacht in Ireland.

Mount Palomar Observatory An OBSERVATORY near Pasadena, California, USA, run by the California Institute of Technology. At an altitude of 1,700 m (5,580 feet) it is the home of the 200-inch (5.1 m) Hale telescope, an 18-inch (46-cm) Schmidt REFLECTING TELESCOPE, as well as a 48-inch (1.2-m) and a 60-inch (1.5-m) reflector. The dome is 41 m (135 feet) high and weighs 1,000 tonnes.

Mount Rushmore A granite mountain in the Black Hills of South Dakota, USA, rising to 1,745 m (5,725 ft). The colossal heads of US presidents Washington, Jefferson, Lincoln, and Theodore Roosevelt were carved on its face by Gutzon Borglum between 1927 and 1941. The site is a national memorial.

Mount St Helens A volcano in Washington state, north-west USA that erupted in 1980 devastating a huge area of the surrounding countryside and reducing its height from 2,950 m (9,682 ft) to 2,560 m (8,402 ft).

Mount Wilson Observatory An OBSERVATORY in the Sierra Madre mountains near Pasadena, California, USA. The first telescope was a solar COELOSTAT, purchased by Helen Snow. This was followed by two solar tower telescopes, 18.3 m (60 feet) and 45.7 m (150 feet) high, that had their associated spectrographs underground where the temperature was constant. The 100-inch (2.5 m) Hooker telescope was first used in November 1917 and for the next 30 years was the most significant telescope in the world.

Mourne Mountains A range of granite hills in south-eastern Northern Ireland, in County Down. Slieve Donard (853 m, 2,796 ft) is the highest peak in Northern Ireland.

mouse (in the animal kingdom) A rodent considered by some authorities to be a member only of the genus *Mus*, but the name is also applied to many other small rodents. Members of the family Muridae can quite properly be described as mice, but other small rodents are also called mice because of their appearance. Examples of the latter include pocket mice, kangaroo mice, New World mice, dormice, and jumping mice. Within the murid family there is no clear distinction between rats and mice, but large murids tend to be called rats and small ones mice. To the purist, only rodents of the genus *Rattus* are true rats.

There are many murid mice. Some typical examples are the temperate HARVEST MICE and WOODMICE, the African grass and striped mice, the Australian native mice, and the Asiatic tree and spiny mice. The most familiar mouse is the HOUSE MOUSE, which can be a health risk. Some other mice are economically significant as pests of growing crops or stored foodstuffs, particularly in the tropics. Most mice are omnivorous, although predominantly herbivorous, taking insects only incidentally. Mice include some of the smallest of mammals, the pygmy mouse weighing only about 7 g (0.25 ounce).

mouse (in computers) A small device that can be moved with one hand over a flat surface: movements of the mouse are communicated to a computer and cause corresponding movements of a cursor on the screen of a VISUAL DISPLAY UNIT. The mouse can be used for drawing, or for selecting icons or options from a menu.

mousebird (or **coly**) A member of a small family, Coliidae, containing six species of bird, all of which are confined to Africa. Although only a little heavier than sparrows, they look larger because of their greatly elongated tail. They are all pale grey or brown, with marked crests; some have red, blue, or white on the head. They live in small flocks and roost closely together at night.

mouse-tailed bat A BAT that forms a family, Rhinopomatidae, occurring in the Middle East and southern Asia. The three species in the single genus, *Rhinopoma*, are characterized by a very long tail, which is about 6 cm (2.25 inches) long, roughly equal to the length of the body. They roost in large numbers, often in man-made structures, such as the Egyptian pyramids. They are insectivorous and have a seasonal state of torpor when insects become scarce.

Mousterian Of or relating to the flint industries of the Middle Palaeolithic period, named after the site, the Moustier cave in the Dordogne region of France, and dated to *c.*70,000–30,000 BC. They are attributed to the Neanderthal peoples living in Europe and around the Mediterranean.

mouth-organ A free-REED INSTRUMENT, such as the HARMONICA. Asian mouth-organs have bamboo pipes as resonators, the Chinese *sheng* and Japanese *shō* have these arranged in a circle with each reed, in the foot of each pipe, in a wind chamber. The Laotian *khāēn* has its pipes in a double raft, with the reeds in a wind chamber part-way down. Asian mouth-organs are so constructed that a pipe will only sound when a hole in it is closed with a finger, or with wax as a DRONE.

moving cluster See OPEN CLUSTER.

Mozambique (formerly **Portuguese East Africa**) A country situated on the south-east coast of Africa, and bounded by Tanzania, Malawi, Zambia, Zimbabwe, South Africa, and Swaziland.

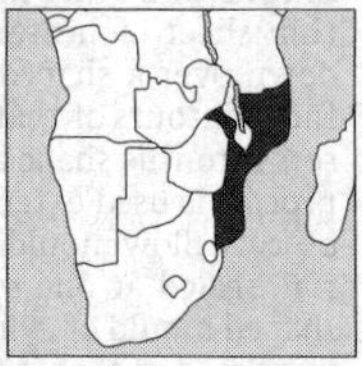

Physical. The Zambezi flows across the middle of the country and the Limpopo across the south. The coastal plain is low and broad, with areas of sand between the marshy river valleys. It is wetter inland, where there are regions of fertile soil covered with tropical forest, before the ground rises northward to rocky plateaux with SAVANNAH vegetation.

Economy. Mozambique's mineral resources include large reserves of coal, iron ore, tantalite, and unknown reserves of natural gas and precious stones. The Cabora Bassa dam on the Zambezi River is one of Africa's largest hydroelectric dams, and electricity is exported to South Africa. Many farms have been collectivized; the main crops are cassava, maize, coconuts, and sugar cane. Shrimps and cashew nuts are the main exports. Industry consists primarily of the processing of local raw materials; an oil-refinery processes imported petroleum.

History. Mozambique was known to medieval Arab geographers as Musambih. According to the Arab historian al-Masudi it was already exporting gold from mines in the interior of what is now ZIMBABWE in the 10th century. Merchants from MOGADISHU had a monopoly for a time, though it was taken over by Kilwa in the 12th century. The Portuguese sacked the port of Sofala in 1505, and built a new town as the seat of a captaincy to control the gold and other trade. Settlers also began to trade in slaves in the 16th century. The present city of Moçambique was begun with a fort in 1508 built by the Portuguese as a refreshment station on the way to GOA. The first inland settlements at Sena and Tete were Arab trading towns, from which they made contact with the Mwene Mutapa and other hinterland rulers until the 19th century.

The Portuguese gradually suppressed all indigenous resistance movements during the 19th century. In 1951, Mozambique became an overseas province of Portugal. In order to rid the country of colonial rule, in 1964 the Marxist–Leninist guerrilla group Frelimo was formed (see FRELIMO WAR). By the mid-1970s Portuguese authority had reached the point of collapse, and in 1975 an independent People's Republic was established under the Frelimo leader Samora Machel. Support for the guerrilla campaigns in Rhodesia and South Africa led to repeated military incursions by troops of those countries, and the establishment of a stable government within the framework of a one-party Marxist state was further hindered by the weak state of Mozambique's agricultural economy. In 1984 Mozambique and South Africa signed a non-aggression pact, the Nkomati Accord; but South African support of rebel groups, funded by Portuguese ex-colonists, continued with some 10,000 well-armed troops operating in the country. In 1989 there was a relaxation of its Marxist-Leninist line by Frelimo, and President Joaquim Chissano agreed to meet Afonso Dhlakama, leader of the rebel Mozambique National Resistance (RENAMO). There was heavy fighting early in 1990, but in November a new constitution took effect. Formal peace talks, brokered by Presidents Mugabe and Moi (of Zimbabwe and Kenya, respectively), were held in Rome and led to acceptance by RENAMO in October 1991 of the new constitution. After a further year of negotiation a peace treaty was agreed in October 1992 and RENAMO became a legitimate political party. Mozambique's first multi-party elections were held in 1994 and Frelimo, under Chissano, was re-elected. In 1995 Mozambique was admitted to the COMMONWEALTH OF NATIONS as a special case, because it has no historical links with Britain. Seventeen years of civil war, together with appalling drought, left Mozambique one of the poorest countries in the world and famine and social unrest continue to threaten its stability.

Capital: Maputo
Area: 802,000 sq km (309,572 sq mi)
Population: 17,889,000 (1995)
Currency: 1 metical = 100 centavos
Religions: Traditional beliefs 47.8%; Christian (mostly Roman Catholic) 38.9% Muslim 13.0%
Ethnic Groups: Makua 47.3%; Tsonga 23.3%; Malawi 12.0%; Shona 11.3%; Yao 3.8%; Swahili 0.8%; Makonde 0.6%; Portuguese 0.2%
Languages: Portuguese (official); Makua; Tsonga; local languages
International Organizations: UN; OAU; SADC; Commonwealth of Nations

Mozart, (Johann Chrysostom) Wolfgang Amadeus (1756–91) Austrian composer. A child prodigy as a harpsichordist, pianist, and composer, he was taken on tours of western Europe by his father Leopold (1719–87). While in Vienna he collaborated with the librettist Da Ponte in the composition of his three comic operas, *The Marriage of Figaro* (1786), *Don Giovanni* (1787), and *Così fan tutte* (1790). His use of music to aid characterization in these works marked an important advance in the development of opera. Early influenced by Haydn, Mozart's work came to epitomize classical music in its purity of form and melody. A prolific composer, he wrote 41 symphonies, 27 piano concertos, 25 string quartets, 16 operas, and a vast quantity of other instrumental and orchestral music.

Mpumalanga See EASTERN TRANSVAAL.

MS-DOS See OPERATING SYSTEM.

Mubarak, (Muhammad) Hosni (Said) (1928–) Egyptian statesman, President since 1981. Appointed head of the Egyptian air force in 1972, Mubarak became Vice-President in 1975 and succeeded President Sadat following the latter's assassination. Although he did much to establish closer links between Egypt and other Arab nations, including distancing himself from Israel when it invaded Lebanon in 1982, he risked division by aligning Egypt against Saddam Hussein in the Gulf War of 1991. After the resurgence of militant Islamic fundamentalism in Egypt in 1992, Mubarak's National Democratic Party government adopted harsh measures to suppress activists.

Mucha, Alphonse (born Alfons Maria) (1860–1939) Czech painter and designer. Based in Paris from 1889, he was a leading figure in the art nouveau movement. He is noted for his flowing poster designs, often featuring the actress Sarah Bernhardt, as in *Gismonda* (1894); with the success of this poster, Mucha was given a six-year commission to design further posters, sets, costumes, and jewellery for the actress.

mucus membrane A membrane that lines the digestive and respiratory tracts as well as the nasal sinuses. It consists of epithelium containing cells that secrete a slimy substance called mucus. The function of the mucus is to protect the surface of the membrane. In the digestive tract it also provides lubrication to assist the flow of food or faeces. In the respiratory tract it traps any particles inhaled with the air.

mud eel See SIREN; CONGO EEL.

Mudéjar ►**1** Any of the Muslims who were allowed to retain their laws and religion in return for their loyalty to a Christian king after the Christian reconquest of the Spanish peninsula from the Moors (11th–15th centuries). After 1492 they were treated with less toleration, dubbed MORISCOS, and forced to accept the Christian faith or leave the country. ►**2** A style of architecture and decorative art of the 12th–15th centuries, combining Islamic and Gothic elements, produced by the Mudéjares. The architecture is characterized especially by the use of the horseshoe arch and the vault; examples can be seen in the churches and palaces of Toledo, Córdoba, and Valencia.

mudpuppy A species of SALAMANDER, *Necturus maculosus*, found in the eastern USA. It does not completely transform into an adult salamander, remaining as a permanent larva. The mudpuppy belongs to the family Proteidae, which includes the olm. It is stout-bodied, and 20–45 cm (8–18 inches) in length, including the tail. It has bright red gills, small eyes, and four toes on both fore- and hind-limbs. An inhabitant of rivers, streams, and lakes, it lays 30–200 eggs, which develop normally into tadpoles that may take up to six years to reach maturity.

mudskipper A fish of the GOBY family that belongs mainly to the genus *Periophthalmus* and is found in inshore waters, especially mangrove swamps and muddy intertidal flats, of the Indian and west Pacific oceans. They frequently leave the water altogether and lie on the mud, or climb the exposed mangrove roots, using their pectoral fins as levers and the pelvic fin sucker to stay in place. Their eyes are placed high on the head and give good all-round vision. They are very alert to predators, skipping away across the mud to hide in the burrows of crabs or returning to water at the first sign of danger.

muezzin See MOSQUE.

mufti See SHARIA.

Mugabe, Robert (Gabriel) (1924–) Zimbabwean statesman, Prime Minister 1980–87 and President since 1987. In 1963 he cofounded the Zimbabwe African National Union (ZANU) and in 1975 became its leader; the following year he formed the Patriotic Front with the leader of the Zimbabwe African People's Union (ZAPU), Joshua Nkomo. Mugabe was declared Prime Minister in 1980 after ZANU won a landslide victory in the country's first post-independence elections. In 1982 he ousted Nkomo from his Cabinet; ZANU and

ZAPU agreed to merge in 1987 and Mugabe became President.

Mughal See MOGUL.

Muhammad (or **Mohammed**) (*c.*570–632) Arab prophet and founder of Islam. He was born in Mecca, where in *c.*610 he received the first of a series of revelations, which became the doctrinal and legislative basis of Islam and which were written down *c.*610–32 as the Koran. His sayings (the Hadith) and the accounts of his daily practice (the Sunna) constitute the other major sources of guidance for most Muslims. In the face of opposition to his preaching he and his small group of supporters were forced to flee to Medina in 622; this flight, known as the Hegira, is of great significance in Islam, and the Islamic calendar (which is based on lunar months) is dated from 622 AD (1 AH). After consolidation of the community in Medina Muhammad led his followers into a series of battles, which resulted in the capitulation of Mecca in 630. He died two years later, having successfully united tribal factions of the Hejaz region into a force that would expand the frontiers of Islam. He was buried in Medina. Islam is now the professed faith of some 1,000 million people.

Muhammad Ahmad See MAHDI.

Muhammad Ali (1769–1849) Ottoman viceroy and pasha of Egypt 1805–49, possibly of Albanian descent. As a commander in the Ottoman army he had overthrown the Mamelukes, Egypt's ruling military caste, by 1811. Although technically the viceroy of the Ottoman sultan, he was effectively an independent ruler and modernized Egypt's infrastructure, making it the leading power in the eastern Mediterranean. In 1841 he and his family were given the right to become hereditary rulers of Egypt, and the dynasty survived until 1952.

Muhammad Ali (born Cassius Marcellus Clay) (1942–) US boxer. He first won the world heavyweight title in 1964 and regained it in 1974 and 1978, becoming the only boxer to be world champion three times. He changed his name in 1964 after converting to Islam. After his retirement in 1981 it was confirmed that he was suffering from Parkinson's disease.

Muhammad Reza Shah Pahlavi (1919–1980) Shah of Iran 1941–79. The son of Reza PAHLAVI, he succeeded on the abdication of his father. After the fall of Mussadegh in 1953 he gained supreme power and with the aid of greatly increased oil revenues, embarked upon a policy of rapid social reform and economic development, while maintaining a regime of harsh repression. In 1962 he introduced a land reform programme to break landlord power. In 1979 he was deposed by a revolution led by the Islamic clergy, notably Ayatollah KHOMEINI, whose supporters were bitterly opposed to the pro-western regime of the Shah. He died in exile in Egypt.

Muir, Edwin (1887–1959) Scottish poet and translator. His collections of poems include *The Labyrinth* (1949). He is also remembered for his translations of Franz Kafka's works, done during his stay in Prague in collaboration with his wife, the novelist Willa Anderson (1890–1970); these appeared in the 1930s and established Kafka's reputation in Britain.

Muir, Jean (Elizabeth) (1933–95) British fashion designer. In 1961 she started producing her own clothing under the name Jane & Jane, establishing her own company, Jean Muir, in 1966, which built an international reputation for women's fashion. Her designs are noted for their classic, restrained, and fluid styles.

Muir, John (1838–1914) Scottish-born US naturalist, a pioneer of environmental conservation. Devoting himself to nature after being injured in an industrial accident, Muir campaigned vigorously for the protection of unspoilt wilderness areas and was largely responsible for the establishment of Yosemite and Sequoia National Parks in California (1890). He wrote several books about the American wilderness, such as *The Mountains of California* (1894).

Mujibur Rahman (known as **Sheikh Mujib**) (1920–75) Bangladeshi statesman, Prime Minister 1972–75 and President 1975. In 1949 he cofounded the Awami (People's) League, which advocated autonomy for East Pakistan. He led the party to victory in the 1970 elections, but was imprisoned in 1971 when civil war broke out. Released in 1972, he became the first Prime Minister of independent Bangladesh. After his failure to establish parliamentary democracy, he assumed dictatorial powers in 1975. He and his family were assassinated in a military coup.

mulberry A small fruit-tree of the genus *Morus*. The black mulberry, *M. nigra*, a tall, deciduous tree growing up to 10 m (33 feet), has been grown in Europe since ancient times, though it is native to western Asia. The delicious purplish berries superficially resemble loganberries. The white mulberry, *M. alba*, is a small tree native to China. Its sweet, pinkish-white fruits are edible, and the bark has been used for making paper, but the white mulberry is grown particularly for its leaves, which are fed to silkworms. Mulberries belong to the family Moraceae.

Muldoon, Sir Robert (David) (1921–92) New Zealand statesman, Prime Minister 1975–84. He became a National Party MP in 1960, serving as deputy Prime Minister for a brief period in 1972 and as leader of the opposition from 1973 to 1974 before becoming Premier the following year. He was chairman of the board of governors for the IMF and World Bank (1979–80) and chairman of the ministerial council for the OECD (1982). His term of office was marked by domestic measures to tackle low economic growth and high inflation.

mule A hybrid between a HORSE and an ass, more especially the offspring of a male ass and a mare. The hybrid from a she-ass and a stallion is often called a hinny. Mules have the shape and size of a horse, and the large head, long ears, and small hoofs of an ass. They are usually sterile, although occasionally a hinny will produce a foal. Mules have great endurance and are sure-footed, making excellent pack or draught animals.

Mull An island of the Inner Hebrides, off the west coast of Scotland; area 950 sq km (367 sq miles). Its chief town is Tobermory and its highest peak in Ben More (966 m, 3,171 ft). Its principal landmark is Duart Castle, home of the Chiefs of the Clan Maclean.

Mullard Radio Astronomy Observatory A radio OBSERVATORY situated at Lord's Bridge near Cambridge, UK, and operated by the University of Cambridge. The technique of INTERFEROMETRY was originally developed by the Cambridge radio astronomers to measure accurate positions of radio sources and was later extended to arrays of telescopes to produce the first detailed maps of radio sources by APERTURE SYNTHESIS. The discovery of pulsars was also made using an interferometer, the 3.6 hectare array.

mullein A plant of the genus *Verbascum*, a large group of chiefly biennial herbs related to antirrhinums, foxgloves, and figworts in the family Scrophulariaceae. They are natives of Europe, Asia, and North Africa, but are also widespread as introduced weeds in other parts of the world. The basal rosettes of large, often grey and woolly leaves, are produced in the first season and the handsome spikes of yellow or reddish-purple flowers, growing up to 2 m (6.5 feet) tall, develop in the second year.

Muller, Hermann Joseph (1890–1967) US geneticist. Realizing that natural mutations were both rare and detrimental, he discovered that he could use X-rays to induce mutations in the genetic material of the fruit fly *Drosophila*, enabling him to carry out many more genetic studies with it. He also recognized the danger of X-radiation to living things, and was concerned about the build-up of genetic mutations in the human population. Muller was awarded a Nobel Prize in 1946.

Müller, Johannes Peter (1801–58) German anatomist and zoologist. He was a pioneer of comparative and microscopical methods in biology. His investigations in physiology included respiration in the foetus, the nervous and sensory systems, the glandular system, and locomotion. Müller also studied the classification of marine animals.

Müller, (Friedrich) Max (1823–1900) German-born British philologist. He is remembered for his edition of the sacred early Sanskrit text the Rig-veda (1849–75); he also promoted the comparative study of Indo-European languages, as well as exploring comparative mythology and religion.

Müller, Paul Hermann (1899–1965) Swiss chemist. Searching for an effective chemical for use in pest control, he synthesized DDT in 1939 and soon patented it as an insecticide. It was immediately successful, especially in controlling lice and mosquitoes, but was withdrawn by most countries in the 1970s when its environmental persistence and toxicity in higher animals was realized. He was awarded a Nobel Prize in 1948.

mullet A fish belonging to either of two unrelated families, the grey mullets of the family Mugilidae, and the red mullets of the family Mullidae. The former are found in all tropical and temperate seas; some species occur as fresh-water fish in parts of the tropics. Greyish in colour, they are broad-headed, torpedo-shaped fishes with two dorsal fins, the first containing only four strong spines. Living in schools, they are most common in shallow water and can be seen browsing on the fine green algae on rocks and harbour walls, and also sucking up mud from the sea-bed. Internally, they have a thick-walled stomach and a very long intestine which allows them to digest algae.

Red mullets, known in North America as goatfishes, are usually red in colour, although many become paler at night. They have two long barbels on the chin that are used as feelers to detect worms, crustaceans, and molluscs buried in the mud and sand. Worldwide in range, they are most abundant in tropical seas.

Mull of Kintyre The southern extremity of the Kintyre peninsula on the west coast of Scotland. It is the nearest point to Ireland on the Scottish mainland.

Mulroney, (Martin) Brian (1939–) Canadian Progressive Conservative statesman, Prime Minister 1984–93. After becoming leader of the Progressive Conservative Party in 1983, he won a landslide victory in the 1984 election. He was re-elected in 1988 on a ticket of free trade with the USA, but stood down in 1993 after the Canadian recession caused his popularity to slump in the opinion polls.

multiple independently targetable re-entry vehicle (MIRV) A package of several WARHEADS, each aimed at a separate target, launched by a single BALLISTIC MISSILE. MIRVs are mounted on a 'bus', which releases each warhead (or re-entry vehicle) in space, with the correct speed and direction. To confuse and overwhelm the enemy's defences, decoy warheads are often mixed with genuine ones, and metallic chaff (radar-reflective particles) is released to blind the radars. The warheads can be guided on to their individual targets with an accuracy of about 100 m (330 feet). Large ballistic missiles like the Soviet Union's SS-18 can carry up to ten re-entry nuclear warheads, each with the explosive power of 50 kilotonnes of TNT.

multiple-mirror telescope (MMT or **segmented mirror telescope**) A REFLECTING TELESCOPE containing a number of small mirrors put together to behave as one large aperture. To collect as much light as possible from celestial objects there is a need for telescopes of very large size, but telescopes with a single large aperture are costly to construct. The multiple-mirror telescope offers a cheaper solution and, although many construction and control problems have to be overcome, successful MMTs have been built. One, on Mount Hopkins in Arizona, consists of six 1.8-m (71-inch) diameter mirrors operating together.

multiple sclerosis A degenerative central nervous system disorder characterized by patchy loss of the outer covering of nerve fibres (myelin sheaths), a process called demyelination; peripheral nerves are not affected. Multiple sclerosis is one of the commonest causes of disability in Britain; the cause is unknown, although a multifactorial origin is suspected. Multiple sclerosis is characterized by remissions and relapses, but the precise course is variable and unpredictable. Symptoms are dependent on the site of demyelination and include sensory loss, weakness in leg muscles, speech difficulties, loss of coordination, visual impairment, and dizziness. Tremor, ataxia, muscle twitching, muscle spasm, incontinence, and impotence may also occur. Symptoms of multiple sclerosis are exacerbated by exercise, temperature increases, and tiredness.

multiple star A group of three or more stars that are so close together that they appear as one to the unaided eye. Normally the components are bound together by gravitation, two of them forming a close BINARY STAR, with a third star (which may itself be a binary) moving in a larger orbit about the system's centre of mass. In some apparent multiple stars, however, one component is an unconnected star nearly in the same line of sight, as in the case of an OPTICAL DOUBLE star.

multiplexing A method of sending several messages simultaneously along the same channel, used mainly in telephony and telegraphy. In frequency-division multiplexing (FDM), suggested by the US inventor Elisha Gray in 1890 and first used during the 1920s, signals of different frequency, each carrying a different message, travel down the cable simultaneously. Complex filters then separate the messages at the receiver. In 1875 the French engineer J.-M.-E. Baudot suggested time-division multiplexing (TDM), in which high-speed samples of several message sources are interleaved. Used with PULSE CODE MODULATION, this system allows many hundreds of telephone channels to use a single OPTICAL FIBRE or COMMUNICATIONS SATELLITE link.

mummers' plays The best known of the British folk plays, mainly associated with Christmas. The extant texts (numbering over 3,000) fall into three categories. The first and largest, the Hero-Combat plays, contain a duel between St George and a pagan knight. The second, the Sword Play, features a slaying with swords by a group of dancers, and in the third, the Wooing Ceremony play, the two main characters are women, played by men. Death, resurrection, and the fool recur in all three. The faces of the cast were often blackened with soot. They were performed regularly until the mid-19th century, and may still be encountered occasionally.

mummy The body of a person or animal embalmed or otherwise treated to ensure its preservation, a practice associated especially with ancient Egypt. It seems to be connected with a belief in life after death, the body being preserved so that the soul could return to it. Artificial methods of preservation were introduced during the Old Kingdom, but the most complex method of embalming was perfected in Dynasty 21 (*c.*1100–950 BC). It continued into the Roman period, until Christianity gradually made it obsolete.

Munch, Edvard (1863–1944) Norwegian painter and engraver. One of the chief sources of German expressionism, he infused his subjects with an intense emotionalism and explored the use of violent colour and linear distortion to express feelings about life and death. Major works include his *Frieze of Life* sequence, incorporating *The Scream* (1893).

Munich (German **München**) An industrial, communications, and commercial city on the River Isar in south-west Germany, capital of Bavaria; pop. (1991) 1,229,050. It is noted for its medieval architecture and as an artistic and cultural centre. It is the home of the Bavarian State Opera Company and Munich Philharmonic. It hosted the Olympic Games in 1972 and is the seat of the European Patent Office. Its industries produce machinery, chemicals, precision instruments, vehicles, and beer. International beer festivals are held each year.

Munich Pact (29 September 1938) The agreement between Britain, France, Germany, and Italy concerning Czechoslovakia. HITLER had long demanded protection for the German-speaking SUDETENLAND and shown readiness to risk war to attain his end. To avert conflict at all costs the British Prime Minister, CHAMBERLAIN, had met Hitler at Berchtesgaden (15 September), and again at Bad Godesberg (23 September), by which time Hitler had extended his demands. He now stipulated the immediate annexation by Germany of the Bohemian Sudetenland and demanded that Germans elsewhere in Czechoslovakia should be given the right to join the THIRD REICH. In a final effort Chamberlain appealed to MUSSOLINI, who organized a conference at Munich where he, Chamberlain, and Hitler were joined by Daladier, the French Premier. No Czech or Soviet representative was invited. Hitler gained most of what he wanted and on 1 October German troops entered the Sudentenland. As part of the agreement, Poland and Hungary occupied areas of Moravia, Slovakia, and Ruthenia. In March 1939 Bohemia and Moravia were occupied by German troops, and the rest of Slovakia became an independent client state; President BENEŠ had resigned, and he left the country. Germany, which now dominated the entire Danubian area, emerged as the strongest power on the mainland of Europe.

Munro, H(ector) H(ugh) See SAKI.

Munster A province of the Republic of Ireland, comprising the south-western counties of Clare, Cork, Kerry, Limerick, Tipperary, and Waterford; area 24,127 sq km (9,319 sq miles); pop. (1991) 1,008,440.

muntjac A small DEER belonging to a subfamily of six species widely distributed in the wild in southern and south-east Asia. The antlers are simple and supported by long, skin-covered pedicels, which continue down the forehead as convergent ridges marked by lines of dark hair. Their coat is deep chestnut in colour, and both sexes have tusk-like canine teeth in the upper jaw that are used for fighting. Reeves's muntjac, *Muntiacus reevesi*, has a loud dog-like bark which is repeated at regular intervals when it is alarmed or disturbed – hence it is commonly called the barking deer. This species has been kept as an ornamental park animal in parts of Europe, and is now feral in many countries there.

muon (in particle physics) A particle produced by the decay of a PION. Muons, like the electrons they resemble, are LEPTONS; they have the same magnitude of charge and spin as electrons, but have a mass over 200 times that of the electron. There are two types of muon, the positive and negative; they are unstable, with an average lifetime of 2 microseconds, and they decay to give NEUTRINOS and either an electron or a positron. Muons are created in the Earth's atmosphere when cosmic rays, which are mostly high energy protons, collide with nuclei of the atoms in the atmosphere. The muons then travel to Earth at a speed very close to the speed of light. Because they are travelling so fast the muons experience the relativistic effect known as TIME DILATION, and their average lifetime becomes 32 microseconds – long enough for them to reach the surface of the Earth. On average, one muon hits each square centimetre of the Earth's surface every minute. Muons belong to the group known as the strange particles, because when they were discovered they didn't seem to fit in with the accepted picture of the nature of matter.

mural A painting, usually large, on a wall or for mounting on a wall as a permanent part of the decoration of a building. An ancient art-form, it was practised by the Minoans and Greeks The classic technique for mural painting is FRESCO, but other methods suitable for damp climates have been used especially in northern Europe. The most successful alternative has been simply to paint in oils on canvas and glue the canvas to the wall. In Asia the traditional method of wall-painting is with glue or dry plaster, but the fresco technique was known there in the 11th and 12th centuries.

Murat, Joachim (*c.*1767–1815) French general, king of Naples 1808–15. One of Napoleon's marshals, Murat made his name as a cavalry commander in the Italian campaign (1800). After he was made king of Naples by Napoleon, he made a bid to become king of all Italy in 1815, but was captured in Calabria and executed.

murder See HOMICIDE.

Murdoch, Dame (Jean) Iris (1919–) British novelist and philosopher, born in Ireland. The author of several philosophical works, Murdoch is primarily known for her novels; many of these portray complex sexual relationships, as in *The Sandcastle* (1957) and *A Severed Head* (1961). Others simultaneously explore the quest for the spiritual life, particularly *The Sea, The Sea* (1978), which won the Booker Prize, and *Nuns and Soldiers* (1980). More recent novels include *The Good Apprentice* (1985), *The Message to the Planet* (1989), and *The Green Knight* (1993).

Murdoch, (Keith) Rupert (1931–) Australian-born US publisher and media entrepreneur. As the founder and head of the News International Communications empire, he owns major newspapers in Australia, Britain, and the USA, together with film and television companies and the publishing firm HarperCollins.

Murillo, Bartolomé Esteban (*c.*1618–82) Spanish painter. He is noted both for his genre scenes of urchins and peasants and for his devotional pictures, which are characterized by delicate colour and ethereal form. Major works include *Two Boys Eating a Pie* (*c.*1665–75) and the *Soult Immaculate Conception* (1678).

Murmansk A fishing and trading port in north-west Russia, on the Kola Peninsula, in the Barents Sea; pop. (1990) 472,000. It is the largest city north of the Arctic Circle and its port is ice-free throughout the year. Its industries include shipbuilding, brewing, timber, and food processing.

Murnau, F. W. (born Frederick Wilhelm Plumpe) (1888–1931) German film director. His revolutionary use of the camera to record and interpret human emotion resulted in films such as *Nosferatu* (1922), in which he used technical effects to produce macabre results. *Der Letzte Mann* (1924) helped establish him as Germany's leading director. Other films include the Hollywood-made *Sunrise* (1927), which won three of the newly founded Oscar awards.

Murray The principal river of Australia, which rises in the Great Dividing Range in New South Wales and flows 2,590 km (1,610 miles) generally north-westwards, forming part of the border between the states of Victoria and New South Wales, before turning southwards in South Australia to empty into the Southern Ocean south-east of Adelaide.

Murray, (George) Gilbert (Aimé) (1866–1957) Australian-born British classical scholar. He is remembered for his rhymed verse translations of Greek dramatists, particularly Euripides. His translations of the latter's *Medea, Bacchae,* and *Electra* were staged in London from 1902, and helped to revive contemporary interest in Greek drama. Murray was also a founder of the League of Nations and later a joint president of the United Nations.

Murray, Sir James (Augustus Henry) (1837–1915) Scottish lexicographer. He was chief editor of the largest of all dictionaries in English, the *Oxford English Dictionary*. Murray did not live to see the dictionary completed; he died after finishing a section of the letter T, two years short of his 80th birthday. Originally issued in instalments between 1884 and 1928 under the title *A New English Dictionary on Historical Principles* (NED), the dictionary was not completed until 1928. A new edition in book-form and on CD-ROM was produced in the 1990s.

Mururoa A remote South Pacific atoll in the Tuamotu archipelago, in French Polynesia, used as a nuclear testing site since 1966.

Musca The Fly, a small CONSTELLATION of the southern sky, introduced by the Dutch navigators Pieter Dirkszoon Keyser and Frederick de Houtman at the end of the 16th century. Its brightest star is of third magnitude but it contains little of note for the casual observer except that part of the Coalsack Nebula intrudes across the border from neighbouring CRUX.

Muscat (Arabic **Masqat**) The capital city of the Sultanate of Oman, a seaport on the south-east coast of the Arabian peninsula adjoining the port of Matrah; pop. (est. 1990) 380,000. Muscat was under Portuguese and then Persian rule until 1798, when a treaty was signed giving links with Britain which lasted until the 1960s.

Muscat and Oman The former name (until 1970) of OMAN.

muscle A body or sheet of tissue that is capable of shortening in length, or contracting. Muscles are used to convert stored chemical energy into mechanical movement. The muscle consists of bundles of fibres, each made from strands, or fibrils, of two types of protein molecules, actin and myosin. These substances are attached to one another in such a way that a change in the chemical conditions surrounding them can alter their structure and make one slide over the other. This involves the use of energy, supplied by a substance called adenosine triphosphate (ATP).

There are three basic types of muscle, each distinguished by the appearance of its fibres when magnified. Striated, or skeletal muscle, which looks banded under the microscope, is used to control movements of the skeletal bones and is usually under voluntary control. Smooth muscle, lacking bands, is found in many internal organs, such as the stomach wall. It is usually under the control of the AUTONOMIC NERVOUS SYSTEM. The last type is cardiac muscle, found only in the walls of the heart. Smooth muscle and cardiac muscle are myogenic (initiate their own contraction).

The energy needs of muscles mean that they are richly innervated with blood vessels, hence their red colour. The blood also removes waste products of the contraction process, particularly a substance known as lactic acid. Striated muscle contractions are initiated by an impulse from a nerve ending. This releases a chemical which makes the membranes of the muscle fibres permeable to certain chemicals. These in turn create the conditions under which contraction occurs. The relaxation of muscles happens when these contraction-causing chemicals are taken back across the membrane.

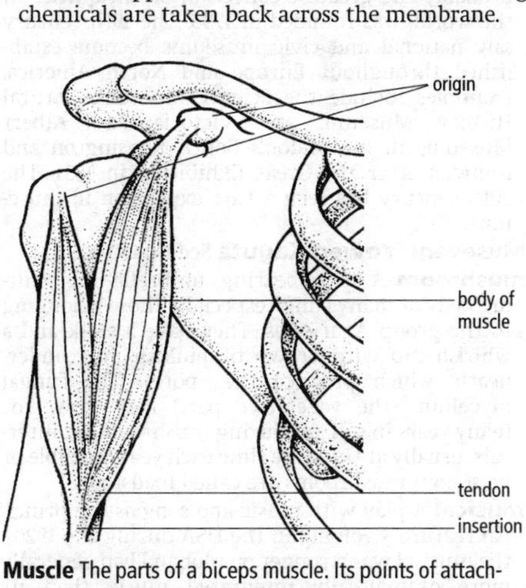

Muscle The parts of a biceps muscle. Its points of attachment are called the origin and the insertion; the latter is the attachment of the muscle to the bone it moves when contracting (in this case, the radius bone of the forearm).

muscovite (in geology) A light, silvery-coloured mineral and a member of the MICA group. It is one of the commonest minerals in igneous, sedimentary, and metamorphic rocks. It occurs as flat plates; specimens 30–50 sq m (36–60 sq yards) in size are recorded from Ontario. It is used for electrical and heat insulation either in sheets or powdered in plaster. Because of its transparency and resistance to heat it makes good furnace windows.

muscular dystrophy A group of muscle diseases, marked by weakness and wasting of selected muscles, in which there is a recognizable pattern of inheritance. The affected muscle fibres degenerate and are replaced by fatty tissue. **Duchenne muscular dystrophy**, which is inherited as a sex-linked recessive character, is nearly always restricted to boys. It usually begins before the age of four, with selective weakness and wasting of the muscles of the pelvic girdle and back. Although the disease cannot be cured, physiotherapy and orthopaedic measures can relieve the disability. The identification of the gene abnormality raises the possibility of gene therapy in the future.

Muses In Greek mythology, the nine daughters of Zeus and Mnemosyne (Memory), each of whom presided over a particular branch of art, literature, or science. Their names and responsibilities vary in different ancient accounts, but are generally given as follows: Calliope (epic poetry), Clio (history), Erato (love poetry and the lyre), Euterpe (lyric poetry and the flute), Melpomene (tragedy), Polyhymnia (hymns), Terpsichore (dance and choral song), Thalia (comedy), and Urania (astronomy).

museum A building or site used for the exhibition and storage of works of art, antiquities, and objects of scientific and historical interest. The origins of museums go back to classical times with the *museion* (Greek, 'temple of the muses') at Alexandria, celebrated for its collection of artefacts and its library. Although there were many private princely collections in, for example, 15th-century Italy, the first modern museum dates back to the foundation of the Ashmolean Museum in Oxford (1683), which was the first public collection in the world. The British Museum, which contains probably the greatest collection of antiquities in the world, was founded in 1753. The 19th century saw national and civic museums become established throughout Europe and North America. Examples include the Science Museum, Natural History Museum, and Victoria and Albert Museum, all in London's South Kensington and founded after the Great Exhibition in 1851. The 20th century has seen a vast expansion in museums.

Museveni, Yoweri Kaguta See UGANDA.

mushroom A spore-bearing, umbrella-like fruiting body of many fungi, especially those belonging to the group Agaricales. They have a stalk and a whitish cap with brown or pinkish gills underneath, which produce the spores. The fungal mycelium (the vegetative part) may grow for many years in soil, producing mushrooms at intervals, usually at the same time each year. Inedible or poisonous mushrooms are called toadstools.

musical A play with music and song as the principal feature. Evolving in the USA during the 1920s, the musical was stronger on plot and had generally more dramatically integrated music than its immediate predecessor, the 'musical comedy'. The first musical of real importance was Jerome Kern's *Show Boat* in 1927. The same year saw the coming of sound to the cinema; a proliferation of film musicals followed, initially dependent on the stage for source material. Composers, such as GERSHWIN, PORTER, BERLIN, Richard RODGERS, and Harold Arlen, followed and challenged Kern's model, and their work was in turn adapted to Hollywood. Meanwhile, musicals were being written especially for the big screen, the spectacular direction of Busby Berkeley opening up new possibilities exploited in the dance musicals of ASTAIRE and Ginger Rogers in the 1930s, such as *Top Hat* (1935), and of KELLY, especially *An American in Paris* (1951) and *Singin' in the Rain* (1952). Stage musicals, such as Frank Loesser's *Guys and Dolls* (1950) and Bernstein's *West Side Story* (1957), became increasingly sophisticated and almost operatic.

In the UK, the musical has also been highly successful, ranging from *No, No, Nanette* (1925) starring Binnie Hale (1900–84) to Andrew LLoyd Webber's *Jesus Christ Superstar* (1971), *Evita* (1978), *Cats* (1981), and *The Phantom of the Opera* (1986).

music-hall A type of entertainment that flourished in Britain during the second half of the 19th and early 20th centuries. The music-hall originated in the 'saloons' of London taverns set apart for 'sing-songs'. Later musical halls provided a varied programme of up to 25 'turns': singers, dancers, comedians, acrobats, jugglers, even dramatic sketches. The early music-halls had a chairman who controlled the proceedings and (unusually for the times) employed women singers and later *comédiennes*, as well as their male counterparts. Some of the music-halls, such as the Alhambra, graduated to revue and the MUSICAL, but many remained the home of twice-nightly variety. With the advent of the cinema, the popularity of the music-hall waned. See also VAUDEVILLE.

musicology The analytical study of music, past and present. The musicologist aims to study the workings of music – how others have composed and performed it – and is not primarily concerned with any direct, practical application. Among the main musicological areas are analysis, editorial work, ethnomusicology, psychology and aesthetics, and the sociology of music.

musique concrète A composition assembled from previously recorded sounds. The sounds may be natural (leaves rustling in the wind) or human-made (cashiers rustling bank-notes). Strictly speaking the sounds should not be modified by electronic means, but the original purity of purpose has been blurred as ELECTRONIC MUSIC has gained ground. The term was first used by Pierre Schaeffer in 1948.

musk deer Any one of three species of small, solitary DEER in the genus *Moschus*, formerly widespread in the forests and scrubland of eastern Asia. Devoid of antlers, they have instead long upper canine teeth. These tusks, used in fights, are 7 cm (3 inches) long in the male, and shorter in the female. The thick coat of dark brown is slightly mottled with grey; the hair is distinctive because of air-filled compartments which enhance insulation. They feed on lichens and mosses, which are chiselled from rock and tree surfaces by spatula-shaped lower incisor teeth. Hunted for centuries for the brown musk contained in a gland near the tail, and used in medicine and perfume, they are now a subject for conservation.

muskeg A swampy area of peat, covered by sphagnum moss and surrounded by coniferous trees, such as spruce. It develops in former lake basins and along river channels in cold, flat areas of the Northern Hemisphere, especially in northern Canada.

muskellunge The largest fish of the PIKE family, *Esox masquinongy*, growing occasionally to a length of 2.4 m (7.75 feet) and a weight of 45 kg (112 pounds). Restricted in its distribution to the Great Lakes of North America and the St Lawrence and

Ohio rivers, it is typically a fish of large waters, especially where aquatic plants grow densely. It is a predatory species, feeding on smaller fishes, with occasional water-birds and mammals featuring in its diet.

musket See FIREARM.

Muskogean A family of Native American languages in south-eastern North America.

musk ox A species of goat-antelope, *Ovibos moschatus*, that lives in the Arctic region of North America. It is more closely related to sheep and goats than to oxen. It stands 1.5 m (5 feet) at the shoulders; the head is long and bears horns curving outwards and downwards and then upwards. The coat is of long black fur and hangs like a fringe around the stocky legs, which, in contrast, have white fur. For most of the year it lives in herds of four to a hundred individuals. The bulls are extremely aggressive in the rutting season and their musk gland exudes a strong smell. A single calf is born and the mother protects it fiercely. Suckling continues for nine months, and the female calves only once every two years.

musk rat A species of aquatic RODENT, *Ondatra zibethicus*. Musk rats look like very large water voles. They are little modified for life in the water, apart from the laterally flattened tail. The musk rat is native to North America. Its soft, dense fur is highly regarded in the trade under the name **musquash** and more of these skins are sold than of any other species. The animals are kept on fur farms and escapes have resulted in the species becoming well established in Europe, where they have become serious pests by undermining river banks with their burrows. The name refers to musky secretions of the male.

Muslim See ISLAM.

Muslim League Political party founded in 1905 to represent the separate interests of the Indian Muslims, who felt threatened by the prospects of a Hindu majority in any future democratic system. The radical nationalist elements in the League forged a pact with the CONGRESS in 1916 on the basis of separate electorates and reserved seats in Muslim minority provinces. A section of the League cooperated with the Congress in the non-cooperation movement. In the provincial elections (1937), the League captured very few Muslim seats, but it succeeded in convincing the Muslim masses that the elected Congress ministries were oppressing Muslims. In 1940 it put forward the demand for an autonomous Muslim homeland, Pakistan, interpreted by its leader, M. A. JINNAH, as an independent state during the transfer of power negotiations between the UK and India. He called for a Direct Action Day in August 1946. Mass rioting followed, whereupon the British and the Congress agreed to partition. The League was virtually wiped out at the first elections in Pakistan.

mussel Perhaps the commonest of all BIVALVE molluscs. Mussels may occur in dense beds several miles long on coastlines and estuaries, wherever there is plentiful suspended food. Like most other bivalves, they filter out this food with their large internal sheet-like gills, and then carry it to their mouths using beating hairs (cilia). They secrete tough byssus threads by which they anchor themselves to the sea-bed. Both horse mussels, *Modiolus modiolus*, and common mussels, *Mytilus edulis*, are extremely abundant between high and low tide-marks. Often, young adult specimens are transported to favourable sites to provide supplies for the seafood industry.

Musset, Alfred de (1810–57) French poet, dramatist, and novelist. His poetry displays the lyricism characteristic of ROMANTICISM, but his best pieces, for example *Les Nuits* (1835–37), have a sharper note of bitterness. Notable among his plays, which were mostly written to be read, is *Lorenzaccio* (1834). His novel *Les Confessions d'un enfant du siècle* (1836) is based on his stormy relationship with George SAND.

Mussolini, Benito (Amilcaro Andrea) (known as 'Il Duce', the leader) (1883–1945) Italian Fascist statesman, Prime Minister 1922–43. Originally a socialist, Mussolini founded the Italian Fascist Party in 1919. Three years later he orchestrated the march on Rome by the Blackshirts and was created Prime Minister, proceeding to organize his government along dictatorial lines. He annexed Abyssinia in 1936 and entered World War II on Germany's side in 1940. Mussolini was forced to resign after the Allied invasion of Sicily in 1943; he was rescued from imprisonment by German paratroopers, but was captured and executed by Italian Communist partisans in 1945, a few weeks before the end of the war.

Mussorgsky, Modest (Petrovich) (or **Moussorgsky**) (1839–81) Russian composer. Most of his best-known works are vocal, his interest in speech rhythms combining with the lyricism of his songs. They include the opera *Boris Godunov* (1874) and *Songs and Dances of Death* (1875–77). He is also noted for the piano suite *Pictures at an Exhibition* (1874). After his death many of his works were completed and altered by Rimsky-Korsakov and others, but recently there has been a tendency to return to Mussorgsky's original scoring.

mustard Any one of a number of European, yellow-flowered, annual plants that give their name to the mustard family, or Cruciferae, a large family with over 3,000 species. This includes many economically important species, such as cabbage and oilseed rape, and many ornamental garden species. White mustard, *Sinapis alba*, is grown as a salad plant, and is eaten as a seedling with cress (as 'mustard and cress'). The seeds of white mustard, brown mustard, *Brassica juncea*, and black mustard, *B. nigra*, are ground to yield mustard flour. When mixed with water, or vinegar, this produces the condiment mustard.

mustard gas A chemical warfare agent, dichloroethyl sulphide [$(ClCH_2CH_2)_2S$], first used by the German Army at Ypres (Belgium) in 1917. It is a colourless oily liquid whose vapour causes painful blistering of the skin and swelling around the eyes, and strips away the mucous membrane of the bronchial tubes. The effects take time to appear, and in severe cases lingering death may take four or five weeks.

mutation A change in the genetic material that may lead to a change in the PHENOTYPE of an organism. The different ALLELES of GENES arise by mutation. There is a notional norm for organisms and any deviation from that norm inherited in a Mendelian fashion is called a mutation. Dwarfism and albinism are examples of mutations in humans.

Point mutations are alterations in one or a few bases in the DNA, leading to an alteration in the amino acid sequence of a protein, which can lead to an altered phenotype. Many such alterations cause no obvious phenotypic change and are only detected as alterations in the net charge of a protein (electrophoretic variants). A second class of mutations are aberrations of CHROMOSOME number or structure. A third class of mutations have been discovered recently and result from the insertion of mobile elements into GENES. These are specific sequences of DNA that can either move themselves or be copied and moved from one site in a chromosome to another in the same or a different chromosome.

Most mutations are either deleterious – they produce an organism less adapted to its environment – or they are neutral, having no effect on the adaptation of the organism to its environment; a few are beneficial. Mutations provide the genetic variation on which NATURAL SELECTION acts. Natural mutations are rare events, but the frequency can be increased by chemicals and radiation.

mute swan The familiar Old World SWAN, *Cygnus olor*, with a gracefully curved neck. The wingbeats of the mute swan produce a musical note. Their orange beaks have black basal knobs. They have been semi-domesticated for centuries, and young birds are still tagged at 'swan upping' ceremonies in Britain.

Mutsuhito See MEIJI TENNO.

mutton bird Either of two different species of petrel. In New Zealand mutton birds are the sooty shearwaters, *Puffinus griseus*; in southern Australia they are the short-tailed shearwaters, *P. tenuirostris*. Fledglings of both are taken from their cavity nests, cooked, and preserved in their own fat as part of the winter diet of the Maoris or Aborigines. Both species of mutton bird nest underground in burrows on offshore islands. The adults are pelagic-feeding.

Muybridge, Eadweard (born Edward James Muggeridge) (1830–1904) British photographer and inventor. Emigrating to the USA at the age of 22 (and changing his name to sound more 'Anglo-Saxon'), Muybridge became a professional photographer in California, taking hundreds of views of the Pacific Coast and Yosemite National Park. Leland Stanford, millionaire governor of California, commissioned him to photograph his favourite horse at full gallop. Having obtained a recognizable silhouette in 1872, he returned to his experiments in 1877, constructing a huge apparatus with 12 cameras actuated by electromagnets at specific intervals. Muybridge went on to photograph many animals in motion, publishing his famous *Human and Animal Locomotion* in 1887. His Zoopraxiscope was the most successful machine for showing movement until Edison introduced his Kinetoscope in 1888.

MVD (Ministry for Internal Affairs) A police organization of the former Soviet Union. Together with the MGB (Ministry of State Security), it replaced the NKVD (People's Commissariat of Internal Affairs) in 1946. The MVD controlled all police forces and administered forced prison camps. During the last years of STALIN's rule it became a significant factor in the Soviet economy, one of its most notorious chiefs being Lavrenti BERIA. The powers of the MGB were extended to supervise and control police agencies throughout the Soviet bloc, and to eliminate all anti-Soviet, anti-communist opposition in the satellite countries. Both agencies were drastically reduced and decentralized between 1953 and 1960, when they were replaced by the KGB.

Myanmar (formerly **Burma**) A country in south-east Asia, with borders (on the west) with India and Bangladesh, on the north-east with China, on the east with Laos, and on the south-east and south with Thailand.

Physical. Myanmar has a long, tropical western coast on the Indian Ocean and is cut off from the rest of Asia by mountains in the north and east. Between the mountains and down the centre of the country run the broad, cultivable valley of the Irrawaddy River and several tributary valleys. To the east is the valley of the Salween River. Climatically it is hot and monsoonal, about 5,000 mm (nearly 200 inches) of rain falling annually along the coast, although in the eastern upland region it is drier and cooler.

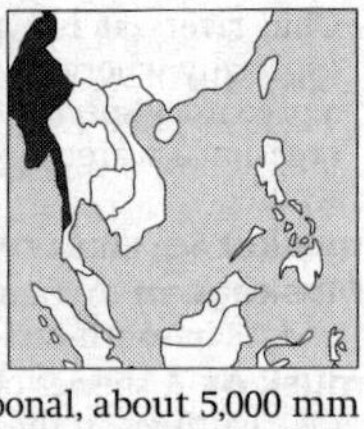

Economy. Myanmar has a broadly based agricultural economy. Crops include sugar cane, pulses, ground nuts, and maize. Major exports are timber, whose production is in the state sector, rice, minerals, and gems. Crude oil is extracted, and production of natural gas is increasing. The small industrial sector includes oil-refining, food-processing, and textiles. Mineral resources include copper, zinc, lead, tin, and silver.

History. There was a Mon kingdom, Prome, in Burma in the 5th century AD. After the arrival of the Burmans in the 9th century there was much hostility between them and the indigenous peoples. Following a period of Mon ascendancy the Burmans of Pagan unified the country for a time (*c*.849–1287). From the Mons an Indian script and Theravada BUDDHISM spread to Pagan and thence throughout Burma. During the 16th century the country was re-united under the Toungoo, but wars against Thai kingdoms and LAOS exhausted it. The last dynasty, the Konbaung, founded by Alaungpaya in 1757, was constantly engaged in wars against Siam, which led to the fall of the Siamese state of Ayuthia in 1767. In 1770 Burma repelled a Chinese invasion. The conquest of ARAKAN brought the Burmese border to the boundary of British India.

Burma was invaded by the British (1824–26; 1852; and 1885). The first two ANGLO-BURMESE WARS led to the cession of territory and the third resulted in the deposition of King Thibaw and the establishment of Upper Burma as a province of British India. In 1931 there was a two-year uprising by the peasantry against European companies, and the Dobama Asi-ayone (Thakin) Party demanded independence. In 1937 Burma became a Crown colony, with a large degree of autonomy, Ba Maw being elected Premier. When Japanese troops moved into Malaya in 1942, a Burma National Army formed under AUNG SAN, was at first ready to welcome the Japanese. This force however defected to the Allies during the later campaign of liberation. Full independence was gained in 1948, Burma electing to remain outside the Commonwealth of Nations. Civil war erupted, with challenges to central government by the Karens of the Irrawaddy Delta and the Chin, Kayah, and Kachin hill tribes. Unu's government succumbed to an army coup in 1962, led by NE WIN. He established an authoritarian state based on quasi-socialist and Buddhist principles, maintaining a policy of strict neutrality. When he retired in 1986, U San Yu became chairman of the governing Burma Socialist Program Party, still faced by intransigent ethnic insurgent groups. In September 1988 General Saw Maung seized power, imposing martial law, and changing the country's name to Myanmar. Its social, economic, and political problems only worsened. During 1989, Aung San's daughter Daw AUNG SAN SUU KYI emerged as a leader of the opposition, but was placed under house arrest. Her party, the National League for

Democracy (NLD), won a two-thirds majority for a constituent assembly in elections in 1990. Saw Maung's State Law and Order Restoration Council (SLORC) refused, however, to allow the assembly to meet and arrested NLD leaders. By now various ethnic separatist guerrilla groups and private armies were roaming the country, some funded by illegal drug traffic. Fighting in the Muslim majority border state of Rakhine between government forces and Rohingya rebels led to some 200,000 Rohingya Muslims fleeing to Bangladesh in 1992. In April 1992 Saw Maung was replaced by his deputy, General Than Shwe. Some degree of political liberalization followed, but the government's emergency powers remained in force, notably order 288, which prohibits meetings of more than five people in a public place. A national convention to coordinate the drafting of a new constitution was inaugurated in 1993, but few meetings were held. Aung San Suu Kyi agreed to hold meetings with SLORC leaders and she was released unconditionally from house arrest in 1995. She was reinstated as leader of the NLD, but the official electoral commission vetoed this decision. The NLD boycotted the national convention, which it claimed was not committed to implementing democratic reform, and was then formally expelled from the convention by SLORC. By mid-1995 15 guerrilla groups had agreed to cease-fires, but the Karens and the Mong Tai Army continued to fight. During 1996 regular mass pro-democracy demonstrations were held outside the house of Aung San Suu Kyi, while the military junta faces growing international criticism over its suppression of legitimate government and its policy of forced labour to work on capital building projects.

Capital: Yangôn (formerly Rangoon)
Area: 676,577 sq km (261,228 sq mi)
Population: 46,527,000 (1995)
Currency: 1 kyat = 100 pyas
Religions: Buddhist 75.2%; Christian 4.9%; Muslim 16.0%; traditional beliefs 1.1%; Hindu 0.5%
Ethnic Groups: Burman 69.0%; Shan 8.5%; Karen 6.2%; Rakhine 4.5%; Mon 2.4%; Chin 2.2%; Kachin 1.4%
Languages: Burmese (official); minority languages; English
International Organizations: UN; Colombo Plan; ASEAN

Mycenae An ancient city in Greece, situated near the coast in the north-east Peloponnese, on a site dominating various land and sea routes. The capital of King Agamemnon, it was the centre of the late Bronze Age Mycenaean civilization. Its period of greatest prosperity was *c.*1400 to 1200 BC, which saw construction of the palace and massive walls of Cyclopaean masonry, including the 'Lion Gate', the entrance to the citadel (*c.*1250 BC). It was destroyed in about 1100 BC by invading Dorians. Systematic excavation of the site began in 1840.

Mycenaean civilization (or **Aegean civilization**) Greek culture that dominated mainland Greece from *c.*1580 BC to *c.*1120 BC, when the invading DORIANS destroyed the citadels of Mycenae and Tiryns. Another important Peloponnesian centre was Pylos, and Mycenaean influence spread as far north as southern Thessaly. In *c.*1450 Mycenaeans seem to have conquered KNOSSOS in Crete, and traders travelled widely to Asia Minor, Cyprus, and Syria. It seems that they also sacked Troy *c.*1200, though the duration and scale of the expedition was doubtless exaggerated by the poet HOMER in his epic, the *Iliad*. Finds from the early period bear witness to considerable wealth and a high artistic skill.

mycorrhiza The symbiotic association of fungi with the roots of a plant in which the plant supplies the fungus with organic compounds and the fungus improves the efficiency of nutrient take-up by the plant roots. Many plants, such as heathers and orchids, cannot grow without their mycorrhizal fungus. There are many different kinds of mycorrhizal association. In the ectomycorrhiza of trees, the rootlets are surrounded by a sheath of fungal tissue, which is sometimes also connected to a fungal fruit-body, such as the fly agaric. Endomycorrhizal associations are those in which the bulk of the mycorrhiza is present inside the plant roots.

myelin A complex fatty material, formed from protein and phospholipid, that forms a sheath around the large nerve fibres of vertebrates (and some invertebrates). The material is produced by Schwann cells at regular intervals along the nerve fibre and by acting as an insulator, increases the speed of conduction of impulses along the fibre.

Mykonos (Greek **Míkonos**) A rocky Greek island in the Aegean Sea, one of the Cyclades; area 85 sq km (33 sq miles); pop. (1981) 4,850. Its chief town and port is Mykonos. Manganese, wine, grain, and figs are produced. It is a popular tourist resort.

mynah bird A bird of the genus *Acridotheres*, belonging to the starling family, Sturnidae. They originated in Asia, but some, particularly the common mynah, *A. tristis*, have been introduced to a wide variety of warmer parts of the world by man. Thrush-sized, blackish or brownish birds, often with bright yellow legs and beak and with conspicuous pale patches in the wings, mynahs are perhaps best known for their ability to mimic the calls of other birds. The common mynah is a popular cage-bird and can be taught to mimic human speech.

myocardial infarction See CORONARY THROMBOSIS.

myriapod A member of an informal group of ARTHROPODS consisting of two classes, chilopods (CENTIPEDES) and diplopods (MILLIPEDES), which comprise some 10,500 species. They are characterized by having legs of similar shape on virtually every segment. Unlike insects, their CUTICLE is not waxy and waterproof, and their fine breathing tubes cannot be closed by valves. This makes them very prone to water-loss; hence they are most frequently found living in dark and humid places beneath stones and humus. They rely on scents and vibrations to explore their twilight world, as they lack the elaborate compound eyes of insects. Most types of myriapod are herbivores, but true centipedes are predatory.

Myron (fl. *c.*480–440 BC) Greek sculptor. Only two certain copies of his work survive, the best known being the *Discobolus* (*c.*450 BC), a figure of a man throwing the discus, which demonstrates a remarkable interest in symmetry and movement.

myrtle A tree or shrub of the genus *Myrtus*, which gives its name to the large family Myrtaceae, containing some 3,000 species of small shrubs and trees. The European myrtle, *M. communis*, is an evergreen shrub of southern Europe and western Asia. The family is mainly centred on tropical and subtropical regions and includes *Eucalyptus* and cloves. The bog myrtle, *Myrica gale*, is an unrelated shrub.

Mysore ▶**1** The former name (until 1973) of the Indian state of Karnataka. ▶**2** A city in the Indian state of Karnataka, former capital of the princely state of Mysore; pop. (1991) 652,250. It is the second-largest city in the state and is noted for the production of silk, incense, and sandalwood oil.

mystery play A popular dramatic representation of scenes from the Old and New Testaments, performed in many towns across Europe from the 13th to the 16th centuries (and, later, in Roman Catholic Spain and Bavaria). They seem to have developed gradually from aspects of the Easter Mass in Latin into civic occasions in the local languages, usually enacted on Corpus Christi, a holy feast day from 1311. In Islam, there is the Shiite passion play (*ta'ziya*), usually performed during the mourning month of Muḥaram, especially for the commemoration of the murder of Husain. The play re-enacts in emotive detail the tragic death of Husain, and is often accompanied by street processions and public expressions of grief, such as self-flagellation.

mysticism The belief that a person can achieve unity with God or some other form of ultimate reality. It is found typically in a RELIGION that conceives of transcendence as an unseen but essential unity of all that exists. Thus, mystical ideas, practices, and experiences are central to BUDDHISM, HINDUISM (see ADVAITA HINDUISM) and DAOISM. Mysticism may also be found in religions that conceive of transcendence as radically other than the world, but in such cases it is often the subject of dispute, as in ISLAM (see SUFISM), Judaism (see KABBALAH), and CHRISTIANITY. These disputes are the result of mystics in these communities valuing individual experiences even when they do not confirm authoritative beliefs. A wide variety of practices is associated with mystical experiences: most important is MEDITATION, but other techniques of concentration including contemplative prayer are also recommended. Subject to more dispute is the mystical use of hallucinatory drugs, alcohol, and sexual activity.

Mystics, the Spanish mystical writers of whom St Teresa of Avila (1515–82) and St John of the Cross (1542–91) are the most notable. Their work, linked to a process of spiritual ferment and reform within the Roman Catholic Church, testifies to a deep-felt spiritual condition.

myth A traditional story about the past, often including religious or fantastic elements. Myths of some sort can be found in all societies, although they may function in different ways. They may be attempts to explain the origins of the Universe and of mankind (see CREATION MYTH), the development of political institutions, or the reasons for RITUAL practices; on the other hand, they may simply be told for the love of a good story. Myths often describe the deeds of gods or supernatural beings, or of heroes, like the trickster, who have supernatural powers that enable them to change from human to animal form, or to perform extraordinary deeds. Anthropologists have spent a greatdeal of time trying to differentiate myth from history, but it is clear that history can serve the same functions as myth, and the two types of tale about the past blur into one another. Theorists like FRAZER regarded myths as a form of early religious or scientific thought. This approach was later criticized by MALINOWSKI, who saw myth as providing a justification for the social order. The Romanian-US historian of religion Mircea Eliade (1907–86) regarded myth as a religious phenomenon, man's attempt to return to the original act of creation. LÉVI-STRAUSS has argued that it is not the content but the structure of myth which is important, since it reveals universal mental processes. In PSYCHOLOGY, myths are regarded as an important basis for human behaviour. Both FREUD and JUNG made extensive use of myths in their work. Whatever the theories regarding the origin and functions of myths, they remain fundamental to the human consciousness. **Mythology** is the study of such myths. Classical mythology is concerned with the myths of ancient Greece and Rome.

Mytilene (Greek **Mitilíni**) The chief town and port of the Greek island of Lesbos in the Aegean Sea; pop. (1991) 23,970.

myxomatosis An infectious viral disease of rabbits and hares, which is usually fatal. However, some strains of rabbits develop resistance to the disease. Myxomatosis was used by Australia and the UK in the 1950s to reduce the rabbit population, because rabbits were causing significant damage to crops.

Mzilikazi (*c*.1796–1868) NDEBELE leader. The first great ruler of the Ndebele, he united his people into a nation under his leadership. He became a war leader under SHAKA, King of the Zulu, but rebelled in 1822. He led his people away from Zululand to what is now the western Transvaal, and then settled with his subjects in the area of Bulawayo. In 1837 he fled north, subduing the Shona, and ruling the Ndebele until his death.

N

Naas The county town of Kildare in the Republic of Ireland, on the road from Dublin to Cork; pop. (1991) 11,140. It was the seat of the kings of Leinster whose royal palace lay on the North Mote. There are racecourses at Naas and at nearby Punchestown.

Nabataean A member of an ancient Arabian people speaking a form of Aramaic strongly influenced by Arabic. Originally a nomadic Arab tribe, they formed an independent state (312–63 BC), prospering from control of trade routes between southern Arabia and the Mediterranean, which converged at their capital Petra (now in Jordan). Their culture reflects Babylonian, Arab, Greek, and Roman influence in its speech, religion, art, and architecture. From 63 AD they became allies and vassals of Rome, and in 106 AD Trajan transformed their kingdom into the Roman province of Arabia.

Nablus A town in the Israeli-occupied West Bank, 66 km (41 miles) north of Jerusalem; pop. (est. 1984) 80,000. It is close to the site of the Canaanite city of Shechem, important in ancient times because of its position at the centre of an east-west route through the mountains of Samaria. The university of Al-Abjah is located here, and oil and soap are manufactured.

Nabokov, Vladimir (Vladimorovich) (1899–1977) Russian-born US novelist and poet. After writing a number of novels in Russian, Nabokov turned to writing in English in 1941. He is best known for *Lolita* (1958), his witty and erudite novel about a middle-aged European man's obsession with a 12-year-old American girl. Other works include *Pale Fire* (1962) and *Ada: A Family Chronicle* (1969). He was also a keen lepidopterist and wrote a number of papers on the subject. *Conclusive Evidence* (1951) revised as *Speak, Memory* (1966) is a brilliant poetic autobiography.

Nadar (pseudonym of Gaspard Felix Tournachon) (1820–1910) French photographer. Nadar was a Parisian journalist and caricaturist before he took up photography in 1853 in partnership with his brother Adrien. In 1860 he opened his own studio. In 1874 he lent this studio to the Impressionists for their first exhibition. Always eager to experiment, Nadar took the first aerial photographs (from a balloon), photographed in the sewers and catacombs of Paris, and, as early as 1860, equipped his studio with electric light.

Nader, Ralph (1934–) US lawyer and reformer. He initiated a campaign on behalf of public safety that gave impetus to the consumer rights movement of the 1960s onwards. His views on defective car design, set out in *Unsafe at Any Speed* (1965) led to Federal legislation on safety standards. Nader was also a moving force behind legislation concerning radiation hazards, food packaging, and the use of insecticides.

nadir That point on the CELESTIAL SPHERE opposite the ZENITH. It is 90 degrees away from the horizon and is approximately the direction in which a plumb-bob hangs. Because the Earth is not spherical the direction of the plumb-bob nadir would not in general pass through the Earth's centre.

NAFTA See NORTH AMERICAN FREE TRADE AGREEMENT.

naga A serpent-geni figure in the mythologies of Hinduism, Jainism, and Buddhism. As water gods, nagas inhabit the bottoms of rivers, lakes, and seas, in splendid, jewel-studded palaces ever alive with dancing and song. In temple architecture, nagas stand guard at the portals of shrines. In South India nagakals, stones decorated with a single serpent or an entwined serpent-pair, are set up as votive offerings by women desiring offspring.

Nagaland A state in the far north-east of India, on the border with Myanmar (Burma), created in 1962 from the former Naga Hills district of Assam and neighbouring areas; area 16,579 sq km (6,404 sq miles); pop. (1991) 1,215,570; capital, Kohima. There is a strong local separatist movement.

Nāgārjuna (*c.*150–250 AD) The first important Buddhist philosopher and founder of the Mādhyamika sect, a branch of MAHAYANA Buddhism. His major achievement was the philosophical justification of a middle way which directly concurred with the teachings of the BUDDHA.

Nagas A group of tribes in the densely forested state of Nagaland, in north-eastern India. The Nagas, who consist of different cultural and linguistic groupings, live in small hill-side villages, and practise SHIFTING CULTIVATION, as well as some hunting and gathering.

Nagasaki A city and port in south-west Japan, on the west coast of the island of Kyushu; pop. (1990) 444,620. Visited by the Portuguese in 1545, it was the first Japanese port to open up to western trade. On 9 August 1945, three days after the first atomic bomb attack on HIROSHIMA, Nagasaki became the next target. The hilly terrain protected the population of 230,000 from the full effects of the explosion, but 40,000 people were killed and tremendous destruction caused. On the following day Japan surrendered and the ceasefire began on 15 August, the official surrender finally being signed on 2 September. Nagasaki now specializes in shipbuilding and heavy engineering.

Nagorno Karabagh See ARMENIA; AZERBAIJAN.

Nagoya A port and city in central Japan, capital of Aichi prefecture in the Chubu region of Honshu Island; pop. (1990) 2,154,660. It is the fourth-largest city in Japan. Landmarks include Nagoya Castle and the Atsuta Shrine. It has iron and steel works, and aircraft, automobile, and chemical industries.

Nagpur A city in the state of Maharashtra, central India, on the Nag River; pop. (1991) 1,661,400. It was a centre of the Chanda dynasty of aboriginal Gonds and capital of the Central provinces. An administrative and commercial centre with textile industries.

Nagy, Imre (1896–1958) Hungarian Communist statesman, Prime Minister 1953–55 and 1956. During his first term in office he introduced liberal policies, pushing for greater availability of consumer goods and less collectivization, but was forced to resign. Back in power in 1956, he announced Hungary's withdrawal from the Warsaw Pact and sought a neutral status for his country. When the Red Army moved in later that year to crush the uprising Nagy was removed from office and executed by the new regime under János Kádár.

Naiad In Greek mythology, a water nymph living in fresh water, such as brooks, fountains, and springs. Sea water nymphs were called Oceanids.

nail The horny covering of the tip of a finger or toe. Hooves or claws are their equivalent in some vertebrates. They develop in the same way as skin but advance from specialized regions of dividing cells, nail roots, which are mostly covered by skin. Nails rest on thin skin but are tucked beneath finer skin along their sides. The half-moon mark, or lunula, on the base of the nail is the limit of firm body attachment to nail roots. In humans, nails grow at a fairly regular rate of half a millimetre (0.02 inch) a day. Claws are used for grooming and scratching as well as the retention of prey.

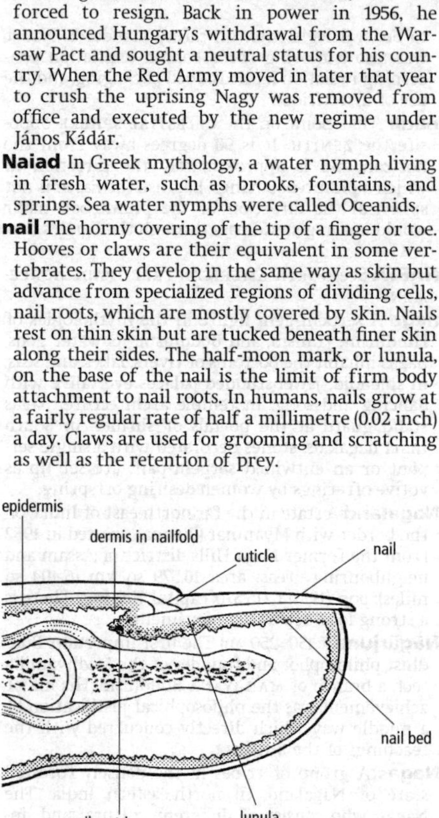

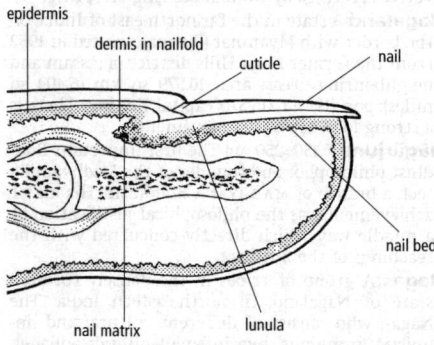

Nail Section through a fingertip and nail. As the nail grows, it slides forward over the nail bed.

Naipaul, Sir V(idiadhar) S(urajprasad) (1932–) Trinidadian novelist and travel writer of Indian descent, resident in Britain since 1950. He is best known for his satirical novels, mostly set in Trinidad, such as *A House for Mr Biswas* (1961). Naipaul's *In a Free State* (1971) won the Booker Prize for its sharp analysis of issues of nationality and identity. His travel books include *An Area of Darkness* (1964), about a visit to India.

Nairnshire (or **Nairn**) A former county of north-east Scotland, on the Moray Firth. From 1975 to 1996 it was a district of Highland Region with an administrative centre in the town of Nairn which lies at the mouth of the River Nairn.

Nairobi The capital of Kenya, situated at an altitude of *c*.1,680 m (5,500 ft) on the central Kenya plateau; pop. (est. 1989) 1,346,000. Originally a railhead camp on the Ugandan Railway in the 1890s it has been capital since 1905. It is now Kenya's administrative, communications, and economic centre with many light industries and tourist facilities.

naïve art Painting (and to a much lesser degree sculpture) produced in sophisticated modern societies but lacking conventional representational skills. Colours are characteristically bright and non-naturalistic, perspective non-scientific, and the vision childlike. Interest in the freshness and directness of vision of outstanding naïve artists, such as Henri ROUSSEAU developed in France in the early years of the 20th century, and since then many other naïve artists, for example Grandma MOSES in the USA, have won critical recognition.

Najaf (or **An Najaf**) A city in southern Iraq, on the Euphrates, 144 km south of Baghdad; pop. (est. 1985) 242,600. It contains the shrine of Ali, the prophet Muhammad's son-in-law, and is a holy city of the Shiite Muslims.

Nakhichevan A predominantly Muslim autonomous republic within Azerbaijan, situated on the borders of Turkey and northern Iran and separated from Azerbaijan by a narrow strip of Armenia; area 5,500 sq km (2,120 sq miles); pop. (1990) 300,400. Persian from the 13th to the 19th centuries, it became part of Russia in 1828 and an autonomous republic of the Soviet Union in 1924. In 1990 it was the first Soviet territory to declare unilateral independence since the 1917 revolution, and along with Nagorno-Karabakh it was subsequently the focal point of conflict between Armenia and Azerbaijan.

Nakir and Munkar In Islamic belief, the two angels who interrogate newly buried corpses about the Prophet Muhammad. Those who answer correctly are said to receive air from Paradise, while incorrect responses are met with beatings and ever-increasing pressure by the angels on the grave of the corpse.

Namib Desert A desert of south-west Africa. It extends for 1,900 km (1,200 miles) along the Atlantic coast, from the Curoca River in south-west Angola through Namibia to the border between Namibia and South Africa. Alluvial diamonds of high quality are mined in the southern area.

Namibia (formerly **South-West Africa**) A country in southern Africa with borders on Angola in the north, Botswana in the east, and South Africa in the south.

Physical. In the north-east of Namibia a long sliver of territory, the Caprivi Strip, reaches between Angola and Botswana to Zambia. In the west the Namib Desert stretches down the Atlantic Ocean coast; in the east is the Kalahari. The higher land between is also hot and arid and has no permanent rivers.

Economy. Poor rainfall limits agriculture to livestock-raising, although fishing, millet, maize, and wheat are also important. Exports are dominated by uranium and diamonds. Diamonds are found near the Orange River in the extreme south. There are also deposits of tungsten, vanadium, tin, copper, and lead. There is a shortage of skilled labour, and manufacturing industry is limited. The economy has not recovered from the devastation of the war for independence, and is still highly dependent on South Africa and multi-national companies.

History. Namibia was occupied by Khoikhoin (Hottentot), San (Bushman), and Herero peoples when Portuguese navigators explored the coastal areas of the country in the late 15th century. German missionaries went there in the 19th century and in 1884 the German protectorate of South-West Africa was established. In 1915, during World War I, it was captured by South African forces, and in 1920 became a LEAGUE OF NATIONS mandated territory under South Africa. In 1946 the UNITED NATIONS refused to allow it to be incorporated into South Africa and ended the mandate (1964), renaming the territory Namibia. In 1971 the International Court of Justice at The Hague ruled that the continued occupation of Namibia by South Africa was illegal and the UN recognized the black nationalist group, SWAPO (South West Africa People's Organization), as the legitimate representative of the people of Namibia. A National Assembly for internal government was established by South Africa in 1979 but SWAPO guerrillas continued to operate from Angola, which South African troops invaded. In 1988 South Africa was persuaded by the UN to negotiate with the SWAPO leader Samuel Nujoma. A Geneva protocol was signed in August and SWAPO won elections in November 1989, with Nujoma becoming President. Namibia gained independence as a multi-party democracy in 1990. Walvis Bay, a major port, remained an enclave of South Africa until 1994, when it was returned to Namibia. Nujoma was re-elected President in 1994.

Capital: Windhoek
Area: 824,292 sq km (317,818 sq mi)
Population: 1,651,000 (1995)
Currency: 1 South African rand = 100 cents
Religions: Lutheran 51.2%; Roman Catholic 19.8%; Dutch Reformed 6.1%; Anglican 5.0%
Ethnic Groups: Ovambo 49.8%; Kavango 9.3%; Herero 7.5%; Damara 7.5%; White 6.4%; Nama 4.8%
Languages: Afrikaans; English; German (official); Ambo; Herero; local languages
International Organizations: Commonwealth; UN; OAS; SADC

Namur (Flemish **Namen**) ▶**1** A province in central Belgium; area 3,666 sq km (1,416 sq miles); pop. (1991) 423,320. ▶**2** The capital of this province, at the junction of the Meuse and Sambre rivers; pop. (1991) 103,440. Its strategic position has made it the site of many battles and sieges, especially in World Wars I and II.

Nanak (known as **Guru Nanak**) (1469–1539) Indian religious leader and founder of Sikhism. He was born into a Hindu family in a village near Lahore. Many Sikhs believe that he was in a state of enlightenment at birth and that he was destined from then to be God's messenger. He learned about both Hinduism and Islam as a child, and at the age of 30 he underwent a religious experience which prompted him to become a wandering preacher. He eventually settled in Kartarpur, in what is now Punjab province, Pakistan; there he built the first Sikh temple. Nanak sought neither to unite the Hindu and Muslim faiths nor to create a new religion, preaching rather that spiritual liberation could be achieved through practising an inward and disciplined meditation on the name of God. His teachings are contained in a number of hymns which form part of the principal sacred scripture of Sikhism, the Adi Granth.

Nanchang The capital of Jiangxi province in south-east China; pop. (1990) 2,471,000. Dating from the 12th century, it is a major centre of industry (aircraft and diesel trucks) and transportation. In 1927 the first Communist uprising against the Kuomintang government took place here.

Nancy The capital of Meurthe-et-Moselle department in the Lorraine region of north-east France, situated on the Meurthe River; pop. (1990) 102,410. It was the seat of the dukes of Lorraine who are buried in the 15th-century Eglise des Cordeliers, and is the administrative, economic, and cultural centre of Lorraine. Industries are based on the Lorraine iron fields and include foundry products and boilers. It is an elegant city with a large university (1970) and academy.

Nanjing (formerly **Nanking**) A city of eastern China, on the Yangtze River, that has served at times as the country's capital and is now the capital of Jiangsu province; pop. (1990) 3,682,000. The 1842 Treaty of Nanking ended the first OPIUM WAR between Britain and China. It gave its name to a type of yellowish cotton cloth known as *nankeen*, and has a notable college of traditional Chinese medicine. It has an integrated iron and steel works, an oil refinery, and many light industries.

Nansei Islands See RYUKYU ISLANDS.

Nansen, Fridtjof (1861–1930) Norwegian Arctic explorer. In 1888 he led the first expedition to cross the Greenland icefields. Five years later he sailed north of Siberia on board the *Fram*, intending to reach the North Pole by allowing the ship to become frozen in the ice and letting the current carry it towards Greenland. By 1895, it had drifted as far north as 84° 4′; Nansen then made for the Pole on foot, reaching a latitude of 86° 14′, the furthest north anyone had been at that time. Nansen became increasingly involved in affairs of state, serving as Norwegian minister in London (1906–08). In 1922 he was awarded the Nobel Peace Prize for organizing relief work among victims of the Russian famine.

Nantes A city and port in western France, capital of the department of Loire-Atlantique in the Pays de la Loire region; pop. (1990) 252,030. Situated at the mouth of the Loire, it was once the leading port of France. It was the scene in 1598 of the signing of the **Edict of Nantes** by Henry IV of France granting toleration to Protestants, revoked by Louis XIV in 1685. It has numerous light industries.

Nantucket An island off the south-east coast of the US state of Massachusetts, south of Cape Cod from which it is separated by the **Nantucket Sound**. First visited by the English in 1602, the town was settled by the Quakers in 1659. It became an important whaling centre in the 18th and 19th centuries; area 122 sq km (47 sq miles).

napalm (*na*phthalene *palm*itate) A thickening agent made from vegetable oils and acids and aluminium. A mixture used in incendiary bombs, comprising thickening agent and PETROL is also called napalm. Napalm was developed in 1942 at the request of the US Army. It is mixed with a flammable jelly which, when ignited, becomes a viscous liquid. It is used in FLAME-THROWERS, or as an incendiary weapon dropped from aircraft in canisters.

naphtha See PETROLEUM REFINING.

naphthalene ($C_{10}H_8$) An AROMATIC hydrocarbon that occurs in coal tar whose structure consists of two fused BENZENE RINGS. It is a white crystalline solid, which burns with a smoky flame. It undergoes reactions more readily than benzene and is employed in the manufacture of phthalic anhydride, $C_8H_4O_3$, used in the production of plasticizers, synthetic resins, and polyesters; other derivatives are used for dyes, drugs, and insecticides.

Napier, John (1550–1617) Scottish mathematician. Napier was the inventor (independently of the German mathematician Joost Bürgi, 1552–1632) of logarithms. His tables, modified and republished by Henry Briggs, had an immediate and lasting influence on mathematics.

Naples (Italian **Napoli**) A city and port on the west coast of Italy, south of Rome; pop. (1990) 1,206,000. Formerly the capital of the Kingdom of Naples and Sicily (1806–60), it is now capital of the province of Naples and the Campania region. A treasure-house of historic buildings and works of art, it is a tourist centre but it also contains the worst slums in Europe. Industrial areas devoted to steel, chemicals, clothing, leather, and foodstuffs encircle the city.

Napoleon Three rulers of France. **Napoleon I** (known as Napoleon; full name Napoleon Bonaparte) (1769–1821) was emperor 1804–14 and 1815. Born in Corsica, he was appointed general of the French Army in Italy in 1796, where he led successful campaigns against Sardinia and Austria to establish a French-controlled republic in northern Italy. Thwarted in his attempt (1798) to create a French empire overseas by Nelson, who defeated the French fleet at the Battle of Aboukir Bay, Napoleon returned to France (1799) and joined a conspiracy which overthrew the Directory. As First Consul he became the supreme ruler of France and over the next four years began his reorganization of the French legal and education systems. He declared himself emperor in 1804, embarking on a series of campaigns known as the NAPOLEONIC WARS. Forced into exile in 1814 (to the island of Elba), he returned briefly to power a year later, but, after his defeat at Waterloo (1815), he was once again exiled, this time to the island of St Helena. **Napoleon II** (full name Napoleon François Charles Joseph Bonaparte) (1811–32) was the son of Napoleon I and Empress Marie-Louise. In 1814 Napoleon I abdicated on behalf of himself and Napoleon II. The Empress took Napoleon II to the court of her father, Austrian emperor Francis I. In 1818 the title Herzog von (duke of) Reichstadt was conferred on Napoleon, but he was given no active political role. **Napoleon III** (full name Charles Louis Napoleon Bonaparte; known as Louis-Napoleon) (1808–73) was emperor 1852–70. A nephew of Napoleon I, Napoleon III came to power after the 1848 revolution, when he was elected President of the Second Republic. In late 1851 he staged a coup, dissolving the Legislative Assembly and establishing a new constitution which was approved by plebiscite, after which the empire was restored and he was confirmed emperor. As emperor, he was noted for his aggressive foreign policy, which included intervention in Mexico, participation in the Crimean War, and war against Austria in Italy. He abdicated in 1870 after the defeat at Sedan in the Franco-Prussian War.

Napoleonic Wars The campaigns carried out between NAPOLEON I and the European powers, including Britain (1796–1815). The first great Italian campaign (1796) under Napoleon secured a series of decisive victories for the French over the Austrians in northern Italy. In 1798 he led an expedition to Egypt, but the British fleet under Admiral NELSON destroyed the French fleet in Aboukir Bay. In 1799 he led an army over the Alps to win the Battle of Marengo (1800) over the Austrians. Britain, apprehensive of Napoleon's threat in the Mediterranean and in continental Europe, was by 1803 once more at war with France. Nelson destroyed the combined Spanish and French fleets at TRAFALGAR (1805), and in the same year Napoleon swung his *grande armée* towards Austria, which, with Russia and Sweden, joined Britain in the Third Coalition. Napoleon's forces encircled the Austrians at Ulm, forcing them to surrender without a battle. Napoleon fought and defeated the emperors of Austria and Russia at the Battle of AUSTERLITZ (1805) and forced Austria to sue for peace. In the following year Prussia joined the Third Coalition but, in a campaign that lasted 23 days, Napoleon broke the Prussian armies at JENA and Auerstädt and accepted the surrender of Prussia. The Russian emperor ALEXANDER I concluded a treaty of friendship and alliance with Napoleon at Tilsit in July 1807. In 1808 a revolt broke out in Spain, which by now was also under French rule. Napoleon sent a large force to quell it, but was confronted by the British army under Sir Arthur Wellesley, later Duke of WELLINGTON. Britain won a series of victories in the PENINSULAR WAR which, though not conclusive, tied up 300,000 French soldiers when they were needed elsewhere. In 1812 Napoleon defeated the Russians at BORODINO and occupied Moscow, but instead of suing for peace, Alexander's forces withdrew further into the country. Napoleon's *grande armée* was forced to retreat from Moscow in the severest winter conditions, which cost the lives of nearly half a million men. After a crushing defeat at LEIPZIG the following year, Napoleon abdicated and retired to Elba (1814). Next year he returned to France and was finally defeated by Wellington and Blücher at the Battle of WATERLOO (1815).

Nara An ancient cultural and religious city on Honshu Island, central Japan, capital of Nara prefecture; pop. (1990) 349,360. It was the first imperial capital of Japan (710–94) and an important centre of Japanese Buddhism. The East Great Temple (Todai-ji), which houses a bronze statue of the Buddha (the largest in Japan), is said to be one of the largest wooden buildings in the world; the 7th-century Temple of Horyu complex, some of the oldest in Japan, is reputed to include the oldest wooden buildings in the world.

Narayan, R(asipuram) K(rishnaswamy) (1906–) Indian novelist and short-story writer. His best-known novels are set in the imaginary small Indian town of Malgudi, and portray its inhabitants in an affectionate yet ironic manner; they include *Swami and Friends* (1935) *The Man-Eater of Malgudi* (1961), and *The Painter of Signs* (1977). His short stories include *Under the Banyan Tree and Other Stories* (1985).

Narayanganj A river port in south-east Bangladesh, on the Lakhya and Dhaleshwari rivers 24 km east of Dhaka (Dacca); pop. (1991) 406,000. Its chief industry is the production of jute.

Narbonne A city in southern France, in Languedoc-Roussillon; pop. (1990) 47,090. It was founded by the Romans in 118 BC, the first Roman colony in Transalpine Gaul. Known as Narbo Martius, it became the capital of the Roman province of Gallia Narbonensis. It was a prosperous port of medieval France until its harbour silted up in the early 14th century. Landmarks include a Roman bridge and amphitheatre and the 13th–14th-century cathedral of St Just.

narcissus Any of the varieties of bulbous plants of the genus *Narcissus* in which the petals are united to form a small cup, as opposed to the trumpet shape of daffodils. The flowers may be borne singly on the flower stem or in clusters. Hundreds of garden varieties have been produced, in which the size and colour of the cup vary considerably.

Narcissus In Greek mythology, a beautiful youth who spurned the love of the nymph Echo and in punishment was made to fall in love with his own reflection; he pined away gazing at himself in a pool and at his death was changed into the flower bearing his name NARCISSUS.

narcotic A drug that induces drowsiness, stupor, or insensibility. Narcotics include the OPIOIDS, i.e. derivatives of opium (such as morphine) and synthesized compounds with morphine-like properties. They are powerful ANALGESICS, used in medicine. A narcotic in the legal sense is any illegal addictive drug that causes euphoria and leads to dependence, including cocaine and cannabis.

narrowboat See BARGE; CANAL.

Narvik An ice-free port on the north-west coast of Norway opposite the Lofoten Islands; pop. (1990) 18,640. It lies north of the Arctic Circle and is linked by rail to the iron-ore mines of northern Sweden.

narwhal A species of TOOTHED WHALE, *Monodon monocerus*, that lives almost exclusively in Arctic and North Atlantic waters. The bull is unmistakable because of the very long, spirally fluted tusk, in the upper jaw. The narwhal itself may be as much as 6 m (20 feet) long and its tusk may project a further 2.7 m (8.8 feet). It does not appear to use its tusk as a weapon, although it may serve in battles for possession of females. It is greyish in colour with darker mottling along the sides and back, and it feeds on fishes, squids, and crustacea.

NASA (National Aeronautics and Space Administration) A civilian agency formed in 1958 to coordinate and direct the whole of aeronautical and space research in the USA. Its headquarters are in Washington, DC. As well as collaborating with industry and universities, NASA also maintains and develops its own installations. Among the latter are the Ames Research Center, California; the Goddard Space Flight Center, near Washington, DC; the Houston Manned Space Flight Center, and the Jet Propulsion Laboratories.

Naseby A village in Northamptonshire, scene of the last major battle (1645) of the main phase of the English Civil War, in which the last Royalist army in England, commanded by Prince Rupert and the King himself, was comprehensively defeated by the larger and better organized New Model Army under Fairfax and Oliver Cromwell. Following the destruction of his army Charles I's cause collapsed completely; the monarchy was never so powerful again.

Nash, John (1752–1835) British town planner and architect. Under the patronage of the Prince Regent (later George IV), he planned the layout of Regent's Park (1811–25), Regent Street (1826–*c.*1835; subsequently rebuilt), Trafalgar Square (1826–*c.*1835), and many other parts of London. The Nash terraces in Regent's Park and Carlton House Terrace in Green Park are among his best works. He also began the reconstruction of Buckingham Palace (*c.*1821–30), for which he designed the Marble Arch, again for George IV. In Brighton he redesigned the Royal Pavilion in an oriental style for the king.

Nash, (Frederic) Ogden (1902–71) US poet. He is noted for his sophisticated light verse, comprising puns, epigrams, highly asymmetrical lines, and other verbal eccentricities. His verse appeared in many collections from 1931 onwards.

Nash, Paul (1889–1946) British painter and designer. He won renown for his paintings as an official war artist in World War I; these recorded scenes of devastation in a modernist style. From 1928 the influence of surrealism resulted in a number of enigmatic pictures based on dreams or suggestive landscape motifs, as in *Equivalents for the Megaliths* (1935). A war artist again in World War II, he depicted the aftermath of the Battle of Britain, notably in *Totes Meer* (1940–41).

Nash, Richard (known as **Beau Nash**) (1674–1762) Welsh dandy. Master of Ceremonies in Bath from 1704, he established the city as the centre of fashionable society and was an arbiter of fashion and etiquette in the early Georgian age.

Nashe, Thomas (1567–1601) English pamphleteer, prose writer, and dramatist. After writing several anti-Puritan pamphlets, he wrote his best-known work *The Unfortunate Traveller* (1594), a medley of picaresque narrative and pseudo-historical fantasy.

Nashville The state capital of Tennessee, USA, a port on the Cumberland River; pop. (1990) 510,780 (with Davidson). First settled in 1779 and known as Fort Nasborough, its name was changed to Nashville nearly 50 years later. The Grand Ole Opry House is the world's largest broadcasting studio.

Nasmyth, James (1808–90) British engineer. He designed and built a number of steam-driven machines, and went on to manufacture railway locomotives. He is best known, however, for his invention of the steam hammer (1839), a major innovation for the forging industry. Nasmyth also became interested in astronomy, particularly the Moon, producing a map of it in 1851 and a book 23 years later.

Nassau The capital of the Bahamas in the West Indies, a port on the island of New Providence; pop. (1990) 172,000. Once frequented by pirates, it is now a popular winter tourist resort and banking centre. Many international companies have registered offices in Nassau.

Nasser, Gamal Abdel (1918–70) Egyptian colonel and statesman, Prime Minister 1954–56 and President 1956–70. He was the leader of a successful military coup to depose King Farouk in 1952, after which a republic was declared with Muhammad Neguib (1901–84) as its President. Nasser deposed Neguib in 1954, declaring himself Prime Minister; two years later he announced a new one-party constitution, becoming President shortly afterwards. His nationalization of the Suez Canal brought armed conflict with Britain, France, and Israel in 1956; he also led Egypt in two unsuccessful wars against Israel (1956 and 1967). With considerable Soviet aid he launched a programme of domestic modernization, including the building of the High Dam at Aswan. The lake created in 1960 after the building of the Aswan Dam is called **Lake Nasser**. It is 500 km (300 miles) long.

nasturtium A variety of the plant species *Tropaeolum majus*, an annual climbing plant with rounded leaves and large orange flowers, found wild in Peru. Together with perennial species, such as canary creepers, *T. peregrinum*, they form the family Tropaeolaceae, containing about 90 species from the mountainous parts of South and Central America. Nasturtiums are very popular summer-flowering garden plants. The young leaves were at one time used in salads and the green fruits may be used as a substitute for capers. They are not to be confused with the genus *Nasturtium*, which includes watercress, from the mustard family.

Natal A former province (until 1994) of the Republic of South Africa, between the Indian Ocean and the Drakensberg Mountains; area 91,355 sq km (35,286 sq miles); pop. (1991) 2,074,150; capital, Pietermaritzburg. It was first settled by British traders in 1823, then by Boers, becoming a Boer republic in 1893. Annexed by the British to Cape Colony in 1845, it became a separate colony in 1856 and acquired internal self-government in 1893. It became a province of the Union of South Africa in 1910. In 1994 the province became part of the new region of KwaZulu-Natal.

Natchez A North American Indian tribe of the Hokan-Natchez linguistic group, originally living in the lower Mississippi valley.

Nathan The Hebrew prophet who condemned King David's seduction of Bathsheba, likening it to the theft of the poor man's sole ewe lamb. Nathan's advice ensured that Solomon, son of David and Bathsheba, rather than Adonijah, succeeded to the kingdom on David's death.

National Academy of Sciences (NAS) A US institution founded in 1863, under Congressional charter, as a non-governmental organization to advance science and its applications, and to advise the government on scientific matters. In 1916 it created the National Research Council to effect a wider representation of scientists and engineers in its affairs. The NAS is currently divided into some 20 sections, covering the principal physical and biological sciences, as well as social, economic, and political sciences. In 1964 a parallel National Academy of Engineering was created under its charter.

national anthem A hymn, song, or march authorized by government as the official expression of patriotic sentiment in words and music. The oldest national anthem is the British 'God Save the (King) Queen'. Its origins and authorship are obscure, but its popularity dates from the landing of the Young Pretender, 1745, when it was introduced in London theatres and widely taken up as an expression of loyalty to King George II.

national debt (or **public debt**) The debt of a country's government, created through borrowing by the public sector. Some of the debt is typically in marketable form (government securities) and some non-marketable (national savings deposits and certificates). It may be held by residents or non-residents of the country in question. Interest on the debt is paid principally from tax revenues. The PUBLIC SECTOR borrowing requirement (approximately equal to the budget deficit) represents the yearly addition to the national debt.

National Gallery An art gallery in London's Trafalgar Square that houses the pre-eminent collection of paintings in the UK. It was opened in 1824 in a building in Pall Mall, moving to its present premises, built by William Wilkins (1778–1839), in 1838. The Sainsbury Wing, designed by Robert Venturi, was added in 1991.

National governments The British coalition governments (1931–35). In August 1931 a financial crisis led to a split within the Labour government, nine ministers resigning rather than accepting cuts in unemployment benefits. The Liberal leader Herbert Samuel suggested that the Prime Minister, MACDONALD, create a 'government of national salvation', by inviting Conservatives and Liberals to replace them, and the first National government was formed on 24 August. An emergency budget was introduced, which increased taxes and proposed to reduce both benefits and public sector salaries. Britain abandoned the GOLD STANDARD and FREE TRADE, adopting a policy of protection. The Labour Party split, supporters of the government being regarded as traitors to socialism. In October MacDonald won a general election and formed a second National government, but its balance was now strongly towards the Conservative Party. The governments of Stanley BALDWIN (1935–37) and Neville CHAMBERLAIN (1937–40) retained the term National, but they were effectively Conservative governments.

National Health Service (NHS) See HEALTH SERVICES.

national insurance (or **social insurance**) A state insurance scheme financed by compulsory contributions from employee and employer. It seeks to provide economic protection against various risks, including sickness and unemployment. Such schemes help to fund social provision within the WELFARE STATE. Pioneered in Germany by BISMARCK, national insurance schemes were introduced in other European countries, including Britain (1911), and in New Zealand before World War I, for state assistance in sickness, accident, unemployment, and old age. In Britain as a result of the BEVERIDGE Report (1942), national insurance was extended to all adults in employment.

nationalization The policy of taking land, firms, or whole industries into public ownership and running them under government-appointed management. Since the early years of the 20th century, nationalization was a declared aim of Labour parties in developed countries, while statist policies in developing countries also favoured nationalization as a means of development and political independence. The typical nationalized industry is a public utility (such as electricity, gas, water, post, and telecommunications), partly because these may be natural MONOPOLIES and partly because these industries form part of a country's infrastructure. Many critics now claim that nationalized industries perform badly because of a lack of competition and recommend PRIVATIZATION. In the UK, most public utilities were nationalized by the Labour government after World War II and privatized in the 1980s and 1990s by the Conservatives.

national park An area of natural beauty protected from farming or industrial use by the government in order to preserve its landscapes, plants, and animals in their natural state for public enjoyment. A national park differs from a NATURE RESERVE in that the latter sets out to protect certain animals and plants (many of them endangered species) for their own sake.

The aims of national parks vary from one nation to another, the emphasis being placed on land or wildlife or both and on preserving cultural sites.

National Physical Laboratory (NPL) A UK government research centre founded in 1900 in the London suburb of Teddington to undertake work useful to industry as a whole and to standardize UNITS. It is comparable with the Max Planck Society for the Promotion of Sciences in Germany and the National Institute of Standards and Technology in the USA. The laboratory has a research staff of around 200 and comprises six divisions, handling electrical science; materials applications; mechanical and optical metrology; numerical analysis and computer science; quantum metrology; and radiation science and acoustics. The Laboratory also undertakes appropriate contract research for industry. It houses the British Calibration Service, the National Testing Laboratory Accreditation Scheme, and the National Corrosion Service.

national theatre A permanent, state-subsidized theatre. The oldest national theatre is the

Comédie-Française in Paris, founded in 1680 by Louis XIV; this was followed by five other French national theatres. The British National Theatre (first suggested by GARRICK) was founded only in 1961, and moved into its own premises on the South Bank of the Thames in 1976. The building, designed by Denys Lasdun, is a vast complex housing three theatres (the Lyttelton, the Olivier, and the Cottesloe). Its first director was Laurence OLIVIER, who was succeeded by Peter HALL in 1973. The Royal Shakespeare Company, formed in 1961, virtually ranks as a second national theatre.

National Trust, The An independent charity founded in the UK in 1895 by philanthropist Octavia Hill (1838–1912) to preserve for the nation places of historic interest or natural beauty. Acts of Parliament define its rights and duties, including the unique right to declare its holdings inalienable in perpetuity. Supported by the subscriptions of 2,000,000 members, gifts, legacies, and the required endowments of given properties, it protects and opens to the public 230 houses and gardens, 240,000 hectares of countryside, and 550 miles of coastline in England, Wales, and Northern Ireland.

NATO (or **Nato**) See NORTH ATLANTIC TREATY ORGANIZATION.

Natta, Giulio (1903–79) Italian industrial chemist. While Director of the Milan Institute of Industrial Chemistry, he initiated a programme for the production of synthetic RUBBER. As consultant to the firm Montecatini, he advised them to purchase the rights for commercial development of ZIEGLER'S low-pressure process for making POLYTHENE, from which he developed POLYPROPYLENE as an analogous new plastic. He also devised processes for polymerizing styrene and butene. He shared the Nobel Prize for chemistry with Ziegler in 1963.

natterjack The smaller and rarer of the two native British TOADS, *Bufo calamita*, which occurs throughout western and central Europe. The natterjack is usually greenish above with darker markings and a central yellow stripe (occasionally absent) on the back. Male natterjacks have a loud ratchet-like call, the sound carrying for considerable distances. They are short-limbed, and run rather than hop, leaving characteristic 'tank-tracks' in sand. They are typically found in sandy habitats, often with midwife toads.

natural gas A FOSSIL FUEL found trapped in the Earth, often in association with PETROLEUM. Natural gas was probably first noticed in prehistoric times, burning in association with petroleum seepage. It is only since World War II that use of natural gas has grown rapidly, because of the development of pipeline transport and underground storage. Also important was the development of large new natural gas fields, such as those in the North Sea, Russia, Canada, and Algeria. Natural gas is now the world's second most important fuel, after petroleum.

Natural gas is obtained by the same basic methods as petroleum (see PETROLEUM EXPLORATION). Some wells produce natural gas alone; others produce petroleum as well as natural gas. Liquid petroleum generally contains much dissolved natural gas, which separates as the petroleum reaches the surface, and can be removed in a separator at the oil well. Gas is moved from the well by pipeline to a cleaning and processing plant and on to a GAS GRID or storage facility. Since the 1960s there has been increasing success in storage and transport by tanker of LIQUEFIED NATURAL GAS.

Natural gas consists mainly of METHANE and ethane, and generally occurs with smaller proportions of PROPANE and BUTANE. 'Wet' natural gas has a significant proportion of the latter two gases, plus some heavier HYDROCARBONS, which may cause uneven burning and gumming up of pipes. 'Drying' of the gas is achieved by compression and cooling to condense out heavier hydrocarbons, or by dissolving them in an oil solvent. This process produces LIQUID PETROLEUM GAS (LPG). In addition to its importance as a heating fuel in homes and industry, natural gas is widely used in ELECTRICITY GENERATION. It is also important as a feedstock in producing hydrogen, PLASTICS, and PETROCHEMICALS.

naturalization The process of satisfying the legal conditions for acquiring a new nationality. The conditions, which vary widely between states, lay down eligibility criteria, such as period of residence, linguistic proficiency, and knowledge of the CONSTITUTION. In some countries, new nationals are permitted to retain their original nationality and thus hold dual nationality.

natural law (in philosophy) Unchanging moral principles common to all people by virtue of their nature as human beings. The existence and nature of natural law has been much discussed by theorists throughout the ages. ARISTOTLE believed that there were universal and immutable laws laid down by nature, while the medieval theologian St Thomas AQUINAS regarded natural law as the part of divine law that is discoverable through human reason. According to such theories, human laws derive their validity from natural law, and if a law conflicts with moral values, it is not fit to be regarded as a law. Later theorists developed the idea of natural rights, based on natural law. Since World War II there has been renewed interest in natural law ideas, and some contemporary theorists have stressed the essential relationship between legal and moral values. Most people today would regard the HUMAN RIGHTS elucidated in the Universal Declaration of Human Rights as natural rights.

natural selection The process of differential survival and reproduction that enables EVOLUTION to take place. The concept was invented by DARWIN, and is the accepted explanation both of evolution and of the fact that organisms are well adapted for living in their natural surroundings.

The argument is that organisms produce more offspring than can survive. Thus, there will be competition for survival. Only those organisms that are well designed for survival will live to reproduce. If the characteristics that enabled them to survive are inherited, then the organisms of the next generation will resemble the successful members of the previous generation. Thus, the organisms best fitted for survival are selected by nature for reproduction. As environments change, so also do the factors that make one individual better 'fitted' than another to reproduce. The constant selection, or survival of the 'fittest', is the force that drives evolution.

Natural selection has been confirmed by observation, and studied by experiment. In a population of peppered moths, *Biston betularia*, for example, of which some were better camouflaged than others, birds have been seen to eat more of the poorly camouflaged type. This results in evolution towards an increase in the proportion of better-camouflaged moths. The agent of natural selection, in this example, is visual hunting by birds. Even a very slight advantage of one individual over another is sufficient to cause changes in the population.

nature reserve A natural area that may be managed to maintain its original state or to avoid a SUCCESSION. They are usually set up to protect a particular type of habitat, such as heathland, and the species normally inhabiting the area. Commercial gain is usually unimportant. Visiting may be restricted. A warden is often present to ensure minimum disturbance.

Nauru A tiny island country just south of the Equator in the south-west Pacific Ocean, between longitudes 166° and 167° E.

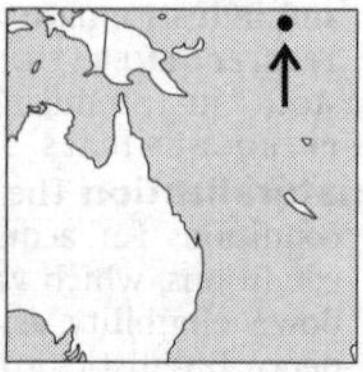

Physical. Nauru is a coral island, with a band of fertile land around the coast rising to a central plateau.

Economy. Nauru's wealth lies in phosphate deposits derived from guano, the excrement of seabirds, which is used as manure. The supply of phosphates is almost exhausted and money has been invested abroad to provide an alternative source of revenue in the future.

History. Nauru was settled by various Polynesian peoples who travelled there from other islands before being discovered by the British in 1798. In 1899 a British company, the Pacific Islands Company based in Sydney, found that the island comprised the world's richest deposits of phosphate of lime. The company began mining the deposits in 1906. From 1888 to 1914 the island was part of Germany's Marshall Islands protectorate. Thereafter, apart from three years of Japanese occupation during World War II, Nauru was a trust territory of Britain, Australia, and New Zealand, before achieving independence and a limited membership of the Commonwealth in 1968. In 1993 Australia, Britain, and New Zealand agreed to pay compensation for the damage done to the island by the extensive mining of phosphates.

Capital: Yaren (de facto: there is no official capital)
Area: 21 sq km (8.2 sq mi)
Population: 10,000 (1995)
Currency: 1 Australian dollar = 100 cents
Religions: Nauruan Protestant Church 43%
Ethnic Groups: Nauruan 61%; other Pacific islanders 27%; Asian 9%; European 3%
Languages: Nauruan; English
International Organizations: Commonwealth; South Pacific Forum

Nautical Almanac See ROYAL GREENWICH OBSERVATORY.

nautical mile An international unit of distance used in navigation, equal to one minute of arc on a great circle or 1,852 m (6,080 feet).

nautilus (in zoology) See PAPER NAUTILUS; PEARLY NAUTILUS.

Navajo (or **Navaho**) A North American Indian people belonging to the Athapaskan linguistic group and native to New Mexico and Arizona. Their name is derived from a Spanish word for 'people with big fields' and their reservation is the largest in the USA. They number 220,000 (1990) and are the largest American Indian tribe.

Navan The county town of Meath in the Republic of Ireland, situated at the junction of the Boyne and Blackwater rivers; pop. (1991) 3,410. It is one of Ireland's leading centres for the manufacture of furniture.

Navarino Bay A bay off Pylos in the Peloponnese of southern Greece, scene of a decisive naval battle in the struggle for Greek independence from the Ottoman empire fought in 1827. Britain, Russia, and France sent a combined fleet, which destroyed the Egyptian and Turkish fleet in the last great battle fought by wooden sailing ships.

Navarre A former Franco-Spanish kingdom in the Pyrenees, Navarre achieved independence in the 10th century under Sancho III, but during the Middle Ages fell at various times under French or Spanish domination. The southern part of the country was conquered by Ferdinand V in 1512, while the northern part passed to France in 1589 through inheritance by Henry IV.

navel (or **umbilicus**) The scar formed in mammals soon after birth by healing at the site of severence of the umbilical cord. In the womb this carries blood between the floating foetus and the PLACENTA.

navigation The planning and directing of a vehicle or person along a set course or route, avoiding collision. For much of history navigation has been a skill used predominantly at sea, but in the 20th century air and space navigation have become important. Navigational aids are also sometimes used on land. Early navigation was concerned almost exclusively with course-finding: most early seafarers followed coastlines, and avoided the open sea. The Phoenicians and the Polynesians were among the earliest ancient peoples to use celestial bodies to navigate, to a limited extent, out of sight of land. There was a gradual development of instruments, which made navigation at sea progressively more accurate. These were the MAGNETIC COMPASS for direction finding; the ASTROLABE, CROSS-STAFF, and SEXTANT for celestial navigation; the ship's LOG for speed measurement; the lead line for depth measurement, and the CHRONOMETER for the determination of longitude.

Since the advent of aviation in the early 20th century, other devices, such as the GYROCOMPASS, RADAR, SONAR, INERTIAL NAVIGATION, NAVIGATION SATELLITES, and radio aids to navigation have made it possible to monitor a vehicle's position continuously. The increasing density of air and sea traffic has made continuous monitoring essential in order to avoid collisions: most civilian aircraft, for example, must now follow strict flight plans that specify course, speed, and cruising heights. Many navigational functions have been automated, with on-board computers monitoring position and course.

navigation satellite A radio aid to navigation using artificial SATELLITES orbiting the Earth. Such satellites are used by ships, aircraft, missiles, or land vehicles (especially military vehicles) to find their position, height, and speed. The first practical system in operation was developed by the US Navy and known as Transit. It became available for commercial use in 1967. A more sophisticated US system is the Navstar Global Positioning System (GPS). The GPS satellites carry atomic CLOCKS and daily transmit their position and time to ground stations. The Soviet Union had its own system, and there are also commercial systems that operate using existing COMMUNICATIONS SATELLITES. The GPS has 18 satellites in uniformly spaced geostationary orbits above the Earth. It can give continuous positions accurate to about 20 m (70 feet), heights accurate to about 30 m (100 feet), and speeds accurate to about 0.1 m/s. Commercial navigational receivers that use signals from GPS are now being used to make small navigational devices (about the size of a playing card) accurate to within 100 m (330 feet).

Navratilova, Martina (1956–) Czech-born US tennis player. Her major successes include nine Wimbledon singles titles (1978–79; 1982–87; 1990) and eight successive grand slam doubles titles. She retired in 1994.

navy A fleet of ships and its crew, organized for war at sea. In the 5th and 4th centuries Athens and Corinth relied on TRIREMES (galleys with three banks of oars) and high-speed manoeuvrable quinqueremes (five-banked galleys) were developed by the Macedonians. At the Battle of SALAMIS an Athenian fleet won a decisive victory over the Persians, established Greek control over the eastern Mediterranean, and the fleet remained the crucial basis of Athenian supremacy. The Roman empire, though essentially a land-based power, fought Carthage at sea in the First PUNIC WAR, and gained control of the Mediterranean.

Navies were needed to protect trading vessels against pirates: the BYZANTINE EMPIRE maintained a defensive fleet to retain control over its vital trade arteries. In England, King ALFRED created a fleet in the 9th century in defence against Scandinavian invasions. The CINQUE PORTS supplied the English navy from the 11th to the 16th centuries and it was organized and enlarged under successive Tudor monarchs. The Italian city-states kept squadrons of galleys and adapted carracks (merchant ships) to defend their ports against the Ottoman Turks and the Battle of LEPANTO saw a Christian fleet decisively beat the Ottomans. The 17th century saw naval reorganization in England under PEPYS, and the Dutch and French also expanded their fleets as trade and colonial expansion accelerated in the 18th century.

From the early Middle Ages the warship altered from being a converted merchant ship, modified by the addition of 'castles', fortified with land artillery, and manned by knights, into a specially armed vessel. By the 14th century ships were being fitted with guns and by the 16th century special warships were being built with heavy armaments. Success or failure in battle, however, was determined by tactical skill as all sailing ships were at the mercy of the wind.

At the time of the NAPOLEONIC WARS, naval vessels were sailing ships, built of wood and armed with cannon that fired broadsides. They engaged at close quarters and ratings were armed with muskets and hand-grenades. Following the Battle of TRAFALGAR (1805), the British navy dominated the oceans of the world for a century. Change came slowly. Steam power replaced sail only gradually, while in 1859 the French navy pioneered the protection of the wooden hull of a ship with iron plates (IRONCLADS). With the development of the iron and steel industry in the late 19th century, rapid advances were made in ship design and the armament of ships. At the same time the submarine, armed with torpedoes, emerged as a fighting vessel. When Germany challenged the supremacy of the British navy, the latter responded with the huge steel DREADNOUGHT battleships (1906), equipped with guns with a range of over 32 km (20 miles). During World War I the German submarine (U-boat) fleet was only checked by the CONVOY SYSTEM to protect Allied merchant shipping, but the major British and German fleets only engaged in the inconclusive Battle of JUTLAND (1916). Between the wars aircraft were rapidly developed and naval warfare in World War II was increasingly fought by aircraft from aircraft carriers, particularly in the great naval battles of the Pacific Campaign. Since World War II, the development of submarines armed with long-range nuclear missiles has reduced the number of surface ships and revolutionized naval strategy as submarines are difficult to detect and destroy. Most countries retain fleets of small, fast vessels for coastal patrol. The USA and the former Soviet Union, however, competed in the size and armament of their navies. The FALKLANDS WAR (1982) revealed the extent to which there remained a place for a conventional navy, but also showed how exposed surface ships were to missile attack. During the GULF WAR the navies of the Allied forces played an important strategic role. Six aircraft carriers provided launch sites from which air strikes against Iraqi ground targets were made.

Naxalite Movement An Indian revolutionary movement named after the village of Naxalbari in the Himalayan foothills in West Bengal, where it first began. The theoretician and founder of the movement, Charu Majumdar, a veteran communist, broke away from the Communist Party of India (Marxist) and established the Communist Party of India (Marxist-Leninist). The CPI (M-L) first organized several armed risings of landless agricultural labourers, especially in eastern India in 1967. It subsequently developed into an urban guerrilla movement, especially in Calcutta. Its programme of terror was suppressed with considerable violence. The CPI (M-L) eventually split up into several factions, one of which adopted a policy of participating in constitutional politics, but Naxalite atrocities continued into the early 1990s.

Naxos A Greek island in the southern Aegean, the largest of the Cyclades, famous in mythology as the island upon which Theseus abandoned Ariadne; area 428 sq km (165 sq miles). At the centre of the island is Mt Zas (Zévs), which rises to 1,004 m (3,295 ft) and is the highest peak in the Cyclades. Wine, citrus fruit, olives, figs, pomegranates, and corn are produced, and emery and marble are quarried. Its chief town is Naxos.

Nazarene A native of Nazareth in Israel. However, writers in the 4th century called Christians of Jewish race in Syria Nazarenes. They continued to obey much of the Jewish Law but were otherwise orthodox Christians using a version of the Gospel in Aramaic.

Nazarenes A group of young, idealistic German painters of the early 19th century who believed that art should serve a religious or moral purpose and desired to return to the spirit of the Middle Ages. The nucleus of the group was established in 1809 when six students at the Academy of Fine Arts in Vienna formed an association called the Brotherhood of St Luke, named after the patron saint of painting. The name Nazarenes was given to them derisively because of their affectation of biblical dress and hairstyles.

Nazareth (Hebrew **Nazerat**) A historic town in lower Galilee in present-day northern Israel; pop. (1982) 39,000. It was mentioned in the Gospels as the home of Mary and Joseph, is closely associated with the childhood of Jesus, and is a centre of Christian pilrimage.

Nazca (or **Nasca**) A culture developed on the southern Peruvian coast *c.*200 BC–600 AD, eventually eclipsed by the expansion of the Huari culture of central Peru in the 7th century. In the extremely dry environment its settlements and population remained modest, but its craftsmen produced a long sequence of pottery styles, with animal and human figures. It also produced large drawings of animals, abstract designs, and straight lines on the coastal plain, by clearing and aligning the surface stones to expose the underlying sand; their purpose is uncertain, but may have been religious.

Nazi A member of the Nationalsozialistische Deutsche Arbeiterpartei or National Socialist German Workers' Party. It was founded in 1919 as the German Workers' Party by a Munich locksmith, Anton Drexler, adopted its new name in 1920, and was taken over by HITLER in 1921. The Nazis dominated Germany from 1933 to 1945. In so far as the party had a coherent programme it consisted of opposition to democracy and a fascist belief in a one party state. It promulgated totally spurious theories of the purity of the Aryan race and consequent ANTI-SEMITISM, allied itself to the old Prussian military tradition, and encouraged an extreme sense of nationalism, inflamed by hatred of the humiliating terms inflicted on Germany in the VERSAILLES PEACE SETTLEMENT. Nazi ideology, to the extent that it had one, made garbled use of the racist theories of the Comte de GOBINEAU, the national fervour of Heinrich von Treitschke, and the superman theories of Friedrich Nietzsche. It was given dogmatic expression in Hitler's *Mein Kampf* (1925). The success of the Nazis in dominating completely what had previously been regarded as a civilized country is to some extent explained by the widespread desperation of Germans over the failure of the WEIMAR REPUBLIC governments to solve economic problems and by a growing fear of BOLSHEVIK power. Through Hitler's oratory, Germans in the 1930s appeared to accept his naive, corrupt, and absurdly fallacious arguments. Only after Hitler had obtained power by constitutional means was the THIRD REICH established. Rival parties were banned, and the army, industry, and the banks supported Hitler in his insane plan to launch Germany on a war of conquest. By now virtually the whole German nation was behind him and the few that weren't were either murdered or frightened into acquiescence.

Over six million Jews, Russians, Poles, and others were incarcerated and exterminated in German CONCENTRATION CAMPS. The German Nazi Party was disbanded in 1945 after it had led Germany into a humiliating defeat, and its revival was officially forbidden by the Federal Republic of Germany.

Ndebele A BANTU-speaking Zulu people, branches of which are found in Zimbabwe (where they are better known as **Matabele**) and in the Transvaal.

N'Djamena The capital and river port of Chad, at the junction of the Chari and Logone rivers; pop. (1993) 530,965. Founded by the French in 1900, it was known as Fort Lamy until 1973. A communications and food-processing centre (groundnuts and meat chilling). There is a university and regional museum.

Neagh, Lough A shallow lake in Northern Ireland, the largest freshwater lake in the British Isles with noted fisheries; area 381.7 sq km (147.4 sq miles). It is fed by several streams, the largest of which is the River Bann.

Neanderthals A hominid race that lived in Europe, the Near East, and Central Asia from about 130,000 to 30,000 years ago. No people with characteristic ('classic') Neanderthal features are known from Africa or the Far East. They are named after the Neander valley near Düsseldorf in Germany where part of a skeleton was discovered in 1856. Neanderthals flourished particularly during the last Ice Age and were adapted for living in cold environments. Called *Homo neanderthalensis*, their features included heavy bones, strong musculature, large brow ridges across a sloping forehead, and larger brains than those of fully modern people. Neanderthals were probably the first people to have burial rites. Flint tools of MOUSTERIAN type are usually found with their remains and characterize the Middle PALAEOLITHIC period.

The part played by Neanderthals in later human evolution is controversial. The most widely held view is that none were our direct ancestors. A study of DNA undertaken in 1996 indicated that the Neanderthals were a separate species and neither evolved into modern humans nor interbred with other early humans but became extinct. An alternative opinion is that at least some interbreeding between Neanderthals and modern humans took place. See also HOMO SAPIENS.

neap tides The weak TIDES that occur twice a month, during the first and third quarters of the Moon's phases, when the influences of the Sun and Moon on the movement of the oceans counteract each other. High tides are lower, and low tides higher, than at other times in the lunar month.

Nebraska A state in the central USA to the west of the Missouri River; area 200,350 sq km (77,355 sq miles); pop. (1990) 1,578,385; capital, Lincoln. The largest cities are Omaha and Lincoln. Nebraska is also known as the Cornhusker, Beef, or Tree Planter State. Acquired as part of the Louisiana Purchase in 1803, it became the 37th state of the USA in 1867. It is a leading producer of grain, cattle, and pigs and has oil and natural gas resources. Its chief landmarks are Scotts Bluff National Monument, Agate Fossil Beds National Monument, Chimney Rock National Historic Site, and the Homestead National Monument of America.

Nebuchadnezzar (*c.*630–562 BC) King of Babylon 605–562 BC. He rebuilt the city with massive fortification walls, a huge temple, and a ziggurat, and extended his rule over ancient Palestine and neighbouring countries. In 586 BC he captured and destroyed Jerusalem and deported many Israelites from Palestine to Babylon (the Babylonian Captivity, which lasted until 539 BC).

nebula An extended patch of hazy light or darkness in a fixed position with respect to the stellar background. Nebulae are usually classified as diffuse (condensations of gas and dust), planetary, or supernova remnants. **Diffuse nebulae** can be bright or dark. Bright nebulae can occur as fairly compact structured regions or they can extend in delicate filamentary wisps over several degrees of the sky. The brightness of the nebular material is due either to light reflected from it (a reflection nebula) or, if a very hot star is nearby, as in a Strömgren sphere, to direct emission of ELECTROMAGNETIC RADIATION from atoms (mainly hydrogen) ionized by the star (an **emission nebula**). The most famous example of an emission nebula is the Orion Nebula. Information regarding the gas density and its composition may be derived from the spectra of such objects. **Dark nebulae** contain thick clouds of dust and gas which obscure and absorb light from stars beyond or within them. PLANETARY NEBULAE, of which about a thousand are known, have nothing to do with planets but are hazy expanding shells of gas surrounding a central very hot star, probably ejected by the star. SUPERNOVA remnants, assumed to be material ejected from supernova explosions, are also bright emission nebulae. The most famous is the CRAB NEBULA, the result of a supernova explosion witnessed by the Chinese in 1054.

Necker, Jacques (1732–1804) Swiss-born banker. He began work as a bank clerk in Switzerland, moving to his firm's headquarters in Paris in 1750. He rose to hold the office of director-general of

French finances on two occasions. During Necker's first term (1777–81), his social and administrative reform programmes aroused the hostility of the court and led to his forced resignation. While in office for a second time (1788–89), he recommended summoning the States General, resulting in his dismissal on 11 July 1789. News of this angered the people and was one of the factors which resulted in the storming of the Bastille three days later.

nectarine A variety of peach, *Prunus persica* var. *nupersica*. These fruit-trees produce distinctive smooth-skinned fruits, which are smaller and more brightly coloured than those of the peach tree, with white or yellow flesh. The trees are less hardy than peaches and are grown in protected positions when in cooler temperate areas.

Needham, Joseph (1900–95) British scientist and historian. He studied biochemistry and published an influential *History of Embryology* (1934), but had a diverse range of interests, especially that of scientific achievement in China. He is best known for his seven-volume *Science and Civilization in China* (begun in 1954). In 1924 he was appointed fellow of Gonville and Caius College, Cambridge, and was Master there (1966–76).

needlefish See GARFISH.

Needles, the A group of rocks in the sea off the west coast of the Isle of Wight, England.

Nefertiti (14th century BC) Wife and queen of AKHENATEN, Pharaoh of Egypt. She was a devoted worshipper of the Sun god Aten, whose cult was the only one permitted by her husband. She fell from favour, and was supplanted by one of her six daughters. She is known to posterity through inscriptions, reliefs, and above all a fine limestone bust which was found at ancient Akhetaton (modern Tell el-Amarna).

Negev, the An arid region of strategic importance forming most of southern Israel, between Beersheba and the Gulf of Aqaba, on the Egyptian border. Large-scale irrigation projects have greatly increased the fertility of the region and there are many kibbutz settlements. Mineral resources include natural gas and copper.

negligence (in COMMON LAW) The breach of a duty of care owed by one person to another. Many duties of care are well established: motorist to other road-users; employer to employee; manufacturer to consumer; doctor to patient. However, the concept is flexible and allows the courts to hold that a duty of care exists between parties who stand in a sufficiently proximate relationship to one another, such as a building society surveyor and the purchaser of a house. The duty of care is breached when the defendant's failure to take reasonable care causes foreseeable damage to the plaintiff. The growth of liability INSURANCE has led to courts being increasingly ready to find breaches of reasonable care, and actions for negligence have become the major means by which accident victims receive compensation.

Negro, Rio Three rivers in South America. **▶1** A major river of northern South America that rises as the Guainia in eastern Colombia and flows about 2,255 km (1,400 miles) through north-west Brazil before joining the Amazon near Manaus. **▶2** A river of central Argentina formed in the eastern foothills of the Andes at the junction of the Neuquén and Limay rivers. It flows *c*.645 km (400 miles) eastwards through the province of Rio Negro to empty into the Atlantic near Viedma. **▶3** The principal river of Uruguay, rising in southern Brazil and flowing *c*.805 km (500 miles) south-westwards to meet the Uruguay River near Fray Bentos. It passes through the Embalse del Rio Negro, one of the largest manmade lakes in South America.

Negroids The indigenous peoples of Africa south of the Sahara and their descendants in other parts of the world. Bantu-speaking Negroid pastoralists and crop-growers are traditionally believed to have spread from western to eastern and southern Africa during the past few thousand years but recent evidence suggests that Negroids speaking other languages were in other parts of sub-Saharan Africa much earlier. They may indeed have originated in southern, not western Africa, but this is controversial. Unquestionably, though, they gained knowledge of agricultural techniques and domesticated animals from northern parts of the continent. Negroids are extremely variable in appearance but they can be seen in their most typical form in West Africa; in the east, there has been much intermixing with Hamitic-speaking CAUCASOIDS (for example, Ethiopians and Egyptians); and in the south with the related hunting and gathering San (Bushmen) and the cattle-raising Khoikhoi (Hottentots). The pygmies of Central Africa are of Negroid stock.

Nehemiah A Hebrew leader (5th century BC) who supervised the rebuilding of the walls of Jerusalem (*c*.444) and introduced moral and religious reforms (*c*.432). His work was continued by Ezra.

Nehru, Jawaharlal (known as **Pandit Nehru**) (1889–1964) Indian statesman, Prime Minister 1947–64. An early associate of Mahatma Gandhi, Nehru was elected leader of the Indian National Congress, succeeding his father Pandit Motilal Nehru (1861–1931), in 1929. Imprisoned nine times by the British for his nationalist campaigns during the 1930s and 1940s, he eventually played a major part in the negotiations preceding independence. Nehru subsequently became the first Prime Minister of independent India. He was the father of Indira Gandhi.

Neill, A(lexander) S(utherland) (1883–1973) Scottish teacher and educationist. He is best known as the founder of the progressive school Summerhill, established in Dorset in 1924 and based in Suffolk from 1927. Since its inception, the school has attracted both admiration and hostility for its anti-authoritarian ethos.

Neill, Sam (born Nigel John Dermot) (1947–) New Zealand actor. After working for the New Zealand National Film Unit for six years as a writer and director, he made his feature-film début in *Sleeping Dogs* (1977) going on to star in *The Final Conflict* (1981) and the British TV series *Reilly: The Ace of Spies* (1983). He achieved international recognition with *Jurassic Park* and *The Piano* (both 1993).

Nelson A city and port on the north coast of South Island, New Zealand, situated on an inlet at the head of Tasman Bay; pop. (1991) 47,390. It was founded in 1841 by the New Zealand company and named after the British admiral Lord Nelson.

Nelson, Horatio, Viscount Nelson, Duke of Bronte (1758–1805) British admiral. Nelson's victories at sea during the early years of the Napoleonic Wars made him a national hero. His unorthodox independent tactics (as a commodore under Admiral Jervis) led to the defeat of a Spanish fleet off Cape St Vincent in 1797. In 1798 Nelson virtually destroyed the French fleet in the Battle of Aboukir Bay; he began his notorious affair with Lady Hamilton, the wife of the British envoy to the court of Naples, shortly afterwards, while stationed in Naples. He proceeded to rout the Danes at Copenhagen in 1801, but is best known for his decisive victory over a combined French and Spanish fleet at the Battle of Trafalgar in 1805; Nelson was mortally wounded in the conflict.

Nelson, Willie (1933–) US country singer and songwriter. He built a reputation in Nashville as a prolific and successful songwriter, writing the hit 'Crazy' for Patsy Cline in 1961. After moving to CBS record albums, such as *Red Headed Stranger* (1975), established him as one of the most successful country singers in the world.

nematode See ROUNDWORM.

nemertine See RIBBON WORM.

nemesia A multicoloured variety of South African annual plant of the genus *Nemesia*, a member of the family Scrophulariaceae. There are about 50 species, some of which are low-growing perennial shrubs; others are popular garden plants of temperate regions.

Nemesis In Greek mythology, the goddess of retribution or vengeance. According to Hesiod, Nemesis was a child of Night. She was a personification of the gods' resentment at, and consequent punishment of, defiance (*hubris*) towards themselves.

Nennius (fl. *c.*800) Welsh chronicler. He is traditionally credited with the compilation or revision of the *Historia Britonum*, a collection of historical and geographical information about Britain, including one of the earliest known accounts of King Arthur.

neoclassicism The dominant artistic movement in European art and architecture in the late 18th and early 19th centuries, characterized by a desire to re-create the spirit and forms of the art of Ancient Greece and Rome. In France it permeated what are known as the LOUIS XVI style, the Régence, the DIRECTOIRE, and the EMPIRE STYLE. In Britain it was reflected in the ADAM style, HEPPLEWHITE and SHERATON in furniture, and it constituted one of the main elements of the REGENCY. The main theorists of the movement were J. J. WINCKELMANN in Germany and in France Antoine Quatremère de Quincy, whose book *An Essay on the Nature and Means of Imitation in the Fine Arts* was published in English in 1837. The pioneers in architecture were Ange-Jacques Gabriel in France, who built the Place de la Concorde in 1754 and whose Petit Trianon at Versailles was regarded as the most perfect example of 'Attic' in French architecture. SOUFFLOT, was also instrumental in introducing the new Classicism into plans for reconstructing Paris.

In painting its chief initiator was A. R. Mengs, who influenced such artists as Benjamin WEST from the USA, Gavin Hamilton from Scotland, and (through Joseph-Marie Vien) its greatest exponent, DAVID in France. Among sculptors whose work was of wide general influence were CANOVA, THORVALDSEN, Jean-Baptiste Pigalle, Jean-Antoine Houdon, and FLAXMAN. In the decorative arts neoclassicism repudiated the asymmetry of ROCOCO, substituting for it a strict axial symmetry, and relying mainly on motifs of Classical origin such as medallions, trophies, urns, tripods, and masks.

Neoclassicism in music is a style that adopts techniques, gestures, or forms from music of an earlier period. It refers particularly to early 20th-century composers who rejected the Romantic expressiveness of late 19th-century composers, and looked instead to 17th- and 18th-century works for their inspiration. The influence of STRAVINSKY's neoclassical scores was felt by many composers in Paris between the wars, among them POULENC, Martinů, HONEGGER, SZYMANOWSKI, and COPLAND. In Germany its leading proponent was HINDEMITH.

Neoclassicism in literature emerged earlier from the rediscovery of ancient critical writings (especially those of Aristotle and of HORACE) in the 16th century. As a doctrine and a system of styles it flourished in late 17th-century France, notably in the works of RACINE and BOILEAU, and in a moderated form in the English AUGUSTAN AGE.

neo-Darwinism The current theory of evolution, formulated between 1920 and 1950, that updates classical Darwinism by including modern information about genes and chromosomes that was unavailable to DARWIN. This has enabled the source of genetic variation upon which natural selection works to be explained in great detail.

neodymium (symbol Nd, at. no. 60, r.a.m. 144.24) A LANTHANIDE element that occurs in monazite and is used with other lanthanides in misch metal and lighter flints.

neo-Freudian Denoting an influential group of psychoanalytic theorists inspired by, but differing from, FREUD. Loosely, it includes JUNG, Melanie KLEIN, and Wilhelm Reich (1895–1957). Frequently, however, it is restricted to those who rejected Freud's model of human development as the manifestation of instinctual drives and their often unsatisfactory suppression through fear of retribution. In contrast, they emphasized that individuals develop through a process of integration into a social and cultural world, which may be benign rather than hostile. They also denied that early infant–parent relationships exclusively caused the healthy or unhealthy development of personality, and they did not accept Freud's doctrine of the UNCONSCIOUS MIND. The Austrian Alfred ADLER viewed people's behaviour as explicable in terms of the goals they adopt and their general attempt to develop their capacities and overcome a sense of their own imperfection and inferiority. The US psychoanalyst Harry Stack Sullivan (1892–1949) saw personality as a matter of how people relate to others throughout their lives, with adolescence a particularly important time in development.

Neogene Period The later of the two geological periods into which the TERTIARY PERIOD can be divided. (The other is the Palaeogene.) The Neogene Period comprises the MIOCENE and PLIOCENE EPOCHS.

neogothic See GOTHIC REVIVAL.

neo-Impressionism A movement in French painting that was both a development from IMPRESSIONISM and a reaction against it. Like the Impressionists, the neo-Impressionists (of whom SEURAT was the most important) were fundamentally concerned with the representation of light and colour, but whereas Impressionism was spontaneous, neo-Impressionism was based on scientific principles and resulted in highly formalized compositions. By using dots of pure colour carefully placed next to each other on the canvas (a technique called POINTILLISM) the Neo-Impressionists hoped to achieve a more luminous effect than if the same colours had been mixed together. Seurat's paintings do indeed convey a vibrating intensity of light, which he combined with a magnificent solidity and clarity of form. Neo-Impressionism, which was launched at the final Impressionist exhibition in 1886, was a short-lived movement, but it had a significant influence on several major artists of the late 19th and early 20th centuries, notably GAUGUIN, van GOGH, MATISSE, and TOULOUSE-LAUTREC.

Neolithic Of or relating to the later part of the Stone Age, when ground or polished stone weapons and implements prevailed. The Neolithic period also saw the introduction of agriculture and the domestication of animals. Sometimes called the 'Neolithic Revolution', this part of the Stone Age saw humans change from being dependent on nature to controlling it, at least partially and indirectly. The change led to the establishment of settled communities, accumulation of food and wealth, and heavier growth of population. In the Old World, agriculture began in the Near East by the 8th millennium BC and had spread to northern Europe by the 4th millennium BC.

neon (symbol Ne, at. no. 10, r.a.m. 20.18) A colourless, odourless gas; it is one of the NOBLE GASES and forms no chemical compounds. Neon is found in minute proportions in the Earth's atmosphere. It is obtained by the FRACTIONAL DISTILLATION of liquid air. It is used in GAS-DISCHARGE LAMPS, where it gives a bright orange-red glow, in gas LASERS, and as a cryogenic (very-low-temperature) refrigerant.

neoplatonists Followers of PLOTINUS (*c*.205–70) and other thinkers of the school of PLATO in the 3rd century AD. They searched for an intellectually 'respectable' basis for the act of reasonable religious belief. God, described as the 'One' or 'Absolute', was the unifying factor making sense of Plato's two worlds – thought and reality, the mental or 'ideal' and the physical. Mystical experience brought man closer to the 'One'. JULIAN turned to this doctrine from Christianity, AUGUSTINE of Hippo from MANICHAEISM.

neoromanticism A movement in British painting and other arts, in the period from about 1935 to 1955, in which artists looked back to certain aspects of 19th-century ROMANTICISM, particularly the 'visionary' landscape tradition of BLAKE and Samuel PALMER, and reinterpreted them in a more modern idiom. The best known of these painters and illustrators are Paul NASH, John PIPER, and Keith Vaughan. Certain painters working in France in the 1930s, who typically painted dreamlike imaginary landscapes with mournful figures, are also sometimes called neoromantics.

neoteny A form of development, common among salamanders (notably the AXOLOTL), in which part or all of the process is slowed so that an animal develops more slowly than did its ancestors. This results in the animal resembling, in some aspects, a juvenile stage of its ancestor, and it may retain some juvenile features throughout life (a condition known as **paedomorphosis**). Since juvenile forms are often less specialized than adult forms, neoteny may offer evolutionary advantages.

Nepal A south Asian country among the peaks and southern slopes of the Himalayas, sandwiched between China (Tibet) and India.

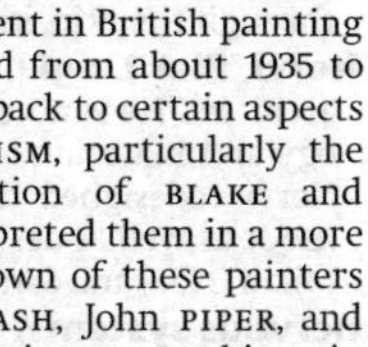

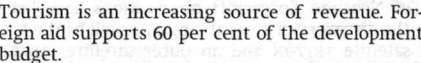

Physical. Nepal contains the highest mountains in the world. The peaks are in the north; below the snowline rivers run through turfy valleys and fine forests of evergreen, oak, and chestnut before reaching the warm, wet plains of the south. Here the natural vegetation is tropical.

Economy. Much of the land is not cultivable and deforestation is a major problem. However, the economy is primarily agrarian, with principal crops of rice, sugar cane, maize, and wheat. Industry is limited mainly to agricultural processing. Tourism is an increasing source of revenue. Foreign aid supports 60 per cent of the development budget.

History. Nepal's first era of centralized control was under the Licchavi dynasty, from about the 4th to the 10th centuries. Buddhist influences were then dominant, but under the Malla dynasty (10th–18th centuries) Hinduism became the dominant religion. In 1769 a Gurkha invasion brought to power the present ruling dynasty. From their capital at Kathmandu they wielded absolute power over the indigenous Nepalese tribes. Their incursion into north-west India led to a border war (1814–16) and to territorial concessions to the British (Treaty of Kathmandu, 1816). Effective rule then passed to a family of hereditary prime ministers, the Ranas, who cooperated closely with the British. Gurkhas were recruited to service in the British and Indian armies. Growing internal dissatisfaction led in 1950 to a coup, which reaffirmed royal powers under the king, Tribhuvan (1951–55). His successor, King Mahendra (1955–72), experimented with a more democratic form of government. This was replaced once more with monarchic rule (1960), which continued under his son, King Birendra Bir Bikram (1972–). Following pro-democracy demonstrations and mass arrests from 1989 onwards, the king agreed to legalize political parties, and granted a new constitution in November 1990, establishing a bi-cameral parliament; the first democratic election, in May 1991, was won by the Nepali Congress Party (NCP) led by Girija Prasad Koirala, with the United Communist Party of Nepal (UCPN) forming the official opposition. The government was accused of corruption and economic mismanagement in 1994 and was brought down by a vote of no-confidence. A UCPN-led coalition was formed following elections, but disputes within the government led to its collapse in 1995. A right-wing coalition government was then formed, led by the NCP.

Capital: Kathmandu
Area: 147,181 sq km (56,827 sq miles)
Population: 20,093,000 (1995)
Currency: 1 Nepalese rupee = 100 paisa (or pice)
Religions: Hindu 89.5%; Buddhist 5.3%; Muslim 2.7%; Jain 0.1%
Ethnic Groups: Nepalese 58.4%; Bihari 18.7%; Tharu 3.6%; Tamang 3.5%; Newar 3.0%
Languages: Nepali (official); Bihari; Tamang
International Organizations: UN; Colombo Plan

Nepali The official language of Nepal, spoken also in parts of north-east India. It belongs to the Indic branch of the Indo-European family of languages.

nephrite See JADE.

nephron See KIDNEY.

Neptune (in mythology) The Roman god of the sea, associated with Poseidon in Greek mythology. He is often represented carrying a trident.

Neptune (in astronomy) The eighth PLANET from the Sun, and the third most massive in the Solar System. Neptune was discovered in 1846 by the German astronomers Johann Galle and Heinrich d'Arrest while trying to verify the computations of LE VERRIER, who predicted that an undiscovered outer planet was perturbing the motion of Uranus. ADAMS had independently arrived at the same result. However, deviations of the observed motion of the planet from the computed one started to appear, and this led astronomers to search for another more remote planet. This planet, PLUTO, was found in 1930 not far from the predicted position but it does not fully account for the variations in Neptune's orbit. Observations by VOYAGER 2 have greatly expanded our knowledge of Neptune. Spacecraft observations have led to the discovery of several rings. As well as the large satellite TRITON and an outer satellite, NEREID, there are also six more satellites of small to medium size, all very close to the planet, which were discovered by Voyager.

neptunium (symbol Np, at. no. 93, r.a.m. 237) The first synthetic transuranic element to be produced (in 1940) by bombarding uranium with neutrons. It is an ACTINIDE, the most stable isotope of which (Np-237) has a half-life of 2.2×10^6 years.

Nereid An outer satellite of Neptune, discovered by the Dutch-American astronomer Gerard Kuiper in 1949. It has the highest orbital eccentricity (0.75) of all natural satellites and a semi-major axis of about 5.5 million km. Photographed at poor resolution by VOYAGER 2 in 1989, it has an irregular shape, a diameter of about 300 km, and an albedo of 0.14.

nerine A South African plant of the genus *Nerine*, part of the family Amaryllidaceae, of which 18 species are known. Their bulbs have a cycle of growth and rest which corresponds to the wet and dry seasons, with attractive and brightly coloured flowers appearing at the onset of the rains.

Nernst, Walther Hermann (1864–1941) German physical chemist, who in 1906 proposed the 'heat theorem' embodied in the third law of thermodynamics. This states that the ENTROPY change of a pure crystalline solid approaches zero as the temperature approaches ABSOLUTE ZERO. Nernst also investigated the specific heat capacities of solids at low temperatures and explained the explosion between hydrogen and chlorine on exposure to light. He was awarded the Nobel Prize for chemistry in 1920.

Nero (full name Nero Claudius Caesar Augustus Germanicus) (37–68 AD) Roman emperor 54–68. The adopted son and successor of Claudius, he became infamous for his cruelty following his ordering of the murder of his mother Agrippina in 59. His reign was marked by wanton executions of leading Romans and witnessed a fire that destroyed half of Rome in 64. A wave of uprisings in 68 led to his flight from Rome and his eventual suicide.

Neruda, Pablo (born Ricardo Eliezer Neftalí Reyes) (1904–73) Chilean poet and diplomat. He adopted the name Neruda as his pseudonym in 1920 after the Czech poet Jan Neruda (1834–91), later changing his name by deed poll (1946). From 1927 to 1952 he spent much of his life abroad, either serving in diplomatic posts or as a result of his membership of the Chilean Communist party, which was outlawed in 1948. His major work, *Canto General* (completed 1950), was originally conceived as an epic on Chile and was later expanded to cover the history of all the Americas from their ancient civilizations to their modern wars of liberation. He was awarded the Nobel Prize for literature in 1971.

Nerva, Marcus Cocceius (*c*.30–98 AD) Roman emperor 96–98. Appointed emperor by the Senate after the murder of the autocratic Domitian, he returned to a liberal and constitutional form of rule.

nerve A bundle of **nerve fibres** and supporting tissues, enclosed in a connective-tissue sheath. Nerves provide a means of communication between the central nervous system and all the other tissues and organs of the body. They are present in virtually all multicellular animals. Each fibre is the elongated portion of a nerve cell (see NEURONE); it carries unidirectional signals to and from the brain independently of neighbouring fibres in the nerve. It is surrounded by a sheath of insulating material (myelin), produced by a special type of cell, to prevent electrical interference between adjacent fibres in the nerve. Signals carried in the fibre are called impulses because they travel as discrete bursts of electrical activity. Each burst is followed by a short period when no further impulses can travel along the nerve. These 'spaces' enable information to be coded into bursts, similar in principle to Morse code. Information from the receptor end of the nerve fibre is thus coded into burst patterns, eventually to be translated into appropriate action by the brain. The junction between two nerve fibres is called a synapse, and the transfer of impulses is mediated by the release of chemicals called NEUROTRANSMITTERS across the gap of the synapse. Amplification or modification of the information can occur at this point. Most fibres split into several smaller fibres at their ends, enabling each neurone to communicate with many other fibres.

nerve gas A chemical warfare agent that attacks the nervous system. The first nerve gas, discovered by the German scientist Gerhard Schracher in 1936, was tabun. Sarin and soman were similar agents developed in Germany during World War II. These three agents plus VX, which was discovered by British researchers in the mid-1950s, are the main families of nerve gas stockpiled today. They are all organophosphorous compounds, and inhibit the body's breakdown of acetylcholine, a compound that chemically transmits impulses between nerve fibres. Hence, neural commands, including commands to the lungs, cannot be transmitted, inducing respiratory failure. Nerve gases are absorbed through the skin, killing the victim in minutes.

Nervi, Pier Luigi (1891–1979) Italian engineer and architect. He is noted as a pioneer of new technology and materials, especially reinforced concrete. Nervi codesigned the UNESCO building in Paris (1953), as well as designing the Pirelli skyscraper in Milan (1958) and San Francisco cathedral (1970).

nervous system A network of NERVES specialized to carry signals between parts of the body. The central nervous system, including the brain and spinal cord, relates the input and output conveyed through the peripheral nervous system. In higher animals, some REFLEXES are situated within the spinal cord, reflecting the segmental organization of the invertebrate nervous system. Other reflexes pass through the brain, where, in addition, more complex processing is possible. The AUTONOMIC NERVOUS SYSTEM also has central and peripheral components. Its activity is entirely reflex, but it can be influenced by other parts of the brain. See also NEUROLOGY AND NEUROSURGERY.

Nesbit, E(dith) (1858–1924) British novelist. She is best known for her children's books, including *The Story of the Treasure Seekers* (1899), *Five Children and It* (1902), and *The Railway Children* (1906). Nesbit was also a founder member of the Fabian Society.

Nestor In Homeric legend, the eldest of the Greek kings at the Trojan War. He was an elder statesman figure, garrulous but wise, counselling moderation in the quarrel of the leaders.

Nestorian Church (or **East Syrian**, **Chaldean**, or **Assyrian Church**) An Oriental CHRISTIAN CHURCH. It has about 170,000 members, who are found mostly in Iraq, Iran, Syria, and the USA, where the Patriarch resides. The liturgical language is Syriac.

Netanyahu, Binyamin (1949–) Israeli Likud statesman, Prime Minister since 1996. Leader of the right-wing Likud coalition since 1993, he narrowly defeated Shimon Peres in the elections of 1996. His attempts to maintain the impetus of the Middle-East peace process has met with a number of obstacles.

netball A seven-a-side ball game related to BASKETBALL, usually played outdoors and almost exclusively by girls and women, mainly in the UK and Commonwealth countries. The court is 30 m (100 feet) long by 15 m (50 feet) wide and divided into three equal areas. The goal, an open net, is mounted on a 3 m (10 feet) high post at each end, surrounded by a semicircular shooting circle 5 m (16 feet) in radius. The game is played between two teams, each consisting of seven players. Each player has a designated position and may only enter limited areas of the court. Only the goal-shooter (GS) and goal-attack (GA) may shoot at goal.

Netherlands, **the** A European country on the North Sea. It is also known informally as HOLLAND, although this properly refers only to two western provinces.

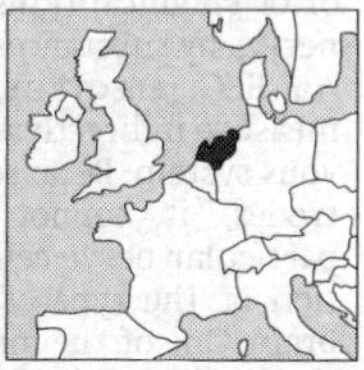

Physical. Bounded by Germany on the east and Belgium on the south, the Netherlands is built up of sediment brought by the Rhine, Meuse, and other rivers. Everywhere, except for the extreme southern corner, is low and flat, much of the land being below sea-level. The coast, partly protected by a chain of sandbanks, has several estuaries and a large lagoon, the IJsselmeer, partly reclaimed from the Zuider Zee. The sediment is rich and supports a great variety of horticulture and livestock farming. Inland, however, there are peat bogs and patches of heath, forested to help keep the sand in place. The climate is temperate maritime, although gales and heavy fogs are not unknown.

Economy. Trade, banking, and shipping have traditionally been important to the economy, which is now primarily industrial. Many raw materials are imported; petroleum products and chemicals are the principal exports. The manufacturing base includes electrical and other machinery, textiles, and food-processing. Of native minerals, natural gas extraction is substantial and a major source of domestic energy. An ongoing programme of maritime land reclamation has increased total land area.

History. The area was conquered as far north as the River Rhine by the Romans; the Franks and Saxons moved in during the early 5th century. After the collapse of the Frankish empire in the mid-9th century, there was considerable political fragmentation. Consolidation began under the 14th- and 15th-century dukes of BURGUNDY, and in 1477 the whole of the Low Countries passed to the House of HABSBURG. In 1568 the Dutch Revolts against Spanish Habsburg rule began. The independence of the United Provinces of the Netherlands (the northern provinces, which formed a self-governing federation) was finally acknowledged at the Peace of WESTPHALIA (1648). During the 17th century it was a formidable commercial power, and it acquired a sizeable DUTCH EMPIRE. It began to decline after the ANGLO-DUTCH WARS and the protracted wars against LOUIS XIV's France. From 1795 to 1814 the Netherlands came increasingly under the control of France. During those years Britain took over the colonies of Ceylon (now Sri Lanka) and Cape Colony in South Africa, important trading posts of the Dutch East India Company. At the settlement of the Congress of VIENNA the entire Low Countries formed the independent kingdom of the Netherlands (1815). Despite the secession in 1830 of BELGIUM, the Netherlands flourished under the House of Orange, adopting in 1848 a constitution based on the British system. It remained neutral during World War I, suffered economic difficulties during the Great DEPRESSION, and was occupied by the Germans during World War II, when many Jews were deported to CONCENTRATION CAMPS. Until World War II it was the third largest colonial power, controlling the Dutch East Indies, various West Indian islands, and Guiana in South America. The Japanese invaded the East Indian islands in 1942 and installed SUKARNO in a puppet government for all INDONESIA. In 1945 he declared independence and four years of bitter war followed before the Netherlands transferred sovereignty. Guiana received self-government as SURINAM in 1954 and independence in 1975, but Curaçao and other Antilles islands remained linked to the Netherlands. Following the long reign of Queen WILHELMINA (1890–1948) her daughter Juliana (1909–) became queen. She retired in 1980 and her daughter succeeded her as Queen Beatrix (1938–). The Netherlands was a founder member of the European Community, and of NATO. Since 1945 the Netherlands has been ruled by a succession of coalition governments. Its strong export-led economy suffered a recession in the early 1990s with an increase in unemployment.

Capital: Amsterdam
Area: 41.863 sq km (16,163 sq mi)
Population: 15,487,000 (1995)
Currency: 1 guilder (florin) = 100 cents
Religions: Roman Catholic 36.0%; non-religious 32.6%; Dutch Reformed Church 18.5%; Reformed Churches 8.4%
Ethnic Groups: Netherlander 96.0%; Turkish 1.0%; Moroccan 1.0%
Languages: Dutch (official); minority languages
International Organizations: UN; OECD; NATO; EU; Council of Europe; CSCE

Netherlands Antilles A dependency of the NETHERLANDS comprising five islands in the CARIBBEAN.

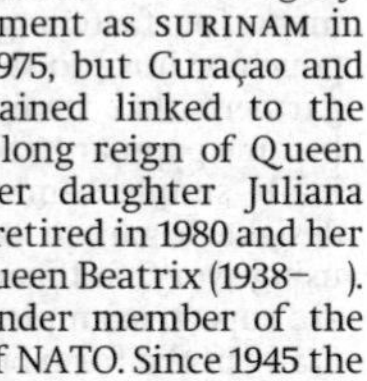

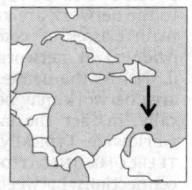

Physical. The islands of Sint Eustatius, the southern part of Sint Maarten (Saint Martin), and Saba fom the northern part of the group. They are part of the Lesser Antilles. The islands of Aruba, Bonaire, and Curaçao are much further south, lying off the coast of Venezuela. Aruba formed part of the group until 1986 but now has special status.

Economy. Tourism is the main source of revenue. Bonaire and Curaçao have petroleum refining, storage, and transshipment industries, which developed to support Venezuela's oil industry. Curaçao also produces liqueur.

History. Aruba, Bonaire, and Curaçao were inhabited by Arawak Indians when they were discovered in 1499 by Alonzo de Ojeda and claimed for Spain. The Spanish settled the islands in 1527, killed the local population, and brought in slaves. The northern islands were inhabited by fierce Carib Indians when they were discovered by COLUMBUS in 1493. The Dutch took possession of Aruba, Bonaire, and Curaçao in 1643 and, except for some short periods of British control during the Napoleonic Wars, they have remained in Dutch possession. The northern islands changed hands many times but finally passed to the Dutch at the beginning of the 19th century. The islands (including Aruba) became known as the Netherlands Antilles in 1845. They became fully autonomous in domestic affairs in 1954. An independence movement grew during the 1970s and 1980s, but the islands opted to remain part of the Netherlands. Aruba withdrew from the group in 1986 with full independence promised by 1996. However, in 1994 this decision was changed and Aruba has remained part of the Netherlands.

Capital: Willemstad
Area: 800 sq km (308 sq mi)
Population: 197,000 (1993)
Currency: 1 Netherlands Antilles guilder = 100 cents
Religions: Roman Catholic 83.8%; Reformed tradition 3.3%; Methodist 3.2%; non-religious 2.6%; Seventh-day Adventist 1.5%; Jewish 0.3%
Ethnic Groups: Mixed 84.0%; White 6.0%
Languages: Dutch (official); English; Papiamento

netsuke A small toggle used in Japan as an attachment for fastening articles (such as a tobacco pouch or inro) to the sash of the man's kimono, a garment that traditionally had no pockets. They became popular in the 17th century and were originally simple bamboo rings, but more elaborate designs began to be made in the 18th century, using ivory and many other materials. The finest are superb examples of miniature sculpture, generally in the form of human or animal figures.

nettle A plant that is either 'stinging' or 'dead'. The stinging nettles belong to the genus *Urtica*, with about 50 species armed with single-celled stinging hairs. The swollen tips of these hairs break off at the slightest touch, releasing an irritant mixture of formic acid and enzymes. They belong to the family Urticaceae, which is found worldwide. Dead-nettles (*Lamium* species) belong to the mint family; they have no stinging properties but have hairy, nettle-shaped leaves.

network (in computing) The connecting together of separate computer systems so that they can exchange DATA, and sometimes PROGRAMS. The points at which individual systems are connected to the network are known as nodes. There are two main classes of computer network: broad area (wide area) networks and local area networks (LANs). As the name implies, the nodes of a broad area network may be widely dispersed geographically; in fact the largest networks may extend worldwide. Typically, broad area networks utilize TELECOMMUNICATION channels to provide the connections between computers. Local area networks usually link computers or workstations on the same site via coaxial cables or OPTICAL FIBRES. LANs are often used to share expensive PERIPHERALS, such as LASER PRINTERS, or to share a central disk store, known as a file server. Both types of network usually provide ELECTRONIC MAIL facilities to enable users to pass messages to each other.

Neumann, John von (1903–57) Hungarian-born US mathematician and computer pioneer. His contributions ranged from pure logic and set theory to the most practical areas of application. He analysed the mathematics of quantum mechanics, founding a new area of mathematical research (algebras of operators in Hilbert space), and also established the branch of mathematics known as game theory, which has become influential in economics, business, and many other fields. Neumann also helped to develop the US hydrogen bomb, but perhaps his most influential contribution was in the design and operation of electronic computers.

neural network A densely interconnected network of simple computer processing units (neurons) imitating some qualities of the biological nervous system. Unlike traditional computers, neural networks share out the computation simultaneously between many processors (parallel processing), enormously increasing their collective power. Consequently, neural networks are well-suited to the computationally intensive tasks of ARTIFICIAL INTELLIGENCE, for example automatic speech recognition and IMAGE PROCESSING. The behaviour of a neural network is determined by the strength of its interconnections (synapses); large numbers of synapses help the network to recognize patterns in the presence of noise, and enable it to keep working after some of its synapses have been removed. See also ANALOG COMPUTER.

neurology and neurosurgery The study and treatment of disorders of the NERVOUS SYSTEM. Diseases of the nervous system can result from disorders of conduction of an impulse along a nerve, or of chemical transmission of impulses between nerves by substances known as neurotransmitters. An EEG (ELECTROENCEPHALOGRAPH) is used to measure indirectly activity within the central nervous system. Because it records from surface electrodes, it cannot localize activity within a particular nerve cell, but it can provide an indication of the type of activity over an area of the brain. One of the most common diseases affecting conduction of the nerve impulse is MULTIPLE SCLEROSIS. Chemical neurotransmitter abnormalities are responsible for many neurological disorders. For example, a shortage of the transmitter dopamine produces the symptoms of Parkinson's disease, and many scientists think that schizophrenia also has a biochemical basis. Investigation of these disorders has proved difficult, but it has recently become possible to develop weakly radioactive markers (see NUCLEAR MEDICINE), which can be attached either to neurotransmitters themselves or to antibodies that are targeted at receptors for the transmitter substances. This should allow the study of neurotransmitter function in living brains. Some neurological disorders result from tumours within the central nervous system. Localization of such growths has recently been made much easier by the development of new and better imaging techniques such as POSITRON EMISSION TOMOGRAPHY and MAGNETIC RESONANCE IMAGING.

neuron(e) (or **nerve cell**) The basic functional unit of the NERVOUS SYSTEM. This type of cell is specialized to transmit electrical impulses and so carry information from one part of the body to another. Each neurone has an enlarged portion, the **cell body**, containing the nucleus; from the body extend several processes (called **dendrites**) through which impulses enter from their branches. A longer process, the **nerve fibre** (or **axon**), extends outwards and carries impulses away from the cell body. This is normally unbranched except at the nerve ending. The point of contact of one neurone with another is known as a **synapse**. See NERVE.

neurosis A type of MENTAL ILLNESS in which a person persistently over-reacts emotionally and behaves in an inappropriate way, while knowing that it is irrational to do so. By contrast, in PSYCHOSIS, this insight is lost. A common example is a PHOBIA, in which there is a crippling fear of, say, social situations or public places. In more complicated cases there may be periodic DEPRESSION, OBSESSION, impulsiveness, and self-damaging behaviour, including suicidal gestures. In a few cases the neurosis can be traced to a single cause, such as an experience in war or of civilian disaster. However, most neuroses reflect long-standing personality difficulties, and originate in an interaction between early environmental influences (for example, parental deprivation, loss, or abuse) and inherited temperamental factors, such as a strong tendency to ANXIETY that makes the individual more vulnerable to STRESS. The term 'anxiety disorder' is now often preferred to neurosis.

neurotransmitter A chemical substance released from nerve endings to transmit impulses across synapses to other nerves and across the minute gaps between the nerves and the muscles or glands that they supply. Outside the central nervous system the chief neurotransmitter is **acetylcholine**; **noradrenaline** is released by nerve endings of the sympathetic system. In the central nervous system, as well as acetylcholine and noradrenaline, several other substances act as transmitters. See NERVE.

neutrality The status of countries that are not parties to an international conflict. Certain rights and obligations apply; for example, ships of a neutral state are usually allowed to leave a blockaded port, and escaped POLITICAL PRISONERS may seek POLITICAL ASYLUM in the territory of a neutral. More generally, states may acquire a reputation, role, or status as a neutral in international politics (for instance, Ireland, Sweden, and Switzerland). Japan and Germany are not neutral in status, but since World War II their constitutions have forbidden involvement in international conflicts. The US **Neutrality Acts** (1935–39) were laws to prevent the involvement of the country in non-US wars. In a spirit of isolationism, the USA declared that it

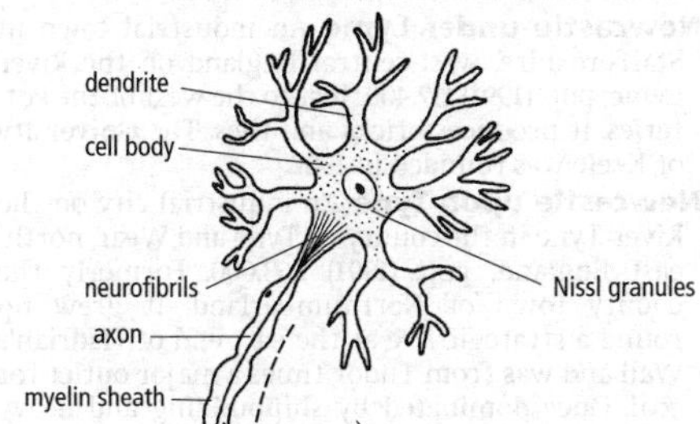

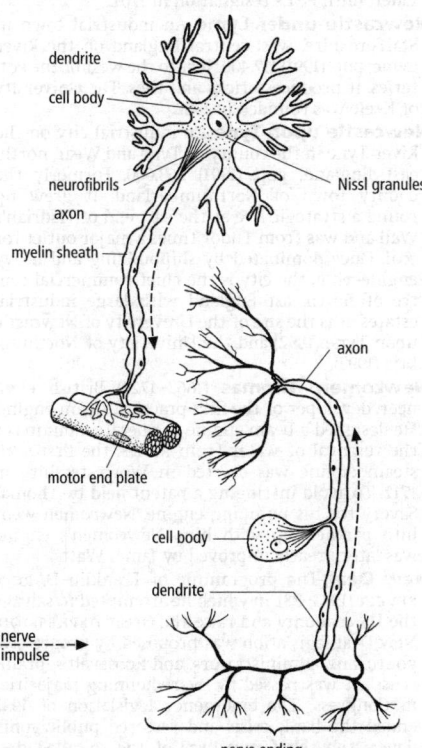

Neurones A motor neurone (above) conducts impulses from the brain to a muscle. A sensory neurone (below) carries impulses from a tissue or organ towards the central nervous system.

would take no stand on issues of international morality by distinguishing between aggressor and victim nations. During 1940 the Roosevelt administration fought for repeal of the Acts on the ground that they encouraged aggression by the AXIS POWERS and ultimately endangered US security. Gradually they were relaxed, before PEARL HARBOR made them irrelevant.

neutralization (in chemistry) The reaction between an ACID and a BASE or alkali, in which a salt and water are formed. The resulting solution is neutral – that is, neither acidic nor alkaline. The positive hydrogen ions of the acid are neutralized by the negative ions from the base. A neutral solution has a pH of 7 (see HYDROGEN ION CONCENTRATION).

neutrino A chargeless elementary particle whose existence was predicted by Wolfgang Pauli in 1930 to avoid the violation of the laws of conservation of energy and momentum in a nuclear process called beta decay. In this radioactive process the electrons or positrons produced are ejected with an observed distribution of energies. Pauli supposed that the remaining energy was given to neutrinos. The existence of the neutrino and its antiparticle (the antineutrino) is now accepted as experimentally confirmed. Three types of neutrino exist, associated respectively with the electron, the muon, and the tau particle. Classed as leptons, neutrinos are weakly interacting. Recently it has been postulated that some of the so-called 'missing mass' in the Universe may be accounted for if neutrinos have some non-zero rest mass although they were originally thought to be massless.

neutron A NUCLEON that is one of the two types of particle (the other being a PROTON) forming the nucleus of an atom. Neutrons are heavy, having almost the same mass as the proton, but they carry no electric charge. The mass of a neutron is 1,838 times that of the electron, and it has a SPIN of $\frac{1}{2}$. While atoms of the same element always have the same number of protons in the nucleus, the number of neutrons can vary; and atoms which have different numbers of neutrons form the ISOTOPES of that element. Neutrons can be emitted by a nucleus when it undergoes radioactive decay or fission. These free neutrons can be absorbed by other nuclei to cause further fission in a chain reaction or to form different isotopes, which may themselves be radioactive. See also NUCLEAR ENERGY.

neutron bomb See NUCLEAR WEAPON.

neutron star A very hot star of exceptionally high density. The density is typically 10^{13}–10^{15} times that of water, and about a million times greater than in a white dwarf. The original electrons and protons of the star's constituent matter have been crushed together, so that its core is composed primarily of neutrons. Neutron stars are thought to be only about 10–20 km in diameter. Consequently they have very low luminosity and are normally impossible to detect. Rotating magnetic neutron stars can, however, be observable as PULSARS. Neutron stars are also thought to be present as components of several X-ray BINARY STARS. They are thought to be the closing stage of STELLAR EVOLUTION in most stars with masses between the CHANDRASEKHAR limit of 1.44 times that of the Sun and about three times the mass of the Sun. Stars of greater mass than this are thought to become BLACK HOLES. Neutron stars are formed by the collapse of the star's core when its nuclear fuel is exhausted, an event that gives rise to a Type II SUPERNOVA outburst.

Nevada A state of the western US, between the Rocky Mountains and the Sierra Nevada, much of which comprises dry, sparsely populated sagebrush desert almost totally in the Great Basin area; area 286,352 sq km (110,561 sq miles); pop. (1990) 1,201,830; capital, Carson City. The largest cities are Las Vegas and Reno. Nevada is also known as the Sagebrush, Silver, or Battleborn State. Acquired from Mexico in 1848, it became the 36th state of the USA in 1864. Its chief landmarks are the Hoover Dam, Great Basin National Park, Lake Tahoe, and Lake Mead National Recreation Area.

Neville, Richard See WARWICK.

Nevis One of the Leeward Islands in the West Indies, forming part of the state of SAINT KITTS AND NEVIS; area 93 sq km (36 sq miles); pop. (est. 1989) 9,000; chief settlement, Charlestown; highest peak, Nevis Peak (985 m, 3,232 ft).

New Age movement A cultural movement covering a broad range of beliefs and activities, all characterized by a rejection of Western values and the promotion of 'holistic' approach to religion, philosophy, and ASTROLOGY. This approach is often linked to a preoccupation with environmental issues and the practice of a range of alternative therapies. Eastern religions, the occult, and parapsychology inform the beliefs of its adherents. Although the movement originated in, and is strongly associated with, California and the West Coast of the USA, its influence spread throughout the USA and northern Europe, and became established in communities, such as Findhorn in Scotland from about the beginning of the 1970s. The lifestyle of New Age travellers, who make only minimal contributions to the mainstream societies that sustain them, seems to derive from aspects of the 'hippie' movement of the 1960s.

New Amsterdam See NEW YORK.

Newark A port and industrial city in New Jersey, USA, on the Passaic River; pop. (1990) 275,220. It is the largest city in the state and has an international airport. First settled in 1666, it is now a major industrial and commercial centre, and specializes in chemicals, beer, electronic equipment, and paints.

New Brunswick A maritime province (from 1867) of south-east Canada, joined to Nova Scotia by the narrow Chignecto Isthmus and separated from Prince Edward Island by the Northumberland Strait; area 73,440 sq km (28,355 sq miles); pop. (1991) 723,900; capital, Fredericton. The largest cities are St John and Moncton. Tourism, fishing, potato farming, dairy farming, forestry, and the mining of potash, zinc, lead, copper, antimony, and bismuth are among its chief industries. Settled by the French and ceded to Britain in 1713, New Brunswick was named by United Empire Loyalists in 1784 after the former German duchy of Brunswick-Lunenburg also ruled by George III.

Newby, (George) Eric (1919–) British travel writer. In 1956 he made the first of a number of expeditions in Central Asia, describing his experiences in *A Short Walk in the Hindu Kush* (1958) and *Slowly Down the Ganges* (1966). His later books include *A Traveller's Life* (1982) and *A Small Place in Italy* (1994). He was travel editor of the *Observer* from 1964 to 1973.

New Caledonia (French **Nouvelle-Calédonie**) An island in the south-west Pacific Ocean, east of Australia, since 1946 forming, with its dependencies, a French Overseas Territory; area 18,575 sq km (7,172 sq miles); pop. (1989) 164,170; official language, French; capital, Nouméa. Rising to a height of 1,639 m (5,377 ft) at Mt Paine, the main island is 400 km (250 miles) long. Also included in the group are the Loyalty Islands, Isles des Pins, Isle Bélep, and the uninhabited Chesterfield and Huon islands. The islands have a mild climate with a wet season from December to March. Coffee, copra, nickel, chrome, and iron ore are the chief exports. It was inhabited for at least 3,000 years before the arrival of Captain James Cook (1774), who named the main island after the Roman name for Scotland. The French annexed the island in 1853, and after the discovery of nickel there (1863) it assumed some economic importance for France. Although there has been a growing separatist movement amongst the minority Kanak people, a referendum in 1987 failed to mobilize enough support for independence from France.

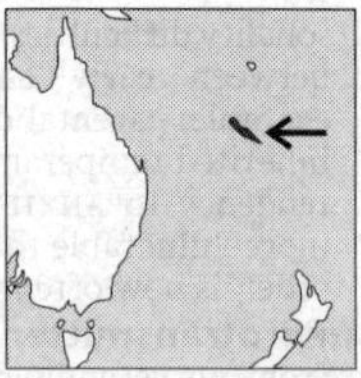

Newcastle An industrial port on the coast of New South Wales, Australia; pop. (1991) 262,160. Founded as a penal colony, it developed as a port and as a centre for the processing of locally-mined coal, copper, lead, and zinc. It has steel mills, shipyards, and chemical industries.

Newcastle, Thomas Pelham-Holles, 1st Duke of (1693–1768) British Whig statesman, Prime Minister 1754–56 and 1757–62. Newcastle succeeded his brother Henry Pelham as Prime Minister on the latter's death in 1754. During his second term in office, he headed a coalition with William Pitt the Elder, until Pitt's resignation in 1761.

Newcastle under Lyme An industrial town in Staffordshire, west-central England on the River Lyme; pop. (1991) 117,400. Just to the west of the Potteries, it produces bricks and tiles. The University of Keele was founded in 1962.

Newcastle upon Tyne An industrial city on the River Tyne in the county of Tyne and Wear, north-east England; pop. (1991) 263,000. Formerly the county town of Northumberland, it grew up round a strategic site at the east end of Hadrian's Wall and was from Tudor times a major outlet for coal. Once dominated by shipbuilding and heavy engineering, the city is the chief commercial centre of north-east England with large industrial estates. It is the site of the University of Newcastle upon Tyne (1852) and the University of Northumbria (1992).

Newcomen, Thomas (1663–1729) British engineer, developer of the first practical steam engine. He designed a beam engine to operate a pump for the removal of water from mines; the first such steam engine was erected in Worcestershire in 1712. To avoid infringing a patent held by Thomas Savery for his pumping engine, Newcomen went into partnership with him. Newcomen's engine was later greatly improved by James Watt.

New Deal The programme of Franklin D. ROOSEVELT (1933–38), in which he attempted to salvage the US economy and raise the Great DEPRESSION. New Deal legislation was proposed by progressive politicians, administrators, and Roosevelt's 'brains trust'. It was passed by overwhelming majorities in Congress. The emergency legislation of 1933 ended the bank crisis and restored public confidence; the relief measures of the so-called first New Deal of 1933–35, such as the establishment of the Tennessee Valley Authority, stimulated productivity; and the Works Project Administration reduced unemployment. The failure of central government agencies provoked the so-called second New Deal of 1935–38, devoted to recovery by measures, such as the Revenue Act, the Wagner Acts, the Emergency Relief Appropriation Act, and the Social Security Act. Although the New Deal cannot be claimed to have pulled the USA out of the Depression, it was important for its revitalization of the nation's morale.

New Delhi See DELHI.

New England ▶**1** A district in north-east New South Wales, the largest area of highlands in Australia. Its chief towns are Tamworth, Armidale, Glen Innes, and Inverell and the Southern Hemisphere's largest granite monolith, Bald Rock, is located near Tenterfield. The **New England National Park** preserves one of the largest remaining areas of rainforest in the state. ▶**2** An area on the north-east coast of the USA, comprising the states of Maine, New Hampshire, Vermont, Massachusetts, Rhode Island, and Connecticut. The name was given to it by the English explorer John Smith in 1614.

New Forest An area of heathland with beech and oak woodland in south Hampshire, England, reserved as Crown property since 1079, originally by William I as a royal hunting area. William II was killed by an arrow when hunting there in 1100. **New Forest ponies**, originally a breed native to the New Forest, have been added to by a variety of different breeds, which roam the forest in wild herds. The area is a noted tourist resort.

Newfoundland ▶**1** A large island at the mouth of the St Lawrence River, Canada, visited by Vikings in *c*.1000, it was explored in 1497 by John Cabot and named the 'New Isle', 'Terra Nova', or more commonly Newfoundland. A colony (Britain's first) was founded by Sir Humphrey Gilbert and in 1949 it was united with Labrador (as Newfoundland and Labrador) as a province of Canada. ▶**2** A province of Canada, comprising the island of Newfoundland and the sparsely inhabited coast and interior of Labrador, eastern Canada; area 404,517 sq km (156,649 sq miles); pop. (1991) 586,470; capital, St John's. South-west Labrador has immense iron deposits and mining and logging are important industries, as are fishing and paper and pulp mills. It gives its name to a large breed of dog with a thick coarse coat.

New France French possessions in North America discovered, explored, and settled from the 16th to the 18th centuries. Its centres were Quebec (founded in 1608) and Montreal (founded in 1642) on the St Lawrence River. In 1712 New France stretched from the Gulf of St Lawrence to beyond Lake Superior and included NEWFOUNDLAND, Acadia (NOVA SCOTIA), and the Mississippi valley as far south as the Gulf of Mexico. It began to disintegrate after the Peace of UTRECHT was signed in 1713, when France lost Acadia, Newfoundland, and Hudson Bay; it ceased to exist as a political entity in 1763 under the terms of the Treaty of PARIS. LOUISIANA, the last French colony on mainland North America, was sold to the USA in 1803.

Newgate A former London prison, originally the gatehouse of the main west gate to the city, first used as a prison in the early Middle Ages and rebuilt and enlarged with funds left to the city by Richard Whittington. Its unsanitary conditions became notorious in the 18th century before the building was burnt down in the anti-Catholic riots of 1780. A new edifice was erected on the same spot soon after but was demolished in 1902 to make way for the Central Criminal Court (known as the 'Old Bailey').

New Granada A former Spanish viceroyalty in north-west South America that comprised present-day Colombia, Ecuador, Panama, and Venezuela.

New Guinea (Indonesian **Irian**) An island of the east Malay archipelago, to the north of Australia, divided between the independent state of Papua New Guinea in the east and the Indonesian province of West Irian in the west. With an area of 789,950 sq km (305,000 sq miles), it is the world's second-largest island.

Newham An inner borough of Greater London, England, on the River Thames; pop. (1991) 200,200. It was created in 1965 from the former boroughs of East Ham and West Ham and parts of north Woolwich and Barking and is both residential and industrial.

New Hampshire A state in the north-eastern USA, bordering on the Atlantic; area 24,032 sq km (9,279 sq miles); pop. (1990) 1,109,250; capital, Concord. Its largest cities are Manchester and Nashua. New Hampshire is also known as the Granite State. It was settled from England in the 17th century and was the first independent colony (1776) before becoming one of the original 13 states of the USA in 1788. The chief industries are tourism, the mining of granite, mica, and feldspar, the production of dairy products, garden crops, fruit, and maple syrup, and the manufacture of footwear, plastics, machinery, electrical goods, and electronic products. Landmarks include the White Mountains, and Lake Winnipesaukee.

New Hebrides The former name (until 1980) of VANUATU.

Ne Win (1911–) Burmese general and socialist statesman, Prime Minister 1958–60, head of state 1962–74, and President 1974–81. An active nationalist in the 1930s, Ne Win was appointed Chief of Staff in Aung San's Burma National Army in 1943. He led a military coup in 1962, after which he established a military dictatorship and formed a one-party state, governed by the Burma Socialist Programme Party (BSPP). He stepped down from the presidency in 1981 and retired as leader of the BSPP after riots in Rangoon in 1988.

New Jersey A state in the north-eastern USA, bordering on the Atlantic; area 20,169 sq km (7,787 sq miles); pop. (1990) 7,730,190; capital, Trenton. It has the highest population density of all the United States with more than 95 per cent of its population living in urban areas. The largest cities are Newark, Jersey City, Paterson, and Elizabeth. New Jersey is also known as the Garden State. Colonized by Dutch settlers and ceded to Britain in 1664, it became one of the original 13 states of the USA. Among its chief industries are tourism, the production of garden vegetables, and the manufacture of chemicals, pharmaceuticals, clothing, and electrical goods. Its principal landmarks are the Delaware Water Gap, Edison National Historic Site, Morristown National Historic Park, and Pinelands National Reserve.

Newlands, John Alexander Reina (1837–98) British chemist who, like MENDELEEV, recognized the periodic nature of the elements. His proposal in 1864 of a 'Law of Octaves', in which similar properties tend to appear after every eighth element, was ridiculed by the Chemical Society. Later, when the significance of his work was appreciated, he was awarded the Davy Medal of the Royal Society.

Newman, John Henry (1801–90) British theologian. He was a leading figure in the Oxford Movement, a group of people who in the 1830s attempted to reform the Church of England by restoring the high-church traditions, and became a prominent convert (1845) to Roman Catholicism. The publication in 1841 of *Tract 90*, which argued that the Thirty-nine Articles of the Church of England could be reconciled with Roman Catholic doctrine, caused a major scandal. In 1846 he went to Rome, where he was ordained priest. A gifted writer, in 1864 he published *Apologia pro Vita Sua*, a justification of his spiritual evolution. He was created cardinal in 1879. His cause for beatification is being examined in Rome.

Newman, Paul (1925–) US actor and film director. Among his many films are *Butch Cassidy and the Sundance Kid* (1969) *The Sting* (1973), *The Color of Money* (1987), for which he won an Oscar, *Mr and Mrs Bridge* (1990), and *Nobody's Fool* (1994). He has also directed several films, including *Rachel, Rachel* (1968) and *The Glass Menagerie* (1987).

Newmarket A town in Suffolk, south-east England, between Cambridge and Bury St Edmunds; pop. (1991) 16,498. It is a noted horseracing centre and headquarters of the Jockey Club.

New Mexico A state in the south-western USA, to the south of Colorado and bordering on Mexico west of the Rio Grande; area 314,925 sq km (121,593 sq miles); pop. (1990) 1,515,070; capital, Santa Fe. The largest city is Albuquerque. New Mexico is also known as the Sunshine State. It was obtained from Mexico in 1848 and 1853 and became the 47th state of the USA in 1912. A major centre of energy research, New Mexico is rich in natural resources, which include oil, gas, uranium, potassium salts, copper, zinc, lead, molybdenum, gold, and silver. Its chief landmarks are the Carlsbad Caverns National Park, the Chaco Culture National Historic Park, and El Morro, Bandelier, Picos, Salinas, White Sands, and Gila Cliff Dwellings National Monuments.

New Model Army The English ROUNDHEAD force established by Parliamentary ordinance on 15 February 1645. A single army of 22,000 men, it was formed largely from the uncoordinated Roundhead forces of the first phase of the ENGLISH CIVIL WAR. Its first commander-in-chief was FAIRFAX, with Philip Skippon commanding the infantry and, after the Self-Denying Ordinance, Oliver CROMWELL in charge of the cavalry. Derided at first by the Cavaliers as the 'New Noddle Army', it consisted of regularly paid, well disciplined, and properly trained men, who became known as the Ironsides. Promotion was by merit. Resounding victories, such as NASEBY and PRESTON won the war for the Roundheads. The army was inextricably involved in national developments until the Restoration. Religious and political radicalism quickly permeated its ranks, with LEVELLER influence particularly strong between 1647 and 1649. The army was responsible for PRIDE'S PURGE (1648), and formed the basis of government in the following years.

New Orleans A city and river port in south-east Louisiana, USA, on the Gulf of Mexico and the Mississippi River; pop. (1990) 496,940. Named in honour of the Duc d'Orléans, Regent of France, it was founded by Jean Baptiste Le Moyne in 1718. Steamboats first sailed up river to Natchez in 1812; the St Louis Cathedral is the oldest cathedral in the USA. The city is noted for its annual Mardi Gras celebrations and for its association with the origins of Jazz. It has shipbuilding and chemical industries. Tourism is also important.

New Orleans, Battle of (8 January 1815) A battle in the WAR OF 1812, fought outside the city of New Orleans. A numerically superior British attempt led by Sir Edward Pakenham to seize New Orleans was brilliantly repelled by US forces commanded by Andrew JACKSON. The battle proved of little military significance, the Treaty of GHENT having formally ended the war two weeks earlier, but Jackson's triumph made him a national hero.

Newport ▶**1** An industrial town and county borough in south-east Wales, on the River Usk; pop. (1991) 129,900. ▶**2** The chief town of the Isle of Wight, off the south coast of England; pop. (1991) 20,574. Parkhurst Prison is situated nearby.

New Providence The principal island of the Bahamas in the West Indies; area 207 sq km (80 sq miles); pop. (1990) 171,540. Its chief settlement is the port of Nassau, capital of the Bahamas.

New Right An intellectual movement of the 1970s and 1980s that sought to reformulate the basis of right-wing opposition to SOCIAL DEMOCRACY and SOCIALISM. New Right thinkers, whose influence was greatest in the USA and the UK, drew in varying proportions upon the ideas of LIBERTARIANISM and CONSERVATISM. The libertarian strain could be seen in their defence of the FREE MARKET, and their belief that the role of government had been over-extended and now needed to be reduced. This meant, for example, the PRIVATIZATION of firms and industries owned by the state, monetarist policies, and a shift away from the WELFARE STATE towards private insurance as a way of coping with ill health and old age. The conservative strain appeared in their strong commitment to law and order, and in their belief that the family unit needed to be strengthened.

Newry An industrial port in County Down, at the head of the River Newry estuary in the south-east of Northern Ireland; pop. (1981) 19,400. From ancient times it occupied a strategic position on the main hill crossing into Ulster from Dublin and the south. The town is intersected by canals built in the 18th century and St Patrick's Church (1578) is said to be the oldest Protestant church in Ireland. Its proximity to the Republic made it a centre of sectarian violence.

news agency (US **wire service**) A local, national, or international organization that collects reports and photographs from staff correspondents and supplies them by telephone link or SATELLITE to subscribing NEWSPAPERS or BROADCASTING companies. News agencies play a key role in the production line that turns events into news. The big four international news agencies are Associated Press and United Press International based in the USA, Agence France-Presse in France, and Reuters in the UK. TASS, once the chief news agency of the former Soviet Union, is under challenge from the independent Interfax. TASS became Itar-Tass following the collapse of the Soviet Union in 1991.

New South Wales A state of south-east Australia, first colonized from Britain in 1788 and federated with the other states of Australia in 1901; area 810,428 sq km (309,433 sq miles); pop. (1991) 5,940,800; capital, Sydney. Australia's most populous state, it was originally the name of the entire colony. The plains of the west are semiarid grazing land, but there is richer wheat and grazing country in the central and coastal areas. The main agricultural products are meat, cereals, fruit, wine, dairy products, and wool. There are extensive coal deposits near Newcastle and Wollongong, and silver, lead, and zinc at Broken Hill.

newspaper A daily or weekly publication containing news, comment, information, and other features. Most newspapers are paid for, but ADVERTISING is an important source of revenue, and provides most of it in US newspapers. 'Free newspapers' are financed entirely by advertising and carry no cover price. Although the pre-eminence of newspapers as a news medium has been challenged, first by RADIO, then by TELEVISION, and although a trend towards fewer newspapers targeted at a narrower audience is often apparent, they remain popular and influential. By the 1970s newspapers in the UK divided between the 'quality' broad-sheet press carrying news and analysis, and the popular tabloid (half-sheet) papers largely devoted to gossip, sensationalism, and entertainment. Although they can lead to high-quality, enterprising JOURNALISM, the circulation wars that break out between newspapers can have a damaging effect on the journalism offered: what are seen as over-simplification, STEREOTYPING, and invasion of privacy have led to many complaints.

newt An amphibian of the family Salamandridae, which also includes the true salamanders. European newts of the genus *Triturus* form a distinct group of species. They are terrestrial for part of the year, but enter the water, usually a pond or lake, to breed in the spring. At this time, the males become generally brighter in colour, and some species, such as the crested newt, *Triturus cristatus*, develop a crest of skin along the back and tail. Male alpine newts, *T. alpestris*, are strikingly coloured, having plain red-orange bellies, bordered with sky blue, and a low cream and black spotted crest. Courtship in newts is elaborate, the male displaying to the female. Eggs are laid singly, attached to aquatic plant leaves.

New Territories That part of the territory of Hong Kong lying to the north of the Kowloon peninsula and including the islands of Lantau, Tsing Yi, and Lamma; area 950 sq km (367 sq miles). Under the 1898 Convention of Peking the New Territories (comprising 92 per cent of the land area of Hong Kong) were leased to Britain by China for a period of 99 years; they reverted to China in 1997.

New Testament See BIBLE.

newton (symbol N) The SI UNIT of force, named in honour of Isaac NEWTON, who first established the relationship between force and motion. One newton is defined as the force that gives a mass of 1 kg an acceleration of 1 m/s^2.

Newton, Sir Isaac (1642–1727) English mathematician and physicist. He was the greatest single influence on theoretical physics until Einstein. His most productive period was in 1665–67, when he retreated temporarily from Cambridge to his isolated home in Lincolnshire during the Great Plague. He discovered the binomial theorem, and made several other contributions to mathematics, notably differential calculus and its relationship with integration. A bitter quarrel with Leibniz ensued as to which of them had discovered calculus first. In his major treatise, *Principia Mathematica* (1687), Newton gave a mathematical description of the laws of mechanics and gravitation (see NEWTON'S LAW OF GRAVITATION; NEWTON'S LAWS OF MOTION) and applied these to planetary and lunar motion. For most purposes Newtonian mechanics has survived even the introduction of relativity theory and quantum mechanics, to both of which it stands as a good approximation. Another influential work was *Opticks* (1704), which gave an account of Newton's optical experiments and theories, including the discovery that white light is made up of a mixture of colours. In 1699 Newton was appointed Master of the Mint; he entered Parliament as MP for Cambridge University in 1701, and in 1703 was elected president of the Royal Society.

Newtonian telescope See REFLECTING TELESCOPE; TELESCOPE.

Newton's law of gravitation One of the most far-reaching and important physical laws. It states that every particle of matter attracts every other particle of matter with a force proportional to the product of the particles' masses and inversely proportional to the square of the distance between them. Together with NEWTON'S LAWS OF MOTION, the law of gravitation, published in 1687, laid the foundations for subsequent major advances in physics and astronomy.

Newton's laws of motion Three laws of motion that are fundamental to the understanding of classical mechanics. The first law states that every body continues in a state of rest or uniform motion in a straight line unless it is acted upon by an external force. The second law states that the rate of change of MOMENTUM of a body is proportional to the applied force and acts in the same direction. If the mass of the body remains constant this law equates force F with the product of mass m and acceleration a, according to the equation $F = ma$. It thus provides a definition of force. The third law states that for every applied force, or action, there is an equal force, or reaction, which acts in the opposite direction; concisely expressed action and reaction are equal and opposite. The crucial consideration when applying Newton's laws is that they only hold relative to inertial frames of reference – that is, frames of reference that are at rest or moving with constant velocity. Since the Earth itself is rotating, it does not strictly provide an inertial frame, although in local problems the effect of this is negligible. When considering the flight of a space rocket, however, the Earth's rotation must be taken into account. Newton's laws, however, do not explain some of the phenomena observed in planetary motion. A more sophisticated theory is needed to explain motion at speeds close to that of light, and the behaviour of objects close in size to atoms. RELATIVITY theory and QUANTUM THEORY have been developed to deal with these situations.

New York A state of the USA, bordering on the Atlantic, the second most populous US state; area 127,189 sq km (49,108 sq miles); pop. (1990) 17,990,455; capital, Albany. The largest cities are New York, Buffalo, Rochester, Yonkers, Syracuse, and Albany. New York is also known as the Empire State. Settled by the Dutch, it was surrendered to the British in 1664 and in 1788 became one of the original 13 states of the USA. Its principal landmarks include the Statue of Liberty, Manhattan Island, the Finger Lakes, the Hudson River, and the Adirondack Forest.

New York City A city and port in the US state of New York, on the Atlantic Ocean at the mouth of the Hudson River; pop. (1990) 7,322,560. It is the richest and most populous city of the USA, containing the financial centre Wall Street, industries of every kind, several universities, an opera house, art galleries, museums, and the headquarters of the United Nations. Its many famous skyscrapers include the Empire State Building (381 m, 1,250 ft high) and the twin towers of the World Trade Center (411 m, 1,350 ft high). The Hudson River and Manhattan Island were discovered in 1609, and in 1626 Dutch colonists purchased Manhattan from the Indians for 24 dollars' worth of trinkets, establishing a settlement there, which they called New

Amsterdam. In 1664 the English naval officer who received the Dutch surrender renamed it in honour of the Duke of York (later James II), who was at that time Lord High Admiral of England. In 1789 George Washington took his oath as first President of the USA in New York. The city has two international airports (La Guardia and J. F. Kennedy) and is divided into five boroughs (Bronx, Brooklyn, Manhattan, Queens, and Staten Island).

New York City Ballet US ballet company formed by writer Lincoln Kirstein and choreographer BALANCHINE. Kirstein persuaded Balanchine to move to the USA in 1934 as director of the School of American Ballet. From this arose the American Ballet in 1935, which after various transformations (Ballet Caravan, 1936; Ballet Society, 1946) became the resident company of the New York City Center for Music and Drama, mounting chiefly works by artistic director Balanchine and co-director ROBBINS. The company rapidly gained an international reputation, combining European tradition with American contemporaneity. It moved to the New York State Theater at the Lincoln Center in 1964.

New Zealand A country situated over 1,900 km (1,180 miles) south-east of Australia, comprising the North Island and the South Island together with many smaller islands in the south-west Pacific Ocean.

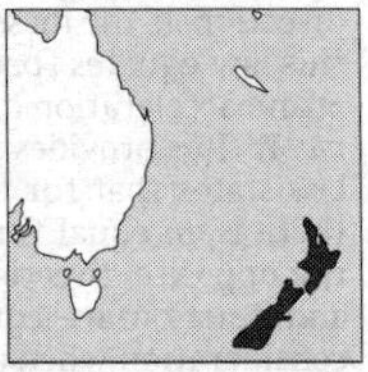

Physical. The two main islands, separated by the fairly narrow Cook Strait, together stretch north-east to south-west over a distance of some 1,600 km (1,000 miles). The boundary between the Indian (Indo-Australian) plate and the Pacific plate passes just south of North Island and diagonally through South Island. Movements along the boundary are responsible for many of the earthquakes of the region. Mostly the islands lie in the path of WESTERLIES which bring mild, wet weather across the Tasman Sea; but North Cape can be very warm while snow is falling on Stewart Island in the extreme south. Mixed arable and grazing land, with deciduous and evergreen forest, can be found throughout, and both main islands have reserves of coal. Natural gas is found near Mount Egmont on North Island, while many of the beaches are black with iron ore. The snow-capped Southern Alps, with Mount Cook in the centre, run the length of the South Island. High glaciers and narrow lakes lie among them; and their forested south-western slopes fall to the edges of still fiords, as in Fiordland National Park. From the eastern slopes rivers, harnessed for hydroelectricity, rush through stony, grey-green foothills to the wide Canterbury Plains. Here there are great sheep runs, extending south into Otago.

Economy. New Zealand has a largely agricultural economy with major exports of meat, wool, and butter. The economy was affected by the loss of preferential treatment by the UK, once the chief trading partner, when the UK joined the EC in 1973. New Zealand imports most manufactured goods and suffers from a balance of payments deficit. In 1984 economic reforms reduced government control of the economy and cut welfare provision. By the 1990s the net public debt had diminished. Most indigenous woodlands are protected National Parks, though commercial forestry is a thriving industry. Hydroelectricity is the basis of power generation, and supplies a large bauxite smelter. There is also some geothermal electricity production. Limited mineral deposits of iron, gold, salt, clay, and pumice are exploited. An oil refinery manufactures petrochemicals and there is some light industry. A treaty for closer economic relations aiming at the gradual introduction of a free market has been signed with Australia.

History. First peopled by the Polynesian MAORI from about 800 AD, European contact began in 1642 with the exploration of the Dutch navigator Abel Tasman. Captain James Cook, in successive explorations from 1769, thoroughly charted the islands, and brought them within the British ambit. Commercial colonization began from New South Wales in Australia and from the New Zealand Association (later Company) (1837) of E. G. WAKEFIELD. Humanitarian pressures contributed to the decision formally to annexe the islands as the colony of New Zealand in 1840 on the basis that the rule of law was necessary to regulate Maori-settler relations (Treaty of WAITANGI). In 1846 the British government conferred a limited constitution (rescinded in 1848) on New Zealand, divided into the provinces of New Munster and New Ulster, and in 1852 granted the islands representative government. Responsible self-government came in 1856. Settlement of the South Island prospered, assisted by the GOLD RUSHES of the 1860s. In the North Island, following the rapid acquisition of Maori land by settlers and by the government, the population was drawn into the disastrous ANGLO-MAORI WARS, following which most Maori land was settled. Regulations of 1881 restricted the influx of Asians, who were resented as a threat to the ethnic purity of the New Zealand people. They were confirmed by the Immigration Restriction Act (1920), whose terms were gradually liberalized. The property qualification for voting was abolished and women were enfranchised in 1893. In 1931 New Zealand became an independent dominion, although it did not choose to ratify the Statute of WESTMINSTER formally until 1947. In 1891–1911 (under the Liberal-Labour Party) and 1935–47 (under Labour) New Zealand won a world reputation for state socialist experiment, providing comprehensive welfare and education services. New Zealand actively supported the Allies in both World Wars, enjoying political stability and a high standard of living. After World War II it concentrated its defence policy on the Pacific and Far East, participating in ANZUS (1951–86) and sending a military force to Vietnam. Following British accession to the European Community (1973), New Zealand strengthened its trading links with Australia and its Pacific neighbours. When the LABOUR PARTY returned to power in 1984 it adopted a non-nuclear policy leading to withdrawal from ANZUS. The National Party under Jim Bolger won the election of 1990 at a time of economic recession. It confirmed Labour's non-nuclear stance, but introduced stringent social welfare cuts, ending free state education and introducing health charges for all. The National Party was re-elected in 1993 and in 1996 but lost its majority and Bolger formed coalition governments. Maori activists continued to demand compensation for land seized illegally by European settlers and the government agreed to pay compensation to the Waikato tribe in 1994 and to the Tainui tribal federation in 1995; in 1996 large tracts of South Island were granted to the Ngai Tahu tribe.

Capital: Wellington
Area: 267,844 sq km (103,415 sq mi)
Population: 3,568,000 (1995)
Currency: 1 New Zealand dollar = 100 cents

Religions: Anglican 24.3%; Presbyterian 18.0%; non-religious 16.4%; Roman Catholic 15.2%; Methodist 4.7%
Ethnic Groups: European origin 82.2%; Maori 9.2%; Pacific Island Polynesian 2.9%
Languages: English, Maori (both official)
International Organizations: UN; Commonwealth; OECD; South Pacific Forum; Colombo Plan

Ney, Michel (1768–1815) French marshal. He was one of Napoleon's leading generals, and after the Battle of Borodino (1812) became known as 'the bravest of the brave'. He commanded the French cavalry at Waterloo (1815), but after Napoleon's defeat and final overthrow he was executed by the Bourbons despite attempts by Wellington and other allied leaders to intervene on his behalf.

Ngata, Sir Apirana Turupa (1874–1950) New Zealand Maori leader and politician. As Minister for Native Affairs he devoted much time to Maori resettlement. Believing firmly in the continuing individuality of the Maori people, he sought to preserve the characteristic elements of their life and culture, including tribal customs and folklore, and emphasized pride in Maori traditions and history.

Ngorongoro Crater A huge extinct volcanic crater in the Great Rift Valley, north-east Tanzania, 326 sq km (126 sq miles) in area. It is the centre of a wildlife conservation area, established in 1959, which includes the Olduvai Gorge.

Niagara River and Falls A river forming part of the US–Canadian border, famous for its spectacular waterfalls. The river issues from Lake Erie and flows generally northward for 56 km (35 miles) to Lake Ontario. It is navigable on its upper course for some 32 km (20 miles), then forms a series of rapids before it splits into two above Goatland on the falls. The Canadian or Horseshoe Falls are more than twice as broad but slightly lower than the American Falls over which the cataract tumbles vertically for 50 m (167 feet).

Niamey The capital of the state of Niger in West Africa, on the River Niger; pop. (1994) 410,000. It is a river port and trade centre at an important road junction and was developed by the French who made it capital of the colony of Niger in French West Africa in 1926.

Nibelung In Germanic mythology, a member of a Scandinavian race of dwarfs, owners of a hoard of gold and magic treasures, who were ruled by Nibelung, king of Nibelheim (land of mist). In the epic poem, *The Nibelungenlied* (*c.*1205), a Nibelung is any supporter of Siegfried, the subsequent possessor of the hoard, as well as any of the Burgundians who stole it from him.

Nicaea An ancient city in Asia Minor, on the site of modern Iznik, important in Roman and Byzantine times. It was the site of two ecumenical councils of the Church. The first, the Council of Nicaea in 325, condemned Arianism and produced the Nicene Creed. The second, in 787, condemned the iconoclasts.

Nicaragua The largest country in Central America, bounded on the north by Honduras and on the south by Costa Rica.

Physical. Nicaragua has a south-western-facing coast on the Pacific Ocean and a longer, eastward-facing one on the Caribbean Sea, the Mosquito Coast. In the west are fertile plains and volcanic mountains. The climate is tropical. In the north are forested hills, and in the south-west two great lakes. The country is subject to earthquakes, being near the junction of crustal plates.

Economy. The civil war has devastated the economy, which has also suffered from US attempts to enact a trade blockade and suspend foreign aid. There have been shortages of most goods and very high inflation. The economy is principally agricultural, with coffee, cotton, beef, and bananas the principal exports. There is also some gold-mining. Other mineral resources are silver and copper. Manufacturing industry includes food-processing, petroleum-refining, textiles, and cement.

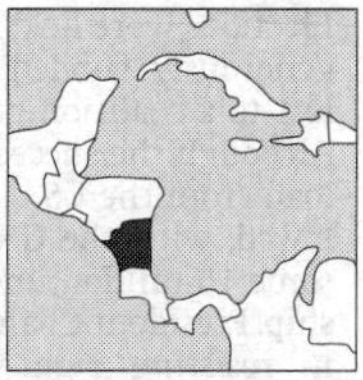

History. The first inhabitants of Nicaragua were Indians from South America who settled on the coast. From the 10th century AD peoples from Mexico began to immigrate into the region. The first Spanish colonization was undertaken by Francisco Hernándes de Córdoba, who founded the towns of Granada on Lake Nicaragua and León on Lake Managua in 1524. One of the main Indian tribes converted to Christianity, which enabled the Spanish to take control of the area with ease. Administratively part of the viceroyalty of New Spain and the captaincy-general of Guatemala, Nicaragua grew slowly. It depended upon agriculture, which developed substantially in the 18th century. The country achieved its independence from Spain in 1821. Nicaragua was briefly annexed into the Mexican empire of Agustín de Iturbide, and with the collapse of that experiment formed part of the United Province of CENTRAL AMERICA until becoming independent again in 1838. In 1848 the British seized San Juan del Norte, known as the Mosquito Coast, after a tribe of American Indians, the Miskito. In 1855 a US adventurer, William Walker, seized control of the country and made himself President (1856–57). His ousting helped unite the country, which made peace with Britain and recognized a separate Mosquito kingdom. The 20th century opened with the country under the vigorous control of the dictator José Santos Zelaya, who extended Nicaraguan authority over the Mosquito kingdom. The USA, apprehensive of his financial dealings with Britain, supported the revolution which overthrew him in 1907. The US presence, including two occupations by the marines, dominated the country until 1933. In 1937 Nicaragua fell under the control of Anastasio SOMOZA, who ruled until his assassination in 1956. He was succeeded by his son Luis (1957–63), and then by the latter's brother, General Anastasio Debayle Somoza (1967–72, 1974–79). In 1962 a guerrilla group, the Sandinista National Liberation Front, was formed. It gained increasing support from the landless peasantry and engaged in numerous clashes with the National Guard, ending in civil war (1976–79). Once established as a ruling party, the Sandinistas, led by Daniel Ortega, expropriated large estates for landless peasants. The dispossessed and exiled owners of the estates then organized opposition to the regime, recruiting a 'Contra' rebel army, funded and organized by the CIA. Mines and forests were nationalized and relations with the USA deteriorated. In 1981 US aid ended and the regime was accused of receiving aid from Cuba and the Soviet Union. The REAGAN administration sought increasing support from the US Congress to give aid to the exiled Contra forces in Honduras and Miami, but was seriously embarrassed by exposure in 1986–87 of illegal diversion of money to the Contras from US sale of arms to Iran. When President Bush took office in 1989 direct military funding to the Contras ended.

Elections were held in 1990 with opposition groups generously funded by the USA. The Sandinistas lost to a coalition group led by Violeta Chamorro. Although she succeeded in winning a $300 million loan from the USA, severe economic recession followed, with the GNP falling by 5.5 per cent and some 1.5 million unemployed, causing great hardship. President Chamorro only narrowly succeeded in resisting right-wing pressure for *haciendas*, confiscated by the Sandinistas, to be returned to their former owners. In 1992 there were violent clashes between re-armed Contras and Sandinista 're-Compas'. A cease-fire agreement was reached in 1994. In 1996 Chamorro resigned, and the conservative Arnaldo Alemán defeated Ortega in presidential elections.

Capital: Managua
Area: 130,700 sq km (50,464 sq mi)
Population: 4,340,000 (1995)
Currency: 1 cordoba = 100 centavos
Religions: Roman Catholic 88.3%; other (mostly Baptist, Moravian, and Pentecostal) 11.7%
Ethnic Groups: Mestizo 77.0%; White 10.0%; Black 9.0%; Amerindian 4.0%
Languages: Spanish (official); Amerindian languages
International Organizations: UN; OAS

Nice A resort city on the French Riviera, capital of the department of Alpes-Maritimes in the Provence-Alpes-Côte d'Azur region of south-eastern France; pop. (1990) 345,670. Situated on the Baie des Anges, an inlet of the Mediterranean, Nice is the fifth-largest city in France. It was annexed from the kingdom of Sardinia in 1860. A leading resort on the French Riviera it has a university and a flourishing trade in fruit and flowers.

niche (in ecology) The place of an organism in its HABITAT, in relation to all of its environmental and resource needs. The fundamental niche is the full range of conditions within which an organism can function and multiply in the absence of competitors, while the realized niche is that part of a fundamental niche to which an organism is actually restricted by competitors and interacting species.

Nicholas Two tsars of Russia. **Nicholas I** (1796–1855), brother of Alexander I, reigned 1825–55. He pursued rigidly conservative policies, maintaining serfdom and building up a large secret police force to suppress radical reformers. He was largely concerned with keeping the peace in Europe, but his expansionist policies in the Near East led to the Crimean War, during which he died. **Nicholas II** (1868–1918), son of Alexander III, reigned 1894–1917. He proved incapable of coping with the dangerous political legacy left by his father and was criticized for allowing his wife Alexandra (and her favourites, especially Rasputin) too much influence. Previously resistant to reform, after the disastrous war with Japan (1904–05) the tsar pursued a less reactionary line, but the programme of reforms which was introduced was not sufficient to prevent the disintegration of the tsarist regime under the strain of fresh military disasters during World War I. Nicholas was forced to abdicate after the Russian Revolution in 1917 and was shot with his family a year later.

Nicholas, St (4th century) Christian prelate. Little is known of his life, but he is said to have been bishop of Myra in Lycia; his supposed remains were taken to Bari in SE Italy in 1087. He became the subject of many legends and is patron saint of children, sailors, and the countries of Greece and Russia. In late medieval Europe he became identified with Father Christmas; the cult of Santa Claus (a corruption of his name) arose in North America in the 17th century from the Dutch custom of giving gifts to children on his feast day (6 December), a practice now usually transferred to Christmas.

Nicholson, Ben (1894–1982) British painter. A pioneer of British abstract art, he met Piet Mondrian in 1933 and from that time produced painted reliefs with circular and rectangular motifs. These became his main output, together with purely geometrical paintings.

Nicholson, Jack (1937–) US actor. He made his film début in 1958, but it was not until he appeared in *Easy Rider* (1969) that he gained wide recognition. He went on to act in such diverse films as *Five Easy Pieces* (1970), *The Shining* (1980), and *A Few Good Men* (1992), and won Oscars for *One Flew Over the Cuckoo's Nest* (1975) and *Terms of Endearment* (1983). His more recent films include *Batman* (1989) and *Wolf* (1994).

nickel (symbol Ni, at. no. 28, r.a.m. 58.71) A hard, grey-white, ferromagnetic metal and one of the TRANSITION METALS. It occurs naturally in pentlandite and pyrrhotite. The crude ore is roasted to give the oxide, which is then reduced to the metal with carbon. Purification is carried out by ELECTROLYSIS or the Mond process, during which it is converted to the volatile nickel carbonyl, $Ni(CO)_4$. The metal is hard, malleable, ductile, and resistant to corrosion, so is widely used to plate objects made from steel and copper. It is also the constituent of many important ALLOYS, such as stainless STEEL, NIMONICS, Monel metal, permalloy, nickel silver, nichrome, and INVAR. Finely divided nickel is an important industrial CATALYST. Chemically nickel resembles iron and cobalt with a usual valency of 2.

nickel silver See ALLOY.

Nicklaus, Jack (William) (1940–) US golfer. Since the start of his professional career in 1962, he has won more than 80 tournaments: major titles include six wins in the PGA championship, four in the US Open, and three in the British Open.

Nicobar Islands See ANDAMAN AND NICOBAR ISLANDS.

Nicodemus The Pharisee and member of the Sanhedrin, who was a secret disciple of Jesus. He protested at Jesus' unjust trial before the Sanhedrin and, after the crucifixion, brought spices for his enbalming, helping Joseph of Arimathea to lay his body in the tomb.

Nicosia (Greek **Lefkosia**) The capital of Cyprus, divided since 1974 into Greek and Turkish sectors; pop. (est. 1993) 186,400. Situated on the Pedias River in the centre of the island, Nicosia was known as Ledra in ancient times. Its old walled town centre includes St Sophia Cathedral, now a mosque. Nicosia has many light industries, such as textiles, cigarettes, and footwear.

Nicotiana A mainly tropical American plant genus with about 45 known species, called tobacco plants. They are mostly annual or perennial herbs with large rosettes of sticky leaves and tall spikes of tubular flowers. *Nicotiana tabacum* is the parent species, from which the many varieties of TOBACCO have been developed. All species, members of the potato family Solanaceae, contain the poisonous substance nicotine, which has useful properties as an insecticide. Most have fragrant flowers, which open at night, but colourful, day-flowering varieties of *N. alata* have been bred.

niello A black compound (typically sulphur, silver, lead, and copper) used as a decorative inlay on metal surfaces. Both the process of making such an inlay and a surface or object so treated are also known as niello. Typically it was used to decorate small luxury items, such as silver snuff-boxes, cups, boxes, knife handles, and belt buckles. Niello work is still produced in India and the Balkans.

Nielsen, Carl August (1865–1931) Danish composer. A major figure in the development of modern Scandinavian music, he gained his first success in 1888 with his *Little Suite* for string orchestra. His six symphonies (1890–1925) form the core of his achievement; other major works include the opera *Maskerade* (1906), concertos, and the organ work *Commotio* (1931).

Niemeyer, Oscar (1907–) Brazilian architect. He was an early exponent of modernist architecture in Latin America and was influenced by Le Corbusier, with whom he worked as part of the group which designed the Ministry of Education in Rio de Janeiro (1937–43). His most significant individual achievement was the design of the main public buildings of Brasilia (1950–60) within the master plan drawn up by Lúcio Costa.

Niemöller, Martin (1892–1984) German Protestant churchman. A U-boat commander in World War I, he became a priest in 1924. In 1933 he founded the Pastors' Emergency League to help combat rising discrimination against Christians of Jewish background. His courageous opposition to the Nazification of the Church led to his confinement in a CONCENTRATION CAMP (1938–45). A pacifist, he became president of the World Council of Churches (1961–68).

Niepce, Joseph Nicéphore (1765–1833) French inventor of the first effective photographic process (see PHOTOGRAPHY). In 1816 he recorded the view from his workshop window on paper sensitized with silver chloride. The image was negative, however, and he tried unsuccessfully to produce a positive from it. In 1826 he coated pewter plates with bitumen of Judaea, an asphalt that hardens and becomes insoluble in water when exposed to light. Areas on which bright light fell became hardened, while those corresponding to shadows could be dissolved in water. Exposure times were long (about 8 hours), but a distinct and permanent picture was achieved. In 1829 DAGUERRE persuaded Niepce to enter into a partnership to develop the photographic process, but Niepce died before the process was perfected.

Nietzsche, Friedrich (1844–1900) German philosopher. Nietzsche, who trained as a philologist, is in the first instance distinguished by the extraordinary literary quality of his writings, which he regarded as inseparable from their philosophical content. Originally under the influence of SCHOPENHAUER, Nietzsche's first book, *The Birth of Tragedy* (1872), identified in Greek tragedy, with whose spirit he associated Wagner's operas, an artistic mode of salvation. In subsequent works, such as *Beyond Good and Evil* (1886), Nietzsche pursued a devastating critique of religious and ethical (particularly Christian) conceptions of life, arguing for a 'revaluation of all values'. The concept of the 'will to power' played an important part in Nietzsche's view that metaphysical systems are to be evaluated not in terms of their truth or falsity, but in terms of the kind of will to which they give expression, and their role in promoting or suppressing the value of life.

Niger A large, landlocked West African country surrounded by Algeria, Libya, Chad, Nigeria, Benin, Burkina Faso, and Mali.

Physical. The River NIGER flows through the country in the extreme south-west, and the northern tip of Lake Chad lies in the extreme south-east. From these points the land rises through dry SAVANNAH and thin, thorny scrub to sandy desert and the high plateaux of the SAHARA.

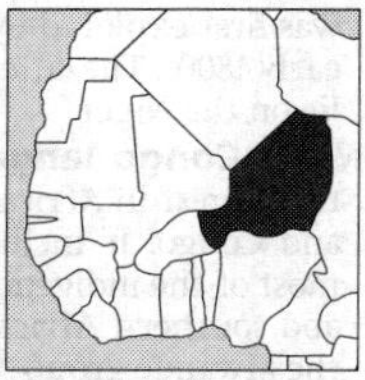

Economy. Agriculture is the principal economic activity, concentrating on livestock (the second largest export) and the cultivation of millet, ground-nuts, sorghum, and other arable staples. Drought has continued to be a problem. Uranium accounts for almost three-quarters of exports, with livestock and vegetables also exported; other mineral reserves are phosphates, tin, and coal, and unexploited reserves of iron, oil, gold, and copper. Industry is mainly textiles, cement, and mining.

History. Archaeological evidence shows that the area was inhabited in the PALAEOLITHIC period. The TUAREGS occupied parts of Niger in the 11th century AD and their kingdom of Agadès grew during the 15th century. In the 17th century the Zerma established an empire around the River Niger. The HAUSA, who had been moving into the area since the 14th century, expanded their territory during the 18th century, displacing the Tuaregs. In 1804 the FULANI, ancient competitors for Hausa land, defeated the Hausa in a war and established the kingdom of Sokoto. The French first arrived in 1891, but the country was not fully colonized until 1914. A French colony (part of FRENCH WEST AFRICA) from 1922, it became an autonomous republic within the FRENCH COMMUNITY in 1958 and fully independent in 1960, but there were special agreements with France, covering finance, defence, technical assistance, and cultural affairs. From 1974, it was governed by a Supreme Military Council, and all political associations were banned. Political activity was re-legalized in 1988. In 1989, under President Ali Saibou, a new constitution was approved by referendum, which set up a new ruling council. Saibou remained opposed to establishing multi-party democracy but strikes and demonstrations throughout 1990 prompted him to agree to implement reforms. Following a National Conference in 1991 a transitional government was formed. A multi-party constitution was approved by a referendum in 1992 and in 1993, following open elections, a coalition government took office and Mahamane Ousmane became President. In 1995 a peace agreement was made with ethnic Tuareg rebels, based in the north of Niger, who had been clashing with government forces since 1991. In January 1996 army officers staged a coup, throwing Ousmane out of office. After pressure from France a presidential election was held, which was won by the military leader Ibrahim Mainassara.

Capital: Niamey
Area: 1,267,000 sq km (489,062 sq mi)
Population: 9,151,000 (1995)
Currency: 1 CFA franc = 100 centimes
Religions: Sunni Muslim 80.0%; traditional beliefs 20.0%
Ethnic Groups: Hausa 54.1%; Songhai, Zerma, and Dendi 21.7%; Fulani 10.1%; Tuareg 8.4%; Kanuri 4.2%; Teda 0.2%
Languages: French (official); Hausa; Songhai; local languages
International Organizations: UN; OAU; Franc Zone

Niger A river in north-west Africa that rises on the north-east border of Sierra Leone and flows in a great arc for 4,100 km (2,550 miles) north-east to Mali, then south-east through western Niger and Nigeria, before turning southwards to empty through a great delta into the Gulf of Guinea. It was first explored by Mungo Park in the 1790s and early 1800s. The cities of Bamako and Mopti in Mali lie on the Niger.

Niger-Congo languages A group of languages, the largest in Africa, named after the rivers Niger and Congo. It includes the languages spoken by most of the indigenous peoples of western, central, and southern Africa; the important Bantu group, the Mwande group (West Africa), the Voltaic group (Burkina), and the Kwa group (Nigeria) which includes Yoruba and Ibo.

Nigeria A large West African country consisting of a federation of 21 states, with the highest population (95 million) of any African country.

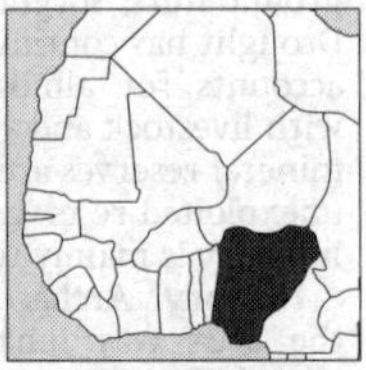

Physical. Nigeria has a southward-facing coast and is bounded by Benin on the west, Niger and Chad on the north, and Cameroon on the east. The sandy coast is bordered by mangrove swamp, inland of which there is a low plain with tropical rain forest spreading up the valleys of the Niger to the north-west and the Benue to the east. Here the climate is hot and very wet; to the west and north it becomes drier as the ground rises through open woodland and SAVANNAH to plateau land. The central Jos Plateau rises to 1,800 m (5,900 feet) with open grassland, but north of this the ground falls away to thorn-covered desert from which, in winter, blows the cool, dusty HARMATTAN.

Economy. Oil accounts for 97.9 per cent of Nigeria's exports (1992); other minerals include abundant supplies of natural gas, iron ore, coal, lead, and zinc. Heavy investment in petroleum and other industries such as steel, cement, and vehicles was halted by the drop in world oil prices in the mid-1980s, but led to a massive foreign debt ($41 billion in 1989) and the neglect of agriculture. IMF-backed austerity measures were introduced. These included cuts in subsidies and the development of traditional cash crops such as cocoa, cotton, and ground-nuts, and staple crops such as millet, sorghum, plantains, and cassava to reduce dependence on food imports. The austerity measures were achieving some degree of success by the early 1990s, but political instability during the mid-1990s has affected the economy badly.

History. The earliest known culture in Nigeria was the Nok culture, which existed from about the 6th century BC to the third century AD. Many different peoples have moved into the region; there are over 250 ethnic groups still living in Nigeria. The kingdom of KANEM-BORNU rose during the 11th century and fell during the 14th century. Islam was introduced to the area during the 13th century. The Portuguese arrived in the 15th century and established a slave trade, supported by the people of the kingdom of BENIN. The British were involved in the slave trade by the 17th century. The HAUSA people broke away from the SONGHAI kingdom and began to mingle with the nomadic FULANI, some of whom settled in Hausa towns. In the early 19th century a Fulani empire emerged. The kingdom of Benin and the YORUBA empire of Oyo occupied southern Nigeria.

The island of Lagos was a centre for the slave trade when this was banned by the British in 1807. The British had to use military force to stop the slave ships. In 1851 the British attacked and burnt the city of Lagos and ten years later bought it from King Dosunmu, administering it first from Freetown, Sierra Leone, and then from the Gold Coast (Ghana), until in 1886 a separate protectorate (later colony) of Lagos was formed. Explorers worked their way inland, but until the discovery of quinine (1854) to provide protection against malaria, the region remained known as 'the white man's grave'. During the second half of the 19th century trading companies were established, forming the Royal Niger Company in 1886, which was then taken over by the British Colonial Office to become the Niger Coast protectorate in 1893. Following the conquest of the kingdom of Benin, this became the protectorate of Southern Nigeria (1900). The protectorate of Northern Nigeria was proclaimed in 1900. In 1906 the colony of Lagos was absorbed into the southern protectorate and in 1914 the two protectorates were merged to form the largest British colony in Africa, which, under its governor Frederick Lugard, was administered indirectly by retaining the powers of the chiefs and emirs of its 150 or more tribes. In Northern Nigeria Muslim chiefs of the Fulani tribes maintained a conservative rule over the majority of the country's Hausa population. In the West, the Yoruba dominated; the Ibo tribe was centred in the East.

Under the constitution of 1954 a federation of Nigeria was created, consisting of three regions: Northern, Eastern, and Western, together with the trust territory of Cameroons and the federal territory of Lagos. In 1960 the federation became an independent nation within the COMMONWEALTH OF NATIONS, and in 1963 a republic. In 1967 the regions were replaced by twelve states, further divided in 1976 into nineteen states. Oil was discovered off Port Harcourt and a movement for Ibo independence began. In January 1966 a group of Ibo army majors murdered the federal Prime Minister, Sir Alhaji Abubakar Tafawa BALEWA, the Premiers of the Northern and Western regions, and many leading politicians. In July a group of northern officers retaliated and installed General GOWON as Head of State. A massacre of several thousand Ibo living in the North followed. Attempts to work out constitutional provisions failed, and in May 1967 the military governor of the Eastern region, Colonel Ojukwe, announced his region's secession and the establishment of the republic of BIAFRA. Civil war between the Hausa and Ibo peoples erupted, and Biafra collapsed in 1970. General Gowon was deposed in 1975. In 1979 the military government organized multi-party elections. Corruption and unrest precipitated more military takeovers, in 1983 and 1985, when General Ibrahim Babangida became Head of State. Progress towards restoration of full civilian rule was threatened by outbreaks of violence between Shiite Islamic fundamentalists and Christians. Political parties were re-legalized in 1989, but only two parties were allowed to register for elections, both having manifestos devised by the government. Open presidential elections in 1993 were, according to unofficial reports, won by Moshood Abiola, but Babangida annulled the elections, prompting serious social unrest. Babangida resigned and handed power over to another military government, promising that an elected civilian government would be installed in 1994. Abiola fled the country and sought international aid; he and his supporters continued to protest that the 1993 elections had been free and fair. The social and political crisis continued and Sanni Abacha took over as head of state in November 1993. He dismantled many existing political institutions and re-instituted the 1979 military constitution, but continued to insist that a civilian government would eventually be installed. Abiola returned to Nigeria to campaign for democracy and was arrested in 1994. In 1995 the government announced that civilian rule could not be introduced before 1997, but lifted the ban on political activity. However, in October 1995 nine pro-democracy activists were charged with murder and executed, provoking international outrage. As a result, Nigeria was suspended from the Commonwealth. Social unrest has persisted.

Capital: Lagos
Area: 923,768 sq km (356,669 sq mi)
Population: 95,434,000 (1995)
Currency: 1 naira = 100 kobo
Religions: Muslim 45.0%; Protestant 26.3%; African indigenous and traditional 17.2%; Roman Catholic 12.1%
Ethnic Groups: Hausa 21.3%; Yoruba 21.3%; Ibo 18.0%; Fulani 11.2%; Ibibio 5.6%; Kanuri 4.2%; Edo 3.4%; Tiv 2.2%; Ijaw 1.8%; Bura 1.7%; Nupe 1.2%
Languages: English (official); Hausa; Yoruba; Ibo; local languages
International Organizations: UN; Commonwealth (suspended in 1995); ECOWAS; OAU; OPEC

Nigerian Civil War See BIAFRA.

nightingale A bird of either of two species of the genus *Erithacus* of the thrush family, Turdidae. Nightingales are smallish and rather nondescript brown birds, 15 cm (6 inches) in length with a reddish-chestnut tail. They breed in much of Europe and western Asia, mostly in wooded country, but spend the winter in Africa. Seeking a breeding site on or close to the woodland floor, they make a small nest of leaves and lay four or five dark olive-brown eggs. Their food consists of insects and small fruits. The European nightingale, *E. megarhynchos*, is particularly famous for its beautiful song, frequently heard at night as well as in the day, and the inspiration of much poetry.

Nightingale, Florence (1820–1910) British nurse and medical reformer. She became famous during the Crimean War for her attempts to publicize the state of the army's medical arrangements and improve the standard of care. In 1854 she took a party of nurses to the army hospital at Scutari, where she improved sanitation and medical procedures, thereby achieving a dramatic reduction in the mortality rate; she became known as 'the Lady of the Lamp' for her nightly rounds. She returned to England in 1856 and devoted the rest of her life to attempts to improve public health and hospital care.

nightjar A bird of the family Caprimulgidae, which has a worldwide distribution with the exception of the cold polar areas, although it is only a summer visitor to high-latitude temperate areas. Most of the species are the size of thrushes, although two species have elongated tail feathers of 65 cm (26 inches) or more. Their plumage is mottled with soft greys, blacks, buffs, and white, making them extremely well camouflaged as they sit on the ground. They feed on flying insects at night or dusk, aided by their large eyes and enormous gapes, which enable them to open their mouths very wide to snap up their prey. They have distinctive, often very repetitive calls which carry long distances. Several species are named by the sound of their calls, for example whip-poor-Will, *Caprimulgus vociferus*, and chuck-Will's-widow, *Caprimulgus carolinensis*. The female lays either one or two well-camouflaged eggs on the ground, without any nesting material. The European nightjar, *Caprimulgus europaeus*, was popularly called the goatsucker from the erroneous belief that it sucked milk from goats in the night.

night monkey A New World monkey, *Aotus trivirgattus*, with large eyes; it is also known as the owl-faced monkey or douroucouli. The only nocturnal monkey, it seems to be blinded by daylight. In the day it remains hidden in hollow trees, coming out at sunset to prowl in search of insects, eggs, birds, and fruit. It has a long tail, which is not prehensile, and is grey-brown in colour with three black stripes along the head. It ranges from Guyana to Brazil and Peru.

nightshade Any of certain species within the potato family, Solanaceae. The deadly nightshade, *Atropa belladonna*, is a tall perennial plant with black cherry-like fruits. Although cultivated for the drugs hyoscyamine and atropine, the whole plant is extremely poisonous, the roots particularly so. The specific name refers to its former use by ladies to dilate the pupils of the eyes in the belief that this enhanced their beauty. Atropine is still used to make examination of the eye easier. Woody nightshade, *Solanum dulcamara*, is a perennial climber with clusters of purple flowers followed by red fruits. The black nightshade, *Solanum nigrum*, is an annual plant with small black fruits, found as a weed of cultivated land the world over. Enchanter's nightshade, *Circaea lutetiana*, is an unrelated, small perennial plant related to the willowherb.

nihilism The total rejection of authority as exercised by the church, the state, or the family. More specifically, the doctrine of a Russian extremist revolutionary party active in the late 19th and early 20th centuries. In their struggle against the conservative elements in Russian society, the nihilists justified violence, believing that by forcibly eliminating ignorance and oppression they would secure human freedom. The government of ALEXANDER II repressed the revolutionaries severely, and they sought vengeance by assassinating the emperor near his palace on 13 March 1881. After 1917 the small and diffuse cells of nihilists were themselves destroyed by better coordinated revolutionaries.

Nijinsky, Vaslav (Formich) (1888–1950) Russian dancer and choreographer. He trained in St Petersburg, and joined DIAGHILEV's Ballets Russes (1909–17). As a dancer he was known for his athleticism in FOKINE's *Spectre de la Rose* (1911), his characterization in *Petrushka* (1911), and for his choreographic and interpretive powers in *L'Après-midi d'un faune* (1912). He was an innovative choreographer; the distorted, inturned movement and violent rhythms of *Le Sacre du printemps* (1913) to Stravinsky's score outraged Paris, although it was in tune with MODERNISM. Mental illness ended his career prematurely.

Nile The longest river in the world, flowing northward from Lake Victoria in East Africa for over 6,400 km (4,000 miles) to the Mediterranean Sea. The lower Nile, the centre of Egyptian civilization for thousands of years, has the longest record of annual floods of any river. The upper Nile, in contrast, was little known before the 19th century, when the search for the river's source preoccupied European explorers. The Victoria, the Albert, then the Mountain Nile flow northward from Lakes Victoria and Albert into the immense Sudd marshes of southern Sudan, where it loses enormous quantities of water through evaporation and from which it emerges calmly, with little seasonal variation in volume. At Khartoum the White Nile is joined by the Blue Nile from the Ethiopian mountains, the north-westward course of the Blue Nile being relatively short and steep – and with a strong summer peak in flow produced by monsoon rains over the mountains. Below Khartoum, the whole river shows this dramatic flood peak. Until recently, Egyptian agriculture was maintained by an annual inundation of fields in the lower valley, with floodwater, silt, and dissolved minerals. Between Khartoum and Aswan, the river flows down six cataracts in a narrow valley bordered by desert. The Aswan high dam at the First Cataract now impounds the vast Lake Nasser, which extends southward to the Second Cataract. This dam controls the Nile's flood, allowing year-round irrigation and electricity generation. One consequence is that the silt that used to be carried into the DELTA, an intensely cultivated zone more than 180 km (110 miles) wide, no longer arrives in sufficient quantities to compensate for erosion by the sea; so the whole delta is now gradually shrinking.

Nile, Battle of the (1 August 1798) A naval battle fought at Aboukir Bay on the Mediterranean coast of Egypt, in which a British fleet defeated a French fleet. The French admiral had anchored his fleet of 13 vessels in the bay. He believed his ships to be safe from attack, but NELSON, the British commander, was able partially to encircle the French fleet. Nine French ships were taken or destroyed, including the flagship *L'Orient*. This conclusive victory established Nelson's prestige, destroyed NAPOLEON's plans for Egypt, and encouraged the signing of the second coalition against France.

nilgai (or **bluebuck**) A species of large antelope, *Boselaphus tragocamelus*, found on the lightly wooded hills of India. The bull has short, smooth, keeled horns, and an iron-grey coat. The female is smaller, without horns, and tawny in colour; the calves are also tawny. Small groups of four to ten cows, calves, and young bulls are found together; adult bulls are solitary or live in bachelor groups.

Nilo-Saharan languages A group of languages spoken in east-central Africa around the southern Nile, Chari, and Niger rivers. The group is a small one, and speakers are often found in 'islands' surrounded by other languages. The largest member is Eastern Sudanic, which includes the group of languages known as Nilotic. Nilotic languages are spoken in southern Sudan, Uganda, western Kenya, and northern Tanzania. Nubian is also an Eastern Sudanic language, spoken along the Nile south of Aswan.

Nilsson, (Märta) Birgit (1918–) Swedish operatic soprano. She made her Swedish début in 1946, gaining international success in the 1950s. She was particularly noted for her interpretation of Wagnerian roles, and sang at the Bayreuth Festivals between 1953 and 1970. Her repertoire also included the operas of Richard Strauss and Verdi.

nimbostratus A low, thick, dark rain cloud.

nimbus A cloud, such as cumulonimbus and nimbostratus, as opposed to the general cumulus and stratus, from which precipitation is falling or about to fall. Nimbus clouds are the darkest, often inky in appearance (due to the density of water droplets they contain). When moving fast, with a lower edge broken by vortex-like wisps, a nimbus cloud generally indicates a squall.

Nîmes A city in southern France, capital of the department of Gard in the Languedoc-Roussillon region; pop. (1990) 133,600. It is noted for its many well-preserved Roman remains. It also gave its name to a type of cloth known as denim (de Nîmes), which was originally produced there, and the manufacture of textiles and clothing is still the principal local industry.

nimonic (US **superalloy**) A proprietary name for various nickel-based alloys that have excellent resistance to oxidation and creep at high temperatures, where steel has little strength. Developed during the 1940s for gas-turbine engines, they were originally based on nickel with 20 per cent chromium and small amounts of other elements. Modern nimonics are much more complex and may contain large amounts of cobalt, rhenium, tantalum, molybdenum, or iron, and smaller quantities of aluminium and titanium.

Nimrod A legendary biblical figure, the 'mighty hunter', and descendant of Cush. As King of Shinar and founder of the Babylonian Empire, Nimrod's dominion of the world was alleged, in Hebrew tradition, to have been acquired through his possession of the garments worn by Adam and Eve. To him is attributed the building of the Tower of Babel, caused by his desire to dominate heaven, too. Assyria was sometimes referred to as the land of Nimrod.

Nin, Anaïs (1903–77) US writer. Born in Paris, she lived in the USA between 1914 and 1920, after which she returned to Europe and studied psychoanalysis. She started writing in 1932, publishing her first novel *House of Incest* in 1936. She returned to the USA in 1940 and produced collections of short stories, essays, novels, and erotica. She is perhaps best known for her ceaselessly introspective *Diaries* (1966–81).

Nineveh An ancient city located on the east bank of the Tigris, opposite the modern city of Mosul in northern Iraq. It was the oldest city of the ancient Assyrian empire and its capital during the reign of Sennacherib (704–681 BC) until it was destroyed by a coalition of Babylonians and Medes in 612 BC. A famous archaeological site, it was first excavated by the French in 1820 and later by the British; it is noted for its monumental Neo-Assyrian palace, library, and statuary as well as for its crucial sequence of prehistoric pottery.

Nine Years War (1688–97) Also known as the War of the Grand Alliance, a conflict that resulted from French aggression in the Rhineland, and that subsequently became a power struggle between LOUIS XIV of France and WILLIAM III of Britain. In 1688 when French armies invaded Cologne and the Palatinate, the members of the League of Augsburg took up arms. Meanwhile William had driven JAMES II from the throne of England and in 1689 a Grand Alliance of England, the United Provinces, Austria, Spain, and Savoy was formed against France. The French withdrew from the Palatinate. James II, supported by French troops, was defeated in Ireland at the battle of the BOYNE. In 1690 the French navy won a victory off Beachy Head, but in 1692 was defeated at La Hogue, though their privateers continued to damage allied commerce. The French campaigns in north Italy and Catalonia were successful, but the war in the Spanish Netherlands became a stalemate as one lengthy siege succeeded another. William's one success was the retaking of Namur. The war was a severe defeat for France, despite a good military performance, because its financial resources were not equal to those of Britain and the United Provinces. Peace was finally concluded by the Treaty of Ryswick.

Ninian, St (*c.*360–*c.*432) Scottish bishop and missionary. According to Bede he founded a church at Whithorn in SW Scotland (*c.*400) and from there evangelized the southern Picts.

Niobe In Greek mythology, a queen of Thebes

whose children were killed by Apollo and Artemis to punish her for her boastfulness. Niobe was turned into a stone figure that wept tears.

niobium (symbol Nb, at. no. 41, r.a.m. 92.91) A dense silvery-grey TRANSITION METAL, originally called columbium, occurring naturally in the ores columbite and pyrochlore. Its most important use is in superconducting magnets, the windings being made from alloys of niobium and tin or niobium and titanium, containing about 75 per cent niobium. Small amounts of niobium are added to stainless STEEL to form stable carbides, enabling the steel to be welded.

nipa palm A PALM, *Nypa fruticans*, of mangrove swamps and estuaries from southern India to the Pacific. It has leaves several metres long arising from a creeping stem, which forks regularly like a seaweed. The fruits are different from those of most other palms in that they float and the plant is thereby dispersed by ocean currents. Nipa palms are the oldest palms known from the fossil record and one of the seven earliest ANGIOSPERM plants. They were much more widely dispersed in past geological eras.

Nipkow disc A disc containing an array of small holes that spiral inwards towards the centre. Invented by the German engineer Paul Nipkow in 1884, it formed the basis of a mechanical scanning process in early TELEVISION cameras. As the disc is rotated, each hole traces out a line across the image, and the amount of light passing through the aperture varies in proportion to the brightness of that part of the image.

Niro, Robert De See DE NIRO.

nirvana (Sanskrit, 'extinguished' or 'blown out') Describing the state of bliss entered into by enlightened or liberated beings, before or after death. In HINDUISM, nirvana is the release from endless rebirths (SAMSARA) into the highest form of consciousness in which the soul finds union with BRAHMAN. In BUDDHISM it is the perfect suspension of volition and cognition, and the removal of all traces of personal emotion.

nitrate A salt of nitric acid that contains the nitrate ion, NO_3^-. In the soil nitrates are formed from ammonium compounds and atmospheric nitrogen and are essential to plant growth. They are found in vast quantities as Chilean saltpetre (potassium nitrate). Industrially they are produced from the neutralization of nitric acid by a base, such as ammonia. All are solid ionic compounds and nearly all are soluble in water. They are used in explosives (particularly ammonium nitrate), as a source of oxygen, and as fertilizers. The widespread use of synthetic nitrate fertilizers has often given cause for concern. Excess amounts of nitrates entering the HYDROLOGICAL CYCLE may cause ecological imbalance with possible harmful consequences.

nitre See POTASSIUM NITRATE.

nitric acid (HNO_3) A colourless corrosive liquid that vaporizes to give red or yellow fumes owing to the presence of nitrogen dioxide. The nitrogen dioxide is formed by thermal decomposition of the nitric acid. In aqueous solution it is both a strong ACID and a powerful oxidizing agent (see OXIDATION AND REDUCTION). Nitric acid is made industrially by the two-stage oxidation of AMMONIA to nitrogen dioxide, which is then absorbed in water to form nitric acid. It is used in the manufacture of explosives, dyes, drugs, plastics, and fertilizers.

nitrile An organic compound of the general formula R–CN, where R is an ALKYL OF ARYL GROUP. The carbon atom and the nitrogen atom of the FUNCTIONAL GROUP are joined by a triple bond. Nitriles therefore undergo addition reactions: for example, in the presence of hydrogen and a catalyst, they are converted to primary amines, $R{-}CH_2NH_2$. They also undergo HYDROLYSIS, in the presence of either acid or alkali, firstly to form the amide $RCONH_2$ and then the corresponding carboxylic acid RCOOH.

nitrocellulose (or **cellulose nitrate**) A highly flammable compound formed when cellulose materials (usually waste cotton fibres and woodpulp) are treated with concentrated NITRIC ACID. The extent of the reaction between the cotton and acid can be varied to give a range of compounds, from the highly explosive gun-cotton to the flammable collodion cotton or pyroxilin. Nitro-cellulose is unstable, and can decompose explosively. To counteract this tendency, the French chemist P.-M.-E. Vieille added stabilizing chemicals to produce a safe firearm propellant (1884), the first of the smokeless powders. These are now used worldwide as propellants in cartridges and other ammunition. Some smokeless powders (for example, cordite) also contain NITROGLYCERINE. Collodion cotton and other less reactive forms of nitrocellulose are used chiefly in lacquers. They also form the basis of one of the earliest plastics, CELLULOID.

nitrogen (symbol N, at. no. 7, r.a.m. 14.01) A colourless, odourless gas that makes up about 78 per cent of the Earth's atmosphere by volume. In its free state it consists of diatomic molecules, N_2. It is produced on a large scale by the fractional distillation of liquid air, having a lower boiling point (−196°C, −385°F) than air's other main component, oxygen. It is an extremely unreactive element, forming metal nitrides only at high temperatures; even so, it forms a wide range of compounds, which are of vast importance, for example in photography, and as dyestuffs, explosives, and polymers. It is used in the manufacture of ammonia and nitric acid, and also where an inert atmosphere is required. Liquid nitrogen is an important coolant. Nitrogen is an essential element for all life-forms: plants use it to build amino acids, proteins, and enzymes, and ammonium compounds and nitrates are therefore widely used as fertilizers. Some bacteria can convert nitrogen gas directly from the atmosphere into nitrogen compounds; this process is called nitrogen fixation (see NITROGEN CYCLE). Large quantities are used to produce ammonia by the HABER–BOSCH PROCESS.

nitrogen cycle A BIOGEOCHEMICAL CYCLE involving the element nitrogen. Nitrogen is extremely unreactive and can be used, or 'fixed', only by certain types of bacteria (including some cyanobacteria). These organisms are able to convert nitrogen gas into ammonia (NH_3), which they use to make amino acids, proteins, nucleic acids, and other nitrogenous compounds. Leguminous plants, such as peas, beans, and clover, form a symbiotic association with *Rhizobium* bacteria, developing root nodules in which these nitrogen-fixing bacteria can live. Nitrogen fixation also occurs during thunderstorms when lightning generates nitrous oxide (NO) and nitrogen dioxide (NO_2) gases in the air; the gases dissolve in rainwater to form nitrates (NO_3^-) in the soil.

All plants take up nitrates from which they produce all their essential nitrogenous compounds. Some of this nitrogen is lost when leaves, seeds, and fruits are shed, but most remains trapped until the plants die or are eaten. Animals obtain their nitrogenous substances directly or indirectly

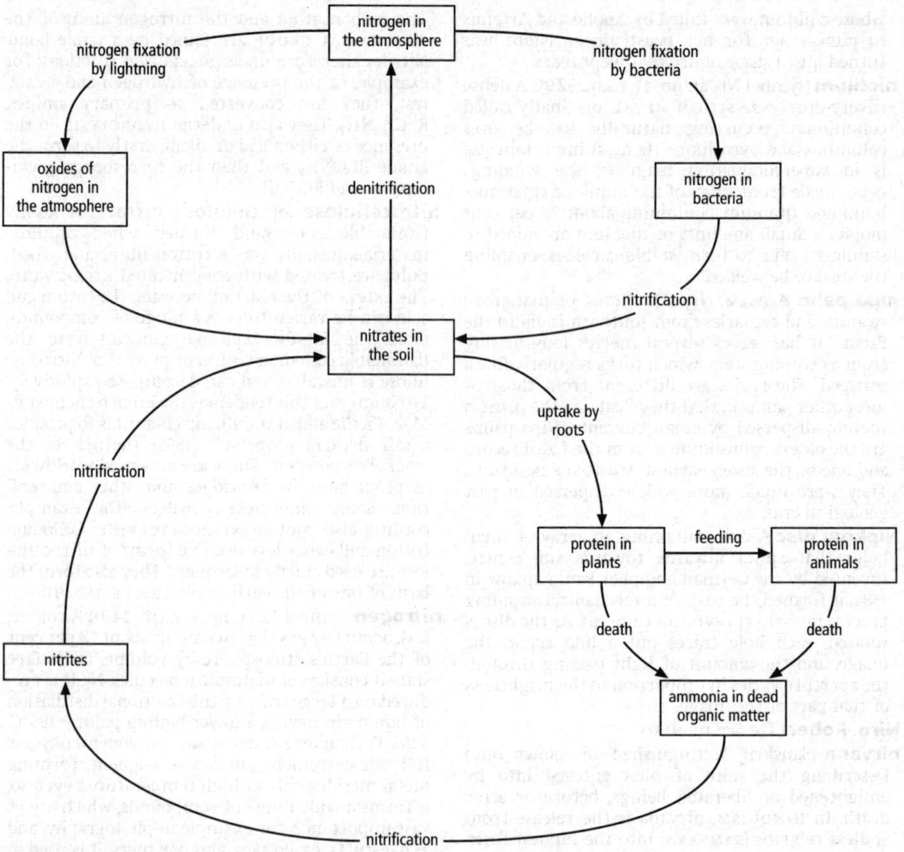

Nitrogen cycle Nitrogen flows continuously between the gases in the atmosphere and the nitrates in the soil. From the soil, nitrates are taken up by plants, which are subsequently eaten by animals.

from plants and excrete excess nitrogen in their faeces and urine. These substances and the dead bodies of all organisms are acted on by decomposing and nitrifying bacteria, which convert ammonia into nitrate, ultimately resulting in the return of nitrates to the soil. Denitrifying bacteria, which live in waterlogged soils, use nitrate for RESPIRATION, producing nitrogen gas, which is released to the atmosphere to complete the cycle. Modern agriculture may disturb the natural balance by adding nitrate fertilizer to the soil, much of which is washed out into rivers.

nitrogen dioxide (NO_2) A poisonous brown gas with a pungent smell. It is a FREE RADICAL, having an odd number of electrons, and in consequence it is magnetic. It supports combustion and is an acidic oxide, dissolving in water to form a mixture of nitrous and nitric acids. On cooling it liquefies and pairs of molecules combine to form nitrogen tetroxide, used as an oxidant in rocketry.

nitroglycerine A powerful explosive, sometimes known as blasting oil, formed when a mixture of concentrated NITRIC and SULPHURIC ACIDS acts upon GLYCEROL. It was invented by the Italian chemist Ascanio Sobrero in 1846. Nitroglycerine is a colourless, oily liquid with a sweet, burning taste, which is extremely sensitive to detonation by shock. Its great sensitivity makes it hazardous both to manufacture and to handle. Great precautions have to be taken to avoid detonation. It is used in the manufacture of the more easily handled explosives DYNAMITE and GELIGNITE; it is also used medically to ease the pain of angina.

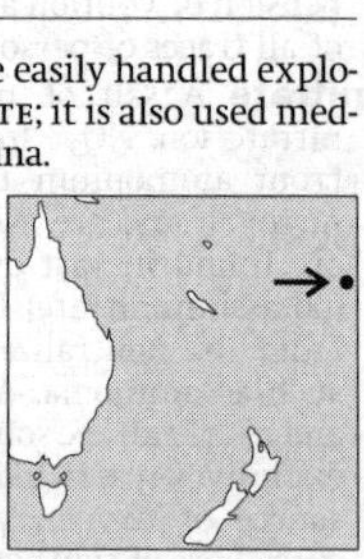

Niue An island territory in the South Pacific to the east of Tonga; area 263 sq km (101 sq miles); pop. (1991) 2,239; capital, Alofi. Sighted by Captain Cook in 1774 and annexed by New Zealand in 1901, the island achieved self-government in free association with New Zealand in 1974. It is the largest coral island in the world. The island's chief export is coconut cream.

Niven, David (born James David Graham Nevins) (1909–83) British film actor, who played many parts epitomizing the English gentleman. His films include *Wuthering Heights* (1939) and *Separate Tables* (1958), for which he won an Oscar. Later films include *The Guns of Navarone* (1961) and *Candleshoe* (1977). His two volumes of autobiography, *The Moon's a Balloon* (1972) and *Bring on the Empty Horses* (1975), were widely read.

Nixon, Richard (Milhous) (1913–94) US Republican statesman, 37th President of the USA 1969–74. He served as Vice-President under Eisenhower (1953–61), narrowly losing to John F. Kennedy in the 1960 presidential election. In his first term of office he sought to resolve the Vietnam War; the negotiations were brought to a successful conclusion by his Secretary of State, Henry Kissinger, in 1973. Nixon also restored Sino-American diplomatic relations by his visit to China in 1972. He was elected for a second term in November of that year, but it soon became clear that he was implicated in the WATERGATE scandal, and in 1974 he became the first President to resign from office, taking this action shortly before impeachment proceedings began. He was granted a pardon by President Ford for any crimes he may have committed over Watergate. He returned to politics in 1981 as a Republican elder statesman.

Nkomo, Joshua (Mqabuko Nyongolo) (1917–) Zimbabwean statesman. In 1961 he became the leader of ZAPU; in 1976 he formed the Patriotic Front with Robert Mugabe, leader of ZANU, and was appointed to a Cabinet post in Mugabe's government of 1980. Dismissed from his post in 1982, he returned to the Cabinet in 1988, when ZANU and ZAPU agreed to merge, and was Vice-President 1990–96.

Nkrumah, Kwame (1909–72) Ghanaian statesman, Prime Minister 1957–60, President 1960–66. The leader of the non-violent struggle for the Gold Coast's independence, he became first Prime Minister of the country when it gained independence as Ghana in 1957. He declared Ghana a republic in 1960 and proclaimed himself President for life in 1964, banning all opposition parties; Nkrumah's dictatorial methods seriously damaged Ghana's economy and eventually led to his overthrow in a military coup.

NKVD (initial Russian letters for 'People's Commissariat for Internal Affairs') The Soviet secret police agency responsible from 1934 for internal security and the labour prison camps, having absorbed the functions of the former OGPU. Mainly concerned with political offenders, it was especially used for STALIN's purges. Its leaders were Yagoda (1934–36) Yezhov (1936–38), and BERIA until 1946, when it was merged with the MVD (Ministry of Interior). After Beria's fall in 1953 the Soviet secret police was placed under the KGB (Committee of State Security).

No See JAPANESE DRAMA.

Noah (or **Noe**) A biblical patriarch who, forewarned by God because of his blameless piety, built a great ark or ship and, together with his family and with the creatures he took on board, survived the Flood sent to punish the wickedness of the human race. According to the Book of Genesis the whole of mankind descends from Noah's sons, Shem, Ham, and Japheth. The rainbow, which manifested itself after the Flood, was the visible sign of God's future protection of mankind against catastrophe. In Islam Nūh (Noah) is regarded as a Prophet Messenger (*nabī rasūl*). The story of Nūh is told in the Koran in various *Suras*, and greatly embellished in Islamic legend.

Nobel, Alfred Bernhard (1833–96) Swedish chemist and engineer. He was interested in the use of high explosives, and after accidents with nitroglycerine he invented the much safer dynamite (1866), followed by other new explosives. He took out a large number of patents in a variety of disciplines, making a large fortune, which enabled him to endow the **Nobel Prizes**. See Appendix.

nobelium (symbol No, at. no. 102, r.a.m. 259) A synthetic transuranic element belonging to the ACTINIDE group. Although seven isotopes are known the most stable isotope has a half-life of only 55 seconds. It is named after Alfred NOBEL.

Noble Eightfold Path A central Buddhist teaching that outlines the practical paths towards the extinction of desire and suffering, thus attaining NIRVANA or release from endless rebirth (SAMSARA). It is the last of the FOUR NOBLE TRUTHS, as defined by the BUDDHA. It is also known as the Middle Way. The Path leads out of the vicious circle of existence and up the creative spiral of enlightenment.

noble gases (or **inert gases, rare gases**) The elements of Group 18 (formerly Group 0) of the PERIODIC TABLE, namely helium, neon, argon, krypton, xenon, and radon. Except for ARGON, they are only present in the atmosphere at trace levels. Their inertness, or chemical unreactivity, is a result of their completely filled outer shells (see VALENCY); only a few compounds of the heavier elements are known – for example, xenon difluoride, XeF_2.

noctuid moth See OWLET MOTH.

nocturne A musical composition that suggests a romantic view of the night. In the 18th century compositions known as *notturni* were played as evening entertainments. In the 19th century the Irish pianist and composer John FIELD called his short piano pieces of a dreamy, romantic nature nocturnes. Such pieces involve an expressive melody accompanied by the ripple of broken chords in the left hand. CHOPIN's examples are particularly fine and, like Field's, owe much to the *bel canto* singing style of Italian opera. Other composers have also described their music with night associations as nocturnes. Debussy's *Three Nocturnes* are orchestral tone-pictures; Britten's *Nocturne* is a song-cycle to poems about night.

noddy A TERN of the genera *Anous, Procelsterna*, or *Gygis*, widely distributed in warm seas. Common, or brown, noddies, *Anous stolidus*, have dark plumage in striking contrast to the white tern, *G. alba*, and the blue-grey noddy, *P. cerulea*. All lay single eggs, usually in small nests on cliffs or in trees.

Noether, Emmy (1882–1935) German mathematician. She simplified and extended the work of her predecessors, particularly Hilbert and Dedekind, on the properties of rings. She lacked status in what was then a man's world, and her position at Göttingen remained insecure and unsalaried until terminated by the anti-Semitic laws of 1933. Nevertheless, she exercised an enormous influence, and inaugurated the modern period in algebraic geometry and abstract algebra.

Nolan, Sir Sidney Robert (1917–93) Australian painter. He is chiefly known for his paintings of famous characters and events from Australian history, especially his 'Ned Kelly' series (begun in 1946). He has also painted landscapes and themes from classical mythology, such as his 'Leda and the Swan' series of 1960.

nomadism The diverse traditional ways of life practised by peoples who move regularly from place to place to ensure a source of food and livelihood. Constantly on the move, nomads fall into three broad categories. First, some HUNTER-GATHERERS move at varying intervals in search of plants and game. Secondly, transhumance is practised by pastoralists (tenders of flocks or herds), such as the KURDS, BASQUES, or NUER, who move their livestock back and forth on a seasonal or periodic basis from relatively fixed points, commonly between mountain pastures in the summer and valley pastures in the winter, or wet- and dry-season pastures. Thirdly, tinker or trader nomads, such as GYPSIES or TUAREG, move on a regular basis to trade or practise small crafts. Traditionally, many nomadic peoples have elaborate lineage-based systems of KINSHIP.

nomenclature in biology A system in which any species of organism has one correct name, by which it is internationally known. The system stems from the work of the Swedish naturalist LINNAEUS.

The language of biological nomenclature is Latin, the language of science in Linnaeus's day, and the correct name of a SPECIES is the basis of the system. This name, called the scientific name, is composed of two words, the generic name, printed with an upper-case first letter, and the specific name, with a lower-case first letter. This system of naming is called binomial nomenclature. The whole scientific name, which is always printed in italic, may be followed by the name of the first user and the date of first use, although these are not obligatory.

nominalism A philosophical view that denies the existence of abstract objects and universals, holding that these are not required to explain the significance of words apparently referring to them. Nominalism holds that all that really exists are particular, usually physical, objects, and that properties, numbers, and sets (for instance) are not further things in the world, but merely features of our way of thinking or speaking about those things that do exist. In making claims about what there really is, nominalism is a thesis about existence (see ONTOLOGY); but it also involves views about meaning related to reductionism.

Non-Aligned Movement A grouping of 110 countries and liberation movements established in 1961 for the purpose of building closer political, economic, and cultural cooperation in the Third World.

Nonconformist (or **Dissenter**) A Protestant who did not conform to the disciplines or rites of the Anglican Church. Nonconformists include a number of groups. The PURITANS wished to purify the Church from within, while the PRESBYTERIANS were specific in their demands for the replacement of organization by bishops for a system of elected elders. The separatists under Robert BROWNE left the Anglican Church entirely. All Nonconformists were subject to penalties; the PILGRIM FATHERS emigrated to escape persecution. During the Civil War Nonconformists (especially CONGREGATIONALISTS and Baptists) fought on the Parliamentary side and the Restoration Settlement (1660) enacted harsh measures against all Nonconformist groups. The 1662 Act of Uniformity deprived them of freedom of worship and subsequent persecution led to a further exodus to North America. In 1681 Pennsylvania was founded as a refuge for QUAKERS. The Toleration Act (1689) brought some improvements in England, but until the 19th century Nonconformists were debarred from holding political office.

non-electrolytes Compounds that when molten or in solution do not conduct electricity – that is, do not undergo ELECTROLYSIS. They consist of molecules, and not ions; they are usually compounds of two or more non-metals. Simple examples are methane and ethanol.

non-metals These constitute about a fifth of all known elements. They are to be found in the top right-hand portion of the PERIODIC TABLE and at room temperature are all solids or gases. For instance nitrogen, oxygen, phosphorous and sulphur are all typical examples: the exception is bromine, which is a liquid. They tend to form negative ions, have acidic oxides, and are generally poor conductors of heat and electricity, due to the essentially covalent nature of their bonding, which means that there are no free electrons to act as conductors.

non-verbal communication The ways in which information is conveyed between individuals face to face in addition to or instead of speech. conversation between individuals is invariably (and often involuntarily) accompanied by non-verbal communication: posture and position, eye contact, gaze direction, facial expressions, and gesticulations. 'Body language' of this kind may reinforce the message conveyed by speech, or it may subtly contradict it (as when eye contact is avoided, for instance). Much body movement is involuntary, but we also make use of voluntary gestures, recognized actions performed in order to express a meaning, such as shrugging the shoulders, giving a thumbs-up sign, or pointing. There are worldwide similarities in facial expression of emotion. However, in the case of certain gestures there may be significant differences in meaning from one culture or community to another. For example, joining the thumb and index fingers to form a circle may signify approval, disapproval, or an overt sexual invitation. Where such gestures are widely recognized they often replace speech entirely, as is also the case in systems, such as SIGN LANGUAGE for the deaf.

Nootka (or **Aht**) A North American Indian tribe of the Wakashan linguistic group living on the northwest coast of British Columbia, on Vancouver Island. They were traditionally accomplished fishermen and boat builders.

Nore mutiny (May 1797) A mutiny by sailors of the British navy stationed at the Nore anchorage in the Thames estuary. Encouraged by the earlier SPITHEAD MUTINY, they demanded improvements in their conditions, the removal of unpopular officers, a greater share in prize money, and, under the influence of their ringleader, Richard Parker, certain radical political changes. This time the Admiralty would make no concessions and eventually the mutineers surrendered. About 19 men, including Parker, were hanged. Alarm at the mutiny probably contributed to the decisive defeat of Grey's parliamentary reform motion of May 1797.

Norfolk A fertile agricultural county (cereals, sugar-beet, cattle, and poultry) on the east coast of England, with numerous fishing ports and coastal resorts. Area 5,375 sq km (2,076 sq miles); pop. (1991) 736,700; county town, Norwich. The county is divided into seven districts.

Norfolk Broads see BROADS.

Norfolk Island An island in the Pacific Ocean, off the east coast of Australia, administered since 1913 as an external territory of Australia; area 34.5 sq km (13.3 sq miles); pop. (1991) 1,912. Occupied from 1788 to 1814 as a penal colony, the island was settled by the descendants of the mutineers from the *Bounty* in 1856. Descendants of the mutineers are known as 'Islanders' and those of Australian, New Zealand, or UK descent as 'mainlanders'.

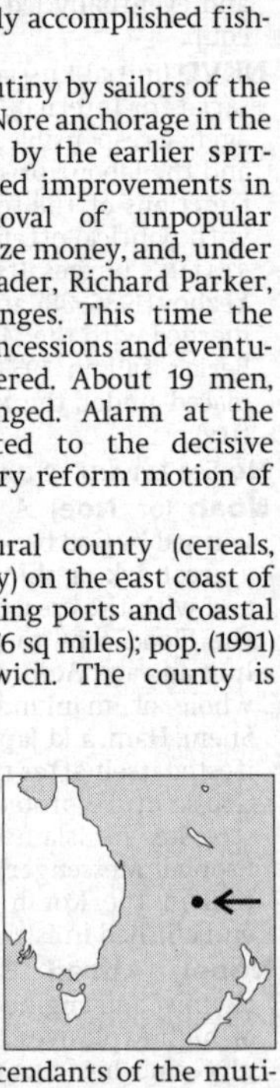

Noriega, Manuel (Antonio Morena) (1940–) Panamanian statesman and general, head of state 1983–89. He was Panama's head of intelligence (1970) becoming Chief of Staff and de facto head of state in 1983. He was charged with drug trafficking by a US grand jury in 1988; US support for his regime was withdrawn, relations worsened, and a year later President George Bush sent US troops into the country to arrest Noriega. He eventually surrendered and was brought to trial and convicted in 1992.

Norma The Level, a CONSTELLATION of the southern sky, introduced by the 18th-century French astronomer Nicolas Louis de Lacaille. It represents a surveyor's level, although Lacaille originally drew it as a set square and ruler. It lies in the Milky Way but its brightest stars are of only fourth magnitude and there are no outstanding objects of interest.

Norman An inhabitant or native of NORMANDY, France, a descendant of a mixed Scandinavian ('Northmen') and Frankish people established there in early medieval times. The area, secured by Rollo in 912 from Charles III of France, was inadequate for settlement since inheritance laws left younger sons without territory; land hunger provided the impetus towards conquest and colonization. Under Duke William the Normans conquered England (1066), and later Wales, Ireland, and parts of Scotland as well as large areas of the Mediterranean. Their expansion southwards, led by a spirited adventurer Robert Guiscard, was initially as mercenaries fighting the Muslims but they soon controlled much of Europe. In 1154, the year of Roger II of Sicily's death and HENRY II's accession to the English throne, Norman power was at its height, witnessed in the highly efficient governments of Sicily and England, which were renowned in Europe for their sophisticated legal and administrative systems.

Norman, Greg(ory John) (1955–) Australian golfer. He turned professional in 1976 and subsequently won the world match-play championship three times (1980; 1983; 1986) and the British Open twice (1986; 1993).

Norman, Jessye (1945–) US operatic soprano. She made her début in Berlin (1969) and subsequently performed in the major European opera houses, appearing in New York for the first time in 1973. Her repertoire includes both opera and concert music and she has given notable interpretations of the works of Wagner, Schubert, and Mahler.

Norman Conquest The period beginning in 1066 with Duke William of Normandy's victory over the English at the Battle of HASTINGS. As WILLIAM I (1066–87) he established a military superiority over the English, rebellions were crushed (1067–71), and about 5,000 castles were constructed by the time of his death. England's frontiers were protected, first by marcher lords and then through conquest. Ruthless attention to detail characterized the Norman approach to government. English institutions were either retained and developed (such as the treasury, the king's council, the king's peace, sheriffs, and the shire system) or replaced with Norman versions. Not all changes were popular with the English, who had already lost heavily in terms of status, land holdings, and public office. Taxation was heavier, forest laws were harsh and outside the common law. Norman efficiency produced the unique survey recorded in DOMESDAY BOOK (1086), though it owed a great deal to existing English records. The language of government and of the court was Norman French. England prospered commercially: its towns grew, as did its population. Many of these developments would probably have arisen without Norman rule – as is also true of the reorganization of the English Church under Archbishop LANFRANC – but the rapid nature of these changes owed most to the Norman Conquest. In architecture the Norman style, characterized by rounded arches and heavy pillars was introduced after the Conquest.

Normandy A former province in north-western France, originally the home of Celtic tribes, and part of the kingdom of CLOVIS. It was in Neustria under MEROVINGIAN rule and suffered from Viking invasions in the 9th century. The Viking Rollo accepted it in 912 as a FIEF from the French king, who was powerless to prevent its falling to the Vikings, and the present name derives from those invaders. They accepted Christianity and adopted the French language but Norman expansion meant that their power rivalled that of the French kings.

In 1066 Duke William of Normandy conquered England, becoming WILLIAM I. The duchy was recovered for France by Philip Augustus in 1204, but fell once more to England in the Hundred Years War. After the Battle of Formigny in 1450 it was permanently reunited with France.

Normandy Campaign (June–August 1944) An Allied counter-offensive in Europe in World War II. A series of landings were made on the beaches of Normandy, France, beginning on 6 June 1944 (D-Day). Five beaches had been designated for the Allied invasion, code-name 'Operation Overlord', for which General EISENHOWER was the supreme commander. British and Canadian troops fought across the eastern beaches, the US forces the western. Allied airforces destroyed most of the bridges over the Seine and the Loire, preventing the Germans from reinforcing their forward units. On D-Day plus 14 two vast steel-and-concrete artificial harbours (code-name 'Mulberry') were towed across the English Channel. One was sunk by a freak storm, but the second was established at Arromanches, providing the main harbour for the campaign. Meanwhile 20 oil pipelines (code-name 'Pluto' – pipe line under the ocean) were laid across the Channel to supply the thousands of vehicles now being landed.

The US forces under General BRADLEY had cut off the Cotentin Peninsula (18 June), and accepted the surrender of Cherbourg. The British army attacked towards Caen, securing it after heavy fighting (9 July) before advancing on Falaise. US troops broke through the German defences to capture the vital communications centre of Saint-Lô, cutting off the German force under ROMMEL. The Germans launched a counter-attack but were caught between the US and British armies in the 'Falaise Gap' and lost 60,000 men in fierce fighting. Field-Marshal Model, transferred from the Eastern Front, was unable to stem Patton's advance, which now swept across France to Paris, while Montgomery moved his British army up the English Channel. Paris was liberated by General Leclerc on 26 August, and Brussels on 3 September. By 5 September more than two million troops, four million tonnes of supplies, and 450,000 vehicles had been landed, at the cost of some 224,000 Allied casualties. See illustration p. 982.

Norse The official language of Norway. **Old Norse** was the Germanic language of Norway and its colonies down to the 14th century. It is the ancestor of the Scandinavian languages and is most clearly preserved in the saga literature of Iceland.

Norseman See VIKING.

North, Frederick, Lord (1732–92) British Tory statesman, Prime Minister 1770–82. He sought to

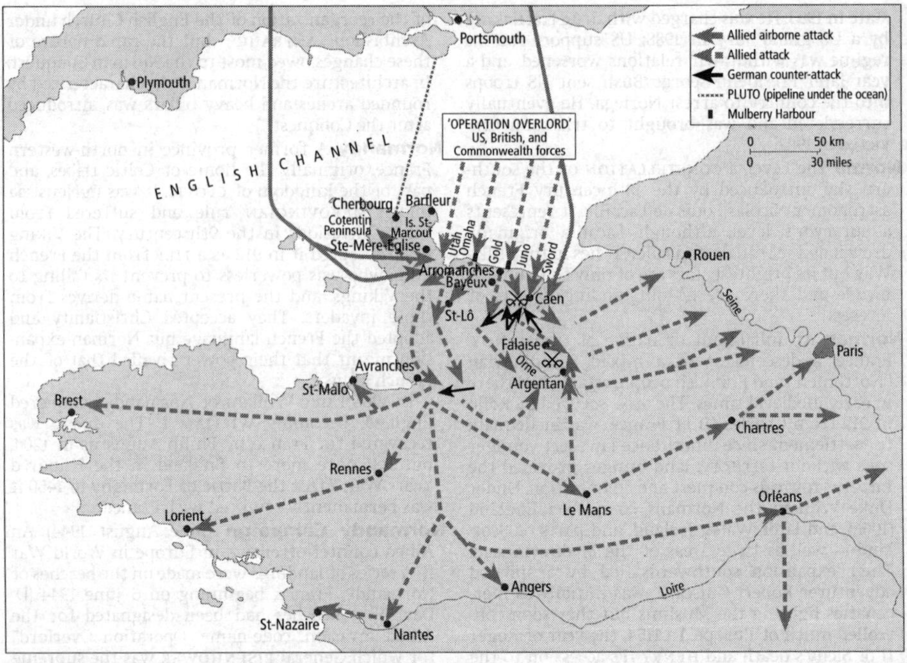

Normandy Campaign This campaign finally destroyed Hitler's Germany. Beginning on 6 June 1944, a series of landings on the Normandy beaches by some 2 million Allied troops under General Eisenhower swept through France against fierce opposition, liberating Paris on 26 August 1944. It was not until 7 May 1945, however, that Germany surrendered.

prevent the War of American Independence, but was regarded as responsible for the loss of the American colonies. This, together with allegations that his ministry was dominated by the influence of George III, led to his resignation in 1782.

North African Campaigns (June 1940–May 1943) A series of military campaigns in Africa in World War II. When Italy declared war in June 1940, General WAVELL in Cairo with 36,000 Commonwealth troops attacked first, the Italians giving up Sidi Barrani, Tobruk, and Benghazi between September 1940 and January 1941. In July 1940 the Italians had occupied parts of the Sudan and British Somaliland, but in January 1941 the British counter-attacked and on 6 April 1941 Ethiopia and all of Italian East Africa surrendered, thus opening the way for Allied supplies and reinforcements to reach the Army of the Nile. In March 1941 General ROMMEL attacked, and the British withdrew, leaving TOBRUK besieged. Under General AUCHINLECK, an offensive (Operation Crusader) was planned. At first successful, the campaign swung back and forth across the desert, both German and British tank casualties being high. Tobruk fell in June 1942 and the British took up a defensive position at El ALAMEIN in July. From there in October the reinforced 8th Army of 230,000 men and 1,230 tanks now under General MONTGOMERY launched their attack, and Rommel fell back to Tunisia. Meanwhile 'Operation Torch' was launched, an amphibious landing of US and British troops (8 November) under General EISENHOWER near Casablanca on the Atlantic and at Oran and Algiers in the Mediterranean. It was hoped to link up with FREE FRENCH forces in West Africa. The Vichy French troops of General DARLAN at first resisted, but after three days acquiesced. From November 1942 to May 1943 German armies, although reinforced, were being squeezed between the 8th Army advancing from the east and the Allied forces advancing from the west. On 7 May Tunis surrendered. Some 250,000 prisoners were taken, although Rommel skilfully succeeded in withdrawing the best troops of his Afrika Korps to Sicily.

North America The northern half of the American landmass, connected to South America by the Isthmus of Panama, bordered by the Atlantic Ocean to the east and the Pacific Ocean to the west. The southern part of the continent was colonized by the Spanish in the 16th century, while the eastern coast was opened up by the British and French in the 17th century, rivalry between the two ending in British victory during the Seven Years War. The American colonies won their independence in the War of American Independence (1775–83), while Canada was granted its own constitution in 1867. The 19th century saw the gradual development of the western half of the continent, the emergence of Mexico as an independent state, and the growth of the United States as a world power. The USA has progressively dominated the continent, both economically and politically, Canada having a very small population relative to its size and Mexico sharing, albeit to a much lesser extent, the problems of its Central American neighbours to the south. The total population of North America is *c*.367 million people.

North America Nebula A widespread distribution, 2 degrees across, of stars and nebular material in the constellation of Cygnus. The NEBULA closely resembles the shape of the North American continent. In good seeing conditions it is visible in binoculars, though its structure is best seen by photography.

North American Free Trade Agreement

(NAFTA) An economic pact permitting free trade between the USA, Canada, and Mexico. NAFTA extends a free trade agreement made between the USA and Canada in 1988. The treaty was signed in 1992, ratified in 1993, and took effect in 1994. It provides for the complete removal on all trade tariffs between the member countries, with tariffs on agricultural products to be phased out. Chile applied to join and in 1994 negotiations over its admittance began.

North American Indians The original AMERICAN INDIAN inhabitants of North America, who migrated from Asia from about 30,000 years ago. By the time of European colonization, the Indian population was probably under 900,000, mostly living along the coasts rather than in the barren interior. They lived in small villages, which, except in the south-west, were organized round hunting, with agriculture a secondary activity. The overall social organization was that of the tribe, and warfare between tribes was endemic. Conflict with British and French settlers in the north-east forced the Indians inland, as did clashes with the Spanish in the south-west. The acquisition of horses from Europeans increased the number of nomadic Indians on the Great Plains. The major tribes are usually divided geographically, North-eastern Woodland (for example, ALGONQUIAN, DELAWARE, IROQUOIS), South-east (e.g. CHEROKEE, CHOCTAW, CREEK), Great Plains (e.g. BLACKFOOT, COMANCHE, and DAKOTA INDIANS), Desert-west (e.g. APACHE, PUEBLO, NAVAHO), Far west (e.g. Paiute), Pacific North-west (e.g. Chinook), and Mountain or Plateau (e.g. Nez Percé).

Northampton The county town of Northamptonshire in central England, on the River Nene; pop.

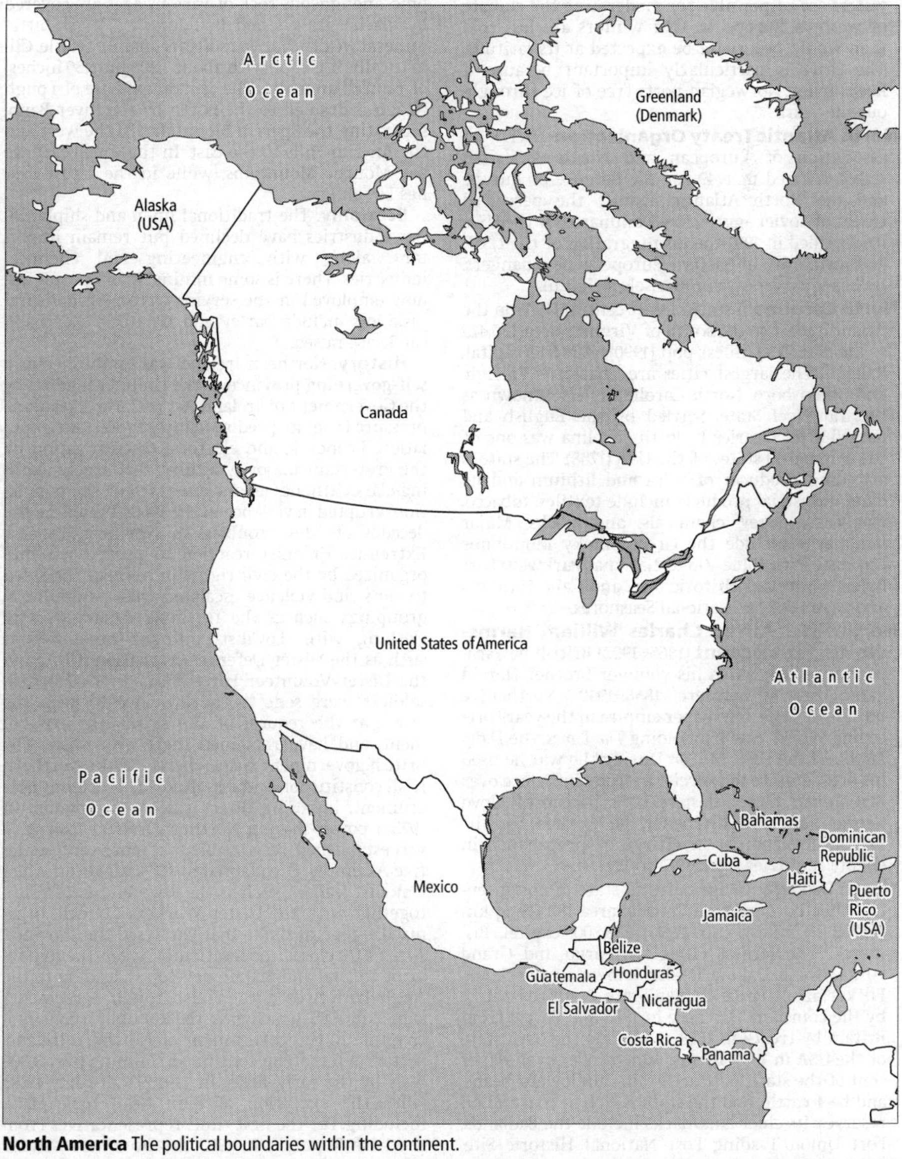

North America The political boundaries within the continent.

(1991) 180,567. Shoemaking was for long the principal industry, succeeded by engineering; there is also a major cattle-market. Northampton is increasingly becoming a dormitory town for London commuters.

Northamptonshire A county of central England; area 2,367 sq km (914 sq miles); pop. (1991) 568,900; county town, Northampton. The county is divided into seven districts.

North Atlantic Co-operation Council (NACC) An international defence and security organization formed in December 1991 at the end of the Cold War. It includes the 16 NATO member-states, the Baltic States, five former Warsaw Pact countries, and Russia.

North Atlantic Drift A broad, slow-moving surface current, a continuation of the GULF STREAM, flowing across the North Atlantic Ocean and towards the Arctic Ocean. Its relatively warm waters are responsible for moderating the climate of western Europe, so that winters are less cold than would otherwise be expected at its latitude. The Drift is particularly important because it keeps many Norwegian ports free of ice throughout the year.

North Atlantic Treaty Organization (NATO) An association of European and North American states, formed in 1949 for the defence of Europe and the North Atlantic against the perceived threat of Soviet aggression. Dominated by the USA, it identified in 1991 the disintegration of the USSR and instability in Eastern Europe as new dangers. Its headquarters are in Brussels, Belgium.

North Carolina A state of east-central USA, on the Atlantic coast to the south of Virginia; area 136,413 sq km (52,669 sq miles); pop. (1990) 6,628,640; capital, Raleigh. The largest cities are Charlotte, Raleigh, and Greensboro. North Carolina is also known as the Tar Heel State. Settled by the English and named after Charles I, North Carolina was one of the original 13 states of the USA (1788). The state is a leading producer of mica and lithium and its chief industrial products include textiles, tobacco, furniture, paper, chemicals, and bricks. Major landmarks include the Great Smoky Mountains National Park, Blue Ridge National Parkway, Fort Raleigh National Historic Site, and Cape Hatteras and Cape Lookout National Seashores.

Northcliffe, Alfred Charles William Harmsworth, 1st Viscount (1865–1922) British newspaper proprietor. With his younger brother Harold (later Lord Rothermere, 1868–1940), Northcliffe built up a large newspaper empire in the years preceding World War I, including *The Times*, the *Daily Mail*, and the *Daily Mirror*. During the war he used his press empire to exercise a strong influence over British war policy; despite his criticism of Lloyd George and Lord Kitchener, he worked for the British government in charge of propaganda in enemy countries from 1917 to 1918.

North Dakota An agricultural state in north-central USA, bordering on Canada; area 183,119 sq km (70,702 sq miles); pop. (1990) 638,800; capital, Bismarck. The largest cities are Fargo and Grand Forks. North Dakota is also known as the Sioux, Flickertail, or Peace Garden State. Acquired partly by the Louisiana Purchase in 1803 and partly from Britain by treaty in 1818, it became the 39th state of the USA in 1889. Farms, which cover over 90 per cent of the state, produce grain, sunflowers, beans, and beef cattle, and the state is rich in coal and oil reserves. Its chief landmarks include the Badlands, Fort Union Trading Post National Historic Site, Theodore Roosevelt National Park, and Knife River Indian Villages National Historic Site.

Northeast Passage A passage for ships eastwards along the northern coast of Europe and Asia, from the Atlantic to the Pacific via the Arctic Ocean, sought for many years as a possible trade route to the East. It was first navigated in 1878–79 by the Swedish Arctic explorer Baron Nordenskjöld (1832–1901).

Northern Cape A province of western South Africa, formerly part of Cape Province; pop. (1995) 742,000; capital, Kimberley.

Northern Ireland A unit of the UNITED KINGDOM comprising the six north-eastern counties of Ulster; area 14,121 sq km (5,452 sq mi); pop. (est. 1992) 1,610,000; capital, Belfast.

Physical. Structurally, it is a south-westward extension of Scotland, separated by the North Channel of the Irish Sea. Sedimentary, metamorphic, and igneous rock of various ages are covered by glacial gravels and boulder clay; it has little mineral wealth, but the soils are mainly fertile. Climatically, it is cool, with about 1,300 mm (50 inches) of rainfall annually. The central expanse of Lough Neagh is drained to the north by the River Bann, separating the Sperrin Mountains to the west and the Antrim Hills to the east. In the south-east are the Mourne Mountains, while in the south-west lies Lough Erne.

Economy. The traditional linen and shipbuilding industries have declined but remain important, along with engineering and chemical industries. There is some mining. Many people are now employed in the service sector. Agricultural products include barley and potatoes; sheep and cattle are raised.

History. Northern Ireland was established as a self-governing province of the United Kingdom by the Government of Ireland Act (1920) as a result of pressure from its predominantly Protestant population. Economic and electoral discrimination by the Protestant majority against the largely working-class Catholics (about one-third of the population) erupted in violence in the 1960s, heralding the decades of 'the Troubles' in Northern Ireland. Extremist Unionist reaction to protest marches organized by the civil rights movement (1968) led to riots, and violence escalated with paramilitary groupings such as the IRISH REPUBLICAN ARMY clashing with 'Loyalist' militant organizations such as the Ulster Defence Association (UDA) and the Ulster Volunteer Force (UVF). In 1969 British soldiers were sent to the province to keep the peace, at the request of the STORMONT government, and have remained there ever since. The British government suspended (1972) the Northern Irish constitution and dissolved the Stormont government, imposing direct rule from London. In 1973 a power-sharing Northern Ireland Executive was established, responsible to a more representative Assembly. It collapsed in 1974, however, when Unionist leaders, such as the Reverend Ian Paisley, together with the Ulster Workers Council, organized a general strike that paralysed the province. After 1979 closer cooperation between the Republic of Ireland and Britain developed, leading to the Anglo-Irish Accord (the Hillsborough Agreement), signed in 1985, which gave the Republic a consultative role in the government of Northern Ireland. Sectarian terrorism continued, claiming over 3,000 lives by the early 1990s. In 1991–92 all-party talks (with the exception of Sinn Fein) took place, including, for the first time, representatives from the Irish Republic. In 1993 the DOWNING STREET

DECLARATION was signed by John MAJOR and Albert Reynolds, the Prime Minister of the Republic of Ireland, paving the way for negotiations with Sinn Fein (as well as other political groups) on condition that they commit themselves to peaceful and democratic means. In 1994 the IRA declared a 'complete cessation' of military activities, which was followed by similar declarations by Loyalist paramilitary groups. However, little progress was made in peace negotiations during 1995 as a result of the UK government's refusal to negotiate with Sinn Fein until decommissioning of IRA weapons took place. In February 1996 the IRA broke the cease-fire by launching bomb attacks on London and Manchester. Sinn Fein was then excluded from the talks, which began in June 1996, but was admitted, following a new IRA cease-fire, in September 1997. In January 1998 the British and Irish governments issued, as a basis for negotiation, a joint document containing proposals for the future government of Northern Ireland, including: (1) a Northern Ireland Assembly to be elected by proportional representation, (2) a north–south ministerial council linking the two parts of Ireland, and (3) an intergovernment council linking assemblies in Northern Ireland, Scotland, and Wales with representatives of the British and Irish governments. In April 1998 a peace agreement based on these proposals was signed by the British and Irish prime ministers and the leaders of the negotiating parties.

Northern Marianas A self-governing territory in the north-west Pacific, comprising the MARIANA ISLANDS with the exception of the southernmost, Guam; area 477 sq km (184 sq miles); pop. (1990) 43,345; languages, English (official), Malayo-Polynesian languages including Chamorro, Woleian, and Filipino; capital, Saipan. The Northern Marianas, which comprise the islands of Saipan, Tinian, Rota, Pagan, Agrihan, Alamagan, and 10 uninhabited islands, are constituted as a self-governing commonwealth in union with the USA.

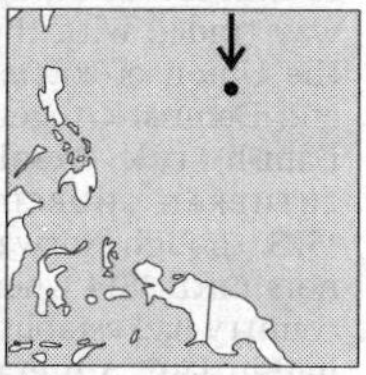

Northern Province A province of South Africa created in 1994 from part of the former province of Transvaal; pop. (1995) 5,397,200. Its capital is Pietersburg.

Northern Rhodesia The former name (until 1964) of ZAMBIA.

Northern Territory A territory of north-central Australia; area 1,346,200 sq km (519,969 sq miles); pop. (1991) 167,800; capital, Darwin. Annexed by the state of South Australia in 1863, the administration was taken over by the Commonwealth of Australia in 1911 and in 1978 it became a full self-governing member within the Commonwealth. It is a major source of minerals including uranium, lead, silver, zinc, and bauxite. Cattle-ranching is carried on in the semiarid scrubland. One-third of the territory is Aboriginal land.

Northern War (1700–21) A conflict between Russia, Denmark, and Poland on one side, and Sweden opposing them, during which, in spite of the victories of CHARLES XII, Sweden lost its empire and Russia under PETER I became a major Baltic power. By the treaties of Stockholm (1719, 1720) Bremen and Verden were ceded to Hanover and most of Pomerania to Prussia. After further Russian naval successes, the Treaty of Nystadt, which ended the war, gave Russia Sweden's Baltic provinces.

North Island The northernmost and less populated of the two main islands of New Zealand, separated from South Island by Cook Strait; area 114,383 sq km (44,180 sq miles); pop. (1991) 2,553,410.

North Korea See KOREA, NORTH.

North Minch See MINCH.

North Ossetia See OSSETIA.

North Pole The northern end of the Earth's axis, at 90° N, longitude 0°. Lying below the ice-covered Arctic Ocean, this geographic North Pole itself is about 4,087 m (13,410 feet) below sea-level. At the surface six months of daylight follow six months of darkness; and at the height of summer, snow on the ice melts into shallow pools and there may even be some rain. The Pole does not coincide with the north magnetic pole, which is in the Canadian Arctic, or with the geomagnetic North Pole, the northern end of the Earth's geomagnetic field (about 78° 30′ N 69° 00′ W). The geographic Pole was first reached by the US explorers Robert Peary and Matthew Henson by dog sleigh (1909).

North Saskatchewan See SASKATCHEWAN.

North Sea The sea lying between Great Britain and northern Europe. An arm of the Atlantic Ocean, it is about 1,000 km (600 miles) from north to south and 640 km (400 miles) wide, being linked to the Atlantic north of Scotland and by the Strait of Dover in the south-west. In the east it connects with the Baltic Sea. The Rhine, Elbe, Thames, Trent and many other rivers all drain into it; the courses of these rivers continue on the sea-bed, relics of the time when it was all above sea-level. It has an average depth of only 93 m (less than 300 feet), and there are several shallow areas where the water is a mere 20 m (65 feet) deep. The dissolved nutrients are good for fish, and below the sediment are the hydrocarbons that produce the UK's and Norway's reserves of oil and gas. The shallowness and shape of the North Sea has a profound effect on the tides that enter from the north, increasing their amplitude. The NORTH ATLANTIC DRIFT keeps the sea moderately warm.

Northumberland A county in the extreme north-east of England; area 5,031 sq km (1,943 sq miles); pop. (1991) 300,600; county town, Morpeth. The former industries of coal-mining and shipbuilding have declined and the county's economy now depends on tourism and light industry. Northumberland is divided into six districts.

Northumberland, John Dudley, Earl of Warwick, Duke of (*c.*1502–53) Ruler of England on behalf of Edward VI (1551–53). As Earl of Warwick he sought to undermine SOMERSET's power and was created Duke of Northumberland in 1551 shortly before ordering Somerset's imprisonment and execution. Though posthumous tradition condemned Northumberland as an evil schemer, his regime promoted stability. He terminated the unsuccessful wars against France and Scotland initiated by Somerset and introduced several important financial reforms. Northumberland brought about his own downfall by trying to ensure the succession of Lady Jane GREY. He was executed and MARY, Henry VIII's daughter, succeeded to the throne.

Northumbria An ancient Anglo-Saxon kingdom of north-east England and south-east Scotland extending from the Humber to the Forth. The name refers to persons living to the north of the Humber and has been revived in modern times by organizations, such as the 'Northumbria Authority', an area of police administration in north-east England.

North Vietnam See VIETNAM.

North-West Frontier The mountainous area,

inhabited by PATHAN and Baluchi peoples, forming the part of Pakistan that abuts Afghanistan. Under British rule from 1849 to 1947, after 1947 the Pakistan government withdrew military forces from tribal territory.

North-west Frontier Province A province of north-west Pakistan; area 74,521 sq km (28,784 sq miles); pop. (est. 1985) 12,290,000; capital, Peshawar. The North-west Frontier is watered by the Indus and is linked to Afghanistan by the Khyber Pass.

Northwest Passage Sea routes through the Arctic archipelago, north of Canada and along the northern coast of Alaska between the Atlantic and the Pacific Oceans. Martin FROBISHER was the first European to explore the eastern approaches (1576–78). In 1610 Henry HUDSON discovered Hudson Bay while seeking a northern route to the Orient. In 1616 William BAFFIN discovered Baffin Bay, through which the passage was finally discovered. A transit of the passage was first accomplished (1903–06) by the Norwegian explorer Roald AMUNDSEN.

North-West Province A province of South Africa created in 1994 from part of the former province of Transvaal; pop. (1995) 3,351,800. Its capital is Klerksdorp.

Northwest Territories The part of Canada lying north of the 60th parallel, west of Hudson Bay, and east of the Rocky Mountains; area 3,426,320 sq km (1,322,909 sq miles); pop. (1991) 57,650; capital, Yellowknife. For the most part it consists of vast, inhospitable, and sparsely inhabited forests and tundra. It includes the islands of the Canadian Arctic and is administratively divided into the districts of Fort Smith, Inuvik, Kitikmeot, Keewatin, and Baffin. It was administered by the Hudson's Bay Company from 1670 and transferred by Britain to Canada in 1870. In the past fur-trapping and fishing were the only occupations of the largely Inuit population. Mining of gold, silver, lead, zinc, and cadmium are now important.

Northwest Territory (or **Old Northwest**) A region and former territory of the USA lying between the Mississippi and Ohio rivers and the Great Lakes. It was acquired in 1783 after the War of American Independence and now comprises the states of Indiana (1800), Ohio (1803), Michigan (1805), Illinois (1809), and Wisconsin (1836).

North Yorkshire A county in north-east England; area 8,312 sq km (3,210 sq miles); pop. (1991) 698,800; administrative centre, Northallerton. It was formed in 1974 from parts of the former North, East, and West Ridings of Yorkshire. It is divided into eight districts.

Norway A country forming the north-western part of Scandinavia in northern Europe.

Physical. Norway's extensive coast, fringed with innumerable small islands, stretches from the Arctic Ocean to the North Sea. Inland it borders on Sweden (a long boundary), Finland, and Russia. It is mountainous, rising to 2,470 m (8,104 feet) in the Jotunheimen range. In the north, it is light all 24 hours in high summer – and equally dark in winter. Its warm climate is caused by the Gulf Stream, which usually keeps the FIORDS from freezing. The south is barren moorland plateau cut by forested valleys.

Economy. Norway has one of the world's largest reserves of aluminium, though the main resource is North Sea oil and natural gas; north in the Arctic the Svalbard (Spitsbergen) archipelago, contains rich deposits of coal. The extraction of North Sea oil and natural gas increased sharply in the 1970s and 1980s, and they made up about half of exports in the 1990s. Most electricity is generated by hydroelectric sources. Norway's annual fish catch is the second highest in Europe after that of the former Soviet Union. Norway has an industrial economy, exporting aluminium and ferrous metals, machinery, ships, chemicals, and paper. Fur production and conifer forestry are significant. Mineral resources include iron ore, copper, zinc, and lead. Agriculture is limited since only 3 per cent of land area is cultivable. Norway's defiance of an international ban on whaling has angered environmentalists.

History. Norway was inhabited in prehistoric times by primitive hunting communities. Rivalry between chiefs, and the desire for land provoked excursions by the Norwegian VIKINGS as far as England, Greenland, and Iceland. Political organization strengthened under Harald Fairhair (*c*.900) and under OLAF I, who brought Christianity. OLAF II furthered the work of Christian conversion, but was killed in a battle with the Danes. Danish rule (1028–35) followed, and thereafter civil war, and, in 1066, an unsuccessful expedition to assert Harald Hardrada's claim to the English throne. The reign of HAAKON IV brought order and, from 1254, Norway traded with the HANSEATIC LEAGUE. In 1397 the Union of KALMAR brought Norway, Sweden, and Denmark together under a single monarch. Danish rule resulted in conversion to the LUTHERAN CHURCH. The Union was dissolved in 1523, though Norway was ruled by Danish governors until 1814 when it was ceded to Sweden. The country had established its own parliament (Storting) in 1807. A literary revival and a new national consciousness brought demands for complete independence. Responsible government was granted in 1884, and universal male suffrage in 1898. Finally, union with Sweden was unilaterally declared dissolved in June 1905, and Prince Charles of Denmark elected as HAAKON VII. A Liberal Party government introduced women's suffrage and social reform, and maintained neutrality during WORLD WAR I. In WORLD WAR II, the Germans invaded, defeating Norwegian and Anglo-French forces at Narvik in 1940 and imposing a puppet government under Vidkun QUISLING. In 1945 the monarchy, and a Labour government, returned. Norway withdrew its application to join the EUROPEAN ECONOMIC COMMUNITY (1972) after a national referendum, while the exploitation of North Sea oil in the 1970s gave a great boost to the economy. Norway had been a founding member of EFTA in 1960, but by 1990 64 per cent of its export revenue was coming from the EC trade, and only 15 per cent from EFTA. Hence Norway was a leading negotiator for the establishment of the European Economic Area in February 1992. Gro Harlem Brundtland (1939–), author of the report on sustainable development worldwide, *Our Common Future* (1987), led four minority Labour governments (1981; 1986–89; 1990–93; 1993–) until her resignation in 1996; she was succeeded as Prime Minister by Thorbjoern Jagland. Norwegians voted against joining the European Union in a referendum held in 1994. King Olav V (1957–91) was succeeded by his son, Harald V.

Capital: Oslo
Area: 323,878 sq km (125,050 sq mi)
Population: 4,360,000 (1995)

Currency: 1 krone = 100 ore
Religions: Church of Norway (Evangelical Lutheran) 88.0%; Penticostalist 1.0%
Ethnic Groups: Norwegian 98.0%; Danish 0.3%; US 0.3%; British 0.2%; Swedish 0.2%; Pakistani 0.2%
Languages: Norwegian (official)
International Organizations: UN; NATO; EFTA; OECD; Council of Europe; CSCE

Norway lobster See DUBLIN BAY PRAWN.

Norwegian The official language of Norway, spoken by its 4 million inhabitants, which belongs to the Scandinavian language group. During the Middle Ages Danish gradually replaced Norwegian as the language of the upper classes in Norway, the peasants continuing to speak Norwegian, and there are still two separate forms of the modern language, *Bokmål* or *Riksmål*, the more widely used (also called Dan-Norwegian), a modified form of the Danish language used in Norway after its separation from Denmark (1814) following four centuries of union, and *Nynorsk* (new Norwegian, formerly called *Landsmål*), a literary form devised by the Norwegian philologist Ivar Aasen (died 1896) from the country dialects most closely descended from Old Norse, and considered to be a purer form of the language than Bokmål.

Norwich The county town of Norfolk in east England, on the River Wesum near its junction with the Yare; pop. (1991) 121,000. It has many old buildings including a cathedral founded in 1096 and is the home of the University of East Anglia (1963). It is a market and light industry centre.

nose An important organ in air-breathing vertebrates, particularly mammals. It serves two distinct purposes, first to clean and warm inhaled air and, secondly, to provide the sense of smell. In its roof there is a moist membrane in which lie nerve endings. These are receptive to different chemical substances, which dissolve in the fluid on the membrane, and signal olfactory sensations to the brain. Compared to most mammals, the human sense of smell is very poorly developed. The nose is used by most vertebrates to find food, to scent danger from predators, and to recognize other individuals, as in mating. Mammals deprived of the sense of smell die.

Most mammals warm incoming air by passing it over moist scroll bones inside the nose. These are kept warm by a rich blood supply. In many mammals, especially those of arid regions, the nasal membranes act as water conservation devices by trapping condensation from exhaled air.

no-see-um See MIDGE.

Nostoc A genus of CYANOBACTERIA. The organisms consist of photosynthetic cells; at the ends of chains, and less commonly within chains, are specialized colourless cells, called heterocysts, within which nitrogen fixation occurs (the trapping of nitrogen from the atmosphere for use as a nutrient). *Nostoc* species occur in rivers and on wet rocks or soils; free-living species, along with other cyanobacteria, are important contributors to fertility in some tropical topsoils. *Nostoc* species also form associations with other organisms, which benefit from their ability to fix nitrogen; they occur in many LICHENS, for example, and in association with some LIVERWORTS, CYCADS and GUNNERAS.

Nostradamus (born Michel de Nostredame) (1503–66) French astrologer and physician. His predictions, in the form of rhymed quatrains, appeared in two collections (1555; 1558). Cryptic and apocalyptic in tone, they were given extensive credence at the French court, where Nostradamus was for a time personal physician to Charles IX. Their interpretation has continued to be the subject of controversy into the 20th century.

notary (from Latin *notarius*, 'one who takes notes of judicial proceedings') An official who is authorized to perform certain legal formalities. A notary's functions encompass drawing up and certifying documents and contracts, administering oaths, and taking sworn statements for use in court proceedings. In some countries, notaries belong to an independent profession, while in others they are civil servants.

notch flute An end-blown flute with a notch, either v-shaped or u-shaped with a rounded or square bottom, into which players direct the airstream. The notch is inherently more efficient than the plain end of simple end flutes, and notch flutes are found in many parts of the world.

notornis (or **takahe**) A large chicken-sized flightless bird, *Porphyrio mantelli*, which belongs to the rail family and resembles a moorhen. It is mainly bright blue in colour with a wide range of iridescent sheens; its heavy beak, the frontal shield above it, and the legs are bright red. It is found only on the South Island of New Zealand, where it lives in hilly grasslands. It is very rare, possibly due to competition for grasses (its staple food) with the introduced red deer. It makes a simple nest on the ground and lays one or two cream-coloured eggs.

Notre-Dame The Gothic cathedral church of Paris, situated on the Ile de la Cité (an island in the Seine). Begun in 1163 and effectively finished by 1250, it is dedicated to the Virgin Mary. It is especially noted for its innovatory flying buttresses, sculptured façade, and great rose windows with 13th-century stained glass.

Nottingham The county town of Nottinghamshire in central England, on the River Trent; pop. (1991) 261,500. Its castle was the headquarters of Richard III before the Battle of Bosworth Field in 1485 and the standard of Charles I was raised here at the outset of the Civil War in 1642. The University of Nottingham was founded in 1948. It developed as an industrial town in the 19th century producing lace, hosiery, tobacco, and bicycles.

Nottinghamshire A county in central England; area 2,161 sq km (835 sq miles); pop. (1991) 980,600; county town, Nottingham. The county is divided into eight districts.

Notting Hill Gate A residential area of west-central London, to the north of Holland Park, whose West Indian community holds a popular annual street carnival.

Nouakchott The capital of Mauritania, founded on the site of a small village in 1958; pop. (est. 1994) 850,000. It has a power-station, Africa's first desalination plant, and a deep-water harbour for the export of copper ores.

Nouméa The capital of the island of New Caledonia in the Pacific Ocean; pop. (1994) 65,000. Formerly called Port de France, it became the capital of the French overseas territory of New Caledonia in 1854 and was a penal colony from 1864 to 1897.

nouveau roman (French, 'new novel') The work of a group of French novelists who came to prominence during the 1950s. The authors usually thus classified are Alain Robbe-Grillet (*La Jalousie*, 1957), Michel Butor (*La Modification*, 1957), Nathalie Sarraute (*Le Planétarium*, 1959), Claude Ollier (*La Mise en scène*, 1958), Robert Pinget (*L'Inquisitoire*, 1963), Jean Ricardou (*La Prise de Constantinople*, 1965), and Claude Simon (*Histoire*, 1967). For the new novelists any authorial interpretation is arbitrary: there is no ultimate meaning behind existence, only the subjective experience of individuals. They were first identified as a group by Jean-Paul SARTRE.

Nouvelle Vague (French, 'New Wave') A group of French film directors, who in the late 1950s began to react against the established French cinema and to make more individual films. Some of its members – TRUFFAUT, Claude Chabrol (1930–), and GODARD (1930–) – had written for the film review *Cahiers du cinéma*, which promoted the same ideas; but the first films in this category were Louis Malle's (1932–95) *Ascenseur pour l'échafaud* (Frantic) and *Les Amants* (both 1958) – the latter being considered extremely erotic. Chabrol, whose films often depicted violence, directed *Le Beau Serge* (1958) and *Les Cousins* (1959). Truffaut made *Les Quatre Cents Coups* (1959) and Alain RESNAIS (1922–) broke new ground with *Hiroshima mon amour* (1959). Godard was another innovator, who in *A bout de souffle* (Breathless, 1960) used hand-held cameras, jump-cuts, and real locations. The movement's influence soon waned, and its leading directors – apart from Godard – gravitated to the commercial cinema.

nova A CATACLYSMIC VARIABLE star that suddenly increases in brightness by 7–19 MAGNITUDES but returns to its previous magnitude after some months. Novae are usually binary stars in which one member is a WHITE DWARF with a very close companion. Gas is drawn from its companion on to the surface of the white dwarf where it erupts in a nuclear fusion explosion throwing off a shell of gas. A nova outburst in a given system may erupt several times at intervals of perhaps tens of thousands of years but in a few **recurrent novae** (subtype NR) between two and six eruptions have been detected within a few decades. Unlike a SUPERNOVA, a nova eruption does not greatly damage the star. About 30 nova outbursts are thought to occur each year in the Galaxy, but most are either missed or concealed by interstellar dust clouds in the plane of the Galaxy.

Nova Lisboa The former name (until 1978) of HUAMBO.

Nova Scotia A province of eastern Canada, comprising the peninsula of Nova Scotia and the adjoining Cape Breton Island; area 55,490 sq km (21,425 sq miles); pop. (1991) 899,940; capital, Halifax. It was settled by the French in the early 18th century, who named it Acadia. It changed hands several times between the French and English before being awarded to Britain in 1713, when it was renamed and the French settlers expelled (mostly to Louisiana). It became a province of Canada in 1867. Iron, coal, steel, lumber, and fish are its chief products.

novel An extended fictional story in prose, with at least one character involved in some form of plot or sequence of events; normally, several characters are presented in relationships with one another within a social setting. However, the novel is extremely flexible, which has made it the most important and popular literary genre in the modern age. Novels may be distinguished from romances by their more realistic characters and events, and from NOVELLAS by their length, but the boundaries here are indistinct. Although there are some precedents in the ancient world, the fully developed tradition of the novel in the West is relatively young: it is usually dated back to the first part of Cervantes's *Adventures of Don Quixote* (1605). La Fayette's *La Princesse de Clèves* (1678) began the distinguished line of French novels. The first significant novel in English was Aphra BEHN's *Oroonoko* (*c.*1688), but Defoe's *Robinson Crusoe* (1719) is often regarded as the origin of the modern tradition. The classic period of the novel was the 19th century: the age of Austen, Balzac, Dickens, Melville, Flaubert, George Eliot, Tolstoy, Dostoyevsky, and Zola. Since the radical experiments of 20th-century MODERNISM and the NOUVEAU ROMAN, the novel continues to flourish. Among the many specialized forms of novel are the detective and epistolatory varieties, the GOTHIC, HISTORICAL, and PICARESQUE NOVELS, and the BILDUNGSROMAN.

novella A short prose fiction; from the Italian word for 'novelty'. The tales in Boccaccio's *Decameron* (1349–53) are the most celebrated early *novelle*. Goethe revived the form in 1795, and it has remained an important genre in German literature, known as the *Novelle*. In English, a novella consists of stories mid-way, in length and complexity, between a short story and a NOVEL, focusing on a single chain of events with a surprising turning point. Conrad's *Heart of Darkness* (1902) is a fine example; James and Lawrence also wrote novellas.

Novello, Ivor (born David Ivor Davies) (1893–1951) British composer, actor, and dramatist. In 1914 he wrote 'Keep the Home Fires Burning', which became one of the most popular songs of World War I. Later he composed and acted in a series of musicals, including *Glamorous Night* (1935), *The Dancing Years* (1939), and *King's Rhapsody* (1949).

Noverre, Jean-Georges (1727–1810) French choreographer and dance theorist. A great reformer, he stressed the importance of dramatic motivation in ballet and was critical of the overemphasis hitherto placed on technical virtuosity. His work, especially as set out in *Lettres sur la danse et sur les ballets* (1760), had a significant influence on the development of ballet.

Novgorod A city in north-west Russia, on the Volkhov River; pop. (1990) 232,000. Claimed as Russia's oldest city, it was first chronicled in 859 and settled by the Varangian chief Rurik in 862, becoming one of the earliest Russian principalities. It was a major commercial and cultural centre of medieval eastern Europe, developing important trade links with Constantinople, the Baltic, Asia, and the rest of Europe. It was ruled by Alexander Nevski between 1238 and 1263. A rival with Moscow for supremacy during the 14th and 15th centuries, it was finally defeated by Ivan the Great in the 1470s. From the 17th century the city became less prominent. Novgorod has many light industries including chinaware, furniture, bricks, and food products.

Novotný, Antonín (1904–75) Czechoslovak Communist statesman, President 1957–68. In 1921 he became a founder member of the Czechoslovak Communist Party, rising to prominence when he played a major part in the Communist seizure of power in 1948. He was appointed First Secretary of the Czechoslovak Communist Party in 1953, and became President four years later. A committed Stalinist whose policies caused much resentment, he was ousted by the reform movement in 1968.

Nubecula Major See MAGELLANIC CLOUDS.

Nubecula Minor See MAGELLANIC CLOUDS.

Nubia An ancient region of southern Egypt and northern Sudan, which includes the Nile valley between Aswan and Khartoum. Nubia fell under ancient Egyptian rule from the time of the Middle Kingdom, soon after 2,000 BC, and from about the 15th century BC was ruled by an Egyptian viceroy.

The country was Egyptianized, and trade (especially in gold) flourished. By the 8th century BC, however, as Egypt's centralized administration disintegrated, an independent Nubian kingdom emerged, and for a brief period extended its power over Egypt. Nubia's capital about 600 BC was Meroe, near Khartoum. Much of Nubia is now drowned by the waters of Lake Nasser, formed by the building of the two dams at Aswan. Nubians constitute an ethnic minority group in Egypt.

Nubian Desert The eastern part of the Sahara Desert lying between the Nile and the Red Sea in north-east Sudan.

Nubian sandstone A coarse-grained sedimentary rock found extensively on the Arabian–Nubian Shield in Saudi Arabia and North Africa. It is CRETACEOUS in age and was deposited on top of the Precambrian basement complex of GNEISSES and SCHISTS that make up the Arabian–Nubian Shield.

nuclear energy Energy derived from nuclear FISSION or FUSION. In nuclear fission, the nucleus of a heavy ATOM is split into two pieces of comparable size; in fusion, two or more relatively light nuclei combine to form a heavier one. Both these processes involve the release of very large amounts of energy. The energy of nuclear reactions has been harnessed for both peaceful and military purposes (see NUCLEAR POWER; NUCLEAR REACTOR; NUCLEAR WEAPONS). Controlled nuclear fusion, however, has yet to be achieved. Experiments investigating radioactivity and atomic structure in the late 19th and early 20th centuries led to the idea of a small, dense nucleus at the centre of the atom, and the detection of the neutron as a component of this nucleus. An experiment by Otto Hahn and Fritz Strassman in 1938 involved the bombardment of uranium with neutrons. They discussed the results of their experiments with MEITNER, who put forward the theory that they had split the uranium atom into two pieces. Her calculations showed that the total mass of the fission fragments was slightly less than the mass of the uranium that they came from: the mass difference had been converted to energy. Einstein had predicted that mass could be converted into energy in his equation $E=mc^2$ (E is energy, m is mass, and c is a constant, the speed of light). Even though the mass loss in this fission reaction was tiny, the amount of energy released was great, because the value of c^2 is extremely large (about 9×10^{16} m^2/s^2). The discovery of fission led to a flurry of activity by scientists to unlock the energy of the atom. FERMI'S ATOMIC PILE demonstrated the self-sustaining CHAIN REACTION in which neutrons released by the fission of uranium atoms could be used to split more uranium atoms. It provided the basis for the design of nuclear reactors, and the peaceful use of nuclear power. It also became apparent that an uncontrolled chain reaction could be used in an atomic bomb. The MANHATTAN PROJECT was set up to build such a device, and in July 1945 the first atomic bomb was successfully demonstrated. Further research after World War II showed that fusion of atomic nuclei could release even more energy. A vast programme of research led to the development of the hydrogen bomb in 1952.

nuclear fuel A material used to fuel a NUCLEAR REACTOR. In the thermal reactors used for nuclear-power generation the fuel is some form of URANIUM: this may be either uranium metal or uranium dioxide. For some reactor types the fuel is enriched to increase the proportion of fissionable uranium-235 (U-235). FAST BREEDER REACTORS use a fuel that is either a mixture of uranium dioxide and plutonium dioxide, or an artificial ISOTOPE of uranium, U-233, made from the element thorium.

nuclear magnetic resonance (NMR) See MAGNETIC RESONANCE IMAGING.

nuclear medicine The use of injected radioactive substances to diagnose disease, particularly cancer. RADIOACTIVE ISOTOPES (radioisotopes) with short half-lives can produce images or other diagnostic records of parts of the body when used in conjunction with a detector. The radioisotopes 'label' substances metabolized in ordinary physiological functions. For example, in thyroid scans, abnormal functioning can be diagnosed by injecting radioactive iodine into the blood system and mapping its distribution in body tissues. In the gamma camera, gamma-rays emitted by injected isotopes produce tiny scintillations of light in large sodium iodide crystals held above the organ being investigated. Magnified and converted into electrical signals, these scintillations can be analysed by a computer and displayed as sophisticated images. In cardiac imaging, radioactive drugs are used to highlight loss of function in diseased hearts.

nuclear power Power, usually electricity, generated using a NUCLEAR REACTOR. The principles of the nuclear reactor were first demonstrated in the ATOMIC PILE built in 1942 by FERMI. Until the end of World War II further development of nuclear power was almost exclusively military, but after the War several countries, notably the USA, the UK, Canada, France, and the Soviet Union, began research into the use of nuclear energy for power generation. By 1994 there were over 400 nuclear power-stations operating in 31 countries, generating over 300 GW of power per annum, about 7 per cent of world consumption (see ENERGY RESOURCES). The USA and France were the largest producers, with France generating over 75 per cent and the USA 20 per cent of their electricity from nuclear power.

The future of the use of nuclear power for electricity generation is extremely difficult to predict. Arguments against the further development of nuclear power centre on four main points: the fear of future nuclear catastrophes such as the major accident at CHERNOBYL; the tremendous storage and safety problems for future generations posed by the highly radioactive wastes from nuclear fuel (see WASTE MANAGEMENT); PLUTONIUM generated in particular by fast breeder reactors is a raw material of NUCLEAR WEAPONS; and the problem that without reprocessing there is unlikely to be enough uranium in the world to fuel conventional reactors into the long-term future. However, the threat of global warming as a result of the combustion of fossil fuels (all of which produce carbon dioxide in vast quantities) has spurred interest in both renewable energy sources and the extension of safe nuclear power.

nuclear reactor An assemblage designed to sustain controlled nuclear FISSION (the splitting of the nucleus of a heavy atom into two lighter fragments) with the object of extracting energy from the process. The fuel for most reactors is some form of URANIUM, the only natural material that can sustain nuclear fission. Nuclear reactors generate large quantities of heat, beta- and gamma-RADIATION, and large numbers of neutrons. Research reactors are used to test the effect of neutron bombardment on materials, and some reactors generate PLUTONIUM for the manufacture of NUCLEAR WEAPONS, but the most common use of reactors is for generation of power, in particular electricity (see NUCLEAR POWER). Reactors fall broadly into two categories: thermal reactors and fast breeder reactors. In thermal reactors, rods of nuclear fuel are embedded in a moderator, a material that slows down neutrons emitted in the fission process. Slow neutrons are more effective in producing fission, so the moderator sustains the nuclear CHAIN REACTION. The best moderating material is deuterium, an ISOTOPE of hydrogen, but normal ('light') water and graphite are also used. In FAST BREEDER REACTORS, no moderating material is used, but the uranium fuel is enriched: the proportion of fissionable material in the fuel is increased, so that the chain reaction can be sustained even with high-energy, fast neutrons. Control of the chain reaction in both types of reactor is usually by means of control rods, made of a material, such as cadmium or boron, with a high neutron absorption (although some reactors are controlled by insertion or withdrawal of the fuel rods). With the control rods completely inserted into the reactor core, neutrons are absorbed before they can produce fission, and the chain reaction is stopped. As the rods are removed, the reactivity of the core increases. Removal of heat from the reactor core is important both in controlling the chain reaction and for obtaining power from the reactor. The heat absorbed by the coolant is used to generate steam, which in turn drives turbine-powered generators. The material used must be a suitable coolant in terms of temperature range and heat-transfer properties, and must also have low neutron absorbency so as not to affect the chain reaction. In the MAGNOX REACTOR, and its successor the **advanced gas-cooled reactor** (AGM), gas is used as a coolant. In the PRESSURIZED-WATER REACTOR (PWR) ordinary water is the coolant, and in the fast breeder reactor liquid sodium is the coolant. The whole reactor must be shielded to prevent the escape of radiation, and elaborate safety systems are incorporated into the reactor design to prevent any escape of fission products or coolants. The PIUS (Process Inherent Ultimate Safety) reactor, a design proposed by the Swedish firm ASEA-ATOM, avoids problems of human error and mechanical breakdown by immersing the whole reactor in a huge pool of water containing borate, an efficient neutron absorber. Any problem in the cooling system of the reactor allows the borated water to flood the reactor core, causing power to fall, without the intervention of an operator or any electromechanical device. Despite safety arrangements, nuclear breakdowns and accidents have occurred, notably at THREE MILE ISLAND and CHERNOBYL.

Nuclear Test-Ban Treaty (1963) An international agreement not to test nuclear weapons in the atmosphere, in outer space, or under water, signed by the USA, the Soviet Union, and the UK (but not France). On 1 July 1968 the UK, the USA, and the Soviet Union signed a Non-Proliferation Treaty, which was endorsed by 59 other states. China carried out underground nuclear tests during 1994–95 and declared it would continue testing. France received international condemnation for carrying out a series of six tests in the south Pacific (1995–96) but then announced a permanent end of French tests. In 1996 member nations began signing a permanent test-ban treaty, which will not become legally binding unless all the nuclear nations sign.

nuclear weapon An explosive device that owes its destructive power to the energy released by nuclear FISSION OF FUSION. These devices include the atomic bomb, the hydrogen bomb, and the neutron bomb. The power, or yield, of nuclear weapons is expressed as the weight of the explosive TNT that would be required to produce an equivalent explosive power. (Thus, a 20-kilotonne bomb would have the same effect as 20,000 tonnes of TNT.) A typical nuclear explosion releases about half its energy as shock and blast, a third as heat, and the rest as RADIATION. Almost all immediate casualties would be caused by blast, heat, or flying debris. Long-term radiation casualties would depend on the amount of FALL-OUT. A NUCLEAR WINTER might result from a large-scale nuclear war.

Nuclear weapons were developed in the USA during World War II under the code name MANHATTAN PROJECT. The first device, an atomic bomb, was exploded in New Mexico in July 1945. The following month, the USA dropped two atomic bombs, code-named Little Boy (a uranium bomb) and Fatman (a plutonium bomb), on the Japanese cities Hiroshima and Nagasaki, killing over 100,000 people outright. These are the only instances of nuclear weapons having been used against an

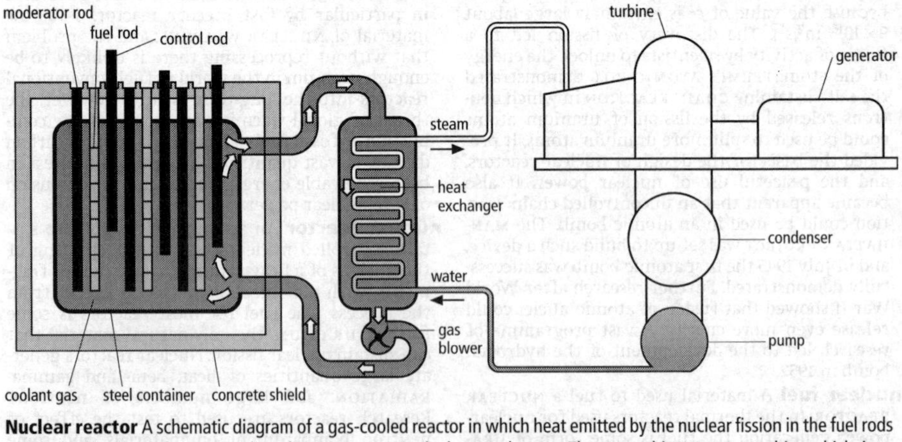

Nuclear reactor A schematic diagram of a gas-cooled reactor in which heat emitted by the nuclear fission in the fuel rods is absorbed by the coolant gas and used to raise steam in the heat exchanger. The steam drives a steam turbine which, in turn, drives the generator, as in a fossil-fuel power station. The neutrons emitted by the fuel rods are slowed down in the moderator, as slow neutrons are required to sustain a chain reaction. The control rods, when lowered into the reactor, absorb neutrons and can slow the reaction or bring it to a halt.

enemy. In 1952, the USA tested the world's first hydrogen bomb, developed by TELLER and his associates, which had an explosive power of 10.4 megatonnes, more than 1,000 times greater than Little Boy's.

Broadly, modern nuclear weapons fall into three categories: strategic weapons, with a range of 5,500 km (3,400 miles) or more; intermediate or theatre weapons, with ranges of 1,000–5,500 km (620–3,400 miles); and short-range weapons, with an effective range of up to 1,000 km (620 miles). Aircraft provided the only delivery system for nuclear weapons until the late 1950s, when the BALLISTIC MISSILE first entered service.

Hydrogen bombs rely on the fusion of two heavy ISOTOPES of hydrogen – either two molecules of deuterium or deuterium with tritium – to form helium atoms. Temperatures of about 10^7°C are needed to sustain a fusion reaction, and these can be achieved by using an atomic bomb as a trigger.

A special type of fission–fusion bomb is the 'neutron bomb'. An enhanced-radiation weapon, in which most of the yield is released as high-energy neutrons, it has an effective range wider than that of a conventional nuclear bomb of similar yield and is designed to kill or disable people by radiation, rather than destroy the surroundings by shock or blast. It was developed by the USA in the 1970s as a tactical weapon.

nuclear winter The possible global cooling that might follow a nuclear war in which large numbers of NUCLEAR WEAPONS were exploded. Extensive fires would produce thick smoke, blocking out sunlight and resulting in severe climatic changes, in particular much lower temperatures. These effects, caused by smoke particles reaching the stratosphere, would be catastrophic to animal and plant life and would last for several years.

nucleic acid A substance, such as DNA or RNA, found in the cells of all living organisms, where it is responsible for protein synthesis and for the cell's hereditary characteristics. Both of these substances consist of long chains of NUCLEOTIDE subunits; RNA molecules are usually single-stranded but DNA is usually double-stranded. In most organisms (except bacteria), DNA is largely confined to the nucleus of the cell; small amounts are found in the mitochondria and chloroplasts. RNA is most commonly found in the cytoplasm.

nucleons Collectively, the two kinds of particle that form the NUCLEUS of an atom. These are the proton, which is positively charged, and the neutron, which has zero charge.

nucleophile A reagent that reacts with a centre of low electron density. The word means 'nucleus lover' and implies that a nucleophile will react with any region of positive charge. This requires that they should themselves possess a region of high electron density, or negative charge. Thus all nucleophiles have at least one LONE PAIR of electrons in their outer shells. They can possess an overall negative charge, an example being the hydroxide ion, OH^-. Alternatively, they can be neutral molecules, containing atoms of different ELECTRONEGATIVITY. An example is ammonia, NH_3, in which nitrogen is the more electronegative element. There is thus a concentration of electron density on the nitrogen atom, which also possesses a lone pair, and therefore the nitrogen atom acts as a nucleophile.

nucleotide A subunit of a nucleic acid. Each nucleotide consists of a five-carbon sugar linked to a phosphate group and an organic, nitrogenous base. In RNA the sugar is ribose, whereas in DNA it is deoxyribose. The nitrogenous base may be adenine, cytosine, guanine, or thymine in DNA; adenine, cytosine, guanine, or uracil in RNA. When RNA is transcribed from DNA, the nitrogenous base uracil is substituted for thymine.

nucleus (in biology) The structure in higher (eukaryotic) CELLS that contains the CHROMOSOMES. It is surrounded by a double MEMBRANE with pores, which allow the transfer of molecules between the CYTOPLASM and the interior of the nucleus. In dividing cells, the individual chromosomes are condensed and easily visible, but normally they are uncoiled and form a substance called chromatin, which fills the nucleus. Some cells, such as bacteria and mammalian red blood cells, lack a nucleus.

nucleus (in astronomy) The central solid region of a comet or the core of a galaxy.

nucleus (in physics) The central, massive part of an atom. It is made up of a certain number of PROTONS, which are positively charged, and usually a larger number of neutral particles, the NEUTRONS. The atomic nuclei of a particular element always contain the same number of protons but can have differing numbers of neutrons, nuclei containing different numbers of neutrons being called ISOTOPES of that element. In most naturally occurring elements the nuclear particles are tightly bound together by the strong interaction and the nucleus is stable. However, in radioactive nuclei the binding is not so strong: particles such as electrons and ALPHA PARTICLES, or radiation (GAMMA RAYS) may be emitted, and the nucleus then decays into the nucleus of another element.

nudibranch See SEA SLUG.

nuée ardente An incandescent cloud of gas, volcanic ash, and larger particles ejected from a VOLCANO during an eruption. The cloud is typically emitted horizontally from the volcano and travels at great speed down its flanks. In recent times the Mount Saint Helens eruption produced a nuée ardente, but the most famous example is that of Mount Pelée in the Antilles, where in 1902 a cloud of incandescent ash accompanying a glowing avalanche overwhelmed the town of Saint Pierre in Martinique, killing 30,000 people.

Nuer A people of south-eastern Sudan speaking a language of the Nilotic sub-group of the Eastern Sudanic group of Nilo-Saharan languages.

Nuffield, William Richard Morris, 1st Viscount (1877–1963) British motor manufacturer and philanthropist. Working in Oxford, he started by building bicycles. In 1912 he opened the first Morris automobile factory there and launched his first car the following year. Morris Motors Limited was formed in 1926, the year of the first MG (Morris Garage) models. In later life he devoted his considerable fortune to philanthropic purposes; these include the endowment of Nuffield College, Oxford (1937), and the creation of the Nuffield Foundation (1943) for medical, social, and scientific research.

Nuffield Radio Astronomy Laboratories See JODRELL BANK.

Nullarbor Plain A vast arid plain in south-west Australia, comprising a slab of uplifted limestone that stretches inland from the Great Australian Bight. It contains no surface water, with sparse vegetation, and is almost uninhabited. Considered to be the world's largest flat surface in bedrock, its name was coined in 1865 from the Latin *nullus arbor* ('no tree'). The Nullarbor Plain is crossed by the Eyre Highway and the Transcontinental Railway which includes the longest section of straight track in the world – 500 km (310 miles).

numbat (or **banded anteater**) A marsupial, *Myrmecobius fasciatus*, that lives in eucalyptus woods in south-west Australia. A reddish pouchless creature with a long tail and white stripes across its back, it feeds on ants and termites using its sticky tongue.

number A value representing a particular quantity. The written forms of numbers we use today are based on the system the Arabs found in India and introduced to Europe in the 14th century (see ARABIC NUMERALS). Gradually it replaced the Roman system, I, II, III, IV, ..., which has no zero and required the abacus for computation (see ROMAN NUMERALS). Cardinal or natural numbers are those used for counting: 1, 2, 3, ... Integers include the natural and the corresponding negative numbers: 0, ± 1, ± 2, ... Rational numbers are formed when one integer is divided by another: 1/2, 7/11, etc.; and they cannot be listed in numerical order, because between any two there are an infinite number of other fractions. Irrational numbers cannot be expressed as a fraction; they include π, $\sqrt{2}$, and e, the base of natural logarithms. All these together form the REAL NUMBERS. COMPLEX NUMBERS are an extension of the reals, of the form $a + ib$, where a and b are real numbers and i is the square root of –1. The concept of number is always being broadened, and many differences of opinion have arisen as to whether a particular collection of numbers – for example, negative or complex – should be accepted as numbers.

numerical control (NC) A method of automatic control of a machine-tool. Originally, numerical control involved the use of punched cards or punched tape; instructions were contained in the position of the holes, which were sensed by mechanical, pneumatic, or optical means. This principle dates back to the JACQUARD loom of 1801 and to the paper rolls used in pianolas. More recently MICROPROCESSOR control of machine-tools (computer numerical control or CNC) has been developed. This allows the most intricate shapes to be produced automatically. Sophisticated methods of driving and controlling the various machine movements are required, using SERVOMECHANISMS and sensors for tool position, speed, and acceleration.

Nunn, Trevor (Robert) (1940–) British stage director. He was artistic director of the Royal Shakespeare Company 1968–87. He also directed a number of Lloyd Webber musicals, including *Cats* (1981) and *Aspects of Love* (1989).

nunnery The building that houses a community of religious women. The word 'nun' is reserved for those living under strict vows of poverty, obedience, and chastity. Religious orders for women date from the 4th century and by the 11th century all communities lived lives devoted to prayer, reading, and work (spinning and weaving). From the 16th century sisterhoods were founded for active work, such as teaching and nursing. All communities were abolished in England at the Reformation but some were refounded in the 19th century.

Nuremberg (German **Nürnberg**) A city of Bavaria in southern Germany, on the Pegnitz River; pop. (1991) 497,500. It was a leading cultural centre in the 15th and 16th centuries. In the 1930s the Nazi Party congresses and the annual Nazi Party rallies were held there and in 1945–46 it was the scene of the NUREMBERG TRIALS, in which Nazi war criminals were tried by international military tribunal. After the war the city centre was carefully reconstructed, because its cobbled streets and timbered houses had been reduced to rubble by Allied bombing. It is an important commercial and industrial centre manufacturing electrical equipment, machinery, and food products. It also has major publishing and printing establishments.

Nuremberg Trials (1945–46) An international tribunal for Nazi war criminals. The trials were complex and controversial, there being few precedents for using international law relating to the conduct of states to judge the activities of individuals. The charges were: conspiracy against peace, crimes against peace, violation of the laws and customs of war, crimes against humanity. As a result of the trials several Nazi organizations, such as the GESTAPO and the SS, were declared to be criminal bodies. Individual judgments against the 24 wartime leaders included death sentences, imprisonment, and not guilty. Ten prisoners were executed, while GOERING and Ley committed suicide. Rudolf HESS was sentenced to life-imprisonment.

Nureyev, Rudolf (1939–93) Russian-born ballet-dancer and choreographer. He defected to the West in 1961, joining the Royal Ballet in London the following year; it was there he began his noted partnership with Margot Fonteyn. Thereafter he danced the leading roles of the classical and standard modern repertory and choreographed many others, including *La Bayadère* (1963). He became a naturalized Austrian citizen in 1982, and was artistic director of the Paris Opéra Ballet 1983–89. He died of Aids.

nurse A person who has completed a programme of basic nursing education and is qualified in his or her country to practise nursing. In Britain, the United Kingdom Central Council for Nursing, Midwifery and Health Visiting is the registering body and is responsible for the regulation of these professions in the interest of the public. Students of nursing undertake a three-year course to qualify as a registered nurse (RN).

nursery education See PRIMARY EDUCATION.

nursery rhyme A traditional verse or verses chanted to infants by adults as an initiation into rhyme and verbal rhythm. Most are hundreds of years old, and derive from songs, proverbs, riddles, BALLADS, street cries, and other kinds of composition originally intended for adults, which have become almost meaningless outside their original contexts. Their origins are often obscure, but several, such as 'Humpty-Dumpty' and 'Hush-a-by-baby' are claimed to make covert references to political or social events. The earliest surviving printed collections are *Tom Thumb's Pretty Song Book* (1744) and *Mother Goose's Melody* (*c.*1765).

nurse shark See CARPET SHARK.

nut (in botany) A particular type of FRUIT in which the wall enclosing the seed (pericarp) is a hard, woody shell, and does not split open when the seed is ripe. However, the term nut is used for any firm, oil-rich kernel, usually surrounded by a hard shell. Of those commonly eaten in temperate regions, only the hazel nut, filbert, and sweet chestnut are, strictly speaking, nuts. Acorns and beechmast are also true nuts. Others, such as Brazil nuts, cashew nuts, pistachios, and macadamia nuts, are really seeds with a hard shell derived from the seed coat (testa), not from the pericarp. They mostly develop inside true fruits, an exception being the cashew. Peanuts are seeds enclosed within a pod, this being a form of pericarp. Walnuts, pecans, almonds, and coconuts are all seeds of DRUPE fruits. Betel nuts, widely chewed in India, are the seeds of a palm, and contain a mild narcotic. Pine nuts are the seeds of pine trees, notably those of the stone pine, native to the Mediterranean region.

Nut The sky goddess of ancient Egypt. Usually portrayed as a naked, giant woman, her arched back, supported by Shu, the air, contained the heavens. Day and night were accounted for in terms of solar birth. The Sun entered the mouth of Nut each evening, passing during the night through her body. In the morning, it was born again from her womb.

nutation A small oscillation superimposed on the PRECESSION of the Earth's axis. The orbit of the Moon is inclined to the ECLIPTIC by 5.1 degrees so that, as the Moon orbits the Earth, it exerts a small torque on the equatorial bulge of the Earth in addition to the main torque from the Sun and Moon that produces luni-solar precession. This results in an additional oscillation, called nutation, being superimposed on the precession, and makes the Earth's north and south poles each trace out a wavy circular path. It amounts to a few arc seconds and the main period of nutation is about 13 days.

nuthatch A bird of the family Sittidae that occurs in Europe, Asia, and North America, mostly in forest. The 25 species range in size from that of a warbler to that of a large sparrow, and are grey or greenish-blue above and paler below, often with dark caps, eye-stripes, or other facial patterns. They have very short tails and longish, straight beaks. They run up and down tree trunks and along branches, probing behind bark for insects. In autumn some species store seeds behind the bark of trees for use as food during the winter. They nest in holes in trees, often plastering the hole with mud to reduce the size of the entrance to prevent larger birds and mammals preying upon their eggs or young.

nutmeg The large brown seed of the tree *Myristica fragrans*, 20 m (75 feet) or more in height, which is native to the Molucca Islands of Indonesia. It belongs to a family, Myristicaceae, of tropical rainforest trees with 380 species spread throughout the tropics. The fleshy fruits resemble large apricots. After drying, the nutmeg is marketed either whole or in a powdered form and used as a flavouring. The trees are either male or female and in plantations about 10 per cent male plants must be planted to ensure pollination of the female flowers. The seed is surrounded by a red-coloured, fleshy network called the mace, which is also used as a flavouring.

nutria See COYPU.

nutrient An inorganic or organic chemical essential as a nourishing substance for the maintenance of life. Both autotrophic and heterotrophic organisms require inorganic chemicals, or mineral salts. The basic elements of all nutrients are ultimately recycled in an ECOSYSTEM.

Plant nutrients, usually mineral salts, are categorized as macro- or micronutrients. Macronutrients are required in large quantities and include nitrogen, phosphorus, and potassium. Micronutrients, such as copper, zinc, and molybdenum, are essential but may be toxic if present in large amounts. Heterotrophs vary in their requirements, but vertebrates require a balanced diet incorporating carbohydrates, fats, proteins, and small quantities of vitamins and certain minerals.

Nutrient deficiency can cause poor growth, deformity, malfunctioning, and sterility. A range of characteristic DEFICIENCY DISEASES is recognized in humans.

nutrition See FOOD AND NUTRITION.

Nuuk The capital of Greenland, a port on the Davis Strait; pop. (est. 1994) 12,480. It was known by the Danish name Godthåb until 1979 and is the oldest Danish settlement. It has fish canning and freezing plants.

Nyasa, Lake (in Malawi **Lake Malawi**) A lake in east-central Africa, the third-largest lake in Africa; area 28,879 sq km (11,150 miles). About 580 km (360 miles) long, it forms most of the eastern border of Malawi with Mozambique and Tanzania. Its name means 'lake' and is due to a misunderstanding by the missionary-explorer David Livingstone who named the lake in 1859.

Nyasaland The name of MALAWI until it gained independence in 1966.

Nyborg A port on the east coast of Fyn Island, Denmark, at the head of the Nybord Fjord; pop. (1990) 18,200.

Nyerere, Julius Kambarage (1922–) Tanzanian statesman, President of Tanganyika 1962–64 and of Tanzania 1964–85. He was an active campaigner for the nationalist movement in the 1950s, forming the Tanganyika African National Union (1954). He served as Prime Minister of Tanganyika following its independence in 1961 and became President a year later. In 1964 he successfully negotiated a union with Zanzibar and remained President of the new state of Tanzania until his retirement.

Nykøping A port on the Baltic Sea, capital of Södermanland county in south-east Sweden; pop. (1990) 65,900. An atomic research centre is nearby.

nylon A synthetic PLASTIC, one of a class of polymers known as polyamides. Nylon was developed by CAROTHERS in the USA during the 1930s. It was first manufactured as a fibre, by extrusion of the molten polymer through a spinneret (see SPINNING). As a textile fibre it is used in several ways. Where the appearance of silk is wanted, or great strength is needed (as in rope), groups of filaments, or even single filaments may be used as continuous-filament yarns for weaving, knitting, and sewing. For other uses, continuous-filament yarns are textured or crimped to give both bulk and extensibility. Alternatively, filaments may be extruded as 'tow', consisting of up to 500,000 filaments. After stretching, the tow is cut or broken into short lengths and (alone or in blends with natural fibres) is spun into yarn on cotton, wool, or flax systems of spinning. Nylon is now also manufactured as sheeting, coatings, and in moulded form, and has a number of industrial applications, for example, for wire insulation, gearwheels, bearings, and reinforcement in tyres. A class of plastics related to nylon are the **aramids**. These are LIQUID CRYSTAL polymers based on polyamides that form extremely strong fibres, used principally in FIBRE-REINFORCED PLASTICS and other COMPOSITES. Aramids were discovered by a research team at the Du Pont Company, USA, in the late 1960s: the best known example is Kevlar.

Nyman, Michael (1944–) British composer. His collaborations with the film director Peter Greenaway established him as a leading film composer. His works, such as the score for Jane Campion's *Piano* (1993), have a distinctive style that synthesizes strands from many periods.

nymphs In Greek and Roman mythology, minor goddesses conceived as beautiful maidens associated with particular places or types of place; Dryads lived in woods, Naiads in fresh water, and Oceanids in the sea.

O

Oahu An island of Hawaii in the Pacific Ocean, between the islands of Molokai and Kauai; area 1,526 sq km (589 sq miles); pop. (est. 1988) 838,500. Its chief town is Honolulu. Tourism and the production of sugar and pineapples are major industries. It is the third-largest of the Hawaiian islands and chief island of the state. It is the site, at Pearl Harbor, of a US naval base, which suffered a surprise attack by the Japanese in December 1941, which brought the USA into World War II.

oak A tree or shrub of the genus *Quercus*, belonging to the same family as beeches and sweet chestnuts, Fagaceae. This genus contains some 450 species that occur in northern temperate zones, and on mountains in the tropics. Cool temperate species are usually deciduous and have leaves with lobed edges. Almost half of the total number of *Quercus* species live in warmer temperate regions and are usually evergreen, such as the holm oak, *Q. ilex*, of southern Europe. Oak trees have their male catkins and inconspicuous female flowers on the same tree and produce their fruit in the form of a nut called an acorn. The most common species of northern Europe is the common, or pedunculate, oak, *Q. robur*, while the durmast, or sessile oak, *Q. petraea*, is found on upland acidic soils. In addition to a hard durable timber, some species, such as the cork oak, *Q. suber*, also provide cork. Several unrelated trees are called oaks in the timber trade, such as the silky oak, *Grevillea robusta*, a relative of the PROTEA.

oak apple gall (or **oak apple**) A large, soft, spherical growth found on the terminal buds of oak trees (*Quercus* species). The growths develop in the summer as a response to the presence of the larvae of a species of GALL WASP, *Biorhiza pallida*. Winged males and wingless females emerge in the autumn from the oak apple gall. The eggs of this generation are laid on oak roots and these larvae cause a different type of gall. From these, wingless females, without males, emerge in the spring to climb the tree and lay eggs in terminal buds, and their larvae stimulate the formation of oak apples again. Oak apples are often confused with marble galls, which are spherical and produced by a different species of gall wasp.

Oakland An industrial port on the east side of San Francisco Bay in western California, USA; pop. (1990) 372,240. Industries include electronics, cars, shipbuilding, and chemicals.

Oakley, Annie (full name Phoebe Anne Oakley Mozee) (1860–1926) US markswoman. In 1885 she joined Buffalo Bill's Wild West Show, of which she became a star attraction for the next 17 years, often working with her husband, the marksman Frank E. Butler. The musical *Annie Get Your Gun* (1946), with music by Irving Berlin, was based on her life.

Oak Ridge A city in east Tennessee, USA, on the Black Oak Ridge and the Clinch River, built during World War II to house people working on the production of uranium 235 for the world's first atomic bomb; pop. (1990) 27,310. Derestricted in 1949, it is now the home of the American Museum of Science and Energy.

oarfish A species of fish, *Regalecus glesne*, distributed worldwide in the open sea, living mainly in mid-water at depths of 300–600 m (975–1,950 feet). Its long, compressed, silvery body, up to 7 m (23 feet) in length, and deep red fins may have given rise to some reports of sea-serpents, when the fish was near the surface. It feeds mainly on small, mid-water euphausid shrimps.

OAS See ORGANIZATION DE L'ARMÉE SECRÈTE; ORGANIZATION OF AMERICAN STATES.

oasis A fertile area in a desert, with a spring or well of water which normally originates as GROUNDWATER. Oases can occur in any desert. They vary in size from small areas to vast regions of naturally watered or irrigated land. The source of the water may be more than 800 km (500 miles) away, usually falling as rain and carried to the oasis in layers of rock beneath the surface. In sandy deserts they are usually found where DEFLATION has lowered the surface to a level that enables the water-table to be reached.

oat An important cereal, *Avena sativa*, particularly in cool, moist regions of North America and northern Europe. An oat crop can tolerate poor or acid soils, but not drought. It is grown mainly as a livestock food, and may be harvested unripe and fed fresh, or as silage. It is more usually fed to livestock as crushed or rolled ripe grain. Relatively little is now used as human food, the grain having a high proportion of husk that is not easily removed. Some is used to produce oatmeal and porridge oats.

Oates, Lawrence Edward Grace (1880–1912) British soldier and explorer, who joined Captain SCOTT's expedition to the South Pole (1910–12). Having reached the Pole, the expedition found itself in trouble on the return journey. Oates, badly frostbitten, crawled out of their tent to his death in order not to slow the party down. In fact they all died and Oates' gallant act was only revealed when Scott's diary was found.

Oates, Titus (1649–1705) English clergyman and conspirator. He is remembered as the fabricator of the Popish Plot, a fictitious Jesuit plot that supposedly involved a plan to kill Charles II, massacre Protestants, and put the Catholic Duke of York on the English throne. Convicted of perjury in 1685, Oates was imprisoned in the same year, but was subsequently released and granted a pension.

OAU See ORGANIZATION OF AFRICAN UNITY.

Ob The principal river of the west Siberian lowlands and one of the largest rivers in Russia. Rising in the Altai Mountains, it flows generally north and west for 3,650 km (2,287 miles) before entering the **Gulf of Ob** (or Ob Bay), an inlet of the Kara Sea and part of the Arctic Ocean. The river is frozen for six months of the year but is nevertheless an important trade and transport route. Flooding occurs annually in its middle section.

Oban A small port and tourist resort on the west coast of Scotland opposite the island of Mull; pop. (1981) 8,110. There are ferry services to the Inner and Outer Hebrides.

Oberammergau A village in the Bavarian Alps of south-west Germany, site of the most famous of the few surviving Passion plays. It has been performed every tenth year (with few exceptions) from 1634 as a result of a vow made during an epidemic of the plague, and remains entirely amateur, the villagers dividing the parts among themselves and being responsible also for the production, music, costumes, and scenery; pop. (1983) 4,800.

Oberon (or **Alberon**) (in mythology) King of the elves in French medieval legend. As Alberich, he is king of the dwarfs in medieval German tales. A member of the Nibelung, he steals the magic gold from the Rhine maidens. In English Tudor literature, Oberon's queen is Titania, the name also given by Ovid to Diana and Circe as descendants of the Titans.

Oberon (in astronomy) The outermost known satellite of Uranus, discovered by William HERSCHEL in 1787. It has a nearly circular orbit above the equator of Uranus at 583,520 km from the planet's centre. It is about 1,500 km in diameter and its density of 1,500 kg/m^3 suggests that the interior contains a mixture of ice and rock.

obesity A condition in which excess fat accumulates in the body, usually in subcutaneous tissues. It is said to occur if a person is more than 20 per cent above the average recommended weight for that person's sex, age, and height. The cause is almost invariably a result of the consumption of more food than is required to sustain that person's daily energy requirements. Obesity is the most common nutritional disorder in Western societies and can have serious consequences for the cardiovascular system. A frugal diet and daily exercise are the obvious remedies.

objet trouvé (French, 'found object') An object found by an artist and displayed as it is, or with only minimal alteration, as a work of art. The practice began with the Dadaists and SURREALISTS. Marcel DUCHAMP gave the name 'ready-made' to a similar type of work in which the object chosen for display is a mass-produced article selected at random.

oblast A first order administrative division in Russia equivalent to a region. There are 49 oblasts and one autonomous oblast in Russia.

oblateness A measure of the degree to which the ELLIPSOID shape of a planet or other celestial body departs from a sphere. It is the fraction obtained by dividing the difference between the equatorial and polar diameters by the equatorial diameter. The oblateness of the Earth results from the CENTRIFUGAL FORCE created by its rotation, which is greatest at the Equator and zero at the poles. The result is that the polar diameter is slightly shorter than the equatorial diameter, causing a bulge at the Equator. The oblateness of the Earth is 1/297, while that of Saturn is 1/1.95.

obliquity of the ecliptic See ECLIPTIC.

oboe A soprano woodwind musical instrument played with a double reed, invented around 1660–70 as an indoor replacement for the SHAWM. The early oboe's broad, comparatively gentle sound meant that parts might often be played by more than one oboist. The bore later became narrower, especially in France, the sound approaching the piercing sweetness of the modern oboe. Since the oboe responded well to cross-fingering (closing one or more finger-holes below the lowest open hole to flatten the PITCH by a semitone), as late as 1800 two keys sufficed, but keywork became more complex in the 19th century; leaders in this development were the Triéberts, father and son. There were two other important sizes of Baroque oboe, an alto in A (the *oboe d'amore*), and tenors in F of several types. One was identical with the treble but larger; another, with a bulb bell, was the ancestor of the COR ANGLAIS; the third, with a flared bell, was presumably that called the *oboe da caccia*.

Obote, (Apollo) Milton (1924–) Ugandan statesman, Prime Minister 1962–66, President 1966–71 and 1980–85. After founding the Uganda People's Congress in 1960, he became the first Prime Minister of independent Uganda. Overthrown by Idi Amin in 1971, he returned from exile nine years later and was re-elected President. Obote established a multi-party democracy, but was removed in a second military coup in 1985.

O'Brien, Edna (1932–) Irish novelist and short-story writer. Her novels include the trilogy *The Country Girls* (1960) *The Lonely Girl* (1962), and *Girls in Their Married Bliss* (1964), which follows the fortunes of two Irish girls from their rural, convent-educated early years to new lives in Dublin and later in London. Among her collections of short stories is *Lantern Slides* (1990).

O'Brien, Flann (pseudonym of Brian O'Nolan) (1911–66) Irish novelist and journalist. He gained recognition as a novelist with his first book *At Swim-Two-Birds* (1939), an exploration of Irish life combining naturalism and farce which employed an experimental narrative structure much influenced by James Joyce. Writing under the name of Myles na Gopaleen, O'Brien contributed a satirical column to the *Irish Times* for nearly 20 years.

observatory (in astronomy) Any site from which astronomical observations and measurements are made. Instruments at most observatories detect ELECTROMAGNETIC RADIATION, and each site tends to specialize in observations at a particular band of wavelengths. The main instruments in most modern observatories are large optical TELESCOPES housed in protective domed buildings, or RADIO TELESCOPES. The light collected by such telescopes is recorded by CAMERAS, image detectors using CHARGE-COUPLED DEVICES, or other instruments, and analysed to retrieve the information it carries from distant astronomical objects.

obsession A morbid preoccupation that occurs in several types of mental disorder, including PSYCHOSIS, where it may take on a delusional quality. However, it most commonly forms part of obsessive–compulsive NEUROSIS in which the person knows the obsession is irrational, but is unable to control an endlessly recurrent, intrusive thought, such as doubt ('Am I *really* sure I locked the door?')

or fear of harming others. Obsessional states are usually grouped, as anxiety-based disorders, alongside PHOBIAS and, although much more resistant to change, they are often treated with similar methods of BEHAVIOUR THERAPY.

obsidian (or **pitchstone**) The most common type of volcanic glass, is a shiny black IGNEOUS ROCK with no crystal structure. It has a characteristic conchoidal fracture and is formed by the rapid cooling of granite magma. It was once used as the raw material for rock wool. See also FLINT.

obstetrics and gynaecology The branches of medicine concerned, respectively, with childbirth and the diseases of women. Before 1700 childbirth was attended by a midwife and a group of female assistants. Surgeons were called only in an emergency. Obstetric forceps began to be widely used in the 1730s, predominantly by male practitioners. Thereafter obstetrics developed rapidly and became an accepted part of medical practice. Gynaecology emerged as a speciality during the mid- to late-19th century, and eventually it became a new speciality, as signalled by the establishment of the Royal College of Obstetricians and Gynaecologists in London in 1929. Thereafter obstetrics gradually moved away from home deliveries and general practice and became dominated by hospital specialists.

Technology in the modern sense came late to obstetrics and gynaecology, but recent advances have been considerable. Relatively recent advances in obstetrics include epidural analgesia (an injection of local anaesthetic around the spinal cord); ULTRASOUND for antenatal imaging of the foetus; techniques such as AMNIOCENTESIS for the detection of foetal abnormalities; and *in vitro* fertilization techniques in the management of some forms of infertility. Pregnancy testing can now be done at home on a urine sample, and during labour the foetal heart-beat and the frequency of labour contractions can be continuously monitored in graphic form by the technique of cardiotocography.

In gynaecology, laparoscopy (see ENDOSCOPY) is already established as a technique for diagnosis and sterilization; it is now being extended to include surgery of the uterus, in which it may replace, at least in some cases, the standard techniques of hysterectomy. Other techniques include CERVICAL SCREENING for the detection of the pre-cancerous state, and examination of the neck of the womb and upper vagina with a colposcope (a type of endoscope). The colposcope can also be used to treat cervical cancer by cauterizing cancerous tissue using laser light.

ocarina A musical instrument, an egg-shaped vessel-flute invented by Giuseppe Donati in Italy in the 1860s, with two thumb- and eight finger-holes, and a duct mouthpiece extending to one side. It is commonly made in earthenware, but porcelain examples exist. It is usually regarded as a toy, but instruments have been made in sets of different sizes, sometimes with a tuning-plunger, and ocarina bands were popular in the late 19th and early 20th centuries in Europe and the USA, where the instrument was also called a sweet potato.

OCAS See ORGANIZATION OF CENTRAL AMERICAN STATES.

O'Casey, Sean (1880–1964) Irish dramatist. Encouraged by W. B. Yeats, he wrote a number of plays, including *The Shadow of a Gunman* (1923) and *Juno and the Paycock* (1924), which were successfully staged at the Abbey Theatre, Dublin. They deal with the lives of the Irish poor before and during the civil war that followed the establishment of the Irish Free State.

Occam, William of See WILLIAM OF OCKHAM.

Occitan The Provençal language.

occlusion (in meteorology) The final stage in the life of a DEPRESSION. The cold front moves at a faster speed than the warm front that precedes it, and may eventually overtake it. Then it may push both the warm air and the warm front off the ground, displacing it to form a cold occlusion. On the ground warm air is replaced by cold air. Alternatively it may lift the warm air off the ground by running up the less steeply sloping warm front, leaving the warm front in contact with the ground and forming a warm occlusion. On the ground cold air is replaced by less cold air.

occultation The interruption of the light from a star or other celestial object when a nearer, Solar System body passes in front. Properties of both objects can be derived from details of how the light extinguishes and restores. Occultation of a star by the Moon's dark limb can indicate the local slope of the lunar mountains, and possibly reveal the angular diameter of the occulted star and whether it is a multiple star. Celestial bodies can also be totally or partially obscured during an ECLIPSE or a TRANSIT.

occupational disease Any disease closely identified with a specific occupation. Probably the largest class of occupational diseases are lung complaints, such as silicosis and asbestosis, caused by inhalation of dust particles of various kinds. Many countries have strict legislation requiring employers to protect workers from known hazards. However, risks are not always recognized or acknowledged until victims appear in statistically significant numbers.

ocean The continuous sheet of salt water that surrounds the land masses of the continents, filling the great depressions of the Earth's surface. It occupies 71 per cent of the surface of the globe and is generally considered as made up of four major areas, which in order of size are the Pacific, Atlantic, Indian, and Arctic oceans. The first three of these extend into the waters of the Antarctic, which can be regarded as a distinct Southern Ocean. The oceans are an essential part of the natural environment, not only because they provide food and fuel and a means of communication but because they are the ultimate source of all water on the globe and supply the moisture that reaches the continents as rain; it is through the HYDROLOGICAL CYCLE that they influence the climates of the continents.

ocean basin A saucer-like depression of the seabed. It may vary in size from a relatively minor feature of the continental margin to a vast, structural division of the deep ocean. The bottom may be of solid rock, igneous or sedimentary, or of unconsolidated silt, clay, or mud, deposited over the years. On average a basin will be some 3 km (2 miles) deep in mid-ocean but many hundreds of kilometres broad – a very shallow saucer.

ocean current A distinct and generally horizontal flow of seawater in a given direction. Ocean currents may form permanent circulatory systems, or gyres, as in the Atlantic and Pacific oceans, or they may be relatively short-lived phenomena affecting only limited areas, particularly along coasts. They may be caused by the drag exerted on the surface by prevailing winds, which can be permanent or seasonal; or by tidal motion, which is periodic; or by the discharge of rivers. They may be affected by differences in water density, determined by temperature and salinity (just as air temperatures affect the direction and strength of wind). Ocean currents, such as the GULF STREAM, KUROSHIO, and PERU CURRENT have a profound influence on climates, particularly in coastal regions.

Oceania The islands of the central and south Pacific and adjacent seas lying between the Tropic of Cancer in the north and the southern tip of New Zealand in the south. It includes the islands of Australia, New Zealand, Polynesia (French Polynesia, Line Islands, Pitcairn, Samoa, Tonga, and Tuvalu), Micronesia (Caroline Islands, Guam, Kiribati, the Marianas, and Marshall Islands), and Melanesia (Fiji, New Caledonia, Papua New Guinea, Solomon Islands, Vanuatu); area 8,500,000 sq km (3,300,000 sq miles).

oceanic ridge That part of the ocean floor through which magma rises from the mantle of the Earth. A mid-oceanic ridge stretches the length of the Atlantic Ocean from north to south.

Ocean Island See BANABA.

oceanography The study of the seas and oceans, which is concerned not only with their structures and the water they contain but also with their climates, flora, and fauna. It embraces hydrography but is wider in scope; in particular it involves the theory of PLATE TECTONICS. Because the world's climate is driven by interaction between the ocean, the atmosphere and the land, oceanography is a vital element in the study, and hence prediction, of climatic change. Most nations now have institutes of oceanography, and exchange observations.

ocean trench A deep depression in the ocean floor at a subduction zone where one tectonic plate dives beneath another.

Oceanus In Greek mythology, the name of a river that was supposed to encircle the Earth and also of a Titan who was god of this river and the father of all water nymphs and river gods.

ocelot (or **painted leopard**) A mammal of the cat family, *Felis (Panthera) pardalis*, that has a buff-coloured coat with black spots and stripes on the legs. It is found in the forests of Central and South America, where it hunts small mammals and reptiles by night.

Ockham, William of See WILLIAM OF OCKHAM.

Ockham's razor See ONTOLOGY.

O'Connell, Daniel (known as **'the Liberator'**) (1775–1847) Irish nationalist leader and social reformer. His election to Parliament in 1828 forced the British government to grant Catholic Emancipation in order to enable him to take his seat in the House of Commons, for which Roman Catholics were previously ineligible. In 1839 he established the Repeal Association to abolish the union with Britain; O'Connell was arrested and briefly imprisoned for sedition in 1844.

O'Connor, Feargus Edward (1794–1855) Irish radical politician and Chartist leader. He was elected Member of Parliament for County Cork in 1832 as a supporter of Daniel O'CONNELL but lost his seat in 1835. In 1837 he founded a radical newspaper the *Northern Star* in England, and it was largely through his tireless energy and his ability as an orator that CHARTISM became a mass movement. After a term of imprisonment for seditious libel, he was elected Member of Parliament for Nottingham in 1847.

O'Connor, (Mary) Flannery (1925–64) US novelist and short-story writer. She drew on her Catholic upbringing in her two Gothic novels, *Wise Blood* (1952) and *The Violent Bear It Away* (1960). She also won acclaim for short stories notable for their dark humour and grotesque characters; they are published in collections such as *A Good Man Is Hard to Find, and Other Stories* (1955).

octane number A measure of the efficiency with which a specific grade of PETROLEUM performs in a PETROL ENGINE. It is the percentage by volume of iso-octane in an iso-octane and heptane mixture that produces the same amount of engine KNOCK as the petrol under test, as measured in the same test engine.

Octans The Octant, a CONSTELLATION that encompasses the south celestial pole. It was introduced by the 18th-century French astronomer Nicolas Louis de Lacaille and represents the navigator's octant, a forerunner of the sextant. The closest naked-eye star to the south celestial pole is Sigma Octantis, magnitude 5.5. The brightest stars in Octans are of fourth magnitude.

Octavian See AUGUSTUS.

October Revolution See RUSSIAN REVOLUTION (1917).

octopus A CEPHALOPOD that has entirely lost its ancestral molluscan shell, leaving a rounded bag-like body suited to a cave-dwelling life. It can use jet propulsion, but more often crawls slowly over surfaces using its eight suckered tentacles. It feeds mostly on crabs and other shellfish, grasping them with its tentacles, biting with strong beak-like jaws, and injecting a poison. Paralysed prey is taken back to the den for feeding. To assist hunting, the octopus can learn complex behaviours, retaining new information in its elaborate brain, which rivals that of many vertebrates in respect of its capacity. Mating behaviour is also complicated, with ritual colour changes. Females brood the large eggs, and generally die thereafter.

Octopuses usually prefer warmer seas, but even there never gain the sizes credited to them in legend; the body rarely exceeds 40 cm (16 inches) in width, though the arms may be up to 5 m (16 feet) long.

Odense A port in eastern Denmark on the island of Fyn, the third-largest city in the country; pop. (1991) 177,640. It is linked by ship canal to Odense Fjord, where there is a major shipyard. It has sugar-refining and food-processing industries.

Oder (Czech and Polish **Odra**) A river of central Europe that rises in the Sudetes Mountains in the west of the Czech Republic and flows 907 km (567 miles) northwards through western Poland to meet the River Neisse, where it forms the border between Poland and Germany before emptying into the Baltic Sea. This frontier, known as the **Oder–Neisse Line**, was adopted at the POTSDAM conference in 1945.

Odessa (Ukrainian **Odesa**) A city and port on the south coast of Ukraine, on the Black Sea; pop. (1990) 1,106,400. It is a resort as well as a commercial and naval port and was the scene of the 1905 worker's revolution led by sailors from the battleship *Potemkin*. It is the home base of the Russian whaling fleet; its industries include steel, shipbuilding, chemicals, and food processing.

Odets, Clifford (1906–63) US dramatist. He was a founder member in 1931 of the avant-garde Group Theatre, which followed the naturalistic methods of the Moscow Art Theatre and staged his best-known play, *Waiting for Lefty* (1935). His plays of the 1930s (especially *The Golden Boy*, 1937) reflect the experiences of the Depression, often displaying a strong sense of social issues.

Odin The chief deity of Norse mythology, husband

of Frigg and father of seven sons, including Balder and Thor. To acquire wisdom, he entered a near-death state by suspending himself on the World Tree, Yggdrasill, for nine days and nights. Identified with the Anglo-Saxon Woden (hence Wednesday from Woden's day) and the Germanic Wotan, Odin was god of the wind, war, magic, and poetry, leader of souls and king of the Aesir.

odometer An instrument for measuring large distances, for example in surveying roads. It consists of a large wheel (whose exact circumference is known) attached to a handle, so that it can be pushed or pulled along the distance to be measured. The number of revolutions of the wheel are registered on a meter and thus the distance travelled can be calculated. The milometer incorporated in the SPEEDOMETER of a motor car is a type of odometer.

Odysseus (Roman name **Ulysses**) In Greek mythology, one of the heroes of the Trojan War, the son of Laertes, king of Ithaca. After the fall of Troy, he spent ten years trying to reach home, frustrated by Poseidon (whose son Polyphemus the Cyclops was blinded by Odysseus) and other hazards (see CALYPSO; CIRCE; SIRENS). These episodes, and Odysseus' final return from Troy and subsequent vengeance on the suitors of his faithful wife, Penelope, are recounted in the *Odyssey*, an epic poem by HOMER.

Odyssey See HOMER.

OECD See ORGANIZATION FOR ECONOMIC COOPERATION AND DEVELOPMENT.

Oedipus In Greek mythology, the son of Laius, king of Thebes, and his wife Jocasta. He was abandoned as a child because of a warning by Apollo that he would kill his father and marry his mother. He was rescued and later unwittingly fulfilled both predictions; when he found out the truth of his birth, he blinded himself and went into exile.

Oedipus complex The repressed sexual feelings of a boy for his mother, combined with aggressive feelings for his father. According to Freudian psychoanalytical theory the desire is normal and is made unconscious by repression. The name comes from the plight of OEDIPUS, who unwittingly married his mother, Jocasta. The equivalent feelings of a girl for her father is sometimes called the **Electra complex**.

Oersted, Hans Christian (1777–1851) Danish physicist who in 1820 discovered that an ELECTRIC CURRENT has a magnetic effect. He noticed the deflection of a compass needle placed near a wire carrying a current. The **oersted**, a unit for magnetic field strength, was named after him. This has been replaced in SI UNITS by the AMPERE per metre.

oesophagus (or **gullet**) In mammals, a tube stretching from the pharynx, behind the nose and mouth, to the stomach. Its muscular wall is lined by a layer of mucus-covered cells. Food is retained in the lower end of the gullet by a sphincter (muscle ring) which opens at intervals for the gullet to squeeze its contents into the stomach. In RUMINANTS the lining of the gullet is especially tough so that their coarse diet does not damage its wall. In these animals food is returned from the stomach via the gullet to the mouth for the chewing of the cud.

oestrogens A group of female steroid hormones (including oestriol, oestrone, and oestradiol) that control female sexual development. Oestrogens are synthesized mainly in the ovaries; small amounts are also produced in the adrenal cortex, the testes, and the placenta. Oestrogens are administered to treat adverse menopausal symptoms (see HORMONE REPLACEMENT THERAPY). Synthetic oestrogens are also a major constituent of oral CONTRACEPTIVES.

Offa (died 796) King of Mercia 757–96. After seizing power in Mercia in 757, he expanded his territory to become overlord of most of England south of the Humber. Offa is chiefly remembered for constructing the frontier earthworks called OFFA'S DYKE.

Offaly A county of the Republic of Ireland, in the province of Leinster, east of the River Shannon; area 1,997 sq km (771 sq miles); pop. (1991) 58,450; capital, Tullamore.

Offa's Dyke A series of earthworks running the length of the Welsh border from near the mouth of the Wye to near the mouth of the Dee, built or repaired by OFFA (king of Mercia 757–96) to mark the boundary established by his wars with the Welsh.

Offenbach, Jacques (born Jacob Eberst) (1819–80) German composer, resident in France from 1833. Offenbach is associated with the rise of the operetta, whose style was typified by his *Orpheus in the Underworld* (1858). He is also noted for his opera *The Tales of Hoffmann* (1881), based on the stories of E. T. A. Hoffmann and first produced after Offenbach's death.

Offenbach am Main An industrial city in the state of Hesse, west Germany, on the River Main; pop. (1991) 115,790. Noted for its leather craft, the city's chief landmark is a 16th-century Renaissance palace. It is also the headquarters of the German Meteorological Service.

offset lithography (or **offset litho**) The most widely used variant of LITHOGRAPHY, in which the greasy image is first 'offset' from an alternately inked and dampened plate cylinder on to a rubber-covered blanket cylinder. The image is then transferred under pressure on to the paper conveyed on an impression cylinder. This offset process enables relatively rough surfaces to carry fine printing, while the all-rotary action permits high printing speeds. Offset litho is almost universally used for work up to the highest quality on a range of machines. These may print on individual sheets, or may use a large roll (web) of paper. Web offset printing machines are extremely fast, and are particularly suitable for large print runs (for example, national newspapers).

Ogaden A desert region in south-east Ethiopia, largely inhabited by Somali nomads. Successive governments of neighbouring Somalia have laid claim to the territory which they call Western Somalia.

OGPU (initial Russian letters for 'United State Political Administration') A security police agency established in 1922 as GPU and renamed after the formation of the SOVIET UNION (1923). It existed to suppress counter-revolution, to uncover political dissidents, and, after 1928, to enforce COLLECTIVIZATION of farming. It had its own army and a vast network of spies. It was absorbed into the NKVD in 1934.

Ohain, Hans Pabst von (1911–) German engineer and pioneer of jet propulsion. He studied at Göttingen University under the physicist Ludwig Prandtl, considered the father of aerodynamics. In 1936 von Ohain joined the Heinkel aircraft company, where he developed a design he had already made for a JET ENGINE. By 1939 a working engine had been built, and was installed in the Heinkel He. 178, the world's first jet aircraft.

O'Higgins, Bernardo (*c.*1778–1842) Chilean revolutionary leader and statesman, head of state 1817–23. The son of a Spanish officer of Irish origin, he was educated in England, where he first became involved in nationalist politics. On his return to Chile he led the independence movement and, with the help of José de San Martín, liberator of Argentina, led the army, which triumphed over Spanish forces in 1817, paving the way for Chilean independence the following year. For the next six years he was head of state (supreme director) of Chile, but then fell from power and lived in exile in Peru for the remainder of his life.

Ohio A state in the north-eastern USA, bordering on Lake Erie; area 107,044 sq km (41,330 sq miles); pop. (1990) 10,847,115; capital, Columbus. The largest cities are Columbus, Cleveland, Cincinnati, and Toledo. Ohio is also known as the Buckeye State. Acquired by Britain from France in 1763 and by the USA in 1783, it became the 17th state of the USA in 1803. It is a leading industrial state, producing motor vehicles, steel, rubber, and machinery and is rich in natural resources such as coal, oil, clay, salt, gypsum, and cement.

Ohio A major river of east-central USA that is formed at the junction of the Allegheny and Monongahela rivers at Pittsburgh, Pennsylvania. It flows 1,578 km (981 miles) generally south-westwards past Cincinnati to join the Mississippi at the frontier between the states of Illinois, Kentucky, and Missouri. From its source at the head of the Allegheny River it is 2,101 km (1,306 miles) long.

ohm (symbol Ω) The SI UNIT of electrical resistance, defined as the resistance between two points on a conductor when a constant potential difference of one volt, applied between these points, produces a current of one ampere in the conductor. It is named after the German physicist, Georg Simon OHM.

Ohm, Georg Simon (1789–1854) German physicist. He published two major papers in 1826, which between them contained the law that is named after him. **Ohm's law** states that the electric current flowing in a conductor is directly proportional to the potential difference (voltage), and inversely proportional to the resistance. Applying this to a wire of known diameter and conductivity, the current is inversely proportional to length. The units OHM and *mho* are also named after him.

oil, crude See PETROLEUM.

oil beetle A soft-bodied, black BEETLE with no hind-wings and the front wing-covers reduced. It exudes an oily, evil-smelling fluid from its joints when alarmed. The larvae are parasitic on solitary bees or grasshoppers and pass through several different stages. Along with BLISTER BEETLES, oil beetles comprise the family Meloidae, with some 2,000 species found worldwide.

oilbird (or guacharo) A bird, *Steatornis caripensis*, which is an aberrant relative of the nightjars, placed in a family of its own, Steathornithidae. It inhabits tropical forests of northern South America. It is the only nocturnal fruit-eating bird and probably finds its food by using its sense of smell. It nests in colonies in the near-total darkness of caves and finds its way by echo-location. This involves emitting a series of clicks and timing how long the echoes take to return, rather after the manner of bats. It lays two to four eggs and the young remain in the nest for up to four months.

oil painting Painting with PIGMENTS mixed with certain types of oil, which harden on exposure to the air. Linseed oil is the best known, but poppy oil and walnut oil have also been used. It was long believed that oil painting was invented by Jan van EYCK, but it is now known that its origins are older and obscurer. Van Eyck, however, showed the medium's flexibility, its rich and dense colour, its wide range from light to dark, and its ability to achieve both minute detail and subtle blending of tones. Since the 16th century oil colour has been the dominant painting medium in Europe. In the 20th century ACRYLIC PAINT has become a serious rival to oil paint.

oil plant A plant that stores oils or fats as a food reserve, usually in its seeds but sometimes (oil palm and olive) in the surrounding fruit wall. Most plants do this to a limited extent, but the 30 or so species exploited commercially contain between 40 and 65 per cent of oil in their fruits or seeds. About 90 per cent of the world's production comes from 12 species. Soya bean, cotton (seed), groundnut, and sunflower are the main sources, plus oilseed rape, coconut (copra), oil palm, linseed, sesame, olive, castor, and safflower, in that order of importance. Invariably the oil is extracted by some means of milling or pressing.

oils, animal and vegetable See FATS AND OILS; OIL PLANT.

Oisín (or **Ossian**) Legendary Irish warrior-poet. A member of Fianna Éireann, an élite corps of huntsmen skilled in poetry, he was lured by a fairy princess to Tír na n Óg, the Land of the Young. There he lived happily for 300 years. Wishing to return to Ireland, the fairy woman warned him to remain mounted on his white horse and not let his foot touch Irish soil. The horse slipped, Oisín fell to the ground, and his body instantly shrivelled into that of a blind old man.

Oistrakh, David (1908–74) Russian violinist. Having won the prestigious Brussels Competition (1937), Oistrakh was unable to make his debut in the UK, France, and the USA until the 1950s on account of World War II. He was the dedicatee and first performer of Shostakovich's First (1955) and Second (1967) Concertos. A brilliant interpreter of the 19th-century concerto, he was one of the greatest violinists of his day. His son **Igor Oistrakh** (1931–) is also a noted violinist and conductor.

okapi A species in the giraffe family, *Okapia johnstoni*, discovered in 1900. It lives in deep forests of the upper Congo in the equatorial zone of Africa. The neck is much shorter than that of the giraffe. It is 1.5 m (5 feet) tall at the shoulders. Only the male has horns, covered for most of their length with hair. The neck and body are a rich dark brown, the head is cream-coloured, and the limbs and hindquarters are unique with slantwise stripes of black and white, while the lower part of the limbs is white. The tail, up to 45 cm (18 inches) long, ends in a tuft of hair. Like the giraffe, it has a long, prehensile tongue with which it browses on the leaves of the forest trees.

O'Keeffe, Georgia (1887–1986) US painter. One of the pioneers of MODERNISM in the USA, she was a member of the circle around the photographer and gallery owner Alfred STIEGLITZ, whom she married in 1924. She is best known for her near-abstract paintings based on enlargements of flower and plant forms, works of great elegance and rhythmic vitality, whose sensuous forms are often sexually suggestive. Her inspiration derived from the landscapes and natural forms of the American South-West and New Mexico.

Okhotsk, Sea of The north-west branch of the Pacific Ocean, bordering north-east on the Kamchatka Peninsula of Siberia, the Kuril Islands, the Japanese island of Hokkaido, and Sakhalin Island. The sea, which covers an area of 1,583,000 sq km (611,000 sq mi), has a mean depth of 777 m (2,549 feet). Strong currents flow through it; it is covered in dense fog during the summer and is ice-bound from November to June.

Okinawa ▶1 A region of southern Japan in the southern Ryuku Islands; area 2,246 sq km (867 sq miles); pop. (1990) 1,222,000; capital, Naha. **▶2** The largest of the Ryuku (Nansei) Islands, in southern Japan. It was captured from the Japanese in World War II by a US assault in April–June 1945. With its bases commanding the approaches to Japan it was a key objective. After the war it was retained under US administration until 1972.

Oklahoma A state in south-central USA, lying west of Arkansas and north of Texas; area 181,186 sq km (69,956 sq miles); pop. (1990) 3,145,585; capital, Oklahoma City. The largest cities are Oklahoma City and Tulsa. Oklahoma is also known as the Sooner State (so-called from those who entered before April 1889 – the set time for legal settlement). It was acquired from the French as part of the Louisiana Purchase in 1803 and during 1834–89 was declared Indian Territory in which Europeans were forbidden to settle. It became the 46th state of the USA in 1907. Oklahoma produces large quantities of natural gas, oil, coal, limestone, wheat, cotton, peanuts, and livestock products.

Oklahoma City The state capital of Oklahoma, USA, on the North Canadian River; pop. (1990) 444,720. First settled during the land rush of 1889, the city is situated on one of the country's largest oilfields, first discovered in 1928. Its chief industries are meat-packing, grain-milling, cotton-processing, and the manufacture of iron, steel, electronics, and oil equipment. In 1995 a government office was destroyed by a terrorist bomb, killing 168 citizens.

okra An erect annual plant, *Abelmoschus esculentus*, up to 2 m (6.5 feet) tall. Okra is native to tropical Africa, though it is now grown throughout the lowland tropics. A relative of cotton, hollyhocks, and mallows, it belongs to the genus *Hibiscus*. It is grown for its fruits, long, ridged pods also known as lady's fingers or quambo. These grow up to 30 cm (1 foot) in length and are harvested while still green. The plant has showy yellow flowers with some red patterning.

Olaf Five kings of Norway. **Olaf I Tryggvason** (969–1000) reigned 995–1000. According to legend he was brought up in Russia, being converted to Christianity and carrying out extensive Viking raids before returning to Norway to be accepted as king. He jumped overboard and was lost after his fleet was defeated by the combined forces of Denmark and Sweden at the Battle of Svöld, but his exploits as a warrior and his popularity as sovereign made him a national legend. **Olaf II Haraldsson** (canonized as St Olaf) (*c.*995–1030) reigned 1016–30. Notable for his attempts to spread Christianity in his kingdom, Olaf was forced into exile by a rebellion in 1028 and killed in battle at Stiklestad while attempting to return. He is the patron saint of Norway. Feast day, 29 July. **Olaf III Haraldsson** (died 1093) reigned 1066–93. **Olaf IV Haakonson** (1370–87) reigned 1380–87. **Olaf V** (full name Olaf Alexander Edmund Christian Frederik) (1903–91) reigned 1957–91.

Olbers' paradox The question formulated by the German philosopher Heinrich Olbers (1758–1840), who asked why the sky is dark at night if the Universe is infinite with luminous bodies to be seen at all distances in every direction. The paradox was resolved in the 1920s with the birth of COSMOLOGY. It is, in fact, the recession of the galaxies that shifts the wavelength of the light from stars of distant galaxies and keeps the night dark. This provides additional evidence for the expansion of the Universe.

old-age benefit A SOCIAL SECURITY benefit paid to those above retirement age. Some form of old-age benefit is to be found in about 130 of the world's countries, but in many, especially developing countries, only a small minority (often government employees) are covered. Some old-age benefits are paid on the basis of contributions (social insurance) and others on the basis of right, or of need (social assistance). In countries in which such benefits are widely available, they have contributed to a substantial improvement in the well-being of older people, an increase in their independence from other family members. Traditionally, the sum paid has been linked either to the subsistence cost of living in the country, or to the previous income (and contributions) of the recipient. The recent tendency is to combine the two, by paying a flat-rate benefit to everyone, and an earnings-related supplement. Those who can afford to do so often supplement their state benefits with occupational pensions (to which they and their employers have contributed) and pensions derived from private INSURANCE. The rapid increase in the numbers of old people across the world and the proportionate decrease in the working population have raised concerns about the future financing of old-age benefits. Many schemes are financed in such a way that current workers and employers directly provide the funds from which pensioners are paid, in the expectation that future generations will do the same. If a shrinking work-force is unable or unwilling to provide funds, a cut in benefit levels or eligibility, or a rise in the retirement age, however unpopular, may become unavoidable.

Old Bailey The popular name for the Central Criminal Court, formerly standing in an ancient bailey of London city wall. The present court, trying offences committed in the City and the Greater London Area, and certain other offences, was built in 1903–06 on the site of Newgate Prison.

Oldenburg A market town and river port in Lower Saxony, north-west Germany, on the River Hunte west of Bremen; pop. (1991) 145,160. It lies on the Coastal Canal and has a university founded in 1970. Oldenburg was formerly the residence of the counts of Ammerland and from 1918 to 1933 was capital of the state of Oldenburg.

Oldfield, Bruce (1950–) British fashion designer. In 1973 he became a freelance designer, working for the New York department store Bendel's and sketching for Yves St Laurent. He displayed his first collection in London in 1975 and gained an international reputation for his ready-to-wear designs and his lavish evening dresses.

Oldham An industrial town in Greater Manchester, north-west England, north-east of Manchester; pop. (1991) 100,000. Its industries produce textiles and electronics.

Oldowan The oldest tradition of human toolmaking, named after the simple stone tools found at OLDUVAI GORGE but now known from many other early human occupation sites in Africa. The oldest certain stone tools, from the Hadar and Omo regions in Ethiopia and from the east of the Democratic Republic of Congo, were made between 2.5 and 2 million years ago, probably by HOMO HABILIS. Usually, the toolmaker started with a large cobble, probably picked out of a stream bed, and flaked it with a hammerstone into the required shape. The detached flakes were also trimmed and put to use. Several distinct types of Oldowan tools were made and were probably used for different tasks. A more advanced tradition, Developed Oldowan, occurs also at Olduvai Gorge around 1.5 million years ago, the maker probably being HOMO ERECTUS.

Old Pretender, the James STUART, son of James II of England and Ireland (James VII of Scotland).

Old Sarum A hill in Wiltshire, southern England, 3 km (2 miles) north of Salisbury. It was the site of an ancient Iron Age settlement and hill fort which was later occupied by Romans, Saxons, and Normans, who built a castle and a town. It became a bishopric but fell into decline after a dispute in 1220 when the new cathedral and town of Salisbury were established to the south. The site of Old Sarum became deserted and the original cathedral was demolished in 1331. Until the Reform Act of 1832 Old Sarum was a 'rotten borough' with only a handful of electors, returning two Members of Parliament.

Old Testament See BIBLE.

Olduvai Gorge A gorge in Northern Tanzania, 48 km (30 miles) long and up to 90 metres (300 ft) deep. The exposed strata contain numerous fossils spanning the full range of the Pleistocene period. Most importantly, the Gorge has provided the longest sequence of hominid presence and activity yet discovered anywhere in the world, with fossils, stone-tool industries, and other evidence of hominid activities that date from *c.*2.1–1.7 million years ago for the oldest dated deposits to *c.*22,000 years ago for the most recent fossil-bearing deposits. The hominids found at individual sites within the gorge include *Australopithecus boisei* (the *Zinjanthropus* fossils), *Homo habilis*, and *Homo erectus*.

Old Vic The popular name of a London theatre, opened in 1818 as the Royal Coburg and renamed the Royal Victoria Theatre in honour of Princess (later Queen) Victoria in 1833. Under the management of Lilian Baylis from 1912 it gained an enduring reputation for its Shakespearean productions. From 1963 to 1976 it was the home of the National Theatre Company. In 1982 the theatre was bought by the Canadian Ed Mirvish.

Old World Europe, Asia, and Africa, or that part of the world known by the ancients to exist.

oleander (or **rosebay**) A plant of the genus *Nerium*, which is part of a family (Apocynaceae) of about 1,500 mainly tropical trees, shrubs, and lianas, including FRANGIPANI and PERIWINKLE. Oleanders are atypical in that they are native to waterside habitats in the Mediterranean area. The common oleander, *Nerium oleander*, is a shrub with narrow leaves, typical of stream-side plants (rheophytes). It has large white or pink flowers and is often cultivated, but all parts of it are poisonous.

oleum (or **Nordhausen acid**) Fuming sulphuric acid, a solution of sulphur trioxide, SO_3, in pure sulphuric acid, H_2SO_4. Oleum contains the compound $H_2S_2O_7$ (disulphuric(VI) acid or pyrosulphuric acid). It is formed in the production of sulphuric acid by the CONTACT PROCESS. When water is added to oleum, pure sulphuric acid is re-formed.

Oligocene Epoch The third of the geological epochs of the TERTIARY PERIOD, spanning the period of time from 36.6 to 23.7 million years ago. It was a time of falling temperature and general retreat of the seas.

oligopoly (in economics) A market structure comprising a small number of firms. Oligopolists may have MONOPOLY power, and the ability to affect price and to make super-normal PROFITS. The main characteristic of oligopoly is that when firms make decisions on price and output levels, they take into account the expected decisions or reactions of competing firms. Thus they frequently avoid competing on price, preferring instead to compete in other ways (for example ADVERTISING), and occasionally to form CARTELS.

olive A narrow-leaved, greyish, evergreen tree of the genus *Olea*, with over 35 species in warm temperate and tropical regions. Olives belong to the same family, Oleaceae, as lilac, jasmine, and ash trees. The common olive, *O. europaea*, is native to the Mediterranean area and is also cultivated in the dry subtropics; it grows up to 20 m (65 feet) in height, and produces oil-rich black fruits, or olives. The tree is tolerant of arid, stony, infertile soils, and fruiting is favoured by dry summers and cool winters, particularly near the sea, where the crop is protected from extremes of temperature. Italy is the largest producer of olives, followed by the USA (principally California), Spain, and France.

When ripe, the black fruits contain up to 60 per cent of oil, which is extracted by crushing and pressing and is valued as cooking and salad oil. About 10 per cent of the crop is harvested unripe or green and pickled in brine. Both ripe and unripe olives have an inherent bitterness, which is removed by soaking in an alkaline solution.

Oliver, Isaac (*c.*1568–1617) English miniaturist of Huguenot origin, his father (a goldsmith) being a refugee from religious persecution in France. Oliver trained under Nicholas Hilliard and later became his main rival, finding much patronage at court after the turn of the century. His style was more naturalistic than that of Hilliard, using light and shade to suggest three dimensions and generally dispensing with the emblematic adornments beloved of the Elizabethan age. Oliver's son, **Peter** (1594–1647), was also a miniaturist.

Olives, Mount of The highest point in the range of hills to the east of Jerusalem. It is a holy place for both Judaism and Christianity and frequently mentioned in the Bible. The Garden of Gethsemane is located nearby and its slopes have been a sacred Jewish burial ground for centuries.

Olivier, Laurence (Kerr), Baron Olivier of Brighton (1907–89) British actor and director. He made his professional début in 1924 and subsequently performed most of the major Shakespearian roles; he was also director of the National Theatre 1963–73. His films include *Wuthering Heights* (1939) and *Rebecca* (1940), as well as adaptations of Shakespeare; he produced, co-directed, and starred in *Henry V* (1944) and directed and starred in *Hamlet* (1948) and *Richard III* (1955). The Olivier Theatre, part of the National Theatre, is named in his honour. He was married to Vivien Leigh from 1940 to 1961 and to Joan Plowright (1929–) from 1961 until his death.

olivine A group of rock-forming minerals, particularly common in igneous rocks that are poor in silica. The olivines range in composition from magnesium silicate, Mg_2SiO_4, to iron silicate, Fe_2SiO_4; these are named forsterite and fayalite respectively. They are hard, and typically olive-green in colour. Crystals of gem quality are known as peridot.

olm An aquatic, cave-dwelling SALAMANDER, *Proteus anguinus*, found in underground lakes and streams in north eastern Italy and Yugoslavia. The adult, which is a permanent 'larva', has a slender, cylindrical body up to 30 cm (12 inches) long, including a crested tail. It has large, feathery, pinkish gills, poorly developed eyes, only three toes on the fore-limbs and two toes on the hind-limbs, and is pale, usually whitish in colour. It often lives deep underground, sometimes living for as long as 25 years, and lays between 12 and 70 eggs. When only a few eggs are produced these may be retained in the body and live young are produced. The olm is a member of the same family as the American mud-puppy.

Olmec ▶1 A member of a prehistoric people inhabiting the coast of Veracruz and western Tabasco on the Gulf of Mexico *c*.1200–100 BC, who established what was probably the first developed civilization of Mesoamerica. They are noted for their sculptures, especially the massive stone-hewn heads with realistic features and round helmets, and small jade carvings featuring a jaguar. **▶2** A member of a native American people living in the highlands of Mexico or migrating to the Gulf coast during the 12th century. Their name is derived from a Nahuatl word meaning 'people of the rubber (-tree) country'.

Olympia A site in western Greece. It was the location of the most important shrine to the god Zeus (see GREEK RELIGION). An oracle of Zeus was there and every four years a festival of competitive games was held in his honour. Archaeologists have recovered much, most notably many of the sculptures of the temple of Zeus (5th century BC), and also the workshop where the gold and ivory statue of Zeus was created by the Athenian Phidias probably in the 430s BC.

Olympic Games A world festival of sport inspired by the ancient Greek games held at OLYMPIA. The first Olympiad is dated 776 BC, though the games were said to have begun before then. Originally local, before long they began to attract Greeks from much further afield. They were greatly expanded from a one-day festival of athletics and wrestling to, in 472 BC, five days with many events, including horse and chariot racing, wrestling, and a race in full armour. Winners received olive wreathes as their prizes, and they brought much glory to their cities. Theodosius stopped the games in 393 AD. The modern version owes its existence to Baron de Coubertin, a French aristocrat, and was conceived as a championship for amateur sportsmen to be staged every four years. For the first Games in 1896, athletes from 12 nations travelled to Athens to compete in GYMNASTICS, ATHLETICS, CYCLING, FENCING, lawn TENNIS, shooting, swimming, WEIGHTLIFTING, and WRESTLING. Apart from intervals for the two World Wars, the Games have continued ever since, at a variety of venues. In 2000 Sydney will host the 27th Olympic Games in the modern series. A separate Winter Olympics began in 1924, at first held in the winter months preceding the summer Games but now held two years after the summer Games. Women's athletic events were introduced in 1928.

Olympus, Mount ▶1 A mountain in Cyprus, in the Troodos range. Rising to 1,951 m (6,400 ft), it is the highest peak on the island. **▶2** A mountain in north-east Greece at the eastern end of the range dividing Thessaly from Macedonia. In Greek mythology it was the home of the gods and the court of Zeus; height 2,917 m (9,570 ft).

Om In Buddhism, Hinduism, and Jainism, a mystic syllable, a universal affirmation, considered the most sacred mantra (Sanskrit, 'instrument of thought'). It represents several important triads: the three spheres of heaven, air, and Earth; the three major Hindu gods, Vishnu, Shiva, and Brahma; the three sacred Vedic scriptures, *Samaveda*, *Yaruveda*, and *Rigveda*; and the triad composed of the gods Vishnu and Lakshmi, and the worshipper him- or herself.

Omagh The county town of Tyrone, Northern Ireland, situated amidst outlying hills of the Sperrin Mountains where the Drumragh and Camowen rivers join to form the Strule; pop. (1981) 14,630.

Omaha A city in eastern Nebraska, USA, on the Missouri River; pop. (1990) 335,795. The largest city in the state, Omaha was settled in 1854 and named after an Indian tribe. It developed into a major livestock and grain market and meat-packing centre after the arrival of the railway in 1865.

Omaha A North American Indian Tribe of the Siouan-Dhegiha linguistic group, originally occupying the Mississippi valley near St Louis and later the plains and prairies of Nebraska.

Oman (formerly **Muscat and Oman**) A country occupying the eastern corner of Arabia.

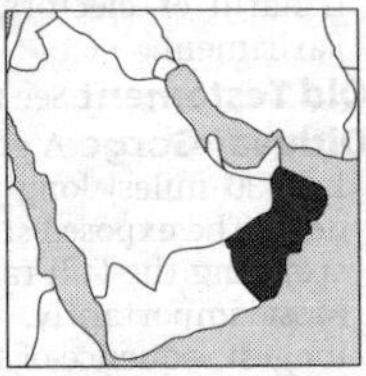

Physical. Oman has a coast on the Arabian Sea, and inland it borders on Saudi Arabia and Yemen. Mountains rise steeply from a narrow coastal plain to a plateau which merges into the desert of the 'empty quarter' or Rub al-Khali.

Economy. Crude oil and natural gas are important exports and sources of government revenue, but Oman is not a member of OPEC. The manufacturing base includes oil-refining, copper-smelting, and the manufacture of cement and motor vehicles. The coastal plain is fertile, supporting crops of dates, coconuts, bananas, and sugar cane. The climate is hot, but cattle can be bred on the mountains and camels in the oases.

History. Oman was a trading outpost of Mesopotamia, settled by Arabs in the 1st century AD. It was conquered for Islam in the 7th century. Expelling Portuguese incursions by 1650, the Omanis created a maritime empire with possessions as distant as MOMBASA and ZANZIBAR and trade contacts with south-east Asia. By 1754 Ahmad ibn Said had expelled Turkish invaders and founded the sultanate that still rules Oman. Under Said ibn Sultan Sayyid Oman was the most powerful state in Arabia in the early 19th century, controlling Zanzibar and the coastal regions of Iran and Baluchistan (now mainly in Pakistan). Tension frequently erupted between the sultan of Oman and the interior tribes. Oil, now the country's major product, began to be exported in 1967. In 1970 the present ruler, Sultan Qaboos bin Said (1940–), deposed his father Said bin Taimur in a palace coup. An uprising by left-wing guerrillas, the Popular Front for the Liberation of Oman, was defeated in 1975. A member of the Arab League, Oman managed to remain largely unaffected by both the IRAN–IRAQ WAR and the GULF WAR. In 1996 Sultan Qaboos decreed Oman to be an hereditary absolute monarchy.

Capital: Muscat
Area: 300,000 sq km (120,000 sq mi)

Population: 2,163,000 (1995)
Currency: 1 Omani rial = 1,000 baiza
Religions: Muslim 86.0%; Hindu 13.0%
Ethnic Groups: Omani Arab 77.0%; Indian 15.0%; Pakistani (mostly Baluchi) 3.5%; Bengali 2.5%
Languages: Arabic (official); minority languages
International Organizations: UN; Arab League; GCC

Oman, Gulf of An inlet of the Arabian Sea, connected by the Strait of Hormuz to the Persian Gulf.

Omar I (*c*.581–644) Muslim caliph 634–44. In early life an opponent of Muhammad, Omar was converted to Islam in 617. After becoming caliph he began an extensive series of conquests, adding Syria, Palestine, and Egypt to his empire. He was assassinated by a Persian slave.

Omar Khayyám (died 1123) Persian poet, mathematician, and astronomer. He is remembered for his *rubáiyát* (quatrains), translated and adapted by Edward Fitzgerald in *The Rubáiyát of Omar Khayyám* (1859); the work contains meditations on the mysteries of existence, expressing scepticism regarding divine providence and a consequent celebration of the sensuous and fleeting pleasures of the earthly world.

ombudsman (Swedish, 'agent' or 'representative') A person responsible for investigating complaints against government officials. The office originated in Sweden in 1809. The late 20th century has seen an explosion in the number of countries with ombudsmen, perhaps stimulated by the increasing activities of public bureaucracy and by the readiness of members of the public to complain: ombudsmen are now established in Australia, Canada, Denmark, Finland, New Zealand, Sweden, the UK, some states of the USA, and elsewhere. Ombudsmen are impartial and independent of the government of the day.

Omdurman A city in central Sudan, on the White Nile opposite Khartoum and the seat of the National Assembly; pop. (1983) 526,290. It was capital of the Mahdist state of Sudan following the British recapture of Khartoum in 1885 and scene of Kitchener's decisive victory over the Mahdi's successor, the Khalifa, in 1898, which marked the end of the Dervish uprising. It has large markets and specializes in gold and silver jewellery.

Omsk A city and major river port in west Siberia, Russia, at the junction of the Om and Irtysh rivers; pop. (1990) 1,159,000. Situated on the Trans-Siberian Railway, its industries produce oil, grain, textiles, and machinery.

Onassis, Aristotle (Socrates) (1906–75) Greek shipping magnate and international businessman. The owner of a substantial shipping empire, he was also the founder of the Greek national airline, Olympic Airways (1957). In 1968 he married Jacqueline Kennedy (see ONASSIS, JACQUELINE).

Onassis, Jacqueline Lee Bouvier Kennedy (known as 'Jackie O') (1929–94) US First Lady. She worked as a photographer before marrying John F. Kennedy in 1953. Her term as First Lady, which began in 1961, was cut short by the President's assassination in 1963. She married Aristotle Onassis in 1968 and after being widowed for a second time in 1975 pursued a career in publishing.

onchocerciasis A roundworm infection caused by *Onchocerca volvulus*, also called river blindness, which is transmitted by the bite from a female black fly of the genus *Simulium*. Onchocerciasis occurs in tropical regions of Africa, southern Arabia, and South America and is one of the main causes of blindness in these regions. Worms reside in muscles and the outer layer covering joints (joint capsule); numerous motile embryonic forms that reside in the skin (microfilariae) are released by the adult worm. Initial symptoms include itching and skin rash. Eye involvement causes inflammation and blindness if untreated.

oncology See CANCER AND CANCER THERAPY.

Ondaatje, (Philip) Michael (1943–) Canadian writer, born in Sri Lanka. He emigrated to Canada in 1962, and in 1967 became a university lecturer. In his works, which include poetry, novels, and an autobiography *Running in the Family* (1982) he compels the reader to see reality as transient. In 1992 his novel *The English Patient* was awarded the Booker Prize, becoming a highly acclaimed film in 1996.

O'Neill, Eugene (Gladstone) (1888–1953) US dramatist. He achieved recognition with his first full-length play, *Beyond the Horizon* (1920), which won a Pulitzer Prize. Among his many other plays are the trilogy *Mourning Becomes Electra* (1931), in which he adapted the theme of Aeschylus' *Oresteia* to portray the aftermath of the American Civil War; *The Iceman Cometh* (1946), a tragedy about a collection of bar-room derelicts; and *Long Day's Journey into Night* (performed and published posthumously in 1956), a semi-autobiographical tragedy portraying mutually destructive family relationships. He was awarded the Nobel Prize for literature in 1936.

onion A vegetable that probably originated in central Asia and was cultivated in ancient Egypt, India, and China. Onions are now widespread in all temperate areas, and the USA, Japan, and Europe are the greatest centres of production. All varieties of onion are derived from a single species, *Allium cepa*, and are naturally perennial plants. They belong to the monocotyledonous family Liliaceae, which includes lilies, tulips, leeks, and asparagus. The onion plant has a very short stem from which a number of sheathing leaves arise. Towards the end of the first season food is stored in the leaf-bases to form a swollen bulb. The pungently flavoured bulbs are harvested when dormant and keep well over a long period. The crops may be grown direct from seed, or from small bulbs or 'sets'. Young plants, known as spring onions or scallions, are eaten as a salad vegetable.

Ono, Yoko (1933–) US musician and artist, born in Japan. She was an established avant-garde performance artist when she met John LENNON, whom she married in 1969. They collaborated on experimental recordings, such as *Unfinished Music No. 1: Two Virgins* (1969) and performed together in the Plastic Ono Band; Ono also recorded her own albums, starting with *Approximately Infinite Universe* (1973). After Lennon's murder in 1980 she continued her solo career with 1981's *Season of Glass*.

Onsager, Lars (1903–76) Norwegian-born US chemist who extended the laws of thermodynamics to irreversible processes and derived an expression for the equivalent conductance of an electrolyte. He provided a theoretical basis for the gaseous-diffusion method of separating uranium-235 from the more common uranium-238, making possible the production of nuclear fuel. In 1968 he was awarded the Nobel Prize for chemistry.

Ontario A province of eastern Canada, between Hudson Bay and the Great Lakes; area 1,068,580 sq km (412,581 sq miles); pop. (1991) 10,084,885; capital, Toronto. Its largest cities are Toronto, Hamilton, Ottawa, London, and Windsor. Settled by the French and English in the 17th century, Ontario was ceded to Britain in 1763, and became a province in 1867. It is the second-largest and most populous of the provinces of Canada with a strong economic base rooted in finance, service industries, agriculture, mining, and the manufacture of vehicles, aircraft, transport equipment, and high tech goods.

Ontario, Lake The smallest and most easterly of the Great Lakes of North America, lying on the border between Ontario in Canada and New York State; area 19,001 sq km (7,336 sq miles); area on the Canadian side of the border, 10,388 sq km (4,010 sq miles); maximum depth 244 m (800 ft). It is linked to Lake Erie in the south by the Niagara River and the Welland Ship Canal and to the Atlantic by the St Lawrence River. The chief cities on its shores are Hamilton and Toronto in Canada, and Rochester in the USA. Pollution of the lake has reduced commercial fishing.

ontological argument An argument first presented by St ANSELM (1033–1109), claiming to establish the existence of God A PRIORI, that is, in a way that depends only on the concept of God, and draws on no factual premiss. The ontological argument is thus contrasted with various cosmological arguments, which seek to demonstrate the existence of God as creator from the existence or order of the natural world. Anselm's argument held that God is the most perfect conceivable being; that a God who exists in reality is of greater perfection than one who exists only as a conception in man's mind; and that therefore God, as the zenith of perfection, must exist in reality. The argument was repeated by DESCARTES, and criticized by KANT, who questioned whether we may, as the argument presupposes, think of existence as a feature something might have or lack.

ontology The philosophical study of the nature of being. Although this can be taken to be the study of what it is for anything to exist at all, as in HEIDEGGER's work, ontological questions are also concerned with what, in particular, exists. Thus our common-sense ontology would include the material objects with which we interact (such as trees, tables, and mountains), but should it also contain abstract mathematical entities (sets and numbers) or the sub-atomic entities of the theoretical sciences (such as protons and muons)? Closely linked is the question of reductionism. For example, can minds be reduced to bodies, or mathematics to LOGIC? A major question is how we are to decide ontological issues. **Ockham's razor**, the principle, formulated by William of OCKHAM in about 1340, that we should not multiply entities beyond necessity, is generally thought of as a principle in the theory of knowledge or EPISTEMOLOGY, and was used as such by RUSSELL. But in recent philosophy this has also often been linked to questions of meaning, as in LOGICAL POSITIVISM.

onyx A type of QUARTZ used as a semi-precious stone and consisting of silica and opal. It is a variety of chalcedony composed of white and brown bands. Sardonyx has white and brownish-red bands. The chief localities of onyx are India and South America.

oolite A limestone composed of OOLITHS. Oolites are common rocks, of all ages. Those of Jurassic age are valuable as building stones.

oolith The particles of which oolitic limestone is made. These are small, spherical concretionary bodies ranging in diameter from 0.25 mm to 2 mm (0.01–0.4 inch). They are usually composed of calcium carbonate in the form of CALCITE, although present-day forms may be ARAGONITE. They are thought to be produced by the rolling about of grains on the sea floor so that consecutive layers of calcium carbonate are gradually built up; and they are forming at the present time in warm shallow waters such as those of the Bahamas and the Red Sea. Those over 2 mm in diameter are known as pisolites.

Oort, Jan Hendrik (1900–92) Dutch astronomer. His early measurements of the proper motion of stars enabled him to prove that the Galaxy is rotating, and to determine the position and orbital period of the Sun within it. Oort was director of the observatory at Leiden for 25 years, during which time he was involved in the discovery of the wavelength of radio emission from interstellar hydrogen, and noted the strong polarization of light from the Crab Nebula. He also proposed the existence of a cloud of incipient comets beyond the orbit of Pluto, now named after him (see OORT–ÖPIK CLOUD).

Oort–Öpik Cloud A cloud of COMETS thought to encircle the edge of the Solar System. Long-period comets seem to originate in the deep recesses of space. Both the Estonian astronomer Ernst Öpik and the Dutch astronomer Jan H. Oort wondered if they were either objects that were loosely bound to the Solar System or interstellar visitors. Oort suggested that the Sun was surrounded by a spherical cloud of 100 billion comets orbiting the Sun every 1–30 million years. At their outermost points they were between 20,000 and 200,000 astronomical units from the Sun. As the nearest star at present is only 270,700 astronomical units away, a star approaching the Sun in the past could have penetrated this cloud and gravitationally perturbed some of the comets. About half of these would have entered the inner planetary regions.

ooze A fine-grained organic deposit that accumulates in the deep parts of the ocean floor, and contributes to the flatness of some ABYSSAL PLAINS. Oozes are made up mainly of the calcareous and siliceous skeletons and shells of marine plants and animals (such as diatoms, foraminifera, and coccoliths), and they accumulate extremely slowly, usually no more than a few centimetres in a thousand years. In the Pacific Ocean the thickness of the ooze is up to 1,000 m (over 3,000 feet) thick, and probably represents 100 million years of deposition.

opacity In astrophysics, a quantity that characterizes the absorption or scattering of ELECTROMAGNETIC RADIATION as it passes through a gas or PLASMA. In high-opacity material a PHOTON travels only a short distance (its **free path**) before it is absorbed or scattered; in contrast the free path is long if the opacity is low. The opacity of the plasma in the interiors of stars is one of several factors that influence the structure and evolution of a star, because the ease with which photons can carry away energy affects the star's core temperature and thus its rate of thermonuclear energy generation. The SPECTRUM of the light emitted by a star is influenced by the opacity of its outer layers, or atmosphere. Opacity, which is related to optical depth, can vary with the wavelength of the radiation so that more power is radiated at wavelengths for which the opacity is low.

opah (or **moonfish**) A deep-bodied, little-known, oceanic fish, *Lampris guttatus*, which is brilliantly coloured, deep blue on the back with a pinkish belly, and rounded milk-white blotches on the body and blood-red fins. It grows to over 1.5 m (5 feet) in length and can weigh up to 50 kg (110 pounds). Despite its stout appearance, it is an exceptionally fast swimmer and feeds on squids and mid-water fishes. It probably lives in mid-water at depths of 100–400 m (325–1,300 feet), but most of the specimens studied have been either accidentally captured by commercial trawlers or stranded on the beach.

opal A form of silica with varying amounts of water. It is formed at low temperatures from water containing silica, and occurs in fissures in igneous rocks and in nodules in sedimentary rocks. Relatively soft and amorphous, it is easily damaged and should not be immersed in liquid. A 'play' of colours is a characteristic of opals; a white or black opal displaying blue, red, green, or orange flashes, although a yellow 'fire' opal may not flash. New South Wales and Queensland in Australia are the common sources of supply, and Hungary is the oldest, but opals are also found in Mexico, Honduras, and Nevada (USA).

Op art A type of abstract art that exploits certain optical phenomena to cause a work to seem to vibrate, pulsate, or flicker. Many of the devices employed by practitioners of Op art are based upon the well-known visual illusions to be found in standard textbooks of perceptual psychology, and the Op artist seeks maximum geometrical precision to evoke an exactly prescribed retinal response. The style developed in the mid-1960s, and leading exponents include Victor VASARELY and Bridget RILEY.

OPEC (Organization of Petroleum Exporting Countries) An international organization seeking to regulate the price of oil. The first moves to establish closer links between oil-producing countries were made by Venezuela, Iran, Iraq, Kuwait, and Saudi Arabia in 1949. In 1960, following a reduction in the oil price by the international oil companies, a conference was held in Baghdad of representatives from these countries, when it was decided to set up a permanent organization. This was formed in Caracas, Venezuela, the next year. Other countries later joined: Qatar (1961), Indonesia (1962), Libya (1962), United Arab Emirates (1967), Algeria (1969), Nigeria (1971), Ecuador (1973), and Gabon (1975). Ecuador left OPEC in 1993 and Gabon withdrew in 1996.

The organization rose to prominence in the mid-1970s after it virtually quadrupled the price of oil over a three-month period at the end of 1973. However, the influence of OPEC on world oil prices declined slightly as Western industrialized countries, such as Norway and the UK, began to exploit their own oil resources, found alternative forms of fuel, or initiated programmes to cut the use of energy. The Organization of Arab Petroleum Exporting Countries (OAPEC), based in Kuwait, was established in 1968, to coordinate the different aspects of the Arab petroleum industry, and safeguard its members' interests.

Opel, Wilhelm von (1871–1948) German motor manufacturer. In 1898 he and his brothers converted their grandfather's bicycle and sewing-machine factory to car production, launching their first original model in 1902. After World War I the company became the first in Germany to introduce assembly-line production and manufactured more than a million cars. Opel sold control of the company to the US manufacturer General Motors in 1929.

open-cast mining The MINING of ores from the earth without tunnelling. This requires a large ore deposit on or very near the surface, which can be broken up by EXPLOSIVES. The resulting debris is then removed by a variety of heavy excavating equipment, such as mobile power shovels and DRAG-LINES, or continuous bucket-and-wheel EXCAVATORS feeding conveyor belts. The ore is then transported directly to processing plants.

open cluster A star CLUSTER found mainly in or near the plane of the Galaxy and therefore often called a **galactic cluster**. The members of an open cluster have very similar velocities through space but ultimately, although the stars in the cluster had a common origin, the individual stars will be dispersed by the gravitational attractions of the galactic centre and interstellar clouds. If the cluster is near enough to the Solar System the stars' PROPER MOTIONS can be determined. For this reason, a nearby open cluster is also called a **moving cluster**. If these motions are plotted on the CELESTIAL SPHERE they are directed at a point known as the convergent point. From a knowledge of the stars' angular distances from the convergent point and their RADIAL VELOCITIES, the distance of the cluster can be calculated. An open cluster usually consists of no more than a few hundred stars. Well-known examples are the Pleiades and the Hyades. Most open clusters are made up of young stars only a few million years old though in the thousand or so open clusters known, there are some whose member stars are much older.

open-hearth furnace (or **Siemens–Martin furnace**) A furnace used for making steel from a mixture of scrap-iron and pig-iron, for glass-making, and in several other industrial processes. The iron or other material is placed in a shallow hearth, and heated by a mixture of fuel-gas and air burnt above it. Waste gases leaving the furnace give up much of their heat to the incoming fuel-gas and air in a heat regenerator. As a result, the temperature of the flame in the hearth reaches about 1,650°C. The open-hearth furnace was first developed by C. W. SIEMENS, and steel production using a mixture of scrap- and pig-iron was developed by Pierre-Emile Martin in 1864.

Open University See DISTANCE EDUCATION.

opera A dramatic composition of which music and singing are essential parts. Although music has been used in association with drama since the days of ancient Greece, the idea of conveying a story entirely in terms of words and music belongs to the end of the 16th century. Its evolution is usually credited to a group of poets, musicians, and intellectuals who met as a Society (the Camerata) in Florence from 1580. In the hope of emulating ancient practice they invented opera (an abbreviation for *opera in musica*). The earliest surviving example, *Eurydice* (1600), has music by Giulio Caccini (*c.*1545–1618) and Jacopo Peri (1561–1633). MONTEVERDI, the first opera composer of genius, used recitative together with a wide variety of musical resources in his first opera, *Orpheus* (1607). In France the first major operatic composer was LULLY. He established the *tragédie héroïque*, with simpler librettos and a more restrained vocal style than in Italian opera. Meanwhile in Rome at the beginning of the 18th century, a group of noblemen and dramatists sought to purify the operatic tradition, writing a series of librettos on uplifting themes. The most important librettist in this *opera seria* style was Pietro Metastasio (1698–1782), but some of the finest *opera seria* were written in London by HANDEL. Because *opera seria* librettos excluded any comic elements, in Italy the more sophisticated *opera buffa* style developed. In Germany, MOZART took the conventions of Italian opera to a high point in *Idomeneo* (1781). In such operas as *The Marriage of Figaro* (1786) and *Don Giovanni* (1787) his inventiveness proved unsurpassed. After Mozart, the divisions between *opera seria* and the various forms of *opera buffa* became blurred. With the 19th century, opera began to have stronger national characteristics. Italian opera, in the hands of ROSSINI, BELLINI, and DONIZETTI, remained true to vocal melody (see BEL CANTO) and finally achieved its apotheosis in the dramas of VERDI. Germany, responding to the spirit of ROMANTICISM, veered towards folklore and fantasy. It also laid greater emphasis on the role of the orchestra, culminating in WAGNER's music-dramas, which dispensed with aria and recitative in favour of a network of LEITMOTIFS. Overt nationalism, reflecting folk-music subjects, came to the fore in the second half of the 19th century in composers from Russia (GLINKA, MUSSORGSKY, BORODIN, RIMSKY-KORSAKOV, and TCHAIKOVSKY) and Czechoslovakia (SMETANA, DVOŘÁK and JANÁČEK). At the end of the century a taste for realistic subjects, first manifest in Bizet's *Carmen* (1875), took root among Verdi's successors – particularly MASCAGNI and PUCCINI. In Germany, meanwhile, Richard STRAUSS followed Wagner with music-dramas of an expressionist type (*Salome*, 1903–05). Opera in the 20th century has embraced many styles, from the ATONALITY of BERG's *Wozzeck* (1925) to the JAZZ of GERSHWIN's *Porgy and Bess* (1935), the impressionism of DEBUSSY's *Pelléas et Mélisande* (1902) to the astringent NEOCLASSICISM of STRAVINSKY's *The Rake's Progress* (1951). Modern innovative works include *Peter Grimes* (1945) and *Billy Budd* (1951) by Benjamin BRITTEN, *Bomarzo* (1964) and *Beatrix Cenci* (1971) by Alberto Ginastera (1916–83), and György LIGETI's *Le Grand Macabre* (1978). Philip GLASS has composed operas in a minimal style, including *Einstein on the Beach* (1976) and *Akhnaten* (1984).

operating system The software that manages the resources of a computer system, independent of the use to which the computer is put. In addition to controlling the operation of HARDWARE, the operating system also manages the transmission of data to and from MEMORY, the disk drives, and PERIPHERALS such as keyboards, displays, and PRINTERS. Widely used operating systems include MS-DOS (MicroSoft Disk Operating System), OS/2, and UNIX.

operational research (or **operations research**, OR) The application of mathematical, scientific, and engineering techniques to model and improve the operation of complex systems involving people, machines, and information. OR thus has much in common with systems engineering. Operational research emerged in the UK during World War II as an interdisciplinary attempt to solve wartime logistical problems. Since then it has been applied to many planning and scheduling problems in industrial, commercial, and public sectors – often using the mathematical technique known as linear programming. OR provides a set of techniques that can be applied to business problems using some form of quantitative representation as an aid to (but not as a substitute for) decision-making. The aim of operational research is to find optimal courses of action using such methods as project management (see CRITICAL PATH METHOD) and simulation techniques. One example of OR is the control of traffic flow within a city.

operetta A light-hearted, small-scale OPERA. Spoken dialogue is used to link the arias and ensembles. Operettas range in complexity from simple plays-with-music to works that involve most aspects of true OPERA, other than recitative (melodic speech). Among the notable composers of operetta are OFFENBACH, Johann STRAUSS, LEHÁR, and GILBERT and SULLIVAN. Similar also is the musical comedy of the early 20th century and the present-day MUSICAL, the difference being largely that of period style and the precise amount and weight of music involved.

ophicléïde A keyed brass musical instrument invented by Halari in 1817 as a bass key-BUGLE to replace the SERPENT (as the name, French-Greek for keyed serpent, suggests). It was widely used in orchestras and military bands in the 19th century, but was eventually replaced by the TUBA.

Ophiuchus The Serpent Holder, a CONSTELLATION on the celestial equator, one of the 48 sky figures known to the ancient Greeks. It represents the mythical healer Aesculapius, visualized holding a serpent (the constellation SERPENS). Its brightest star is second-magnitude Alpha Ophiuchi, known as Rasalhague from the Arabic meaning 'head of the serpent bearer'.

ophthalmic surgery The branch of SURGERY concerned with the eyes. The ancient practice of couching cataracts (displacing a damaged lens downwards into the eye) was widespread until the 18th century. However, the treatment of eye disease was not accepted into mainstream medicine until the 19th century, when specialist hospitals were founded. The invention of the OPHTHALMOSCOPE in 1851 aided diagnosis, while local anaesthetics (particularly cocaine after 1884) and asepsis made more complex operations possible. Thereafter, forms of cataract, squint, glaucoma (raised pressure within the eye), and retinal disorder all gradually became amenable to surgery. Technological developments, such as the operating microscope, titanium instruments for microsurgery, and, in the last decade, artificial (polymethyl methacrylate) lens implants have greatly improved results. Knifeless techniques including DIATHERMY, cryosurgery (localized freezing and hence destruction of unwanted tissues), and, since 1962, LASERS have also played an important role.

ophthalmoscope An instrument for viewing the internal structures of the eye. Looking through the pupil, the specialist can see the retina and is able to diagnose eye disorders and some general conditions, such as diabetes and high blood pressure. The modern ophthalmoscope was invented by the German physicist and physiologist Hermann von Helmholtz in 1851, and was the first type of instrument to allow direct visualization of the interior of a living organ.

Opie, **John** (1761–1807) British painter. His work includes portraits of contemporary figures, such as Mary Wollstonecraft, and history paintings, such as *The Murder of Rizzio* (1787).

opinion poll A sample survey of public opinion on a topic of current concern. The sample of the population questioned can either be random, or one which is designed to reflect the social, educational, or vocational proportions of the population as a whole (quota sample). The study of statistics in elections (psephology) is used to calculate the margins of error and to assess the accuracy of the inferences made from the sample to the population as a whole. Opinion polls have been criticized for failing to provide a true picture of public opinion, for invading people's privacy, or even for influencing public opinion itself, by creating a 'bandwagon' effect.

opioid Any compound with morphine-like pharmacological activity. Opioids include **opiates**, i.e. compounds that occur naturally in the OPIUM POPPY, such as morphine and codeine, and their synthetic derivatives, such as heroin (diamorphine) and methadone, as well as structurally unrelated compounds. Opioids used in medicine are called opioid analgesics, which are used for the relief of mild to severe pain; for example, codeine may be used for mild to moderate pain, and morphine for moderate to severe pain. Opioid analgesics are very effective, although they may cause dependence, tolerance, and withdrawal symptoms following prolonged use. Side-effects of opioids include nausea, vomiting, constipation, respiratory depression, low blood pressure, and drowsiness. Opioids also induce euphoria, which accounts for their misuse as illegal drugs.

opium poppy A widely distributed, summer-flowering annual plant, *Papaver somniferum*, of the poppy family, Papaveraceae. It is grown in hot, dry climates, including parts of Europe and east Asia, for the drug opium, which is extracted from its sap. The raw material is refined to produce medically important pain-killing drugs, including morphine and codeine. See OPIOID.

Opium Wars (1839–42; 1856–60) Two wars between Britain and China. In the early 19th century British traders were illegally importing opium from India to China and trying to increase trade in general. In 1839 the Chinese government confiscated some 20,000 chests of opium from British warehouses in Guangzhou (Canton). In 1840 the British Foreign Secretary, Lord PALMERSTON, sent a force of 16 British warships, which besieged Guangzhou and threatened Nanjing and communications with the capital. It ended with the Treaty of NANJING (1842). In 1856 Chinese officials boarded and searched a British flagged ship, the *Arrow*. The French joined the British in launching a military attack in 1857, at the end of which they demanded that the Chinese agree to the Treaty of Tianjin in 1858. This opened further ports to Western trade and provided freedom of travel to European merchants and Christian missionaries inland. When the emperor refused to ratify the agreement, Beijing was occupied, after which, by the Beijing Convention (1860), the Tianjin Agreement was accepted. By 1900 the number of treaty ports had risen to over 50, with all European colonial powers, as well as the USA, being granted trading concessions.

Oporto (Portuguese **Porto**) The principal city of Northern Portugal, near the mouth of the River Douro; pop. (1991) 310,640. It was a busy port before it was silted up. However, wine, including port wine which takes its name from the city, is still exported. Oporto is the centre of an industrial region producing chemicals, electrical equipment, tyres and other car parts, textiles, and soap. Prince Henry the Navigator (1394–1460) was born in Oporto.

opossum A New World MARSUPIAL of the family Didelphidae, though some Australian PHALANGERS are loosely called opossums, as are members of the separate family of South American RAT OPOSSUMS. There are some 75 species of didelphid opossums, most of which live in Central or South America. Some show convergence with placental mammals in resembling mice or shrews and there is an 'otter' in the form of the yapok, or water opossum, *Chironectes minimus*. Most opossums are small or medium-sized mammals, with the Virginia, or common opossum, *Didelphis virginiana*, being the largest at up to 5.5 kg (12 pounds). It is noted for its habit of feigning death, or 'playing possum', when attacked.

Oppenheimer, (Julius) Robert (1904–67) US physicist. He was appointed in 1942 as Director of the MANHATTAN PROJECT, based at Los Alamos, New Mexico, which in 1945 made the first atomic bomb. In 1953, at the height of the witch-hunting campaign led by the US Senator Joseph McCarthy, Oppenheimer was excluded from sensitive research on the grounds that he had Communist sympathies, but subsequently (1963) he was unreservedly rehabilitated.

optical activity A property possessed by certain crystals and solutions of rotating the plane of polarization of polarized light. The activity is called dextrorotatory if the rotation is clockwise when facing the light, and laevorotatory when it is anticlockwise. It occurs when a molecule exists in two mirror-image forms that cannot be superimposed on one another. These are called ENANTIOMERS or optical isomers; one is dextrorotatory (the *d*-isomer), the other laevorotatory (the *l*-isomer), and the optical activity of a substance depends on the proportion in which the two are present. Various methods exist for denoting the molecular configuration of optical isomers. Commonly, molecules are said to be D- or L-isomers if they are derived from a simple precursor that is a *d*- or *l*-form, respectively. Note that the D-form of a compound need not necessarily be dextrorotatory. A mixture containing both isomers in equal proportions is called a RACEMIC MIXTURE. Optical activity occurs in molecules possessing CHIRALITY.

optical character recognition (OCR) A technique for providing computers with input data directly from text or other symbols printed on paper, obviating the need for keying in the information. OCR systems generally use PHOTOCELLS or a modified television camera to scan the text. The signal is then fed to the computer. In most systems the computer identifies each character by matching it with stored characters, but advanced systems use ARTIFICIAL INTELLIGENCE techniques to improve accuracy. Some typefaces are specially designed to be read by computer, and are often used on financial documents, such as cheque-books.

optical double Two stars that, by chance, appear to be close together because they lie nearly along the same line of sight. An optical double is not a true BINARY STAR: the two stars may in reality be very far apart so that they are not under each other's gravitational attraction.

optical fibre A thin transparent fibre of glass or plastic that allows the transmission of light. Light can be retained within the fibre if the core is covered with a material (cladding) of a lower refractive index: the core–cladding boundary acts as a mirror, reflecting the light continuously back into the core. A light source, usually a LASER, can be modulated, and can carry a large number of channels each of enormous BANDWIDTH (due to its very high frequency), and can be multiplexed. An additional advantage is that optical-fibre transmission is not vulnerable to electrical INTERFERENCE, a problem associated with conventional electrical cable and radio. Major rewiring of the UK telephone system with optical fibres began in 1982, and there are now several transoceanic optical-fibre cables.

optical glass See GLASS.

optics The scientific study of light and vision. The two major branches of optics are **geometrical optics**, which is concerned with the geometry of light rays in an optical system, and **physical optics**, dealing with the properties of light and its interaction with matter.

opuntia See PRICKLY PEAR.

Opus Dei (Latin, 'work of God') A Roman Catholic organization founded in 1928 by the Spanish priest Josemaria Escrivá de Balaguer (1902–75). Members, of whom there are 76,000 worldwide, may be either priests or lay people. Particularly active in General Franco's Spain (1939–75), the organization has exercised a controversial and largely conservative influence on public affairs. It maintains a number of educational establishments, including the Universities of Pamplona and Navarre. There is a separate branch for women, segregation of the sexes being an important principle. Opus Dei emphasizes the austere aspect of Catholicism; members follow a range of ascetic practices, which include daily 'mortification' (self-flagellation), and celibacy is encouraged. The movement has attracted considerable criticism for its secrecy and authoritarianism, but Pope John Paul II is a supporter – he beatified de Balaguer in 1992.

ora See KOMODO DRAGON.

orache A member of the plant genus *Atriplex*, of which there are several species. Oraches are tall-growing plants or small shrubs of the sea coast, often covered with a powdery meal and bearing small flowers. The leaves of some species have been used as a substitute for spinach and as a cure for gout.

oracle A place consulted for advice or prophecy. There were many oracles in the ancient Greek world, most notably at DELPHI, Didyma on the coast of Asia Minor, Dodona in Epirus, and OLYMPIA. The most famous non-Greek oracle was that of the Egyptian Ammon at Siwah oasis in the Sahara, identified by the Greeks with Zeus and consulted by Alexander the Great in 331 BC. Apollo was the god most favoured as a giver of oracles though many other deities presided over oracular shrines. Consultations usually concerned religious matters but were also used by leaders seeking support for political or military actions.

Oran (Arabic **Wahran**) A port and industrial city on the Mediterranean coast of Algeria; pop. (1989) 664,000. A former provincial capital of the Ottoman Turks and a French naval base, Oran is the second-largest city in Algeria. Its industries include chemicals, textiles, cement, and food processing.

orange A widely cultivated CITRUS FRUIT. The sweet orange, *Citrus sinensis*, cultivated for thousands of years in China, is now grown wherever a suitable Mediterranean-type climate exists. Its juice contains up to 12 per cent sugar and 1 per cent citric acid (the least acid of all citrus fruits) and is rich in vitamin C. The sour, or Seville, orange, *C. aurantium*, from south-east Asia, is too bitter to be eaten fresh and has a citric acid content of about 3 per cent. It is valued for marmalade production and is an important crop of the Seville area of Spain.

Orange The ruling house (in full Orange-Châlons) of the principality centred on the small city of Orange, southern France. The city grew up around its Roman monuments, which include a semicircular theatre and a triumphal arch. In the 11th century it became an independent countship, and from the 12th century its rulers were vassals of the Holy Roman Emperor and came to style themselves 'princes'.

After 1530 the related house of Nassau-Châlons succeeded to the title, and in 1544 William of Nassau-Dillenburg (1533–84) became Prince of Orange and subsequently, as William I (the Silent), statholder in the Netherlands. His younger son, Maurice of Nassau (1567–1625), assumed the military leadership of the Dutch Revolts in 1584. Until the late 18th century the Orange dynasty continued to play a major part in the politics of the United Provinces. The principality itself was conquered by Louis XIV (1672) and incorporated into France by the Treaty of Utrecht (1713), but the title of Prince of Orange was retained by WILLIAM III, who became King of England, Scotland, and Ireland in 1689.

Orange, William of William III of England, Scotland, and Ireland. See WILLIAM.

Orange Free State (name since 1994 **Free State**; Afrikaans **Vrystaat**) A province in central South Africa, situated to the north of the Orange River; area 127,993 sq km (49,437 sq miles); pop. (1991) 1,929,370; capital, Bloemfontein. First settled by Boers after the Great Trek from Cape Colony (1836–38), it was annexed by Britain in 1848 but restored in 1854 to the Boers, who established the Orange Free State Republic. It was re-annexed by Britain in 1900, as the Orange River Colony, was given internal self-government in 1907, and became a province of the Union of South Africa in 1910, as the Orange Free State. It remained a province following local government reorganization in 1994. Grain, livestock, gold, and oil from coal are its chief products.

Orange River The longest river in South Africa, which rises in the Drakensberg Mountains in north-east Lesotho and flows generally westward for 2,173 km (1,350 miles) across almost the whole breadth of the continent before entering the Atlantic on the frontier between Namibia and South Africa. The river is much used for irrigation and the Orange River Scheme for hydroelectric power and irrigation was begun in 1963. There are rich alluvial diamond beds at the mouth of the river.

orang-utan A large APE, *Pongo pygmaeus*, related to chimpanzees, gorillas, and man. It is the largest fruit-eater in the world and is known to eat at least 200 species of fruit. It lives in lowland, tropical rain forests of Borneo and Sumatra, usually within river boundaries or mountain ranges, where it is an endangered species.

The prominent flanges of fat at the side of the face are very striking in large adult males. The jaws project forward from the face, the eyebrow ridge is only slightly pronounced, and the eyes and ears are small. The coat is shaggy, especially over the shoulders and arms. The fur varies in colour from shades of orange to purplish-blackish-brown, becoming darker with age. When extended the arms may span 2.4 m (7.8 feet) and their length is exaggerated because the standing height of the animal is only 1.4 m (4.5 feet). The female is smaller, standing only 1.06 m (3.5 feet) in height and weighing only half as much as the male. Sexual maturity is reached at about ten years of age and, after an elaborate courtship, mating occurs in the trees. The baby is born after a gestation period of eight months, and it is nursed for two to three years.

oratorio A religious musical composition for solo singers, chorus, and orchestra, which is designed to be sung without scenery or costumes. Oratorios originated in the plays given in the Oratory of St Philip Neri in Rome during the second half of the 16th century. The first true oratorio was CAVALIERI's *Representation of Soul and Body* (1600). Later contributors to its development include Carissimi, Alessandro SCARLATTI, SCHÜTZ, HANDEL, HAYDN, MENDELSSOHN, ELGAR, and TIPPETT. As oratorio developed, the chorus assumed more and more importance. This in turn led to the establishment of amateur choral societies. Until the end of the 18th century, oratorio was regarded as an alternative to opera (opera could not be performed during Lent).

Orbison, Roy (1936–88) US singer and composer. He began by writing country-music songs for other artists, establishing himself as a singer with the ballad 'Only the Lonely' (1960). Further hits followed, including 'Crying' (1961), 'Blue Bayou' (1963), and 'Oh, Pretty Woman' (1964), which was one of the best-selling singles of the 1960s.

orbital (in atomic physics) A pattern of electronic charge density in the space surrounding an atom. An orbital corresponds to at most two electrons, and it may be visualized as a kind of fuzzy cloud: where the cloud is dense there is a high probability of an electron being present; where it is thin the probability is small. The shape of the orbitals depends on the QUANTUM NUMBERS of the electrons concerned and can be calculated from the SCHRÖDINGER EQUATION. When atoms form molecules, atomic orbitals on each atom overlap to form molecular orbitals. Electrons in these orbitals are labelled by a different set of quantum numbers. They are valuable to the understanding of the chemical bonding and the precise arrangement of atoms in molecules.

Orcadian A native of the Orkney Islands off the north coast of Scotland.

Orcagna (born Andrea di Cione) (*c*.1308–68) Italian painter, sculptor, and architect. His painting represents a return to a devotional, brightly coloured style in opposition to Giotto's naturalism; his work includes frescos and an altarpiece in the church of Santa Maria Novella, Florence (1357). His only known sculpture is the tabernacle in the church of Or San Michele, Florence (1359). He was an advisor on the construction of Florence Cathedral and chief architect of Siena Cathedral in the period 1358–62.

orchestra A body of musical instruments grouped together in families with a view to achieving a balanced sound. The orchestra may be a large group of mixed instruments (the standard symphony orchestra of 100 players or more), or a small group (such as a chamber orchestra of 16 to 30 players). It can consist of strings only (the string orchestra), though for historical reasons groups of woodwind and/or brass with no strings are usually called bands. Gradually the 18th-century orchestra began to take shape, until by the end of the century it was fairly generally established that it should consist of a balanced group of strings; two each of woodwind; two horns and two trumpets; and a pair of kettledrums. The history of the orchestra in the 19th century is largely one of expansion. Much of this was made possible by a radical change or adaptation in the construction and playing mechanism of instruments to meet the acoustic requirements of a larger auditorium. By the end of the century a typical orchestra generally employed over 100 players as compared to the 40 or so that would have been usual in the 1820s. In recent years composers have begun to specify unorthodox layouts in order to emphasize particular features of their music – often conceived with spatial or theatrical effects in mind.

orchestration The art of scoring music for an ORCHESTRA or band, or of arranging music that was originally composed for another medium. When writing orchestral music, composers think directly in terms of orchestral sound. In this sense orchestration is an integral part of composition. Music conceived in terms of specific orchestral colour may lose much of its effect when transcribed for different instruments. Orchestration assumed an increasing importance in the art of composition from the mid-18th century.

orchid A member of the plant family Orchidaceae, of which there are possibly 30,000 species, making it one of the world's largest flowering-plant families. Orchids are found on all continents, with the exception of Antarctica, and occur in a wide vari-

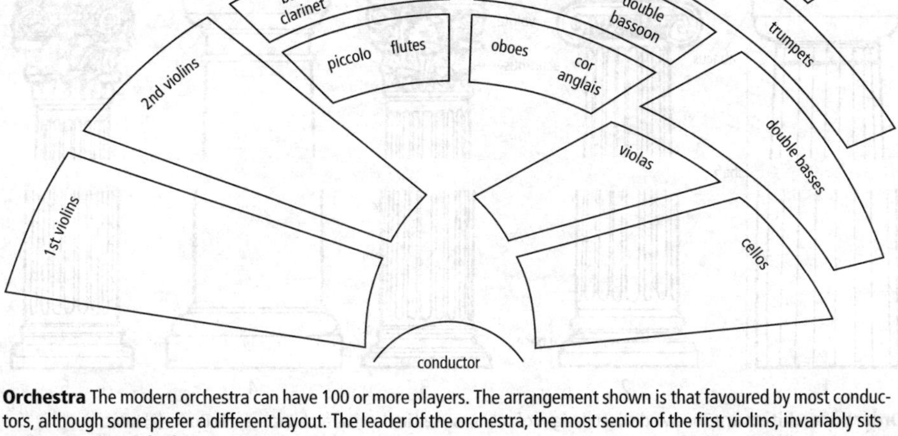

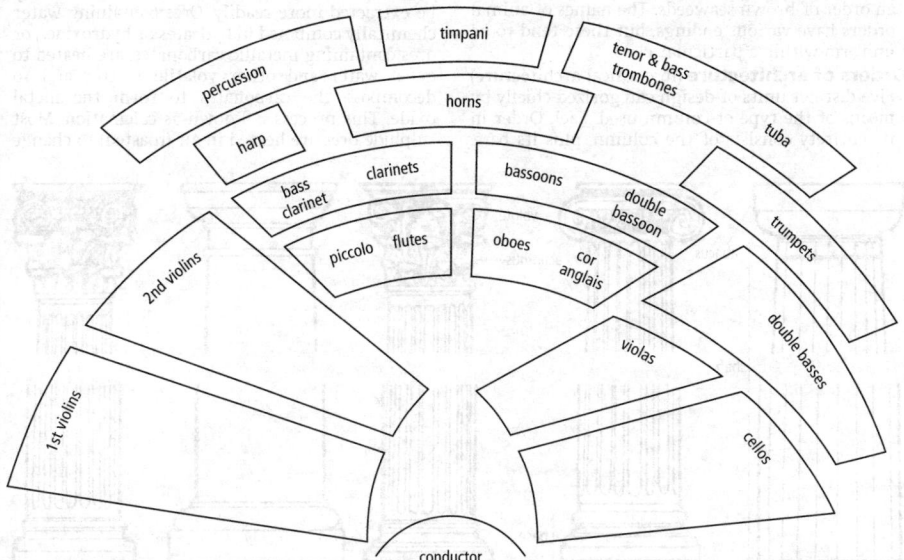

Orchestra The modern orchestra can have 100 or more players. The arrangement shown is that favoured by most conductors, although some prefer a different layout. The leader of the orchestra, the most senior of the first violins, invariably sits on the immediate left of the conductor.

ety of habitats ranging from tropical forests to semi-deserts.

They vary greatly in form and habit. Some have swollen stems (pseudobulbs), others, such as *Vanilla*, have climbing stems, while some live on the branches of tropical trees (i.e. are EPIPHYTES). Most species have green leaves or stems (containing chlorophyll), but certain species, such as the European bird's-nest orchid, *Neottia*, have no chlorophyll, and obtain their nutrients from soil humus. The flowers of orchids, which vary considerably, are adapted for pollination by a great variety of insects. The seeds, which are dust-like, are produced in large numbers and are wind-dispersed. In the wild, they require the association of a certain kind of fungus in order to germinate.

Orchids have been cultivated by gardeners for a long time, and many thousands of artificial hybrids have been produced.

orchis An ORCHID of the genus *Orchis*. About 35 species are known, of which 23 are European and the remainder mainly from Asia. The leaves and flower stems are produced annually from an underground, tuberous rootstock and the flowers, which are relatively small, are far less showy than the tropical epiphytic orchids. The tubers of some have medical and culinary uses. Many species are rare and endangered.

Orczy, Baroness Emmusca (1865–1947) Hungarian-born British novelist. Her best-known novel is *The Scarlet Pimpernel* (1905), telling of the adventures of an English nobleman smuggling aristocrats out of France during the French Revolution.

order In the classification of animals and plants, a category that ranks below a CLASS and is made up of FAMILIES. Many orders, particularly if they include two or more distinctive clusters of families, may be divided into suborders. The members of each order or suborder have characteristics indicating common evolution by descent, and generally have more in common than all members of larger groups. The Latin names of plant orders are usually indicated by the ending -ales, as in Fucales, an order of brown seaweeds. The names of animal orders have various endings, but these tend to be uniform within a particular class.

Orders of architecture (in classical architecture) Five distinct units of design categorized chiefly by means of the type of column used. Each Order in its entirety consists of the column, plus its base, plinth, or pedestal (if any), its CAPITAL, and its entablature (the decorative horizontal member that surmounts it). The Greeks had three Orders; Doric, Ionic, and Corinthian, named after regions of Greece in which they are said to have been first used. The Corinthian style is the slimmest and most richly decorated. The Doric is the stoutest and least decorated. The Romans added two more: Tuscan, a starker form of Doric; and Composite, the richest of all, which combines features of Ionic and Corinthian. The Orders were discussed by VITRUVIUS, and from the Renaissance their proportions and detailing were codified and illustrated in numerous architectural treatises.

Ordnance Survey (OS) An official survey organization in the UK, originally under the control of the Master of the Ordnance, preparing large-scale detailed maps of the whole country. Its headquarters is in Southampton.

Ordovician Period The second of the periods in the PALAEOZOIC ERA, spanning the time interval from 505 to 438 million years ago. It follows the Cambrian and precedes the Silurian. Many Ordovician sediments are deep-water muds, clays, and limestones; and all the animals are marine. The graptolites (colonial organisms, now extinct) diversified greatly, as did the cephalopods. The period saw the first vertebrates (jawless fish) in North America and the onset of the Caledonian OROGENY with the opening of the proto-Atlantic.

ore A naturally occurring mineral from which metals or other useful elements can be extracted. Even the richest ores contain some admixture of valueless minerals, collectively called GANGUE, from which the mineral of value must be separated. After MINING or quarrying, ores are usually pulverized so that lighter particles of gangue can be washed away, leaving the denser metal-bearing particles. If the metal-bearing particles are magnetic, they can be extracted by magnetic ore separation (see also ORE FLOTATION). Once concentrated, the ores are often treated chemically to convert them into substances from which the metal may be extracted more readily. Ores containing water chemically combined in hydrates or hydroxides, or ores containing metallic carbonates, are heated to expel water and other volatile matter and to decompose the carbonates to form the metal oxide. This process is known as calcination. Most sulphide ores are heated in air (roasted) to change

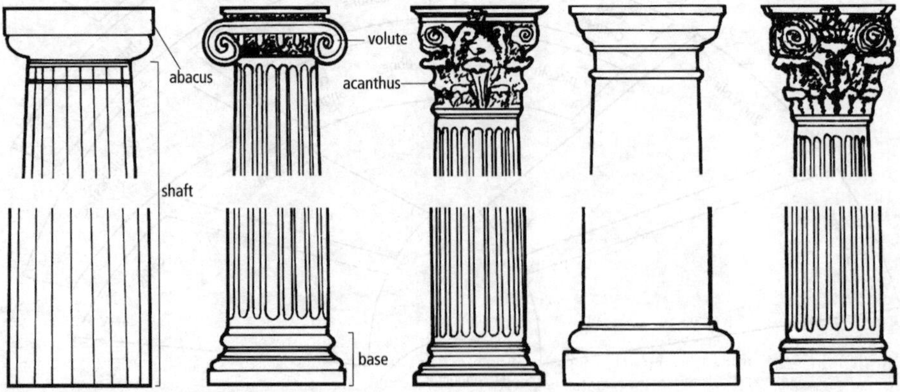

Orders of architecture The five distinct designs of columns used in classical architecture. (1) Doric. (2) Ionic. (3) Corinthian. (4) Tuscan. (5) Composite.

the sulphides to oxides and to expel sulphur as sulphur dioxide. After this preparation the ore is subjected to SMELTING.

ore flotation A process for removing metal ORE from unwanted material (gangue), such as earth, clay, sand, and rocks, before SMELTING. Finely crushed ore is agitated in water containing chemicals that form a surface froth. Particles of metal ore stick to this froth, while unwanted materials sink to the bottom of the water. Careful control of the acidity and concentration of the mixture is required for maximum effectiveness.

Oregon A state in north-west USA, on the Pacific coast, to the west of the Snake River; area 251,419 sq km (97,073 sq miles); pop. (1990) 2,842,320; capital, Salem. The largest cities are Portland, Eugene, and Salem. Oregon is also known as the Beaver State. It was occupied jointly by British and Americans until 1846, when it was ceded to the USA, and became the 33rd state of the USA in 1859. Timber processing, salmon-fishing, and fruit-growing are its leading industries.

Oregon Trail A route across the central USA, from the Missouri across to Oregon, some 3,000 km (2,000 miles) in length, which took the average emigrant train six months to complete. It was used chiefly in the 1840s by settlers moving west.

Orestes In Greek mythology, the son of Agamemnon and Clytemnestra. With his sister Electra, Orestes avenged his father's murder by killing his mother and her lover.

Orff, Carl (1895–1982) German composer and educationalist. In 1924 he helped found the Munich Güntherschule for gymnastics, music, and dance, which led to the development of Orff-Schulwerk (1930), through which he expounded his ideas for a practical course of music study. The simple tunes and hypnotically repetitive rhythms of his secular cantatas, such as CARMINA BURANA (1937) and *Catulli Carmina* (1943), based on medieval poems, brought him immense popularity.

organ A keyboard musical instrument sounded by air in pipes. On small organs, from their invention in around 250 BC in Alexandria to the medieval portative organ, when KEYS were depressed, tracker-rods moved perforated plates to admit air to pipes. In the 15th century, further rods linked the keys through greater distances to pallets (air reservoirs) at the foot of the pipes. Stops, which control which row of pipes sound, were used on the surviving Roman organ at Budapest in Hungary, but knowledge of this device was lost. When stops were re-invented, in the 15th century, the disadvantage of the tracker action was that as further ranks of pipes were added to increase or alter the sound, the action grew heavier. The pneumatic lever, perfected before 1840, alleviated this problem, and the tubular-pneumatic action, replacing trackers by tubes down which air could travel, allowed the organ keyboards to be separated from pipework; the invention of the electro-pneumatic action in 1861 allowed still further separation. All early pipes were flues, similar in principle to DUCT FLUTES. The regal, with small beating reeds, existed by 1500, and was followed by pipes with reeds. By the early 1600s, Baroque organs, with the separate sections of *Hauptwerk, Brustwerk, Positive*, and *Pedal*, were firmly established. Pedals were rare in Britain until the 19th century. In that century organs grew ever larger, but since the 1920s there has been a tendency to return to late 17th-century specifications, allowing improved performance of Baroque music but precluding the playing of much 19th-century organ music. In the modern **electric organ** pipes are dispensed with and notes are produced by electronic oscillators and amplified through loudspeakers.

organic chemistry The chemistry of the compounds of carbon. Carbon is unique in the very large number of compounds it can form; over 90 per cent of all known chemical compounds contain carbon. Much of the chemistry of living organisms (biochemistry) constitutes organic chemistry as the compounds involved consist largely of carbon. In addition organic compounds usually contain hydrogen and may contain other elements, such as oxygen, nitrogen, chlorine, and fluorine. As there are so many organic compounds it is important that they are named systematically so that they can readily be identified. The internationally accepted rules for naming organic compounds include the following. The name of a compound consists of an optional prefix, a stem, and a suffix. The suffix denotes the HOMOLOGOUS SERIES to which the compound belongs; for example -ane denotes alkane, -anol denotes alcohol, and -anal denotes aldehyde. The stem denotes the number of carbon atoms in the longest carbon chain in the molecule; thus meth- denotes one carbon atom, eth- two carbon atoms, prop- three carbon atoms and but- four carbon atoms. The optional prefix contains information about positioning and other features of the molecule. As an example, in the two isomers with molecular formula C_4H_{10}, the isomer $CH_3CH_2CH_2CH_3$ is called butane, while the other isomer $(CH_3)_3CH$ is 2-methylpropane. The suffix indicates an alkane. The longest carbon chain has only three atoms, denoted by the syllable prop-. The fourth carbon is in a methyl ($-CH_3$) group attached to the second carbon in the three-carbon chain; hence the prefix 2-methyl-. For a compound of any complexity the systematic name becomes too cumbersome for ordinary use. A name that is only partly systematic may be used instead, such as neohexane (systematic name 2,2-dimethylbutane). These are called trivial names.

organic farming A method of farming that aims to operate without using artificial FERTILIZERS, PESTICIDES, or other AGROCHEMICALS. Many different strategies are adopted to combat pests. Growing crops and grazing livestock in a balanced rotation prevents pest and parasite build-up (see CROP ROTATION). Hedgerows, mixed plant breaks (strips of grass, herbs, and wild flowers within fields), and companion planting (mixing certain non-crop plants with the main crop) all encourage predators that feed on pests. Mixed cropping (for example, oats with clover) hinders weeds, and disease-resistant plant strains are used wherever possible. Planting can also be timed to avoid the period during which weeds and pests are most active. (See also BIOLOGICAL PEST CONTROL.) Manure and COMPOST are used to fertilize the soil, with added nutrients, such as rock phosphate, seaweed, and other natural fertilizers. In contrast to FACTORY FARMING, animals are allowed to mature without growth hormones and are stocked at low levels. Antibiotics are not used as prophylactics (as in much conventional farming), but only in case of sickness in the animal. Deep-rooting herbal mixes sown in grazing areas provide mineral-rich pasture for livestock and help maintain a good soil structure.

Organic farming is labour-intensive and produces lower crop yields, but in the West it supplies a niche market of those willing to pay extra for what they believe to be healthier and more environmentally friendly products.

Organization de l'Armée secrète (OAS) A French secret terrorist organization based in Algeria, formed in 1961. Its aim was the destruction of the French Fifth Republic in the interest of French colonial control of Algeria. It plotted an unsuccessful assassination attempt on President DE GAULLE in 1962. Its action had little effect on the French government, which by now was determined to grant independence to Algeria. Subsequent riots in Algiers were suppressed, and the OAS itself eliminated (1963) by the capture or exile of its leaders.

Organization for Economic Co-operation and Development (OECD) An international organization of Western developed countries established in 1961 for the purpose of promoting economic and social welfare and stimulating aid to developing countries. It replaced the Organization for European Economic Co-operation which was established in 1948. There are 25 member-states and the headquarters of the organization is in Paris.

Organization of African Unity (OAU) An association of African states founded in 1963 for mutual cooperation and the elimination of colonialism. Comprising 53 states in 1994, its headquarters are in Addis Ababa, Ethiopia.

Organization of American States (OAS) An association of 35 American and Caribbean states. Originally founded in 1890 for largely commercial purposes, it adopted its present name and charter in 1948. Its aims are to work for peace and prosperity in the region and to uphold the sovereignty of member-nations. Its General Secretariat is based in Washington, DC, USA.

Organization of Central American States (OCAS) (1951–60) A regional grouping comprising Costa Rica, El Salvador, Guatemala, Honduras, and Nicaragua. Established in 1951, its purpose was to establish the CENTRAL AMERICAN COMMON MARKET. This goal was reached in 1960, but OCAS members cooperated on little else. The San Salvador Charter (1962) expanded the trade and fiscal provisions of the original treaty, envisaging permanent political, economic, and defence councils.

Organization of the Petroleum Exporting Countries See OPEC.

organometal A compound in which a metal atom is bonded to one or more carbon atoms. The TRANSITION METALS form large numbers of organometallic compounds, which usually involve the metal in a low oxidation state or valency. There are several types of organic compounds that can act as LIGANDS to metal atoms. ALKYL OF ARYL GROUPS can bond to a metal atom, as for example in the compound tetraethyl lead, $Pb(C_2H_5)_4$, which is used as an ANTIKNOCK compound in petrol. Alkenes, alkynes, and benzene and its derivatives can also bond: for instance, chromium dibenzene, $Cr(C_6H_6)_2$, is an example of a compound in which the metal atom is literally sandwiched between the two planar benzene molecules. As the metal is generally in a low oxidation state, organometallic compounds are usually susceptible to oxidation. Therefore they are prepared and studied in the absence of oxygen. It is found that many organometallic compounds can act as CATALYSTS, especially in reactions involving organic molecules. An example is the Ziegler catalyst used in the polymerization of ethane.

organ-pipe coral A CORAL, *Tubipora musica*, with a skeleton of parallel tubes, each containing one feeding POLYP, making it look very like a set of organ-pipes, often bright orange or red. It has a fleshy covering when alive, and eight tentacles per polyp, a typical feature of octocorals. It is common in shallow Indo-Pacific reefs.

organ transplant See TRANSPLANT SURGERY

organum The earliest form of POLYPHONY, known since the late 9th century. In the earliest type of organum all the voices moved in parallel. The melody (PLAINSONG) was therefore being sung simultaneously at different pitches, beginning with octaves and then embracing fourths and fifths. This would seem to suggest that organum probably arose quite naturally out of people with different voice ranges attempting to sing the same melody. The movement of organum parts eventually (12th century) became freer, so that the parallel effects were no longer strictly maintained. This freedom led, in turn, to the development of COUNTERPOINT. A 15th-century version of organum, involving parallel thirds and sixths and particularly loved by British composers, such as John Dunstable, is known as fauxbourdon or faburden.

Origen (*c*.185–*c*.254) Christian scholar and theologian, probably born in Alexandria. Of his numerous works the most famous was the *Hexapla*, an edition of the Old Testament with six or more parallel versions. He recognized literal, moral, and allegorical interpretations of Scripture, preferring the last. His teachings are important for their introduction of Neoplatonist elements into Christianity but were later rejected by Church orthodoxy.

original sin In CHRISTIANITY, the doctrine that the SIN of Adam, the first man, has been inherited by all humanity, and confers a tendency to do wrong. The concept of original sin is not explicitly set out in the BIBLE, but was firmly established in the writings of St AUGUSTINE. It has served Christianity as an explanation for what is seen as the imperfection of the human condition. Christians believe in redemption from sin through JESUS CHRIST's death on the cross, and the SACRAMENT of Baptism symbolizes the washing away of this sin, through acceptance into the Church. Jesus Christ and, according to Roman Catholics, the Virgin Mary, are believed to be free of original sin.

Orinoco A river in northern South America, which rises in south-east Venezuela and flows 2,060 km (1,280 miles) in a great arc through Venezuela, entering the Atlantic Ocean by a vast delta. For part of its length it forms the border between Colombia and Venezuela.

oriole A member of the bird family Oriolidae. Orioles, of which there are 28 species, occur in most of the warmer areas of the Old World. The name is probably derived from the Latin 'aureolus', meaning golden or yellow. The males of many species are yellow or rich brown with black wings and head markings. The females are darker, often olive-green. Orioles live in wooded country and nest high up in trees. Many have very beautiful, flute-like calls.

This name is also often used for the species of the New World family Icteridae, which includes the American blackbirds. Most are thrush- to crow-sized, and predominantly black (especially the males; the females may be brown), often with striking patches of red or yellow in the wings and tail. Most live in wooded country although some, such as the bobolink, dickcissel, and the meadowlarks, live in open country. They are insectivorous, fruit- or seed-eating birds, some being serious pests of soft fruit and rice. Many of those breeding in North America migrate to warmer areas for the winter. The cowbirds are parasitic, laying their eggs in the nests of other birds. Many of these 'New World' orioles breed in colonies and some, such as the oropendolas, *Psarocolius* species, weave long, tube-like nests hanging from the branches of trees.

Orion (in Greek mythology) A giant and hunter of Boeotia, the subject of various legends, according to which he was deprived of sight by Dionysus, or killed by Artemis (either from jealousy because he was loved by Eos, the Dawn, or because he challenged her to throw the discus against him), or stung to death by a scorpion, by the same goddess's design, while ridding the Earth of wild beasts. Another story is that he pursued the Pleiades and both he and they were turned into constellations.

Orion (in astronomy) The Hunter, a prominent CONSTELLATION on the celestial equator, one of the 48 constellations recognized by the ancient Greeks. The brightest stars in Orion are BETELGEUSE and RIGEL. A line of three stars marks **Orion's Belt**, and beneath the belt lies **Orion's Sword** and the **Great Nebula in Orion** (M42), containing the TRAPEZIUM star group. South of Zeta Orionis lies the HORSEHEAD NEBULA. The Orionid METEOR SHOWER radiates from the constellation every October.

Orissa A state in eastern India, on the Bay of Bengal, formerly the ancient region of Odra; area 155,707 sq km (60,142 sq miles); pop. (1991) 31,512,070; capital, Bhubaneswar. Formerly an outlying district of Bengal Presidency and later part of Bihar, Orissa became a separate province in 1936. It merged with Mayurbhanj and became a state in 1949. The state is rich in minerals and is India's leading producer of chromite. Rice, oilseed, sugar-cane, and turmeric are cultivated.

Orkney Islands (or **Orkneys**) A group of over 70 islands off the north-east tip of Scotland (the principal islands are Mainland and Hoy), constituting an Islands Area of Scotland; area 976 sq km (377 sq miles); pop. (1991) 19,450; chief town, Kirkwall. Colonized by the Vikings in the 9th century, they were ruled by Norway and Denmark until 1472 when they came into Scottish possession (together with Shetland) as security against the unpaid dowry of Margaret of Denmark after her marriage to James III. Fishing, livestock, and servicing the North Sea oil industry are the chief occupations.

Orlando A city in central Florida, USA; pop. (1990) 164,690. It was a camp-ground for soldiers during the Seminole Indian War (1835–42) and then a trading post that developed into a city after the arrival of the railroad in 1880. It trades in citrus fruit and winter vegetables and is a popular winter resort with an international airport. Nearby tourist attractions include the John F. Kennedy Space Center, Sea World, and Disney World.

Orleans (French **Orléans**) A city in central France, on the Loire, capital of the department of Loiret; pop. (1990) 107,965. It was conquered by Julius Caesar in 52 BC and by the 10th century was one of the most important cities in France. In 1429 it was the scene of Joan of Arc's first victory over the English during the Hundred Years War. The city trades in wine, vegetables, and grain. Tourism is also important.

Orléans, Duc d' A title borne by younger princes of the French royal family from the 14th century. Charles VI of France bestowed the duchy of Orléans on his brother Louis (1392). Louis's grandson became LOUIS XII of France. His great-grandson became FRANCIS I and the Valois-Orléans ended with the death of HENRY III in 1589. Philippe (1674–1723) of the second Bourbon-Orléans branch of the family became Regent of France in 1715 during the minority of LOUIS XV. His great-grandson Louis Philippe Joseph ('Philippe Égalité') succeeded to the title in 1785. He was a supporter of the French Revolution from its beginnings, and in June 1789 he organized the 47 nobles who joined the Third Estate. In 1792 he voted for the death of the king but his eldest son, afterwards King Louis-Philippe, had him arrested, with all the remaining Bourbons, accused of conspiracy, and guillotined (1793).

Orly A suburb of Paris, France, in the department of Val-de-Marne, with an international airport located 14 km (9 miles) south-west of the city centre.

ormolu (from French *dorure d'or moulu*, 'gilding with gold paste') A form of gilded bronzework used in various ways in the applied arts, particularly for the ornamentation of furniture. Strictly ormolu is made by mixing powdered gold with mercury, brushing the resulting paste on to the bronze, and then firing the object so treated to make the mercury evaporate, leaving a layer of gold on the surface. It was an expensive procedure, used for luxury objects and reached its highest technical and artistic level in 18th-century France. Apart from furniture, it was used for candlesticks, chandeliers, clock-cases, and so on. Some products of simpler and cheaper processes are also described as ormolu.

Ormoz A variant of HORMUZ.

ornithology The study of BIRDS, which includes the investigation of their behaviour, biology, and biogeography. The physics of bird FLIGHT has been studied in detail, and birds have been used extensively in investigations of animal behaviour. Bird MIGRATION has always intrigued ornithologists and much information about their travels has been obtained by banding or ringing birds, and by tracking them on radar.

orogenesis See MOUNTAIN BUILDING.

orogeny Movements on the Earth's surface that involve the folding of sediments, faulting, and metamorphism. See MOUNTAIN BUILDING.

Orpheus In Greek mythology, a musician of sublime artistry; he played the lyre so beautifully that he could charm wild animals and even trees and rocks. He married Eurydice, a Dryad. When Eurydice died, Orpheus went down to Hades to recover her. By his music he induced Persephone to let Eurydice go, on condition that he should not look back at her. He failed, and lost her. Later, he was torn to pieces by the Maenads and his head, still singing, reached the Isle of Lesbos.

Orphism (or **Orphic Cubism**) A movement in French painting that developed out of CUBISM in about 1912. The word 'Orphism' was applied to the movement by the writer Apollinaire, and the reference to ORPHEUS reflected the desire to bring a new element of lyricism and colour into the austere intellectual Cubism of Picasso, Braque, and Gris. Among the leading practitioners were Robert DELAUNAY and Frank Kupka (1871–1957). Orphism was short-lived, but it was particularly influential on German painting.

orrery A large complex, usually clockwork, model of the Solar System. It is named after Charles Boyle, Fourth Earl of Orrery, who commissioned one from John Rowley in 1712. Usually the Sun is represented by a large central brass ball and the ivory planets and their attendant satellites are supported on radiating pivots. The clockwork mechanism drives the planets around the Sun at the correct rate and the system is adjusted to show the celestial positions of the planets at a given time. Smaller geared orreries became popular in the 18th and 19th centuries. On some orreries the planets can be replaced by a Sun-Earth-Moon system, which shows the form of the Moon's orbit.

Ortega (Saavedra), Daniel (1945–) Nicaraguan statesman, President 1985–90. He joined the Sandinista National Liberation Front (FSLN) in 1963, becoming its leader in 1966. After a period of imprisonment he played a major role in the revolution which overthrew Anastasio Somoza in 1979. He headed a provisional socialist government from this date, later gaining the presidency after the Sandinista victory in the 1984 elections, but his regime was constantly under attack from the US-backed Contras. He lost power to an opposition coalition following elections in 1990.

Ortega y Gasset, José (1883–1955) Spanish philosopher. In 1910 he was appointed to the chair of metaphysics at Madrid University. An existentialist thinker, he became one of the most influential figures in 20th-century Spanish thought, and in 1923 he founded the magazine *Revista de occidente*, which introduced northern European ideas to Spanish intellectuals. His many academic works include *The Revolt of the Masses* (1930), in which he proposed leadership by an intellectual élite.

orthodontics See DENTISTRY.

Orthodox Church The Eastern or Greek Church, having the Patriarch of Constantinople as its head, and the national Churches of Russia, Romania, etc. in communion with it. Separation from the Western Church came in the 4th century, originally through cultural and political factors, focused from the 5th century onwards on differences of doctrine and ritual, and took formal effect in 1054 when the Pope and the Patriarch of Constantinople excommunicated each other. In the latter part of the 20th century the Orthodox Churches have taken an active part in the ecumenical movement; the mutual excommunication of 1054 was abolished in 1965.

Orthodox Judaism A major branch within JUDAISM teaching that the TORAH contains all the divine revelation that Jews require. Religious practice demands the strict observance of 613 rules (*mitzvot*), which govern moral behaviour, dress, religious customs, diet, work, observance of the Shabbat (SABBATH), and personal hygiene. When interpretation of the Torah is required, reference is made to the TALMUD, whose religious authority is second only to the Torah. Unlike modern movements (Liberal, Reform, and Conservative Judaism), which they do not recognize, Orthodox Jews maintain the separation of sexes in synagogue worship. There is only an Orthodox rabbinate in Israel, with the result that all official religion in that country is Orthodox controlled. While many Orthodox Jews support ZIONISM, they deplore the secular origins of the movement and the fact that ISRAEL is not a fully religious state.

orthopaedics A branch of surgery specializing in the treatment of bone and joint disorders. Orthopaedics as a speciality began in 1741, when the French surgeon Nicolas André suggested that the skeletal deformities of adults started in childhood, and embarked on a study of how to treat them. The discovery of X-RAYS in 1895 had an almost immediate impact on orthopaedic medicine, allowing orthopaedic surgeons to diagnose accurately fractures and other conditions of the skeletal system. ANTIBIOTICS and IMMUNIZATION have almost eradicated diseases, such as tuberculosis and poliomyelitis, that formerly caused many of the deformities described by André. Artificial hips (see HIP REPLACEMENT) and other joints (such as knee, shoulder, and elbow) are widely used to replace those worn out by osteoarthritis and other diseases. A valuable tool for examining joints internally and performing small operations is the optical fibre arthroscope.

ortolan A small bird, *Emberiza hortulana*, that is a member of the BUNTING family, and breeds over much of Europe and western Asia, favouring open country with trees. It migrates southwards for the winter and has long been prized as a delicacy in some countries.

Orton, Arthur (known as 'the Tichborne claimant') (1834–98) British butcher. In 1852 he emigrated to Australia, but returned to England in 1866 claiming to be the heir to the wealthy Tichborne estate; he asserted that he was the eldest son of the 10th baronet, who was presumed lost at sea, and convinced the lost heir's mother that he was her son. After a long trial he lost his claim and was tried and imprisoned for perjury.

Orton, Joe (born John Kingsley Orton) (1933–67) British dramatist. He wrote a number of unconventional black comedies, notable for their examination of corruption, sexuality, and violence; they include *Entertaining Mr Sloane* (1964), *Loot* (1965), and the posthumously performed *What the Butler Saw* (1969). Orton was murdered by his homosexual lover, who then committed suicide.

Oruro The chief mining city of western Bolivia, capital of the department of Oruro; pop. (1990) 208,700. Tin, silver, antimony, and tungsten are mined.

Orvieto An ancient town in the Paglia valley, Umbria, central Italy; pop. (1990) 21,575. It has been occupied since Etruscan times and lies at the centre of a noted wine-producing area. The principal landmark is a 13th-century cathedral.

Orwell, George (pseudonym of Eric Arthur Blair) (1903–50) British novelist and essayist. Born in Bengal, he returned to Europe in 1928. His work is characterized by his concern with social injustice; after living as a vagrant in London, he described his experiences in *Down and Out in Paris and London* (1933); he also wrote about the plight of the unemployed in *The Road to Wigan Pier* (1937), and fought for the Republicans in the Spanish Civil War. His best-known works are *Animal Farm* (1945), a satire on Communism as it developed under Stalin, and *Nineteen Eighty-Four* (1949), an account of a future state in which every aspect of life is controlled by Big Brother.

oryx Any one of three species of antelope with almost straight, slender horns placed immediately behind the eyes. The oryx or gemsbok, *Oryx gazella*, has a cream-coloured coat and chocolate 'stockings'. The face has dark eye- and nose-stripes, and often a dark forehead patch. This pattern accentuates the length of the head. The animal can be up to 1.2 m (4 feet) tall at the shoulder, with horns up to 1 m (3.3 feet) long.

The scimitar-horned oryx, *O. dammah*, is one of the most threatened antelopes. Its survival may depend upon the establishment and maintenance of reserves with adequate protection. The majority of the wild population is found in Niger, and to some extent in Chad, and it is extinct north of the Sahara. It breeds well in captivity, and captive-bred stock could be returned to herds in reserves. The Arabian oryx, *O. leucoryx*, once roamed the deserts of Arabia, Syria, and Mesopotamia in large numbers; today it is extinct in the wild. Fortunately, a herd was established in 1962 to prevent its extinction, and it has been reintroduced into Oman. An inhabitant of wild, arid areas, it is one of the few large mammals that can exist for very long periods without water.

Osaka A port, commercial, and cultural city in central Japan, on Honshu Island, chief city of Kinki Region; pop. (1990) 2,642,000. It is the third-largest city in Japan and lies on the north-east shore of Osaka Bay. A great commercial centre during the Edo period, the city was largely destroyed during World War II and later rebuilt. It is a centre of transport with ferry links to Kyushu and Shikoku with many light industries including tourism.

Osborne, John (James) (1929–94) British dramatist. His first play, *Look Back in Anger* (1956), ushered in a new era of kitchen-sink drama; its hero Jimmy Porter was seen as the archetype of contemporary disillusioned youth, the so-called 'angry young man'. Later plays include *The Entertainer* (1957), *Luther* (1961), *A Patriot for Me* (1965), and *Déjà vu* (1991). He also wrote two volumes of autobiography, *A Better Class of Person* (1981) and *Almost a Gentleman* (1991).

oscillator A circuit that converts direct-current power into a periodic, alternating-current waveform of constant frequency. These waveforms can include sine waves, square waves, and saw-tooth waves, which have several different applications. A simple low-frequency, square-wave oscillator circuit, for example, could be used to flash a light on and off. At radio frequencies, sine-wave oscillators provide 'carrier' signals on which radio and television images may be transmitted during broadcasting (see MODULATION). MICROWAVE COOKERS incorporate a magnetron as a microwave oscillator. All oscillators incorporate a TRANSISTOR, thermionic valve, or similar device, plus a resonant circuit that determines the oscillation frequency.

oscilloscope An instrument that can provide a visual display of the electrical signals passing through a circuit on a CATHODE-RAY TUBE screen. Oscilloscopes are used in the design and testing of electronic circuits, and are especially useful for the display of high-frequency alternating-current signals. The signals are used to deflect the electron beam of the cathode-ray tube, and the beam traces a continuous wave-form on the screen. Typical oscilloscopes can monitor signal FREQUENCIES in the range from 10 to 100 million Hz. They may be equipped with storage facilities to capture very high-speed or short-lived electronic events.

osier See WILLOW.

Osiris One of the most important gods of ancient Egypt, originally perhaps connected with fertility. In mythology he was king of Egypt, killed by his jealous brother Set who dismembered his body. Osiris' sister-wife, Isis, gathered the pieces and reassembled them as the first mummy with the aid of Anubis, breathing new life into his corpse as goddess of magical powers, and conceiving from Osiris a son, Horus, through her function as fertility goddess. Osiris, magically revived, ruled the dead in the underworld as king of the dead, symbolizing resurrection and regeneration, whilst his son Horus ruled the living. During the Old Kingdom, deceased pharaohs were identified with Osiris, but later all the dead could be termed an 'Osiris'.

Osler, Sir William (1849–1919) Canadian-born physician and classical scholar. He was professor of medicine at four universities, and his *Principles and Practice of Medicine* (1892) became the chosen clinical textbook for medical students. At Johns Hopkins University, Baltimore, he instituted a model teaching unit in which clinical observation was combined with laboratory research.

Oslo The capital, chief port, and largest industrial centre of Norway, on the south coast at the head of Oslofjord; pop. (1990) 458,360. Founded in the 11th century, it was known as Christiania from 1624 to 1924 in honour of Christian IV of Norway and Denmark, who rebuilt the city after it had been destroyed by a fire. It became capital of independent Norway in 1905. It is a cultural centre with theatres, museums, and art galleries and exhibitions. Its university was founded in 1811. Oslo's industries include shipbuilding, chemicals, electrical equipment, metal products, machine tools, textiles, and food processing.

Osman I (or **Othman**) (1259–1326) Turkish conqueror, founder of the Ottoman (Osmanli) dynasty and empire. After succeeding his father as leader of the Seljuk Turks in 1288, Osman reigned as sultan, conquering NW Asia Minor. He assumed the title of emir in 1299.

osmium (symbol Os, at. no. 76, r.a.m. 190.2) A TRANSITION METAL in the platinum group and one of the densest elements known. It is found in nature in osmiridium and as a sulphide and is used for hardening alloys. When combined with oxygen at high temperature it gives osmium tetroxide, OsO_4, which is a commonly used biological stain and fixative.

osmosis The diffusion of water or another solvent through a selectively permeable MEMBRANE. This membrane is like a sieve, allowing solvent molecules, which are small, to pass through it, but preventing larger molecules dissolved in the solvent from passing through. If a selectively permeable membrane separates two solutions of different concentrations, solvent molecules pass through the membrane from the side of lesser concentration to the side of greater concentration. This tends to equalize the concentrations on either side of the membrane.

Cells and bacteria can be ruptured, for experimental purposes, by osmotic shock. For example, if red blood cells, which are normally found in blood plasma, are placed in pure water, then the cell walls allow the water to diffuse inwards, and the cells swell and eventually burst. Osmosis is of great importance in many processes that occur in animals and plants. It controls the intake of water by the hairs on plant roots, and the production of urine in the kidney. The turgidity of plant cells is due to their maintaining a difference in pressure across their cell walls. Water enters their concentrated cell contents and effectively 'inflates' the cell.

osprey (or **fish hawk**) A bird of prey, *Pandion haliaetus*, which is widespread throughout the world on lakes and sea coasts, breeding on all the continents except Antarctica and South America. Eagle-like in size and disposition, it specializes in catching fish close to the surface, spotting these prey from a height, diving with wings folded, and entering the water with clawed feet forward ready to grasp. The pads and claws are rough to facilitate holding; surprisingly large fish can be lifted and carried to the nest. For a time extinct in Britain, ospreys are now returning slowly; individual nests are carefully guarded each season against egg-hunters. The single species of osprey is placed in a unique family, the Pandionidae.

Ossetia A region of the central Caucasus, divided into ▶**1 North Ossetia** A republic of the Russian Federation; area 8,000 sq km (3,088 sq miles); pop. (1990) 638,000; capital, Vladikavkaz. Under a new constitution it adopted the name Alania in 1994. ▶**2 South Ossetia** A former autonomous region of Georgia; area 3,900 sq km (1,506 sq miles); pop. (1990) 99,000; capital, Tskhinvali. South Ossetia has been the scene of ethnic conflict with the Georgians and is currently (1995) governing itself under a Russian-brokered peace, although the Georgian Supreme Soviet voted in 1990 to abolish its former autonomous status.

Ossian See OISÍN.

Ostade, Adriaen van (1610–85) Dutch painter and engraver. He is thought to have been a pupil of Frans Hals, and his work chiefly depicts lively genre scenes of peasants carousing or brawling in crowded taverns or barns. His brother and pupil, Isack (1621–49), was also a painter, particularly of winter landscapes and genre scenes of peasants outside cottages or taverns.

Ostend (Flemish **Oostende**; French **Ostende**) A port and resort on the North Sea coast of West Flanders in north-west Belgium; pop. (1991) 68,500. It is a major ferry port with links to Dover.

osteomyelitis Inflammation of the bone marrow as a result of infection, a hazard that occurs following exposure of the marrow during joint surgery following compound fractures. It can also be caused by blood-borne microorganisms, commonly in the shaft of a long bone of children. It causes severe pain, swelling, fever, and general illness. It is usually treatable by antibiotics. If not treated **chronic osteomyelitis** can result.

osteopathy See COMPLEMENTARY MEDICINE.

osteoporosis Weakness and brittleness of the bones, which occurs in the elderly and in women after the menopause. HORMONE REPLACEMENT THERAPY is useful in preventing osteoporosis in post-menopausal women.

Ostia An ancient city and harbour situated on the western coast of Italy at the mouth of the River Tiber. It was the first colony founded by ancient Rome and was a major port and commercial centre. Now located about 6 km (4 miles) inland, it was buried and its ruins were preserved, by the gradual silting up of the River Tiber.

Ostpolitik (German, 'eastern policy') The Federal Republic of GERMANY's opening of relations with the Eastern bloc in the 1970s. It was a reversal of West Germany's refusal to recognize the legitimacy of the German Democratic Republic (East Germany), as propounded in the Hallstein Doctrine (1955). The policy of Ostpolitik was pursued with particular vigour by Willy BRANDT, as Chancellor of the Federal Republic. A General Relations Treaty (1972) normalized relations between the two Germanys, while treaties between West Germany and both the Soviet Union and Poland gave formal recognition to the Oder-Neisse frontier (1970–72).

Ostrava An industrial city in the Moravian lowlands of the central Czech Republic; pop. (1991) 327,550. It is capital of the North Moravian region, and is situated in the coal-mining region of Upper Silesia. Founded in 1267, coal was first mined near here in 1767. The city has heavy industries based on steel and a large chemicals industry.

ostrich A flightless bird, *Struthio camelus*, which is the sole member of its family, Struthionidae, although it has been suggested that a subspecies, *S. c. molybdophanes*, should be classified as a separate species. It is the largest living bird and occurs only in Africa. The male stands up to 2.5 m (8 feet) tall and weighs up to 120 kg (270 pounds); it has a long, bare, pinkish neck and long, bare legs, with pink thighs. The feathers are loosely structured, and black in colour, except for white feathers in the rudimentary wings and in the tail. The female is a little smaller and has brown instead of black plumage. She lays her eggs in simple scrapes in the ground, each egg being up to 20 cm (8 inches) long and weighing up to 1.3 kg (3 pounds). The tail and wing plumes have long been valued for headdresses and the bird is now kept on farms for this purpose and also for its meat.

Ostrogoths The eastern GOTHS on the northern shores of the Black Sea. They became vassals of the HUNS whose westward migration displaced them and under ATTILA they were defeated by Roman and barbarian allied armies on the CATALAUNIAN FIELDS, 451 AD. Forty years later THEODORIC established a kingdom in Italy. After the murder in 533 of Theodoric's daughter, who was the regent of Italy, JUSTINIAN's general BELISARIUS twice invaded and defeated them, and the Ostrogothic kingdom was crushed by Narses in 552.

Ostwald, Friedrich Wilhelm (1853–1932) German physical chemist. He did much to establish physical chemistry as a separate discipline, and is particularly remembered for his pioneering work on catalysis. He also worked on chemical affinities, the hydrolysis of esters, and electrolytic conductivity and dissociation. After retiring Ostwald studied colour science, and developed a new quantitative colour theory. He was awarded the Nobel Prize for chemistry in 1909.

Oswald, Lee Harvey (1939–63) US alleged assassin of President KENNEDY at Dallas, Texas, in 1963. He was arrested but before he could be tried, he was himself killed by another civilian, Jack Ruby. Many theories have been aired that Oswald had accomplices, but the WARREN Commission concluded that he had acted on his own.

Oswald of York, St (died 992) English prelate and Benedictine monk. He rose first to become bishop of Worcester and then Archbishop of York. He founded several Benedictine monasteries and, along with St Dunstan, was responsible for the revival of the Church and of learning in 10th-century England. Feast day, 28 February.

Othman See OSMAN I.

Otho, Marcus Salvius (32–69 AD) Roman emperor January–April 69. He was proclaimed emperor after he had procured the death of Galba in a conspiracy of the praetorian guard. Otho was not recognized as emperor by the German legions; led by their candidate, Vitellius, they defeated his troops and Otho committed suicide.

Otis, Elisha Graves (1811–61) US inventor and manufacturer. He produced the first efficient elevator with a safety device in 1852; it consisted of a mechanical hoist for carrying machinery to the upper floors of a factory, with a device to prevent it from falling even if the lifting cable broke. In 1857 he installed the first public elevator for passengers in a New York department store.

O'Toole, (Seamus) Peter (1932–) Irish-born British actor. He began his career at the Bristol Old Vic Theatre (1955–58) and after a season with the Royal Shakespeare Company came to international prominence as a film star in *Lawrence of Arabia* (1962). His other films include *Goodbye Mr Chips*

(1969), *The Stunt Man* (1980), *The Last Emperor* (1987), and *Rebecca's Daughters* (1992).

otorhinolaryngology The study of the diseases of the ear, nose, and throat. The need for surgery in otorhinolaryngology has been much reduced by the use of ANTIBIOTICS, but it is still needed to treat the many diseases that arise from infections and require the removal of tonsils and the drainage of sinuses. Examination and diagnosis have been greatly advanced by the introduction of small, hand-held OTOSCOPES, and electronic AUDIOMETERS for analysing hearing loss. Technological advances and the development of MICROSURGERY have made it possible to repair the fine structures of the middle ear and to produce HEARING AIDS and cochlear implants.

otoscope (or **auriscope**) An instrument using reflected light to examine the eardrum and parts of the ear external to it. Invented in 1860 by the German physician Anton von Tröltsch, it is now employed routinely to diagnose infection of the middle ear chamber (interior to the eardrum) and certain chronic conditions leading to deafness.

Ottawa The federal capital of Canada, a city in Ontario on the Ottawa River (a tributary of the St Lawrence) and the Rideau Canal; pop. (1991) 313,990; 920,860 (metropolitan area). Founded in 1827, it was named Bytown in honour of Colonel John By (1779–1836), builder of the Rideau Canal. The city received its present name in 1855 and was chosen as capital (of the United Provinces of Canada) by Queen Victoria in 1857. In 1867 the first Canadian parliament met here after the founding of the Dominion of Canada. The city contains government offices, parliament buildings, national museum and library, and public archives.

otter Any one of some 12 species of carnivore in the weasel family, Mustelidae, with worldwide distribution except in polar regions and oceanic islands. Long-bodied and streamlined with short limbs and webbed paws, otters have a wide, flexible tail and rich brown, waterproof fur. They inhabit rivers and freshwater lakes, and are some of the fastest aquatic mammals, cruising at 10 km/hour (6 miles per hour). When swimming, they can shut their nose and remain submerged for four minutes or more without coming up for air. Otters feed mostly on fish, usually the rather sluggish species. Male otters are larger than females and may be about 1.4 m (4.6 feet) long. There are usually two or three cubs in a litter. They are blind and toothless at birth, and the mother cares for them. Otters of the genus *Lutra*, which includes the Eurasian otter, *L. lutra*, the Oriental short-clawed otter, *Aonyx cinerea*, and the Cape clawless otter, *A. capensis*, catch their food with their jaws, though most otters use their front limbs. One species, the sea otter of North America, *Enhydra lutris*, is marine, and feeds on shellfish, which it opens by using pebbles as tools.

Otto, Nikolaus August (1832–91) German engineer. Otto's name is given to the four-stroke cycle on which most petrol engines for cars work. His patent of 1876 was invalidated ten years later when it was found that Alphonse-Eugène Beau de Rochas (1815–93) had described the successful cycle earlier, so enabling other manufacturers to adopt it.

Otto I (known as **Otto the Great**) (912–73) King of the Germans 936–73, Holy Roman emperor 962–73. As king of the Germans he carried out a policy of eastward expansion from his Saxon homeland and defeated the invading Hungarians in 955. He was crowned Holy Roman emperor in 962 and began to establish a strong imperial presence in Italy to rival that of the papacy.

Ottoman empire The Muslim empire of the Turks (1299–1922), established in northern Anatolia by OSMAN I and expanded by his successors to include all of Asia Minor and much of south-east Europe. Ottoman power received a severe check with the invasion of Tamerlane in 1401, but expansion resumed several decades later, resulting in the capture of Constantinople in 1453. The empire reached its zenith under Suleiman I (1520–66), dominating the eastern Mediterranean, including North Africa, and threatening central Europe, but thereafter it began to decline. Still powerful in the 17th century, it had, by the 19th century, become the 'sick man of Europe', eventually collapsing in the early 20th century. See map p. 1018.

Otway, Thomas (1652–85) English dramatist. After failing as an actor he wrote for the stage and achieved success with his second play, *Don Carlos* (1676), a tragedy in rhymed verse. He is now chiefly remembered for his two blank verse tragedies, *The Orphan* (1680) and *Venice Preserved* (1682).

Ouagadougou The capital city of Burkina in West Africa; pop. (1985) 442,220. Formerly capital of the Mossi empire, it was taken by the French in 1896. It is linked by rail to the port of Abidjan in the Côte d'Ivoire. Its principal buildings combine African and French architectural styles. There is a large, new sports stadium.

Oudenarde (Flemish **Oudenaarde**; French **Audenarde**) A town in the province of East Flanders, Belgium, scene of a victory (1708) of allied British and Austrian troops under MARLBOROUGH and Prince Eugene over the French in the War of the SPANISH SUCCESSION: pop. (1991) 27,160.

Ouida (pseudonym of Marie Louise de la Ramée) (1839–1908) British novelist. She lived mostly in Italy, and wrote 45 novels often set in a fashionable world far removed from reality and showing a spirit of rebellion against the moral ideals that were prevalent in much of the fiction of the time. Her books include *Under Two Flags* (1867), *Folle-Farine* (1871), and *Two Little Wooden Shoes* (1874).

Ouse The name of several rivers in England. ▶**1** A river in south-east England that rises in the Weald of West Sussex and flows 48 km (30 miles) south-eastwards to the English Channel at Newhaven. ▶**2** A river in Yorkshire formed at the junction of the Ure and Swale. It flows 92 km (57 miles) south-eastwards through York to join the River Trent which then becomes the Humber Estuary. ▶**3 Great Ouse** A river that rises in Northamptonshire and flows 257 km (160 miles) eastwards through East Anglia to the Wash near King's Lynn. ▶**4 Little Ouse** A river of East Anglia, which forms a tributary of the Great Ouse. For much of its length it marks the border between Norfolk and Suffolk.

outcrop (in mining and geology) The exposed area of a stratum or vein of rock on the Earth's surface; generally, the surface area of a stratum or vein of rock whether it is exposed or not.

outer planets Any of the major PLANETS beyond the asteroid belt, that is, Jupiter, Saturn, Uranus, Neptune, and Pluto. Their composition is very different from the INNER PLANETS and, with the exception of Pluto, they are gas giants retaining a significant fraction of the hydrogen and helium of the original nebula from which all the planets were formed. Apart from Pluto, they all have complex natural satellite systems.

output device (in computing) A PERIPHERAL that

communicates information from a computer system to users. The most common output devices are PRINTERS and VISUAL DISPLAY UNITS: they can provide both text and GRAPHICS data output. Graphics printers are commonly used, for example, in COMPUTER-AIDED DESIGN and to present business statistics in pictorial form on paper. Output devices are controlled by interfaces that communicate with the host computer. Interfaces to electromechanical devices under computer control are often required in ROBOTICS, and speech synthesizers present output in a way that simulates a human voice.

ouzel See RING-OUZEL.

Oval, the A cricket ground in Lambeth, London, headquarters of the Surrey Cricket Club and venue for test matches.

ovary ▶**1** One of the two female reproductive organs in animals that produce the egg cell, or OVUM. In mammals they produce single or multiple egg cells at regular intervals. In humans this involves the release of a single egg from one of a pair of ovaries after 28 days. After another 28 days the other ovary in its turn releases an egg, and so on. Occasionally more than one egg will be released at once. The release of eggs in all mammalian ovaries is controlled by HORMONES, some of which are produced by the ovary itself. The ovaries of invertebrates can consist of several parts, each capable of continuously producing eggs. See REPRODUCTION. ▶**2** The part of a flower of a plant that encloses the ovules, destined to become seeds. It is usually associated with the style and stigma; these organs, situated inside the flower, trap and encourage pollen to grow down into the ovary, where FERTILIZATION occurs.

ovenbird (or **horuero**) A member of a South and Central American family, Furnariidae, which contains some 217 species. The name also applies to

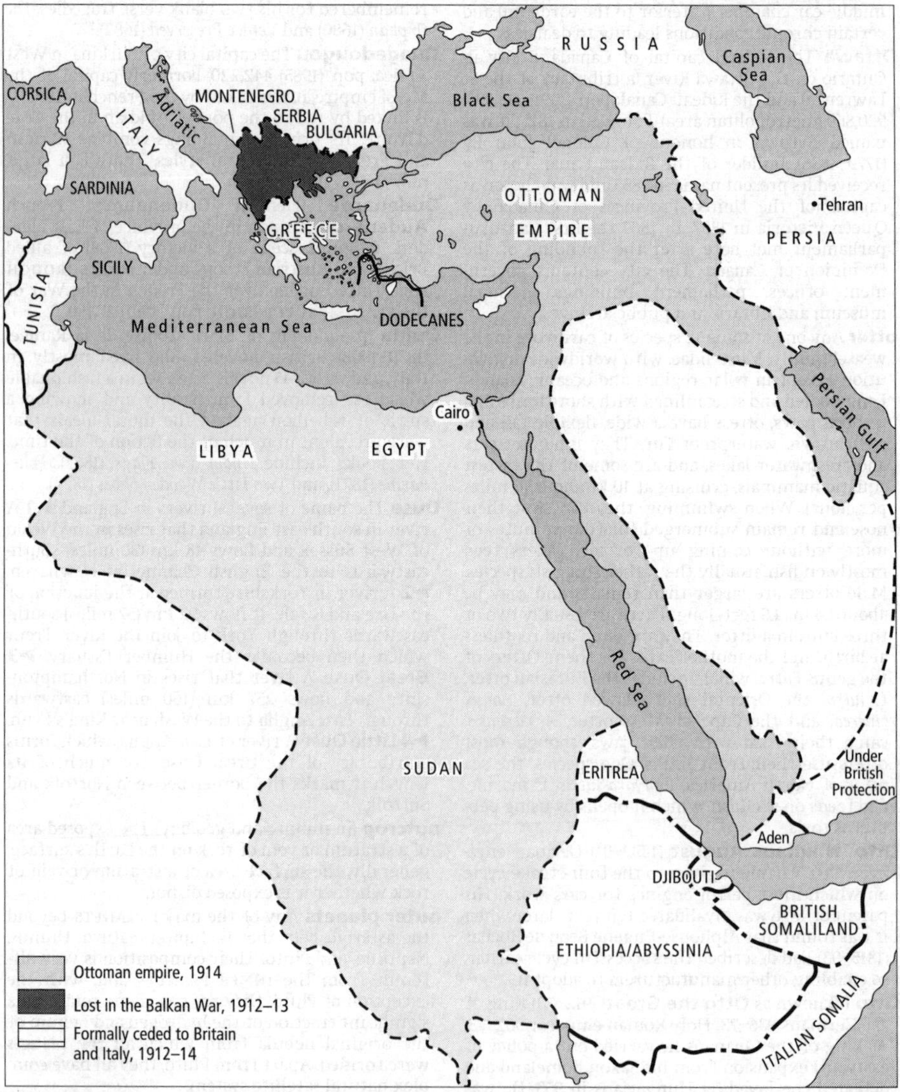

Ottoman empire

Seiurus aurocapillus of the family Fringillidae, which occurs in North American deciduous woodland from British Columbia to northern South America. Varying in size from that of a warbler to that of a large thrush, most ovenbirds are uniform brown in colour, with pale underparts. Their wings are short and rounded, and their beaks slender, and occasionally curved. They live in a wide variety of habitats from forest to semi-desert. Their nests are usually domed, built of sticks or mud. Some, such as the red, or rufous, ovenbird, *Furnarius rufus*, build a round nest with a side entrance; this sets very hard and looks rather like a simple clay oven, hence their name.

Overbury, Sir Thomas (1581–1613) English poet and courtier. He is remembered for his 'Characters', portrait sketches on the model of those of Theophrastus, published posthumously in 1614. On the pretext of his refusal of a diplomatic post he was sent to the Tower of London. There he was fatally poisoned by the agents of Frances Howard, Lady Essex, whose marriage to his patron Robert Carr (afterwards Earl of Somerset) he had opposed.

overpopulation An excess of people in relation to the resources available to sustain them. The UN's forecast of population growth suggests that between 1990 and 2025 the world's population will increase from 5.3 billion to 8.5 billion. Almost all of this increase will occur in the developing countries of Asia, Africa, and Latin America. By the late 1980s, 67 nations with 85 per cent of the developing world's population officially considered their growth rates too high. The UN Population Fund now argues that environmental degradation is the gravest immediate threat posed by overpopulation, rather than shortages of food, fuel, and minerals as previously thought. The UN Population Fund believes that only development can stabilize the world's population and calls for sanitation, EDUCATION, health care, and FAMILY PLANNING in order to reduce FERTILITY RATES. However, the youthful age structure of the world's population and the opposition of the Roman Catholic Church to family planning, especially in South America, mean that overpopulation is one of the severest challenges facing the planet.

overture A one-movement orchestral introduction to an OPERA, ORATORIO, or play; also a concert work in the same form. Concert overtures, also frequently programmatic in content, became popular in the 19th century, while at the same time the purely operatic overture was sometimes replaced by a less formal prelude, as in Wagner's music-dramas. Operas in the 20th century have usually dispensed with the overture altogether.

Ovid (full name Publius Ovidius Naso) (43 BC–*c*.17 AD) Roman poet. He was a major poet of the Augustan period, particularly known for his elegiac love-poems (such as the *Amores* and the *Ars Amatoria*) and for the *Metamorphoses*, a hexametric epic which retells Greek and Roman myths in roughly chronological order. His irreverent attitudes offended Augustus and in 8 AD he was exiled to Tomis (modern Constanţa), on the Black Sea, where he continued to write elegiac poems describing his plight; these are collected in the *Tristia*.

ovum The female egg cell in animals. Before development, it usually has to undergo FERTILIZATION by a male sex cell, or SPERM. Unlike normal body cells, the nucleus of an ovum contains only half of the genetic material, or CHROMOSOMES, required for full development. Some animals can produce individuals without fertilization of the ovum, but such offspring are sterile. Fertilized mammalian ova develop within the mother, whereas birds and reptiles lay fertilized ova, which develop outside the body. In fishes and amphibians ova are deposited outside the body and fertilized externally by the male.

Owen, David (Anthony Llewellyn), Baron Owen of the City of Plymouth (1938–) British politician. After serving as Foreign Secretary (1977–79) in the Labour government he became increasingly dissatisfied with the Labour Party's policies, and in 1981 broke away to become a founding member of the Social Democratic Party (SDP). He led the SDP from 1983 to 1987, resigning to form a breakaway SDP when the main party decided to merge with the Liberals; he eventually disbanded this party in 1990. In 1992 he was appointed the EC's chief mediator in attempts to solve the crisis in the former Yugoslavia.

Owen, Sir Richard (1804–92) British anatomist and palaeontologist. A qualified surgeon, Owen was superintendent of natural history at the British Museum for 28 years and planned the new Natural History Museum in South Kensington. He made important contributions to the taxonomy and understanding of the evolution of monotremes and marsupials, flightless birds, and fossil reptiles, and coined the word *dinosaur* in 1841. Owen is chiefly remembered for his opposition to Darwinism and to its defender T. H. Huxley, because he did not accept that natural selection was sufficient to explain evolution.

Owen, Robert (1771–1858) Welsh social reformer and industrialist. A pioneer socialist thinker, he believed that character is a product of the social environment. He founded a model industrial community centred on his cotton mills at New Lanark in Scotland; this was organized on principles of mutual cooperation, with improved working conditions and housing together with educational institutions provided for workers and their families. He went on to found a series of other cooperative communities; although these did not always succeed, his ideas had an important long-term effect on the development of British socialist thought and on the practice of industrial relations.

Owen, Wilfred (1893–1918) British poet, one of the most important poets of World War I. Already a scrupulous craftsman, he was much encouraged in his poetry by SASSOON, with whom he found himself recuperating in a military hospital. Most of his best work was written during the last year of the war. He was killed in action in France, a week before the armistice. His poems have a bleak and indignant realism ('What passing bells for these who die like cattle?') and emotional drama ('"I am the enemy you killed, my friend"'). Several of his poems were used for BRITTEN's *War Requiem* (1962).

Owens, Jesse (born James Cleveland Owens) (1913–80) US athlete. In 1935 he equalled or broke six world records in 45 minutes, and in 1936 won four gold medals (100 and 200 metres, long jump, and 4 × 100 metres relay) at the Olympic Games in Berlin. The success in Berlin of Owens, as a black man, outraged Hitler, who was conspicuously absent when Owens's medals were presented.

owl A nocturnal bird of prey belonging to an order made up of two families united by many common features. All have soft, cryptically coloured plumage, rounded wings, and a short tail. The beak is small and curved, and the legs are often feathered. Like all birds of prey, their feet are strongly clawed for grasping and lifting. Owls fly remarkably silently, characteristically striking at prey on the ground. Accuracy is achieved by very good nocturnal vision and directional hearing through asymmetrically set ears. They usually swallow their prey whole and regurgitate indigestible matter, such as bones and feathers.

Owls scream, hoot, whistle, and click in conversation. Their courtship is often noisy, conducted over their large territories by night. Nests are untidy collections of sticks, often taken over from other species. Most owls lay two to five white eggs, though the number is variable and may exceed a dozen. The eggs hatch asynchronously, giving the best opportunities of survival to the earliest hatchlings.

One family, Tytonidae, includes about ten species of barn owls, distinguishable by their heart-shaped mask. The other family, Strigidae, includes the remaining 120 or so species, ranging widely in size, habits, and geographical distribution. From the smallest pygmy owls to the largest eagle owls, all are unmistakably owls. Though seldom seen by day, they are common birds in every kind of habitat.

owlet moth (or **noctuid moth**) A small to medium-sized, night-flying moth, often dull brown in colour and well camouflaged, matching the stereotyped idea of a moth. Some, however, are day-flying and brightly coloured. They form the largest family of Lepidoptera, known as the Noctuidae, which includes some 20,000 species. The majority have a wing-span of 2–4 cm (0.75–1.5 inches), but one of the largest of all moths, the giant owl moth, *Thysania agrippina*, with a wing-span of 30 cm (12 inches), is a noctuid. Other common species of noctuid include the angle shades moth, *Phlogophora meticulosa*, and the large yellow underwing, *Noctua pronuba*.

ox-bow lake (or **cut-off**) A shallow, curved lake found on flat FLOODPLAINS. Ox-bows are parts of old loops which have been abandoned by MEANDERING rivers and which are now slowly silting up and being invaded by vegetation. They usually form one at a time, as a river cuts a new channel across the neck of land between the two ends of a meander. Really big floods, however, can sometimes cause a river to cut a completely new course on its floodplain, leaving large numbers of meanders to become ox-bows.

Oxbridge Oxford and Cambridge universities regarded together, especially in contrast to newer universities.

OXFAM (Oxford Committee for Famine Relief) British charity founded in Oxford in 1942 to relieve suffering caused by poverty or natural disasters. Most of its aid is now directed at Third World countries.

Oxford A city in central England, on the River Thames, the county town of Oxfordshire, the seat of a major English university organized as a federation of colleges, and an industrial city; pop. (1991) 109,000. A university (*studium generale*) was organized there soon after 1167. The first colleges were founded in the 13th century – University (1249), Balliol (1263), and Merton (1264). The University includes the BODLEIAN LIBRARY. Other landmarks include the Radcliffe Camera (1737), the Sheldonian Theatre (1644–48), and the Ashmolean Museum (1845). There are many ancient churches and Christ Church Cathedral is early 13th century. Apart from Oxford University, the city also has Oxford Brookes University (1992). Oxford has always been a market town. Printing and publishing are also long-established industries but the automobile industry in the eastern part of the city brought it commercial prosperity.

Oxford Movement See NEWMAN, JOHN HENRY.

Oxfordshire A county of south-central England; area 2,608 sq km (1,007 sq miles); pop. (1991) 553,800; county town, Oxford.

oxidation and reduction Two important classes of chemical reaction. Literally, oxidation means the addition of OXYGEN, and reactions in which materials combine with oxygen are oxidations. The substance causing the oxidation is called an **oxidizing agent**. Combustion is an oxidation process, involving the rapid, high-temperature oxidation of fuels. This definition has been extended to include reactions in which atoms in the reacting materials can be shown to lose electrons. Reduction is the opposite of oxidation, that is, reactions in which oxygen is removed by a **reducing agent**. This definition has likewise been extended to include reactions in which atoms in the reacting materials gain electrons. Although oxidation and reduction are often described as separate processes, in fact in any oxidation-reduction reaction both processes occur simultaneously, since if one reactant is oxidized, another must be reduced.

oxide A compound of oxygen with another element, formed when the other element reacts with oxygen in the air, usually during heating or burning. There are several types. Acidic oxides are mostly those of non-metals and are covalent in character; when soluble in water they form acid solutions. Basic oxides are mostly those of metals and are ionic in character, consisting of the oxide ion O^{2-}, the peroxide ion O_2^{2-}, or the superoxide ion O_2^{-}; when soluble in water they form alkalis, and they neutralize acids to form a salt and water. Amphoteric oxides react both with strong acids and with strong bases, while neutral oxides react with neither. Mixed oxides contain metals in more than one oxidation state.

oxidizing agent See OXIDATION AND REDUCTION.

oxisol A clayey soil formed as a result of intense weathering in tropical or subtropical areas on land surfaces that have been stable for a long time. Oxisols are generally many metres thick and tend to lack distinct HORIZONS. Their bright red, yellow, or yellowish-brown colour is due to the abundance of iron in the profile. They contain little humus, because organic matter is rapidly destroyed in hot climates, and therefore crumble apart very easily, despite the presence of clay. These soils are generally not very fertile. Oxisols occur throughout tropical South America and Africa.

Oxus The ancient name for the AMU DARYA.

oxygen (symbol O, at. no. 8, r.a.m. 15.9994) A colourless, odourless gas, and the most abundant element on Earth, occurring in the crust, in fresh water and sea-water, and in the atmosphere, of which it forms 21 per cent by volume. Oxygen belongs to Group 16 (formerly VIB) of the PERIODIC TABLE. It exists both as the highly reactive molecule O_2 and, especially in the upper atmosphere, as the even more reactive O_3, or OZONE. As the element involved in respiration and a product of photosynthesis, it is essential to most forms of life. Oxygen is slightly denser than air and has a boiling-point of −183°C (−361°F). It is manufactured by the fractional distillation of liquid air, from which the nitrogen content is distilled first. Industrially it has many uses, such as in welding, metal-cutting, explosives, and rocket fuels. It is necessary for combustion and will relight a glowing splint, a simple laboratory test for oxygen. As an oxidizing agent it combines with all other elements, except the NOBLE GASES, and with many compounds.

oxygen cycle A BIOGEOCHEMICAL CYCLE in which the element OXYGEN circulates between living organisms and the non-living environment. The primeval atmosphere of the Earth contained very little oxygen, but with the evolution of photosynthetic organisms it became an important part of the atmosphere. Over many millions of years its concentration has gradually increased to the present level of 21 per cent by volume. Virtually all of this oxygen was formed by PHOTOSYNTHESIS carried out by CYANOBACTERIA, and later by green plants. Oxygen is removed from the atmosphere by the aerobic respiration of living organisms, by the burning of fossil fuels, and by the formation of oxides. Respiration and the burning of fossil fuels produce carbon dioxide gas, which can be used again for photosynthesis, which in turn releases oxygen into the atmosphere to complete the cycle. The oxygen cycle parallels the CARBON CYCLE in most respects.

oxymoron A figure of speech that combines two usually contradictory terms in a compressed paradox: 'bittersweet', 'living death'. Oxymoronic phrases, such as Milton's 'darkness visible', were especially cultivated in 16th- and 17th-century poetry.

oxytocin A hormone produced by the pituitary gland of pregnant women that causes contraction of the womb during labour and stimulates milk flow from the breasts.

oyster A BIVALVE mollusc of the order Ostreoida encountered in vast natural or cultivated beds in coastal shallows throughout the world. Prized everywhere as food, some forms are also valued for pearl production.

Oysters live with their flattened, left shell valve underneath, whereas the upper valve assumes rough and often bizarre shapes, according to the currents and sediments where they grow, unlike the beautifully sculptured symmetry of the valves of cockles or scallops.

Tiny pearls can occur in all oysters, but are rarely of value in temperate species, being made of irregular, chalky shell material rather than the special smooth nacre with which true pearl oysters coat intrusions. Most Western oyster farmers therefore concentrate on raising large meaty specimens, keeping at bay predators and other competing bivalves which encroach on the beds.

oystercatcher (or **sea-pie**, **kleeper**) A large, portly, pied or all-black wading bird with a long, blunt, scarlet bill. The bill is laterally flattened like knife-blades and used to hack at and lever open bivalves (though not oysters in Britain). The loud 'kleep' call, often uttered in flight, is distinctive. Generally seen on the sea-shore, oystercatchers are sometimes found in large flocks outside the breeding season. They belong to the family Haematopodidae, in which there are four species. The common oystercatcher, *Haematopus ostralegus*, is widely distributed. The New Zealand oystercatcher, *Haematopus finschi*, breeds along the rivers of the South Island. Others occur in places as far apart as Iceland and China.

Ozawa, Seiji (1935–) Japanese conductor. In 1959 he won an international conducting competition and since then has been based chiefly in North America; he was the conductor of the Toronto Symphony Orchestra (1965–70) and in 1973 became music director and conductor of the Boston Symphony Orchestra.

ozone A form of OXYGEN in which each molecule is composed of three atoms instead of two (triatomic oxygen, O_3). It is a pale blue gas with a pungent, burning smell (which is rarely present in seaside air). However, it does occur naturally as a result of the reaction between oxygen and solar ultraviolet radiation, forming a layer (the **ozonosphere** or **ozone layer**), which spans most of the STRATOSPHERE surrounding the Earth. Ozone is constantly being produced and constantly being destroyed within this layer. The reactions involved have been shown to be affected by the presence of certain gases, namely nitrogen oxides and CHLOROFLUOROCARBONS (CFCs). These gases are produced as a result of human activities and give rise to areas of ozone depletion or 'holes' in the ozone layer. The most immediate result is reduction in the protective effect of the ozone layer against harmful ultraviolet radiation from the Sun. Scientists and environmentalists have been urging that a total ban be placed on the production of CFCs to prevent irreparable damage.

ozonosphere See OZONE.

P

paca A large South American RODENT weighing up to 10 kg (22 pounds), closely related to the AGOUTI with which it shares the family Dasyproctidae. The two species, *Cuniculus paca* and *C. taczanowskii*, are pig-like in appearance although with a rounded muzzle. They prefer tropical forests and lie up during the day in burrows, which they leave in the evening to forage for roots, grasses, and fallen fruits. They take readily to water and can swim well.

pacemaker A device used to correct an abnormal or irregular heart rate. Implantable pacemakers date from the 1960s. They comprise a pulse generator, inserted under the skin of the shoulder or abdomen, which delivers minute, regular electrical impulses via a connecting wire to an electrode touching the heart. These impulses stimulate the heart muscle to contract, thus regularizing the heartbeat.

Pachelbel, Johann (1653–1706) German composer and organist. In 1695 he became organist of St Sebald's church in his native Nuremberg, a post he held until his death. His compositions, which influenced Bach, include 78 chorale preludes, 13 settings of the Magnificat, and his best-known work, Canon and Gigue in D for three violins and continuo.

Pacific Ocean The world's largest ocean, covering one-third of the Earth's surface (181,300,000 sq km, 70 million sq miles). It separates Asia and Australia from North and South America and extends from Antarctica in the south to the Bering Strait (which links it to the Arctic Ocean) in the north. It was named by its first European navigator, Magellan, because he experienced calm weather there. It reaches a maximum depth of 11,034 m (36,200 ft) in the Challenger Deep in the Mariana Trench.

pacifism The belief that war is never justifiable, no matter how good the cause or how great the threat to one's country. Pacifism springs either from religious faith, as in the case of QUAKERS, or from a humanist belief in the sanctity of life; the religious underpinning can be seen in works such as Tolstoy's *Christianity and Pacifism* (1883). In its purest form it prohibits all use of violence, even in self-defence. In this century many states have respected the beliefs of pacifists by recognizing CONSCIENTIOUS OBJECTION as a ground for refusing CONSCRIPTION.

Pacino, Al(fred) (1940–) US film actor. Nominated for an Oscar eight times, he first achieved recognition with *The Godfather* (1972) and *The Godfather Part II* (1974). Other films include *Scarface* (1983), *Dick Tracy* (1990), *Scent of a Woman* (1992), for which he won an Oscar, and *Carlito's Way* (1993).

Packer, Kerry (Francis Bullmore) (1937–) Australian media entrepreneur. He launched a number of Australian sport initiatives, notably the 'World Series Cricket' tournaments (1977–79) for which he claimed exclusive television coverage rights. As part of these tournaments Packer engaged many of the world's leading cricketers in defiance of the wishes of cricket's ruling bodies, precipitating a two-year schism in international cricket.

paddlefish Either of two species of fishes belonging to the family Polyodontidae. Paddlefish are so-named because of their long, blunt and flattened snout, which looks like a paddle or lolly-stick. The American paddlefish, *Polyodon spathula*, and a relative from China, *Psephurus gladius*, are the only members of their family, and are related to the sturgeons. Living in the Mississippi River system, the American paddlefish grows to 2 m (6.5 feet) and feeds on plankton, principally small or larval crustaceans which it catches by swimming with its huge mouth open.

paddle worm See BRISTLEWORM.

Paderewski, Ignacy Jan (1860–1941) Polish pianist, composer, and statesman, Prime Minister 1919. He became one of the most famous international pianists of his time and also received acclaim for his compositions, which include the opera *Manru* (1901). He was the first Prime Minister of independent Poland, but resigned after only ten months in office and resumed his musical career. In 1939 he served briefly as head of the Polish government in Paris, before emigrating to the USA in 1940 when France surrendered to Germany.

Padua (Italian **Padova**) A city in Venetia, northeast Italy, capital of the province of Padua; pop. (1990) 218,190. The city, first mentioned in 302 BC as Patavium, was the birthplace of the Roman historian Livy (59 BC–17 AD). A leading cultural city from the 11th century, it was ruled by the Cararra family from 1318 until 1405, when it passed to Venice. The modern city is an agricultural, commercial, and industrial centre specializing in motorcycles, agricultural machinery, electrical goods, and textiles.

paediatrics The medical specialty concerned with illness in infants and children, from birth to adolescence. It requires detailed knowledge of genetics, obstetrics, and the psychological development of children and an understanding of parents and parenthood, the management of handicaps, and the relationship between social conditions and child health, in addition to the treatment and prevention of the illnesses to which infants and children succumb.

Paganini, Niccolò (1782–1840) Italian violinist and composer. From the age of 13, Paganini toured throughout Europe and composed difficult pieces to demonstrate his virtuosity. In Paris in 1833 he commissioned BERLIOZ to write a viola piece but rejected the resulting work, *Harold in Italy*, because it gave him too little to play.

Page, Sir Frederick Handley (1885–1962) British aircraft designer. In 1909 he founded Handley Page Ltd, the first British aircraft manufacturing company. He is noted for designing the first twin-engined bomber (1915), as well as the Halifax heavy bombers of World War I.

Paglia, Camille (Anna) (1947–) US cultural critic. Her first book, *Sexual Personae* (1990), brought her to public attention, with its controversial pro-capitalist and anti-feminist examination of art and decadence through the ages. She has remained in the public eye through her active self-promotion and the publication of subsequent essay collections, *Sex, Art, and American Culture* (1992) and *Vamps and Tramps* (1994).

Pagnol, Marcel (1895–1974) French dramatist, film director, and writer. As a director Pagnol is best known for the film trilogy comprising *Marius* (1931), *Fanny* (1932), and *César* (1936), cinematic adaptations of his own plays. In 1946 Pagnol became the first film-maker to be elected to the Académie française. His novels include *La Gloire de mon père* (1957) and *Le Château de ma mère* (1958); the films *Jean de Florette* and *Manon des Sources* (both 1986) were based on Pagnol's *L'Eau des collines* (1963).

pagoda tree See FRANGIPANI.

Pago Pago The chief port of American Samoa, on the Pacific island of Tutuila at the west end of Pago Pago Harbour; pop. (1990) 4,000. Acquired by the USA in 1872, it originally served as a mid-ocean coaling station. The seat of administration lies further east at Fagatogo on the south side of the harbour.

Pahlavi, Muhammad Reza Shah See MUHAMMAD REZA SHAH PAHLAVI.

Pahlavi, Reza (born Reza Khan) (1878–1944) Shah of Iran 1925–41. An army officer, he took control of the Persian government after a coup in 1921. In the absence of the reigning monarch, Reza Khan was elected shah by the National Assembly in 1925. He abdicated in 1941, following the occupation of Iran by British and Soviet forces, passing the throne to his son MUHAMMAD REZA SHAH PAHLAVI.

pain An unpleasant sensation mediated by the nervous system that assists in the recognition of injury or disease so that protective mechanisms can be put into action. There are at least two types of nerve fibres responsible for relaying pain impulses to the brain. Fast fibres are responsible for sharp pain, and in certain instances they precede a reflex avoiding action. Slow fibres are responsible for dull, aching pain.

One or both types of nerve fibre may be responsible for the sensation of pain in a particular situation.

Paine, Thomas (1737–1809) British political writer. After emigrating to America in 1774, he wrote the pamphlet *Common Sense* (1776), which called for American independence and laid the ground for the Declaration of Independence. On returning to England in 1787, he published *The Rights of Man* (1791), defending the French Revolution in response to Burke's *Reflections on the Revolution in France* (1790). His radical views prompted the British government to indict him for treason and he fled to France. There he supported the Revolution but opposed the execution of Louis XVI. He was imprisoned for a year, during which time he wrote *The Age of Reason* (1794), an attack on orthodox Christianity.

paint A substance for decorating or protecting a surface, consisting typically of a liquid mixture of PIGMENT (colouring matter) and medium (oil, water, etc.) that dries to form a hard coating. The nature of the medium determines the qualities and appearance of the paint. In OIL PAINTING the medium is a vegetable oil; in TEMPERA it is egg yolk (or sometimes the whole egg); and in WATERCOLOUR the medium is usually gum arabic, which is soluble in water.

Early paints generally consisted of linseed oil (see DRYING OIL) as the medium, plus a metal oxide powder as the pigment. Modern paints are more complex. The media contain synthetic resins, of which a variety are now available. The development of water-soluble media gave rise to EMULSION PAINTS. Modern paints also contain extenders – salts, such as calcium and barium sulphate, which have little covering power but are used to supplement expensive pigments and to improve the brushability of the paint and the mechanical strength of the dried film. New solvent-free paints currently under development contain no hydrocarbons, which cause AIR POLLUTION. Instead a free-flowing binder, such as Vernonia oil, is used.

painted-lady butterfly A member of the BRUSH-FOOTED BUTTERFLY family, occurring worldwide. Many are migratory; the species occurring in Britain in summer, *Cynthia cardui*, is pinky-orange with black and white markings, and flies fast and powerfully. Every year this species spreads throughout Europe from its winter base in the Mediterranean region and North Africa, and migrates south in autumn. There are nine species of painted-lady butterfly; seven are found in America, and one in Australia, whereas *C. cardui* is worldwide in distribution.

painted snipe A member of a distinct family of SNIPES, the Rostratulidae, comprising two species of tropical and subtropical wading birds. They look like true snipes but have shorter beaks and fly weakly with legs dangling, like rails. The females are bigger and more brightly coloured than the males and are the dominant partners. The greater painted snipe, *Rostratula benghalensis*, occurs in swampy areas of the Old World, whereas the American painted snipe, *R. semicollaris*, is confined to South America.

Paisley A town in Renfrewshire, central Scotland, to the west of Glasgow; pop. (1991) 75,500. It developed around a Clunaic abbey founded by the Stewarts in 1163. A centre of hand-weaving by the 18th century, it became famous during the 19th century for its distinctive shawls, woven in imitation of the highly prized shawls imported from Kashmir in India. The University of Paisley (formerly Paisley College of Technology) was established in 1992.

Paisley, Ian (Richard Kyle) (1926–) Northern Irish clergyman and politician. He was ordained as a minister of the Free Presbyterian Church in 1946, becoming its leader in 1951. Paisley first became politically active in the 1960s and was elected MP for North Antrim in 1970. A co-founder of the Ulster Democratic Unionist Party (1972) he has been a vociferous and outspoken defender of the Protestant Unionist position in Northern Ireland. Paisley became a Member of the European Parliament in 1979.

Paiute A tribe of North American Indians of the Uto-Aztecan linguistic group, originally occupying the Great Basin of Utah, Nevada, and eastern California and numbering *c.*11,000 (1990).

Pakistan A country in the north-west of the Indian sub-continent, bounded by Iran on the west, Afghanistan on the north-west, China on the north-east, and India on the east.

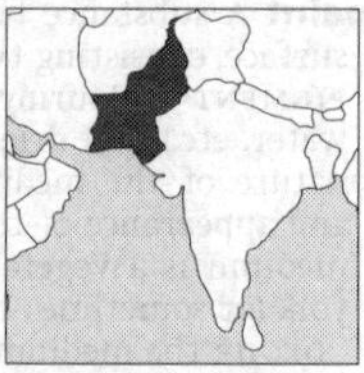

Physical. The Hindu Kush, Karakoram, and Himalaya mountain ranges ring the north of Pakistan. Other ranges sweep down its western side to the Arabian Sea. Below them is the long, broad valley of the Indus. The North-West Frontier Province, containing the strategically important Khyber Pass, is very high. To the south is the plateau of the Punjab, or Panjab, meaning 'five rivers', watered by the tributaries of the Indus. Wheat is grown here; but elsewhere the climate is hot and arid, despite a summer monsoon, and the land is dependent on irrigation. To the east is the Thar Desert. Between the Sind Desert, which covers part of the Indus delta, and Baluchistan in the western hills, there are large reserves of natural gas and some oil, which is also present in the Punjab.

Economy. Pakistan has a mainly agricultural economy, the main exports being raw and processed cotton, cotton fabrics, and rice. However, Pakistani workers abroad earn more foreign currency than do exports. Other crops include sugar cane, wheat, and maize. Livestock-raising is also substantial. Textiles are an important part of industry and contribute substantially to exports. Other industry includes cement, fertilizer, chemicals, and food-processing.

History. Prior to 1947, Pakistan formed part of INDIA. Following the British withdrawal from the Indian sub-continent in 1947, Pakistan was created as a separate state, comprising the territory to the north-east and north-west of India in which the population was predominantly Muslim. The 'Partition' of the subcontinent of India led to unprecedented violence between Hindus and Muslims, costing the lives of more than a million people. Seven and a half million Muslim refugees fled to both parts of Pakistan from India, and ten million Hindus left Pakistan for India. Muhammad Ali JINNAH, president of the MUSLIM LEAGUE, became the new state's first governor-general. The country's liberal constitution was opposed by the orthodox Muslim sector, and in 1951 the Prime Minister, Liaqat Ali Khan, was assassinated by an Afghan fanatic. In 1954 a state of emergency was declared and a new constitution adopted (1956). When attempts to adopt a multi-party system failed, Ayub Khan (1907–74) imposed martial law (1958). His decade of power produced economic growth, but also political resentment. The two wings of Pakistan were separated by a thousand miles of Indian territory. Allegations by the Bengalis in East Pakistan against West Pakistan's disproportionate share of the state's assets led to demands by the Awami League, led by MUJIBUR RAHMAN, for regional autonomy. In the ensuing civil war (1971), the Bengali dissidents defeated a Pakistani army, with Indian help, and established the new state of BANGLADESH (1971). In 1970 the first ever general election brought to power Zulfikar Ali BHUTTO, leader of the Pakistan People's Party, who introduced constitutional, social, and economic reforms. In 1977 he was deposed, and later executed. The regime of General ZIA UL-HAQ (1977–88) committed Pakistan to an Islamic code of laws. With the Soviet invasion of Afghanistan in 1979, over 3 million refugees entered Pakistan. Although martial law was lifted in 1986, with the promise of a return to democracy, Zia's regime ended with his assassination. A general election in December 1988 brought back to power the Pakistan People's Party, led by Zulfikar Ali Bhutto's daughter Benazir BHUTTO; but her government was short-lived, collapsing in 1990 on charges of corruption. Bhutto's successor Mian Mohammad Nawaz Sharif, leader of the Islamic Democratic Alliance, won an absolute majority in the Assembly. His government initiated a policy of further 'Islamization', but Sharif himself was criticized for his pro-Western position during the GULF WAR. In 1993, Benazir Bhutto was returned to office to head a coalition government, which was again dismissed, in 1996, on grounds of corruption. Sharif was re-elected President in 1997.

Capital: Islamabad
Area: 796,095 sq km (307,374 sq mi)
Population: 140,497,000 (1995) (includes Afghan refugees and Jammu and Kashmir residents)
Currency: 1 Pakistan rupee = 100 paisa
Religions: Muslim 96.7%; Christian 1.6%; Hindu 1.5%
Ethnic Groups: Punjabi 48.2%; Pashto 13.1%; Sindhi 11.8%; Saraiki 9.8%; Urdu 7.6%
Languages: Urdu (official); Punjabi; Sindhi; Pashtu; English
International Organizations: UN; Commonwealth; Colombo Plan

Palade, George Emil (1912–) Romanian-born US cell biologist, discoverer of RIBOSOMES. He studied medicine in Bucharest, then moved to the USA where, using electron microscopy, he proved that the MITOCHONDRIA were the sites of energy production in a cell. He also showed that ribosomes are the sites of protein synthesis. He shared a Nobel Prize for physiology and medicine in 1974.

Palaeocene Epoch The first of the geological epochs of the TERTIARY PERIOD, spanning the time-interval from 66.4 to 57.8 million years before the present and preceding the Eocene. Great changes took place and conditions were very different from those of the preceding CRETACEOUS Period. The sudden diversification of the mammals is a notable feature of the Epoch.

Palaeogene Period The earlier of the two geological periods into which the TERTIARY PERIOD can be divided. (The other is the Neogene.) It comprises the Palaeocene, Eocene, and Oligocene epochs.

Palaeolithic (US **Paleolithic**) The earlier part of the STONE AGE, when primitive stone implements were used; a period, which extends from the first appearance of artefacts, some 2.5 million years ago, to the end of the last ice age *c.*10,000 BC. It has been divided into the **Lower Palaeolithic**, with the earliest forms of mankind and the presence of hand-axe industries, ending *c.*80,000 BC, the **Middle Palaeolithic** (or Mousterian), the era of Neanderthal man, ending *c.*33,000 BC, and the **Upper Palaeolithic**, which saw the development of *Homo sapiens*.

palaeomagnetism The field of GEOPHYSICS concerned with the measurement and interpretation of remnant magnetism or the record of the Earth's past magnetic field. Valuable information concerning CONTINENTAL DRIFT and the successive positions (or wandering) of the palaeomagnetic pole have been obtained through palaeomagnetic studies.

palaeontology The study of past life on the

Earth, based on the evidence of FOSSILS. As well as being concerned with individual organisms, it provides information for evolutionary studies and palaeoecology (the study of ancient ecosystems). In addition, fossils can be clues to other aspects of the Earth's history, such as geography and climate.

Palaeontology is indispensable to the geologist because it helps to indicate the relative age of rocks. Fossil invertebrates are commonly used for this purpose, and different groups of these are used in the dating of different geological periods.

palaeosol An ancient soil that developed on a former land surface during a longish period in the geological past. Palaeosols are generally formed under different environmental conditions from those influencing present-day soils in the same area and therefore tend to have different characteristics from modern soils. Although some have remained at the surface, it is common to find them buried beneath more recent sediments.

Palaeozoic Era One of the four eras into which geological time is subdivided. It spans the period of time from 570 to 245 million years ago. It consists of the Cambrian, Ordovician, Silurian, Devonian, Carboniferous (in America the Mississippian and Pennsylvanian), and Permian Periods. The Cambrian to the Silurian constitute the Lower Palaeozoic; the Devonian to the Permian the Upper Palaeozoic. The Palaeozoic saw the development of many marine and terrestrial plants and animals.

palate The roof of the mouth, which consists of two parts. The **hard palate**, at the front of the mouth, is covered by mucous membrane. The **soft palate**, further back, is a movable fold of mucous membrane that tapers at the back of the mouth to form the **uvula**, a fleshy flap.

palatinate A territory formerly under the jurisdiction of a Count Palatine, an official or feudal lord having locally authority that elsewhere only belonged to a sovereign. Palatinates existed in the later Roman empire, in Germany, and in England, where they extended over the earldom of Chester, the duchy of Lancaster, and other territories.

Palau see BELAU.

pale A distinct area of jurisdiction, often originally enclosed by a palisade or ditch. Pales existed in medieval times on the edges of English territory – around CALAIS (until its loss in 1558), in Scotland (in Tudor times), and, most importantly, as a large part of eastern Ireland (from HENRY II's time until the full conquest of Ireland under ELIZABETH I); the actual extent of the Irish pale depended on the strength of the English government in Dublin. CATHERINE II (the Great) in 1792 made a Jewish pale in the lands she had annexed from Poland: Jews had to remain within this area, which ultimately included all of Russian Poland, Lithuania, Belorussia (now Belarus), and much of the Ukraine.

Palermo The capital of the Italian island of Sicily, a port on the north coast of the island in a bay of the Tyrrhenian Sea; pop. (1990) 734,240. Founded as a trading post by the Phoenicians during the 8th century BC and later settled by the Carthaginians, it was taken by the Romans in 254 BC. It was conquered by the Arabs in 832 AD, becoming in 1072 the capital of Sicily, which was then a Norman kingdom. The city is rich in works of art. Industries include shipbuilding, textiles, cement, and tourism.

Palestine A territory in the Middle East on the eastern coast of the Mediterranean Sea, also called the 'Holy Land' because of its links with Judaism, Christianity, and Islam. It has seen many changes of frontier and status in the course of history, and contains several places sacred to Christians, Jews, and Muslims. In biblical times Palestine comprised the kingdoms of Israel and Judaea. The land was controlled at various times by the Egyptian, Assyrian, Persian, and Roman empires before being conquered by the Muslims in 634 AD. It remained in Muslim hands, except for a brief period during the Crusades (1098–1197), until World War I, being part of the Ottoman empire from 1516 to 1917, when Turkish and German forces were defeated by the British at Megiddo. The name 'Palestine' was used as the official political title for the land west of the Jordan mandated to Britain in 1920. Jewish immigration was encouraged by the Balfour Declaration of 1917, and increased greatly in 1948 when the State of ISRAEL was established. The name Palestine continues to be used, however, to describe a geographical entity, particularly in the context of the struggle for territory and political rights of Palestinian Arabs displaced when Israel was established.

Palestine Liberation Organization (PLO) A political and military body formed in 1964 to unite various Palestinian Arab groups in opposition to the Israeli presence in the former territory of PALESTINE. From 1967 the organization was dominated by al-FATAH, led by Yasser ARAFAT. The activities of its radical factions caused trouble with the host country, Jordan, and, following a brief civil war in 1970, it moved to Lebanon and Syria. In 1974 the organization was recognized by the Arab nations as the representative of all Palestinians. The Israeli invasion of Lebanon (1982) undermined its military power and organization, and it regrouped in Tunisia. Splinter groups of extremists, such as the 'Popular Front for the Liberation of Palestine' and the 'Black September' terrorists, have been responsible for kidnappings, hijackings, and killings both in and beyond the Middle East. In 1988 Arafat persuaded the movement to renounce violence, and its governing council recognized the State of Israel. Since then the PLO has been accepted by an increasing number of states as being a government-in-exile. In 1993 Arafat became chair of the Palestinian National Authority administering the West Bank and the Gaza Strip.

Palestinians An Arabic-speaking people who formed the indigeneous population of PALESTINE before the establishment of the State of Israel. It is estimated there are 5.25 million Palestinians worldwide, of whom over 1 million live in the territory known as the West Bank (of the River Jordan), which was annexed by Jordan in 1950 and was under Israeli occupation from 1967 to 1994. A further half a million live in the territory known as the Gaza Strip, which was administered by Egypt until it too was occupied by Israel in 1967. There are Palestinian refugee camps in Israel, Jordan, Lebanon, and Syria: there are an estimated 929,000 Palestinian refugees in Jordan (where, in all, Palestinians account for about half the population); there are 302,000 refugees in Lebanon, and 280,000 in Syria; and Palestinians are scattered as migrant workers in both professional and menial jobs throughout the world, but particularly in the Gulf States. Deprived of their historic homeland, the Palestinians recognize as their sole legitimate representative the PALESTINE LIBERATION ORGANIZATION (PLO).

Palestrina, Giovanni Pierluigi da (*c.*1525–94) Italian composer. He composed several madrigals, but is chiefly known for his sacred music, notably 105 masses and more than 250 motets. His music is characterized by its control of counterpoint; major works include the *Missa Papae Marcelli* (1567).

Palgrave, Francis Turner (1824–97) British critic and poet. He is best known for his anthology *The Golden Treasury of Songs and Lyrical Poems in the English Language* (1861). He compiled other anthologies, wrote several volumes of verse, and was professor of poetry at Oxford from 1886 to 1895.

Pali See INDO-IRANIAN LANGUAGES.

Palissy, Bernard (*c.*1510–90) French potter. From the late 1550s he became famous for richly coloured earthenware decorated with reliefs of plants and animals. From about 1565 he enjoyed royal patronage and was employed by the court.

Palladianism A style of architecture based on the buildings and publications of the 16th-century Italian architect Andrea PALLADIO. 'Palladianism' usually refers to a movement that dominated British architecture from about 1715 to about 1760. During this period Palladio was admired by influential figures, such as Lord BURLINGTON and William KENT, and the exuberant Baroque style associated with Wren (in his late years), Vanbrugh, and Hawksmoor gave way to one characterized by symmetry, methodical regularity, and classical correctness of detail. In Britain Palladianism was almost entirely confined to domestic architecture; interiors were often richly decorated compared with the sober exteriors. It then began to merge with the more severe and archaeologically spirited NEOCLASSICISM in the 1760s, but at about the same time it was taken up in America, where it enjoyed a long and fruitful popularity.

Palladio, Andrea (1508–80) Italian architect. He led a revival of classical architecture in 16th-century Italy, in particular promoting the Roman ideals of harmonic proportions and symmetrical planning. He designed many villas, palaces, and churches; major buildings include the church of San Giorgio Maggiore in Venice (1566 onwards). His theoretical work *Four Books on Architecture* (1570) was the main source of inspiration for the style known as PALLADIANISM.

palladium (symbol Pd, at. no. 46, r.a.m. 106.42) A ductile and malleable silvery-white platinum metal. The element occurs in association with other platinum metals. It dissolves in concentrated nitric acid and hot sulphuric acid and is the most reactive of the platinum metals. Its main use is as an industrial CATALYST, particularly in reactions involving hydrogen. It is also used in some electrical components, and forms the alloy white gold with gold.

Pallas The second-largest ASTEROID, discovered in 1802 by the German astronomer Heinrich Olbers. Pallas interacts gravitationally with CERES and this has enabled the mass of Pallas to be measured as $(2.15 \pm 0.43) \times 10^{20}$ kg. In 1978 an occultation of star SAO 85009 by Pallas led to a diameter measurement of 538 ± 12 km

palm A tree belonging to the Palmae, a family of 2,500 species of woody MONOCOTYLEDONS. Palms occur mainly in the tropics, with a few extending into the Mediterranean region, subtropical China, and New Zealand. Most are unbranched with a terminal head of pinnate (divided) leaves, like the coconut, or fan-shaped leaves like the talipot. Other palms sucker from the base, like the sago palms, or are branched, like the doum palm of Africa, *Hyphaene thebaica*, or the NIPA PALM, *Nypa fruticans*, whose stem creeps along the ground. The rattans are climbing plants, or LIANAS. Some palms, like the talipot, flower once and die, others flower several times from lateral shoots. *Lodoicea maldivica* of the Seychelles has the largest seed of any plant and one of the largest of all known leaves. All palms produce DRUPES, juicy like the date, or fibrous like the coconut.

Palma (in full **Palma de Mallorca**) An industrial port, resort, and capital of the Balearic Islands, chief town of the island of Majorca; pop. (1991) 308,620. It was founded as a Roman colony in 276 BC. Palma exports fruit and wine, and has many light industries in addition to being a tourist centre.

palm-chat A sparrow-sized bird, *Dulus dominicus*, found only on the West Indian islands of Hispaniola and Gonave, which is placed in its own family, Bombycillidae. It is greenish and brown above, with pale, heavily streaked underparts, and has a broad and heavy beak for feeding on berries. Several pairs build a communal nest of twigs, though each pair has a separate entrance.

palm civet Any one of some seven species of carnivore making up a subfamily intermediate between genets and mongooses, but more closely related to the former. There is an African species, *Nandinia binotata*, but most occur in tropical Asia. They are arboreal and, although they certainly occur in palm trees, they are by no means confined to them. Their diet consists of small mammals, birds, and insects but they do not take much vegetable matter apart from some fruit. Another closely related subfamily consists of the five species of banded palm civets, which are similar in all respects to the palm civets.

Palme, (Sven) Olof (Joachim) (1927–86) Swedish statesman, Prime Minister 1969–76 and 1982–86. He became leader of the Social Democratic Socialist Workers' Party in 1969. His electoral defeat in 1976 marked the end of 44 continuous years in power for the Social Democratic Party. He was killed by an unknown assassin during his second term of office.

Palmer, Arnold (Daniel) (1929–) US golfer. His many championship victories include the US Masters (1958; 1960; 1962; 1964) the US Open (1960), and the British Open (1961–62).

Palmer, Samuel (1805–91) British painter and etcher. From 1824 his friendship with William Blake resulted in the mystical, visionary landscape paintings, such as *Repose of the Holy Family* (1824), for which he is best known. He was leader of The Ancients (a group of artists so called because of their love of the medieval), who were inspired by Blake's mysticism. Later, after a visit to Italy (1837–39), he devoted himself to more conventional pastoral works.

Palmerston, Henry John Temple, 3rd Viscount (1784–1865) British Whig statesman, Prime Minister 1855–58 and 1859–65. He left the Tory Party in 1830 to serve with the Whigs as Foreign Secretary (1830–34; 1835–41; 1846–51). In his foreign policy Palmerston was single-minded in his promotion of British interests, declaring the second Opium War against China in 1856, and overseeing the successful conclusion of the Crimean War in 1856 and the suppression of the Indian Mutiny in 1858. He maintained British neutrality during the American Civil War.

palmetto (originally **palmito**) The dwarf fan palm, *Chamaerops humilis*. The name is also used for other palms, notably *Sabel palmetto*, a fan palm of the southern USA which reaches 25 m (80 feet). The dwarf fan palm is the only palm native to the European mainland, being found in the western

Mediterranean region, where it is typical of the short leathery-leaved vegetation known as *garigue*.

Palm Springs A popular desert oasis and fashionable resort city in the desert area of southern California, USA; pop. (1990) 40,180. Occupying an area once inhabited by the Agua Caliente Indians, its mineral springs were discovered by stage-coachers and railroad surveyors, and a spa hotel was eventually built in 1886.

Palm Sunday The Sunday before Easter that commemorates Christ's last ride into Jerusalem, when the people threw palm leaves in his path. It is the start of Holy Week.

Palmyra An ancient Syrian city that rose to prosperity in the 1st century BC by organizing and protecting caravans crossing the desert between Babylonia and Syria. It was probably incorporated within the Roman empire in 17 AD, but rose to its greatest power in the 3rd century AD under King Odaenathus (died 267) and his second wife, Zenobia. The latter at one point ruled Syria, Egypt, and almost all of Asia Minor, but by 273 AURELIAN had captured her and destroyed Palmyra.

Palomar, Mount A mountain in southern California, USA, north-east of San Diego, that rises to a height of 1,867 m (6,126 ft). It is the site of an astronomical observatory, which contains a large telescope developed by the US astronomer George Hale.

Pamir Mountains (or **Pamirs**) A mountain system of central Asia, centred in Tajikistan and extending into Kyrgyzstan, Afghanistan, Pakistan, and western China. The system's highest peak, in Tajikistan, rises to 7,495 m (24,590 ft).

pampas Large treeless plains in central Argentina and southern Uruguay, South America, dominated by bunch grasses and occasional 'monte' shrub vegetation. Cattle were introduced onto the wide flat grasslands in the 16th century and in the 19th century the pampas were settled by immigrant farmers from Europe. The Argentinian pampas are responsible for almost the entire agricultural production – meat and grain – of the country.

pampas grass A plant that is native to tropical and temperate South America. There are six species of pampas grass in the genus *Cortaderia*. The plants are large perennials with long, narrow leaves and tall silky-plumed flower-heads. *C. selloana* is the common kind frequently cultivated as an ornamental garden plant. The sexes are separate, and female plants produce larger flower spikes than the males. The plant may reach some 2 m (6.5 feet) when in flower.

Pamplona A city in northern Spain, capital of the former kingdom and modern region of Navarre, known in Roman times as Pompaelo ('city of Pompey'); pop. (1991) 191,110. Situated on the River Arga, on a route over the Pyrenees to France, the city is noted for its Gothic cathedral and fiesta of San Fermin, held there in July, which is celebrated with the running of bulls through the city streets.

Pan In Greek mythology, the god of flocks, herds, woods, and fields, represented as an ugly but merry man with the legs and usually the horns and ears of a goat. He played the pan-pipes, which he invented, and his musical skills helped him to seduce the nymphs he constantly pursued (he was regarded as a personification of Lust).

Pan-Africanism A movement seeking unity within Africa. It became a positive force with the London Pan-African Conference of 1900. An international convention in the USA in 1920 was largely inspired by the Jamaican Marcus GARVEY. The invasion of Ethiopia by Italy in 1935 produced a strong reaction within Africa, stimulating anti-colonial nationalism. The Pan-African Congress in Manchester in 1945 was dominated by Jomo KENYATTA and Kwame NKRUMAH, and by the 'father of Pan-Africanism', the American W. E. B. DU BOIS. In 1958 a conference of independent African states was held in Accra, followed by two further conferences in Monrovia in 1959 and 1961. In 1963 in Addis Ababa 32 independent African nations founded the ORGANIZATION OF AFRICAN UNITY, by which time Pan-Africanism had moved from being an ideal into practical politics.

Panama A tropical country occupying the narrow isthmus linking Central and South America, bounded by Costa Rica to the west and Colombia to the east.

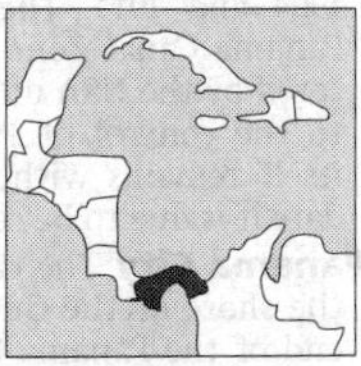

Physical. Along the length of the country runs a range of hills, through the centre of which was cut the pass, for the PANAMA CANAL. The Canal gives access to shipping from the Caribbean in the north to the Pacific in the south. The land is fertile, supporting coffee on the higher ground and sugar cane on the coastal plains.

Economy. International finance and shipping are of importance due to Panama's position as a world trade centre. The principal agricultural exports are bananas, shrimps from the coastal waters, and coffee; there are substantial, as yet unexploited, copper reserves, and some light industry, mostly food-processing. There is a petroleum refinery, but its products are of declining importance.

History. Panama was visited in 1501 by the Spaniard Rodrigo de Bastidas. It was explored more thoroughly in 1513 by Vasco Núñez de BALBOA, the first Spaniard to see the Pacific Ocean. Portobello on the Caribbean coast served as the principal port for the trade of the viceroyalty of Peru. In the 18th century, Panama became part of the viceroyalty of NEW GRANADA. In 1821 the country gained independence from Spain as a province of Gran Colombia. Despite nationalist insurrections against Colombia in the 19th century, the area only became independent as the republic of Panama in 1903 as a protectorate of the USA. The latter had aided Panama's struggle in return for a Panamanian concession to build a canal across the isthmus and a lease of the zone around it to the USA. The volatile, élite-dominated politics which have characterized Panama during much of the 20th century have led to its occupation by US peace-keeping forces in 1908, 1912, 1918, and 1989. From 1968 to 1981, General Omar Torrijos controlled Panama, working to diversify the economy and reduce US sovereignty over the Canal Zone, an object of long-standing national resentment. In 1977 he signed the Panama Canal Treaties, but was killed in 1981. In 1988 General Manuel Noriega seized power. A US military invasion in December 1989 deposed him and installed Guillermo Endara as President, placing Noriega on trial in the USA for drug trafficking; he was convicted in 1992. Widespread strikes took place against Endara's government, which itself was accused of involvement with drug rings. In 1991 a new constitution abolished the armed forces. A general election in 1994 led to Ernesto Pérez Balladares becoming president.

Capital: Panama City
Area: 77,082 sq km (29,762 sq mi)
Population: 2,631,000 (1995)

Currency: 1 balboa = 100 centesimos (US$ also in circulation)
Religions: Roman Catholic 84.0%; Protestant 4.8%; Muslim 4.5%; Baha'i 1.1%; Hindu 0.3%
Ethnic Groups: Mestizo 62.0%; Black and mixed 19.0%; White 10.0%; Amerindian 6.0%; Asian 2.0%
Languages: Spanish (official); English creole; Amerindian languages
International Organizations: UN; OAS; Non-Aligned Movement

Panama Canal A canal about 80 km (50 miles) long and 150 m (490 ft) wide, across the isthmus of Panama, connecting the Atlantic and Pacific Oceans. Its construction, begun by Ferdinand de Lesseps in 1881 but abandoned through bankruptcy in 1889, was completed by the USA between 1904 and 1914. The surrounding territory, the Panama Canal Zone or Canal Zone, was administered by the USA until 1979, when it was returned to the control of Panama. Control of the canal itself remains with the USA until 1999, at which date it is due to be ceded to Panama.

Panama City The capital of Panama, situated on the shore of the Gulf of Panama near the Pacific end of the Panama Canal; pop. (1990) 584,800. The old city was destroyed by the Welsh buccaneer Henry Morgan in 1671. The new city, built in 1674 on a site a little to the west, became capital of Panama in 1903, when the republic gained its independence from Colombia. The city, which developed rapidly after the opening of the Panama Canal in 1914, has industries, which produce clothing, chemicals, and plastics.

Pan-Americanism The movement towards economic, military, political, and social cooperation among the 21 republics of South, Central, and North America. The first Pan-American conference was held in 1889 in Washington, DC, to encourage inter-American trade as well as the peaceful resolution of conflicts in the region. The seventh conference (Montevideo 1933) was important because the USA, in harmony with Franklin D. ROOSEVELT's 'Good Neighbor' policy, finally adopted the long-espoused Latin American principle of non-intervention, while the conference at Buenos Aires in 1936 adopted a treaty for the peaceful resolution of conflicts between American states. The Conference at Chapultepec (1945) agreed on a united defence policy for the signatory nations. At the conference held in Bogotá in 1948, the ORGANIZATION OF AMERICAN STATES (OAS) was established, transforming the Pan-American system into a formal regional organization within the framework of the United Nations.

pancreas (or **sweetbread**) A large gland that lies in the mammalian abdomen. It contains two separate types of cell. One group manufactures digestive juices, which enter the small intestine via ducts. The other type consists of isolated patches of cells, called islets of Langerhans, scattered among the digestive juice-secreting cells and their ducts. The islets together form an ENDOCRINE GLAND and secrete their products into the bloodstream. These endocrine cells are responsible for the production of the hormones insulin, used to treat diabetes, and glucagon.

panda (or **giant panda**) *Ailuropoda melanoleuca*, a member of the BEAR family that was adopted as the symbol of the World Wildlife Fund (now called the World Wide Fund for Nature). With its black body, white head, black ears, and black 'spectacles', it has a most endearing appearance. It lives high in the mountains of southwestern China and eastern Tibet, where it moves overland with a lumbering gait on its flat, bear-like feet. Perhaps surprisingly, it is quite agile and climbs trees. It lives in dense forests of bamboo on which it feeds almost exclusively and of which it must ingest a prodigious amount to obtain its nourishment. Compare RED PANDA.

Pandit, Vijaya (Lakshmi) (1900–90) Indian politician and diplomat. After joining the Indian National Congress, led by her brother Jawaharlal Nehru, she was imprisoned three times by the British (1932; 1941; 1942) for nationalist activities. Following independence she led the Indian delegation to the United Nations (1946–48; 1952–53) and was the first woman to serve as president of the United Nations General Assembly (1953–54). She was High Commissioner to the UK (1955–61).

Pandora In Greek mythology, the first woman on Earth, sent by Zeus as a punishment for Prometheus' crime of stealing fire from the gods. Zeus gave Pandora a box which, when opened, let out all the ills that have since beset mankind; Hope, however, remained inside it as a comfort.

Pangaea The great supercontinent that divided to form LAURASIA and GONDWANA, so named by Alfred WEGENER, who proposed that Pangaea began to split up as a result of CONTINENTAL DRIFT in the JURASSIC Period, and that the fragments eventually became the continental masses we know today.

pangolin A toothless mammal found in the tropical regions of the Old World, and belonging to the family Manidae and order Pholidota. Pangolins are the only mammals with scales; those of the great ground, or giant pangolin, *Manis gigantea*, are 7.5 cm (3 inches) long and 13 cm (5 inches) wide. The seven species of pangolin, four in Africa, and three in Asia, have a small head, a long, tapering body, and broad, heavy tail. The head and body of the giant pangolin is 85 cm (33 inches) long and the tail is up to 80 cm (31 inches). It moves slowly, dragging the heavy tail; if threatened, it curls into a ball and so is protected by the sharp-edged scales. It feeds on insects, usually ants or termites, and after tearing open a nest will mop them up with its long, thin, sticky tongue.

Pankhurst, Mrs Emmeline (1858–1928) British suffragette. In 1903 Emmeline and her daughters **Christabel** (1880–1958) and **(Estelle) Sylvia** (1882–1960) founded the Women's Social and Political Union, with the motto 'Votes for Women'. Following the imprisonment of Christabel in 1905, Emmeline initiated the militant suffragette campaign and was responsible for keeping the suffragette cause in the public eye until the outbreak of World War I.

panpipes (or **syrinx**) A musical instrument, a series of tubes, each of different length, blown as end-flutes or via ducts, usually fixed together in a raft or bundle. (The name derives from the myth of Pan and the nymph Syrinx, who became a clump of reeds to escape him.) Some peoples, for example the Lithuanians and the South African Venda, have a player for each tube.

pansy See VIOLET.

panther See PUMA.

pantomime A British theatrical entertainment that derives its name (though not its character) from the Roman *pantomimus*. Associated with Christmas, it developed from the HARLEQUINADE. Traditional fairy-tales form the basis for a mixture of songs, dances, slapstick, topical jokes, magic, and spectacle. The principal boy is traditionally played by a girl in tights, while the comic old woman, the dame, is usually played by a male comedian in a wig.

Paolozzi, Sir Eduardo (Luigi) (1924–) Scottish

artist and sculptor, of Italian descent. He was a key figure in the development of pop art in Britain in the 1950s. His work is typified by mechanistic sculptures in a figurative style, often surfaced with cog wheels and machine parts, as in *Japanese War God* (1958).

Papa See RANGI AND PAPA.

papacy The office of the pope (Bishop of Rome), derives its name from the Greek *papas* and Latin *papa*, which are familiar forms of 'father'. In early times many bishops and even priests were called popes, but in the Western Church the word gradually became a title and restricted to the Bishop of Rome; Pope Gregory VII in 1073 forbade its use for anyone except the Bishop of Rome. The traditional enumeration lists 265 holders of the office, excluding ANTIPOPES, beginning with St PETER and reaching to the present holder John Paul II. The basis of papal authority derives from St Peter's position of leadership among the 12 Apostles, given him by Jesus Christ, the early tradition that he came to Rome and was martyred there. The papal claim to extend its jurisdiction over all Christian Churches was a major cause of various Churches breaking with Rome, notably the ORTHODOX CHURCH definitively in 1054, and the Protestant Churches at the time of the REFORMATION in the 16th century.

Papal States A part of central Italy held between 756 and 1870 by the Catholic Church, corresponding to the modern regions of Emilia-Romagna, Marche, Umbria, and Latium. Taken from the Lombards by the Frankish king Pepin III, the states were given to the papacy as a strategy to undermine Lombard expansionism. Greatly extended by Pope Innocent III in the early 13th century and by Pope Julius II in the 16th century, they were incorporated into the newly unified Italy in 1860 and 1870. Their annexation to Italy deprived the papacy of its temporal powers until the Lateran Treaty of 1929 recognized the sovereignty of the Vatican City.

papaya (or **pawpaw**) A rapid-growing, soft- or hollow-stemmed small tree, *Carica papaya*, with a crown of large, segmented evergreen leaves. Of Central American origin, it is widespread as a garden plant throughout the tropics but rarely cultivated on a larger scale. It gives its name to the small family Caricaceae, comprising 30 species of tropical trees; other *Carica* species also produce edible fruit. The orange or yellow fruits of the papaya are eaten fresh, canned, or made into drinks. Immature fruits may be cooked as vegetables. The latex of the tree contains the useful enzyme, papain, which breaks down protein, and is used to prevent cloudiness in beer, to shrink-proof wool and silk, and as a meat tenderizer.

Papeete The capital of French Polynesia, situated on the north-west coast of the Pacific Island of Tahiti; pop. (1988) 78,800. The town developed as a tourist centre after the building of an airport in 1959.

Papen, Franz von (1879–1969) German politician. A member of the Catholic Centre Party, he had little popular following, and his appointment as Chancellor (1932) came as a surprise. To gain NAZI support he lifted the ban on the BROWNSHIRTS, but HITLER remained an opponent. Attempts to undermine Nazi strength failed and he resigned. He persuaded HINDENBURG to appoint Hitler (January 1933) as his Chancellor, but as Vice-Chancellor he could not restrain him. He became ambassador to Austria (1934), working for its annexation (ANSCHLUSS) in 1938, and to Turkey (1939–44). He was tried as a war criminal (1945) but released.

paper manufacture The conversion of suitable fibres into rolls and sheets of paper. Wood-pulp for making paper varies in its manufacture according to how the fibre is extracted, but a general method involves cooking woodchips with chemicals in a digester, then passing the pulp through a disc refiner, which mechanically separates the fibres. The resulting pulp is washed (and sometimes bleached), screened for impurities, and then beaten (refined) again with additives to give the paper the required properties. The pulp is then about 98 per cent water, yet it forms a continuous web of paper on the wire of the paper-making machine. The paper web is dried and then calendered, a process in which it passes between a series of heated, polished metal rollers, which impart a smooth finish to the paper.

paper nautilus A small floating OCTOPUS of the genus *Argonauta*, which has no true molluscan shell. Mature females secrete a beautiful, thin-walled, chalky egg-case using the expanded tips of two tentacles. This is used as a brood-chamber and carried by the female once eggs are laid. It is usually large enough to be used as a shelter by the female, who can retreat fully inside; the tiny males also occasionally cohabit.

papier mâché (French, 'chewed paper') A material made of pulped paper mixed with glue (and sometimes sand), which can be moulded when moist and hardens when baked to form a strong but light substance that can be polished and painted. It is used in a great variety of ways: for household objects, such as trays and boxes; for light furniture (sometimes inlaid with mother-of-pearl); for window displays and theatrical decorations; for architectural mouldings imitating plasterwork; and even as a building material.

papillon See DOG.

Pappus (known as **Pappus of Alexandria**) (fl. *c.*300–350 AD) Greek mathematician. Little is known of his life, but his *Collection* of six books (another two are missing) is the principal source of knowledge of the mathematics of his predecessors. They are particularly strong on geometry, to which Pappus himself made major contributions. Fragments of other works survive.

paprika See CAPSICUM.

Papua The south-eastern part of the island of New Guinea, now part of the independent state of Papua New Guinea.

Papua New Guinea A country consisting of the eastern half of the island of New Guinea north of Australia, together with the Bismarck Archipelago and other adjacent islands in the south-west Pacific Ocean. The western half of the island of New Guinea forms the province of Irian Jaya, part of INDONESIA.

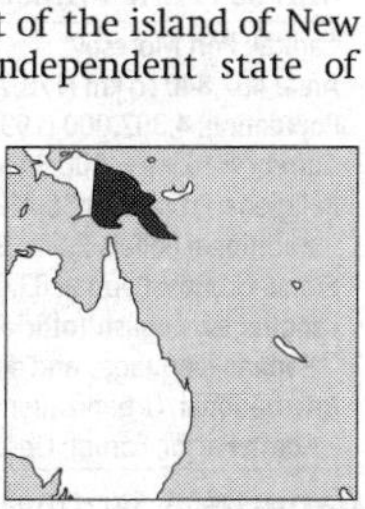

Physical. The mainland is divided by a central range of mountains rising to 4,509 m (14,762 feet) at Mount Wilhelm. A low-lying plain is drained by the Fly River in the south-west, and there are active volcanoes in the east. The climate is tropical and monsoonal, with heavy rainfall and temperatures ranging from 10°C to 32°C (50°F to 95°F), according to altitude.

Economy. Papua New Guinea exploits extensive copper and substantial gold deposits, and together these account for half of the country's exports. There are also petroleum reserves. Coffee, timber, cocoa, and palm oil are significant exports, and tropical fruits grow in abundance. Tuna-fishing is also important. Other agriculture includes bananas, coconuts, yams, and sugar cane. Industry is limited mainly to food-processing. Australia contributes one-fifth of the annual budget in direct aid. High unemployment is a long-term problem.

History. Contact with Europe goes back to the 16th century, when the Portuguese Jorge de Meneses named the island Ilhas dos Papuas (Malay, 'frizzy-haired') and the Spaniard Ortiz Retes christened it New Guinea because he was reminded of the Guinea coast of Africa. In 1828 the Dutch annexed the western half of the island, followed, in 1884, by the German and British division of the eastern half. In 1904 the British transferred their territory, now called Papua, to Australia, and at the outbreak of World War I an Australian expeditionary force seized German New Guinea (Kaiser-Wilhelmsland). During World War II Australian troops fought off a determined Japanese invasion. Formal administrative union of the area as Papua New Guinea was achieved in 1968. Self-government was attained in 1973 and in 1975 Papua New Guinea became an independent nation within the Commonwealth. A defence treaty with Australia was negotiated and democratic political activity, by graduates of the University of Port Moresby (founded 1965), quickly developed. Secessionist demands from some of the offshore islands, especially Bougainville, became a key issue facing the coalition government of Rabbie Namaliu (1990–92), troops being landed on Bougainville in May 1992. Namaliu's government was defeated in the 1992 general election and Paias Wingti was elected Prime Minister of another coalition government. During the early 1990s relations between Papua New Guinea and Indonesia, which had been strained throughout the 1980s over the conflict in Irian Jaya, improved. In 1994 Wingti was forced from office and replaced by Julius Chan. Although a cease-fire was agreed between the government and the Bougainville Revolutionary Army, subsequent peace talks broke down and fighting resumed. In 1997 the use of foreign mercenaries to suppress the rebellion led to a mutiny by the army and the resignation of Chan; Bill Skate replaced him as Prime Minister.

Capital: Port Moresby
Area: 462,840 sq km (178,704 sq mi)
Population: 4,302,000 (1995)
Currency: 1 kina = 100 toea
Religions: Protestant 58.4%; Roman Catholic 32.8%; Anglican 5.4%; traditional beliefs 2.5%; Baha'i 0.6%
Ethnic Groups: Papuan 83.0%; Melanesian 15.0%
Languages: English (official); Tok Pisin; about 700 Melanesian and Papuan languages and dialects
International Organizations: UN; Commonwealth; Colombo Plan; South Pacific Forum; Observer status at ASEAN

papyrus A writing material prepared in ancient Egypt from the pithy stem of the aquatic plant *Cyperus papyrus*, from which paper takes its name. Fresh stalks of the grass gathered from the River Nile were teased out with a needle to give strands of damp fibre. These strands were laid out in two crossed layers on a moistened board and compacted in a press, their juice and the added moisture bonding them together. After drying, the sheets so formed would accept writing in ink.

parabola One of the three kinds of CONIC SECTION. It is a U-shaped curve obtained by slicing a cone parallel to its slant side. A parabola can also be

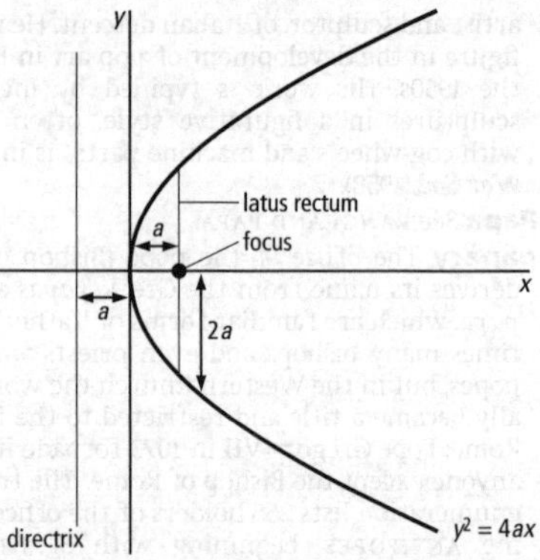

Parabola The distance between the focus and the directrix is 2a; the equation of the curve is $y^2 = 4ax$ if the vertex of the curve is at the origin and the curve is symmetrical about the x-axis.

described as the locus of points in a plane whose distance from a fixed point, the focus, equals that from a fixed line, the directrix. The simplest algebraic equation of a parabola is $y = x^2$, or in polar coordinates, $r = 1/(1 - \cos\theta)$. The property of a **parabolic mirror** to reflect through the focus all light travelling parallel to its axis has proved useful in reflecting telescopes, while the converse property (producing a parallel beam of light by a source at its focus) is made use of in torches and car headlights.

Paracelsus (born Theophrastus Phillipus Aureolus Bombastus von Hohenheim) (*c*.1493–1541) Swiss physician. He developed a new approach to medicine and philosophy condemning medical teaching that was not based on observation and experience. He introduced chemical remedies to replace traditional herbal ones, and gave alchemy a wider perspective. Paracelsus saw illness as having a specific external cause rather than being caused by an imbalance of the humours in the body, although this progressive view was offset by his overall occultist perspective.

paracetamol See ANALGESIC.

parachute A rectangular or umbrella-shaped device that allows a person or load attached to it to descend slowly from a height, especially from a BALLOON or AEROPLANE. The first human parachute descent was made in 1797, when Jacques Garnerin parachuted from a balloon over Paris. Folding parachutes were first used in the USA in 1880, and towards the end of World War I aviators first used parachutes to escape from their aeroplanes. Early parachutes were made of canvas, and later silk. Modern parachutes comprise many separate panels of nylon, so that tears are confined to a small area. Until recently parachutes were umbrella-shaped, but parafoils (air-filled AEROFOILS) are now common. In addition to their use as safety devices, parachutes are used for sport, for aerial drops of supplies and equipment, and as braking devices (drogues) for landing aircraft or other vehicles.

paradox A self-contradictory statement. In LOGIC paradoxes arise when all of a set of premisses are asserted to be true but the conclusion deduced from these premisses negates one or more of them. The best-known paradox is that of the Liar, where Epimenedes, the Cretan, claims 'all Cretans are liars' (Cretans never speak the truth). However,

Epimenedes, being a Cretan, must have lied when making this claim, so if it is a lie (false) then it must be true. If Epimenedes spoke the truth when he made the claim then he is a truthful Cretan, so if it is true then it must be false.

paraffin ▶**1** (US **kerosene**) A mixture of liquid hydrocarbons, now obtained chiefly from petroleum, but in the past also obtained from coal, shale, and wood. In the early years of PETROLEUM REFINING during the latter half of the 19th century, paraffin represented the most important petroleum fraction, because of its use as a fuel in lamps. With the introduction of electric lighting at the end of the 19th century, demand dropped sharply and its use was confined largely to paraffin heaters. However, as the main constituent of AVIATION FUEL for jet engines, it has shown a marked resurgence during the latter half of the 20th century. ▶**2** The former name for an ALKANE.

paraffin wax A mixture of high-molecular-weight HYDROCARBONS (straight-chain alkanes) obtained from PETROLEUM REFINING. About 90 per cent of the wax used commercially is recovered from petroleum. It is used to make polishes, wax crayons, and candle wax (a mixture of paraffin wax with alcohols and acids); in the moulding of sculptured bronzes; and for waterproofing wood and paper products.

Paraguay A landlocked country in south-central South America, bordered by Bolivia and Brazil on the north and Argentina on the south.

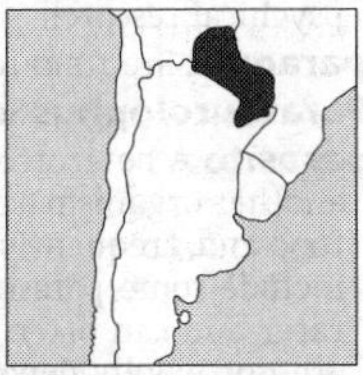

Physical. The navigable Paraguay River, running down the middle of the country, joins the Paraná and provides access to the sea. In the west is the Gran Chaco, a region of black, fertile earth which provides rich pasture and hardwood forests. In the east, the land rises to a low range of forested hills, to the south of which there are swamps and palm-fringed, shallow lakes. Here it can be very damp, with rainfall averaging about 1,800 mm (71 inches) a year.

Economy. Paraguay has a primarily agricultural economy, with cotton and soya beans the principal exports, and subsistence crops of cassava and maize. The construction of the Itaipú dam (1985), the world's largest hydroelectric project, benefited the economy, but high inflation and debt remain a problem. Industry is restricted to textiles, food-processing, and cement. Mineral resources are limited.

History. Paraguay was part of Spain's Rio de la Plata territory from the founding of the capital Asunción in 1537. It was only sparsely settled by Spaniards and was dominated by Jesuit mission villages among the Guaraní Indians until their suppression in 1767. The country achieved its independence (1811) when local Paraguayan military leaders led a bloodless revolt against the Spanish governor. The dictator José Gaspar Rodriguez de Francia ruled the new republic from 1813 to 1840, but the rest of the 19th century was dominated by corruption, coups, and chronic bankruptcy. Francisco Solano López led the country to disaster in the Paraguayan War (1864–70). Political turmoil continued into the 20th century with the exception of the presidency of the liberal Edvard Schaerer (1912–17), which was marked by foreign investment and economic improvements. In the CHACO WAR (1932–35), Paraguay won from Bolivia the long-contested territory believed to have oil reserves. In 1954 General Alfredo Stroessner, supported by the USA, seized power. A massive hydroelectric scheme (the Itaipú dam) was begun and some progress made in settling landless peasants; but cattle exports to Europe fell, the economy declined, and the regime became increasingly brutal. Stroessner lost US support and was deposed in 1989. Elections brought General Andrés Rodríguez to office as President. A liberal party, *Asunción Para Todos* (APTO) emerged, but, with military backing, Rodríguez and his Colorado Party retained power. Paraguay's first multi-party elections were held in 1993, with the civilian Juan Carlos Wasmosy being elected President.

Capital: Asunción
Area: 406,752 sq km (157,048 sq mi)
Population: 4,828,000 (1995)
Currency: 1 guaraní = 100 céntimos
Religions: Roman Catholic 96.0%; Protestant 2.0%
Ethnic Groups: Mestizo 90.0%; Amerindian 3.0%; German 1.7%
Languages: Spanish (official); Guaraní
International Organizations: UN; OAS

parakeet A bird belonging to any of three separate groups of the parrot family. The first includes six birds of the genus *Cyanoramphus*, which occur in New Zealand and a number of other Pacific islands. The second group belongs to the genus *Psittacula*, with 13 species, found mainly on Indian ocean islands and in south-east Asia. The third group belongs to the genera *Brotogeris*, *Forpus*, and *Bolborhynchus*, with 19 species from Central and South America. All are smallish, though some, with the exception of the New World species, have long tails. The rose-ringed parakeet, *P. krameri*, is a common cage-bird which has escaped and become established in the wild in a number of countries, including England.

parallax The apparent displacement of two objects relative to one another when the observer changes his or her viewpoint. The angular shift in direction is called the parallactic angle and the distance of the object can be measured if a suitable baseline of known length is used, the directions of the object being measured from each end of the baseline. This is essentially the surveyor's method of triangulation. Within the Solar System a suitably long baseline is the radius of the Earth, about 6,378 km. The angle subtended at a Solar System object by the Earth's radius at right angles to the direction of the object is the **geocentric parallax** of the object. Most parallaxes are measured in minutes or seconds of arc, so great are the distances to Solar System objects. Even the Moon, the Earth's nearest natural neighbour, has a geocentric parallax of only about 1 degree.

parallels of latitude See LATITUDE AND LONGITUDE.

paralysis Loss or impairment of the sensory or motor function of nerves caused by disease or injury of the nervous system, which results in the inability to feel sensations or initiate movement in the affected part. Paresis is partial, incomplete paralysis. Flaccid paralysis is paralysis with additional loss of tendon reflexes and impaired muscle tone. Spastic paralysis is paralysis with increased tendon reflexes and muscle tone. The extent of paralysis depends on the site of damage, and the area normally innervated by the damaged nerve supply. Hemiplegia is complete paralysis of one side of the body, and may occur following a stroke. Diplegia is paralysis of matching parts on both sides of the body. Paraplegia is paralysis of the lower part of the body, including the legs, which may occur following spinal cord damage caused by injury, cancer, or other diseases. Quadriplegia is paralysis of the arms and legs.

Paramaribo The capital of Surinam, a port on the Atlantic at the mouth of the Surinam River; pop. (est. 1993) 200,920. Founded by the French in 1540, it became capital of British Surinam in 1650, but was placed under Dutch jurisdiction in 1816. Its port trades in bauxite, coffee, fruit, and timber.

Paramecium A genus of freshwater, ciliated PROTOZOANS, and part of the phylum Ciliophora (ciliates). These protozoans are slipper-shaped, about 0.15 mm (0.005 inch) long, and swim actively, engulfing small food particles via mouth and gullet. The surface of all species of *Paramecium* is covered with beating cilia, all interconnected and coordinated, and with trichocysts, tiny toxic barbs, which are discharged into prospective predators or used for anchorage. All ciliates, including *Paramecium*, can reproduce by asexual division, when they simply divide into two halves. Most species can also undergo sexual reproduction by a process called conjugation; two sexually compatible types come together and fuse, eventually dividing into new daughter cells once genetic material has been exchanged.

paramedic A partially qualified person who plays a part in the health care system. Some paramedical workers have substantial training and play a leading role in PRIMARY HEALTH CARE: nurses in some parts of the world carry out basic medical techniques previously performed by doctors. Another group (often known as 'barefoot doctors') are normally recruited from the population they are to serve and are briefly trained for specific functions, such as checking children for IMMUNIZATION or administering malaria medicines. The country most closely associated with the barefoot doctor is China, where millions of peasants were recruited as the basis of a decentralized post-revolutionary health system. In the health care system of a developed country, the paramedic might be a laboratory analyst, radiographer (who operates X-ray machines for diagnosis and treatment), physiotherapist, speech therapist, or pharmacist. New paramedical occupations are constantly evolving: for example, some ambulance staff have been trained to use portable life-saving equipment and do some work once done only by doctors in casualty departments. Their growth has been rapid in recent years, encouraged partly by concerns over the rising cost of medical care.

parameter (in mathematics) A quantity that may have various values but is constant in any particular situation or example. For instance, in the general form of a quadratic function $ax^2 + bx + c$, a, b, and c are parameters, whereas x is the variable. It also means a variable in terms of which the coordinates of a point are expressed. The parametric equations of a circle with radius r are $x = \cos\theta$, $y = r\sin\theta$, and θ is the parameter. In statistics, parameter refers more specifically to a numerical characteristic of a population – for example, the mean or the variance – in contrast to a statistic, which refers to a sample taken of it.

In physics, a parameter is any variable quantity that characterizes a system.

Paraná A river of South America, rising in south-east Brazil and flowing about 3,300 km (2,060 miles) southwards before meeting the River Plate estuary in Argentina. For part of its length it follows the south-east frontier of Paraguay.

paranoia A form of mental disorder in which a person has an exaggerated degree of mistrust in others, in extreme cases a feeling of being persecuted, usually accompanied by a feeling of self-importance. Paranoid ideas may form part of the more general disintegration of thinking found in SCHIZOPHRENIA. More common among men, paranoid delusions bear a disconcerting resemblance to the beliefs propagated by some religious or political leaders. In the 20th century, both Hitler and Stalin expressed paranoid ideas, and murdered those they perceived as persecutors.

paraplegia See PARALYSIS.

parapsychology The study of human experience and behaviour based on the belief that people may gain knowledge or control of their environment in paranormal ways, i.e. by means that cannot be explained by known mechanisms. Landmark experiments were described in Joseph B. Rhine's *Extrasensory Perception* (1934). Participants tried to name the shape printed on a card when neither they nor anyone else was looking at the target card (clairvoyance), when someone else was looking at it (telepathy), or before the cards were shuffled and one shown (precognition). Researchers reported some successful demonstrations of these abilities, which do not, however, seem reliable. Rhine also reported that some people could will dice to fall one way rather than another (psychokinesis). These results do not persuade sceptics, who allege that non-supportive findings tend to be suppressed in psychical research.

paraquat See HERBICIDE.

Parasaurolophus See DINOSAUR.

parasite A heterotrophic organism living in or on another organism (the host), from which it obtains food and, frequently, shelter. Many animal groups include some parasites. Parasitic plants are much rarer and can often photosynthesize so that they are not wholly dependent on their host for food. Occasionally the host may be killed but a 'true' parasite is so well adapted to its host that this is unusual. Ectoparasites live on the outside of their host. Endoparasites may live in the cells of their host (intracellular) or within its body cavities and fluids (extracellular).

Reproduction presents great problems for endoparasites. A secondary host may be used to carry the parasite from one primary host to the next. The mosquito *Anopheles* carries the parasitic protozoan *Plasmodium*, which causes malaria in humans. Most endoparasites need to produce thousands of eggs to ensure that some of their offspring are passed on to other hosts. The endoparasitic ROUNDWORM *Ascaris lumbricoides* can produce 250,000 eggs a day. Some endoparasites are self-fertilizing hermaphrodites, or simply reproduce parthenogenetically, as in APHIDS or parasitic wasps (ICHNEUMON FLIES).

parathyroid glands Two pairs of small endocrine glands lying behind, or embedded within, the thyroid gland. They produce **parathyroid hormone**, which causes a release of calcium from the bones into the blood in response to a fall in the level of calcium in the blood. Deficiency of this hormone can cause muscle spasms and cramps.

parchment (or **vellum**) An animal skin, especially that of a goat, sheep, or calf, prepared to take writing or painting. Rough skins were used up to the 2nd century BC when, at Pergamum (now Bergama in Turkey), smooth skins were prepared by repeated scrapings, first with a blunt iron tool and then with a sharpened scraper. Parchment is now a general term for smooth, thick, high-grade paper made to resemble traditional parchment.

pardolote See FLOWERPECKER.

Paris In Greek mythology, a Trojan prince, son of Priam, of whom it was predicted at his birth that he would bring destruction to Troy. He was left to die, but was brought up by the shepherds who rescued him. He grew into the most handsome of mortal men and was appointed judge in the dispute among the goddesses Aphrodite, Athena, and Hera as to who was the most beautiful. All three tried to bribe Paris and he succumbed to Aphrodite, who promised him the most beautiful woman in the world. This was Helen, and Paris' abduction of her caused the Trojan War. In the war, Paris – a skilful archer – killed Achilles, but he was himself killed by an arrow shot by Philoctetes.

Paris The capital and political, commercial, and cultural centre of France, situated on the River Seine; pop. (1990) 2,175,200. An early settlement on the small island in the Seine, known as the Ile de la Cité, was inhabited by a Gallic people called the Parisii. It was taken by the Romans, who called it Lutetia, in 52 BC. In the 5th century AD it fell to the Frankish king Clovis, who made it his seat of power. It declined under the succeeding Merovingian kings, but was finally established as the capital in 987 under Hugh Capet. The city was extensively developed during the reign of Philippe-Auguste (1180–1223) and organized into three parts; the island of the *cité*, the Right Bank, and the Left Bank. During the reign of Francis I (1515–47) the city expanded again, its architecture showing the influence of the Italian Renaissance. The city's neoclassical architecture characterizes the modernization of the Napoleonic era. This continued under Napoleon III, when the bridges, parks, and boulevards of the modern city were built under the direction of Baron Haussmann. The city's chief landmarks are the Eiffel Tower (1889), Hôtel des Invalides (1671–76), the Arc de Triomphe (1806–36), Pompidou Centre (1977), the Louvre (begun 1546 but largely 17th century), and the 12th–13th-century Notre-Dame Cathedral. Its many workshops manufacture luxury articles of clothing, perfume, and jewellery, whilst heavy industry, such as the making of cars and trucks, is located in the suburban areas. Paris is the transport and communications focus of western Europe with three airports, a large river port, and seven main railway stations.

Paris, Commune of (15 March–26 May 1871) A revolutionary government in Paris. It consisted of 92 members, who defied the provisional government of Thiers and of the National Assembly. The Commune, which had no connection with communism, was an alliance between middle and working classes. Suspicious of royalist strength and opposing the armistice made with Prussia, the Communards wanted to continue the war and were determined that France should regain the principles of the First Republic. With the victorious German army encamped on the hills outside Paris, government troops were sent to remove all cannons from the city. They were bitterly resisted; Paris, demanding independence, broke into revolt. Thiers decided to suppress the revolt ruthlessly. For six weeks Paris was bombarded by government troops and its centre destroyed. Early in May its defences were breached and a week of bitter street fighting followed. Before surrendering, the Communards murdered their hostages, including the Archbishop of Paris. Over 20,000 people were massacred by the government forces, leaving France deeply divided.

Paris, Matthew See MATTHEW PARIS.

Paris, Peace of (1783) The treaty that concluded the American War of INDEPENDENCE. It was mainly engineered by John Jay, Benjamin FRANKLIN, and the Earl of Shelburne, and was damaging to Spain, which regained only Florida. The peace recognized American independence, gave it north-eastern fishing rights, and attempted (unsuccessfully) to safeguard creditors, protect loyalists, and settle the frontier between Canada and the USA. These failures led to 30 years' friction, especially in the NORTHWEST TERRITORY, where Britain retained forts in retaliation, and led to the War of 1812.

parish The smallest unit of ecclesiastical and administrative organization in England. In the 7th and 8th centuries regional churches ('minsters') were founded, staffed by teams of priests who served large 'parochiae' covering the area of perhaps five to 15 later parishes. These were broken up during the 10th to 12th centuries as landowners founded local churches for themselves and their tenants, though it was only in the 12th century that the territories which these served crystallized into a formal parochial system.

parity See SYMMETRY.

Park, Mungo (1771–1806) Scottish explorer. He undertook a series of explorations in West Africa (1795–97), among them being the navigation of the Niger. His experiences were recorded in his *Travels in the Interior of Africa* (1799). He drowned on a second expedition to the Niger (1805–06).

Park, Nick (1958–) British animator. Nick Park has won Oscars for three films which he wrote, directed, and animated using clay models. The films, starring part-time inventor Wallace and his dog Gromit, are *A Grand Day Out* (1992) *The Wrong Trousers* (1993), and *A Close Shave* (1995). Park first became known with *Creature Comforts* (1990), a humorous look at what zoo animals might think of their surroundings.

Park Chung Hee (1917–79) South Korean statesman, President 1963–79. In 1961 he staged a military coup that ousted the country's democratic government. Two years later he was elected President, assuming dictatorial powers in 1971. Under Park's presidency South Korea emerged as a leading industrial nation, with one of the world's highest rates of economic growth. He was assassinated by Kim Jae Kyu (1926–80), the head of the Korean Central Intelligence Agency.

Parker, Charlie (full name Charles Christopher Parker; known as 'Bird' or 'Yardbird') (1920–55) US saxophonist. From 1944 he was based in New York, where he played with Thelonious Monk and Dizzy Gillespie and became one of the key figures of the bebop movement. He is noted especially for his recordings with Miles Davis in 1945.

Parker, Dorothy (Rothschild) (1893–1967) US humorist, literary critic, short-story writer, and poet. She was a leading member of the Algonquin Round Table, a circle of writers and humorists that met in the 1920s and included James Thurber. From 1927 Parker wrote book reviews and short stories for the *New Yorker* magazine, becoming one of its legendary wits. As a poet, she made her name with the best-selling verse collection *Enough Rope* (1927).

Parkinson, James (1755–1824) British surgeon and palaeontologist. He was author of *An Essay on the Shaking Palsy* (1817), describing **Parkinson's disease**, which is a disorder of ageing people characterized by trembling. His work on fossils culminated in the publication of *Organic Remains of a Former World* (3 vols., 1804–11).

Parlement A sovereign judicial authority in France, the chief being in the capital, PARIS. First established in the 12th century, this functioned as a court of appeal, and as a source of final legal rulings. There were also provincial *Parlements*, those of Toulouse, Bordeaux, Rouen, Aix, Grenoble, Dijon, and Rennes. Political importance derived from their power to register royal edicts, and to remonstrate against them. This power could be overidden by the king, either by order or by *lit de Justice* (a personal intervention).

Parliament, British The supreme LEGISLATURE in Great Britain and Northern Ireland, comprising the sovereign, as head of state, and the two chambers, the HOUSE OF COMMONS and the HOUSE OF LORDS. Together, these chambers comprise the Palace of Westminster.

Beginning in the 13th century as simply a formal meeting of the king and certain of his officials and principal lords, Parliament became partly representative, as in Simon de MONTFORT's Parliament (1265), which contained commoners (knights of the shire and burgesses of the boroughs) who were elected in their locality, and in Edward I's MODEL PARLIAMENT (1295).

Until the 16th century, both chambers grew in importance *vis-à-vis* the crown, as it came to be accepted that their approval was needed for grants of taxation; HENRY VIII effected the English REFORMATION through the long-lived Reformation Parliament (1529–36). Kings such as Charles I tried to manage without summoning a parliament (1629–40), but by the 17th century the Commons had made themselves indispensable. Charles I had to call Parliament in 1640 in order to raise money, and Parliament, led by John Pym, led the opposition to him. The Parliamentary side won the ENGLISH CIVIL WAR, and at the end of the COMMONWEALTH period it was the members of the House of Commons who negotiated the RESTORATION of Charles II (1660) and the accession of WILLIAM III and Mary (1688). The legislation enacted in the GLORIOUS REVOLUTION of 1688–89 and the Act of SETTLEMENT (1701) settled the relationship of crown, Lords, and Commons definitively and made clear the ultimate supremacy of the Commons.

Present-day workings of Parliament may be summarized as follows. The Prime Minister and the cabinet (a selected group of ministers from either House) are responsible for formulating the policy of the government. Acts of Parliament in draft form, known as Bills, each of which have to be 'read' (debated) three times in each House, are referred in the House of Commons (and occasionally in the House of Lords) for detailed consideration to parliamentary standing or select committees. The sovereign's powers of government are dependent on the advice of ministers, who in turn are responsible to Parliament. The monarch's prerogatives, exercised through the cabinet or the Privy Council, include the summoning and dissolution of Parliament. The Treaty of Rome, which Britain accepted in 1972 when joining the EUROPEAN COMMUNITY (now the European Union), provided for a gradual development of Community institutions. The British parliamentary system was adopted by many European countries and by most member countries of the COMMONWEALTH OF NATIONS when they gained dominion status or independence.

Parma A city in northern Italy, on the River Parma and the Via Emilia, the second city of Emilia-Romagna after Bologna; pop. (1990) 193,990. Founded by the Romans in 183 BC, it became a bishopric in the 9th century AD and capital of the duchy of Parma and Piacenza in about 1547. Its Teatro Farnese (1618) was one of the first purpose-built theatres in Europe. Parma gives its name to Parmesan, a hard dry type of cheese originally made there, and Parma hams.

Parmenides (fl. 5th century BC) Greek philosopher. Born in Elea in SW Italy, he founded the Eleatic school of philosophers and was noted for the philosophical work *On Nature*, written in hexameter verse. In this he maintained that the apparent motion and changing forms of the Universe are in fact manifestations of an unchanging and indivisible reality.

Parmigianino (born Girolamo Francesco Maria Mazzola) (1503–40) Italian painter. A follower of Correggio, he made an important contribution to early mannerism with the graceful figure style of his frescos and portraits. His works include *Self-Portrait in a Convex Mirror* (1524) and *Madonna with the Long Neck* (1534).

Parnassus, Mount (Greek **Parnassós**) A mountain in central Greece, which rises just north of Delphi to a height of 2,457 m (8,064 ft). Held to be sacred by the ancient Greeks, as was the spring of Castalia on its southern slopes, it was associated with Apollo and the Muses and regarded as a symbol of poetry.

Parnell, Charles Stewart (1846–91) Irish nationalist leader. Elected to Parliament in 1875, Parnell became leader of the Irish Home Rule faction in 1880, and, through his obstructive parliamentary tactics, successfully raised the profile of Irish affairs. In 1886 he supported Gladstone's Home Rule bill, following the latter's conversion to the cause. He was forced to retire from public life in 1890 after the public exposure of his adultery with Mrs Katherine ('Kitty') O'Shea (1840–1905).

parole (or **release on licence**) The release of a prisoner before expiry of the sentence, on the promise of good behaviour. Depending upon the jurisdiction, a prisoner may apply for parole after serving either a minimum amount of time in custody or a certain proportion of his or her sentence. It differs from remission in that it is discretionary, and the parolee must keep to the conditions of release, which will include supervision by a PROBATION officer, or face recall to prison to serve the unexpired portion of his or her sentence.

Paros A Greek island in the southern Aegean, in the Cyclades. It is noted for its fine-textured translucent white marble, which has been quarried here since the 6th century BC; area 195 sq km (75 sq miles). Its chief town is Paros (Paríkia).

Parr, Katherine (1512–48) Sixth and last wife of Henry VIII. Having married the king in 1543, she influenced his decision to restore the succession to his daughters Mary and Elizabeth (later Mary I and Elizabeth I). Soon after Henry's death in 1547 she married Thomas, Baron Seymour of Sudeley, but died after bearing his daughter.

parrot A bird of a very large family, Psittacidae, containing about 330 species, which occur in most of the warmer areas of the world. The family includes parrots, budgerigars, love-birds, parakeets, lorikeets, cockatoos, and macaws. The majority are forest-dwelling species. They vary in size from the tiny buff-faced pygmy parrot, *Micropsitta pusio*, 8.5 cm (3.5 inches) long, from the lowland forest of New Guinea, to the hyacinth macaw, *Anodorhynchus hyacinthinus*, 1 m (3.25 feet) long, from tropical South America.

parrot disease See PSITTACOSIS.

parrotfish A brightly coloured fish of the family Scaridae, which lives on reefs in shallow tropical and subtropical seas. Their teeth are fused to form beak-like tooth plates joined at the midline, while in the back of the throat there are an upper pair of pharyngeal teeth and a single lower set of teeth. These grind up the algae and soft coral rock, which the fish bites off with its powerful front 'beak'. Parrotfishes are responsible for the erosion of many coral reefs. About 70 species are recognized, mostly small and less than 45 cm (18 inches) in length. However, since the two sexes are often differently coloured (the males usually being brighter), and in many species females change sex as they age, there has been much confusion about exactly how many species there are.

Parry, Sir (Charles) Hubert (Hastings) (1848–1918) British composer. He is noted for his choral music, including the cantata *Blest Pair of Sirens* (1887). Parry's best-known work, however, is his setting of William Blake's poem 'Jerusalem' (1916), which has acquired the status of an English national song.

parsec A unit of distance employed in astronomy, equal to that distance at which a star would have a trigonometric PARALLAX of 1 arc second. The word parsec is a contraction of 'parallax-arc second'. One parsec is equivalent to 3.086×10^{16} m, 206,265 ASTRONOMICAL UNITS, or 3.26 LIGHT-YEARS.

Parsi (or **Parsee**) Indian followers of the ancient Persian religion of ZOROASTRIANISM. The Parsis emigrated to India from Iran in about the 8th–10th centuries, to avoid persecution by Muslims. Their belief and worship are based on the *avesta*, the scripture attributed to ZARATHUSTRA (628–*c*.551 BC). Parsis are monotheists but they subscribe to the dualist belief that the Earth is a battleground for the forces of good (*Ahura Mazda*) and evil (*Angra Mainyu*). Religious practice includes the fire temple, where a sacred flame is kept alight, and the tower of silence, upon which the dead are left exposed. Parsis in India live chiefly in Bombay and surrounding areas. In Iran, a sect called the Gabars, numbering about 25,000, maintains the traditions of Zoroastrianism. There are also significant Parsi communities outside India, for example in London.

parsley A biennial herb, *Petroselinum crispum*, which probably originated in southern Europe, but has been cultivated for so long that this is uncertain. It is a member of the carrot family, Umbelliferae. The wild form has a plain, deeply segmented leaf, but the cultivated form has curled and crisped segments. The leaves are used whole or finely chopped as a garnish in a variety of dishes.

parsnip A vegetable derived from a wild biennial species, *Pastinaca sativa*, of the Umbelliferae, or carrot family, that occurs throughout Europe and western Asia. The parsnip has been cultivated for its uniquely flavoured roots since ancient times and has been introduced throughout the world. The tapered yellowish roots contain both sugar and starch, hence their sweet flavour.

Parsons, Sir Charles (Algernon) (1854–1931) British engineer, scientist, and manufacturer. He patented and built the first practical steam turbine in 1884, a 7.5-kW engine designed to drive electricity generators. Many such machines were installed in power stations, and their output was later increased by adding a condenser and using superheated steam. Parsons also developed steam turbines for marine propulsion, the experimental vessel *Turbinia* (which can still be seen in Newcastle) creating a sensation by its unscheduled appearance at a British naval review in 1897. He was also interested in optics, manufacturing searchlight reflectors, large reflecting telescopes, and optical glass.

Parsons, Talcott (1902–79) US sociologist who synthesized the ideas of FUNCTIONALISM and attempted to establish a system of analysis that could encompass all aspects of human behaviour. Parsons emphasized the shared values that make it possible for people to live together. He further argued that the different parts of a society, such as its educational and political systems, play distinctive roles in maintaining its equilibrium. Among his major writings are *The Structure of Social Action* (1937) and *The Social System* (1951).

parthenogenesis A mode of reproduction that involves the development of an unfertilized egg. Animals or plants using this method of reproduction produce offspring that have the usual two pairs of chromosomes per cell but are genetically identical to the parent. Parthenogenetic reproduction may alternate with normal sexual reproduction in plants, such as dandelions, and in animals, such as APHIDS.

Parthenon The temple of Athene Parthenos ('the maiden'), built on the Acropolis at Athens in 447–432 BC by Pericles to honour the city's patron goddess and to commemorate the recent Greek victory over the Persians. Designed by the architects Ictinus and Callicrates with sculptures by Phidias, including a colossal gold and ivory statue of Athene (known from descriptive accounts) and the Elgin Marbles now in the British Museum, the Parthenon was partly financed by tribute from the league of Greek states led by Athens, and housed the treasuries of Athens and the league.

Parthia An ancient Asian kingdom to the south-east of the Caspian Sea, which from *c*.250 BC to *c*.230 AD ruled an empire stretching from the Euphrates to the Indus, with Ecbatana as its capital. The Parthian culture contained a mixture of Greek and Iranian elements and the Parthians were superb horsemen, original and competent in warfare.

particle accelerator A machine used in nuclear physics research to accelerate charged, subatomic particles, such as protons and electrons. These are used to bombard and fragment atomic nuclei, providing information about the structure of matter. The higher the energy of bombardment, the more effective the fragmentation. They are also used commercially to generate high-energy X-rays and gamma rays for industrial and medical radiography, and for RADIOTHERAPY. Accelerator energies are typically measured in millions of electron-volts (MeV).

partita In the late 16th century and the 17th, one of a set of musical variations, as in the titles of a number of volumes of instrumental (especially keyboard) music. Italian and, later, other composers customarily based sets of variations ('parti' or 'partite') on the bass lines of well-known tunes, such as the *folia* or *romanesca*. In late 17th-century Germany it came to be an alternative title for a SUITE. In the 18th century it could be applied loosely to any sort of multi-movement instrumental piece of the suite or sonata type.

Parton, Dolly (Rebecca) (1946–) US singer and songwriter. She is best known as a country-music singer; in the mid-1960s she moved to Nashville and had her first hit in 1967 with 'Dumb Blonde'. Her other hits include 'Joshua' (1971) and 'Jolene' (1974). She has also had a number of film roles.

partridge A bird of which there are a number of species in the pheasant family, Phasianidae, not all closely related, but all medium-sized and short-tailed. They live on the ground in open country and some, such as the Himalayan snow partridge, *Lerwa lerwa*, live high in mountains. All have short, stubby beaks and eat seeds, other vegetation, and also some insects. The European, Hungarian, or grey partridge, *Perdix perdix*, is an important gamebird and has been widely introduced in North America.

part-song A work for several voices (male, female, or mixed) usually, but not always, sung without accompaniment. Though part-songs may make use of COUNTERPOINT, the movement of parts is likely to be more restricted and the real interest concentrated in the top line. Part-songs are often verse-repeating.

Parvati See DEVI.

pascal (symbol Pa) The SI UNIT of pressure equal to one newton per square metre. The unit is named after Blaise Pascal.

Pascal, **Blaise** (1623–62) French mathematician, physicist, and religious philosopher. A child prodigy, before the age of 16 he had proved an important theorem in the projective geometry of conics, and at 19 constructed the first mechanical calculator to be offered for sale. He discovered that air has weight, confirmed that vacuum could exist, and derived the principle that the pressure of a fluid at rest is transmitted equally in all directions. He also founded the theory of probabilities, and developed a forerunner of integral calculus. He later entered a Jansenist convent, where he wrote two classics of French devotional thought, the *Lettres provinciales* (1656–57), directed against the casuistry of the Jesuits, and *Pensées* (1670), a defence of Christianity.

PASCAL See COMPUTER LANGUAGE.

Pashto The Iranian language of the Pathans, the official language of Afghanistan, spoken by some 10 million people there and another 6 million in north-west Pakistan. It is an Indo-Iranian language and, like Persian, is written in a form of the Arabic script.

Pasolini, **Pier Paolo** (1922–75) Italian film director and novelist. Following World War II Pasolini became a Marxist and moved to Rome, where he lived in the city's slums. He drew on his experiences there first for his novels and then his films, including his directorial début, *Accattone!* (1961). Pasolini became recognized for his controversial, bawdy literary adaptations, such as *The Gospel According to St Matthew* (1964) and *The Canterbury Tales* (1973). He was murdered in a Rome suburb.

pasque-flower A perennial plant, *Pulsatilla vulgaris*, with finely divided leaves and purplish cup-shaped flowers, so called because it flowers at Easter. Pasque-flowers are related to buttercups and columbines, which share the same genus. These medicinally useful plants usually grow in chalk grassland throughout Europe and western Asia. Larger-flowered varieties with violet and reddish petals have been developed as garden plants.

passacaglia See CHACONNE.

Passchendaele (or **Passendale**) A village in western Belgium, in West Flanders south of Bruges. During World War I it marked the furthest point of the British advance in the Ypres offensive of 1917 and was the scene of heavy loss of life.

passenger pigeon A now extinct species of dove, *Ectopistes migratorius*, that was formerly one of the most abundant of all bird species, living in huge flocks in North America. Due to a combination of over-hunting and destruction of its woodland habitat, it had become extinct in the wild by about 1900. The last one died in captivity in 1914.

passerine See BIRD.

passion flower, **passion fruit** See PASSION VINE.

passion play A religious play representing the life and crucifixion of Jesus of Nazareth. Performances of such plays are recorded in Europe from the early 13th century. Some formed part of the cycles of MYSTERY PLAYS, others were performed separately, usually on Good Friday. The most famous example today is the *Passionsspiel* still performed by the villagers of OBERAMMERGAU in Bavaria.

passion vine A plant of the family Passifloraceae, which includes 600 species of vines, trees, shrubs, and herbaceous plants, found in the tropics and subtropics. The genus *Passiflora*, with 400–500 species, includes many that are woody climbers with edible fruit (called passion fruit), such as the GRANADILLAS. The purple passion flower, *P. edulis*, and its cultivars are grown in many parts of the world for their round or egg-shaped, aromatic fruit. Most species of *Passiflora* have very distinctive flowers with conspicuous central filaments forming a corona. The flower was once regarded as a symbol of Christ's Passion – hence the name. Several species of *Passiflora* are cultivated as ornamental climbers.

passive resistance Non-violent opposition to a ruling authority or government. It frequently involves a refusal to cooperate with the authorities or a defiant breach of laws and regulations and has been a major weapon of many nationalist, resistance, and social movements in modern times. One of the most successful campaigns was that waged by GANDHI against British rule in India, when widespread civil disturbances and protests persuaded the British to make major concessions. Gandhi's example was an inspiration for the CIVIL RIGHTS movement in the USA from the 1950s, where passive resistance, large-scale demonstrations, and the deliberate breaking of segregation laws brought considerable improvements for the black population.

Passos, **John Dos** See DOS PASSOS.

Passover (Hebrew *Pesach*, 'Feast of Unleavened Bread') A major Jewish festival celebrated in spring (March–April) and lasting eight days. It marks God's angel 'passing over' the houses of the enslaved Jews in Egypt, which had been marked with the blood of a lamb, thus saving their first-born from death and allowing them to escape to the desert. Houses are thoroughly cleaned to remove all leaven (raising agent for bread, such as yeast), because traditionally the Jews ate unleavened bread before their Exodus, having had no time to let it rise. The Seder ('order') meal occurs on the first and second nights. In commemorating the Exodus from slavery, Passover recalls and renews what Jews believe to be the unique historical identity of the Jewish people and their destiny to be saved by God, a destiny emphasized by a series of questions about the meaning of the festival, which must be asked by the youngest present. The answers are found in the *Haggadah*, or narrative, on the Passover story.

pastel A drawing or painting material consisting of a stick of colour made from powdered PIGMENTS mixed with just enough resin or gum to bind them. Pastel is applied directly to paper, and thus the colour as applied represents the final result – no allowance has to be made for changes during drying. Pastel has the disadvantage of being fragile and easily dislodged from the paper. This can be counteracted by using a fixative, though this reduces the brilliance of the colour.

Pasternak, Boris (Leonidovich) (1890–1960) Russian poet, novelist, and translator. On the eve of the Russian Revolution in 1917 he wrote the lyric poems *My Sister, Life* (1922), which established his reputation when published. In the 1930s he started work on the novel *Doctor Zhivago* (1957), a testament to the experience of the Russian intelligentsia during the Revolution. It was banned in the Soviet Union until 1988 but was published abroad; in 1958 Pasternak was awarded the Nobel Prize for literature, but was forced to refuse it under pressure from the Soviet authorities.

Pasteur, Louis (1822–95) French chemist and bacteriologist. His early work, in which he discovered the existence of dextrorotatory and laevorotatory forms of sugars, was of fundamental importance in chemistry, but he is popularly remembered for his 'germ theory' (1865) – that each fermentation process could be traced to a specific living microorganism. Following the success of his introduction of PASTEURIZATION, he developed an interest in diseases. Pasteur isolated bacteria infecting silkworms, finding methods of preventing the disease from spreading. He then isolated the bacteria causing anthrax and chicken cholera, made vaccines against them, and pioneered vaccination against rabies using attenuated virus.

pasteurization A method of FOOD PRESERVATION, particularly for DAIRY PRODUCTS, in which the product is heated to and maintained at a certain temperature (for example 72°C for milk) for a specific time, before being quickly cooled. The process (named after PASTEUR) reduces the bacterial content and activity within a product without unduly affecting its taste or appearance. In wine treated this way the yeast responsible for souring will be destroyed, but not the yeast necessary for FERMENTATION. Pasteurization of milk destroys any tuberculosis bacteria present and improves the milk's storage life, but some bacteria remain. The vitamin C content of milk is slightly reduced by pasteurization.

pastoralist A herder, such as the LAPPS in Europe or the MAASAI in Africa. Many pastoralists practise forms of NOMADISM. Transhumance, or seasonal movement back and forth (for example, the Lapps' move from lowland pasture in the winter to highland pasture in the summer), is a form of pastoralism, and tends to be practised by sheep, reindeer, and goat herders; it is also found among the yak herders of Tibet.

Patagonia A region of South America, in southern Argentina and Chile. Consisting largely of a windswept arid plateau, it extends from the Colorado River in central Argentina to the Strait of Magellan and from the Andes to the Atlantic coast. The region is barren except in the river valleys where grapes and fruit are farmed. Sheep are raised by the descendants of Welsh settlers who came here in the 19th century. Oil production has become increasingly developed. It takes its name from the *Patagon*, a Native American people alleged by 17th–18th-century travellers to be the tallest known people.

Pataliputra The ancient name for PATNA.

patella (or **kneecap**) See LEG.

patent A government authority to an individual or organization, conferring the exclusive right to make, use, or sell a specified invention for a limited time (commonly 20 years in the UK). Patents thus form part of general INTELLECTUAL PROPERTY legislation, like COPYRIGHT, or the registration of TRADEMARKS. Medieval letters patent conferred by a sovereign granted monopolistic control of specific goods to an individual; the earliest evidence of these is from 14th-century Italy. The exclusive monopoly is not conferred automatically, as in the case of copyright; patentees must define and disclose the invention to their national Patent Office, which investigates as far as possible whether the invention is new and non-obvious, and then publishes the application. Protection only has effect in the country in which application has been made, but patents can also be applied for through the Patent Co-operation Treaty, an international system for the multiple filing of patent applications, or the European Patent Convention, which grants protection to an invention in all countries that are parties to the convention. The World Intellectual Property Organization (WIPO), a specialized agency of the UNITED NATIONS, is working towards a treaty setting the norms for patent protection.

Pater, Walter (Horatio) (1839–94) British essayist and critic. He came to fame with *Studies in the History of the Renaissance* (1873), which incorporated his essays on the then neglected Botticelli and on Leonardo da Vinci's *Mona Lisa*; it had a major impact on the development of the Aesthetic Movement. Pater's other works include *Marius the Epicurean* (1885), which develops his ideas on 'art for art's sake'.

Pathan A Pashto-speaking people inhabiting north-west Pakistan and south-east Afghanistan.

Pathé, Charles (1863–1957) French film pioneer. In 1896 he and his brothers founded a company that dominated the production and distribution of films in the early 20th century; it also initiated the system of leasing (rather than selling) copies of films. The firm also became internationally known for its newsreels, the first of which were introduced in France in 1909.

Pathet Lao Laotian communist movement. In the independence struggle after World War II, Pathet Lao forces cooperated with the VIETMINH against French colonial power. After the Geneva Agreement (1954), it emerged as a major political and military force within Laos, seeking the alignment of their country with communist China and North Vietnam. Between the mid-1950s and mid-1970s the Pathet Lao and its political wing, the Neo Lao Hak-sat (Patriotic Party of Laos) under the leadership of Prince Souphanouvong, waged a prolonged political and military struggle for power with non-communist government forces, eventually emerging triumphant with the formation of the People's Democratic Republic of Laos in 1975.

pathogen Any disease-producing microorganism. Pathogenic organisms are parasites, and include a diverse range of bacteria, viruses, fungi and protozoa. If the host's defences are low because of a drop in the efficiency of their immune system through illness, they are susceptible to microorganisms known as **opportunistic pathogens**, which would not normally cause disease in a healthy host. See also COMMUNICABLE DISEASE.

pathology The study of disease processes. Pathology encompasses the study of the causes, mechanisms, effects, and consequences of disease processes. It is studied by examining diseased tissues and samples of body fluids, in addition to sophisticated techniques of analysis. Pathology also combines its knowledge with other specialities, such as IMMUNOLOGY and TOXICOLOGY, for a fuller understanding of disease processes.

Patmore, Coventry (Kersey Dighton) (1823–96) British poet. His most important work is *The Angel in the House* (1854–63), a sequence of poems in praise of married love.

Patmos A Greek island in the Aegean Sea, in the Dodecanese. It is believed that St John was living there in exile (from 95 AD) when he had the visions described in Revelations; area 34 sq km (13 sq miles); its chief town is Hora.

Patna The capital of the state of Bihar in northern India, on the south bank of the Ganges; pop. (1991) 1,098,570. Known as Pataliputra, it was the capital between the 5th and 1st centuries BC of the Magadha kingdom and in the 4th century AD of the Gupta dynasty. After this it declined and had become deserted by the 7th century It was refounded in 1541 by the Moguls, becoming a prosperous city and viceregal capital. Lying at the centre of a rice-growing region.

Paton, Alan (Stewart) (1903–88) South African writer and politician. He is best known for his novel *Cry, the Beloved Country* (1948), a passionate indictment of the apartheid system. Paton helped found the South African Liberal Party in 1953, later becoming its president until it was banned in 1968.

patriarchy The authority and control of men over women, the converse of MATRIARCHY. The concept of patriarchy, according to which men control the social institutions and the dominant ideology, has been seen as the general, perhaps the universal, condition of society. For some apologists, patriarchy is justified by the different reproductive functions of men and women. Gender, the FAMILY, and the processes of socialization can all be viewed in terms of patriarchy: the traditional view of the family as consisting of father-provider and mother-carer, each fulfilling their allotted tasks, is thought to be influential in reinforcing gender stereotypes in children.

patrician A privileged landed aristocrat of early republican Rome. The patricians (or 'fathers') gathered after the expulsion of TARQUIN to guide the state. Supported by revered tradition they were hereditary members of the SENATE. They monopolized all magistracies and priesthoods but during the 'struggle of the Orders' with the plebeians they were forced to share power with them – in 367 BC the consulship was open to plebeians. Thereafter a 'plebeian nobility' arose, which together with the patricians formed the ruling class. Their ranks were thinned and their influence waned in the late republic but the ancient names still carried prestige.

Patrick, St (5th century) Apostle and patron saint of Ireland. His *Confession* is the chief source for the events of his life. Of Romano-British parentage, he was captured at the age of 16 by raiders and shipped to Ireland as a slave; there he experienced a religious conversion. Escaping after six years, probably to Gaul, he was ordained and returned to Ireland in about 432. Feast day, 17 March.

Patton, George Smith (1885–1945) US general. In World War II Patton commanded a corps in North Africa and then the 7th Army in Sicily. He lost his command in 1944 after a publicized incident in which he hit a soldier suffering from battle fatigue, but later led the 3rd Army in the NORMANDY CAMPAIGN. His tendency to make rapid military advance, at times with no regard for supporting units or allies, became evident in 1944 in his spectacular sweep through France, across the Rhine, and into Czechoslovakia. As military governor of Bavaria, he was criticized for his leniency to Nazis. He was killed in a road accident while commanding the US 15th Army.

Paul III (born Alessandro Farnese) (1468–1549) Italian pope 1534–49. He excommunicated Henry VIII of England in 1538, instituted the order of the Jesuits in 1540, and initiated the Council of Trent in 1545. Paul III was also a keen patron of the arts, commissioning Michelangelo to paint the fresco of the *Last Judgement* for the Sistine Chapel and appointed him architect of St Peter's.

Paul, Les (born Lester Polfus) (1915–) US jazz guitarist. In 1946 he invented the solid-body electric guitar for which he is best known; it was first promoted in 1952 as the Gibson Les Paul guitar. In the 1950s he wrote and recorded a number of hit songs with his wife, Mary Ford (1928–77), such as 'Mockin' Bird Hill' (1951).

Paul, St (known as **Paul the Apostle**; born Saul of Tarsus) (died *c*.64) Missionary to the Gentiles. Of Jewish descent, he was brought up as a Pharisee and at first opposed the followers of Jesus, assisting at the martyrdom of St Stephen. On a mission to Damascus, he was converted to Christianity after a vision and became one of the first major Christian missionaries and theologians. His missionary journeys are described in the Acts of the Apostles. Paul's radical understanding of the Christian message provoked hostility, and a riot against him on a visit to Jerusalem led to his arrest by the Roman authorities. He was eventually taken to Rome, where he is thought to have died a martyr's death. Several of Paul's letters to early Christian groups have been preserved in the New Testament of the Bible. Through them his influence on Christian life and thought has been greater than that of any other of the first Christians. Feast day, 29 June.

Pauli, Wolfgang Ernst (1900–58) Austrian-born US physicist who made a major contribution to the theoretical study of energies of electrons in the atom. In 1924 he enunciated the exclusion principle that no more than two electrons can occupy the same ORBITAL in an atom. If they do so, they must have opposite SPINS and therefore different energies. In 1931 he postulated the existence of a new elementary particle, later discovered, called the NEUTRINO. In 1945 he won the Nobel Prize for physics and in 1946 became a US citizen.

Pauling, Linus Carl (1901–94) US chemist, who made major advances in almost all areas of chemistry. His most famous discoveries were the 'α-helix' and 'pleated sheet' protein structures, and the cause of sickle cell anaemia. He aroused controversy with his pacifist rejection of nuclear weapons, for which he was awarded the Nobel Peace Prize in 1962 to add to his Prize for chemistry in 1954.

pavan A dance of Italian origin, possibly from Padua. Popular in the 16th and 17th centuries, it was in duple TIME and fairly stately in character. The pavan was usually paired with the quicker-moving GALLIARD.

Pavarotti, Luciano (1935–) Italian operatic tenor. He made his début as Rudolfo in Puccini's *La Bohème* in 1961, and achieved rapid success in this and a succession of other leading roles, including Edgardo in Donizetti's *Lucia di Lammermoor* and the Duke in Verdi's *Rigoletto* (both 1965). He has been widely acclaimed for his bel canto singing.

Pavese, Cesare (1908–50) Italian novelist, poet, and translator. He is best known for his last novel *La Luna e i falò* (1950), in which he portrays isolation and the failure of communication as a general human predicament. Pavese also made many important translations of works written in English, including novels by Herman Melville, James Joyce, and William Faulkner. He committed suicide in 1950.

Pavia A university city of Lombardy in northern Italy, situated at the junction of the Ticino and Po rivers; pop. (1990) 80,070. It is capital of the province of Pavia. Formerly confined within medieval city walls, its industrial development dates from the late 19th century. Light industries include food processing, agricultural machinery, textiles, and sewing machines.

Pavlov, Ivan (Petrovich) (1849–1936) Russian physiologist. He was awarded a Nobel Prize in 1904 for his work on digestion, but is best known for his later studies on the conditioned reflex. He showed by experiment with dogs how the secretion of saliva can be stimulated not only by food but also by the sound of a bell associated with the presentation of food, and that this sound comes to elicit salivation when presented alone. Pavlov applied his findings to show the importance of such reflexes in human and animal behaviour.

Pavlova, Anna (Pavlovna) (1881–1931) Russian dancer, resident in Britain from 1912. As the prima ballerina of the Russian Imperial Ballet she toured Russia and northern Europe in 1907 and 1908. Her highly acclaimed solo dance *The Dying Swan* was created for her by Michel Fokine in 1905. After brief appearances with the Ballets Russes in 1909, Pavlova made her New York and London débuts the following year. On settling in Britain, she formed her own company.

Pavo The Peacock, a CONSTELLATION of the Southern sky introduced by the Dutch navigators Pieter Dirkszoon Keyser and Frederick de Houtman at the end of the 18th century. Its brightest star is Alpha Pavonis, magnitude 1.9, named Peacock after the constellation itself.

Pawnee A tribe of North American Indians of the Hokan-Caddoan linguistic group, originally occupying the plains and prairies of Nebraska.

pawpaw See PAPAYA.

Paxton, Sir Joseph (1801–65) British gardener and architect. He became head gardener to the Duke of Devonshire at Chatsworth House in Derbyshire in 1826, and designed a series of glass-and-iron greenhouses. He later reworked these, making the first known use of prefabricated materials, in his design for the Crystal Palace for London's Great Exhibition in 1851.

Paz, Octavio (1914–98) Mexican poet and essayist. His poems are noted for their preoccupation with Aztec mythology, as in *Sun Stone* (1957). He is also known for his essays, particularly *The Labyrinth of Solitude* (1950), a critique of Mexican culture, and *Postscript* (1970), a response to Mexico's brutal suppression of student demonstrators in 1968. Paz was awarded the Nobel Prize for literature in 1990.

PC ▶**1** Personal computer. See MICROCOMPUTER. ▶**2** Politically correct. See POLITICAL CORRECTNESS.

pea A climbing, annual plant of the genus *Pisum*, with terminal leaflets modified into tendrils. It gives its name to the pea family, Leguminosae (LEGUMES), one of the largest plant families, with over 17,000 species of trees, shrubs, climbers, and herbaceous plants. This worldwide family includes BEANS, PEANUTS, VETCHES, and ACACIAS. Their characteristic features include divided leaves, a single carpel on the flower, root nodules containing nitrogen-fixing bacteria, and seeds that are held inside pods.

Several species of pea have been cultivated since prehistoric times but only *P. sativum* is widely grown now. It probably originated in the Middle East. The pods contain numerous seeds, which vary in size and form according to variety. Mangetout peas have tender pods, which can be eaten whole if they are picked before the seeds swell.

peach A small, deciduous tree that originated in China as *Prunus persica*. This species has been cultivated throughout the warm, temperate zone of the Old World since ancient times and has given rise to many varieties. Closely related to the almond and cherry, the peach belongs to the rose family along with apples, pears, and many other shrubs, herbs, and trees. The velvety skin of the peach fruit is greenish-white, or yellow, often flushed with red. The flesh also varies from white to yellow, according to variety. Some varieties of the peach tree are grown for their ornamental white, pink, or red flowers, but all require warmth for satisfactory culture. The NECTARINE is one of the most distinct varieties of peach.

peacock (or **peafowl**) A bird of the genus *Pavo*, which contains three species in the pheasant family, Phasianidae. The male common peacock, *Pavo cristatus*, came originally from India and Sri Lanka and is famous for its beautiful train of multicoloured feathers, which it fans during courtship. This is a noted example of sexual selection, in which a trait becomes more pronounced because it advertises mate quality.

Peacock, Thomas Love (1785–1866) British novelist and poet. He is chiefly remembered for his prose satires, including *Nightmare Abbey* (1818) and *Crotchet Castle* (1831), lampooning the romantic poets.

peacock butterfly A species of BRUSH-FOOTED BUTTERFLY, *Inachis io*, with large spectacular eyespots; it occurs throughout Eurasia and is common almost everywhere that its larval food plant (nettles) thrives. If threatened by a bird, the peacock butterfly orientates the eye-markings towards the attacker and makes a hissing noise by rubbing the wings together.

peacock moth See EMPEROR MOTH.

peacock worm See FANWORM.

Peak District A limestone plateau at the southern end of the Pennines in Derbyshire, England, rising to a height of 636 m (2,088 ft) at Kinder Scout. A national park was established in 1951 over 1,404 sq km (542 sq miles) of the Peak District.

Peake, Mervyn (Laurence) (1911–68) British novelist, poet, and artist, born in China. He is principally remembered for the trilogy comprising *Titus Groan* (1946), *Gormenghast* (1950), and *Titus Alone* (1959), set in the surreal world of Gormenghast Castle. Peake was also a notable book illustrator.

peanut (or **groundnut, monkeynut**) An annual LEGUME, *Arachis hypogaea*, of South American origin widely cultivated throughout the tropical and subtropical areas of the world. The wrinkled fibrous pods contain two to four red or brown seeds with white flesh, harvested from below soil level. After fertilization, the flowering stalks grow downwards into the soil where the seed pod develops, perhaps safe from predators. This habit has earned the plant the alternative name of groundnut. The seeds are extremely nutritious, containing about 30 per cent protein and up to 50 per cent oil, and are rich in vitamins B and E. The whole seeds (for they are not true nuts) may be cooked, as in tropical Africa, or eaten raw or roasted, with the skins removed, as in the USA and Europe. The edible oil is important in world trade and is widely used for cooking, for margarine, and for soaps and lubricants. The protein-rich seed residue is widely used in animal feeding after the oil has been extracted or expelled.

peanut worm See SIPUNCULID.

pear A tree that has been grown throughout Europe and western Asia since the earliest historical times. There are several wild species, but cultivated pears are all descended from *Pyrus communis*, a large, deciduous, long-lived tree, growing up to 15 m (49 feet) in height, which is slow to bear fruit. Pears belong to the rose family and are related to the apple, cherry, and peach. Pears are now often grafted on to quince rootstocks so that they fruit earlier. The green fruits of pears are classified as dessert fruit, cooking pears, or perry pears, which are crushed and used to produce a type of cider.

Pearl Harbor A harbour on the Pacific island of Oahu, in Hawaii, the site of a major US naval base, where a surprise attack on 7 December 1941 by Japanese carrier-borne aircraft, inflicted heavy damage and brought the USA into World War II.

pearl mussel An elongate, slightly kidney-shaped, fresh-water BIVALVE of the genus *Margaritifera*, cultivated in Roman times because they often produce tiny pearls in the body wall in response to an irritating parasite.

pearl oyster An oyster that occurs in warmer Pacific seas, and produces the finest natural pearls by coating any foreign object intruding within their shell valves with the same iridescent mother-of-pearl material, called nacre, that lines their shells. All BIVALVES do this, but in most types the resultant pearl will be very irregular, or fuses to the shell itself, so becoming commercially useless. Pearl oysters, such as *Pinctada margaritifera* and *P. mertensi*, can be 'seeded' artificially, producing valuable pearls within three years.

pearly nautilus The only CEPHALOPOD mollusc with an external shell, *Nautilus macromphalus*. The shell is secreted as a spiralled series of gas-filled buoyancy chambers. It can be found in the tropical Pacific from the surface down to 500 m (1,600 feet). The animal occupies the most recently made shell chamber, with its 38 tentacles projecting. During its nocturnal feeding activities, the nautilus usually swims backwards.

Pears, Sir Peter (1910–86) British operatic tenor. Pears was celebrated in his own right as a singer of oratorio, lieder, and opera, but it is for his lifelong partnership with Benjamin Britten that he is particularly known. Pears created the title roles in most of Britten's operas, notably *Peter Grimes* (1945). With Britten he founded and organized the annual Aldeburgh Festival from 1948.

Pearson, Karl (1857–1936) British biologist and mathematician who wrote *The Grammar of Science* (1892), which stimulated a generation of young scientists. He applied statistical measurement to the Darwinian theory of evolution by natural selection. Later in his life, his energy was a prime factor in the establishment of statistical laboratories throughout the USA and Europe.

Pearson, Lester Bowles (1897–1972) Canadian diplomat and Liberal statesman, Prime Minister 1963–68. As Secretary of State for External Affairs (1948–57) he headed the Canadian delegation to the United Nations, served as chairman of NATO (1951), and acted as a mediator in the resolution of the Suez crisis (1956), for which he received the Nobel Peace Prize in 1957. Pearson became leader of the Liberal Party in 1958; he resigned as Prime Minister and Liberal Party leader in 1968.

Peary, Robert Edwin (1856–1920) US explorer. He made eight Arctic voyages before becoming the first person to reach the North Pole, on 6 April 1909.

Peasants' Revolt (1381) A social uprising in England. Widespread unrest caused by repressive legislation, such as the Statute of Labourers (1351) was brought to a head by the imposition of the POLL TAX of 1380. The revolt drew support from artisans, VILLEINS, and the destitute. Men from Kent and Essex, led by Wat TYLER and John BALL, entered London, massacring some merchants and razing the palace of the Duke of Lancaster. The young king Richard II promised the men the abolition of serfdom, cheap land, and free trade. The rebels then occupied the Tower of London and beheaded the Archbishop and the king's Treasurer. The king persuaded the rebels to disperse, promising them further reforms. Tyler was murdered by the enraged Mayor of London, and the militant bishop of Norwich crushed the rebels in East Anglia. The government re-established control and reneged on the monarch's promise. The revolt succeeded only as a protest against the taxation of the poor and the further levying of the Poll Tax.

Peasants' War (1524–26) A mass revolt of the German lower classes during the REFORMATION. It began in south-west Germany and spread down the River Rhine and into Austria. Frustrated by economic hardships, the rebels were encouraged by radical PROTESTANT preachers to expect a second coming of Jesus Christ and the establishment of social equality and justice. They raided and pillaged in uncoordinated bands, driving LUTHER to condemn them in his fierce broadsheet *Against the thieving and murdering hordes of the peasants* (1525). Luther also supported the army of the Swabian League under Philip of Hesse, which helped to crush the main body of insurgents at Frankenhausen. Over 100,000 rebels were eventually slaughtered.

peat A dark brown deposit consisting of the compressed, partly carbonized remains of plants. It represents an early stage in the formation of lignite and more bituminous forms of COAL, being formed less than 1 million years ago. If dried out, peat will burn, although it produces ammonia fumes. Peat is also cut for use as a soil enricher in horticulture. It is common in Canada, and northern and central Europe, and forms in swampy areas. The decaying organic matter may, in marshlands, emit an inflammable gas (phosphine), whose spontaneous combustion gives rise to the phosphorescent light (*ignis fatuus*) seen hovering over peaty ground.

pecan A large tree, *Carya illinoensis*, that grows up to 60 m (195 feet) tall. It is found along streams in the arid areas of Mexico and southern-central USA. In North America it is now widely cultivated in orchards, where it is kept pruned to 15 m (48 feet). A relative of the walnut in the family Juglandaceae, the fruit of the pecan is a nut with a smooth red shell and a sweet flesh.

peccary A member of the family Tayassuidae, and the New World equivalent of the PIG. There are three species found in South and Central America. They are forest animals that travel in groups of a few to 300 individuals. They dig for tubers and roots, and also eat fruit and small animals, including snakes. The collared peccary, *Tayassu tajacu*, occurs from sea-level up to altitudes of 5,500 m

(18,000 feet). It has thick, coarse, bristly hair, grizzled in colour, with a light-coloured 'collar' almost encircling the body at the shoulders. The peccary reaches a height of 50 cm (20 inches) at the shoulders. The white-lipped peccary, *T. pecari*, and Chacoan peccary, *Catagonus wagneri*, are larger, and live in tropical and thorny forests respectively.

Peck, (Eldred) Gregory (1916–) US actor. He made his screen début in 1944. His many films range from the thriller *Spellbound* (1945) to the western *The Big Country* (1958). Peck won an Oscar for his role as the lawyer Atticus in the literary adaptation *To Kill a Mockingbird* (1962). Later films include *The Omen* (1976) and *The Old Gringo* (1989).

pectin A carbohydrate combined with cellulose that occurs in the cell walls of plants. Normally present in an insoluble form, in ripening fruits and tissues affected by certain diseases it changes into a soluble form, causing the tissues to soften. The jelly-like soluble form of pectin is an essential ingredient in jam-making, causing the jam to set.

pedalfer A zonal soil formed in an area with more than 60 cm (25 inches) of rain a year, where moisture for LEACHING is therefore abundant. Soluble salts are washed out of the soil, which is, therefore, characteristically abundant in iron and aluminium. Soils of this sort are widespread throughout the eastern USA. PODZOLS, ALFISOLS, and OXISOLS are examples of pedalfer soil.

pediment (in geomorphology) A broad plain of eroded bedrock surrounding upland in deserts and semi-deserts. There is usually a very sharp change in slope angle between the upland and the even-surfaced pediment, which generally has a gradient of less than 11°. While some pediments show the bare rock, most have at least a thin covering of ALLUVIUM, which gets gradually thicker away from the upland, until an alluvial plain called a 'bajada' is formed.

pedipalp An important paired structure in ARACHNIDS, which is situated just behind the jaws. In spiders the pedipalps are used by the male for sperm transfer, and are enlarged and knob-like resembling boxing gloves. The space within the knob is filled with sperm by dipping it into a globule of semen previously deposited on a tiny silken mat, after which the filled pedipalp is inserted into the female.

In scorpions and false scorpions the pedipalps are modified as the pincers. In mites and ticks they are reduced in size and used as additional mouthparts or lost altogether.

pedocal A zonal soil formed in relatively dry climates where evaporation rates are high and rainfall is generally less than 60 cm (25 inches) a year. In these conditions soluble salts, such as calcium carbonate, are not removed by LEACHING but accumulate within the profile, making the soil alkaline. Soils of this sort are widespread throughout the western USA. Desert soils, BROWN SOILS, and ARIDISOLS are all examples of pedocals.

pedology (from Greek *pedon*, 'ground') The scientific study of the soil. Soil is an important natural resource that supports the growth of plants for food, timber, and many other purposes. Certain types of soil can be used as building material, while others contain valuable mineral deposits. An understanding of how soil forms and why it differs from place to place is essential if man is to make the best of agriculture, forestry, etc.

Peeblesshire A former county of Scotland, the greater part of which is now part of Scottish Borders local government area (unitary authority). From 1975 to 1996 it was included in Tweeddale District in the Borders Region. Its county town was Peebles.

PEEK (polyether etherketone) See COMPOSITE.

Peel, Sir Robert (1788–1850) British Conservative statesman, Prime Minister 1834–35 and 1841–46. During his second term as Home Secretary (1828–30) Peel established the Metropolitan Police (and gave his name to the nicknames *bobby* and *peeler*). As leader of the new Conservative Party he affirmed his belief in moderate electoral reform in the Tamworth Manifesto (1834). His repeal of the Corn Laws in 1846, however, split the Conservatives and forced his resignation. In the last years of his career he came to support the Whig policies of free trade.

Pegasus (in Greek mythology) A winged horse that sprang from the blood of Medusa the Gorgon when Perseus killed her. Pegasus was ridden by Perseus when he rescued Andromeda, and by Bellerophon when he killed the Chimaera.

Pegasus (in astronomy) The Winged Horse, a CONSTELLATION of the northern sky, one of the 48 constellations known to the ancient Greeks. It represents the forequarters of the mythical horse, and it is the seventh-largest constellation. Its body is outlined by the four stars of the **Square of Pegasus**: Alpha, Beta, and Gamma Pegasi and Alpha Andromedae.

pegmatite An extremely coarse-grained igneous rock with crystals that may be up to several metres (tens of feet) in length. The composition varies, but granite pegmatites are the most common and are usually referred to simply as pegmatites.

Pei, I(eoh) M(ing) (1917–) US architect, born in China. His name is associated with monumental public buildings, in which simple geometric forms are placed in dramatic juxtaposition. Major works include the John F. Kennedy Memorial Library at Harvard University (1964), the east wing of the National Gallery of Art, Washington, DC (1971–78), and the glass and steel pyramid in the forecourt of the LOUVRE, Paris (1989).

Peirce, Charles Sanders (1839–1914) US philosopher and logician. One of the founders of American pragmatism, he proposed a theory of meaning in which the meaning of a belief or an idea is to be understood by the actions, uses, and habits to which it gives rise. Logic was central to Peirce's philosophic concerns. He also pioneered the logic of relations, in which he argued that induction is an indispensable correlative of deduction, and, as a formal logician, discovered the quantifier shortly after Gottlob FREGE.

Peisistratus See PISISTRATUS.

Peking See BEIJING.

Peking Man The numerous remains of *Homo erectus pekinensis* (originally *Sinanthropus pekinensis*) found at ZHOUKOUDIAN near Peking (now Beijing) in China since 1927. The term is often used for all HOMO ERECTUS fossils from China.

pekin robin See BABBLER.

Pelagius (*c*.360–*c*.420) British or Irish monk. He denied the doctrines of original sin and predestination, defending innate human goodness and free will. His beliefs were opposed by St Augustine of Hippo and condemned as heretical by the Synod of Carthage in about 418.

pelargonium A perennial plant or small shrub native to South Africa, often with scented leaves and large, colourful flowers. Pelargoniums are often called GERANIUMS, although they do not belong to the genus of this name. The genus *Pelargonium*, along with true geraniums (*Geranium* species), forms a major part of the family Geraniaceae, with some 750 species of subtropical and temperate-region plants.

Pelé (born Edson Arantes do Nascimento) (1940–) Brazilian footballer. He played for Brazil at the age of 17, scoring twice in his country's victory in the World Cup Final of 1958. In all he appeared 111 times for Brazil, scoring 97 goals, including one in the 1970 World Cup Final victory. Regarded as one of the greatest footballers of all time, he ended his career with New York Cosmos (1975–77) and is credited with over 1,200 goals in first-class soccer.

Pelée, Mount An intermittently active volcano on the island of Martinique, in the West Indies. Its eruption in 1902 destroyed the town of St Pierre, which at that time was the island's capital, killing its population of some 30,000 and rendering a large area a complete wasteland. It rises to a height of 1,397 m (4,583 ft).

Pelham, Henry (1696–1754) British Whig statesman, Prime Minister 1743–54. After serving in Sir Robert Walpole's Cabinet from 1721 onwards, he replaced him as Premier, and introduced a period of peace and prosperity by bringing to an end the War of the Austrian Succession (1740–48).

pelican A member of a family of water-birds allied to boobies and cormorants, the Pelecanidae, and well known for its very large beak and extraordinary throat pouch. They appear ponderous creatures, but are majestic and spectacular both in flight and on the water. The brown pelican of North America, *Pelecanus occidentalis*, catches fish by plunging into the water from above like a booby, but most species are surface-feeders, dipping their heads under water or scooping prey up in their throat pouches. Pelicans are gregarious birds; they often hunt in parties, roost communally, and usually nest in colonies. The eight species are widely distributed in warmer latitudes.

Pelletier, Pierre-Joseph (1788–1842) French chemist. He specialized in plant products, and began with a study of gum resins and pigments. He is best known as the founder of alkaloid chemistry, having isolated a number of alkaloids for the first time with his friend Joseph-Bienaimé Caventou (1795–1877). Pelletier and Caventou also isolated the green pigment of leaves and gave it the name *chlorophyll*.

pellitory A slender, perennial herbaceous plant that belongs to the stinging-nettle family, Urticaceae. The common European pellitory of the wall, *Parietaria judaica*, is a plant used medicinally for complaints of the bladder. As its name suggests, it typically grows on walls.

Peloponnese, the (or **Peloponnesus**; Greek **Pelopónnisos**) The mountainous southern peninsula of Greece, connected to the mainland by the Isthmus of Corinth and comprising the departments of Corinth, Achaia, Elis, Arcadia, Argolid, Messenia, and Laconia; area 21,321 sq km (8,235 sq miles); pop. (1991) 1,077,000. Patras is the largest city. Its Greek name means 'Island of Pelops'.

Peloponnesian War The war waged between Athens and Sparta and their respective allies between 431 and 404 BC. Sparta invaded Attica with its allies in 431, but PERICLES had persuaded the

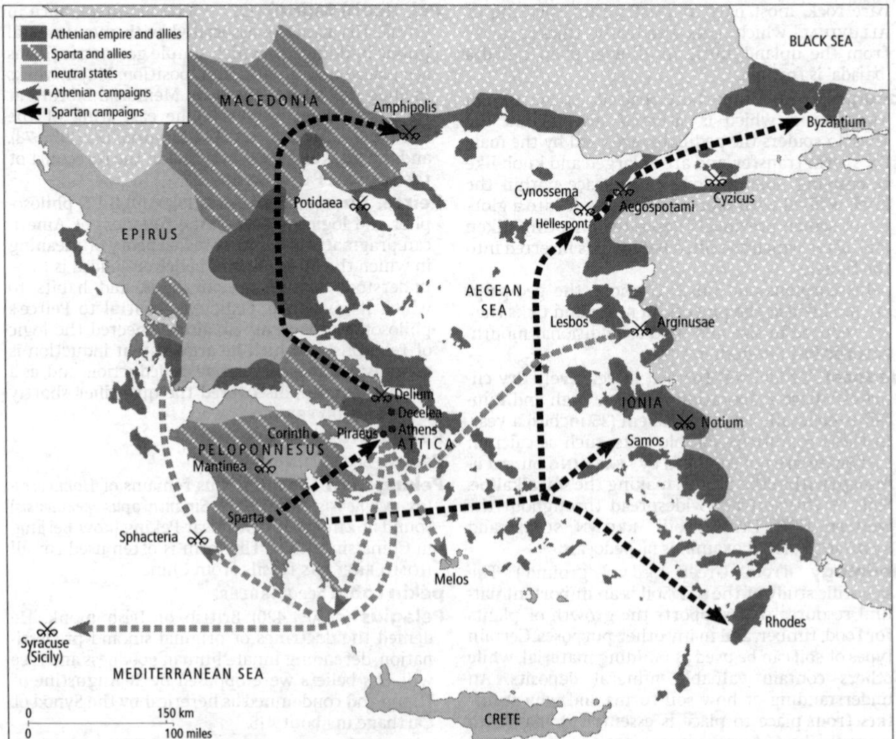

Peloponnesian War Sparta, a powerful land force, overran Attica in 431 BC. Athens, strong at sea, could not be defeated until its fleet was captured at Aegospotami in 404 BC.

Athenians to withdraw behind the 'long walls', which linked Athens and its port of Piraeus, and avoid a land-battle with Sparta's superior army. Athens relied on its fleet of TRIREMES to raid the Peloponnese and guard its empire and trade-routes. It was struck a serious blow by an outbreak of plague in 430, which killed about a third of the population, including Pericles. Nevertheless the fleet performed well and a year's truce was made in 423 BC.

The Peace of Nicias was concluded in 421 BC, but Alcibiades orchestrated opposition to Sparta in the Peloponnese, though his hopes were dashed when Sparta won a victory at Mantinea in 418. He was also the main advocate of an expedition to Sicily (415–413), aimed at defeating Syracuse, that ended in complete disaster for Athens. War was formally resumed in 413 BC. Athenian fortunes revived, with naval victories at Cynossema (411), Cyzicus (410), and the recapture of Byzantium (408). There was a further victory at Arginusae in 406. From then on, Persian financial support for Sparta and the strategic and tactical skills of the Spartan LYSANDER tilted the balance. Sparta's victory at Aegospotami and its control of the Hellespont starved Athens into surrender in April 404. An oligarchic coup followed immediately, supported by Sparta, and the reign of terror of the 'Thirty Tyrants', but democracy was restored in 403.

pelota A group of handball games derived from the French *jeu de paume* and especially popular in Latin America. In *rebot*, a five-a-side game played in the Basque provinces, players catch the ball in a wicker basket attached to the wrist and hurl it back against the end wall of the court. The speed of the ball makes it one of the fastest of all ball games. *Jai alai*, which is extremely popular in Mexico and Florida, is another variant of pelota.

Pelton wheel See WATER TURBINE.

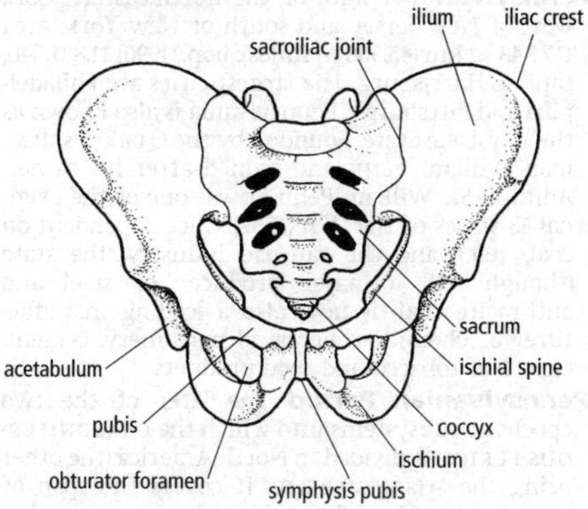

Pelvis The human pelvis is formed by the hip bones (ilium, ischium, and pubis) and the sacrum and coccyx of the spine.

pelvis The lower part of the abdomen in most vertebrates, or more specifically the bony structure formed by the hip bones and lower part of the spine. It is shaped differently in male and female. In the female, the pelvis is broader and the central space rounder, wider, and with smoother walls, for the easier exit of the foetus. Measurement of skeletal pelvic remains can reveal the sex of the individual. The pelvic contents consist of internal male or female sex organs, the bladder, and the rectum.

Pembrokeshire A county of south-west Wales, which was incorporated into the county of Dyfed between 1974 and 1996; pop. (1996) 117,000. Its county town is Haverfordwest.

PEN (Poets, Playwrights, Editors, Essayists, Novelists) An international association of writers, founded in London in 1921. Membership of the association is open to all writers who subscribe to its principles. PEN fights for FREEDOM OF EXPRESSION and against CENSORSHIP throughout the world, supporting those who have been imprisoned or harassed for speaking out against their governments, or for publishing unpopular views; it raises money for refugee writers; and it promotes the translation of works by its members.

Penderecki, Krzysztof (1933–) Polish composer. His music frequently uses unorthodox effects, including sounds drawn from extra-musical sources and note clusters, as in his *Threnody for the Victims of Hiroshima* (1960) for 52 strings. Penderecki's many religious works include *Stabat Mater* (1962), a fusion of conventional and avant-garde elements, and the *Polish Requiem* (1980–84).

pendulum A weight suspended from a fixed point and able to swing freely under the influence of gravity. In about 1602, GALILEO discovered that, for small amplitudes, the time of swing (t) of a pendulum is dependent only on its length (l) and not on its amplitude or the size of the weight, i.e. $t = 2\pi (l/g)$, where g is the acceleration of free fall. He realized that this had great possibilities for the measurement of time, and pendulums began to be used for astronomical observations. In 1657, Christiaan Huygens patented an invention using a pendulum to regulate the mechanism of a CLOCK. Pendulum clocks remained the most accurate time keeping devices until the introduction of the quartz clock in 1929.

Penelope In Greek mythology, the faithful wife of Odysseus. During his absence she was wooed by many suitors; unwilling to repulse them outright, she prevaricated by saying that before marrying she had first to finish weaving the robe on her loom, which she worked every day and then unpicked each night until Odysseus returned.

Penghu See PESCADORES.

penguin A flightless seabird with 17 living species in the family Spheniscidae. Confined entirely to the Southern Hemisphere, they range from the Galápagos penguin, *Spheniscus mendiculus*, to those of Antarctica (emperor and Adélie). Emperors, *Aptenodytes forsteri*, are the largest, standing 1 m (3 feet), and blue or fairy penguins, *Eudyptula minor*, are the smallest at 20 cm (8 inches). Their modified wings act as flippers to propel them through the water; webbed feet and stiff tail feathers act as a rudder. Food includes fish and swimming or floating crustaceans; larger species dive for bottom-feeding fish and squid. Most nest colonially, some in huge colonies. Tropical species nest under cover, some in burrows and caves.

penicillin Any of various ANTIBIOTICS produced naturally by moulds of the genus *Penicillium*, or synthetically, and able to prevent the growth of certain disease-causing bacteria. In 1928 Alexander FLEMING isolated the first penicillin, from the mould *Penicillium notatum*. In 1939 FLOREY and CHAIN at Oxford, UK, began an investigation of penicillin as part of a wider study of antibiotic action. They showed that it had unique properties: minimal toxicity to animal tissues and an antibacterial activity far greater than that of other drugs. Penicillin first became available in 1941, and it was used to treat military casualties during World War

II. Penicillins are still widely used in certain situations, for example, in the treatment of some forms of meningitis. However, not all bacteria are sensitive to the drug, and even those that are may develop permanent resistance, though this has been countered to some extent by the use of chemically altered varieties.

penillion Traditional Welsh music-making, in which a singer improvises a poem (or makes use of existing words) as a COUNTERPOINT to a well-known melody played on the harp. The harp always starts first with a plain statement of the melody and then accompanies the voice with a set of improvised variations. Singer and harpist (usually the same person) then end together.

Peninsular War (1807–14) One of the NAPOLEONIC WARS, fought in Spain and Portugal. War was caused by NAPOLEON's invasion of Portugal (1807) in order to compel it to accept the CONTINENTAL SYSTEM. In 1808 the conflict spread to Spain, whose king was forced to abdicate, Napoleon's brother Joseph Bonaparte being placed on the throne. In June the Spanish revolted and forced the French to surrender at Baylen, whereupon Joseph fled from Madrid. In August Wellesley (later the Duke of WELLINGTON) landed in Portugal and routed a French force at Vimeiro and expelled the French from Portugal. In November Napoleon personally went to Spain, winning a series of battles, including Burgos, and restoring Joseph to the throne. British hopes of pushing the French out of Spain were dashed in January 1809, after MOORE's retreat to Corunna. Despite his victory at Talavera, Wellesley withdrew to Lisbon. Here he built a strong defensive line, which he centred at Torres Vedras. In 1810 Napoleon sent Massena to reinforce Soult and drive the British into the sea. Massena attempted to lay siege to Torres Vedras, but after four months his army, starved and demoralized, was forced to retreat. Soult, jealous of Massena's command, was slow in coming to his support, but managed to capture Badajoz. Wellington, who had pursued Massena and defeated him at Almeida, withdrew from invading Spain and turned to face Soult. During 1812 Wellington recaptured Badajoz and after defeating Massena's replacement, Marmont, at Salamanca, entered Madrid. The following year he defeated Joseph at the decisive Battle of Vitoria. He went on to defeat Soult at Orthez and Toulouse (1814), having driven the French out of Spain.

penis The male copulatory organ in mammals and some birds and reptiles, or a similar organ in some invertebrates, including slugs and snails. In mammals, in which it is also the urinatory organ, the penis is essentially a tube, called the urethra, surrounded by spongy, erectile tissue. In some, including humans, the tip is expanded into a cone-shaped structure called a glans, which is covered by the prepuce, an extension of skin lined by mucous membrane which keeps it moist.

The urethra connects to the bladder and is used to void urine. It is also used as a duct to transfer sperm from the testes into the female vagina during copulation, when the organ is erect. Erection of the penis is caused by blood entering the cavernous spaces within membrane-bound tissue but being prevented from leaving by contraction of all draining veins.

With the exception of man, most primates, rodents, and several other animal groups, have a bone, called a baculum, within the erectile tissue. In animals erection is most usually caused by olfactory stimuli coming from a receptive female. In man, erection is under voluntary as well as emotional control. The glans is liberally supplied with sensory nerves which when stimulated by friction within the vagina lead to the forceful ejection of semen.

penis worm A small, sluggish, seashore creature of which only eight species are known. It is placed in a separate phylum, Priapulida, because of its unique body structure. Its body is cucumber-shaped, with a protrusible proboscis at the front and, in *Priapulus bicaudatus*, two frilly 'gills' at the back.

Penis worms burrow in soft sand, feeding on passing invertebrates, such as polychaete worms, using spines around the tip of their proboscis. They are simply built worm-like animals, lacking segmentation, blood vessels, or eyes, and have a primitive nervous system. They have been found off the coasts of North America and Siberia, and in the Baltic sea and Antarctic waters. There is still controversy about which other groups of animals may be their nearest relatives.

Penn, William (1644–1718) English Quaker, founder of Pennsylvania. He was imprisoned in the Tower of London in 1668 for writing in defence of Quaker practices. Acquitted in 1670, he was granted a charter to land in North America by Charles II (1682), using it to found the colony of Pennsylvania as a sanctuary for Quakers and other Nonconformists in the same year. Penn also co-founded the city of Philadelphia.

Pennines (or **Pennine Chain**) A range of hills in northern England extending northwards from the Peak District in Derbyshire to the Scottish border. Described as the 'Backbone of England', its highest peak is Cross Fell (893 m, 2,930 ft). A long-distance footpath known as the **Pennine Way** stretches for 402 km (251 miles) along the full length of the Pennines.

Pennsylvania A state of the north-eastern USA, west of New Jersey and south of New York; area 117,348 sq km (45,308 sq miles); pop. (1990) 11,881,640; capital, Harrisburg. The largest cities are Philadelphia and Pittsburgh. Pennsylvania is also known as the Keystone State. Founded by the Quaker statesman William PENN and named after his father, Admiral Sir William Penn, it was one of the original 13 states of the USA (1787). Once dependent on coal, steel, and the railroad industry, the state (though still a major producer of steel and anthracite coal) is now also a leading manufacturer of chemicals, electrical machinery, cement, cigar leaf tobacco, and food products.

Pennsylvanian Period The later of the two epochs or subsystems into which the CARBONIFEROUS PERIOD is divided in North America (the other being the MISSISSIPPIAN). It covers the span of time from 320 to 286 million years ago, and is named after its most famous exposures in the state of Pennsylvania, USA.

penny post See HILL, SIR ROWLAND.

pennyroyal A small-leaved plant, which is a creeping member of the mint family, Labiatae. Its botanical name, *Mentha pulegium*, is from the Latin *pulex*, meaning flea, indicating its reputation for discouraging these pests. From the leaves is produced pennyroyal tea, an old remedy for coughs and colds. The species is native to Europe, Asia and north Africa.

penny whistle See FLAGEOLET.

pension See OLD-AGE BENEFIT.

Pentagon, the The headquarters of the US Department of Defense, near Washington, DC.

Built in 1941–43 in the form of five concentric pentagons, it covers 13.8 hectares (34 acres) and is one of the world's largest office buildings.

pentameter A verse line of five metrical units ('feet') or, in English verse, five stresses. The iambic pentameter (see IAMBIC VERSE) is the most important METRE in the English literary tradition. Greek and Latin pentameters were dactylic, comprising two half-lines of two and a half feet each.

Pentateuch See TORAH.

pentathlon An athletic contest derived from the ancient OLYMPIC GAMES, now reserved for women. Contestants earn points from their performance in five events: 100 m hurdles; shot; high jump; long jump; and 200 m.

Pentecost, Jewish and Christian festivals occurring 50 days after PASSOVER and EASTER respectively. The Jewish festival celebrates the giving of the Ten Commandments and is the continuation of an ancient Hebrew harvest festival. The Christian festival, also called Whit Sunday, commemorates the descent of the Holy Spirit on to the disciples. It marks the end of Eastertide.

Pentecostal Movement A part of the CHARISMATIC MOVEMENT among PROTESTANTS, which started at the beginning of the 20th century. Pentecostalists believe the modern Church should display the same spiritual gifts as the early Church, and advocate what is called 'Baptism in the Holy Spirit', the power of healing, prophesying, and 'speaking in tongues' (the uttering in a heightened spiritual state, of incomprehensible syllables). Usually they hold conservative evangelical beliefs. Pentecostal Churches have over 35 million full members, and are particularly strong in Latin America. In the UK there are two main groups: the Assemblies of God and the Elim Church.

pentstemon (or **penstemon**) A perennial plant of the genus *Pentstemon*, mostly native to North and Central America. Pentstemons belong to the foxglove family, Scrophulariaceae. The name refers to the flower's five stamens (four fertile and one abortive stamen). The stem bases are often woody and this gives a low shrubby habit to some species. The tubular flowers, which are often large and colourful, make them popular as garden plants.

penumbra See ECLIPSE.

Penzance A resort town in Cornwall, south-west England; pop. (1981) 19,600. There is a sea link and helicopter links with the Scilly Isles.

Penzias, Arno Allan (1933–) US astrophysicist, born in Germany. With Robert Wilson he discovered the cosmic background radiation coming from space, which supports the BIG BANG THEORY. For this work Penzias and Wilson shared the 1978 Nobel Prize for physics with Peter Kapitza.

peony A perennial, tuberous-rooted, herbaceous plant or small woody shrub. Peonies form the family Paeoniaceae, which contains only the genus *Paeonia* with 33 species. They are widely distributed in Europe, Asia, China, and northwest America. The large and colourful flowers of most species make them popular as garden plants. Many ornamental varieties have been bred from the herbaceous species *P. lactiflora* and *P. officinalis*, while the shrubby tree peonies are derived from *P. suffruticosa*, the moutan and other species.

Pepin Three Frankish 'mayors of the palace' under MEROVINGIAN rule who gave rise to the Carolingian dynasty. **Pepin I** of Landen was mayor of Austrasia, and his son **Pepin II** of both Austrasia and Neustria, the two most important parts of the Merovingian kingdom. **Pepin III**, the Short, was the grandson of the latter and son of CHARLES MARTEL. He ousted the last Merovingian, Childeric III, in 751 and was crowned King of the Franks. A close ally of the papacy, he defended it from Lombard attacks and made the Donation of Pepin which was the basis for the PAPAL STATES. He added Aquitaine and Septimania to his kingdom, which passed, on his death in 768, to CHARLEMAGNE and Carloman.

pepper (or **true pepper**) A perennial, woody climbing shrub, *Piper nigrum*, native to southwest India and now cultivated as a crop in most parts of south-east Asia, Brazil, and Madagascar. It belongs to a family of small tropical trees, shrubs, and climbers, Piperaceae, containing around 2,000 species. Historically it has been the most important of spices, known even to the ancient Greeks and Romans. It is still universally used as a condiment and flavouring in all kinds of savoury dishes.

Flourishing only in hot, wet, tropical climates with a long rainy season, the pepper plant produces red fruits borne in long clusters. Black pepper is made from the dried, whole fruits which become black and wrinkled and are known as peppercorns. White pepper, a less pungent form, is produced if the fleshy red outer skin is removed before drying. The pungency is caused by various resins and a yellow alkaloid, piperine. See also SWEET PEPPER.

peppered moth A species of moth in the family Geometridae, *Biston betularia*, which rests by day on tree trunks where the usual black-mottled white colour form of *B. b. typica* acts as camouflage among lichens. In industrial areas, where tree trunks are blackened and bare, an all-black form, *B. b. carbonaria*, is more frequent, a phenomenon known as industrial melanism. This moth is one of the few documented cases of 'evolution' in response to a change in its environment.

peppermint A hybrid between water MINT and spear mint, widely cultivated in Europe, North Africa, and America. Unlike other mints, it is prized for its oil, which is distilled from fresh flowering plants and used in cordials and confectionery. The oil is mildly antiseptic and is also used to treat indigestion.

pepper-shrike A bird belonging to the family Laniidae, which contains only two species, both of which occur in Central and South America. They are around 15–18 cm (6–7 inches) long, olive-green above and yellow or white below, with grey cheeks and orange and brown eyestripes. They have stout, hooked beaks with which they eat insects and fruit.

pepsin See STOMACH.

peptic ulcer See ULCER.

Pepys, Samuel (1633–1703) English diarist and naval administrator. He is particularly remembered for his *Diary* (1660–69), an important record of contemporary events, such as the Great Plague (1665–66), the Fire of London (1666), and the sailing of the Dutch fleet up the Thames (1665–67). The *Diary* was written in code and was first deciphered in 1825. Pepys became secretary of the Admiralty in 1672 but was deprived of his post in 1679 and committed to the Tower for his alleged complicity in Titus Oates's fabricated Popish Plot However, he was reappointed in 1684 and became president of the Royal Society in the same year.

perception (in philosophy) The sensory process enabling knowledge of the external world to be obtained. The philosophical problem of perception is epistemological: how to justify perceptual claims to knowledge? This question is not answered by psychology, which already assumes the existence of an external world. The main difficulty consists in showing why we should trust our perceptual experiences, given that we have apparently identical, but illusory, kinds of experience, such as dream and hallucination. Philosophical theories of perception include representational realism, which says that external objects are hypothesized in order to explain and match our experiences, and phenomenalism, according to which external objects are in fact nothing but bundles of experiences.

perception (in psychology) The processes intervening between sensation and the mental organization of the experience (cognition). Common sense urges us to trust our senses, but scientists are familiar with visual illusions and other errors in perception. The initial sensation involves changes in the nerve cells close to the source of the stimulus, and also selection between stimuli. In vision, for example, different distributions of radiant energy give rise to the experience of hue (red, yellow, violet), brightness, and saturation. At the other extreme, our ability to recognize, remember, and describe objects depends on how we name them. Furthermore, perception may be influenced or determined by language. Attempts to understand the early stages of perception are often linked to characteristics of neurological processes. Thus the fact that any coloured patch can be matched by combinations of only three different lights probably results from the three classes of photoreceptor that mediate colour vision. There have been attempts to pursue this approach further, either to find out how different neural transformations affect our experience or to find the neurophysiological states corresponding to specific perceived objects. Other attempts to describe perceptual processes in psychological terms are usually too vague to produce testable predictions. Some approaches suggest that 'unconscious inference' links our experience, for example of the distance of an object to both the size of its image on the retina and our knowledge of the object's actual size.

Perceval, Spencer (1762–1812) British Tory statesman, Prime Minister 1809–12. He was shot dead in the lobby of the House of Commons by a bankrupt merchant who blamed the government for his insolvency.

perch Either of two species of freshwater fishes of the family Percidae. The European perch, *Perca fluviatilis*, is found across the Eurasian land mass from Ireland to Siberia. A similar, but distinct, species, the yellow perch, *P. flavescens*, ranges across northern North America. Both are very distinctive fishes with a large, spiny dorsal fin, bold dark bars across the body and blood-red pelvic and anal fins. They are typical fishes of lowland rivers and lakes, often swimming in small schools, although large specimens tend to be solitary. They feed on invertebrates when young, but eat larger prey as they grow, including fishes and often young perch. Breeding takes place in late spring, the eggs being shed in long strings and wound among plants, tree roots, or branches lying in the water. They are popular fishes with anglers, and are a common food-fish on the European continent.

percussion instruments Musical instruments that are sounded by striking with a hand or stick or by shaking. Drums usually have a tensioned skin, struck by a hammer; they include the orchestral timpani, side drums, snare drums, and base drums. Other solid percussion instruments which sound by being struck include the triangle, gong, cymbals, bells, glockenspiel, and xylophone. Of these only the timpani, bells, glockenspiel, and xylophone produce sounds of a definite pitch.

Percy A family of marcher lords of medieval England with lands in Northumberland. **Henry de Percy** (1341–1408), 1st Earl of Northumberland, was the first of the family to be of major importance in the defence of England's northern frontier. The earl's son, **Sir Henry Percy** ('Hotspur') (1364–1403), was a hero of the Battle of Otterburn. When Henry

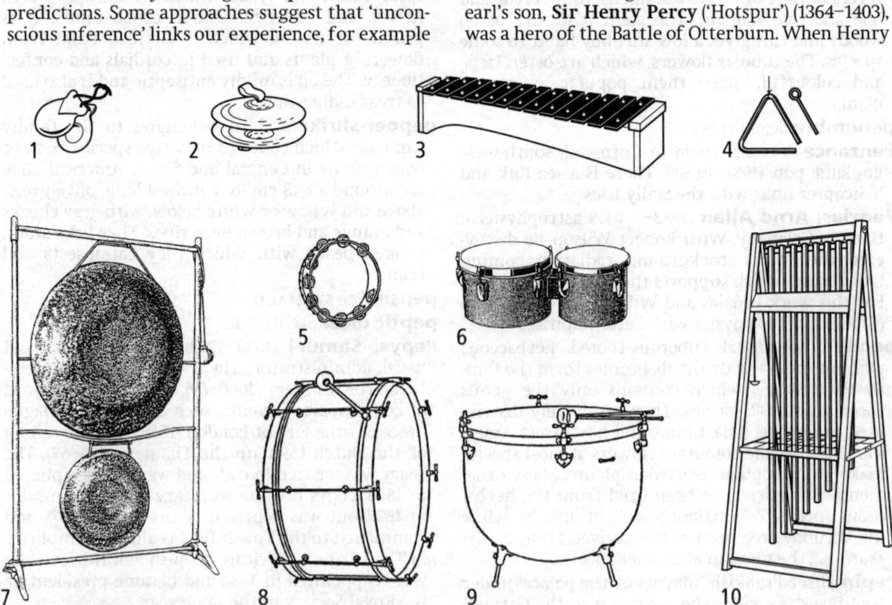

Percussion instruments (1) Castanets. (2) Cymbals. (3) Xylophone. (4) Triangle. (5) Tambourine. (6) Bongo drums. (7) Tam-tams (bronze gongs). (8) Bass drum. (9) Kettledrum (timpano). (10) Tubular bells.

of Bolingbroke landed in the north of England in 1399, the earl and Hotspur helped assure him of the crown; they were well rewarded, but within four years their greed for more offices or money led them into open rebellion. Hotspur and his uncle Thomas, Earl of Worcester, were killed at SHREWSBURY in 1403. Five years later Earl Henry invaded England from Scotland, but he too was killed and his estates were forfeited.

Subsequently restored to their estates, later generations of the family resumed their role as guardians of the northern frontier and rivals of the Nevilles. The male line ended in 1670, but the earldom passed in the female line to Sir Hugh Smithson (1715–86) who took the name of Percy and in 1766 was created Duke of Northumberland.

peregrine A species of large FALCON, *Falco peregrinus*, with some 19 subspecies recognized throughout the world. They are noted for their swift, versatile flight and spectacular hunting of birds on the wing, characteristics which endear them to falconers. They live on open ground, sea coasts, and other areas where birds are plentiful, northern populations following their prey southward in winter. Two to four eggs are laid.

Père Lachaise A cemetery in Paris, France, named after the confessor of Louis XV, Père Lachaise, who enlarged a former Jesuit building on the site. Amongst those buried within its walls are Honoré de Balzac, Frédéric Chopin, Colette, Edith Piaf, Gioacchino Rossini, and Oscar Wilde.

Perelman, S(idney) J(oseph) (1904–79) US humorist and writer. In the early 1930s he worked in Hollywood as a scriptwriter, notably on some of the Marx Brothers' films. From 1934 his name is linked with the *New Yorker* magazine, for whom he wrote most of his short stories and sketches. Towards the end of his life he lived in London.

perennial A plant that lives for more than two years (as opposed to ANNUALS and BIENNIALS). In a garden sense, perennials are usually herbaceous plants with perennial rootstocks which annually produce new flowering shoots above the ground. Woody perennials retain a permanent framework of branches while the climbing kinds may be herbaceous or woody.

Peres, Shimon (born Szymon Perski) (1923–) Israeli statesman, Prime Minister 1984–86 and 1995–96. Born in Poland, he emigrated to Palestine in 1934. Labour Party leader since 1977, Peres became head of a coalition government with the Likud Party in 1984, later serving as deputy to Yitzhak Shamir. As Foreign Minister from 1992 he played a major role in negotiating the PLO–Israeli peace accord (1993) and shared the 1994 Nobel Peace Prize with Yitzhak Rabin and Yasser Arafat. He replaced Rabin as Prime Minister after the latter's assassination, only to be narrowly defeated in the elections of 1996 by Binyamin Netanyahu.

perestroika See GLASNOST.

Pérez de Cuéllar, Javier (1920–) Peruvian diplomat. He served as Secretary-General of the United Nations from 1982 to 1991, and played a key role in the diplomatic aftermath of the Falklands War (1982) and in ending the Iran–Iraq War (1980–88). His efforts to avert the Gulf War in 1990 raised his international standing.

perfume A fragrant liquid giving a pleasant smell, especially to the body. Perfumes have been known and used for thousands of years. Until recently, they comprised only natural materials, but advances in natural product chemistry have made it possible to synthesize the active ingredients. Perfumes are usually alcoholic solutions of substances that have an attractive smell. On application, body heat causes the alcohol to evaporate quickly, leaving the fragrant substances on the skin to evaporate gradually over several hours.

Pergamum See BERGAMA.

peri (or **pari**) In Persian mythology, a benign female spirit, endowed with grace and beauty. Peris, as a race of superhuman beings, were thought in earlier mythology to be attractive but demonic creatures.

Pericles (*c.*495–429 BC) Athenian statesman and general. A champion of Athenian democracy, he pursued an imperialist policy and masterminded Athenian strategy in the Peloponnesian War. He commissioned the building of the Parthenon in 447 and promoted the culture of Athens in a golden age that produced such figures as Aeschylus, Socrates, and Phidias. He died of the plague that struck Athens in 430.

peridot A gem-quality crystal of OLIVINE, pale green in colour. Gem crystals have been found in lava on Saint John's Island (Red Sea), in Arizona (USA), and in Myanmar (Burma).

peridotite An intrusive IGNEOUS ROCK that is rich in the dark mineral OLIVINE. PYROXENE and other FERROMAGNESIAN MINERALS may also be present. The rock is usually dark green with large crystals, which are enriched with accessory rare metals.

perigee The point in the orbit of the Moon or of an artificial Earth satellite where it is nearest to the Earth's surface. Compare APOGEE.

perihelion The point on a planet's orbit about the Sun where the planet is nearest to the Sun. The Earth is at perihelion on 3 January. Compare APHELION.

period (in physics) The time interval between recurrent events. The period of an oscillation or wave is the time taken to complete one cycle, usually measured in hertz. In astronomy, periods are ascribed to rotational spins of bodies, orbital revolutions, solar magnetic phenomena, and pulsations within stellar atmospheres.

period (in chemistry) See PERIODIC TABLE.

period (in geology) See GEOLOGICAL TIMESCALE.

periodic law A law first proposed by Dimitri MENDELEEV, which now states that if the chemical elements are arranged in order of atomic number (the number of protons in the nucleus), then elements with related properties occur at regular intervals. By placing elements with related properties in vertical columns. Mendeleyev was able to construct the PERIODIC TABLE.

periodic table An arrangement of the chemical elements in order of increasing atomic number – that is, the number of protons in their nuclei. In the traditional form of the table the elements were arranged horizontally in seven rows called **periods**; the first period consisted of two elements (hydrogen and helium), the second of eight elements (lithium to neon), the third of eight elements (sodium to argon), the fourth of 18 (potassium to krypton), and so on. In this form of the table, it was customary to divide the main groups into subgroups A and B. These were numbered from IA to VIIA and from IB to VIIB with Group 0 for the noble gases. The TRANSITION METALS were placed in a block in the centre of the table. There was considerable confusion about the numbering of groups, in particular the designation of which sets of elements belong to A or B subgroups. Consequently, it was decided to number the groups across the table from Group 1 to Group

18. Atoms that form positive IONS are represented to the left of each period, and the electronegative ones to the right. When the elements are arranged in this way, they fall into columns called **periodic groups**; and it is found that elements occurring in the same group resemble each other chemically: thus all the noble gases appear in the extreme right-hand group, which is called Group 0. This pattern occurs because the properties of an element depend primarily on the number of electrons in its outermost (valence) shell. Each shell can only hold a fixed number of electrons. When the shell becomes full, a new shell is started and a new period in the table is begun. The table's arrangement therefore reveals information on the electronic configuration of atoms. See also Appendix.

period-luminosity law The relation between the periods of pulsating stars and their intrinsic brightness or absolute MAGNITUDE. The first such law was established by the US astronomer Henrietta Leavitt in 1912 by observing CEPHEID VARIABLE STARS in the Magellanic Clouds. Refinements have since been made to the law to allow for there being distinct luminosity types of Cepheid.

peripheral (in computing) A device that is connected to a computer system but is not part of the CENTRAL PROCESSING UNIT or associated MEMORY. Common peripherals include OUTPUT DEVICES, such as PRINTERS and plotter units, disk drives, INPUT DEVICES, such as keyboards attached to VISUAL DISPLAY UNITS, and MODEMS.

periscope An optical instrument that deflects light, allowing the user to see over obstacles, round corners, or into inaccessible places. Their main use is in tanks and submarines. The simplest periscope uses two parallel mirrors or prisms to reflect light through two right angles, displacing the beam by the distance separating the reflectors. Lenses arranged as a telescope can be included to magnify the scene. Submarine periscopes obtain a wide field of view using a series of lenses inside a tube of rectangular section, with telescope arrangements at the top and bottom.

peristalsis A wavelike movement that occurs in some of the body's tubular organs, especially the intestines. It occurs involuntarily and is induced by distension of the walls. Immediately behind the distension the circular muscles of the tube contract. In front of the distension the circular muscles relax and the longitudinal muscles contract, pushing the contents of the tube forward. Peristalsis is the process that forces food through the digestive system.

peritonitis Inflammation of the membrane that covers the abdominal cavity and the organs within the cavity (peritoneum). Peritonitis is usually caused by bacterial infection arising from perforation of the gastro-intestinal tract. Some causes of peritonitis include APPENDICITIS, perforated peptic ulcer, and perforation of the colon. Peritonitis can be localized or diffuse; symptoms include severe abdominal pain, tenderness, vomiting, fever, low blood pressure, increased heart rate, dehydration, and failure of intestinal PERISTALSIS (paralytic ileus). Complications associated with peritonitis include SHOCK and abdominal abscess. Treatment of the underlying cause is essential before treatment of peritonitis.

periwinkle (plant) A plant of the species *Vinca* or *Catharanthus*, both members of the same family (Apocynaceae) as oleander. The first is a genus of shrubs and climbers of Eurasia, some of which are grown in gardens; the second comprises tropical shrubby plants, mostly native to Madagascar. The Madagascar periwinkle, *C. roseus*, is one of the commonest of tropical weeds. ALKALOIDS found in the plant have been used in the treatment of leukaemia in children.

periwinkle (animal) See WINKLE.

perjury (in COMMON LAW) The making of a false statement while under oath in a COURT OF LAW, before a tribunal, or in front of someone having power at law to hear evidence. The statement must be materially important, and made wilfully rather than through inadvertence.

Perkin, Sir William Henry (1838–1907) British chemist and pioneer of the synthetic organic chemical industry. At the age of 18 he prepared the first synthetic dyestuff, mauve, which is made from aniline. The discovery was made by accident when he was trying to synthesize the drug quinine. He and his father then set up a factory to make mauve, which was used for textiles and postage stamps, and other synthetic dyes.

permafrost Frozen ground whose temperature does not rise above 0°C (32°F) for at least 12 months. It occurs wherever temperatures are low enough, even under the shallow, cold waters of the Arctic Ocean. Usually only the sub-surface layer is permafrost and there is an active layer at the surface, which thaws in warmer weather. Any disturbance of the ground surface – particularly the removal of insulating vegetation or global warming – is likely to cause permafrost to thaw and the active layer to deepen, releasing energy. If the subsurface contains ice which then melts, there may be sinking or collapse, which can tilt or swallow buildings and fracture roads, airstrips, and pipelines.

permalloy See ALLOY.

permeability (or **magnetic permeability**) The ratio of the MAGNETIC FLUX density (B) in a substance to the external field strength (H), i.e. $\mu = B/H$, where μ is the permeability. The permeability of free space, μ_0, also called the **magnetic constant**, has the value $4\pi \times 10^{-7}$ henry per metre. The **relative permeability** of a substance, μ_r, is given by, $\mu_r = \mu/\mu_0$.

Permian period The last of the geological periods of the PALAEOZOIC ERA, extending in time from 286 to 245 million years ago. It follows the CARBONIFEROUS and comes before the TRIASSIC. A period characterized in many parts of the world by hot deserts, it saw the extinction of many marine animals (for example, trilobites and primitive corals) and the proliferation of reptiles.

permittivity According to COULOMB's law, if two charges Q_1 and Q_2 are separated by a distance r in a vacuum, the force F between them is given by $F = Q_1Q_2/r^2 4\pi\varepsilon_0$, where ε_0 is called the absolute permittivity of free space, or the **electric constant**. It has the value 8.854×10^{-12} farad per metre. If the medium between the charges is anything other than a vacuum, the electric constant is replaced by ε, the **absolute permittivity** of the medium. The **relative permittivity** (formerly called the **dielectric constant**) of a medium, ε_r, is given by $\varepsilon_r = \varepsilon/\varepsilon_0$.

Pernambuco See RECIFE.

Perón, Eva (full name María Eva Duarte de Perón; known as 'Evita') (1919–52) Argentinian politician. After pursuing a successful career as a radio actress in the 1930s and 1940s, she married Juan PERÓN and became de facto Minister of Health and of Labour. Idolized by the poor, she organized female workers, secured the vote for women, and earmarked substantial government funds for social welfare. She was nominated for the vice-presidency in 1951, but was forced by the army to withdraw. She died the following year from cancer.

Perón, Juan Domingo (1895–1974) Argentinian soldier and statesman, President 1946–55 and 1973–74. He participated in the military coup organized by pro-Fascist army officers in 1943, and was elected President in 1946, when he assumed dictatorial powers. He won popular support with his programme of social reform, but, after the death of his second wife, Eva PERÓN, the faltering economy and his conflict with the Roman Catholic Church led to his removal and exile in 1955. Following a resurgence by the Peronist Party in the early 1970s, Perón returned to power in 1973, but died in office.

peroxide A chemical compound containing linked pairs of oxygen atoms (–O–O–) or containing the O_2^{2-} ion, the simplest example being hydrogen peroxide (H_2O_2). The oxygen-oxygen link is a weak bond and can be broken by ultraviolet radiation, which starts and catalyses many reactions in the atmosphere and in nature. Peroxides are used as rocket fuels, in solution as bleaches for wool and hair, and as antiseptics.

Perpendicular style The third of the three stages into which English Gothic architecture is conventionally divided, following Early English and Decorated. It originated in about 1330 and lasted well into the 16th century, merging into TUDOR architecture. The name derives from the dominance of straight lines in window tracery and in the decorative panels that spread over wall surfaces, creating great unity of effect. The regular panelling extended also to VAULTS in the form known as the fan vault. The greatest masterpieces of the style include three chapels dating from the late 15th and early 16th centuries: St George's Chapel, Windsor Castle; Henry VII's Chapel, Westminster Abbey; and King's College Chapel, Cambridge. The Perpendicular style is unique to England, late Gothic developing in other directions elsewhere in Europe. See GOTHIC ART AND ARCHITECTURE.

perpetual motion The motion of a hypothetical machine that, once set in motion, would run for ever unless subject to an external force or to wear. Such a machine is contrary to the basic laws of thermodynamics. This, however, has not deterred ingenious inventors, and in the 19th century the US Patent Office refused patents for perpetual motion machines unless accompanied by models, some of which are now exhibited in the SMITHSONIAN INSTITUTION. The British Patent Office banned such patents in 1949.

Perpignan A city of southern France near the Spanish frontier in the north-eastern foothills of the Pyrenees, capital of the department of Pyrénées-Orientales; pop. (1990) 108,050. A centre of food processing and tourism, it was the fortified capital of the old province of Roussillon.

Perrault, Charles (1628–1703) French writer. He is remembered for his *Mother Goose Tales* (1697), containing such fairy tales as 'Sleeping Beauty', 'Little Red Riding Hood', 'Puss in Boots', 'Bluebeard', and 'Cinderella'. They were translated into English by Robert Samber in 1729.

Perrin, Jean-Baptiste (1870–1942) French physicist who made detailed studies of Brownian motion. From his observations he determined a value for the Avogadro constant (see MOLE). He also demonstrated that cathode rays carry a negative charge. He was awarded the Nobel Prize for physics in 1926.

Perry, Fred(erick John) (1909–95), British tennis player. He began his career as a table-tennis player, winning the world singles championship in 1929. In tennis, his record of winning three consecutive singles titles at Wimbledon (1934–36) was unequalled until the success of Björn BORG.

Perseids A METEOR SHOWER that reaches its peak about 12 August each year, but its meteors can be seen for about three weeks around this date. At least a dozen historic records are known of this shower between 36 AD and 1451.

Persephone In Greek mythology, a beautiful goddess, the daughter of Zeus and Demeter, goddess of agriculture. She was carried off by the god Hades and made queen of the Underworld. Demeter sought her everywhere, lighting her torches at the fires of Mount Etna, while the Earth became barren at her neglect. Though Zeus yielded at length to Demeter's lamentations, Persephone could not be entirely released from the lower world because she had eaten some pomegranate seeds there. She was allowed to spend part of each year on Earth and the remainder in Hades.

Persepolis The ceremonial capital of the ACHAEMENID empire. A festival of tribute was held there each year, it was the burial place of the kings, and its treasury was a repository of enormous wealth. The city was captured, looted, and burnt in 331 BC by Alexander the Great's troops. Excavation of the palaces – built by DARIUS I and XERXES—and other buildings, while confirming the destruction that took place, has also revealed some magnificent examples of Achaemenid art and architecture, particularly the bas-reliefs.

Perseus (in Greek mythology) A hero, the son of Zeus and Danae (a mortal). He killed Medusa the Gorgon and rescued and married Andromeda, who had been held captive by the sea-monster Cetus.

Perseus (in astronomy) A CONSTELLATION of the northern sky, one of the 48 constellations known to the ancient Greeks. It represents the mythical hero PERSEUS. Alpha Persei is a yellow supergiant of magnitude 1.8, surrounded by a scattered cluster of stars. Beta Persei is the famous eclipsing binary ALGOL, marking the Gorgon's head carried by Perseus.

Pershing missile A two-stage solid-fuel nuclear missile used by the US army. A surface-to-surface weapon, it is fired from a launcher vehicle and has a range of 740 km (400 miles). It is named after General John J. Pershing (1860–1948), a US general who commanded the US forces in World War I.

Persia See IRAN.

Persian The language of ancient Persia or modern Iran (officially, Farsi), spoken by over 25 million people in Iran and Afghanistan. It belongs to the Indo-Iranian language group and is attested from the 6th century BC when Old Persian was the language of the Persian Empire, which at one time spread from the Mediterranean to India. Old Persian was written in cuneiform, but in the 2nd century BC the Persians created their own alphabet (Pahlavi), which remained in use until the Islamic conquest in the 7th century; since then Persian or Farsi has been written in the Arabic script.

Persian Gulf (or **Arabian Gulf**, **the Gulf**) An arm of the Arabian Sea to which it is connected by the Strait of Hormuz and the Gulf of Oman, separating the Arabian peninsula from mainland Asia. It is a major shipping and supply route, linking the oil-producing countries of the Middle East to the outside world.

Persian language See INDO-IRANIAN LANGUAGES.

Persian wars See GREEK-PERSIAN WARS.

persimmon A deciduous tree that grows up to 13 m (43 feet) tall and is native to warm temperate regions. Persimmons belong to the genus *Diospyros*, which includes some 200 species, mostly tropical and evergreen, and are in the same family as ebony, Ebenaceae.

Persis The ancient name of the province of Fars in south-west Iran.

personal computer See MICROCOMPUTER.

personality The stable differences between people in social, emotional, and motivational characteristics. The most common approaches to personality in psychology are trait theories, which attempt to show that people do have a limited number of stable characteristics, which exist in a different degree in everyone. Most models of personality development are fairly deterministic, differing only about the relative importance of experience and heredity.

personality disorder The state of individuals who do not suffer from a clearly identifiable mental illness but who nevertheless show a profound defect of character and temperament that notably interferes with their social relations. There is no agreement about their causes. Some categorizations of personality disorder are purely descriptive, recognizing, for instance, aggressive or dependent types. Others imply parallels between personality types and psychiatric disorders which they resemble. For example, schizoid personality is supposed to share some lesser features of SCHIZOPHRENIA, such as social withdrawal and difficulty in expressing feelings. Other recognized types are obsessional, hysterical, paranoid, and an antisocial set of traits often referred to as sociopathic or PSYCHOPATHIC.

perspective A system for representing spatial recession on a flat or shallow surface. In Western art, perspective, variously known as geometric, linear, mathematical, optical, Renaissance, or scientific perspective, was developed in Florence in the 15th century by BRUNELLESCHI and put into practice by such artists as MASACCIO and UCCELLO. It is based on using the apparent convergence of parallel lines as they recede from the spectator to try to create in a picture an illusion of the same kind of spatial relationships that we see in the real world, with objects appearing to diminish in size the further away they are. Such perspective was one of the cornerstones of European art for almost five centuries after its invention. The art of primitive peoples and of some highly cultivated cultures (for example, the ancient Egyptians and Chinese) tends to ignore or underplay perspective. See also AERIAL PERSPECTIVE.

Perspex See POLYMETHYL METHACRYLATE.

Perth The capital of the state of Western Australia, on the estuary of the River Swan, the leading commercial and transportation centre of west coast Australia; pop. (1991) 1,018,700. Founded in 1829, it developed rapidly after the discovery of gold and the opening of Fremantle harbour in 1897. The port exports refined oil, wheat, and wool. Perth has two universities: Western Australia (1911) and Murdoch (1975).

Perth A royal burgh at the head of the Tay estuary in eastern Scotland, administrative centre of Perth and Kinross; pop. (1991) 41,450. The Scottish Reformation was initiated here in 1559 after a sermon by John Knox. It holds an annual arts festival in May.

Perthes, Jacques Boucher de See BOUCHER DE PERTHES.

Perthshire A former county of central Scotland, now part of Perth and Kinross local government area (unitary authority). From 1975 to 1996 it was part of Perth and Kinross District, Tayside Region.

perturbation See CELESTIAL MECHANICS.

Peru A country on the Pacific coast of South America, bounded by Ecuador and Colombia on the north, Brazil and Bolivia on the east, and Chile on the south.

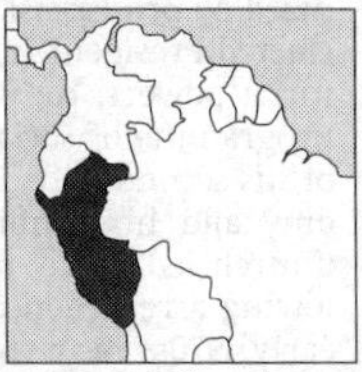

Physical. The north-east of the country is in the upper Amazon basin and comprises equatorial rain forest. In stark contrast, the south-west half is occupied by the Andes mountain ranges, whose snow-capped peaks rise to over 6,500 m (21,000 feet). Between the ranges are plateau areas of wide, rock-strewn slopes, the high mountain lake, Titicaca, in the extreme south-east, and many valleys used for cultivation and the rearing of livestock. Here also minerals are found in rich profusion. The coastal plain is arid and mostly desert, cooled by the PERU CURRENT and subject to dense mists.

Economy. High inflation and a large foreign debt have caused economic problems for Peru. Exports include copper, zinc, lead, and silver. There is a wide range of agriculture, and Peru is almost self-sufficient in food, with crops such as potatoes, rice, and sugar. Llamas and sheep provide wool for export. One of the world's leading producers of fishmeal, Peru has a well-established manufacturing sector which includes petroleum products, although oil production is declining. There is widespread illegal cultivation of coca, which is sent to Colombia for processing into cocaine.

History. Peru was the site of a succession of complex cultures and states from *c*.1000 BC: Chavín in the central Highlands, Mochica on the northern coast, NAZCA on the southern coast, and TIAHUANACO round Lake Titicaca in the Andes. Between *c*.600 AD and 1000 Huari in the central Andes conquered a small 'empire', and the CHIMÚ state rose on the northern coast *c*.1000. The INCAS were another such group, based round CUZCO, who began their regional expansion *c*.1200 and eventually conquered a vast empire stretching from Chile to Ecuador during the 15th century. Spanish invader Francisco PIZARRO's defeat of ATAHUALPA in 1532 was followed by rivalry for control and led eventually to direct rule by the Spanish crown. Inca revolts continued for nearly 50 years. The vice-royalty, with its capital at Lima, attempted to placate the various factions but was not in reasonable control until the mid-16th century. Further Inca insurrections occurred in 1780, led by Tupac Amarú, and in 1814.

In 1821 José de SAN MARTÍN captured Lima, proclaiming an independent republic and issuing a constitution (1823). In 1824 José de SUCRE won the Battle of Ayacucho, and Spanish troops were withdrawn. Political quarrels in the new republic led to an invitation to Simón BOLÍVAR to accept the powers of a dictator. He tried unsuccessfully to bring Peru into his state of Gran Colombia (which comprised present-day Colombia, Ecuador, and Venezuela). A long period of civil war followed, the situation stabilizing under President Ramón CASTILLA (1844–62), who ended slavery, established an education system, and promoted the extraction of guano (natural nitrates and phosphates produced from sea-bird droppings), which brought immediate prosperity but was soon exhausted. The loss of nitrate revenue and the cost of the War of the Pacific (1879–84) led to national bankruptcy in 1889. Civilian politics had emerged in the 1870s with two parties, the Democrats and the Civilians, alternating in office. The latter, led by Augusto Leguia, held power (1908–30), introducing progressive legislation and settling the Tacna–Arica Dispute. After World War I a radical group, the Alianza Popular Revolucionaria Americana (APRA), led by Haya de la Torre, sought to obtain greater participation in politics by the Indians. President Manuel Prado, elected in 1939, aligned Peru with US policies in World War II. Terry Belaúnde gained office in 1963. In 1968 a left-wing military junta seized power, seeking to nationalize US-controlled industries. A more moderate junta succeeded in 1975, and in 1979 elections were again held. In 1980 Belaúnde was re-elected President, when a new constitution was established. In the face of severe economic problems Belaúnde succeeded in re-democratizing the country, and in 1985 President Alan Garcia was elected. Confronted by massive rescheduling requirements for Peru's foreign debts, his regime imposed an austerity programme and engaged in a guerrilla war against a strong ultra-left Maoist group, *Sendero Luminoso* ('Shining Path'). His APRA Party did badly in the 1990 elections, when the son of Japanese immigrants, Alberto Keinya Fujimori of the Cambio 90 Party, was elected President. The austerity measures which he continued resulted in protests, with strikes and guerrilla attacks across the country. In September 1992, however, his government won a resounding victory against terrorism, by capturing and imprisoning Abimael Guzmán, who had founded and led *Sendero Luminoso* since 1970. A new constitution was introduced in 1993, and Fujimori was re-elected in 1995.

Capital: Lima
Area: 1,285,216 sq km (496,225 sq mi)
Population: 23,489,000 (1995)
Currency: 1 inti = 100 centimos
Religions: Roman Catholic 92.4%
Ethnic Groups: Quechua 47.0%; Mestizo 32.0%; European 12.0%; Aymara 5.0%
Languages: Spanish, Quechua (both official); Aymara
International Organizations: UN; OAS; Andean Group

Peru Current (or **Humboldt Current**) A broad, shallow, slow-moving body of cool water flowing northward along the western coast of South America. In this region prevailing winds blow surface waters away from the coast, causing an upwelling of cold sub-surface waters to replace them. Upwelling brings nutrient-rich water to the surface, and this encourages the growth of phytoplankton, the tiny floating plants that fish feed on. The region is therefore rich in marine life and an important fishing area. If the position of the Peru Current changes, as it sometimes does with an EL NIÑO occurrence, upwelling is inhibited, and this has serious effects on the local fishing industries.

Perugia A medieval city in central Italy, on the Tiber, the capital of Perugia province and chief city of Umbria; pop. (1990) 150,580. Founded by the Etruscans, it was occupied by the Romans from 310 BC. Taken by the Lombards in the late 6th century, it was contested over the succeeding centuries by powerful local families. It flourished in the 15th century as a centre of the Umbrian school of painting. A papal possession from 1540, it became a part of united Italy in 1860. It has many fine medieval buildings and has two universities one the Italian University for Foreigners. The economy is dependent on tourism and confectionery.

Perugino, Pietro (born Pietro Vannucci) (*c.*1445–1523) Italian painter. He worked mainly in Perugia, but also in Rome (he painted frescos in the Sistine Chapel) and Florence. He was a fine portraitist as well as a fresco painter, but he is best known for his altar-pieces. At his best he has the authority of a great master, and the harmony and spatial clarity of his compositions and his idealized physical types influenced the young RAPHAEL, who worked in his busy studio.

Peruvian art See SOUTH AMERICAN INDIAN ART.

Pescadores, the (or **Fisherman Isles**; Chinese **Penghu**) A group of 64 small islands (of which 24 are inhabited) in the Taiwan Strait (Formosa Channel) between Taiwan and mainland China; area 127 sq km (49 sq miles); pop. (1991) 120,000. The majority of the population live on Penghu Island whose chief town is Makung.

Peshawar The capital of North-West Frontier Province, in Pakistan; pop. (1981) 555,000. Mentioned in early Sanskrit literature, it is one of Pakistan's oldest cities. Under Sikh rule from 1834, it was occupied by the British between 1849 and 1947. Situated at a strategic location near the Khyber Pass, which leads into Afghanistan, it is a major road, rail, and military centre.

Pestalozzi, Johann Heinrich (1746–1827) Swiss educational reformer. He pioneered education for poor children and had a major impact on the development of primary education. His theory and method are set out in *How Gertrude Teaches Her Children* (1801). Pestalozzi's work is commemorated in the International Children's Villages named after him; the first, for war orphans, was established at Trogen in Switzerland in 1946.

pesticide A natural or synthetic AGROCHEMICAL used to kill organisms that are harmful to cultivated plants or to animals. HERBICIDES are used to kill weeds, INSECTICIDES act against insect pests, and FUNGICIDES are anti-fungal agents. Pesticides are designed as far as possible to be effective against a specific pest in a particular context, to avoid unwanted toxic effects in other organisms. However, many pesticides are toxic to humans in large doses, or after long-term exposure. In some countries, certain pesticides have been banned because of their toxic effects or their persistence in the food chain. Methods of BIOLOGICAL PEST CONTROL are also being developed, either to reduce or to replace pesticide use.

PET (polyethene terephthalate) See PLASTICS.

Pétain, (Henri) Philippe (Omer) (1856–1951) French general and statesman, head of state 1940–42. He became a national hero in World War I for halting the German advance at Verdun (1916) and later became Commander-in-Chief of French forces (1917). In World War II he concluded an armistice with Nazi Germany after the collapse of French forces in 1940 and established the French government at Vichy (effectively a puppet regime for the Third Reich) until German occupation in 1942. After the war Pétain received a death sentence for collaboration, but this was commuted to life imprisonment.

pétanque (or **boules**) A ball-and-target game similar to lawn bowls. The wooden jack is thrown by a player in the chosen starting circle to a point between 6 and 10 m (19.5 and 33 feet) distant. The players then toss metal balls (weighing between 620 g and 800 g/22 and 28 ounces) in an attempt to place them as close as possible to the jack. Play resumes with the winner throwing the jack from its position in the previous game. Unlike lawn bowls, pétanque may be played along village streets or in back yards.

Peter I (known as **Peter the Great**) (1672–1725) Tsar of Russia 1682–1725. After the death of his half-brother Ivan in 1696 Peter I assumed sole authority and launched a policy of expansion along the Baltic coast. Modernizing his armed forces he waged the Great Northern War (1700–21) against Charles XII of Sweden, and went on to annex Estonia and Latvia, as well as parts of Finland, following the defeat of the Swedish monarch. Peter I's introduction of extensive government and administration reforms were instrumental in transforming Russia into a significant European power. In 1703 he made St Petersburg his capital.

Peter, St (died *c.*64 AD) Originally named Simon, the leader of the Apostles who followed JESUS CHRIST. Jesus named him Cephas (Aramaic, 'rock'; Greek *petra*, 'rock') to signify his key role in establishing the early Christian Church. After the death of Jesus, Peter was the undisputed leader of the Church, preaching, and defending the new religious movement. He was the first to accept Gentiles (non-Jews) into the Church but later disagreed with St PAUL over the admission of Gentiles. It seems certain that Peter spent the last years of his life in Rome and was probably crucified during NERO's persecution of 64. The PAPACY traces its origins back to Peter and the ROMAN CATHOLIC CHURCH identifies him as the founder and first bishop of the church of Rome. He is regarded as the keeper of the gate to heaven; his attribute is a set of keys. Feast day, 29 June.

Peterborough An industrial city in Cambridgeshire, east-central England, on the River Nene; pop. (1991) 148,800. It has a 12th-century cathedral and has been developed as a planned urban centre since the late 1960s. The city has agricultural and brick-making industries.

Peterhead A fishing port and North Sea oil base on the coast of Aberdeenshire, north-east Scotland; pop. (1981) 17,085.

Peterloo massacre (16 August 1819) A violent confrontation in Manchester, England, between civilians and government forces. A large but peaceable crowd of some 60,000 people had gathered in St Peter's Fields to hear the radical politician Henry 'Orator' Hunt address them. After he had begun speaking the local magistrates sent in constables to arrest him. In the mistaken belief that the crowd was preventing the arrest, the magistrates ordered a body of cavalry to go to the assistance of the constables. In the ensuing riot 11 civilians were killed and over 500 injured.

Peterson, Oscar (Emmanuel) (1925–) Canadian jazz pianist and composer. He toured with the US impresario Norman Granz (1918–) from 1949, becoming internationally famous in the 1960s, when he often appeared with Ella Fitzgerald. During this period he usually led a trio with a bass and guitar. In the 1970s he frequently played the piano solo, recording the album *My Favourite Instrument* (1973).

Peterson, Roger Tory (1908–96) US ornithologist and artist. Peterson produced his first book for identifying birds in the field in 1934, introducing the concept of illustrating similar birds in similar postures with their differences highlighted. The book was the forerunner of his *Field Guide to the Birds* (1947), the first of the famous Peterson field guides published in the USA and elsewhere.

Peter's pence A tax formerly paid annually to the papacy. First stated as compulsory in 787, it was levied in England from the 10th century at the rate of one penny per householder. It was revived by WILLIAM I as a single lump sum of £200 for the whole of England. It was abolished in England in 1534 during the Reformation.

Peter the Great See PETER I.

Peter the Hermit (*c.*1050–1115) French monk. His preaching on the First Crusade was a rallying cry for thousands of peasants throughout Europe to journey to the Holy Land; most were massacred by the Turks in Asia Minor. Peter later became prior of an Augustinian monastery in Flanders.

Petipa, Marius (Ivanovich) (1818–1910) French ballet-dancer and choreographer, resident in Russia from 1847. He became principal dancer for the Russian Imperial Ballet in St Petersburg in 1847 and first ballet master in 1869. Petipa choreographed more than 50 ballets, collaborating closely with Tchaikovsky on the premières of *Sleeping Beauty* (1890) and *The Nutcracker* (1892).

Petit, Roland (1924–) French dancer and choreographer. His works have a strong sense of theatre and offer rich collaborative possibilities. He spans musical comedy as well as ballet and has worked with many European companies, latterly the Ballet de Marseilles. He is best known for his own choreography, such as the chic *Carmen* (1949).

Petition of Right (1628) A document drawn up by opposition members of the English Parliament, led by COKE. It came at the time of Charles I's wars against France and Spain, and the lengthy quarrel over tunnage and poundage. It stated parliamentary grievances and forbade illegal unparliamentary taxation, the forced billeting of troops, the imposition of martial law, and arbitrary imprisonment. Charles did assent to the Petition but it was a limited parliamentary victory and did nothing to curb Charles's unconstitutional rule during the 11 years of government without Parliament.

Petra An ancient city in modern Jordan. It was the capital of the Nabataeans (an Arab tribe) from the 4th century BC to the 2nd century AD. Its prosperity was derived from the caravan trade from southern Arabia, but declined after its annexation by the Romans in 106 AD. The remains of the city, accessible only by a single narrow entrance cut through steep rocks, are extensive and spectacular, particularly the tombs and temples carved in the pink rock of the hills.

Petrarch (born Francesco Petrarca) (1304–74) Italian poet. His reputation is chiefly based on his lyrical poetry, in particular the *Canzoniere* (*c.*1351–53), a sonnet sequence in praise of a woman he calls Laura; this was to be a major source of inspiration for the English sonnet writers, such as Thomas Wyatt and Philip Sidney. Petrarch was also an important figure in the rediscovery of classical antiquity, together with his friend Boccaccio, initiating the revived study of Greek and Latin literature and writing most of his works in Latin. In 1341 Petrarch was crowned Poet Laureate in Rome.

petrel A seabird belonging to one of three families: the Procellariidae (true petrels and shearwaters), Hydrobatidae (storm petrels), and Pelecanoididae (diving petrels). All are oceanic seabirds, with characteristic tubular nostrils, which help to drain the salt glands positioned close to the eyes. Nearly 100 species are known, over half of them prevalent in temperate or cold latitudes of the Southern Hemisphere. Most species are highly social, nesting colonially and feeding together in huge floating 'rafts'. All species lay a single white egg, tending it for the unusually long incubation period of six to seven weeks. Petrels range in size from tiny storm petrels and diving petrels of the species *Pelecanoides*, 15 cm (6 inches) long, to the giant petrel, *Macronectes giganteus*, with wings spanning 2 m (6 feet) or more.

Petrie, Sir (William Matthew) Flinders (1853–1942) British archaeologist and Egyptologist. After fieldwork at Stonehenge in the 1870s he began excavating the Great Pyramid at Giza in 1880, pioneering the use of mathematical calculation and precise measurement in field archaeology. In his excavations in Egypt and Palestine Petrie also became the first to establish the system of sequence dating, now standard archaeological practice, by which sites are excavated layer by layer and historical chronology determined by the dating of artefacts found *in situ*.

petrochemical Any of the enormous range of chemicals produced from petroleum by further processing after PETROLEUM REFINING or extraction from NATURAL GAS. Fuels, lubricating oils, tars, and natural gas go direct from a refinery for end use. The remaining substances are known as petrochemicals. The first petrochemical was probably CARBON-BLACK, made from natural gas in the 1850s. For most of the next hundred years, COAL-TAR was the main raw material for making organic chemicals and plastics.

Petrograd A former name (1914–24) of ST PETERSBURG.

petrol (US **gasoline**) A volatile oil that readily produces an explosive mixture with air, the fuel used in most INTERNAL-COMBUSTION ENGINES. Petrol is graded according to its ANTIKNOCK quality – its evenness of burning inside an engine. Most petrol is a blend of about 25 HYDROCARBONS, constantly checked and varied to maintain the correct octane number. Adding LEAD TETRAETHYL improves the octane number, but causes lead pollution from car exhausts. Its use is, therefore, being increasingly discouraged. Unleaded petrol still causes emissions of toxins, such as carbon monoxide and hydrocarbons. CATALYTIC CONVERTERS and other devices have been used to reduce these emissions.

petrol engine An INTERNAL-COMBUSTION ENGINE fuelled by petrol in which combustion is initiated by a spark-plug (see IGNITION SYSTEM). Petrol engines have a wide variety of applications, but the most important is as the power unit for the MOTOR CAR. At the centre of the engine are a number of cylinders, each containing a piston. There may be from two to 12 cylinders in a car engine, but most commonly there are four. Most car engines use OTTO's four-stroke cycle. One or two inlet valves on the cylinder head admit the fuel–air mixture from the CARBURETTOR or the injection mechanism, while an exhaust valve or valves releases the exhaust gases after combustion into the exhaust system. These valves are opened and closed by cams on a camshaft, which is driven by a chain or gears from the CRANKSHAFT at half the crankshaft speed. Most modern engines use overhead valves (OHV) and many have one or two overhead camshafts (OHC). Each cylinder also has a spark-plug for ignition of the fuel–air mixture. Because useful work is done on only the third stroke of the four-stroke cycle, a FLYWHEEL is needed on the crankshaft to maintain rotation and smooth out speed fluctuations. In a four-cylinder engine, the power strokes of the pistons are staggered so that on each stroke one of the cylinders is supplying power to the crankshaft.

Some smaller engines, for example marine outboard and small MOTOR-CYCLE engines, use a simpler two-stroke cycle. Instead of valves, the two-stroke engine uses inlet and exhaust ports in the sides of the cylinder, which are covered and uncovered at appropriate points in the engine cycle. Two-stroke engines have advantages of lightness and smoothness, but they are less efficient, and the exhaust is more polluted. Under optimum conditions, modern four-stroke engines can achieve thermal efficiencies of around 30 per cent. However, a DIESEL ENGINE can reach a peak efficiency of 40 per cent.

petroleum A complex mixture, consisting mainly of HYDROCARBON gases and oils, formed in the upper strata of the Earth by the fossilization of vegetable matter over a period of millions of years. It is generally found trapped between layers of impervious rock, usually in the spaces in a layer of porous rock or sand. In China in about 200 BC, petroleum was encountered in digging salt wells; within a few hundred years the petroleum was being used, both for lighting and as a fuel. In the middle of the 19th century, the need for lighting fuel led to the development of the petroleum industry. Since about 1900, the invention of the PETROL ENGINE and the DIESEL ENGINE and the subsequent growth of motor transport has caused the industry to grow very rapidly. Petroleum now provides a large proportion of the world's energy for transport, and has also become the source of thousands of PETROCHEMICALS.

petroleum exploration Petroleum seeping out at the Earth's surface was first extracted as a fuel in prehistoric times, but systematic exploration and recovery dates from 1859, when a well was drilled at Oil Creek in Pennsylvania, USA, near a site of surface seepage.

Exploration for potential traps (reservoirs) now generally starts with aerial or satellite surveying using such devices as gravity meters or magnetometers. Likely trap locations are selected for follow-up with seismography. In this technique, shock waves are generated at the surface using explosives, and measurement of the behaviour of these waves in the Earth provides information on the underlying rock formations. The next stage is to select sites for test drilling. A DRILLING RIG is used to bore a hole through possible oil-bearing locations. Information is collected at each stage of drilling, and the depth of productive rock formations is measured. If the test shows that production will be economic, the well is completed by lining it with concrete. At each productive layer, the concrete is pierced with explosive, and the hole linked to the surface with a narrow pipe called a production string.

The method of recovering the oil depends on the pressure in the trap. Often, well production starts with enough natural pressure to bring up the oil. As the oil stock declines, pressure drops, and artificial methods of lifting it may be needed. Various kinds of pump may be used, or gas lift may be possible. This involves forcing natural gas bubbles to rise up the well, drawing the petroleum up by their buoyancy like the air-powered water circulator in an aquarium. The amount of oil produced by a well can be increased by injecting gas or water to increase reservoir pressure.

petroleum jelly See PETROLEUM REFINING.

petroleum refining The processes used to produce fuels, chemicals, and gas by treatment of PETROLEUM. Petroleum has been known for thousands of years, but systematic separation of its components has only been carried out for just over a century. Initially, petroleum was refined almost entirely to produce fuels. Since World War II the use of refinery products as a source of PETROCHEMICALS has become more important, but over 90 per cent of crude petroleum is still used for fuel.

Petroleum refining consists of separating HYDROCARBONS into various groups of similar compounds. The groups are distinguished by their boiling-points, and they are separated by FRACTIONAL DISTILLATION. A group of hydrocarbons with similar boiling-points is called a fraction. Fractions for which there is little demand may be converted to other fractions by later refinery processes. Refinery gas is the petroleum fraction with the lowest boiling-point, and does not condense in a fractional distillation column. Propane and butane may be extracted from refinery gas to make LIQUID PETROLEUM GAS. The residual gas, containing mainly hydrogen, methane, and ethane, is used as a fuel to operate the refinery. The most economically important product of petroleum refining is the range of fractions called PETROL, which boils at 30–140°C. Light petrol condenses at boiling-points of 30–80°C, right at the top of the fractionation column. It is used to make fuel for petrol engines. Next down the column, at boiling-points of 80–190°C, naphthas are drawn off. Individual naphthas are separated and used to make solvents, and as a raw material in producing many organic chemicals. Much of the naphtha fraction is reformed for use in petrol. The fraction next below the naphthas in the fractionation column condenses at boiling-points of 190–250°C. This fraction contains the kerosenes, which include PARAFFIN, traditionally burnt with a wick for heating and lighting but now more important for making AVIATION FUEL for jet aircraft. The final group of fractions condensing in the column is DIESEL OIL, or gas oil, with boiling-points in the range 250–350°C. Their main use is in DIESEL ENGINES. Heavier oil which does not evaporate in the initial fractional distillation passes through the bottom of the column and are used in LUBRICATING OILS and petroleum jelly.

petrology The scientific study of rocks, their mineral composition, texture, occurrence, and origin. The study is concerned with the origin and mode of formation of all rocks, sedimentary, igneous, and metamorphic. Within the subject, petrography is concerned with the description of rocks, and petrogenesis with their origin.

Petronius, Gaius (known as **Petronius Arbiter**) (died 66 AD) Roman writer. Petronius is generally accepted as the author of the *Satyricon*, a work in prose and verse satirizing the excesses of Roman society. Only fragments of the *Satyricon* survive, most notably that recounting a tastelessly extravagant banquet held by Trimalchio, a character bearing some resemblance to Nero. According to Tacitus, Petronius was 'arbiter of taste' at Nero's court. Petronius committed suicide after being accused of treason by Nero.

petty sessions See HUNDRED.

petunia A colourful, large-flowered annual plant of the genus *Petunia*, related to the tobacco plant, *Nicotiana*, and the potato. The genus contains over 30 species of annuals or perennials, all from South America. The garden petunias are chiefly hybrids between *P. integrifolia* and *P. nyctaginiflora*.

Pevsner, Antoine (1886–1962) Russian-born sculptor and painter who became a French citizen in 1930. He was the elder brother of Naum GABO and like him one of the pioneers of CONSTRUCTIVISM. Until he settled in Paris in 1923 he had been a painter, but he turned to sculpture, at first working mainly in plastic and then in welded metal. His work was important in spreading Constructivist ideas to Western artists.

Pevsner, Sir Nikolaus (1902–83) British art historian, born in Germany. His *Outline of European Architecture* (1942) and *The Buildings of England* (1951–74) are well-known and highly regarded works.

pewter An ALLOY of tin known since the 3rd century AD. Pewter originally consisted of four parts tin to one part lead. Modern pewter, however, contains no lead, being roughly 92 per cent tin with 5 per cent antimony and 3 per cent copper. It has a white lustre and is resistant to corrosion. During the Middle Ages it was extensively used for utilitarian goods, including plates, bowls, drinking vessels and, during the 16th century, it began to be used for similar items intended for decoration, 'display pewter'. In the 19th century new raw materials and techniques made it more or less obsolete for practical purposes, but it continues to be used for decorative wares.

peyote A small, round cactus, *Lophophora williamsii*, native to the Rio Grande Valley, Mexico, and central Texas, which is the source of the hallucinogenic drug mescaline. Unlike most cacti it does not possess spines. It has religious significance to the Peyote Indians.

pH See HYDROGEN ION CONCENTRATION; PH METER.

phagocyte See LEUCOCYTE.

phalanger (or **cuscus**) A MARSUPIAL belonging to the family Phalangeridae. Phalangers are often called 'opossums', but this name is used specifically for the very different South American OPOSSUMS. The family Phalangeridae does however contain four species known as brush-tail possums.

Phalangers have a wide distribution throughout Australasia and include some ten species, the majority of which are lemur-like, such as the black-spotted cuscus, *Phalanger rufoniger*. Most species of cuscus and brushtail possums are herbivorous, although some species also eat insects. The common brush-tail possum, *Trichosurus vulpecula*, was introduced to New Zealand as a potential fur species but has done much damage to native trees by its feeding. It also carries tuberculosis which may infect cattle.

phalarope A small WADING BIRD making up three species with lobed feet and needle-like beaks. Habitual swimmers, they sit high in the water and spin like tops to stir up food in shallows. The males, smaller and less colourful than the females, incubate the eggs and care for the young. Wilson's phalarope, *Steganopus tricolor*, is not in the same genus as the other phalaropes, which are species of *Phalaropus*.

phanerogam A seed-bearing plant. Phanerogams consist of two main groups: the ANGIOSPERMS and the GYMNOSPERMS. Their common feature is that they reproduce, and are dispersed, by means of seeds as opposed to the spores of CRYPTOGAMS. The seed contains the developing plant embryo and a store of food for the initial growth of the germinating plant. The whole seed is enclosed within a hard protective coat, or testa.

Phanerozoic Age A period of geological time comprising the PALAEOZOIC, MESOZOIC, and CAINOZOIC (Cenozoic) Eras. It began approximately 590 million years ago at the start of the Cambrian Period and is marked by the accumulation of sediments containing the remains of animals with mineralized skeletons.

pharaoh A king of ancient EGYPT. The Egyptians themselves only used the term in this way from 950 BC onwards. The pharaoh was thought of as a god, the son of Osiris ruling on Earth, and acted as an intermediary between gods and men. He wielded immense power as the religious, civil, and military leader of the country.

Pharisee A member of a religious party in ancient Israel that set great store by observance of every detail of the Jewish law. They tended to be rather isolated from other Jews and came into conflict with JESUS CHRIST whose compassion was often at odds with their dry legalism, as is clearly documented in the Gospels of the BIBLE. They continued to have enormous influence on Jews – being more popular than the conservative, aristocratic SADDUCEES – and on the development of Judaism after the destruction of the Second Temple of Jerusalem in 70 AD.

pharmaceutics The science of preparing and dispensing medicines. DRUGS are designed by pharmaceutical chemists, who test them on animals and investigate their mode of action. They are manufactured and distributed by the pharmaceutical industry, and dispensed by pharmacists, who sell them as medicines. See also PHARMACOLOGY.

pharmacology The study of the actions of DRUGS on the body. Until the 20th century most pharmacological knowledge was derived from a few observations by physicians on the effects of drugs given to their patients. Now, however, experimental work on animals has enabled scientists to classify drugs by their actions, to describe relationships between the structure of a drug and the actions it exerts, and even to predict (if not always with confidence) the effects that a newly synthesized drug will have. More recently, computers have been used to display the conformation of substances before they are synthesized and to model their probable biological properties.

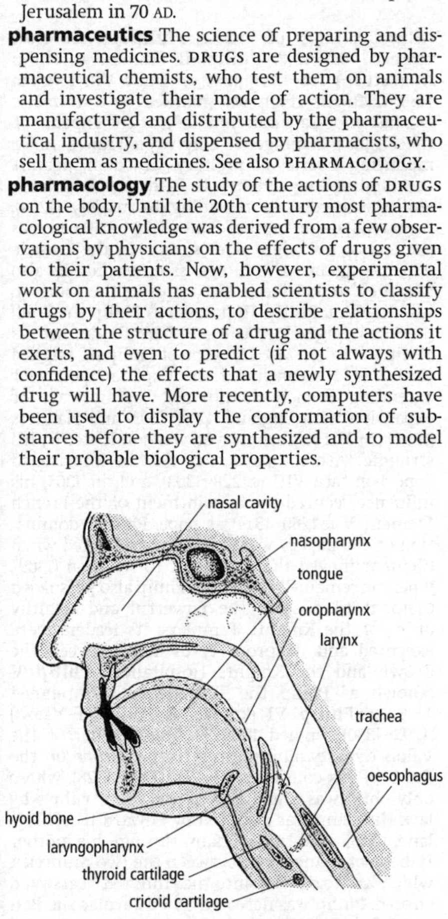

Pharynx In humans the pharynx is divided into the nasopharynx, oropharynx, and laryngopharynx.

pharynx The muscular tube, lined with mucous membrane, that extends from the back of the mouth to the oesophagus (gullet) and larynx. It acts as a passageway for food between the mouth and the gullet and also conducts air from the nasal cavity to the larynx. Inflammation of the pharynx, called **pharyngitis**, is often the cause of a sore throat.

phase In astronomy, the fraction of a body's apparent disc that is illuminated. For example, the cycle of the phases of the Moon occurs because of the changing angle between the Earth, the Moon, and the Sun, together with the fact that the Moon has no light of its own and shines by light reflected from the Sun. At any moment, only half of the Moon's surface reflects light and only when the Moon is in opposition is the whole of the illuminated half presented towards the Earth giving a **full Moon**. At other times within its lunation only a fraction of the illuminated half can be seen. When over half the illuminated face is visible the Moon is said to be **gibbous**. Earthshine is sometimes seen near **new Moon** when the Moon is in conjunction.

phases of matter The states in which matter can exist in which it has different physical properties while retaining the same chemical composition. For example, water (H_2O) can exist as a solid (ice), a liquid (water) or a gas (steam). These different states are known as the three phases of matter. Two further states are considered to be different phases of matter: these are PLASMA and LIQUID CRYSTAL.

pheasant A gamebird that belongs to the family Phasianidae, containing about 183 species found all over the world, with the exception of southern South America, areas of high latitude, and the dry areas of North Africa and the Middle East. The name is used specifically for *Phasianus colchicus*. There is a great range in size in birds of the pheasant family, from the smallest quails, which are up to 13 cm (5 inches) long, to the long-tailed peacocks, up to 2 m (6.5 feet) long, including their tails. The females of most species are mottled brown in colour, which serves to camouflage them when they incubate their eggs on the ground. The males are often brilliantly coloured, with long, elegant tails. The family also includes francolins, wood-quails, partridges, and jungle-fowl.

phenol (or **carbolic acid**, C_6H_5OH) A colourless, low-melting-point, crystalline solid. Dilute phenol solutions were used as disinfectants and for cauterization in 19th-century hospitals; modern antiseptics (for example, trichlorophenol, TCP) are phenol derivatives. Carbolic soap for household cleaning contains phenol. Although it was first extracted from COAL-TAR in 1834, phenol is now more commonly synthesized from BENZENE. Commercially it is used in the manufacture of nylon dyes, drugs, perfumes, photographic developers, explosives, and thermosetting plastics. Phenol is the simplest example of a whole class of aromatic alcohols, also known as **phenols**, in which a hydroxyl group is bonded to a carbon atom that forms part of an aromatic ring. The phenols differ from aliphatic alcohols in that the hydrogen atom on the hydroxyl group is acidic.

phenol-formaldehyde resin A thermosetting PLASTIC produced by the polymerization of phenol (C_6H_5OH) and methanal (formaldehyde, HCHO). In alkaline conditions the reaction produces a viscous resin that forms a hard, intractable material on heating. In acid conditions a type of resin called novolak is produced. This can be ground to a fine powder and dissolved in solvents for use as a varnish, or mixed with fillers and binders and moulded under pressure, whereupon additional polymerization takes place, producing an insoluble, infusible material. The first phenol-formaldehyde resin to be produced commercially was **Bakelite**.

phenomenology A philosophical method developed by the philosopher Edmund HUSSERL and widely employed in CONTINENTAL PHILOSOPHY. The key tenet of phenomenology, defined in *Cartesian Meditations* (1931), is that philosophical truth is to be obtained by examining the nature and content of consciousness. Phenomenological investigation emphasizes that consciousness is intentional, and employs the 'phenomenological reduction', an operation that enables us to suspend belief in, or 'bracket', the existence of the things we have consciousness of, such as the external world. This is not undertaken with a view to promoting SCEPTICISM about the external world, but in order to focus on what survives such a reduction: namely, pure consciousness. Husserl's phenomenology was never brought to completion, but it led directly to EXISTENTIALISM.

phenotype The physical expression of a particular GENOTYPE; for example, in tall and short pea plants. Because of dominance and recessiveness, different genotypes may give the same phenotype. For example, the homozygous and heterozygous combinations of the ALLELES T and t, TT and Tt, represent different genotypes, but both give the same tall phenotype. The phenotype can also be altered by the environment (see ADAPTATION).

pheromone A highly volatile HORMONE-like chemical secreted by an animal in order to influence the behaviour of another individual of the same species. Pheromones work at minute concentrations and can be released from special glands, or simply discharged from the body in perspiration, urine, or faeces. They function as a chemical signalling system, of particular importance in the life of insects. Pheromones play a very important part in the sexual behaviour of many animals. Other functions of pheromones include territory marking, trail marking in ants, and alarm signalling, particularly in fish and tadpoles. Similar scents designed to have effects on other species of animal are called allomones.

Use is now being made of pheromones in pest control: they are used to attract male insects, which are then killed. Because they are highly specific, pheromones lack the damaging side-effects of INSECTICIDES. Examples of their successful use include the control of cotton boll-weevil (*Anthonomus grandis*) in Pakistan, and the cotton leafworm alabama (*Alabama argillacea*) in Peru.

Phidias (5th century BC) Athenian sculptor. In about 447 he was appointed by Pericles to plan and supervise building on the Acropolis in Athens. His own contributions to the project included a colossal gold-and-ivory statue of Athene Parthenos for the Parthenon (*c.*438), which has not survived; he also supervised the carving of the Elgin Marbles. He is also noted for his vast statue of Zeus at Olympia (*c.*430), which was one of the Seven Wonders of the World.

Philadelphia The chief city of Pennsylvania, USA, a deep-water port at the junction of the Delaware and Schuylkill rivers; pop. (1990) 1,585,580. First settled by Swedes in the 1640s, it is now the second-largest city on the east coast and fifth-largest in the USA, with industries producing vehicle parts, electrical machinery, clothes, carpets, scientific instruments, and cigars.

Philby, Kim (full name Harold Adrian Russell Philby) (1912–88) British Foreign Office official and spy. While chief liaison officer at the British Embassy in Washington, DC (1949–51) he was suspected of being a Soviet agent and interrogated, but in the absence of firm evidence against him Philby was merely asked to resign. He defected to the USSR in 1963, and in the same year it was officially revealed that he had spied for the Soviets from 1933. He became a Soviet citizen in 1963 and was appointed a general in the KGB.

Philip Five kings of ancient Macedonia, notably Philip II and Philip V. **Philip II** (known as Philip II of Macedon) (382–336 BC), father of Alexander the Great, reigned 359–336. He unified and expanded ancient Macedonia, as well as carrying out a number of army reforms, such as the introduction of the phalanx formation. His victory over Athens and Thebes at the Battle of Chaeronea in 338 established his hegemony over Greece. He was assassinated as he was about to lead an expedition against Persia. **Philip V** (238–179 BC) reigned 221–179. His expansionist policies led to a series of confrontations with Rome, culminating in his defeat in Thessaly in 197 and his resultant loss of control over Greece.

Philip Six kings of France. **Philip I** (1052–1108) reigned 1059–1108. **Philip II** (known as Philip Augustus) (1165–1223), son of Louis VII, reigned 1180–1223. His reign was marked by a dramatic expansion of Capetian influence, at the expense of the English Plantagenet empire in France. After mounting a series of military campaigns against the English kings Henry II, Richard I, and John, Philip succeeded in regaining Normandy (1204), Anjou (1204), and most of Poitou (1204–05). Towards the end of his reign, after success in the crusade (1209–31) against the Albigensian heretics, he also managed to add fresh territories in the south to his kingdom. **Philip III** (known as Philip the Bold) (1245–85) reigned 1270–85. **Philip IV** (known as Philip the Fair) (1268–1314), son of Philip III, reigned 1285–1314. He continued the Capetian policy of extending French dominions, waging wars of expansion with England (1294–1303) and Flanders (1302–05). His reign, however, was dominated by his struggle with the papacy; in 1303 he imprisoned Pope Boniface VIII (*c.*1228–1303), and, in 1305, his influence secured the appointment of the French Clement V (*c.*1260–1314) as pope. Philip's domination of the papacy was further consolidated when Clement moved the papal seat to Avignon (1309), where it remained until 1377. Philip also persuaded Clement to dissolve the powerful and wealthy order of the Knights Templars; its leaders were executed and its property divided between the Crown and the Knights Hospitallers. **Philip V** (known as Philip the Tall) (1293–1322) reigned 1316–22. **Philip VI** (known as Philip of Valois) (1293–1350) reigned 1328–50. The founder of the Valois dynasty, Philip came to the throne on the death of his cousin Charles IV (1294–1328), whose only child was a girl and barred from ruling by law. His claim was disputed by Edward III of England, who could trace a claim through his mother Isabella of France. War between the two countries, which was to develop into the Hundred Years War, ensued. Philip was defeated by Edward at the Battle of Crécy (1346).

Philip Five kings of Spain. **Philip I** (known as Philip the Handsome) (1478–1506) reigned 1504–06. Son of the Holy Roman emperor Maximilian I of Habsburg (1459–1519), Philip married the infanta Joanna, daughter of Ferdinand of Aragon and Isabella of Castile, in 1496. After Isabella's death he ruled Castile jointly with Joanna, establishing the Habsburgs as the ruling dynasty in Spain. **Philip II** (1527–98), son of Charles I, reigned 1556–98. Philip married the second of his four wives, Mary I of England, in 1554, and came to the throne following his father's abdication two years later. His reign came to be dominated by an anti-Protestant crusade which exhausted the Spanish economy. He failed to suppress revolt in the Netherlands (1567–79), and although he conquered Portugal in 1580, his war against England also proved a failure, an attempted Spanish invasion being thwarted by the defeat of the Armada in 1588. **Philip III** (1578–1621) reigned 1598–1621. **Philip IV** (1605–65) reigned 1621–65. **Philip V** (1683–1746), grandson of Louis XIV, reigned 1700–24 and 1724–46. The selection of Philip, a Bourbon, as successor to Charles II, and Louis XIV's insistence that Philip remain an heir to the French throne, gave rise to the threat of the union of the French and Spanish thrones and led to the War of the Spanish Succession (1701–14). Internationally recognized as king of Spain by the Peace of Utrecht (1713–14), Philip reigned until 1724, when he abdicated in favour of his son Louis I (1707–24), but returned to the throne following Louis's death in the same year.

Philip, Prince, Duke of Edinburgh (1921–) Husband of Elizabeth II. The son of Prince Andrew of Greece and Denmark (1882–1944), he married Princess Elizabeth in 1947; on the eve of his marriage he was created Duke of Edinburgh. He served in the Royal Navy until Elizabeth's accession in 1952.

Philip, St (1st century) One of the 12 Apostles. According to John, he was born in Bethsaida, answered Christ's call, and was instrumental in the call of St Nathanael (probably Bartholomew the Apostle). According again to John, he participated in the miracle of the loaves and the fishes, therefore acquired the symbol of loaves in medieval art. Feast day (in the Western Church), May 11.

Philip Augustus Philip II of France. See PHILIP (kings of France).

Philip II of Macedon Philip II of Macedonia. See PHILIP (kings of Macedonia).

Philip II of Spain See PHILIP (kings of Spain).

Philip of Valois Philip VI of France. See PHILIP (kings of France).

Philippi (Greek **Fílippoi**) A city of ancient Macedonia, the scene in 42 BC of the two battles in which Antony and Octavian defeated Brutus and Cassius. The ruins lie close to the Aegean coast in north-eastern Greece, near the port of Kaválla (ancient Neapolis).

Philippines A country in south-east Asia comprising over 7,000 islands between the Pacific Ocean and the South China Sea.

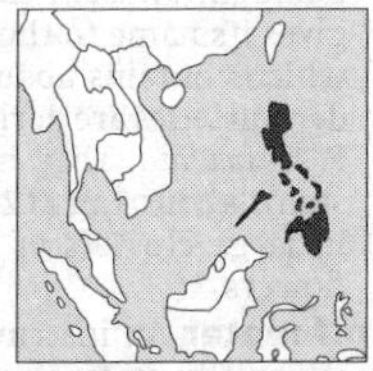

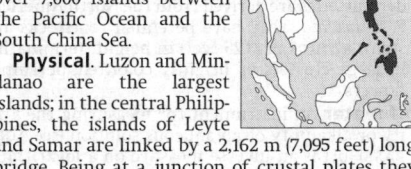

Physical. Luzon and Mindanao are the largest islands; in the central Philippines, the islands of Leyte and Samar are linked by a 2,162 m (7,095 feet) long bridge. Being at a junction of crustal plates they contain volcanoes and are subject to earthquakes; and as they are in the path of two MONSOONS there is rain for most of the year. The climate is tropical throughout the year. Many of the islands are mountainous and heavily forested with teak, ebony, and sandalwood. Bamboo and coconut palms grow in profusion.

Economy. The economy of the Philippines is predominantly agricultural, but manufacturing industry such as textiles, chemicals, electric machinery, and food-processing is expanding. Mineral resources include coal, nickel ore, copper, chromite, iron, silver, and gold. The principal exports are electronics and clothing; sugar cane, bananas, timber, and coconuts are the major cash crops, while rice, maize, and tobacco are also grown. There is widespread poverty, and land reform is an important issue.

History. The original Negrito inhabitants of the Philippines were largely displaced by waves of Malay peoples migrating from Yunnan province in south-west China after *c*.2000 BC. By 1000 AD the islands were within the south-east Asian trade network. By the 16th century Islam was advancing from Mindanao and Sulu into the central islands and Luzon. After Spaniards under MAGELLAN visited the islands (1521), Spanish seamen discovered how to return eastbound across the Pacific to Mexico. In 1543 they named the islands after Prince Philip (later PHILIP II of Spain). In 1564 Miguel de Legazpi, with 380 men, set out from Mexico to establish a settlement, Christianize the Filipinos, open up commerce with East Asia, and secure a share of trade in the MOLUCCAS. A settlement was made in 1565 at Cebu in the western Visayas, but the Spaniards moved their headquarters to Manila in 1571. Manila became the centre for a trade in Chinese silks with Mexico, in return for Mexican silver dollars. From there Spanish influence and control spread out through the Philippine island chain, particularly assisted by missionary activity. Christian outposts founded by Dominicans, Franciscans, and Augustinians grew into towns. Revolts against the harsh treatment of Filipinos by the Spanish were frequent, particularly in the 17th century. During the SEVEN YEARS WAR the British occupied Manila for two years.

In 1896, a nationalist uprising against the Spanish colonial authorities broke out in Manila, led by José Rizal. After the outbreak of the Spanish–American War in 1898, General Emilio AGUINALDO, acting with the support of the USA, declared the country's independence. After Spain's defeat, however, the nationalists found themselves opposed by the Americans, and after a brief war (1899–1901), the islands passed under US control. Internal self-government was granted in 1935, and, after the Japanese occupation during World War II, the Philippines became an independent republic in 1946 under the Presidency of Manuel Roxas, with the USA continuing to maintain military bases. Successive administrations proved incapable of dealing with severe economic problems and regional unrest. In 1972, using the pretext of civil unrest, in particular the communist guerrilla insurgency conducted by the New People's Army in Luzon, and violent campaigns of Muslim separatists, the Moro National Liberation Front, in the southern Philippines, President MARCOS declared martial law, assuming dictatorial powers. While the Marcos regime achieved some success in dealing with both economic problems and guerrilla activities, the return to democratic government was never satisfactorily achieved and corruption was widespread, epitomized in the amassing of huge personal fortunes by the Marcos family. After the murder of the opposition leader, Benigno Aquino Jr, in 1983, resistance to the Marcos regime coalesced behind his widow Corazon Aquino and the United Nationalist Democratic Organization. US support for the Marcos government waned and in 1986, after a disputed election and a popularly backed military revolt, Marcos fled, and Corazon Aquino became President in his place, restoring the country to a fragile democracy. When she came into office it is estimated that 70 per cent of the population of the Philippines remained below the poverty line, while the eruption of Mount Pinatubo in 1991 caused immense damage. There were no less than six attempted military coups against President Aquino, who refused to stand for re-election. She was succeeded in 1992 by her ex-Defence Secretary Fidel Ramos, who completed arrangements for the withdrawal of US forces from Subic Bay and other military and naval installations. In 1994, Ramos announced a coalition with the main opposition party, in order to facilitate passage of a common legislative programme and in 1996 a peace agreement with Muslim rebels was made.

Capital: Manila
Area: 300,000 sq km (115,800 sq mi)
Population: 70,011,000 (1995)
Currency: 1 Philippine peso = 100 centavos
Religions: Roman Catholic 84.1%; Aglipayan Philippine Independent Church 6.2%; Muslim 4.3%; Protestant 3.9%
Ethnic Groups: Tagalog 29.7%; Cebuano 24.2%; Ilocano 10.3%; Hiligaynon Ilongo 9.2%; Bicol 5.6%; Samar-Leyte 4.0%; Pampango 2.8%; Pangasinan 1.8%
Languages: English, Pilipino (based on Tagalog) (both official); Cebuano; Ilocano; local languages
International Organizations: UN; Colombo Plan

Philip the Bold Philip III of France. See PHILIP (kings of France).

Philip the Fair Philip IV of France. See PHILIP (kings of France).

Philip the Good (1396–1467) Duke of Burgundy 1419–67. His first act as Duke of Burgundy was to forge an alliance with HENRY V of England and to recognize him as heir to the French throne. He was a powerful ally: by the early decades of the 15th century his territories included Namur (acquired 1421), Holland and Zeeland (1428), Brabant (1430), Luxembourg (1435); the bishoprics of Liege, Cambrai, and Utrecht were under Burgundian control. Under Philip the Burgundian court was the most prosperous and civilized in Europe. He founded an order of CHIVALRY, the Order of the Golden Fleece, and patronized Flemish painters.

Philip the Handsome Philip I of Spain. See PHILIP (kings of Spain).

Philip the Tall Philip V of France. See PHILIP (kings of France).

Philistines A non-Semitic people, originally a group of the SEA PEOPLES, who settled in southern PALESTINE in the 12th century BC. Having established five cities – Ashdod, Askelon, Ekron, Gath, and Gaza – they gained control of land and sea routes and proved a formidable enemy to the Israelites, inflicting defeats on Samson and SAUL. King DAVID, however, gained decisive revenge (*c.*1000 BC) and from then on Philistine power declined until they were assimilated with the CANAANITES.

Philoctetes In Greek mythology, a warrior, famous for his prowess with bow and arrows (which he had inherited from Hercules). On his way to the Trojan War he was bitten by a serpent and abandoned on the island of Lemnos because of his terrible cries and the stench from his fetid wound. After many years the Greeks were told in a prophecy that Troy would not fall without Philoctetes' help, so he was rescued from Lemnos and healed by Machaon. Philoctetes killed Paris with his arrow, thus helping to bring about the downfall of Troy.

philosophy (Greek, 'love of wisdom') The use of reason and argument in the search for truth and the nature of reality, especially of the causes and nature of things and of the principles governing existence, PERCEPTION, human behaviour, and the material Universe. Philosophical activities can also be directed at understanding and clarifying the concepts, methods, and doctrines of other disciplines, or at reasoning itself and the concepts, methods, and doctrines of such general notions as truth, possibility, knowledge (EPISTEMOLOGY), necessity, existence (ONTOLOGY and METAPHYSICS), and proof. Philosophy has many different areas, classified according to the subject-matter of the problems being addressed; thus, philosophy of mind is concerned with such questions as 'how does the mental interact with the physical?'; philosophy of mathematics with such questions as 'what constitutes a proof?'; of RELIGION ('does God exist?'); of science ('what constitutes good evidence for a hypothesis?'); of ETHICS; of POLITICS; and indeed of any other discipline. The first philosophers were also the first scientists, people who asked questions about the physical world and who attempted to answer them by observation (see EMPIRICISM) and reasoning (see RATIONALISM) rather than by appealing to magic or to a God of some kind. Major areas in which philosophy can be applied to the problems of everyday life are moral and political philosophy, especially in MEDICAL ETHICS, such as the prevention of conception and the enhancement of fertility. In such cases very deep moral problems arise, the solutions to which require sustained and critical examination of what is right and what is wrong.

Phiz (pseudonym of Hablot Knight Browne) (1815–82) British illustrator. He was apprenticed to an engraver, but turned to etching and watercolour painting. In 1836 he was chosen to illustrate Dickens's *Pickwick Papers*, and took his pseudonym to complement Dickens's 'Boz'. He illustrated many of Dickens's works, including *Martin Chuzzlewit* and *Bleak House*.

phloem Plant tissues making up vessels involved in the movement, or translocation, of food substances around the plant. They do so by using chemical energy to transport substances up or down the plant, from the leaves to the roots, or vice versa. In woody plants the phloem vessels constitute the innermost layer of the bark.

phlox An annual or perennial herb or shrub of the genus *Phlox*, from temperate America and Eurasia, which takes its name from the Greek word for flame (in allusion to the colour of its flowers). It gives its name to the phlox family, Polemoniaceae, which contains about 300 species. The many garden varieties are derived from the North American *P. paniculata*. They have perennial rootstocks and stems about 1 m (3.25 feet) in height, terminating in large clusters of brightly coloured, perfumed flowers.

pH meter An instrument for measuring the acidity or alkalinity of an aqueous solution (see ACID; BASE). pH is an inverse measure on a logarithmic scale of the HYDROGEN ION CONCENTRATION of a solution. In a pH meter, hydrogen ion concentration is measured electrically: the solution whose pH is being measured forms part of an electrochemical cell (see BATTERY) containing a standard or reference electrode of known pH, with which the pH of the unknown solution is compared.

Phnom Penh The capital of Cambodia, a port at the junction of the Mekong, Bassac, and Tonlé Sap rivers; pop. (est. 1994) 920,000. Founded by the Khmers in the 14th century, it succeeded Angkor as capital in the mid-15th century. During the 1970s and 1980s its population fluctuated dramatically, first in response to an influx of refugees after the spread of the Vietnam war to Cambodia, and second when the Khmer Rouge took over the city in 1975 and forced its population of 2.5 million into the countryside as part of a radical social programme. The city was repopulated after the arrival of the Vietnamese in 1979.

phobia A type of ANXIETY disorder in which there is an unfounded or disproportionate fear of, and consequent urge to avoid, some object or situation. Specific phobias, for example of snakes or spiders, are common and not necessarily disabling in everyday life. Of more concern in PSYCHIATRY is agoraphobia, a fear of public places, which may limit the person's freedom of movement. In treatment by BEHAVIOUR THERAPY, patients confront a series of increasingly potent examples of what they fear. When they can cope with the less terrifying encounters they move on to those they find worse. The patients are often also taught relaxation techniques or other strategies to overcome the build-up of anxiety.

Phobos The inner satellite of Mars, discovered by the US astronomer Asaph Hall in 1877. Its orbit is 9,830 km from the planet's centre. Phobos has an irregular shape, with a mean radius of about 11 km and a density of 2,200 kg/m^3. Images from the VIKING probes showed a dark, heavily cratered and REGOLITH-covered surface.

Phoebe A satellite of Saturn, discovered by the US astronomer William Pickering in 1898. Its orbit has a semi-major axis of about 13 million km and Phoebe moves in the opposite direction to Saturn's orbital motion. VOYAGER images have revealed a nearly spherical shape of diameter 220 km and a patchy surface with low albedo (0.06).

Phoenician A Semitic people of ancient Phoenicia in southern Syria, of unknown origin, but culturally descended from the Canaanites of the 2nd millennium BC, who occupied the coastal plain of modern Lebanon and Syria in the 1st millennium BC and derived their prosperity from trade and manufacturing industries in textiles, glass, metalware, carved ivory, wood, and jewellery. Their trading contacts extended throughout Asia, and reached westwards as far as Africa (where they founded Carthage), Spain, and possibly Britain. The Phoenicians continued to thrive under Assyrian and then Persian suzerainty until 322 BC, when the capital, Tyre, was sacked and the country incorporated in the Greek world by Alexander the Great.

phoenix A sacred bird of Egyptian and oriental myth, said to renew itself every few hundred years from the ashes of a pyre of flames on which it placed itself. The phoenix, used in literature as a symbol of death and resurrection, is alleged to resemble an eagle, but with red and gold plumage. As a sacred symbol of Egypt, the phoenix represented the Sun, which sinks each night and rises again each morning.

Phoenix A CONSTELLATION of the southern sky, introduced by the Dutch navigators Pieter Dirkszoon Keyser and Frederick de Houtman at the end of the 16th century. It represents the mythical PHOENIX that was reborn from its own ashes. Alpha Phoenicis, its brightest star, is of second magnitude.

Phoenix The capital and largest city of Arizona, USA; pop. (1990) 983,400. Founded in 1870, it became territorial capital in 1889 and remained the capital when Arizona became a state in 1912. Phoenix is now a centre for information technology and the manufacture of computers and aircraft, its dry climate also making it a popular winter resort.

phoneme See PHONOLOGY.

phonetics The analysis of speech sounds as physical entities from the point of view of their production (atriculatory phonetics), transmission (acoustic phonetics), and perception (auditory phonetics). Sounds (or phones) are broadly classified as vowels and consonants. Vowels are further described in articulatory terms with respect to the degree of mouth opening, and the positions of the tongue and the lips. Consonants are described with reference to the manner in which the air passes through the vocal tract and the participating speech organs. Many of the applications of phonetics depend on accurate written records (transcriptions) of spoken texts. These use phonetic alphabets to represent the sound systems of individual languages. The International Phonetic Alphabet (IPA), a British invention of 1889, is a widely used example.

phonology A branch of LINGUISTICS investigating the organization of sounds in LANGUAGES. Its major insight is that different sounds may count as a single sound within a language. For example, the *p* sound in *pill* differs from the *p* sound in *spill*: only the former is aspirated, followed by a short puff of air. This difference never distinguishes one word from another in English and the speakers are unaware of it. A number of sounds that count as a single sound in this way are known as a **phoneme**. Speech can largely be analysed as a sequence of phoneme segments, but speech also has features extending beyond one segment, notably intonation and tone. Intonation refers to the patterns of pitch or melody performing various grammatical and semantic functions. Tone is a similar feature of individual words, distinguishing one word from another, in so-called tone languages such as Chinese and the Niger–Congo languages.

phosgene (or **carbonyl chloride**, $COCl_2$) A gaseous chemical warfare agent that attacks the respiratory system, first used by the German Army in 1915. When inhaled, phosgene corrodes the lungs, making lesions in the membrane and causing fluid congestion. Death is by asphyxiation.

phosphate (PO_3^{4-}) Any salt or ester of PHOSPHORIC ACID. Phosphates occur in a number of natural deposits, including guano and the phosphates of sodium, potassium, and calcium; specifically, rock phosphate (phosphorite). The deposits are sedimentary material both of marine origin (phosphate salts precipitated directly from sea water) and, more commonly, formed on land (bones or guano). Extensive supplies occur in several countries, notably Morocco, Algeria, Tunisia, and China. Synthetic phosphates are used chiefly as FERTILIZERS, to supply the essential element PHOSPHORUS in the form of superphosphate and triple phosphate. They are also used in washing powders, water softeners, baking powder, and processed foods and drinks.

phosphorescence The emission of light from a substance after it has been exposed to and excited by some form of radiation. It occurs because the energy from the original radiation is absorbed by the charge cloud of electrons in the atoms of the substance and this distorts the shape of the cloud. When the radiation is removed the cloud reverts to its original shape and in so doing the energy is re-emitted in the form of light. When this happens immediately the phenomenon is called FLUORESCENCE, but in certain types of atom there is a time-lag and the material continues to glow for a time until the charge clouds of all the atoms have returned to their normal pattern. Materials that exhibit phosphorescence are called **phosphors** and they are used to produce the picture on a television tube: the original excitation is produced by a beam of electrons which strikes the phosphor momentarily, causing it to emit light of a particular colour. Phosphorescence is also used more widely to include any emission of light by a cold object, for example by fireflies (more properly called **bioluminescence**).

phosphoric acid (or **orthophosphoric acid**, H_3PO_4) A colourless, crystalline solid, usually encountered as a syrupy concentrated solution. It is manufactured industrially by treating phosphate rock with dilute SULPHURIC ACID, filtering, and concentrating the filtrate by evaporation. Its main uses are in the manufacture of PHOSPHATES and for rust-proofing STEEL before painting.

phosphorus (symbol P, at. no. 15, r.a.m. 30.97) A non-metal in Group 15 (formerly VA) of the PERIODIC TABLE, which exists as several ALLOTROPES. White phosphorus is waxy and catches fire spontaneously in air, and so it is normally stored under water; it is used in the making of rat poisons. The second form, red phosphorus, is a dark red powder, non-poisonous, and generally more stable; it is used to make match heads. Red phosphorus is obtained industrially by heating calcium phosphate with sand and coke in an electric furnace. Black phosphorus is prepared by heating the white form under pressure; it has a layer structure and is also stable. Phosphorus occurs in nature only in a combined state, mainly as PHOSPHATES, in limestones, bone beds, and guano. The mineral apatite, found in igneous rocks, is the major source. Extraction is by heating with coke and silica; the phosphorus is distilled off and condensed under water. Of its compounds, the oxide is a white powder used as a drying agent, and the phosphates are used for making fireworks and smoke bombs and as fertilizers and detergents. The element is essential to life: it is needed for the formation of bones and teeth, and for the chemistry of respiration and reproduction.

Photius (*c.*820–*c.*891) Byzantine scholar and patriarch of Constantinople. His most important work is the *Bibliotheca*, a critical account of 280 earlier prose works and an invaluable source of information about many works now lost.

photocell A TRANSDUCER that converts light into electrical energy. Originally a photocell was a photoelectric cell, in which light of a suitable wavelength falling on the cell results in the emission of electrons, and, in the presence of a small driving voltage, the flow of electric current. Such a cell can be used to measure light intensity. A photocell is now more commonly a photoconductive cell, which only becomes conductive when illuminated. Photodiodes and photovoltaic cells may also be called photocells. A photodiode produces a current when its cathode is illuminated, while a photovoltaic cell (see SOLAR CELL) generates a potential difference or voltage on exposure to light. Photocells are often used to detect the passage of an object (in door-opening sensors, burglar alarms, etc.): most commonly, the photocell is illuminated by a thin beam of light, and passage of an object between the light and the photocell produces an interruption in the photocurrent.

photochemical reaction A chemical reaction initiated by light that will not proceed in the absence of light. An important naturally occurring photochemical reaction is PHOTOSYNTHESIS. Photography is based on a photochemical reaction initiated when light-sensitive substances on the film are exposed to light.

photochromic lens A glass lens used in sunglasses that darkens when exposed to sunlight and clears again when light levels fall. The glass contains minute crystals of silver halide, so small that the glass is normally transparent. The blue and ultraviolet light in sunlight temporarily turns parts of the crystals into silver, which absorbs light and darkens the glass.

photocopier A device for making duplicates (photocopies) of documents using **xerography**, a dry electrostatic process in which a pattern of electric charge is induced when light falls on a layer of semiconducting material on a conducting surface. Toner powder sprayed onto this material sticks to the highly charged areas, and is transferred to the paper copy, where it is fixed by heating. Most photocopiers are designed to reproduce only black-and-white images, but colour photocopiers – which scan the document with red, green, and blue filters – are becoming increasingly common. It is also possible to insert a screen into the photocopier to mimic the HALF-TONE PROCESS for images with intermediate tones.

photoelectric cell See PHOTOCELL.

photoelectric effects The interaction of ELECTROMAGNETIC RADIATION with matter, especially solids. Irradiation of most materials with PHOTONS of ultraviolet light or radiation of shorter wavelength results in the emission of electrons; some substances exhibit the phenomenon with visible light also. This is called photoemission. The energy of the photons is given up to the emitted electrons, which are called photoelectrons and can constitute a current in an electric circuit. The energy of the electrons depends on the frequency of the light; its intensity affects only the number emitted. These observations led Albert Einstein to develop further Max Planck's ideas of the QUANTUM THEORY. Photoemission has led to development of the PHOTOCELL. Other photoelectric effects are photoconduction and the photovoltaic effect. In photoconduction the electrons released act as additional charge carriers within the material and so the electrical resistance decreases. This is particularly effective in SEMICONDUCTORS, and the phenomenon is used in several devices for detecting not only visible light but also infrared radiation. In the photovoltaic effect, light falling on pairs of materials, such as selenium on a metal plate, will generate an electromotive force, as in a cell, producing a current. As the basis of several light-sensitive devices it is one of the principles being used to harness solar energy in order to produce electricity.

photography The recording of a permanent image by the action of light, or other ELECTROMAGNETIC RADIATION, upon a sensitive medium.

The basic photographic process has changed little since the late 19th century, although photographic EMULSIONS have been greatly improved, and the CAMERA has undergone radical changes. The image of the object to be photographed is focused on to the film through the camera's LENS SYSTEM. After exposure to light the film is developed in a series of chemical processes to obtain a negative image, from which positive photographic prints are then made by exposing light-sensitive paper through the negative. In a reversal system, the film from the camera is processed to produce a positive slide rather than a negative image.

photogravure See GRAVURE PRINTING.

photometry The measurement of the brightness of light, used in astronomy and physics. The earliest estimates of stellar brightness were naked-eye observations by HIPPARCHUS and Ptolemy, which formed a basis for the logarithmic MAGNITUDE scale invariably used in modern astronomical photometry. Most professional photometry uses **photometers** consisting of a telescope with an electronic detector at the eyepiece; the measurements are corrected for the absorbing and scattering effects of the Earth's atmosphere. A series of differently coloured filters is used to sample the light from the celestial object under study. The wavelengths (colours) passed by the filters are carefully chosen to reveal characteristic spectral lines, such as absorption lines in stars and galaxies, and emission lines and bands in gaseous nebulae and comets. Magnitudes from different filters are usually compared and interpreted as a COLOUR INDEX, which is a ratio and thus independent of the actual light levels or the distance to the object. In recent years the photometry of galaxies and other extended objects has been enormously improved as CCD CAMERAS have displaced photography.

photomultiplier A device for detecting extremely low light levels. The photomultiplier is a type of ELECTRON tube with a cathode (negative electrode) that emits electrons when light falls on it. Electrons emitted from the cathode are accelerated towards the first of a series of anodes (positive ELECTRODES) called dynodes. The dynode is made from a material that emits several electrons in response to each electron received from the cathode. Each subsequent dynode multiplies the number of electrons emitted. This 'avalanche effect' results in a measurable electrical current being produced from an initially very small light input.

photon A 'packet' or quantum of ELECTROMAGNETIC RADIATION. Max PLANCK showed that radiation can be emitted or absorbed by a system only in certain fixed amounts or quanta. These may be considered as small indivisible packets or units of energy, or as particles of zero mass. The energy of a photon depends on its frequency and is equal to $h \times$ frequency, where h is the Planck constant (6.6×10^{-34} joule second). Thus, for example, a photon at a radio frequency is of much lower energy than a gamma-ray photon. If energetic enough, a photon can ionize atoms. Photons are required to explain phenomena, such as the PHOTOELECTRIC EFFECT, that require light to have particle character. See also WAVE-PARTICLE DUALITY.

photosphere Those layers of a star's atmosphere from which most of the light is emitted, and where many of the spectral lines are formed. The photosphere is usually very thin relative to the size of a star; a representative thickness is one-thousandth of the stellar radius. The PLASMA temperature drops through the photosphere as the distance from the centre of the star increases, and then rises in the overlying and more transparent CHROMOSPHERE and CORONA. In the particular case of the Sun, it is the thinness of the solar photosphere that gives the Sun its apparently sharp edge. In fact the photosphere is frequently thought of as the surface of the Sun.

photosynthesis The utilization of light energy from the Sun to produce food in the form of CARBOHYDRATES. It is a process carried out by all plants and algae and certain bacteria, using special pigments, called CHLOROPHYLLS, which can absorb the radiant energy of the Sun and convert it to chemical energy. This chemical energy is used to make sugars from the gas carbon dioxide and water. In this sense 'food' is simply stored energy, capable of being released either within the plant at a later date, or utilized by animals.

In plants, the chlorophylls are contained in small 'packets', called chloroplasts, in the surface layers of leaves and young stems. Some algae and bacteria have additional red, blue, or brown photosynthetic pigments called phycobilins, which function in a manner similar to chlorophyll.

phototypesetting See TYPESETTING.

Phrygia An ancient region of west-central Asia Minor, to the south of Bithynia. Centred on the city of Gordium west of present-day Ankara, it dominated Asia Minor after the decline of the Hittites in the 12th century BC, reaching the peak of its power in the 8th century under King Midas. Conquered by the Cimmerians *c.*760 BC, it was eventually absorbed into the kingdom of Lydia in the 6th century BC.

phylloxera A plant BUG belonging to the homopteran family Phylloxoridae. The most notorious species is the grape phylloxera, *Phylloxera vitifolia*, which is closely related to APHIDS and has a similarly complex life cycle. The insect feeds on grape vines, causing the formation of galls on leaves and roots that eventually destroy the plant. Native to North America, it spread to Europe in the 19th century, when it ravaged the wine industry in France and Germany.

phylum One of the first group of divisions into which KINGDOMS of living organisms are classified. In general, phyla are groups that show no evolutionary relationship to others except in that all have the basic characters of the kingdom. All phyla are subdivided into CLASSES, although in the animal kingdom some large phyla, notably the Chordata and Arthropoda, are divided first into subphyla. In traditional systems of plant classification, groups at the level of phyla are called divisions, and their Latin names are distinguished by the ending -phyta.

physical chemistry The branch of chemistry concerned with the effect of chemical structures on physical properties. It includes molecular kinetics, reaction rates, chemical thermodynamics, electrochemistry, photochemistry, and spectroscopy.

physical geography The branch of geography that deals with the natural features of the Earth's surface.

physics The study of the properties and interactions of matter and energy; it differs from chemistry in dealing less with particular substances and more with matter in general, although there are areas of overlap, as in PHYSICAL CHEMISTRY. Physics originally was the systematic study of all nature, both animate and inanimate: what is now called science and was formerly called natural philosophy. Only in the 17th and 18th centuries did it become restricted first to the study of inanimate matter and then, with the separate development of chemistry, to the present-day classical physics, which includes optics, acoustics, mechanics, thermodynamics, and electromagnetism. In the 20th century the most far-reaching contributions came from QUANTUM THEORY and RELATIVITY, which have led to knowledge about the Universe at the smallest scale (QUARKS) and the largest (cosmology and the 'big bang'). Modern aspects of the subject include nuclear physics, particle physics, solid state physics, and astrophysics.

physiology The study of the functioning of living organisms and their component parts. It is closely associated with both anatomy (the structure of living organisms) and biochemistry (the chemical reactions taking place in living organisms).

physiotherapy The treatment of muscles and joints by physical means. It promotes healing more quickly than rest alone, with minimal restriction of movements. For example, massage increases blood supply, reduces swelling due to oedema (water retention), and relieves pain. It is very valuable following sports injuries. In older people it relieves pain resulting from everyday injuries and helps alleviate joint stiffness and arthritis. It can also be used to relieve the pain from muscular tension.

phytogeography Plant geography or the study of the geographical distribution of plants.

pi (symbol π) In geometry pi has been defined historically in two different ways. The ratio of the circumference of any circle to its diameter is always the same. The ratio of the area of any circle to that of the square on its radius is also always a constant. Both constants have the same value commonly approximated by 3.142 or 22/7. It has been evaluated to billions of decimal places by computer. Pi is both an IRRATIONAL NUMBER and a TRANSCENDENTAL NUMBER.

Piaf, Edith (born Edith Giovanna Gassion) (1915–63) French singer. She acquired her name in 1935, when a cabaret impresario called her *la môme piaf* ('little sparrow'), referring to her small size. She became known as a cabaret and music-hall singer in the late 1930s, touring Europe and the USA in the 1940s. She is especially remembered for her defiant and nostalgic songs, some of which she wrote herself, including 'La Vie en rose'. Other songs include 'Je ne regrette rien'.

Piaget, Jean (1896–1980) Swiss psychologist. Piaget's work centred on the thesis that children initially lack intellectual and logical abilities, which they acquire through experience and interaction with the world around them. They then proceed through a series of fixed stages of cognitive development, each being a prerequisite for the next. His books include *The Origin of Intelligence in Children* (1954).

piano (or **pianoforte**) A KEYBOARD musical instrument with strings struck by hammers, so called because it plays both piano (softly) and forte (loudly), unlike the HARPSICHORD. Bartolomeo Cristofori invented the first true piano around 1700. It met with little success because the light strings then available were more suitable to plucking (as in the harpsichord) than striking. Only after 1750 did musicians prefer pianos to harpsichords, by which time technological advances had brought heavier strings. The problem of higher tensions required by the heavier strings was finally resolved when, in 1825, Alpheus Babcock patented the full iron frame. Grand pianos always existed, but square pianos (actually oblong) were popular for domestic use for about a century from about 1750. Uprights were introduced late in the 18th century. By about 1870 the piano had reached its modern form, but changes, especially to the tone in Japan and the USA, continued. In the 19th century the mechanical **pianola** (or player piano) was invented. This was controlled by a perforated roll of paper regulating the airflow to pneumatically operated hammers. The bellows were either operated by pedals or, later, by electric motor. The pianola was extremely popular in the 1920s, before the widespread use of the gramophone and the modern electronic player piano. In the electronic piano, the familiar seven-and-a-quarter octave keyboard is used to produce sounds resembling a struck string by electronic means.

pianola See PIANO.

pibroch See PIOBAIREACHD MUSIC.

Picardy (French **Picardie**) A region of northern France centred on the former province of this name and comprising the departments of Aisne, Oise, and Somme; area 19,399 sq km (7,493 sq miles); pop. (1990) 1,810,690. Its chief town is Amiens.

picaresque novel A story comprising the adventures of a *picaro* (Spanish, 'rogue'), usually a quick-witted servant who has several masters in succession. The form originated in 16th-century Spain, and was imitated by Grimmelshausen in Germany and by Defoe and Smollett in England. More loosely, stories without a complex plot, that follow a sequence of episodes involving an unchanging central character are also called picaresque. In this sense, Cervantes' *Don Quixote* (1605) and Fielding's *Tom Jones* (1749) are called picaresque, although they do not fit the stricter Spanish meaning.

Picasso, Pablo (1881–1973) Spanish painter, sculptor, and graphic artist, resident in France from 1904. His prolific inventiveness and technical versatility assured his position as the dominant figure in avant-garde art in the first half of the 20th century. The paintings of Picasso's Blue Period (1901–04) used melancholy blue tones to depict social outsiders. These gave way to his Rose Period (1905–06), in which circus performers were represented in pinks and greys. *Les Demoiselles d'Avignon* (1907), with its rejection of naturalism signalled the emergence of cubism, which he developed with Georges Braque and others from 1908 to 1914. The 1920s and 1930s saw the evolution of a neoclassical figurative style, designs for Diaghilev's Ballets Russes, and the evolution of semi-surrealist paintings using increasingly violent imagery. Notable examples include *The Three Dancers* (1935) and *Guernica* (1937), his response to the destruction of the Basque capital by German bombers in the Spanish Civil War.

Piccadilly A street in central London, England, stretching from Hyde Park eastwards to **Piccadilly Circus**. It is noted for its shops, the Ritz Hotel, Burlington House (home of the Royal Academy), and Burlington Arcade. The aluminium statue of Eros or 'Christian Charity' at the centre of Piccadilly Circus was erected in honour of the 7th Earl of Shaftesbury (1801–85) who was responsible for developing much of the property in the area.

Piccard, Auguste 1884–1962) Swiss scientist and explorer. In 1931 he began his exploration of the stratosphere by balloon, reaching a height of 16,940 metres (55,577 feet) in 1932. From 1948 his interest turned to the depths of the ocean, which with his son **Jacques Piccard** (1927–), he explored in his bathyscaphe, *Trieste*. In the Mediterranean he reached a depth of 3,100 metres (10,171 feet) and later in the Pacific a depth of 10,917 metres (35,817 feet).

piccolo A half-size FLUTE, sounding an octave higher than written. Because it is played in the orchestra by a flautist, its development has paralleled that of the flute save that it has rarely acquired the C-footkeys; its lowest note is normally the D a ninth above middle C.

pickerel A small member of the PIKE family, Esocidae, found only in eastern North America. Two species are known, the chain pickerel, *Esox niger*, and the redfin or grass pickerel, *E. americanus*, the latter being divided into two subspecies. They are similar to the pike in many ways but not in size, the chain pickerel growing to 75 cm (30 inches) and the grass pickerel to 38 cm (15 inches). Both feed on small crustaceans and insect larvae, and eat fishes once they are longer than 10 cm (4 inches). They live in slow-flowing, heavily weeded streams and lakes.

picketing A form of INDUSTRIAL ACTION in which people stand outside a workplace in order to discourage other employees from going into work where other workers are on strike. Pickets may try to prevent deliveries to or from the workplace from crossing the picket line. Secondary picketing is picketing by workers at a workplace other than that of those directly involved in a dispute. Flying pickets move rapidly from one site to another to add their support to other workers.

Pickford, Mary (born Gladys Mary Smith) (1893–1979) Canadian-born US actress. She was a star of silent films, usually playing the innocent young heroine, as in *Rebecca of Sunnybrook Farm* (1917) and *Pollyanna* (1920). In 1919 she co-founded the film production company United Artists; she was married to one of the other founders, Douglas Fairbanks, between 1919 and 1936.

Pict A member of an ancient people, of disputed origin and ethnological affinities, who formerly inhabited parts of northern Britain. In Roman writings (*c.*300 AD) *Picti* ('painted people') was used to describe the hostile tribes occupying the area north of the Antonine Wall. According to chroniclers the Pictish kingdom was united with the Scottish under Kenneth MacAlpine in 843, and the name of the Picts as a distinct people gradually disappeared.

Pictor The Painter's Easel, a CONSTELLATION of the southern sky, introduced by the 18th-century French astronomer Nicolas Louis de Lacaille. Its brightest star is of only third magnitude.

piddock A BIVALVE of the family Pholadidae, which gains protection against predators by burrowing into rocks, clay, or even masonry foundations of man-made structures. The shell valves gape open towards the front and back of the animal, allowing the foot to protrude for burrowing and the siphons to be extruded for irrigating the burrow with clean water. The foot holds the piddock in its burrow while the shell valves rock back and forth to scrape rock away.

pidgin and creole languages (respectively, from a Chinese corruption of English 'business' and Spanish *criollo*, 'native') Two related types of LANGUAGE. A pidgin is a grammatically, lexically, and functionally simplified form of the dominant language. Well-known pidgins have been derived from English, French, and Portuguese. Pidgin English was formerly widely used by Chinese people talking to Europeans. Neo-Melanesian is another form of pidgin English spoken in New Guinea. Creoles are pidgins based on English, French, or Dutch spoken in the West Indies as a mother tongue. The status of creoles is the same as that of other natural languages, but their history is different.

Piedmont (Italian **Piemonte**) A region of north-west Italy in the foothills of the Alps, comprising the provinces of Alessandria, Asti, Cuneo, Novara, Torino, and Vercelli; area 25,400 sq km (9,810 sq miles); pop. (1990) 4,357,230; capital, Turin. It is watered by the River Po. Dominated by Savoy from 1400, it became part of the kingdom of Sardinia in 1720 and the kingdom of Italy in 1861. It was the centre of the movement for a united Italy in the 19th century.

Pierce, Franklin (1804–69) US Democratic statesman, 14th President of the USA 1853–57. His presidency saw the rise of divisions within the country over slavery and the encouragement of settlement in the north-west. His support for the Kansas–Nebraska Act lost him the support of northern Democrats and any chance of renomination in 1856.

Piero della Francesca (*c.*1415–92) Italian painter. He worked in a number of cities, including Florence and Arezzo, and was influenced by the work of Masaccio and Uccello. He is best known as a panel and fresco painter, and among his major works is a fresco cycle in Arezzo depicting the story of the True Cross (begun 1452).

Piero di Cosimo (*c.*1462–*c.*1521) Italian painter, one of the most unconventional of the Florentine artists of the RENAISSANCE. He painted religious works and portraits, but is best known for a novel type of painting – fanciful mythological scenes inhabited by fauns, centaurs, and primitive men. ANDREA DEL SARTO was his pupil.

Pierre The state capital of South Dakota, USA, on the east bank of the Missouri River; pop. (1990) 12,900. It was first settled in 1880 and lies at the geographic centre of the state.

Pierrot A stock character in the French and British theatres, based on the comic servant mask of Pedrolino in the *commedia dell'arte*, and featured in the HARLEQUINADE. Simple-minded and awkward, with a whitened face, he wore a long-sleeved loose white garment with a ruff and floppy hat. Pierrot was transformed into a pathetic and lovesick character by Deburau, the French MIME artist.

Pietermaritzburg A city in the province of KwaZulu-Natal, South Africa, situated in the foothills of the Drakensberg Range; pop. (1991) 228,550. Founded in 1838 by Cape Colony Boers, it was named in honour of the Boer leaders Piet Retief and Gert Maritz who were killed by Zulus. It was capital of the former province of Natal from 1843 (when it was annexed by the British) to 1994.

Pietersburg The capital (since 1994) of Northern Transvaal, South Africa, an agricultural and mining centre north-east of Pretoria; pop. (1985) 29,000.

piezoelectric effect A phenomenon discovered by the brothers Pierre and Jacques Curie in 1880. They found that crystals of quartz gave rise to a small voltage when compressed or stretched. Applications include piezoelectric MICROPHONES, and the crystal pickups used in some record-players. In many CLOCKS and WATCHES the reverse effect is used – an alternating voltage causes a crystal to expand and contract rhythmically, thus providing the constant frequency needed for accuracy.

pig A member of the family Suidae, which contains nine species, widely distributed in the Old World. They are members of the large order Artiodactyla (even-toed ungulates) but, unlike most other members of this order, they are non-RUMINANTS. The pig family includes wild BOARS, BUSH PIGS, babirusas, and wart hogs. All are terrestrial and their modest-sized body is covered with bristles. All have an elongated head which terminates in a snout. This is a tough, mobile, disc-like plate of cartilage, reinforced with a small bone to withstand the stresses exerted when it is used for pushing, lifting, digging, and breaking through tangled brush. Their canine teeth are tusk-like and grow upwards and outwards. They are omnivores. See also PIG FARMING.

pigeon A bird of the DOVE family, Columbidae, with an almost worldwide distribution. This family contains about 280 species ranging in size from about 15 cm (6 inches) long for the smallest species, to large-crowned pigeons from New Guinea, *Goura cristata*, which are almost the size of a small turkey, 80 cm (32 inches) long. Pigeons have a wide range of plumage colours, especially greys and greyish-browns, though the 20 or so species of fruit pigeons are predominantly green. The typical pigeon beak is of medium length, but thinnish. Most species are monogamous and live in pairs during the breeding season, though many aggregate into flocks, sometimes of considerable size, at other times of the year.

All species are herbivorous, eating leaves, seeds, or fruits. Pigeons build flimsy nests of twigs, usually in the branches of trees, but sometimes in holes in trees, on rock ledges, or on the ground. Most species lay one or two white eggs. The young are raised on pigeon's milk, a product of the cell walls of the parents' crop, for the first few days, followed by increasing amounts of vegetable material.

pigeon-racing The sport of breeding and training pigeons to race from a common release-point back to their loft. On arrival, the owner removes a coded race-ring from the bird's leg and places it in a timing clock to record its performance. Pigeon-racing is especially popular in northern England, Belgium, and Germany, where individual owners, known as fanciers, join a local club. To give the birds an equal chance and minimize the effects of changing wind-forces during a race, each club has a small fixed radius of membership.

pig farming The rearing of pigs to produce pork and bacon for human consumption: for pork they are slaughtered at 70–90 kg (155–200 pounds) and for bacon at 80–100 kg (175–220 pounds). Among large animals, pigs offer the most meat in relation to their volume. They may be factory-farmed or raised free-range: traditional pig breeds remain highly prized for the quality of their meat. Sows have a gestation period of about 114 days, and litters average ten piglets. They can therefore produce 20 piglets or more each year, from the age of 12 months.

Piggott, Lester (Keith) (1935–) British jockey. He was champion jockey nine times between 1960 and 1971 and again in 1981 and 1982; he won the Derby a record nine times. He made a comeback as a jockey in 1990 after a period of imprisonment for tax irregularities (1987–88).

pig-iron See IRON.

pigment A substance that imparts colour to another substance or mixture, a basic ingredient of PAINTS, INKS, DYES, and COSMETICS. With the exception of some naturally occurring organic pigments, such as chlorophyll, which dissolve in organic SOLVENTS, most pigments are insoluble in water and organic solvents. Examples of pigments include metal oxides, such as iron oxide (red-brown), naturally occurring earths that are easily ground into fine powders (for example, sienna and ochres), metal powders, such as aluminium dust (silvery), metal salts, such as lead chromate (chrome yellow), amorphous carbon (black), and insoluble dyes, such as Prussian blue. Most pigments that were once derived from natural sources are now manufactured synthetically.

pigmy moth A tiny moth of the family Nepticulidae, occurring worldwide, with a wing-span between 3 mm (0.125 inch) and 10 mm (0.5 inch). The wings are hairy, and the fore-wings usually dark and metallic coloured. The caterpillars are leaf-miners, most constructing a mine with a characteristic shape.

pika (or **cony**) A mammal of the family Ochotonidae in the order Lagomorpha, which otherwise includes only rabbits and hares. They resemble rabbits in their dentition and in the habit of eating their night-time droppings. Unlike the rabbits, however, they have short ears, hind-legs that are not much longer than the front ones, and they lack a tail. They are unique among mammals in making hay in the late summer for use in the winter, for they do not hibernate. Grasses and other vegetation are carried to rocks exposed to the Sun and, when dry, they are stored in piles at the entrance of their burrows or under rock overhangs. The 14 species range from the Urals to Japan in temperate Asia and there are two North American species, the collared pika, *Ochotona collaris*, and the North American pika, *O. princeps*.

pike A slender freshwater fish of the genus *Esox*, in the family Esocidae, with dorsal and anal fins placed close to the tail fin, and a pointed head. There are five species across northern Europe, Asia, and North America in slow-flowing rivers and lakes. Pike are predatory fishes, eating mainly aquatic insect larvae and crustaceans when young but later eating other fishes with the occasional duck or mammal. They typically lie in wait for prey close to vegetation, camouflaged by their mottled coloration, and make sudden charges, the huge teeth in the lower jaw grasping the prey.

pike-perch (or **zander**) A European fish, *Lucioperca lucioperca*. Its original range was in central and eastern Europe, but it has been introduced in France, the Netherlands, and England. A slender-bodied relative of the perch, it has a long-based, spiny dorsal fin. Feeding mostly at dawn and dusk, it is an efficient predator of smaller fishes and competes successfully with both perch and pike.

Pilate, Pontius (died *c.*36 AD) Roman prefect of Judaea *c.*26–*c.*36. Little is known of his life; he is chiefly remembered for presiding at the trial of Jesus Christ and sentencing him to death by crucifixion, as recorded in the New Testament. Pilate was later recalled to Rome to stand trial on charges of cruelty, having ordered a massacre of the Samaritans in 36. According to one tradition he subsequently committed suicide.

pilchard A member of the herring family. The European species, *Sardina pilchardus*, is called a pilchard when adult and a sardine when immature. This species occurs throughout European seas (except the Baltic) although it is uncommon north of Britain. It is a schooling fish living from the surface to a depth of 55 m (180 feet) and feeding on plankton. Other species of pilchard are abundant off southern Africa and Australia, and these belong to the genus *Sardinops*, as does the Californian or Pacific sardine, *S. caeruleus*.

pilgrimage A journey, usually lengthy, to visit a religious shrine or site.

Most religions have traditional pilgrimage sites, such as sacred rivers, shrines, or buildings. Christian pilgrimage was initially made to sites connected with the life of JESUS CHRIST (principally Jerusalem, also a sacred site for Jews and Muslims), and Muslim obstruction of this custom helped to provoke the CRUSADES.

Pilgrimage to the Kaaba at MECCA, well established in pagan Arabia, was incorporated into

ISLAM, the detailed rites being based on MUHAMMAD's own practice. Every Muslim tries to undertake the pilgrimage to Mecca at least once in a lifetime. The *hajj* (Arabic, 'pilgrimage'), undertaken only in the twelfth month of the Muslim calendar, became highly organized, with special caravans and guides. In addition, Karbala and Najaf in Iraq are sacred to Shiite Muslims.

In India, pilgrimage was often linked to Hindu festivals and associated with rivers, such as the Ganges, or sacred cities, such as VARANASI (Benares). The Golden Temple at Amritsar in the Punjab is a pilgrimage site for Sikhs. In China and Japan mountains, such as Mount Tai and Mount Fujiyama, were early favoured as sites for BUDDHIST pilgrimage. Mendicants and scholars often adopted pilgrimage as a permanent way of life.

Pilgrimage of Grace (1536–37) A series of rebellions in the northern English counties, the most significant of which was led by Robert Aske, a lawyer. He managed, briefly, to weld together the disparate grievances of his socially diverse followers. The main causes of concern were the religious policies of Thomas CROMWELL, notably the Dissolution of the MONASTERIES, although the rebels stressed their loyalty to HENRY VIII. Severe retribution followed, as Henry authorized the execution of about 200 of those involved, including Aske.

Pilgrim Fathers The 102 founders of the Plymouth plantation in America, who had travelled from Plymouth in England in the *Mayflower* in 1620. Some of them had been persecuted as separatists from the Church of England, and the nucleus of them had fled from Scrooby in Nottinghamshire in 1608 to Holland. In 1618 they obtained backing from a syndicate of London merchants and permission to settle in Virginia. On the voyage, having no charter, they subscribed to a covenant for self-government, the Mayflower Compact. They made landfall at Cape Cod, Massachusetts, in December and decided to settle there. Only half the party survived the first winter.

Pillars of Hercules The two promontories known in ancient times as Calpe and Abyla and now known as the Rock of Gibraltar and Mount Acho in Ceuta. Situated opposite one another at the eastern end of the Strait of Gibraltar, they were held by legend to have been parted by the arm of Hercules and were regarded as marking the limit of the known world.

pill beetle A small, drab, almost spherical beetle of the family Byrrhidae, with some 270 species distributed worldwide. It lives at the roots of grass or moss and under stones. When disturbed, pill beetles draw their antennae and legs close to the body and feign death; in this state they are difficult to detect.

pill bug See WOODLOUSE.

pilot fish A species of oceanic fish, *Naucrates ductor*, worldwide in distribution in tropical and subtropical seas, which occasionally occurs in cool temperate seas. It belongs to the same family as the HORSE MACKEREL, and like it is streamlined in body shape, but has five to seven broad, dark blue bars on its sides; it grows to 70 cm (28 inches) in length. Pilot fishes have the habit of swimming close to larger animals, such as sharks and turtles, and often accompany sailing ships, usually keeping slightly below but close to the front of the animal or ship. As juveniles they swim close to floating weeds and jellyfishes.

Piltdown Man Supposed fossil remains 'discovered' by Charles Dawson in 1908–13 in gravels in the hamlet of Piltdown in East Sussex, England. The association of a modern-looking skull, ape-like jaw, and extinct animal bones provided just the missing link in human evolution being keenly sought at the time. It was not until 1953 that '*Eoanthropus dawsoni*' was shown by scientific tests to be a forgery.

pimento (or **allspice**) A small tropical tree, *Pimenta officinalis*, belonging to the myrtle family, Myrtaceae. It is native to the West Indies and tropical Central America and the powdered, dried, unripe berries are used to flavour foods. An oil is extracted from the berries, and another from the leaves. These are used in toilet preparations, soap, and hair tonics, and bay oil is obtained from a closely related species.

pimpernel A plant belonging to the genus *Anagallis*, of which the best-known European species is the scarlet pimpernel, *A. arvensis*. This tiny annual, with bright red, pink, or even blue flowers, is also called poor man's weather-glass because the flowers open only in fine weather. The genus contains 28 species, all of which are restricted to northern temperate regions. They belong to the primrose family, Primulaceae. The Mediterranean species, *A. linifolia*, is a perennial in its native habitat but is often grown in gardens as an attractive annual with several colour forms.

pinchbeck See BRASS.

Pindar (*c*.518–*c*.438 BC) Greek lyric poet. His surviving works include four books of odes (the *Epinikia*) celebrating victories won in athletic contests at Olympia and elsewhere. The odes are often in the form of choral hymns.

pine An evergreen conifer of the genus *Pinus*, of which there are 70–100 species in the north temperate zones and mountains of the tropics. Together with silver firs, spruces, hemlock spruces, Douglas firs, cedars, and larches, they make up the main family of conifers, Pinaceae. All pines produce resin and have female cones, which take two to three years to ripen after pollination. The wind-blown pollen is produced in such quantities that it can turn rain yellow and leave a scum on standing water. Pines are important constituents of northern temperate forests and are widely planted for timber throughout the world.

pineal gland (or **pineal body**) A small ball of tissue attached to the brain of vertebrates. In some vertebrates, such as frogs and sharks, this organ contains sensory cells that respond to light and in these animals acts like a third 'eye' under the surface of the skin. In mammals it is apparently devoid of nerve cells, but consists of secretory cells, which are activated by fibres of the AUTONOMIC NERVOUS SYSTEM. The cells contain serotonin, which is converted to a hormone, melatonin. The amounts of melatonin in the gland, brain fluids, and PLASMA fluctuate in a 24-hour rhythm, peaking during darkness, and it is thought that melatonin and serotonin work together to regulate the sleep cycle.

pineapple A plant, *Ananas comosus*, of South American origin, cultivated particularly in Hawaii, Malaysia, Thailand, and other tropical areas. It belongs to the family Bromeliaceae (see BROMELIAD). The short-stemmed perennial plants have a spiral of large, sword-shaped leaves, topped by a swollen stem carrying between 100 and 200 flowers. Their fruits join together to produce the large, pine-cone-shaped, sweetly flavoured fruit, which contains about 15 per cent sugar and is rich in vitamins A, B, and C.

pine marten See MARTEN.

Pinero, Sir Arthur Wing (1855–1934) British dramatist. His first serious play, *The Profligate* (1889), concerned the double standards for men and women, which became a recurring theme for many of his plays, including *Lady Bountiful* (1891), the first of his 'social' plays, and his most lasting success *The Second Mrs Tanqueray* (1893).

pink A plant belonging to a large genus, *Dianthus*, in the family Caryophyllaceae. This large family of over 2,000 species has a worldwide distribution and includes many popular garden plants, including *Gypsophila* and campions. Pinks are species of *Dianthus* occurring naturally or as hybrids. The carnation is a form of *D. caryophyllus*, while the 'garden pink' is derived from *D. plumarius*. Both parent species are native to Europe and have been selectively bred for over 300 years to produce the garden pinks and carnations.

Pinkerton, Allan (1819–84) Scottish-born US detective. He emigrated to the USA in 1842, and in 1850 he established the first US private detective agency (in Chicago), becoming famous after solving a series of train robberies. In the early years of the American Civil War (1861–62) he served as chief of the secret service for the Union side. His agency was later involved in anti-trade union activity, particularly in the coal industry (1877).

pink-footed goose A species of goose, *Anser brachyrhynchus*, that can be distinguished from the larger bean and greylag geese by the darker head and neck, black and pink beak, and pink legs. They breed in Greenland, Iceland, and Spitzbergen and winter in western Europe, including Britain, where they are the most numerous visiting goose.

Pinochet (Ugarto), Augusto (1915–) Chilean general and statesman, President 1974–90. He became Commander-in-Chief of Chile's armed forces in 1973 and in the same year masterminded the military coup that overthrew President Allende. He imposed a repressive military dictatorship until forced to call elections (December 1989), giving way to a democratically elected President in 1990.

pintail A slender, long-necked dabbling DUCK, *Anas acuta*, widespread in the Northern Hemisphere. The drake (male) is mainly grey, with a chocolate and white head, neck, and breast. Both sexes have pointed tails, but the drake's is greatly elongated, and needle-like.

Pinter, Harold (1930–) British dramatist, actor, and director. His plays are associated with the Theatre of the Absurd and are often marked by a sense of brooding menace; they include *The Birthday Party* (1958) *The Caretaker* (1960), *Party Time* (1991), *Moonlight* (1993), and *Ashes to Ashes* (1996). He has also written screenplays, including the film version of John Fowles's *The French Lieutenant's Woman* (1981) and *The Trial* (1993).

pinworm (or **threadworm**) A ROUNDWORM that is a parasite in the gut of vertebrates and invertebrates. The human pinworms, *Enterobius vermicularis*, are a common, but relatively harmless, parasite of children throughout the world. They pass from child to child as eggs derived from foods or by hands contaminated with the faeces of an infected individual.

pinyin See ALPHABET; SINO-TIBETAN LANGUAGES.

piobaireachd music (Scots Gaelic, 'piping'; Anglicized as **pibroch**) The 'great music' of the Scottish Highland BAGPIPE, contrasting with the 'small music', represented by military music, airs, and dances. It was developed from the early 16th century as a form of ceremonial music played at highland courts, clan gatherings, and battles, the names of the main classes – salute, lament, march, gathering – reflecting this.

pion An atomic particle belonging to the class known as MESONS. In 1935 the Japanese physicist Hideki YUKAWA suggested that the strong nuclear INTERACTION could be regarded as the result of an interchange of certain particles between nucleons. These particles are now called pions. There are two types of pion: the charged pions, which can be either positively or negatively charged and have a mass 273 times that of the electron; and the neutral pions, which have a mass 264 times that of the electron. Pions have a lifetime of 30 nanoseconds.

pipe and tabor The original one-man dance band, used throughout Europe from the 13th century. The pipe is played with the left hand, and the TABOR, strapped to the left shoulder, wrist, or forearm, is struck with the right. The pipe has only three holes, two finger-holes and one thumb-hole, enough to fill the gaps between the overblown harmonics.

pipefish Any of about 150 species of long thin fish of the family Syngnathidae, which are relatives of the sea horses and like them are slow swimmers. They are found in marine and brackish water in all but the polar seas, although they occur most abundantly in the tropics. A few species, principally in south-east Asia, live in fresh water. Mostly they are found in shallow seas down to a depth of 90 m (295 feet) but a few live at the surface of the open sea, often in association with floating seaweed.

Piper, John (1903–92) British painter and designer. His early paintings were abstract, but in the 1930s he turned to a romantic naturalism. During World War II he was one of the artists commissioned to depict the results of air raids on Britain. He is best known for watercolours and aquatints of buildings (such as those depicting Windsor Castle, 1941–42) and stained glass for Coventry and Llandaff cathedrals.

pipe snake See CYLINDER SNAKE.

pipette A graduated glass tube for delivering accurate quantities of a liquid. It is a standard piece of laboratory equipment. The liquid was originally sucked up by mouth, but rubber bulbs with control valves are now used. Automatic or 'Oxford' pipettes draw up liquid by a plunger mechanism into a disposable tip: depression of the plunger dispenses a fixed quantity of liquid.

pipistrelle A small to medium-sized insectivorous BAT of the genus *Pipistrellus*, family Vespertilionidae. There are some 47 species, found in most parts of the world except South America. The common pipistrelle, *P. pipistrellus*, is the commonest bat in Britain and is the one most often found roosting in attics and seen flying just before dusk.

pipit Any one of about 34 species of bird of the genus *Anthus*, belonging to the WAGTAIL family. All are small, 15–18 cm (6–7 inches) long, greyish or greenish above, and paler below; many of them are heavily streaked. Most have white outer tail feathers. They have a worldwide distribution, and live in open country or on the edge of woods, usually nesting on the ground.

Piraeus The chief port of Athens in ancient and modern Greece, situated on the Saronic Gulf 8 km (5 miles) south-west of the city; pop. (1991) 182,670. Used as a port by the ancient Athenians, it was connected to the city by the 'long walls', two parallel walls built in the 5th century BC. It was destroyed by the Roman general Sulla in 86 BC. Extensive development in the 19th century led to its modern status as the principal seaport of Greece. It has oil refining and shipbuilding industries as well as chemicals and textiles.

Pirandello, Luigi (1867–1936) Italian dramatist and novelist. His plays challenged the conventions of naturalism and had a significant influence on the development of European drama, anticipating the anti-illusionist theatre of Brecht. Of his ten plays the best known include *Six Characters in Search of an Author* (1921) and *Henry IV* (1922). Among his novels are *The Outcast* (1901) and *The Late Mattia Pascal* (1904). He was awarded the Nobel Prize for literature in 1934. He profoundly influenced the existentialist pessimism of ANOUILH and SARTRE, as well as the absurdist comedy of IONESCO and BECKETT and the religious verse-drama of ELIOT.

Piranesi, Giovanni Battista (1720–78) Italian engraver. His interest in classical Roman architecture is reflected in his prints, in which he relied on atypical viewpoints and dramatic chiaroscuro to aggrandize its power and scale. His *Prisons* (1745–61) extended this imagery into the realms of fantasy.

piranha A predatory fish in the same family as the characins and tetras, the Characidae, but confined to the tropical fresh waters of South America. Piranhas are deep-bodied, disc-shaped fishes of the genera *Serrasalmus*, *Rooseveltiella*, and *Pygocentrus*, with a blunt head, a moderately long dorsal fin, and an adipose fin near the tail. Their most notable features are the teeth and jaws. The teeth are triangular in the lower jaw, but have several cusps in the upper; all are pointed and razor-sharp, while the jaws are strong with powerful muscles. Piranhas live in shoals and eat fishes, and can quickly strip all the flesh from a large, disabled fish, leaving only the bones.

Pisa A city in Tuscany, west-central Italy, capital of Pisa province; pop. (1990) 101,500. The city is noted for the 'Leaning Tower of Pisa', an eight-storey circular bell-tower which leans about 5 m (17 ft) from the perpendicular over its height of 55 m (181 ft), part of this inclination dating from its construction at the end of the 12th century. Formerly situated on the coast, it was an important Etruscan town and a naval base in Roman times, becoming a powerful maritime city-state in the Middle Ages. It now lies about 10 km (6 miles) inland, as a result of the silting of the Arno on which it stands. Its university dates from the mid-14th century, and it was the birthplace of Galileo in 1564. Pisa's modern industries include engineering, glassware, pharmaceuticals, clothing, and tourism.

Pisan, Christine de See DE PISAN.

Pisanello (born Antonio Pisano) (*c*.1395–*c*.1455), Italian painter and medallist. He worked mainly in Verona and his successful career also took him to Rome and numerous courts of northern Italy. Pisanello was the finest portrait medallist of his period and arguably of the whole Renaissance. With GENTILE DA FABRIANO he is also regarded as the foremost representative of the INTERNATIONAL GOTHIC style in Italian painting, though few of his paintings survive. There are still, however, a good many of his drawings in existence.

Pisano, Andrea (*c*.1290–*c*.1348) Italian sculptor. He is notable as the creator of the earliest pair of bronze doors for the baptistery at Florence (completed 1336). His son **Nino** (died *c*.1368) was one of the earliest sculptors to specialize in free-standing life-size figures.

Pisano, Nicola (*c*.1220–*c*.1278) Italian sculptor. His work departed from medieval conventions and signalled a revival of interest in classical sculpture. His best-known works are the pulpits in the baptistery at Pisa (*c*.1255–60) and in Siena cathedral (1265–68). His son, **Giovanni** (*c*.1250–*c*.1314), was also a sculptor, whose works include pulpits in the church of Santa Andrea in Pistoia (completed 1301) and Pisa Cathedral (1302–10), and the richly decorated façade of Siena cathedral.

Pisces The Fishes, a CONSTELLATION of the zodiac. In mythology it represents Venus and her son Cupid who jumped into the river Euphrates to escape from the monster Typhon and were turned into fishes; in the sky the tails of the two fishes are visualized tied together by a cord. Alpha Piscium (Alrescha, Arabic for 'cord') is a close binary star of fourth and fifth magnitudes.

Piscis Austrinus (or **Australis**) The Southern Fish, a CONSTELLATION of the southern sky, one of the 48 constellations known to the ancient Greeks. It is depicted as a fish drinking the flow of water from the urn of Aquarius, and supposedly represents the Syrian fertility goddess Derceto who fell into a lake and was saved by (or changed into) a fish.

Pisistratus (or **Peisistratus**) (*c*.600–*c*.527 BC) Tyrant of Athens. He seized power in 561 and after twice being expelled ruled continuously from 546 until his death. As ruler he reduced aristocratic power in rural Attica and promoted the financial prosperity and cultural pre-eminence of Athens.

Pissarro, Camille (1830–1903) French painter and graphic artist, one of the leading figures of IMPRESSIONISM. The only artist who exhibited at all eight Impressionist exhibitions, he was looked upon as an inspirational teacher. His large output consisted mainly of landscape paintings, and when – from about 1895 – failing eyesight caused him to give up painting in the open, he produced many town views from windows in Paris.

pistachio A nut that comes from a small evergreen tree, *Pistacia vera*, related to the mango in the family Anacardiaceae, and native to the Near East and western Asia. It has been cultivated there and in the Mediterranean area for up to 4,000 years. Male and female flowers are on separate trees and from the latter are obtained the pleasant but mild nuts (in fact a seed, not a true nut) with green kernels.

pistol A FIREARM small enough to be fired with one hand. The earliest pistols (16th century) were wheel-locks (see FIREARM) and were used primarily by cavalry, who found the two-handed musket too unwieldy while riding a horse. Flint-locks replaced the wheel-locks at the end of the 17th century. In the early 19th century percussion ignition was introduced, as for other firearms. Towards mid-century several inventors, among them COLT, developed repeating pistols incorporating a revolving cylinder with five or more chambers, each of which could be loaded with a percussion cap and a round of ammunition. At the beginning of the 20th century, automatic pistols were developed, using a blow-back system of operation. A slide, pushed back by surplus propellant gases after the bullet has left the barrel, forces open the breech to eject the spent CARTRIDGE. A spring at the base of the magazine forces the next round into the breech.

Pitcairn Islands A British dependency comprising a group of volcanic islands in the South Pacific, east of French Polynesia; area 4.6 sq km (1.75 sq miles); pop. (1995) 54. The colony's only settlement is Adamstown, on Pitcairn Island, the chief island of the group (which also includes the uninhabited

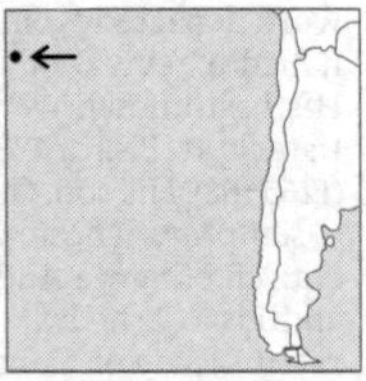

islands of Henderson, Ducie, and Oeno). Pitcairn Island was discovered in 1767 by a British naval officer, Philip Carteret, and named after the midshipman who first sighted it. It remained uninhabited until settled in 1790 by mutineers from HMS *Bounty* and their Tahitian companions, some of whose descendants still live there.

pitch (in music) The height or depth of a musical note as perceived by the ear. The pitch of a note is measured by its frequency. Most instruments are tuned to note A, set at an internationally agreed concert-pitch of 440 hertz (vibrations per second). It replaced the standard of 435 hertz set by the French government in 1859. Before that date pitches differed from place to place. Pitch can be notated in the form of a scale, or described by a series of letter-names (A, B, C, D, E, F, G) or syllables (doh, ray, me, fah, soh, la, te, doh).

pitch See COAL-TAR.

pitchblende See URANINITE.

pitcher plant A CARNIVOROUS PLANT with leaves or leaf-parts modified as pit-fall traps, into which insects are attracted, ensnared, and utilized as a source of food.

This way of life has evolved in three different families of plant. The genus *Nepenthes*, with some 70 species, forms its own family of jungle plants of India, Australasia, and Madagascar. Their pitchers may be up to 30 cm (12 inches) deep, and contain up to 2 litres (3.5 pints) of water. The family Sarraceniaceae contains 17 species, divided into three genera, of North or South American species. Their narrow pitchers may reach 15 cm (6 inches) in some species, and are attractively coloured. The Australian flycatcher plant, *Cephalotus follicularis*, is the sole representative of the exclusively Australian family Cephalotaceae. Its pitchers, which reach 5 cm (2 inches) in depth, have lids, or hoods.

Pitman, Sir Isaac (1813–97) British inventor of a shorthand system. Inspired by the phonetic shorthand system designed in 1786 by Samuel Taylor (1749–1811), Pitman devised his own system, published as *Stenographic Sound Hand* (1837). Pitman shorthand, first adopted (in the USA) in 1852, is still widely used in the UK and elsewhere.

Pitt, William, 1st Earl of Chatham (known as **Pitt the Elder**), (1708–78) British Whig statesman. He became Secretary of State (effectively Prime Minister) in 1756 and headed coalition governments 1756–61 and 1766–68. He brought the Seven Years War to an end in 1763 by using a successful maritime strategy to defeat France. He also masterminded the conquest of French possessions overseas, particularly in Canada and India. He was the father of Pitt the Younger.

Pitt, William (known as **Pitt the Younger**) (1759–1806) British statesman, Prime Minister 1783–1801 and 1804–06. The son of Pitt the Elder, he became Prime Minister at the age of 24, the youngest ever to hold this office. He restored the authority of Parliament, introduced financial reforms, reduced the enormous national debt he had inherited, and reformed the administration of India. With Britain's entry into war against France (1793), Pitt became almost entirely occupied with the conduct of the war and with uniting European opposition to France. Having secured the Union of Great Britain and Ireland in 1800, he resigned in 1801 over the issue of Catholic Emancipation (which George III refused to accept). He returned as Premier in 1804 after hostilities with France had been resumed, and died in office.

pitta A forest-dwelling bird that inhabits warm areas of the Old World including Africa, south-east Asia, and Australia. It comprises some 31 species in the family Pittidae. In shape and size pittas are rather like short-tailed, long-legged thrushes. Most species are strikingly coloured, with patches of blue, red, green, or black, many having turquoise blue on the wing or bright red under the tail. They hop around the forest floor catching a wide variety of small animals. They build a domed nest, made of twigs, on or close to the ground.

Pitt-Rivers, Augustus Henry Lane Fox (1827–1900) British archaeologist and anthropologist. In 1882 he retired from the army and began a series of excavations of the prehistoric, Roman, and Saxon sites on his Wiltshire estate. He donated his collection of weapons and artefacts to found the ethnological museum in Oxford that bears his name.

Pittsburgh An industrial city at the junction of the Allegheny and Monongahela rivers in south-west Pennsylvania, USA; pop. (1990) 369,880. The city, originally named Fort Pitt after the British statesman, William Pitt the Elder, was founded in 1758 on the site of a former French settlement. A coal-mining and steel-producing town for many years, it is now a centre of high technology.

pituitary gland (or **hypophysis**) The most important of the vertebrate ENDOCRINE GLANDS, despite its small size. It lies in a bony pocket at the base of the skull. The anterior lobe consists of six specialized cell groups, each producing a different hormone. Outputs of these hormones can be adjusted individually by specific releasing factors, which are transported in blood from the hypothalamus. The endocrine functions of sex glands, thyroid glands, and adrenal glands are regulated in this manner. Other hormones secreted by the anterior pituitary include somatrophin (growth hormone), which controls the growth of bone and muscle, and prolactin, which controls milk production by mammary glands.

The posterior lobe is attached to the brain by a short stalk containing neurosecretory fibres from the hypothalamus. Some of these release vasopressin (anti-diuretic hormone, or ADH) to act rapidly on the reabsorption of water by the kidney; others release oxytocin, a hormone that causes milk ejection when teats are pulled.

pit viper A venomous snake with folding fangs. There are some 60 species living in the New World, where they are spread diversely, and in certain regions of Asia. They detect their prey (such as mammals) by using heat-sensitive pit organs that are situated on the head between the eye and the nostril. Some of the most feared snakes of the tropical Americas, such as the fer-de-lance, jararaca, and bushmaster, belong to this group. Other pit vipers include the rattlesnakes, the copperheads, and cottonmouths or water moccasins. Many of the Asiatic pit vipers are tree-dwelling. Pit vipers belong to the family Crotalidae and give birth to live young.

Pius XII (born Eugenio Pacelli) (1876–1958) Pope 1939–58. He upheld the neutrality of the Roman Catholic Church during World War II, maintaining diplomatic relations with both Allied and Axis governments. After the war there was criticism of his failure to condemn Nazi atrocities and of his apparent ambivalence towards anti-Semitism, for which the Vatican made a formal apology in 1997.

Pius XII took steps to counter the rise of Communism in postwar Italy, threatening to excommunicate its supporters.

pivot See LEVER.

Pizan, Christine de See DE PISAN.

Pizarro, Francisco (*c*.1478–1541) Spanish conquistador. In 1531 he set out from Panama to conquer the Inca empire in Peru. Crossing the mountains, he defeated the Incas and in 1533 executed their emperor Atahualpa (born 1502) setting up an Inca puppet monarchy at Cuzco and building his own capital at Lima (1535). He was assassinated in Lima by supporters of his rival Diego de Almagro (1475–1538).

placenta ▶**1** An organ within the UTERUS that provides the developing embryo with nutrients. It is connected to the embryo via the UMBILICAL CORD. The mass of cells and blood vessels that form the placenta permit food and oxygen to be transferred from the mother to the embryo through a cell barrier. Waste-products from the embryo pass across the placenta into the mother's bloodstream for excretion. ▶**2** The tissue that connects a seed to the inside of a fruit in a plant.

placoderm A member of a group of ancient, extinct fishes, living from around 400 to 200 million years ago. They were among the first fishes to evolve true biting jaws and are often known as the ancient jawed fishes. The head and front part of the body were covered in heavy bony plates for protection, and they had a pair of pelvic fins similarly encased in bone.

plagioclase Any of a series of minerals of the FELDSPAR group with a varied composition ranging from sodium aluminium silicate (albite) to calcium aluminium silicate (anorthite). They form a series with a continuous gradation in their physical properties between albite and anorthite. Intermediate members are known as oligoclase, andesine, labradorite, and bytownite. Plagioclase feldspars are common constituents of igneous rocks.

plague A number of epidemic diseases, particularly the infectious bubonic plague caused by bacteria in fleas carried by rodents. The form known as the BLACK DEATH swept through Europe during 1346–50: England may have lost as much as half its population, with severe long-term consequences. In 1665 London was afflicted by the GREAT PLAGUE, which carried off at least 70,000 victims.

plaice A species of FLATFISH, *Pleuronectes platessa*, with both eyes on the right side of the head and orange-red spots on the coloured side. It is a European species, which is common in shallow coastal water from the tideline down to 50 m (162 feet), and prefers sandy bottoms but will live on mud or gravel. It eats a wide range of bottom-living animals, especially molluscs. It has stronger teeth on the underside of the jaws than above. Spawning takes place in late winter; the eggs float near the surface, hatching in 10–20 days.

Plaid Cymru A political party devoted to the cause of Welsh nationalism. Founded in 1925 as Plaid Genedlaethol Cymru (Welsh Nationalist Party), it seeks to ensure independent recognition for WALES in matters relating to its culture, language, and economy. It became active in the 1960s and 1970s, but its hope that Wales would be able to have a separate representative assembly was rejected by a referendum in Wales in 1979. In 1997 a further referendum voted narrowly in favour of a representative assembly with limited powers.

Plains of Abraham A plateau in Quebec City, eastern Canada, scene of the decisive battle for North America in 1759. The British Army under General Wolfe surprised the French defenders by scaling the heights above the city under cover of darkness, and the city fell. The battle led to British control over Canada, but both Wolfe and the French commander Montcalm died of their wounds.

plainsong The traditional ritual melody of the Western Christian Church. In the form in which it is said to have been codified by Pope Gregory the Great (*c*.540–604) it is known as Gregorian chant. Plainsong developed during the early years of Christianity under the influence of a great many musical sources, including those of the Jewish synagogue and ancient Greece. It consists of a single melodic line, designed to be sung in unison and without accompaniment according to the free rhythms of speech. It is therefore written down without recourse to bar lines. It has its own system of notation, employing a stave of four lines, instead of the later five, and the early form of notation known as neumes. During the period of choral POLYPHONY, plainsong was often woven into the fabric of new compositions in the form of a *cantus firmus* (Latin, 'fixed' or 'given song'), which the other melodic lines would move around and generally make reference to. A similar and equally important body of chant is attached to the rite of the Eastern Orthodox Church, established at Constantinople in the 4th century. This Byzantine rite is widely practised throughout the Near East and in the Slavonic countries, including Russia.

planarian A free-living FLATWORM belonging to the class Turbellaria. Planarians can be found in almost any pond or stream, their tiny flat bodies gliding along with the aid of cilia on the undersurface and their heads, often with two or more simple eyes, waving from side to side 'tasting' the water. They can also swim by undulating their bodies. Other planarians live in marine environments, and a few occur in wet soils. Planarians have a small protusible pharynx, which is used for feeding on detritus and tiny invertebrates.

Planck, Max (Karl Ernst Ludwig) (1858–1947) German theoretical physicist, who founded the quantum theory. He published fundamental papers on thermodynamics before taking up the problem of black-body radiation. In 1900 he announced his **Planck's law**, according to which electromagnetic radiation from heated bodies was not emitted as a continuous flow but was made up of discrete units or quanta of energy, the size of which involved a fundamental physical constant (Planck's constant). The quantum concept was immediately used to explain atomic structure and the photoelectric effect. It has since become the basis for much of modern physics. Planck was awarded the 1918 Nobel Prize for physics.

planet A non-luminous body in space that forms from the gas and dust around a star and that shines only by reflected light. This includes all bodies from just a few kilometres across, such as the ASTEROIDS or minor planets, up to objects with a mass ten times that of JUPITER. Above that mass, the body's central temperature is sufficient to commence nuclear reactions and it then becomes a STAR. Planets may be composed mainly of either rocky and metallic materials, for example MERCURY, VENUS, EARTH, and MARS, or gaseous materials, for example Jupiter, SATURN, URANUS, and NEPTUNE. Planetary systems are formed by the same process that forms stars. A huge cloud of cold gas and dust slowly condenses to form a disc. The heavily condensed central portion heats up to form a new star while the material in the disc condenses into a number of much smaller bodies. If the major body exceeds a mass ten times that of Jupiter, it too becomes a star, forming a BINARY STAR system. However, if the disc forms a family of smaller bodies, a planetary system is produced. Those planets close to the central star are strongly heated and lose their light gaseous materials to form small rocky terrestrial planets. Those farther from the central star retain more of their light materials to produce large gaseous planets.

Our own SOLAR SYSTEM is thought to have formed in this way some 4.6 billion years ago. Several planets orbiting other stars have now been detected from periodic wobbles they induce in the motion of their central star. Planetary systems are probably a common phenomenon in the Universe.

planetarium A large domed room or building that houses a projector that forms images of the planets and other celestial bodies on the dome. The projector can be geared so that it shows the daily movement of the Sun, Moon, planets, and stars in a few minutes and can therefore show how the sky appeared to an observer in the past or will appear in the future. It can also be adjusted so that it takes into account the PRECESSION of the equinoxes and changes in the observer's latitude and longitude.

planetary nebula A hot tenuous gas shell surrounding certain faint but hot stars and having a planet-like appearance in the telescope. The luminous shells are found to be expanding and cooling on time-scales of 10,000 years or so, and may be produced in the final stage of a star's decay to the WHITE DWARF state. Similar features are shown by Wolf–Rayet stars.

plane tree A tree belonging to the genus *Platanus*, which includes some ten species of deciduous trees of which eight are native to the southwest USA and Mexico. The most widely cultivated species are the oriental plane, *P. orientalis*, from southeastern Europe, and the buttonwood, or American plane, *P. occidentalis*, of eastern North America. The London plane is believed to be a hybrid between these two species. Because it is one of the most pollution-tolerant of all trees, it is widely planted in towns. It has a thin, flaky bark and fruits which resemble drumstick heads on short ropes. In North America some species are commonly called sycamores, a name reserved for a type of maple in Europe. Plane trees belong to the family Platanaceae.

plankton The assemblage of microscopic organisms, both algae (phytoplankton) and animals (zooplankton), that drift passively in the surface waters of seas and fresh water. Their location is mainly dependent on currents and water clarity, as the plants require sunlight for PHOTOSYNTHESIS. The diatoms, tiny algae, and small animals drift freely; larger animals swim independently. In marine plankton, these animals include representatives of virtually every marine group; some are totally planktonic, others only during their larval stages. Plankton is the basis of all aquatic food-chains. The algae photosynthesize and are eaten by planktonic animals that fall prey to larger invertebrates, fishes, and even whales. Dead plankton sinks, and becomes food for detrital feeders.

planned economy (or **command economy**) A form of economy in which (most) resources are allocated centrally by government, rather than by MARKETS. All land and CAPITAL in such an economy is owned by the state, and factories are given resources to reach specified targets. The distribution of income is likewise determined centrally. Eastern Europe, the Soviet Union, and China in the period 1945–90 were closest to this definition of a planned economy, although in some sectors markets and private enterprise continued to exist (in particular in AGRICULTURE and the black economy or informal sector). The main problems associated with central planning are chronic inefficiency, rigidity in resource allocation, the costs of a large bureaucracy, and lack of incentives for workers and managers. State power over the economy is also associated with authoritarian government and lack of individual freedom. See also MIXED ECONOMY.

plant A living organism, composed of many cells, whose LIFE CYCLE alternates between a haploid gametophyte and a diploid sporophyte generation. Most plants produce their own food from water, carbon dioxide, mineral salts, and sunlight. They do this by the process of PHOTOSYNTHESIS and are often called autotrophs, meaning 'self-feeding'.

Groups normally considered as plants (kingdom Plantae) include liverworts, mosses, ferns, and seed plants. See also Appendix.

Plantagenet English dynasty descended from the counts of Anjou in France and rulers of England from 1154 to 1485, when the TUDOR line began. The unusual name arose from the sprig of broom plant, *Genista*, that Geoffrey (1113–51), Count of Anjou, wore on the side of his cap. It was Geoffrey's son Henry who became HENRY II (ruled 1154–89) of England and established the Plantagenet dynasty, although it is customary to refer to the first three monarchs Henry II, RICHARD I (ruled 1189–99), and JOHN (ruled 1199–1216), as Angevins (descendants of the House of Anjou). The line was unbroken until 1399 when RICHARD II was deposed and died without an heir. The throne was claimed by Henry Bolingbroke, Earl of Lancaster, Richard's cousin and the son of John of GAUNT (Edward III's third son). In becoming king as HENRY IV he established the LANCASTRIAN branch of the dynasty which was continued by HENRY V (ruled 1413–22) and HENRY VI (ruled 1422–61, 1470–71).

The second branch of the family, the House of YORK, claimed the throne through Anne Mortimer, the great-granddaughter of Lionel (Edward III's second son), who had married the father of Richard, Duke of York. The Yorkist claim succeeded when Edward, Richard's son, became EDWARD IV (1461–70, 1471–83) and was in turn followed by EDWARD V (ruled 1483) and Richard III (ruled 1483–85). In contending for the crown the Houses of Lancaster and York and their supporters resorted to civil war, known as the Wars of the ROSES (1455–83), and to murder (of Henry VI, the Duke of Clarence, and Edward V). The Plantagenet line was ousted by HENRY VII.

plantain A perennial or occasionally annual plant of the genus *Plantago*, with low-growing rosettes of leaves and slender spikes of inconspicuous flowers. Out of the 253 species in the plantain family, Plantaginaceae, 250 belong to the genus *Plantago*. They are found in all temperate regions, and on mountains in the tropics. Some species are troublesome weeds on lawns, since the leaves can grow below the reach of mower blades.

Plantation of Ireland See IRELAND; ULSTER.

plant classification. Within the plant kingdom the most basic division is between plants that produce seeds, the PHANEROGAMS, and those which reproduce by spores, the CRYPTOGAMS. Cryptogams with multicellular sex organs, but no clear differentiation of vegetative organs into roots, stems, and leaves, are mosses and liverworts (bryophytes), whereas those with such a clear differentiation are ferns, clubmosses, and horsetails (known collectively as pteridophytes in traditional classification systems). Phanerogams are split into GYMNOSPERMS, in which the seeds are not enclosed in a protecting carpel, and ANGIOSPERMS, in which they almost always are. See also NOMENCLATURE IN BIOLOGY; Appendix (for table).

plantcutter Any one of three species of bird in a family of their own, Phytotomidae. They are found in Peru, Chile, Bolivia, and northwestern Argentina, where they inhabit open, bushy country. They are sparrow-sized, brownish or greyish with dark streaks above, the underparts and the top of the head being a dull red. The beak is finch-like, short and stout, and they feed mainly on fruit and seeds.

plant hormone (or **growth substance**) A substance that, like an animal HORMONE, is produced in one part of the organism and acts on distant target cells. There are several types of growth substances. **Auxins** have many functions in the plant, including growth promotion by cell elongation, flower initiation, sex determination, and fruit growth. A second group of hormones, the **gibberellins**, promote a number of effects including bolting (elongation of plant stems), breaking of seed dormancy, and fruit set. A third hormone is **ethylene**, which promotes fruit ripening.

plant propagation The natural process by which desirable plant stocks are bred from the parent stock. Many annual crops, including CEREALS, are propagated almost entirely from seed. The method is cheap and reliable, and numerous offspring are obtained from a single parent. Other crops are propagated vegetatively, the method employed varying with species. ROOT-CROPS naturally propagate themselves via underground organs, and in some yam cultivars the capacity for seed production has disappeared completely. Cocoa and tea are propagated from leaf cuttings, bananas from suckers, mango and CITRUS crops by GRAFTING. In nutmeg, in which fruit is borne solely on female trees, vegetative propagation eliminates the production of male trees, which have no commercial value. Vegetative propagation allows cloning of high-yielding individuals of a species.

plasma (in physics) A gas containing a large number of positively and negatively charged particles – usually positive IONS and free electrons in roughly equal numbers. This state can occur if a gas is in an intense electric field or if it is raised to extremely high temperatures. In addition, the charged particles themselves can interact magnetically and electrically. The outer regions of the Sun consist of a plasma of hydrogen and plasmas are created in thermonuclear reactors. It is sometimes regarded as the fourth PHASE OF MATTER.

plasma (in physiology) The fluid-based part of the blood. It is a water-based solution of substances, such as glucose, amino acids, salts, antibodies and vitamins. The dissolved substances form a reservoir of raw materials that can be tapped by tissue cells according to their needs. The plasma fraction of blood also carries waste products, such as urea, until they are removed by the excretory organs. In human beings, plasma forms about 55 per cent of blood volume, the remainder being mostly blood cells.

Plassey (or **Palashi**) A village northwest of Calcutta in West Bengal, India, scene of a British victory in 1757, when a very small British army under Robert Clive defeated a much larger force under the Nawab of Bengal, Siraj-ud-Daula, partly because Clive had previously bribed some of the Indian generals. The victory established British supremacy in Bengal.

plaster A soft, pliable mixture applied to surfaces

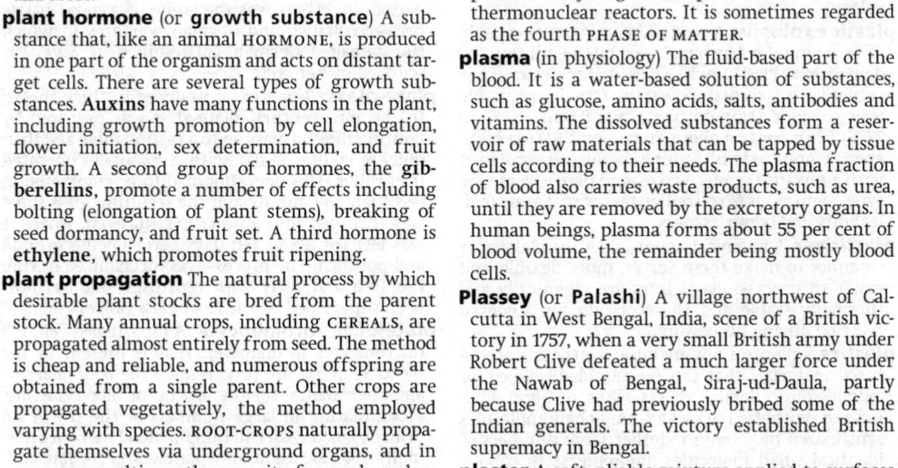

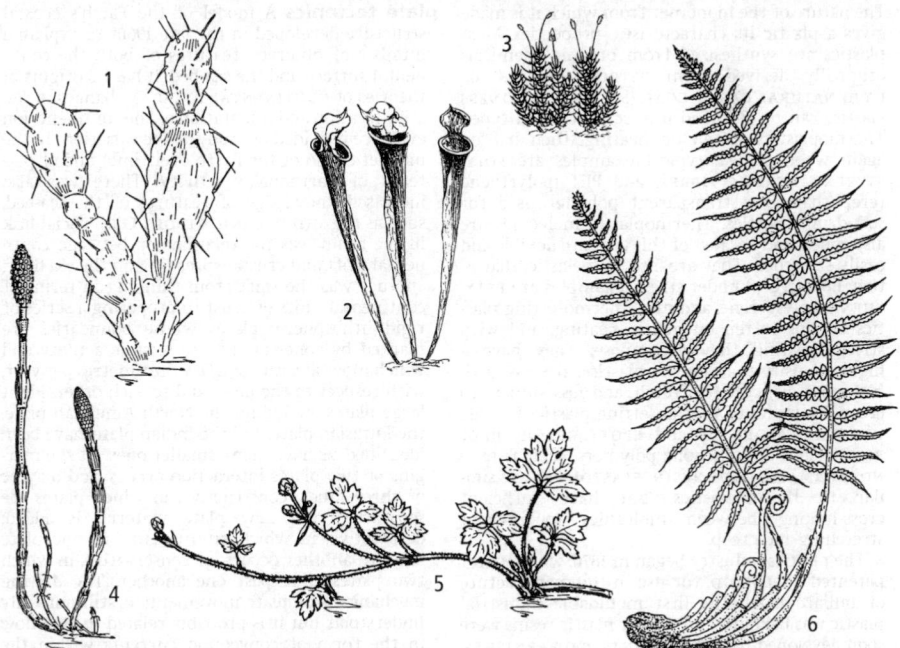

Plants Representatives of the major groups of plants. (1) Prickly pear cactus (a succulent flowering plant). (2) Pitcher plant (a carnivorous flowering plant). (3) Polytrichum moss. (4) Horsetail. (5) Buttercup. (6) Male fern.

such as walls, which hardens to give a smooth, easily cleaned finish. In the 20th century, GYPSUM has largely replaced LIME as a plaster for interior work; other constituents include sand, PORTLAND CEMENT, and hair. Plaster surfaces can be decorated by incising patterns in the wet plaster or by fixing precast mouldings of fibrous plaster (reinforced gypsum). Plasterboard – a replacement for lath and plaster – has a gypsum core strengthened with paper facings.

plastic bullet A BULLET made of rigid plastic, designed for practice firing or to disperse crowds without causing fatal injuries (although they can be fatal at close range). Bullets for riot control are large calibre (37 mm) and are fired from adapted RIFLES or purpose-built weapons, using small CARTRIDGES of propellant to restrict the bullet's flight velocity.

plastic explosive A putty-like EXPLOSIVE capable of being moulded by hand, used by the military for demolition. Plastic explosives differ from other explosives of similar power in remaining usable over a wider temperature range (from −57°C to 77°C). They contain about 80 per cent RDX (a high-energy, non-toxic nitramine explosive) combined with a mixture of oils, waxes, and plasticizers. One type, 'Semtex', is favoured by terrorists for its malleability and odourlessness.

plasticizer A chemical agent added to plastics or ceramics to make them softer, more flexible, and easier to process. Plasticizers are chemically and thermally stable and therefore do not undergo reaction during processing.

plastics A group of non-metallic, synthetic, carbon-based materials that can be moulded, shaped, or extruded into flexible sheets, films, or fibres. Plastics are synthetic POLYMERS, long-chain molecules synthesized by joining together large numbers of identical small molecules (monomers). In copolymers, more than one species of monomer is used. The nature of the monomer from which it is made gives a plastic its characteristic properties. Most plastics are synthesized from organic chemicals originally derived from PETROCHEMICALS, or from NATURAL GAS or COAL. (See also SILICONES.) Plastics can be classified into several broad types. Thermoplastics soften on heating, then harden again when cooled: typical examples are POLYSTYRENE, ACRYLIC FIBRES, and PET (polyethene terephthalate), a transparent polymer used for soft-drinks bottles. Thermoplastic molecules are also coiled, and because of this they are flexible and easily stretched. They are also viscoelastic, that is, they flow (creep) under stress. Examples are POLYTHENE, polystyrene, and PVC. Thermosetting plastics do not soften on gentle heating, and with strong heating they decompose. They have a higher density than thermoplastics, are less flexible, more difficult to stretch, and less subject to creep. Examples of thermosetting plastics include UREA-FORMALDEHYDE and EPOXY RESINS, most POLYESTERS, and phenolic polymers, such as PHENOL-FORMALDEHYDE RESIN. ELASTOMERS are similar to thermoplastics, but have sufficient cross-linking between molecules to prevent stretching and creep.

The plastics industry began in 1870, when HYATT patented CELLULOID, for use in the manufacture of billiard balls. The first mouldable industrial plastic was Bakelite, and similar plastic resins were soon developed for use in PAINTS and VARNISHES. Laminated plastics quickly followed Bakelite, and in 1912 PVC was first produced from the vinyl chloride monomer.

plastic surgery The branch of surgery concerned with the reconstruction of deformed or damaged parts of the body. **Cosmetic surgery** is concerned only with improving the appearance of the patient, but most plastic surgery involves the treatment and repair of burns and accident damage as well as the correction of such congenital defects as harelip and cleft palate. Great advances in plastic surgery were made in World War II as a result of experience with war wounds.

Plate, River (Spanish **Río de la Plata**) A wide estuary on the Atlantic coast of South America at the border between Uruguay and Argentina, formed by the confluence of the rivers Paraná and Uruguay. The cities of Buenos Aires and Montevideo lie on its shores. Its name refers to the export of silver (Spanish *plata*) in the Spanish colonial period. In 1939 it was the scene of a naval battle between British and German warships in which the damaged German battleship *Graf Spee* was scuttled by her crew.

plate-glass Clear GLASS produced in thick sheets. In the 18th century, plate-glass was prepared by pouring molten glass on to a casting table and then quickly rolling it flat with a manually operated iron roller. This operation had to be completed in less than one minute and the resulting glass sheet was then put into an ANNEALING oven, where it was left for about ten days before being ground and polished. The process was mechanized during the 19th and early 20th centuries, but has now been superseded by the float glass process.

platelet (or **thrombocyte**) A disc-shaped cell, 1–2 micrometres in diameter, that is present in the blood. Platelets are produced by the bone marrow and are essential for the process of blood clotting, accumulating in large numbers at the site of an injured blood vessel. In human blood there are normally 150–400 thousand platelets per cubic millimetre of blood.

plate tectonics A model of the Earth's crustal structure developed in the late 1960s to explain a number of observed features of both the continental surface and the sea-bed. It has its origins in theories of CONTINENTAL DRIFT, of changes in relative location and orientation of the continents (on evidence provided by study of the variations in the magnetic field of the Earth over time), and of patterns of earthquake activity. There was also increased knowledge of features of the sea-bed, such as the MID-OCEANIC RIDGES. One crucial link in the chain was the relationship between continental drift and crustal spreading on the sea floor; another was the shift from thinking in terms of continental units of crust to proposing a series of rigid lithospheric plates whose boundaries are marked by zones of intense seismic activity and which move at a rate of a few centimetres per year, with respect to the poles and to each other. Eight large plates, including the North American plate, the Eurasian plate, and the Indian plate, have been identified, as have many smaller ones. At the margins of two plates interaction occurs, and may be of three kinds: constructive, in which plates are separating and new plate material is added; destructive, in which SUBDUCTION of one plate beneath another occurs; or conservative, in which two plates slide past one another. The driving mechanism for plate movements is still not fully understood, but it is probably related to heat flow in the form of convection currents within the mantle.

Plath, Sylvia (1932–63) US poet. She moved to Britain after studying in the USA and married the

British poet Ted HUGHES in 1956. Her first poetry collections *A Winter Ship* and *The Colossus* were published in 1960. Her life was marked by periods of severe depression and her work is notable for its controlled and intense treatment of extreme and painful states of mind. After separating from her husband in 1962, she committed suicide in 1963; it was only after the posthumous publication of *Ariel* (1965) that she gained wide recognition. She also wrote a novel, *The Bell Jar* (1963).

platinum (symbol Pt, at. no. 78, r.a.m. 195.09) A silvery-white, very malleable and ductile TRANSITION METAL long known in South America. Although sparse and therefore precious, it occurs naturally in the form of fine black grains in alluvial deposits of heavy sands and in heavy metal sulphide ores from which it can be readily obtained by reduction. Unaffected by simple acids and fusible only at very high temperatures, it is used in jewellery, electrical contacts, and in laboratory equipment that comes into contact with corrosive liquids and gases. As a finely divided black powder called 'platinum black' it is employed as a CATALYST in hydrogenation reactions. Platinum hexafluoride, PtF_6, is a powerful oxidizing agent.

Plato (*c*.429–*c*.347 BC) Greek philosopher. He was a disciple of Socrates and the teacher of Aristotle, and he founded the Academy in Athens. His system of thought had a profound influence on Christian theology and Western philosophy. His philosophical writings, which cover metaphysics, politics, and ethics, are presented in the form of dialogues, with Socrates as the principal speaker; they include the *Symposium* and the *Phaedo*. An integral part of his thought is the theory of 'ideas' or 'forms', in which abstract entities or *universals* are contrasted with their objects or *particulars* in the material world. Plato's political theories appear in the *Republic*, in which he explored the nature and structure of a just society. He proposed a political system based on the division of the population into three classes, determined by education rather than birth or

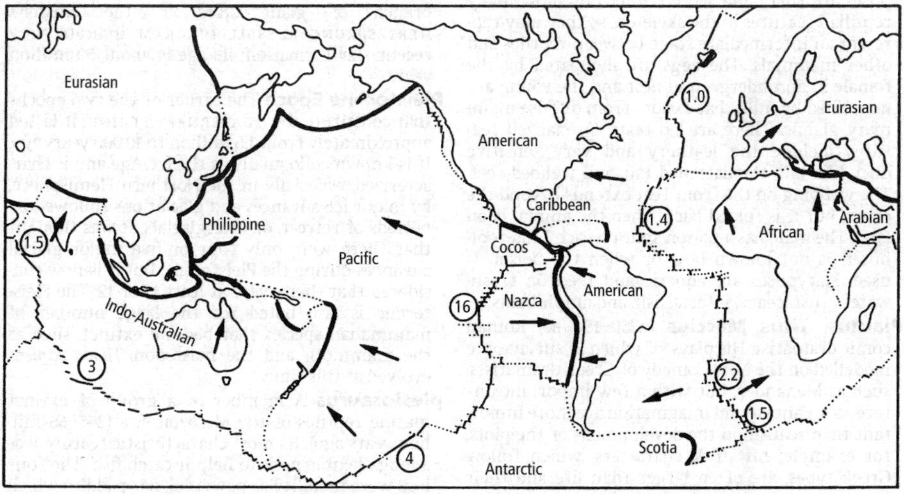

1

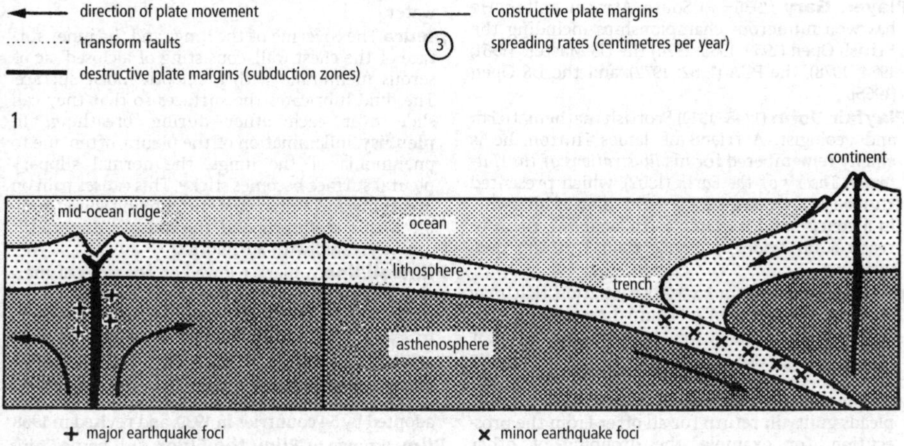

2

Plate tectonics (1) The lithospheric plates. (2) A cross-section showing two zones of earthquake activity. On the left is a constructive plate margin, where two plates are drawing apart a mid-ocean ridge. On the right is a destructive plate margin, where the oceanic plate is being subducted below the continental plate.

wealth: rulers, police and armed forces, and civilians.

platy Any one of a group of freshwater or brackish-water tropical aquarium fishes. The name derives from the genus in which they were formerly placed, *Platypoecilia*. The male has the first rays of the anal fin modified to transfer sperm to the female, who gives birth to live young. They originate in the Atlantic coastlands of Central America, where they live in swamps, pools, and slowly flowing rivers.

platyhelminth A member of the phylum Platyhelminthes, which contains three classes of FLATWORMS: the free-living Turbellaria (PLANARIANS), and the parasitic Trematoda (known as FLUKES) and Cestoda (TAPEWORMS).

platypus (or **duck-billed platypus**) A primitive mammal, *Ornithorhynchus anatinus*, found in eastern Australia and Tasmania. It is a member of the subclass Monotremata, together with the echidnas, distinguished by their egg-laying habits. Platypuses are furry and secrete milk but show many reptilian features in the skeleton, so they may represent an intermediate stage between reptiles and other mammals. The eggs are incubated by the female in an underground nest and the young are nourished by milk that exudes from diffuse mammary glands. There are no teats. Specialized features include the leathery and very sensitive duck-like bill, the flattened tail, and webbed feet. The webbing on the front feet extends beyond the claws, but it is folded back when the animal is on land. The male has a poison spur on each hind-foot, but it is not known how or when the poison is used. Platypuses are aquatic and feed on freshwater crustaceans, insects, fish, and amphibians.

Plautus, Titus Maccius (*c*.250–184 BC) Roman comic dramatist. His plays, of which 21 survive, are modelled on the New Comedy of Greek dramatists, such as Menander, but with a few important differences. Fantasy and imagination are more important than realism in the development of the plots, for example; his stock characters, which follow Greek types, are often larger than life and their language is correspondingly exuberant.

Player, Gary (1936–) South African golfer. He has won numerous championships including the British Open (1959; 1968; 1974) the US Masters (1961; 1974; 1978), the PGA (1962; 1972), and the US Open (1965).

Playfair, John (1748–1819) Scottish mathematician and geologist. A friend of James Hutton, he is chiefly remembered for his *Illustrations of the Huttonian Theory of the Earth* (1802), which presented Hutton's views on geology – and some of his own – in a concise and readable form, enabling them to reach a far wider audience than Hutton's own writings.

plea bargaining (in law) A negotiation that may affect the outcome of a criminal case. It can take several forms. A judge may let it be known that if the accused pleads guilty, he will receive a lower sentence. In other cases, the PROSECUTION and defence reach an agreement by which the accused pleads guilty in return for an offer from the prosecution (for example, the dropping of other charges, which may be more serious, or the prosecution's influence in requesting a lighter sentence). Plea bargaining is common in the USA; it has the advantage of securing admissions in cases that might be difficult to prove, but can result in the prosecution habitually abandoning more serious charges, which may undermine the administration of justice.

plebs The common people of ancient Rome, including the poor and landless. In the early republic they were excluded from office and from intermarriage with PATRICIANS. The political history of the early republic reflects largely their increasingly organized claim for greater political participation, which was rewarded by the concession of eligibility for the consulship in 367 BC. During the 'Struggle of the Orders' in the 5th and 4th centuries BC the office of TRIBUNE became a watchdog over the activities of the traditional SENATE.

Pleiades A CLUSTER of some 500 stars in the constellation of Taurus of which seven (the **Seven Sisters**) or more are visible to the naked eye. The Pleiades is a classic open cluster sharing a common space velocity. There are between three and ten times as many stars per unit volume of space as there are in the vicinity of the Sun. These are Population I stars. The remnants of the NEBULA from which the stars were formed and the absence of a branch of giant stars in the cluster's HERTZSPRUNG–RUSSELL DIAGRAM indicate very recent star formation; its age is about 50 million years.

Pleistocene Epoch The earlier of the two epochs that constitute the QUATERNARY PERIOD; it lasted approximately from 1.6 million to 10,000 years ago. It is known colloquially as the Ice Age and is characterized, especially in the Northern Hemisphere, by major ice advances and glaciations followed by periods of retreat, or interglacials. It was thought that there were only four or five major glacial advances during the Pleistocene, but it is now considered that there were at least 11 or 12. The Pleistocene is also noted for the large number of mammalian species that became extinct, such as the mammoth and the mastodon. *Homo sapiens* evolved at this time.

plesiosaurus A member of a group of extinct marine reptiles of the Mesozoic Era (245–66 million years ago). Its most characteristic feature was a long, flexible neck to help it catch fish. The four legs were modified as powerful, flat paddles which beat up and down to propel the body through the water.

pleura The covering of the lungs and the inner surface of the chest wall, consisting of a closed sac of serous membrane with a smooth moist surface. The fluid lubricates the surfaces so that they can slide over each other during breathing. In **pleurisy**, inflammation of the pleura, often due to pneumonia of the lungs, the normal slippery pleural surface becomes sticky. This causes pain on breathing and a characteristic rubbing sound audible with a stethoscope. If the cause is bacterial it can be treated with antibiotics.

Plimsoll line A mark painted on the sides of merchant ships to show the maximum depth to which a ship may be loaded. It allows variations according to season and location. Named after the politician Samuel Plimsoll (1824–98), a merchant and shipping reformer, it was made compulsory in the UK in 1875. An internationally agreed loading line was adopted by 54 countries in 1930, and revised in 1968.

Pliny (known as **Pliny the Elder**; full name Gaius Plinius Secundus) (23–79) Roman lawyer, historian, and naturalist. Of his many works only the 37 volumes of his *Natural History* survive, a valuable compendium of ancient scientific knowledge blended with folklore and anecdote. He died while leading a rescue (and research) party on the stricken coastline near POMPEII, during the eruption of Vesuvius.

Pliny (known as **Pliny the Younger**; full name Gaius Plinius Caecilius Secundus) (61–112) A senator and consul, nephew of the Elder PLINY. A close friend of TRAJAN and TACITUS, he governed Bithynia (in present-day Turkey). His 'Letters', which are really essays, give a detailed picture of the lifestyle adopted by wealthy Romans of his class. Other letters, written after 100, provide the only detailed accounts of the eruption of Vesuvius in 79, in which his uncle perished, and the devastation of Campania of which he was a youthful eyewitness.

Pliocene Epoch The last of the geological epochs of the TERTIARY PERIOD, extending from 5.3 to 1.6 million years ago. It was a time when the temperature was falling and many of the species of mammals that had flourished earlier were becoming extinct. Both marine and freshwater Pliocene deposits are found in Europe. Those of the UK are shelly sands (the 'Crags' of East Anglia) and gravels.

PLO See PALESTINE LIBERATION ORGANIZATION.

Plotinus (*c*.205–70 AD) Philosopher, probably of Roman descent, the founder and leading exponent of Neoplatonism. Neoplatonism was a religious and philosophical system based on elements from Plato, Pythagoras, Aristotle, and the Stoics, with overtones of Eastern mysticism. It was the dominant philosophy of the pagan world from the mid-3rd century AD until the closing of the pagan schools by Justinian in 529, and also strongly influenced medieval and Renaissance thought. Plotinus studied in Alexandria and later Persia before finally settling in Rome in 244 and setting up a school of philosophy. His writings were published after his death by his pupil Porphyry.

Plough The pattern formed by seven stars of URSA MAJOR. This shape is also known as the **Big Dipper**. All seven stars are bright; a good test of eyesight is to attempt to see the middle star (MIZAR) in the handle of the Plough as double. In our present era Merak and Dubhe, the two stars farthest away from the handle, point to the star POLARIS (the Pole Star).

Plovdiv An industrial and commercial city and market town in central Bulgaria on the River Maritsa, the second-largest city in Bulgaria; pop. (1990) 379,080. A city of ancient Macedonia from 341 BC, when it was conquered by Philip II of Macedon, it became part of Roman Thrace in 46 AD and was taken by the Turks in 1364. Known to the Greeks as Philippopolis ('Philip's city') and to the Romans as Trimontium, it assumed its present name after World War I. Landmarks include a Roman amphitheatre and medieval buildings. Industries include machinery, textiles, footwear, electrical goods, and foodstuffs.

plover A member of a large subfamily, Charadriinae, of 56 species of WADING BIRDS with a cosmopolitan but mainly tropical range. They differ from sandpipers in having short, straight beaks, thick necks, and boldly patterned plumages, frequently with a dark band across the breast and/or tail. Typically, they inhabit open country near water, and lay their eggs in a shallow scrape in the ground, protecting them and their young by feigning injury. The main genera are: the lapwings; the golden plovers, remarkable for the long migrations made by the American species; and the sand plovers, which include small shore-birds like the ringed plover.

plum A tree of the cherry genus, *Prunus*, which occurs wild throughout the Northern Hemisphere. A number of different species of *Prunus* have contributed to the development of the modern plums. They are small, deciduous trees, often grown as bushes, with small, white flowers and fleshy, short-stalked fruits containing a single, hard-shelled seed. The European plums were developed from crosses between the native BLACKTHORN and the cherry plum, *P. cerasifera*, of western Asia. They vary in skin colour (greenish-yellow, yellow, red to purple) and season of ripening (late July to late September). Cooking plums are more acidic than dessert types. Certain varieties, more suited to the warmer temperate areas, are grown to produce prunes, the purple-skinned fruit being dried on the tree or artificially. Other important species are the American plum and the Japanese plum. The greengage and damson are both types of plum.

plumbago A plant belonging to a genus, *Plumbago*, of some 12 woody herbs and scramblers of warm regions, which are part of the same family, Plumbaginaceae, as sea lavender and thrift. They have glandular hairs on the outer surface of the fruit which are thought to aid their dispersal by animals. Many members of this genus and family are grown in gardens as climbers or small shrubs.

plume moth A moth of the family Pterophoridae, usually with the wings divided into several hair-fringed lobes, and long legs, giving an extremely fragile appearance. Most are greyish, yellow, or brown, and they fly feebly at dusk. The twenty-plume moth, *Orneodes hexadactyla*, with each wing divided into six lobes, belongs to another family, the Orneodidae.

pluralism (in politics) A condition in which POWER is diffused throughout society with no single group controlling all decisions. A pluralist state is one in which decision-making is divided among many independent groups: for example, government ministers, civil servants, interest groups, and local officials. Like exponents of élitism, who believe that power is concentrated in the hands of an élite, advocates of pluralism acknowledge that, even in a DEMOCRACY, decisions are made by a small minority, but they maintain that no single group should dominate all decisions. They also believe that individuals should have an opportunity to become involved in making decisions, even if they often choose not to do so.

Plutarch (*c*.46–126 AD) Greek writer and philosopher of wide-ranging interests. His extant works include rhetorical pieces, philosophical treatises, and, most memorably, his *Parallel Lives*, paired biographies of famous Greeks and Romans. He was concerned to highlight the personal virtues (and sometimes vices) of his subjects, and the result has been an inspiration to later writers, most notably Shakespeare in his Roman plays.

Pluto The outermost PLANET of the Solar System, discovered by the US astronomer Clyde Tombaugh in 1930. Pluto's perihelion lies inside the orbit of Neptune and this, together with its small size and mass, suggests that Pluto may have originally been a satellite of Neptune. Also remarkable is the fact that Pluto has a comparatively large satellite CHARON, which might have split from it following a shattering impact. Pluto and Charon always keep the same face turned towards each other. Pluto's mean density of about 2,000 kg/m^3 suggests that its interior is a mixture of rocks, water ice, and methane ice; in fact, methane has been identified on the surface by PHOTOMETRY and spectrophotometry. Pluto's brightness changes with its rotation rate of 6.4 days due to bright patches on the surface.

plutonic rock See IGNEOUS ROCK.

plutonium (symbol Pu, at. no. 94, r.a.m. 244) One of the TRANSURANIC ELEMENTS and a member of the actinides. It was synthesized in 1940 and used in the atomic bomb dropped on Nagasaki in 1945. There are traces of the element in uranium ores, but it is produced on a larger scale from uranium-238 in nuclear reactors; in this process a U-238 atom absorbs a neutron to form Pu-239. All the isotopes are radioactive, plutonium-239 having a HALF-LIFE of 24,360 years. Above a certain critical size, plutonium-239 can initiate a nuclear explosion; 1 kilogram has an energy potential of about 10^{14} joules. It is used as a nuclear fuel in the form of alloys. Plutonium-238, obtained from neptunium, is employed as a nuclear power source in space exploration.

Plymouth The capital of the island of Montserrat in the West Indies, abandoned following the volcanic eruption of Chance Peak in 1997; pop. (1991) 3,500.

Plymouth A port, naval base, and commercial centre in south-west England, on the Devon coast; pop. (1991) 238,800. It was from here that Sir Francis Drake set sail in 1588 to attack the Spanish Armada, and he and other Elizabethan explorers set out from Plymouth Sound. In 1620 the PILGRIM FATHERS sailed from Plymouth to North America in the *Mayflower*. Plymouth University (formerly Polytechnic South West) was established in 1992.

Plymouth Brethren A strict Protestant group, so called because of their early establishment in Plymouth, England, by John Nelson Darby (1800–82) in 1831. The Brethren underwent a major division in 1849, becoming what are known as the 'Exclusive Brethren' and the 'Open Brethren', the latter being the less rigorous. They advocate adult Baptism and reject clergy.

Plymouth plantation See PILGRIM FATHERS.

plywood See LAMINATE.

pneumonia Inflammation of the lungs resulting in the production of exudate that fills up the air sacs (alveoli), causing the exclusion of air, and the formation of a solid mass (consolidation). Pneumonia is commonly caused by bacterial infection, although it may be caused by viruses, fungi, and protozoa (e.g. *Pneumocystis carinii* pneumonia in Aids patients). Common causative bacteria include *Streptococcus pneumoniae*, *Klebsiella pneumoniae*, and *Staphylococcus aureus*; less commonly encountered microorganisms include *Legionella pneumophilia*. Pneumonia may be localized and confined to a complete lobe or lobule of the lung. Bronchopneumonia is inflammation of the bronchi and bronchioles causing consolidation in adjacent lobules of the lungs and results in diffuse pneumonia. Symptoms of pneumonia include painful cough, fever, and blood in the sputum. Complications of pneumonia include MENINGITIS and lung abscess. Pneumonia, which was once a common cause of death, is now treated with antibiotics (if it is bacterial).

Po A river in northern Italy. Italy's longest river, it rises in the Cottian Alps near the border with France and flows 668 km (415 miles) eastwards to meet the Adriatic in a wide delta east of Ferrara.

poa grass A species of grass in the genus *Poa*. They are identified by a prefix, such as bulbous, alpine, wood, and annual. *P. annua* (annual poa) is possibly the commonest grass weed of cultivation and is found throughout the world. Meadow species, such as smooth meadow-grass, *P. pratensis*, are useful for grazing stock and hay production, while others with narrow leaf-blades are used for lawns.

Pocahontas (*c*.1595–1617) North American Indian 'princess', the daughter of Powhatan, Chief of the Indians in the JAMESTOWN region of Virginia. Captain John Smith claimed that she saved him from torture and death in 1607. To cement Anglo-Indian relations, she was married to the colonist John Rolfe in 1614 with the Christian name of Rebecca. He took her to England, where she was presented at court, but she died of smallpox.

pochard A member of a tribe of mainly freshwater bay ducks of genera *Netta* and *Aythya*, that collect food from the shallow river- or lake-bed, or from underwater vegetation. Like other diving ducks they patter along the surface of the water before taking off. The 16 species of bay ducks include several called pochard and tufted ducks.

pocket mouse A member of a family of 65 species of RODENTS, restricted to the New World. They can be divided into two habitat groups: the kangaroo rats (*Dipodomys* species), kangaroo mice (*Microdipodops* species), and pocket mice (*Perognathus* species) live in hot, dry habitats of North America; the spiny pocket mice (*Heteromys* and *Liomys* species) live in tropical rain forests of Central and northern South America. They all eat seeds and other vegetable material and are usually active at night.

pod The fruit characteristic of the Leguminosae, or pea family, though other fruit types may be included. Pods usually split down one side to expose a row of seeds, though some, like the peanut, are indehiscent (do not burst open).

Podgorica (or **Podgoritsa**) The capital of the republic of Montenegro in the Balkans; pop. (1991) 117,875. A New Town, from 1948 until 1992 it was named Titograd in honour of Marshall Tito, former president of Yugoslavia. It has tobacco and aluminium industries.

podzol A zonal soil that occurs in the taiga or boreal forest regions of the world, where winters are cold, summers are relatively short, and the

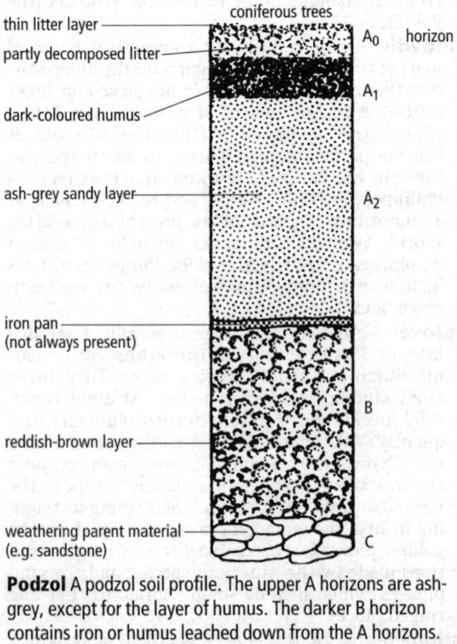

Podzol A podzol soil profile. The upper A horizons are ash-grey, except for the layer of humus. The darker B horizon contains iron or humus leached down from the A horizons. The C horizon contains the parent material.

yearly rainfall between 500 and 800 mm (20 and 30 inches). The rainfall is sufficiently great to cause LEACHING of even relatively insoluble minerals, such as iron and aluminium from the upper part of the soil. This leaching results in the formation of a bleached, pale-coloured zone, which may also be depleted of clay. The substances leached accumulate lower down the profile, where they may become cemented to form a HARDPAN (for example, an iron pan). Podzols are found in moorland areas of the UK, in mid-Canada, and in parts of Siberia.

Poe, Edgar Allan (1809–49) US short-story writer, poet, and critic. He spent most of his life in poverty and ill health. His fiction and poetry are Gothic in style and characterized by their exploration of the macabre, the fantastic, and the grotesque. His most famous short stories include the Gothic romance 'The Fall of the House of Usher' (which appeared in *Tales of the Grotesque and Arabesque*, 1840) and 'The Pit and the Pendulum' (1843), while his poems include 'The Raven' (1845) and 'Annabel Lee' (1849). His story 'The Murders in the Rue Morgue' (1841) is often regarded as the first detective story in English literature. His critical writings include 'The Poetic Principle' (1850), which anticipated many of the concerns of the Aesthetic Movement ('art for art's sake').

Poet Laureate An honour given to a British poet who is appointed to write poems for state occasions and who receives a stipend as an officer of the Royal Household. Dryden was the first to be given the title officially in 1668. Wordsworth, Tennyson, Robert Bridges, Cecil Day-Lewis, and John Betjeman have been among later holders of the title, which at present is held by Ted HUGHES.

poetry Language sung, chanted, spoken, or written according to some pattern of recurrence which emphasizes the relationships between words on the basis of sound as well as sense: this pattern is almost always a rhythm or METRE, which may be supplemented by RHYME or alliteration or both. The demands of verbal patterning usually make poetry a more condensed medium than prose or everyday speech, often permitting unusual orderings of words within sentences, and sometimes involving the use of special words and phrases ('poetic diction') peculiar to poets. Poetry is usually characterized by a more frequent and elaborate use of figures of speech, principally METAPHOR and SIMILE.

pogrom (Russian, 'riot' or 'devastation') A mob attack approved or condoned by authority, frequently against religious, racial, or national minorities – most often against Jews. The first occurred in the Ukraine following the assassination of ALEXANDER II (1881). After that, there were many pogroms throughout Russia, and Russian Jews began to emigrate to the USA and western Europe often giving their support to HERZL's ZIONIST campaign. After the revolution of 1905, ANTI-SEMITIC persecutions increased. Conducted on a large scale in Germany and eastern Europe after Hitler came to power they led ultimately to the HOLOCAUST.

Poincaré, Jules-Henri (1854–1912) French mathematician and philosopher of science. Poincaré made far-reaching contributions to pure and applied mathematics. He worked extensively on differential equations, which enabled him to transform celestial mechanics, and was one of the pioneers of algebraic topology. By 1900 he was proposing a relativistic philosophy, suggesting that it implied the absolute speed of light, which nothing could exceed.

poinsettia See SPURGE.

Pointe-à-Pitre The chief port and commercial capital of the French overseas territory of Guadeloupe, on the south-west coast of the island of Grande-Terre; pop. (1994) 26,000.

Pointe-Noire The chief seaport of the Republic of Congo, an oil terminal on the Atlantic coast of West Africa; pop. (1995) 576,200. It exports timber, cotton, palm-oil, groundnuts, and coffee, and has shipbuilding, food-processing, and plywood industries.

Pointers See URSA MAJOR.

pointillism A technique of painting, used by the NEO-IMPRESSIONISTS, in which dots (French, *points*) or small touches of pure, unmixed colour are methodically applied to the canvas so that when viewed from an appropriate distance they seem to react together optically, creating more vibrant effects than if the same colours were physically mixed together. SEURAT, the leading pioneer and greatest exponent of the technique, preferred the term 'divisionism'.

poison ivy A climbing shrub, *Rhus toxicodendron*, with aerial roots, native to North America. Although it resembles ivy, it is a species of SUMAC and is related to cashew and mango rather than to true ivy. Like many other members of its family, when touched it provokes a severe skin reaction, producing painful blisters and sores. Its ally, poison oak, *R. radicans*, has similar properties.

Poisson, Siméon-Denis (1781–1840) French mathematical physicist. Early in his career he began applying the integration of differential equations to problems in physics, an approach that he used for many years with great effect. He added to the work of Laplace and Lagrange on planetary motions, and went on to study electrostatics, heat, elasticity, and magnetism. Perhaps his major contributions were in probability theory, in which he greatly improved Laplace's work and developed several concepts that are now named after him.

Poitier, Sidney (1924–) US actor and film director. He won an Oscar for his performance in *Lilies of the Field* (1963) and became the first African-American superstar actor. In the 1970s he began directing films such as *Uptown Saturday Night* (1974) and *Ghost Dad* (1990), and after ten years away from acting he reappeared in *Little Nikita* (1988) and *Sneakers* (1992).

Poitiers A city in west-central France, the capital of the department of Vienne and chief town of the Poitou-Charentes region; pop. (1990) 82,500. It was capital of the former province of Poitou and the location of a number of important battles; here the Merovingian king Clovis defeated the Visigoths under Alaric in 507, Charles Martel halted the Saracen advance in 732, and Edward the Black Prince defeated the French in 1356.

pokeweed (or **pokeberry**, **poke root**) A plant belonging to the genus *Phytolacca*. This forms part of the family Phytolaccaceae, which includes some 125 species of trees, shrubs, woody climbers, and herbaceous plants of mainly tropical and subtropical regions of the New World.

Poland A country on the North European Plain with a Baltic Sea coast and bounded by Germany on the west, Russia, Lithuania, Belarus, and Ukraine on the east, and the Czech Republic and Slovakia on the south.

Physical. The North European Plain is sandy in places, marshy in others and requires careful culti-

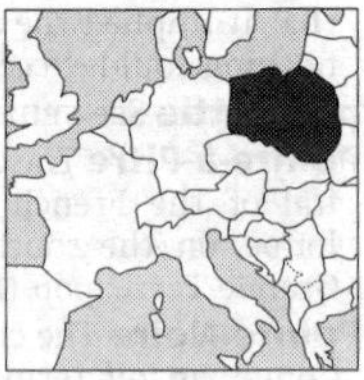

vation, although inland it is well drained by the Odra (Oder), Vistula, and other rivers. The climate is continental, with wide ranges of temperature. There are many small forests of spruce and fir, which increase in size as the land rises through rolling hills and richer land to the Carpathian Mountains in the south-east.

Economy. After the collapse of communism, Poland has made the transition to a market economy; however, the economic problems this has engendered include high inflation, a large budget deficit, and high foreign debt. In late 1989, an economic reform package, introduced to gain IMF support, reduced wages and removed price subsidies. The Polish stock exchange was opened in late 1989 and some privatizations have been completed. The majority of agricultural land is in private hands, wheat, rye, barley, oats, potatoes, and sugar-beet being the main crops. Mineral resources include coal (from some of the largest bituminous and lignite coal fields in the world), copper, iron, silver, sulphur, lead and natural gas. Industry is hampered by power shortages and high fuel prices, and financial problems have delayed the nuclear energy programme. Loss-making industries, such as steel, and ship-building have been heavily subsidized at the expense of other areas. Coal, clothing, iron and steel products, metals and agricultural products are the main exports.

History. Poland became an independent kingdom in the 9th century and was Christianized under Miezko I (962–92). Unity was imposed under Ladislas I (1305–33) and Casimir the Great, who improved the administration, and the country's defences, and encouraged trade and industry. Jagiellon rule (1386–1572) culminated in the brief ascendancy of Protestantism, and achievement in the arts and sciences. The 16th century saw Poland at its largest, after Lithuania was incorporated (1447, 1569), stretching from the Baltic to the Black Sea. However, the weakness of a hereditary monarchy took effect and despite the victories of John Casimir (1648–68) and John Sobieski (1674–96), internal decline and foreign attack undermined Polish independence, and much territory was ceded to Sweden and Russia. Ravaged by the Great Northern War and the War of the Polish Succession, it lost its independence in the 18th century. From 1697 the Electors of Saxony took the title of king and partition between Russia, Austria, and Prussia followed in 1772. Brief resistance under KOSCIUSZKO resulted in two further partitions in 1793 and 1795, mainly to the benefit of Catherine the Great's Russia, and Poland became effectively a protectorate of Russia.

Following the treaties of Tilsit in 1807 Napoleon created the Grand Duchy of Warsaw, under the King of Saxony, introducing the CODE NAPOLÉON, but retaining serfdom and the feudal nobility. The duchy collapsed after the Battle of LEIPZIG and at the Congress of VIENNA, when Poland was represented by Count Czartoryski, parts of the duchy reverted to Prussia and Austria, but the bulk became the kingdom of Poland, which had its own administration but with the Russian emperor Alexander I as king. Revolutions took place in 1830, 1846–49, and 1863. Serfdom was ended in 1864, but policies of repression followed in both Russian and Prussian Poland. This did not, however, prevent the development of political parties demanding democratic government. After World War I in 1918 full independence was granted and Poland became a republic. War against Bolshevik Russia (1920–21) was followed by the dictatorship of Marshal Pilsudski. Poland was to have access to the port of Danzig (Gdańsk) via a POLISH CORRIDOR. The status of Danzig and the existence of this corridor provided an excuse for the Nazi invasion in 1939, which precipitated World War II. As a result of the Nazi–Soviet Pact, Poland lost territory to both countries. After 1945 two million Germans left East Prussia (now in Poland) for the Federal Republic of Germany, and Poles, mainly from those Polish territories annexed by the Soviet Union, were resettled in their place. Following the WARSAW UPRISING a provisional Polish government was established under Red Army protection, which cooperated with STALIN to bring the country within the Soviet bloc. Political opposition was neutralized, and in 1952 a Soviet-style constitution was adopted. In 1956 Polish workers went on strike to protest against food shortages and other restrictions. Under Wladyslaw Gomulka (1956–70) rigid control by the government was maintained, leading to further strikes (1970). The election of a Polish pope, Karol Wojtyla, as John Paul II in 1978, strengthened the influence of the ROMAN CATHOLIC CHURCH in the country. Strikes, organized by the Free Union of the Baltic Coast resulted in the formation of SOLIDARITY at Gdańsk. Martial law was imposed by Prime Minister General Wojciech Jaruzelski (1981–82), military tribunals continuing to operate after it officially ended. By 1987 the government was in crisis and put forward plans for limited decentralization of the economy; the ban on Solidarity was lifted, and round-table talks with all groups, including the Roman Catholic Church, began. A new constitution was agreed and multi-party politics were legalized in 1989; in December 1990 Lech WALESA was elected President. Friendship treaties were made with newly united Germany and post-Marxist Russia and with France. In spite of recession, a private sector in the economy grew rapidly. The influence of Solidarity began to wane, and in June 1992 Walesa appointed his first non-Solidarity Prime Minister, Waldemar Pawlak, of the Polish Peasant Party. In 1993, the former Communist Party emerged as the largest single party in elections, forming a government under Józef Oleksy. The last Russian troops stationed in Poland left the country in 1994. Walesa was defeated by the former Communist Aleksander Kwasniewski in presidential elections in 1995. Solidarity won legislative elections in 1997 and headed a coalition goverment led by Jerzy Buzek.

Capital: Warsaw
Area: 312,683 sq km (120,727 sq mi)
Population: 38,641,000 (1995)
Currency: 1 zloty = 100 groszy
Religions: Roman Catholic 95.0%
Ethnic Groups: Polish 98.7%; Ukrainian 0.6%; German and other 0.7%
Languages: Polish (official); minority languages
International Organizations: UN; CSCE; Council of Europe; North Atlantic Co-operation Council

Polanski, Roman (1933–) French film director, of Polish descent. Born in France, he grew up in Poland, where he pursued a career as an actor from the age of 14 and directed the film *Knife in the Water* (1962), which established his international reputation. He subsequently worked in Hollywood, having success with such films as *Rosemary's Baby* (1968) and *Chinatown* (1974). He left the USA for

France in 1977 under threat of prosecution for drug and sex offences. His later films, including *Tess* (1979) and *Frantic* (1988), have not had the success of his earlier titles. His second wife, Hollywood actress Sharon Tate (1943–69), was one of the victims of a multiple murder by followers of the cult leader Charles Manson.

polar bear A single species of bear, *Thalarctos maritimus*, which is one of the largest carnivorous animals in the world. A mature male can reach a length of 2.75 m (9 feet) and a height of 1.5 m (5 feet) at the shoulders. The female is smaller but otherwise similar in appearance. The polar bear lives amongst the ice-floes of the Arctic and has even travelled to Iceland and Greenland. It is quite at home in the water. The coat of dense, long fur is white tinged with yellow. The feet are heavily haired to provide insulation and give a grip on the cold, slippery ice of its habitat. It has better vision than most bears and a good sense of smell, both essential in searching for prey in such a bleak region. Its favourite foods are seals and walrus cubs, but caribou, foxes, birds, shellfish, and any other form of animal life is eaten.

polar coordinates (in mathematics or geology) An alternative system to the more familiar CARTESIAN COORDINATES for locating points in a plane. The reference line of the system is a rightward-pointing horizontal line with end-point O, the origin or POLE. The first coordinate of a point is its distance from the origin, and the second is the angle that the line from the point to the origin makes with the reference line, measured anticlockwise from the latter. The basis of polar coordinates is thus a distance and an angle rather than two distances. The coordinates are customarily written (r, θ), where $r \geq 0$ and is the distance from the origin, and θ, with $0 \leq \theta > 360°$, is the angle.

polarimeter An apparatus to study and measure the way polarized light (light in which the light waves vibrate in only one plane) is affected by substances. Polarized light is passed through a solution of the substance, and any rotation of the plane of polarization is detected by examining the light in the emergent beam. Polarimeters are used in the qualitative and quantitative analysis of some organic chemicals, particularly sugars.

Polaris (or **Pole Star**) A VARIABLE STAR of second magnitude that lies within one degree of the north celestial pole. Found in the constellation of Ursa Minor, it is also known as Alpha Ursa Minoris. It is a MULTIPLE STAR whose bright component is a SUPERGIANT star, which is itself a spectroscopic BINARY STAR with a period of 30 years. The fainter companion is a ninth-magnitude DWARF STAR moving in a very wide orbit about the spectroscopic binary.

polarization The restriction of the waves of ELECTROMAGNETIC RADIATION, including light and radio waves, to one plane or one direction. This property is not directly perceived by the eye but can be detected, in the case of light, by the behaviour of the light after it has interacted with various materials called polarizers (see POLARIMETER). Two polarizers in line, with one being rotated, can produce darkness at some angles of rotation but not at others. The first polarizer the light meets allows through only radiation vibrating in a particular direction at right angles to the direction of propagation of the light. If the second polarizer is placed so that it would allow through only light vibrating at right angles to that particular direction, then none of the light transmitted by the first polarizer is able to pass through the second. The measurement of the degree of polarization of electromagnetic radiation coming from any celestial object reveals valuable information not only about that object but also about any material lying between the object and observer.

polarography The measurement of low concen-

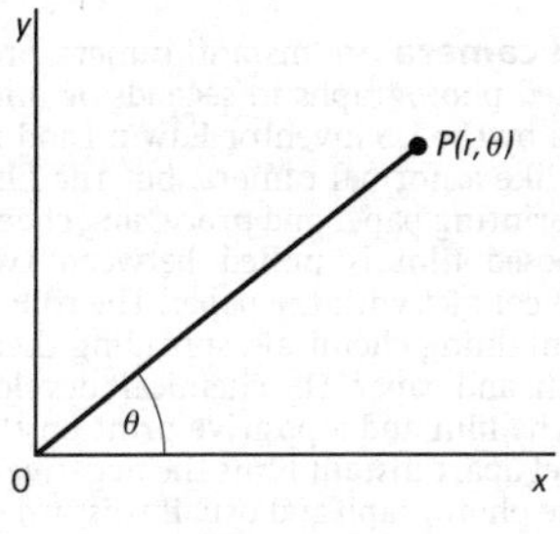

1

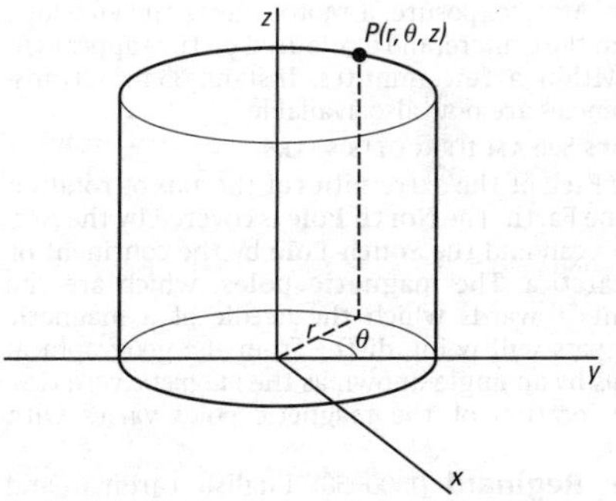

2

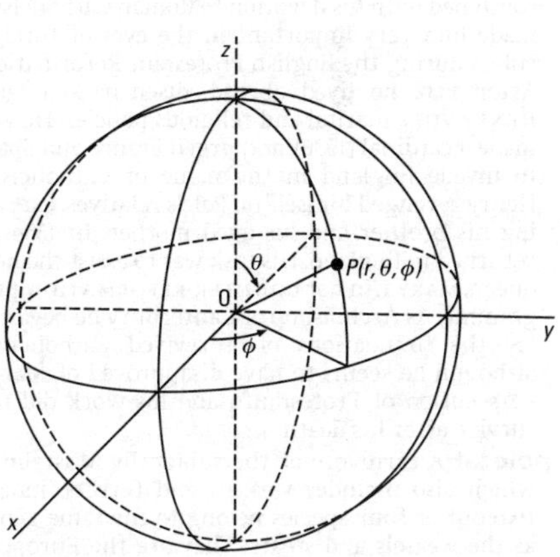

3

Polar coordinates (1) Two-dimensional coordinates of the point P are (x,y) in Cartesian coordinates and (r,θ) in polar coordinates. (2) In three-dimensional cylindrical polar coordinates the point P is regarded as lying on the surface of a cylinder. Its coordinates are then (r,θ,z). (3) Alternatively, three-dimensional coordinates can be given in spherical coordinates with the point P lying on the surface of a sphere. The coordinates are then given in terms of r and two angles, i.e. (r,θ,φ).

trations of dissolved substances. Polarography uses an apparatus in which the current flowing through a solution between two electrodes – a reference ANODE kept at constant potential, and a dropping mercury CATHODE – is measured at different voltages. The constituents of the solution can be analysed from the resulting current-voltage curve.

Polaroid Land camera An 'instant' camera producing processed photographs in seconds or minutes, developed by the US inventor Edwin Land in 1947. It works like a normal camera, but the film pack includes printing paper and processing chemicals. The exposed film is pulled between two rollers while in contact with the paper. The rollers break a pod containing chemicals, spreading them between the film and paper. The chemicals develop a negative on the film and a positive print on the paper. With peel-apart instant films the negative is peeled from the photograph and usually discarded. More popular for amateur use are film packs in which the negative, print, and processing chemicals are permanently sealed inside a plastic envelope. After exposure, a motor ejects the envelope from the camera, and a coloured picture appears in it within a few minutes. Instant 35-mm transparencies are now also available.

polars See AM HERCULIS STARS.

pole Each of the extremities of the axis of rotation of the Earth. The **North Pole** is covered by the Arctic Ocean and the **South Pole** by the continent of Antarctica. The **magnetic poles**, which are the points towards which the needle of a magnetic compass will point, differ from the geographical poles by an angle known as the *magnetic variation*. The location of the magnetic poles varies with time.

Pole, Reginald (1500–58) English cardinal and Archbishop of Canterbury. He held a YORKIST claim to the throne of England through his mother, the Countess of Salisbury. This high birth, combined with his devotion to Roman Catholicism, made him very important in the eyes of foreign rulers during the English Protestant Reformation. After 1532 he lived abroad, disenchanted with HENRY VIII's marital and religious policies. He was made a cardinal (1536), and urged France and Spain to invade England in the name of Catholicism. Henry revenged himself on Pole's relatives, executing his brother and his aged mother. In 1554 he returned to England. His task was to assist the new queen, MARY I, in her COUNTER-REFORMATION programme. As Archbishop of Canterbury he began to lay the foundations of a revived Catholicism, although he seems to have disapproved of Mary's persecution of Protestants, and his work did not survive after his death.

polecat A carnivore of the subfamily Mustelinae, which also includes weasels and ferrets; indeed two out of four species belong to the same genus as the weasels and stoats. They are the European polecat, *Mustela putoris*, and the steppe polecat, *M. eversmanni*, of eastern Europe. The others are the marbled polecat, *Vormela peregusna*, and the African polecat or zorilla, *Ictonyx striatus*. The American SKUNK is sometimes called a polecat. The European polecat is found in forests throughout Europe, with the exception of Scandinavia. It is a nocturnal predator, preying on hares, small rodents, birds, and invertebrates. It is noted for the foul-smelling secretions from its anal glands.

Pole Star See POLARIS.

police A body of civilian officers with responsibility for upholding the law and maintaining public order through crime prevention and crime investigation. In London the Magistrates' Court at Bow Street pioneered from *c.*1750 a system of unarmed uniformed 'runners' (the Bow Street Runners) employed to apprehend criminals. These were developed by Sir Robert PEEL in 1829 by the formation of the London Metropolitan Police Force, soon copied in most other major British cities. Police forces have since been adopted by almost all nation-states. In some countries, the national police force is supplemented by regional or local bodies, or by groups set up for particular purposes, such as riot control, serious crime detection (for example, the US Federal Bureau of Investigation, or FBI). Military police forces are given the same powers as civilian police in respect of service personnel. Most police services make a distinction between uniformed and plain-clothes operations; the former patrol the streets and act as a first line of defence against crime, while the latter are detectives who investigate crime, and who often have close links with INTELLIGENCE and COUNTER-INTELLIGENCE SERVICES. See also INTERPOL; POLICE STATE.

police state A state in which a national police organization, often secret, is under the direct control of an AUTHORITARIAN government, whose political purposes it serves, sometimes to the extent of becoming a state within a state. The inhabitants of a police state experience restrictions on their mobility, and on their freedom to express or communicate political or other views, which are subject to police monitoring or enforcement. In some cases, the exercise of police control is supported by systems, such as internal passports or internal exile, or by punishment camps; likewise, there is often a strict system of censorship and extensive secrecy.

poliomyelitis A central nervous system infection by the poliomyelitis virus, which is transmitted by ingestion of food or water contaminated with human sewage containing the virus; it is more common in conditions associated with poor sanitation. Poliomyelitis is more common in developing countries.

In most cases, only a mild illness with fever and headache is seen, and individuals have obtained immunity once they recover. However, in more severe disease, symptoms return after remission; fever, headache, drowsiness, nausea, vomiting, diarrhoea, and loss of appetite are common. Flaccid PARALYSIS may develop and in children may affect the limbs and cause deformities. Paralysis of the respiratory muscles is a life-threatening complication. Active IMMUNIZATION is an effective measure in the prevention of poliomyelitis and has largely eliminated the disease from developed countries.

Polish The language of Poland, which belongs to the Slavonic language group and is spoken by its 38 million inhabitants, by Poles in the Baltic States and Belarus, and by some 2,500,000 people in the USA.

Polish Corridor A former region of Poland, which extended northwards to the Baltic coast and separated East Prussia from the rest of Germany. A part of Polish Pomerania in the 18th century, the area had since been subject to German colonization. It was granted to Poland after World War I to ensure Polish access to the coast. Its annexation by Germany in 1939, with the German occupation of the rest of Poland, precipitated World War II. After the war the area was restored to Poland.

Politburo The highest policy-making committee of the former USSR and its satellites. The Soviet Politburo was founded, together with the Ogburo (Organizational Bureau), in 1917 by the BOLSHEVIKS to provide leadership during the RUSSIAN REVOLUTION. Both bureaux were later re-formed to control all aspects of Soviet life.

political asylum The protection given by a state to a political REFUGEE from another country. The 1951 UN Convention Relating to the Status of Refugees defines as a refugee a person who, 'owing to well-founded fear of being persecuted for reasons of race, religion, nationality, membership of a particular social group or political opinion, is outside the country of his nationality and is unable or, owing to such fear, is unwilling to avail himself of the protection of that country...or...to return to it'. The Convention does not guarantee a right to asylum; strictly speaking, in INTERNATIONAL LAW, the right of asylum is not the individual's but the state's to grant protection in its sovereign territory. However, the Convention does declare that a refugee should be expelled only on grounds of national security and should not be returned to a territory where his or her life or freedom is threatened.

political correctness The concept that racism, sexism, or other prejudices should not be allowed expression in colloquial language. While it would not be acceptable, i.e. politically correct, to describe someone as 'working like a nigger' or to say that one had been 'jewed out of one's money', the concept of political correctness can be stretched to unreasonable limits by those who find the word 'mankind' sexist. Perhaps the criterion should be that one should not use words or idioms that disparage, even by implication, a minority group.

political party A permanent organization that aims to occupy positions of authority within the state, usually but not always through electoral means. In contrast to an interest group, a party seeks to form the government and not just to influence it. Parties are a response to the emergence of the mass electorate. With the extension of the FRANCHISE, parties had to develop a modern organization and a coherent set of policies in order to cultivate electoral support. Parties exist in almost all countries, except where they are banned or suppressed. They may be based on ethnic, religious, or regional identifications or on differing IDEOLOGIES. Political parties, whether they operate under two-party or multiparty systems, are necessary for the creation of a viable democratic government, and have become an indispensable feature of politics in the modern world. One-party political systems are invariably totalitarian.

political prisoner A person detained or imprisoned because of his or her political beliefs or activities, under laws designed to restrict dissent or opposition. Given the nature of the 'offence' concerned, such detention or imprisonment often takes place under emergency powers, without trial or appeal; likewise, release of political prisoners is often less a reflection of legal processes than of political change. Perhaps the world's best-known political prisoner of recent times is Nelson Mandela, who was held in South Africa from 1963 to 1990, having originally been convicted of involvement in subversive activities carried out by the African National Congress. Political prisoners who have not espoused violence are also sometimes referred to as prisoners of conscience, and form part of the concern of pressure groups, such as AMNESTY INTERNATIONAL. In some countries, classification of prisoners as political may be a matter of serious dispute, as for example, in Northern Ireland, since it may confer certain privileges not available to criminal offenders.

politics The study and practice of government and the exercise of authority on a national scale. Efforts are made to influence, gain, or wield POWER at various levels of government, both internally and internationally, rather than in private settings and associations. Modes of political activity are highly diverse, varying from dispute resolution and formal elections to the threat or use of outright coercion or force. The degree to which people can engage in political activity also varies in different countries: in open societies, individuals have more freedom to participate in the exercise of political power than in closed societies, where such power is restricted to small groups.

Polk, James Knox (1795–1849) US Democratic statesman, 11th President of the USA 1845–49. His term of office resulted in major territorial additions to the USA: Texas was admitted to the Union in 1845, and the successful outcome of the conflict with Mexico resulted in the annexation of California and the south-west two years later.

polka A traditional round-dance from Bohemia that became popular in European ballrooms in the early 19th century. It was in quick duple TIME, with steps on the first three beats and a small hop on the fourth. The polka figures as a typical Johann Strauss dance, but is also found in the concert music of Smetana and Dvořák It continues to be used in both folk and ballroom settings.

pollack A fish, *Pollachius* (or *Gadus*) *pollachius*, of the cod family, Gadidae, distinguished by its brownish-green back shading to yellowish-green on the sides, and by its lack of a chin barbel. It occurs off the Atlantic coast of Europe and in the western Mediterranean, swimming in schools near rocky reefs and wrecks in depths of 5–200 m (19–650 feet). It feeds on fishes and large quantities of crustaceans. Spawning takes place in early spring in deep water; both the eggs and larvae float at the surface and drift inshore. Young fishes are common in shallow water in midsummer.

pollen Grains containing minute male 'plants' encased in a tough wall. This is often characteristically shaped or ornamented so that in many cases the pollen grain's parent plant can be identified. The wall's function is to protect the male GAMETES from desiccation or other injury during their passage to the female gametes in POLLINATION. Pollen grains are produced by structures called stamens in angiosperms. In late spring and early summer, pollen, particularly from wind-pollinating plants like conifers and grasses, may be so copiously produced as to cause scums on ponds. Some people are sensitive to high levels of airborne pollen and have an allergic reaction known as HAY FEVER.

pollen-feeding moth See GOLD MOTH.

pollination The process prior to fertilization in plants in which pollen grains are brought into contact with ovules in GYMNOSPERMS, or stigmas in ANGIOSPERMS. The effective agents may be wind, as in many trees and in grasses, water, as in some aquatics, or animals, particularly insects, such as bees. Most plants promote the transfer of pollen from one plant to another. This is called cross-pollination and produces offspring with a genetic make-up in between that of their parents. The pollen-producing structures often mature well before the ovule, or stigma, is ready to receive pollen; this prevents plants from becoming self-pollinated. There are many exceptions to this rule, however; some plants use only self-pollination, while others can use both types.

Pollock, (Paul) Jackson (1912–56) US painter. His earlier work shows the influence of surrealist painters, such as Joan Miró, but he later became a leading figure of abstract expressionism and from 1947 onwards developed the style known as ACTION PAINTING. Fixing the canvas to the floor or wall, he poured, splashed, or dripped paint on it, covering the whole canvas and avoiding any point of emphasis in the picture. He was killed in a car accident; he had earlier been treated for alcoholism and in 1938 suffered a mental breakdown.

poll tax A tax levied on every poll (or head) of the population. Poll taxes were granted by the English House of Commons in 1377, 1379, and 1380. The third of these poll taxes, for one shilling from every man and woman, was acknowledged as a cause of the PEASANTS' REVOLT. The community charge (1988–93) was a poll tax that replaced domestic rates. See also TAXATION.

pollution Contamination of any kind, but especially of the environment. The introduction into the environment of substances that are detrimental to human health, to other animals, to plants, and to the planet itself is an inescapable feature of industrialization and overpopulation. However, pollution has become a cause of widespread concern in the late 20th century. Pollution can be classified according to whether it affects the air, water, or land, but other classifications are also possible, for example, pollution may be chemical, physical, or thermal. Pollution can include excessive noise (for example, from an airport or motorway), which has few long-term effects; it may be local, such as smelting slag, or global, such as radioactive FALL-OUT. Other large-scale pollutants may effect climatic changes or damage trees and other plant life. Most commonly pollution can be attributed to specific chemical substances. For example, sulphur compounds from fossil fuels cause ACID RAIN; carbon dioxide emissions from car exhausts and other sources are responsible for the GREENHOUSE EFFECT; PESTICIDES, such as DDT, can enter the food chain; and such compounds as the CHLOROFLUOROCARBONS (CFCs), used as aerosol propellants, are depleting the stratospheric OZONE layer that protects the Earth from excessive ultraviolet radiation. Pollution can arise through failure adequately to control normal processes, as when untreated sewage is discharged into the sea, or excessive nitrate fertilizers are leached from the soil into water supplies (see EUTROPHICATION); or it may be caused by some major disaster, such as at the CHERNOBYL nuclear power-station in Ukraine, the BHOPAL chemical works in India, or an oil spillage from a damaged tanker. See also AIR POLLUTION; WATER POLLUTION.

polo A ball-and-goal game of Central Asian origin played on horseback by teams of four. Players attempt to hit a wooden ball with the side of a mallet through a pair of goal posts on a grass field 182.88 m by 274.32 m (200 yards by 300 yards). The game, which is divided into four to eight chukkas of seven minutes each, is as much a test of horsemanship as of ball-playing skills.

Polo, Marco See MARCO POLO.

polonaise A stately processional dance, developed from its peasant origins by the Polish aristocracy during the 17th century. In its stylized 18th-century version the phrase-lengths are short, rhythmic, and repetitive, and start always on the first beat of the bar.

polonium (symbol Po, at. no. 84, r.a.m. 210) A radioactive element; it is a highly active alpha-emitter with a HALF-LIFE of 103 years for the most stable isotope, polonium-209. The element occurs in trace amounts in uranium deposits. Polonium-210 is made artificially and is used in satellites as an energy source. Polonium was discovered by Marie CURIE in pitchblende and named after Poland, her country of birth.

Pol Pot (born Saloth Sar) (*c.*1925–98) Cambodian Communist leader, Prime Minister 1976–79. From 1968 he led the Khmer Rouge, becoming Prime Minister soon after its seizure of power in 1975. During his regime the Khmer Rouge embarked on a brutal reconstruction programme in which more than 2 million Cambodians died. Overthrown in 1979, Pol Pot led the Khmer Rouge in a guerrilla war against the new Vietnamese-backed government until his official retirement from the leadership in 1985.

polyanthus See PRIMROSE.

Polybius (*c.*200–*c.*118 BC) Greek historian. After an early political career in Greece, he was deported to Rome. His 40 books of *Histories* (only partially extant) chronicled the rise of the Roman Empire from 220 to 146 BC.

polycarbonate Any of a class of thermoplastic POLYMERS in which the monomer units are linked through carbonate groups. Polycarbonates have a unique combination of strength, stiffness, toughness, high softening temperature and processability. Their only drawback is their susceptibility to attack by organic solvents. Applications include safety helmets, street-lighting, protective windows, and electrical terminals.

Polycarp, St (*c.*69–*c.*155) Greek bishop of Smyrna in Asia Minor. His dates are uncertain but he was probably the leading Christian figure in Smyrna in the mid-2nd century. He was arrested during a pagan festival, refused to recant his faith, and was burnt to death. His followers buried his remains and wrote an account of his martyrdom, which provides one of the oldest such records to survive. Feast day, 23 February.

Polyclitus (5th century BC) Greek sculptor. He is known for his statues of idealized male athletes. His best known surviving works are Roman copies of the *Doryphoros* (spear-bearer) and the *Diadumenos* (youth fastening a band round his head). His other works include a large gold and ivory statue of the goddess Hera.

polyester fibre A synthetic POLYMER fibre made by the same melt-spinning process as NYLON fibres. Whinfield discovered the polyester fibre Terylene in 1941, some six years after CAROTHERS discovered nylon. The two fibres have much in common: both are strong and durable, and both are used in large amounts worldwide to make clothing, either alone or in blends with natural fibres.

polygamy A form of MARRIAGE in which more than one spouse is permitted. The most common form, **polygyny**, permits a man to have more than one wife. This occurs in some Muslim countries and in some Christian sects, on the grounds that it was the form of marriage practised in the Old Testament. It also occurs in some African countries. Usually it is restricted to leaders of communities and others with sufficient resources to support more than one wife and their many children. It is not permitted in developed countries, because it implies a diminished status to women. The reverse of this argument has made **polyandry**, the form of marriage permitting a woman to have more than one husband, relatively rare, although not unknown in some primitive societies.

polygon A closed, geometric figure in the plane, all of whose sides are straight and only intersect at the corners (the vertices) in pairs. The number of edges, vertices, and angles is constant for any type of polygon. A regular polygon has equal sides and equal angles: common examples are equilateral triangles and squares. Circles can be regarded as at the limit of regular polygons, as the number of sides tends to infinity.

polygraph A machine for detecting and recording physiological activity, such as pulse rate and blood pressure, popularly known as a 'lie detector'. The polygraph is attributed to British physiologist James Mackenzie, who built the first apparatus in 1892. It is used in police work and in recruitment for high-security jobs, although its reliability is disputed.

polyhedron A closed solid figure, all of whose faces are POLYGONS. Regular polyhedra have faces that are congruent and there are only five possible forms: the tetrahedron, a pyramid with four equilateral triangular faces; the hexahedron, a cube with six square faces; the octahedron, with eight equilateral triangular faces; the dodecahedron, with 12 regular pentagonal faces; and the icosahedron, with 20 equilateral triangular faces.

polymer A compound composed of MACROMOLECULES, formed from a chain of repeating simple chemical sub-units (monomers). Natural organic polymers include proteins, DNA, and latexes, such as rubber; while diamond, graphite, and quartz are examples of inorganic natural polymers. Synthetic polymers include inorganic compounds, such as glass and concrete, but the great majority are PLASTICS. The polymer is formed from monomers under the influence of heat, pressure, or the action of a CATALYST. The exact nature of the polymer produced depends on the nature of the monomer (or monomers) and the conditions of polymerization. Two classes of polymers are usually recognized. In condensation polymers (for example, POLYURETHANE), the joining together of the monomers involves the elimination of a small molecule, commonly water. In the second, addition polymers, the monomers join together without elimination of a small molecule; examples are POLYTHENE and POLYSTYRENE. Copolymers are made by the combination of two or more different monomers in the same polymer chain. The properties of a copolymer can be varied by altering the relative amounts of the different monomers. The ABS (acrylonitrile–butadiene–styrene) family of plastics are copolymers: uses include telephone and computer body shells and piping.

polymethyl methacrylate A PLASTIC composed of POLYMERS of methyl methacrylate. It is sold in the UK under the brand name of Perspex. Polymethyl methacrylate is transparent, and is lighter and more impact-resistant than glass. It is used as a replacement for glass in many applications, for example aircraft domes, optical instruments, roofing, and lighting fixtures.

Polynesia A region of the central Pacific, lying to the east of Micronesia and Melanesia and containing the easternmost of the three great groups of Pacific islands, including New Zealand, Hawaii, the Marquesas Islands, Samoa, the Cook Islands, and French Polynesia. **Polynesians** show close affinity in physical features, language, and culture, and probably spread from a focal centre in the area of Samoa and Tonga within the past 3000–2000 years. The principal immigration of Maoris from the Marquesas into New Zealand, is dated to about 1350 AD, though it was not the first.

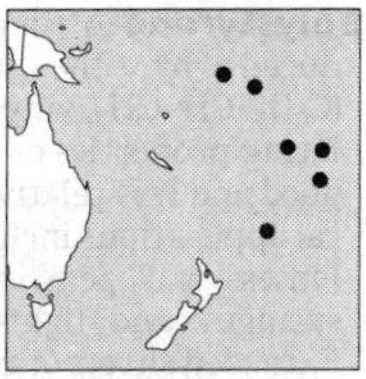

The origins of Polynesians are controversial. Some authorities, on the basis of their fair skin coloration, wavy hair, and stocky build relate them to the CAUCASOIDS; they have also been regarded as close to the Melanesians. Probably the widest held view is that they are a distant offshoot of a MONGOLOID population in south-east Asia.

polynomial An expression in algebra that contains several terms added together (or subtracted), especially where the terms have different POWERS. The following expression $7x^3 + 4x^2 + 5x - 3 = 79$ is a polynomial equation of degree 3 (the degree is determined by the x term(s) with the highest power). The number in front of each x term is its coefficient (here it is 7 for the x^3 term). Polynomials have an important place in mathematics. Elementary shapes, such as circles, ellipses, parabolas, etc. (see CONIC SECTIONS), are described mathematically by polynomial equations; POWER SERIES, such as the BINOMIAL EXPANSION, are polynomials; and some families of polynomials, for example, the Hermite and the Legendre polynomials, are solutions to certain DIFFERENTIAL EQUATIONS that arise in science and engineering.

polyp Any sedentary invertebrate of the phylum Cnidaria with radial symmetry, living singly or in a colony, and catching food in its waving tentacles. Polyps include such creatures as sea anemones, hydras, and corals, all of which are rather plant-like in appearance. The polyp phase of these animals can be a larval or an adult stage. In some jellyfish the polyp is the sedentary larval stage, developing into a free-swimming 'umbrella' with tentacles beneath. Such forms are called medusae and are the dispersive stage of polyp-bearing animals.

Polyphemus See CYCLOPS.

polyphony Music in which several strands of melody are combined simultaneously. Polyphony consists of a horizontal combination of melodies, as opposed to homophony, which emphasizes the topmost melody, supported by accompanying HARMONIES. The great polyphonic period is usually defined as from about 1200 to 1650, but polyphony has survived to the present day as one of music's essential techniques.

polypody A fern of the genus *Polypodium*. Rather variable in appearance, the fronds of *Polypodium* can reach 40 cm (16 inches) long depending on species; they are herring-bone shaped and bear rows of round, orange-brown spore-cases. The fronds remain green through the winter and only die back when new ones appear in spring.

polypropylene A tough, lightweight, rigid thermoplastic (see PLASTICS) made by the polymerization of high-purity propene (propylene) gas in the presence of an organometallic CATALYST at relatively low temperatures and pressures. It is widely used for domestic containers and appliances because it is cheap, and will withstand hot water, detergents, and harsh treatment. Other typical applications include some automotive parts, pipes, rope, nets, and carpets and other heavy-duty textile products. See also NATTA.

polystyrene A thermoplastic (see PLASTICS) produced by the polymerization of styrene (C_6H_5–CH=CH_2, vinyl benzene). The electrical insulating properties of polystyrene are outstandingly good and it is relatively unaffected by water. Typical applications include light fixtures, toys, bottles, lenses, ball pens, capacitor dielectrics, medical syringes, and light-duty industrial components. Extruded sheets of polystyrene are widely used for packaging, envelope windows, and photographic film. Its resistance to impact can be improved by the addition of rubber modifiers. Polystyrene can be readily foamed; the resulting expanded polystyrene is used extensively for packaging.

polytetrafluoroethene See PTFE.

polythene (or **polyethene**, **polyethylene**) A thermoplastic (see PLASTICS) made from ETHENE. It was first developed in the 1930s in the UK, by the polymerization of ethene at a pressure of 2,000 bar, at 200°C. This produced a highly branched, low-density polythene (LDPE). An unbranched, relatively high-density form (HDPE) was synthesized in the 1950s using a complex catalyst. Polythene is a white waxy solid with very low density, reasonable strength and toughness, but low stiffness. It is easily moulded and has a wide range of uses in containers, packaging, pipes, coatings, and insulation.

polyunsaturated fatty acid See FATS AND OILS.

polyurethane Any of a family of thermosetting resins (see PLASTICS) produced by reacting compounds containing an isocyanate group (–N=C=O) with organic compounds containing hydroxyl (–OH) groups. Polyurethanes are made in many forms, ranging from flexible and rigid foams to rigid solids and highly abrasion-resistant products. They can be shaped by EXTRUSION or MOULDING. The flexible foams are used for upholstery. Rigid urethane foams are excellent heat insulators: they are used to insulate the low-temperature fuel in rocket motors, and most domestic refrigerators. As coating resins and varnishes, the urethanes provide an exceptional degree of toughness and hardness, plus flexibility and chemical resistance. Polyurethane elastomers are useful synthetic RUBBERS. Other typical products include gearwheels, shock mounts, pulleys, industrial lorry tyres, drive belts, and synthetic leather.

polyvinyl chloride See PVC.

pome A false FRUIT consisting of a central 'true' fruit surrounded by swollen tissue derived from a flower-stalk. Apples, pears, and quinces are examples, the 'core' being the true fruit.

pomegranate Either of two species of deciduous bush, or small tree, which form their own plant family, Punicaceae, containing just one genus, *Punica*. One species, *P. protopunica*, is native to an island near south Yemen, while the other, *P. granatum*, is native to the area between the Balkans and the Himalayas. This is the species now widely cultivated wherever there are hot, dry summers and cool winters, as in California and the Mediterranean area. The fruit has a leathery, brown to red skin and contains many seeds in a pink, juicy, somewhat acid pulp.

pomelo See GRAPEFRUIT.

Pomerania A territory around the River Oder with the Baltic to the north. Its name derives from a SLAV tribe that settled there in the 5th century. From 1062 to 1637 it enjoyed much independence, ruled by its dukes, but after the Peace of Westphalia in 1648 it was divided between Sweden and Brandenburg. In 1770 Prussia acquired most of Swedish Pomerania.

Pomeranian See DOG.

Pompadour, Jeanne Antoinette Poisson, Marquise de (1721–1764) Mistress of LOUIS XV of France from 1745. She came from the world of wealthy officials and bankers, and was a lively witty woman, on friendly terms with the *philosophes* of the ENLIGHTENMENT. The people blamed her for the extravagance of the court and the disasters of the SEVEN YEARS WAR, but her political influence has probably been exaggerated.

pompano A fish belonging to the same family as the horse mackerel, Carangidae. Most are placed in the genus *Trachinotus*, and the name is in wide use in North America. They are deep-bodied, rather blunt-snouted fishes with long-based dorsal and anal fins. They are especially abundant in shallow water and moderate depths near reefs, and swim in schools, feeding on crustaceans and small fishes. Most species grow to a length of 50 cm (20 inches). Pompanos are well known as a good-tasting food-fish.

Pompeii An ancient city in western Italy, south-east of Naples. The life of the city came to an abrupt end following an eruption of Mount Vesuvius in 79 AD, as described by Pliny the Younger (and in which his uncle, the Elder Pliny, perished). The city lay buried for centuries beneath several metres of volcanic ash until excavations of the site began in 1748. The well-preserved remains of the city include not only buildings and mosaics but wall-paintings, furniture, graffiti, and the personal possessions of the inhabitants, providing an unusually vivid insight into the life, art, and architecture of the period.

Pompey (known as **Pompey the Great**; full name Gnaeus Pompeius Magnus) (106–48 BC) Roman general and statesman. His greatest achievements were the suppression of the Mediterranean pirates (66), and the defeat of Mithridates in the east (63). He formed the First Triumvirate with Caesar and Crassus in 60, but disagreement with Caesar resulted in civil war. Pompey was defeated at the battle of Pharsalus, after which he fled to Egypt, where he was murdered.

Pompidou, Georges Jean Raymond (1911–74) French statesman. He served in the RESISTANCE MOVEMENT in World War II and, from 1944, became an aide and adviser to DE GAULLE. While the latter was President, Pompidou held the post of Prime Minister (1962–68) and played an important part in setting up the Evian Agreements. The strikes and riots of 1968 prompted de Gaulle's resignation (1969) and Pompidou was elected President. In a swift and decisive policy change he devalued the franc, introduced a price freeze, and lifted France's veto on Britain's membership of the EUROPEAN ECONOMIC COMMUNITY. See also CENTRE POMPIDOU.

Ponce de León, Juan (*c.*1460–1521) Spanish explorer. He accompanied Columbus on his second voyage to the New World in 1493 and later became governor of Puerto Rico (1510–12). He landed on the coast of Florida in 1513, claiming the area for Spain and becoming its governor the following year.

Pondicherry A French colony (1674–1954), in south-east India, originally established by the FRENCH EAST INDIA COMPANY. It provoked Dutch and British rivalry, and was captured several times in the 18th-century trade struggles. It survived the collapse of the French East India Company to remain the administrative centre for French interests in India throughout the British Raj era.

pond skater An elongate, blackish BUG that lives

on the surface film of ponds and streams. There are over 200 species of pond skater in the family Gerridae. They lay their eggs in batches on water plants below the surface and both young and adults are carnivorous, usually feeding on other insects trapped by the surface-tension of the water. A few, such as *Halobates*, belong to that small number of insect species to live on the sea.

pond snail A snail that can be found in almost every freshwater habitat, ranging from tiny spire-shaped species, such as *Hydrobia*, to the giant ram's-horn snails, *Planorbis*. While most breathe by gills and are related to winkles and whelks (prosobranchs), some are amphibious lung-breathers (pulmonate snails), having adapted from land-dwelling ancestors and reverted to freshwater life. These often act as hosts to parasites of vertebrates, such as liver flukes. A few pond snails give birth to live young, but most species lay gelatinous egg-masses on aquatic vegetation.

pondweed The common name for plants belonging to the monocotyledonous family Potamogetonaceae, though they may be of a great variety of species. The family includes the genus *Potamogeton*, of which about 50 species are known with a worldwide distribution. Most are submerged aquatics, with slender stems and pale green to brownish, almost translucent, leaves. In keeping with many plants adapted to live below water-level, the tissues are not strengthened by the substance lignin, and collapse on removal from the water. They are to be found in still and running water. Some species spread with great rapidity and may eventually prove troublesome in lakes, filtration plants, and drainage systems. Some species have two kinds of leaves, broad, floating ones and narrower, submerged ones.

Ponte, Lorenzo Da See DA PONTE.

Pontiac (*c*.1720–69) Leader of a North American Indian tribal confederacy, and chief of the Ottawa Indians, for many years allies of the French. After the French defeat in 1759 and British occupation of their forts, he managed to confederate many ALGONQUIAN tribes, fearful of British expansion and intransigence. Spurred by religious enthusiasm, Ottawa, Ojibwa, Potawatomi, Wyandot, Shawnee, and Delaware tribesmen rose in a concerted frontier attack from the Great Lakes to Virginia in May 1763. Only Detroit and Fort Pitt held out and 200 settlers were killed, many in western Pennsylvania. British punitive expeditions weakened the confederacy, and in 1766 Pontiac made peace. He was murdered in 1769 near St Louis by hired Indian assassins.

Pontius Pilate See PILATE, PONTIUS.

Pontus An ancient region of northern Asia Minor, on the Black Sea coast north of Cappadocia. Established as an independent kingdom by the end of the 4th century BC, it reached the height of its powers between 120 and 66 BC under Mithridates VI. At this time it dominated the whole of Asia Minor, but by the end of the 1st century BC it had been defeated by Rome and absorbed into the Roman Empire.

pony A small horse, standing less than 1.47 metres (14.2 hands) to the top of the withers. Most native breeds of ponies have been crossed with thoroughbred or Arab stock. They have been used as pack animals and for riding, especially by children, and for pony trekking.

Pony Express (1860–61) Horse-borne mail delivery system in the 19th-century US west. It was founded in 1860 by the Missouri freight company of Russell, Majors, and Waddell to prove that there was a viable alternative to the southern route into California for the transportation of overland mail. It operated between St Joseph, Missouri, and Sacramento, California, using a relay of fresh ponies and riders, and took two weeks to cover the full distance of nearly 3,200 km (2,000 miles). High costs made the operation unprofitable, and the coming of the telegraph made it unnecessary.

poodle See DOG.

pool A form of billards that originated in the USA, but is now also common in Europe. It is played on a table 1.4 × 2.7 metres (4.5 × 9 feet) with six pockets. Numbered coloured balls are used, which have to be potted with a cue ball.

Poona See PUNE.

Poor Laws Legislation that provided the basis for organized relief and welfare payments, originating in England in the 16th century. They gradually reduced the charitable obligations placed upon ecclesiastical institutions, guilds, and other private benefactors in the Middle Ages. With the Dissolution of the MONASTERIES an important source of charity was abolished. Originally only those physically incapable were deemed worthy of charity and able-bodied beggars were dealt with harshly. However, a statute passed in 1576 recognized that men fit and willing to work might be genuinely unable to find employment and were in need of support. Three categories of poor were subsequently recognized: sturdy beggars or vagabonds, regarded as potential trouble-makers, the infirm, and the deserving unemployed. In 1834 a Poor Law Amendment Act tried to end the giving of assistance outside the workhouse; it established the principle that all citizens should have the right to relief from destitution through accommodation. The workhouses were run by locally elected Boards of Guardians, who raised money through a poor-rate. The system proved inadequate in the growing cities, where the Guardians sometimes resorted to relief without the guarantee of accommodation. The Poor Law was gradually dismantled by social legislation of the 20th century, particularly that of the Liberal governments (1906–14) by important Acts in 1927, 1929 (when Boards of Guardians were abolished), 1930, 1934 (when Unemployment Assistance Boards were created), by SOCIAL SECURITY legislation following the BEVERIDGE Report (1942), and by the establishment of the WELFARE STATE.

pop art A movement in art based on the imagery of consumerism and popular culture – comic books, advertisements, packaging, and images from television and the cinema were among the sources used. The movement began in the mid-1950s and flourished until the early 1970s, chiefly in the USA and Britain. In the USA, where its most famous exponents were Andy WARHOL and Roy LICHTENSTEIN, it was seen initially as a reaction against the seriousness of ABSTRACT EXPRESSIONISM. Pop art could also be disturbing or macabre. In Britain, where David HOCKNEY (early in his career) and Peter Blake were among the leaders, pop art was generally less aggressive than in the USA.

pope In Western Christianity, the bishop of Rome (residing in VATICAN CITY); as the head of the Holy See he is the supreme leader of the ROMAN CATHOLIC CHURCH. Within the Roman Catholic Church, the pope is believed to be the spiritual descendant of St Peter, leader of Jesus' disciples, and his title 'Vicar of Christ' expresses a claim to universal jurisdiction over all Christians. In recent years, the pope has become an increasingly visible figure, travelling throughout the world on missions to strengthen the Roman Catholic faith and assert the relevance of the Christian message.

In the EASTERN ORTHODOX CHURCH, the patriarch of Alexandria is sometimes called the pope, and the title may be used of any priest.

Pope, Alexander (1688–1744) English poet. His *Essay on Criticism* (1711), a poem on the art of writing, drew him to the attention of Addison's literary circle; he later associated with Jonathan Swift, John Gay, and others. Among Pope's other major works are the mock-heroic *The Rape of the Lock* (1712; enlarged 1714), the philosophical poem *An Essay on Man* (1733–34), and the *Epistle to Dr Arbuthnot* (1735), a fierce and ironic attack on his critics. He published an edition of Shakespeare's plays (1725). Pope also made notable translations of the *Iliad* (1715–20) and the *Odyssey* (1726).

Popish Plot (1678) An alleged conspiracy by Roman Catholics to kill Charles II of England and replace him as king by his Roman Catholic brother, James, Duke of York. The plot was invented by Titus Oates, an Anglican priest, who asserted that a massacre of Protestants and the burning of London were imminent. The plot achieved credibility because of SHAFTESBURY's willingness to use Oates as a means to secure James's exclusion from the throne. A nationwide panic ensued during which more than 80 innocent people were condemned before Oates was discredited. He was punished for perjury, but survived to receive a pension from WILLIAM III.

poplar A tree of the genus *Populus*, allied to the willows in the family Salicaceae and native to northern temperate regions. There are 35 species, all deciduous, with simple leaves and flowers in pendulous catkins. The female catkins produce seeds covered in down, hence their name of cottonwood in North America. The seeds are dispersed by wind. The trees are fast-growing and relatively short-lived, the timber being much used for pulp, matches, and other small objects. In plantations, the most commonly cultivated poplars are hybrids between the European black poplar, *P. nigra*, and the American eastern cottonwood, *P. deltoides*. The spire-shaped Lombardy poplar, *P. nigra* var. 'Italica', is a popular ornamental species. The aspen, *P. tremula*, a tree native to Europe, has leaves distinctive for their 'trembling' in the slightest breeze.

Popocatépetl A dormant volcano in Mexico, 72 km (45 miles) south-east of Mexico City, rising to a height of 5,452 m (17,887 ft).

Popper, Sir Karl Raimund (1902–94) Austrian-born British philosopher. He was originally associated with the logical positivist group the Vienna Circle, but was highly critical of the emphasis placed by logical positivism on verification. In *The Logic of Scientific Discovery* (1934) he posits instead that scientific hypotheses can never be finally confirmed as true and are acceptable only in so far as they manage to survive frequent attempts to falsify them. He is also known for his criticism of the historicist social theories of Plato, Hegel, and Marx, as, for example, in *The Open Society and its Enemies* (1945). He left Vienna on Hitler's rise to power and eventually settled in England, where he was a professor at the London School of Economics (1949–69).

poppy A plant of the family Papaveraceae, with over 400 species of mainly temperate distribution. The chief genera are *Papaver* and *Meconopsis*, each having about 40 species. To the former belong the corn or field poppy, and the oriental, opium, and Iceland poppies. They have divided leaves, a milky sap (latex) and large, colourful flowers. Among other genera for which this name is used are *Eschscholzia* (California poppy), *Glaucium* (horned poppy), *Argemone* (Mexican poppy), and *Romneya* (tree poppy).

Popular Front A political coalition of left-wing parties in defence of democratic forms of government believed threatened by right-wing fascist attacks. Such coalitions were made possible by the strategy adopted by the COMINTERN in 1934. In France such an alliance gained power after elections in 1936, under the leadership of Léon BLUM, who implemented a programme of radical social reforms. In Spain the Popular Front governments of Azaña, Caballero, and Negrin were in office from 1936 to 1939, and fought the SPANISH CIVIL WAR against FRANCO and the Nationalists. A Popular Front government ruled in Chile (1938–47).

population (in ecology) All the representatives of one species that live and breed at a particular site. This distinguishes it from a flock, or swarm, which is usually part of a much larger interbreeding population.

population, world The number of people alive in the world at a given time. Between the collapse of the Roman empire in the 5th century AD and the late 18th century world population appears to have remained fairly stable, with high death rates and occasional plagues. In the late 18th and 19th centuries in Europe there was an unprecedented rise in population, largely because of improved public health and control over infectious disease. In 1803 Thomas MALTHUS propounded the theory that the rapidly growing population would soon increase beyond the capacity of the world to feed it, and that controls on population were therefore necessary to prevent catastrophe. Japan instituted the first modern official birth-control policy after World War II, setting an example that other countries followed, with China now having the strictest birth-control policy in the world. Since 1950 there has been a population explosion in Asia, Africa, and Latin America, with a total world population rising from 2.5 billion in 1950 to 5.3 billion in 1990. By 2000 AD world population is expected to reach 6 billion. The UN forecasts that by the year 2025 it will reach 8.5 billion. It is predicted that 3 billion of these additional people will live in Africa, Asia, and Latin America, and only 200 million in the developed regions.

To combat the suffering and deprivation resulting inevitably from world overpopulation, in 1965 the United Nations Population Commission recommended that member nations should be given technical support in providing birth control, especially in the developing nations. According to some estimates, doubling the amount currently spent on family planning in the Third World would save the lives of over 5 million babies and 250,000 mothers each year. Such measures are resolutely opposed by the Roman Catholic Church.

population density The number of people relative to the territory in which they live. Over the world's land surface it surpassed 400 persons per 1,000 ha in the early 1990s. Hong Kong, Macau, and Singapore, with rates of over 44,000 per 1,000 ha, have the highest densities in the world.

populism A style of politics that claims to represent the true feelings and aspirations of the people in contrast to the prevailing political establishment. Populist leaders often stand outside existing POLITICAL PARTIES and attempt to mobilize the people directly by articulating grievances against the ruling élite or against foreigners.

porbeagle A large, heavily built shark, *Lamna cor-*

nubica, which ranges across the whole of the North Atlantic region and possibly also the Southern Hemisphere. It lives close to the surface, migrating northwards in summer but rarely coming close inshore. It is a very powerful swimmer, with a broad, deep tail and a body temperature higher than the surrounding sea. It feeds mainly on fishes and squids. Despite its size of up to 3 m (9.75 feet) long, it is not dangerous to man.

porcelain A CERAMIC made from china clay (kaolin) and feldspar (china-stone), closely related to POTTERY but fired at a much higher temperature to produce a fine, hard, translucent, white material. Porcelain was first made during the Tang dynasty (618–907 AD) in China, where a combination of easily accessible raw materials and superior KILN design resulted in the ceramic industry being many centuries in advance of the West.

In Europe a soft-paste porcelain, made solely from clay and ground glass and fired at 1,200°C, was produced in an effort to duplicate Chinese porcelain. This material was not a true porcelain, being much less hard and fine. The first true European porcelains were developed by BÖTTGER at Meissen in Germany in 1708, but large-scale porcelain manufacture did not begin in the West until new deposits of kaolin were found, such as those in Cornwall, England. These were fired at a temperature of 1,450°C. The first major Western development was the discovery of bone china by the British potter Josiah Spode in about 1800. Spode added calcined bone to hard paste mixes to produce a hybrid porcelain, still widely used in the UK. Porcelain is also a useful engineering ceramic, with properties similar to ALUMINA, that is used in many electrical insulating applications.

porcupine A large RODENT characterized by quills, or spines, which are modified hairs, though they are not well developed in all species. There are two distinct families, both with 11 species, the Old World porcupines (Hystricidae) and those of the New World (Erethizontidae). The largest species, and the one with the best-developed spines, is the crested or African porcupine, *Hystrix cristata*, which weighs up to 27 kg (60 pounds). The other African genus of porcupine, the brush-tailed, is much smaller at about 3 kg (7 pounds). The Asian porcupines, such as the Asiatic brush-tailed porcupine, *Atherurus macrourus*, are more like typical rodents in appearance, and the Bornean long-tailed porcupine, *Trichys lipura*, has only rudimentary spines. The New World porcupines are markedly more arboreal than those from the Old World and have less well-developed spines. Two species have a prehensile tail (*Coendou* species). There is only one North American species, *Erethizon dorsatum*, which extends as far north as the Arctic ocean.

porgy A North American SEA BREAM. Ten species are recognized on the Atlantic coast and one on the Pacific coast. Most of them are deep-bodied fishes, and possess a single dorsal fin. They have well-developed teeth in the jaws, those in the sides being blunt, crushing teeth. They are bottom-dwelling, living close to reefs as well as on open sandy and muddy bottoms. Most are carnivores, eating sea-urchins, molluscs, and crustaceans, but some also eat plants. They are good food species.

Porifera See SPONGE.

pornography The exhibition or description of sexual activity in the printed word, films, or the visual arts, which is intended to stimulate erotic rather than aesthetic feelings. Some pornography, defined as 'tending to deprave or corrupt', is regarded by the law as obscene, although different countries have varying standards and different ways of controlling the publication and sale of pornography. Pornographic material may range from 'soft' pornography, which produces normal arousal, to 'hard-core' pornography, which may involve sadistic violence against women, bestiality (sexual intercourse between a person and an animal), and paedophilia (sexual desire directed towards children). While soft pornography is often seen as harmless by liberal opinion that is disinclined to curb freedom of expression by banning it, hard-core pornography can be regarded as encouraging violence against women and children by depicting them as willing victims of pain and humiliation. The causal connection between pornography and violent and sexual crimes has been hotly debated, however.

porphyry (or **porphyrite**) Any medium- to coarse-grained IGNEOUS ROCK in which large, well-formed crystals are surrounded by a mass of much finer crystals. Hard white and purple rocks used by sculptors is also loosely called porphyry.

Porphyry (born Malchus) (*c*.232–303) Neoplatonist philosopher. Born in Tyre, he studied first at Athens. He then moved to Rome, where he became a pupil of Plotinus, whose works he edited after the latter's death. Porphyry's own works include *Against the Christians*, of which only fragments survive.

porpoise The smallest marine mammal, with some six species in the family Delphinidae, found in the north temperate zones, the west Indo-Pacific, and the coastal waters of southern South America. These TOOTHED WHALES are often found near the coast and in estuaries, and sometimes swim upriver for many miles. They may reach a length of up to 2.25 m (7.3 feet). They are black above and white below, with a low dorsal fin and small flippers. Superb swimmers, they will pursue shoals of herrings, sardines, and mackerel. Mating takes place in the summer and gestation lasts until the following June or July. The calf is large, being about half the length of its mother; it is suckled with extremely rich milk. The harbour or common porpoise, *Phocoena phocoena*, is found around the coasts of Europe and in the North Atlantic and Pacific oceans.

Porsche, Ferdinand (1875–1952) Austrian car designer. In 1934, with backing from the Nazi government, he designed the Volkswagen ('people's car'), a small economical car with a rear engine, developed and produced in great numbers before and after World War II. Porsche's name has since become famous for the high-performance sports and racing cars produced by his company, originally to his designs.

Porsenna, Lars (or **Porsena**) (6th century BC) A legendary Etruscan chieftain, king of the town of Clusium. He was summoned by Tarquinius Superbus after the latter's overthrow and exile from Rome and as a result laid siege to Rome but was ultimately unsuccessful in capturing the city.

Portal, Charles Frederick Algernon, Viscount Portal of Hungerford (1893–1971) Marshal of the Royal Air Force. In 1915 he joined the Royal Flying Corps, and by 1937 he was an air vice-marshal and Director of Organization at the Air Ministry. In 1940 he was placed in charge of Bomber Command. The aircraft available had technical deficiencies, especially in navigation, but by carrying the BOMBING OFFENSIVE into Germany, they disrupted munitions factories, power plants, and railway junctions. While introducing technical improvements, he pressed for a policy of 'area bombing' to replace that of specific targets. After the war he became Controller of Atomic Energy in Britain (1945–51).

Port Arthur A city in south-east Texas, USA, on Lake Sabine; pop. (1990) 58,720. Once an anchorage for the pirate Jean Lafitte, the area around Port Arthur was settled by French Acadians in the 18th century. In 1895 it was chosen as the Gulf terminus of the Kansas City, Pittsburg and Gulf Railroad and a city was founded. In addition to shipping and chemical industries, Port Arthur is the largest petroleum-refining centre in the USA.

Port-au-Prince The capital of Haiti, a port on the west coast of the island of Hispaniola in the West Indies; pop. (est. 1992) 1,255,080. Founded by the French in 1749, it became capital of the new republic in 1806, when it was called Port Republicain. Sugar, rum, and textiles are its chief products.

Port Elizabeth A seaport and beach resort on the coast of Eastern Cape, South Africa, on Algoa Bay; pop. (1991) 853,200. Settled in 1820 on the site of a British fort (Fort Frederick), it was named after the wife of the acting governor of the province. Largely developed since the creation of the rail link with Kimberley, the city now produces a wide range of goods including steel, textiles, and vehicles.

Porter, Cole (1892–1964) US songwriter. He made his name with a series of Broadway musicals during and after the 1930s; these include *Anything Goes* (1934) and *Kiss me, Kate* (1948). He also wrote songs for films, including *Rosalie* (1937) and *High Society* (1956). Among his best-known songs are 'Let's Do It', 'Night and Day', and 'Begin the Beguine'.

Porter, Katherine Anne (1890–1980) US short-story writer and novelist. Her collections of short stories include *Pale Horse, Pale Rider* (1939) and *Collected Short Stories* (1965), for which she won a Pulitzer Prize. Her novel *Ship of Fools* (1962) is an allegorical treatment of a voyage from Mexico to Germany during the period of the rise of Nazism.

Porter, Peter (Neville Frederick) (1929–) Australian poet, resident chiefly in England since 1951. His early collections, such as *Poems, Ancient and Modern* (1964) provide a sharply satiric portrait of London in the 1960s. His later work became increasingly meditative, complex, and allusive. Other collections include *English Subtitles* (1981) and *The Automatic Oracle* (1987).

Port Harcourt The principal seaport of south-east Nigeria, on the River Bonny at the eastern edge of the Niger delta; pop. (1991) 371,000. Established just before World War I as an outlet for coal from the Enugu coalfields, it was named after the British statesman Sir William Harcourt. It has many industries including steel and aluminium products, tyres, paint, and vehicle assembly.

Port Jackson shark A shark, *Heterodontus philippi*, a member of a small family of rather primitive sharks, often called bullhead sharks, which are found only in shallow water in the Indo-Pacific region. Living off southern Australia, it is similar to the Californian horn shark, *H. francisci*, growing to a length of 1.5 m (5 feet). Its body is deep and heavy, with spines in front of the dorsal fins, and its teeth are distinctive, being sharp in the centre of the jaws and rounded, for crushing, at the sides. The teeth are well adapted to a diet of sea urchins, molluscs, and crustaceans, all hard-shelled prey. These sharks lay their eggs in spirally twisted egg-cases which have a tendril at each corner; these tangle in seaweeds.

Portland, Isle of A rocky limestone peninsula on the Dorset coast of England, south of Weymouth. Its southernmost tip is known as the **Portland Bill**. Stone from its quarries (known as **Portland stone**) is a famous building material that was used by Wren for St Paul's Cathedral.

Portland cement The most widely used hydraulic CEMENT. Named from a supposed resemblance to natural Portland stone, it was developed by Joseph Aspdin of Wakefield, England, and patented in 1824. It is made by SINTERING together chalk or limestone and clay in a rotary kiln. The resulting ash is then finely ground with GYPSUM.

Port Laoise (or **Portlaoighise**) The county town of Laois in the Irish province of Leinster, 80 km (50 miles) south-west of Dublin; pop. (est. 1990) 9,500. Formerly known as Maryborough, it the site of a top-security prison.

Port Louis A seaport in the Indian Ocean, capital of the island of Mauritius; pop. (est. 1993) 143,510. Founded in 1735, it developed as a trading port after the construction of the Suez Canal.

Port Mahon See MAHÓN.

Portmeirion A resort town on Tremadog Bay, north Wales, created as a 'folly' in Italian style by the Welsh architect Clough Williams Ellis.

Port Moresby The capital of Papua New Guinea, situated on the south coast of the island of New Guinea, on the Coral Sea; pop. (1990) 193,240. Rubber, gold, and copra are exported.

Pôrto Alegre A major port and commercial city in south-eastern Brazil, capital of the state of Rio Grande do Sul; pop. (1991) 1,263,400. Situated at the north-western end of the Lagoa dos Patos, a lagoon separated from the Atlantic by a sandy peninsula, it is accessible to ocean-going ships via the port of Rio Grande. It has shipyards, meat-packing plants, and foundries, and many light industries.

Port-of-Spain The capital of Trinidad and Tobago, a port on the west coast of the Caribbean island of Trinidad, situated on the Gulf of Paria in the crook of the Charaguaramas peninsula; pop. (1990) 46,000. First visited by Columbus in 1498, it replaced St Joseph as capital in 1757. It is the commercial and industrial centre of the island.

Porto Novo The capital of Benin, a port on the Gulf of Guinea close to the border with Nigeria; pop. (1992) 179,140. Formerly a centre of the Portuguese slave-trade, it was for many years, until independence in 1960, a trading port of French West Africa. It is being replaced by Cotonou, which has better links to the sea and with the interior, as the administrative and commercial centre.

portraiture The art of depicting likenesses of individual people. The earliest surviving portraits of individuals are probably the faces painted on the surfaces of Egyptian sarcophagi. In the Western world, portraiture was well known to the ancient Greeks and was developed by the Romans to become a major art-form, both in the form of painting and the more durable sculpted bust. Portraiture became virtually extinct during much of the Middle Ages, reviving in the 15th century when, in both Italy and northern Europe, portraits began to be included in religious compositions. In Italy 15th-century portraits were often in pure profile, but Leonardo, Raphael, and Titian introduced much greater variety of pose and expression. The secularization of art in northern Europe after the Reformation gave great encouragement to secular portrait painters, such as Holbein and the 17th century witnessed the work of such masters as Van Dyck, Rembrandt, Rubens, and

Velázquez. The 18th century saw Britain's greatest age for the portrait, with Hogarth, Gainsborough, Raeburn, Ramsay, Reynolds, and Romney. Photography posed a major threat in the 19th century, but portraiture has survived, as a minority artform with the work of such masters as Jacob Epstein, Graham Sutherland, and Lucian Freud.

Port Said A duty-free seaport and summer resort of Egypt, at the north end of the Suez Canal; pop. (1991) 449,000. It was founded in 1859 in association with the building of the Suez Canal by the khedive Said Pasha after whom it is named. On the opposite bank is Port Fouad, built in 1926 and named in honour of King Fouad (1868–1936). It was severely damaged in the 1967 war with Israel, but largely reconstructed in 1975. It has chemical, tobacco, and textile industries.

Portsmouth A port, naval base, and tourist city on the south coast of England, in Hampshire; pop. (1991) 174,700. The naval dockyard was established there in 1496. There are ferry links with the Isle of Wight, the Channel Islands, and France; Nelson's flagship HMS *Victory* and the Tudor warship *Mary Rose* can be visited here. It has several museums, a cathedral dating back to the 12th century, and many engineering industries. Portsmouth University (formerly Portsmouth Polytechnic) was formed in 1992.

Port Stanley See STANLEY.

Port Sunlight A town on the south bank of the Mersey in north-west England, built in 1888 as a model village for the employees of Lever Brothers 'Sunlight' soap factory at Birkenhead near Liverpool.

Portugal A west European country on the Atlantic west coast of the Iberian peninsula, flanked by Spain on the north and east. The Atlantic archipelago of the AZORES and MADEIRA are also part of Portugal.

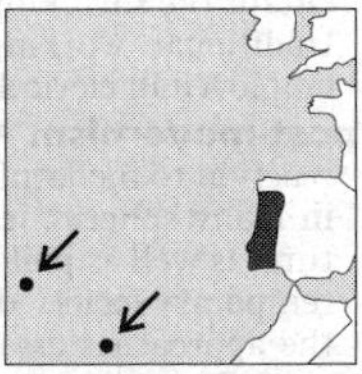

Physical. Half of the country lies on the edge of the high and ancient Iberian plateau, in a region of rugged hills, lakes, and deep gorges. Winters are cold here, and there is moderate rainfall. Much of the region is covered with forests of pine and cork-oak, and from it flow three great rivers – the Douro, Tagus, and Guadiana – which water the flat and sandy coastal plain. Here it is warm, although still fairly dry; vineyards flourish, as do cereals and citrus fruits.

Economy. One of the poorest countries in Western Europe, Portugal has a mixed economy, with a large agricultural sector. Fishing is important, with a substantial annual sardine catch; Portugal is the world's largest producer of cork. PYRITES form the country's main mineral resource, although there are also deposits of several other metallic ores as well as sodium and coal. Manufacturing industries include the principal exports of clothing, machinery, footwear, textiles, and chemicals. Tourism is important, and Portuguese workers abroad contribute substantially to foreign earnings. Portugal has also benefited from EU development aid.

History. Portugal was settled by Celtic tribes from *c.*500 BC, and during Roman domination was known as 'Lusitania'. Periods of Gothic and Moorish control followed the collapse of the Western Roman empire, and Portugal struggled to develop a distinct identity until the papacy recognized the kingship of Alfonso I in 1179. In 1249 the Portuguese completed the reconquest of their country from the MOORS. Then, after a series of unsuccessful wars against Castile, peace was at last concluded in 1411, and under the ruling house of Avis (1385–1580) the vast overseas Portuguese empire took shape. On the expiry of the Avis dynasty, PHILIP II of Spain became king by force. The Spanish union lasted until 1640, when the native House of BRAGANZA was swept to power by a nationalist revolt. During the relatively peaceful and prosperous 18th century, close links were established with England. In the wake of the disastrous Lisbon earthquake (1755) the dynamic minister Pombal exercised the powers of an enlightened despot. During the NAPOLEONIC WARS the Prince Regent John (King John VI from 1816), together with the Braganza royal family, fled to Brazil. Here he met demands for political and economic freedom, Brazil emerging peacefully as an independent empire in 1822. Through most of the rest of the 19th century there was considerable political instability until 1910, when a republic was established. In 1926 there was a military coup which was followed in 1932 by the establishment of SALAZAR as Prime Minister, Minister of Finance, and virtual dictator (1932–68), strongly supported by the Roman Catholic Church. Portugal supported the Allies in World War I and in World War II remained theoretically neutral while allowing the Allies naval and air bases. GOA, Diu, and Damao were lost to India in the 1960s, but MACAO in South China was retained. Salazar's autocratic policies were continued by Marcello Caetano until a military coup in 1974. Increasingly bitter guerrilla warfare had developed in Portuguese Africa, especially in ANGOLA and MOZAMBIQUE. These gained independence in 1975, although both experienced civil war, while the state of GUINEA-BISSAU was created in 1974. After two years of political instability at home, a more stable democracy began to emerge following the election of Antonio Eanes as President in 1976. Moderate coalition governments both left and right of centre have alternated, all struggling with severe economic problems. President Mario Soares was elected in 1986, having been Prime Minister since 1983. He was re-elected President in 1991, with Anibal Cavaço Silva of the Social Democrat Party as Prime Minister. Portugal joined the European Community in 1986. In the general election of 1995, the Socialist Party under António Guterres won power and in 1996 Jorge Sampaio was elected President.

Capital: Lisbon
Area: 92,389 sq km (35,672 sq mi)
Population: 9,906,000 (1995)
Currency: 1 escudo = 100 centavos
Religions: Roman Catholic 95.0%; Protestant 1.0%; Jewish 0.1%
Ethnic Groups: Portuguese 99.0%; Angolan 0.2%; Cape Verdean 0.2%
Languages: Portuguese (official)
International Organizations: UN; OECD; NATO; Council of Europe; EU; CSCE

Portuguese The official language of Portugal, its territories and former colonies and of Brazil, where it was taken by 15th-century explorers. It is a Romance language, most closely related to (but clearly distinct from) Spanish, with over 10 million speakers in Portugal and over 150 million in Brazil.

Portuguese Congo A former name for CABINDA, an exclave of Angola to the north of the mouth of the Congo River.

Portuguese East Africa The former name of MOZAMBIQUE in Africa.

Portuguese Guinea The former name of GUINEA-BISSAU in West Africa.

Portuguese man-of-war *Physalia physalis*, a colonial coelenterate. A colony produces different types of individual which, by cooperating together, resemble a large jellyfish. One modified individual secretes a gas-filled float, and the other individuals produce feeding tentacles that hang from this, the whole structure reaching 30 cm (12 inches) across. Each individual is either a modified POLYP or a medusa, and those specialized for feeding have tentacles reaching several metres down. These kill fish on contact and draw their dead bodies upwards to the feeding polyps. The tentacles are capable of inflicting painful stings on bathers. Other individuals are adapted for reproduction.

Portuguese West Africa The former name of ANGOLA in Africa.

Poseidon In Greek mythology, the god of the sea, of earthquakes, and of horses. He was a brother of Zeus. The Romans identified him with the water-god Neptune.

positive discrimination (US **affirmative action**) Policies that aim to counteract the inferior position of groups that have been subjected to DISCRIMINATION, especially in terms of employment, EDUCATION, and access to housing. Supporters of positive discrimination maintain that past negative discrimination against certain groups means that to achieve equality of opportunity they must be given preferential treatment. This may entail, for example, giving a job or university place to a black candidate who is less well qualified than a white candidate. Opponents of positive discrimination argue that it is unjust and leads to resentment in the majority population, thereby increasing antagonism.

positivism See COMTE; SOCIAL SCIENCES.

positron An antiparticle (see ANTIMATTER) of an electron, having the same mass but a positive charge. Positrons occurring in cosmic-ray showers exist only briefly. They soon collide with electrons and are thus annihilated, producing two or three PHOTONS. A positron can form a short-lived stable system with an electron, somewhat analogous to a hydrogen atom. This is called a positronium. Its HALF-LIFE is of the order of 10^{-7} second.

positron emission tomography (PET) A technique of NUCLEAR MEDICINE used to monitor physiological and biochemical change within the body. A substance 'labelled' with a RADIOACTIVE ISOTOPE having a short half-life is administered to the patient and its distribution is traced. The substance is chosen for its capacity to be metabolized in the part of the body under examination; for example, labelled fluoro-deoxyglucose can make visible glucose metabolism in the brain. PET was developed in the 1970s and, like COMPUTERIZED TOMOGRAPHY, it relies on a computer to produce the final image.

possum An Australian MARSUPIAL belonging to any one of several families. The pygmy possums of the family Burramyidae comprise seven species, including the pygmy glider, *Acrobates pygmaeus*. The 16 species of ringtail possums are grouped in the family Pseudocheiridae and, like most possums, are nocturnal tree-dwellers. Like many other species, members of this family are leaf or sap eaters, unlike the striped possums (*Dactylopsila*) of the family Petauridae (gliders), which are insectivorous. A specialized possum in a unique family is the honey possum, *Tarsipes rostratus*. This small shrew-like marsupial, up to 8 cm (3 inches) in body length, feeds exclusively on nectar and pollen. Other possums include the brush-tail possums, which are PHALANGERS.

posthorn A valveless brass musical instrument used throughout Europe on mail coaches. In Britain it was a short, straight instrument, a shorter version of the coach horn, which has now become standardized in A♭ for playing Koenig's *Posthorn Galop* (1844) in dance bands. On the Continent of Europe it was a coiled instrument, which can still be seen on postage stamps and post boxes.

Post-Impressionism Various trends in painting, particularly in France, that developed from IMPRESSIONISM or in reaction against it in the period from about 1880 to about 1905. The term was first used by the British critic Roger Fry. The ways in which Post-Impressionist artists rejected the naturalism and preoccupation with momentary effects of Impressionism varied greatly; SEURAT and the NEO-IMPRESSIONISTS, for example, concentrated on a more scientific analysis of colour; CÉZANNE was concerned with pictorial structure; GAUGUIN explored the symbolic use of colour and line; and van GOGH was the fountainhead of EXPRESSIONISM.

post-industrial society A hypothetical society whose economy is based on the production of services rather than manufactured goods. The concept was elaborated by US sociologist Daniel Bell in his *The Coming of Post-Industrial Society* (1973). According to Bell, a post-industrial society (the USA is taken to be a model) places a high value on 'knowledge' and most of its citizens are well educated. The reduction in industrial production entails the shrinking and eventual abolition of the traditional working class, most citizens being employed in clerical or professional jobs.

post-modernism A contemporary movement in reaction to modernism, which has been influential in many spheres: it has influenced art and literature, as well as philosophy and the analysis of contemporary society, deconstructionism being one of the approaches associated with it (see DECONSTRUCTION). The concept came into common use in the 1970s in the context of **post-modernist architecture**. In post-modernist buildings, warmer more familiar vernacular materials, such as red brick, replaced the brutal undressed concrete of modernism. However, more generally, post-modernism opposes all systems of thought and meaning from traditional RELIGION to scientific reason, Freudian analysis to MARXISM – anything with claims to absolute truth. Post-modernist writings (such as Salman Rushdie's *Satanic Verses* (1988) and Umberto Eco's *Foucault's Pendulum* (1988)) are characterized by their emphasis on the meaninglessness of all 'higher truths', a constant merging of fact and fiction, reality and image. Post-modernism's critics express scepticism about what they see as its pretentious jargon and its cynical and superficial approach to understanding the world.

postmortem (or **autopsy**) The detailed examination of a dead body, usually to determine the cause of death (if it is uncertain), to provide information about a disease or condition that is poorly understood, or to detect and explore any criminal activities that might have caused the death. Permission of the relatives is required before a postmortem can be carried out unless a coroner at an inquest considers the death to have been sudden and of unexplained cause or unless the police request a postmortem before the inquest.

potash (or **potassium carbonate**, K_2CO_3) A term misleadingly used to describe potassium, as in 'potash feldspar'. Potassium carbonate used to be obtained as an alkaline substance by leaching vegetable ashes and evaporating the solution in iron – hence the name, 'pot ash'. Caustic potash is potassium hydroxide, KOH.

potassium (symbol K, at. no. 19, r.a.m. 39.10) An ALKALI METAL, similar in properties to SODIUM, obtained either by the electrolysis of molten potassium chloride or by the reaction of metallic sodium with molten potassium chloride. Potassium tarnishes quickly in air and reacts violently with water, producing a lilac flame, and so is stored under paraffin to avoid contact with water vapour. Potassium is produced on a small scale only, offering few advantages over the much cheaper sodium. Compounds of potassium are important as fertilizers, in the production of soft soaps, in the manufacture of GUNPOWDER and photographic chemicals, and in extracting GOLD and SILVER from their ores. When it is alloyed with sodium, the molten mixture has a high specific HEAT CAPACITY, which makes it useful as a coolant in nuclear reactors.

potassium hydroxide (or **caustic potash**, KOH) A white, crystalline BASE that is readily soluble in water, giving a strong alkali. It is prepared in the laboratory by reacting potassium with water and industrially by the electrolysis of potassium chloride solution. Its chemical properties are similar to SODIUM HYDROXIDE, NaOH, although it is more soluble; it is used in making liquid soap and as an electrolyte in batteries.

potassium nitrate (KNO_3) A white crystalline salt, also known by the older names of nitre and saltpetre. The salt is not naturally abundant and is therefore synthesized by fractional crystallization from a solution of sodium nitrate, $NaNO_3$, and potassium chloride, KCl. It is used in the manufacture of fireworks, gunpowder, and types of glass.

potassium permanganate ($KMnO_4$) A dark purple crystalline solid; the intense colour is due to the permanganate ion MnO_4^-. It is soluble in water and is a powerful oxidizing agent. It is useful in titrations because its colour changes when all the permanganate is reduced. This means the analysis requires no indicator.

potato *Solanum tuberosum*, one of the most important food crops of the family Solanaceae, thus related to the tomato. Potatoes are grown throughout the world, particularly in cool, temperate regions, for their swollen tubers which act as storage organs for carbohydrate food reserves. A perennial plant, the potato is cultivated from fresh tubers (seed potatoes), planted each spring. Many varieties exist, differing in their season of use, skin colour, flesh colour, flesh texture after cooking, and tuber shape.

Potemkin, Gregory (1739–91) Russian soldier and favourite of CATHERINE II. He was a man of great energy and an able administrator, who extended Russian rule in the south, carried out a series of army reforms, annexed the Crimea in 1783, and built a Black Sea fleet and a naval base at Sevastopol. In the war with the Turks he was made army commander and died in a year of Russian military victory. The battleship named after this soldier is famous for the mutiny that occurred on it in 1905. This incident persuaded the Emperor to agree to the election of a Duma.

potential difference (p.d.) The difference in electric potential between two points in an electric field. It is defined by the work that must be done to move a unit charge from one to the other. In SI UNITS it is measured in joules per coulomb, or VOLTS (V), and potential difference is commonly called voltage. See ELECTRICITY AND MAGNETISM.

potential energy The ability of an object to do work because of its position. For an object of mass m kg that is h metres above the surface of the Earth, the potential energy will be mgh, where g is the ACCELERATION of free fall. In SI UNITS it is measured in joules. The concept of potential energy can be applied to a wide range of situations in which there is a potential for work to be done – for example, in a stretched spring awaiting release. Its potential energy is converted to KINETIC ENERGY as the spring is released and returns rapidly to its original length. In astronomy, a planet in orbit about the Sun has potential energy and kinetic energy, continuously transferring one into the other as its distance from the Sun varies.

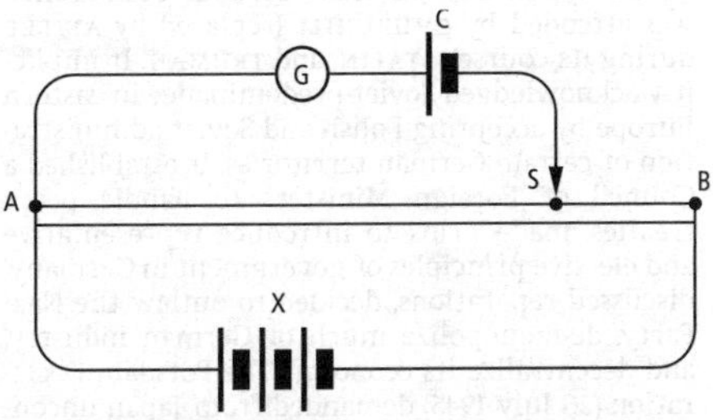

Potentiometer To determine the e.m.f. of the cell C, the sliding contact S is moved along the potentiometer wire AB until the galvanometer reading is zero. At this point the e.m.f. of C is exactly balanced by that of the accumulator X. The e.m.f. of cell C is then the e.m.f. of the accumulator multiplied by the ratio AS with zero galvanometer reading to the value of AS when X is used in place of C.

potentiometer A variable RESISTOR for electric circuits, similar to a RHEOSTAT. The potentiometer is also used for the accurate measurement of an unknown electrical potential or electromotive force (e.m.f): the unknown voltage is connected in a circuit with a source of known voltage, and the two voltages are balanced using the potentiometer. The unknown voltage can be calculated from the known voltage and the potentiometer setting.

potholing The activity of descending through potholes (funnel-shaped holes in limestone, usually where cracks in the rock meet) into underground drainage passages to follow the course of streams. Potholing can be dangerous but is becoming increasingly popular.

potlatch A ritual based on gift exchange found among American Indians of the north-west Pacific region. Potlatches were ritual feasts in which competitors for positions of status sought to outdo each other by giving ever more lavish gifts. The arrival of Europeans in the area during the 19th century, and the changes this brought to the local economy, caused a huge escalation in the scale of potlatches. Large quantities of European trade goods like blankets were not only given away but were also publicly destroyed to force a rival to equal the gesture.

Potomac A river of the eastern USA, which rises in the Appalachian Mountains in West Virginia and flows about 459 km (285 miles) through Washington, DC, into Chesapeake Bay on the Atlantic coast.

potoo (or **tree night-hawk**) A bird making up five species in the family Nyctibiidae, which inhabit the northern half of South America, parts of Central America, and the Caribbean. They are about the size of a crow, and beautifully camouflaged in browns, buffs, greys, and blacks. Their beaks are small, but, like the nightjar, the gape is enormous and used for catching insects at night. They lay their single egg on a broken stump of a tree, incubating it by sitting vertically above it, looking like an extension of the stump.

Potsdam The capital city of the state of Brandenburg in Germany, situated just west of Berlin on the Havel River; pop. (1991) 139,025. During the 17th and 18th centuries it was the summer residence of the electors of Brandenburg and the Prussian royal family. It developed during the reign of Frederick II (1740–86) who built the palace and park of Sans Souci. In August 1945 it was the site of a conference of US, Soviet, and British leaders, following the end of the war in Europe. This **Postdam Conference** was attended by CHURCHILL (replaced by ATTLEE during its course), STALIN, and TRUMAN. It implicitly acknowledged Soviet predominance in eastern Europe by accepting Polish and Soviet administration of certain German territories. It established a Council of Foreign Ministers to handle peace treaties, made plans to introduce representative and elective principles of government in Germany, discussed reparations, decided to outlaw the Nazi Party, de-monopolize much of German industry, and decentralize its economy. The Potsdam Declaration (26 July 1945) demanded from Japan unconditional surrender. Potsdam is an educational and industrial centre with locomotives, textiles, and food-processing industries.

Potter, Beatrice See WEBB, SIDNEY.

Potter, (Helen) Beatrix (1866–1943) British writer of children's stories. She is known for her series of animal stories, illustrated with her own delicate watercolours, which began with *The Tale of Peter Rabbit* (first published privately in 1900). She was also a respected biologist and botanical illustrator.

Potter, Dennis (Christopher George) (1935–94) British television dramatist. He began suffering from a crippling form of psoriasis in the 1960s, after which he wrote his most acclaimed works, the series *Pennies from Heaven* (1978) and *The Singing Detective* (1986). Both use popular songs of the 1920s, 1930s, and 1940s to contrast the humdrum or painful realities of everyday life. Other plays include *Blue Remembered Hills* (1979), in which adults played the parts of children, and the controversial *Brimstone and Treacle* (1976). In 1996, after Potter's death, his last works *Karaoke* and *Cold Lazarus* were screened jointly by two otherwise competing TV stations, BBC1 and Channel Four, in tribute to the writer.

Potteries, the A district in the upper Trent Valley of north Staffordshire, central England, in which the English pottery industry developed and reached a peak during the life of Josiah Wedgwood (1730–95). It was the setting for many of the novels of Arnold Bennett (1867–1931).

potter wasp See MASON WASP.

pottery Objects made from clay and hardened (fired) by heating. Pottery was one of the earliest technologies to be developed (*c*.7000 BC), because the raw material, clay, was widely available and easily shaped. The craft of potmaking probably originated independently in several places. The earliest pottery was sun-dried, but wood-burning KILNS were soon developed. Pottery was revolutionized by the invention of the potter's wheel, which probably came into use in the 4th millennium BC. All pottery can be divided into three basic categories: EARTHENWARE is the oldest and simplest type of pottery; stoneware, made by firing the pot at a temperature high enough to vitrify the outer surface, is harder and more durable; while PORCELAIN is equally hard but finer and translucent. The surface of a pot can be coated with a glaze before baking or firing to make it water-impermeable.

potto Either of two species of primate belonging to the same family as the lorises and bushbabies. They live in trees in the rain forests of West and central Africa. The short limbs and grasping hands and feet are used to cling tightly to branches. The potto, *Perodicticus potto*, and the golden potto, or angwantibo, *Arctocebus calabarensis*, are nocturnal animals which grow up to 32 cm (13 inches) in body length, with a tail 1–5 cm (0.5–2 inches) long. Both have thick fur, brownish-grey to brownish-red on the back, paler on the underside. The gestation period lasts for about five months and there is usually a single offspring. The baby crawls immediately on to the mother, who carries it until it is self-sufficient. Pottos eat insects, leaves, birds' eggs and other small animals, and have large forward-facing eyes, well adapted to seek prey at night.

pouched mouse Any of various mouse-like MARSUPIALS in Australia, usually species of the genus *Sminthopsis*, which includes the fat-tailed mouse, or dunnart, *S. crassicaudata*. Other mouse-like marsupials often called pouched mice include the kultarr, *Antechinomys laniger*, a jerboa-like animal, and the mulgara, *Dasycerus cristicauda*. All are members of the family Dasyuridae and tend to be insectivorous and carnivorous.

Poulenc, Francis (Jean Marcel) (1899–1963) French composer. He was a member of the group Les Six. The influence of Satie can be seen particularly in his adoption of the idioms of popular music, such as jazz. His work is also characterized by a lyricism heard especially in his many songs and in such instrumental works as the sonatas for flute (1957) and oboe (1962). He also wrote a series of lyrical and contrapuntal sacred choral pieces, while his works for the theatre include the opera *Dialogues des Carmélites* (1957) and the ballet *Les Biches* (1923).

poultry Domesticated birds, particularly those farmed for their eggs or meat, such as CHICKENS, turkeys, ducks, and geese. All domestic breeds of duck are descendants of the mallard, *Anas platyrhynchos*. The domestic goose has been derived primarily from the wild greylag goose, *Anser anser*, though in eastern Asia the so-called Chinese goose, *Anser cygnoides* (not a wild species), is a domestic derivative of the swan goose. The Egyptian goose, *Alopochen aegyptiacus*, was widely domesticated in ancient Egypt but has now been replaced by other domestic strains. Other main species that have been domesticated for their eggs or flesh are guineafowl, pigeons, and peafowl.

poultry farming The farming of POULTRY for meat and eggs. Poultry farming began with the domestication of Indian jungle-fowl, ancestor of the modern hen, in about 3200 BC. Both egg and meat production used free-range geese, turkeys, ducks, and hens until the late 19th century, when poultry farms were first established. Broiler production, the keeping of chickens and turkeys in a controlled environment under artificial daylight to maximize production, originated in the USA. Intensive egg and meat production followed, with specialist birds bred for each purpose and controlled by hormone-enriched feeds. Poultry farming has changed the chicken from an expensive luxury to an affordable meal for many families throughout the world. However, animal welfare groups have highlighted the keeping of chickens in battery cages as one of the most cruel forms of FACTORY FARMING.

Pound, Ezra (Weston Loomis) (1885–1972) US poet and critic. He went to Europe in 1908 and co-founded the imagist movement, rejecting romanticism and seeking clarity of expression through the use of precise images. Collections of poetry from this period include *Ripostes* (1912). He also contributed to the magazine of the vorticist movement, *Blast* (1914–15). Work from this later period includes *Hugh Selwyn Mauberley* (1920) and the long (unfinished) series of *Cantos* (1917–70). In 1925 he settled in Italy; he was charged with treason in 1945 following his pro-Fascist radio broadcasts during World War II, but was adjudged insane and committed to a mental institution until 1958.

Poussin, Nicolas (1594–1665) French painter. Regarded as the chief representative of French classicism in art and a master of the grand manner, he was extremely influential in the development of French art. From 1624 he lived mostly in Rome and was influenced by the work of Italian painters, particularly Titian and Raphael. In the 1630s and 1640s he developed in his painting a harmony and sense of order suffused with a rich colour sense. His subject-matter included biblical scenes (*The Adoration of the Golden Calf*, *c.*1635), classical mythology (*Et in Arcadia Ego*, *c.*1655), and historical landscapes.

powder metallurgy The fabrication of objects from powdered metal by compressing the powder into the desired shape and then heating (SINTERING) to a temperature below the melting-point of the metal. The powder particles weld to form a solid. For small components this is often more economical than CASTING, which involves machining and scrap loss, and, in the case of metals with high melting-points, there is a considerable saving of energy. This process also permits the manufacture of porous components and the production of an 'alloy' from mutually insoluble materials.

Powell, Anthony (Dymoke) (1905–) British novelist. He is best known for his sequence of twelve novels, *A Dance to the Music of Time*, beginning with *A Question of Upbringing* (1951) and ending with *Hearing Secret Harmonies* (1975). These novels are a satirical and panoramic portrayal of the fortunes of the English upper middle classes between the World Wars.

Powell, (John) Enoch (1912–98) British politician. He was a classical scholar before World War II, joining the Conservative Party in 1946. After serving as Minister of Health (1960–63) he attracted public attention in 1968 with his condemnation of multiracial immigration into Britain; as a result he was dismissed from the shadow Cabinet. Powell also opposed British entry into the Common Market, resigning from the Conservative Party in 1974 on this issue. He later served as an Ulster Unionist MP (1974–87).

Powell, Michael (Latham) (1905–90) British film director, producer, and screenwriter. Having made his directing début in 1931, he co-founded the Archers Company in 1942 with the Hungarian scriptwriter Emeric Pressburger (1902–88). Their films are visually striking and often fantastic, and include *The Tales of Hoffman* (1951), *The Red Shoes* (1948), and the controversial *Peeping Tom* (1960).

power (in physics) The rate of doing work, or, alternatively, the rate of transfer of energy. If one machine does the same amount of work as another, but in half the time, it has twice the power. Power is a SCALAR quantity measured in WATTS, a watt being one joule per second. Light bulbs and most other domestic electric devices are rated in terms of their wattage, to denote the rate at which they consume electrical energy. A 2 kilowatt electric fire will consume 2 kW every hour, the cost of this energy being quoted in pence per kilowatt-hour (3.6×10^6 joules).

power (in mathematics) The product obtained when a number is multiplied by itself a certain number of times. The third power of 2, or two to the power of three, is $2 \times 2 \times 2$, written 2^3, that is 8. The sixth power of 10, written as 10^6, is $10 \times 10 \times 10 \times 10 \times 10$, or 1,000,000.

power series A mathematical SERIES in which each term contains a power of x. For example, $x - x^3/3! + x^5/5! - x^7/7! + \ldots$ is a power series that converges for all values of x and gives numerical values equal to sin x if x is in radians (the notation 3!, or FACTORIAL 3, $= 3 \times 2 \times 1$). A power series is an infinite POLYNOMIAL. Isaac NEWTON believed his work on power series, particularly the BINOMIAL EXPANSION, to be among his most significant mathematical achievements.

power-station A place in which electric power is produced. ELECTRICITY GENERATION accounts for about a quarter of world energy consumption, with coal providing over half the input and smaller contributions from HYDROELECTRICITY, oil, nuclear power, and gas. In almost all present systems, the conversion to electric power is by means of a turbo-generator: a rotating GENERATOR driven by a TURBINE. (Exceptions such as SOLAR CELLS make only a very small contribution.) In hydroelectric or TIDAL ENERGY plants the driving power comes from flowing water, in GAS-TURBINES from hot combustion gases, in wind farms from the wind, and in all other types from superheated steam, which is produced either by burning fossil fuels or in a NUCLEAR REACTOR. Power stations using COMBINED-CYCLE TECHNOLOGY have both gas and steam turbines, while the waste heat from some power-stations is used for space-heating (see COMBINED HEAT AND POWER GENERATION). The first public station offering electricity for sale to private consumers (Holborn Station, in London) was commissioned in 1882. The turn of the century saw the first megawatt (million-watt) systems, with STEAM-TURBINES replacing the older engines. BOILERS became more efficient with the introduction of pulverized coal (1919) and improved HEAT EXCHANGERS. Output reached 100 MW in the 1930s and over 1,000 MW from a single turbo-generator by 1970. The electricity produced per tonne of coal rose from 200 kWh to over 2,000 kWh. Nevertheless, even the best modern plant can achieve only 30–40 per cent EFFICIENCY. Other emissions also cause concern. Electrostatic precipitators remove much of the fine ash from flue gases, but the high cost and technical problems have limited the introduction of desulphurization to remove acid gases (see ACID RAIN). A FLUIDIZED-BED FURNACE is able to reduce both these emissions, but not the carbon dioxide, a necessary by-product of fossil fuel burning that is a major contributor to the GREENHOUSE EFFECT. The cleanest forms of power-stations are those that make use of hydroelectric power or of wind farms. Emissions from nuclear power-stations are minimal but they create problems of nuclear-waste disposal.

Powys An inland county of Wales, formed in 1974 from the former counties of Montgomeryshire, Radnorshire, and most of Breconshire; area 5,077 sq km (1,960 sq miles); pop. (1991) 116,500; county town, Llandrindod Wells. It is divided into three districts.

Prado The Spanish national art gallery in Madrid. Established in 1818 by Ferdinand VII and Isabella of Braganza, it houses the greatest collection in the world of Spanish masters – Velasquez, El Greco, Zurbarán, Ribera, Murillo, Goya – as well as important examples of Flemish and Venetian art collected as a result of political ties with these countries in the reigns of Charles V, Philip II, and Philip IV. The gallery takes its name from the *prado* or meadow that once surrounded it.

praetorian Originally a bodyguard for a Roman general or 'praetor'. In 27 BC AUGUSTUS established nine cohorts of such troops in and near Rome. They were an élite, better paid than legionaries, serving shorter engagements and with many privileges. They also became 'king makers' since their support was essential for gaining high political office. At least four prefects became emperor before CONSTANTINE abolished them early in the 4th century.

pragmatism A US philosophical tradition, originally developed by Charles Peirce (1839–1914) and then extended by, amongst others, JAMES and DEWEY. Its main claims, easily caricatured, are that statements only have meaning to the extent that they can affect our actions, and that truth is, ultimately, what works for a scientifically sophisticated community. It thus has strong affinities with, but is more subtle than, positivism.

Prague (Czech **Praha**) The capital of the Czech Republic and former capital of Czechoslovakia (1918–1992), on the River Vltava; pop. (1991) 1,212,000. The Bohemian king and Holy Roman emperor Charles IV made it the capital of Bohemia in the 14th century. It was the scene of religious conflict in the early 15th century between the followers of John Huss and the Catholic Church, and again in the 17th century when, in response to the oppression of the ruling Catholic Habsburgs, the Protestant citizens threw Catholic officials from the windows of Hrdčany Castle. This event, known as the **Defenestration of Prague** (1618), contributed to the outbreak of the Thirty Years War. The city was invaded in 1968 by Soviet troops, an action that crushed the attempts at liberal reform introduced by the government of Alexander Dubček in a period known as the Prague Spring. It is a popular tourist destination with industries that include chemicals, engineering, and pharmaceuticals.

Praia The capital of the Cape Verde Islands, a port situated on the south coast of the island of São Tiago; pop. (1990) 62,000.

prairie A grassland on the great level tracts of land in central North America, formerly occupied by herds of buffalo and now mostly converted to the cultivation of cereals. See also PRAIRIE SOIL.

prairie-chicken (or **prairie-hen**) Either of two species of bird of the genus *Tympanuchus*, part of the GROUSE family. Both lesser and greater prairie-chickens live in North America in grass prairies. About the size of chickens, they are heavily barred, brown birds. The males display communally, by inflating large air-sacs (red in the lesser, orange in the greater) in the side of the neck. The females tend the eggs and chicks.

prairie dog A GROUND SQUIRREL of the genus *Cynomys*. The five species are all small, fat rodents of the open plains and Rocky Mountain region of North America. They feed upon green vegetation or, if that is scarce, upon roots, and will also eat insects when these reach plague proportions. From four to six young are born in May in an underground nest, and at four weeks they emerge to begin feeding on plants. The black-tailed prairie dog, *C. ludovicianus*, is about 30 cm (1 foot) long with a tail of 8 cm (3 inches) and is buff or cinnamon in colour apart from its tail. The white-tailed prairie dog, *C. leucurus*, is smaller and, apart from the white tip to its tail, resembles its relative.

prairie soil (or **brunizem**) A zonal soil in sub-humid grassland areas in which rainfall is between 600 and 1,000 mm (25 and 40 inches) a year. The presence of abundant organic matter causes the surface HORIZONS of this soil to be very dark, and there is a gradual shading into lighter-coloured lower horizons with less humus. Although some of the more soluble soil components, particularly calcium, may be washed downwards, the rainfall in sub-humid areas is insufficient to cause excessive LEACHING. Like CHERNOZEMS, which they resemble, these soils are very fertile. They occur extensively in the corn-growing areas of Iowa and southern Minnesota, USA.

Prandtl, Ludwig (1875–1953) German physicist. Prandtl is remembered for his studies of both aerodynamics and hydrodynamics. He established the existence of the boundary layer (a layer of more or less stationary fluid immediately surrounding an immersed and moving object), and made important studies on streamlining. The **Prandtl number** is a dimensionless group used in these studies.

praseodymium (symbol Pr, at. no. 59, r.a.m. 140.9077) A LANTHANIDE element first isolated in 1885 by C. A. von Welsbach. Its only non-radioactive isotope is Pr-151. It is used in mischmetal and as a catalyst.

pratincole Any one of eight species of bird of the genus *Glareola*, which belong to a family, Glareolidae, of WADING BIRDS that also includes the COURSERS. They are widespread in warm areas of the Old World, living in open country, often near to water. They are brown, short-legged, long-winged birds, resembling very large swallows as they catch their insect prey on the wing. They lay two to four eggs in a shallow scrape on the bare ground.

prawn Any of the larger, inshore, decapod CRUSTACEANS of the suborder Dendrobranchiata, which contains the SHRIMPS, especially those with a long projection (rostrum) between the eyes. Prawns tend to live below tide-level in winter, but are found in rock-pools in the summer, and some species move up estuaries, burrowing in the sand. They have a sharply bent abdomen and usually lack enlarged pincers, as they feed only on small pieces of vegetation and debris. The common edible prawn, *Leander serratus*, 5–8 cm (2–3 inches) long, has a saw-edged rostrum and occurs in temperate seas.

Praxiteles (mid-4th century BC) Athenian sculptor. Although only one of his works, *Hermes Carrying the Infant Dionysus*, survives, he is regarded as one of the greatest Greek sculptors of his day. Other examples of his work survive in Roman copies or are known from their descriptions by writers; they include a statue of Aphrodite, which represents the first important female nude in sculpture.

praying mantis A large insect in which the first segment of the thorax is elongate and the front legs are modified for seizing prey. Mantids sit on plants in a 'praying' position until prey appears.

The females sometimes eat the males during mating. They are one of two major divisions of the order Dictyoptera, the other being the cockroaches. There are around 1,300 species of mantids, found mainly in the tropics and subtropics.

Precambrian Era The period before the PHANEROZOIC, hypothetically including all the Earth's history from some 4,600 million years ago to 570 million years ago. It is subdivided into the ARCHAEAN and PROTEROZOIC eons. Characteristically exposed in continental interiors (SHIELDS), the Precambrian was once considered to be devoid of organic life but it is now known to contain a variety of organisms, including algae, microfossils, and, in the late Precambrian, traces of animals.

pre-cast concrete A CONCRETE product or component made prior to fixing it in its final location. The alternative is to cast the concrete in its permanent position. Pipes, masonry blocks, kerbs, paving slabs, posts, floor planks, bridge beams, and similar components are usually manufactured in a pre-casting factory. Large wall-panels, stair flights, and system buildings may be made on the construction site itself.

precedent A judicial decision containing a statement of a legal principle, which is authoritative not only in that case but also in future cases. The power of courts to make law through precedents operates only in CASE LAW systems. Generally, decisions of higher courts are said to bind lower courts. Precedent operates more rigidly in the UK than in the USA, where JUDICIAL REVIEW of legislation for inconsistency with an entrenched CONSTITUTION gives courts the freedom to re-interpret the constitution without being strictly bound by precedent.

precession The 'wobbling' motion of a rapidly spinning body or gyroscope in which the axis of rotation slowly sweeps out a cone of circular cross-section. Astronomically the term is used for the precession of the EQUINOXES, the movement of the equinoxes westward round the ecliptic as the axis of the spinning Earth slowly rotates about its mean or average position. In the same way as a top wobbles or precesses about the vertical, so the Earth wobbles about the perpendicular to the plane of its orbit. Its axis is inclined at an angle of 23° 27′ to this perpendicular, and it rotates about it slowly, once every 26,000 years. The cause is the gravitational attraction of the Sun and Moon on the Earth's equatorial bulge (its OBLATENESS).

precipitation (in meteorology) The rain, snow, sleet, or hail falling through the atmosphere to the ground. It occurs when particles which have formed in a CLOUD have grown too large for upcurrents of air within the cloud to support them. In cumulonimbus (heaped) clouds, such as arise in tropical revolving storms, precipitation results from convection. The clouds form fairly rapidly, and the rates at which condensation occurs and precipitation falls are rarely equal. The result is showers, often short-lived and of varying intensity. Nimbostratus (layered) cloud, on the other hand, is usually formed by ADVECTION, as, for example, when air travels over a colder land or sea surface, or by the orographic effect of its flow up hillsides. The result may be a light but persistent drizzle, the rates of condensation and fall being equal. In DEPRESSIONS, air rises because of the horizontal convergence of two air masses. The types of cloud will depend on the nature of the associated front. A warm front will have a thick layer of cloud and may give steady and continuous precipitation. A cold front may include cumulonimbus and give heavier and more intense precipitation. It is an essential part of the HYDROLOGICAL CYCLE.

precipitation (in chemistry) The formation, in a solution, of solid particles that fall to the bottom as a precipitate. It may occur as a result of a chemical reaction between two solutions, or a solution and a gas, to form one or more products insoluble in the solvent. Alternatively the state of a solvent may be changed so that the solubility of the solute in it is reduced. Precipitation is frequently used to extract metal ions from solution. The process of quantitative gravimetric analysis is based upon the production of highly pure and easily separable precipitates. Precipitation methods are also used in separations, using filters or centrifuges, and to show end-points in titrations.

pre-Columbian art See SOUTH AMERICAN INDIAN ART.

predestination The belief that all aspects of life and AFTERLIFE are foreordained by God. In Christian THEOLOGY, this belief is not incompatible with the notion of FREE WILL: God predestines to salvation those whose future faith and merits he foreknows. The doctrine of predestination is closely linked to that of God's grace: only through divine grace, God's free favour, can man be saved. Islamic belief in the predetermined will of Allah (*qadar*) is similarly fatalistic, but in practice the devout Muslim attempts to bring his behaviour into line with the will of Allah, in order to retain responsibility for his actions. The Hindu notion of KARMA differs from that of predestination, in that appropriate behaviour in this life determines the quality of future REINCARNATIONS.

pre-eclampsia High BLOOD PRESSURE in a pregnant woman, which may be accompanied by fluid retention and the presence of protein in the urine. The condition requires treatment to reduce the blood pressure and plenty of rest. Severe or untreated pre-eclampsia may progress to the more serious condition of **eclampsia**, characterized by convulsions.

preference shares See SHARE.

Pregl, Fritz (1869–1930) Austrian chemist who was given the Nobel Prize for chemistry in 1923 for his work on microchemical methods of analysis. Until the early part of the 20th century, analysis in organic chemistry required large quantities of pure compounds. Pregl refined combustion analysis so that only milligrams were required, and the techniques he devised contributed greatly to subsequent progress.

pregnancy The period during which an EMBRYO or foetus develops within the body of a female mammal. It covers the time from fertilization of a female ovum by a male spermatozoon until birth, and is also known as gestation. In the human female, this period is normally about 266 days or, more conveniently, 40 weeks from the last menstrual period. In other mammals, the gestation period varies. In rabbits it takes between 30 and 43 days. In horses it takes a much longer period of 330–380 days. The period is relatively fixed in each species.

pregnancy test A urine test to detect the presence of the hormone human chorionic gonadotrophin (HCG), which is produced during pregnancy. The first hormone test, published in 1928, involved injecting samples of the woman's urine into immature female laboratory mice. Pregnancy was diagnosed if the animals' reproductive organs became fully developed. Modern home pregnancy tests use MONOCLONAL ANTIBODIES to detect the same hormone.

prehistory The period before written records, when the only source of evidence about early societies is archaeology. It thus covers an immense period of time, linking evolutionary biology, archaeology, and history. The subject begins with the study of early humans, and can be said to have lasted down to recent times in remote parts of the world. It is divided into the STONE AGE (PALAEOLITHIC, MESOLITHIC, and NEOLITHIC), the BRONZE AGE, and the IRON AGE. History, based on written records began *c.*3000 BC in Egypt and Mesopotamia.

prelude A piece of music that acts as an introduction to something else. Thus a SUITE may commence with a prelude, an OPERA may begin with one, or a FUGUE may be preceded by one. In the 19th century the term was used as a title for short piano pieces. Chopin, Debussy, and Rachmaninov, among others, published books of preludes.

Preminger, Otto (Ludwig) (1906–86) Austrian-born US film director. He was a theatre and film director in Vienna before moving to New York, where he was a director on Broadway and with Twentieth Century Fox (1941–51). He then made a series of independent productions, including the influential films *The Moon is Blue* (1953), *The Man with the Golden Arm* (1955), and *Bonjour Tristesse* (1959). His later films included *Exodus* (1960), *Hurry Sundown* (1966), and *The Human Factor* (1979).

Pre-Raphaelite Brotherhood A small group of young English artists formed in 1848 who took their name from their desire to revive the sincerity and simplicity of early Italian painting (before the time of Raphael). The nucleus was formed by three fellow students – HOLMAN HUNT, MILLAIS, and ROSSETTI. They chose religious or other morally uplifting themes; their desire for fidelity to nature was expressed through detailed observation and the use of a clear, bright, sharp-focus technique. At first the group was bitterly attacked (their work was thought to be not only unidealized but even sacrilegious in representing biblical characters as ordinary people), but their fortunes improved after the critic RUSKIN publicly defended them in 1851. However, the group had virtually disbanded by 1853, as the individual artists went their separate ways, only Holman Hunt remaining true to the original doctrines throughout his career.

Presbyterian A Protestant Christian who subscribes to the anti-episcopal theories of Church government, and usually to the doctrines of John CALVIN. Presbyterian Churches oppose state intervention in religious affairs and advocate the primacy of the Bible as a rule of faith.

Reformed and Presbyterian Churches all over the world made various adaptations to the original Calvinist pattern, but they remained essentially similar. Government of Presbyterian Churches is by elected representative bodies of ministers and elders. The first Presbyterian Church to be organized on a national basis was in 16th-century France; its members became known as HUGUENOTS, and they played a large part in provoking the French Wars of Religion. Reformed congregations contributed to the Dutch Revolt, and once the Netherlands secured independence from Catholic Spain the Reformed Church became established there. Elsewhere in Europe, many congregations managed to survive the COUNTER-REFORMATION. In 1628 a Dutch Reformed Church was organized on Manhattan Island. The first American Presbyterian Church was founded in Philadelphia in 1706. The official Church of Scotland, with 1.25 million members, is one of the largest of the Presbyterian Churches.

pre-school education See PRIMARY EDUCATION.

Prescott, John (Leslie) (1938–) British Labour politician, Deputy Prime Minister since 1997 and secretary of state for the environment, transport, and the regions. Formerly a merchant seaman (1955–63) and union official, he was first elected to parliament in 1970, becoming deputy leader of the Labour Party in 1994.

president A non-monarchical head of state, a post which may also be combined with executive power and responsibilities. In constitutional states, presidents are chosen in various ways; the most common methods are election by the LEGISLATURE, by an electoral college, or by direct popular election. The main distinction is between presidential and parliamentary types of executive. In parliamentary systems, a presidential head of state has a mainly ceremonial role, receiving ambassadors, formally appointing ministers, conferring honours, and so forth. Such a president sometimes exercises significant choice among party leaders in the formation of a new government, as in Germany, for instance. Under presidential systems, by contrast, the president is usually elected separately from the legislature for a fixed term of office. He is chief executive and commander-in-chief of the armed forces, as well as head of state. The US government is headed by such a president. The French Fifth Republic is a constitutional hybrid in which the president is a directly elected head of state, sharing executive authority with a PRIME MINISTER appointed by him but who is also accountable to the national assembly. In many undemocratic regimes, on the other hand, the president is an autocrat, usually backed by the armed forces, and sustained by a combination of force, corruption, and electoral fraud.

Presley, Elvis (Aaron) (1935–77) US rock-and-roll and pop singer. He was the dominant personality of early rock and roll, known particularly for the vigour and frank sexuality of his style. He first gained fame in 1956 with the success of such records as 'Heartbreak Hotel' and 'Blue Suede Shoes', attracting a worldwide following. After doing his national service in the army he made a number of films during the 1960s, resuming his personal appearances at the end of the decade, mostly in Las Vegas. He lived much of his life in his Memphis mansion Graceland. He died young, probably as the result of drug dependence, becoming a cult figure.

Pressburg The German name for BRATISLAVA.

Pressburger, Emeric See POWELL, MICHAEL.

pressgang A detachment of sailors empowered to seize men for service in the British navy. The use of the pressgang had been sanctioned by law since medieval times but the practice was at its height in the 18th century. All able-bodied men were liable for impressment, although in fact the pressgangs confined their attention to the seaport towns, where they were able to find recruits with suitable experience. The navy continued to rely on the pressgangs until the 1830s, when improvements in pay and conditions provided sufficient volunteers. The system was also used to a lesser extent by the army but discontinued after 1815.

pressure The force per unit area experienced on a surface. **Atmospheric pressure** is the force produced by the weight of all the air above the spot, so the greater the altitude the less is the pressure. The pressure of a solid on a solid is in proportion to the size of the area of contact. The pressure in a liquid is the product of its density and the depth multiplied by the ACCELERATION of free fall.

The SI UNIT of pressure is the pascal (Pa), which is defined as 1 newton per square metre. Atmospheric pressure at sea-level has the value of 101,325 Pa. In meteorology a commonly used unit is the millibar (mb), which is equal to 100 Pa. Thus atmospheric pressure can be stated, in this form, as 1013.25 mb. A unit that is used in some barometers, and in the measurement of blood pressure, is the millimetre of mercury (mmHg); atmospheric pressure is given as 760 mmHg, this being the height of a column of mercury that the atmosphere can support under standard conditions.

pressure-cooker A sealed saucepan that cooks food rapidly at elevated temperatures by the generation of steam pressure. At higher pressures, the temperatures at which liquids boil increase, thus allowing food to be cooked faster. The pressure-cooker was introduced in 1679 by the French physicist Denis Papin. Modern pressure cookers consist of a large metal saucepan and removable lid sealed together with a rubber gasket. The internal pressure rises, elevating the boiling temperature of the water to around 130°C. A steady pressure is maintained by a weighted safety-valve that allows excess steam to escape.

pressure gauge An instrument for measuring the pressure of a liquid or gas. Mechanical devices include the aneroid BAROMETER, and the Bourdon gauge, in which the distortion of a curved tube moves a needle round a dial. Other pressure gauges balance the pressure to be determined against the pressure of a column of liquid (usually mercury). Devices for measuring very low pressures include the Pirani gauge, which measures the thermal conductivity of a gas (this increases with pressure), and the Penning gauge, which measures the electrical conductivity of an ionized gas.

pressurized-water reactor (PWR) The type of NUCLEAR REACTOR widely used for NUCLEAR POWER generation. These reactors use normal water under high pressure, as opposed to heavy water, both as a reactor coolant and as a moderator (see FISSION, NUCLEAR). The reactor core and the water are contained within a cylindrical pressure vessel: after being heated in the reactor core the water passes to a heat exchanger, where its heat is transferred to a secondary coolant. The boiling-water reactor (BWR) is similar to the PWR, but the circulating water is allowed to boil, and is used to power steam-turbines directly rather than using a secondary coolant.

Prester John (from Greek *presbyter*, 'priest') A legendary Christian ruler to whom successive generations of Crusaders looked for help against the growing power of Islam. First mentioned in a 12th-century German chronicle, he was variously identified as a Chinese prince, the ruler of Ethiopia, and, in a papal appeal of 1177, as 'illustrious and magnificent King of the Indies'.

Preston The county town of Lancashire, north-west England, on the River Ribble; pop. (1991) 126,200. A spinning and weaving centre since the 15th century, it was the site in the 18th century of the first English cotton mills. The University of Central England (formerly Lancashire Polytechnic) was established here in 1992. Preston has numerous industries including aircraft, heavy goods vehicles, textiles, and chemicals.

pre-stressed concrete CONCRETE in which a stress has been induced prior to its incorporation into a structure. It was first developed by Freyssinet in 1928. Normally, a compressive stress is induced in the tension zone of a beam. When subjected to working load, the net stress to be carried by the concrete will be the difference between the pre-stress and the working-load stress. In pre-tensioned, pre-stressed concrete, steel wires are tightened between the ends of a pre-casting mould. After placing, the concrete binds to the wires and prevents them from returning to their original length when the mould is removed, thus inducing compression in the concrete. In post-tensioned pre-stressed concrete, ducts are cast in the member. When the concrete has matured, high-tensile steel wires, rods, or cables are threaded through the ducts, tightened by hydraulic jacks, and anchored at each end, again inducing compression.

Prestwick A village and international airport near Ayr on the west coast of Scotland.

Pretender See STUART, CHARLES EDWARD (The Young Pretender); STUART, JAMES (The Old Pretender).

Pretoria The administrative capital of the Republic of South Africa, in the province of Gauteng; pop. (1991) 1,080,180. It was founded in 1855 by Marthinus PRETORIUS, the first president of the South African Republic, and named after his father, Andries W. J. PRETORIUS. It was until 1994 capital of the Transvaal. It has iron and steel, car assembly, railway, and machinery industries.

Pretoria-Witwatersrand-Vereeniging The former name for GAUTENG in South Africa.

Pretorius, Andries (Wilhelmus Jacobus) (1798–1853) Boer leader and general. After several frontier campaigns against the Xhosa he took part in the GREAT TREK, and became commandant-general of the Boers after Piet Retief's murder (1838). He defeated the Zulu at the BLOOD RIVER (1838). In 1847 he organized protests against the British annexation of the land between the Orange and Vaal, but in 1848 he was defeated at Boomplaats by Sir Harry Smith, when the Orange River Sovereignty was established. In 1852 he was instrumental in negotiating the Sand River Convention, which recognized the land beyond the Vaal as the South African Republic (TRANSVAAL).

Pretorius, Marthinus Wessel (1819–1901) Boer statesman. He was President of the South African Republic (TRANSVAAL) 1857–71, having followed his father, Andries PRETORIUS, in the GREAT TREK. After fighting the ZULU, he became one of the four Transvaal commandant-generals, and was elected President. He was also elected President of the Orange Free State (1859–63). His claim to diamond fields (1867) on the Vaal River brought him into conflict with British interests. Following the annexation of the Transvaal by Britain in 1877 he was imprisoned. With the outbreak of the First BOER WAR (1880–81) he proclaimed with KRUGER and Joubert a new Boer republic (January 1881). After the victory of Majuba Hill, he was a signatory of the Treaty of Pretoria, which re-established the independent states of Transvaal and Orange Free State.

Prévert, Jacques See CARNÉ, MARCEL.

Previn, André (George) (1929–) German-born US conductor, pianist, and composer. He is most famous as a conductor, notably as chief conductor with the London Symphony Orchestra (1968–79), the Pittsburgh Symphony Orchestra (1976–86), and the Royal Philharmonic Orchestra (1987–91). He has also composed musicals, film scores, and orchestral and chamber works, and is a noted jazz and classical pianist.

Prévost d'Exiles, Antoine-François (known as **Abbé Prévost**) (1696–1763) French novelist. He became a Benedictine monk in 1721 and was ordained as a priest five years later. He is remembered for his novel *Manon Lescaut* (1731), the story of a mutually destructive passion between a nobleman and a *demi-mondaine*, which inspired operas by MASSENET and PUCCINI.

Prez, Josquin des See DES PREZ.

Priam In Greek mythology, the king of Troy at the time of the Trojan War, the husband of Hecuba and the father of Hector and Paris. Priam was killed when Troy fell to the Greeks.

prices and incomes policy A policy that attempts by regulation or persuasion to influence changes in money prices and incomes, in order to curb or prevent INFLATION. By contrast, fiscal and monetary policies influence pay settlements and prices only indirectly. Incomes policy, which may also be used to redistribute income, typically involves government agreements with TRADE UNIONS and industry to restrain increases in pay and prices. This approach, besides being of questionable long-term effectiveness, carries potential dangers of misallocation of resources by interfering with the price system. Incomes policies were once much favoured as a means of combating inflation, but are largely discredited in favour of FREE MARKET approaches.

prickleback See BLENNY.

prickly pear The common name for the 300 or so species of CACTUS in the genus *Opuntia*, which includes the Indian fig, *O. ficus-indica*. Most species bear large pear-shaped, prickly fruits, from which their name is derived. They are native to northern South and Central America, but many species have been introduced to other parts of the world. Several species are now well established in South Africa and were once a serious weed in Australia.

Pride's Purge (6 December 1648) An English army coup in the aftermath of the ENGLISH CIVIL WAR, in which Members of Parliament (the exact number is uncertain but it was more than 100) who wished to reach an agreement with Charles I were forcibly excluded from the House of Commons by Colonel Thomas Pride, a Puritan army officer. The remaining members continued to sit in the Commons, forming the RUMP PARLIAMENT.

Priestley, J(ohn) B(oynton) (1894–1984) British novelist, dramatist, and critic. His first major success came with the picaresque novel *The Good Companions* (1929); this was followed by many other novels, including the more sombre *Angel Pavement* (1930). His plays include *Time and the Conways* (1937) and the mystery drama *An Inspector Calls* (1947). During and after World War II he was a popular radio broadcaster on current affairs.

Priestley, Joseph (1733–1804) British scientist and theologian. Priestley was the author of about 150 books, mostly theological or educational. His chief work was on the chemistry of gases, a number of which he managed to isolate, including ammonia, sulphur dioxide, nitrous oxide, and nitrogen dioxide. Priestley's most significant discovery was of 'dephlogisticated air' (oxygen) in 1774; he demonstrated that it was important to animal life, and that plants give off this gas in sunlight. In his theological writings he maintained a Unitarian position. His support of the French Revolution provoked so much hostility that he settled in the USA in 1794.

primary colours In painting, those colours – blue, red, and yellow – that cannot be made from mixtures of other colours. Two primaries mixed together form a **secondary colour**, red and yellow making orange, red and blue making purple, and yellow and blue making green. A related term is 'complementary colour'; blue is the complementary of orange (made up of the other two primaries), red is the complementary of green, and yellow is the complementary of purple. In a scientific context however, **primary additive colours** are those required to give all the colours of the spectrum, including white light, when mixed in the correct proportions. Many such combinations exist but the set used most frequently, especially in television and photography, is red, green, and blue.

primary education The initial stage of education for children between the ages of, typically, 6 and 11 and concentrating on skills such as LITERACY and numeracy. Primary, or elementary, education differs from **pre-school education** in its greater emphasis on formal study, and from SECONDARY EDUCATION in the less specialized nature of the instruction offered. Over half the school time is spent on reading, writing, arithmetic, and speaking aloud. Elements of history, geography, nature study, science, and social studies may be integrated into this approach, and there may be periods of physical education, music, art, drama, and religious instruction. Primary education is compulsory in the industrialized world. In recent decades there has been a huge increase in enrolment in developing countries, where four out of five children of primary school age are now enrolled.

primary elections Elections for the selection of candidates for public office, most significantly for the US presidency. They are held by the state and the results are legally binding. There are both 'open' and 'closed' presidential primaries. In the former, any adult voter in a state may take part, regardless of his or her own party preference. In the latter, only those who are registered members of the party may vote.

primary health care The health care with which patients first come into contact. It is seen by the World Health Organization as the linchpin of health services. In affluent countries, it is normally provided by a general medical practitioner. In the developing world, it is delivered through PARAMEDICS with varying amounts of training. Most medical problems can be dealt with at the primary health care level, including the diagnosis and treatment of common ailments, advice, and preventive measures, such as IMMUNIZATION. However, hospital-based care still consumes a larger proportion of health budgets in all countries. The success of primary health care has two components: its effectiveness in relieving minor ailments and the appropriateness of its referrals to hospitals in more difficult ilnesses.

primate A member of an order of placental mammals, Primates, primitively with arboreal habits, an omnivorous diet, and comparatively unspecialized teeth. They have dextrous, grasping hands and feet with the first and second digits usually being opposable. Instead of claws, their fingers and toes are equipped with nails, with sensitive pads on the tips of their digits. They have forward-looking large eyes with stereoscopic vision, and a large brain.

Most primates are specialized for an arboreal

life, and the few that live mainly on the ground are descended from tree-living forms. Primates have been most successful in tropical and sub-tropical areas, where most of the 181 species occur. There are two main suborders: the prosimians, which include lemurs, bushbabies, and pottos; and the anthropoids, which include tarsiers, marmosets, tamarins, monkeys, apes, and humans.

prime meridian A fixed circle, on the surface of a planet or satellite, which passes through its POLES and from which longitude (see LATITUDE AND LONGITUDE) can be measured east or west. Thus the **longitude** of a place is the angular distance of the place's meridian east or west from the prime meridian. The **latitude** of the place is its angular distance north or south of the body's equator measured along its meridian. The prime meridian on Earth (or Greenwich meridian) passes through the original ROYAL GREENWICH OBSERVATORY.

prime minister (or **premier**, **chief minister**) The member of a government charged with speaking for it in the principal chamber of the LEGISLATURE. Where the head of state is a constitutional monarch without significant executive powers, the prime minister is effectively the head of the executive branch, initiating policies and making decisions, even though in constitutional theory he or she merely 'advises' the monarch. Where the head of state is a ceremonial PRESIDENT, the chief executive is again normally the prime minister. In some countries, however, such as France, executive power is shared between president and prime minister.

prime mover An original natural or mechanical source of motive power, rather than a machine that only transmits power or transforms it into another form. Thus any form of heat ENGINE is a prime mover because it generates mechanical power from a source of heat. An electric motor is not a prime mover because it merely converts electric power generated elsewhere into mechanical power output.

prime number A whole number other than 1 that has no divisors (factors) other than 1 and itself; the first prime numbers being 2, 3, 5, 7, and 11. All other whole numbers (called composite) can be expressed as a number of primes multiplied together, and this process is called prime decomposition.

primitive art The art of all societies outside the great Western and Oriental civilizations. For example, Pre-Columbian American is usually regarded as primitive art although much of it was produced by peoples who had highly developed cultures. Primitive art may also be regarded as a synonym for NAÏVE ART.

primitive moth A tiny, brilliantly coloured, day-flying moth of the family Eriocraniidae, less than 12 mm (0.5 inch) in wing-span. The proboscis is short, and unlike most moths they have rudimentary jaws. Females of the European species lay eggs in slits in leaves, usually birch, and the legless caterpillars are leaf-miners. They pupate in the ground.

Primo de Rivera, Miguel (1870–1930) Spanish general and statesman, head of state 1923–30. He came to power after leading a military coup in 1923, when he assumed dictatorial powers with the consent of Alfonso XIII. The decline of the economy contributed to his forced resignation in 1930. His son, José Antonio Primo de Rivera (1903–36), founded the Falange in 1933 and was executed by Republicans in the Spanish Civil War.

primordial fireball See COSMOLOGY.

primrose The common name for several of the 500 or so species in the plant genus *Primula*, which includes cowslips, *P. veris*, true oxlips, *P. elatior*, and other species or hybrids known as primulas. The common primrose, *P. vulgaris*, is a spring-flowering perennial, native to western Europe and Asia Minor. Like most other *Primula* species, it produces a rosette of leaves at ground level and flowers held on stalks. The common primrose hybridizes naturally with the cowslip to produce the false, or common oxlip, *P. vulgaris* × *veris*. Similar hybrids between these parents also give rise to the garden variety of polyanthus. The auricula, *P. auricula*, has ear-shaped leaves (hence its name) and is much cultivated as a florist's flower.

The primrose gives its name to the family Primulaceae, comprising some 1,000 species of mainly northern temperate region plants. Relatives of the primroses include the shooting stars, *Dodecatheon* species, PIMPERNELS, and CYCLAMENS.

Primrose League An organization founded by Sir Drummond Wolf and Lord Randolph CHURCHILL in 1883, devoted to the cause of Tory democracy. The League used the emblem of DISRAELI's favourite flower to focus on his concept of Conservatism. This involved defence of traditional features of British life, but also a wish to broaden support for Conservatism by showing its capacity to improve living and working conditions for the masses.

Prince (full name Prince Rogers Nelson) (1958–) US rock, pop, and funk singer, songwriter, and musician. An eccentric, prolific performer, Prince has been responsible for an extremely varied output since the release of his first album in 1978, much of it overtly sexual but also frequently humorous. He is perhaps best known for the album and film *Purple Rain* (1984). In 1993 he announced that he was no longer to be known as Prince, but rather by an unpronounceable symbol.

Prince Edward Island The smallest province of Canada, cradled in the southern part of the Gulf of Saint Lawrence; area 5,660 sq km (2,185 sq miles); pop. (1991) 129,765; capital Charlottetown. Unlike the mainland, on the other side of the Northumberland Strait, it is almost devoid of hills and there is much farmland, the soil of which is characteristically red.

Prince of Wales See CHARLES, PRINCE.

Princes in the Tower The young sons of Edward IV; Edward, Prince of Wales (born 1470) and Richard, Duke of York (born 1472), supposedly murdered in the Tower of London in or shortly after 1483. In 1483 Edward reigned briefly as Edward V on the death of his father but was not crowned; he and his brother were taken to the Tower of London by their uncle (the future Richard III). Richard was appointed Protector and the princes disappeared soon afterwards. They are generally assumed to have been murdered, but whether at the instigation of Richard III (as Tudor propagandists claimed) or of another is not known; two skeletons discovered in 1674 are thought to have been those of the princes.

Princess Royal, the See ANNE, PRINCESS.

Princeton A town in west New Jersey, USA, named in 1724 in honour of William III, Prince of Orange-Nassau; pop. (1990) 12,020. From June to November 1783 Princeton was the capital of the USA. It is the site of the fourth-oldest US university, founded in 1756, and the Institute for Advanced Study (1930), where EINSTEIN spent his last years.

printed circuit (or **printed circuit board**, PCB) An assembly of electronic components on a sheet of material (usually fibreglass), in which the interconnections between components are made by copper-based tracks integral with the board. These tracks are formed by coating the board with copper, then photographically depositing a protective coating over the track areas. The board is then etched to remove the unprotected copper. Components are attached by soldering them to the copper tracks at specified positions. In most contexts printed circuits now contain INTEGRATED CIRCUITS instead of individual components.

printer (in computers) An OUTPUT DEVICE for providing printed text and sometimes graphics from a computer. A number of types of printer are in common use. The first used were impact printers, in which the characters were formed by striking an inked ribbon onto the paper as in a conventional typewriter. The daisy-wheel printer is an example. In a dot-matrix printer, the characters are formed by combinations of dots. Early dot-matrix printers formed the characters by striking needles against a ribbon. In INK-JET PRINTING, printers use tiny nozzles to spray the ink on to the paper. The best quality printers are LASER PRINTERS, which resemble photocopiers in their operation.

printing The process of reproducing copies of text, pictures, or designs on to a suitable material, such as paper, board, plastic, or metal, usually by pressing an inked image against the material being printed. Early civilizations in the Far East developed the first known forms of printing. In the 8th century the Chinese produced a million copies of Buddhist texts using WOOD-BLOCKS, and there is evidence of printing from movable wooden (and later metal) type in China and Korea from the 11th century. In the West, monks used wood-blocks in the late 14th century to print pictures of the saints. However, GUTENBERG in Germany initiated the real development of European printing in the 1450s through his invention of a TYPESETTING mould for casting individual metal letters.

During the next three centuries, artists, typefounders, artisans, and printers all contributed to advances in the design and quality of printing. Various non-relief printing processes, such as LITHOGRAPHY and GRAVURE, were also developed. However, output remained relatively low because of the need to redistribute type before setting it again, the slowness of hand presses, and the need to dampen paper before printing on it. The 19th century brought a surge of mechanical inventiveness, which included the development of the platen press, in which a plate presses the paper against the type; the flat-bed cylinder press, in which an inked frame carrying the metal type (known as a forme) moves beneath a cylinder carrying the paper; and the rotary press, using curved printing plates that rotate against paper that is sheet-fed (individual sheets) or reel-fed (continuous sheet). Late in the 19th century, advances were made in the technologies of TYPESETTING, with the development of Linotype and MONOTYPE, of STEREOTYPING, and of illustration. The principles of the HALF-TONE PROCESS, OFFSET LITHOGRAPHY, colour printing, and photography for platemaking were also laid down during this period, so that by the beginning of the 20th century most of the basic forms of LETTERPRESS, lithographic, and INTAGLIO printing had been established. Between the two World Wars print engineering was much improved, and photographic methods grew in importance, while modern electronics have made a major impact since 1950.

Modern typesetting and ELECTRONIC SCANNING can rapidly provide digitized forms of image (see DIGITIZATION) that can be stored on computer, manipulated, transmitted by satellite, and reproduced on film or paper worldwide. Platemaking and printing machines, many of them computer-controlled, can produce quality work at speeds of up to 10,000 sheets per hour, or between 20,000 and 60,000 impressions (copies) per hour on reel-fed presses (see OFFSET LITHOGRAPHY). Bookbinding and print finishing have also become increasingly automated to keep pace with the increase in print speeds.

Priscian (full name Priscianus Caesariensis) (6th century AD) Byzantine grammarian. He taught Latin in Constantinople and his *Grammatical Institutions* became one of the standard Latin grammatical works in the Middle Ages.

prism A transparent, geometric body, usually triangular in section, having refracting surfaces at acute angles to each other. A simple triangular-section prism can be used to spread light into a spectrum of colours; this was demonstrated by Isaac NEWTON. Other prisms are used to deflect a light path or to invert an image, as in BINOCULARS, a PERISCOPE, or the view-finder of a single-lens CAMERA.

Priština A city in southern Serbia, capital of the province of Kosovo; pop. (1991) 108,000. A former capital of Serbia, it is situated on the eastern edge of the Kosovo Field where the Serbians failed to arrest the advance of the Turks in 1389. It remained under Turkish control until 1912. It is an administrative, educational, and communications centre with textile, metal, and electrical industries.

Pritchett, Sir V(ictor) S(awdon) (1900–97) British writer and critic. He is chiefly remembered as a writer of short stories; collections include *The Spanish Virgin and Other Stories* (1930). Among his critical works are *The Living Novel* (1946) and *Lasting Impressions* (1990). He is also noted for his novels and for two volumes of autobiography, *A Cab at the Door* (1968) and *Midnight Oil* (1971).

privateer A licensed sea-raider in time of war, who had government-issued letters of marque or reprisal to attack enemy shipping. Privateers were often employed in European wars in the 16th and 17th centuries by the English, French, and Dutch, and they later became common in the West Indies, North America, and the Indian Ocean during imperial conflicts. The Americans resorted to widespread privateering during the Wars of Independence and 1812, and the South followed this example during the Civil War. They were internationally abolished by the Declaration of Paris (1856).

private law See PUBLIC LAW.

private sector Those parts of the economy neither owned by the state nor under the direct control of government. Thus it includes households, all privately owned businesses, and non-profit-making organizations, such as charities and private research institutes. See also PUBLIC SECTOR.

privatization The total or partial transfer of ownership of resources from the PUBLIC SECTOR to the PRIVATE SECTOR. Typically it involves some combination of the sale of SHARES, withdrawal of government control, and the contracting out of government-purchased services to private producers. The motives for privatization may be budgetary, economic (to remove inefficiency), or political (to diminish the economic role of the state and to widen share ownership). Advocates of privatization argue that it enhances efficiency, consumer choice, and quality of service, reduces political interference, and raises CAPITAL. With the growth in popularity of FREE-MARKET ideas, privatization has become widespread, replacing earlier socialist policies on which it was thought the state should control many industries for reasons of public interest. Governments in Western Europe committed themselves to privatization in the early 1980s because the apparent inefficiency, inertia, and excessive cost of state-run nationalized industries. By the 1990s it had become an equally central part of economic liberalization in the formerly socialist states of the Eastern bloc. When important public services, such as water or electricity have been privatized, new systems of regulation to ensure accountability and consumer protection and to prevent profiteering have proved necessary.

privet A shrub of the Old World genus *Ligustrum*, which contains 50 species belonging to the same family as lilacs, olives, and ashes, Oleaceae. The wild privet of Europe, *L. vulgare*, was formerly much used for hedging, but it has been displaced by the Japanese *L. ovalifolium*, a plant that is tolerant of pollution.

probability A measure of the relative likelihood of an event occurring. An impossibility is said to have a probability of 0, whereas a certainty has probability 1. In between are events that are more or less probable. The basis of probability theory is first to assign numerical values to some simple events, often on the basis of equal likelihood, and then to find ways to calculate more complicated probabilities from them. Probability attempts to quantify the inherent but predictable variability in many real-life situations and is the foundation of certain modern physical theories, such as thermodynamics and QUANTUM THEORY.

probate The formal confirmation of a WILL granted by the appropriate authority to the person (the executor) entrusted with distribution of the assets of the person making the will (the testator). This is normally granted on application by the executor. Where a will is disputed, proof must take place in a formal probate action. In some jurisdictions there is a specific Court of Probate, but in England the High Court is responsible.

probation A sentence imposed by a COURT OF LAW by which an offender is supervised by a **probation officer** for a fixed period as an alternative to other community penalties or to imprisonment. The court may impose additional requirements, such as residence at a hostel or treatment for a mental disorder. The aim of probation is both to assist the offender and to control his or her criminal behaviour. Although this mixture of COUNSELLING and surveillance is inherently fraught with conflict, many offenders complete their orders successfully. Probation is frequently used in dealing with young offenders (see JUVENILE DELINQUENCY). If the offender fails to comply with the order, he or she may be returned to court and given another sentence.

proboscis monkey A species of Old World monkey, *Nasalis larvatus*, that is confined to Borneo, where it dwells in forest regions close to water. It will sit for long periods of time on a branch or travel in small troops and can swim well. Its call is a drawn-out, resonant honk. A herbivore, it feeds on leaves and fruit. About 75 cm (2.5 feet) long, it has a reddish coat with some grey hair on the limbs and lower back. It is remarkable for the extremely long nose in the male, which can be 75 mm (3 inches) in length and reach below the chin.

proboscis worm See RIBBON WORM.

processor See CENTRAL PROCESSING UNIT; MICROPROCESSOR.

Procopius (*c*.500–*c*.562) Byzantine historian, born in Caesarea in Palestine. He accompanied Justinian's general BELISARIUS on his campaigns between 527 and 540. His principal works are the *History of the Wars of Justinian* and *On Justinian's Buildings*. The authenticity of another work, the *Secret History*, has often been doubted but is now generally accepted; it is a virulent attack on Justinian, his policy, and his officials, and also contains comments on the dubious morals of the Empress Theodora.

Procyon A nearby first-magnitude BINARY STAR in the constellation of Canis Minor, and also known as Alpha Canis Minoris. It comprises a subgiant or dwarf star somewhat hotter than the Sun and with about eight times its luminosity, with an eleventh-magnitude white dwarf companion in a 41-year orbit. The distance of Procyon is 3.5 parsecs.

production (in economics) The process of transforming RESOURCES (inputs of FACTORS OF PRODUCTION) into outputs of GOODS and services. In economic theory, the production function represents the technological relationship between the maximum amount of output that can be produced from various combinations of inputs. Given input prices with a production function, a firm's cost curves (showing production costs per unit of output) can be derived; and thence, once the firm's objective (for example, PROFIT maximization) and the demand conditions facing the firm are known, its level of output is also determined.

productivity The amount of output produced per unit of input of a FACTOR OF PRODUCTION. Where total output is measured, productivity measures the rate of output (for example, output per worker-hour). Average productivity is the ratio of total output to total input of the factor in question. Marginal productivity measures the additional output from an additional unit of factor input. Increases in productivity, which are an important source of economic growth, may come about as a result of technological advance in CAPITAL or as a result of altered working practices.

profile (in geology) A vertical section through the soil from the surface down to the parent material. All the successive horizontal layers, or HORIZONS, which make up the soil are displayed in such a section. The depth of the profile varies from soil to soil, as do the degree of horizon development and the characteristics of the various horizons. CHERNOZEMS, for example, have very deep profiles, each with a thick, black, highly organic upper horizon, while desert soils are relatively shallow, with poorly defined horizons and little organic matter. Many soils, then, have characteristic profiles by which they are recognizable.

profit (in economics) The difference between sales revenue and production COSTS. Economists classify profit into normal profit and excess or supernormal profit. Normal profit is the level of profit which makes it just worthwhile for an entrepreneur to stay in business in the long run; it is equivalent to the opportunity cost of CAPITAL and of the entrepreneur's time. While an accountant includes normal profit in the definition of profit, an economist tends to include it in costs of production. Therefore, economic profits represent excess or super-normal profits, which act as a market signal, attracting new firms into an industry so long as there is perfect competition.

Profumo, John (Dennis) (1915–) British Conservative politician. In 1960 he was appointed Secretary of State for War under Harold Macmillan. Three years later news broke of his relationship with the mistress of a Soviet diplomat, Christine Keeler, raising fears of a security breach and precipitating his resignation.

program (in computing) A set of coded instructions (the SOFTWARE) to control the operation of a COMPUTER or other machine. For example, utility programs perform tasks usually related to the OPERATING SYSTEM. Since the CENTRAL PROCESSING UNIT only processes MACHINE CODE, programs written in a high-level computer language or assembly language must be translated into machine code before execution. See also ALGORITHM.

programme music Music that attempts to tell a story, evoke an atmosphere, or in some way illustrate a non-musical event. The term originated with Liszt's SYMPHONIC POEMS, though the practice of writing descriptive music was established long before that, and received a particular impetus from the needs of OPERA to illustrate dramatic situations. Most programme music, however – even that of such a master of description as Richard Strauss – requires to be supplemented by some verbal clue (a title or a 'programme note'). Music that is not descriptive is said to be **abstract**.

programming language See COMPUTER LANGUAGE.

Prohibition era (1920–33) The period of national prohibition of alcohol in the USA. A culmination of the Temperance Movement, it began when the Eighteenth Amendment to the Constitution went into effect by the passing of the Volstead Act (1919). Despite the securing of some 300,000 court convictions between 1920 and 1930, drinking continued. Speakeasies (illegal bars) and bootlegging (illegal distilling of alcohol) flourished. The success of such gangsters as Al CAPONE, who controlled the supply of illegal alcohol, led to corruption of police and city government. After the Wickersham Commission in 1931 reported that the prohibition laws were unenforceable and encouraged public disrespect for law in general, the Eighteenth Amendment was repealed by the Twenty-First Amendment. A number of states and counties retained full or partial prohibition, but by 1966 no state-wide prohibition laws existed.

projection, map Any method used to map the curved surface of the Earth on to a plane surface with the minimum of distortion. Simple graphical projections can be made by fitting a plane surface around a sphere in a variety of ways, for example, as a cylinder or cone. If the detail on the sphere is now projected on to the plane surface, the points at which it touches the sphere are mapped without distortion, while elsewhere there is some distortion of scale, bearing, shape or area. Most projections used in the making of MAPS AND CHARTS use mathematical methods based on simple graphical projections but with their formulae adjusted in some way. Probably the best-known projection is that of Gerardus MERCATOR.

projector (in photography) A device for shining an enlarged image (still or moving) on to a screen. All projectors work on the same basic principle. A light source is used to illuminate an image which is held accurately in position, while a lens focuses an enlarged version of this image on to a screen. Most modern still projectors are designed to be used with transparencies (slides) made on 35-mm FILM. To create the illusion of movement, cine-projectors have to show a rapid succession of images at a regular speed, keeping each image steady on the screen for an instant. An intermittent claw mechanism and a rotating shutter are used to achieve this, as in a CINE-CAMERA.

prokaryote An organism that, in contrast to a EUKARYOTE, has no defined nucleus and only a very limited range of cell organelles, such as ribosomes. The DNA of a prokaryote is organized into a simple, usually circular, chromosome, that lies free in the cytoplasm. BACTERIA are prokaryotes.

Prokofiev, Sergei (Sergeevich) (1891–1953) Russian composer. By the age of 13 he had already written operas, sonatas, and piano pieces. In 1918 Prokofiev emigrated to the USA; he lived there and in Paris before returning to the Soviet Union in 1933. Notable works include seven symphonies, the operas *The Love for Three Oranges* (1919) and *War and Peace* (1941–43), the *Lieutenant Kijé* suite (1934), and the ballet music for *Romeo and Juliet* (1935–36). He also wrote *Peter and the Wolf* (1936), a young person's guide to the orchestra in the form of a fairy tale.

prolactin A hormone produced by the pituitary gland that is required by mammals for lactation. In other animals this protein hormone has a variety of other functions, including growth, reproduction, and the salt–water balance.

proletariat See MARXISM.

promethium (symbol Pm, at. no. 61, r.a.m. 145) A radioactive element formed in certain nuclear reactions. The most stable isotope has a half-life of only 17.7 years and the element is therefore unknown on Earth, although its spectrum has been detected in starlight.

Prometheus In Greek mythology, a Titan who made the first man from clay and stole fire from the gods to give to mankind. In revenge for the theft, Zeus chained Prometheus to a rock, where his liver was eaten every day by an eagle, only to grow again every night. Hercules eventually rescued him.

prominent moth A member of the family Notodontidae, worldwide in distribution, which includes the kitten moth, *Furcula* species, the PUSS MOTH, and the LOBSTER MOTH. When the insect is at rest, projecting tufts of scales at the middle of the hind margin of each fore-wing are brought together, forming a prominence above the centre of the sloping wings. Prominent moths are stout-bodied, white, greyish or brownish, with pale hind-wings and long, narrow fore-wings, camouflaged as bark or wood. The caterpillars characteristically have one or more humps on their backs, and tend to rest with the hindpart, and occasionally also the fore-part, somewhat elevated. They feed on the leaves of a variety of trees.

pronghorn (or **prongbuck**) A species of even-toed ungulate (hoofed mammal), *Antilocapra americana*, found in semi-arid regions of western North America. It is the only surviving representative of the family Antilocapridae, which was once widespread in that continent. The pronghorn is the only horned animal that sheds the horn sheath each year, and the only one with branched horns (as opposed to antlers). The male can reach a height of up to 1 m (3.25 feet) at the shoulders; the female is smaller. The coat is brown, and the underside of the body and neck and part-way up each side is white. The neck is banded and the cheeks are white. The rump has a patch of long, white hairs that are erectile and act as a warning signal to others. The females give birth to twin fawns after a gestation period of eight months.

propaganda The attempt to shape or manipulate people's beliefs or actions by means of information (true or false), arguments, or symbols. Propaganda may be printed, broadcast, or visual. All governments engage more or less in propaganda activities, describing them in many cases as public information programmes, sometimes with a totally cynical disregard for the truth. In the 1930s, the German Nazis, led by Hitler's minister of propaganda, Joseph GOEBBELS, conducted a highly skilful propaganda campaign that indoctrinated the German people with bogus racial theories, urged them to seek world domination, and excluded them from hearing what the rest of the world thought of them. The success of this campaign in persuading some 80 million Germans to embark on World War II may only have been possible because it reflected at least some aspects of their own aspirations. Culpability for the obscenities perpetrated by the Third Reich cannot, therefore, be laid exclusively at the feet of its leaders.

propane ($CH_3CH_2CH_3$) A HYDROCARBON obtained from natural gas or from PETROLEUM REFINING; propane is the third member of the ALKANE series. It is a colourless flammable gas that is readily liquefied by compression and cooling. In pressurized containers it constitutes an important industrial and domestic fuel (see LIQUID PETROLEUM GAS). In particular, it is being increasingly used for welding torches and as a cheaper alternative to petrol in specially adapted automobile engines. It is also used in the synthesis of ethene, which in turn is used as the starting material for the chemical synthesis of POLYTHENE and many other polymers.

propanone (or **acetone**, CH_3COCH_3) A colourless, low-boiling-point, highly flammable liquid with a characteristic pungent odour. It was originally made by distilling wood, but is now produced commercially by fermentation of corn or molasses, or by controlled oxidation of HYDROCARBONS. It is widely used as a solvent for NITROCELLULOSE, ETHYNE (acetylene), and varnishes; as a remover of paint, varnish, and fingernail polish; and in the manufacture of drugs.

propellant See EXPLOSIVE; ROCKET MOTOR.

propeller A power-driven rotating hub fitted with helical blades that propels an aeroplane or ship by its rotation. The AEROFOIL section and overall shape of each propeller blade acts to accelerate a stream of air or water through the propeller disc, thus providing thrust. Early ship's propellers were two-bladed, but multi-bladed designs soon evolved to improve efficiency. Earlier designs were fixed pitch, that is, the propeller blades met the water at a fixed angle. Fixed-pitch propellers are optimally efficient when the ship is travelling at one particular speed: variable-pitch propellers have therefore been evolved, in which the blade angle adopts optimally to the changing speed of the vessel. More recently several other forms of propeller have come into use, for example, the cycloidal or Schneider propeller, used on some tugs and large ferries, which is vertically mounted and requires no rudder.

Aeroplane propellers are larger than marine screw-propellers, since air is a much less dense medium, and much larger volumes must be accelerated to obtain adequate thrust. Propellers are more efficient than JET ENGINES at speeds below about 800 km/h (500 mph). For most propeller-driven aircraft variable-pitch propellers are used. Contra-rotating propellers are used with some more powerful engines: in these, two propellers rotate in opposite directions on the same axis, counteracting the twisting force induced by a single propeller.

proper motion The intrinsic angular motion of a star across the sky relative to the background of more distant stars. The VELOCITY of a star moving through space with respect to the Sun is a vector, which can be resolved into its RADIAL VELOCITY along the line of sight and its transverse velocity at right angles to this across the line of sight. The proper motion is a result of the star's transverse speed through space, in contrast to its PARALLAX which is an apparent motion arising from the Earth's orbit about the Sun.

Propertius, Sextus (*c.*50–*c.*16 BC) Roman poet. His four books of elegies are largely concerned with his love affair with a woman whom he called Cynthia, though the later poems also deal with mythological and historical themes.

prophet A person regarded as speaking from divine inspiration or predicting future events. The prophets of the Old Testament strove to instil a moral vision into Jewish belief and practice, and later provided Christianity with a prophetic ideal, in the person of JESUS CHRIST. The 'gift of prophecy' continues to be a feature of charismatic Christian movements, and 'inspired utterances' are also characteristic of Quakerism. In Islam, MUHAMMAD is regarded as the Prophet, who, through the angel Gabriel, received and revealed the KORAN, the divine word of Allah.

proportional representation (PR) An electoral system that seeks to give parties a share of seats proportional to the number of votes cast for them. Apart from the UK, Canada, and the USA, most liberal democracies use some form of PR rather than majoritarian representation. In a PR system, the size of a constituency is critical. Each constituency has several seats, and the more seats it has, the more proportional the outcome is likely to be. A common form of PR is the list system. In this, the elector casts a vote for a POLITICAL PARTY's entire list of candidates; the number of seats eventually awarded to a party is determined by the number of votes its list receives. However, in practice, most list systems also allow voters some choice between the candidates of the party they vote for. Belgium, Finland, Italy, Norway, and Switzerland are examples of countries using the list system. The other main form of PR is the single transferable vote, as used in Ireland and Malta. Here, voters rank candidates in order of preference, and complex computations are necessary in order to achieve a result. The main characteristic of this system is that it emphasizes candidates, rather than parties. Whichever form of PR is adopted, however, the normal result is that no party wins a majority of seats in the legislature, often resulting in COALITION GOVERNMENTS.

proscenium See THEATRE.

prosecution The act of bringing a criminal charge in court. The function of the prosecutor is to act on behalf of the state in the best interests of justice. In France, prosecution is conducted by officers of a branch of the CIVIL SERVICE, while in the USA, states have their own prosecutors (district attorneys), who are usually elected to office. In England and Wales the Crown Prosecution Service (CPS) was set up in 1985 to ensure the separation of investigation and prosecution, for both of which the police had formerly been responsible. Once a person has been charged with an offence by the police, the CPS decides whether there is sufficient evidence for a prosecution, and whether it would be in the public interest. In Scotland the role of the CPS is undertaken by the **procurator fiscal** (see SCOTS LAW).

prospecting Exploration in search of mineral deposits. Prospecting techniques can be broadly divided into two categories: direct and indirect. The former includes study of existing geological maps and guides to ORES, supplemented by surface examination in the field, which may involve exploratory probes by drilling or trenching. If a potentially workable vein outcrops at the surface, an estimate must be made of how far it extends; it may, for example, end abruptly in a major fault, plunging too deep to be followed. Samples of ore must be analysed to see whether working the vein is economically worthwhile. Indirect techniques include looking for surface signs of underlying ore, such as rock staining or a distinctive pattern of vegetation. For example, outcrops of the enormous copper–cobalt deposits of the Democratic Republic of Congo and Zambia support a characteristic flora of metal-tolerant plants. Modern methods include magnetic surveys on the ground and from the air; seismic probes (see PETROLEUM, exploration, and recovery); analysis of gas that has seeped up through the overlay; and observation from Earth resources satellites in space. Certain elements, notably uranium and thorium, can be located by their radioactivity using a Geiger–Müller counter. See also MINING; QUARRYING.

Prost, Alain (1955–) French motor-racing driver. He was the first Frenchman to win the Formula One world championship (1985); he won the championship again in 1986, 1989, and 1993, after which he retired from racing. Since 1987 Prost has held the record for the most Grand Prix victories.

prostaglandin One of a group of hormone-like substances present in many body tissues and fluids. Derived from long-chain fatty acids, they cause contraction of the womb, dilation of blood vessels, and modification of some hormonal activity. They are released in the process causing inflammation; aspirin relieves pain by inhibiting their synthesis. Synthetic prostaglandins are used to induce labour or cause abortion, to treat peptic ulcers, and in the treatment of newborn babies with heart disease.

prostate gland A male gland that opens into the urethra just below the bladder. It secretes an alkaline fluid during ejaculation that forms part of the semen. In some elderly men the gland becomes enlarged, obstructing the neck of the bladder and impairing urination. This condition is treated surgically by **prostatectomy**, often performed through the urethra (transurethral resection).

prosthesis An artificial replacement for part of the body, which may be functional, structural, or both. Some prostheses, such as cardiac PACEMAKERS or HIP REPLACEMENTS, are surgically implanted. Others are worn, such as HEARING AIDS, dentures, or artificial limbs.

prostitution The sale and purchase of sexual relations. Most prostitutes are women, although there are male and homosexual prostitutes; the system of prostitution, however, is almost exclusively organized by men. The attitude of the law to prostitution varies in different jurisdictions. In some it is illegal; in others, it is not in itself unlawful, but certain activities associated with it, such as soliciting, kerb-crawling, brothel-keeping, and 'living off immoral earnings', are illegal; in others it is lawful and subject only to medical controls. Prostitution, which has always been an attribute of human societies (especially those in which sexual activity is controlled), is usually motivated by poverty or by a need to support a drug habit; in some places, poverty has generated vast numbers of prostitutes (many of them children) in the growing trade of 'sex tourism' and CHILD SEXUAL EXPLOITATION. While some prostitutes claim to provide a public service, health authorities all over the world are concerned that their activities, and those of their clients, contribute to the rapid spread of the AIDS virus and to other sexually transmitted diseases.

protactinium (symbol Pa, at. no. 91, r.a.m. 231) A radioactive ACTINIDE that occurs in pitchblende as a decay product of uranium. It has no uses and was first discovered by Lise MEITNER and Otto HAHN in 1917.

protea An evergreen shrub, one of some 130 species in the genus *Protea*, mostly from the Cape region of South Africa. They form part of the family Proteaceae, containing over 1,000 species of shrubs and trees distributed throughout the Southern Hemisphere. *Protea* species have inflorescences that consist of many flowers enclosed in coloured bracts. One of the most spectacular is the king or giant protea, *P. cynaroides*, with flower-heads measuring almost 30 cm (1 foot) across. Such robust flowers are suited for pollination by sunbirds, which feed on the nectar. Other species of the family Proteaceae, such as those of the Australian genus *Banksia*, are pollinated by small nocturnal animals.

protected species Those plants and animals protected by law from collection or interference by humans. The protection may be temporary, perhaps lasting only for the breeding season, as for many gamebirds and freshwater fish, or it may be permanent, where a particularly valuable or ENDANGERED SPECIES is given local, national, or international protection throughout the year. This protection may be worldwide, as for Steller's albatross, or limited to certain countries in regions where a threat exists. Several whales and fishes have been protected, as an aid to their conservation, by internationally agreed, annual catch quotas. Many species are indirectly protected through living in NATURE RESERVES or wildlife parks.

protectionism The use by government of any measure designed to restrict international trade or to give artificial assistance to domestic producers at the expense of their foreign competitors. It most commonly involves attempts to reduce imports by tariffs, QUOTAS, and other barriers. Non-tariff barriers also include health and safety regulations, bias in government purchasing, and 'voluntary export restraint' (VER) agreements, among others. Export taxes similarly restrict trade, while export and producer subsidies give a cost advantage to domestic firms. The GATT (General Agreement on Tariffs and Trade) is an international agreement intended to reduce trade restrictions worldwide.

protective coloration (or **defensive coloration**) Animal coloration arising as a result of NATURAL SELECTION for protection against predators. Insects show a diverse range of protective coloration strategies, which include CAMOUFLAGE, WARNING COLORATION, and MIMICRY. Protective colours may also form part of defensive DISPLAYS, as in flash and startle coloration.

Protectorate, English (16 December 1653–25 May 1659) The rule of England established by Oliver CROMWELL. Unable to work with the BAREBONES

PARLIAMENT, Cromwell entrusted a council of army officers with the task of drawing up a new constitution. The resulting Instrument of Government made Cromwell Lord Protector, monarch in all but name, who would share power with a single House of Parliament elected by Puritans. Politically it was a failure. Cromwell could not work with his first Protectorate Parliament, so he divided England into 11 military districts ruled by army officers known as major-generals. This was so unpopular that he reverted to parliamentary rule through the second Parliament of the Protectorate in 1656. Although the Protectorate was successful in foreign policy and notable for religious toleration of all faiths other than Roman Catholicism, its stability depended on Cromwell's personal qualities. After his death in 1658 it did not take long for the army to remove Richard CROMWELL, his successor, bringing the Protectorate to an end in 1659 in preparation for the RESTORATION of Charles II.

protein A molecule composed of long chains of AMINO ACIDS linked by peptide bonds. Proteins make up about half of the dry weight of the bodies of living organisms. The 'primary' structure of a protein is the order, or sequence, of amino acids in it; different proteins have different primary structures. The amino acid sequence determines the final three-dimensional shape of the protein molecule. The 'secondary' structure of a protein is the regular three-dimensional folding of the polypeptide chain, formed, for example, by hydrogen-bonding between regions of the chain. The commonest secondary structure is a right-handed spiral shape, called an α-helix; this occurs in proteins, such as keratin from hair, horns, nails, and wool, and helps to explain the physical properties of these structures. Globular proteins have rounded, compact, soluble molecules produced by an additional folding process involving interaction between different parts of an already regularly folded, 'secondary' level structure; this gives the molecule its 'tertiary' structure. Globular proteins include enzymes, antibodies, and many other types. Some proteins, such as haemoglobin, show 'quaternary' structure, in which complete, 'tertiary' level molecules are fitted together to make a larger protein assembly.

In the human diet, proteins are needed to repair or replace existing molecules, or for growth, but may also be exploited as an energy source.

Proterozoic A division of PRECAMBRIAN time: the time-interval from 2,500 million years ago to the end of the Precambrian (570 million years ago).

Protestant A member or adherent of any of the Christian bodies that separated from the ROMAN CATHOLIC CHURCH at the REFORMATION. The term was coined after the imperial Diet summoned at Speyer in 1529, and derives from the 'Protestatio' of the reforming members against the decisions of the Catholic majority. These adherents of the Reformation were not merely registering objections: they were professing their commitment to the simple faith of the early Church, which they believed had been obscured by the unnecessary innovations of medieval Roman Catholicism. Since then, Protestants are those who accept the principles of the Reformation, as opposed to Catholic or Orthodox Christians. LUTHER, ZWINGLI and CALVIN founded the largest of the original Protestant branches, and there were other more radical groups, such as the Anabaptists (see ANABAPTISTM).

All the early Protestants shared a conviction that the BIBLE was the only source of revealed truth and it was made available to all in vernacular translations. While not all Protestants agree on all the issues, most reject papal authority and repudiate TRANSUBSTANTIATION, PURGATORY, special veneration of the Virgin Mary, and invocation of the saints. The importance of the sacraments is also diminished, with only baptism and the Eucharist being accepted by most. In England, members of both the established ANGLICAN COMMUNION and the various NONCONFORMIST Churches are usually regarded as Protestants.

Proteus In Greek mythology, a sea-god who had the power of assuming different shapes to escape capture. If he was captured, however, he would use his gift of prophecy to answer questions about the future.

protocol (in computing) A set of rules determining the formats by which information may be exchanged between different computer systems. Protocols for data communication are set by international bodies, such as the International Standardization Organization (ISO) and the International Telegraphy and Telephone Consultative Committee (CCITT), a branch of the INTERNATIONAL TELECOMMUNICATION UNION.

Protoctista One of the five major KINGDOMS of living organisms, including algae, protozoa, and slime moulds, all of which are EUKARYOTES. Protoctists typically comprise single cells or aggregations of similar cells.

proton A NUCLEON that is one of the two types of particle (the other being a neutron) forming the nucleus of an atom. A proton has a mass of 1.67×10^{-27} kg (about 1,836 times that of the electron) and a spin of 1/2. The number of protons in the nucleus determines its total positive charge and in a neutral atom this charge is exactly balanced by the negative charge of the electrons round the nucleus. The atomic number (also called the **proton number**) of an ELEMENT is given by the number of protons in the nucleus. Different ISOTOPES of an element contain the same number of protons but different numbers of neutrons. The nuclei of hydrogen atoms are isolated protons, and in nuclear and particle physics they are accelerated to very high energies to act as bombarding particles to initiate nuclear reactions.

proton–proton reaction The dominant nuclear FUSION reaction in main-sequence stars whose central temperature is below 1.8×10^7 K. The proton–proton reaction creates helium-3 from hydrogen via two intermediate stages in which deuterium and helium-3 are produced together with NEUTRINOS and gamma rays. The Sun's central temperature is 1.6×10^7 K and so is low enough to sustain the proton–proton reaction. Hotter main-sequence stars are fuelled by the CARBON-NITROGEN CYCLE.

protoplasm See CYTOPLASM.

protozoan A simple unicellular organism. Protozoa literally means 'first animals', and it was probably from such life-forms that the animal kingdom evolved. Most living protozoans, which are a vast, diverse assemblage of one-celled non-photosynthetic organisms, are very far from simple, being themselves the product of lengthy evolution. There are at least 50,000 species of protozoans, which together with algae and the slime moulds are included in the kingdom Protoctista.

Protozoans are incredibly diverse in habits. FLAGELLATES, RADIOLARIANS, and FORAMINIFERA are abundant in plankton, while AMOEBAS and ciliates (e.g. *Paramecium*) occur in fresh water. Many protozoans are parasitic (causing dysentery, sleeping sickness, and malaria), or symbiotic. In fact, examples of protozoa can be found eating almost anything, which reflects their amazing adaptability.

protractor See GONIOMETER.

proturan A member of an order of minute white wingless insects, Protura, comprising some 200 species, each not more than 2 mm (0.125 inch) long, and found in humus-rich soils throughout most of the world. Proturans have piercing mouthparts and no eyes or antennae. The first of three pairs of legs are held forward to serve as sensory organs. They probably feed by sucking nutrients from the hyphae of fungi.

Proudhon, Pierre Joseph (1809–65) French social philosopher and journalist. His criticism of Napoleon III (Louis-Napoleon) and the Second Republic led to his imprisonment from 1849 to 1852; he later spent a period (1858–62) in exile in Belgium. His writings exercised considerable influence on the development of anarchism and socialism in Europe. He is chiefly remembered for his pamphlet *What is Property?* (1840), which argued that property, in the sense of the exploitation of one person's labour by another, is theft. His theories were developed by his disciple Bakunin.

Proust, Joseph Louis (1754–1826) French analytical chemist. He is remembered mainly for proposing the law of constant proportions, which demonstrates that any pure sample of a chemical compound (such as an oxide of a metal) always contains the same elements in fixed proportions. Berzelius later established the connection between this and John Dalton's atomic theory, giving Proust full credit, though some exceptions to the law were found many years later.

Proust, Marcel (1871–1922) French novelist, essayist, and critic. The son of a Roman Catholic doctor and his cultivated Jewish wife, he moved in fashionable Paris society during the 1890s. However, he was severely incapacitated by asthma and became a virtual recluse after his mother's death in 1905. He devoted the remainder of his life to writing his novel *Á La Recherche du temps perdu* (published in seven sections between 1913 and 1927). Influenced by the philosophy of Henri BERGSON, and the theories of Sigmund FREUD, the work traces the life of the narrator from childhood to middle age; its central theme is the recovery of the lost past and the releasing of its creative energies through the stimulation of unconscious memory. The strong autobiographical element includes a preoccupation with the theme of homosexuality. The novel is often regarded as one of the greatest works of fiction in any language.

Prout, William (1785–1850) British chemist and biochemist. He was trained as a physician, and carried out analyses of urine, gastric juices, and foodstuffs. In theoretical chemistry he developed the hypothesis that hydrogen is the primary substance from which all other elements are formed, and if the atomic weight of hydrogen is regarded as unity the weights of all other elements are exact multiples of it. Although this hypothesis was later found to be incorrect, it stimulated research in atomic theory, and in modern particle physics the hydrogen nucleus (proton) is indeed considered a fundamental particle.

Provence A former province of south-east France, on the Mediterranean coast east of the lower Rhône. Settled by the Greeks in the 6th century BC, the area around Marseilles became, in the 1st century BC, part of the Roman colony of Gaul. It was united with France under Louis XI in 1481 and is now part of the region of Provence-Alpes-Côte d'Azur. In Roman times *Provincia* was southern Gaul, the first Roman province to be established outside Italy.

Provençal (or **Occitan**, **Langue D'Oc**) A Romance language spoken in Provence, southern France, closely related to French, Italian, and Catalan. In the 12th–14th centuries it was the language of the troubadours and cultured speakers of southern France, but the subsequent spread of the northern dialects of French led to its gradual decline despite attempts to revive it.

Providence The capital of the state of Rhode Island, USA, on the Providence River; pop. (1990) 160,730. The town was founded in 1636 as a haven for religious dissenters by Roger Williams who had been banished for his views from the colony at Plymouth and was grateful that 'God's merciful providence' had led him to this spot. Originally a farming town, it developed as a maritime centre, its clippers sailing to China and the West Indies. Now a centre for jewellery, engineering, and metal manufactures.

Proxima Centauri A variable eleventh-magnitude red DWARF STAR, our Solar System's nearest stellar neighbour, at a distance of 1.3 parsecs in the constellation of Centaurus. It was discovered by the British astronomer Robert Innes in 1915 from its large PROPER MOTION, which it shares with ALPHA CENTAURI, 2.2 degrees away in the sky.

Prunus See CHERRY; PLUM.

Prussia A former kingdom of Germany, which grew from a small country on the south-east shores of the Baltic to an extensive domain covering much of modern north-east Germany and Poland. The forested area to the east of the Vistula, originally inhabited by a Baltic people known as the Prussians, was taken in the 13th century by the Teutonic Knights, and in the 16th century it became a duchy of the Hohenzollerns, passing in 1618 to the electors of Brandenburg. The kingdom of Prussia, proclaimed in 1701, with its capital at Berlin, grew in the 18th century under Frederick the Great to become a dominant power. After victory in the Franco-Prussian War of 1870–71, Prussia under Wilhelm I became the nucleus of the new German Empire created by Bismarck. With Germany's defeat in World War I, the Prussian monarchy was abolished and Prussia's supremacy came to an end.

Przewalski's horse See HORSE.

psalm A sacred song or hymn, especially the Hebrew verses in the biblical Book of Psalms, sometimes attributed to King David. These psalms have long formed a central part of the Jewish liturgy, and notably in the English translation attributed to Miles Coverdale (*c.*1488–1569) found in the *Book of Common Prayer* (1662), have also had an important place in Christian worship and in English religious poetry.

psaltery A musical instrument, consisting of a flat soundbox with strings (plucked with fingers or plectra) running across it. It was widely used in the Middle Ages: from the 10th century it had the triangular shape of a harp, and from the 13th century it had an isosceles trapezoid shape with the non-parallel sides curving inwards. A later version of the instrument halved this, producing a shape identical, in miniature, to the HARPSICHORD, which is a mechanized psaltery.

psephology See OPINION POLL.

pseudoscorpion (or **false scorpion**) A tiny

ARACHNID, usually less than 4 mm (0.16 inch) long, living among humus, bark, and soil, worldwide. The 2,000 or so species, making up the order Pseudoscorpiones (Chelonethida), are rarely seen, though they are quite common. They resemble true scorpions but lack the long abdomen and sting, and are much smaller. The PEDIPALPS are modified as pincers, bearing poison glands; hence the false scorpions carry their sting not in their tails but in their arms. They build silk nests for over-wintering and for protection when moulting.

psittacosis (or **parrot disease**) An infectious disease caused by the bacterium *Clamydia psittaci*. The symptoms include fever, cough, and severe muscular pains. The infection is endemic in birds, especially parrots, canaries, and poultry, all of which may be carriers although they have no symptoms. The condition responds to some antibiotics.

Psyche (Greek, 'soul') In Roman fable, a princess of outstanding beauty loved by Cupid. Their love was initially thwarted by Cupid's mother, Venus, who was jealous of Psyche's beauty. Cupid placed her in a remote palace, but only visited her in total darkness and forbade her to see him. One night she lit a lamp and discovered that the figure sleeping at her side was the god of love himself. A drop of oil from her lamp fell on him and Cupid awoke in anger at her disobedience. He fled, and Psyche wandered the Earth in search of him. Finally Jupiter made her immortal and gave her in marriage to Cupid.

psychiatry A branch of medicine concerned with the study and treatment of MENTAL ILLNESS. The conditions coming within its scope are mainly those in which there is no established damage to, or disease of, the brain (these are the province of neurology) and include PSYCHOSES, such as SCHIZOPHRENIA; NEUROSES, such as PHOBIAS; DEPRESSION; DEMENTIA; DRUG ABUSE; and PERSONALITY DISORDERS. Psychiatrists, who are medically qualified and generally work with other professionals, such as psychiatric nurses, CLINICAL PSYCHOLOGISTS and social workers, offer varied treatments. These include treatment by PSYCHOTROPIC DRUGS, electroconvulsive therapy (ECT) (for some forms of depression), BEHAVIOUR THERAPY, FAMILY THERAPY, GROUP THERAPY, PSYCHOTHERAPY, and individual COUNSELLING and support. In 1977 the psychiatrists' international body, the World Psychiatric Association, promulgated the Declaration of Hawaii, a set of ethical guidelines to promote high standards and prevent the misuse of psychiatry, not least in countries in which political dissenters are diagnosed as mentally ill and incarcerated.

psychoanalysis A theory of and therapy for the mental disorders known as NEUROSES, and a general theory of PERSONALITY and emotional development constructed almost entirely by FREUD. The therapy is one-to-one, over an extended period, and investigates the interaction between the conscious and, by free association of ideas, the unconscious mind, bringing to light repressed fears and conflicts. To this end, two hour-long weekly sessions with the analyst, lasting for several years, are not uncommon. The theory has been of enormous influence in 20th-century thinking and culture. It gives a central role to the drives of INSTINCT and the way that socialization may pervert such drives through too much indulgence or control. Psychoanalysis stresses that instincts and emotions may remain, unacknowledged, in the UNCONSCIOUS and profoundly affect thought and behaviour. Freud believed that instincts from childhood onwards revolve round physical gratification and are broadly sexual. Subsequently, however, he suggested that we have destructive as well as sexual instincts. The Austrian-British psychoanalyst Melanie KLEIN took this idea of *thanatos* (death) and *eros* (love) much further; her work with children is probably the most important contribution to psychoanalysis after Freud. In *The Ego and the Id* (1923), Freud proposed a tripartite division of the personality into ego ('I'), id ('it'), and super-ego. The id is unconscious and contains primitive emotions and drives. The super-ego contains ideals and moral values. The ego steers between the two, trying to reconcile their demands and the constraints of the real world. It is the seat of consciousness, but its DEFENCE MECHANISMS are not conscious processes. Later NEO-FREUDIAN theorists placed more stress on development of the ego and less on the unconscious and sexual motivation (JUNG rejected the centrality of the latter). The theory of psychoanalysis, is now regarded as having fundamental conceptual weaknesses. Many of its claims are impossible to test by experiment, or, where tested, have not been confirmed. Psychoanalytical therapy seems less effective than many less time-consuming and expensive forms of treatment, such as PSYCHOTHERAPY, BEHAVIOUR THERAPY, and other treatments offered by PSYCHIATRY.

psycholinguistics A branch of LINGUISTICS concerned with the ways in which human beings process LANGUAGE and especially with how they plan and produce utterances and perceive and interpret the utterances of others. Psycholinguistics is sometimes seen as including the study of LANGUAGE development and CLINICAL LINGUISTICS.

psychology 'The science of mental life', in the words of William JAMES, one of its great figures. Psychology concerns both the normal and abnormal workings of the mind, whereas PSYCHIATRY only deals with the latter. The earliest scientific psychology was the study in the 19th century of sensory PERCEPTION. This and other major psychological problems were defined earlier by the philosophers LOCKE and HUME, who theorized about emotion, motivation, sensation, MEMORY, and understanding. Progress in mid-20th-century psychology centred on LEARNING theories, especially those of BEHAVIOURISM, associated with WATSON, and SKINNER. These derived general laws of learning from animal experiments on the control of behaviour through CONDITIONING. This work has had important applications in CLINICAL PSYCHOLOGY and the treatment of psychiatric illness. However, in the 1950s behaviourism's oversimplified conceptual base and sacrifice of realism to experimental rigour came to seem increasingly inadequate. This was one reason for the rise of humanistic psychology. Technological advances are helping to overcome these problems: it is now possible to record the activities of the brain in various ways; knowledge of genetics has increased dramatically; and computers assist in statistical analysis. Computers have also provided a reference point for COGNITIVE PSYCHOLOGY, which since World War II has become the dominant area of research. It grew out of work on memory and problem-solving, and from the analogy with computers (see ARTIFICIAL INTELLIGENCE). It concerns itself with those questions for which behaviourism appeared manifestly inadequate: LANGUAGE development, and the nature and development of human thought and knowledge. Cognitive psychology shares its ancestry in German GESTALT PSYCHOLOGY with modern SOCIAL

PSYCHOLOGY, the other major development since World War II. Social psychology addresses such topics as prejudice, relationships, and misunderstandings of ourselves and others. It has also been influenced by ETHOLOGY. Psychology finds application in industry, ADVERTISING, EDUCATION, child-rearing, and, through clinical psychology, in the diagnosis and treatment of psychiatric illness.

psychopathic personality A persistently antisocial individual whose abnormally aggressive or irresponsible behaviour cannot be ascribed to low intelligence but stems from a PERSONALITY DISORDER that can rarely be resolved by treatment. There is no agreement as to its causes. Characteristic of the disorder are a failure to make loving relationships, impulsive actions, a lack of guilt, and a failure to learn from adverse experiences. Although many psychopaths are superficially charming, they have a striking indifference to the feelings of others.

psychosis Serious forms of MENTAL ILLNESS in which thinking and feeling become so aberrant that the individual loses a grip on reality, may suffer HALLUCINATIONS and delusions (as in PARANOIA), yet fails to appreciate that anything is wrong. The symptoms can be a sign of brain damage, due for example to longstanding ALCOHOL ABUSE, or the result of taking such drugs as LSD. Otherwise the symptoms are most likely to indicate that the person is suffering from SCHIZOPHRENIA or MANIC DEPRESSION, the two most common forms of psychosis. Psychosis can be contrasted with NEUROSIS, in which the individual is fully aware of his or her irrational behaviour or emotional reactions. It has been said that neurotics believe that two and two make four, but are worried by the conclusion, while psychotics have every confidence in their belief that two and two make five.

psychosomatic disorders Bodily diseases caused at least in part by psychological stress. Examples are some forms of ulcer, asthma, and skin complaints. Some argue that all illness is partly psychosomatic. This belief accounts for the popularity of certain forms of alternative medicine using such psychological techniques such as relaxation.

psychotherapy The treatment of emotional or behavioural problems by psychological means, often in one-to-one interviews or small groups. Modern PSYCHOANALYSIS and cognitive therapies concentrate on the patient's beliefs. Other therapies, such as those within humanistic psychology, attend to the patient's emotional state or sensitivity. The distinction, however, is not clear-cut, as all these therapies involve intense exploration of the patient's conflicts, and most rely on the emotion generated in therapy as a force in the patient's recovery. In contrast, BEHAVIOUR THERAPIES derive from the view that neurosis is a matter of maladaptive CONDITIONING and concentrate on modifying patients' behaviour.

psychotropic drug Any member of a large group of substances used in the treatment of psychological disorders. They are classified according to the conditions for which they are given. **Antipsychotic drugs** (or major TRANQUILLIZERS), such as phenothiazines, may be given for severe psychotic disorders, such as schizophrenia and mania. Minor tranquillizers, of which the most popular are the benzodiazepines, are effective in anxiety states. **Antidepressants** are used to relieve severe depression and are classified according to their chemical structure (for example, tricyclic antidepressants) or their biochemical actions (for example, monoamine oxidase (MAO) inhibitors and SSRIs – selective serotonin reuptake inhibitors). The mode of action of psychotropic drugs can sometimes give information about the nature of the disease in which they are effective, although many such hypotheses depend on an over-simplified view of an exceedingly complicated subject, and have not stood the test of time. Nevertheless, the discovery and marketing of psychotropic drugs is now an important branch of pharmaceutics over the last 20 years. Psychotropic drugs are sometimes used in conditions other than mental disease: for example, the benzodiazepines may be used to treat some forms of epilepsy.

ptarmigan Any of three species of bird in the genus *Lagopus*, belonging to the grouse family. They live in northern temperate areas of both Old and New Worlds, usually on treeless moorland or on mountains. All species of ptarmigan moult into a white plumage in winter so as to be well camouflaged in the snowy areas in which they live. They may shelter from extremely cold nights by digging burrows in the snow. They are herbivorous, living on shoots and leaves.

Pterandon See PTERODACTYL.

Pteraspis A primitive JAWLESS FISH that lived in fresh or brackish water in early Devonian times (around 390 million years ago). The front of the body was covered in thick plates of dermal bone which tapered in the front to form a long snout. The eyes were large and placed on either side of the head shield. *Pteraspis* had no fins, but bony spines were used as substitutes. The tail was covered in diamond-shaped scales and was well developed and flexible. No fossils of the internal skeleton have been found but it is assumed that it was made of cartilage.

pteridophyte In traditional classification systems, a plant of the division Pteridophyta, which includes FERNS, HORSETAILS, and CLUBMOSSES. They were grouped together because they are all flowerless plants with true stems, leaves, and roots, and have an organized system of XYLEM. They show marked alternation of generations (see LIFE CYCLE), the first being a non-sexual, spore-bearing generation, and the second being a sexual generation that produces GAMETES.

pterodactyl (or **pterosaur**) One of a group of extinct flying reptiles which lived in the Mesozoic Era (245–66.4 million years ago), at the same time as the dinosaurs. The fourth finger of each hand was greatly elongated and supported a flight membrane. As a further adaptation to 'flight', the skeleton was extremely lightly built. They probably flew mainly by gliding. *Pteranodon*, an advanced pterodactyl, had a wing-span of nearly 8 m (26 ft).

PTFE (polytetrafluoroethene) A thermoplastic (see PLASTICS) made from the monomer tetrafluoroethene (CF_2=CF_2). It has a very high resistance to attack by chemicals, stability at high temperatures, and a very low coefficient of friction. It is used for its low-friction properties as a coating on cooking equipment, gaskets, skis, chemical apparatus, and laboratory ware, and on handling equipment for food and drugs. It is also used in high-temperature cable and wire insulation.

Ptolemies The Macedonian dynasty that ruled Egypt from 323 to 30 BC. **Ptolemy I** was an officer of Alexander the Great who, after the king's death, was appointed satrap of Egypt. He proclaimed himself king in 304, and by the time of his death in 283–82 he had established control over Cyprus, Palestine, and many cities in the Aegean and Asia

Minor. The reigns of the Ptolemies who succeeded him were characterized externally by struggles with the SELEUCIDS for control of Syria, Asia Minor, and the Aegean; and internally by dissatisfaction and rebellion among the native Egyptians. Contact with the rising power of Rome came to a head during the reign of CLEOPATRA VII, whose liaison with MARK ANTONY led ultimately to defeat at Actium, suicide, and the annexation of Egypt by Octavian.

Ptolemy (*c*.90–168) Greek astronomer and geographer. His major work, known by its Arabic title (*Almagest*), was a textbook of astronomy based on the geocentric system of Hipparchus. Ptolemy's teachings had enormous influence on medieval thought, the geocentric view of the cosmos being adopted as Christian doctrine until the late Renaissance. The *Almagest* included detailed tables of lunar and solar motion with eclipse predictions, and a catalogue giving the positions and magnitudes of 1,022 stars. Ptolemy's *Geography*, giving lists of places with their longitudes and latitudes, was also a standard work for centuries, despite its inaccuracies.

puberty The stage of human development when the output of hormones from the GONADS increases sufficiently for reproduction to be possible. Its onset usually occurs between 10 and 16 years in girls, and 11 and 15 years in boys, though this is variable. It is associated with a period of rapid bodily growth and the gradual appearance of the secondary sexual characteristics. In boys the scrotum, testes, and penis enlarge, hairs grow on face and body, and the voice breaks. In girls the breasts enlarge, the hips broaden, the distribution of body fat changes, and MENSTRUATION begins.

public finance See PUBLIC SECTOR.

public health A speciality within MEDICINE that aims to identify and prevent the environmental and social causes of ill health. It is based on EPIDEMIOLOGY, the study of disease within a population. The traditional concerns of public health include sanitation and WATER SUPPLY, air and noise POLLUTION, food hygiene, nutrition, housing conditions, and the health and safety of people at work. More recently, public health doctors have also examined the health consequences of social problems such as UNEMPLOYMENT and poverty.

public law That part of the law that deals with the functions, duties, and powers of state bodies, the relationships between state bodies, and the relationships of state bodies with private individuals and organizations. Public law includes rules of the CONSTITUTION and administrative law, together with much of the law of civil liberties. It is recognized in many societies that the special functions of state bodies necessitate different treatment from that which citizens normally receive in the area of **private law**, which governs the relations between individuals or bodies. In the UK, there is less distinction between public and private law than in some other countries, such as France.

public ownership See NATIONALIZATION.

public relations (PR) The management of the public's perception of a business or other organization. PR emerged in the early 20th century as a distinct occupation serving big business corporations in the USA; it was pioneered by Edward L. Bernays, author of *The Engineering of Consent*. Much PR activity is directed at journalists; it therefore operates indirectly, as opposed to ADVERTISING or MARKETING direct. PR techniques include the press conference, where journalists are invited to listen to a statement, ask questions, then report; and the written press release.

public sector The part of the economy under direct national or local government control as contrasted with the PRIVATE SECTOR. On the production side, it comprises public services, such as nationalized industries, and public (state-owned) corporations. On the spending side, government expenditure includes government outlays on goods and services together with transfer payments, such as pensions and SOCIAL SECURITY payments. Some of the outlays are on what economic theory calls public or collective goods, that is goods whose consumption by one individual does not preclude consumption by others, such as street lighting and national defence. It may also supply merit goods, such as education, if it considers that private-sector provision would be inadequate to the needs of society. The public sector is financed by taxation. **Public finance** is concerned with fiscal policy and the effects of taxation.

public sector borrowing requirement (PSBR; US **government sector deficit**, **combined budget deficit**) The amount the government needs to borrow to finance its budget deficit in any given period, typically a year. The PSBR is equal to the public sector financial deficit (government expenditure minus taxation) plus government lending to other sectors. A negative PSBR is known as a public sector debt repayment (PSDR). See also NATIONAL DEBT.

publishing The commissioning, editing, production, and marketing of printed materials, such as books, periodicals, journals, specialized magazines, and works of music. The publisher coordinates the activities of the author, editor, printer, and bookseller. Modern publishing houses have developed different departments specializing in editing, manufacturing, design, accounting and marketing, and distribution, while the printing and binding is often done in a country with lower costs. The great innovation of the paperback book, pioneered by Allen Lane and his Penguin imprint, increased the market for a wide variety of literature.

A development that now challenges traditional publishing is the growth in new technologies for the storage, transmission, and distribution of data. Microcomputers with specialized programs and laser printers facilitate desk-top publishing (DTP), which cuts out expensive typesetting and makes even very short runs of highly specialized work economic to produce. DTP is now a growing area in the field of INFORMATION TECHNOLOGY.

More far-reaching in its effects is the development of the publishing of books in electronic form – either as COMPACT DISCS (CDs) or other types of disc or on-line through the INTERNET. This particularly applies to reference books – especially dictionaries and encyclopedias, many of which are now routinely published as both books and CDs. CDs are often cheaper than large sets of books, although they cannot be used without a relatively expensive multimedia computer; it is this factor that has restricted their sales. For this, and other reasons, most publishers expect paper books to coexist with CDs.

Puccini, Giacomo (1858–1924) Italian composer. He established his reputation with his third opera, *Manon Lescaut* (1893). Puccini's sense of the dramatic, gift for melody, and skilful use of the orchestra have ensured that his works remain among the most popular in the repertoire. Several others followed, including *La Bohème* (1896), *Tosca* (1900), *Madama Butterfly* (1904), *Girl of the Golden*

West (1910), and *Turandot*, which was completed by a pupil after his death and produced in 1926.

Puck (Irish **púca**; Welsh **pwcca**) The 16th-century English name for a mischievous demon or goblin, also known as Robin Goodfellow and Hobgoblin, and commonly believed to haunt, in a variety of shapes, the countryside. As Puck he appears in Shakespeare's *A Midsummer Night's Dream* (1595). In earlier superstition he was considered an evil demon, luring travellers off their path and young girls to disaster.

Pueblo A member of certain North American Indian peoples occupying a pueblo settlement. Their prehistoric period is known as the Anasazi (Pueblo) culture. The Chaco Culture National Historical Park in New Mexico, USA, embraces the remains of over 80 prehistoric communities of the Pueblo culture, which was centred at Chaco Canyon.

Pueblo Alto A city in central Chile, situated to the south-east of Santiago; pop. (1991) 187,370.

Puerto Rico An island commonwealth in the CARIBBEAN, between Hispaniola and the Virgin Islands.

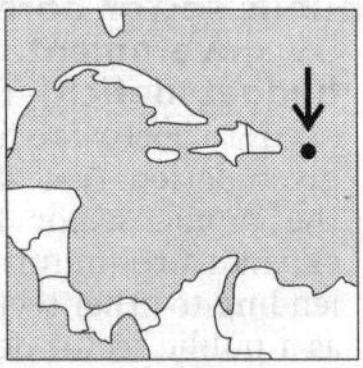

Physical. The west-east length of Puerto Rico is some 180 km (112 miles), while its north-south width is about 60 km (37 miles) at the widest point. Its climate is tropical: hot and very wet, with occasional storms and hurricanes. The coast offers good harbours and the coastal plains are fertile, yielding sugarcane, sweet potatoes, and maize. In the interior highlands rise to 1,220 m (4,000 feet) and more; coffee and tobacco are grown on their slopes.

Economy. The mainstays of the Puerto Rican economy are tourism and manufacturing industry, the major products being chemicals, food products, electrical goods, and machinery. Chemicals, metals, and foodstuffs are the main exports, almost all to the USA. Agriculture is of declining importance, with dairy, livestock, and cereals the principal products. Mineral resources are scanty.

History. Originally known as Boriquén, Puerto Rico was discovered by Columbus in 1493. Encouraged by tales of gold from the indigenous Arawak Indians, his companion, Juan PONCE DE LEÓN, was granted permission by the Spanish crown to colonize the island. In 1508 he founded the settlement of Caparra and in 1509 he was made governor. Caparra was abandoned and the settlement moved to nearby San Juan in 1521, to take better advantage of the bay for trading. By the end of the 16th century the Arawak were virtually extinct from European-introduced diseases and exploitation. In the 17th and 18th centuries the island remained important for its sugar and tobacco plantations, worked by imported black slaves, and as a key to Spain's defence of its trading interests in the Caribbean and Atlantic against France, Britain, and Holland.

Puerto Rico was maintained by Spain as a garrison protecting trade routes until the loss of Mexico in 1821 removed its strategic importance. In 1887 the Autonomist Party was founded to protect home rule under Spanish sovereignty. In 1898, during the Spanish–American War, the island came under US military rule and was ceded to the USA at the end of the war. In 1917 an Act of the US Congress (Jones Act) declared Puerto Rican inhabitants to be US citizens. Since the 1940s, with a decline in the sugar industry, there have been successful efforts at industrialization and diversification of the economy. Muñoz Marín (1898–1980) was the first elected governor (1948–64), being re-elected three times. In 1952 the Commonwealth of Puerto Rico was proclaimed, and ratified by a plebiscite. The party which has dominated politics since then, the Popular Democratic Party (PPD), has supported the status quo, while urging greater autonomy. Its rival, the New Progressive Party (PNP) would like the island to become the fifty-first state of the USA. There is also a small Independence Party, but the violent separatist organization, the FALN, has had little support on the island. The UN has regularly urged a plebiscite to decide the island's future. In 1993, Puerto Ricans voted to retain their country's status as a self-governing commonwealth, thereby rejecting both independence and US statehood.

Capital: San Juan
Area: 9,104 sq km (3,515 sq mi)
Population: 3,725,000 (1995)
Currency: 1 US dollar = 100 cents
Religions: Roman Catholic 85.0%; Protestant 5.0%
Ethnic Groups: Hispanic 75.0%; Black 15.0%; mixed 10.0%
Languages: Spanish; English (both official)
International Organizations: CARICOM

puff adder A stoutly built VIPER, *Bitis arietans*, up to about 1.4 m (5 feet) in length, from Africa and western Arabia. It lives in all of sub-Saharan Africa, with the exception of rain forest. Although nocturnal, puff adders often bask during the day. If disturbed, they make loud hissing (puffing) noises. In southern Africa, such vipers as the puff adder account for 80 per cent of all bites by venomous snakes, but the mambas account for a greater number of deaths. The puff adder is a close relative of the GABOON VIPER, *B. gabonica*.

puffball The spore-bearing structure of fungi of the order Lycoperdales. The powdery mass of dry spores develops inside a hollow ball of fungal tissue, which is white or buff. When ripe this has a hole at the top from which clouds of spores are puffed when the puffball is struck. The giant puffball, up to 100 cm (3 feet) across, is one of the largest fungal fruiting bodies known.

puffbird A bird of Central and South America making up a family, Bucconidae, of some 32 species found mostly in forests, where they sit upright on perches and fly out after insects. An exception is the swallow-winged puffbird, *Chelidoptera tenebrosa*, a longer-winged species which spends more time in the air than the others. In general, puffbirds are thick-set, black, brown, grey, and white birds with long, strong beaks (often yellow or red). They nest in holes in banks or in the ground.

pufferfish (or **blowfish**) A fish well-known for its ability to inflate its stomach with water or air (in which case it floats helpless at the surface). There are about 130 species in the family Tetraodontidae, mostly tropical and subtropical, coastal sea fishes, with a few living in the open ocean and others living in fresh water in Africa and south-east Asia.

puffin Any of three species of bird of the family Alcidae, making up a tribe of AUKS with coloured beaks and occasionally head plumes. They nest colonially in burrows dug with feet and bill, and feed by swimming and diving. Atlantic puffins, *Fratercula arctica*, breed on North Atlantic and Arctic coasts, while three other species inhabit the northern Pacific.

Pugin, Augustus Welby Northmore (1812–52) British architect and designer. He converted to Roman Catholicism in 1835 and became the main champion of the GOTHIC REVIVAL; he believed that the Gothic style was the only proper architectural style because of its origins in medieval Christian society. Among his chief contributions to architecture and design is his work on the external detail and internal fittings for the Houses of Parliament designed by Sir Charles Barry. Pugin's views, set out in such works as *Contrasts* (1836), influenced John Ruskin and ultimately the Arts and Crafts Movement.

Puglia The Italian name for APULIA.

pug moth A small moth of the family Geometridae, which rests with its wings spread away from the body and pressed flat. Its LOOPER caterpillars mostly feed inside flowers or seed pods, although some eat leaves, and a Hawaiian species has recently been found to catch and eat flies. The pupae of most pug moths are brightly coloured and are formed in silken cocoons in the ground.

puja (Sanskrit, 'worship') Religious observance within HINDUISM, usually involving worship offered to a god or goddess. Personal acts may include lighting incense, giving offerings to the deity, prayer, and the recitation of MANTRAS. Communal acts of worship, conducted by priests or *pujaris*, consist of three elements: *havan*, the offering of fire, *ārti*, worship using lights, and the distribution of *prashad* ('edible grace'), the left-over food that has been offered to the god.

Pulitzer, Joseph (1847–1911) Hungarian-born US newspaper proprietor and editor. A pioneer of campaigning popular journalism, he owned a number of newspapers, including the *New York World*. Through his journalism he aimed to remedy abuses and reform social and economic inequalities. He made provisions in his will for the establishment of the annual **Pulitzer Prizes** for achievements in journalism and literature.

pulsar A rapidly spinning NEUTRON STAR emitting a narrow rotating beam of radiation, and detected as a pulsing radio source if the beam sweeps across the Earth. A pulsar may also be a source of gamma-ray, X-ray, and optical pulses. A pulsar has a strong MAGNETIC FIELD, whose axis is at an angle to that of rotation. Electrons spiralling around the magnetic field lines emit SYNCHROTRON RADIATION in the direction of the magnetic axis, giving rise to the observed beams. The first pulsars were discovered in 1967 and several hundred are now known. Their periods range from 0.001 seconds to over 4 seconds.

pulsating variable See VARIABLE STAR.

pulse ▶**1** A series of waves of dilation passing along an artery as a result of the pressure of blood caused by the pumping action of the left ventricle of the heart. It is easily detected in man by feeling the radial artery near the wrist. The average pulse rate of the resting adult is between 60 and 80 pulses per minute. ▶**2** In physics, a variation in a quantity for a brief time or a series of such variations with a regular square waveform.

pulse code modulation (PCM) A method of DIGITIZATION and MODULATION of an information signal. The information signal is sampled frequently and the instantaneous value is coded in digital form. Each coded sample is then transmitted as a group of pulses of light (in optical fibres), electricity (in copper cables), or radio waves (for free-space transmission). PCM lends itself to MULTIPLEXING, and is used extensively in TELEPHONY. A similar technique is used in digital audio searching on tape or COMPACT DISC.

Pulu TIGLATH-PILESER III, king of Assyria.

puma (or **cougar**, **mountain lion**, **panther**) A species in the CAT family, *Felis concolor*, which ranges over the whole of North and South America. It lives in a wide variety of habitats from sea-level to altitudes of up to 4,000 m (13,000 feet). It resembles a slender lioness and may reach a length of 2.9 m (9.5 feet), about a third of which is tail. In colour the short, close fur varies from yellowish-brown to red, the underparts are white, the ridge of the back and the tail are usually marked by a darker line, and the tail is black-tipped. A solitary animal, which avoids humans, it can travel 48–80 km (30–50 miles) when hunting. It feeds on a wide variety of prey from deer to slugs and snails. Breeding occurs only every two to three years, when one to six kittens are born in a den after a gestation period of three months. The kittens are not fully independent until about two years of age. Pumas have a life-span of about 18 years.

pumice A volcanic rock formed when (usually acid) lava is expelled violently into the air during the initial gas-rich phase of an eruption. When solidified it contains many holes, which make the rock very light; it can be carried long distances in the air and sea. Its main use is as an abrasive.

pump A machine used to transport, raise, or compress fluids. The earliest pumps were used to lift water from wells: a type of reciprocating lift pump was known in Egypt from the 2nd century BC; other early devices for pumping water were WATER WHEELS and the Archimedean screw. During the Middle Ages reciprocating pumps were reinvented for pumping water from mines, and in the 19th century many different types of rotary pump were developed. In the 20th century there has been a proliferation of pump types for a wide range of uses. They may be positive displacement pumps, in which fluid by a rotor is displaced either mechanically or by another fluid; kinetic (rotodynamic) pumps, in which motion is imparted to the fluid; or electromagnetic pumps, in which electromagnetic force is used to move or compress the fluid. Most pumps are of the positive displacement or kinetic variety.

pumped storage A method of ENERGY STORAGE using electric power to pump water from a lower reservoir to an upper one. The stored water can then be released to generate HYDROELECTRICITY. Pumped storage is not in itself a source of energy, but it increases the efficiency with which other sources are used. Demand for electricity fluctuates continuously, but POWER-STATIONS, particularly nuclear-power plants, run most economically with a steady output. Storing the surplus during times of low demand for use when demand rises can therefore improve the overall efficiency of the network.

pumpkin The fruit of certain plants of the genus *Cucurbita*; the name is used in Europe for a variety of *C. maxima*, and in North America for a variety of *C. pepo*. Both are orange in colour and only the European pumpkin is invariably round. Pumpkins are typical members of the family Cucurbitaceae, which includes cucumbers, melons, marrows, and others. The family contains around 700 species, all typically perennial, climbing or trailing plants which produce rotund fruits with a leathery skin.

punctuated equilibrium A theory of EVOLUTION proposing that plant and animal species usually arose relatively quickly (in less than 100,000 years), rather than through a process of gradual change (as postulated in Darwinian theory). It cites as evidence the discontinuities observed in the fossil records of certain animal groups (e.g. ammonites).

Pune (formerly **Poona**) An industrial city of western India, in Maharashtra state; pop. (1991) 2,485,000. A former capital of the Maharattas, it was a military and administrative centre under British rule from 1817. Its chief products include firearms, pharmaceuticals, machinery, and textiles.

Punic wars The three wars fought in the 3rd and 2nd century BC between Rome and Carthage, so named from 'Poenicus' ('Dark skin' or 'Phoenician'). The contest was for control of the Mediterranean Sea. Rome emerged as victor from each war.

The First (264–241 BC) was fought largely at sea. Rome expanded its navy and took control of Sicily. Corsica and Sardinia were seized a few years later. HAMILCAR, father of HANNIBAL, led the defeated side. The Second (218–201) arose from Hannibal's invasion of Italy from Carthaginian bases in Spain via the Alps. He led a huge force including elephant squadrons. Rome suffered disastrous defeats, most notably in the mists by Lake Trasimene and at CANNAE. Italy was overrun by Hannibal but the Italian tribes did not rise against Rome. The strategy of the dictator FABIUS prevented further losses. In a long-drawn-out series of campaigns Hannibal's extended lines of supply were threatened by defeats in Sicily and Spain and the brilliant generalship of SCIPIO. HASDRUBAL, Hannibal's brother, was defeated on the Italian mainland in 207. By 203 Hannibal, who had no effective siege engines, was summoned to withdraw to Africa to defend Carthage itself, now threatened by Scipio. Pursued by Scipio he was defeated at Zama in 202 and the Carthaginians were forced to accept humiliating terms the following year. Spain was acquired as a provincial territory by Rome.

In 149 BC at a peak of its territorial expansion and at the insistence of CATO, Rome intervened in an African dispute to side with Numidia against Carthage. In the Third War (149–146) the Younger SCIPIO besieged and destroyed Carthage utterly, sowed the site with symbolic salt, and declared Africa a Roman province.

Punjab ▶1 (or **the Punjab**) A region of north-west India and Pakistan, a wide fertile plain traversed by the Indus and its five tributaries (Jhelum, Chenab, Ravi, Beas, and Sutlej) which give the region its name (Hindustani *pañj* five, *āb* waters). Under Muslim influence from the 11th century, the region became a centre of Sikhism in the 15th century and, after the capture of Lahore in 1799 by Ranjit Singh, a powerful Sikh kingdom. It was annexed by the British in 1849 and became a part of British India. In the partition of 1947 it was divided between Pakistan and India. The Indian state of Punjab was divided in 1966 into the two states of Punjab and Haryana. **▶2** A province of Pakistan; area 205,334 sq km (79,310 sq miles); pop. (1981) 47,292,000; capital, Lahore. **▶3** A state of India; area 50,362 sq km (19,452 sq miles); pop. (1991) 20,190,795; capital, Chandigarh.

Punjabi See INDO-IRANIAN LANGUAGES.

pupa The resting stage in the complete METAMORPHOSIS of many insects, which comes between the larva and adult. Pupae show the outlines of the appendages of the adults, but only some abdominal muscles are functional. These are enough for some, like mosquito pupae, to swim, but most do not move about. Pupae fall into two groups: those in which the appendages are closely stuck to the body, like butterflies, and those in which they are free, like beetles. Most pupae are contained in silken cocoons or earthen cells, but those of two-winged flies live inside the hardened and darkened last larval skin, or puparium.

puppetry Entertainment in which inanimate figures are manipulated by humans to give an impression of spontaneity. The hand or glove puppet is the simplest and most familiar. The puppets are held above the head of the puppeteer, who stands inside a booth – as in the British Punch and Judy show. Hand puppets are limited in size and gesture, and only two characters can normally be shown at a time. A marionette is a type of puppet controlled from above by fine threads attached to the limbs, shoulders, head, and back. These are much less limited than hand puppets and have been used for the performance of full-length plays and operas. There are hand-puppets in China; in India, where they were once very common, they survive mainly in Kerala. Rod puppets, still used in India and Java, are full-length figures. Controlled from below, they are slow and measured in their movements. The *bunraku* puppets of JAPANESE DRAMA are about two-thirds life-size; they carry controlling mechanisms in their backs. The (visible) operators work in teams, no puppet being workable by one operator alone. Indian string puppets, now mostly used for the 'dance of the dolls', are manipulated somewhat differently. A form of puppetry used for political satire on television uses rubber caricatures of political leaders, and puppets are also used to provide children's entertainment.

Puppis The Stern, a CONSTELLATION of the southern sky. It was originally part of the ancient Greek constellation Argo Navis, the ship of the Argonauts, until 1763 when the French astronomer Nicolas Louis de Lacaille divided that large constellation into three; the other parts are CARINA and VELA. Its brightest star is Zeta Puppis, named Naos which is Greek for 'ship'. With a magnitude of 2.3, it is one of the hottest stars known.

Puranas Collections of Hindu legends and traditions in Sanskrit. They are regarded as divinely inspired texts, each glorifying a particular god, but are also encyclopedias of secular as well as religious knowledge. Most were composed by 1000 AD, but with many additions later. The most popular is the *Bhagavatapurana* ('Purana of the Blessed Lord'), containing the life of Krishna.

Purbeck, Isle of A peninsula on the Dorset coast of southern England extending into the English Channel, with Poole Bay to the north. It is noted for its hard polished limestone (**Purbeck marble**) used in making pillars, effigies, etc. The **Purbeck Hills** are a range of chalk hills that cross the peninsula from east to west. Britain's first mainland marine reserve protects the kelp beds and coralline seaweeds of the gently shelving Kimmeridge ledges.

Purcell, Henry (1659–95) English composer. He enjoyed royal patronage and was organist for Westminster Abbey (1679–95) and the Chapel Royal (1682–95). He composed many choral odes and songs for royal occasions as well as sacred anthems for the Chapel Royal. His main interest was in music for the theatre; he composed the first English opera, *Dido and Aeneas* (1689), moving away from the tradition of the masque, breaking new dramatic ground and accommodating a wide emotional range. He also composed the incidental music for many plays, while his instrumental music includes a series of *Fantasias* for the viol (1680).

purdah (from Persian, 'curtain') The seclusion of women in Islamic society. In the early Muslim period the Persian and Byzantine practice of secluding women was adopted. The KORAN does not stipulate seclusion, although it prescribes modesty for both men and women, which is reflected in the *chuddar*, an all-enveloping black garment worn by some Muslim and Hindu women. In the fundamentalist revival of Islam in some countries (notably Iran) during the 1980s, the use of the *chuddar* again became obligatory. However, elsewhere in contemporary Muslim society the seclusion and rights of women are important issues, which are debated in the context of a return to the SHARIA and the rights and wrongs of westernization.

purgatory In Roman Catholic and Orthodox Christian doctrine, the state of existence or condition of a soul which still needs purification from venial (pardonable) sin before being admitted to heaven. It is believed that souls in purgatory can be helped by the prayer and good works of the faithful. Those who die unrepentant, having totally and deliberately rejected God, are said to go direct to hell.

Purim (known as the 'Feast of Esther') A Jewish festival celebrating the legendary foiling by Esther, the beautiful Jewish wife of the Persian king, of his countrymen's plot to slaughter the Persian Jews. *Pur* means 'lot', and recalls the casting of lots by the vizier Haman to set the date for their annihilation. Thanks to Esther the plot was uncovered and the fateful date was chosen by the Jews to trigger the slaughter of the Persians. Readings from the Book of Esther commemorate the salvation of the Persian Jews.

Puritan A member of the more extreme English Protestants who were dissatisfied with the Anglican Church settlement and sought a further purification of the English Church from ROMAN CATHOLIC elements. Their theology was basically that of John CALVIN. At first they limited themselves to attacking 'popish' (Roman Catholic) practices – church ornaments, vestments, and organ music – but from 1570 extremists attacked the authority (episcopacy) of bishops and government notably in the Martin Marprelate tracts. However, James I resisted their attempts to change Anglican dogma, ritual, and organization, voiced at the HAMPTON COURT CONFERENCE. In the 1620s some emigrated to North America, but it was the policies of LAUD and Charles I in the 1630s that resurrected the Puritan opposition of the 1580s. The doctrine of Predestination (that God ordains in advance those who shall receive salvation) became a major source of contention between the Puritans, for whom it was a fundamental article of faith, and the Arminians who rejected it. Religion was a key factor leading to the outbreak of civil war in 1642. Puritanism was strong among the troops of the NEW MODEL ARMY and in the 1640s and 1650s, with the encouragement of Cromwell, Puritan objectives were realized. After the Restoration they were mostly absorbed into the Anglican Church or into larger NONCONFORMISTS groups and lost their distinctive identity.

purple emperor butterfly A dark brown butterfly with a white band and spots; males have a rich purple or blue iridescence. There are several species of the genus *Apatura*, within the BRUSH-FOOTED BUTTERFLY family, which occur in Europe and Asia, with one British species. They are powerful fliers, generally soaring high above the treetops, but are attracted down by carrion. The adults never visit flowers, feeding instead on honeydew.

purpura A skin rash resulting from bleeding into the skin from small blood vessels. Senile purpura is a harmless condition of the elderly. However, purpura may also occur in younger people as a result of defects in the capillaries or to a deficiency of blood PLATELETS. Henoch-Schönlein purpura occurs in young children and is characterized by red weals and a purple rash on the buttocks and elsewhere, due to bleeding from inflamed capillaries.

pus A yellow fluid, containing lipids, proteins, cell debris, and bacteria. It is formed from the decomposition of cells destroyed by neutrophil LEUCOCYTES in the blood, which migrate to infected tissues as a defence against invading bacteria. Boils, abscesses, etc., contain pus.

Pusan A seaport on the south-east coast of the Korean peninsula, the second-largest city and principal port of South Korea; pop. (1990) 3,797,570. It has shipyards, as well as iron and steel, machinery, and textiles industries.

Pusey, Edward Bouverie (1800–82) British theologian. In 1833, while professor of Hebrew at Oxford, he founded the Oxford Movement together with John Henry Newman and John Keble; he became leader of the Movement after the withdrawal of Newman (1841). His many writings include a series of *Tracts for the Times* and a statement of his doctrinal views *The Doctrine of the Real Presence* (1856–57).

Pushkin, Aleksandr (Sergeevich) (1799–1837) Russian poet, novelist, and dramatist. His revolutionary beliefs and atheistic writings led to his dismissal from the civil service and eventual internal exile; he was rehabilitated in 1826 after the accession of Nicholas I. A leading figure in Russian literature, he wrote prolifically in many genres; his first success was the romantic narrative poem *Ruslan and Ludmilla* (1820). Other notable works include the verse novel *Eugene Onegin* (1833), and the blank-verse historical drama *Boris Godunov* (1831). He was fatally wounded in a duel with his wife's admirer.

Puskas, Ferenc (1927–) Hungarian footballer. A striker, he came to prominence in the celebrated Hungarian national team of the early 1950s. In 1956 he left Hungary to play for Real Madrid, scoring four goals in their 1960 European Cup Final victory and a hat trick in the corresponding 1962 final, in which Real Madrid lost.

puss moth A fat-bodied, furry moth, *Cerura vinula*, with white fore-wings delicately etched with grey. The caterpillars are green with a white-edged, purplish-brown saddle and a forked tail; when irritated, they rear up, exposing a red false face, protrude a pair of lashing threads from the tail, and squirt formic acid. The family to which the puss moth belongs, Notodontidae, comprises the PROMINENT MOTHS.

putrefaction The DECOMPOSITION of organic materials, usually anaerobically (without the presence of oxygen), by bacteria. The breakdown of protein substances in a deoxygenated environment leads to the formation of compounds with unpleasant odours: it releases gaseous products which are subject to further oxidation, such as methane. An example is the smell produced by the breakdown of proteins in rotting meat.

Puttnam, Sir David (Terence) (1941–) British film director. After a series of polished low-budget features Puttnam directed the internationally acclaimed *Chariots of Fire* (1981), which won four Oscars. Its success enabled him to explore human and moral dilemmas on a larger scale in such films as *The Killing Fields* (1984) and *The Mission* (1986). He became chairman and chief executive of Columbia

Pictures in 1986, but returned to Britain a year later. Later films include *Memphis Belle* (1990), *Meeting Venus* (1991), and *Being Human* (1993).

Puyi (or **P'u-i**) (1906–67) Last QING emperor of China 1908–12. Proclaimed emperor at the age of two by the empress dowager CIXI (his great aunt), he reigned until the CHINESE REVOLUTION forced his abdication in 1912. He continued to live in the imperial palace until forced to flee by a local warlord to Tianjin in 1924. After the Japanese seizure of Manchuria, Puyi was placed at the head of the puppet state of MANCHUKUO. Deposed and captured by Soviet forces in 1945, he was later handed over to the communist Chinese, and eventually allowed to live out his life as a private citizen.

PVC (polyvinyl chloride) A thermoplastic (see PLASTICS) made from vinyl chloride (chloroethene, C_2H_3Cl), itself derived from ETHENE. PVC is a colourless solid with outstanding resistance to water, alcohols, and concentrated acids and alkalis. It is obtainable as granules, solutions, lattices, and pastes. When compounded with PLASTICIZERS, it yields a flexible material more durable than RUBBER. It is widely used for cable and wire insulation, in chemical plants, and in the manufacture of protective garments. Blow MOULDING of unplasticized PVC (uPVC) produces clear, tough bottles which do not affect the flavour of their contents. uPVC is also used for drains and other types of tube or pipe.

PVD (physical vapour deposition) See VAPOUR DEPOSITION.

PWR See PRESSURIZED-WATER REACTOR.

Pygmalion In Greek mythology, a king of Cyprus who fell in love with the statue of a beautiful woman (in some accounts he carved it himself). He prayed to Aphrodite to give him a wife as beautiful as the statue, and the goddess brought the statue to life; Pygmalion married the woman so created (sometimes called Galatea).

pygmy A widely scattered peoples characterized by their shortness of stature. The most notable of these are the Mbuti, who live in the Ituri Forest of the Congo. They are HUNTER-GATHERERS, but they also have social and economic ties with agricultural peoples living at the edge of the forest. The Mbuti are subservient in their relations with these neighbours, but when they live among themselves in the forest, their society is remarkably egalitarian.

pygopodid A legless LIZARD belonging to a family found in Australia. These snake-like creatures do not burrow into the soil like many similar families of legless lizards, but hunt other species of lizards for food. The widespread Burton's legless lizard, *Lialis burtonis*, grows to 30 cm (12 inches) in length.

Pym, Barbara (Mary Crampton) (1913–80) British novelist. During the 1950s she wrote a number of novels dealing satirically with English middle-class village life, including *Excellent Women* (1952) and *Less than Angels* (1955). Having endured a period of unfashionability in the 1960s and 1970s, she published more novels, including *Quartet in Autumn* (1977), which gained her fresh recognition.

Pynchon, Thomas (Ruggles) (1937–) US novelist. He is an elusive author who shuns public attention, while his works, experimental and often esoteric, abandon the normal conventions of the novel. They include *V* (1963), *The Crying of Lot 49* (1966), *Gravity's Rainbow* (1972), the collection of short stories *Slow Learner* (1984), and *Vineland* (1989).

Pyongyang The capital of North Korea, on the Taedong River; pop. (est. 1994) 2,000,000. The oldest city on the Korean peninsula, it was first mentioned in records of 108 BC. It fell to the Japanese in the late 16th century and was devastated by the Manchus in the early 17th century. It developed as an industrial city during the years of Japanese occupation, from 1910 to 1945. It is North Korea's principal industrial centre with iron and steel, machinery, railway, and textile industries.

pyramid A monumental structure especially characteristic of ancient Egypt, often built as a royal tomb and usually made of stone, with a square base and sloping sides meeting centrally at an apex. At first the pharaohs were buried in underground chambers over which were built rectangular *mastabas*; these were stone structures housing the food and accoutrements the pharaoh would need in the afterlife. Although all the interior tombs were sealed, often with elaborate devices to prevent entry, all the pyramids were robbed of their valuables in antiquity. The first pyramid was that constructed for King Zoser at Saqqara by IMHOTEP *c.*2700 BC, the so-called Step Pyramid which has six enormous steps and is over 60 m (197 ft) high. Most of the best known pyramids date from the Old Kingdom (*c.*2700–2200 BC), though some were built during the eleventh and twelfth dynasties (*c.*2050–1750 BC). The pyramids of Khufu, Khafre, and Menkaure at Giza are a spectacular illustration of the skill of Egyptian architects – and of the state's ability to organize a large workforce. The Great Pyramid of Giza, constructed of enormous stone blocks of up to 200 tonnes in weight, is estimated to have required a labour force equivalent to about 84,000 people employed for 80 days a year for 20 years.

Stepped pyramids known as ziggurats survive from the 3rd millennium BC in Mesopotamia. Stepped-pyramid structures were also built as bases for temples in pre-Columbian Central America. These were erected by the MAYAS, AZTECS, and TOLTECS, for the most part between 250 AD and 1520. The Temple of the Sun in TEOTIHUACÁN in Mexico is perhaps the most impressive.

Pyramus and Thisbe The tragic Babylonian lovers of classical legend, immortalized in Shakespeare's *A Midsummer Night's Dream* (*c.*1595). As related by the poet Ovid, the lovers, forbidden to marry, planned to elope. Pyramus killed himself when he mistakenly thought that Thisbe had been devoured by a lion, and Thisbe killed herself on finding Pyramus dead. Their blood was said to have turned the mulberries on a nearby tree, previously white, to red.

Pyrenees (French **Pyrénées**; Spanish **Pirineos**) A range of mountains extending along the border between France and Spain from the Atlantic coast to the Mediterranean. Its highest point is the Pico de Aneto in Spain (3,404 m, 11,168 ft). The Gouffre de la Pierre St Martin below the Pic d'Arlas is one of the deepest caves in the world and the Grotte Casteret is the highest ice cave in Europe. The glacier on the north side of the Pico de la Maladetta is the largest ice field in the Pyrenees.

pyrethrum A group of perennial, herbaceous plants now included in the *Chrysanthemum* genus. The garden forms are derived from *C. coccineum*, a variable species from Iran and the Caucasus, and have divided, fern-like leaves and large daisy-like flowers in red, pink, or white. The INSECTICIDE pyrethrum is produced from the closely related *C. cinerariifolium*.

pyrite (or **iron pyrites**) An iron sulphide mineral (FeS_2), yellow-gold in colour, and with a cubic crystal form (also known as fool's gold). It is hard and will spark if hit with a hammer. It is currently used in the production of sulphuric acid, but it has been mined as an ore of sulphur.

pyroclast A fragment of lava that has been ejected from a volcano and blown into the atmosphere. When ejected in a molten state pyroclasts quickly cool and form PUMICE, scoria, volcanic bombs, or hairs. If already solid when ejected they produce ashes and ignimbrites. Rocks that are formed in this way are **pyroclastic rocks**.

pyroxene A mineral group that includes some of the most common rock-forming silicates. The group contains six main members (enstatite, ferrosilite, diopside, augite, pigeonite, and jadeite) of varying chemical formulae, most of which combine magnesium and calcium with iron or aluminium (or both) in the silicate structure. Pyroxenes occur both in igneous and in metamorphic rocks.

Pyrrho (*c.*365–*c.*270 BC) Greek philosopher. Regarded as the founder of scepticism, he established the Pyrrhonic school of philosophy at Elis. He held that certainty of knowledge is impossible and that true happiness must therefore come from suspending judgement.

Pyrrhus (*c.*318–272 BC) King of Epirus *c.*307–272. After invading Italy in 280, he defeated the Romans at Asculum in 279, but sustained heavy losses, hence a **Pyrrhic victory** is one in which the cost to the victor is excessive.

Pythagoras (*c.*580–500 BC) Greek philosopher, born at Samos. Pythagoras is said to have discovered the numerical ratios determining the intervals of the musical scale, leading to his attempt at interpreting the entire physical world in terms of numbers, and founding their systematic (and mystical) study. His followers were known as Pythagoreans. It is probable that the well-known **theorem of Pythagoras** (that in a right-angled triangle the square on the hypotenuse is equal to the sum of the squares on the other two sides) was discovered by the later Pythagoreans in southern Italy. In astronomy, his analysis of the courses of the Sun, Moon, and stars into circular motions was not set aside until the 17th century. Pythagoras also founded a secret religious, political, and scientific sect in Italy: the Pythagoreans held that the soul is condemned to a cycle of reincarnation, from which it may escape by attaining a state of purity.

Pytheas (*fl.* 300 BC) Greek navigator, geographer, and astronomer; the first Greek to visit and describe the Atlantic coast of Europe and the British Isles. Born at Massalina, Gaul (Marseilles, France), Pytheas sailed from the Mediterranean into the Atlantic, stopping at the Phoenecian city of Gades (Cadiz, Spain), and on to Belerium (Land's End, England) where he visited the tin mines of Cornwall, famous in the ancient world. Claiming to have explored a large part of the British Isles on foot, he accurately estimated its circumference as 6,400 km (4,000 miles). He was one of the first to fix LATITUDES by observing the Sun's altitude at a given time of day, to note that the Pole Star is not at the true pole, and to realize that TIDES are connected with the Moon.

python Any one of about 20 species of snake of the family Boidae, which occur in warm regions from Africa to Australia, and are absent from the Americas and Madagascar, where they are replaced by BOAS. They resemble boas in retaining claw-like vestigial hind-limbs, but differ in being egg-layers (boas bear live young). The female pythons coil their bodies over the eggs for the six- to eight-week incubation period. Pythons are found in a wide range of habitats: some species live close to water and are extremely fast swimmers; many climb trees and bushes. They feed mainly on small mammals and birds, which they kill by constriction. Their upper and lower jaws are well endowed with teeth, which are backward-pointing and, although not venom-producing, will hold prey firmly in the mouth. Most pythons have heat-sensitive sensitive pits in their upper lips, similar in function to the facial pit of PIT VIPERS, which assist the snake to locate its prey. The reticulated (or royal) python, *Python reticulatus*, from Asia, is the largest snake of the Old World, growing to a length of 10 m (33 feet).

Pyxis The Compass, a CONSTELLATION of the Southern Hemisphere, introduced by the 18th-century French astronomer Nicolas Louis de Lacaille and representing a ship's magnetic compass. Its brightest stars are of only fourth magnitude.

Q

Qaddafi See GADDAFI.

Qatar A country of Arabia. It is bounded by Saudi Arabia inland and BAHRAIN to its west.

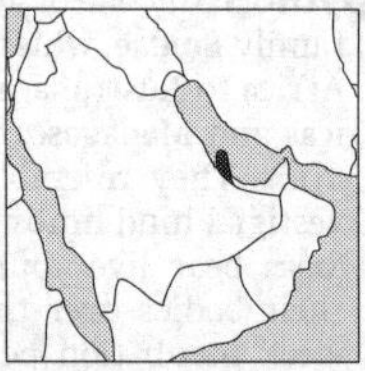

Physical. Qatar is a hot arid country occupying a peninsula of desert on the southwest of the Persian Gulf.

Economy. The economy and exports of Qatar are dominated by crude oil, which is present in very large quantities both on-shore and off-shore. Industries include oil-refining, gas liquefaction, fertilizers, cement, and steel. Due to its oil wealth the country has one of the highest per capita incomes in the world. In 1987, native Qataris constituted less than a quarter of the total population, the remainder being immigrant workers.

History. Historically linked with Bahrain, Qatar was under Bahraini suzerainty for much of the 19th century. In 1872 it came under Ottoman suzerainty, but the Ottomans renounced their rights in 1913. In 1916 Qatar made an agreement with Britain which created a *de facto* British protectorate. Oil was discovered in 1939 and exploited from 1949. The agreement with Britain was terminated in 1968 and Qatar became fully independent in 1971, under a constitution by which the Emir, Shaikh Khalifa bin Hamad al-Thani would govern as Prime Minister. Qatar provided bases for UN forces in the GULF WAR, after which it strengthened its links with Iran. In 1995 the Emir was overthrown in a bloodless coup by his son, Shaikh Hamad bin Khalifa al-Thani, who embarked on a programme of liberal reforms. This has caused mounting tension with Bahrain and Saudi Arabia and led to an attempted coup in 1996.

Capital: Doha
Area: 11,337 sq km (4,377 sq mi)
Population: 579,100 (1995)
Currency: 1 Qatar riyal = 100 dirhams
Religions: Muslim (mainly Sunni) 92%; Christian 6.0%; Hindu 1.0%; Baha'i 0.2%
Ethnic Groups: South Asian 34.0%; Qatari Arab 20.0%; other Arab 25.0%; Iranian 16.0%
Languages: Arabic (official); South Asian languages; Persian
International Organizations: UN; Arab League; OAPEC

Qattara Depression An extensive, low-lying and largely impassable area of desert in north-east Africa, to the west of Cairo. Falling to 133 m (436 ft) below sea-level, it extends over *c*.18,100 sq km (7,000 sq miles).

Qin (or **Ch'in**) (221–206 BC) China's first imperial dynasty. It was founded by Prince Zheng, ruler of the ZHOU vassal state of Qin. Unlike rival Chinese states, Qin used cavalry not chariots in battle and early adopted iron weaponry. It ensured a regular food supply by developing a system for land irrigation. Based in Shaanxi, it began to expand its territories *c*.350 BC. Under Zheng, it overthrew the Eastern Zhou and conquered (256–221 BC) all Zhou's former vassal states. Zheng then took the title Huangdi and is best known as Shi Huangdi (First Emperor). He died in 210 BC and his dynasty was overthrown four years later. From that time, though China was sometimes fragmented, the concept of a united empire prevailed. From Qin is derived the name China.

Qing (or **Ch'ing**) (1644–1912) The last dynasty to rule China. Its emperors were MANCHUS. In 1644 a MING general, Wu Sangui, invited Manchu Bannermen massed at Shanhaiguan, the undefended eastern end of the Great Wall of China, to expel the bandit chieftain Li Zicheng from Beijing. The Bannermen occupied the city and proclaimed their child-emperor 'Son of Heaven'. Resistance continued for up to 30 years in south China. Chinese men were forced to braid their long hair into a queue or 'pigtail'. But Qing rule differed little from that of Chinese dynasties. It emphasized study of the Confucian classics (see CONFUCIAN LITERATURE) and the Confucian basis of society (see CONFUCIANISM). The empire of China reached its widest extent, covering Taiwan, Manchuria, Mongolia, Tibet, and Turkistan. The Qing regarded all other peoples as barbarians and their rulers as subject to the 'Son of Heaven', and were blind to the growing pressure of the West. Under KANGXI (1654–1722) and Qianlong (1736–96) China was powerful enough to treat the outside world with condescension.

Thereafter, however, the authority of the dynasty was reduced. Faced with major internal revolts, most notably the TAIPING REBELLION (1850–64) and a succession of Muslim uprisings in the far west, the Qing proved unable to contend simultaneously with increasing intrusions from western powers interested in the economic exploitation of China. Humiliating defeat in the SINO-JAPANESE WAR (1894–95) and the BOXER RISING (1900) weakened Qing power, and after the CHINESE REVOLUTION OF 1911, the last Qing emperor PUYI was forced to abdicate in 1912.

quadrant Probably the earliest astronomical instrument to be used at sea, consisting of a flat plate in the shape of a quarter-circle, with a plumb-line suspended from the apex. The handheld quadrant is held in a vertical plane with the right angle away from the eye and the curved edge downwards. One of the straight edges is equipped with a pair of metal pinhole sights, which are aligned with an astronomical object and the hanging cord reads off the altitude of this object above the horizon on the circular scale. It was used in the 15th century to measure the altitude (height above the horizon) of a celestial body, usually the pole star.

quadratic equation An algebraic equation in which the highest power of the variable is two; it has the general form $ax^2 + bx + c = 0$, which has two ROOTS $x = [-b \pm (b^2 - 4ac)^{1/2}]/2a$. The sum of the roots is $-b/a$ and their product is c/a.

Quadruple Alliance An alliance formed in 1813 by Britain, Prussia, Austria, and Russia that committed them to the defeat of Napoleon. At the Battle of LEIPZIG (1813) Napoleon was decisively defeated.

quagga An extinct subspecies of the plains ZEBRA, *Equus burchelli*, which once lived in southern Africa. It has been exterminated by man, the last survivor having died in a Dutch zoo in 1883. It was much less prominently striped than other plains zebras, and the hind region was almost plain coloured.

quahog See CLAM.

quail A small bird belonging to the pheasant family, Phasianidae. Quails are short-tailed, and measure no more than 25 cm (10 inches) in length. The best known of the New World species are the bobwhite, *Colinus virginianus*, and the California quail, *Lophortyx californica*; both of which are brownish above, and mottled and barred below. They also have striking black and white face patterns, the California quail having a black plume standing vertically on the top of its head and curving slightly forwards. The best-known Old World species is the common quail, *Coturnix coturnix*, a species that has a wide range over Europe, Asia, and much of southern Africa. The European birds migrate over the Mediterranean to Africa for the winter. The Japanese quail, *Coturnix japonica*, is known to preferentially mate with distant relatives.

Quakers (formal name **The Society of Friends**) A Christian body that rejects the formal structures of CREED and SACRAMENTS and usually of clergy and LITURGY, emphasizing instead the individual's search for 'inner light'. Founded by the Englishman George FOX in the 17th century, the Quakers became convinced that their 'experimental' discovery of God – sometimes featuring trembling or quaking experiences during meetings – would lead to the purification of all Christendom. The name 'Quaker' was originally a term of contempt but is now widely used.

By 1660 there were more than 20,000 converts, and missionaries were at work in Ireland, Scotland, Wales, and the American colonies. They continued to grow in number, despite severe penalization from 1662 to 1689 for refusing to take oaths, attend Anglican services, or pay tithes. After considerable debate, they evolved their present form of organization, with regular monthly, quarterly, and annual meetings.

In 1681 William PENN founded the American Quaker colony of PENNSYLVANIA, and Quaker influence in the colony's politics remained paramount until the American War of Independence.

quality control A system for ensuring that predetermined standards are met in a process. A number of stages can be involved: a check that materials received for the production process are of sufficient quality and consistency; a check that quality standards are being maintained during the production process; finally, a check that the finished product meets quality standards, carried out by inspecting a sample of each production batch (see MASS PRODUCTION). Modern techniques have concentrated on two areas to improve quality: the human and the mechanistic. Following Japanese methods, staff may be formed into 'quality circles' representing all grades of workers and concentrating together on the improvement of quality in specific areas. Total quality management (TQM) is a development of quality control in which these human factors are stressed. Quality control is a vital activity. If defective products are not detected before delivery, not only are costs incurred, but the organization's reputation may suffer. The concept of **servqual** provides a marketing strategy in which a high level of service to the customers is combined with high and consistent quality of the product.

quango (quasi-autonomous non-governmental organization) A special agency or body, often of a regulatory nature, ostensibly of independent standing, and typically straddling the public-private boundary in the economy. Quangos usually receive financial support from the government, which makes senior appointments. Examples include broadcasting authorities and supervisory bodies in the service industries. The proliferation of quangos reflects recognition that private interests need to be regulated for the public good in certain situations.

Quant, Mary (1934–) British fashion designer. She was a principal creator of the '1960s look', launching the miniskirt in 1966 and promoting bold colours and geometric designs. She was one of the first to design for the ready-to-wear market, and her styles, created especially for the young, did much to make London a leading fashion centre.

quantity theory of money (in economics) A theory of the price level summarized in the equation developed by the economist FISHER: MV = PT, where M is the MONEY SUPPLY, V is velocity (the speed at which money circulates round the economy), P is the general price level, and T represents the total volume of goods and services transacted. The equation in itself is an identity. The quantity theory assumes T and V to be (approximately) constant, so that P is proportional to, and determined by, M. MONETARISTS interpret the equation as indicating that INFLATION (a rise in P) is caused by the money supply (M) growing faster than the economy's capacity to produce goods and services (T). The theory has been criticized on a number of grounds: for instance, that neither V nor T are constant, and that M cannot be adequately monitored or controlled by the authorities.

Quantock Hills (or **the Quantocks**) A range of hills north of Taunton in Somerset, south-west England, rising to a height of 385 m (1,261 ft).

quantum mechanics The general mathematical technique used to calculate the way atomic and subatomic particles move when they are acted on by FORCES, especially those produced by electromagnetic fields. It is particularly useful for predicting the energies of electrons in their charge clouds surrounding the nucleus of the ATOM. The size and shape of the charge cloud can also be determined. The principle underlying the mathematics is that the particle is represented by a wave that can either extend over a large distance or be a short pulse localized at one place. The AMPLITUDE of the wave at any point is a measure of the probability that the particle will be at that point, and the wavelength of the wave is a measure of its momentum (and hence its energy): the shorter the wavelength, the greater the momentum. Since a wave must always extend a certain distance, be it large (for an extended wave) or small (for a pulse), it follows that the position of a particle it represents cannot be fixed or known precisely; and this can be seen as one explanation of the UNCERTAINTY PRINCIPLE.

quantum number Any of the integral or half-integral numbers used to express the magnitude (in terms of the PLANCK constant) of physical quantities that cannot be subdivided, especially those of an electron in its charge cloud around the nucleus of an atom, but also of all the other ELEMENTARY PARTICLES. The numbers give a measure of various attributes of a particle, some of which could be envisaged in terms of the properties of macroscopic bodies. For electrons these attributes are angular momentum (denoted by *l*), magnetic moment (*m*), and spin (*s*), because in many ways they obey the same rules as these quantities in the macroscopic world. In particle physics, however, further attributes or quantum numbers are required in order to account for all the phenomena. These cannot be associated with anything with which we are familiar. This has resulted in the use of such terms as charm, strangeness, and colour, which bear no relation to the everyday meaning of these words.

quantum theory The theory based on the existence of quanta of energy. It originated with the ideas of Max PLANCK and Albert EINSTEIN in the early years of the 20th century. Planck suggested that electromagnetic energy is quantized, i.e. it can be gained or lost only in discrete quanta or packets called PHOTONS. This enabled him to explain the spectral distribution of the radiation emitted by a BLACK BODY at any given temperature. Einstein took the idea a step further in 1905 and proposed that all forms of energy exist as quanta, and this notion was used with success by him and by the Dutch physicist Peter Debye (1884–1966) to calculate the energy of vibrating atoms and the HEAT CAPACITY of solids. These ideas were extended by Neils BOHR when he proposed that the electrons surrounding the nucleus of the atom could only have quantized amounts of angular momentum. His theory postulated a set of precise orbits for these electrons, each orbit having a special energy. If an electron moved from an orbit of high energy to one of lower energy its excess energy would be emitted as a single quantum of radiation with a particular frequency. The sharp spectral lines emitted by atoms were explained by this theory and for hydrogen and other simple atoms there was close correlation between the Bohr values and experimental values. In spite of the success of the theory, however, it was not wholly satisfactory because it was unable to explain why the angular momentum of the electron should be quantized and also why the electrons orbiting the nucleus did not continuously emit radiation, which was the prediction of classical electromagnetic theory. These objections were overcome in a new theory which used QUANTUM MECHANICS and other more sophisticated mathematical techniques. These still predicted the set of fixed energies the electrons are permitted to have; but the idea that they travel in orbits round the nucleus was replaced by the concept of a statistical cloud, or ORBITAL, which indicated the probable position of an electron at any instant. Each orbital corresponds to a particular energy determined mainly by the electrical charge of the nucleus, electrons in the orbitals nearer the nucleus having a lower energy than those in orbitals further away. Each electron is normally constrained to occupy a single orbital, and there is a limit to the number of electrons that can simultaneously exist in one orbital. If there is a vacancy in an orbital of low energy, an electron from a higher-energy orbital can move into the lower-energy orbital; its excess energy, *E*, is emitted as a single photon of a particular frequency ν. The frequency is given by the relation: $E = h\nu$, where *h* is the Planck constant and has a value of 6.626196×10^{-34} J s. These processes of electron transitions between orbitals are responsible for the visible radiation emitted by STARS. Quantum theory also describes the internal behaviour of atomic nuclei and how they combine by nuclear FUSION, the source of energy in most stars.

quarantine The time during which a person or animal is kept in isolation because they have, or are suspected of having, an infectious disease. The quarantine period is usually somewhat longer than the incubation period of the disease, so that if no symptoms appear during quarantine the person can be regarded as free of the infection. All domestic animals imported into the UK have to remain in quarantine for six months; this policy has been effective in preventing rabies from occurring in the UK. Quarantine (from French *quarantaine*) was originally the 40-day period during which a ship suspected of carrying people with an infection had to wait at sea before docking.

quark (in particle physics) The constituents of the ELEMENTARY PARTICLES known as hadrons. Six main types of quark have been established, and these are labelled by 'flavours': u (up), d (down), c (charmed), s (strange), t (top), and b (bottom or beauty). The hypothesis is elaborate. The u, c, and t quarks have an electric charge of +2/3 of the charge on an electron, and the d, s, and b quarks a charge of −1/3. Each of these types is subdivided into three further groups, which are labelled with 'colours': r (red), b (blue), and g (green). (The choice of all these names is quite arbitrary, and is not related to the usual meanings of these words.) Thus there are 18 types of quark, and for each there is a corresponding antiquark, making a total of 36 types in all. All the hadrons known can be accounted for by a suitable combination of quarks. For example, the proton, with a charge of +1, is uud (2/3 + 2/3 − 1/3); the neutron, with zero charge, is udd. The quarks are held together by INTERACTIONS mediated by yet another set of particles, called gluons. All quarks have a spin of either +1/2 or −1/2, and thus a particle consisting of three quarks, called a baryon, will have a half-integral spin (1/2, 3/2, and so on). A particle composed of two quarks, a meson, will have either zero or integral spin (+1, −1). Free individual quarks do not appear to exist, they can only occur in combination with other quarks to form particles.

quarrying The extraction of granite, limestone, slate, or other stone from an open working. The process of obtaining coal and metallic ore from surface workings is known as OPEN-CAST MINING. There are two distinct types of quarrying. One involves the preparation of blocks of specific size and shape (dimension-stone quarrying) for building, paving, memorial stones, and so on. The second is the production of crushed and broken stone, for road-making and other civil engineering purposes, and for use in some chemical and metallurgical processes. For dimension-stone a first requirement is suitable deposits of uniform colour and texture. Explosives can be used only sparingly because of their shattering effect, and much of the stone is cut out with mechanical saws. Drilling-and-broaching is a method in which a row of holes is drilled close together; the solid areas between the holes are then broken down, using a broaching tool, to complete the cut. In quarrying for crushed stone, explosives are freely used and thousands of cubic metres may be thrown down in one firing. The stone is then taken away to be crushed and graded.

quartz One of the commonest minerals of the Earth's crust (12 per cent by volume), being pure silica or silicon dioxide (SiO_2). It can occur in crystal form (single crystals weighing as much as 130 kg or 290 pounds have been recorded), as concretionary masses, or as fine-grained coloured nodules. In pure form, referred to as rock-crystal, it is transparent and colourless, but more commonly it is white or translucent. Semiprecious coloured quartz can be blue, smoky, rose, yellow, or AMETHYST. Quartz occurs in both intrusive and extrusive igneous rocks. It is an extremely important mineral for industry because of the PIEZOELECTRIC EFFECT; it is used also as an abrasive, in paints, for carving, and as semiprecious gemstones.

quartz clock, **quartz watch** See CLOCKS AND TIME MEASUREMENT; WATCH.

quartzite A metamorphosed quartz-rich sandstone, typically produced by recrystallization at fairly high temperatures. Quartzites are pale in colour, often white. Highly durable, they are used in the building industry as a construction material. They are widespread in occurrence and very common in the Scottish Highlands. Quartzite is also sometimes used for unmetamorphosed quartz sandstones, or orthoquartzites.

quasar (or **quasi-stellar object**) A star-like object that emits the energy of hundreds of normal galaxies. Its original name, 'quasi-stellar object', has been shortened to 'quasar'. The nature of quasars is not well understood. They exhibit very large RED SHIFTS of their spectral lines, so if the Hubble Law is applied, such objects must be the farthest known objects in the Universe. One theory suggests they are the highly luminous centres of galaxies in which BLACK HOLES drag material into them by their massive gravitational fields. Some quasars exhibit significant and rapid changes in luminosity.

Quasimodo, **Salvatore** (1901–68) Italian poet. His early work was influenced by French symbolism. Major collections include *Water and Land* (1930) and *And It's Suddenly Evening* (1942). His later work is more extrovert and concerned with political and social issues. He was awarded the Nobel Prize for literature in 1959.

quassia A tree of which there are 40 species in the genus *Quassia*, native to the tropics, particularly the Americas. They are evergreen, the most important being quassia wood or bitter quassia, *Q. amara*, a tree 6 m (20 feet) tall with divided leaves. Its bitter wood and root was formerly much used in medicine.

Quaternary Period The period of geological time that follows the TERTIARY. It comprises the PLEISTOCENE and the Holocene Epochs and spans the interval of time from 1.6 million years ago until the present day. The earlier part of the Quaternary is notable for the widespread glaciations that affected Europe and America and for changes in sea-level. *Homo sapiens* evolved during this period.

quatrain A verse STANZA of four lines, usually rhymed. The quatrain is the most commonly used stanza in most European languages. Most BALLADS and many HYMNS are composed in quatrains in which the second and fourth lines rhyme (ABCB or ABAB). A different rhyme-scheme known as the 'envelope stanza' (ABBA) was used by Tennyson in *In Memoriam* (1850). The rhyming four-line groups that make up the first eight or 12 lines of a SONNET are also known as quatrains.

Quebec (French **Québec**) ▶**1** A heavily forested province in eastern Canada; area 1,667,926 sq km (594,860 sq miles); pop. (1991) 6,895,960; chief cities, Quebec and Montreal. Originally inhabited by the Algonquin and Cree peoples, it was settled by the French from 1608, ceded to the British in 1763, and became one of the original four provinces in the Dominion of Canada in 1867. The majority of its residents are French-speaking and its culture is predominantly French. It has a certain amount of political independence from the rest of Canada, and is a focal point of French–Canadian nationalism, a movement that advocates independence for Quebec. A national referendum in 1992 rejected constitutional changes that included increasing Quebec's autonomy. Complete independence was again rejected, by an extremely narrow margin, in a provincial referendum in 1995. Its chief industries include oil and mineral refining, meat processing, and the manufacture of paper, pulp, iron and steel, motor vehicles, and dairy products. ▶**2** Its capital city, a port on the St Lawrence River, and industrial, cultural, and tourist centre; pop. (1991) 167,000; 645,550 (metropolitan area). Founded by the French explorer Champlain in 1608, it became capital of the royal province of New France in 1663. The city was eventually captured from the French by a British force under General James Wolfe in 1759 (see PLAINS OF ABRAHAM) and it became capital of Lower Canada (the mainly French-speaking region of Canada around the St Lawrence River) in 1791. Laval University, based on a seminary founded in 1663 by Quebec's first bishop, is the oldest French university in North America and the Basilica of Sainte-Anne-de-Beaupré stands on the oldest pilgrimage site (1658) in North America. The French Canadian Carnaval de Québec with its famous snow sculptures is held every February. Industries include shipbuilding and the manufacture of pulp and paper.

Quebec Liberation Front A French Canadian separatist movement. Set up in the early 1960s, it launched a terrorist and bombing campaign to secure the separation of QUEBEC Province from Canada. The Front de Libération du Québec (FLQ) was greatly encouraged when DE GAULLE used the separatist slogan *Vive le Québec Libre* (Long Live Free Quebec) while visiting Canada in 1967. But its terrorist activities proved unpopular; much more support was given to the constitutional Parti Québecois, which won a majority of the seats in the Quebec legislative assembly in 1976 and remains an important force in the province.

Quechua (or **Quichua**) An Amerindian people of Peru and neighbouring parts of Bolivia, Chile, Colombia, and Ecuador whose group of related languages is one of the two official languages of Peru.

Queen, **Ellery** The pseudonym of the cousins Frederic Dannay (1905–82) and Manfred Lee (1905–71), US writers of detective fiction. Their many detective novels, featuring the detective also called Ellery Queen, include *The French Powder Mystery* (1930). They went on to found and edit *Ellery Queen's Mystery Magazine* (1941).

Queen Anne style An English architectural style considered typical of the reign of Queen Anne (1702–14), or more loosely of the period *c.*1660–*c.*1720. It is a style mainly of domestic architecture, characterized by a Dutch-influenced use of red brick in basically rectangular designs, out of which the Georgian style grew. In the late 19th century the Queen Anne style was revived, often in a more elaborate and rich way, by Richard Norman Shaw and other architects. The Queen Anne style of furniture, dating from the first 20 years of the 18th century, is characterized by the use of walnut veneers, often with herringbone inlays, cabriole legs, and curved outlines.

Queen's Counsel (QC) See BARRISTER.

Queensland A state comprising the north-eastern part of Australia; area *c.*1,727,000 sq km (667,050 sq miles); pop. (1991) 2,999,900; capital, Brisbane. Originally established in 1824 as a penal settlement, it was constituted a separate colony in 1859, having previously formed part of New South Wales, and was federated with the other states of Australia in 1901. Mainly an agricultural state producing cattle, sugar-cane, wheat, and tropical fruits. There are huge deposits of coal, bauxite, copper, lead, silver, and zinc. Oil and natural gas are also exploited.

Quercia, Jacopo della (*c.*1374–1438) Italian sculptor of the Sienese School. He was one of the outstanding figures of his time in Italian sculpture, alongside DONATELLO and GHIBERTI. His major works included a public fountain for Siena (now, much damaged, in the loggia of the Palazzo Pubblico there), and reliefs on the portal of San Petronio, Bologna, commissioned in 1425 and left unfinished at his death. The figures have a directness and strength that won the admiration of Michelangelo when he visited Bologna in 1494.

quetzal A member of the trogon family of birds, Trogonidae. They live in tropical forests of Central and South America. The size of a small crow, they are brilliant green above and red below. By far the most striking is the resplendent quetzal, *Pharomachrus mocinno*, in which the male's upper tail-coverts are brilliant iridescent green, and extend for some 60 cm (2 feet) beyond the tail. They sit motionless on branches just below the canopy of the forest to attack passing insects and to pluck fruits off trees. They nest in holes in trees, laying two to four pale eggs.

Quetzalcóatl Literally 'quetzal-bird snake' – hence 'feathered serpent' – one of the chief gods of ancient Mesoamerica (Mexico and northern Central America). Quetzalcóatl was also the official title of the AZTEC high priest. As a god he was known throughout Mesoamerica and was called Kukulkán by the MAYA. Images and temples to him appear at early sites, such as as TEOTIHUACÁN, but he was especially revered *c.*700–1520.

Quezon, Manuel Luis (1878–1944) Filipino statesman, president (1935–44). He followed AGUINALDO in the Philippine wars against Spain and the USA (1896–1901). Later he served in the Philippines Assembly and became resident commissioner for the Philippines in Washington (1909–16). His successful conduct in this post made him a national hero and he was elevated to the office of President of the Philippine Senate. In 1935 he became first President of the newly constituted Philippine Commonwealth and ruled his country dictatorially until forced into exile by the Japanese invasion in 1942. He headed a government in exile in the USA until his death, and was succeeded by his Vice-President, Sergio Osmena.

Quezon City A city on the island of Luzon in the northern Philippines; pop. (1990) 1,667,000. Situated on the outskirts of Manila, Quezon City was established in 1940 and named after Manuel Luis QUEZON, the first President of the republic. From 1948 to 1976 it was the capital of the Philippines. It has a very large university founded in 1908.

Quiberon Bay A bay on the east side of the Quiberon Peninsula on the Côte Sauvage (Wild Coast) of the department of Morbihan in Brittany, north-west France. It was the scene of a naval battle, in November 1759 during the Seven Years War, in which the French were defeated by the British under Hawke and Boscawen.

quicklime See CALCIUM OXIDE.

quicksand An area of loose wet sand that easily yields to pressure and readily engulfs any heavy object from the surface. Quicksands are pools of water partially filled with sand, with an underlying layer of impervious clay or rock. They are found in estuaries or along flat stretches of streams or beaches. In some places they may result from the agitation of strong currents or tides, reverting to a normal and harmless part of the beach when the agitation has gone.

quince A tree or shrub native to southern Europe and Asia, closely related to JAPONICA and other plants of the rose family. The common quince, *Cydonia oblonga*, has been grown in Europe since Roman times for its golden-yellow, pear-shaped, aromatic fruits. Somewhat hard and too acidic to be a dessert fruit, they are used to make jam or jelly. The quince is also used as a rootstock for pears. Ornamental quinces belong to the genus *Chaenomeles*, and are small hardy shrubs, which produce attractive pink, red, or white flowers.

Quincey, Thomas De See DE QUINCEY.

Quine, Willard Van Orman (1908–) US philosopher and logician. A radical critic of modern empiricism, Quine took issue with the philosophy of language proposed by Rudolf Carnap, arguing that 'no statement is immune from revision' and that even the principles of logic themselves can be questioned and replaced. In *Word and Object* (1961) he held that there is no such thing as satisfactory translation. He also developed the work on the foundations of mathematics begun by Frege and Russell, specializing in the theory of sets, published in *Set Theory and Its Logic* (1963).

quinine See CINCHONA.

Quintilian (full name Marcus Fabius Quintilianus) (*c.*35–*c.*100 AD), Roman rhetorician. Born in Spain, he spent some years in Rome practising advocacy and teaching the art of public speaking. His learning and experience are distilled in *Training of an Orator*, which survived as an admired textbook in the Middle Ages and Renaissance.

Quisling, Vidkun Abraham Lauritz Jonsson (1887–1945) Norwegian fascist leader. An army officer, he founded the fascist Nasjonal Samling (National Unity) Party, and in 1940 helped Hitler to prepare the conquest of Norway. He became head of a new pro-German government and was made Premier in 1942. He remained in power until 1945, when he was arrested and executed. By this time 'Quisling' had become a derogatory term to describe traitors who supported invaders of their countries.

Quito The capital of Ecuador and its educational, cultural, and political centre, situated just south of the equator at an altitude of 2,850 m (9,350 ft) at the foot of Pichincha volcano in the Andes; pop. (est. 1995) 1,401,400. Built on the site of a pre-Columbian settlement taken by the Spanish in 1533, Quito gave its name to a Spanish presidency which became the independent republic of

Ecuador in 1830. It has diverse light industries and handicrafts, a historic cathedral, and two universities.

Qumran A region on the north-western shore of the Dead Sea in the Israeli-occupied West Bank, site of caves in which the Dead Sea scrolls were found (1947–56) and of the settlement of an ancient Jewish community (probably the Essenes) to whom these manuscripts belonged.

quotas (in economics) A limit on physical quantity, most commonly set upon output or imports. A CARTEL, such as OPEC, may allocate a quota to each producer in order to restrict supplies and keep the product price up to an agreed or target level. The success of such a strategy depends upon the willingness of individual producers to remain within their agreed quota. In international trade, a country or common market may set a maximum level of imports of a specified good in a given time (see PROTECTIONISM). Quotas may be preferred to tariffs if a country wants the absolute volume of imports to be kept below a certain level.

Qu Yuan (*c.*340–*c.*278 BC) China's first known poet. Qu is traditionally credited with the authorship of *Songs of the South* (*Songs of Chu*), a collection of elegiac poems from Chu, one of the Warring States. It is quite likely that he wrote *On Encountering Sorrow* (*Li Sao*), an allegory in which a spiritual quest represents the search for recognition of statesmanlike virtues. His death by drowning when he heard that Chu had been overthrown by the rival Warring State of Qin is still commemorated in China at the Dragon Boat Festival. The genre of poetic writing created by Qu Yuan was cultivated for more than five centuries.

Qwaqwa (or **QwaQwa**) A former homeland established by South Africa for the South Sotho people; pop. (1985) 183,000; capital, Phuthaditjhaba. Situated in the Drakensberg Mountains in Orange Free State, Qwaqwa was designated a self-governing national state in 1974.

R

Ra See RE.

Rabat The capital of Morocco, an industrial port with textile industries on the Atlantic coast on the south bank of the Oued Bou Regreg; pop. (1993) 1,220,000. It is one of the four Imperial Cities of Morocco and was founded by the Almohad dynasty in the 12th century when a fortified monastery *ribat* known as Ribat el Fath (Arabic, 'fort of victory') was built on the site of a Oudaida settlement. The new city was built after 1912 by General Lyautey during the period of the French protectorate.

rabbi (Hebrew, 'master') A Jewish religious teacher, and, after the Temple's destruction in 70 AD, any ordained exponent of Jewish Law (see TALMUD). Rabbi Judah (135–217 AD), compiler of the authoritative MISHNAH, is considered the rabbinic exemplar. The rabbi is not a priest and there is usually not a rabbi at every synagogue; he may conduct services and be invited to preach sermons, but he is not essential in, for example, Orthodox marriages. Rabbis are responsible for the religious instruction of the young, and are expected to marry and have children as an example to the community. Liberal, Reform, and Conservative Judaism now permit the ordination of women rabbis, but Orthodox Judaism does not.

rabbit A member of the mammalian order Lagomorpha, which also contains hares and pikas. There are two principal groups: the Old and New World rabbits. Of three species of Old World rabbit the most familiar is the European rabbit, *Oryctolagus cuniculus*, from which domestic rabbits are descended. Its original range was around the Mediterranean region but, through introductions, its distribution is now worldwide except for the tropics. New World rabbits, which include seven species of cottontails among a total of 14 species, occur southwards from southern Canada.

rabbit-eared bandicoot (or **bilby**) An Australian MARSUPIAL, *Macrotis lagotis* or *M. leucra*, so called because of its long rabbit-like ears and hopping gait. They are about the size of rabbits and live in burrows but otherwise are not similar, with their pointed snouts, long tails, and insectivorous diet.

rabbitfish A fish of the family Siganidae, widespread in the Indian and Pacific oceans, so-called because of the blunt snout and rabbit-like appearance of the jaws. About ten species are known, all shallow-water reef fishes, which feed on algae. The spines on the dorsal, anal, and pelvic fins (each pelvic fin has two spines) have a toxic mucus, which can cause painful wounds.

Rabelais, François (*c.*1494–1553) French satirist. He spent a period in his early life as a Franciscan monk; he also later worked as a physician. He is remembered for his sequence of allegorical works parodying medieval learning and literature, attacking asceticism, and affirming humanist values. These are marked by coarse humour and an imaginative and exuberant use of language, and include *Pantagruel* (*c.*1532) and *Gargantua* (1534). His influence on English literature has been widespread, though particularly marked on Butler, Swift, Sterne, and Joyce.

rabies A central nervous system infection caused by the rabies virus, which can infect a wide range of animals, such as dogs, foxes, raccoons, and vampire bats. It is transmitted by a bite or contact with saliva of infected animals; man is most commonly infected by a dog bite. In the UK, rabies has been eradicated by the application of strict QUARANTINE rules; in Europe, the fox is the main source of infection.

The virus enters the nervous system and makes its way to the brain along nerve fibres; hydrophobia is a characteristic symptom, with panic attacks and violent spasm of the diaphragm and larynx in response to the sight or sound of water. Rabies is invariably fatal. A vaccine is available for active IMMUNIZATION of people at high risk. Rabies immunoglobulin for passive immunization is also available and is used in people bitten by an animal suspected of carrying the rabies virus.

Rabin, Yitzhak (1922–95) Israeli general and statesman. Rabin was chief of staff of the Israeli army 1964–68, commanding the Israeli Defence Forces in the SIX-DAY WAR of June 1967 against Israel's Arab neighbours. As leader of the Labour Party, he was Prime Minister from 1974 until 1977. He regained leadership of the party and the premiership in 1992, and in the following year signed a peace accord with Yasser ARAFAT of the PALESTINE LIBERATION ORGANIZATION. This agreement brought Rabin the Nobel Peace Prize in 1994 (jointly with Arafat and Israeli Foreign Minister Shimon Peres). Arab and Jewish ultra-nationalists remained opposed to the settlement; while attending a peace rally in Tel Aviv in 1995, Rabin was assassinated by a Jewish right-wing extremist.

race A group, population, breed, or variety within a SPECIES, although because of difficulties in its definition race is rarely used in a scientific context.

Race is also sometimes used to divide humanity into different groups according to real or imagined common descent. Such divisions are usually based on physical characteristics, such as skin and hair colour, and shape of eyes and nose, which are related to the geographical origins of a particular group. In the 19th century, it was believed that human beings could be unambiguously classed as members of particular races, and that social and cultural differences could be explained on racial grounds. In the early 20th century Franz BOAS put forward the theory that racial typing on a purely physical basis was arbitrary and argued the cultural origin of mental differences. His approach became generally accepted, though the Nazis, who produced entirely spurious theories of race, burned his book. Human variation continues to be studied but the notion of 'race' as a rigid classification or genetic system has largely been abandoned.

raceme See FLOWER.

racemic mixture (in chemistry) A mixture of equal proportions of the two ENANTIOMERS of a compound showing OPTICAL ACTIVITY. One is dextrorotatory, rotating the plane of polarized light to the right as it passes through; the other is laevorotatory, rotating it to the left by a corresponding amount. The effects cancel and the mixture shows no optical activity.

Race Relations Act (1976) British Act of Parliament. It repealed the Acts of 1965 and 1968, strengthened the law on racial discrimination, and extended the 1968 ban on discrimination to housing, employment, insurance, and credit facilities. The Act also established (1977) a permanent Race Relations Commission to eliminate discrimination and to promote equality of opportunity and good relations between different racial groups within Britain, which by then had become a multiracial society, with the immigration of large numbers of Asians and West Indians. The Public Order Act of 1986 contained six offences of inciting racial hatred, while the Criminal Justice Act (1994) included a provision against racial harassment in its offence dealing with threatening behaviour.

Rachel One of the four Jewish matriarchs; the beloved second wife of Jacob. Tricked by his avaricious maternal uncle, Laban, into first marrying her elder sister, Leah, Jacob served him 14 years before marrying the younger Rachel. Childless for many years, Rachel eventually bore Joseph. She died giving birth to Benjamin.

Rachmaninov, Sergei (Vasilevich) (1873–1943) Russian composer and pianist, resident in the USA from 1917. He was a celebrated pianist and is primarily known for his compositions for piano, in particular the Prelude in C sharp minor (1892), the Second Piano Concerto (1901), and the *Rhapsody on a Theme of Paganini* (1934) for piano and orchestra. He also wrote three other piano concertos, as well as three symphonies and three operas. Rachmaninov, the last of the great Russian romantic composers, still commands large audiences.

Racine, Jean (1639–99) French dramatist. The principal tragedian of the French classical period, he drew on many different sources, including Greek and Roman literature (*Andromaque*, 1667; *Iphigénie*, 1674; *Phèdre*, 1677) and the Bible (*Athalie*, 1691). Like his contemporary Corneille he wrote within the constraints of the rules governing tragic composition that were derived from Aristotle, in particular observance of the three unities of time, place, and action.

racism The belief that human attributes are determined by race or ethnic group, often expressed as an assertion of superiority by one race or group over another, and prejudice against members of a different group. Often race is confused with culture, so that dislike of certain cultural practices is used to condemn a racial group as a whole. Racism is often an underlying issue in the political and economic factors that lead to world wars and strife. It is explicit in some political ideologies, such as that of the German NAZIS, whose belief that fair-haired Nordic peoples were superior to Jews and other 'non-Aryans' led to the GENOCIDE of millions of Jews, Slavs, and gypsies during Nazi rule (1933–45). Although these views are now totally discredited, racist policies have also been responsible for political systems such as apartheid in South Africa, which kept different races apart. Even where it is not institutionalized, a furtive racism may still have a great influence, affecting the access to education or employment that is given to ethnic groups.

racket A small double-reed musical instrument producing low notes. A series of bores drilled in one piece of wood or ivory are linked together by channels carved in the end caps, so that a single tube zigzags up and down, compressing a long tube into a short space. Renaissance rackets were cylindrically bored like CRUMHORNS.

Rackham, Arthur (1867–1939) British illustrator. He established his reputation as an artist of high imagination and Gothic invention with his edition of the Grimm brothers' *Fairy Tales* (1900). Rackham's best-known pictures appear in books, such as *Rip Van Winkle* (1905) and *Peter Pan* (1906), and were displayed in many galleries worldwide.

racoon A carnivore of the genus *Procyon*, which is related to coatis and kinkajou. They give their name to the family Procyonidae. Racoons range from southern Canada to northern South America. There are six species, of which the most widespread in the USA is the common racoon, *Procyon lotor*. They are heavily furred, with a long bushy tail, and their pelts are valued in trade. Racoons are found near water and take much of their food from streams, particularly frogs, crayfish, and fish. They also eat insects, small mammals, and a certain amount of vegetable matter, such as seeds and nuts.

radar (*ra*dio *d*etection *a*nd *r*anging) A device for remotely determining the direction, range, or presence of objects using centimetric radio waves. It is used in AIR-TRAFFIC CONTROL, for navigation by ships, aircraft, and some MISSILES, and in warning and detection systems. It provides a means of detecting objects over quite long distances or when visibility is poor. The principle of radar was first discovered in 1904 by the Austrian Karl Hülsmeier. In 1935 R. M. Page in the USA constructed a radar device that was used to determine the positions of aircraft. A comprehensive radar system, then called radio direction finding (RDF), was developed independently in the UK from 1935 by WATSON-WATT and others. The invention in 1939 of the magnetron, a THERMIONIC VALVE capable of producing pulsed radio waves of very high (microwave) frequencies, made radar a practical proposition, and it played a decisive role in World War II. From 1945 radar became commercially available.

Radar measures the distance of an object from a radar transmitter by timing the interval between the transmission of a pulse of radio waves and the reception of the echo of the pulse from the object. The distance can be calculated from the time interval because the speed of the radio waves (the speed of light) is known. The pulses of radio waves are usually directed in a narrow beam from the transmitting ANTENNA, enabling the bearing of the object to be determined. Usually, the radar antenna rotates continuously, so that the radar beam is scanned through 360 degrees. The positions of objects detected by the radar are normally displayed on a plan position indicator (PPI), in which the radar transmitter is at the centre of the screen, and the objects detected appear as bright spots or areas of light.

radar astronomy The transmission of radio waves to nearby astronomical objects and analysis of the echoes received. Since the strength of the radar echo from an astronomical object varies inversely as the fourth power of the distance, radar astronomy is restricted to investigation of the Solar System. Echoes have been received from seven planets and some of their major satellites using the world's largest RADIO TELESCOPES, including the 305 m (1,000 foot) diameter telescope at the Arecibo Radio Observatory, Puerto Rico. Such studies yield data on the topography of planets and on the properties of the material several metres below the surface, since echoes can usually be detected from depths of up to about ten wavelengths.

Radcliffe, Mrs Ann (1764–1823) British novelist. She was a leading exponent of the Gothic novel and influenced the work of other writers, including Byron, Shelley, and Charlotte Brontë. Her novels include *The Mysteries of Udolpho* (1794) and *The Italian* (1797).

Radhakrishnan, Sir Sarvepalli (1888–1975) Indian philosopher and statesman, President 1962–67. A teacher of philosophy at Mysore, Calcutta, and Oxford universities, he introduced some of the main ideas of classical Indian philosophy to the West. Major works include *Indian Philosophy* (1923–27) and *Eastern Religions and Western Thought* (1939). Radhakrishnan was Indian ambassador to the Soviet Union (1949–52) before returning to India in 1952 to become Vice-President under Nehru; he was elected President ten years later.

radial velocity The component of a star's intrinsic VELOCITY along the line of sight. It may be determined from the DOPPLER effect by measuring the shift in optical or radio spectral lines. Any measurement of radial velocity is made relative to the Earth and so an allowance must be made for the Earth's motion about the Sun.

radian The plane angle subtended at the centre of a circle by an arc that is equal in length to the radius of the circle. The whole circumference of a circle subtends at its centre an angle of 2π radians, thus $360° = 2\pi$ radians.

radiant The point on the CELESTIAL SPHERE from which a METEOR appears to come. The radiant is also the common point from which a METEOR SHOWER seems to radiate, but in this case the effect is one of perspective, because in reality all the METEOROIDS in a specific METEOR STREAM are moving along parallel paths.

radiation See ELECTROMAGNETIC RADIATION.

radiation, nuclear Energetic particles, or energy, emitted by RADIOACTIVE ISOTOPES, or during nuclear FISSION or FUSION. Radioactive ISOTOPES decay in specific ways by emitting certain particles, or quanta of energy. The three most common ways are by alpha-, beta-, and gamma-radiation. Alpha-radiation, for example from URANIUM, is the emission of positively charged alpha particles (two neutrons plus two protons), which are equivalent to the nucleus of a helium atom. Alpha-radiation has a range of a few centimetres in air, and can be deflected by electric or magnetic fields. Beta-radiation is the emission of beta particles, electrons moving at high speed. Beta-radiation has a range in air of many centimetres and is strongly deflected by an electric or magnetic field. Gamma-radiation consists of photons (high-frequency ELECTROMAGNETIC RADIATION with no mass or charge), and is not deflected in an electric or magnetic field. It has a range of many centimetres even in lead.

radiation, thermal The transfer of heat by electromagnetic waves, as distinct from the other two mechanisms of heat transfer, CONDUCTION and CONVECTION. Thermal or INFRARED RADIATION has wavelengths longer than those of visible light and frequencies very similar to those of the vibrations of atoms in liquids and solids. It can therefore be absorbed by atoms to increase the amplitude of their vibration and hence their energy: thus they become hotter. The ability of a body to absorb radiation, however, depends very much on its surface condition. Radiation is reflected most efficiently by shiny, light-coloured surfaces, and absorbed most efficiently by matt black ones. Heat from the Sun reaches the Earth as electromagnetic waves travelling through space.

radiation belts Regions of ionized particles surrounding planets possessing magnetic fields. Electrically charged particles originating from the Sun become trapped in the planet's magnetic field to form one or more doughnut-shaped rings about the planet. In the Earth's case, the belts are known as the VAN ALLEN radiation belts.

radiation sickness Any acute illness resulting from exposure to radioactive substances or other sources of ionizing radiation, e.g. X-rays or gamma rays. Very high doses cause death within hours by damaging the central nervous system. Lower doses, which may also prove ultimately fatal, cause immediate symptoms of vomiting and diarrhoea, followed by bleeding, hair loss, and damage to the bone marrow.

radio The transmission of information by means of ELECTROMAGNETIC RADIATION in the FREQUENCY range 3 kHz to 40,000 MHz, WAVELENGTH range 1 cm to more than 1 km (0.4 inch to 0.6 mile). The radio-frequency spectrum is arbitrarily divided into a number of WAVEBANDS, from very low frequencies (long wavelengths) to ultra-high and microwave frequencies (short wavelengths). Sections of the spectrum have been allocated by international agreement to use for telegraph, telephonic speech, and radio and television broadcasting.

In order to be transmitted, the information in a radio signal is used to modulate (see MODULATION) a radio-frequency wave. The modulated radio signal is then amplified, and a transmitting ANTENNA projects as much as possible of the radio-frequency energy into space. The signals are picked up by the aerial of a RADIO RECEIVER tuned in to the wavelength of the transmission. In 1864 the British physicist James Clerk Maxwell predicted the existence of electromagnetic radiation and its ability to travel through space at the speed of light. HERTZ confirmed Maxwell's theories experimentally in 1888, but it was MARCONI who developed these discoveries to provide a means of communication. In 1896 he transmitted a radio signal from Penarth, South Wales, to Weston-super-Mare, England; in 1901 he transmitted the letter 's' in Morse code across the Atlantic from Poldhu in Cornwall, England, to St Johns, Newfoundland, Canada.

Marconi's broadcasts were telegraphic signals rather than sound transmissions. Early in the 20th century Reginald FESSENDEN developed amplitude modulation, which made it possible to transmit sound by radio. In 1906 he made a music transmission that was picked up by several wireless operators and was claimed as the first radio broadcast. These innovations led to the development of simple crystal RADIO RECEIVERS after World War I. By 1921 regular programmes were being transmitted from eight stations in the USA; the BBC was transmitting in the UK by 1923, and by 1925 there were 600 radio stations worldwide.

radioactive dating See RADIO-CARBON DATING; RADIOMETRIC DATING.

radioactive isotope (or **radioisotope**) An unstable chemical ISOTOPE that decays to a lighter element with the emission of RADIATION. Very few naturally occurring elements are radioactive (examples are URANIUM and RADIUM), but radioactive isotopes of many common elements occur naturally in minute quantities. Other radioactive materials have been produced artificially through nuclear FISSION: examples are PLUTONIUM, strontium-90, and caesium-137. Radioactive decay occurs because the nuclei of these elements are unstable. The rate of this decay can vary enormously: the half-life (the time taken for half of a given mass of the material to decay) of a radioactive isotope may vary from over a billion years to a tiny fraction of a second. Radioactive elements have a variety of uses. Uranium and plutonium are NUCLEAR FUELS and provide materials for NUCLEAR WEAPONS. The rate of decay of radioactive isotopes, such as carbon-14, can be used in RADIOMETRIC DATING to estimate the age of rocks, fossils, and other artefacts. Small quantities of radioactive material can be used to 'tag' a compound, so that its presence can be detected using a radiation detector.

radioactive waste disposal See WASTE MANAGEMENT.

radioactivity A phenomenon discovered in 1896 by Henri BECQUEREL, who noticed that uranium salts continuously emitted radiation that affected a wrapped photographic plate. Uranium is described as a naturally radioactive material; others include radium, discovered by Marie CURIE in 1898, thorium, and radon. The radiation from a radioactive material is called nuclear radiation (see RADIATION, NUCLEAR), because it is emitted by the nuclei of its atoms. The nuclei are unstable; they disintegrate at random, shooting out tiny particles of matter (ALPHA PARTICLES or BETA PARTICLES) sometimes accompanied by bursts of wave energy (GAMMA RAYS). The process of disintegration is called radioactive decay, and it releases energy which ultimately ends up as heat. In general, radioactive decay fundamentally alters atoms, changing one element into another. This, in turn, may itself be radioactive, and so on. Uranium, after a series of such decay processes, ultimately becomes lead, which is stable. Several other decay series of this type exist in nature. Some materials become radioactive when bombarded with nuclear radiation, a phenomenon discovered by Irène Curie and Jean-Frédéric JOLIOT in 1934.

radio astronomy The study of the extraterrestrial Universe by analysing its radio-wavelength signals. Radio astronomy complements and extends knowledge obtained by conventional optical astronomy and is particularly sensitive to the emissions from objects, such as the remnants of exploding stars or the explosions of very distant radio galaxies. An important class of **radio sources**, celestial sources of radio waves, was found that did not appear to be associated with any optical object. Only with the advent of the interferometer RADIO TELESCOPE, which measured the position of radio sources with high precision, was it possible to begin identifying them, by the simultaneous use of the largest optical telescopes. Even relatively intense radio sources are associated with galaxies at the limit of visibility in Earth-bound optical telescopes. Even with the best optical techniques using the largest optical telescopes some 30 per cent of the brightest thousand or so radio sources remain unidentified. In 1962, QUASARS were discovered; these were an entirely new type of extragalactic object, which had many of the radio properties of radio galaxies but in an optical telescope they looked like stars and hence were given the name quasi-stellar objects or quasars. In fact they are intensely active galaxies with luminosities exceeding radio galaxies by factors of up to 10^4, if their distances are as indicated by their measured red shifts. Indeed, because of

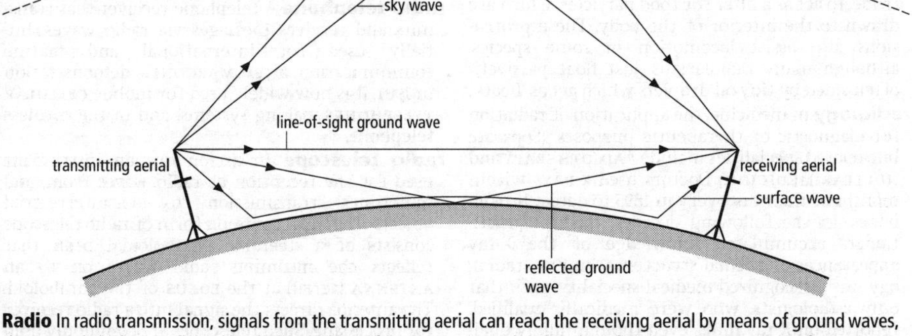

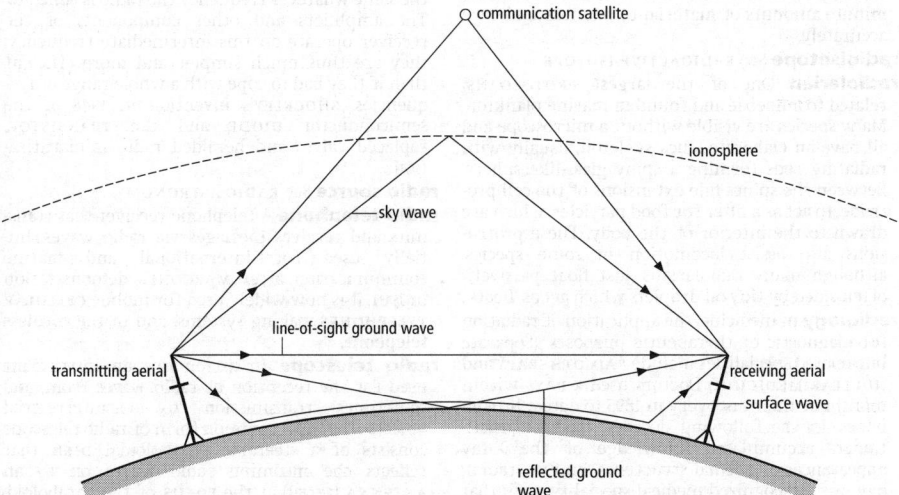

Radio In radio transmission, signals from the transmitting aerial can reach the receiving aerial by means of ground waves, sky waves (which are reflected by the ionosphere of the upper atmosphere), or by reflection or retransmission from a communication satellite.

their high luminosity and exceptionally large red shifts, their distances have been called into question. It is argued by some astronomers that their red shift may not be cosmological, that is, caused by the expansion of the Universe, but may be produced by some as yet unrecognized physical process.

radio-carbon dating A method of dating organic materials, based on the decay of the RADIOACTIVE ISOTOPE carbon-14 to nitrogen-14. This method of dating was invented by LIBBY in 1947. Living material contains the carbon ISOTOPES carbon-14 (C-14) and carbon-12 (C-12) in equilibrium with the same isotopes in the atmosphere. When an organism dies, however, it no longer takes in carbon dioxide from the atmosphere and the C-14 begins to decay to nitrogen-14, at a known rate. By measuring the C-14: C-12 ratio in an organic artefact, its age (up to a limit of about 40,000 years) can be determined.

radio galaxy A source of radio waves identified with an optically visible galaxy and partly distinguished from a normal galaxy by its high radio power output. A radio galaxy, such as CYGNUS A, often reveals a single source with two lobes or a double source with the optical object located between the two sources of radio-frequency radiation. The energy generation mechanism of radio galaxies is not understood.

radiography The process or technique of producing images of an opaque object on photographic film or on a fluorescent screen by means of radiation (either particles or electromagnetic waves of short wavelength, such as X-rays and gamma rays). The photograph produced is called a **radiograph**. The process is widely used in RADIOLOGY, using X-rays.

radioimmunoassay A type of biochemical assay using antibodies 'tagged' with a RADIOACTIVE ISOTOPE to measure how much chemical or protein is present in a blood sample or other specimen. The antibodies will attach very specifically to one type of molecule (for example, a hormone such as thyroxine). The amount of combined hormone–antibody complex can then be determined from the quantity of radioactivity in a sample. Using very sensitive instruments, this technique enables minute amounts of material to be measured very accurately.

radioisotope See RADIOACTIVE ISOTOPE.

radiolarian One of the largest PROTOZOANS, related to amoebae and found in marine plankton. Many species are visible without a microscope and all have an elaborate silica skeleton, usually with radiating rods forming a spiny glass-like sphere. Between the spines fine extensions of the cell protrude, to act as a filter for food particles, which are drawn to the interior of the body. These protrusions also assist locomotion in some species, although many radiolarians just float passively, often aided by tiny oil droplets which act as 'floats'.

radiology In medicine, the application of radiation for diagnostic or therapeutic purposes. (Separate but related specialities include RADIOTHERAPY and NUCLEAR MEDICINE.) Doctors used X-RAYS within months of their discovery in 1895 to detect broken bones. In the following decades, medical practitioners accumulated knowledge of the X-ray appearances of normal structures. By 1948, radiology was a recognized medical speciality, such that only radiologists, who were medically qualified, reported on X-ray films, even though highly qualified radiographers were (and still are) responsible for taking most of the X-ray pictures (see RADIOGRAPHY). X-rays have also been used to screen symptomless people for disease, most notably in the anti-tuberculosis campaigns of the 1940s and 1950s. Some parts of the body do not show clearly on an X-ray, however, and so techniques have been developed for injecting such parts with non-toxic, radio-opaque substances (contrast media). For example, barium sulphate is commonly given orally to reveal the upper or lower gut.

Radiology now incorporates sophisticated techniques such as COMPUTERIZED TOMOGRAPHY, as well as imaging methods that do not use ionizing radiation, such as ULTRASOUND and MAGNETIC RESONANCE IMAGING.

radiometric dating (or **isotopic dating**) A method for determining the age of a rock by measuring the amount of a RADIOACTIVE ISOTOPE, either in the rock as a whole or in a mineral contained in it, and comparing it with the amount of the stable 'daughter' isotope that it decays into. It is necessary to know accurately the HALF-LIFE of the element concerned – that is, the time required for half the nuclei originally present to decay. The measured ratio of parent to daughter element can then be used in conjunction with the half-life to calculate the age of the specimen.

radio receiver A device that detects modulated RADIO signals and converts them into sound. Originally, this consisted of a tuned circuit to select the appropriate radio-frequency modulated carrier wave from all the other signals picked up by the ANTENNA (aerial). This radio-frequency signal was passed to a crystal RECTIFIER to separate the audio-frequency signal from the radio-frequency carrier. The audio-frequency signal was converted to sound waves in a set of headphones. This simple device was greatly improved by J. A. FLEMING's invention of the THERMIONIC VALVE in 1904, which enabled DE FOREST in 1906 to produce the triode valve. This device enabled signals to be amplified sufficiently to operate a loudspeaker.

Modern radio receivers operate on the superheterodyne principle. In such receivers, the rectified radio signal is mixed with a signal from an oscillator inside the radio, to give an intermediate signal. The frequency of this intermediate signal is the same whatever frequency the radio is tuned to. The amplifiers and other components of the receiver operate on this intermediate frequency: they are thus much simpler and more efficient than if they had to cope with a whole range of frequencies. SHOCKLEY's invention in 1948 of the semiconductor DIODE and the TRANSISTOR, replaced valves and heralded radio miniaturization.

radio source See RADIO ASTRONOMY.

radio-telephone A telephone receiver that transmits and receives messages via radio waves. Initially used for international and marine communication after MARCONI's demonstration in 1901, it is now widely used for mobile CELLULAR TELEPHONES, paging systems, and in the cordless telephone.

radio telescope In astronomy, an instrument used for the reception of radio waves from, and sometimes transmission to, extraterrestrial objects. The most common form of radio telescope consists of a steerable paraboloidal DISH that reflects the incoming radio waves on to an ANTENNA (aerial) at the FOCUS of the paraboloid. The antenna directs the signal into a radio receiver for processing. Such telescopes are commonly used for RADIO ASTRONOMY and RADAR ASTRONOMY, and are frequently used for communicating with a satellite or spacecraft. Another form of radio telescope, used at long radio wavelengths or to gain very high resolution, depends for its operation on INTERFEROMETRY. It comprises an array of aerials or dish telescopes, each of which receives a signal from the radio source. The resolution depends on the distance between the farthest aerials (baseline) and resolutions much higher than those obtained from existing dish or optical telescopes have been achieved by using APERTURE SYNTHESIS with intercontinental baselines.

radiotherapy (or **radiation therapy**) The use of ionizing electromagnetic radiation, such as X-rays and gamma rays, for the treatment of disease, particularly CANCER. Before the late 1920s radium in hollow needles was often inserted into tumours, but since then controlled irradiation from a distance of a metre or more (teletherapy) has been the favoured approach, bombarding the cancerous cells with radiation. X-ray tubes have been superseded first by RADIOACTIVE ISOTOPES, such as radium and cobalt-60, and later by PARTICLE ACCELERATORS. In some cases radiotherapy is combined with surgery or cytotoxic-drug therapy. The critical factor in all radiotherapy is dosage, since normal tissues are also sensitive to radiation. Tumour sites can now be accurately identified using techniques, such as COMPUTERIZED TOMOGRAPHY, and modern apparatus can deliver a precise, localized dose of radiation. Adverse effects are also reduced by the use of multiple, lower-intensity dosages.

radio waves See ELECTROMAGNETIC RADIATION.

radish A popular salad vegetable, *Raphanus sativus*, various forms of which are cultivated in most parts of the world. The small red or white, pungent, swollen roots vary in shape from round to cylindrical. They are relatives of cabbage, turnip, and other members of the mustard family.

radium (symbol Ra, at. no. 88, r.a.m. 226.03) A rare, white, radioactive element discovered by Marie and Pierre CURIE in 1898 in the mineral pitchblende, which is the chief ore. The last member of the ALKALINE EARTH METALS, it reacts with water and tarnishes in air. It has several isotopes that are members of radioactive decay sequences, the most stable, radium-226, having a HALF-LIFE of 1,620 years before decaying to the gas radon. The discovery of radium led to numerous crucial experiments on radioactivity, paving the way for the rapid advances in atomic physics in the 20th century. Until the 1920s radium was used in RADIOTHERAPY.

radius See ARM.

radius vector See KEPLER'S LAWS.

Radnorshire A former county of eastern Wales. It became part of Powys in 1974.

radon (symbol Rn, at. no. 86, r.a.m. 222) The heaviest NOBLE GAS. It occurs naturally and has been noticed to increase in groundwater before seismic activity. It is highly radioactive and produced by the radioactive decay of heavy elements, such as radium. The most stable isotope, radon-222, has a HALF-LIFE of 3.825 days and is used in tracer studies.

Raeburn, Sir Henry (1756–1823) British portraitist. His vigorous style could be extremely effective in conveying the character of rugged Highland chiefs or local legal worthies. He painted some sensitive portraits of women and had a penchant for vivid and original lighting effects.

Raeder, Erich (1876–1960) German admiral. He was Admiral Hipper's chief of staff in World War I, and from 1928 was commander-in-chief of the German navy, secretly rebuilding it in violation of the VERSAILLES PEACE SETTLEMENT. In the 1930s he elaborated his 'Z-Plan' for building a fleet capable of challenging Britain, but World War II began before this was achieved. He resigned and was replaced by Doenitz in January 1943, after Hitler became outraged by the poor performance of the surface fleet against Allied convoys. His part in unrestricted U-boat warfare led to his post-war imprisonment after trial at NUREMBERG.

raffia A tropical PALM, *Raphia farinifera*, which yields the material used for tying up plants, or for handicrafts. The fibre is stripped from the upper surface of the youngest leaflets. There are several species, all with gigantic leaves. In parts of Africa they provide the principal material used in local house-building, the stalks providing the framework and the leaves the roofing.

Raffles, Sir (Thomas) Stamford (1781–1826) British colonial administrator. Born in Jamaica, he joined the East India Company in 1795, becoming Lieutenant General of Java in 1811. He later served as Lieutenant General of Sumatra (1818–23), during which time he persuaded the company to purchase the undeveloped island of Singapore (1819) and undertook much of the preliminary work for transforming it into an international port and centre of commerce.

Rafsanjani, Ali Akbar Hashemi (1934–) Iranian statesman and religious leader, President 1989–97. A supporter and former pupil of Ayatollah Khomeini, in 1978 he helped organize the mass demonstrations that led to the shah's overthrow the following year. In 1988 he helped to bring an end to the Iran–Iraq War, having persuaded Khomeini to accept the UN's peace terms. When Khomeini died in 1989 Rafsanjani emerged from the ensuing power struggle as Iran's leader. He sought to improve Iran's relations with the West, and kept his country neutral during the Gulf War of 1991.

ragfish A single species, *Icosteus aenigmaticus*, which is the only representative of its family; it lives in the North Pacific, on both the Asian and North American coasts. Although it grows to a length of at least 2 m (6.5 feet), its bones contain very little calcium, and so are somewhat flexible. This gives it its peculiarly floppy (rag-like) appearance out of water. Young fishes live in inshore waters near the surface and are brownish in colour; the adults live in mid-water in the open ocean.

Raglan, FitzRoy James Henry Somerset, 1st Baron (1788–1855) British soldier. Joining the army in 1804, he served as aide-de-camp to Arthur Wellesley (Duke of WELLINGTON) during the PENINSULAR WAR, and lost an arm at the Battle of Waterloo. Appointed to lead the British expeditionary force in the CRIMEAN WAR, he won a victory at Inkerman (5 November 1854) with French assistance, but was criticized for his general conduct of the campaign.

ragtime A type of US popular music which flourished from about 1890 to 1920 in parallel with the emergence of JAZZ. Its main characteristic is a syncopated melody over a steady beat in the accompaniment, generally in 2/4 time. Scott JOPLIN was the first ragtime composer to write the music down.

ragworm See BRISTLEWORM.

ragwort A plant of the genus *Senecio*, itself part of the sunflower family. Common ragwort, *S. jacobaea*, is a tall perennial with yellow flowers, a weed of waste places and pastures which, because of its poisonous nature, is avoided by grazing animals. The so-called Oxford ragwort, *S. squalidus*, is one of the most rapidly spreading alien weeds in Europe. It is an annual, branching plant from Sicily, with yellow, daisy-like heads, and fruits supported by silky hairs, facilitating dispersal by wind.

Rahman See ABDUL RAHMAN, TUNKU.

rail A member of a large family of birds, Rallidae, which includes crakes, gallinules, and coots. A typical rail is a chicken-like marsh bird with long legs, which dangle below it in flight, short rounded wings, and a stubby tail. Its beak can be long, short, or conical. Many rails, such as the corncrake, *Crex crex*, live on the ground in thick vegetation and, because of their reluctance to fly, are rarely seen. Familiar European species are the moorhen, *Gallinula chloropus*, the coot, *Fulica atra*, and the water rail, *Rallus aquaticus*.

rail-bus A simple form of passenger railway vehicle. In the UK it comprises essentially two passenger-carrying vehicle bodies joined back-to-back and mounted on a four-wheel underframe, housing the engine, transmission, and running gear. The simple design results in considerable weight-saving compared with conventional vehicles. Rail-buses of a similar basic design are used throughout the world on branch lines; they may be operated together in multiple-unit trains.

railways, history of The advent of railways brought together the technology of the STEAM-ENGINE, developed in the early 18th century, and the horse- or human-powered wagon-ways used in mining since the 16th century. Richard TREVITHICK was the first to build a STEAM LOCOMOTIVE to run on such wagon-ways (1804); other steam-locomotive pioneers, also British, were John Blenkinsop (1783–1831), William Hedley (1779–1843), and George STEPHENSON. Early locomotives were handicapped by the weakness of the available railway track: it was not until technical advances were made in track construction that the railway became truly practical.

The Stockton and Darlington Railway (1825) was the first to carry both freight and passengers. In 1830 it was followed by the Liverpool and Manchester Railway, the line that heralded the beginning of the railway era using Stephenson's *Rocket* as locomotive. There followed a period of rapid expansion and development of railways throughout the world. By 1847, 250,000 navvies were employed in railway construction in the UK, and in the USA, where railroad companies were the main agents of westward expansion, nearly 34,000 km (21,100 miles) of railway were constructed between 1850 and 1860. By the end of the century railway networks covered Europe, the USA, Canada, and parts of imperial Russia. In Europe cheap and easy travel helped to break down provincial differences, while in Switzerland and the Mediterranean the holiday industry steadily developed. Railways were important for both sides in the American Civil War, for moving troops and supplies. The first electric locomotive was demonstrated in Berlin in 1879. Electric traction was commercially applied first on suburban and metropolitan lines, but was quickly adopted for UNDERGROUND RAILWAYS. One of the earliest users of electric locomotives on main-line routes was Italy, where a line was opened in 1902.

The railways proved strategically important on all fronts in World War I. After the war many railway companies grouped together as national railway systems or large geographical concerns. In the late 1930s the steam locomotive reached its zenith, but electric locomotives were already in widespread use in Europe and Scandinavia, and main-line diesel locomotives were coming into service in the USA. In this period road and air transport began to challenge the railways.

Following World War II there was a period of reconstruction: new steam locomotives were introduced in the UK and mainland Europe, and new diesels were also under test. Steam locomotive production ended in the USA in the 1950s, and in Europe in the 1960s, and, as the competition from roads increased, there were major cutbacks in the rail network. In Japan in 1964, the high-speed *shinkansen* or 'bullet' trains began operation, running on specially developed track at speeds of up to 210 km/h (130 mph). At around the same period experiments began using GROUND GUIDANCE-SYSTEMS other than conventional track.

In the last quarter of the 20th century, railway construction worldwide started to grow again, though in developed countries few new lines were built. In Europe, notably in France and more recently Germany, other HIGH-SPEED TRAINS have been developed. There has also been a considerable investment in commuter trains and light railway rapid-transit systems to ease congestion on roads and pollution. A new development in Jakarta, Indonesia, is the Aeromovel, a light, engineless train powered by compressed air blown through a duct below the track. New underground railways have been built in some of the newer large cities (for example, the Metro in Mexico City), while in China the railway network is growing at a rate of some 1,000 km (600 miles) per year. The Channel Tunnel rail link between England and France began to operate in 1994. Following a model adopted by Sweden in the early 1990s, Britain privatized its rail network in the mid-1990s.

rain Atmospheric PRECIPITATION consisting of water droplets at least 0.5 mm (0.02 inch) in diameter (anything less being drizzle). They may reach a size of 5 mm (0.2 inch) and more by COALESCENCE or by the melting of large snowflakes; at some point they can no longer be supported within the cloud in which they form; they then fall. EVAPORATION while falling determines their size on reaching the ground. The intensity and duration of rainfall are dependent on the type of cloud that harbours it. Steady and persistent rain is generally associated with nimbostratus (layered) cloud, which forms at FRONTS; the cloud is caused by the uplift and cooling of warm, moist air, and the resulting precipitation is called frontal rain. Cumulonimbus (heaped) cloud, which is more likely to provide an intense though short-lived downpour, is formed by CONVECTION. Moist air, warmed at ground level, rises, expands, and is cooled adiabatically to dew-point. The resulting precipitation is known as convectional rain.

rainbow A phenomenon formed in the atmosphere through the REFRACTION and internal REFLECTION of sunlight by falling raindrops. Well-developed rainbows consist of a bright primary bow, with red on the outside, followed by orange, yellow, green, blue, indigo, and violet on the inside. A less intense secondary bow, in which the colour sequence is reversed, can form outside the primary bow and one or more faint bows inside it. All the bows have their centre on a line from the Sun through the observer. Rainbows can only be seen while standing with one's back to the Sun, facing the illuminated raindrops.

rainbow trout A species of fish, *Salmo gairdneri*, a

member of the salmon family, Salmonidae. It is native to the rivers and lakes of the western coast of North America from northern Mexico to Alaska, but has been introduced to the rest of North America and other temperate regions of the world. In the north of its native range, it is migratory and, although breeding in fresh water, spends part of its life in the sea (when it is known as a steelhead trout). Heavily spotted on back and fins, the rainbow trout has an iridescent streak along its side. It feeds on insects, their larvae, and crustaceans, and large specimens eat other fishes. Preferring clean, cool water it is nevertheless tolerant of low oxygen levels and this has made it suitable for intensive culture in fish farms as a food species.

rain forest An area of vegetation that occurs mostly in tropical and subtropical regions with adequate rainfall. Rain forests also occur in the temperate, northwest coastal areas of the USA and New Zealand. The trees in such forests are evergreen and often very tall.

Tropical rain forest is probably the richest of all vegetation types in terms of the number of plant and animal species involved and is notable for the high proportion of LIANAS and EPIPHYTES. It represents a huge resource in terms of timber, drugs, and other produce, but is rapidly disappearing through overexploitation of a few species. The remaining forest species are neglected or burnt. Once destroyed, tropical rain forest cannot always be re-established as severe soil erosion occurs after the plant-cover is removed.

rain frog A member of a group of small African frogs that belong to the family Microhylidae, with almost spherical bodies, short limbs, and a very short snout. They live in burrows throughout most of the year, emerging to feed on termites and

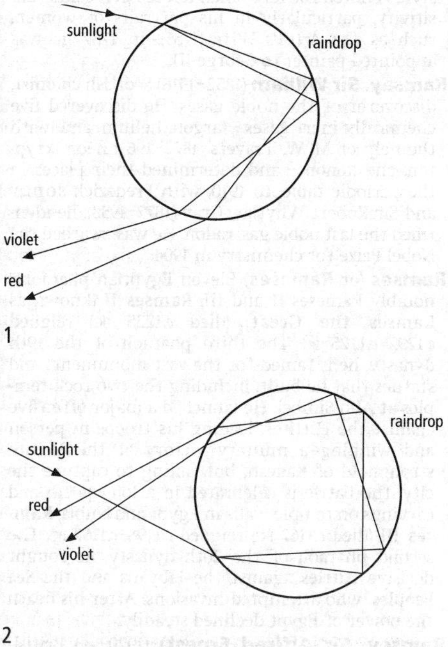

Rainbow (1) The primary bow is formed by refraction and a single internal reflection of sunlight in a droplet of rain. (2) A secondary bow (with the colours reversed) occurs if there are two internal reflections within the water droplet.

to breed when the first rains fall in southern Africa. The male rain frogs are considerably smaller than the females. During mating, the male becomes glued to the female's back by his throat, chest, and fore-arms. If it is threatened, the rain frog is able to inflate its body and exude sticky droplets, which deters most predators.

rain gauge See METEOROLOGICAL INSTRUMENT.

Rajasthan A state in western India to the east of Pakistan and south of the Punjab; area 342,239 sq km (132,190 sq miles); pop. (1991) 43,880,640; capital, Jaipur. It was formed as the Union of Rajasthan in 1948 from the former region of Rajputana. In 1956 additional territory was added and its name became simply Rajasthan. The western part of the state consists largely of the Thar Desert and is sparsely populated. It is rich in minerals, such as gypsum, rock phosphate, silver, asbestos, copper, mica, and felspar.

Rajput (Sanskrit, 'son of a king') The predominantly landowning class, also called Thakurs, living mainly in central and northern India, who claim descent from the Hindu Ksatriya (warrior) caste. Many leading clans are of royal lineage, but others include cultivators of Sudra (menial) caste. Their clans are divided into four lines: Solar, Lunar, Fire, and Snake.

Rakosi, Matyas (1892–1971) Hungarian politician. He played an important role in the Hungarian communist revolution led by Béla KUN in 1919. After four years in Moscow (1920–24), Rakosi returned to Hungary but was later arrested, to be released only in 1940. In 1944 he became First Secretary of the Hungarian Communist Party and during this time established a ruthless Stalinist regime. He was Prime Minister (1952–53). Opposition to his Stalinist policies led to his resignation as Party Secretary and return to the Soviet Union in 1956. The brutality of his secret police contributed to the HUNGARIAN REVOLUTION of 1956.

raku A type of Japanese pottery invented in Kyoto in the 16th century specifically for the tea ceremony. Raku vessels are made of lead-glazed earthenware and are moulded by hand rather than thrown on a potter's wheel. Some have simple decoration, but generally they depend for their effect on irregularity of shape, expressing the individuality of the maker's hand, and on beauty of colour and texture.

Raleigh The capital of the US state of North Carolina; pop. (1990) 207,950. Laid out in 1792, the city was named after Sir Walter RALEIGH. It is a research centre for the electronic, chemical, and food-processing industries and is home to an annual convention of whistlers. It is at the heart of a major tobacco-growing region.

Raleigh, Sir Walter (or **Ralegh**) (*c*.1552–1618) English explorer, courtier, and writer. A favourite of Elizabeth I, he organized several voyages of exploration and colonization to the Americas, including an unsuccessful attempt to settle Virginia (1584–89) and a journey up the Orinoco River in search of gold (1595); from his travels he brought back potato and tobacco plants to England. Raleigh was imprisoned in 1603 by James I on a charge of conspiracy, but released in 1616 to lead a second expedition up the Orinoco in search of the fabled land of El Dorado. He returned empty-handed after a clash with some Spanish settlers, and was subsequently executed on the original charge.

RAM See MEMORY (computer).

Rama The seventh incarnation or *avatar* of the Hindu god Vishnu as the son of King Dasharatha of

Oudh, descendant of an ancient solar dynasty. His incarnation was Vishnu's response to the threat of the demon-king Ravana's power in Sri Lanka.

Ramadan The ninth month of the Islamic calendar, commemorating the revelation of the KORAN; Ramadan is prescribed as a time of fasting for all healthy Muslims. Fasting, which fulfils *Sawm*, one of the five PILLARS OF ISLAM, occurs throughout the daylight hours and includes abstinence from tobacco and sexual intercourse as well as food and drink. Only the young, pregnant or nursing mothers, or the sick are exempt.

Ramakrishna (born Gadadhar Chatterjee) (1836–86) Indian yogi and mystic. In his teachings he condemned lust, money, and the caste system, and preached that all religions leading to the attainment of mystical experience are equally good and true. His doctrines were spread widely in the USA and Europe by his disciple Vivekananda.

Raman, Sir Chandrasekhara Venkata (1888–1970) Indian physicist. He discovered the RAMAN EFFECT, an important proof of QUANTUM THEORY. He also studied vibrations and sound, and the theory of musical instruments. In optics he went on to investigate the properties of crystals and minerals and the physiology of colour vision. Raman was awarded the 1930 Nobel Prize for physics.

Raman effect The change in wavelength that occurs when light is scattered discovered in 1928 by Sir Chandrasekhara RAMAN. According to the QUANTUM THEORY, light consists of photons, each with a wavelength depending on its energy. When scattering occurs, photons strike and are deflected by gas molecules. This alters the motion of the molecules, and they may absorb or release energy. Scattered photons then have a different energy from the original photons, and therefore a different wavelength.

Ramanujan, Srinivasa Aaiyangar (1887–1920) Indian mathematician. Largely self-taught, he was a mathematical genius who produced a number of original discoveries in number theory and power series. Collaborating with G. H. Hardy (1877–1947) in Cambridge, he made what is probably his most important contribution – a theorem concerning the partition of numbers into a sum of smaller integers.

Ramayana ('The Goings of Rama') One of the two great epics of SANSKRIT literature. Its 24,000 verses, attributed to Valmiki, narrate Prince Rama's banishment from Ayodhya, his life of exile in the forest, his wife Sita's abduction by Ravana, the demon king of Lanka, his rescue of Sita aided by the monkey god Hanuman, and their triumphant return home. In the figures of Rama and Sita, ideals of courage, faithfulness, duty, and obedience are portrayed.

Rambert, Dame Marie (born Cyvia Rambam) (1888–1982) British ballet-dancer, teacher, and director, born in Poland. In 1913 she joined Diaghilev's Ballets Russes as a teacher of eurhythmics, moving to London in 1917. Rambert later formed the Ballet Club (1930), which became known as the **Ballet Rambert** (1935). For over 50 years the company, under her direction, promoted new British ballets and young choreographers and dancers, such as her pupil Frederick Ashton. In 1986 it changed its name to the Rambert Dance Company.

rambutan See LITCHI.

Rameau, Jean-Philippe (1683–1764) French composer, musical theorist, and organist. In 1722 he published his influential *Treatise on Harmony*. He is best known for his four volumes of harpsichord pieces (1706–41); noted for their bold harmonies and textural diversity, these consist largely of genre pieces with descriptive titles, such as 'La Poule'. Rameau also wrote many operas, including *Castor and Pollux* (1737).

Rameses See RAMSES.

Ramillies A village north of Namur in Brabant, Belgium, scene of a battle in 1706 at which Marlborough defeated the French under Villeroi. The French losses were five times greater than Marlborough's. He went on to overrun much of Flanders and Brabant.

ram-jet A JET ENGINE with no compressor, in which air is drawn in and compressed by the forward motion of the engine. It has no moving parts, and is essentially a shaped duct (sometimes called a 'flying drainpipe'), consisting of an intake section which acts as a compressor by slowing down the entering air, a combustion chamber in which fuel is added and burnt, and a nozzle section in which the stream of hot gas is accelerated to give a high-speed exhaust jet. The jet provides propulsive thrust in a manner similar to that of a rocket. The device has found limited application because it only functions at speeds in excess of Mach 2 and therefore has to be launched by a rocket.

Ramón y Cajal, Santiago (1852–1934) Spanish physician and histologist. He identified the neuron as the fundamental unit of the nervous system, but argued (incorrectly) that the axons end only in the brain and do not join up with other axons or neurons. Ramón y Cajal shared a Nobel Prize with Camillo Golgi in 1906.

Ramsay, Allan (1713–84) Scottish portrait painter. From the late 1730s he was based in London, where he became much in demand as a portraitist. His style is noted for its French Rococo grace and sensitivity, particularly in his portraits of women, such as *The Artist's Wife* (1755). In 1767 he was appointed painter to George III.

Ramsay, Sir William (1852–1916) Scottish chemist, discoverer of the noble gases. He discovered five chemically inert gases – argon, helium, and (with the help of M. W. Travers, 1872–1961) neon, krypton, and xenon – and determined their places in the periodic table. In 1910, with Frederick SODDY and Sir Robert Whytlaw-Gray (1877–1958), he identified the last noble gas, radon. He was awarded the Nobel Prize for chemistry in 1904.

Ramses (or **Rameses**) Eleven Egyptian pharaohs, notably Rameses II and III. **Ramses II** (known as **Ramses the Great**) (died *c.*1225 BC) reigned *c.*1292–*c.*1225 BC. The third pharaoh of the 19th dynasty, he is famed for the vast monuments and statues that he built, including the two rock temples at Abu Simbel. He launched a major offensive against the Hittites, leading his troops in person and winning a military victory at the Hittite stronghold of Kadesh, but failing to capture the city; the battle is celebrated in a long poem and carvings on temple walls in Egypt and Nubia. **Ramses III** (died *c.*1167 BC) reigned *c.*1198–*c.*1167 BC. The second pharaoh of the 20th dynasty, he fought decisive battles against the Libyans and the Sea Peoples, who attempted invasions. After his death the power of Egypt declined steadily.

Ramsey, Sir Alf(red Ernest) (1920–) British footballer and manager. He played as a defender for Southampton before moving to Tottenham Hotspur in 1949. He also played for England, winning 31 caps. As a manager he took Ipswich Town from the third division to the first division championship (1962). He then managed England (1963–74), winning the World Cup in 1966.

Ramsgate A resort town and fishing port on the coast of Kent, south-east England, made popular in the 19th century following a visit by George IV; pop. (1991) 37,895. There are ferry links with France and Belgium.

ramshorn snail A gastropod MOLLUSC with a flat, spiralled shell unlike the asymmetric coil of more typical snails, found in fresh water browsing among dense weeds. The many species of ramshorn snails breathe via a 'lung' within the mantle cavity. They also have blood that contains the respiratory pigment HAEMOGLOBIN; this enables them to live in stagnant waters.

Rance A river of Brittany, north-west France, that flows into the English Channel near St Malo. A dam (the **Rance barrage**) and power station built 1960–67 harness the tidal power of 13-m (44-ft) tides at the mouth of the river and was the first in the world to do so. Its 24 turbogenerators are capable of producing 240 MW.

Rand See WITWATERSRAND.

Rand, Ayn (born Alissa Rosenbaum) (1905–82) US writer and philosopher, born in Russia. Emigrating to the USA in 1926, she became known for her novels *The Fountainhead* (1943) and *Atlas Shrugged* (1957). She developed her philosophy of 'objectivism' in *For the New Intellectual* (1961), arguing for 'rational self-interest', individualism, and laissez-faire capitalism.

Rangi and Papa In Oceanian mythology, the sky and the Earth, progenitors of all gods and all creatures. According to Maori legend their separation by their son, the sky god Tane, gave rise to mankind's affliction with storms and floods. Papa and Rangi's sorrow at their separation is the origin of summer mists, dew, and ice.

Rangoon (Burmese **Yangon**) The capital Myanmar (Burma), a seaport on the Rangoon River, one of the mouths of the Irrawaddy; pop. (1983) 2,458,710. The city was named Yangon ('the end of war') in 1755 when King Alaungpaya captured the riverside village of Dagon from the Mons. It was officially renamed Yangon in 1989. Rebuilt by the British on a grid system after the Second Anglo-Burmese War it became the capital in 1885, its chief landmark being the Shwedagon Pagoda, built over 2,500 years ago to house eight sacred hairs of the Buddha. The commercial and industrial centre of Myanmar, its exports of rice, teak, oil, and rubber have declined since independence.

Ranjit Singh (known as 'the Lion of the Punjab') (1780–1839) Indian maharaja, founder of the Sikh state of Punjab. After succeeding his father as a Sikh ruler at the age of 12, he seized Lahore from the Afghans in 1799 and proclaimed himself maharaja of Punjab in 1801. He proceeded to make the state the most powerful in India, securing the holy city of Amritsar (1802) and expanding his control north-west with the capture of Peshawar (1818) and Kashmir (1819). At the end of the Sikh Wars, which followed his death, most of his territory was annexed by Britain.

Ranjitsinhji Vibhaji, Sir Kumar Shri, Maharaja Jam Sahib of Navanagar (1872–1933) Indian cricketer and statesman. He made his cricketing début for Sussex in 1895, going on to score a total of 72 centuries as a batsman for Sussex and England (when he was popularly known as 'Ranji'). In 1907 he succeeded his cousin as maharaja of the state of Navanagar and promoted a number of modernization schemes to improve the state's infrastructure. He was knighted in 1917.

Rank, J(oseph) Arthur, 1st Baron (1888–1972) British industrialist and film executive, founder of the Rank Organization. In the 1930s he became interested in films when, as chairman of a flour-milling business and a Methodist Sunday school teacher, he realized that they could be an ideal medium for spreading the Gospel. He founded the film production and distribution company known as the Rank Organization in 1941. Under his chairmanship it went on to own or control the leading British studios and cinema chains in the 1940s and 1950s.

Rann of Kutch See KUTCH, RANN OF.

Ransom, John Crowe (1888–1974) US poet and critic. He studied at Oxford University and then taught at Vanderbilt University 1914–38, during which time he published *Poems About God* (1919). With the book *The New Criticism* (1941) he started a school of criticism that rejected the Victorian emphasis on literature as a moral force and advocated a close analysis of textual structure in isolation from the social background of the text.

Ransome, Arthur (Michell) (1884–1967) British novelist. Ransome is best known for his children's classics, such as *Swallows and Amazons* (1930) and *Great Northern?* (1947), which depict the imaginative world of children, while reflecting a keen interest in sailing, fishing, and the countryside.

ranunculus See BUTTERCUP.

Rao, P(amulaparti) V(enkata) Narasimha (1921–   ) Indian statesman, Prime Minister 1991–96.

Raoult, François Marie (1830–1901) French chemist considered one of the founders of physical chemistry. He formulated **Raoult's law**, which relates the vapour pressure of a solution to the number of molecules of solute dissolved in it. This law explains the lowering of the FREEZING-POINT and the raising of the BOILING-POINT of a solvent by the addition of a solute and provides a method for calculating the relative molecular masses of dissolved substances.

rape (or **oilseed rape**) A plant that is a variety of the species *Brassica napus*. It belongs to the mustard family, and is an annual plant, grown either to be grazed by cattle or, increasingly in recent years, for its oil-rich seeds. Autumn or spring sown, the 1 m (3.25 feet) tall plant produces masses of yellow flowers. Up to 40 per cent of the seed is oil, and is used in the manufacture of margarine and cooking oils.

rape (in law) The crime of having sexual intercourse with a person (usually female but sometimes male) who has not freely given consent. Rape is considered a violent CRIME as well as a sexual offence. Evidence suggests that in as many as half of all rapes, the attacker is already known to the victim, and, furthermore, that most rapes are planned and systematic. Rape is difficult to prove in law, since it is usually one person's word against another's: conviction hinges on proving that the victim has not consented and that the attacker realized this. Under British law, sexual assaults against males (by an attacker of either sex) were not recognized as rape until 1994.

Raphael (born Raffaello Sanzio) (1483–1520) Italian painter and architect. He was a leading figure of the High Renaissance in Italy. From 1504 to 1508 he worked a good deal in Florence, where he painted a series of small madonnas distinguished by a serenity of expression. On moving to Rome in 1508 he was commissioned to paint the frescos in various papal rooms in the Vatican (1509). At this time he worked on further madonnas, including his best-known altarpiece the *Sistine Madonna* (*c.*1513). He was also an important architect and was put in charge of the work on St Peter's Basilica in Rome (1514).

rare-earth element See LANTHANIDE.

rare gas See NOBLE GAS.

Rarotonga A mountainous island in the South Pacific, the chief island of the Cook Islands. Its chief town, Avarua, is the capital of the Cook Islands.

Rasmussen, Knud Johan Victor (1879–1933) Danish Arctic explorer and ethnologist, born in Greenland of part-Inuit descent. In 1921–24 he undertook a polar journey from Baffin Island to the north-east corner of Siberia by dog-sledge, making a scientific study of virtually every Inuit tribe in the region. As well as his valuable cartographic, archaeological, and ethnographic studies, he published translations of Inuit mythology and song.

raspberry A prickly, deciduous bush belonging to the genus *Rubus*, related to the blackberry and other fruit bushes within the rose family. Raspberries are cultivated commercially in parts of Europe and western North America. The fruit is made up of an aggregate of many single-seeded fruitlets, characteristically separating from the conical white core when it is picked. These fruits are usually red, but yellow and black-fruited types also occur. Raspberries are perennial plants with upright, slightly prickly canes, and the fruit is usually borne on two-year-old canes.

Rasputin, Grigori (Efimovich) (1871–1916) Russian monk. Originally a Siberian peasant, he came to exert great influence over Tsar Nicholas II and his family during World War I by claiming miraculous powers to heal the heir to the throne, who suffered from haemophilia. His appropriation of ecclesiastical, political, and military powers, with the support of the Empress Alexandra during Nicholas's absence, combined with a reputation for debauchery, steadily discredited the imperial family and was one of the main causes of the Russian Revolution. Rasputin was eventually assassinated by a group loyal to the tsar.

Ras Shamra See UGARIT.

Rastafarian A sect of Jamaican origin believing that African Americans are the chosen people, that the late Emperor Haile Selassie of Ethiopia was God Incarnate, and that he will secure their repatriation to their homeland in Africa. Ras Tafari (Amharic, *ras* chief) was the title by which Haile Selassie was known from 1916 until his accession in 1930.

rat A RODENT belonging to a widespread group of the family Muridae. This family also includes mice, but several other subfamilies, including the Cricetomyinae, Otomyinae, and Rhizomyinae are called rats. Most usually, however, a rat is a member of the genus *Rattus*, of which there are 63 species with a worldwide distribution.

Two species are of particular economic importance because of their destructive feeding habits and their role in the transmission of disease. These are the black rat, *Rattus rattus*, and the brown rat, *R. norvegicus*, but as the colour varies in either species, the alternative names of ship rat and common rat are preferred. The former was distributed throughout the world by ships. It arrived in Britain during the 11th century and was the species implicated in the Black Death of the Middle Ages. The common rat, a native of China, arrived in Europe around 1729, rapidly displacing the ship rat.

Diseases spread by rats include plague, typhus, leptospirosis, toxoplasmosis, and food poisoning.

Ratana, Tahupotiki Wiremu (1873–1939) Maori political and religious leader. A Methodist farmer, he founded the Ratana Church (1920), an interdenominational movement whose aim was to unite Maoris of all tribes. Its doctrine of faith-healing and many unorthodox rituals led to a rift with other Christian denominations in 1925. Politically Ratana struggled for Maori rights by pressing for full implementation of the Treaty of Waitangi.

ratel (or **honey badger**) A badger-like carnivore, closely related to true BADGERS, that occurs throughout most of Africa and southern Asia as far east as the Bay of Bengal. The single species, *Mellivora capensis*, is also known as the honey badger on account of its habit of breaking open the nests of wild bees. It is omnivorous and extremely aggressive; although only about 12 kg (26 pounds) in weight, it has been known to drive lions away from their kill.

rate of a reaction See CHEMICAL REACTION.

ratfish See CHIMAERA.

rationalism A broad philosophical position characterized by the claim that REASON is, in some way, a source of knowledge. This claim can mean either that reason provides A PRIORI concepts (or innate ideas), which can give the content of knowledge, or, more simply, that sense-experience gives the content, which then has to be corrected, and justified, by reason. Rationalist is the common label for 17th-century philosophers, such as DESCARTES, LEIBNIZ, and SPINOZA. Traditionally, rationalism stands opposed to EMPIRICISM, in which experience provides all of our concepts, and is the ultimate source of justification of knowledge claims. Philosophers, such as KANT, attempted to synthesize the insights of the two.

rat kangaroo A small MARSUPIAL belonging to the same family as the large kangaroos. They are called rat kangaroos mainly because of their small size: they do not look much like rats except for one species from Queensland. Most of the ten species have kangaroo-like hind-limbs, which, although relatively short, are used for hopping.

rat opossum (or **shrew opossum**) A member of the family Caenolestidae, a group of five species of small South American MARSUPIALS confined to the Andes. They have long tails like rats, but their pointed snouts give them a closer resemblance to shrews. Like shrews, they are insectivorous. The females lack the marsupial pouch.

rat-tail A deep-water marine fish found in all oceans, of which there are around 250 species. They are blunt-headed and have an extremely long tail, a short, high dorsal fin, and a many-rayed but low anal fin. They make up their own family, the Macrouridae, and are distantly related to cod. They are near-bottom feeders, and possibly the most abundant fishes in the deep ocean.

rattan A climbing PALM, notably many of the 200 species of the genus *Calamus*, particularly common in the forests of tropical Asia. Rattans include some of the longest known organisms, some exceeding 100 m (330 feet). They climb upwards as a host tree grows, and collapse as it decays; then, the growing tip climbs up again as a new host grows into the canopy, and so on. Many are fiercely armed with thorns. Their major importance is in the manufacture of cane furniture, an important forest export of such countries as Indonesia and Malaysia.

Rattigan, Sir Terence (Mervyn) (1911–77) British dramatist. His plays include *The Winslow Boy* (1946), concerning a father's fight to clear the name of his accused son, *The Browning Version* (1948), about a repressed and unpopular schoolmaster, and *Ross* (1960), based on the life of T. E. Lawrence. He also wrote screenplays for several films, including *The Yellow Rolls Royce* (1965).

Rattle, Sir Simon (Denis) (1955–) British conductor. He made his reputation as principal conductor with the City of Birmingham Symphony Orchestra, a post which he held from 1980 until 1991, when he became the orchestra's music director (until 1996). He is noted particularly for his interpretation of works by early 20th-century composers such as Mahler, and as a champion of new music.

rattlesnake A venomous snake of the PIT VIPER group, the family Crotalidae, confined to the Americas, where distribution extends from southern Canada to northern Argentina and Uruguay. Their most remarkable feature is the rattle at the end of the tail. The rattle consists of horny interlocking segments and makes a buzzing sound when vibrated rapidly. New segments are added to the rattle each time the snake's skin is shed; barring damage, the older the specimen the longer the rattle. The purpose of the rattle is to warn other animals of the snake's presence and prevent it from being accidentally trampled on. The rattle is thus defensive: when the snake is alarmed, it shakes its tail.

Large rattlesnakes feed mainly on small mammals; smaller forms tend to prefer lizards. All species bear their young alive. There are two main subgroups of rattlesnakes: the pygmy rattlesnakes of the genus *Sistrurus*, which grow to 60 cm (2 feet) and have small rattles, and the larger rattlesnakes of the genus *Crotalus*, which can reach 2.4 m (8 feet) in length.

Rauschenberg, Robert (1925–) US artist. During the 1950s and 1960s he produced a series of 'combine' paintings, such as *Charlene* (1954) and *Rebus* (1955), which incorporate three-dimensional objects such as nails, rags, and bottles. His work has also included theatre design and choreography, and he combined art with new technology in pieces such as *Soundings* (1968).

Ravel, Maurice (Joseph) (1875–1937) French composer. His early music was influenced by impressionism and the piano music of Liszt, but his mature works have a distinctive tone colour as well as an ironic flavour derived from the use of unresolved dissonances. Major works include the ballet *Daphnis and Chloë* (1912), staged by Diaghilev's Ballets Russes, the opera *L'Enfant et les sortilèges* (1925), and the orchestral works *La Valse* (1920) and *Boléro* (1928). He also wrote chamber music and piano music, including two piano concertos (1930, for left hand only, and 1931).

raven Any of ten species of bird of the genus *Corvus*, part of the crow family. The best-known member of the group is the common raven, *C. corax*, a glossy blue-black bird that may grow to 65 cm (26 inches) in length. Its hoarse croak has given it the reputation of being a bird of ill omen. Ravens are found in virtually every country of the world, with the largest number of species in Australia.

Ravenna A historic tourist city near the Adriatic coast in the Emilia-Romagna region of north-east-central Italy; pop. (1991) 136,720. An important centre in Roman times, Ravenna became the capital of the Ostrogothic kingdom of Italy in the 5th century and afterwards served as capital of the Byzantine Empire of Italy. It became an independent republic in the 13th century and then a papal possession in 1509, remaining in papal hands until 1859. The discovery of natural gas nearby in the 1950s has led to the development of refining and petrochemical industries.

Rawalpindi An industrial city in Punjab province, northern Pakistan, in the foothills of the Himalayas; pop. (1981) 928,000. A former military station controlling the routeways to Kashmir, it was interim capital of Pakistan 1959–67 during the construction of Islamabad. It has an oil refinery and numerous industries.

Rawls, John (1921–) US philosopher. He is the author of *A Theory of Justice* (1972), which invokes the philosophical concept of social contract and attacks the utilitarian doctrine of subjugating individual needs to the more pressing claims of the general good, arguing for principles to be formulated that guarantee basic liberties.

ray A member of a moderately large order, Rajiformes, containing some 300 species of CARTILAGINOUS FISHES. They are related to the sharks but are distinguished from them by having the five or six paired gill-openings on the underside of the head and the eyes and spiracles on top, and by the enormous development of the pectoral fins, which join onto the head. These features make them suited to life on the sea-bed; in particular, the dorsal spiracles mean they can pump water over the gills without raising themselves from the sea-bed. However, several rays, notably the manta rays and eagle rays, have adopted a mid-water to surface lifestyle.

Rays have evolved in several ways. Most numerous are those of the family Rajidae (known as SKATES), which lay eggs in rectangular capsules. The electric ray family, which includes TORPEDOES, is heavy-bodied with large dorsal and tail fins, and powerful electric organs in the head and back region (skates also produce weak electric currents). There are several small families of STINGRAY, including the South American river sting-rays, which are the only cartilaginous fishes to live in fresh water. SAWFISHES are a family of unmistakable rays with their long, serrated snouts.

Ray, John (1627–1705) English naturalist. His principal interest was botany, and his major work was the three-volume *Historia Plantarum* (1686–1704). He toured Europe with F. Willoughby (1635–72) in search of specimens of flora and fauna. Ray was the first to classify flowering plants into monocotyledons and dicotyledons, he established the species as the basic taxonomic unit.

Ray, Man (born Emmanuel Rudnitsky) (1890–1976) US photographer, painter, and film-maker. He helped to found the New York Dada movement before moving to Paris in 1921 and becoming a leading figure in the European Dada and surrealist movements. Ray pioneered the photogram or 'rayograph', placing objects on sensitized paper and exposing them to light; he later applied the technique to film-making.

Ray, Satyajit (1921–92) Indian film director. His first film, *Pather Panchali* (1955), won a prize at Cannes and brought Indian films to the attention of Western audiences. Filmed in neo-realist style and set in his native Bengal, it formed part of a trilogy completed by *Aparijito* (1956) and *Apur Sansar* (1959). His other films include *Kanchenjunga* (1962), for which he also wrote the music, and *The Home and the World* (1984).

Rayleigh, John William Strutt, 3rd Baron (1842–1919) British physicist. He published a major work on acoustics, *The Theory of Sound*, and carried out pioneering work on atmospheric airglow and black-body radiation. He was director of the Cavendish Laboratory after James Maxwell, his researches including the establishment of electrical units of resistance, current, and electromotive force. He worked with William Ramsay from 1894, and their accurate measurement of the constituents of the atmosphere led to the discovery of argon and other inert gases. In 1904 Rayleigh was awarded the Nobel Prize for physics.

rayon The first successful manufactured fibre, made from CELLULOSE and patented by CROSS in 1892. There are two main categories of rayon: viscose and acetate. Both are made from natural cellulose, usually wood-pulp or cotton linters (very short fibres), and both are made into filaments by extrusion through spinnerets (see NYLON). Cellulose is dissolved in caustic soda (SODIUM HYDROXIDE) for making viscose and in PROPANONE when making acetate rayon, extruded as a solution (wet SPINNING) and subsequently coagulated. The wet-spinning process for viscose rayon was patented in 1892 by CROSS and BEVAN. As with synthetics, rayon fibres are made in varying degrees of fineness and are used both as short or staple fibre (alone or in blends) and as long, continuous filament yarn.

razorbill An AUK, *Alca torda*, of the North Atlantic and Arctic oceans, breeding from France to Greenland. The deep bills, upright stance, and diving habit of razorbills make them the closest northern equivalent to penguins. Their head and back are black and their underparts white. They nest colonially on cliffs, raising a single chick, which leaves the nest before its wings are fully feathered. Razorbills feed mainly on small fishes and plankton.

razor-shell A long, rectangular BIVALVE belonging to the family Solenidae, shaped like an old-fashioned cut-throat razor. It is specialized for burrowing in sand of coastal waters and can escape from predators at speed by a very efficient digging action. Normally only the feeding siphons, used to filter out detritus for food, are exposed at the surface of sandy beaches; if the animal senses vibrations in the sand it stops feeding and rapidly digs downwards until danger passes.

Re (or **Ra**) In Egyptian mythology, god of the Sun and of creation. He is depicted most frequently as a falcon-headed man with a Sun disc on his head, but can also be seen as a ram-headed man. His chief cult centre was On (Heliopolis), from whence emerged the Heliopolitan creation myth. During the Amarna Period (*c.*1353–1335 BC), the heretic Pharaoh Akhenaten chose to worship the visible Sun's disc, which is called the Aten, a form of the god Re. By the 5th dynasty (*c.*2495–*c.*2345 BC) every Pharaoh claimed to be both the son of Re, and even Re himself.

reactance The opposition, measured in ohms (Ω), of a reactor (a CAPACITOR or an inductor) to alternating current. Unlike resistance (see RESISTOR), reactance varies with the frequency of the alternating current; the reactance of an inductor increases with increasing frequency, while that of a capacitor decreases. See also IMPEDANCE.

Reade, Charles (1814–84) British novelist and dramatist. He is remembered for his historical romance *The Cloister and the Hearth* (1861); set in the 15th century, it relates the adventures of Gerard, father of Erasmus.

Reading The county town of Berkshire in southern England, on the River Kennet near its junction with the Thames; pop. (1991) 122,600. It has a university (1926) and the remains of a 12th-century Clunaic abbey in which Henry I is buried. It is a market and residential town with numerous light industries including electronics, engineering, biscuits, and seeds.

Reading An industrial and commercial city in south-east Pennsylvania, USA; on the Schuylkill River; pop. (1990) 78,380. Founded in 1748 on land purchased from the Lenni-Lenape Indians by William Penn, it was named Reading by his sons Thomas and Richard after their former home in England. It was an early iron-production centre making ordnance during both the Revolutionary and Civil Wars. A farmstead near here was the birthplace in 1734 of the frontiersman Daniel Boone.

Reagan, Ronald (Wilson) (1911–) US Republican statesman, 40th President of the USA 1981–89. He was a Hollywood actor before entering politics and becoming governor of California (1966–74). In 1981, at the age of 69, he became the oldest-ever President of the USA. During his presidency military expenditure was increased, the Strategic Defense Initiative was launched, taxes and spending on social services were reduced, and the national budget deficit rose to record levels. An intermediate nuclear forces non-proliferation treaty with the USSR was signed in 1987.

realism (in the arts) The artistic representation of some aspect of everyday life (usually in painting, cinema, drama, or the novel) to produce a convincingly lifelike effect. In the broad sense, realism is a characteristic of many writers and artists, DEFOE and VERMEER, for instance, before the 19th century, but the novels of BALZAC and the paintings of COURBET helped to inspire a self-consciously realist trend in late 19th-century French culture, which spread to the rest of Europe and the USA and developed into naturalism. The novels of FLAUBERT, notably *Madame Bovary* (1857), George ELIOT, and TOLSTOY, and the plays of IBSEN and SHAW usually show the best features of realism. In the 20th century, realism tended to be eclipsed by various movements, CUBISM, EXPRESSIONISM, MODERNISM, and others, which challenged the conventional reproduction of external reality. In Italy, however, an important group of 'neorealist' film-makers such as ROSSELLINI, had a worldwide impact from the late 1940s with their use of outdoor locations, amateur actors, and 'documentary' styles, which in turn influenced the CINÉMA-VÉRITÉ of the French NOUVELLE VAGUE.

realism (in philosophy) A view of any subject area or range of judgements holding that truth and falsity in that area is determined by how things stand in the world, independently of our opinions, or the evidence we can have for those opinions. Various philosophical doctrines have opposed realism in particular areas: emotivism is a form of anti-realism about morality; instrumentalism is an anti-realist attitude to scientific theories. A principal motivation for anti-realist views has been the difficulty of explaining how we can come to know the realist's completely independent facts.

real numbers The numbers corresponding to the points on an infinitely long straight line. They include positive and negative whole numbers (−1, 7, 416, for example), fractions (1/2, 99/100), and all the numbers in between, including IRRATIONAL NUMBERS. Two real numbers are required to define COMPLEX NUMBERS.

real time (computing) The computer analysis of events as they happen rather than data stored for later processing. Real-time computing is extremely important in the automatic control of, for example, vehicles or machinery, where decisions need to be executed as soon as possible after an event has occurred.

reason (or **rationality**) The faculty of making judgements and inferences. Reason may be divided into theoretical and practical reason. Theoretical reason aims at true belief; practical reason aims at right action. The operations of reason can also be divided into DEDUCTION and INDUCTION, and can to some extent be formally described by LOGIC. Reason is distinguished from other faculties, such as PERCEPTION, emotion, and imagination. The relative power of reason and desire is a central philosophical question; HUME claimed that practical reason can only ever be the 'slave of the passions'. Possession of reason is often said to provide the essential difference between man and other members of the animal kingdom. DESCARTES described human reason as 'universal', meaning that a being that has reason is not limited to a fixed stock of responses, and connected the faculty of reason with the ability to use LANGUAGE. The existence of reason provides a major challenge for a naturalistic view of persons.

Réaumur, René Antoine Ferchault de (1683–1757) French scientist. He compiled a list of France's arts, industries, and professions, and, as a consequence, suggested improvements in several manufacturing processes. He is chiefly remembered for his thermometer scale, now obsolete, which set the melting-point of ice at 0° and the boiling-point of water at 80°. Réaumur also carried out pioneering work on insects and other invertebrates.

rebec A bowed musical instrument of the Middle Ages and Renaissance. The body was carved and hollowed from a solid block of wood, with a thin belly of spruce or similar wood laid over the hollow. The back was normally rounded, so that the instrument looked like an elongated half-pear. In the Renaissance rebecs were used principally for dance music, with a family of sizes. The three-stringed treble was the most important, and was one of the ancestors of the violin. Rebecs still exist today as folk instruments, especially in Eastern Europe.

Rebecca One of the four Jewish matriarchs, wife of Isaac, and sister of Laban, mother of the twin brothers Esau and Jacob. Rebecca devised the deception of the blind and aged Isaac which enabled Jacob, her favourite, to obtain his father's blessing and become the traditional ancestor of the people of Israel.

Recent Epoch (in geology) See HOLOCENE EPOCH.

receptacle See FLOWER.

recession (in economics) A period of underemployment of RESOURCES in an economy, as a result of a temporary reduction in aggregate demand. It is now technically defined as two consecutive quarters of falling output. It is normally viewed as a phase of the TRADE CYCLE – the typical cyclical fluctuation of aggregate demand relative to supply potential. A slump is a severe recession. Economic DEPRESSION is the term used to denote a more sustained period of UNEMPLOYMENT.

Recife (formerly **Pernambuco**) A port and tourist resort on the Atlantic coast of Pernambuco state, north-east Brazil; pop. (1991) 1,298,230. Situated at the mouth of the River Capibaribe, it is state capital and a leading port of the north-east. It was the original capital of Brazil 1537–49. Recife exports primary products from its hinterland and has sugar refineries and cotton mills.

reciprocating engine Any engine in which a sliding piston is constrained to move to and fro (or up and down), usually transmitting power via a crankshaft and connecting-rod to a rotating flywheel. The earliest STEAM-ENGINES were reciprocating BEAM-ENGINES, later replaced by crankshaft engines. GAS-ENGINES, PETROL ENGINES, STIRLING engines, and DIESEL ENGINES are normally reciprocating engines, although some Diesels, are turbines and some petrol engines, such as the Wankel engine, are ROTARY ENGINES.

recitative See OPERA.

recombinant DNA See GENETIC ENGINEERING.

Reconstruction Acts (1867–68) Legislation passed by the US Congress dealing with the reorganization of the South in the aftermath of the AMERICAN CIVIL WAR. The question of the treatment of the defeated CONFEDERACY raised conflicting priorities between reconciliation with white Southerners and justice for the freed slaves. In 1866 an impasse developed between President Andrew JOHNSON, and the Republican majorities in Congress. In 1867 Congress passed, over the President's veto, a Reconstruction Act that divided the South into military districts, and required the calling of a new constitutional convention in each state, elected by universal manhood suffrage. The new state governments were to provide for black suffrage and to ratify the Fourteenth Amendment as conditions for readmittance to the Union. Further Reconstruction Acts were passed in the following 12 months to counter Southern attempts to delay or circumvent the implementation of the first measure.

record A thin plastic disc on which sound is recorded as a horizontally undulating pattern on the inside of a continuous groove which spirals inwards from the outer part of the disc. The first record was produced by Emil Berliner in 1887, for his GRAMOPHONE. Large-scale reproduction was developed in 1894. Berliner also pioneered the use of electro-forming techniques for the large-scale reproduction of records. In this process the master disc is first made electrically conductive and then plated with either nickel or copper, making a negative mould. After separation from the master the negative can be used directly in a plastic-moulding press. For commercial quantities of records, positive copies of the master, called stampers, are used to make thousands of records. Early records were made of shellac to rotate on gramophone turntables at 78 r.p.m. From the 1950s these were replaced by vinyl plastic records (rotating at 45 r.p.m. or 33 r.p.m.). These records were lighter, more resilient, and had better moulding characteristics. From the 1960s the record began to be replaced by the audiocassette and in the 1980s by the COMPACT DISC.

recorder A musical instrument, a DUCT FLUTE. The recorder is a special form of FLAGEOLET, with, in the Renaissance, one thumb- and eight fingerholes, the lowest being duplicated to be accessible to either little finger. Renaissance recorders were in one piece and, initially, cylindrical in bore. By the late 16th century the inversely conical bore, narrowing towards the foot, had been introduced, resulting in increased range and improved tuning of the upper notes. Around 1660–70 the Baroque form of the recorder was devised at the French court; this was in three sections, head, body, and foot. Because the foot could be turned, the duplicated hole was unnecessary. The conicity was increased, extending the range and improving the tuning. It is this form that is now commonly used.

record player See GRAMOPHONE.

recrystallization The process of purifying or improving the quality of a crystalline substance by repeated crystallization. With each crystallization, fresh solvent is used to dissolve the substance, and some impurities are left behind as undissolved solid. The solution is then filtered and evaporated until crystallization begins; other impurities will be left in the used solvent.

rectifier A device that passes current in one direction only, offering a low resistance to signals of one polarity, but a very high resistance to signals of the opposite polarity. The commonest rectifiers are solid-state DIODES, which except for large currents, have replaced thermionic diodes. Rectifiers are used in power supplies as the first stage of converting alternating-current signals into direct-current signals; the second stage typically being a smoothing circuit. Rectifiers are also used to detect radio and television signals.

rectum The terminal part of the large intestine of animals in the posterior part of the pelvic cavity. It functions as a store for faeces before they are voided through a ring of voluntary muscle known as the anal sphincter.

recycling The processing of waste so that it can be recovered and reused. Historically, recycling has largely been carried out for economic reasons, but recently its value in reducing the depletion of natural resources has been emphasized. Recycling items of domestic refuse also helps reduce the growing problem of waste disposal. Metals, such as scrap steel, are returned to the steel mill for reprocessing. Recycling of paper has become important in view of accelerating DEFORESTATION. French, German, Japanese, and Norwegian authorities have taken steps to set up stable markets for recycled paper. Glass is also recycled, often being first sorted into colours. Some 3 million tonnes of glass are recycled annually in Europe. Road materials, such as asphalt and concrete, can be planed off the road, heated, mixed, and relaid. Thermoplastics can quite easily be recycled if the waste is a fairly pure sample of one plastic, but recycling of mixed plastics gives poor results. Some manufacturers of engineering plastics for the motor car and aerospace industry design plastic products that are easier to recycle.

red admiral butterfly A velvety brown, BRUSH-FOOTED BUTTERFLY of the genus *Vanessa*, originally called a 'red admirable', with red bands on the fore- and hind-wings: the fore-wing apex is white-spotted black. Its caterpillars usually feed on plants of the nettle family. The common red admiral, *V. atalanta*, occurs throughout Europe, Asia, North Africa, and North America. Other species are more restricted in their distribution, such as the blue admiral, *V. canace*, of south-east Asia.

Red Army Soviet army formed by TROTSKY as Commissar for War (1918–25) to save the BOLSHEVIK revolution during the RUSSIAN CIVIL WAR. For trained officers, Trotsky had to rely on former officers of the Imperial Army. After HITLER's invasion of the Soviet Union (1941) the Red Army became the largest in the world – reaching five million by 1945. Precise figures remain unknown, but Red Army casualties in World War II have been estimated as high as seven million men. The name fell into disuse shortly after World War II and was replaced by that of Soviet Armed Forces, which in turn adopted the titles of the independent republics after the breakup of the Soviet Union in 1991.

red-backed vole See BANK VOLE.

Red Baron, the See RICHTHOFEN.

Redbridge A borough of north-east Greater London, England, that includes the suburbs of Chigwell, Ilford, Wanstead, and Woodford; pop. (1991) 220,600. Primarily residential, it is also an important commercial and light industrial centre. It includes much of Epping Forest within its boundaries.

red bug A BUG of the family Pyrrhocoridae, contrastingly marked with red or orange and black. Most are flattened, plant-feeding bugs, although some resemble ants, and at least one is carnivorous. They include the cotton stainers, *Dysdercus* species, widely distributed in warm countries, which pierce cotton bolls to feed on the seeds, thereby admitting a fungus which stains the fibres. They are serious pests in India and North America.

Red Cross International agency concerned with the alleviation of human suffering. Its founder, the Swiss philanthropist Henri Dunant (1828–1910), horrified by the suffering he saw at the Battle of Solferino, proposed the formation of voluntary aid societies for the relief of war victims. In 1863 the International Committee of the Red Cross was established and in the following year 12 governments signed the GENEVA CONVENTION. This drew up the terms for the care of soldiers and was extended to include victims of naval warfare (1906), prisoners of war (1929), and, 20 years later, civilians. Its conventions have now been ratified by almost 150 nations. Its flag is a red cross on a white background. In Muslim countries the cross is replaced by a red crescent. The International Red Cross was awarded Nobel Peace Prizes in 1917 and 1944.

red currant A European native shrub, *Ribes rubrum*, which like its close relative, the black currant, belongs to the family Grossulariaceae. Cultivated types may be either derived directly from *R. rubrum* or from crosses with other *Ribes* species. These crosses have produced a variety of fruit colours ranging from red to white. The white currant, for example, is often preferred as the fruit is less acid. In contrast to black currant, the fruit is produced on the older wood.

red deer A species of deer, *Cervus elephas*, widely distributed in North America (where it is known as the **wapiti** or **elk**), Europe, and Asia. In summer the coat is a rich red-brown colour, becoming a greyish-brown in winter. The stag may have a shoulder height of up to 1.4 m (4.6 feet) with antlers up to 1 m (3.25 feet). Only the stags bear antlers; these are cast each year and become progressively more complex, reaching full development when the stag is six years old.

For most of the year the sexes are segregated. In the rutting season, each stag collects a harem of hinds and guards them and his territory against all challengers. About eight months after mating, the hind leaves the herd and gives birth to a single calf. Some hinds bear each year, others only in alternate years. The calf is suckled for 12 months.

Redding, Otis (1941–67) US soul singer. Despite never achieving a major US pop success until after his death, Redding was one of the most influential soul singers of the late 1960s. It was not until an appearance at the Monterey pop festival in 1967 that he gained widespread recognition; he died in a plane crash the following December.

redfish A fish of the genus *Sebastes*, which belongs to the scorpionfish family. The name is used for the three North Atlantic species, especially for a fish otherwise known as the ocean perch, *Sebastes marinus*. In the North Pacific, where there are more than 60 species of *Sebastes*, they are known as **rockfishes**, although similar in all other respects to the redfish. Most species are thickset, with large heads, and spiny dorsal and anal fins, and are red in colour. Different species live at different depths from the shoreline down to 1,000 m (3,250 feet).

Redford, (Charles) Robert (1936–) US film actor and director. He made his name playing opposite Paul Newman in *Butch Cassidy and the Sundance Kid* (1969), co-starring again with him in *The Sting* (1973). Other notable films include *The Great Gatsby* (1974), *All the President's Men* (1976), and *Out of Africa* (1986). Redford won an Oscar as the director of *Ordinary People* (1980), and was nominated for one for *Quiz Show* (1994).

red giant A GIANT STAR that is also a late-type star. The LUMINOSITIES of typical giant stars range from 50 times that of the Sun at SPECTRAL CLASS G5 to 1000 times at class M5. Most red giants are of spectral class K or M. Highly evolved stars of spectral classes C and R, which are found only among the giant and SUPERGIANT stars, are much rarer. Several bright naked-eye stars are red giants, including Aldebaran, Arcturus, and Pollux.

Redgrave A family of British actors. **Sir Michael (Scudamore)** (1908–85) was a well-known stage actor, who played numerous Shakespearian roles as well as appearing in other plays, notably in the title role of *Uncle Vanya* (1963). He also starred in such films as *The Browning Version* (1951) and *The Importance of Being Earnest* (1952). His elder daughter **Vanessa** (1937–) has had a successful career in the theatre and cinema: her films include *Mary Queen of Scots* (1972), *Julia* (1976), for which she won an Oscar, and *Howard's End* (1992). His son **Corin** (1939–) is also an actor, as is his younger daughter **Lynn** (1944–), who has made a number of stage and screen performances, is best known for the film *Georgy Girl* (1966). Vanessa's two daughters **Joely** (1958–) and **Natasha Richardson** (1963–) are both actresses.

red grouse The British and Irish subspecies of the willow grouse or willow ptarmigan, *Lagopus lagopus*, which is a member of the grouse family. In all other subspecies the wings are white and much of the body plumage turns white in winter, but in red grouse the wings and body plumage stay a dark reddish-brown all the year round. The red grouse lives on open moorland and eats mainly heather shoots, though the growing chicks eat many insects.

Red Guards Militant young supporters of MAO ZEDONG during the Chinese CULTURAL REVOLUTION (1966–69). Taking their name from the army units organized by Mao in 1927, the Red Guards, numbering several million, provided the popular, paramilitary vanguard of the Cultural Revolution. They attacked supposed reactionaries, the Communist Party establishment, China's cultural heritage, and all vestiges of Western influence, maintaining the momentum of the movement through mass demonstrations, a constant poster war, and violent attacks on people and property. Fighting between opposing Red Guard groups led to thousands of deaths. After the Cultural Revolution, many were sent into the countryside for forced 're-education'.

red lead (or **dilead(II) lead(IV) oxide**, Pb_3O_4) A scarlet crystalline powder, an oxide of LEAD, used in making storage batteries, paints, ceramic products, and flint glass. It is formed by heating yellow lead oxide in air at 400–500°C. Red-lead paint provides particularly effective rust protection for ironwork.

Redmond, John (Edward) (1856–1918) Irish politician. He succeeded Charles Parnell as leader of the Irish Nationalist Party in the House of Commons (1891–1918). The Home Rule Bill of 1912 was introduced with his support, although it was never implemented because of World War I.

Redon, Odilon (1840–1916) French painter and graphic artist. He was a leading exponent of symbolism, and an important forerunner of the surrealists, especially in his early work, which chiefly consisted of charcoal drawings of fantastic, often nightmarish, subjects. He began to use colour from about 1890 onwards, becoming known for his richly coloured pastels depicting flowers, mythological subjects, and portraits.

red panda (or **lesser panda**) A species, *Ailurus fulgens*, of the racoon family Procyonidae. It is found in an area from the Himalayas to south China. It has long, luxuriant fur of a deep, rich chestnut colour, except for the face, which is white with a narrow, dark stripe running from the eyes to the corners of the mouth. The tail is ringed with bands alternately light and dark. In many ways this animal resembles a racoon. At night it forages for bamboo shoots, grass roots, acorns, and fruit. It usually rests in trees during the day, with its long bushy tail curled round its body. See also PANDA.

Red Sea A long narrow landlocked sea separating Africa from the Arabian Peninsula. It is linked to the Indian Ocean in the south by the Gulf of Aden and to the Mediterranean in the north by the Suez Canal. Its chief ports are Port Sudan, Massawa, Jeddah, and Hodeida.

redshank Either of two Old World species of SANDPIPER with scarlet legs. The white rump and hind border of the wing are conspicuous in flight. The typical call of the common redshank, *Tringa totanus*, is a musical 'tew-hew-hew', falling in pitch. When on the ground, they frequently bob their heads up and down in characteristic sandpiper fashion. The spotted redshank, *T. erythropus*, occurs in northern Europe and winters in Africa and China.

red shift A shift in spectral lines of celestial bodies towards the red end of the spectrum as a consequence of the DOPPLER effect. Light from the more distant objects in the Universe, such as galaxies and quasars, is red-shifted and this observation has to be incorporated into any theory of COSMOLOGY. The usual explanation of the red shift is that it is due to the expansion of the Universe. It is now generally accepted that the extremely large red shift of quasars is a consequence of their very large distances from the Earth and these objects are therefore used by astronomers to give information about the Universe both at great distances and at earlier epochs, since the light has taken many millions of years to reach the Earth.

red spider mite One of the commonest orchard and greenhouse pests. They are herbivorous MITES belonging to the family Tetranychidae, and they possess needle-like mouthparts with which they pierce plant cells and suck out juices. Their tiny resistant eggs are attached to plants by silk. There may be several generations per year depending upon temperature. Adults move between crops by 'parachuting' on silk threads.

red squirrel See SQUIRREL.

redstart A small bird making up two groups, one belonging to the New World WARBLERS family, Parulidae, and the other to the Old World CHATS of the family Muscicapidae. The first group includes 11 species of the genus *Myioborus* and the American redstart, *Setophaga ruticilla*. The *Myioborus* species are found mainly in Central and South America, though the painted redstart, *M. pictus*, occurs in North America. All are brilliant red and black, often with white wing and tail markings. The Old World redstarts belong to the genus *Phoenicurus*. These birds have orange-red tails and black, grey, or red bodies. Although widespread in Eurasia, most occur in the mountain ranges of Asia.

reduction (in chemistry) See OXIDATION AND REDUCTION.

redwing (or **red-winged thrush**) A species of THRUSH, *Turdus iliacus*, which is widely distributed across the cooler parts of Europe and Asia. It is about 20 cm (8 inches) long, brown above, with a whitish eye-stripe, and pale with dark streaks below. There are orange-red patches on its flanks and under the wings, which are clearly visible when it flies. It feeds largely on insects and worms in summer, but takes many berries and fruits in winter.

redwood A tall North American conifer of the genera *Sequoia* or *Sequoiadendron*, each of which has one species. The Sierra redwood, *Sequoiadendron giganteum*, is also known as the mammoth tree, wellingtonia, giant sequoia, or big tree. It reaches some 98 m (over 320 feet) with a trunk diameter of up to 24 m (79 feet) and a mass of 2,000 tons, and is native to the Sierra Nevada hills of California. The coast redwood, *Sequoia sempervirens*, is one of the tallest known trees, reaching 112 m (368 feet) in height. It is native to southern California and produces a valuable soft, fine-grained timber, much in demand for building construction and carpentry. This has led to the loss of many of these trees, with the consequence that they are now conserved in forest refuge areas. Both species of redwood are very long-lived; some Sierra redwoods are considered to be 3,500 years old. They are relic species of a once much more numerous group of conifers.

reed A moisture-loving grass. Reeds belong mainly to the genus *Phragmites*. Three species are known, two of which are tropical, from Argentina and Asia, while the common reed, *P. communis*, is distributed widely throughout the temperate regions of the world. All colonize ditches, streams, and pond and lake margins, by means of perennial rhizomes from which arise leafy stems up to 4 m (13 feet) in height. In Europe, the common reed has long been used for thatching the roofs of houses, fencing, and furniture-making.

Reed, Sir Carol (1906–76) British film director. He made a succession of celebrated films in the post-war years, including *The Fallen Idol* (1948) and *The Third Man* (1949), both with screenplays by Grahame GREENE. Among his notable later films are *The Outcast of the Islands* (1952) and the musical *Oliver!* (1968), for which he won an Oscar.

Reed, Lou (full name Lewis Allan Reed) (1942–) US rock singer, guitarist, and songwriter. Reed led the Velvet Underground, an influential group probably best known for their first album, *The Velvet Underground and Nico* (1967) produced in association with Andy Warhol. His best-known solo recordings are the song 'Walk on the Wild Side' and the album *Transformer* (both 1972).

Reed, Walter (1851–1902) US physician. He worked mainly in the US Army Medical Corps, and finally headed the Yellow Fever Board (1900–01), based in Cuba. His group proved that the disease was transmitted by the mosquito *Aëdes aegypti*, and then showed that the agent responsible was a virus – the first to be recognized as the cause of a human disease. The mosquito's breeding places were successfully attacked, and a vaccine was developed some years later.

reedfish See BICHIR.

reed instruments Musical instruments whose sound is generated by a vibrating reed (usually made from plants such as *Arundo donax*, but also of other materials, including metal and slips of wood). Reeds are either beating or free, and beating reeds are either single or double. free reeds are so called because they vibrate freely to and fro in a closely fitting slot; unlike all other reeds they are sounded both by blowing and sucking. Single reeds are either a tongue cut in a tube of cane, attached at one end, as on some BAGPIPES and zummāras, or a slip of cane attached to a mouthpiece, as on CLARINETS and SAXOPHONES. The tongue beats against the body of the tube, and the slip of cane against the edges of the mouthpiece. Double reeds for OBOES and BASSOONS are two slips of cane beating against each other. On many SHAWMS, double reeds are flattened pieces of plant stem, so that the two sides beat against each other. With all reeds, the vibrations of the reed are transmitted to the column of air inside the instrument, which then produces a musical sound. The behaviour of WIND INSTRUMENTS is controlled by the shape of the bore, not by the type of reed.

reed warbler Any one of about 25 species of bird of the genus *Acrocephalus*, belonging to the Old World WARBLER family, Sylviidae. Varying in size from 13 to 20 cm (5 to 8 inches), they are mostly dull olive-green birds, though a few are buff and streaked. They live in thick vegetation, such as reed-beds and scrub, and often make their presence known by characteristic, powerful songs. The marsh warbler, *A. palustris*, is a great mimic of other birds' songs.

reef A mass of rock that generally occurs in relatively shallow coastal waters. The top of the reef usually projects above the surface of the sea, at least during low-water periods, although it may be permanently, though shallowly, submerged. While reefs may be made of solid rock or pebbles, they are more commonly formed from organic material. The most common type of reef is made of coral, the accumulated skeletons of coral polyp colonies. Coral reefs are particularly common in tropical seas.

referendum An electoral device that enables voters to express their opinion directly on an issue. A government may call a referendum in order to test public opinion, or to decide questions that cut across party lines, such as issues involving morality (for example, DIVORCE) or CONSTITUTION (for example, membership of the EU).

reflecting telescope (or **reflector**) In astronomy, a TELESCOPE utilizing a large concave mirror, referred to as the primary mirror, to collect light from a celestial object and bring it to a FOCUS. NEWTON believed there was no practical way of overcoming chromatic ABERRATION in the REFRACTING TELESCOPE of his time, and so built a reflecting telescope, now known as a **Newtonian**

telescope, in 1668. Since then, as the technology of casting and grinding large mirrors developed, the size of the primary mirror has increased. In addition, a number of different ways of viewing the image have been devised.

reflection The return of all or part of a beam of particles or waves when it strikes a smooth surface. All types of wave – light, sound, heat – may be reflected from a suitable surface; and provided none of the wave enters the surface, all the energy remains within the reflected wave. The two laws of reflection are based on the concept of a line, the normal, perpendicular to the reflecting surface and meeting it where the incident ray meets the surface. Then the reflected ray lies in the plane defined by the incident ray and the normal; and the angle between the reflected ray and the normal (the angle of reflection) is the same as that between the incident ray and the normal (the angle of incidence).

reflex A built-in involuntary response of the NERVOUS SYSTEM to a variety of external or internal stimuli. The simplest reflex involves two NEURONES: a sensory nerve cell with a receptor, and a motor neurone connected to a muscle or a gland. The sensory neurone transmits a signal directly to the motor neurone, through a connection within the brain, or in the spinal cord. This signal is known as a reflex arc.

Reform Acts A series of legislative measures that extended the franchise in 19th- and 20th-century Britain. The Reform Act of 1832 eliminated many anomalies, such as ROTTEN BOROUGHS, and enfranchised the new industrial towns, which had hitherto been unrepresented. The Reform Act of 1867 doubled the size of the electorate and gave many urban working-class men the vote. However, agricultural labourers and domestic servants had to wait a further 17 years to be enfranchised: the Reform Act of 1884 increased the electorate to about five million. The Representation of the People Act (1918) gave the vote to all men over the age of 21 and conceded some of the demands of the SUFFRAGETTES by enfranchising women over 30, but on a property qualification. Universal adult suffrage for everyone over 21 was finally achieved in the UK in 1928, when women between the ages of 21 and 30 secured the right to vote and the property qualification was abolished. In 1969 the voting age was lowered to 18.

Reformation The 16th-century movement for reform of the doctrines and practices of the ROMAN CATHOLIC CHURCH, ending in the establishment of Protestant, or REFORMED, CHURCHES.

The starting point of the Reformation is often given as 1517, when the German theologian Martin LUTHER launched his protest against the corruption of the papacy and the Roman Catholic Church, although he was breaking no new controversial ground. In fact, most of the Reformation movements laid stress, not on innovation, but on return to a primitive simplicity. Luther's theological reading led him to attack the central Catholic doctrines of transubstantiation, clerical celibacy, and papal supremacy. He also called for radical reform of the religious orders. By 1530 the rulers of Saxony, Hesse, Brandenburg, and Brunswick, as well as the kings of Sweden and Denmark had been won over to the reformed beliefs. They proceeded to break with the Roman Church, and set about regulating the churches in their territories according to Protestant principles.

In Switzerland, the Reformation was led first by ZWINGLI, who carried through antipapal, antihierarchic, and antimonastic reforms in Zurich. After his death the leadership passed to CALVIN, in whose hands reforming opinion assumed a more explicitly doctrinal and revolutionary tone. Calvinism became the driving force of the movement in western Germany, France, the Netherlands, and Scotland, where in each case it was linked with a political struggle. Calvinism was also the main doctrinal influence within the Anglican Church. In Europe the reforming movement was increasingly checked and balanced by the COUNTER-REFORMATION. The religious wars came to an end with the conclusion of the THIRTY YEARS WAR (1618–48).

Reformed Churches All PROTESTANT Churches, but especially those in the tradition of the French Protestant theologian John CALVIN. They emphasize that the Bible contains all that is necessary for salvation, and traditionally hold that God in his absolute power through PREDESTINATION wills who is to be saved or damned, though many Reformed Churches have modified this strict doctrine. Many countries have their own Reformed Churches; there are about 20 million full members in all.

Reform Judaism A movement founded in Germany by Zachariah Frankel (1801–75) in reaction to the perceived laxity of Liberal JUDAISM. Frankel questioned the wholly divine inspiration of the TORAH, whilst retaining observance of some Jewish laws and traditions. In the UK, Reform Jews might be regarded as being on the 'right' of the Liberal or Progressive movement. In the USA, Reform Judaism refers to the whole of the Liberal tradition, brought across by German immigrants in the 19th century. American Reform Jews are roughly equivalent to British Liberal Jews.

refracting telescope (or **refractor**) In astronomy, a TELESCOPE in which a large lens, known as the **objective**, acts as a light collector by focusing a beam of light from a celestial object into an image. The earliest astronomical refractor was developed by GALILEO in 1609. From 1609 to 1668, when NEWTON invented the REFLECTING TELESCOPE, the refractor was the only type of telescope employed in astronomy. Since then it has under-

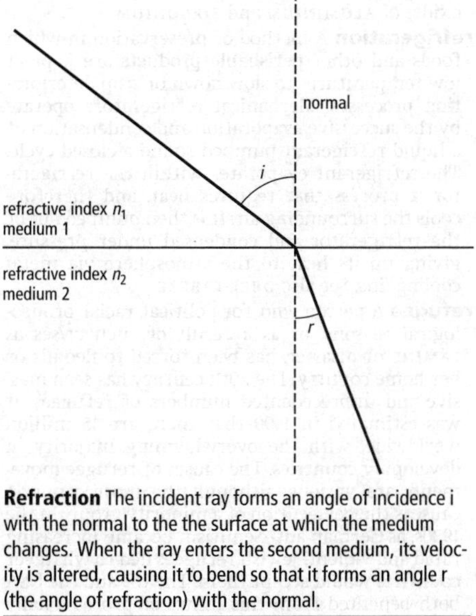

Refraction The incident ray forms an angle of incidence i with the normal to the the surface at which the medium changes. When the ray enters the second medium, its velocity is altered, causing it to bend so that it forms an angle r (the angle of refraction) with the normal.

gone a process of continual development. Although, in 1756, the British optician John Dolland showed that the defects of refractors, such as chromatic ABERRATION, could be corrected, it was eventually realized that lenses for refractors were impossible to make beyond a certain size. Thus the largest refractor in use still remains the 40-inch (1.02 m) telescope completed in the 19th century at the YERKES OBSERVATORY.

refraction The change in direction of a wave when it enters another medium, as for example when light passes from air to glass. If the direction of the ray is exactly at right angles to the surface no refraction occurs; but in all other cases the ray is bent towards the normal (an imaginary line perpendicular to the surface) when it enters a denser medium, and is bent away from it when it leaves. The angle between the normal and the refracted ray is called the angle of refraction, and this is related to the angle of incidence by a quantity called the REFRACTIVE INDEX (*n*) (see SNELL'S LAW). Refraction occurs with all forms of electromagnetic radiation, because the waves travel at slightly different speeds in different media. The principle is used optically in the design of lenses and prisms. See illustration p. 1139.

refractive index A value by which the capacity of a material to cause REFRACTION is measured. It is the ratio of the speeds of a wave in two different media (one of them usually being air or a vacuum), and is chiefly used of light. Between air and glass the refractive index is about 1.6, and between air and water at 25°C (77°F) it is about 1.3: that is, light travels 1.3 times as fast in air as in water. Light of different wavelengths is refracted by different amounts. This is the effect known as dispersion; it is responsible for the ability of a prism to separate the lines of atomic spectra.

refractory A substance that can withstand very high temperatures. Refractories are used to line KILNS, BLAST-FURNACES, incinerators, and other high-temperature environments. They must be unreactive at high temperatures and have good load-bearing properties. Oxides of the minerals magnesite and dolomite are important refractories used in steel furnaces and cement kilns. Other widely used refractories are SILICON CARBIDE and oxides of ALUMINIUM and ZIRCONIUM.

refrigeration A method of preservation in which foods and other perishable products are kept at low temperatures to slow down or stop deterioration processes. Mechanical refrigerators operate by the successive evaporation and condensation of a liquid refrigerant pumped round a closed cycle. The refrigerant evaporates within the refrigerator, a process that requires heat, and therefore cools the surrounding air. It is then pumped out of the refrigerator and condensed under pressure, giving up its heat to the atmosphere via metal cooling fins. See also DEEP-FREEZE.

refugee A person who, for political, racial, or ideological reasons, or as a result of such crises as FAMINE or disaster, has been forced to flee his or her home country. The 20th century has seen massive and unprecedented numbers of refugees; it was estimated in 1990 that there are 15 million worldwide, with the overwhelming majority in developing countries. The causes of refugee movements are various, although the most common cause is the persecution of a minority group. In the 1930s, as German anti-Semitism became increasing rabid and violent, Jewish refugees fled to whatever countries would accept them. The UK and the USA both benefited from this influx of professionally qualified Jews (including most of the physicists who created nuclear weapons). In the post-war period, refugees from the former Eastern bloc from the 1950s to the 1970s were likely to be regarded as defectors possessing valuable intelli-

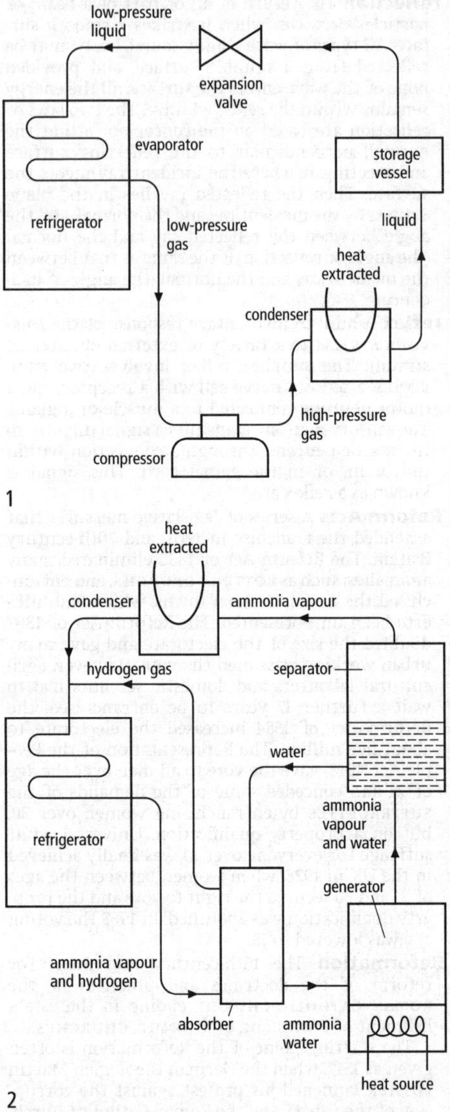

Refrigeration (1) In the vapour-compression cycle, the refrigerant (a volatile liquid) passes to an evaporator, where it boils, extracting the latent heat required from the refrigeration chamber. The vapour is then compressed so that both its temperature and pressure rise. The compressed vapour then passes to a condenser, where the liquid formed releases its latent heat to the atmosphere. The liquid then passes to a storage vessel before passing through an expansion valve, enabling it to enter the evaporator again as a low-pressure liquid. (2) In the vapour-absorption cycle there is no pump and energy is supplied in the form of heat. The refrigerant is usually ammonia liberated from a water solution and moved through the evaporator by a stream of hydrogen gas under pressure.

gence, whereas the response in Europe and North America to growing numbers of refugees from developing countries was to apply increasingly restrictive admissions policies. Even if refugees are successful in obtaining legal status, the problems in rebuilding a satisfactory social and economic life are huge. The office of the UN High Commissioner for Refugees and other agencies attempt to mitigate immediate problems, such as lack of food and housing. In the long term, however, the future of many refugees is bleak.

Regency, the The period in Britain from 1811 to 1820 when the Prince of Wales, later GEORGE IV, acted as regent for his father, GEORGE III, who had become insane. Among the major events of the Regency were the WAR OF 1812 involving Britain and the USA, the successful conclusion of the NAPOLEONIC WARS, and the Congress of VIENNA (1814–15). In Britain the post-war period was marked by a slump in the economy, which caused much social unrest. The Tory government used severe measures to quell popular discontent, which culminated in the PETERLOO MASSACRE of 1819. See also REGENCY STYLE.

Regency style In Britain, the style of architecture, decoration, costume, and furniture characteristic of the REGENCY (1811–20) and by extension the period during which the former Prince Regent ruled as George IV (1820–30) and more loosely for the first three decades of the 19th century. There was in fact no one style during this period; NEO-CLASSICISM (Greek rather than Roman in inspiration) was predominant, but there were also strains of Gothic, ROCOCO, Egyptian, and Chinese (see CHINOISERIE) influence. The building most closely associated with the Prince Regent himself, is John NASH's remodelling of the Royal Pavilion at Brighton (1815–21), in an exotic oriental style. Nash also designed Regent Street and Regent's Park in London, naming them in honour of his patron.

reggae See CARIBBEAN MUSIC.

Regina The capital of the Canadian province of Saskatchewan, situated at the centre of the wheat-growing plains of central Canada; pop. (1991) 191,690 (metropolitan area). It was founded on the site of a hunters' camp known as Pile o' Bones and was renamed in 1882 in honour of Queen Victoria; its name means 'queen' in Latin. In addition to being Canada's agrarian capital, it has a major oil refinery and steelworks.

Regiomontanus, Johannes (born Johannes Müller) (1436–76) German astronomer and mathematician. He was probably the most important astronomer of the 15th century, and worked in Venice, Buda (Hungary), Nuremberg, and finally Rome. Regiomontanus completed a translation of Ptolemy's *Mathematical Syntaxis*, with revisions and comments, and wrote four monumental works on mathematics (especially trigonometry) and astronomy.

register (in computing) See CENTRAL PROCESSING UNIT.

regolith On the Earth, the mantle of loose, unconsolidated material that overlies solid rock, the bedrock on continental land surfaces. It consists of rock-waste, formed by the mechanical and chemical breakdown of the bedrock, and superficial deposits such as alluvium, till, volcanic ash, loess, and wind-blown sands. The soils which subsequently develop on this loose material are part of the regolith.

On other bodies in the Solar System it is the layer of rock-dust and rock fragments that covers most of the lunar surface and the surface of other waterless planets and satellites.

regosols The immature soils developed on recently formed sediments, such as dune sands, wind-blown loess deposits, and glacial tills. Although the upper part of the PROFILE may be modified by the presence of organic matter, these soils are too young for distinct horizons to have formed.

regression analysis (in mathematics) The method used to find the relationship that holds between two variables when a number of pairs of values for them are known. It corresponds to drawing the best curve through a collection of points on a graph, referred to as a scatter diagram, and finding its equation, called the regression equation. The most usual form of equation is a 'line of best fit', where 'best' is determined by the LEAST SQUARES METHOD.

Rehoboam King of ancient Israel *c.*930–*c.*915 BC, son of Solomon. His reign witnessed the secession of the northern tribes and their establishment of a new kingdom under Jeroboam, leaving Rehoboam as the first king of Judah (1 Kings 11–14).

Reich, Steve (Michael) (1936–) US composer. His work at the San Francisco tape music centre (1964–65) and the study of West African and Balinese music helped mould his concept of MINIMAL MUSIC, in which the repetition of short phrases in a simple harmonic field creates a hypnotic effect far removed from traditional Western procedures. *Drumming* (1971) and *The Desert Music* for chorus and orchestra (1984) are typical of his style.

Reichstag (German, 'imperial parliament') The legislature of the GERMAN SECOND EMPIRE and of the WEIMAR REPUBLIC. Its role was confined to legislation, being forbidden to interfere in federal government affairs and having limited control over public spending. Under the WEIMAR REPUBLIC it enjoyed greater power as the government was made responsible to it. On the night of 27 February 1933 the **Reichstag fire** occurred. GOERING and GOEBBELS allegedly planned to set fire to the building, subsequently claiming it as a communist plot. The arsonist was a half-crazed Dutch communist, Marinus van der Lubbe. The subsequent trial was an embarrassment as the accused German and Bulgarian communist leaders were acquitted of complicity and only van der Lubbe was executed. But the fire had served its political purpose. On 28 February a decree suspended all civil liberties and installed a state of emergency, which lasted until 1945. Elections to the Reichstag were held on 5 March 1933, but by the Enabling Act of 23 March 1933 the Reichstag effectively voted itself out of existence.

Reign of Terror See FRENCH REVOLUTION; REVOLUTIONARY WARS.

reincarnation The postulated rebirth of the human soul in another form after death. It is most commonly associated with Indian thought, but is also found amoung Australian ABORIGINE peoples, and in African traditional religions. In HINDUISM, a single soul or ATMAN is subject to an endless cycle of births, deaths, and rebirths, through the process of SAMSARA. In BUDDHISM, however, the concept of 'non-self' (*anatta*), one of the Three Marks of Existence, is a central belief. There is no personal or transcendent soul, and therefore no continuing spiritual entity. Rebirth is explained through the process of DEPENDENT ORIGINATION, in which each embodied existence, conditioned by karma, is linked to the next.

reindeer (or **caribou**) A species of deer, *Rangifer tarandus*, found in the northern parts of Eurasia and in equivalent regions of North America and Greenland. It is the only deer in which both sexes have antlers; even fawns of two months have small spiky antlers. The adult is large, standing up to 1.5 m (5 feet) at the shoulder, and is usually brown to grey with a paler mane. It is the most migratory and sociable of the deer, travelling in herds of thousands of individuals over long distances. Many subspecies exist, especially in North America, where it is known as the caribou.

The reindeer is the only domesticated member of the deer family and is used in Scandinavia for riding, and pulling sledges. It also provides meat and milk and other dairy products. Its hide is used for clothing and shoes. It lives further north than any other hoofed animal, even entering the Arctic Circle.

reindeer moss The common name for *Cladonia rangiferina*. It is not a moss, but a lichen, which grows as clumps of branched, grey stems, up to about 8 cm (3 inches) tall. It is abundant in the Arctic regions and is grazed by reindeer.

reinforced concrete See CONCRETE.

Reinhardt, Django (born Jean Baptiste Reinhardt) (1910–53) Belgian jazz guitarist. He became famous in Paris in the 1930s for his original improvisational style, blending swing with influences from his gypsy background. In 1934, together with violinist Stephane GRAPPELLI, he formed the Quintette du Hot Club de France and went on to make many recordings with the group until they disbanded in 1939. Reinhardt also toured the USA with Duke Ellington in 1946.

Reinhardt, Max (born Max Goldmann) (1873–1943) Austrian theatre director and impresario. He dominated the theatre in Berlin during the first two decades of the 20th century with his large-scale productions of such works as Sophocles' *Oedipus Rex* (1910) and Vollmöller's *The Miracle* (1911). Reinhardt also helped establish the Salzburg Festival, with Richard Strauss and Hugo von Hofmannsthal, in 1920.

Reith, John (Charles Walsham), 1st Baron (1889–1971) Scottish administrator and politician, first general manager (1922–27) and first director-general (1927–38) of the BBC. He played a major part in the growth and developing ethos of the BBC, refusing to treat broadcasting simply as a means of entertainment and championing its moral and intellectual role in the community. Reith later served in various Cabinet posts during World War II. In 1948 the BBC established the **Reith Lectures**, broadcast annually, in his honour.

relative atomic mass (r.a.m.; formerly **atomic weight**) The mass of one atom of an element expressed in terms of the mass of an atom of the ISOTOPE carbon-12, defined to be exactly 12 atomic mass units (a.m.u.). On this scale the relative atomic mass of hydrogen is 1.0079, and of uranium is 238.03. The values are the weighted means of the relative atomic masses of each naturally occurring isotope. Each isotope has its own characteristic atomic mass.

relative density (formerly **specific gravity**) See DENSITY.

relative molecular mass (formerly **molecular weight**) The mass of one molecule of a substance divided by one-twelfth of the mass of an atom of the carbon-12 isotope. The relative molecular mass is calculated by adding up the RELATIVE ATOMIC MASSES of the atoms in the molecule, as given by the MOLECULAR FORMULA.

relativity, general theory of A theory of gravitation published in 1915 by EINSTEIN, this was a sequel to the special theory (see RELATIVITY, SPECIAL THEORY OF) and dealt with accelerated relative motion. This theory reformulated the concept of a gravitational field, relating it to the CURVATURE of SPACE-TIME produced by the presence of matter. This is in contrast to NEWTON'S LAW OF GRAVITATION in which the mass of a body produces a force of attraction. A particle in the neighbourhood of a mass follows a trajectory called a geodesic, which, for most practical situations, is indistinguishable from the path the particle would take under Newtonian gravitation. Einstein postulated that the effects experienced or the laws of nature deduced by an observer in a laboratory under a uniform gravitational force would be equivalent if the observer and the laboratory were instead subjected to a suitable acceleration. Einstein went on to formulate the so-called **field equations** by which the space-time curvature produced by a gravitational field can be found.

The general theory of relativity is now firmly established, being supported by all known tests to the present date and is crucial to the understanding of BLACK HOLES.

relativity, special theory of A theory put forward by EINSTEIN in 1905 that has completely changed our understanding of the Universe. Einstein reassessed the laws of physics as experienced by observers in inertial frames, that is, observers moving with a fixed velocity not subject to acceleration. The theory involves the speed of light, c, which Einstein assumed to be the same in a vacuum for all such observers. No matter what their speeds were and even if a source of light had a large speed with respect to the observer, the speed of light from it to the observer would be unaltered. He deduced that all physical laws and the numerical constants in those laws were the same in every inertial frame. In the theory, where events and properties in inertial frames are compared, a quantity $\beta = \sqrt{[1-(v/c)^2]}$ appears, where v is the relative speed between inertial frames, for example between the source of light's inertial frame and the observer's. This quantity β produces differences between classical Newtonian physics and Einsteinian physics, noticeable only when v approaches c. Because in everyday life speeds are always tiny compared to the speed of light, the quantity β is very nearly equal to 1 so that Newtonian physics is indistinguishable from Einsteinian. It is only recently that observational experiments have shown that the physical world agrees with Einstein rather than Newton. For example, synchrotrons, which accelerate charged particles of **rest mass** m_0 to speeds close to that of light, have to take into account the growing mass $m = m_0\ \beta$ of the particles as they spiral round; in this context m is called the **relativistic mass**. A further consequence is that no particle with a non-zero mass can ever achieve the speed of light since at that speed it would have infinite mass.

In developing his theory, Einstein also deduced that mass m and energy E were related by the equation $E = mc^2$. This equation describes the rate at which energy can be extracted from nuclear reactions taking place in nuclear reactors and in the stars. In the cores of the stars the fusion of hydrogen atoms into helium atoms involves the annihilation of mass and its transformation into radiant energy.

relay An electromechanical device used to switch one or more signals under the control of other signals. A typical relay consists of an ELECTROMAGNET that, when energized, is able to open or close other contacts. Relays have largely been superseded by solid-state switches, such as TRANSISTORS, but they are still used for switching high-voltage signals.

A relay, or repeater, is also a signal booster circuit that amplifies weak signals in international telecommunication circuits to make them audible (see TELEPHONY). Undersea telecommunications cables and television broadcast networks are fitted with relays at regular intervals.

relief (in art) A sculpture that projects from a background surface rather than standing freely. According to the degree of projection, reliefs are generally classified as high (*alto relievo*), medium (*mezzo relievo*), or low (*basso relievo* or bas relief).

religion A system of beliefs that involves a supernatural power, usually a GOD who created the Universe. In most religions God the creator is also God the judge, who takes an interest in what is happening in the Universe he created. In religions that postulate such a personal God, faith in the system of beliefs and adherence to its principles is rewarded by a blissful future existence (heaven for Jews, Christians, and Muslims), while a tormented future existence (hell) is regarded as the lot of the faithless. In Buddhism, the faithful can expect to escape from human existence and the cycle of rebirth in which Hindus believe. Most societies have sought to give order and meaning to life through some form of religion. Usually religion is associated with social institutions that have professional attendants, such as a temple or church with its priests, who are seen as guardians and preservers of the system of beliefs; such institutions give religion a public character. Religions provide many individuals with great comfort and for some, the idea of a Universe without a transcendent creator is unthinkable. However, for the atheist, the concept seems both unnecessary and devisive. Moreover, it is evident that the more strongly adherents of a particular religion believe in its precepts, the more fiercely do they react to those with different beliefs. This has made the interplay of world religions one of the most bloody aspects of human history.

Religion, Wars of See WARS OF RELIGION, FRENCH.

religious drama See MORALITY PLAY; MYSTERY PLAY; PASSION PLAY.

Remarque, Erich Maria (1898–1970) German-born US novelist. His first novel, *All Quiet on the Western Front* (1929), was a huge international success and was made into a film in 1930. The book and its sequel *The Road Back* (1931) were banned by the Nazis in 1933 and he emigrated to the USA in 1939, becoming a US citizen in 1947. Remarque's other novels, all dealing with the horror of war and its aftermath, include *Spark of Life* (1952) and *A Time to Live and a Time to Die* (1956).

Rembrandt (full name Rembrandt Harmensz van Rijn) (1606–69) Dutch painter. After working at first in his native Leiden, he moved to Amsterdam, where he made his name as a portrait painter with the *Anatomy Lesson of Dr Tulp* (1632). With his most celebrated painting, the *Night Watch* (1642), he used chiaroscuro to give his subjects a more spiritual and introspective quality, a departure which was to transform the Dutch portrait tradition. Rembrandt is especially identified with the series of more than 30 self-portraits painted from 1629 to 1669, a sustained exercise in self-analysis. His prolific output also included many religious, genre, and landscape paintings, drawings, and etchings. Although his name remained well known after his death, it was not until the romantic period that Rembrandt was recognized as a supreme artist.

remora A marine fish found in all tropical oceans, of which there are about eight species, all members of the family Echeneidae. They have an elongate, streamlined body with a flattened head, on the top of which is a large sucking disc (formed by the modified first dorsal fin, the rays of which cross the head like slats of a Venetian blind). This disc is used to attach the fish to large sharks, manta rays, bony fishes, turtles, and even whales, on which they ride. Some remora species are found only on certain hosts, others, like the sharksucker, *Echeneis naucrates*, attach to several kinds of host. Most remoras eat small fishes which they catch by swimming free of their host; a few eat the skin parasites of their host.

Renaissance (French, 'rebirth') The intellectual and artistic flowering that began in Italy in the 14th century, culminated there in the 16th century, and greatly influenced other parts of Europe. The notion of a rebirth refers to a revival of the values of the classical world. The idea was brilliantly characterized by ALBERTI, himself an architect, painter, scientist, poet, and mathematician, and in LEONARDO DA VINCI. BRUNELLESCHI is considered the first Renaissance architect; from his interest in Roman remains he created buildings that could be compared with the finest ancient examples. Other major architects included BRAMANTE, regarded by contemporaries as the most successful architect of the High Renaissance, and PALLADIO. In sculpture, it was DONATELLO in the early 15th century who assimilated the spirit of ancient sculpture. GHIBERTI, Michelangelo, and others revealed new possibilities of expression that had been unknown to antiquity. In painting, fidelity to nature became a central concern to early Renaissance painters, such as Giotto and MASACCIO, who brought scientific vigour to the problems of representation, while the invention of PERSPECTIVE assisted in the realistic portrayal of nature. Michelangelo, Raphael, Titian and others broke new ground by introducing the human figure, naturalistically depicted, into their paintings. Florence in the period around 1425 was the cradle of the Renaissance, but by the early 16th century – the 'High Renaissance' – Venice and Rome were equally important. The ideals and imagery of the Italian Renaissance did not generally begin to spread to the rest of Europe until about 1500. DÜRER was the outstanding artist of the 'Northern Renaissance', making it his mission to transplant the new Italian ideas on to German soil. Out of the art of the High Renaissance there developed a style characterized by a sense of extreme elegance and grace, which became known as MANNERISM.

In literature the Renaissance was led by humanist scholars and poets, notably PETRARCH, DANTE, and BOCCACCIO in Italy. Poetry and prose began to be written in the vernacular instead of Latin, and the invention of printing contributed to the spread of ideas. Among the notable writers of the Renaissance beyond Italy are ERASMUS in the Netherlands; MONTAIGNE and RABELAIS, and the poets of the Pléiade in France; Lope de VEGA and CERVANTES in Spain; and Edmund SPENSER, Sir Philip SIDNEY, SHAKESPEARE, and Sir Francis

BACON in Britain. The Renaissance profoundly affected the presentation and content of theatrical production. Dramatists introduced classical form and restraint into their works, which were to be codified, notably in France, with greater severity than in classical times. The Renaissance had far-reaching consequences in many other fields. The impulse to explore the world led to the voyages of discovery of DÍAZ, DA GAMA, and MAGELLAN. These in turn led to advances in geography and cartography and the colonization of new lands. The astronomers COPERNICUS, KEPLER, and GALILEO proposed new theories about the movement of the planets, and advances were made in biology, chemistry, physics, and medicine. The Flemish anatomist VESALIUS wrote *De humani corporis fabrica* (1543), an influential anatomical treatise. The new spirit of enquiry also affected perception of the Church and paved the way for reform.

Renaissance music (*c.*1320–*c.*1600) During this time, composers such as Guillaume de MACHAUT, Jacopo da Bologna (fl. 1340–60), and Francesco Landini (*c.*1325–97) composed a range of music, particularly secular POLYPHONY for a courtly culture, that expressed emotions and moods quite as clearly as the painting of their time. Around 1400, the hitherto separate traditions of French and Italian song appear to have coalesced, partly in the hands of Johannes Ciconia (*c.*1375–1412), born in Liège but working mainly in Italy; and the years between about 1420 and 1540 are largely dominated by Franco-Flemish composers who benefited from the opportunities provided by the rich Italian courts. The earliest substantial repertory of independent idiomatic instrumental music was for the lute, starting just before 1500; but there is also a considerable repertory of instrumental part-music from the 16th century, the surviving printed sources evidently aimed at a growing amateur market. Sacred music, which had experienced a decline in the 14th century, appears to have received a new stimulus in the 1420s from the English repertory and particularly DUNSTABLE whose music was widely admired on the Continent and influenced the most resourceful and fascinating genius of 15th-century music, DUFAY. The major achievement of the later Renaissance in music is the polyphonic mass cycle: after some hesitant starts, this tradition really began around 1450 at the hands of Dufay; in the next generation it was further evolved by Josquin DES PREZ, perhaps the most glorious and pure composer of the Renaissance: and the tradition continued through to the 100-odd masses of PALESTRINA.

Renan, (Joseph) Ernest (1823–92) French historian, theologian, and philosopher. A major figure in 19th-century French theology and philosophy, he provoked a controversy with the publication of his *Vie de Jésus* (1863), which rejected the supernatural element in the life of Jesus. His belief that the future of the world lay in the progress of science found expression in *L'Avenir de la science* (1890).

Renault, Louis (1877–1944) French engineer and motor manufacturer. Together with his brothers he established the original Renault company in 1898 and became known for designing and manufacturing a series of racing cars. In 1918 the company produced its first tank; Renault subsequently expanded the firm's range to incorporate industrial and agricultural machinery, as well as further military technology. In 1944 Renault was imprisoned, accused of collaborating with the Germans; he died before the trial began. His company was nationalized in 1945 and subsequently became one of France's leading car manufacturers.

Renault, Mary (pseudonym of Mary Challans) (1905–83) British novelist, resident in South Africa from 1948. Her reputation is based on her historical novels set in ancient Greece and Asia Minor. They include two novels recalling the legend of Theseus (*The King Must Die*, 1958; *The Bull from the Sea*, 1962) and a trilogy recounting the story of Alexander the Great (*Fire from Heaven*, 1970; *The Persian Boy*, 1972; *Funeral Games*, 1981).

Rendell, Ruth (Barbara), Baroness (1930–) British writer of detective fiction and thrillers. She is known as the creator of Chief Inspector Wexford, who appears in a series of detective novels starting with *From Doon with Death* (1964). Rendell is also noted for her psychological crime novels, including *A Judgement in Stone* (1977) and – under the pseudonym of Barbara Vine – *A Dark-Adapted Eye* (1986) and *The Brimstone Wedding* (1996).

renewable energy resource See ENERGY RESOURCES.

Renfrewshire A local government area of central Scotland on the south side of the River Clyde; area 261 sq km (101 sq miles); pop. (est. 1996) 177,000. Its administrative centre is Paisley. In 1975 the historic county of Renfrewshire became a district of Strathclyde Region; in 1996 it was divided into the local government areas of Renfrewshire, East Renfrewshire, and Inverclyde.

Rennes An industrial city of Brittany in northwest France, capital of the department of Ille-et-Vilaine; pop. (1990) 203,530. It was established as the capital of a Celtic tribe, the Redones, from whom its derives its name, later becoming the capital of the ancient kingdom of Brittany. The city was partially rebuilt after a great fire in 1720. Industries include car assembly, electric and electronic equipment, chemicals, and clothing. It is a cultural and educational centre with two universities, an agricultural college, and a medical school.

rennet An extract obtained from the stomach of cows, used in cheese making. It contains the enzyme renin, that causes milk to coagulate.

Rennie, John (1761–1821) Scottish civil engineer. He is best known as the designer of the London and East India Docks (built *c.*1800), the Inchcape Rock lighthouse (1807–*c.*1811), and Waterloo Bridge, Southwark Bridge, and London Bridge (1811–31).

Reno A city in the US state of Nevada, on the Truckee River; pop. (1990) 133,850. Settled in 1859 and named in honour of General J. L. Reno, it developed after the arrival of the Union and Central Pacific Railroad in 1868 as a centre for trade in livestock, grain, timber, and cement. Reno also has a reputation for gambling and for its liberal laws enabling quick marriages and divorces.

Renoir, (Pierre) Auguste (1841–1919) French painter. One of the early impressionists, he developed a style characterized by light, fresh colours and indistinct, subtle outlines. In his later work he concentrated on the human, especially female, form. His best-known paintings include *Le Moulin de la galette* (1876), *Les Grandes Baigneuses* (1884–87), and *The Judgement of Paris* (*c.*1914).

Renoir, Jean (1894–1979) French film director, son of Auguste RENOIR. His early films made in France in the 1930s, including *La Grande Illusion* (1937), concerning prisoners of war in World War I, and *La Règle du jeu* (1939), a black comedy about a weekend shooting-party. After spending World War II in the USA, he returned to Europe, where he made such films as *Le Déjeuner sur l'herbe*, which had an important influence on the *nouvelle vague* film directors of the 1960s.

reparations Compensation payments for damage done in war by a defeated enemy. They were a condition of the armistice for World War I, and part of the VERSAILLES PEACE SETTLEMENT. After World War II reparations took the form of Allied occupation of Germany and Japan. Britain, France, and the USA ended reparation collections in 1952. In the aftermath of the Gulf War (1991), the UN Compensation Commission obliged Iraq, whose invasion of Kuwait had precipitated the conflict, to pay reparations to war victims.

repeater See RELAY.

repertory theatre A theatre staging a repertoire of plays in rotation, rather than a single play. The system was once adopted in all theatres, but became unpopular with the advent of the touring company and the long run. Unsuccessful efforts were made in Britain at the beginning of the 20th century to revive it, but the term came merely to signify a theatre that presented its own productions for limited runs. 'True' repertory is still staged by the Royal Shakespeare Company, the National Theatre, and seasonal theatres in Britain, and by subsidized theatres on the Continent of Europe and elsewhere.

repetitive strain injury (RSI) Pain with associated loss of function in a limb resulting from repeated movements or sustained static loading on the part. The hand, wrist, and arm are the most commonly affected limbs. It can occur with violinists, computer operators, and others making awkward or continually repeated movements. Some sufferers have successfully sued their employers for negligence.

reprocessing, nuclear See NUCLEAR FUEL.

reproduction The process enabling species to continue even though individuals die. This is achieved by passing on genes to the next generation either by asexual or sexual reproduction.

In asexual reproduction there is only one parent. One or several cells develop and detach from the parent to give a new individual genetically identical to the parent (a CLONE). Single-celled organisms, such as amoebae, often divide by splitting into equal halves (binary fission). Asexual reproduction is largely confined to microorganisms, invertebrates (male bees develop from unfertilized eggs), and plants, although rare asexual reproduction occurs in all vertebrate groups except birds and mammals. Asexual reproduction in plants is called vegetative reproduction.

Sexual reproduction usually involves two parent organisms that produce reproductive cells (GAMETES) by MEIOSIS. Each gamete contains half of the parent's genetic information. During fertilization, a pair of gametes fuse, forming a zygote. This zygote develops into a new individual that possesses some of the characteristics of each parent. Isogamy is the condition in which both gametes are equal, and occurs in some lower organisms. Anisogamy is more common, with unequal gametes, the smaller coming from the male parent, the larger from the female. In most organisms the gametes are produced by sex organs (GONADS).

Hermaphrodite animals, such as the earthworm, possess both male and female gonads but normally cannot fertilize themselves. Plants may be unisexual or bisexual and some are able to fertilize themselves, while others have mechanisms preventing self fertilization. Many plants and some invertebrates can reproduce both sexually and asexually.

reptile A member of a class of vertebrates, Reptilia, generally with dry, scaly skins, whose representatives include the TURTLES, the Lepidosauria (the TUATARA, LIZARDS, AMPHISBAENIDS, and SNAKES), and the Archosauria (CROCODILES, PTERODACTYLS and DINOSAURS). Reptiles are extraordinarily diverse, and share with mammals and birds the ability to produce eggs, which contain amniotic membranes that enclose the developing embryo in a bag of fluid. Reptiles, birds, and mammals are therefore collectively called amniotes. The amniote egg represents an important difference from the reproductive patterns that occur in most amphibians, in that hatchling reptiles are miniature replicas of their parents, and this way, the aquatic, larval (tadpole) stage is omitted. Reptiles, however, resemble amphibians in being cold-blooded, that is, their body temperature primarily depends on absorbing heat from the environment. Birds and mammals, in contrast, are warm-blooded. See illustration p. 1146.

Repton, Humphry (1752–1818) British landscape gardener. Repton's reconstructions of estates often used regular bedding and straight paths close to the house, but his parks were carefully informal after the model of Capability Brown. Important designs include the park at Cobham in Kent (*c*.1789–*c*.1793) and the house and grounds at Sheringham Hall in Norfolk (1812–19).

republic A state in which supreme power is held by the people, their elected representatives, or by an elected or nominated PRESIDENT rather than a

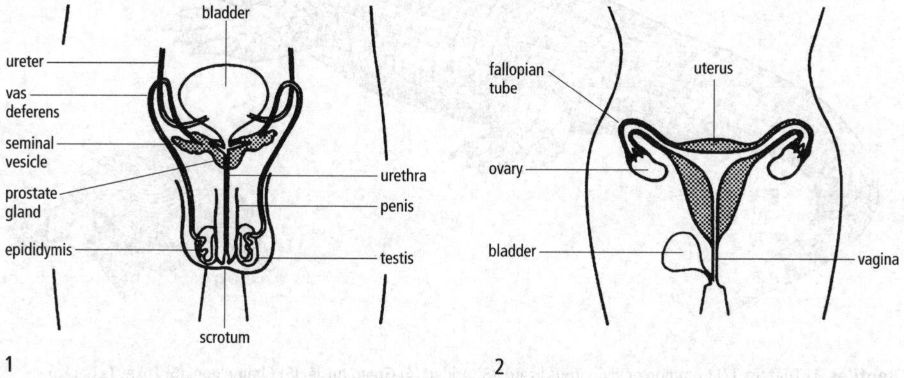

Reproduction (1) The human male reproductive system. (2) The human female reproductive system.

Reptiles (1) Tuatara. (2) Common or viviparous lizard. (3) Adder. (4) Green turtle. (5) Chameleon. (6) Tokay (a gecko). (7)Terrapin. (8) American alligator. (9) Tortoise.

monarch. The head of state in a republic is normally a president, either directly or indirectly elected. A republican head of state may also be chief executive, but the office may be simply a ceremonial position. Republican forms of government have a long history, dating from ancient Greece and Rome. Though the powers of government nominally derive from the people, a republic is not necessarily democratic.

Republican Party A major political party in the USA. The present Republican Party was formed in 1854, being precipitated by the Kansas–Nebraska Act and by the agitation of the Free Soil Party; it brought together groups opposed to slavery but supporting a protective trade tariff. The party won its first presidential election with Abraham LINCOLN in 1860 and from then until 1932 lost only four such contests, two each to CLEVELAND and Woodrow WILSON. Under more recent Republican Presidents NIXON, FORD, and REAGAN, it became associated with military spending and a forceful assertion of US presence worldwide, especially in Central America. Strongly backed by corporate business, it nevertheless failed to maintain a grip on Congress, which usually had a Democratic majority even when the President was Republican. However, this trend was reversed in 1994, when the Republicans gained control of both the Senate and the House of Representatives for the first time in 40 years.

requiem The Roman Catholic MASS for the dead, beginning with the Introit *Requiem aeternam dona eis Domine* ('Give them eternal rest, O Lord') sung while a priest approaches the altar for the Eucharist. The text follows the main outline of the normal mass, but omits the more joyful sections (the *Gloria* and *Credo*) and includes the 13th-century sequence *Dies irae, dies illa* (Latin, 'Day of wrath, day of judgement').

resistance (in electricity) The ratio of the POTENTIAL DIFFERENCE (p.d. or voltage) across a conductor to the electric current flowing through it. The unit of measurement is the ohm (Ω), this being the resistance of a conductor requiring a potential difference of 1 volt across its ends to produce a current of 1 ampere. For a given metal conductor at constant temperature the value is the same whatever the current (OHM's law), but rises if the temperature rises. Any conductor possessing resistance gives off heat when a current flows through it. The effect is described by JOULE's law.

resistance movements Underground movements that fought against Nazi Germany and Japan during World War II. Their activities involved publishing underground newspapers, helping Jews and prisoners-of-war to escape, conveying intelligence by secret radios, as well as committing acts of sabotage. In occupied Europe there were often deep divisions between communist and non-communist organizations, notably in France, where the MAQUIS was active, as well as in Belgium, Yugoslavia, and Greece. Communist parties had at first remained passive, but following the German invasion of the Soviet Union (June 1941), they formed or joined underground groups. Dutch, Danish, and Norwegian resistance remained unified and worked closely with London, where in 1940 the British Special Operations Executive (SOE) was set up to coordinate all subversive activity, both in Europe and the Far East, and to supply arms and equipment by secret air-drops. In the Far East clandestine operations were carried out through British and US intelligence organizations. Much of their effort was devoted to intelligence gathering, psychological warfare, and prisoner-of-war recovery, while the actual sabotaging of selected installations and communication lines was conducted by native-born, nationalist, and often communist-inspired guerrillas.

resistor An electrical device that opposes electrical current flow. Resistors employed in electronics are usually constructed from carbon or metal films. The value of the resistance of a resistor, in ohms (Ω), is usually depicted on its body as a series of coloured rings. The values of resistance may vary from 10 Ω to 10 MΩ or higher. Resistors are used in electrical and electronic circuits as a means of controlling the current flow through the circuit, or a part of it.

Resnais, Alain (1922–) French film director. He was one of the foremost directors of the *nouvelle vague*. Throughout his career Resnais has collaborated with writers, such as Marguerite Duras, notably in *Hiroshima mon amour* (1959) and Alain Robbe-Grillet, in *L'Année dernière à Marienbad* (1961). More recent films include *Mon oncle d'Amérique* (1980) and *L'Amour à mort* (1984).

resolving power The ability of a TELESCOPE to separate two close objects, such as the components of a binary star. For a RADIO TELESCOPE, the wavelengths collected are so large compared with those of visible light that even a very large instrument, such as the JODRELL BANK Lovell telescope, which has a dish of 76.2 m (250 feet) in diameter, has poor resolving power. This is overcome by coupling two or more radio dish telescopes together to employ the principle of INTERFEROMETRY, as in the multi-element radio linked interferometer network (MERLIN) and the VERY LARGE ARRAY.

resonance The oscillation of a body when it is subjected to a vibration whose FREQUENCY is the same as its own natural frequency (or some multiple of it). A similar phenomenon occurs in electric circuits, and this is employed in oscillators and radios; tuning consists in altering the resonant frequency of the receiver.

resources (in economics) Those scarce elements used for producing GOODS and services. They are: land, LABOUR, and CAPITAL. Land is normally defined to include all naturally occurring resources as well as the use of land surface area. Labour includes the efforts of workers, managers, and entrepreneurs. Capital comprises goods used in the production process. Skilled or qualified labour is often described as incorporating human capital. See also FACTORS OF PRODUCTION.

Respighi, Ottorino (1879–1936) Italian composer. He is best known for his suites the *Fountains of Rome* (1917) and the *Pines of Rome* (1924), based on the poems of Gabriele d'Annunzio and influenced by Rimsky-Korsakov, his former composition teacher, in their orchestration. In addition to writing nine operas he arranged Diaghilev's ballet *La Boutique fantasque* (1919) from Rossini's original music.

respiration The energy-yielding metabolic process in living animals and plants, and in many, but not all, microorganisms. The energy generated is derived from food molecules, and the process requires an externally supplied oxidizing agent – usually oxygen. In a sequence of biochemical reactions, a food molecule is broken down to simpler molecules, and the energy released is harnessed in the form of ATP. For example, glucose, the most common energy-yielding food molecule, is broken down into carbon dioxide and water via GLYCOLY-

SIS, KREBS' CYCLE and an ELECTRON TRANSPORT CHAIN.

Some microorganisms can, in the absence of oxygen, use oxidizing agents other than oxygen for respiratory purposes: this is known as **anaerobic respiration**. For example, some bacteria can use nitrate, sulphur, sulphate, or carbon dioxide. FERMENTATION is a type of anaerobic respiration. Many microorganisms carry out anaerobic respiration in the absence of oxygen but switch to the more efficient (in terms of energy generation) **aerobic respiration** when oxygen is available.

In animals, aerobic respiration depends on an efficient system for supplying the necessary oxygen and removing the waste-product carbon dioxide. This is accomplished by a large respiratory surface, such as LUNGS or GILLS, together with an efficient circulatory system to transport oxygen from the respiratory surface to the tissues, and carbon dioxide in the reverse direction. The process of breathing and getting oxygen to cells is called **external respiration**, and the energy-releasing biochemical reactions, which occur mostly within the MITOCHONDRIA, are called **internal** or **cellular respiration**.

respirator A device providing artificial respiration by mechanical means, used in the treatment of respiratory disease and paralysis, and in ANAESTHESIA. The 'iron lung', which was extensively used in the poliomyelitis epidemics of the 1930s and 1950s, consisted of a sealed box enclosing the whole patient except for the head. The rhythmic removal of air from the box forces the patient to take in air through the nose or mouth (negative-pressure ventilation). In positive-pressure ventilation, air is forced into the lungs, usually through a close-fitting tube in the trachea. Modern respirators are essential both to anaesthetic techniques and to the INTENSIVE-CARE UNIT. They now use sophisticated electronics to monitor the patient's own breathing efforts and can vary the depth, rate, and pattern of respiration.

rest mass See RELATIVITY, SPECIAL THEORY OF.

Restoration (1660) The re-establishment in England and Scotland of the Stuart monarchy by placing Charles II, the exiled son of Charles I, on the throne. The Restoration was accompanied by the revival of the Church of England, the growth of Cavalier fortunes (although those who had sold their estates to pay fines could not get them back), and a flourishing cultural and social life. The Restoration did not restore the absolute authority of the Stuart monarchy, as Charles II was soon to discover.

Restoration comedy A type of social COMEDY of manners that flourished in London after the RESTORATION of the monarchy in 1660. It is characterized by glittering, cynical, licentious, and extravagant language and plot. Women's roles, until then played by boys, were taken by actresses, the most notable among them being Nell Gwynne, the leading comedienne of the King's Company.

restriction enzyme An enzyme obtained from bacteria, that cuts (cleaves) DNA molecules into specific short sections. They are widely used in GENETIC ENGINEERING

restrictive practice An agreement to limit competition or output in industry. Restrictive trade agreements between firms may be formal or informal. Examples are CARTELS and price agreements, which set prices higher than would otherwise occur, in order to extract MONOPOLY profits. Members of TRADE UNIONS and certain professions may benefit from procedures that restrict competition between those doing the same kind of work. Some restrictive practices are banned, but some, such as certain state monopolies or CLOSED SHOPS, may be allowed if they are considered to be in the public interest.

resurrection Rising from the dead. The resurrection of JESUS CHRIST, as recounted in the New Testament, is a crucial doctrine of Christianity because it is believed that, through Jesus' triumph over death, all Christians have the opportunity to share in the AFTERLIFE. The idea of resurrection is found in ancient Near Eastern religions, and both the Greeks and Romans believed in the immortality of the soul. The Christian doctrine of resurrection is based on Jewish prophecies of resurrection found in the Old Testament; both Muslims and Zoroastrians hold similar beliefs in the resurrection of the dead before the Day of Judgement.

retail price index (RPI; or **cost-of-living index**) A measure of changes in the average price level of goods and services. The RPI is a base-weighted index measuring changes in the cost of a basket of household goods bought in the base year. Each item in the basket is given a share or 'weight' in the overall index, according to its importance in the average base-year household budget. Family expenditure surveys are carried out at intervals, to monitor changes in spending patterns and thus facilitate updating of the items in the RPI sample of goods.

Reticulum The Net, a small CONSTELLATION of the southern sky introduced by the 18th-century French astronomer Nicolas Louis de Lacaille to represent the reticle used in his telescope for measuring star positions. Zeta Reticuli is a pair of fifth-magnitude stars similar to the Sun, divisible with binoculars or even the naked eye.

retina See EYE.

retinopathy Any non-inflammatory disease of the light-sensitive layer within the eye (retina). **Diabetic retinopathy** is a complication of DIABETES MELLITUS, and is characterized by abnormalities of the blood vessels within the retina and can result in blindness. **Hypertensive retinopathy** occurs following prolonged hypertension and results in thickening of the blood vessels of the retina; in more severe cases, haemorrhage may occur, and production of exudate is associated with visual impairment and blindness in severe cases. **Retinitis pigmentosa** is an inherited disease characterized by degeneration of the retina. Initial symptoms include night blindness; progression leads to complete blindness. **Retinal detachment** is the separation of the retina from the eye; it may be associated with injury, haemorrhage, exudate, or may be of unknown cause.

retriever See DOG.

retrograde motion See SATELLITE, natural.

retrovirus A virus containing RNA that is able to convert its genetic material into DNA by means of the enzyme reverse transcriptase. This conversion enables the virus to become integrated into the DNA of the host cell. Retroviruses include the Aids virus (HIV) and some viruses believed to cause cancer. They are also used as vectors in gene therapy.

Reuben The eldest son of Jacob and Leah, and ancestor of the tribe of Reuben, one of the ten Israelite tribes later taken captive by the Assyrians. In the Bible he is depicted as being more merciful than the other brothers to his half-brother Joseph.

Réunion A volcanically active, subtropical island in the Indian Ocean east of Madagascar, one of the

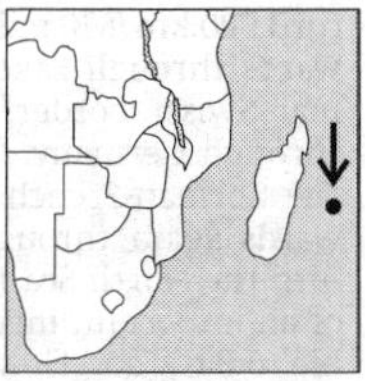

Mascerene Islands; area 2,512 sq km (970 sq miles); pop. (1990) 596,700; capital, Saint-Denis. A French possession since 1638, the island became an overseas department of France in 1946 and an administrative region in 1974. Its chief export is sugar.

Reuter, Paul Julius, Baron von (born Israel Beer Josaphat) (1816–99) German pioneer of telegraphy and news reporting. After establishing a service for sending commercial telegrams in Aachen (1849), he moved his headquarters to London, where he founded the news agency Reuters.

Revere, Paul (1735–1818) US patriot and silversmith. He was one of the demonstrators involved in the Boston Tea Party of 1773, the protest at the imposition of tax on tea by Britain. Two years later he made his famous midnight ride from Boston to Lexington to warn fellow American revolutionaries of the approach of British troops; the journey is immortalized in Longfellow's poem 'Paul Revere's Ride' (1863).

reverse fault A fracture in which the rocks on opposite sides of a FAULT have moved in such a way that the beds on one side overlap in the vertical plane those on the other. Horizontal distances between points on opposite sides of the fault are reduced by the fault-movement and vertical distances are increased.

reversing layer See CHROMOSPHERE.

revolution (in politics) The transformation of a political system or regime through a relatively rapid and concentrated process, often but not always accompanied by political violence. It is distinguished from a *coup d'état*, which refers to the sudden overthrow of a government, and not of the political system as a whole. The American and French Revolutions of 1776 and 1789 established the assumption that a radical break with previous governmental patterns was central to revolution; the Bolshevik Revolution of 1917 in Russia further established that such transformation should extend to the social, economic, and cultural aspects of the state concerned.

revolution (in astronomy) Usually the orbital revolution of one body about another, as for example the Moon about the Earth or the Earth about the Sun (revolution of the Earth). The time taken for one revolution with respect to the stellar background is the sidereal period of revolution.

Revolutionary Wars (1792–1802) A series of wars in Europe following the FRENCH REVOLUTION. In 1791 Louis XVI attempted unsuccessfully to escape from France to Germany, to win support from Austria and Prussia. In April 1792 France declared war on Austria, which then ruled Belgium (the Austrian Netherlands). A series of French defeats followed until, on 20 September, an invading Prussian army was defeated at Valmy. In February 1793 war was declared against Britain, Spain, and the United Provinces of the Netherlands. For a year a **Reign of Terror** operated in France, but, at the same time, under the skill of CARNOT, armies had been steadily raised and trained. At first the aim was to consolidate the frontiers of France along the 'natural frontiers' of the Rhine and the Alps, but from 1795, these armies were to conquer Europe. A number of brilliant young officers emerged, for example Bernadotte (later CHARLES XIV of Sweden), Barthélemy Joubert (killed in battle 1799), and above all NAPOLEON BONAPARTE. All the Netherlands were conquered, Belgium being annexed, and the Republic of Batavia created from the United Provinces; French armies advanced across the Rhine and into South Germany. Switzerland was made into the Helvetic Republic (1798). In 1796–97 Napoleon took an army into Italy, defeated the Austrians at Arcola and occupied Venice, creating the Cisalpine and Ligurian Republics. In 1798 he led an expedition to Egypt, but the British fleet under NELSON destroyed his fleet at Aboukir Bay, and Napoleon returned to Paris. Meanwhile Austrian and Russian troops had re-occupied Italy and in 1799 Napoleon again marched across the Alps to defeat the Austrians at Marengo. At the same time General Moreau won a second great victory at Hohenlinden. The peace treaties of Lunéville (1801 with Austria) and Amiens (1802 with Britain) were then negotiated, ending the Revolutionary Wars.

Revolutions of 1848 A series of revolutions in western and central Europe. Revolution erupted first in France, where supporters of universal suffrage and a socialist minority under Louis BLANC caused the overthrow of the July Monarchy of LOUIS PHILIPPE and established the Second Republic. In most German states there were popular demonstrations and uprisings, and a movement for an elected national parliament to draft a constitution for a united Germany. Rioting in Austria caused the flight of both METTERNICH and the emperor, and the formation of a constituent assembly and the emancipation of the peasantry. A movement for Hungarian independence, headed by KOSSUTH, led to a short-lived republican government from Budapest for all Hungarian lands; but Magyar refusal to consider independence for its own minorities resulted in an insurrection by Croat, Serb, and Transylvanian forces and in Hungary's defeat by Austrian and Russian forces. In the Italian states there was a series of abortive revolutions which led to the temporary expulsion of the Austrians and the flight of Pope Pius IX from Rome, but the united, democratic republic dreamt of by MAZZINI did not come about. A Pan-Slav Congress in Prague inspired Czech nationalist demonstrations to demand autonomy within a federal Austria. By 1849 counter-revolutionary forces had restored order, but the concept of absolute monarchy and the feudal rights of a land-owning aristocracy had been tacitly abandoned.

revolver See PISTOL.

Reykjavik The capital of Iceland, a port on Faxa Bay; pop. (1990) 97,570. It was the first place on Iceland to be settled and is the world's northernmost capital city. It takes its name (Icelandic, 'smoky bay') from the steam that was seen to rise from nearby geothermal features. It is the base of the fishing fleet and has fish-processing, metal-working, printing, and clothing industries.

Reynaud, Paul (1878–1966) French politician. He was Finance Minister 1938–40, and Prime Minister in the emergency of 1940, but, having appointed PÉTAIN and WEYGAND, he was unable to carry on the war when these two proved defeatist. He resigned in mid-June 1940. After the war he was Finance Minister (1948) and Vice-Premier (1953) in the Fourth Republic. He assisted in the formation of the Fifth Republic, but later quarrelled with DE GAULLE.

Reynolds, Albert (1933–) Irish Fianna Fáil statesman, Taoiseach (Prime Minister) 1992–94. He was involved with John Major in drafting the DOWNING STREET DECLARATION (1993), intended as the basis of a peace initiative in Northern Ireland.

Reynolds, Sir Joshua (1723–92) British painter. He became the first president of the Royal Academy (1768), and through his professional and social prestige succeeded in raising the status of painting in Britain. Reynolds sought to raise portraiture to the status of history painting by adapting poses and settings from classical statues and Renaissance paintings (as in *Mrs Siddons as the Tragic Muse*, 1784). His theories were presented in the *Discourses* delivered annually at the Royal Academy (1769–90).

Reza Shah See PAHLAVI.

Rhaeto-Romance (or **Rhaeto-Romanic**) Any of the Romance dialects of south-east Switzerland and western Austria, especially Romansh and Ladin.

rhea Either of two species of large, flightless bird of the family Rheidae, confined to South America. Somewhat similar to ostriches, rheas are long-legged, long-necked birds with a loose covering of feathers on the body, standing up to 1.5 m (5 feet) tall and weighing up to 25 kg (55 pounds). They escape from their enemies by running rapidly. The males are polygamous, up to six females laying their eggs in the male's nest. He then incubates them and looks after the young.

Rhea (in astronomy) A satellite of Saturn, discovered by Giovanni Domenico CASSINI in 1672. It has a nearly circular equatorial orbit at 527,000 km from the planet's centre. Its diameter is 1,530 km and its density is 1,300 kg/m^3. The latter value implies a predominantly water ice composition.

Rheims (French **Reims**) An ancient cathedral city in the department of Marne, north-east France, chief city of the Champagne-Ardenne region; pop. (1990) 185,160. The building of its famous cathedral began in 1211 and was completed about a century later. Most of the city was destroyed in World War I but has since been rebuilt. It is the centre of the Champagne wine industry.

rhenium (symbol Re, at. no. 75, r.a.m. 186.2) A rare TRANSITION METAL extracted from flue dusts. It is silvery grey and was first detected from its X-ray spectrum in 1925. It has a very high melting-point (3,180°C, or 5,755°F) and is chemically similar to manganese. The element is hard and resistant to wear and corrosion. Its uses include alloy steels, fountain-pen nib points, high-temperature THERMOCOUPLES, electrical components, and as a catalyst.

rheostat A variable RESISTOR. Rheostats are generally used in higher-power circuits. The commonest form consists of a large bare-wire COIL, along which a movable terminal can slide. As the terminal is moved, a smaller or larger portion of the coil is incorporated into the circuit, and the resistance in the circuit is thus increased or decreased.

rhesus factor (or **Rh factor**) A group of antigens that can occur on the surface of red blood cells and form the basis of the rhesus blood group system. Most people are Rh-positive, i.e., they have the rhesus factor. Those that do not have it (some 17% of the population) are rhesus-negative. Incompatibility between Rh-positive and Rh-negative blood cause transfusion reactions and haemolytic disease of the newborn. The factor is therefore tested for. It is named after the RHESUS MONKEY in which the factor was first recognized.

rhesus monkey A monkey, *Macaca mulatta*, that lives in large colonies in forests in south Asia. It can grow up to 60 cm (2 feet) long and is used in medical research.

Rhine A river of Western Europe that rises in the Rheinwaldhorn glacier in the Swiss Alps and flows for 1,320 km (820 miles) to the North Sea, first westwards through Lake Constance, forming the German-Swiss border, then turning northwards through Germany, forming the southern part of the German-French border, before flowing westwards again through the Netherlands to empty into the North Sea near Rotterdam. It forms part of an important inland waterway network navigable to Basle and flows through several major cities including Basle, Mannheim, Mainz, Cologne, and Düsseldorf. It carries large loads of freight especially between the Ruhr area and Rotterdam. It is heavily polluted but nevertheless a popular destination for tourists much influenced by its legends and its famous vineyards and castles.

Rhineland The region of western Germany through which the Rhine flows, especially the part to the west of the river. The area was demilitarized as part of the Versailles Treaty in 1919 but was reoccupied by Hitler in 1936. It was recaptured in 1945 by US troops during World War II and now forms part of Germany.

rhinoceros A huge, ungainly creature equalling the hippopotamus as the second largest land mammal. The largest of five species in the family Rhinocerotidae, the white or square-lipped rhinoceros, *Ceratotherium simum*, stands 2 m (6.5 feet) at the shoulders, and its horn may reach a length of 1.5 m (5 feet). The head is massive and armed with one or two horns, these being formed from a consolidated mass of hair. The huge body is covered with scantily haired hide, the legs are thick, and the three-toed feet have a horny sole. Their uneven number of toes relates them to horses in the order Perissodactyla.

The black or hook-lipped rhino, *Diceros bicornis*, once common in Africa south of the Sahara, is today found only in East Africa. It browses, using its prehensile upper lip to grasp and draw twigs and leaves into its mouth. It can reach a speed of 56 km/hour (35 miles per hour) in spite of its bulk and relatively short legs. About 18 months after mating, one calf is born. The lifespan is probably about 25 years.

The white rhino is found in central Africa. The Indian or greater one-horned rhino, *Rhinocerus unicornis*, is found in Asia, and its thick, almost hairless, hide is folded into large plates or shields. The Javan or lesser one-horned rhino, *R. sondaicus*, is similar to the Indian but smaller, being only 1.4 m (4.5 feet) in height. The Sumatran or Asiatic two-horned rhino, *Dicerorhinus sumatrensis*, is similar in size to the Javan rhino.

rhizome A swollen underground STEM bearing roots and some scale-leaves as well as the aerial parts of the plant. There is no clear distinction between rhizomes and CORMS or stem TUBERS, and some, such as those of *Iris*, grow at ground-level. Rhizomes act as storage organs during adverse periods, such as winter in temperate regions or dry seasons in the tropics.

Rhode Island A state in the northeastern USA, on the Atlantic coast, settled from England in the 17th century; area 3,140 sq km (1,212 sq miles); pop. (1990) 1,003,460; capital, Providence. The smallest of the 50 states, it is also known as the Ocean State and was one of the original 13 states of the USA.

Rhodes (Greek **Ródhos**) A Greek island in the south-east Aegean, off the Turkish coast, the largest of the Dodecanese Islands and the most easterly island in the Aegean; area 1,398 sq km (540 sq miles); pop. (1991) 98,450. Rhodes flourished in the late Bronze Age, becoming a significant trading nation and dominating several islands in the

Aegean. It came under Byzantine rule in the 5th century. Throughout the 14th and 15th centuries under the Knights of St John it was a centre for the struggle against Turkish domination, eventually falling under Turkish administration in 1522, which lasted until 1912 when it was ceded to Italy. In 1947, following World War II, it was awarded to Greece.

Rhodes, Cecil (John) (1853–1902) British-born South African statesman, Prime Minister of Cape Colony 1890–96. He went to South Africa in 1870, where he became a successful diamond prospector, and 20 years later owned 90 per cent of the world's production of diamonds. Entering politics in 1881, he expanded British territory in southern Africa, annexing Bechuanaland (now Botswana) in 1884 and developing Rhodesia from 1889 onwards through the British South Africa Company, which he founded. While Premier, Rhodes was implicated in the Jameson Raid into Boer territory (1895) and forced to resign. In his will he established the system of Rhodes Scholarships to allow students from the British Empire (now the Commonwealth), the USA, and Germany to study at Oxford University.

Rhodes, Wilfred (1877–1973) British cricketer. An all-rounder, he played for Yorkshire (1898–1930) and for England (1899–1926), scoring almost 40,000 runs during this time and taking 4,187 first-class wickets, more than any other player.

Rhodesia ▶1 The former name of a large territory in central-southern Africa, divided into Northern Rhodesia (now Zambia) and Southern Rhodesia (now Zimbabwe). The region was developed by and named after Cecil RHODES, through the British South Africa Company, which administered it until Southern Rhodesia became a self-governing British colony in 1923 and Northern Rhodesia a British protectorate in 1924. From 1953 to 1963 Northern and Southern Rhodesia were united with Nyasaland (now Malawi) to form the federation of Rhodesia and Nyasaland. **▶2** The name adopted by Southern Rhodesia when Northern Rhodesia left the Federation in 1963 to become the independent republic of Zambia.

Rhodesia and Nyasaland, Federation of See CENTRAL AFRICAN FEDERATION.

rhodium (symbol Rh, at. no. 45, r.a.m. 102.91) A silvery, unreactive platinum metal. The element occurs in association with other platinum metals in cupro-nickel deposits and is used mainly as an alloying addition to strengthen platinum or palladium, and in THERMOCOUPLES. It is also used in plating jewellery, making searchlight reflectors, and in electroplating. Rhodium is also used as a catalyst in ethanoic acid production.

rhododendron An evergreen or deciduous shrub or tree of the genus *Rhododendron*, which comprises some 850 species in the north temperate zone, the mountains of tropical Asia, and the Arctic. They have large flowers varying from white and yellow to red and pink and the evergreen species have glossy, dark green leaves. Like most of their relatives in the heather family, Ericaceae, they are pollinated by bees and birds. Some are very stout trees with massive stems and big buds and leaves, while others are low creeping shrubs, and some are EPIPHYTES. **Azaleas** are species, mostly deciduous, of *Rhododendron*, and are widely cultivated for their flowers, often as hybrid forms.

Rhône A river in south-west Europe that rises in the Swiss Alps and flows 812 km (505 miles), at first westwards through Lake Geneva into France, then to Lyon, where it turns southwards, passing Avignon, to the Mediterranean Sea west of Marseilles, where it forms a wide delta that includes the Camargue region. South of Lyon it has been developed for hydroelectric power and irrigation, and in order to improve navigation.

rhubarb A perennial plant belonging to the genus *Rheum*, with very large leaves arising from a substantial rootstock, producing a supply of leaf stalks over a long period of the year. Forced rhubarb is produced from rootstocks lifted in the winter and placed in the dark. Although referred to as a fruit, rhubarb is really a vegetable, since it is the long, fleshy leaf stalks that are eaten. The fresh leaves must not be eaten as they contain a high level of oxalic acid, a poison to humans. Rhubarb is related to sorrel and docks in the family Polygonaceae.

rhyme The identity of sound between syllables or words, usually at the end of verse lines, but sometimes (in 'internal rhyme') within the same line. Normally the last stressed vowel and all sounds following it make up the rhyming element: this can be a monosyllable (*love / above*), known as 'masculine' rhyme, or two syllables (as in the 'feminine' rhyme wh*ether / together*), or even trisyllabic (*sing to me / bring to me*). Rhyme is not essential to poetry: many languages rarely use it, and in English it finally replaced alliteration as the structuring principle of verse only in the late 14th century.

rhyolite A light, fine-grained igneous rock formed by the rapid cooling of lava rich in silica; it is widespread in the south-western USA and in other volcanic regions. When heat-treated it is used as a thermal and acoustic insulator. Pumice, pitchstone, and obsidian are all forms of rhyolite.

Rhys, Jean (pseudonym of Ella Gwendolen Rees Williams) (1890–1979) British novelist and short-story writer, born in Dominica. Her novels include *Good Morning, Midnight* (1939) and *Wide Sargasso Sea* (1966); the latter, set in Dominica and Jamaica in the 1830s, recreates Charlotte Brontë's *Jane Eyre* from the point of view of Mrs Rochester, the 'mad woman in the attic'.

rhythm and blues The style of music that grew out of the BLUES tradition as it developed among African American musicians in the northern industrial cities of the USA in the 1950s and 1960s. The typical 'R & B' band was made up of a rhythm section (drums, bass, electric guitar, and piano), and a leading player (either vocalist or guitarist), often with the support of a vocal backing group. Rhythm and blues was a significant influence on the early development of rock and roll (see ROCK MUSIC).

rib A flat, curved bone forming part of the rib-cage in all vertebrates, the number of ribs being progressively reduced in the higher forms. They are jointed to the VERTEBRAE behind, and the front ends are joined to the sternum by springy cartilages, which allow the chest to be expanded and compressed by muscle action. In the cavities of the ribs there is red, blood-forming marrow. The ribs, within the structure of the rib-cage, are interconnected by muscles. Some pull the ribs together during breathing out, others pull the ribs apart during inhaling.

Ribbentrop, Joachim von (1893–1946) German Nazi politician. A close associate of Hitler, Ribbentrop served as Foreign Minister from 1938 to 1945. During his ministry, he signed the non-aggression pact with the Soviet Union (1939). He was convicted as a war criminal at the Nuremberg trials and hanged.

ribbonfish A fish of the family Trachipteridae, found in all oceans. They are elongate and very compressed mid-water inhabitants of the open ocean, living in depths of 300–700 m (1,975–2,275 feet). They are usually bright silver in colour with reddish fins, but their biology is little known. There are about seven species, of which the North Atlantic dealfish, *Trachipterus arcticus*, is one of the largest, growing to 2.5 m (8 feet).

ribbon worm (or **bootlace worm**, **proboscis worm**) An invertebrate comprising some 650 species in the phylum Nemertini. Ribbon worms are often very long, and sometimes brightly coloured, and can be found in tangled knots under sea-shore rocks, or in shallow water of temperate seas throughout the world. A few species live in fresh water, or are terrestrial in the tropics. These animals have no COELOM, are unsegmented, and move by slow undulations of the body, or by gliding. All have a long proboscis, sometimes barbed, which can be shot out to catch prey; some use it to grasp nearby objects and pull their bodies along after it.

Ribera, **José de** (or **Jusepe**) (known as 'Lo Spagnoletto', 'the little Spaniard') (*c*.1591–1652) Spanish painter and etcher, resident in Italy from 1616. He is best known for his paintings of religious subjects and for his genre scenes; these are noted for their dramatic chiaroscuro effects and for their realistic depiction of torture and martyrdom. Important works include the *Martyrdom of St Bartholomew* (*c*.1630).

ribosome A small spherical organelle within the cytoplasm of a cell. Ribosomes are the site of protein synthesis and consist of a type of RNA and a protein.

Ricardo, **David** (1772–1823) British political economist who, with Adam SMITH, founded British classical economics. In 1819–23 he was an MP, supporting FREE TRADE, a return to the GOLD STANDARD, and the repeal of the CORN LAWS. He is best remembered for his *Principles of Political Economy and Taxation* (1817), arguing that the value of a commodity is related to amount of labour required to make it – a premise later adopted by Karl MARX. He also formulated the law of comparative advantage in international trade.

Ricci, **Sebastiano** (1659–1734) Italian decorative painter. He is generally considered a member of the Venetian School, but he travelled extensively in Italy and elsewhere before settling in Venice in 1717. He had a gift for vivid colouring, and his career was important in spreading knowledge of Italian decorative painting. Little of the decorative work he did in England survives, but there are examples at Chelsea Hospital and Burlington House (now the Royal Academy). He often worked in partnership with his nephew **Marco Ricci** (1676–1730), who was primarily a landscape painter.

rice A tropical annual grass, *Oryza sativa*, which provides the staple cereal diet of half the world's population and is second only to wheat in terms of total output. Rice is an Asian species, and is unique among cereals as it is usually cultivated in standing water (paddy fields), the rice stems being adapted to allow oxygen to pass downwards to supply the waterlogged root system. It is an invaluable crop in the high-rainfall regions of the tropics and subtropics. Rice cultivation is also important in Central and South America. Hillside fields may be terraced to retain water. Upland rice, or dry rice, is grown on hills where the paddy-field system is impossible but rainfall is sufficiently high. Rice is always established from seed, and the best yields are obtained by transplanting nursery-raised seedlings, a process carried out by hand in most parts of the world. Rice is cut before the crop is fully ripe, threshed, and polished to remove the grain husk. Several harvests can be gathered each year. Most of the production, which is highly labour intensive, is carried out by peasant farmers and sharecroppers; in some cases control over the water supply, and the resources to build extensive irrigation systems become a political issue.

Rice, **Sir Tim(othy Miles Bindon)** (1944–) British lyricist and entertainer. He came to public attention as the co-writer, with Andrew Lloyd Webber, of a number of hit musicals, including *Joseph and the Amazing Technicolor Dreamcoat* (1968) *Jesus Christ Superstar* (1970), and *Evita* (1976). He later moved into new partnerships with lyrics for productions such as *Chess* (1984), and in 1994 won the second of his two Oscars for best original film song with 'Can You Feel the Love Tonight', a collaboration with Elton John, from *The Lion King*.

Rich, **Buddy** (born Bernard Rich) (1917–87) US jazz drummer and band-leader. At the age of 16 he joined the band of clarinettist Joe Marsala, and subsequently played for band-leaders such as Artie Shaw and Tommy Dorsey. He formed his own band in 1946, which he reduced to a smaller group in 1951, but fronted another large band in 1966 and toured extensively until his death.

Richard Three kings of England. **Richard I** (known as Richard Coeur de Lion or Richard the Lionheart) (1157–99), son of Henry II, reigned 1189–99. Richard's military exploits made him a medieval legend, but meant that he spent most of his reign absent from his kingdom, leading to a growth in the power of the barons. Soon after succeeding his father he left to lead the Third Crusade, defeating Saladin at Arsuf (1191), but failing to capture Jerusalem. He was taken prisoner on his way home in 1192 by Duke Leopold of Austria (1157–94) and subsequently held hostage by the Holy Roman emperor Henry VI (1165–97), only being released in 1194 following the payment of a huge ransom. After later embarking on a campaign against Philip II of France, Richard was fatally wounded during the siege of the castle of Châlus. **Richard II** (1367–1400), son of the Black Prince, reigned 1377–99. On his accession as a minor the government was placed in the hands of selected nobles, dominated by his uncle John of Gaunt. During this time Richard helped to put down the Peasants' Revolt, but was soon facing a threat to his power from rebel nobles; in 1389 he asserted his right to rule independently of his protectors and later executed or banished most of his former opponents (1397–98). However, his confiscation of John of Gaunt's estate on the latter's death provoked Henry Bolingbroke's return from exile to overthrow him. **Richard III** (1452–85), brother of Edward IV, reigned 1483–85. During the Wars of the Roses he served as a commander in the Battle of Tewkesbury (1471), which restored Edward IV to the throne. After his brother's death he served as Protector to his nephew Edward V, who, two months later, was declared illegitimate on dubious grounds and subsequently disappeared (See PRINCES IN THE TOWER). As king, Richard ruled with some success for a brief period, before being defeated and killed at Bosworth Field (1485) by Henry Tudor (later Henry VII). Historical opinion on the popular picture of Richard as a hunchbacked cutthroat usurper is still divided; many modern historians argue that he was demonized as part of Tudor propaganda.

Richard, Sir Cliff (born Harry Rodger Webb) (1940–) British pop singer, born in India. Influenced by rock and roll, he formed his own group the Drifters (later called the Shadows) in 1958, recording, such songs as 'Living Doll' (1959) and 'Bachelor Boy' (1961) with them. Richard went on to act in several films, mainly musicals such as *Expresso Bongo* (1960) and *Summer Holiday* (1962). He left the Shadows in 1968, and in the 1970s became a born-again Christian; he has since combined a successful pop career with evangelism.

Richard Coeur de Lion RICHARD I of England.

Richard of York See YORK, RICHARD PLANTAGENET, 3RD DUKE OF.

Richards, Frank (pseudonym of Charles Hamilton) (1876–1961) British writer for boys' magazines. He wrote under many pseudonyms, inventing some 50 fictional public schools. The best known was Greyfriars School, where the exploits of Billy Bunter, Harry Wharton, and co. entertained the readers of *Magnet* and *Gem* from about 1907 to the start of World War II.

Richards, Sir Gordon (1904–86) British jockey. He was champion jockey 26 times between 1925 and 1953.

Richards, I(vor) A(rmstrong) (1893–1979) British literary critic and poet. In 1929 he became a fellow of Magdalene College, Cambridge, and was appointed professor of English at Harvard in 1944. His works include *Principles of Literary Criticism* (1924) and *Practical Criticism* (1929).

Richards, Viv (full name Isaac Vivian Alexander Richards) (1952–) West Indian cricketer. Born in Antigua, he made his début for the West Indies in 1974, and captained the team from 1985 until 1991, a period during which his country dominated international cricket. He scored more than 6,000 runs during his test career. He also played county cricket in England for Somerset (1974–86) and Glamorgan (1990–93).

Richardson, Sir Ralph (David) (1902–83) British actor. He established himself as a leading actor with the Old Vic in London in the early 1930s. He played many Shakespearian roles, as well as leading parts in plays, such as Harold Pinter's *No Man's Land* (1975) and films, such as *Oh! What a Lovely War* (1969).

Richardson, Samuel (1689–1761) British novelist. His first novel, *Pamela* (1740–41), was entirely in the form of letters and journals and was responsible for popularizing the epistolary novel. He experimented further with the genre in *Clarissa Harlowe* (1747–48), which explored moral issues in a detailed social context with psychological intensity.

Richard the Lionheart RICHARD I of England.

Richelieu, Armand Jean du Plessis (1585–1642) French cardinal and statesman. From 1624 to 1642 he was chief minister of Louis XIII, dominating French government. He destroyed the power base of the Huguenots in the late 1620s and set out to undermine the Habsburg empire by supporting the Swedish king Gustavus Adolphus in the Thirty Years War, involving France from 1635. In the same year, Richelieu was also responsible for establishing the Académie française.

Richler, Mordecai (1931–) Canadian novelist. Much of his work reflects his Jewish upbringing in Montreal. His best-known novel is probably his fourth, *The Apprenticeship of Duddy Kravitz* (1959); other works include the satirical *The Incomparable Atuk* (1963), *St Urbain's Horseman* (1971), and *Solomon Gursky was Here* (1989).

Richmond The capital of the US state of Virginia, a port on the James River; pop. (1990) 203,060. Richmond became state capital in 1780. During the American Civil War it was the Confederate capital from 1861 until its capture in 1865. In addition to producing tobacco products, paper, aluminium, chemicals, textiles, and machinery, it is the seat of the Virginia Commonwealth University and the University of Richmond.

Richmond upon Thames A residential borough of Greater London, England, on the Thames; pop. (1991) 154,600. Hampton Court Palace and the Royal Botanic Gardens at Kew are located here. There are the remains of a Tudor royal palace in which Queen Elizabeth I died in 1603, and White Lodge in Richmond Park is also strongly associated with the British royal family.

Richter, Charles Francis (1900–85) US geologist. Richter worked mainly in California, becoming professor of seismology at the California Institute of Technology in 1952. He devised the **Richter scale** for measuring the strength of earthquakes in 1935, basing it on the amplitude of the waves produced. The scale from 0 to 10 is logarithmic, so that an increase of one point represents a tenfold increase in amplitude, with the release of about 30 times more energy. A figure of 2 on the Richter scale records a barely perceptible tremor; one measuring 8 or more is a major earthquake causing extensive damage in a built-up area.

Richthofen, Manfred, Freiherr von (known as 'the Red Baron') (1882–1918) German fighter pilot. In World War I he initially fought in the cavalry, but transferred to the flying corps, joining a fighter squadron in 1915 and flying a distinctive bright red aircraft. He was eventually shot down, probably by Allied infantrymen, after destroying 80 Allied planes.

ridge (in meteorology) A short-lived area of high surface pressure that is elongated in form. Over land or sea ridges may be accompanied by strong breezes, although the weather is fair or fine. The opposite of a ridge is a trough.

Ridley, Nicholas (*c*.1500–55) English Protestant bishop and martyr. He became one of Thomas Cranmer's chaplains in 1537 and, during the reign of Edward VI, was appointed bishop of Rochester (1547) and then of London (1550). During this period, he emerged as one of the leaders of the Reformation, opposing the Catholic policies of Edward's sister and successor Mary I, for which he was later imprisoned (1553) and burnt at the stake in Oxford.

Rie, Lucie (1902–95) British potter, born in Austria. In 1938 she went to England as a refugee. The following year she established a studio, and went on to influence a generation of British potters. Her pottery and stoneware are found in collections worldwide. She was made a Doctor of the Royal Academy of Arts in 1969.

Riefenstahl, Leni (full name Bertha Helene Amalie Riefenstahl) (1902–) German film-maker and photographer. She is chiefly known for two films which she made during the 1930s; *Triumph of the Will* (1934) a powerful depiction of the 1934 Nuremberg Nazi Party rallies, and *Olympia* (1938), a two-part documentary of the 1936 Berlin Olympic Games. She was not a Nazi Party member and insisted on full control over these films, but outside Germany her work was regarded as Nazi propaganda.

Riel, Louis (1844–85) Canadian political leader. He

headed the rebellion of the Metis at Red River Settlement (now in Manitoba) in 1869 to protest against the planned transfer of the territorial holdings of the Hudson's Bay Company to Canadian jurisdiction, a move that the Metis feared would result in the loss of some of their land to Anglo-Protestant settlers. Having formed and headed a provisional government, Riel oversaw negotiations for acceptable terms for union with Canada, including the establishment of the province of Manitoba. He was executed for treason after leading a further rebellion of the Metis in the Saskatchewan valley (1884–85).

Riemann, (Georg Friedrich) Bernhard (1826–66) German mathematician. He studied under Karl Gauss at Göttingen and became professor there. He founded Riemannian geometry, which is of fundamental importance to both mathematics and physics. The *Riemann hypothesis*, about the complex numbers which are roots of a certain transcendental equation, remains one of the unsolved problems of mathematics.

rifle A FIREARM with a gun barrel that has rifling (internal grooves that impart spin to the BULLET) for greater accuracy. The first rifles (late 18th century) were identical to the muzzle-loading flintlock muskets of their day except for their longer, rifled barrels. The improvement in accuracy was such that, by the middle of the 19th century, the armies of most European nations equipped their soldiers with rifled muskets. At about the same time, a percussion cap replaced the flintlock, and breech-loading rifles were developed. Different methods of operation were employed, but the commonest type was the bolt-action rifle. Automatic rifles harness some of the propellant gases produced in firing to drive back the bolt immediately after a round has been fired. The spent cartridge is ejected, and a new round is automatically inserted. In early semi-automatic rifles the trigger was pulled for each round. Fully automatic weapons now merely require the trigger to be kept pulled; they will then fire continuously until the magazine is emptied.

Rif Mountains (or **Er Rif**) A mountain range of northern Morocco, running parallel to the Mediterranean for about 290 km (180 miles) eastwards from Tangier to near the Algerian frontier. Rising to over 2,250 m (7,000 ft), it forms a westward extension of the Atlas Mountains. The retreat of Berber tribesmen who have often been in revolt against occupying authorities.

rift valley A valley bounded by two roughly parallel faults formed when the rocks at its base moved downwards. See GREAT RIFT VALLEY.

Riga The capital of Latvia, a port at the mouth of the Daugava River on the Gulf of Riga, an inlet of the Baltic Sea; pop. (1990) 916,500. Founded in *c.*1190 and becoming a member of the Hanseatic League in 1282, Riga developed as a major Baltic trading centre in the Middle Ages. The medieval old town contains many imposing buildings. Modern industries include shipbuilding and marine engineering, chemicals, textiles, and electronics.

Rigel A star in the constellation of Orion, and also known as Beta Orionis, with an apparent magnitude of 0.12. It is a hot SUPERGIANT multiple star at an estimated distance of 400 parsecs, with about 140,000 times the luminosity of the Sun, and is thus one of the most luminous stars known.

right ascension See CELESTIAL SPHERE.

rights issue See SHARES.

right whale A WHALEBONE WHALE making up a family of three species, distinguished from all other whales by the absence of a dorsal fin, and by grooves on the throat and chest. Included in this family is the common right whale, *Balaena glacialis*, the bowhead whale, *B. mysticetus*, and the pygmy right whale, *Caperea marginata*. This last is the smallest, being only about 6 m (20 feet) long; it is very rare and found only in the waters of the Southern Hemisphere. Colour varies from black to slate-grey according to species.

Right whales have very large heads and are rich in whalebone, with some 500 plates of baleen hanging from the roof of the mouth, the longest plate being about 2 m (7 feet). The body is rather chunky with a velvety appearance and in *B. glacialis* and *B. mysticetus* is up to 15 m (50 feet) long. When the right whale surfaces to expire, the spout is double and is directed forwards and upwards about 4.5 m (15 feet) in the air. The common right whale has several subspecies, each given common names according to its location.

Rigil Kentaurus See ALPHA CENTAURI.

Rijeka (Italian **Fiume**) A port on the Adriatic coast of Croatia, once the largest port of Yugoslavia; pop. (1991) 167,900. Once a Roman settlement and later occupied by Slavs in the 7th century, Rijeka was the leading naval port of the Austro-Hungarian empire prior to 1918. It has shipyards and oil refineries.

Rijksmuseum The national gallery of the Netherlands, in Amsterdam. Established in the late 19th century and developed from the collection of the House of Orange, it now contains the most representative collection of Dutch art in the world.

Riley, Bridget (Louise) (1931–) British painter. A leading exponent of op art, she worked with flat patterns of lines, dots, and geometrical forms, initially in black and white and later in colour, to create optical illusions of light and movement. Notable paintings include *Movement in Squares* (1961) and *Fall* (1963).

Rilke, Rainer Maria (pseudonym of René Karl Wilhelm Josef Maria Rilke) (1875–1926) Austrian poet, born in Bohemia. Two trips to Russia (1899–1900) inspired him to write the *Book of Hours* (1905), written from the perspective of a Russian monk. Rilke's conception of art as a quasi-religious vocation culminated in the hymnic lyrics for which he is best known: the *Duino Elegies* and *Sonnets to Orpheus* (both 1923).

Rimbaud, (Jean Nicholas) Arthur (1854–91) French poet. Rimbaud wrote his most famous poem, 'Le Bateau ivre', at the age of 17. In the same year he began a passionate relationship with the poet Paul Verlaine, which partly inspired his collection of symbolist prose poems *Une Saison en enfer* (1873). In this and *Les Illuminations* (*c.*1872; published 1884), he explored the visionary possibilities of systematically 'disorientating the senses'.

Rimini A port, resort, and cultural centre on the Adriatic coast of Emilia-Romagna region, northeast Italy; pop. (1990) 130,900. It is situated at the crossroads of the Via Emilia, the Via Flaminia, and the Via Popilia on the site of the Roman town of Arminum which was founded in 268 BC. Rimini passed to the Papal States in 1509 and was annexed to the kingdom of Italy in 1860.

Rimsky-Korsakov, Nikolai (Andreevich) (1844–1908) Russian composer. He achieved fame with his orchestral suite *Scheherazade* (1888) and his many operas drawing on Russian and Slavonic folk tales, notably *Sadko* (1896) and *The Golden Cockerel* (1906–07); the latter was based on Pushkin's poem lampooning autocracy and was banned in Russia until 1909. Rimsky-Korsakov was also a noted orchestrator, completing works by composers, such as Borodin and Mussorgsky.

ring-dove See WOODPIGEON.

ringhals See RINKALS.

ringlet butterfly A BROWN butterfly of several genera occurring in many countries, with caterpillars that feed on grasses. Ringlet butterflies have prominent white-centred black spots near the edge of the otherwise brown wings, on both upper- and under-sides. Some species have conspicuous yellow-ringed eye-spots near the apex of the wings, but others, such as the genus *Erebia*, have only small black spots. The spots to which the name ringlet refers act as deflection marks during attacks by birds.

ring-ouzel A species of bird, *Turdus torquatus*, belonging to the thrush family, which breeds in northern parts of Europe and winters further south, often on moorland or in open forest. The male is greyish-black with a white crescent across its breast; the female is browner with a smaller crescent.

ring-tailed cat (or **miner's cat**) A species of carnivore, *Bassaricus astutus*, related to the racoons. It is found in Mexico and the southwestern USA as far as Alabama and Oregon, where it lives in dry, rocky habitats. It is racoon-like in appearance with a tail banded with grey and dark brown rings, and feeds on small mammals, insects, and fruit.

The **cacomistle**, *Bassaricus sumichrasti*, is a similar species which occurs in Central America.

ringworm (or **tinea**) An infection of the skin with one of a variety of FUNGI. It causes a mild inflammation, with redness and scaling, which may spread outwards, leaving a more normal central area, and thus forms a ring (hence the name). It was once a common infection of the scalp in children and difficult to treat, but modern drugs have largely removed the problem. When it occurs between the toes, ringworm infection is called athlete's foot, or tinea pedis.

rinkals (or **ringhals**) A species of venomous snake, *Haemachatus haemachatus*, mainly restricted to eastern parts of southern Africa. It is nocturnal in its habits and eats mammals, birds, and toads. The rinkals is a species of spitting COBRA, which, when threatened, as a defensive reaction may spray venom for distances of up to 3 m (9.75 feet) into the eyes of an intruder, causing at least temporary blindness.

Rio de Janeiro The chief port, second-largest city, the cultural, financial, and commercial centre, and former capital of Brazil; pop. (1991) 5,480,770. Situated on Guanabara Bay (an inlet of the Atlantic Ocean), the skyline of the city is dominated by Sugar Loaf Mountain and by Corcovado on which stands the statue of 'Christ the Redeemer'. Copacabana beach and the district of Ipanema are popular resorts. Its buildings range from beautiful 18th-century churches to famous modern architecture, which contrasts with the huge shanty-towns or *favelas* clinging to steep hillsides around the city. The capital was eventually transferred to Brasilia in 1960.

Rio Grande A river of North America which rises in the Rocky Mountains of south-west Colorado and flows 3,030 km (1,880 miles) generally south-eastwards to the Gulf of Mexico. It forms the US–Mexico frontier from El Paso to the sea.

Río Muni The part of Equatorial Guinea that lies on the mainland of West Africa; area 26,016 sq km (10,049 sq miles). Its chief town is Bata.

Riot Act An Act to prevent civil disorder passed by the British Parliament in 1715. The Act made it a serious crime for anyone to refuse to obey the command of lawful authority to disperse; thus the Act imposed upon the civil magistrates the dangerous duty of attending a riot, or a large meeting which might become riotous, and reading the Riot Act. Frequent use was made of the Act in the 18th century. Its use declined in the 19th century and it was repealed in 1911.

Risorgimento (*c.*1831–61) (Italian, 'resurrection' or 'rebirth') A period of political unrest in ITALY, during which the united kingdom of Italy emerged. Much of Italy had experienced liberal reforms and an end to feudal and ecclesiastical privilege during the NAPOLEONIC WARS. The restoration of repressive regimes led to uprisings in Naples and PIEDMONT (1821), and in Bologna (1831), then part of the Papal States. Following the French JULY REVOLUTION in 1830, Italian nationalists began to support MAZZINI and the YOUNG ITALY movement. In this they were encouraged by the liberal Charles Albert, who succeeded to the throne of Sardinia, and became ruler of Piedmont in 1831. In 1847 Count CAVOUR started a newspaper, *Il Risorgimento*; this had a considerable influence on Charles Albert, who in 1848 tried to drive the Austrians out of Lombardy and Venetia. He was defeated at Custozza (1848) and Novara (1849) and abdicated. He was succeeded by his son VICTOR EMANUEL II. During the REVOLUTIONS OF 1848 republicans held power briefly in Rome, Florence, Turin, and Venice and hoped to create a republic of Italy, but were also defeated. Under the guidance of Cavour, Prime Minister of Piedmont from 1852, the French emperor NAPOLEON III was encouraged to ally with Piedmont, in return for promises of Nice and a part of the Alpine region of Savoy, and Austria was defeated in the battles of MAGENTA and Solferino in 1859. Austria evacuated Lombardy and much of central Italy. GARIBALDI liberated Sicily, marched north and almost reached Rome. Plebiscites were held and resulted in a vote to accept Victor Emanuel II as first King of Italy (1861).

rites of passage See RITUAL.

ritual Various forms of stylized human behaviour, often, but not always, religious. Ritual is closely linked to MAGIC, MYTH, and RELIGION, and includes activities such as initiation, CIRCUMCISION, MARRIAGE, and funerals. In addition it is an important feature of political organization in most societies. One important group of rituals are **rites of passage**, which involve a transition from one status or position in society to another. The collective action in rituals can create a powerful response both in the participants and in those watching, whether they be mourners at a funeral, cheering crowds at a royal wedding, or spectators at a football match. The French sociologist Émile DURKHEIM thought that ritual made people aware of the collective power of society over the individual, and that rituals were a necessary source of social integration.

river A copious natural stream of water flowing in a channel to the sea. A typical stream may rise near a watershed, or from a spring, or from a limestone cave or the melting end of a glacier. Seeking the steepest and shortest course downward, it cuts its way through soft rock, carrying the loosened particles with it. Joined by tributaries, its cutting power increases. Gullies become canyons or, if mass wasting erodes the sides, broad valleys are created over the years; the further it travels the more its load increases. The stream may enter a lake, from which it emerges with its speed diminished; but joined by more tributaries it now becomes a river. The work of erosion continues, but DEPOSITION now begins in earnest. In its lower reaches, where the gradient is less, there is more likelihood of MEANDERING. Melting snows or heavy rain may cause the river to flood: alluvium is deposited on the FLOODPLAIN. Finally the river enters its DELTA or meets, in its estuary, the tides of the sea. The form of a typical river depends not only on geology (especially the permeability of rock) but also on climate. In arid regions streams are ephemeral. Channels fed by melting mountain snow are generally dry in winter but swollen in spring and early summer, while in Mediterranean and some continental climates summer is the season when they are dry. In temperate regions rivers rise in winter and occasionally flood. In tropical and especially monsoon regions, the regime is one of seasonal variations in the discharge of rivers.

Rivera, Diego (1886–1957) Mexican painter. His monumental frescos of the 1920s and 1930s were a part of a revival of fresco painting in Latin America and the USA. Rivera's largest and most ambitious mural was a history of Mexico for the National Palace in Mexico City; begun in 1929 and unfinished at his death, it explicitly sought to construct a sense of nationalist and socialist identity.

river blindness (or **onchocerciasis**) An infestation with a species of parasitic ROUNDWORM, *Onchocerca volvulus*. It causes inflammation of the skin, since the body responds to the worms' presence by forming fibrous nodules around them. Migration of their larvae into the eye causes blindness. It derives its name from the fact that the worms are transmitted by black flies, *Simulium damnosum*, which keep close to the rivers in which they breed. It is a serious cause of blindness in some parts of Africa. Other forms also occur in Central and South America.

river dolphin Any one of five species of TOOTHED WHALE found in fresh or brackish waters of rivers of southern Asia and tropical South America. There are river dolphins called Ganges, *Platanista gangetica*, Indus, *P. minor*, whitefin, *Lipotes vexillifer*, Amazon, *Inia geoffrensis*, and La Plata, *Pontoporia blainvillei*. All have a long, narrow beak and jaws studded with teeth, are blind or nearly so, and small, being 1.5–3 m (5–10 feet) long. The La Plata river dolphin travels and breeds in small schools in the estuaries of large rivers along the coast of South America. The whitefin dolphin is found only in the Yangtze and lower Fuchunjian rivers of China.

Riviera, the Part of the Mediterranean coastal region of southern France and northern Italy, extending from Cannes to La Spezia, famous for its scenic beauty, fertility, and mild climate, and with many fashionable resorts.

Riyadh (Arabic **Ar Riyad**) The capital and commercial centre of Saudi Arabia, situated at an oasis on a high plateau in the Central Province (Nejd). The poor central area with its bazaars is surrounded by the modern suburbs built since the 1950s.; pop. (est. 1988) 2,000,000.

Rizzio, David (1533–66) Italian-born secretary and adviser to MARY, QUEEN OF SCOTS. He entered service at court in 1561 and by 1564 he had become her Secretary: he possibly arranged her marriage to his friend DARNLEY. By March 1566 'Seigneur' David's arrogant monopoly of power, combined with fears of his being a papal agent, led to his assassination. Darnley, who suspected him of adultery with Mary, was involved in the plot.

RNA (ribonucleic acid) A NUCLEIC ACID molecule consisting of a long chain of NUCLEOTIDE subunits. The subunits are joined in a sequence which, in cellular organisms, is precisely determined by

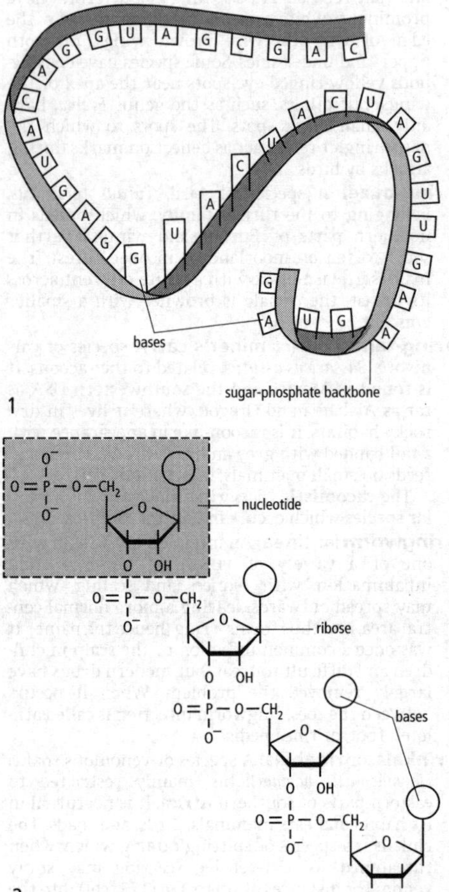

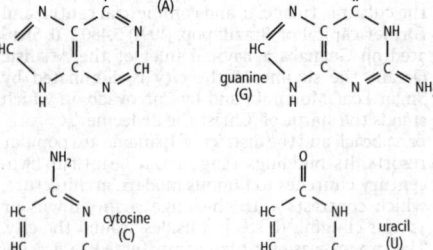

RNA (1) The single-stranded structure of an RNA molecule. (2) Detail of the molecular structure of the sugar-phosphate backbone. (3) Molecular structure of the four bases of RNA.

the DNA of the cell: that is, RNA is transcribed (copied) directly from the DNA.

In cells, there are three main types of RNA, all of which are involved in the synthesis of proteins: messenger RNA (mRNA), transfer RNA (tRNA) and ribosomal RNA (rRNA). Messenger RNA carries the coded instructions for making proteins; in the cytoplasm it becomes attached to ribosomes, cell components upon which protein synthesis takes place. Transfer RNA molecules each contain 74–95 nucleotides; they occur in the cytoplasm of the cell. They are responsible for the correct positioning of amino acids as proteins are assembled. Each type of tRNA recognizes a particular sequence of three nitrogenous bases (a codon) on the mRNA, to which it becomes attached; the other end of the tRNA carries a specific amino acid which thus becomes incorporated in the correct location in the growing protein chain. The process of building a protein from amino acids according to the sequence of codons in the mRNA is called translation. Ribosomal RNA is the major structural and functional component of ribosomes; each ribosome contains three different types of rRNA, which differ, for example, in size.

RNA also occurs in many viruses as the sole genetic material of the virus. In some of these, the so-called RETROVIRUSES (such as the Aids virus), the RNA is reverse-transcribed into DNA within a host cell, the DNA then becoming integrated with the host chromosome; more virus RNA can then be transcribed from this DNA intermediate. However, in most RNA viruses DNA is never made, the RNA being duplicated directly during the life cycle of the virus.

roach (fish) A species in the carp family, *Rutilus rutilus*, widely distributed in western and central Europe. Because of its popularity as an anglers' fish it has been introduced to many areas outside its natural range. Living in lowland rivers and lakes, it is relatively undemanding of water quality and adaptable to different foods. The roach thrives in large ponds, reservoirs, and even slightly polluted water. It eats insects, crustaceans, snails, and plants. It spawns in late spring, shedding its yellow eggs on plants where they hatch in 9–12 days. The roach is distinguished by its moderately deep body, bluish or greeny-brown back, silvery sides, and orange to red pelvic and anal fins.

roach (insect) See COCKROACH.

roadrunner A bird of the species *Geococcyx*, belonging to the CUCKOO family, found in semi-desert areas of North and Central America. They are heavily streaked, brown birds with shaggy crests, long tails, and powerful legs; they usually run instead of flying. They feed on lizards and other small animals. Their nest of twigs is usually built low down in a bush or cactus and in it they lay three to five eggs.

Road Town The capital of the British Virgin Islands, situated on Road Harbour on the island of Tortola; pop. (est. 1991) 6,330. It takes its name from the 'road' or open anchorage, a term used in the 17th century.

Roaring Forties That part of the southern oceans between 40° and 50° south, where strong westerly winds predominate. The seas in similar latitudes to the north of the equator in the North Atlantic are sometimes given the same name.

Robbe-Grillet, Alain (1922–) French novelist. He established himself as a leading exponent of the avant-garde *nouveau roman* in the 1950s; his first novel *The Erasers* (1953) was an early example of the form, which rejected the plot, characters, and omniscient narrator central to the traditional novel. Among his later fictional works are *The Voyeur* (1955) and *Jealousy* (1957). His theories on fiction appeared in his collection of essays *Towards a New Novel* (1963). He also wrote screenplays in which he explored the visual potential of his fictional techniques, most notably that for *L'Année dernière à Marienbad* (1961).

robber crab See COCONUT CRAB.

robber fly A medium-sized to large fly, some of which are robust and hairy, most with a long, narrow abdomen, which preys on other insects. Robber flies make up a family, Asilidae, of some 4,000 species. The legs are long and strong and, on close examination, the head is grooved between the eyes, and the face bearded. Some catch their food in flight using the legs as a scoop; others lie in wait and pounce. The proboscis is horny and is used to pierce the prey and suck its juices. Eggs are laid in damp soil, rotting wood, or similar places, and larvae eat decaying plant material.

Robbins, Jerome (1918–) US ballet-dancer and choreographer. He choreographed a long series of successful musicals including *The King and I* (1951) *West Side Story* (1957), and the *Fiddler on the Roof* (1964). Although chiefly inspired by jazz and modern dance, he has also created a number of ballets with music by classical composers.

Robert Three kings of Scotland. **Robert I** (known as Robert the Bruce) (1274–1329) reigned 1306–29. He led the Scottish campaign against Edward I after the death of Sir William Wallace. His subsequent campaign against Edward II culminated in victory at Bannockburn (1314). He then went on to re-establish Scotland as a separate kingdom, negotiating the Treaty of Northampton (1328), which committed the Plantagenets to recognizing his title as king of Scotland and relinquishing their claims to overlordship. **Robert II** (1316–90), grandson of Robert the Bruce, reigned 1371–90. He was steward of Scotland from 1326 to 1371, and the first of the Stuart line. **Robert III** (born John) (*c.*1337–1406), son of Robert II, reigned 1390–1406. Before ascending the throne, he was involved in an accident in which the kick of a horse made him physically disabled. As a result, his reign was marked by a power struggle amongst members of his family during which Scotland was chiefly ruled by his brother Robert, Duke of Albany (*c.*1340–1420).

Roberts, Frederick Sleigh, 1st Earl Roberts of Kandahar (1832–1914) British Field Marshal. He won a Victoria Cross in 1858 for his part in suppressing the Indian Mutiny and commanded the British army in its victory at Kandahar (1880), which ended the Second Afghan War (1878–80). As Commander-in-Chief (1899–90) during the Second Boer War, he planned the successful march on the Boer capital of Pretoria (1900).

Robert the Bruce ROBERT I of Scotland.

Robeson, Paul (Bustill) (1898–1976) US singer and actor. His singing of 'Ol' Man River' in Jerome Kern's musical *Showboat* (1927) established his international reputation. Noted for his rich and resonant bass voice, he gave many recitals of spirituals. As an actor, Robeson was particularly identified with the title role of *Othello*, which he performed to great acclaim in London (1930) and on Broadway (1943). He was a prominent African American activist, and had his passport revoked in 1950 because of his Communist affiliations.

Robespierre, Maximilien François Marie Isidore de (1758–94) French revolutionary. Robespierre was the leader of the radical Jacobins in the National Assembly and, as such, backed the execution of Louis XVI and implemented a successful purge of the moderate Girondists (both 1793). Later the same year he consolidated his power with his election to the Committee of Public Safety (the revolutionary governing body 1793–94) and his appointment as president of the National Assembly. Robespierre was guillotined for his role in the Terror, although he had objected to the scale of the executions.

Robey, Sir George (born George Edward Wade) (1869–1954) British comedian and actor. From the 1890s, he performed in music-halls and was billed as the 'Prime Minister of Mirth'. He later appeared in films such as Laurence Olivier's *Henry V* (1944).

robin Originally the European robin redbreast, *Erithacus rubecula*, a small bird of the thrush family, widely distributed in Europe. It is brown with an orange-red breast. This bird is regarded with great affection in Britain and is commonly portrayed on Christmas cards. Pioneer settlers in many other parts of the world tended to call any local small bird with a red breast a robin and hence the name is used for other birds in most parts of the world, especially the American robin, *Turdus migratorius*, the African scrub robins of the genus *Cercotrichas*, and the Australian robins, especially those of the genus *Petroica*.

Robin Hood The legendary English outlaw who stole from the rich to give to the poor. He is traditionally represented as the unjustly outlawed Earl of Huntingdon, fighting the corrupt administration of King JOHN and his local officer the sheriff of Nottingham from Sherwood Forest. The earliest literary evidence of Robin appears in William Langland's poem *Piers Plowman* (written *c.*1367–86). The fullest account of his exploits, given in the late medieval *Lytell Geste of Robyn Hode* (printed *c.*1495), locates him in Barnsdale, Yorkshire. Robin's sympathies for the plight of the gentry, not just the peasantry, are best understood in the context of 14th-century disenchantment with royal justice. Post-medieval ballads give Robin Hood companions in Sherwood Forest, among them his mistress Maid Marian, and his friends Friar Tuck, Little John, Will Scarlett, and Allan-a-Dale.

Robinia A genus of some 20 species of deciduous trees or shrubs native to eastern North America and Mexico. Along with acacias and laburnum, they are part of the pea family. The locust tree, or false acacia, *Robinia pseudacacia*, is widely planted in the Old World for timber, but it readily naturalizes and has become a weed in many places. This and other species are cultivated for their feathery foliage and pretty pea-flowers.

Robinson, Edward G. (born Emanuel Goldenberg) (1893–1972) Romanian-born US actor. After playing the part of Rico Bandello in the gangster film *Little Caesar* (1930), he went on to appear in a string of similar films in the 1930s. He later played a wider range of screen roles, such as the father in Arthur Miller's *All My Sons* (1948). His later films include *The Cincinnati Kid* (1965). Robinson was also a noted art collector.

Robinson, (William) Heath (1872–1944) British cartoonist and illustrator. He is best known for his humorous drawings, through which he achieved worldwide fame. He lampooned the machine age by inventing absurdly complicated, jerry-built 'Heath Robinson contraptions' to perform elementary or ridiculous actions, such as serving peas to diners or putting mites into green cheese. He also provided more conventional illustrations for editions of *Don Quixote* (1897) and *Twelfth Night* (1908).

Robinson, Mary (Terese Winifred) (1944–) Irish Labour stateswoman, President 1990–97. She was called to the bar in 1967 and entered politics in 1969, when she became a member of the Irish Senate. In 1990 she became Ireland's first woman President. She was noted for her platform of religious toleration and for her liberal attitude to abortion, divorce, and homosexuality. In 1997 she became UN Commissioner for Human Rights.

Robinson, Smokey (born William Robinson) (1940–) US soul singer and songwriter. His group the Miracles were one of the first signings to the Motown label. They had a series of successes with songs written by Robinson, such as 'Tracks of my Tears' (1965) and 'Tears of a Clown' (1970). Robinson also wrote many songs for other Motown artistes, for example 'My Guy' (1964) for Mary Wells. He left the Miracles in 1972 to embark on a solo career and to work for Motown.

Robinson, Sugar Ray (born Walker Smith) (1920–89) US boxer. He was world welterweight champion 1946–51 and middleweight champion 1951 (twice), 1955, 1957, and 1958–60.

robotics The science and technology of machines designed to function in place of a human being, especially to carry out tasks automatically. The word robot (from the Czech *robota*, 'compulsory service') was coined by the playwright Karel Čapek in 1920. Practical robotics was first formulated by the British inventor C. W. Kenward in 1957, and subsequently exploited in the USA for industrial automation to handle parts for die casting, injection moulding, and metal-cutting machines. A robot that could manipulate a tool (for painting) was first used in Norway in 1966, and in the USA, robots were developed for spot-welding on assembly lines. Since then, there has been a continual evolution towards robots of greater precision, such as the Japanese selective compliance assembly robot arm (SCARA).

Rob Roy (born Robert Macgregor) (1671–1734) Scottish outlaw. His escapades as a highland cattle thief and opponent of the government's agents on the eve of the Jacobite uprising of 1715 were popularized in Sir Walter Scott's novel *Rob Roy* (1817).

Robsart, Amy (1532–60) English noblewoman, wife of Robert DUDLEY, Earl of Leicester. Her mysterious death at a country house near Oxford aroused suspicions that her husband (the favourite of Queen Elizabeth I) had had her killed so that he could be free to marry the queen. Sir Walter Scott's novel *Kenilworth* (1821) follows this version of her fate.

Robson, Dame Flora (1902–84) British actress. She was noted for her screen performances of historical parts, such as the Empress Elizabeth in *Catherine the Great* (1934) and Queen Elizabeth I in *Fire Over England* (1937). Her many acclaimed stage roles included Mrs Alving in Ibsen's *Ghosts* (1959).

Roche limit The minimum distance from the centre of a planet at which small solid particles orbiting in the neighbourhood of the planet can combine and form a sizeable satellite. Outside this distance their mutual gravitational attraction exceeds the tidal force (see TIDE) of the planet, whereas inside this limit tidal forces overcome the gravitational attraction between the particles and prevent them combining. The Roche limit, named after the French mathematician Edouard Roche who defined it in 1846, is approximately 2.46 times the planetary radius provided the densities of the particles and the planet are equal.

Rochester A town in Kent, south-east England, on the Medway; pop. (1991) 23,971. It has an 11th-century castle and 12th-century cathedral.

Rochester ▶1 A city in south-east Minnesota, USA; pop. (1990) 70,745. It is a noted medical centre and home of the world-famous Mayo clinic founded in 1889 by Charles and William Mayo. **▶2** An industrial city in the US state of New York, a port on the Genesee River near its outlet to Lake Ontario; pop. (1990) 231,640. Its industries include photographic, optical, and dental equipment.

Rochester, John Wilmot, 2nd Earl of (1647–80) English poet and courtier. Infamous for his dissolute life at the court of Charles II, he wrote many sexually explicit love poems and, with his social and literary verse satires, is regarded as one of the first Augustans. Famous works include his *Satire Against Mankind* (1675).

rock The various kinds of hard, solid substances in and underneath the ground. In geology the word 'rock' is used for loose, unconsolidated deposits, such as sand and gravel, as well as for hard, solid rocks like granite and slate. Rocks are classified according to the way in which they were formed. IGNEOUS ROCKS have formed from magma, or molten material; most SEDIMENTARY ROCKS are made up of particles that have been transported and deposited elsewhere; METAMORPHIC ROCKS have been formed from earlier rocks, either igneous or sedimentary, that have been changed by pressure or heat, or both.

rock-crystal A pure form of QUARTZ that is colourless and of exceptional transparency. It is much used for optical and scientific instruments and polishes well for jewellery. Occurring in IGNEOUS ROCKS, it is found mainly in Brazil, although the USA, Britain, Japan, Madagascar, Switzerland, and Hungary also have sources of supply. The creation of small decorative objects from rock-crystal, is found in many parts of the world. It was much used in the ancient world (Egypt, Greece, Rome, and the Middle East) for jewellery and for various types of drinking vessels and ornaments. Since then, the best-known rock-crystal carving has been in Renaissance Italy and Bohemia.

Rockefeller, John D(avison) (1839–1937) US industrialist and philanthropist. One of the first to recognize the industrial possibilities of oil, Rockefeller established the Standard Oil Company (1870) and by the end of the decade exercised a virtual monopoly over oil refining in the USA. Early in the 20th century he handed over his business interests to his son, **John D(avison) Rockefeller Jr.** (1874–1960), and devoted his private fortune to numerous philanthropic projects, such as the establishment of the Rockefeller Foundation (1913). His son's many philanthropic institutions include the Rockefeller Center in New York (1939).

rocket motor A motor that propels a vehicle forward by expelling combustion gases from nozzles at the rear. It differs from a JET ENGINE in that it carries its own oxidizer, allowing the motor to operate in the absence of an air supply. Rocket motors have been extensively applied in SPACEFLIGHT but they can also be used to power MISSILES, aeroplanes, and cars. The forward force acting on a rocket (its thrust) is produced because the combustion of fuel within the rocket exerts a great pressure on the walls of the combustion chamber, except where the gases escape at the rear. The resulting unbalanced force on the front wall of the chamber propels the rocket forward. The magnitude of the thrust depends on the mass and velocity of the expelled gases. Rocket motors may use solid or liquid fuel. Solid fuels contain an oxidizer intimately mixed with the fuel. Liquid fuel motors are more complex, as the fuel and oxidizer are stored separately and then mixed in the combustion chamber, but they are more controllable than solid fuel motors. Liquefied oxygen and hydrogen are the most common liquid fuels.

The earliest use of rockets was in China, where war rockets propelled by GUNPOWDER were used as incendiary devices, probably by 1300 AD. Their use in war and as FIREWORKS reached Italy in the 14th century and France in the 15th century. Having seen rockets in India, the English artillery expert William Congreve (1772–1828) developed a more powerful gunpowder rocket with a range of 2,750 m (9,030 feet), which was first used against France in 1806. At the end of the 19th century a Russian schoolteacher, Konstantin Tsiolkovsky, proposed the use of liquid rockets to power spacecraft. In the USA, in 1926, GODDARD launched the first liquid-fuelled rocket; meanwhile, in Germany and the Soviet Union, experimenters worked on solid-fuelled rockets for cars and aeroplanes as well as on liquid-fuelled rockets. In the 1930s rocket research in Germany was supported by the military authorities. Here, von BRAUN led a team that built rocket weapons, culminating in the V2 rocket (1942), the first BALLISTIC MISSILE. Subsequent liquid-fuelled rockets were developed from the V2. As the cold war intensified, efforts were directed towards building rocket-powered MISSILES to carry nuclear warheads. *Sputnik 1*, the world's first artificial satellite (1957), and *Explorer 1*, the USA's first satellite (1958), were both launched by modified ballistic missiles. Von Braun, by now leading the team in the USA, built the giant *Saturn V* rocket that took the APOLLO PROGRAMME to the Moon in 1969; from 1971 the Soviet Union's rockets launched SPACE STATIONS, equipped for prolonged occupation, into Earth orbit. Economy has now dictated the development of reusable rocket-powered spacecraft, such as the SPACE SHUTTLE.

rockfish See REDFISH.

rockling Any of about 20 species of fish belonging to the cod family, Gadidae, similar to the ling in body shape, but much smaller, growing up to 50 cm (20 inches) in length. They have two, three, or four barbels round the mouth and another on the chin. Most species live close to the sea-bed or near the shore among rocks.

rock lobster See CRAWFISH.

rock music (originally **rock and roll**) A popular music form originating in the USA in the 1950s. Rock and roll grew out of the African American RHYTHM AND BLUES music, which in the mid-1950s was being taken up by white COUNTRY MUSICIANS, such as Bill HALEY, Buddy HOLLY, and Elvis PRESLEY. 'Rock around the Clock' (1955) by Bill Haley and the Comets, was the first rock and roll record to achieve mass popularity. In Britain in the early 1960s there was an explosion of musical talent: groups such as the Rolling Stones and The Who played music that drew heavily on rock and roll and African American music. The first of these groups to gain international recognition was the BEATLES. By the 1970s rock was part of the music establishment. The late 1970s saw the advent of punk, which caught some of the raw energy of rock and roll. During the late 1980s and 1990s rock music became ever more diverse and eclectic, with no one style predominant.

rock rose A low-growing, slender-stemmed shrub of spreading or mat-forming habit. The plant genera to which it belongs, *Helianthemum* and *Cistus*, are both part of the rock rose family, Cistaceae, containing around 165 species. Of these, about 70 species of *Helianthemum* and 20 of *Cistus* are known from Europe, Asia, and North America. The perennial garden varieties with an extensive range of colours have mainly been produced from the European *H. nummularium* and other closely related species.

rock salt See HALITE.

Rockwell, Norman (Percevel) (1894–1978) US illustrator. Rockwell's often sentimental depictions of small-town American life made him one of the most popular artists in the USA. He was an illustrator for several major periodicals, including *Life* and the *Saturday Evening Post*, for whom he created 317 covers (1916–63).

Rocky Mountains (or **Rockies**) The chief mountain system of North America, which extends for *c.*4,800 km (3,000 miles) from the US–Mexico border to the Yukon Territory of northern Canada. It separates the Great Plains from the Pacific Coast and forms the Continental Divide. Several peaks rise to over 4,300 m (14,000 ft), the highest being Mount Elbert in Colorado (4,399 m, 14,431 ft).

Rocky Mountain spotted fever (or **tick fever**) One of a group of infections resembling TYPHUS. It is caused by *Rickettsia rickettsii*, a microorganism infecting rodents and other small mammals. In spite of its name, it occurs in South as well as North America and is transmitted to man by TICKS. The fever responds to antibiotic treatment.

Rococo A style of art and architecture that emerged in France in about 1700 and spread throughout Europe in the 18th century. It was characterized by lightness, grace, playfulness, and intimacy and was both a development of and a reaction against the weightier style in BAROQUE ART. In painting, the first great master of the Rococo style was WATTEAU, and the painters who most completely represent the lighthearted spirit of the mature Rococo style are BOUCHER and FRAGONARD. In architecture the Rococo style was much more suitable for interior decoration, with asymmetrical curves and pretty decorative motifs prevailing, than for exteriors, but something of its refinement and charm can be seen even in such a regular and relatively unadorned building as GABRIEL's Petit Trianon (1763–69) at Versailles. In Britain the style was confined mainly to the applied arts, such as furniture and silversmithing, but aspects of it can be seen in the painting of HOGARTH, for example, or of GAINSBOROUGH, whose delicacy of characterization and sensitivity of touch are thoroughly in the Rococo spirit. Rococo lasted longest in Central Europe, where it flourished until the end of the 18th century, but in France and most of the rest of Europe the tide of taste began to turn against it in the 1760s. By then it was coming to be considered frivolous, and it was ousted by the serious NEOCLASSICAL style.

Roddick, Anita (Lucia) (1943–) British businesswoman. In 1976 she opened her first shop, selling cosmetics with an emphasis on environmentally conscious products made from natural ingredients and not tested on animals. This developed into the Body Shop chain, which by the late 1980s comprised several hundred outlets in the UK and abroad.

rodent A member of a large order of mammals, Rodentia, containing around 1,700 species. Few are bigger than a squirrel, although the largest, the South American capybara, is the size of a sheep. Rodents are primitive mammals showing few departures from the body plan of the first mammals. They are found in all parts of the world except Antarctica and are mainly terrestrial, although a few, such as the beaver, are aquatic. Many of them are of great economic importance either because they are pests or because they provide a desirable product such as fur. Some are used extensively as human food, particularly in the tropics. Rodents are recognized by the single pair of front teeth (incisors) in each jaw. These teeth are chisel-like and the cutting edge is maintained by the upper and lower pairs working against each other. The cheeks can be drawn in behind the front teeth so that material being gnawed falls out of the mouth and is not swallowed.

Rodgers, Richard (Charles) (1902–79) US composer. Together with librettist Lorenz Hart (1895–1943), he created such musicals as *The Girl Friend* (1926). After Hart's death, Rodgers collaborated with Oscar HAMMERSTEIN II on a succession of popular musicals, including *Oklahoma!* (1943), *Carousel* (1945), *South Pacific* (1949), and *The Sound of Music* (1959).

Rodin, Auguste (1840–1917) French sculptor. His first major work, *The Age of Bronze* (1875–76), was considered so lifelike that Rodin was alleged to have taken a cast from a live model. By 1880 he had been publicly commissioned to create *The Gate of Hell* for the Musée des arts décoratifs; it remained unfinished at his death and its many figures inspired such independent statues as *The Thinker* (1880) and *The Kiss* (1886).

Rodney, George Brydges Rodney, 1st Baron (1719–92) British admiral. He gained his early naval expertise with HAWKE at Finisterre in 1747, and at Le Havre in 1759, where he destroyed the French flotilla in the SEVEN YEARS WAR. His greatest victory was at the Battle of Les Saintes, 1782, in the West Indies, where he restored British supremacy at sea in the closing stages of the American War of INDEPENDENCE.

Rodrigo, Joaquín (1901–) Spanish composer. Blind from the age of 3, he studied in Valencia (1920–23) and with Paul Dukas in Paris (1927–32). His *Concierto de Aranjuez* (1939) for guitar and orchestra is written in a colourful 'Spanish' style that has earned it the status of a modern classic. Rodrigo also composed concertos in a similar style for piano, violin, cello, and flute.

Roe, Sir (Edwin) Alliott Verdon (1877–1958) British engineer and aircraft designer. He built the first British seaplane to take off from the water and (in 1912) the first aircraft with an enclosed cabin. With his brother H. V. Roe he founded the Avro Company and built a number of planes, of which the Avro 504 trainer biplane was the most successful; in 1928 he formed the Saunders-Roe Company to design and manufacture flying boats. Roe also invented anti-dazzle car headlights.

roe deer A species of small DEER, *Capreolus capreolus*, with a wide distribution in Europe, the Middle East, and northern Asia. It inhabits the edges of forests, open wood, or scrubland, which provides thick cover during the day. It is active mainly at night, when it browses on leaves, and eats berries, fungi, and grass. The smallest of the European deer, the buck is usually about 73 cm (29 inches) at the shoulders, and its antlers are 22 cm (9 inches) long. Only the male has antlers and these are shed at the beginning of winter. Shortly afterwards the new antlers form rapidly, their size and complexity increasing until the buck is about four years old. Twins are usual and are born in the spring. The fawn has a pale brown coat flecked with white, providing it with excellent camouflage.

Roeg, Nicholas (Jack) (1928–) British film director. His work is often unsettling and impressionistic, and uses cutting techniques to create disjointed narratives. His films include *Performance* (1970) *Walkabout* (1970), *Don't Look Now* (1972), *The Man Who Fell to Earth* (1975), *Castaway* (1986), and *The Witches* (1990).

Roentgen See RÖNTGEN.

Rogers, Ginger (born Virginia Katherine McMath) (1911–95) US actress and dancer. She is best known for her dancing partnership with Fred ASTAIRE; from 1933 they appeared in a number of film musicals, including *Top Hat* (1935), *Swing Time* (1936), and *Shall We Dance?* (1937). Rogers's solo acting career included the film *Kitty Foyle* (1940), for which she won an Oscar.

Rogers, Richard, Baron (1933–) British architect, born in Italy. He was a leading exponent of high-tech architecture and founded his own practice, Team 4, in 1963. He gained international recognition in the 1970s for the Pompidou Centre in Paris (1971–77), which he designed in partnership with the Italian architect Renzo Piano (1937–) and which featured ducts and pipes on the outside of the building. Rogers's Lloyd's Building in London (1986) followed a similarly original high-tech design. He designed the MILLENNIUM Dome in Greenwich.

Roget, Peter Mark (1779–1869) British scholar. He worked as a physician but is remembered as the compiler of *Roget's Thesaurus of English Words and Phrases*, which he completed after his retirement and which was first published in 1852. The work, which has been revised many times since, is a dictionary of synonyms using Roget's innovative classification of words according to underlying concept or meaning.

Rolland, Romain (1866–1944) French novelist, dramatist, and essayist. His interest in genius led to biographies of Beethoven (1903), Michelangelo (1905), and Tolstoy (1911), and ultimately to *Jean-Christophe* (1904–12), a cycle of ten novels about a German composer. These epitomize the literary form known as the *roman-fleuve* and in their portrayal of the composer's friendship with a Frenchman symbolized Rolland's desire for harmony between nations. He was awarded the Nobel Prize for literature in 1915.

roller A bird belonging to the family Coraciidae, which is widespread in warmer parts of the Old World. The 11 species of rollers vary in size from that of a large thrush to that of a crow. They are brightly coloured, many with dark blue in the wings and pinkish brown or turquoise blue on the bodies. A few have elongated outer tail feathers. They are birds of open country, sitting conspicuously on branches, preying upon large insects, lizards, and other small animals with their powerful, brownish, slightly hooked beaks. They nest in holes in trees or banks and get their name from their tumbling display flight.

roll-on, roll-off ship (or **ro-ro ship**) See CAR FERRY.

Rolls, Charles Stewart (1877–1910) British motoring and aviation pioneer. He was one of the founder members of the Royal Automobile Club (RAC) in 1897 and the Royal Aero Club (1903). In 1906 he and Henry ROYCE formed the company Rolls-Royce Ltd., with Royce as chief engineer and Rolls as demonstrator–salesman. The company became a major producer of aircraft engines and luxury motor cars; after becoming bankrupt in 1971 it was formed into two separate companies. Rolls was the first Englishman to fly across the English Channel, and made the first double crossing in 1910 shortly before he was killed in an air crash, the first English casualty of aviation.

ROM See MEMORY (computer).

Romains, Jules (born Louis Farigoule) (1885–1972) French novelist, dramatist, and poet. His works are the illustration of his theory of *unanimisme*, according to which mankind achieves its fullest expression in the group rather than the individual. His views emerge first in *La Vie unanime* (1908), a collection of poems, and later in *Knock* (1923), a play about a doctor who persuades a healthy village community that it is in reality ridden with illness. *Les Hommes de bonne volonté* (1932–47) is a 27-volume revue of French society from 1908 to 1933.

Roman art The art of the Roman Empire from *c.*6th century BC to *c.*5th century AD. Etruscan art and the later stage of GREEK ART were the most important of the various roots from which Roman art sprang. Among its greatest achievements is architecture. The advance of Roman over Greek architecture is in the use of the ARCH and the VAULT. These were first used in engineering constructions, such as bridges, aqueducts, and viaducts, and were later used in palaces, theatres, and other buildings. The BASILICA, used as a law-court, place of assembly, or market-hall, greatly influenced later Byzantine architecture. No less important were the achievements of Roman architecture in the design of THEATRES and AMPHITHEATRES. Two of the most famous Roman buildings are in Rome: the Colosseum (*c.*75–82 AD) and the Pantheon (118–28 AD). Patterns and pictures in MOSAIC first appear on floors, but later also on walls in place of paintings. Ceilings were often decorated with relief designs in stucco. Compared with their splendid architectural achievements the sculpture of the Romans seems somewhat weak and derivative. Portraiture, however, is one of the most characteristic and important achievements of every period of Roman art. In many ways Roman art can be seen as a continuation of HELLENISTIC ART, and achieved much the same in the minor and luxury arts, silversmithing, glass-blowing and cutting, and the working of precious stones and ivory, and in the major works of sculpture and architecture.

Roman Britain (43–410 AD) The period during which most of Britain was part of the ROMAN EMPIRE. Britain was first visited by the Romans under Julius CAESAR during the GALLIC WARS. It was then the home of Gallic tribes and later a refuge for defeated allies of VERCINGETORIX. CLAUDIUS invaded Britain in 43 AD, attracted by the island's minerals and grain. At first the Belgic tribes were subdued as far north as the FOSSE WAY. The frontier was then extended into native Celtic territories and established by the building of HADRIAN's Wall. Native culture absorbed many Roman ways: enlarged former tribal capitals adopted a Roman lifestyle. Army veterans settled there after discharge, as did traders, scholars, craftsmen, and soldiers from all parts of the Roman empire. Universally acknowledged Christian bishoprics were established. Roman villas, ROMAN ROADS, and titles abounded, but little Latin was spoken and the people remained essentially Celtic. In 406 and 409 the Britons rebelled against Roman rule. The Romans withdrew from Britain in 410. The period of Roman decline and the early history of the Saxon kingdoms remains obscure.

Roman Catholic Church The Christian Church that acknowledges the pope as its head, especially that which has developed since the REFORMATION. It has an elaborately organized hierarchy of bishops and priests. Popes are traditionally regarded as successors to St Peter, to whom Christ entrusted his power. In doctrine the Roman Catholic Church is characterized by strict adherence to tradition combined with acceptance of the living voice of the Church and belief in its infallibility. The classic definition of its position was made in response to the Reformation at the Council of Trent (1545–63). During this period the Catholic Church responded to the challenge of Protestantism by the movement known as the COUNTER-REFORMATION, which brought about various reforms and a draconian tightening of Church discipline (see INQUISITION). During the Enlightenment the Church increasingly saw itself as an embattled defender of ancient truth, a belief that culminated in the proclamation of Papal Infallibility in matters of doctrine in 1870. The 20th century has seen a great change as the Church has become more open to the world, a change given effect in the decrees of the 2nd Vatican Council (1963–65). The papacy of JOHN PAUL II (1978–), however, has been marked by his resistance to change in the teaching of the Church on the controversial issues of contraception, abortion, divorce, homosexuality, and the celibacy of the priesthood. In all these issues, especially the first, the Church has maintained a position seriously at odds with generally enlightened 20th-century views. For Christians of other denominations and for the members of other religions, the reluctance of the Vatican to accept change has marginalized its moral authority.

Romance languages The group of European languages descended from Latin, of which the main languages are French, Spanish, Portuguese, Italian, and Romanian. With the spread of the Roman Empire, Latin was introduced as the language of administration; with its decline the languages of separate areas began to develop in different ways, and the Latin from which they developed seems to have been not the classical Latin of Rome but the informal Latin of the soldiers.

Roman Empire The area of the Old World conquered and controlled during the period of Roman history from 27 BC, when Octavian took the power of what was effectively a constitutional monarch with the title of Augustus, until the barbarian invasions of the 4th–5th centuries, which followed the death of Constantine and ended with the overthrow of the last Roman emperor, Romulus Augustulus, in 476 AD. At its greatest extent Roman rule or influence extended from Armenia and Mesopotamia in the east to the Iberian peninsula in the west, and from the Rhine, Danube, and British Isles in the north to Egypt and provinces on the Mediterranean coast of North Africa. The empire was divided by Theodosius (395 AD) into the Western or Latin and Eastern or Greek Empire, of which the Eastern lasted until 1453 and the Western, after lapsing in 476, was revived in 800 by Charlemagne and continued to exist as the Holy Roman Empire until 1806.

Romanesque The style of architecture and art that prevailed throughout most of Europe in the 11th and 12th centuries. The most obvious characteristic of the Romanesque architecture was a massiveness of scale. Architects looked to Roman buildings to solve the question of how to build stone ceilings or VAULTS over the large spaces they created. Initially barrel vaults (built like a tunnel) were used, but these were eventually supplanted by rib vaults, which instead of being of solid, heavy masonry utilized a skeleton-like framework of intersecting arches (ribs) with a comparatively thin and light infilling of stone between them. The need to provide a stable support for vaults encouraged the massive strength of construction and solidity of wall typical of Romanesque architecture. Common to Romanesque architecture everywhere was the use of the round ARCH (as in Roman buildings), giving way to the pointed arch as GOTHIC ART AND ARCHITECTURE developed later. Romanesque architecture in Britain is often called Norman, because it is associated so closely with the Norman conquest of 1066. The most notable example of Romanesque church architecture in Britain is Durham Cathedral, begun in 1093.

Castles built of stone made their appearance during the Romanesque period, constructed in the form of keeps or huge central towers that served as the chief living quarters of a castle and the final line of defence. A famous example is the keep at the Tower of London, built for William the Conqueror in 1078–87.

Originally applied to architecture, Romanesque has also been used to describe painting and other arts of the period. However, comparatively little large-scale painting, mostly of church murals, has survived (originally the churches of the period would have been alive with colour). Nevertheless, many manuscript illuminations have come down to us and the art of stained glass was perfected during the Romanesque period. There are also some fine Romanesque mosaics, particularly in Italy. A remarkable work of pictorial art of the period is the wall-hanging embroidered on linen, the BAYEUX TAPESTRY.

Romania An east European country with its east coast on the Black Sea; it is bounded by Ukraine and the republic of Moldova on the north and east, Hungary and Serbia on the west, and Bulgaria on the south.

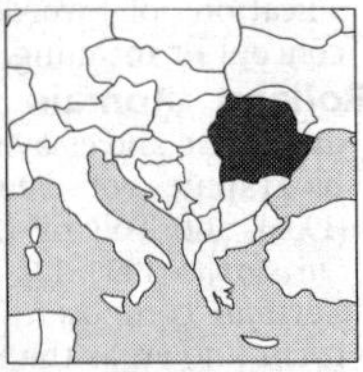

Physical. Roughly half of Romania is mountainous. The Carpathians, curving from the north-west, meet the Transylvanian Alps in the centre of the country, where rainfall is heavy and there are large forests. Moldoveanu, at 2,543 m (8,343 feet) is the highest point. The rest of the country is plain, much of it providing the richest soil in Europe. Here summers are very warm, and winters are very cold, with biting winds. The Danube forms the southern border as it flows east to its delta on the Black Sea.

Economy. Despite the fall of the repressive communist regime of Nicolae Ceausescu in December 1989, social and economic conditions remain bleak. The policy of promoting exports regardless of domestic needs to pay off foreign debt has caused massive hardship. Ceausescu's 'systemization' programme, which forced resettlement in towns, ostensibly to free land for agricultural use, has been reversed, and collective and state farms have been privatized in the hope of boosting food supplies. Romania is moving towards a market economy, and many businesses have been freed from state control. Principal crops are maize, wheat, rye, potatoes, sugar-beet, plums, and apples; mineral resources include coal, iron ore, petroleum, and natural gas. Despite heavy subsidies at the expense of agriculture, industry is in great need of modernization. Major industries are metallurgical, mechanical engineering, and chemicals, with mineral fuels, machinery, and transport equipment the principal exports.

History. Although the regions known as Moldavia and Walachia were part of the OTTOMAN EMPIRE from the 15th century onwards, Turkish domination was increasingly challenged by both Russia and Austria. In 1812 Russia gained control of north-east Moldavia (present-day Moldova). During the next 40 years Romanian nationalism precipitated many insurrections against the Turks. Following the CRIMEAN WAR, during which the region was occupied by Russia, Walachia and Moldavia proclaimed themselves independent principalities; in 1861 they united to form Romania, electing a local prince, Alexander Cuza, as ruler. On his deposition (1866) Prince Carol Hohenzollen-Sigmaringen was elected. At the Congress of BERLIN independence was recognized, and Prince Carol crowned king as CAROL I (1881–1914). His pro-German policy led in 1883 to Romania's joining the Triple Alliance of 1882 (Germany, Austria, and Italy). In World War I Romania remained neutral until, in 1916, it joined the Allies. At the VERSAILLES PEACE SETTLEMENT the country was rewarded with the doubling of its territories, mainly by the addition of Transylvania from Hungary. Carol I was succeeded by Ferdinand I (1914–27) and then by CAROL II (1930–40), who imposed a fascist regime. He was forced to cede much territory to the AXIS POWERS in 1940. Romanian forces cooperated with the German armies in their offensives (1941–42), but after the battle of STALINGRAD the Red Army advanced and Romania lost territory to the USSR and Bulgaria. A communist regime was established in 1948 and for the next 20 years the country became a Soviet satellite. A much greater degree of independence was restored during the presidency of Nicolae Ceausescu (1967–89), whose rule became increasingly brutal and autocratic. Stringent economic measures had to be enforced in 1987. During 1989 a movement towards democracy culminated in a violent revolution and the execution of the President and his wife on Christmas Day. A National Salvation Front (NSF) was formed, led by Ion Iliescu, who was elected President. He and many of his colleagues had been communists, and popular demonstrations against the government were brutally put down. Ethnic violence against Hungarians in Transylvania, and against the large indigenous gypsy population increased. In spite of opposition from groups such as the Democratic Convention of Romania (CDR), Iliescu retained power in the 1992 presidential election, having secured a $748 million IMF loan. In 1995 the Chamber of Deputies enacted a Mass Privatization law affecting over 3,000 businesses. In 1996 Iliescu was defeated in presidential elections by the CDR candidate, Emil Constantinescu.

Capital: Bucharest
Area: 237,500 sq km (91,699 sq mi)
Population: 22,693,000 (1995)
Currency: 1 leu = 100 bani
Religions: Romanian Orthodox 70.0%; Greek Orthodox 10.0%; Muslim 1.0%
Ethnic Groups: Romanian 86.0%; Hungarian 9.0%; gypsy 4.0%; German and other 1.0%
Languages: Romanian (official); Hungarian; Romany
International Organizations: UN; CSCE; North Atlantic Co-operation Council

Romanian The official language of Romania, the only Romance language spoken in eastern Europe, which developed from the Latin introduced by Trajan when he conquered the area in the 2nd century AD and has kept its Latin character, being lightly influenced by the Slavonic languages. It is spoken by over 20 million people in Romania itself and by the majority of the population of Moldova.

Roman law The body of law developed in Rome between about 150 BC and 250 AD and codified by the Emperor JUSTINIAN in 529 in his *Corpus Juris Civilis* ('Body of Civil Law'). Roman law re-emerged in the 11th century as a popular subject of study in the Italian universities; later it evolved into the common core of the CIVIL LAW (or Romano-Germanic law) family of legal systems, which established itself in the lands of the Holy Roman Empire. The ideas of Roman law were dominant in the French CODE NAPOLÉON, adopted in 1804, and in later civil codes adopted in Germany, Switzerland, and Austria. The codification movement appealed to the perceived higher rationality of Roman law as providing a logically consistent set of principles and rules for solving disputes.

Romanov The ruling house of Russia from 1613 until the Revolution of 1917. After the Time of Troubles (1604–13), a period of civil war and anarchy, Michael Romanov was elected emperor and ruled until 1645, to be followed by Alexis (1645–76) and Fyodor (1676–82). Under these emperors Russia emerged as the major Slavic power. The next emperors established it as a great power in Europe: PETER I (the Great) (1689–1725) and CATHERINE II (the Great) (1762–96) were the most successful of these rulers.

Roman numerals The numbering system devised by the ancient Romans, using letters of the alphabet. It survived until the 9th century, after which it was gradually replaced by the much more versatile system of ARABIC NUMERALS. The Roman numerals are: I = 1, V = 5, X = 10, L = 50, C = 100, D = 500, M = 1000. Intermediate numbers are given by repetition or combination of these seven basic letters (e.g. 3 = III, 7 = VII, 25 = XXV, 180 = CLXXX). Roman numerals have no symbol for zero, making computation very difficult.

Roman religion The religion of the Roman republic and empire. In its developed form it came to have much in common with GREEK RELIGION, although it contained elements of Etruscan and other native Italian regional beliefs and practices. The Roman gods mirrored those of Greece: Jupiter = Zeus, Juno = Hera, Neptune = Poseidon, Minerva = Athene, Diana = Artemis, Mars = Ares, Mercury = Hermes, and so on; but it too had its array of minor deities. Romans also possessed domestic shrines of the spirits of the household (Lares and Penates). Although CHRISTIANITY became the official religion of the empire from the late 4th century AD, pagan beliefs and practices proved tenacious in many areas, especially away from the cities, and in many places the Christian Church had often to take over Roman festivals and hallowed shrines or sites under a new guise.

Roman republic (Latin *respublica*, 'common wealth') The political form of the Roman state for 400 years after the expulsion of TARQUIN. The rule of a sole monarch yielded to the power of a landed aristocracy, the PATRICIANS, who ruled through two chief magistrates or consuls and an advisory body, the ROMAN SENATE.

The city of Rome could operate as a 'public concern' as long as the small landed aristocracy managed the state. But, with overseas expansion, generals had to be given power to deal with problems abroad. Their substantial independence threatened republican tradition with its corporate government and brief periods of high office for individuals in rotation. Eventually the generals simply ignored the law, which required generals to lay down their commands on returning to Italian soil. The last of these commanders-in-chief, Octavian, achieved a settlement that appeared to combine republican institutions with personal military power. The ROMAN EMPIRE succeeded the republic.

Roman roads A systematic communications network originating in the Italian peninsula joining Rome to its expanding empire. The APPIAN WAY was the first major stretch, leading into Samnite territory. The Via Flaminia, constructed in 220 was the great northern highway to Rimini. For travellers landing from Brindisi the Egnatian Way continued overland through Greece and on to Byzantium. By the 1st century AD three roads crossed the Alps and the Domitian Way went from the Rhône valley to Spain. Every province had such roads which served military and commercial purposes. In Britain major highways fanned out from Londinium (London), some now known by their Anglo-Saxon names: WATLING STREET and ERMINE STREET. Designed with several thick layers they were drained by side ditches, and maintained by engineers.

Roman Senate The assembly of the landed aristocracy and PATRICIANS, which originated in the royal council of the kings of Rome. Entry widened to include those of plebeian origin by the late 4th century BC. A membership of 600 established by SULLA was standard although it rose to 900 in CAESAR's time. This advisory body consisted of hereditary (patrician) and life (conscript) members, the latter being ex-magistrates. It was summoned by the consuls as chief magistrates and passed decrees, which were ratified by the people in assembly. It was expected that all magistrates would submit proposals to the Senate before putting them to the people. This procedure began to be flouted from the time of the Gracchi onwards. Its power was real but informal, based on prestige and wealth. Even the emperors made at least the token gesture of consulting the 'Fathers'. Until the 3rd century AD all bronze coinage carried the mark 'By Consultative Decree of the Senate'.

Romansh (or **Rumansh**) The Rhaeto-Romanic dialects, especially as spoken in the Swiss canton of Grisons.

Romanticism A Western attitude to art and human creativity that dominated much of European culture in the first half of the 19th century. Romanticism has shaped much subsequent developments in the arts. In its most coherent early form, as it emerged from the 1790s in Germany and Britain, and from the 1820s in France and elsewhere, it is known as the Romantic Movement. Its chief emphasis was upon freedom of individual self-expression. The restraint and balance valued in the 18th-century in imitation of classical models as well as the ordered rationality of the ENLIGHTENMENT, were abandoned in favour of emotional intensity, often taken to extremes of rapture, nostalgia, or sentimentality. The creative imagination occupied the centre of Romantic views of art, which replaced the rules of convention with the principle of natural growth and free development.

The emergence of Romanticism can be attributed to several developments in late 18th-century culture, the most significant being the STURM UND DRANG phase of German literature, the primitivism of ROUSSEAU, the cult of the GOTHIC NOVEL, and the taste for the sublime and picturesque. This new German thinking spread via COLERIDGE to Britain and via Mme de STAËL to France, eventually shaping American Transcendentalism. English Romanticism had emerged independently with BLAKE's then little-known anti-Enlightenment writings of the 1790s and with the landmark of WORDSWORTH's 1800 Preface to *Lyrical Ballads*. Romanticism thus began as a literary movement in which LYRIC poetry underwent a major revival led by Wordsworth, KEATS, PUSHKIN, Giacomo Leopardi, HEINE, and others. The astonishing personality of BYRON provided de MUSSET, LERMONTOV, and other admirers with a model of the Romantic poet as tormented outcast.

In music, a continuous Romantic tradition can be traced from BEETHOVEN (a Romantic hero, although predominantly classical in style) through to Rachmaninov, MAHLER, and Richard STRAUSS in the early 20th century, embracing styles as divergent as those of Schubert, Schumann, Liszt, Chopin, Brahms, Wagner, and Tchaikovsky. The operas and ballets of the period featured folk-tales, pastoral scenes, and the unashamed passion associated with unrequited love. In the visual arts, the boundaries of Romanticism stand out less clearly: the 18th-century taste for the 'wildness' of mountain scenery and for 'picturesque' ruins preceded any clearly identifiable Romantic school of painting. Indeed there is no dominant Romantic visual style; instead there is an acceptance of personal vision, notably in TURNER's use of light and colour, and in the sombre symbolic landscapes of FRIEDRICH. The controversial French artists GÉRICAULT and DELACROIX stood out as Romantics with the violent energy of their paintings; both admired the quieter Romantic landscapes of CONSTABLE. Other significant Romantic artists include FUSELI, John Martin, and the poet-engraver Blake. The nostalgia of the PRE-RAPHAELITES and of the GOTHIC REVIVAL in architecture may also be seen as Romantic.

Romany The distinctive language of the gypsies, which shares common features with Sanskrit and the later Indian languages (indicating an origin in the Indian subcontinent), with regional variations reflecting the incorporation of loanwords and other local linguistic features absorbed in their travels.

Romberg, Sigmund (1887–1951) Hungarian-born US composer. He wrote a succession of popular operettas, including *The Student Prince* (1924), *The Desert Song* (1926), and *New Moon* (1928).

Rome A city on the River Tiber, the capital of Italy and bishopric of the pope; pop. (1990) 2,791,350. It was at the heart of the ROMAN REPUBLIC and then the ROMAN EMPIRE. Several traditions surround its foundation on seven low hills. One legend said that the twins, ROMULUS (after whom the city was supposedly named) and Remus, suckled by a wolf, began the first settlement on the Palatine Hill. The date 753 BC became accepted and is well supported by archaeological excavation. ETRUSCAN remains, dating from the TARQUINS (*c.*650–500 BC) have been discovered. The expansion of provinces under the republic and early empire brought wealth to Rome. AUGUSTUS was said to have turned a city of brick into one of marble, and successive emperors added palaces, arches, columns, and temples. NERO burnt much of it, hoping, it was said, to rebuild it and rename it after himself. As the empire declined, Rome was attacked by GOTHS and VANDALS. By then it was politically overshadowed by CONSTANTINOPLE, the capital of the Eastern

Roman empire. During the Middle Ages Rome emerged as the seat of the papacy and the capital of Western Christianity. It became a centre of the RENAISSANCE and was largely rebuilt in the Baroque style in the 17th century. The city was sacked in 1527 and again in 1798. Rome remained under papal control until the unification of Italy in 1870; it became the capital of the new country the following year. From this time until 1929, when Mussolini created the VATICAN CITY State, there was a longstanding dispute between the Church and State over the incorporation of the papal states into Italy. Rome's many famous ruins and buildings include the Forum, the Colosseum, St Peter's, the Villa Borghese, and countless monuments, academies, and fountains. Its university was founded in 1303 and its music academy in 1584. Its economy depends to a large extent on tourism.

Rome, Treaties of (1957) Two international agreements signed in Rome by Belgium, France, Italy, Luxembourg, the Netherlands, and the Federal Republic of Germany. They established the EUROPEAN ECONOMIC COMMUNITY and Euratom (the European Atomic Energy Community). The treaties included provisions for the free movement of labour and capital between member countries, the abolition of customs barriers and cartels, and the fostering of common agricultural and trading policies. New members of the European Community are required to adhere to the terms of these treaties. The MAASTRICHT TREATY was planned as a development of the Rome Treaties.

Rommel, Erwin (known as 'the Desert Fox') (1891–1944) German Field Marshal. Rommel was posted to North Africa in 1941 after the collapse of the Italian offensive, and, as commander of the Afrika Korps, he deployed a series of surprise manoeuvres and succeeded in capturing Tobruk (1942). After being defeated by Montgomery at El Alamein (1942), he was ordered home the following year to serve as Inspector of Coastal Defences. He was forced to commit suicide after being implicated in the officers' conspiracy against Hitler in 1944.

Romney, George (1734–1802) British portrait painter. Based in London from 1762, he rivalled Thomas Gainsborough and Sir Joshua Reynolds for popularity in the late 18th century. From the early 1780s he produced more than 50 portraits of Lady Hamilton in historical poses.

Romney Marsh A level tract of reclaimed land in southern England, on the coast of Kent between Hythe and Rye. Once completely covered by the sea, drainage began in Roman times and the area became known for its pastureland and for the fine quality wool from its sheep.

Romulus The legendary founder of Rome. He and his twin brother **Remus** were the children of a Vestal Virgin who had been ravished by Mars; they were abandoned to die, but were suckled by a she-wolf and brought up by a herdsman. In 753 BC Romulus is said to have founded Rome; he killed Remus, who had ridiculed him by jumping over the beginnings of the city wall. After his death, Romulus was regarded as a god and was identified with the god Quirius.

rondo A musical form in which a main section returns several times during the course of the movement. In between these recurring sections are passages of contrasting material. The main section always returns in the same key, and is supplied with a memorable tune.

Röntgen, Wilhelm Conrad (or **Roentgen**) (1845–1923) German physicist, the discoverer of X-rays. He was a skilful experimenter and worked on a variety of topics. In 1895 Röntgen observed that a nearby fluorescent screen glowed when a current was passed through a Crookes' vacuum tube. He investigated the properties of the radiation responsible, which he called 'X-rays', and produced the first X-ray photograph (of his wife's hand). He was awarded the first Nobel Prize for physics in 1901. The former unit of dose of ionizing radiation, the **röntgen**, is named after him. It is the dose that produces ions of one sign carrying a charge of 2.58×10^{-4} coulomb per kilogram of pure dry air.

rook A species of bird, *Corvus frugilegns*, belonging to the CROW family. It is about 50 cm (18–19 inches) long and has a black plumage with an iridescent sheen. The adult has a bare, whitish area on the face. Rooks breed throughout Europe and Asia and nest in colonies called rookeries in the tops of trees.

Rooney, Mickey (born Joseph Yule Jr.) (1920–) US actor. From childhood he appeared in a great many films, starting with *Not to Be Trusted* (1926). He played Andy Hardy in a series of 16 comedy drama films over 20 years about the Hardy family, the USA's favourite fictional characters during World War II. Other films include the musical *Babes in Arms* (1939), the comedy *The Human Comedy* (1943), for both of which he received Oscar nominations, and *The Black Stallion* (1979).

Roosevelt, (Anna) Eleanor (1884–1962) US humanitarian and diplomat. She was the niece of Theodore Roosevelt, and married Franklin D. Roosevelt in 1905. She was involved in a wide range of liberal causes, including civil and women's rights. After her husband died in 1945 she became a delegate to the United Nations, and, as chair of the UN Commission on Human Rights, played a major role in drafting the Declaration of Human Rights (1948).

Roosevelt, Franklin D(elano) (known as 'FDR') (1882–1945) US Democratic statesman, 32nd President of the USA 1933–45. Roosevelt's early political career was curtailed by his contraction of polio in 1921; in spite of the disease, he resumed public life in a wheelchair in 1928 and received the Democratic presidential nomination in 1932. His New Deal package of economic measures (1933) helped to lift the USA out of the Great Depression, and after the American entry into World War II he played an important part in the coordination of the Allied war effort. In 1940 Roosevelt became the first US President to be elected for a third term in office, and he subsequently secured a fourth term. He was the joint author, with Winston Churchill, of the Atlantic Charter (1941), a declaration of eight common principles in international relations that was intended to guide a postwar peace settlement.

Roosevelt, Theodore (known as 'Teddy') (1858–1919) US Republican statesman, 26th President of the USA 1901–09. He was elected Vice-President in 1900, succeeding William McKinley in 1901 following the latter's assassination. At home Roosevelt was noted for his antitrust laws, while abroad he successfully engineered the US bid to build the Panama Canal (1904–14) and won the Nobel Peace Prize in 1906 for negotiating the end of the Russo-Japanese War.

root (in botany) The organ through which a plant absorbs water and mineral nutrients. Roots also serve to anchor the plant in the soil. Generally they are underground, though some are aerial, and they lack chlorophyll. If there is one major swollen root with small offshoots, it is known as a tap-root. If there are many roots of equal size, the plant has a fibrous root system. If there are several swollen roots, as in the dahlia, they are known as root tubers. Roots are usually covered at their growing points with fine hairs, called **root hairs**. These are the site of water and mineral uptake; the rest of the root is covered with a tough 'skin' equivalent to the bark in woody plants.

root (in mathematics) ▶**1** One of two or more equal factors of a number. The *r*th root of the number *n*, written $\sqrt[r]{n}$, is the number that gives *n* when it is raised to the *r*th power. If r is 2, it is known as a square root, e.g. 4 is the **square root** of 16, i.e. $4^2 = 16$ (or $\sqrt{16} = 4$). If $r = 3$, the root is called the **cube root**, e.g. 2 is the cube root of 8. ▶**2** The solution of an equation. See QUADRATIC EQUATION.

root-crop A plant grown for its high-yielding underground roots, tubers, or bulbs. Root-crops are rich in carbohydrate and highly digestible; they are grown for human consumption, sugar extraction, and stock feeding. The world's main root-crops are staple foods: potato in temperate regions, sweet potato and yam, taro, and cassava in tropical areas. Root-crops consumed as fresh vegetables, such as carrots and the onion group, are prized for their flavour more than for their dietary contribution. SUGAR-BEET production is important in Europe and the area of beet sown has markedly increased in recent years. The pulp left after sugar extraction provides feed for livestock, as do other root-crops: fodder beet, mangels, and turnips.

root-mean-square (r.m.s.) The square root of the MEAN of the squares of a set of values. It has important applications in physics. For example, the pressure exerted by a gas depends on the r.m.s. of the speeds of its molecules; also an alternating current has the same heating effect as a steady current equal to its r.m.s. value.

rorqual A WHALEBONE WHALE making up the family Balaenopteridae, with a dorsal fin and longitudinal grooves below the throat and chest. There are six species, the four most important being the blue whale or Sibbald's rorqual, *Balaenoptera musculus*, the FIN WHALE or common rorqual, the sei whale or Rudolph's rorqual, *B. borealis*, and the HUMPBACKED WHALE. The majority feed on small crustaceans and krill, but some will also take small fishes. Females give birth once every two to three years to a single calf after a gestation period of ten to eleven months.

Rosa, Salvator (1615–73) Italian painter and etcher. His reputation is chiefly based on his landscapes, often peopled with bandits and containing scenes of violence in wild natural settings; their picturesque and 'sublime' qualities were an important influence on the romantic art of the 18th and 19th centuries.

Rosario A port on the Paraná River in east-central Argentina; pop. (1991) 1,096,000. It is Argentina's largest inland port and the largest city in the province of Santa Fé. Settled in 1725, it developed as an outlet for agricultural produce from the pampas. Its industrial products include steel and machinery.

Roscius (full name Quintus Roscius Gallus) (died 62 BC) Roman actor. He achieved phenomenal success as a comic actor during his lifetime and later became identified with all that was considered best in acting; many notable English actors from the 16th century onwards were nicknamed in reference to him.

Roscommon ▶**1** A county in the north-central part of the Republic of Ireland, to the west of the River Shannon in the province of Connaught; area 2,463 sq km (951 sq miles); pop. (1991) 51,880. ▶**2** Its county town; pop. (1991) 17,700. Named after St Coman who founded a monastery here, it has a 13th-century castle and an abbey which was established by the King of Connaught in 1253.

rose A shrub of the genus *Rosa*, consisting of some 250 species native to the north temperate zone and mountains of the tropics. Most have rather pithy stems with thorns. The flowers are followed by brightly coloured false fruits called hips, fleshy receptacles formed from the stalk beneath the flower. The true fruits are the 'seeds' within.

The rose family, Rosaceae, is one of the largest families of woody or herbaceous species with over 3,370 species distributed worldwide. It includes many large and showy garden plants, such as rowans, cotoneasters, and japonicas, as well as many fruit-bearing species, such as apples, plums, cherries, and strawberries. Virtually all species have simple flowers, producing sufficient quantities of pollen to attract insect pollinators.

Roseau The capital of Dominica in the West Indies, at the mouth of the Roseau River; pop. (1991) 15,850. It takes its name from the French word for the reeds that used to grow there.

rosebay willowherb See WILLOWHERB.

Rosebery, Archibald Philip Primrose, 5th Earl of (1847–1929) British Liberal statesman, Prime Minister 1894–95. He succeeded Gladstone as Premier after the latter's retirement and subsequently alienated Liberal supporters as a result of his imperialist loyalties during the Second Boer War (1899–1902).

rosechafer A white-flecked, metallic-green CHAFER of the genus *Cetonia*, slightly smaller than a cockchafer; a member of the family Scarabaeidae. Its larvae live in the soil feeding on roots, and the adults feed in the hearts of roses. Some tropical species are very brightly coloured.

rosefinch A bird grouped in the genus *Carpodacus* of the finch family, Fringillidae. Although most of the 20 or so species occur in Eurasia, a few, such as the common house finch, *C. mexicanus*, are widespread in the New World. As their name suggests, the males are usually largely or partly pink in colour; the females tend to be greyish-brown above, paler and heavily streaked below. All rosefinches feed primarily on seeds for most of the year, but bring insects to their young.

rosemary A densely leaved, evergreen shrub of the genus *Rosmarinus*, belonging to the mint family. It is native to dry, Mediterranean scrub regions, where it grows up to 2 m (6.5 feet) tall. It has been cultivated in Europe for several centuries as a culinary herb. Commercially, it is valuable as the source of an oil used in perfumes, shampoos, and soaps. Several varieties, developed from the common rosemary, *Rosmarinus officinalis*, are also used as ornamental plants.

Rosenberg Julius (1918–53) US spy who, with his wife **Ethel Rosenberg** (1915–53), was convicted and executed for passing information concerning atomic weapons to Soviet agents. They became the first American civilians to be sentenced to death for espionage by a US court. The only seriously incriminating evidence had come from a confessed spy, and the lack of clemency shown to them was an example of the intense anti-communist feeling that gripped the USA in the 1950s.

rose of Jericho A small, annual plant, *Anastatica*

hierochuntica, of the mustard family, Cruciferae. If dried out by drought, the shrivelled plant can resume its form when wetted. The inward curling of the branches of the dried, mature plant allows it to be blown across the deserts of its native Syria, thus dispersing its seeds.

Roses, Wars of the (1455–85) A protracted struggle for the throne of England, lasting for 30 years of sporadic fighting. These civil wars grew out of the bitter rivalry between two aspirants to the throne – Edmund BEAUFORT (1406–55), Duke of Somerset, of the House of Lancaster (whose badge was a red rose), and Richard, 3rd Duke of YORK (whose badge was a white rose); the former was a close supporter of HENRY VI and MARGARET OF ANJOU, while Richard of York became their opponent. In 1455 Richard gained power by winning the first Battle of ST ALBANS; a whole series of private enmities and disputes was now absorbed into a bitter and openly fought civil war. Richard of York was killed at the Battle of WAKEFIELD (1460), and Henry VI's supporters, the LANCASTRIANS, won a further victory at the second Battle of St Albans (February 1461), yet their hesitations allowed Richard's son Edward to gain the throne a month later as EDWARD IV, the first YORKIST king of England. In September 1470 a Lancastrian invasion restored Henry VI to the throne (although power was effectively exercised by 'the kingmaker', Richard Neville, Earl of WARWICK), but in April 1471 Edward regained it by the victory of BARNET. Most of the remaining Lancastrian leaders were killed at TEWKESBURY in May 1471, but the struggle ended only in 1485 when Henry Tudor defeated RICHARD III at BOSWORTH FIELD. HENRY VII married Edward IV's eldest daughter, Elizabeth of York, in order to unite the two factions. The wars weakened the power of the nobility and after a bid for the throne from Lambert SIMNEL in 1487, there were no serious challenges to the TUDOR dynasty.

Rosetta stone A piece of black basalt bearing inscriptions that provided the key to the deciphering of Egyptian HIEROGLYPHS. It was found in 1799 by a French soldier during Napoleon's occupation of Egypt, and contained three inscriptions, in Greek, in Egyptian demotic, and in Egyptian hieroglyphics. Comparative study of the three texts, which date from 196 BC, was undertaken by Thomas Young and Jean-François Champollion, the latter finally unlocking the secrets of hieroglyphics in 1821–22. The stone is housed in the British Museum in London.

Rosh Hashanah (Hebrew, 'beginning of the year') A two-day Jewish festival accepted as marking the religious new year in the seventh month Tishri (usually falling in September or October). A ram's horn, or shofar, is blown 100 times as a call to repentance and spiritual self-examination. The festival is also known as a Day of Judgement, a time for each Jew to review his or her standing with God. It is also traditionally the anniversary of the creation, and of the birthdays of Abraham, Isaac, and Jacob. The following day is a fast day and is the first of Ten Penitential Days of repentance and forgiveness, which culminate in YOM KIPPUR.

Rosicrucian A member of certain secret societies who venerated the emblems of the Rose and the Cross as symbols of Jesus Christ's resurrection and redemption. Rosicrucians claimed to possess secret wisdom passed down from the ancients, but their origin cannot be dated earlier than the 17th century. The anonymous *Account of the Brotherhood* published in Germany in 1614 may well have launched the movement. It narrated the tale of a mythical German knight of the 15th century, Christian Rosenkreutz, who travelled extensively to learn the wisdom of the East, and then founded the secret order. Robert Fludd subsequently helped to spread Rosicrucian ideas. In later centuries many new societies were founded under this name.

Ross, Diana (1944–) US pop and soul singer. She made her name as the lead singer of the Supremes, with whom she recorded many hit singles. She left the group in 1969 and became a successful solo artist, recording songs such as 'Remember Me' (1971). She has also appeared in several films, including *Lady Sings the Blues* (1973), for which she received an Oscar for her role as the jazz singer Billie Holiday.

Ross, Sir James Clark (1800–62) British explorer. He discovered the north magnetic pole in 1831, and headed an expedition to the Antarctic from 1839 to 1843, in the course of which he discovered Ross Island, Ross Dependency, and the Ross Sea, all named after him. He was the nephew of Sir John ROSS.

Ross, Sir John (1777–1856) British explorer. He led an expedition to Baffin Bay in 1818 and another in search of the North-west Passage between 1829 and 1833, during which he surveyed King William Land, the Boothia Peninsula, and the Gulf of Boothia. He was the uncle of Sir James Clark ROSS.

Ross, Sir Ronald (1857–1932) British medical officer who discovered, while serving in India, the final link that brought malaria under control. His proof that it was transmitted by mosquitoes helped to show how yellow fever, sleeping sickness, typhus, plague, and other epidemic diseases are spread. He was awarded a Nobel Prize in 1902.

Ross and Cromarty A former county of northern Scotland, from 1975 to 1996 a district of Highland Region, stretching from the Moray Firth to the North Minch. It is now part of Highland unitary authority.

Ross Dependency Part of Antarctica administered by New Zealand. It was explored in 1841 by Sir James ROSS, after whom it is named, and brought within the jurisdiction of New Zealand in 1923. Its land area is estimated at 413,540 sq km (159,730 sq miles) and permanent ice shelf at 336,770 sq km (130,077 sq miles). There are no permanent inhabitants, but in January 1957 the New Zealand Antarctic Expedition established Scott Base on Ross Island.

Rossellini, Roberto (1906–77) Italian film director. He is known for his neorealist films, particularly his quasi-documentary trilogy about World War II, filmed using a mainly non-professional cast; this comprises *Open City* (1945), *Paisà* (1946), and *Germany, Year Zero* (1947).

Rossetti, Christina (Georgina) (1830–94) British poet. She contributed several poems to the Pre-Raphaelite journal *The Germ* in 1850. Influenced by the Oxford Movement, Rossetti wrote much religious poetry reflecting her High Anglican faith, although she also wrote love poetry and children's verse. Marked by technical virtuosity, a sense of melancholy, and recurrent themes of frustrated love and premature resignation, her work includes the verse collection *Goblin Market and Other Poems* (1862). She was the sister of Dante Gabriel ROSSETTI.

Rossetti, Dante Gabriel (full name Gabriel Charles Dante Rossetti) (1828–82) British painter and poet. He was a founder member of the PRE-RAPHAELITE BROTHERHOOD (1848), and encouraged the movement to make links between painting and literature, basing many of his paintings on the work of the Italian poet Dante and on Arthurian legend. In his later career, however, he concentrated on dreamy and idealized images of women, including *Beata Beatrix* (*c*.1863) and *The Blessed Damozel* (1871–79); the latter took its subject from his poem of 1850. From 1861 Rossetti was associated with William Morris's firm Morris & Company. He was the brother of Christina ROSSETTI.

Rossini, Gioacchino Antonio (1792–1868) Italian composer. He wrote more than 30 operas, of which the best known are the comic opera *The Barber of Seville* (1816) and the grand opera *William Tell* (1829). He was one of the creators of the Italian bel canto style of singing, together with Bellini and Donizetti. His later religious music included the *Stabat Mater* (1842) and the *Petite Messe solennelle* (1863).

Ross Sea A large arm of the Pacific forming a deep indentation in the coast of Antarctica. It was first explored in January 1841 by an expedition led by Sir James ROSS, after whom many features of this area are named. At its head is the **Ross Ice Shelf**, the world's largest body of floating ice, which is approximately the size of France. On the eastern shores of the Ross Sea lies Ross Island, which is the site of Mount Erebus and of Scott Base, established by New Zealand in 1957.

Rostand, Edmond (1868–1918) French dramatist and poet. His reputation is chiefly based on his poetic drama *Cyrano de Bergerac* (1897), which romanticized the life of the 17th-century soldier, duellist, and writer Cyrano de Bergerac.

Rostov-on-Don An industrial port and cultural, scientific, and transportation centre in southern Russia on the River Don near its point of entry into the Sea of Azov; pop. (1990) 1,025,000. Built around a fortress erected in the 18th century, it developed as a major centre for the export of grain in the 19th century before becoming an important manufacturing city. It has ship and locomotive repair yards, and numerous light industries.

Rostropovich, Mstislav (Leopoldovich) (1927–) Russian-born cellist, pianist, and conductor, resident in the USA. Rostropovich gave the first London performance of Shostakovich's First Cello Concerto (1960). His friend Britten composed the Cello Sonata and the *Cello Symphony* (1963) for him. As a pianist, he frequently accompanies his wife, the Russian-born soprano singer Galina Vishnevskaya (1926–). Rostropovich is also an operatic and symphonic conductor.

rotary engine An INTERNAL-COMBUSTION ENGINE that generates rotary motion directly, rather than converting reciprocating motion through a crankshaft. The most successful example has been the Wankel engine, developed by the German engineer Felix Wankel in 1959. Instead of a piston the engine has a three-lobed rotor, which rotates within an oval casing containing inlet and exhaust ports for fuel. As the rotor revolves, the three spaces between the rotor and the casing execute a four-stroke cycle similar to that of a normal PETROL ENGINE. The engine has found only limited application due to difficulties in obtaining a seal between the rotor and the outer casing.

A new rotary engine design, the Rotorcam, uses conventional cylinders and pistons arranged radially outwards from a central axis. The engine, developed by the US inventor Jerome Murray, is more efficient, can run on a variety of fuels, and requires fewer gears than a conventional engine.

Roth, Philip (1933–) US novelist and short-story writer. His first collection, *Goodbye, Columbus* (1959), set the pattern for a succession of novels featuring observation of Jewish-American mores and contemporary sexuality in a personal style, culminating in the popularly successful *Portnoy's Complaint* (1969), a man's confessions to his psychoanalyst. Later works include *Zuckerman Bound* (1985) and *The Counterlife* (1987).

Rotherhithe Tunnel A road tunnel in south-east England, under the Thames east of Wapping in London. Built in 1904–08 to a design by Maurice Fitzmaurice, it links Rotherhithe on the south side of the river with Shadwell on the north.

Rothko, Mark (born Marcus Rothkovich) (1903–70) US painter, born in Latvia. In the late 1940s, he became a leading figure in colour-field painting, creating canvases consisting of hazy and apparently floating rectangles of colour, usually arranged vertically and in parallel, with the intention of absorbing the spectator in an act of contemplation. His works include a series of paintings for the Seagram Building in New York, notably *Black on Maroon* (1958), which were never installed and which Rothko gave to the Tate Gallery in London.

Rothschild, Meyer Amschel (1743–1812) German financier. He was the founder of the Rothschild banking-house in Frankfurt and financial adviser to the landgrave of Hesse. By the time of his death, his firm had already conducted significant financial transactions for a number of European governments. He had five sons, all of whom entered banking, setting up branches of the organization across western Europe. Notable among them was **Nathan Meyer**, Baron de Rothschild (1777–1836), who founded a bank in London (1804) and became a British citizen; Nathan's son, **Lionel Nathan**, Baron de Rothschild (1808–79), was Britain's first Jewish MP. Lionel's son **Nathan** (1840–1915) was the first Jewish British peer. Later generations, while maintaining their connection with the bank, have been notable patrons of the arts and some have been scientists.

rotifer (or **wheel animalcule**) A member of the phylum Rotifera, containing around 1,500 species of tiny invertebrates taking their name from a ciliated crown that can appear to rotate. This 'crown' can be used to suck planktonic organisms into the mouth of sessile rotifers, or as a locomotory organ in free-living species. They are among the tiniest of multicellular animals, often no bigger than protozoa, yet they contain numerous tissues with complex sensory organs and eyes, and show elaborate behaviour and locomotory patterns. Some have very beautiful skeletal coverings.

Rotorua A city and tourist town on North Island, New Zealand, on the south-west shore of Lake Rotorua; pop. (1991) 53,700. Situated at the centre of a region of volcanic lakes, thermal springs, and geysers, it became a fashionable spa town in the early 20th century.

rotten borough A British Parliamentary borough whose population had virtually disappeared by 1832. At that time there were more than 50 such boroughs with two Members of Parliament. Among the most notorious were Old Sarum with a handful of electors and Dunwich, mostly submerged under the North Sea. They were abolished by the REFORM ACT of 1832.

Rotterdam An industrial city and the principal port of the Netherlands, in the province of South Holland at the junction of the Rotte and the

Nieuwe Maas rivers; pop. (1991) 582,270. Its expansion dates from the completion in 1890 of the New Waterway linking it with the Hook of Holland, and in 1966 the opening of the Europort harbour made it one of the world's largest ports. Shipbuilding, engineering, oil refining, and the manufacture of petrochemicals and electronic goods are important industries.

Rouault, Georges (Henri) (1871–1958) French painter and engraver. Although he exhibited with the Fauves in 1905, he is chiefly associated with expressionism. His best-known paintings are characterized by the use of vivid colours and simplified forms enclosed in thick black outlines, reflecting the influence of his apprenticeship to a stained-glass window-maker (1885–90). A devout Roman Catholic, from the 1930s he turned increasingly towards religious subject-matter; notable among such works is *Christ Mocked by Soldiers* (1932).

Rouen A major river port on the Seine in north-west France, the capital of the department of Seine-Maritime in Upper Normandy (Haute-Normandie); pop. (1990) 105,470. Known during Roman times as Rotomagnus, Rouen was in English possession from the time of the Norman Conquest (1066) until captured by the French in 1204, becoming the medieval capital of Normandy. It returned briefly to English rule (1419–49) after its capture by Henry V during the Hundred Years War. In 1431 Joan of Arc was tried and burnt at the stake here. Badly damaged during World War II but now restored, it has metal, chemical, drugs, and textile industries, as well as tourism.

roulette A gambling game played in casinos worldwide, although it was developed in the casino at Monte Carlo. A small ball is thrown in a clockwise direction into a horizontal wheel that is spinning counter-clockwise. The wheel spins in a housing with 37 (or sometimes 38) numbered compartments (0 and 1–36 or 0 and 00, plus 1–36). A green baize board next to the wheel enables players to lay their bets on the number of the compartment into which they expect the ball to come to rest. The use of alternate red and black numbered compartments enables players to make bets ranging from even odds (red or black, odd or even, over or below 18) to 35–1 on a single number. Between these extremes players can make bets of virtually any odds by backing groups of numbers.

rounders A bat-and-ball game played mainly in Britain and said to be a forerunner of BASEBALL. Two teams of nine take turns to bat and field, and a match consists of two innings each. The batter uses a rounded stick and faces up to the bowler, who delivers the hard leather ball with an under-arm action from a square 7.5 m (25 feet) away. The batter tries to hit the ball forward of his or her square and runs to first post or further, continuing if possible to fourth post and scoring a rounder. Fielders can dismiss batters by catching a hit on the full or touching the ball to a post before the batter can reach it.

Roundheads Puritans and Parliamentarians during the ENGLISH CIVIL WAR. It originated as a term of abuse, referring to the Puritans' disapproval of long hair and their own close-cropped heads. Roundhead strength during the Civil War lay mainly in southern and eastern England.

roundworm (or **nematode**) A member of the largest phylum of worm-like animals, Nematoda, with over 10,000 species. Many species are so tiny that they pass unnoticed, although they may be extraordinarily abundant in soils or within other organisms. They include free-living species, usually less than 1 mm (0.04 inch) in length, which occur in soil, sea water and fresh water, but by far the most common are the parasitic species. All have a cylindrical body, bounded by a single muscle layer and a tough CUTICLE. They feed on other smaller animals or bacteria, or may simply swallow food from tissues of their host. Many serious parasites or pests are roundworms, such as EELWORMS in plants, and HOOKWORMS, LUNGWORMS, and elephantiasis-producing filaria in mammals. Virtually all groups of animals and plants have at least one roundworm parasite associated with them. Many, such as PINWORMS, are relatively harmless and widespread. Others, such as the large *Ascaris*, which grows up to 30 cm (12 inches), live in the gut of vertebrates such as pigs and humans, where they may weaken the host if present in large numbers.

Rousseau, Henri (Julien) (known as 'le Douanier', 'the customs officer') (1844–1910) French painter. After retiring as a customs official in 1893, he devoted himself to painting, although it was only after his death that he was recognized as a notable naive artist. Fantastic dreams and exotic jungle landscapes often form the subjects of his bold and colourful paintings. Famous works include the *Sleeping Gypsy* (1897) and *Tropical Storm with Tiger* (1891).

Rousseau, Jean-Jacques (1712–78) French philosopher and writer, born in Switzerland. From 1750 he came to fame with a series of works highly critical of the existing social order; his philosophy is underpinned by a belief in the fundamental goodness of human nature, encapsulated in the concept of the 'noble savage', and the warping effects of civilization. In his novel *Émile* (1762) Rousseau formulated new educational principles giving the child full scope for individual development in natural surroundings, shielded from the corrupting influences of civilization. His *Social Contract* (1762) anticipated much of the thinking of the French Revolution. Rousseau is also noted for his *Confessions* (1782), one of the earliest autobiographies.

Rousseau, (Pierre Étienne) Théodore (1812–67) French painter. He was a leading landscapist of the BARBIZON School and placed great importance on making preliminary studies for studio paintings out of doors, directly from nature. His works typically depict the scenery and changing light effects of the forest of Fontainebleau, and include *Under the Birches, Evening* (1842–44).

rove beetle A BEETLE of the large family Staphylinidae, which has an estimated 27,000 species throughout the world. They are small to medium-sized, elongate, with short wing-covers; the large hind-wings are elaborately folded beneath them. The whole of the abdomen is thus exposed. Many species fly readily. Both adults and larvae are active carnivores and are an important part of the soil fauna. They include the familiar devil's coach-horse beetles.

rowan A tree of the genus *Sorbus*, which also includes white-beams, *S. aria*, and the wild service tree, *S. domestica*. It belongs to the family Rosaceae. Most rowans have divided leaves with small, toothed leaflets. Their flowers are produced as clusters and are followed by red, yellow, or white berries, depending upon species. The European rowan, *S. aucuparia*, also known as the mountain ash, is a tree some 18 m (60 feet) in height and is native to Europe and western Asia. Species of *Sorbus* hybridize readily and can produce a large number of intermediate varieties.

Rowe, Nicholas (1674–1718) British dramatist. He is best known for his tragedies *Tamerlane* (1701) and *The Fair Penitent* (1703). The latter, marked by pathos and suffering, provided Mrs Siddons with one of her most celebrated roles.

rowing The worldwide sport of propelling an oared boat faster than its rivals. In sculling, the rower pulls two oars, and in ordinary rowing one oar. Racing boats are long and slender, and fitted with sliding seats and outriggers to hold the oars. Main competitions, or regattas, feature races for single and double sculls, coxed and coxless pairs (with and without a separate steersman), coxless fours, quadruple sculls (coxed and coxless), and eights. The world's most famous boat race is the annual Putney to Mortlake contest on the River Thames between the eights of Oxford and Cambridge Universities.

Rowlandson, Thomas (1756–1827) British painter, draughtsman, and caricaturist. He is remembered for his many watercolours and drawings satirizing Georgian manners, morals, and occupations. His best-known illustrations feature in a series of books known as *The Tours of Dr Syntax* (1812–21).

Rowntree A family of English business entrepreneurs and philanthropists. **Joseph** (1801–59) a grocer, established several Quaker schools. His son **Henry Isaac** (1838–83) founded the family cocoa and chocolate manufacturing firm in York; Henry's brother **Joseph** (1836–1925) became a partner in 1869 and subsequently founded three Rowntree trusts (1904) to support research into social welfare and policy. The latter's son **B(enjamin) Seebohm** (1871–1954), chairman of the firm from 1925 to 1941, conducted surveys of poverty in York (1897–98; 1936).

Roxburghshire A former county of SE Scotland. From 1975 to 1996 Roxburgh constituted an administrative district of Borders Region; it is now part of Scottish Borders unitary authority.

Royal Academy of Arts, London The national art academy of Britain, founded in 1768 with the aim of raising the status of the artistic professions and arranging exhibitions of works attaining an appropriate standard of excellence. Its first President was Sir Joshua REYNOLDS. Until the late 19th century it was the most influential art institution in Britain, but it then came under attack as a bastion of orthodox mediocrity opposed to creative innovation, and the New English Art Club was set up to challenge its domination. The Academy still enjoys considerable prestige, however; its annual summer exhibition is a popular social event, and it regularly organizes historical exhibitions of the highest quality.

Royal Ballet Britain's national ballet company. It began as the Vic-Wells Ballet in 1931 under the direction of Ninette DE VALOIS and with the encouragement of Lilian BAYLIS. By 1946 it had moved from Sadler's Wells Theatre to the Royal Opera House and in 1956 was granted a royal charter. With a repertoire grounded in the 19th-century classics it has staged numerous works by British choreographers and nurtured such dancers as Dame Margot Fonteyn, Dame Antoinette Sibley, and Sir Anthony Dowell. A subsidiary company, the Birmingham Royal Ballet, was established in Birmingham in 1990.

Royal Geographical Society A learned geographical society whose headquarters are based in Kensington, London, and whose function is to advance exploration and research and promote geographical knowledge. Founded in 1830, it took over the work of the Africa Association. It promotes geographical research and exploration by means of symposia, lectures, the presentation of prestigious awards. Academic papers are published in the *Geographical Journal* and articles of more popular appeal are published under licence in the *Geographical Magazine*.

Royal Greenwich Observatory (RGO) An OBSERVATORY founded by King Charles II and built by Christopher Wren in 1675 on the foundations of Greenwich Castle in a royal park east of London. Its original purpose was to produce accurate star charts and EPHEMERIDES of lunar and planetary motions so that they could be used at sea to enable longitude to be calculated correctly. The first director and Astronomer Royal was John FLAMSTEED. In 1767 the observatory began publishing the annual *Nautical Almanac*, a compendium of navigational information, which is still being produced. The meridian at Greenwich of the Airy Transit Circle, an instrument for determining times of TRANSIT of stars, has become the PRIME MERIDIAN of the world, separating the eastern hemisphere from the western hemisphere. The transit of the mean Sun across the Greenwich Meridian is the basis for GREENWICH MEAN TIME (GMT) on which the international time zone system is based. In 1946 Herstmonceux Castle in Sussex was purchased and the observatory moved there over the following years. In the early 1980s the Isaac Newton Telescope was relocated to La Palma Observatory in the Canary Islands and by 1990 the observatory staff had moved to Cambridge (UK) from where the Isaac Newton telescope can be remotely controlled.

Royal Institution A body founded in London in 1799 by the Anglo-American Benjamin Thompson, 'to teach the application of science to the common purposes of life'. In effect, the Royal Institution has devoted itself primarily to scientific research, and to the presentation of science to non-scientific audiences. The change of emphasis resulted from the work of DAVY (from 1801) and FARADAY (from 1813) at the Institution. They were followed in the 19th century by men of equal distinction, including John Tyndall, famous for research on heat; James Dewar, inventor of the VACUUM FLASK; and John Strutt (Lord RAYLEIGH), discoverer of argon. In the 20th century W. H. BRAGG and his son W. L. Bragg, who conducted early research into X-RAY crystallography, succeeded one another as directors.

Royal Society (of London for Improving Natural Knowledge) One of the world's oldest and most prestigious scientific societies. The first such society in Britain, it was founded in 1660 as a fellowship of some 40 natural philosophers meeting in London, and received its first Royal Charter from Charles II in 1662. Its *Philosophical Transactions* (1665–) was the first permanent scientific journal. Among its earliest members were BOYLE, HOOKE, PEPYS, WREN, and NEWTON. Among more literary members were DRYDEN, EVELYN, and AUBREY. In 1848 the Society became wholly scientific: only those who had made a distinguished contribution to the sciences were eligible for election as Fellows of the Royal Society (FRS). The Fellowship now numbers around 1,100, including about 100 Foreign Members.

royal waterlily (or **Victoria waterlily**) A freshwater aquatic plant, *Victoria amazonica*, belonging to the family Nymphaeaceae. This is one of three tropical South American species in the genus *Victoria*, named in honour of Queen Victoria. It has very large tray-like, floating leaves up to 2 m (6.5 feet) in diameter. The large white flowers, some 30 cm (12 inches) across, remain open for only two days and the petals turn pinkish-red on the second day.

Royce, Sir (Frederick) Henry (1863–1933) British engine designer. He founded the company of Rolls-Royce Ltd. with Charles Stewart ROLLS in 1906, previously having established his own successful electrical manufacturing business and designing and building his own car and engine. He became famous as the designer of the Rolls-Royce Silver Ghost car and later also became known for his aircraft engines, which were used to power planes in World Wars I and II. In the post-war era Rolls-Royce has built many jet engines.

Ruanda-Urundi See BURUNDI.

rubber (natural) A natural ELASTOMER obtained from the latex of several plants, but chiefly from the Brazilian rubber tree (*Hevea brasiliensis*). Rubber trees are grown by plantation farming methods, with 90 per cent of the world's production coming from south-east Asia, particularly Malaysia and Indonesia. A tall tree growing to 25 m (81 feet) in height, *Hevea brasiliensis* belongs to the SPURGE family, Euphorbiaceae, and is related to the castor-oil plant. It is a native of the Amazon basin. A short diagonal incision is made into the bark of the tree to allow the latex to run out into a collecting cup. The latex is treated with acid so that the rubber particles coagulate and settle into thin sheets. These can then be separated from the residual liquid. Alternatively the latex can be processed in a CENTRIFUGE to yield a concentrate.

The natural rubber is very soft, inelastic, and perishes rapidly on contact with air. Working the rubber between rollers, masticating it, and treating it with sulphur (VULCANIZATION) generates a material with greater elasticity and resilience than any other solid. It is used extensively in the production of tyres and also in combination with fabrics to produce WATERPROOF cloth for use in raincoats and groundsheets. Vulcanization with excess sulphur produces a rigid plastic called ebonite. Foam rubber, made by frothing latex and vulcanizing it, is used as padding in upholstery and other applications.

rubber (synthetic) A range of compounds manufactured to reproduce the properties of natural RUBBER. The first synthetic rubber was a POLYMER of dimethyl butadiene (C_4H_6) manufactured in Germany during World War I. Many different synthetic rubbers are now in use, the most widespread being rubber produced by polymerization of butadiene with styrene. For many purposes this rubber can directly replace natural rubber, and it has better resistance to ageing, cracking, and abrasion than the natural product. However, it has poor strength and resilience, and in some applications (notably tyre treads) it is mixed with natural rubber. Another synthetic rubber is butyl rubber, which is exceptionally impermeable to gases and is used for inner tubes and the inner linings of tubeless tyres. Other examples of synthetic rubbers include polychloroprene (neoprene), used in the cable and wire industry, and oil-resistant nitrile rubbers, for gaskets and for the ink-spreading rollers on printing machines. Some forms of SILICONES, POLYURETHANE, and PTFE are also used as synthetic rubbers.

Rubbra, (Charles) Edmund (1901–86) British composer and pianist. He wrote 11 symphonies, of which the fifth (1947–48) is the most frequently performed; the ninth, the *Sinfonia Sacra* (1971–72), is in the nature of a choral passion. He also wrote two masses (1945; 1949) and many songs.

Rubens, Sir Peter Paul (1577–1640) Flemish painter. The foremost exponent of northern Baroque, he spent a period of time in Italy (1600–08), where he studied the work of such artists as Titian and Raphael, before settling in Antwerp and becoming court portraitist in 1609. He quickly gained fame as a religious painter with altarpieces, such as *The Descent from the Cross* (1611–14). On a visit to England (1629–30) he was knighted by Charles I and executed several commissions for him, including a series of decorative ceilings at the Banqueting Hall in Whitehall. In addition to his portraits, Rubens is perhaps best known for mythological paintings featuring voluptuous female nudes, as in *Venus and Adonis* (*c.*1635).

Rubicon A small stream in north-east Italy near San Marino that flows into the Adriatic, marking the ancient boundary between Italy and Cisalpine Gaul. By taking his army across it (i.e. outside his own province) in 49 BC Julius Caesar committed himself to war against the Senate and Pompey.

rubidium (symbol Rb, at. no. 37, r.a.m. 85.47) A silvery white, highly reactive ALKALI METAL used in photoelectric cells. It was discovered by the German chemist Robert Bunsen and was named after the dark red colour of its flame in a flame test.

Rubinstein, Anton (Grigorevich) (1829–94) Russian pianist and composer. Touring and studying in Europe from 1840, Rubinstein settled in St Petersburg (1858) where he founded the Conservatory in 1862. He toured the USA (1872–73) and visited Britain several times. One of the greatest pianists of his day, his playing compared with that of LISZT, Rubinstein was a prolific composer, although only the *Melody in F* for piano is remembered.

Rubinstein, Artur (1888–1982) Polish-born US pianist. He first came to public attention with his Berlin début in 1900 at the age of 12, when he played the Mozart Concerto in A major. Thereafter he toured extensively in Europe as well as the USA and made many recordings, including the complete works of Chopin. He became a US citizen in 1946.

Rubinstein, Helena (1882–1965) US beautician and businesswoman. Born in Poland, she trained in medicine there before going to Australia in 1902, where she opened her first beauty salon. Her success enabled her to return to Europe and open salons in London (1908) and Paris (1912), and later to go to the USA and open salons in New York (1915) and elsewhere. After World War I her organization expanded to become an international cosmetics manufacturer and distributor.

ruby A gem species of CORUNDUM (Al_2O_3; aluminium oxide), varying in colour from deep crimson to pale rose-red. As crystals rubies are usually six-sided prisms, the rare 'star' rubies having internal cavities which reflect light after cutting. Pigeon-blood rubies come from Myanmar (Burma), which has the best stones. Those from Sri Lanka are normally paler, and those from Thailand darker.

rudbeckia See CONEFLOWER.

rudd A species of fish, *Scardinius erythrophthalamus*, closely related to the roach but distinguished by its steeply angled mouth, bronzy-yellow sides, and deep, blood-red pelvic and anal fins. It is widely distributed in western and central Europe, but is less adaptable than the roach, and feeds mainly on surface-living insects and crustaceans. It lives in lowland lakes and back-waters of rivers, often among dense vegetation, and grows to 40 cm (16 inches).

Rudolph, Paul (1918–) One of the leading post-war US architects. He was a pupil of GROPIUS at Harvard, and his early buildings reflect BAUHAUS ideas, but he came to develop a more independent sense of form. His best-known work is the Art and Architecture Building at Yale University (1958–64) in Brutalist concrete (see BRUTALISM). His other work has included urban planning, houses, embassies, and government and civic buildings.

ruff A species of bird, *Philomacus pugnax*, within the Old World sandpiper family. It is notable for the extraordinary, variably coloured ruffs and ear-tufts developed by the males in the breeding season. These can be erected and feature prominently in courtship display, which takes place in special arenas called leks, where the males congregate. The smaller females are traditionally called 'reeves'.

rugby See FOOTBALL.

Rugby A cattle-market and engineering town in Warwickshire, central England, on the River Avon 19 km (12 miles) south-west of Coventry; pop. (1991) 61,106. Rugby School, where the game of Rugby football was developed in the early 19th century, was founded here in 1567.

Ruhr A former major region of coal-mining and heavy industry in North Rhine-Westphalia, western Germany. It is named after the River Ruhr, which rises in the Rothaargebirge Mountains and flows westwards for 233 km (145 miles) to meet the Rhine near Duisburg. World recession has forced diversification in the eastern area where light industries have developed. Petrochemical industries continue in the west.

Ruisdael, Jacob van (c.1628–82) Dutch landscape painter. Born in Haarlem, he painted the surrounding landscape from the mid-1640s until his move to Amsterdam in 1657, where he spent the rest of his life. His typical subject-matter was forest scenes, seascapes, and cloudscapes.

Ruiz de Alarcón y Mendoza, Juan (1580–1639) Spanish dramatist, born in Mexico City. His most famous play, the moral comedy *La Verdad sospechosa*, was the basis of Corneille's *Le Menteur* (1642).

ruminant A herbivorous hoofed mammal that feeds on plants and regurgitates a food bolus for further mastication, known as chewing the cud. The ability to ruminate not only provides for better utilization of the food but has the added advantage that the time needed for grazing, in an open dangerous environment, is reduced to a minimum. The characteristic feature of these animals is the huge rumen, or storage pouch, which is part of the stomach. The rumen contains symbiotic microorganisms that break down the cell walls of the plants before the food bolus is returned to the mouth. Examples of ruminants are chevrotains, deer, giraffes, okapis, pronghorns, cattle, sheep, goats, bison, and antelopes.

Rump Parliament The remnant of the English LONG PARLIAMENT, which continued to sit after PRIDE'S PURGE (1648). In 1649 it ordered Charles I's execution, abolished both monarchy and House of Lords, and established the COMMONWEALTH. Its members were mostly gentlemen, motivated by self-interest, and its policies were generally unpopular. Oliver CROMWELL expelled the Rump in April 1653. Six years later it was recalled to mark the end of the PROTECTORATE; in 1660 the members excluded by Pride were readmitted, and the Long Parliament dissolved itself in preparation for the RESTORATION of the monarchy.

Rum Rebellion (1808) A revolt in Australia, when colonists and officers of the New South Wales Corps (later known as the Rum Corps because of its involvement in the rum trade) overthrew Governor William BLIGH. It was fuelled by Bligh's drastic methods of limiting the rum traders' powers and his attempts to end the domination of the officer clique, while an immediate cause was the arrest of the sheep-breeder John Macarthur in his role as liquor merchant and distiller. The officers induced the commander, Major George Johnston, to arrest Bligh as unfit for office. When Governor MACQUARIE took office in 1810, the Corps was recalled, George Johnston was court-martialled in England and cashiered in 1811. Bligh, although exonerated, was removed from office.

Rundstedt, (Karl Rudolf) Gerd von (1875–1953) German field-marshal. He was called from retirement in 1939 to take command in the Polish and French campaigns of World War II. In 1941 he commanded the invasion of the Soviet Union but was dismissed after he had withdrawn from Rostov against Hitler's orders, in order to improve his chances of resisting a Soviet counter-offensive. From 1942 to 1945 he commanded the forces occupying France and launched the Battle of the Bulge in the ARDENNES campaign in December 1944. Relieved of his command in March 1945, he was captured by US troops in May but released in 1949 on grounds of ill health.

rune A written character used in Norse and some other Germanic languages. It derives from the Gothic word *runa*, a mystery, and was often associated with magic. The letters are thought to be a modified form of the Etruscan or Roman characters; earliest examples date from the 3rd century. The **runic alphabet** of 24 characters is known as the *futhark* from its first six letters *f*, *u*, *th*, *a*, *r*, *k*.

Runnymede A meadow at Egham on the south bank of the Thames near Windsor, Surrey. It is famous as the place in which King John signed the MAGNA CARTA in 1215. There are memorials here to this event and to Commonwealth airmen and to John F. Kennedy.

Runyon, (Alfred) Damon (1884–1946) US author and journalist. He is best known for his short stories about New York's Broadway and underworld characters, written in colourful New York slang. His collections include *Guys and Dolls* (1932), which formed the basis for the musical of the same name (1950).

Rupert, Prince (1619–82) English Royalist general, son of Frederick V, elector of the Palatinate, and nephew of Charles I. Born in Bohemia, he went to England and joined the Royalist side just before the outbreak of the Civil War in 1642. He made his name in the early years of the war as a leader of cavalry, but after a series of victorious engagements was defeated by Parliamentarian forces at Marston Moor (1644) and Naseby (1645). He later lived chiefly in France until the Restoration (1660), when he returned to England and commanded naval operations against the Dutch (1665–67 and 1672–74). In 1670 Rupert became the first governor of the Hudson's Bay Company in Canada. He was deeply interested in art and science, and was also responsible for the introduction of mezzotint engraving into England.

rush A monocotyledonous plant of the family Juncaceae. Rushes occur worldwide, with the exception of the tropics, and form a family of some 400 species. Most are perennial, with rhizome-like rootstocks bearing grass-like or tubular leaves. They are plants of bog or marshy habitats and, though they have little value as ornamental plants, they were frequently used at one time as floor-covering and for basket- and mat-weaving. Unrelated plants using the name include the flowering rush, *Butomus umbellatus*, which is the sole member of its family, and bulrush, *Typha* species, a genus in the family Typhaceae.

Rushdie, (Ahmed) Salman (1947–) Indian-born British novelist. He was educated in England and became a British citizen in 1964. His Booker Prize-winning novel *Midnight's Children* (1981) views the development of India since independence through the eyes of a telepathic child. His later novel *The Satanic Verses* (1988), with its portrayal of a figure that many identified with Muhammad, was regarded by Muslims as blasphemous; in 1989 Ayatollah Khomeini issued a fatwa condemning Rushdie to death and he has since lived in hiding. He has since published *Imaginary Homelands* (1991), a collection of essays, and *The Moor's Last Sigh* (1995), a novel.

Rushmore, Mount See BLACK HILLS.

Ruskin, John (1819–1900) Influential British critic and art theorist, also a talented water-colourist. His literary output was enormous and he had a remarkable hold over public opinion, as he showed when he defended the PRE-RAPHAELITES in 1851. In the second half of his life he devoted himself to philanthropic work (using his inherited fortune) and to writing on economic and political questions. His eloquence in linking art with the daily life of the workman had affinities with the views of William MORRIS. He was a proponent of craftsmanship against the innovations of mass production that followed the Industrial Revolution.

Russell, Bertrand (Arthur William), 3rd Earl Russell (1872–1970) British philosopher, mathematician, and social reformer. His work on mathematical logic was extremely influential; his major work in this field being *Principia Mathematica* (1910–13), written with A. N. Whitehead. His philosophical views underwent continual development and revision; however, he wrote several books in the empiricist tradition (such as *Our Knowledge of the External World*, 1914) and was a principal proponent of neutral monism (a denial of the duality of matter and mind). During World War I Russell became widely known as a conscientious objector; he also campaigned for women's suffrage and in his nineties took a leading role in CND. He was awarded the Nobel Prize for literature in 1950.

Russell, George William (1867–1935) Irish poet. He met W. B. Yeats in 1886 and became interested in theosophy and mysticism; the first of several volumes of verse (published under the pseudonym AE) appeared in 1894. After the performance of his poetic drama *Deirdre* (1902) Russell became a leading figure in the Irish literary revival. His interests extended to public affairs and he edited *The Irish Homestead* (1905–23) and *The Irish Statesman* (1923–30).

Russell, Henry Norris (1877–1957) US astronomer and astrophysicist, who developed the work of HERTZSPRUNG in graphical form in what is now known as the HERTZSPRUNG–RUSSELL DIAGRAM. Russell believed that this diagram represented a sequence of stellar evolution, a view no longer accepted. He carried out spectroscopic analyses to determine the constituent elements of stars, and he discovered that the Sun contained much more hydrogen than had been expected.

Russell, John, 1st Earl Russell (1792–1878) British Whig statesman, Prime Minister 1846–52 and 1865–66. As a member of Lord Grey's government (1830–34), he was responsible for introducing the Reform Bill of 1832 into Parliament. He became Prime Minister when Sir Robert Peel was defeated (1846) and later served as Foreign Secretary in Lord Aberdeen's coalition government (1852–54); Russell's second premiership ended with his resignation when his attempt to extend the franchise again in a further Reform Bill was unsuccessful.

Russell, Ken (born Henry Kenneth Alfred Russell) (1927–) British film director. After making a series of increasingly unconventional biographical films on composers for the BBC he gained an international reputation with a lavish screen adaptation of D. H. Lawrence's *Women in Love* (1969). His films are characterized by their extreme imagery, often attracting controversy for their depiction of sex and violence. His prolific output includes *The Devils* (1971), *The Rainbow* (1989), and the television film *Lady Chatterley* (1993).

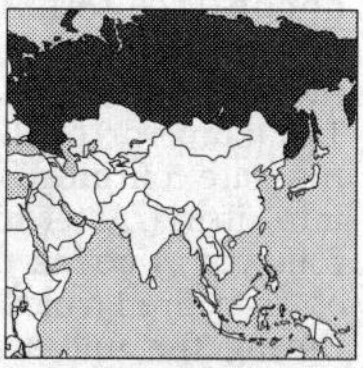

Russia (official name **Russian Federation**) A country in northern Asia and eastern Europe. Its borders touch Norway and Finland in the north, Poland in the north-west, Estonia, Latvia, Lithuania, Belarus, and Ukraine in the west, Georgia, Azerbaijan, Kazakhstan, Mongolia, China, and Korea in the south; its maritime borders meet the Baltic Sea, Black Sea, the inland Caspian Sea, the Arctic, and the Pacific. It is separated from Alaska in the north-east by the Bering Strait.

Physical. The largest country in the world, Russia spans 11 time zones and 160 degrees of longitude – nearly halfway around the Earth. It extends from the Gulf of Finland in the west to the peaks of Kamchatka in the east, from the frozen islands of Novaya Zemlya in the north to the warm Black Sea, the Caucasus Mountains, and the Pamirs and other ranges bordering China and Mongolia in the south. The north–south trending Ural Mountains divide European from Asian Russia. The plateaus and plains of Siberia make up most of the area to the east. To the west of the Urals extends the North European Plain. Great rivers include the Volga flowing south to the Caspian Sea, the Ob, Yenisei, and Lena draining north into the Arctic Ocean, and the Amur entering the Pacific Ocean to the east. East of the Lena is an area of mountains stretching from the Verkhoyanska to the Anadyr Range, which is half the size of Europe. Lake Baikal is Eurasia's largest, and the world's deepest, lake. Across the country extend belts of tundra (in the far north), forest, steppe, and fertile areas.

Economy. Since the collapse of communism and the end of the Soviet Union, Russia has embarked on a difficult transition to a free-market economy by freeing prices and introducing measures for privatization and land reform. However, chronic food shortages have been worsened by the disintegration of distribution systems and lack of confidence in the monetary system. Potentially of enormous wealth, Russia has rich mineral resources, with huge deposits of coal, iron ore, gold, platinum, copper, diamonds, and other metals, and, in Siberia, the world's largest reserves of petroleum and natual gas. Heavy industry, such as machinery, automobile production, paper and wood industries, and chemicals, dominates the economy, with mining and oil refineries also of importance. There is also light industry such as textiles and food-processing. Half the agricultural produce of the former Soviet Union was grown in Russia: the principal crops are grain and livestock, as well as commercial crops such as sunflower seeds, sugar-beet, and flax. Russia controls the former Soviet Central Bank but it shares responsibility for the Soviet Union's foreign debt with other former Soviet republics. The ownership of certain Soviet assets such as foreign exchange and gold is disputed.

History. In the 9th century the house of Rurik began to dominate the eastern Slavs, establishing the first all-Russian state with its capital at KIEV. This powerful state accepted Christianity in about 985. However, decline had set in long before the Mongols established their control over most of European Russia in the 13th century.

Following the collapse of Mongol rule in the late 14th century, the principality of Muscovy emerged as the pre-eminent state. Gradually it absorbed formerly independent principalities such as NOVGOROD (1478), forming in the process an autocratic, centralized Russian state. IVAN the Terrible was the first Muscovite ruler to assume the title of Tsar (Emperor) of all Russia (1547). During his reign the state continued its expansion to the south and into Siberia. After his death a period of confusion followed as BOYAR families challenged the power of Theodore I (ruled 1584–98) and Boris GODUNOV. During the upheavals of the Time of Troubles (1604–13), there were several rival candidates to the throne which ended with the restoration of firm rule by Michael Romanov. The ROMANOV dynasty resumed the process of territorial expansion, and in 1649 established peasant serfdom. In the early 18th century PETER I transformed the old Muscovite state into a partially Westernized empire, stretching from the Baltic to the Pacific.

From this time onward Russia played a major role in European affairs. Under the empresses ELIZABETH I and CATHERINE II, it came to dominate POLAND, and won a series of victories against the Ottoman Turks. In 1798–99 the Russians joined Great Britain, Austria, Naples, Portugal, and the Ottoman empire to fight against NAPOLEON. The Treaty of Tilsit (1807) enabled it to acquire FINLAND from Sweden, while the early Russo-Turkish Wars led to territorial acquisitions in Bessarabia and the Caucasus. Following Napoleon's defeat, the Treaty of VIENNA (1815) confirmed Russia and Austria as the leading powers on the continent of Europe. Attempts at liberal reform by the DECEMBRISTS were ruthlessly suppressed, and Russia helped Austria to quell Hungarian nationalist aspirations in the REVOLUTIONS OF 1848. Rivalry of interests, especially in south-east Europe, between Russia and the Western powers led to the CRIMEAN WAR. Serfdom was abolished in 1861, and attempts at changes in local government, the judicial system, and education were partially successful, though they fell short of the demands made by the Populists and other radical reform groups. In the late 19th century Russian expansionism, curtailed by the Congress of BERLIN, led to its abandonment of the Three Emperors' League and, later, to a Triple Entente with Britain and France (1907). Defeat in the unpopular RUSSO-JAPANESE WAR led to the RUSSIAN REVOLUTION of 1905. A DUMA (Parliament) was established, and its Prime Minister, Stolypin, attempted a partial agrarian reform. The beginning of the 20th century saw a rapid growth in Russian industry, mainly financed by foreign capital. It was among the urban concentration of industrial workers that the leftist Social Democratic Party won support, although it split after 1903 into BOLSHEVIKS and Mensheviks. Support for Balkan nationalism led Russia into WORLD WAR I. The hardship which the war brought on the people was increased by the inefficient government of NICHOLAS II. A series of revolts culminating in the RUSSIAN REVOLUTION of 1917 led to the overthrow of the Romanov dynasty and to the RUSSIAN CIVIL WAR, after which the SOVIET UNION was established in 1922.

The Russian republic was by far the largest of the Soviet republics, with 70 per cent of the population. In 1978 it received a new constitution as the Russian Soviet Federal Socialist Republic (RSFSR), consisting of six territories, forty-nine provinces, five autonomous regions, and sixteen autonomous republics. The Communist Party of the Soviet Union maintained firm control over the federation until the late 1980s, when pressures developed for greater independence. In 1990 a new constitution created a Russian Congress of People's Republics and a Russian Supreme Soviet, of which Boris YELTSIN was elected Chairman on a ticket of multi-party democracy and economic reform. In June 1991 he was elected President of the Federation by popular vote. Following the disintegration of the Soviet Union and the resignation of President GORBACHEV in December, Russia became an independent sovereign state. It took the leading role in forming a new body, the Commonwealth of Independent States (CIS), which most of the former Soviet republics joined. Problems facing Russia in the early 1990s included tensions between autonomous republics, ethnic conflicts, the redeployment of military and naval forces and equipment, and of nuclear weapons, and a rapidly collapsing economy. Following endorsement of Yeltsin's economic reforms in a national referendum in 1993, communists staged an unsuccessful coup against his administration. Yeltsin suspended parliament and ruled by presidential decree. In December 1993, elections to the Federal Assembly saw the rise of the far-right Liberal Democratic Party of Russia under its nationalist leader Vladimir Zhirinovsky. In 1994 serious unrest broke out in the Caucasian region of Chechnya, where Muslim Chechens declared an independent republic. Although invading Russian forces devasted the capital, Grozny, resistance continued; despite sporadic peace talks the status of Chechnya had not been resolved by mid-1996. In the mid-1990s, Yeltsin's position was further weakened by failing health and by the Communist Party's victory in parliamentary elections in 1995. Although he was re-elected President in 1996, his authority appeared to be on the wane.

Capital: Moscow
Area: 17,075,000 sq km (6,590,950 sq mi)
Population: 147,168,000 (1995)
Currency: 1 rouble = 100 kopeks
Religions: Eastern Orthodox; Jewish; Muslim; and other minorities
Ethnic Groups: Russian 82%; Tatar 4%; Ukrainian, Mordvin, Lapp, Chuvash, Bashkir, Polish, German, Udmurt, Mari, Yakut, and Ossete minorities
Languages: Russian (official); minority languages
International Organizations: UN; CSCE; Commonwealth of Independent States; North Atlantic Co-operation Council

Russian The official language of Russia, the most important of the Slavonic languages, spoken as a first language in Russia and by people of Russian origin in the former republics of the Soviet Union. It is written in the Cyrillic alphabet, the invention of which is attributed to St Cyril (*c.*827–69).

Russian art The art and architecture of Russia and, from 1921 until 1991, of the Soviet Union. Russian art originated among the Slav-speaking people who settled in the 7th century AD in the great central plain contained by the rivers Dnieper and Volga. In the 10th century the Slav rulers adopted Christianity, which then formed the core of the nation's culture. Its people, strongly influenced by BYZANTINE ART, built churches and monasteries and adorned them with scenes from the scriptures painted on the interior walls as well as upon individual panels and icons. In architecture, the churches had, like their Byzantine models, three aisles and a dome; but the Russians soon began experimenting with the shape of the dome until, in the 12th century, they had evolved the characteristic onion shape. The Mongol occupation of Russia (mid-13th–end 14th century) arrested the growth of Russian art. It revived, however, during the 15th century, when the most important centre of art was Novgorod. Among other architectural innovations was the wooden 'iconostasis' (stand for icons), a screen to separate the altar in the apse from the body of the church. Throughout the 14th and 15th centuries, religious paintings of outstanding quality were produced, for example the work of Andrey Rublyov. In Novgorod, the rigid Byzantine style gave place to a gentleness inspired by slight contact with Italian art. The medieval style of religious painting came to a sudden end when Peter the Great (1682–1725) Westernized Russia and transferred his capital from Moscow to St Petersburg. Since Russian artists could not instantly produce secular, Westernized art, Peter employed foreign artists from Holland, Italy, Germany, and France grafting an alien art on the indiginous art. Crafts, on the other hand, were little influenced by Western ideas, but retained their original flamboyance and their medieval forms. In the 19th century artists threw their skill into the social battle for reform, producing numerous paintings with a moral message. This movement was rejected at the turn of the century by a group of artists, known as 'The World of Art' group, which set out to revive artistic quality under the banner of 'Art for Art's Sake'. They created many paintings of fine quality, and made their influence felt in every branch of art. In the early 20th century Russian painters, sculptors, and theatre designers were in the vanguard of ABSTRACT ART, most notably in the movements called CONSTRUCTIVISM and SUPREMATISM. After the Revolution, however, the state disapproved of experimental art and encouraged 'SOCIALIST REALISM'. The disintegration of the Soviet Union after 1990 led to experimentation in new artforms, and an expression of artistic consciousness no longer ruled from Moscow.

Russian Civil War (1918–21) A conflict fought in Russia between the anti-communist White Army supported by some Western powers, and the RED ARMY of the Soviets in the aftermath of the RUSSIAN REVOLUTION of 1917. It is sometimes referred to as the War of Allied Intervention. Counter-revolutionary forces began organized resistance to the BOLSHEVIKS in December 1917, and clashed with an army hastily brought together by TROTSKY. In northern Russia a force made up of French, British, German, and US units landed at Murmansk and occupied Archangel (1918–20). Nationalist revolts in the BALTIC STATES led to the secession of Lithuania, Estonia, Latvia, and Finland, while a Polish army, with French support, successfully advanced the Polish frontier to the Russian Ukraine, gaining an area not re-occupied by the Soviet Union until World War II. In Siberia, where US and Japanese forces landed, Admiral Kolchak acted as Minister of War in the anti-communist 'All Russian Government' and, with the aid of a Czech legion made up of released prisoners-of-war, gained control over sectors of the Trans-Siberian Railway. He, however, was betrayed by the Czechs and murdered, the leadership passing to General Denikin, who sought to establish (1918–20) a 'United Russia' purged of the BOLSHEVIKS. In the Ukraine Denikin mounted a major offensive in 1919, only to be driven back to the Caucasus, where he held out until March 1920. In the Crimea the war continued under General Wrangel until November 1920. A famine in that year caused further risings by the peasants against the communists, while a mutiny of sailors at Kronstadt was suppressed by the Red Army. To win the war, LENIN imposed his ruthless policy of 'war communism'. Lack of cooperation between counter-revolutionary forces contributed to their final collapse and to the establishment of the SOVIET UNION.

Russian literature Literature written in the Russian language. From its beginnings in the late 10th century until the 18th it was largely the written record of the doctrines and official views of the Eastern Orthodox Church. It was invariably anonymous and derived from Byzantine models. It was probably the late 12th century that produced the much debated work of Old Russian literature, the epic *The Lay of Igor's Campaign*. The Renaissance had no profound cultural effect on Russia. Secular literature, notably satirical tales, began to appear in the 17th century. It was only with the foundation of St Petersburg and the impact of the European ENLIGHTENMENT in the 18th century that modern literature began. The 18th century saw the introduction, following French and German models of neoclassical literature. A vital role was performed by LOMONOSOV, who attempted to systematize poetic diction. The first important Russian poet was Gavriil Derzhavin. The 18th century saw the first attempts to collect the oral legacy of Russian folklore. The satirical play, *Wit Works Woe* (1822) by Aleksandr Griboyedov (1795–1829) created a gallery of now proverbial characters and some of the most oft-quoted lines in the Russian language. PUSHKIN's work contained the seeds of subsequent developments in all the genres of the 19th and early 20th centuries. His wide use of folklore and of the living language brought literature within reach of a much wider public, while LERMONTOV introduced a more passionate note. Both poets were influenced by Western ROMANTICISM. After this, verse went into a decline, the novel emerging as the leading genre of the national literature. Of formative influence were the short stories and novels of GOGOL. However, it was the novels of TOLSTOY, DOSTOEVSKY, and TURGENEV that brought Russia to the forefront of literature. The scope of realistic composition was refined by CHEKHOV in his short stories and dramas, which rank among the masterpieces of European literature. Symbolist and post-Symbolist Russian poets born between 1880 and 1895 brought about an unprecedented flowering of poetry. During the Symbolist period GORKY and others kept alive the classic tradition of SOCIAL REALISM that was drawn upon when Soviet literature, with its mandatory doctrine of Socialist Realism, was created in the 1930s. The imposition of Party controls led to a new specifically Soviet literature, centred in the novel. However, literary talent was always pitted against political dogma, as in the work of Osip Mandelstam, Anna AKHMATOVA, and BULGAKOV, whose novel, *The Master and Margarita* remains the best-known work of that period. Since the Revolution there has been an unbroken tradition of unofficial writing, sometimes 'self-published' (*samizdat*), sometimes sent abroad for publication, and sometimes hidden, awaiting a more favourable environment ('writing for the drawer'). Soviet literature was revitalized with the Khrushchev 'thaw', which began after 1956 and lasted until the mid-1960s by the flourishing of the work of such writers as YEVTUSHENKO. Under Brezhnev, official literary policy was tightened when it became apparent, principally through the SOLZHENITSYN case, that dissident writers could not be silenced. Increasingly, they were exiled from the USSR. The policies of Gorbachev after 1985 and the subsequent fall of communism led to a regeneration of literary life, with many previously banned works being permitted publication.

Russian Revolution (1905) A conflict in Russia between the government of NICHOLAS II and industrial workers, peasants, and armed forces. Heavy taxation had brought mounting distress to the poor, and Russia's defeat in the RUSSO-JAPANESE WAR aggravated discontent. A peaceful demonstration in St Petersburg was met with gunfire from the imperial troops. Mutiny broke out on the battleship *Potemkin*, and a soviet or council of workers' delegates was formed in St Petersburg. The emperor yielded to demands for reform, including a legislative DUMA. The SOCIAL DEMOCRATS continued to fight for a total overthrow of the system, and were met with harsh reprisals. Democratic freedoms were curtailed and the government became increasingly reactionary.

Russian Revolution (1917) The overthrow of the government of NICHOLAS II in Russia and its replacement by BOLSHEVIK rule under the leadership of LENIN. It was completed in two stages – a liberal (Menshevik) revolution in March (February, old style), which overthrew the imperial government, and a socialist (Bolshevik) revolution in November (October, old style). A long period of repression and unrest, compounded with the reluctance of the Russian people to continue to fight in World War I, led to a series of violent confrontations aiming to overthrow the existing government. The revolutionaries were divided between the liberal intelligentsia, who sought the establishment of a democratic, Western-style republic, and the socialists, who were prepared to use extreme violence to establish a MARXIST proletarian state in Russia. In the March Revolution strikes and riots in Petrograd (St Petersburg), supported by imperial troops, led to the abdication of the emperor and thus to the end after more than 300 years of Romanov rule. A committee of the DUMA (Parliament) appointed the liberal Provisional Government under Prince Lvov, who later handed over to the Socialist revolutionary KERENSKY. He faced rising opposition from the Petrograd Soviet of Workers' and Soldiers' Deputies. The October Revolution was carried through in a nearly bloodless coup by the Bolsheviks under the leadership of Lenin. Workers' Councils (SOVIETS) took control in the major cities, and a cease-fire was arranged with the Germans. A Soviet constitution was proclaimed in July 1918 and Lenin transferred the government from Petrograd to Moscow. The RUSSIAN CIVIL WAR continued for nearly three more years, ending in the supremacy of the Bolsheviks and in the establishment of the SOVIET UNION.

Russo-Japanese War (1904–05) An important conflict over control of Manchuria and Korea. The Japanese launched a surprise attack on Russian warships at anchor in the naval base at Port Arthur (now Lüshun), Manchuria, without declaring war, after Russia had reneged on its agreement to withdraw its troops from Manchuria. Port Arthur fell to the Japanese, as did Mukden, the capital of Manchuria. The Russian Baltic fleet sailed 28,000 km (18,000 miles) from its base to the East China Sea, only to be destroyed in the Tsushima Straits by the Japanese fleet led by Admiral Togo Heihashiro (1846–1934). This was the first Japanese defeat of a Western power both on land and at sea. The war was ended by the Treaty of PORTSMOUTH. For Russia, it was a humiliating defeat, which contributed to the RUSSIAN REVOLUTION of 1905.

rust Hydrated iron oxide, reddish-brown in appearance and basically of the formula FeO_2H. It is a product of the CORROSION of iron and steel caused by moist air. The rate of its formation is increased by the presence of sodium chloride and by atmospheric pollutants generally. The prevention of rust requires either a protective coating (paint, zinc plating, etc.) or alloying the iron or steel with certain metals to form stainless STEEL

rust fungus A parasitic fungus of the order Uredinales which attacks plants, causing disease. Many rust fungi have complex life-cycles involving the formation of several different kinds of spores. Typically, at some stage during the life-cycle, rust-red spores form in patches on the leaves and stems of diseased plants. Cereal rusts, such as wheat rust, *Puccinea graminis*, can reduce crop yields, and the fungal infection can spread rapidly when a crop of a susceptible species is grown over a large area. Clouds of spores are then produced which travel on the wind. Rust fungi are very host-specific: each species of fungus infects only one or two species of plant. In some fungi, two host plants are necessary, for example in *Puccinia graminis*, which is the causal agent of black-stem rust in wheat, some stages infect wheat, others barberry (*Berberis*), and both plants are necessary for completion of the rust life-cycle.

rutabaga See SWEDE.

Ruth The Moabite great-grandmother of King David, ancestress through Joseph of Jesus and central figure in the biblical Book of Ruth. The Gentile Ruth, although widowed, remained faithful to her Hebrew mother-in-law Naomi, and came with her to Bethlehem. There her wealthy kinsman, Boaz, struck by her beauty and devotion, married her.

Ruth, Babe (born George Herman Ruth) (1895–1948) US baseball player. He played for the Boston Red Sox (1914–19) and the New York Yankees (1919–35); he set the record for the most home runs (714), which remained unbroken until 1974.

ruthenium (symbol Ru, at. no. 44, r.a.m. 101.07) A shiny, grey, brittle element with a high melting-point (2,310°C, 4,890°F). Ruthenium is a platinum metal and occurs in association with other platinum metals as fine black grains in alluvial deposits. It is harder than other platinum metals and is used in electrical alloys and jewellery.

Rutherford, Sir Ernest, 1st Baron Rutherford of Nelson (1871–1937) New Zealand physicist. He is regarded as the founder of nuclear physics, and worked mainly in Britain. He established the nature of alpha and beta particles, and (with Frederick Soddy) proposed the laws of radioactive decay. He later concluded that the positive charge in an atom, and virtually all its mass, is concentrated in a central nucleus. In 1919 Rutherford announced the first artificial transmutation of an element; he had changed nitrogen atoms into oxygen by bombarding them with alpha particles. He was awarded the Nobel Prize for chemistry in 1908.

Rutherford, Dame Margaret (1892–1972) British actress. She is chiefly remembered for her roles as a formidable but jovial eccentric; they include Miss Prism in *The Importance of Being Earnest*, which she played on stage in 1939 and on film in 1952. Among her other films are *Passport to Pimlico* (1949), several film versions of Agatha Christie novels in which she played Miss Marple, and *The VIPs* (1963), for which she won an Oscar.

rutherfordium (symbol Rf, at. no. 104, r.a.m. 263) A transactinide element first synthesized in the USA in 1974. It was named in 1994 after Lord RUTHERFORD, despite a claim to have detected it in 1964 made by Soviet scientists, who named it **kurchatovium**, after the Soviet physicist Igor Vasilievich KURCHATOV.

Rutland A former county in the East Midlands of England that became part of Leicestershire in 1974. The smallest county in England, it was reinstated as a unitary authority in 1997. **Rutland Water** is one of the largest artificial reservoirs in the UK.

Rwanda A small country in east central Africa. It is bounded in the west by the Democratic Republic of Congo and Lake Kivu, on the north by Uganda, on the east by Tanzania, and on the south by Burundi.

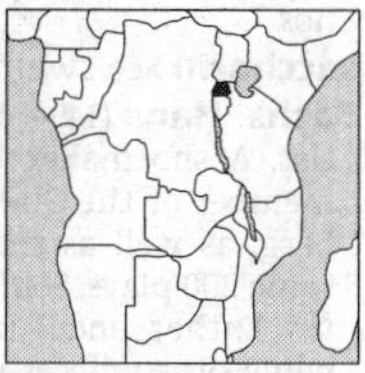

Physical. Rwanda occupies a mountainous region where the equatorial climate is modified by the altitude. Set on the eastern edge of the Great Rift Valley, at the head of Lake Tanganyika, it is also volcanic.

Economy. Rwanda is one of the poorest countries in the world. Subject to drought and famine and with a high incidence of parasitic and other diseases, it has one of the highest population densities in Africa and a high birth-rate. Coffee and tea are the main exports, and plantains, sweet potatoes, and cassava are staple crops. The principal mineral resource is cassiterite (a tin ore), but exports are at a standstill since the collapse in world tin prices. Other mineral resources include wolframite, gold and unexploited natural gas reserves. Limited manufacturing industry comprises mostly food-processing.

History. Rwanda obtained its present boundaries in the late 19th century under pastoral Tutsi kings who ruled over the agriculturalist Bahutu (Hutu). In 1890 Germany claimed it as part of German East Africa. Belgian forces took it in 1916, and administered it under a League of Nations mandate. Following civil war (1959) between the Tutsi and Hutu tribes, Rwanda was declared a republic in 1961 and became independent in 1962. The now dominant Hutu forced large numbers of Tutsi into exile, but after the accession to power of President Juvénal Habyarimana in 1973 domestic stability improved. In 1975 Habyarimana's party, the National Revolutionary Movement for Development (MRND) declared itself the sole legal political organization; he was re-elected in 1978, 1983, and 1988. In October 1990 Uganda-based rebels of the Front Patriotique Rwandaise (FPR), many of whose members were Tutsi, invaded. Belgian and French forces helped to repel them, while the OAU negotiated. In 1991 a new constitution legalized opposition parties, but the FPR refused to participate. In 1992 a coalition government was formed pending a general election, but Tutsi–Hutu tension persisted. In 1994, Habyarimana was assassinated. Massacres of Tutsis by the Hutu-dominated army ensued, reigniting the civil war. The FPR emerged victorious, but this provoked millions of Hutus to flee the country for fear of reprisals.

Capital: Kigali
Area: 26,338 sq km (10,169 sq mi)
Population: 6,700,000 (1995)
Currency: 1 Rwanda franc = 100 centimes
Religions: Roman Catholic 65.0%; traditional beliefs 17.0%; Protestant 9.0%; Muslim 9.0%
Ethnic Groups: Hutu 90.0%; Tutsi 9.0%; Twa 1.0
Languages: Rwanda, French (both official); Swahili
International Organizations: UN; OAU

Rydberg, Johannes Robert (1854–1919) Swedish physicist who established (1890) a general equation linking the various wavelengths of light emitted by hot hydrogen gas. The equation contains a constant now called the **Rydberg constant**.

Ryder, Sue, Baroness Ryder of Warsaw and Cavendish (1923–) British philanthropist. After World War II she co-founded an organization to care for former inmates of concentration camps; later known as the Sue Ryder Foundation for the Sick and the Disabled, it expanded to provide homes for the mentally and physically disabled in the UK and elsewhere in Europe. Ryder married the philanthropist Leonard CHESHIRE in 1959, and is a trustee of the Cheshire Foundation.

Ryder Cup A cup awarded to the winners of a professional golf tournament between teams from the USA and Europe. Originally presented by Samuel Ryder, a British businessman, in 1927 to the winners of teams of US and British professional golfers, the tournament was widened in 1979 when the British opened their team to European players. The contest takes place every other year.

rye A cereal plant, *Secale cereale*, cultivated in central Europe since Roman times. Like oats, it is thought to have been selected from grass seeds carried unintentionally with wheat as its cultivation spread from western Asia. It was more successful than wheat in central Europe, being more tolerant of the cold winters.

Ryle, Gilbert (1900–76) British philosopher. He was professor of metaphysical philosophy at Oxford 1945–68. A prominent figure in linguistic philosophy, he held that philosophy should identify 'the sources in linguistic idioms of recurrent misconstructions and absurd theories'. His most famous work, *The Concept of Mind* (1949), is a strong attack on the mind-and-body dualism of Descartes. He was a cousin of the astronomer Sir Martin RYLE.

Ryle, Sir Martin (1918–84) British astronomer. He carried out pioneering work in radio astronomy in the 1950s, when he produced the first detailed sky map of radio sources. His demonstration that remote objects appeared to be different from closer ones helped to establish the big bang as opposed to the steady-state theory of the Universe. Ryle was Astronomer Royal 1972–82 and was awarded the Nobel Prize for physics in 1974.

Ryukyu Islands (or **Nansei Islands**) A chain of more than 70 islands in the western Pacific, stretching for about 960 km (600 miles) from the southern tip of Kyushu Island, Japan, to Taiwan. The largest island is Okinawa. Part of China in the 14th century, the archipelago was incorporated into Japan in 1879. The islands were placed under US military control in 1945 and returned to Japan in 1972.

S

Saadi See SADI.

Saarbrücken An industrial city in western Germany, the capital of Saarland, on the River Saar close to the border with France; pop. (1991) 361,610. Situated at the centre of a large coal-mining region, its industries produce coke, machinery, rubber, metal goods, and optical equipment.

Saarland A state of western Germany, on the frontiers with France and Luxembourg; area 2,570 sq km (1,062 sq miles); pop. (1991) 1,076,880; capital, Saarbrückenchmid

. It is traversed by the River Saar and has rich deposits of coal and iron ore. Between 1684 and 1697 and again between 1792 and 1815 the area belonged to France. After World War I, until 1935, it was administered by the League of Nations. A plebiscite in 1935 – and a referendum after World War II – indicated the desire on the part of the population to be part of Germany. The area became the 10th German state in 1959.

Sabah A state of Malaysia, comprising the northern part of Borneo and some offshore islands; area 73,613 sq km (28,433 sq miles); pop. (1990) 1,470,200; capital, Kota Kinabalu. A British Protectorate (North Borneo) from 1888, it gained independence and joined Malaysia in 1963. Mount Kinabalu (4,094 m, 13,431 ft) is the highest peak in Borneo and south-east Asia.

sabbath (Hebrew *shabbat*, 'rest') The Jewish weekly holy day, beginning at sunset on Friday and ending at sunset on Saturday, during which time no work is permitted (except in liberal traditions), in obedience to the Fourth Commandment. Among Orthodox Jews the prohibition of work is taken to ban any creative or causal activity, such as writing, travelling, or switching on an electric light. Ritual is based primarily in the home, although SYNAGOGUE attendance is usual on both days.

Sabin, Albert Bruce (1906–93) US virologist born in Russia, who developed a live oral vaccine against poliomyelitis. Sabin's vaccine, consisting a weakened live strain of the virus, has largely replaced SALK's earlier killed virus.

Sabines A tribe native to the foothills of the Apennines north-east of Rome. According to tradition they joined the earliest settlement of Rome in the 8th century BC. Legend relates how the Romans abducted the Sabine women during a festival; an army was raised to take revenge but the women appeared on the battlefield with new-born babies and the two sides were reconciled. They became Roman citizens only after conquest.

sable A species of MARTEN, *Martes zibellina*, that inhabits the coniferous forests of central Siberia. It hunts in the trees for squirrels, birds, and eggs, but also eats berries and seeds. It is noted for its fine, dark fur, which is valuable in the fur trade.

sabretoothed tiger An extinct member of the cat family that lived during the late Tertiary Era. Species such as *Smilodon* evolved a pair of huge upper canine teeth while reducing the lower canines. Their main food was probably large, tough-skinned animals, such as elephants and rhinos.

saccharin See SWEETENER, ARTIFICIAL.

Sachs, Hans (1494–1576) German poet and dramatist. A shoemaker by trade, he was a renowned member of the Guild of Meistersingers in Nuremberg, as well as the prolific author of verse and some 200 plays. Some of his poetry celebrated Martin Luther and furthered the Protestant cause, while other pieces were comic verse dramas. Forgotten after his death, he was restored to fame in a poem by Goethe, and Wagner made him the hero of his opera *Die Meistersinger von Nürnberg* (1868).

sackbut The English name, used from the 15th to the 18th centuries, for the TROMBONE, which is Italian for large trumpet. Derived from the French *saqueboute* ('pull-push'), sackbut is now used to distinguish earlier models of trombone from later instruments.

Sackville-West, Vita (full name Victoria Mary Sackville-West) (1892–1962) British novelist and poet. Her works include the long poem *The Land* (1927), notable for its evocation of the English countryside, and the novel *All Passion Spent* (1931). She is also known for the garden which she created at Sissinghurst in Kent and for her friendship with Virginia Woolf; the central character of Woolf's novel *Orlando* (1928) is said to have been based on her.

sacrament A religious ceremony or act regarded as an outward sign of spiritual grace. In CHRISTIANITY, the sacraments are the seven rites of Baptism, Confirmation, the Eucharist, Penance, Ordination, Anointing of the Sick (formerly called Extreme Unction), and Matrimony. Both the ROMAN CATHOLIC and EASTERN ORTHODOX CHURCHES accept all these as sacraments, whereas most PROTESTANT Churches give this name to only two of them, the Eucharist and Baptism, which were, they believe, actually ordained by Jesus Christ himself; the QUAKERS and SALVATION ARMY accept no form of 'outward observance' of the sacraments.

Sacramento ▶**1** A river of northern California, USA, which rises near the border with Oregon and flows some 611 km (380 miles) southwards to San Francisco Bay. ▶**2** The capital of the US state of California, situated 115 km (72 miles) north-east of

San Francisco, on the Sacramento River; pop. (1990) 369,365. Founded during the gold-rush of 1848 on the site of John Sutter's New Helvetia Colony, it became state capital in 1854 and the western terminus of the Pony Express in 1860. It is linked to Suison Bay by a (43-mile) channel. Missile development industries, market gardening, and army and airforce bases are the main employers.

Sadat, (Muhammad) Anwar al- (1918–81) Egyptian statesman, President 1970–81. He broke with the foreign policies of his predecessor President Nasser, for example by dismissing the Soviet military mission to Egypt, removing the ban on political parties, and introducing measures to decentralize Egypt's political structure and diversify the economy. He later worked to achieve peace in the Middle East, visiting Israel (1977), and attending talks with Prime Minister Begin at Camp David in 1978, the year they shared the Nobel Peace Prize. Also in that year he founded the National Democratic Party, with himself as leader. He was assassinated by members of the Islamic Jihad.

Saddam Hussein See HUSSEIN.

Sadducee A member of a sect that rivalled the PHARISEES in ancient Israel. The Sadducees were drawn mostly from the rich landowners, and were naturally conservative, but by the time of JESUS CHRIST they had declined considerably from their previously dominant position. Nevertheless they still held a number of priesthoods and were a powerful voice in the SANHEDRIN.

Sade, Donatien Alphonse François, Marquis de (1740–1814) French writer and soldier. His career as a cavalry officer was interrupted by prolonged periods of imprisonment for cruelty and debauchery. While in prison he wrote a number of sexually explicit works, which include *Les 120 Journées de Sodome* (1784), *Justine* (1791), and *La Philosophie dans le boudoir* (1795). **Sadism** refers to the sexually deviant practices he described.

Sadi (or **Saadi**) (born Sheikh Muslih Addin) (*c.*1213–*c.*1291) Persian poet. His principal works were the collections known as the *Bustan* (1257) and the *Gulistan* (1258); the former is a series of poems on religious themes, while the latter is a mixture of poems, prose, and maxims concerning moral issues.

Sadler's Wells Theatre A London theatre so called because in 1683 Thomas Sadler exploited a medicinal spring in his garden as a pleasure-garden, which became known as Sadler's Wells. A wooden music room built there in 1685 became a theatre in 1753, whose stone-built successor remained in use until 1906. In 1927 Lilian Baylis took over the derelict building, erecting a new theatre which opened in 1931. Here both the Sadler's Wells Opera Company (now the English National Opera) and the Sadler's Wells Royal Ballet (now the Birmingham Royal Ballet) were founded.

safety-belt (or **seat belt**) A restraining strap or harness used to secure a person against injury that might result from sudden deceleration as in an aeroplane or car accident. Early lap safety-belts allowed the upper body and head to be catapulted forward. The modern design is the three-point inertia-reel belt. This allows free movement in normal travelling, but any sudden deceleration activates a ratchet and pawl mechanism, which locks the safety-belt strap and restrains the wearer. Up to 50 per cent of injuries can be prevented by safety-belt use.

safety-glass See GLASS.

safety-valve A device invented by the French physicist Denis Papin in 1679 to guard against excessive pressure in a BOILER or pipe system. The valve itself is usually of the poppet type, mushroom-shaped, similar to those used in internal-combustion engines. It is designed to lift suddenly when a critical pressure is reached and to close sharply when the pressure lowers.

safflower An annual or perennial plant or shrub with spiny leaves and yellow flowers, native to the Mediterranean region. Safflowers belong to the genus *Carthamus*, part of the sunflower family, and yield an edible oil. *C. tinctorius* is known as the saffron thistle because of its spines and its flowers, which yield yellow or red dyes.

saffron The flavouring and colouring obtained from the orange-red stigmas of the Asian saffron crocus, *Crocus sativus*. It is very expensive to produce, as 150,000 flowers are needed to yield 1 kg (2 pounds 3 ounces) of saffron.

saga Various kinds of prose tales composed in medieval Scandinavia and Iceland and written down from the 12th century to the 14th. These usually tell of heroic leaders, early Norse kings, 13th-century bishops, or of the heroic settlers of Iceland in the 9th and 10th centuries; others, such as the *Vǫlsunga saga*, relate earlier legends.

Sagan, Carl (Edward) (1934–96) US astronomer. He specialized in studies of the planets Mars and Venus, and in 1968 became director of the Laboratory of Planetary Studies at Cornell, dealing with information from space probes to those planets. Sagan showed that amino acids can be synthesized in an artificial primordial soup irradiated by ultraviolet light – a possible explanation for the origin of life on Earth. In 1983 he and several other scientists put forward the concept of a nuclear winter as a likely consequence of global nuclear war.

Sagan, Françoise (pseudonym of Françoise Quoirez) (1935–) French novelist, dramatist, and short-story writer. Her first novel *Bonjour Tristesse* (1954) and subsequent novels explore the transitory nature of love. Other novels include *Un Certain sourire* (1956) and *Aimez-vous Brahms?* (1959). She has since written a biography of Sarah Bernhardt, as well as several plays, including *Zaphorie* (1973).

sage A low-growing shrub, *Salvia officinalis*, belonging to the mint family. It is native to arid areas of southern Europe, though it is cultivated as a culinary herb in other, cooler regions. Its greyish, velvety leaves are distinctly flavoured. Variegated forms of sage are also used as ornamental plants (see SALVIA).

Sagitta The Arrow, the third-smallest CONSTELLATION. It lies in the northern half of the sky and was one of the 48 figures known to the ancient Greeks; it represents an arrow that, according to various myths, was shot by Apollo, Hercules, or Cupid.

Sagittarius The Archer, a CONSTELLATION of the zodiac, one of the 48 constellations known to the ancient Greeks who identified it as Crotus, a son of Pan and the inventor of archery. Sagittarius contains rich Milky Way star fields towards the centre of the Galaxy; the exact centre of the Galaxy is believed to coincide with the radio source Sagittarius A.

sago A starch product obtained from the trunks of two species of sago palm of the genus *Metroxylon*, and sometimes from other monocotyledons, as well as certain cycads. The trees are cut down just before flowering and the trunks split to remove the pulp. These palms occur in the lowland swamps of Papua New Guinea and in parts of Indonesia, providing a staple food for the Papuans and a useful substitute for rice in other areas.

Sahara A vast desert in North Africa, the largest in the world, covering an area of about 9,065,000 sq km (3,500,000 sq miles) and extending from the Atlantic in the west to the Red Sea in the east. It is bounded in the north by the Mediterranean Sea and the Atlas Mountains and in recent years it has been increasing its southerly extent into the SAHEL.

Sahel A belt of dry savanna on the southern margin of Africa's Sahara Desert. It stretches some 5,000 km (3,125 miles) from Senegal and Mauritania on the Atlantic coast to the Red Sea coast of Sudan and Eritrea. The area, which covers some 20 per cent of Africa's land surface, was the first to bring the problem of desertification to world attention. Droughts have caused widespread famine among its pastoral peoples in recent years.

Said, Edward W(adi) (1935–) US critic, born in Palestine. A professor of English and comparative literature at the University of Columbia, he came to public notice with *Orientalism* (1978) a study of Western attitudes towards Eastern culture. In *The Question of Palestine* (1985), Said defended the Palestinian struggle for political autonomy and has since played an active role in moves to form a Palestinian state. Other works include *Culture and Imperialism* (1993), a critique of Western culture.

Saigon The former name of HO CHI MINH CITY.

sailfish A fish of the Atlantic, Indian, and Pacific oceans, *Istiophorus platypterus*, which migrates with seasonal warming of the sea. It is easily recognized by its long, pointed snout, which is rounded in cross-section, and its very high, sail-like dorsal fin. It is dark blue on the back and the dorsal fin is cobalt blue and ornamented with rounded dark spots. It grows to a length of 3.5 m (11.5 feet).

sailing ships and boats Water-going vessels using sails as a means of propulsion. Ships with a single square sail were built in Egypt some 5,500 years ago: the earliest vessels were made of papyrus reeds. The sail acted as a supplement to crews of oarsmen, and steering-oars over the stern guided the boat. This combination of oars and sail predominated in the Mediterranean and northern Europe for several thousand years. In other parts of the Mediterranean, wooden ships were being built by about 2000 BC. They were nearly all narrow to facilitate rowing, and this design continued to be important in the development of WARSHIPS. In the eastern Mediterranean, broader, shorter merchant ships were developed in which the sail was the main method of propulsion. During Greek and Roman times the long ships for war and the round ships for trade continued to improve: the Greeks perfected a form of the oared GALLEY (the trireme), while the Romans built larger merchant ships, some carrying a small mast and sail forward of the mainmast. From around the 6th century the LATEEN RIG largely replaced the square sail in the Mediterranean until the late Middle Ages.

In China and south-east Asia, sailing vessels developed along different lines. The Chinese JUNK, a large, flat-bottomed vessel with a rudder placed on the centre-line, had sails that could be hauled about, to allow the ship to sail into the wind. In the 15th century junks were larger, stronger, and more seaworthy than any European ships of the period.

Northern ships, such as the cog, were perhaps the earliest European vessels to employ a rudder. The cog was initially a single-masted, square-rigged merchant ship with raised 'castles' at the fore and stern for defence, and was used throughout northern Europe from the 13th to the 15th century. In the Mediterranean, some of these characteristics were copied in the carrack, a large three-masted merchant ship that first appeared in the 16th century. A later development from the carrack was the GALLEON. During the 15th century the three-masted, square-rigged ship evolved out of a merging of the shipbuilding technologies of the Mediterranean and the north. This type became the basic pattern for ships for the next 300 years.

During the 18th century the fore-and-aft rig, long used in smaller boats, became increasingly important in ships (for example, in SCHOONERS). By the late 18th century two-masted ships, such as the BRIG, were becoming more important. From the mid-19th century, STEAMSHIPS offered serious

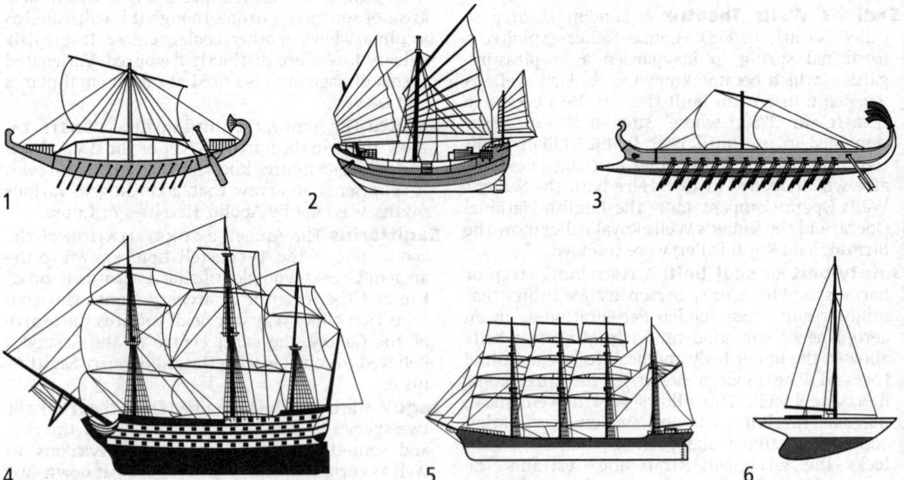

Sailing ships and boats (1) Egyptian trading ship (c.1500 BC). (2) Junk (c.500 BC). (3) Greek trireme with sails and three banks of oars (c.500 BC). (4) 18th-century ship-of-the-line, armed with over 100 guns. (5) Four-masted barque, used as a grain ship in the late 19th and early 20th centuries. (6) Bermuda sloop, the common rig on modern sailing boats.

competition to sail and by 1880 had all but made sailing ships obsolete.

Sailing as a sport increased in popularity early in the 20th century, with the use of fore-and-aft rigged YACHTS and smaller DINGHIES. The size of boat ranges from a small 3 m (10 feet) long dinghy to ocean cruisers of 23 m (75 feet) or more, capable of sailing round the world. See AMERICA'S CUP.

sainfoin A perennial, leafy LEGUME, *Onobrychis sativa*, with a deep taproot, widely grown in North America and Europe. It is a valuable crop for hay, particularly for race-horses.

Sainsbury, John James (1844–1928) British grocer. He opened his first grocery store in London in 1875. After his death the business was continued by members of his family, developing into the large supermarket chain bearing the Sainsbury name.

saint (from Latin *sanctus*, 'holy') A person of remarkable holiness or powerful religious example. In the early Christian Church, all members were referred to as saints. The MARTYRS were considered to be first in rank among the saints. Most religions recognize the status of holy men and women, from Hindu sadhus to Theravada Buddhist *arahats* and Mahayana Buddhist BODHISATTVAS. ISLAM, however, specifically rejects the notion of sainthood, although there are popular local cults of saints, *wali*, particularly in Sufi and Shia practice.

St Agnes, St Barnabas, and other saints See AGNES, ST; BARNABAS, ST; etc.

St Albans A cathedral city in Hertfordshire, England, on the River Ver; pop. (1991) 80,376. The city developed around the abbey of St Albans, which was founded in Saxon times on the site of the martyrdom in 304 AD of ALBAN, a Christian Roman from the nearby Roman city of Verulamium. The ruins of ancient Verulamium lie within the modern city. The cathedral, mostly 11th century, incorporates Roman bricks and tiles.

St Andrews A university town in east Scotland, on the North Sea coast of Fife; pop. (1991) 14,050. It was the ecclesiastical capital of Scotland until the Reformation. Its university, founded in 1411, is the oldest in Scotland and the Royal and Ancient Golf Club is the ruling authority on the game of golf. There are remains of a castle, cathedral, and medieval town wall.

St Bartholomew's Day Massacre (23–24 August 1572) An event that marked a turning-point in the French WARS OF RELIGION. The Catholic GUISE faction prevailed upon Catherine de Medici to authorize an assassination of about 200 of the principal HUGUENOT leaders. Parisian Catholic mobs used these killings as a pretext for large-scale butchery, until some 3,000 Huguenots lay dead, and thousands more perished in the 12 provincial disturbances that followed. COLIGNY was killed in Paris, while HENRY IV of Navarre saved himself by avowing the Catholic faith. Catherine's reputation as a mediator was damaged by the massacre.

St Bernard See DOG.

St Bernard Pass Either of two passes across the Alps in southern Europe. The Great St Bernard Pass, on the border with south-west Switzerland and Italy, rises to 2,469 m (8,100 ft). The Little St Bernard Pass, on the French-Italian border south-east of Mont Blanc, rises to 2,188 m (7,178 ft). Both are named after the hospices founded on their summits in the 11th century by the French monk St BERNARD.

St Christopher and Nevis See SAINT KITTS AND NEVIS.

Sainte-Beuve, Charles Augustin (1804–69) French critic and writer. He is chiefly known for his contribution to 19th-century literary criticism, in which he concentrated on the influence of social and other factors in the development of authors' characters; his critical essays were published in collected form as *Causeries du lundi* (1851–62) and *Nouveaux lundis* (1863–70). He also wrote a study of Jansenism (*Port-Royal*, 1840–59) and was an early champion of French romanticism.

Saint Elmo's fire An electrical discharge sometimes seen during THUNDERSTORMS around high projecting objects, such as the mast of a ship. It occurs because an electric field, concentrating round the sharp projection, has become large enough to produce IONS in the air, which glows as a result. Saint Elmo was a patron saint of sailors and his 'fire' was believed to give protection against storms.

Saint-Exupéry, Antoine (Marie Roger de) (1900–44) French writer and aviator. His best-known work is probably the fable *The Little Prince* (1943). He drew on his experiences as a commercial and air-force pilot in novels such as *Night Flight* (1931). He was shot down and killed while on active service in North Africa during World War II.

St George's The capital of the island of Grenada in the West Indies, situated on a ridge between St George's Harbour and the Caribbean Sea; pop. (1990) 4,440. The port is named after George III.

St George's Channel A channel linking the Irish Sea with the Atlantic Ocean and separating Ireland from mainland Britain.

St Gotthard Pass A high pass rising to an altitude of 2,108 m (6,916 ft) in the Lepontine Alps of southern Switzerland, linking Andermatt and Airolo. Beneath it is a 15-km (9-mile) railway tunnel (constructed in 1872–80) and a road tunnel (opened in 1980).

St Helena A solitary island of volcanic origin in the South Atlantic, a British dependency, famous as the place of Napoleon's exile (1815–21) and death; area 122 sq km (47 sq miles); pop. (1997) 5,644; chief town, Jamestown. St Helena was discovered by the Portuguese navigator Joao da Nova Castella who named it after the mother of Constantine the Great. The island was held by the East India Company from 1659 until 1834 when it became a British colony, and is now administered by a Governor assisted by a Legislative Council.

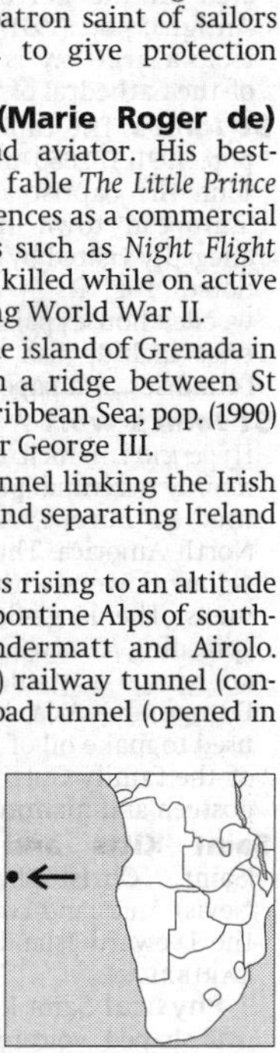

St Helens, Mount A volcanic peak in the Cascade Range, south-west Washington, USA. A dramatic eruption in May 1980 killed 100 people and reduced the height of the mountain from 2,950 m (9,578 ft) to 2,560 m (8,312 ft).

St Helier A market town and resort on the south coast of the island of Jersey on St Aubin's Bay; pop. (1991) 28,120. The town, which is the administrative centre of Jersey, is named after a 6th-century Christian saint who is said to have had a hermitage nearby.

St Ives School A group of British painters who concentrated their activities in the fishing port of St Ives on the north Cornish coast. It was popular with painters from the late 19th century, but it was only after Barbara HEPWORTH and Ben NICHOLSON settled there in 1939 that a colony of artists was established. In 1993 the Tate Gallery opened a small gallery in St Ives, some of which is devoted to the St Ives School. The studio potters Bernard LEACH and Michael Cardew (1901–83) were also based for some time at St Ives.

St James's Palace The old Tudor palace of the monarchs of England in London, built by Henry VIII on the site of an earlier leper hospital dedicated to St James the Less. The palace was the chief royal residence in London from 1697 (when Whitehall was burnt down) until Queen Victoria made Buckingham Palace the monarch's London residence. The Court of St James's is the official title of the British court, to which ambassadors from foreign countries are accredited.

St John, Order of See KNIGHT HOSPITALLER.

St John's The capital of Antigua and Barbuda, situated on the north-west coast of the island of Antigua; pop. (1991) 21,510. The town, which overlooks a large bay, is dominated by the twin towers of the Cathedral of St John the Divine (1845).

St John's The capital of Newfoundland, Canada; pop. (1991) 171,860 (metropolitan area). Named after John the Baptist and claiming to be the oldest 'European' town in North America, the site was allegedly visited by John Cabot in 1497. The town is noted for its traditional square, flat-roofed, wooden houses painted in different colours. Industries include fish processing, shipbuilding, iron foundries, and paper.

St John's wort A plant belonging to the genus *Hypericum*, which contains about 300 species of mainly perennial plants and shrubs widely distributed in Europe, Asia Minor, China, Japan, and North America. The shoots terminate in heads of yellow flowers with a central cluster of long stamens. The large-flowered varieties, such as the spreading *H. calycinum* and the shrubby *H. patulum* are grown as garden plants. *H. perforatum*, from Europe and Asia, has medicinal uses and is also used to make oil of St John's wort. They form part of the family Guttiferae which includes the mangosteen and mammy apple.

Saint Kitts and Nevis (Saint Christopher and Nevis) An island country in the Leeward Islands of the CARIBBEAN.

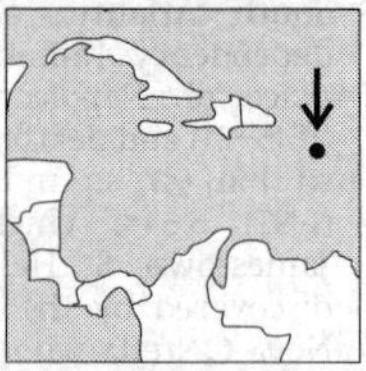

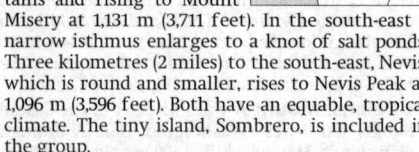

Physical. Saint Kitts is an oval-shaped volcanic island crossed by rugged mountains and rising to Mount Misery at 1,131 m (3,711 feet). In the south-east a narrow isthmus enlarges to a knot of salt ponds. Three kilometres (2 miles) to the south-east, Nevis, which is round and smaller, rises to Nevis Peak at 1,096 m (3,596 feet). Both have an equable, tropical climate. The tiny island, Sombrero, is included in the group.

Economy. Agriculture has been replaced by tourism as the main source of revenue, and both manufacturing and service industries are developing. The chief crops are sugar cane, coconuts, and fruit, and the leading industries are food-processing, electronics, and clothing. Foodstuffs and machinery are the leading exports.

History. Originally inhabited by Caribs, the islands were visited by Christopher Columbus in 1493, who named the larger island Saint Christopher. English settlers in the early 17th century shortened the name to Saint Kitts; this was the first successful English colony in the Caribbean. The islands, together with Anguilla, were united as a single colony in 1882. In 1958, they joined the West Indies Federation. Anguilla became a separate British dependency in 1980, while Saint Kitts and Nevis gained independence within the British Commonwealth in 1983. Nevis has its own legislature and retains the right to secede from Saint Kitts at any time should it so choose. In 1996 the issue of secession was being considered.

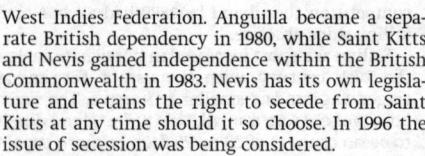

Capital: Basseterre
Area: 269.4 sq km (104.0 sq mi)
Population: 39,400 (1995)
Currency: 1 East Caribbean dollar = 100 cents
Religions: Anglican 32.6%; Methodist 28.8%; Moravian 8.7%; Roman Catholic 7.2%
Ethnic Groups: Black 90.5%; mixed 5.0%; East Indian 3.0%; White 1.5%
Languages: English (official)
International Organizations: UN; OAS; Commonwealth

Saint Laurent, Yves (Mathieu) (1936–) French couturier. He was Christian Dior's assistant from 1953 and after Dior's death in 1957 succeeded him as head designer. His fashions at this time reflected youth culture, and included a 'beatnik' look of turtle-neck sweaters and black leather jackets. He opened his own fashion house in 1962; four years later, he launched the first of a worldwide chain of Rive Gauche boutiques to sell ready-to-wear garments. From the 1970s he expanded the business to include perfumes and household fabrics.

St Lawrence A river of North America flowing 1,287 km (800 miles) from Lake Ontario past Montreal and Quebec City to the **Gulf of St Lawrence**, an inlet of the Atlantic Ocean. The **St Lawrence Seaway**, which includes a number of artificial sections to bypass rapids, enables ocean-going vessels to navigate the entire length of the river and Great Lakes and is 3,768 km (2,342 miles) long. It is a major transport corridor of North America and was inaugurated by Canada and the USA in 1959. Bypassing Niagara Falls, the Welland Canal overcomes the 100 m (326 ft) difference in levels by means of a staircase of seven locks. The Lachine rapids between Lake Ontario and Montreal, with a further 75 m (246 ft) drop, are bypassed by an additional series of locks.

St Louis A city and port in Missouri, USA, a major transportation centre on the Mississippi River; pop. (1990) 396,685. Founded as a fur trading post in 1764, the city was dedicated to Louis XV of France by Pierre Laclede who named it after his 'name' saint, Louis IX of France. It is one of the world's largest markets for wool, timber, and pharmaceuticals and its industries produce beer, chemicals and transportation equipment in addition to processing iron, lead, zinc, copper, aluminium, and magnesium.

Saint Lucia An island country, one of the Windward Islands of the CARIBBEAN.

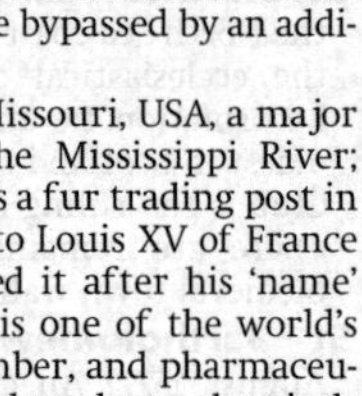

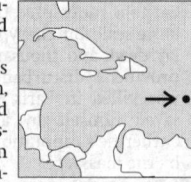

Physical. Saint Lucia is 43 km (27 miles) in length, roughly oval-shaped, and picturesquely rugged, rising to Morne Gimie at 959 m (3,145 feet). In the south-west is the dormant volcano Qualibou with its solfataras (boiling sulphur springs). The twin peaks of the Pitons have fine volcanic cones. The fertile volcanic valleys and coastal plains are well watered and the interior has virgin forests and mineral springs. There is a fine harbour.

Economy. Tourism is an important source of revenue, but agriculture is still predominant. Timber, bananas, cocoa, copra, and coconuts are all grown. Manufactured goods include paper products and clothing, both exported, and there is a food-processing industry.

History. The Arawak Indians, the earliest inhabitants of Saint Lucia, were driven out by Carib Indians before Europeans arrived. The British failed in their attempts to colonize the island in 1605 and 1638 and the French settled it, making a treaty with the Caribs in 1660. Saint Lucia changed hands several times before being ceded to Britain in 1814. A representative local government was established in 1924 and Saint Lucia was a member of the Federation of the West Indies from 1958 until 1962. Saint Lucia became an independent member of the British Commonwealth in 1979, after 12 years of internal self-government. The island has been governed since independence by the United Workers' Party. Its economy was severely affected by the fall in prices for bananas (its chief export) in the European market in 1993. Saint Lucia is a member of the CARIBBEAN COMMUNITY AND COMMON MARKET (CARICOM).

Capital: Castries
Area: 617.4 sq km (238.4 sq mi)
Population: 143,000 (1995)
Currency: 1 East Caribbean dollar = 100 cents
Religions: Roman Catholic 85.6%; Seventh-day Adventist 4.3%; Anglican 2.7%
Ethnic Groups: Black 87.0%; mixed 9.1%; East Indian 2.6%; White 1.3%
Languages: English (official); English and French creoles
International Organizations: UN; OAS; CARICOM; Commonwealth

St Mark's Cathedral A church in Venice, its cathedral church since 1807, built in the 9th century to house the relics of St Mark brought from Alexandria, and rebuilt in the 11th century. It is lavishly decorated with mosaics (11th–13th centuries) and sculptures.

St Moritz A resort and winter-sports centre in Graubünden canton, south-east Switzerland, at an altitude of 1,822 m (5,980 ft). The village of lies on the north shore of the small lake of St Moritz. The chief skiing areas lie on the slopes of Piz Corvatsch (3,303 m, 10,837 ft), Piz Nair (3,057 m, 10,030 ft), and Corviglia (2,486 m, 8,156 ft). The Winter Olympics of 1928 and 1948 were held here.

St Paul The capital of the US state of Minnesota, on the Mississippi River; pop. (1990) 272,250. Founded in 1840 and originally known as Pig's Eye, it prospered on river trade and became capital of the Minnesota Territory in 1849 and the state in 1858. Today St Paul is a major manufacturing and distribution centre for north-central USA. Together with its twin city, Minneapolis, it is a centre for printing, publishing and the production of electronics, computers, trucks, and building materials.

St Paul's Cathedral A Baroque cathedral on Ludgate Hill, London, England, built between 1675 and 1711 by Sir Christopher Wren to replace the medieval cathedral largely destroyed in the Great Fire of 1666. Its crypt has the tombs of Nelson and Wellington.

St Peter's Basilica The Roman Catholic basilica in the Vatican City, Rome, the largest church in Christendom. The present 16th-century building replaced a much older basilican structure erected by Constantine on the supposed site of St Peter's crucifixion. A succession of architects (Bramante, Raphael, Peruzzi, Sangallo) in turn made drastic changes in the design; the dome closely follows a design of Michelangelo.

St Petersburg The second-largest city in Russia, a port near the mouth of the River Neva; pop. (1990) 4,467,000. Founded by Peter the Great in 1703 as a trade outlet to the Baltic, it was capital of Russia from 1712 until 1918 when it was replaced by Moscow. It was called Petrograd (1914–24) and Leningrad (1924–91). Its chief landmarks include the 18th-century Winter Palace (including the Hermitage), the Fortress of Peter and Paul, and the Cathedral of St Isaac. It is a leading industrial city with engineering, shipbuilding, metal refining, chemicals, and many light industries.

St Pierre and Miquelon A group of eight small islands in the North Atlantic, south of Newfoundland, which form the last remnants of the once extensive French possessions in North America; area 242 sq km (93 sq miles); pop. (1990) 6,390; chief town, St Pierre. Since 1985 the islands, whose chief export is fish, have been a Territorial Collectivity of France.

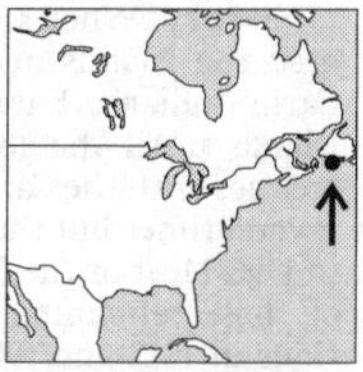

Saint-Saëns, (Charles) Camille (1835–1921) French composer, pianist, and organist. He was organist at the church of the Madeleine in Paris (1858–77) and played an important role in the city's musical life. His works include operas (notably *Samson et Dalila*, 1877) and oratorios, but he is probably now best known for his Third Symphony (1886), the symphonic poem *Danse macabre* (1874), which was the first orchestral piece to use a xylophone, and the *Carnaval des animaux* (1886).

Saint-Simon, Claude-Henri de Rouvroy, Comte de (1760–1825) French social reformer and philosopher. In reaction to the chaos engendered by the French Revolution he developed a new theory of social organization and was later claimed to be the founder of French socialism. His central theory was that society should be organized in an industrial order, controlled by leaders of industry, and given spiritual direction by scientists. His works, which greatly influenced figures such as John Stuart Mill and Friedrich Engels, include *Du système industriel* (1821) and *Nouveau Christianisme* (1825).

Saint-Simon, Louis de Rouvroy, Duc de (1675–1755) French writer. He is best known for his *Mémoires*, a detailed record of court life between 1694 and 1723, in the reigns of Louis XIV and XV.

St Sophia (or **Sancta Sophia**; Turkish **Ayasofia** or **Hagia Sophia**) A church at Constantinople (now Istanbul), dedicated to the 'Holy Wisdom' (i.e. the Person of Christ), built by order of Justinian and inaugurated in 537. It replaced an earlier church built by Constantine the Great in 326 and was designed to surpass all other buildings. The key monument of Byzantine architecture, it has an enormous dome. In 1453, on the day of the Turkish invasion, it was converted into a mosque; the interior mosaics were covered and partly destroyed, and minarets were added. It was used as a mosque until 1935, when ATATÜRK converted it into a museum.

St Swithin's Day See SWITHIN, ST.

Saint Vincent and the Grenadines An island country in the Windward Islands of the CARIBBEAN, consisting of the main island of Saint Vincent and two islets of the Grenadines.

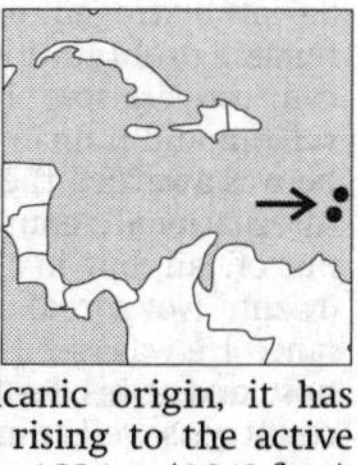

Physical. The main island, Saint Vincent, is 29 km (18 miles) long. Of volcanic origin, it has forested, rugged mountains rising to the active volcano of Mount Soufrière at 1,234 m (4,048 feet).

There are picturesque valleys and fertile well-watered tracts. While the climate is tropical, there are hurricanes and occasional earthquakes.

Economy. Luxury tourism is an important source of revenue, with exports headed by agricultural products such as bananas and vegetables. Manufacturing industry includes food-processing and electronics.

History. When Christopher COLUMBUS discovered the islands in 1498 they were inhabited by Carib Indians. Europeans did not colonize the islands until the 18th century when they made treaties with the Caribs. The islands changed hands several times but the British finally gained control in 1796. Most of the Caribs were deported and most of those remaining were killed in volcanic eruptions in 1812 and 1902. The British brought many African slaves to the islands, and after the abolition of slavery in 1834 many Portuguese and Asian labourers were brought in to work on sugar-cane plantations. The country was a British colony from 1871 until 1956 when colonial rule was ended. Part of the Federation of the West Indies (1958–62), Saint Vincent and the Grenadines became fully independent in 1979. The country has been governed since 1984 by the right-wing New Democratic Party.

Capital: Kingstown
Area: 389.3 sq km (150.3 sq mi)
Population: 112,000 (1995)
Currency: 1 East Caribbean dollar = 100 cents
Religions: Anglican 36.0%; Methodist 20.4%; Roman Catholic 19.3%; Seventh-day Adventist 4.1%; Plymouth Brethren 3.9%
Ethnic Groups: Blacks 74.0%; mixed 19.0%; White 3.0%; Amerindian 2.0%; East Indian 2.0%
Languages: English (official); English creole
International Organizations: UN; OAS; CARICOM; Commonwealth

saithe pollock See COALFISH.

saker falcon A large FALCON of eastern Europe and Asia, *Falco cherrug*, which winters in the eastern Mediterranean region, Arabia, and northeast Africa. Dark-plumaged, it is otherwise similar in most respects to the peregrine, being a fierce and skilled hunter of birds on the wing. Unlike the peregrine it is adapted to life in dry, hot, desert conditions.

Sakha, Republic of The official name of YAKUTIA in the Russian Federation.

Sakhalin An elongated Russian island, roughly 1,000 km (620 miles) long and oriented north–south, in the Sea of Okhotsk. It is separated from the Pacific coast of Siberia by the Tatar Strait and from the Japanese island of Hokkaido by La Perouse Strait. The northern part of the island, opposite the delta of the Amur, is relatively low-lying and includes the Manchili Plain – a tundra environment. The remainder comprises subdued mountain ranges. Crabs, herrings, cod, and salmon are fished; other industries include petroleum extraction, coal mining, and lumbering.

Sakharov, Andrei (Dmitrievich) (1921–89) Russian nuclear physicist. Having helped to develop the Soviet hydrogen bomb, he campaigned against nuclear proliferation and called for Soviet–American cooperation. He fought courageously for reform and human rights in the USSR, for which he was awarded the Nobel Peace Prize in 1975. His international reputation as a scientist kept him out of jail, but in 1980 he was banished to Gorky (Nizhni Novgorod) and kept under police surveillance. He was freed (1986) in the new spirit of glasnost, and at his death he was honoured in his own country as well as in the West.

Saki (pseudonym of Hector Hugh Munro) (1870–1916) British short-story writer and journalist. He wrote political satire for the *Westminster Gazette* and was correspondent for the *Morning Post* in Poland, Russia, and Paris. He was best known for his short stories, which were collected in *Reginald* (1904) and other volumes, including *Reginald in Russia* (1910), *The Chronicles of Clovis* (1911), *Beasts and Super-Beasts* (1914), and *The Square Egg* (1924). They include the satirical, the macabre, and the supernatural. He also wrote a novel, *The Unbearable Bassington* (1912). He was killed in France in World War I.

Saladin (Arabic name Salah-ad-Din Yusuf ibn-Ayyub) (1137–93) Sultan of Egypt and Syria 1174–93. He invaded the Holy Land and reconquered Jerusalem from the Christians (1187), and, for a period, resisted the Third Crusade, the leaders of which included Richard the Lionheart. He was later defeated by Richard at Arsuf (1191) and withdrew to Damascus, where he died.

Salam, Abdus (1926–96) Pakistani theoretical physicist. He worked on the interaction of subatomic particles, and independently developed a unified theory to explain electromagnetic interactions and the weak nuclear force. In 1979 he shared the Nobel Prize for physics, the first Nobel laureate from his country.

Salamanca A city on the River Tormes in the Castilla-León region of western Spain, capital of Salamanca province; pop. (1991) 185,990. It was the scene of a victory of the British under Wellington over the French in 1812, during the Peninsular War. It is an agricultural centre with industries producing pharmaceuticals, textiles, and rubber goods.

salamander An animal belonging to the order Caudata, of tailed AMPHIBIANS. The true salamanders, belonging to the family Salamandridae, include the newts and such species as the fire salamander, *Salamandra salamandra*. Typically, true salamanders are lizard-like, although the skin is not scaly. Most species have a tadpole, or larval, stage, though some species, such as the European fire salamander, give birth to fully metamorphosed (transformed) young. Some species of 'false' salamander, such as the olm and the blind salamanders from Texas and Georgia, USA, remain as permanent larvae, which are capable of breeding in the larval state. Salamanders are principally a northern temperate group of amphibians, found in North America, Europe, North Africa, and Asia.

Salamis An island in the Saronic Gulf in Greece. In the straits between it and the western coast of Attica the Greek fleet under Themistocles crushingly defeated the Persian fleet of Xerxes in 480 BC at the **Battle of Salamis**.

Salazar, Antonio de Oliveira (1889–1970) Portuguese statesman, Prime Minister 1932–68. While Finance Minister (1928–40), he formulated austere fiscal policies to effect Portugal's economic recovery. During his long premiership, he ruled the country as a virtual dictator, firmly suppressing opposition and enacting a new authoritarian constitution along Fascist lines. Salazar maintained Portugal's neutrality throughout the Spanish Civil War and World War II.

Salem ►**1** A city and port in north-east Massachusetts, USA; pop. (1990) 38,090. First settled in 1626, it became a centre of shipbuilding and was until 1812 a major port of the China trade. It was the scene of a series of celebrated witchcraft trials in 1692, when 19 witches were tried and executed. ►**2** The capital of the US state of Oregon, on the

Willamette River; pop. (1990) 107,790. Settled by missionaries in 1841, it became state capital in 1859. Its industries produce processed food and high-tech equipment.

Salerno A port and centre of light industries on the coast of Campania, south-west Italy, 48 km (30 miles) south-east of Naples; pop. (1990) 151,370. It is capital of the province of Salerno and has a noted university and medical school. Heavy fighting occurred in World War II, after an Allied landing here in 1943. Nearby are the ruins of the ancient Greek city of Paestum.

Salford An industrial city in Greater Manchester, England; pop. (1991) 79,755. Engineering and the manufacture of textiles, chemicals, and electrical goods are its chief industries. It has a university (1967) founded in 1896 as the Royal Technical Institute.

Salic law The legal code of the Salian FRANKS, which originated in 5th century Gaul. It was issued by CLOVIS (465–511) and reissued under the CAROLINGIANS. It contained both criminal and civil clauses and provided for penal fines for offenders. It also laid down that daughters could not inherit land and was later used in France and in some German principalities to prevent daughters succeeding to the throne.

Salieri, Antonio (1750–1825) Italian composer. His output includes more than 40 operas, four oratorios, and much church music. He lived in Vienna for many years and taught Beethoven, Schubert, and Liszt. Salieri was hostile to Mozart and an unlikely story arose that he poisoned him.

Salinger, J(erome) D(avid) (1919–) US novelist and short-story writer. He is best known for his colloquial novel of adolescence *The Catcher in the Rye* (1951). His other works include *Franny and Zooey* (1961).

Salisbury A market town in Wiltshire, southern England, noted for its 13th-century cathedral whose 14th-century spire is the highest in England (123 m, 404 ft) and whose clock is one of the oldest still working. The cathedral library houses one of the four copies of the MAGNA CARTA; pop. (1991) 39,268. The Roman name for Salisbury was Sorbiodonum, abbreviated in medieval times to Sarum. The modern city of Salisbury is also known as New Sarum. Old Sarum, site of an Iron Age fort and early cathedral, was abandoned in 1220, when the 'new' cathedral was built in New Sarum.

Salisbury The former name (until 1980) of HARARE, capital of Zimbabwe.

Salisbury, Robert Arthur Talbot Gascoigne-Cecil, 3rd Marquess of (1830–1903) British Conservative statesman, Prime Minister 1885–86, 1886–92, and 1895–1902. His main area of concern was foreign affairs; he was a firm defender of British imperial interests and supported the policies that resulted in the Second Boer War (1899–1902).

Salisbury Plain A large area of open-undulating chalky downland in Wiltshire, southern England, part of which is a military training area. STONEHENGE stands on Salisbury Plain and there are many other minor prehistoric remains.

saliva A juice containing an enzyme (ptyalin, or salivary amylase), salts, and mucus. It is formed by the salivary glands and lubricates the lining membranes and contents of the mouth so that swallowing becomes possible. It dissolves substances, such as sugar, which increases sensations of taste. Ptyalin breaks down starches into sugars.

Salk, Jonas Edward (1914–95) US microbiologist. He worked in the early 1950s on developing a safe vaccine for polio, first having to devise a method of growing the virus in chick embryos and then killing the virus to make it harmless. After 1954, the vaccine was successfully injected into millions of people. It has now been largely replaced by the oral SABIN vaccine. Salk was director of the Salk Institute at the University of California 1963–75.

Sallust (full name Gaius Sallustius Crispus) (86–35 BC) Roman historian and politician. As a historian he was concerned with the political decline of Rome after the fall of Carthage in 146 BC, to which he accorded a simultaneous moral decline. His chief surviving works deal with the Catiline conspiracy and the Jugurthine War.

salmon Any of seven species of migratory fish that breed in fresh water and migrate to the sea to feed and mature, returning to spawn between one and four years later. The Atlantic salmon, *Salmo salar*, breeds in rivers in Europe and North America, and many travel to the seas around Greenland for their feeding migration. In the North Pacific region there are six species of salmon, all members of the genus *Oncorhynchus*, which are distinguished from the Atlantic species by the greater number of rays in the anal fin. Many of these, like the sockeye, *O. nerka*, and the king or chinook salmon, *O. tshawytscha*, are important commercial fishes for canning, but all salmon are valuable food-fishes. They feed on crustaceans and other fishes while in the sea and grow rapidly. All the Pacific salmon die after spawning in the gravelly shallows of rivers, as do many Atlantic salmon, but some of the latter survive to spawn two or three times.

Salmonella A genus of rodlike bacteria that inhabit the intestines of animals and man and can cause several diseases. *S. paratyphi* causes paratyphoid and *S. typhi* causes typhoid fever. *S. typhimurium* is a common cause of food poisoning. Other species infect other animals and birds.

Salome The stepdaughter of HEROD Antipas and daughter of Herodias. Struck by the gracefulness of her dancing, Herod Antipas offered to reward her with whatever gift she desired. Prompted by her mother, she asked for and received the head of John the Baptist, who had objected to Herodias's marriage to Herod, who was her uncle.

Salonica see THESSALONÍKI.

Sālote Tupou III See TONGA.

salpiglossis A plant of the genus *Salpiglossis*, from Chile, related to the potato but more ornamental. *S. sinuata*, a large-flowered annual species with a great deal of colour variation, is grown as a pot plant in greenhouses or as an outdoor border plant in temperate regions.

salsify *Tragopogon porrifolius*, a member of the sunflower family with large, attractive, purplish flower-heads resembling those of a dandelion. Sometimes grown as an ornamental, it flowers in its second year. A native of southern Europe, it is more commonly grown for its carrot-like, white roots, which may be eaten boiled, baked, or in soups and are said to resemble oysters in taste. The young leaves of this 'oyster plant' are sometimes used in salads.

salt (in chemistry) A type of compound formed by reaction between ACIDS and BASES. Salts are usually crystalline IONIC COMPOUNDS. A typical example is SODIUM CHLORIDE ($NaCl$, also known as common salt), which can be formed by the reaction between hydrochloric acid (HCl) and sodium hydroxide ($NaOH$).

SALT See STRATEGIC ARMS LIMITATION TALKS.

Salt Lake City The capital and largest city of the US state of Utah, on the Jordan River near the southern shore of the Great Salt Lake; pop. (1990) 159,940. Founded in 1847 by Brigham Young for the Mormon community, the city is the world headquarters of the Church of Jesus Christ of Latter-Day Saints. Its industries produce processed food, electronic goods, aerospace equipment, agricultural chemicals, and refined minerals.

salt-marshes Flat, poorly drained areas of land subject to periodic or occasional inundation by salt water. They are commonly situated along sheltered, low-lying coasts, although they can also occur inland in salt lake basins. Coastal salt-marshes generally form in protected environments behind shingle bars and sand-pits; but they can also form in the sheltered parts of estuaries when silt and mud are deposited during times of slack water between the tides.

saltpetre See POTASSIUM NITRATE; NITRATES; GUNPOWDER.

Salvador (or **Bahia**) A port on the Atlantic coast of north-east Brazil, capital of the state of Bahia; pop. (1991) 2,075,270. Founded in 1549, Salvador and its surrounding sugar-cane plantations were the economic heartland of colonial Brazil. It was capital until 1763 and after Lisbon, the second city of the Portuguese empire. Salvador is divided into the historic hilltop site of the original settlement (Cidade Alta) and the commercial, financial, and port district (Cidade Baixa). Oil refining and the production of petrochemicals are its chief industries, the bulk of which are located in Brazil's first planned industrial park (Centro Industrial de Aratu).

Salvation Army An international Protestant evangelical and charitable organization, founded in London in 1865 by William BOOTH as the Christian Revival Association. Preaching in the slums of London, Booth used unconventional methods to win people to Christianity, insisting on militant teetotalism and revivalism. In 1878 his mission took on the name Salvation Army, run on military lines, and with a fundamentalist approach to religion. The Army placed emphasis on welfare work and devoted much time to helping the destitute. It expanded rapidly not only in Britain but also overseas; in the USA Ballington Booth, a son of the founder, set up (1896) a splinter group, the Volunteers of America. The Salvation Army offers a successful missing persons bureau.

salvia A member of a large genus, *Salvia*, of annual, biennial, or perennial plants or small shrubs, with about 500 species. They are distributed throughout temperate and subtropical regions and belong to the mint family. Many species are used as decorative plants in the greenhouse and garden, while some, such as SAGE, are culinary herbs. Varieties of *S. splendens*, with compact spikes of scarlet flowers, are treated as half-hardy annuals in temperate regions.

Salyut See SPACE STATION.

Salzburg ▶1 A federal state of central Austria that takes its name from the rich deposits of salt that have been mined for centuries in the Salzburg Alps; pop. (1991) 483,880. **▶2** Its capital city, noted for its music festivals, one of which is dedicated to the composer Mozart who was born in the city in 1756; pop. (1991) 143,970.

samādhi (Sanskrit, 'making firm', 'putting together') The highest goal of YOGA, representing a total absorption or concentration upon the object of MEDITATION. In BUDDHISM, *samādhi* is a stage of meditation, and the last stage of the NOBLE EIGHTFOLD PATH.

Samaria The ancient capital of the northern kingdom of the Hebrews in central Palestine, now occupied by the village of Sabastiyah in the West Bank north-west of Nablus. Built in the 9th century BC, it was captured in 721 BC by the Assyrians and resettled with people from other parts of their empire (2 Kings 17,18). In New Testament times Samaria was rebuilt and greatly enlarged by Herod the Great. It is the alleged burial place of John the Baptist.

Samaritans ▶1 The people of ancient Samaria. They adopted a form of Judaism, but were disliked by the Jews. Only a small number of Samaritans survive (in Nablus). **▶2** A voluntary organization founded in 1953 by the Rev. Chad Varah (1911–) to listen to (on the telephone or face-to-face) those who are suicidal or in despair. The Samaritans offer a 24-hour service in some 200 centres in the UK manned by over 23,000 trained volunteers. A nonreligious charity, it offers confidential, anonymous, and nonprofessional support to anyone in distress. Many overseas branches are affiliated to its associated organization Befrienders International.

samarium (symbol Sm, at. no. 62, r.a.m. 150.36) A LANTHANIDE element discovered spectroscopically in 1879. It occurs in monazite and bastnaesite; it is used in the form of its oxide (Sm_2O_3) in special glasses and some lasers.

Samarkand (Uzbek **Samarqand**) A city in the Uzbekistan, Central Asia; pop. (1990) 369,900. One of the oldest cities in Asia, Samarkand was destroyed by Alexander the Great in 329 BC but later rose to fame as the centre of the silk trade. It was destroyed again by Genghis Khan in 1221 but later became the capital of Tamerlane's empire. By 1700 it was almost deserted, but in 1868 it was taken by Russia and in 1924 was incorporated into the Uzbek Soviet Socialist Republic, briefly becoming its capital. Its chief industries are the production of cotton and silk.

samba A dance from Brazil. It has two distinct forms: the rural samba, which has African influences and a complicated rhythmic structure; and the urban samba, known as the 'samba-carioca', a more popularized form developed in the dance-halls of Rio de Janeiro.

samizdat (Russian, 'self publishing') Unofficial writings circulated in the former Soviet Union and Eastern bloc, expressing the views of dissident groups and individuals in defiance of official censorship and controls. The samizdat movement took shape in the 1950s and was intensified following the death of Stalin and the 'thaw' of the mid-1950s.

Samnite wars A succession of wars fought between the southern neighbours of Rome, the Samnites and the Latins. The first war (343–341 BC) was brief, but the second (326–304) was more protracted. Roman troops experienced the humiliation of having to walk like slaves under a yoke of spears after their defeat at the Caudine Forks. The APPIAN WAY was begun in 312 to assist communications between Rome and the war area. Gauls joined against Rome in the third of the wars (298–290), but were defeated. The Samnites were consistently hostile to Rome. They helped HANNIBAL in the second PUNIC WAR and revolted for the last time in the Social War of 90, after which they became allies of MARIUS. SULLA crushed them and devastated their homelands.

Samoa A group of islands in Polynesia. The group

was divided administratively in 1899 into American Samoa in the east and German Samoa in the west. The latter, mandated to New Zealand in 1919, gained independence in 1962 as WESTERN SAMOA. See also AMERICAN SAMOA.

Samos A Greek Island in the eastern Aegean Sea, close to the west coast of Turkey; area 476 sq km (184 sq miles); pop. (1991) 41,850; chief town, Vathy. An important commercial centre in the 7th century BC, Samos has as its chief monument of antiquity the Heraion or Sanctuary of Hera, and it is said to be the birthplace of the Greek philosopher Pythagoras. Wine, tobacco, timber, and olive oil are its chief products.

Sampras, Pete (1971–) US tennis player who won the US Open in 1990 (shortly after his 19th birthday) and 1993. He was singles champion of Wimbledon for three consecutive years (1993–1995) and again in 1997.

samsara (Sanskrit, 'journeying through') A central notion within HINDUISM and BUDDHISM denoting the way in which successive lives are determined by the laws of KARMA. In Hinduism, the soul continues to be reborn in a variety of forms, according to its actions in past lives, until release (*moksha*) is achieved. Buddhism rejects the existence of the soul but clearly recognizes a spiritual link between successive lives (see DEPENDENT ORIGINATION).

samskāra (Sanskrit, 'making perfect') Personal rites of passage and purification within HINDUISM. There are 16 *samskāras*, beginning with rituals connected with conception, pregnancy, and birth; they continue by marking each stage of life, until the final set of ceremonies after death.

Samson Judge of Israel, the Hebrew hero whose legendary strength reputedly came from his long hair, which, as a Nazirite, he had vowed to God never to cut. Bribed by the enemies of his people, the Philistines, Delilah seduced him and cut it off, enabling him to be captured, blinded, and imprisoned in Gaza. He regained his strength as his hair grew and he exacted revenge by pulling down the pillars of the temple of the Philistines, destroying himself and those who had mocked him.

Samuel (11th century BC) Israelite leader and prophet. He was the last leader (judge) of the tribes of ISRAEL before the establishment of hereditary kingship. Ruling during a period of PHILISTINE domination of Israel, he rallied his people in opposition to them. He was instrumental in creating the monarchy by anointing SAUL as the first King of Israel. Samuel provided Saul with prophetic advice until they had a disagreement over his priestly duties, and he then anointed DAVID as the next king.

samurai (from Japanese, 'those who serve') Warrior retainers of Japan's daimyo (feudal lords). Prominent from the 12th century, they were not a separate class until Hideyoshi limited the right to bear arms to them, after which they became a hereditary caste. Their two swords were their badge. Their conduct was regulated by *Bushido* (Warrior's Way), a strict code that emphasized the qualities of loyalty, bravery, and endurance. Their training from childhood was spartan. Their ultimate duty when defeated or dishonoured was *seppuku*, ritual self-disembowelment.

Sana'a (or **San'a**) The capital of the Republic of Yemen and of the former Yemen Arab Republic (1967–90); pop. (est. 1993) 926,600. It lies inland on a high plateau 2,286 m (7,500 ft) above sea-level. It is claimed by the Arabs to be the world's oldest city. Its medina is one of the largest completely preserved walled city centres in the Arab world, many of its decorated tower houses being over 400 years old. It is a noted centre of handicrafts and also has a textile factory and iron foundry.

San Andreas fault A fault line or fracture of the Earth's crust extending for some 965 km (600 miles) through the length of California, USA. Seismic activity is common along its course and is ascribed to movement of two plates of the Earth's crust – the eastern Pacific plate and the North American plate – which abut in this region. The city of San Francisco lies close to the fault; its devastating earthquake of 1906 and further convulsions in 1989 and 1994 are all attributed to this fault.

San Antonio An industrial city in south-central Texas, USA, on the San Antonio River; pop. (1990) 935,930. The Mission San Antonio de Valero (the Alamo) was founded here in 1718 and a military post was established by the Spanish Governor of the Province of Texas. The Alamo was defended by Texan heroes during the Mexican siege of 1836. Amongst its most prominent landmarks is the 229-m (750-ft) high Tower of the Americas. Its industries produce, beer, aircraft, electronic equipment, textiles, and chemicals.

San Cristóbal The capital of the state of Táchira in western Venezuela is a commercial and industrial centre, situated in the northern Andes on terraces overlooking the River Torbes; pop. (1991) 220,700; 364,730 (metropolitan area). Textiles, ceramics, leather goods, cement, and tobacco are produced.

sanctions Coercive or punitive measures taken by one or more countries (or an international organization) against another to force a change in policy or to secure fulfilment of international obligations. Such measures may involve BOYCOTT and the complete or partial interruption of economic and cultural links, communications, and diplomatic relations. The UNITED NATIONS SECURITY COUNCIL is empowered to order mandatory sanctions against an offending country.

sand Grains of rock and mineral particles (often quartz grains) with sizes between 2 and 0.0625 mm (about 0.08–0.0025 inch). It results from the disintegration of rocks by weathering and erosion, especially in dry climates, and may be formed by the action of the sea, by rivers, by wind action, or by the melt-waters of glaciers. It is used to make glass and, mixed with lime and gravel, cement.

Sand, George (pseudonym of Amandine-Aurore Lucille Dupin, Baronne Dudevant) (1804–76) French novelist. In 1831 she left her husband to lead an independent literary life in Paris. Her earlier romantic novels, including *Lélia* (1833), portray women's struggles against conventional morals; she later wrote a number of pastoral novels (for example *La Mare au diable*, 1846). Among her other works are *Elle et lui* (1859), a fictionalized account of her affair with the poet Alfred de Musset (1810–57), and *Un Hiver à Majorque* (1841), describing an episode during her ten-year relationship with the composer Chopin.

sand-dollar A flat, disc-shaped SEA URCHIN that has lost the regular spherical symmetry of its relatives. Sand-dollars are often biscuit-like, only the five-rayed marking on the surface revealing their ECHINODERM affinities. Some have slits or notches in their internal skeleton (test), and the spines are usually very short to allow efficient burrowing by the many specialized hydraulic tube-feet.

sand-eel (or **sand-lance**) A small fish of the family Ammodytidae, of which 12 species are known.

The family is best represented in the northern Atlantic, where there are eight species. They are long, slender fishes with a pointed head, protuberant lower jaw, long dorsal and anal fins, and a forked tail. The largest is the European greater sand-eel, *Ammodytes*, growing to 32 cm (13 inches). It burrows in clean sand but feeds on planktonic organisms. All sand-eels are eaten by fishes and seabirds.

sanderling A species of small SANDPIPER, *Calidris alba*, which has chestnut and white plumage while breeding in the Arctic, and white and grey plumage for the winter migration to the southern continents. They are exceedingly active birds, following the tideline to feed upon shrimps and molluscs stranded by the receding waves.

sand fly A small, blood-sucking fly of the genus *Phlebotomus*, which can inflict painful bites. Sand flies are found in warm countries, and are notorious as VECTORS for various disease organisms, including those that cause kala-azar and oriental sores in South America, northern Africa, and southern Asia.

sandgrouse A bird, making up a separate family, Pteroclididae, of which there are 16 species, all resembling ground-living pigeons. They live in arid or semi-arid areas of Africa, Europe, and western Asia. They are not related to true GROUSE. Their upper parts are usually well camouflaged in mottled greys and browns, but their undersides may have bolder markings such as yellow, reddish-brown, or black. They often fly in large flocks, and regularly move long distances at dusk or dawn to reach water. They lay two or three eggs in a simple scrape in the ground. When they are rearing young, the males of several species transport water back to the chicks soaking their belly feathers which absorb the water and enable the chicks to drink without leaving their desert homes. Sandgrouse feed mainly on fruits, berries, and seeds.

sandhopper (or **beach flea**) A terrestrial AMPHIPOD that lives among driftwood or other debris along the strandline of the sea-shore, digging short burrows amongst the dead seaweed and scavenging. Sandhoppers scull rapidly along the sand, and can jump using a rapid flick of the abdomen. One species, *Talorchestia*, 2 cm (0.8 inch) long, can leap a distance of 1 m (3 feet). They have well-developed eyes, and they use the angle of the Sun and polarization of its light to locate their normal zone on the beach.

Sandhurst The Royal Military Academy, Sandhurst: a training college, now at Camberley, Surrey, for officers for the British Army. It was formed in 1946 from an amalgamation of the Royal Military College at Sandhurst in Berkshire (founded 1799) and the Royal Military Academy at Woolwich, London (founded 1741).

San Diego An industrial city and US naval port on the Pacific coast of southern California; pop. (1990) 1,110,550. The San Diego de Alcalá Mission (1769) was the first to be established in California. It has large aerospace, electronic and shipbuilding industries and is a processing centre for a very productive agricultural area. Its climate, beaches and historical attractions are the basis of its tourist industry. San Diego is also a cultural, educational, and medical centre.

Sandinista Liberation Front See NICARAGUA.

Sand Island See MIDWAY ISLANDS.

sand lizard A species of LIZARD found over much of Europe, extending to central Asia. It is a stout species, growing up to 19 cm (7.5 inches) in length, and is a representative of the family Lacertidae. This family includes many familiar European species, such as the viviparous, or common, lizard, *Lacerta vivipara*, and the green lizard, *Lacerta viridis*. In England it is a protected species found on sandy heathland and dunes, but in other parts of its range it also occurs on embankments, and in hedgerows and fields.

sand martin Any of four species of martin in the genus *Riparia*, members of the swallow family, Hirundinidae. The most common sand martin, *R. riparia*, is known in the New World as the bank swallow. It breeds over wide areas of Europe, Asia, and North America, migrating southwards to the tropics in winter. It is a small bird, 12 cm (5 inches) long, brown above and whitish below with a brown breast-band. Sand martins are insectivorous and get their name from building nests (often in colonies of considerable size) in the banks of rivers, sand quarries, etc.

sandpiper A WADING BIRD of the family Scolopacidae, allied to godwits, curlews and snipe, and comprising some 75 species. Strictly, the name refers to members of the genera *Tringa* and *Calidris*. Sandpipers are generally small, brown and white birds, which are 15–30 cm (6–12 inches) long; some species are slender with long beaks and legs, like the redshank, others are dumpy and short-legged like. the dunlin. The common sandpiper and some others prefer inland habitats, but the majority are birds of the estuary and seashore. Unlike their relatives in the plover family, which are largely tropical, the sandpipers are mainly northern in distribution. Some species are known as peeps in North America.

Sandringham House A holiday residence of the British royal family, north-east of King's Lynn in Norfolk. The estate was acquired in 1861 by Queen Victoria for Edward VII, then Prince of Wales.

sandstone An important class of SEDIMENTARY ROCK, consisting of consolidated deposits of material, predominantly sand-sized. Usually rich in quartz grains, sandstones can be cemented by various materials, including silica and calcium carbonate. They form in various ways. Some, such as ARKOSES, form by the accumulation of material weathered from pre-existing rocks (terrigenous sandstones). Most are formed in the sea; some are deposited in freshwater lakes; others are the products of wind action (having formed as DUNES) or have been deposited from glacial meltwaters. Some, such as GREYWACKES, are the products of rapid deposition. Many varieties of sandstone are quarried and used as building stone or crushed for building aggregate.

sand wasp A solitary wasp of the family Sphecidae that digs burrows in sand. Some species provision each burrow with a single large caterpillar before laying an egg and then sealing the burrow. Others go on providing food as the larva grows, showing early traces of social behaviour. Some adult sand wasps are quite large insects with a very thin 'stalk' joining their abdomen to the thorax.

Sandwich Islands The former name of the Pacific islands of HAWAII.

San Francisco A city and seaport on the Pacific coast of California, USA, with a magnificent land-locked harbour entered by a channel called the Golden Gate; pop. (1990) 723,960. Built on a series of hills, the original settlement dates from the founding of a mission in 1776. Under Mexican rule it was known as Yerba Buena, but after it had been taken by the US Navy in 1846 its name was changed to

San Francisco. It grew rapidly after the 1848 gold-rush, and in 1869 it became the western terminus of the first transcontinental railroad. In 1906 it was badly damaged by a severe earthquake and again in 1989 (see SAN ANDREAS FAULT). It is a leading US financial and cultural centre, and the beauty of its setting and its climate make it an attractive residential city. It is a major centre of trade with eastern Asia and the Pacific. Industries include shipbuilding, oil refining, metals, chemicals, and foodstuffs.

Sanger, Frederick (1918–) British biochemist. Sanger worked mainly for the Medical Research Council, becoming a divisional head of the Molecular Biology Laboratory at Cambridge in 1961. He worked first on the structure of proteins, determining the complete amino-acid sequence of insulin in 1955, and later on the structure of nucleic acids, establishing the complete nucleotide sequence of a viral DNA in 1977. Sanger twice received the Nobel Prize for chemistry, in 1958 and 1980.

Sanger, Margaret (Higgins) (1883–1966) US birth-control campaigner. Her experiences as a nurse from 1912 prompted her two years later to distribute the pamphlet *Family Limitation* in defence of birth control. Legal proceedings were initiated against her for disseminating 'obscene' literature, but these were dropped in 1916. In the same year she founded the first US birth-control clinic in Brooklyn, serving as its president for seven years. She also set up the first World Population Conference in Geneva in 1927 and became the first president of the International Planned Parenthood Federation in 1953.

Sanhedrin (from Greek *synedrion*, 'council') The supreme court of the JEWISH PEOPLE, headed by the high priest, before the fall of JERUSALEM in 70 AD. It was probably founded around the 2nd century BC. Under the Romans its jurisdiction covered Palestinian Jews in civil and religious matters, though capital sentences required Roman confirmation.

San José The capital of Costa Rica; pop. (1995) 318,765. Founded in 1737 and made capital of the newly independent state of Costa Rica in 1823, it is laid out in a grid plan. It is a trade centre for coffee, cocoa, and sugar.

San Juan The capital and chief port of the island of Puerto Rico; pop. (1990) 437,745. Its main industry is tourism but it also manufactures clothing, cigars, and cigarettes, rum, and refined sugar. It has the oldest church in continuous use in the Americas (San José, founded 1523), and a school of tropical medicine.

San Marino, Republic of A tiny landlocked country near the Adriatic Sea in east-central Italy.

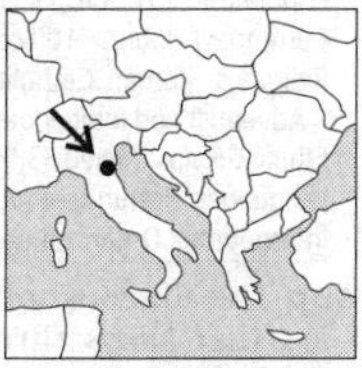

Physical. San Marino lies at the foot of the Apennine Mountains. It is entirely surrounded by Italian territory.

Economy. The economy is dominated by tourism and agriculture, with postage stamps an important source of foreign currency. Building stone from Mount Titano is exported.

History. First chronicled in the 4th century AD, San Marino was an independent commune by the 12th century. After Italy became a nation-state in 1862, it guaranteed San Marino its independence. The country's parliament is headed by two captains-regent, who are elected every six months.

Capital: San Marino
Area: 61.19 sq km (23.63 sq mi)
Population: 24,900 (1995)
Currency: 1 San Marino lira = 100 centesimi
Religions: Roman Catholic 95.0%
Ethnic Groups: Sammarinesi 85.8%; Italian 13.8%
Languages: Italian (official)
International Organizations: UN; CSCE; Council of Europe

San Martín, José de (1778–1850) Argentinian soldier and statesman. Having assisted in the liberation of his country from Spanish rule (1812–13) he went on to aid Bernardo O'Higgins in the liberation of Chile (1817–18). He was also involved in gaining Peruvian independence, becoming Protector of Peru in 1821; he resigned a year later after differences with the other great liberator Simón Bolívar.

San Pedro Sula The second-largest city in Honduras, capital of the department of Cortés in the Ulúa valley; pop. (est. 1991) 325,900. It is a trade centre for coffee, bananas, sugar, and timber, and has steel mills, textiles, plastics and many light industries which, together with good communications, make it central America's fastest-growing town.

sansa A musical instrument with a number of flexible tongues, usually made of iron but sometimes of reed, fixed to a board or box and plucked with thumbs and forefingers. Used all over sub-Saharan Africa, either by itself or accompanying singing, it has many names; approximations to *sansa, mbira, likembe*, and *kalimba* are the commonest.

San Salvador The capital of El Salvador, at an altitude of 680 m (2,230 ft) on the Acelhuate River; pop. (1992) 422,520; 1,522,120 (Greater Metropolitan area). The San Salvador volcano rises to 1,885 m (6,184 ft) to the north-west. It is principally concerned with processing the locally grown coffee but has many light industries.

sans-culotte Originally, a member of the volunteer republican 'army' of the early FRENCH REVOLUTION. 'Sansculotte' ('without knee-breeches'), was chosen by the revolutionaries to describe the labourer's loose-fitting linen garment worn by their supporters. During the Reign of Terror public functionaries styled themselves *citoyens sansculottes*, with a distinctive costume: *pantalon* (long trousers), *carmagnole* (short-skirted coat), red cap of liberty, and *sabots* (wooden clogs).

Sanskrit The ancient language of Hindus in India, belonging to a branch of the Indo-European family of languages. It flourished in India as the language of learning for more than three millennia, well into the 19th century, but has been gradually eclipsed by English and the modern Indian languages (e.g. Hindi, Bengali, Gujarati) to which, as a spoken language, it gave rise, and is now used only for religious purposes. It is written in the Devanagari script.

Sansovino, Jacopo (born Jacopo Tatti) (1486–1570) Italian sculptor and architect. He was city architect of Venice from 1529, where his buildings include the Palazzo Corner (1533) and St Mark's Library (begun 1536), all of which show the influence of his early training in Rome and the development of classical architectural style for contemporary use. His sculpture includes the colossal statues *Mars* and *Neptune* (1554–56) for the staircase of the Doges' Palace.

Santa Cruz A leading commercial city in the agricultural central region of Bolivia, capital of the department of Santa Cruz; pop. (1992) 694,610. Founded by the Spanish in 1561 as Santa Cruz de la Sierra, the city proved vulnerable to attack by local

Indians and was moved westwards to its current site at the end of the 16th century. It has expanded rapidly since the building of road and rail links in the 1950s and 1960s. It exports oil and natural gas.

Santa Cruz de Tenerife The capital of the Canary Islands and chief city of the island of Tenerife; pop. (1991) 191,970. Admiral Nelson lost his arm in a naval action near here in 1797. The port trades in fruit and acts as a refuelling centre. It is also a popular holiday resort.

Santa Fe (or **Santa Fé**) The capital of the US state of New Mexico, at the foot of the Sangre de Cristo (Spanish, 'blood of Christ') Mountains; pop. (1990) 55,860. Founded in 1610 by Don Pedro de Peralta as the seat of Spanish governors, it claims to be the oldest capital city in the USA. The Palace of the Governors is the oldest public building in continuous use in the USA. Santa Fe was the scene of a Pueblo Indian revolt in 1680 and was captured by US troops in 1846. Nearby are the San Ildefonso Pueblo, Santa Fe National Forest, and Pecos National Monument. It is an administrative and tourist centre.

Santayana, George (born Jorge Augustin Nicolás Ruiz de Santayana) (1863–1952) Spanish philosopher and writer. He was educated at Harvard, where he became professor of philosophy in 1907. He then moved to England in 1912, before settling in Rome in 1924. He wrote a number of philosophical works, including *The Realms of Being* (1924), and was also known for his poetry and his best-selling novel *The Last Puritan* (1935).

Santiago The capital of Chile, on the River Mapocho; pop. (1992) 5,180,750. It was founded in 1541 by Pedro de Valdivia and is the country's chief centre of industry, producing chemicals, textiles, and foodstuffs. It has also been the focus of cultural development of Chile since colonial times with libraries, museums, theatres, and three universities. Its cathedral was founded in 1558.

Santiago de Cuba The second-largest city on the island of Cuba, capital of a province of the same name; pop. (est. 1992) 432,900. Founded in 1514, it was moved to its present site in south-east Cuba in 1588 and was for 40 years capital of the island. The town has a strong French heritage that dates back to the influx of 30,000 French planters during the Haitian revolt of 1791. It is a seaport handling iron, manganese, copper, sugar, rum, and tobacco, and has textile mills, distilleries, and an oil refinery.

Santo Domingo The capital and chief port of the Dominican Republic, on the River Ozama; pop. (est. 1991) 2,055,000. Founded in 1496, it is the oldest European city in the Americas and was the seat of the Viceroys of the Americas in the early 1500s. From here the Spanish conquistadors departed on their expeditions to explore the mainland of the New World. Devastated by an earthquake in 1562, it was known as Ciudad Trujillo from 1936 to 1961. It has two universities and its 16th century cathedral has one of the reputed tombs of Christopher Columbus.

Santos A city and port in the state of São Paulo, southern Brazil, on the Atlantic coast to the south of São Paulo; pop. (1991) 428,920. It is one of the largest ports in Brazil handling about half of both exports and imports. It has oil refineries and chemical industries.

Sanusi Popular name for the *Sanusiyyah*, a Muslim brotherhood. It was founded in Mecca in 1837 as a Sufi religious order by an Algerian, Sidi Muhammad al-Sanusi al-Idrisi, but in *c.*1843 he retired to the desert in Cyrenaica. The movement spread in LIBYA under the son and grandson of al-Sanusi; by 1884 there were 100 *zawiyas* or daughter houses, scattered through North Africa and further afield. It became important politically in both world wars, becoming more militant and attacking the British occupation of Egypt in World War II, and opposing the Italians in Libya. When Libya became independent in 1951, the leader of the order at that time, Idris I, became the country's first king.

São Paulo ▶1 A state in south-eastern Brazil; area 248,256 sq km (95,890 sq miles); pop. (1991) 31,546,470. **▶2** Its capital, the largest city in Brazil and second-largest metropolitan area in South America; pop. (1991) 9,627,000. Founded in 1554 by Jesuits, it developed during the 19th and 20th centuries into the leading commercial city of South America, and the financial, cultural, and industrial centre of Brazil. Its manufactures include motor vehicles, heavy machinery, electrical equipment, pharmaceuticals, chemicals, textiles, and foodstuffs. It has four universities, a medical school, law school, art galleries, and publishing houses.

São Tomé and Príncipe A country comprising two islands and several islets, lying on the Equator in the Gulf of Guinea, off the coast of West Africa.

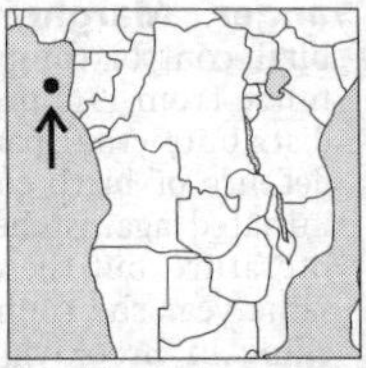

Physical. The two main islands are volcanic and both have coastal lowlands rising to central mountainous regions. The island of Principé lies about 144 km (90 miles) north of São Tomé. Tropical rainforests cover most of the islands.

Economy. The economy was centrally planned until the mid-1980s, when severe drought and worsening economic conditions, including a drop in world cocoa prices, prompted the government to seek Western aid and reduce state controls. The main export is cocoa, followed by copra. Industry is restricted to food-processing. Since agriculture concentrates on cash crops for exports, most food is imported.

History. The islands were probably uninhabited when they were discovered by the Portuguese in 1471 and were annexed by Portugal in 1522. Independence was gained in 1975, with Portugal's withdrawal from all its African colonies. Multi-party democracy was instituted under a new constitution in 1990. In 1995, President Miguel Trovoada was deposed by Cuban-trained rebel forces but was swiftly restored to power.

Capital: São Tomé
Area: 1,001 sq km (386 sq mi)
Population: 131,000 (1995)
Currency: 1 dobra = 100 centimos
Religions: Roman Catholic 84.0%; remainder mainly Seventh-day Adventist and indigenous Evangelical Church
Ethnic Groups: Mixed 43.0%; African 51.0%
Languages: Portuguese (official); Portuguese creole
International Organizations: UN; OAU

sap The aqueous solution of mineral salts and sugars that flows through the PHLOEM and XYLEM of seed plants. It may be tapped and eaten fresh, for example as with maple syrup, or fermented into alcoholic drinks, like pulque from *Agave* species in Mexico or various toddies from palms throughout the tropics.

Sapir, Edward (1884–1939) German-born US linguistics scholar and anthropologist. One of the founders of American structural linguistics, he carried out important work on American Indian languages and linguistic theory. His book *Language*

(1921) presents his thesis that language should be studied within its social and cultural context. According to the **Sapir-Whorf hypothesis**, in which Sapir collaborated with his pupil **Benjamin Lee Whorf** (1897–1941), a culture's language embodies the way in which it understands the world and dictates how those who use that language think about the world. This may be due to structural factors, such as the way time is expressed in verb tenses, as well as to more superficially obvious features such as vocabulary.

sapodilla A 20 m (65 feet) tall, evergreen tree, *Manilkara zapota*, native to Mexico and Central America but now widespread in the tropics. It is part of the family Sapotaceae, which contains 800 species of trees yielding timber, latex, or edible fruits. The yellow-brown flesh of the ripe apple-sized fruit (sapodilla plum) is prized for its sugary flavour, but the tree is better known for the gum known as chicle obtained by collecting a milky latex from cuts in the trunks. Chicle gum is used to form the basis of natural chewing-gum, and was used as such by the Aztecs.

sapphire A gem species of CORUNDUM (Al_2O_3; aluminium oxide). Sapphires are extremely hard and are normally of a transparent blue colour (although they can be almost any other colour except red – then they are RUBIES). The best deposits are found in igneous rocks in Sri Lanka, Myanmar (Burma), Australia, and Montana, USA.

Sappho (early 7th century BC) Greek lyric poet. She was renowned in her own day and became the centre of a circle of women and young girls on her native island of Lesbos. The surviving fragments of her poetry, written in her local dialect, are mainly love poems, dealing with such subjects as passion, jealousy, and enmity. Many of her poems express her affection and love for women, and have given rise to her association with female homosexuality, from which the words *lesbian* and *Sapphic* derive.

saprophyte An organism that does not produce its own organic compounds through photosynthesis, but obtains them from other dead organisms as food. Saprophytic fungi and bacteria are important in FOOD CHAINS as they help decompose dead plants or animals and recycle nutrients. The word 'saprotroph' is now preferred for these organisms as 'saprophyte' implies that they are plants (reflecting obsolete systems in which fungi and bacteria were classified as plants).

Saqqara A vast necropolis of ancient Memphis, Egypt, 24 km (15 miles) south-west of Cairo. It has monuments dating from the early dynastic period (3rd millennium BC) to the Graeco-Roman age, including the step pyramid of Djoser (*c.*2700 BC), the earliest type of pyramid and the first known building entirely of stone.

saraband See SUITE.

Saracen ▶**1** An Arab or Muslim at the time of the Crusades. ▶**2** A nomad of the Syrian and Arabian desert.

Saragossa (Spanish **Zaragoza**) An industrial city on the River Ebro in northern Spain, the capital of Aragon; pop. (1991) 614,400. A former seat of the kings of Aragon, its chief landmark is the Aljafareria Moorish palace. The heroic exploits during the siege of Saragossa (1808–09) of Maria Augustín, the Maid of Saragossa, are described in Byron's poem *Childe Harold*. It has engineering, sugar-refining, and wine-making industries.

Sarah (or **Sarai**) One of the four Hebrew matriarchs, the wife of Abraham. Sarah accompanied Abraham in his desert wanderings from Ur to Canaan. Presented there by Abraham as his sister rather than his wife, she was taken into the harems of the Egyptian pharaoh and the Philistine king, Abimelech. After giving birth to Isaac at over 90, Sarah became jealous of Hagar, her Egyptian handmaid, for having given birth to Abraham's son Ishmael, and had both cast out into the desert to die.

Sarajevo The capital city of BOSNIA-HERCEGOVINA; pop. (est. 1993) 200,000. The heir apparent to the Austro-Hungarian throne, Archduke FRANCIS FERDINAND, was assassinated here in 1914, an event that triggered World War I. In the fighting that followed the republic's declaration of independence from the former YUGOSLAVIA in 1992, Sarajevo was besieged and bombarded by Bosnian Serb forces. The siege was broken in 1995 and a peace accord was signed. It has many factories, research centres, a university and over 100 mosques.

Saransk The capital of the republic of Mordvinia in eastern European Russia; pop. (1990) 316,000. Founded as a fortress town in 1680, it is now an industrial and transportation centre specializing in machine building.

Sarasota A resort town with beach, fishing, and golfing facilities in western Florida, USA, on the Gulf of Mexico; pop. (1990) 50,960. The first golf course in Florida was established here in 1886.

Saratoga Springs A city and spa in east New York state, USA; pop. (1990) 25,000. First settled in 1773 around natural geysers and springs, the town became one of the best-known resorts in North America during the 19th century. Near this city two battles, now commemorated in the Saratoga National Historic Park, were fought (1777) in the War of American Independence. The Americans were victorious in both, and in the second battle, the British forces under General Burgoyne, were decisively defeated.

Sarawak A state of Malaysia on the north-west coast of Borneo; area 124,449 sq km (48,068 sq miles); pop. (1990) 1,669,000; capital, Kuching. Administered by the Brooke dynasty of 'white rajahs' from 1841, Sarawak became a British protectorate in 1888 and a Crown Colony in 1946. In 1963 it became a member of the independent Federation of Malaysia. Its chief exports are timber, oil, and rubber.

sardine See PILCHARD.

Sardinia A large island in the western Mediterranean Sea, now part of Italy, lying just south of the smaller island of Corsica; area 24,090 sq km (9,305 sq miles); pop. (1990) 1,664,370; capital, Cagliari. The island was given to the House of Aragon in 1297 by the pope. It passed to Spain in the 15th century, Austria in the early 18th century, and the House of Savoy in 1720. The kingdom of Sardinia gradually extended over most of Italy and in 1861 Victor Emmanuel II of Sardinia was proclaimed king of Italy. The island's chief products are tobacco, wine, olives, coal, and minerals, such as magnesium, zinc, and lead.

Sargasso Sea A region of the western Atlantic Ocean between the Azores and the West Indies, around latitude 35° N, so called because of the prevalence in it of floating sargasso seaweed. It is the breeding-place of eels from the rivers of Europe and North America.

Sargent, John Singer (1856–1925) US painter. Born in Florence, he travelled and studied widely in Europe in his youth. In the 1870s he painted some impressionist landscapes, but it was in portraiture that he developed the bold brushwork typical of his style, which reflects the influence of Manet, Hals, and Velázquez. He was much in demand in Parisian circles, but following a scandal over the supposed eroticism of *Madame Gautreau* (1884) he moved to London, where he dominated society portraiture for more than 20 years. In World War I he worked as an official war artist.

Sargent, Sir (Henry) Malcolm (Watts) (1895–1967) British conductor and composer. He is remembered particularly for his involvement with the BBC Promenade Concerts, for which he was responsible from 1948 until his death. Sargent conducted a number of ensembles, including the Liverpool Philharmonic Orchestra (1942–48), and in 1950 was appointed conductor of the BBC Symphony Orchestra.

Sargon I See AKKAD.

Sargon II (died 705 BC) King of Assyria 721–705. He was probably a son of Tiglath-pileser III, and is thought to have been named after the semi-legendary King Sargon. He is famous for his conquest of a number of cities in Syria and Palestine; he also took ten of the tribes of Israel into a captivity from which they are believed never to have returned, becoming known as the Lost Tribes of Israel (2 Kings 17:6).

Sark One of the Channel Islands, a small island lying to the east of Guernsey; area 5 sq km (2 sq miles). Divided by an isthmus into Little and Great Sark, it has had its own parliament ruled by a Seigneur/Dame since the reign of Elizabeth I. The island has no towns or motor cars and its residents pay no income tax. It is very popular in the summertime with tourists ferried across from Guernsey.

Saros A period between similar ECLIPSES of the Sun and Moon. The Babylonians of the 2nd–1st millennia BC discovered from their eclipse records that eclipses of the Sun and Moon occur in almost exactly similar detail in a period of 18 years and 10 or 11 days. This period of time, called the Saros, is almost equal to 223 lunations (6,585.32 days) and 19 SYNODIC PERIODS of the Moon's node (6,585.78 days).

sarsaparilla The dried underground parts of at least eight South American monocotyledonous plant species of *Smilax*, a genus of some 350 species of woody or herbaceous climbers with hooks or tendrils. This genus provides many extracts considered of importance in medicine.

Sarto, Andrea del (born Andrea d'Agnolo) (1486–1531) Italian painter. He worked chiefly in Florence, where among his works are fresco cycles in the church of Santa Annunziata (such as *Nativity of the Virgin*, 1514) and a series of grisailles in the cloister of the Scalo (1511–26) depicting the story of St John the Baptist. His work displays a feeling for tone and harmonies of colour, while the gracefulness of his figures influenced the mannerist style of his pupils Pontormo and Vasari.

Sartre, Jean-Paul (1905–80) French philosopher, novelist, dramatist, and critic. While studying at the Sorbonne in 1929 he began his lifelong association with Simone de Beauvoir; they founded the review *Les Temps modernes* in 1945. A leading exponent of existentialism, he was originally influenced by the work of Martin Heidegger; his later philosophy deals with the social responsibility of freedom, and attempts to synthesize existentialism with Marxist sociology. His works include the treatise *Being and Nothingness* (1943), the novel *Nausée* (1938), the trilogy *Les Chemins de la liberté* (1945–49), and the plays *Les Mouches* (1943) and *Huis clos* (1944). In 1964 he declined the Nobel Prize for literature.

Sarum See SALISBURY.

Saskatchewan A province of central Canada situated between the 49th and 60th parallels of latitude; area 652,330 sq km (251,866 sq miles); pop. (1991) 988,930; capital, Regina. Its largest settlements are Regina, Saskatoon, and Moose Jaw. and its highest point is in the Cypress Hills (1,392 m, 4,567 ft). Settled by the Hudson's Bay Company, it became a province of Canada in 1905. It is the largest wheat producer in Canada and also produces rapeseed, oats, rye, barley, copper, zinc, coal, potash, oil, and natural gas.

Saskatoon An industrial city in Saskatchewan, central Canada, on the South Saskatchewan River; pop. (1991) 211,020 (metropolitan area). It was first settled as a temperance colony in 1882 by Ontario Methodists and is now the largest city in the province, the seat of the University of Saskatchewan (1907), and one of Canada's leading mining and high-tech cities.

sassafras Any of three species of deciduous tree of the genus *Sassafras*, relatives of the avocado, bay laurels, and cinnamon in the family Lauraceae. The name is also used for an oil derived from roots of the American sassafras, *Sassafras albidum*, a tree with simple leaves, native to North America, and reaching a height of some 30 m (100 feet) in the wild. It was formerly used in medicine or to kill lice and treat insect-stings. It is still important in scent-making.

Sassanid A dynasty founded by Ardashir I ruling the Persian empire from 224 AD until driven from Mesopotamia by the Arabs (637–51).

Sassoon, Siegfried (Lorraine) (1886–1967) British poet and prose writer, known for his anti-war poetry and fictionalized autobiographies. He enlisted in World War I and was seriously wounded in France. He published his anti-war poetry, *The Old Huntsman* (1917) and *Counter-Attack* (1918), while he was still in the army. He was sent to a military sanatorium where he met Wilfred OWEN, whose works he published after Owen was killed at the front. A strong attachment to the countryside is seen in his post-war works, notably his semi-autobiographical trilogy beginning with *Memoirs of a Fox-Hunting Man* (1928).

Sassoon, Vidal (1928–) British hairstylist. After opening a London salon in 1953, he introduced the cut and blow-dry. Ten years later he created a hairstyle that was short at the back and long at the sides; first modelled at a Mary Quant fashion show, it became known as the 'Sassoon Cut'.

Satan (Hebrew, 'adversary') See DEVIL.

Satavahana A dynasty that ruled the north-west DECCAN of India, probably from the late 1st century BC until the 4th century AD. Its greatest king, Gautamiputra Satakarni (106–130 AD), consolidated his hold over the north-west Deccan, and extended his sway from coast to coast. Under his successors, Satavahana power gradually declined and had been entirely lost by the early 4th century.

satellite, artificial Usually an unmanned spacecraft orbiting the Earth or any other large body in space. The first artificial satellite, Sputnik 1, was launched on 4 October 1957. The USA's first satellite, *Explorer 1*, flew in February 1958; it carried instruments that revealed the presence of radiation belts around the Earth. Since then over 5,000 satellites have been launched, several hundred of which are currently operational. They include METEOROLOGICAL SATELLITES, SCIENTIFIC SATEL-

LITES and EARTH RESOURCES SATELLITES, MILITARY SATELLITES, COMMUNICATIONS SATELLITES, and NAVIGATION SATELLITES. The orbit of a satellite may be elliptical or circular, and its height above the Earth's surface and angle to the equator vary depending on its purpose. Most communications satellites have a geostationary orbit, an equatorial orbit at a height of 35,800 km (22,300 miles). At this height a satellite orbits once every 24 hours, so that its position relative to the Earth's surface remains constant. Power for the equipment aboard a satellite is usually provided by SOLAR PANELS and back-up batteries, though some satellites have small nuclear reactors. Information from a satellite's instruments is relayed to ground stations by a microwave radio link. Satellites also transmit radio signals that allow them to be tracked from Earth.

satellite, natural Any natural body that orbits around a planet. The 60 known satellites of the Solar System span a wide range of sizes. The seven largest are the Earth's MOON, the four GALILEAN SATELLITES of Jupiter, TITAN, and TRITON. These each exceed 2,500 km in diameter and are really small 'worlds', with complex geological histories and sometimes even an atmosphere. All the other satellites have sizes comparable to those of the ASTEROIDS, namely from about 10–1,500 km Natural satellites also display a variety of other characteristics. Their compositions can be rocky or icy, their shapes can vary from nearly spherical to very irregular, and their surfaces may be very ancient and heavily cratered or may still be subjected to changes originating in their interiors.

satellite broadcasting The re-transmission via satellite of TELEVISION and RADIO broadcasts, transmitted from the Earth back to distant points on the Earth's surface. Satellite broadcasts reach the individual television receiver via microwave frequencies or cable from ground stations, or from a direct broadcasting satellite (DBS), via small 'backyard antenna' dishes (see SATELLITE DISH). Satellites can make news, sporting, and other images available to worldwide audiences of over a billion people. Future developments may be in direct broadcasts to rural areas (of potential benefit in developing countries), and delivery of high-definition images (HDTV).

satellite dish A dish-shaped ANTENNA sending and receiving radio signals to and from satellites. The dish collects and focuses the signals on to a receiver; they are then amplified and converted for use. Major ground station dishes are usually around 30 m (100 feet) in diameter, while domestic TELEVISION dishes can be as little as 30 cm (12 inches) across.

Satie, Erik (Alfred Leslie) (1866–1925) French composer. His genius lay in his ability to use extremely simple means, often involving repetition, to produce works of great originality. He also made use of snatches of music-hall songs, jazz, and *objets trouvés* such as typewriters and a revolver. Satie was associated with the composers known as Les Six; he was also admired and championed by COCTEAU; they collaborated on a provocatively unconventional ballet, *Parade* (1924). His work had a liberating influence on later composers.

satsuma See MANDARIN.

Saturn (in mythology) In Roman mythology, a god of agricultural plenty, later identified with the Greek god Cronus. His festival was the Saturnalia, celebrated from 17 to 19 December, during which presents were given.

Saturn (in astronomy) The sixth PLANET from the Sun and the outermost planet clearly visible with the unaided eye. Saturn is the second largest planet in the Solar System. Some of its main physical characteristics suggest a resemblance to JUPITER but the results of spacecraft investigations have shown that there are also important differences between the two planets. Saturn, like Jupiter, is mostly composed of light elements, such as hydrogen and helium, and has an overall density less than that of water. It has an inner rocky core of about 10–20 times the mass of the Earth, roughly the same size as the core of Jupiter. **Saturn's rings** are well known and were explored in great detail by the VOYAGER missions. The particles composing the ring system are made of ice, with the main rings finely subdivided into hundreds of ringlets, some of which are elliptical. The visibility of the ring system changes in a 29.5-year cycle. When presented edge-on to the Earth, the rings cannot be seen well. The satellite system is composed of 17 bodies, of which the innermost ones orbit at the outskirts of the ring system, having strong gravitational interactions with the rings themselves. Proceeding outwards there is a group of icy satellites of small to intermediate size, some of which strongly influence each other's orbits. TITAN is the second-largest satellite of the Solar System and has a substantial atmosphere.

Satyr In Greek mythology, a type of creature of the woods and hills, mainly human in form, but with some bestial aspect, usually the legs of a goat. Lustful and fond of revelry, satyrs often attended Dionysus. The Roman equivalent were fauns.

Saud The ruling family of Saudi Arabia. Originally established at Dariyya in Wadi Hanifa, Nejd, in the 15th century, its fortunes grew after 1745 when Muhammad ibn Saud allied himself with the Islamic revivalist Abd al-Wahhab (see WAHHABISM), who later became the spiritual guide of the family. The first wave of Saudi expansion ended with defeat by Egypt in 1818, but Saudi fortunes revived under Abd al-Aziz ibn Saud (*c.*1880–1953), who captured Riyadh (1902), and other territories that formed the kingdom of SAUDI ARABIA in 1932. Abd al-Aziz was succeeded by his sons Saud (1953–64), FAISAL IBN ABD AL-AZIZ (1964–75), Khalid (1975–82), and Fahd (1982–), as rulers of the richest oil state in the world.

Saudi Arabia A country in south-west Asia occupying most of the peninsula of Arabia.

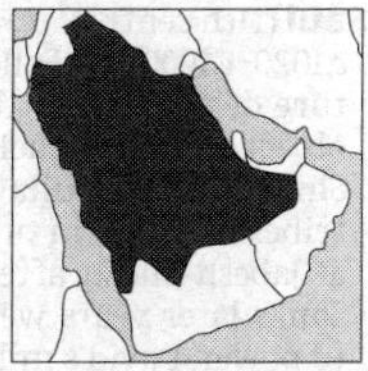

Physical. Most of Saudi Arabia is set on a plateau of deserts, which rises to mountains in the south and falls away to a low plain in the east. It is dry, hot, and often windy. The ground varies between rock, gravel, and bare sand, and little grows except in the oases and along the Red Sea coast, where slight seasonal rain makes possible the cultivation of dates and a few cereals.

Economy. With a quarter of the world's oil reserves, the Saudi economy and exports are dominated by crude oil, extracted mainly by the state-owned ARAMCO company. Oil-refining, and the manufacture of cement, fertilizers, and steel, are the main areas of industry. Agriculture suffers from poor rainfall and moving sands, but investment in irrigation and livestock production has resulted in self-sufficiency in some foodstuffs. The natural resources of the former Neutral Zone with Kuwait are shared.

History. Saudi Arabia was formed from territories assembled by the SAUD family, who were followers of WAHHABISM, and proclaimed as the kingdom of Saudi Arabia in 1932. The early years of the kingdom were difficult, when revenues fell as a result of the declining Muslim pilgrim trade to Mecca and Medina. An oil concession was awarded to the US firm Standard of California in 1933 and oil was exported in 1938. In 1944 the oil company was re-formed as the Arabian American Oil Company (ARAMCO), and Saudi Arabia was recognized as having the world's largest reserves of oil. Since the death of Abd al-Aziz ibn Saud (1953) efforts have been made to modernize the administration by the passing of a series of new codes of conduct to conform both with Islamic tradition and 20th-century developments. The Saudi Arabian Minister for Petroleum and Natural Resources, Sheikh Ahmad Yemani, ably led the OPEC in controlling oil prices in the 1970s. King Fahd succeeded to the throne after the death (1982) of his half-brother, Khalid. There were various Saudi initiatives for peace in the Middle East in the 1980s, and that of 1989 finally resolved the crisis in LEBANON by the Taif Accord. In 1990 the UN sent troops to protect Saudi oil fields from Iraqi invasion. The GULF WAR which followed had de-stabilizing social effects, with pro-democracy liberals and Islamic fundamentalists voicing criticism of the regime of King Fahd. In 1992 King Fahd announced the creation, by royal decree, of a Consultative Council, comprising 60 members chosen by the King every four years. The council, inaugurated in 1993, was to have an advisory and not a legislative function, as the King expressed his view that democracy was not suited to the Gulf region. King Fahd also denounced the spread of Islamic fundamentalism, while international concern was raised over the abuse of human rights and the incidence of public executions in Saudi Arabia.

Capital: Riyadh (royal); Jiddah (administrative); Mecca (religious)
Area: 2,240,000 sq km (865,000 sq mi)
Population: 17,880,000 (1995)
Currency: 1 Saudi riyal = 100 halalah
Religions: Muslim (mostly Sunni) 98.8%; Christian 0.8%
Ethnic Groups: Saudi Arab (including Bedouin 27.0%) 82.0%; Hemeni Arab 9.6%; other Arab 3.4%
Languages: Arabic (official)
International Organizations: UN; Arab League; GCC; OAPEC; OPEC

Saul (11th century BC) The first King of the Israelites *c.*1020–*c.*1000 BC. Following the PHILISTINES' capture of the Ark of the Covenant (the most sacred object of the Israelites) and the destruction of Shiloh and its ruling priesthood, Saul united the tribes of Israel in order to defeat the Ammonites at Jabesh-Gilead, after which he was crowned king. Saul's later years were dominated by DAVID's rise to power. David's military successes and friendship with Saul's son Jonathan provoked Saul's jealousy, and he banished David. When Saul and Jonathan were killed fighting the Philistines at Mount Gilboa, David assumed leadership of the tribe of Judah.

Saul of Tarsus The original name of St PAUL.

Saurischia See DINOSAUR.

Saussure, Ferdinand de (1857–1913) Swiss linguistics scholar. He is one of the founders of modern linguistics and his work is fundamental to the development of structuralism. Departing from traditional diachronic studies of language, he emphasized the importance of a synchronic approach, treating language as a system of mutually dependent and interacting signs. He also made a distinction between *langue* (the total system of language) and *parole* (individual speech acts), and stressed that linguistic study should focus on the former.

Savage, Michael Joseph (1872–1940) New Zealand statesman. Settling in New Zealand in 1907, he joined the Labour Party on its foundation, entering Parliament in 1919, and becoming deputy-leader in 1923. He took over as leader in 1933 on the death of Harry Holland, and became Prime Minister in 1935 after Labour's landslide victory. Savage is best remembered for his insistent advocacy of the Social Security Act and was one of the most popular of the country's political leaders.

savannah (or **savanna**) Level areas of grassland interspersed with isolated trees. It occupies a belt between tropical forests and grassland and is a particularly common vegetation type in southern and East Africa.

Savannah A city and port on the Savannah River in the US state of Georgia, noted for its Georgian colonial architecture; pop. (1990) 137,600. Founded in 1733 by General James E. Oglethorpe, it originally prospered on tobacco and cotton. In 1819 the SS *Savannah* sailing from here to Liverpool was the first steamship to cross the Atlantic. Chemicals, petroleum, rubber, timber, and plastics are its main industries.

Savery, Thomas (*c.*1650–1715) English engineer. He took out a number of patents, notably one for an engine to raise water 'by the Impellent Force of Fire' (1698) – the first steam engine. Its use of high-pressure steam, however, made it dangerous, and only a few were actually used (at low pressure) in water mills. However, Savery's patent covered the type of engine developed by Thomas Newcomen, who was therefore obliged to join him in its exploitation.

Savonarola, Girolamo (1452–98) Italian preacher and religious reformer. A Dominican monk and strict ascetic, in 1482 he moved to Florence, where he attracted great attention for his passionate preaching denouncing immorality, vanity, and corruption within the Church, and for his apocalyptic prophecies. He became virtual ruler of Florence (1494–95), but made many enemies, and in 1495 the pope forbade him to preach and summoned him to Rome. His refusal to comply with these orders led to his excommunication in 1497; he was hanged as a heretic.

savory Either of two herbs of the genus *Satureja*, members of the mint family. Summer savory, *S. hortensis*, is a fragrant annual herb well known in Roman times, whose leaves and young shoots are used in combination with other culinary herbs. Winter savory, *S. montana*, is also of Mediterranean origin, with similar culinary uses, but it differs in being a small, woody, perennial, bushy plant.

Savoy A former duchy of south-east France bordering on north-west Italy, ruled by the counts of Savoy from the 11th century although frequently invaded and fought over by neighbouring states. In 1720 Savoy was formed with Sardinia and Piedmont into the Kingdom of Sardinia. In the mid-19th century Sardinia served as the nucleus for the formation of a unified Italy, but at the time of unification (1861) Savoy itself was ceded to France. It now comprises the departments of Haute-Savoie and Savoie.

sawfish A CARTILAGINOUS FISH of the genus *Pristis*, within the RAY order. There are about six species and all have a very elongate snout, along the sides of which are large teeth. Although usually inshore fishes of tropical and subtropical oceans, they are often caught in estuaries and even in fresh water. The 'saw' is used mainly for stirring up the bottom mud in search of buried crustaceans, worms, and molluscs. The greater, or small-toothed, sawfish, *P. pectinata*, is found in all tropical oceans and can grow up to 7.7 m (25 feet) in length.

sawfly (or **horntail**) An insect of the order Hymenoptera, distinguished from others of the same order (such as ants, bees, and wasps) by the absence of a narrow 'waist' between thorax and abdomen, and the consequent tubular or flattened appearance. Many of the 2,000 or so species have a saw-edged ovipositor through which eggs are inserted into plant tissues. Most are black, or black and yellow.

Saxe-Coburg A former duchy of Bavaria in central Germany whose heirs became the ruling dynasty of Belgium and (through Prince Albert, consort of Queen Victoria) of Britain during the 19th century.

saxhorn A family of valved brass musical instruments, from sopranino in B♭ to subcontrabass in E♭, invented by Adolphe Sax from 1845 onwards. This was the first homogenous family to include cornet, tenor, baritone, and tuba, and although the smaller instruments were initially made in trumpet shape, eventually all were made upright like tubas.

saxifrage A member of a large group of mainly alpine plants from the mountains of the Northern Hemisphere, but extending into the Andes of South America. They belong to the large and widespread family Saxifragaceae, which contains some 1,250 species. They mostly form rosettes of leaves, which may be hairy or succulent. The flowers vary considerably in colour from white through yellow, pink, and red; some are solitary, others appear in long, arching panicles.

Saxons Germanic tribes, possibly named from their single-edged *seax* ('sword'). Under pressure from the migrating FRANKS they spread from their homelands on the Danish peninsula into Italy and the Frisian lands and engaged in piracy on the North Sea and English Channel between the 3rd and 5th centuries. They appear to have entered Britain, together with ANGLES and JUTES as mercenaries in the late period of the Roman occupation. By the 5th century their settlements had marked the beginning of ANGLO-SAXON England. Their name survives in Wessex ('West Saxons'), Essex ('East Saxons'), and Sussex ('South Saxons') in England, as well as in Saxony in Germany.

Saxony ▶1 A former province of east-central Germany on the upper reaches of the Elbe, earlier part of the large kingdom of Saxony. **▶2** A state of the Federal Republic of Germany revived following the reunification of Germany in 1990; area 18,337 sq km (7,083 sq miles); pop. (1991) 4,678,880; capital, Dresden.

Saxony-Anhalt (German **Sachsen-Anhalt**) A state of the Federal Republic of Germany, on the plains of the Elbe and the Saale rivers; area 20,445 sq km (7,897 sq miles); pop. (1991) 2,823,320; capital, Magdeburg. Created in 1990, it corresponds to the former duchy of Anhalt and the central part of the former kingdom of Saxony.

saxophone A single-reed musical instrument of conical bore made, usually, of brass, and invented by Adolphe Sax in about 1842 by combining a clarinet mouthpiece with approximately the tubing and keywork of an OPHICLÉÏDE. Saxophones were originally made in two sets, from sopranino to contrabass, in F and C for orchestral use and in E♭ and B♭ for military bands. Only the latter set is now seen.

Sayers, Dorothy L(eigh) (1893–1957) British novelist and dramatist. She is chiefly known for her detective fiction featuring the amateur detective Lord Peter Wimsey; titles include *Murder Must Advertise* (1933) and *The Nine Tailors* (1934). She also wrote religious plays (such as *The Devil to Pay*, 1939).

Say's Law See CLASSICAL ECONOMICS.

Sayyid dynasty Muslim rulers of the Delhi sultanate in northern India 1414–51. They seized power from the Tughluqs, but never equalled their predecessors' imperial pretensions. Rival neighbours soon threatened their claims even in the north, and in 1448 their last sultan abandoned Delhi, to be replaced three years later by the Afghan Lodis.

scabies A communicable infection by the scabies mite, *Sarcoptes scabiei*, which is transmitted by close bodily contact with an infected individual. The female mite burrows into the skin where it lays eggs, which hatch and mature into adults. Parts of the body most commonly affected include the genitals and the areas between fingers, although spread to all parts of the body may occur. Symptoms include severe itching, which may be an ALLERGY to the mite. Scabies is treated relatively easily, although close family contacts may also require treatment and clothing and bedding must be washed to prevent reinfection.

scabious An annual or perennial plant of the genus *Scabiosa*, which forms part of the family Dipsacaceae. The name is derived from the Latin *scabies*, itch, alluding to the reputation of the plants for curing this condition. Over 50 species are known within the genus. The Dipsacaceae, which also includes teasel, has some 350 species in Europe, Asia, and Africa. Some species of *Scabious*, such as the annual *S. atropurpurea* and the perennial *S. caucasica*, are popular as garden plants.

scad See HORSE MACKEREL.

Scafell Pike The highest peak in England, in the Lake District in Cumbria, rising to a height of 978 m (3,210 ft).

scalars (in mathematics) Quantities having only magnitude, and no direction. A scalar quantity is one that can be measured by a scalar: examples are length and temperature. If a direction is associated with a scalar it becomes a VECTOR. Scalars can multiply vectors, and two vectors can be multiplied to give a scalar.

scale (in zoology) One of a mass of bony or horny plates that cover the outer surfaces of reptiles and some fishes. The wings of some insects, such as butterflies or moths, are covered in 'scales', which are really modified, flattened, cuticular bristles.

scale (in music) A series of musical notes arranged in ascending or descending order of PITCH. Western music recognizes two pitch differences: a large step, the tone, and a half-step, the semitone. Other cultures recognize even smaller steps, but the Western ear is not readily able to accept them. The Western scale is based on the octave, first recognized by Pythagoras in about 550 BC. He found that dividing a string's length in half raised the pitch by an octave and made this the most important relationship. Different divisions in the length of the string gave him the fourth and fifth, and later the intervals between these. A scale that proceeds in 12 equal steps, all semitones, is called a **chromatic scale**. Scales that proceed in seven steps (five tones and two semitones) are **diatonic scales**. These are reckoned major and minor according to the sequence of tones and semitones (for variations in the exact tuning of the intervals see TEMPERAMENT). The starting-note (tonic) of each scale is used to identify the KEY it represents and therefore its TONALITY.

scale insect A member of a superfamily (Coccoidea) of plant-feeding BUGS with 'normal' insect-like winged males and wingless, squat, scale-like females. The minute, first stage larvae are active in both sexes, but at the first moult those destined to be females become inactive, or sessile, often losing all appendages and secreting a coating of wax and a scale, which may entirely cover them. Under this scale the female remains until fully mature and ready to produce eggs. The females are thus fixed to their food plants for life, and look like an excrescence of it. Scale-insects are among the most damaging of all insect pests, although a few species, such as the lac insect, *Laccifer lacca*, of India, which secretes a resinous substance (shellac) used as varnish, produce substances that are valuable to man.

scale worm A polychaete ANNELID belonging to the family Polynoidae or Sigalionidae. It has plate-like extensions of its upper surface, which overlap like tiles on a roof. Most species occur in shallow waters around sea coasts, and many are COMMENSAL with other animals.

Scaliger, Julius Caesar (1484–1558) Italian-born French classical scholar and physician. Appointed physician to the bishop of Agen, he settled in France and became a French citizen in 1528. Besides polemical works directed against Erasmus (1531, 1536), he wrote a long Latin treatise on poetics, a number of commentaries on botanical works, and a philosophical treatise. His son, **Joseph Justus Scaliger** (1540–1609), was a leading Renaissance scholar, often regarded as the founder of historical criticism. His edition of Manilius (1579) and his *De Emendatione Temporum* (1583) revolutionized understanding of ancient chronology.

scallop A BIVALVE mollusc of the family Pectinidae, highly prized as food, which lives on sandy sea-beds throughout most of the world's seas. The two shell valves have wavy or 'scalloped' edges, covering many tiny eyes and feelers on the edge of the scallop's mouth (body folds). When these detect predators like starfish the valves are clapped together to jet water out, and the scallop 'jumps' away to safety. Like all bivalves, scallops are filter-feeders.

scaly-tailed squirrel A gliding RODENT making up the family Anomaluridae, unrelated to the flying squirrels or other true squirrels. Scaly-tailed squirrels live in the forests of central, eastern, and West Africa and all but one of the seven species has a web of skin between the limbs. The scaly underside of the tail helps them to grip tree trunks.

scampi See DUBLIN BAY PRAWN.

Scandinavia That part of north-western Europe forming a peninsula bounded by the Arctic Ocean in the north, the Atlantic in the west, the Baltic in the south, and the Gulf of Bothnia in the east. Although the peninsula comprises only Norway and Sweden, Scandinavia also includes Denmark, Iceland, and Finland in a wider cultural and literary context.

Scandinavian The North Germanic branch of the Indo-European family of languages, including Danish, Norwegian, Swedish, and Icelandic, all descended from Old Norse.

scandium (symbol Sc, at. no. 21, r.a.m. 44.96) One of the Group III metals, found in many of the ores of the lanthanides in Scandinavia, from which its name originates. It is extracted from these ores by precipitation. The metal is fairly reactive; it is used to strengthen alloys but otherwise it has very few industrial uses.

scanner See ULTRASOUND.

Scapa Flow A stretch of sea in the Orkney Islands, Scotland. In May 1919 the terms of the VERSAILLES PEACE SETTLEMENT were submitted to the Germans, who protested vigorously. As an act of defiance, orders were given under Admiral von Reuter to scuttle and sink the entire German High Seas Fleet, then interned at Scapa Flow. In October 1939 the defences of Scapa Flow were penetrated when a German U-boat sank HMS *Royal Oak*. The naval base was closed in 1957 but the anchorage at Flotta at the southern entrance to Scapa Flow became the centre of the oil industry in Orkney.

scapula See ARM.

scarab A member of a large family (Scarabaeidae) of heavy and often colourful beetles, which includes CHAFERS, HERCULES BEETLES, and the famous sacred scarab, *Scarabeus sacer*, worshipped by the ancient Egyptians. Adult sacred scarabs make and roll balls of dung, sometimes coated with clay, for larval food. Their eggs are laid in buried balls of dung. There are some 2,000 species of scarab beetle throughout the world.

Scarlatti, (Pietro) Alessandro (Gaspare) (1660–1725) Italian composer. He was an important and prolific composer of operas, more than 70 of which survive; in them can be found the elements which carried Italian opera through the Baroque period and into the classical. He also established the three-part form of the opera overture which was a precursor of the classical symphony. His many other works include cantatas, masses, and oratorios. His son, **(Giuseppe) Domenico Scarlatti** (1685–1757) was a prolific composer of keyboard music, writing more than 550 sonatas for the harpsichord. His work made an important contribution to the development of the sonata form and did much to expand the range of the instrument.

scarlet fever A communicable infection caused by strains of toxin-producing Group A β-haemolytic streptococci, which is transmitted from an individual with scarlet fever by inhalation of infected droplets derived from coughing or sneezing; it may also be transmitted via contact with inanimate objects handled by the carrier (fomites). Scarlet fever most commonly occurs in children and is characterized by sore throat, pain on swallowing, increased heart rate, fever, headache, and vomiting. Subsequently, a skin rash develops, which initially begins behind the ears and spreads to the rest of the body including the arms, neck, chest, and back; itching is not associated with the rash. Contracting scarlet fever usually confers lifelong immunity against subsequent reinfection.

scatter diagram See REGRESSION ANALYSIS.

scattering The random changes in direction of waves when they encounter a material made of particles of various sizes. Both sound waves and ELECTROMAGNETIC RADIATION can be scattered if they meet appropriately sized particles. The reddening of objects near the horizon is due to atmospheric particles scattering blue light better than red, which is also the reason that the sky is blue.

scaup Any of three species of POCHARD. The New Zealand scaup, *Aythya novaeseelandiae*, is purplish black, while the other two species look like tufted ducks, except that the drakes have grey backs and no tuft. The greater scaup, *A. marila*, is marine, with a circumpolar breeding range, whereas the lesser scaup, *A. affinis*, is a North American bird, which prefers inland habitats.

Scelidosaurus See DINOSAUR.

scepticism Any philosophical position maintaining that our beliefs about a certain subject-matter cannot be justified. EPISTEMOLOGY, the philosophical theory of knowledge, has often been regarded as the search for an effective answer to scepticism. Global scepticism is concerned with all our beliefs about the external world, and claims that we can have no knowledge of the way that the world really is. Local scepticism is more specific, and only claims that beliefs in a certain area, such as ETHICS, cannot be justified.

Scheele, Carl Wilhelm (1742–86) Swedish chemist. He was a keen experimenter, working in difficult and often hazardous conditions; he discovered a number of substances including glycerol and a green gas that was later named chlorine. He is also noted for his discovery of oxygen in 1773, which he named 'fire air', although he did not publish his findings until after the publication of Joseph Priestley's work in 1774.

Scheherazade See SHAHRAZAD.

Scheldt (or **Schelde**; French **Escaut**) A river that rises in northern France and flows 432 km (270 miles) through Belgium into the Netherlands where it meets the North Sea. The city of Antwerp lies upon it.

scherzo (Italian, 'joke') A light-hearted, fast-moving musical movement, which succeeded the MINUET as the standard third movement in SYMPHONIES and SONATAS. Scherzo-like movements can be found in Haydn's music, but it was Beethoven who established the scherzo's symphonic validity. Like the old minuet and trio, the scherzo usually has a contrasting middle section – the symphonic movement becoming a scherzo and trio.

Schiaparelli, Elsa (1896–1973) Italian-born French fashion designer. She settled in Paris and opened her own establishment in the late 1920s. She introduced padded shoulders in 1932, and the vivid shade now known as 'shocking pink' in 1947. She later expanded her interests into ready-to-wear fashions and ranges of perfume and cosmetics.

Schiaparelli, Giovanni Virginio (1835–1910) Italian astronomer. He studied the nature of cometary tails, and showed that many meteors are derived from comets and follow similar orbits. He observed Mars in detail, identifying the southern polar ice cap and features which he called 'seas', 'continents', and 'channels' (*canali*). The last was mistranslated as 'canals', beginning a long-running controversy about intelligent life on Mars.

Schiele, Egon (1890–1918) Austrian painter and draughtsman. He was influenced by KLIMT and ART NOUVEAU, but soon developed a distinctive style. His best-known works are his drawings of nudes (including self-portraits), which have an explicit and disturbing erotic power. He died of influenza when he was beginning to achieve international acclaim, and has since been recognized as one of the greatest Expressionist artists.

Schiller, (Johann Christoph) Friedrich von (1759–1805) German dramatist, poet, historian, and critic. His early work was influenced by the *Sturm und Drang* movement; his mature work established him as a major figure, with Goethe (with whom he formed a long-standing friendship), of the Enlightenment in Germany. His first major work was the historical drama in blank verse *Don Carlos* (1787). His other historical plays include the trilogy *Wallenstein* (1800), which drew on his historical studies of the Thirty Years War, *Mary Stuart* (1800), and *William Tell* (1804). Among his best-known poems are 'Ode to Joy', which Beethoven set to music in his Ninth Symphony, and 'The Artists' (both written *c.*1787). His many essays on aesthetics include *On Naive and Reflective Poetry* (1795–96), in which he contrasts his poetry with that of Goethe.

Schindler, Oskar (1908–74) German industrialist. In 1940 he established an enamelware factory in Cracow, Poland, employing Jewish workers from the city's ghetto. After the Nazi evacuation of the ghetto in 1943, Schindler exercised his financial influence to protect his employees from being sent to Plaszów, a nearby labour camp. In 1944 he compiled a list of more than 1,200 Jews from Plaszów and his own factory to be relocated at a new armaments factory in Czechoslovakia, thereby saving them from death in concentration camps. Schindler's life and role in rescuing Polish Jews are celebrated in the novel *Schindler's Ark* (1982), by Thomas Keneally, and the film *Schindler's List* (1993), directed by Steven Spielberg.

schism See ROMAN CATHOLIC CHURCH.

schist A relatively coarse-grained METAMORPHIC ROCK with dark and light minerals (especially micas) arranged in wavy bands about 0.5 cm (0.25 inch) thick. Schists are typical products of regional metamorphism of intermediate grade. Schists can be derived from many sedimentary rocks (but most commonly from clays or silts). They can consequently vary in physical appearance. They are common throughout the world and predominate in older rocks.

schistosomiasis See BILHARZIA.

schizanthus A colourful, showy annual plant of the genus *Schizanthus*. The 15 species of *Schizanthus* are mainly native to parts of South America, and are related to the potato and tobacco plant. *S. pinnatus* and its varieties are popular garden plants.

schizophrenia A MENTAL ILLNESS in an acute episode of which the symptoms may include delusions, hallucinations, such as imaginary voices, and bizarre behaviour. Many who experience an acute episode recover well, but if the disease becomes chronic, the mental torment drives some sufferers to become apathetic and withdrawn, while others become unpredictable, demanding, and sometimes aggressive. The risk of SUICIDE is high. The causes of schizophrenia are unknown, but research suggests that it arises from a disturbance in the biochemical balance in the brain triggered by stress, hormonal changes, or other factors in predisposed individuals. The predisposition is sometimes inherited. Drug treatment can control symptoms but not cure the illness.

Schlegel, August Wilhelm von (1767–1845) German poet and critic. In 1798 he became professor of literature and fine art at Jena, before periods in Berlin (1801–04) and Bonn (1818), where he was professor of literature until his death. He was prominent in the romantic movement and stands at the beginning of art history and comparative philology. His translations of Shakespeare are still used on the German stage.

Schleswig-Holstein A state of north-west Germany; area 15,729 sq km (6,075 sq miles); pop. (1991) 2,648,530; capital, Kiel.

Schlick, Moritz (1882–1936) German philosopher and physicist. From 1922 he was professor of inductive sciences at Vienna. In the late 1920s he formed the Vienna Circle, a group of young empiricist thinkers who laid the foundations of LOGICAL POSITIVISM. He had a relatively modest output, his major works including *General Theory of Knowledge* (1918). He was murdered by one of his graduate students.

Schliemann, Heinrich (1822–90) German archaeologist. A former businessman with an amateur interest in archaeology, he was determined to discover the location of the ancient city of Troy, and in 1871 began excavating the mound of Hissarlik on the NE Aegean coast of Turkey. He discovered the remains of a succession of nine cities on the site, identifying the second oldest as Homer's Troy (and romantically naming a hoard of jewellery 'Priam's Treasure'), although he had in fact uncovered a pre-Homeric site. He subsequently undertook significant excavations at Mycenae (1876) and at other sites in mainland Greece.

Schmidt, Helmut (1918–) German statesman. A member of the Social Democratic Party, he was elected to the Bundestag (Parliament of the Federal Republic of Germany) in 1953. He was Minister of Defence (1969–72) and of Finance (1972–74). Elected federal Chancellor in 1974, following the resignation of Willy BRANDT, he served for a second period (1978–82), during which he increasingly lost the support of the left wing of his party and of the Green Party.

Schmidt telescope See TELESCOPE.

Schneider Trophy A trophy awarded 1913–31 to the most seaworthy and fastest seaplanes. The trophy was presented by the French financier Jacques Schneider and was eventually won outright by the UK. The Spitfire and its engine, the Rolls Royce Merlin, of World War II were derived from the seaplane designed for this competition.

Schoenberg, Arnold (1874–1951) Austrian-born US composer and music theorist. His major contribution to modernism is his development of the concepts of atonality and serialism. He introduced atonality into the final movement of his second string quartet (1907–08) and abolished the distinction between consonance and dissonance in his *Three Piano Pieces* (1909). From these experiments he evolved a serial system of composition, in which a fixed series of notes, especially the 12 notes of the chromatic scale, are used to generate the harmonic and melodic basis of a piece and are subject to change only in specific ways: the third and fourth movements of the *Serenade* (1923) for seven instruments and bass voice are the first clear examples of this technique. He was a professor of music in Vienna and in Berlin until 1933 when, after condemnation of his music by Hitler because he was Jewish, he emigrated to the USA, becoming a US citizen in 1941. He continued to develop his serial techniques and his work influenced such composers as his pupils Berg and Webern.

scholasticism The educational tradition of the medieval 'schools' (universities) which flourished in the 12th and 13th centuries. It was a method of philosophical and theological enquiry, which aimed at a better understanding of Christian doctrine by a process of definition and systematic argument.

The writings of Aristotle (translated from Greek into Latin by BOETHIUS) and of St AUGUSTINE played a crucial part in the development of scholastic thought. Scholastics did not always agree on points of theology; AQUINAS and DUNS SCOTUS argued from different standpoints. Scholasticism declined in the later Middle Ages; in the 14th century the writings of WILLIAM OF OCKHAM challenged the scholastic position by stressing the opposition between faith and reason.

Schönbein, Christian Friedrich (1799–1868) German chemist who explored the properties of NITROCELLULOSE. In 1845–46, while Professor of Chemistry at Basel University, Switzerland, he developed both the highly explosive gun-cotton, and also cellulose nitrate, a much less reactive substance that can be moulded and shaped. Schönbein patented these in the UK in 1846.

schooner A fore-and-aft rigged sailing vessel whose foremast is the same length as, or shorter than, the mainmast, which is situated towards the rear. In the late 19th and early 20th centuries schooner design culminated in two forms. Grand Banks schooners were fast, two-masted vessels used for fishing on the Newfoundland Grand Banks, similar designs now being used as YACHTS; larger schooners, some with as many as seven masts, were built as bulk carriers.

Schopenhauer, Arthur (1788–1860) German philosopher. In his main work, *The World as Will and Representation* (1818), Schopenhauer took KANT's idealist metaphysics as his starting-point. He accepted Kant's thesis that the external world is constituted by our minds, and in this sense is a 'representation'. But he denied that the world as it is in itself is unknowable and identified it instead with 'will'. Will in Schopenhauer's sense is a blind, surging force, without purpose or direction. This, he argued, vindicates a profoundly pessimistic view of human life, to which art and aesthetic contemplation provide a partial antidote.

Schreiner, Olive (Emilie Albertina) (1855–1920) South African novelist. She is best known for *The Story of an African Farm* (1883), a tragic novel of feminist protest set in the veld in which she grew up. Two other novels, *From Man to Man* (1927) and *Undine* (1929), appeared after her death. Her political views are expounded in *Woman and Labour* (1911).

Schrödinger, Erwin (1887–1961) Austrian theoretical physicist. In the 1920s he founded the study of wave mechanics, deriving the SCHRÖDINGER EQUATION. Professor of physics at Berlin from 1927, Schrödinger left Germany after the Nazis came to power in 1933, returning to Austria in 1936 but fleeing again after the *Anschluss* of 1938 and finally settling in Dublin. He wrote a number of general works, including *What is Life?* (1944), which proved influential among scientists of all disciplines. He shared the Nobel Prize for physics in 1933.

Schrödinger equation The fundamental equation of QUANTUM MECHANICS, derived by Erwin SCHRÖDINGER. The equation relates the energy of the electron to the field in which it is situated. It has many possible solutions; however, since quantum theory allows electrons to have only certain specific energies, only some of the solutions are allowed. As well as enabling the energy of electrons to be calculated, the Schrödinger equation also gives a mathematical parameter known as the WAVEFUNCTION, which is represented by the Greek letter psi (ψ). The wavefunction enables the probability of an electron being at a particular place at a particular time to be predicted. This enables the likely position of an electron in the field of a nucleus to be calculated, enabling the shape of the orbitals that electrons occupy in atoms to be determined.

Schubert, Franz (1797–1828) Austrian composer. While his music is associated with the romantic movement for its lyricism and emotional intensity, it belongs to the classical age of Haydn and Mozart. During his brief life he produced more than 600 songs, nine symphonies, 15 string quartets, and 21 piano sonatas, as well as operas and church music. His lieder include the songs 'Gretchen am Spinnrade' (1814) and 'Erlkönig' (1815; 'Erl-King'), in addition to such song cycles as *Die Schöne Müllerin* (1823) and *Winterreise* (1827). Among his other significant works are the String Quintet in C major (1828), the 'Trout' piano quintet (1819), and the Ninth Symphony ('the Great C Major') (1828).

Schulz, Charles (1922–) US cartoonist. He is the creator of the 'Peanuts' comic strip (originally entitled 'Li'l Folks') featuring a range of characters including the boy Charlie Brown and the dog Snoopy. The comic strip was first published in 1950 after Schulz sold the rights to United Features Syndicate, and it later appeared in many publications around the world.

Schumacher, E(rnst) F(riedrich) (1911–77) German economist and conservationist. His reputation is chiefly based on his book *Small is Beautiful: Economics as if People Mattered* (1973), which argues that economic growth is a false god of Western governments and industrialists, and that mass production needs to be replaced by smaller, more energy-efficient enterprises. Schumacher also worked to encourage conservation of natural resources and supported the development of intermediate technology in developing countries.

Schumann, Robert (Alexander) (1810–56) German composer. He was a leading romantic composer and is particularly noted for his songs and piano music. He drew much of his inspiration from literature, writing incidental music for Byron's *Manfred* (1849) and setting to music poems by Heinrich Heine and Robert Burns. Notable among his piano pieces are the miniatures *Papillons* (1829–31), *Carnaval* (1834–35), and *Waldszenen* (1848–49), the Fantasy in C major (1836), and the Piano Concerto in A minor (1845). His other works include four symphonies and much chamber music. He spent the last two years of his life in a mental asylum. His wife, **Clara Schumann** (1819–96), was the daughter of Friedrick Wieck, with whom Schumann studied. She was a remarkable pianist and very capable composer, who lived on to support their children and champion his music.

Schuman Plan (9 May 1950) A proposal drafted by Jean Monnet and put forward by the French Foreign Minister Robert Schuman. It aimed initially to pool the coal and steel industries of France and the Federal Republic of Germany under a common authority, which other European nations might join. The Plan became effective in 1952 with the formation of the European Coal and Steel Community, to which Italy, Belgium, Holland, and Luxembourg as well as France and West Germany belonged. Britain declined to join. Its success ultimately led to the formation of the EUROPEAN ECONOMIC COMMUNITY.

Schuschnigg, Kurt von (1897–1977) Austrian statesman. He became Chancellor following the murder of DOLLFUSS (1934). He considered his main task to be the prevention of German absorption of Austria. Although an Austro-German Agreement (July 1936) guaranteed Austrian independence, Hitler accused him of breaking it. In February 1938 Hitler obliged him to accept Nazis in his cabinet. His attempt to hold a plebiscite on Austrian independence was prevented and he was forced to resign. On 12 March German troops invaded Austria without resistance in the ANSCHLUSS.

Schütz, Heinrich (1585–1672) German composer and organist. He is regarded as the first German Baroque composer and his work reflects the influence of periods spent in Italy, for example in the settings of *Psalms of David* (1619). He composed much church music and what is thought to have been the first German opera (*Dafne*, 1627; now lost).

Schwann, Theodor Ambrose Hubert (1810–82) German physiologist. He is chiefly remembered for his support of cell theory, showing that animals (as well as plants) are made up of individual cells, and that the egg begins life as a single cell. He also isolated the first animal enzyme, pepsin, recognized that fermentation is caused by processes in the yeast cells, and discovered the cells forming the myelin sheaths of nerve fibres (**Schwann cells**). Schwann became disillusioned following criticism of his work by chemists, emigrated to Belgium at the age of 28, and withdrew from scientific work.

Schwarzenegger, Arnold (1947–) Austrian-born US actor. Schwarzenegger won several body-building titles before retiring to concentrate on acting and appearing in the highly successful *Conan the Barbarian* (1982). He went on to play a number of action roles, such as that of *The Terminator* (1984), before attempting to diversify in films, such as the comedy *Kindergarten Cop* (1990) and the spy thriller *True Lies* (1994).

Schwarzkopf, Dame (Olga Maria) Elisabeth (Friederike) (1915–) German-born British operatic soprano. She made her début in Berlin in 1942, and went on to become especially famous for her recitals of German lieder and for her roles in works by Richard Strauss, such as *Der Rosenkavalier*.

Schwarzschild radius The distance from the centre of a BLACK HOLE within which the gravitational field is so strong that not even ELECTROMAGNETIC RADIATION can escape from it. It was first calculated by the German astronomer Karl Schwarzschild in 1916.

Schweitzer, Albert (1875–1965) German theologian, musician, and medical missionary, born in Alsace. He decided to devote the first 30 years of his life to learning and music and the remainder to the service of others. His main contribution to theology was his book *The Quest for the Historical Jesus* (1906), which emphasized the importance of understanding Jesus within the context of the Jewish apocalyptic thought of his day. In 1913 he qualified as a doctor and went as a missionary to Lambaréné in French Equatorial Africa (now Gabon), where he established a hospital and lived for most of the rest of his life. He was awarded the Nobel Peace Prize in 1952.

sciatica A pain that spreads from the lower back down the leg. It is usually caused by an intervertebral disc protruding laterally onto the roots of the sciatic nerve, the longest nerve in the body. Treatment is by bed rest, or in severe cases by surgical intervention.

science fiction A literary genre in which imaginative fiction is created using an extrapolation of scientific knowledge into the fields of fantasy. Extraterrestrial life forms, space travel, and a liberal misuse of the concept of time are common components of the genre. Early precedents include Mary SHELLEY's *Frankenstein* (1818), but true modern science fiction begins with VERNE's *Voyage au centre de la terre* (1864) and WELLS's *The Time Machine* (1895). Once uniformly dismissed as pulp trash, science fiction, or SF as its devotees call it, gained greater respect from the 1950s, with the work of such writers as Isaac Asimov, Ray Bradbury, Arthur C. Clarke, and John Wyndham. Among other important writers are J. G. Ballard, Philip K. Dick, Frank Herbert, Ursula Le Guin, William Gibson, Kurt Vonnegut, and Walter M. Miller Jr. SF is also popular in the cinema: notable films include LANG's *Metropolis* (1927), KUBRICK's *2001: A Space Odyssey* (1968), *Star Wars* (1977) and its sequels, and *Alien* (1979) and its sequels. Many SF television series have been extremely successful and the genre has also inspired video games, plays, and musicals.

Science Museum A UK museum instituted in 1853 as the National Museum of Science and Industry. It now houses one of the world's great collections relating to the history of science and technology. Until 1909 it was associated with London's Victoria and Albert Museum, dedicated to fine and applied art. Its main collections are at South Kensington in London, along with the Science Museum Library, which specializes in the history of science and technology. It also includes the Wellcome Museum of the History of Medicine, the National Railway Museum in York, and the National Museum of Photography, Film, and Television in Bradford.

scientific satellite Artificial SATELLITE used for studying the Earth and the space around it, and for collecting light and other radiation from the Sun and distant astronomical objects. Instruments on the satellite detect gamma rays, X-rays, and ultraviolet or infrared radiation, relaying data to ground stations for processing.

Scientology A religious system based on the teachings of the US science-fiction writer, L. Ron Hubbard (1911–86). The Church of Scientology, which evolved from a type of psychotherapy called 'Dianetics', was established in 1955. Its teachings combine 'psychotherapy' with aspects of CHRISTIANITY, HINDUISM, and BUDDHISM. The basic belief is that humans are immortal beings called Thetans, who progress towards enlightenment through a process of REINCARNATION. In order to rediscover the Thetan within, members undergo 'auditing', a rigorous interview process, including lie-detector tests, to increase self-awareness. Controversially, the results are stored for future reference and guidance; the financial demands that Scientology makes on its members have also aroused controversy.

scilla A plant of the genus *Scilla*, part of the lily family. Over 100 species have been recorded, chiefly from Europe, Asia, and the Mediterranean region, but extending into southern Africa. They are mainly spring-flowering, with white, blue, or greenish flowers. The blue-flowered *S. siberica* and *S. bifolia* can be naturalized in gardens.

Scilly Isles A group of islands in the UK. The Scilly Isles comprise a cluster of about 40 small islands and granite rocks lying 45 km (28 miles) from the south-west tip of England. Only five – St Mary's, Tresco, St Martin's, Bryher, and St Agnes – are large enough for habitation, and none is more than 4 km (2.5 miles) long. The climate, influenced by the Gulf Stream, is mild enough for the cultivation of subtropical plants.

scintillation See SCATTERING.

Scipio Aemilianus (full name Publius Cornelius Scipio Aemilianus Africanus Minor) (*c.*185–129 BC) Roman general and politician. He achieved distinction in the third Punic War, and blockaded and destroyed Carthage in 146. His successful campaign in Spain (133) ended organized resistance in that country. Returning to Rome in triumph, he initiated moves against the reforms introduced by his brother-in-law Tiberius Gracchus. Scipio's sudden death at the height of the crisis gave rise to the rumour that he had been murdered.

Scipio Africanus (full name Publius Cornelius Scipio Africanus Major) (236–*c.*184 BC) Roman general and politician. His aggressive tactics were successful in concluding the second Punic War, firstly by the defeat of the Carthaginians in Spain in 206 and then by the defeat of Hannibal in Africa in 202; his victories pointed the way to Roman hegemony in the Mediterranean. His son was the adoptive father of Scipio Aemilianus.

scorpion The most primitive ARACHNID, perhaps the first arthropod to adapt to life on land. About 800 species are known, most common in tropical areas. Most are secretive and nocturnal. Most species are 3–10 cm (1–4 inches) long, but fossil species grew to almost 90 cm (35 inches). The oval, front part of the body of a scorpion bears eight legs, pincer-like PEDIPALPS, and jaws, while the mobile abdomen bears the barbed sting. To humans, the venom of most species is merely an irritant, although several species, notably *Androctonus australis* of the Sahara region, have venom powerful enough to kill. The poison is mostly used on insects sought as food. To avoid mistakes during mating, scorpions use elaborate courtship dances to avoid each other's sting. After hatching, youngsters ride on the mother's back for safety.

scorpionfish A fish of the family Scorpaenidae, found mainly in tropical and warm temperate seas. Scorpionfishes are bottom-dwelling, are often found in rocky areas, and are well camouflaged to match their surroundings by colouring as well as by the presence of numerous flaps of skin on the head and body. Many of the 330 species have glands which secrete venom at the bases of the sharp fin spines, and can inflict very painful wounds. In general they are stout-bodied with a large head which has a strong bony ridge on the cheek; the head is often spiny. They eat a wide range of fishes and crustaceans, and rarely grow larger than 50 cm (20 inches).

scorpionfly An insect belonging to the order Mecoptera, which derives its name from the upturned, bulbous end to the abdomen which characterizes the males of some of the 400 or so species. All have a head which extends downwards into a beak bearing the biting jaws. Scorpionflies differ little from fossils some 250 million years old. Some feed on dead or dying insects and occasionally fruit, and the minute, wingless, snow flea, *Boreus hyemalis*, eats the mosses among which it lives. Another species catches insects with its hindlegs while hanging by the front pair. The larvae are scavengers in soil or leaf litter.

Scorpius The Scorpion, a CONSTELLATION of the zodiac, representing the scorpion that stung Orion to death. Its brightest star is ANTARES. Beta Scorpii, called Graffias from the Latin meaning 'claws', is divisible into a double of third and fifth magnitudes through small telescopes. Near this star lies the bright X-ray source Scorpius X-1.

Scorsese, Martin (1942–) US film director. He made his directorial début in 1968, but first gained recognition five years later with *Mean Streets*, a realistic study of New York's Italian community, focusing on the plight of a group of friends entangled in a web of crime and violence. The film marked the beginning of Scorsese's long collaboration with the actor Robert De Niro, which continued in such films as *Taxi Driver* (1976) *Raging Bull*

(1980), *GoodFellas* (1990), and *Casino* (1995). Other films include the *The Last Temptation of Christ* (1988) and *The Age of Innocence* (1993).

scorzonera A perennial plant of the sunflower family with yellow, dandelion-like flowers, native to central and southern Europe. The black-skinned, fleshy tap-roots of *Scorzonera hispanica* may be boiled and eaten as a vegetable, like those of its close relative, salsify. Like chicory, it is the source of a coffee substitute and the fresh young leaves may be used in salads. *S. humilis*, a species not used as a vegetable, is commonly known as viper's grass.

scoter Any of three species of bulky, blackish, sea duck allied to the eiders. Like them, scoters are birds of the far north. Most of the common scoters, *Melanitta nigra*, and all the velvet scoters, *M. fusca*, which are seen in Britain, are winter visitors.

Scotland The northern part of Great Britain and of the United Kingdom; area 77,167 sq km (29,805 sq miles); pop. (1991) 4,957,300; capital, Edinburgh. Sparsely populated until Celtic peoples arrived from the Continent during the Bronze and Early Iron Age, the inhabitants of Scotland were named the Picts by the Romans, who established a northerly line at the ANTONINE WALL for about 40 years. An independent country in the Middle Ages, after the unification of various small Dark Age kingdoms of the Picts, Scots, Britons, and Angles between the 9th and 11th centuries, Scotland successfully resisted English attempts at domination but was amalgamated with her southern neighbour as a result of the union of the crowns in 1603 and of the parliaments in 1707. Broadly divided into Highland and Lowland regions, Scotland has a heavily indented west coast with numerous islands to the west (Inner and Outer Hebrides) and north (Orkney and Shetland Islands). The Highlands to the north and the Southern Uplands north of the English border are sparsely populated, the greater proportion of the Scottish population being concentrated in the Central Lowlands between the Firth of Clyde and the Firth of Forth. Oil and natural gas, agricultural produce, timber, textiles, whisky, paper, and high-tech electronic goods are amongst its chief industrial products. Scotland is divided into 32 administrative regions (unitary authorities). A referendum on devolution was held in 1997 in which the electorate overwhelmingly voted in favour of a measure of devolution. This will include a Scottish parliament with 129 MPs to be elected by proportional representation and to begin sitting in 2000. It will have powers to make laws on domestic matters and to vary the basic rate of income tax by up to 3p.

Scotland Yard The headquarters of the London Metropolitan Police, situated from 1829 to 1890 in Great Scotland Yard, a short street off Whitehall in London, from then until 1967 in New Scotland Yard on the Thames Embankment, and from 1967 in New Scotland Yard, Broadway, Westminster.

Scots (or **Dalriads**) Celtic Irish settlers, in what is now Scotland. In the early 6th century AD they settled Argyll (Ar Gael) after two centuries of raiding the coasts of Britain and Gaul. They overcame the northern PICTS in the Highlands and introduced the Celtic Gaelic language. The name 'Scotia' (Scotland), formerly a name for Hibernia (Ireland) passed to the land of CALEDONIA and the territories of all the Picts.

Scots law The law applicable in Scotland, which remains resistant to the dominant influence of English law within the UK legal system. Scots law came under early Anglo-Saxon–Norman influence in the feudal period (11th to 13th centuries), but Scotland's later political and cultural alliance with France led to the importation during the 14th to 16th centuries of ROMAN LAW doctrines by Scottish law students returning from continental universities. The separate Scottish legal system, court structure, and procedures have still been preserved, despite the union of the two kingdoms in 1603 and of the two parliaments in 1707. Scots law is more highly systematized, relying, like other CIVIL LAW systems, more on general principles (such as the law of obligations) than on CASE LAW and PRECEDENT. The chief inferior courts in Scotland are sheriff courts, with both a civil and a criminal jurisdiction. The sheriff is the title of the JUDGE, and the public prosecutor is known as the **procurator fiscal**. The **Lord Advocate** is the chief law officer in Scotland, with ultimate responsibility for Crown prosecutions. The superior Scottish civil court is the Court of Session, and the superior criminal court is the High Court of Justiciary. The supreme Scottish civil court is the House of Lords, sitting in London, and consisting usually of three English judges and two Scottish judges.

Scots pine A conifer, *Pinus sylvestris*, native to Europe and Asiatic Russia. Natural Scots pine forests still persist in parts of Scotland, though most of the trees seen in the British Isles have been introduced by man from European continental stocks. Its reddish, flaking, young bark is characteristic, and its timber is valued for carpentry and general building construction.

Scott, Sir George Gilbert (1811–78) British architect. He attracted controversy for his restoration of medieval churches and in 1858 came into conflict with Palmerston over the design for the new Foreign Office, for which Scott was ultimately compelled to adopt an Italianate style; his Albert Memorial in London (1863–72) reflects more accurately his preferred aesthetic. His grandson **Sir Giles Gilbert Scott** (1880–1960) also worked as a revivalist architect and is best known for the Gothic Anglican cathedral in Liverpool (begun in 1904, completed in 1978).

Scott, Sir Peter (Markham) (1909–89) British naturalist and artist. He was particularly interested in wildfowl and their conservation, and in 1946 founded the Wildfowl Trust at Slimbridge in Gloucestershire. He was well known as a wildfowl artist and a presenter of natural history programmes on television, and he became increasingly involved in conservation worldwide. He was the son of the explorer Robert Falcon SCOTT.

Scott, Ridley (1939–) British film director. With such films as *Alien* (1979) Scott established himself as one of modern cinema's foremost visual stylists. In the influential *Blade Runner* (1982) he fused the medieval with the technological to create the image of a dirty, overcrowded, and run-down future. His later films include *Thelma and Louise* (1991). His brother **Tony Scott** (1944–) is also a successful film director, responsible for such works as *Top Gun* (1986) and *True Romance* (1993).

Scott, Sir Robert Falcon (1868–1912) British explorer and naval officer. As commander of the ship *Discovery* he led the National Antarctic Expedition (1900–04), surveying the interior of the continent and charting the Ross Sea. On a second expedition (1910–12) Scott and four companions made a journey to the South Pole by sled, arriving there in January 1912 to discover that the Norwegian explorer Amundsen had beaten them to their goal by a month. Scott and his companions died on the journey back to base, and their bodies and diaries were discovered by a search party eight months later. Scott, a national hero, was posthumously knighted. He was the father of the naturalist and artist Sir Peter SCOTT.

Scott, Sir Walter (1771–1832) Scottish novelist and poet. Among his novels are *Waverley* (1814), *Old Mortality* (1816), *Ivanhoe* (1819), and *Kenilworth* (1821). His poetry was influenced by medieval French and Italian poetry, and by contemporary German poets; he collected and imitated old Borders tales and ballads, while among his original works are the romantic narrative poems *The Lay of the Last Minstrel* (1805) and *The Lady of the Lake* (1810).

Scottish-Gaelic literature Literature in the native tongue of Scotland. Scottish Gaelic remained linked to Irish Gaelic until the 17th century, and early versions of Scottish tales, sagas, and poetry are to be found in the manuscripts of early IRISH LITERATURE. They are distinctive for their simplicity and terseness of style, and for their colour and richness of imagery. In the Fenian cycle, which became prominent in *c.*1330, the poet sings of nature and love in BALLAD-form, and the Fenian legends have survived to modern times. The earliest extensive anthology of heroic tales and ballads written in literary Gaelic was *The Book of the Dean of Lismore*, compiled in the Strathclyde region between 1412 and 1526, and containing works by Scottish and Irish authors from 1310 to 1520. After the rise of Presbyterianism in Scotland in the 16th century, Scottish Gaelic evolved a separate literature. Popular songs in stressed METRES have survived from the early 17th century. These are the work songs or walking songs used as an accompaniment to manual labour. The 17th century saw the high point of Scottish Gaelic literature. Some of the poetry and prose of the period has been preserved in the *Black* and the *Red Books of Clanranald* written by members of the MacMhuirich bardic family, whose work spans nearly 500 years from the 13th century to the 18th. Among the best-known poets of the 17th century were Mary Macleod (*c.*1615–*c.*1706) and the blind harper, An Clarsair Dall. Gaelic printing in the 18th century, greatly influenced by the first Scottish Gaelic book of secular poetry, *Resurrection of the Ancient Scottish Tongue* (1751) by Alexander Macdonald, produced valuable collections of poetry and social satire. Little literature appeared in the 19th century, but a 20th-century movement to free Gaelic poetry from its traditional conventions has kept the medium alive in the works of writers such as Sorley MacLean (1911–).

Scottish National Party (SNP) A Scottish political party, formed in 1934 from a merger of the National Party of Scotland and the Scottish Party. The party gained its first parliamentary seat in 1945 at a by-election in Motherwell. In the October 1974 general election 11 of its candidates won parliamentary seats. In 1979 a referendum in Scotland on a Scottish representative assembly failed to elicit the required majority, and in the 1979 general election all but two of the candidates were defeated. Three were elected in 1987 and in 1992. In the 1997 election the SNP held six seats. The SNP were not initially in favour of the Scottish parliament proposed by the Labour Party, but now accept it as a first step to full independence.

scrambler An electronic device that ensures the security of transmitted speech, data, and video information. Speech scramblers either split the frequency spectrum into groups and interchange them, or digitally code the sound, and as for data scramblers, add a fixed pre-arranged code. Video scramblers modify the synchronization signal at the start of each television line.

scrapie An infectious disease of the central nervous system of sheep and goats. Symptoms appear some two years after infection. The first symptoms are an itch that causes the animals to scrape themselves against trees, fences, etc. The following stage involves drowsiness and the staggering gait resulting from paralysis of the legs. The disease is usually fatal six months after the appearance of the first symptoms. It is related to BOVINE SPONGIFORM ENCEPHALOPATHY (BSE) in cattle and CREUTZFELDT-JAKOB DISEASE (CJD) in humans.

screamer A goose-like bird belonging to a family, Anhimidae, of three species, which are confined to South America. They are members of two genera, *Anhima* and *Chauna*. They are large and slightly turkey-like, mainly black or grey above and light grey or white below. They carry a sharp spur on the leading edge of the wing. Although they do not resemble ducks, they are thought to be related to them. Screamers live in marshes and have rather long toes to support their weight on the soft ground. They eat vegetable matter and build a shallow nest of reeds in which they lay three to six white eggs. The young leave the nest soon after hatching. Screamers have a powerful, far-carrying call which is the origin of their name.

scree (or **talus**) A mass of debris, comprising loose fragments of rock that covers a steep, bare slope or is piled up in a conical or fan-shaped mass at its foot. The particles are detached from the rock walls by the action of rain and frost, and they fall or slide downslope until they interlock with other fragments. Active scree slopes are bare of vegetation, since their surface is constantly disturbed by new falls of debris, bouncing downslope. They also tend to show a definite zoning of material, with the largest blocks travelling furthest and forming the lower portions of the scree.

screening See HEALTH SCREENING.

screen printing A printing process in which the image is formed using a stencil on a fine mesh screen (originally silk), through which ink is forced by a squeegee on to the paper or substrate underneath. Screen-printing (adapted from the ancient technique of stencilling) was first used in the 19th century for transferring patterns on to pottery and textiles. Modern screen-printing is very versatile, utilizing photo-mechanical stencils on screens of manufactured fibre and stainless steel in both flat and rotary machinery. It is particularly used for advertising material, posters, packaging, plastic containers, clothing, and other difficult printing surfaces.

Scriabin, Aleksandr (Nikolaevich) (or **Skryabin**) (1872–1915) Russian composer and pianist. He wrote symphonies, symphonic poems, and numerous pieces for the piano, including sonatas and preludes. Much of his later music reflects his interest in mysticism and theosophy, especially his third symphony *The Divine Poem* (1903) and the symphonic poem *Prometheus: The Poem of Fire* (1909–10), which is scored for orchestra, piano, optional choir, and 'keyboard of light' (projecting colours on to a screen).

scripture See BIBLE.

scrub-wren See WARBLER.

sculpin See BULLHEAD.

Sculptor The Sculptor, a CONSTELLATION of the southern sky introduced by the 18th-century French astronomer Nicolas Louis de Lacaille to represent a sculptor's workshop. Its brightest stars are of only fourth magnitude.

sculpture The branch of art concerned with the production of three-dimensional representational or abstract objects. Techniques used include stone-carving, WOODCARVING, and bronze CASTING, as well as the production of pottery and porcelain figures. In the history of Western art sculpture reached a zenith in the work of the ancient Greek sculptors PHIDIAS, PRAXITELES, and Scopas. During the medieval period sculpture, much of it ecclesiastical, was largely anonymous, with sculptors rising to prominence again during the Renaissance. In Florence during this period DONATELLO and MICHELANGELO were the outstanding innovators, and later BERNINI's style epitomized the sculpture of the high Baroque. CANOVA and THORVALDSEN in the 18th century were the two most prominent exponents of a Neoclassical style. In the 19th century the major figure was RODIN, who owed much to the realist movement. The development of modern sculpture was greatly influenced by African sculpture, with its intention of portraying a spirit or feeling instead of a naturalistic depiction. Important figures in the modern movement include EPSTEIN, MOORE, and HEPWORTH. Other artists rejected carving and modelling; the movement towards constructions, led by PICASSO and the CONSTRUCTIVISTS, set the style for much work in the field. GABO and CALDER examined the possibilities of KINETIC ART, such as mobiles, while the minimalist movement has pared works down to their basic geometrical forms, and other sculptors have experimented with the use of different materials, particularly various metals and plastics.

scurvy A disease caused by a deficiency of vitamin C (ascorbic acid). The symptoms include swollen, bleeding gums, subcutaneous bleeding, and the opening of previously healed wounds. It is easily cured by the administration of vitamin C tablets. It is prevented by including fresh vegetables and fruit in the diet and is now rarely seen. It was formerly a hazard of sailors on long voyages, who had no access to fresh vegetables and fruit.

Scutum The Shield, the fifth-smallest CONSTELLATION. It lies just south of the celestial equator. Scutum was introduced by Johannes Hevelius (1611–87) in honour of the King of Poland. Its brightest stars are of only fourth magnitude.

Scylla In Greek mythology, a female sea-monster who lived in a cave opposite the whirlpool **Charybdis** (traditionally they were situated in the Straits of Messina between Italy and Sicily). In seeking to avoid one of the dangers, sailors ran the risk of being killed by the other – hence 'to be between Scylla and Charybdis' means to be between two equally dangerous situations.

Scythia An ancient country on the north shore of the Black Sea. Its inhabitants were an Indo-European people of Central Asian origin, skilful horsemen and craftsmen, known for their distinctive 'animal style' art. They were eventually absorbed by the Goths and other immigrants during the 3rd and 2nd century BC.

SDI See STRATEGIC DEFENSE INITIATIVE.

sea The expanse of salt water that covers most (70.98 per cent) of the Earth's surface and surrounds its land masses. It covers an estimated 362,033,000 sq km (139,835,000 sq miles). Excluding the major oceans of the world, the largest sea is the South China Sea. Some large inland salt lakes are also called seas, such as the Caspian Sea, Aral Sea, Dead Sea, and Salton Sea. The average salinity of seawater is about 35 parts per thousand (by mass), but can rise to 55 ppt, as in the Red Sea, or fall to less than 10 ppt, as in parts of the Baltic Sea. The main salts formed by evaporation of seawater are calcium carbonate, calcium sulphate, and the chlorides of sodium, potassium, and magnesium. See also DESALINATION.

sea anemone A solitary POLYP usually less than 5 cm (2 inches) long, though some reef-dwelling forms reach 1 m (3 feet) across. Sea anemones can be spectacularly coloured, especially in tropical waters. As members of the phylum Cnidaria, they all have radial bodies bearing tentacles. Anemones catch small invertebrates or fishes by paralysing them with stinging cells (nematocysts) on their tentacles. The prey is then pushed into the large digestive cavity inside the sea anemone. While most animals succumb to the anemone poisons (some even being painful to humans), a few creatures, such as the fish *Amphiprion*, have special defences enabling them to live within the mass of tentacles, cleaning the anemone in return for protection and bits of food.

sea bass See BASS.

Seaborg, Glenn (Theodore) (1912–) US nuclear chemist. During 1940–58 Seaborg and his colleagues at the University of California, Berkeley, produced nine of the transuranic elements (plutonium to nobelium) by bombarding uranium and other elements with nuclei in a cyclotron; he coined the term ACTINIDE for the elements in this series. Seaborg and his early collaborator Edwin McMillan (1907–91) shared the Nobel Prize for chemistry in 1951, and Seaborg was chairman of the US Atomic Energy Commission 1962–71.

sea bream A fish of the family Sparidae, which also includes the North American porgies and Australian snappers. They are marine fishes, especially abundant in tropical and warm temperate seas but also occurring in temperate regions. They are deep-bodied, fully scaled on head and body, with spiny dorsal and anal fins. Their teeth are specialized according to their diet and can be either strong and sharply pointed, blunt and rounded, or flat. The red sea bream, *Pagellus bogaraveo*, of European and North American coastal waters, is a typical example of this group.

sea cow A member of an order of mammals, Sirenia, that is now largely extinct. There are two genera and four living species, three species of MANATEE of the Atlantic (comprising the family Trichechidae) and one species of DUGONG (family Dugongidae) of the Pacific and Indian oceans. A fifth species, the enormous Steller's sea cow, was discovered in 1741 in the Bering sea, but became extinct 27 years later. The population was isolated and virtually imprisoned on Bering Island, as any attempt to leave would have led to their death from large marine predators.

sea cucumber A worm-like leathery creature, belonging to a class, Holothuroidea, of ECHINODERMS. Its internal skeleton is reduced to small, calcareous ossicles or spicules, and tube-feet are concentrated around the mouth for feeding, or in rows below for walking. Most sea cucumbers live within crevices or burrows. When they are disturbed they eject entangling gummy strands (hence their other name of 'cotton-spinners'), or even their own guts. In some countries these animals are dried as 'trepang', valued as a food. Most common species are 10–30 cm (4–12 inches) long but some Pacific species can reach 1 m (3 feet) in length and 60 cm (2 feet) in diameter.

sea duck A BAY DUCK that spends much of its life at sea or on coastal waters. Sea ducks find their food, principally molluscs, on the sea-bottom. Typical sea ducks include the EIDERS, SCOTERS, and the LONG-TAILED DUCK.

sea eagle Any of the eight species of *Haliaeetus* that occur thinly across northern Europe, Asia, and North America. Among the largest of the eagles, they are typically found on islands or mainland close to the coast, where fishes are readily obtainable. Arctic populations migrate south in winter when the sea freezes.

sea fan A GORGONIAN coral with a regular flattened branching pattern which results in a fan-like structure, often 50 cm (20 inches) across. Each POLYP within the colony catches small suspended animals from the sea water, and usually the fans span the prevailing current. They occur mostly in warmer seas, and are familiar in marine aquaria. They tend to harbour a variety of encrusting organisms, which obscure their beautiful latticed outlines.

sea-floor spreading The movement of the tectonic plates that form the floors of the oceans away from the MID-OCEANIC RIDGES. According to PLATE TECTONICS it is the process by which oceans are formed and enlarged. Magma – molten igneous rock – rises through fissures at the mid-oceanic ridge to solidify (usually below the sea) and fill the gaps that are left as the plates move apart. New crust is thus formed. As a result of sea-floor spreading, the age of the rocks of the ocean floors increases as one travels away from the axis of a mid-oceanic ridge. The sea floors on each side of a mid-oceanic ridge are characterized by magnetic anomalies that are arranged in bands parallel to the axis of the ridge and are symmetrical with respect to it. They are interpreted as representing the direction of the Earth's magnetic field at the time when the rocks crystallized.

sea gooseberry (or **comb jelly**) A strange, floating marine animal with some 90 species worldwide, forming the phylum Ctenophora. Their name describes their ovoid jelly-like shape, and the regular rows of cilia that provide propulsion. They also have a pair of trailing tentacles, which bear adhesive cells to trap plankton. This simple structure suggests links with the sea anemones and jellyfish. Sea gooseberries are often luminescent, and sometimes become stranded in shimmering masses on coastlines.

sea holly Either of two totally unrelated plants. The sea holly of Europe and Mediterranean coasts is *Eryngium maritimum*, a member of the carrot family. This is a glaucous, spiny-leaved perennial with attractive grey-blue stems and leaves, and blue flowers. The leaf colour is the result of a waxy secretion which enables the plant to withstand wind and salt spray. Other *Eryngium* species are cultivated as garden plants.

The Asian sea holly, *Acanthus ebracteatus*, belongs to the family Acanthaceae. Its leaves are used to make a cough medicine popular in Malaysia.

sea horse A fish that, with the pipefish, makes up the family Syngnathidae. These fish have tails curved forwards, and their heads are inclined forwards. They swim upright, propelled by an undulating dorsal fin, and can anchor themselves by means of the tail. The male carries the eggs in an abdominal pouch. The Australian leafy sea-horse, *Phyllopteryx foliatus*, grows up to 30 cm (12 inches) long and is unusual in having fleshy growths on its body which mimic seaweed, a feature which it shares with the sea dragon, *Phycodurus eques*.

sea kale A member of the mustard family, *Crambe maritima*, native to the sea-cliffs and shores of western Europe. The leaf stalks, if blanched, may be boiled, and although somewhat bitter they have a nutty flavour.

seal Any of 19 species of carnivorous mammal belonging to the family Phocidae in the order Pinnipedia. Seals superficially resemble sea lions, but are better adapted to marine life with their small tail and hind feet not adapted for locomotion, and also in having only vestigial external ears. They feed mainly on marine invertebrates and fish, and are found in all oceans, mainly in high latitudes, and in central Asia. There are four subfamilies: monk seals, Monachinae, the oldest group and a protected species; crab-eater seals, Lobodontidae; hooded seals, Cystophorinae; and common seals, Phocinae, including ringed seals.

sea lily (or **crinoid**) A stalked relative of the FEATHER-STAR, now largely extinct with only about 80 species remaining, all in deep waters. The sea lilies comprise part of a class, Crinoidea, of ECHINODERMS, which flourished in Palaeozoic seas, their feathery arms filtering out abundant planktonic food. Some of the fossil sea lilies had stalks 25 m (80 feet) long.

sea lion A marine mammal belonging to the family Otariidae in the order Pinnipedia; it lives both on land and in the water. There are 14 species of sea lions, or eared seals, found in the North and South Pacific, the South Atlantic, and other southern waters. The Californian sea lion, *Zalophus californianus*, and the northern fur seal, or sea-bear, *Callorhinus ursinus*, are found in the Northern Hemisphere. The remaining species live in the Southern Hemisphere. All sea-lions have a streamlined body with paddle-like limbs, the digits of which are joined by a web. The adults are entirely at home in the sea but the young have to learn how to swim. The largest male may reach a length of 3 m (10 feet); the females are smaller. They range in colour from the dark chocolate-brown of the Californian to the greyish-yellow of the Australian sea lion, *Neophoca cinerea*. Sea lions are quite mobile on land: they can rotate their hind-limbs forward to support their body and can even climb cliffs. Herd-living, they are more sociable than the seals. In the breeding season harems are formed and territories defended. The pups are suckled for at least three months.

sea lizard (or **Darwin's lizard**) A large marine IGUANA, *Amblyrhynchus cristatus*, which basks, sometimes in large aggregations, among lava rocks on the shores of the Galápagos Islands. Sea lizards are essentially herbivorous, feeding on seaweeds for which they often have to dive. Submergence time may vary from about three minutes in shallow water to about one hour in deeper water. They are large, stocky lizards growing to 1.2 m (4 feet) in length, and have a crest running from the neck to the tail. They lay two or three eggs in tunnels dug in sandy beaches.

sea mat See MOSS ANIMAL.

sea moth Any of six species of small fish found only in the tropical Indian and West Pacific oceans. They belong to the family Pegasidae, and grow up to about 14 cm (6 inches) long. The body is oddly shaped, broad and flat at the front, then tapering toward the tail. The body appears to be encased in rings of bony plates. The snout is almost duck-billed, while the pectoral fins are large and like moths' wings. Usually brown in colour, they live mainly on sandy bottoms.

sea mouse A beautifully iridescent marine animal of the genus *Aphrodite*, which is a polychaete ANNELID. Seen from below, the segmentation and stout bristly paddles on which it walks reveal its true worm identity. But from above, the sea mouse is covered by scales and long, glistening hairs, and when moving along half-buried in sand it resembles a rather sluggish mouse, with very colourful fringes. Sea mice are related to SCALE WORMS.

sea otter A species of OTTER, *Enhydra lutris*, that lives along the shores of the west coast of America, swimming and floating among beds of seaweed. A single pup is born in a nest of floating kelp, and lives entirely at sea. It is able to swim at 16 km/hour (10 miles per hour) and may dive to a depth of 30 m (100 feet) or more in search of food. It feeds on sea urchins, crustaceans, cuttlefish, mussels, and other shellfish. It is one of the few tool-using mammals: it will rest a stone on its chest and crush clams and sea urchins against it.

Sea Peoples (or **Peoples of the Sea**) Groups of people who encroached on the Levant and Egypt by land and by sea in the late 13th century. Their identity is still being debated. In the Levant they are associated with destruction; the Egyptians were successful in driving them away. Some, including the Philistines, settled in Palestine.

sea perch (or **surf perch**) A fish of the family Embiotocidae, with about 23 species native to the North Pacific, and one species found in fresh water in California. Most are around 25 cm (10 inches) in length and are deep-bodied fishes with large scales and a spiny dorsal fin. They live in shallow coastal water, often among the kelp beds. The male has a fleshy modified anal fin, which acts as an intromittent organ (for transferring sperm); these fishes give birth to live young.

seaplane An aeroplane that can land and take off from water; it differs from a **flying boat** in that it has a conventional fuselage supported by floats rather than a floating hull. They are used in Canada and other areas where lakes abound; in the winter the floats are often replaced by skis.

Searle, Ronald (William Fordham) (1920–) British artist and cartoonist. He is best known for his humorous drawings, his most famous creations being the schoolgirls of St Trinian's, who became the subjects of four films (starting with *The Belles of St Trinians*, 1954) and a number of books. He was a contributor to *Punch* magazine from 1949.

sea scorpion (or **eurypterid**) An extinct, aquatic, freshwater arthropod, thought to be a true ARACHNID. Sea scorpions were common in fresh water during the Ordovician to Permian eras (505–245 million years ago), and were rapacious carnivores. Some species achieved a very large size, up to 3 m (10 feet) long, and their main prey must have included contemporary species of fishes.

sea slug (or **nudibranch**) A gastropod MOLLUSC of the order Nudibranchia, related to the snail but usually with a reduced or absent shell. The exposed flattened body is often brilliantly coloured, signalling to predators the possession of distasteful or toxic secretions and so conferring protection. A few species even eat sea anemones and acquire their prey's stinging cells, which are then stored in projections on the back to be used for the sea slug's own defence. Most species breathe through filamentous projections, which are often brightly coloured.

sea snake A snake belonging to the family Hyrophiidae, which mainly occurs in the shallow tropical seas of south-east Asia and northern Australia, although some of the 50 or so species are more wide-ranging. Sea snakes are poisonous, their venom apparatus being similar to that of COBRAS. The majority are totally aquatic, and they give birth to live young, but some less specialized species lay eggs on land. They have several marine adaptations, such as paddle-shaped tails and valvular nostrils (often on top of the snout), and glands under the tongue which are modified for the elimination of excess salt.

sea spider A marine animal, quite commonly found, especially around rocks and pilings, though it is often overlooked. It resembles a spider, having eight to twelve legs, and its 600 or so species form the arthropod class Pycnogonida. Sea spiders are remotely related to the arachnids. Curiously, they have reproductive organs in their legs, and males have special egg-bearing limbs. The male gathers eggs as the female lays them, cementing them together and carrying the spherical mass until hatching-time.

sea squirt A sessile animal of the chordate subphylum Urochordata (or Tunicata), found in shallow seas. Sea squirts resemble a bag of jelly, with a hard outer coat which has two openings where water is drawn in and out during filter feeding. Despite this primitive (and sometimes colonial) way of life, sea squirts are quite advanced animals, sharing with ACORN WORMS and LANCELETS some features that are also found in vertebrates. These features are most obvious in the larvae, which are tadpole-like and swim actively, using propulsive muscular tails.

seat-belt See SAFETY-BELT.

SEATO See SOUTH-EAST ASIA TREATY ORGANIZATION.

Seattle A port and industrial city in the state of Washington, the largest city in the north-western US; pop. (1990) 516,260. Situated on Elliott Bay, between Puget Sound and Lake Washington, its economy is based on tourism, the world's biggest aircraft industry, serving as a provisioner for Alaska, and trading in products from its surrounding forests, farms and waterways.

sea urchin The only ECHINODERM to have a complete rigid test (an internal shell), the five arms having joined to give a spherical shell. From this, spines and protective tiny claws (sometimes poisonous) protrude upwards, while the tube-feet mostly emerge below to allow walking. The sea urchin's mouth is armed with five elaborate rasping jaws to scrape up algae, the whole structure being referred to as the Aristotle's lantern. Sea urchins belong to the class Echinoidea. Most are regular in shape, ranging from 1–40 cm (0.4–16 inches) across; but a few asymmetrical burrowing forms occur, such as sand-dollars, heart urchins, and sea potatoes. Some species commonly burrow beneath sandy beaches.

sea water See DESALINATION; SEA.

seaweeds Marine ALGAE, ranging in size from a few centimetres to many metres long. They may be green, red, or brown and the different coloured, photosynthetic pigments are accompanied by differences in life cycle, construction, and habitat. The largest are the brown algae, or brown seaweeds, including the KELPS and wracks, which are anchored to rocks on the sea-bed by a strongly adhesive disc, the hold-fast, while their fronds move in the water currents. Green seaweeds, such as the edible sea lettuce, *Ulva lactuca*, often grow in brackish water. The purple-red seaweeds, such as the laver, *Porphyra umbiliacus*, and the red dulse, *Rhodymenia palmata*, are edible, while others are used as fertilizers, as grazing for sheep in some areas, and as sources of iodine and alginates.

sebaceous gland See SKIN.

Sebastapol (Russian **Sevastopol**) A fortress and Black Sea naval base near the southern tip of the Crimea peninsula, southern Ukraine; pop. (1990) 361,000. It was the focal point of military operations during the Crimean War, falling eventually to Anglo-French forces in September 1855 after a year-long siege. It is port to the Black Sea fleet over which Russia and Ukraine have been in dispute.

second ▶1 The SI UNIT of time. The second was first defined in terms of astronomical parameters, such as the day (one revolution of the Earth on its axis). However, such parameters vary slightly, so the second had to be redefined in terms of an unvarying parameter. It is now defined as equal in duration to 9,192,631,770 periods of the radiation corresponding to the transition between two hyperfine levels of the ground state of the caesium-133 atom. **▶2** A unit of angle, equal to one sixtieth of a MINUTE.

secondary colour See PRIMARY COLOUR.

secondary education The instruction of children from the age of about 11, on leaving primary school, to the time when they enter employment or continue into higher or vocational education. In most industrialized countries, nearly all children receive their secondary education free, at least to the lower grades (in many developing countries, schooling for the majority does not continue beyond the age of 12). Current teaching in Europe and North America attempts broadly to develop the intellect, with the teacher dominating the learning process through lecturing, demonstrations, questioning, and debate. More recently, a method that attempts to anticipate employment needs has been gaining ground. In this, education is process led, that is, in conjunction with a firm foundation in the humanities, social sciences, and the natural sciences, pupils are encouraged to develop skills and attitudes which mirror social needs and employment opportunities.

Second Reich See GERMAN SECOND EMPIRE.

secretary bird The sole member of the family Sagittariidae, *Sagittarius serpentarius*, found in open country over much of Africa south of the Sahara. It stands up to 1.5 m (5 feet) high and has pale grey plumage except for black wings and thighs. The feathers of the loose crest look rather like quills stuck behind the ear, and may be the origin of the name. It is long legged and runs about on the ground, catching snakes, small mammals, large insects, and lizards. It is related to the birds of prey and, like many of them, builds nests of branches in the tops of trees and has two or three young at a time.

security A document issued by firms, institutions, and governments giving the owner of the security certain property rights and/or the right to receive INTEREST or DIVIDENDS. Securities are commonly traded on STOCK EXCHANGES. Types of securities include fixed-interest-bearing securities, normally representing debts, such as DEBENTURES, preference SHARES, and BONDS (including GILT-EDGED SECURITIES and other government securities); and variable income securities, essentially SHARES (also called equities).

Security Council See UNITED NATIONS SECURITY COUNCIL.

Sedan A town on the River Meuse in the department of Ardennes, north-east France; pop. (1990) 22,400. Its bastions and ramparts date back to the 15th century. It was the site of the decisive battle (1870) in the Franco-Prussian War, in which the Prussian army succeeded in surrounding a smaller French army under Napoleon III and forcing it to surrender. This marked the end of the Second Empire.

sedative See PSYCHOTROPIC DRUG.

sedge A perennial monocotyledonous plant with rhizomatous or creeping rootstocks, solid triangular stems, and grass-like leaves. Sedges belong to the genus *Carex*, with over 1,000 species widely distributed throughout the temperate, Arctic, and Antarctic regions of the world. The family Cyperaceae, to which they belong, contains over 4,000 species, some of which are referred to as reeds or even 'grasses'. They have little ornamental or economic value, though *C. arenaria*, from Europe and Siberia, is useful for stabilizing loose sands and grows mostly on sea-shores. Sweet sedge, *Acorus calamus*, is a member of the arum family and is botanically unrelated to the true sedges.

Sedgemoor A plain in Somerset, scene of a battle (1685) in which MONMOUTH, who had landed on the Dorset coast as champion of the Protestant party, was defeated by James II's troops. Monmouth himself was captured, and was executed soon afterwards.

sedge warbler A species of bird, *Acrocephalus schoenobaenus*, in the family of Old World WARBLERS. It breeds in damp areas and wet ditches over wide areas of Europe and western Asia and spends the winter in Africa. It is a small brownish, heavily streaked bird, 12.5 cm (5 inches) long, and has a conspicuous whitish eye-stripe.

Sedgwick, Adam (1785–1873) British geologist. He was based in Cambridge and specialized in the fossil record of rocks from North Wales, assigning the oldest of these to a period that he named the Cambrian. Sedgwick also amassed one of the greatest geological collections.

sedimentary rock A solid deposit that has been laid down by water, wind, ice, or gravity. The material of which sedimentary rocks are composed has usually been transported from its source. They have accumulated at or near the Earth's surface at normal temperatures and pressures, and are thus distinguished from igneous rocks, which have originated as MAGMA in a molten or semi-molten state, and from METAMORPHIC ROCKS, which have been produced by the effects of heat or pressure. Many sedimentary rocks were deposited in water in which the transported material was in a state of suspension or solution. After deposition they have been consolidated. Some, such as LOESS, were deposited by the wind; some, such as boulder clay, are the result of glacial action; some have simply accumulated in place. Sediments can be divided into three groups: clastic rocks, chemical precipitates, and organic sediments. Of these, clastic sediments are the most abundant. They are made up of fragments of pre-existing rocks. Clays, sands, and gravels are in this category. Chemical precipitates include some limestones and deposits formed by the evaporation of lakes or seawater. These deposited rocks include gypsum and halite (rock-salt). Organic sediments are those formed largely of the remains of once-living organisms: examples are coal, oil shale, and limestones made mainly of fossil material. By volume, sedimentary rocks make up only 5 per cent of the known crust of the Earth, compared with 95 per cent of igneous rocks. They are, however, exposed on over two-thirds of the Earth's land surface, forming thin but extensive deposits. The commonest types are shales, sandstones, and limestones. The earliest known sedimentary rocks came from the Barberton Mountain Land of South Africa; these have been dated as 3,500 million years old.

seed The product of FERTILIZATION in plants, consisting of a plant embryo surrounded by a protective seedcoat. In seeds of ANGIOSPERMS the embryo is embedded in fleshy tissue known as endosperm, which provides a store of food for the developing embryo, and in some species, for the seedling after germination. In many plants, the food reserves are stored in the cotyledons, which are the first leaves of the seedling. There may be up to four layers in the seed's protective coat, but more frequently there are two, known as the testa (outer) and tegmen (inner). A third layer, the aril, is sometimes present as a fleshy layer enveloping the whole or part of the seed. The testa and tegmen may be toughened by different layers of tissue, giving protection to the seed from desiccation and crushing. Seeds vary in size from those that are dust-like, such as those produced in millions in the capsules of orchids, to those of the palm, *Lodoicea maldivica*, which weigh several kilograms each. They are often dispersed within a FRUIT.

seed dressing The application of a FUNGICIDE or PESTICIDE to seeds to protect them from damage. Chemicals may be applied to prevent attack by fungus during storage or to repel birds at the time that seeds are most susceptible, just after sowing and whilst the first shoots are developing.

Seeger, Pete (1919–) US folk musician and songwriter. In 1949 he formed the folk group the Weavers, with whom he recorded a series of best-selling protest songs. From the early 1950s he followed a solo career and was prominent in the US folk revival. Among his most famous songs are 'If I Had a Hammer' (*c*.1949) and 'Where Have All the Flowers Gone?' (1956). Seeger fell under suspicion during the McCarthy era and was not cleared of all charges until 1962.

Seferis, George (Georgios Stylianou Seferiades) (1900–71) Greek poet. He was born in Smyrna, whose destruction in 1922 (in the aftermath of the Greco-Turkish war) left a lasting sense of pessimism in his poetry. His career as a diplomat brought him into contact with European culture, and he consequently became one of the first MODERNIST poets in Greece. Greekness is central to his poetry, particularly in *Mythistorema* (1935). His later collections, such as the three 'Logbooks' and his poem 'The Thrush', extend the breadth and depth of his preoccupations. He was awarded the Nobel Prize for literature in 1963.

Seghers, Hercules (*c*.1589–*c*.1633) Dutch painter and etcher of landscapes. Little is known of his life and only about a dozen paintings survive that are confidently attributed to him. Seghers certainly influenced REMBRANDT, who collected his work. Seghers's etchings are perhaps even more original than his paintings.

segmented mirror telescope See MULTIPLE-MIRROR TELESCOPE.

Segnosaurus See DINOSAUR.

Segovia, Andrés (1893–1987) Spanish guitarist and composer. He was largely responsible for the revival of interest in the classical guitar, elevating it to the status of a major concert instrument. He made a large number of transcriptions of classical music, including Bach, to increase the repertoire of the instrument, and also commissioned works from contemporary composers, such as Manuel de Falla.

Seine A river of northern France flowing 761 km (473 miles) from its source on the limestone Plateau de Langres in Burgundy to the English Channel near Le Havre. It drains a region of northern France known as the Paris Basin and the cities of Troyes, Paris, and Rouen lie along its course.

seismograph An instrument for detecting and measuring movement of the ground due to earthquakes or explosions. Most modern instruments incorporate some sort of pendulum, but they additionally involve an electromagnetic recording device. In a strain seismograph, two firmly anchored piers are connected by a fused-quartz tube containing a transducer, a device which measures the strain on the tube due to Earth movement. The newest high-precision seismometers have at their centre a leaf spring with a weight attached at one end. An electronic force detector senses any motion of the weight.

seismology The scientific study of EARTHQUAKES and the resultant waves and shocks within the Earth. These waves are generated by earthquakes or man-made explosions and a collection of well-distributed SEISMOGRAPHS enable the nature and time of arrival of the waves to be recorded. Three types of waves occur, these being the compressional waves (P-waves, involving a push-pull movement along the direction of propagation), the shear waves (S-waves, involving perpendicular movement), and the longitudinal waves (L-waves) that travel along the surface. All travel at different speeds and suffer different degrees of absorption. The wave velocity increases with rock density and the waves are refracted, that is, bent when the density changes. Wave characteristics can be interpreted in terms of the subsurface structure of the crust and mantle and also the physical conditions acting on these rocks. The outer boundary of the Earth's core provides a major seismic discontinuity because, being liquid, the S-waves cannot travel through it.

Selene In Greek mythology, the Moon, the daughter of Hyperion and the Titaness Theia. She is sometimes identified with Artemis.

selenium (symbol Se, at. no. 34, r.a.m. 78.96) A METALLOID element in Group 16 (formerly VIB) of the periodic table; it occurs in several different ALLOTROPES including a metallic form. It occurs as an impurity in sulphide ores, from which it can be recovered. The stable, grey selenium allotrope contains chains of selenium atoms whose conductivity is increased by light; it is used as a photoconductor in photoelectric cells (see PHOTOELECTRIC EFFECTS). It is also used in PHOTOCOPIERS and alternating-current RECTIFIERS, in colouring glass red, in ceramic glazes, and in hardening steel. It is an essential trace element and is present in some garlic-smelling plants.

selenography The mapping of the Moon. This subject started with the invention of the telescope, the first telescopic maps being produced by GALILEO and by the British astronomer Thomas Harriot in 1611. The large light and dark areas were named after watery expanses, such as oceans, seas, and lakes, and the various states of the climate and weather, for example, Mare Frigoris. Features, such as craters and mountains, were associated with famous philosophers, scientists, mathematicians, and astronomers. The development of photography in the mid-19th century eventually led to the production of new atlases by the Dutch–US astronomer Gerard Kuiper, the US physicist David

Alter, and the Japanese astronomer Shotaro Miyamoto. The first maps of the far side of the Moon were made after the Soviet Luna 3 spacecraft produced photographs in 1959. Detailed lunar mapping has continued with images from Orbiter and APOLLO missions. Selenography was transformed after the Moon landings of ALDRIN and ARMSTRONG in 1969. Samples brought back by this and subsequent missions have given the science a firm foundation in fact.

Seles, Monica (1973–) US tennis player, born in Yugoslavia. She became the youngest woman to win a grand slam singles title with her victory in the French Open in 1990, and in 1991 she was the youngest woman to win the Australian Open. Her career was interrupted in 1993 when she was stabbed on court by a fan of her rival Steffi Graf, but she returned to play in 1995, winning the Australian Open in 1996.

Seleucid The Hellenistic dynasty founded by Seleucus I Nicator, one of the generals of Alexander the Great, ruling over Syria and a great part of western Asia 312–64 BC. Its capital was at Antioch.

Selfridge, Harry Gordon (1858–1947) US-born British businessman. In 1906 he came to England and began to build the department store in Oxford Street, London, that bears his name; it opened in 1909.

Seljuk A Turkish dynasty that ruled Asia Minor in the 11th–13th centuries, successfully invading the Byzantine Empire and defending the Holy Land against the Crusaders.

Selkirk, Alexander (or **Selcraig**) (1676–1721) Scottish sailor. While on a privateering expedition in 1704, Selkirk quarrelled with his captain and was put ashore, at his own request, on one of the uninhabited Juan Fernandez Islands in the Pacific, where he remained until he was rescued in 1709. His experiences later formed the basis of Daniel Defoe's novel *Robinson Crusoe* (1719).

Selkirkshire A former county in the Scottish Borders, from 1975 to 1996 included in the Ettrick and Lauderdale District of Borders Region. Its county town was Selkirk.

Sellafield An industrial site near the coast of Cumbria, north-west England, formerly the site of a Royal Ordnance Factory and now belonging to British Nuclear Fuels. It was the scene in 1957 of a fire which caused a serious escape of radioactivity. The site was known as **Windscale** between 1947 and 1981.

Sellers, Peter (1925–80) British comic actor. He made his name in *The Goon Show*, a British radio series of the 1950s, with Spike Milligan and Harry Secombe. Sellers then turned to films, starring in many comedies, such as *The Lady Killers* (1955), *I'm All Right Jack* (1959), and *Dr Strangelove* (1964). In the 'Pink Panther' series of films of the 1960s and 1970s, he played the role of the French detective Inspector Clouseau, for which he is best known. His last films included *Being There* (1979).

Selous, Frederick Courteney (1851–1917) British explorer, naturalist, and soldier. He first visited South Africa in 1871 and spent the following ten years in exploration and big-game hunting in south central Africa. From 1890 he was involved in the British South Africa Company, negotiating mineral and land rights for the British (see also RHODES).

selvas The equatorial rainforest of the Amazon basin in South America.

Selye, Hans Hugo Bruno (1907–82) Austrian-born Canadian physician. He showed that environmental stress and anxiety could result in the release of hormones that, over a long period, could produce many of the biochemical and physiological disorders characteristic of the 20th century. Selye's theory had a profound effect on modern medicine, and he became a popularizer of research on stress.

Selznick, David O(liver) (1902–65) US film producer. Based in Hollywood from 1926, he produced such films as *King Kong* (1933) for RKO and *Anna Karenina* (1935) for MGM. In 1936 he established his own production company, Selznick International, with which he produced such screen classics as *Gone with the Wind* (1939) and *Rebecca* (1940).

semantics A branch of LINGUISTICS studying meaning. For some linguists it is concerned with all aspects of meaning, but for others it is concerned only with those aspects that are independent of context. Context-dependent aspects of meaning such as politeness or conversational interaction, are in this view regarded as belonging to the province of pragmatics. On either view, it deals with such matters as ambiguity, where an expression (word, phrase, or sentence) has more than one meaning; synonymy, where two expressions mean the same; and entailment, where one sentence follows from another. It draws on work in LOGIC and PHILOSOPHY.

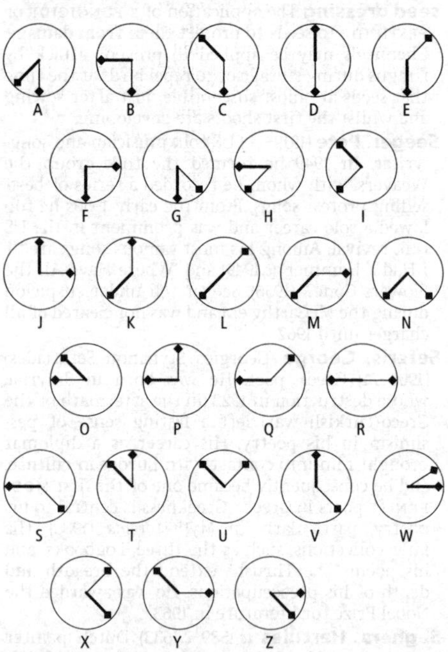

Semaphore The arrows indicate the position of the arms for each letter of the alphabet. The thick lines represent the right arm, the thin lines the left arm.

semaphore A coded means of visual communication using different positions of two movable arms to represent different letters of the alphabet. Semaphore was originally transmitted by a relay of machines erected on towers on hills; the system was invented by CHAPPE in 1794 for the French Army. The most common form of semaphore involves the sender holding a flag in each hand. Railway signal systems have also used a type of semaphore.

Semarang A commercial city and capital of the

province of Central Java, Indonesia; pop. (1990) 1,249,200. Ceded to the Dutch in 1677, it was formerly the seat of the Dutch governor of the North-East Provinces. Once the leading port of Indonesia, its harbour gradually silted up. The northern harbour area is the city's commercial centre, while the hillier southern district (called Candi) is a residential quarter. It has shipbuilding and textile industries.

semen The watery fluid containing sperms that is ejaculated from the penis of vertebrates. The fluid is a mixture of secretions produced by the prostate and other accessory glands of the male reproductive tract. It acts as a supporting medium for sperms, providing them with the sugar fructose, which is converted to energy by the sperms. It also includes prostaglandins, which act on the womb and may assist transport of the sperms.

semiconductor A material that conducts electricity much better than an insulator, such as glass, but not nearly so well as a conductor, such as metal. Unlike metals, their conductivity increases when the temperature is raised rather than when it is reduced. The increase in conductivity occurs because the extra thermal energy available at higher temperatures enables the electrons bound to atoms to break away. They escape, and move freely in the material. The greater the number of free electrons the more electrical charge can be transported, and so the conductivity increases. The electrical conductivity of such materials is also increased by 'doping' – that is, by the addition of small traces of certain impurities – because introduced elements may either contribute extra electrons, or reduce the number of electrons, for the conduction process. If elements producing extra electrons are used the conduction is said to be n-type (n for negative). If the number of electrons is reduced 'holes' are created and the conduction is p-type. A hole behaves as if it were an electron with a positive charge. The elements germanium and silicon are widely used in SEMICONDUCTOR DEVICES and impurities, such as arsenic, antimony, or phosphorous, may be added to form extrinsic semiconductors; boron, aluminium, or gallium may be added to form intrinsic semiconductors.

semiconductor device A solid-state device, such as a TRANSISTOR or a DIODE, that is made from a SEMICONDUCTOR material such as SILICON, GERMANIUM, or gallium arsenide. The simplest semiconductor device is the diode, in which there is one p–n junction between a region of p-type semiconductor and a region of n-type material. Variants of this basic junction are employed in all other semiconductor devices. A TRANSISTOR has three differently doped regions and two junctions (p–n–p or n–p–n), while a thyristor has three junctions. However, once switched on, the device will continue to pass current even when the gate circuit is broken. Semiconductor devices made from gallium arsenide (GaAs) can work at higher frequencies than silicon-based devices, and they can both detect and emit light. Such devices are currently used in high-frequency microwave circuits, and are likely to become important in OPTICAL FIBRE communications. New organic POLYMERS developed recently have semiconducting properties suitable for the manufacture of electronic devices. See also CIRCUITS, ELECTRICAL AND ELECTRONIC; INTEGRATED CIRCUIT.

Seminole A North American Indian tribe of the Muskogean linguisitic group, originally a branch of the Creek tribe who migrated from Georgia to Florida in the 18th century. Most were resettled in Oklahoma in the 19th century. Today they number *c.*14,000.

semiotics The study of natural and artificial signs and sign systems. It postulates that communication is a code. For example, in LANGUAGE, signs such as sounds and words are arranged in a particular manner, following rules of GRAMMAR, into a speech system. Other communication systems include gesturing (see NON-VERBAL COMMUNICATION), the structure of MYTHS, symbolic rites, styles in clothing, and food customs. The semiotic approach to LANGUAGE was advocated by SAUSSURE, but other linguists have rejected it as descriptively inadequate.

Semiramis In Greek legend, the daughter of a Syrian goddess, and second wife of Ninus, king of Assyria, with whom she founded Nineveh. After Ninus' death, Semiramis is alleged to have ruled for many years, conquering many lands and founding the city of Babylon. At her death she vanished from the Earth in the shape of a dove and was thereafter worshipped as a deity. The historical figures behind the legend are thought to be two powerful Assyrian queen-mothers, Sammuramat (9th century BC) and Naqi'a (7th century BC).

Semite Any of the peoples supposed to be descended from Shem, son of Noah (Genesis 10: 21 ff.), including especially the Jews, Arabs, Assyrians, and Phoenicians.

Semitic languages An important group of languages spoken throughout North Africa, the Arabian peninsula, and the Middle East. All modern Semitic languages are descendants of the Western branch of the language. The Eastern group was extremely important in antiquity, however; Akkadian (which later developed into Babylonian and Assyrian) was the language of Mesopotamia during the first two millennia BC. The CUNEIFORM tablets bearing these languages were deciphered in the 19th century. Western Semitic falls into two branches, South and Central. South Semitic has two main languages: Tigrinya (spoken in Tigre and Eritrea) and Amharic, the official language of Ethiopia (13 million speakers). Central Semitic includes Arabic, Hebrew, Phoenician, and Aramaic. By far the largest Semitic language is Arabic (over 150 million native speakers). There are two varieties: classical Arabic, the language of Islam, has remained virtually unchanged since the 7th century AD, and is an Arab LINGUA FRANCA. Colloquial Arabic consists of the numerous modern dialects. Hebrew has a long history: the Jewish scriptures were written in biblical Hebrew between about 1200 and 200 BC, but the language had declined by the end of the 6th century BC and was almost supplanted by Aramaic by the time of Jesus. However, the language was maintained by Jews down the centuries as a religious language, and was resurrected (with modifications) at the beginning of the 20th century. It is now the official language of 4 million Israelis. Aramaic has a descendant called Syriac, which has 300,000 Middle Eastern speakers. Phoenician is now extinct, but was important in the first millennium BC. Semitic is part of Afro-Asiatic, a larger group which includes ancient Egyptian, Berber, Chadic, and Cushitic.

Semmelweis, Ignaz Philipp (born Ignác Fülöp Semmelweis) (1818–65) Hungarian obstetrician who spent most of his working life in Vienna. He discovered the infectious character of puerperal fever, at the time a major cause of death following childbirth. Semmelweis demonstrated that the infection was transmitted by the hands of doctors who examined patients after working in the dissecting room, and advocated rigorous cleanliness and the use of antiseptics.

Senanayake, Don Stephen (1884–1952) Sinhalese statesman, Prime Minister of Ceylon (now Sri Lanka) 1947–52. In 1919 he co-founded the Ceylon National Congress, and during the 1920s and 1930s held ministerial positions on Ceylon's legislative and state councils. He became Prime Minister in 1947, and the following year presided over Ceylon's achievement of full dominion status within the Commonwealth.

Senate, US The second, or upper, chamber of the US Congress, representing the 50 states of the union. The powers and composition of the Senate are set out in Article I of the US Constitution, and the Senate first met in 1789. Senators, two from each state, have six-year terms and were chosen by the state legislatures until 1913, when the Seventeenth Amendment provided for their direct election. The terms of one-third of the Senators expire every two years. A Senator must be at least 30 years old, must have been a US citizen for not less than nine years, and must be a resident of the state he or she represents. The Vice-President presides over the Senate, voting only in the case of a tie. The Senate must ratify all treaties, confirm important presidential appointments, and take a part in legislation. See also ROMAN SENATE.

Seneca A subgroup of the Iroquois North American Indian people of New York State, USA, one of the Iroquois League or Five Nations of the Iroquois.

Seneca, Marcus Annaeus (known as **Seneca the Elder**) (*c.*55 BC–*c.*39 AD) Roman rhetorician, born in Spain. Seneca is best known for his works on rhetoric, only parts of which survive, including *Oratorum Sententiae Divisiones Colores* and *Suasoriae*. His son, **Lucius Annaeus Seneca** (known as **Seneca the Younger**) (*c.*4 BC–65 AD) was a Roman statesman, philosopher, and dramatist. Born in Spain, he was banished to Corsica by Claudius in 41, charged with adultery; in 49 his sentence was repealed and he became tutor to Nero, through the influence of Nero's mother and Claudius' wife, Agrippina. Seneca was a dominant figure in the early years of Nero's reign and was appointed consul in 57; he retired in 62. His subsequent implication in a plot on Nero's life led to his forced suicide. As a philosopher, he expounded the ethics of Stoicism in such works as *Epistulae Morales*. Seneca also wrote nine plays.

senecio Any of about 2,000 species of plant with a worldwide distribution, making up the genus *Senecio*, part of the sunflower family, and the genus to which RAGWORTS belong. In habit they vary considerably and include small annuals, such as *Senecio vulgaris* (groundsel), desert succulents, climbers, and the giant *S. grandifolius* from Mexico, which grows to over 5 m (18 feet) in height. In the mountains of East Africa are found strange tree-like forms, which have adapted to survive the extremes of temperature between night and day. Several shrubby species, such as *S. laxifolius* are valuable garden shrubs, while the Canary Island *S. cruentus* is the parent of the pot plant called cineraria.

Senegal A West African country with an Atlantic coast.

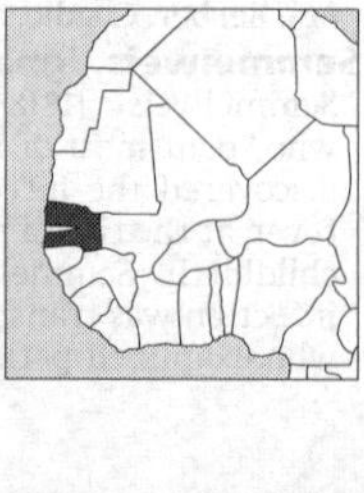

Physical. Senegal surrounds the Gambia and is itself bounded inland by Mauritania, Mali, Guinea, and Guinea-Bissau. Its most westerly point (and that of continental Africa) is Cape Verde, formed by a volcano, to the north of which the coast is straight and sandy and offers a cool, dry climate. Inland there is SAVANNAH, sparser in the north than in the south, which is wetter; the south of the country has a marshy coast. In winter the drying HARMATTAN wind blows from the interior.

Economy. The predominantly agricultural economy has been weakened by drought and low world prices for agricultural exports. The principal exports are fish, ground-nuts, and phosphates. Other crops include sugar-cane, millet, rice, and cotton. Mineral resources include phosphates, and unexploited reserves of iron ore, and gold. Industry includes ship repair and oil-refining in Dakar, and food-processing.

History. Senegal has been part of several ancient empires, including those of GHANA, MALI, and SONGHAI. The Tukulor, one of Senegal's seven main ethnic groups, converted to Islam in the 11th century, but animism remained widespread until the middle of the 19th century. Portuguese navigators explored the coast of Senegal in 1445. Founded by France in the 17th century, the colony of Senegal was disputed by Britain in the Napoleonic Wars. The interior was occupied by the French governor L. L. Faidherbe (1854–61); in 1871 the colony sent its first Deputy to the French Assembly. It became part of French West Africa in 1895, and in 1958 it was made an autonomous republic within the FRENCH COMMUNITY. It became part of the Federation of MALI (1959–60). Under the leadership of Léopold Sédar Senghor it became independent in 1960. It briefly federated with The GAMBIA as Senegambia (1982–89). In 1980 Abdou Diouf succeeded Léopold Senghor as President within a multi-party system. Relations between Senegal and MAURITANIA deteriorated sharply in 1989 following the killing of hundreds of Senegalese residents in Mauritania and the expulsion of thousands more. A virtual frontier war lasted through 1990, while both the OAU and President Mubarak of Egypt tried to mediate. Faced with the problems arising from ethnic tension, President Diouf formed a power-sharing coalition government in 1991 which succeeded in restoring a degree of order, diplomatic relations being resumed with Mauritania in 1992. Meanwhile a separatist movement had developed within Casamance in southern Senegal. Diouf was re-elected in early 1993. Violence by the separatists marred the presidential election, but a cease-fire agreement was concluded later in the year. Despite French and IMF aid, the Senegalese economy was on the verge of bankruptcy; a currency devaluation took place early in 1994. In 1995 the cease-fire agreement was breached by the Casamance separatists, but further peace talks were planned.

Capital: Dakar
Area: 196,722 sq km (75,955 sq mi)
Population: 8,312,000 (1995)
Currency: 1 CFA franc = 100 centimes
Religions: Sunni Muslim 91.0%; Roman Catholic 5.6%; traditional beliefs 3.2%
Ethnic Groups: Wolof 38.0%; Fulani-(Peul-)Tukulor 22.0%; Serer 19.0%; Diola 7.0%; Mande 7.0%
Languages: French (official); Wolof; other local languages
International Organizations: UN; OAU; Franc Zone

senescence The normal and inevitable effects of ageing, which are not caused by acquired disease or injury. It is thought that senescence arises when an organism fails to adapt to changes in the environment. The failure occurs over a relatively protracted period largely, it is believed, as a result of errors of replication of DNA caused by mutations that occur to the genetic material. The longer an organism lives, the greater is its exposure to such mutations.

Senna, Ayrton (1960–94) Brazilian motor-racing driver. He won the Formula One world championship in 1988, 1990, and 1991. He died from injuries sustained in a crash during the Italian Grand Prix in 1994.

Sennacherib (died 681 BC) King of Assyria 705–681. The son of Sargon II, he devoted much of his reign to suppressing revolts in various parts of his empire, including Babylon, which he sacked in 689. In 701 he put down a Jewish rebellion, laying siege to Jerusalem but sparing it from destruction (according to 2 Kings 19:35) after an epidemic of illness amongst his forces. He rebuilt and extended the city of Nineveh and made it his capital, and also initiated irrigation schemes and other civil engineering projects.

Sennett, Mack (born Michael Sinnott) (1880–1960), Canadian-born US film producer and director, known as the 'King of Comedy'. He was the inspiration behind the Keystone Company from its foundation in 1912 until 1917, developing the use of slapstick in crazy, irreverent short films almost always involving a final chase, and introducing the legendary Keystone Kops. He worked with notable comedians such as KEATON and Mabel Normand (1894/5–1930).

sensitive plant A small shrubby perennial, *Mimosa pudica*, from tropical America, belonging to the pea family. Its leaves are divided into many leaflets, which quickly fold together when the plant is touched. This sensitivity and movement of plant leaves also occurs in other plant species within the pea family, such as *Neptunia*, or in other families such as the genus *Biophytum* in the family Oxalidaceae.

sensor Any device that detects, records, or measures a physical property, such as temperature, sound, light, or radio waves. A very wide variety of devices, ranging from MASS SPECTROMETERS to SMOKE DETECTORS and burglar alarms may be described as sensors. Many sensors detect some form of electromagnetic radiation or other form of WAVE: examples include the PHOTOCELL for detecting light, the MICROPHONE for sound, and the GEIGER–MÜLLER COUNTER for nuclear radiation. They are usually also TRANSDUCERS, converting the incoming energy into an electrical signal. Sensors are often associated with some sort of SERVO-MECHANISM, which can operate a control system on the basis of the information from the sensor.

Seoul The capital of the Republic of Korea, on the Han River; pop. (1990) 10,627,790. It was the capital of the Korean Yi dynasty from the late 14th century until 1910, when Korea was annexed by Japan. Extensively developed under Japanese rule, it became capital of South Korea in 1945. Largely rebuilt since its destruction during the Korean War, its chief landmarks are the Namsan Tower, the Royal Ancestral Shrines, the 15th-century Changdok Palace, and the Kyongbok Palace, which houses the National Museum. It has textile manufacturing, agricultural processing, railway repair works, tanneries, and many light industries.

separation of powers A classic doctrine of liberal government, usually associated with the French philosopher Montesquieu (1689–1755), although the tripartite division was earlier suggested by ARISTOTLE and LOCKE. In *The Spirit of the Laws* (1748), Montesquieu set out that the three branches of government – the LEGISLATURE, the executive, and the JUDICIARY – should be constitutionally separate from each other, both in function and in persons. The doctrine is enshrined in the US Constitution, which provides a formal separation of Congress, President, and Supreme Court. The separation, however, is not total and some collaboration, especially between President and Congress, is necessary if the system is to work. In the UK, the executive, formed from the majority in Parliament, dominates the legislature. The judiciary, however, is largely independent of legislative and executive processes, although the head of the judiciary, the Lord Chancellor, is a member of the CABINET (executive) as well as the presiding officer of the HOUSE OF LORDS (legislature).

Sephardi (from Hebrew, 'sefarad', Spain) A member of the southern branch of the JEWISH PEOPLE. They number 17 per cent of the world's Jewish population, and many are resident in Israel, where they formed over half the population until the influx of Soviet Jews in the 1990s. Sephardi Jews were resident in Portugal and Spain until their expulsion in 1492, when they settled elsewhere in Europe (especially Holland), North Africa, and the lands of the Ottoman Empire. Sephardic Jews speak Ladino, a form of medieval Spanish with Hebrew elements, and they preserve the Babylonian Jewish traditions rather than the Palestinian traditions of the ASHKENAZIM.

septicaemia The presence of bacteria, or toxins produced by them, in the blood; septicaemia is a serious and life-threatening condition in the absence of treatment. Bacteria may originate from infection elsewhere in the body; common sites include the skin, throat, colon, and urinary tract. Other points of entry include surgical wounds and intravenous lines used for the administration of drugs and fluids. Bacteria in the blood may be transported to other organs, such as the heart, liver, kidneys, bones, and brain, which may result in secondary infections of these organs. Symptoms include fever, diarrhoea, and vomiting; hypotension and life-threatening SHOCK may follow. Early treatment is essential.

septic tank A small-scale SEWAGE treatment installation for a single building or small group of houses. Waste water passes through underground chambers, where the solids settle and are decomposed by anaerobic bacteria. The resulting effluent is further treated, normally by subsoil IRRIGATION. The tank requires desludging every year. A **cesspit** is a watertight underground chamber for storing sewage, which needs emptying more frequently than a septic tank.

sequence (in mathematics) An ordered list of mathematical terms. The Fibonnacci numbers, 1, 1, 2, 3, 5, 8, 13, ... form a sequence in which each term is the sum of the two preceding terms. A linear sequence is one in which each term is obtained by adding a constant to the previous term. See SERIES.

Sequoia See REDWOOD.

Sequoia National Park A national park in the Sierra Nevada, California, USA, established in 1890 to protect groves of giant red-wood trees. Located within the park are Mt Whitney (4,418 m, 14,495 ft), the highest mountain in the USA outside Alaska, and the General Sherman Tree which is the world's largest living tree (83 m, 272 ft high; 11.2 m, 37 ft diameter at its greatest girth).

Seraphic Doctor See BONAVENTURA, ST.

Serapis The supreme god of the Graeco-Roman

period, worshipped during the reign of Ptolemy I Soter (*c*.304 BC). He combined elements of Egyptian gods with those of the Greeks, providing a recognizable deity for the ruling Greeks to worship in Egypt. Serapis is the assimilation of Osiris and Apis (the sacred bull of Ptah at Memphis), depicted in Greek style as a man with long curly hair and beard, also wearing a ram's horns.

Serbia (Serbo-Croat **Srbija**) A Balkan republic which, with Montenegro, forms the remnant of the former six-member Federal Republic of Yugoslavia; area 88,361 sq km (34,129 sq miles); pop. (1981) 9,313,700; capital, Belgrade. Serbia includes the nominally autonomous provinces of Vojvodina and Kosovo. An independent state as early as the 6th century, it was conquered by the Turks in the 14th century. With the decline of Ottoman power in the 19th century, the Serbs successfully pressed for independence, finally winning nationhood in 1878. Subsequent Serbian ambitions to found a South Slav nation state brought the country into rivalry with the Austro-Hungarian empire and eventually contributed to the outbreak of World War I. Despite early successes against the Austrians, Serbia was occupied by the Central Powers and was, after the end of hostilities, absorbed into the new state of Yugoslavia. With the secession of four out of the six republics from the collective state in 1991–92, Serbia struggled to retain the viability of Yugoslavia and found itself internationally isolated as a result of armed conflict with neighbouring Croatia, involvement in the civil war in Bosnia, and the suppression of Albanian nationalism in Kosovo. In late 1995 the governments of Serbia, Croatia, and Bosnia-Hercegovina accepted a US-brokered peace settlement.

Serbo-Croat (or **Serbo-Croatian**) The language of the Serbs and Croats, generally considered to be one language (the differences between Serbian and Croatian are cultural rather than linguistic). Serbian is spoken by 10 million Serbs who belong to the Eastern Orthodox religion and so use the Cyrillic alphabet; Croat is spoken by five million Croats who are Roman Catholic and use the Roman alphabet.

Serengeti A vast plain lying to the west of the Great Rift Valley in Tanzania. In 1951 a national park was created to protect large numbers of migrating wildebeest, zebra, and Thomson's gazelle.

serf An unfree medieval peasant under the control of the lord whose lands he worked. As villeins or servants of a lord they represented the bottom tier of society. They were attached to the land and denied freedom of movement, freedom to marry without permission of their lord, and were obliged to work on their lord's fields, to contribute a proportion of their own produce, to surrender part of their land at death, and to submit to the justice and penalties administered by their lord in the manorial court in the case of wrongdoing. The lord had obligations to his serfs (unlike slaves), most notably to provide military protection and justice.

Serfdom originated in the 8th and 9th centuries in western Europe and subsequently became hereditary. In much of western Europe the system was undermined in the 14th century by the BLACK DEATH and starvation resulting from war, which led to acute labour shortages. Commutation of their labour for cash meant that the lord became a rentier and the serf a tenant; in the PEASANTS' REVOLT in England (1381) the main demand was for the abolition of serfdom and the substitution of rent at 4 pence an acre for services. However, in the eastern regions of Germany and Muscovy, the increased power of the nobility led to consolidation of serfdom. It was formally abolished in France in 1789, but lingered in Austria and Hungary till 1848, and was abolished in Russia only in 1861.

Sergius, St (Russian name Svyatoi Sergi Radonezhsky) (1314–92) Russian monastic reformer and mystic. He founded the monastery of the Holy Trinity near Moscow re-establishing monasticism, which had been lost in Russia as a result of the Tartar invasion; altogether he founded 40 monasteries. His political influence was also considerable: he stopped four civil wars between Russian princes, and inspired the resistance which saved Russia from the Tartars in 1380. Feast day, 25 September.

serialism (or **twelve-note technique**) A system of musical composition associated with SCHOENBERG, whose 'method of composing with 12 notes which are related only to one another' was developed during the 1920s as an explanation of what was giving avant-garde music its sense of 'order' at a time when the old TONAL SYSTEM had either broken down or been seriously weakened. Instead of the ordered hierarchy of the KEY system, serialism treats all 12 notes of the chromatic SCALE as being of equal importance. The basis of each composition is a 'series' of 12 chromatic notes, taken in any order, but without repetition, and formed into a 'note row'. The note row, transposed if necessary, or used in inversion or backwards, and so on, therefore becomes the source of the composition. The notes may be used melodically or harmonically, but a strict sequence must be maintained. It is the order that confirms their identity. Thus, notes 3, 5, and 7, may be heard simultaneously or consecutively, but not before notes 4 and 6 have been sounded. Many composers have found Schoenberg's theory inspiring, but not all have applied it with the same rigour.

seriema Either of two species of bird of the family Cariamidae, related to the cranes, and confined to grassland areas of central South America: the red-legged seriema, *Cariama cristata*, and the black-legged seriema, *Chunga burmeisteri*. They are tall, thin birds standing 75–90 cm (30–36 inches) tall, and are greyish above, paler below. They usually run rather than fly. They eat a wide range of insects and other small animals as well as some fruits. They build simple nests of twigs in a bush and rear two or three young at the same time.

series (in mathematics) A SEQUENCE of terms connected by an operation. For instance, the sequence $a, ar, ar^2, ar^3, \ldots$ combines to form the geometric series $a + ar + ar^2 + ar^3 + \ldots$, in which each term is a constant multiple of the previous term. In the arithmetic series $b + (b + d) + (b + 2d) + (b + 3d) \ldots$, each term is formed by *adding* a constant to the previous term. CONVERGENT SERIES and DIVERGENT SERIES have particular characteristics. POWER SERIES have regularly increasing powers of a variable, while MACLAURIN's series is a means of expanding a function.

serow Either of two species of goat-antelope. The mainland serow, *Capricornis sumatrensis*, frequents the forest lands on the mountain slopes of northern India, Myanmar (Burma), and China, at heights of up to 4,000 m (13,000 feet). It is an elusive, agile animal, and if discovered can leap 4.5–6 m (15–20 feet). As it makes off through the thickets, it utters a loud, angry, whistling snort. In the rutting season rams often 'horn' the trees, making the surface of the horns smooth. It will take readily to water and can swim well. The Japanese serow, *C.*

crispus, is similar in appearance but is adapted to the lower temperatures of Japan and Taiwan.

Serpens The Serpent, a CONSTELLATION straddling the celestial equator, one of the 48 constellations known to the ancient Greeks. It represents a huge snake held in the hands of Ophiuchus who was a healer credited with the ability to bring people back to life, and the fact that snakes shed their skin was a symbol of rebirth. Serpens is a unique constellation because it is split into two halves, the head and the tail, either side of OPHIUCHUS; however, it is regarded as a single constellation. Its brightest star, third-magnitude Alpha Serpentis, is known as Unukalhai, from the Arabic meaning 'serpent's neck'.

serpent In music, a wooden horn with finger-holes, built in sinuous shape. Serpents were used in churches to support the bass voices from around 1600, and in military and other wind bands from about 1740, by which time three keys had been added for chromatic notes. As orchestras grew larger, the serpent was introduced, and it appears in scores up to the middle of the 19th century, after which it was replaced by the TUBA.

serpentine A soft magnesium silicate mineral that is green or greenish black. There are two main varieties, antigorite and chrysotile, the latter being the major source of manufactured asbestos. Serpentine is formed by the alteration during metamorphism of OLIVINE and PYROXENE. It is used for ornamental purposes.

serpent star See BRITTLE STAR.

service tree See ROWAN.

servo-mechanism The means of powered automatic control of a larger system; this involves amplification of low-power command signals (mechanical, electrical, hydraulic, or other) so that they can control the motion of heavy equipment. An example of a servo-mechanism is the power steering used on some motor vehicles. Typically the position (and often also velocity and acceleration) of the device being controlled is measured by a SENSOR and fed back to a controller, usually as an electrical signal. The controller then generates the control action needed to correct any error via an actuator (power source), such as a servo-motor. Applications of servo systems include satellite-tracking systems, and the control (in three dimensions) of the position and velocity of a moving robot arm.

servqual See QUALITY CONTROL.

sesame An ancient oil plant of African origin, principally grown in the drier areas of India, China, Mexico, Myanmar (Burma), and the Sudan. True sesame, *Sesamum orientale*, is one of 50 species in the sesame family, Pedaliaceae, and the most important as a commercial crop. It is an erect, hairy annual, 2 m (6.5 feet) tall, which develops white to purplish, bell-shaped flowers that produce capsules containing small white, brown, or black seeds. The edible oil that forms 50 per cent of the seeds is used for cooking, and in the manufacture of margarine. Husked seeds are traditionally used for garnishing cakes, confectionery, and bread, particularly in Mediterranean countries. The expellers or extractors remaining after removal of the oil are used as animal feed.

set (in mathematics) A collection of objects, each member of the collection being called an element. A set can be a collection of anything, but it must be precisely defined. Frequently elements of sets are abstract, for example numbers or points. A set is denoted by a capital letter and its elements by

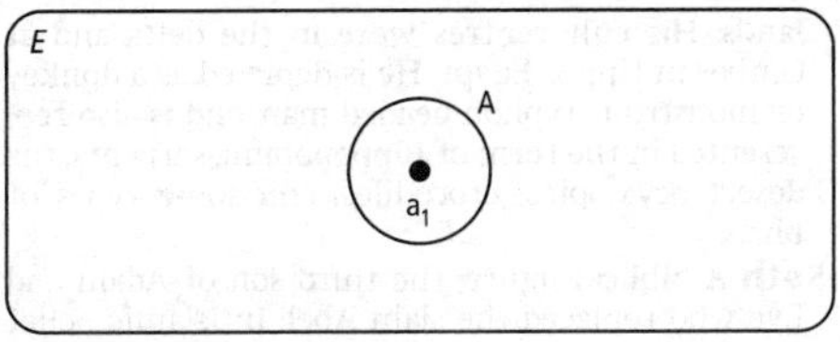

1

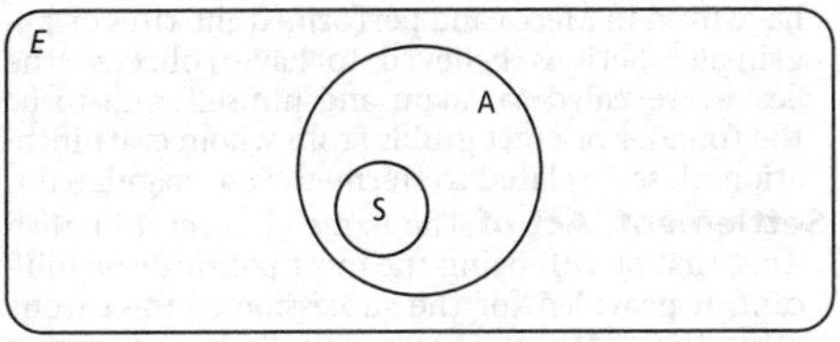

2

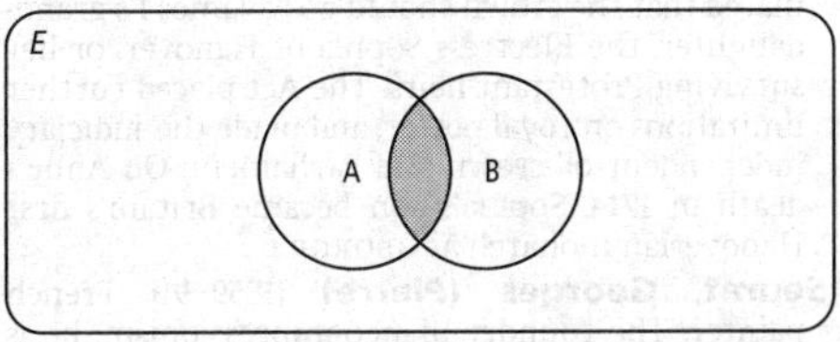

3

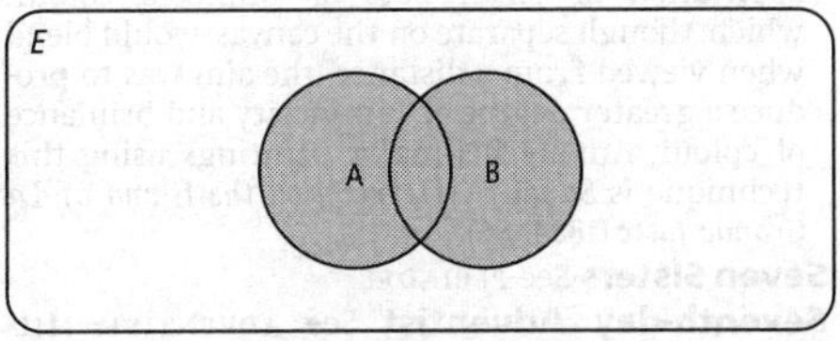

4

Sets (1) A set A is a collection of elements, a_1, a_2, etc. $a_1 \in A$ means that a_1 belongs to the set A. (2) If S is a subset of the larger set A, this is written $S \supset A$. (3) The intersection of two sets A and B is written $A \cap B$, meaning that it contains all the elements common to both A and B. (4) The union of two sets A and B, written $A \cup B$, is the set containing all the elements of A and all the elements of B.

small letters. Thus a set A is a collection of elements $a_1, a_2, a_3, \ldots, a_n$ and this is written $A = \{a_1, a_2, a_3, \ldots, a_n\}$, where the elements are contained within curly brackets. The symbol $\in$ is used to show that a particular element belongs to the set, thus $a_2 \in A$. The set containing no elements is the null or empty set $\varnothing$. That containing all elements is the universal set. Set S is a subset of the larger set A if all its elements are also in A, written as $S \supset A$. The union of two sets A and B, written as $A \cup B$, is the set containing all elements of A and all elements of B. The intersection of two sets A and B, written as $A \cap B$, is the set of all elements which are both in A and B. If $A \cap B = \varnothing$, then A and B are said to be disjoint.

Georg CANTOR introduced the concept of a set as an object of mathematical study, and set theory now attempts to provide a language, notation, and setting within which to do mathematics.

Set (or **Seth**, **Sutekh**) In Egyptian mythology, the god of the forces of chaos and of the hostile desert lands. His cult centres were in the delta and at Ombos in Upper Egypt. He is depicted as a donkey or monstrous typhon-headed man, and is also represented in the form of hippopotami, serpents, the desert oryx, pigs, crocodiles, and some types of birds.

Seth A biblical figure, the third son of Adam and Eve who replaced the slain Abel. In Islamic belief Seth (Shith, Shath) is a Prophet Messenger (*nabī rasūl*) and the executor of Adam's will, who was instructed by Adam how to worship God. Said to have lived in Mecca and performed the rites of pilgrimage, Seth is believed to have collected the 'leaves' revealed to Adam and himself, and to be the founder of craft guilds from whom craft initiation, closely related to Hermeticism, originated.

Settlement, Act of The name of several English Acts, that of 1701 being the most politically significant. It provided for the succession to the throne after the death of Queen ANNE's last surviving child, and was intended to prevent the Roman Catholic Stuarts from regaining the throne. It stipulated that the crown should go to James I's granddaughter, the Electress Sophia of Hanover, or her surviving Protestant heirs. The Act placed further limitations on royal power, and made the judiciary independent of crown and Parliament. On Anne's death in 1714, Sophia's son became Britain's first Hanoverian monarch as GEORGE I.

Seurat, Georges (Pierre) (1859–91) French painter. The founder of neo-impressionism, he is chiefly associated with pointillism, which he developed during the 1880s. The technique involved the application of small dots of unmixed colour, which, though separate on the canvas, would blend when viewed from a distance; the aim was to produce a greater degree of luminosity and brilliance of colour. Among his major paintings using this technique is *Sunday Afternoon on the Island of La Grande Jatte* (1884–86).

Seven Sisters See PLEIADES.

Seventh-day Adventist See ADVENTIST; MILLENARIANISM.

Seven Weeks War See AUSTRO-PRUSSIAN WAR.

Seven Wonders of the World The seven most spectacular man-made structures of the ancient world. The earliest extant list of these dates from the 2nd century; traditionally they comprise (1) the pyramids of Egypt, especially those at Giza; (2) the Hanging Gardens of Babylon; (3) the Mausoleum of Halicarnassus; (4) the temple of Diana (Artemis) at Ephesus in Asia Minor, rebuilt in 356 BC; (5) the Colossus of Rhodes; (6) the huge ivory and gold statue of Zeus at Olympia in the Peloponnese, made by Phidias *c.*430 BC; (7) the lighthouse built by Ptolemy II *c.*280 BC on the island of Pharos outside the harbour of Alexandria. Only the pyramids still exist.

Seven Years War (1756–63) A wide-ranging conflict involving Prussia, Britain, and Hanover fighting against Austria, France, Russia, Sweden, and Spain. It continued the disputes left undecided after the treaty of AIX-LA-CHAPELLE, and was concerned partly with colonial rivalry between Britain and France and partly with the struggle for supremacy in Germany between Austria and Prussia. Fighting had continued in North America with the Braddock expedition. Each side was dissatisfied with its former allies and in 1756 FREDERICK II of Prussia concluded the Treaty of Westminster with Britain. This made it possible for MARIA THERESA of Austria and her minister Count von Kaunitz to obtain an alliance with France (known as the 'diplomatic revolution') by the two treaties of Versailles in 1756 and 1757; she was also allied with Elizabeth of Russia. At first the advantage was with the French and Austrians, but in July 1757 PITT the Elder came to power in England and conducted the war with skill and vigour. In November Frederick II won his great victory of Rossbach over the French, and in December he defeated the Austrians at Leuthen. Frederick was hard pressed in 1758, but he defeated the Russians at Zorndorf and Ferdinand of Brunswick protected his western flank with an Anglo-Hanoverian army. In 1759 WOLFE captured Quebec, Ferdinand defeated the French army at MINDEN, and HAWKE destroyed the French fleet at QUIBERON BAY. In India CLIVE had won control of Bengal at Plassey, and in 1760 Montreal was taken. Admiral BOSCAWEN successfully attacked the French West Indies. In 1761 Spain entered the war and Pitt resigned. The death of Elizabeth of Russia eased the pressure on Frederick, as her successor Peter III reversed her policy. All were ready for peace, which was concluded by the Treaty of PARIS in 1763: overall England and Russia were victorious.

Severn The longest river of Britain, rising on Mount Plynlimon in eastern Wales and flowing about 320 km (200 miles) to the Bristol Channel. It is crossed by the two Severn Bridges, the first opened in 1966 and the second in 1996.

Severus, Septimius (full name Lucius Septimius Severus Pertinax) (146–211) Roman emperor 193–211. He was active in reforms of the imperial administration and of the army, which he recognized as the real basis of imperial power. In 208 he took an army to Britain to suppress a rebellion in the north of the country, and later died at York.

Seville (Spanish **Sevilla**) A port and industrial city in southern Spain, on the Guadalquivir River; pop. (1991) 683,490. It is capital of Andalusia and has a 15th-century Gothic cathedral. Wines, fruit, olives, and cork are exported. Arms, textiles, machinery, and chemicals are manufactured. Seville is the capital of bull-fighting in Spain. It gives its name to a bitter orange used to make marmalade.

Sèvres A suburb of south-west Paris, France, on the edge of the Saint-Cloud park; pop. (1990) 22,060. Sèvres porcelain was first made at a factory founded in 1738 in the Château de Vincennes, east of Paris. This factory moved to Sèvres in 1756 and three years later was purchased by Louis XV to save it from closure; thereafter it became a subsidized royal venture. In 1793 the French Republic took over the factory; it created a sophisticated style at the beginning of the 19th century, but the great designs faded and the factory took to producing copies of the 18th-century wares.

Sèvres, Treaty of (1920) A treaty, part of the VERSAILLES PEACE SETTLEMENT, signed between the Allies and Turkey, effectively marking the end of the OTTOMAN EMPIRE. Adrianople and most of the hinterland to Constantinople (now Istanbul) passed to Greece; the Bosporus was internationalized and demilitarized; a short-lived independent ARMENIA was created; Syria became a French mandate; and Britain accepted the mandate for Iraq, Palestine, and Transjordan. The treaty was rejected by Mustafa Kemal ATATÜRK, who secured a redefinition of Turkey's borders by the Treaty of Lausanne (see VERSAILLES PEACE SETTLEMENT).

sewage All the liquid discharged into the sewer from a household, including human waste and the water used for washing and food preparation. In the UK each person produces on average 180 litres of sewage daily. Sewage may also include surface or storm water from pavements and roads, which may be disposed through a separate system. Waste water from industrial processes is now commonly treated separately from sewage.

In a combined sewage-treatment system, both sewage and storm water are carried to the plant; in separate systems, untreated storm water is discharged directly to the nearest watercourse. Sewage treatment is divided into a series of stages. Preliminary treatment involves the removal of gross solids – oil, grease, and grit. In primary treatment the sewage passes slowly through sedimentation tanks, where larger particles sink to the bottom as a sludge. Chemicals may be added to encourage smaller particles to coagulate. Sewage discharged into the sea may receive only preliminary and perhaps primary treatment, although this procedure is now discouraged. Discharges into inland waters also undergo secondary (biological) treatment. In this, dissolved and colloidal organic material are oxidized by microorganisms, such as BACTERIA. The bacteria may be layered on percolating filters over which the sewage flows, or mixed with the sewage by a vigorous aeration device (the activated sludge process). If the receiving watercourse is used for domestic supply, or is very susceptible to pollution, it undergoes tertiary treatment (polishing), involving the removal of residual organic matter, suspended solids, pathogens, nutrients, such as nitrogen and phosphorus, and toxic metals. Separated sludge is dewatered by filtration, compaction, drying, or withdrawal of water using a vacuum. The sludge is then stabilized, and disposed of in landfill, farmland, or by incineration. New, stricter controls on sewage treatment being introduced in both Europe and the USA have led to research into new treatment methods. Promising developments include the use of reed-beds to detoxify sewage, peat or lignite to absorb pathogenic bacteria and other materials, bacteria immobilized in a solid medium, such as carbon powder, and ultrafiltration membranes (see FILTRATION), fine enough to remove viruses.

sewellel See MOUNTAIN BEAVER.

sewing-machine A machine for stitching together leather, textiles, and other materials. From about the middle of the 18th century, there was growing interest in creating sewing-machines. HOWE of Massachusetts, USA, constructed a lockstitch machine and patented it in 1846, but it was SINGER, also of Massachusetts, who five years later produced the first practicable domestic sewing-machine. Most domestic and industrial lockstitch sewing-machines today are direct descendants of Singer's machine and use the same mechanism of stitch formation. Machines are now generally powered by electricity rather than by hand or treadle. Other machines can make single-thread or two-thread chain-stitches, which are used where an extendable seam is required (as in knitted fabrics). More complex machines can carry out overlocking, machine embroidery, button sewing, and buttonhole making.

sex hormones The steroid hormones that are responsible for controlling sexual development and reproductive function. In women they are mainly produced by the ovaries and are called oestrogens (which include oestriol, oestrone, and oestradiol) and progesterone. In men they are mainly products of the testes and are called androgens (including testosterone and androsterone).

sexism See DISCRIMINATION.

Sextans The Sextant, a CONSTELLATION on the celestial equator, introduced by the Polish astronomer Johannes Hevelius (1611–87) to represent the sextant with which he measured star positions. It is exceedingly faint (its brightest star is only of magnitude 4.5) and it contains no objects of particular interest.

sextant A light, portable instrument with a graduated arc of 60 degrees used for measuring the angular distance between two objects, most commonly the altitude (angle above the horizon) of a celestial body. The observer looks through a small telescope at the horizon (or a small spirit bubble if the horizon is obscured). A mirror on a movable arm above the telescope is adjusted to reflect the light from the Sun or other body on to a half-silvered mirror and back into the telescope, so that the observer seems to see the body sitting on the horizon. The angle of the sextant arm at this correct adjustment is half the altitude of the celestial body.

sexual harassment Unwanted attention or intimidation, usually directed by men against women, which may range from leering and suggestive remarks to unwanted pressure for sexual favours, molesting, sexual assault, and even RAPE. Taking action against harassment may be difficult, since sexual harassment is not a criminal offence unless it goes as far as sexual assault or RAPE. Many trade unions and women's groups have campaigned for codes of practice within workplaces and institutions, and sex DISCRIMINATION legislation may be used to obtain redress against some forms of harassment.

sexually-transmitted disease (STD; formerly **venereal disease**) A COMMUNICABLE DISEASE usually or primarily spread by sexual contact, which can be homosexual, heterosexual, or both. Sexual transmission may be the sole mode or one of a number of modes of transmission of a sexually transmitted disease. Besides GONORRHOEA and SYPHILIS, there are many extremely prevalent but less serious infections, such as genital HERPES SIMPLEX VIRUS INFECTION and chlamydia. Such diseases are difficult to contain: their stigma may prevent people seeking treatment; both partners must be treated; and, in their early stages, the diseases may be virtually symptom-free, especially in women, so that one carrier may unwittingly infect several partners before seeking treatment. With the use of antibiotic and sulphonamide drugs, few people die of the bacterial STDs today, but untreated gonorrhoea or chlamydial infections are a significant cause of INFERTILITY in both women and men, as well as causing miscarriages, stillbirths, and birth defects. Viral infections, notably AIDS and HIV infection, but also HEPATITIS B and genital herpes, are more difficult to treat.

Seychelles A country comprising an archipelago in the Indian Ocean.

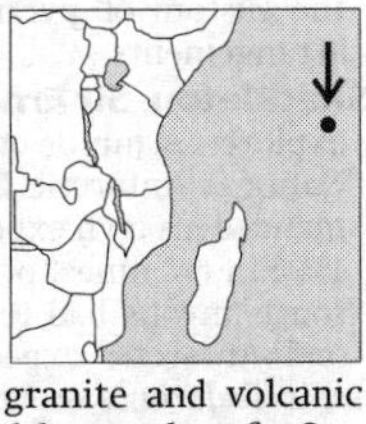

Physical. The Seychelles consists of 92 islands lying 4°S of the Equator and some 1,500 km (930 miles) from the east African coast. The islands are variously composed, the larger being of granite and volcanic rocks, sometimes surrounded by coral reefs. One group, of which Mahé at 142 sq km (55 sq mi) is the largest, is mainly hilly; another outlying group is mostly flat. The climate is warm and wet.

Economy. Tourism is the mainstay of the economy. The main exports are fish and copra.

History. The islands were uninhabited until colonized by the French. They were discovered in 1609 by an expedition of the British East India Company and formally annexed to France in 1756. They were captured from the French by Britain in 1810 during the Napoleonic Wars and were administered from MAURITIUS before becoming a separate crown colony in 1903. The islands gained universal suffrage in 1970, becoming an independent republic in 1975. In 1977 there was a coup, the Prime Minister, France-Albert René proclaiming himself President, and being re-elected in 1989. In 1991 he ended his resistance to the legalization of opposition parties. Multi-party elections held in 1993 resulted in a landslide victory for René's Seychelles People's Progressive Front.

Capital: Victoria
Area: 453 sq km (175 sq mi)
Population: 75,000 (1995)
Currency: 1 Seychelles rupee = 100 cents
Religions: Roman Catholic 90.9%; other Christian (mostly Anglican) 7.5%; Hindu 0.7%
Ethnic Groups: Seychellois creole (mixture of Asian, African, and European) 89.1% Indian 4.7%; Malagasy 3.1%; Chinese 1.6%; British 1.5%
Languages: Creole, English, French (all official)
International Organizations: UN; Commonwealth; OAU

Seyfert galaxy A type of GALAXY distinguished by the violent activity at its centre. First discovered by the US astronomer Carl Seyfert in 1943, over 100 examples have since been found. It is possible that Seyfert galaxies, with their bright nuclei and ejection of hot gas from their centres, are temporary stages in the lives of normal galaxies.

Seymour, Edward See SOMERSET, EDWARD SEYMOUR, 1ST EARL OF HERTFORD AND DUKE OF.

Seymour, Jane (*c.*1509–37) Third wife of HENRY VIII and mother of EDWARD VI. She married Henry in 1536 and finally provided the king with the male heir he wanted, although she died 12 days afterwards.

Seymour, Lynn (1939–) Canadian ballet-dancer. From 1957 she danced for the Royal Ballet in London, performing principal roles in ballets choreographed by Kenneth MacMillan (1929–92) and Frederick Ashton. Her most acclaimed roles came in Ashton's *Five Brahms Waltzes in the Manner of Isadora Duncan* and *A Month in the Country* (both 1976). Seymour later worked as artistic director of the Bavarian State Opera in Munich (1978–80).

s-'Gravenhage See THE HAGUE.

Shabaka (known as **Sabacon**) (died 698 BC) Egyptian pharaoh of the 25th dynasty, reigned 712–698 BC. He succeeded his brother Piankhi as king of Cush in about 716; four years later he conquered Egypt and founded its 25th dynasty. A conservative ruler, he promoted the cult of Amun and revived the custom of pyramid burial in his own death arrangements.

Shackleton, Sir Ernest Henry (1874–1922) British explorer. A junior officer on Robert Falcon Scott's National Antarctic Expedition (1900–04), he commanded his own expedition in 1909, getting within 155 km (97 miles) of the South Pole (the farthest south anyone had reached at that time). On a second Antarctic expedition (1914–16), Shackleton's ship *Endurance* was crushed in the ice. He and his crew eventually reached an island, from which he and five others set out in an open boat on a 1,300-km (800-mile) voyage to South Georgia to find help. In 1920 he led a fourth expedition to the Antarctic, but died of a heart attack on South Georgia.

shad A fish of the herring family, most species of which belong to the genus *Alosa*. In general they resemble large, deep-bodied herrings, sometimes growing to 60 cm (25 inches) in length, and with a notch in the upper jaw. Many species, such as the European twaite shad, *A. fallax*, are migratory and spawn in rivers after migrating from the sea. Most feed on plankton but the North American hickory shad, *A. mediocris*, eats small fishes. The gizzard shads are not members of this genus, but are close relatives.

shaddock The largest CITRUS FRUIT, *Citrus maxima*, up to 30 cm (12 inches) in diameter. The shaddock is also known as pummelo (not to be confused with pomelo, a West Indian name for grapefruit). It is coarse-skinned and rather bitter and, although not grown extensively anywhere, it is grown throughout Asia as a dessert fruit.

shaduf (or **shadoof**) An ancient Middle Eastern water-lifting device, still widely used in many countries. It comprises a beam pivoted in the fork of a vertically fixed branch. At one end the beam carries a bucket on a rope, and at the other a counterweight just heavier than the filled bucket. The operator pulls the beam down to fill the bucket, which is then raised by the counterweight.

Shaftesbury, Anthony Ashley Cooper, 1st Earl of (1621–83) English statesman. He entered Parliament in 1640 as a royalist supporter, but changed sides in 1643, eventually becoming a member of CROMWELL's council of state. In 1660 he was one of the Commissioners of the Convention Parliament who invited Charles II to return, and Charles rewarded him with the Chancellorship of the Exchequer. After CLARENDON's fall he became one of the CABAL, but was dismissed in 1673 because of his support for the TEST ACT and his unwavering opposition to Roman Catholicism. He became leader of the opposition, and used the POPISH PLOT to try to exclude the Roman Catholic James, Duke of York, from the succession (the Exclusion Crisis), but his political failure led him to flee into exile in 1682.

Shaftesbury, Anthony Ashley Cooper, 7th Earl of (1801–85) British philanthropist and social reformer. He was a dominant figure of the 19th-century social reform movement, inspiring much of the legislation designed to improve conditions for the large working class created as a result of the Industrial Revolution. His reforms included the introduction of the ten-hour working day (1847); he was also actively involved in improving housing and education for the poor.

shag An alternative name for CORMORANT, widely used in New Zealand and Australia. In Britain a shag is more specifically the green cormorant, *Phalacrocorax aristotelis*, to distinguish it from the common cormorant, *P. carbo*.

shaggy ink cap An AGARIC fungus of the genus *Coprinus*, whose fruiting bodies, or 'toadstools', commonly appear in autumn among grass on rich soil. White at first, the gills underneath the cap later break down into a fluid that looks like ink because it is full of black spores. The breakdown of the fruiting body helps to disperse the spores. The majority of species grow in rich soils, often favouring dung heaps or compost.

Shah, Karim Al-Hussain See AGA KHAN.

Shah, Reza See PAHLAVI.

Shah Jahan (1592–1666) MOGUL emperor of India 1628–58. He extended Mogul power, notably in the Deccan, and rebuilt the capital at Delhi. His buildings there and in Agra, notably the Taj Mahal, built as a shrine for his wife, mark the peak of Indo-Muslim architecture. His severe illness in 1657 caused a succession war between his four sons in which AURANGZEB, the third son, killed his rivals, imprisoned his father in the Agra palace, and seized the throne. On his death Shah Jahan was buried with his wife in the Taj Mahal.

Shahrazad (or **Scheherazade**) The wife of the Sultan Shahriyar, legendary king of Samarkand. As narrator of the tales of *The Thousand and One Nights*, Shahrazad's own story provides the framework for the tales believed to have been taken from the lost book of Persian folk tales, *Hazar Afsānah* ('Thousand Tales'). From the first night of their marriage onwards, Shahrazad sets out to break the practice of the king of having his brides executed after the consummation of their marriage. She entertains him with tales each night for 1,001 nights, firing his curiosity by interrupting each tale at a crucial moment in the narrative, and postponing the continuation until the next night.

Shaka (or **Chaka**) (*c*.1787–1828) Zulu chief. After seizing the Zulu chieftaincy from his half-brother in 1816, he reorganized his forces and waged war against the Nguni clans in SE Africa, subjugating them and forming a Zulu empire in the region. Shaka's military campaigns led to a huge displacement of people and a lengthy spell of clan warfare in the early 1820s. He was subsequently assassinated by his two half-brothers.

Shaker (or **Shaking Quaker**) A member of a religious sect, so-called because of their uncontrolled jerkings in moments of religious ecstasy. They were a revivalist group and held many QUAKER views although they left the Quaker movement in 1747. Ann Lee, who joined in 1758, declared herself the female Christ and, inspired by visions, established a community near Albany in New York colony in 1774. The community prospered and Shakers gained a reputation in New England as skilled craftsmen. **Shaker furniture**, made of high quality materials in austere styles, reflecting their way of life, has retained a high reputation. The sect reached a peak of about 6,000 members in the 1820s, but a decline set in after 1860.

Shakespeare, **William** (known as 'the Bard (of Avon)') (1564–1616) English dramatist whose works translated and performed throughout the world, have made him the most famous and quoted of English writers. He was born a merchant's son in Stratford-upon-Avon in Warwickshire and in about 1582 married Anne Hathaway, with whom he had three children. Some time thereafter he went to London, where he pursued a career as an actor, poet, and dramatist. He probably began to write for the stage in the late 1580s; although his plays were widely performed in his lifetime, many were not printed until the First Folio of 1623. His plays are written mostly in blank verse and include comedies (such as *A Midsummer Night's Dream* and *As You Like It*); historical plays, including *Richard III* and *Henry V*; the Greek and Roman plays, which include *Julius Caesar* and *Antony and Cleopatra*; the so-called 'problem plays', enigmatic comedies which include *All's Well that Ends Well* and *Measure for Measure*; the great tragedies, *Hamlet*, *Othello*, *King Lear*, and *Macbeth*; and the group of tragicomedies with which he ended his career, such as *The Winter's Tale* and *The Tempest*. He also wrote more than 150 sonnets, published in 1609, as well as narrative poems such as *The Rape of Lucrece* (1594).

Shakti (Sanskrit, 'power', 'energy') A name of the Great Goddess or Devī, one of the most important of the monotheistic deities worshipped by Hindus. As the Earth mother she is the object of widespread popular devotion in India. She is also the consort of SHIVA, but is worshipped independently of him. In her benevolent aspect she is known as Umā, Pārvatī, or Ambikā (little mother), while in her fearful and destructive aspect she appears as Kālī or Durgā (see DEVI).

shale A sedimentary CLAY laid down in thin layers, that can easily be split apart: shales disintegrate in water. They are made up of mineral grains (quartz, feldspar, and mica) of microscopic size, together with clay particles and larger fragments of rock. Shales are very common and probably represent almost half of all sedimentary rocks. Oil shales contain so much decayed organic matter that they readily ignite, like bitumen.

shale oil Oil obtained by the application of heat to certain oil-bearing sedimentary rocks (oil-shales). Unlike crude PETROLEUM, shale oil is not accumulated in a reservoir but is distributed throughout pores in the rock. Heat (generally in the form of steam) is required to make the oil flow in a recoverable stream. The bulk of the world's petroleum reserves exist in the form of shale oil, the world's largest known deposits being the Athabasca tar sands, along the Athabasca River in Alberta, Canada. The BITUMEN in the sands has been used as a petroleum source since the 1960s, but the high cost of recovery has in general limited the exploitation of shale-oil.

shallot A variety of the common onion, *Allium cepa*, which forms a spreading clump of new bulbs from a single planted bulb. The bulbs are smaller than those of the onion but are used in the same way. They are milder in flavour and are widely cultivated in many parts of the world, including the tropics, but particularly in Europe and the USA.

Shalmaneser III (died 824 BC) King of Assyria 859–824. Most of his reign was devoted to the expansion of his kingdom and the conquest of neighbouring lands. According to Assyrian records (though it is not mentioned in the Bible) he defeated an alliance of Syrian kings and Ahab, king of Israel, in a battle at Qarqar on the Orontes in 853 BC. His other military achievements included the invasion of Cilicia and the capture of Tarsus.

shamanism A religious practice focused on specific individuals, known as shamans, who claim to be able to act as mediums between the human and the supernatural. Although shaman is originally a Siberian word, it is used in a wide variety of contexts in Africa, Asia, and the Americas. Typically male, shamans combine both religious and healing functions, and their authority derives from personal religious experience, such as spirit possession, rather than from an institutional role. Shamanic experiences can involve the use of hallucinogenic drugs, or sensory deprivation or stimulation, which some shamans claim will assist them in establishing contact with the spirit world.

Shamir, **Yitzhak** (born Yitzhak Jazernicki) (1915–) Israeli statesman, Prime Minister 1983–84 and 1986–92. Born in Poland, he emigrated to Palestine in 1935. On Menachem Begin's retirement in 1983, Shamir became Premier, but his Likud party was narrowly defeated in elections a year later. As Prime Minister of a coalition government with Labour, he sacked Shimon Peres in 1990 and formed a new government with a policy of conceding no land to a Palestinian state. Under his leadership Israel did not retaliate when attacked by Iraqi missiles during the Gulf War of 1991, thereby possibly averting the formation of a pro-Saddam Hussein Arab coalition.

Shandong (formerly **Shantung**) A province of eastern China on the Yellow Sea; area 153,300 sq km (59,212 sq miles); pop. (1990) 84,893,000; capital, Jinan. A leading industrial and agricultural province, its chief products are maize, wheat, cotton, fruit, vegetables, tobacco, livestock, and silk.

Shang A dynasty that ruled China during part of the 2nd millennium BC, probably 16th–11th centuries BC. The discovery of inscriptions on more than 100,000 tortoise shells confirmed literary references to the existence of the Shang dynasty, which witnessed the perfection of the wheel, the use of chariots in warfare, bronze casting, and the carving of jade and ivory.

Shanghai A port on the estuary of the Yangtze River, the largest city in China; pop. (1990) 7,780,000. Formerly an enclave for western traders, Shanghai is now the country's leading industrial centre and gateway to the great Yangtze basin of central China. Its industries include shipbuilding, oil refining and the manufacture of textiles, electronics, bicycles, radios, and televisions. The port of Shanghai handles the major share of China's foreign and coastal trade.

Shankar, Ravi (1920–) Indian sitar player and composer. Already an established musician in his own country, from the mid-1950s he embarked on tours of Europe and the USA giving sitar recitals, doing much to stimulate contemporary Western interest in Indian music. He founded schools of Indian music in Bombay (1962) and Los Angeles (1967).

Shankly, William (known as 'Bill') (1913–81) Scottish-born football manager and footballer. Shankly played as a wing-half for Carlisle United and Preston North End, with whom he won the FA Cup in 1938, and won five international caps. He managed a number of clubs, including Carlisle, before becoming manager of Liverpool (1960–74). There he created a strong team that had outstanding success in Britain and Europe.

Shannon The chief river of Ireland, flowing 390 km (240 miles) southwards through Lough Allen, Lough Ree and Lough Derg to its estuary on the Atlantic coast between Co. Clare and Co. Limerick.

Shannon, Claude Elwood (1916–) US engineer. He was a pioneer of information theory, which has become vital to the design of both communication and electronic equipment. He also investigated digital circuits, and was the first to use the term *bit* to denote a unit of information.

Shansi See SHANXI.

Shantung See SHANDONG.

Shanxi (formerly **Shansi**) A province of north-central China, on the eastern edge of the loess plateau to the south of Inner Mongolia; area 157,100 sq km (60,680 sq miles); pop. (1990) 28,759,000; capital, Taiyuan. Wheat, maize, sorghum, coal, and chemical fertilizers are the chief products.

Shapley, Harlow (1885–1972) US astronomer. He studied globular star clusters, using CEPHEID VARIABLES within them to determine their distance. He then used their distribution to locate the likely centre of the Galaxy and infer its structure and dimensions.

share A SECURITY issued by a COMPANY to raise long-term CAPITAL. The ordinary shareholders of a JOINT-STOCK COMPANY are its owners. In proportion to the shares they own, they are entitled to voting rights (to elect the directors of the company), to DIVIDENDS, and to the proceeds that remain from the liquidation of the company after all other creditors have been repaid in the event of bankruptcy. Preference shareholders take priority over ordinary shareholders in this event. They also receive their fixed dividend before any dividend can be paid to ordinary shareholders. To raise capital, a company may offer new shares through an issuing house. Alternatively, it may avoid the high cost of such an issue by seeking new capital from existing shareholders; this is known as a rights issue. A scrip issue (or share split) raises no new capital but merely alters the denomination of the company's shares, facilitating transactions in the shares in smaller lots. A convertible issue is a way of raising loan capital that gives the option of conversion to shares.

sharecropping A form of land tenancy in which a landlord allows land to be used in return for a share of the tenant's crops or labour. Sharecropping is found all over the world, especially among peasant societies in developing countries; for example, it is widespread in many parts of Asia, especially in rural areas of high population densities.

share index A financial INDEX formed by selecting a number of shares of prominent companies traded on a stock exchange and comparing the daily average price of these shares with the average price on a stated date in the base year. A weighted average is usually taken (i.e. it takes into account the volume of each share traded). In the UK, the Financial Times has a range of share indexes, the most widely used being the Financial Times–Stock Exchange 100 Share Index (known as FOOTSIE).

Sharia (from Arabic, 'path') The law of Islam. The *sharia* is the way of life prescribed for Muslims, based on the KORAN and the HADITH. The *sharia*, the path of religion, contains, and is sometimes identified with *fiḳh*, jurisprudence, or the science of the *sharia* worked out by the four orthodox schools in Sunni Islam and by Imam Jafar Sādiq (*c.*700–65) and other *imams* in Shiite Islam. Although the *sharia* has no codification as in some Western law systems, the *fiḳh* books may be considered the equivalent of law books. Legal opinions based on *fiḳh* known as *fatwas* are given by scholars known as *muftis*. In Iran and Saudi Arabia, the *sharia* is the basis of the legal system, with special religio-legal bodies to ensure its correct application in all areas of government. The question of the reintroduction of all or part of the *sharia* as happened in Iran and Sudan, is an issue for many Muslim countries, causing heated debate in some cases between Islamic fundamentalists and Islamic modernists. Pakistan announced plans to make the *sharia* the supreme law of the land in 1991, whereas in Algeria the authorities closed down the pro-*sharia* Islamic Salvation Front in early 1992.

Sharjah (Arabic **Ash-Shariqah**) The third-largest of the member-states of the United Arab Emirates, comprising three enclaves on the Gulf of Oman coast (Khor Fakkan, Dibba Hisn, and Kalba); area 2,600 sq km (1,000 sq miles); pop. (1995) 400,300. It has for centuries been a home base for the trading Qawasim tribe whose fleet was destroyed by the British in 1819. Oil and gas have been exploited since their discovery in the early 1970s and industries also produce petrochemicals, steel products, and cement.

shark One of a group of large marine CARTILAGINOUS FISHES whose skeleton is hardened by deposits of calcium. The upper jaw is not fused with the skull, and the teeth, arranged in rows, are not fused with the jaw bones; as each outer row of teeth wears out it is replaced by a new inner row.

They lack the air float, or swim bladder, of bony fish. The intestine has a spiral arrangement to increase its absorptive surface. The body of all sharks is tube-shaped like a torpedo, and the upper lobe of the tail fin is longer than the lower. Their skin is covered with tooth-like dermal denticles, which give it a rough texture. Male sharks have pelvic claspers, which act as guides for spermatozoa when these are inserted into the female cloaca to fertilize the eggs. Most species give birth to fully formed young, though some, such as the RAYS, lay their eggs in horny capsules. Sharks are predatory, mostly eating other fishes, but a few species (whale shark and basking shark) feed on plankton. They are marine creatures, although a few species enter rivers and lakes in tropical areas, occurring both inshore and in the deep sea; but they are rare in polar regions. About 300 species are known, mostly moderate to large in size, with the WHALE SHARK, the largest known fish, growing to 18 m (60 feet) in length.

Sharma, Shankar Dayal (1918–) Indian statesman, President since 1992. A member of the Congress party, Sharma served as Vice-President 1987–92.

Sharp, Cecil (James) (1859–1924) British ethnomusicologist, who devoted himself to the collection, publication, and performance of the folk dance and folk-song of the British Isles. His collection of nearly 5,000 examples includes many that he had collected in the USA (1916–18). Sharp's example and enthusiasm had a crucial influence on the music of Holst and Vaughan Williams.

sharpbill A bird found in Central America and much of South America, *Oxyruncus cristatus*. It is classified as the sole member of the family Oxyruncidae. The size of a large sparrow, it is olive-green above with a small brownish-black crest, which usually conceals some orange-red feathers in the centre of the crown. It has a straight, slightly broad beak with which it eats fruit. The sharpbill makes a nest of twigs high in forest trees; however, its breeding habits are mostly unknown. The first nest was only found in 1980.

Sharpeville massacre (21 March 1960) An incident in the South African township of Sharpeville. The police opened fire on a demonstration against APARTHEID laws, killing 67 Africans, and wounding 180. There was widespread international condemnation, and a state of emergency was declared in South Africa. 1,700 persons were detained, and the political parties, the AFRICAN NATIONAL CONGRESS and Pan-Africanist Congress were banned. Three weeks later a white farmer attempted to assassinate the Prime Minister, Verwoerd, and, as pressure from the Commonwealth against the apartheid policies mounted, South Africa became a republic and withdrew from the Commonwealth (1961).

Shatt al-Arab (Iranian **Arvand River**) A river of south-east Iraq, formed by the confluence of the Tigris and Euphrates rivers, flowing about 195 km (120 miles) south-east to the Persian Gulf. It is an important access route to the oil ports of Iran and Iraq between which it forms an international boundary.

Shaw, Artie See JAZZ.

Shaw, George Bernard (1856–1950) Irish dramatist and writer. He moved to London in 1876 and began his literary career as a critic and unsuccessful novelist. His first play was performed in 1892. His best-known plays combine comedy with intellectual debate in challenging conventional morality and thought; they include *Man and Superman* (1903), *Major Barbara* (1907), *Pygmalion* (1913), *Heartbreak House* (1919), and *St Joan* (1923). He wrote lengthy prefaces for most of his plays, in which he expanded his philosophy and ideas. A socialist, he joined the Fabian Society in 1884 and was an active member during its early period, championing many progressive causes, including feminism. He was awarded the Nobel Prize for literature in 1925.

shawm A double-reed musical instrument of conical bore, producing a loud and penetrating sound. The earliest evidence for such an instrument is Etruscan, around 480 BC. Thereafter it appears only spasmodically, but from the 6th century, in Sassanid Persia, it became a standard instrument in the Near East. By the end of the 17th century the shawm was extinct in mainstream European music. However, it survives as a folk instrument in southern Europe, from Brittany to the Balkans, and as a leading instrument in North Africa and Nigeria and throughout the Middle, Near, and Far East. The shawm is usually blown with circular breathing, inhaling through the nose while blowing from the cheeks.

Shawnee A North American Indian tribe, the southernmost of the Algonquian speaking peoples, originally living in the Tennessee River valley but later occupying reservations in Oklahoma.

Shearer, Moira (born Moira Shearer King) (1926–) British ballet-dancer and actress. As a ballerina with Sadler's Wells ballet from 1942 she created roles in a number of works by Sir Frederick Ashton. She is perhaps best known for her portrayal of a dedicated ballerina in the film *The Red Shoes* (1948). Her later acting career included roles in plays by Shaw and Chekhov.

shearwater A long-winged PETREL belonging to several genera in the family Procellaridae. They have a swooping, wave-skimming flight and feed on surface-feeding fishes and marine organisms in large mid-ocean or offshore flocks. Some species dabble at the surface; others dive and swim powerfully under water, using their webbed feet as paddles and wings part-extended as hydrofoils. They nest colonially on cliffs and screes or in tussock-screened burrows, feeding by day and returning to the nests after dark to avoid aerial predators. The fledglings of some southern species are much in demand for their oil and rich meat (MUTTON BIRDS).

sheathbill Either of two species of small, white, pigeon-like birds of the sub-Antarctic and southern South American coasts, making up a family of their own, Chionidae. The name derives from a horny sheath covering the base of the bill. They scavenge on shores and in the breeding colonies of penguins and other seabirds. The yellow-billed sheathbill, *Chionis alba*, inhabits Atlantic coasts, while the black-billed sheathbill, *C. minor*, is found on the most southerly islands of the Indian Ocean. Combative though gregarious, they feed in small groups, eating seaweeds, flotsam, and abandoned eggs and chicks of other birds. A single chick is usually reared.

Sheba The Biblical name of Saba, an ancient country in south-west Arabia, famous for its trade in gold, frankincense, and spices. The **Queen of Sheba** visited King Solomon in Jerusalem and in some accounts their union produced Nebuchadnezzar. This visit is also referred in the Koran and embellished in Islamic legend. The Hebrew word is the name of the people (Sabaeans), but was erroneously assumed by Greek and Roman writers to be a place name.

Sheene, Barry (born Stephen Frank Sheene) (1950–) British racing motorcyclist. He won the 500 cc. world championship in 1976 and 1977.

sheep A RUMINANT mammal of the genus *Ovis* in the cattle family (Bovidae), closely related to goats. Sheep have transversely ribbed horns which tend to curl in spirals, with the points turning outwards as they rise. Wild sheep, of which there are six species, do not have the thick, woolly coats of domesticated breeds. They include the BIGHORN, the MOUFLON, and the ARGALI. The domestication of sheep for the production of milk, meat, leather, wool, and lanolin goes far back into antiquity. The ewes usually produce one or two lambs, although five have been recorded; they are born woolly and open-eyed. The gestation period is about 21 weeks. The sheep is the first mammal to have been cloned (1997; see CLONE).

sheep-ked See LOUSE FLY.

sheep-tick (or **castor bean tick**) Probably the commonest TICK in temperate areas, *Ixodes ricinus*. It occurs mainly on sheep and cattle, but occasionally bites humans and smaller mammals. The eggs hatch in autumn, but the six-legged larva waits until spring to find a host. It then feeds, falls off, and moults into a larger eight-legged larva which survives for a year without feeding. A year later feeding again occurs, leading to maturity. Bean-like adults are found in the third year, mating on sheep and cattle. The males then die, and the females continue the cycle by laying batches of eggs in crevices in the ground. Redwater fever in cattle and louping in sheep may be transmitted by this tick.

Sheffield An industrial city in South Yorkshire, England, on the River Don; pop. (1991) 500,500. From medieval times it was noted for metal-working, and became famous, especially for the manufacture of cutlery and silverware. The establishment of a works by Henry Bessemer in 1859 made it a centre for the production of steel and steel goods including tools and machinery. It is the site of the University of Sheffield (1905) and Sheffield Hallam University (formerly Sheffield Polytechnic).

Sheffield plate Metalware made of copper coated on one or both sides with a layer of silver, the two metals being fused by heat. This process for producing a cheap substitute for solid silver was invented in the early 1740s by Thomas Boulsover, a Sheffield cutler. From about 1840 Sheffield plate was rapidly superseded by ELECTROPLATING, which was less attractive but cheaper as the layer of silver coating the copper was much thinner.

shelduck A member of a genus of six species of Old World dabbling DUCKS. They have a goose-like character, being slower on the wing than typical ducks, and rather heavily built. The plumage of the sexes is nearly the same. The common shelduck, *Tadorna tadorna*, is a large black and white bird banded with chestnut, with a red beak and pink legs. It is sometimes referred to as the **sheldrake**. It inhabits estuaries and coasts, where it breeds in burrows in sand dunes. Of the other five species the chestnut-orange ruddy shelduck, *T. ferruginea*, of the southern Palearctic region, is the most widespread.

shell (in zoology) A hard outer covering found in many animal groups, with a great range of shapes and structures, some very different from the familiar sea shells formed by molluscs. Polyps may secrete external shells to become corals, and sea urchins also have shells, just beneath their skins. But it is molluscs and arthropods that are particularly renowned for their hard outer coverings. Molluscs have an incomplete shell, into which the soft body can be withdrawn, whereas the arthropods always have a complete, jointed, armour-plating which covers their bodies. Even when well adapted to a lifestyle, shells can be a hindrance. The complete arthropod shell or EXOSKELETON makes it necessary for the animal to moult periodically to allow growth, and even the incomplete molluscan shell, which permits growth at the edges, may cause problems by precluding fast predatory movements, so the CEPHALOPOD molluscs have evolved by reducing or completely losing their shells.

shell (in warfare) ARTILLERY ammunition filled with explosive. Early shells were cannon-balls hollowed out and filled with gunpowder. Following the Crimean War (1854–56), a new kind of shell was developed for rifled breech-loading guns. It was essentially a cylinder with a rounded nose, similar to a modern shell. Steel became the standard material for shells in the 20th century. During World Wars I and II many types of specialist shells were developed. They included illumination, smoke, anti-aircraft, armour-piercing, anti-tank, naval, and gas shells (see CHEMICAL AND BIOLOGICAL WARFARE).

Shelley, Mary (Wollstonecraft) (1797–1851) British writer. The daughter of William Godwin and Mary Wollstonecraft (who died a few days after her birth), she eloped with the poet Shelley in 1814, becoming his second wife in 1816. She is chiefly remembered as the author of the Gothic novel *Frankenstein, or the Modern Prometheus* (1818). Her other works include further novels, short stories (some with science-fiction elements, others Gothic or historical), and an edition of her husband's poems (1830).

Shelley, Percy Bysshe (1792–1822) British poet. He was a leading figure of the romantic movement, with radical political views, which are often reflected in his work. After the collapse of his first marriage in 1814 he eloped abroad with Mary Godwin and her stepsister (Clare Clairmont), marrying Mary in 1816; after a stay on Lake Geneva close to Lord Byron, they settled permanently in Italy two years later. Major works include the political poems *Queen Mab* (1813) and *The Mask of Anarchy* (1819), *Prometheus Unbound* (1820), a lyrical drama on his aspirations and contradictions as a poet and radical, lyric poetry (for example 'Ode to the West Wind', 1820), the essay *The Defence of Poetry* (1821), vindicating the role of poetry in an increasingly industrial society, and *Adonais* (1821), an elegy on the death of Keats. Shelley was drowned in a boating accident.

shellfish Any aquatic invertebrate with a shell, especially those that are edible. It includes both crustaceans and molluscs. In the first group are lobsters, crabs, shrimps, and prawns; in the latter cockles, winkles, mussels, and their relatives. In some countries other groups, such as sea urchins and marine worms, may also be valued as edible shellfish. In **shellfish farming** crustaceans and molluscs are cultivated, mostly in sea-water. Farming supplements shellfish fishing, rather than replacing it. Worldwide production of crustaceans, mainly shrimps, now exceeds half a million tonnes per year. Crustaceans are carnivores, and food needs to be provided for them, but their high market price means that farming is still profitable. Farmed molluscs, such as mussels, oysters, and clams, are generally herbivores. They feed on naturally occurring phytoplankton and need no additional feeding. More than 4 million tonnes of molluscs are produced per year.

Shenandoah River One of the most scenic rivers of the eastern USA. Some 240 km (150 miles) long, it is formed between the Allegheny and Blue Ridge mountains by the union of its two headstreams, North Fork and South Fork. Its valley with orchards and pasture then runs north-east and the river joins the Potomac at Harper's Ferry. The **Shenandoah National Park** lies to the south-east in the Blue Ridge uplands.

Shenyang (formerly **Mukden**) The fourth-largest city in China, an important Manchu city between the 17th and early 20th centuries and now the capital of Liaoning province; pop. (1990) 4,500,000. It lies at the hub of the densest railway network in China and is a major industrial centre producing machine tools and mining equipment.

sherardizing A process for protecting iron and steel from CORROSION by coating with zinc. It was named after the British chemist Sherard Cowper-Coles (1867–1936). The object to be coated is heated in a sealed container with zinc powder at a temperature between 350 and 450°C. The coating consists largely of a zinc-iron alloy, which is thin enough not to interfere with any pattern or design on the original article. (Compare GALVANIZING.)

Sheraton, Thomas (1751–1806) British cabinet-maker and furniture designer. No furniture by his own hand has been identified, and his fame rests on his publications, the most important of which is *The Cabinet-Maker and Upholsterer's Drawing Book* (1791–94). The designs were much used by furniture-makers in Britain and the USA, and Sheraton's name has come to be used as a label for the prevailing style in furniture around 1800.

Sheridan, Richard Brinsley (Butler) (1751–1816) Anglo-Irish dramatist and Whig politician. The most celebrated of his plays are *The Rivals* (1775), with Mrs Malaprop among its characters, and *The School for Scandal* (1777), both comedies of manners. He wrote many more plays, including *A Trip to Scarborough* (1777), and *The Duenna* (1775), both musical plays. In 1780 he was elected to Parliament, where he proved himself to be a brilliant orator and held senior government posts. He was also a friend of the Prince Regent. In 1813 he was arrested for debt and three years later he died in poverty.

sheriff (from Old English, 'shire-reeve') The chief representative of the crown in the shires (counties) of England from the early 11th century, taking over many of the duties previously performed by ealdormen. Sheriffs assumed responsibility for the fyrd, royal taxes, royal estates, shire courts, and presided over their own court, the Tourn. They abused these powers, as an inquest of 1170 showed, when many were dismissed. However, by *c.*1550 the office had become purely civil, as a result of the proliferation of specialist royal officials (Coroners, 1170, Justices of the Peace, 1361, LORDS LIEUTENANT, 1547).

Sherman, William Tecumseh (1820–91) US general. He held various commands in the American Civil War from its outset in 1861, and in March 1864 succeeded Ulysses S. Grant as chief Union commander in the west. He set out with 60,000 men on a march through Georgia, during which he crushed Confederate forces and broke civilian morale with his policy of deliberate destruction of the South's sources of supply. In 1869 he was appointed commander of the US army, a post he held until his retirement in 1884.

Sherpa A Himalayan people living on the borders of Nepal and Tibet. Skilled in mountaineering, the Sherpas have acted as porters for many Himalayan expeditions. The Sherpa Tensing Norgay, with Edmund Hillary, was the first to reach the summit of Everest (1953).

Sherrington, Sir Charles Scott (1857–1952) English physiologist. His researches contributed greatly to understanding of the nervous system, particularly concerning motor pathways, sensory nerves in muscles, and the areas innervated by spinal nerves. He introduced the concept of reflex actions and the reflex arc and was the first to apply the term *synapsis* (later *synapse*) to the junction of two nerve cells. Sherrington shared a Nobel Prize in 1932.

Sherwood Forest The remnants, near Ollerton, of a once large forest that extended over Nottinghamshire, central England. It has associations with the exploits of the legendary Robin Hood. Part of the forest is now protected within a country park that contains some of the oldest and largest oaks in Britain.

Shetland An Islands Area of Scotland consisting of the Shetland Islands, a group of about 100 islands north-east of the Orkneys (the principal islands are Mainland, Yell, Unst, and Fetlar); area 1,433 sq km (533 sq miles); pop. (1991) 22,020; administrative headquarters, Lerwick. The islands were settled by Norsemen in the 9th century and became Scottish only in 1472. They are noted for the production of textiles (especially hand knitwear) and have become an important base for the exploitation of oil and gas in the North Sea, the oil terminal at Sullom Voe being the largest in Europe. The islands are linked by ferries, and by sea and air to the mainland of Scotland. Tourism is now an important industry.

Shevardnadze, Eduard (Amvrosievich) (1928–) Georgian statesman, head of state of Georgia since 1992. He became a candidate member of the Soviet Politburo in 1978 and a full member in 1985. In the same year Shevardnadze was appointed Minister of Foreign Affairs under Mikhail Gorbachev, a position he retained until his resignation in 1990. While in office, Shevardnadze supported Gorbachev's commitment to détente and played a key role in arms control negotiations with the West. In 1992 Shevardnadze was elected head of state of his native Georgia, following the toppling of President Zviad Gamsakhurdia (1939–94).

Shia (or **Shiah**) One of the two main branches of Islam. Shiites reject the first three Sunni Caliphs and regard Ali as Muhammad's first successor. They followed a succession of imams, whom they believed to possess a Divine Light giving them special wisdom in matters of the faith and community of believers. The more orthodox Sunnis did not recognize Shi'ism as a legitimate school of Islam until 1959. Shia Muslims number some 90 million worldwide and are dominant in Iran, Iraq, Bahrain, and parts of Lebanon.

shield (in geology) A large region on the continental plates of the Earth's crust that has remained relatively stable over long periods of geological time. Shields are very old, usually PRECAMBRIAN, and are made up of igneous and metamorphic rocks surrounded by sedimentary platforms. Although very much worn down they are unaffected by later mountain building. Known also as cratons, they exist at or near the centres of all continental plates, away from the volcanic and earthquake zones of the plate boundaries. The Canadian and Western Australian shields are examples.

shieldbug A shield-shaped BUG, which is often brightly coloured or conspicuously marked. Some shieldbugs can produce a pungent odour and are also known as stink bugs. The majority belong to the family Pentatomidae, which contains over 2,500 species; they can be distinguished by their large triangular scutellum (an extension of the thorax, between or covering the leathery wing-bases). Some shieldbugs take other insects for food, but the majority feed on plants. The harlequin bug, *Tectocoris diophthalmus*, which belongs to the family Scutelleridae, is a pest of cabbage and related crops in North America. Some species of shieldbug inhabiting tropical regions can grow to lengths of up to 3 cm (1.25 inches).

shield excavator (or **tunnelling shield**) A machine used when excavating a TUNNEL in soft ground to provide temporary support at the face. Invented by M. I. BRUNEL, the shield is a short, rigid cylinder of the same profile as the tunnel and has platforms from which the face is excavated. As the shield cuts the face, the tunnel is lined with concrete segments. The shield then advances by pushing against the completed lining behind it. A closed shield, which excludes water by the presence of compressed air, is used when excavating in waterlogged ground.

shifting cultivation A form of agriculture now usually practised in tropical conditions. Also known as slash-and-burn or swidden, it involves cutting small clearings in virgin forest, burning the wood to create ash for fertilizer, and then using the land for ARABLE FARMING. When the soil is exhausted, a new plot of land is sought and cleared: if left long enough, the original plot will return to forest. Shifting cultivation has been the basic mode of subsistence in all parts of the world for thousands of years, but recent population increases in some areas, and the use of shifting cultivation for growing crops for sale or barter, rather than subsistence, have led to a drastic shortening of the fallow cycle, and a rapid degeneration of the soil.

shih-tzu See DOG.

Shiite See SHIA.

Shikoku The smallest of the four main islands of Japan, comprising the prefectures of Ehime, Kagawa, Kochi, and Tokushima; area 18,795 sq km (7,260 sq miles); pop. (1990) 4,195,000; chief city, Matsuyama. Its highest peak is Ishizuchi (1,980 m, 6,496 ft).

Shilton, Peter (1949–) British footballer. He played in goal for Leicester City, Stoke City, Nottingham Forest (with whom he won the League Championship in 1978 and successive European Cups in 1979 and 1980), Southampton, and Derby, and made a UK record 1000th league appearance in 1996. With England he won a record 125 caps (1970–90).

shingle A mass of water-worn, rounded pebbles or cobbles, usually mixed with gravel and varying widely in size – from 20 to 200 mm (0.5 to 8 inches) in diameter – and occurring on the higher parts of beaches. It is carried there by powerful waves during storms; and since normal waves cannot move material of this size it tends to accumulate, forming ridges parallel to the shore. Shingle ridges sometimes form off shore as spits or bars and are usually made of resistant materials such as flint.

shingles (or **herpes zoster**) A viral infection caused by the varicella-zoster virus, which is also responsible for chickenpox; it is reactivation of the virus, which remains latent in nerves following chickenpox in childhood, that causes shingles. Therefore, shingles itself cannot be transmitted, although chickenpox can be contracted from an individual with shingles. Symptoms include a rash along the route marked by the nerve, which is commonly on one side of the trunk. Severe nerve pain (neuralgia) is the first symptom, which subsides as the rash remits, but may persist, especially in the elderly. If the eye nerves are involved, blindness may occur.

Shinto (Chinese/Japanese, 'the Way of the Spirits') A Japanese religion dating from prehistoric times, based on the worship of ancestors and nature-spirits. Things that inspire awe – twisted trees, contorted rocks, dead warriors – are believed to enshrine *kami* ('spirits'). In early times each clan had its *kami*. With the supremacy of the YAMATO, its Sun-goddess, Amaterasu, enshrined at the temple at Ise, became paramount. Shinto is tolerant and adaptable, laying emphasis on high standards of behaviour and on daily rituals, rather than on doctrine. Shinto offers no code of conduct, no philosophy. It stresses ritual purity; at simple shrines worshippers rinse hands and mouth, bow, and offer food and drink.

The name Shinto was adopted in the 6th century AD to distinguish it from Buddhist and Confucian cults. There is no official Shinto scripture, although the *Kojiki* (Records of Ancient Matters) and *Nihon-gi* (Chronicles of Japan), 8th-century compilations based on oral tradition, contain myths and stories about creation and the gods. During the 5th century AD, the spread of CONFUCIANISM introduced ANCESTOR WORSHIP to Shinto, and in the 6th century BUDDHIST beliefs became incorporated into the ancient religion.

During the 19th century the rise of the unified Japanese state saw the development of state Shinto: the emperor came to be worshipped as a descendant of the Sun-goddess Amaterasu. State Shinto was not classed as a religion but as a code of conduct requiring loyalty and obedience to the divine emperor; it informed all public life and encouraged extreme nationalism, until it was rescinded by the emperor (under US pressure) in 1945. It was replaced by the older form, shrine Shinto, the worship of *kami* in shrines or sanctuaries, tended by priests. In the home, the *kami* are housed within a *kamidana*, or 'godshelf'. Personal worship involves purification rites and daily prayers to the *kami*. Shinto is regarded as the religion of life, while Buddhism is seen as that of death; marriages are therefore celebrated according to Shinto tradition, while people generally choose Buddhist rites for funerals.

ship Any large seagoing vessel. The earliest seagoing vessels were probably used about 60,000 years ago by the colonizers of Australia. Their craft were probably CANOES or rafts, propelled by paddles. Later, oars and then sails were developed. With the advent of sail power, SAILING SHIPS AND BOATS became the predominant form of power at sea, and remained so until the mid-19th century. STEAMSHIPS were developed throughout the 19th century, and in the 20th century motor ships were introduced, generally powered by DIESEL ENGINES or sometimes steam turbines for large vessels. Until the 19th century most ships were built of wood, but in 1839 the development of techniques of using MAGNETIC COMPASSES in iron-hulled ships made seagoing iron ships possible. The use of iron, and later steel, for shipbuilding led to changes in hull design and growth in ship size.

Since the early 19th century, but particularly in

the late 20th century, ships have grown in size. A ship's size is measured in several ways. Merchant ships are usually referred to in terms of gross or net tonnage, a measurement of their capacity rather than their weight. Displacement tonnage, measured by the amount of water the ship displaces, is the chief size-measurement method for WARSHIPS.

ship money Originally, an occasional sum of money paid by English seaports to the crown to meet the cost of supplying a ship to the Royal Navy. Charles I revived the tax in 1634, while he was ruling without Parliament. From 1635 he extended it to the inland towns, and raised up to £200,000 a year as a result. In 1637 John Hampden was taken to court for refusing to pay and claimed that Charles needed Parliament's approval to levy such a regular tax. The judges decided by 7 to 5 in Charles's favour, but the narrowness of the victory encouraged widespread refusal to pay tax afterwards. The LONG PARLIAMENT made ship money illegal in 1641.

ship-to-ship missile See MISSILE.

shipworm A BIVALVE mollusc of the species *Teredo*. The typical two-piece molluscan shell is much reduced in shipworms, forming the scraping drills enabling the animal to burrow into wood. The unprotected wormlike body and siphons follow behind the shell, secreting a chalky lining to the burrow. Shipworms filter food from water via the siphons, but also digest wood while burrowing, and therefore pose real problems to wooden boats and pilings.

Shiraz A city in the Zagros Mountains of south-west-central Iran, capital of Fars province; pop. (1991) 965,800. It was a leading city of the medieval Islamic world and capital of Iran from 1753 to 1794. An important cultural centre since the 4th century BC, the city is noted for the school of miniature painting based there between the 14th and 16th centuries, and for the manufacture of carpets. The surrounding area is noted for its wine, the city lending its name to a variety of grape.

shire Formerly, the main unit of local administration in England. Shires evolved as territorial units in Wessex in the 9th century, replacing the Roman system of provinces. They were extended over a wider area of England by ALFRED the Great and his heirs as administrative and political units. The English shire system reveals many different evolutionary processes. Some were based on former kingdoms (Kent, Sussex, Essex); others on tribal subdivisions within a kingdom (Norfolk and Suffolk); others were created during the 10th-century reconquest of the DANELAW or as territories centred on towns (Oxfordshire, Warwickshire, Buckinghamshire, etc.). England north of the River Tees was not absorbed into the shire system until the Norman Conquest when shires were re-styled 'counties'.

Shiva (Sanskrit, 'the kind or auspicious one') One of the most important of the monotheistic deities found in the Hindu tradition. With BRAHMA and VISHNU, Shiva forms the Hindu trinity (*trimurti*). Sometimes called Rudra (Sanskrit, 'howler'), Shiva may have evolved from an Aryan deity, who was the dreaded god of the storm and of the dead. Shiva is worshipped in several apparently contradictory aspects, whose combination gives emphasis to his incomprehensible transcendence. He is seen as a giver of blessings, and is also a symbol of sensuality, represented by the lingam or phallus. On the other hand, he is sometimes depicted as an ascetic, seated in meditation in the Himalayas. Shiva is also the god of destruction and dissolution. In his manifestation as Shiva Natarāja, the four-armed Lord of the Dance, he tramples on the forces of ignorance and chaos, and keeps creation in balance. His female consort appears variously as Pārvatī (see DEVI), Durgā, or Kālī, and he is sometimes also paired with the Great Goddess, SHAKTI. In benevolent aspect he lives with Pārvatī in the Himalayas and rides his bull, Nandi. In human form he is often shown with three eyes, wearing a skull necklace entwined with writhing snakes, and carrying a trident. Shaivism, the cult of Shiva, is, with Vaishnavism and Shaktism, one of the three main forms of HINDUISM.

Shivaji (or **Sivaji**) (1627–80) Indian raja of the Marathas 1674–80. In 1659 he raised a Hindu revolt against Muslim rule in Bijapur, southern India, inflicting a crushing defeat on the army of the sultan of Bijapur. Shivaji was later captured by the Mogul emperor Aurangzeb, but escaped in 1666 and proceeded to expand Maratha territory. He had himself crowned raja in 1674; during his reign he enforced religious toleration throughout the Maratha empire and blocked Mogul expansionism by forming an alliance with the sultans in the south.

shock A life-threatening condition characterized by inadequate output of blood from the heart, occurring in conjunction with compensatory mechanisms of blood vessel constriction and reduced supply to the kidneys and other organs; blood vessel constriction maintains blood supply to vital organs, such as the brain, although the supply is markedly reduced. Hypovolaemic shock occurs when there is massive fluid loss, as in severe haemorrhage, burns, and diarrhoea, and infections, such as PERITONITIS and SEPTICAEMIA, which cause dilatation of blood vessels as a result of bacterial toxins or tissue breakdown products. Cardiogenic shock occurs when the cardiac output is reduced, which may occur in severe heart disease and THROMBOSIS with pulmonary embolism. Anaphylactic shock is an intense allergic reaction (see ALLERGY), which commonly occurs in conjunction with skin reactions and respiratory difficulties.

The onset of shock may be gradual or sudden; symptoms include hypothermia, sweating, weakness, cold skin, rapid but weak heart rate, and low blood pressure. Reduced blood supply to the kidneys causes a marked drop in urine production (known as oliguria), and acute kidney failure may also occur. The patient may be conscious, but confusion and irritability are common. Prompt and effective treatment is essential.

shock absorber (or **damper**) The device in the SUSPENSION SYSTEM of a vehicle whose function is to damp out oscillation. The spring is the means of absorbing shocks due to the wheel passing over an irregularity, but without dampers the result would be uncomfortable oscillation. Originally dampers were solid, of a friction type, which gave poor dynamic control and wore badly. Hydraulic dampers are now used, which consist of a piston sliding inside a cylinder filled with oil, the flow of which is controlled by spring-loaded valves. In this way a resistance to motion in either direction is provided.

Shockley, William (Bradford) (1910–89) US physicist. He worked mainly at the Bell Telephone Laboratories, where he organized a group to research into solid-state physics. By 1948 they had developed the transistor, which was eventually to replace the thermionic valve, and Shockley shared with his co-workers the Nobel Prize for physics in

1958. He was appointed professor of engineering science at Stanford in 1963, and later became a controversial figure because of his views on a supposed connection between race and intelligence.

shoe-bill See WHALE-HEADED STORK.

shogunate A Japanese institution under which government was in the hands of a *Sei-i dai-shogun* ('barbarian-conquering great general'). The shoguns exercised civil and military power in the name of emperors, who became figure-heads. The shogunate as a form of government originated with Minamoto Yoritomo's appointment without any limit to his authority (1192). After he died the HOJO regents took control of affairs, but in theory they remained subject both to the emperor and the shogun. During the Ashikaga period the shoguns were independent of any other authority though their rule was ineffective. Under the TOKUGAWA the power of the shogunate was decisive in national politics. Japan had been effectively ruled by the Tokugawa since the beginning of the 17th century, but from the 1840s it was progressively undermined by political pressures unleashed by increasing foreign incursions into Japanese territory. Resistance to the shogunate's conservative policies coalesced around advocates of a return to full imperial rule, and between 1866 and 1869 the Tokugawa armies were gradually defeated by an alliance of provincial forces from Choshu, Satsuma, and Tosa acting for the Meiji emperor, who formally resumed imperial rule in January 1868.

Sholes, Christopher Latham (1819–90) US printer and inventor of the modern TYPEWRITER. From 1867 he directed most of his attention to the possibility of a mechanical writing machine. The concept was not new, but Sholes's type-bar machine was the first to achieve technical success. He patented it in 1868, but failed to achieve backing for manufacture and marketing. He sold his rights to the Remington Arms Company in 1875.

Sholokhov, Mikhail (Aleksandrovich) (1905–84) Russian novelist. His epic novel *And Quiet Flows the Don*, published in four books between 1928 and 1940, was heralded as a powerful example of Socialist Realism and has become a classic of Soviet literature. Sholokhov was awarded the Nobel Prize for literature in 1965.

Shona A group of Bantu people living in south-east Africa between the Indian Ocean and Botswana. About three-quarters of the people of Zimbabwe are Shona.

shooting star (in astronomy) See METEOR.

shooting star (in botany) See PRIMROSE.

shore bird See WADING BIRD.

short-eared owl A species of medium-sized, dull-brown OWL, *Asio flammeus*, with scarcely visible eartufts and rounded wings which span a metre (over 3 feet). Cosmopolitan in distribution, they prefer rolling country, particularly marshy or wet heath. In such habitats they may be resident throughout the year, but some short-eared owls migrate annually from tundra regions to northern temperate areas. Their food is mostly small mammals and birds, often hunted by day. They nest on the ground, and usually lay between two and six eggs.

shorthand (or **stenography**) Any system for rapid WRITING, usually used for the transcription of spoken language by abbreviating the letters or the sounds of words, and replacing frequent words and expressions by single signs. It is used to record speech in business, JOURNALISM, and elsewhere. In 1837 the Englishman Isaac Pitman published a phonetic shorthand system which is still widely used in the UK. In the USA, the shorthand system developed in 1888 by the Irish-born US inventor John Gregg is most common. Twentieth-century shorthand systems have tended to use normal alphabetic characters: they are easy to learn and to transcribe, but they are slower than other systems.

Stenotypy is a typed shorthand using a limited keyboard, used widely in the USA for recording court proceedings.

shorthorn grasshopper A medium to large insect of the superfamily Acridoidea of GRASSHOPPERS, which has antennae not much longer than the length of its head. There are almost 10,000 species worldwide including the LOCUSTS. In most species the males stridulate by rubbing a row of pegs on the hind-legs against a thickened vein on the front wings. The sound is a series of chirps, not so long or loud as that of longhorn grasshoppers. The females have short ovipositors and lay pods of eggs by inserting the abdomen deep in the soil. They feed mostly on grasses, although a few eat broad-leaved plants.

short-wave radiation See ELECTROMAGNETIC RADIATION.

Shoshone A North American Indian tribe of the Uto-Aztecan linguistic group, originally occupying the Great Basin from the eastern Oregon desert to southern Colorado.

Shostakovich, Dmitri (Dmitrievich) (1906–75) Russian composer. He was a prolific composer whose works include 15 symphonies, concertos, operas, and many chamber works, although it is for the symphonies that he is most renowned. Shostakovich developed a highly personal style and, although he experimented with atonality and 12-note techniques, his music always returned to a basic tonality. The failure of his music to conform to Soviet artistic ideology earned him official condemnation, especially during the Stalinist period. His later work, particularly the last symphonies and string quartets, written after Stalin's death when the strictures on artistic freedom were less tight, became increasingly sombre and intense.

shotgun A smooth-bore FIREARM that shoots clusters of pellets, which fly out of the muzzle in a diverging pattern. Shotguns are one- or two-barrelled, shoulder weapons with a short range – up to about 45 m (150 feet). Repeating shotguns were developed in the 1880s. Some incorporate a pump slide that opens the breech to discharge the CARTRIDGE and then reloads from the magazine; others have a lever which is pushed away from the stock. US soldiers in World War I found repeating shotguns very effective in attacks on trenches. Today, the shotgun is used by many police forces, and for shooting small targets, such as birds. The sawn-off shotgun, which is a notorious criminal weapon, has the choke at the end of the barrel removed, allowing the shot to spread more quickly.

shott A shallow lake and marshy area found in hot desert areas, particularly in North Africa. Shotts receive water from rainfall or rivers or groundwater, but tend to dry up in summer. Because of the high temperatures and the fast evaporation, the salts in the water are concentrated, producing brackish conditions and leaving a sheet of salt crystals at the surface when the shott dries out.

shoveller A dabbling DUCK, easily distinguished by its outsize, spoon-shaped beak. The drake of the common shoveller, *Anas clypeata*, has a green head, white and chestnut underparts, and a large blue wing-patch. It is chiefly found in shallow freshwater habitats and is widely distributed in the Northern Hemisphere.

showboat A floating theatre which travelled down the rivers of the USA, bringing entertainment to areas newly colonized. The first true showboat was launched about 1831. It travelled annually down the Ohio and Mississippi from Pittsburgh to New Orleans, giving mainly one-night stands. Showboats became extremely popular and spread to other rivers, mostly staging MELODRAMA and comedy; usually they were pushed by tugs and had three decks. They disappeared during the Civil War but later returned, being destroyed eventually by the Depression, the cinema, and the opening of more polished city theatres.

shrapnel Specialized anti-personnel SHELLS. Shrapnel was developed by the British lieutenant Henry Shrapnel, in 1784. The shells incorporated lead balls as well as the regular gunpowder filling. The FUSE was timed to explode the shell over enemy troops, scattering the lead into their ranks. High-explosive shells largely replaced shrapnel after World War II. Shrapnel now more commonly describes the fragments of exploding bombs or shells.

shrew An INSECTIVORE belonging to the family Soricidae, although the name is also used for other insect-eating mammals, such as ELEPHANT SHREWS. Most shrews are small, and one, the pygmy white-toothed shrew, *Suncus etruscus*, has the distinction of being the smallest living mammal, weighing only 2 g (less than 0.1 ounce). Shrews are characterized by a pointed snout, dense fur, and often a strong, musky odour emanating from glands on the flanks. They are usually solitary, burrowing, terrestrial animals, but a few are adapted for an aquatic life. Water shrews, such as the American *Sorex palustris*, have fringes of hair on the feet and tail which help them to swim. Air trapped in the fur gives them buoyancy. These and some other shrews produce venom in the saliva. All shrews are insectivorous or carnivorous and some will take carrion and vegetable matter in their diet.

Shrewsbury The country town of Shropshire in western England, on the River Severn; pop. (1991) 64,219. A former seat of the princes of Powys, it was absorbed into the kingdom of Mercia in the 8th century. It has many medieval buildings and light industries.

shrike Any of about 70 species of bird of the family Laniidae. The great majority occur in Africa, with some others in the Old World. Two species occur in North America, the great grey shrike, *Lanius excubitor*, and the loggerhead shrike, *L. ludovicianus*. The latter reaches Central America, but is absent from South America and Australasia. They vary in size from that of a small thrush to that of a small crow and are often strikingly coloured in blacks, greys, and whites. Some of the tropical species are brilliantly coloured with red, green, and yellow. Their beaks are powerful and slightly hooked. They perch on bushes and pounce on passing insects, small birds, and other small animals. They often impale surplus food on thorns, retiring to their larder later; hence an alternative name of butcher birds.

shrimp A small, laterally compressed CRUSTACEAN of the suborder Dendrobranchiata, related to crabs and lobsters (decapods); the suborder also includes the PRAWNS. Shrimps have an elongate abdomen and a fanlike tail, which are rapidly flexed for swimming. The antennae are very long and whiplike, and the animals feed on tiny marine organisms. The European shrimp, *Crangon vulgaris*, is trawled for food. The name 'shrimp' is also used for other elongate swimming crustaceans, such as EUPHAUSID SHRIMPS and MANTIS SHRIMPS.

shrimp fish Any of four species of fish of the family Centricidae, found in the tropical Indo-Pacific ocean. They are small, rarely exceeding 15 cm (6 inches) in length, and are slender and compressed, with a long snout and the second dorsal and tail fins displaced on to the underside of the body. They swim vertically in the water in a head-down posture. One species has been reported to live in underwater caves.

Shropshire A west-Midland county of England; area 3,490 sq km (1,348 sq miles); pop. (1991) 401,600; county town, Shrewsbury. Shropshire is divided into six districts.

shrub A woody plant less than 10 m tall, without the obvious trunk of a tree but with a number of basal shoots, giving a bushy appearance. There is no clear distinction between shrubs and trees: species such as hawthorn, hazel, or birch may grow from a shrub into a tree. Shrubs include a number of crops, such as tea, coffee, and blackcurrants, and have great importance in horticulture, particularly as hedging plants.

Shute, Nevil (born Nevil Shute Norway) (1899–1960) British novelist. After World War II he settled in Australia, which provides the setting for his later novels; among the best known are *A Town Like Alice* (1950) and *On the Beach* (1957), which depicts a community facing gradual destruction in the aftermath of a nuclear war.

shutter (in photography) A device in a CAMERA that controls the length of time during which light is able to reach the FILM. Shutter speed and APERTURE together control the amount of exposure to light that the film receives. Modern shutters are of two main types: focal-plane and leaf. The focal-plane shutter forms an integral part of the camera and is positioned at the focal plane (immediately in front of the film). When the shutter is activated, two blinds move across the film, the width of the gap between them determining the shutter speed. Leaf shutters consist of a number of thin, overlapping metal blades which open to form a diaphragm of a particular aperture, and then close after exposure.

sial The former name for material of the upper part of the EARTH's crust: the layer that makes up the bulk of the continents but is relatively thin under the oceans. It consists of rocks (granite, for example) that are rich in silica (Si) and aluminium (Al), lying above the SIMA.

Siam The name until 1939 of THAILAND.

Siamese The former name for THAI.

Siamese fighting fish See FIGHTING FISH.

Sian See XIAN.

Sibelius, Jean (born Johan Julius Christian Sibelius) (1865–1957) Finnish composer. He is best known for the series of seven symphonies spanning the years 1898 to 1924. His affinity for his country's landscape and legends, especially the epic *Kalevala*, expressed themselves in a series of symphonic poems including *The Swan of Tuonela* (1893), *Finlandia* (1899), and *Tapiola* (1925); he also wrote a violin concerto (1903) and more than 100 songs. An eighth symphony, completed in 1929, was destroyed by the composer, who virtually ceased composing after 1926 – partly through self-doubt and lack of sympathy with contemporary trends in music, and partly because of heavy drinking.

Siberia (from Tatar, 'Sleeping Land') The vast northern, central, and eastern region of northern Asia, which extends from the Ural Mountains in Russia, eastward to the Pacific and from the Arctic Ocean southward to Mongolia and China. Nearly one-third of Siberia is within the Arctic Circle. Here, and especially along the coastal plain, there is tundra; here also is the northern edge of the taiga or coniferous forest which stretches in a wide but irregular belt across the region. It extends over an area of about 12,800,000 sq km (4,950,000 sq miles). There are three natural divisions. The west Siberian plain, abutting the Ural Mountains, is low-lying and very flat. It occupies the great basins of the Ob and Yenisei rivers, which flow from the southern mountains through steppe and marshland. The climate here is continental, with warm, arid summers and extremely cold winters. The central Siberian plateau rises to over 1,000 m (3,300 feet) and is more undulating. It contains grazing land and is drained by the Lena and its tributaries. Lake Baikal, the world's deepest lake, lies in a RIFT VALLEY in the south and is frozen during winter. Eastern Siberia is mountainous, much of it volcanic, and contains enormous deposits of gold, iron, nickel, mica, bauxite, graphite, and coal.

Sibyl Any ancient Greek or Roman prophetess. They sometimes had individual names, for example Herophile (also known as the Erythraean Sibyl, from her birthplace Erythrae), who prophesied to Hecuba before the Trojan War.

Sichuan (or **Szechuan**) A province of west-central China; area 567,000 sq km (219,000 sq miles); pop. (1990) 107,218,000; capital, Chengdu. Surrounded by mountain ranges, the Chengdu Plain produces rice, wheat, maize, sugar cane, and beans.

Sicilian Vespers An uprising and massacre in Sicily, which began at the time of vespers (the evening church service) on Easter Tuesday in 1282. It marked the end of the rule of the ANGEVINS in the island and of their dynastic ambitions in Italy. Charles I of Anjou had received the Kingdom of the Two Sicilies from Pope Urban IV in 1266 and to claim it had defeated the Hohenstaufen Manfred, son of the Holy Roman Emperor Frederick II. His rule was extremely harsh, enforcing heavy taxation, and the French occupation was generally hated. Within a month all the French had been killed or forced to flee and the crown was later given to Pedro III of Aragon, who thwarted Angevin attempts at reoccupation, and who passed the crown to his son Frederick III of Sicily.

Sicily (Italian **Sicilia**) A large triangular island in the Mediterranean Sea, separated from the 'toe' of Italy by the narrow Strait of Messina. It forms, with the neighbouring islands of Lipari, Egadi, Ustica, and Pantelleria, a region of Italy comprising the provinces of Agrigento, Caltanissetta, Catania, Enna, Messina, Palermo, Ragusa, Siracusa, and Trapani; area 25,706 sq km (9,929 sq miles); pop. (1990) 5,196,820; capital, Palermo. Settled successively by Phoenicians, Greeks, and Cartheginians, it became a Roman province in 241 BC after the first Punic War. After various struggles Sicily and southern Italy became a Norman kingdom towards the end of the 11th century. It was conquered by Charles of Anjou in 1266, but the unpopularity of the Angevin regime led to the uprising known as the SICILIAN VESPERS and the establishment in Sicily of the Spanish House of Aragon in its place; southern Italy remained under Angevin rule until reunited with Sicily in 1442. In 1816 the two areas were officially merged when the Spanish Bourbon Ferdinand styled himself King of the Two Sicilies. The island was liberated by Garibaldi in 1860 and finally incorporated into the new state of Italy. The Sicilian economy is predominantly agricultural. Tourism is important.

Sickert, Walter Richard (1860–1942) British painter, of Danish and Anglo-Irish descent. He was a pupil of Whistler and also worked with Degas. His subjects were mainly urban scenes and figure compositions, particularly pictures of the theatre and music-hall and drab domestic interiors, avoiding the conventionally picturesque. His best-known painting, *Ennui* (1913), portrays a stagnant marriage.

sickle-cell anaemia An inherited blood disease that affects some people of African descent, but that also occurs in the Mediterranean region and India. It occurs when the sickle-cell gene has been inherited from both parents, causing an abnormal type of HAEMOGLOBIN to form. When the blood is deprived of oxygen, this haemoglobin precipitates in the red cells, forming crystals that distort the cells into a characteristic sickle shape. These sickle cells are removed from the blood by the spleen, causing anaemia and jaundice. There is no satifactory treatment, causing a high mortality in affected children. The **sickle-cell trait**, which occurs when the faulty gene is inherited from only one parent, causes no symptoms but confers some protection from malaria, which may explain the gene's high frequency in areas plagued by malaria.

Sì dà Tiānwáng (or **Sì dà Jıngāng**, 'the Four Great Diamond Kings'; Japanese **Shitennō**, 'the Four Heavenly Kings') In Buddhism, the guardians of the Universe and controllers of the four elements (fire, air, earth, water). Often seen as immense images bearing symbols (which vary according to the country) and in full armour, at the entrance to temples, the four deities are said to have helped Gautama Buddha at important stages of his life.

Siddons, Mrs Sarah (née Kemble) (1755–1831) British actress. The sister of John Kemble, she made her first, unsuccessful, London appearance in 1775; she then toured the provinces and made a successful return to the London stage in 1782, where she became an acclaimed tragic actress, noted particularly for her role as Lady Macbeth. She retained her pre-eminence until her retirement in 1812.

siderolite See METEORITE.

sidewinder A small RATTLESNAKE, *Crotalus cerastes*, that occurs in the south of the USA and in Mexico. Its name reflects its sideways looping slither, which enables it to move rapidly over loose sand. Usually brown or grey, it can grow up to 75 cm (2 feet) long.

Sidney, Sir Philip (1554–86) British poet and soldier. Generally considered to represent the apotheosis of the Elizabethan courtier, he was a leading poet and patron of poets, including Edmund Spenser. His best-known work is *Arcadia* (published posthumously in 1590), a prose romance including poems and pastoral eclogues in a wide variety of verse forms.

SIDS (sudden infant death syndrome) See COT DEATH.

Siegfried (or **Sigurd**) In Germanic mythology, a hero of outstanding strength, beauty, and courage, who killed the dragon Fafnir with a magic sword. Sprayed with the dragon's blood, Siegfried became invulnerable except when a leaf settled between his shoulders. He learned the language of the birds and overcame the dwarf Nibelungs, taking their treasure and the magic ring that he gave to Brunhild after rescuing her. He was killed at Brunhild's instigation after he married Kriemhild, sister of the Burgundian king, Gunther. The 13th-century Icelandic *Volsunga Saga* tells a similar story with Sigurd, Brynhild, Gudrun, and Gunnar, corresponding to the Germanic characters. See also NIBELUNG.

Siegfried Line The line of defence constructed along the western frontier of Germany before World War II.

Siemens, Ernst Werner von (1816–92) German electrical engineer. He developed electroplating and an electric generator using an electromagnet; he set up a factory that manufactured telegraph systems and electric cables and pioneered electrical traction. His brother **Karl Wilhelm Siemens** (Sir Charles William Siemens, 1823–83) moved to England, where he developed the open-hearth steel furnace and designed the cable-laying steamship *Faraday*, and also designed the electric railway at Portrush in Northern Ireland. A third brother **Friedrich Siemens** (1826–1904) worked both with Werner in Germany and with Charles in England; he applied the principles of the open-hearth furnace to glassmaking.

Siemens–Martin furnace See OPEN-HEARTH FURNACE.

Siena A city of Tuscany in west-central Italy, noted for its medieval architecture and for its school of Gothic art, which flourished in the 13th–14th centuries; pop. (1990) 57,745. It has a university founded in 1240 and a vast cathedral dating from the 13th century. The city gives its name to sienna, a ferruginous earth used as a pigment in paint. The annual *Palio* horse-races in the main square take place in July and August.

Sierra Leone A tropical West African country with a south-west-facing Atlantic coast and a fine natural harbour, surrounded inland by Guinea and Liberia.

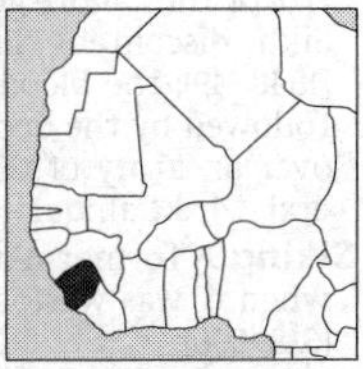

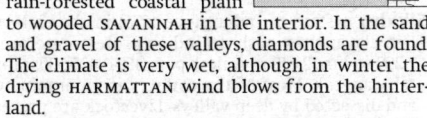

Physical. Swamps spread up river valleys, through a rain-forested coastal plain to wooded SAVANNAH in the interior. In the sand and gravel of these valleys, diamonds are found. The climate is very wet, although in winter the drying HARMATTAN wind blows from the hinterland.

Economy. The leading exports are rutile, diamonds, bauxite, cocoa, and coffee; smuggling of gold and diamonds is widespread. Iron-ore mines are inactive due to lack of financing. In agriculture, the main cash crops are cocoa and coffee, and the main staple crops are cassava, rice, and plantains. Industry is confined to food-processing and other light industry.

History. The Portuguese navigator Pedro de Cintra reached it in 1462, at about the time the Temne, its chief inhabitants, were reaching the coast. During the 16th and 17th centuries the slave trade and piracy attracted many Europeans, including English, so that the coast has a very mixed population. In 1772 Britain declared that any escaped slave who came to Britain would automatically become free. In 1787 the Anti-Slavery Society bought the coastal territory from the local ruler as a haven for slaves found destitute in Britain. British philanthropists organized their transport to Cape Sierra Leone, where Freetown was established. In 1791 Alexander Falconbridge formed a transport company, the Sierra Leone Company, landing the first colonists at Freetown in 1792. It became a crown colony in 1808. After 1815 British warships who captured slave ships brought freed captives there. During the 19th century the hinterland of Sierra Leone was gradually explored and in 1896 it became a British protectorate, which remained separate from the colony of Freetown until 1951. The country gained its independence under Prime Minister Sir Milton Margai (1895–1964) in 1961, but after his death electoral difficulties produced two military coups before some stability was restored by the establishment of a one-party state under Dr Siaka Stevens. Food shortages, corruption, and tribal tensions produced serious violence in the early 1980s, and in 1985 Stevens retired in favour of Major-General Joseph Saidu Momoh. As head of state, he retained a civilian cabinet with the All People's Congress (APC) the sole legal party; its rule was deeply corrupt. In April 1992 an army coup, led by Captain Valentine Strasser, ousted Saidu Momoh and formed a National Provisional Defence Council, committed to the elimination of corruption and the restoration of the economy. Although the ban on political parties imposed in 1992 was lifted in 1995, actions by rebel forces opposed to the government intensified. In 1996 Strasser was ousted by his deputy, Captain Julius Bio, who took over as head of state. In March 1996 democratic elections were won by Ahmad Tejan Kabbah who became President of a civilian government. This government was overthrown in a military coup in 1997, but Nigerian forces retook the capital in 1998 and the President was reinstated.

Capital: Freetown
Area: 71,740 sq km (27,699 sq mi)
Population: 4,509,000 (1995)
Currency: 1 leone = 100 cents
Religions: Traditional beliefs 51.5%; Sunni Muslim 39.4%; Protestant 4.7%; Roman Catholic 2.2%; Anglican 1.2%
Ethnic Groups: Mende 46.0%; Temne 45.0%
Languages: English (official); Krio (English creole); Mende; Temne, other local languages
International Organizations: UN; OAU; ECOWAS; Commonwealth

Sierra Madre The chief mountain system of Mexico, stretching from the US frontier in the north-west to the Gulf of Tehuantepec in the south-east. It is divided for most of its length into the **Sierra Madre Occidental** in the west and the **Sierra Madre Oriental** in the east, and to the south of Mexico City and west of Oaxaca the **Sierra Madre del Sur** extends along the Pacific coast. Rising to 5,699 m (18,697 ft) near Orizaba, Citaltépetl is the highest peak in the Sierra Madre.

Sierra Nevada ▶1 A mountain range in Andalusia, southern Spain rising to 3,480 m (11,411 ft) at Mulhacén. **▶2** A mountain range in California, USA, that rises sharply from the Great Basin in the west and descends gradually into the central valley of California. Its highest point is Mt. Whitney (4,418 m, 14,495 ft).

Sigismund (1368–1437) Holy Roman Emperor 1411–37, king of Hungary 1387–1437, Germany 1411–37, Bohemia 1419–37, and Lombardy 1431–37, the last emperor of the House of Luxemburg. In 1396 he was defeated by the Turks at Nicopolis but went on to acquire and secure a large number of territories and titles in a long and violent reign, which featured warfare with the HUSSITES, Venetians, and rivals for the thrones of Hungary and Germany. An orthodox Catholic, he acted severely against the Hussites, and put pressure on the pope to call a council at CONSTANCE to end the Hussite Schism; Sigismund promised Huss safe-conduct to attend the council, which subsequently ordered his death.

Signac, Paul (1863–1935) French NEO-IMPRESSIONIST painter; SEURAT's chief disciple. In his paintings he used mosaic-like patches of pure colour (as opposed to Seurat's pointillist dots), mostly of seascapes. In 1899 he published *D'Eugène Delacroix à néo-impressionisme*, in which he upheld the idea of painting with scientific precision.

significant figures Digits giving an approximation of stated accuracy to a number. Reduction to *n* significant figures is obtained by counting *n* + 1 digits from the left, beginning at the first non-zero digit of the number. The last figure counted is used to round off the *n*th digit, and the remaining digits are replaced by zeros where necessary. Thus 271,493, 51.73259, 0.00516001 reduced to four significant figures become 271,500, 51.73, and 0.005160 respectively. (Note that 0.00516001 itself has six significant figures.)

Sign language Finger spelling used to represent letters of the alphabet for the deaf.

sign language An independent linguistic system used by the deaf. It is a system of hand shapes and movements in relation to the upper part of the signer's body. The complexity of its GRAMMAR (the rules of sign and sentence formation) and expressiveness equals that of spoken languages. Sign languages have their own DIALECTS, undergo linguistic change, and for some are acquired as their native tongue. Among the many different, mutually unintelligible sign languages, the American Sign Language (ASL) is the most widespread. Finger spelling and cued speech which aids LIP-READING are alternative forms, which are 'parasitically' dependent on spoken language.

Sihanouk, Norodom (1922–) Cambodian king 1941–55 and since 1993, Prime Minister 1955–60, and head of state 1960–70 and 1975–76. Two years after Cambodian independence (1953) Sihanouk abdicated in order to become Premier, passing the throne to his father Prince Norodom Suramarit (died 1960). On his father's death, Prince Sihanouk proclaimed himself head of state, a position he retained until a US-backed military coup ten years later. Sihanouk was reinstated by the Khmer Rouge in 1975, only to be removed the following year. After serving as President of the government-in-exile (1982–89), he was appointed head of state by the provisional government and subsequently crowned for the second time (1993).

Sikhism A monotheistic religion founded in the Punjab in the 15th century by Guru Nanak. It combines elements of Hinduism and Islam, accepting the Hindu concepts of karma and reincarnation but rejecting the caste system, and has one sacred scripture, the Adi Granth. The tenth and last of the series of gurus, Gobind Singh, prescribed the distinctive outward forms (the so-called five Ks) – long hair (to be covered by a turban) and uncut beard (*kesh*), comb (*kangha*), short sword (*kirpan*), steel bangle (*kara*), and short trousers for horse-riding (*kaccha*). Originating as a religion, Sikhism became a militant political movement in the Punjab, where most of the world's 18 million Sikhs live.

Sikh Wars (1845–49) Two conflicts between the Sikhs of Lahore and the English EAST INDIA COMPANY. The First Sikh War (1845–46) took place when Sikh troops crossed the Sutlej River into British India. After the drawn battles of Mudki and Firuzshah, the British defeated the Sikhs at Aliwal and Sobraon. By the Treaty of Lahore (1846) Britain obtained the cession of the Jullundar Doab, took Kashmir for Gulab Singh, and established control of the Lahore government through a Resident. Sikh discontent led to the Second Sikh War (1848–49); the bloody Battle of Chillianwallah was followed by the decisive British victory at Gujerat over an army of 60,000 Sikhs. The governor-general, Lord Dalhousie, annexed the Punjab in 1849.

Siking A former name of the Chinese city of Xian when it was western capital of the Tang dynasty (618–906).

Sikkim A state of India (since 1975) in the eastern Himalayas, previously an Indian protectorate; area 7,299 sq km (2,819 sq miles); pop. (1991) 405,500; capital, Gangtok. Most of the country is mountainous and dissected by deep valleys. Livestock are grazed on lower slopes and grain, fruit, and vegetable crops grown in the valleys. There are handicraft industries including the weaving of cotton.

Sikorski, Vladislav (1881–1943) Polish general and statesman. He commanded divisions against the BOLSHEVIKS (1919–20) and during 1922–23 headed a non-parliamentary coalition government in Poland. In 1939 he fled to France and organized a Polish army in exile that fought with the Allies in World War II. As head of the exiled Polish government in London he succeeded in maintaining tolerable relations with Moscow until news of the KATYN massacre broke. During his ascendancy Polish prisoners-of-war in the Soviet Union were recruited to form the 'Polish Army in Russia' under General Wladyslaw Anders to fight with the Allies. He was killed in an air crash, which formed the subject of a controversial play by HOCHHUTH.

Sikorsky, Igor (Ivanovich) (1889–1972) Russian-born US aircraft designer. He studied aeronautics in Paris before returning to Russia to build the first large four-engined aircraft, the Grand, in 1913. After experimenting unsuccessfully with helicopters he emigrated to New York, where he established the Sikorsky Aero Engineering Co. and produced many famous amphibious aircraft and flying boats. Sikorsky again turned his attention to helicopters, personally flying the prototype of the first mass-produced helicopter in 1939, and was closely associated with their subsequent development.

silage An animal FEEDSTUFF produced when any fodder crop, but predominantly grass, is cut green, pressed, and preserved by its own partial FERMENTATION in an airtight SILO or storage pit. If sealed, the silage partially ferments to a slightly sour mixture, after which the contents remain stable. More recently, chemicals have been added to aid the ensiling process. Large BALERS are used to bale fresh-cut grass, which when sealed into a plastic bag makes high-grade silage without the need for expensive storage facilities. The advantages of silage-making over haymaking are that it is much less labour intensive, the nutritional quality of silage is higher than that of hay, and, as it is not dependent on dry weather, the crop may be harvested at the best time in its growing cycle.

Silbury Hill An ancient prehistoric earthwork near Avebury in Wiltshire, southern England, 40 m (130 ft) high. It is believed to be the largest man-made mound in Europe.

Silesia (Czech **Slezsko**; Polish **Śląsk**) A region of central Europe (now largely in south-west Poland), an ancient district and duchy, partitioned at various times between the states of Prussia, Austria-Hungary, Poland, and Czechoslovakia. Lying to the north of the Sudeten Mountains and Western Carpathians and drained by the Oder, it is a largely agricultural and forested lowland region with extensive coal and mineral resources.

silica (or **silicon dioxide**, SiO_2) The most abundant constituent of the Earth's crust, occurring in many types of rocks, both in its pure form and as a constituent of SILICATES. There are three main crystalline forms: QUARTZ, tridymite, and cristobalite, the last two being rare, and found only in acidic volcanic rock. In each the silicon atom is bound tetrahedrally to four oxygen atoms, but their crystalline structures are all very different. Crypto-crystalline forms, that is forms where the crystals are too small to be seen under a conventional microscope, include chert, chalcedony, and opal. Silica is tough and has a high melting-point, which makes it useful in the manufacture of refractory materials. It is the raw material of the glass industry, and as a colloid or gel is widely used as a binder and adsorbent.

silicates A very widely occurring group of compounds containing silicon, oxygen, and one or more metals. Natural silicates form the major part of most rocks and of many minerals. All silicates are based on the SiO_4 tetrahedron, although there is a vast range of structures adopted (according to which they are classified). They vary in composition from the relatively simple minerals, such as zircon, $ZrSiO_4$, to infinite three-dimensional arrays of SiO_4 units in which the oxygen atoms form bridges between the silicon atoms. Typical natural silicates include a number of gemstones, talc, clay, and mica. Portland cement contains a large proportion of calcium silicates.

silicon (symbol Si, at. no. 14, r.a.m. 28.09) A browny-black METALLOID element in Group 14 (formerly IVB) of the PERIODIC TABLE. The element has a giant molecular structure similar to that of diamond. It is the second most abundant element after oxygen and forms nearly 28 per cent of the Earth's crust. It is found in a wide range of SILICATES. Industrially it is formed by the reduction of SILICA, SiO_2, with carbon or calcium carbide, CaC_2, in an electric furnace. When it is purified further, it is used to manufacture silicon chips (see INTEGRATED CIRCUIT) in electronics; and when very small quantities of boron or phosphorus are added (doping), it is used as a SEMICONDUCTOR in transistors. Silicon forms stable compounds in which it shows a valency of 4. SILICON CARBIDE (carborundum) crystals, SiC, are manufactured as abrasives. Solutions of SILICATES are obtained by reacting the element with alkalis. Synthetic polymers can be formed of silicon, carbon, hydrogen, and oxygen; they are called silicones and are oily liquids, resins, or rubbery solids, widely used as waxes and water repellents.

silicon carbide (or **carborundum**, SiC) A very common ABRASIVE material, manufactured by fusing a mixture of carbon and sand or silica (SiO_2) in an electric furnace. It is almost as hard as diamond, and is used in fine powder form as a high-melting-point, wear-resistant CERAMIC used for REFRACTORY materials and abrasive tools. Silicon-carbide fibres are made for use in COMPOSITES, and silicon-carbide films can be formed by VAPOUR DEPOSITION as wear-resistant coatings.

silicon chip See INTEGRATED CIRCUIT.

silicon dioxide See SILICA.

silicone Any of a family of POLYMERS in which the central backbone or chain is made up of silicon and oxygen atoms. (PLASTICS and natural organic polymers have a central backbone of carbon atoms.) Silicones are water-repellent, resistant to heat and are used in applications in which this property offsets their greater cost. Examples include greases for lubrication, rubber-like sheeting for gaskets, and thermosetting, insulating varnishes for coating and laminating.

silicon nitride (Si_3N_4) A very hard, stiff, and light CERAMIC, which retains its properties up to very high temperatures. It is of particular importance in mechanical engineering because of its creep resistance. It is made by the reaction of silicon with nitrogen gas at high temperatures, or by VAPOUR DEPOSITION reactions between ammonia (NH_3) and chlorosilanes (for example, $SiCl_4$).

Silicon Valley The industrial area between San Jose and Palo Alto in Santa Clara County, California, USA, which is a noted centre for computing and the manufacture of electronics. So called, because silicon is the basis of modern electronics.

silk The fibre produced for its cocoon by the SILKWORM, and the fabric made from the fibre. Silk is made by soaking the cocoons in hot water to soften the glutinous matter, the 1–3 km (0.6–1.9 miles) of twin silk filaments which constitute each cocoon are unwound (reeled) and dried in skein form. Silk thread to be used as WARP in weaving is known as tram. It is made by combining the twin filaments from several skeins by drawing them through warm water and then through a small metal orifice which both removes adherent impurities and compacts the thread. It is then further compacted on throwing machines, which are used for twisting continuous filaments. Silk thread to be used as WEFT is known as organzine. It is processed in a similar way to tram except that it is twisted only lightly and in the opposite direction. Silk damaged during reeling is unsuitable for throwing, and is made into YARN by cutting it into lengths and SPINNING it in the same way as cotton, linen, and wool. Before this can be done, all the natural gums must be removed from the silk by FERMENTATION treatment or by boiling in an aqueous soap solution.

Historically, commercial silk production was confined to China and Japan (still the leading producers) and India, but it has also been attempted in Europe and North America.

silk moth See SILKWORM.

Silk Road (or **Silk Route**) An ancient caravan route linking China with the West, used from Roman times onwards and taking its name from the silk that was a major Chinese export. By this route Christianity and (from India) Buddhism reached China. A 'North Road' skirted the northern edge of the Taklimakan Desert before heading westwards into Turkestan (and thence to the Levant), while a 'South Road' followed a more southerly route through the high passes of the Kunlun and Pamir mountains into India. A railway (completed in 1963) follows the northern route from Xian to Urumchi and into Kazakhstan.

silk-screen printing See SCREEN PRINTING.

silkworm The caterpillar of the silk moth, which extrudes SILK from mouth glands and uses it to weave cocoons within which it pupates. The common silk moth, *Bombyx mori*, a native of China, has been domesticated for centuries and no longer occurs in the wild. The caterpillars are fed on mulberry leaves; adults neither feed nor fly. Before the silk is wound off, the pupae are killed by immersion in hot water. Each cocoon yields up to 900 m (over 0.5 mile) of thread.

Silk moths belong to the family Saturniidae. Caterpillars of many species other than *B. mori* also produce silk (which is often called shantung or tussore silk), but none is as commercially important as that of the common silk moth.

silky flycatcher A bird of a subfamily of some four species which are closely related to waxwings in the family Bombycillidae. They are found in the southwestern USA and Central America and have a sparrow-sized body, with a crested head and a longish tail 18–25 cm (7–10 inches). Their plumage is blackish, grey, or brown with yellow markings, and white in the tail and wings. They live in bushy country and feed on berries and insects.

sill A sheet-like body of igneous rock that has been injected concordantly (along bedding planes) into surrounding rocks while still in a molten state. Sills are usually composed of medium-grained rock, often DOLERITE.

Sillitoe, Alan (1928–) British writer. His fiction is notable for its depiction of working-class provincial life; his first novel *Saturday Night and Sunday Morning* (1958) describes the life of a dissatisfied young Nottingham factory worker, while the title story in *The Loneliness of the Long-Distance Runner* (1959) portrays a rebellious Borstal boy. He has also published volumes of poetry, short stories, and plays.

silo A pit or circular tower for the storage of SILAGE or grain. Silos can be made from wire mesh lined with plastic, but are most commonly tall, metal-skinned towers with a non-corrosive fused-glass or porcelain lining. The tower is filled from the top, and emptied from the bottom. Inside the sealed chamber bacterial FERMENTATION of the stored grain takes place until the concentration of fermentation products becomes too high for it to continue. Carbon dioxide gas evolved during fermentation prevents oxidative decay of the silage or grain.

silt An aggregate of mineral grains or rock fragments with diameters ranging from 0.0625 to 0.002 mm (0.0025–0.00008 inch). In technical contexts, silt also refers to soils made up of silt-sized particles. The silt grade is larger in grain size than CLAY but smaller than SAND.

Silurian In geological time, the third period of the Palaeozoic era, following the Ordovician and preceding the Devonian, lasting from about 438 to 408 million years ago. The first land plants and the first fish (with jaws) appeared during this period.

silver (symbol Ag, at. no. 47, r.a.m. 107.87) A brilliant white, malleable, TRANSITION METAL. It has the highest known electrical conductivity; and is one of the so-called precious metals. It occurs widely in nature – mostly in South Africa and Russia – both in sulphide ores and as the native or free metal. Silver can be extracted from ores before smelting, by treating with cyanide and then displacing with zinc, or by amalgamating with mercury followed by distillation. It normally shows a VALENCY of 1, although silver oxide, AgO, does exist; this is a black solid with a complex structure containing monovalent and trivalent silver ions. A dark silver sulphide forms when silver tarnishes in air because of the presence of sulphur compounds. The metal is used for ornaments and jewellery. Copper and brass objects are coated with silver by ELECTROPLATING. Large amounts of silver halide are used in photographic FILM.

silver bromide (AgBr) A pale yellow solid, with a melting-point of 420°C (788°F), produced when hydrobromic acid, HBr, is added to a solution of a silver salt. It is found naturally as the mineral bromyrite. It is photosensitive and is used in photography.

silverfish (or **bristletail**) An elongate, tapering, wingless insect, up to 1.2 cm (0.5 inch) long, and covered with silvery scales. Silverfish comprise the order Thysanura, with over 550 species distributed worldwide. The antennae are long and there are three long appendages at the tail-end. They are harmless commensals of humans, living in damp places, such as cracks around sinks, and feeding on scraps of food and paper. The eggs are laid in the cracks and the young resemble the adults, except that the scales are not developed. The firebrat, *Thermobia domestica*, is a cosmopolitan example.

silver nitrate ($AgNO_3$) A caustic compound important as an analytical reagent and as an antiseptic. It is used in the commercial preparation of other silver salts, particularly the silver halides, especially SILVER BROMIDE, used in photographic emulsions. In the laboratory it is used in the volumetric determination of halides, cyanides, and thiocyanates, and to indicate the presence of reducing agents. Silver nitrate is soluble in water, alcohol, and many other organic solvents. When heated to temperatures above 310°C (590°F), silver is produced.

silverpoint A method of drawing using a fine silver rod, pointed at one end, on prepared paper. Other metals – copper, gold, lead – may be used, but silver is the most common. It produces an attractive fine grey line that oxidizes to a light brown. The strength of tone can hardly be varied at all and the technique demands great certainty of purpose and hand.

silverside A mostly small, coastal and inshore marine fish, which is abundant in tropical and warm temperate seas. A substantial number of the 180 or so species, however, live in fresh water especially in Central America, New Guinea, and Australia. They all belong to the family Atherinidae, and are recognized by two widely separated dorsal fins, large scales, moderately big eyes, and a mouth opening at the top of the head. All species have a prominent silvery LATERAL LINE. They spawn in shallow water, the eggs of many species having short adhesive threads on their surface.

sima The former name for material of the layer of rocks 6–7 km (about 4 miles) thick that make up the lower portion of the EARTH's crust. The sima forms most of the ocean floors, and in this context it can be thought of as representing rocks with the composition of BASALT, which are relatively rich in silicon and magnesium (si + ma). The sima at depth below the continents (underneath the SIAL) is thought to approximate more closely to DIORITE than basalt in composition.

Simenon, Georges (Joseph Christian) (1903–89) Belgian-born French novelist. He is best known for his series of detective novels featuring Commissaire Maigret, who was introduced in 1931. Maigret relies on his understanding of the criminal's motives rather than scientific deduction to solve crimes and the novels show considerable insight into human psychology.

Simeon Stylites, St (*c.*390–459) Syrian monk. After living in a monastic community he became the first to practise an extreme form of ascetism, which involved living on top of a pillar; this became a site of pilgrimage.

simile An explicit comparison between two different things, actions, or feelings, using the words 'as' or 'like': 'I wandered lonely as a cloud' (Wordsworth). A very common figure of speech in both prose and verse, simile is more tentative and decorative than METAPHOR. The 'epic similes' of Homer and other epic poets are sustained comparisons of two complex actions, for instance the charging of an army and the onset of storm-clouds.

Simla (or **Shimla**) A hill station in northern India, capital of the state of Himachal Pradesh; pop. (1991) 109,860. It was the summer capital of British India (1864–1947), and is now a summer resort and army headquarters.

Simnel, Lambert (*c.*1487–*c.*1525) English royal PRETENDER. Although he was actually a joiner's son certain YORKISTS pretended or believed that he was Edward of Warwick, son of the murdered George, Duke of CLARENCE, and on 24 May 1487 he was crowned in Dublin as Edward VI. Next month he was brought to England, but the Yorkists were defeated and HENRY VII, showing mercy, gave him employment in the royal kitchens.

Simon, (Marvin) Neil (1927–) US dramatist. Most of his plays are wry comedies portraying aspects of middle-class life; they include *Barefoot in the Park* (1963) *The Odd Couple* (1965), and *Brighton Beach Memoirs* (1983). Among his musicals are *Sweet Charity* (1966) and *They're Playing Our Song* (1979).

Simon, Paul (1942–) US singer and songwriter. He formed a folk-rock partnership with his school friend **Art Garfunkel** (1941–), which first made its mark with the album *Sounds of Silence* (1966). Further achievements were the soundtrack music to the film *The Graduate* (1968) and the song 'Bridge Over Troubled Water' (1970) from the album of the same name. The duo split up in 1970 and Simon went on to pursue a successful solo career, recording albums such as *Graceland* (1986), which featured many black South African musicians, and *The Rhythm of the Saints* (1990). He has also acted in films, including Woody Allen's *Annie Hall* (1977).

Simon, St (known as **Simon the Zealot**) An Apostle. According to one tradition he preached and was martyred in Persia along with St Jude. Feast day (with St Jude), 28 October.

Simone Martini See MARTINI, SIMONE.

Simonides (*c.*556–468 BC) Greek lyric poet. He wrote for the rulers of Athens, Thessaly, and Syracuse; much of his poetry, which includes elegies, odes, and epigrams, celebrates the heroes of the Persian Wars, and includes verse commemorating those killed at Marathon and Thermopylae.

simony The buying and selling of spiritual or Church benefits. It is taken from the name of Simon Magus who, according to an account in the New Testament of the Bible, tried to buy spiritual powers from St Peter. It came to mean the purchase of any office or authority within the ROMAN CATHOLIC CHURCH. The Church's policy that its benefices should not be sold for money was often jeopardized because many secular lords claimed that they were theirs to dispose of as they wished. Wealthy families bought offices for their members and used them as a form of patronage. Simony was one of the abuses criticized at the time of the REFORMATION.

simple harmonic motion A to-and-fro motion in which the acceleration and deceleration of the moving body is always proportional to its distance from the centre of the oscillation. The most familiar example is the motion of a spring when it is stretched and then released. Simple harmonic motion is described mathematically by the equation $d^2x/dt^2 = -\Omega x^2$, and arises whenever there is a force proportional to distance. Here x is the distance from the centre of the motion, t is time, and Ω is a constant. The solution of this equation is $x = A \sin(\Omega t) + B \cos(\Omega t)$, where A and B are constants. This shows that Ω is 2π times the frequency of the motion. Given a point moving round a circle at a constant speed, the projection of its position on to a diameter moves back and forth along that diameter with simple harmonic motion, and Ω is the angular speed of the point round the circle.

Simplon (Italian **Sempione**) A pass in the Bernese Alps of southern Switzerland linking Brig in the Swiss canton of Valais with Domodosola in Italy. Reaching an altitude of 2,028 m (6,591 ft), the road through the pass was built by Napoleon in 1801–05. The nearby railway tunnel (1922) connecting Switzerland and Italy is 19 km (12 miles) long.

Simpson, Sir James Young (1811–71) Scottish surgeon and obstetrician. He discovered the usefulness of chloroform as an anaesthetic by experimentation on himself and his colleagues shortly after the first use of ether. Simpson was also a distinguished antiquarian and historian, publishing monographs on archaeology and the history of medicine.

Simpson, O(renthal) J(ames) (1947–) US football player, actor, and celebrity. He was arrested in 1994, accused of murdering his wife and her male companion, but was acquitted after a lengthy, high-profile trial. An outstanding player of American football, he joined the Buffalo Bills in 1968 as a running back. In 1975 he scored a record 23 touchdowns in one season. As an actor he has appeared in numerous films including the *Naked Gun* series (1988, 1991, and 1994).

Simpson, Wallis (née Warfield) (1896–1986) US wife of Edward, Duke of Windsor (Edward VIII). Her relationship with the king caused a national scandal in 1936, especially in view of her impending second divorce, and forced the king's abdication. The couple were married shortly afterwards and she became the Duchess of Windsor. She remained in France after her husband died and lived as a recluse until her death.

Simpson Desert A desert in central Australia, situated between Alice Springs and the Channel Country to the east. It was named in 1929 after A. A. Simpson, who was President of the Royal Geographical Society of Australia at that time.

sin A notion within Judaism, Christianity, and Islam implying deliberate disobedience against the known will of God. In a wider sense it can indicate any moral evil or failure to live up to some moral law, but more specifically it applies to those religions that worship a personal deity. Judaism, Christianity, and Islam explain mankind's fallen state and the presence of evil on the basis of ORIGINAL SIN: Adam, the first man, misused his FREE WILL in choosing to eat the forbidden fruit of the tree of knowledge, and as a result mankind became predisposed to sin. Roman Catholic theology distinguishes between this original sin and what it calls actual sin: evil acts performed in thought, word, or deed. Traditionally the seven deadly sins are pride, covetousness, lust, anger, gluttony, envy, and sloth. Practices to remove sins or repent from them include Baptism, Confession, and periods of abstinence and repentance, such as YOM KIPPUR and LENT.

Sinai A peninsula, mostly desert, at the north end of the Red Sea, now part of Egypt; area 65,000 sq km (25,000 sq miles). In the south is Mount Sinai, where according to the Bible (Exodus 19–34), the Ten Commandments and the Tables of the Law were given to Moses by God. At its foot is the Greek Orthodox monastery of St Catherine, built on the alleged site of the burning bush, and housing the remains of St Catherine of Alexandria, miraculously transported to Sinai after her execution. It has been a focus of conflict between Arabs and Jews and was occupied by Israel from 1967 to 1982, when it was returned to Egypt under a treaty signed in 1979.

Sinatra, **Frank** (full name Francis Albert Sinatra) (1915–) US singer and actor. He began his long career as a singer in 1938 performing with big bands on the radio, becoming a solo star in the 1940s with a large teenage following; his many hits include 'Night and Day' and 'My Way'. Among his numerous films are *From Here to Eternity* (1953), for which he won an Oscar.

Sinclair, **Sir Clive (Marles)** (1940–) British electronics engineer and entrepreneur. Sinclair founded a research and development company and launched a range of innovative products including pocket calculators, wrist-watch televisions, and personal computers. A three-wheeled electric car, the C5, powered by a washing-machine motor, failed to achieve commercial success.

Sinclair, **Upton (Beall)** (1878–1968) US novelist and social reformer. Sinclair first came to prominence with *The Jungle* (1906), his graphic exposure of the conditions in Chicago's meat-packing industry. Sinclair became a socialist as a young man and in 1907 attempted to found an experimental Utopian commune in New Jersey, which was destroyed by fire. He agitated for social justice in 79 books, including the 11-volume 'Lanny Budd' series (1940–53).

Sind A province of southern Pakistan, formerly part of British India after its acquisition by Britain in 1843; area 140,914 sq km (54,428 sq miles); pop. (est. 1985) 21,682,000; capital, Karachi.

sine The ratio of the length of the side opposite the angle in a right-angled triangle to that of the hypotenuse. The values of the sine function vary between +1 and −1. It is one of the primary trigonometric functions and its definition can be extended to all numbers, including complex ones.

sinfonia See SYMPHONY.

Singapore A south-east Asian island state.

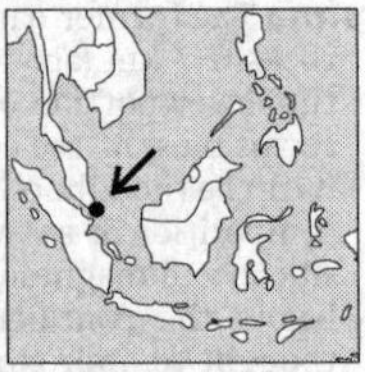

Physical. Singapore comprises an island at the southern end of the Malay Peninsula, only 2° N of the Equator. The climate is hot and damp, and the land is naturally swampy. The country comprises a large, low-lying island, about 40 km (25 miles) wide by 22 km (14 miles) from north to south, and many much smaller ones. Its chief physical resource is a magnificent natural harbour.

Economy. The port of Singapore is one of the largest in the world and entrepôt trade has long been important. Manufacturing industry, including shipbuilding, electronics, and refining of imported crude oil, has been developed, and Singapore is a leading financial centre. Tourism is significant, and although agriculture is relatively unimportant, rare orchids and exotic fish are valuable exports. The principal exports are machinery, petroleum products, communications equipment, and clothing. Singapore has among the world's largest capital reserves; and there is high government spending on social services, with some 20 per cent of the budget used for education.

History. The island of Singapore was formerly known as Tumasik or Temasek. It was inhabited mainly by fishermen and pirates before becoming part of the Sumatran empire of Srivijaya. It then passed to the Majapahit empire in the 14th century and then to the Ayutthaya empire of Siam. In the 15th century it became part of the Malacca empire, and subsequently came under Portuguese and then Dutch control.

The island was acquired for the English EAST INDIA COMPANY by Sir Stamford RAFFLES in 1819 from the sultan of JOHORE, and rapidly developed into an important trading port. In 1867 Singapore was removed from British Indian administration to form part of the new colony of the STRAITS SETTLEMENTS, its commercial development, dependent on Chinese immigrants, migrants, proceeding alongside its growth as a major naval base. In 1942 it fell to Japanese forces under General Yamashita and remained in Japanese hands until the end of World War II. The island became a separate colony in 1946 and enjoyed internal self-government from 1959 under the leadership of Lee Kuan Yew (1923–). It joined the Federation of MALAYSIA in 1963, but Malay fears that its predominantly Chinese population would discriminate in favour of the non-Malays led to its expulsion in 1965. A member of the COMMONWEALTH OF NATIONS, and the ASSOCIATION OF SOUTH-EAST ASIAN NATIONS, it has maintained close ties with Malaysia and Brunei. The People's Action Party has governed since 1965, with Lee Kuan Yew as the world's longest-serving Prime Minister (1965–90). Lee Kuan Yew resigned in 1990, filling the role of Senior Minister. He was succeeded as Prime Minister by Goh Chok Tung.

Capital: Singapore
Area: 622 sq km (240 sq mi)
Population: 2,989,000 (1995)
Currency: 1 Singapore dollar = 100 cents

Religions: Buddhist 28.3%; Christian 18.7%; Muslim 16.0%; Taoist 13.4%; Hindu 4.9%
Ethnic Groups: Chinese 77.0%; Malay 15.0%; Indian and Sri Lankan 6.0%
Languages: Malay, Mandarin, Tamil, English (all official); Chinese
International Organizations: UN; Colombo Plan; Commonwealth; ASEAN

Singer, Isaac Bashevis (1904–91) Polish-born US novelist and short-story writer. His work, written in Yiddish but chiefly known from English translations, blends realistic detail and elements of fantasy, mysticism, and magic to portray the lives of Polish Jews from many periods. Notable titles include the novels *The Magician of Lublin* (1955) and *The Slave* (1962) and the short-story collection *The Spinoza of Market Street* (1961). He was awarded the Nobel Prize for literature in 1978.

Singer, Isaac Merrit (1811–75) US inventor of the domestic SEWING-MACHINE. Engaged to repair a sewing-machine, he quickly devised an improved version, which he patented in 1851. He began manufacture, but found himself in conflict with an earlier inventor, HOWE, to whom he had eventually to pay royalties. Nevertheless, it was Singer's machine, improved in a number of patents up to 1863, which came into general use worldwide.

single-cell protein (SCP) Dried cells of algae, bacteria, yeasts, or fungi that are rich in protein. These cells can provide foodstuffs cheaply from such raw materials as oil, methane, molasses, or sewage. FERMENTATION of microorganisms and substrate in a bioreactor can give high yields of SCP, which requires little processing apart from drying. Production of SCP animal feeds is competitive with other sources, but so far economic production of SCP for human consumption has not been achieved.

singularity A point in space at which the curvature of space is effectively infinite, a situation said to occur in a BLACK HOLE. In such circumstances the laws of physics are no longer applicable. An EVENT HORIZON surrounding the black hole or singularity prevents observation of events within that horizon because no matter or energy can escape from it.

Sinhalese (or **Singhalese**) An Aryan people deriving from northern India and forming the majority of the population of Sri Lanka. Their language, spoken by 9 million people in Sri Lanka, is descended from Sanskrit and was brought by settlers from northern India in the 5th century BC; its alphabet resembles that of the Dravidian languages of southern India.

Sinkiang See XINJIANG.

Sinn Fein (Gaelic, 'we ourselves') An Irish political party dedicated to the creation of a united Irish republic. Originally founded by Arthur GRIFFITH in 1902 as a cultural revival movement, it became politically active and supported the EASTER RISING in 1916. Having won a large majority of seats in Ireland in the 1918 general election, Sinn Fein Members of Parliament, instead of going to London, met in Dublin and proclaimed Irish independence in 1919. An independent parliament (Dáil Éireann) was set up, though many of its MPs were in prison or on the run. Guerrilla warfare against British troops and police followed. The setting up of the IRISH FREE STATE (December 1921) and the partition of Ireland were bitterly resented by Sinn Fein, and the Party abstained from the Dáil and the Northern Ireland parliament for many years. Sinn Fein is now the political wing of the Provisional IRISH REPUBLICAN ARMY and has the support of the uncompromising Irish nationalists. In 1994, following a peace initiative by the Irish and British governments, Sinn Fein President Gerry Adams announced a complete IRA cease-fire. This was broken in February 1996, due to Sinn Fein's refusal to commit the IRA to decommissioning weapons as a precondition to negotiation, and Sinn Fein were excluded from talks on the future of Northern Ireland that began in June 1996. They were admitted to the talks in 1997, following a further cease-fire, and signalled their support for the peace agreement reached in 1998 (see NORTHERN IRELAND).

Sino-Japanese War (1894–95) War fought between China and Japan. After Korea was opened to Japanese trade in 1876, it rapidly became an arena for rivalry between the expanding Japanese state and neighbouring China, of which Korea had been a vassal state since the 17th century. A rebellion in 1894 provided a pretext for both sides to send troops to Korea, but the Chinese were rapidly overwhelmed by superior Japanese troops, organization, and equipment. After the Beiyang fleet, one of the most important projects of the Self-Strengthening Movement, was defeated at the battle of the Yellow Sea and Port Arthur (now Lüshun) captured, the Chinese found their capital Beijing menaced by advancing Japanese forces. They were forced to sign the Treaty of Shimonoseki, granting Korean independence and making a series of commercial and territorial concessions which opened the way for a Japanese confrontation with Russia, the other expansionist power in north-east Asia.

Sino-Tibetan A language group that includes Chinese, Burmese, Tibetan, Nepalese, and Thai. They are tonal languages, but the exact relationships between them are far from clear.

sintering The welding together of powdered particles of a substance or mixture by heating to a temperature below the melting-point of the components. The particles stick together and form a sinter. The process is used in POWDER METALLURGY and also as a treatment for iron ore in which a mixture of fine ore and high-grade coal (or coke) powder is sintered for use in a BLAST-FURNACE. The porous glass used in laboratory filtering equipment is made by sintering small glass granules.

Sintra (or **Cintra**) A town in central Portugal, formerly the summer residence of the Portuguese royal family; pop. (1981) 20,000. Its chief landmarks are the National Palace, the gardens of Montserrate, and the hilltop Pena Palace.

Sinuiju A city on the Yalu River in western North Korea, capital of North Pyongan province; pop. (est. 1984) 500,000. It is an industrial port, which has chemicals and aluminium industries.

Sioux (Siouan **Dakota**) A group of North American Indian tribes originally occupying the plains and prairies. With a population in the 19th century of more than 30,000, it was one of the largest tribes in North America.

sipunculid A member of the phylum Sipunculida, containing some 330 species of marine animals, sometimes called 'peanut worms', as smaller species resemble unshelled peanuts if they have their proboscis withdrawn. But many are larger than this, up to 75 cm (30 inches) long, and all have a proboscis which bears tentacles. Sipunculids mostly live in burrows on muddy shores, gathering food from the mud with their tentacles, though a few bore into corals or live in mollusc shells. These worms have a COELOM, like the

ANNELIDS to which they are probably related, but lack segmentation and are slow burrowers.

siren A SALAMANDER belonging to a unique group usually classed in the family Sirenidae, though some biologists consider them to belong to a separate order of AMPHIBIANS. There are only three species, all found in the southern USA: two in the genus *Siren* and one in the genus *Pseudobranchus*. They are eel-like and permanently aquatic, retaining many larval characteristics, such as the lack of a pelvic girdle and hind-limbs, and retention of a pair of feathery gills. The fore-limbs are minute and the jaw margins are horny. When the shallow ditches, swamps, and ponds which they inhabit dry up, they are able to survive by living in mud burrows, protected by a mucous cocoon.

Sirens In Greek mythology, two (or in some accounts three) sea-nymphs who – by the irresistible beauty of their singing – lured sailors to destruction on a rocky coast. When his ship was about to pass their island, Odysseus ordered his men to stop their ears with wax but left his own unblocked and had himself lashed to the mast so that he could be the only person to experience the beauty of their singing and live to tell the tale. According to one account, the Sirens killed themselves in vexation at his escape.

Sirius The brightest star visible to the naked eye (after the Sun) and one of our nearest stellar neighbours. Located in the constellation of Canis Major, and also known as Alpha Canis Majoris or the **Dog Star**, its magnitude is −1.46.

sirocco (or **scirocco**) **▶1** A hot, dry Saharan wind that blows northwards to the northern shores of the Mediterranean. **▶2** A warm, sultry rainy wind in southern Europe.

sisal (or **sisal hemp**) A useful FIBRE plant, native to Central America. Sisals are species of AGAVE, and produce the strong, durable fibres named after the plants. Most important are *A. sisalana* and *A. fourcroydes*. Sisal is grown in many tropical countries, including Brazil, Haiti, and several parts of Africa, including the largest producer, Tanzania. Sisal fibre is woven into matting, fishing nets, cordage, and other such products.

siskin A small bird, *Carduelis spinus*, that is a member of the finch family, Fringillidae. Siskins are widespread in the Northern Hemisphere and also occur in Central and South America. They are greenish-yellow with bright yellow markings in the wings and tail, resembling their close relative the greenfinch (*C. chloris*). The males tend to be brighter than the females and have black caps. Siskins live in woods and forests and eat the seeds of trees. Other species of *Carduelis* include the GOLDFINCHES.

Sisley, Alfred (1839–99) French impressionist painter, of English descent. His development towards impressionism from his early Corot-influenced landscapes was gradual and greatly indebted to Monet. He is chiefly remembered for his paintings of the countryside around Paris in the 1870s, with their concentration on reflecting surfaces and fluid brushwork; like Monet, he also painted the same scenes under different weather conditions.

Sistine Chapel A chapel in the Vatican, built by Pope Sixtus IV, containing Michelangelo's painted ceiling and his fresco of the Last Judgement, and also frescos by Botticelli, Ghirlandaio, and others. It is used for the principal papal ceremonies and also by the cardinals when meeting for the election of a new pope.

Sisulu, Walter (1912–) South African politician. Violently opposed to apartheid, he became secretary-general of the African National Congress (ANC) in 1949. When the ANC was declared illegal, Sisulu was imprisoned with MANDELA and others. He was not released until 1989, when DE KLERK legalized the ANC; Sisulu subsequently became deputy president (1991–94) of the ANC.

Sisyphus In Greek mythology, a cunning king of Corinth who, for his various crimes, was, after his death, sentenced to eternal punishment in Hades. He was made to roll a large stone to the top of a hill, only for it to roll down again, so that he had to toil uphill endlessly.

sitar One of the most important musical instruments of the classical music of the northern Indian sub-continent, a long-necked lute with four main plucked strings and three plucked as a rhythmic DRONE; 12 sympathetic strings are plucked occasionally. The strings can be pulled sideways along the curved metal frets, varying the pitch up to a fifth. The strings vibrate on a flat area of the bridge, which enriches the sound.

sitatunga (or **marsh buck**) An antelope species, *Tragelaphus spekei*, related to the kudu, living in the swamps and water courses of central and East Africa. It swims, dives, and even travels considerable distances under water. Its feet are adapted for life near water, for the halves of the slender hoofs spread widely when walking or running, leaving a V-shaped spoor (track). The male may reach 1.2 m (4 feet) at the shoulders, has spiral horns 90 cm (3 feet) long, and brown hair with stripes. The female is hornless, and she and the young are bright chestnut in colour with white stripes and spots.

Sitting Bull (Sioux name Tatanka Iyotake) (*c*.1831–90) Sioux chief. As the main chief of the Sioux peoples from about 1867, he resisted the US government order of 1875 forcibly resettling the Sioux on reservations; when the US army opened hostilities in 1876, Sitting Bull led the Sioux in the fight to retain their lands, which resulted in the massacre of General Custer and his men at Little Bighorn. In 1885 he appeared in Buffalo Bill's Wild West Show, but continued to lead his people; becoming an advocate of the Ghost Dance cult, he was killed in an uprising.

Sitwell, Dame Edith (Louisa) (1887–1964) British poet and critic. Light-hearted and experimental, her early verse, like that of her brothers, **Sir Osbert** (1892–1969) and **Sir Sacheverell** (1897–1988), marked a revolt against the prevailing Georgian style of the day. In 1923 she attracted attention with *Façade*, a group of poems in notated rhythm recited to music by William Walton. Her later verse is graver and makes increasing use of Christian symbolism.

SI units (Système International d'Unités) A system of UNITS proposed in 1960 as a rational and coherent replacement for the older CGS (centimetre, gram, second) system. It has since been widely adopted throughout most of the world. The SI system defines seven basic units: the METRE (m), the basic unit of length; the SECOND (s), the unit of time; the KILOGRAM (kg), mass; the AMPERE (A), electric current; the KELVIN (K), thermodynamic temperature; the CANDELA (cd), luminous intensity; and the MOLE (mol), amount of substance. All other units of measurement are defined with reference to these seven: for example, the definition of the NEWTON (the SI unit of force) is the force required to impart an acceleration of 1 m/s to a mass of 1 kg. See also Appendix.

Sivaji See SHIVAJI.

Six, Les A group of young French (and Swiss) composers who, under the influence of SATIE and COCTEAU, had rejected the German ROMANTICISM of WAGNER as well as the IMPRESSIONISM of DEBUSSY. They were AURIC, Louis Durey (1888–1979), HONEGGER, MILHAUD, POULENC, and TAILLEFERRE. Although they soon went their separate ways, their music shared such elements as syncopated rhythms and dry sonorites. They were first so called by the French critic Henri Collet in 1920.

Six Counties, the The Ulster counties of Antrim, Down, Armagh, Londonderry, Tyrone, and Fermanagh, which since 1922 have comprised the province of Northern Ireland.

Six-Day War (5–10 June 1967) Arab–Israeli war, known to the Arabs as the June War. The immediate causes of the war were the Egyptian request to the UN Emergency Force in Sinai to withdraw from the Israeli frontier, the increase of Egyptian forces in Sinai, and the closure of the Straits of Tiran (the Gulf of Aqaba) to Israeli shipping. An

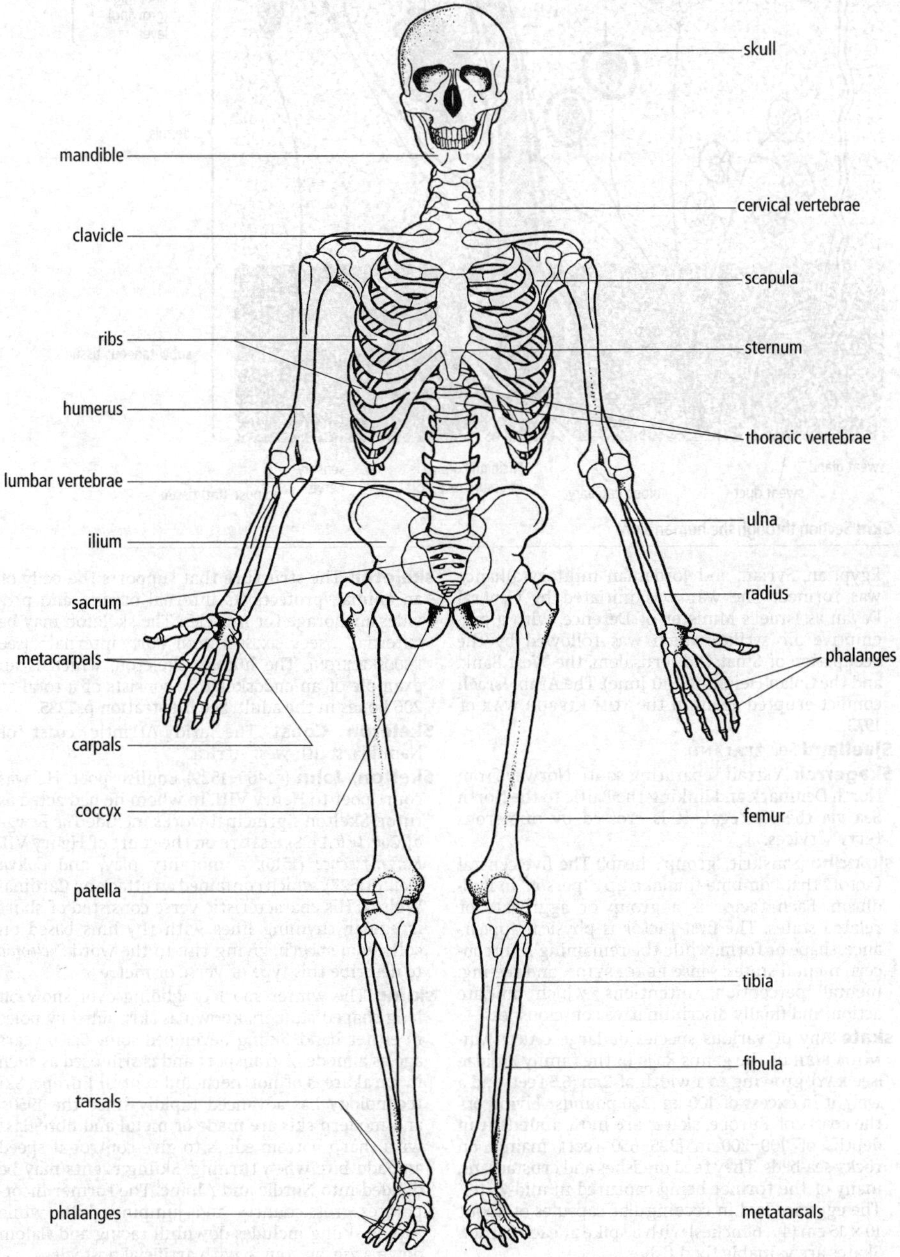

Skeleton The human skeleton.

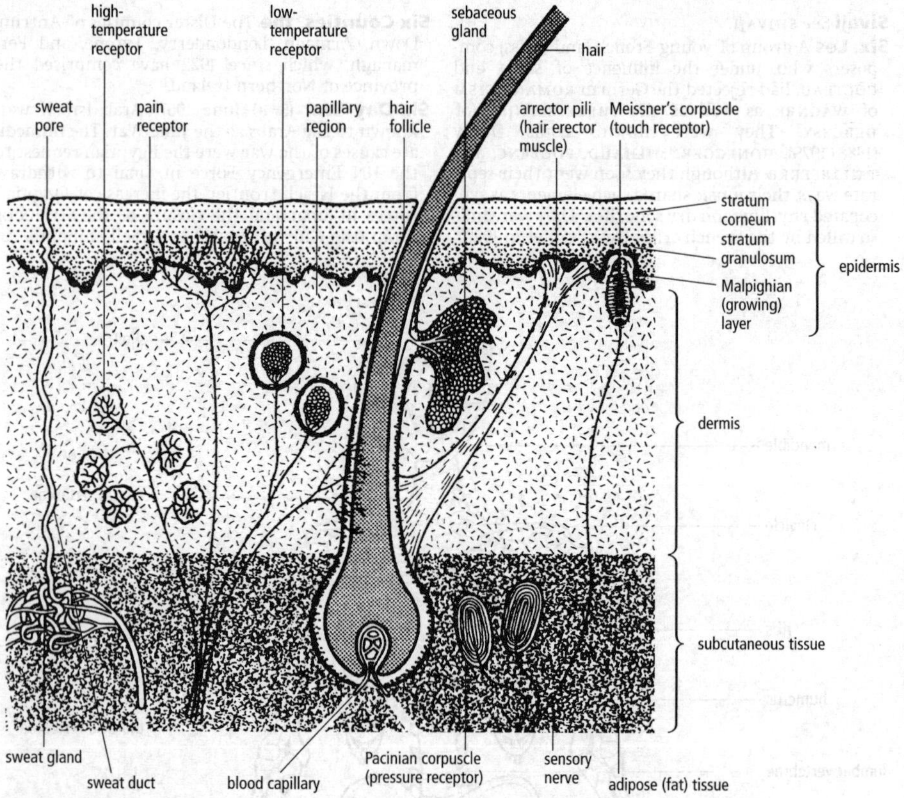

Skin Section through the human skin.

Egyptian, Syrian, and Jordanian military alliance was formed. The war was initiated by General Dayan as Israel's Minister of Defence, with a pre-emptive air strike, which was followed by the occupation of Sinai, Old Jerusalem, the West Bank, and the Golan Heights (9–10 June). The Arab–Israeli conflict erupted again in the YOM KIPPUR WAR of 1973.

Sjaelland See ZEALAND.

Skagerrak A strait separating south Norway from North Denmark and linking the Baltic to the North Sea via the Kattegat. It is crossed by numerous ferry services.

skandha (Sanskrit, 'group', 'heap') The five central factors that combine to make up a 'person' in Buddhism. Each factor is a group or aggregate of related states. The first factor is physical appearance, shape or form, while the remaining four concern mental states: sense PERCEPTION and feeling; mental perception; intentions which initiate action; and finally discriminative consciousness.

skate Any of various species of large CARTILAGINOUS FISH of the genus *Raja* in the family Rajidae (see RAY), growing to a width of 2 m (6.5 feet) and a weight in excess of 100 kg (220 pounds). Living off the coasts of Europe, skates are most abundant in depths of 100–200 m (325–650 feet), mainly on rocky sea-beds. They feed on fishes and crustaceans, many of the former being captured in mid-water. The eggs are laid in rectangular capsules of about 10 × 15 cm (4 × 6 inches) with a spike at each corner. Skates are valuable food-fishes.

skating See ICE SKATING.

skeleton The structure that supports the body of an animal, protects its internal organs, and provides anchorage for muscles. The skeleton may be external (see EXOSKELETON) or internal (see ENDOSKELETON). The human skeleton, which is an example of an endoskeleton, consists of a total of 206 bones in the adult. See illustration p. 1235.

Skeleton Coast The arid Atlantic coast of Namibia, south-west Africa.

Skelton, John (*c*.1460–1529) English poet. He was court poet to Henry VIII, to whom he had acted as tutor. Skelton's principal works include *The Bowge of Courte* (*c*.1498), a satire on the court of Henry VII, *Magnificence* (1516), a morality play, and *Collyn Cloute* (1522), which contained an attack on Cardinal Wolsey. His characteristic verse consisted of short irregular rhyming lines with rhythms based on colloquial speech, giving rise to the word *Skeltonic* to describe this type of verse or metre.

skiing The winter sport of gliding over snow on long shaped runners known as skis, aided by poles in either hand. Skiing developed some 5,000 years ago as a mode of transport and is still used as such in rural areas of northern and central Europe. Ski technology has advanced rapidly since the 1950s, and modern skis are made of metal and fibreglass with sharp bottom edges to give control at speed and add bite when turning. Skiing events may be divided into Nordic and Alpine. The former incorporates cross-country and jumping skills, while Alpine skiing includes downhill racing and slalom down a zigzag course with artificial obstacles.

skimmer Any of three species of large, tern-like

bird belonging to the family Rhynchopidae, 40–45 cm (16–18 inches) long, with a greatly enlarged, flexible lower mandible. They feed by skimming over smooth water with their beak cutting the surface, catching small fish, insects, and crustaceans. Large flocks feed and roost together. Skimmers live in Africa, India, and the Americas.

skin The surface covering of all vertebrates formed of two layers: the outer surface layer, the **epidermis**, and the **dermis** underneath. The epidermis is formed of a single, or multiple, layer of cells which can be replaced if it is damaged or worn away. The epidermis of terrestrial vertebrates consists of many cell layers; those on the surface progressively die and turn into dry scales. These are constantly shed as the result of wear and tear, being replaced from the basal living cells by division. The underlying dermis is formed of a mesh-work of tough fibrous tissue interlaced with elastic fibres. It is very strong and resistant to injury. Within the dermis there are numerous blood vessels and nerve endings, which when stimulated give rise to the sensations of touch, pressure, warmth, cold, and pain. The skin may bear SCALES, FEATHERS, or HAIR, and the epidermis may be modified to form CLAWS or hoofs. In amphibians, the skin acts as an air-breathing surface. Within the skin of some mammals are SWEAT GLANDS, producing sweat which helps to cool the body through evaporation. However, other mammals, such as dogs and cats, lose heat via the mouth (panting). Among the hair follicles in skin lie **sebaceous glands**, producing an oil (sebum) which protects the skin and maintains its waterproof qualities.

skink A lizard of a very large family, Scincidae, comprising over 600 species, which are very widely distributed but most numerous in the tropical areas. They are mainly ground-dwelling and burrowing lizards. The smaller species usually eat insects, but the larger ones often subsist partly on plant material. They usually have cylindrical bodies, mostly with smooth scales that are reinforced by internal bony plates (osteoderms).

Skinner, Burrhus Frederic (1904–90) US psychologist. He promoted the view that the proper aim of psychology should be to predict, and hence be able to control, behaviour. He demonstrated that arbitrary responses in animals could be obtained by using reinforcements – rewards and punishments. He applied similar techniques in both clinical and educational practice, devising one of the first teaching machines, and was involved in the development of programmed learning.

skipjack See CLICK BEETLE.

skipper A mostly small, moth-like butterfly that beats its wings fast in rapid, darting flight. Skippers make up the family Hesperiidae, with over 3,500 species. Their wings are small in relation to the robust, hairy body; the antennae are widely separated, and often have a narrow hooked tip. Some species rest with the wings flat over the body, but most hold the hind-wings flat and tilt the fore-wings at an angle. The caterpillars, many of which feed on grasses, have a narrow section, like a neck, behind the head. They spin shelters among the leaves of the food plant, within which they later pupate. They are cosmopolitan in distribution and the butterflies of some tropical species are colourful with long 'tails' to the hind-wings.

Skopje The capital of the Former Yugoslav Republic of Macedonia, on the River Vardar; pop. (1994) 440,500. An ancient city founded by the Romans, it was under Turkish control from the late 14th until the 20th century. In 1963 it was badly damaged by an earthquake that killed over 1,000 people. It is a communications hub and industrial centre with chemicals, metalwares, glass and steel making, and textiles.

skua Any of five species of brown or mottled, gull-like bird that make up their own family, Stercorariidae. They are found in both hemispheres at high latitudes. Predatory on smaller birds and mammals, they also catch fish and krill at sea, migrating long distances between breeding seasons. Skuas steal food from other birds.

skull The hollow skeleton of the head in vertebrates, comprising a series of flat, jointed bones, usually immovable except for that of the lower jaw. The bones of the skull can be roughly divided into the cranium, which houses the brain, and the face. It is supported by the spine and moved by the muscles of the neck. The cranium in humans consists of eight bones which between them form a 'box' with the mechanical rigidity to resist crushing. Holes in the base and sides allow entry of the spinal cord and blood vessels. The facial bones, of which there are 14 in humans, have sockets and cavities for the nose, eyes, and ears. In human

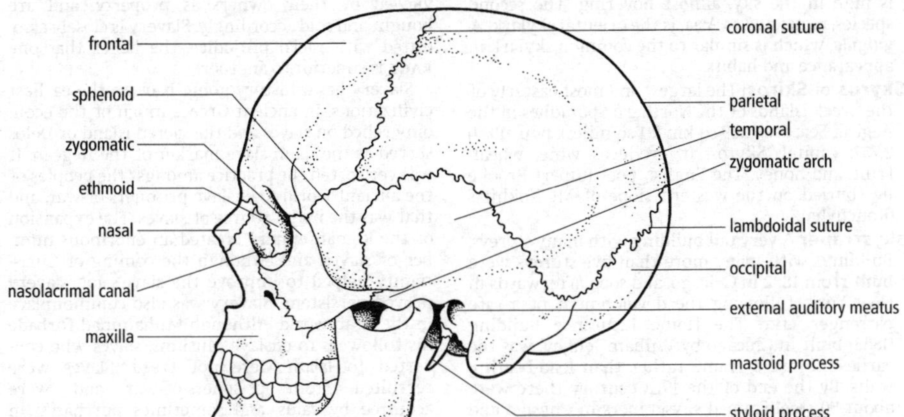

Skull The bones making up the human skull.

babies there are membraneous spaces between the bones of the skull vault which allow the head to mould during birth and the brain to reach full maturity before the bones join. Between the main joints, or sutures, are small additional (sutural) bones which suggest that the brain could grow yet larger in the course of evolution.

skunk A small mammal belonging to the weasel family, Mustelidae, and well known for its foetid secretions, which can be ejected forcibly from the anal glands towards an attacker. In addition to its strong smell, the secretion has irritant properties and is an effective deterrent to would-be predators. There are 13 species of skunk, all of which have bold black and white patterns in the fur, which are clearly warning signals. The commonest species is the striped skunk, *Mephitis mephitis*, whose range extends from Canada to Mexico. The closely related hooded skunk, *M. macroura*, is limited to the southern USA and Central America. Other species are the four species of spotted skunks (*Spilogale*) of North and Central America and the seven species of hog-nosed skunks (*Conepatus*), whose range extends from the southern USA into South America. All skunks feed on insects and small vertebrates, as well as some plant material, and most lie up in burrows during the winter.

Skye The largest of the Inner Hebrides in north-west Scotland. It has a heavily indented coastline and much of the island is mountainous, especially the rugged Cuillin Hills. During the 1880s the island crofters were in the forefront of the battle to win rights to land. The chief settlements are Portree and Broadford, and Dunvegan, which is reckoned to be the oldest continuously inhabited castle in Britain, is the seat of the chief of the Clan Macleod. The island gives its name to a small long-bodied short-legged long-haired slate or fawn coloured variety of Scotch terrier. The principal occupations are crofting and sheep farming but tourism is also important.

Skylab See SPACE STATION.

skylark Either of two species of bird in the LARK family, Alaudidae. The common skylark, *Alauda arvensis*, is widely distributed in Europe and Asia, where it lives in open, grassy country. About the size of a sparrow, it is a streaky brown bird with white outer tail feathers and a very slight crest. Although undistinguished to look at, the skylark is famous for its beautiful song, given when the bird is high in the sky, almost hovering. The second species, restricted to Asia, is the oriental skylark, *A. gulgula*, which is similar to the common skylark in appearance and habits.

Skyros (or **Skiros**) The largest and most easterly of the Greek islands of the Northern Sporadhes in the Aegean Sea; area 209 sq km (81 sq miles); pop. (1981) 2,757; capital, Skyros. It produces wine, wheat, fruit, and honey. The English poet Rupert Brooke lies buried on the western slope of Mt Kokhílas (Konchylia).

skyscraper A very tall building with many storeys. Buildings with many more than five storeys were built from 1882 in Chicago, and soon afterwards in New York, following the development of a safe passenger LIFT. The Home Insurance Building (1883) built in Chicago by William Jenney, was the earliest to use a frame rather than load-bearing walls. By the end of the 19th century there were about 50 steel-framed skyscrapers in Chicago and New York, up to 118 m (386 feet) high, most with thin, masonry, non-load-bearing external walls. Skyscrapers steadily increased in height up to the 381-m (1,250-feet) high Empire State Building (New York, 1931), their structures remaining as steel skeleton frames with masonry walls. Modern skyscrapers, such as the World Trade Center, New York, have steel and concrete hull-and-core structures. The central core – a reinforced concrete tower – contains lift shafts, staircases, and vertical ducts. From this core, the concrete and steel composite floors span on to a steel perimeter structure; a lightweight aluminium and glass CURTAIN WALL encloses the building. This type of construction is the most efficient so far designed against wind forces. It is used in the 109-storey Sears-Roebuck Tower in Chicago, completed in 1974, which is 443 m (1,454 feet) high and was the tallest skyscraper in the world until 1996. Petronas Towers in Kuala Lumpur, Malaysia, was completed in 1996 and stands 450 m (1,476 feet) high. However, even taller skyscrapers are being built in China and Hong Kong.

slaked lime See CALCIUM HYDROXIDE.

slate A shiny, dark grey rock with pronounced cleavage – that is, it splits easily. Slate is the product of low-grade regional metamorphism of fine-grained sediments, such as clays and shales. They cleave easily into many thin slices because of the parallel arrangement of fine-grained, flaky clay minerals in the rock as a result of lateral pressure during metamorphism. Slate is used for roofing and flooring. Classic slate areas are North Wales and the Vosges, France.

slater See WOODLOUSE.

Slav A member of a group of peoples in Central and Eastern Europe speaking **Slavonic languages** including Russian, Ukraninian, Belorussian, Polish, Czech, Slovak, Slovenian, Serbian, Croatian, and Bulgarian. The common Slavonic language from which they are all descended probably broke away from the main Indo-European family before Christian times. They have many characteristics in common: nouns and adjectives are highly inflected (Russian and Polish have as many as seven cases), verbs have few tenses but preserve an ancient distinction (called aspect) between actions thought of as finished or limited in time and those regarded as continuous. The two principal alphabets used are the Cyrillic and Latin.

Slave Kings See MAMELUKE.

slavery The ownership of one person by another, who controls the slave's life and labour. Slaves are viewed by their owners as property, and are bought and sold accordingly. Slavery is closely associated with racial prejudice, the belief that one RACE is superior to another.

Slavery has a history going back to the earliest civilizations. In ancient Greece much of the economy relied on slaves and the sacred island of Delos served as the main slave market of the Aegean. It was very often the practice amongst the peoples of the ancient world to enslave prisoners-of-war, and that was the major source of slaves. The expansion of the Roman empire created an enormous number of slaves, and although the coming of Christianity helped to improve the slave's lot, slavery proved persistent. Slavery was also commonplace in the Arab world. Although Muhammad forbade his followers to enslave Muslims, slaves who converted to Islam were not freed. Slaves were recruited from prisoners-of-war and were acquired by raids, and sometimes purchases, in Europe, Asia, and Africa. Slaves served a variety of purposes, including labour, military service, domestic duties, and many enslaved women were treated as concubines. The Arab slave trade was abolished as a result of international pressure in the 19th century.

One of the most significant periods of slavery was the use of African slave labour in the plantations of the Caribbean and the southern states of the USA during the 18th and early 19th centuries. In this period it is thought that 9.5 million Africans were transported as slaves to the New World. The cruelty of slave traders and plantation owners finally succumbed to the persuasiveness of such humanitarians as William WILBERFORCE in Britain (1834) and 30 years later in the USA, having been one of the causes of the Civil War.

During World War II the Germans made extensive use of slave labour. Able-bodied Jews, Russians, Slavs and others to whom the Germans believed themselves to be superior were forced to work as slaves. After the war, the word 'slave' was defined by the UN as anyone who cannot voluntarily withdraw his or her labour; the UN estimates that some 200 million such slaves exist, principally in Asia, Africa, and South America, where bonded labourers (persons who bind themselves over for a fixed period to pay off a debt or earn a fixed sum) and child slavery are widespread.

sleep A natural state of torpor and a lowering of consciousness associated with changes in the patterns of electrical waves recorded from the brain (electroencephalograms). The body's relaxation is induced by graded switching off of the nerves which activate postural and other muscles. Sleep consists of alternating periods of 'deep' sleep and a type characterized by rapid eye flickering. It is during the latter phase that dreams occur. The biological need for sleep is not understood, but all species of mammal undergo regular periods of it, though these periods vary with age, species, and, under natural conditions, with the seasonal changes of day length. See also DREAM.

sleeping sickness See TRYPANOSOMIASIS.

slide-rule A hand-held device for rapid mathematical calculation of multiplications or divisions, now superseded by the electronic CALCULATOR. The first known slide-rule was made by Robert Bissaker in England in 1654. The slide-rule consists of an accurately machined ruler, usually engraved with a number of logarithmic scales, together with a sliding central strip. Calculations are made by moving the strips and the result is indicated on the ruler's scale.

Sligo A county of western Ireland, in Connaught province; area 1,795 sq km (693 sq miles); pop. (1991) 54,740.

Slim, William Joseph, 1st Viscount (1891–1970) British field-marshal. He commanded an Indian division in the 1941 conquest of the VICHY French territory of Syria. In early 1942 he joined the BURMA CAMPAIGN, and in 1943 took command of the 14th Army. After the victory at Kohima he pushed down the Irrawaddy River to recapture Rangoon and most of Burma. After the war he became Chief of the Imperial General Staff (1948–52) and governor-general of Australia (1953–60).

slime mould One of a group of single- to multi-celled organisms, traditionally classified as fungi but having characteristics of both plants and animals. They reproduce by spores, yet their cells can move like an amoeba and feed by ingesting particles of food. In a widely used modern classification system slime moulds are placed in the kingdom PROTOCTISTA.

slit-faced bat See HISPID BAT.

Sloane, Sir Hans (1660–1753) British physician and naturalist who bequeathed to his country a library and collections which formed the nucleus of the British Museum. Physician to the governor of Jamaica, he returned to Britain with several hundred plants. He succeeded Sir Isaac Newton as President of the Royal Society in 1727, when he also became physician to George II.

sloe See BLACKTHORN.

sloop In modern usage, a YACHT carrying a mainsail and a single foresail or jib. Historically, other types of ship have been called sloops. In the late 17th century a sloop was a single-masted merchant vessel, similar in rig to the modern sloop. In the early 18th century the largest British warships that were not SHIPS of the line were referred to as sloops. During World War I, sloops became specialized escort vessels even though they were steam-powered rather than sailing ships. By World War II these types of warships were known as frigates, and sloop acquired its modern meaning.

sloth A mammal of the order Edentata, which also includes the armadillo. Sloths are fully adapted to tree life. The limbs are long, especially the fore-limbs, and the digits carry hooked claws which allow the animal to hang upside-down from the branch of a tree. As the name suggests, the sloths are very lethargic. They differ from all other mammals in that their body temperature is low and variable between 24 and 37°C (75–98°F). Sloths feed upon foliage and their teeth have a grinding surface; the stomach is divided into several compartments as that of the ruminants. Three-toed sloths, of which there are three species, have three curved claws on their fore-limbs, while the two species of two-toed sloths have only two. Both have three claws on their hind-limbs, are about 60 cm (2 feet) long, and have thick coarse hair of a drab brown or grey colour. The presence of algae, growing in their fur, gives them a greenish tinge which helps them blend into their surroundings. A single young is born in the summer months and it clings to the mother's belly.

Slovakia A central European republic, formerly part of CZECHOSLOVAKIA.

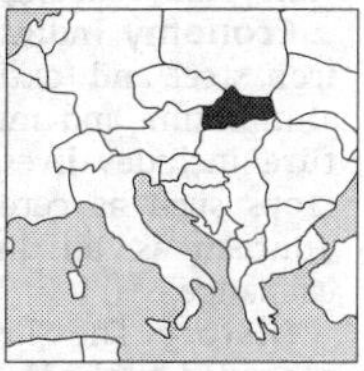

Physical. Slovakia is surrounded by Poland to the north, Ukraine to the east, Hungary to the south, and Austria and the Czech Republic to the west. The Carpathian mountains dominate the country reaching a height of 2,655 m (8,711 feet) at the Gerlach Shield in the High Tatras. Some steppe grasslands are to be found in the south-eastern lowlands; one third of the country is cultivated and two-fifths is covered in forest. The Danube briefly forms the border between Slovakia and Hungary flowing towards Bratislava and finally on to the Black Sea.

Economy. Industry is in urgent need of modernization, and is hampered by the need to import energy, as the potential for hydroelectric power has not yet been exploited. Motor vehicles, glass, armaments, footwear, and textiles are the main exports. IMF resources have been made available to stabilize the transition to a market economy. Slovakia's mineral resources include iron ore, copper, magnesite, lead, zinc, and lignite. There are also numerous mineral springs.

History. A land belonging to the Hungarian crown since medieval times, Slovakia experienced an upsurge in nationalism in the late 18th and early 19th centuries. A final break with Hungary was made with the collapse of the Austro-Hungarian empire after World War I; Slovakia entered into union with the Czech lands. However, resentment at centralized control from Prague led to a declaration of autonomy within a federal Czecho-Slovak state on the eve of the Nazi annexation of Czechoslovakia in 1938; this was followed by nominal independence under German protection. With the end, in 1990, of the communist regime that had controlled Czechoslovakia since 1948, Slovak demands for independence grew and the Slovak Republic (with its capital at Bratislava) came into being on 1 January 1993 without conflict. Michal Kováč was elected President and the nationalist leader Vladimir Meciar became Prime Minister. Problems have been experienced in restructuring the Slovak economy, which was geared to labour-intensive heavy industry under the influence of Stalinism in the 1950s. Tensions remain between the Slovak majority and the ethnic Hungarian minority population.

Capital: Bratislava
Area: 49,035 sq km (18,928 sq mi)
Population: 5,355,000 (1995)
Currency: 1 koruna = 100 haléřů
Religions: Roman Catholic 63.8%; non-religious 26.7%; Protestant 7.9%; Orthodox 0.6%; other 0.6%
Ethnic Groups: Slovak 86.6%; Czech 1.2%; Hungarian 10.9%; other 1.3%
Languages: Slovak, Czech (both official); Hungarian; Romany; other minority languages
International Organizations: UN; CSCE; Council of Europe

Slovenia A small country in south-east Europe.

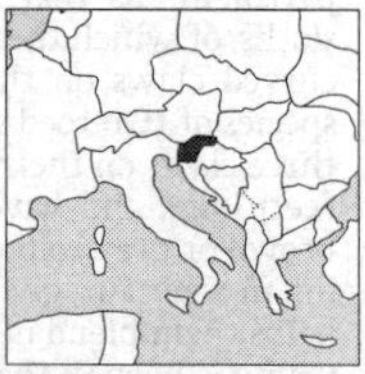

Physical. Slovenia is bordered by Austria to the north, Hungary to the east, Italy to the west, and Croatia to the south and east. It has an outlet to the Adriatic Sea. The country is largely mountainous and wooded, with deep and fertile valleys and coal and extensive mineral reserves.

Economy. Industry is well developed, including iron, steel, and textiles. Deposits of coal, lead, zinc, aluminium, and mercury are exploited. Agriculture includes livestock-rearing, viticulture, and crops such as cereals, sugar-beet, and potatoes. Tourism is an important source of foreign exchange.

History. The Slovenes are a west Slavonic people, ruled by the Habsburgs from the 14th century until 1918. After World War I the majority of the Slovene people were incorporated into the new kingdom of Serbs, Croats, and Slovenes, later YUGOSLAVIA. In 1941 their lands were divided between Italy, Hungary, and the THIRD REICH. In 1945, 1947, and 1954, areas of the Istrian peninsula, including parts of the Free Territory of TRIESTE, were incorporated into the Republic of Slovenia within the Federal Republic of Yugoslavia. The most economically and educationally advanced of the Slav republics, Slovenes are predominantly Roman Catholic, with a strong Western heritage. During 1989 pressure began to mount for independence, and a coalition of six parties, the Democratic Opposition of Slovenia (DEMOS) emerged. In May 1990 it formed a non-communist government under President Milan Kučan, and in July declared independence, confirmed by a referendum in December. There was intermittent fighting between Slovene partisans and units of the Yugoslav army during 1990, before Serbia tacitly accepted the situation. In April 1992 DEMOS split, and the Liberal Democrats under Janez Drnovsek formed a government. Kučan was re-elected President later that year. New coalition governments, led by the Liberal Democrats, were formed in 1993 and again in 1996.

Capital: Ljubljana
Area: 20,251 sq km (7,897 sq mi)
Population: 1,971,000 (1995)
Currency: 1 tolar = 100 stotin
Religions: Roman Catholic 90.0%
Ethnic Groups: Slovene 90.0%
Languages: Slovenian (official)
International Organizations: UN; CSCE

Slovenian See SLAV.

slow worm A species of limbless LIZARD, *Anguis fragilis*, readily distinguishable from snakes by having movable eyelids. Slow worms occur over most of Europe (including Britain but not Ireland) to southwest Asia and parts of North Africa. They are found mainly in thickly vegetated localities, resting by day under stones, logs, and other Sun-warmed objects. Their diet comprises mainly small slugs, earthworms, and insect larvae. Largest individuals may attain 50 cm (1.6 feet) in total length but most are smaller. Captive specimens have lived over fifty-four years.

slug A member of the same class (Gastropoda) of MOLLUSCS as snails and periwinkles that has mostly lost the coiled shell typical of this class. Slugs are therefore active only during damp periods when there is no danger of drying out. On dry days their streamlined shape lets them shelter in crevices, protected by foul-tasting slime to deter hungry birds. In hot spells they retreat underground, and can survive the loss of 80 per cent of their body fluid. They feed on vegetable matter, using a ribbon of very fine teeth which rasps plant leaves and stems. Some species also eat earthworms and other species of slugs.

Small Magellanic Cloud See MAGELLANIC CLOUDS.

smallpox A viral infection by the variola virus. As a result of international efforts by the World Health Organization and active IMMUNIZATION, the world was declared smallpox-free in 1980; the last known case was in Somalia in 1977 and there were two cases acquired in the laboratory in 1978. Smallpox was transmitted by contact with infected people. There were no other animal or insect reservoirs of infection, and humans could also not be asymptomatic carriers of disease. These factors helped in the eradication of smallpox. Symptoms of smallpox included fever, muscle pain, nausea, and vomiting; a pustular rash appeared after four or five days, characterized by crops of vesicles. Severe disease was invariably fatal. Small quantities of smallpox vaccine are held for laboratory staff at two designated laboratories that maintain the smallpox virus.

smell An important sense used by some animals to help locate food, find a mate, and define territories. Smell is usually considered to involve airborne substances, while taste implies food, but both senses rely on the reception of chemical substances in the surrounding air or in food. Molecules arriving at the olfactory organs (often in the NOSE) trigger nerves to send electrical messages to the smell centres in the brain. Some fish, such as the carp, have smell receptors on the body surface. In insects, the receptors for smell and taste are often concentrated in the antennae but may occur in almost any other body surface. The elaborate branched antennae of some moths can detect a single molecule of the female's scent or PHEROMONE. Amphibians and reptiles have smell detectors in the roof of the mouth, where incoming air carries the scents. Snakes extend their forked tongue to pick up airborne molecules, then retract it and insert it into the cavities, where the olfactory organs lie.

Humans do not have a well-developed sense of smell but are still able to discriminate several thousand different odours. Other mammals, such as the cats and dogs, make greater use of smells. They mark out their territory with urine and the female signals her sexual receptivity by odour. Some animals, such as salmon, use water-borne scent to locate their stream of origin, to which they return and spawn.

smelting The process by which an ore concentrate is fused (melted) at high temperatures to extract a matte or impure metal. Usually a FLUX is added to remove impurities as a slag. In the smelting of iron ore, COKE is added to the blast-furnace to reduce the oxide to iron metal.

Smetana, Bedřich (1824–84) Czech composer. Regarded as the founder of Czech music, he was dedicated to the cause of Czech nationalism, as is apparent in his operas (for example *The Bartered Bride*, 1866) and in the cycle of symphonic poems *My Country* (1874–79). He also contributed to the cause through his work as conductor of the National Theatre in Prague. He died in an asylum after suffering ten years of deteriorating health as a result of syphilis, which had left him completely deaf in 1874.

smew The smallest of the MERGANSERS, *Mergus albellus*. The drake is white marked with black, with a white crest; the female is chestnut, white, and grey. They breed in the northern Palearctic region, nesting in holes in trees, and spend winter on lakes, ponds, and rivers throughout Europe and central Asia.

Smirke, Sir Robert (1780–1867) British architect. He began his career designing country houses in a medieval style, but turned mainly to public buildings, becoming a distinguished exponent of the Greek Revival. His masterpiece is the British Museum in London (1823–46) – huge, majestic, and austere. (The famous domed reading-room in the centre of the museum was built to the design of his brother, **Sydney Smirke** (1798–1877), in 1854–57.)

Smith, Adam (1723–90) Scottish economist and philosopher. He is regarded by many as the founder of modern economics, and his work marks a significant turning-point in the breakdown of mercantilism and the spread of laissez-faire ideas. Smith retired from academic life to write his *Inquiry into the Nature and Causes of the Wealth of Nations* (1776), establishing theories of labour, distribution, wages, prices, and money, and advocating free trade and minimal state interference in economic matters.

Smith, Bessie (1894–1937) US blues singer. She became a leading artist in the 1920s and made more than 150 recordings, including some with Benny Goodman and Louis Armstrong. She was involved in a car accident and died after being refused admission to a 'whites only' hospital.

Smith, David (Roland) (1906–65) US sculptor. He allied his metal-working skills with an enthusiasm for cubism, and in particular the work of Picasso, to produce his first steel sculpture in 1933. The recurring motifs of human violence and greed characterize his early work, including *Pillars of Sunday* (1945). In the late 1950s and 1960s these give way to a calmer, more monumental style, reflected in works such as the *Cubi* series.

Smith, F(rederick) E(ldwin) See BIRKENHEAD, 1ST EARL OF.

Smith, Ian (Douglas) (1919–) Rhodesian statesman, Prime Minister 1964–79. He founded the white supremacist Rhodesian Front (renamed the Republican Front in 1981) in 1962, becoming Prime Minister and head of the white minority government two years later. In 1965 he issued a unilateral declaration of independence (UDI) after Britain stipulated that it would only grant the country independence if Smith undertook to prepare for black majority rule. He eventually conceded in 1979 and resigned to make way for majority rule; after the country became the independent state of Zimbabwe he remained active in politics, leading the Republican Front until 1987.

Smith, Joseph (1805–44) US religious leader and founder of the Church of Jesus Christ of Latter-Day Saints (the Mormons). In 1827, according to his own account, he was led by divine revelation to find the sacred texts written by the prophet Mormon, which he later translated and published as the Book of Mormon in 1830. He founded the Mormon Church in the same year and established a large community in Illinois, of which he became mayor. He was murdered by a mob while in prison awaiting trial for conspiracy.

Smith, Dame Maggie (full name Margaret Natalie Cross, née Smith) (1934–) British actress. Her performances in the theatre began with the revue *Share My Lettuce* (1957) and subsequently encompassed a wide range of classical and modern plays, including a solo performance as Virginia Woolf in *Virginia* (1981). Her many films include *The Prime of Miss Jean Brodie* (1968), for which she won an Oscar, *A Room with a View* (1986), and *The Secret Garden* (1993).

Smith, Stevie (pseudonym of Florence Margaret Smith) (1902–71) British poet and novelist. Although she first attracted notice with her novel *Novel on Yellow Paper* (1936), she is now mainly remembered for her witty, caustic, and enigmatic verse, often illustrated by her own comic drawings. Collections include *A Good Time Was Had by All* (1937), *Not Waving But Drowning* (1957), and the posthumous *Collected Poems* (1975).

Smith, Sydney (1771–1845) British Anglican churchman, essayist, and wit. He is notable for his witty contributions to the periodical the *Edinburgh Review* and as the author of the *Letters of Peter Plymley* (1807), which defended Catholic Emancipation.

Smith, William (1769–1839) British land-surveyor and self-taught geologist, one of the founders of stratigraphical geology. Working initially in the area around Bath, he discovered that rock strata could be distinguished on the basis of their characteristic assemblages of fossils, and that the identity of strata exposed in different places could thereby be established. Smith later travelled extensively in Britain, accumulating data which enabled him to produce the first geological map of the whole of England and Wales.

Smithfield A part of London containing the city's principal meat market. Formerly an open area situated just outside the north-west walls of the City of London, it was used as a horse and cattle market, as a fairground, and as a place of execution.

Smithsonian Institution The oldest US foundation for scientific research, established by Congress in 1838 and opened in 1846 in Washington, DC. It originated in a £100,000 bequest in the will of James Smithson (1765–1829), British chemist and mineralogist, for 'an establishment for the increase and diffusion of knowledge among men'.

smithsonite An ore of zinc (zinc carbonate, $ZnCO_3$), formerly known as calamine. Greenish-white, brownish, or grey, it is a hard, dense mineral formed by the action of water rich in zinc sulphate on carbonate rocks. It is found mainly in Colorado, USA, and Kazakhstan. Calamine lotion is made up of zinc carbonate and ferric oxide (Fe_2O_3).

smog Fog intensified by smoke which commonly reduces visibility to around 4 m (12–15 feet). It forms in urban and industrial areas if the atmosphere contains large enough quantities of dust particles to permit condensation to occur before the air becomes saturated.

smoke detector A device to give warning of a fire by detecting the presence of smoke. They are now often found in private houses as well as industrial premises. The device is a sensitive PHOTOCELL. When the intensity of light falling on the cell is diminished by smoke, an alarm sounds. In principle, smoke detectors have the advantage over thermal devices of giving warning before a dangerous temperature rise occurs.

smokeless powder See NITROCELLULOSE.

smoking Inhaling the smoke of tobacco leaves. Tobacco contains the drug nicotine, which is a stimulant and can be addictive, as well as tar and other toxic substances. Smoking has been proved to cause lung CANCER and cancers of the mouth, larynx, and oesophagus; chest diseases, such as bronchitis and emphysema; and to contribute to HEART DISEASE. Women smokers have a higher risk of diseases of the circulatory system, particularly if smoking is combined with the contraceptive pill; smoking during pregnancy may put the unborn baby at risk, or lead to lighter birth weight.

Smolensk An industrial city and transportation centre in western Russia, a port on the River Dnieper; pop. (1990) 346,000. Of strategic importance, the city has been sacked, burned, and devastated in wars from the 13th to the 20th century. Industries include timber, engineering, glass, food, and textiles, especially flax.

Smollett, Tobias (George) (1721–71) Scottish novelist. His novels are picaresque tales characterized by fast-moving narrative and humorous caricature; they include *The Adventures of Roderick Random* (1748), *The Adventures of Peregrine Pickle* (1751), and the epistolary work *The Expedition of Humphry Clinker* (1771). Among his other works are *A Complete History of England* (1757–58) and translations of Voltaire and Cervantes.

smooth snake A non-venomous species of COLUBRID SNAKE, *Coronella austriaca*, from Europe and Asia Minor. Its length only exceptionally exceeds 80 cm (2.6 feet). It occurs mainly in dry, sunny localities, where other reptiles, such as lizards, form its main food. In England the smooth snake is rare, being restricted to a few heathland localities in the south, and is a protected species. It gives birth to up to 15 live young.

smut fungus A parasite that grows inside plants and produces a mass of dark, smut-like spores. In 'loose smut' of wheat these spores are produced in place of grain as the ear ripens. Like RUST FUNGI, there are numerous species, each with specific hosts.

Smuts, Jan Christiaan (1870–1950) South African statesman and soldier, Prime Minister 1919–24 and 1939–48. He led Boer forces during the Second Boer War, but afterwards supported Louis Botha's policy of Anglo-Boer cooperation and was one of the founders of the Union of South Africa. During World War I he led Allied troops against the Germans in East Africa (1916); he later attended the peace conference at Versailles in 1919 and helped to found the League of Nations. He then succeeded Botha as Prime Minister. After World War II Smuts played a leading role in the formation of the United Nations and drafted the preamble to the UN charter.

Smyrna See IZMIR.

snail Any of numerous MOLLUSCS, most familiar as garden animals, but also including sea snails and pond snails. All are characterized by the coiled shell, which encloses and protects their body. Snails, together with a few uncoiled forms, such as abalones and limpets, and the shell-less slugs, constitute the largest class, Gastropoda, of molluscs, with 35,000 species. Most snails creep about on a broad flat foot, leaving trails of mucus, and feed by scraping up algae with a ribbon of renewable tiny teeth. The highly successful land snails breathe with a special lung, and can close the shell with a lid (operculum) to conserve water. Some species have shells designed to reflect heat and combat desiccation so well that they even survive in deserts.

snake An elongate REPTILE of which there are 2,500 species in the suborder Serpentes (or Ophidia). Snakes are generally limbless, although claw-like hind-limb vestiges occur in some primitive groups. Most have enlarged, wide scales on the underside of the body, but these are reduced or absent in many totally aquatic groups, such as sea snakes, wart snakes, and some burrowing species. Snakes lack movable eyelids, the eyes of most species being covered by a transparent spectacle (brille), and this feature separates them from lizards. In some burrowing species of snake the eye is small and covered by the head-scales. Most snakes have remarkably mobile jaw-bones which, together with stretchable throat skin, enable them to swallow prey that is much wider than their own head.

Three categories (or superfamilies) of snakes may be recognized: Scolecophidia, which includes blind snakes and thread snakes; Henophidia, a group with some primitive characteristics and including boas, pythons, cylinder snakes, sunbeam snake, and shield-tail snakes, and Caenophidia, or higher snakes, including colubrids, elapids (such as cobras, mambas, coral snakes, kraits, and sea snakes), and vipers.

snakebird See DARTER.

snakefly An insect characterized by the elongation of the front of the thorax into a 'neck'. Snakeflies form the insect order Megaloptera, along with alder flies. Their larvae are terrestrial and are found in wooded regions. Females use a long, thin ovipositor to lay eggs in crevices in bark. Adults and larvae are predatory.

snakehead fish A freshwater fish of the family Channidae, with a cylindrical body, a broad head, a wide mouth, and heavy scales, giving the impression of a snake's head. There are about ten species, all native to tropical Africa and south-east Asia. They have an accessory breathing organ in the upper part of the gill chamber by means of which they can breathe air, and they frequently live in swamps. Some species grow to 1 m (3.25 feet) long.

snake-necked turtle A TURTLE of the families

Chelidae and Pelomedusidae, with some 30 species that are found in South America, Australia, and New Guinea. The common name is based on some species, such as the Australian snake-necked turtle, *Chelodina longicollis*, with a neck almost as long as the shell. A long neck is an advantage for reaching prey and also enables the turtle to breathe air from above the surface of the water while remaining on the bottom of a pool.

snapdragon See ANTIRRHINUM.

snapper A predatory, marine fish belonging to the family Lutjanidae, containing some 230 species. They occur in all the tropical oceans except the eastern Pacific and occasionally swim up estuaries. They are moderately deep-bodied fishes, with a rather long, concave profile, and a spiny dorsal fin continuous with a second dorsal fin. They have strong sharp-pointed teeth in the front of the jaws and eat a wide range of fishes, crustaceans, and octopuses. They are important food-fish for man, although in the Caribbean their flesh may be poisonous, due to the build-up of toxins ingested from algal-eating fishes that the snappers in turn have eaten.

snapping turtle A freshwater, New World species of TURTLE of the family Chelydridae, with a large head, a strong jaw, and a rough shell. The alligator snapping turtle, *Macrochelys temmincki*, is exceptionally large, and can weigh more than 90 kg (200 pounds). The smaller common snapping turtle, *Chelydra serpentina*, does not often exceed 25 kg (55 pounds), but is particularly aggressive, especially when encountered on land. The strong jaws of these turtles, which are endowed with sharp, horny ridges (turtles lack teeth), can sever a man's finger.

Snell's law One of the two laws of REFRACTION. It states that when light passes from one medium to another, denser, medium (for example from air to glass), the sine of the angle of incidence (the angle between the incident ray and the normal) bears a constant ratio to the sine of the angle of refraction. The ratio is the REFRACTIVE INDEX of the denser medium in relation to the lighter one (air or vacuum). It was formulated by Willebrord Snell (1591–1626) in 1623.

snipe A member of a group of medium-sized WADING BIRDS in the family Scolopacidae, notable for long, straight beaks with which they locate and swallow underground prey. The position of their eyes gives them an extra-wide field of vision, useful in avoiding predators. They inhabit marshland and, when disturbed, tend to crouch until almost trodden upon before rising. In the breeding season some species, including the widely represented common snipe, *Gallinago gallinago* (which is known as Wilson's snipe in North America), perform spectacular switchback display flights in which bleating or drumming noises are made by outer tail feathers during dives. There are about 20 species of snipe.

snipefish A marine fish belonging to a family, Macrorhamphosidae, containing about ten species, which usually live in tropical and subtropical seas. Snipefishes are related to the pipefishes and have a similar long, tubular snout, but are deeper-bodied and have a long spine in the first dorsal fin. Most species are small, few growing as long as 30 cm (12 inches), and generally they are rose-pink in colour.

snoek A valuable food-fish, *Thyristes atun*, found off the coasts of South Africa and southern Australia, where it is known as barracouta. It also occurs in the open sea all round the Southern Hemisphere. The snoek is a migratory fish travelling in large schools, and feeding on smaller fishes and euphausid crustaceans. Although superficially resembling the mackerels, it belongs to a separate family, which includes mostly open-ocean fishes. Its body is slender, the spiny dorsal fin is long-based, and it has finlets behind both the dorsal and anal fins; its teeth are large, numerous, and sharp. It grows to 1.5 m (5 feet) in length.

snooker A development of BILLIARDS played mainly in the UK. The table is set with 15 red balls and six colours. Players use a white cue ball to pot, in sequence, first a red then a colour, continuing in a prescribed manner until the table is cleared. Professional snooker commands large television audiences. Pool (or pocket billiards) is a variant of snooker that is popular in the USA. There are 15 numbered balls that must be potted in sequence by the cue ball.

Snorri Sturluson (1178–1241) Icelandic historian and poet. A leading figure of medieval Icelandic literature, he wrote the *Younger* or *Prose Edda* (a handbook to Icelandic poetry, with prosodic and grammatical treatises, quotations, and prose paraphrases from old poems) and the *Heimskringla*, a history of the kings of Norway from mythical times to the year 1177.

snow The result of water vapour condensing on ice crystals in a cloud, which usually occurs when the air temperature in the lowest 300 m (825 feet) of the atmosphere is near freezing point. It falls when the aggregations so formed are too heavy to remain suspended in the cloud and do not have time to melt before reaching the ground; it rarely falls if the air temperature is above 4°C (39°F). The aggregation of crystals to form large, branching, hexagonal snowflakes occurs most effectively between 0°C and −4°C (32°F and 25°F) in clouds that contain large quantities of water vapour but a relatively small number of crystals. Below −4°C snowflake sizes generally decrease with decreasing temperature, especially when formed in clouds composed entirely of ice crystals (powder snow). With temperatures below −30°C (−22°F), snowflakes form when the individual crystals collide and interlock or stick together. Most heavy snowfalls are associated with the layered clouds of very active FRONTS.

Snow, C(harles) P(ercy), Baron (1905–80) British novelist. He is best known for his sequence of 11 novels, *Strangers and Brothers* (1940–70), which includes *The Corridors of Power* (1963) and other fictional studies of life in the Civil Service and in the academic and scientific communities.

snowberry Any of 11 or so shrubs of the genus *Symphoricarpos*, native to North America and western China, especially the North American *S. alba*. It is a deciduous shrub with simple leaves, small pinkish flowers, and spherical white fruits about 1 cm (0.5 inch) in diameter. These shrubs belong to the same family as elders and honeysuckles, Caprifoliaceae.

Snowdon A mountain in Gwynedd, north-west Wales. Rising to 1,085 m (3,560 ft) in **Snowdonia National Park** (1951), it is the highest mountain in Wales.

Snowdon, Antony Armstrong-Jones, 1st Earl of (1930–) British photographer, who was formerly married (1960–78) to Princess Margaret. In 1965 he designed the Aviary of London Zoo and has produced a number of photographic books, including *Venice* (1972).

snowdrop A perennial plant of the genus *Galan-*

thus, in the daffodil family (Amaryllidaceae), which grows from bulbs. The four species of snowdrop flower in early spring and are native to woods and scrubland in Europe. Their small pendulous white flowers, held about 18 cm (7 inches) high, consist of six petals, the three inner ones each having a green patch. The common snowdrop, *G. nivalis*, has been selected by breeders to produce double-flowered forms, which are popular as garden plants.

snow flea See SCORPIONFLY.

snow goose A large, pure white goose, *Anser caerulescens*, with black wing-tips, or, in its dark form, grey with a white head and neck. The bill and legs are pink. They breed in the Arctic tundra and move southwards to North America in winter, sometimes visiting Europe accidentally.

snow leopard One of the most beautiful species of big CAT, *Panthera uncia*, that lives in the Himalayas above the timber-line at altitudes of 1,800–5,500 m (6,000–18,000 feet). To combat the cold, the snow leopard has a superb coat of deep, soft fur, pale grey or creamy buff in colour, which is ornamented with large black rosettes or broken rings. It is 60 cm (2 feet) tall at the shoulder and 1.9 m (6.25 feet) long. It is a shy, nocturnal animal; little is known about it except that wild sheep, goats, marmots, and domestic stock fall prey to it.

snowy owl A species of large, white or grey-spotted OWL of the northern tundra, *Nyctaea scandica*, with a wing-span of 1.5 m (5 feet). Nesting in the far north, they migrate to subarctic and temperate latitudes in winter. Females are darker and slightly larger than males. They nest on the ground, laying four or five eggs, and their success at raising chicks depends on the availability of rodents. Large numbers of foxes and predatory skuas and gulls also affect their breeding success.

Soane, Sir John (1753–1837) British architect. After initial training in England and Italy he was appointed architect of the Bank of England in 1788, where he developed a characteristic neoclassical style. By 1810 his style had become more severe, avoiding unnecessary ornament and adopting structural necessity as the basis of design. At his death he left to the nation the marvellously eccentric house he built for himself in Lincoln's Inn Fields, London (1812–13), to form Sir John Soane's Museum.

soap A cleaning agent, comprised of sodium or potassium salts of fatty acids, made by treating FATS AND OILS with ALKALI. A mixture of fat or oil and SODIUM HYDROXIDE solution is heated by steam in huge soap pans until all the fat has been broken down. The soap is separated from the mixture by the addition of concentrated sodium chloride solution ('salting out'). The crude soap floats on the surface of the mixture. The liquid underneath is called 'lye', and is a solution of GLYCEROL (from the fat), sodium hydroxide, and salt. The glycerol is valuable and is recovered. The soap is further treated or 'fitted' with sodium hydroxide solution, sodium chloride solution, or water to bring it to the desired smooth consistency. The resulting molten soap is then pumped off and left to solidify. Perfume and colouring are added. Soap made from animal fat (sheep and cattle) must be used with hot water because it is only slightly soluble in cold water. Soap made from vegetable oils (coconut and palmkernel) can be used in cold or warm water. The cleaning action is identical to that of DETERGENTS, but soaps are less effective in hard water. Metallic soaps (salts of calcium, magnesium, lithium, copper, and zinc) are used in greases and lubricating oils.

soapwort A perennial plant, *Saponaria officinalis*, related to the carnation in the family Caryophyllaceae. The leaves, when bruised, release a sap that can be used as a substitute for soap.

Sobers, Sir Garfield St Aubrun (known as 'Gary') (1936–) West Indian cricketer. Born in Barbados, he first played for the West Indies in 1953. Four years later he hit a record test score of 365 not out, which stood until beaten by Brian Lara in 1994. He was captain of the West Indies (1965–72) and of Nottinghamshire (1968–74). During his test career he scored more than 8,000 runs and took 235 wickets, bowling in three different styles; he was also a fine fielder. In 1968 Sobers became the first batsman in first-class cricket to hit all six balls of an over for six.

Sobieski, John See JOHN III.

Sobrero, Ascanio See NITROGLYCERINE.

socage In Anglo-Saxon and Norman England, a free tenure of land which did not require the tenant to perform military service. He might pay a rent in cash or in kind, and perform some ploughing on his lord's estates. He was liable to pay the three feudal dues – 20 shillings when the lord's son came of age and when the lord's daughter married, and one year's rent to redeem his lord from captivity. In contrast to military tenure, no restrictions attached to the inheritance of the tenure nor to the marriage of the heir.

soccer See FOOTBALL.

Social Chapter See MAASTRICHT TREATY.

social class Any of the groups into which a population can be divided according to birth, education, wealth, occupation or lifestyle. The specific groups into which the population is divided depends to a certain extent on the nature of the population. However, evidence from across the world suggests that social class divisions based on occupation and economic standing are to be found in every society. In the UK, birth and education have traditionally formed the basis of division, although the development of state education for all since World War II has weakened these divisions. In the USA, where state education for all is the norm, the divisions tend to be defined mostly by wealth (see CLASS STRUGGLE).

In the 1960s the retailing and marketing industry in the West began to classify potential customers in social grades A to E: A, higher managerial, administrative, or professional; B, intermediate managerial, administrative, or professional; C1, supervisory or clerical, and junior managerial, administrative, or professional; C2, skilled manual workers; D, semi-skilled and unskilled manual workers; and E, state pensioners, casual, or lowest-grade workers.

social contract ▶**1** An agreement among the members of a society to acknowledge the authority of a set of rules or a political regime. It was an expression used by the philosophers HOBBES, LOCKE, and ROUSSEAU in their examination of the nature of the state's authority over the invidual. Social contract theories became popular in the 16th and 17th centuries as a means of explaining the rightful origin of government and hence the political obligations of subjects. Postulating an original state of nature without political authority, contract theorists such as Hobbes (*Leviathan*, 1651) and Locke (*Two Treatises of Government*, 1689), argued that it would be in each person's interest to agree to the establishment of government. Hobbes considered man without government to be in such a state of fear that he will accept authority to gain security. Locke believed that man is guided by reason and conscience even in a state of nature and that in accepting government he still retained natural rights. Locke's view influenced the makers of the American Constitution: JEFFERSON held that the preservation of natural rights was an essential part of the social contract. Rousseau disagreed with Locke's description of the state of nature and thought that man, a 'noble savage' in his natural state, acquired a civic sense only when part of a democratic community. More recently the social contract tradition has been revived, especially by RAWLS (*A Theory of Justice*, 1971), to address problems of distributive justice, and by public choice theorists to establish the limits of state activity. ▶**2** (or **social compact**) An agreement between the UK Labour government in 1974 and the trade unions, in which wage restraint was accepted provided the government agreed to certain social and industrial reforms. It was replaced in 1975 by specific limits to wage increases.

social democracy A form of society in which democratic political methods are used to create greater social equality through the redistribution of resources. At the beginning of the 20th century, social democracy was virtually synonymous with SOCIALISM. After the break with COMMUNISM in the 1920s, however, social democratic parties were distinguished by their commitment to parliamentary DEMOCRACY and their moderate programmes of social change. They gradually abandoned their commitment to public ownership of industry (see NATIONALIZATION), seeking instead to make capitalist economies work in a fairer way by implementing equality of opportunity and by using progressive taxation to provide SOCIAL SECURITY and welfare programmes for the poorer members of society. Most Western societies since World War II have adopted social democratic policies to some degree, with the Scandinavian countries going furthest in this direction.

Social Democrat A member of a political party that supports SOCIAL DEMOCRACY. Wilhelm Liebknecht and August Bebel in Germany first used the term in founding the German Social Democratic Labour Party (1869). In 1875 it was fused with the German Workers' Association, founded (1863) by Ferdinand Lasalle, to form the Social Democratic Party (SDP) of Germany. Other parties followed, for example in Denmark (1878), Britain (1883; Henry Hyndman's Social Democratic Federation), Norway (1887), Austria (1889), the USA (1897), and Russia (1898), where a split came in 1903 into BOLSHEVIK and Menshevik factions. In other countries, for example France, Italy, and Spain, the term Socialist Party was more common. The German SDP was the largest party in the Weimar Republic, governing the country until 1933, when it was banned. It was reformed in West Germany after World War II, with a new constitution (1959), ending all Marxist connections. It entered a coalition with the Christian Democrats in 1966, and headed a coalition with the Free Democrats between 1969 and 1982. In East Germany a revived SDP campaigned for office in 1990, following the collapse of the communist regime. In Sweden the SDP, socialist and constitutional in outlook, has been the dominant party since the 1930s, although it was out of office from 1976 to 1982 and from 1991 to 1994. In Britain four prominent members of the Labour Party resigned in 1981 to form a short-lived, moderate Social Democratic Party (see LIBERAL DEMOCRATS).

socialism A political theory of social organization advocating limits on the private ownership of industry. The word first appeared in France and Britain in the early 19th century. It covers a wide range of positions from COMMUNISM at one extreme to SOCIAL DEMOCRACY at the other. Most socialists believe that the community as a whole should own and control the means of production, distribution, and exchange to ensure a more equitable division of a nation's wealth, either in the form of state ownership of industry (see NATIONALIZATION), or in the form of ownership by the workers themselves. They have also often advocated replacing the market economy by some kind of PLANNED ECONOMY. The aim of these measures is to make industry socially responsible, and to bring about a much greater degree of equality in living standards. In addition, socialists have argued for provision for those in need, as in the WELFARE STATE. Socialism as a political ideal was revolutionized by Karl MARX in the mid-19th century, who tried to demonstrate how CAPITALIST profit was derived from the exploitation of the worker, and argued that a socialist society could be achieved only by a mass movement of the workers themselves. Both the methods by which this transformation was to be achieved and the manner in which the new society was to be run remained the subject of considerable disagreement and produced a wide variety of socialist parties.

These debates have been somewhat overshadowed in recent years by the question of whether socialism is viable at all as an alternative to capitalism. Most Western socialists now opt for SOCIAL DEMOCRACY, others for market socialism. It is only in certain developing countries that traditional socialist aims still attract support.

social ownership See NATIONALIZATION.

social psychology The study of how people understand, influence, and relate to one another. It covers topics of great political and social importance, including AGGRESSION, ALTRUISM, attitude, CONFORMITY, communication, person perception, persuasion, relationships, sexual behaviour, and social understanding. During the 1970s and 1980s the last two (cognitive) topics have probably been the most researched. Social psychology emerged as a distinct area of research after World War II, primarily in the USA. Among the major figures were Theodor Adorno (1903–69), on prejudice, and Fritz Heider (1896–1988) and Solomon Asch on person perception and conformity. In general, US social psychology has been individualistic, stressing environmental rather than innate determinants of behaviour. Modern European social psychologists have attempted to develop theories of collective rather than individual phenomena. In France, for instance, Serge Moscovici has modified DURKHEIM's claim that central ideas affecting individuals' thought and behaviour derive from their culture.

Social Realism A form of art that makes overt social or political comment, generally through scenes taken from seamy or depressing aspects of contemporary life. Essentially a 20th-century concept, it is to be distinguished from **Socialist Realism**, the name given to the officially approved style in the Soviet Union involving acceptance of the Communist Party line in a traditional academic style.

social sciences Branches of the study of human society and social relationships. The disciplines usually encompassed, at least in some of their aspects, are: ANTHROPOLOGY, DEMOGRAPHY, ECONOMICS, GEOGRAPHY, POLITICAL SCIENCE, PSYCHOLOGY, and SOCIOLOGY.

social security A system of financial maintenance organized by government to protect individuals against the loss of earnings resulting from sickness, UNEMPLOYMENT (unemployment benefit), old age (OLD-AGE BENEFIT), and other misfortunes; to meet medical costs; and to give support to families with children (CHILD BENEFIT). Schemes have developed in industrialized countries since the late 19th century in response to the emergence of a large class of factory workers dependent on the regular payment of wages.

By the 1970s almost the entire population of industrialized countries was protected to a greater or lesser extent by social security schemes. However, with social security receipts accounting for a quarter of GDP in some countries, governments have raised insurance contributions and reduced benefits while boosting the importance of occupational and personal insurance. In many countries, including the USA and the UK, social security provision was reduced in scope during the 1980s, as costs rose. Increasing longevity of the population and long-term structural unemployment mean that governments of many developed countries will continue to have to grapple with escalating social security costs.

Most developing countries have neither the money nor the administrative infrastructure for social security systems. Consequently, their citizens are vulnerable to the financial consequences of natural disasters and personal misfortune.

social services State welfare services delivered in kind rather than cash. These can include HEALTH SERVICES, EDUCATION, social care, and, in some countries, housing, food supplements, and employment services. In many parts of the world, the state is closely involved in planning and monitoring its social services, but permits a multiplicity of public, private, and voluntary organizations to supply them. In industrialized countries, if services are designed for universal use, such as the UK's National Health Service and the French education system, public pressure for high standards is likely and national solidarity may be reinforced, but costs are high. If services are selective, resources may be concentrated on those in most need, but determining eligibility can be administratively complex, and there is a danger of creating inferior, stigmatized services, as has happened with welfare housing in the USA.

Society Islands A group of Pacific islands in French Polynesia, including Tahiti; area 1,535 sq km (593 sq miles); pop. (1988) 162,570. They were named by Captain Cook (who visited the islands in 1769) in honour of the Royal Society and in 1844 became a French protectorate.

Society of Friends See QUAKERS.

sociobiology The study of the biological bases of social behaviour in humans and animals. In the 1940s and 1950s ETHOLOGY set out to explain behaviour in terms of its evolutionary history and adaptive function. Sociobiology grew up round discussions of various apparent anomalies of DARWIN's evolutionary theory, such as ALTRUISM. Sociobiological assumptions about adaptiveness and biological selfishness in human behaviour, however, are fraught with difficulties because human culture may act as a buffer against evolutionary mechanisms and moral or legal prescriptions determine some of our actions. Nevertheless sociobiology attempts to explain aspects of human sexuality and parental behaviour as well as altruism.

sociology The systematic study of the development, structure, and functioning of society. The late 19th-century writings of MARX, WEBER, and DURKHEIM laid the foundations of sociology. All three analysed many facets of their own societies, in the more general context of observing the causes and consequences of the transition from traditional pre-industrial life to modern societies. The fundamental postulate of sociology is that human beings act not by their own free decisions taken rationally, but under the influence of history and culture, and the expectations and demands of others: human beings are both the products and the makers of their societies. Sociologists are less concerned with the characteristics of individuals than with patterns of behaviour that recur irrespective of the individuals involved. During the 20th century, sociologists have been particularly interested in the influence of role, status, SOCIAL CLASS, and POWER on experience and behaviour, in the FAMILY and in the community; in the factors that contribute to cohesion and conflict; in social structure and social stratification; and in social problems, such as CRIME, DRUG ABUSE, and domestic violence. There are many approaches to sociology, from the FUNCTIONALISM of PARSONS to the MARXISM of the FRANKFURT SCHOOL. Although some sociologists are primarily theorists, others attempt to provide evidence to support theories by analysing data provided by interviews, surveys, etc. Sociological findings are used increasingly by governments and businesses, such as ADVERTISING and PUBLIC RELATIONS.

Socrates (469–399 BC) Greek philosopher. His interests lay not in the speculation about the natural world engaged in by earlier philosophers but in pursuing questions of ethics. He was the centre of a circle of friends and disciples in Athens and his method of inquiry (the *Socratic method*) was based on discourse with those around him; his careful questioning was designed to reveal truth and to expose error. Although he wrote nothing himself, he was immensely influential; he is known chiefly through his disciple Plato, who recorded Socrates' dialogues and teachings in, for example, the *Symposium* and the *Phaedo*. Charged with introducing strange gods and corrupting the young, Socrates was sentenced to death and condemned to take hemlock, which he did, spurning offers to help him escape into exile.

soda ash See SODIUM CARBONATE.

Soddy, Frederick (1877–1956) British physicist. He worked with Ernest Rutherford in Canada on radioactive decay and formulated a theory of isotopes, the word *isotope* being coined by him in 1913. He also assisted William Ramsay in London in the discovery of helium. Soddy wrote on economics, and later concentrated on creating an awareness of the social relevance of science. He was awarded the Nobel Prize for chemistry in 1921.

sodium (symbol Na, at. no. 11, r.a.m. 22.99) A soft, silvery metal, the sixth most abundant element in the Earth's crust. It occurs naturally in sea water and salt deposits and is manufactured by the electrolysis of a molten sodium chloride (SALT) – calcium chloride mixture in a Downs cell, which is designed to keep the products of the electrolysis apart and so prevent the reformation of sodium chloride. The chemistry of sodium is dominated by the great ease with which it forms the monovalent ion, Na^+. Sodium metal reacts with oxygen and extremely violently with water, and must therefore be stored under liquid paraffin. Wire made from sodium metal is used to dry hydrocarbon SOLVENTS in chemical laboratories. Sodium is also used in the production of the metals titanium and zirconium, and to make sodium peroxide (a powerful bleach) and sodium cyanide (used in metal extraction and electroplating). It is used in sodium lamps for motorways because its yellow light penetrates fog and mist well. Another important use of sodium is as a molten coolant in fast breeder NUCLEAR REACTORS. Other important sodium compounds are SODIUM CARBONATE and SODIUM HYDROXIDE.

sodium bicarbonate See SODIUM HYDROGENCARBONATE.

sodium borate See BORAX.

sodium carbonate (Na_2CO_3) A white, crystalline compound. The commercial form, soda ash, is manufactured by the Solvay (ammonia–soda) process. In this a solution of sodium chloride, NaCl, in water (brine) has ammonia, NH_3, added to it, and then carbon dioxide, CO_2, is bubbled through. The sparingly soluble sodium hydrogencarbonate, $NaHCO_3$, is precipitated and is then decomposed to sodium carbonate on heating. The decahydrate, $Na_2CO_3.10H_2O$, is known as washing soda; it effloresces to form the monohydrate on standing. Sodium carbonate reacts with water to give a weakly alkaline solution containing sodium hydroxide, NaOH, and sodium hydrogencarbonate, $NaHCO_3$. In industry it has many uses including bleaching, water-softening, and the making of soap, detergents, and glass. It is also used in PETROLEUM REFINING and textile manufacture. Some soda ash is found naturally in mines, and in the beds of dry lakes, especially in Lake Magadi, Kenya, and in California, USA.

sodium chloride (or **common salt**, NaCl) A white water-soluble crystalline solid with a melting-point of 801°C (1,474°F). It is essential for the maintenance of the chloride ion balance in the body and is used to flavour food. It can be extracted from seawater by solar evaporation in salt pans, but the major source is underground rock-salt deposits derived from ancient seas. These can be mined using high explosives to break up the rock: crushed rock-salt for de-icing roads in winter (by lowering the freezing-point of water) is obtained in this way. Salt for use in the chemical industry is obtained by pumping water down into rock-salt deposits. The salt dissolves and is carried to the surface in solution (brine), while insoluble impurities remain underground. Sodium chloride is used as a starting material for the production of many important chemicals including SODIUM HYDROXIDE, SODIUM CARBONATE, CHLORINE, and HYDROCHLORIC ACID.

sodium hydrogencarbonate (or **sodium bicarbonate**, $NaHCO_3$) A white powder, soluble in water and stable in dry air. On heating to 270°C (518°F) it decomposes to sodium carbonate (Na_2CO_3) and carbon dioxide (CO_2). It is prepared by the same process used to obtain SODIUM CARBONATE. It has numerous commercial uses, for example, in fire extinguishers and effervescent drinks and in BAKING POWDER.

sodium hydroxide (or **caustic soda**, NaOH) A white, translucent, hygroscopic solid, which forms a strongly alkaline solution in water. The solution attacks glass slowly and reacts with carbon dioxide from the air to form SODIUM CARBONATE. Industrially, it is produced by the electrolysis of brine in very large quantities using the CASTNER–KELLNER CELL. Sodium hydroxide is an important starting material for the manufacture of many other chemicals; it is also used in the production of rayon and other textiles, paper and pulp, aluminium, petrochemicals, soaps, and detergents. It is a standard laboratory reagent.

sodium hypochlorite (NaOCl) A soluble salt formed, together with sodium chloride, NaCl, when chlorine, Cl_2, is bubbled through cold sodium hydroxide (NaOH) solution. Aqueous NaOCl is used as an antiseptic and as a bleach.

sodium silicates A range of salts, each having a different sodium:silicon ratio. The most important is the mixture known as water-glass, which is formed by dissolving SILICA in sodium hydroxide, NaOH, under pressure. This is a colourless viscous liquid used in various printing processes and as an adhesive, preservative, and cleaning agent.

Sodom and Gomorrah In the Old Testament, two of the five cities of the plain, possibly now covered by the shallow waters near the southern end of the Dead Sea. Notorious for the corrupt lives led by their citizens and for the perverted sexual acts in which they indulged, the inhabitants of both cities, with the exception of Lot and his family, were destroyed by 'brimstone and fire' rained on them by God.

Sofia (or **Sophia**, **Sofiya**) The capital of Bulgaria, situated midway between the Adriatic and the Black Sea on a plain to the south of Mt Vitosha; pop. (1990) 1,220,900. Settled in ancient times by Thracian tribes who used its mineral springs, it was named Serdica by the Romans and Triaditsa by the Byzantines. Held by the Turks between the 14th and late 19th centuries, it became capital of the newly independent Bulgarian state in 1879. It is now Bulgaria's principal industrial, transportation, and cultural centre. Its chief industries are metallurgy, engineering, chemicals, textiles, and food processing. It has an opera house, art galleries and museums, and a university.

softball A version of BASEBALL. It is played with a smaller diamond, a shorter bat, and a ball which is not soft but larger and heavier than a baseball, with a circumference of 30 cm (12 inches). The effect of the smaller playing area is to speed up the action, and the larger ball, delivered at speed with an underarm action from 14 m (46 feet) for men and 12 m (40 feet) for women, gives the pitcher a greater advantage over the batter. In high-class games, scores therefore tend to be low. Each team of nine plays seven innings, and the principles of play are similar to those in baseball. Softball began in the USA and since the 1960s has spread to many countries.

soft coral A fleshy or leathery coelenterate of the order Alcyonacea, found in most seas, which forms colonies up to 1 m (3 feet) across in Indo-Pacific reefs. Soft corals differ from other CORALS in lacking massive calcium carbonate skeletons, gaining support from their own soft rubbery bodies instead (though there may be some chalky spicules). They are usually irregular in shape, with lobes and projections, and one common type, *Alcyonium*, is aptly named dead men's fingers. They belong to the octocorals – each POLYP within the coral has eight tiny tentacles which can be withdrawn if the animal is disturbed.

soft-shelled turtle A turtle of the family Trionychidae, in the genus *Trionyx*, which occurs in North America, Africa, Asia, and western Indonesia. Its shell is covered with a layer of leathery skin, unlike the horny, shell covering of most other turtles. It is mainly aquatic in habits and has a snout extended into a snorkel-like proboscis, used for breathing air from the water surface whilst the rest of the body remains submerged. Its lips, which conceal the jaw surfaces, are fleshy and soft, and its main food is crayfish, aquatic insects, and molluscs.

software Computer PROGRAMS, and sometimes also DATA, as opposed to HARDWARE. All computer systems comprise both hardware and software, the hardware performing tasks and operations under the control of a sequence of instructions provided by the software.

Soho A district centred around Soho Square in the West End of London, England, noted for its clubs, bars, bistros and restaurants. Popular with immigrants since the 17th century, Soho was associated with the avant-garde literary and artistic set in the 1950s, subsequently gaining a reputation for its sleazy nightlife. It has a large Chinese community.

soil The disintegrated rock with an admixture of organic matter that covers much of the Earth's surface and is capable of supporting plant growth. While the nature of the weathered rock or sediment forming the basic material determines its mineral content, climate often determines its texture; decayed vegetation provides its organic material in the form of humus, and topography influences the thickness of its PROFILE between surface and bedrock from place to place. The fertility of soils depends upon the availability of nutrients to plants. Both waterlogging by the exclusion of air, and acidity, inhibit the microorganisms that recycle elements in leaf litter, and so impoverish the soil progressively. Removal of vegetation by cultivating annual crops, over-grazing or destroying forests can, in adverse climates, have disastrous effects on many types of soil. The science of PEDOLOGY now helps to prescribe a soil's suitability for a food, fibre, or timber crop.

soil erosion The removal of soil particles, usually by running water or wind, from any part of the Earth's surface. It refers particularly to hillsides and to the loss of the upper-most layers of soil, which are often the most fertile. This is a major problem in the modern world, for not only does soil erosion destroy valuable farmland but the material removed can choke rivers and irrigation channels and can bury crops under a layer of dust or mud. On land laid bare it takes a long time for natural processes to re-create the top-soil. The chief cause is removal or reduction of the protective covering of vegetation. This not only allows wind, rain, and frost to break up the surface but also reduces the ability of the ground to absorb water, so that overland flow is encouraged, creating rills, which can rapidly grow into gullies or ravines. While severe erosion also occurs naturally, particularly as a result of climatic changes, in many parts of the world today it results from unwise farming practices.

soil mechanics The science of the engineering properties of soils as opposed to rocks. When designing foundations, the engineer assesses the bearing capacity of the soil and the likely settlement of the structure. Earthwork projects, such as embankments and cuttings, and the assessment of soil pressures on retaining walls all rely on soil mechanics. For tunnel-building and excavation predictions of earth pressures and water flow are required for the design of supports and water-control techniques.

Sokhumi See SUKHUMI.

Solano See LEVANTER.

solar cell (or **photovoltaic cell**) A device for producing electric power directly from light. It consists of two layers of SEMICONDUCTOR material, the upper layer being sufficiently thin for light to penetrate to the boundary, where electrons are released and allow a current to flow. Selenium photovoltaic cells were first introduced in the 1920s and the present silicon devices in the 1950s. Their relatively high cost, and low power output have limited their use to low-power applications (light meters, pocket calculators, and so on), and situations in which other sources are not available (lightships, spacecraft, remote houses, or defence installations). New materials, such as gallium arsenide, may, however, prove cheaper and more efficient.

solar constant See SOLAR RADIATION.

solar cycle See SUNSPOTS.

solar eclipse See ECLIPSE.

solar energy See SOLAR POWER.

solar flare See FLARE.

solar furnace An arrangement for achieving very high temperatures by focusing solar radiation. A parabolic mirror concentrates the radiation on the central focus. To track the Sun, an array of tiltable flat mirrors is often used, reflecting the sunlight into the parabola. Solar furnaces have achieved temperatures of over 3,000°C.

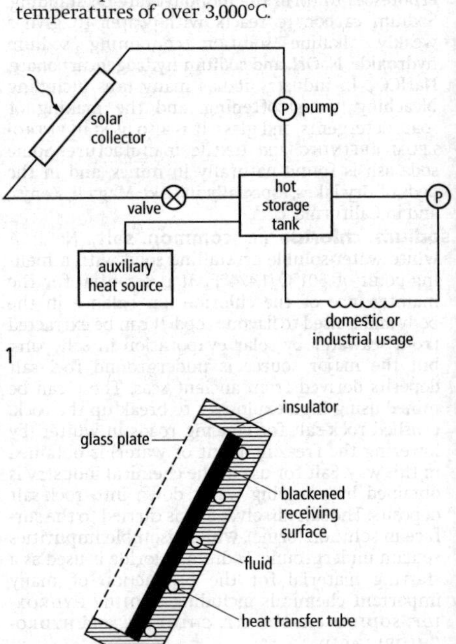

Solar panel (1) Water pumped through the solar collector is warmed by the Sun's rays and stored in a tank, which is subsequently heated further by an auxiliary heat source. (2) The solar collector has a blackened receiving surface through which the water is piped.

solar panel A flat or concave panel designed to collect solar energy to provide heat; alternatively, a sheet of SOLAR CELLS. Solar heating panels are a development of a simple hot-water system consisting of a black hosepipe coiled on the roof and connected to the water supply. The modern panel absorbs solar radiation through a black surface in close contact with pipework, through which a fluid circulates. A sheet of glass in front of the panel and insulating material surrounding it reduce heat losses.

solar parallax The angle subtended by the Earth's

equatorial radius at the centre of the Sun, at the time when the Earth is at its mean distance from the Sun. The value of this PARALLAX angle is about 8.8 arc seconds. The radius of the Earth (6,378.164 km) divided by the solar parallax in radians (4.26×10^{-5} radians) gives the ASTRONOMICAL UNIT (1.50×10^{8} km), that is, the average distance from the Earth to the Sun.

solar power Power derived from solar energy. The total radiation reaching the Earth from the Sun is equivalent to about 20,000 times the world's current rate of energy consumption and the intensity at the Earth's surface is about 1 kilowatt per square metre (about 80% of the solar constant; see SOLAR RADIATION). Solar energy originates in nuclear FUSION in the Sun's interior and travels through space as ELECTROMAGNETIC RADIATION. It is the ultimate source of nearly all the world's ENERGY RESOURCES, and 'passive' solar heating is a major factor in maintaining temperatures in buildings. However, solar energy appears in estimates of energy consumption only when harnessed in some way, for example, in SOLAR CELLS, SOLAR FURNACES, and solar-powered vehicles. Research in solar power has tended to focus on the generation of electricity from solar radiation. However, new research into the direct use of the thermal energy of the Sun seems very promising. Developments in transparent insulation materials (TIMs), which transmit light but also provide good heat insulation, could be used to cut heating costs for buildings by a large amount, and also to heat water. See also SOLAR PANEL.

solar radiation All the radiation that comes from the Sun. Most of it is in the form of visible and near-visible light, although the whole spectrum of ELECTROMAGNETIC RADIATION is emitted. The quantity reaching the Earth is denoted by the **solar constant**. This is the solar energy per second falling on 1 square metre of a surface at a distance from the Sun's centre equal to the mean distance to the Earth. It has the value 1.36 kW m^{-2} s^{-1}. About 80 per cent of this energy reaches the Earth's surface and the majority of it has a wavelength of 3.8 to 10×10^{-7} m. In addition to electromagnetic radiation, the Sun also emits streams of energetic charged particles (see SOLAR WIND), such as electrons, especially from solar flares. Some of these are trapped in the VAN ALLEN belts and they are believed to be responsible for magnetic storms.

Solar System The collection of planets, satellites, asteroids, comets, and cosmic dust particles that are mostly in elliptical, coplanar orbits around the Sun. The total mass of the Solar System is around 450 times the mass of the Earth and about 1/750 of the mass of the Sun. About three-quarters of that mass is concentrated in the gaseous giant planet Jupiter. COSMOGONY, the study of the origin of planets, indicates that the cloud of gas and dust that condensed to form the Solar System must have had a mass a few hundred times greater than that of the present system. The planets formed about 4.6 billion years ago and in the early days suffered a great deal from bombardment by asteroids. The rate of these collisions has decreased by about 2,000 times since then. The surface temperature of the planets decreases roughly as the inverse square root of their distance from the Sun. The inner planets, Mercury, Venus, Earth, and Mars have a rock and metal composition, low relative mass, and few satellites. The Moon is unusual in as much as it has a mass of 1/81 of that of Earth. Only Charon, Pluto's satellite, compared to Pluto's mass, has a larger ratio. Phobos and Deimos, the two small satellites of Mars, are thought to be captured asteroids. The outer planets, Jupiter, Saturn, Uranus, and Neptune, have rock-metal cores of ten to 20 or so times the mass of the Earth and are surrounded by huge atmospheres of hydrogen and helium gas. These planets have large collections of orbiting satellites and all have ring systems, although the rings of Saturn are by far the most elaborate. Pluto, the outermost planet, has a mass of only one-quarter that of the Moon and is probably an escaped satellite. There was relatively little matter in the preplanetary nebula in the region of Pluto and it would have taken a long time for a planet to form at that distance from the Sun. It is therefore probable that there are no major planets beyond Neptune. However, many astronomers believe that a large spherical shell of comets, the OORT–ÖPIK CLOUD, surrounds the planetary sys-

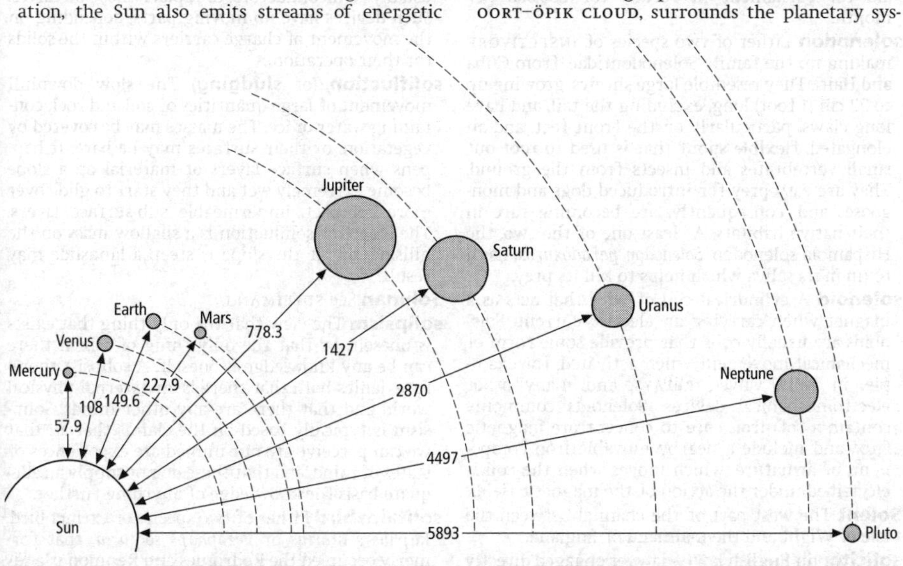

Solar System Nine planets revolve around the Sun. The diagram shows the radius of each orbit. The sizes of the planets are drawn approximately to scale.

tem and extends almost one-third of the way to the nearest stars. Therefore the planetary system probably has a radius of only about 40 times that of the Earth's orbit, whereas the distance to the nearest stars is some 270,000 times the radius of the Earth's orbit.

solar wind A stream of charged particles, mainly protons and electrons, that are ejected from the Sun into the interplanetary medium. The solar wind escapes from holes in the hot CORONA and forms the heliosphere, which can reach distances of about 100 astronomical units from the Sun. The effect of the solar wind is vividly seen in the tail of a comet. The tail, which is always directed away from the Sun, is formed by the solar wind sweeping material out from the nucleus of the comet.

sole A FLATFISH of the family Soleidae, of worldwide distribution in tropical and temperate seas, almost always found in shallow water. They are slender-bodied, with the dorsal fin beginning on the snout and continuing almost to the tail fin; the anal fin is almost as long, but the other fins are small. Soles have both eyes on the left side of the head (they undergo a metamorphosis like all flatfishes) and the mouth is often twisted. On the blind side of the head there are elaborate sensory organs. The Dover sole, *Solea solea*, is a European fish, living on the sea-bed. It is most common on sandy or muddy bottoms, and usually feeds at night on small crustaceans and worms. It is an important food-fish and grows to a length of 60 cm (2 feet). Several members of the sole family are found on the Atlantic coast of North America. See also LEMON SOLE.

Solemn League and Covenant (1643) The agreement between the English Parliament and Scottish COVENANTERS during the ENGLISH CIVIL WAR. It undertook that the Presbyterian Church of Scotland was to be preserved, and the Anglican Church was to be reformed. The Scots soon realized that Presbyterianism would not be imposed on England by the specially established Westminster Assembly of Divines. This put considerable strain upon the other aspect of the agreement: Scottish military aid for Parliament in return for £30,000 per month.

solenodon Either of two species of INSECTIVORE making up the family Solenodontidae, from Cuba and Haiti. They resemble large shrews, growing up to 32 cm (1 foot) long, excluding the tail, and have long claws, particularly on the front feet, and an elongated, flexible snout that is used to root out small vertebrates and insects from the ground. They are easy prey for introduced dogs and mongooses and, consequently, are becoming rare in their native habitats. At least one of the two, the Hispaniola solenodon, *Solenodon paradoxurus*, has a toxin in its saliva which helps to kill its prey.

solenoid A cylindrical coil of wire that acts as a magnet when carrying an electric current. Solenoids are usually coils that provide some form of mechanical movement when activated, for example, in bells, valves, RELAYS, and many other electromechanical devices. Solenoids commonly contain a soft-iron core to concentrate magnetic flux, and include a nearby movable iron component, or armature, which moves when the coil is electrified under the action of the magnetic field.

Solent The west part of the channel between the Isle of Wight and the mainland of England.

solicitor (in English law) A lawyer engaged directly by a client to carry out legal administrative work (such as conveyancing or drafting of wills), or to give advice on the LAW. A solicitor has a right of audience in inferior courts, but in higher courts, must instruct a BARRISTER to represent the client. Under reforms enacted in 1990, however, solicitors who have the relevant advocacy qualification have rights of audience in the higher courts.

solid One of three most common PHASES OF MATTER, the others being liquids and gases (see PLASMA; LIQUID CRYSTALS). Solids are characterized by having a fixed size and shape as long as the temperature does not change. This is because the forces between the atoms or molecules making up a solid are strong enough to resist the disruptive effect of their thermal vibrations. There are two main types: CRYSTALS (such as common salt or sugar) in which the atoms are arranged in a regular pattern throughout the material, and amorphous solids (such as glass) in which the atomic positions are irregular. Whereas crystals have definite melting-points at which they become liquids, amorphous solids tend first to become pliable on heating.

Solidarity (Polish **Solidarnosc**) An independent trade-union movement in Poland. It emerged after a wave of strikes at Gdańsk in 1980 organized by the Free Union of the Baltic Coast. Demands included the right to a trade union independent of Communist Party control. Under its leader Lech WALESA membership rose rapidly, as Poles began to demand political as well as economic concessions. In 1981 the Prime Minister, General Jaruzelski, proclaimed martial law and arrested the Solidarity leaders, outlawing the movement in 1982. In 1989 the government, under pressure from both Left and Right, sponsored round-table talks from which Solidarity emerged as the dominant political organization. In 1990 Walesa was elected President of the republic; but ideological differences soon emerged and the movement broke up into a number of separate political parties, only one, a minority party, retaining the name *Solidarnosc*.

solid-state device An electronic component or device that uses the electronic properties of solids, usually semiconductors, to replace those of valves. Such devices have no moving parts, depending on the movement of charge carriers within the solids for their operation.

solifluction (or **sludging**) The slow downhill movement of large quantities of soil and rock containing water or ice. The masses may be covered by vegetation, or their surfaces may be bare. It happens when surface layers of material on a slope become extremely wet and they start to glide over more compact, impermeable sub-surface layers. The effect of solifluction is a shallow mass on the hillside, but if the slope is steep a landslide may result.

Soliman See SULEIMAN I.

solipsism The view that the only thing that exists is oneself, or that the only thing of which there can be any knowledge is oneself. A solipsist therefore denies both that there is an external physical world and that there are any other minds. Solipsism is typically based on the claims that all that we can perceive are our immediate experiences or states of mind, and that these do not supply an adequate basis for knowledge of anything further.

solitaire bird Either of two species of extinct bird, *Raphus solitarius* or *Pezophaps solitaria*, that formerly occupied the Rodrigues and Réunion islands in the Madagascar group. They were related to the DODO and similarly were completely flightless; in size and general form they resembled a large turkey. By 1761, both species had become extinct.

solmization A musical notation in which the notes of the diatonic SCALE are designated by syllables and manual signs. The system was introduced by Guido d'Arezzo in the 11th century, but is more familiar as the 'tonic sol-fa' system, established by John Curwen in 1853. The tonic sol-fa syllables are: doh, ray, me, fah, soh, la, ti, doh.

Solomon Son of David, king of ancient Israel *c.*970–*c.*930 BC. During his reign he extended the kingdom of Israel to the border with Egypt and the Euphrates, and became famous both for his wisdom and for the magnificence of his palaces. In 957 he built the Temple of Jerusalem. The discontent of some Israelites forced to labour on his building schemes or to pay levies to finance them culminated in the secession of the northern tribes, who formed a separate kingdom (*c.*930–721 BC) but were carried away to captivity in Babylon. In the Bible Solomon is traditionally associated with the Song of Solomon, Ecclesiastes, and Proverbs; the Wisdom of Solomon in the Apocrypha is also ascribed to him.

Solomon Islands An island country in the south-west Pacific.

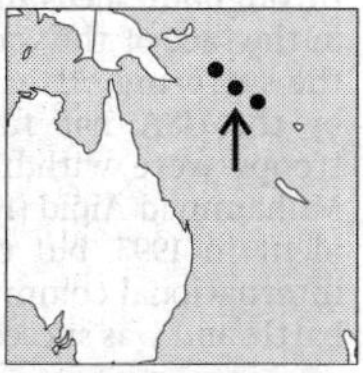

Physical. The Solomon Islands form a large archipelago comprising a double chain of six large and many smaller islands, lying between 5° and 13° S of the Equator. The largest island, Bougainville, together with a few others in the north-west, is part of PAPUA NEW GUINEA; all the rest constitute a country in which the most important island is Guadalcanal. Lying at the edge of the Pacific plate, the region is subject to earthquakes; and there are volcanoes on the main islands.

Economy. The soil is generally fertile and cocoa and tobacco are grown, although the main resource is copra – dried coconut kernels, from which oil can be squeezed. Timber and palm oil are exported. Fishing is also important.

History. Occupied for at least 3,000 years, European missionaries and settlers arrived throughout the 18th and 19th centuries, and in 1885 the German New Guinea Company established control of the north Solomons. Britain declared a protectorate over the southern islands in 1893. During World War II the Solomons witnessed fierce battles between Japanese and Allied forces. The Solomon Islands became an independent member of the COMMONWEALTH OF NATIONS on 7 July 1978. Solomon Mamaloni (Prime Minister since 1989) faced severe criticism during 1991 for allegedly ignoring the constitution and seeking to rule without a mandate. Following an election in 1993, the independent Francis Billy Hilly became Prime Minister. His short-lived administration ended in late 1994, when Mamaloni again won power. Relations with Papua New Guinea continued to be strained. After elections in 1997 a new government was formed, with Batholomew Ulufa'alu as Prime Minister.

Capital: Honiara
Area: 28,370 sq km (10,954 sq mi)
Population: 382,000 (1995)
Currency: 1 Solomon Islands dollar = 100 cents
Religions: Protestant 75%; Roman Catholic 19%; Baha'i 0.4%; other 2.9%
Ethnic Groups: Melanesian 94.2%; Polynesian 3.7%; other Pacific islander 1.4%
Languages: English (official)
International Organizations: UN; Commonwealth; South Pacific Forum

Solomon's seal A perennial plant of the genus *Polygonatum*, part of the lily family, with a stout, rhizomatous rootstock, producing annual stems 1 m (3.25 feet) in height with clusters of pendent white flowers in the axils of the paired leaves. Virtually all are native to Europe and Asia.

Solon (*c.*630–*c.*560 BC) Athenian statesman and lawgiver. One of the Seven Sages listed by Plato, he is notable for his economic, constitutional, and legal reforms, begun in about 594. He revised the existing code of laws established by Draco, making them less severe; for example, he abolished the punishment of slavery for debt and reserved the death penalty for murder. His division of the citizens into four classes based on wealth rather than birth with a corresponding division of political responsibility laid the foundations of Athenian democracy.

solstice The time during which the Sun is furthest from the equator. At the **summer solstice** the Sun is furthest north from the equator, about 21 June in the Northern Hemisphere. At the **winter solstice** the Sun is furthest south from the equator, about 22 December in the Northern Hemisphere.

Solti, Sir Georg (1912–97) Hungarian-born British conductor. From 1961 to 1971 Solti revivified Covent Garden as musical director, and took British nationality in 1972. Solti commenced a long association with the London Philharmonic Orchestra in 1973, but his appointment as conductor of the Chicago Symphony Orchestra (1969–91) brought him his greatest fame. He was appointed director of the Salzburg Easter Festival in 1992.

solute A substance (solid, liquid, or gas) that will dissolve in a solvent, forming a SOLUTION. Whereas the solubility of solids usually increases with temperature, that of gases usually decreases with temperature but increases with pressure. Solutes differ from one another in their degree of solubility in any particular solvent.

solution A liquid formed when one substance becomes completely dispersed in another substance. Solutions are homogeneous – that is, they have the same composition throughout. Solutions are formed by dissolving SOLUTES in SOLVENTS. An aqueous solution is one in which water is the solvent. One containing only a small quantity of a solute is said to be dilute, one with a large quantity is concentrated, and one with as much as possible is saturated. Some alloys are solutions of metals in each other, the process having taken place in the molten state; they are called solid solutions.

Solvay, Ernest (1838–1922) Belgian industrial chemist. In 1861 he developed a process (the **Solvay process**) for the manufacture of SODIUM CARBONATE (soda ash) to replace the LEBLANC process. Subsequently he made great improvements to the process, establishing several manufacturing plants.

solvent A liquid that can dissolve other substances, forming a SOLUTION. Substances may dissolve in some solvents but not others: a useful guide is 'like dissolves like', i.e. polar solvents generally dissolve materials composed of IONS, whereas non-polar solvents will generally dissolve materials composed of uncharged molecules. Water is the most common polar solvent. Liquid HYDROCARBONS (e.g. ethanol and toluene) are non-polar solvents used in the petrochemical and polymer industries as well as for degreasing and cleaning purposes. Chlorinated hydrocarbons (e.g. chloroform and trichloromethane) are good non-polar solvents, but their use may be a health risk. ALCOHOLS, esters, and ketones are non-polar solvents used extensively in industry.

Solway Firth An inlet of the Irish Sea, formed by the estuary of the Esk and Eden rivers, separating Cumbria (England) from Dumfries and Galloway (Scotland).

Solzhenitsyn, Aleksandr (Isaevich) (1918–) Russian novelist. In 1945 he was imprisoned for eight years in a labour camp for criticizing Stalin and spent another three years in internal exile before being rehabilitated. After his release he was allowed to publish his first novel, *One Day in the Life of Ivan Denisovich* (1962), describing conditions in a labour camp. In 1963, however, he was again in conflict with the authorities and thereafter was unable to have his books published in the Soviet Union. He was deported to West Germany in 1974 following the publication abroad of the first part of his trilogy *The Gulag Archipelago* in 1973; the first Russian-language edition appeared in 1989. Solzhenitsyn lived in the USA until returning to Russia in 1994. He was awarded the Nobel Prize for literature in 1970.

Somali A Hamitic Muslim people of Somalia in north-east Africa, speaking a language that belongs to the Cushitic branch of the Hamito-Semitic family of languages (see CUSHITIC LANGUAGES) and is the official language of Somalia.

Somalia A country on the so-called 'horn' in the north-east of Africa.

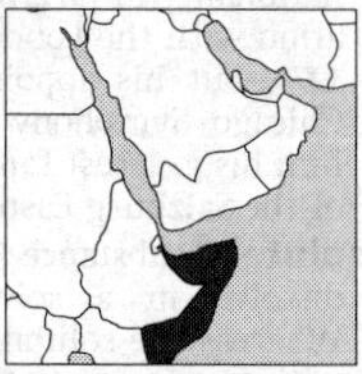

Physical. Somalia has north and south-east coasts on the Gulf of Aden and the Indian Ocean and borders Ethiopia and Kenya inland. Along its north coast, desert plains rise by steep-cliffed ridges to the red sandstone hills of a northern plateau. There it is hot and arid, the only vegetation being thin thornscrub. The south of the country is lower and has one permanent river, the Juba, as a source of irrigation.

Economy. One of Africa's poorest countries and heavily dependent on foreign aid, Somalia has suffered from drought, flooding, famine, civil war, and high foreign debt in recent years. The main exports are livestock and bananas; other crops are sugar-cane, maize, and sorghum. Industry is confined mainly to processing agricultural products, although imported petroleum is refined. Mineral resources include lead, gold, zircon, coal, uranium, and kyanite, but most of these are not fully exploited.

History. The kingdom of Punt, mentioned in ancient Egyptian writings, probably occupied the area of Somalia's northern and eastern coastline. Muslim Arabs and Persians established trading routes in the area between the 7th and 10th centuries AD. Somali nomads had lived in the interior area from at least the 10th century AD and Galla peoples lived in the south and west of the country. After the British occupied Aden (now in Yemen) in 1839 European exploration of the region commenced. The area of the 'horn' of Africa was divided between British, French and Italian spheres of influence in the late 19th century. The modern Somali Republic is a result of the unification in 1960 of the former British Somaliland Protectorate and the Italian Trusteeship Territory of Somalia. From then onwards Somalia was involved in border disputes with Kenya and Ethiopia. In 1969 President Shermarke was assassinated in a left-wing coup and the Marxist Somali Revolutionary Socialist Party took power, renaming the country the Somali Democratic Republic under the dictatorship of General Muhammad Siyad Barrah (*c*.1911–95). There followed 21 years of one-man rule, with a sharply deteriorating economy and an escalating civil war. Fighting broke out in 1988 between government forces and rebel groups, the most important of which being the Somali National Movement (SNM). The country, already hit by drought, now descended into what has been described as the world's 'worst man-made disaster', as refugees fled the insurgents and famine and disease took their toll. Siyad Barrah fled office in January 1991, forming a breakaway grouping, the Somali National Front. The SNM proclaimed a Somaliland Republic in the north reviving the republic that had briefly succeeded the former British Somaliland protectorate and repudiating a union with ex-Italian Somalia. By mid-1992 some six million people were facing starvation, as UN troops were deployed against rival warlords throughout the country and relief agencies tried, in the face of the warlords' opposition, to alleviate the suffering. After UN peace-keeping forces, led by the USA, had failed to maintain a cease-fire, troops were withdrawn by March 1995. General Muhammad Aidid (1936–96) declared himself President in 1995, but this was not accepted by the international community. In 1996 he was killed in battle and was succeeded by his son, Hussein Aidid.

Capital: Mogadishu
Area: 637,000 sq km (246,000 sq mi)
Population: 6,734,000 (1995)
Currency: 1 Somali shilling = 100 cents
Religions: Sunni Muslim 99.8%; Christian 0.1%
Ethnic Groups: Somali 98.3%; Arab 1.2%; Bantu 0.4%
Languages: Somali, Arabic, English (official); Italian; Swahili
International Organizations: UN; OAU; Arab League

Somerset A county of south-west England; area 3,452 sq km (1,333 sq miles); pop. (1991) 459,100; county town, Taunton. Somerset is divided into five districts.

Somerset, Edward Seymour, 1st Earl of Hertford and Duke of (*c*.1506–52) Protector of England and effective ruler of England on behalf of EDWARD VI 1547–49. On the death of HENRY VIII in 1547 Edward Seymour (brother of Jane SEYMOUR) took the titles of Duke of Somerset and Lord Protector and won an immediate military success against Scotland at the Battle of Pinkie. His attempts to enforce the use of a Protestant English Prayer Book by Act of Uniformity (1549) sparked off the Western Rising. KETT'S REBELLION, coinciding with discontent among magnates grouped around his rival, the Earl of Warwick (later the Duke of NORTHUMBERLAND), led to his downfall. He was overthrown in 1549 and executed on the orders of Northumberland in 1551.

Somme A river of north-east France that rises in the department of Aisne and flows 245 km (153 miles) into the English Channel near St Valéry-sur-Somme. It was the scene of heavy fighting in World War I, especially in July–November 1916. In this most terrible battle of the war the Allies lost 600,000 men and gained a few kilometres of mud.

Somoza A family dynasty that dominated NICARAGUA from the 1930s until 1979. **Anastasio Garcia Somoza** (1896–1956) engineered a successful coup against the liberal regime and took over the presidency in 1936, exercising dictatorial control until his assassination in 1956. Somoza family rule continued under his sons **Luis** and **Anastasio (Tachito) Somoza Debayle** (1956–63, 1967–79, respectively). The Somozas used the National Guard to eliminate political opposition while they accumulated vast amounts of Nicaragua's agrarian and industrial resources. Military and economic assistance from the USA helped maintain the Somozas in power until 1979, when economic problems and world outcry against human rights abuses undermined Tachito's control and the SANDINISTA NATIONAL LIBERATION FRONT took power.

sonar (*so*und *na*vigation and *r*anging) A method used to find the position, speed, or nature of an object at sea using sound. It was initially developed for use by warships in detecting submarines during World War II, and was originally known as ASDIC (from Allied Submarine Detection Investigation Committee). Active sonar works in a similar way to RADAR, transmitting a pulse of sound and measuring the time taken for the echo to return from the object. The use of a narrow transmission beam enables the object's bearing to be calculated. Furthermore, changes in the frequency of the returning echo can be measured, and give some indication of the object's speed and direction, using the DOPPLER principle. An echo-sounder is a specialized type of active sonar used for depth measurement. Passive sonar operates by using a listening device to determine the direction of an underwater sound. The sound may give clues as to the nature of the object, for example, a ship's engine or the call of a whale. In warfare, passive sonar has the advantage of not betraying the presence of the listener.

sonata A musical work in several movements for piano, or for piano and one other instrument. In the 16th century any music played by instruments was called a sonata, as opposed to the CANTATA, which was sung. During the 17th century instrumental works divided into five or more contrasting sections were known as sonatas, but by the early 18th century the sonata had become a work in several separate movements, similar to the suite. Such sonatas were of two kinds: the *sonata da chiesa* (Italian, 'church sonata'), some of whose movements were of a more serious nature, and the *sonata da camera* (Italian, 'chamber sonata'), whose movements followed dance patterns. These types merged and their movements acquired the structural sophistications of the 18th century to become the three- and four-movement sonatas of Haydn, Mozart, and Beethoven.

The **sonata form** evolved during the early part of the 18th century from the BINARY form. The basis of the form is KEY relationship, in which separate themes may be set in contrasting keys and ultimately reconciled by a restatement of all the thematic material in the main key of the overall structure. The form proceeds in three stages. First is the exposition, in which two main themes are set out in closely related but contradictory keys – a first subject (or subjects) in the tonic (main) key of the movement, followed by a second subject (or subjects) in a related key (the dominant in major keys and the relative major in minor keys). A frequent practice is to make the second subject more lyrical than the first, which is likely to be vigorous and emphatic. This section is usually repeated, and then flows directly into the second, development section, in which the material is worked in free fantasia, modulating through various keys, but finally leading to a third recapitulation section, in which the original thematic material is restated entirely in the main (tonic) key of the movement. A coda may provide a more decisive ending. Sonata form remained the usual form for the first movement of sonatas and symphonies until the principles of TONALITY were challenged at the end of the 19th century.

Sondheim, Stephen (Joshua) (1930–) US composer and lyricist. He became famous with his lyrics for Leonard Bernstein's *West Side Story* (1957) and later wrote both words and music for a number of musicals, including *A Funny Thing Happened on the Way to the Forum* (1962), *A Little Night Music* (1973), and *Sweeney Todd* (1979).

Song (or **Sung**) A dynasty of Chinese emperors ruling from 960 to 1279, between the Tang and Yuan periods. During the Song Dynasty art and literature flourished and paper money was invented.

Songhai A Muslim empire of West Africa founded by Berbers in the 8th century and extending its influence over the middle Niger until the 16th century. In the 17th century it broke up into a number of smaller states.

song thrush A species of bird, *Turdus philomelos*, belonging to the thrush family, which is widely distributed over Europe and western Asia. Closely related to the redwing, *T. iliacus*, the song thrush is a duller brown, lacking the redwing's conspicuous eye-stripe and having pale orange under the wing instead of orange-red. It has a musical song, containing notes or phrases copied from other birds. Each phrase is usually repeated two or three times.

sonnet A LYRIC poem of 14 iambic PENTAMETER lines (or lines of 12 syllables in French, 11 in Italian). Originating in Italy, the sonnet was established by Petrarch as a major form of love poetry, and adopted in France and England in the late 16th century. Sidney, Spenser, and Shakespeare wrote outstanding sequences of sonnets, while Donne and Milton extended its subject-matter to religion and politics. Keats, Wordsworth, and Baudelaire revived the form in the 19th century. The rhyme-schemes of the sonnet follow two basic patterns: the Italian or Petrarchan sonnet comprises an 'octave' of two QUATRAINS, rhymed ABBAABBA, and a 'sestet' usually rhymed CDECDE or CDCDCD, with a 'turn' in the poem's argument between octave and sestet (although Milton and some other poets dispensed with this). The English or Shakespearian sonnet comprises three quatrains and a COUPLET, rhymed ABABCDCDEFEFGG, delaying the 'turn' until the final couplet; a variant of this, the Spenserian sonnet, rhymes ABABBCBCCDCDEE.

Sontag, Susan (1933–) US writer and critic. She established her reputation as a radical intellectual with a series of essays collected in *Against Interpretation* (1966). In the 1970s Sontag made two films and won critical acclaim for her study *On Photography* (1976) and her collection of essays *Illness as Metaphor* (1979); the latter was prompted by her experiences as a cancer patient. Her more recent works include the collection of essays *Under the Sign of Saturn* (1980), the novel *The Volcano Lover* (1992), and the play *Alice in Bed* (1993).

Sophia See SOFIA.

sophist (from Greek *sophistes*, 'wise man') An itinerant professional teacher in Greece, the Greek colonies in Sicily, and southern Italy in the 5th century BC. Sophists offered instruction in a wide range of subjects and skills considered necessary for public life, rhetoric in particular, in return for fees. By questioning the nature of gods, conventions, and morals, and by their alleged ability to train men 'to make the weaker argument the stronger' through rhetoric, they aroused some opposition. Their readiness to argue either cause in a dispute brought them condemnation from PLATO as self-interested imitators of wisdom lacking any concern for the truth.

Sophocles (*c.*496–406 BC) Greek dramatist. He is one of the trio of major Greek tragedians, with Aeschylus and Euripides. His seven surviving plays are notable for their addition of a third actor to the previous two (in addition to the chorus), thus allowing a greater complexity of plot and fuller depiction of character, and for their examination of the relationship between mortals and the divine order. The plays include *Antigone*, *Electra*, and *Oedipus Rex* (also called *Oedipus Tyrannus*).

Sopwith, Sir Thomas (Octave Murdoch) (1888–1989) British aircraft designer. During World War I he designed a number of planes, including the famous fighter biplane the Sopwith Camel, which were built by his Sopwith Aviation Company (founded 1912). During World War II, as chairman of the Hawker Siddeley company, he was responsible for the production of such aircraft as the Hurricane fighter.

Sorbonne Originally, a theological college founded in Paris by Robert de Sorbon, chaplain to Louis IX *c.*1257 and later, the faculty of theology in the University of Paris, suppressed in 1792. It was made a state university by Napoleon, it is now the seat of the faculties of science and letters of the University of Paris. Situated in the Place de la Sorbonne, on the Left Bank.

sorghum *Sorghum vulgare*, one of the most valuable cereals in the semi-arid areas of the tropics, being more resistant to drought than maize. Of African origin, it has been the staple cereal in parts of Africa and Asia for thousands of years. It is a variable, annual grass up to 4 m (13 feet) tall, bearing a large terminal flower head. The round grains vary in colour from white or yellow to red, brown, or even black. The lighter-coloured types are preferred for eating, the more bitter dark-coloured types being used for beer. Sorghum flour is usually made into a porridge. In the southern Great Plains of the USA, a dwarf sorghum with compact heads is widely grown for livestock food.

sorrel Any of several low-growing perennial plants of the widespread genus *Rumex*. They are closely related to DOCKS and are members of the rhubarb family, Polygonaceae. The common European sorrel, *R. acetosa*, has arrow-shaped leaves which can be used as a green salad vegetable. A related species, *Oxyria digyna*, known as the mountain sorrel, belongs to the same family.

Sotho A subdivision of the Bantu people that includes tribes living chiefly in Botswana, Lesotho, and the Transvaal.

soul music A development of RHYTHM AND BLUES, dating from the late 1960s. Primarily the music of African American performers (white performers' versions being known as blue-eyed soul), it combines the driving rhythms of ROCK MUSIC with the emotional fervour of gospel songs and BLUES. The style is characterized by an impassioned improvisatory delivery by featured vocalists (for example, Aretha Franklin, Ray Charles, Otis Redding, James Brown), or saxophonists (for example, Grover Washington Jr.), and vocal devices, such as sudden shouts, sobs, and cries.

sound (or **acoustics**) Longitudinal pressure WAVES that travel through elastic media (gases, liquids, or solids). Sound waves are caused by a source vibrating to and fro and causing successive compressions and rarefactions in the medium; hence sound cannot travel in a vacuum. Sound waves are received by the ear and interpreted as a sensation by the brain. The frequencies of sonic waves detectable by humans fall within the range 15 hertz to 20,000 hertz. Some animals can detect sound at considerably higher frequencies. Simple sounds are characterized by simple waveforms, high and low PITCH of sound corresponding to high and low frequencies, whereas in speech and music there are complex waveforms containing a number of frequencies. In a musical note these frequencies are HARMONICS and bear a simple relation to one another. The ear is a sensitive organ and can detect intensities (measured in DECIBELS) varying by a factor of 10^{12} from the softest to the loudest sounds. It is pitch and loudness, rather than frequency and intensity, that are the sensations registered in the brain. The intensity (energy) of the lowest note on a piano must be a million times as great as that of middle C if it is to sound as loud to the ear.

The transmission of sound waves depends on the nature of the medium, which affects both the SPEED OF SOUND and the extent to which it is absorbed as it travels. Sound travels faster through liquids than through gases, and even faster through solids. Its speed also varies in proportion to temperature (sound travels faster through a hot medium than through a cold one) and pressure (at an altitude of 10,000 m, 32,800 feet, the speed of sound is about 13 per cent slower than at sea-level). The wavelength is equal to the speed divided by the frequency; doubling the frequency of a musical note (raising it an octave) requires that the length of the string or pipe producing it must be halved. Middle C (256 Hz) has a wavelength of 3.93 m (12.9 feet) in air. The conversion of sound waves into electrical impulses, and vice versa, is the basis of most SOUND RECORDING AND REPRODUCTION equipment, and of sound transmission by RADIO or TELEPHONY. See also SONAR; ECHO-SOUNDING.

sound barrier See SUPERSONIC FLIGHT.

sound recording and reproduction Sound recording techniques involve the transcription of audible air vibrations on to a storage medium, such as MAGNETIC TAPE; sound reproduction reverses the process, converting the stored information back to sound. Sound can be stored on mechanical (RECORDS), magnetic (tape), or optical (film sound-track, COMPACT DISC) media; associated equipment includes AMPLIFIERS, LOUDSPEAKERS, and MICROPHONES. The earliest sound-recording device was the mechanical (acoustic) GRAMOPHONE – electrical recording methods were not introduced until the 1920s. Optical sound reproduction was first used for film sound-tracks in 1923, using a process developed by DE FOREST. Early sound recordings were made with an acoustical horn, which concentrated sound on to a diaphragm connected to a cutting stylus. The stylus cut a groove – the variations of which corresponded to the vibrations of the diaphragm – in a wax master record. In 1924 an all-electric recording system was perfected by H. C. Harrison of the Western Electric Company, USA, in which MICROPHONES were used to collect the sound, and the resulting signal was amplified electrically before driving an electrical disc-cutting head. However, recording still had major limitations, notably the time limit of 4.5 minutes imposed by the 78 r.p.m. shellac record. The situation was improved by the introduction of the long-playing vinyl record in 1948, but the real breakthrough did not come until

1949, when TAPE RECORDERS were first used to make a master recording, from which discs could be cut later. Recordings of virtually any length could now be made, and the ease with which magnetic tape could be edited meant that restarts or retakes became possible. The advent of multi-track tapes meant that each instrument or sound could be recorded on its own track, and the relative levels of each track could be balanced electrically after recording. Many other innovations in recording have followed since the introduction of magnetic tape. Digital recording techniques (see DIGITIZATION) can produce recordings of extremely high fidelity, and provide more flexibility than analog techniques. For example, a poor recording can be digitally remastered and surface noise can be removed. Monophonic recordings can be split into two tracks to give STEREOPHONIC REPRODUCTION using digital techniques. In modern sound reproduction the sound is digitally encoded on COMPACT DISCS from which any part of the disc can be accessed accurately and almost instantly.

Soûr See TYRE.

soursop *Annona muricata*, a member of a family, Annonaceae, of small, tropical American trees that produce compound fruits with a custard-like flavour. The **sweetsop** or **custard-apple**, *A. reticulata*, belongs to the same genus. Pollination in all of them is carried out naturally by beetles, and ultimately large green, spiny fruits are produced. The flesh of the fruit ripens as a pulp and is eaten also by bats, squirrels, and monkeys. Soursop is cultivated for this fruit, but being very sensitive to cold, it succeeds only in the warmest climates.

Sousa, John Philip (1854–1932) US composer and conductor. He became director of the US Marine Band in 1880, and then formed his own band in 1892. His works include more than 100 marches, for example *The Stars and Stripes Forever*, *King Cotton*, and *Hands Across the Sea*. The **sousaphone** (see TUBA), invented in 1898, was named in his honour.

South Africa A country occupying most of the southern part of the African continent.

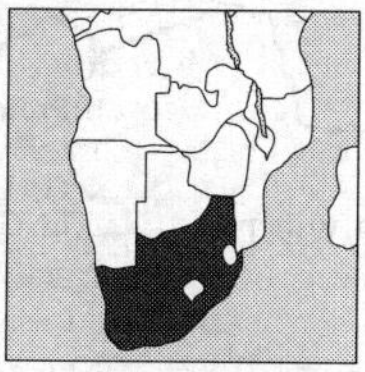

Physical. In the north the country is bounded by Namibia, Botswana, Zimbabwe, Mozambique, and Swaziland. Southward, the Orange Free State region partly surrounds Lesotho, which forms an enclave. In the east are boundaries with Mozambique, Swaziland, and Lesotho. From Cape Agulhas in the extreme south to the Limpopo River in the extreme north-east is a distance of about 1,600 km (1,000 miles). Two great rivers, the Orange and its tributary the Vaal, traverse the country from the Drakensberg Mountains in the east to the Atlantic in the west, while many shorter rivers run south and east into the Indian Ocean. There are rolling grasslands, or veld, and deserts. The climate varies widely, from warm dry summers in the south-west to hot wet ones on the eastern coast, and (according to altitude) to winter frosts on high ground in the north.

Economy. The country has a wealth of minerals, including diamonds, gold, platinum, iron ore, lime, uranium, and coal. There are also reserves of natural gas. Gold and other metal products are the chief exports. Industry is highly developed, and includes metal production, chemicals, engineering, and food-processing. Arms production is also important. Agriculture is vulnerable to droughts and inadequate irrigation; the main crops are cereals, sugar, and fruit, and livestock-raising is also important. International trade and sporting sanctions were imposed in protest against apartheid; sporting and EC sanctions were lifted in 1991 and 1992 respectively. World recession and low commodity prices have also had adverse effects. There is endemic poverty and high unemployment among black South Africans who, under the apartheid regime, were deprived of access to social services such as health care and education. The Southern African Customs Union links South Africa to Botswana, Lesotho, and Swaziland.

History. South Africa was occupied by the San (Bushmen) and Khoikhoin (Hottentots) about 10,000 years ago. BANTU-speaking peoples had moved into the area and developed mining industries, trading along the east coast of Africa, by the time European exploration began in the 15th century. A Dutch colony was established in 1652; the settlers were at first known as BOERS and later as AFRIKANERS. At first the San and Khoikhoin associated and intermarried with the Boers, but later the Khoikhoin were displaced by the Boers and forced to become labourers on their farms. The San withdrew into mountainous areas. Some Boers known as *trekboers*, moved inland and encountered the XHOSA people, who had a settled, agricultural society. By the end of the 18th century frontier wars had broken out between the Xhosa and the Boers.

Britain established a colony in 1806 and fought with the Bantu-speaking peoples. In the 1830s large numbers of Boers moved northwards in the GREAT TREK. The Boers refused to form a federation with the British, leading to the BOER WARS. The republics of TRANSVAAL and ORANGE FREE STATE were defeated by the British and were united with the British colonies of CAPE and NATAL in 1910 to form the Union of South Africa, a self-governing DOMINION of the British crown. Politically dominated by its small white minority, South Africa supported Britain in the two World Wars, its troops fighting on a number of fronts. After 1948 the right-wing Afrikaner-dominated National Party formed a government. It instituted a strict system of APARTHEID, intensifying discrimination against the disenfranchised non-white majority. This policy entailed brutal repression of dissent (see SHARPEVILLE MASSACRE).

South Africa became a republic (1960) and left the Commonwealth (1961); the AFRICAN NATIONAL CONGRESS was banned and its leaders, including Nelson MANDELA, imprisoned. Although its economic strength allowed it to dominate the southern half of the continent, the rise of black nationalism both at home and in the surrounding countries (including the former mandated territory of NAMIBIA) produced increasing violence and emphasized South Africa's isolation in the diplomatic world. In 1985 the regime of P. W. Botha began to make some attempts to ease tension by interpreting apartheid in a more liberal fashion. This failed, however, to satisfy either the increasingly militant non-white population or the extremist right-wing groups within the small white élite. In 1986 a state of emergency was proclaimed and several thousands imprisoned without trial. The domestic and international sides of the problem remained inseparable, with South African troops fighting against SWAPO guerrillas in Namibia and Angola, and support by surrounding states for the forces of the outlawed African National Congress producing a series of cross-border incidents. In 1988 the US Congress voted to support the 'Front Line' African states in their demand for international sanctions. President Botha retired in 1989 and his successor President DE KLERK began the quest for racial reconciliation. Following the repeal of apartheid legislation in July 1990 sanctions were eased and South Africa re-admitted to international sport. In December 1991 delegations from the government, the National Party, the Democratic Party, the South African Communist Party, ANC, Inkatha, and from the Indian and Coloured communities, joined to form the Convention for a Democratic South Africa (CODESA). Its deliberations through 1992 were interrupted by a number of violent racial incidents, and it was fiercely attacked by the neo-fascist Afrikaner Resistance Movement. The government was replaced in 1993 by a multi-party Transitional Executive Council. The country's first multi-racial elections were held in 1994, with the ANC emerging as clear victors. Nelson Mandela became President and de Klerk Deputy President, leading a coalition government of national unity. The same year, South Africa was admitted to the ORGANIZATION OF AFRICAN UNITY and rejoined the Commonwealth. In 1996 a permanent multi-racial democratic constitution was adopted. De Klerk and the National Party withdrew from the coalition government in order to form the official opposition.

Capital: Pretoria (executive) Bloemfontein (judicial) Cape Town (legislative)
Area: 1,123,226 sq km (433,680 sq mi)
Population: 41,465,000 (1995)
Currency: 1 rand = 100 cents
Religions: Christian 59.0%; Bantu Churches 17.0%; Hindu 2.0%; Muslim 1.0%; Jewish 1.0%
Ethnic Groups: Zulu 23.8%; White 18.0%; Coloured 10.5%; North Sotho 9.8%; Xhosa 9.7%; South Sotho 7.3%; Tswana 5.7%; Asian 3.3%
Languages: Afrikaans; English; Zulu; Sotho; Xhosa; Ndebele; Pedi; Swazi; Tsonga; Tswana; Venda (all official)
International Organizations: UN; OAU; Commonwealth; SADC

South America The southern half of the American land mass, connected to North America by the Isthmus of Panama, bordered by the Atlantic Ocean to the east and the Pacific Ocean to the west; area 17,800,000 sq km (6,900,000 sq miles); pop. (est. 1990) 296,716,000. The fourth largest of the continents and occupying 13 per cent of the world's land surface, South America can be divided into six physiographic regions, (1) the Andes, a series of mountain ranges that stretch the entire length of the west coast from Colombia to the tip of Chile; (2) the Guiana and Brazilian Highlands, the uplifted remains of an earlier continental mass; (3) the Orinoco Basin, a lowland region between the Venezuelan Andes and the Guiana Highlands; (4) the Amazon basin, which stretches from the eastern foothills of the Andes to the Atlantic Ocean; (5) the Pampa-Chaco plain of Argentina, Paraguay, and Bolivia; (6) the Patagonian plateau, a series of rugged terraces that rise up from the Atlantic towards the southern Andes. South America's largest cities are Buenos Aires, São Paulo, Rio de Janeiro, Bogotá, Santiago, Lima, and Caracas. Colonized largely by the Spanish in the 16th century (although the British, Dutch, and Portuguese were particularly active in the north-east), much of the

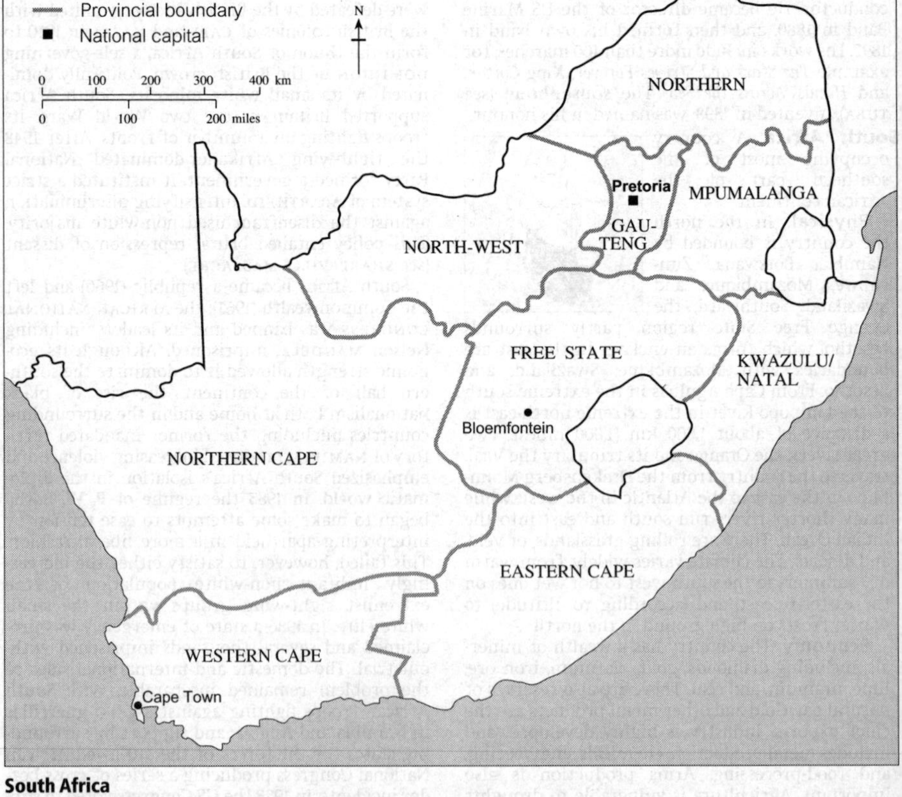

South Africa

continent remained part of Spain's overseas empire until liberated under the leadership of Bolivar and San Martin in the 1820s. Both culturally and ethnically the continent is now a mixture of indigenous Indian and imported Hispanic influences, modified slightly by North European and North American penetration in the 19th and 20th centuries. Although many South American countries are still hampered by economic underdevelopment and political instability, a minority have emerged as world industrial powers in their own right.

South American Indian art The art and architecture of the native inhabitants of South America, particularly in the period before the Spanish conquest in the 16th century, often known as **Pre-Columbian art**. In artistic terms the vast area of South America divides into two fairly clear zones: firstly, the central Andean and adjacent Pacific coastal area, which is now mainly within the modern state of Peru; secondly, all the other areas. These include the northern Andean civilizations of Colombia, such as the Tairona, Quimbaya, and Muisca, all known for the remarkable metalworking techniques, particularly in goldwork. The Andean civilization is associated above all with the Incas, who, by the 15th century, had established a far-flung empire linked by a road system that was superior even to that of the Romans. There were settled communities before 2000 BC, but the earliest distinct Andean culture, called Chavín, flourished from about 900 BC to about 200 BC. It is named after the great ruin of Chavín de Huántar in the north-eastern highlands of Peru, which includes a

South America The political boundaries within the continent.

large temple complex built with well-cut stone blocks and decorated with relief carvings. The Chavín people also produced pottery, goldwork, and textiles. Probably the most remarkable textiles were those made in the Paracas culture, named after the Paracas Peninsula, about 161 km (100 miles) south of Lima. This culture, which began at about the same time as the Chavín culture and lasted until about 400 AD, is divided into two main phases: Paracas Cavernas, so-called because the dead were buried in caverns; and the later Paracas Necropolis, when the dead were buried in cemeteries. In the Paracas Necropolis culture corpses were wrapped in sumptuous burial cloths, many of which have survived in good condition in the dry soil.

Of the other Andean cultures that flourished before the Incas the best known are the Mochica and the Chimú. The Mochica culture, which flourished from about 200 BC to about 600 AD, is named after the great archaeological site at Moche on the coast of northern Peru. This includes the remains of the 'Pyramid of the Sun', the largest ancient building in South America. Their pottery, especially their jugs in the form of realistic portraits of heads, mark the high point of Pre-Columbian ceramics. Until it was absorbed by the Incas in 1470, the Chimú culture dominated northern Peru. Their capital, Chan Chan, was built of mud-brick buildings in a well-planned layout. The Chimú also excelled in gold and silver metalwork.

The Incas have much in common with the Aztecs of Mexico: they emerged at about the same time, quickly established a mighty empire, and then totally succumbed to the Spanish *conquistadores*. Much more is known about the Incas than about any of the earlier cultures of South America, for although they had no system of writing (the Maya were the only Pre-Columbian people who had), a great deal of their oral tradition was recorded by contemporary Spanish chroniclers. 'Inca' means 'king' or 'prince', and the Incas saw their history in terms of the succession of rulers from the foundation of a dynasty in about 1200. Their great period lasted only about a century, from *c*.1438, when Pachacutec (or Pachacuti) became ruler, until 1532, when Francisco Pizarro landed and assumed power virtually unopposed. The Inca state was highly regimented, and the Incas were among the greatest builders in history, their achievements being all the more remarkable for having been achieved without the knowledge of the wheel. Many of their great walls are still visible in the city of Cuzco (formerly the Inca capital), where they have often been used as the foundations for later buildings. The most famous Inca site, however, is MACHU PICCHU, set in remote mountains about 80 km (50 miles) north-west of Cuzco.

Southampton An industrial city, seaport, and resort on the south coast of England, situated on a peninsula between the estuaries of the Rivers Test and Itchen in Hampshire; pop. (1991) 194,400. It is a major UK port with container traffic, ferry links to the Isle of Wight and the Continent, and oil refineries. It is the site of the University of Southampton (1952).

South Australia A state comprising the central-southern part of Australia; area 984,000 sq km (380,069 sq miles); pop. (1991) 1,454,000; capital, Adelaide. In 1836 it was constituted as a hybrid of a Crown colony and chartered colony, to which no convicts were to be sent. After financial collapse it lost its semi-independent status and became a regular Crown colony in 1841. It was federated with the other states of Australia in 1901. It has a large area of irrigated farmland producing grain, vegetables, tobacco, wine, and livestock. Leading industrial products include wood products, paper, processed food, textiles, chemicals, and metal goods.

South Carolina A state of the USA on the Atlantic coast between North Carolina and Georgia; area 80,582 sq km (31,113 sq miles); pop. (1990) 3,486,700; capital, Columbia. Its largest cities are Columbia, Charleston, North Charleston, and Greenville. South Carolina is also known as the Palmetto State. Its industries produce textiles, chemicals, asbestos, wood pulp, and steel products, and agricultural crops include peaches, tobacco, cotton, and peanuts. Settled by the Spanish and English in the 16th–17th centuries and named after Charles I, it became one of the original 13 states of the USA in 1789. Its chief landmarks are the Fort Sumter and Conagree Swamp National Monuments, the Charles Pinckney and Ninety Six National Historic Sites, Cowpens National Battlefield, and Kings Mountain National Military Park.

South China Sea See CHINA SEA.

South Dakota A state in the north-central USA, bounded by North Dakota, Minnesota, Nebraska, Iowa, Wyoming, and Montana; area 199,730 sq km (77,355 sq miles); pop. (1990) 696,000; capital, Pierre. The largest city is Sioux Falls. South Dakota is also known as the Coyote or Sunshine State. Once dominated by Sioux Indians, it was acquired partly by the Louisiana Purchase in 1803. Organized as a territory in 1861 and settled a year latter by those who took up the offer of free land under the Homestead Act, it was the scene of a gold-rush in 1874 and joined the Union as the 40th state in 1889. South Dakota is a leading producer of agricultural crops such as grain, sunflower seed, and livestock, and minerals such as gold, silver, beryllium, uranium, and bentonite. Its principal features are the Missouri River, the Badlands, and the Black Hills which are the highest hills east of the Rockies and include Mt Rushmore, Jewel Cave National Monument, and Wind Cave National Park.

South-East Asia Treaty Organization (SEATO) A defence alliance established in 1954 for countries of south-east Asia and part of the south-west Pacific, to further a US policy of containment of Communism. Its members were Australia, Britain, France, New Zealand, Pakistan, the Philippines, Thailand, and the US. The organization was dissolved in 1977.

Southern African Development Community (SADC) An organization of southern African countries whose principal goals are to promote regional integration and encourage economic develoment. The SADC was formed in 1992, in the light of political changes in South Africa, as a successor to the **Southern African Development Co-ordination Conference** (SADCC).

In 1992 moves towards ending apartheid had been made in South Africa and the members of the SADCC decided to replace the organization with the SADC, concentrating on promoting economic and social progress in the region. In 1994 South Africa had abolished apartheid and was admitted to the SADC. In 1995 Mauritius joined and plans to create a regional free-trade zone were announced.

Southern Cross See CRUX.

Southern Crown See CORONA AUSTRALIS.

Southern Fish See PISCIS AUSTRINUS.

Southern Ocean The body of water surrounding

the continent of Antarctica, comprising the southern part of the three oceans: the Pacific, the Atlantic and the Indian. It lies south of the ROARING FORTIES but is nevertheless the world's stormiest ocean. A cold and dense water mass (Antarctic Bottom Water) forms around the continent, particularly over the CONTINENTAL SHELF of the Weddell Sea. In summer many icebergs break off from the continental ice sheet, and float north to latitude 55° S and even further. The main resource at present is an abundant supply of krill (planktonic crustaceans), which is being increasingly harvested.

Southern Rhodesia See ZIMBABWE.

Southern Triangle See TRIANGULUM AUSTRALE.

Southey, Robert (1774–1843) British poet. Associated with the Lake Poets, he wrote a number of long narrative poems including *Madoc* (1805), but is best known for his shorter poems, such as the antimilitarist ballad the 'Battle of Blenheim' (1798), and for his biography the *Life of Nelson* (1813). Southey was made Poet Laureate in 1813.

South Georgia A sub-Antarctic, mountainous island under British administration, approximately 1,300 km (800 miles) east of the Falkland Islands in the South Atlantic Ocean. It is 4,100 sq km (1,600 sq mi) in area and rises to 2,915 m (9,564 feet) at Mount Paget. The island comprises Palaeozoic and Mesozoic sedimentary rocks and is part of the Scotia Ridge.

South Glamorgan A former county of south Wales on the Bristol Channel, bounded by Mid Glamorgan to the north and west and Gwent to the east. It was created in 1974 and in 1996 was replaced by the county of Cardiff and the county borough of Vale of Glamorgan.

South Island The larger of the two principal islands of New Zealand, separated from North Island by the Cook Strait; area 151,215 sq km (58,406 sq miles); pop. (1991) 881,540 (25 per cent of the total population of New Zealand). Its chief urban areas are Christchurch, Dunedin, and Invercargill. Dominated by the Southern Alps, which extend the entire length of the island and are flanked to the east by the fertile Canterbury Plains, South Island's chief products are grain, sheep, fruit, and timber.

South Korea See KOREA, SOUTH.

South Orkney Islands A group of uninhabited islands in the South Atlantic, lying to the north-east of the Antarctic Peninsula and including the islands of Coronation, Inaccessible, Laurie, and Signy. Discovered by Captain G. Powell in 1821, they are now administered as part of the British Antarctic Territory; area 620 sq km (240 sq miles).

South Pole A geographical site at 90° S, longitude 0°, the southern end of the Earth's axis, where six months of daylight follow six months of darkness. Situated in central ANTARCTICA where the ice-cap is 2,722 m (8,930 feet) thick, the pole is altogether 2,922 m (9,816 feet) above sea-level. At this height no free water is to be seen. It never rains, and even in summer a thermometer stuck 15 m (50 feet) into the snow will register −50°C (−58°F). It does not coincide with the south magnetic pole, which occurs 1,600 km (1,000 miles) distant, near the edge of the continent in Adélie Land.

South Sandwich Islands A group of small islands in the South Atlantic Ocean, under British administration, lying north of the Weddell Sea and 760 km (470 miles) south-east of South Georgia. They are part of the Scotia Ridge. As a consequence they possess some active volcanic cones, and the ocean floor descends steeply eastward to a deep trench.

South Saskatchewan See SASKATCHEWAN.

South Sea Bubble An English financial disaster in which the South Sea Company took over most of the National Debt in 1720 and needed a rise in the value of the shares of the Company. This was achieved not by past trading profits, but by rumours of future ones. Some politicians and even members of the court were bribed with cheap or free South Sea Company shares to promote the company's interests. The shares increased ten-fold in value, and expectations of high dividends rose accordingly. When confidence collapsed, the South Sea Company's shares fell to less than 10 per cent of their peak value, and thousands of investors were ruined. Sir Robert WALPOLE began his long period of office by saving the company and restoring financial stability, and managed to limit the political damage to two of George I's ministers who had been implicated in the scandal.

South Shetland Islands A group of uninhabited islands in the South Atlantic, lying immediately north of the Antarctic Peninsula. Discovered in 1819 by Captain W. Smith, they are now administered as part of the British Antarctic Territory.

South Uist See UIST.

South Vietnam See VIETNAM.

South-West Africa See NAMIBIA.

South West Africa People's Organization See SWAPO.

South Yemen A former country on the south-west Arabian peninsula. It declared its independence in 1967 and, after long negotiations, amalgamated in 1989 with the Yemen Arab Republic to form YEMEN.

South Yorkshire A metropolitan county of northern England created in 1974; area 1,560 sq km (602 sq miles); pop. (1991) 1,249,300. It comprises four districts.

Soutine, Chaïm (1893–1943) French painter, born in Lithuania. After emigrating to Paris in 1913, he was closely associated with a group of painters that included Chagall and Modigliani. A major exponent of expressionism, Soutine evolved a style distinguished by bright colours, vigorous brushstrokes, and impasto, imbued with a feverish emotional content. During the 1920s he produced pictures of grotesque figures, with twisted faces and deformed bodies. From 1925 he increasingly painted still lifes, including plucked fowl and flayed carcasses.

sovereignty Supreme and independent authority over a given territory. Sovereignty is usually vested in the people of the territory, who delegate it to the government administering the state on their behalf. Internally, sovereignty implies a legitimate source of rule within society, above which there is no higher authority. This can in practice diverge from and conflict with the actual power of a ruling élite. A stable and legitimate system of government requires both the right to control a society and the means for doing so. Externally, the claim to sovereign control of a given territory is normally recognized by other sovereign states either *de facto* (because it exists in fact) or *de jure* (by right). In practice, INTERNATIONAL LAW imposes restrictions upon the sovereign power of states, which are not allowed to act simply as they please within their territory.

Soviet Union (official name **Union of Soviet Socialist Republics**) A former federation of 15 republics occupying the northern half of Asia and part of Eastern Europe, comprising Russia, Belorussia (Belarus), Ukraine, the Baltic States (Estonia, Latvia, and Lithuania), Georgia, Armenia, Moldova (Moldavia), Azerbaijan, Kazakhstan, Kirghizia, Turkmenistan, Tajikistan, and Uzbekistan; area 22,402,076 sq km (865,279 sq miles); capital, Moscow. Created as a Communist state after the 1917 revolution, the Soviet Union was the largest country in the world. Its agricultural and industrial production were increased, often by brutal means, until the devastation caused by World War II. In the post-war era it emerged as one of the two antagonistic superpowers, rivalling the USA, in the polarization of the Communist and non-Communist worlds. Attempts to reform its centrally planned economy during the 1980s led to a rise in nationalist feeling and unrest in the republics, some of which began to seceded from the Union which was finally dissolved in 1991.

sow bug See WOODLOUSE.

Soweto A predominantly black urban area, southwest of Johannesburg in South Africa; pop. (1991) 596,600. In January 1976 black schoolchildren demonstrated against legislation proposing to make Afrikaans the compulsory language of instruction, and police broke up the demonstration, using guns and tear gas. This triggered off a wave of violence; by the end of 1976 some 500 Blacks and Coloureds, many of them children, had been killed by the police. The plans for compulsory teaching in Afrikaans were dropped. Thereafter, until the multi-racial elections of 1994 that ended white minority rule, the anniversary of the demonstration was marked by further unrest.

soya bean An annual LEGUME, *Glycine max*, native to southwest Asia, and the most important food legume in China, Korea, Japan, and Malaysia. The soya bean was first grown commercially in the USA in 1924, and North America now produces 40 per cent or more of the world's output. Because of its long history of cultivation, thousands of varieties are now known, each adapted to a different use. It is one of many beans used in Chinese cookery, either fresh, as whole beans, or fermented to give soy sauce. The dried seeds can be ground into protein-rich flour, useful as an ingredient of ice cream or mixed with wheat flour for baking. The seeds contain up to 50 per cent protein and 25 per cent oil. This oil is used for margarine and cooking oils. The protein-rich residue, left after oil extraction, is an invaluable source of vegetable protein, used mainly as a livestock feed, but increasingly incorporated into human diets as a replacement for animal protein.

Soyinka, Wole (1934–) Nigerian dramatist, novelist, and critic. He made his name in 1959 with the play *The Lion and the Jewel*. His writing often uses satire and humour to explore the contrast between traditional and modern society in Africa, and combines elements of both African and European aesthetics. His works include the novel *The Interpreters* (1965) the play *Kongi's Harvest* (1964), and the collection of poems and other writings *The Man Died* (1972), a record of his time spent serving a sentence as a political prisoner 1967–69. In 1986 Soyinka became the first African to receive the Nobel Prize for literature.

Spaak, Paul-Henri (1899–1972) Belgian statesman. Entering Parliament as a socialist in 1932, he was Prime Minister 1938–39 and 1947–49, and became the first President of the UNITED NATIONS General Assembly and of the consultative assembly of the COUNCIL OF EUROPE (1949–51). A firm supporter of a united Europe, he put forward proposals that formed the basis of the EUROPEAN ECONOMIC COMMUNITY.

space The three-dimensional extent of the physical Universe. For scientific purposes this volume of the Universe is associated with the fourth dimension of time, making up a four-dimensional SPACE-TIME.

Space also refers to any region of the Universe that is empty of matter, such as interplanetary space, interstellar space, or intergalactic space. These regions, however, contain dust and gas, though in very small densities.

In recent times, mathematicians have represented space not as a container in the Euclidean manner, but as a finite sphere, our conceptions of which depend upon choosing one geometry in which to interpret our observation. These views culminated in the work of Albert EINSTEIN, who showed that space–time has its own geometry, which he incorporated into his general theory of RELATIVITY.

space exploration In 1903 the Russian physicist Konstantin Tsiolkovsky was developing ideas for space rockets fuelled by liquefied gas and by 1926 Robert Goddard in the USA had successfully designed the first liquid-fuelled rocket. There followed considerable German research into rockets, culminating in the launch of the V-2 rocket in 1944. In 1957 the Soviet Union surprised the USA by putting the first artificial satellite, Sputnik I, in orbit; this was followed by the US Explorer I in 1958. Yuri Gagarin was the first man in space in 1961, followed by John Glenn in 1962. In 1961 President KENNEDY proposed the APOLLO PROGRAMME to achieve a manned lunar landing by 1970, and in 1969 Neil Armstrong and Edwin ('Buzz') Aldrin landed on the Moon. The Soviet Union concentrated on unmanned flights, Luna IX achieving a soft landing on the Moon in 1966. In the early 1970s space stations were launched by both the USA and the Soviet Union, and in 1975 an Apollo capsule linked up with a Soviet Soyuz capsule. Unmanned flights have been made to Venus and Mars, while the US probe, VOYAGER 2, launched in 1977, reached Neptune in 1989. In 1981 the USA launched a space shuttle, the first reusable space craft, but its commercial and scientific programme was interrupted for two years by the explosion of the shuttle, *Challenger*, on lift-off in 1986. In 1986 the giant Soviet modular space station, MIR, was launched, with astronauts being ferried to the station by Soyuz spacecraft, followed in 1987 by the placing in space of the powerful Energiya station. The Hubble space telescope, which can produce images of other solar systems, was launched from a US shuttle in 1990. Its faulty mirror limited observations until it was repaired by astronauts in the space shuttle *Endeavour* in 1993. An international space station, Freedom, conceived by the USA in 1984, was due to become operational in the late 1990s. Space technology has resulted in numerous applications, and telecommunication satellites have greatly improved global COMMUNICATIONS; while meteorological satellites provide advance weather information, and reconnaissance satellites register the Earth's resources and military information.

space-flight, principles of The theoretical and practical aspects of manned space programmes or robot travel beyond the Earth's atmosphere. The atmosphere extends to a height of 320 km (200 miles): for a spacecraft to travel beyond this and achieve an orbit (a condition in which the craft's forward momentum balances gravitational attraction, and it circles the Earth), it must attain a veloc-

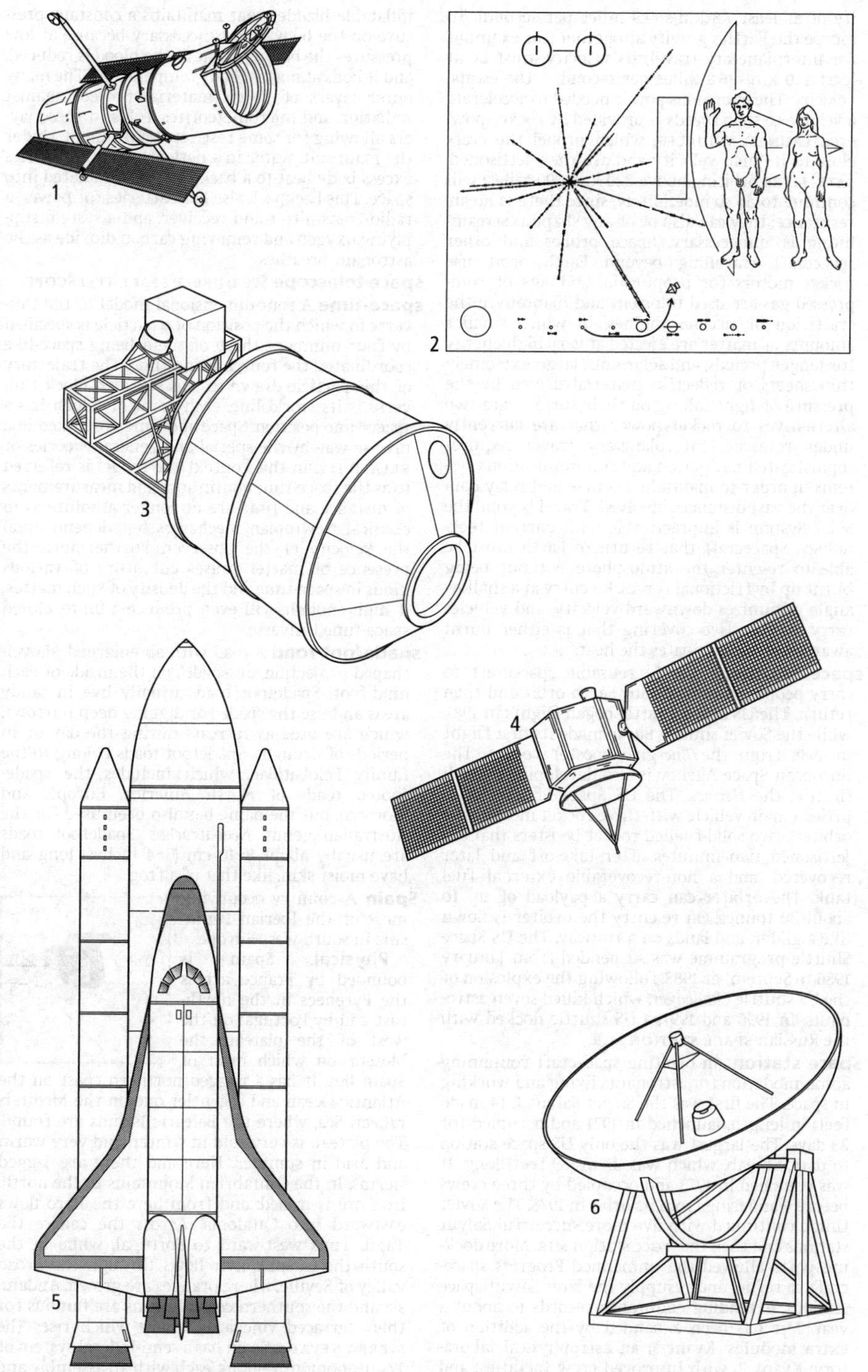

Space exploration (1) The Hubble Space Telescope, launched in 1990. (2) Panels fixed to Pioneer 10 and 11 space probes to identify the Earth and its inhabitants to any extraterrestrial intelligent beings who may find them. (3) Spacelab 3, a manned space laboratory for studying conditions of near weightlessness, was launched in 1985. (4) Communications satellite showing solar panels for collecting solar energy by means of arrays of solar cells. (5) The US space shuttle, which became operational in 1981. The orbiting vehicle can carry a payload of 30 tonnes, and on re-entry glides back to land on a runway. (6) Dish-aerial space telescope, used as a ground receiving station in communicating with spacecraft.

ity of at least 7.8 km/s (4.9 miles per second). To escape the Earth's gravity altogether (for example, for interplanetary travel) its velocity must be at least 11.0 km/s (6.8 miles per second) – the escape velocity. The enormous power needed to accelerate a vehicle to such speeds is provided by rocket-powered LAUNCH VEHICLES, which propel the craft close to its final velocity and are then jettisoned. SATELLITES orbiting above 320 km (200 miles) will continue to do so indefinitely, since there is no air resistance; they can also be of any shape as streamlining is unnecessary. Space probes and other spacecraft travelling beyond Earth orbit use rocket motors for propulsion, and jets of compressed gas are used to orient and manœuvre the craft. Ion or plasma engines, in which smaller amounts of matter are ejected at very high energy for longer periods, and solar sails, large, extremely thin sheets of reflective material driven by the pressure of light falling on their surface, are two alternatives to rocket power that are currently under research. Interplanetary travel requires sophisticated navigation and communications systems in order to maintain a course and relay data over the vast distances involved. Travel beyond the Solar System is impracticable with current technology. Spacecraft that return to Earth must be able to re-enter the atmosphere without being burnt up by frictional forces. Re-entry at a shallow angle minimizes downward velocity, and vehicles carry a protective covering that is either burnt away slowly or dissipates the heat.

space shuttle A partly reusable spacecraft to carry people and cargo into Earth orbit and then return. The US Space Shuttle began flights in 1981, while the Soviet shuttle *Buran* made its first flight in 1988 from the *Energiya* booster rocket. The European Space Agency is also developing a small shuttle, the *Hermes*. The US Space Shuttle comprises a main vehicle with three rocket motors (the orbiter), two solid-fuelled rocket boosters that are jettisoned two minutes after take-off and later recovered, and a non-recoverable external fuel tank. The orbiter can carry a payload of up to about 30 tonnes. On re-entry the orbiter is flown like a glider, and lands on a runway. The US Space Shuttle programme was suspended from January 1986 to September 1988, following the explosion of the US shuttle *Challenger*, which killed seven astronauts. In 1996 and 1997, a US shuttle docked with the Russian SPACE STATION MIR.

space station An orbiting spacecraft containing accommodation for astronauts living and working in space. The first was the Soviet Salyut 1, 14 m (46 feet) in length, launched in 1971 and occupied for 23 days. The largest was the only US space station to date, Skylab, which was 27 m (89 feet) long. It was launched in 1973 and occupied by three crews before wandering from its orbit in 1978. The Soviet Union continued with five more successful Salyut stations and then the space station MIR. More docking ports allowed the unmanned Progress spacecraft to refuel and resupply the later Salyut space stations, extending endurance records to about a year. Mir has been expanded by the addition of extra modules: Kvant 1, an astrophysical laboratory; Kvant 2, with improved crew facilities; and Kristall, designed for producing semiconducting materials in space. Space stations open up new areas of study in astronomy and Earth resources, and the weightless conditions facilitate processing of crystals, alloys, and pure drugs.

spacesuit A sealed suit that enables an astronaut to survive in space. The inner layer of the suit is an inflatable bladder that maintains a constant pressure on the body: this is necessary because at low pressures the boiling-point of the blood is reduced, and it boils at normal body temperature. The many outer layers of tough material protect against radiation and micrometeorites, folds in these layers allowing for some restricted movement. Under the main suit, water in a network of tubes carries excess body heat to a backpack to be radiated into space. This backpack also has batteries for power, a radio transmitter and receiver, and a system supplying oxygen and removing carbon dioxide as the astronaut breathes.

space telescope See HUBBLE SPACE TELESCOPE.

space-time A four-dimensional model of the Universe in which the position of a particle is specified by four numbers, three of them being space-like coordinates, the fourth being time. The trajectory of this particle drawn in this so-called block Universe is its world line, each point of which has a space-time position. Space and time are linked in a precise way by the special and general theories of RELATIVITY; in this context the model is referred to as the space-time continuum and measurements of distance and time are no longer absolute as in classical Newtonian mechanics but depend upon the velocity of the observer. Furthermore, the presence of matter causes curvature of various kinds in space-time and the density of such matter, if high enough, will even produce a finite, closed space-time Universe.

spadefoot toad A toad with an enlarged, shovel-shaped projection, or 'spade', on the inside of each hind-foot. Spadefoot toads usually live in sandy areas and use the spade for digging deep burrows, which are used as retreats during the day or in periods of drought. Spadefoot toads belong to the family Pelobatidae, which includes the spade-footed toads of North America, Europe, and Morocco, but the name has also been used for the Australian genus, *Neobatrachus*. Spadefoot toads are usually about 8–10 cm (3–4 inches) long and have moist skin, like that of a frog.

Spain A country occupying most of the Iberian Peninsula in south-west Europe.

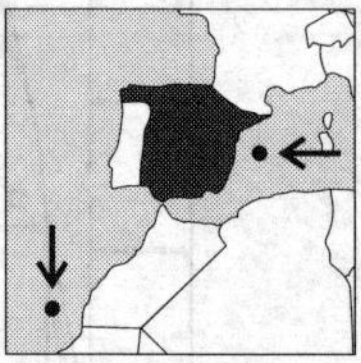

Physical. Spain is bounded by France across the Pyrenees in the north-east and by Portugal on the west of the plateau, the Meseta, on which most of Spain lies. It has a rugged northern coast on the Atlantic Ocean and a gentler one on the Mediterranean Sea, where the Balearic Islands are found. The plateau is very cold in winter, and very warm and arid in summer. Here and there are jagged sierras. In the Cantabrian Mountains to the north, iron ore is mined; and from here the Ebro flows eastward into Catalonia. Across the centre the Tagus runs west-ward to Portugal, while in the south the Guadalquivir flows through the broad valley of Seville, where oranges are grown. Andalusia and the southern coastal plains are famous for their terraced vineyards, above which rises the SIERRA NEVADA. Spain has a semi-federal system of 17 autonomous regions, each with an assembly and government. In the Basque and Catalan regions local nationalist parties have formed governments, but there are continuing internal tensions caused by demands for greater autonomy. Spanish territory includes Ceuta, Melilla, Alhucemas, Chafarinas, and Peŋtild.ón de Vélez in North Africa, which are the subject of territorial disputes with

Morocco, and the Canary and Balearic Islands. The sovereignty of GIBRALTAR is disputed with the UK.

Economy. Spain has a broadly based manufacturing sector, which has experienced rapid growth in recent years. Tourism makes a substantial contribution to the economy. Exports include motor vehicles, iron and steel, zinc, petroleum products, and chemicals. Agriculture remains important and concentrates on grains, tomatoes, citrus, and livestock-raising. Mineral resources include iron ore, zinc, and lead. Spain has had a consistently high level of unemployment and a weak system of social security.

History. Spain has been inhabited for at least 20,000 years, and supported at least two early cultures. Celtic peoples began to migrate into Spain during the 9th century BC. Spain began to come under Roman control after 206 BC, after a period of Carthaginian domination. Roman rule was followed, after 415 AD, by that of the VISIGOTHS, who were themselves toppled by Muslim invaders from Morocco (711–18). Moorish Spain reached its zenith under the UMAYYAD dynasty of al-Andalus (736–1031). During the subsequent political fragmentation, Christian kingdoms became consolidated where Muslim power was weakest, in the north: ARAGON and CASTILE were the most significant of these. By 1248 Christian reconquest had been so successful that only GRANADA remained in Muslim hands. FERDINAND II of Aragon and ISABELLA I of Castile united their respective kingdoms in 1479, reconquered Granada in 1492, and went on to establish unified Spain as a power of European and world significance. (See SPANISH NETHERLANDS.) Under their rule the vast SPANISH EMPIRE overseas began to take shape, and under their 16th-century successors, CHARLES V and PHILIP II, Spain enjoyed its 'golden age'. Decline set in during the 17th century, the end of Habsburg rule came in 1700 when Philip V became the first Bourbon monarch. The accession of Philip V led to the War of the SPANISH SUCCESSION (1701–14), in which Spain lost many of its lands in Europe.

In the early 19th century Spain suffered as a result of the NAPOLEONIC WARS and briefly came under French control (1808–14). This defeat encouraged revolution in South America, resulting in the SPANISH–SOUTH AMERICAN WARS OF INDEPENDENCE, which led to the emergence as independent countries of Argentina, Bolivia, Peru, Venezuela, and Mexico. Spain subsequently remained peripheral and undeveloped in a Europe which was fast becoming industrialized. From 1814 the absolutist monarchy was involved in a struggle with the forces of liberalism, and from 1873 to 1875 there was a brief republican interlude. In 1898 the Spanish–American War resulted in the loss of Puerto Rico, the Philippines, and Guam, while Cuba, which had been more or less in revolt since 1868, became a US protectorate in 1903. In 1923 General Miguel PRIMO DE RIVERA established a virtual dictatorship, which was followed by another republican interlude (1931–39), scarred by the savage SPANISH CIVIL WAR (1936–39). Nationalist victory resulted in the dictatorship of General Francisco FRANCO (1939–75). His gradual liberalization of government during the late 1960s was continued by his successor Juan Carlos I, who established a democratic constitutional monarchy. Separatist agitation, often violent, by ETA, an organization seeking independence for the Basque provinces, continued throughout the period. Of its remaining colonies Spain granted independence to Spanish Sahara in 1976, which was divided between Morocco and Mauritania. King Juan survived attempted military coups in 1978 and 1981, and

Spain

from 1982 a series of stable, left-of-centre governments were established under Prime Minister Felipe González. Spain joined the EC in 1986. Pressure for greater Catalan autonomy continued. González was defeated in elections in 1996 but the winning right-wing Popular Party gained no overall majority and formed a coalition government, led by José María Aznar.

Capital: Madrid
Area: 504,750 sq km (194,885 sq mi)
Population: 39,188,000 (1995)
Currency: 1 peseta = 100 céntimos
Religions: Roman Catholic 97.0%
Ethnic Groups: Spanish 73.0%; Catalan 16.0%; Galician 8.0%; Basque 2.0%
Languages: Spanish (Castilian) (official); Catalan; Galician; Basque
International Organizations: UN; EU; NATO; OECD; Council of Europe; CSCE

Spallanzani, Lazzaro (1729–99) Italian physiologist and biologist. A priest as well as a keen traveller and collector, he is known for his experiments on a wide variety of subjects. He explained the circulation of the blood and the digestive system of animals, showed that fertilization can result only from contact between egg and seminal fluid, demonstrated that protozoa do not appear as a result of spontaneous generation, and studied regeneration in invertebrates. Spallanzani also worked on various problems in the physical and Earth sciences.

spaniel See DOG.

Spanish The language of Spain and Spanish America, the most widely spoken of the Romance languages, with many Arabic words dating from the time when the Moors dominated Spain (8th–15th centuries); there are in all about 250 million speakers. It is the official language of Spain, Mexico, and every Central and South American republic except Brazil, Guyana, Surinam, and Belize, and is widely spoken in the islands of the Greater Antilles, the southern states of the USA, and, decreasingly, in the Philippines. In sound it is very like Italian, with a strong 'r' sound and with many masculine words ending in -o and feminine words in -a; the ñ sound is characteristic. A variety of Spanish known as Ladino is spoken in Turkey and Israel by descendants of Jews expelled from Spain in 1492.

Spanish Armada A large naval and military force that PHILIP II of Spain sent to invade England at the end of May 1588. It consisted of 130 ships, carrying about 8,000 sailors and 19,000 infantrymen, under the command of the inexperienced Duke of Medina Sidonia. The Spanish fleet was delayed by a storm off Corunna, and was first sighted by the English naval commanders on 19 July, then harassed by them with long-range guns, until it anchored off Calais. Unable to liaise with an additional force from the Low Countries led by FARNESE, its formation was wrecked by English fireships during the night and as it tried to escape it suffered a further pounding from the English fleet before a strong wind drove the remaining vessels into the North Sea and they were forced to make their way back to Spain round the north of Scotland and the west of Ireland. Barely half the original Armada returned to port.

Spanish Civil War (1936–39) A military struggle between left- and right-wing elements in Spain. After the fall of PRIMO DE RIVERA in 1930 and the eclipse of the Spanish monarchy in 1931, Spain was split. On the one hand were such politically powerful groups as the monarchists and the FALANGE, on the other were the Republicans, the Catalan and Basque separatists, socialists, communists, and anarchists. The elections of February 1936 gave power to a left-wing POPULAR FRONT government, causing strikes, riots, and military plots. In July 1936 the generals José Sanjurjo and Francisco FRANCO in Spanish Morocco led an unsuccessful coup against the republic, and civil war began. In 1937 Franco's Nationalists overran the Basque region, which supported the Republicans in the hope of ultimate independence. Franco then divided the Republican forces by conquering territory between Barcelona and Valencia (1938). The Republicans, weakened by internal intrigues and by the withdrawal of Soviet support, attempted a desperate counter-attack. It failed, and Barcelona fell to Franco (January 1939), quickly followed by Madrid. Franco became the head of the Spanish state and the Falange was made the sole legal party. The civil war inspired international support on both sides: the Soviet Union gave military supplies to the Republicans, while Italy and Germany supplied men to the Nationalists. Bombing of civilians by German pilots and the destruction of the Basque town of Guernica (1937) became the symbol of fascist ruthlessness and inspired one of Picasso's most famous paintings. As members of the INTERNATIONAL BRIGADES, left-wing and communist volunteers from many countries fought for the Republican cause. The war cost about 750,000 Spanish lives.

Spanish empire The overseas territories which came under Spanish control from the late 15th century onwards. They included the Canaries, most of the West Indian islands, the whole of central America, large stretches of South America, and the Philippines. Christopher COLUMBUS laid the foundations of the empire with his four voyages (1492–1504) in search of a western route to the Orient. Then the CONQUISTADORES followed, colonizing by force in MEXICO, PERU, and elsewhere in the New World. As the wealth of these lands became apparent, private enterprise gradually gave way to direct rule by Spain. The gold and silver from the New World made 16th-century Spain the richest country in Europe, under Emperor Charles V. The colonies themselves were eventually divided into viceroyalties: New Spain (1535), PERU (1569), NEW GRANADA (1717), and Rio de la Plata (1776). The Spanish empire ended in the first quarter of the 19th century with the SPANISH–SOUTH AMERICAN WAR OF INDEPENDENCE.

Spanish fly A blue or green BLISTER BEETLE and member of the family Meloidae, whose adults feed on privet and ash in Mediterranean countries. The dried, bright green wing-cases of one species, *Lytta vesicatoria*, were once used in medicine for raising blisters. If taken internally, they can be dangerously poisonous.

Spanish Inquisition A council authorized by Pope Sixtus IV in 1478 and organized under the Catholic monarchs FERDINAND II and ISABELLA I of Spain to combat heresy. Its main targets were converted Jews and Muslims, but it was also used against WITCHCRAFT and against political enemies. The first Grand Inquisitor was TORQUEMADA. Its methods included the use of torture, confiscation, and burning at *autos-da-fé*. It ordered the expulsion of the Jews in 1492, the attack on the Moriscos (Muslims living in Spain who were baptized Christians but retained Islamic practices) in 1502, and, after the REFORMATION attacked all forms of Protestantism. In the 16th century there were 14 Spanish branches and its jurisdiction was extended to the colonies of the New World, including Mexico and Peru, and to the Netherlands and Sicily. Its activities were enlarged in the reign of PHILIP II, who favoured it as a COUNTER-REFORMATION weapon. It was suppressed and finally abolished in the 19th century.

Spanish mackerel A species of fish, *Scomberomorus maculatus*, of the tuna family, Scombridae, which inhabits tropical Atlantic waters. It has a rather slender body with a long-based, spiny, first dorsal fin, and is deep blue on the back, with silvery sides and belly adorned with yellow to orange spots. It grows to 1.2 m (4 feet) in length and lives near the surface, often in shallow coastal water, and enters estuaries. It is regarded as a fine game-fish by anglers. The name Spanish mackerel is also used in Britain for a smaller mackerel-like fish, *Scomber japonicus*, which is known as chub mackerel in North America.

Spanish Netherlands The southern provinces of the Netherlands ceded to PHILIP II of Spain in the Union of Arras (1579), during the Dutch Revolts. These lands originally included modern Belgium, Luxembourg, part of northern France, and what later became part of the United Provinces of the Netherlands. Although Philip II still intended to re-subjugate the rebellious northern provinces, he granted the sovereignty of the Spanish Netherlands to his daughter Isabella and her husband the Archduke Albert (1598). During the Twelve-Year Truce (1609–21) and the unsuccessful war against the United Provinces (1621–48), the region enjoyed only nominal independence from Spain. A great deal of territory was lost to LOUIS XIV of France during the wars of the 17th century, including Artois and part of Flanders. On the expiry of the Spanish Habsburg dynasty in 1700, the region came under French rule until 1706, when it was occupied by the British and Dutch. By the Peace of UTRECHT (1713) it passed under the sovereignty of the Austrian Habsburg Holy Roman Emperors.

Spanish–South American Wars of Independence (1810–25). The roots of the wars of independence are to be found in the attempts made by Spain after 1765 to re-establish imperial control over its American colonies (see SPANISH EMPIRE). This was resented by the Creoles (colonial descendants of Spanish settlers), whose political authority, economic prosperity, and sense of national identity were threatened. Creoles in Spanish America achieved *de facto* economic independence, and with the abdication of FERDINAND VII (1808), political independence. In 1811 the first declarations of independence were made. Initially the movements were hampered by a counter-revolutionary drive by Spanish royalists. In 1816 Simón BOLÍVAR returned to Venezuela from exile and united with José Antonio Páez and the Ilaneros (plainsmen) of the interior. With the assistance of British mercenaries Bolívar crossed the Andes and won the battle of Boyaca, and proclaimed the United States of COLOMBIA (1819). The victories of Carabobo (1821) and Pichincha (1822) brought Venezuela and Ecuador into the Colombian Federation. Bolívar then linked up with the independence movement in the south under the leadership of SAN MARTÍN, who had crossed the Andes from the United Provinces of La Plata (Argentina) and won the battles of Chabuco (1817) and Maipo (1818) and liberated Chile. Both movements now closed in on the bastion of the Spanish empire, Peru. The battles of Junin and Ayacucho (1824) were the final victories in the liberation of the continent.

Spanish Succession, War of the (1701–13) A conflict that arose on the death of the childless Charles II of Spain in 1700. One of his sisters had married LOUIS XIV, the other Emperor Leopold, so both the French BOURBONS and the Austrian HABSBURGS claimed the right to rule the Spanish empire, which included the southern Netherlands, Milan, Naples, and most of Central and South America. Before Charles II's death WILLIAM III took a leading part in negotiations to pre-empt the crisis, and a partition treaty was signed (1698) between LOUIS XIV and William, that Spain and its possessions would be shared out between France, Austria, and Joseph Ferdinand, the 7-year old Elector of Bavaria, grandson of Leopold. Charles II meanwhile left all of Spain's empire to Joseph Ferdinand. When he died, Louis and William signed a second partition (1699). However, Charles II left a will bequeathing his whole empire to Louis XIV's second grandson, the future Philip V. Louis accepted this will and, instead of allaying European fears of French domination, intervened in Spanish affairs, seized the Dutch barrier fortresses, recognized JAMES II's son as King of England, and refused to make it impossible for Philip also to inherit the French throne.

In 1701 William III formed a grand alliance of the English and Dutch with the Austrian emperor and most of the German princes to put the rival Austrian candidate, the Archduke Charles, on the throne; Savoy and Portugal later joined the alliance. William died in 1702 and the war therefore became Queen Anne's War. Fighting took place in the Netherlands, Italy, Germany, and Spain. France's only allies were Bavaria and the people of Castile, who supported Philip V while Catalonia declared for the Archduke Charles. MARLBOROUGH and Eugène of Savoy won a series of brilliant victories, including BLENHEIM. France was invaded in 1709 and the allies were stronger at sea, taking Gibraltar, in 1704. The war came to an end because Castile would not abandon Philip V and when Marlborough fell from power the new Tory government in England began the negotiations, which led to the Peace of UTRECHT (1713).

Spanish Town The second-largest town of Jamaica, 19 km (12 miles) west of Kingston; pop. (1991) 110,380. The capital of Jamaica until 1872, it is now a centre of sugar and food processing.

spanworm See LOOPER.

Spark, Dame Muriel (1918–) Scottish novelist. Her novels include *Memento Mori* (1959) a comic and macabre study of old age, and *The Prime of Miss Jean Brodie* (1961), a sardonic portrait of an emancipated Edinburgh schoolmistress and her favourite pupils. In 1954 Spark converted to Roman Catholicism; her awareness of the parodoxes and ironies of the faith informs much of her work, particularly her novel *The Mandelbaum Gate* (1965). Her later novels include *A Far Cry from Kensington* (1988) and *Symposium* (1990).

sparrow Any one of many small birds, especially those that are streaky brown and have short, stout beaks for eating seeds. The family of true sparrows, Passeridae, contains about 20 species of the genus *Passer*. These are Old World in origin, but some, especially the house or English sparrow, *P. domesticus*, have spread widely in man-made habitats around the world. They nest in holes or in thick vegetation, building untidy nests. The other main group contains about 50 species of several genera in the bunting family, all occurring in the New World. Most of these are smaller than the house sparrow, but the fox sparrow, *Passerella iliaca*, is almost the size of a thrush. Most are brownish or greyish birds, many heavily streaked below; others have chestnut or black head markings. All are primarily seed-eating, though they may feed insects to their young.

sparrow hawk A broad-winged HAWK of the genus *Accipiter*, especially the European sparrow hawk, *A. nisus*. This species is found in woodland and forests throughout much of Eurasia, and is a stealthy hunter of birds, insects, and other small prey. It uses the cover of woodland edges to swoop on sparrows, pigeons, and other birds feeding on open ground. Twig nests are built in trees and between four and seven eggs are laid, the males feeding the females throughout incubation. Many sparrow hawks die of insecticide poisoning. In the USA, sparrow hawks are usually *Falco sparverius*.

Sparta (Greek **Spartí**) A city in the southern Peloponnese in Greece, capital of the department of Laconia; pop. (1991) 13,000. In ancient Greece, Sparta was a powerful city-state, capital of the state of Laconia. Invading Dorian Greeks occupied Laconia *c.*950 BC, and by about 700 BC the Spartans had emerged as the dominant element among them, with a large slave class of helots working on the land. Sparta had also, in the late 8th century, defeated and annexed the territory of Messenia, its western neighbour, reducing its population to helotry and dividing its land among the full Spartiate citizens. The stark austerity, militarism, and discipline of Spartan society were traditionally ascribed to a single great legislator, Lycurgus, variously dated *c.*900 and *c.*700 BC; it is likeliest that the fully developed Spartan system took shape somewhere between 700 and 600 BC.

From the 6th century, Sparta became the hub of an alliance comprising most of Peloponnesian and Isthmian states except its traditional rival, Argos; but many of these allies in the 'Peloponnesian League' were little more than puppets of Sparta. Sparta led the successful Greek resistance in the GREEK-PERSIAN WARS, but later came into protracted conflict with ATHENS in the PELOPONNESIAN WAR. Its final victory in 404 BC left it dominant in Greece and the Aegean; but after crushing defeats by Thebes at Leuctra (371) and Mantinea (362) and the loss of Messina it declined in importance.

Spartacus (died *c.*71 BC) Thracian slave and gladiator. He led a revolt against Rome in 73, increasing his army from some 70 gladiators at the outset to several thousand rebels. He was eventually defeated by Crassus in 71 and crucified.

Spartakist Movement A group of German radical socialists. Led by Karl Liebknecht and Rosa LUXEMBURG, it was formed in 1915 in order to overthrow the German imperial government and replace it with a communist regime. Spartakist was a pseudonym used by Liebknecht in calling on the modern 'wage slave' to revolt like the Roman gladiator Spartacus. In December 1918 the Spartakists became the German Communist Party and attempted to seize power in Berlin. In January 1919, Gustav Noske, as leader of the armed forces, ordered the suppression of all radical uprisings throughout Germany. Within days, a second rebellion in Berlin was brutally crushed and the two leaders murdered without trial. There was a further Spartakist rising in the Ruhr in 1920.

Spassky, Boris (Vasilyevich) (1937–) Russian chess player. He became both international grandmaster and junior world champion in 1953. In 1969 he won the world championship, but was faced with hostility in his homeland after losing his title to the American Bobby Fischer in 1972. He lived in Paris from 1975, and played for France in the 1984 Olympics. In a rematch with Fischer in 1992 he was again defeated.

spawn The eggs of aquatic animals (especially fish and some amphibians, but also some molluscs and crustaceans) when they are expelled in a mass. The egg is composed of stored food material in the form of yolk and fat (mostly oil droplets) surrounded by albumin and covered with a thin shell.

spearfish See MARLIN.

spear mint See MINT.

special relativity See RELATIVITY, SPECIAL THEORY OF.

species In the classification of organisms, the rank below the GENUS, forming the basic unit of classification. A species is usually considered to include a group of individuals capable of interbreeding with each other to produce fertile offspring, and kept apart from other species by genetic, geographical, or other barriers. It may include many distinct subspecies, varieties, or races. Cultivars (named varieties of plants) developed by selection or hybridization are also included, provided they produce viable offspring. In biological NOMENCLATURE, Latin names of species are usually in two parts, as in man's specific name, *Homo sapiens*; a third word may be added to indicate a subspecies or another division below the level of the species.

specific heat capacity See HEAT CAPACITY.

spectacles A pair of LENSES in a frame, worn in front of the eyes to correct defective sight, or for protection. Spectacle lenses are made from shatterproof plastic or glass; sometimes they are PHOTOCHROMIC LENSES or coated to reduce reflections or protect the eye from ultraviolet light. They curve away from the eye to ensure accurate correction over the whole lens. Concave lenses correct near sight, when the eye focuses light in front of the retina, and convex lenses correct far sight, where the eye's focus is behind the retina. A cylindrical lens can often correct astigmatism, caused by the front surface of the eye curving unevenly. Bifocal lenses have two areas, for distance vision at the top and near vision at the bottom. Protective spectacles include sunglasses, and safety goggles to protect the eyes from chemicals or flying particles. CONTACT LENSES can replace spectacles.

Spector, Phil (1940–) US record producer. In 1961 he formed a record company and pioneered a 'wall of sound' style, using echo and tape loops. He had a succession of hit recordings in the 1960s with girl groups, such as the Ronettes and the Crystals, produced 'River Deep – Mountain High' for Ike and Tina Turner (1966), and worked on the last Beatles album, *Let it Be* (1970).

spectral classes A system of classifying stars by their SPECTRUM, first introduced by Angelo Secchi in the 1860s. His original classification as a series of letters, A, B, C, and so on has been rearranged as knowledge of stellar structure has improved. The **Harvard classification**, introduced in the 1890s by Harvard astronomers, was further developed by E. C. Pickering and A. J. Cannon into its present form in the 1920s. The colour of a star indicates its surface temperature and stars are now arranged in order of decreasing temperature, the classes in that order being O, B, A, F, G, K, M, R, N, and S. Each class is divided into ten steps, as for example A0 to A9.

spectrometer In astronomy, an instrument attached to an optical telescope in order to obtain the SPECTRUM of a celestial object. It normally uses a diffraction grating to disperse or spread the light into its component colours. Older instruments employ glass prisms and some special designs have elements such as Fabry–Perot interferometers. The spectrum is recorded on a photographic plate or is stored electronically by a solid state device such as a CCD CAMERA.

spectroscopic binary See BINARY STAR.

spectroscopy The branch of physics concerned with analysis of electromagnetic spectra. When electromagnetic radiation is reflected or scattered by a substance it is changed in a way that is characteristic of the substance. Analysing the wavelengths in the scattered or reflected light (that is, its SPECTRUM) can give information about the substance. This information depends on the radiation involved. Visible-light spectra give information about the electron ENERGY LEVELS in atoms, enabling the atoms to be identified. This is used in chemistry and in astronomy: spectra of the visible light from stars can be analysed to find out which atoms are present in the stars. Infrared radiation can cause molecules to bend, rotate or vibrate, so infrared spectra give information about the structure of molecules. Radio-frequency spectra from outer space are analysed to give information about distant quasars and pulsars. Spectra can be made of parameters other than wavelength: for example the mass spectrum of a substance gives information about the mass and abundance of its components.

The simplest **spectroscope** splits incident visible light into spectral lines that can be observed by the human eye. In spectrochemical analysis, the substance under investigation is heated, so that it emits radiation. Each component of the substance emits a characteristic radiation, and this can be used as a means of identification. The radiation is passed through a DIFFRACTION grating or a PRISM to separate it into its constituent wavelengths. Detectors are then used to observe or record details of the spectrum, and instruments can be used to measure the wavelengths and intensities of spectral lines. A permanent record of the results (a **spectrograph**) may be made to allow more detailed analysis. Comparison of the spectrum with the spectra of known, pure, substances allows the components to be identified and, with quantitative analysis, their relative proportions determined. This offers an extremely sensitive method of analysis of chemical substances, and automated spectroscopic procedures are now used routinely in laboratories.

spectrum (pl. **spectra**) A pattern of the amount or intensity of a parameter over a range of values: for example, the number of particles of a particular mass over a range of values of mass; or the intensity at each wavelength of light consisting of a range of wavelengths. Thus the pattern of colours obtained when white light is passed through a prism is a spectrum of wavelengths. The same pattern of colours is produced by a diffraction grating or, in the sky, by raindrops (the RAINBOW). The colours are conventionally described as red, orange, yellow, green, blue, indigo, and violet. The spectrum arises as a result of the different REFRACTIVE INDEX of glass for different wavelengths present in white light. The spectrum produced by sunlight contains many dark lines because certain wavelengths in the light from the Sun are strongly absorbed by its outer layers, so that they are missing from the spectrum. The resulting pattern of lines is called an **absorption spectrum**. When a substance is heated or subjected to an electrical discharge it may give out light. If this light is passed through a prism a pattern of bright lines against a dark background is produced – an **emission spectrum**. In both cases the particular wavelengths absorbed or emitted are those for which the PHOTONS have an energy equal to the difference between two electron ENERGY LEVELS. Each element, therefore, has its own characteristic spectrum. See SPECTROSCOPY.

speech The human faculty for the verbal exchange of ideas, using language. Sound is generated by forcing air out of the lungs against the resistance provided by the vocal cords (LARYNX). This sets up vibrations in the air-flow that produce sound, which is modified by changing the position of the lips and tongue to produce the elementary speech sounds. Different sequences of the basic sounds produce words. Learning to do this accurately in childhood requires normal hearing and normal control of the muscles in the throat, mouth, and tongue by the brain. See also LANGUAGE.

speed of light The speed at which ELECTROMAGNETIC RADIATION travels through free space (in a vacuum). It has a value of 299,792,458 metres (186,281 miles) per second and is a universal constant. The speed of light is slightly less in the atmosphere. It has a special significance in relativity theory in three respects: it is absolute – that is, its value (c) is independent of the motion both of its source and of the observer; it is impossible to accelerate anything to this speed, since doing so would require an infinite amount of energy; and it provides the link between mass (m) and energy (E) in the equation $E = mc^2$.

speed of sound The speed at which SOUND waves travel through a medium. For air at a temperature of 0°C (32°F) this is 331 metres per second (1,087 feet per second). As the temperature increases, the density of the air decreases and this enables the sound waves to travel faster; thus at 18°C (64°F) it is 342 m/s (1,123 feet per second). The speed of sound is much higher in liquids and solids: in water, for example, it is over four times greater than in air.

speedometer An instrument for measuring the speed of a vehicle. It consists of a pointer attached to an aluminium ring, which surrounds a permanent magnet. The magnet is connected to the propeller shaft or front axle of the vehicle, and rotates when the vehicle is in motion, the speed of its rotation being proportional to the vehicle's speed. As the magnet rotates, eddy currents are produced, which induce a second magnetic field. The interaction of the two fields produces a turning force in the ring, and the pointer is swung over a graduated speed scale. The ring is attached to a restraining spring, so that it cannot turn a full circle. Speedometers usually include ODOMETERS to indicate the mileage travelled.

speedwell A plant of the genus *Veronica*, which belongs to the foxglove family, Scrophulariaceae. They are annual or perennial plants, often with prostrate or creeping stems, opposite leaves, and spikes of blue or occasionally white flowers. The species are found in a variety of habitats – streamsides, woodlands, meadows, as weeds in lawns, and at fairly high altitudes on mountains. They are chiefly from the temperate regions of the Northern Hemisphere. This genus formerly included a large number of evergreen shrubs, most of them native to New Zealand; these have now been classified as the genus *Hebe*.

Speer, Albert (1905–81) German Nazi leader. He was the official architect for the Nazi Party, designing the grandiose stadium at Nuremberg (1934). An efficient organizer, he became (1942) Minister for

Armaments and was mainly responsible for the planning of Germany's war economy, marshalling conscripted and slave labour in his *Organization Todt* to build strategic roads and defence lines. He was imprisoned after the war.

Speke, John Hanning (1827–64) British explorer. From 1854 to 1858 he accompanied Sir Richard Burton on expeditions to trace the source of the Nile. They became the first Europeans to discover Lake Tanganyika (1858), after which Speke went on to reach a great lake which he identified as the 'source reservoir' of the Nile; he called it Lake Victoria in honour of the queen.

Spence, Sir Basil (1907–76) British architect. He assisted LUTYENS on the Viceroy's House, New Delhi. From 1930 he worked mainly as a designer of houses, and became a leading figure in his profession. He is best known for his rebuilding of the bombed Coventry Cathedral (1954–62). Spence was particularly involved with new housing and university projects in the 1950s and 1960s. His controversial cavalry barracks in Knightsbridge (1970) was criticized for the effect its tower had on London's Hyde Park skyline.

Spencer, Herbert (1820–1903) British philosopher and sociologist. He was an early adherent of evolutionary theory, which he set down in his *Principles of Psychology* (1855). Spencer embraced Darwin's theory of natural selection proposed four years later, coined the phrase the 'survival of the fittest' (1864), and advocated social and economic laissez-faire. He later sought to synthesize the natural and social sciences in the *Programme of a System of Synthetic Philosophy* (1862–96).

Spencer, Sir Stanley (1891–1959) British painter. He is best known for his religious and visionary works in the modern setting of his native village of Cookham in Berkshire. Famous works include the painting *Resurrection: Cookham* (1926), the series of military murals for the Sandham Memorial Chapel at Burghclere in Hampshire (1927–32), and the sequence of panels portraying the Clyde shipyards during World War II when he was an official war artist.

Spender, Sir Stephen (1909–95) British poet and critic. His *Poems* (1933) contained both personal and political poems including 'The Pylons', which lent its name to the group of young left-wing poets of the 1930s known as the 'Pylon School'; its members used industrial imagery in their work and included W. H. Auden, C. Day Lewis, and Louis MacNeice. In his critical work *The Destructive Element* (1935), Spender defended the importance of political subject-matter in literature. He later wrote the autobiography *World Within World* (1951), giving an account of his association with the Communist Party.

Spengler, Oswald (1880–1936) German philosopher. His fame rests on his book *The Decline of the West* (1918–22), in which he argues that civilizations undergo a seasonal cycle of about a thousand years and are subject to growth, flowering, and decay analogous to biological species.

Spenser, Edmund (*c.*1552–99) English poet. His first major poem was the *Shepheardes Calendar* (1579) in 12 eclogues. He is best known for his allegorical romance the *Faerie Queene* (1590; 1596), celebrating Queen Elizabeth I. The poem is written in the stanza invented by Spenser (later used by Keats, Shelley, and Byron) with eight iambic pentameters and an alexandrine, rhyming *ababbcbcc*. He also wrote the marriage poem *Epithalamion* (1594).

sperm The male equivalent of the OVUM, produced in vast numbers by the TESTIS. A sperm cell has a head containing the NUCLEUS with half the normal number of CHROMOSOMES. Attached to the head is a tail, which propels the sperm towards the ovum. Only one sperm head penetrates the ovum wall and fertilizes the ovum, after which development of the egg commences.

spermaceti See SPERM WHALE.

sperm whale The largest of the TOOTHED WHALES. The three species in the family Physeteridae range through all the seas, migrating north and south with the seasons. The large, almost square head is a striking feature of these mammals. Much of the head is taken up by the 'case', a transformed and expanded region of the right nostril, filled with **spermaceti**. This is liquid at body temperature but forms a white wax when cooled. Spermaceti may be important in controlling buoyancy, particularly during prolonged and deep dives. It is used commercially in medicines, perfume, candles, and confectionery. The sperm whale, *Physeter macrocephalus*, can reach depths of 1,200 m (4,000 feet). It can remain below the surface for as long as 50 minutes, after which it spends ten minutes at the surface. It feeds largely on squids and cuttlefish; a large male eats a total of some 99,800 kg (110 US tons) of these cephalopods in a year. The male can reach a length of 19.8 m (65 feet) and is larger than the female. A single calf of up to 4.8 m (16 feet) in length is born after a gestation period of about 14.5 months; it may be suckled for as long as two years. The two other species, the pygmy sperm whale, *Kogia breviceps*, and dwarf sperm whale, *K. sinus*, are much smaller, the largest reaching 3.4 m (11 feet) in length. They occur in warmer seas than the sperm whale.

Spezia, La A naval and commercial seaport on the Mediterranean coast of Liguria, north-west Italy, capital of La Spezia province; pop. (1990) 103,000. It developed after the transfer of the naval dockyard from Genoa. There is a ferry link with Corsica.

sphagnum A MOSS of the genus *Sphagnum* that forms large areas of peat bog in wet, upland regions, especially in acid and nutrient-poor conditions in which few other plants can thrive. They have a uniquely spongy structure so that the hummocks (carpets) of sphagnum plants retain water. The damp, nutrient-poor conditions in which these mosses grow rule out rapid decomposition of dead plant material; instead, layers of peat develop. Sphagnum is used as poultry litter, in orchid composts, and as an emergency surgical dressing.

sphalerite See ZINC SULPHIDE.

sphinx A mythological creature with a lion's body and human head, an important figure in ancient Egyptian and Greek culture. To the ancient Egyptians the sphinx was a representation of the Pharaoh with a lion's body (the Pharaoh was endowed with the vigour of the bull and the lion) and with a man's head, wearing the traditional striped head-cloth. The best known of these statues is the monumental sphinx at Giza (*c.*2613–2494 BC), bearing the face of Khephren (4th dynasty) and probably positioned by his pyramid as a guardian. Later tradition identified this sphinx as Haurun, a Canaanite god, and Harmachis, a form of Horus, probably because the statue faces eastwards towards the rising Sun.

In Greek mythology, the sphinx was a monster with a woman's bust and the body of a winged lion. She devoured all who could not solve the riddle disclosed to her by the Muses, namely: 'What is it that has one voice, walks on four legs in the morning, on two at midday, and on three in the evening?'

Oedipus alone gave the answer, 'man', who crawls on all fours as an infant, walks upright in his prime, and in old age leans on a stick. The sphinx thereupon destroyed herself.

sphinx moth See HAWKMOTH.

sphygmomanometer An instrument for measuring arterial blood pressure. The most common type, which was devised by the Italian Scipione Riva-Rocci in 1896, consists of a rubber cuff fastened round the upper arm and attached to a MANOMETER. The cuff is inflated until the pulse at the elbow cannot be detected with a STETHOSCOPE, giving the systolic pressure (the pressure produced by the heart in contraction). The diastolic pressure (when the heart is between contractions) is found by releasing pressure until the pulse is again audible. Recently, electronic devices for blood pressure measurement have been introduced.

Spica A first-magnitude VARIABLE STAR in the constellation of Virgo, and also known as Alpha Virginis. It is a spectroscopic BINARY STAR with a period of four days, comprising two hot DWARF STARS.

Spice Islands See MOLUCCAS.

spider The commonest ARACHNID, found in huge numbers everywhere except in the Antarctic, with up to 2 million in any acre of meadow. There are 35,000 known species, many only 1 mm (0.04 inch) long, but a few tarantulas have bodies 10 cm (4 inches) in length. Most spiders are carnivores, and are the only invertebrates that trap flying insects. Those using silk to catch prey employ it as tripwires, webs, or even lassos. All spiders rely mainly on touch and vibration to sense their prey, as their eyes are simple, and capable only of discriminating between night and day. They all use venom to paralyse prey, though only a few can pierce human skin. Ground-hunting species of jumping spiders have eight prominent eyes and are very agile.

Silk is spun from six glands, of varying thickness and stickiness. It is the strongest material made by any invertebrate, and hardens as it is stretched. Spiders use it not only for trapping but also for insulating their homes, wrapping their eggs, and dispersal by parachuting into the air.

spider crab A crustacean that has a triangular or pear-shaped body with a projection between the eyes, and very long legs. Spider crabs include the decorator crabs, which camouflage their shells with a forest of other sessile organisms. The giant of the group is the Japanese spider crab with a leg-span up to 4 m (13 feet). Most spider crabs are entirely marine, quite common in rock-pools but always difficult to spot.

spider monkey Any of four species of New World monkey in the genus *Ateles*, found in the tropical forests of Central and South America from southern Mexico to Bolivia. They live in the upper branches of trees and are remarkably acrobatic, able to take a flying leap of 9 m (30 feet). Spider monkeys eat fruit, flowers, insects, and birds. They are easily recognizable by their light, slender body, long spidery limbs, and tail of 60 cm (2 feet), a little longer than the head and body together. The tip of the tail is naked and can grasp firmly anything it touches, acting almost like a hand. The coarse, woolly fur of the long-haired spider monkey, *Ateles belzebuth*, and the black spider monkey, *A. paniscus*, is entirely black, while in the brown-headed spider monkey, *A. fusciceps*, and black-handed spider monkey, *A. geoffroyi*, it can be reddish-brown.

spiderwort A perennial herbaceous plant, *Tradescantia virginiana*, of the monocotyledonous family Commelinaceae. It has grass-like leaves and clusters of bright blue flowers each composed of three petals. Some species are popular flower-border or house plants.

Spielberg, Steven (1947–) US film director and producer. He established a wide popular appeal with films concentrating on sensational and fantastic themes, such as *Jaws* (1975) *Close Encounters of the Third Kind* (1977), and *ET* (1982), which he also produced. He later directed a series of adventure films, notably *Raiders of the Lost Ark* (1981) and *Indiana Jones and the Temple of Doom* (1984). Other films include *Jurassic Park* (1993), which like his earlier film *ET* broke box-office records, and *Schindler's List* (1993), which won seven Oscars, including that for best director and best picture.

Spillane, Mickey (pseudonym of Frank Morrison Spillane) (1918–) US writer. He wrote a series of enormously popular detective novels during the late 1940s and early 1950s, which emphasized sadistic violence rather more than mystery. He wrote the screenplay and starred in the film of his book *The Girl Hunters* (1962). His other books include *My Gun Is Quick* (1950), *The Big Kill* (1951), and *The Twisted Things* (1966).

spin (in atomic physics) An attribute of some ELEMENTARY PARTICLES giving them intrinsic angular momentum and a magnetic moment, so that they behave like tiny bar magnets. It is impossible to say whether particles are indeed spinning in the ordinary sense of the word, but spin is a convenient label for referring to these properties of a particle. Spin (or absence of it) is one of the distinguishing characteristics of an elementary particle. It was first discovered in the electron.

spina bifida A congenital disorder characterized by a developmental abnormality resulting in defective closure of the spinal column. A sac protrudes from the defect and contains the nerves, part of the spinal cord, covering membranes (meninges), and cerebrospinal fluid. The defect commonly occurs in the lower spine. The location and extent of the defect determine the nature of the manifestations. PARALYSIS of variable extent is common; associated symptoms include incontinence. Sensory loss may also occur. Increased amounts of cerebrospinal fluid within the brain (hydrocephalus) and other developmental abnormalities may also be present. Surgery is necessary to close the defect; however, paraplegia and incontinence are common residual abnormalities. This disorder can now be detected prenatally by AMNIOCENTESIS.

spinach A vegetable, *Spinacia oleracea*, widely cultivated in temperate regions for its leaves, which are rich in protein. It belongs to the same family as sugar beet, beetroot, and mangels, Chenopodiaceae.

spinach beet A variety of *Beta vulgaris*, the species that also includes BEETROOT and SUGAR BEET. This vegetable is grown for its succulent leaves throughout most of the year. Spinach-like, but milder in flavour and also known as perpetual spinach and leaf beet, they can be eaten whole, including the long, green stalk.

spinal cord See NERVOUS SYSTEM; SPINE.

spindle tree A member of the cosmopolitan genus *Euonymus*, which comprises some 175 species of deciduous trees and shrubs. The common spindle tree, *Euonymus europaeus*, is typical of the genus in having scarlet fruits which split open to reveal orange seeds. Some other species have winged or spiny fruits. The wood has been used to make spindles, and burnt to produce high-quality charcoal. Spindle trees make up the family Celastraceae.

spine (or **backbone**) A series of small bones (VERTEBRAE) making up a flexible column in vertebrates, which extends down the long axis of the body, providing skeletal support. The **spinal cord**, one of the major parts of the central NERVOUS SYSTEM, runs within the spine, inside the neural arch of each vertebra. The spine protects the spinal cord and permits the animal's body to twist and turn, and varies from species to species.

In lower vertebrates, all the vertebrae are very similar and their parts are barely fused. In higher vertebrates, however, the vertebrae are modified into five different types supporting different parts of the body: seven cervical vertebrae (supporting the neck), 12 thoracic (thorax, rib-cage), five lumbar (lower back), five fused sacral vertebrae (pelvic girdle), and the caudal (tail) vertebrae, reduced to the coccyx in humans. The vertebrae articulate with one another and are so arranged that spine movements are limited in degree and direction. Cervical vertebrae can move backwards and forwards, and the first two (atlas and axis) are articulated so as to permit rotation of the head. Thoracic vertebrae can move forwards, and rotate upon one another to a very limited extent, but cannot move backwards. Lumbar vertebrae can only flex and extend upon one another to a limited extent. The vertebrae are separated by shock-absorbing DISCS of cartilage. The human spine is so constructed that it has three natural curvatures. The cervical vertebrae form a forward convex curve, the thoracic a backward curve, and the lumbar a forward curve.

spinet A musical instrument, in English usage from the 17th century, comprising a small wing-shaped domestic version of the HARPSICHORD, with strings running diagonally away from the keyboard. However, spinet was earlier used to mean the VIRGINALS and sometimes the harpsichord itself. As with the virginals there was only one rank of strings, and normally only one keyboard.

spinning The process of making a YARN or thread. This may involve the compaction and twisting of long polymer fibres, as for example, in SILK processing. Alternatively, it may be by the alignment and twisting together of short (staple) fibres, such as cotton or wool. The spinning of staple fibres into yarn is a very ancient craft. Essentially it consists of disentangling and aligning the fibres (carding), drawing them out to provide an assembly to give a yarn of the required thickness, and then providing a twist to form a coherent structure. Early manual methods included the **spindle and distaff**, consisting of a cleft staff (distaff) and a cylindrical spinning implant (spindle), which were used in Europe until the Middle Ages and are still widely used in Third World countries. The **spinning-wheel**, essentially the same as the distaff and spindle except that the spindle is driven by a cord from a wheel, was invented in India and introduced into Europe in the 14th century. It was faster than hand-spinning, and gave a more uniform yarn. In the late 18th century the INDUSTRIAL REVOLUTION promoted a spate of inventions relating to spinning: HARGREAVES's spinning-jenny, ARKWRIGHT's water-frame, CROMPTON's mule spinning frame, and efficient mechanical CARDING MACHINES to provide fibre for the spinning frames. By the beginning of the 19th century these developments had been combined into a low-cost, mechanized system for staple yarn manufacture, which is essentially the same as those now in use.

Spinoza, Baruch de (or **Benedict de**) (1632–77) Dutch philosopher, of Portuguese Jewish descent. His unorthodox views led to his expulsion from the Amsterdam synagogue in 1656. Spinoza rejected the Cartesian dualism of spirit and matter in favour of a pantheistic system, seeing God as the single infinite substance, the immanent cause of the Universe and not a ruler outside it. His *Ethics* (1677) sought to formulate a metaphysical system that was mathematically deduced. Spinoza espoused a determinist political doctrine, arguing that the individual surrenders his or her natural rights to the state in order to obtain security.

spiny ant-eater See ECHIDNA.

spiny dormouse An oriental dormouse, *Platacanthomys lasiurus*, from southern India. It is similar to the common dormouse in appearance, with its long bushy tail, and is about the same size, but it has sharp spines protruding from the fur on its back. The animal lives in trees and feeds on fruits and seeds.

spiny-headed worm An animal comprising some 500 species in the phylum Acanthocephala. They are endoparasites, usually 1–2 cm (0.25–0.75 inch) long. The juvenile acanthocephalans are parasitic initially within arthropods or crustacea, and are passed on to their primary vertebrate host when their intermediate host is eaten by the vertebrate. Inside the vertebrate host the larvae encyst and attach themselves to the intestine wall using a strongly spined proboscis. Spiny-headed worms have no gut and feed by direct uptake of the host's fluids across their body wall. Females may produce millions of eggs, which pass out of the vertebrate host in faeces.

spiny rat A member of the cavy-like RODENT family Echimyidae; most, but not all, of the 56 species have spiny or bristly hairs in the fur. Some have pointed snouts, large ears, and long tails that give them a close similarity to true rats. All are Central or South American. Some are arboreal but others live in burrows. They are herbivorous.

spiny rock lobster See CRAWFISH.

Spiraea A genus of some 100 species of deciduous shrubs native to the north temperate zone and extending as far south as Mexico. They have heads of small white, pink, or reddish flowers, and many species are cultivated as garden plants. As members of the rose family they are closely related to very similar species in the genera *Aruncus* and *Filipendula*. Some of these and species of *Astilbe*, in the saxifrage family, are commonly referred to as 'spiraea' because of their similar flowers.

spiral galaxy A galaxy exhibiting spirally coiled arms of dust, gas, and stars springing from a central nucleus. It is one of the most common types of galaxy and is labelled So to SC in the HUBBLE CLASSIFICATION. The majority of spiral galaxies possess two arms arising from opposite sides of the nucleus. In general, the stars within the arms are young Population I stars.

spiritual A religious song of the African American peoples of the southern states of the USA, but probably derived from the evangelist hymns of the white settlers. The words serve a double purpose: as a temporary distraction from the pains of slavery, and as a heartening, subversive symbol of defiance through identification with the biblical Israelites escaping from the tyranny of Egypt.

spiritualism A movement with the belief that the spirits of the dead can communicate with the living by means of a medium, a person regarded as sensitive to the spirit world. It is an ancient belief, common to many religions. Many followers of spiritualism are anxious to obtain evidence of life after death, or to make contact with the spirits of loved ones who have died. Psychic phenomena common at seances include clairvoyance, telepathy, and trance states, while physical manifestations include table turning, automatic writing, levitation, and the appearance of ectoplasm, a viscous substance supposed to emanate from the body of the medium during a trance. Spiritualist beliefs and practices have been attacked both by established Churches, which regard spiritualism as dabbling in the occult, and by those who believe that spiritualist manifestations are based on trickery and sleight of hand. See also PARAPSYCHOLOGY.

Spirogyra A genus of filamentous green ALGAE commonly found in fresh water as skeins of fine green threads. The threads consist of individual cells attached end-to-end. Inside each cell is one or more ribbon-like, spirally arranged chloroplast(s), hence the name *Spirogyra*. Growth occurs by simple transverse division of cells, and sexual reproduction occurs by fragmentation of threads. Occasionally, *Spirogyra* undergoes sexual reproduction: two threads lie alongside each other, and the contents of each cell in one strand pass through a temporary 'tunnel' into the corresponding cell of the other strand. The donor thread thus becomes an empty shell, while the recipient thread undergoes a series of changes before resistant 'spores' are released, eventually to produce new threads.

Spithead mutiny A mutiny by sailors of the British navy based at Spithead, on the southern coast of Britain. In April 1797 the fleet refused to put to sea, calling for better pay and conditions, including the provision of edible food, improved medical services, and opportunities for shore leave. The Admiralty, acknowledging the justice of the sailors' grievances and fearing that the mutiny would spread further agreed to their demands and issued a royal pardon.

Spitsbergen See SVALBARD.

spittlebug See FROGHOPPER.

Spitz, Mark (Andrew) (1950–) US swimmer. He won seven gold medals in the 1972 Olympic Games at Munich and set 27 world records for free style and butterfly (1967–72).

spleen The abdominal organ concerned with maintaining the proper condition of the blood in most vertebrates. It is a fibrous capsule, which encloses developing white blood cells (lymphocytes). It also contains numerous phagocytic cells (capable of engulfing foreign matter or bacteria) and has an extensive, slowly moving blood supply. In mammals, it lies in the upper left part of the abdomen. It acts as a blood purifier and reconditioner and adds lymphocyte defence cells to the circulation. In mammals other than man, the spleen has a muscular capsule, which contracts during exercise in order to augment the blood supply to the muscles.

Split A seaport, cultural centre, and resort on the Adriatic coast of Croatia; pop. (1991) 189,300. Founded as a Roman colony in 78 BC, it contains the ruins of the palace of the emperor Diocletian, built in about 300 AD.

Spock, Benjamin McLane (known as **Dr Spock**) (1903–98) US paediatrician and writer. His manual *The Common Sense Book of Baby and Child Care* (1946) challenged traditional ideas of discipline and rigid routine in child rearing in favour of a psychological approach and influenced a generation of parents after World War II. He was sent to prison in 1968 for helping draft-dodgers during the Vietnam War. Many of his ideas are no longer accepted.

Spode, Josiah (1755–1827) British potter. Having inherited the pottery founded by his father in Stoke-on-Trent, he invented what became standard English bone china by combining china clay with bone ash. Much of his characteristic work done around the turn of the 19th century consisted of elaborate services and large vases, ornately decorated and gilded.

sponge An animal of the phylum Porifera, of which there are 10,000 species. Sponges have no mouth, digestive cavity, nerves, muscles, locomotion, or true behaviour. They consist of aggregates of cells formed into hollow bodies, which may be grouped into colonies. With the exception of 150 freshwater species, the vast majority of sponges are marine. Most form small and irregular encrusting masses on rocks, although some may reach 1 m (3 feet) across. They occur in a wide range of colours. Sponges survive on the food particles brought by water currents, which enter the colony through pores all over their surface. The whole structure is supported by skeletal spicules of chalk or silica, or by a network of fibres. This system is apparent in the natural bath sponge when the living cell contents have been dissolved away.

spoonbill A large, chiefly freshwater marsh bird of the family Threskiornithidae, especially *Platalea leucorodia*, akin to ibises, with unusual flattened spoon-tipped beaks. Mainly tropical or subtropical, they breed in colonies, often building stick nests in trees. The five Old World species are white, but the single American species, the roseate spoonbill, *Ajaia ajaia*, is rosy pink.

Spooner, William Archibald (1844–1930) British clergyman and Oxford don. He is remembered for his eccentric transposition of the initial letters of words, which have become known as **Spoonerisms** (for example, 'the dear old Queen' becomes 'the queer old Dean').

spore A microscopic reproductive structure produced by bacteria, algae, protozoa, fungi, and some plants. They are only just visible to the naked eye, but can be seen as clumps on the underside of fern leaves or under the cap of fungi. Unlike seeds, they contain only a few cells and no embryo, but still grow into new individuals. Most are liberated into the air and travel long distances in air currents, although most algae and some fungi have spores that can swim in water using beating hairs, or flagellae. Other kinds of spores lie dormant where they are produced; dormant spores of bacteria are the longest-surviving living material, resistant to extremes of temperature and drought. Those of the bacterium *Bacillus anthracis*, which causes ANTHRAX, can survive up to 50 years.

sprat A small fish, *Sprattus spattus*, in the herring family, which is found in coastal waters around Europe. Its maximum length is 16 cm (6 inches). It is an abundant, schooling fish, usually found near the surface, and is often common in estuaries and bays. Sprats spawn in spring and summer; the eggs and larvae are planktonic and the young fishes drift into coastal waters as they develop. The young are eaten as WHITEBAIT and the adults are eaten either fresh or smoked, or they may be canned as brisling. They superficially resemble small herring, as their back is green, shading to silver on the sides.

Spratly Islands (Chinese **Nansha**; Vietnamese

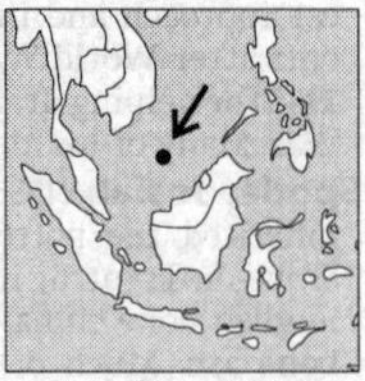

Truong Sa; Philippino **Kalayaan**) A group of islets and coral reefs in the South China Sea between Vietnam and Borneo. Dispersed over a distance of some 965 km (600 miles) and commanding the sea route between Singapore and Japan, the islands are claimed in whole or in part by China, Taiwan, Vietnam, the Philippines, and Malaysia. Oil was discovered beneath its waters in 1976 and in 1988 it was the scene of a brief naval engagement between Chinese and Vietnamese forces.

spreadsheet An APPLICATIONS PROGRAM for a computer that can rapidly perform arithmetical calculations on many values. Spreadsheets are widely used in business and accountancy for the generation of financial statements and business projections. The spreadsheet is divided into a set of rows and columns, the intersections of which form large numbers of 'cells'. A typical spreadsheet program may permit 2,048 rows and 256 columns. Numerical values and formulae are entered by the user in any cell and mathematical operations can be performed on the contents of the cells.

spring A place from which water emerges from underground. Natural springs occur where WATER-TABLES intersect the ground surface or where underground rivers emerge from caves and passages in limestone or lavas. Caused by the positioning of permeable and impermeable rock in such a way that the latter forces the water to surface, they are known as **artesian springs** if it emerges under pressure.

springbok (or **springbuck**) A species of GAZELLE, *Antidorcas marsupialis*, about 76 cm (30 inches) tall at the shoulders. On its back is a fold of skin, which is turned inside out to display an array of white hairs when the animal is startled. This serves as a signal to others in the herd. Huge herds once roamed the plains of South Africa, but persistent hunting has reduced their numbers and range.

spring equinox See EQUINOX.

Springfield An administrative, commercial, medical, and insurance centre, the capital of the US state of Illinois since 1837; pop. (1990) 105,230. First settled in 1819, it was named after a spring on the land of Elisha Kelly, its first resident.

springhaas (or **springhare**) An African RODENT, *Pedetes capensis*, the sole representative of the family Pedetidae. It resembles and hops like a small bushy-tailed kangaroo. About 4 kg (9 pounds) in weight, it is prized by the African Bushmen for its flesh. Its distribution is disjunct, with one population in southern Africa and another in East Africa. It lives in dry, sandy country, digging extensive burrow systems, and is nocturnal and herbivorous.

Springsteen, Bruce (1949–) US rock singer, songwriter, and guitarist. He is noted for his songs about working-class life in the USA and for his energetic stage performances. Major albums include *Born to Run* (1975) and *Born in the USA* (1984).

springtail A minute, wingless insect whose abdomen contains only six segments, over 2,000 species of which form the order Collembola. The fourth abdominal segment bears a double appendage which is held at rest under a catch on the third segment. When this catch is released, the springtail jumps high into the air. The first segment of the abdomen bears a long tube, which is used either to absorb water, or as an adhesive organ to help springtails climb steep surfaces. They feed mostly on fungi and plant detritus and are the most abundant animals in the upper layers of the soil. A few, including the lucerne flea, *Sminthurus viridis*, live on plant leaves, while others can live on the surface film of fresh or salt water.

spring tide See TIDE.

spruce A conifer of the genus *Picea*, which belongs to the pine family. They are evergreen trees with hard, sharp leaves, or needles. Their cones are soft, leathery cylinders, which hang from branches. The Norway spruce (also called Christmas tree), *Picea abies*, found from the Pyrenees to the Arctic Circle, provides valuable timber, resin, and turpentine. There are 50 other species of spruce, of which many are grown for their timber and ornament. The red spruce, *P. rubens*, black spruce, *P. mariana*, and the white spruce, *P. glauca*, of North America, are used for pulp, especially newsprint. A species planted widely in Europe for timber and pulp is the Sitka spruce, *P. sitchensis*.

spurge A plant of the genus *Euphorbia*, which has over 1,000 species, widely distributed throughout the temperate and tropical regions of the world and showing great variation in size and form. The succulent kinds (often devoid of true leaves) from southern and southwest Africa include *E. grandidens*, a spiny cactus-like tree up to 12 m (39 feet) in height, and *E. globosa* from the Cape Province, a dwarf cylindrical-stemmed succulent only a few centimetres (two or three inches) high. The leafy herbaceous species from Europe and the Mediterranean region are often used as garden border plants, while *E. pulcherrima* from Mexico is the popular Christmas pot plant called **poinsettia**. All have a poisonous milky latex. The family to which this genus belongs, the Euphorbiaceae, contains over 5,000 species of mostly tropical plants.

Sputnik A series of Soviet SATELLITES. *Sputnik 1* was the first artificial satellite to orbit the Earth, in October 1957. *Sputnik 2* carried the first animal into space, the dog Laika. The main purpose of *Sputniks 1* to *10* was to prepare for a manned space flight. Subsequent *Sputniks* (*11* to *24*) were also called *Cosmos*.

square root See ROOT.

squash (vegetable) The edible fruits of several species and varieties of *Cucurbita*, belonging to the pumpkin family. Summer squash consists of varieties of *C. pepo*, the young fruits of various shapes and colours being used as vegetables (including marrows). Winter squash consists of the mature fruits of several species, which keep well in frost-free conditions and form invaluable food for livestock and man.

squash (sport) A fast-paced racket-and-ball game played in an enclosed rectangular court measuring 9.75 m (32 feet) by 6.4 m (21 feet). From a small square on one side of the court, the server hits the small rubber ball against the front wall so that it rebounds into the back half of the other side of the court. The receiver returns the ball, and the rally continues until one player either fails to reach the ball before it has bounced twice or hits it out of bounds. First to score nine points wins the game, and only the server may score; if the server loses a point, service passes to the other player. In the American (as opposed to the International) game, the court is almost a metre narrower, the ball is harder, the game is up to 15 points, and points count irrespective of service. A variant of squash that is becoming extremely popular in the USA is racketball. This is game played in a completely

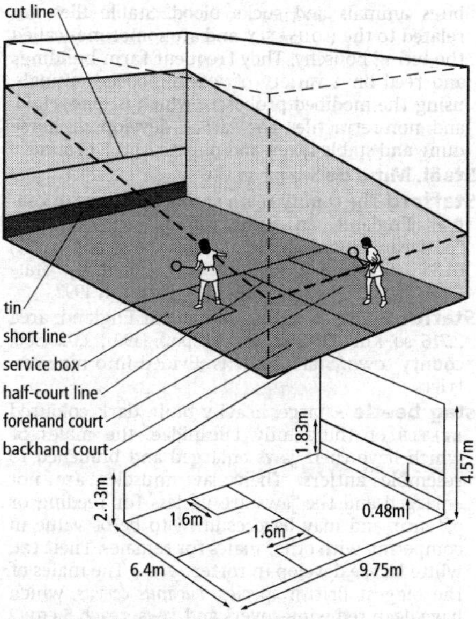

Squash The dimensions of the court.

enclosed indoor court, roughly the size of a squash court. The rackets are like tennis rackets but with much shorter handles, and the rubber ball (which is larger than a squash ball) is very bouncy. Unlike squash, the ball can bounce off the ceiling, but otherwise scoring and mode of play are quite similar.

squid The commonest CEPHALOPOD mollusc: a sinuous, torpedo-shaped animal usually up to 50 cm (20 inches) long. Squids have eight arms and two larger tentacles at the front, all bearing suckers, and a rear fin giving stability as they squirt water out of their siphon for jet propulsion. The shell is reduced to an internal, transparent, horny 'pen', so-called because of its resemblance to a quill pen. Large schools of squids can eat considerable numbers of shrimp and fishes and may even threaten man's offshore catches. The rare giant squids, *Architeuthis* species, can be 18 m (60 feet) long, and are the largest known invertebrates. There are also 'flying squids', which can glide briefly above the waves.

squirrel A diurnal RODENT of the large family Sciuridae, which in addition to the familiar **tree squirrels** includes the burrowing GROUND SQUIRRELS and the gliding **flying squirrels** among the 267 species. Squirrels are widely distributed throughout the world. The typical tree-dwelling squirrels build nests in holes and have long bushy tails. They include the Eurasian red squirrel, *Sciurus vulgaris*, and the American grey squirrel, *S. carolinensis*, which has displaced the red species in many regions. Tree squirrels are very agile, leaping from branch to branch, so that it is not surprising that some have evolved into flying squirrels of which there are many species. The largest, of the genus *Petaurista*, are reputed to glide for up to 450 m (1,500 feet) and to be able to change direction in flight. The largest tree-living species is the Indian giant squirrel, *Ratufa indica*, which weighs up to 3 kg (7 pounds), and the smallest, only 7 cm (3 inches) long, is the African pygmy squirrel, *Myosciurus pumilio*.

squirrelfish Any of about 50 species of spiny marine fish of the family Holocentridae, which live in all tropical oceans. They are distinguished by the massive spines in the dorsal, anal, and pelvic fins, rough-edged scales and, in many species, a long spine on the lower edge of the cheek; they have large eyes. Many are red in colour, and most are nocturnal, hiding in crevices and caves in reefs during the day.

Sri Lanka (formerly **Ceylon**) A pear-shaped island country in the Indian Ocean off the south-east coast of India.

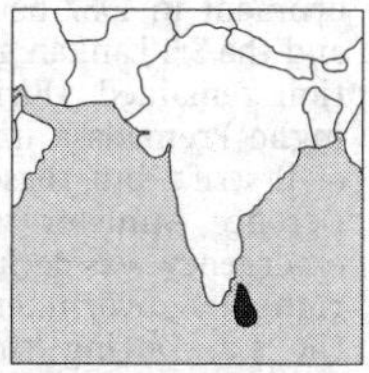

Physical. Sri Lanka has very broad coastal plains which rise at the centre to highlands 2,000 m (6,560 feet) high and more. The climate is monsoonal, with very heavy rainfall; but while the plains are always hot and sticky, the hills are cooler and less humid. At high altitudes the scenery is beautiful, with mixed forests, streams, and waterfalls. On the lower slopes tea is grown; and on the well-rivered plains there are rubber-trees, coconut palms, and paddy fields. The flat stretches of coast contain many palm-fringed beaches.

Economy. The economy is largely agrarian, with exports of tea, rubber, precious stones, and coconut products. Manufacturing industry includes textiles, cement, and petroleum-refining. Remittances from emigrant workers are significant, as was tourism until it was disrupted by the civil war.

History. Sri Lanka's early history was shaped by Indian influences and its modern identity by three phases of European colonization. The origins of the dominant Sinhalese racial group go back to Indo-Aryan invaders from north India, whose successors dominated the north central plain from the 5th century BC until about 1200 AD. During the 2nd century BC BUDDHISM spread, following the conversion of the reigning king. An outstanding ruler was Parakramabahu I (1153–86), who exercised strong military and administrative leadership and also reformed the quarrelling Buddhist sects. However, intermittent invasions from south India gradually created an enclave of Tamil Hindu power on the northern Jaffna peninsula and the north-eastern coast. The centre of Sinhalese and Buddhist civilization gradually shifted south-westwards, and political power was divided between a number of kingdoms.

European contacts began in the early 16th century when Portuguese merchants, profiting from the internal disunity, gained trading privileges on the west coast. Dutch traders gradually supplanted Portuguese influence in the 17th century, but were replaced by British forces in 1796. When the embattled interior kingdom of Kandy fell in 1815, the entire island came under the control of the British, who called it Ceylon. In the early 20th century the middle class was pressing for self-government. A new constitution was established in 1931, but racial tensions prevented its full implementation. The island, although now granted an element of self-government, remained a crown colony until 1948, when it was granted independence as a dominion within the COMMONWEALTH OF NATIONS. A government was established by the United National Party under Don SENANAYAKE, who was succeeded (1952) by his son, Dudley Senanayake. The Socialist Sri Lanka Freedom Party was in power from 1956 to 1965, and Solomon BANDARANAIKE was its dominant force until his death in 1959. His widow, Sirimavo Bandaranaike, succeeded him as Prime

Minister (1960–65, 1970–77, 1994–). A new constitution in 1972 established the island as the Republic of Sri Lanka. Tensions have re-emerged between the majority Sinhalese, traditionally Buddhist, and the minority Tamil, chiefly Hindu, who had come from southern India and live in northern Sri Lanka. A cease-fire was arranged by the Indian government in 1987 between Tamil guerrilla groups and the Sri Lankan government, but a tense situation remained. During 1989–90 President Ranasinghe Premadasa initiated all-party talks to end civil strife, but these again failed and in 1991 the Defence Minister was assassinated. A state of emergency was declared, but violations of human rights by government forces led to suspension of UK aid. During the years 1990–91 civil strife claimed some 12,000 lives. Although peace talks were again initiated in April 1992, they made little progress. Meanwhile the Sri Lankan economy rapidly declined. President Premadasa was assassinated in 1993. Chandrika Kumaratunga, daughter of Solomon and Sirimavo Bandaranaike, was elected Prime Minister in 1994. Later in the same year, Kumaratunga became President and was succeeded as Prime Minister by her mother. Peace negotiations and a cease-fire between the Government and Tamil guerrillas in 1994 were abandoned, and renewed fighting erupted in 1995. Despite a successful assault by government forces on the Tamil guerrilla stronghold in the Jaffna peninsula in the north of the island, fighting has continued.

Capital: Colombo (President and judiciary); Sri Jayewardenepura Kotte (Prime Minister and legislature)
Area: 65,610 sq km (25,332 sq mi)
Population: 18,090,000 (1995)
Currency: 1 Sri Lankan rupee = 100 cents
Religions: Buddhist 70.0%; Hindu 15.0%; Christian 8.0%; Muslim 7.0%
Ethnic Groups: Sinhalese 74.0%; Tamil 18.0%; Moor 7.0%
Languages: Sinhalese, Tamil (both official); English
International Organizations: UN; Commonwealth; Non-Aligned Movement; Colombo Plan

Srinagar The summer capital of the state of Jammu and Kashmir in north-west India, a crafts, textile-manufacturing, and tourist city on the Jhelum River north-west of the Pir Panjal Range; pop. (1991) 595,000.

SS (*Schutzstaffel*; German, 'protective echelon') The élite corps of the German Nazi Party. Founded (1925) by HITLER as a personal bodyguard, the SS was schooled in absolute loyalty and obedience, and in total ruthlessness towards opponents. From 1929 until the dissolution of the THIRD REICH in 1945 the SS was headed by Heinrich HIMMLER, who divided it mainly into two groups: the Allgemeine SS (General SS), and the Waffen-SS (Armed SS). Subdivisions of the SS included the GESTAPO and the Sicherheitsdienst, in charge of foreign and domestic intelligence work. The Waffen-SS administered the CONCENTRATION CAMPS. After the fall of the Third Reich, Himmler committed suicide and the whole corps was condemned by the court at the Nuremberg trials.

stabilizer A device used to minimize the rolling (side-to-side) motion of a ship at sea. One type is the fin stabilizer, a continuously adjusting fin projecting from the side of the vessel, which opposes and thus minimizes rolling. An onboard GYROSCOPE senses deviations of the ship from the vertical; these deviations are opposed by the action of the fins. Other types of stabilizer utilize the inertia of a specially shaped tank of fluid carried on board to oppose the ship's rolling action.

stable fly A true FLY of the genus *Stomoxys*, which bites animals and sucks blood. Stable flies are related to the HOUSEFLY, and are sometimes called the biting housefly. They frequent farm buildings and feed on a variety of warm-blooded animals, using the modified proboscis, which is long, rigid, and non-retractile. The larvae develop in horse dung and stable litter, and pupate in the ground.

Staël, Mme de See DE STAËL.

Stafford The county town of Staffordshire in central England, an industrial town producing footwear, chemicals, and electronics; pop. (1991) 61,885. Staffordshire University (formerly Staffordshire Polytechnic) was established in 1992.

Staffordshire A county of central England; area 2,716 sq km (1,049 sq miles); pop. (1991) 1,020,300; county town, Stafford. It is divided into nine districts.

stag beetle A large, heavily built, dark coloured BEETLE of the family Lucanidae, the males of which have their jaws enlarged and branched to resemble antlers. Their jaw muscles are not enlarged and the jaws are useless for feeding or offence, and may be presumed to be of value in competing with other males for females. Their fat, white larvae develop in rotten wood. The males of the biggest British species, *Lucanus cervus*, which have deep red wing-covers and jaws, reach 5 cm (2 inches) in length and are the heaviest British insects. Most of the 750 species of stag beetles are tropical insects.

stage-coach See CARRIAGES AND COACHES.

stag's horn fern A fern belonging to the genus *Platycerium*. The 17 species are widely distributed in the tropics and subtropics of the Old World. Although they are all EPIPHYTES, some species of stag's horn fern also grow on steep cliffs. They are characterized by two types of fronds: an upright, undivided type, adapted to clasp the host; and a spore-bearing divided type (the stag's horn), which droops downwards.

stained glass Glass that has been given translucent colour in any of various ways, used particularly for creating pictorial designs in church windows. The art began in the service of the Christian Church and is of Byzantine origin, but in its most characteristic development and its highest achievements it is essentially an art of Western Christendom. Medieval windows are generally made up of hundreds of small pieces of glass of varied colours and shapes held together by strips of lead. Windows of any size were made up of several panels so treated, and these were set in a framework of iron ('armature') that served not only as a support against wind pressure, but also to accentuate the main lines of the design of the window. In the 20th century many noteworthy artists have designed stained-glass windows, among them CHAGALL, MATISSE (notably at Vence in the South of France), and John PIPER in England.

Stainer, Sir John (1840–1901) British composer. He is remembered for his church music, including hymns, cantatas, and the oratorio *Crucifixion* (1887).

stainless steel See STEEL.

stalactites Stony pendants formed by precipitation of calcium carbonate from slowly dripping water. They hang down like icicles from the ceilings of caves or even the arches of bridges.

stalagmites Pillars of calcium carbonate deposited on the floor of a cave. Like STALACTITES, they are formed by the precipitation of calcium carbonate from water dripping from the roof of the cave. They are usually found underneath stalactites but are thicker. In time a stalactite and stalagmite may meet and form a continuous column reaching from the roof of the cave to the floor.

Stalin, Joseph (born Iosif Vissarionovich Dzhugashvili) (1879–1953) Soviet statesman, General Secretary of the Communist Party of the USSR 1922–53. Born in Georgia, he joined the Bolsheviks under Lenin in 1903 and co-founded the party's newspaper *Pravda* in 1912, adopting the name 'Stalin' (Russian, 'man of steel') by 1913; in the same year he was exiled to Siberia until just after the Russian Revolution. Following Lenin's death he became chairman of the Politburo and secured enough support within the party to eliminate TROTSKY as a contender for the leadership. By 1927 he was the uncontested leader of the party, and in the following year he launched a succession of five-year plans for the industrialization and collectivization of agriculture; as a result some 10 million peasants are thought to have died, either of famine or by execution. His purges of the intelligentsia in the 1930s along similarly punitive lines removed all opposition, while his direction of the armed forces led to victory over Hitler 1941–45. After 1945 he played a large part in the restructuring of postwar Europe and attempted to maintain a firm grip on other Communist states; he was later denounced by Khrushchev and the Eastern bloc countries.

Stalingrad See VOLGOGRAD.

Stalingrad, Battle of (1942–43) A long and bitter battle in World War II in which the German advance into the Soviet Union was turned back. During 1942 the German 6th Army under General von Paulus reached the key city of Stalingrad (now Volgograd) on the Volga. Soviet resistance continued, with grim and prolonged house-to-house fighting, while sufficient Soviet reserves were being assembled. The Germans were prevented from crossing the Volga and in November Stalin launched a winter offensive of six Soviet armies under Marshalls ZHUKOV, Koniev, Petrov, and Malinovsky. By January 1943 the Germans were surrounded and von Paulus surrendered, losing some 330,000 troops killed or captured. This defeat marked the end of German success on the Eastern Front.

stamen The structure in a flower that produces POLLEN grains, consisting of a stalk (filament) and a terminal head (anther), which contains the pollen-producing cells. They are arranged in one or more whorls, rarely spirals, around the ovary in bisexual flowers.

Stamford Bridge, Battle of (25 September 1066) A battle at a village on the River Derwent in Yorkshire, north-east England, in which HAROLD II of England defeated a large invading army under his exiled brother Tostig and the King of Norway, Harald Hardrada, both of whom were killed. Harold's army marched south from Stamford to face the Norman invasion and fight the Battle of HASTINGS.

standard deviation The most common measure of the spread, or dispersion, of a statistical sample, indicating how far the values, taken as a whole, vary from the sample MEAN, $\bar{x}$. It is the square root of the VARIANCE, which is itself the arithmetic mean of the squares of the deviation from the sample mean. The standard deviation $s = \sqrt{[1/n\ \Sigma(x_i - \bar{x})^2]}$. It is measured in the same units as the data.

standard temperature and pressure (STP) Standard conditions for quoting volumes of gases, i.e. 0°C and 1 atmosphere pressure (101,325 pascals).

standing wave A wave in which the positions of the nodes and antinodes stay in the same place. For example, when a stretched string is plucked at its central point the antinode remains at the midpoint of the string and the nodes are at the fixed ends. Standing waves (sometimes called stationary waves) are also set up when air is blown through the tube of a musical instrument.

Stanford, Sir Charles Villiers (1852–1924) Dublin-born British composer and educationalist. Among his works are a choral setting of Tennyson's *Revenge* (1886), but his music is seen at its best in the comic opera *Shamus O'Brien* (1896) and in his church music.

Stanford-Binet Scale See BINET, ALFRED.

Stanhope, Lady Hester Lucy (1776–1839) British traveller. She kept house for her uncle William Pitt the Younger from 1803 to 1806, becoming a distinguished political hostess. Stanhope was granted a pension on Pitt's death and later set out for the Middle East (1810), settling in a ruined convent in the Lebanon Mountains four years later. She participated in Middle Eastern politics for several years, but eventually died in poverty after her pension was stopped by Lord Palmerston.

Stanislaus, St (Polish name Stanisław) (1030–79) Patron saint of Poland. He became bishop of Cracow in 1072 and, as such, excommunicated King Boleslaus II (1039–81). According to tradition, Stanislaus was murdered by Boleslaus while taking Mass. Feast day, 11 April (formerly 7 May).

Stanislavsky, Konstantin (Sergeevich) (born Konstantin Sergeevich Alekseev) (1863–1938) Russian theatre director and actor. In 1898 he founded the Moscow Art Theatre and became known for his innovative productions of works by Chekhov and Maxim Gorky. He trained his actors to take a psychological approach and use latent powers of self-expression; his theory and technique of acting were later adopted in the USA and developed into the system known as method acting.

Stanley (or **Port Stanley**) The chief port and town of the Falkland Islands, situated on the island of East Falkland; pop. (1991) 1,557. Originally named Port William, Stanley replaced Port Louis as the capital of the Falklands in 1843. During the Argentine occupation of 1982 it was renamed four times in the space of six weeks, being known as Puerto Rivero, Puerto de la Isla Soledad, Puerto de las Islas Malvinas, and Puerto Argentino.

Stanley, Sir Henry Morton (born John Rowlands) (1841–1904) British explorer. As a newspaper correspondent he was sent in 1869 to central Africa to find the Scottish missionary and explorer David LIVINGSTONE; two years later he found him on the eastern shore of Lake Tanganyika. After Livingstone's death, Stanley continued his exploration, charting Lake Victoria (1874), tracing the course of the Congo (1874–77), mapping Lake Albert (1889), and becoming the first European to discover Lake Edward (1889). Stanley also helped establish the Congo Free State (now Democratic Republic of Congo), with Belgian support, from 1879 to 1885.

Stanleyville The former name (1882–1966) of KISANGANI.

Stanneries, the The tin-mining areas of west Devon and east Cornwall in south-west England. Its name is derived from the Latin *stannum* ('tin'). Until 1896 the region had its own 'stannary courts' which met in the open air at Crockern Tor on Dartmoor.

Stansted The site, in north Essex, south-east England, of London's third international airport. It was originally a World War II US Airforce base. Its £400 million airport complex was designed by Sir Norman Foster and opened in 1991. There is a railway link with Liverpool Street Station in central London.

stanza A group of verse lines with a set pattern of METRE and RHYME, which is repeated throughout a poem, each stanza having the same number of lines. Stanzas, sometimes loosely referred to as 'verses', are usually separated by spaces in printed poems. The commonest stanza is the QUATRAIN; Boccaccio, Chaucer, and Spenser introduced stanzaic patterns of greater intricacy.

star A self-luminous gaseous body, such as our own Sun. Stars are formed from the gas and dust that exists in the vast spaces between them, whereas planets form from material in orbit around a young star. The Milky Way GALAXY contains some 100 billion stars. The stars are traditionally grouped into CONSTELLATIONS, but for the most part they are unconnected and are at greatly differing distances. The brightest stars in each constellation are usually designated by letters of the Greek alphabet, and many have proper names, most of which were given by Islamic astronomers. Fainter stars are designated by their number in a catalogue.

Apart from the Sun, stars are at great distances from the Earth; the nearest, Proxima Centauri, is 1.3 parsecs or 40 million million kilometres away. Consequently most stars appear as fixed points of light that cannot be seen as discs by even the largest telescopes.

Much can be learnt about stars by studying their spectra (see SPECTROSCOPY). They can be classified according to their temperature and luminosity. Most stars derive their energy from nuclear fusion, though in some the Kelvin-Helmholtz contraction releases gravitational energy. WHITE DWARFS are powered by thermal energy, and NEUTRON STARS by rotational energy. Stellar evolution can be conveniently summarized on the HERTZSPRUNG–RUSSELL DIAGRAM.

Stara Planina See BALKAN MOUNTAINS.

starch The main food storage compound of plants. It is a mixture of two different CARBOHYDRATES of the polysaccharide group, amylose and amylopectin. Amylose contains 250–300 glucose subunits linked to form a long right-handed spiral shape, or helix. Amylopectin is very similar except that it has a branching structure. Following PHOTOSYNTHESIS, starch grains are deposited in the cytoplasm of many plant cells, particularly in seeds, and in storage organs, such as potato tubers. The starch is hydrolysed by enzymes called amylases to sucrose for transport in plants and, after being further broken down into GLUCOSE, provides a large proportion of the daily energy requirement in animals. Starch itself is used in pastes, for stiffening paper and fabrics, and as a filler in pills.

Star Chamber An English court of civil and criminal jurisdiction primarily concerned with offences affecting crown interests, noted for its summary and arbitrary procedure. It was long thought to have had its origin in a statute of 1487; in fact, however, since the reign of EDWARD IV the court of Star Chamber had been developing from the king's council acting in its judicial capacity into a regular court of law. It owed its name to the fact that it commonly sat in a room in the Palace of Westminster that had a ceiling covered with stars. Its judges specialized in cases involving public order, and particularly allegations of riot. Its association with the royal prerogative, and Charles I's manipulation of legislative powers in the making of decrees during the period of his personal rule, made it unpopular in the 17th century and caused its abolition by the LONG PARLIAMENT in 1641.

starfish The most familiar of the ECHINODERMS, with over 1,600 species found in marine habitats worldwide. Like many other echinoderms, they show a five-rayed symmetry. The five arms each bear hundreds of tiny coordinated suction feet. Together these may exert enough force to pull open a bivalve. The starfish then everts its own stomach into the prey, releasing digestive enzymes, before sucking up the resulting soup through its ventral mouth. Starfish can be brightly coloured, often bearing elaborate spines and miniature claws. In the tropics, where they may reach 1 m (3 feet) across, their colours may be quite startling. In some burrowing species, such as the cushion stars, the arms are so reduced that the body forms a five-sided pad. Starfish belong to the subclass Asteroidea.

starling A bird of the Old World family Sturnidae, containing about 110 species. Mostly thrush-sized, they tend to have an iridescent sheen on black, purple, or green plumage. This family also includes the mynahs, which are well known as mimics and are kept as cage-birds. The common starling, *Sturnus vulgaris*, originated in the Old World but has been introduced to many other parts of the world, including North America. About 20 cm (8 inches) long, it is blackish with pale speckles and a purple or green sheen. In the breeding season the normally black beak turns yellow.

Starling, Ernest Henry (1866–1927) British physiologist. Studying the digestive system, he demonstrated the existence of peristalsis, and showed that a substance secreted by the pancreas passes via the blood to the duodenal wall, where it stimulates the secretion of digestive juices. He coined the term *hormone* for such substances, and founded the science of endocrinology. Starling also studied the theory of circulation, the functioning of heart muscle, and fluid exchange at capillary level.

star of Bethlehem Any of several perennial plants of the genus *Ornithogalum*, in the lily family, Liliaceae, native to Europe and northern Africa. The clusters of green and white flowers of *O. umbellatum* are produced in spring and early summer and open only when the Sun shines. The bulbs were formerly much valued as a source of food, eaten both raw and cooked.

star of David A six-pointed star consisting of two equilateral triangles superimposed on each other. A symbol of considerable antiquity, it has been associated with Judaism since the 17th century. A yellow star of David had to be worn by Jews in Germany and German-occupied Europe during the years preceding the Holocaust. A blue star of David now appears on the Israeli flag.

Starr, Ringo (born Richard Starkey) (1940–) British rock and pop drummer. He replaced Pete Best in the Beatles in 1962, by which time he was already an experienced professional drummer. In 1966 he sang the hit 'Yellow Submarine', which later formed the basis of a cartoon film (1969). After the band's split (1970) he pursued a solo career.

START See STRATEGIC ARMS REDUCTION TALKS.

state of matter See PHASES OF MATTER.

States-General (or **Estates-General**) Usually a gathering of representatives of the three estates of a realm: the Church; the nobility; and the commons (representatives of the corporations of towns). They met to advise a sovereign on matters of policy. The name was applied to the representative body of the United Provinces of the Netherlands in their struggle for independence from Spain in the 16th century.

In France, it began as an occasional advisory body, usually summoned to register specific support for controversial royal policy. It was developed by Philip IV who held a meeting in 1302 to enlist support during a quarrel with the pope, but throughout the 14th century it was rarely convoked and the first proper States-General in France was in 1484 in the reign of Louis XI.

stationary waves See STANDING WAVES.

Stations of the Cross See CROSS.

statistical mechanics A branch of physics in which statistical methods are applied to the microscopic constituents of matter in order to predict its macroscopic properties. In classical statistical mechanics each particle is regarded as occupying an exact position and to have an exact momentum at any instant. The MAXWELL-BOLTZMANN DISTRIBUTION gives the probable distribution of such particles. In quantum statistics these assumptions cannot be made as a result of the HEISENBERG uncertainty principle, which led to BOSE-Einstein statistics and FERMI-Dirac statistics.

statistics The classification and study of collections of data and their interpretation in mathematical terms. Statistics are often used in order to draw an inference or calculate a measure, called a statistic. Analysis is made of a population (in the most general sense) and sometimes predictions of changes are made in terms of PROBABILITY. Normally a representative sample is taken, large enough for it to be generalized to the whole. In descriptive statistics the data are summarized and the population described. Inferential statistics normally proposes a null hypothesis and then endeavours to disprove it. Because no sample can be guaranteed to be representative, statisticians need to indicate confidence limits, using calculations of mean and VARIANCE.

Statius, Publius Papinius (*c.*45–96 AD) Roman poet. He flourished at the court of Domitian and is best known for the *Silvae*, a miscellany of poems addressed to friends, and the *Thebais*, an epic concerning the bloody quarrel between the sons of Oedipus. His work, which often uses mythological or fantastical images, was much admired in the Middle Ages.

Statue of Liberty See LIBERTY, STATUE OF.

statute law Law contained in enactments of the supreme legislative body in a jurisdiction. Proposed legislation is usually introduced in draft, and if approved (with or without amendment) in the manner provided for under the constitution, becomes law. Statute law usually overrides all other sources of law such as CASE LAW and CUSTOMARY LAW. Exceptions are any entrenched constitutional provisions or, in member states of the European Communities, provisions of Community law which have direct effect in member states.

Stauffenberg, Claus, Graf von (1907–44) German army colonel who planted the bomb under the conference table at Hitler's headquarters on 20 July 1944, in an attempt to assassinate him. Known as the **July Plot**, this assassination attempt was organized by a number of senior German officers. However, the attempt failed and Hitler was only slightly injured. Stauffenberg and his fellow conspirators were executed.

Steady State theory Any theory of COSMOLOGY postulating that the Universe is the same in all places and at all times. The Steady State theory of Bondi, HOYLE, and Gold requires that matter is continually being created. Although it is one of the most appealing theories it cannot satisfactorily explain the radio source counts and the MICROWAVE BACKGROUND RADIATION and is now generally discredited.

steam distillation A process in which steam is passed into a mixture that is to be distilled. Direct external heating often causes local overheating and decomposition. This is avoided in steam DISTILLATION because the steam condenses, giving up its latent heat of vaporization evenly throughout the mixture, eventually causing the mixture to boil and distillation to occur. An example of its use is in the purification of ESSENTIAL OILS.

steam-engine The first effective heat ENGINE, in which steam from a BOILER is used to drive a piston in a cylinder. Although the ancient Greeks built small steam-powered models (see STEAM-TURBINE), the first successful steam-engine was the BEAM-ENGINE, developed by NEWCOMEN in 1712 for pumping water out of mines. It was improved by Smeaton and further developed by WATT, who in 1769 introduced a condenser separate from the cylinder and made many other improvements. TREVITHICK in Cornwall and EVANS in the USA developed high-pressure steam-engines that exhausted into the atmosphere rather than to a condenser. These could produce the same power and efficiency in a much smaller and lighter unit, making portable engines possible. The first STEAM LOCOMOTIVE, developed by Trevithick, was built in 1804. STEAMSHIPS were first built in the late 18th and early 19th century; they continued to develop throughout the 19th century. Compound engines, in which steam is expanded in two stages, originated with the UK engineer Jonathan Hornblower in 1781. The triple-expansion engine became standard for marine use, in which fuel economy is important, in the late 1880s. Large steam-engines were used to drive workshops and mills, while an engine with a high rotational speed, needed for electricity generation, was designed by P. W. Willans. By 1900 the steam-engine was a versatile power unit but within a very few years it had largely given way to STEAM-TURBINES, which could work at higher speeds, and the INTERNAL-COMBUSTION ENGINE, which was lighter and more efficient.

steam locomotive A railway locomotive powered by a STEAM-ENGINE. The first steam locomotive was built in 1804, by TREVITHICK. Between 1804 and the building of the *Rocket* in 1829 by R. STEPHENSON, the basic layout for most subsequent steam locomotives was evolved. Hot gases from a water-jacketed fire-box pass into a BOILER made up of a large number of copper tubes; the gases heat water circulating around the tubes and turn it into steam. The steam passes into a pair of double-acting cylinders, which drive the powered wheels through connecting-rods. The spent steam is exhausted through a chimney to the atmosphere, the draught from the exhaust being used to draw the fire-box fire. Fuel (usually coal) and water are carried in a tender behind the locomotive (except on the tank locomotive). Later improvements included superheating the steam, using three or four cylinders instead of two, and (in the compound steam locomotive) using the steam from the high-pressure cylinders to drive a set of low-pressure cylinders. However, even the most advanced designs had a thermal EFFICIENCY of only about 6 per cent. It was this low efficiency and the growing cost of the labour-intensive maintenance that led to the development of diesel and electric locomotives to replace them.

steamship A ship powered by a STEAM-ENGINE. During the late 18th century numerous trials of steam-powered vessels were carried out in France, Britain, and the USA. The steamship *Charlotte Dundas* of 1802 was intended as a canal steamer, but was withdrawn after four days because of fears that its wash would erode the canal banks. The first commercially successful steamers were FULTON's steamer *North River* (*Clermont*) in the USA (1807) and the British engineer Patrick Bell's *Comet* in Scotland (1812). By the mid-1820s paddle-wheel steamers were carrying passengers on rivers and short sea runs in North America and Europe, and navies were beginning to use steam for smaller warships. The marine PROPELLER was developed in the late 1830s, and was widely adopted by navies in the 1840s. By then, steam was replacing sail for carrying passengers and mail on all but the longest oceanic routes. With the introduction of steam colliers in the 1850s, steam also began to take over in cargo-carrying. As steam-engines became more reliable and efficient, the use of steamships continued to grow. As a result of the introduction of the triple-expansion engine at the end of the 1880s, steam tramp ships became the dominant general-purpose cargo carriers, and ships no longer carried sails for assistance and safety. The demonstration of the STEAM-TURBINE by PARSONS in 1897 led to a change from the reciprocating steam-engine to turbine power. Many of the large LINERS of the early 20th century used steam-turbines. In the early 20th century the marine DIESEL ENGINE made its appearance, and has steadily increased in importance, although steam-turbines are still used in some large ships.

steam-turbine An ENGINE that uses the thermal energy of steam produced in a BOILER to drive a TURBINE at high speed. Jets of steam from nozzles around the periphery of the turbine impinge on the turbine blades, causing them to turn. Steam-turbines can work at high rotational speeds and generate high powers from a relatively small unit. Their major use is in ELECTRICITY GENERATION; for a time they were also important marine engines. They have the advantage over GAS-TURBINES in that they can be built in much larger capacity units: power outputs from the largest turbines may exceed 1,000 MW.

steel An alloy of IRON and CARBON, of immense importance in all developed countries. It is strong and stiff, but corrodes easily through rusting, although **stainless steel** (usually containing 18 per cent chromium and 8 per cent nickel) and other special steels resist CORROSION. The amount of carbon in a steel influences its properties considerably. Steels of low carbon content (mild steels) are quite ductile, and are used in the manufacture of sheet iron, wire, and pipes. Medium-carbon steels containing 0.2–0.4 per cent carbon are tougher and stronger and are used in railway tracks, structural steel, and boiler plates. Both mild and medium-carbon steels are suitable for FORGING and WELDING. High-carbon steels contain 0.4–1.5 per cent carbon, are hard and brittle, and are used in cutting tools, surgical instruments, razor blades, springs, and cutlery. Tool steel, also called silver steel, contains about 1 per cent carbon and is strengthened and toughened by quenching and TEMPERING. The inclusion of other elements affects the properties of the steel. MANGANESE gives extra strength and toughness, whereas 4 per cent silicon steel is used for transformer cores or electromagnets. The addition of **chromium** and nickel gives extra strength and corrosion resistance. Heating in the presence of carbon- or nitrogen-rich materials is used to form a hard surface on steel (case-hardening). High-speed steels, which are extremely important in machine-tools, contain chromium and TUNGSTEN plus smaller amounts of VANADIUM, MOLYBDENUM, and other metals.

Steel, David (Martin Scott), Baron (1938–) British politician, leader of the Liberal Party 1976–88. He was jointly head (with David Owen) of the alliance between the Liberals and the Social Democratic Party 1981–87, and supported the merger of the two parties to form the Social and Liberal Democratics (later renamed the Liberal Democrats).

steel band A type of percussion ensemble, originating in the Caribbean, comprising instruments made from discarded oil drums. One end of the drum is beaten down to form a basin, and areas of it are beaten up into domes. Each section produces its own note when tapped, and is then tuned by further beating with a hammer. There are six basic types of drum: the rhythm pan, which has two sections; the melody pan, which has 25; the second pan, with 14 sections; the cello pan, with nine; and the bass pan with five. Bands composed of a set of steel drums are capable of amazing versatility, playing music ranging from CALYPSO and carnival music to arrangements of Western classical pieces.

Steele, Sir Richard (1672–1729) Irish essayist and dramatist. He founded and wrote for the periodicals the *Tatler* (1709–11) and the *Spectator* (1711–12), the latter in collaboration with Joseph Addison; both had an important influence on the manners, morals, and literature of the time. Steele also launched the short-lived periodical the *Guardian* (1713), to which Addison contributed.

Steer, Philip Wilson (1860–1942) British painter. With SICKERT (his friend and contemporary), Steer was the leader in his generation of those progressive British artists who looked to French artists, in his case DEGAS and MONET, for inspiration. He trained in Paris in 1882–84, and in the late 1880s and early 1890s he produced works (mainly beach scenes and seascapes) that are remarkable for their great freshness and subtle handling of light. After about 1895 Steer's work became more conventional and more closely linked with the English tradition of landscape painting.

Stefan, Joseph (1835–93) Austrian physicist who established the law linking the temperature of an object and the rate at which it radiates energy. According to **Stefan's Law** the total power P emitted per unit surface area, in watts per square metre, is given by $P = \sigma T^4$, where $\sigma = 5.67 \times 10^{-8}$ W m^{-2} K^{-4} is the Stefan-Boltzmann constant, and T is the thermodynamic temperature of the black body.

Stegocerus See DINOSAUR.

Stegosaurus See DINOSAUR.

Stein, Gertrude (1874–1946) US writer. From 1903 she lived mainly in Paris, where during the 1920s and 1930s her home became a focus for the avant-garde, including such writers as Ernest Hemingway and Ford Madox Ford and such artists as Matisse. In her writing, Stein developed an esoteric stream-of-consciousness style, whose hallmarks include use of repetition and lack of punctuation. Her best-known work is *The Autobiography of Alice B. Toklas* (1933), in which her long-standing American companion Alice B. Toklas (1877–1967) is made the ostensible author of her own memoir.

Steinbeck, John (Ernst) (1902–68) US novelist. His work is noted for its sympathetic and realistic portrayal of the migrant agricultural workers of California, as in *Of Mice and Men* (1937) and *The Grapes of Wrath* (1939). His later novels include *East of Eden* (1952). Steinbeck was awarded the Nobel Prize for literature in 1962.

Steiner, Rudolf (1861–1925) Austrian philosopher, founder of anthroposophy. He joined Annie Besant's theosophist movement in 1902, but ten years later broke away to found his own Anthroposophical Society. Steiner proposed that spiritual development had been stunted by over-attention to the material world and that to reverse this process it was necessary to nurture the faculty of cognition. His society is noted for its contribution to child-centred education, and particularly for its Steiner schools for children with learning difficulties, operating in many parts of the Western world.

Steinway, Henry (Engelhard) (born Heinrich Engelhard Steinweg) (1797–1871) German piano-builder, resident in the USA from 1849. His name is used to designate pianos manufactured by the firm which he founded in New York in 1853.

Stella, Frank (Philip) (1936–) US painter. In the late 1950s he reacted against the subjectivity of abstract expressionism and became an important figure in minimalism, painting a series of all-black paintings. He later experimented with shaped canvases and cut-out shapes in relief.

stellar evolution The study of the life history of stars. Stars are believed to be formed by the collapse under GRAVITATION of material, mainly hydrogen, in NEBULAE. They heat up through the Kelvin-Helmholtz contraction, and when their central temperature reaches about 10 million K they begin to draw their energy from nuclear fusion, converting hydrogen to helium in the CARBON-NITROGEN CYCLE. Such stars are called DWARF STARS, and are found on the main sequence in the HERTZSPRUNG–RUSSELL DIAGRAM. This stage lasts a million years or less in the most massive stars, or about 10^{10} years for such stars as the Sun. It continues until the mass of helium at the star's core reaches the Schönberg-Chandrasekhar limit. Hydrogen burning then continues in a shell surrounding the core, and the star begins to evolve towards the GIANT STAR stage, with increasing radius and decreasing surface temperature. Stars with a mass greater than 0.4 times that of the Sun can go on to convert helium to carbon, and carbon to heavier elements by nuclear synthesis. Eventually the star exhausts its nuclear fuel. Most stars shed their outer layers, exposing the helium-rich core, which becomes a WHITE DWARF. In massive stars, the core may collapse in a SUPERNOVA explosion, forming a NEUTRON STAR or even a BLACK HOLE. Such a collapse is thought to occur if the star's mass remains greater than the CHANDRASEKHAR limit.

stellar parallax See PARALLAX.

stellar populations The classification, introduced by BAADE, of stars into two main classes. **Population I** contains young blue SUPERGIANTS, while **Population II** contains old RED GIANTS. Such populations show a marked preference for various parts of the Galaxy, with Population I stars being found in open, galactic CLUSTERS and the spiral arms (see SPIRAL GALAXY) while Population II stars make up globular clusters and are also found in the region of the galactic centre. Population II stars seem to have only traces of the heavy elements in their make-up in contrast to Population I stars, which may have up to ten times more. This is consistent with the belief that the INTERSTELLAR MEDIUM is being continually enriched by the ejection of heavy elements created in SUPERNOVA explosions.

Steller, Georg Wilhelm (1709–46) German naturalist and geographer. Working for a period as a physician with the Russian army, Steller became a research member of Vitus Bering's ill-fated second expedition to Kamchatka and Alaska. Following their shipwreck on Bering Island (1741) he made a large collection of specimens but had to abandon it; however, he later described many new birds and mammals, several of which (including the extinct giant sea cow) now bear his name. Steller later died of fever in Siberia at the age of 37.

stem The part of a plant that bears the leaves and flowers (or other reproductive structures) and contains vascular tissue (XYLEM and PHLOEM). Stems are usually aerial but may be subterranean, as in RHIZOMES, BULBS, and CORMS. Stems are green in their early stages of growth, and photosynthesize; in leafless succulents they may continue to photosynthesize. With age, they acquire more strengthening tissue and, in some perennials, accumulate deposits of wood, forming woody stems and branches, or a thick trunk in trees.

Stendhal (pseudonym of Marie Henri Beyle) (1783–1842) French novelist. His two best-known novels are *Le Rouge et le noir* (1830), relating the rise and fall of a young man from the provinces in the France of the Restoration (1814), and *La Chartreuse de Parme* (1839), set in a small Italian court in the same period. Both are notable for their psychological realism and political analysis.

Sten gun See SUB-MACHINE-GUN.

Steno, Nicolaus (born Niels Steensen) (1638–86) Danish anatomist and geologist. He proposed several ideas that are now regarded as fundamental to geology – that fossils are the petrified remains of living organisms, that many rocks arise from consolidation of sediments, and that such rocks occur in layers in the order in which they were laid down, thereby constituting a record of the geological history of the Earth. Steno also recognized the constancy of crystal form in particular minerals. He later became a bishop.

Stephen (*c.*1097–1154) Grandson of William the Conqueror, king of England 1135–54. Stephen seized the throne of England from MATILDA a few months after the death of her father Henry I. Having forced Matilda to flee the kingdom, Stephen was confronted with civil war following her invasion in 1139; although captured at Lincoln (1141) and temporarily deposed, he ultimately forced Matilda to withdraw from England in 1148. However, the year before he died Stephen was obliged to recognize Matilda's son, the future Henry II, as heir to the throne.

Stephen, St (died *c.*35 AD) Christian martyr. He was one of the original seven deacons in Jerusalem appointed by the Apostles. He incurred the hostility of the Jews and was charged with blasphemy before the Sanhedrin and stoned, so becoming the first Christian martyr. Saul (the future St Paul) was present at his execution. Feast day (in the Western Church), 26 December; (in the Eastern Church), 27 December.

Stephen, St (*c.*977–1038) King and patron saint of Hungary, reigned 1000–38. The first king of Hungary, he united Pannonia and Dacia as one kingdom, and took steps to Christianize the country. Feast day, 2 September or (in Hungary) 20 August.

Stephenson, George (1781–1848) British engineer, the father of railways. He started as a colliery engineman, applied steam power to the haulage of coal wagons by cable, and built his first locomotive in 1814. He became engineer to the Stockton and Darlington Railway, and in 1825 drove the first train on it using a steam locomotive of his own design. His son **Robert Stephenson** (1803–59) assisted him in the building of engines and of the Liverpool to Manchester railway, for which they built the famous *Rocket* (1829) – the prototype for all future steam locomotives. Robert became famous also as a bridge designer, notably of major bridges at Menai Strait and Conwy in Wales, Berwick and Newcastle in northern England, Montreal in Canada, and in Egypt.

steppe The vast areas of flat grasslands in eastern Europe and Asia that have been largely altered as a result of cultivation and extensive grazing by livestock. In their natural state they varied from the meadow steppes of the northern forest edge to the semidesert grasslands of central Asia.

stereochemistry The study of the three-dimensional structure of molecules. Stereochemical considerations are important in both ISOMERISM and studies of the mechanisms of chemical reactions. Implicit in a mechanism is the stereochemistry of the reaction; in other words, the relative three-dimensional orientation of the reacting particles at any time in the reaction.

stereophonic reproduction A recording technique that attempts to re-create the spatial effect a listener would usually experience at a live performance (for example, the sounds of different instruments emanating from different regions in an orchestra). The first stereophonic demonstration involved relaying a live Paris Opera performance to the Paris Exposition in 1881. Stereophonic recording, first proposed in 1931 by BLUMLEIN, was achieved by recording the signals from two microphones at a live performance on the two sides of a record groove. Stereo RECORDS were first marketed in 1958.

stereophotography The making of stereoscopic photographs – a pair of photographs of a scene taken from slightly different viewpoints, which give a three-dimensional effect when seen through a viewer (a stereoscope). The photographs are shot simultaneously by a stereo-camera, which has two identical lens systems separated by several centimetres, mimicking the separation of the eyes. The stereoscope allows each eye to see only one of the two photographs: this gives the image an impression of depth. Stereophotography was first popular in the late 19th century; a major use today is in aerial surveys, where it allows height measurement from photographs.

stereotype (in printing) A LETTERPRESS PRINTING plate made by taking a thick paper mould of the original composed metal type and illustration blocks under pressure. Molten, lead-based metal that hardens quickly is poured into the mould to produce the plate. The back of the plate is then planed to a uniform thickness. To fit rotary presses, stereotypes are cast in a curve.

sterilization The practice of making medical equipment free from microbiological contamination, and hence greatly reducing the incidence of infection in patients. Heat sterilization using boiling water, steam, or steam under pressure in autoclaves has replaced the earlier, chemical methods of ANTISEPSIS. Other agents, including ethylene oxide and certain gas mixtures, are suitable for sterilizing more complex equipment. Disposable items such as dressings, needles, and hypodermic syringes are supplied pre-packed and sterilized (sometimes by gamma irradiation) by the manufacturer. See also ASEPSIS.

Sternberg, Josef von (born Jonas Sternberg) (1894–1969) Austrian-born US film director. He is best known for his films with Marlene Dietrich, beginning with the German-made *The Blue Angel* (1930), about the destruction of a middle-aged professor through sexual dependence. The remaining films, made in the USA, were *Morocco* (1930), *Dishonored* (1931), *Shanghai Express* and *Blonde Venus* (both 1932), *The Scarlet Empress* (1934), and *The Devil is a Woman* (1935).

Sterne, Laurence (1713–68) Irish novelist. He worked as a clergyman in the north of England before publishing the first two volumes of his best-known work *The Life and Opinions of Tristram Shandy* in 1759. Seven subsequent volumes appeared between 1761 and 1767. Both praised for its humour and condemned for its indecency at the time, *Tristram Shandy* parodied the developing conventions of the novel form and used devices – including a distinctive fluid narrative – which anticipated many of the stylistic concerns of modernist and later writers. He suffered from tuberculosis and after 1762 spent much of his time in France and Italy, later writing *A Sentimental Journey Through France and Italy* (1768).

steroids and steroid treatment Steroids are a large group of fat-soluble compounds, having a basic structure of 17 carbon atoms arranged in four linked rings. Steroids are widely distributed in living organisms and include SEX HORMONES, corticosteroids (hormones produced by the cortex of the ADRENAL GLANDS), VITAMIN D, and sterols such as CHOLESTEROL. Therapeutically, corticosteroids are used as anti-inflammatory agents and immunosuppressants in the treatment of a wide range of diseases, including auto-immune diseases, and in TRANSPLANT SURGERY. Applied to the eye or skin, they are relatively safe to use, since little is absorbed into the body. However, large doses taken orally over long periods can produce serious side-effects. These include a reduced ability of the body to repair injury and resist infection, and a loss of calcium from the bones. **Anabolic steroids** are derived from the male hormone, testosterone. They cause the deposition of protein in tissues, and were formerly given to aid convalescence. They are sometimes taken by athletes and weight-lifters for their muscle-building properties, but can cause serious damage to the liver. Large amounts may lead to bouts of aggressive behaviour, or even death. Steroids form the active ingredients of most oral contraceptive pills.

stethoscope A diagnostic instrument for listening to sounds inside the body. Invented by LÄENNEC in 1816, it became accepted when the view was established that disease was localized in organs of the body, and was not due to an imbalance of bodily humours. Early monaural stethoscopes (for one ear) were wooden tubes about 30 cm (1 foot) long, but these were superseded by the binaural stethoscope from the 1890s. Stethoscopes are mostly used in the diagnosis of lung and heart conditions, but also in OBSTETRICS, and together with the SPHYGMOMANOMETER to measure blood pressure.

Stevenage A town in Hertfordshire, south-east England, built as a New Town in 1946; pop. (1991)

76,064. It has light industries including aircraft and electronic equipment.

Stevens, Wallace (1879–1955) US poet. He spent most of his working life as a lawyer for an insurance firm, writing poetry privately and mostly in isolation from the literary community, developing an original and colourful style. Collections of his work include *Harmonium* (1923), *Man with the Blue Guitar and Other Poems* (1937), and *Collected Poems* (1954), which won a Pulitzer Prize.

Stevenson, Robert Louis (Balfour) (1850–94) Scottish novelist, poet, and travel writer. He suffered from a chronic bronchial condition and spent much of his life abroad, notably in the South Seas. Stevenson made his name with the adventure story *Treasure Island* (1883). His other works include the novel *The Strange Case of Dr Jekyll and Mr Hyde* (1886) and a series of Scottish romances including *Kidnapped* (1886) and *The Master of Ballantrae* (1889). He is also known for *A Child's Garden of Verses*, a collection of poetry first published as *Penny Whistles* in 1885.

Stewart, Jackie (born John Young Stewart) (1939–) British motor-racing driver. He was three times world champion (1969; 1971; 1973).

Stewart, James (Maitland) (1908–97) US actor. He made his screen début in 1935. Notable films include *The Philadelphia Story* (1940), which earned him an Oscar, Alfred Hitchcock's *Rear Window* (1954) and *Vertigo* (1958), and westerns, such as *The Man from Laramie* (1955).

Stewart, Rod(erick David) (1945–) British rock singer and songwriter. A recognized figure of London's rhythm and blues community in the mid-1960s, Stewart began a solo recording career in 1969 while also singing with the band the Faces. In 1971 his single 'Maggie May' and album *Every Picture Tells a Story* topped the singles and album charts in both Britain and the USA. His later hits include 'Sailing' (1976) and 'Do You Think I'm Sexy?' (1978).

Stewart Island New Zealand's third largest island, 32 km (20 miles) south of the South Island, across the Foveaux Strait. It has a rugged and deeply indented coastline and a mountainous interior, rising to Mount Anglem at 980 m (3,210 feet) in the north. It measures 63 km (39 miles) long and 32 km (20 miles) wide, and the climate is cool. Tin and feldspar are found.

stick insect (or **walking stick**) A large, elongate, green or brown insect, making up the order Phasmida along with the LEAF INSECTS. In most species the female is wingless and the males, if they occur, are winged. They live in warm climates and are protectively coloured and camouflaged to look like twigs. Most feed on the leaves of trees and drop their eggs to the ground singly. Those that feed on or near the ground are among the bulkiest insects known, growing up to 30 cm (12 inches) in length. Many species are parthenogenetic, producing fertile eggs without mating and rarely producing males.

stickleback A fish of a small family, Gasterosteidae, which is confined to the Northern Hemisphere, with species living in fresh, brackish, and sea water. Eight species are known, and most are moderately elongate and scaleless with a series of separate spines (3–16 depending on species) along the back, and a single spine forming each pelvic fin. Best known is the three-spined stickleback, *Gasterosteus aculeatus*, found in fresh water in both North America and Europe, and in the sea in the northern part of their range. It grows to 5 cm (2 inches) in length and feeds mainly on small crustaceans. It breeds in early summer in a nest made by the male.

Stieglitz, Alfred (1864–1946) US photographer, critic, and gallery director. Founder of the Photo-Secession, Stieglitz edited *Camera Notes* (1897–1902) and *Camera Work* (1903–17) and directed the Little Galleries of the Photo-Secession (1905–17), showing not only photography but the work of most of the important figures in European avant-garde art. Throughout his life he organized art exhibitions and, though a fine photographer was finally most important for his role in shaping the art of photography – particularly pictorialist photography – in 20th-century America.

stifftail A member of a distinctive group of mainly nocturnal, freshwater BAY DUCKS, possessing stiff tails with which they steer under water. On the surface they often swim with tails cocked. They belong to the tribe Oxyurini of the duck family, Anatidae. Typical is the ruddy duck, *Oxyura jamaicensis*, an American bird introduced into Britain: the drake is chestnut, black, and white with a blue beak. The largest stifftail is the Australian musk duck, *Biziura lobata*, whose male has a big fleshy lobe beneath its beak, and performs complicated communal courtship displays.

Stijl, De (Dutch, 'the style') A group of mainly Dutch artists founded in 1917 and also the name of the journal they published to set forth their ideas. The artists involved, the most famous of whom was MONDRIAN, sought laws of equilibrium and harmony that would be applicable to life and society as well as art, and their style was one of austere abstract clarity. Their ideas had considerable influence between the two World Wars, but more on architecture and design (notably at the BAUHAUS) than on painting and sculpture.

stilt Any of nine species of wading bird in the same family as AVOCETS, Recurvirostridae, but with straighter beaks and longer legs. The black-winged stilt, *Himantopus himantopus*, has an almost cosmopolitan distribution. It is black and white with exaggeratedly gangly, pink legs which trail behind the tail in flight. Australia has the only species of stilt in the genus *Cladorhynchus*, the banded stilt, *C. leucocephalus*.

Stilton A village in Cambridgeshire, England, 10 km (6 miles) south-west of Peterborough. It gives its name to a strong, rich cheese, often with blue veins, originally made at various places in Leicestershire and formerly sold to travellers in Stilton at the Bell Inn, a coaching inn on the Great North Road from London.

stingray A CARTILAGINOUS FISH of the family Dasyatidae, most abundant in tropical and warm temperate seas (see RAY). They have a long, serrated-edged spine at the base of the tail, which is used as a defensive weapon. The spine has venom in grooves on its surface, which makes wounds very painful; large stingrays have killed humans who have stepped on them. In Britain the Atlantic stingray, *Dasyatis sabina*, is mainly a summer migrant, but it does occur all round the coast, and grows to a length of 1 m (3.25 feet). Similar species occur on both the Atlantic and Pacific coasts of North America.

stink bug See SHIELDBUG.

stinkhorn A fungus with a fruiting body that exudes a distasteful aroma in some species. The powerful and pervasive smell attracts flies, which carry away the slimy greenish mass of spores. In the common stinkhorn, *Phallus impudicus*, these fruiting bodies are borne on a stalk about 10–20 cm (4–8 inches) high, which develops at remarkable speed from an egg-like structure at ground-level. The dog stinkhorn, *Mutinus caninus*, has a pale pink finger-like fruiting body.

Stirling A royal burgh to the south of the River Forth in central Scotland, administrative centre of Stirling unitary authority; pop. (1991) 27,900. The town is dominated by Stirling Castle which stands on a volcanic outcrop and was a regimental depot until 1964. It is the site of the University of Stirling founded in 1967.

Stirling, Sir James (1926–) British architect. He came to prominence with his original, high-tech design for the Engineering Department at Leicester University (1959–63). His grand and imposing designs include the Neuestaatsgalerie in Stuttgart (1977), which is regarded as his most accomplished and sophisticated work. Other designs include the controversial Number 1 Poultry, Mansion House Square, London (1985).

Stirling, Robert (1790–1878) Scottish engineer and Presbyterian minister. In 1816 he was co-inventor (with his brother) of a type of external-combustion engine using heated air, and both the engine and the heat cycle that it uses are named after him. The **Stirling engine** consists of a hot and a cold cylinder, containing two enclosed, oscillating pistons phased about 90 degrees apart. The passage between the two cylinders contains a regenerator, a matrix of fine passages whose function is to act as a heat exchanger. Heat applied to the hot cylinder causes the gas to expand, doing work; the gas is cooled by the regenerator on its way to the cold cylinder, where it is compressed before being heated again on its way back to the hot cylinder. It achieved a modest success in the 1890s but development lapsed until 1938, and it has not achieved commercial success despite postwar efforts using pressurized helium.

stoat A species of carnivore, *Mustela erminea*, related to weasels. Its range extends throughout Eurasia and North America with little variation in appearance. The stoat is a small carnivore – the male at 230 g (8 ounces) is very much heavier than the 120 g (4 ounce) female – but it is capable of overpowering prey much bigger than itself, such as rabbits. It also takes birds and small mammals. Northern populations of stoats turn white in winter (see ERMINE).

stock (in commerce) See SECURITY.

stock exchange A MARKET in which SECURITIES are bought and sold. Most large cities have stock exchanges. The world's largest stock exchanges are to be found in New York (Wall Street), Paris (the Bourse), Frankfurt, Tokyo, and London. All stock exchanges make it possible for firms to raise long-term CAPITAL by issuing securities to investors, who can then use the stock exchange to sell their securities when they wish. Investors normally buy and sell through brokers, and in most stock exchanges deals are now conducted using computers.

Stockhausen, Karlheinz (1928–) German composer. After studying with Olivier Messiaen (1952) he co-founded the new electronic music studio of West German Radio, creating works such as *Gesang der Jünglinge* (1956), in which the human voice is combined with electronic sound. Later works include the serialist *Gruppen* (1955–57) for three orchestras, influenced by Anton Webern, and *Momente* (1962). With *Donnerstag* (1980), Stockhausen embarked on his *Licht* cycle of musical ceremonies, meant to be performed on each evening of a week; four further parts of the cycle had been completed by 1994.

Stockholm The capital of Sweden, a seaport situated on the mainland and several islands at the outflow of Lake Mälar into the Baltic; pop. (1990) 674,450. The Old Town, situated on the islands of Staden, Helgeandsholmen, and Ryddarholmen, was fortified in the 13th century. It is Sweden's economic, administrative, tourist, and cultural centre. It has shipbuilding and port industries as well as machinery, textiles, motor vehicle, and electrical industries. It has two universities, a school of economics, and numerous academies.

Stockport An industrial town in the metropolitan county of Greater Manchester, England, 10 km (6 miles) south-east of Manchester; pop. (1991) 130,000. The Goyt and Tame rivers join here to form the Mersey. Granted a charter in 1220, the town developed as a cotton-spinning centre in the 19th century.

Stockton-on-Tees An industrial town in Cleveland, north-east England, on the River Tees; pop. (1991) 170,200. It developed after the opening of the Stockton–Darlington railway in 1825 (the first passenger rail service in the world) and now has industries engaged in engineering, and the manufacture of chemicals.

Stoic A member of a philosophical school founded by Zeno of Citium *c.*300 BC, who taught in the *Stoa Poikile* (painted colonnade in Athens (hence the name)). Zeno's followers propounded various metaphysical systems, united chiefly by their ethical implications. All were variants on the pantheistic theme that the world constitutes a single, organically unified and benevolent whole, in which apparent evil results only from our limited view. Their philosophy had at its core the beliefs that virtue is based on knowledge; reason is the governing principle of nature; individuals should live in harmony with nature. The vicissitudes of life were viewed with equanimity: pleasure, pain, and even death were irrelevant to true happiness.

stoichiometry The ratios in which the reactants in a chemical reaction combine to form the products. For example, two MOLES of hydrogen react with one mole of oxygen, giving two moles of water. The stoichiometric equation summarizes this as $2H_2 + O_2 \rightarrow 2H_2O$. In stoichiometric compounds, the elements are present in simple whole number ratios: for example, the ratio is one to one in hydrogen chloride, HCl. In contrast, iron sulphide, Fe_xS, is a nonstoichiometric compound, x taking a range of values slightly less than one.

Stoke-on-Trent A pottery-manufacturing city on the River Trent in Staffordshire, England; pop. (1991) 244,800. It is the home of the University of Keele (1962).

Stoker, Abraham (known as 'Bram') (1847–1912) Irish novelist and theatre manager. He was secretary and touring manager for the actor Henry Irving from 1878 to 1905, but is chiefly remembered as the author of the vampire story *Dracula* (1897).

Stokes, Sir George Gabriel (1819–1903) British physicist who made important advances in the studies of FLUORESCENCE, sound, and fluid flow. He noted that most fluorescent materials emit light radiation of a longer wavelength than that received, and he established a law describing the absorption of energy as sound waves pass through a medium. He is probably best remembered, however, for **Stokes' law** of fluid resistance, which states that the resisting force acting on a sphere moving smoothly through a liquid or gas is in direct proportion to the velocity and to the radius of the sphere.

Stokowski, Leopold (1882–1977) British-born US conductor, of Polish descent. He is best known for arranging and conducting the music for Walt Disney's film *Fantasia* (1940), which brought classical music to a wide variety of cinema audiences by means of cartoons.

STOL (Short Take-Off and Landing aircraft) Aeroplanes capable of a short take-off and landing. This is usually achieved by the extension on landing and take-off of special slats and flaps on the wing (see FLIGHT, PRINCIPLES OF MANNED) to increase its lift at low speeds. STOL aircraft are particularly useful if the area of an AIRPORT is limited, as at London's Dockland Airport. Such an airport is called a Stolport. Examples of STOL aircraft include the De Havilland DHC-7 AIRLINER, and the Swedish Saab-37 Viggen air defence FIGHTER.

stomach The first part of the intestines to receive food and start digestion in most animals. The stomach is essentially a holding place for food, where it can be mixed with hydrochloric acid and the protein-digesting enzyme, pepsin. That of fishes, amphibians, and reptiles is tube-like. In birds the stomach's function of food storage may be taken away by the expansion of the lower part of the oesophagus into a crop. The stomachs of mammals fall into one of two general types, those of carnivorous or omnivorous groups, and those of herbivores, including RUMINANTS. The human stomach is of the general non-ruminant type, and roughly J-shaped. A muscular ring, the pyloric sphincter, forces the partly digested food into the first part of the small intestine.

stone (or **calculus**) (in pathology) An abnormal hard mass that may form in many of the ducts in the body, but most commonly in the gall-bladder as GALLSTONES, and in the urinary tract or kidneys. Kidney stones result from the precipitation of calcium oxalate. This substance is normally held in supersaturated solution, and may precipitate out to form hard, spherical stones under certain conditions. A stone often causes severe pain, especially when passing down the ureter. Small stones may be passed spontaneously, but larger ones need to be surgically removed.

Stone, Oliver (1946–) US film director, screenwriter, and producer. His adaptation of the novel *Midnight Express* (1978) for the screen won him his first Oscar. He became known for his political films indicting recent American history, such as *JFK* (1991), and especially those about the Vietnam War: examples are *Platoon* (1986) and *Born on the Fourth of July* (1989), for both of which he won an Oscar for best director.

Stone Ages Those periods of the past when metals were unknown and stone was used as the main material for missiles, as hammers, for making tools for such tasks as cutting and scraping and, later, as spear heads. Hard, fine-grained stone was the material most suitable for flaking. Although the best locally available would have been the material of first choice, stone needed for special purposes was occasionally brought from long distances, even by early toolmakers of up to 2 million years ago as at OLDUVAI GORGE and KOOBI FORA in eastern Africa. Flint is popularly associated with flaked stone tools, especially in Europe, but in Africa, where flint is rare, quartz, chert, and volcanic rocks, such as basalt and obsidian (natural glass), were the materials worked long before early Europeans used flint. In Europe, three Stone Ages are recognized – the Old Stone Age (PALAEOLITHIC), the Middle Stone Age (MESOLITHIC), and the New Stone Age (NEOLITHIC). In other parts of the world, different subdivisions are used. The Stone Ages are followed by the BRONZE and IRON AGES. This division of prehistory into three chronological stages, defined by the main material used for tools (stone, bronze, and iron) – the Three Ages System – was first put to practical use for classifying archaeological material in Denmark in 1819. As it spread to other countries, it became necessary to subdivide the three ages. All human societies lived by hunting and gathering until the development of agriculture.

stonechat A member of the thrush family, *Turdidae*, which occurs mainly in Asia. All are small, dark brown or black birds, 12.5–17.5 cm (5–7 inches) long, with white or chestnut marks and pale or white underparts. They live in open bushy country and sit conspicuously on perches from which they pounce on their insect prey. The best-known species is the common stonechat, *Saxicola torquata*, which is widely distributed across Europe, Asia, and Africa. Its call sounds like two stones being knocked together. Many other species in the thrush family are called chats and include rockchats, cliffchats, and bushchats.

stonecrop A member of the large family of SUCCULENT PLANTS, Crassulaceae, especially any species of *Sedum*, some of which are popular as rock-garden plants. Stonecrops live in extreme environments: some species of *Sedum* and *Sempervivum* (houseleek) are frost-resistant alpines; some species of *Kalanchoe* and *Crassula* live in desert regions.

stone-curlew (or **thick-knee**, **dikkop**) Any of nine species of bird in the family Burhinidae. Related to the other WADING BIRDS, these birds are found in many parts of the Old and New Worlds. They inhabit open, bushy, stony, or sandy country, often away from coasts. They are long-legged, well camouflaged in mottled brown and grey, usually with conspicuous white marks in the wings which are only visible in flight. Most species of stone-curlew are active at dusk or at night, when they feed on a wide range of animal foods.

stone fish A relative of the scorpionfishes but belonging to the family Synanceiidae. There are several species, confined to the shallow inshore waters of the tropical Indian and western Pacific oceans, which live hidden in coral or among rubble on the bottom. Two species of the genus *Synanceia* are well known for their highly poisonous spines in the dorsal fin. If disturbed the fish erects the spines, which, if trodden upon, automatically inject venom into the wound, which then becomes agonizingly painful. Although deaths are rare from stone fish stings, a wound can lead to amputation of the affected limb.

stonefly A small to medium-sized insect with long antennae and usually a pair of tail filaments. Stoneflies make up the order Plecoptera, with over 1,600 species found particularly in cooler regions of the Northern and Southern Hemispheres. They rest with the wings flat or wrapped around the body. Their aquatic nymphs, which also have two tail filaments, are found beneath stones; most are herbivorous, some carnivorous.

Stonehenge A unique megalithic monument on Salisbury Plain in Wiltshire, England. Its alleged connection with the Druids dates from the 17th century, when people's ideas about what constituted 'the past' were very vague. In the 12th century it was believed to be a monument over King Arthur's grave; other theories have attributed it to the Phoenicians, Romans, Vikings, and visitors from other worlds; modern theory inclines to the view that it was a temple. Scientific study and excavation have identified three main constructional phases between *c.*3,000 BC and *c.*1,500 BC, i.e. it was completed in the Bronze Age. The circular bank and ditch, double circle of 'bluestones' (spotted dolerite), and circle of sarsen stones (some with stone lintels), are concentric, and the main axis is aligned on the midsummer sunrise – an orientation that was probably for ritual rather than scientific purposes. It is believed that the 'bluestones' were transported from the Prescelly Hills, Pembrokeshire, Wales, a distance of 320 km (200 miles).

Stopes, Marie (Charlotte Carmichael) (1880–1958) British scientist and writer on parenthood and birth control. She was appointed lecturer in palaeobotany at Manchester University in 1904 and then taught at Imperial College in London. It was, however, her books, particularly *Married Love* (1918) and *Wise Parenthood* (1918), with her clear views on birth control, that made her famous. With her second husband, H. Verdon-Roe, she founded a clinic for birth control in London in 1921. Her activities roused opposition but also steadily increasing support among the medical profession and the general public.

Stoppard, Sir Tom (born Thomas Straussler) (1937–) British dramatist, born in Czechoslovakia. His best-known plays are comedies, which often deal with metaphysical and ethical questions and are characterized by verbal wit and the use of pastiche. His first successful play, *Rosencrantz and Guildenstern are Dead* (1966), was based on the characters in *Hamlet*; other works include *Jumpers* (1972), *Travesties* (1975), *The Real Thing* (1982), *Arcadia* (1993), *Indian Ink* (1995), and *The Invention of Love* (1997).

stork A member of a family of some 17 species of birds, Ciconiidae, closely related to herons. They are widespread in both the Old and New Worlds, though only one, the wood stork, *Mycteria americana*, occurs in North America. Standing up to 1.5 m (5 feet) high, they are long-legged, long-necked birds, primarily black and white, often with red legs and beaks. They mostly live in damp, marshy ground and eat fish and amphibians. Some, such as the European white stork, *Ciconia ciconia*, are migrants, arriving in their northern breeding grounds in spring. This species has for long been associated with the bringing of good luck (or babies) and for that reason is encouraged to nest on roof tops.

Stormont A suburb of Belfast and former seat of the parliament of NORTHERN IRELAND; pop. (1991) 5,950. Created by the Government of Ireland Act (1920) as a subordinate body to Westminster, the Stormont Parliament was dominated by the ULSTER UNIONIST PARTY until, following the breakdown in law and order in the late 1960s it was suspended in 1972. Direct rule from Westminster was imposed, to be administered by civil servants of the Northern Ireland Office based in Stormont Castle.

storm petrel A small, brown and white PETREL, 12–25 cm (5–10 inches) long, which feeds in flocks over rough seas, picking small fishes and crustaceans from the surface. Seven species breed in the Southern Hemisphere, and over a dozen in the north, usually in burrows on islands. All are members of the family Hydrobatidae.

Stowe, Harriet (Elizabeth) Beecher (1811–96) US novelist. She won fame with her anti-slavery novel *Uncle Tom's Cabin* (1852), which was successfully serialized 1851–52, and strengthened the contemporary abolitionist cause with its descriptions of the sufferings caused by slavery. Other works include the controversial *Lady Byron Vindicated* (1870), which charged the poet Byron with incestuous relations with his half-sister.

Strabo (*c.*63 BC–*c.*23 AD) Historian and geographer of Greek descent. His only extant work, *Geographica*, in 17 volumes, provides a detailed physical and historical geography of the ancient world during the reign of Augustus.

Strachey, (Giles) Lytton (1880–1932) British biographer. A prominent member of the Bloomsbury Group, he achieved recognition with *Eminent Victorians* (1918), which attacked the literary Establishment through satirical biographies of Florence Nightingale, General Gordon, and others. Other works include a biography of Queen Victoria (1921) and *Elizabeth and Essex* (1928).

Stradivari, Antonio (*c.*1644–1737) Italian violin-maker. He devised the proportions of the modern violin, altering the bridge and reducing the depth of the body to produce a more powerful and rounded sound than earlier instruments. About 650 of his celebrated violins, violas, and violoncellos are still in existence.

strain (in physics) The deformation of a body that is subjected to a STRESS. The strain on a body subjected to a tensile stress is the extension per unit length that results, this is called the **longitudinal strain**. The change in volume per unit volume when a body is compressed is called the **bulk strain**.

strain gauge An instrument to measure the deformation of a material subjected to stress. It consists essentially of a fine zigzagged wire attached to a backing sheet, which is fixed to the object being tested. The wire is incorporated in an electric circuit. Under tensile stress the wire is stretched, and its length increases, thus decreasing its diameter. This increases its electrical resistance, and the change in resistance can be equated to the strain produced.

Straits Settlements Former British crown colony comprising territories bordering on the strategic Malacca Strait in south-east Asia. The three English East India colonies of Penang, Malacca, and SINGAPORE were combined in 1826 as the Straits Settlements. After 1858, they passed to British Indian control, and in 1867 became a crown colony, to which Labuan was added in 1912. The colony was dismantled in 1946, Singapore becoming a separate colony and Penang, Malacca, and Labuan joining the Malayan Union.

strangeness (in physics) A property of certain nuclear particles (HADRONS) produced in high-energy interactions, so called because the particles decayed much more slowly than expected. Strangeness is now recognized as one of the six distinct types, or FLAVOURS, of QUARKS.

Strasberg, Lee (born Israel Strassberg) (1901–82) US actor, director, and drama teacher, born in Austria. As artistic director of the Actors' Studio in New York City (1948–82), he was the leading figure in the development of method acting in the USA. Among his pupils were Marlon Brando, James Dean, Jane Fonda, and Dustin Hoffman.

Strasbourg An industrial, and commercial city at the Ill River and Rhine confluence Alsace, north-east France, capital of the department of Bas-Rhin; pop. (1990) 255,940. It is a river port with canal connections. It has an 11th–15th century Gothic cathedral. Its many industries include metal-casting, machinery, and oil and gas refining. Meetings of the Council of Europe and sessions of the European Parliament are held in this city.

strata Layers of SEDIMENTARY ROCK. The layering, or bedding, can result from changes in the process of deposition: pauses in deposition, for example, or changes in the type of material or the rate at which it is deposited. The thickness of a single stratum may range from a millimetre (0.04 inch) to metres (tens of feet).

Strategic Arms Limitation Talks (SALT) Agreements between the USA and the Soviet Union, aimed at limiting the production and deployment of nuclear weapons. A first round of meetings (1969–72) produced the SALT I Agreement, which prevented the construction of comprehensive anti-ballistic missile (ABM) systems and placed limits on the construction of strategic (i.e. intercontinental) ballistic missiles (ICBM) for an initial period of five years. A SALT II Treaty, agreed in 1979, sought to set limits on the numbers and testing of new types of intercontinental missiles, but it was not ratified by the US Senate. New STRATEGIC ARMS REDUCTION TALKS (START) began in 1982.

Strategic Arms Reduction Talks (START) Discussions aimed at nuclear ARMS CONTROL between the USA and the Soviet Union (after 1991, between the USA and the four republics of the former Soviet Union that inherited nuclear weapons – Belarus, Ukraine, Russia, and Kazakhstan). START negotiations began in 1982, but were suspended by the Soviet Union at the end of 1983 in protest at US deployment of intermediate nuclear missiles in Western Europe. Resuming in 1985, the talks eventually led to the signing of the treaty known as START I in July 1991, which committed the USA and the Soviet Union to a 30 per cent reduction in their nuclear weapons stockpiles. The four nuclear states that emerged from the break-up of the Soviet Union acceded to START I in November 1993. In the interim, Russia and the USA had signed START II in January 1993, which provided for the dismantling of two-thirds of each country's strategic nuclear warheads.

Strategic Defense Initiative (SDI; known as 'Star Wars') A research and development programme intended to provide a multi-layer ANTI-BALLISTIC MISSILE space defence system for the USA. It was initiated by President Reagan in 1983 and was based on the use of new weapons, including high-powered LASER WEAPONS and particle beams fired from space platforms, to eliminate ballistic missiles, ideally early in flight before they have released their warheads. However, the programme was regarded as excessively expensive; the Bush administration reduced the funding and in 1991 it was scaled down and renamed GPALS (Global Protection Against Limited Strikes). This is based on deployment of approximately 1,000 small interceptor missiles in space, an equal number of ground-based anti-missile missiles in the USA, and mobile ground missiles in several other parts of the world. A new type of gun, the rail gun, which uses electromagnetic forces to propel a projectile or shell at extremely high velocities, is being developed as a further layer of defence. Following the end of the COLD WAR, the Russian President, Boris Yeltsin, proposed a joint global defence system incorporating the Star Wars technology to shield the world from nuclear attack.

Stratford-upon-Avon A market town on the River Avon in Warwickshire, England, where William Shakespeare was born and is buried; pop. (1991) 22,231. Shakespeare's birthplace, the school he probably attended, and his wife's home are preserved and visited annually by many tourists. The riverside Royal Shakespeare Theatre presents regular performances of Shakespeare's plays.

Strathclyde A local government region in western Scotland from 1975 to 1996; its capital was Glasgow. In 1996 it was abolished and administration passed to 12 unitary authorities.

stratigraphy (or **historical geology**) The study of STRATA, especially their character, their sequences, and the relationships between them. For the most part it deals with sedimentary rocks, but LAVAS can also be treated stratigraphically. The subject has two main aspects: lithostratigraphy, which is concerned with establishing the sequences of the rocks, and chronostratigraphy, which is concerned with correlating rocks of the same age in different places, chiefly by means of the fossils they contain. A fundamental principle is that of superposition: younger rocks rest on older, provided that they have not been disturbed by Earth movements. Starting from these principles, geologists have since built up a picture of the sequence of stratified rocks and have classified into larger and smaller units – systems, series, and stages – corresponding to the units of GEOLOGICAL TIME. Stratigraphical studies also enable the geography of past times to be reconstructed. Palaeogeographical maps can be drawn to show the distribution of land and sea and other geographical features that existed at some specified time in the geological past. Stratigraphy is of particular importance in exploration for oil and coal.

stratosphere A layer of atmospheric air above the troposphere extending to about 50 km (31 miles) above the Earth's surface, in which the lower part changes little in temperature with height. The boundary between the STRATOSPHERE and the MESOSPHERE at a height of about 60 km (38 miles) is called the **stratopause**. It is the layer at which the air temperature stops increasing with height. Its temperature is about 10°C and is caused in the main by the absorption of solar ultraviolet radiation by OZONE. The ozone at the stratopause shields the Earth's inhabitants from harmful ultraviolet radiation.

stratus cloud A generally shapeless, grey, layered form of cloud that forms at 500 m (1,600 feet) or below. When very low-lying, it is often the cause of fog. The layers commonly develop in stable conditions and light winds by ADVECTION, as moist air passes over a colder surface, though dense and multi-layered stratus several hundred metres deep may accumulate in the vicinity of FRONTS.

Strauss, Johann (known as **Strauss the Elder**) (1804–49) Austrian composer. He was a leading composer of waltzes from the 1830s, although probably his best-known work is the *Radetzky March* (1838). His son **Johann** (known as **Strauss the Younger**) (1825–99) became known as 'the waltz king', composing many famous waltzes, such as *The Blue Danube* (1867) and *Tales from the Vienna Woods* (1868). He is also noted for the operetta *Die Fledermaus* (1874).

Strauss, Richard (1864–1949) German composer. From the mid-1880s he composed a succession of symphonic poems, including *Till Eulenspiegels Lustige Streiche* (1895) and *Also Sprach Zarathustra* (1896). His reputation grew as he turned to opera, exploring polytonality in *Salome* (1905) and *Elektra* (1905). The latter marked the beginning of his collaboration with the librettist Hugo von Hofmannsthal; together they produced such popular operas as *Der Rosenkavalier* (1911). Despite the magnificence of much of his later music, including the operas *Ariadne on Naxos* (1912, revised 1916), *The Woman without a Shadow* (1918), *Arabella* (1933), and *Daphne* (1938), Strauss's genius seemed to falter with World War II. Often regarded as the last of the 19th-century romantic composers, Strauss retained his romanticism to the end of his long career, notably in *Four Last Songs* (1948) for soprano and orchestra.

Stravinsky, Igor (Fyodorovich) (1882–1971) Russian-born composer. He made his name as a composer for Diaghilev's Ballets Russes, writing the music for the ballets *The Firebird* (1910) and *The Rite of Spring* (1913); both shocked Paris audiences with their irregular rhythms and frequent dissonances. Stravinsky later developed a neoclassical style, typified by the ballet *Pulcinella* (1920) and, ultimately, the opera *The Rake's Progress* (1948–51), based on William Hogarth's paintings. In the 1950s he experimented with serialism in such works as the cantata *Threni* (1957–58). Resident in the USA from the outbreak of World War II, Stravinsky became a US citizen in 1945.

strawberry A perennial, trailing plant of the genus *Fragaria*, belonging to the rose family. The wild European wood or alpine strawberry, *F. vesca*, was once cultivated for its richly flavoured, small, dark red fruits. All modern cultivated varieties have been developed from two American species, *F. chiloensis* from the Pacific seaboard, and *F. virginiana* from eastern America, introduced to Europe in the 18th century. The strawberry plant has a crown of leaves, and produces runners that take root, eventually to produce new plants. The 'fruit' consists of the swollen red flower base (receptacle); the true fruits are the tiny pips that are embedded on its surface.

strawberry tree An evergreen tree of the genus *Arbutus*, native to Europe, western Asia, and North America. Strawberry trees belong to the heather family, Ericaceae, and are closely related to cranberry and blueberry. Of the 12 species, the common strawberry tree, *A. unedo*, is perhaps most familiar as a species native to the Mediterranean. It is also found in parts of western Ireland. The tree produces a bitter strawberry-like fruit which is edible but rarely eaten, although it is used in liqueurs, notably in Portugal. The madroña of North America, *A. menziesii*, produces a useful wood.

streamlining The shaping of an object so that it offers the least possible resistance to a flow of air, water, or other fluid. A non-streamlined object moving through a fluid creates eddies and turbulence, which cause drag on the object. The rounded, smooth shapes of many aeroplanes, motor vehicles, and boats are designed to produce a smooth, regular flow of fluid around them, thus minimizing drag and improving efficiency. Optimal streamlined shapes tend to be long ellipses tapering in the direction of flow, for example, an AEROFOIL cross-section. At supersonic speeds this optimal shape changes, and a sharper front end is required.

stream of consciousness A method of representing the mental processes of fictional characters as a continuous blending of sense-perceptions, thoughts, feelings, and memories, as if they were recorded directly without the author's intervention, sometimes without punctuation. This technique, also known as 'interior monologue', was pioneered by Dorothy Richardson in *Pilgrimage* (1915–38), by PROUST in *À la recherche du temps perdu* (1913–27), by JOYCE in *Ulysses* (1922), and further developed by Virginia WOOLF in *Mrs Dalloway* (1925) and Faulkner in *The Sound and the Fury* (1929). It has become a common device in modern fiction.

Streep, Meryl (born Mary Louise Streep) (1949–) US actress. After her screen début in 1977 she became a leading star in the 1980s. She won an Oscar for her part as a divorcée in *Kramer vs. Kramer* (1980). Her other films include *The French Lieutenant's Woman* (1981), *Sophie's Choice* (1982), for which she won a second Oscar, *Out of Africa* (1986), *She-Devil* (1990), and *Death Becomes Her* (1992).

street theatre See COMMUNITY THEATRE.

Streicher, Julius (1885–1946) German Nazi leader and propagandist. Originally a school-teacher, he expounded his anti-Semitic views in his periodical *Der Stürmer*. He was Party leader (*Gauleiter*) in Franconia (1933–40), and continued to function as a propagandist. He was sentenced to death at the NUREMBERG TRIALS and subsequently hanged.

Streisand, Barbra (Joan) (1942–) US singer, actress, and film director. She became a star in 1964 in the Broadway musical *Funny Girl*, winning an Oscar in 1968 for her performance in the film of the same name. She later played the lead in *A Star is Born* (1976) which she also produced; the film's song 'Evergreen', composed by Streisand, won an Oscar. She took other starring roles in films, such as *Yentl* (1983), which she also produced and directed. Her later films include *The Prince of Tides* (1992).

strelitzia See BIRD OF PARADISE FLOWER.

stress (in psychology) An unusually high demand on physical, emotional, or mental strength. Stress is a major health issue of modern society. Although the physical effects of stress, such as HEART DISEASE, hypertension, lowered immunity, and gastric ulcers, are important, lower levels of stress – measurable in changed activity of the heart, brain, and hormonal system – also impair people's health, satisfaction, and efficiency. Early investigations concentrated on physical stressors, such as extreme temperature, noise, illness, and injuries. More recent studies have emphasized the impact of factors such as work-load, crowding, bereavement, and poor relationships. Research shows the importance of perceptions of control over the source of stress.

stress (in physics) The force per unit area exerted on a body causing a STRAIN in that body. In **tensile stress** the force tends to stretch the body, while in **bulk stress** the body tends to be compressed. **Shear stress** tends to twist a body.

strike (in labour relations) See INDUSTRIAL ACTION.

Strindberg, (Johan) August (1849–1912) Swedish dramatist and novelist. Although best known outside Scandinavia as a dramatist and precursor of expressionism in the theatre, Strindberg was also a leading figure in the naturalist movement in literature; his satire *The Red Room* (1879) is regarded as Sweden's first modern novel. His earlier plays, also naturalistic in style, depict a bitter power struggle between the sexes, notably in *The Father* (1887) and *Miss Julie* (1888). His later plays are typically tense, symbolic, psychic dramas; the trilogy *To Damascus* (1898–1904) and, more particularly, *A Dream Play* (1902), introduced expressionist techniques and are of major importance for the development of modern drama.

stringed instruments A musical instrument in which the sound is created by a stretched string. All are coupled systems; as strings produce very faint sounds, a resonator is needed. Usually this is a box (VIOLINS and GUITARS, etc.), but it may be a

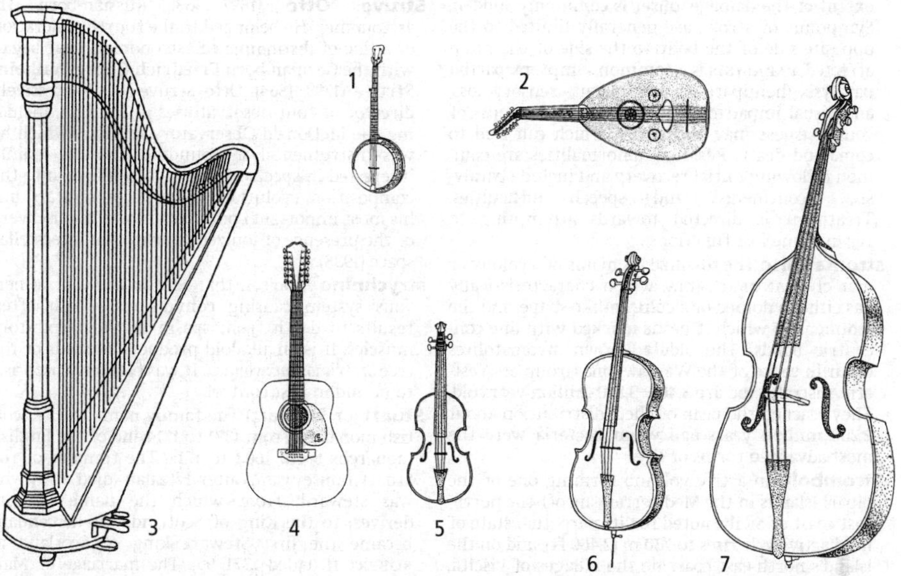

Stringed instruments (1) Banjo. (2) Lute. (3) Harp. (4) Spanish guitar. (5) Viola. (6) Cello. (7) Double bass.

board (some ZITHERS and PIANOS), or the player's mouth (some musical bows), and some modern instruments have complex electrical amplification systems. There are many ways of making a string vibrate. The simplest, and oldest, is plucking it. Another is striking it (DULCIMERS and pianos). A third is stroking it with a BOW (violins, etc.), or a wheel (HURDY-GURDIES). A fourth is blowing it (AEOLIAN HARPS). A fifth, only possible with steel strings, is with electromagnets (some electronic instruments). A string's pitch is determined by its length, mass, and tension. To avoid the resonator twisting under unequal string tension, it is desirable for all the strings to be at nearly the same tension. This is achieved by varying either the length or mass (thickness) of the strings, or both. There are limits to the practicable length of strings, and on instruments with a great many, such as pianos, some must be longer than others. The strings of violins must obviously all be the same length, and only their mass and tension differ. Once it vibrates, the pitch of the string can be varied. The normal way is by shortening the vibrating length by stopping it part-way along. Another, as on some Indian instruments, including the SITAR, and the blues guitar, is by altering the tension of the string while playing.

string theory (in atomic physics) The quantum physics of elementary particles assumes that the particles have no size: that is, they exist as points with no dimensions. This assumption has been very useful, but it is inappropriate in some circumstances, for example at very high energies or over very short distances. String theory claims to provide a description of particles that is appropriate for these and all other circumstances. In string theory particles are not points, but are one-dimensional objects, which can be thought of as strings – though, unlike everyday string, they have length but no thickness. There are two types of string: the open, which are curves, and the closed, which are loops. The length of the strings is defined by a relationship between the fundamental quantities Planck's constant, the speed of light, and the gravitation constant; it has the value 1.6×10^{-33} cm. String theories appear to avoid the difficulties that other theories have with the inclusion of gravity in GRAND UNIFIED THEORIES. A further development of string theory, called superstring theory, looks promising in this regard. String theory was first proposed by Jöel Scherk and John Schwartz in 1974.

stroboscope An instrument that intermittently illuminates a rotating or vibrating object to study its motion or determine its rotational or vibrational speed. It consists of a light that gives a rapid series of flashes of very short duration (typically one-millionth of a second). If the speed of the flashes is close to the speed of rotation or vibration of the object being studied, the object will appear to slow down and can be examined: adjusting the flash speed so that the object appears stationary will give its exact rotational or vibrational speed. The stroboscope is also used in high-speed photography to obtain very short exposures.

Stroheim, Erich von (1885–1957) Austrian-born US actor and director. Of the nine films he directed and scripted (or co-scripted), all but the first two suffered from studio interference, largely because of their extravagance and excessive length. The first three, *Blind Husbands* (1918), *The Devil's Passkey* (1919), and *Foolish Wives* (1921), were witty comedies of adultery. His other films include *Greed* (1923), originally seven hours long; *The Merry Widow* (1925); *The Wedding March* (1926); and *Queen Kelly* (1928), which was halted when only one-third finished, and never shown in the USA. He was forced to end his career as it began, playing stiff-backed Prussians, notably in Renoir's *La Grande Illusion* (1937).

stroke (or **apoplexy**) Brain damage caused by loss of blood supply either as a result of a blood clot (THROMBOSIS) or brain haemorrhage. Precipitating factors include ARTERIOSCLEROSIS, high blood pressure, cerebral ANEURYSM, and excessive alcohol consumption. Symptoms of stroke are dependent on the area of the brain damaged and to the extent of the damage; onset is commonly sudden. Symptoms of stroke are generally limited to the opposite side of the body to the side of the brain affected. PARALYSIS is a common symptom; partial paralysis (hemiparesis), hemiplegia, sensory loss, and visual impairment may occur. Sudden loss of consciousness may also occur, which can lead to coma and death. Residual abnormalities are common following initial recovery and include paralysis, incontinence, and speech difficulties. Treatment is directed towards attempting to regain some lost functions.

stromatolite The fossilized remains of a colony or mat of CYANOBACTERIA, which characteristically has either a domed or a column-like shape, and the sediment in which it lies is marked with fine concentric bands. The oldest known stromatolites occur in rocks of the Warrawoona Group of Western Australia and are 3,400–3,500 million years old. They reached the peak of their distribution about 2,200 million years ago when bacteria were the most advanced forms of life.

Stromboli An active volcano forming one of the Lipari Islands in the Mediterranean, off the north-east coast of Sicily, noted for its perpetual state of mild activity. It rises to 750 m (2,460 ft), and on the island's north-east coast lie the villages of Piscità, Ficogrande, and San Vincenzo which are popular with tourists.

strong force (in atomic physics) One of the four fundamental FORCES of nature. It is carried by PIONS, and is responsible for holding hadrons together to form nuclei. The strong force is by far the strongest of the fundemental forces, but it is effective only over very short distances. See also INTERACTIONS.

strontium (symbol Sr, at. no. 38, r.a.m. 87.62) A silvery-white malleable element, a member of the ALKALINE EARTH METALS, and a good conductor of electricity. Its principal sources are strontianite ($SrCO_3$) and celestine ($SrSO_4$). The metal is obtained by ELECTROLYSIS of fused strontium chloride, $SrCl_2$, or by high-temperature reduction of strontium oxide, SrO. Its chemical properties are similar to those of calcium and barium; it reacts vigorously with water and on heating with hydrogen, oxygen, nitrogen, and the halogens. Its compounds are used in fireworks and flares, which colour red. The isotope strontium-90 is present in nuclear fall-out and represents a danger to health. It is radioactive with a HALF-LIFE of as long as 28 years and, because it is chemically similar to calcium, becomes incorporated within bone.

structuralism A method of study in which the phenomenon to be analysed is seen as comprising a system of structures, which are regarded as more important than the isolated elements that make them up. Structuralism derives from the linguistic theories of SAUSSURE in the early 20th century. Saussure regarded language as a vast network of structures; he broke it down into its minimal components (linguistic units, such as phonemes and words), which could be defined only in relation to other such units. Saussure's linguistic theories were applied by the anthropologist LÉVI-STRAUSS in his study of MYTH, KINSHIP, and totemism, which he analysed as though they were language systems. He believed that the structures he identified corresponded to structures inherent in the human mind. Structuralism came to be applied to other areas, such as SOCIOLOGY and literary criticism.

Strutt, John William See RAYLEIGH.

Struve, Otto (1897–1963) Russian-born US astronomer. He belonged to the fourth generation of a line of distinguished astronomers that began with the German-born **Friedrich Georg Wilhelm Struve** (1793–1864). Otto Struve was successively director of four observatories in the USA, including the McDonald Observatory in Texas which he was instrumental in founding. He was mainly interested in spectroscopic investigations into the composition, evolution, and rotation of stars, but his most important contribution was his discovery of the presence of ionized hydrogen in interstellar space (1938).

strychnine A poison that acts on the central nervous system causing convulsions, which often results in death from spasm in the respiratory muscles. It is an alkaloid produced in seeds of the tree *Strychnos nux-vomica*. It was formerly used as a tonic and in pest control.

Stuart (or **Stewart**) The family name of the Scottish monarchs from 1371 to 1714 and of the English monarchs from 1603 to 1714. The founder of the Stuart house was Walter Fitzalan (died 1177) who was steward (from which the name Stewart derives) to the King of Scotland. His descendant became the first Stewart king of Scotland as ROBERT II (ruled 1371–90). The marriage of Margaret Tudor, daughter of HENRY VII, to JAMES IV linked the royal houses of Scotland and England, and on the death of ELIZABETH I without heirs in 1603, James VI of Scotland succeeded to the English throne as JAMES I. The Stuarts lost the throne temporarily with the execution of Charles I in 1649, regaining it with the RESTORATION of Charles II in 1660. The GLORIOUS REVOLUTION (1688) sent JAMES II into exile and the crown passed to his daughter Mary and her husband William, then to his second daughter ANNE. Her death without heirs in 1714 resulted in the replacement of the Stuart house by the house of HANOVER headed by George I. Supporters of the exiled house of Stuart were known as JACOBITES. After the failure of the FIFTEEN and the FORTY-FIVE (1715 and 1745) rebellions the Stuart cause faded, and George III felt able to grant a pension to the last direct Stuart claimant, Henry, Cardinal York, who died in 1807.

Stuart, Charles Edward (known as **the Young Pretender** or 'Bonnie Prince Charlie') (1720–88) Pretender to the British throne, son of James Stuart. He led the Jacobite uprising of 1745–46 (see FORTY-FIVE), gaining the support of the Highlanders, with whom he invaded England and advanced as far as Derby. However, he was driven back to Scotland by the Duke of Cumberland and defeated at the Battle of Culloden (1746). He later died in exile in Rome.

Stuart, James (Francis Edward) (known as **the Old Pretender**) (1688–1766) Pretender to the British throne, son of James II (James VII of Scotland). He arrived in Scotland too late to alter the outcome of the FIFTEEN Jacobite uprising and left the leadership of the 1745–46 uprising to his son Charles Edward STUART.

Stuart, John McDouall (1815–66) Scottish explorer. He was a member of Charles STURT's third expedition to Australia (1844–46), and subsequently crossed Australia from south to north and back again, at his sixth attempt (1860–62).

Stuart, Mary See MARY, QUEEN OF SCOTS.

Stubbs, George (1724–1806) British painter and engraver. Known for the anatomical accuracy of his depictions of animals, he established his reputation with the book *Anatomy of the Horse* (1766), illustrated with his own engravings. He is particularly noted for his sporting scenes and paintings of horses and lions, for example, the *Mares and Foals in a Landscape* series (*c.*1760–70).

Stubbs, William (1825–1901) British historian and ecclesiastic. He wrote the influential *Constitutional History of England* (three volumes 1874–78), which charted the history of English institutions from the Germanic invasion to 1485. He was also bishop of Chester (1884–88) and of Oxford (1888–1901).

stupa In Buddhist (and also Jain) architecture, a solid, dome-like monument erected to enshrine relics of the Buddha or some other holy personage or to mark a sacred spot. Typically the stupa was surrounded by a railing with four gateways (as with the Great Stupa at Sanchi). The form spread throughout the Buddhist world, developing into complex architectural forms in, for example, Borobudur in Java. In Tibetan art the equivalent of the stupa is the chorten.

sturgeon A fish of an order that has many primitive features, and lives in fresh and salt water of the Northern Hemisphere. They are distinguished by the heterocercal tail (in which the vertebrae continue up the upper lobe), a mainly cartilaginous skeleton, and the presence of a spiral valve in the gut (a primitive feature also seen in sharks). Most are large fishes with rows of large bony plates along the back and sides. The beluga, *Huso huso*, of the Black Sea grows to about 5 m (16 feet). The European sturgeon, *Acipenser sturio*, reaches a maximum 3.5 m (11.5 feet) and migrates up rivers to spawn. Its eggs are used as the delicacy caviar.

Sturm und Drang (German, 'storm and stress') A German literary movement of the 1770s using as its preferred medium the theatre. Influenced partly by the exaltation of freedom and nature by J.-J. ROUSSEAU, it represents a reaction against the exclusive value placed by the ENLIGHTENMENT on the intellect and refined civilization at the expense of emotion, instinct, fantasy, and natural genius. Stylistically and structurally innovative, the plays frequently criticize contemporary social and political conditions in extravagant terms, for example, GOETHE in *The Sorrows of Young Werther* (1774), and SCHILLER in *The Robbers* (1781).

Sturt, Charles (1795–1869) British explorer of Australia who surveyed its largest river system and opened up the south for settlement. In 1828–29 he examined the marshes of the Macquarie and discovered the Darling and Murray Rivers. From Adelaide in 1844–45 he discovered the Sturt Desert and Cooper's Creek. He was also a good administrator, rising to the post of colonial secretary before he retired in 1851 and returned to England.

Stuttgart A motor-manufacturing city and river port in Baden-Württemberg, south Germany, on the Neckar River; pop. (1991) 591,950. It was the capital of the former kingdom of Württemberg. In addition to vehicles its industries produce textiles, paper, machinery, electronic goods, photographic products, and precision equipment.

stylops A small, strange insect, perhaps related to beetles, but placed in the order Strepsiptera with about 370 species in the family Stylopidae. The young and most females are sac-like internal parasites, usually in solitary bees. The males enjoy a brief free life of active flight, fertilizing the females within their hosts. Females of a few species are briefly free-living, but wingless.

Styracosaurus See DINOSAUR.

Styx In Greek mythology, one of the nine rivers of the underworld, over which Charon ferried the souls of the dead.

subduction (in geology) The process in which tectonic plates of oceanic LITHOSPHERE descend back into the Earth's mantle along margins between adjoining plates. The **subduction zone** itself is marked by a zone of deep-focus earthquakes, and its surface expression is commonly an island arc or OCEAN TRENCH or both. The location of the deep-focus of an earthquake may be referred to as the hypocentre, and the point at the Earth's surface overlying this the epicentre. See also PLATE TECTONICS.

subgiant See GIANT STAR.

sublimation (in chemistry) The process by which a solid is converted on heating directly into a gas, without going through a liquid state. Only a small number of solids sublime, carbon dioxide, CO_2 and IODINE, I_2, being examples. Some solids that do melt to form a liquid still evaporate quite rapidly if kept below their melting-points; iodine and sulphur are examples. This is also sublimation, and can be used as a method of purification.

sub-machine-gun A small MACHINE-GUN that does not require a rest from which to fire it. Sub-machine-guns commonly fire ammunition of the same calibre as that used by pistols. Most operate on the blow-back system, in which the rear of the barrel is closed by a bolt that is held in place by a spring. On firing, the seal is maintained until the bullet leaves the barrel; what remains of the propellant force then pushes back the bolt, opening the breech and permitting the spent CARTRIDGE to be ejected and a new round inserted. The **Sten gun** of World War II was a 9 mm sub-machine-gun designed by Sheppard and Turpin. Some four million Sten guns were produced at a cost of £1.50 each.

submarine A vessel, especially a warship, capable of operating under water and usually equipped with torpedoes, missiles, and a periscope. The essential requirements are an ability to lose and regain positive buoyancy; a means of underwater propulsion that does not use oxygen; and a hull sufficiently strong to withstand the pressure of water at depth. The earliest practicable designs were French and American. They all had the same basic features: ballast tanks, which were flooded when diving and emptied when surfacing; electric motors for underwater propulsion, with steam or petrol (later diesel) engines to recharge the batteries and for surface propulsion; and usually an internal hull with a circular cross-section to withstand high pressures. The TORPEDO provided submarines with an effective weapon, and they were soon adopted by many navies. During World Wars I and II submarines played an extremely important role in sinking enemy shipping. In 1954 nuclear-powered submarines were introduced; a nuclear power-plant provides heat to drive steam-turbines, which then generate electricity for propulsion and other power applications. Nuclear submarines can remain submerged almost indefinitely, travel at speeds of up to 30 KNOTS, operate at great depth, and fire intercontinental BALLISTIC MISSILES while submerged. See also INERTIAL NAVIGATION; SUBMERSIBLE.

submersible A SUBMARINE operating under water for short periods. One of the most widely used types is the lockout submersible. Its crew (normally two people) work at normal atmospheric pressure, but a separate, pressurized chamber, carries one or more divers (see DEEP-SEA AND DIVING TECHNOLOGY). Such craft are used for repair and inspection work, particularly on marine oil rigs. For work at great depths, submersibles with remotely controlled robot arms can be used. Increasingly, such submersibles are without a crew, and are remotely piloted from the surface. See also BATHYSPHERE.

subsidence The downward movement of a block of rock relative to the surrounding area. It is normally associated with faulting or with the removal or erosion of underlying beds, and can be caused by human activities (mining) or by natural agencies: solution (cave collapse) or erosion (sea cliff collapse).

In meteorology, subsidence is the widespread, slow descent of air. It is particularly associated with ANTICYCLONES. It results from the chilling of the surface layers of air by conduction from a cold ground surface and by long-wave radiation losses, or from high-level horizontal CONVERGENCE. Air tends to become warmer and its relative HUMIDITY decreases as it subsides.

subsistence crop See SHIFTING CULTIVATION.

substitution reaction See CHEMICAL REACTIONS.

subtropical Describing regions with a near-tropical climate or, more precisely, those areas lying between the Tropic of Cancer and 40°N and the Tropic of Capricorn and 40°S.

succession (in biology) The series of ecological COMMUNITIES that appear or become extinct as an area changes from bare ground to a mature ECOSYSTEM. Primary succession develops at sites not previously colonized, such as new islands formed by marine volcanoes. Secondary succession takes place where clearance has occurred, often on land cleared by man or fires. The first species to colonize a site are known as 'pioneers', and include annual species of plants and migratory animals. When established, these progressively modify the nutrient status and condition of the soil, enabling other species to colonize; competition usually then excludes the pioneers. Further modification of the site admits more species, and eventually a dynamically stable climax is established with one or two species dominant. The climax vegetation in many parts of the world is forest, but where water is in short supply or grazing animals are abundant this may be grassland. The whole succession (sere) is directional and predictable.

The first animals and plants to colonize an area typically produce a lot of seed or offspring, grow quickly, and are small in size. Climax species of plants and animals are usually long-lived, large organisms, which produce few fruits or young, which they may endow with large food reserves to maximize survival.

succubus See INCUBUS.

succulent plant A plant, such as the cactus, adapted to grow successfully in arid, saline, or desert regions. Succulent plants have evolved tissues modified for water storage, enabling them to survive long periods of drought. These modified tissues include stems and leaves. Typical stem-storage species include the cactus-like *Euphorbia canariensis*, with swollen spiny stems up to 7 m (23 feet) in height. Others include *Stapelia*, the BAOBAB tree of tropical Africa, and *Nolina* of Mexico, with a swollen stem base resembling an elephant's foot. Leaf succulents show great variety of form, ranging from the diminutive rounded leaves of the STONECROPS to the large fleshy leaves of the African ALOES, and the sword-like leaves of the AGAVES of Central and South America.

Suchow See XUZHOU.

sucking louse A small insect of the order Siphunculata, which is rarely longer than 5 mm (0.25 inch), but the largest LOUSE of mammals. Sucking lice pierce the skin and feed on blood or cell contents. They are flattened and usually live at the base of hairs, cementing their eggs, or nits, to them. The 300 or so species occur on humans and many other mammals. They are transferred to new hosts mostly by contact between hosts when young, but also by sexual intercourse. They are highly successful parasites. Although a few such as the human louse, *Pediculus humanus*, can carry diseases, most are harmless, but intensely irritating. The body louse and head louse are subspecies of *P. humanus*.

Suckling, Sir John (1609–42) English poet, dramatist, and Royalist leader. He lived at court from 1632 and was a leader of the Cavaliers during the English Civil War. His poems include 'Ballad upon a Wedding', published in the posthumous collection *Fragmenta Aurea* (1646). According to John Aubrey, Suckling invented the game of cribbage.

Sucre The legal capital and seat of the judiciary of Bolivia, situated at an altitude of 2,700 m (8,860 ft) in the Andes; pop. (1992) 130,950. Prior to the arrival of the Spanish it was known as Charcas and was the indigenous capital of the valley of Choque-Chaca, a name corrupted to Cuquisaca and given to the city by the Spanish. Bolivia's Declaration of Independence was signed in the Legislative Palace in 1825 when the city's name was changed to Sucre in honour of General Antonio José de SUCRE, second-in-command to Simon Bolívar and an advocate of independence for the region. It is a major agricultural centre supplying the altiplano mining region, and has an oil refinery.

Sucre, Antonio José de (1795–1830) Venezuelan revolutionary and statesman, President of Bolivia 1826–28. Sucre served as Simón Bolívar's Chief of Staff, liberating Ecuador (1822), Peru (1824), and Bolivia (1825) from the Spanish. The first President of Bolivia, Sucre resigned following a Peruvian invasion in 1828; he was later assassinated. The Bolivian judicial capital Sucre is named after him.

sudden infant death syndrome (SIDS) See COT DEATH.

Sudan A country in north-east Africa which takes the name of the great belt of open SAVANNAH crossing Africa south of the Sahara. Sudan extends from Ethiopia to Cape Verde. The site of many ancient kingdoms, including those of MALI, SONGHAI, and GHANA, Sudan was crossed by BERBER trade routes.

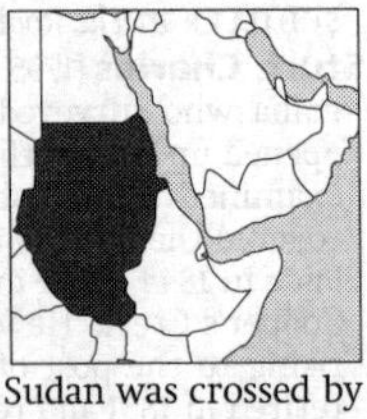

Physical. Sudan has Egypt on its northern boundary, a coast on the Red Sea, and boundaries also with Ethiopia, Eritrea, Kenya, Uganda, the Democratic Republic of Congo, the Central African Republic, Chad, and Libya. The largest country on the African continent, it has equatorial forest in the south and the Nubian Desert in the north; and its whole length is traversed from south to north by the River Nile. The mid-south contains the Sudd swamps with islands of vegetation scattered among the reeds and tall papyrus grass. There is a region of SAVANNAH, and near the junction of the Blue and White Niles cotton is grown under irrigation on the wide clay plains of the Gezira. Further north are areas covered with acacia bushes, the source of gum arabic. In the extreme north years may pass without rain, and the only cultivation is on the river's banks.

Economy. The civil war, drought, and flooding have devastated the economy, which is also crippled by massive foreign debt ($13.5 billion in 1990), and have led to famine in the south among both Sudanese and the several million refugees from Ethiopia and Chad. The distribution of food aid has been seriously hampered by the war. Agriculture is the principal economic activity, with cotton, gum arabic, and sesame the main exports. Sugar cane, sorghum, and livestock are the other main products. The war has stopped exploitation of oil reserves; other resources include silver, chromite, lead, mica, asbestos, talc, tungsten, diamonds, uranium, copper, zinc, iron ore, and gold. Industry is limited to oil-refining and processing agricultural products such as sugar and cotton.

History. Nubian culture was established in northern Sudan about 30,000 years ago. Most of Nubia gradually came under the control of Egypt from about 4,000 BC. Nubia formed part of the kingdom of Cush, which lasted from the 11th century BC to the 4th century AD. From about the 6th century AD missionaries established Christianity in the area. From the 13th century Arab nomads began immigrating into Sudan and eventually took control of the Christian areas.

In 1800 northern Sudan consisted of the Muslim empire of the Funji, where an Islamic revival was occurring. The Funji were conquered by Mehemet Ali from Egypt (1820–23). In 1874 Khedíve Ismail, viceroy of Egypt, offered the post of governor of the Egyptian Sudan to Charles GORDON. His anti-slave administration was not popular. In 1881 Muhammad Ahmad declared himself MAHDI and led an Islamic rebellion in the Sudan. Britain occupied Egypt in 1882 and invaded the Sudan where Gordon was killed (1885). The Mahdists resisted Anglo-Egyptian forces until Kitchener defeated them at Omdurman in 1898. The following year an Anglo-Egyptian condominium was created for the whole Sudan under a British governor. A constitution was granted in 1948 but in 1951 King Farouk of Egypt proclaimed himself King of Sudan. After his fall, Egypt agreed to Sudan's right to independence; self-government was granted in 1953 and full independence in 1956. North–South political and religious tension undermined stability until General Nimeiri achieved power in 1969 and negotiated an end to the civil war in the south in 1972. Peace broke down again in the early 1980s with the collapse of the economy, widespread starvation, and a renewal of separatist guerrilla activity in the south. Nimeiri was overthrown by the army in April 1985, and a brief civilian coalition government was formed under Sadiq al-Mahdi. But civil war continued; the Sudan People's Liberation Army (SPLA) militarized much of the south, while the Muslim Brotherhood's National Islamic Front (NIF) strengthened its hold in the north. A military coup by General Omar Hassan Ahmad al-Bashir in 1989 was followed by a ban on all political parties. The early 1990s saw an influx of several million refugees from Ethiopia and Chad. The continuing civil war, drought, and flooding led to large-scale destitution and famine. The strongly Islamic Bashir regime has been accused of sponsoring fundamentalist terrorism, particularly in the neighbouring country of Egypt.

Capital: Khartoum
Area: 2,503,890 sq km (966,757 sq mi)
Population: 28,098,000 (1995)
Currency: 1 Sudanese pound = 100 piastres = 1,000 millimes
Religions: Sunni Muslim 73.0%; traditional beliefs 16.7%; Roman Catholic 5.6%; Anglican 2.3%
Ethnic Groups: Sudanese Arab 49.1%; Dinka 11.5%; Nuba 8.1%; Beja 6.4%; Nuer 4.9%; Azande 2.7%; Bari 2.5%; Fur 2.1%; Shilluk 1.7%; Lotuko 1.5%
Languages: Arabic (official); Dinka; Nuba; other local languages
International Organizations: UN; OAU; Arab League

Sudetenland An area of Bohemia in the Czech Republic adjacent to the German border, allocated to the new state of Czechoslovakia after World War I despite the presence of three million German-speaking inhabitants. The Sudetenland became the first object of German expansionist policies after the Nazis came to power, and, after war was threatened, was ceded to Germany as a result of the Munich Agreement of September 1938. In 1945 the area was returned to Czechoslovakia, and the German inhabitants were expelled and replaced by Czechs.

Suetonius (full name Gaius Suetonius Tranquillus) (*c.*69–*c.*150 AD) Roman biographer and historian. His surviving works include *Lives of the Caesars*, covering Julius Caesar and the Roman emperors who followed him, up to Domitian.

Suez (Arabic **Suweis**) A port in north-eastern Egypt, situated on the Red Sea at the southern end of the SUEZ CANAL; pop. (1991) 376,000. It is the control centre for the Canal with refuelling facilities and two oil refineries.

Suez Canal A shipping canal 171 km (106 miles) long and without locks connecting the Mediterranean (at Port Said) with the Red Sea, constructed in 1859–69 by Ferdinand de Lesseps. The canal, now important for Egypt's economy as providing the shortest route for international sea traffic travelling between Europe and Asia, came under British control after Britain acquired majority shares in it, at Disraeli's instigation, in 1875; after 1888 Britain acted as guarantor of its neutral status. It was nationalized by Egypt in 1956 and an Anglo-French attempt at intervention was called off after international protest (see SUEZ WAR). It has been enlarged to take ships of almost any draught.

Suez War (1956) A military conflict involving British, French, Israeli, and Egyptian forces. It arose from the nationalization of the SUEZ CANAL Company by Egypt in 1956. When attempts to establish an international authority to operate the Canal failed, Britain and France entered into a military agreement with Israel. The latter, concerned at the increasing number of *fedayeen* or guerrilla raids, was ready to attack Egypt. On 29 October Israel launched a surprise attack into Sinai, and Britain and France issued an ultimatum demanding that both Israel and Egypt should withdraw from the Canal. This was rejected by President NASSER. British and French planes attacked Egyptian bases, and troops were landed at Port Said. Under pressure from the USA, with the collapse of the value of sterling, and mounting criticism of most other nations, the Anglo-French operations were halted and their forces evacuated. A UN peace-keeping force was sent to the area. The US Secretary of State, J. F. Dulles, formulated the short-lived Eisenhower Doctrine (1957), offering US economic and military aid to Middle East governments whose independence was threatened. Israeli forces were withdrawn in March 1957 after agreement to install a UN Emergency Force in Sinai and to open the Straits of Tiran to Israeli shipping.

Suffolk A county of eastern England; area 3,797 sq km (1,466 sq miles); pop. (1991) 629,900; county town, Ipswich. The county, which gives its name to a black-faced breed of sheep and a breed of draft horse, is divided into seven districts.

suffrage See FRANCHISE; WOMEN'S SUFFRAGE.

suffragette A member of a British militant feminist movement that campaigned for the right of adult British women to vote in general elections. The Women's Social and Political Union, which was founded by Emmeline PANKHURST in 1903, gained rapid support, using as its weapons attacks on property, demonstrations, and refusal to pay taxes. There was strong opposition to giving women the vote at national level, partly from calculations of the electoral consequences of enfranchising women. Frustration over the defeat of Parliamentary bills to extend the vote led the suffragettes to adopt militant methods to press their cause; Parliamentary debates were interrupted, imprisoned suffragettes went on strike, and one suffragette, flinging herself in front of the king's horse in the 1913 Derby horse-race, was killed. These tactics were abandoned when Britain declared war on Germany in 1914 and the WSPU directed its efforts to support the war effort. In 1918, subject to educational and property qualifications, British women over 30 were given the vote (the age restriction was partly to avoid an excess of women in the electorate because of the deaths of men in the war). In 1928 women over 21 gained the vote.

Sufism Muslim MYSTICISM, from the word for the simple woollen garment (*suf*) worn by early ascetics. Sufism arose in the early Islamic period as a reaction against the strict formality of orthodox teaching, and was organized into orders from the 12th century. Seeking personal union with God, Sufis eschew the formal rituals and orthodox learning of the *ulama* (the doctors of sacred law and theology) in favour of esoteric practices and teachings from sheikhs, whose personal powers equip them to set initiates on the path to communion with God. Sufis have included outstanding poets, such as the Persian Rumi, scholars, such as al-Ghazzali, and massive brotherhoods, among them the Qadiriyya and Tijaniyya. The central aim of Sufism is to know God directly; ASCETICISM and meditational practices, such as *dhikr* (recitation) and *sama'* (dance), are amongst the most common Sufi practices. Sufism has been influenced by the beliefs of other faiths, amongst them neo-Platonism and BUDDHISM, but is deeply rooted in Islamic spiritualism.

sugar A water-soluble CARBOHYDRATE, which often has a sweet taste, including simple sugars, such as GLUCOSE, fructose, and ribose; slightly more complex sugars, such as maltose, lactose, and sucrose (table sugar); and trisaccharide sugars, such as raffinose. Sugars are small molecules, commonly containing between three and twelve carbon atoms. Glucose and fructose are hexose (six-carbon) sugars that form the immediate energy source for most animals and plants, respectively. Other common sugars, such as sucrose, maltose (found in malt), and lactose (found in milk) are combinations of two hexose sugars. Sugars play a wide variety of roles in organisms: they are important constituents of DNA, and form part of some glycoproteins and lipids (FATS AND OILS). Simple sugars are also the building blocks for much larger carbohydrates, such as STARCH and cellulose.

sugar beet A variety of *Beta vulgaris*, the species that also gives rise to beetroot. Up to 20 per cent of the large, whitish, conical, swollen roots can be made up of the sugar, sucrose, and they are an alternative source to sugar-cane in temperate regions (see SUGAR PROCESSING). This crop was developed in about 1800 and large quantities are now grown in central and eastern Europe, Britain, and the USA. It is a member of the family Chenopodiaceae.

sugarbird Either of two South African species of bird of the family Promeropidae, unique to southern Africa. Although the body is only the size of a small thrush, the males in particular have long tails, which are up to 45 cm (18 inches) long. They are greyish-brown birds with flashes of bright yellow underneath the bases of the tail, and long, curved beaks. They specialize in feeding on protea flowers, taking both nectar and insects on the blooms.

sugar cane A perennial grass, *Saccharum officinarum*, from south-east Asia, where it has been cultivated for thousands of years. It was introduced into the Caribbean by Spanish explorers of the 15th and 16th centuries. Its solid stems, up to 6 m (19.5 feet) high, are rich in extractable sugar (sucrose). More than half of the world's sugar supply comes from this species. The main areas of production are Brazil, Cuba, Mauritius, the Caribbean, Hawaii, and Australia. Commercial production is concentrated in large plantations, as expensive machinery is needed to culture, harvest, and extract the sugar (see SUGAR PROCESSING). Crops are propagated from stem cuttings and are usually harvested after burning to remove unwanted leaves.

sugar processing The production of crystalline sugar from SUGAR CANE or SUGAR BEET. Sugar is extracted from cane by rolling it to release the juices. Lime is added to clear the liquid, and gradual evaporation drives water from the juice. As the concentration of sugar increases, crystals form; these are separated from the waste **molasses** in a centrifuge. The raw sugar is light or dark brown in colour, depending upon the amount of molasses that is extracted with it. The molasses is a thick brown uncrystallized bitter syrup left over from the refining process. It is used as an animal feed, a starting material for making industrial alcohol, and is fermented to make rum. The process of extracting sugar from beet begins by slicing the root and heating it in water to which lime has been added. The resultant juice is then evaporated in a vacuum until the sugar crystallizes, the crystals being separated in a centrifuge. Waste sugar-beet fibres are used as fuel or in livestock feed; they also provide the raw material for fibreboard.

Sui A dynasty of emperors ruling China from 589 to 618, between the period of The Three Kingdoms and the Tang Dynasty. Reuniting the country, the Sui emperors built the Grand Canal.

suicide The intentional killing of oneself. In some societies, suicide used to be regarded as praiseworthy, or obligatory in certain circumstances, as for instance the Japanese *seppuku* or hara-kiri, ritual disembowelling in order to escape humiliation or demonstrate loyalty, or the Hindu practice of suttee, the voluntary burning of a widow after her husband's death. On the other hand, suicide is forbidden in Islam, Judaism, and Christianity. For centuries in Christian countries, suicide was considered a crime, and those who committed it were refused burial in consecrated ground. Criminal penalties for attempting suicide were only abolished in 1961 in England and Wales, and it is still a crime to help someone to commit suicide. The Voluntary Euthanasia Society has campaigned for the right to assist a suicide, particularly in cases where terminal illness is involved (see EUTHANASIA). Unsuccessful suicide attempts may be deliberately unsuccessful, a 'cry for help', or they may well lead to a future, fatal attempt. Organizations, such as the SAMARITANS, listen sympathetically to the distress of the suicidal.

suite (in music) A composition consisting of contrasted movements. Although suite did not emerge until the middle of the 16th century, the form originated in the much earlier practice of performing dances in contrasted pairs – the stately PAVAN followed by the lively GALLIARD, and so on. When adapted as purely instrumental music (usually for keyboard), such pairings became the basis of an extended work – the Baroque dance suite. The 17th-century dance suite had four dances as its almost invariable framework: the ALLEMANDE, the COURANTE, the saraband, and the GIGUE. Optional dance movements included MINUET, gavotte, bourrée, passepied, and rigaudon. Most of the movements were in simple BINARY FORM. Within the suite the various movements were usually based on one key, though modulations could occur within the individual movement. As the earliest effective way of providing extended instrumental works, the suite is the forerunner of most of the instrumental forms of the 18th and 19th centuries, including the overture, the concerto grosso, the solo concerto, and the symphony. Once superseded by these SONATA forms, however, the suite became simply a collection of contrasting movements, assembled perhaps from the incidental music to a play, or from outstanding sections of an opera or ballet.

Sukarno, Achmad (1901–70) Indonesian statesman, President 1945–67. One of the founders of the Indonesian National Party (1927), he was Indonesian leader during the Japanese occupation (1942–45) and led the struggle for independence, which was formally granted by the Netherlands in 1949. From the mid-1950s his dictatorial tendencies aroused opposition. He was alleged to have taken part in the abortive Communist coup of 1965, after which he steadily lost power to the army, being finally ousted two years later.

Sukhumi (Georgian **Sokhumi**) The capital of the autonomous republic of Abkhazia in Georgia, a port and resort on the east coast of the Black Sea; pop. (1991) 121,700. In the aftermath of the breakup of the Soviet Union in 1991 it was the focus of armed conflict between Georgian and separatist Abkhazian forces, which seized it in September 1993. This led to a mass exodus of Georgians.

Sukkur A commercial and industrial city on the River Indus in the province of Sind, south-east Pakistan; pop. (est. 1991) 350,000. Nearby is the Sukkur Barrage, nearly 1.6 km (1 mile) long, completed in 1932, built across the river and feeding irrigation canals, which direct its water to over 12 million hectares (5 million acres) of the Indus valley. It is a centre for trade with Afghanistan and has varied textile industries.

Sukuma A Bantu people of north-west Tanzania, the largest tribal group in the country. They depend for their livelihood on cattle herding and cotton, which is largely sold in the town of Mwanza on Lake Victoria.

Sulawesi A large island of Indonesia, east of Borneo, formerly called Celebes; area 189,216 sq km (73,084 sq miles); pop. (1993) 13,279,000. It is the third-largest of the Greater Sundas and Ujung Pandang is its chief port and largest city. Beyond a narrow coastal fringe the island has a mountainous interior rising to 3,225 m (10,580 ft) at Mount Sonjol.

Suleiman I (or **Soliman**, **Solyman**) (*c.*1494–1566) Sultan of the Ottoman Empire 1520–66. The Ottoman Empire reached its fullest extent under his rule; his conquests included Belgrade (1521), Rhodes (1522), and Tripoli (1551), in addition to those in Iraq (1534) and Hungary (1562). This and the cultural achievements of the time earned him the nickname in Europe of 'Suleiman the Magnificent'. He was also a noted administrator, known to his subjects as 'Suleiman the Lawgiver'.

Sulla (full name Lucius Cornelius Sulla Felix) (138–78 BC) Roman general and politician. Having come to prominence as a result of military successes in Africa, Sulla became involved in a power struggle with Marius, and in 88 marched on Rome. After a victorious campaign against Mithridates VI Sulla invaded Italy in 83, ruthlessly suppressing his opponents. He was elected dictator in 82, after which he implemented constitutional reforms in favour of the Senate, resigning in 79.

Sullivan, Sir Arthur (Seymour) (1842–1900) British composer. Although he composed much 'serious' music, his fame rests on the 14 light operas he wrote in collaboration with the librettist W. S. GILBERT, many for Richard D'Oyly Carte's company at the Savoy Theatre.

sulphates Compounds containing the ion SO_4^{2-}; they can be made by neutralizing sulphuric acid. Potassium sulphate, K_2SO_4, and ammonium sulphate, $(NH_4)_2SO_4$, are water-soluble; they are used in fertilizers. Calcium sulphate, $CaSO_4$, occurs naturally as gypsum, and forms plaster of Paris on heating.

sulphides The compounds formed between sulphur and other elements. All the metals except gold and platinum combine with sulphur to form sulphides, many of which are insoluble in water. They frequently occur naturally and constitute many important metal ores. Sulphur also forms covalent sulphides with many non-metals, such as hydrogen sulphide, H_2S, and carbon disulphide, CS_2.

sulphites The series of salts containing the SO_3^{2-} ion, in which sulphur has a valency of 4. They correspond to the putative sulphurous acid, H_2SO_3. Solutions of the alkali metal sulphites are used as reducing agents.

sulphonamide Any organic compound consisting of an amide of sulphuric acid, in particular a class of drugs that were the first of the modern chemotherapeutic agents. The sulphonamide Prontosil was discovered by DOMAGK in 1935, and was widely employed during World War II. The sulphonamides inhibit the growth of bacteria, rather than killing them, and organisms easily develop resistance to these drugs. They can also have severe side effects. Consequently, for most purposes they have been superseded by ANTIBIOTICS.

sulphur (US **sulfur**; symbol S, at. no. 16, r.a.m. 32.06) A yellow non-metallic element in Group 16 (formerly VIB) of the PERIODIC TABLE that exists in two different ALLOTROPES, both of which are yellow. It occurs naturally both in the free state and in sulphides and sulphates, and is found chiefly around hot springs, and in volcanic regions. Sedimentary deposits are found in Texas and Louisiana, USA. It is extracted, sometimes from considerable depths, by melting with superheated steam; the liquid sulphur collects in a pool and is then pumped to the surface almost chemically pure. This is the FRASCH PROCESS. It is also found in some natural gas as hydrogen sulphide, H_2S, and in sedimentary rocks, such as gypsum. It is principally used in the production of SULPHURIC ACID by the CONTACT PROCESS. It is also used in the VULCANIZATION of rubber, in the manufacture of GUNPOWDER, and to produce carbon disulphide, a valuable solvent. Sulphur dioxide is a toxic gas formed when sulphur burns in air, which is used to bleach straw and wool. It is a major cause of AIR POLLUTION and ACID RAIN. Hydrogen sulphide, an extremely toxic gas with a characteristic smell of bad eggs, is produced in large amounts at petroleum refineries. Pollution is reduced by controlled burning, in which one-third is burned to sulphur dioxide, which then reacts with the remaining two-thirds to produce water and sulphur.

sulphur dioxide (SO_2) A colourless, poisonous gas with a characteristic, choking pungency. A typical acidic oxide, dissolving solving in water to form sulphurous acid, H_2SO_3. It is used to prepare sulphur trioxide, SO_3, in the manufacture of sulphuric acid, H_2SO_4, and in bleaching and food preservation. As a by-product of the combustion of fossil fuels containing sulphur, particularly coal, it is a major air pollutant, dissolving in water in the atmosphere and oxidizing to sulphuric acid to give ACID RAIN that can cause severe environmental damage.

sulphuric acid (or **oil of vitriol**, H_2SO_4) A colourless, corrosive, oily liquid. In its concentrated form it is a strong oxidizing agent and is used to dehydrate many compounds. When it is diluted, a process that requires great care as it is violently exothermic, it readily dissociates and has all the properties of a strong ACID. It is mainly manufactured by the CONTACT PROCESS in which sulphur dioxide, SO_2, is passed over a catalyst to give sulphur trioxide, SO_3, which is then dissolved in the acid already produced to give OLEUM (or fuming sulphuric acid). This is then diluted to give concentrated sulphuric acid (98 per cent H_2SO_4, 2 per cent H_2O). Sulphuric acid is the most widely produced industrial chemical. It is used in the production of ammonium sulphate and soluble phosphate fertilizers; in petroleum refining to remove impurities from gasoline and kerosene; in the pickling of steel to clean its surface before galvanizing or plating; in the production of dyes, drugs, and disinfectants; and in the manufacture of textiles, paints, pigments, plastics, explosives, and lead storage batteries.

sumac A shrub or tree of the genus *Rhus*, of which there are some 250 species in the subtropics and warm, temperate regions, including the POISON IVY. The leaves of the common sumac, *R. coriaria*, of the Mediterranean, are ground up for use in dyeing and tanning. Familiar in gardens is the fast-growing stag's-horn sumac, *R. typhina*, from North America, a species whose leaves are tinted a deep red in the autumn.

Sumatra (or **Sumatera**) A large island of Indonesia, separated from the Malay peninsula by the Strait of Malacca; area 424,760 sq km (164,000 sq miles); pop. (est. 1993) 39,232,800. Its largest city and port is Medan and its indigenous people include a dozen ethnic groups who speak some 20 dialects. Sumatra's interior is covered by dense rainforest; much of the eastern half of the island is swampland. It produces rubber and timber for export and its oil and other minerals provide three-quarter's of Indonesia's income.

Sumer Southern Mesopotamia, the region inhabited by Sumerian-speaking people from the 4th millennium BC, which was later known as Babylonia.

Sumerian A people speaking a non-Semitic language and civilization native to Sumer in the 4th millennium BC. The Sumerians were a hybrid stock speaking an agglutinative language related structurally to Turkish, Hungarian, Finnish, and several Caucasian dialects. As the first historically attested civilization they are credited with the invention of cuneiform writing, the sexagesimal system of mathematics, and the socio-political institution of the city-state with bureaucracies, legal codes, division of labour, and a money economy. Their art, literature, and theology had a profound cultural and religious influence on the rest of Mesopotamia and beyond, which continued long after the Sumerian demise *c.*2,000 BC, as the prototype of Akkadian, Hurrian, Canaanite, Hittite, and eventually, biblical literature. Two of their main cities were Ur and Lagash.

summer solstice That time, about 21 June, when the Sun, moving along the ECLIPTIC, is at its maximum northerly distance from the celestial equator. The Sun's declination is then 23 degrees 26 minutes and lies in the zodiacal constellation of Cancer. The Sun passes directly through the ZENITH at noon on the Tropic of Cancer. The Earth's Northern Hemisphere then has its longest period of daylight and shortest period of darkness; the Southern Hemisphere has its shortest period of daylight and longest period of darkness.

sumo See WRESTLING.

Sun The star around which the Earth orbits. An ordinary main-sequence star of SPECTRAL CLASS G2 (see HERTZSPRUNG–RUSSELL DIAGRAM), the Sun is a self-luminous gaseous mass, comprising some 71 per cent hydrogen and 26 per cent helium by mass, having an absolute visual MAGNITUDE of +4.83 and an effective surface temperature of 5,770 K. At the solar centre, the temperature rises to 1.5 $\times 10^7$ K to provide the pressure necessary to support the overlying mass against gravity which, at the Sun's radiating surface (the PHOTOSPHERE), is 27 times that of the Earth. This high temperature also sustains, by the nuclear FUSION of hydrogen into helium, a solar radiation output which totals 3.8×10^{26} watts emanating from the photosphere.

The mass of the Sun is 1.99×10^{30} kg and the mean radius of the approximately spherical photosphere is 7.0×10^5 km. Solar rotation is observed in the motions of surface features, such as sunspots, in the photosphere and overlying layers. The mean rotation period is 25.4 days about an axis inclined at 7.25 degrees to the ECLIPTIC but ranges from 25 days at the solar equator to 41 days near the poles.

The importance of the Sun to mankind lies in its proximity to the Earth, the mean distance being about 150 million km, or 1 astronomical unit. In consequence, the solar radiation maintains terrestrial conditions, particularly the Earth's surface temperature, within habitable limits, as well as providing daytime illumination directly and nocturnal illumination by reflection from the Moon. Solar energy is the ultimate source of all the energy we utilize, except nuclear energy.

sunbird A bright, metallic-coloured bird comprising 105 species in the family Nectariniidae, found mainly in Africa, but also in the warmer parts of Asia, with one species in Australia. They are mostly small birds, 9–12.5 cm (4–5 inches) long, though a few are larger and some have very long tails. They are mostly coloured brilliant metallic blues, greens, or reds, though a few are dull green. Their beak is long and curved for reaching into flowers to obtain nectar and some species also take small insects and spiders.

sun-bittern A bird, *Eurypyga helias*, that inhabits the forested edges of marshes and streams in tropical South and Central America. It is the sole member of its family, Eurypygidae, and is related to the rails, being about chicken-sized with thinnish legs and a longish beak. The wing, when spread, shows a big circular, Sun-like patch of black, chestnut, and white; this is shown in display and is the origin of the bird's name. It feeds on insects and other small animals.

Sunderland An industrial city in Tyne and Wear, north-east England, a port at the mouth of the River Wear; pop. (1991) 286,800. Formerly a centre of shipbuilding, it now produces chemicals, electronics, furniture, and vehicles. The University of Sunderland (formerly Sunderland Polytechnic) was established in 1992.

sundew A CARNIVOROUS PLANT of the genus *Drosera*, which, together with the VENUS'S FLY-TRAP, belongs to the family Droseraceae. They have rounded or elongated leaves provided with long, stalked glands which secrete a sticky mucilage. Insects are attracted to these leaves and ensnared. Sundews may be plants of bogs or sandy habitats where nitrogen and other nutrients are in short supply: the insects they catch are a valuable supplement to their nutrition. About 70 species of sundew are found throughout the world.

sundial A device for measuring the apparent solar TIME by the shadow of a rod or triangular edge cast by the Sun on a scaled dial. It consists of two parts, the **gnomon** and the **plate**. The gnomon is the rod or triangular edge and acts as the indicator. It is set parallel to the spin axis of the Earth. The geometry is such that the angle that the gnomon makes with the horizontal is equal to the latitude of the sundial. The gnomon is always in the north–south plane. The markings forming the scaled dial on the plate depend on its orientation. The sundial suffers from two problems. If its position is, say, x degrees of longitude west of the time meridian it reads $4x$ minutes slow; if it is east it reads fast. Secondly, the equation of time has to be taken into account. See CLOCKS AND TIME MEASUREMENT.

sunfish A fish belonging to one of two quite unrelated groups. The marine sunfishes are members of the family Molidae, found in all the tropical and temperate oceans. Although rather uncommon, a few of the five species can weigh over 1,000 kg (2,200 pounds) each. The ocean sunfish, *Mola mola*, is one of the most abnormally shaped fishes. Its dorsal and anal fins are set well back on the body on either side of a much reduced caudal fin. The body is disc-shaped and appears to be all head. The ocean sunfish eats marine invertebrates such as jellyfish.

Freshwater sunfishes belong to the family Centrarchidae, of which there are 32 species, confined to the rivers and lakes of North America (although introduced to other parts of the world). Most are deep-bodied, often brightly coloured, with a continuous dorsal fin, the first section of which is spiny. Few of them grow larger than 20 cm (8 inches) in length, but all build nests in river- or lake-beds, in which the eggs, when laid, are defended by the male. Several species, such as the green sunfish, *Lepomis cyanellus*, range from Canada to Mexico.

sunflower A tall annual, *Helianthus annuus*, reaching 2.5 m (8 feet) in height and giving its name to the sunflower family, Compositae. This includes daisies, asters, ragworts, dahlias, and many other familiar plants, and is one of the largest families of flowering plants, with over 25,000 species. Sunflowers have large, yellow flower-heads, which produce oil-rich seeds, and are grown in warm temperate areas and at medium altitudes in the tropics. The main producers are Russia, followed by southern and eastern Europe, and Argentina. Harvested by hand or machine, the seeds, containing up to 40 per cent oil, are threshed and crushed to yield a high-quality table or cooking oil, used also in the manufacture of margarine. Inferior grades of oil are used for soap, paints, and varnish. *H. annuus*, together with perennial species of *Helianthus*, are also widely grown for their ornamental flowers.

Sung The dynasty which ruled in China 960–1279.

Sun King The nickname of LOUIS XIV of France.

Sunni (from Arabic *sunna*, 'tradition') The belief and practice of mainstream, as opposed to SHIA, ISLAM. Sunni Muslims, constituting over 80 per cent of all believers, follow the *sunna*, or rules of life, the exemplary practice of MUHAMMAD, based on the *hadith* collected in the *Sihah Satta*, six authentic books of Tradition. The Sunna, variously translated as 'custom', 'code', or 'usage', means whatever Muhammad, by positive example or implicit approval, demonstrated as the ideal behaviour for a Muslim to follow. It therefore complements the KORAN as a source of legal and ethical guidance.

sun spider An ARACHNID of the unique order Solifugae, named for their habit of being active in full sunlight. Sun spiders are also called wind scorpions because they run extremely fast. They are found mostly in hot, dry areas in India, the Caribbean, western USA and northern Mexico, though six of the 800 species can be found in Europe. They resemble large spiders, but have enormous jaws, which can project upwards. They feed on small animals, captured by the PEDIPALPS and torn apart by the jaws. Mating necessitates the male's subduing the female by stroking, until he can deposit his sperm.

sunspots Dark spots visible on the surface of the Sun. Sunspots have been recorded since ancient times and are now recognized as regions of the PHOTOSPHERE cooled some 2,000 K below their surroundings through insulation by strong magnetic fields of about 2,000 gauss. Sunspots have a relatively dark central area (the umbra) surrounded by a lighter outer region (the penumbra). The flow of gas from the umbra to the penumbra is described by the Evershed effect. The numbers and latitudes of sunspots vary in an 11-year period, known as the **solar cycle** or **sunspot cycle**. The basic 11-year cycle has longer-term variations superimposed upon it.

sunstroke (or **heatstroke**) A dangerous rise in body temperature due to inadequate heat loss by sweating in a hot environment. Excessive exertion before acclimatization and dehydration are factors often involved. In extreme cases it may be fatal unless alleviated by giving the patient drinks, or cooling his body.

Sun Yat-sen (or **Sun Yixian**) (1866–1925) Chinese KUOMINTANG statesman, provisional President of the Republic of China 1911–12 and President of the Southern Chinese Republic 1923–25. Generally regarded in the West as the father of the modern Chinese state, he spent the period 1895–1911 in exile after an abortive attempt to overthrow the Manchus. During this time he issued an early version of his influential 'Three Principles of the People' (nationalism, democracy, and the people's livelihood) and set up a revolutionary society which became the nucleus of the Kuomintang. He returned to China to play a vital part in the revolution of 1911 in which the Manchu dynasty was overthrown. After being elected provisional President, Sun Yat-sen resigned in 1912 in response to opposition from conservative members of the government and established a secessionist government at Guangzhou. He reorganized the Kuomintang along the lines of the Soviet Communist Party and began a period of uneasy cooperation with the Chinese Communists before dying in office.

supercharger A compressor used to increase the amount of air admitted to an INTERNAL-COMBUSTION ENGINE cylinder during the admission stroke. It enables more fuel to be burnt, so increasing the power output. Originally superchargers were mechanically driven from the crankshaft, but now most are driven by a turbine utilizing the power of the exhaust gas. The combination of a directly coupled turbine and compressor is known as a turbo-charger, and is widely used in DIESEL ENGINES. Petrol engines for high-performance cars are also sometimes turbo-charged.

superconductivity A property displayed by certain metals and alloys when their temperature is lowered to within a few degrees of ABSOLUTE ZERO. It was first discovered by the Dutch physicist Heika Kamerlingh Onnes in 1911. The electrical resistance of these metals suddenly vanishes, which makes them ideal for the manufacture of coils and CABLES that do not dissipate power. Superconductivity also makes possible the manufacture of extremely powerful but very small electromagnets; however, the effect may be destroyed by the presence of a magnetic field, in some cases only a fraction of a TESLA. It was not until 1960 that materials were discovered to remain superconducting in fields powerful enough to allow exploitation. Among them are a niobium–titanium alloy, which remains superconducting in fields of up to 10 tesla, and a compound of niobium and tin, Nb_3Sn, which continues operating up to 20 tesla. Such substances are now widely used in the manufacture of very powerful electromagnets used in medical instrumentation. In 1987 several research groups discovered a class of electroceramics that exhibit superconductivity at much higher temperatures than previously known. When developed, these may make available the benefits of superconductivity on a large scale. According to the BSC theory of superconductivity, put forward by J. Bardeen, L. N. Cooper, and J. R. Schriefer in 1957, a moving electron in a crystal lattice causes a slight lattice distortion, which can affect a second passing electron. Cooper showed that in superconductors, current is carried by such electron pairs (**Cooper pairs**). Because the total momentum of a Cooper pair is unchanged by the interaction between one of the electrons and the lattice, the electron flow continues indefinitely.

superfluidity The property of a liquid at a very low temperature that enables it to flow without friction. Both isotopes of helium possess this property. The **lamda point** (temperature at which superfluidity occurs) of ^{4}He is 2.172K, whereas for ^{3}He it is 0.00093K. Helium below the lamda point in a beaker defies gravity by flowing up the walls of the vessel spontaneously.

supergiant A star of very high LUMINOSITY (6,000 to 250,000 or more times that of the Sun), large diameter (20 to 500 or more times that of the Sun), and low mean density (from one hundredth to one ten-millionth that of water). Supergiants are rare and no supergiant is near enough to determine its distance directly by measuring its trigonometric PARALLAX. Owing to their high luminosity, however, there are several supergiants among the bright naked-eye stars, including Antares, Betelgeuse, Deneb, and Rigel.

superheterodyne See RADIO RECEIVER.

Superior, Lake One of the five Great Lakes of North America and the largest freshwater lake in the world; maximum depth 405 m (1,329 ft); area 84,243 sq km (32,526 sq miles); area on the Canadian side of the border, 29,888 sq km (11,540 sq miles). The cities of Duluth and Thunder Bay lie on its shore and it is linked to Lake Huron by the St Mary's River.

supernova A star that explodes and temporarily brightens by 20 MAGNITUDES or more. A supernova is a more destructive event than a NOVA and can be classified in two ways. Type I supernovae are old, small stars that have few heavy elements. The explosion usually destroys the star completely leaving only a supernova remnant of expanding gas. They are probably WHITE DWARF components of BINARY STARS that undergo detonation by nuclear FUSION. Type II supernovae are massive young stars that have exhausted the available elements for energy generation and whose cores collapse to form a NEUTRON STAR or BLACK HOLE, ejecting a shell of gas as they do so. The material ejected from a Type II supernova eventually enriches the interstellar medium with heavy elements.

superoxide A compound that contains the O_2^- ion. Superoxides are generally yellow in colour at room temperature, but as they are cooled many undergo a reversible phase transition, accompanied by a colour change to white. The ALKALI METALS all form ionic superoxides when they are dissolved in liquid ammonia and oxidized with oxygen gas. Chemically, superoxides are both strong oxidizing agents and strong bases, and are thus extremely corrosive.

superphosphate A fertilizer containing the $H_2PO_4^{2-}$ ion, made by treating phosphate rock with sulphuric acid.

supersonic flight The flight of an aircraft or missile at speeds greater than that of sound (Mach 1). For many years aeroplanes had difficulty in achieving supersonic speeds even in a dive. This was because at around the speed of sound the air-flow around an aeroplane is compressed into a shock wave (often heard on the ground as a 'sonic boom'). Such shock waves cause excessive drag and create large stresses on the aircraft. The first aeroplane to achieve supersonic flight was a US rocket-engined Bell X-1, on 14 October 1947. Its design was modelled on that of a bullet, which was known to travel faster than sound. Modern supersonic aircraft are designed with a sharply pointed nose and smaller, swept-back wings. At speeds above Mach 2, heating due to air friction becomes appreciable, and special materials must be used in aircraft construction (see also HYPERSONIC FLIGHT). Nearly all supersonic aircraft are military vehicles; the only exception being the supersonic airliner Concorde.

superstrings See STRING THEORY.

supply and demand, law of The economic principle that in a competitive market there is an equilibrium price at which the amount supplied of a good will tend to equal the amount demanded. Typically, as the price of a good increases, the quantity demanded decreases, and the quantity supplied increases, so there will normally be one price at which supply equals demand, this is the equilibrium price. Apart from certain exceptions, if demand is greater than supply, then some consumers will be willing to pay more for the good, and firms will be able to charge higher prices whilst still being able to sell all their output. This leads to a rise in the price of the good, which in turn stimulates supply and reduces the quantity demanded (thus reducing the excess demand). The process continues until supply and demand are equal. Conversely, if supply is greater than demand, suppliers will tend to undercut each other and price will fall, raising demand and reducing supply until, again, supply equals demand.

Suprematism A Russian ABSTRACT ART movement, developed by MALEVICH from about 1913 and officially launched by him in 1915. His Suprematist paintings were the most radically pure abstract works created up to that time, for he limited himself to basic geometrical shapes and a narrow range of colour, reaching the ultimate distillation of his ideas in a series of paintings of a white square on a white background, after which he announced the end of Suprematism.

surface tension A property of liquids resulting from unbalanced forces of attraction between the constituent atoms or MOLECULES near the surface. Whereas forces within the liquid pull in all directions, the net force at the surface is inwards, pulling the molecules together so that they form an elastic skin. It acts at all boundaries, and has energy associated with it. Drops of a liquid are spherical because, for any given volume, a sphere has the smallest surface area. Surface tension falls as temperature rises; and it differs with different liquids, those with a high degree displaying the greatest capillary action (see CAPILLARITY). A **surfactant** is a substance that causes a change in the surface tension of a liquid. Often called 'wetting agents', surfactants usually lower the surface tension, allowing the liquid to interact with, and wet, solids. DETERGENTS are surfactants, enabling dirt particles to become detached from fabrics and suspended in water.

surface-to-air missile (SAM) See MISSILE.

surface-to-surface missile (SSM) See MISSILE.

surfactant See SURFACE TENSION.

surgeonfish See UNICORN FISH.

surgery The physical repair of diseased or injured organs and tissues. Scrolls from ancient Egypt and China describe surgical instruments and the use of splints to set broken bones. Early Hindu medicine included several complex surgical operations. However, as recently as 150 years ago surgery was a dangerous and unpleasant practice, since anaesthetics were restricted to alcohol and opium, and fatal infections produced mortalities of over 90 per cent in some hospitals. Recent surgical triumphs have only been made possible by modern anaesthetic practices. These have now advanced to the point where it is possible to keep a patient alive while such vital organs as the heart and lungs are removed (as in TRANSPLANT SURGERY). Other important developments include the use of antiseptics and antibiotics to control infection and intravenous fluids and BLOOD TRANSFUSIONS to restore blood and other body fluids lost during operations.

Modern techniques rely heavily on new tools and devices, such as the OPTICAL FIBRE ENDOSCOPE to examine bowels, renal tracts, and joints. In minimally invasive (or 'keyhole') surgery, laparoscopy (insertion of a rigid tube through the abdominal wall), when combined with endoscopy, can be used to perform minor operations without opening the abdomen. ULTRASOUND is used to aid diagnosis, and has been used in gallstone removal (see LITHOTRIPSY). Finely focused LASERS are used to cut and cauterize tissue. Other recent devices include artificial joints, lens implants for the eye, and PACEMAKERS for the heart.

suricate See MEERKAT.

Surinam A country on the north-east coast of South America, known until 1948 as Dutch Guiana.

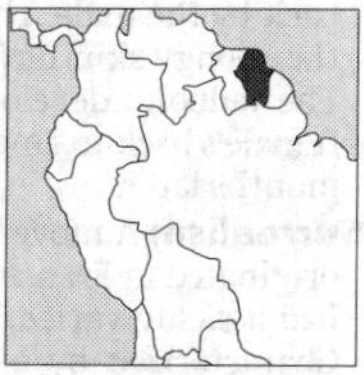

Physical. Surinam is sandwiched between Guyana and French Guiana, with Brazil to the south. The climate is equatorial: hot and very wet. Thick forest covers most of the interior, which rises to highlands in the centre. Rice and sugar cane can be grown on the coast.

Economy. Dutch and US aid, on which the economy depends, was suspended in 1980, following a military coup, but was restored in 1988 after democratic elections. Surinam's exports are dominated by bauxite and its aluminium products but production was disrupted by civil war. Bauxite-smelting and food-processing are the main industries. There are considerable mineral reserves, especially iron ore and gold. Agriculture is restricted to the alluvial coastal area, rice being the main crop.

History. Surinam's name is taken from the name of its earliest inhabitants, the Surinen, who had been driven out of the area by other South American Indians by the time Europeans arrived. Surinam was claimed by Spain in 1593 but was colonized by the Dutch from the beginning of the 17th century. The territory alternated between British and Dutch control until the Netherlands received it in a treaty settlement of 1815. In the 17th century African slaves had begun to be imported. By the late 19th century plantation labour was recruited from India and Java. The ethnic diversity of Surinam resulted in increasing racial and political strife after World War II. In 1954 Surinam became an equal partner in the Kingdom of the Netherlands, and full independence was granted in 1975. After several years of party strife the military took over in 1980. In 1986 an extended guerrilla protest by the Surinamese Liberation Army (SLA) was launched, organized from the jungle in neighbouring French Guyanne. In 1988 civilian rule was restored, following elections, but the military retained great influence. In 1990 a new military coup was staged, but in 1991 a coalition of opposition parties, the New Front for Democracy and Development, led by Ronald Venetiaan, won elections. A peace agreement with the SLA was made in 1992. Drug trafficking, gun-running, and money laundering all remained problems. After elections in 1996 a new coalition government led by the National Democratic Party was formed, and Jules Wijdenbosch was elected President.

Capital: Paramaribo
Area: 163,820 sq km (63,251 sq mi)
Population: 430,000,000 (1995)
Currency: 1 Suriname guilder = 100 cents
Religions: Hindu 27.0%; Roman Catholic 23.0%; Muslim 20.0%; Protestant (mostly Moravian) 19.0%
Ethnic Groups: East Indian 35.0%; Creole 32.0%; Indonesian 15.0%; African (bush negro) 10.0%; Amerindian 3.0%; Chinese 3.0%; European 1.0%

Languages: Dutch (official); English; Sronan Tongo; Spanish; Hindi; Javanese; Chinese; local Amerindian and pidgin languages
International Organizations: UN; OAS

Surinam toad A species of completely aquatic and rather bizarre-looking toad, *Pipa pipa*. The body is flattened, the head triangular, and the toes of the forefeet have star-shaped tips. Its mating behaviour is remarkable, and involves the fertilized eggs being pressed into the spongy skin of the female's back by the male. These eggs are then engulfed by the spongy skin until a 'cap' has grown over each. The tadpoles develop inside these pockets on the female's back to emerge as tiny toads three to four months later.

Surrealism A movement in art and literature that originated in France in the 1920s and subsequently had a richly varied influence on Western culture. Characterized by a fascination with the bizarre, the incongruous, and the irrational, it was a many-sided movement, but its essential aim was to try to liberate the creative powers of the unconscious mind by overcoming the dominance of reason. The group's objectives were partially anticipated by DADA, a more extreme movement, which flourished between about 1916 and 1922. André BRETON, the main founder and theoretician of Surrealism, said its purpose was 'to resolve the previously contradictory conditions of dream and reality into an absolute reality, a superreality'. Surrealism became the most widely disseminated and controversial aesthetic movement between the wars, spreading not only throughout Europe, but also to the USA, where many artists migrated during the war years. Its methods and techniques continued to influence artists in many countries. It was, for example, a fundamental source for ABSTRACT EXPRESSIONISM.

Surrey A largely residential county of south-east England; area 1,679 sq km (648 sq miles); pop. (1991) 997,000; county town, Guildford. Surrey is divided into 11 districts.

Surtees, Robert Smith (1805–64) British journalist and novelist. He is remembered for his comic sketches of Mr Jorrocks, the sporting Cockney grocer, collected in *Jorrocks's Jaunts and Jollities* (1838); its style, format, and illustrations by 'Phiz' were to influence Dickens's *Pickwick Papers*. Other famous caricatures, all set against a background of English fox-hunting society, include Mr Soapy Sponge of *Mr Sponge's Sporting Tour* (1849; 1853).

Surtsey A small island to the south of Iceland, which rose from the sea during a volcanic eruption in 1963. It is named after the Norse god Surtur, who was appointed to set fire to the Earth the day the gods fall.

surveillance (technological) The monitoring of behaviour from a distance by means of electronic equipment or other technological means. A major feature of security service activities during the 20th century has been the use of technological means to gather information on the opinions or activities of citizens with or without their consent. Such means include telephone tapping, powerful directional microphones, and various forms of loudspeaker devices or 'bugs'. Because surreptitious surveillance threatens privacy, in most countries it is subject to legal controls, and can be employed only under a warrant issued by a specified authority, such as a judge in the USA and Australia, or a special tribunal in Germany. Electronic tagging is a form of non-surreptitious surveillance consisting of a device attached to convicted offenders allowing their whereabouts to be monitored, for example, during the last months of a prison sentence, before complete release. Another common means of surveillance is the use of closed-circuit television systems in public places as a means of detecting and deterring crime. See also DATA PROTECTION.

surveying The determination of position, form, and boundaries of an area of land by measuring distances and angles. Conventionally, a topographic survey is one used to produce MAPS covering large areas at scales smaller than about 1:10,000. A cadastral survey, at a scale of perhaps 1:500, is used for engineering and building projects and shows accurately the extent and measurement of every plot of land. In such a survey, the horizontal features of the land are surveyed by triangulation. Details on the land, such as irregular boundaries and buildings, are measured as perpendiculars (offsets) from the principal lines. A THEODOLITE focused on a calibrated staff can be used to measure relative heights, while electronic devices employing LASERS or infrared emitters give accurate, long-distance length measurement.

suspension bridge A BRIDGE suspended by vertical rods (hangers) from cables supported by towers on each bank. The cables are anchored to the bank behind the towers and loads are distributed evenly among the hangers by a stiffening girder beneath the roadway (deck). A related bridge type is the cable-stayed bridge, in which spans are supported on either side of a high tower by cables fanning out from the tower to points along the deck. Although early bridges used rope or iron chains, most modern bridges use wire for the suspension cables.

suspension system A system to enable the wheels of a land vehicle to support its body without transmitting to the body all the shocks arising from irregularities in the road. Road vehicles had no suspension until the development of systems for use on horse-drawn CARRIAGES, in which the carriage body was suspended by leather braces from curved wooden or iron members. In about 1804, elliptical springs were developed for coaches.

Most modern cars have suspension systems using helically coiled steel springs, which are designed with the required amount of flexibility for a particular load. Usually a SHOCK ABSORBER is contained within the spring, the combined unit being known as a McPherson strut. Railway wagons and lorries formerly used heavy-duty leaf springs for suspension, but springs that use compressed air are now becoming usual on these vehicles.

Sussex A former county of southern England, now divided into East and West Sussex.

Sutherland A former county of Scotland, from 1975 to 1996, when it was abolished, a district of Highland Region.

Sutherland, Graham (Vivian) (1903–80) British painter. During World War II he was an official war artist, who concentrated on depicting the devastation caused by bombing. Among his portraits are those of Somerset Maugham (1949) and Sir Winston Churchill (1954); the latter was considered unflattering and was destroyed by Churchill's family. His postwar work included the tapestry *Christ in Majesty* (1962), designed for the rebuilt Coventry cathedral.

Sutherland, Dame Joan (1926–) Australian operatic soprano. Noted for her dramatic coloratura roles, she is best known for her performance of the title role in Donizetti's *Lucia di Lammermoor* in 1959.

Suttee See CREMATION.

Sutton Hoo An estate in Suffolk, England, site of a group of barrows, one of which was found (1939) to cover the remains of a Saxon ship burial (or perhaps a cenotaph; no body was discovered) of the 7th century AD. The timbers had decayed and only their impression was left in the soil, with the iron bolts still in place, and in the centre was a magnificent collection of grave goods, including exotic jewellery, an iron standard, decorated shield, bronze helmet, and Merovingian gold coins.

Suva The capital of Fiji (since 1882), situated on the Pacific island of Viti Levu; pop. (1986) 71,600. It is a port with a deep-water harbour that receives cargo and cruise ships.

Suyin, Han (pseudonym of Elizabeth Comber) (1917–) Chinese-born British writer and doctor. Born to a Chinese father and Belgian mother, she came to England in 1939 and trained as a doctor. Her autobiographical novel *A Many Splendoured Thing* (1952) brought her to public attention. She has written an acclaimed five-volume series of autobiography and Chinese history, the first volume of which was *The Crippled Tree* (1965).

Suzman, Helen (1917–) South African politician, of Lithuanian Jewish descent. In 1953 she became an MP for the opposition United Party, before becoming one of the founders of the anti-apartheid Progressive Party in 1959. In the elections two years later she was the only Progressive candidate to be returned to parliament, and from this time until 1974 she was the sole MP opposed to apartheid. Suzman was awarded the UN Human Rights Award in 1978; she retired in 1989.

Svalbard A group of islands, comprising **Spitsbergen** and other groups, in the Arctic Ocean about 640 km (400 miles) north of Norway, to which country they have belonged since 1925; area 62,000 sq km (24,000 sq miles); pop. (1995) 3,700. There are important coal and mineral deposits.

Sverdlovsk See YEKATERINBURG.

Swabia (German **Schwaben**) A former German duchy, now divided between Germany, Switzerland, and France.

Swahili ▶**1** A Bantu people of Zanzibar and the adjacent coast of Africa. ▶**2** Their language, a Bantu language of the Niger-Congo group with a vocabulary heavily influenced by Arabic. It is the most important language in East Africa, spoken also in the central and southern regions and expanding rapidly to the west and north, and while it is the first language of only about a million people it is used as a common language by about 20 million who speak different mother tongues. It is the official language of Kenya and Tanzania.

swallow A bird of the family Hirundinidae, with a worldwide distribution except for cold areas at high latitudes. The long-tailed species are often referred to as swallows and the short-tailed ones as MARTINS. Swallows are mostly small, less than 15 cm (6 inches) long; a few species are larger or have long tail feathers. Many are glossy blue-black or greenish above and pale below, and a number have bright reddish-chestnut patches on the breast or head. They are almost exclusively insectivorous, catching their prey on the wing. As a result they cannot survive in most temperate areas in winter because there are no insects available, and so they migrate. Some, such as the common or barn swallow, *Hirundo rustica*, nest in close association with man.

swallowtail butterfly A mainly tropical butterfly with between 621 and 641 species in the family Papilionidae, which contains some of the largest and most beautiful butterflies in the world. Many have 'tails' on the hind-wings. They are found mainly in forests, but the abundant citrus swallowtail, *Papilio demodocus*, of Africa, and the related chequered swallowtail, *P. demoleus*, of southern Asia and Australia, both intricately patterned in black and yellow, frequent gardens and plantations, where their caterpillars eat citrus leaves, and may be pests. The caterpillars of swallowtails usually have an eversible forked process, often red, behind the head, which releases a pungent aroma.

Swammerdam, Jan (1637–80) Dutch naturalist and microscopist. Qualified in medicine, he preferred to commit himself to research. He worked extensively on insects, describing their anatomy and life history and classifying them into four groups. A pioneer in the use of lenses, Swammerdam was the first to observe red blood cells. He also provided an elegant demonstration of the fact that muscles do not change in volume during motion.

swamp eel See CUCHIA.

swan A bird of the family Anatidae, which also includes geese and ducks. They are generally bigger than geese, the largest being over 1.5 m (5 feet) long, and have longer necks which assist them to feed on underwater vegetation, although they also graze on land. Their flight is ponderous, with slow, regular wing-beats. The seven species of swans have pure white adult plumage, with the exception of the black swan, *Cygnus atratus*, in Australia and the black-necked swan, *C. melanocoryphus*, in South America. The sexes are alike: 'cob' refers to male, 'pen' to female.

Swan, Sir Joseph Wilson (1828–1914) British physicist and chemist. He was a pioneer of electric lighting, devising in 1860 an electric light bulb consisting of a carbon filament inside a glass bulb; he worked for nearly 20 years to perfect it. In 1883 he formed a partnership with Thomas Edison to manufacture the bulbs. Swan also devised a dry photographic plate, and bromide paper for the printing of negatives.

Swanscombe Man An early inhabitant of Britain, named after a village in Kent, England, where three skull bones were discovered in river gravels in 1935, 1936, and 1955. They belong to an adult individual, probably a young woman, dated at around 250,000 years ago. The skull seems closely related to a similar skull from Steinheim in Germany; both probably represent late neanderthals (*Homo neanderthalensis*) or *Homo heidelbergensis*.

Swansea (Welsh **Abertawe**) A city in South Wales, at the mouth of the River Tawe; pop. (1991) 182,100. Swansea developed rapidly in the 19th century based on the export of anthracite coal and a major tin-plate and associated steel industry. This has now declined and been succeeded by light industries and tourism; the popular Gower peninsula is within the city boundaries. Swansea has one of the University Colleges of Wales (1982). The county of Swansea, created in 1996, includes the conurbation and some of the surrounding countryside.

Swanson, Gloria (born Gloria May Josephine Svensson) (1899–1983) US actress. She was the most highly paid star of silent films in the 1920s; with her own production company, Swanson Productions, she made such films as *Sadie Thompson* (1928) and *Queen Kelly* (1928). Swanson is perhaps now chiefly known for her performance as the fading movie star Norma Desmond in *Sunset Boulevard* (1950).

SWAPO (South West Africa People's Organization) A nationalist organization formed in South West Africa (NAMIBIA) in 1964–66 as the South African government extended formal authority in the region. Driven from the country, SWAPO, under the presidency of Sam Nujoma, began a guerrilla campaign, operating largely from neighbouring Angola. Efforts by the United Nations failed to find an agreeable formula for Namibian independence and the guerrilla war continued until 1988. SWAPO won the first general election in November 1989. In the first post-independence elections in Namibia, in 1994, SWAPO secured a two-thirds majority in the National Assembly.

swastika (from Sanskrit *svastika*, 'conducive to well-being') An emblem in the form of an even-length cross, with the arms bent at right angles, clockwise or anti-clockwise. A symbol of prosperity and good fortune, it was used in ancient Mesopotamia, in early Christian and Byzantine art, in South and Central America, and among the Hindus and Buddhists of India. In 1910 the German poet Guido von List proposed the swastika (German, *Hakenkreuz* 'hooked cross') as a symbol for all ANTI-SEMITIC organizations in the mistaken belief that it was Teutonic in origin. The NAZI PARTY adopted it in 1919, incorporated it (1935) into the national flag of the THIRD REICH, and made it a symbol of German national depravity.

Swazi A people of mixed stock inhabiting Swaziland and parts of eastern Transvaal in the Republic of South Africa. The Swazi language, which is of the Niger-Congo group, is one of the official languages of Swaziland.

Swaziland A small country of southern Africa.

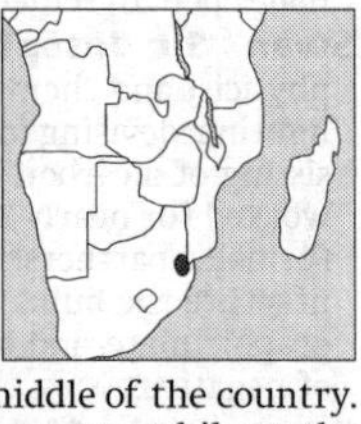

Physical. Swaziland is landlocked by South Africa on three sides and by Mozambique on the east. In the west are well-watered hills rich in iron ore, and from them run several rivers to the dry veld in the middle of the country. Here a variety of crops can be grown, while on the lower plains in the east there is livestock farming, together with the cultivation of sugar cane.

Economy. The economy is heavily dependent on South Africa; many Swazis find work in South African mines, and much of Swaziland's electricity is imported from South Africa. The land is fertile, and sugar, citrus fruit, pineapples, and cotton are grown for export. Maize and livestock are important locally, and the forestry industry produces wood-pulp for export. Tourism is increasing. Industry concentrates on processing agricultural products. Coal, diamonds, gold, and asbestos are mined and exported, but the falling world market for asbestos has led to unemployment.

History. Swaziland takes its name from the Swazis, who probably moved into the area during the 16th century. The name is thought to have been given to the people in 1836 when Mswati (Mswazi) II became king. A South African protectorate from 1894, Swaziland came under British rule in 1902 after the Second BOER WAR, retaining its monarchy. In 1968 it became a fully independent kingdom under Sobhuza II (1921–82). Revisions of the constitution in 1973 in response to requests from its Parliament, and again in 1978, gave the monarchy wide powers. All political parties were banned under the 1978 constitution. As a result, King Mswati III, who succeeded in 1986, faced increasing demands (1991–92) for the introduction of democracy. Parliamentary elections were held on a non-party basis in 1993, but were widely held to be undemocratic. After pro-democracy protests in 1996, the king agreed to review the ban on political parties.

Capital: Mbabane (administrative); Lobamba (royal and executive)
Area: 17,364 sq km (6,704 sq mi)
Population: 913,000 (1995)
Currency: 1 lilangeni = 100 cents
Religions: Protestant 37.3%; African indigenous churches 28.9%; traditional beliefs 20.9%; Roman Catholic 10.8%
Ethnic Groups: Swazi 84.3%; Zulu 9.9%; Tsonga 2.5%; Indian 0.8%; Pakistani 0.8%; Portuguese 0.2%
Languages: English, Swazi (both official); Zulu; local languages
International Organizations: UN; OAU; Commonwealth; SADC

sweat gland A tubular gland in the SKIN that supplies a watery solution (**sweat**), the evaporation of which cools the body. The rate of sweating is controlled by the brain and related to body temperature. Sweat glands are well developed in primates, horses, and camels. Two million or so of these glands are distributed in human skin.

swede (or **rutabaga**) One of the two BRASSICAS that are commonly grown for their swollen roots (the other is the turnip). The swede, *Brassica napus*, is cultivated for both human and livestock food. It can be distinguished from the less frost-resistant turnip by the swollen, ridged neck with its leaf scars. Purple-, white-, or yellow-skinned, the flesh is normally orange-yellow, but can be whitish. Swedes are best suited to cool, moist, temperate climates such as parts of northern and western Europe.

Sweden A country in northern Europe occupying the southern and eastern (the largest) part of the Scandinavian peninsula.

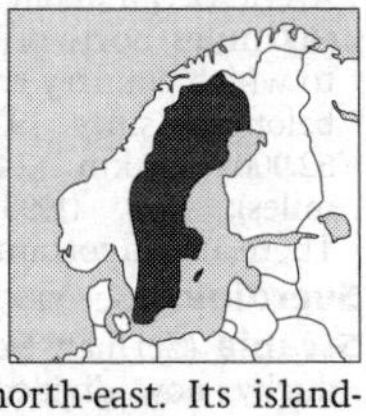

Physical. Sweden has a long, mountainous boundary with Norway on the north-west and a shorter one with Finland on the north-east. Its island-fringed coasts are on the Baltic Sea and the Kattegat, the channel to the North Sea. Sweden's islands include Gotland and Öland in the Baltic Sea. The northern part of the country is within the Arctic Circle. There are glaciers in the mountains, which everywhere are heavily forested with conifers. Parallel rivers fall to the Baltic Sea (Gulf of Bothnia) in rapids and falls, many of which have hydroelectric power stations, and forming at intervals long lakes. High-grade iron ore is found here, together with many other minerals. A region of hummocky hills and huge lakes lies to the south of the mountain range, and then the land rises again to a rocky, forested plateau. The southern coastal plain is extremely fertile; and the largest island, Gotland, has splendid beaches.

Economy. Sweden has an industrial economy based on the exploitation of abundant natural and mineral resources. Major exports include machinery, motor vehicles, paper, iron, and steel. A leading producer of iron ore, the country also has deposits of copper, lead, and zinc. Commercial forestry is important, though threatened by acid rain, as are the wood-pulp, sawmill, and paper industries. Electricity is generated almost entirely from nuclear and hydroelectric sources, but it is planned that the nuclear programme be discontinued by 2010. Agriculture has declined in importance, although livestock and dairy-farming are still substantial.

History. The country's earliest history is shrouded in legend, but Suiones tribesmen are mentioned by Tacitus and were probably the founders of the first unified Swedish state. Swedish VIKINGS were active in the Baltic area, and also ventured into Russia and the Arab caliphate of Baghdad. Christianity was introduced in the 9th century but the whole population was not converted until much later. In the 13th century parts of Finland and Karelia were occupied, but from 1397 to 1523 Sweden belonged to the Danish-dominated Union of KALMAR. Gustavus Vasa led the successful revolt which ended in independence for Sweden, a national crown for himself and his dynasty, and the introduction of the LUTHERAN CHURCH as the state religion. During the 16th and 17th centuries Sweden expanded territorially and achieved considerable political status, thanks largely to the efforts of GUSTAVUS ADOLPHUS and Axel Oxenstierna. The high point was reached after the Treaty of WESTPHALIA, during the reign of Charles X (1654–60), but the strains of maintaining a scattered empire began to tell during the reign of CHARLES XII (1682–1718). After the NORTHERN WAR (1700–21) the empire was dismembered, and a form of parliamentary government then prevailed until the coup of Gustavus III in 1771 who remained in power until 1792.

During the NAPOLEONIC WARS Sweden joined the Third Coalition against France (1805), but France defeated Russia, and the latter in turn took Finland from Sweden as compensation (1809). In that year the pro-French party in the Swedish estates overthrew the existing monarch, Gustav IV, and elected the aged and childless Charles XIII (1809–18). In 1810 they invited Jean-Baptiste Bernadotte to become crown prince. He subsequently ruled as CHARLES XIV (1818–44), and his descendants have remained monarchs of Sweden ever since. From 1814 to 1905 Norway was united with Sweden. Pursuing a policy of non-alignment, Sweden kept out of both World Wars, and by the 1950s it had developed into one of the world's wealthiest and most socially progressive states with an extensive social welfare system. A long Social Democrat hegemony was challenged during the 1970s, but regained by Olof Palme (1982–86), until his assassination. Sweden has played a central role in UN peace-keeping missions. It hosted the conference in 1959 resulting in EFTA, but in 1991 it applied to join the EUROPEAN COMMUNITY and became a member of the European Union in 1995. The Moderate Unity Party under Carl Bildt came to power in 1991, committed to reduction in public expenditure on welfare provision, particularly health and education. Social Democrat leader Ingvar Carlsson, who had succeeded Olof Palme as Prime Minister in 1986, regained power in 1994, but handed over power to Göran Persson in 1996.

Capital: Stockholm
Area: 449,964 sq km (173,732 sq mi)
Population: 8,826,000 (1995)
Currency: 1 Swedish krona = 100 ore
Religions: Church of Sweden (Evangelican Lutheran) 90.0%
Ethnic Groups: Swedish 90.0%; Finnish 3.1%; Lapp minority
Languages: Swedish (official); minority languages
International Organizations: UN; EU; Council of Europe; CSCE

Swedenborg, Emanuel (1688–1772) Swedish scientist, philosopher, and mystic. As a scientist he anticipated in his speculative and inventive work later developments, such as the nebular theory, crystallography, and flying machines. He became increasingly concerned to show by scientific means the spiritual structure of the Universe. However, a series of mystical experiences (1743–45) prompted him to devote the rest of his life to expounding his spiritual beliefs. His doctrines, which blended Christianity with elements of both pantheism and theosophy, were taken up by a group of followers, who founded the New Jerusalem Church in 1787.

Swedish The official language of Sweden, spoken by its 8.8 million inhabitants, by another 300,000 in Finland (where it is one of the two official languages), and by 600,000 in the USA. It belongs to the Scandinavian language group.

sweet corn A form of MAIZE, shorter than most other strains, but differing principally in that its grains store mainly sugar rather than starch. As the cobs are harvested well before the grains are fully ripe, it can be grown, at least in sheltered areas, in cool, temperate regions such as Britain.

sweetener, artificial Any substance other than a SUGAR that is capable of producing a sweet taste. One of the most widely used artificial sweeteners is saccharin, discovered by the US chemists Ira Remsen and Constantine Fahlberg in 1879, and found to be 500 to 600 times sweeter than sugar. It was considered to be inert and therefore harmless, but some research suggests that it may have toxic properties when fed in large doses to rats. In recent years a more popular alternative has been found, aspartame. This is the product of two naturally occurring amino acids, phenylalanine and aspartic acid.

sweet pea An annual climbing plant of the pea family with large, sweetly scented flowers on long stalks. Sweet peas have been developed as garden and florists' flowers by selective breeding from the Italian species *Lathyrus odoratus*. This species was first introduced to England from southern Italy in 1699. Variously coloured varieties were in existence by 1900, when frilled and waved-petal forms appeared and became instantly popular.

sweet pepper A variety of *Capsicum annuum*, a species that also gives rise to some paprikas and pimentos, and belongs to the family Solanaceae. Native to tropical America, it is now widespread in the tropics generally and, like its relative the tomato, is often grown under glass in temperate areas. The fruits are usually red or green, up to 25 cm (10 inches) long, and vary in their shape from more or less spherical to long and narrow. Varieties differ in their pungency, but all are mild compared to the chilli.

sweet potato A root crop harvested from the vine-like, climbing plant, *Ipomoea batatas*, related to BINDWEED and morning glory in the family Convolvulaceae. It is native to South America and was taken, via 16th-century Spain, to Asia, where it is now an important crop. Its elongated, swollen tubers have a red or purplish skin and white or yellow flesh which is rich in starch. In the USA, it is often wrongly referred to as a yam.

Sweyn I (or **Sven**; known as **Sweyn Forkbeard**) (died 1014) King of Denmark *c.*985–1014. From 1003 he launched a series of attacks on England, finally driving the English king Ethelred the Unready to flee to Normandy at the end of 1013. Sweyn then became king of England until his death five weeks later. His son Canute was later king of England, Denmark, and Norway.

swift A bird making up a family, Apodidae, containing 66 species with a worldwide distribution except for colder areas at high latitudes. The family also contains the swiftlets, spinetails, and needletails. Like SWALLOWS, they are insectivorous, catching all their prey on the wing, so they have to be summer visitors to many temperate areas. They are slightly larger than swallows, and are mostly black or black and white. They often nest in colonies and some, such as the edible-nest swiftlet, *Collocalia fuciphaga* (the bird whose nest is used for the Chinese bird's nest soup), live in enormous numbers in caves.

Swift, Jonathan (known as **Dean Swift**) (1667–1745) Irish satirist, poet, and Anglican cleric. He was born in Dublin, a cousin of John Dryden, and divided his life between London and Ireland. His *Journal to Stella* (1710–13) gives a vivid account of life in London, where he was close to Tory ministers. In 1713 he was made Dean of St Patrick's in Dublin, where he wrote his satirical work, *Gulliver's Travels* (1726), a fantastic tale of travels in imaginary lands. He also involved himself in Irish affairs and wrote many political pamphlets, such as *A Modest Proposal* (1729), ironically urging that the children of the poor should be fattened to feed the rich. His poems include the *Verses on the Death of Dr Swift* (1739), in which he reviews his life with pathos and humour.

swift moth A moth that differs from most in the way the fore- and hind-wings are held together, and in having similar venation in both wings. They comprise the family Hepialidae, with 300 or so species, best represented in Australia, but widely distributed throughout the world. Their caterpillars tunnel into wood or feed on roots of a wide variety of plants, and the pupae have a flexible, spined abdomen with which they work their way to the surface when the adults are ready to emerge. The largest European species is the ghost moth, *Hepialus humili*, which gets its name from the brilliant white upper wings of the male. These dance up and down in the air above vegetation and seem to appear and disappear alternately as their upper wing surfaces reflect the moonlight. There are many species in Australia; the bent-wing, *Zelotypia stacyi*, has a wing-span of 19 cm (7.5 inches) and its caterpillars tunnel destructively in eucalyptus trees.

swim bladder An air-filled sac that lies above the intestine of BONY FISHES. Its role is to maintain the buoyancy of the fish by effectively reducing the fish's weight at different depths of water. The swim bladder is either filled with air through a connection with the mouth, or filled with gases passed from the blood system into, or out of, the swim bladder. In lungfishes the swim bladder functions as a lung.

Swinburne, Algernon Charles (1837–1909) British poet and critic. Associated with Dante Gabriel Rossetti and the Pre-Raphaelites, he came to fame with *Atalanta in Calydon* (1865), a drama in classical Greek form, which was praised for its metrical finesse. In *Songs Before Sunrise* (1871), Swinburne expressed his hatred of authority and his support for Mazzini's struggle for Italian independence. As a critic he contributed to the revival of contemporary interest in Elizabethan and Jacobean drama and produced influential studies of William Blake and the Brontës.

Swindon An industrial town in Wiltshire, southern England; pop. (1991) 145,263. It is a centre of the high-tech and motor industries and is a major warehousing and distribution centre. Swindon developed into a 'railway town' when it was chosen by Brunel in 1841 as the site of a major railway works. The 'old' town has a large railway museum.

swing See JAZZ.

swing-wing aeroplane (or **variable geometry aeroplane**) An aeroplane that has its wings pivoted so that the angle of sweep can be altered in flight. It can thus take off and land at slower speeds (and hence on shorter runways) than otherwise similar aircraft, with the wings extended out from the fuselage. In flight, the wings can be swung back at a sharper angle for efficient SUPERSONIC FLIGHT. Examples include the General Dynamics F-111 and Panavia Tornado fighter-bombers.

Swithin, St (or **Swithun**) (died 862) English ecclesiastic. He was chaplain to Egbert, the king of Wessex, and bishop of Winchester from 852. The tradition that if it rains on St Swithin's day it will do so for the next 40 days may have its origin in the heavy rain said to have occurred when his relics were to be transferred to a shrine in Winchester cathedral. Feast day, 15 July.

Switzerland A country in central Europe, consisting of a Federation of 23 cantons; three cantons are subdivided making a total of 26 administrative units.

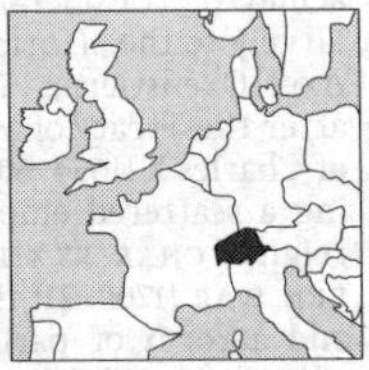

Physical. Switzerland is surrounded by France, Germany, Italy, and the tiny country of Liechtenstein. It is Europe's loftiest country with the Alps stretching across the whole of its southern half. The rivers Rhône and Rhine rise here and form broad valleys. Below the forested mountain slopes, snow-covered all winter, the land is fertile and the summer temperature is warm. Northward the country stands on a hilly plateau which contains the Swiss lakes and rises again in the north-west to the Jura Mountains, a region important for dairying and forestry, and with vineyards on the southern slopes.

Economy. Switzerland is a prosperous country with the highest GDP per capita in the world. Major exports include machinery, electrical goods, instruments, watches, textiles, and pharmaceuticals. Tourism and international finance and banking are important. Agriculture is mainly livestock- and dairy-farming.

History. Switzerland was occupied by the Celtic HELVETII in the 2nd century BC. Its position astride vital Alpine passes caused the area to be invaded by the Romans, Alemanni, Burgundians, and Franks before it came under the control of the Holy Roman Empire in the 11th century. In 1291 the cantons (Swiss confederacies) of Uri, Schwyz, and Unterwalden declared their independence of their Habsburg overlords, and the alliance for mutual defence was later joined by Lucerne, Zürich, and Bern. During the 15th century this Swiss Confederation continued to expand, and it fought successfully against Burgundy, France, and the Holy Roman Empire, creating a great demand for its soldiers as mercenaries. During the REFORMATION and COUNTER-REFORMATION, its political stability was undermined by civil warfare, but in 1648 the Habsburgs acknowledged its independence in the Treaty of WESTPHALIA.

In 1798 French Revolutionary armies entered the country and established the Helvetic Republic. But at the Congress of VIENNA (1815) Swiss control was restored and the European powers guaranteed the confederation's neutrality. In 1847 a separate Roman Catholic league within the federation, the

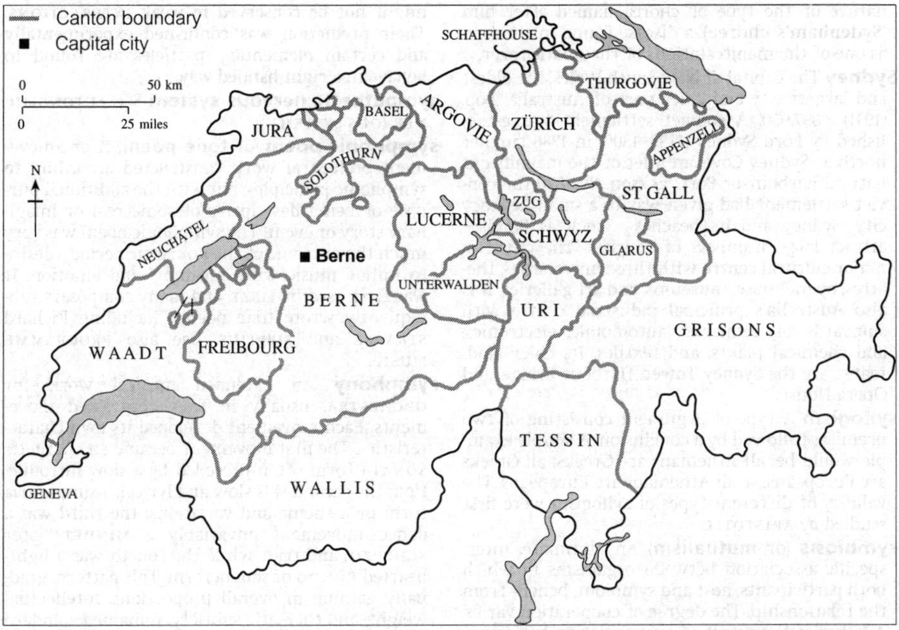

Switzerland

Sonderbund, was formed after radicals took power in one of the cantons. After a brief civil war, peace and stability were restored by the new, democratic, federal constitution of 1848. During World War I the country maintained its neutrality despite the contradictory affections of the French and German sections of its population. In World War II the Swiss again preserved their armed neutrality, and have continued since then to enjoy a high level of economic prosperity. In 1979 the 22 cantons of the confederation were joined by the new Canton of Jura. Women were not allowed to vote on a federal basis until 1971, and suffrage remains restricted in some cantons. Because of its long tradition of neutrality, the International Red Cross and the League of Nations were both based in Switzerland, as are many UN agencies. In 1992 it rejected by referendum membership of the European Economic Area, thus freezing its government's application to the EUROPEAN COMMUNITY (now the European Union), which is still being considered.

Capital: Berne
Area: 41,293 sq km (15,943 sq mi)
Population: 7,039,000 (1995)
Currency: 1 Swiss franc = 100 centimes
Religions: Roman Catholic 48.0%; Protestant 44.0%; Jewish 0.3%
Ethnic Groups: German 65.0%; French 18.4%; Italian 9.8%; Spanish 1.6%; Romansch 0.8%; Turkish 0.6%
Languages: French, German, Italian (all official); minority languages
International Organizations: OECD; EFTA; Council of Europe; CSCE

sword A hand weapon with a metal blade and a handle (hilt) with a handguard. The history of the sword began in the Bronze Age when bronze-casting enabled a weapon heavier and longer than the flint knife to be produced. The blade of a sword can be designed to cut, to thrust, or both, and it may be given a single or a double edge. Many different kinds of swords have been made: the sabre, the Indian *tulwar*, and the Japanese *katana* are all examples of cutting swords; the rapier and the Turkish *kilj* are thrusting swords; the Roman *gladius* and most swords of medieval Europe were cut-and-thrust weapons. The sword, of all hand weapons, has remained the longest in use. Swords of modified design are used in FENCING.

swordfish A species of large BONY FISH, *Xiphias gladius*, of worldwide distribution in temperate and warm temperate seas. It is a heavily built fish with a high, but short, first dorsal fin and a broad tail, but its most distinctive feature is the long sword-like snout, which is flattened like a sword. Active, strong swimmers, they eat a wide range of smaller fishes and squids, which are captured in the mouth, not impaled on the sword. Living in the upper 1,000 m (3,250 feet) of the sea, they are often sighted near the surface. The swordfish is captured for food, but has become scarce in recent years.

swordtail A popular tropical aquarium fish, *Xiphophorus helleri*, which originated in Mexico and Guatemala, where it is native to mountain streams as well as still waters on the coastal plains. It is a member of the family Poeciliidae, hence related to guppies, platys, and mollies, and gives birth to well-developed young. The male has a structure called a gonopodium, formed from some of the rays of the anal fin, with which sperm is transferred to the female. Only males have the characteristic, coloured, sword-like, long rays of the tail fin. Females occasionally change sex after producing a few broods, and grow the distinctive sword tail.

sycamore Any of various trees. The sycamore of the Bible was a fig, *Ficus sycomorus*. In Britain, the sycamore is one of the MAPLES, *Acer pseudoplatanus*, native to southeast Europe but widely introduced elsewhere. In North America the name is used for PLANE TREES.

Sydenham, Thomas (*c*.1624–89) English physician. He was known as 'the English Hippocrates', because of his contemporary reputation as a physician and his scepticism towards theoretical medicine. He emphasized the healing power of nature, made a study of epidemics, wrote a treatise on gout (from which he suffered), and explained the nature of the type of chorea named after him (**Sydenham's chorea**), a disease found in children as one of the manifestations of rheumatic fever.

Sydney The capital of New South Wales, the oldest and largest city and chief port of Australia; pop. (1991) 3,097,950. A convict settlement was established by Lord Sydney (1733–1800) in 1788 further north at Sydney Cove, an inlet of the magnificent natural harbour of Port Jackson. By 1820 the convict settlement had given way to a small Regency city. Sydney and its beaches – such as Bondi – attract large numbers of tourists. The city is a major cultural centre with three universities, theatres, opera house, museums, and art galleries. It is also Australia's principal industrial centre with shipyards, oil refineries, automobile, electronics, and chemical plants, and textiles. Its chief landmarks are the Sydney Tower, Harbour Bridge, and Opera House.

syllogism A type of argument consisting of two premises followed by a conclusion. A simple example would be: all Athenians are Greeks; all Greeks are Europeans; so all Athenians are Europeans. The validity of different types of syllogism were first studied by ARISTOTLE.

symbiosis (or **mutualism**) Any intimate, interspecific association between organisms in which both participants, host and symbiont, benefit from the relationship. The degree of cooperation varies. A lichen is the result of an association between a unicellular alga and a fungus. The alga gains nutrients, protection, and anchorage, and the fungus obtains carbohydrates from its photosynthesizing partner. Another example of symbiosis involves herbivorous animals, such as RUMINANTS, and the cellulose-digesting microorganisms that gain protection and food in their alimentary canals. The relationship between leguminous plants (LEGUMES) and nitrogen-fixing bacteria is an example of plant symbiosis.

Symbolist movement An art movement that flourished particularly in France in the 1880s and 1890s, based on the belief that the function of art is not simply to describe but to suggest, by means of symbols, the transcendent reality behind the surface appearance of things. In literature it had its origins in the work of Baudelaire and developed partly in reaction to the naturalism of such writers as Zola. Symbolist drama was written by MAETERLINCK, CLAUDEL, and JARRY, whose work anticipated the ideas of the SURREALISTS. In art the Symbolist movement reacted against the naturalistic aims of the Impressionists. Its artists believed that colour and line in themselves could express ideas, and preferred suggestion and evocation to direct description. Although chiefly associated with France, such diverse artists as BURNE-JONES and MUNCH are regarded as part of the movement in its broadest sense, while in literature its influence was widespread, extending to Russia, where it stimulated a revival of poetry in the early 20th century in works by such figures as BLOK and Bely.

symmetry The property of remaining invariant under certain changes (for example, of orientation in space, of the sign of the electric charge, of parity, or of the direction of time flow). It is from natural symmetries that some fundamental laws of nature arise. Examples are the laws of conservation of momentum and energy. However, in 1956 the Chinese-born physicists Tsung Dao Lee (1926–) and Ning Chen Yang (1922–) suggested that **parity** (the notion that both left-handed and right-handed phenomena occur equally in nature) might not be conserved in weak INTERACTIONS. Their prediction was confirmed experimentally and certain elementary particles are found to behave in a right-handed way.

sympathetic nervous system See AUTONOMIC NERVOUS SYSTEM.

symphonic poem (or **tone-poem**) A one-movement orchestral work constructed according to symphonic principles, but with the additional purpose of being descriptive of some real or imaginary story or event. The symphonic poem was very much the outcome of the Romantic period's desire to imbue music with 'meaning' and emotion. It was first used by LISZT, and many composers subsequently wrote tone poems, including Richard STRAUSS and SIBELIUS. See also PROGRAMME MUSIC.

symphony An extended musical work for ORCHESTRA, usually in four contrasted movements. Each movement developed its own characteristics. The first movement became an energetic SONATA form often preceded by a slow introduction; the second was slow and lyrical, a simple aria form or a theme and variations; the third was a dance movement (invariably a MINUET (later SCHERZO) and trio); while the fourth was a lighthearted RONDO or sonata form. This pattern, gradually gaining in overall proportions, intellectual weight, and thematic subtlety, remained standard throughout the 19th century. Following the example of Beethoven's Ninth Symphony (1823), some composers (such as Mendelssohn and Mahler) introduced voices into their symphonies, some (Vaughan Williams, Britten) writing symphonies entirely for chorus and orchestra. The symphony has remained perhaps the greatest of all challenges to a composer's skill and imagination.

synagogue (from Greek, 'bringing together') The Jewish place of worship, originally called the *beth ha knesset*, 'house of assembly'. Synagogues also provide religious instruction and are centres of legal authority. Synagogues arose after the Babylonian Exile (586 BC) and after the destruction of the Temple (70 AD) they spread rapidly, forming and remaining a focal point for Jewish life. Synagogues may be of any shape, but internally the central focus is the Ark (*Aron ha-kodesh*). This is a cupboard in the wall facing Jerusalem, which contains the scrolls of the Law (see TORAH). Above the Ark are two tablets with the first two words of each of the Ten Commandments inscribed upon them. A light, the *ner tamid* ('lamp of perpetual light'), is suspended in front of it and represents both God's presence and the continuity of Judaism. During a service a scroll is removed from the Ark and transferred to a reading desk (*bimah*), from where it is read aloud. In ORTHODOX JUDAISM the sexes are separated, singing is unaccompanied, and services are in Hebrew. REFORM JUDAISM (Conservative Judaism in the USA) and LIBERAL JUDAISM (Reform in the USA) may allow family seating and musical accompaniment, and part of the service may be in a language other than Hebrew.

synapse See NERVE.

synapsid A member of an extinct group of reptiles from which the mammals evolved. The earliest synapsids were the pelycosaurs, best known from North America, or species such as *Dimetrodon incisivus*, distinctive for the large 'sail' along its spine, which appeared about 300 million years ago. These were superseded by the more advanced therapsids. These gradually became more and more like mammals; the first known mammals evolved from the therapsids about 190 million years ago as small rodent-like animals, such as *Morganucodon*.

synchronous motor See ELECTRIC MOTOR.

synchrotron See PARTICLE ACCELERATOR.

synchrotron radiation ELECTROMAGNETIC RADIATION emitted by an electron moving at a high speed in a magnetic field. Some of the light coming from the Crab Nebula is generated by this synchrotron mechanism from electrons spiralling in the mesh of magnetic fields within the nebula. The phenomenon occurs in synchrotron PARTICLE ACCELERATORS in which electrons move at speeds approaching the speed of light.

syncline A geological FOLD structure in the form of a through or inverted arch, produced by the downfolding of stratified rocks. Each side of the fold dips in towards the centre; the younger rocks thus crop out in the centre of the syncline and the older rocks on its flanks. A syncline is the opposite of an ANTICLINE.

Synge, (Edmund) J(ohn) M(illington) (1871–1909) Irish dramatist. Between 1898 and 1902 he lived with the peasant community on the Aran Islands, an experience that inspired his plays *Riders to the Sea* (1905) and *The Playboy of the Western World* (1907). The latter caused outrage and riots at the Abbey Theatre, Dublin, with its explicit language and its implication that Irish peasants would condone a brutal murder.

synodic period The time interval between successive similar positions of a body with respect to the Sun and Earth. The synodic period of a planet, for example, is the time between two successive identical planetary configurations of opposition or conjunction. The synodic period for the Moon it is the time between successive PHASES of full Moon or new Moon.

syntax See GRAMMAR.

synthesis See CHEMICAL REACTION.

synthesizer (in music) An electronic apparatus that changes electrical impulses into sound according to instructions given by the operator through a keyboard and a series of switches and variable controls. The sound is thus created by entirely artificial means and may differ completely from, or imitate more or less exactly, normal instrumental or vocal sound. Every aspect of synthesized sound can be controlled: pitch, intensity, tone-colour, quality of attack, duration, dynamics, and so on. The results can be recorded on tape for later reproduction, or played 'live' during a performance.

synthetic fibre A fibre made from synthetic materials. In contrast to RAYONS and other manufactured fibres derived from naturally occurring POLYMERS, synthetic fibres are polymeric molecules, usually PLASTICS, manufactured from simpler chemical materials (often PETROCHEMICALS). The fibres are 'spun' by EXTRUSION of liquid polymer through the fine holes of a spinneret (see SPINNING). There are many types, but the POLYESTERS, ACRYLIC FIBRES, and the polyamides or NYLONS are the most common. They are used principally in TEXTILES, but nylon and polyester fibres also have industrial applications, where strength and durability are required. Other important synthetics are spun fibres of POLYTHENE and POLYPROPYLENE. These are used in large quantities for carpets and other floor-coverings, for rot-resistant sacking, for nets, cord, and rope. Since problems with dyeing these materials have been overcome, they have also increasingly been used for woven and knitted fabrics. Polyurethane and other synthetic, rubber-like fibres are used in the making of elastic, and for manufacturing stretch fabrics such as Lycra. CARBON FIBRES are used in the manufacture of light, strong composite materials.

synthetic fuel Any liquid fuel made from coal. There are two processes. In the synthesis process, the coal structure is completely destroyed to produce a gas mixture which, in its passage over a catalyst, is synthesized to gasoline, diesel fuel, and methanol. The **Fischer–Tropsch process** (invented in 1925 by Franz Fischer, 1852–1932, and Hans Tropsch, 1830–1935), which operates this route, is the only coal liquefaction process in commercial operation. In the liquid solvent extraction (LSE) method, crushed coal is heated with a coal-derived solvent and is then reacted with hydrogen to give a liquid product rich in aromatics and suitable for REFORMING to valuable fuels at low cost and with available refinery techniques. The LSE process is more efficient and cheaper but the synthesis process can use cheaper, high ash, coal.

syphilis A chronic, communicable, SEXUALLY TRANSMITTED DISEASE resulting from bacterial infection by *Trepenoma pallidium*. Syphilis is communicable during the first two years of acquiring the infection. Long-term antibacterial treatment is necessary to prevent its manifestations. Initially, an ulcer (chancre) develops at the infection site, usually the genitals (primary syphilis); it heals without treatment in two to six weeks. Secondary syphilis develops six to eight weeks later with the appearance of a skin rash and highly communicable spots (papules) in between skin folds. This is followed by a latent period of many years. Tertiary syphilis, which is a non-communicable stage, occurs after ten or more years with soft, tumour-like lesions (gumma) on the buttocks, face, legs, bones, connective tissue, and mucous membrane of the mouth, which resolve after a prolonged time. Quaternary syphilis may occur after 20–30 years and effects include cardiovascular involvement and damage to heart and blood vessels, which can be life-threatening.

Syracuse (Italian **Siracusa**) A port and tourist centre on the south-east coast of Sicily; pop. (1990) 125,440. Founded by the Corinthians *c.*734 BC, it was a flourishing centre of Greek culture especially in the 5th–4th centuries BC under its rulers Dionysius the Elder and Dionysius the Younger. It has petrochemical plants and food-processing industries.

Syria A country in the Middle East at the eastern end of the Mediterranean Sea.

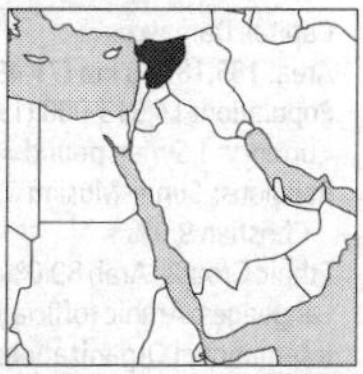

Physical. Bounded on the north by Turkey, on the east by Iraq, on the south by Jordan, and on the south-west by Israel and Lebanon, Syria has a narrow coastal plain with a Mediterranean climate: citrus fruit and tobacco can be grown. Behind a range of hills the Asi (Orontes) River runs northward, along a RIFT VALLEY; and beyond that the ground rises to a plateau of steppe, where cotton can be grown. This merges into hot, dry desert, relieved only by the upper Euphrates, which runs across the country. In the extreme north-east there is oil.

Economy. Although still largely agricultural, with sheep- and goat-raising the primary agricultural activities, Syria is becoming more industrialized and has benefited in recent years from rising oil exports. Other exports are textiles, clothing, and chemicals. Mineral resources include petroleum, phosphates, salt, and gypsum, and manufacturing industry includes textiles, cement, and chemicals.

History. Syria was settled successively by the Akkadians, Arameans, and Canaanites, and formed a valuable province of successive empires, from the Phoenicians to the Byzantines. After the Arab conquest of the 630s, Damascus became the brilliant capital of the Arab caliphate under the UMAYYADS from 661 to 750, but subsequently Syria became a province of other rulers, such as the FATIMIDS and the MAMELUKES of Egypt. It became a province of the OTTOMAN EMPIRE in 1516, and after the Turkish defeat in World War I Syria was mandated to France. Controlled by VICHY France at the outbreak of World War II, the country was invaded and occupied by British and FREE FRENCH forces, and declared its independence in 1941. Political stability proved elusive, with three army-led coups in 1949 and others in 1951 and 1954. An abortive union with Egypt in the UNITED ARAB REPUBLIC provided no solution and was terminated by a further army coup. A leading political grouping, the Ba'ath Socialist Party, remained split by personal and ideological rivalries, though one successful and two abortive coups in 1963 did see a swing to policies of nationalization. Further coups in 1966 and 1970 saw the eventual emergence of General Hafiz al-Assad as the leader of a new regime, capable not only of crushing internal opposition but also of asserting significant influence over neighbouring war-torn Lebanon. But, aspiring to a role of regional dominance, Syria suffered major reverses in the 1967 SIX-DAY WAR and the YOM KIPPUR WAR of 1973 against Israel. It was deeply involved in the civil war in LEBANON (1975–89), and remained generally antagonistic towards Iraq, sending troops to defend Saudi Arabia in 1990 in the GULF WAR. In December 1991 a reconciliation took place with the PLO, when Yasser ARAFAT visited Damascus. Relations with other Arab League states were improved and Syria took a cautious part in the Middle East peace negotiations of 1992, President Assad having been re-elected in March. Unlike its former allies in the Six-Day War (Egypt and Jordan) Syria has not undertaken any rapprochement towards Israel. However, with the peace agreements between Israel and the PLO and Israel and Jordan (1993; 1994), President Assad came under increasing pressure to reach an accommodation with Israel.

Capital: Damascus
Area: 185,180 sq km (71,498 sq mi)
Population: 14,313,000 (1995)
Currency: 1 Syrian pound = 100 piastres
Religions: Sunni Muslim 72.0%; Alawi (Shia) 11.0%; Druze 3.0%; Christian 9.0%
Ethnic Groups: Arab 89.0%; Kurdish 6.0%; Armenian and other 4.0%
Languages: Arabic (official); minority languages
International Organizations: UN; Arab League; OAPEC

Syriac The liturgical language of the Maronite and Syrian Catholic Churches, the Syrian Jacobite Church, and the Nestorian Church. It is descended from the Aramaic spoken near the city of Edessa (now Urfa) in south-east Turkey from shortly before the Christian era, and was extensively used in the early Church owing to the active Christian communities in those parts. After Greek it was the most important language in the eastern Roman Empire until the rise of Islam in the 8th century. The Syriac alphabet developed from a late form of Aramaic used at Palmyra in Syria.

syringa See LILAC.

systems analysis The investigation, analysis, design, implementation, and evaluation of an information system, usually with the aim of computerizing some human activity. First, the problem to be solved (for example, the computerization of a business's accounting system) must be accurately defined. The existing system is then investigated to understand how it works, using techniques such as FLOW CHARTS and decision tables. Next, the results of the investigation are analysed and used as the basis for the design of a new system, making optimum use of the available computer hardware, software, and staffing resources.

Szechwan See SICHUAN.

Szent-Györgyi, Albert von (1893–1986) Hungarian-born US biochemist. After working in various countries Szent-Györgyi returned to Hungary in 1930 and then emigrated to the USA in 1947. He isolated a substance from both adrenal glands and plant material that became known as ascorbic acid, which was later identified with vitamin C. He later worked on the biochemistry of muscle, in particular the mechanisms of cellular respiration and fibre contraction. Szent-Györgyi was awarded a Nobel Prize in 1937.

Szilard, Leo (1898–1964) Hungarian-born US physicist and molecular biologist. Working in Germany before World War II, he developed an electromagnetic pump that is now used for coolants in nuclear reactors. He fled the Nazis, first to Britain, where he suggested the idea of nuclear chain reactions, and then to the USA, where he became a central figure in the Manhattan Project to develop the atom bomb. After the war Szilard turned to experimental and theoretical studies in molecular biology and biochemistry.

Szymanowski, Karol (Maciej) (1882–1937) Ukrainian-born Polish composer. His earliest works were influenced by BRAHMS and Richard STRAUSS, but from 1915 the influence of DEBUSSY and RAVEL began to be evident. His best-known works are the Third Symphony ('The Song of the Night', 1916), the First Violin Concerto (1916), and the opera *King Roger* (1924). Later works, such as the *Stabat Mater* (1926) and the Symphonie Concertante for piano and orchestra (1932), drew on folk sources.

T

Tabernacles, Feast of Jewish autumn festival lasting eight days. It recalls the offerings made by Jews at the end of the harvest and God's care for the Jews during the period in the wilderness after the Exodus (*c.*1300 BC) living in tabernacles, that is, portable dwellings. During this festival meals are eaten in a *sukkah* (a hut made of branches, leaves, etc.).

tableland A plateau or extensive elevated region with a level surface.

Table Mountain A spectacular flat-topped mountain overlooking and Cape Town in South Africa, rising to a height of 1,087 m (3,563 ft). Its summit is 3 km (2 miles) long and has served as a landmark to seamen since the Portuguese navigator Bartholomew Diaz sailed this way in 1488.

table tennis A miniature indoor version of TENNIS, played with small bats and a hollow plastic ball on a tabletop with a central net. A full-sized table measures 2.7 m (9 feet) by 1.5 m (5 feet). Games are up to 21 points, and players serve in sequences of five points then change over. Skilled players use cut and spin to swerve the ball through the air and make it deviate or accelerate on bouncing. In recent years China has been the dominant nation, with other top players emerging from Korea, Japan, France, Russia, Croatia, and Belarus.

taboo A system of ritual prohibitions forbidding contact with certain things or people. Taboo is originally a Polynesian word, but has been extended to refer to anything forbidden. In 19th-century ANTHROPOLOGY, the idea of taboo was usually associated with the food prohibitions of totemism, and the marriage prohibitions of INCEST.

tabor A musical instrument, the drum of the PIPE AND TABOR, always with a snare (a strand of gut) on the struck head. Tabors vary in size. In the 13th century they were small; by the 16th they were larger, but by the late 19th the English Morris tabor was so small that a child's toy drum was often used instead.

Tabriz The capital of the province of East Azerbaijan, north-west Iran, on the River Talkheh; pop. (1991) 1,089,000. Formerly known as Tauris, it was capital of Armenia in the 3rd century AD and from the 13th century was the administrative and commercial centre of the Persian empire. Its industries now produce carpets, metal castings, and cotton and silk textiles.

tachinid fly See BRISTLE FLY.

Tacitus (full name Publius, or Gaius, Cornelius Tacitus) (*c.*56–*c.*120 AD) Roman historian. His major works on the history of the Roman Empire, only partially preserved, are the *Annals* (covering the years 14–68) and the *Histories* (69–96). They are written in a concise style, pervaded by a deep pessimism about the course of Roman history since the end of the Republic.

Tadmur (or **Tadmor**) See PALMYRA.

tadpole The larval stage of frogs and toads. Tadpoles have a combined head and body, usually round or oval in shape, and a well-developed tail; they do not resemble the adult. In other amphibians the larva *is* like the adult except that it has feathery gills. Not all frogs and toads have a free-living tadpole stage; some undergo direct development, such as the SURINAM TOAD and the African viviparous toad, *Nectophrynoides* species, both of which produce fully formed young which are miniatures of their parents. In some species the tadpole stage is passed inside the egg.

Taft, William Howard (1857–1930) US Republican statesman, 27th President of the USA 1909–13. His presidency is remembered for its dollar diplomacy in foreign affairs and for its tariff laws, which were criticized as being too favourable to big business. Taft later served as Chief Justice of the Supreme Court (1921–30).

Tagalog (or **Filipino, Pilipino**) The principal language group of the people of the Philippine Islands, a Malayo-Polynesian language heavily influenced by Spanish with some adaptations from Chinese and Arabic.

Tagore, Rabindranath (1861–1941) Indian writer and philosopher. His poetry pioneered the use of colloquial Bengali instead of the archaic literary idiom then approved for verse; his own translations established his reputation in the West, and he won the Nobel Prize for literature in 1913 for *Gitanjali* (1912), a set of poems modelled on medieval Indian devotional lyrics. He also wrote philosophical plays, novels such as *Gora* (1929), and short fiction which often commented on Indian national and social concerns. He was knighted in 1915, an honour he renounced after the Amritsar massacre (1919).

Tagus (Spanish **Tajo**; Portuguese **Tejo**) A river of the Iberian peninsula that rises in the Sierra de Gudar in eastern Spain and flows westwards into Portugal where it turns south before flowing into the Atlantic near Lisbon; length, *c.*1,000 km (625 miles).

Tahiti One of the Society Islands of French Polynesia in the South Pacific, administered by France; area 1,042 sq km (402 sq miles); pop. (1988) 115,820; capital, Papeete. Its highest peak is Mt Orohena (2,237 m, 7,339 ft). In 1767 Captain Samuel Wallis was the first European to visit Tahiti, which was ruled by the Polynesian Pomare dynasty until 1880 when the island became part of a French Colony. It is the largest island in French Polynesia. It produces tropical fruit and its beauty attracts many tourists.

taiga Slow-growing coniferous forest in northern regions, especially in Siberia where it lies between tundra and forest-steppe.

Taiji (or **T'ai-chi**) (Chinese, 'Great Ultimate', literally, 'ridge beam') In Chinese philosophy, an expression of supreme or ultimate reality; the fundamental force from which spring YIN AND YANG and all creation. The notion was first mentioned in the *yijing* and was borrowed by Zhu Xi (Chu Hsi), a founder of neo-CONFUCIANISM, who used it to define the unity of matter and the structure of the Universe.

Tai languages A group of around 60 closely related languages spoken in Thailand and Laos, as well as in northern Myanmar (Burma) and Assam to the west, and northern Vietnam and southern China to the east. Spoken by over 60 million people, the languages fall into three sub-groups: North, Central, and South-West. South-West Tai has by far the largest number of speakers, since it includes Thai and Lao, the two biggest languages in the group.

tailed frog An amphibian, *Ascaphus truei*, unique among frogs and toads in that the male has a tail-like extension of the cloaca (the common reproductive-excretory tract), which acts as a copulatory organ, preventing sperm loss during mating in the fast-flowing streams of North America where it lives. Tadpole development is slow in the cold water of these streams and between one and three years may pass before the tadpoles are transformed into juvenile frogs. Some authorities place the tailed frog in a family on its own, Ascaphidae, while others group it with three 'tail-less' species which belong to the genus *Leiopelma*, from New Zealand.

Tailleferre, Germaine (1892–1983) French composer and pianist. She was a pupil of Ravel and later became a member of the group Les SIX. Her works include concertos for unusual combinations of instruments, including one for baritone, piano, and orchestra.

Tainan A city on the south-west coast of Taiwan; pop. (1991) 690,000. It is the oldest city on the island and was capital of Taiwan 1684–1887. Now industrialized it produces metals, textiles, and machinery.

taipan A relatively slender-bodied, rather MAMBA-like snake, *Oxyuranus scutulatus*, up to 3.4 m (11 feet) long. It occurs in coastal areas of northern and northeastern Australia and in southern parts of New Guinea. One of the world's most venomous snakes, when threatened, a taipan is capable of striking at an intruder with considerable speed and ferocity. It eats small mammals.

Taipei The largest city and capital of Taiwan since the Nationalists under Chiang Kai-shek were forced to flee from the mainland of China in 1949; pop. (1991) 2,718,000. It is a commercial and cultural, as well as administrative centre. Its major industries include metals, engineering, chemicals, wood and paper products, textiles, printing, and foodstuffs.

Taiping Rebellion (1850–64) Revolt against the Chinese QING dynasty. Led and inspired by Hong Xiuquan (1813–64), who claimed to be the younger brother of Jesus Christ, the Taiping Rebellion began in Guangxi province. It developed into the most serious challenge to the Qing, bringing most of the central and lower Yangtze region under rebel control, and costing 20 million lives. The rebels captured Nanjing in 1853 and established their capital there before launching an unsuccessful attack on Beijing. Taiping resistance was crushed with the capture of Nanjing in 1864, Hong Xiuquan having died in the siege, but the Qing regime never really recovered from the long civil war.

Taiwan (official name **Republic of China**) A country (not recognized by most other countries and not a member of the UN) comprising a large island and several much smaller ones off the south-east coast of China.

Physical. The main island is almost 370 km (230 miles) long from north to south and 130 km (81 miles) wide from west to east. Climatically it is very warm and wet in summer and cooler in winter. High mountains running most of its length, richly forested with camphor, oak, cypress, and cedar, drop steeply eastward to the Pacific Ocean. Westward many rivers flow through plains bearing sugar cane, paddy, and tropical fruits.

Economy. Taiwan is a newly industrializing country with very high growth rates based on exports of manufactured goods, particularly to the USA. Textiles, electronic goods, and information technology are the principal exports. Agriculture, with sugar cane and rice as the main crops, is of little importance, and mineral resources are limited, though silver and gold are mined and there are deposits of coal, oil, sulphur, and iron. Taiwan's economic success has been achieved at the cost of considerable environmental degradation.

History. Portuguese explorers called it **Formosa** ('the Beautiful Island'). Sparsely populated by a non-Chinese people, it was long a Chinese and Japanese pirate base. In the 17th century the Dutch (1624) and the Spaniards (1626) established trading posts, the Dutch driving out the Spaniards in 1642. With the fall of the MING dynasty in 1644 opponents of the QING started to settle on the island and in 1661 'Koxinga' (Zheng Chenggong), a Ming patriot, expelled the Dutch. It was conquered by the QING in 1683 and for the first time became part of China. Fighting continued between its original inhabitants and the Chinese settlers into the 19th century. Taiwan was occupied by Japan as a result of the Treaty of Shimonoseki in 1895 and remained under Japanese control until the end of World War II. The island was occupied by the Chinese forces of CHIANG KAI-SHEK in September 1945, but Taiwanese resentment at the administration of Chiang's governor Chen Yi produced a revolt which had to be put down by force of arms. When the CHINESE CIVIL WAR began to turn against the KUOMINTANG in 1948, arrangements were made to transfer Chiang's government to Taiwan, a move completed in the following year, and by 1950 almost two million refugees from the mainland had also arrived on the island. Supported militarily by the USA, Taiwan maintained its independence from communist China, as the Republic of China, and, until expelled in 1971, sat as the sole representative of China in the United Nations. Chiang Kai-shek remained its President until his death in 1975, and was succeeded by his son, Chiang Ching-kuo. He died in 1988 and was succeeded by President Lee Teng-hui. Since the 1950s Taiwan has undergone dramatic industrialization, becoming one of the world's major industrial nations. In 1986 the creation of new political parties was legalized, but with strict regulations governing their policies. Martial law, in force since 1949, was replaced in 1987 by the slightly less severe National Security law. Pro-democracy demonstrations during the late 1980s and early 1990s led to further political reforms. The first full multi-party elections since 1949 were held in 1992 and were won by the Kuomintang. The Kuomintang has consistently opposed full independence for Taiwan and sought reunification with the mainland, but only if the mainland regime rejects communism. Negotiations between the two countries have been sporadic and generally unproductive, but in 1991 Taiwan officially ended its state of war with communist China. In 1993 a formal structure for further negotiations on economic and social issues was agreed but relations between the two countries have remained tense. By 1995 Taiwan had been recognized as a separate nation by 29 countries. In 1996 Taiwan's first democratic presidential elections were won by the incumbent, Lee Teng-Hui.

Capital: Taipei
Area: 36,000 sq km (13,900 sq mi)
Population: 21,268,000 (1995)
Currency: 1 New Taiwan dollar = 100 cents
Religions: Buddhist 43.0%; Daoist 21.0%; Christian 7.0%; Muslim 0.5%
Ethnic Groups: Taiwanese 84.0%; Mainland Chinese 14.0%; Aborigine (Indonesian) 2.0%
Languages: Mandarin Chinese (official); Chinese dialects

Taiyuan A city in northern China, capital of Shanxi province; pop. (1990) 1,900,000. Its industries manufacture, iron, steel, machinery, chemicals, textiles, and electricity.

Taizong (or **T'ai-tsung**) (596–649) Second Tang Emperor of China 627–49. He was renowned for his military prowess, scholarship, and concern for people. He was a patron of Xuanzang, the Buddhist pilgrim who, in 645, brought back from India Buddhist scriptures, which he translated into Chinese.

Tajik A people of Central Asia descended from Persian-speaking Iranians. They preserved their cultural identity in the face of successive Mongol and Turkic conquests by occupying high mountain valleys to the south of the Syr Darya.

Tajikistan A country bounded by China on the east and Afghanistan on the south, one of the highest regions of central Asia.

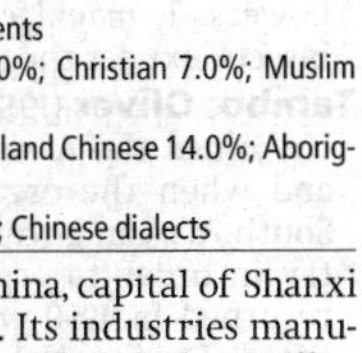

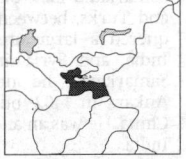

Physical. The Pamir mountains occupy a third of Tajikstan while the Alai range stretches across its centre. Below the snow-line the slopes are generally great stretches of bare red and grey rocks, broken by alpine meadows, the forests near the tree-line being of firs and juniper.

Economy. Tajikstan is the poorest of the former Soviet republics, despite its considerable mineral resources, which include coal, zinc, lead, molybdenum, petroleum, and natural gas; mining and extraction of these are the principal heavy industries. Light industry includes a number of textile mills to process cotton, which is the chief agricultural crop. Silk, fruit, wheat, and natural oils are also produced and cattle are raised. Tajikistan's valleys support vineyards, orchards, and fields of cereal and cotton, while hydroelectricity is available from river power.

History. Tajiks were originally of Iranian stock, but were conquered by Arab people during the 7th and 8th centuries AD. Large numbers of Turkic people moved into the area, which came under the control of the Uzbek khanate of Bukhara from the 15th to the mid-18th century and was then conquered by the Afghans. By 1868 the whole area had been conquered by the Russians and proclaimed a protectorate. Following the Russian Revolution a Bukharan People's Soviet Republic was proclaimed in 1920. This however was conquered by the Red Army, and a confused situation lasted until 1929 when the Tajik Soviet Socialist Republic was formed, which in 1936 joined the Soviet Union. During 1990 opposition parties were legalized. In September 1991 independence was proclaimed and Tajikistan joined the COMMONWEALTH OF INDEPENDENT STATES (CIS). By 1992, polarization between a nationwide Islamic majority and a Russian minority based in the capital Dushanbe and the industrialized north had developed. There were armed skirmishes, with Russian troops still stationed in the country becoming involved. In that year President Rakhmon Nabiyev was removed from office by force. Fighting between government forces and Muslim rebels was halted by a cease-fire in 1994, but sporadic violence has continued. A new constitution was approved in 1994 and Imamoli Rakhmanov, who had been acting head of state since 1992, was elected President. Legislative elections in 1995 resulted in victory for the ruling (formerly Communist) party.

Capital: Dushanbe
Area: 143,100 sq km (55,240 sq mi)
Population: 5,832,000 (1995)
Currency: 1 rouble = 100 tanga
Religions: Sunni Muslim; Eastern Orthodox; Ismaili minority
Ethnic Groups: Tajik 62.0%; Uzbek 23.0%; Russian 7.0%
Languages: Tajik (Persian) (official); Russian; minority languages
International Organizations: UN; CSCE; Commonwealth of Independent States; North Atlantic Co-operation Council

Taj Mahal A mausoleum at Agra in northern India, by the River Jumna. Completed *c.*1648, it was built by the Mogul emperor Shah Jahan in memory of his favourite wife who had borne him 14 children. Set in formal gardens, the domed building in white marble is reflected in a pool flanked by cypresses.

takahe See NOTORNIS.

Takamine Jokichi (1854–1922) Japanese industrial chemist. In 1887 he left government service to establish a factory making superphosphate fertilizer. He later developed a process for making the starch-digesting enzyme diastase. In 1901 he was the first to isolate a pure hormone, adrenalin.

takin An unusual-looking and rare species of antelope, *Budorcas taxicolor*, which combines features of the ox, goat, and antelope. It is a close relative of the musk ox, and characteristically has eyes high in its head, and curving horns at the top of the forehead. The takin lives in the rough mountainous country of the Himalayas, western China, and Korea, at elevations of 2,500–4,300 m (8,000–14,000 feet). It is a heavy-looking animal, some 90 cm (3 feet) high at the shoulder, and has a shaggy coat of yellowish hair. It spends its days in thickets near the timber-line, from which it emerges at dusk and dawn to feed on the grassy slopes.

Talbot, (William Henry) Fox (1800–77) British pioneer of photography. Working at the family seat of Lacock Abbey in Wiltshire, he produced the first photograph on paper in 1835. Five years later he discovered a process for producing a negative from which multiple positive prints could be made. Apart from patenting a number of other photographic processes and publishing two of the earliest books illustrated with photographs, he also made contributions to mathematics and deciphered cuneiform scripts.

talc (or **talcum**) A common magnesium silicate mineral, $Mg_3Si_4O_{10}(OH)_2$, which is extremely soft and soapy to the touch. The product of the alteration of magnesium compounds, it is found most commonly in metamorphic rocks. It never occurs as distinct crystals, but always as light-grey masses. Large deposits exist in Styria (Austria) and Madras (India). It is used in powder form in the paper, rubber, textile, paint, and cosmetic industries.

Taliesin See WELSH-LANGUAGE LITERATURE.

talipot palm A PALM from India, *Corypha umbraculifera*, which can grow to 24 m (75 feet) tall. It then produces a terminal inflorescence several metres (yards) in height, after which it dies. The large leaves have been used as umbrellas and for thatching, and also as a writing material.

Tallahassee The capital of the US state of Florida, situated in the north-west of the state; pop. (1990) 124,770. Settled in 1824, it was the only capital city east of the Mississippi not captured by Union forces during the American Civil War. It is the seat of Florida State University (1857) with industries that include publishing, printing, food processing, and the manufacture of timber products.

Talleyrand (full name Charles Maurice de Talleyrand-Périgord) (1754–1838) French statesman. Foreign Minister under the DIRECTORY from 1797, he was involved in the coup that brought Napoleon to power, and held the same position under the new leader (1799–1807); he then resigned office and engaged in secret negotiations to have Napoleon deposed. Talleyrand became head of the new government after the fall of Napoleon (1814) and recalled Louis XVIII to the throne. He was later instrumental in the overthrow of Charles X and the accession of Louis Philippe (1830).

Tallinn A commercial and ferry port on the Gulf of Finland, capital of Estonia; pop. (1990) 505,100. It was known as Revel until 1917. The upper town is dominated by Lutheran and Orthodox cathedrals and a lower town surrounded by medieval walls. Industries include shipbuilding, machinery, electrical equipment, textiles, and chemicals.

Tallis, Thomas (*c.*1505–85) English composer. Organist of the Chapel Royal jointly with William Byrd, he served under Henry VIII, Edward VI, Mary, and Elizabeth I. In 1575 he and Byrd were given a 21-year monopoly in printing music, and in that year published *Cantiones Sacrae*, a collection of 34 of their motets. Tallis is known particularly for his church music, especially the 40-part motet *Spem in Alium*.

Talmud (Hebrew, 'study') The compilation of scholarly interpretations and commentaries on Jewish oral law codified in the MISHNAH. The destruction of the Temple in Jerusalem (70 AD) and the growth of DIASPORA prompted a vigorous effort to preserve traditional teachings. Judah Ha-Nasi *c.*200 AD compiled the Mishnah, an organized summary of the oral tradition. This, together with subsequent commentary, the *Gemara*, constitutes the Talmud. There are two major versions: the Palestinian or Jerusalem Talmud (completed *c.*400 AD) and the Babylonian Talmud (completed *c.*500 AD). Both are based on the same Mishnah, but the Babylonian Talmud is more extensive and considered more authoritative. The Talmud is primarily a legal compilation, but it also includes non-legal sections, known as *Haggadah* (narratives). The standard version of the Talmud prints part of the Mishnah and the relevant Talmud on each page. Summaries of Talmudic teachings were subsequently prepared by such scholars as MAIMONIDES in the 12th century and Joseph Caro in the 16th century. The Talmud is the basis of later codifications of Jewish law (*Halakhah*), the most influential of which is Caro's *Shulhan Arukh* ('Laid Table') (1565). Study of the Talmud has been central to Jewish intellectual and religious life ever since its compilation.

talus See SCREE.

tamandua See ANTEATER.

tamarind A tree of the family Caesalpiniaceae, *Tamarindus indica*, or its dried fruit. Although it grows in seasonally dry areas throughout the tropics, its origin is unknown. The tart fruit, consisting of brown pods, is used as a flavouring and a food preservative, and is also used in medicine; the timber is valuable.

tamarisk A shrub or tree belonging to the genus *Tamarix*, containing some 90 species distributed throughout Eurasia, many of them growing in soils with high levels of salt. They give their name to the tamarisk family, Tamaricaceae, which has some 120 species. Most are rather wispy shrubs with fine, hair-like leaves and spikes of tiny flowers. *T. mannifera*, when punctured by scale insects, exudes the manna used by the bedouin.

Tambo, Oliver (1917–93) South African politician. He joined the African National Congress in 1944, and when the organization was banned by the South African government (1960) he left the country in order to organize activities elsewhere; he returned in 1990 when the ban on the ANC was lifted. During Nelson Mandela's long imprisonment he became acting president of the ANC (1967) and president (1977), a position he held until 1991, when he gave it up in favour of the recently released Mandela. Tambo remained as ANC national chairman until his death.

tambourine A shallow, single-headed drum with miniature cymbals in the frame to add a jingle. It was used in the Middle Ages and as a folk instrument. It came into the orchestra from the military band in the 19th century, to give an Arab, Spanish, or Italian flavour; later it became an instrument in its own right.

Tamerlane (or **Tamburlaine**) (born Timur Lenk, 'lame Timur') (1336–1405) Mongol ruler of Samarkand 1369–1405. Leading a force of Mongols and Turks, between about 1364 and 1405 he conquered a large area including Persia, northern India, and Syria and established his capital at Samarkand; he defeated the Ottomans near Ankara in 1402, but died during an invasion of China. He was an ancestor of the Mogul dynasty in India.

Tamil A people inhabiting southern India, Sri Lanka, and Malaysia speaking Tamil, a Dravidian language that is one of the official languages of Sri Lanka.

Tamil Tigers A Tamil separatist movement in Sri Lanka, formed in the 1970s to protest against the treatment of the Tamil minority. They seek an independent homeland for Tamils in northern Sri Lanka, for which purpose they have trained several forces.

Tammany Hall Headquarters of a political organization in New York City. Founded in 1789, it was named after a late 17th-century Indian chief, and based its rites and ceremonies on pseudo-Indian forms. It acquired, under the control of Aaron BURR, a political importance that endured until the 1950s. The word Tammany became synonymous with machine politics, graft, corruption, and other abuses in city politics.

Tampico A principal seaport of the Gulf of Mexico, in Tamaulipas state, east Mexico, on the Pánuco River; pop. (1990) 271,640. It is a major oil port and fish-processing centre, and a popular resort.

tam-tam See GONG.

tanager Any of about 235 species of birds in the family Emberizidae, native to the New World, mainly to Central and South America. A few are summer migrants to North America. Most are sparrow- to thrush-sized, though one or two species are slightly larger. They are like sparrows in shape, with stoutish beaks, and many are brilliantly coloured red, yellow, or blue. They live in a wide variety of habitats from rain forest to open scrub and eat a wide range of fruits and insects.

Tananerive The former name (from 1895 to 1976) of ANTANANARIVO, capital of Madagascar.

Tang The dynasty which ruled in China from 618 to *c*.906, a period noted for territorial conquest and great wealth and regarded as the golden age of Chinese poetry and art.

Tanganyika See TANZANIA.

Tanganyika, Lake A lake in East Africa on the frontier between Tanzania, the Democratic Republic of Congo, Zambia, and Burundi; area 32,764 sq km (12,650 sq miles). It is the deepest and second-largest lake in Africa. The chief towns on its shores are Bujumbura (capital of Burundi), Kigoma, Ujiji, and Kalémie (formerly Albertville). In 1858 the explorers Richard Burton and John Speke were the first Europeans to encounter it, and the famous meeting between Livingstone and Stanley took place at Ujiji in 1871.

Tange, Kenzo (1913–) Japanese architect. His work reflects the influence of Le Corbusier and is characterized by the use of modern materials, while retaining a feeling for traditional Japanese architecture. During the 1950s he built a number of civic buildings in Brutalist style, including the Peace Centre at Hiroshima (1955). Later buildings, such as the National Gymnasium in Tokyo (built for the 1964 Olympics), make use of dynamic, sweeping curves.

tangent (in geometry) A straight line that touches a curve. A tangent to any of the CONIC SECTIONS does not intersect the curve anywhere else, whereas a straight line may touch and later cut the graph of, for example, a cubic function. The tangent to the graph of any function at a point is the limit approached as two points of intersection of a straight line with the curve coalesce. It equals the slope of the curve at that point. A tangent plane is the equivalent notion for surfaces in three-dimensional space. The derivative of the function evaluated at that point gives a number which is the value of the **trigonometrical tangent** of the angle between the tangent line and the horizontal. The trigonometrical tangent of an angle in a right-angled triangle is the length of the side opposite the angle divided by the length of the adjacent side which is not the hypotenuse.

tangerine See MANDARIN.

Tangier (or **Tanger**) A seaport of Morocco, situated nearly opposite Gibraltar and commanding the western entrance to the Mediterranean; pop. (1993) 307,000. It had its beginning in the Roman port and town of Tingis, but the present walled city was built in the Middle Ages by the Moors. From 1904 until 1956 (except for five years in World War II) the zone was under international control. In 1956 it passed to the newly independent monarchy of Morocco. It became a free port in 1962 and is today a commercial, cultural, and tourist centre.

tank A heavy, enclosed, armoured fighting vehicle that moves on CATERPILLAR TRACKS. Tanks were first used in action in 1916 during the Battle of the Somme (France). By 1918 the design included a central turret on top of the chassis, which replaced the frontal or side gun-mountings of most early tanks. The tank's tactical role largely changed from ARTILLERY support for infantry to the defeat of other tanks. Tanks are driven by internal-combustion engines, and have all-round armour, with the thickest plating at the front of the hull. They are now usually armed with a large-calibre ANTI-TANK GUN (105–120 mm, 4.1–4.7 inches) carried in a turret. Some tanks can also fire missiles, and most carry two or three MACHINE-GUNS.

tanker A ship designed to carry bulk liquid cargoes, especially crude oil, at sea. The tanker hull is almost completely taken up by several large tanks, separated by narrow transverse compartments as a safety measure. The earliest tankers were built in the late 19th century. Until 1956 their size, around 30,000 tonnes, was dictated by the limitations of the SUEZ CANAL. Closure of the canal due to local wars in 1956 and 1967, coupled with huge increases in the demand for oil stimulated by worldwide growth in the use of motorized transport, led to vastly bigger **supertankers** of 400,000–500,000 tonnes. Tankers are also designed and built for the transport of liquefied gas and, on a smaller scale, of wine.

Tannhäuser (*c*.1200–*c*.1270) German poet. In reality a Minnesinger (an aristocratic poet-musician who performed songs of courtly love), he became a legendary figure as a knight who visited Venus' grotto and spent seven years in debauchery, then repented and sought absolution from the pope. He is the subject of Wagner's opera *Tannhäuser* (1845). The real Tannhäuser's surviving works include lyrics and love poetry.

tanning The process by which animal hides are made into leather. Tanning displaces water from the interstices of the hide's protein fibres, and binds the fibres together. The oldest tanning method, still widely used, is vegetable tanning, in which the hide is soaked in a liquid rich in **tannin** (a derivative of phenol present in the bark and leaves of trees). In mineral tanning, the hide is soaked in a solution of mineral salts, usually of chromium. This process is much faster than vegetable tanning and is used particularly for light leathers. Oil tanning uses fish or other oils or fats. Synthetic tanning agents are also widely used. After the leather has been tanned, it is dried, dyed, lubricated with oils and greases, and then dried again. Final finishing involves stretching and softening the leather, and coating the surface to resist abrasion and cracking.

Tannu-Tuva See TUVA.

Tansen (*c*.1500–89) Indian musician and singer. He is regarded as the leading exponent of northern Indian classical music. A native of Gwalior, he became an honoured member of the court of Akbar the Great, and was noted both for his skill as an instrumentalist and as a singer. Many legends arose about his life and musical achievements.

tantalum (symbol Ta, at. no. 73, r.a.m. 180.95) A heavy grey TRANSITION METAL. It occurs with niobium in the mineral tantalite, which has the formula $(Fe,Mn)(Nb,Ta)_2O_6$. Tantalum alloys are used for dental and surgical instruments and for spinnerets for SYNTHETIC FIBRE production. It is added to STEELS to prevent weld-decay and improves the performance of nickel alloys in gas-turbines. Sintered tantalum is used for electrolytic CAPACITORS. Tantalum forms an extremely hard carbide, which is used as an abrasive and in cutting tools for machining steel.

Tantalus In Greek mythology, a king of Lydia, son of Zeus and a nymph. At first the intimate friend of the gods, he offended them and was banished to Tartarus, the prison beneath the underworld. Here he was set in a pool of water, which always receded when he tried to drink from it, and under trees whose branches the wind tossed aside when he tried to pick their fruit (hence the word 'tantalize').

tantra (Sanskrit, 'loom') An esoteric tradition in both HINDUISM and BUDDHISM, which, through magical texts (MANTRAS), MEDITATION, and rituals, leads the practitioner to spiritual liberation and supernatural powers. In Hinduism, tantric practice, which may involve indulgence in normally forbidden taboos, is designed to awaken the energy of SHAKTI. Tantric Buddhism or Vajrayana ('Diamond Vehicle') is an important element in TIBETAN BUDDHISM. Meditation is based upon medical, occult, and astrological texts, as well as on mantras, *mudras* (symbolic hand gestures), and mandalas (visual aids such as sacred diagrams).

Tanzania A country in East Africa, consisting of the former republic of Tanganyika and the island of ZANZIBAR.

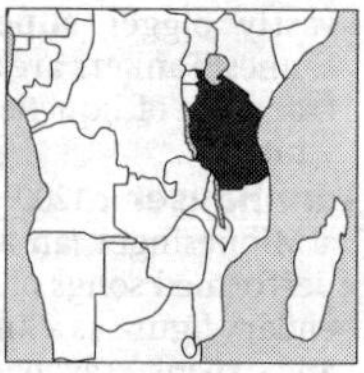

Physical. Tanzania is bounded by Kenya and Uganda on the north, Rwanda, Burundi, and the Democratic Republic of Congo on the west, and Zambia, Malawi, and Mozambique on the south. It has a coast on the Indian Ocean and several islands; Pemba and Zanzibar islands both have a degree of autonomy. A hot, wet coastal plain rises through thick forest and areas planted with sisal to a warm plateau. Here it is drier, and the soil is poor; but to the north is Mount Kilimanjaro, below which the soil is volcanic and coffee can be grown. In the extreme north is Lake Victoria, round which cotton is cultivated, diamonds are found, and animals roam in the Serengeti National Park. Lake Tanganyika lies along the western border, and Lake Malawi in the south, both in the western arm of the Great Rift Valley.

Economy. In recent years Tanzania has shifted from socialist principles in economic planning to IMF-backed liberalization policies, and is making the transition to a multi-party system. Agriculture is the mainstay of the economy, which is dependent on foreign aid, but export cash crops of coffee, cotton, tea, sisal, cashew-nuts, and cloves have all been adversely affected by drought and falling commodity prices. Cassava and maize are the main staple crops. Mineral resources include diamonds, gold, iron ore, coal, oil, and phosphates; there are unexploited natural gas reserves. Industry, mostly state-owned, is limited, with food-processing, textiles, oil- and metal-refining the principal sectors.

History. In the first millenium BC northern mainland Tanzania was inhabited by Caucasoid peoples, probably from Egypt. Bantu-speaking peoples from western Africa moved into the region and were established there by about 500 AD. Arab slave merchants settled along the coast, clashing occasionally with Portuguese explorers, who first arrived in the late 15th century. German missionaries went to Tanganyika (mainland Tanzania) in the 1840s and were followed by German colonists. By 1907 Germany had taken full control of the country. Tanganyika became a British mandate after World War I, and a trust territory, administered by Britain, after World War II. It became independent in 1961, followed by Zanzibar in 1963. The two countries united in 1964 to form the United Republic of Tanzania under its first President, Julius NYERERE. In the Arusha Declaration of 1967 Nyerere stated his policy of equality and independence for Tanzania. In 1975 the Tan–Zam railway line was completed. Tanzania helped to restore democracy in Uganda in 1986 and gave strong support to political exiles from Zimbabwe, Angola, and Namibia. Nyerere was succeeded by President Ndugu Ali Hassan Mwinyi, who was re-elected in 1990 and whose years in office saw a marked revival of the economy with its very considerable potential. In June 1992 he ended 27 years of one-party rule by the legalization of opposition parties. During 1994 and 1995, some 800,000 refugees from civil war and ethnic violence in the neighbouring countries of RWANDA and BURUNDI fled to Tanzania; some Tanzanian politicians called for their repatriation. Internal tensions also grew in this period, particularly in Zanzibar, where the ruling party encountered growing opposition from Islamic fundamentalists. Multi-party elections, held in November 1995, saw the Party for the Revolution retain power, with Benjamin Mkapa becoming the country's new President.

Capital: Dar es Salaam
Area: 945,037 sq km (364,881 sq mi)
Population: 28,072,000 (1995)
Currency: 1 Tanzanian shilling = 100 cents
Religions: Christian 34.0%; Muslim 33.0%; traditional beliefs and other 33.0%
Ethnic Groups: Nyamwezi and Sukuma 21.1%; Swahili 8.8%; Hehet and Bena 6.9%; Makonde 5.9%; Haya 5.9%
Languages: Swahili, English (both official); Sukuma; local languages
International Organizations: UN; OAU; Commonwealth; Non-Aligned Movement; SADC

Taoism See DAOISM.

tapaculo A small bird, the 29 species of which make up the family Rhinocryptidae, restricted to Central and South America. The family name refers to their covered nostrils. They are mostly brown, grey, or black in colour and most have short tails which are useless in flight. Most species are ground-living, and tend to run rather than fly. They live in a wide variety of habitats from dense grassland to forest scrub, although most are confined to mountain forests.

tape recorder A machine that records and replays sound on MAGNETIC TAPE. During recording the sound is converted by a microphone into an oscillating electrical signal, which when passed through the coils of an electromagnet produces an equivalent magnetic field. As it passes the electromagnet (the recording head), the magnetic tape becomes magnetized in a pattern reflecting the sound being recorded. On replay the magnetic pattern on the tape induces in a second electromagnet (the replay head) an electrical signal which, after amplification, drives a loudspeaker. The Danish engineer Valdemar Poulsen invented the earliest tape recorder in 1898, which recorded sound on a wire. Subsequent developments have included plastic tape in 1935, stereophonic recording in 1958, and DOLBY SYSTEMS to reduce surface hiss from cassettes in 1966. For domestic music systems, COM-

PACT DISCS (CDs) have largely replaced tape recordings.

tapestry Any heavy ornamental fabric used as a wall-hanging or upholstery fabric; more correctly, it is a hand-woven textile in which the design is formed by lengthwise threads (wefts) inserted over and under the crosswise threads (warps) according to the requirements of colour. The design is thus an integral part of the material, rather than something superimposed on it. Tapestries have been woven in every continent, the silk tapestries of Asia being particularly fine. In Europe, France has the richest tradition in the art, with particularly well-known factories at Arras, Aubusson, Beauvais, and Paris (the GOBELINS manufactory). In the 20th century leading Modernist artists, including Matisse, Braque, and Picasso, used tapestry as a medium, while one of the most ambitious tapestries of the century, 'Christ in Glory', was designed in 1962 by Graham Sutherland for Coventry Cathedral in Britain. See also BRUSSELS TAPESTRIES; WEAVING.

tapeworm A highly specialized invertebrate animal that lives inside the guts of vertebrates, and reaches 12 m (40 feet) in length in some species. Tapeworms form a class, Cestoda, of FLATWORMS. The head bears suckers and hooks for gripping. The rest of the body consists of flat, square sections linked like a segmented tape. Each of these sections is packed with reproductive organs. They have no gut, as they can absorb the host's food directly across their specialized body wall. Mature segments rupture and release eggs via the host's faeces. These eggs are eaten in contaminated food by other animals, often a specific secondary host. The larvae grow within the secondary hosts, which can be vertebrate or arthropod, and return to their main host when the secondary host is eaten by the larger main host. Hence, eating undercooked meats which harbour tapeworm larval cysts can cause debilitating tapeworm infestation in humans. Many species have complex life-cycles with unique adaptations to ensure that some larvae eventually reinfect their main host.

tapioca See CASSAVA.

tapir A large, brown, or black and white ungulate (hoofed) mammal which comprises a family (Tapiridae) of four species, found in northern South America and Malaya. The snout and upper lip are elongated to form a short, flexible trunk, with terminal nostrils. The trunk is used to draw twigs, leaves, and branches into the mouth.

tar See COAL-TAR; PETROCHEMICAL.

Tarabulus See TRIPOLI.

Tarantino, Quentin (Jerome) (1963–) US film director, screenwriter, and actor. Tarantino came to sudden prominence with the gangster thriller *Reservoir Dogs* (1992), which he followed in 1994 with *Pulp Fiction*. Both aroused controversy for their amorality and violence, but also won much admiration for their wit, style, and structure. Tarantino also wrote the script for the similarly violent film *True Romance* (1993).

tarantula A spider belonging to the family Theraphosidae with long, hairy legs, notorious for its fist-sized body and its diet. Tarantulas can prey on small vertebrates, but normally eat invertebrates. North American species are not venomous, unlike species in the Southern Hemisphere, but most have irritant hairs. They live in burrows, but hunt nocturnally, relying mainly upon vibration to locate their prey.

Tarawa The capital of Kiribati, a densely populated Pacific Island, formerly one of the Gilbert Islands; pop. (1990) 28,800. Government offices are mostly located at Bairiki and the international airport at Bonriki.

tardigrade See WATER BEAR.

Tarkovsky, Andrei (Arsenevich) (1932–86) Russian film director. He rejected the constraints of socialist realism in the post-Stalin era in favour of a poetic, impressionistic, and personal style that brought his works criticism from the Soviet authorities. He won critical acclaim with *Ivan's Childhood* (1962), *Andrei Rublev* (1966), *Solaris* (1972), and *Stalker* (1979). His final film, *The Sacrifice* (1986), won the special grand prize at Cannes.

taro A valuable crop of the wet, humid, tropical areas of Asia and Polynesia, where it is grown for its short, swollen, underground stems (corms) that yield a highly digestible starchy food. It belongs to the genus *Colocasia*, part of the monocotyledonous family Araceae. Also known as dasheen, true taro, *C. esculenta*, is a native of Asia. It has large leaves similar in size and shape to those of its relative the arum lily.

tarot A set of 78 playing cards from which the modern 52-card pack is derived. It originated in Italy in the 14th century as 22 cards consisting of the Fool (joker) and 21 numbered cards representing natural elements, vices, and virtues. These were combined with 56 number cards in four suits representing nobility, clergy, merchants, and peasants. The tarot pack was primarily used in fortune telling.

tarpon A huge oceanic fish, *Tarpon atlanticus*, living in the tropical Atlantic and occasionally moving northwards in warm seasons. It grows to 2.4 m (7.8 feet) in length. A similar species in the Pacific, *Megalops cyprinoides*, grows to only 1.5 m (5 feet). Both belong to the family Megalopidae. They are large silvery fishes with big scales and a single dorsal fin, the last ray of which forms a streamer. They live and breed in the upper waters of the open sea. The young, however, are found close inshore in lagoons, estuaries, and often in the oxygen-poor waters of mangrove swamps.

Tarquin The fifth and the seventh Etruscan kings of Rome, **Priscus** (616–579 BC) and **Superbus** (534–510 BC), both subjects of legend and tradition. The stories were largely symbolic, contrasting the decadence of the monarchy with the idealism of the new ROMAN REPUBLIC. After this time the word 'king' was used by the Romans as a term of political abuse.

tarragon A southern European plant, *Artemisia dracunculus*, belonging to the family Compositae. It spreads by underground runners, and its leaves are used as a culinary herb.

tarsal See FOOT.

tarsier Either of three species of nocturnal prosimian PRIMATE inhabiting the East Indies and placed in a separate family, Tarsiidae. The adults are 15 cm (6 inches) long and have tails 25 cm (10 inches) long, which are hairless except for a tuft at the tip. The head is round, with a short face and comparatively large, rounded ears. The close-set, forward-facing eyes are enormous, as in most nocturnal creatures. The tarsiers hunt insects among the trees where they live. Adhesive pads on the fingers and toes allow these animals to cling firmly to smooth surfaces as they leap vertically from branch to branch. When on the ground, they travel with the same type of movements. The female bears a single young.

tartan See CLAN.

Tartar (or **Tatar**) ▶**1** A member of any of numerous mostly Muslim and Turkic tribes inhabiting various parts of European and Asiatic Russia, especially parts of Siberia, Crimea, North Caucasus, and districts along the Volga. ▶**2** A member of the mingled host of Central Asian peoples, including Mongols and Turks, who under the leadership of Genghis Khan overran and devastated much of Asia and eastern Europe in the early 13th century, and under Tamerlane (14th century) established a large empire in central Europe with its capital at Samarkand.

Tashkent The capital of the Central Asian republic of Uzbekistan, in the western foothills of the Tien Shan Mountains; pop. (1990) 2,094,000. The city has been a centre of culture, trade, and transportation since ancient times. It is now a major industrial centre producing machinery, textiles, chemicals, furniture, and foodstuffs. It suffered a major earthquake in 1966 and had to be rebuilt.

Tasman, Abel (Janszoon) (1603–*c*.1659) Dutch navigator. In 1642 he was sent by Anthony van Diemen (1593–1645, the Governor-General of the Dutch East Indies) to explore Australian waters; that year he reached Tasmania (which he named Van Diemen's Land) and New Zealand, and in 1643 arrived at Tonga and Fiji. On a second voyage in 1644 he also reached the Gulf of Carpentaria on the north coast of Australia.

Tasmania The smallest state of the Commonwealth of Australia, consisting of one large mountainous island and several smaller islands (including King, Flinders, and Bruny) situated south-east of the continent from which it is separated by the Bass Strait; area 68,331 sq km (26,393 sq miles); pop. (1991) 469,200; capital, Hobart. Like mainland Australia, Tasmania has many unique species of plants and animals, and was inhabited since prehistoric times by Aborigines, most of whom were wiped out by the new settlers. The first European explorer to arrive there (in 1642) was Abel TASMAN, who called the island Van Diemen's Land, a name which it bore until 1855. Claimed for Britain by Captain Cook and later settled by a British party from New South Wales in 1803, it became a separate colony in 1825 and was federated with the other states of Australia in 1901. In 1869 Tasmania was the first colony in the British Empire to make education compulsory. The islands' chief products are meat, fruit, grain, dairy produce, timber, paper, and minerals such as tin, copper, and zinc.

Tasmanian devil A species of carnivorous MARSUPIAL, *Sarcophilus harrisi*, that once roamed over much of Australia but now survives only in Tasmania. Despite its name, it is no more fearsome than any other carnivorous mammal. Rather bear-like in appearance, it is about 90 cm (3 feet) long and has a black coat with irregular blotches of white hair. A land animal, it haunts the edges of rivers and beaches in search of food. It will take crabs, frogs, and small mammals, but can attack and kill animals larger than itself. At night it calls with a low, yelling growl followed by a snarling cough. Like all marsupials, the female has a pouch in which the young are carried until they are too large; the mother then builds a nest for them.

Tasmanian wolf (or **thylacine**) A species of MARSUPIAL, *Thylacinus cynocephalus*, that has been eliminated throughout most of Australia, but may still survive in Tasmania, although the last sighting of it there was in 1936. It is the largest of the flesh-eating marsupials, being some 165 cm (5.4 feet) long, including the tail of 50 cm (1.6 feet). Brown in colour, it has 16–18 chocolate-brown stripes across its back. The head is rather dog-like with a long, pointed muzzle, and broad, rounded ears. During the day the Tasmanian wolf remains in its lair in the rocks, waiting until dusk before venturing out in search of wallabies or other marsupials to prey upon. The female has a pouch large enough for four babies.

Tasman Sea Part of the South Pacific lying between Australia and New Zealand; it merges into the Coral Sea in the north and the Southern Ocean in the south. About 1,900 km (1,200 miles) in width, it contains the Tasman Basin with the Ulladullah Trough and Thomson Deep at 5,944 m (19,502 feet) in the west. The ridge that rises to the island of Tasmania is to the south-west and the Lord Howe Ridge to the north-east. The warming East Australian Current enters from the north, while across the south cold WESTERLIES blow.

Tasso, Torquato (1544–95) Italian poet and dramatist. He entered the service of the dukes of Este at Ferrara, where from an early age he wrote poetry and produced his pastoral drama *Aminta* (1573). His poem *Jerusalem Delivered* (1574) intended to give Italy a religious EPIC. Tasso's epics and critical works had a great influence on English literature, notably on Spenser, Milton, Dryden, and Gray, while Byron and Goethe wrote works on his tragic life.

taste The sensation experienced when specialized nerve endings in the tongue and pharynx, known as taste buds are activated by substances dissolved in the saliva. The taste buds react selectively to various substances and some animals have taste buds that respond to pure water. Humans possess four basic tastes: sweet, sour, bitter, and salt.

Tata An Indian Parsi commercial and industrial family. It is one of the two (with the BIRLAS) most important merchant families in modern India. The family began in Far East trade, but diversified their operations creating, under Jahangir Ratanji Dadabhai Tata (1904–93), an airline which later became Air India.

Tatar Republic (or **Republic of Tatarstan, Tataria**) A republic of the Russian Federation, in the middle valley of the Volga and its tributaries; area 68,000 sq km (26,265 sq miles); pop. (1990) 3,658,000; capital, Kazan. Inhabited by Bulgars since the 5th century, the region was conquered by the Mongols, under Genghis Khan, in the 13th century, becoming a Tatar Khanate. In 1552, after a fierce struggle with Ivan the Terrible, it was absorbed into the Russian empire and in 1920 was constituted as an autonomous republic of the USSR. On the breakup of the Soviet Union in 1991 it refused to sign the new Federation Treaty with Russia, voting to become an independent state in 1992. Its chief products are oil, coal, timber, grain, and textiles.

Tate, Nahum (1652–1715) Irish dramatist and poet, resident in London from the 1670s. He wrote a number of plays, chiefly adaptations from earlier writers; he is especially known for his version of Shakespeare's *King Lear*, in which he substituted a happy ending. He also wrote the libretto for Purcell's *Dido and Aeneas* (1689) and (with John Dryden) the second part of *Absalom and Achitophel* (1682). He was appointed Poet Laureate in 1692.

Tate Gallery A national gallery of British art at Millbank, London, which originated in the dissatisfaction felt at the inadequate representation of English schools in the National Gallery. The Tate Gallery, opened in 1897, was built at the expense of

(Sir) Henry Tate (1819–99), a sugar manufacturer, to house the collection presented by him (in 1890) and other works accumulated by various bequests to the nation. In the 20th century modern foreign paintings and sculpture (both British and foreign) were added. On foundation the gallery was subordinate to the National Gallery, but it was made fully independent in 1954. New Tate Galleries have been opened in Liverpool (1988; in the Albert Docks) and St Ives, Cornwall (1993).

Tati, Jacques (born Jacques Tatischeff) (1908–82) French film director and actor. Although he made only five full-length films, he became internationally known as a comic actor with his performances as Monsieur Hulot, a character which he introduced in his second film *Monsieur Hulot's Holiday* (1953). Subsequent films featuring the character include the Oscar-winning *Mon oncle* (1958).

Tatra Mountains (or **Tatras**) The highest range of the Carpathians in east-central Europe. The High Tatra on the frontier between Slovakia and Poland rises to 2,655 m (8,710 ft) at Gerlachovsky, the highest peak in Slovakia. The Low Tatra to the south-west rises to 2,043 m (6,703 ft) at Dumbier, also in Slovakia.

Tatum, Art(hur) (1910–56) US jazz pianist. He was born with cataracts in both eyes and as a result was almost completely blind throughout his life. He first became famous in the 1930s as a musician of great technical accomplishment; he performed chiefly in a trio with bass and guitar or as a soloist.

Taunton The county and market town of Somerset, south-west England, on the River Tone; pop. (1991) 55,855. Founded *c.*705 as a West Saxon stronghold against the Celts, its castle dates from the 12th century. It has textile and clothing industries as well as cider-making.

Taupo, Lake The largest lake of New Zealand, occupying a volcanic depressions in central North Island; area 619 sq km (239 sq miles). It receives the River Tongariro and its chief outlet is the River Waikato. The townships of the Taupo region are popular resort and fishing centres.

Tauranga A seaport and industrial town on the Bay of Plenty, North Island, New Zealand; pop. (1991) 70,800. It is one of the largest export ports of New Zealand, handling timber, pulp, and newsprint.

Taurus The Bull, a CONSTELLATION of the zodiac. In mythology it represents the bull into which Zeus turned himself to abduct Princess Europa. Only the front half of the bull is depicted in the sky. Its eye is marked by the red giant ALDEBARAN, and its horns are tipped by second-magnitude Beta Tauri (also known as Elnath, Arabic for 'the butting one') and third-magnitude Zeta Tauri. Near Zeta Tauri lies the CRAB NEBULA.

Tavener, John (1944–) British composer. He studied under Lennox BERKELEY, coming to public notice with his cantata *The Whale* (1966). His opera *Thérèse* (1979) also brought critical acclaim. His later works, such as *Mary of Egypt* (1992), have been influenced by liturgical music of the Russian Orthodox Church.

Taverner, John (*c.*1490–1545) English composer. He was the first master of the choristers at Cardinal College (now Christ Church), Oxford (1526–30), where choral music on a large scale was encouraged. He wrote a number of fine masses, such as the six-part *Corona spinea* and *Gloria tibi Trinitas*. His smaller-scale masses, including the well-known one on the 'Western Wynde' melody, point the way to the simpler style of church music.

tawny owl A species of OWL, *Strix aluco*, common in woodlands throughout much of Eurasia. They have also taken readily to parks, nesting as successfully on buildings as in hollow trees and dense undergrowth. They are small, heavily barred, brown owls with rounded wings and tail. Their main prey consists of rodents and other small mammals, though birds are taken when abundant. Clutches of four or more spherical white eggs are laid; males do most of the hunting throughout the incubation and brooding periods.

taxation The compulsory transfer of money (taxes) to the central or local government from individuals, firms, and other groups, normally on an annual basis. Taxation has several roles. First, it provides income for the government. Secondly, taxation may be used, together with government expenditure, to alter the distribution of income and WEALTH. A progressive tax is one that reduces inequality (taking an increasing proportion of income as income rises), and a regressive tax is one which increases inequality (taking a decreasing proportion of income as income rises). Thirdly, taxation can be used to change relative prices of GOODS and services and so affect demand patterns. Fourthly, changes in tax can be used to influence aggregate demand. Taxes can be classified into direct and indirect taxes. Direct taxes are those levied on individuals and companies, and include capital gains tax, corporation tax, income tax, inheritance tax, poll tax, property tax, and wealth tax. Indirect taxes are those levied on expenditure, and include CUSTOMS AND EXCISE duties, sales tax, and VALUE-ADDED TAX.

taxonomy The science or practice of naming and classifying organisms. See NOMENCLATURE IN BIOLOGY; PLANT CLASSIFICATION; KINGDOM; PHYLUM; CLASS; ORDER; FAMILY; GENUS; SPECIES.

Tay A river of Scotland that rises on the slopes of Ben Lui as the Fillan and flows 192 km (120 miles) eastwards through Loch Dochart and Loch Tay before entering the North Sea in a wide estuary known as the **Firth of Tay**. From its source at the head of the Fillan it is the longest river in Scotland.

tayberry A soft hybrid fruit obtained by crossing the American blackberry, variety 'Aurora', with a raspberry. It was introduced to cultivation in about 1980. The deep purple fruits, up to 4 cm (1.5 inches) long, have a rich flavour. The quick-growing, prickly plants are cultivated like blackberries or loganberries.

Taylor, Elizabeth (1932–) US actress, born in England. She began her career as a child star in films such as *National Velvet* (1944). She went on to star in many films, including *Cat on a Hot Tin Roof* (1958), *Who's Afraid of Virginia Woolf?* (1966), for which she won an Oscar, and *The Mirror Crack'd* (1980). She has been married eight times, including twice to the actor Richard Burton, with whom she starred in a number of films, notably *Cleopatra* (1963).

Taylor, Jeremy (1613–67) English Anglican churchman and writer. He was chaplain to Charles I during the English Civil War and lived chiefly in Wales until the Restoration, when he was appointed bishop of Down and Connor (1660). Although a celebrated preacher in his day, he is now remembered chiefly for his devotional writings, especially *The Rule and Exercises of Holy Living* (1650) and *The Rule and Exercises of Holy Dying* (1651).

Taylor, Zachary (1784–1850) US Whig statesman, 12th President of the USA 1849–50. He became a national hero after his victories in the war with Mexico (1846–48). As President, he came into conflict with Congress over his desire to admit California to the Union as a free state (without slavery). He died in office before the problem could be resolved.

Tayside A local government region in eastern Scotland from 1975 to 1996; its administrative centre was Dundee. It was abolished in 1996 and replaced by three unitary authorities: Angus, Dundee, and Perth and Kinross.

Tblisi (formerly **Tiflis**) The capital of the Republic of Georgia, a city on the River Kura in the Caucasus, between the Caspian and Black Seas; pop. (1991) 1,267,500. It developed in ancient times as a trading centre on the route between Europe and the East and is said to be one of the world's oldest cities. Its industries include chemicals, petroleum products, locomotives, machine tools, and electrical equipment.

Tchaikovsky, Pyotr (Ilich) (1840–93) Russian composer. He is especially known as a composer of the ballets *Swan Lake* (1877), *Sleeping Beauty* (1890), and *The Nutcracker* (1892), the First Piano Concerto (1875), and the overture *1812* (1880); other notable works include the operas *Eugene Onegin* (1879) and *The Queen of Spades* (1890), six symphonies, a violin concerto, and chamber music. His music is characterized by great lyrical passages and, especially in his later symphonies (including his sixth symphony, the 'Pathétique', 1893), melancholy. His death was officially attributed to cholera, but there is now a theory that he took poison because of a potential scandal arising from an alleged homosexual relationship.

tea An evergreen shrub, *Camellia sinensis*, in the family Theaceae, and suited to hill slopes in the tropics with good rainfall and acid soils. The infusion produced by its leaves is drunk regularly by half of the world's population, particularly in India, south-east Asia, and the Far East, where it has been cultivated for thousands of years. Although tea was not introduced to Europe until after coffee drinking had become established, it found particular favour in Britain, which now imports nearly one third of the total production. India is the main producer, followed by Sri Lanka and China.

Two forms of tea are grown: the hardier narrow-leaved China type, and the larger-leaved Assam type. The two terminal leaves of the young shoots yield the highest-quality tea, though up to four such leaves may be harvested per shoot. The leaves are steamed, rolled, and dried rapidly to produce the green tea popular in the Far East, or withered, fermented to release the drug caffeine, and carefully but rapidly dried to develop the flavour and colour of the more familiar black tea. Most commercial teas are blends of leaves of different qualities from various sites.

teak A tall tree of seasonally dry forest in Myanmar (Burma), Thailand, Malaysia, Indonesia, and India. It has been planted commercially elsewhere, particularly in Africa and the Caribbean. The timber is hard and durable, rather oily, and is used in shipbuilding and for furniture. Teak is strictly only timber from the tree *Tectona grandis* (family Verbenaceae), but a number of timbers with similar qualities derived from quite unrelated kinds of trees are also known as teak.

teal Any of various species of DUCK, mostly small dabblers. Typical is the green-winged teal, *Anas crecca*, a species noted for its small size and rapid flight. Tight flocks of this species are formed outside the breeding season, and manoeuvre in the air with the agility of waders.

tear-gas Any of a group of gases that affect the mucous membranes of the eyes, causing irritation and copious watering. Tear-gases are usually organic halogen compounds, the most widely used being Mace gas (alpha-chloroacetophenone) and CS gas (1-*ortho*-chlorophenyl-2,2-dicyanoethene). Tear-gases are designed principally as riot-control agents, and are used in this role by police forces in many countries.

teasel A biennial or perennial plant with tall spiny stems and leaves. In the common teasel, *Dipsacus fullonum*, the leaf bases form a cup in which water collects, preventing climbing insects, such as ants, from pillaging the nectar and pollen of the flowers. The fuller's teasel, *D. sativus*, is a cultivated kind with hooked spines on the flower-heads. These are used in the textile industry to tease or raise the nap of cloth. They belong to the same family as scabious, Dipsacaceae.

technetium (symbol Tc, at. no. 43, r.a.m. 98.91) A grey TRANSITION METAL formed from the neutron bombardment of molybdenum, and discovered in waste fission products. It was the first artificially produced element, and there are still no known terrestrial sources. Technetium has 16 radioactive isotopes, one of which is used in diagnostic tracer work.

Technicolor See CINEMATOGRAPHY.

technology The techniques of engineering and applied science for commercial and industrial purposes. Many fundamental technologies – the SMELTING and working of metals, SPINNING and weaving of textiles, and the firing of clay, for example – were empirically developed at the dawn of civilization, long before any concept of science existed. With the advent, in about 3000 BC, of the first major civilizations in EGYPT and Mesopotamia, many new technologies were developed – irrigation systems, road networks and wheeled vehicles, a pictographic form of writing, and new building techniques. Other civilizations subsequently became important technological centres, notably those of GREECE and Rome, the Arab empire of the 7th to 10th centuries, and the Mayan, Aztec, and Toltec civilizations of the American continent. In the mid-16th century the focus of technological change shifted to Europe, with the beginning of the Scientific Revolution.

By the late 17th century, technology essentially meant engineering. During the 19th century science began to create many new technologies, such as ELECTRICITY GENERATION AND SUPPLY and PHOTOGRAPHY. The trend continued into the 20th century, especially with the development of road vehicles, the petrochemical industry, plastics, RADIO and TELEVISION, SOUND RECORDING AND REPRODUCTION, SYNTHETIC FIBRES, a wide range of pharmaceutical products, NUCLEAR POWER, and the advent of COMPUTERS and INFORMATION TECHNOLOGY. Since the 1970s POLLUTION and the depletion of ENERGY RESOURCES have caused increasing public concern. This has led to the growth of alternative technologies, with an emphasis on renewable energy sources, RECYCLING of raw materials, and the conservation of energy.

tectonics The study of the structure of the Earth's crust or of a particular region of it, especially with respect to the folding, faulting, and other movements that have taken place, either on a large or on a small scale. PLATE TECTONICS is concerned with the movement of continents, with SEA-FLOOR SPREADING, and with the other processes that are entailed in the creation and destruction of crustal material.

Teesside An urban area in north-east England, on the estuary of the River Tees. It includes the towns of Stockton-on-Tees, Redcar, Thornaby, and Middlesbrough.

teeth See TOOTH.

Teflon See PTFE.

Tegucigalpa The largest city and capital of Honduras, situated in the highlands of south-central Honduras; pop. (est. 1991) 670,100. It was founded as a gold and silver mining town in the 16th century by the Spanish and became capital in 1880. It produces textiles, chemicals, and processed foods.

Teheran Conference (28 November–1 December 1943) A meeting between CHURCHILL, ROOSEVELT, and STALIN in the Iranian capital. Here Stalin, invited for the first time to an inter-Allied conference, was told of the impending opening of a Second Front to coincide with a Soviet offensive against Germany. The three leaders discussed the establishment of the UNITED NATIONS after the war, and Stalin pressed for a future Soviet sphere of influence in the BALTIC STATES and Eastern Europe, while guaranteeing the independence of Iran.

Tehran (or **Teheran**) The capital and largest city of Iran, situated in the southern foothills of the Elburz Mountains; pop. (1994) 6,750,000. In 1788 it replaced Ispahan (Esfahan) as capital of Persia and in the 20th century the city was modernized by Reza Shah. Industries include the manufacture of textiles, chemicals, and tobacco.

Teilhard de Chardin, Pierre (1881–1955) French Jesuit philosopher and palaeontologist. He is best known for his theory, blending science and Christianity, that man is evolving mentally and socially towards a perfect spiritual state. His views were held to be unorthodox by the Roman Catholic Church and his major works (such as *The Phenomenon of Man*, 1955) were published posthumously.

Te Kanawa, Dame Kiri (Janette) (1944–) New Zealand operatic soprano, resident in Britain since 1966. She made her début in London in 1970 and since then has sung in the world's leading opera houses, especially in works by Mozart, Richard Strauss, and Verdi.

tektite A small glassy object found in certain localized areas of the Earth's surface. These areas include the southern half of the Australian continent, Indo-Malaysia, Côte d'Ivoire, Czech Republic, and Texas. Tektites have many different ages. For example, the Australites are 610,000 years old and the Moldavites are 14.7 million years old. Many scientists think that tektites were formed by the fusion of terrestrial material during the impact of giant METEORITES, but some believe they were created by explosive volcanoes on the Moon.

Tel Aviv A city on the Mediterranean coast of Israel; pop. (est. 1993) 357,100. Founded in 1909 by Russian Jewish immigrants as a small residential suburb of the port of Jaffa, Tel Aviv became capital of Israel (1948–50). Industries include the manufacture of textiles, sugar, and chemicals.

telecommunications The communication of information (usually audio, visual, or computer data) over a distance. Early techniques included signal fires and SEMAPHORE; modern systems include TELEPHONY, TELEX, FAX, RADIO, TELEVISION, and COMPUTER. Over short distances electrical telegraph or telephone signals can be transmitted via two-wire telephone lines without additional processing. For longer distances, various techniques of MODULATION and/or coding at the transmitter, followed by demodulation or decoding at the receiver, are employed. Transmission may be to a single receiver or it may be broadcast to many individual receivers; it may be direct or switched through a complex NETWORK. Until recently most telecommunications systems were analog in form, but now the message signal commonly undergoes DIGITIZATION at the transmitter, using PULSE CODE MODULATION or similar techniques: it is then decoded into usable form (sound, print, video) at the receiver. The widespread digitization of telecommunications signals has begun a trend in many countries towards the combination of hitherto separate systems into a single Integrated Services Digital Network (ISDN). It has also resulted in the convergence of computing and telecommunications (see INFORMATION TECHNOLOGY). Because of the complexity of modern telecommunications systems, standardization bodies such as the INTERNATIONAL TELECOMMUNICATIONS UNION (ITU), and the International Organization for Standardization (ISO) have taken on great importance. See also COMMUNICATIONS SATELLITE.

telegraphy The transmission of information by coded electrical impulses, transmitted along wires and received manually or by machine. Telegraph channels require only a narrow frequency BANDWIDTH, and can be multiplexed to allow many transmissions along one line, so telegraphy is a cheap and efficient communications medium. In the mid-19th century equipment designed by MORSE in the USA transmitted information along a single wire, using the MORSE CODE: a similar electric telegraph was developed by COOKE in the UK. Initially, skilled operators were needed to code and send messages, but subsequently telegraphic transmission and reception became mechanized (see TELEPRINTER). Submarine CABLES provided the first transatlantic telecommunications link in 1866, but most telegraph signals today are carried by telephone lines or radio waves. FAX and TELEX are the most common modern telegraphic systems.

Telemann, Georg Philipp (1681–1767) German composer and organist. His prolific output includes 600 overtures, 44 Passions, 12 complete services, and 40 operas; his work reflects a variety of influences, particularly French composers, such as Lully. In his lifetime his reputation was far greater than that of his friend and contemporary J. S. Bach.

teleology Explanation by reference to ends, purposes, or function. In Aristotle the value of teleological explanations rests on his metaphysical doctrine of forms, the fundamental kinds into which all things fall, and which define their proper ends. Without some metaphysical underpinning, the use of such explanations is hard to justify; in particular, the mechanistic world-view characteristic of much of modern science emphasizes efficient causation and seems to leave little room for purposefulness. The great achievement of DARWIN's theory of evolution was to show how some teleological explanations in biology could be rested on a mechanistic foundation. How far this kind of reconciliation is possible is a continuing issue in the philosophy of science.

telephone exchange A common connecting point for the telephone lines through which calls to and from receivers in a particular area are routed. The first automatic telephone exchange was invented by a US undertaker, Almon Strowger, and became operational in 1897. In the 1920s and 1930s such automatic electromechanical switchboards were introduced in Europe and North America. Electromechanical exchanges have now largely been replaced by electronic switchboards, which serve similar functions but are smaller, faster, more reliable, more flexible, and cheaper. Newer connection systems integrate subscribers not only to telephones but also to numerous other facilities and databases.

telephony The transmission of speech via an electrical signal between one telephone receiver and another, the signal being transmitted either along a CABLE or by RADIO or OPTICAL-FIBRE transmission. Alexander Graham BELL patented the first telephone receiver and transmitter in the UK and the USA during 1876 and demonstrated it in Philadelphia. Transmission between receivers was electrical, along wires, the signal being a copy of the sound wave. Telephony quickly developed into a sophisticated communications system over fairly short distances; by 1887 there were over 100,000 telephone subscribers worldwide. Further development took place more slowly. Underground and submarine cables were introduced in cities and for crossing water. Inductors at regular intervals along a telephone line were found to reduce distortion over long distances, and later repeaters, which boosted or amplified the telephone signal, were introduced. Transatlantic telephone transmission relied on high-frequency RADIO TRANSMISSION until 1956, because submarine cable links were not sufficiently reliable. COMMUNICATIONS SATELLITE links using microwaves are now used for many international calls. Optical-fibre cables are a recent introduction; they give virtually noise-free transmission. Another recent development has been the DIGITIZATION of telephone signals. Digital signals can be multiplexed easily, and PULSE CODE MODULATION offers a way of transmitting the digital signals with minimal noise or distortion. Telephone circuits now also carry TELEX, FAX, ELECTRONIC MAIL, and TELEVISION SIGNALS in a form that can be fed directly into appropriate receivers. Additionally, they are used to enable computers to communicate over large distances.

teleprinter (US **teletypewriter**) A device that transmits messages entered through its keyboard and prints the messages at the receiver. Invented in the 1900s as the printing telegraph (see TELEGRAPHY), the first teleprinter exchange was not available until the 1930s. Originally, relays converted the message into electric signals; subsequent developments concentrated on various methods of displaying the message prior to transmission, enabling operators to check for errors and perhaps store the message. Such methods included punched tape, printing on gummed tape for telegrams, magnetic tape, or more recently computer disks and VISUAL DISPLAY UNITS.

telescope An instrument used to view magnified images of distant objects. Optical telescopes collect and focus light to produce images. RADIO TELESCOPES use arrays of ANTENNAE or concave metal dishes to collect radio waves from objects in space. Optical telescopes were probably first manufactured in about 1608 by the Dutch spectacle-maker Hans Lippershey, though their invention pre-dates this. They soon became astronomy's most important instrument, and now also form part of binoculars, gunsights, and periscopes. REFLECTING TELESCOPES use concave mirrors, and REFRACTING

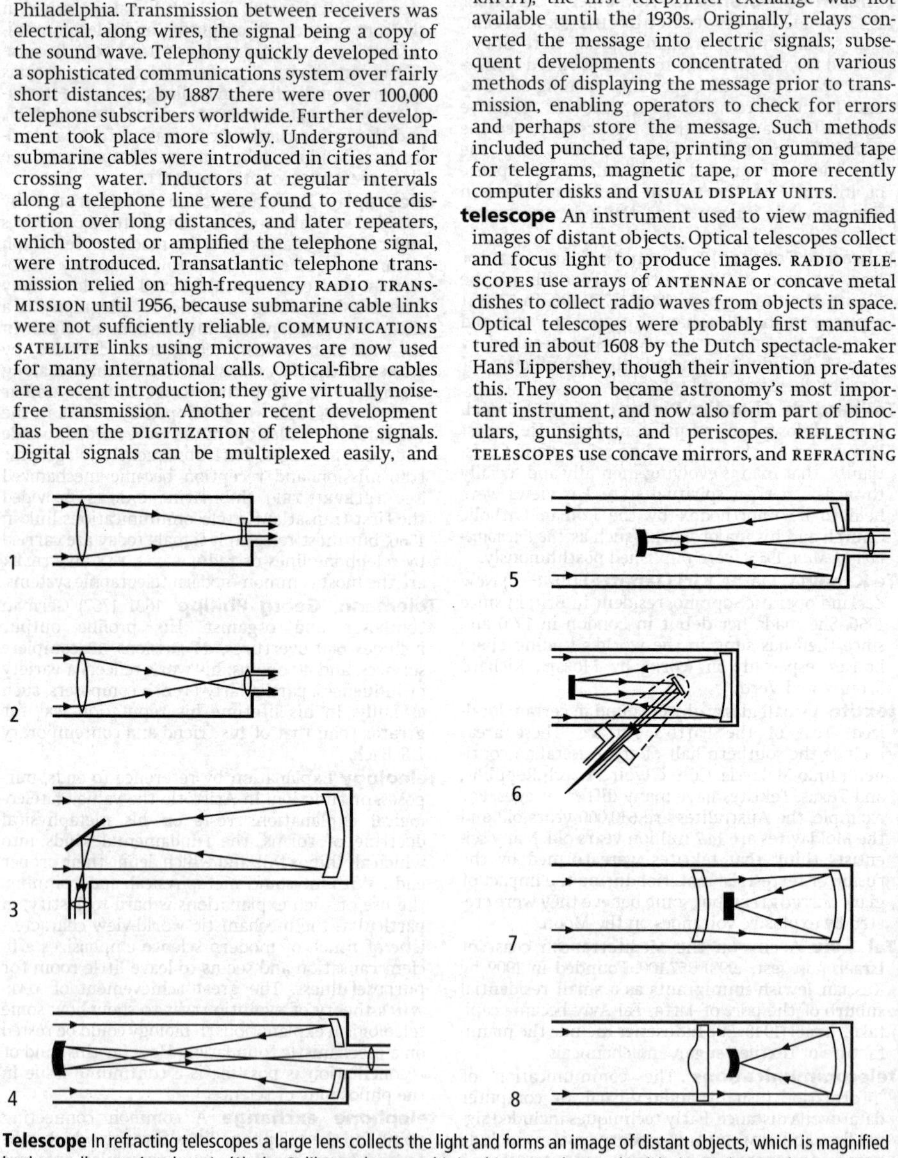

Telescope In refracting telescopes a large lens collects the light and forms an image of distant objects, which is magnified by the smaller eyepiece lens. In (1), the Galilean telescope, this is a biconcave lens and in (2), the Keplerian telescope, it is a biconvex lens. Telescopes of this kind are used for both terrestrial and astonomical purposes. In reflecting telescopes, used in astronomy, a large concave mirror collects the light; the simplest (3) is the Newtonian telescope, in which the image formed by the mirror is enlarged by a convex lens. The same principle is used in (4) the Gregorian telescope, (5) the Cassegrain telescope, (6) the coudé telescope, and (7) the Maksutov telescope, each using a different optical system. In (8), the Schmidt telescope, a corrective lens is used to widen the field of view.

TELESCOPES use convex LENSES to collect light from distant objects, focusing it to form an inverted, real image. This image acts as a close object for the eyepiece lens, which forms a magnified but inverted virtual image of it. In astronomy a photographic plate, or more recently a CHARGE-COUPLED DEVICE, often replaces the eyepiece. Telescopes for terrestrial uses have extra lens systems (prisms in binoculars) to give an upright image. The illustration shows the optical layout of a number of telescopes.

Telescopium The Telescope, a CONSTELLATION of the southern sky introduced by the 18th-century French astronomer Nicolas Louis de Lacaille. Its brightest stars are of only fourth magnitude.

teletext A television-based information system. Teletext is a VIDEOTEX service, transmitting information in the unused area (usually the top four lines) of a normal television signal. By using a special decoder attached to the television set, this information becomes visible on the entire screen as pages of text and graphics.

television A system for converting visual images (and accompanying sound) into an electrical signal that can be transmitted, either through an electrical cable or on a radio WAVEBAND, to receivers that reproduce the images on a screen. Transmission of all the visual information of a moving scene requires a **television camera** which electronically scans the scene and divides it into 300,000 or more elements, for each of which an electrical impulse, proportional to the amount of light in that area of the scene, is emitted. In order to depict rapid motion smoothly, 25 of these scans must be made each second (30 scans in the USA). Motion is simulated by a rapid succession of still scenes, as in a cine-camera. A television system must thus transmit more than four million electrical impulses per second in order to give a detailed, moving image on the television screen. For transmission, the television signal is modulated (see MODULATION): a very large BANDWIDTH is needed to transmit all the information from a moving picture. The transmitted signal is picked up by the household television ANTENNA and reassembled in the TELEVISION RECEIVER, which reconstructs the images so quickly that the eye is unaware that they have been assembled sequentially. See illustration p. 1320.

In 1923 Vladimir ZWYORKIN patented the iconoscope, an electronic scanning television camera that provided the basis for the modern camera. By 1935 Germany had a regular broadcasting service, though the picture quality was poor. In the UK, the BBC began broadcasting in 1927, using Baird's black-and-white mechanical system: in 1937 they began the world's first high-quality public television broadcasting service, using an electronic system developed by Alan BLUMLEIN. Colour broadcasts did not become viable until 1953, when a standardized electronic system compatible with existing black-and-white receivers was developed in the USA. This system, known as the NSTC system, is currently used in the USA and Japan. Elsewhere two other systems – SECAM (used in France and the Soviet Union) and PAL (used by most of Europe) – have been developed. More recent developments in television technology include the growth of CABLE TELEVISION; the introduction of stereo sound; and satellite television, in which microwave transmissions are broadcast via COMMUNICATIONS SATELLITES either directly to domestic satellite dishes, or to ground stations for relay via cable. New developments include high-definition television (HDTV) broadcasting, in which the television images are made up of over 1,000 scanning lines instead of the current 525 or 625, and the transmission of television pictures as digital rather than analog signals. Japanese analog HDTV (Hi-Vision) television receivers were first sold in 1990. See also VIDEO RECORDER; VIDEOTEX.

television camera See TELEVISION.

television receiver An apparatus for receiving TELEVISION signals, either from an antenna or an electrical cable, and converting the video and sound information into a picture on a screen, with accompanying sound. In a black-and-white receiver the phosphor-coated screen of a CATHODE-RAY TUBE is scanned by an electron beam. The scanning pattern is a series of parallel, near-horizontal lines that start at the top left-hand corner of the screen. Where the beam strikes the screen the phosphor glows for a moment, the intensity of the glow being proportional to the strength of the electron beam. The electron beam is controlled by information from the television signal, which regulates the strength of the electron beam as it scans, thus causing changes in light intensity on the screen corresponding to those in the original image. In a colour television receiver each portion of the screen contains microscopic dots of red, green, and blue phosphor. The receiver carries a separate electron beam for each phosphor. Thus three separate primary colour images are formed on the screen simultaneously, but because the dots that form each image are so small and uniformly distributed, the eye combines the three images to produce a full-colour picture. In most modern receivers the picture is formed of either 525 or 625 lines. Recently small LIQUID CRYSTAL receivers, which do not require a tube and can therefore be much slimmer, have been developed, and research is continuing into replacing the single, large CATHODE-RAY TUBE (CRT) with thousands of very small CRTs, which are more compact and require less power.

telex An international communications network designed on a similar basis to the telephone network, to carry telegraphic messages between TELEPRINTERS. For simple messages telex has the advantage over FAX that one telex message can be transmitted to several receivers simultaneously. In 1985 an improved telex system was launched, which can use any public communications network, and is faster and cheaper.

Telford A town in Shropshire, west-central England, on the River Severn 52 km (33 miles) north-west of Birmingham; pop. (1991) 115,000. Designated a New Town in 1963, it comprises the settlements of Dawley, Oakengates, and Wellington and has diverse light industries. It is named after the engineer Thomas Telford.

Telford, Thomas (1757–1834) Scottish civil engineer. He built hundreds of miles of roads, especially in Scotland, more than a thousand bridges, and a number of canals. Among his most important achievements are the London to Holyhead road, including the suspension bridge crossing the Menai Strait (1819–26), the Caledonian Canal across Scotland (opened 1822), and the Göta Canal in Sweden. He was the first president of the Institution of Civil Engineers (founded 1818).

Tell, William A legendary hero of the liberation of Switzerland from Austrian oppression, who refused to pay homage to the Austrians and was forced to shoot an arrow at an apple placed on the head of his son; this he successfully did. The events are placed in the 14th century, but there is no evidence for a historical person of this name.

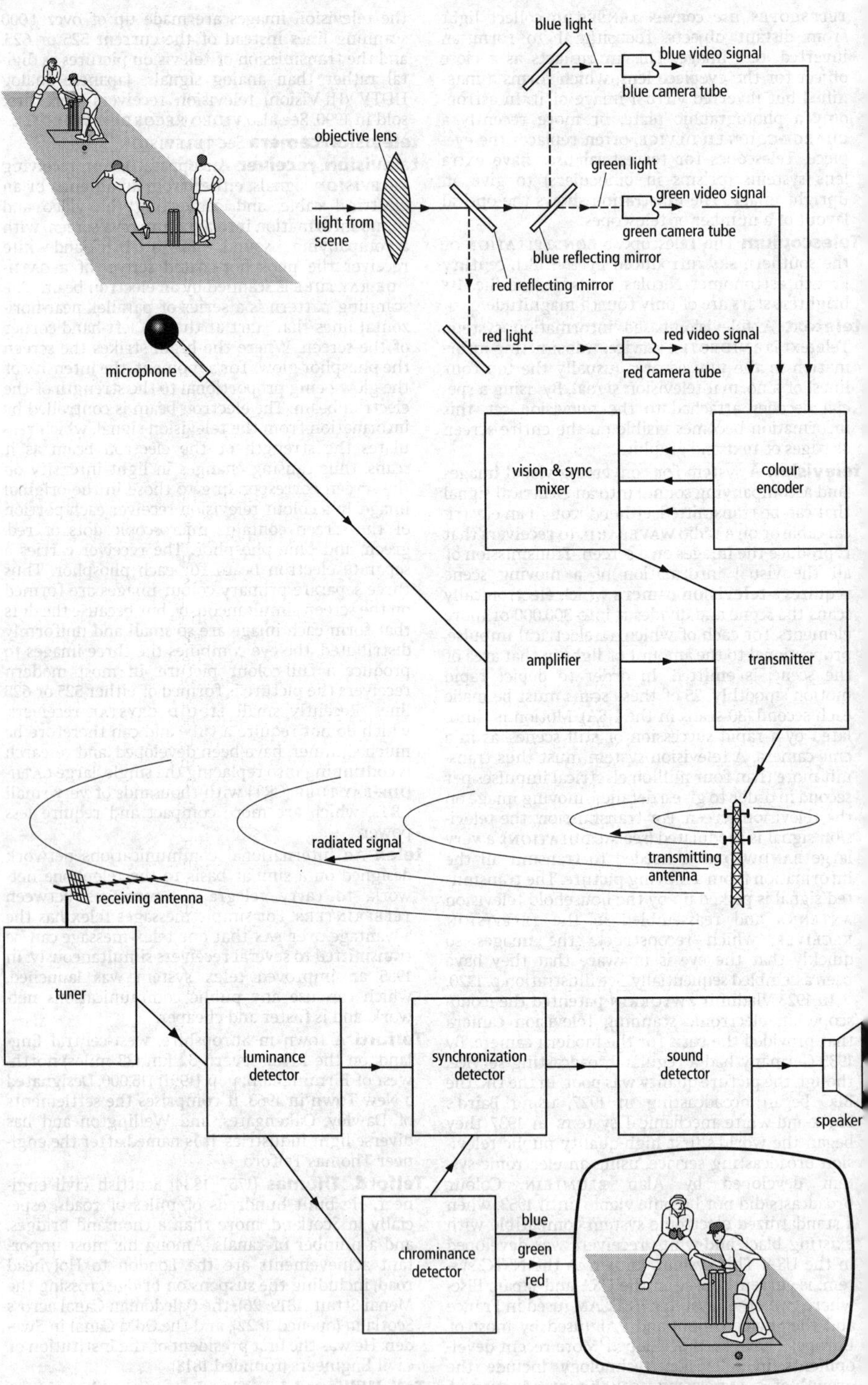

Television The camera creates a video signal representing the scene by splitting the scene into red, green, and blue images. This is merged and synchronized with the audio signal from the microphone. These amplified signals are passed to the transmitting antenna enabling them to be picked up by the receiving antenna. The scene is recreated on the screen and the speakers of the television set.

Teller, Edward (1908–) Hungarian-born US physicist. After moving to the USA in the 1930s he worked on the first atomic reactor, later working on the first atom bombs at Los Alamos. Teller studied the feasibility of producing a fusion bomb, and work under his guidance after World War II led to the detonation of the first hydrogen bomb in 1952. His own studies on fusion were mainly theoretical and later concerned with its peaceful use, though he was a forceful advocate of the nuclear deterrent.

tellurium (symbol Te, at. no. 52, r.a.m. 127.60) A METALLOID element in Group 16 (formerly VIB) of the periodic table. It has a grey 'metallic' form composed of infinite chains of tellurium atoms. A SEMICONDUCTOR, it shows greater conductivity in certain directions, according to the alignment of the atoms. Its compounds are toxic. The chief use of tellurium is in the VULCANIZATION of rubber. It is also used to colour glass, to increase the hardness of lead in battery plates, and to improve the machinability of stainless steel.

Telstar See COMMUNICATIONS SATELLITE.

tempera Any paint in which the PIGMENT is dissolved in water and mixed (tempered) with an organic gum or glue. Egg tempera was the most important technique for PANEL PAINTING in Europe from the beginning of the 13th century until the end of the 15th, when it began to be overtaken by oil. Tempera painting has had a revival in the late 19th and 20th centuries, Andrew Wyeth being a noted exponent.

temperament (in music) The adjustment of intervals involved in the various systems used in tuning the notes of the octave. In the acoustically 'pure' or 'untempered' SCALE that arises in the natural harmonic series, the semitones vary very slightly in size. These differences pose no problems to singers, or to instruments (such as the violin family) that can vary their PITCH at will, but they do pose problems with instruments (such as the keyboard) in which the pitch is fixed as part of their construction. With fixed-pitch instruments it was not possible to pass satisfactorily from one KEY to another until tuning in equal temperament had been adopted in the 17th century by the French mathematician Mersenne. In this the octave is made up of twelve equal semitones in which each interval is slightly out of tune, but still acceptable to the average ear. The advantages of equal temperament was demonstrated by Bach in his *Well-Tempered Clavichord* (1722), a collection of 48 preludes and fugues in all keys.

temperature See HEAT AND TEMPERATURE.

temperature measurement See THERMOMETER.

tempering A heat treatment applied to steel and certain alloys. Fully hardened steel, made by quenching from a high temperature, is too hard for many applications and is also brittle. Tempering, which involves reheating to an intermediate temperature and cooling slowly, reduces this hardness. Tempering temperatures depend on the composition of the steel, but are frequently between 100 and 650°C; higher temperatures give a softer, tougher product.

Tempest, Dame Marie (born Mary Susan Etherington) (1864–1942) British actress. Though trained as a singer she made her name in comedy, becoming noted for her playing of elegant middle-aged women; the role of Judith Bliss in *Hay Fever* (1925) was created for her by Noel Coward.

Templar See KNIGHT TEMPLAR.

Temple, Shirley (1928–) US child star. In the 1930s she appeared in a succession of films, often adapted from children's classics (such as *Rebecca of Sunnybrook Farm*, 1938). Later, as Shirley Temple Black, she became active in Republican politics, represented the USA at the United Nations, and served as ambassador in various countries.

Temple, William (1881–1944) British churchman and educationalist. He became a priest in 1909 and was Archbishop of Canterbury 1942–44. He worked with R. A. (later Lord) BUTLER on his Education Bill which became law in 1944. He also sought to secure a greater sense of common purpose between the different religious denominations and his work led to the foundation of the WORLD COUNCIL OF CHURCHES.

tench A fish of the genus *Tenca*, in the CARP family, widely distributed in Europe and central Asia. It is a deep greeny-brown in colour with bronze sides, and has small scales and rounded fins. A bottom-living fish, it prefers muddy lakes and rivers with dense vegetation, and can survive with little oxygen.

Ten Commandments (or **Decalogue**) The religious and moral laws given by God to Moses on Mount Sinai, according to the Old Testament. They constitute the convenant between God and the Jewish people; obedience to these Commandments would ensure that the Jews would enjoy a privileged relationship with God as His chosen people. As set out in Exodus 20: 1–17 they are: the Jewish God shall be unique; the Jews shall have no other gods or idols; the name of God shall not be taken in vain (misused); the Sabbath must be respected as a holy day; parents must be honoured; murder is forbidden; adultery is forbidden; theft is forbidden; false evidence against another must not be given; coveting the possessions of others is forbidden. These injunctions were carved on two tablets of stone, and kept in the Ark of the Covenant. They are accepted as a moral basis for all Jews and Christians, although according to the New Testament they also apply to all humans.

Tenerife A volcanic island, belonging to Spain, in the Atlantic Ocean off the north-west coast of Africa, the largest of the Canary Islands and popular holiday resort; area 2,059 sq km (795 sq miles); pop. (1990) 771,000. Dominated by the volcanic peak of Mt Teide (3,718 m, 12,198 ft), its chief town is Santa Cruz.

Teng Hsiao-p'ing See DENG XIAOPING.

Teniers, David (known as **David Teniers the Younger**) (1610–90) Flemish painter. The son of the painter **David Teniers the Elder** (1582–1649), he worked chiefly in Antwerp and Brussels, and from 1651 was court painter to successive regents of the Netherlands. His many works include peasant genre scenes in the style of Brouwer, religious subjects, landscapes, and portraits.

Tennant, Charles (1768–1838) British chemical industrialist of Scottish extraction who invented bleaching powder. His apprenticeship to a weaver made him familiar with the method of bleaching cotton by exposure to sunlight. He investigated faster bleaching methods using chemicals, and in 1799 took out a patent for a process to manufacture bleaching powder from chlorine and slaked lime (calcium hydroxide). This was an immediate success.

Tennessee A state in central south-eastern USA, lying to the south of Kentucky between the Mississippi River and the Smoky Mountains; area 109,152 sq km (42,144 sq miles); pop. (1990) 4,877,185;

capital, Nashville. The largest cities are Memphis, Nashville, Knoxville, and Chattanooga. It is also known as the Volunteer State. Ceded by Britain to the USA in 1783, Tennessee became the 16th state of the Union in 1796. The floodplain between the Mississippi and Tennessee rivers is dominated by corn, tobacco, and cotton fields while central Tennessee is 'blue-grass' country largely given over to livestock grazing. Its industries produce chemicals, textiles, electrical goods, and processed food.

Tennessee A river of the USA that rises in headstreams in eastern Tennessee and flows 1,049 km (652 miles) south-westwards into Alabama, then north into Tennessee again before joining the Ohio River in Kentucky. The river is used extensively as a source of irrigation water and hydroelectric power, the **Tennessee Valley Authority** (TVA; formed by Congress in 1933) having converted it into a chain of lakes held back by nine major dams.

Tenniel, Sir John (1820–1914) British illustrator and cartoonist. He is known chiefly for his illustrations for Lewis Carroll's *Alice's Adventures in Wonderland* (1865) and *Through the Looking Glass* (1871). He also worked as a cartoonist for the magazine *Punch* between 1851 and 1901.

tennis, lawn A racket-and-ball game. It is generally played outdoors, but indoor courts are becoming increasingly popular. The court measures 23.77 m (78 feet) by 8.23 m (27 feet) for singles with a pair of 'tramlines' at the side for doubles. The server stands on the baseline and serves the ball, usually with an overarm action diagonally across the net into the receiver's right-hand court. The players rally until the ball hits the net and remains on the hitter's side, bounces twice, or goes out of play without bouncing in the court. The server then serves into the receiver's left-hand court. Players need four points to win a game, scored as 15, 30, 40, and game. If they level at 40, deuce is called, and one player must win two clear points to take the game. Players need six games and a lead of two games to win a set. If the set continues to 6–6, a tie-break is called. Women's matches are played over three sets and men's championships usually over five. The most prestigious championships take place in Paris (French Open), London (Wimbledon), New York (US Open), and Melbourne (Australian Open). Lawn tennis derives from the ancient game of **real** (or royal) **tennis** or (in France) *jeu de paume*. This is a racket-and-ball game played in an indoor court.

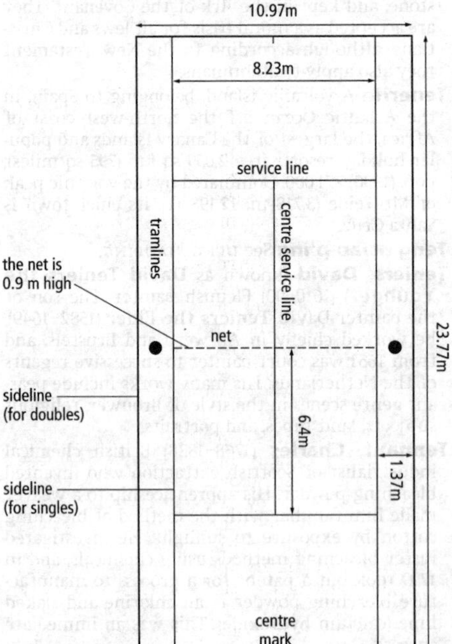

Tennis The dimension of a lawn tennis court. For doubles games the posts supporting the net are placed outside the doubles sidelines.

Tennyson, Alfred, 1st Baron Tennyson of Aldworth and Freshwater (1809–92) British poet. His first poems, published in the early 1830s, include 'Mariana', 'The Lotos-Eaters', and 'The Lady of Shalott'; a later collection (1842) included 'Morte d'Arthur', the germ of *Idylls of the King* (1859). His reputation was established by *In Memoriam*, a long poem concerned with immortality, change, and evolution, written in memory of his friend Arthur Hallam (1811–33); although begun in about 1833, it was not published until 1850. The same year he was made Poet Laureate; thereafter he enjoyed considerable celebrity and was one of the most popular poets of his day, publishing 'The Charge of the Light Brigade' in 1854 and *Maud* in 1855. His later works include the collection *Tiresias and Other Poems* (1885) and several dramas.

Tenochtitlán Literally 'place of the Tenochca', the island capital of the AZTECS in Lake Texcoco, now modern Mexico City. Traditionally founded in *c.*1345, it grew to a population of *c.*300,000 by the early 16th century. It was laid out in a grid of streets and canals round a huge ceremonial precinct of pyramids, temples, and palaces, and surrounded by artificial islands of gardens called *chinampas*. Three wide causeways stretched out across the lake to the mainland. As the hub of the Aztec empire, its capture by CORTÉS on 13 August 1521 was rapidly followed by complete capitulation.

tenrec A member of a family, Tenrecidae, of insectivores confined to Madagascar and the nearby Comoro Archipelago. In the absence of other insectivores, the tenrecs have evolved into a range of some 34 species that resemble insectivores elsewhere. This tendency is most marked in the 'hedgehog' tenrecs, such as the greater hedgehog tenrec, *Setifer setosus*, but there are also shrew-like tenrecs, others like water shrews, and three species of rice tenrecs, *Oryzarictes*, which have the habits and something of the appearance of a mole. The common tenrec, *Tenrec ecaudatus*, resembles the New World opossums.

tensor (in mathematics) An extension of the notion of a VECTOR. A vector associates any direction in space with a scalar, which is the component of the vector in that direction. A tensor by analogy allows the association of any direction with a vector. The state of stress at a given point in a solid object is represented by a tensor. In four-dimensional space, particularly the SPACE-TIME continuum of the special theory of relativity, tensor analysis is of considerable importance.

tent caterpillar A caterpillar, such as that of the lackey moth, *Malacosoma neustria*, that lives gregariously in or on silken webs, spun over the bushes or trees which serve as its food plant. Two species are abundant and regarded as pests in North America. The eastern tent moth, *M. americana*, builds conspicuous tents and feeds particularly on orchard trees; the forest tent moth, *M.*

disstria, constructs webs on forest trees such as oak, which are used as platforms for resting.

Tenzing Norgay (1914–86) Sherpa mountaineer. In 1953, as members of the British Expedition, he and Sir Edmund Hillary were the first to reach the summit of Mount Everest.

Teotihuacán The largest city of pre-Columban America, about 40 km (25 miles) north-east of Mexico City. Built *c.*300 BC it reached its zenith *c.*300–600 AD, when it was the centre of an influential culture, but by 650 it had declined as a major power and was sacked by the invading Toltec *c.*750. Among its monuments are the pyramids of the Sun and Moon and the temple of Quetzalcóatl. The ruins of the city were rediscovered in the 15th century by the Aztecs who founded the new city of TENOCHTITLÁN nearby.

terbium (symbol Tb, at. no. 65, r.a.m. 158.92) A silvery, soft LANTHANIDE element discovered in 1843 by C. G. Mosander (1797–1858). It occurs in monazite, and the oxide (Tb_2O_3) is used in phosphors for television tubes.

Terence (born Publius Terentius Afer) (*c.*190–159 BC) Roman comic dramatist. His six surviving comedies are based on the Greek New Comedy; set in Athens, they use the same stock characters as are found in Plautus, but are marked by a more realistic treatment of character and language, and a greater consistency of plot. Terence's work had an influence on the development of Renaissance and Restoration comedy.

Teresa, Mother (or **Theresa**) (born Agnes Gonxha Bojaxhiu) (1910–97) Roman Catholic nun and missionary, born in what is now Macedonia of Albanian parentage. In 1928 she went to India, where she devoted herself to helping the destitute. In 1948 she became an Indian citizen and founded the Order of Missionaries of Charity, which became noted for its work among the poor and the dying in Calcutta. Her organization now operates in many other parts of the world. Mother Teresa was awarded the Nobel Peace Prize in 1979.

Teresa of Ávila, St (1515–82) Spanish Carmelite nun and mystic. She combined vigorous activity as a reformer with mysticism and religious contemplation. Seeking to return the Carmelite Order to its original discipline and observances, she instituted the 'discalced' reform movement, establishing the first of a number of convents in 1562 and encouraging St John of the Cross to found a similar monastic order. Her spiritual writings include *The Way of Perfection* (1583) and *The Interior Castle* (1588). Feast day, 15 October.

Teresa of Lisieux, St (or **Thérèse**) (born Marie-Françoise Thérèse Martin) (1873–97) French Carmelite nun. After her death from tuberculosis her cult grew through the publication of her autobiography *L'Histoire d'une âme* (1898), teaching that sanctity can be attained through continual renunciation in small matters, and not only through extreme self-mortification. Feast day, 3 October.

Tereshkova, Valentina (Vladimirovna) (1937–) Russian cosmonaut. In June 1963 she became the first woman in space; her spacecraft returned to Earth after three days in orbit.

terminal velocity The constant speed obtained by an object when moving under gravity with no reactant force acting on it. For instance, when an object falls through air, the air resistance on it increases as its speed increases. Eventually, the air resistance balances the object's weight. The object then continues to travel downward with a constant terminal velocity.

termite (or **white ant**) A social insect unrelated to true ants, forming the order Isoptera with 1,900 species. Termites are found in all warm countries, where no wooden structure is safe from their feeding activities. Foraging workers move in soil-covered runways, as protection from desiccation. Most species eat wood or dead wood and harbour symbiotic flagellate protozoa in their guts, which digest cellulose. Other species eat vegetable matter or debris; a few attack live plants. Many species eat soil, digesting its organic component and building the excreted clay into rock-hard mounds above their nests which may be several metres tall and are a feature of African and South American grasslands. Colonies consist usually of a king and queen, sterile, wingless workers and soldiers, and developing nymphs. All castes include males and females. Periodically, winged reproductives are produced and leave the nest in swarms, to mate and found new colonies. Colony composition is regulated chemically by the exchange of regurgitated food and saliva; the queen's faeces also pass among the colony and inhibit the production of reproductives. Some queens live for ten years, grow enormously large, and lay an egg every two seconds.

tern A slender gull-like bird with narrow wings and a forked tail. They hover over water, picking up small fish with forceps bills. Their tribe, Sternini, of the family Laridae, includes 32 species of black-capped true terns, *Sterna* species, and four species of NODDIES, *Anous* species.

terracotta (Italian, 'baked earth') Baked clay that has not been glazed. Terracotta is a form of earthenware, but from ancient times it has been used for statues (usually small-scale) and architectural ornaments. Terracotta is also a reddish-brown colour.

terrapin An edible TURTLE of the family Emydidae, especially the diamond back terrapin, *Malaclemys terrapin*. This species occurs along the east coast of North America, from Massachusetts to Mexico, in salt or brackish water.

In Britain a terrapin is virtually any small, mainly freshwater, turtle, especially those imported from America as pets, such as the red-eared, or pond, terrapin, *Pseudemys scripta*.

territory (in ecology) The space defended by an organism or a group, using DISPLAY or AGGRESSION, against others of the same species. It may be either temporary or permanent. Many birds establish territories for nesting, as do some fishes, such as the stickleback. Territories may be large or small. A pride of lions may occupy territories several square kilometres in extent. The gannet in large breeding colonies maintains a territory of only about 1.5 sq m (5 sq feet). When the young of a species become mature they are usually driven off to establish their own territories.

terrorism The use of violent and intimidating acts, especially for political ends. Terrorism has been used most commonly by revolutionary groups, whose objective is the overthrow of a particular state authority, and by nationalist groups seeking national self-determination.

Techniques of terrorism involve bombing and shooting attacks against property and individuals, the ASSASSINATION of significant persons associated with the established government or security forces, hostage-taking, and hi-jacking of aircraft, trains, ships, and buses. The major objectives of terrorism are: to keep a particular cause in the forefront of public consciousness; to pressure the political authorities to concede the terrorists' demands by inducing a state of public fear; and to induce a government to betray its own commitment to freedom and democracy by imposing illiberal security measures in order to contain such violence.

International collaboration against terrorism has not proved easy since it involves the close cooperation of legal and police authorities from many different states, which may have different international interests. The European Convention on the Suppression of Terrorism (1977), the 'Trevi system' of cooperation among EC members (1976), which has now spread to Council of Europe states, the Tokyo summit declaration on terrorism in 1986, and the participation of the former Soviet Union in anti-terrorist collaboration have all helped to establish a climate of international cooperation.

Terry, Dame Ellen (Alice) (1847–1928) British actress. A member of a theatrical family, she had a beautiful voice, which was widely acclaimed. In 1878 she began her famous partnership with Henry IRVING, playing most of the Shakespearian heroines as well as contemporary roles. In 1906 she appeared as Lady Cicely Waynflete in Shaw's *Captain Brassbound's Conversion*, a role created for her.

Tertiary The first period in the Cenozoic geological era, so-called because it follows the Mesozoic, which was formerly also called *Secondary*. It lasted from about 65 to 2 million years ago, and comprises the Palaeocene, Eocene, Oligocene, Miocene, and Pliocene epochs. World temperatures were generally warm except towards the close of the period, and mammals evolved rapidly, becoming the dominant land vertebrates.

Tertullian (born Quintus Septimius Florens Tertullianus) (*c.*160–*c.*240) Early Christian theologian. Born in Carthage after the Roman conquest, he converted to Christianity *c.*195. His writings (in Latin) include Christian apologetics and attacks on pagan idolatry and Gnosticism. He later joined the millenarian heretics the Montanists, urging asceticism and venerating martyrs.

tesla (symbol T) The SI UNIT of magnetic flux density or magnetic induction, named in honour of Nikola TESLA. MAGNETIC FLUX, or total quantity of magnetic field in a given area, is measured in webers (Wb). A concentration of magnetic flux of 1 weber per square metre (at right angles to the flux) gives a magnetic flux density of 1 tesla.

Tesla, Nikola (1856–1943) Croatian-born US electrical engineer and versatile inventor. He worked as an engineer in Budapest before emigrating to the USA in 1884. For a short time he worked with EDISON on direct-current electric GENERATORS and motors. He then transferred to WESTINGHOUSE and concentrated on alternating-current devices. He developed the first alternating-current induction motor in 1888, and the Tesla coil (1891), which is widely used in radio and television sets. He ultimately became a recluse and died in poverty.

Test Acts Laws that made the holding of public office in Britain conditional upon subscribing to the established religion. Although Scotland imposed such a law in 1567, the harsh laws against recusants in England were sufficient in themselves to deter Roman Catholics and dissenters from putting themselves forward for office. But in 1661 membership of town corporations, and in 1673 all offices under the crown, were denied to those who refused to take communion in an Anglican church. In 1678 all Catholics except the Duke of York (the future JAMES II) were excluded from Parliament. In the 18th century religious tests in Scotland were not always enforced, except for university posts, and in England the test could be met by occasional communion, but this was not possible for Roman Catholics. The Test Acts were finally repealed in 1829, and university religious tests were abolished in the 1870s and 1880s.

testis The organ of male animals that produces SPERM, present in most vertebrates as a pair, the testes. In adult male mammals they are called **testicles** and lie outside the abdomen in the scrotum (see REPRODUCTION). They develop inside the abdominal cavity, where they always remain in such mammals as the elephant, but in other mammals they descend through the abdominal wall into the scrotum at about the time of birth. Within the scrotum in the adult the testicles lie in small isolated cavities. Testicles in the scrotum are at a lower temperature than that of the body core, which is required for the normal development of sperm.

testosterone See SEX HORMONES; STEROIDS AND STEROID TREATMENT.

test-tube baby See IN VITRO FERTILIZATION.

tetanus (or **lockjaw**) An infectious disease due to the effect on the spinal cord of a toxin produced by the bacterium *Clostridium tetani*. This is most commonly contracted through the contamination of wounds by spores of the bacterium, naturally present in soil. The resistant spores may remain latent for long periods in soil. The condition, which is characterized by painful cramps, is always serious and often fatal. Inoculation with modified toxin gives good protection.

Tétouan (or **Tetuán**) A city in the Rif Mountains of northern Morocco, formerly the capital of Spanish Morocco; pop. (1993) 272,000. It has light industries and tourist attractions.

tetra A group of fishes (CHARACINS) popular as aquarium fishes. Tetras mostly live in tropical South America (although other characins also occur in Africa), and they are small, active, and beautifully coloured. They all possess an adipose fin on the back just in front of the tail. Possibly the best-known species is the neon tetra, *Paracheirodon innesi*, found in the upper Amazon. Most other tetras belong to the genus *Hyphessobrycon*.

tetracycline See ANTIBIOTIC.

Teuton A member of a north European tribe mentioned in the 4th century BC and combining with others to carry out raids on north-eastern and southern France during the Roman period until heavily defeated in 102 BC.

Teutonic Knight A member of a military and religious order whose full title was the Order of the Knights of the Hospital of St Mary of the Teutons in Jerusalem. Founded in 1190 at Acre, it was made up of knights, priests, and lay brothers and was active in Palestine and Syria, though its members retreated to Venice when the Crusaders failed to contain the Muslims. The Holy Roman Emperor Frederick II employed the order as missionaries to overcome and convert the pagans beyond the north-eastern border of the empire and in this they were very successful, gaining Prussia in 1229.

In 1234, though in practice independent, they declared that they held the lands they had conquered as a fief from the pope. Joining with the Livonian Order, they continued to advance around the Baltic coast, amassing huge territories, but their progress was checked decisively when they were defeated at Tannenberg in 1410 by King Ladislas of Poland. In 1525 the Grand Master, Albert of Brandenburg, became a Lutheran, resigned his office, and the order was declared secular, and it remained an order under the control of the Electors of Brandenburg.

Tewkesbury, Battle of (4 May 1471) A battle in the Wars of the ROSES fought between EDWARD IV fresh from his victory as BARNET and the Lancastrian forces of Margaret of Anjou. Margaret's forces were defeated and her son, Prince Edward, was among those killed.

Texas A state in the southern USA, bordering on Mexico and the Gulf of Mexico and lying to the south of Oklahoma between New Mexico and Louisiana; area 691,030 sq km (266,807 sq miles); pop. (1990) 16,986,510; capital, Austin. The largest cities are Houston, Dallas, San Antonio, Austin, and Fort Worth. It is also known as the Lone Star State. Mountainous in the south-west, the greater part of northern and western Texas is open range. Plantations of rice, sugar cane and cotton lie to the east and in the valley of the Rio Grande are citrus groves. It is a major producer of cattle, sheep, cotton, oil, gas, and minerals such as sulphur, helium, graphite, and bromine. The area was opened up by Spanish explorers (16th–17th centuries) and formed part of Mexico until it became an independent republic in 1836 and the 28th state of the USA in 1845. Amongst its chief landmarks are the Big Bend and Guadalupe National Parks, the Johnson Space Centre at Houston, Padre Island National Seashore, and the Palo Alto Battlefield National Historic Site.

Texas Rangers A para-military US police force. The Texas Rangers were first organized in the 1830s to protect US settlers in Texas against Mexican Indians. After the formation of the republic of TEXAS (1836), they were built up by HOUSTON as a mounted border patrol of some 1,600 picked men. They became renowned for their exploits against marauders and rustlers in the heyday of the great CATTLE drives after the AMERICAN CIVIL WAR.

textile All types of natural and manufactured FIBRES, filaments, YARNS and fabrics together with a wide variety of products made from fibres or fibre-based materials. The earliest textile fibres were based on quite coarse materials, such as grasses, reeds, and rushes. They were used in prehistoric times to make screens, BASKET-WORK, fishing nets, matting, and ropes. Later, techniques for using finer natural materials, such as flax, jute, and animal hair were developed. From the third millennium BC other fibres, notably COTTON, WOOL, and SILK, were increasingly exploited. Towards the end of the 19th century, the first significant manufactured fibres were produced: these were the RAYONS, regenerated from natural cellulose. From the 1930s onwards SYNTHETIC FIBRES based on polymeric materials were developed. These included NYLONS, POLYESTER and ACRYLIC FIBRES, and polyolefins.

Textile fibres are converted into yarn by SPINNING. Fibres of different types may be spun together to form blends, for example, polyester and cotton, or wool and nylon. Yarns are then used to make fabrics by such processes as weaving on a LOOM, KNITTING, or felting (see FELT). Textile-finishing processes are then often applied, to give the fabric particular properties. Some of these processes (for example, dyeing) may be used on raw fibres, yarns or complete articles. The variety of textile products is almost endless.

texturized vegetable protein (TVP) See FOOD TECHNOLOGY.

Tezcatlipoca (Nahuatl, 'smoking mirror') The all-powerful chief deity of Aztec mythology, but probably of Toltec origin. Credited with several aspects, Tezcatlipoca was the Sun-god turned into a tiger by Quetzalcóatl, his constant opponent; as patron of warriors he was identified with Huitzilopochtli. He is often depicted as one-footed, the other having been bitten off by the monster, Earth, as Tezcatlipoca raised him from the primeval waters.

Thackeray, William Makepeace (1811–63) British novelist, born in Calcutta. He worked in London as a journalist and illustrator after leaving Cambridge University without a degree. All of his novels originally appeared in serial form; he established his reputation with *Vanity Fair* (1847–48), a vivid portrayal of early 19th-century society, satirizing upper-middle class pretensions through its central character Becky Sharp. Later novels include *Pendennis* (1848–50), *The History of Henry Esmond* (1852), and *The Virginians* (1857–59). In 1860 Thackeray became the first editor of the *Cornhill Magazine*, in which much of his later work was published.

Thai The official language of Thailand, a tonal language of the Sino-Tibetan language group. Thai-speaking groups include the Shan, Lue, and Phutai, but it is the language of the Central Thai that is taught in schools and used in government.

Thailand (formerly **Siam**) A country in south-east Asia bounded by Myanmar (Burma), Laos, and Cambodia, and, in the south, Malaysia.

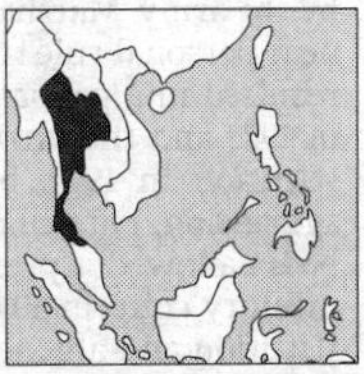

Physical. The country extends more than halfway down the Malay Peninsula and its north–south length is over 1,600 km (1,000 miles). The north is hilly and covered with dense forest, including teak. In the centre is a great, low-lying plain threaded with rivers which drain into the Gulf of Thailand. This is densely cultivated, with paddy fields which yield fish as well as rice; while further south, on the peninsula, rubber is grown. The climate is hot and monsoonal, and wetter in the west than in the east.

Economy. A newly industrializing country, Thailand has experienced high economic growth in recent years, based on exports of textiles and machinery and agricultural products such as rice, tapioca, and rubber. Mining and industry are replacing agriculture as the leading economic activities. Mineral resources include tin, lead, iron ore, lignite, tungsten, antimony, fluorspar, and petroleum. Rice, once the leading export, dominates agricultural production; other crops include sugar cane, cassava, maize, and rubber. Teak production is also important and tourism a significant earner of foreign exchange. Rapid industrial growth concentrated around Bangkok has strained Thailand's infrastructure.

History. The Thais, akin to the Shans and Lao, originated in the Yunnan province of south-west China. Their name means 'free'. MONGOL pressure accelerated their southward movement from Yunnan. They set up kingdoms in Sukhotai and Chiengmai, formerly under KHMER rule, became Theravada BUDDHISTS, and adopted an Indian script. About 1350 Ayuthia became the capital of a new Thai kingdom which, after prolonged fighting, captured ANGKOR in 1431. Ayuthia ruled much of Cambodia and at times Tenasserim and nothern Malaya. Wars with Burma, whose kings coveted Ayuthia's sacred white elephants, brought no lasting loss of Thai territory.

Among Europeans who became active in

Ayuthia the French were dominant. In 1684 Thai envoys presented LOUIS XIV with elephants, rhinoceroses, and a letter engraved on gold. The Burmese finally destroyed Ayuthia in 1767. Under the leadership of General Taskin, the Burmese were expelled from Siam by about 1777. His successor, General Chakri (later Rama I) founded the Chakri dynasty and established Bangkok as his capital. The Chakri dominated much of LAOS and northern Malaya and succeeded in maintaining their country's independence through a policy of conciliation, ceding their vassal state in Laos and Cambodia to France in the late 19th and early 20th centuries. In the reigns of Mongkut (1851–68) and CHULALONGKORN (1868–1910) Thailand achieved substantial modernization in both the administrative and economic spheres. The middle class produced by the modernization process became intolerant of absolute royal rule, and an economic crisis in 1932 produced a bloodless coup which left the Chakri dynasty on the throne but transferred power to a constitutional government. Although technically allied to Japan during World War II, Thailand retained western friendship because of prolonged guerrilla resistance to Japanese forces. Until the early 1970s the country was largely ruled by the army, Marshal Pibul Songgram maintaining near personal rule from 1946 to 1957. Severe rioting resulted in a partial move to civilian government in 1973 and the introduction of a democratic constitution in 1974, but the threat of communist aggression, particularly on its borders with Cambodia allowed a pronounced military influence. A military coup in 1991 was followed by a new constitution and a general election in 1992. Commander-in-chief General Suchinda Kraprayoon was appointed Prime Minister, and he imposed a military crackdown. This resulted in riots, arrests, and the killing of demonstrators, before King Bhumibol (succeeded 1946) was able to restore stability by a political compromise; Suchinda resigned and civilian political parties were re-legalized. Further elections in September 1992 were won by a coalition of pro-democracy parties; the leader of the Democrat Party, Chuan Leekpai, became Prime Minister. Elections in 1996 were won by a six-party coalition; Chavalat Yongchaiyudh, leader of the largest party, New Aspiration, became prime minister.

Capital: Bangkok
Area: 513,115 sq km (198,115 sq mi)
Population: 58,791,000 (1995)
Currency: 1 baht = 100 satang
Religions: Buddhist 95.0%; Muslim 4.0%; Christian 1.0%
Ethnic Groups: Siamese 54.0%; Lao 28.0%; Chinese 11.0%; Malay 4.0%; Khmer 3.0%
Languages: Thai (official); Lao; Chinese; Malay; Mon-Khmer languages
International Organizations: UN; ASEAN; Colombo Plan

thalassaemia An inherited disease characterized by impaired haemoglobin production. The most common type of thalassaemia is beta thalassaemia, which is characterized by failure of effective red cell production because the cells do not mature, and chronic ANAEMIA. There are two subtypes of beta thalassaemia, which are called beta thalassaemia major and beta thalassaemia minor. Beta thalassaemia major is life-threatening and characterized by profound anaemia; symptoms occur during the first year of life. Blood transfusions are necessary for survival. Beta thalassaemia minor is a mild form of the disease, which may be asymptomatic.

Thales (*c.*624–*c.*545 BC) Greek philosopher, mathematician, and astronomer, of Miletus. He was one of the Seven Sages listed by Plato and was held by Aristotle to be the founder of physical science; he is also credited with founding geometry. He proposed that water was the primary substance from which all things were derived, and represented the Earth as floating on an underlying ocean; his cosmology had Egyptian and Semitic affinities.

thallium (symbol Tl, at. no. 81, r.a.m. 204.37) A soft, white, lead-like metal in Group 13 (formerly IIIB) of the PERIODIC TABLE, named after the intense green spectral line (Greek *thallos*, green shoot) that identifies the element. It occurs naturally in crookesite and lorandite, often found with sulphur and selenium ores. Its compounds are used to make optical glass of high refractive index. The metal and its salts are poisonous and are used as pesticides.

Thames A river of southern England, flowing eastwards 338 km (210 miles) from the Cotswolds in Gloucestershire through London to the North Sea. In Oxfordshire known as the Isis, the Thames is the largest river in England, having a width of *c.*700 m at Gravesend. Oxford, Reading, and London lie on the river, across which a flood barrier to protect London was completed at Woolwich in 1982.

thane (or **thegn**) A nobleman of Anglo-Saxon England. Their status, as determined by their wergild, was usually 1,200 shillings. In return for their services to the crown they received gifts of land, which became hereditary. The king's thanes, members of the royal household, were required to do military service, attend the WITAN, and assist in government.

Thanet, Isle of The easternmost peninsula of Kent, south-east England, including the resort and residential towns of Ramsgate, Broadstairs, and Margate. It was formerly separated from the mainland by the Wantsum Channel.

Thant, U (1909–74) Burmese statesman and third Secretary-General of the United Nations 1961–71. He entered the Burmese diplomatic service in 1948 and served at the United Nations from 1957. In 1961 he succeeded Dag HAMMARSKJÖLD as Secretary-General. He filled the post with great distinction, his achievements including assistance in the resolution of the CUBAN MISSILE CRISIS and the admission of communist China to full UN and Security Council membership in 1971.

Thar Desert (or **Great Indian Desert**) A desert region to the east of the Indus River in the Rajasthan and Gujarat states of north-west India and the Punjab and Sind regions of south-east Pakistan. It covers *c.*259,000 sq km (100,000 sq miles). The 650-km (400-mile) Indira Gandhi Canal (completed in 1986) brings water from the snow-fed rivers of Himachal Pradesh to the desert regions of Rajasthan.

Thatcher, Margaret (Hilda), Baroness Thatcher of Kesteven (1925–) British Conservative stateswoman, Prime Minister 1979–90. She became Conservative Party leader in 1975 and in 1979 was elected the country's first woman Prime Minister; she went on to become the longest-serving British Prime Minister of the 20th century. Her period in office was marked by an emphasis on monetarist policies and free enterprise, privatization of nationalized industries, and legislation to restrict the powers of trade unions. In international affairs she was a strong supporter of the policies of President Reagan. She was well known for determination and resolve (she had been dubbed 'the Iron Lady' as early as 1976), especially in her handling of the Falklands War of 1982. She resigned after a leadership challenge and was created a life peer in 1992.

theatre A building or outdoor area for the performance of plays and similar entertainments. The earliest recorded theatres were in Ancient Greece, and evolved from the worship of Dionysus (see GREEK THEATRE). They were set on hillsides around which were ranged semicircular tiers of seats, with a circular area (orchestra) containing the altar at the foot, where the CHORUS performed. The Roman theatre seldom used sloping ground, and the lofty stage building formed a single unit with the semicircular auditorium, both rising to the same height. The actors performed on a raised stage, the front of which was usually decorated with reliefs. The outer walls of the auditorium were composed of several storeys, each formed by a row of arches. Huge amphitheatres, such as the Roman Colosseum, resembled double theatres, with an arena in the middle. The theatres of Renaissance Italy were modelled on the Roman and Greek, but were covered. The curtained proscenium arch between the auditorium and stage was introduced, and the audience occupied what had been the orchestra. The platform stage of the Elizabethan theatre later became the apron stage (in front of the proscenium arch), which formed the acting area of the Restoration theatre, with proscenium doors on each side through which the actors entered and exited. The apron stage was retained in 18th-century Georgian theatres, but the actors gradually moved back behind the proscenium arch among the scenery. By the early 19th century the apron stage had disappeared and the 'picture-frame' stage reigned supreme. Many theatres were built during the 19th century; exteriors improved, interiors grew more luxurious. Modern theatres often incorporate the picture frame and the open stage. The popular theatre-in-the-round ensures intimacy between actors and audience, especially in 'promenade' productions in which the actors mingle with a standing audience. Flexible staging, which can be adapted for various styles of presentation, is popular with fringe groups and in the small studio theatres attached to many large theatres or forming part of arts complexes. Many theatrical performances are also given in public houses and other buildings never intended for theatrical events, and on the streets.

Thebes ▶**1** A city of Upper Egypt, about 675 km (420 miles) south of modern Cairo, that was the capital of ancient Egypt under the 18th Dynasty (*c.*1550–1290 BC). Its monuments (on both banks of the Nile) were the richest in the land, with the town and major temples at LUXOR and KARNAK on the east bank, and the necropolis, with tombs of royalty and nobles, on the west bank. It was already a tourist attraction in the 2nd century AD. ▶**2** (Greek **Thívai**) A city of Greece, in Boetia, about 74 km (46 miles) north-west of Athens, leader of the whole of Greece for a short period after the defeat of the Spartans at the Battle of Leuctra in 371 BC.

Themistocles (*c.*528–462 BC) Athenian statesman. He was instrumental in building up the Athenian fleet, which under his command defeated the Persian fleet at Salamis in 480. In the following years he lost influence, was ostracized in 470, and eventually fled to the Persians in Asia Minor, where he died.

theocracy A society governed by priests, or one whose government is heavily influenced by religious leaders. Originally it meant a system in which divine law was the basis of all humanly enacted law, and in which religious and political hierarchies were merged, as in Tibet until Chinese occupation in 1951. There are no theocracies in this strict sense in the modern world.

Theocritus (*c.*310–*c.*250 BC) Greek poet, born in Sicily. Little is known of his life but he is thought to have lived on the island of Kos and in Alexandria as well as Sicily. He is chiefly known for his bucolic idylls, hexameter poems presenting the song-contests and love-songs of imaginary shepherds. These poems were the model for Virgil's *Eclogues* and for subsequent pastoral poetry.

theodolite An optical SURVEYING instrument used for measuring angles in the horizontal or vertical plane. A TELESCOPE with internal cross-hairs for sighting the target pivots up and down within a frame (trunnion); the trunnion and telescope can also be rotated horizontally. The theodolite is mounted on a tripod. A spirit-level on the instrument is used for levelling it. Angles are read off circular scales to an accuracy of fractions of a degree. The theodolite is used for triangulation (see SURVEYING) in road- and tunnel-making, and other civil engineering work.

Theodora (*c.*500–48) Byzantine empress, wife of Justinian. She is reputed (according to Procopius) to have led a dissolute life in her early years. She later became noted for her intellect and learning and, as Justinian's closest adviser, exercised a considerable influence on political affairs and the theological questions of the time.

Theodorakis, Mikis (1925–) Greek composer. His prolific output includes the ballet *Antigone* (1958) and the well-known score for the film *Zorba the Greek* (1965). In 1964 he was elected as a member of the Greek Parliament, but in 1967 was imprisoned by the new military government for his left-wing political activities. He was released in 1970 after worldwide protests and re-elected to Parliament in 1981. His later work includes the opera *Kostas Kariotakis* (1985).

Theodoric (known as **Theodoric the Great**) (*c.*454–526) King of the Ostrogoths 471–526. He invaded Italy in 488 and completed its conquest in 493, establishing a kingdom with the capital at Ravenna. At its greatest extent his empire included not only the Italian mainland, but Sicily, Dalmatia, and parts of Germany.

Theodosius, Flavius (known as **Theodosius the Great**) (349–95 AD), Roman emperor in the East 379–94 and sole emperor 394–95. The son of a famous general, Count Theodosius, Gratian appointed him co-emperor in 378. After failing to defeat the GOTHS he formed a treaty with them in 382. He was a champion of strict political and religious orthodoxy. His two sons, Arcadius and Honorius, succeeded him.

theology (from Greek, 'the study of God') The study of beliefs concerning God, including the study of scripture, PHILOSOPHY, comparative religion, and church history. Theology may be practised in the context of all religions, but has flourished most in the monotheistic religions, JUDAISM, ISLAM, and, in particular, CHRISTIANITY. In both Judaism and Islam, the codification of religious law (see TALMUD; SHARIA) has been considered a separate discipline and has often taken precedence over theology. Both religions lay stress on the indivisible unity of God and his unknowability by humans, and their theologians were not therefore as exercised with the problem of God's nature as were Christian theologians. In Christianity, however, the interaction between ideas of essentially Jewish provenance and the Greco-Roman world, and the systematic attempts to define Jesus' relationship to God the Father and the Holy Spirit (see TRINITY), the relationship of divine and human nature in the person of Jesus, and the significance of his birth, crucifixion, and resurrection, have led to a long history of theological argument.

Theophrastus of Eresos (*c.*372–287 BC) Greek philosopher. He wrote a *History of Plants* and *Causes of Plants*, which influenced botanical science into the Middle Ages, and bequeathed his garden for the benefit of his students.

theosophy (Greek, 'divine wisdom') A religious philosophy claiming insight into the nature of God and the Universe through direct experience, making use of such means as MYSTICISM, MEDITATION, occult practices, and hidden meanings in sacred texts. Theosophists include Neoplatonists and Gnostics, but they are now more generally identified with members of the Theosophical Society, founded in New York by Helena Blavatsky (1831–91). The ideas of the society were heavily influenced by HINDUISM and its base moved to India, where its leading exponents was Annie Besant (1847–1933).

Theravada (Pali, 'teaching of the elders') One of the most important groupings within BUDDHISM, predominant in Sri Lanka and south-east Asia. It is also known as Southern Buddhism. The Theravada school takes as its canon of scripture the *tripitaka*, written in Pali, which contains the original teachings of the BUDDHA: the FOUR NOBLE TRUTHS, the NOBLE EIGHTFOLD PATH, and the doctrine of DEPENDENT ORIGINATION. Theravada differs from the other great school, the MAHAYANA, in its emphasis on individual, rather than universal enlightenment.

Thérèse of Lisieux, St See TERESA OF LISIEUX, ST.

thermal A rising current of warm air produced when air near the ground becomes unstable as a result of daytime heating. Thermals often reach 3,000 m (10,000 feet) and are associated with the development of cumulus and cumulonimbus cloud. See also GLIDER.

thermal conductivity See CONDUCTION, THERMAL.

thermionic valve A type of electron tube used in electronic circuits to achieve amplification and switching. Thermionic emission was first noted by EDISON in 1883, when he modified an ordinary light bulb by introducing an extra conductor close to the filament. An electric current flowed through the vacuum between the filament (the CATHODE) and the conductor (the ANODE). This current resulted from free electrons emitted by the heated filament. FLEMING and DE FOREST followed up Edison's finding, and invented the thermionic diode and triode. The diode can pass current in one direction but not in the other (rectification). The properties of a diode can be modified by the addition of extra electrodes (grids) between the anode and cathode. The triode, the pentode, and other valves formed in this way were used in radio and television, as well as in other electronic devices, until they were replaced in the 1950s by SEMICONDUCTOR devices, which are smaller, cheaper, more reliable, and use less power. However, specialized valves such as the CATHODE-RAY TUBE, klystron, and magnetron are still used for specific applications.

thermocline A layer of water in which there is a greater decrease in temperature as depth increases than is found in the layers above or below it. Such layers are found both in the ocean and in large lakes. In the oceans, there is a permanent thermocline between the relatively warm waters of the wind-mixed surface layer above and the cold deep water below. The top of the thermocline usually occurs at a depth between 200 and 300 m (600 and 985 feet), although it is at relatively shallow depths near the Equator, where there is a marked decrease in temperature over a quite moderate vertical distance. In mid-latitudes the thermocline occurs at greater depths and the change in temperature is less marked. Near the poles it develops close to the surface of the water.

thermocouple A thermoelectric device used mainly for measuring temperatures, especially high temperatures, remotely. If wires made of two different metals are joined at their ends, and the two junctions are kept at different temperatures, an electric potential is generated and a current proportional to the temperature difference will flow in the circuit. This is the **thermoelectric effect**, which can be used to measure temperature differences using a millivoltmeter. One junction is placed at the point at which the temperature is to be measured, and the other is maintained at some fixed reference temperature, usually that of melting ice (0°C). Although nearly all pairs of metals show the thermoelectric effect, only a few are used in practical instruments. For accurate measurement up to 1,700°C, a junction of pure PLATINUM with platinum–rhodium ALLOY is used; a cheaper junction of chrome and aluminium alloys can be used up to 1,300°C. For lower temperatures, thermocouples using iron and constantan (up to 700°C) or copper and constantan (up to 400°C) are in common use.

thermodynamics The branch of physics concerned with the nature of heat and its association with other forms of energy. It has its basis in three laws. The first states that energy in a system cannot be created or destroyed, it can only be changed from one form to another. Thus, when work is done compressing a gas, its molecules move about faster and it gets hotter; when it expands, it does work on its surroundings and cools. The second law states that heat always flows from a body at a high temperature to one at a lower temperature, and it is impossible for heat from a cool body to flow of its own accord into a hot body, making it hotter still. The third law states that the differences in ENTROPY between different states of a substance approach zero as ABSOLUTE ZERO is approached. The practical consequence is that it is impossible to cool a body to absolute zero: it is a limit that can only be approached. An additional law, known as the zeroth law, states that if two systems are each in thermal equilibrium with a third system then they are in thermal equilibrium with each other.

thermodynamic temperature See HEAT AND TEMPERATURE; KELVIN.

thermoelectric device Any system which makes use of thermoelectric effects. The effects, first observed in the 19th century, are twofold. If an electric current flows in a circuit consisting of different metals, it is observed that some junctions become cooler and others warmer (the Peltier effect). Conversely, if the junctions are heated or cooled, a voltage is generated. This second effect (the Seebeck effect) has been used for over a century in THERMOCOUPLES. More recently, the much greater output obtained with semiconducting materials has led to the development of thermoelectric power supplies. Although not economic for general use, these have the advantage of having no moving parts and have found application in spacecraft and heart pacemakers, the heat input in both cases coming from an encapsulated radioactive source. The reverse effect, thermoelectric cooling, has a number of technological applications where a compact device without moving parts is required.

thermography The production, by electronic or photographic means, of diagnostic images showing the different heat levels of an object. In medicine, thermography can be used to detect 'hot spots' caused, for example, by cancer of the breast, but results have proved unreliable. Its use for assessment of rheumatic conditions has been much more successful.

thermometer An instrument for measuring temperature. A liquid-in-glass thermometer depends on the thermal expansion of a liquid in a tube. Depending on the temperature range to be measured, a variety of liquids is used. Alcohol and pentane (coloured to make them visible) are used for very low temperatures, but the commonest liquid is mercury. The first mercury thermometer was made by the German physicst G. D. FAHRENHEIT. The principle and design of the thermometer are both simple. The liquid is contained in a bulb at the end of an evacuated glass capillary tube, into which it extends. When the temperature rises, the liquid in the bulb expands, and is forced further up the tube, the rise being proportional to the temperature increase. By recording the position of the liquid at certain fixed points – notably the melting-point of ice (0°C) and the boiling-point of water (100°C) – a graduated scale can be calibrated so that ambient temperatures can be measured. This scale of temperature is called the **Celsius scale**, devised by the Swedish astronomer Anders Celsius in 1742. In 1848 the British physicist William Thomson (Lord Kelvin) devised the thermodynamic temperature scale, based on the degree now known as the KELVIN.

Since the 19th century other physical properties that vary with temperature, such as electrical resistance and the thermoelectric effect (see THERMOCOUPLE), have been used for temperature measurement. Many modern thermometers are designed for specific applications and temperature ranges. Cryogenic (low-temperature) thermometers include types made from doped SEMICONDUCTORS, used for ranges from 0.2 to 20 K (−272.8 to −253°C). Thermistors – small beads or cylinders of semiconductors or complex metal oxides – can measure temperatures ranging from 4 to 600 K (−269 to 327°C). For high temperatures, radiation thermometers such as the optical pyrometer are used: these need not touch the material being monitored, and can measure temperatures up to 1,800 K (1,527°C). The lowest temperature theoretically possible is −273.15°C, a point known as ABSOLUTE ZERO. In scientific work, temperatures are normally expressed in kelvins. The kelvin scale uses Celsius degrees but counts them from absolute zero, so that 0°C = 273.15 K.

thermonuclear bomb See NUCLEAR WEAPON.

thermonuclear reactor See FUSION, NUCLEAR.

thermoplastic See PLASTIC.

Thermopylae A pass in Greece, about 200 km (120 miles) north-west of Athens, originally narrow but now much widened by the recession of the sea. It was the scene of the heroic defence (480 BC) against the Persian army of Xerxes by 6,000 Greeks including 300 Spartans under their commander Leonidas.

thermosetting plastic See PLASTIC.

Thermos flask See VACUUM FLASK.

thermosphere The outermost part of Earth's atmosphere, extending from the top of the MESOPHERE at a height of about 80 km (50 miles) to outer space. It is a region in which the temperature increases with height, reaching several thousand degrees.

thermostat A device that maintains a system at a pre-set constant temperature. Modern thermostats are of two main types: on–off and gradual-action thermostats. The former, introduced at the beginning of the 20th century, usually incorporates a BIMETALLIC STRIP, which bends as the temperature changes, and can be used to open or close electrical contacts or valves to maintain a predetermined temperature. A typical gradual-action thermostat is used in the 'regulo' thermostat for gas cookers, introduced in the UK in 1923. In this, a rod of invar alloy (with a very small coefficient of thermal expansion) is welded to a brass tube located within the oven. The brass expands with heat, causing the invar rod to move and control a valve regulating the supply of gas to the burners. Thermostats are used in many control applications, including central heating systems, electric irons, refrigerators, greenhouses, and washing-machines.

Theseus In Greek mythology, one of the greatest of heroes, especially venerated in Athens, of which city he became king. His most famous feat was, with the aid of Ariadne, killing the Minotaur.

Thesiger, Sir Wilfred (Patrick) (1910–) British explorer. He made his first expedition at the age of 23, living with the Ethiopian Danakil tribe. In 1935 he joined the Sudan Political Service, and he fought in Africa during World War II. He explored Saudi Arabia and Oman from 1945 to 1950, and from 1960 onwards travelled and lived in East Africa. He described his adventures in a number of books, including *Arabian Sands* (1959) and *The Marsh Arabs* (1964).

Thespis (6th century BC) Greek dramatic poet. He is regarded as the founder of Greek tragedy, having been named by Aristotle as the originator of the role of the actor in addition to the traditional chorus. Actors are called **thespians** after Thespis.

Thessaloníki (or **Salonica**; Latin **Thessalonica**) A seaport in north-eastern Greece, capital of the modern Greek region of Macedonia; pop. (1991) 378,000. Founded in 316 BC by Cassander, king of Macedon, and named after his wife, it became the capital of the Roman province of Macedonia and an important city of Byzantium. It fell to the Turks in 1430, remaining a part of the Ottoman empire until 1912. It was the scene of a joint Anglo-French campaign in support of Serbia during World War I and is now a major port and the second-largest city in Greece. It is also a university city, a NATO base, and a major industrial centre with oil refineries, engineering, and textile plants.

thickhead (or **whistler**) Any of about 46 species of bird in the family Pachycephalidae. All are found in wooded areas of India, south-east Asia, and Australasia. Most are small, less than 20 cm (8 inches), though some are up to 25 cm (10 inches) long. The majority are dull grey and brown, or may, like the golden whistler, *Pachycephala pectoralis*, have bright yellow underparts. They are mainly insectivorous.

thick-knee See STONE-CURLEW.

Third Reich (1933–45) The period covering the NAZI regime in GERMANY.

Third World The undeveloped countries of the world. Of French origin (*le Tiers-Monde*), the expression formed part of a UN classification in which the developed capitalist countries were the First World and the developed Communist countries were the Second World. It is now more usual to refer to **developing countries**.

thirst A sensation aroused by the need for water, which is essential for the survival of many terrestrial vertebrates. Its function is to stimulate an urgent search for water to replace the deficit in the body fluids. Thirst cannot be referred to a particular sense organ or part of the body, although dryness of the mouth, tongue, and throat usually accompanies it. Thirst is extreme in certain medical conditions, such as diabetes or cholera, when the body's fluid volume is severely reduced.

Thirty-Nine Articles The set of doctrinal formulae first issued in 1563 and finally adopted by the ANGLICAN COMMUNION in 1571 as a statement of its position. Many of the articles allow a wide variety of interpretation. They had their origin in several previous definitions, required by the shifts and turns of the English Reformation. The Ten Articles (1536) and Six Articles (1539) upheld religious conservatism, but the Forty-Two Articles (1553), prepared by CRANMER and Ridley, were of markedly Protestant character, and they provided the basis of the Thirty-Nine Articles.

Thirty Years War (1618–48) A series of conflicts, fought mainly in Germany, in which Protestant–Catholic rivalries and German constitutional issues were gradually subsumed in a European struggle. It began in 1618 with the Protestant Bohemian revolt against the future emperor FERDINAND II; it embraced the last phase of the Dutch Revolts after 1621; and was concentrated in a Franco-Habsburg confrontation in the years after 1635.

By 1623 Ferdinand had emerged victorious in the Bohemian revolt, and with Spanish and Bavarian help had conquered the PALATINATE of FREDERICK V. But his German ambitions and his Spanish alliance aroused the apprehensions of Europe's Protestant nations and also of France. In 1625 Christian IV of Denmark renewed the war against the Catholic imperialists, as the leader of an anti-Habsburg coalition organized by the Dutch. After suffering a series of defeats at the hands of Tilly and Wallenstein, Denmark withdrew from the struggle at the Treaty of Lübeck (1629), and the emperor reached the summit of his power.

Sweden's entry into the war under GUSTAVUS ADOLPHUS led to imperial reversals. After Gustavus was killed at Lützen (1632), the Swedish Chancellor Oxenstierna financed the Heilbronn League of German Protestants (1633), which broke up after a heavy military defeat at Nördlingen in 1634. In 1635 the Treaty of Prague ended the civil war within Germany, but in the same year France, in alliance with Sweden and the United Provinces, went to war with the Habsburgs. Most of the issues were settled after five years of negotiation at the Treaty of WESTPHALIA in 1648, but the Franco-Spanish war continued until the Treaty of the Pyrenees in 1659.

thistle Any of various spiny-leaved, annual or perennial plants of the sunflower family. The very troublesome weeds spear and creeping thistle belong to the genus *Cirsium*. Some thistles are used as garden plants, notably the globe thistles (genus *Echinops*). Others are used as animal fodder in the young and non-spiny stage.

Thistlewood, Arthur See CATO STREET CONSPIRACY.

Thom, Alexander (1894–1985) Scottish expert on prehistoric stone circles. Thom was a qualified engineer and was employed first at Glasgow University and later (as professor) at Oxford. In the 1930s he began a detailed survey of the stone circles of Britain and Brittany. He found that they were constructed using units of measurement, which he dubbed the 'megalithic yard' and 'megalithic inch'. His chief books are *Megalithic Sites in Britain* (1967) and *Megalithic Lunar Observatories* (1971).

Thomas, Dylan (Marlais) (1914–53) Welsh poet. He moved to London in 1934 and worked in journalism and broadcasting while continuing to write poetry. He won recognition with *Deaths and Entrances* (1946), and continued his success with such works as *Portrait of the Artist as a Young Dog* (1940; prose); *Adventures in the Skin Trade*, an unfinished novel, was published posthumously in 1955. Shortly before his death in New York of alcohol poisoning, he narrated on radio his best-known work, *Under Milk Wood*, a portrait of a small Welsh town, interspersing poetic alliterative prose with songs and ballads.

Thomas, (Philip) Edward (1878–1917) British poet. He wrote mostly journalistic prose and reviews before being encouraged by Robert Frost in 1914 to concentrate on writing poetry; most of his work was written while serving in World War I and was published posthumously after he was killed at Arras in 1917. His work offers a sympathetic but unidealized depiction of rural English life, adapting colloquial speech rhythms to poetic metre.

Thomas, St An Apostle. He said that he would not believe that Christ had risen again until he had seen and touched his wounds (John 20:24–29); the story is the origin of the nickname 'doubting Thomas'. According to tradition he preached in SW India. Feast day, 21 December.

Thomas à Kempis (born Thomas Hemerken) (*c.*1380–1471) German theologian. Born at Kempen, near Cologne, he became an Augustinian canon in Holland. He wrote a number of ascetic treatises and is the probable author of *On the Imitation of Christ* (*c.*1415–24), a manual of spiritual devotion.

Thompson, Benjamin, Count von Rumford (1753–1814) American-born British scientist, soldier, civil servant, and founder of the Royal Institution (1799), who is remembered chiefly for his observations (1798) on the relationship between work and heat. Noting that a brass gun barrel continuously gave out heat when drilled with a blunt borer, he concluded that the heat produced by the motion of the borer, was a form of motion and was not some invisible liquid form of matter, 'caloric', released from the metal. His ideas were later developed by James JOULE, and came to form the basis of the first law of THERMODYNAMICS.

Thompson, Daley (1958–) British athlete. He won a number of major decathlon titles in the 1980s, including gold medals in the Olympic Games of 1980 and 1984.

Thompson, Emma (1959–) British actress and screenwriter. Although noted at first for her versatile comic talent, she later built a reputation as a serious actress. In 1989 she appeared in Kenneth BRANAGH's film of *Henry V*, and married Branagh the same year; the couple separated in 1995. Her other films include *Howard's End* (1992) for which she won an Oscar for best actress, *Carrington* (1995), and *Sense and Sensibility* (1995), for which she also wrote the Oscar-winning screenplay.

Thompson, Flora (Jane) (1876–1947) British writer. She is remembered for her semi-autobiographical trilogy *Lark Rise to Candleford* (1945), which evokes through the childhood memories and youth of 'Laura' a vanished world of rural customs and culture. It was originally published in three parts as *Lark Rise* (1939), *Over to Candleford* (1941), and *Candleford Green* (1943).

Thompson, Francis (1859–1907) British poet. His best-known work uses powerful imagery to convey intense religious experience, and includes the poems 'The Hound of Heaven' and 'The Kingdom of God'. He published three volumes of verse (1893–97) and much literary criticism in periodicals. He died from the combined effects of opium addiction and tuberculosis.

Thomson, Elihu (1853–1937) British-born US electrical engineer and inventor. Thomson registered some 700 patents, including a successful alternating-current motor, high-frequency generators and transformers, and a method of electrical welding. He was also the first to suggest the use of helium gas to prevent the 'bends' in deep-sea diving.

Thomson, James (1700–48) Scottish poet. His poem in four books *The Seasons* (1726–30) anticipated the romantic movement in its treatment of nature; the text was adapted for Haydn's oratorio of that name (1799–1801). He also co-wrote the masque *Alfred* (1740) with David Mallet (*c*.1705–65); it contains the song 'Rule, Britannia', whose words have been attributed to him.

Thomson, James (1834–82) Scottish poet. He is chiefly remembered for the poem 'The City of Dreadful Night' (1874), a powerful evocation of a half-ruined city where the narrator encounters tormented shades wandering in a Dantesque living hell, presided over by Melancolia.

Thomson, Sir Joseph John (1856–1940) British physicist, discoverer of the electron. While professor of physics at Cambridge (1884–1918) he consolidated the reputation of the Cavendish Laboratory. From his experiments on the deflection of cathode rays in magnetic and electric fields, Thomson deduced that he was dealing with particles smaller than the atom. These he initially called *corpuscles* and later *electrons*, a word coined by the Irish mathematical physicist George Johnstone Stoney (1826–1911). Thomson received the 1906 Nobel Prize for physics for his researches into the electrical conductivity of gases. His son **Sir George Paget Thomson** (1892–1975) shared the 1937 Nobel Prize for physics for his discovery of electron diffraction by crystals while professor of physics at London's Imperial College.

Thomson, Roy Herbert, 1st Baron Thomson of Fleet (1894–1976) Canadian-born British newspaper proprietor and media entrepreneur. In 1931 he opened his own radio station in northern Ontario. He then built up his North American press and radio holdings before acquiring his first British newspaper, the *Scotsman*, in 1952, the year he settled in Britain. He subsequently added the *Sunday Times* (1959) and *The Times* (1966) to his acquisitions, by which time the Thomson Organization had become an international corporation, with interests in publishing, printing, television, and travel.

Thomson, Tom (full name Thomas John Thomson) (1877–1917) Canadian painter. A pioneering artist of Canada's wilderness, he began sketching in Algonquin Park, Ontario, in the spring of 1912, returning there in subsequent summers. Major paintings include *Northern Lake* (1913), *The West Wind* (1917), and *The Jack Pine* (1917). Thomson's premature death at Canoe Lake, Algonquin Park, remains a mystery.

Thomson, William, 1st Baron Kelvin (1824–1907) British mathematician and physicist born in Belfast who made major advances in the science of THERMODYNAMICS, which he applied to his work on the age of the Earth. In 1848 he proposed a thermodynamic temperature scale, now called the KELVIN scale, based on energy considerations rather than the properties of any particular substance. Three years later, he put forward principles that were to form the basis of the second law of thermodynamics.

Thor The Norse god of the Sun and of thunder, the son of Odin, an enemy to the race of giants but benevolent to mankind. The attribute most commonly associated with him is thunder and lightning, which he created by casting his hammer Mjollnir to Earth. Thor's day (Thursday) was considered propitious for marriages.

thorax In the higher terrestrial vertebrates, the area between the head and the abdomen that contains the heart and lungs. In mammals, the thorax is separated from the abdomen by the DIAPHRAGM. The thorax of insects is made up of three segments: the prothorax, mesothorax and metathorax, from which arise three pairs of legs and up to two pairs of wings, where developed. The thorax of ARACHNIDS and CRUSTACEANS is fused with the head into a single cephalothorax.

Thoreau, Henry David (1817–62) US essayist and poet. Together with his friend and mentor Ralph Waldo Emerson he is regarded as a key figure of the philosophical, religious, and social movement Transcendentalism. He is best known for his book *Walden, or Life in the Woods* (1854), an account of a two-year experiment in self-sufficiency when he built a wooden hut by Walden Pond, near his home town of Concord, Massachusetts, and sought to live according to his ideals of simplicity and closeness to nature. His essay on civil disobedience (1849), in which he argues the right of the individual to refuse to pay taxes when conscience dictates, influenced Mahatma Gandhi's policy of passive resistance.

thorium (symbol Th, at. no. 90, r.a.m. 232.04) A soft, ductile, radioactive metal. Thorium is alloyed with magnesium to improve its performance at high temperatures. Thorium oxide (ThO_2) is an important catalyst, and is added to some creep-resistant alloys. Although one of its isotopes (thorium-232) can undergo FISSION, thorium is not currently used as a nuclear fuel.

thorn apple A plant, *Datura stramonium*, having long, pinkish, trumpet-shaped flowers and spiny fruit capsules. It is one of ten species of poisonous plants and shrubs of the genus *Datura*. They are related to the potato and occur widely in the tropics and warm temperate regions, especially the New World. Several American species are naturalized throughout the world and include the thorn apple. Some tropical species have large pendent flower trumpets and are called angel's trumpets or moon flowers (on account of their strong scent at night).

thornbill See WARBLER.

Thorndike, Dame (Agnes) Sybil (1882–1976) British actress. She gave notable performances in a wide range of Shakespearian and other roles; she was particularly memorable in the title part of the first London production of George Bernard Shaw's *St Joan* (1924). From the 1920s she appeared in a number of films, including *Nicholas Nickleby* (1947).

Thorvaldsen, Bertel (or **Thorwaldsen**) (*c*.1770–1844) Danish neoclassical sculptor. From 1797 he lived and worked chiefly in Rome, where he made his name with a statue of Jason (1803); other major works include the tomb of Pius VII at St Peter's in Rome (1824–31) and a monument to Byron in Trinity College, Cambridge (1829).

Thoth (or **Djehuty**) In Egyptian mythology, originally a Moon-god, depicted mostly as an ibis-headed man, but also as an ibis or squatting baboon, and in all cases wearing a Sun disc and Moon crescent on his head. Thoth was the scribe of the gods, recording their dictates, transmitting wisdom through writing, science, and mathematics, acting as impartial arbitrator in disputes, and recording the result of the Weighing of the Hearts ceremony performed before Osiris in the afterlife. As god of wisdom, he uttered words that sprang into life, thus animating the first beings.

Thrace (Greek **Thráki**) **▶1** An ancient country lying west of Istanbul and the Black Sea and north of the Aegean, now part of modern Turkey, Greece, and Bulgaria. It extended as far west as the Adriatic but the Thracians retreated eastwards between the 13th and 5th centuries BC under pressure from the Illyrians and Macedonians. Conquered by Philip II of Macedon in 342 BC it later became a province of Rome. The region was ruled by the Ottoman Turks from the 15th century until the end of World War I, but northern Thrace was annexed by Bulgaria in 1885. In 1923 all of Thrace east of the Maritsa River was restored to Turkey. **▶2** A region of modern Greece, in the north-east of the country; area 8,578 sq km (3,313 sq miles); pop. (1991) 337,530; capital, Komotiní.

Thrale, Mrs Hester Lynch (latterly **Piozzi**) (1741–1821) British writer. She and her husband became great friends of Dr Johnson, who lived for several years at their house in Streatham Place in London. Three years after her husband's death in 1781 she married the Italian musician Gabriel Piozzi amid much opposition from family and friends, especially Johnson, who ended their intimacy. Among her writings are her *Anecdotes of Dr Johnson* (1786), and a number of poems.

thrasher A member of the MOCKINGBIRD tribe, Minimi, of the family Sturnidae. There are 16 species in five genera. All live in the New World. Most species resemble rather short-winged, long-tailed thrushes. Their beaks are often curved, and are used to collect insects and seeds. They inhabit woodland and are essentially ground-feeders.

threadfin A mainly marine and brackish-water fish of the family Polynemidae, found in all tropical and subtropical seas; a few of the 35 species are found in rivers. They are distinguished by their two-part pectoral fins, each of which has long anterior rays separate from the main fin. Bottom-living, they feed on crustaceans and fishes; most are relatively small fishes but the Asiatic threadfin, *Eleutheronema tetradactylum*, grows to 1.8 m (6 feet).

Threadneedle Street A street in the City of London, England, containing the premises of the Bank of England (the Old Lady of Threadneedle Street). It is possibly named after a tavern with the arms of the Needlemakers.

thread snake Any of about 50 species of snake in the family Leptotyphlopidae, occurring in Africa, parts of Asia, and the New World. They are similar in external appearance and burrowing habits to BLIND SNAKES, but differ in having teeth only on the lower jaws. They are short (the family contains some of the shortest known snakes) and very slender, and feed mainly on termites.

threadworm See PINWORM.

Three Mile Island An island in the Susquehanna River near Harrisburg, Pennsylvania, USA, site of a nuclear power station. In 1979 an accident caused damage to uranium in the reactor core, an incident that provoked strong opposition to the expansion of the nuclear industry in the USA and precipitated a reassessment of safety standards.

thrips (or **thunder fly**) A very small insect belonging to the order Thysanoptera, most of the 3,000 species having narrow wings fringed with long hairs. Generally they are plant-feeders with sucking mouthparts. The females either have a delicate ovipositor, or a long cylindrical terminal segment to the abdomen, and no ovipositor. Wingless species live in the surface of soils, while the winged ones are abundant in flowers. Many species cause considerable damage and are important VECTORS of plant virus diseases.

thrombosis The formation of a blood clot (thrombus) within a blood vessel, commonly a deep leg vein, which is usually caused when venous circulation becomes static; predisposing factors include major surgery and immobility, obesity, injury, varicose veins, impaired blood clotting mechanisms, and pregnancy. There are often no local symptoms, although the calf may ache and become hot and red; in some cases, severe pain may occur. The thrombus may be transported to the lungs leading to blockage of a blood vessel (embolism) of the lungs. Thrombosis in superficial veins is characterized by local pain and redness; it does not result in embolism. Thrombosis in arteries supplying the brain is a common cause of STROKE; thrombosis in arteries supplying the heart (coronary arteries) causes CORONARY THROMBOSIS.

thrush A bird belonging to the family Turdidae, containing about 300 species of birds with worldwide distribution. Thrushes vary in size from species about the size of the European robin, 14 cm (5 inches), to those 32 cm (13 inches) in length. They include the BLUEBIRD, the NIGHTINGALE, the STONECHAT, and the WHEATEAR. They live in a wide variety of habitats from open desert to thick forest. Many are primarily insectivorous, though they also take berries and fruits.

The true thrushes belong to the subfamily Turdinae. These are mostly among the larger species of the family, such as the American robin, *Turdus migratorius*, and the European BLACKBIRD and SONG THRUSH. Many tend to be brownish or greyish above and heavily streaked below, though the large Himalayan whistling thrush, *Myiophoneus caeruleus*, is blackish with a bright blue gloss.

thrush (or **candidiasis**) A common fungal infection of the vagina and mouth, caused by *Candida albicans*. It produces red itching patches and often occurs when patients are receiving broad-spectrum antibiotics. It is treated effectively with antifungal drugs, such as nystatin.

Thucydides (*c*.455–*c*.400 BC) Greek historian. He is remembered for his *History of the Peloponnesian War*, an account of a conflict in which he fought on the Athenian side. The work covers events up to about 411 and presents an analysis of the origins and course of the war, based on painstaking inquiry into what actually happened and including the reconstruction of political speeches of such figures as Pericles, whom he greatly admired.

thug (from Hindi *thag*, 'swindler') A devotee of the Hindu goddess Kali, who was worshipped through ritual murder and sacrifice of travellers. The thuggee centre was in remote central India, where victims were strangled. Eradication of the brotherhoods was difficult because of the secrecy of the cult. It was largely suppressed in the 1830s by the detective skills of William Sleeman, appointed to the task by Lord William BENTINCK. Indians welcomed the intervention, and there has been no revival, but the term passed into the English language.

thulium (symbol Tm, at. no. 69, r.a.m. 168.934) A LANTHANIDE element discovered in 1879 by P. T. Cleve. It is the least abundant of the lanthanides, but the radioactive isotope Tm-169 is used in some X-ray equipment.

thunder The sound that accompanies the violent expansion of air when it is rapidly heated along the path of a LIGHTNING flash. The rumbling is caused by the time difference between the sounds originating from nearer and further parts of the flash. A thunderbolt occurs when the flash occurs so close to the place of observation that the sound seems simultaneous. There is no rumble, only a crack. Thunder is rarely heard more than 15 to 25 km (10 to 15 miles) from the lightning that causes it.

thunder fly See THRIPS.

thunderstorm A local storm accompanied by LIGHTNING and thunder and normally precipitation in the form of heavy rain or hail. The precondition for such storms is usually the formation of irregular, cellular groups of CUMULONIMBUS cloud, a fully developed cell being upwards of 1.5–8 km (1–5 miles) in diameter and 7,500 m (25,000 feet) in vertical extent. Each cell may generate thunder and lightning, together with precipitation, for 15 to 20 minutes, persistent thunderstorms resulting from the development of successive cells. Intensive squalls may be produced, and TORNADOES are also associated with thunderstorms in many parts of the world.

Thurber, James (Grover) (1894–1961) US humorist and cartoonist. In 1927 he began his long association with the *New Yorker* magazine, in which he published many of his essays, stories, and sketches. Among his many collections are *My Life and Hard Times* (1933) and *My World – and Welcome to It* (1942), which contains the story 'The Secret Life of Walter Mitty'.

Thuringia (German **Thüringen**) A densely forested state of the Federal Republic of Germany, lying to the north of the Ore Mountains; area 16,251 sq km (6,277 sq miles); pop. (1991) 2,572,070; capital, Erfurt. From 1946 to 1989 it formed part of East Germany.

thyme An aromatic plant of the Old World genus *Thymus*. They are members of the family Labiatae. A few are grown as culinary herbs and several more as ornamental plants. Garden thyme, *T. vulgare*, is a low, evergreen, bushy species from the mountain slopes of the western Mediterranean region, with strongly aromatic leaves. Lemon thyme, *T. citriodorus*, has a distinct but milder lemon scent. Variegated thymes with grey or golden leaves are grown for their decorative qualities, while creeping thymes, with red, pink, or white flowers, are cultivated as garden plants.

thymus gland An organ found at the base of the neck of vertebrates. Consisting mainly of lymphoid tissue similar to the spleen, tonsils, and LYMPH NODES, it enlarges from birth to puberty, shrinking gradually during adult life. It plays an important part in the development of an individual's IMMUNITY to foreign substances and tolerance of its own tissue components.

thyristor See SEMICONDUCTOR DEVICE.

thyroid gland An ENDOCRINE GLAND in the neck of vertebrates, containing two kinds of secreting tissue. Thyroxine, a hormone containing iodine, is secreted at a rate controlled by a PITUITARY GLAND hormone called thyrotrophin. It is required for the development and growth of the nervous system, and also increases heat production in most metabolizing tissues. Deficiencies in hormone output cause GOITRE, while excesses cause overheating and extreme restlessness. The second hormone, calcitonin, is secreted when blood calcium levels are higher than normal.

Tiahuanaco The ruins of a pre-Incan city in Bolivia, situated to the south of Lake Titicaca in the southern highlands of the Central Andes at an altitude of *c.*3,965 m (13,000 ft). The site is noted for its classic stone architecture and carving which includes the famous Gateway of the Sun, a huge monolith cut from a single block of andesite.

Tiananmen Square See BEIJING; CHINA.

Tianjin (formerly **Tientsin**) The third-largest city in China, a port on the Hai River; pop. (1990) 7,790,000. It is the leading port of northern China and a special economic zone producing iron, steel, chemicals, motor vehicles, carpets, machinery, and consumer goods such as bicycles and sewing machines. The city preserves much of its 19th-century colonial architecture.

Tianjin, Treaty of (1858) See OPIUM WARS.

Tian Shan (or **Tien Shan**) A mountain system stretching for 3,000 km (1,800 miles) across central Asia in Xinjiang, China, and Kyrgyzstan. It is bounded to the north by the plains of Dzungaria and south Kazakhstan and overlooks the great Tarim Basin to the south-east, part of the Alai range forming its south-western extremity. Relief is extreme: the highest peaks such as Pobedy at 7,439 m (24,406 feet) contrast with deep basins such as the Turfan Depression to the east, 154 m (505 feet) below sea-level. Glaciers fall from crest lines to valleys, the largest, Inylchek, extending for 60 km (37 miles) on the western slopes of the Khan–Tengri massif.

Tiber (Italian **Tevere**) A river of central Italy, upon which Rome stands, flowing 405 km (252 miles) westwards from the Tuscan Apennines to the Tyrrhenian Sea at Ostia.

Tiberias A resort town on the Sea of Galilee (**Lake Tiberias**), north-east Israel. Built *c.*20 AD, it was named after the Roman emperor Tiberius and following the destruction of Jerusalem in the 2nd century it became a leading Jewish centre of learning. It is noted for its hot springs and as the site where the Jewish Talmud was edited.

Tiberius (full name Tiberius Julius Caesar Augustus) (42 BC–37 AD) Roman emperor 14–37 AD. He was the adopted successor of his stepfather and father-in-law Augustus, under whom he had pursued a distinguished military career. As emperor he sought to continue his stepfather's policies but became increasingly tyrannical and his reign was marked by a growing number of treason trials and executions. In 26 he retired to Capri, never returning to Rome.

Tibet (Chinese **Xizang**) A mountainous region of Asia to the north of the Himalayas, occupying the highest plateau in the world with an average elevation of 4,000 m (13,123 ft), an autonomous region of China; area 1,228,000 sq km (474,314 sq miles); pop. (1990) 2,196,000; capital, Lhasa. Ruled by Buddhist lamas since the 7th century, Tibet was conquered by the Mongols in the 13th century and the Manchus in the 18th century China extended its authority over Tibet in 1951 but only gained full control after crushing a revolt in 1959 during which the country's spiritual leader, the Dalai Lama, made his escape into India. Many of Tibet's monasteries and shrines were destroyed in an unsuccessful attempt to change national culture and consciousness. Almost completely surrounded by mountain ranges, Tibet is the source of some of Asia's largest rivers including the Yangtze, Salween, and Mekong.

Tibetan The language of Tibet, spoken by about 2 million people there, a similar number in neighbouring provinces of China, and a million people in Nepal. It belongs to the Sino-Tibetan language group and is most closely related to Burmese. Its alphabet is based on that of Sanskrit and dates from the 7th century.

Tibetan Buddhism A distinctive form of MAHAYANA Buddhism found in Tibet. The predominant sect, the Yellow Hats, is headed by the DALAI LAMA, who is both a religious and political leader. Tibetan Buddhists revere the BODHISATTVA of Compassion, Avalokiteshvara, and they believe that each Dalai Lama is his REINCARNATION. Much of the ritual of Tibetan Buddhism is based on the esoteric tradition of TANTRA, as well as the ancient SHAMANISM of the earlier Bon religion of Tibet. Worship includes the recitation of MANTRAS and prayers, and the singing of hymns to the accompaniment of horns and drums. The Tibetan canon of scripture includes the *Kangur* and the *Tenjur* (further commentaries). The *Tibetan Book of the Dead* (*Bardo Thödröl*) describes consciousness between death and rebirth.

Tibeto-Burman languages See SINO-TIBETAN LANGUAGES.

tibia See LEG.

Tibullus, Albius (*c.*50–19 BC) Roman poet. He is known for his elegiac love poetry and for his celebration of peaceful rural life in preference to the harsh realities of military campaigning.

Tichborne claimant See ORTON.

tick An ARACHNID that, together with the MITES, makes up the order Acarina. Ticks, which are larger than mites, are entirely parasitic on vertebrates, though they attach to the host only when feeding. They have specialized, hooked mouthparts, and suck out the host's blood, adding an anticoagulant to stop it clotting. Their own body expands enormously as they feed. After feeding, ticks usually drop off the host, rest for a while, and moult. As much as a year may pass before they need another meal, when they climb up vegetation to find another passing host. Ticks mate on the host, and females deposit waxy egg-masses after they leave the host. The newly hatched, six-legged larvae must feed twice, often on different hosts, before they achieve maturity as adult ticks. In some areas ticks are important carriers of disease in livestock; the common SHEEP-TICK can cause serious disorders of sheep and cattle. Tick-borne diseases in humans include some forms of TYPHUS.

tidal bore A steep-fronted wave that occurs periodically in certain rivers and estuaries where the tidal range is particularly large. They are caused by constriction of the advancing flood or flood-tide as it enters a long, narrow, relatively shallow inlet. As water driven by this tide piles up against the flow of the river current, a large, turbulent wall-like wave of water is formed. The wave is travelling faster than waves may normally travel into such shallow water, and so is analogous to a 'sonic boom', which occurs when a pressure disturbance is forced to travel faster than the speed of sound. This solitary wave moves upstream at a speed of up to 16 km (10 miles) an hour. It gradually diminishes in height as it loses energy and eventually dies away, but this may be after many kilometres.

tidal energy The energy carried by the regular tidal movement of the sea. Tidal energy could in principle supply a significant amount of the world's energy needs, but economic factors limit its use to coastlines where the tidal range is particularly great. Of the many methods proposed for extracting tidal energy, only one has been widely used, whether for ancient tide-mills or modern POWER-STATIONS. The rising water enters an enclosed basin through sluices in a dam or barrage; the sluices are then closed, the sea-level outside falls and the captured water flows out, driving WATER WHEELS or WATER TURBINES. The tidal cycle of about 12.5 hours and the fortnightly cycle of maximum and minimum range (springs and neaps) pose a problem in maintaining a regular power supply, and have led to ideas for more complex systems – with several basins for instance, or using PUMPED STORAGE. The RANCE barrage and two smaller schemes in Russia and China are the only existing operational tidal power installations.

tide A regular rise and fall of the surface of the sea in response to the gravitational attraction of the Moon (also the Sun, but to a much lesser degree). This attraction causes the water of the oceans to bulge out slightly on that part of the Earth facing the Moon and on that part directly opposite; the daily rotation of the Earth through these bulges appears to us as a rise and fall in sea-level. The attraction is strongest when the Earth, Moon, and Sun are in line (at full or new Moon), a condition known as **syzygy**, giving **spring tides**; and weakest when they are at right angles, (during the Moon's first and last quarters), giving NEAP TIDES. The corresponding horizontal movement of water is a current, a **tidal stream**, which is usually semi-diurnal (two flood- and two ebb-tides in slightly more than a day) although diurnal tides occur in many places. Tidal ranges from mean sea-level also vary around the world.

Tien Shan See TIAN SHAN.

Tientsin See TIANJIN.

Tiepolo, Giovanni Battista (1696–1770) Italian painter. One of the leading artists of the Rococo style, he painted numerous frescos and altarpieces in Italy, Germany, and Spain, assisted on many commissions by his two sons. His painting is characterized by dramatic foreshortening, translucent colour, and settings of theatrical splendour. His works include the *Antony and Cleopatra* frescos in the Palazzo Labia, Venice (*c.*1750), and the decoration of the residence of the Prince-Bishop at Würzburg (1751–53). In 1762, at the request of Charles III, he moved to Madrid where he spent the rest of his life, working on the ceilings of the Royal Palace and the royal chapel at Aranjuez.

Tierra del Fuego An archipelago separated from the southern tip of South America by the Strait of Magellan and the name of its main island. Visited by Magellan in 1520, its name in Spanish meaning 'land of fire', it is now divided between Chile and Argentina.

Tiffany, Louis Comfort (1848–1933) US glass-maker and interior decorator. He was the son of Charles Louis Tiffany (1812–1902), who founded the New York jewellers Tiffany and Company. A leading exponent of American art nouveau, he established an interior decorating firm in New York in 1881 which produced stained glass and mosaic in a distinctive style, as well as iridescent glass vases and lamps.

Tiflis See TBLISI.

tiger The largest member of the CAT family. The single species, *Panthera tigris*, resembles the lion but lacks a mane and has a striped coat. This coat provides camouflage in the forests and dense underbush. Tigers can swim, taking readily to water, and can leap 4 m (15 feet) in one bound. Under cover of darkness, they hunt prey, which include deer, livestock, etc. There are eight subspecies, including the Indian or Bengal, Siberian, and Caucasian tigers.

tiger beetle A medium-sized, colourful BEETLE, with strong jaws, a member of the family Cicindelidae. The wing-covers are often metallic blues, reds, or greens. The larvae live in vertical burrows in the ground and have specialized mouthparts which resemble gin-traps. Both larvae and adults are ferocious predators and usually occur in dry habitats. There are 2,000 or so species throughout the warmer regions of the world.

tigerfish A large African CHARACIN that has a slender-body with a high, first dorsal fin and a separate adipose fin, and large silvery scales with a dusky line along each row. The teeth of tigerfishes are large and fang-like, forming a single row on each side of the mouth, and are visible when the jaws are closed. They are avid predators on smaller fishes and eat large numbers of practically all the active mid-water fishes in their habitats. Two species are widespread in Africa: the giant tigerfish, *Hydrocynus goliath*, which grows to 1.8 m (6 feet) and may attain 70 kg (154 pounds) in weight, and *H. vittatus* which grows to 1 m (3.25 feet) and is found in the Nile, Niger, Congo, and Zambezi rivers.

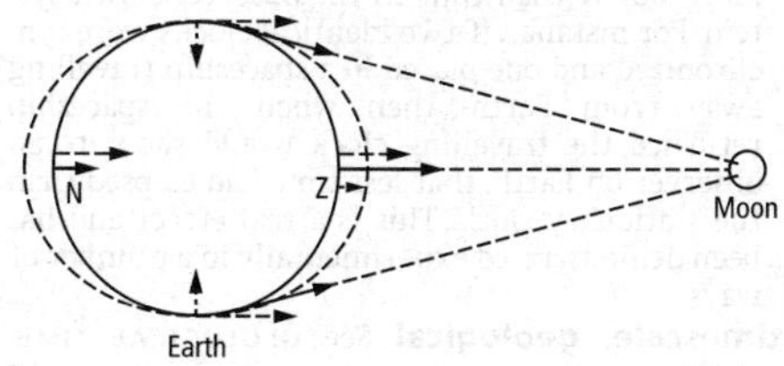

1

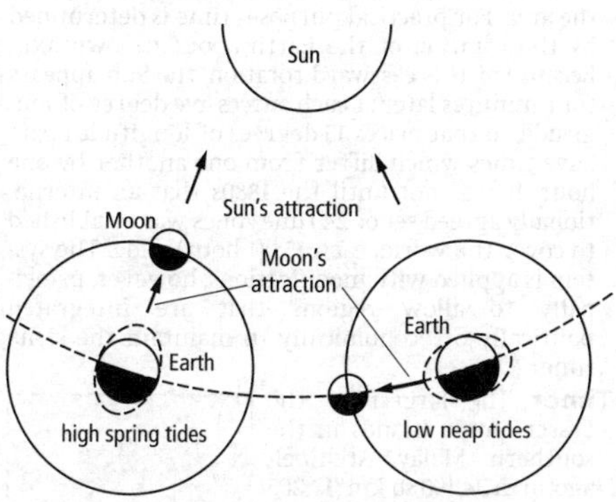

2

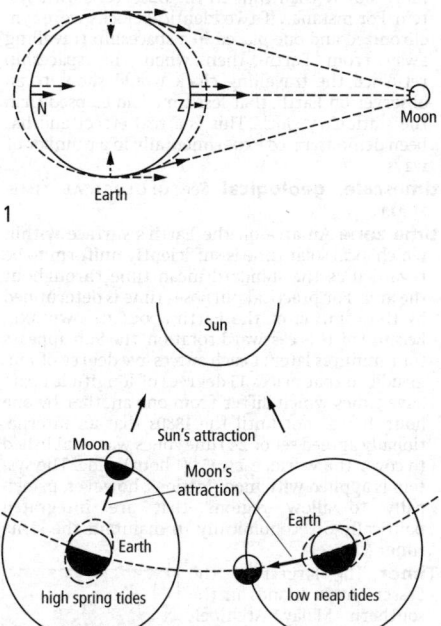

Tide (1) The resultant gravitational force between the Moon and various points on the Earth (solid lines) are shown as the vector sums of the tide-generating forces (broken lines) and a constant force that is the same at all points on the Earth and is created by the Moon's attraction on the Earth's centre. At the zenith Z, the resultant is greater than at the nadir N, because Z is closer to the Moon than N. (2) The Moon and the Sun act together to produce high spring tides but the attractive forces are at right angles when causing the low neap tides.

tiger moth A stout-bodied, brightly coloured, conspicuously patterned moth of the family Arctiidae, which is distributed worldwide and contains about 3,500 species. Many tiger moths are combinations of yellow, red, orange, black, and white. They are unpalatable or poisonous to predators, deriving some toxins from the food plants of the caterpillar and manufacturing others themselves. The garden tiger moth, *Arctia caja*, of Europe, Asia, and North America, has black and white fore-wings and blue-spotted, red hind-wings, which it displays if attacked. Its hairy caterpillars, often referred to as woolly-bears, feed on plants such as nettles, dandelions, and docks.

tiger snake A species of swamp-loving snake, *Notechis scutatus*, up to about 2 m (6.5 feet) in length, found in southern parts of Australia. Its coloration is variable, but it commonly possesses cream or yellow cross-bands. The tiger snake is highly venomous, and if threatened it flattens its neck and body and may strike aggressively. The African back-fanged snake, *Telescopus semiannulatus*, is also known as the tiger snake.

Tiglath-pileser Three kings of Assyria, notably Tiglath-pileser I and II. **Tiglath-pileser I** reigned *c.*1115–*c.*1077 BC. He extended Assyrian territory further into Asia Minor, taking Cappadocia and reaching Syria, as well as expanding his kingdom to the upper Euphrates and defeating the king of Babylonia. **Tiglath-pileser III** (known as Pulu) reigned *c.*745–727 BC. He brought the Assyrian empire to the height of its power, subduing large parts of Syria and Palestine, and, towards the end of his reign, conquering Babylonia and ascending the Babylonian throne under the name of Pulu.

Tigris The more easterly of the two rivers of Mesopotamia, 1,900 km (1,180 miles) long, rising in the mountains of eastern Turkey and flowing through Iraq to join the Euphrates, forming the Shatt al-Arab which flows into the Persian Gulf. The city of Baghdad lies upon it. Its waters have supplied large irrigated areas since earliest times.

tilapia An edible CICHLID fish, native to Africa, belonging to the genus *Tilapia* and related genera. They have been widely introduced to other parts of the tropics, where they are intensively farmed. All are freshwater fishes growing to a length of 25–30 cm (10–12 inches).

Tilbury A port on the north bank of the River Thames in Essex, the principal port of London and south-east England.

Tillich, Paul (Johannes) (1886–1965) German-born US theologian and philosopher. He proposed a form of Christian existentialism, outlining a reconciliation of religion and secular society, as expounded in *Systematic Theology* (1951–63).

Timbuktu (or **Tombouctou**) A town in the Gao region of northern Mali in West Africa, situated to the north of the River Niger; pop. (1976) 20,500.

Founded by the Tuareg in the 11th century, it became a centre of Muslim learning and as the southern end of a trans-Saharan caravan route and meeting place for the nomadic people of the Sahara, noted for its market in gold and slaves.

time The concept of the duration between events. Time may be measured astronomically either with reference to the stars or to the Sun. The former, called **sidereal time**, is conceptually simpler. Local sidereal time is defined with respect to the stars. For example, the sidereal DAY is essentially the time of one apparent revolution of the CELESTIAL SPHERE. More precisely, sidereal time is the hour angle of the vernal EQUINOX. The PRECESSION of the equinoxes, and sometimes NUTATION, are allowed for but these effects are very small, so that sidereal time is almost entirely dependent on the Earth's rotation.

Civil timekeeping is based on **solar time**, which is defined in terms of the position of the Sun in the sky. This depends both on the Earth's rotation and on its orbital motion. While the Earth's axial rotation appears uniform, its orbital motion is not, because its orbit is elliptical. A further complication arises because of the inclination of the Earth's equator to its orbit. For these reasons, the Sun itself is not a suitable point of reference for solar time. Instead, a fictitious body called the **mean Sun** is adopted, which moves above the equator at a uniform rate. The **mean solar time** is then defined with respect to the position of the mean Sun. It is the hour angle of the mean Sun plus 12 hours, so that 12.00 corresponds to noon. The mean solar time on the Greenwich Meridian is chosen as a world standard and is called **Universal Time** (UT) or GREENWICH MEAN TIME. Civil time used in different parts of the world generally differs from UT only by an exact number of hours or half-hours.

In 1952 a new time-scale was introduced called **Ephemeris Time** (ET). This is a modified solar time-scale correcting variations in the Earth's rotation rate. It is defined to correspond to the uniform time that occurs in the motion of the Solar System, and it is independent of the Earth's rotation. ET is used to predict the positions of the Sun, Moon, and planets, but it can be determined only with difficulty after observations of these bodies have been analysed. By contrast, UT is readily accessible, as it is directly related to sidereal time obtained from TRANSIT observations of the stars. At present ET is about 55 seconds ahead of UT.

Irregularities in the Earth's rotation rate can now be measured directly by timing transit observations with atomic clocks. Atomic time-scales have been available since 1956 and **International Atomic Time** (TAI) was introduced in 1972. This is the most precisely determined time-scale available. It is not an astronomical time-scale, as its basic unit, the SI second, is defined from atomic processes but in such a way that it does not differ significantly from the ephemeris second. It is conceivable that an astronomical time-scale, such as ET, might not be uniform compared with an atomic time-scale. This would involve a variation in the gravitational constant and, as yet, no such variation has been established. For practical purposes, the two time-scales are in step and ET = TAI + 32.18 seconds.

Recent theoretical developments in physics have brought about a revolution in our way of thinking about time. Most notably, whereas it had always been assumed that SPACE and time were separate dimensions, modern science now combines them into a single four-dimensional space–time continuum. Moreover, the idea that an interval of time has a definite duration, the same for all observers, is not accepted in relativity theory; intervals have to be defined in terms of SPACE also in order to pinpoint them in the space–time continuum. See also TIME DILATION.

time and tempo (in music) Musical time is the underlying pattern of beats in a piece of music, shown (in Western music) by means of two figures arranged one above the other. The upper figure indicates the number of beats in each bar, and the lower figure the type of beat. Thus 2/4 indicates a two-beat pattern of crotchet values, while 3/4 indicates a pattern of three such beats. These signs, called time signatures, are placed at the beginning of a piece of music and again wherever the metre changes. According to whether the beat itself can be divided into halves and quarters, or thirds and sixths, we speak of simple time and compound time. Tempo refers to the speed at which music is taken. This is usually indicated by standard Italian terms placed at the beginning of a piece of music, and again wherever the speed changes. They can be backed up by METRONOME marks indicating the number of beats per second.

time dilation The principle that intervals of time are not absolute but are relative to the motion of the observers. Time, in a moving system appears, to an observer who is standing still, to be passing more slowly than time in the observer's own system. For instance, if two identical clocks were synchronized and one placed in a spaceship travelling away from Earth, then when the spaceship returned the travelling clock would show, to an observer on Earth, that less time had elapsed than the stationary clock. This is a real effect and has been demonstrated experimentally in a number of ways.

timescale, geological See GEOLOGICAL TIMESCALE.

time zone An area on the Earth's surface within which local solar time is sufficiently uniform to be regarded as the standard mean time throughout the area. For practical purposes time is determined by the rotation of the Earth about its own axis. Because of this eastward rotation, the Sun appears four minutes later at each successive degree of longitude, so that places 15 degrees of longitude apart have times which differ from one another by one hour. It was not until the 1880s that an internationally agreed set of 24 time zones was established to cover the world, each 15° (1 hour) wide. The system is applied with modifications, however, principally to allow regions that are integrated politically or economically to maintain the same time.

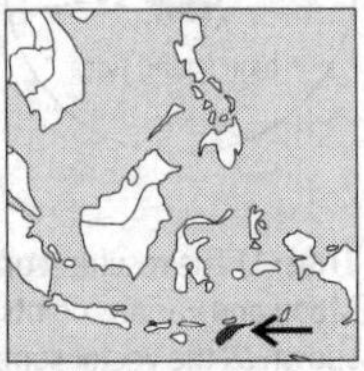

Timor The largest of the Lesser Sunda Islands in the southern Malay Archipelago; area 34,190 sq km (13,205 sq miles). The island was formerly divided into Dutch **West Timor** and Portuguese **East Timor**. In 1950 West Timor was absorbed into the newly formed Republic of Indonesia, becoming part of the province of Nusa Tenggara Timur (chief town, Kupang). In 1975 East Timor briefly declared itself independent from Portugal but was invaded and occupied by Indonesia. In 1976, against the wishes of the inhabitants, Indonesia formally annexed East Timor and administered it as the province of Timur Timur or Loro Sae (chief town, Dilí); area 14,874 sq km (5,745 sq miles); pop. (est. 1993) 808,300. A number of anti-Indonesian resistance movements continue to fight for independence.

Timor Sea The part of the Indian Ocean between Timor and north-west Australia.

Timothy, St (1st century AD) In the New Testament, Paul's companion and 'son in the faith'. The son of Eunice, a Judean Christian, Timothy was found in Lystra by Paul, circumcized to placate the Jews, and left in charge of the church in Ephesus. Said to have been killed in a riot after denouncing the worship of Artemis, Timothy became a Christian saint and martyr. Feast Day, 22 or 26 January.

timothy grass A strong-growing European grass species, *Phleum pratense*. It is a valuable perennial meadow plant for grazing and hay production, and consequently has been distributed widely as a cultivated plant.

timpani The orchestral and military kettledrums, introduced to Europe from Turkey via Hungary in the late 15th century. Originally played in pairs on horseback, two remained the normal number when they came into the orchestra, as a bass to the trumpets, in around 1600. A third was added in the 19th century, and four are now normal. Timpani are the only orchestral drums that are tuned to definite pitches, formerly by various types of hand-turned screws, now by a pedal so that players can tune while playing.

Timur See TAMERLANE.

tin (symbol Sn, at. no. 50, r.a.m. 118.69) A metal in Group 14 (formerly IVB) of the PERIODIC TABLE, which occurs as three ALLOTROPES. The ordinary 'white tin', β-Sn, is malleable and ductile, and when a bar of tin is bent, a distinctive 'tin cry' is heard as the crystal structure breaks. Below 13°C (55°F) 'grey tin', α-Sn, is the stable form, but the change from white tin into grey tin takes place only at much lower temperatures unless some grey tin is already present. When the change does occur the tin crumbles into a powder, and this is called 'tin plague' or 'tin pest'. The presence of impurities in commercial tin normally prevents this happening. Above 161°C (342°F), it exists as the brittle γ-Sn. The major ORE is cassiterite, SnO_2, which after some initial purification is reduced by SMELTING with carbon to form the metal. Tin is refined by reheating to melting-point in a furnace with an inclined hearth; the purer tin flows down the slope, leaving impurities in the dross. It can be further purified by ELECTROLYSIS. The main use of tin is in the production of tin plate. Tin plate is used in the manufacture of a wide variety of cans and utensils, although many of these are now made from aluminium. Most tin plate is now produced by electroplating, which requires less tin than the original process of dipping the sheet in molten metal, and gives a better coating. Tin is also used in the production of various alloys, such as solder, BRONZE, and type metal. Some alloys with niobium exhibit SUPERCONDUCTIVITY. Tin compounds are used in the manufacture of opaque glasses and enamels, and as MORDANTS in dyeing. Tin(II) fluoride (SnF_2) is the additive in fluoride toothpastes, Tin(II) chloride, $SnCl_2$, the most important compound, is used as a reducing agent and as a mordant in dyeing. Chemically, tin exhibits valencies of 2 and 4. It resists attack by water but is dissolved by strong acids and alkalis.

tinamou A bird belonging to the family Tinamidae, which contains 47 species found in South and Central America. Varying from quail- to chicken-size, tinamous look rather like gamebirds, but are not closely related to them. They are well camouflaged in greys and browns, usually barred or spotted, and have powerful legs and very short tails. They live on the ground in forests or in bushy grassland feeding mainly on vegetable matter, though they also eat some insects. Their flight is very poor, which may be caused by the small size of their heart and lungs.

Tinbergen, Jan (1903–94) Dutch economist. In 1969 he shared with Ragnar Frisch the first Nobel Prize for economics, awarded for his pioneering work on econometrics. He was the brother of the zoologist Niko Tinbergen.

Tinbergen, Niko(laas) (1907–88) Dutch ethologist. He studied many aspects of animal BEHAVIOUR including COURTSHIP and mating behaviour, CAMOUFLAGE and LEARNING. One of his major discoveries was that males use menacing gestures to avoid physical conflict and injury. He believed that by analysing animal behaviour, human behaviour could be better understood. In 1973 he was awarded the Nobel Prize for physiology and medicine with LORENZ and von FRISCH.

tinea See RINGWORM.

tinnitus See MÉNIÈRE'S DISEASE.

Tin Pan Alley Originally a district of New York City (28th Street, between 5th Avenue and Broadway) where many songwriters, arrangers, and music publishers were based. The district gave its name to the American popular music industry between the late 1880s and the mid-20th century, particularly to such composers as Irving Berlin, Jerome Kern, George Gershwin, Cole Porter, and Richard Rogers. Denmark Street in London is also sometimes called Tin Pan Alley.

Tintagel A village on the coast of northern Cornwall, with ruins of a castle that was a stronghold of the Earls of Cornwall from *c.*1145 until the 15th century It is the traditional birthplace of King Arthur.

Tintern Abbey A ruined 12th-century Cistercian abbey on the River Wye near Chepstow in Monmouthshire, south-east Wales, immortalized in a poem written by William Wordsworth in 1798.

Tintoretto (born Jacopo Robusti) (1518–94) Italian painter. He acquired his name because his father was a dyer (Italian *tintore*). Based in Venice, Tintoretto gained fame with the painting *St Mark Rescuing a Slave* (1548), whose bright colours were influenced by Titian. From this time, his work was typified by a mannerist style, including unusual viewpoints, striking juxtapositions in scale, and bold chiaroscuro effects. Primarily a religious painter, he is best known for the huge canvas *Paradiso* (1588–90) in the main hall of the Doges' Palace in Venice, and for his paintings of the life of the Virgin, the life of Christ, and the Passion (1565–87) in the halls of the Scuola di San Rocco, also in Venice.

Tipperary A county of central Ireland, in the province of Munster; divided into North and South Ridings whose administrative centres are at Nenagh and Clonmel; area 4,254 sq km (1,643 sq miles); pop. (1991) 133,620.

Tippett, Sir Michael (Kemp) (1905–97) British composer. He established his reputation with the oratorio *A Child of Our Time* (1941), which drew on jazz, madrigals, and spirituals besides classical sources. He is also noted for five operas, for all of which he also wrote the libretti; these include *The Midsummer Marriage* (1955). Among his other works are the oratorio *The Mask of Time* (1983), four symphonies, and several song cycles.

Tirana (Albanian **Tiranë**) The capital of Albania, situated on the Ishm River in central Albania; pop. (1990) 244,200. Founded by the Turks in the 17th century, it became capital of Albania in 1920. Laid out by Italian architects before World War II, it has been greatly expanded under Communist rule since 1946 with light industries and a hydroelectric power-station.

Tirol See TYROL.

Tirpitz, Alfred von (1849–1930) German grand-admiral. As Secretary of State for the Navy (1897–1916) his first Navy Bill in 1898 began the expansion of the German navy and led to the naval race with Britain. In 1907 he began a large programme of DREADNOUGHT-class battleship construction. During World War I he made full use of submarines, but following the sinking of the LUSITANIA (1915), unrestricted submarine warfare was temporarily abandoned. The policy was resumed in 1917, resulting in US entry into the war.

Tissot, James (1836–1902) French painter and etcher. He achieved success with his scenes of contemporary life, in both Paris and London, where he lived from 1871 to 1882. In 1885 he underwent a religious conversion after going into a church to 'catch the atmosphere for a picture', and thereafter he devoted himself to religious subjects, his biblical illustrations proving enormously popular.

tissue A group of CELLS and associated nerves and blood vessels which perform a particular function. Together tissues make up a living creature. For example, in vertebrates, skin, muscles, and bones are all tissues making up a limb. The extent to which any tissue will grow is determined both genetically and as the result of environmental influences.

tit A bird that makes up three separate families. The first is the Aegithalidae (the long-tailed tits and bushtits), a family of very small, longish-tailed birds, which occur in Europe, Asia, and North and Central America. The largest are only about 14 cm (5.5 inches) long, of which more than half is tail; they weigh about 6 – 8 g (0.2 – 0.3 ounce). Most are black, grey, brown, and white, although the common long-tailed tit, *Aegithalos caudatus*, has pink in its plumage. They are primarily insectivorous.

The family Remizidae (the penduline tits) contains 12 species, four of which are found only in Africa and one, the verdin, *Auriparus flaviceps*, in North and Central America. They are only slightly larger than the long-tailed tits, mostly dull greenish or greyish in colour.

The third family is the Paridae, the true tits or chickadees, a group of about 65 species with a worldwide distribution except for Australia and South America. Most are small, less than 14 cm (5.5 inches) long, and brown, grey, and white (some have blue and yellow markings), often with a white-cheeked pattern on the head; a few have crests. Agile, active birds, some are common in gardens at bird-feeders. They eat insects in the summer, but will eat seeds in winter.

Titan The largest satellite of Saturn, discovered by the Dutch astronomer Christian Huygens in 1665. The diameter of its solid body is 5,150 km, slightly smaller than that of GANYMEDE, but Titan also has an impenetrable atmosphere 200 km thick. The surface pressure is about 1.5 times that of the Earth's and the temperature is about 94 K. Methane, ethane, and argon are the main atmospheric constituents. The mean density of Titan is 1,880 kg/m^3 indicating the presence of a rocky core surrounded by an icy mantle.

Titania A satellite of Uranus, discovered by William HERSCHEL in 1787. It has a nearly circular equatorial orbit about Uranus at 435,910 km from the planet's centre. It is about 1,600 km in diameter and its density of 1,600 kg/m^3 suggests that the interior contains a mixture of ice and rock. Photographed by VOYAGER 2, its icy surface shows many small craters, a few large impact basins, and an extensive network of faults up to 5 km deep.

titanium (symbol Ti, at. no. 22, r.a.m. 47.90) A commonly occurring TRANSITION METAL that occurs naturally in rutile, TiO_2, and in ilmenite, $FeTiO_3$, as well as in much organic matter. It is present in meteorites and in the Sun, and the rock obtained by the Apollo 11 lunar mission contained up to 12 per cent of the metal. It has a high melting-point and is resistant to corrosion. Titanium alloys are used extensively in aerospace technology and other applications requiring lightness and high strength. Titanium is also used for HIP REPLACEMENTS as it is not attacked by body fluids. Titanium dioxide is a white solid used as a pigment in PAINT, and as a filler in paper, soap, and rubber. Titanium nitride is used to form a hard coating on steel cutting tools.

Titans In Greek mythology, six sons and six daughters of Uranus (Heaven) and Gaia (Earth); they were the older generation of gods who were overthrown by the Olympian gods, led by Zeus. Some of their children (notably Atlas and Prometheus) were also regarded as Titans.

tithe (Old English, 'tenth') A payment made by parishioners for the maintenance of the church and the support of its clergy. Levied by the early Hebrews and common in Europe after the synods of Tours (567) and Mâcon (585), tithes were enforced by law in England from the 10th century. They were divided into three categories – praedial (one-tenth of the produce of the soil), personal (one-tenth of the profits of labour and industry), and mixed (a combination of the produce of animals and labour). They were abolished finally in England in 1936.

Titian (born Tiziano Vecellio) (*c.*1488–1576) Italian painter. The most important painter of the Venetian school, he was first a pupil of Bellini, and completed a number of Gorgione's unfinished paintings after his death in 1510. Titian subsequently experimented with vivid colours; his *Madonna with Saints and Members of the Pesaro Family* (1519–*c.*1528) was innovative in not having the Madonna in the centre of the picture. He also painted many sensual mythological works, including *Bacchus and Ariadne* (*c.*1522–23). His portraits were notable for the characterization of their sitters; he was appointed court painter by the Holy Roman emperor Charles V in 1533.

Titicaca, Lake A lake in the Andes of South America, straddling the frontier between Peru and Bolivia. At an altitude of 3,809 m (12,497 ft), it is the highest large navigable lake in the world; area 8,288 sq km (3,200 sq miles).

Tito (born Josip Broz) (1892–1980) Yugoslav Marshal and statesman, Prime Minister 1945–53 and President 1953–80. Born in Croatia, he served in the Austro-Hungarian army during World War I and was captured by the Russians in 1915. After escaping, he fought with the Bolsheviks in the Russian Revolution and became an active Communist organizer on returning to his country in 1920. Tito responded to the German invasion of Yugoslavia (1941) by organizing a Communist resistance movement using guerrilla tactics. His success in resisting the Germans earned him Allied support and he emerged as head of the new government at the end of the war. Tito defied Stalin over policy in the Balkans in 1948, proceeding to establish Yugoslavia as a non-aligned Communist state with a federal constitution. He was made President for life in 1974.

Titograd The name of PODGORICA from 1948 until 1992.

Titus (full name Titus Vespasianus Augustus; born Titus Flavius Vespasianus) (39–81 AD) Roman emperor 79–81, son of Vespasian. In 70 he ended a revolt in Judaea with the conquest of Jerusalem. Titus also helped to complete the Colosseum and provided relief for the survivors of the eruption of Vesuvius in 79.

Titus, St (1st century AD) Greek churchman. A convert and helper of St Paul, he was traditionally the first bishop of Crete. Feast day (in the Eastern Church) 23 August; (in the Western Church) 6 February.

Tivoli A city of Latium near Rome in central Italy, noted for its waterfalls formed on the Aniene River and for its villas which include the Villa of Hadrian, the Villa Gregoriana, and the Villa d'Este; pop. (1990) 55,030.

TNT (2,4,6-trinitrotoluene) An important high EXPLOSIVE, discovered by J. Wilbrand in 1863. It is a yellow, crystalline solid with a low melting-point. TNT has low shock sensitivity and even burns without exploding. This makes it easy and safe to handle and cast. However, once detonated, it explodes violently. It is manufactured by treating toluene (obtained from petroleum) with a mixture of concentrated nitric and sulphuric acids.

toad An AMPHIBIAN of the order Anura, especially one belonging to the genus *Bufo* (true toads). These toads have stout bodies, short limbs, and a dry, warty skin. They are found in all continents of the world with the exception of Antarctica. Among the better-known species are the common toad, *B. bufo*, the natterjack toad, *B. calamita*, and the giant or marine toad, *B. marinus*, introduced into Australia to control the cane beetle, an agricultural pest which attacks sugar-cane.

Toads of other genera include the MIDWIFE TOAD, the SPADEFOOT TOADS, the SURINAM TOAD, and the MEXICAN BURROWING TOAD.

toadfish A member of the family Batrachoididae, which contains about 50 species of mainly marine fishes occurring in shallow tropical seas. They are blunt-headed fishes with a large mouth, and two dorsal fins, the first of which has two or three sharp spines (in some species these spines are hollow and have venom glands). Most toadfishes are dull coloured but a few are brightly marked. Some are capable of making loud noises underwater.

toadstool The spore-bearing structure or fruiting body of certain FUNGI belonging to the basidiomycete order Agaricales. A toadstool, like a mushroom, has a stalk and a cap, on the underside of which are the spore-producing gills or pores. There is no biological difference between mushrooms and toadstools, but inedible or poisonous fungi are usually called toadstools.

tobacco An annual or short-lived perennial plant, *Nicotiana tabacum*, which produces a spiral of large leaves on a stout stem about 2 m (6.5 feet) tall. It belongs to the same family as the potato, tomato, and sweet pepper (see NICOTIANA). Native to tropical America, it is now cultivated throughout the world, with the USA being the largest producer. Tobacco plants may be harvested whole, or individual leaves may be picked as they mature. The leaves are then air-, fire-, or flue-cured. After curing, the leaves must be held for a time in humid conditions before they can be further processed. During this fermentation process the aroma develops and levels of the drug nicotine decrease. Cured leaves are used in the manufacture of cigars, cigarettes, pipe tobacco, and snuff. One other species of *Nicotiana* is cultivated for its high nicotine content (up to 9 per cent of the leaf), which is extracted for use as an INSECTICIDE, though its toxicity is a severe disadvantage.

Tobacco smoke, particularly from cigarettes, is a direct cause of lung and other cancers, and SMOKING is the single most important avoidable cause of cancer in humans.

tobacco hornworm See HAWKMOTH.

tobacco mosaic virus A virus that attacks tobacco and other plants of the family Solanaceae, causing dead patches on their leaves. It is typical of the many viruses that attack plants in that it contains only RNA as its chromosomal material. The viral particles of tobacco mosaic virus are rod-like and can be transmitted by insects which feed on infected plants.

Tobago See TRINIDAD AND TOBAGO.

Tobruk (Arabic **Tubruq**) A port on the Mediterranean coast of north-east Libya; pop. (1984) 94,000. Tobruk was the scene of fierce fighting during the North African campaign in World War II. It was captured by the Germans in June 1942 and recaptured by the British in November 1942.

Todd, Mark James (1956–) New Zealand equestrian. He won individual gold medals for three-day eventing in the Olympic Games of 1984 and 1988, and was ranked number one in the world in 1984, 1988, and 1989.

Todd River A river of central Australia that rises in the Macdonnell Ranges and flows 320 km (200 miles) south-eastwards through Alice Springs to the Simpson Desert. It flows only in wet years and its dry bed is the scene of the occasional 'Henley-on-Todd Regatta' in which boats are carried by runners.

tody A bird belonging to the family Todidae, containing five species of the genus *Todus*, found only on Caribbean islands. Small birds, about 10 cm (4 inches) long, they are brilliant green above, and pale greyish or white below with a red chin patch. The Jamaican tody, *Todus todus*, is also referred to as the robin redbreast by locals. They live in wooded country, making sallies from perches to catch flying insects. They nest in holes in banks and lay two to five white eggs.

Togo A West African country lying between Ghana and Benin.

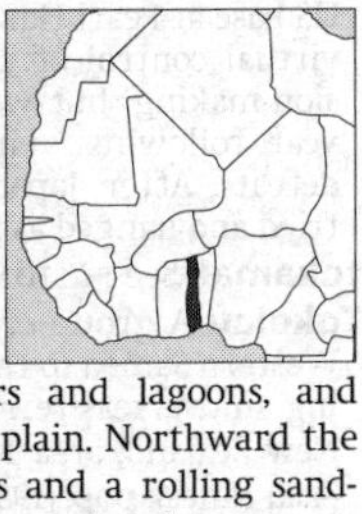

Physical. Togo has a southern coastline on the Gulf of Guinea of only 56 km (35 miles) but extends inland for over 560 km (350 miles) to Burkina Faso. The tropical coast has sand-bars and lagoons, and inland there is a fertile clay plain. Northward the land rises to low mountains and a rolling sandstone plateau, where it is drier and cooler.

Economy. Drought and falling world commodity prices have affected the economy adversely and loss of income has been exacerbated by a high foreign debt. Agricultural crops for export include cocoa, coffee, and cotton, and staple crops include cassava, maize, and sorghum. Livestock-raising is also of importance. Mining includes phosphates (the principal export), salt, and marble, while industry concentrates on food-processing and cement production. There are also reserves of bauxite and iron ore.

History. Togo's earliest known inhabitants were Gur-speaking Voltaic peoples in the north and Kwa peoples in the south. The Ewé immigrated during the 14th–16th centuries and the Ane (Mina) entered the region in the 17th century. Part of Togo's slave coast was controlled by Denmark during the 18th century and the area formed a buffer zone between the Ashanti and DAHOMEY kingdoms. Annexed by Germany in 1884 as a colony, Togoland was mandated between France and Britain after World War I. The western British section joined GHANA on the latter's independence in 1957, and became known as the Volta region. The remainder of the area became a UN mandate under French administration after World War II and achieved independence, as Togo, in 1960. After two civilian regimes were overthrown in 1963 and 1967, Togo achieved stability under President Gnassingbe Eyadema, who in 1979 was elected executive President, as the sole candidate, and re-elected in 1986. Following violent demonstrations early in 1991, he agreed to legalize political parties. The situation, however, deteriorated, with troops loyal to Eyadema taking the Prime Minister hostage. There was some fighting and further deterioration during 1992, as plans were made for a new constitution and elections. In 1993, Eyadema won the country's first multi-party presidential elections. In the following year, the ruling and opposition parties formed a coalition government. Early in 1994, fighting around the capital, Lomé, left 58 people dead; Togo's relations with Ghana, which was blamed for harbouring insurgents, worsened as a result.

Capital: Lomé
Area: 56,785 sq km (21,925 sq mi)
Population: 4,138,000 (1995)
Currency: 1 CFA franc = 100 centimes
Religions: Traditional beliefs 58.8%; Roman Catholic 21.5%; Muslim 12.0%; Protestant 6.8%
Ethnic Groups: Ewé-Adja 43.1%; Tem-Kabre 26.7%; Gurma 5.0%; Kebu-Akposo 3.8%; Ana-Ife (Yoruba) 3.2%; non-African 0.3%
Languages: French (official); Ewé; Kabre; local languages
International Organizations: UN; OAU; ECOWAS; Franc Zone

Tojo, Hideki (1884–1948) Japanese military leader and statesman, Prime Minister 1941–44. By 1937 he had risen to Chief of Staff of the Japanese army of occupation in Manchuria, and was appointed Minister of War in 1940. Shortly after becoming Premier in 1941 he initiated the Japanese attack on the US base at Pearl Harbor. By 1944 Tojo had assumed virtual control of all political and military decision-making, but was forced to resign later that year following a number of Japanese military defeats. After Japan's surrender in 1945 he was tried and hanged as a war criminal.

tokamak See FUSION, NUCLEAR.

Tokelau A group of islands between Kiribati and Western Samoa in the western Pacific Ocean, forming an overseas territory of New Zealand; area 10 sq km (4 sq miles); pop. (1986) 1,690. Chief settlement, Nukunonu. It comprises the three low-lying atoll islands of Atafu, Nukunonu, and Fakaofo. Formerly part of the Gilbert and Ellice Colony, the group was transferred to New Zealand administration in 1926, incorporated as part of New Zealand in 1949, and named Tokelau in 1976.

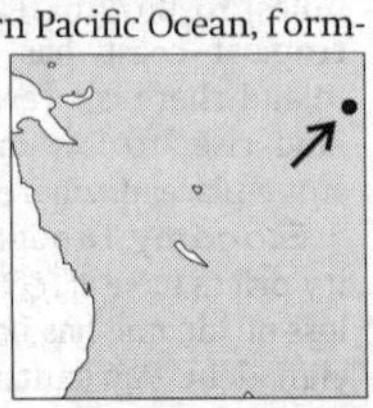

Tokugawa The last Japanese SHOGUNATE (1603–1867). Tokugawa Ieyasu, its founder, ensured supremacy by imposing severe restrictions on the daimyo (feudal lords). To avoid the effects of European intrusion, Christianity was proscribed in 1641 after the suppression of the Christian Shimabara rebellion and all foreigners except a few Dutch and Chinese traders at Nagasaki were excluded. Japanese were forbidden to go overseas. Interest in European science and medicine increased during the rule of Tokugawa Yoshimune.

There followed 250 years of almost unbroken peace and economic growth. An economy based largely on barter became a money economy. An influential merchant class emerged whilst some daimyo and their SAMURAI were impoverished; some married into commercial families. The shogunate was faced with growing financial difficulties but under its rule educational standards improved dramatically.

Tokyo The capital of Japan, situated on the Kanto plain, east-central Honshu Island; pop. (1990) 8,163,000. The city was formerly called Edo and was the centre of the military government under the Shoguns; it was renamed Tokyo in 1868 when it became the imperial capital. One of the largest cities in the world, it is the centre of government, commerce, and industry in Japan. It was devastated by an earthquake in 1923 and by bombing during World War II; its chief landmarks are the Imperial Palace and adjoining gardens, and Buddhist temples and shrines. Tokyo is also Japan's leading educational centre with over 100 universities and colleges, numerous museums, libraries, and art galleries. It has diverse heavy and light industries.

Toledo An ancient city of Toledo province in the Castilla-La Mancha region, central Spain, situated on the River Tagus; pop. (1991) 63,560. It was the Spanish capital 1087–1560, and was long famous for the manufacture of finely-tempered sword-blades.

Toleration Act (1689) The granting by the English Parliament of freedom of worship to dissenting Protestants, who could not accept the authority or teaching of the Anglican Church. Dissenters were allowed their own ministers, teachers, and places of worship subject to their taking oaths of allegiance and to their acceptance of most of the THIRTY-NINE ARTICLES. The TEST ACTS, which deprived dissenters of public office remained, but from 1727 annual indemnity acts allowed them to hold local offices. Roman Catholics were excluded from the scope of the Act, and had to rely on failure to enforce the penal laws.

Tolkien, J(ohn) R(onald) R(euel) (1892–1973) British novelist and academic, born in South Africa. Professor of Anglo-Saxon and later of English language and literature at Oxford University, Tolkien is famous for the fantasy adventures *The Hobbit* (1937) and *The Lord of the Rings* (1954–55), in which an imaginary land (Middle Earth) is peopled by hobbits and other mythical beings. *The Silmarillion*, an account of the mythology and early history of Middle Earth, was published posthumously (1977).

Tolpuddle A village in Dorset, England, made famous by the **Tolpuddle Martyrs**, six farm labourers who attempted to form a union to obtain an increase in wages and were sentenced in 1834 to seven years' transportation on a charge of administering unlawful oaths. Their harsh sentences caused widespread protests, and two years later they were pardoned and repatriated from Australia.

Tolstoy, Leo (Russian name Count Lev Nikolaevich Tolstoi) (1828–1910) Russian writer. He is best known for the novels *War and Peace* (1863–69) and *Anna Karenina* (1873–77). The former is an epic tale of the Napoleonic invasion and the lives of three aristocratic families; the latter describes a married woman's passion for a young officer and her tragic fate. Tolstoy subsequently espoused a moral code based on love of humankind, renouncing property, and repudiating organized religion, for which he was excommunicated by the Russian Orthodox Church in 1901.

Toltec A Nahuatl-speaking people who dominated central Mexico *c*.900–1200. They were a warrior aristocracy, whose period of domination was violent and innovative. The Toltec founded or developed cities (their capital was Tula), but were unable to consolidate their hold on the conquered area, which developed into a number of states, mostly independent. In the 12th–13th centuries famine and drought (perhaps caused by climatic changes) brought catastrophe, and the disunited area fell to invading tribes from the north.

Toluca (in full **Toluca de Lerdo**) A commercial and industrial city on the central plateau of Mexico, capital of the state of Mexico; pop. (1990) 487,630. It lies at the foot of the extinct volcano Nevado de Toluca and at 2,680 m (8,793 ft) is the highest of Mexico's state capitals. Founded in 1530 by Hernan Cortés, its Indian market is said to be the largest in Mexico. It has car, machinery-making, and food-processing industries.

toluene (or **methylbenzene**, $C_6H_5CH_3$) An aromatic, flammable liquid hydrocarbon consisting of a methyl group bonded to a BENZENE RING. It is obtained from petroleum and used as a solvent. Nitrating toluene yields TNT, widely used as an explosive.

tomato An annual plant with weak, trailing stems. Tomatoes arose from the species *Lycopersicon esculentum* in tropical Central and South America. They belong to the family Solanaceae, along with potato, tobacco, sweet pepper, and aubergine. Grown for the round or egg-shaped, red or yellow, smooth-skinned fruits, a wide range of types have been produced and cultivated. Tomatoes are grown throughout the warmer areas of the world, or in heated glasshouses in cool temperate regions.

Tombaugh, Clyde William (1906–97) US astronomer. His chief interest was in the search for undiscovered planets, which he carried out mainly at the Lowell Observatory in Arizona. His extensive examination of photographic plates led to his discovery of the planet Pluto in 1930. Tombaugh subsequently discovered numerous asteroids.

Tombouctou See TIMBUKTU.

tomography In diagnostic RADIOLOGY, a technique that produces a sharp image of a layer within the body while deliberately blurring structures at other depths. In the original device (1921), the effect was achieved by mounting the X-ray tube and a photographic plate at opposite ends of a lever, thus showing the body structures in one plane. In COMPUTERIZED TOMOGRAPHY, POSITRON EMISSION TOMOGRAPHY, and certain applications of ULTRASOUND, a similar effect is created by electronic and software techniques rather than by photomechanical means.

Tompion, Thomas (*c*.1639–1713) English clock and watchmaker. He made one of the first balance-spring watches to the design of Robert Hooke, and for the Royal Greenwich Observatory he made two large pendulum clocks, which needed winding only once a year. Tompion also collaborated with Edward Barlow (1636–1716) in patenting the horizontal-wheel cylinder escapement needed to produce flat watches.

Tomsk An industrial city, river port and educational centre of Russia on the River Tom in west-central Siberia; pop. (1990) 506,000. It produces machine tools, electrical equipment, machinery, timber, and chemicals.

tonality The relationship in music between PITCHES, with particular reference to those pitches that govern the relationship of all the other notes of a major or minor SCALE. Music written in accordance with the principles of tonality (Western music of, roughly, 1600–1900) assumes three such notes: a tonic (or 'key note'), a dominant, five degrees above it, and a subdominant, five degrees below. In the KEY of C major these would be C, G, and F. These notes govern the cycle of keys that form the basis of the tonal system. ATONALITY denies the necessity for key-relationships of this kind.

Tone, (Theobald) Wolfe (1763–98) Irish nationalist. In 1791 he helped found the Society of United Irishmen, which lobbied for parliamentary reform. In 1794 he went to France to induce a French invasion of Ireland to overthrow English rule. The invasion failed, and during the Irish insurrection in 1798 Tone obtained only limited French support. He was captured by the British and committed suicide in prison.

tone-poem See SYMPHONIC POEM.

Tonga (or **Friendly Islands**) An island country bordering the Tonga Trench in the South Pacific Ocean.

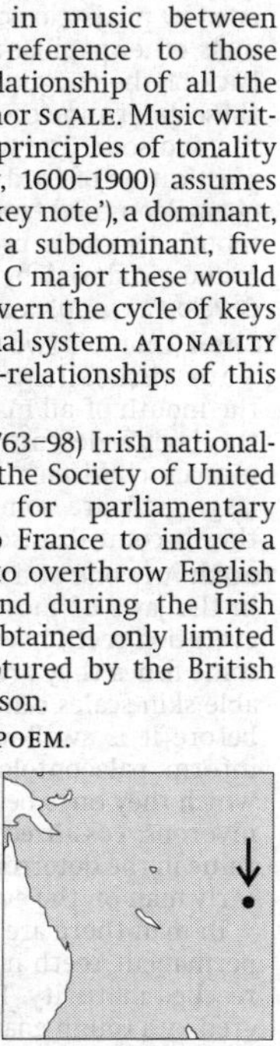

Physical. Tonga comprises over 150 islands, most of them too small for habitation and even the largest, Tongatapu, measuring a mere 40 km (25 miles) by 16 km (10 miles). Some are coral and some volcanic, with active craters.

Economy. Oil has been discovered, the only other natural resource being a fertile soil, used for the cultivation of coconuts and bananas.

History. Austronesian-speaking peoples inhabited the islands from at least 1000 BC. By the 13th century Tongans ruled islands as far flung as Hawaii. Named the Friendly Islands by Captain James Cook, who visited them in 1773, the country was soon receiving missionaries. King George Tupou I (1845–93) unified the nation and gave it a constitution. In 1900 his son signed a treaty, making the islands a self-governing British protectorate. During World War II Queen Sālote Tupou III (1900–65) placed the island's resources at the disposal of the Allies; she was succeeded by her son, Taufa'ahau Tupou IV, in 1965. In 1968 British controls were reduced, and in 1970 Tonga became independent within the COMMONWEALTH OF NATIONS. Tonga's first political party was founded in 1994, with an agenda for democratic reform of the constitution.

Capital: Nuku'alofa
Area: 749.9 sq km (289.5 sq mi)
Population: 100,400 (1995)
Currency: 1 pa'anga = 100 seniti
Religions: Free Wesleyan 43%; Roman Catholic 16%; Mormon

12.1%; Free Church of Tonga 11%; Church of Tonga 7.3%; other 10.6%
Ethnic Groups: Tongan 95.5%
Languages: Tongan, English (both official)
International Organizations: Commonwealth

Tongatapu The main island of Tonga in the South Pacific; area 259 sq km (100 sq miles). Its chief town is Nuku'alofa, capital of Tonga. Tourism and the production of fruit and vegetables are the main economic activities.

tongue A muscular, very flexible organ arising from the floor of the mouth in all vertebrates, except bony fishes. It is covered with mucous membrane, the upper surface of which is roughened by projections: the filiform papillae. In mammals, other papillae are found around the sides and back of the tongue to support taste-buds. In man these determine the recognition of salt, sweet, bitter, and sour. The tongue is not only used for the mastication of food but, for instance in the case of chameleons and frogs, can be projected out of the mouth to catch prey. It is also used to modify sound produced by the voice box, so helping to develop a complex system of communication.

tonsil One of two masses of lymphoid (LYMPH NODE) tissue situated in the pharynx at the back of the mouth of all mammals. They make up part of the body's defence system against infection. In human children, the tonsils are comparatively large, and are sometimes surgically removed if they become diseased.

tooth Any one of a set of hard structures situated in the jaws of most vertebrates. In the course of evolution teeth have become highly specialized. In some fishes they are merely modified and replaceable skin scales called denticles, used to hold prey before it is swallowed alive. Fossilized teeth can inform palaeontologists whether the animal to which they once belonged was herbivorous or carnivorous. Fossilized teeth have also been of great value in the determination of the place of apes and early man on the evolutionary tree.

In man there are only two sets of teeth and the permanent teeth no longer grow after they have reached maturity. The teeth of mammals are covered by a tough enamel layer overlying a bone-like material called dentine. The tooth root has a hollow canal along which nerves and blood vessels pass. In a living animal the tooth is attached by a spongy bone-like substance, cementum, and only a small part of the tooth protrudes above the gums.

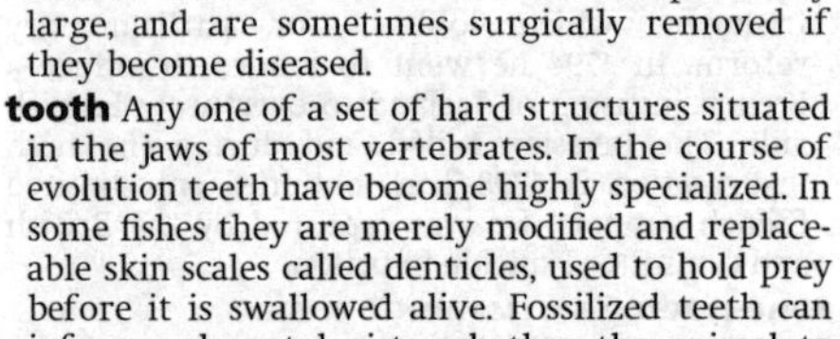

Tooth The permanent teeth of humans, which replace the primary, or 'milk', teeth. The incisors and canines are for biting; the premolars and molars are specialized for chewing and grinding.

toothcarp See KILLIFISH.

toothed whale A whale of the suborder Odontoceti, which is smaller and more varied in form than the WHALEBONE WHALES. The adults have as many as 180 triangular, rather shark-like teeth, a dorsal fin, and two longitudinal grooves on the throat, and the BEAKED WHALES have a distinct beak. Best known of these whales is the killer whale, *Orcinus orca*, distinguished by its black and white markings. It travels in schools of up to 40 animals which will attack and kill other, smaller, whales, seals, and dolphins. Other toothed whales feed on fish, squids, and octopuses. The largest of the 66 species is the SPERM WHALE. Others include the beluga, narwhal, dolphin, and porpoise.

toothwort A perennial plant of the genus *Lathraea*, which lacks normal leaves and chlorophyll and is parasitic on the roots of shrubs or trees. The common toothwort, *L. squamaria*, parasitizes the roots of hazel, elm, and beech. A plant of woodlands and hedgerows throughout Europe and Asia, it appears above ground in the spring as short spikes of dull white flowers. It belongs to the BROOMRAPE family, Orobanchaceae.

topaz An aluminium silicate mineral much prized for its gold-coloured crystals. It is a very hard but fragile mineral found in a variety of colours (yellow, blue, red, green). It occurs in acid igneous rocks, in pegmatite and tin veins, and also in alluvial sands. The largest and finest crystals (up to 270 kg, or 600 pounds, in weight) come from Minas Gerais (Brazil); yellow gemstones are mined in Myanmar (Burma) and Sri Lanka.

Topeka The capital of the US state of Kansas, situated on the Kansas River; pop. (1990) 119,880. Established as a railway town in 1854 and state capital in 1861, it was developed as a terminus and general office of the Atchison, Topeka, and Santa Fe Railroad. Industries include printing, grain milling and the manufacture of tyres, cellophane, and steel products.

top-minnow See KILLIFISH.

topology A branch of GEOMETRY that studies the geometrical properties remaining invariant under continuous transformations. It was developed when mathematicians accepted that Euclidean geometry was not the only way to describe spaces. Most of Euclid's concepts are not topological invariants. A straight line can be twisted; a circle can be squashed into an oval; an area can be stretched to twice its size. A ring or torus, on the other hand, can be stretched and twisted but will always possess one hole; a sheet will always have two surfaces and cannot be continuously transformed into a sphere which has only one surface, or into two sheets with four surfaces altogether. These are topologically invariant properties. This view of geometry allows much of mathematics to be simplified, in that the study of one topological space, for example the sphere, is in fact relevant to all spaces with no edges. Two spaces are said to be topologically equivalent if it is possible to change from one to the other and back again in a continuous way – that is, without cutting or tearing. Unusual objects of particular interest to topologists include the MÖBIUS STRIP, which has only one edge and one face, and the Klein bottle, which is formed by passing the neck of a bottle through the side to join a hole in the base, and has only one side. The study of topology includes the theory of SETS and has applications in the analysis of complicated electrical networks.

topsoil The upper part of the soil, rich in organic matter and plant nutrients. Also called the A-HORIZON of the soil profile, it is the most important part of the soil from the gardener's or farmer's viewpoint, because its quality determines how well plants will grow. LOAMS are the best kind of topsoil for most purposes.

tor A mass of exposed bedrock, standing abruptly above its surroundings. The block is an undisturbed, weathered piece of bedrock, not an erratic carried by a glacier. Tors are common on hard rocks with relatively widely spaced JOINTS – the granites of Devon and Cornwall, UK, for example, or the schists of central Otago, New Zealand – but they can occur on similarly massive sedimentary rocks, especially sandstones.

Torah (from Hebrew, 'teaching') The essential doctrines, law, and narratives of JUDAISM, held to be God's fullest truth for mankind. In a narrow sense, the Torah refers only to the Pentateuch, the first five books of the BIBLE, which are believed to have been revealed to Moses on Mount Sinai. The Pentateuch is kept in scroll form (*sepher Torah*) in all SYNAGOGUES and readings from it form part of the Jewish liturgy. The Torah may also include the oral law compilations and commentaries of the TALMUD and the MISHNAH.

tormentil Any of certain species of the plant genus *Potentilla*, which is part of the rose family. Most *Potentilla* species are perennials native to Europe and Asia. Common tormentil, *P. erecta*, is a plant of open habitats on heaths, fens, and mountains. It has a thick rootstock, leaves composed of four to five leaflets, and slender flower stems with yellow flowers. Common tormentil has long been valued for its medicinal properties for treating stomach disorders, and was also formerly used for tanning or staining leather.

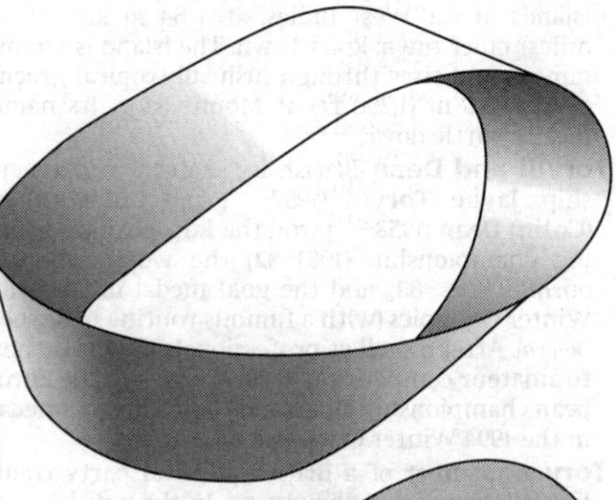

1

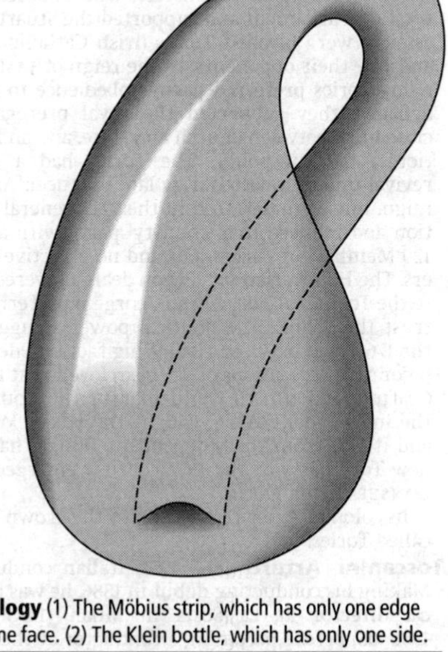

2

Topology (1) The Möbius strip, which has only one edge and one face. (2) The Klein bottle, which has only one side.

tornado A destructive rotating wind generated by massive storm clouds (cumulonimbus) in which the central part of the cloud rotates. The rotation extends downwards, emerging below the cloud base. It is dangerous only if it touches the ground. Tornadoes can happen anywhere but many are associated with the meeting of warm moist air from the Gulf of Mexico and cold air from the western USA. They occur most frequently in northern Texas, Oklahoma, Kansas, and Missouri.

Toronto The capital of Ontario and largest city in Canada, situated on the north shore of Lake Ontario at the mouth of the River Don; pop. (1991) 635,400; 3,893,050 (metropolitan area). Founded in 1793 and laid out in the style of a European city, it was christened York, but in 1834 was renamed Toronto, a name derived from a Huron Indian word meaning 'meeting place'. It developed into a major industrial, financial, and cultural centre on the St Lawrence Seaway. Its industries include iron and steel, electrical equipment, farming machinery, and aircraft.

torpedo A cigar-shaped, self-propelled underwater missile used by warships and SUBMARINES that explodes on impact with a ship; also a similar device dropped from an aircraft. In 1867 Robert Whitehead, a British engineer, developed the Whitehead locomotive torpedo, which carried an explosive warhead and was powered by compressed air. By the start of World War I torpedoes propelled by an engine burning an air, water vapour, and oil mixture could reach speeds of 44 KNOTS over a range of about 3.5 km (2.2 miles). They were held at the required depth by a hydrostatic valve, and directed by a preset, gyroscopically controlled rudder. Between 1936 and 1940 Japan produced the Long Lance torpedo, driven by liquid oxygen, and at about the same time acoustic homing torpedoes were developed. Modern torpedoes all possess passive or active homing mechanisms or are remotely guided (see GUIDED MISSILE), while miniaturization has brought lightweight torpedoes fired from aircraft for use as anti-submarine weapons.

torpedo-boat A type of small warship developed during the 1870s and designed to discharge TORPEDOES from above-water tubes. The first effective torpedo-boat was Britain's HMS *Lightning*, modified in 1879 for torpedo discharge. Other navies developed similar vessels, and by the 1890s they were so successful that a new type of small warship, the torpedo-boat DESTROYER, was evolved to counter their threat. During World War I a smaller type of fast torpedo-boat with INTERNAL-COMBUSTION ENGINES was produced. This vessel was developed during World War II into a successful high-speed weapon. Similar boats in use today are generally classed as fast patrol boats.

torpedo fish The largest of the electric RAYS, *Torpedo mobiliana*, which can grow to a length of 1.8 m (6 feet). It occurs on both sides of the North Atlantic and off the coasts of South Africa, mainly on sand and mud bottoms. The torpedo fish is a member of the family Torpedinidae. It has powerful electric organs, which generate a current of 8 amps at 220 volts, but the power of the shocks lessens if repeated quickly. It feeds on fishes, which are stunned by the electric current.

torque (or **moment of force**) The tendency of a force to rotate a body to which it is applied. Torque is specified with regard to a specific axis of rotation and is an important quantity in the measurement of the power of an ENGINE or other rotating body, since the power is measured as torque multiplied by angular VELOCITY (speed of rotation). It can be measured using a DYNAMOMETER.

Torquemada, **Tomás de** (1420–98) Spanish Dominican friar. He acted as the ruthlessly cruel first Grand Inquisitor of the SPANISH INQUISITION. As such he was responsible for directing its early activities against Jews and Muslims in Spain, and in fashioning its methods, including the use of torture and burnings.

Torrens, **Lake** A salt lake in Australia, the second-largest of the salt lakes of South Australia, occupying the rift valley to the west of the Flinders Range. It is named in honour of Sir Robert Torrens (1780–1864), chairman of the South Australia Commission to manage land sales and emigration.

Torres Strait A channel linking the Arafura Sea and Coral Sea and separating the north tip of Queensland, Australia, from the island of New Guinea. It is named after Luis Vaez de Torres, captain of one of the ships that in 1606 sailed along the south coast of New Guinea. The Torres Strait Islands, which lie within 96 km (60 miles) of the coast of Australia, were annexed to Queensland in 1872. Of largely Malaysian descent, the Torres Strait Islanders engage in pearl fishing.

Torricelli, **Evangelista** (1608–47) Italian mathematician and physicist, a disciple of Galileo whom he succeeded as mathematician to the court of Tuscany. A law or theorem that bears his name deals with the velocity of liquids flowing under the force of gravity from orifices. His most important invention was the mercury barometer in 1643, with which he demonstrated that the atmosphere exerts a pressure. He was the first person to produce a sustained vacuum.

Tórshavn The capital of the Faeroe Islands, situated on the island of Strømø; pop. (1994) 13,680. Now a North Atlantic fishing port, it was the site of an Alting (parliament) established here in the 9th century.

tort (from medieval Latin *tortum*, 'wrong') A breach of duty, other than a breach of contract, leading to liability for DAMAGES or in certain circumstances an injunction. The aim of the law of tort is to secure COMPENSATION for personal injury or damage to property, as well as to protect other interests, such as reputation or privacy. COMMON LAW SYSTEMS tend towards a proliferation of individual torts, whereas systems based on CIVIL LAW, in which a tort is usually called a **delict**, have recourse to a general principle of responsibility, which operates in the majority of cases. In addition to compensating the victim, the law of tort also encourages those whose activities carry risks for society (such as drivers of cars, or manufacturers of potentially dangerous products) to undertake them with care. Those whose activities carry special risks are in some legal systems subject to strict liability. Even in the codified systems of the civil law, but particularly in common law systems, tort law is largely judge-made law, and liability is subject to judicial perceptions of the correct limits of personal responsibility.

Tortelier, **Paul** (1914–90) French cellist. He made his concert début as a cellist in 1931, achieving international recognition after World War II. He was noted for his interpretations of Bach and Elgar, and also gave recitals with his wife and children. Tortelier was appointed professor at the Paris Conservatoire in 1957, where Jacqueline du Pré was among his pupils.

tortoise A largely herbivorous TURTLE that occurs, usually in dry habitats, in most warm regions of the world, with the exception of Australia. The greatest range of species occurs in Africa. Tortoises have rather short, broad feet and elephantine hind-legs that are cylindrical in shape. Their shells have hard, horny coverings. As additional protection, the front legs have thick scales over the part that remains exposed when the tortoise retracts into its shell; in the hind region, only the tail and the soles of the feet are incompletely retracted.

Some of the largest living tortoises are found on oceanic islands, especially the Galápagos Islands in the eastern Pacific, and Aldabra in the western Indian ocean. Each of the bigger islands in the Galápagos had its own distinctive population of tortoises at one time. On islands with sparse food resources, rather small forms of tortoise evolved, with long legs and a characteristic saddle-backed shell (elevated above the neck) which enabled them to reach and browse on taller vegetation.

tortoiseshell butterfly See BRUSH-FOOTED BUTTERFLY.

Tortola The principal island of the British Virgin Islands in the West Indies; area 54 sq km (21 sq miles); chief town, Road Town. The island is mountainous and rises through lush subtropical greenery to 366 m (1,200 ft) at Mount Sage. Its name means 'turtle dove'.

Torvill and Dean British ice-skaters. In partnership, **Jayne Torvill** (1957–) and **Christopher (Colin) Dean** (1958–) won the European ice-dancing championship (1981–82) the world championships (1981–83), and the gold medal in the 1984 Winter Olympics (with a famous routine to Ravel's *Boléro*). After a spell as professionals they returned to amateur competition in 1994, winning the European championship again and then a bronze medal in the 1994 Winter Olympics.

Tory A member of a British political party traditionally opposed to the WHIGS. In the political crisis of 1679 royalist supporters, who opposed the recall of Parliament and supported the Stuart succession, were labelled Tories (Irish Catholic brigands) by their opponents. In the reign of JAMES II many Tories preferred passive obedience to open defiance; they supported the royal prerogative, close links between church and state, and an isolationist foreign policy. The Tories had a brief revival under Robert Harley late in Queen Anne's reign, but were defeated in the 1715 general election and reduced to a 'country' party with about 120 Members of Parliament and no effective leaders. The Hanoverian succession dealt a severe blow to the Tories, as George I and George II preferred to trust the Whigs. The political power struggle in the 1760s was between rival Whig factions, despite pejorative accusations of Toryism levelled at BUTE, Grafton, and NORTH. William PITT the Younger, the independent Whig, fought the Foxite Whigs, and it was from the independent Whigs that the new Tory party of the 19th century emerged. See CONSERVATIVE PARTY.

In colonial America loyalists to the crown were called Tories.

Toscanini, **Arturo** (1867–1957) Italian conductor. Making his conducting début in 1886, he was musical director at La Scala in Milan (1898–1903; 1906–08) before becoming a conductor at the Metropolitan Opera, New York (1908–21). Toscanini later returned to La Scala (1921–29). Among the works he premièred were Puccini's *La Bohème* (1896) and *Turandot* (1926).

total eclipse See ECLIPSE.

totalitarianism A political system in which all individual activities and social relationships are subject to surveillance and control by the state. The idea originated in the 1930s and 1940s, with Nazism under Hitler, FASCISM under Mussolini, and COMMUNISM under Stalin: one-party government headed by a single powerful individual; promotion of an official IDEOLOGY; and extensive use of terror tactics by the secret police. A totalitarian regime is a specifically modern form of AUTHORITARIAN STATE, requiring as it does an advanced technology of social control. Some observers (most notably ARENDT) have explained the emergence of such regimes with reference to the growth of mass society: where the bonds of community break down, atomized individuals can be mobilized by the propaganda of political leaders. Features of totalitarianism are to be found in a number of developing countries governed by authoritarian regimes.

totem An animal or species regarded as the original ancestor of a particular CLAN. Totemism is often associated with RITUAL observances and prohibitions on eating the flesh of the animal concerned. The symbol of the totemic animal may be tattooed on the skin as a body adornment, represented in masks, or carved on poles. At one time, totemism, which is found in Australia, Melanesia, North America, and other parts of the world, was believed to be the original, primitive form of all RELIGION. The most recent theory of totemism is that of LÉVI-STRAUSS, who argues that totemism is one aspect of the general human desire to classify and order the world.

toucan A member of the family Ramphastidae, comprising about 37 species of birds, all of which live in forests in Central and South America. About the size of a crow, they are usually black or green, with white, red, or yellow patches. They are famous for their enormous and brightly coloured beaks, which they use for reaching fruit at the extremities of branches. They also eat large insects, lizards, and other small animals. They nest in holes in trees.

touchstone A black, fine-grained siliceous stone used for assaying gold and silver. The gold or silver is rubbed on the stone to produce streaks, which are compared with streaks made by metals of known purity. The comparison is made easier by treating the streaks with nitric acid, which dissolves impurities and leaves streaks of metal only. The method is not reliable for silver, but is still used today for assaying gold.

Toulon A port and naval base on the Mediterranean coast of southern France, capital of the department of Var in the Provence-Alpes-Côte d'Azur region; pop. (1990) 170,170. Developed in the 17th century by Louis XIV, it is one of the world's leading naval ports.

Toulouse A city of south-west France on the River Garonne, capital of the department of Haute-Garonne in the Midi-Pyrénées region; pop. (1990) 365,930. It was the capital of the Visigoths (419–507), and later the chief town of Aquitaine and of the Languedoc; its university was founded in 1229. Toulouse is now a centre of the aerospace and electronics industries.

Toulouse-Lautrec, Henri (Marie Raymond) de (1864–1901) French painter and lithographer. Toulouse-Lautrec's reputation is based on his colour lithographs from the 1890s, depicting actors, music-hall singers, prostitutes, and waitresses in Montmartre: particularly well known is the *Moulin Rouge* series (1894). His work is noted for its calligraphic line and flatness, influenced by Japanese prints.

tourmaline Any of several silicate minerals containing sodium, calcium, iron, magnesium, and other metals. These minerals are very hard and dense, and are normally found in prismatic crystals. Found in many igneous and metamorphic rocks, they are used as semiprecious stones.

Tour de France See CYCLING.

Tours An industrial city in west-central France, capital of the department of Indre-et-Loire; pop. (1990) 133,400. Situated on the Loire, it is a centre of light industry, data processing, and the wine trade.

Toussaint L'Ouverture, Pierre Dominique (*c.*1743–1803) Haitian revolutionary leader. Brought up a slave in the western part of Hispaniola (now Haiti), in 1791 he became one of the leaders of a rebellion that succeeded in emancipating the island's slaves by 1793. In 1797 he was appointed Governor-General by the revolutionary government of France, and led the drive to expel the British and Spanish from western Hispaniola. In 1801 he took control of the whole island, establishing his own constitution, but the following year Napoleon (wishing to restore slavery) ordered his forces to regain the island; Toussaint was eventually taken to France, where he died in prison.

Tower Hamlets An inner borough of Greater London, England, on the River Thames; pop. (1990) 153,500. It was created in 1965 from the East End boroughs of Bethnal Green, Poplar, and Stepney which, in medieval times, were hamlets belonging to the Tower of London. Wapping, Millwall, Limehouse, and Bow all lie within the borough.

Tower of London A fortress by the River Thames just east of the City of London. The oldest part, the White Tower, was begun in 1078. It was later used as a State prison, and is now a repository of ancient armour and weapons and other objects of public interest, including the Crown jewels (which have been kept there since the time of Henry III).

Townes, Charles Hard (1915–) US physicist. Following work on radar in World War II he investigated the quantum electronic effects associated with microwave radiation. His development of microwave oscillators and amplifiers led to his invention of the maser in 1954. Townes later showed that an optical maser (a laser) was possible, though the first working laser was constructed by others. He shared the Nobel Prize for physics in 1964.

Townsend, Mount A mountain rising to 2,214 m (7,251 ft) north of Mount Kosciusko in the Australian Alps, New South Wales. It is the second-highest peak in Australia.

Townsville An industrial port and resort town of Queensland, on the north-east coast of Australia; pop. (1991) 101,400 (with Thuringowa). It was founded in 1864 by J. M. Black who was commissioned by the merchant and cotton-grower Robert Towns to develop an outlet for produce from the north. It developed rapidly after the discovery of minerals at Mount Isa in the 1870s and is now a point of access for touring the Great Barrier Reef.

toxicology The study of the isolation and identification of drugs and chemicals from tissues, body-fluids, proprietary preparations, post-mortem material, and other sources. The aim is to determine the presence and role of substances in situations such as fatalities, drug misuse (especially in sport) disease, environmental hazards, and for protecting public health. A range of sophisticated techniques are employed to provide an accurate measure of the content of substances within samples.

toxic shock syndrome A state of shock as a result of septicaemia. The commonest cause is a retained foreign body (such as a tampon) combined with the presence of staphylococci. The condition can be life threatening if not treated with antibiotics, fluid replacement, etc.

toxin A poison produced by a living organism, especially a bacterium. In such diseases as tetanus, the toxin is produced by the bacteria within the body. In botulism the toxin is produced in contaminated food eaten by the victim. Some toxins can be useful, for example, penicillin is a toxin produced by certain fungi that kill bacteria.

toxoplasmosis A disease of mammals and birds caused by the protozoan *Toxoplasma gondii*, which is usually transmitted to humans by eating undercooked meat or by contact with cat faeces. Symptoms are generally mild but can be serious in patients with a reduced immune response.

Toynbee, Arnold (Joseph) (1889–1975) British historian. He is best known for his 12-volume *Study of History* (1934–61), in which he surveyed the history of different civilizations, tracing in them a pattern of growth, maturity, and decay and concluding that contemporary Western civilization is in the last of these stages.

Trabzon (formerly **Trebizond**) A commercial city and port of north-east Turkey, on the Black Sea at the mouth of the Degirmen River; pop. (1990) 143,940. Traditionally founded by Greek colonists in 756 BC, its ancient name was Trapezus. From 1204 to 1461 it was the capital of an empire established by Alexis Comnenus. It is now capital of the province of Trabzon, and exports food products and tobacco.

trace element A chemical element needed in the body of an organism in very small amounts, usually 100 parts per million or less. They are essential components of certain ENZYMES and other proteins, and include copper, iodine, iron, cobalt, chromium, silicon, manganese, and zinc. Copper is needed for the enzyme cytochrome oxidase, which forms part of the electron transport chain in aerobic organisms. Iron is needed during the manufacture of chlorophyll in plants, for cytochrome proteins, and as part of haemoglobin. Many trace elements are toxic in larger quantities and are usually supplied by a well-balanced diet.

trace fossil A sign of animal activity that has been preserved in hardened sedimentary rock. These include trails, burrows, and tracks such as footprints. Because similar traces can be made by quite different animals, they are classified according to their type rather than the specific animals which may have caused them. From trace fossils geologists can calculate such things as the abundance of life in a particular sediment and rates of sedimentation. The study of trace fossils is called ichnology.

tracery Decorative stonework (or more rarely brickwork) set in the upper part of windows, and by extension to describe similar ornament applied to other architectural features or, for example, furniture. Tracery is one of the most characteristic features of medieval architecture after about 1200 and its variations or absence have been used to classify different stages of the Gothic style, notably EARLY ENGLISH, DECORATED, and PERPENDICULAR in Britain. See also GOTHIC ART AND ARCHITECTURE.

trachea (or **windpipe**) A tube that starts below the LARYNX in mammals and ends in the thorax as it divides into two bronchi. The trachea is lined with hair-like cilia, and is moistened by mucus. The cilia beat so that foreign particles are wafted outwards, towards the pharynx. The tube is kept open, and resists crushing by means of rings of CARTILAGE in its walls.

trachoma See BLINDNESS.

tracked vehicle See CATERPILLAR TRACK.

traction-engine A mobile steam-powered vehicle used for haulage, for agricultural purposes, or as a mobile power source. The earliest portable steam engines were not self-powered but were pulled by teams of horses. Self-propelled engines were first built in 1834 by Walter Hancock (UK) but they gained little popularity. By the late 19th century, traction-engines were in use on many farms, but by World War I they were being replaced by TRACTORS. Some traction-engines continued to be used for heavy road haulage until World War II.

tractor A motor vehicle used to haul agricultural machinery and for general farm work. Modern tractors derive from steam-powered TRACTION-ENGINES. The first petrol-engined tractor was made in 1892 in the USA, and by World War II tractors were well established. Modern tractors use either two- or four-wheel drive, and have caterpillar tracks or large, rubber-tyred wheels. A major feature is the power take-off, which can be either an extension of the tractor's transmission system or an independent drive. This can power a wide range of agricultural machines. Hydraulically powered, rear-mounted arms on the tractor are used to raise and lower such implements as harrows and ploughs, controlling the depth to which they penetrate the soil.

Tracy, Spencer (1900–67) US actor. After his screen début in 1930, he won his first Oscar seven years later for his performance in *Captains Courageous*. Tracy formed a successful film partnership with Katharine Hepburn, co-starring with her in films such as *Adam's Rib* (1949) and *Guess Who's Coming to Dinner* (1967).

trade cycles (or **business cycles**) Regular cyclical fluctuations in the level of aggregate demand, and hence of national income. The cycle consists of boom, recession, depression, recovery, and a return to boom conditions. The amplitude of each phase of the cycle can sometimes be lessened by means of stabilization policies. The causes of trade cycles vary. Many theoretical models focus on fluctuations in the level of investment by firms as the cause of the cycles. However, changes in investment may themselves stem from several different causes, including demand 'shocks' (such as the jump in world oil prices in 1973–74, which affected other components of demand besides investment) and sudden changes in monetary policy and INTEREST rates.

trademark An identification symbol (name and/or logo) legally registered or established by use in order to distinguish the goods of a particular manufacturer. Such a device may be one of the manufacturer's most effective marketing tools, and therefore it is protected by INTELLECTUAL PROPERTY laws. A trademark need not be registered if it has become well established, but registration gives an immediate right to prevent someone else making use it. A service mark is the same sort of device as a trademark, but it applies to services rather than manufactured goods.

Tradescant, John (1570–1638) English botanist and horticulturalist. He was the earliest known collector of plants and other natural history specimens, and took part in a number of collecting trips to Western Europe, Russia, and North Africa. Tradescant was later employed as gardener to Charles I and set up his own garden and museum in Lambeth, London. His son **John** (1608–62) had similar interests and added many plants to his father's collection, which was eventually bequeathed to Elias Ashmole.

Trades Union Congress (TUC) An organization of British trade unions. It was founded in 1868 with the purpose of holding national conferences on trade union activities. In 1871 it set up a Parliamentary Committee to advance the interests of unions with Members of Parliament. From 1889 onwards, it began to be more politically militant and in 1900 helped to found the Labour Representation Committee, known from 1906 as the LABOUR PARTY, with whom it has had links ever since. The General Council, elected by trade union members, replaced the Parliamentary Committee in 1920. The Congress can urge support from other unions, when a union cannot reach a satisfactory settlement with an employer in an industrial dispute, but it has no powers of direction. After the GENERAL STRIKE relations between the Congress and government (of whatever party) were cautiously conciliatory. It was closely involved in British industrial planning and management during World War II and under successive Labour and Conservative governments until 1979. Since then it has tended to be on the defensive, particularly against legislation designed by Margaret Thatcher's governments of the 1980s to weaken trade union power.

trade union An organized association of workers in a particular trade or profession. Unions represent employees in negotiations with employers. In the USA they are referred to as labor unions. In Britain in the late 18th century groups and clubs of working-men in skilled trades developed, to regulate admission of apprentices and sometimes to bargain for better working conditions. During the wars with France (1793–1815) COMBINATION ACTS suppressed any such activity, but on their repeal in 1824 limited trade union activity became possible in certain crafts. By 1861 a number of trade unions of skilled workers existed in Britain, forming the TRADES UNION CONGRESS (TUC) in 1868, gaining some legal status in 1871, and the right to picket peacefully in 1875. With the development of MASS-PRODUCTION methods in the industrialized countries large numbers of semi-skilled and unskilled workers were recruited, and from the 1880s attempts were made to organize these into unions. These attempts were more successful in Britain and in Europe than in the USA, where cheap immigrant labour was for long available. Unions emerged in Australia and New Zealand and in other British dominions in the 19th century. As industrialization proceeded in other countries so trade unions developed, although in South Africa trade union activity among black workers was illegal until 1980. In the former Soviet Union and communist Eastern Europe 90 per cent of industrial workers belonged to government-controlled unions. Elsewhere, union membership fluctuates with political and economic vicissitudes, especially in developing countries, where it ranges from under 10 per cent (India) to over 40 per cent (Algeria).

Trade unions are funded by membership subscriptions and are usually run by an elected executive and full-time officials, and elected workplace representatives (shop stewards in Britain). Their main economic objectives are to attain good wages, good working conditions, and secure employment for their members. Trade unions aim to achieve their workplace INDUSTRIAL RELATIONS objectives through COLLECTIVE BARGAINING, supported when necessary by INDUSTRIAL ACTION. A significant development since World War II has been the increasing participation of trade unions in government and tripartite bodies at national or industry level (see CORPORATISM).

trade wind A constant wind blowing towards the equator from the north-east or south-east. The name was originally applied to any wind that 'blows trade', i.e. in a constant direction.

Trafalgar A cape on the coast of Cadiz province, southern Spain, near which a decisive battle of the Napoleonic Wars was fought on 21 October 1805. The British fleet under Nelson (who was killed in the action) achieved a decisive victory over the combined fleets of France and Spain, which were attempting to clear the way for Napoleon's projected invasion of Britain.

tragedy In the Western tradition, a drama (or sometimes, prose fiction) that represents the disastrous downfall of a central character. The tragedies of Aeschylus, Euripides, and Sophocles are the most impressive works of GREEK THEATRE. From them Aristotle arrived at a very influential definition of tragedy in his *Poetics* (4th century BC): the imitation of an action that is serious and complete, achieving a catharsis through incidents arousing pity and terror. The tragic effect usually depends on our awareness of admirable qualities in the protagonist, which are wasted in the unavoidable disaster. The Roman tragedian Seneca set the pattern followed by English playwrights from Thomas Kyd's *The Spanish Tragedy* (1586) to Webster's *The Duchess of Malfi* (1623) in their violent 'tragedies of blood'. The major achievements in tragedy of this period are Shakespeare's *Hamlet*, *Othello*, *Macbeth*, and *King Lear*. In 17th-century France Corneille and Racine wrote tragedies modelled more closely on Greek examples, usually observing the 'unities' of time, place, and action, which dramatic theorists claimed to derive from Aristotle. Tragedy declined in the 18th and 19th centuries, and the validity of its modern revival by Ibsen, Tennessee Williams, and Miller is much disputed.

Traherne, Thomas (1637–74) English prose writer and poet. His major prose work *Centuries*, originally published in 1699, faded into obscurity until it was rediscovered on a London bookstall along with some poems in manuscript form in 1896; it was republished as *Centuries of Meditation* (1908). Its account of his early intuitions constitutes an important contribution to the portrayal of childhood experience in English literature. His poems were republished as *Poetical Works* (1903).

Trajan (born Marcus Ulpius Traianus) (*c*.53–117 AD) Roman emperor 98–117. Born in Spain, he was adopted by Nerva as his successor. Trajan's reign is noted for the DACIAN WARS (101–06), which ended in the annexation of Dacia as a province; the campaigns are illustrated on Trajan's Column in Rome. He was also an efficient administrator and many public works were undertaken during his reign.

Tralee The county town of Kerry in the Republic of

Ireland, a port at the mouth of the River Lee where it enters Tralee Bay; pop. (1991) 17,200. St Brendan the Navigator (484–577), patron saint of Kerry, was born to the west of Tralee near the port of Fenit. Tralee is the headquarters of the Folk Theatre of Ireland.

tram (US **streetcar**) A passenger vehicle that operates on rails laid along public roads. Originally horse- or steam-hauled, trams now operate electrically, usually by means of overhead wires or a third rail buried beneath the track. They often work in multiple units of two to four cars, all of which may be powered. As the European cities in which most trams operate have grown larger, tramlines have been built leading off the public roads into the suburbs. This avoids congestion and allows the trams to reach speeds approaching those of commuter trains. Trams are frequently allowed to run through pedestrianized areas because they are quiet and non-polluting. In the USA, the famous San Francisco streetcars are cable-hauled. See also TROLLEYBUS.

tranquillizer A drug having a calming effect. Tranquillizers calm and relax patients with less sedative and hypnotic actions than other drugs. 'Major' tranquillizers (now called antipsychotics; for example, chlorpromazine) are used to treat severe psychotic disorders, such as mania and schizophrenia. 'Minor' tranquillizers are effective against anxiety and insomnia; an example is diazepam, the best-known formulation of which is Valium. Prolonged use of minor tranquillizers may produce dependence, but overdoses are far less dangerous than overdoses of the BARBITURATES, which they largely replaced. See also PSYCHOTROPIC DRUG.

transcendental meditation See MEDITATION.

transcendental numbers The numbers that are not solutions of any POLYNOMIAL equation with integer coefficients; they are thus not algebraic and not rational because any rational number p/q is a root of the linear equation $qx = p$. Since $\sqrt{2}$ is a solution of the equation $x^2 - 2 = 0$, the transcendentals are not equivalent to the IRRATIONAL NUMBERS but form a subset of them.

Trans-Dniester A region of Eastern Moldova (Moldovia) lying between the Dniester River and the border with Ukraine. Its population is Slav-dominated with ethnic Russians and Ukranians together outnumbering ethnic Moldovans. A separatist movement emerged in the 1980s, and in 1994 the region was granted special autonomous status. Its chief city is Tiraspol.

transducer Any device that converts one form of energy into another. Generally, transducers are SENSORS, providing an electrical output in response to some physical variable, such as pressure, temperature, humidity, acidity, sound intensity, light intensity, or chemical constitution. However, some transducers, for example, RELAYS and LOUDSPEAKERS, function as actuators, providing a defined physical output for some defined electrical input. Transducers are selected for their function, dynamic range (the maximum response they can give), linearity (how faithfully the output follows the input), resolution (the smallest input that will create an output), and accuracy. Some transducers can now be fabricated directly on to a silicon chip as part of an INTEGRATED CIRCUIT.

transformer An electrical device that can provide a low-voltage supply from a high-voltage, alternating-current (a.c.) power source (step-down), or a high-voltage supply from a low-voltage a.c. source (step-up). It comprises two interacting coils, the primary and secondary coils, wound on a core of magnetically 'soft' iron (see MAGNET). Alternating current supplied to the primary coil induces a current in the secondary coil (see ELECTROMAGNETIC INDUCTION). The ratio of primary and secondary voltages is determined by the number of turns on each coil: for example, if the secondary carries twice the number of turns of the primary, it will supply double the voltage. Transformers have many applications. For example, in mains electricity supply, a.c. power is transmitted at high voltage, and transformers are used to step this high voltage down to mains domestic voltage. Radio, television, and computer circuits usually require further transformers that are incorporated in the equipment.

transgenic organism An organism that has had its GENOME modified by the addition of foreign DNA, usually from a different species. The DNA is incorporated into a VECTOR, which integrates into the host genome. In the case of dicotyledonous plants the vector is derived from the bacterium *Agrobacterium tumifaciens*, which causes crown gall. Using this vector, genes have been incorporated into plants to enable them to produce their own insecticides and resistance to herbicides. Transgenic farm animals have been produced, which yield milk containing therapeutic proteins. See also GENETIC ENGINEERING.

transhumance See NOMADISM; PASTORALIST.

transistor A three-terminal, solid-state SEMICONDUCTOR DEVICE used in electronic circuits to provide amplification or as a high-speed switch. Transistors, which were first developed in 1948 by SHOCKLEY and colleagues, have largely replaced thermionic valves in electronic circuits. They may be used individually, or as part of an INTEGRATED CIRCUIT. There are two principal types of transistor, the bipolar transistor and the field-effect transistor (FET). The bipolar transistor consists of a sandwich of three regions of doped semiconductor, the emitter, the base, and the collector. The emitter and collector are connected into a circuit carrying a large current, while the base and emitter form a circuit that can carry a much smaller current in the reverse direction. No current can flow in the emitter–collector circuit if the base–emitter circuit is off. However, a small current flow in the base circuit 'turns on' the transistor and allows a much larger current (50–100 times greater) to flow in the emitter–collector circuit. Bipolar transistors can operate at very high speeds, and for this reason are used in radio circuits. They are also used in AMPLIFIERS. FETs can be of several types. A common type comprises a channel of n-type material through some p-type material. The channel can act as a conducting path for electrons, the input being known as the source, and the output as the drain. A third electrical connection, the gate, is made to the p-type material between the source and the drain. A small voltage applied to the gate acts to 'squeeze' electrons in the n-type material into a narrower channel, thus making it harder for current to flow between the source and drain. Varying the voltage on the gate therefore controls current flow along the n-type channel. Field-effect transistors can be made much smaller than bipolar transistors, and they are therefore used in random-access computer MEMORY and other circuits with a high density of components.

transit (in astronomy) The passage of a celestial body across a reference line. For example, it can refer to the time when a star or an artificial satellite crosses the MERIDIAN of an observatory, or an inner planet is seen to cross the face of the Sun, or a Jovian satellite is seen to cross the disc of the planet.

transition metals (or **d-block elements**) The elements that occur in the block in the middle of the PERIODIC TABLE, from scandium to zinc, from yttrium to cadmium, and from lanthanum to mercury. Their atomic structures all have partially filled d-shells, which give rise to their typical properties of variable VALENCY, colour, MAGNETISM and complex ion formation. They use the penultimate electron shell, as well as the outermost shell, in bonding. All are hard and strong, have high melting- and boiling-points, and are good conductors of heat and electricity. The uses of the transition metals vary widely; iron is used for construction, copper for wiring and coinage, gold and silver for jewellery, and nickel and platinum as catalysts. Many of the metals are alloyed to improve their properties: for example, iron is mixed with carbon and many metals to give steels, and copper and zinc are mixed to form brass.

Transjordan The former name of an area of Palestine east of the River Jordan, held under British mandate after the breakup of the Ottoman empire at the end of World War I. It became an independent state in 1946 as the Hashemite Kingdom of Jordan.

Transkei A former independent tribal homeland of the Xhosa people in South Africa, granted self-government in 1963, but united with Eastern Cape province in 1994.

translocation (in genetics) A rearrangement of genetic information, in which a piece of one chromosome is relocated on another chromosome. Translocations are frequently reciprocal; for example, simultaneous breaks in chromosomes two and three could be repaired by joining two with three, and vice versa. When such a segment is relocated at a different position on the same chromosome, the rearrangement is referred to as a transposition.

transmitter See RADIO; TELEVISION.

transpiration The evaporation of water from the aerial parts of plants, mostly from the leaves, but also from stems, flowers, and fruits. The impermeable CUTICLE covering these structures is designed to prevent desiccation, but is perforated by pores (stomata, or lenticels) to allow gases through for PHOTOSYNTHESIS and RESPIRATION. Evaporation also occurs through these pores, generating a continuous upward flow from the roots to replace water lost. Transpiration helps to cool the plant in hot weather, and minerals are carried up from the roots in the transpiration stream. In conditions of drought and high atmospheric humidity, stomata close, reducing transpiration. Warmth and wind speed up the process. Transpiration rates are greatest during daylight hours. It forms part of the HYDROLOGICAL CYCLE.

transplant surgery The practice of replacing diseased organs or tissues with healthy ones taken from another part of the patient's body (such as skin grafts), or from another person (for example, heart transplants). Normally, transplanted organs taken from another person are treated by the body as a foreign tissue and are destroyed by the patient's immune system (see IMMUNOLOGY). This rejection tendency is much reduced if the donor and recipient are of a similar tissue type, and by using special drugs to suppress the immune response, it is possible to prevent rejection altogether. See also GRAFTING.

transponder A radio receiver and transmitter that transmits in response to predetermined sig-

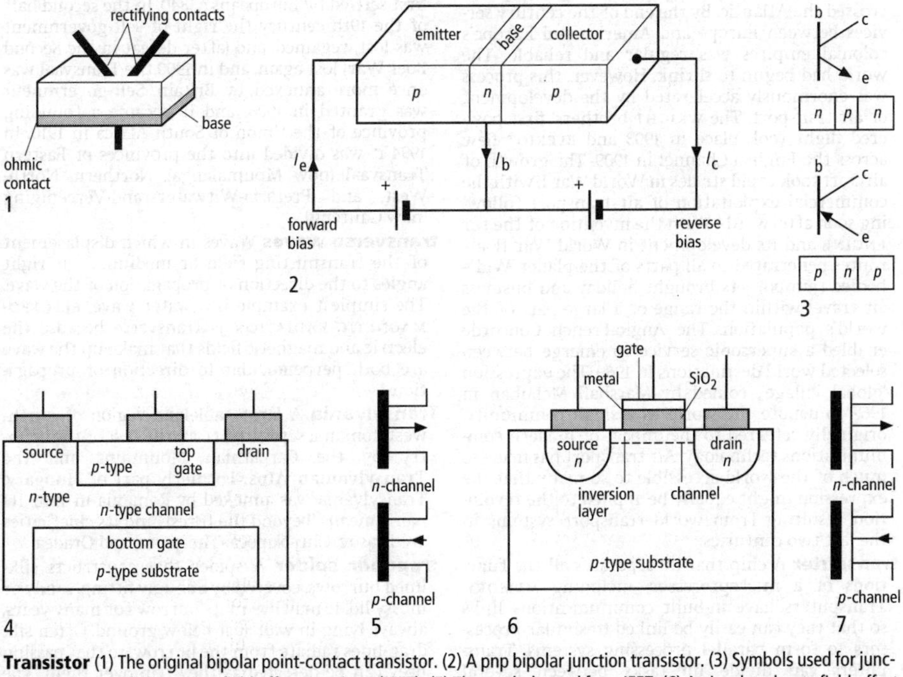

Transistor (1) The original bipolar point-contact transistor. (2) A pnp bipolar junction transistor. (3) Symbols used for junction transistors. (4) A junction field-effect transistor (JFET). (5) The symbols used for a JFET. (6) An insulated-gate field-effect transistor (IGFET). (7) The symbols used for an IGFET.

nals. In COMMUNICATIONS SATELLITES, transponders receive information signals from Earth carried on one microwave frequency, and transmit them back after amplification on another, lower microwave frequency.

transport The movement of people and goods from one place to another. Until the beginning of the 19th century the horse (and other animals) were relied on for land transport, while wind and muscle-power provided the energy for transport on water. As a result of the INDUSTRIAL REVOLUTION and the development of the STEAM-ENGINE, the first passenger and goods railway (between Stockton and Darlington) opened in 1825. By 1851 there were rail networks in 17 other countries, including the 650 km (404 mile) link between Moscow and St Petersburg in Russia. (See also RAILWAYS, HISTORY OF.) It was not until the end of the century, however, that road transport by internal-combustion engine was developed. By 1890 both DAIMLER and BENZ were selling motorized dog carts, but it was FORD's mass-produced Model T automobile (1909) that heralded the replacement of the horse as a means of personal transport on land. Between the horse and the car, one significant invention provided a convenient, if somewhat limited form of personal transport. This was the BICYCLE, invented in 1839, but not really widely popular until the development of pneumatic tyres in 1899. Since the 1960s the bicycle, as a pollution-free form of urban transport, has had an active resurgence. The development of the railways and, above all, the MOTOR CAR, enormously increased individual mobility by the beginning of the 20th century. This had far-reaching effects on the structure of society, not the least of which was the growth of the suburbs.

On water, STEAMSHIPS began tentatively to transform river and coastal transport early in the 19th century and by 1838 the first steamship had crossed the Atlantic. By the end of the century services between Europe and America and Europe's colonial empires was regular and reliable. The world had begun to shrink. However, this process was enormously accelerated by the development of air transport. The WRIGHT brothers' first powered flight took place in 1903 and BLÉRIOT flew across the English Channel in 1909. The growth of aircraft took rapid strides in World War I, with the commercial exploitation of air transport following soon afterwards. With the invention of the JET ENGINE and its development in World War II, air routes penetrated to all parts of the planet. Wide-bodied (jumbo) jets brought holiday and business air travel within the range of a large part of the world's population. The Anglo-French Concorde enabled a supersonic service to emerge between selected world destinations in 1969. The expression 'global village', coined by Marshall McLuhan in 1967 to denote the world as a small community, originally referred to the impact of modern communications technology. Air transport has made so much of the world accessible to so many that the expression might equally be applied to the revolution resulting from world transport systems in the last two centuries.

transputer A chip that incorporates all the functions of a microprocessor, including MEMORY. Transputers have in-built communications links so that they can easily be linked to similar processors to form parallel processing systems. Transputers can divide up tasks between several identical processors, enabling them to handle large amounts of data very quickly. Arrays of transputers are used to run applications where a significant increase in speed over conventional computers is required.

Trans-Siberian Railway A railway built in 1891–1904 from Moscow east around the southern end of Lake Baikal to Vladivostok on the Sea of Japan, a distance of 9,311 km (5,786 miles). It opened up Siberia and advanced Russian interest in east Asia. A major extension to the north of Lake Baikal (the Baikal–Amur Mainline) was completed in 1984 and stretches 3,102 km (1,952 miles) from Ust-Kut in east Siberia to the Pacific coast.

transubstantiation The Christian doctrine that the bread and wine used in the sacrament of the Eucharist are transformed into the body and blood of Christ, who is therefore present at the Mass. This doctrine was reaffirmed by the Council of Trent in 1545–63 and is still accepted by Roman Catholics although not by most Protestants.

transuranic elements The elements that come after uranium in the PERIODIC TABLE – that is, with atomic numbers greater than 92. The 16 transuranic elements known are all radioactive and, as they decay to other elements in times much less than the lifetime of the Universe, none occurs naturally. They are made by bombarding a heavy nucleus with a light nucleus; at first neutrons and helium nuclei were used, but recently heavier nuclei, such as iron, have been employed. Such elements as neptunium and plutonium have become important in producing nuclear energy, and have been manufactured in quite large quantities, but the later elements are extremely unstable; in some cases only small numbers of atoms have been produced.

Transvaal A former province of the Republic of South Africa, lying north of the Orange Free State and separated from it by the River Vaal. Its capital was Pretoria. Inhabited by Ndebele Africans, it was first settled by Europeans *c.*1840. In the second half of the 19th century the right of self-government was lost, regained, and (after defeat in the Second Boer War) lost again, and in 1900 the Transvaal was once more annexed by Britain. Self-government was granted in 1906, and it became a founding province of the Union of South Africa in 1910. In 1994 it was divided into the provinces of Eastern Transvaal (now Mpumalanga), Northern, North-West, and Pretoria-Witwatersrand-Vereeniging (now Gauteng).

transverse waves Waves in which displacement of the transmitting field or medium is at right angles to the direction of propagation of the wave. The simplest example is a water wave. ELECTROMAGNETIC RADIATION is transverse because the electric and magnetic fields that make up the wave are both perpendicular to direction of propagation.

Transylvania A large tableland region of north-west Romania separated from the rest of the country by the Carpathian Mountains and the **Transylvanian Alps**. Formerly part of Hungary, Transylvania was annexed by Romania in 1918. Its name means 'beyond the forest' and its chief cities are Brasov, Cluj-Napoca, Timişoara, and Oradea.

trapdoor spider A spider that constructs silk-lined burrows, covered by a snugly fitting, sandy or mossy lid. It may live in its burrow for many years, always lying in wait just below ground. Often silk drag-lines radiate from the burrow, so that passing prey can be detected as they trip over them. The trapdoor spider jumps out and pierces the animal with its jaws, injecting poison, then drags the

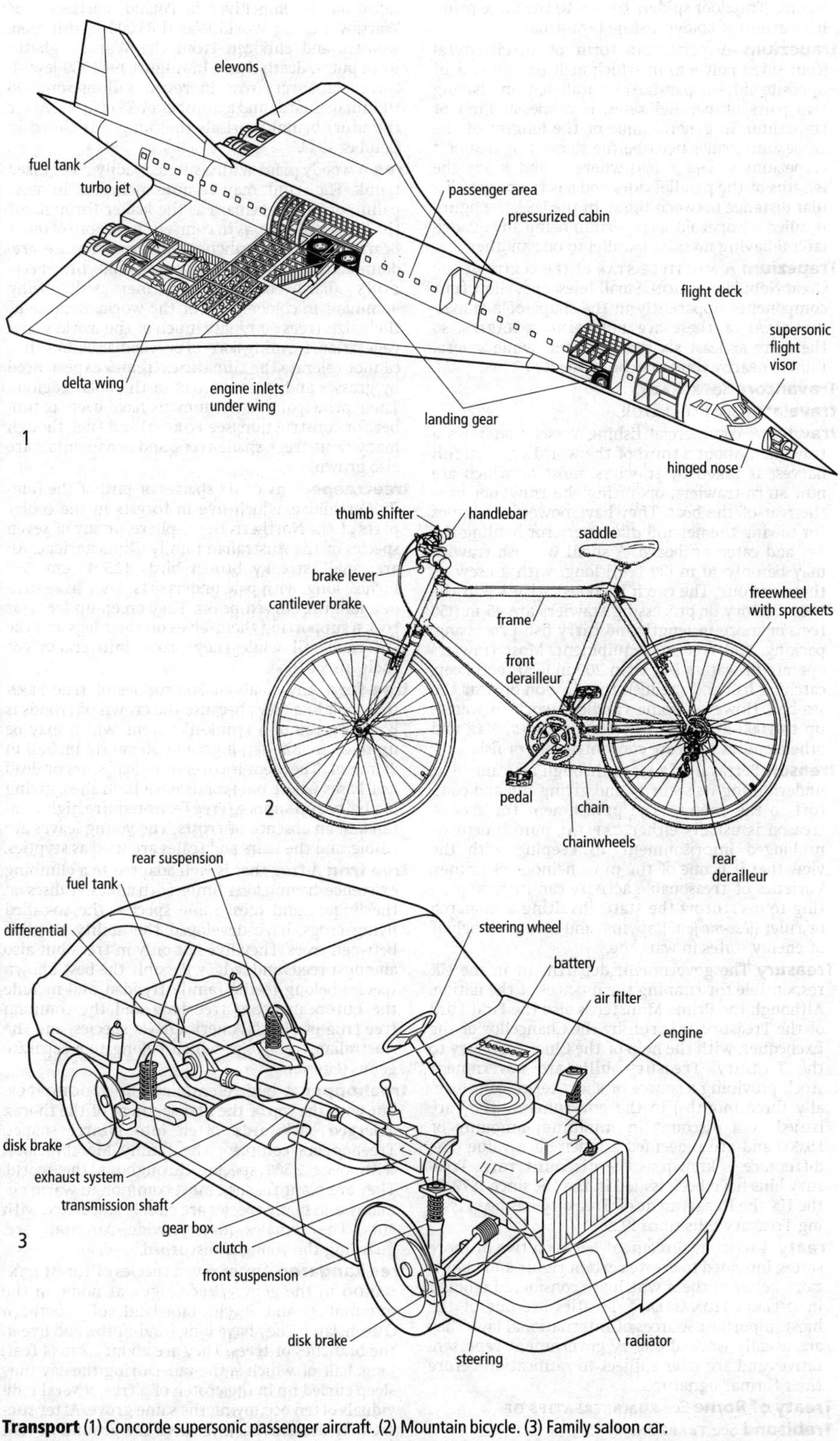

Transport (1) Concorde supersonic passenger aircraft. (2) Mountain bicycle. (3) Family saloon car.

paralysed victim back to the burrow to feed on at leisure. Trapdoor spiders belong to the same primitive group of spiders as the tarantulas.

trapezium A particular form of quadrilateral (four-sided polygon) in which at least one pair of opposite sides is parallel. A parallelogram, having two pairs of parallel sides, is a special kind of trapezium. In general none of the lengths of the trapezium's sides need be the same. The area of a trapezium is $\frac{1}{2}(a + b)h$, where a and b are the lengths of the parallel sides and h is the perpendicular distance between them. In the USA the figure is called a trapezoid, a trapezium being any quadrilateral having no sides parallel to one another.

Trapezium A MULTIPLE STAR at the centre of the Great Nebula in ORION. Small telescopes show four components, apparently in the shape of a trapezium. Two of these are ECLIPSING BINARIES, so there are at least six stars present, while several fainter nearby stars may be connected.

Travancore See KERALA.

travelator See ESCALATOR.

trawler A commercial fishing vessel that tows a trawl-net. About a third of the world's annual fish harvest is taken by trawlers, most of which are now stern-trawlers, operating the trawl-net over the rear of the boat. They have powerful engines for towing the net and machinery for hauling the net and catch on board. A small wet-fish trawler may be only 10 m (30 feet) long, with a crew of three or four. The catch is cooled with ice in the hold. Factory or processing trawlers are 45 m (150 feet) or more in length and carry fish processing, packing, and freezing equipment. Most trawlers operate in waters less than 200 m (650 feet) deep, catching fish and shellfish that live on or near the sea-bed. However, some trawlers work in waters up to 1,000 m (3,300 feet) deep, using SONAR and other sensors to locate concentrations of fish.

treason Betrayal of a state through acts aimed at undermining its security and giving 'aid and comfort to the enemy'. The punishment for acts of treason is usually either CAPITAL punishment or prolonged imprisonment, in keeping with the view that it is one of the most heinous of crimes. Varieties of treasonable activity can include plotting to overthrow the state, insulting a monarch or ruler (*lèse-majesté*), spying, and acting on behalf of enemy states in wartime.

Treasury The government department in the UK responsible for running the finances of the nation. Although the Prime Minister is also the First Lord of the Treasury, it is run by the Chancellor of the Exchequer, with the help of the Chief Secretary to the Treasury. **Treasury bills** are government stock providing a source of short-term loans (usually three months) to the government. They are issued at a discount in minimum amounts of £5,000 and are redeemed at their face value. The difference is known as the **discount rate**. Treasury bills have been issued in the UK since 1877. In the UK the Department of Treasury has been issuing Treasury bills since 1929.

treaty A written agreement between two or more states, intended to create certain rights and obligations between them which are considered binding in INTERNATIONAL LAW. Treaties are one of the most important sources of international law. They are usually worked out by government representatives and are later subject to ratification before their formal signature.

Treaty of Rome See ROME, TREATIES OF.

Trebizond See TRABZON.

Treblinka The site of a German concentration camp on the Bug River in Poland, north-east of Warsaw. During World War II 85,000 Jewish men, women, and children from the Warsaw ghetto were put to death there. In August 1943 700 Jewish forced labourers rose in revolt killing some 15 Ukranian guards and a number of SS officers. After the usual brutal reprisals the camp was closed in October 1943.

tree A woody plant with a single readily recognized trunk. The trunk may be unbranched, as in most palms, or it may remain as the leader throughout the life of the tree, as in conifers, but more often it bears a crown of branches. Modern trees are predominantly conifers (softwoods) and DICOTYLEDONS (hardwoods), the former still being dominant in colder parts of the world. Because of their size, trees dominate much of the world's land vegetation, forming forests or woodlands, but they cannot tolerate the climatic extremes experienced by grasses and CRYPTOGAMS in the polar regions. Their principal uses to humans have been as timber for construction (see FOREST) and fuel, though many fruit-trees, shade-trees, and ornamentals are also grown.

treecreeper Any of six species of bird of the family Certhiidae, which live in forests in the cooler parts of the Northern Hemisphere, or any of seven species of the Australian family Climacteridae. All are small, streaky brown birds 12.5–17 cm (5–7 inches) long, with pale underparts. They have slender, longish, curved beaks. They creep up trees (or rocks) supporting themselves on their legs and the stiffened tail while they probe into cracks for their insect food.

tree fern Any of about 800 species of true FERN that look like trees because the crown of fronds is borne on top of a trunk-like stem, which may be up to 25 m (82 feet) high and 30 cm (12 inches) in diameter. The stem is covered in leaf scars or dead leaf bases where old fronds have been shed, giving it a hairy appearance. Tree ferns require high rainfall and an absence of frosts. The young leaves are edible, and the hairs and scales are used as styptics.

tree frog A frog that is well adapted to a climbing existence, having long limbs with adhesive discs on the fingers and toes. Some species, the so-called flying frogs, have developed the ability to glide between trees. They live not only in trees but also amongst reeds and sedges. Possibly the best-known species belong to the family Hylidae, and include the European green tree frog and the common tree frog of North America (*Hyla* species) and the Australian tree frogs, which belong to a separate genus (*Litoria*).

treehopper A bug resembling the FROGHOPPER, but with the top of the first segment of the thorax enlarged backwards, often into bizarre shapes. Treehoppers comprise the family Membracidae, with over 2,500 species throughout the world. They are plant-feeders, most common in warm climates, and many species are closely associated with ants. The females may provide parental care, guarding the young if disturbed.

tree kangaroo Any of seven species of forest KANGAROO in the genus *Dendrolagus*, at home in the mountains and high tableland of northern Queensland. They have long hind-limbs, and live in the branches of trees. They are about 1.2 m (4 feet) long, half of which is the tail. During the day they sleep curled up in the crotch of a tree, several individuals often occupying the same grove. After sunset they descend backwards to the ground to visit

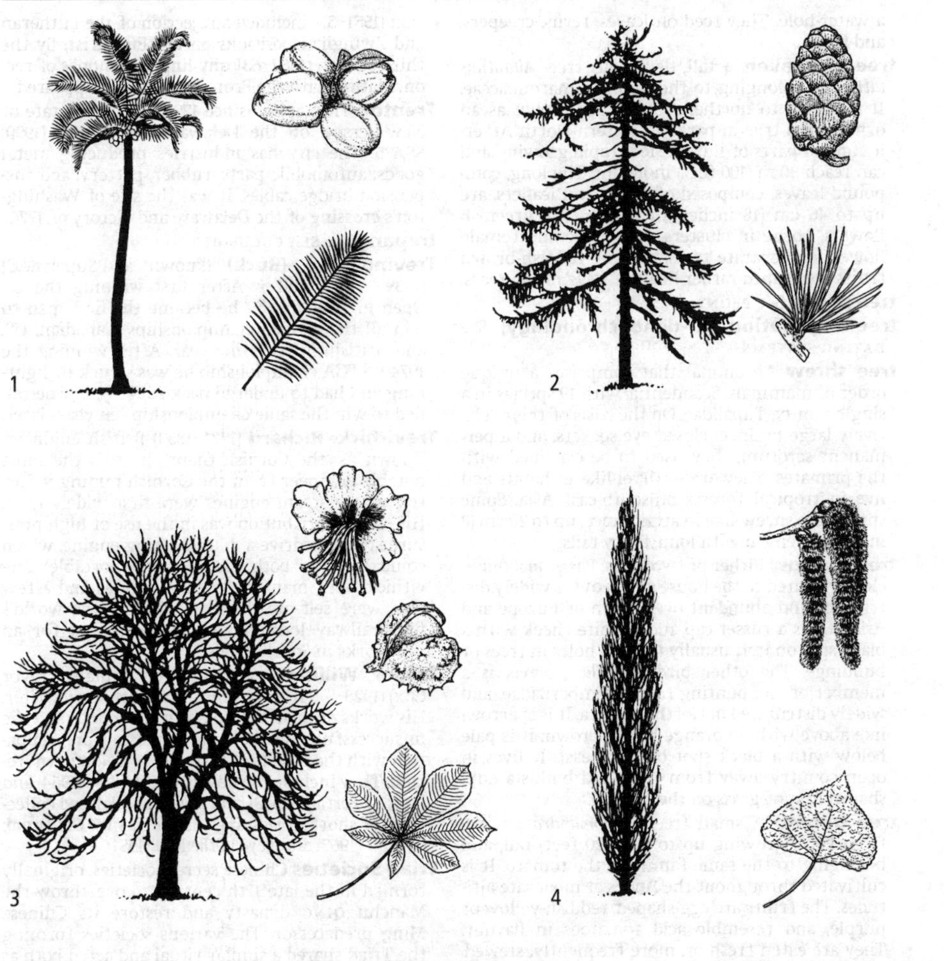

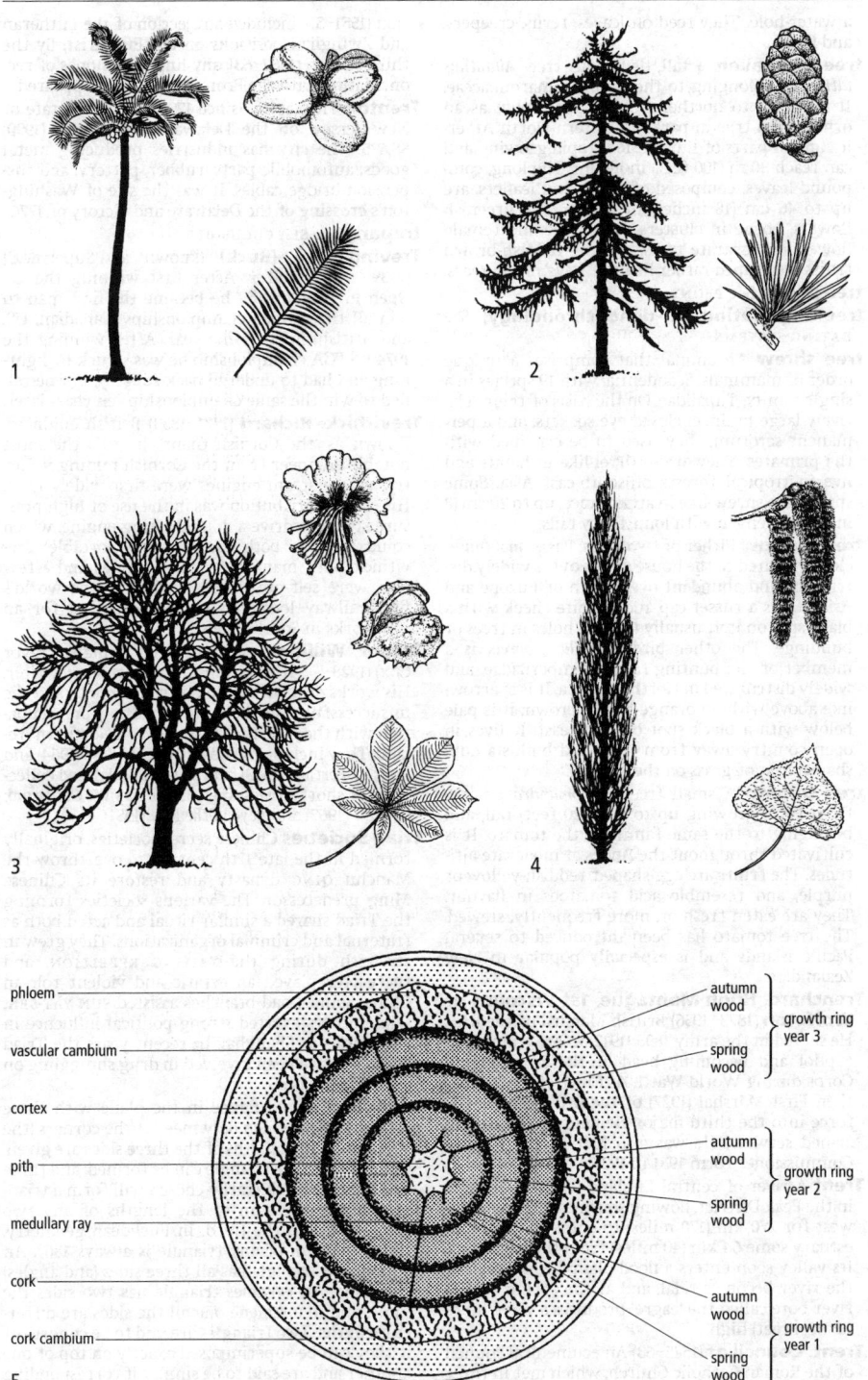

Trees (1) Coconut palm, with details of fruits and a leaf. (2) European larch, with details of a cone and a cluster of leaves. (3) Horse chestnut, with details of a flower, fruit, and leaf. (4) Lombardy poplar, with details of catkins and a leaf. (5) Transverse section through a three-year-old tree trunk. Each growth ring consists of large xylem vessels forming spring wood and small vessels forming autumn wood, both produced by division of the vascular cambium. The cork cambium divides to produce cork, forming the outer layer of the bark. The medullary rays consist of cells that store and transport food materials.

a water-hole. They feed on leaves, ferns, creepers, and fruit.

tree of heaven A tall, deciduous tree, *Ailanthus altissima*, belonging to the family Simaroubaceae. It is native to northern China but grown as an ornamental tree in parks in eastern North America and in parts of Europe. It is rapid growing and can reach 30 m (100 feet) in height. The long, compound leaves, composed of 15–30 oval leaflets, are up to 46 cm (18 inches) in length. The greenish flowers, borne in clusters, have male and female flowers on separate trees, and the reddish-brown fruits are shaped rather like the 'keys' of ash trees.

tree peony See PEONY.

tree-ring dating (or **dendochronology**) See DATING SYSTEMS.

tree shrew An animal that comprises a unique order of mammals, Scandentia, with 19 species in a single family, Tupaiidae. On the basis of their relatively large brain, enclosed eye sockets, and a permanent scrotum, they used to be classified with the primates. They are squirrel-like in habits and live in tropical forests of south-east Asia. Some species are shrew-like in appearance, up to 20 cm (8 inches) in length with long, furry tails.

tree sparrow Either of two birds. *Passer montanus*, closely related to the house SPARROW, is widely distributed and abundant over much of Europe and Asia. It has a russet cap and a white cheek with a black spot on it. It usually nests in holes in trees or buildings. The other bird, *Spizella arborea*, is a member of the bunting family, Emberizidae, and widely distributed in North America. It is sparrow-like above with an orange-brown crown; it is pale below with a black spot on its breast. It lives in open country away from trees and builds a cup-shaped nest of grass on the ground.

tree tomato A small tree, *Cyphomandra betacea*, from Peru, growing up to 6 m (20 feet) tall, and belonging to the same family as the tomato. It is cultivated throughout the Andes at moderate altitudes. The fruits are egg-shaped, reddish-yellow or purple, and resemble acid tomatoes in flavour. They are eaten fresh or, more frequently, stewed. The tree tomato has been introduced to several Pacific islands and is especially popular in New Zealand.

Trenchard, Hugh Montague, 1st Viscount of Wolfeton (1873–1956) British Marshal of the RAF. He served in the army 1893–1912 before training as a pilot and becoming head of the Royal Flying Corps during World War I. As Chief of Staff (1918) then First Marshal (1927) of the RAF he built the force into the third major element of the British armed services. He was also Metropolitan Police Commissioner form 1931 to 1935.

Trent A river of central England with headwaters in the Peak District, flowing south-east then north-west for 270 km (170 miles) to enter the Humber estuary some 64 km (40 miles) from the North Sea. Its valley soon enters a flood-plain; below Newark the river becomes tidal, and at the spring tides a river bore called the 'eagre' produces a wave up to 1.2 m (4 feet) high.

Trent, Council of (1545–63) An ecumenical council of the Roman Catholic Church, which met in three sessions in the city of Trento (anglicized to Trent) in northern Italy. It defined the doctrines of the Church in opposition to those of the REFORMATION, reformed discipline, and strengthened the authority of the papacy. Its first session (1545–47) produced a ruling against LUTHER's doctrine of justification by faith alone. The brief second session (1551–52) included a rejection of the Lutheran and Zwinglian positions on the Eucharist. By the third session (1562–63), any lingering hopes of reconciliation with the Protestants had disappeared.

Trenton The capital (since 1790) of the US state of New Jersey, on the Delaware River; pop. (1990) 88,675. The city has industries producing metal goods, automobile parts, rubber, pottery, and suspension-bridge cables. It was the site of Washington's crossing of the Delaware and victory of 1776.

trepang See SEA CUCUMBER.

Trevino, Lee (Buck) (known as 'Supermex') (1939–) US golfer. After first winning the US Open in 1968, in 1971 he became the first man to win all three Open championships (Canadian, US, and British) in the same year. After winning the 1974 US PGA championship he was struck by lightning and had to undergo back surgery, but he rallied to win the same championship ten years later.

Trevithick, Richard (1771–1833) British engineer. Known as 'the Cornish Giant', he was the most notable engineer from the Cornish mining industry, where steam engines were first widely used. His chief contribution was in the use of high-pressure steam to drive a double-acting engine, which could then be both compact and portable. Trevithick built many stationary engines and a few that were self-propelled – including the world's first railway locomotive (1804), designed for an ironworks in South Wales.

Trevor, William (pseudonym of William Trevor Cox) (1928–) Irish novelist and short-story writer. His works deal with the elderly, the lonely, and the unsuccessful, and show an increasing preoccupation with the effects of terrorism on Northern Ireland. They include the novels *The Old Boys* (1964) and *Fools of Fortune* (1983), and several acclaimed collections of short stories, such as *The Day We Got Drunk on Cake* (1967) and *Beyond the Pale* (1981).

Triad Societies Chinese secret societies, originally formed in the late 17th century to overthrow the Manchu QING dynasty and restore its Chinese Ming predecessor. The various societies forming the Triad shared a similar ritual and acted both as fraternal and criminal organizations. They grew in strength during the TAIPING REBELLION, and thereafter played an erratic and violent role in China. Some Triad branches assisted SUN YAT-SEN, while others exerted strong political influence in such cities as Shanghai. In recent years the Triad Societies have been involved in drug smuggling on a worldwide basis.

triangle A closed figure in the plane with three straight sides, which only meet at the corners (the vertices). If the lengths of the three sides are given, only one possible triangle can be formed; and three line segments arbitrarily chosen will form a triangle only if the sum of the lengths of any two always exceeds the third. In Euclidean geometry, the angle sum of any triangle is always 180°. An equilateral triangle has all three sides (and angles) the same. An isosceles triangle has two sides the same, and in a scalene one all the sides are different lengths. Two triangles are said to be congruent if they can be superimposed exactly on top of one another and are said to be similar if corresponding angles are the same. A right-angled triangle is one containing an angle of 90° The area of any triangle is always 0.5 × base × height. It is possible to discuss spherical triangles where the sides are parts of great circles, that is circles on the surface of a sphere which have the same radius as the sphere. In this geometry, the angle sum of any triangle is not constant but always greater than 180° and the only similar triangles are those that are also congruent.

Triangulum The Triangle, a CONSTELLATION of the northern sky, one of the 48 figures known to the ancient Greeks, who called it Deltoton. Its brightest stars are of third magnitude.

Triangulum Australe The Southern Triangle, a CONSTELLATION of the southern sky introduced by the Dutch navigators Pieter Dirkszoon Keyser and Frederick de Houtman in the late 16th century. Its brightest star, Alpha Trianguli Australis, named Atria, is of second magnitude.

Trianon, Treaty of See VERSAILLES PEACE SETTLEMENT.

Triassic The earliest period of the Mesozoic era, following the Permian and preceding the Jurassic, lasting from about 248 to 213 million years ago. Dinosaurs became numerous during this period, which also saw the appearance of the first mammals. The geological strata of this period are divisible into three groups.

tribunal A body, other than an ordinary COURT OF LAW, appointed to adjudicate on disputed matters, for example between a citizen and a government department, or between individuals. Examples in the UK are social security tribunals and industrial tribunals, which hear disputes between employers and employees. There are also tribunals set up to enforce discipline within professional groups, such as doctors. In the UK tribunals are usually presided over by a legally qualified chairman, but they are largely composed of laymen, and are conducted less formally than courts of law. The tribunal's decisions, while based on rules of law, often concern broad discretionary issues and require members to bring their own experience to bear in reaching their conclusions.

tribune In ancient Rome, ten tribunes were elected to protect PLEBS from PATRICIANS; they were empowered to veto decisions of magistrates and, later, the Senate's decrees. They could also propose legislation of their own. Roman emperors also took the title of tribune, which gave them the constitutional rights of tribunes and a popular image. Military tribunes were senior officers of legions, also elected. The Latin word *tribunus* was derived from *tribus*, tribe, indicating 'of the people'.

triceratops One of the bird-hipped DINOSAURS. Triceratops was a quadrupedal plant-eater, and its head bore three powerful horns. A distinctive frill of bone extended from the skull back over the neck region to serve as protective armour. It was among the last living dinosaurs, becoming extinct some 65 million years ago.

Trier (French **Trèves**) A city in the wine-producing Moselle region of Rhineland-Palatinate in western Germany; pop. (1991) 98,750. Established by a Germanic tribe, the Treveri, *c.*400 BC, Trier is one of the oldest cities in Europe. The Roman town of Augusta Treverorum was founded in 15 BC by the Emperor Augustus. Later it became a seat of the Roman emperor. It was a powerful archbishopric from 815 until the 18th century, but fell into decline after the French occupation in 1797. Trier, in addition to its vast wine cellars has steel, textile, and precision instruments industries.

Trieste A city of north-east Italy, the largest seaport on the Adriatic and capital of Friuli-Venezia Giulia region; pop. (1990) 231,050. Formerly held by Austria, Trieste was annexed by Italy after World War I and retained in 1954 following a failed attempt by the UN to make the area a Free Territory. Oil refining and shipbuilding are amongst its chief industries.

triggerfish A member of a family, Balistidae, containing perhaps 120 species of mainly tropical marine fishes. They have deep, compressed bodies with heavy, smooth scales, and two dorsal fins, the first of which contains strong spines. The large front spine is blunt and strong and is locked into position by the third spine (which has to be depressed first before the front spine is lowered, thus acting as a trigger).

trigonometry A branch of mathematics concerned with the measurement of triangles. It was founded by Hipparchus in the 2nd century BC. It is based on the sine (o/h), cosine (a/h), and tangent (o/a) of the angle θ opposite the right angle in a right-angle triangle, where h is the hypotenuse, a is the side adjacent to θ, and o is the side opposite θ. In any triangle, the cosine rule states that $c^2 = a^2 + b^2 - 2bc \cos A$, where a side and its corresponding angle are labelled with the same letter. The sine rule states that $a/\sin A = b/\sin B = c/\sin C$. Spherical trigonometry, the associated study of spherical triangles whose sides are parts of GREAT CIRCLES rather than straight lines, is a more complex field of study with major uses in navigation and astronomy.

trilobite An extinct arthropod common from the Cambrian to Permian eras (570–245 million years ago). Trilobites had a single head shield, and some species had insect-like compound eyes and antennae. This was followed by more than 20 short body segments, each bearing a pair of jointed legs on the underside. They lived in marine habitats and were 2–30 cm (1–12 inches) in length.

Trinidad and Tobago An island country in the south-east corner of the CARIBBEAN Sea, the larger island, Trinidad, lying only 11 km (7 miles) off the northern coast of South America.

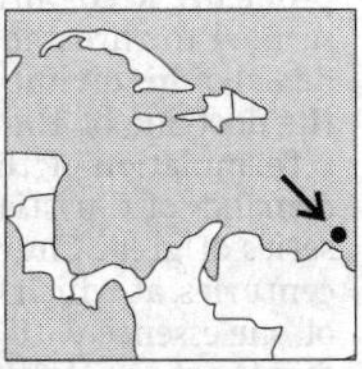

Physical. The country is hot and, in the summer, wet. Trinidad measures about 80 km (50 miles) by 60 km (37 miles). In the south-west is the great Pitch Lake, a basin of bitumen; and across the north of the island is a range of low mountains which contains the Maracas Falls. The densely forested hills of Tobago, to the north-east, are the ridge of an otherwise submerged mountain range.

Economy. The economy is dominated by oil, which, with petroleum products, accounts for the majority of exports. There are also large reserves of natural gas and asphalt. The industrial sector includes an oil refinery, steelworks, and chemicals. With declining oil revenues, tourism, which is comparatively undeveloped, is being encouraged as an alternative source of foreign exchange. Agriculture has been neglected and many staples are imported, although cocoa, sugar, and citrus are grown.

History. The islands were originally inhabited by Arawak and Carib Indians. Trinidad was discovered by Columbus in 1498 during his third voyage. Trinidad was claimed by Spain but left to its indigenous CARIBS until 1532, when settlement was begun. As it lacked precious metals it remained largely ignored until 1595, when Sir Walter RALEIGH landed there for ship repairs and sacked the newly founded town of San José; the Dutch raided it in 1640, and the French in 1677 and 1690. Sugar and tobacco plantations were established in the 17th century, worked by imported African slaves. In 1797, during war between England and Spain, a British squadron entered the Gulf of Paria but met little resistance before the island surrendered. In 1802 it was officially ceded to Britain under the Treaty of Amiens. In 1962, the country became an independent member of the British Commonwealth and, in 1976, a republic. The first Prime Minister of the new republic was Eric Williams, founder of the People's National Movement (PNM). Trinidad's first President, Ellis Clarke, was succeeded in 1987 by Noor Mohammed Hassanali. In the same year Tobago achieved full internal self-government. An attempted coup by black Muslim militants in 1990 failed. The PNM, led by Patrick Manning, won a general election held in December 1991. General elections in 1995 produced no overall winner and Basdeo Panday became Prime Minister, leading a coalition.

Capital: Port of Spain
Area: 5,128.4 sq km (1,980.1 sq mi)
Population: 1,265,000 (1995)
Currency: 1 Trinidad and Tobago dollar = 100 cents
Religions: Roman Catholic 32.2%; Hindu 24.3%; Anglican 14.4%; Muslim 5.9%; Presbyterian 3.7%; Pentecostal 3.4%
Ethnic Groups: Black 40.8%; East Indian 40.7%; mixed 16.3%; White 0.9%; Chinese 0.5%; Lebanese 0.1%
Languages: English (official)
International Organizations: UN; Commonwealth; OAS; CARICOM

Trinity A central doctrine of Christianity: that GOD is one substance, but three persons, Father, Son, and Holy Spirit. This doctrine is not found explicitly in the New Testament, although some threefold formulas are used. Early Christian creeds used Trinitarian language, but this raised theological problems. Recognition of JESUS CHRIST's divinity seemed to threaten Christian monotheism, while denial of his divinity put salvation in doubt. Hence the doctrine of the Trinity represents the radical reformulation of the doctrine of God to meet the demands of Christian faith. It was formulated in a series of great Church councils in the 3rd and 4th centuries, at which first the Son was declared to be of one essence with the Father, and later the equal dignity of the Holy Spirit was affirmed.

triode See DE FOREST; THERMIONIC VALVE.

Triple Alliance (1882) A secret alliance between Germany, Austria, and Italy signed in May 1882 at the instigation of BISMARCK. The three powers agreed to support each other if attacked by either France or Russia. It was renewed at five-yearly intervals, but Italy reneged in 1914 by not coming to the support of the Central Powers.

triple-alpha process A nuclear FUSION reaction occurring in the later stages of a star's life when the central temperature has risen to 10^8 K. Three alpha particles or helium nuclei fuse to form a carbon-12 atom in a process in which energy is released.

triple point The set of conditions in which a gas, a liquid, and a solid can all exist together in equilibrium. There is only one temperature and pressure at which this can occur for any particular substance. The triple point of water (H_2O) is 0.01°C (32.02°F) at 101,325 pascals (atmospheric PRESSURE). This value forms the basis of the definition of the KELVIN and the thermodynamic temperature scale.

triple star A MULTIPLE STAR containing three components, normally bound together by gravitation. Two of the stars form a close BINARY STAR, with the third star moving in a larger orbit about the system's centre of mass. In some apparently triple stars, however, one component is an unconnected star lying nearly in the same line of sight, as in the case of an OPTICAL DOUBLE star.

Tripoli (Arabic **Trâblous**) A Mediterranean seaport in north-west Lebanon; pop. (1988) 160,000. It is capital of the province of Ash Shamal and second-largest city in Lebanon. It stands on the site of the Phoenician city of Oea. It was the terminus for the pipeline from the Iraqi oilfields and has an oil refinery.

Tripoli (Arabic **Tarabulus**) The capital, chief port, commercial, industrial, and communications centre of Libya; pop. (1984) 990,700. Founded by Phoenicians in the 7th century BC, it became the chief city of Tripolitania. It was held successively by Romans, Vandals, Arabs, the Spanish, the Knights of St John, the Ottoman Turks, and Italians, and was a base of the Barbary pirates in the 18th and early 19th centuries. It was an important base for the Axis powers during World War II. Its manufactures include textiles, tobacco, and processed food.

Tripolitania The coastal region surrounding Tripoli in Libya in which the Phoenicians established the three colonies of Leptis Magna, Sabratha, and Oea (now Tripoli).

triptych A painting (or less commonly a carving) in three compartments side by side, the lateral ones ('wings') usually being subordinate to the central one, and often hinged to fold over it. Like the DIPTYCH and the polyptych, the triptych was a common form for altar-pieces in the Middle Ages and Renaissance.

trireme The principal warship of antiquity from the 6th to the late 4th century BC. A type of GALLEY with three banks of oars, it was lightly built for speed and manoeuvrability and unable to venture very far from land; each trireme carried a crew of some 200 men, the majority being rowers. They were probably seated three to a bench, the bench being angled so that each rower pulled a separate oar. A beak of metal and wood was set at the front of the galley, ramming being the principal aim of the steersman. Athens' fleet of triremes played a major part in the Greek victory at SALAMIS and was instrumental in controlling the ATHENIAN EMPIRE.

Tristan de Cunha An island group in the South Atlantic Ocean lying at latitude 37° S on the Mid-Atlantic Ridge. It consists of three small volcanic islands: Tristan, Inaccessible, and Nightingale. Tristan rises to about 2,100 m (6,900 feet) and has a circumference of 34 km (21 miles) at its base. Bleak and barren though it is in appearance, potatoes and wheat can be grown and livestock can be reared on its tussocky turf. The group is a dependency of the British colony of Saint Helena.

Tristram In Celtic mythology, a Cornish knight who, disguised as the minstrel Tantris, was healed by the Irish Queen Iseult. Later he was by mistake given a love-potion intended for her daughter, Iseult, and her betrothed, the king of Cornwall. Tristram and Iseult were bound thereafter in endless passion; they were nevertheless forced to part and Tristram eventually married a Breton princess. On being fatally wounded, however, it was to his great love, Iseult, that he appealed for help. Tristram died when he was wrongly told that his beloved Iseult was not on board the ship approaching Brittany. The myth was incorporated into Arthurian legend in the 13th century and formed the basis of Wagner's opera *Tristan und Isolde*.

tritium (T or ^{3}H) The isotope of hydrogen with mass number 3; its nucleus consists of a proton and two neutrons. It is found in less than 1 part in 10^{17} of the gas but can be made in nuclear reactors. Tritium has a HALF-LIFE of 12.4 years, decaying to helium-3 with the emission of beta-particles. Its main use is as a tracer in radioactive labelling.

Triton (in Greek mythology) A sea-god, son of Poseidon (Roman name, Neptune). More loosely, a type of merman – half-man, half-fish. Tritons are usually shown blowing wind instruments made of conch-shells.

Triton (in astronomy) The largest satellite of Neptune, discovered by the British amateur astronomer William Lassell in 1846. Somewhat smaller than the Earth's Moon, Triton orbits Neptune in the opposite direction to Neptune's orbital motion and with a significant inclination to Neptune's equator. This suggests that Triton may be a captured satellite, whose initially highly elliptical orbit was subsequently shrunk and made circular by the effects of TIDES. The average density of about 2,000 kg/m^3 is very close to that of Pluto, implying that a mixture of ice and rock forms the interior below the icy crust. In general Triton and Pluto are probably very similar objects.

trogon A bird, the 39 species of which comprise the family Trogonidae, which inhabit the tropical forests of the Americas, Africa, and Asia. These birds are about the size of a thrush or small crow, except for the QUETZAL. They are mostly metallic green above with yellow or red underparts. They sit very still beneath the forest canopy and fly out after insects or to pluck fruit. They nest in hollow trees.

troll In Norse mythology, originally a member of the supernatural race of giants associated with Thor's battles. In later folklore trolls came to be seen as dwarfs, who live in caves and mountains, credited with skilful craftsmanship but limited intelligence.

trolleybus An electric bus running on wheels on the road, but obtaining its power from overhead cables. The first trolleybus service began in Germany in 1901, and trolleybuses are still operated in Moscow and a few other cities. Trolleybuses are quiet, pollution-free, and have rapid acceleration, but they lack the flexibility of the motor bus, having to follow the overhead cables. The high costs of electricity supply and cable maintenance make the trolleybus expensive to operate. Nevertheless, there is currently a revival of interest in their use.

Trollope, Anthony (1815–82) British novelist. He worked for the General Post Office in London, Ireland, and other parts of the world from 1834 to 1867, during which time he introduced the pillar-box to Britain. Trollope established his reputation as a writer with his fourth novel *The Warden* (1855), the first of the six 'Barsetshire' novels, which also include *Barchester Towers* (1857) and *The Last Chronicle of Barset* (1867). Set in an imaginary English West Country and with recurring characters, they portray a solid rural society of curates and landed gentry. Another novel sequence, the six political 'Palliser' novels, was published 1864–80. Trollope was a prolific writer, publishing travel books, biographies, and short stories as well as 47 novels.

trombone A brass musical instrument. It obtains PITCHES between the notes of the harmonic series by lengthening the tube by means of an extending slide. It was the only fully chromatic BRASS INSTRUMENT before valves were invented. Valve trombones have been made for military use and for other circumstances in which extending slides is difficult. Up to the 18th century the English name was SACKBUT, used now to distinguish earlier models from modern.

trompe-l'oeil (French, 'deceives the eye') A technique used in painting that is intended to deceive the spectator into thinking that the object or scene depicted exists in three dimensions, rather than being a two-dimensional representation. Such virtuoso displays of skill often have a humorous intent, and stories of visual trickery are common in artists' biographies.

Trondheim A fishing port and the second-largest city in Norway, capital of Sør-Trøndelag county; pop. (1991) 138,060. Formerly known as Nidaros, Trondheim is situated on a peninsula in west-central Norway. Founded by Olaf I Tryggvason, it was the capital of Norway during the Viking period, later becoming a pilgrimage centre as the burial place of Olaf II Haraldsson (St Olaf) who died in battle nearby in 1030. Since 1814 Norwegian monarchs have been proclaimed in Trondheim Cathedral, which was built over the tomb of St Olaf.

tropic The parallel of latitude 23° 27′ north (**tropic of Cancer**) or south (**tropic of Capricorn**) of the equator at which the Sun is overhead respectively around 21 June and 22 December. The region between the tropics of Cancer and Capricorn is known as **the Tropics**.

tropical year See YEAR.

tropic-bird (or **boatswain bird**) Any of three species of seabird in the genus *Phaethon*, widespread over warm tropical and subtropical seas, usually wherever there are flying-fish, their main food. Distinguished by very long central tail feathers, they fly low over the sea singly or in pairs, plunging for fish and squid. They nest on trees or in burrows, usually on islands, rearing single chicks which both parents tend. They belong to the family Phaethontidae.

troposphere The lowest layer of the Earth's atmosphere. The cold atmospheric gases that lie on top of the relatively warm surface of the planet are heated by CONVECTION, so that the hot regions of the lower atmosphere rise up bodily through a region of higher density and the transfer their thermal energy to the cooler overlying regions. The troposphere contains about 70 per cent of the total mass of the Earth's atmosphere and much of it is dominated by stratus, cumulus, and altocumulus clouds. All weather occurs within it, so the air is in continual motion, with horizontal airflows and vertical currents. It varies in height according to season, being thinner in winter when the air is densest. In summer it extends for about 8 km (5 miles) above the poles and for about 18 km (11 miles) above the Equator, over which the air is most rarefied. Temperature decreases with altitude by about 6.5°C per km (18.8°F per mile), until the **tropopause**, the boundary between the troposphere and stratosphere, is reached.

Trotsky, Leon (born Lev Davidovich Bronstein) (1879–1940) Russian revolutionary. Joining the Bolsheviks in 1917, he helped to organize the October Revolution with Lenin, and built up the Red Army that eventually defeated the White Russian forces in the Russian Civil War. After Lenin's death he alienated Stalin and others with his view that socialism within the Soviet Union could not come about until revolution had occurred in western Europe and worldwide. Trotsky was eventually defeated by Stalin in the struggle for power, being expelled from the party in 1927 and exiled in 1929. After settling in Mexico in 1937, he was murdered three years later by a Stalinist assassin.

troubadour A lyric poet or MINSTREL in the 11th century in southern France, particularly in Provence. Their poetry dealt with courtly love, CHIVALRY, religion, and politics, but usually the matter was heavily disguised in formal, decorative language. Much of it was heretical, and in the 13th century many of its devotees were persecuted.

trout A fish of the salmon family, which is native across Europe and in Atlantic coastal waters, but has been introduced to many other parts of the world as a sporting and food-fish. Brown trout, *Salmo trutta*, live in rivers and lakes. Sea trout, which are a form of *S. trutta*, are silvery and migrate to the sea to feed. They spawn in winter, the eggs being laid in redds hollowed out in river gravel and hatching in six to eight weeks. Young trout eat insects, insect larvae, and crustaceans; large trout eat fishes too. They require cool water with high oxygen levels. The North American rainbow trout, *S. gairdneri*, has a purple band along each side.

trout perch A freshwater fish, *Percopsis omiscomaycus*, living in the back waters of lowland rivers and in shallow lakes in parts of North America. It grows to about 20 cm (8 inches) in length and is slender-bodied, with weak spines in the dorsal and anal fins and a small adipose fin. It feeds on aquatic insects, small crustaceans, and molluscs, and spawns over gravel-beds in late spring and early summer.

Troy (Turkish **Truva**; Latin **Ilium**) In Homeric legend, the city of King Priam, which was besieged for ten years by the Greeks in their endeavour to recover Helen, wife of Menalaus, who had been abducted. It was believed to be a figment of Greek legend until a stronghold called by the Turks Hissarlik, in Asiatic Turkey near the Dardanelles, was identified as the site of Troy by the German archaeologist H. Schliemann, who in 1870 began excavations of the mound which proved to be composed of 46 strata, dating from the early Bronze Age to the Roman era. The stratum known as Troy VII, believed to be that of the Homeric city, was sacked *c.*1210 BC. Again destroyed *c.*1100 BC, the site was resettled by the Greeks *c.*700 BC and finally abandoned in the Roman period.

Troyes, Chrétien de See CHRÉTIEN DE TROYES.

Trucial States Seven Arab sheikdoms on the Persian Gulf, which since 1971 have been known as the United Arab Emirates. It refers to the maritime truce made with Britain in 1836 (and subsequently renewed and extended) by which local rulers undertook to abstain from maritime warfare.

Truck Acts Measures passed by the British Parliament in the 19th century regarding the method of payment of wages. Certain employers paid their workmen in goods or in tokens, which could be exchanged only at shops owned by the employers – the so-called truck system. The Truck Act of 1831 listed many trades in which payment of wages must be made in coins. It was amended by an Act of 1887, which extended its provisions to cover virtually all manual workers. In 1896 a further Act regulated the amounts that could be deducted from wages for bad workmanship. The Payment of Wages Act of 1960 repealed certain sections of the Truck Acts to permit payment of wages by cheque.

Trudeau, Pierre (Elliott) (1919–) Canadian Liberal statesman, Prime Minister of Canada 1968–79 and 1980–84. A committed federalist, Trudeau made both English and French official languages of the Canadian government (1969). During his second term, in 1980, a provincial referendum rejected independence for Quebec; Trudeau also presided over the transfer of residual constitutional powers from Britain to Canada in 1982.

Trueman, Fred(erick Sewards) (1931–) British cricketer. A fast bowler, he played for England from 1952 until 1965, during which time he became the first bowler to take 300 test wickets (1964) and took 307 wickets overall. He also played for his home county, Yorkshire (1949–68), taking a total of 2,304 wickets in first-class games. After retiring from the sport he became a cricket commentator and journalist.

Truffaut, François (1932–84) French film director. He was an influential film critic in the 1950s and originated the idea of the director as 'auteur'. In 1959 he directed his first feature film, *Les Quatre Cents Coups*, a work that established him as a leading director of the *nouvelle vague*. He acted and collaborated in the scriptwriting of this and many of his other films, among which are *Jules et Jim* (1961), *La Nuit américaine* (1973; *Day for Night*), which won an Oscar for best foreign film, and *The Last Metro* (1980).

truffle A FUNGUS belonging to the order Tuberales, only found underground. The fruiting body, which is often referred to as the truffle, is usually round and pitted, and 1–7 cm (0.5–3 inches) in diameter. Several species are highly esteemed delicacies, particularly the Périgord truffle, *Tuber melanosporum*, and are usually found under oak or beech trees. Many have a strong smell and attract animals, such as rabbits and squirrels, which help disperse them by digging them up. In France, trained dogs or pigs are used to find them by their smell.

Trujillo, Rafael (born Rafael Leónidas Trujillo Molina; known as 'Generalissimo') (1891–1961) Dominican statesman, President of the Dominican Republic 1930–38 and 1942–52. Although he was formally President for only two periods, he wielded dictatorial powers from 1930 until his death. His dictatorship was marked by some improvement in social services and material benefits for the people, but also by the deployment of a strong and ruthless police force to crush all opposition. He was assassinated in 1961.

Truk (or **Chuuk**) One of the four Federated States of Micronesia in the western Pacific Ocean, comprising 14 volcanic islands and numerous atolls all lying within a reef-fringed lagoon; area 127 sq km (49 sq miles); pop. (est. 1990) 53,700; administrative centre, Moen. The Truk lagoon is one of the largest in the world.

Truman, Harry S (1884–1972) US Democratic statesman, 33rd President of the USA 1945–53. As Vice-President, he automatically took office on Franklin Roosevelt's death in 1945. One of his first actions was to authorize the use of the atom bomb against Hiroshima and Nagasaki in 1945 to end the war with Japan. At home Truman put forward an extensive social programme, which was largely blocked by Congress, although racial segregation in the armed forces and in federally funded schools was ended. His expression in 1947 of what became known as the **Truman Doctrine** (the principle that the USA should give support to countries or peoples threatened by Soviet forces or Communist insurrection) was seen by the Communists as an open declaration of the cold war. In 1948 his administration introduced the Marshall Plan of emergency aid to war-shattered European countries and helped to establish NATO the following year. He later involved the USA in the Korean War.

trumpet A brass musical instrument. In the 13th century European trumpets were straight, but by the late 1300s they were often folded in an S-shape. In the 15th century they were folded with a loop of tubing, often with a long mouthpiece-stem sliding in the first length, allowing players to produce some chromatic notes. The normal Baroque trumpets played only natural HARMONICS, and could play melodically only in the high register. At the end of the 18th century, the key trumpet was invented, for which Haydn and Hummel both wrote concertos, and in England there was a new slide trumpet with its slide in the back bow. The latter became the English orchestral trumpet. Elsewhere, valve trumpets were used from the mid-19th century, usually in F; only towards the end of the 19th century were they reduced in length to form the modern B♭ instrument.

trumpeter swan The largest and rarest of the SWANS, *Cygnus buccinator*, named for its bugle-like calls. They have only recently been saved from extinction by conservationists. Except for their black bills they are very like whooper swans and inhabit northwestern America.

trumpetfish Any of three species in the family Aulostomidae, all distantly related to the pipefishes. They occur in the Indo-Pacific, and parts of the Atlantic. All are long-bodied, with long tubular snouts and a series of separate spines along the back. They are slow swimmers and live on reefs and in shallow water, catching fishes and shrimps by stealth.

trunkfish A member of the family Ostraciontidae, related to the triggerfishes and pufferfishes. They are also called boxfishes, because of the specialized scales that cover the head and body in a shell-like covering. They are found in all tropical oceans, mainly in shallow water. Slow swimmers, moving mainly by paddle-like motions of the fins, they are protected from predators by their box-like armour and by a toxin that they secrete.

Truro A cathedral and tourist city and county town of Cornwall, south-west England, on the River Truro; pop. (1991) 18,966. Its granite-built cathedral was founded in 1879.

trust (in law) An arrangement in which funds or assets are managed by one person (known as a trustee) for the benefit of another (a beneficiary). In England, the trust developed in the COMMON LAW SYSTEM in the court of EQUITY, and there is no direct equivalent in CIVIL LAW systems. The duties of the trustee are determined both by the general law and by the express instructions of the person who established the trust. The trustee is ostensible owner of the trust property but must keep the trust property separate from his own assets, must invest and preserve it, and distribute income from it in accordance with the terms of the trust. Historically, a trust facilitated the holding of family property over several generations. It is now used to minimize taxation, as a way in which ownership of land can be shared, and as a means by which funds are held for a charitable purpose. In the UK, a trust also refers to a financial institution, such as an investment trust, which facilitates STOCK EXCHANGE trading by small-scale investors. In the USA, a trust is a group of COMPANIES who form a CARTEL to fix prices or restrict competition. US legislation to break up cartels are called **anti-trust laws.**

trusteeship (in politics) A system devised after World War II by the UNITED NATIONS for administering certain non-self-governing territories, notably former Japanese and Italian colonies. UN trusteeship is modelled on the mandates system established by the League of Nations after World War I. Reports on trust territories are submitted to the UN Trusteeship Council, whose role is to superintend their transition to self-government. As a result of the decolonization process virtually all such territories have achieved independence, with the exception of certain small US-administered Pacific islands.

Truth, Sojourner (previous name Isabella Van Wagener) (*c.*1797–1883) US evangelist and reformer. Born into slavery, she was sold to a man named Isaac Van Wagener, who set her free in 1827. She became a zealous evangelist and in 1843 changed her name and travelled across the USA. Her preaching in favour of black rights and women's suffrage drew large crowds, her fame grew, and in 1864 she was received at the White House by Abraham Lincoln.

Truva See TROY.

trypanosomiasis A protozoal infection caused by organisms of the genus *Trypanosoma*. African trypanosomiasis (**sleeping sickness**) is caused by *T. brucei*; two subtypes are encountered in different parts of Africa, *T. brucei gambiense* and *T. brucei rhodesiense*. The infection is transmitted by the bite of a TSETSE FLY; symptoms include fever, malaise, itching, and anaemia. Progression leads to hallucinations, drowsiness, convulsions, and coma. It can be fatal if it is not treated in its early stages.

American trypanosomiasis (**Chagas' disease**) is caused by *T. cruzi*, which occurs in Central and South America, and is transmitted by bugs. Symptoms include fever, weakness, facial swelling, and the enlargement of the liver and spleen. A chronic phase begins after many years causing heart disease and dilatation of the gastro-intestinal tract. This type of trypanosomiasis can be successfully treated.

tsetse fly A dark brown or yellowish blood-sucking fly of the genus *Glossina*, occurring in tropical Africa. The adults act as VECTORS for the protozoan parasites that cause sleeping sickness (TRYPANOSOMIASIS) in man and nagana in cattle and horses. They are woodland insects, each of the 21 species of *Glossina* requiring particular conditions of temperature and humidity to provide suitable conditions for mating, breeding, feeding, and sheltering. Large wild mammals are their usual source of blood. Slaughter of wild animals and bush clearance are the principal means of control.

Tshombe, Moise (Kapenda) (1920–69) African leader in the Belgian Congo. He founded the Conakat political party, which advocated an independent but loosely federal Congo. He took part in talks that led to Congolese independence in 1960, but then declared the province of Katanga independent of the rest of the country. He maintained his position as self-styled President of Katanga (1960–63) with the help of white mercenaries and the support of the Belgian mining company, Union Minière. Briefly Prime Minister of the Congo Republic (1964–65), he was accused of the murder of LUMUMBA, and of corruptly rigging the elections of 1965, and fled the country when General MOBUTU seized power. In 1967 he was kidnapped and taken to Algeria, where he died in prison.

Tsiolkovsky, Konstantin (Eduardovich) (1857–1935) Russian aeronautical engineer. His early ideas for aircraft and rockets were not officially recognized until after the Russian Revolution, though his proposal for the use of liquid fuel in rockets predated Robert Goddard's successful rocket flight by nearly 40 years. During the 1920s Tsiolkovsky carried out pioneering theoretical work on multi-stage rockets, jet engines, and space flight.

Tskhinvali The capital town of the South Ossetian autonomous region in the Republic of Georgia, in the Caucasus north-west of Tbilisi.

tsunami A long, high sea wave caused by underwater earthquakes of 5.5 or more on the Richter Scale, or by other disturbances, such as volcanoes, landslides, or the calving of very large icebergs from glaciers.

Tuareg A group of BERBERS, relatively few in number, who roam over a vast territory in North Africa. In the past they criss-crossed the Sahara in their caravans, trading between the Mediterranean and the Sahel, and subsisting on dates and millet, which they traded for their livestock. Traditional Tuareg society is hierarchical and feudal, the different castes being mutually interdependent. Traditionally it is Tuareg men who go veiled, not the women. In recent years the NOMADISM of the Tuareg has been threatened both by trading restrictions and by Sahelian droughts. There have been militant Tuareg uprisings in Niger (1991–95) and Mali (1990–93).

tuatara An unusual, primitive, lizard-like reptile, *Sphenodon punctatus*, which lives only on some rocky islands off the coast of New Zealand, where it is protected by law. The tuatara is the sole survivor of an order, Rhynocephalia, of reptiles that flourished in the Triassic Period (220–250 million years ago). It is active at lower body temperatures than other reptiles and has a very slow rate of growth so that it is not sexually mature until it is 20 years old, and may live more than 100 years. The tuatara lives in burrows which it either constructs itself or takes over from excavating birds, such as petrels and shearwaters. Their eggs take 12–15 months to hatch.

tuba A musical instrument, a bass valved BUGLE in F, with three valves, developed in the 1820s and then known as a bombardon. A fourth and then a fifth valve were added to fill the octave between the first two harmonics. A further advance was the development of the BB♭ tuba, a fifth lower (CC for orchestral use). Because upright tubas are heavy to carry on the march, the spirally coiled helicon, whose weight rests of one shoulder, was invented in 1845. This led to the sousaphone, which projects the sound forward instead of sideways.

tube-mouth fish A species of fish related to the wrasses, and forming the family Odacidae. The tube-mouth fish resembles a pipefish, being extremely long and slender. It lives among seaweeds on the coasts of southern Australia and grows to a length of 40 cm (16 inches).

tuber A swollen plant organ, usually produced underground and derived from roots, as in the dahlia, or from underground stems, as in the potato. They act as storage organs and several have been exploited for food. Compare RHIZOME.

tuberculosis A communicable infection most commonly caused by *Mycobacterium tuberculosis*. Tuberculosis is associated with poor living conditions, such as nutritional deficiency, and inadequate housing, and is therefore more prevalent in developing countries where standards of medical care are inadequate. Transmission of tuberculosis is by inhalation of infected droplets. Initially, primary tuberculosis occurs, which is characterized by infection of the lungs causing the tuberculosis lesion (tubercle); it may be mild and asymptomatic, although cough, fever, breathing difficulties, loss of appetite, and weight loss may occur. The primary infection commonly resolves within a few weeks, but it may progress. In some cases, the microorganism infects other organs and tissues via the blood stream, which is called miliary tuberculosis; lesions may occur in the brain (MENINGITIS), bones, skin, heart, joints, and kidneys. Treatment is by the long-term administration of antibacterial drugs; treatment renders patients non-infective very quickly, and isolation may only be required when children are at risk of infection. Active IMMUNIZATION is an effective measure in the prevention of tuberculosis.

Tubman, William Vacanarat Shadrach (1895–1971) Liberian statesman, President 1944–71. A member of an Americo-Liberian family, he was elected to the Liberian Senate in 1930 and became President in 1944. He encouraged economic development to remove Liberia's financial dependence on the USA and successfully integrated the inhabitants of the country's interior into an administration.

Tubuai Islands (or **Austral Islands**) A 1,300-km (800-mile) chain of volcanic islands in the southern Pacific Ocean forming part of French Polynesia; area 148 sq km (57 sq miles); pop. (1988) 6,500. The principal islands are Tubuai, Rimatara, Rurutu, Rapa, and Raivavae and the chief settlement and port is Mataura (on Tubuai).

tubular bell A metal tube used instead of a church bell. Twelve tubes, covering a full octave, can hang on a stand occupying about one square metre or yard of floor, and can be moved by two people. The same number of real bells would weigh 30–40 tonnes and occupy a large space. The tubes are hung with 'white' notes in front and 'black' behind, and are struck with rawhide hammers.

Tucana The Toucan, a CONSTELLATION of the southern sky introduced by the Dutch navigators Pieter Dirkszoon Keyser and Frederick de Houtman in the late 16th century. Beta Tucanae is a binocular double star of fourth and fifth magnitudes.

tuco-tuco A cavy-like RODENT of a family with a wide distribution in southern South America, Ctenomyidae. There are some 38 species in the genus *Ctenomys*, found from sea-level to 4,000 m (13,000 feet) up the Andes. They are gopher-like in habit, constructing extensive burrows. They weigh up to 700 g (1.5 pounds) and are entirely herbivorous, feeding mostly at night on roots as well as leaves and seeds.

Tucson A resort city in south-east Arizona, USA, on the Santa Cruz and Rillito rivers; pop. (1990) 405,390. Founded by the Spanish in 1775, the Presidio of Tucson was built to withstand Apache Indian attacks. It is the seat of the University of Arizona (1885). Copper, cotton, and cattle are traded and nearby are the Coronado National Forest and Biosphere 2, a glass-enclosed self-sustaining model of the Earth's ecosystems.

Tudjman, Franjo (1922–) Croatian politician, president of Croatia as a federal republic of Yugoslavia 1990–92 and as an independent state since 1992. Imprisoned in the 1970s and 1980s for his advocacy of Croatian independence, he led the Croatian forces in the fight against the Serb-led Yugoslavian army (1991–92) and involved Croatian forces in the civil war in Bosnia-Hercegovina. He was re-elected president in 1997, although the election was criticized for his total control of the media.

Tudor The English royal house that began as a family of Welsh gentry. Its fortunes started to rise when HENRY V's widow, Katherine of Valois, married Owen Tudor (*c.*1400–61), her clerk of the wardrobe. He was executed after the YORKISTS' victory of Mortimer's Cross (1461) during the Wars of the Roses, but his son Edmund (*c.*1430–56), Earl of Richmond, married Margaret BEAUFORT, and their son Henry was thus a descendant, though illegitimately, of the House of Lancaster. His claim to the throne became more acceptable after the death of HENRY VI's son Edward in 1471, and RICHARD III's loss of the nobility's support paved the way for Henry's invasion of England and taking of the throne as HENRY VII in 1485.

Henry safeguarded his claim to the throne by marrying Elizabeth of York, the Yorkist heiress: she bore him eight children, although four died in infancy. Arthur died soon after marrying Catherine of Aragon, and it was his younger brother who succeeded to the throne, as HENRY VIII. Of his children, his only son, EDWARD VI, died in his youth. His elder daughter MARY died in 1558 after a childless marriage to Philip II of Spain, and ELIZABETH never married. With Elizabeth's death (1603) the House of Tudor ended, and the throne passed to James VI of Scotland, of the House of STUART.

Tudor architecture The architecture characterized by the buildings erected in Britain under the TUDOR dynasty, that is, from the accession of Henry VII in 1485 to the death of Elizabeth I in 1603. This period encompasses the final flowering of the PERPENDICULAR style. It is expressed mainly in secular architecture (collegiate as well as domestic), for church building in Britain had virtually ended by the Reformation. The most characteristic building material was brick, often patterned by the use of contrasting colours or used to create splendid decorative chimney stacks. Outstanding examples include Hampton Court Palace, begun by Cardinal Wolsey in 1515; Compton Wynyates in Warwickshire, one of the most idyllically beautiful of English country houses, built by Sir William Compton; and the Great Gate of Trinity College, Cambridge, completed in 1533. Architecture of the later Tudor period is often called 'Elizabethan' (Elizabeth I reigned 1558–1603). In this period stone is used more often for major buildings, and houses become more grandiose.

tufa (or **calc tufa**) A calcareous deposit. It is normally white, although it can be stained many colours. It occurs as spongy, porous masses deposited from springs and river waters rich in calcium carbonate. A common deposit of limestone regions, it fills cracks, fissures, and joints in rock as well as cementing gravels.

tufted duck An Old World species of POCHARD. *Aythya fuligula* is very common in Europe, where it nests on islands in lakes and ponds, and forms large flocks outside the breeding season. The drake is black and white, and has a thin tuft drooping behind its head, unlike its relative the scaup.

tug A small, powerful vessel used in harbours and elsewhere for aiding large vessels to move in confined spaces, for towing at sea, for fire-fighting, and for salvage and rescue. There are several types of tug. Harbour tugs are usually around 250 tonnes and develop a power of up to 1,900 kW; ocean-going tugs are much larger (2,000 tonnes) and may develop over 11,200 kW. With the immense amount of power available from modern engines, there is the real risk of turning a tug over unless the pull is kept accurately over the stem or stern.

Tuileries A French royal residence in Paris built in the 16th century. In June 1792 during the FRENCH REVOLUTION crowds forced their way into the palace, and on 10 August it was attacked, the Swiss Guard was massacred, and the royal family took refuge with the Assembly. The palace was burned down in the 19th century, but the formal gardens laid out in the 17th century remain.

Tula The ancient capital (980–1168) of the Toltecs in Mexico, usually identified with a site near the town of Tula in Hidalgo state, central Mexico.

tulip A perennial plant belonging to the genus *Tulipa*, part of the LILY family. With the onset of the growing period the bulbs produce variously shaped leaves or leafy stems which terminate in showy flowers. Over 100 species are known, from Europe, Asia, and North Africa, ranging from small, multiflowered alpines to species with large and colourful solitary flowers. They have been popular as garden and greenhouse plants since the introduction of *T. suaveolens* to Europe in 1572. Dutch plant breeders were mainly responsible for the early varieties, which resulted in the tulip mania of the 1630s, when vast sums were paid for single bulbs of new hybrids. Modern varieties are now divided into several classes according to habit and flowering time.

tulip tree Either of two species of *Liriodendron*, which are members of the magnolia family. The tulip tree, *L. tulipifera*, is native to North America from Nova Scotia to Florida, and the Chinese tulip tree, *L. chinense*, is native to central China. Both are deciduous trees, which may reach 60 m (190 feet) in height, and have tulip-like flowers as their name suggests. The American tulip tree has fine-grained, light yellow timber which is used in carpentry.

Tull, Jethro (1674–1741) English agriculturalist. He had a profound effect on agricultural practice with his invention of the seed drill (1701), which could sow seeds in accurately spaced rows at a controlled rate. This made possible the control of weeds by horse-drawn hoe, reducing the need for farm labourers.

Tulsidas (*c.*1543–1623) Indian poet. He was a leading Hindu devotional poet, who is chiefly remembered for the *Ramcaritmanas* (*c.*1574–77), a work consisting of seven cantos based on the Sanskrit epic the Ramayana. The poet's expression of worship or bhakti for Rama led to the cult of Rama (rather than that of Krishna) dominating the Hindu culture of northern India.

tumour An abnormal growth in the tissues of the body, which may be benign or malignant. **Benign tumours** are characterized by growth at one site only, which is often by slow cell division, which may stop. They are structurally distinct and well demarcated; cells are normal and resemble the cells of the tissue from which they originated; the cellular structure is regular, and function of the tissues may also be retained. Benign tumours are covered by a capsule and have a good blood supply and supportive structures. They may be harmless, but compression of adjacent tissues or occlusion of an organ may cause severe effects.

Malignant tumours are characterized by rapid cell division and growth that rarely stops, and may spread and invade adjacent tissues; commonly, cells show partial or complete loss of function and bear little resemblance to the tissue cells from which they originated. A malignant tumour is not enclosed by a capsule and has an arbitrary and poor blood supply and supportive structures. Malignant tumours are never harmless and cause extensive damage (see CANCER AND CANCER THERAPY).

tuna A medium to large marine fish of the family Scombridae, which also includes the mackerel. Tunas are oceanic fishes, and most abundant in tropical and warm temperate seas, but they migrate into cooler waters in the warm seasons. They live near the surface and are active, predatory fishes, feeding on a wide range of surface-living fishes and squids. They all have a spindle-shaped body with a pointed head, two dorsal fins, and a broad tail fin. The first dorsal fin slots into a groove on the back, and the second, like the anal one, ends in a series of small finlets. Tunas are immensely powerful swimmers, and have a body-temperature higher than that of the surrounding water. The most common species in the Atlantic is the blue-fin tunny, or tuna, *Thunnus thynnus*, which grows up to 4 m (13 feet) in length; it migrates northwards into Norwegian waters in summer.

Tunbridge Wells (or **Royal Tunbridge Wells**) A spa and commuter town in Kent, south-east England; pop. (1981) 58,140. Founded in the 1630s after the discovery of iron-rich springs by Lord North in 1606, the town was visited by Queen Victoria and in 1909 given its 'Royal' prefix.

tundra A vast, level, treeless Arctic region usually with a marshy surface and underlying permafrost, dominated by low-growing herbaceous plants, dwarf shrubs, grasses, sedges, lichens, and mosses.

tungsten (symbol W, at. no. 74, r.a.m. 183.85) A lustrous silvery white TRANSITION METAL, taking its name from the Swedish for 'heavy stone'. Also known as wolfram, it occurs naturally as wolframite, (Fe, Mn) WO_4, together with traces of stolzite, $PbWO_4$, and scheelite, $CaWO_4$. Important deposits occur in the USA, Russia, and China; commercially the metal is obtained by reducing tungsten oxide, WO_3, with hydrogen or carbon. It has the highest melting-point, 3,410°C (6,170°F), the lowest vapour pressure, and above 1,000°C (1,832°F) the highest tensile strength of any metal. Moreover, it is very resistant to corrosion, and is only slightly attacked by acids. Its main uses are in steel alloys, as filaments in light bulbs, in television and X-ray tubes, and in tungsten carbide tips for drilling and cutting tools.

Tunis The capital of Tunisia, situated near the Mediterranean coast of North Africa; pop. (1984) 596,650. The ruins of Carthage and the Bardo National Museum are nearby and the city itself contains a large number of ancient monuments. It is linked by a deep-water channel to the new port of La Goulette. Its industries include smelting and railway workshops and there are numerous handicrafts and light industries.

Tunisia A country on the North African coast, sandwiched between Algeria and Libya, which has its southern part in the Sahara.

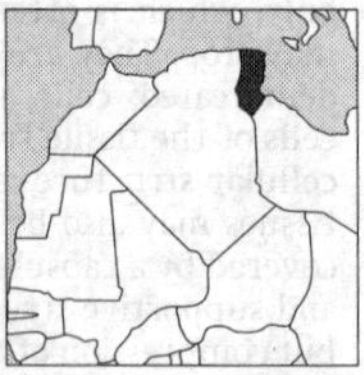

Physical. The coastal climate is Mediterranean. In the north-west of the country are hills, mostly covered in scrub though containing forests of cork-oak. Southward it becomes hotter and drier. Salt marshes cover the central belt, where there are also large phosphate deposits. The south is sandy but contains oases.

Economy. Crude oil is the mainstay of Tunisia's economy, but falling production has caused economic problems. Other mineral resource include phosphate, iron ore, zinc, and lead. There is natural gas off-shore. Agriculture, though adversely affected by drought and locust plagues in recent years, is well developed, producing cereals, olives, grapes, dates, and citrus. Food-processing, oil, and phosphates are the chief manufacturing industries. Tourism also plays an important part in the economy.

History. Tunisia has been the strategic centre of the Mediterranean. PHOENICIANS came first *c.*1000 BC; and, traditionally, CARTHAGE, seat of a sea-borne empire, was founded here in 814 BC. BERBER caravans came north to exchange produce for imports. Carthage fell in 146 BC, and, despite Berber resistance, Rome made the province of Africa Proconsularis rich in corn, olives, and vines. VANDALS from Spain took it in 429, but BYZANTIUM recovered it in 533. The Berbers, nevertheless, held the interior, giving way only when the Arabs built Kairouan as an inland base to control Africa. The caliphate was replaced by an independent local dynasty, the Aghlabids, in 800, until 909, when the FATIMIDS took Kairouan. Another local dynasty, the Zirids, replaced them when they moved to Cairo in 969. In revenge, the Fatimids sent thousands of Arab tribesmen to lay waste the country. In the 12th century the Normans from Sicily held some towns, until the ALMOHADS expelled them. Then another local dynasty, the Hafsids (1228–1574) emerged, taking Algiers (1235) and Tlemcen (1242). In 1270 they repulsed the Crusaders under St LOUIS. From 1574 until 1881 the Regency of Tunis owed nominal allegiance to the Ottomans, but after 1612 a dynasty of Beys established itself. The Bey of Tunis became increasingly independent and CORSAIRS operated from Tunis, leading to the Tripolitan War with the USA. A period of great prosperity ended when the corsairs and the slave trade were suppressed (1819). During the 19th century, the Bey's control weakened and, in 1881, France declared Tunisia a protectorate. The rise of nationalist activity led to fighting between the nationalists and the colonial government in the 1950s. Habib BOURGUIBA, the nationalist leader, was imprisoned, but was released (1955) when the country achieved independence. The Bey of Tunis abdicated (1956) and the country became a republic led by Bourguiba and the neo-Destour Party. In the 1970s the government's refusal to allow the formation of other political parties caused serious unrest, while subsequent attempts at liberalization were interrupted by fresh outbreaks of rioting in 1984–85. Bourguiba was deposed (1987) and succeeded by President Zine el-Abidine Ben Ali, who introduced a multi-party system in 1988 and was re-elected in 1994. The Islamic fundamentalist party al-Nahdah, however, was suppressed in 1990, and there were violent incidents throughout 1991. Tunisia took a neutral stance over the GULF WAR, as a result of which both Kuwait and Saudi Arabia withdrew investments and the USA cut aid. From 1982 it provided a refuge for the PLO until a peace agreement was made with Israel (1993).

Capital: Tunis
Area: 154,530 sq km (59,664 sq mi)
Population: 8,896,000 (1995)
Currency: 1 Tunisian dinar = 1,000 millimes
Religions: Sunni Muslim 99.4%; Christian 0.3%; Jewish 0.1%
Ethnic Groups: Arab 98.2%; Berber 1.2%; French 0.2%; Italian 0.1%
Languages: Arabic (official); French
International Organizations: UN; OAU; Arab League; Maghreb Union

tunnel An underground passage for use by road or railway vehicles, or in MINING, or for water supply or sewage. Tunnels in hard rock are generally self-supporting and are made by drilling, blasting, mucking out, and fixing temporary supports if required. If a smooth profile is required, a permanent concrete lining is built in sections. In soft ground, where the tunnel cannot fully support itself, the permanent lining is usually fixed as the tunnel is excavated. In the 19th and early 20th centuries, brickwork linings were employed, but they took a long time to construct. Their use has been superseded by the prefabrication of linings built from cast IRON or PRE-CAST CONCRETE segments. Tunnels in soft ground are usually excavated with a tunnel boring machine (TBM), which was developed from the SHIELD EXCAVATOR. Shallow tunnels may be built by the cut-and-cover method, used particularly in urban streets. A section of road is excavated, perhaps after the construction of diaphragm walls to support adjacent structures. When that section of the tunnel has been built, the excavation is covered over and work proceeds to the next section. For tunnels under shallow water the immersed tube technique is widely used. The tunnel structure is prefabricated in short lengths in a dry dock, and each section is sealed, making it buoyant. It is then towed out and sunk into a trench dredged in the sea- or river-bed, where it is jointed by divers to the previous section, sealed, and covered over. The most spectacular tunnelling achievement in the world is the Anglo-French CHANNEL TUNNEL.

tunnelling (in atomic physics) The passage of minute particles through apparently impassable force barriers. Tunnelling is explained by QUANTUM MECHANICS. For example, an electron held in position by an electric field has the characteristics of a wave as well as a particle. At the point at which the particle aspect of the electron hits the barrier, the wave aspect – which is spread out – may spread into the barrier and, if the barrier is thin enough, out the other side. Since this wave is an indication of the probability of finding the particle at a certain place (see WAVEFUNCTION), there is a probability that the particle will appear on the other side of the barrier. Tunnelling has been observed experimentally, and explains a number of phenomena, including some properties of semiconductors and the escape of alpha particles from unstable nuclei.

tupelo A deciduous tree or shrub of the genus *Nyssa*, native to North America and the Far East. Several species are grown for their durable wood. The trunk of the black gum, or tupelo, *N. sylvatica*, may reach 30 m (100 feet) in length. It is native to swampy and other poorly drained ground in eastern North America. The water tupelo or cotton gum, *N. aquatica*, of the southeastern USA, withstands flooding of up to 2 m (6.5 feet) or more of water.

Tupolev, Andrey Nikolayevich (1888–1972) Soviet aeronautical engineer. He was a pupil of Nikolay Zhukovsky, the father of Soviet aviation. He was responsible for more than 100 military and civilian aircraft, from the all-wood single-seater ANT-1 (1922) to the supersonic Tu-22 bomber (1961). Tupolev also designed GLIDERS, hydroplanes, and TORPEDO-BOATS. His main rival was ILYUSHIN.

turaco (or **touraco**, **plantain-eater**) A bird belonging to the family Musophagidae, which contains about 23 species related to the cuckoos. The name strictly applies to the 17 species of *Tauraco* and *Musophaga*. All occur in Africa south of the Sahara, and most live in forest, though a few are found in open savannah. Their body-size is similar to that of a crow, but they have long tails. Most species are glossy blue-black or green with red and yellow markings, but some are greyish-brown and white. They eat mainly fruits, but also some insects.

turbine A machine that converts the energy stored in a fluid into mechanical energy. It comprises a rotor with one or more rows of shaped blades: fluid is directed on to the blades, causing them to move and thus rotate the rotor. WATER WHEELS and WINDMILLS are simple turbines that have been used for many centuries; more recent developments include WATER TURBINES, used in hydroelectricity generation and STEAM-TURBINES used to generate electricity in thermal and nuclear power stations. GAS TURBINES are used in a variety of applications, including the aircraft JET ENGINE. Small, high-speed turbines are used in pneumatic tools such as dental drills, and in gas-liquefaction plants expansion turbines are used to remove energy from hot gases, thus cooling them.

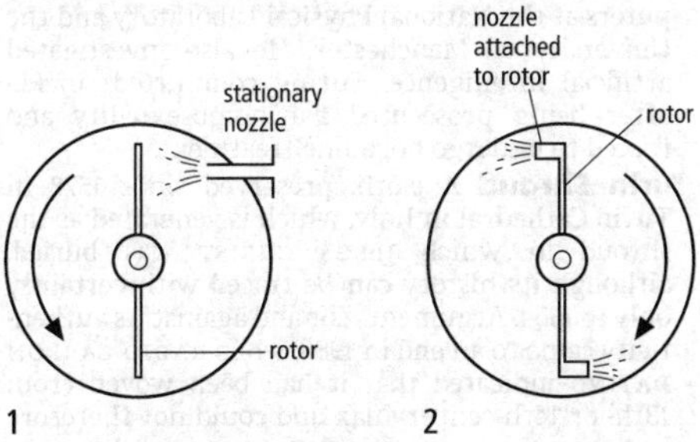

Turbine (1) In the impulse turbine a high-pressure low-velocity fluid is expanded through stationary nozzles and directed onto the blades of a rotor. Some of the kinetic energy of the jet is converted into the rotational kinetic energy of the rotor. (2) In the reaction turbine the discharge nozzles are attached to the rotor. The reaction of the fluid jet on the rotor arms causes the rotation.

turbocharger See SUPERCHARGER.

turbofan, **turbojet**, **turboprop** See JET ENGINE.

turbot A species of FLATFISH, *Scophthalmus maximus*, which has a very broad body with a large head, and large, bony tubercles in the skin instead of scales. Widely distributed in European seas, it lives on gravel and coarse sand from the shoreline to depths of about 80 m (260 feet). It feeds mostly on other fishes.

turbulence Fluid flow (gas or liquid) that undergoes irregular fluctuations or mixing. In a turbulent flow the motion continually changes in both magnitude and direction; almost all mixing of fluids is therefore turbulent. The rate of many fast chemical reactions in solution is determined by the degree of turbulence in the mixing of the reagents, and in the combustion chambers of engines there is always turbulent mixing of the fuel with air. Streamlining is important in reducing the turbulence of the flow around an object, especially in the design of aircraft.

Turcoman See TURKOMAN.

Turgenev, Ivan (Sergeevich) (1818–83) Russian novelist, dramatist, and short-story writer. From the 1850s he spent much of his life abroad, especially in Paris and Baden-Baden. His play *A Month in the Country* (1850) was followed by the prose work *A Sportsman's Sketches* (1852), which condemned the institution of serfdom. He subsequently wrote a series of novels examining individual lives to illuminate the social, political, and philosophical issues of the day, as in *Rudin* (1856) and *Fathers and Sons* (1862); in the latter, Turgenev depicted the rise of nihilism in Russia through his hero Bazarov.

Turin (Italian **Torino**) An industrial city on the River Po in north-west Italy, capital of the Piedmont region; pop. (1990) 991,870. Turin was the capital of the kingdom of Sardinia from 1720. A centre of the Risorgimento in the 19th century, it was the first capital of a unified Italy (1861–64). Its industries produce motor cars, iron and steel, textiles, electrical goods, and food products. The city's Romanesque cathedral contains the TURIN SHROUD.

Turing, Alan (Mathison) (1912–54) British mathematician. He developed the concept of a theoretical computing machine in 1937, a key step in the development of the first computer. Turing carried out important work on code-breaking during World War II, after which he worked on early computers at the National Physical Laboratory and the University of Manchester. He also investigated artificial intelligence. Turing committed suicide after being prosecuted for homosexuality and forced to undergo hormone treatment.

Turin Shroud A cloth, preserved since 1578 in Turin Cathedral in Italy, which is venerated as the shroud in which JESUS CHRIST was buried, although its history can be traced with certainty only to 1354. Arguments for and against its authenticity came to an end in 1988, when RADIO-CARBON DATING indicated that it had been woven from 13th- or 14th-century flax and could not therefore be authentic.

Turkana, Lake (formerly **Lake Rudolf**) A salt lake with no outlet set in a barren landscape in north-west Kenya and Ethiopia; area 6,405 sq km (2,474 sq miles). Sometimes known as the Jade Sea, it was explored in 1888 by Count Teleki who named it Lake Rudolf in honour of the Crown Prince of Austria. Hominid remains have been found on its shores.

turkey A gamebird belonging to the family Meleagrididae, related to pheasants and grouse. Turkeys formerly inhabited woodland in North and Central America but because of over-hunting, their natural ranges are much reduced. They are powerfully built birds with dark greenish-grey feathers edged with black. The male of the common turkey, *Meleagris gallopavo*, has a large protuberance on its neck. The bird grows to 1.25 m (4 feet), and has been extensively domesticated, with many breeds available. The turkey was almost certainly introduced direct to western Europe by the Spanish, very soon after Columbus discovered America, and did not come by way of Turkey as its name might suggest.

Turkey A country partly in Asia and partly in Europe.

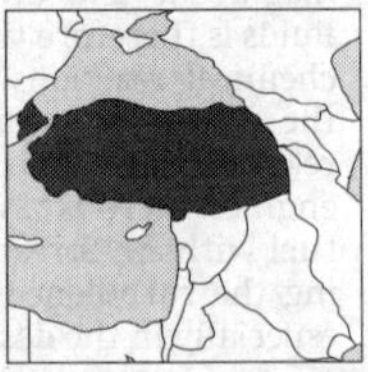

Physical. The Asian and European parts of Turkey are separated by the Bosporus, the Sea of Marmara, and the channel of the Dardanelles. The smaller, European part is bounded by Bulgaria and Greece. The much larger Asian part comprises the whole of Asia Minor and is known as Anatolia. It has the Black Sea on the north, Georgia, Armenia, and Iran on the east, Iraq and Syria on the south, and coasts on the Mediterranean and Aegean seas. Here the coastal plains are fertile, as are the valleys leading to them; but the plateau above is less so. Very warm in summer and cold in winter, rugged and mountainous in the east, it is a place of forests and lakes, arid deserts, and poor grazing for goats and sheep. Its largest river, the Kizil Irmak, is saline for nearly half its course to the Black Sea. In the east rise the Tigris and Euphrates rivers. The plateau is subject to devastating earthquakes, however, lying as it does at a junction of crustal plates.

Economy. Turkey has an expanding industrial sector and prospering agriculture. Although exports, which include textiles, fruit, vegetables, and metals, have risen, high inflation has threatened economic stability as has rapid population growth and rural exodus to the towns. One of the world's four largest chrome producers, Turkey has rich mineral deposits of coal, antimony, copper, iron ore, sulphur, lead, and zinc. Tourism is expanding, and remittances from Turkish workers abroad are an important source of foreign exchange.

History. Modern Turkey evolved from the OTTOMAN EMPIRE, which was finally dissolved at the end of World War I. By the Treaty of SÈVRES at the Versailles Peace Conference parts of the east coast of the Aegean around the city of Izmir (Smyrna) were to go to Greece, and the Anatolian peninsula was to be partitioned, with a separate state of ARMENIA created on the Black Sea. The settlement triggered off fierce national resistance, led by Mustafa Kemal. A Greek army marched inland from Izmir, but was defeated. The city was captured, Armenia occupied, and the new Treaty of Lausanne negotiated. This recognized the present frontiers, obliging some one and a half million Greeks and some half-million Armenians to leave the country (July 1923). In October 1923 the new Republic of Turkey was proclaimed, with Kemal as first President. His dramatic modernizing reforms won him the title of ATATÜRK, 'Father of the Turks'. The one-party rule of his Republican People's Party continued under his lieutenant Ismel Inonu until 1950, when in the republic's first open elections, the free-enterprise opposition Democratic Party entered a decade of power, ending with an army coup. Civilian rule was resumed in 1961, but there was a further period of military rule (1971–73). Atatürk's neutralist policy had been abandoned in 1952 when Turkey joined NATO. Relations with allies, however, were strained by the invasion of CYPRUS (1974). A US trade embargo resulting from this was only lifted in 1978. Tension between left-wing and right-wing factions, hostility to Westernization by the minority Shiites, who seek to enforce Islamic puritanism, and fighting between Turks, Kurds, and Armenians, continued to trouble the country. A military coup, led by General Kenan Evren, overthrew the civilian government of Suleiman Demirel. Under Presidents Evren (1982–87) and Turgut Özal (1987–93) some political stability developed, with rather more concern for human rights. Martial law was lifted in 1987 and the state of emergency ended in 1988, some political parties having been legalized, including a neo-fascist Nationalist Workers' Party. The Kurdish Workers' Party, claiming to speak for Turkey's 12 million Kurds, continued its armed campaign for an independent KURDISTAN. Turkey contributed to the GULF WAR, and claimed a loss of revenue of some $6,200 million as a result. During 1991–92 it sought to establish a Black Sea Economic Prosperity Zone with former republics and satellites of the Soviet Union. Civilian rule was resumed in 1991, with the re-election of Suleiman Demirel at the head of a coalition. 1993 saw the election of Tansu Çiller (1946–), Turkey's first woman Prime

Minister, and Demirel became President. However, the secular nature of the Turkish state became increasingly challenged by the rise of Islamic fundamentalism. In 1995 a military offensive was launched against the Kurds in northern Iraq, and unrest within the country led to the collapse of Çiller's government. The pro-Islamist Welfare Party won subsequent elections but the two major centre-right parties formed an anti-Islamist coalition. This collapsed in 1996 and a coalition led by the Welfare Party was formed. This coalition resigned in 1997 and was replaced by a new one led by the centre-right Motherland Party. In 1989 the European Community postponed consideration of Turkey's application for membership (1987), in part as a result of its human rights violations.

Capital: Ankara
Area: 779,452 sq km (300,948 sq mi)
Population: 62,526,000 (1995)
Currency: 1 Turkish lira = 100 kurush
Religions: Muslim (principally Sunni) 99.0%; Eastern Orthodox 0.3%; other Christian and Jewish 0.5%
Ethnic Groups: Turkish 85.7%; Kurdish 10.6%; Arab 1.6%; Greek, Armenian, and other 2.1%
Languages: Turkish (official); Kurdish; Arabic
International Organizations: UN; OECD; NATO; Council of Europe; CSCE

turkey-vulture A heavily built, New World VULTURE, *Cathartes aura*, found in North and South America, distributed sparsely but widely over mountains and woodlands. They are dark green-brown with a bare red head and neck, and have a wingspan of 2 m (6.5 feet). In flight they use upcurrents to soar while they search out carrion, but farmers destroy them for their predation on lambs and sheep. Two chicks are raised in caves or tree nests.

Turkic A group of about 20 Ural-Altaic languages (including Turkish) spoken in Turkey, Iran, and Central Asia.

Turkish The official language of Turkey spoken by over 50 million people, the most important of the Turkic group. It was originally written in Arabic script but changed over to the Roman alphabet in 1928.

Turkistan (or **Turkestan**) A region of central Asia east of the Caspian Sea extending over Turkmenistan, Uzbekistan, Kyrgyzstan, Tajikistan, the southern part of Kazakhstan, and the western part of Xinjiang province in China. Forming a major geographic frontier between East and West, it includes parts of the Pamir and Tien Shan mountains, the Kyzl-kum and Kara-kum deserts, and the Fergana valley of Uzbekistan. Between 1918 and 1924 there existed in the USSR a Turkistan Autonomous Soviet Republic. Following the collapse of the Soviet Union in 1991, the independent republics of Central Asia have sought to maintain economic and social alliances.

Turkmen A people of Central Asia speaking Turkoman, a Turkic branch of the Altaic family of languages. For centuries a tribal people, the main groups are the dominant Tekke tribe of central Turkmenistan, the Ersry in the south-east, and the Yomud in the west. They constitute 73 per cent of the population of Turkmenistan.

Turkmenistan A country lying east of the Caspian Sea and north of Iran.

Physical. Turkmenistan is in an arid region; it contains the greater part of the Kara Kum desert, which has important mineral resources. Low-lying and hot, the oases produce cotton and mulberry trees (for silkworms), while livestock roam the semi-desert areas in search of sparse grass. Oil and natural gas are found in the west, on the Caspian coastal plain.

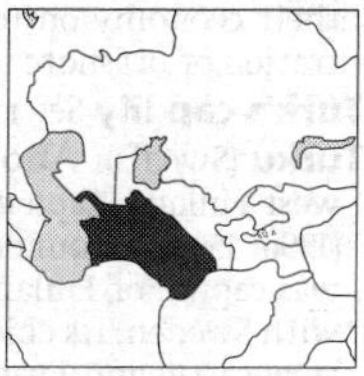

Economy. Turkmenistan is rich in mineral resources, including coal, sulphur, silver, cotton, lead, high-grade petroleum, and natural gas. Other heavy industry concentrates on chemicals, engineering, and metal-processing; light industry includes carpet-making and food- and textile-processing. Agriculture is largely dependent on irrigation; cotton is the chief crop, and karakul sheep, horses, and camels are raised. Silk is also an important product.

History. Turkmen never experienced political unity until conquered by the Russians in 1869. Even then fierce resistance lasted until 1881, and there was a rebellion in 1916. In 1918 a Social Revolutionary Transcaspian Republic was proclaimed. It was briefly supported by British troops until April 1919, after which it was conquered by the Red Army. In 1924 the Turkmen Soviet Socialist Republic was formed, and incorporated into the Soviet Union in 1925. It declared its sovereignty in August 1990 and its independence in October 1991. Turkmenistan joined the COMMONWEALTH OF INDEPENDENT STATES (CIS) in 1991. A new constitution in March 1992 increased the powers of its executive President Saparmuradi Niyazov, and allowed only ethnic Turkmen to work in state enterprises. The extension of President Niyazov's term of office was approved in a referendum in 1994. Legislative elections later that year were won by the former communists, renamed the Turkmen Democratic Party.

Capital: Ashkhabad
Area: 488,100 sq km (186,400 sq mi)
Population: 4,081,000 (1995)
Currency: 1 manat = 100 tenesi
Religions: Sunni Muslim; Eastern Orthodox; Baha'i
Ethnic Groups: Turkmen 72.0%; Russian 9.0%; Uzbek 9.0%; Kazakh minority
Languages: Turkoman (offical); Russian; minority languages
International Organizations: UN; CSCE; Commonwealth of Independent States; North Atlantic Co-operation Council

Turkoman (or **Turcoman**) The official language of Turkmenistan in Central Asia, spoken by the various Turkic peoples of that country.

Turks Originally nomads from TURKISTAN. During the 6th century AD they controlled an empire stretching from Mongolia to the Caspian Sea. With the conquest of western Turkistan in the 7th century by the ABBASIDS, many were converted to Islam and moved westwards, retaining their distinctive language and culture. In the 11th century, under the SELJUKS they replaced the Arabs as rulers of the Levant and Mesopotamia, then expanded north-west at the expense of BYZANTIUM. The rival house of Osman continued this trend, founding the OTTOMAN empire, which endured for 600 years, and embraced most of the Middle East, North Africa, and the Balkans.

Turks and Caicos Islands A British dependency in the Caribbean, a group of over 30 subtropical islands (of which 6 are inhabited) about 80 km (50 miles) south-east of the Bahamas; area *c.*500 sq km (193 sq miles); pop. (1990) 12,350; capital, Cockburn Town (on the island of Grand Turk). Once an important source of salt, the islands now depend for

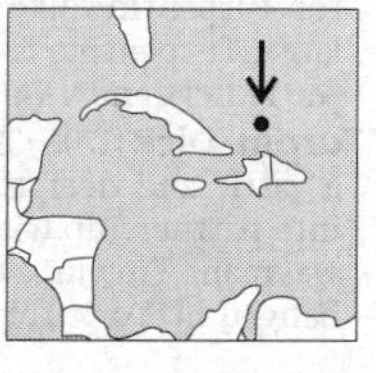

their economy on tourism, fishing, and the registration of offshore financial companies.

Turk's cap lily See LILY.

Turku (Swedish **Åbo**) An industrial port in south-west Finland, capital of Turku-Pori province; pop. (1990) 159,180. Founded in the 11th century, Turku was capital of Finland until 1812. It has ferry links with Sweden. Its chief landmarks are the 13th-century castle and Evangelical-Lutheran cathedral. It has two universities, one Finnish-speaking and one Swedish-speaking. Its industries include shipyards, engineering, textiles, and clothing.

turmeric A plant, *Curcuma longa*, closely related and similar in growth to the ginger plant in the family Zingiberaceae. The spice for which it is cultivated is, like ginger, obtained from swollen underground stems. The strong yellow colour of curry is principally provided by turmeric, which also yields a yellow-orange dye used in Asia and Europe to dye natural fibres. An ancient Asian crop, it is grown in India, China, Indonesia, and the Caribbean, wherever the climate is hot and moist.

Turner, J(oseph) M(allord) W(illiam) (1775–1851) British painter. The originality of his work and the extent to which it anticipated later styles, such as impressionism and abstract art made him a highly controversial figure in his day. He made his name with stormy seascapes, such as *The Shipwreck* (1805), and landscapes painted in the grand Italian style of Claude Lorrain, as in *Crossing the Brook* (1815). From 1819 Turner made several visits to Italy and became increasingly concerned with depicting the power of light, using primary colours – especially yellow. In the 1830s and 1840s he adopted watercolour techniques for his 'colour beginnings' in oil, which he later worked up to finished paintings, notably in *Norham Castle* (*c.*1845). He is perhaps best known for *Rain, Steam, Speed* (1844) and for *The Fighting Téméraire* (1838).

Turner, Tina (born Anna Mae Bullock) (1939–) US rock and soul singer. In 1958 she married musician Ike Turner (1931–) and started singing with his band. They had such hits as 'River Deep – Mountain High' (1966) but despite Tina's dynamic vocals and stage presence her husband maintained rigorous control over the group's act. Tina Turner divorced her husband in 1976 and built her own career, becoming an international superstar with the release of the album *Private Dancer* (1984).

turnip A BRASSICA root crop, *Brassica rapa*, similar to the swede and equally useful as a vegetable and for livestock feed. Grown mainly for their swollen roots, some varieties (stubble turnips) are particularly fast-growing and can be grazed while the roots are fairly small by sheep or cattle. The leaves are bright green and rough in contrast to the smooth bluish-green leaves of the swede. The round roots are white- or yellow-skinned with either a green- or purple-tinged top. Turnips are an ancient European crop, known since prehistoric times and now widespread throughout the world.

turpentine A strong-smelling, naturally occurring oil obtained by STEAM DISTILLATION of the resin exuded by coniferous trees. Conifers are 'milked' for turpentine like rubber trees are milked for latex. Turpentine is used as a solvent and as a base for PAINTS and VARNISHES.

Turpin, Dick (1706–39) British highwayman. He was a cattle and deer thief in Essex before entering into partnership with Tom King, a notorious highwayman. Turpin eventually fled north and was hanged at York for horse-stealing. His escapades were celebrated in the popular literature of the day.

turquoise A copper aluminium phosphate mineral found as light green-blue masses in nodules or veins. It is hard and opaque, shines with a waxy lustre, and is formed by alteration of aluminium-rich rock. Valued as a semi-precious stone, it is also used as an ornamental material. The best sources of turquoise are in Nishapur in Iran, Sinai in Egypt, and New Mexico in the USA.

turtle A member of an order of REPTILES, Chelonia, which includes TORTOISES and TERRAPINS. They are distinguished by a relatively short, broad body, enclosed in a box of bony plates, which are commonly covered in a horny material or, in some families, such as soft-shelled turtles, a layer of leathery skin. They are known from fossils as far back in time as the late Triassic Period (200 million years ago). All living forms lack teeth; instead they have sharp-edged, horny beaks. These are modified into broader ridged beaks in species which crush their food. All species are egg-layers, even the most aquatic turtles still needing to return to land for this purpose.

Tuscany (Italian **Toscana**) A region of west-central Italy comprising the provinces of Arezzo, Firenze, Grosseto, Lucca, Livorno, Massa-Carrara, Pisa, Pistoia, and Siena; area 22,989 sq km (8,879 sq miles); pop. (1990) 3,562,525; capital, Florence. Its many medieval towns and art treasures ensure its popularity with tourists. It is predominantly a farming area with Chianti wine a special product, but there are also important industries: wool at Prato; steel at Piombino; motor scooters at Pontedera; clothing in Arezzo; and marble at Carrara. Modern Tuscany corresponds to the greater part of ancient Etruria.

tusk A hard structure formed by the elongation of teeth, usually of the incisor or canine. Perhaps best known, because of their size, are those of the elephant, where the incisor and the canine teeth have become reduced to a single pair of upward-curving tusks. These may be up to 3.2 m (10.5 feet) long in an African elephant. The mammoths had even larger tusks, up to 5 m (16.5 feet). The male narwhal has a single tooth which grows continuously, to form a spirally twisted tusk up to 2.7 m (8.8 feet) long. This tusk may be used in sparring with other males. Pigs have persistently growing canine teeth which form tusks in the male. The males of the walrus and some deer also have tusks developed from canine teeth.

Tussaud, Madame (born Marie Grosholtz) (1761–1850) French founder of Madame Tussaud's waxworks, resident in Britain from 1802. After taking death masks in wax of prominent victims of the French Revolution, she toured Britain with her wax models, which came to include other famous and topical people. In 1835 she founded a permanent waxworks exhibition in Baker Street, London, which moved to Marylebone Rd after a fire in 1925.

tussock grass Any of various grasses with a tufted, compact habit of growth, especially *Deschampsia flexuosa*, a perennial species with a wide distribution in Europe, Asia Minor, Japan, North America and Africa. Its long, wavy flowering stems arise from dense tufts of leaves raised above ground-level. It is a plant of wet meadows, acid heaths, moors and open woodlands, and has little agricultural value.

tussock moth A medium-sized moth of the family Lymantridae, the hairy caterpillars of which bear prominent clumps or tussocks of coloured hairs on their backs. The hairs are irritant, the bright colours advertising this to potential predators, and are incorporated into the cocoon at pupation. Adults never feed, their mouthparts being VESTIGIAL ORGANS. The family includes the gold-tail, *Euproctis similis*, and vapourer moths, *Orgyia* species. The gold-tail and the closely related brown-tail, *E. chrysorrhoea*, can reach pest proportions, and their larval hairs can cause skin irritation in humans. The gypsy moth is another important pest species of trees.

Tutankhamun (died *c.*1352 BC) Pharaoh of Egypt *c.*1361–1352 BC. Little is known about his reign; his importance is largely that his tomb in the VALLEY OF THE KINGS escaped looting in antiquity. Hidden by rubble from the construction of a later tomb, it was found almost intact by the British archaeologist Howard Carter and his patron, Lord Carnarvon, in 1922. Tutankhamun's mummified body was inside three coffins, the inner one of solid gold; over his face was a magnificent gold funerary mask, and the burial chamber housed a unique collection of jewellery and weapons.

Tutu, Desmond (Mpilo) (1931–) South African clergyman. He served as General Secretary of the South African Council of Churches (1979–84), becoming a leading voice in the struggle against apartheid, calling for economic sanctions against South Africa and emphasizing non-violent action. He was awarded the Nobel Peace Prize in 1984, and in the following year he became Johannesburg's first black Anglican bishop. He was archbishop of Cape Town 1986–96.

Tuva (or **Tuva Republic**) A republic in southern Siberia, in the Russian Federation, on the frontier with Mongolia; area 170,500 sq km (65,855 sq miles); pop. (1990) 314,000; capital, Kyzyl. A mountainous region that includes the upper basin of the Yenisei River, Tuva was formerly part of the Chinese Empire (1757–1911), falling under Tsarist Russia in 1914. As the Tuvinian People's Republic, popularly known as **Tannu Tuva**, it was independent from 1921 until annexed in 1944 by the USSR, which gave it the status of an autonomous oblast and then an autonomous republic (1961). Following the breakup of the Soviet Union in 1991 it maintained its autonomous status within the Russian Federation. The Tuvans are a Turkic-speaking people and are largely pastoralists. The republic's resources include livestock, gold, cobalt, asbestos, and hydroelectric power.

Tuvalu A country comprising a scattered archipelago of small islands between Kiribati and Fiji in the South Seas.

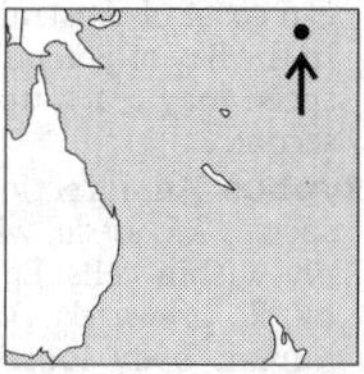

Physical. Funafuti is the chief island in the group, which numbers nine, all of them coral atolls and not exceeding a height of approximately 6 m (20 feet) above sea level. The islands experience high temperatures and heavy rainfall and the vegetation consists mainly of coconut palms.

Economy. Tuvalu is almost entirely dependent on foreign aid. The only export is copra, but sales of postage stamps also bring in foreign currency.

History. The first settlers probably came from Samoa and Tonga in the 14th century AD. The islands were sighted by Spanish explorers in the 16th century. They were formerly called the Ellice Islands after a 19th-century British shipowner, Edward Ellice. In the 19th century whalers, traders, missionaries, and 'blackbirders' (KANAKA catchers) for the QUEENSLAND sugar plantations began to take an interest in these atolls, which the British were to include in the Gilbert and Ellice Islands Protectorate in 1892. In 1974 the Ellice Islanders, who are of Polynesian descent, voted to separate from the Micronesian Gilbertese. They achieved independence in 1978, establishing a constitutional monarchy. The USA claims sovereignty over four of the islands. In 1995 Tuvalu removed the Union Jack from its flag as a first step towards the possible renunciation of the British monarch as head of state.

Capital: Fongafale (on Funafuti)
Area: 23.96 sq km (9.25 sq mi)
Population: 9,400 (1995)
Currency: 1 Tuvalu dollar = 100 cents; Australian currency is also legal tender
Religions: Church of Tuvalu 97%
Ethnic Groups: Tuvaluan 91.2%; other Pacific islander 7.2%
Languages: Tuvaluan; English
International Organizations: Commonwealth

Twain, Mark (pseudonym of Samuel Langhorne Clemens) (1835–1910) US novelist and humorist. After working as a river pilot on the Mississippi he established a reputation as a humorist with early work including *The Innocents Abroad* (1869), a satirical account of an American cruise to the Mediterranean. He is best known for the novels *The Adventures of Tom Sawyer* (1876) and *The Adventures of Huckleberry Finn* (1885); both works give a vivid evocation of Mississippi frontier life, faithfully capturing Southern speech patterns and combining picaresque adventure with moral commentary.

Tweed A river flowing largely through the Southern Uplands of Scotland for a distance of 155 km (97 miles) before entering the North Sea at Berwick-upon-Tweed in north-east England. It rises at Tweedswell and is a famous salmon-fishing river.

Twickenham A residential district in the Greater London borough of Richmond-upon-Thames. It contains the English Rugby Football Union ground and Hampton Court Palace.

Twiggy (full name Leslie Lawson, née Hornby) (1949–) British fashion model and actress. At the age of 17 she epitomized the London fashion scene of the swinging sixties with her cockney accent and long thin legs, usually accentuated by miniskirts. Her film debut in *The Boy Friend* (1971) earned her sufficient praise to enable her to appear in several other films. Her autobiography, *Twiggy*, was published in 1975.

twilight In astronomy, the two periods, in the morning and the evening, when the Sun is set, but the centre of its disc is less than 18 degrees below the horizon. Near midsummer, astronomical twilight lasts continuously all night at latitudes greater than about 48.5 degrees, as then, even at midnight, the Sun is less than 18 degrees below the horizon.

twister See TORNADO.

two-party system A pattern of party competition in which two leading POLITICAL PARTIES dominate national politics and alternate in forming the government. Such a pattern, usually associated with the first-past-the-post system of government, is found in the UK and the USA. Minor parties may attract a fair amount of support, but because of this electoral system, the best they can hope for is to hold the balance of power in a COALITION GOVERNMENT.

two-stroke engine See PETROL ENGINE.

Tycho Brahe See BRAHE.

Tyler, John (1790–1862) US Whig statesman, 10th

President of the USA 1841–45. Successor to William Henry Harrison as President, he was noted for securing the annexation of Texas (1845). Throughout his political career Tyler advocated states' rights, and his alliance with Southern Democrats on this issue helped to accentuate the divide between North and South in the years leading up to the American Civil War.

Tyler, Wat (died 1381) English leader of the Peasants' Revolt of 1381. After capturing Canterbury, he led the rebels to Blackheath and took London. During a conference with the young king Richard II he put forward the rebels' demands (including the lifting of the newly imposed poll tax), to which Richard consented. At a later conference in Smithfield he was killed by the Lord Mayor of London and several other royal supporters.

Tyndale, William (*c.*1494–1536) English translator and Protestant martyr. Faced with ecclesiastical opposition to his project for translating the Bible into English, Tyndale went abroad in 1524, never to return to his own country; his translation of the New Testament (*c.*1525–26) was published in Germany. He then translated the Pentateuch (1530) and Jonah (1531), both of which were printed in Antwerp. Tyndale's translations later formed the basis of the Authorized Version. In 1535 he was arrested in Antwerp on a charge of heresy, and subsequently strangled and burnt at the stake.

Tyndall, John (1820–93) Irish physicist. He is best known for his work on heat, studying such aspects as the absorbance and transmission of heat by gases and liquids and the thermal conductivity of solids. Tyndall also worked on diamagnetism, glaciers, the transmission of sound, and the scattering of light by suspended particles, becoming the first person to explain the blue colour of the sky (the **Tyndall effect**), according to which blue light is more strongly scattered than red light because the scattered intensity is related to the fourth power of the wavelength.

Tyne and Wear A metropolitan county of north-east England; area 540 sq km (209 sq miles); pop. (1991) 1,087,000; county town, Newcastle upon Tyne. It is divided into five districts.

typesetting Assembling metal or photographic forms of letters into words to a pre-arranged format. The process began in Europe in about 1450 when GUTENBERG cut matrices and developed a mould for the metal casting of individual letters that could be hand-assembled. Until the mid-1800s, all typesetting was done by hand, with the compositor (typesetter) picking letters from sectioned trays or cases, assembling them into lines in a composing stick, and then storing the lines on shallow, tray-like 'galleys' for correcting and page make-up. The 19th century saw the development of mechanical typesetting systems, which greatly speeded up the process. MONOTYPE produced lines of individual letters, while Linotype set words in solid lines. Pages of metal type may be used directly for printing, or they may provide a mould for platemaking. After World War II, phototypesetting developed, at first using mechanical typesetters that exposed letters on to film through negative letter images. Then, to increase the speed of letter selection, rotating discs carrying the negatives and working in conjunction with timed flashes of light were introduced; later developments included other forms of image projection. Recently, COMPUTERS have been used to capture original text on disk, store digital letter founts (different styles of letter), or control a LASER beam to set the type required on to film or paper at very high speed. Page make-up may involve pasting up individual pages of text and illustration by hand, but in the more modern electronic page make-up printing plates are made photographically from the completed pages (camera-ready copy) or by laser imaging from computer files.

typewriter A desk-top machine with keys for producing print-like characters. Workable typewriting machines first appeared in the early 1800s, but enjoyed little commercial success until the Remington Arms Company (USA) marketed in 1874 a design bought from SHOLES. Most Western typewriters have 46 character keys while shift keys allow for two different characters on each key, producing a total of 92 characters plus an interword space. Mechanical typewriters gave way to electrical and electronic models, with a spinning 'golf-ball' or 'daisy-wheel' typehead. In most contexts the typewriter has now been replaced by the WORD PROCESSOR.

typhoid and paratyphoid fever Communicable bacterial infections caused by *Salmonella typhii* (typhoid fever) and *S. paratyphii* A, B, and C (paratyphoid fever). Transmission is by ingestion of water or food contaminated with human sewage containing the microorganisms. Initial symptoms of typhoid fever occur when the microorganism gains entry into the blood and include headache, fever, and abdominal pain. Constipation is common, although in children, diarrhoea and vomiting may occur initially. These symptoms resolve in about seven days, and are followed by the appearance of a rash on the abdomen and back, diarrhoea replacing constipation, nose bleeds, and a dry cough. Persistent fever as a result of toxin production is common, which may also cause drowsiness and confusion. During the third week, unless treatment has begun, increasing toxin production causes delirium, coma, and death. Paratyphoid fever follows a similar course, although symptoms may be abrupt in onset and illness is generally milder than typhoid fever. Isolation and effective treatment are essential to prevent spread and complications. Active IMMUNIZATION provides some protection against typhoid fever, but preventive measures are essential.

typhoon An intense tropical revolving storm that occurs in the western Pacific Ocean and the China Seas, chiefly during July to October. It is known as a HURRICANE in the Caribbean, on the north-eastern coast of Australia, and in the Atlantic regions. In the Bay of Bengal it is often called a CYCLONE. Its speed may reach up to 60 m/s (nearly 200 feet per second).

typhus An infection by microorganisms of the species *Rickettsia*, which can only grow and multiply within cells. Epidemic typhus fever is caused by *R. prowazeki*, which is transmitted by the human body louse (*Pediculosis humanus corporis*) from its faeces, gaining entry by scratching, skin abrasion, and inhalation. Endemic typhus fever is caused by *R. mooseri*, which is transmitted by fleas from its faeces gaining entry by scratching. Symptoms include fever, headache, back pain, constipation, a skin rash, and inflammation of the bronchi; progression may lead to deafness, incontinence, delirium, and impaired consciousness. In the absence of treatment, life-threatening complications can occur.

Tick-borne typhus is caused by *R. rickettsii* (causing rocky mountain spotted fever), which occurs in America and South America; *R. conori*, which occurs in parts of Africa; and *R. australis*, which occurs in parts of Australia. Scrub typhus is caused by *R. tsutugamushi*, which occurs in the Far East, parts of Asia and Australia, and the Pacific Islands.

typography ▶**1** The art of printing from movable type. ▶**2** The design of printed matter, including choice of paper, finished size, specification of type, and the arrangement of text and illustrations. Typography as a separate branch of design began in the late 19th century among 'art compositors'. In the 1920s and 1930s it became common for the layout of printed matter to be specified by a graphic designer. The invention in recent decades of electronic means of transmitting typefaces to the printed surface or screen has led to the evolution of many new typefaces, and visually acceptable ways of combining text and images to convey information.

Tyr (Anglo-Saxon **Tiw**) In Norse and Germanic mythology, a war-god and deity of athletes. Identified with Mars, 'Tiw's day' became Tuesday, corresponding to the Roman *martis dies* (day of Mars). Cited variously as the son of Frigg, Odin, and Hymir, Tyr chained Fenrir, the wolf-son of Loki, and his hand was bitten off. He is doomed to die at Ragnarök, slaying Garm, the watchdog at the entry to Hel, the world of the dead.

Tyrannosaurus A lizard-hipped DINOSAUR, the largest of the carnivores, standing 6 m (20 feet) high, and completely bipedal, the front legs being reduced. Their jaws were large and powerful and armed with dagger-like teeth, indicating that they were carnivores.

tyre A rubber covering, usually inflated, fitted to the outer rim of a WHEEL to protect it from excessive wear, and to give a cushioned ride. The tread (that part of the tyre in contact with the road surface) may carry a pattern of grooves or projections to improve traction or road-holding. Before the development of tyres, metal rims protected wheels; later, solid rubber tyres in a metal channel were used, the first being made by the British inventor Thomas Hancock in 1846 for light horse-drawn vehicles and BICYCLES. Pneumatic tyres were first patented in 1845 by the British engineer Robert Thomson; they were first produced commercially in 1888 by DUNLOP. However, the pneumatic tyre was not generally adopted until the invention of the dished wheel-rim, patented in 1890 by the British engineer C. K. Welch. By 1916 pneumatic tyres were standard on most passenger vehicles and lorries. Modern motor-car tyres are generally tubeless and radially built, comprising rubberized fabric with steel reinforcement.

Tyre (Arabic **Soûr**) A city and Mediterranean seaport in Lebanon, in Al Janub province 80 km (50 miles) south of Beirut; pop. (1988) 14,000. Once a major commercial centre of the Phoenicians, it was noted for its silk garments, glassware, and purple dye.

Tyrol (German **Tirol**) An Alpine province of western Austria, the southern part of which was ceded to Italy after World War I; area 12,647 sq km (4,885 sq miles); pop. (1991) 630,350; capital, Innsbruck. The South Tyrol, which remained Italian after 1945, maintains close economic ties with the provinces of Tyrol and Vorarlberg in Austria.,

Tyrone A county of Northern Ireland to the west of Lough Neagh; area 3,136 sq km (1,211 sq miles); pop. (1981) 143,880; county town, Omagh.

Tyrrhenian Sea A part of the Mediterranean Sea bounded by mainland Italy, Sicily, Sardinia, Corsica, and the Ligurian Sea.

Tyson, Mike (full name Michael Gerald Tyson) (1966–) US boxer. He became undisputed world heavyweight champion in 1987, winning the WBA, WBC, and IBF titles, and successfully defended his position until 1990, when he was beaten by Buster Douglas. He was imprisoned in 1992 for rape; after his release in 1995 he defeated Frank Bruno in 1996 to win the WBA title but lost the title to Evander Holyfield later that year. In a further contest with Holyfield in 1997 Tyson bit off a piece of Holyfield's ear, for which he was disqualified, and subsequently banned from boxing.

Tyumen A city in the west Siberian lowlands of Russia, on the Tura River; pop. (1990) 487,000. Regarded as the oldest city in Siberia, it lies on the Trans-Siberian Railway and is a link between rail and river transport. It is the centre of the oil province of Tyumen.

U

UAE See UNITED ARAB EMIRATES.

Ubangi The chief northern tributary of the Congo River in central Africa. It is formed at the junction of the Bomu and Uele rivers and flows 1,060 km (660 miles) west and south to join the Congo near Mbandaka on the frontier between the Republic of Congo and the Democratic Republic of Congo.

Uccello, Paolo (born Paolo di Dono) (*c.*1397–1475) Italian painter. His nickname (*uccello*, 'bird') is said to refer to his love of animals, especially birds. He was based largely in Florence and is associated with the early use of perspective in painting. His surviving works include three long panels on the *Battle of San Romano* (*c.*1455) and *The Hunt*, noted for its atmosphere of fairy-tale romance.

Udmurtia (or **Udmurt Republic**) A republic of the Russian Federation, to the north of the Tatar Republic and north-west of Bashkortostan; area 42,100 sq km (16,261 sq miles); pop. (1990) 1,619,000; capital, Izhevsk. The land of the Udmurts (or Votyaks) was annexed by Russia in the 16th century and became the Votyak autonomous oblast in 1920 and the Udmurt autonomous oblast in 1932. In 1934 it was designated an autonomous republic of the Soviet Union. The Udmurts, who account for some 30 per cent of the population, speak a language of the Finno-Ugric linguistic group.

Ufa The capital of the republic of Bashkortostan in the Russian Federation, an industrial city in the Ural Mountains at the junction of the Belaya and Ufa rivers and near the Volga–Urals oilfields; pop. (1990) 1,094,000. It has machinery, chemicals, timber, electric, and electronic industries.

UFO (Unidentified Flying Object) Sightings of unidentified objects above the Earth's surface that a wide variety of people claim to have seen. Many thousands of sightings of these objects have been reported all over the world in the past 50 years. Careful investigations by various agencies have satisfactorily explained about 93 per cent of authentic sightings as aeroplanes, high-flying meteorological balloons, the planet Venus, phenomena due to temperature inversions, and so on. There is no reliable evidence that the remaining 7 per cent are spacecraft of extraterrestrial origin, as some observers claim.

Uganda A landlocked country in East Africa, bounded by Sudan on the north, Kenya on the east, Tanzania and Rwanda on the south, and the Democratic Republic of Congo on the west.

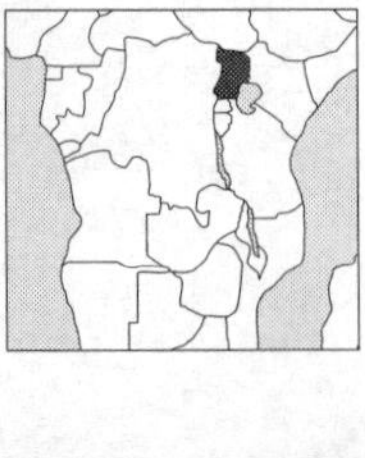

Physical. Uganda's tropical climate is alleviated by its height, most of it being over 1,000 m (3,300 feet) above sea-level; and over one-sixth of its area is water. Between lakes Victoria (the source of the Nile), Kyoga, and Albert in the southern half of the country are hills with richly fertile slopes and valleys. Round the Ruwenzori Range (the 'Mountains of the Moon') in the south-west, and the old volcanic Mount Elgon in the east, coffee is grown. The SAVANNAH country in the north supports cotton and grain.

Economy. Despite falling world prices for coffee, which accounts for about 95 per cent of the country's exports, Uganda has experienced a considerable degree of economic recovery in the last ten years. Other cash crops are cotton, tea, and maize, and there are livestock-raising, fishing, and subsistence crops of cassava, cereals, plantains, and yams. Mineral resources include copper, mining of which has ceased, apatite, tin, tungsten, and unexploited iron-ore reserves. Industry concentrates on agricultural processing. However, economic reform has prompted considerable grants from the IMF.

History. During the 18th and 19th centuries the kingdom of Buganda on Lake Victoria became the dominant power in the area under its kabaka (king) Mutesa I. He welcomed the explorers SPEKE and STANLEY, hoping for protection against Arab slave and ivory traders. Following Mutesa's death tensions developed between Christians and Muslims, and also between British and German interests. In 1890 there was an Anglo-German agreement that the area be administered by the British, and the newly formed British East Africa Company placed Buganda and the western states Ankole and Toro under its protection. In 1896 the British government took over the protectorate. After World War II nationalist agitation for independence developed, with Mutesa II being deported. In 1962 internal self-government was granted. Uganda was to be a federation of the kingdoms of Ankole, Buganda, Bunyoro, Busoga, and Toro. In September the Prime Minister, Milton OBOTE, renounced this constitution and declared Uganda a republic. Mutesa II was elected first President, but in 1965 he was deposed by Milton OBOTE, who became President himself, only to be deposed in turn by General Idi AMIN DADA (1971). Amin's rule was tyrannical and racist, including the expulsion of Uganda's Asian residents, an economically vital group of entrepreneurs. In 1980, after the invasion by Tanzanian forces and Ugandan exiles, Amin fled the country. Obote returned in 1981, but his failure to restore order led to a coup in 1985, the resulting military regime being overthrown by the National Resistance Army of Yoweri MUSEV-

ENI, who became President in 1986. Under his presidency Uganda tried to recover from the disastrous years of 1971–80, which had ruined the economy and cost hundreds of thousands of lives. Extensive loans by the World Bank and IMF required demobilization of the armed forces. However, with growing insurgence in the north of Uganda during 1995–96 by the terrorist group, the Lord's Resistance Army, military strength has had to be increased once more. The ban on political parties, imposed when Museveni took power, was renewed in 1992 and endorsed in a new constitution in 1995. In 1994, non-party elections to the Constituent Assembly were won by Museveni's supporters. Museveni won the country's first presidential election in 1996.

Capital: Kampala
Area: 241,040 sq km (93,070 sq mi)
Population: 18,659,000 (1995)
Currency: 1 Uganda shilling = 100 cents
Religions: Roman Catholic 49.6%; Protestant 28.7%; traditional beliefs 15.0%; Muslim 6.6%
Ethnic Groups: Ganda 17.8%; Teso 8.9%; Nkole 8.2%; Soga 8.2%; Gisu 7.2%; Chiga 6.8%; Lango 6.0%; Rwanda 5.8%; Acholi 4.6%
Languages: English (official); Swahili; Ganda; local languages
International Organizations: UN; OAU; Non-Aligned Movement; Commonwealth

UHF See WAVEBAND.

Uist Two small islands (**North Uist** and **South Uist**) of the Outer Hebrides of Scotland, lying to the south of Lewis and Harris; separated from each other by Benbecula and from the island of Skye by the Little Minch. The chief settlements and ferry ports are Lochmaddy (on North Uist) and Lochboisdale (on South Uist).

Ujjain A city of west-central India in the state of Madhya Pradesh, on the River Shipra; pop. (1991) 367,150. It is one of the seven holy cities of Hinduism, where the God Siva is said to have triumphed over the demon ruler of Tripuri by changing the name of his capital from Avantika to Ujjaiyini ('one who conquers with pride').

Ujung Pandang (formerly **Macassar**, **Makassar**, or **Makasar**) The chief seaport of the Sulawesi Islands of Indonesia, situated on the west coast of Sulawesi's southern peninsula; pop. (1990) 944,370. It is capital of the province of South Sulawesi and was formerly a major port of south-east Asia which, as Makassar, gave its name to an oil once used for the hair. It is an important commercial centre.

ukiyo-e (Japanese, 'pictures of the floating world') The dominant movement in Japanese art of the 17th to 19th centuries. It refers to the subjects from transient everyday life, with its ever-shifting fashions, favoured by print-makers at this time, including such celebrated artists as Hiroshige, HOKUSAI, and UTAMARO. Favourite subjects were theatre scenes and prostitutes and bath-house girls. Prints were originally in black outline only, then hand-tinting became the custom, and colour printing was established by the 1760s. They caught the attention of avant-garde French artists in the second half of the 19th century, influencing the Impressionists and POST-IMPRESSIONISTS with their flat decorative colour and expressive pattern.

Ukraine A country comprising a large region of eastern Europe stretching from the Carpathian Mountains to the Donetz River and bounded on the south by the Black Sea. To the east are Poland, Slovakia, Hungary, Romania and Moldova; to the west, Russia.

Physical. Northern Ukraine is a continuation of the low plains, woods, and marshes of Belarus. To the south, and forming three-quarters of the region, is the treeless steppe: a vast plain of rich black soil with occasional low hills, deep ravines of streams, and the great Dnieper River flowing down the centre. In the extreme south is the CRIMEA, a peninsula with a milder climate than the steppe, which is snow-covered in winter and very warm in summer.

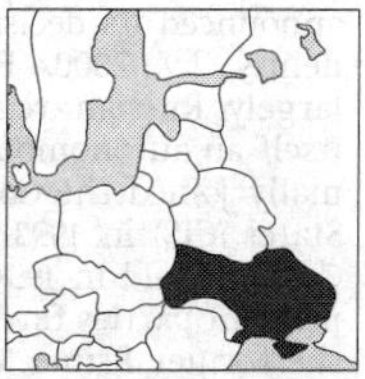

Economy. After independence Ukraine undertook measures to reduce its economic interdependence with Russia and the other former Soviet republics, including an agreement to import Iranian oil and natural gas to replace Russian supplies. Mineral resources are abundant and varied, including iron ore, coal, manganese, bauxite, salt, and some petroleum. Other than mining, heavy industry includes iron and steel production, machinery and transport equipment, aircraft, chemicals, and consumer goods. Food-processing, notably sugar, sunflower oil, and wine, and textiles are important light industries. Grain is the most important agricultural product, followed by potatoes, vegetables, fruit, and grapes; industrial crops are sunflower seeds, sugar-beet, and flax. Agriculture has suffered greatly because the nuclear accident at Chernobyl in 1986 contaminated large tracts of the rich steppe land, rendering it uncultivable. Despite increasing economic problems, the IMF has approved several loans to Ukraine to aid economic reform.

History. Originally inhabited by Neolithic settlers in the Dnieper and Dniester valleys, Ukraine was overrun by numerous invaders before Varangian adventurers founded a powerful Slav kingdom based on KIEV in the 9th century. Mongol conquest in the 13th century was followed in the 14th century by Lithuanian overlordship until 1569, when Polish rule brought serfdom and religious persecution, which produced an exiled community of Cossacks who resisted both Polish and Russian domination. With the partition of Poland in 1795 the region, including the Crimea, under OTTOMAN control from 1478, came under Russian control, a situation which lasted until the break-up of the Soviet Union in 1991. Yet Ukrainian nationalism, despite repression, remained strong. In 1918 independence was proclaimed, but by 1922 the area had been conquered by Soviet forces, to become the Ukrainian Soviet Socialist Republic. Stalin imposed COLLECTIVIZATION on the region, which suffered grievously from his purges. It was devastated during the German occupation of 1941–44, although many nationalists welcomed the Germans. Territorial gains from Romania, eastern Poland, and Slovakia completed the union of all Ukrainian lands into one republic by 1945, the Crimea being added in 1954. By 1990 strong pressure had built up for independence from the Soviet Union, and the Ukraine Supreme Soviet formally declared independence in August 1991, with overwhelming support in a referendum. Multiparty elections followed, with Leonid Kravchuk elected president. The 20 per cent Russian minority was placed under no pressure; at the same time, negotiations took place with Russia over naval and military armed forces, Ukraine declaring itself a nuclear-free zone. The Chernobyl nuclear power-station disaster of 1986 had left thousands of square kilometres of its countryside permanently contaminated; the Ukrainian government has announced its decision to close the plant permanently by 2000. Following independence, the largely Russian region of the Crimea declared itself an autonomous region in 1992. Ukraine formally joined the Commonwealth of Independent States (CIS) in 1993. In elections to the Supreme Council, held in 1994, both communists and independent parties fared well. Later in the same year, the former Prime Minister Leonid Kuchma, who advocated economic reform and closer links with Russia, replaced Kravchuk as President. Relations with Russia remained tense, as Ukraine continued to dispute the autonomy of Crimea. A new constitution abolishing Soviet-style institutions and consolidating democracy was adopted in June 1996.

Capital: Kiev
Area: 603,700 sq km (171,700 sq mi)
Population: 52,003,000 (1995)
Currency: 1 hryvnya = 100 kopiykas
Religions: Eastern Orthodox; Ukrainian Catholic; Jewish minority
Ethnic Groups: Ukrainian 73.0%; Russian 22.0%; Belarussian, Moldovan, and Polish minorities
Languages: Ukrainian (official); Russian; minority languages
International Organizations: UN; CSCE: Commonwealth of Independent States; North Atlantic Co-operation Council

ukulele A miniature four-stringed GUITAR, which originated in Hawaii but derived from the small Portuguese guitar-type instrument the *machete*, which had been carried to the Philippines in the 16th century and had travelled thence to Hawaii.

Ulan Bator (or **Ulaanbaatar**) The capital of Mongolia, a city on the River Tola founded in 1639 as a monastery town; pop. (1990) 575,000. It changed its name from Urga to Ulan Bator in 1924, three years after becoming capital of Communist-ruled Mongolia. It has cultural facilities including a university and state circus. Its main industries are food processing, textiles, and the manufacture of building materials.

Ulanova, Galina (Sergeevna) (1910–98) Russian ballet-dancer. In 1928 she joined the Kirov Ballet, transferring to the Bolshoi company in 1944. She gave notable interpretations of 19th-century ballets, such as *Swan Lake* and *Giselle*, and also danced the leading roles, composed especially for her, in all three of Prokofiev's ballets. During the 1950s she became well known in the West through touring with the Bolshoi Ballet. After her retirement as a dancer in 1962 she remained with the company as a teacher.

ulcer A localized erosion and destruction of the protective layer of organs and tissue, such as the skin and mucous membranes of the gastro-intestinal tract. This results in the exposure of underlying tissue. Peptic ulceration, commonly due to bacterial infection by *Helicobacter pylori* and treatable by antibiotics, occurs in the lower part of the oesophagus, stomach (gastric ulcer), and duodenum (duodenal ulcer), which are caused by reduced defence mechanisms, increased production of acid and digestive enzymes, or both. Acute erosive ulceration (stress ulcers) is the presence of multiple ulcers in the oesophagus, stomach, and duodenum; they may be caused by stress associated with major surgery, trauma, or burns, or where the mucous membrane has been damaged by excessive alcohol consumption or drugs. Mouth ulcers (aphthous ulceration or stomatitis) affect the mucous membrane of the mouth; they are small and painful. Ulcers may also occur in other parts of the gastro-intestinal tract, as in ulcerative COLITIS.

Skin ulcers are the destruction and erosion of the outer layer of the skin (epidermis), which may be caused by abnormalities of venous circulation (venous ulcers) such as in varicose veins and deep vein THROMBOSIS. Trauma may also cause ulcers; prolonged pressure at one site, such as during bed rest when the patient is unable to turn, may also result in ulceration.

Ulfilas (or **Wulfila**) (*c*.311–*c*.381) Bishop and translator. Believed to be of Cappadocian descent, he became bishop of the Visigoths in 341. Ulfilas is best known for his translation of the Bible from Greek into Gothic (of which fragments survive), the earliest known translation of the Bible into a Germanic language. The translation uses the Gothic alphabet, based on Latin and Greek characters, which Ulfilas is traditionally held to have invented.

Ullswater A lake in the Lake District of Cumbria, north-west England, the second largest lake in England. It is 12 km (7.5 miles) long and reaches a depth of 64 m (210 ft).

Ulm An industrial city on the Danube in Baden-Württemberg, southern Germany; pop. (1991) 112,170. Napoleon defeated the Austrians at the Battle of Ulm in 1805 and the city was the birthplace in 1879 of Albert Einstein. Its Gothic cathedral, founded in 1377, has the highest spire in the world (161 m, 528 ft) Ulm has industries making vehicles, electrical goods, and textiles.

ulna See ARM.

Ulpian (born Domitius Ulpianus) (died *c*.228) Roman jurist, born in Phoenicia. His numerous legal writings provided one of the chief sources for Justinian's *Digest* of 533.

Ulster ▶**1** A former kingdom of IRELAND, lying in the north-east of the island. The kingdom of Ulster reached its zenith in the 5th century AD, at the beginning of the Christian era. During the Anglo-Norman conquest the de Lacey and de Burgh families held the earldom of Ulster from 1205 to 1333. By the 16th century, the O'Neill clan had reasserted its commanding position in the area, until the failure of the Earl of Tyrone's rebellion against ELIZABETH I and her unwelcome religious policy (1594–1601) marked the end of O'Neill supremacy. James I promoted the **plantation** in Ulster of thousands of Presbyterian Scots and Protestant English and many Catholics were forced off their land. These Protestants supported WILLIAM III in his campaign against JAMES II, which culminated in William's victory at the Battle of the BOYNE (1690). At the division of Ireland in 1920–21, six of the nine counties that originally comprised Ulster opted for self-governing status as NORTHERN IRELAND, a province of the UNITED KINGDOM. The remaining three counties of Cavan, Donegal, and Monaghan became part of the Irish Free State (later the Republic of Ireland). The name Ulster is still used (especially by Unionists) to refer to Northern Ireland. ▶**2** A province of the Republic of Ireland comprising the counties of Cavan, Donegal, and Monaghan; area 8,012 sq km (3,095 sq miles); pop. (1991) 232,000.

Ulster Unionist Parties Political parties in NORTHERN IRELAND supporting maintenance of the union with the UK. In 1886 Lord Harlington and Joseph CHAMBERLAIN formed the Liberal Unionists, allying with the Conservatives and pledging to maintain the Union of Ireland with the rest of the United Kingdom. In 1920, with the division of Ireland, the majority party in Northern Ireland was the Unionist wing of the Conservative Party, now calling itself the Ulster Unionists, under Sir James Craig, who was Prime Minister 1921–40. The party, supported by a Protestant electorate, continued to rule under his successors, until the imposition of direct rule from Westminster in 1972. The policy for handling the increased violence between Nationalists and Unionists after the civil rights campaign of 1968 led to divisions in the party, and in 1969 it split into the Official Ulster Unionist Party and the Protestant Unionist Party. The latter, led by the Revd Ian Paisley, was renamed in 1972 the Ulster Democratic Unionist Party, with policies more extreme than those of the Ulster Unionists (led, from 1979 to 1995, by James Molyneaux and from 1995 by David Trimble).

Ulster Volunteers An Irish para-military organization, formed in 1912 to exclude Ulster from the HOME RULE Bill then about to go through Parliament. Its supporters pledged themselves 'to use all means' to resist this. They were given every encouragement by Sir Edward CARSON and several prominent English Conservatives. The Volunteers were drilled and armed: thousands of rifles were smuggled into Ireland for their use. A clash between these Volunteers and the nationalist Irish Volunteers (formed in Dublin in 1913) became probable but was averted by the start of World War I.

ultracentrifuge See CENTRIFUGE.

ultrasound Vibrations in the FREQUENCY range 20 kHz to 1,000 MHz. It is inaudible to humans, but some animals – dogs, bats, and dolphins for example – can hear it. (For humans, audible sound is in the range 15–20,000 Hz.) The effects of such high-frequency vibration on gases, liquids, and solids are diverse and have led to a number of industrial, biological, and medical applications since the 1940s. In medicine, ultrasonography is a diagnostic technique in which sound waves are transmitted into the body by a **scanner** and bounce back from the internal tissues. The reflected sound waves can be detected and displayed as a moving image of an internal organ on a cathode-ray tube. This scanning technique is used widely in OBSTETRICS to examine the foetus and in CARDIOLOGY and cardiac surgery to study heart function. Ultrasound is also used to fragment STONES without the need for surgery (see LITHOTRIPSY).

ultraviolet astronomy The observation of extraterrestrial ultraviolet radiation. Most of this ultraviolet radiation is absorbed by the OZONE layer in the Earth's atmosphere and measurements of it can only be made from rockets and satellites. Important results coming from the ultraviolet domain are on the brightness of stars as seen at these wavelengths, on the shapes of spectral lines, which have indicated the presence of stellar winds, and the discovery of an absorption hump round about 220 nm caused by the dusty grains of the interstellar medium.

ultraviolet radiation ELECTROMAGNETIC RADIATION with wavelength shorter than those of visible light and longer than those of X-rays, approximately 10^{-7} to 10^{-9} metre. The waves near the longer end of the range are called near ultraviolet and are emitted by certain atoms, such as those of mercury, when they are electrically excited. Sunlight contains much near ultraviolet. It is responsible for producing pigmentation (suntan) and vitamin D in the skin. Ultraviolet light can kill certain bacteria, and can cause FLUORESCENCE in certain atoms and molecules, some of which are used in paints.

Ulyanov, Vladimir Ilich See LENIN.

Ulysses See ODYSSEUS.

Umayyad A Muslim dynasty, descended from the Quraish tribe to which the prophet Muhammad belonged, that ruled Islam from *c.*660 to 750 and later ruled Moorish Spain 756–1031.

umbilical cord The tissue that connects the embryo to the PLACENTA in placental mammals. Blood passes from the embryo to the placenta along two arteries, propelled by the embryo's heart. It returns from the placenta via a large umbilical vein to the heart for recirculation. These vessels forming the cord are twisted around one another and resemble a rope. In humans the cord is clamped and cut after birth. Animals bite through it; their saliva contains an enzyme that stops bleeding from the cord after it has been severed.

umbra See ECLIPSE.

umbrella bird Any of three species of bird of the genus *Cephalopterus*, belonging to the COTINGA family. They occur from Costa Rica southwards down South America, living in tropical forest. They are the largest members of the family. All are black in colour and get their name from the umbrella-like thatch of raised feathers on the crown. All the males have a throat wattle, which is covered in black feathers in two species; in the male long-wattled umbrella bird, *C. penduliger*, the wattle may be up to 35 cm (14 inches) long. They eat fruits and insects.

Umbria ▶**1** A district of ancient central Italy. ▶**2** A corresponding region of modern Italy; area 8,456 sq km (3,266 sq miles); pop. (1990) 822,765; capital, Perugia. Taking its name from the ancient Umbri, it is the only region of Italy without a coastline. Predominantly agricultural its medieval hill towns are a favourite tourist destination.

Umm al Qaiwain The second-smallest of the seven states of the United Arab Emirates, situated between Dubai and Ras al Khaimah; area 750 sq km (290 sq miles); pop. (1995) 35,100; capital, Umm al Qaiwain. Its economy is based on pearling, trading, fishing, and agriculture (mostly around the oasis of Falaj al-Mualla).

UN See UNITED NATIONS.

uncertainty principle The principle that it is impossible to make a precise simultaneous measurement of both the position and the momentum of a small particle. The German physicist Werner HEISENBERG showed that the product of the uncertainties in the two quantities must be of the order of Planck's constant, h (6.6×10^{-34} joule second). This is a very small number and it has the consequence that the uncertainties can never be detected for ordinary objects; but they become very important for atoms and smaller particles. See also WAVE-PARTICLE DUALITY.

unconscious mind In PSYCHOANALYSIS, the site of memories and wishes that, according to FREUD, cannot be recalled to consciousness but that continue to influence thought and behaviour. They have not merely been forgotten, but repressed by DEFENCE MECHANISMS because recall is painful. The unconscious contents manifest themselves in DREAMS and in errors of speech ('Freudian slips' of the tongue), or forgetting appointments. Psychoanalytic therapy is based on the belief that the contents of the unconscious cause neurotic symptoms because of this repression. The psychoanalyst aims to help the patient to release unconscious material into consciousness, and, by releasing suppressed feeling to shed them. A more recent concept in COGNITIVE PSYCHOLOGY is that the brain can accept and analyse information unconsciously, rather like the ARTIFICIAL INTELLIGENCE of a computer. This unconscious processing of information is basic to human behaviour.

underground railway (US **subway**) A railway system carrying passengers in tunnels beneath the streets of a city. The first underground ('tube') was opened in London in 1863, and ran from Paddington to Farringdon. It was built by the cut-and-cover method (see TUNNEL). Lines using fully AUTOMATIC TRAIN CONTROL have been developed for some underground systems: the first was the Victoria Line in the London tube system. The Paris Métro, and other systems modelled on it, have introduced trains running on concrete track instead of rails, an example of a GROUND-GUIDANCE SYSTEM. New and extended underground railways, such as the BART (Bay Area Rapid Transit) system in San Francisco, USA, help ease problems of urban transportation.

underwing moth A moth that has brightly coloured hind-wings, which are exposed in flight but concealed by the camouflaged fore-wings at rest. The name is used for a number of different types of moth, but particularly for OWLET MOTHS of the genera *Catocala* and *Noctua*. There are about 100 species of *Catocala* in North America, but only five in the British Isles, including the red underwing, *Catocala nupta*. There are six British species of yellow underwing (*Noctua*), the most common of which is the large yellow underwing, *Noctua pronuba*, whose caterpillars are CUTWORMS, which eat roots, stems, and leaves of a variety of low-growing plants.

unemployment A measure of the proportion of the available work-force without a job. Unemployment tends to affect disproportionately women, young people, seasonal and migrant workers, and unskilled workers. Official statistics are based on various concepts of 'availability for work', but probably underestimate levels of unemployment and underemployment (people who are not, but want to be, fully employed); both these affect developing countries particularly. In developing countries, in Latin America for example, population expansion, out-of-date forms of land tenure and the mechanization of agriculture have driven many people off the land to join growing numbers of urban unemployed. In some industrialized countries (UK, Ireland, and Spain), unemployment was at historically high levels, with the proportion of long-term unemployed rising. In centrally planned or statist economies, government policy was to maintain low or zero levels of unemployment; however, that such statistics are misleading or cushioned by permitting redundant posts to continue to be filled is evidenced by soaring unemployment in eastern Germany, where unemployment figures reached 50 per cent within a year of German reunification in 1990.

UNESCO See UNITED NATIONS EDUCATIONAL, SCIENTIFIC AND CULTURAL ORGANIZATION.

unicorn A mythical animal resembling a horse with a single horn on its forehead. An enigmatic symbol, it was first used in ancient Sanskrit texts. According to Islamic and Western medieval legend it was difficult to capture and could be tamed only by a virgin girl. As the biblical animal of the Old Testament, the unicorn was taken as an allegorized interpretation of the Christian Church, often likened to Christ.

unicorn fish A fish of the genus *Naso*, within the family Acanthuridae. All species of *Naso* live in the tropical waters of the Indo-Pacific and have a protuberant horn on the front of the head when they are adult. They also have two (occasionally one or three) forward-pointing spines on the tail. They feed on the leafy, large algae, which grow around the bases of coral or on broken coral.

In the same family are the 100 or so species of surgeonfish, whose name is derived from the sharp spines on the tail. Most species reach a length of 30 cm (12 inches) and feed on plants and animals living on rocks or coral.

Unification Church A religious movement founded by Sun Myung Moon (1920–) in South Korea in 1954. Members are popularly known as the 'Moonies'. Its theology, found in the *Divine Principle*, claims that a sinless man (often thought to be Moon himself) could save the world and form the kingdom of God on Earth. There are said to be 3 million members. The movement has attracted controversy through its business practices and accusations that it brainwashes new recruits into absolute obedience.

unified field theory See GRAND UNIFIED THEORY.

Uniformity, Acts of A series of English laws intended to secure the legal and doctrinal basis of the ANGLICAN COMMUNION. The first (1549) made the Book of Common Prayer compulsory in church services, with severe penalties on non-compliant clergymen. The second (1552) imposed a revised Prayer Book, which was more Protestant in tone, and laid down punishments for recusants. MARY I had both Acts repealed, but the third (1559) introduced a third Book of Common Prayer and weekly fines for non-attendance at church. The fourth (1662) presented a further revised, compulsory Book. Under its terms some 2,000 non-compliant clergymen lost their benefices, creating the Anglican-NONCONFORMIST breach.

Union, Acts of Laws that cemented the political union of Great Britain and Ireland. Following the complete subjugation of Wales by 1284, the Statute of Rhuddlan, never submitted to a formal Parliament, sanctioned the English system of administration there. Not until 1536 was an Act passed by HENRY VIII, which incorporated Wales with England, and granted for the first time Welsh representation in Parliament. The Stuarts united the thrones but not the governments of England and Scotland in 1603. In 1707 an Act of Union between England and Scotland gave the Scots free trade with England, but in return for representation at Westminster they had to give up their own Parliament. The Protestant Irish Parliament enjoyed independence from 1782 to 1800, when legislation (1 August 1800) was introduced to establish the UNITED KINGDOM of Great Britain and Ireland (1 January 1801).

Union of Soviet Socialist Republics See SOVIET UNION.

unit (of measurement) The name of a quantity, such as second or metre, chosen as a standard for use in measurement or comparison. Units measuring the quantities of mass, distance, area, and volume have existed since early in human history. Early units of linear measurement were often derived from body measurements: the Egyptian cubit, for example (derived *c.*3000 BC), was based on the distance from the elbow to the fingertip. Later, more accurate standards were developed. The Egyptian royal cubit (524 mm, 20.62 inches) was standardized against a master cubit of black marble. Ancient Greek units drew from both the Egyptian and Babylonian systems of weights and measures. The Romans based their units on those of the Greeks. Medieval Europe inherited the Roman system, but in time many regional variations arose. The great European trade fairs of the 12th and 13th centuries forced merchants from different countries to adopt the same units of measurement, but many variations remained in England. In the 18th century the metric system was introduced in France, in the aftermath of the French Revolution. The system was designed to be rational and practical, with each unit being subdivided or multiplied decimally. The metric system spread through Europe and to many other countries during the 19th century, and in the 20th century became the basis for the modern SI UNIT system, now used internationally by the scientific community. In the UK and the USA a system of units, rationalized from the European medieval system, continued to be used for most purposes except scientific work. The UK began a changeover to the metric system in 1965, but the USA still has no national legislation to introduce metric units.

Unitarianism An undogmatic Christian sect based on freedom, reason, tolerance, and a belief in the goodness of human nature. Modern Unitarianism derives from 16th-century PROTESTANT Christian thinkers who rejected the doctrine of the TRINITY and stressed the unity of God. In 1961 the Unitarian Universalist Association was founded in the USA by the union of Unitarianism and Universalism, the latter, founded in 1778, having members of diverse religious opinions.

United Arab Emirates (UAE) A federation of seven sheikhdoms (emirates) occupying the southern (Arabian) coast of the Gulf between Qatar and Oman, together with its offshore islands.

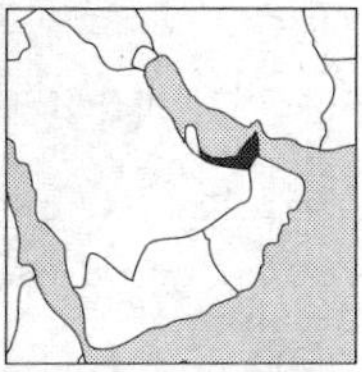

Physical. Abu Dhabi in the west is the largest emirate and also the richest in oil and natural gas. Dubai to the east is the second largest emirate and has oil offshore, as has Sharjah. Further east, Ras al-Khaimah and Fujairah are predominantly agricultural, while Ajman and Umm al-Qaiwain are very small. The terrain throughout the emirates is sandy and low-lying.

Economy. The economy of the UAE is based largely on crude oil, which, with natural gas, dominates exports. In addition, Dubai has a substantial entrepôt trade. Industries include petroleum products, cement, and aluminium-smelting. Agriculture suffers from arid conditions and poor irrigation. There is a large immigrant workforce, mainly of Pakistanis, Indians, and Iranians.

History. The sheikhdoms concluded several treaties with Britain from 1820 onwards. In 1892, they accepted British military protection, becoming known thereafter as the TRUCIAL STATES. The emirates came together as an independent state when they ended their individual special treaty relationships with the British government, and signed a Treaty of Friendship with Britain in 1971. The large oil resources of Abu Dhabi were first discovered in 1958. Each of the rulers of the seven constituent emirates has autonomy in his own state. Since 1979 Sheikh Zayed bin Sultan al-Nahayan of Abu Dhabi has been President of the Federation. The collapse of the Bank of Credit and Commerce cost Abu Dhabi some $10,000 million.

Capital: Abu Dhabi
Area: 77,700 sq km (30,000 sq mi)
Population: 2,195,000 (1995)
Currency: 1 UAE dirham = 100 fils
Religions: Sunni Muslim 80.0%; Shiite Muslim 20.0%; Christian minority
Ethnic Groups: UAE Arab 30.7%; other Arab 56.4%; Pakistani and Indian 10.0%; Iranian 1.7%
Languages: Arabic (official); other immigrant languages
International Organizations: UN; GCC; Arab League; OAPEC

United Arab Republic A political union that existed between Egypt and Syria from 1958 until 1961. It was seen as the first step towards the creation of a pan-Arab union in the Middle East.

United Kingdom (UK) A country in NW Europe consisting of ENGLAND, WALES, and SCOTLAND, and the province of NORTHERN IRELAND. The Channel Islands and the Isle of Man are British Crown dependencies but are not an integral part of the United Kingdom.

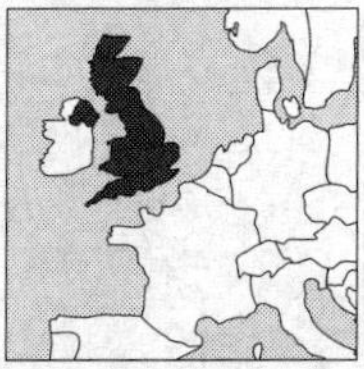

Physical. The United Kingdom consists of Great Britain, a large island off Europe's north-west coast containing England, Scotland, and Wales, and the north east corner of the neighbouring island of Ireland (see BRITISH ISLES). The distance from Land's End on its south-west corner to John o' Groats in the far north is 971 km (603 miles); yet such are the coastal indentations that no part is more than 160 km (100 miles) from the sea. Of its mountains, which lie in the north and west, few are higher than 1,000 m (3,300 feet), while of its rivers none is longer than the Severn at 354 km (220 miles). Within this small compass, however, the geological differences are great. The rocks are of many periods and kinds, with granite and slate, basalt, sandstones, and hard limestone all included. Generally lower in the west than the north, the rocky masses underlie much moorland, generally bare of trees and having for vegetation peat moss, heather, and acid grass in varying proportions. The south of the country, which is warmer and drier than the rest, has hills of chalk and flint or limestone rising to 300 m (less than 1,000 feet). Here the valleys are broad, with sandy soil or clay supporting oak, ash, beech, and chestnut trees. In the east, which is lower and flatter, river gravels and alluvium from the North Sea have produced dark, rich soils. Its principal river, the THAMES, flows into the North Sea.

Economy. The United Kingdom has a heavily industrialized economy with substantial, though declining, offshore oil production in the North Sea; main exports include machinery, chemicals, electrical equipment, petroleum, and steel. Britain is one of the world's largest steel producers, but its wide range of manufacturing industry has declined in recent decades. There is a growing service sector and high-technology industries are being developed. London is an expanding finance and banking centre. The state sector shrank considerably during the 1980s and 1990s owing to policies of privatization. Coal is mined for domestic consumption and electricity generation. Other mineral resources include iron ore, zinc, tin, and lead. Agricultural productivity has been boosted by mechanization and intensive-farming methods.

History. WALES was incorporated into England in the reign of HENRY VIII. In 1604 JAMES I was proclaimed 'King of Great Britain', but although his accession to the English throne (1603) had joined the two crowns of ENGLAND and SCOTLAND the countries were not formally united. In the aftermath of the English Civil War, Oliver Cromwell effected a temporary union between England and Scotland, but it did not survive the RESTORATION. The countries were joined by the Act of UNION (1707) which left unchanged the Scottish judicial system and the Presbyterian church. IRELAND was incorpo-

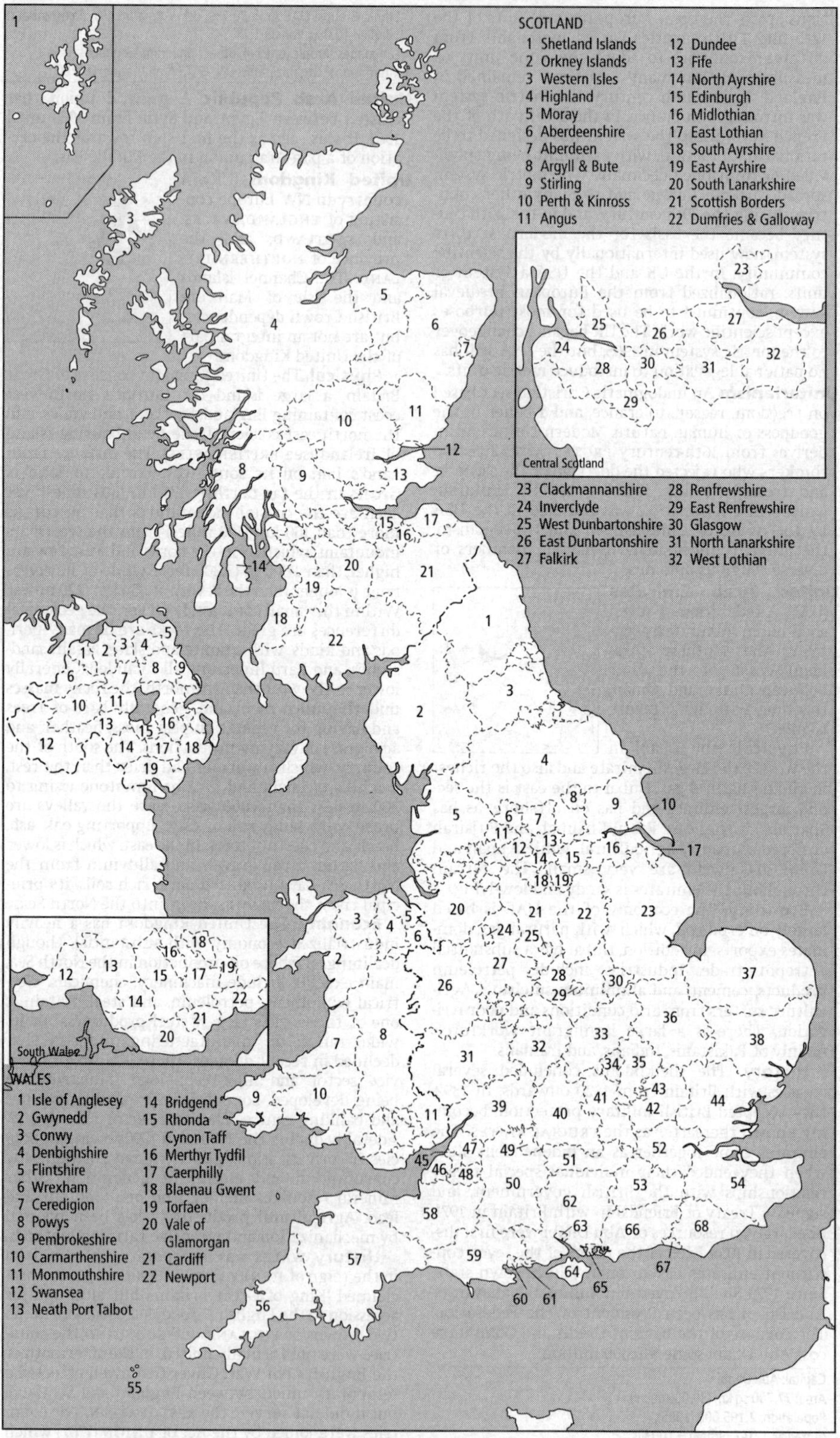

United Kingdom The local government areas (counties and unitary authorities) within the kingdom.

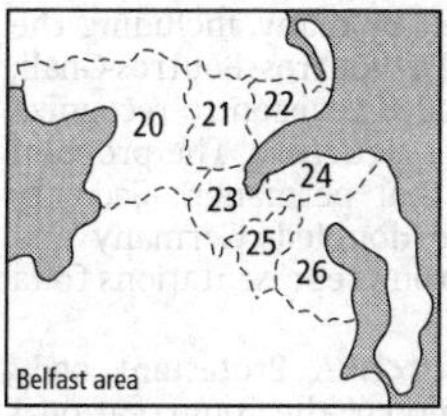

NORTHERN IRELAND

1 Derry City
2 Limavady
3 Coleraine
4 Ballymoney
5 Moyle
6 Strabane
7 Magherafelt
8 Ballymena
9 Larne
10 Omagh
11 Cookstown
12 Fermanagh
13 Dungannon
14 Armagh
15 Craigavon
16 Lisburn
17 Banbridge
18 Down
19 Newry & Mourne
20 Antrim
21 Newtownabbey
22 Carrikfergus
23 Belfast City
24 North Down
25 Castlereagh
26 Ards

ENGLAND

1 Northumberland
2 Cumbria
3 Durham
4 North Yorkshire
5 Lancashire
6 Bradford
7 Leeds
8 York
9 East Riding of Yorkshire
10 Kingston-upon-Hull
11 Calderdale
12 Kirklees
13 Wakefield
14 Barnsley
15 Doncaster
16 North Lincolnshire
17 North East Lincolnshire
18 Sheffield
19 Rotherham
20 Cheshire
21 Derbyhire
22 Nottinghamshire
23 Lincolnshire
24 Stoke-on-Trent
25 Derby City
26 Shropshire
27 Staffordshire
28 Leicestershire
29 Leicester City
30 Rutland
31 Hereford & Worcester
32 Warwickshire
33 Northamptonshire
34 Milton Keynes
35 Bedfordshire
36 Cambridgeshire
37 Norfolk
38 Suffolk
39 Gloucestershire
40 Oxfordshire
41 Buckinghamshire
42 Hertfordshire
43 Luton
44 Essex
45 Bristol
46 North Somerset
47 South Gloucestershire
48 Bath & North East Somerset
49 Swindon
50 Wiltshire
51 Berkshire
52 Greater London (see GREATER LONDON)
53 Surrey
54 Kent
55 Isles of Scilly
56 Cornwall
57 Devon
58 Somerset
59 Dorset
60 Poole
61 Bournemouth
62 Hampshire
63 Southampton
64 Isle of Wight
65 Portsmouth
66 West Sussex
67 Brighton & Hove
68 East Sussex

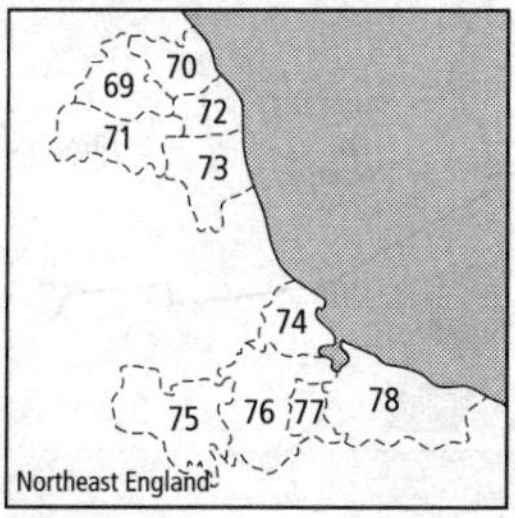

69 Newcastle-upon-Tyne
70 North Tyneside
71 Gateshead
72 South Tyneside
73 Sunderland
74 Hartlepool
75 Darlington
76 Stockton-on-Tees
77 Middlesbrough
78 Redcar & Cleveland

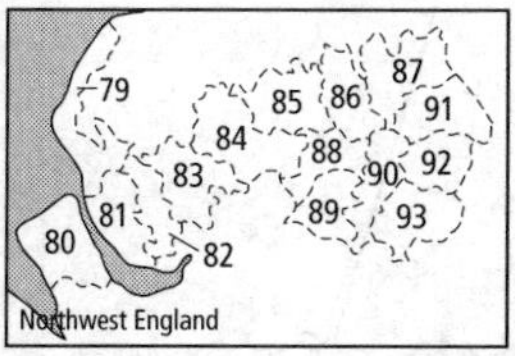

79 Sefton
80 Wirral
81 Liverpool
82 Knowsley
83 St Helens
84 Wigan
85 Bolton
86 Bury
87 Rochdale
88 Salford
89 Trafford
90 Manchester
91 Oldham
92 Tameside
93 Stockport

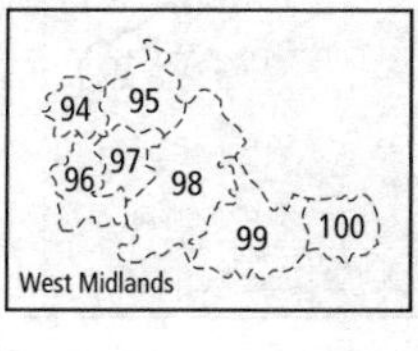

94 Wolverhampton
95 Walsall
96 Dudley
97 Sandwell
98 Birmingham
99 Solihull
100 Coventry

rated into the United Kingdom in 1800 but became independent (except for Northern Ireland) in 1921.

Britain was the first country in Europe to become fully industrialized, developing a predominantly urban, rather than a rural, society by the mid-19th century. A series of parliamentary reform acts, beginning with the REFORM ACT of 1832, steadily increased the power of the HOUSE OF COMMONS compared to that of the monarch and the HOUSE OF LORDS. Under Queen VICTORIA, colonial expansion of the BRITISH EMPIRE reached its height. However, growing pressure for independence from peoples within the empire meant that during the 20th century British dominions and colonies gradually gained independence; most of them elected to join the COMMONWEALTH OF NATIONS, established in 1931. During WORLD WAR I and WORLD WAR II Britain fought against Germany and its allies, emerging from both conflicts on the victorious side. A period of austerity, which began to ease in the 1950s, followed World War II. Since 1967 gas and oil from offshore wells have been commercially produced, creating a major impact on the nation's economy. In 1973 Britain became a member of the European Economic Community, subsequently the EUROPEAN UNION. In 1982 Britain fought the FALKLANDS WAR with Argentina and in 1991 sent troops to support the US-led coalition in the GULF WAR.

The main political parties in Britain are the CONSERVATIVE PARTY, the LABOUR PARTY, and the Liberal Democrats (see LIBERAL PARTY). The Liberals have not been in power since the resignation of LLOYD GEORGE in 1922. During World War II a coalition government under Winston CHURCHILL was formed. The postwar Labour ATTLEE ministries saw the introduction of the National Health Service and the WELFARE STATE, largely on the lines of the BEVERIDGE Report. Labour governments have traditionally been supported by TRADE UNIONS and legislated to nationalize service industries. Subsequent Conservative governments, notably those of Margaret THATCHER and John MAJOR, reversed the procedure by privatizing many publicly owned companies; they also passed laws to restrict the power of the trade unions and restricted public spending. The Labour Party led by Tony BLAIR won the general election of 1997 and formed a new government.

In 1997 referendums favoured devolution for Scotland and a degree of autonomy for Wales. Progress has been made towards resolving the problem of Northern Ireland, which has seen recurrent conflict between Catholic supporters of a united Ireland and Protestant supporters of union with Britain. The latest round of peace talks, involving all the main Northern Irish political parties, began in 1996 and concluded in 1998 with the signing of a peace agreement by the British and Irish governments and the leaders of most of the Northern Irish parties.

Capital: London
Area: 244,110 sq km (94,251 sq mi)
Population: 58,586,000 (1995)
Currency: 1 pound sterling = 100 pence
Religions: Church of England 50%; Roman Catholic 13.0%; Church of Scotland 4.0%; Methodist 2.0%; Baptist 1.0%; Muslim 1.0%; Jewish 0.8%; Hindu 0.75%; Sikh 0.5%
Ethnic Groups: White 94.4%; Asian Indian 1.3%; West Indian 1.0%; Pakistani 0.7%; Chinese 0.2%; African 0.2%; Bangladeshi 0.2%; Arab 0.1%
Languages: English (official); Welsh; Scots-Gaelic; other minority languages
International Organizations: UN; EU; Commonwealth; OECD; NATO; Council of Europe; CSCE

United Nations (UN) An international organization of countries set up in 1945, in succession to the League of Nations, to promote international peace, security, and cooperation, with its headquarters in New York. Its members, originally the countries that fought against the Axis in World War II, numbered 186 in 1995 and include most sovereign states of the world. Administration is by the Secretariat, headed by the Secretary-General. The chief deliberative body is the General Assembly, in which each member-state has one vote; recommendations are passed but the UN has no power to impose its will. The Security Council bears the primary responsibility for the maintenance of peace and security; other bodies carry out the functions of the UN with regard to international economic, social, judicial, cultural, educational, health, and other matters. With the close of the Cold War era UN peace-keeping activities expanded rapidly. Between 1987 and 1993 15 UN peace-keeping operations were initiated compared with a total of 13 missions in the previous 40 years.

United Nations Educational, Scientific and Cultural Organization (UNESCO) A specialized agency of the UNITED NATIONS, founded in 1946 and based in Paris, which promotes international collaboration in education, science, culture, and communication. In education, it supports the spread of literacy, continuing education, and universal primary education; and in science, assists developing countries, and international interchange between scientists. It encourages the preservation of monuments and sites, and of other aspects of culture such as oral traditions, music, and dance. By 1989 UNESCO's 'World Heritage List', designed to protect landmarks of 'outstanding universal value', comprised 315 sites in 67 countries. In the field of communication, UNESCO is committed to the free flow of information. In 1980 its supreme governing body approved a New World Information and Communication Order despite opposition from those who believed it threatened press freedom (see MASS MEDIA). In 1984 the USA (which had been due to supply about a quarter of UNESCO's budget) and in 1985 the UK and Singapore withdrew, alleging financial mismanagement and political bias against Western countries.

United Nations Security Council One of the six principal organs of the UNITED NATIONS, based at UN headquarters in New York, whose prime responsibility is to maintain world peace and security. The Security Council, which first met in January 1946, consists of five permanent members (the USA, Russia, China, France, and the UK), and ten non-permanent members elected by the United Nations General Assembly for two-year terms on a rotating basis. With the changes in the economic and political BALANCE OF POWER since the end of the cold war, a change in the permanent membership to admit Germany, Japan, the EU, or other regional powers, is likely to come under discussion. The Security Council can investigate any international dispute, and recommend ways of achieving a settlement, including 'enforcement measures', such as SANCTIONS, or the use of force by UN members (as, for example, in Somalia in 1992). It is also responsible for peacekeeping forces. Decisions taken by the Security Council require a majority of nine, including all five permanent members. This rule of great power unanimity, usually referred to as the right of veto, had been the cause of controversy. The effectiveness of the Council was improved after the collapse of the Soviet bloc in 1991. By 1992 it was felt by many, including the then Secretary-General Dr Boutros Boutros-Ghali, that its membership needed revision to recognize the current world power-structure. The proposal was advanced, in 1994, that permanent Security Council membership be doubled; Germany and Japan made especially strong representations for a permanent seat.

United Reformed Church A Protestant body formed in 1972 by the union of the Congregational Church of England and Wales and the Presbyterian Church of England. This was the first union of different Protestant denominations in the UK. Traditionally, the Presbyterians were governed by local and national assemblies, while Congregationalism affirmed the independence of local congregations, a principle modified but not abandoned in the United Church. It currently has 12 provinces in the UK, with about 1,100 ministers and 200,000 members.

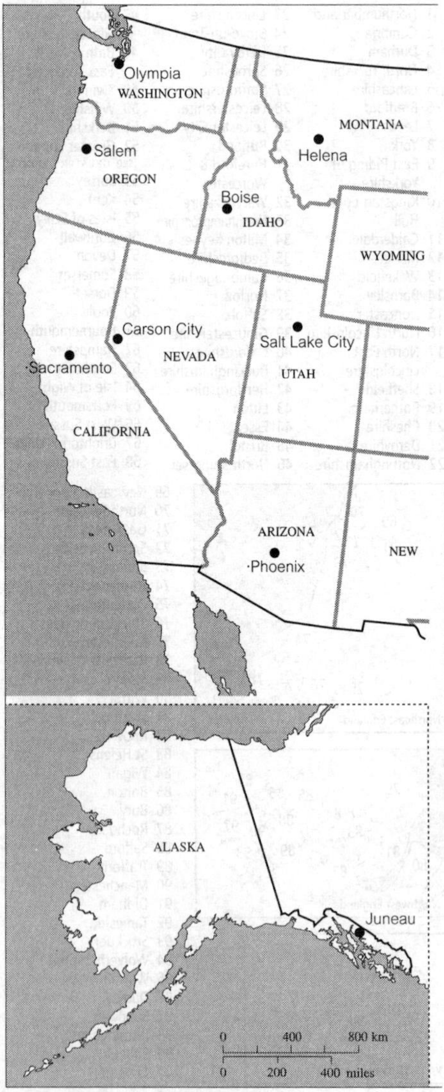

United States of America

United States of America (USA) The world's fourth largest country, comprising the central belt of North America together with Alaska, Hawaii, Puerto Rico, and many small Pacific Ocean islands. Mainland USA is bounded by Canada on the north, generally along latitude 49° N and the Great Lakes, and by Mexico on the south, generally at about 32° N and along the Rio Grande.

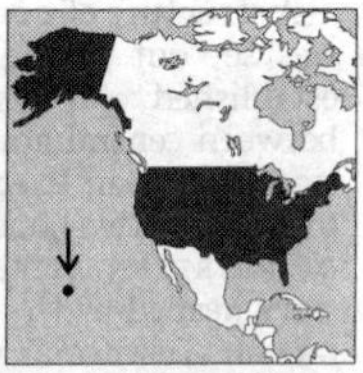

Physical. The USA contains several topographically very diverse regions. The West Coast is a series of mountain ranges with attendant valleys and plateaux running roughly parallel to the climatically mild Pacific coast. In the north, the Cascade Range is cut by the valley of the Columbia River; and here, in Washington and Oregon, there are orchards and mighty softwood forests. In California, the reverse slopes of the Coast Range descend to the lush Sacramento and San Joaquin valleys, which are fringed inland by the snow-capped peaks of the Sierra Nevada. From here the Great Basin of Nevada and parts of Oregon, Idaho, Utah, and California, an arid and rugged plateau containing its own mountain ranges, extends eastward to the Rocky Mountains. The Rockies are the 'Great Divide', the main watershed of the country. Out of their massive ranges in Montana, Wyoming, Colorado, and New Mexico (the Mountain States), emerge the westward-running Snake and Colorado rivers, and the eastward-flowing tributaries of the Mississippi. The Great Plains, occupied by the Dakotas, Nebraska, Kansas, Oklahoma, and Texas, are cut through by the eastward flows and have become a great prairie supporting cattle ranching and wheat cultivation. The prairies extend through the Middle West (including Minnesota, Iowa, Missouri, and north-west Arkansas) to the basin of the Mis-

sissippi, which intersects the country from north to south. The PODZOLS of the northern states in the Middle West (Wisconsin, Michigan, Illinois, Indiana, and Ohio) are well suited to the cultivation of maize and differ greatly from the red and yellow soils of the Deep South. Here, in Louisiana, Mississippi, Tennessee, Alabama, and Georgia, the main crops are cotton, rice, tobacco, and sugarcane. In this region also there are oilfields which extend into the Gulf of Mexico. The peninsula of Florida is renowned for the warmth of its climate and for its citrus fruits. The south-eastern coastal plain, occupied by Virginia, the Carolinas, and eastern Georgia, is drained by the rivers of the Appalachian Mountains and supports much mixed farming. Mountainous New England, the north-eastern region, experiences harsh winters but contains rich pastures and many areas of great natural beauty. Inland, the Great Lakes form a great transport artery and provide hydroelectric power for the northern states.

Economy. The US economy benefits from abundant natural resources and a large internal market. A free-trade treaty was signed with Canada in 1989, and in 1993 the NORTH AMERICAN FREE TRADE AGREEMENT created a free-trade region comprising the USA, Canada, and Mexico. Exports, at only 7.6 per cent of gross domestic product in 1994, show the economy to be largely self-sufficient and comparatively unaffected by global economic trends. However, a surge in imports in the 1980s, particularly from Japan, and the uncompetitiveness of exports have caused a trade deficit which, together with the large federal budget deficit, has aroused worldwide concern. Major exports are electrical goods, machinery, chemicals, motor vehicles, cereals, and aircraft. The USA has a wealth of mineral deposits, including coal, oil, gold, silver, lead, copper, iron ore, zinc, uranium, and phosphates. Regional climatic differences enable agricultural diversity: the main crops are maize and wheat, soya beans, cotton, and tobacco. Fishing, forestry, and livestock are also substantial.

History. The indigenous peoples of North America probably came from Asia across the Bering land bridge over 30,000 years ago. From the territory now occupied by Alaska, they spread out to populate the entire continent (and South America). By 1600 AD, it is estimated that there were around 1.5 million AMERICAN INDIANS in what are now Canada and the USA. European colonization of the eastern seaboard of North America began in the early 17th century, gaining momentum as the rival nations, most notably the British and French, struggled for control of the new territory. The Treaty of PARIS (1763) marked the final triumph of Britain, but by that time the British colonies, stretching from NEW ENGLAND in the north to GEORGIA in the south, had become accustomed to a considerable measure of independence. British attempts to reassert central authority produced first discontent and then open resistance. The First CONTINENTAL CONGRESS met in 1774 to consider action to regain lost rights, and the first armed encounters at Lexington and Concord in April 1775 led directly to full-scale revolt and to the formal proclamation of the separation of the Thirteen Colonies from Britain, as the United States of America, in the DECLARATION OF INDEPENDENCE (4 July 1776). In the American War of INDEPENDENCE, which lasted until 1783, the American cause was assisted by France and Spain. The war ended with the Peace of PARIS (1783), which recognized US independence.

A structure of government for the new country was set out in the Constitution of 1787, which established a federal system, dividing power between central government and the constituent states, with an executive President, a legislature made up of two houses, the SENATE and the HOUSE OF REPRESENTATIVES, and an independent judiciary headed by the Supreme Court (see also CONGRESS). Territorial expansion followed with the LOUISIANA PURCHASE of 1803, the acquisition of Florida in 1810–19, and of TEXAS, California, and the south-west following the MEXICAN–AMERICAN WAR of 1846–48. The western lands of the Louisiana Purchase and those seized from Mexico were at first territories of the USA, administered by officers of the federal government. When the population reached some 60,000 an area of territory negotiated to be admitted to the Union as a new state. The mid-19th century was dominated by a political crisis over slavery and states' rights, leading to the secession of the Southern states and their reconquest in the AMERICAN CIVIL WAR of 1861–65. The final decades of the century saw the westward expansion of European settlement, the purchase of Alaska (1867), and the acquisition of Spanish overseas territories after the Spanish–American War of 1898. In the 20th century the USA has participated in the two World Wars and has gradually emerged from isolationism to become a world power, a process accelerated by the COLD WAR division. After the disintegration of the Soviet Union in 1991 US foreign policy has concentrated on the resolution of major regional disputes and on providing military support for UN peacekeeping operations around the world.

Capital: Washington DC
Area: 9,529,063 sq km (3,679,192 sq mi)
Population: 263,057,000 (1995)
Currency: 1 dollar = 100 cents
Religions: Protestant 49.1%; Roman Catholic 29.6%; other Christian 8.4%; Jewish 2.7%; Muslim 1.9%; Hindu 0.2%; non-religious and atheist 6.8%
Ethnic Groups: European origin (White, of whom Hispanic 6.4%) 83.2%; Black 12.4%; Asian and Pacific Islander 1.5%; Amerindian 0.6%
Languages: English (official); Spanish; numerous minority or immigrant languages
International Organizations: UN; OAS; NATO; OECD; Colombo Plan; Anzus; CSCE; NAFTA

unit trust A UK trust formed to manage a portfolio of investments, especially stocks and shares, in which small investors can buy units. This enables small investors to own part of a diverse portfolio of securities, chosen and managed by professional fund managers. A wide spectrum of trusts caters for those seeking high growth and those seeking high income. In the USA they are called mutual funds.

Universal Time (UT) A system of time measurement formerly based on the diurnal motion of the stars and related to GREENWICH MEAN TIME (GMT). Since 1972 it has been based on International Atomic time, the SI unit of which is the SECOND. This is independent of the Earth's motions.

Universe The collection of all astronomical objects and the space between them. In COSMOLOGY, the properties of model Universes are compared with observations of the real Universe to decide what kind of Universe we live in. It is of unimaginable size (10^{10} light years) and age (10^{10} years), leading to a high expectation (but no proof) that life exists elsewhere.

university A centre of higher education with responsibilities for teaching and research. Higher education expanded at a remarkable rate during the 19th and 20th centuries, and by 1980 some 1,320 universities existed, including some 400 in the USA, together with several thousand colleges and institutes of higher education. By the 1990s there was accelerated university expansion, in part created by the granting of university status to academies of science in the former communist bloc, and by the upgrading of polytechnics and technical colleges to university status in Britain. The Open University system, using radio and television for advanced distance-learning, was launched in Britain in 1969 and has since then been successfully introduced in other countries.

Upanishads (Sanskrit, 'sitting near', i.e. at the feet of a master) A collection of more than 100 HINDU SACRED TEXTS composed in Sanskrit at an uncertain date (probably after about 400 BC). They contain a distillation of the teaching of the VEDAS and the Brahamanas (commentaries on the Vedas) and are therefore known as the VEDANTA ('the end of the Vedas'), but are more philosophical and mystical in character. Scholars identify in the Upanishadic era the first emergence of a concept within HINDUISM of a single supreme God (Brahman), who is knowable by the human self (atman). Hence the BHAGAVADGITA, although part of the later Mahabharata epic, is often classed with the Upanishads as providing the highest and most essential Hindu teaching.

Updike, John (Hoyer) (1932–) US novelist, poet, and short-story writer. He is noted for his quartet of novels *Rabbit, Run* (1960) *Rabbit Redux* (1971), *Rabbit is Rich* (1981), and *Rabbit at Rest* (1990), a small-town tragicomedy tracing the career of an ex-basketball player; the latter two novels were awarded Pulitzer Prizes. Other novels include *Couples* (1968) and *The Witches of Eastwick* (1984).

Upper Palaeolithic See PALAEOLITHIC.

Upper Volta The former name (until 1984) of BURKINA FASO in West Africa.

Uppsala An industrial and cultural city in eastern Sweden, capital of Uppsala county; pop. (1990) 167,500. Founded in 1477, its university is the oldest in northern Europe. There is a 15th-century cathedral. It has machinery, building materials, and pharmaceutical industries.

Ur A city of the SUMERIANS. It was occupied from the 5th millennium BC, and was at one point damaged by a severe flood. By 3000 BC it was one of a number of sizeable Sumerian cities. It was subject to the rule of AKKAD, but emerged *c.*2150 as the capital of a new Sumerian empire, under the third dynasty established by Ur-Nammu. The city was captured by the Elamites *c.*2000, but continued to thrive under the Chaldean kings of Babylon. It was finally abandoned in the 4th century BC.

Uralic A family of languages comprising the Finno-Ugric group and Samoyed, spoken over a wide area in Europe, Asia, and the Scandinavian countries.

Ural Mountains (or **Urals**; Russian **Uralskiy Khrebet**) A mountain range in Russia. It extends 1,600 km (1,000 miles) south from within the Arctic Circle to the Kazakhstan frontier, and forms a natural boundary between Europe and Asia. Its highest peak is Mt Narodnaya (1,894 m, 6,214 ft).

Urals Republic A region of Russia in the Ural Mountains that declared itself independent following the breakup of the Soviet Union in 1991; pop. (1989) 4,731,000; capital, Yekaterinburg. It was the first region to claim a status equivalent to the 21 republics of the Russian Federation, although it is not officially recognized.

uraninite (UO_2) The chief ore of uranium, normally pitch-black in colour, hard, very dense, and radioactive. Found in high-temperature veins of igneous origin, it is associated with thorium, lead, and the rare-earth elements. Large crystals of uraninite are found in Ontario (Canada) and South Africa. In its massive form (pitchblende) it was used in 1898 by the CURIES to identify radium, helium, and polonium, and it is still used as a source of radium.

uranium (symbol U, at. no. 92, r.a.m. 238.03) A dense, white, metallic element, a member of the ACTINIDES; it is radioactive, decaying over a long period to lead. Measurement of the lead content of uranium-containing rocks can be used to date the rock. The importance of uranium stems from its use in producing nuclear energy, both in reactors and in bombs. Naturally occurring uranium consists of three ISOTOPES, of mass numbers 234, 235, and 238. Uranium-235 has an abundance of only 0.71 per cent, but it is the only naturally occurring isotope that can be split by a slow neutron to form smaller nuclei and release energy. The much more abundant (99.28 per cent) uranium-238 is used in breeder reactors to produce PLUTONIUM. Although uranium is probably about 40 times as abundant in nature as silver is, it is not found uncombined. Indeed it occurs only sparingly in ores, the most notable of which are URANINITE, pitchblende, carnotite, and coffinite, a silicate.

Uranus (in Greek mythology) The personification of the heavens and the first ruler of the Universe. The husband of Gaea (Earth) and father of the Titans and Cyclopes, he was overthrown by his son Cronus.

Uranus (in astronomy) The seventh PLANET from the Sun and the fourth most massive planet of the Solar System. Uranus is generally not visible to the naked eye. It was discovered in 1781 by William HERSCHEL who initially thought it was a comet. Because of its slow motion, it became apparent that its orbit was nearly circular, and it was then clear that it was actually a planet. Uranus had, in fact, appeared in contemporary star catalogues but because it moves so slowly, it was thought to be a star. This previous information quickly led to a good knowledge of its orbit. Among the outer planets, Uranus is characterized by several unique properties. Its equator is inclined at 97 degrees to the plane of its orbit, its satellites are all small to medium in size and are in nearly circular equatorial orbits, and it is surrounded by nine very narrow dark rings, some of which are elliptical. Uranus apparently lacks an internal energy source comparable to those of the other outer planets and the line joining its magnetic poles is inclined at about 60 degrees to the rotation axis, a value that is larger than for any other planet.

Urban VIII (born Maffeo Barberini) (1568–1644) Pope 1623–44. He became a cardinal in 1606, and Bishop of Spoleto in 1608. As pope, he canonized Philip Neri and IGNATIUS LOYOLA, condemned Galileo and JANSENISM, and approved a number of new religious orders. In diplomacy, his fears of Habsburg domination in Italy led him to favour France during the THIRTY YEARS WAR. He also extensively fortified the PAPAL STATES, and fought the War of Castro (1642–44) against the north Italian Farnese Duke of Parma. The result was a humiliating defeat which crippled the papal finances and made him bitterly unpopular with the Roman people.

Urdu An Indic language allied to Hindi, which it resembles in grammar and structure, but with a large admixture of Arabic and Persian words, having been built up from the language of the early Muslim invaders, and usually written in Persian script. It is the language of the Muslim population, spoken as a first language by over 5 million people in Pakistan (where it is an official language), as a second language by another 40 million there, and by about 30 million in India.

urea A natural organic compound, formula $(NH_2)_2CO$, which is produced in the liver of mammals following the breakdown of amino acids. It circulates in the blood and is excreted by the kidneys, forming 2–4 per cent of URINE. Industrially produced urea is used as a fertilizer, and for making plastics.

urea-formaldehyde resin A synthetic thermosetting PLASTIC derived from the reaction of urea (carbamide) with formaldehyde (methanal) or its POLYMERS. Its main advantage over phenol-formaldehyde resins, such as Bakelite, is that it has a light coloration. Originally used in decorative applications, it is now used chiefly in such electrical applications as domestic plugs and sockets.

Urey, Harold Clayton (1893–1981) US chemist. He searched for a heavy isotope of hydrogen, discovering deuterium in 1932, and developing a technique for obtaining heavy water. Because of his work on isotope separation he was made director of the atom bomb project at Columbia University during World War II. Urey pioneered the use of isotope labelling; he also developed theories on the formation of the planets and of the possible synthesis of organic compounds in the Earth's primitive atmosphere. He was awarded the Nobel Prize for chemistry in 1934.

Urga The former name (until 1924) of ULAN BATOR.

urine The fluid produced by the KIDNEYS of vertebrates. In aquatic freshwater vertebrates it is produced in large quantities and contains ammonia, in addition to salts and other substances. In birds and reptiles, it is a stiff white paste, due to the inclusion of waste nitrogen in the form of insoluble uric acid. Terrestrial vertebrates produce urine rich in UREA, and salts. The composition and daily volume of urine are adjusted to keep the salt and water content of the body fluids neutral and constant, varying according to an animal's habitat.

urochordate See SEA SQUIRT.

Ursa Major The Great Bear, the third-largest CONSTELLATION, lying in the Northern Hemisphere of the sky. It was one of the 48 constellations known to the ancient Greeks and according to mythology it represents Callisto, a secret love of Zeus who was changed into a bear. Its most distinctive feature is a group of seven stars that form the shape commonly known as the PLOUGH. Two stars in the bowl of the dipper point to the north celestial pole. The **Pointers** are Alpha and Beta Ursae Majoris, named Dubhe and Merak, each of second magnitude. The second star in the handle of the plough is Zeta Ursae Majoris, known as MIZAR.

Ursa Minor The Little Bear, a CONSTELLATION at the north celestial pole, one of the 48 figures known to the ancient Greeks. In mythology it represents Ida, one of the two nymphs who nursed the infant Zeus. The constellation forms a ladle shape that is popularly known as the **Little Dipper**. At the end of the dipper's handle lies the north pole star, POLARIS.

urticaria (or **hives, nettle rash**) An itchy skin eruption of raised flat spots on a reddened background. The usual cause is an allergy, often to an unusual food. When recurrent, and if no provoking cause can be found, it can usually be alleviated by antihistamine drugs.

Uruguay A country in south-east-central South America with a coast on the Atlantic bounded by Argentina on the west and Brazil on the north-east.

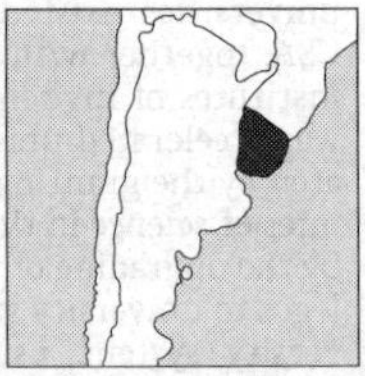

Physical. Uruguay has a coast on the estuary of the River Plate, and the Uruguay River flowing down its western boundary is navigable for some 320 km (200 miles). Tributaries flow westward across the country, which is mainly warm, grassy plain (PAMPAS) supporting cattle and sheep. In the centre and north-east the plain is broken by occasional rocky ridges.

Economy. Uruguay has a predominantly agricultural economy dominated by livestock-rearing. Textiles, wool, and meat are the major exports. Arable crops, particularly cereals and rice, occupy only 10 per cent of agricultural land. Mineral deposits are insignificant (there are some deposits of iron), but hydroelectricity is exported to Brazil, and accounts for some 90 per cent of domestic consumption. Food-processing and textiles are the principal industries.

History. Uruguay was inhabited by various indigenous peoples, such as the Chaná and Charnía, prior to the arrival of Spanish and Portuguese colonists in the 16th century. During the colonial period, it was known as the Banda Oriental and became a part of the Spanish vice-royalty of Rio de la Plata. In 1814 the leaders of the Banda Oriental, notably ARTIGAS, broke with the military junta in ARGENTINA and led a struggle for Uruguayan independence until occupied by Brazil in 1820. In 1825 an independent republic of Uruguay was declared, which was recognized by the treaty between Argentina and Brazil, signed at Rio de Janeiro in 1828. Under a republican constitution, the liberals (*Colorados*, redshirts) and the clerical conservatives (*Blancos*, whites) struggled violently throughout the 19th century for political control. In 1872 the Colorado Party began a period of 86 years in office. During the first three decades of the 20th century, José BATLLE Y ORDÓÑEZ, while in and out of the presidency, helped mould Uruguay into South America's first welfare state. Numerous measures for promoting governmental social services and a state-dominated economy were enacted. In 1958 the elections were won by the Blanco Party. Economic and political unrest plagued the nation throughout the 1960s and saw the emergence of the Marxist terrorist group, the Tupamaros. The military took over in the 1970s, and a return to civilian rule took place in 1985, when Julio Sanguinetti became President. After a long campaign he won a referendum in 1989 in support of an Amnesty Law for political prisoners from the military regime of 1973–85. In 1990 Luis Alberto Lacalle Herrera of the Blanco Party succeeded him, forming a coalition government with the Colorado Party. Sanguinetti was re-elected in 1995. Uruguay has emerged as one of the most prosperous and literate nations in the continent, in spite of falling world commodity prices and high inflation.

Capital: Montevideo
Area: 176,215 sq km (68,037 sq mi)
Population: 3,186,000 (1995)
Currency: 1 Uruguayan new peso = 100 centésimos
Religions: Roman Catholic 60.0%; Jewish 2.0%; Protestant 2.0%
Ethnic Groups: European (Spanish/Italian) 90.0%; Mestizo 3.0%; Jewish 2.0%; mixed 2.0%

Languages: Spanish (official)
International Organizations: UN; OAS

Uruk One of the leading cities of the SUMERIANS. A community occupied the site as early as 5000 BC and in the 3rd millennium BC the city was surrounded by a 9.5-km (6-mile) wall. Excavation has revealed ziggurats dedicated to the two main gods, Anu and Inanna. It continued to be inhabited into Parthian times.

USA See UNITED STATES OF AMERICA.

Ussher, James (1581–1656) Irish theologian, Archbishop of Armagh from 1625. In 1640 he escaped to England on the outbreak of the Irish Rebellion and settled there. He is best remembered for his completely fallacious but long-accepted chronology of scripture (1650–54), which set the date of the creation as 23 October 4004 BC.

USSR See SOVIET UNION.

Ustinov, Sir Peter (Alexander) (1921–) British actor, director, and dramatist, of Russian descent. He has written and acted in a number of plays including *Romanoff and Juliet* (1956) and his many films include *Spartacus* (1960) and *Death on the Nile* (1978). Ustinov is also well known as a mimic, raconteur, broadcaster, and novelist.

Usumbura The former name (until 1962) of BUJUMBARA.

Utah A Rocky Mountain state in the western USA, between Nevada to the west and Colorado to the east; area 219,889 sq km (84,899 sq miles); pop. (1990) 1,722,850; capital, Salt Lake City. It is also known as the Beehive State. The area was ceded to the USA by Mexico in 1848 and was settled by Mormons; statehood was refused until they abandoned their practice of polygamy – a dispute which led to a brief war (1857) of settlers against US troops. Utah became the 45th state of the Union in 1896. It is rich in oil-shale deposits and minerals such as copper, gold, silver, lead, zinc, and molybdenum, and a leading producer of sheep and irrigated crops such as wheat, beans, and alfalfa. Major landmarks include the Arches, Bryce Canyon, Canyonlands, Capitol Reef, and Zion national parks; and Dinosaur, Natural Bridges, Hovenweep, Timpanogos Cave, Cedar Breaks, and Rainbow Bridge national monuments.

Utamaro, Kitagawa (born Kitagawa Nebsuyoshi) (1753–1806) Japanese painter and printmaker. A leading exponent of the UKIYO-E school, he created many books of woodblock prints and was noted for his sensual depictions of women. His technique of portraying his subjects seemingly cut off by the margin of a print was admired by the impressionists.

Ute A North American Indian tribe of the Uto-Aztecan linguistic group, which formerly hunted big game in the Great Basin of western Colorado, eastern Utah, and northern New Mexico, and which gave its name to the US state of Utah.

uterus (or **womb**) Part of the female reproductive system in mammals, consisting of a thick wall of involuntary muscle surrounding a small cavity that connects with the OVARIES via the FALLOPIAN TUBES and with the exterior through a canal in the cervix, a small conical piece of uterus that projects into the vagina (see REPRODUCTION). The uterus is a tube in which the young develop. In many mammals it has two parts, which together enter the birth canal. Embryos develop in both parts, giving multiple pregnancies, as in pigs. In other mammals, the uterus is a single tube and usually contains only one developing offspring. In most mammals the uterus is inactive until the mother comes into season, when the lining membrane increases in thickness. If fertilization does not occur the lining membrane decreases in thickness, being reabsorbed by the blood supply.

In sexually mature females of some apes, and humans, the lining of the uterus undergoes a series of monthly changes related to ovulation. The membrane thickens and the blood supply increases in readiness to receive a fertilized ovum. In the absence of fertilization the membrane is shed, resulting in MENSTRUATION. If fertilized, the ovum embeds in the uterine wall, which gradually enlarges to accommodate the developing baby.

utilitarianism An ethical doctrine expounded by Jeremy BENTHAM and refined by John Stuart MILL. In his *Introduction to the Principles of Morals and Legislation* (1789), Bentham identified the goal of morality as 'the greatest happiness of the greatest number', and claimed that an action is right in so far as it tends to promote that goal. Acting as a pressure group on both Conservative and Liberal governments, they often gave a lead to public opinion. Mill's essay, *Utilitarianism* (1863), gave perhaps the clearest expression to the doctrine.

As a philosophical proposition, utilitarianism is hampered by the fundamental difficulty of comparing quantitatively the happiness of one person with that of another. Nevertheless, it has proved a remarkably persistent doctrine which continues to attract adherents.

Utopianism A form of speculative thinking in which ideal societies are depicted in order to highlight the defects of those we inhabit. The original *Utopia*, published in 1516 by Sir Thomas More, depicted a society whose members lived communally and abstemiously, sharing property, and working under the direction of spiritual leaders. Many 19th-century Utopias were socialist in inspiration, but the genre is not tied to any particular political creed. In the 20th century, so-called 'dystopias' extrapolate present trends to present a nightmarish vision of the future (Huxley's *Brave New World* (1932) and Orwell's *1984* (1949) are examples) in the hope that such developments can be forestalled.

Utrecht A city in the Randstad conurbation of the Netherlands, capital of the province of Utrecht; pop. (1991) 231,230. Situated on a branch of the Lower Rhine, Utrecht is a major transportation, financial, and cultural centre. In 1579 the seven Protestant provinces of the northern Netherlands united under the Union of Utrecht against Spanish rule, and in 1713 the Peace of Utrecht was signed here ending the War of the Spanish Succession.

Utrillo, Maurice (1883–1955) French painter. The son of the French painter Susan Valadon (1867–1938), he was adopted by the Spanish architect and writer Miguel Utrillo in 1891. Utrillo is chiefly known for his depictions of Paris street scenes, especially the Montmartre district; the works of his 'white period' (1909–14), when he made extensive use of white pigment, are considered particularly notable.

Uttar Pradesh A state in northern India, bordering on Tibet and Nepal; area 294,413 sq km (113,717 sq miles); pop. (1991) 139,031,130; capital, Lucknow. Prior to it being renamed Uttar Pradesh in 1950 the greater part of the state comprised the United Provinces of Agra and Oudh. A major producer of sugar and grain, it is rich in minerals including bauxite, coal, copper, and limestone.

Uttley, Alison (1884–1976) British writer. She is remembered for her children's books, particularly the 'Little Grey Rabbit' series (1929 onwards) and the 'Sam Pig' stories (1940 onwards).

Uzbekistan A country in central Asia situated south of Kazakhstan; to the south and east are Turkmenistan, Afghanistan, Tajikistan, and Kyrgyzstan.

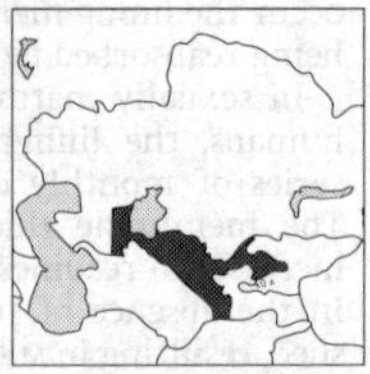

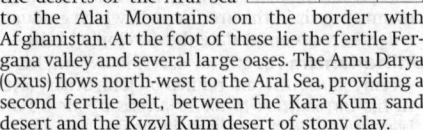

Physical. Uzbekistan stretches south-east from the deserts of the Aral Sea to the Alai Mountains on the border with Afghanistan. At the foot of these lie the fertile Fergana valley and several large oases. The Amu Darya (Oxus) flows north-west to the Aral Sea, providing a second fertile belt, between the Kara Kum sand desert and the Kyzyl Kum desert of stony clay.

Economy. Uzbekistan's principal mineral reserves are natural gas, petroleum, coal, and metal ores (including those of copper and lead), all of which are extracted. Heavy industry focuses on machinery production, particularly for the cultivation and processing of cotton, of which Uzbekistan is the third largest producer in the world. Other agricultural products are silks, fruit, grapes, and livestock, particularly karakul sheep. The increased mechanization of cotton cultivation has cut employment dramatically, and the use of defoliants and pesticides has caused health problems and environmental degradation. In recent decades, aluminium factories have produced uncontrolled wastes that are now affecting fruit-growing areas and livestock.

History. Uzbekistan was the centre of the empire of Genghis Khan, and its two ancient cities of Samarkand and Tashkent flourished with the silk caravan trade. Divided into three khanates, Bukhara, Khiva, and Kokand, it was repeatedly attacked by Russia from 1717 until its annexation in 1876. Its Sunni Muslim Uzbeks were excluded from office by the Russians, and in 1918 staged a rebellion. This was suppressed by the Red Army, and a Soviet Socialist Republic was formed in 1929, which joined the Soviet Union in 1936. After 1989 the republic pressed for independence. The former Communist Party of Uzbekistan, renamed the People's Democratic Party, retained power in the country's parliament following elections in 1990. Uzbekistan declared independence from the Soviet Union in August 1991. However, the commitment of the PDP to democratic reform has been questioned; three major opposition parties are officially proscribed. The banned Islamic Renaissance Party claimed that President Karimov was trying to unseat the Mufti of Tashkent, leader of Islam throughout central Asia. Uzbekistan joined the Commonwealth of Independent States in 1991. However, dissatisfaction at the Russian dominance of this body led Uzbekistan to form an alternative economic union with Kazakhstan and Kyrgyzstan in 1994.

Capital: Tashkent
Area: 447,400 sq km (172,741 sq mi)
Population: 22,886,000 (1995)
Currency: sum
Religions: Sunni Muslim; Eastern Orthodox; Jewish and minority faiths
Ethnic Groups: Uzbek 71.0%; Russian 8.0%; Tatar, Tajik, Ukrainian, and Armenian minorities
Languages: Uzbek (official); Russian; minority languages
International Organizations: UN; Commonwealth of Independent States; CSCE; North Atlantic Co-operation Council

Uzbeks A Turkish-speaking people, Mongol by descent and SUNNI Muslim by religion. They moved through Kazakhstan to Turkistan and Transoxania between the 14th and 16th centuries to trouble the Shiite Safavid rulers of Persia. Initially ruled by the Shaybanids and then the Janids, they later split into dynasties based on Bukhara, Khiva, and Kokand.

V

V1 rocket See CRUISE MISSILE.

V2 rocket See BALLISTIC MISSILE.

Vaal A river of South Africa, the chief tributary of the Orange River. It rises in south-east Transvaal and flows *c.*1,200 km (750 miles) south-westwards to join the Orange River near Douglas. For much of its course it forms the border between Transvaal and Orange Free State.

vaccination (or **inoculation**) The administration of a preparation (**vaccine**) containing microorganisms, or toxins of microorganisms, in order to induce active immunity (see IMMUNIZATION). Vaccines may consist of attenuated microorganisms (live vaccines), such as measles vaccine or BCG vaccine against tuberculosis; dead microorganisms (inactivated vaccines), such as influenza or typhoid vaccine; or toxins that have been detoxified (toxoids), such as tetanus or botulism vaccine, which stimulate the production of ANTIBODIES.

vacuum A space that contains no MATTER. It is impossible to obtain a perfect vacuum as any material surrounding a vacuum will have a VAPOUR PRESSURE and will thus release particles into the vacuum. The nearest approach to a perfect vacuum is space, where the concentration of particles may be as low as one per cubic centimetre, a level of vacuum that is unattainable on Earth.

vacuum distillation A DISTILLATION process for materials that have very high boiling-points or are likely to decompose below their boiling-point. Air is evacuated from the apparatus with a vacuum pump, and the vacuum so formed causes the materials being heated to boil at a temperature lower than they would under normal atmospheric pressure. This enables distillation to take place at lower temperatures. One example of its use is in PETROLEUM REFINING.

vacuum flask (or **Dewar flask**) An insulated container that thermally isolates the contents from its surroundings. The space between the double walls of the flask contains a vacuum, in order to eliminate heat transfer by convection. The walls are made from thin glass to limit heat conduction and are silvered to reduce radiation transfer. The vacuum flask was originally developed in the 1890s by James Dewar for storing liquefied gases at very low temperatures. The modern domestic Thermos flask is used to maintain the temperature of hot or iced drinks.

vacuum pump A device for removing air from laboratory apparatus. The PUMP may be required because the materials to be handled are air-sensitive or because a low pressure is needed – for example, in VACUUM DISTILLATION. A reliable vacuum can be obtained using a motor-driven oil pump. For very low pressures, the additional use of a mercury vacuum pump is required, in which a diffused jet of mercury vapour is injected at the inlet port and drives gas molecules towards the outlet. Another low-pressure pump is the turbomolecular pump, basically a very high-speed TURBINE. In a 'getter' pump, a film of some active substance such as titanium is deposited in the evacuation chamber and reacts chemically with any gas molecules present, thus removing them from the chamber.

Vaduz The capital of the Principality of Liechtenstein, on the River Rhine; pop. (1991) 5,000. Dominated by a medieval castle, the town is a centre for tourism and agricultural trade and has engineering industries. Due to its liberal taxation laws, it is also an international finance centre.

vagina (or **birth canal**) The lowest part of the female reproductive system in mammals. It opens to the exterior via the vulval lips. In virgin females its opening is partly covered by the hymen, a thin, almost bloodless membrane, which is easily ruptured by direct force. The vagina is a muscular tube whose wall is collapsed except when it contains an erect penis or a baby on its way to birth. The neck of the UTERUS, the cervix, projects into the upper part of the vagina. The interior of the vagina is lubricated by secretions of glands stimulated by sexual arousal.

Valdez An ice-free fishing port and oil town in southern Alaska, USA, on Prince William Sound. In 1898 it became a debarkation point for prospectors seeking a duty-free route to the goldfields of the Yukon. In 1964 the town was devastated by an earthquake and in 1989 an oil tanker, the *Exxon Valdez* ran aground in the sound releasing 12 million gallons of crude oil and causing a major environmental disaster.

Valencia ►**1** A region of eastern Spain, comprising the provinces of Alicante, Castellón, and Valencia; area 23,260 sq km (8,940 sq miles); pop. (1991) 3,857,230. ►**2** Its capital, a port on the Mediterranean coast at the mouth of the Turia River; pop. (1991) 777,430. There are car ferries to the Balearic and Canary Islands and industries include shipbuilding and the manufacture of chemicals, textiles, motor vehicles, and metal goods.

valency (or **valence**) The combining capacity of an atom, ion, or radical, equal to the number of hydrogen atoms that will combine with that atom, ion, or radical. For example, nitrogen has a valency of 3, therefore it forms the compound NH_3 (ammonia) with hydrogen. Many elements show more than one valency in their compounds; iron has valencies 2 and 3, and forms two different chlorides, $FeCl_2$

and $FeCl_3$. The valency of an atom is equal to the number of bonds that it forms in COVALENT COMPOUNDS, and to the number of charges it acquires in IONIC COMPOUNDS. Many valencies can be predicted from the PERIODIC TABLE: for instance, elements in Groups 1 and 17 have valency 1, those in Groups 2 and 16 have valency 2, those in Groups 13 and 15 have valency 3, and those in Group 14 have valency 4. There is no such pattern in the transition metals, however, electron shells may be regarded as spherical layers centred on the nucleus, which can contain a fixed maximum number of electrons. The innermost shell, the K-shell or $n = 1$ shell, which contains a maximum of two electrons, is filled first, then the L-shell or $n = 2$ shell, which contains a maximum of eight electrons, is filled, and so on. The last shell to be occupied is usually only partly filled, and this is called the valence shell. The NOBLE GASES are the only elements whose atoms have complete valence shells and they are very stable and unreactive. Other atoms seek the stability of a complete valence shell by gaining or losing electrons.

Valentino, Rudolph (born Rodolfo Guglielmi di Valentina d'Antonguolla) (1895–1926) Italian-born US actor. He became a leading star of silent films in the 1920s, playing the romantic hero in such films as *The Sheikh* (1921) and *Blood and Sand* (1922). After his death from a perforated ulcer thousands of women attended his funeral.

Valera, Eamon de See DE VALERA.

valerian A perennial herbaceous plant with a stoloniferous root-system, divided leaves arranged in pairs, and, typically, heads of pink flowers. It belongs to a family, Valerianaceae, of some 400 species. The common valerian, *Valeriana officinalis*, is native to Europe and Asia. The root of the plant has long been valued for its medicinal properties, chiefly as a sedative. The North American ground orchid, *Cypripedium pubescens*, is also called valerian.

Valerian (full name Publius Licinius Valerianius) (died 260) Roman emperor 253–60. He became emperor following the murder of Gallus (reigned 251–53) and appointed his son Gallienus as joint ruler. During his reign Valerian renewed the persecution of the Christians initiated by Decius. He was captured while campaigning against the Persians of the Sassanian dynasty and died in captivity. Gallienus continued to rule as sole emperor until 268.

Valéry, (Ambroise) Paul (Toussaint Jules) (1871–1945) French poet, essayist, and critic. His poetry, influenced by symbolist poets, such as Mallarmé, and blending lyricism, rich imagery, and intellectual eloquence, includes *La Jeune parque* (1917) and 'Le Cimetière marin' (1922). He later concentrated on prose, publishing essays on a variety of literary, philosophical, and aesthetic subjects. He is also known for his notebooks, published posthumously as *Cahiers* (1958–62).

Valhalla In Scandinavian mythology, the hall in Asgard assigned to heroes who have died in battle, in which they feast with Odin.

Valkyrie (Old Norse, 'chooser of the Slain') In Norse and Germanic mythology, the warrior maidens, chief of whom was Brynhild. They lived with Odin as his attendants and messengers in VALHALLA. The Valkyries rode out on horses through the air and over the seas to fetch the heroes slain in battle whom Odin had selected for their outstanding valour.

Valladolid The capital of Castilla León region in northern Spain, an industrial city at the junction of the Pisguera and Esguera rivers; pop. (1991) 345,260. It was the principal residence of the kings of Castile in the 15th century. Industries include vehicles, railway engineering, tanning, brewing, chemicals, and textiles.

Valletta The capital and chief port of Malta in the Mediterranean; pop. (1987) 102,000; urban harbour area pop. (1992) 102,000. It is named after Jean de Valette, Grand Master of the Knights of St John, who built the town after the siege of 1565. It is a shipbuilding, yachting, and tourist centre with an international airport at Luqa.

valley An elongated and usually interconnecting depression of the Earth's surface. Some valleys are formed by Earth movements and faulting, others (normally U-shaped) by glaciers, and a very few by wind erosion. By far the most, however, are the work of rivers, cutting channels towards the base level of erosion over thousands of millions of years. The valley cut by vertical erosion is usually V-shaped in cross-section and irregular in its course, its gradient being punctuated by sudden drops (waterfalls) and long shelves (lakes).

Valley, The The capital of the island of Anguilla in the West Indies; pop. (1985) 2,000. Situated at the centre of the island, it is served by Wallblake Airport.

Valley of the Kings A narrow gorge in western THEBES containing the tombs of at least 60 pharaohs of the 18th to 20th dynasties (*c.*1550–1050 BC), beginning with Thutmose I. It was a rich hunting-ground for robbers in antiquity, and of those tombs discovered only that of TUTANKHAMUN had not been plundered.

Valois ▶**1** A medieval duchy of northern France now part of the department of Aisne and Oise. ▶**2** The name of the French royal family from the time of Philip VI (1328) to the death of Henry II (1589), when the throne passed to the Bourbons.

Valois, Dame Ninette de See DE VALOIS.

Valparaiso The principal port of Chile and one of the chief ports on the Pacific coast of South America; pop. (1992) 276,740. Its industries include ship repairing, foundries, chemicals, and textiles. Founded by the Spanish in 1536, it is the terminus of the trans-Andean railway. It is subject to severe earthquakes; the last was in 1906.

value-added tax (VAT) An indirect tax on goods or services, calculated as a percentage of their value. The whole cost of the tax is borne by the consumer. Used in many countries, VAT was introduced in the UK in 1973 to replace purchase tax and to become compatible with the EU. It is collected by the Board of Customs and Excise. For most goods and services the rate is 17.5 per cent, although food, childrens' clothes, and books are zero rated.

vampire A legendary creature supposed to suck the blood of a sleeping person. A vampire may be seen as a reanimated corpse, which at night takes on the form of a bat-like demon; once bitten, the victim in turn becomes a vampire. To protect the living, a stake could be driven through the buried corpse, or it was exhumed and burned. Vampires, according to some folklores, cast neither shadow nor mirror-reflection; they appear in mythologies as far apart as Europe (where Count Dracula is the archetypal example), Asia, and Africa. In Hindu mythology, a species of female vampire is commonly held to debilitate a sleeping man by sucking blood from his toes.

vampire bat A bat of the family Desmodontidae

with a reputation as a blood-sucker. They feed on the blood of vertebrates at night, either by landing on them or crawling towards them after alighting on the ground. The very sharp incisor teeth cut a shallow groove and blood is sucked up through the tongue. The wound is almost painless, but the bat's saliva contains an anticoagulant which causes protracted bleeding. Vampire bats are dangerous not because of the loss of blood they cause, but because they can transmit serious diseases, such as rabies. There are three species in the family Desmodontidae, all confined to the New World.

vanadium (symbol V, at. no. 23, r.a.m. 50.94) A brilliant white TRANSITION METAL that occurs naturally in patronite, V_2S_5, vanadinite, $Pb_5(VO_4)Cl$, and crude oil. It is used mainly as a constituent of STEELS, to give strength at high temperatures and corrosion-resistance. It is also added to copper alloys to increase strength and corrosion-resistance, especially in marine environments. Vanadium-aluminium alloys are used in airframe construction, and vanadium oxide, VO, is a good industrial catalyst.

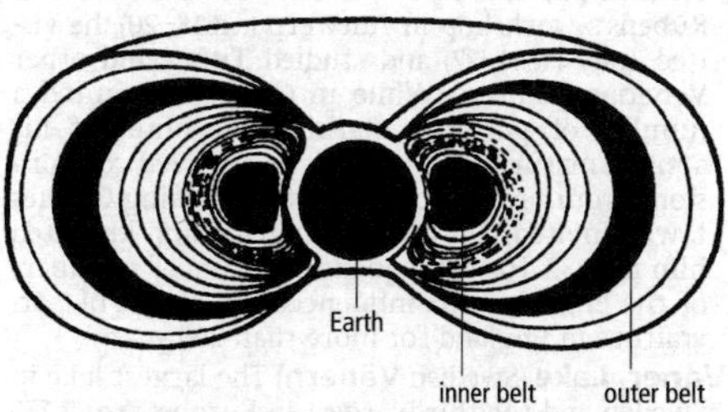

Van Allen belts Two belts of high-energy charged particles trapped in the Earth's magnetic field. The inner (lower) belt lies some 3,000 km (1,875 miles) above the equator and contains electrons and protons. The outer (higher) belt lies at height of 13,000 km (8,125 miles) and contains mainly electrons.

Van Allen, James Alfred (1914–) US physicist. Van Allen was head of physics at Iowa University for 34 years. Expertise in missile technology and electronics led him to use balloons and rockets to study cosmic radiation in the upper atmosphere. The first orbiting satellites in 1958 encountered zones of high radiation, which Van Allen showed were the result of charged particles from the solar wind being trapped in two belts around the Earth, later known as **Van Allen belts**. The lower belt is some 3,000 km (1,875 miles) above the Earth, while the higher belt lies at a height of 13,000 km (8,125 miles).

Vanbrugh, Sir John (1664–1726) English architect and dramatist. In his early life he gained success as a dramatist with his comedies, including *The Relapse* (1696) and *The Provok'd Wife* (1697). After 1699 he became known as an architect and as one of the chief exponents of the English Baroque; major works include Castle Howard in Yorkshire (1699) and Blenheim Palace in Oxfordshire (1705), both produced in collaboration with Nicholas Hawksmoor, and Seaton Delaval Hall in Northumberland (1720).

Van Buren, Martin (1782–1862) US Democratic statesman, 8th President of the USA 1837–41. He was appointed Andrew Jackson's Vice-President in 1832 and became President five years later. His measure of placing government funds, previously held in private banks, in an independent treasury caused many Democrats to join the Whig party.

Vancouver A city and seaport of British Columbia, Canada; pop. (1991) 471,840; 1,602,500 (metropolitan area). Established in the 1860s, it was named in honour of Captain George VANCOUVER, who explored the waters round Vancouver Island in 1792 and whose boat, the *Discovery*, is berthed at Deadman's Island naval base. The city developed after the arrival of the Canadian Pacific Railway into the largest city on the west coast of Canada and the third-largest metropolitan area of Canada. Industries are shipbuilding, fish processing, oil refining, textiles, and diverse light industries.

Vancouver, George (1758–98) British navigator. After accompanying Captain James Cook on his second and third voyages, he took command of a naval expedition exploring the coasts of Australia, New Zealand, and Hawaii (1791–92). He later charted much of the west coast of North America between southern Alaska and California. Vancouver Island and the city of Vancouver are named after him.

Vancouver Island An island off the Pacific coast of British Columbia, Canada, opposite Vancouver; area 31,285 sq km (12,080 sq miles). It is the largest island off the west coast of North America and is separated from the mainland by the Queen Charlotte, Georgia, Johnston, and Juan de Fuca straits. It was made a crown colony in 1866. Its chief city, Victoria, is the capital of British Columbia.

Vandals A Germanic tribe that migrated from the Baltic coast in the 1st century BC. After taking Pannonia in the 4th century they were driven further west by the HUNS. With the Suebi and Alemanni they crossed the Rhine into Gaul and Spain, where the name Andalusia ('Vandalitia') commemorates them. They were then ousted by the Goths. Taking ship to North Africa under Genseric, they set up an independent kingdom after the capture of Carthage. In 455 they returned to Italy and sacked Rome. BELISARIUS finally subjected them in 534.

Van de Graaff, Robert Jemison (1901–67) US physicist. Van de Graaff worked in various countries before he returned to the USA in 1929, moving to the Massachusetts Institute of Technology two years later. He invented the high voltage **Van de Graaff generator** in about 1929, using a hollow sphere to store up a large electrostatic charge, imparted to it by a continuous motorized belt, which is itself continually fed with charge from an external source. This device was improved in later years, being adapted for use as a particle accelerator and as a high-energy X-ray generator for medical treatment and industrial use. See illustration p. 1388.

Vanderbilt, Cornelius (1794–1877) US businessman and philanthropist. Vanderbilt amassed a fortune from shipping and railroads, and from this made an endowment to found Vanderbilt University in Nashville, Tennessee (1873). Subsequent generations of his family, including his son **William Henry Vanderbilt** (1821–85), increased the family wealth and continued his philanthropy.

Van der Post, Sir Laurens (Jan) (1906–96) South African explorer and writer. In 1949 Van der Post was sent to explore Nyasaland (now Malawi) for the British; his book of the journey, *Venture to the Interior* (1952), was the first of several works combining travel writing and descriptions of fauna with philosophical speculation based on his Jungian ideas of the necessary balance between 'unconscious, feminine' Africa, and 'conscious,

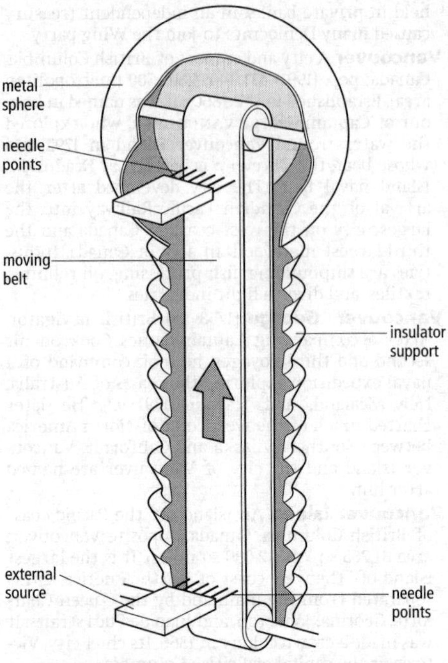

Van de Graaff generator An electrostatic generator used to produce a high voltage. A large metal sphere mounted on a hollow insulated support is fed with charge by a moving belt. In the original type, charge from an external source is sprayed onto the belt by needle points (held at about 10 kV). A similar row of needle points near the top of the belt feeds the charge from the belt to the surface of the sphere. The voltage achieved is proportional to the sphere's radius; a sphere with 1 m radius will produce 1 MV.

masculine' Europe. He developed this theme after travels among the Bushmen of the Kalahari Desert, described in such books as *The Lost World of the Kalahari* (1958).

van der Waals, Johannes Diderik (1837–1923) Dutch physicist who made a detailed study of the liquefaction of gases. In 1879 he proposed an equation, which now bears his name, linking the pressure, volume, and temperature of a gas. The equation is more accurate than Boyle's law or Charles's law (see GAS): it makes allowance for the forces of attraction between the molecules (known as VAN DER WAALS' FORCES) and successfully describes the behaviour of a gas which is nearing a liquid state. He was awarded the Nobel Prize for physics in 1910.

van der Waals' forces A type of weak INTERMOLECULAR FORCE, discovered by VAN DER WAALS in 1873, that exists between all pairs of atoms and molecules that are not chemically bonded; they are important in both liquids and solids. Although the exact nature of van der Waals' forces varies from case to case, in general, the motion of the electrons in one molecule only affects the electrons in another when the molecules are very close, producing an attractive force. The forces increase as the number of electrons in a molecule increases.

van de Velde A family of Dutch painters. **Willem van de Velde the Elder** (1611–93) painted marine subjects and was for a time official artist to the Dutch fleet. He also worked for Charles II. His sons were **Willem van de Velde the Younger** (1633–1707) and **Adriaen van de Velde** (1636–72). Like his father, Willem the Younger was a notable marine artist who painted for Charles II, while Adriaen's works include landscapes, portraits, and biblical and genre scenes.

van de Velde, Henri (Clemens) (1863–1957) Belgian architect, designer, and teacher. He was influenced by the Arts and Crafts Movement and pioneered the development of art nouveau design and architecture in Europe. In 1906 he became head of the Weimar School of Arts and Crafts (which developed into the Bauhaus), Walter Gropius being among his pupils. Van de Velde's buildings include the Werkbund Theatre in Cologne (1914) and his own house near Brussels (1895). He also designed furniture, ceramics, and graphics.

Van Diemen's Land The former name of TASMANIA, Australia. Its name commemorates Anthony van Diemen (1593–1645), Dutch governor of Java, who sent TASMAN on his voyage of exploration.

Van Dyck, Sir Anthony (or **Vandyke**) (1599–1641) Flemish painter. Having worked as an assistant in Rubens's workshop in Antwerp (*c.*1618–20), he visited Italy (1621–27) and studied Titian and other Venetian painters. While in Genoa he painted a number of portraits marking the onset of his artistic maturity. Thereafter he received commissions from several royal clients, including Charles I, who invited Van Dyck to England and knighted him in 1632. His subsequent portraits of members of the English court influenced the course of portraiture in England for more than 200 years.

Vaner, Lake (Swedish **Vänern**) The largest lake in Sweden and the third-largest in Europe; area 3,755 sq km (1,450 sq miles).

Van Eyck, Jan See EYCK, JAN VAN.

van Gogh See GOGH, VINCENT VAN.

vanilla A substance used as a flavouring extracted from the dried pods of a climbing ORCHID, *Vanilla planifolia*, native to tropical Central America. The pods need careful drying: the characteristic odour is absent from the unfermented pod. It is now mainly produced in Madagascar, but Mexico and some other Central American countries are exporters.

van Leyden, Lucas See LUCAS VAN LEYDEN.

van Meegeren, Han (1889–1947) Dutch painter and master forger. Accused of selling old masters to the Germans during the occupation of Holland, he confessed that he had sold the Germans forgeries, which he had painted himself. He also shocked the art world by confessing to having painted the acclaimed *Christ at Emmaus*, which was thought to have been by Vermeer when it was discovered in 1937. He was imprisoned in 1947 as a forger and died in prison.

van't Hoff, Jacobus Hendricus (1852–1911) Dutch chemist who applied the laws of THERMODYNAMICS to chemical reactions. He derived an equation known as the **van't Hoff isochore**, showing the dependence of equilibrium constants on temperature, and showed that the osmotic pressure of a solution varies directly with the temperature. In organic chemistry van't Hoff studied the spatial arrangements of groups attached to a carbon atom. He won the first Nobel Prize for chemistry in 1901.

Vanuatu (formerly **New Hebrides**) A country comprising a double chain of over 80 south-west Pacific Ocean islands between latitudes 13° and 21°S and longitudes 167° and 170°E.

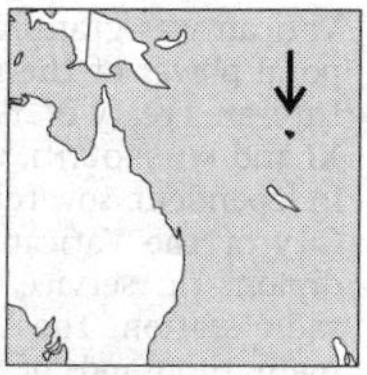

Physical. Only a dozen of Vanuatu's islands are suitable for settlement, the largest being Espíritu Santo, Efate, Malekula, Maewo, Pentecost, Ambrim, Erromanga, and Tanna. Of volcanic origin, they are very hilly. South-east trade winds moderate the heat from May to October.

Economy. Coconuts are the most important cash crop on Vanuatu; copra is the country's major export. The soil on the slopes of the extinct volcanoes that form the island group is suitable for growing coffee, while livestock are grazed on the warm, wet plains.

History. During the 19th century, thousands of the indigenous people of Vanuatu – KANAKAS – were taken to work on sugar plantations in QUEENSLAND, Australia. The population was decimated and took many years to recover. The islands were placed under an Anglo-French naval commission in 1887. In World War II they served as a major Allied base. They became an independent republic and member of the Commonwealth of Nations in 1980.

Capital: Vila
Area: 12,190 sq km (4,707 sq mi)
Population: 168,000 (1995)
Ethnic Groups: mainly Ni-Vanuatu, with European and other minorities
Languages: Bislama; French; English
International Organizations: UN; Commonwealth

vapour deposition A method of manufacturing materials, particularly in the form of thin films, by the deposition of gas or vapour atoms or molecules on a substrate. In chemical vapour deposition (CVD), the gas or vapour decomposes in a surface reaction to form a solid layer: decomposition is activated either by heat or by direct excitation using laser light. CVD is used to manufacture SEMICONDUCTOR DEVICES, wear-resistant ceramic films, diamond films, and ceramic or GLASS FIBRES. In physical vapour deposition (PVD) the vapour, produced by high-temperature evaporation of a solid or liquid in a vacuum, is condensed on to the substrate. PVD is used to manufacture semiconductor devices, and to evaporate thin layers of aluminium on to plastic food packaging films, or on to polycarbonate discs in the manufacture of COMPACT DISCS. A vapour can also be produced at normal temperatures by the technique of sputtering. Sputtering is a physical process in which IONS extracted from an inert gas (for example, ARGON) are accelerated and bombarded upon the solid target material (the CATHODE) that is to be deposited. The target atoms are ejected (vaporized) by this bombardment and deposit on a substrate (the ANODE). Sputtering is used mostly in the deposition of metals that are difficult to deposit by other means.

vapourer moth See TUSSOCK MOTH.

vapour pressure The pressure of the vapour given off by a solid on liquid. For example, damp air contains water vapour and this contributes to the overall pressure of the air. The saturated vapour pressure is the pressure when there is an equilibrium between the liquid and the vapour in contact with it, with as many molecules passing from liquid to vapour as are passing from vapour to liquid. The saturated vapour pressure increases with temperature. If a liquid open to the atmosphere is heated so that its vapour pressure equals that of the atmosphere, the liquid is said to boil.

Varah, (Edward) Chad (1911–) British clergyman. He founded the SAMARITANS in 1953 after recognizing a widespread need for an anonymous and confidential listening service; the organization offers help, particularly over the telephone, to the suicidal and despairing. He was president of Befrienders International (Samaritans Worldwide) from 1983 to 1986 and travelled widely abroad to spread the organization's principles.

Varanasi (or **Benares**) A city in northern India, in the state of Uttah Pradesh, which has long been renowned as a centre of PILGRIMAGE for Hindus from all over India; pop. (1991) 1,026,470. Pilgrims seek ritual purification in the sacred River Ganges and cremate their dead on the ghats (flights of steps), which line the river and on other cremation grounds along the river. The city contains many famous temples and mosques, two Hindu universities, and diverse light industries.

Varèse, Edgard (Victor Achille Charles) (1883–1965) French-born US composer. From the 1920s his music explored modern developments – complex rhythms, strident dissonances, freely developing forms. Such works as *Ionisation* for 13 percussion instruments (1931) look forward to the ELECTRONIC MUSIC that was to concern him in later life. In 1953 the gift of a tape recorder enabled him to create the kind of music he had imagined. *Déserts* (1954) and *Poème électronique* (1958) were fruits of this new resource. His last composition, *Nocturnal*, remained incomplete at his death.

Vargas, Getúlio Dornelles (1883–1954) Brazilian statesman, President 1930–45 and 1951–54. Although defeated in the presidential elections of 1930, Vargas seized power in the ensuing revolution, overthrowing the republic and ruling as a virtual dictator for the next 15 years. He furthered Brazil's modernization by the introduction of fiscal, educational, electoral, and land reforms, but his regime was totalitarian and repressive. He was overthrown in a coup in 1945 but returned to power after elections in 1951. After widespread calls for his resignation, he committed suicide.

Vargas Llosa, (Jorge) Mario (Pedro) (1936–) Peruvian novelist, dramatist, and essayist. His fiction often contains elements of myth and fantasy and has been associated with magic realism; it is frequently critical of the political situation in Peru. Novels include *The Time of the Hero* (1963), satirizing Peruvian society via the microcosm of a corrupt military academy, *Aunt Julia and the Scriptwriter* (1977), and *The War of the End of the World* (1982). He returned to Peru in 1974, after living abroad for many years, and stood unsuccessfully for the presidency in 1990.

variable star A star whose MAGNITUDE changes with time. Over 30,000 such stars have been catalogued and about 80 types and subtypes are recognized. These may be grouped into **intrinsic variables**, whose changes are due to physical processes in or near the stars themselves, and **extrinsic variables**, whose changes are a geometrical effect due to rotation or orbital motion.

variance (in statistics) The square of the STANDARD DEVIATION – that is, the mean of the squares of variations from the arithmetic MEAN. It is of little importance as a descriptive statistic, but the analysis of variance is an important tool for comparing sample groups.

varicose veins Distended veins, usually the superficial veins of the legs in people who are constantly standing. The usual cause is incompetent valves obstructing the blood flow. They can ache, and if suffered over long periods can cause thrombosis or phlebitis. The veins can be removed surgically or sometimes made to shrivel by injection.

varnishes and lacquers A varnish is a transparent solution of a natural or synthetic resin. Natural resins (such as shellac) are dissolved in alcohol (usually industrial methylated spirits) to make spirit varnishes, traditionally used in French polishing. Synthetic resins, such as polyurethane, are dissolved in a drying oil. Varnishes are applied to a material (usually wood) to provide a thin, transparent, and waterproof protective coating. They are also used in printing INKS. Lacquers, too, are film-forming substances (the most common are cellulose lacquers); however, they are dissolved in volatile solvents and dry entirely by evaporation, whereas the drying of varnishes involves OXIDATION as well as evaporation.

Varro, Marcus Terentius (116–27 BC) Roman scholar and satirist. He was a prolific author and although most of his writings are now lost, his prose works are known to have covered many subjects, including philosophy, agriculture, the Latin language, and education. His satires (*Saturae Menippeae*) presented critical sketches of Roman life in a mixture of verse and prose.

Varuna An Indo-Aryan deity, and one of the oldest of the Vedic gods of the *Rig Veda*, the collection of sacred songs that form part of the ancient Vedic literature of India. Originally considered the sovereign lord of the Universe (superseded first by Indra, then by Shiva and Vishnu), and god of law and justice, Varuna became associated in Hinduism with the Moon, where, with Yama the first human, he was lord of the dead. In this capacity he was also guardian of the sacred plant, soma, which was alleged to give strength, wisdom, and immortality. Varuna was a god of justice.

Vasarely, Viktor (1908–97) Hungarian-born French painter. He settled in Paris in 1930 after studying art in Budapest. A pioneer of op art, he began experimenting with the use of optical illusion during the 1930s, although the style of geometric abstraction for which he is best known dates from the late 1940s. His paintings are characterized by their repeated geometric forms and interacting vibrant colours, which create a visually disorientating effect of movement.

Vasari, Giorgio (1511–74) Italian painter, architect, and biographer. He wrote *Lives of the Most Excellent Italian Painters, Sculptors, and Architects* (1550, enlarged 1568), a work that laid the basis for later study of art history in the West. His own work was mannerist in style and includes the vast frescos depicting the history of Florence and the Medici family in the Palazzo Vecchio in Florence, as well as the design of the Uffizi palace.

Vasco da Gama See DA GAMA.

vassal A holder of land by contract from a lord. This tenurial arrangement was one of the essential components of the FEUDAL SYSTEM. The land received was known as a FIEF and the contract was confirmed when the recipient knelt and placed his hands between those of his lord.

VAT See VALUE-ADDED TAX.

Vatican City An independent papal state in Rome, the seat of government of the ROMAN CATHOLIC CHURCH; area 44 hectares (109 acres); pop. (est. 1991) 1,000. Following the RISORGIMENTO, the former Papal States, that is, the modern Italian provinces of Lazio, Umbria, Marche, and parts of Emilia-Romagna, became incorporated into a unified Italy in 1870 while, by the Law of Guarantees (1871), the Vatican was granted extraterritoriality. The temporal power of the POPE was suspended until the Lateran Treaty of 1929, signed between Pope Pius XI and MUSSOLINI, which recognized the full and independent sovereignty of the Holy See in the City of the Vatican. It has its own police force, diplomatic service, postal service, coinage, and radio station. The Vatican is visited annually by many thousands of tourists. A major attraction is the recently restored Sistine Chapel decorated by Michelangelo and others, 1508–12.

Vatican Council See POPE.

vaudeville US entertainment consisting of a succession of short items – singers, dancers, comedians, acrobats, animal acts – and often including star names from the theatre. Dating from the 1880s, it resembled British MUSIC-HALL. Vaudeville developed its own stars, such as the comedian W. C. FIELDS and the 'blackface' artist Lew Dockstader, and survived until the 1930s.

Vaughan, Henry (1621–95) Welsh poet. He was one of the group of Metaphysical poets, whose poems had a distinctive ethereal quality that led them to be described as mystical. His volumes of religious poetry include *Silex Scintillans* (1650, 1655), in which he acknowledges his debt to George Herbert. Among his prose works is *The Mount of Olives, or Solitary Devotions* (1652).

Vaughan, Sarah (Lois) (1924–90) US jazz singer and pianist. She began singing with jazz bands in the early 1940s and was chiefly associated with bebop. She performed as a soloist from 1945, and became internationally famous in the early 1950s.

Vaughan Williams, Ralph (1872–1958) British composer, founder of the nationalist movement in 20th-century English music. From about 1903 he began to collect folk-songs and from 1904 to 1906 was editor of *The English Hymnal*, for which he wrote the celebrated hymn, 'For All the Saints'. His study of English FOLK MUSIC and his interest in English music of the Tudor period dictated the development of his idiom away from the dominant German style of his day. He incorporated modal elements based on folk song and medieval scales, and a new rhythmic freedom of his own, into a highly personal and characteristically English style. Three works – the song cycle *On Wenlock Edge* (1909), the choral *Sea Symphony* (1909), and the *Fantasia on a Theme by Thomas Tallis* (1910) – established him as a composer of major importance. The core of his original talent may be found in his nine symphonies (1909–57) and in the opera *The Pilgrim's Progress* (1949).

vault A three-dimensional arched structure, curved transversely and sometimes lengthwise. It is to be distinguished from the DOME, a doubly curved vault in which the weight acts downwards, while the vault exerts lateral thrust, in the same way as an ARCH. It therefore often requires strong side BUTTRESSES rather than massive walls or piers to support it. Whereas the dome is typically used over a roughly square or circular central space in a building, the vault is often used over a longer space, such as the nave of a church.

Vavilov, Nikolai (Ivanovich) (1887–*c.*1943) Soviet plant geneticist. He travelled extensively on botanical expeditions and amassed a considerable collection of new plants, with the aim of utilizing their genetic resources for crop improvement. He did much to improve the yields of Soviet agriculture, and located the centres of origin of many cultivated plants. However, Vavilov's views conflicted with official Soviet ideology (dominated by the theories of T. D. Lysenko) and he was arrested in 1940, dying later in a labour camp. His reputation was subsequently restored, a research institute being named after him.

VDU See VISUAL DISPLAY UNIT.

Veblen, Thorstein (Bunde) (1857–1929) US economist and social scientist. He is best known as the author of *The Theory of the Leisure Class* (1899), a critique of capitalism in which he coined the phrase 'conspicuous consumption'. This and subsequent works, such as *The Theory of Business Enterprise* (1904), had a significant influence on later economists, such as J. K. Galbraith.

vector (in biology) An organism that carries or is infected by a disease-causing organism, and acts as an agent of transfer for that disease or infection. A vector important to the transfer of disease in humans is the MOSQUITO, mainly known as a carrier of malaria. In GENETIC ENGINEERING, the piece of DNA, usually a plasmid or a bacteriophage, that carries the cloned piece of DNA is also called a vector.

vector (in mathematics) A quantity that has both magnitude and direction, in contrast to SCALARS, which have only magnitude. Velocity is a vector quantity, whereas speed is a scalar. Similarly weight, a downward force, is a vector whereas mass is a scalar. Vectors may be represented by straight lines of suitable length and orientation and used in diagrams to perform calculations. A **parallelogram of vectors** is used in mathematics to determine the sum of two vector quantities. If two vectors are represented in magnitude and direction by two adjoining sides of a parallelogram, their resultant is represented by the diagonal.

Vedanta (Sanskrit, 'the end of the Veda') The teaching of the UPANISHADS (commentaries attached to the VEDAS) and the most influential of the orthodox schools of Hindu philosophy, based on Upanishad doctrine. Vedanta schools share a belief in the supremacy of BRAHMAN, the transmigration of souls (SAMSARA), the desirability of release from the cycle of reincarnation (*moksha*), and the ability of the soul (ATMAN) to direct its own actions and thus determine its status in the next incarnation. Inspired by the idea of the ultimate equality of individual souls, exponents of Vedanta in the 20th century stress the need for social justice and a casteless society.

Vedas (Sanskrit, 'wisdom') The most authoritative of the HINDU SACRED TEXTS, regarded as *shruti*, the product of divine revelation. The basic four collections of *Vedas* consist of the *Rigveda* ('The Veda of Verses'), hymns of praise to the nature gods, particularly Agni, the fire god, and Indra, the warrior god; the *Yajurveda* ('The Veda of Sacrificial Texts'), a collection of sacrificial rites; the *Samaveda* ('The Veda of Chants'), containing the melodies and chants required for special sacrifices; and the *Atharvaveda* ('The Veda of the Fire-Priest') (included later in the canon), which consists of occult formulas and spells. Later on, commentaries were added, stemming from different schools. The *Brahmanas* are detailed explanations of the sacrifices, for the use of priests. The *Aranyakas* are works suitable for the hermit, while the UPANISHADS are mystical and philosophical works. See also VEDANTA.

Vega A star in the constellation of Lyra, also known as Alpha Lyrae, with an apparent magnitude of 0.03. It is a hot DWARF STAR at a distance of 8 parsecs, with about 50 times the luminosity of the Sun.

Vega, Lope de (full name Lope Felix de Vega Carpio) (1562–1635) Spanish dramatist and poet. He is regarded as the founder of Spanish drama and is said to have written 1,500 plays, of which several hundred survive. His dramas cover a wide range of genres from the historical and sacred to contemporary plays of intrigue and chivalry. His other works include epic poems and pastoral romances.

vegetarian A person whose diet does not contain meat, nor in most cases fish. **Vegans** exclude all animal products from their diet, including eggs and dairy foods, and may avoid all use of animal products, such as wool and leather. There are two interconnected arguments for vegetarianism, political and moral. The moral argument, based on the moral status of animals (see ANIMAL RIGHTS), denies man the right to kill them. The political argument measures the high cost in resources of meat production against the background of FAMINE and malnutrition in many countries. There is also a health argument, based on the view of some doctors that excessive fat is unhealthy. Those who regard vegetarianism as unwarranted point out that humans are biologically omnivorous and that vegetarians, especially vegans, can become anaemic and deficient in other dietary respects.

vegetative reproduction See REPRODUCTION.

vein A blood vessel carrying deoxygenated blood back to the heart. An exception to this rule is the pulmonary vein, which carries oxygenated blood from the lungs to the heart. The walls of veins are thinner than those of ARTERIES and they carry blood at lower pressure. They connect with arteries via fine capillaries.

In the leaves of plants, veins are the tissues that conduct water from the roots and soluble organic substances made during PHOTOSYNTHESIS to other parts of the plant (translocation).

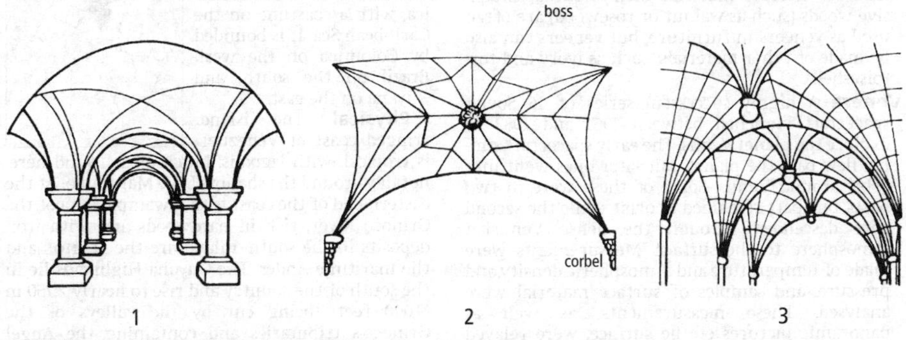

Vaults (1) Groined vault. (2) Ribbed vault. (3) Fan vault.

Vela The Sails, a CONSTELLATION of the southern sky, one of the three parts into which the Greek constellation of Argo Navis was divided by the 18th-century French astronomer Nicolas Louis de Lacaille.

Velázquez, Diego Rodríguez de Silva y (1599–1660) Spanish painter. His early paintings consisted chiefly of naturalistic religious works and domestic genre scenes. After his appointment as court painter to Philip IV in 1623, he painted many notable portraits, which tended towards naturalness and simplicity. Among the best known are *Pope Innocent X* (1650) and *Las Meninas* (*c.*1656). Other notable works include *The Toilet of Venus* (known as The Rokeby Venus, *c.*1651).

Velázquez de Cuéllar, Diego (*c.*1465–1524) Spanish conquistador. After sailing with Columbus to the New World in 1493, he began the conquest of Cuba in 1511; he founded a number of settlements including Havana (1515), and later initiated expeditions to conquer Mexico.

veld (or **veldt**) Treeless open country or grassland in southern Africa, often divided altitudinally into highveld, middleveld, and lowveld. It is an Afrikaans word from the Dutch *veldt*, field.

Velde, van de See VAN DE VELDE.

Velleius Paterculus (*c.*19 BC–*c.*30 AD) Roman historian and soldier. His *Roman History* in two volumes, covering the period from the early history of Rome to 30 AD, is notable for its rhetorical manner and for its eulogistic depiction of Tiberius, with whom Velleius had served in Germany before Tiberius became emperor.

vellum See PARCHMENT.

velocity A VECTOR quantity measuring the movement of an object in a particular direction in a given period. The instantaneous velocity v of an object is given by the derivative of its displacement x over time t, i.e. $v = dx/dt$.

velocity of light See SPEED OF LIGHT.

velocity of sound See SPEED OF SOUND.

velocity ratio (or **distance ratio**) The ratio of the speeds of two points in a mechanism. The simplest example is a first-class LEVER: a force at one end will move a load at the other in a velocity ratio equal to the ratio of the distance of force and load from the pivot.

Venda A former independent homeland created in northern Transvaal, South Africa, for the Vahvenda people, now part of Northern Province. It was designated a self-governing national state in 1973 and an independent republic in 1979 and abolished in 1994.

veneer A thin sheet of material with a decorative or fine finish bonded to the surface of an object made of cheaper material. Rich-coloured, expensive woods (such as walnut or rosewood) are often used as veneers in furniture, but veneers can also be made of other materials, such as ivory and tortoiseshell.

Venera A highly successful series of 16 Soviet spacecraft launched between 1961 and 1983 to explore the planet Venus. The early spacecraft simply flew past the planet, but later ones went into orbit around Venus. Some of these were in two parts: one part remained in orbit while the second part descended through the dense Venusian atmosphere to the surface. Measurements were made of temperature and atmospheric density and pressure, and samples of surface material were analysed. These measurements, as well as panoramic pictures of the surface, were relayed back to Earth via the orbiting module. The major surface features, such as plateaux, mountain ranges, and volcanoes, were mapped by radar from orbiting spacecraft.

venereal disease See SEXUALLY-TRANSMITTED DISEASE.

Venetia (Italian **Veneto**) A region of north-eastern Italy, comprising the provinces of Belluno, Padova, Rovigo, Treviso, Venezia, Verona, and Vicenza; area 18,379 sq km (7,099 sq miles); pop. (1990) 4,398,110; capital, Venice. The region takes its name from the pre-Roman inhabitants, the Veneti, an Italic tribe with their own distinctive language, who inhabited north-east Italy from the 1st millennium BC.

Venetian art The art and architecture of Venice. Culturally it was open to diverse influences and originally looked east to Byzantium, as is seen in the most famous Venetian building – the Basilica of St Mark (see BYZANTINE ART). In the 15th century, led by the BELLINI family, Venice became established as a leading Italian centre for painting. Giovanni Bellini established the Venetian concern for colour rather than drawing as the dominant means of artistic expression. His pupils included GIORGIONE and TITIAN, and the line of great painters was continued to the end of the century by TINTORETTO and VERONESE. Venetian architecture is characterized by the Doge's Palace, with its lacy open stonework, and the St Mark's Libary in an exuberant classical style. In Venetia, the mainland area inland from Venice, the pre-eminent architect PALLADIO built villas and civic buildings, as well as churches in the city itself. By the 17th century, the native genius seemed to have exhausted itself, and most of the best painters in Venice came from elsewhere. Venice, however, can boast one of the finest and most original buildings of the Italian Baroque – the church of Santa Maria della Salute by Longhena. In the 18th century Venice enjoyed its second great flowering of art. TIEPOLO and Giambattista Piazzeta were outstanding among many distinguished decorative painters, who revived the brilliant colours of the 16th century. The engraved *veduti* (views) of the city published by Luca Carlevaris in 1703 are, together with his paintings, the foundation on which CANALETTO and GUARDI built their own popular images of the city. With the rise of NEOCLASSICISM in the late 18th century, the vitality again went from Venetian art, and since the 19th century the city has been more a place of cultural pilgrimage than a creative centre. In the 20th century, however, the Venice Biennale, an international exhibition instituted in 1895 and held every two years, become a show-place for contemporary art.

Venezuela A country on the north coast of South America, with a coastline on the Caribbean Sea. It is bounded by Colombia on the west, Brazil on the south, and Guyana on the east.

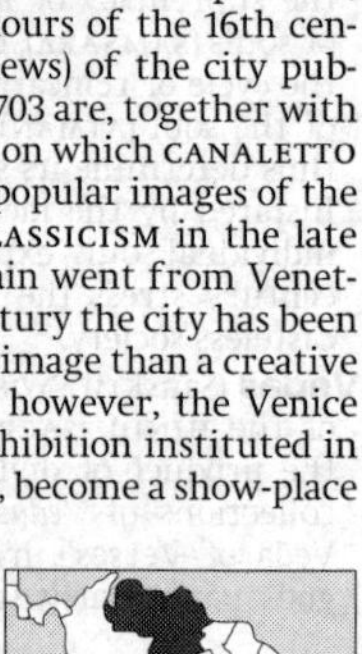

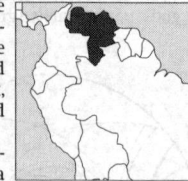

Physical. The island-fringed coast of Venezuela is tropical, with lagoons. Much oil is found here, notably around the shallow Lake Maracaibo. At the eastern end of the coast is the swampy delta of the Orinoco River, rich in hardwoods and with iron deposits in the south. Inland are the LLANOS and the maritime Andes. The Guyana Highlands lie in the south of the country and rise to nearly 2,750 m (9,000 feet), being cut by the valleys of the Orinoco's tributaries and containing the Angel Falls, the highest in the world.

Economy. The Venezuelan economy is dominated by state-owned oil production and associated industries, but production has fallen due to a policy of conservation. Also, attempts have been made to diversify the economy. There are substantial mineral deposits, including bauxite and iron ore, refined by the government-owned steel industry. Although agriculture is potentially rich, Venezuela imports about 60 per cent of its food. The economy has suffered from its over-dependence on oil, high rates of inflation, and foreign debt.

History. Venezuela was visited in 1499 by the explorer Amerigo Vespucci, who gave it its name ('Little Venice') after sighting native houses built on stilts on Lake Maracaibo. It was subsequently colonized by the Spanish. By the mid-18th century wealthy Creoles (Spaniards born in the colony) were protesting against trade restrictions imposed by Madrid. It was in its capital Caracas that the Colombian Independence Movement began (1806), resulting in the creation by Simón BOLÍVAR of Gran Colombia. When this collapsed (1829), Venezuela proclaimed itself a republic under its first President, General José Antonio Páez (1830–43), who, while preserving the great estates, provided a strong administration, allowed a free press, and kept the army under control. The period that followed (1843–70) was politically chaotic and violent. Under President Guzmán BLANCO (1870–88) moves were made towards democracy, with the first election in 1881, and there was growth in economic activity. Despotic government returned under the CAUDILLOS Cipriano Castro (1899–1908) and Juan Vicente GÓMEZ (1909–35). Oil was discovered before World War I, and by 1920 Venezuela was the world's leading exporter of oil. Military juntas continued to dominate until Rómulo Betancourt completed a full term as a civilian President (1959–64), to be peacefully succeeded by Dr Raul Leoni (1964–69). Since then, democratic politics have continued to operate, with two parties, Accion Democratica and Christian Democrat, alternating in power, even though extremists of left and right have harassed them with terrorism. A post-war oil boom brought considerable prosperity, but rising population and inflation caused many problems for President Dr Jaime Lusinchi (1983–88). Falling oil prices and increased drug trafficking were additional problems for his successor Carlos Andrés Pérez, who faced serious riots in 1989 for his austerity measures, and two unsuccessful military coup attempts in 1992. In 1993 Pérez was removed from office and charged with corruption. Elections in December of that year saw Rafael Caldera Rodríguez accede to the presidency.

Capital: Caracas
Area: 912,050 sq km (352,144 sq mi)
Population: 21,884,000 (1995)
Currency: 1 bolivar = 100 centimos
Religions: Roman Catholic 92.0%
Ethnic Groups: Mestizo 69.0%; White 20.0%; Black 9.0%; Amerindian 2.0%
Languages: Spanish (official); Amerindian languages
International Organizations: UN; OAS; OPEC; Andean Group

Venice (Italian **Venezia**) A city of Venetia in north-east Italy, on a lagoon of the Adriatic Sea, built on numerous islands separated by canals and linked by bridges; pop. (1990) 317,840. It was a powerful republic in the Middle Ages, and from the 13th to the 16th century a leading sea-power, controlling trade to the Levant. Its commercial importance declined after the Cape route to India was discovered at the end of the 16th century, but it remained an important centre of art and music (see VENETIAN ART). After the Napoleonic Wars Venice was placed under Austrian rule; it was incorporated into a unified Italy in 1866. Amongst its many fine buildings are St Mark's Church, the 15th-century Doge's Palace, the Bridge of Sighs, and the Church of S Maria della Salute.

Extraction of water from the subsoil has caused massive sinking and flooding problems, which are receiving urgent attention. There is little industry but the city is a tourist centre, with a seaside resort, the Lido, 3 km away on the edge of the lagoon.

Vening Meinesz, **Felix Andries** (1887–1966) Dutch geophysicist. He devised a technique for making accurate gravity measurements with the aid of a pendulum, using it first for a gravity survey of the Netherlands. He then pioneered the use of submarines for marine gravity surveys, locating negative gravity anomalies in the deep trenches near island arcs in the Pacific and interpreting them as being due to the downward buckling of the oceanic crust. This was eventually confirmed; Vening Meinesz, however, never supported the idea of continental drift.

Venn diagram A geometric means for representing relationships between SETS. Each set is represented by a ring and all are drawn within the confines of a rectangle representing the universal set under consideration. The area common to two rings represents their intersection, and the area in the combined region, their union. Shading is often used to focus attention on the particular compound set under consideration. Venn diagrams provide a pictorial image of the operations described in truth tables. They were first proposed by the British logician John Venn (1834–1923).

Venturi, **Robert (Charles)** (1925–) US architect. He reacted against the prevailing international style of the 1960s and pioneered the development of post-modern architecture. Among his buildings is the Sainsbury Wing of the National Gallery in London (1991). His writings include *Complexity and Contradiction in Architecture* (1966).

venturi tube An instrument used to measure the rate of fluid flow, or to draw in liquid from a reservoir. It consists of a tube with a short constriction in the middle designed to cause a drop in pressure in a fluid flowing through it. The rate of fluid flow is measured by attaching a pressure gauge to the constriction. A venturi tube is also used to draw petrol into the CARBURETTOR of a motor car.

Venus (in Roman mythology) The goddess of love and beauty, identified with Aphrodite in Greek mythology. Venus Verticordia was the goddess, worshipped by Roman matrons, who turned married women's hearts to chastity.

Venus (in astronomy) The second major PLANET in order of distance from the Sun. Also known as Hesperus, the **evening star**, or Phosphorus, the **morning star**, Venus can be the brightest object in the sky after the Sun and Moon and follows a near-circular path some 106 million kilometres from the Sun, taking 225 days to complete one orbit. It shows phases in the same way as Mercury and can also pass in front of the Sun during a TRANSIT. In photographs taken with ultraviolet light, it shows dark patches and streaks, which are temporary breaks in the dense lower cloud levels. These race round the planet in only four days, carried by a high-altitude 350 km/h gale, which never abates. The atmosphere is extremely dense and hot, made up of over 90 per cent carbon dioxide.

The surface pressure is 91 times that of the Earth and the global surface temperature is kept permanently at about 475°C by the GREENHOUSE EFFECT. The solid globe, with a mean density of 5,240 kg/m^3, is 12,104 km in diameter and rotates slowly from east to west, that is, in a retrograde manner, with a period of 243 days so that its day is longer than its year. The Soviet spacecraft VENERA 9 and 10 gave the first glimpses of the surface in 1975. Both spacecraft soft-landed and returned panoramic photographs showing hot stony desert landscapes scattered with rocks of all sizes. Recent radar studies suggest that this is typical of the whole planet and show that Venus has a cratered surface.

Venus's fly-trap A CARNIVOROUS PLANT, *Dionaea muscipula*, which Darwin described as 'one of the world's most wonderful plants'. It is native to boglands in North and South Carolina. The modified leaves have two lobes, centrally hinged to form a trap, the margins of which are provided with long spines. The trap is sprung when insects, attracted by the colour and nectar-like secretions, touch trigger-hairs on the inner faces of the trap. These cause extremely rapid bursts of growth in the hinge cells, which culminate in the closing of the trap. The marginal spines prevent escape even before the lobes are completely closed. Glands secrete enzymes that break down the softer parts of the insect and, by absorbing the 'digested' insect juices, the plant is provided with nutrients, such as nitrogen, which are difficult to obtain in bogland habitats.

Vercingetorix (died 46 BC) King of the tribe of the Averni in Gaul. Towards the end of the GALLIC WARS in 52 BC he revolted against Roman occupation and was acclaimed king of the united Gauls. Defeated and captured, he was finally paraded through Rome as a trophy in CAESAR's triumph (46 BC) and then executed.

Verdi, Giuseppe (Fortunino Francesco) (1813–1901) Italian composer. He is remembered for his many operas, which are notable for strong characterization, original orchestration, and memorable tunes. Verdi was a supporter of the movement for Italian unity, and several of his early works were identified with the nationalist cause, including *Nabucco* (1842), with which he established his reputation. Other operas include *Rigoletto* (1851), *La Traviata* (1853), and *Otello* (1887); *Aida*, commissioned to be staged in Cairo to celebrate the opening of the Suez Canal, was delayed due to the Franco-Prussian War and eventually first performed there in 1871. Among his other compositions is Requiem Mass of 1874.

verdin See TIT.

Verdon Roe, Sir Edwin Alliott See ROE.

Verdun A fortified town on the River Meuse in north-east France; pop. (1990) 23,430. Of strategic importance, it was the scene of long and severe battles in World War I (1916), where the French and Germans suffered heavy losses. There are huge war cemeteries and monuments.

Verlaine, Paul (1844–96) French poet. Initially a member of the Parnassian group of poets, he later became prominent among the symbolists, especially with the publication of his influential essay 'Art poétique' (1882). Notable collections of poetry include *Poèmes saturniens* (1867), *Fêtes galantes* (1869), and *Romances sans paroles* (1874), a work characterized by an intense musicality and metrical inventiveness. The last was written in prison, where Verlaine was serving a two-year sentence for wounding his lover, the poet Arthur Rimbaud, during a quarrel.

Vermeer, Jan (1632–75) Dutch painter. He spent his life in his native town of Delft, where he generally painted domestic genre scenes, often depicting a single figure engaged in an ordinary task (for example *The Kitchen-Maid*, *c.*1658). His work is distinguished by its clear design and simple form, and by its harmonious balance of predominant yellows, blues, and greys. His other works include two views of Delft and the *Allegory of Painting* (*c.*1665). His paintings only began to receive full recognition in the later 19th century.

vermiculite A clay mineral formed from mica. It expands to some 20 times its original volume on heating, when the water molecules between layers of silicate evaporate. In this form it is light and water-absorbent. It is used for insulation, growing seedlings, and packaging.

Vermont A state of New England in north-eastern USA, bordering on Canada; area 24,900 sq km (9,614 sq miles); pop. (1990) 562,760; capital, Montpelier. Also known as the Green Mountain State, its largest city is Burlington. Explored and settled by the French during the 17th and 18th centuries, it became an independent republic in 1777 and the 14th state of the USA in 1791. Its chief products are granite, marble, asbestos, slate, talc, and maple syrup. In addition to skiing, fishing, and hunting one of Vermont's principal attractions is the Green Mountain National Forest.

vernacular architecture Buildings made of local materials generally of unknown authorship and following traditional patterns. Typical materials include timber, thatch, wattle and daub, flint, and certain types of brick and stone. Wood was much employed in timber-framing. The distinction between vernacular 'building' and mainstream 'architecture' appeared only after the Renaissance, with the rise of the profession of architect.

vernal equinox See EQUINOX.

Verne, Jules (1828–1905) French novelist. Regarded as one of the first writers of science fiction, in his adventure stories he often anticipated later scientific and technological developments. He explored the possibilities of space travel in *From the Earth to the Moon* (1865) and the use of submarines in *Twenty Thousand Leagues Under the Sea* (1870). Other novels include *Journey to the Centre of the Earth* (1864) and *Around the World in Eighty Days* (1873).

vernier A small movable graduated scale that slides along a fixed scale in order to obtain fractional parts of the divisions on the main fixed scale. It was devised by the French mathematician Pierre Vernier (1580–1637) in 1631.

Verona An ancient city in Venetia, north-east Italy, on the River Adige; pop. (1990) 258,950. Its principal landmarks are the Roman Arena, the medieval Gastelvecchio, the 12th-century cathedral, and the Romanesque San Zeno Maggiore. A tourist centre, Verona has plastic, furniture, and paper industries.

Veronese, Paolo (born Paolo Caliari) (*c.*1528–88) Italian painter. Born in Verona, by about 1553 he had established himself in Venice, where he gained many commissions, including the painting of frescos in a number of churches and in the Doge's Palace. Assisted by a large workshop, he produced numerous paintings, mainly dealing with religious, allegorical, and historical subjects; he is particularly known for his richly coloured feast-scenes (such as *The Marriage at Cana*, 1562). Other notable works include his series of frescos in Palladio's villa at Maser near Treviso (1561).

veronica See SPEEDWELL.

verruca See WART.

Versailles A town south-west of Paris in central France, capital of the department of Yvelines; pop. (1990) 91,030. It is noted for its royal palace, originally built as a hunting lodge for Louis XIII but later extended as a royal seat by Louis XIV. Its architecture is the work of Louis Le Vau, Jules Hardouin-Mansart, and Robert de Cotte. The interiors were designed by Charles Lebrun and the gardens laid out by André Le Nôtre. Versailles was the residence of the French kings until the revolution of 1789. Treaties were signed here ending the War of American Independence (1783) and World War I (1919).

Versailles Peace Settlement (1919–23) Sometimes referred to as the Paris Peace Settlement, a collection of peace treaties between the Central Powers and the Allied powers ending World War I. The main treaty was that of **Versailles** (June 1919) between the Allied powers (except for the USA, which refused to ratify the treaty) and Germany, whose representatives were required to sign it without negotiation.

A second treaty, that of **St Germain-en-Laye** (September 1919), was between the Allied powers and the new republic of AUSTRIA. A third treaty, that of **Trianon** (June 1920), was with the new republic of HUNGARY, in which some three-quarters of its old territories (i.e., all non-Magyar lands) were lost to Czechoslovakia, Romania, and Yugoslavia, and the principle of reparations again accepted. A fourth treaty, that of **Neuilly** (November 1919), was with BULGARIA, in which some territory was lost to Yugoslavia and Greece, but some also gained from Turkey; a figure of £100 million reparations was agreed, but never paid. These four treaties were ratified in Paris during 1920. A fifth treaty, that of **Sèvres** (August 1920), between the Allies and the old OTTOMAN EMPIRE, was never implemented as it was followed by the final disintegration of the empire and the creation by Mustafa Kemal ATATÜRK of the new republic of Turkey. The treaty was replaced by the Treaty of **Lausanne** (July 1923), in which Palestine, Transjordan, and Iraq were to be mandated to Britain, and Syria to France. Italy was accepted as possessing the Dodecanese Islands, while Turkey regained Smyrna from Greece.

vertebra A bone of the vertebrate SPINE, consisting of a circular, thick disc (the centrum) extended on one side to form an arch of bone called the neural arch, through which the spinal cord passes. From this arch extend three bony processes to which muscles are attached. The single dorsal arch and two lateral processes act as sites for muscle attachment. The lateral processes are also interconnected by ligaments and help control movement of the backbone. Differing slightly in shape one to another, the vertebrae are connected via DISCS, which act to cushion shock waves, and prevent jarring of the complete spine.

vertebrate A member of the subphylum Vertebrata, of the phylum Chordata, containing animals with backbones (see SPINE) whose NERVOUS SYSTEMS are differentiated anteriorly into an elaborate brain, housed in a cranium. These animals can be divided into a series of classes: JAWLESS FISH, CARTILAGINOUS FISH, BONY FISH, AMPHIBIANS, REPTILES, BIRDS, and MAMMALS.

vertical take-off and landing aircraft See VTOL AIRCRAFT.

Verulamium See ST ALBANS.

Verwoerd, Hendrik Frensch (1901–66) South African statesman. As Minister of Native Affairs (1950–58) he was responsible for establishing the policy of APARTHEID. He became Nationalist Party leader and Prime Minister (1958–66). During his government, in the aftermath of the SHARPEVILLE MASSACRE, South Africa became a republic and left the Commonwealth. Harsh measures were taken to silence black opposition, including the banning of the AFRICAN NATIONAL CONGRESS. He was assassinated in Parliament.

Very Large Array (VLA) The world's most powerful RADIO TELESCOPE. Situated at Socorro in New Mexico, USA, it consists of 27 radio dishes in a gigantic Y-shaped configuration 36 km (23 miles) across. The telescopes weigh 200 tonnes each, and can be moved to different positions along the arms of the Y using a specially designed transporter. The telescopes are linked to make use of INTERFEROMETRY, with 351 different pairings of telescopes. The VLA was completed in 1980, and is operated by the National Radio Astronomy Observatory.

Very light A flare fired from a hand-held pistol as a signal or to provide temporary brilliant illumination, especially in warfare. It was named after its US inventor, E. W. Very (1847–1910). It resembles a rocket and the colour of the light can be varied by including different metal salts in the charge.

Vesalius, Andreas (1514–64) Flemish anatomist. He wrote *De humani corporis fabrica* ('On the fabric of the human body'; 1543), which was based on actual dissection and examination and became the foundation of modern anatomy. He was later made physician to Emperor Charles V, but died at the age of 49 as the result of a shipwreck.

Vespasian (full name Titus Flavius Vespasianus) (9–79 AD) Roman emperor 69–79 and founder of the Flavian dynasty. A distinguished general, he was acclaimed emperor by the legions in Egypt during the civil wars that followed the death of Nero and gained control of Italy after the defeat of Vitellius. His reign saw the restoration of financial and military order and the initiation of a public building programme, which included the rebuilding of the Capitol and the beginning of the construction of the Colosseum (75).

Vespucci, Amerigo (1451–1512) Italian merchant, navigator, and explorer. While in the service of the king of Portugal, Vespucci made several voyages to the New World and claimed, on dubious authority, to have been the first to sight the mainland of South America (1497). The name America is derived from his first name.

Vesta (in Roman mythology) The goddess of the blazing hearth, identified with Hestia in Greek mythology. In Vesta's temple in Rome, the sacred fire on the state hearth was never allowed to die out, except on 1 March, the start of the new year, when it was ceremonially renewed. The fire was tended day and night by VESTAL VIRGINS.

Vesta (in astronomy) The brightest and third largest ASTEROID, first observed by the German philosopher and astronomer Heinrich Olbers in 1807. Analysis of Vesta using a spectrophotometer indicates that it has a basaltic crust of igneous origin, and therefore an interior made up of several different materials.

Vestal virgin An attendant of VESTA, goddess of fire, hearth, and home. The virgins numbered six, chosen by lot from a short list of aristocratic girls. Under vows of chastity they served for 30 years, dressed as brides, cleaning Vesta's shrine and tending the fire. Unchaste Vestals were buried alive.

They lived in the House of the Vestals in the Forum at Rome, and wills were deposited with them for safekeeping.

vestigial organ The atrophied, functionless remains of what was once, in an earlier evolutionary time, a functional organ. For example, the eyes of many animals that live in caves are vestigial.

Vesuvius (Italian **Vesuvio**) An active volcano near Naples in Italy, 1,277 m (4,190 ft) high. It erupted violently in 79 AD, burying the towns of Pompeii and Herculaneum. The last minor eruption was in 1944.

vetch (or **tare**) A weakly climbing plant of the genus *Vicia*, with end-leaflets modified into tendrils. Vetches are LEGUMES of temperate regions, best suited to chalky soils. They are sometimes grown, either on their own or in a mixture with cereals, to be cut for silage or hay. Many vetches occur as native plants throughout temperate regions, with pink, blue, purple, or yellow flowers.

veterinary medicine The science dealing with the health and welfare of farm and domestic animals. Its practice includes both the treatment of sickness and injury, and preventive medicine. Veterinary surgeons have also been concerned with animal welfare, including the design of buildings to achieve optimum comfort and productivity, as well as the development and administration of drugs and hormones. Understanding of genetics, as well as the development of such techniques as ARTIFICIAL INSEMINATION and embryo transplantation (see IN VITRO FERTILIZATION), have also increased the involvement of veterinary surgeons on the farm. Certain diseases, such as brucellosis and anthrax, are transmitted between animals and humans, and the veterinary surgeon must control and isolate stocks bearing that disease. In addition to its agricultural aspects, veterinary medicine also includes the treatment of domestic pets, and animals, such as horses, kept for sport, breeding, or leisure activities.

VHF See WAVEBAND.

Via Appia See APPIAN WAY.

viaduct A bridge that crosses a valley in a continuous series of small linked arches. In the 19th century, brick or masonry viaducts were the normal means of maintaining the level of a railway across a valley in cases when an embankment would be too high or its base too wide. Viaducts are also used in the approaches to a large-span crossing of a waterway, where the foundations for the piers would be difficult to build. In current practice, pre-stressed concrete beams supported on concrete piers are the most economical construction for a viaduct.

viburnum See GUELDER ROSE.

Vicente, Gil (*c.*1465–*c.*1536) Portuguese dramatist and poet. Vicente is regarded as Portugal's most important dramatist. He enjoyed royal patronage for much of his life, and many of his poems and plays were written to commemorate national or court events. His works (some written in Portuguese, some in Spanish) include dramas on religious themes, farces, pastoral plays, and comedies satirizing the nobility and clergy.

Vichy A spa town in the Auvergne region of central France noted for its effervescent mineral waters; pop. (1990) 28,050. During World War II it was the seat of the VICHY GOVERNMENT.

Vichy government (1940–45) The French government established after the Franco-German armistice in World War II. The Germans having occupied Paris, it was set up under Marshal PÉTAIN in VICHY by the French National Assembly (1940) to administer unoccupied France and the colonies. Having dissolved the Third Republic, it issued a new constitution establishing an autocratic state. The Vichy government was never recognized by the Allies. In 1941 it granted Japan right of access and air bases in Indo-China, from which it was to launch its Malaya and Burma campaigns. It was dominated first by LAVAL, as Pétain's deputy (1940), then by DARLAN (1941–42) in collaboration with Hitler, and once more (1942–44) by Laval as Pétain's successor after German forces moved in to the unoccupied portions of France. After the Allied liberation of France (1944), the Vichy government established itself under Pétain at Sigmaringen in Germany, where it collapsed when Germany surrendered in 1945.

Vico, Giambattista (1668–1744) Italian philosopher. His work championed the philosophy of history rather than the mathematical and scientific philosophy favoured by his contemporaries. In *Scienza Nuova* (1725) he proposed that civilizations are subject to recurring cycles of barbarism, heroism, and reason. Vico argued that these cycles are accompanied by corresponding cultural, linguistic, and political modes. He claimed that in literature, for example, poetry flourishes in the heroic age, while prose enters in the age of reason. His historicist philosophy made an impression on later philosophers, such as Marx and Umberto Eco.

Victor Emmanuel II (1820–78) Ruler of the kingdom of Sardinia 1849–61 and king of Italy 1861–78. His appointment of Cavour as Premier in 1852 hastened the drive towards Italian unification. In 1859 Victor Emmanuel led his Piedmontese army to victory against the Austrians at the battles of Magenta and Solferino, and in 1860 entered the papal territories around French-held Rome to join his forces with those of Garibaldi. After being crowned first king of a united Italy in Turin in 1861, Victor Emmanuel continued to add to his kingdom, acquiring Venetia in 1866 and Rome in 1870.

Victor Emmanuel III (1869–1947) King of Italy 1900–46. He succeeded to the throne after his father's assassination. Under Mussolini, whom he had invited to form a government in 1922 in order to forestall civil war, Victor Emmanuel lost all political power. However, during World War II, after the loss of Sicily to the Allies (1943), he acted to dismiss Mussolini and conclude an armistice. Victor Emmanuel abdicated in favour of his son in 1946, but a republic was established the same year by popular vote and both he and his son went into exile.

Victoria (1819–1901) Queen of Great Britain and Ireland 1837–1901 and empress of India 1876–1901. She succeeded to the throne on the death of her uncle, William IV, and married her cousin Prince Albert in 1840; they had nine children. As queen she took an active interest in the policies of her ministers, although she did not align the Crown with any one political party. She largely retired from public life after Albert's death in 1861, but lived to achieve the longest reign in British history. During her reign Britain's power and prosperity grew enormously. Her golden jubilee (1887) and diamond jubilee (1897) were marked with popular celebration.

Victoria A state of south-east Australia; area 227,600 sq km (87,910 sq miles); pop. (1991) 4,439,400; capital, Melbourne. Originally known as the Port Philip district of New South Wales, it became a separate colony in 1851 and was federated with the other states of Australia in 1901. Rich in mineral resources that include brown coal, gold, gypsum, kaolin, bauxite, and off-shore oil, the state also produces grain, fruit, wine, wool, and dairy produce.

Victoria A port city on the west coast of Canada, provincial capital of British Columbia; pop. (1991) 71,200; 287,900 (metropolitan area). Situated at the southern tip of Vancouver Island, the city was founded in 1843 as a Hudson's Bay Company fort. It was a base for gold prospectors during the gold-rush of 1858 and became provincial capital in 1871. It is a naval and fishing-fleet base with a university. Industries include shipbuilding, timber, paper making, and tourism.

Victoria The business centre, port, and capital of Hong Kong, on the north coast of Hong Kong Island. Victoria Harbour is one of the busiest and greatest natural harbours in the world. The city is connected to Kowloon by ferries and a road tunnel. Central Victoria is Hong Kong's business centre. It is backed by Victoria Peak where crowded tenements give way to the buildings of Government House and the university.

Victoria, Lake (or **Victoria Nyanza**) The largest lake in Africa (69,464 sq km, 26,820 sq miles) and the chief reservoir of the Nile, explored by SPEKE in 1858. Areas of it lie within the boundaries of Uganda, Tanzania, and Kenya.

Victoria, Tomás Luis de (1548–1611) Spanish composer. In 1565 he went to Rome, where he may have studied with Palestrina; he eventually returned to Spain, settling in Madrid in 1594. His music, all of it religious, resembles that of Palestrina in its contrapuntal nature; it includes motets, masses, and hymns.

Victoria and Albert Museum A prestigious museum of applied arts founded in 1853 in Marlborough House in London, to house many of the articles displayed in the Great Exhibition of 1851. When Queen Victoria laid the foundation stone of the present building in South Kensington in 1899, she asked for it to be given its present name.

Victoria Cross (VC) The highest British award for bravery, instituted in 1856 by Queen Victoria for "conspicuous bravery in the face of the enemy". A bronze Maltese cross, until 1942 it was cast from Russian guns captured in the Crimean War.

Victoria Falls A spectacular waterfall 109 m (355 ft) high on the Zambezi River at the border of Zimbabwe and Zambia, explored by David Livingstone in 1855. Originally known as Mosi-oa-tunya ('the smoke that thunders'), it is divided into five main sections: the Eastern Cataract, Rainbow Falls, Devil's Cataract, Horshoe Falls, and Main Falls. The winding gorge below the Falls is crossed by a 198 m (650 ft) road and rail bridge 94 m (310 ft) above the river.

Victoria waterlily See ROYAL WATERLILY.

vicuña A species of LLAMA, *Vicugna vicugna*, related to the alpaca and guanaco. It is less than 90 cm (3 feet) high at the shoulders, and is tawny in colour, with a white bib on the lower neck. The coat is not excessively luxuriant, but because of its silkiness the wool is greatly prized and commands a high price. The vicuña lives at very high altitudes on the slopes of the High Andes, travelling in small herds of 6–12 females, with a lone male as leader. He keeps watch and utters a shrill whistle at the first hint of danger, covering the rear of the retreating herd. Although still found in the wild, it is also domesticated.

Vidal, Gore (born Eugene Luther Vidal) (1925–) US novelist, dramatist, and essayist. His first novel, *Williwaw* (1946), was based on his wartime experiences. His other novels, usually satirical comedies, include *Myra Breckenridge* (1968), *Creation* (1981), and *Hollywood* (1989). Among his plays are *Suddenly Last Summer* (1958). His essays, published in a number of collections, form a satirical commentary on US political and cultural life.

video camera A camera for recording electronically encoded visual images. Video cameras for amateur use are designed to be used with VIDEO RECORDERS. These can be either separate portable units, or more commonly, video-tape cassette recorders incorporated with the camera in devices known as **camcorders**. Recently, the still video camera was introduced, combining ordinary photography with electronic video technology. In both camcorders and still video cameras, the lens focuses images on to a CHARGED-COUPLED DEVICE (CCD). The image is then recorded either on to videotape, or (for a still camera) on to a magnetic disk or COMPACT DISC, which acts as the 'film'. The videotape from a camcorder can be played back on a suitable TELEVISION RECEIVER. Still video images can also be replayed on a television receiver using a computer, or printed out as a hard copy 'photograph' without the need for chemical processing.

videodisc See COMPACT DISC.

video recorder A device that records on magnetic tape or COMPACT DISC the audio and video signals that constitute a TELEVISION programme. In a videotape recorder, the picture is recorded in the same way as a TAPE RECORDER records sound – as magnetic patterns on a tape – but the greater complexity of the video signal necessitates the use of a wide tape and a rotating recording head rather than a fixed one. In the domestic VHS (Video Home System) the rotating drum has only two recording heads, and the tape runs across the drum at an angle, producing a video signal recorded diagonally across the tape. The accompanying soundtrack is synchronized with the pictures by a control signal; sound and control signals are recorded on narrow tracks at the edges of the tape.

videotex Television-based information systems, using COMPUTERS holding extensive DATABASES. One format, called **Viewdata**, is an interactive system enabling the user to conduct a dialogue with a remote computer, using a MICROCOMPUTER, a MODEM, and a telephone link. Viewdata is used in business and leisure, including home shopping and making travel and theatre reservations. Another format of videotex, TELETEX, was developed in the UK in the 1970s and provides information as 'pages', selectable by the viewer, transmitted in unused areas of a standard television signal.

Vienna (German **Wien**) The capital of Austria, situated on the River Danube; pop. (1991) 1,533,180. It was an important military centre (*Vindobona*) under the Romans, and from 1278 to 1918 the seat of the Habsburgs, the rulers of the Austro-Hungarian Empire. It has long been a centre of the arts and especially music, Mozart, Beethoven, Brahms, and Johann Strauss being among the great composers associated with it. The principal landmarks are St Stephen's Cathedral, the Opera House, Schönbrunn Palace, the Hofburg (the residence of the President of Austria), the Spanish Riding School, and the Giant Wheel in the Prater Park. Vienna's geographical position has made it a natural meeting-place for Eastern and Western Europe. It has numerous light industries and is a tourist centre.

Vienna, Congress of (1814–15) An international peace conference that settled the affairs of Europe after the defeat of NAPOLEON. It continued to meet through the HUNDRED DAYS of Napoleon's return to France (March–June 1815). The dominant powers were Austria, represented by METTERNICH, Britain, represented by CASTLEREAGH, Prussia, represented by FREDERICK WILLIAM III, and Russia, represented by ALEXANDER I. TALLEYRAND represented Louis XVIII of France. The Congress agreed to the absorption by the new kingdom of the Netherlands (now Belgium), but otherwise the Habsburgs regained control of all their domains, including Lombardy, Venetia, Tuscany, Parma, and TYROL. Prussia gained parts of Saxony as well as regaining much of Westphalia and the Rhineland. Denmark, which had allied itself with France, lost Norway to Sweden. In Italy the pope was restored to the Vatican and the Papal States, and the Bourbons were re-established in the Kingdom of the Two Sicilies. The German Confederation was established, and Napoleon's Grand Duchy of Warsaw was to be replaced by a restored Kingdom of Poland, but as part of the Russian empire with the Russian emperor also king of Poland. The Congress restored political stability to Europe.

Vientiane The capital and chief port of Laos, on the Mekong River; pop. (1985) 377,400. It has several Buddhist temples including the Great Sacred Stupa which was allegedly first erected in the 3rd century BC to enclose a breastbone of the Buddha.

Vietcong Communist guerrilla organization operating in South Vietnam 1960–75. Opposition to the Saigon-based regime of Ngo Dinh Diem had already produced widespread guerrilla activity in South Vietnam when communist interests founded the National Front for the Liberation of South Vietnam (known to its opponents as the Vietcong) in 1960. As US military support for the Saigon government broadened into the full-scale VIETNAM WAR so Vietcong forces were supplied with arms and supported by North Vietnamese forces brought to the south via the Ho Chi Minh Trail, which passed through neighbouring Laos and Cambodia. They maintained intensive guerrilla operations, and occasionally fought large set-piece battles. They finally undermined both US support for the war and the morale of the South Vietnamese army and opened the way for communist triumph and the reunification of Vietnam in 1975.

Vietminh Vietnamese communist guerrilla movement. Founded in 1941 in south China by HO CHI MINH and other exiled Vietnamese members of the Indo-Chinese Communist Party with the aim of expelling both the French and the Japanese from Vietnam, the Vietminh began operations, with assistance from the USA, against the Japanese in 1943–45 under the military leadership of Vo Nguyen Giap. After the end of World War II, it resisted the returning French, building up its strength and organization through incessant guerrilla operations and finally winning a decisive set-piece engagement at DIEN BIEN PHU in 1954. This forced the French to end the war and grant independence to Vietnam, partitioned into two states, North and South.

Vietnam A country in south-east Asia, shaped like an 'S', bordering on China on the north and Laos and Cambodia on the west, and having long east and south coasts on the South China Sea.

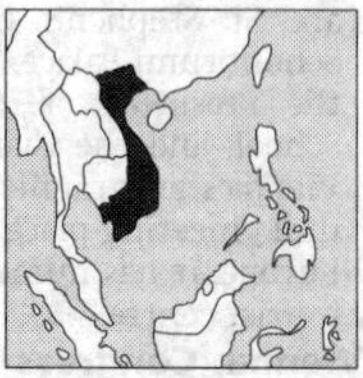

Physical. In the north of Vietnam the Red and Black rivers flow from forested mountains across very warm, wet lowlands spread with paddy-fields. The south is even wetter, with rice being cultivated all down the coastal strip and in the Mekong delta. Rubber and other crops are grown in areas where the ground rises to the central highlands.

Economy. Despite policies of economic liberalization and a decision in 1986 to switch to a free-market economy, the Vietnamese government maintains its adherence to communism. Primarily agricultural, the Vietnamese economy has been badly damaged by war, poor climatic conditions, and a US embargo and veto on Western aid. Once-substantial Soviet aid has ceased, and many of the Vietnamese migrant workers in the former Eastern bloc have returned home. The chief agricultural crops are rice, sugar-cane, tea, coffee, rubber, and fruits, but Vietnam depends on imports to meet its food requirements. There are large reserves of coal, iron ore, manganese, and other minerals, including off-shore oil fields.

History. In 1802 the two states of ANNAM and Tonkin were reunited by the Annamese general Nguyen Anh, who became emperor Gia-Long. Gia-Long was given French assistance and French influence increased in the 19th century. By 1883 Vietnam was part of FRENCH INDO-CHINA, although a weak monarchy was allowed to remain. In World War II the Japanese occupied it but allowed VICHY France to administer it until March 1945. In September 1945 HO CHI MINH declared its independence, but this was followed by French reoccupation and the French Indo-Chinese War. The Geneva Conference (1954), convened to seek a solution to the Indochina conflict, partitioned Vietnam along the 17th parallel, leaving a communist Democratic Republic with its capital at Hanoi in the north, and, after the deposition of the former emperor BAO DAI in 1955, a non-communist republic with its capital at Saigon in the south. Ho Chi Minh, the North Vietnamese leader, remained committed to a united communist country, and by the time the South Vietnamese president Ngo Dinh Diem was overthrown by the military in 1963, communist insurgents of the VIETCONG were already active in the south. Communist attempts to take advantage of the political confusion in the south were accelerated by the infusion of massive US military assistance, and in the late 1960s and early 1970s, the VIETNAM WAR raged throughout the area, with the heavy use of US airpower failing to crush growing communist strength. Domestic pressures helped accelerate a US withdrawal and, after abortive peace negotiations, the North Vietnamese and their Vietcong allies finally took Saigon in April 1975; a united Socialist Republic of Vietnam was proclaimed in the following year. Despite the severe damage done to the economy, Vietnam adopted an aggressively pro-Soviet foreign policy, dominating Laos, invading Cambodia to overthrow the KHMER ROUGE regime (1975–79), and suffering heavily in a brief border war with China (1979). In 1989, Vietnamese troops withdrew from Cambodia. Attempts to reorder society in the south of the country produced a flood of refugees, damaging Vietnam's international standing and increasing its dependence on the Soviet Union. Many of these refugees were from the Chinese minority; known as the 'Boat People,' they fled Vietnam in small boats on the South China Sea. With the disintegration of the Soviet Union in 1991, Vietnam was prompted to normalize relations with China and the USA. A new constitution was adopted in 1992, incorporating major economic and political reforms. However, the Communist

Party of Vietnam retained its dominant position as the sole political party. Relations with the USA continued to improve during 1993–94, with joint investigations taking place into the whereabouts of US servicemen missing in action during the Vietnam War. Economic links were forged with the USA and other countries (e.g. Japan and Britain), notably to exploit oil and natural gas fields in the country's territorial waters.

Capital: Hanoi
Area: 331,688 sq km (128,065 sq mi)
Population: 74,545,000 (1995)
Currency: 1 dong = 10 hao = 100 xu
Religions: Buddhist 55.3%; Roman Catholic 7.0%; Muslim 1.0%
Ethnic Groups: Vietnamese (Kinh) 88.0%; Chinese (Hoa) 2.0%; Tai 2.0%; Khmer 1.0%; Muong 1.0%; Thai 1.0%; Nung 1.0%
Languages: Vietnamese (official); minority languages
International Organizations: UN

Vietnamese language See AUSTRO-ASIATIC LANGUAGES.

Vietnam War (1964–75) The civil war in Vietnam after the commencement of large-scale US military involvement in 1964. Guerrilla activity in South Vietnam had become widespread by 1961, in which year President Ngo Dinh Diem proclaimed a state of emergency. Continued communist activity against a country perceived in the USA as a bastion against the spread of communism in south-east Asia led to increasing US concern, and after an alleged North Vietnamese attack on US warships in the Gulf of Tonkin in 1964, President Johnson was given congressional approval (Tonkin Gulf Resolution) to take military action. By the summer of 1965 a US army of 125,000 men was serving in the country, and by 1967 the figure had risen to 400,000, while US aircraft carried out an intensive bombing campaign against North Vietnam. Contingents from South Korea, Australia, New Zealand, and Thailand fought with the US troops. Although communist forces were held temporarily in check, the war provoked widespread opposition within the USA, and after the Tet Offensive of February 1968 had shaken official belief in the possibility of victory, the bombing campaign was halted and attempts to find a formula for peace talks started. US policy now began to emphasize the 'Vietnamization' of the war, and as increasing efforts were made to arm and train the South Vietnamese army, so US troops were gradually withdrawn. Nevertheless, US forces were still caught up in heavy fighting in the early 1970s and the bombing campaign was briefly resumed on several occasions. US troops were finally withdrawn after the Paris Peace Accords of January 1973, but no lasting settlement between North and South proved possible, and in early 1975 North Vietnamese forces finally triumphed, capturing Saigon (the capital of South Vietnam; renamed Ho Chi Minh City in 1976) on 30 April 1975. The war did enormous damage to the socio-economic fabric of the Indochinese states, devastating Vietnam and destabilizing neighbouring Cambodia (Kampuchea) and Laos.

viewdata See VIDEOTEX.

Vigée-Lebrun, (Marie Louise) Élisabeth (1755–1842) French painter. In 1779 she was commissioned to paint Marie Antoinette, whom she painted about 25 times over the next ten years. Vigée-Lebrun became a member of the Royal Academy of Painting and Sculpture in Paris in 1783. On the outbreak of the French Revolution in 1789 she fled to Italy, where she was acclaimed for her portraits of Lady Hamilton. Vigée-Lebrun worked in many countries throughout Europe, chiefly as a portraitist of women and children, before returning to France in 1810.

Vignola, Giacomo Barozzi da (1507–73) Italian architect. His designs were mannerist in style and include a number of churches in Rome as well as private residences such as the Palazzo Farnese near Viterbo (1559–73). One of his most influential designs was that for the church of Il Gesù in Rome (begun 1568), the headquarters of the Jesuit order; based on Alberti's church of San Andrea, Mantua, it has a Latin cross plan, with the nave broadened and the dome area increased, in accordance with Counter-Reformation ideas and the new importance attached to preaching. He also wrote a significant treatise on the five orders of architecture (1562).

Vigny, Alfred Victor, Comte de (1797–1863) French poet, novelist, and dramatist. From 1822 he published several volumes of verse which reveal his philosophy of stoic resignation; later poems, published posthumously in 1863, assert his faith in 'man's unconquerable mind'. Other works include his historical novel *Cinq-Mars* (1826) and the play *Chatterton* (1835), whose hero epitomizes the romantic notion of the poet as an isolated genius.

Vigo, Jean (1905–34) French film director. He is noted for his experimental films, which combine lyrical, surrealist, and realist elements. These include two short films and the two feature films *Zéro de conduite* (1933) and *L'Atalante* (1934). The former's indictment of repressive authority in a French boarding-school caused it to be banned in France until 1945.

Viking A member of the Scandinavian traders and pirates who ravaged much of northern Europe, and spread eastwards to Russia and Byzantium, between the 8th and 11th centuries. While their early expeditions were generally little more than raids in search of plunder, in later years they tended to end in conquest and colonization. Much of eastern England was occupied by the Vikings and eventually CANUTE, king of Denmark, succeeded to the English throne.

Viking Either of two successful US spacecraft sent to Mars. Launched in 1975, they went into orbit around Mars in 1976 a few months apart. Each consisted of an orbiter and a lander. The orbiters sent about 52,000 pictures of the Martian surface to Earth; they also relayed the information collected by the landers on the surface. Each of the two landers carried two television cameras, a seismometer, a meteorological station, and a small laboratory in which soil samples collected by a sampling arm and scoop could be analysed.

Viking ship The type of vessel used by the VIKINGS for trade and warfare *c.*850–1200 AD. Viking warships were long, open, oared vessels, clinker-built and rowed by 40–80 men. They had a short mast carrying a single square sail that could be braced to allow some measure of travel into the wind. The larger vessels had a part-deck fore and aft. Viking trading ships ('knorrs') were broader in beam and relied on sails much more than on oar power. The Vikings sailed in such vessels as far as VINLAND (Newfoundland) to the west; northern Africa to the south; and the Black Sea to the east.

Vila (or **Port Vila**) The capital of Vanuatu, on the south-west coast of the South Pacific island of Efate; pop. (1992) 20,000.

Villa, Pancho (born Doroteo Arango) (1878–1923) Mexican revolutionary. He played a prominent role in the revolution of 1910–11 led by Francisco Madero (1873–1913), and together with Venustiano

Carranza (1859–1920) overthrew the dictatorial regime of General Victoriano Huerta (1854–1916) in 1914. Later that year, however, he and Emiliano Zapata rebelled against Carranza and fled to the north of the country after suffering a series of defeats. Villa invaded the USA in 1916 but was forced back into Mexico by the US army. He continued to oppose Carranza's regime until the latter's overthrow in 1920. Villa was eventually assassinated.

Villa-Lobos, Heitor (1887–1959) Brazilian composer. At the age of 18 he visited the Brazilian interior collecting folk music. He later wove this music into many of his instrumental compositions, notably the series of 14 *Chôros* (1920–29), scored in the style of Puccini, and the nine *Bachianas brasileiras* (1930–45), arranged in counterpoint after the manner of Bach. Villa-Lobos was a prolific composer, writing at least 2,000 works; he was also a major force in music education in Brazil, founding the Academy of Music in Rio de Janeiro in 1945 and serving as its president until his death.

villein (from Latin *villanus*, 'villager') A medieval peasant entirely subject to a lord or attached to a manor, similar to a SERF. Both groups were part of the MANORIAL SYSTEM which dominated Europe between the 4th and 13th centuries. Villeins provided labour services to the lord (in return for tilling their own strips of land). By the 13th century villeins in England had become unfree tenants. In Europe they had fewer duties and remained essentially free peasants, creating a significant difference in rank to the serfs. By the 15th century, even in England, social and economic changes had blurred the distinctions between free and unfree peasants, leading to a single enlarged class of peasants.

Villiers See BUCKINGHAM, GEORGE VILLIERS, 1ST DUKE OF.

Villon, François (born François de Montcorbier or François des Loges) (fl. *c.*1460) French poet. He is one of the greatest French lyric poets, best known for *Le Lais* or *Le Petit testament* (1456) and the longer, more serious *Le Grand testament* (1461). He was notorious for his life of criminal excess and spent much time in prison. In 1462 he received the death sentence in Paris; when it was commuted to banishment he left the capital and subsequently disappeared.

Vilnius The capital of Lithuania, a city on the River Neris; pop. (1991) 593,000. Dating from the 10th century, it became capital of the former grand duchy of Lithuania in 1323. It fell to Russia in 1795 and between 1920 and 1939 was held by Poland. Under Russian control again, it was capital of the Lithuanian Soviet Socialist Republic from 1944 until it once more became capital of an independent Lithuania in 1991. The city's university was founded in 1579 and has a stormy history. Vilnius was a leading centre of Jewish culture until the German extermination of its large Jewish population in World War II. It has metallurgical and machine industries, as well as chemicals, textiles, and electrical industries.

Vincent de Paul, St (1581–1660) French priest. He devoted his life to work among the poor and the sick and established a number of institutions to continue his work. In 1625 he established the Congregation of the Mission, an organization (also known as the Lazarists) that now has foundations worldwide. In 1633 Vincent de Paul was one of the founders of the Daughters of Charity (Sisters of Charity of St Vincent de Paul), an unenclosed women's order devoted to the care of the poor and the sick. Feast day, 19 July.

Vinci, Leonardo da See LEONARDO DA VINCI.

Vine, Barbara See RENDELL, RUTH, BARONESS.

Vine, Frederick John (1939–) British geologist. Vine worked at Princeton before returning to Britain as reader in environmental science at the University of East Anglia. Developing the hypothesis of sea-floor spreading, Vine and his colleague Drummond H. Matthews (1931–97) reasoned that new rock formed at a mid-ocean ridge should be magnetized according to the prevailing polarity of the Earth, and that successively older rocks further from the ridge should provide a record of changing polarities. Their demonstration (1963) that magnetic data from the Atlantic Ocean supported this hypothesis was a decisive step in establishing the theory of plate tectonics.

vinegar fly See FRUIT FLY.

Vinland A region of North America, probably on or near the northern tip of Newfoundland, discovered and briefly settled in the 11th century by Norsemen under Leif Ericsson. It was so named from the report that grapevines were growing there.

viol A bowed musical instrument created in the 15th century in southern Spain by applying a bow to the guitar-like vihuela. Viols have six strings tuned in fourths and a third, fretted fingerboards, flat backs, and bellies much less arched than those of violins. The function of the frets was to provide every note with something of the quality of an open-string sound. Viols, irrespective of size, are played *a gamba* (Italian, 'on or between the knees').

viola The alto member of the VIOLIN family. There is no standard size, and body lengths vary from 400 mm to 479 mm (15.5–19 inches). It evolved in the mid-17th century, when it was used in orchestras as mezzo-soprano, alto, and tenor, the size of the instrument suiting the range of the music. The tuning was the same for all three, irrespective of size. The **viola da braccio** and the **viola da gamba** (Italian, 'arm viola' and 'leg viola') are terms that came into use in Italy in the 16th century to distinguish between the violin family (*da braccio*) and the viols (*da gamba*). The **viola d'amore** was an 18th-century instrument roughly of viola size, which had sympathetic strings, and was played on the arm, without frets.

violet A perennial plant of the genus *Viola*, which has over 400 species widely distributed in temperate regions. There are white-, purple-, and yellow-flowered kinds. Several species are sweetly scented, including *V. odorata*, the sweet violet of Europe. Violets give their name to the family Violaceae, which has some 900 species including the genus *Viola*. This family contains annual and perennial species and many natural or artificially induced hybrids, such as the garden pansy. Plants of the violet family are characterized by heart-shaped or kidney-shaped leaves, and flowers with five unequally shaped petals.

violin A bowed stringed musical instrument evolved in Italy late in the 15th century by combining the stringing and size of the treble REBEC with the body of the *lira da braccio* (see LIRA). Adding a fourth string, violins retained the character, most suited to dance music, of the rebecs. Like all Renaissance instruments, violins were made in different sizes, from treble (violin) through three sizes of alto (including contralto and tenor VIOLA), and bass (CELLO), to DOUBLE BASS. In violins, as in most stringed instruments, the exact position of the soundpost, a round stick of pine wedged between the belly and back, is crucial to the vibration of the sound as is that of the bass bar, a block of pine glued lengthwise beneath the foot of the bridge.

violoncello See CELLO.

viper A venomous SNAKE of which there are approximately 170 species. There are two main groups of vipers: the New World PIT VIPERS (including the copperhead and rattlesnakes); and the Old World vipers of the family Viperidae (such as the adder, gaboon viper, and puff adder). They are almost worldwide in distribution but are notably absent from the Australian region. They occur in a wide variety of habitats; most are ground-dwelling, many others live in trees, and relatively few are aquatic. The venom production and injection system is highly developed in these snakes. Long, tubular fangs, through which the venom flows, are stored horizontally (parallel with the roof of the mouth) but rotate to a vertical position as the snake strikes.

Viracocha An ancient Peruvian god and chief deity of the Inca empire, believed to inhabit the depths of Lake Titicaca with his sister-wife Mama Cocha. God of water and all life, creator of the Universe and man. Viracocha, according to one of many variations of the myth, was displeased with his first creation, and destroyed it in a deluge. In his subsequent creation he wandered as a beggar, teaching man the rudiments of civilization. He is depicted with the Sun as a crown, rain as tears, and holding thunderbolts.

Virchow, Rudolf Karl (1821–1902) German physician and pathologist, founder of cellular pathology. He saw the cell as the basis of life, and believed that diseases were reflected in specific cellular abnormalities. He set these views out in *Die Cellularpathologie* (1858), thus giving a scientific basis to pathology. Virchow also worked on improving sanitary conditions in Berlin. He also helped to make Berlin a European centre of medicine.

vireo A bird native to the New World, which makes up some 42 species in the family Vireonidae, all living in forests. Vireos are small birds, 9–15 cm (4–6 inches) long; most are greenish, brownish, or greyish above and paler, usually yellow or white, below. Many species have conspicuous pale eye-stripes and white wing-bars. They feed primarily on insects, but also take some fruit. Most of the 12 species that spend the summer in North America migrate southwards for the winter.

Virgil (full name Publius Vergilius Maro) (70–19 BC) Roman poet. Virgil is one of the most important poets of the Augustan period. His first major work was the *Eclogues*, ten pastoral poems, modelled on those of Theocritus, in which the traditional themes of Greek bucolic poetry are blended with contemporary political and literary themes. His next work, the *Georgics*, is a didactic poem on farming, which also treats the wider themes of the relationship of human beings to nature. His last work was the *Aeneid*, an epic poem modelled on Homer, which relates the wanderings of the Trojan hero Aeneas after the fall of Troy. Virgil's works quickly established themselves as influential classics of Latin poetry.

virginals A musical instrument, strictly, a small member of the harpsichord family with both bridges on the soundboard and strings running parallel with the keyboard, popular from the 15th to the 17th century. The HARPSICHORD has also been called the virginals.

Virginia A state on the Atlantic coast of the USA; area 105,586 sq km (40,767 sq miles); pop. (1990) 6,187,360; capital, Richmond. The largest cities are Virginia Beach, Norfolk, Richmond, Newport News, Chesapeake, and Hampton. Virginia is also known as the Old Dominion State or Mother of Presidents. The site of the first permanent European settlement in North America (1607), Virginia was named in honour of Elizabeth I, the 'Virgin Queen'. It was one of the original 13 states of the USA and is now a leading producer of tobacco, peanuts, apples, tomatoes, timber, and coal. Amongst its chief landmarks are the Blue Ridge Mountains, the Shenandoah River, the historic towns of Jamestown, Williamsburg, and Fredericksburg, and the homes of famous statesmen such as George Washington (Mount Vernon), James Monroe (Ashlawn), Thomas Jefferson (Monticello), Robert E. Lee (Arlington House), and Woodrow Wilson (Staunton).

Virginia creeper A tall deciduous climber that clings to its support by discs at the ends of the branches of branched tendrils. Virginia creepers belong to the same family, Vitaceae, as the grape vine and include some 15 species of the genus *Parthenocissus* in Asia and North America. The true Virginia creeper, *P. quinquefolia*, has three or usually five leaflets to each leaf and is native to central and eastern North America. It has been largely replaced in gardens by the Japanese creeper or Boston ivy, *P. tricuspidata*, native to China and Japan. This is often called Virginia creeper but can be distinguished by its lobed leaves, which are not divided into leaflets.

Virgin Islands A group of about 100 islands in the Caribbean Sea between Puerto Rico and the Lesser Antilles, divided between British and US administration.

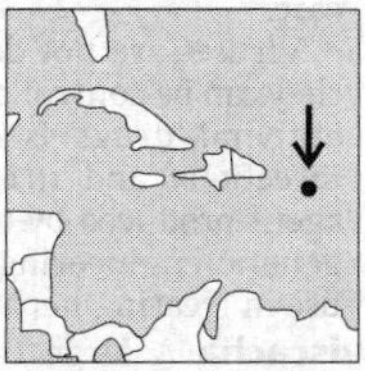

Physical. Saint Croix, Saint Thomas, Saint John, and Tortola are the most important, ranging from 207 sq km (80 sq mi) to 52 sq km (20 sq mi) in area. Most are too small for settlement. They are volcanic in origin and suffer mild earthquakes. The hillsides are grassy and well suited to livestock farming.

History. Although they were visited by Columbus in 1493, effective settlement of the Virgin Islands, primarily by British and Danish planters, did not occur until the 17th century. Descendants of African slaves imported for the sugar plantation economy account for the majority of the population of the islands today. In 1917 Denmark sold its possessions to the USA, which was interested in their strategic value; the **Virgin Islands of the United States** comprises over 50 islands, the largest of which is Saint Croix. The **British Virgin Islands** are a smaller group at the northern end of the Leeward Islands, with Tortola the largest island. From 1872 to 1956 this group was part of the British colony of Leeward Islands, but since 1956 has been administered separately by British governors or administrators who have gradually extended self-government.

Virgin Mary See MARY.

Virgo The Virgin, a CONSTELLATION of the zodiac, and the second-largest constellation of all. In Greek mythology it represents Dike, goddess of justice. Its brightest star is SPICA. Gamma Virginis, named Porrima, consists of a pair of fourth-magnitude yellow stars that orbit each other every 171 years.

virus A minute particle (approximately 20–30

nanometres in size, visible only with an electron microscope) that is capable of infecting a living cell and directing it to make multiple copies of the virus's own components. The host cell may die as a result, as in chickenpox, measles, and influenza, or be transformed in such a way that it multiplies uncontrollably, causing a CANCER. Naked viruses are the simplest, consisting of a nucleic acid, either deoxyribonucleic acid (DNA) or ribonucleic acid (RNA), surrounded by a protective protein layer; they are classified as DNA viruses and RNA viruses. Most viruses, however, including bacteriophages and HIV (human immunodeficiency virus, the cause of AIDS), are more complex and contain a lipoprotein layer surrounding the structure (enveloped viruses), which commonly also have 'spikes' on the outer surface consisting of glycoprotein. These surface proteins are important in infection and may also have antigenic properties, which can be used in active IMMUNIZATION. Enzymes from such viruses have provided key tools for GENETIC ENGINEERING.

Virus particles must enter a cell in order to replicate. Once inside the cell, the nucleic acid is uncovered and inserted into the cell's replicating sites, where viral proteins and nucleic acids are synthesized. After acquisition of the outer membranes, a new virion (fully formed virus) is released ready to infect another cell. DNA viruses and RNA viruses differ in the precise mechanism of replication. Viruses are capable of spontaneous mutation, which alters their genetic structure; this process may make the virus more or less able to cause disease.

Viruses are not destroyed by ANTIBIOTICS, but they can be controlled by VACCINATION. A range of antiviral drugs is effective against some viral infections, and INTERFERON, a natural antiviral agent produced by the body and manufactured by genetic engineering techniques, has found some use in treating hepatitis B and C.

viscacha A large cavy-like RODENT from South America, which belongs to the same family as the chinchillas. The plains viscacha, *Lagostomus maximus*, lives in underground colonies on the Argentinian pampas, emerging at night to feed. The mountain viscachas (*Lagidium* species), of which there are three species, are diurnal and live in rocky country. They have long ears and tails and hop like rabbits. Numbers are declining through human persecution and competition from introduced animals.

Visconti, Luchino (full name Don Luchino Visconti, Conte di Modrone) (1906–76) Italian film and theatre director. Born into an aristocratic family, he became a Marxist and his films reflect his commitment to social issues. He worked for a time with Jean Renoir, the influence of whose naturalistic technique is seen in his first film *Obsession* (1942), which was later regarded as the forerunner of neo-realism. Other notable films include *The Leopard* (1963) and *Death in Venice* (1971). In the theatre Visconti directed many successful dramatic and operatic productions, including works by Jean-Paul Sartre, Jean Cocteau, and Verdi.

viscosity The property of a fluid that determines the ease or difficulty with which it flows. A low viscosity, for example that of a gas, means that the flow through a fine tube will be quite rapid, whereas a high viscosity (as with a thick oil) means that the motion will be sluggish. It manifests itself whenever different parts of a fluid flow at different rates (as in most actual flow), and arises from the INTERMOLECULAR FORCES in the fluid (its 'internal friction'). The stronger these are, the greater the viscosity. If the temperature is raised, the attraction between the molecules is reduced, and so they are able to move more independently of one another. Thus the viscosity of boiling water is only one sixth of the value at the ice point. If two layers of a Newtonian fluid, x distance apart and area A, flow with a relative velocity v, the force between the layers is $\eta Av/x$, where η is the **coefficient of viscosity**. The kinematic viscosity is η/d, where d is the density of the fluid.

Vishnu (Sanskrit, 'all-pervader', 'worker') Originally a minor solar deity but now one of the most important of the deities worshipped by Hindus. Together with BRAHMA the creator and SHIVA the destroyer, Vishnu represents one of the three aspects (trimurti) of Brahman (the Supreme Reality); he is regarded as the preserver of the cosmos and the restorer of moral order, and is said to have appeared in several animal and human earthly incarnations (AVATARS), in particular Rama and Krishna. Vishnu is often portrayed as a blue-skinned youth clad in yellow robes and holding a conch shell, a mace, a disc, and a lotus in his four hands. Vishnu's consort is the goddess of wealth and beauty, Lakshmi. Vaishnavism, the worship of Vishnu, is one of the major forms of modern Hinduism, alongside Shaivism and Shaktism. It is characterized by *bhakti*, or devotion to the god as a means of escape from the cycle of birth, death, and rebirth (SAMSARA).

Visigoth A West Goth, a member of the branch of the Goths who invaded the Roman Empire between the 3rd and 5th centuries and eventually established in Spain a kingdom that was overthrown by the Moors in 711–12.

Vistula (Polish **Wisła**) A river of central Europe that rises in the Carpathians of south-west Poland and flows generally northwards for 940 km (592 miles) before joining the Baltic at Gdansk.

visual binary See BINARY STAR.

visual display unit (VDU) A computer OUTPUT DEVICE that uses a CATHODE-RAY TUBE screen to display information from a computer. Commonly used as a terminal, it is principally designed for text, but most modern types can also be used for GRAPHICS of varying degrees of sophistication. It is an alternative to a computer PRINTER when a permanent record of the output information is not required. In graphics applications, a fast, high-resolution VDU can produce graphical output more quickly than a plotter. Interactive systems and MICROCOMPUTERS now frequently use VDUs.

vitamin A carbon compound needed in small amounts by all organisms for their normal growth and development. Vitamins are a very diverse group of substances, and are not related to each other. Most are needed as COENZYMES in chemical reactions within organisms. Green plants and most microorganisms synthesize their own vitamins, but animals must obtain most types of vitamin in their diets. Two groups of vitamins are distinguished: water-soluble vitamins include the vitamin B complex and vitamin C; and fat-soluble vitamins include vitamins A, D, E, and K. Lack of a vitamin in the diet results in a deficiency disease, for example, scurvy, which results from insufficient vitamin C. Deficiency treatment consists of supplying either the pure vitamin or a food source rich in that vitamin. Excessive intake of vitamins not only does no good but may do harm.

vitamin A (or **retinol**) A fat-soluble vitamin found most plentifully in fish, fish-liver oils, and dairy products, and in a more complex form as carotenoid pigments. It forms an essential part of rhodopsin, the visual pigment in the retina of the eye. This pigment responds to light and initiates impulses in the optic nerve, thus providing the basis of vision. Deficiency in vitamin A leads to poor night vision and to xerophthalmia, a disease in which the conjunctiva becomes dry and liable to infection. Vitamin A cannot be excreted from the body but is stored in the liver; large amounts are toxic and cause an illness which is known as hypervitaminosis A.

vitamin B complex A group of water-soluble vitamins obtained from many foods, but notably yeast, liver, and wheat. Most of them function as COENZYMES. The group includes thiamine (vitamin B_1), riboflavin (vitamin B_2), pyridoxine (vitamin B_6), cobalamins (vitamin B_{12} complex) and niacin (nicotinic acid). Thiamine plays an important role in GLYCOLYSIS and its absence leads to the disease beri-beri. Other B-complex vitamins play similarly important parts in other biochemical reactions throughout the body.

vitamin C (or **ascorbic acid**) A water-soluble vitamin found in citrus fruits and fresh vegetables. Most mammals can synthesize vitamin C, but humans and other primates cannot, and must obtain it from their diet. Its functions include roles in the manufacture of collagen proteins, found in skin, blood vessels, and tendons. Deficiency of the vitamin causes scurvy.

vitamin D (or **calciferol**) A group of fat-soluble vitamins found mainly in dairy products and liver; vitamin D_3 (cholecalciferol) is also produced in the skin following exposure to sunlight. Vitamin D is essential for normal development of the bones, and acts by stimulating calcium and phosphate absorption from the small intestine. Lack of the vitamin in children causes the disease rickets. Like vitamin A, it cannot be excreted and is toxic in large amounts.

vitamin E (or **tocopherol**) A fat-soluble vitamin found principally in wheatgerm and vegetable oils. Its functions in the human body are not fully understood, but it is known to be an ANTIOXIDANT and lack of it is known to cause infertility and wasting of muscle tissue in experimental animals.

vitamin K (or **phylloquinone**) A fat-soluble vitamin present in the leaves of plants and normally produced by some bacteria living in the intestines of humans and other mammals. It is needed for making prothrombin, an essential blood-clotting factor; deficiency leads to defective blood clotting and possible haemorrhage.

Vitellius, Aulus (15–69) Roman emperor. He was acclaimed emperor in January 69 by the legions in Germany during the civil wars that followed the death of Nero. Vitellius defeated his main rival Otho and briefly reigned as emperor but was in turn defeated and killed by the supporters of Vespasian in December of the same year.

Viti Levu The largest of the islands of Fiji in the South Pacific; area 10,429 sq km (4,028 sq miles). Its chief town is Suva, capital of Fiji.

vitrification The formation of glass or a glass-like material, usually by heating. Vitrification is an important step in the SINTERING of most commercial CERAMICS. On heating, a small proportion of the ceramic material melts to form a highly viscous liquid, which draws the ceramic particles together during sintering. On cooling, the viscous phase transforms into a glass, which binds the ceramic together. Glass-ceramics are characterized by a devitrification or crystallization, which occurs on cooling.

Vitruvius (full name Marcus Vitruvius Pollio) (fl. 1st century BC) Roman architect and military engineer. He wrote a comprehensive ten-volume treatise on architecture, largely based on Greek sources. This deals with all aspects of building, including matters such as acoustics and water supply. His influence was considerable, both during his own time and in the Renaissance.

Vitus, St (died *c.*300) Christian martyr. Little is known of his life, but he is said to have been martyred during the reign of Diocletian. He was invoked against rabies and as the patron of those who suffered from epilepsy and certain nervous disorders, including St Vitus's dance (Sydenham's chorea). Feast day, 15 June.

Vivaldi, Antonio (Lucio) (1678–1741) Italian composer and violinist. Throughout his life he worked in an orphanage in Venice as violin teacher and composer, and he composed many of his works for performance there. He emerged as one of the most important Baroque composers. He is best known for *The Four Seasons* (1725) and his surviving operas and solo motets. His other numerous compositions include hundreds of concertos (several of which were later arranged by J. S. Bach) and 73 sonatas. His work has enjoyed a re-evaluation during the 20th century.

Vivekananda, Swami (born Narendranath Datta) (1863–1902) Indian spiritual leader and reformer. He was a disciple of the Indian mystic Ramakrishna and did much to spread his teachings; during his extensive travels he was also responsible for introducing Vedantic philosophy to the USA and Europe. On his return to India in 1897 he founded the Ramakrishna Mission near Calcutta, devoted to charitable work among the poor.

Vladimir I, St (956–1015) Grand Duke of KIEV 978–1015. He was converted to Christianity and married the sister of the Byzantine emperor. By inviting missionaries from Greece into his territories he initiated the Russian branch of the Eastern ORTHODOX CHURCH, which was rapidly established. He was canonized and became the patron saint of Russia.

Vladivostok The principal seaport, cultural centre, and naval base of Russia on the Pacific east coast; pop. (1990) 643,000. It is an eastern terminus of the Trans-Siberian Railway and a base for fishing and whaling fleets. Its industries include oil refining, timber, machinery, and foodstuffs.

Vlaminck, Maurice de (1876–1958) French painter and writer. Largely self-taught, he met Derain and Matisse in the early 1900s and with them became a leading exponent of FAUVISM, painting mainly landscapes. He was later influenced by Cézanne and from about 1908 his colour and brushwork became more subdued. He also wrote novels and memoirs and was a pioneer collector of African art.

VLBI (very long baseline interferometry) A technique for combining signals from widely separated RADIO TELESCOPES in order to study the fine detail of radio sources. Even a large radio telescope has poor RESOLVING POWER compared to that of a small optical telescope, so that long baseline INTERFEROMETRY is used to increase the overall system's resolving power.

Vltava (German **Moldau**) A river of the Czech Republic that rises in the Bohemian Forest and flows *c.*435 km (270 miles) northwards through Prague to join the River Elbe near Melnik.

vocal cords See LARYNX.

vodka The national drink of Poland and Russia, consisting of a spirit distilled from potatoes, barley, or malt. Colourless and almost flavourless, it is drunk neat in Eastern Europe, but usually with orange juice (Screwdriver) or tomato juice (Bloody Mary) in the USA and elsewhere.

Volans The Flying Fish, an inconspicuous CONSTELLATION of the southern sky introduced by the Dutch navigators Pieter Dirkszoon Keyser and Frederick de Houtman in the late 16th century.

volcano A mountain or hill having an opening or openings in the Earth's crust through which lava, cinders, steam, gases, etc., are or have been expelled. They may be active or dormant. Geologists generally group volcanoes into four main types: **cinder cones**, created from gas-charged lava ejected from a single vent and falling as cinders to form a circular or oval cone; **composite volcanoes**, steep-sided symmetrical cones built of alternating layers of lava, ash, and cinders; **shield volcanoes**, built of fluid basaltic lava that slowly creates a massive gently-sloping cone; **lava domes**, formed by viscous lava piling up around a vent. Volcanoes take their name from the Mediterranean island of Vulcan near Sicily, thought in ancient times to be the chimney of the forge of Vulcan, blacksmith of the gods. There are nearly 1,350 active volcanoes in the world, the majority erupting at the boundaries of the Earth's crustal plates. About 60 per cent occur around the Pacific Ocean plate in an area known as the 'Ring of Fire'. The largest active volcano is Mauna Loa on the island of Hawaii.

vole A small RODENT related to hamsters, rats, and mice. Along with the lemmings, they comprise a distinct subfamily (Microtinae), which is distributed throughout the cooler regions of the Northern Hemisphere. About the same size as rats and mice, they can be distinguished by their shorter tails and rounded noses. The largest of the 99 species of vole is the MUSKRAT of America, and the largest Old World species is the WATER VOLE. Both show structural adaptations for an aquatic life.

Volga The longest river in Europe, rising in north-west Russia and flowing 3,531 km (2,194 miles) generally southwards to the Caspian Sea. Navigable for most of its course, it has been linked to the Baltic and the Black Sea to form a major network of trade routes.

Volgograd An industrial city of Russia, a port on the River Volga at the eastern end of the Volga-Don Canal; pop. (1990) 1,005,000. The city was called Tsaritsyn until 1925, and Stalingrad from then until 1961. During World War II it was the scene of a long and bitterly fought battle in 1942–43, in which the German advance in the Soviet Union was halted. Its industries generate hydroelectric power and produce oil, aluminium, textiles, and footwear.

volleyball A handball game played worldwide by two teams of six separated by a net 2.4 m (8 feet) high for men and 2.2 m (7 feet) for women. The court measures 18 m (59 feet) by 9 m (30 feet), and the object is to ground the ball in the opponents' half of the court. The server stands behind the baseline and hits the ball into the opponents' court. A receiver tries to prevent the ball from hitting the ground and passes it to a team-mate, who may then hit it back across the net or set it up for a better-positioned team-mate to hit a winning shot. Opponents meanwhile jump and try to block the return. Only the serving team may score, and the first to gain 15 points (with a lead of two points) wins the set. Matches are decided by the best of three or five sets.

volt (symbol V) The SI UNIT of electric potential, potential difference (p.d.), or e.m.f. A p.d. of 1 volt exists between two points in an electrical conductor if 1 joule of work is done when a charge of 1 coulomb moves between them, or equivalently, if a current of 1 ampere dissipates a power of 1 watt.

Volta A river of West Africa formed in central Ghana by the junction of the headwaters, the Black Volta (Mouhoun), Red Volta (Nazinon), and White Volta (Nakanbe), which rise in Burkina. At Akosombo in south-east Ghana the river has been dammed, creating which is one of the world's largest man-made lakes, completed in 1965. The lake is used for navigation, fishing, irrigation, and the generation of hydroelectric power, which serves the large local aluminium industry.

Volta, Alessandro Giuseppe Antonio Anastasio, Count (1745–1827) Italian physicist. Volta was the inventor of a number of important electrical instruments, including the electrophorus and the condensing electroscope, but is best known for the **voltaic pile** or electrochemical battery (1800) – the first device to produce a continuous electric current. The impetus for this was Luigi Galvani's claim to have discovered a new kind of electricity produced in animal tissue, which Volta ascribed to normal electricity produced by the contact of two dissimilar metals. The unit of electric potential (VOLT) is named after him.

voltaic cell See BATTERY.

voltaic pile See VOLTA, ALESSANDRO GIUSEPPE ANTONIO ANASTASIO, COUNT.

Voltaire (pseudonym of François-Marie Arouet) (1694–1778) French writer, dramatist, and poet. He was a leading figure of the Enlightenment, and frequently came into conflict with the Establishment as a result of his radical political and religious views and satirical writings. He spent a period in exile in England (1726–29) and was introduced there to the theories of Isaac Newton and the empiricist philosophy of John Locke. He also became acquainted with British political institutions, and extolled them as against the royal autocracy of France. Voltaire lived in Switzerland from 1754, only returning to Paris just before his death. Major works include *Lettres philosophiques* (1734) and *Candide* (1758), a satirical tale attacking Leibniz's optimism; he also wrote plays, poetry, and historical works, and was a contributor to the great French *Encyclopédie* (1751–76).

voltmeter A moving-coil or solid-state instrument that measures voltage in an electrical or electronic circuit. Voltmeters are two-terminal devices that, in contrast to AMMETERS, have an extremely high internal resistance. This enables them to take very little current, allowing measurement of the voltage source to be made without disturbing its value.

voluntary organization A non-profit organization operating for the public good. Voluntary organizations range from small local support groups with no paid staff, to large international agencies with paid professionals, such as Save the Children Fund and the World Wide Fund for Nature. Their activities encompass supplying shelters for the homeless, pioneering new services such as hospices for the terminally ill, offering help to people with specific diseases, suicidal tendencies, or marital problems, and campaigning for policy change, such as an end to commercial whaling. Until the 20th century, SOCIAL SERVICES were provided almost entirely by voluntary groups and organizations, often run by religious bodies. In the 20th century their responsibilities have tended to diminish, as the state's have expanded. Scandinavian countries, for example, with well-developed WELFARE STATES, have few voluntary organizations, while most African and Asian countries do not have them, largely because the populace is too poor or uneducated to provide volunteers. In communist countries, voluntary organizations were outlawed on the grounds that the state could meet all needs. The recent trend away from government intervention has led to their growth on the grounds that they can supply services more cheaply than state agencies, give scope for diverse approaches to social problems, harness the sense of social responsibility of unpaid volunteers, and offer choice to service users.

Voluntary Service Overseas (VSO) A British organization founded by Alexander Dickson (1914–) in 1958. Volunteers, such as teachers and doctors, are sent overseas for a two-year period and are provided with accommodation and a living allowance by the host government. VSO pays the air fare and a grant.

von Braun, Wernher Magnus Maximilian See BRAUN, WERNHER MAGNUS MAXIMILIAN VON.

von Frisch, Karl See FRISCH, KARL VON.

Vonnegut, Kurt (1922–) US novelist and short-story writer. His works are experimental in nature and blend elements of realism, science fiction, fantasy, and satire. They include *Cat's Cradle* (1963) and *Slaughterhouse-Five, or The Children's Crusade* (1969), based on the fire-bombing of Dresden in 1945, which Vonnegut himself experienced as a prisoner of war. Among his notable recent writings is the novel *Galapagos* (1985).

von Neumann See NEUMANN.

von Sternberg, Josef See STERNBERG, JOSEF VON.

voodoo A religious practice based in the southern states of the USA, the Caribbean, and Brazil; it is the chief religion of the majority of the people of Haiti. Voodoo was brought to the Caribbean by West African slaves; the name derives from Vodun, 'god', or 'spirit' in the language of the Fon people of Benin. Voodoo combines ANCESTOR WORSHIP and belief in African deities with Roman Catholic elements, dating from the time of colonization. The *loa*, identified as ancestors, saints, or gods, communicate with the individual by spirit possession, during collective worship, presided over by priests or priestesses, which involves song, drumming, ecstatic dance, and ritual sacrifice. Voodoo has become associated in the popular imagination with its use of *obeah*, 'sympathetic' magic practices in which objects or images (such as dolls) are used as substitutes for reality, and beliefs, such as that a sorcerer can raise the corpse of a dead person (*zombi*) to be used as a slave. Such practices are not, however, typical of ordinary voodoo ritualizing. In Haiti the Roman Catholic Church, which for many years denounced voodoo, has come to coexist with it.

Voortrekkers See GREAT TREK.

Vorticism A short-lived British art movement originating just before World War I. The central figure of Vorticism was the artist and writer Wyndham LEWIS, who edited its review – *Blast*. His harsh, angular, mechanistic style was shared by other artists in his circle, among them the sculptors Jacob EPSTEIN and Henri GAUDIER-BRZESKA. Vorticism was strongly influenced by CUBISM and FUTURISM, and the name was coined by the poet Ezra POUND, perhaps in reference to a statement by the Futurist artist Umberto BOCCIONI that all artistic creation must originate in a state of emotional vortex.

Vortigern A legendary 5th-century Romano-British king said by BEDE to have invited HENGIST and Horsa to Britain as mercenaries in an attempt to withstand the raids by the PICTS and the SCOTS. The plan rebounded on Vortigern when Hengist and Horsa turned against him (455) and seized lands in Kent. He was blamed by Gildas for his misjudgement and also for the loss of Britain.

Vosges ►**1** A mountain system of eastern France to the west of the Rhine and separated from the Jura in the south by the Belfort Gap. Its highest peak is the Ballon de Guebwiller (Grand Ballon) which rises to 1,423 m (4,669 ft). ►**2** A department of Lorraine in north-east France; area 5,903 sq km (2,280 sq miles); pop. (1990) 386,260; capital, Épinal.

voting See FRANCHISE.

Voyager Two unmanned US spacecraft designed to explore the GIANT PLANETS. Voyager 1 was launched in 1977 and reached Jupiter in 1979 before using Jupiter's gravitational field to put it on a new trajectory to Saturn, which it reached in 1980. Voyager 1 is now leaving the Solar System. Voyager 2, launched in 1977, reached Jupiter in 1979 before following Voyager 1 to reach Saturn in 1981. It has since passed by Uranus in 1986 and Neptune in 1989. Like Voyager 1 it is destined to leave the Solar System. The Voyager missions have been spectacularly successful in the wealth of new scientific information they have transmitted back to Earth.

VTOL aircraft (Vertical Take-Off and Landing aircraft) An aeroplane capable of taking off and landing without a runway. While HELICOPTERS can be considered as VTOL aircraft, the term is more usually applied to fixed-wing aeroplanes. The most famous development of this principle is the British Aerospace Harrier jump-jet, in which two movable nozzles direct the thrust of its jet engines downwards for take-off.

Vuillard, (Jean) Édouard (1868–1940) French painter and graphic artist. A member of the Nabi Group, he produced decorative panels, murals, paintings, and lithographs; domestic interiors and portraits were his most typical subjects. His early work in particular, with its flat areas of colour, reflects the influence of Japanese prints.

Vulcan (in Roman mythology) An early god of fire and metalworking, identified with Hephaestus in Greek mythology.

Vulcan (in astronomy) A hypothetical planet moving inside the orbit of MERCURY, long searched for by 19th-century astronomers. The existence of Vulcan was assumed to explain the anomalous precession by 43 arc seconds per century of the perihelion of Mercury. Photographic searches, carried out at the beginning of this century, concluded that any object with a Vulcan-type orbit cannot be larger than about 100 km in diameter. However, it is possible that smaller, asteroid-like bodies named **vulcanoids** actually orbit inside Mercury's orbit; they may be best detectable at infrared wavelengths. The anomalous precession of Mercury's perihelion was finally accounted for by Einstein's theory of general RELATIVITY.

vulcanization The reaction of crude rubber with SULPHUR or other suitable agent under intense heat, producing extensive changes in the physical properties of the rubber. Vulcanization results in an increase in cross-linking between the POLYMER molecules in the rubber, which make it more durable and adaptable. The changes in physical properties include decreased plastic flow, reduced surface tackiness, increased elasticity, much greater tensile strength, and considerably less solubility. Recently it has become possible to develop a version of POLYTHENE, which can be vulcanized, giving it increased resistance to deformation.

Vulgate The Latin translation of the Bible adopted by the Council of TRENT (1546) as the official version for the Roman Catholic Church. It was made by St Jerome in the 4th century; it differs from earlier Latin versions in that Jerome translated the Old Testament from Hebrew rather than Greek. The Vulgate formed the basis of the English translation by Ronald Knox (1949).

Vulpecula The Fox, a CONSTELLATION of the northern sky, introduced by the Polish astronomer Johannes Hevelius (1611–87) under the original title of Vulpecula cum Anser, the Fox and Goose.

vulture A bird of which there are 15 species in the HAWK family, Accipitridae, in Africa, Asia, and Europe, and seven American species making up the family Cathartidae. All are heavily built birds, with broad wings and remarkably graceful flight, and a predatory or scavenging habit. LAMMERGEIERS and Andean CONDORS are among the largest, spanning almost 3 m (10 feet) and weighing 4–5 kg (10–12 pounds). The Himalayan GRIFFON VULTURE spans up to 2.8 m (9.2 feet) and weighs a massive 12 kg (26.4 pounds).

Vultures nest in crags or tall trees. Mostly dark-plumaged, they have a generally bare head and neck, a strongly curved beak, a capacious crop and powerful talons. Soaring high on thermals in search of carrion, they follow each other's movements, often landing in flocks to tear a mammal carcass to pieces.

W

Waco A city in central Texas, USA, on the River Brazos; pop. (1990) 103,590. Founded as a ferry-crossing in 1849, it was named after the Waco (Huaco) Indians. In 1993 a ranch near Waco was the scene of a 51-day armed siege in which four government agents and 72 members of the Branch Davidian religious sect were killed. It is a commercial and industrial centre with tyres, glass, and paper manufactures.

Wade, George (1673–1748) British soldier. After serving with distinction in the army in Spain 1704–10, he was posted to the Scottish Highlands in 1724. There he was responsible for the construction of a network of roads and bridges to facilitate government control of the Jacobite clans after the 1715 uprising.

Wade, (Sarah) Virginia (1945–) British tennis player. She won many singles titles, including the US Open (1968), the Italian championship (1971), the Australian Open (1972), and Wimbledon (1977).

wadi A rocky watercourse in North Africa and south-west Asia, dry except in the rainy season.

wading bird (or **wader**) A bird of the order Charadriiformes, which includes the plovers and sandpipers. Typical waders live on the shores of seas, lakes, and rivers, or in marshes, and nest on the ground, and are no larger than thrushes, while the biggest curlews are about 60 cm (2 feet) long including the beak. They are brown, or black and white in colour. They are powerful fliers, many migrating vast distances and, when not breeding, highly gregarious. Their beaks are variously adapted to different ways of collecting food: many of them are very long, for probing mud and sand; some are straight; others curved up or down. In some groups, the legs too are long, to facilitate wading.

In North America these birds are all known as shore birds and the Ciconiiformes are called waders. These are mostly large marsh- and water-birds with long beaks and legs and include herons, storks, ibises, and flamingos.

Wafd (in full **Wafd al-Misri**; Arabic, 'Egyptian Delegation') Egyptian nationalist party. Under the leadership of Zaghlul Pasha it demanded freedom from British rule. When Egypt won nominal independence in 1922, the Wafd demanded full autonomy and control of the SUDAN and the SUEZ CANAL. After 1924 there were frequent Wafdist governments, in conflict with the monarchy. In 1930 the constitution was suspended and Egypt became a royal dictatorship until the Wafdists succeeded in restoring the constitution in 1935. In 1950 the Wafd formed a one-party cabinet and the struggle between King FAROUK and his government intensified. The monarchy fell in 1952 and the new Revolutionary Command Council under Colonel Gamal NASSER dissolved all political parties.

Wagner, (Wilhelm) Richard (1813–83) German composer. He developed an operatic genre, which he called music drama, synthesizing music, drama, verse, legend, and spectacle. In the late 1840s and early 1850s Wagner propounded his theories in a series of essays which polarized European musical opinion for decades. *The Flying Dutchman* (1841) was innovative in using scenes rather than numbers to form the structure. Wagner was forced into exile after supporting the German nationalist uprising in Dresden in 1848; in the same year he began writing the text of *Der Ring des Nibelungen* (*The Ring of the Nibelungs*), a cycle of four operas (*Das Rheingold*, *Die Walküre*, *Siegfried*, and *Götterdämmerung*) based loosely on ancient Germanic sagas. He wrote the accompanying music from 1854 to 1874, during which time he returned to Germany (1860). The *Ring* cycle is notable for its use of leitmotifs and orchestral colour to unify the music, dramatic narrative, and characterization. It was first staged in 1876 at Wagner's new Bayreuth theatre. Other works include the music drama *Tristan and Isolde* (1859), *The Mastersingers of Nuremberg* (1867), the *Siegfried Idyll* (1870) for orchestra, and his last opera *Parsifal* (1882).

Wagram, Battle of (5–6 July 1809) A battle in the NAPOLEONIC WARS fought between the combined French and Italian forces led by NAPOLEON, and the Austrians under the Archduke Charles, at the village of Wagram, near Vienna. Napoleon, determined to offset earlier setbacks, ordered a massive attack on the well-chosen Austrian position. The French, who had been close to defeat, claimed the victory, but their losses outnumbered those of the Austrians. It was followed by the Treaty of Schönbrunn, in which Austria lost territory and agreed to join the CONTINENTAL SYSTEM against Britain.

wagtail A bird of the family Motacillidae, a group of 65 species of birds which also includes the PIPITS. The name is used more specifically for the ten or so species of birds of the genus *Motacilla*, an Old World group of birds. They are mostly small, about 18 cm (7 inches) long including a long tail, though the Indian large pied wagtail, *M. maderaspatensis*, is larger, being 21 cm (8.5 inches) long. Several species are black with white face markings; others are greenish or greyish above with yellow underparts. Most species are primarily insectivorous. Several live in wet or damp areas, and many migrate during the northern winter. They wag their tails as they walk – hence the name.

Wahhabism The doctrine of an Islamic reform movement. Founded by Muhammad ibn 'Abd al-Wahhab (1703–92) in Nejd, Saudi Arabia, it is based on the SUNNI teachings of Ibn Hanbal (780–855), involving puritanism, monotheism and rejection of popular cults, such as the Sufi veneration of saints and tombs, on the grounds that these constitute idolatry. Under the SAUD family, the Wahhabis raided into the Hejaz, Iraq, and Syria, capturing Mecca in 1806. They were crushed by Ottoman forces in a series of campaigns (1812–18), but the SAUD family gradually consolidated its power within the peninsula. The cult was revived by Abd al-Aziz ibn Saud in his bid for power after World War I, but later crushed, as too fanatical, with British help in 1929 at the Battle of Sibilla. Sunni Wahhabism revived after World War II, with the growth of Islamic fundamentalism, and Wahhabi Mujahidin were fierce participants in the Afghan civil war of 1979–89.

Waikato The longest river of New Zealand, flowing north and north-west for 434 km (270 miles) from Lake Taupo at the centre of North Island to the Tasman Sea.

Wailing Wall See WESTERN WALL.

Wain, John (Barrington) (1925–94) British writer and critic. Wain was one of the ANGRY YOUNG MEN of the early 1950s. His first novels, including *Hurry on Down* (1953), are satirical portraits of young people trapped in a stifling middle-class society. He also wrote books of literary criticism, notably *Preliminary Essays* (1957), and poetry characterized by its wit and verbal dexterity. Wain was professor of poetry at Oxford from 1973 to 1978. His later novels include *Young Shoulders* (1982) and *Comedies* (1990).

wait See MINSTREL.

Waitangi The site of a historic house and reserve on the western shore of the Bay of Islands, Northland Region, New Zealand. It was here on 6 February 1840 that the **Treaty of Waitangi** was signed by Maori chiefs and Captain William Hobson representing Queen Victoria. This treaty formed the basis of British annexation of New Zealand. The Treaty House was originally the home of James Busby a pioneer settler who was appointed British Resident in New Zealand in 1832 and the signing of the treaty is celebrated annually as a national holiday (Waitangi Day).

Wajda, Andrzej (1929–) Polish film director. He came to prominence in the 1950s with a trilogy (including *Ashes and Diamonds*, 1958) about the disaffected younger generation in Poland during and after World War II. A recurrent theme in his work is the conflict between individual choice and the march of political events, as in *Man of Iron* (1981), which draws on the early history of the trade-union movement Solidarity, and *Danton* (1983), which traces developments in the French Revolution leading up to the Reign of Terror.

Wakefield The county town of West Yorkshire, England, on the River Calder; pop. (1991) 73,955. A cloth-manufacturing town in medieval times, its modern industrial products include chemicals, textiles, and machinery. The **Battle of Wakefield** (30 December 1460) was fought here in the Wars of the ROSES. The LANCASTRIANS defeated and killed the YORKIST claimant to the throne, Richard, 3rd Duke of York.

Wakefield, Edward Gibbon (1796–1862) British colonial reformer and writer. In 1829 he published his *Letter from Sydney* using information he had obtained while serving a sentence in Newgate gaol in London. Concerned that Australian settlements were failing because land could be acquired so easily, he proposed a 'sufficient price' for land, which would finance the regulated emigration of labourers and oblige them to work to buy their own land. This would give a balanced colonial society and provide some relief to unemployment in Britain. His ideas were taken up and implemented from 1831, with some 70,000 migrants travelling to Australia in the next ten years. In 1837 Wakefield founded the New Zealand Association (later Company). He was largely responsible for the succession of systematic settlements in New Zealand. He wrestled for years for self-government for the colonists, emigrating to New Zealand in 1853.

Wake Island An atoll in the central Pacific Ocean between Hawaii and Guam, comprising the three small islets of Wake, Wilkes, and Peale; area 6.5 sq km (2.5 sq miles). Discovered by Captain William Wake in 1796 and later surveyed by Captain Charles Wilkes, Wake Island was annexed by the USA in 1899. It has been used as a commercial and military air base since 1938 and is administered by the US Department of the Air Force.

Waksman, Selman Abraham (1888–1973) Russian-born US microbiologist. He searched for potential antibiotics in soil microorganisms, discovering the bacterium *Streptomyces griseus* in 1915 and isolating streptomycin from it in 1943. This was developed into the first effective drug against tuberculosis, which became a much less serious public health problem through its use. Waksman was awarded a Nobel Prize in 1952.

Walcott, Derek (Alton) (1930–) St Lucian poet and dramatist. His plays include *Dream on Monkey Mountain* (1967), first staged at the Trinidad Theatre Workshop, which he founded. His poetry, highly charged, vivid, and rhythmical, includes the long epic *Omeros* (1991) based on the Homeric stories and set in his native St Lucia, which won him the Nobel Prize for literature in 1992.

Walden, Paul (1863–1957) Latvian chemist who discovered the inversion reaction named after him. This is a reaction in which a compound showing OPTICAL ACTIVITY can be transformed into its optical isomer. It is of great significance in the theory of the mechanisms of certain reactions.

Waldenses (or **Vaudois**) A Christian religious sect founded by Peter Valdes (died 1217) in the 12th century. Assuming a life of poverty and religious devotion, he founded the 'Poor Men of Lyons' in France. They lived simply and taught from vernacular scriptures. They were persecuted as heretics but survived in southern France and in Piedmont in north-eastern Italy. In 1532 they formed an alliance with the Swiss Reformed Church but were almost destroyed in France, and in 1655 the Piedmontese Waldenses, despite support from Protestant groups, were massacred.

Waldheim, Kurt (1918–) Austrian diplomat and statesman, President 1986–92. He was Secretary-General of the United Nations (1972–81) and, five years later, he stood as the right-wing People's Party candidate for the presidency of Austria; this he secured after a run-off election. During the campaign he denied allegations that as an army intelligence officer he had direct knowledge of Nazi atrocities during World War II; he was subsequently cleared in court of charges relating to his war record.

Wales (Welsh **Cymru**) The western part of Great Britain and a principality of the UNITED KINGDOM.

Physical. Wales measures roughly 225 km (140 miles) from north to south and between 60 and 160 km from west to east, where it borders England. This border region, the Marches, is a stretch of pastureland much broken by hills, woods, and twisting rivers. It rises to the Cambrian Mountains, which stretch down the centre of the country. In the south-east are the Brecon Beacons and coalfields, and in the south-west the Pembroke Peninsula with its rocky coasts. Snowdonia is in the north-west. Wales enjoys an Atlantic maritime climate. Even on the higher peaks snow seldom lies long, for they face the warm westerlies which come in on the NORTH ATLANTIC DRIFT. The water flows into lakes, the largest of which is Bala, and into rivers such as the southward-flowing Towy and Usk. There are deposits of coal and slate and water is an important Welsh resource.

Economy. Coal-mining and steel production were the main economic activities in Wales until the 1980s, when depletion of the coal seams led to closure of most of the mines. Coal mined in South Wales was of extremely high quality and the region was the world's chief exporter of coal in the 19th century. Heavy industry developed close to the mines. In the 1930s unemployment rose dramatically and the government encouraged industrial diversification. There are oil-refining and petrochemical industries, concentrated in South Wales around the deep-water port of Milford Haven. Forestry and farming, especially the rearing of sheep and cattle, have remained important. Tourism is an increasingly significant source of revenue and employment.

History. The population of Wales, which is Celtic in origin, resisted the Romans (who penetrated as far as Anglesey in a campaign against the DRUIDS), and after the departure of the Romans was increased in size by British refugees from the SAXON invaders (*c*.400). By the 7th century Wales was isolated from the other Celtic lands of Cornwall and Scotland. Christianity was gradually spread throughout Wales by such missionaries as St Illtud and St DAVID, but politically the land remained disunited, having many different tribes, kingdoms, and jurisdictions; Gwynedd, Deheubarth, Powys, and Dyfed emerged as the largest kingdoms, one notable ruler being Hwyel Dda (the Good), traditionally associated with an important code of laws.

From the 11th century the Normans colonized and feudalized much of Wales and Romanized the Church, but the native Welsh retained their own laws and tribal organization. There were several uprisings but as each revolt was crushed the English kings tightened their grip. Although LLYWELYN the Great (ruled 1194–1240) recovered a measure of independence, EDWARD I's invasion in 1277 ended hopes of a Welsh state: Llywelyn II was killed in 1282, and in 1301 Edward of Caernavon (EDWARD II) was made Prince of Wales. Thereafter Wales was divided between the Principality, royal lands, and virtually independent marcher lordships. The unsuccessful revolt of Owen GLENDOWER in the early 15th century revived Welsh aspirations, but HENRY VIII, the son of the Welsh HENRY VII, united Wales with England in 1536, bringing it within the English legal and parliamentary systems. Welsh culture was eroded as the gentry and Church became Anglicized, although most of the population spoke only Welsh, given a standard form in the Bible of 1588, until the 19th century. The strong hold of the NONCONFORMISTS, especially of the Baptists and Methodists, made the formal position of the Anglican Church there the dominant question of Welsh politics in the later 19th century, leading to the disestablishment of the Church from 1920. The social unrest of rural Wales, voiced in the Rebecca riots, resulted in significant emigration. The INDUSTRIAL REVOLUTION brought prosperity to South Wales but during the Great DEPRESSION in the 1930s many people lost their jobs. Unemployment was exacerbated by the closure of most of the coalfields by the 1980s and remains a problem despite the introduction of a more diversified industry. Political, cultural, and linguistic nationalism survive, and have manifested themselves in the PLAID CYMRU party, the National Eisteddfod, and Welsh-language campaigns. A Welsh referendum in 1979 voted overwhelmingly against partial devolution from the United Kingdom. A second referendum in 1997 reversed this decision.

Wales, Prince of See CHARLES, PRINCE.

Walesa, Lech (1943–) Polish statesman, President 1990–95. A shipyard worker from Gdańsk, he founded the independent trade union movement SOLIDARITY after a wave of strikes in 1980. Further political agitation led to a total industrial stoppage along the Baltic seaboard, and the government under General Jaruselski was forced to concede the right to organize themselves independently. In 1981 Solidarity was outlawed and Walesa imprisoned. Released in 1982, he forged close links with Pope John Paul II. In 1989 Solidarity was legalized, and in 1990 he was re-elected its chairman. Increasingly on the right wing of the movement and with the full power of the Church behind him, he defeated Tadeusz Mazowiecki in the presidential election of November 1990. Throughout Walesa's term of office, his governments grappled with the economic challenge of moving towards a free-market economy. In December 1995, Walesa was defeated in presidential elections by the former communist Aleksander Kwasniewski.

Walker, Alice (Malsenior) (1944–) US writer and critic. She won international acclaim for *The Color Purple* (1982), an epistolary novel about a young black woman faced with recreating her life after being raped by her supposed father. It won her the Pulitzer Prize and was made into a successful film by Steven Spielberg (1985). Other works include *In Search of Our Mothers' Gardens: Womanist Prose* (1983), a collection of her critical essays, and the novel *Possessing the Secret of Joy* (1992), an indictment of female circumcision.

Walker, John (1952–) New Zealand athlete. He was the first athlete to run a mile in less than 3 minutes 50 seconds (1975) and was also the first to run 100 under-four-minute miles.

walking fern (or **walking leaf**) A fern, *Camptosorus rhizophyllus*, native to North America. Its long, thin fronds taper to points, which readily root themselves to produce new plants. It is unusual among ferns in being adapted to dry conditions: the small plant, which germinates from a spore (the prothallus), is resistant to drought.

walking worm An animal of the phylum Onychophora, with some 65 species, which possibly form the 'missing' link between the soft ANNELID worms and the stiff-legged, cuticle-covered ARTHROPODS. They have legs and a cuticle, yet the body is soft and flexible and the legs are short, stumpy, and unjointed. These little creatures, of which the best known is *Peripatus*, live only in the tropics, on humid forest floors, breathing through tracheae. Their life on land is aided by sticky defensive secretions, and by giving birth to live young.

wallaby One of a diverse assemblage of MARSUPI-

ALS belonging to the KANGAROO family, Macropodidae, but smaller than most kangaroos. They have large hind-feet, strong hind-limbs, and a long tail, and move quickly by jumping. The short-tailed wallaby, or quokka, *Setonix brachyurus*, was once widespread, but is now mostly restricted to two islands off Australia; it is mainly nocturnal, emerging to graze on ground vegetation or browse in the trees after climbing up on to the branches.

The young wallabies are born after a gestation period of a month or so. The single newborn young is very small, about 2.5 cm (1 inch) long. After climbing into the pouch and attaching itself to a teat, the joey remains there for four to six months. It is not weaned until nine or ten months old. The female can mate again the day after birth. If fertilization occurs the resulting embryo develops for a few days but then remains dormant while the pouch is occupied by a previous young. Once the pouch is empty the embryo resumes development and is born 20–25 days later. There are some 36 species of wallabies, including the tammar, *Macropus eugenii*, the spectacled hare, *Lagrostrophus conspicillatus*, and the black wallaby, *Wallabia bicolor*.

Wallace, Alfred Russel (1823–1913) British naturalist, a founder of zoogeography. He independently formulated a theory of the origin of species that was very similar to that of Charles Darwin, to whom he communicated his conclusions. He travelled extensively in South America and the East Indies, collecting specimens and studying the geographical distribution of animals (see WALLACE'S LINE). In 1858 a summary of the joint views of Wallace and Darwin concerning natural selection was read to the Linnaean Society in London, but credit for the theory has been attached somewhat arbitrarily to Darwin.

Wallace, (Richard Horatio) Edgar (1875–1932) British novelist, screenwriter, and dramatist. He is noted for his crime novels, including *The Four Just Men* (1905) and *The Crimson Circle* (1922). Based in Hollywood from 1931, he wrote the screenplay for the film *King Kong*, which was made shortly after his death.

Wallace, Sir William (*c*.1270–1305) Scottish national hero. He was a leader of Scottish resistance to Edward I, defeating the English army at Stirling in 1297. In the same year he mounted military campaigns against the north of England and was appointed Guardian of the Realm of Scotland. After Edward's second invasion of Scotland in 1298, Wallace was defeated at the Battle of Falkirk; he was subsequently captured and executed by the English.

Wallace's Line A boundary line that may be drawn on a map to distinguish between the distinct flora and fauna of south-east Asia and Australasia. The line was originally determined by the naturalist Alfred Russel WALLACE, who noted in his *Malay Archipelago* (1869) that islands to the east of Bali in Indonesia were characterized by an impoverished fauna associated with low rainfall and thorny scrub typical of Australasia while islands to the west had a rich continental fauna associated with high rainfall and tropical vegetation more typical of Asia.

Wallachia (or **Walachia**) A former principality of south-eastern Europe, between the Danube and the Transylvanian Alps, united in 1859 with Moldavia to form Romania.

Wallenberg, Raoul (1912–47) Swedish diplomat. While working as a businessman in Budapest in 1944, he was entrusted by the Swedish government with the protection of Hungarian Jews from the Nazis. Wallenberg helped some 95,000 Jews to escape death by issuing them with Swedish passports. When Soviet forces took control of Budapest in 1945 he was arrested, taken to Moscow, and imprisoned. Although the Soviet authorities stated that Wallenberg had died in prison in 1947, his fate remains uncertain and there were claims that he was still alive in the 1970s.

Waller, Fats (born Thomas Wright Waller) (1904–43) US jazz pianist, songwriter, band-leader, and singer. He composed the songs 'Ain't Misbehavin'' (1928) and 'Honeysuckle Rose' (1929), and was the foremost exponent of the New York 'stride school' of piano playing, which used tenths in the left hand to give a strong bass line.

wallflower A perennial plant of the genera *Cheiranthus* or *Erysimum*, in the mustard family, Cruciferae. The familiar garden varieties in white, yellow, orange, and red have been developed by selective breeding from the European species *C. cheiri*. Although strictly perennial, for garden use they are treated as biennials, being sown in early summer to flower in the spring of the following year. The Siberian wallflower, *E.* × *marshallii*, with yellow or orange flowers, is a hybrid variety which can be treated as a true perennial.

Wallis, Sir Barnes Neville (1887–1979) British inventor. Working for the Vickers company, he pioneered geodetic construction in his designs for the R100 airship (1930) and the Wellington bomber used in World War II. During the war he designed more effective bombs, including the bouncing bomb, used against the Ruhr dams in Germany in 1943. His main postwar work was on guided missiles and supersonic aircraft: he pioneered variable geometry (swing-wing) designs, although these were not fully developed at the time. Altogether he patented more than 140 designs.

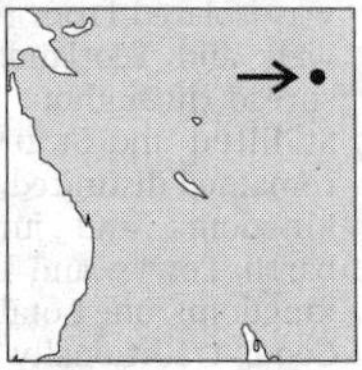

Wallis and Futuna Islands An overseas territory of France comprising two groups of islands (the Iles de Hoorn and the Wallis Archipelago) to the west of Samoa in the central Pacific; area 274 sq km (106 sq miles); pop. (1990) 13,700; capital, Mata-Utu (on Uvea).

Walloonia A French-speaking region of southern Belgium to the south of the Flemish region of Flanders; area 16,841 sq km (6,505 sq miles); pop. (1991) 3,250,000.

Wall Street A street at the south end of Manhattan, New York, where the New York Stock Exchange and other leading US financial institutions are located. The name is used allusively to refer to the US money-market or financial interests. The street is named after a wooden stockade that was built in 1653 around the original Dutch settlement of New Amsterdam.

walnut A tall, deciduous tree, native to southeastern Europe, Central Asia, America, and China, and prized for its dark-coloured timber, used in making furniture. Walnuts belong to the same family as hickories and pecan-nut trees, Juglandaceae, and include 15 species of the genus *Juglans* from America and Asia. The irregularly shaped, wrinkled nut of the common, English, or Persian walnut, *J. regia*, is contained in a hard shell, which in turn is surrounded by a fleshy green layer. High in protein (18 per cent) and fat (60 per cent), these nuts are commercially produced in China, southern Europe, and California, where they are preferred to the stronger flavoured, exceedingly hard-shelled nuts of the native American black walnut, *J. nigra*.

Walpole, Horace, 4th Earl of Orford (1717–97) British writer and Whig politician, son of Sir Robert WALPOLE. He wrote *The Castle of Otranto* (1764), which is regarded as one of the first Gothic novels. Walpole is also noted for his contribution to the Gothic revival in architecture, converting his Strawberry Hill home at Twickenham, near London, into a Gothic castle (*c.*1753–76). He served as an MP from 1741 to 1767.

Walpole, Sir Hugh (Seymour) (1884–1941) British novelist, born in New Zealand. His third novel, *Mr Perrin and Mr Traill* (1911), reflects his experiences as a schoolmaster. He is best known for *The Herries Chronicle* (1930–33), a historical sequence set in the Lake District.

Walpole, Sir Robert, 1st Earl of Orford (1676–1745) British Whig statesman, First Lord of the Treasury and Chancellor of the Exchequer 1715–17 and 1721–42. Walpole is generally regarded as the first British Prime Minister in the modern sense, having presided over the Cabinet for George I and George II during his second term as First Lord of the Treasury and Chancellor. His period of office was marked by peace and considerable prosperity, although Walpole failed to prevent war with Spain in 1739. He was the father of Horace WALPOLE.

walrus A species of SEAL, *Odobenus rosmarus*, which is the sole member of the family Odobenidae. Walruses are found in shallow water round the circumpolar Arctic coasts. Like sea lions, they are able to bring their hind-limbs forward underneath their body, enabling them to move on land. Adult males may reach a length of 3.7 m (12 feet); females are a little smaller. The head is somewhat square in profile, the eyes are small, and external ears are absent. Tusks (the upper canine teeth) are present in both sexes, and grow throughout the life of the animal, sometimes reaching a length of 1 m (3.25 feet) in the male. They are used to dig for clams and other molluscs in the sea-bed. The female reaches sexual maturity at six years and the male a year or two later. Pregnancy occurs probably in every second or third year. Gestation lasts about a year and the young is born in April or May. Walruses still provide much of the meat eaten by Eskimos, but are the subject of conservation measures.

Walsall An industrial town in the west Midlands of England, north-west of Birmingham; pop. (1991) 171,000. During the 17th century it became a noted centre for the manufacture of locks and keys.

Walsingham Either of two villages (Great and Little Walsingham) in Norfolk, east England. Little Walsingham was at one time the most important place of pilgrimage in England; the Shrine of Our Lady of Walsingham commemorated a vision of the Virgin Mary seen here during the reign of Edward the Confessor. The shrine was destroyed in 1538. Part of the Priory and an Anglican shrine still exist.

Walsingham, Sir Francis (*c.*1530–90) English politician. From 1573 to 1590 he served as Secretary of State to Queen Elizabeth I. He developed a domestic and foreign spy network that led to the detection of numerous Catholic plots against Elizabeth I and the gathering of intelligence about the Spanish Armada. In 1586 Walsingham uncovered a plot against Elizabeth involving Mary, Queen of Scots; he subsequently exerted his judicial power to have Mary executed.

Waltham Forest An outer residential borough of Greater London, south-east England, created in 1965 by the merger of the municipal boroughs of Chingford, Leyton, and Walthamstow; pop. (1991) 203,400.

Walton, Ernest Thomas Sinton (1903–95) Irish physicist. In 1932 he succeeded, with Sir John Cockcroft, in splitting the atom. See COCKCROFT.

Walton, Izaak (1593–1683) English writer. He is chiefly known for *The Compleat Angler* (1653; largely rewritten, 1655), which combines practical information on fishing with folklore, interspersed with pastoral songs and ballads. He also wrote biographies of John Donne (1640) and George Herbert (1670).

Walton, Sir William (Turner) (1902–83) British composer. He lived for a time with the Sitwells, and gained fame with *Façade* (1921–23), a setting of poems by Edith Sitwell for recitation. The work of Stravinsky and Hindemith strongly influenced his Viola Concerto (1928–29). Other works include two symphonies, two operas, the oratorio *Belshazzar's Feast* (1930–31), and film scores for adaptations of three Shakespeare plays and for *The Battle of Britain* (1969).

waltz A dance derived from an old Austrian-German peasant dance, the *Ländler*; it first gained popularity in the early 19th century and still exists in the late 20th century in various versions. It was originally a fast dance in 3/4 or 3/8 time with a marked accent on the first beat. Over the years the tempo decreased, although the 'Viennese Waltz', as in the works of the STRAUSS family, has retained much of the earlier fast style. In ballet (and musicals) it is often used as a romantic dance, as in the Tchaikovsky ballet *Swan Lake*.

Walvis Bay The principal port and fishing centre of Namibia on the Atlantic coast of south-west Africa; pop. (1980) 25,000. Formerly part of a British enclave in German South West Africa visited by whalers and fishermen, it was later administered by South Africa as part of Cape Province. In 1994 the South African government transferred the port and offshore Penguin Islands to Namibia. Walvis Bay is linked to the interior by rail.

Wandsworth A largely residential inner borough of Greater London, England, south of the River Thames; pop. (1991) 237,500. It includes the suburbs of Battersea Park, Putney Heath, and Streatham.

Wangaratta A town in the state of Victoria, south-east Australia, at the junction of the Ovens and King rivers; pop. (1991) 15,980. Its industries produce textiles and computer supplies and its air museum (Drage Airworld Museum) houses one of the world's largest collections of flying antique civil aircraft.

Wankel engine See ROTARY ENGINE.

wapiti See RED DEER.

Warbeck, Perkin (1474–99) Flemish claimant to the English throne. Encouraged by Yorkists in England and on the Continent, he claimed to be Edward II's son Richard, Duke of York (who had disappeared in 1483 – see PRINCES IN THE TOWER), in an attempt to overthrow Henry VII. After a series of attempts to enter the country and begin a revolt he was captured and imprisoned in the Tower of London in 1497; he was later executed.

warble fly See BOT FLY.

warbler Any of a wide variety of small, insectivorous birds. The Sylviidae or Old World warblers form a very large family, including about 552 species, a few of which, despite the name, occur in the New World. Most are small, measuring 15 cm (6 inches) or less, though a few are a little larger.

They are usually dull-coloured in browns, greens, and muted yellows, though the so-called scrub warblers of the genus *Sylvia* are quite brightly patterned with black and rich orange-browns. Many of the species which breed in temperate regions migrate southwards for the winter. The group includes the blackcap, chiffchaff, sedge warbler, white-throat, willow warbler, and wood warbler.

The Australian warblers include scrub-wrens and thornbills, and comprise a family (Acanthizidae) of about 68 species, the majority from Australia and New Guinea. Most species are small, dull green, grey, or brown in colour. The New World warblers, or wood warblers, family Parulidae, comprise a group of 115 species, restricted to the New World, the members of which are often brightly marked with yellow, white, orange, red, or blue. They live in a wide range of habitats from forest to bushy grassland. Most of those which breed in North America migrate south to warmer areas for the winter.

Warburg, Aby (Moritz) (1866–1929) German art historian. From 1905 he built up a library in Hamburg dedicated to preserving the classical heritage of Western culture. It became part of the new University of Hamburg in 1919; four years after his death it was transferred to England and housed in the Warburg Institute (part of the University of London).

Warburg, Otto Heinrich (1883–1970) German biochemist. He pioneered the use of the techniques of chemistry for biochemical investigations, especially for his chief work on intracellular respiration. He devised a manometer for this research, enabling him to study the action of respiratory enzymes and poisons in detail. Warburg was awarded a Nobel Prize in 1931, but the Hitler regime prevented him from accepting a second one in 1944 because of his Jewish ancestry.

war crimes Certain activities in war that violate the rules governing the established rules of warfare, as set out in the Hague and GENEVA CONVENTIONS. In most societies, such activities as the killing of prisoners, their torture or enslavement, hostage-taking, and the deportation and killing of civilians are deemed to be war crimes. Present-day attitudes to war crimes have been influenced by the trials at Nuremberg and Tokyo in 1945–46 of German and Japanese wartime leaders. In the course of these proceedings, it was made clear that an individual was to be held responsible for his or her actions even if carrying out the orders of a higher authority. During the Vietnam War (1964–75), US soldiers were indicted on charges of killing civilians; and Iraq's hostage-taking and maltreatment of prisoners during its occupation of Kuwait (1990–91) also led to calls for those responsible to be tried for war crimes. A war crimes tribunal of the INTERNATIONAL COURT OF JUSTICE, the principal judicial organ of the UNITED NATIONS, was convened in 1993 to try people accused of war crimes committed during the conflict in BOSNIA-HERCEGOVINA.

Ward, Mrs Humphry (née Mary Augusta Arnold) (1851–1920) British writer and anti-suffrage campaigner. The niece of Matthew Arnold, she is best known for several novels dealing with social and religious themes, especially *Robert Elsmere* (1888). Although she supported higher education for women, she was an active opponent of the women's suffrage movement, becoming the first president of the Anti-Suffrage League in 1908.

Ward, Sir Joseph George (1856–1930) New Zealand statesman. A minister of the first and successive Liberal cabinets, he was noted for the provision of low-interest credit to farmers. As Prime Minister (1906–12) and in coalition with William Massey (1915–19) he supported empire unity. He won office as Prime Minister again in 1928 as head of the United Party, partly on his reputation as a 'financial wizard', but failed to solve the crises brought on by the Great DEPRESSION.

Warhol, Andy (born Andrew Warhola) (1928–87) US painter, graphic artist, and film-maker of Czech extraction. In 1962 he achieved notoriety when he exhibited stencilled pictures of Campbell's soup cans and sculptures of Brillo soap-pad boxes, rapidly becoming the most famous figure in US POP ART. He was opposed to the concept of a work of art as a piece of craftsmanship and turned out his works like a manufacturer, calling his studio 'The Factory'. From 1965 he concentrated on film-making – his later films gained widespread attention because of their voyeuristic concentration on sex.

Warlock, Peter (born Philip Arnold Heseltine) (1894–1930) British composer, critic, and author. His compositions consist mainly of songs, notable for their sensitive response to the English language. He founded the magazine *The Sackbut* (1920) and wrote about and edited Tudor and Jacobean music. His best-known instrumental work is the collection of dances the *Capriol Suite* (1926), and there is a *Serenade* (in honour of Delius) for strings (1921–22).

warlord Chinese regional military ruler of the first half of the 20th century. Following the death of Yuan Shikai in 1916, China was divided among many local rulers, who derived their power from control of personal armies. In origin, the warlords were mostly former soldiers of the imperial and republican armies, bandits, or local officials. They depended on revenue from towns and agricultural areas in their own spheres of influence to feed the well-equipped troops with which they sought to establish their primacy over local rivals. The most successful generally controlled easily defended areas, and the largest of the many wars between rival cliques of warlords witnessed the mobilization of hundreds of thousands of soldiers. CHIANG KAI-SHEK's Nanjing government (1928–37) re-established central authority over most warlord areas, but military rulers persisted in the far west of China into the 1940s.

warning coloration The conspicuous colour patterns used by well-defended animals to advertise to predators that they are not worth attacking or eating. Warning coloration is a form of PROTECTIVE COLORATION particularly widespread amongst insects, though the distinctive black and yellow banded pattern of the South American ARROW-POISON FROG is a striking example. Although some predators have an instinctive aversion to warning colour patterns, most have to learn the association between the colour pattern and the animal's defence. It is thought that prey species use such gaudy warning colour patterns because they are easier for predators to learn, and are less easily confused with the appearance of palatable prey. In many cases, warning coloration is so effective at deterring predators that other species have evolved similar colour patterns in order to gain the same protection from experienced predators through MIMICRY, even though they may actually be quite harmless.

War of 1812 (1812–15) A war between Britain and the USA. US frustration at the trade restrictions imposed by Britain in retaliation for Napoleon's CONTINENTAL SYSTEM, together with a desire to remove British and Canadian obstacles to US westward expansion, led the US Congress to declare war on Britain (June 1812). The USA–British North American (Canadian) border was the main theatre of war. In July, the US General, William Hull, advanced into Upper Canada, but in early August withdrew to Detroit, which was soon after captured by Major-General Isaac Brock. In October 1812 a second invading US force crossed the Niagara River and stormed Queenston Heights, but it too was driven back by a British force, under Brock, who was killed. In October 1813 another US army under General William Harrison won the Battle of the THAMES, in southwestern Ontario. In November US troops were defeated by a much smaller British force at Crysler's Farm on the St Lawrence. In July 1814, at the Battle of Lundy's Lane, a US force under General Jacob Brown briefly fought at night a British force under General Drummond and then withdrew, after which no more attempts were made to invade Canada. On Lake Erie in September 1813 a US force captured a British squadron of six ships, while the following year (September 1814), in a similar victory on Lake Champlain, a British squadron of 16 ships was forced to surrender. At sea US warships won a series of single-ship engagements, but they were unable to disrupt the British naval blockade, which by 1814 was doing considerable harm to the US economy. In June 1814 a British expenditionary force landed in Chesapeake Bay, Virginia, marching north and burning the new city of Washington. War-weariness now brought the two sides to the conference table and in December 1814 the Treaty of GHENT was signed, restoring all conquered territories to their original owners.

warp The longitudinal threads in woven fabrics, as opposed to the lateral WEFT. Warp threads are subject to high tension and frequent abrasion during weaving on a LOOM. They are also highly stressed during TEXTILE finishing processes. For these reasons, YARNS to be used as warp are generally tightly twisted to give strength and are sized to resist abrasion.

Warren, Earl (1891–1974) US judge. During his time as Chief Justice of the US Supreme Court (1953–69) he did much to promote civil liberties, achieving the prohibition of segregation in US schools in 1954. He is also remembered for heading the commission of inquiry (known as the **Warren Commission**) held in 1964 into the assassination of President Kennedy; the commission found that Lee Harvey Oswald was the sole gunman, a decision that has since been much disputed.

Warren, Robert Penn (1905–89) US poet, novelist, and critic. An advocate of New Criticism, he collaborated with the US critic Cleanth Brooks in writing such critical works as *Understanding Poetry* (1938) and *Understanding Fiction* (1943). Warren also wrote several novels, including *All the King's Men* (1946), and many volumes of poetry; he became the first to win Pulitzer Prizes in both fiction and poetry categories and in 1986 he was made the first US Poet Laureate.

Warrington An industrial town on the River Mersey in Cheshire, England; pop. (1991) 82,812. It was developed as a new town in 1968. It is noted for soap making, brewing, and its new high technology industries.

Warrnambool A coastal resort and former whaling town in the state of Victoria, south-east Australia, situated on Lady Bay south-west of Melbourne; pop. (1991) 23,950. Its Maritime Village is a leading historic landmark of the state.

Warrumbungle National Park A national park on the western slopes of the Great Dividing Range in New South Wales, Australia. Situated 490 km (306 miles) north-west of Sydney, the park protects a diverse scenery stretching from low-lying forest to high peaks covered with snow gums.

Warsaw (Polish **Warszawa**) The capital of Poland, on the River Vistula, and one of Europe's great historical cities; pop. (1990) 1,655,660. Capital of Poland since 1586, the city was systematically razed to the ground (see WARSAW UPRISINGS) with the loss of 700,000 lives during World War II, but has been painstakingly rebuilt. Warsaw is a major cultural centre; it has a university founded in 1818 and the Polish Academy of Sciences. Amongst its chief industries are the manufacture of steel, vehicles, medicines, scientific instruments, and confectionery.

Warsaw Pact A treaty of mutual defence and military aid signed in Warsaw on 14 May 1955 by Communist states of Eastern Europe under Soviet leadership. Established during the era of the Cold War in response to the creation of NATO, it began to break up in 1968 when Albania left and was finally dissolved in February 1991 following the collapse of the Communist system in the Soviet Union and Eastern Europe.

Warsaw Uprising ▶1 A Jewish uprising (February 1943) in Warsaw during World War II. In 1940 the German occupying forces had established a ghetto for 400,000 Jews. After the murder of some 300,000 Jews in Treblinka concentration camp, the remaining 100,000 Jews staged an uprising in which many Germans and Ukrainians were killed. The Germans finally overcame these Jews, put them to death, and razed the ghetto to the ground. **▶2** A Polish insurrection (August–October 1944) in Warsaw in World War II, in which Poles tried to expel the German Army before Soviet forces occupied the city. As the Red Army advanced, Soviet contacts in Warsaw encouraged the underground Home Army, supported by the exiled Polish government in London, to stage an uprising. Polish resistance troops led by General Tadeusz Komorowski gained control of most of the city against a weak German garrison. Heavy German air-raids lasting 63 days preceded a strong German counterattack. The Soviet Army reached a suburb of the city but failed to give help to the insurgents, or allow the western Allies to use Soviet air bases to airlift supplies to them. Supplies ran out and on 2 October the Poles surrendered. The Germans then systematically deported Warsaw's population and destroyed what was left of the city itself. The main body of Poles that supported the Polish government in exile was thus destroyed, and an organized alternative to Soviet political domination of the country was eliminated enabling the Soviet-sponsored Polish Committee of National Liberation to impose a Communist Provisional Government on Poland (1 January 1945) without resistance.

warship A vessel specifically built or adapted for use in war. The earliest types for which there is evidence were Egyptian warships that combined sail and oar propulsion. Around the 2nd millennium BC in the eastern Mediterranean the ram became the major weapon. The oared GALLEY used in this style of fighting was developed further by the Greeks. The galley remained the standard Mediterranean warship until about the 6th century AD, when rams were abandoned. However, the use of oared galleys, later armed with guns, continued in the Mediterranean into the 16th century and beyond.

In northern Europe, the oared, rowing and sailing VIKING SHIP was gradually replaced by vessels with 'castles' in the bow and stern to provide platforms from which fire could be directed against enemy ships. During the 15th century the three-masted, square-rigged ship spread throughout Europe, and from about 1500 ships began to carry CANNON in their hulls. In the Anglo–Dutch war of 1650 the cannon became the ship's main weapon. Thereafter, warships were divided into SHIPS of the line and smaller scouting and auxiliary vessels. With the introduction of steam propulsion and iron ships in the 19th century, armoured IRONCLADS and later BATTLESHIPS replaced the largest wooden warships. Breech-loading guns superseded cannon, and development of the TORPEDO led to the building of TORPEDO-BOATS, as a counter to which the DESTROYER was introduced. By 1900 the first practicable SUBMARINES were being built, and during World War I the AIRCRAFT CARRIER first appeared. After World War II a new type of naval warfare emerged, based on the use of aircraft, submarines, and MISSILES. Important new ship types were guided-missile destroyers, anti-submarine frigates, and specialized amphibious assault craft. Modern naval warfare is highly dependent on electronic equipment, warning and detection systems being as important as the actual weaponry and its guidance systems.

Wars of Religion, French A series of political conflicts in France that took place intermittently between 1562 and 1598. They revolved around the noble families fighting for control of the expiring Valois dynasty, supported on one side by the Huguenots and on the other by the Catholics. After the ST BARTHOLOMEW'S DAY MASSACRE (1572) a party of moderate Catholics emerged led by the Montmorency family. However when the Bourbon Huguenot leader Henry of Navarre became heir to the throne in 1584, the Catholic Holy League grew increasingly militant. The resulting war of 1585–89 ended with Henry of Navarre defeating the Holy League and driving its Spanish allies out of the country. Adopting Catholicism, he became king, as Henry IV, and by the Edit of NANTES (1598) established religious toleration.

wart A benign skin growth caused by infection with the human papillomavirus (a few of which can cause cancer). Common warts often occur on the hands and will disappear spontaneously. **Plantar warts** (or **verrucas**) occur on the feet and can be tender. Warts can be treated with lactic acid or salicylic acid or by cryotherapy with liquid nitrogen.

wart hog See PIG.

wart snake An aquatic snake, the habitat of which ranges from south-east Asia to northern Australia. They comprise a family, Acrochordidae, of two genera (*Acrochordus* and *Chersydrus*) and three species, having robust bodies covered with small, wart-like scales. They are non-venomous, mainly nocturnal forms, that eat fish and give birth to live young. The largest species, the Javan file snake, or elephant-trunk snake, grows to about 2.5 m (8.2 feet) and has peculiarly baggy skin which is known, in the leather trade, as karung.

Warwick The county town of Warwickshire in central England, on the River Avon; pop. (1991) 22,476. Founded in Saxon times, it developed around the great castle of the Earls of Warwick and was largely rebuilt after a fire in 1694. It has a university founded in 1965.

Warwick, Richard Neville, Earl of (known as 'the Kingmaker') (1428–71) English statesman. During the Wars of the Roses he fought first on the Yorkist side, helping Edward IV to gain the throne in 1461. Having lost influence at court he then fought on the Lancastrian side, briefly restoring Henry VI to the throne in 1470. Warwick was killed at the Battle of Barnet.

Warwickshire A midland county of England; area 1,980 sq km (765 sq miles); pop. (1991) 477,000; county town, Warwick. Warwickshire is divided into five districts.

Wash, the An inlet of the North Sea on the east coast of England between Norfolk and Lincolnshire. It receives the Nene, Ouse, Welland, and Witham rivers. Much adjacent land has been reclaimed by dyking and drainage.

washing powder See DETERGENT; SOAP.

Washington A Pacific state of the USA; area 176,479 sq km (68,139 sq miles); pop. (1990) 4,866,690; capital, Olympia. The largest cities are Seattle, Spokane, and Tacoma. Washington is also known as the Evergreen or Chinook State. Occupied jointly by Britain and the USA in the first half of the 19th century, it became the 42nd state of the union in 1889. The state is a major producer of timber, fruit, vegetables, wheat, livestock, fish, and hydroelectric power. Its chief landmarks are Mount Rainier, Mount St Helens, the Coulee Dam, North Cascades National Park, and the Whitman Mission and Fort Vancouver National Historic Sites.

Washington, Booker T(aliaferro) (1856–1915) US educationist. An emancipated slave, he pursued a career in teaching and was appointed head in 1881 of the newly founded Tuskegee Institute in Alabama for the training of black teachers. Washington emerged as a leading commentator for black Americans at the turn of the century and published his influential autobiography, *Up from Slavery*, in 1901. His emphasis on vocational skills and financial independence for blacks rather than on intellectual development or political rights, combined with his support for segregation, brought harsh criticism from other black leaders.

Washington, DC The capital and administrative centre of the USA, coterminous with the District of Columbia; pop. (1990) 606,900. Named after George Washington, in whose presidency it was founded, the city was established in 1790 on land ceded to Congress by Maryland and Virginia. It was planned and partly laid out by a French engineer, Major Pierre Charles L'Enfant, whose work was completed by Major Andrew Ellicott and Benjamin Banneker. Its famous buildings include the Congress building, the Washington Monument and Lincoln Memorial, the Smithsonian Institution, the National Gallery of Art and other museums, the Pentagon, and the White House. Washington is a major cultural centre with five universities and many attractions for the millions of tourists. Its main activity is government service but there are also many business and financial institutions.

Washington, George (1732–99) US soldier and statesman, 1st President of the USA 1789–97. After serving as a soldier 1754–59 in the war against the French, Washington took part in two of the three Continental Congresses held by the American colonies in revolt against British rule (1774 and 1775), and in 1775 was chosen as commander of the army raised by the colonists, the Continental Army. He served in that capacity throughout the

War of Independence, bringing about the eventual American victory by keeping the army together through the bitter winter of 1777–78 at Valley Forge and winning a decisive battle at Yorktown (1781). Washington chaired the convention at Philadelphia (1787) that drew up the American Constitution, and two years later he was unanimously elected President, initially remaining unaligned to any of the newly emerging political parties but later joining the Federalist Party. He served two terms, following a policy of neutrality in international affairs, before declining a third term and retiring to private life.

wasp A carnivorous insect of the order Hymenoptera. In common usage, the name refers specifically to species of the family Vespidae, which are stinging insects usually with black and yellow warning colours. These are also known as social wasps, and include HORNETS; they overwinter as queens, which often hibernate in houses. They make horizontal combs from chewed-up wood, with a surrounding case of paper and a hole at the bottom. The young are fed on masticated insects and, when the first workers emerge, the queens devote themselves to reproduction while the workers forage and enlarge the nest. New queens and males appear in the autumn and mate before the males die off. The old queen also dies when the cold weather starts, and the colony breaks up.

Solitary wasps of other families may show the beginnings of a social life or, such as MASON WASPS, may lead a totally solitary life. The largest suborder of the Hymenoptera is made up of the parasitic wasps, which are known as ICHNEUMON FLIES.

waste management The disposal or utilization of solid or semi-solid wastes. In most Western countries, economic and population growth has resulted in greatly increased amounts of waste. The most common methods of waste disposal in modern times have been sanitary landfill and incineration. Landfill disposal involves dumping and compacting waste in large pits on specially prepared sites. Landfill has been widely used because of its low cost, but the increasing scarcity of suitable sites has increased landfill costs in urban areas. Incineration of waste greatly reduces the volume of material to be disposed of, and the heat generated can be used in DISTRICT HEATING systems: disadvantages are capital and fuel costs, and the pollution caused by incinerator gases. The production of refuse-derived fuel (RDF), made by initial separation of combustible material followed by formation of pellets or **briquettes** is energy-efficient. Up to 40 per cent of domestic waste (mainly metals, glass, and fibrous materials for PAPER MANUFACTURE) could be recycled, although few schemes achieve this in practice. Organic waste can be made into compost, or fermented to produce ethanol or methane. Pilot waste management schemes have been set up that separate waste into several fractions, and process each by a different method.

The disposal of **radioactive waste** material poses special problems as some such wastes will remain radioactive for thousands of years. High-level waste, such as spent NUCLEAR FUELS, need to be stored for years by the nuclear power stations that produce them before disposal. Intermediate-level waste from processing plants is solidified, mixed with concrete, and finally disposed of in concrete chambers in deep mines or below the sea. Low-level wastes, contaminated by traces of radioactivity, are disposed of in the UK by a special company (Nirex Ltd), who bury it in steel drums in concrete lined trenches.

watch A portable instrument for measuring time, usually strapped to the wrist, carried in the pocket, or suspended from the neck. Although portable CLOCKS appeared in the 16th century, pocket or 'fob' watches only became practicable in the late 17th century, with the advent of the coiled spring drive and balance-spring regulator. Many watches incorporated a repeating mechanism, striking the hours and quarter-hours. Watches remained a luxury until 1868, when G. F. Rosskopf, in Switzerland, introduced cheap watches of simplified design. Wrist-watches appeared in the 1880s, originally in response to the demands of fashion. Self-winding watches, responding to movements of the wearer's wrist, appeared in the early 1920s. In the early 1960s electronic watches were introduced, and in 1969 the first quartz electronic watches were manufactured. In the quartz watch, an electronic circuit produces electrical oscillations of precise frequency, which are controlled by the vibrations of a quartz crystal with extreme accuracy. These oscillations are counted and used to advance the hands on a traditional watch face or a digital LIQUID CRYSTAL display once every second. Digital watches often include other functions, such as day and date, stop-watch, and alarm.

water (H_2O) The normal oxide of hydrogen, which covers nearly three-quarters of the Earth's surface and is present in varying degrees in the atmosphere. Pure water freezes at 0°C (32°F), has its maximum density at 4°C (39.2°F), and boils at 100°C (212°F), becoming a gas (steam). Water is remarkable for its heat capacity, chemical stability, and solvent action. The water molecule is a polar molecule – the oxygen atom having a partial negative charge and the hydrogen atoms a partial positive charge. HYDROGEN BONDS between molecules are the cause of some of its unusual properties. For most substances, the solid form is denser than the liquid form. However, ice is less dense than water. As water is cooled below 4°C the hydrogen bonds organize the water molecules into a partially ordered structure in which they are further apart than they are in liquid water at higher temperatures. This structure is fixed once the water freezes, giving ice, which being less dense than water floats on water.

Water is a neutral oxide, forming hydroxides and hydrogen with electropositive metals and acids with non-metallic oxides. Natural water, such as RAIN, is never pure but always contains dissolved substances. Limestone accounts for the HARDNESS OF WATER underground. The most abundant source, seawater, requires desalination before it can be used for drinking, irrigation, or industrial purposes. Of the estimated 1.43×10^{21} kg of water on Earth, 97.4 per cent is in the ocean, 2.0 per cent in the ice-caps, and only 0.6 per cent as fresh water. Rivers return 3.7×10^{16} kg/year of water to the ocean.

Heavy water is water in which one or both of the hydrogen atoms is replaced by an atom of DEUTERIUM. The physical properties of heavy water differ from those of ordinary water because the deuterium atoms are heavier than hydrogen atoms. Heavy water has a higher freezing-point and a higher boiling-point (3.81°C or 38.85°F and 101.42°C or 214.55°F, respectively) and is more viscous. Heavy water is capable of absorbing energy and is therefore used as a moderator in NUCLEAR REACTORS.

water bear (or **tardigrade**) A tiny freshwater animal of the phylum Tardigrada, with a short, plump body and four pairs of stumpy legs. Most of the 350 species live in the water-film surrounding mosses and lichens, although a few species live in marine or freshwater habitats. The terrestrial species have a remarkable capacity to survive drought by shrivelling up completely. As soon as it rains again they revive, and resume their feeding on plant cells. They grow by moulting, before reproducing rapidly and often by PARTHENOGENESIS to give large numbers of females.

Waterbearer See AQUARIUS.

water beetle A BEETLE that lives, both as larvae and adult, in fresh water. Most are carnivorous; for example the great diving beetle, *Dytiscus marginalis*, eats small fish. To enable it to breathe while submerged it keeps a bubble of air under its wing covers, which is replenished by pushing the tail-end of the body through the water surface. It is about 4 cm (1.5 inches) long. The silver water beetle, *Hydrophilus piceus*, is even larger, 5 cm (2 inches) long, but is a plant-feeder. It keeps air on its underside, replenishing it from the head-end. Whirligigs, beetles belonging to the family Gyrinidae, are smaller and spend much time gyrating in groups on the water surface. Water beetles include representatives from several families.

water boatman (or **boat fly**) A freshwater BUG of the family Notonectidae or Corixidae, which swims by using its oarlike hind-legs. Greater water boatmen, *Notonecta glauca*, also known as back swimmers, swim upside down, are fierce carnivores, and feed on tadpoles and young fish. All water boatmen fly actively. Lesser water boatmen, *Corixa* species, of the family Corixidae are plant-feeders which swim with their backs up.

water-closet (WC; or **lavatory**) A device for receiving solid or liquid human waste and passing it into a drain in a water-borne SEWAGE-treatment system. It was invented by the English courtier and writer John Harington in 1589. The waste is flushed out of the bowl into the drain by water, usually discharged around the bowl rim from a small cistern fixed above the pan and connected to it by a pipe. In some countries direct flushing from the mains water supply is allowed. The bowl outlet is shaped to form a water seal ('U-bend'); this retains a small depth of water which prevents odours rising from the drain and the entry of vermin. In more elaborate designs the outlet is shaped so that a siphon is formed when flushing starts, giving more efficient removal of the waste.

water-colour A paint soluble in water or the type of painting in which these water-soluble paints are applied, usually very thinly, allowing the paper to show through. This creates a sparkling luminosity, since the light reflects back from the paper; usually no white colour is used, the paper instead being left untouched for the brightest highlights. Although there were distinguished earlier exponents, such as Dürer and van Dyck, water-colour had its chief flowering in Britain in the 18th and 19th centuries, particularly in the landscape painting of Turner. Opaque water-colour is known as GOUACHE. See also CHINESE ART.

watercress A hardy, aquatic, perennial Eurasian plant, *Nasturtium officinale*, a member of the family Cruciferae. It is widely cultivated as a salad vegetable, its fresh, young shoots having the pungent flavour of mustard and cress and being rich in vitamins. There are two main types grown, the hardier bronze-green varieties and the frost-susceptible dark green varieties. Watercress needs careful cultivation as it thrives only in clean, running water, as found in chalk streams.

water cycle See HYDROLOGICAL CYCLE.

waterfall A stream or river flowing over a precipice or down a steep hillside, usually occurring where water passes over harder rock to an area of softer rock. A large waterfall, or a series of waterfalls, is called a **cataract**. The ANGEL FALLS, on a tributary of the Caroni River in Venezuela, is the world's highest waterfall with a total drop of 979 m (3,212 ft). The highest waterfall in the UK is Eas Coul Aulin in the Highlands of Scotland (201 m, 658 ft); the highest in North America is Yosemite Falls (739 m, 2,425 ft). The Niagara Falls on the USA–Canada frontier has the world's highest mean annual flow of 5,940 cubic metres per second (212,200 cubic feet per second). Waterfalls provide the energy required to produce hydroelectricity.

water fern A diminutive, free-floating FERN of the genus *Azolla*, which covers the surface of pools and slow-moving streams. Sometimes called fairy moss, water ferns are found mainly in tropical and subtropical regions, but a few species reach temperate latitudes; of the five or six species, two are native to the USA and are naturalized in parts of Europe. Their stems bear a series of overlapping, paired leaves, the upper ones floating and green, the lower ones colourless. A few thread-like roots hang into the water, and the upper leaves have cavities inhabited by a symbiotic cyanobacterium, *Anabaena* species, which 'fixes' nitrogen for its host. Water ferns reproduce sexually and vegetatively, parts of the plants being dispersed by water-birds.

water flea See DAPHNIA.

Waterford A county on the south coast of the Irish Republic, in the province of Munster; area 1,839 sq km (710 sq miles); pop. (1991) 91,600; administrative centre, Dungarvan.

Watergate A building in Washington, DC, housing the offices of the Democratic Party, the scene of a bungled bugging attempt by Republicans during the US election campaign of 1972. The attempted cover-up and subsequent enquiry caused a massive political scandal, gravely weakened the prestige of the government, and finally led to the resignation of President Richard NIXON in August 1974 to avoid impeachment (he was subsequently pardoned by the new President, Gerald Ford).

Waterhouse, Alfred (1830–1905) British architect. He designed the Manchester Assize courts (1859) and Town Hall (1869–77) before moving to London, where he designed the Romanesque Natural History Museum (1873–81). His work includes a number of educational buildings, such as Caius College, Cambridge (1868 onwards), and his use of red brick gave rise to the term 'redbrick university'.

water hyacinth See WEED.

waterlily A perennial aquatic plant of the family Nymphaeaceae. The largest genus is *Nymphaea*, with 50 species found in temperate or tropical areas. The temperate ones are hardy, and through hybridization a large number of varieties have been introduced for garden use, in colours ranging from white through yellow and pink to red shades. The rootstock is a thick rhizome, from which arises long, stalked leaves that usually lie flat on the water surface. The tropical species, mainly found in Africa, tropical America, and Australia, have a greater colour range and include blue and purple flowers. The genus *Nuphar*, often called yellow water-lilies, has 25 species native to north temperate regions.

Waterloo A village of Brabant in Belgium, situated 18 km (11 miles) south of Brussels; pop. (1991) 27,860. On 18 June 1815 Napoleon's army was defeated by the British (under the Duke of Wellington) and Prussians. The battlefield can be viewed from the top of the Lion's Mound, a man-made hillock built by the Dutch in 1824–26 with soil obtained when the surrounding land was levelled, and there is a museum in Wellington's former headquarters.

Waterloo A town in south-east Ontario, Canada, adjacent to Kitchener; pop. (1991) 71,200. It is the site of the University of Waterloo (1959).

watermark A faint trade or recognition mark put into some paper during manufacture, visible when held against the light. During PAPER MANUFACTURE, the raised watermark design is carried on a 'dandy' roller positioned over a suction box so that the paper incorporates the design required while it is still semi-liquid. The paper is thinner in the area of the watermark, allowing light to pass through.

water melon A sprawling, annual relative of the cucumber and melon, derived from the tsamma melon, *Citrullus lanatus*, very variable in fruit size, flavour, and flesh colour. Water melons are native to the sandy, tropical areas of Africa, such as the Kalahari, but are grown throughout the tropics and subtropics. Green-fleshed types are used only as stock feed, but the large, red-fleshed types with a higher sugar content are prized as attractive, thirst-quenching fruits.

water-mill See WATER POWER.

water of crystallization A quantity of water chemically incorporated in the crystals of certain IONIC COMPOUNDS. For example, white anhydrous copper(II) sulphate, $CuSO_4$, will absorb moisture from the air, changing into blue hydrated copper(II) sulphate, $CuSO_4.5H_2O$. The five water molecules are referred to collectively as the water of crystallization. Alums contain water of crystallization, a common example being potash alum, $K_2SO_4.Al_2(SO_4)_3.24H_2O$. In this case, water molecules act as LIGANDS, six surrounding each metal ion. The water of crystallization can be removed by heating.

water pollution The fouling or contamination of water resources. Population growth and higher living standards make greater demands on water resources than can be met by the natural HYDROLOGICAL CYCLE. Consequently, in some places the quality of surface and underground fresh water, and of seas and coastal waters, is increasingly impaired. A certain amount of water pollution can be assimilated by dilution or by organisms in the food web adjusting to changes in the water. Beyond that, however, pollution represents a real threat to water quality, health, and the environment. Toxic chemicals, such as the heavy metals cadmium and mercury, produced in some industrial and mining operations and discharged into rivers, lakes, or coastal waters, can kill living organisms and collect in the tissues of fish and shellfish, which then enter the human food chain. Other possibly harmful metal pollutants are aluminium, which is used in water treatment, and lead, used for piping in some older houses, and identified as a cause of brain damage in some children. Organic pollutants of fresh and salt water, such as inadequately treated sewage and animal waste, can threaten fish stocks by reducing the amount of dissolved oxygen available to them, while excessive use of agricultural fertilizers and the release of nitrogen may cause the spread of poisonous algae. Thermal pollution, produced by water used for cooling in power-stations, also reduces oxygen solubility in rivers and lakes; and species diversity is further threatened when streams are choked by otherwise harmless inert solids, resulting from, for example, dredging or land drainage, or by urban rubbish. In developing countries, water pollution from untreated sewage contributes to the spread of cholera and typhoid, as well as being responsible for water-borne, parasitic diseases, such as schistosomiasis and onchocerciasis (river blindness).

water polo A game in which two seven-a-side teams compete, usually in a swimming pool, to score goals with an inflated ball passed between players by throwing. The players must swim; only the goalkeeper is allowed to walk, jump, or punch the ball.

water power The power of moving water. For 2,000 years water has been an important source of mechanical power. It remained the only significant source of stationary power in Europe until the introduction of windmills in the 12th century. Under the Romans there was widespread construction of water-mills. Tide-mills and the floating mills (those floating in a river and worked by the current) were later employed on rivers, such as the Danube and the Seine. With the developing technologies of the Middle Ages, the uses of water power extended, with WATER WHEELS powering flour milling, pumping, cloth manufacture, leather tanning, and the operation of sawmills and forges. The number of mills in England grew from the 5,000 listed in the 'Domesday Book' to a peak of 20,000 before the advent of the steam-engine. After a period of decline, WATER TURBINES used in HYDROELECTRICITY generation brought a revival; this is now the main use of water power. The later 20th century has also brought interest in TIDAL ENERGY and research into the potential of WAVE POWER.

waterproofing A process applied primarily to textiles, to prevent water passing through a fabric, and also to prevent the fabric from absorbing water. Most waterproof fabrics are based on high-strength SYNTHETIC FIBRES and heavy POLYMER coatings. They are being increasingly used in industrial, military, domestic, and leisure applications. Many clothing fabrics are waterproofed by coating them with a thin layer of one of the rubber-like polymers. Because most of these are impermeable to air, perspiration condenses inside the garment. To overcome this difficulty, inherently waterproof but 'breathable' fabrics are tightly woven so that water cannot pass through, but air and water vapour can. These fabrics are usually treated with SILICONES or natural waxes to provide water repellency. An alternative is to coat the fabric with a polymeric finish which has micropores too small to allow the passage of water, but large enough to allow water vapour molecules to pass through. Such a fabric can be layered between outer and lining fabrics, giving a three-layered structure.

water rat Any of various rat-like RODENTS that live near water. True rats can swim but they are not in any way modified for aquatic life. The WATER VOLE is the species most often called a water rat but it is not a true rat. The COYPU is another species sometimes given the name. Water rats in Spanish-speaking Latin America are the marsh rats, *Holochilus* species, of South America.

They have webbed feet and spend much of their time in water, but they are relatives of the voles, and are not rats.

Waters, Muddy (born McKinley Morganfield) (1915–83) US blues singer and guitarist. Based in Chicago from 1943, he became famous with his song 'Rollin' Stone' (1950). In the same year he formed a band, with which he recorded such hits as 'Got My Mojo Working' (1957). Waters impressed new rhythm and blues bands such as the Rolling Stones, who took their name from his 1950 song.

water scorpion An oval-shaped, flattened water BUG belonging to the family Nepidae, which has a long, thin tube at the end of the abdomen and large grasping fore-legs. The tube is used as a 'snorkel' for respiration and, along with the front legs, gives the animals a superficial resemblance to land scorpions. The 150 or so world species are carnivorous, and they lie in wait for prey, which they seize with their front pair of legs.

water shrew Any of various species of SHREW in several different genera. They include the common European water shrew, *Neomys fodiens*, and the American water shrew, *Sorex palustris*, both of which have hairs on the feet and tail that help them to swim. There are also four species of Asiatic water shrews of the genera *Chimarrogale* and *Nectogale*. All live on the land but take much of their prey of insects and small vertebrates under water.

Water Snake See HYDRA.

water softening Treatment to alleviate hardness in water, caused principally by the presence of carbonates and sulphates of calcium and magnesium. These salts form scale in pipes and boilers when heated and make soap lather less effectively. In the lime–soda process, these salts are precipitated by reaction with slaked lime or soda ash and then removed by sedimentation. In the base-exchange process (see ION-EXCHANGE RESIN), the magnesium and calcium ions are exchanged for sodium, which does not form scale. The water behaves as though it were soft, but in fact has the same quantity of dissolved solids. Formerly zeolites (sodium silicates) were used to achieve this exchange, but these have now been largely replaced by synthetic resins cross-linked to polystyrene beads.

waterspout A type of TORNADO occurring at sea that is made up of a spinning column of water extending from the base of a cumulonimbus cloud to the surface of the sea.

water supply and treatment The global use of water doubled between 1940 and 1980, and is projected to double again before 2000. Worldwide, average water consumption can range from about 740 litres per capita per day (l.c.d.) in urban USA, to as little as 1 l.c.d. in parts of Ethiopia or Somalia. Water is supplied from both surface and subterranean sources by a network of pipes, whose capacity must be able to meet domestic, industrial, and agricultural needs, while making a significant allowance for waste due to leaks. Upland reservoirs distant from towns require extensive AQUEDUCTS; intakes from rivers or lakes usually have a local reservoir to provide adequate supply when water levels are low and to allow closure of the intake against any temporary pollution. Deep aquifers (water-carrying rocks) are tapped by WELLS and often provide better-quality water. The first stage of water treatment is to store the water in a reservoir, where the combined action of sedimentation (settling of suspended materials due to gravity) and ultraviolet and visible light substantially eliminates bacteria. However, high-temperature areas in the water in summer can cause algal growth in nutrient-rich waters. To combat this, slow sand filtration has been used since the early 19th century; this relies on a combination of direct filtering and bacterial action within the upper layers of the sand bed. More modern fast filters use chemical treatments, particularly with aluminium sulphate, to coagulate suspended solids before they are removed in a clarifier. Water is commonly disinfected by chlorination, though this can cause an unpleasant taste when certain organic substances are present. After treatment, water is stored in a 'service reservoir', which is either an underground covered tank on high ground or, in flat country, a water tower. This stores a few days' supply and by its height provides pressure for local distribution.

In developing countries, such sophisticated supply and treatment networks exist only on a limited scale, if at all; deficiencies in water supply and sanitation services are the principal reasons for the high incidence of COMMUNICABLE DISEASES in these countries.

water-table A surface below which the ground is completely saturated with water. Above a water-table, water drains downwards under gravity; below, it moves under pressure. Water-tables tend to reflect the form of the land surface: they are higher (though deeper below the surface) under hills, and in valleys are usually at about the same level as the river channels. They may rise or fall with shifts in the rock and the amount of rain received. Where they intersect the surface, SPRINGS, seepages, and rivers occur. When rocks become saturated with water although the layers below them are not completely full, the result may be a perched water-table. Thick layers of rock with high water-tables in which water moves long distances are called aquifers. They are heavily exploited by wells for human use. A lowering of water-tables, especially in coastal areas, is serious if it allows salt water to flood in. Irrigated areas are particularly vulnerable and soils often become too saline to be farmed.

water turbine A type of WATER WHEEL. In early versions (*c*.1820), water entering a vertical central tube was expelled through curved horizontal pipes in the sides. In the modern Francis turbine the water enters through a curved volute (shaped like a snail shell) and guide vanes direct it inwards on to concave vanes on the central rotor. After deflection it discharges along an axial outlet. Power and water speed are controlled by tilting the guide vanes, which means that the water enters under pressure. Machines in which pressure contributes to the driving force are called reaction turbines, in contrast to impulse turbines, such as the Pelton wheel (patented in the USA in 1880 by L. A. Pelton), whose jets are at atmospheric pressure. It has spoon-shaped buckets into which jets of water are directed, and is used for HYDROELECTRICITY installations with a water head of 250 m (800 feet) or more. Francis turbines are used for hydroelectricity generation at medium heads, producing up to 500 MW (million watts) at efficiencies that can exceed 90 per cent. For utilizing TIDAL ENERGY and other low-head situations, the propeller or Kaplan turbine is more efficient, and this axial-flow machine has the additional advantage that its blades can be turned to allow operation in either flow direction.

water vapour Water in the state of a vapour. In the atmosphere it accounts for about 3 per cent of the mass of dry air, its distribution varying considerably in both time and space. It enters the air from sea and land through the processes of evaporation and TRANSPIRATION; and its concentration, as expressed by the relative HUMIDITY of the air, depends on temperature. Water vapour is an essential constituent of the atmosphere. It exerts a fundamental role in controlling the distribution of heat throughout the troposphere by means of its absorption and release of latent heat through the mechanism of the GREENHOUSE EFFECT. It is also fundamental to the formation of clouds and in the condensation process of PRECIPITATION.

water vole A rat-sized VOLE of which there are three species in the genus *Arvicola*, distributed throughout the temperate Old World from Europe to Siberia. They burrow into the banks of streams, so causing damage in some cases, and feed mainly on reeds and grasses, although they will take other vegetation, including root crops. They swim well but are not modified for life in water. They include the European water vole, or water rat, *A. terrestris*.

water wheel A wheel driven by the force of flowing water on blades or buckets around its rim. Water wheels were in use in Asia Minor from at least the second century BC, and probably as early in China. VITRUVIUS (1st century BC) describes an undershot wheel driving a millstone by means of right-angled gears, and a Chinese manuscript of 31 AD describes a horizontal wheel with its vertical shaft connected directly to the stone. A number of technological improvements came with the spread of WATER POWER throughout Europe in Roman and medieval times. The more efficient overshot wheel was introduced, and tilted or curved blades replaced flat blades. Bearings, gears, and belt drives became more sophisticated. Wheel diameters reached 6 m (20 feet); but efficiencies remained low. Rotating at little more than 10 revolutions per minute, the wheels extracted less than two-thirds of the energy of the water and their power output rarely exceeded 10 kW. With the introduction of steam-power in the 18th century, development virtually ceased for over 100 years. Fresh impetus came with the advent of HYDROELECTRICITY, but the demands of faster-running WATER TURBINES have replaced them.

Watford An industrial town in Hertfordshire, south-east England, 26 km (16 miles) north-west of London; pop. (1991) 113,080. Printing, papermaking, and electronics are the chief industries.

Watling Street A north-westerly Roman road of Britain that ran from Dubris (Dover), via Londinium (London) and Verulamium (St Albans), to Deva (Chester). Much of it was built *c.*60–70 AD for the advance north of the FOSSE WAY. Its name derives from the Anglo-Saxon name for Verulamium ('Waeclingacaester').

Watson, James Dewey (1928–) US biologist. Together with Francis CRICK he proposed a model for the structure of the DNA molecule, later recounting the discovery in *The Double Helix* (1968). He shared a Nobel Prize with Crick and Maurice Wilkins in 1962. He became director of the molecular biology laboratory at Cold Spring Harbor on Long Island in 1968, concentrating efforts on cancer research; he also served as director of the National Center for Human Genome Research (1989–92).

Watson, John Broadus (1878–1958) US psychologist, founder of the school of behaviourism. He viewed behaviour as determined by an interplay between genetic endowment and environmental influences, and held that the role of the psychologist was to discern, through observation and experimentation, which behaviour was innate and which was acquired. In seeking an objective study of psychology, he set the stage for the empirical study of animal and human behaviour which was to dominate 20th-century psychology, particularly in the USA.

Watson-Watt, Sir Robert Alexander (1892–1973) British physicist. He produced a system for locating thunderstorms by means of their radio emissions, and went on to lead a team that developed radar into a practical system for locating aircraft. This was improved and rapidly deployed in Britain for use in World War II, in which it was to play a vital role.

watt (symbol W) The SI UNIT of power. The power produced when work is being done at the rate of 1 joule per second. Larger units of power are the kilowatt (kW; 1,000 W), and the megawatt (MW; 10^6 W). The unit is named in honour of the British engineer James WATT.

Watt, James (1736–1819) Scottish engineer. He greatly improved the efficiency of Thomas Newcomen's beam engine by condensing the spent steam in a separate chamber, allowing the cylinder to remain hot. The improved engines were adopted for a variety of purposes, especially after Watt entered into a business partnership with the engineer Matthew Boulton. Watt continued inventing until the end of his life, introducing rotatory engines, controlled by a centrifugal governor, and devising a chemical method of copying documents. He also introduced the term 'horsepower', and the unit of power is named after him.

Watteau, Jean Antoine (1684–1721) French painter, of Flemish descent. An initiator of the Rococo style in painting, he is also known for his invention of the pastoral genre known as the *fête galante*. Watteau deliberately created an imaginary and rather theatrical world; the light-hearted imagery of his painting contrasted with the serious religious and classical subject-matter approved by the Royal Academy of Painting and Sculpture. His best-known painting is *L'Embarquement pour l'île de Cythère* (1717).

wattle See ACACIA.

wattle and daub A traditional method of filling the spaces in the timber frame of a building. Wooden rods were fitted into holes in the horizontal members; withies (tough, flexible branches) were then laced through these to form a wattle (lattice). Mud (daub) was then applied to seal the building against wind and rain.

wattlebird (or **wattled crow**) A bird of the family Callaeidae, which is confined to New Zealand, and was once represented by three species of colourful ground-dwelling birds: the kokako, *Callaeas cinerea*, the saddleback, *Philesturnus carunculatus*, and the huia, *Heteralocha acutirostris*. The South Island kokako is rare or extinct; the South Island saddleback is extinct on the mainland but thrives on some southern offshore islands. The North Island kokako survives in the central North Island, and the North Island saddleback inhabits numerous northern offshore islands. They are about crow-sized. The huia is the most famous wattlebird, but has not been seen since the early 20th century and is probably extinct; the male had a medium-length straight beak, and the female a much longer, strongly curved one.

Watts, George Frederic (1817–1904) British painter and sculptor. His work reflects his view of art as a vehicle for moral purpose; this is most evident in his allegorical paintings such as *Hope* (1886). He is best known for his portraits of public figures, including Gladstone, Tennyson, and John Stuart Mill. He married the actress Ellen Terry in 1864, but the marriage lasted less than a year and the couple were finally divorced in 1877.

Watts, Isaac (1674–1748) British hymn-writer and poet. His songs for children, which included 'How Doth the Little Busy Bee' (1715), anticipated those of William Blake. Watts is also remembered for hymns such as 'O God, Our Help in Ages Past' (1719).

Waugh, Evelyn (Arthur St John) (1903–66) British novelist. His early novels *Decline and Fall* (1928) and *Vile Bodies* (1930) were followed by *Black Mischief* (1932), *A Handful of Dust* (1934), and *Scoop* (1938), stylistically brilliant works of social satire which capture the brittle frivolity of the inter-war generation. *Brideshead Revisited* (1945) was a serious study of a landed family and the recovery of their faith in Roman Catholicism. His wartime experiences in Crete and Yugoslavia inspired his trilogy *Sword of Honour* (1965), in which he analyses the eternal struggle between good and evil, and civilization's fight against barbarism. His son, **Auberon Waugh** (1939–) is also a novelist and journalist. His novels include *Consider the Lilies* (1968) and *A Bed of Flowers* (1971).

wave A periodic disturbance of particles or of space by which many forms of energy propagate away from their source. The energy released by a stone dropped into still water moves outwards as a series of concentric peaks and troughs. All wave motions through a medium are the result of individual particles oscillating about their own fixed point. Waves have three characteristic parameters: the frequency, the number of oscillations per unit time; the amplitude, the size of the oscillation; and the speed at which they travel. The WAVELENGTH is equal to the speed of travel divided by the frequency. Ocean waves in water are called transverse waves because the displacement of the wave peaks and troughs is at right angles to the direction of travel. Sound waves travel as successive regions of compression and rarefaction of the air or other medium. They are therefore called longitudinal waves because the transmitting molecules oscillate back and forth in the same direction as the wave's propagation.

Light, radio waves, and infrared radiation are examples of ELECTROMAGNETIC RADIATION, and require no medium for propagation: they can travel through a vacuum. The wave-like nature of electromagnetic radiation is due to energy oscillating back and forth between a magnetic field and an electrical field as the wave travels. Because the magnetic and electrical fields are perpendicular to the direction of propagation this type of radiation is regarded as transverse wave motion.

Waves can be reflected when they meet an obstacle. SONAR and RADAR send out short pulses of waves, and detect waves reflected back from objects in the wave path. If reflected waves travel back over their original path, the incident and the reflected waves will be superimposed on each other and a stationary pattern of standing waves will be set up. See also INTERFERENCE.

waveband A subdivision of the RADIO region of the ELECTROMAGNETIC RADIATION spectrum. Because radio space is so crowded, sections of the radio-frequency spectrum are designated by the INTERNATIONAL TELECOMMUNICATION UNION for specific uses. Telecommunications systems that require a large BANDWIDTH, such as FM radio and television, use higher-frequency wavebands, which have a large frequency range. Historically, the first wavebands used were the low and medium frequencies. Radio waves of these frequencies can travel around the curvature of the Earth by reflection or refraction (bending) in the ionosphere, a layer of charged or ionized air 50–400 km (30–250 miles) above the Earth. Very high frequency (VHF), ultra high frequency (UHF), and microwave frequencies are not reflected by the ionosphere. Although these frequencies can thus only transmit over a limited range on the ground, they can pass through the ionosphere, which enables them to be used for SATELLITE communications.

wave erosion The destruction or wearing away of the coastline and the removal of loose debris by the action of ocean waves. The erosion can be due both to the force of the waves themselves as they pound on the shore and to the abrasion caused by the fragments of rock and sand particles carried away. The force exerted by a large wave on an exposed coast is nearly 10 tonnes per square metre (one ton per square foot), and may be three times as great during storms. Sandy and soft chalk cliffs can be torn away at a rate of 2 m (7 feet) a year, the material being deposited elsewhere along the coast. A wide beach is the best protection against such erosion, and a shore platform is often the result of it.

wavefunction A mathematical description of the behaviour of a particle that has wave properties. In physics the wavefunction for any particle is called psi, and it can be found from the SCHRÖDINGER EQUATION. The value of the wavefunction associated with a particle at a particular point in space and time is related to the probability of finding the particle there.

waveguide A hollow, conducting, metal tube or pipe used to direct very high frequency electromagnetic radiation, and microwaves in particular. Waveguides are superior to conventional cables, which exhibit too high a loss at these frequencies. The microwaves are propagated along the inside of the waveguide, where they are continually reflected off the inside walls. The width and depth of the waveguide (which is often rectangular in cross-section) are carefully calculated so that one mode, or characteristic wave-form, of the microwave is selectively propagated.

wavelength The distance between equivalent points on adjoining WAVES in a series – between the crests on water waves for example, or the points of maximum compression in sound waves. Sound waves range in wavelength from several metres to one or two centimetres. Electromagnetic waves have the widest range of all, with wavelengths from several kilometres for some radio waves down to less than 10^{-10} metre for gamma radiation. See ELECTROMAGNETIC RADIATION.

Wavell, Archibald Percival, 1st Earl (1883–1950) British field-marshal and viceroy of India. In World War I he served in France (where he lost an eye) and in 1937–39 he commanded the British forces in Palestine. In 1939 he became commander-in-chief in the Middle East and won the victory of Sidi Barrani (1940) over the Italians. In 1941, forced to divert some of his forces to Greece, and facing new German formations, he had to retreat in NORTH AFRICA and was dismissed by Churchill. He then served in India, first as commander-in-chief from 1941, then as viceroy (1943–47), where he made it his main task to prepare India for independence.

wave mechanics See QUANTUM THEORY.

wave-particle duality One of the paradoxes of modern physics is that ELECTROMAGNETIC RADIATION, such as light, seems to be a wave because it exhibits the phenomena of DIFFRACTION and INTERFERENCE, while the PHOTOELECTRIC EFFECT suggests that light also has a particle nature and that its energy is concentrated in small packets or quanta. Conversely, electrons, which seem to be small particles, also show some wave character because they can be diffracted. Such matter waves are called DE BROGLIE waves. This wave-particle duality has been incorporated into the theory of wave mechanics (see QUANTUM MECHANICS; QUANTUM THEORY). See also COMPLEMENTARITY.

wave power Power extracted from the ocean waves, usually for the generation of electricity. In the open ocean, waves a few metres high carry several kilowatts of power for each metre of their width. The first proposal for extracting this power, in 1799, envisaged a huge lever pivoted on the shore and with one end on a pontoon. A century later, the first practical device used the oscillating water in a cliff-face borehole to compress air, which drove a small turbogenerator. This principle is used in the automatic buoys developed in Japan in the 1950s, generating the 100 W needed for a navigation light. In recent years other countries have also investigated systems based on oscillating water columns. Some devices have reached outputs of a few kilowatts, but none is yet economically and technically proven on a large scale. Other types of system studied in the late 1970s, mainly in the UK, included hinged rafts, compressible air-bags, and a chain of cam-shaped rocking devices, known as nodding ducks.

wax Any of a group of pliable carbon-based substances that generally melt between 35°C and 95°C and form hard, glossy films on polishing. Waxes share similar physical properties, but, depending on their origin, differ markedly in their chemical structures. They are allied to FATS AND OILS and contain about 30 carbon atoms. BEESWAX and spermaceti wax (from the SPERM WHALE) have animal origins, whereas small amounts of other specialized waxes are obtained from plants. PARAFFIN WAX accounts for about 90 per cent of the wax used in industry and is extracted from lubricating oil derived from crude petroleum. Large quantities are still used for candle manufacture.

waxbill A small bird of the family Estrilidae, found in Africa, south-east Asia, and Australasia. The large majority of the 130 or so species in the family are less than 12.5 cm (5 inches) in length and many are brightly coloured, often with red or blue. They feed mainly on seeds. They are extremely popular as cage-birds, and one, the Bengalese finch, has been kept in captivity so long that it is no longer like any wild species, though it is probably derived from the white-backed munia, *Lonchura striata*.

waxwing Any of three species of bird in the same family as silky flycatchers, Bombycillidae. They live in temperate areas of the Northern Hemisphere. All are about the size of a small, dumpy thrush with pinkish-brown plumage and a marked crest. The tip of their tail is yellow or red and the inner flight feathers have a curious red waxy tip, hence their name. The European or Bohemian waxwing, *Bombycilla garrulus*, sometimes moves southwards out of its normal range in large numbers when the berries, which it depends upon for food, are in short supply. In the past these occasional migrations were thought to be a prelude to some human disaster, such as plague or war.

Wayne, John (born Marion Michael Morrison; known as 'the Duke') (1907–79) US actor. Associated with the film director John Ford from 1930, Wayne became a Hollywood star with his performance in Ford's western *Stagecoach* (1939). Remembered as the archetypal cowboy hero, he appeared in many other classic westerns, notably *Red River* (1948) and *True Grit* (1969), for which he won an Oscar. Wayne's fierce patriotism was reflected in his other main roles, for example as a US marine in Ford's *Sands of Iwo Jima* (1949) and as Davy Crockett in *The Alamo* (1960), which he also produced and directed.

weak force One of the four fundamental FORCES of nature, which is approximately 10^{10} times weaker than the electromagnetic INTERACTION. It occurs between LEPTONS, in the decay of HADRONS, and is also responsible for the beta decay of particles and nuclei.

wealth (in economics) The stock of assets accumulated by individuals, households, businesses, or nations. These assets can be physical possessions (e.g. land or buildings), financial assets (bank accounts and securities), 'human capital' (people's skills and talents), or natural RESOURCES (mineral deposits). Wealth may be accumulated by saving out of current income or it may be inherited. Wealth, in turn, can create income. For instance, owners of bank deposits are paid INTEREST and shareholders receive DIVIDENDS.

weasel The smallest species of the family Mustelidae, to which they give their name, with a wide distribution in northern temperate regions. The weasels and other species in the genus *Mustela* include the stoat and the European weasel, *M. nivalis* (which is known as the least weasel in North America). Weasels are wholly carnivorous, feeding on mice, voles, and other small animals. They sometimes kill large prey, such as rabbits.

weather The set of atmospheric conditions prevailing at a particular time and place (whereas CLIMATE describes 'average' conditions over a much longer term). It is the combination, experienced locally, of heat or cold, wind or calm, clear skies or cloudiness, high or low pressure, and the electrical state of the atmosphere. In meteorology it is expressed in terms of air temperature and pressure, wind speed and direction, visibility, relative humidity, cloud cover, and precipitation. In most parts of the world definite patterns exist. They may recur on a daily basis (as in equatorial regions), seasonally (as in the subtropics), or over a period of about a week (as in the mid-latitudes, where the movement of short-lived DEPRESSIONS and of ANTICYCLONES controls most weather conditions). See illustration p. 1422.

weather satellite See METEOROLOGICAL SATELLITE.

weaverbird (or **weaver**) A member of a large family, Ploceidae, of some 117 species of finch-like birds. Most of the species are found in Africa, but some occur in Europe and Asia. The females are generally sparrow-like in plumage while the males are often brightly coloured yellow and black. Many breed in colonies, the males weaving elaborate grass nests before using these as a display ground in an attempt to attract the females. The red-billed quelea, *Quelea quelea*, is a major pest of grain crops in many parts of Africa, where a single colony may contain many millions of birds. Weavers also include the buffalo weavers of the genus *Bubalornis*, and widow birds of the genus *Euplectes*.

weathering See DENUDATION.

weaving The art of constructing fabric by inter-

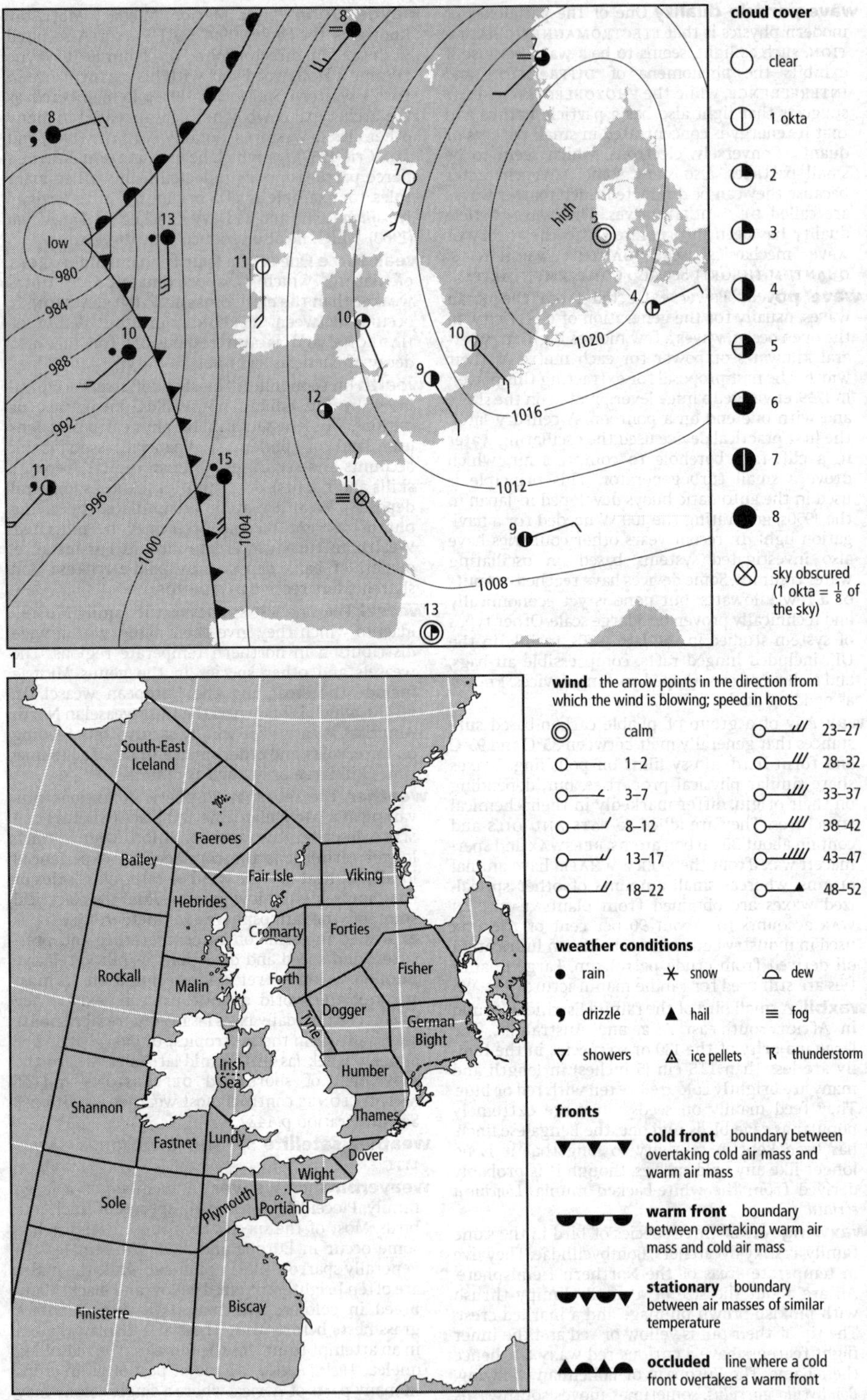

Weather (1) A weather map. The symbols, interpreted in the key, indicate weather conditions. The numbers against the wind symbols show temperature (°C); isobars show atmospheric pressure in millibars. (2) Coastal sea areas around the British Isles. Predictions of weather conditions likely to affect these areas are given in weather forecasts for ocean shipping.

lacing threads. The principal materials used in weaving are wool, SILK, COTTON, linen, and, sometimes, metallic thread. The simplest and most common weave is the plain weave, with a simple alternate over and under structure; such fabrics are often known as calico or tabby, and include muslins and CANVAS. Poplin is a plain weave which has a fine and close warp and much thicker weft. To form a twill weave, sets of warp threads are raised sequentially for successive passages of weft, resulting in diagonal lines on the face of the cloth. To form a herringbone weave, the twill sequence is reversed after a given number of weft insertions. Denim is a twill fabric designed to have extra warp on the face of the fabric to enhance durability. Pile fabrics are woven in such a way that loops of warp or weft yarn form on the face of the fabric. The loops may subsequently be cut, as in velvets, corduroys, and terrys.

Webb, Beatrice See WEBB, SIDNEY, BARON PASSFIELD.

Webb, (Gladys) Mary (1881–1927) British novelist. Her novels, representative of much regional English fiction popular at the beginning of the 20th century, include *Gone to Earth* (1917) and *Precious Bane* (1924). The earthy subject-matter and purple prose typical of her writing were satirized in *Cold Comfort Farm* (1933) by the British novelist Stella Gibbons (1902–89).

Webb, Sidney (James), Baron Passfield (1859–1947) British socialist, economist, and historian. He and his wife, **(Martha) Beatrice Webb** (née Potter) (1858–1943), whom he married in 1892, were prominent members of the Fabian Society, and helped to establish the London School of Economics (1895). Together they wrote several important books on socio-political theory and history, including *The History of Trade Unionism* (1894) and *Industrial Democracy* (1897), as well as founding the weekly magazine the *New Statesman* (1913). Sidney Webb became a Labour MP in 1922 and served in the first two Labour governments.

weber (symbol Wb) The SI unit of magnetic flux equal to the flux linking a circuit of one turn that produces an electromotive force of 1 volt when reduced uniformly to zero in 1 second. It is named after Wilhelm WEBER.

Weber, Carl Maria von (1786–1826) German composer, conductor, and pianist, one of a large family of musicians. The success of his OPERAS *Der Freischütz* (1821) and *Euryanthe* (1823) led to a commission to write an opera for London (*Oberon*, 1826), where he died at the height of his powers. In *Der Freischütz* Weber established the prototype romantic German opera, in which Italianate aria vies with simple, folk-like tunes, all brilliantly orchestrated and set against a background of German legend and the supernatural.

Weber, Max (1864–1920) German economist and sociologist. His writings on the relationship between economy and society established him as one of the founders of modern sociology. In his celebrated book *The Protestant Ethic and the Spirit of Capitalism* (1904), Weber argued that there was a direct relationship between the Protestant work ethic and the rise of Western capitalism. Throughout his work he stressed that the bureaucratization of political and economic society was the most significant development in the modernization of Western civilization. Other works include *Economy and Society* (1922).

Weber, Wilhelm Eduard (1804–91) German physicist. His early researches were in acoustics and animal locomotion, but he is chiefly remembered for his contributions in the fields of electricity and magnetism. Weber proposed a unified system for electrical units, determined the ratio between the units of electrostatic and electromagnetic charge, and devised a law of electrical force (later replaced by Maxwell's field theory). He went on to investigate electrodynamics and the nature and role of the electric charge. The SI unit of magnetic flux is named after him.

Webern, Anton (Friedrich Ernst) von (1883–1945) Austrian composer. He followed the development of the work of his teacher Schoenberg from tonality to atonality; this departure is evident in his 1908–09 setting of songs by the German poet Stefan George (1868–1933). His music is marked by its brevity; the atonal *Five Pieces for Orchestra* (1911–13) lasts under a minute. Together with Berg, Webern became the leading exponent of the serialism developed by Schoenberg. Important serial works include the *Symphony* (1928) and the *Variations for Orchestra* (1940). During World War II his work was denounced by the Nazis. He was shot, accidentally, by a US soldier during the postwar occupation of Austria.

web offset printing See OFFSET LITHOGRAPHY.

web spinner A small, elongate insect of warm climates, which makes up an order, Embioptera, of at least 300 species. Females are always wingless, and males are usually winged. They live gregariously in silken tubes or tunnels, made from silk spun from glands on the front legs. The females guard their eggs, but do not care for the young.

Webster, John (*c.*1580–*c.*1625) English dramatist. He wrote several plays in collaboration with other dramatists but his reputation rests chiefly on two revenge tragedies, *The White Devil* (1612) and *The Duchess of Malfi* (1623). His plays were not popular in his own day; Charles Lamb, in particular, was responsible for his revival in the 19th century.

Webster, Noah (1758–1843) US lexicographer. His *American Dictionary of the English Language* (1828), in two volumes, was the first dictionary to give comprehensive coverage of American usage, and his name survives in the many dictionaries produced by the US publishing house Merriam–Webster.

webworm See GRASS MOTH.

Weddell Sea An arm of the South Atlantic Ocean lying adjacent to Antarctica and to the east of the Antarctic Peninsula. It is named after the British navigator, James Weddell (1787–1834), who visited it in 1823.

Wedekind, Frank (1864–1918) German dramatist. He was a key figure in the emergence of expressionist drama. His play *The Awakening of Spring* (1891) scandalized contemporary German society with its explicit and sardonic portrayal of sexual awakening. Wedekind later attacked the bourgeois sexual code at the turn of the century in his two tragedies *Earth Spirit* (1895) and *Pandora's Box* (1904), both featuring the femme fatale Lulu. The plays form the basis of Berg's opera *Lulu*.

Wedgwood, Josiah (1730–95) British potter. He earned an international reputation with the pottery factories that he established in Staffordshire in the 1760s. These produced both practical and ornamental ware, maintaining high standards of quality despite large-scale production. Wedgwood's designs, and those of his chief designer John Flaxman, were often based on antique relief sculptures and contributed to the rise of neoclassical taste in England. His name is perhaps most associated with the powder-blue stoneware pieces (Jasperware) with white embossed cameos that first appeared in 1775.

weed Any plant growing where it is not wanted. Weeds reduce the yield of desirable plants by competing with them for light, water, and nutrients. Some, like DODDERS, are parasites of crops. Successful weeds either have features very similar to those of the crop or are very difficult to eradicate. The former include unwanted grass species in cereal crops, with seeds of much the same size as the cereals, so that they are gathered with the crop seed. The latter group of weeds produce large numbers of seeds which are spread widely and germinate over a period of years. Some may remain dormant in the soil for many decades. Other features favouring persistence include fragmenting roots, such as those of ground elder and bindweed, and the capacity to withstand herbicides, as in certain species of docks. Aquatic weeds include species which reproduce rapidly through fragmentation, such as the water hyacinth, *Eichhornia crassipes*, in tropical waterways.

weedkiller See HERBICIDE.

weeverfish Any of five species of fish in the family Trachinidae, all marine fishes that live in the inshore waters of Europe and West Africa. They are rather long-bodied and compressed with the mouth strongly oblique and the eyes on top of the head. They stay buried in sand or mud during most of the day but emerge at night to forage in shallow water for crustaceans and worms. The spiny first dorsal fin and the spines on the gill-cover have venom glands, and wounds from these are very painful but not fatal to man. The European lesser weever, *Echiichthys vipera*, grows up to 14 cm (5 inches); it lives close inshore and is responsible for stings on the feet of bathers.

weevil A BEETLE of the family Curculionidae, with some 60,000 species, making them the largest family of insects, and possibly the largest family of any animal. The head of a weevil is elongated at the front to form a snout (rostrum), which may be as long as the rest of the animal. The jaws are at its tip and the antennae, often elbowed and with a terminal club, are about halfway along the snout. They are almost all herbivorous, often feeding on seeds, and the long snout may also be used to bore holes in which to insert eggs. The larvae are legless. Many species, such as the granary weevil, *Sitophilus granarius*, or the cotton boll weevil, *Anthonomus grandis*, are destructive to crops.

weft The lateral (sideways) thread in woven cloth, as opposed to the lengthwise WARP. In weaving on a LOOM and in most fabric construction it is protected by the warp, and so does not need great strength. YARN for weft is lightly twisted to reduce SPINNING costs and to increase the bulk of yarn within the cloth.

Wegener, Alfred Lothar (1880–1930) German meteorologist and geologist. He was the first serious proponent of the theory of CONTINENTAL DRIFT, but this was not accepted by most geologists during his lifetime, partly because he could not suggest a convincing motive force to account for continental movements. It is, however, now accepted as correct in principle. Wegener also wrote a standard textbook of meteorology. He died on the Greenland ice-cap in 1930 during an expedition.

weight (symbol W) The resultant force exerted on a body by the gravitational field in which it is situated. It is a VECTOR quantity since it has direction, unlike MASS, and the SI unit of weight is the newton. Weight is mass times the acceleration of free fall. It decreases with height above the Earth's surface; but nowhere in the universe is unaffected by some gravitational field. However, the effect of WEIGHTLESSNESS occurs with a body that falls freely, such as a parachutist before the parachute is opened or an astronaut in an orbiting spacecraft. See also TERMINAL VELOCITY.

weightlessness The effect of zero GRAVITY. It occurs in free fall. For a person inside a spacecraft that is falling freely, the rate of acceleration of the person and the spacecraft are the same; therefore the person appears to have no weight and floats freely. During most phases of space travel the astronauts are weightless. The human body is not accustomed to this state and on long space flights special exercises must be carried out to ensure that there are no long-term effects. Some Soviet cosmonauts have spent about a year under conditions of weightlessness and it seems that no long-term damage results.

weightlifting A sport and method of training for keep-fit enthusiasts in which both men and women participate. In most competitions, which date back to the ancient Olympic Games, contestants make three attempts to lift a barbell (a metal pole with weights attached to each end) in two styles; in the 'snatch' the barbell is raised above the head in one movement, while in the 'clean and jerk' it is raised first to the chest and then above the head. In **power lifting**, different techniques are used: the 'squat', the 'dead lift', and the 'bench press', all of which rely on sheer strength rather than skill.

Weil, Simone (1909–43) French essayist, philosopher, and mystic. Weil deliberately chose to work in a Renault car factory (1934–35) and to serve in the Spanish Civil War on the Republican side (1936). Two years later she had the first in a series of mystical experiences that were to have a profound influence on her writing; she did not, however, affiliate herself to any established religion. During World War II Weil joined the Resistance movement in England, where she died from tuberculosis. Her reputation is based on autobiographical works, such as *Waiting for God* (1949) and *Notebooks* (1951–56), both published posthumously.

Weill, Kurt (1900–50) German composer, resident in the USA from 1935. In 1926 Weill married the Austrian singer Lotte LENYA, for whom many of his songs were written. He was based in Berlin until 1933 and is best known for the operas he wrote in collaboration with Bertolt BRECHT, political satires, which evoke the harsh decadence of the pre-war period in Germany and which are marked by his direct and harmonically simple style of composition. These include *The Rise and Fall of the City of Mahagonny* (1927) and *The Threepenny Opera* (1928).

Weimar Republic (1919–33) The republic of Germany formed after the end of World War I. On 9 November 1918 a republic was proclaimed in Berlin under the moderate socialist Friedrich Ebert. An elected National Assembly met in January 1919 in the city of Weimar and agreed on a constitution. Ebert was elected first President (1919–25), succeeded by HINDENBURG (1925–34). The new republic had almost at once to face the VERSAILLES PEACE SETTLEMENT, involving the loss of continental territory and of all overseas colonies and the likelihood of a vast reparations debt, the terms being so unpopular as to provoke a brief right-wing revolt, the Kapp putsch. The country was unable to meet reparation costs, and the mark collapsed, whereupon France and Belgium occupied the Ruhr in 1923, while in BAVARIA right-wing extremists (including HITLER and LUDENDORFF) unsuccessfully tried to restore the monarchy. Gustav Stresemann succeeded in restoring confidence and in persuading the USA to act as mediator. The Dawes Plan adjusted reparation payments, and France withdrew from the Ruhr. It was followed in 1929 by the Young Plan. Discontented financial and industrial groups in the German National Party allied with Hitler's NAZI PARTY to form a powerful opposition. As unemployment developed, support for this alliance grew, perceived as the only alternative to communism. In the presidential elections of 1932 Hitler gained some 13 million votes, exploiting anti-communist fears and anti-Semitic prejudice, although Hindenburg was himself re-elected. In 1933 he was persuaded to accept Hitler as Chancellor. Shortly after the REICHSTAG fire, Hitler declared a state of emergency (28 February 1933) and, on Hindenburg's death in 1934, made himself President and proclaimed the THIRD REICH.

Weinberg, Steven (1933–) US theoretical physicist. Weinberg worked at several universities before being appointed professor of physics at the University of Texas. He devised a theory to unify electromagnetic interactions and the weak forces within the nucleus of an atom, for which he shared the Nobel Prize for physics in 1979 with SALAM and GLASHOW. Weinberg's popular work *The First Three Minutes* (1977) is an account of the processes occurring immediately after the big bang.

Weismann, August (1834–1914) German biologist, who expounded a theory of heredity that assumed the continuity of germ plasm. Weismann postulated that germ plasm was transmitted via the GAMETES from one generation to the next, giving rise to body cells. This ruled out the theory of transmission of acquired characteristics.

Weissmuller, John Peter (known as 'Johnny') (1904–84) US swimmer and actor. He won three Olympic gold medals in 1924 and two in 1928. He was the first man to swim 100 metres in under a minute and set 28 world records in freestyle events. He later achieved wider recognition as the star of the Tarzan films of the 1930s and 1940s.

Weizmann, Chaim (Azriel) (1874–1952) Israeli statesman, President 1949–52. Born in Russia, he became a British citizen in 1910. A supporter of Zionism from the early 1900s, Weizmann participated in the negotiations that led to the Balfour Declaration (1917), which outlined British support for a Jewish homeland in Palestine. He later served as president of the World Zionist Organization (1920–31; 1935–46), facilitating Jewish immigration into Palestine in the 1930s. Weizmann also played an important role in persuading the US government to recognize the new state of Israel (1948) and became its first President in 1949.

weka (or **weka rail**) A species of RAIL, *Gallirallus australis*, confined to New Zealand. It is mainly brown in colour and has lost the power of flight. There are four subspecies, but none inhabit both the North and South Islands. *G. a. grevi* is the only weka inhabiting the North Island, and *G. a. scotti* is found on Stewart Island. *G. a. australis* is the only weka in the western South Island, and *G. a. hectori* inhabits the east and has been introduced to Chatham Island.

welding A technique for joining metal parts without using low-melting-point fillers. It provides a stronger joint than either soldering or brazing. The earliest form of welding was forge welding, in which two pieces of red-hot iron were hammered together, a technique now used only by blacksmiths. The modern pressure welding, in which the metal is deformed cold, is used widely for aluminium alloys. However, the most important method is arc welding, in which a continuous electric spark (arc) jumps from a metal rod to the join line where the two parts meet. The high temperature melts the end of the rod and material on either side of the join to form a welded joint. Gas welding uses an oxyacetylene flame, and cold wire is added to the joint as a filler. Originally as important as arc welding, this method is now restricted to specialist sheet fabrication. In resistance welding, a high-current, low-voltage pulse of electricity is applied on opposite sides of the join line. The required heat is generated by the resistance across the joint. Welding on automated robotic assembly lines is by this method. Cracked railway lines are welded with thermite. This is a mixture of aluminium powder and iron oxide that can be ignited to give a violent and spectacular reaction in which the iron oxide is reduced to iron, providing molten iron in a cheap and simple way. There are several specialized welding techniques using lasers, electron beams, and even friction (from rubbing the two parts together) as the heat source.

Welensky, Sir Roy (Roland) (1907–91) Rhodesian statesman. He entered politics in 1938, and founded the Federal Party in 1953, dedicated to 'racial partnership'. He was an advocate of the CENTRAL AFRICAN FEDERATION, which was created largely as a result of his negotiations. He was Prime Minister of the Federation from 1956 to 1963. When the Federation was dissolved (1963) Welensky lost the support of the white Rhodesians, who gave their allegiance to the Rhodesian Front of Ian SMITH.

welfare state A country with a comprehensive system of social welfare funded both by taxation and NATIONAL INSURANCE. The emergence of the strong secular state in 19th-century Europe was characterized by the development of state involvement in education, public health, and housing. Public education systems were first introduced in France and Prussia early in the 19th century, while the need for housing and public health measures accelerated as urbanization increased in Europe. A scheme of social insurance against unemployment, sickness, and old age was pioneered in Germany under BISMARCK, and other European states soon followed. In Britain a similar scheme, together with other social welfare measures, began to be introduced under the Liberal governments (1906–14). Between the wars significant developments towards its establishment took place in New Zealand under the LABOUR PARTY, while F. D. Roosevelt's NEW DEAL in the USA created a series of federal social welfare agencies. In 1942 a report by William BEVERIDGE proposed a comprehensive British system of national social insurance. His proposals were implemented by Clement ATTLEE's Labour government after World War II, which also introduced the National HEALTH SERVICE. In the Soviet Union and East European states welfare provision became an official part of the fabric of society. In the USA, the concept of social welfare support is regarded as being fundamentally at odds with the FREE MARKET economy and so remains highly selective. Sweden is usually taken as the purest example of a welfare state, because of its interventionist labour market policy and integrated health care system, but Belgium and The Netherlands have more generous SOCIAL SECU-

RITY. In a welfare state, the proportion of GNP allocated to social expenditure can rise as high as 40 per cent. In Britain, the heavy public expenditure required to distribute social benefits was increasingly challenged and a fundamental revision of the NHS and the social security system took place in the 1980s and early 1990s under the Conservatives; further reforms were initiated by the 'New Labour' government in the late 1990s.

well A shaft sunk from ground-level to perhaps 50 m (170 feet) below to reach a water-bearing stratum (AQUIFER), usually a porous rock, such as chalk, limestone, or sandstone. Wells may also occur naturally, as fissures in the Earth's crust leading to underground water supplies. Having percolated slowly down from the surface, the water in a deep aquifer is usually of high quality. The upper part of the well is lined where it passes through water-bearing surface strata to prevent contamination by surface water or possibly polluted ground-water. A PUMP is used to raise water to the surface. The water reaches the surface in a rising main of large diameter to minimize friction losses. See also ARTESIAN WELL.

Welles, (George) Orson (1915–85) US film director and actor. Welles formed his own Mercury Theatre company and caused a public sensation in 1938 with a radio dramatization of H. G. Wells's *The War of the Worlds*, whose realism persuaded many listeners that a Martian invasion was happening. Turning to films, he produced, directed, wrote, and acted in the critically acclaimed *Citizen Kane* (1941), based on the life of the newspaper tycoon William Randolph Hearst. Welles was an important figure in the *film noir* genre as shown by such films as *The Lady from Shanghai* (1948), in which he co-starred with his second wife Rita Hayworth. His best-known film performance was as Harry Lime in *The Third Man* (1949).

Wellington The capital of New Zealand, situated at the south-western tip of North Island; pop. (1991) 150,300 (city); 325,680 (urban area). Originally named Port Nicholson when its harbour was first visited by Europeans in 1826, the city was established by the New Zealand Company in 1840 and named after the Duke of Wellington. Many of its major buildings date from the Victorian period. In 1865 the seat of government was moved from Auckland to Wellington. It subsequently developed as a port but being geographically restricted, industrial growth took place in nearby urban areas, such as Hutt Valley and the Porirua basin. Its international airport is located at Rangotai, on the narrow isthmus between Evans and Lyall Bays, 6 km (4 miles) south-east of the city centre. Wellington manufactures vehicles, chemicals, machinery, metal goods, and clothing.

Wellington, Arthur Wellesley, 1st Duke of (known as 'the Iron Duke') (1769–1852) British soldier and Tory statesman, Prime Minister 1828–30 and 1834. Born in Ireland, he served as commander of British forces in the Peninsular War, winning a series of victories against the French and finally driving them across the Pyrenees into southern France (1814). The following year Wellington defeated Napoleon at the Battle of Waterloo, so ending the Napoleonic Wars. During his first term as Prime Minister he granted Catholic Emancipation under pressure from Daniel O'Connell.

wellingtonia See REDWOOD.

Wells A city in Somerset, south-west England, the smallest cathedral city in England; pop. (1991) 9,763. Its English Gothic cathedral was built between 1180 and 1340 and its 13th-century palace of the bishops of Bath and Wells contains the natural wells after which the city is named.

Wells, H(erbert) G(eorge) (1866–1946) British novelist. After studying biology with T. H. Huxley he wrote some of the earliest science-fiction novels, such as *The Time Machine* (1895) and *The War of the Worlds* (1898). These combined political satire, warnings about the dangerous new powers of science, and a hope for the future. In 1903 Wells joined the Fabian Society; his socialism was reflected in several comic novels about lower-middle-class life, including *Kipps* (1905) and *The History of Mr Polly* (1910). He is also noted for much speculative writing about the future of society, particularly in *The Shape of Things to Come* (1933).

Wells, Fargo and Company US transport organization, founded by Henry Wells, William C. Fargo, and associates in 1852 to operate between New York and California. Wells and Fargo established a monopoly west of the Mississippi within a decade, succeeding the PONY EXPRESS as the agency for transporting bullion to eastern markets, and for 20 years dominated the postal service in the West. In 1918 it merged with a number of other concerns to become the American Railway Express Company.

Welsbach, Carl Auer von See AUER.

Welsh The language of Wales belonging to the Brythonic group of the Celtic languages. It is spoken by about 500,000 people in Wales and has a substantial literature dating from the medieval period. When Wales was united with England in 1536 it seemed likely that Welsh would disappear as a living language, but the publication of a Bible in Welsh in 1588 played an important part in preserving it. Although under great pressure from English, Welsh is widely used and taught in Wales as a compulsory part of the National Curriculum to GCSE level, and all official documents are bilingual. It is written phonetically, each letter (except *y*) having one standard sound only.

Welsh-language literature Poetry of the 6th century has survived in 8th-century documents. Among early poets are Aneirin and Taliesin who flourished in the ancient Welsh territories of north Britain, and composed eulogies and religious verse. Among the finest achievements of writing in Welsh are the poems of eulogy associated with the independent princes, the medieval prose tales known as the MABINOGION, and the lyric nature poetry of Dafydd ap Gwilym (*c*.1320–80), which was to influence succeeding generations of poets. A characteristic element of the Welsh bardic tradition was expressed in the strict poetic conventions of *cynhanedd* ('harmony'), a complicated system of accentuation, alliteration, and internal rhyme. A conscious literary use was made of prose by storytellers whose oral tales were recorded in writing. The Reformation and the Tudor policy of encouraging the use of English led to a diminution of appreciation of the Welsh culture. The first Welsh printed book, *Yn y lhyvyr hwnn* ('In this Book', known by its opening words) (1545) was followed by a translation of the Bible into Welsh in 1588. Welsh literature in the 17th century consisted mainly of religious works. Goronwy Owen (1723–69) founded a new school of Welsh poetry, which led to the establishment of local eisteddfods or meetings of competitors to perpetuate the classical forms of Welsh literature. The greatest lyric poet of the 19th century was Ceiriog (John Hughes, 1832–87), while in the 20th century poets and dramatists such as Saunders Lewis (1893–1985) drew increasingly on the rhythms and vocabulary of colloquial speech. The dramatist John Gwyllm Jones (1920–) and the novelist and short-story writer Islwyn Ffowc Elis (1924–) have been innovators in form and subject-matter, and are followed by a younger generation of enthusiastic writers.

Welsh Nationalist Party See PLAID CYMRU.

Welwyn Garden City An industrial town in Hertfordshire, south-east England, to the north-east of St Albans; pop. (1991) 42,087. It was founded by Sir Ebenezer Howard in 1920 and designated a New Town in 1948. It is best known for food products.

Wembley A residential district of west London in the outer borough of Brent, south-east England, site of the famous Wembley Stadium, built for the British Empire Exhibition (1924–25).

Wenceslas (or **Wenceslaus**) (1361–1419) King of Bohemia (as Wenceslas IV) 1378–1419. He became king of Germany and Holy Roman emperor in the same year as he succeeded to the throne of Bohemia, but was deposed by the German Electors in 1400. As king of Bohemia, Wenceslas supported the growth of the Hussite movement, but could not prevent the execution of John Huss in 1415.

Wenceslas, St (or **Wenceslaus**; known as 'Good King Wenceslas') (*c.*907–29) Duke of Bohemia and patron saint of the Czech Republic. He worked to Christianize the people of Bohemia but was murdered by his brother Boleslaus; he later became venerated as a martyr and hero of Bohemia. The story told in the Christmas carol 'Good King Wenceslas', by J. M. Neale (1818–66), appears to have no basis in fact. Feast day, 28 September.

werewolf A mythical being that at times changes from a person to a wolf. Belief in werewolves is found throughout the world; in countries where wolves are uncommon, the creature is said to assume the form of another dangerous animal, such as a tiger or a bear. Traditionally, werewolves are held to be most active at full moon, devouring animals, humans, or corpses. A person who is bitten by a werewolf is turned into one her- or himself.

Werner, Abraham Gottlob (1749–1817) German geologist. He was the chief exponent of the Neptunian theory, which included the belief that rocks, such as granites (now known to be of igneous origin) were formed as crystalline precipitates from a primeval ocean. Although this theory was invalid, the controversy that it stimulated prompted a rapid increase in geological research, and Werner's was probably the first attempt to establish a universal stratigraphic sequence.

Werner, Alfred (1866–1919) French-born Swiss chemist, founder of coordination chemistry. He demonstrated that the three-dimensional structure of molecules was important not just for organic compounds but for the whole of chemistry. In 1893 he announced his theory of chemical coordination, proposing a secondary or residual form of valency to explain the structures of coordination compounds. He was awarded the Nobel Prize for chemistry in 1913.

Wesak (or **Vesak**) The most important of the THERAVADA Buddhist festivals, commemorating the birth, enlightenment, and death (and thus NIRVANA) of the BUDDHA. It is celebrated on the full moon in the lunar month of Wesak (April/May), and it is a time of temple worship, the presentation of alms, and the renewal of vows.

Wesker, Arnold (1932–) British dramatist. His writing is associated with British kitchen-sink drama of the 1950s and his plays, reflecting his commitment to socialism, often deal with the working-class search for cultural identity, as in *Roots* (1959). He is also noted for *Chips with Everything* (1962), a study of class attitudes in the RAF during national service, and *The Merchant* (1977), which reworks the story of Shylock in an indictment of anti-Semitism.

Wesley, John (1703–91) British preacher and co-founder of Methodism. He became the leader of a small group in Oxford, which had been formed in 1729 by his brother **Charles** (1707–88); its members were nicknamed the 'Methodists'. In 1738 John Wesley experienced a spiritual conversion as a result of a reading of Luther's preface to the Epistle to the Romans. He resolved to devote his life to evangelistic work; however, when Anglican opposition caused the churches to be closed to him, he and his followers began preaching out of doors. Wesley subsequently travelled throughout Britain winning many working-class converts and widespread support of the Anglican clergy. Despite his wish for Methodism to remain within the Church of England, his practice of ordaining his missionaries himself (since the Church refused to do so) brought him increasing opposition from the Anglican establishment and eventual exclusion; the Methodists formally separated from the Church of England in 1791.

Wessex The kingdom of the West Saxons, established in Hampshire in the early 6th century and gradually extended by conquest to include much of southern England. Under Alfred the Great and his successors it formed the nucleus for the Anglo-Saxon kingdom of England. The name was revived by Thomas Hardy to designate the south-western counties of England (especially Dorset) in which his novels are set, and is used in the titles of certain present-day regional authorities.

West, Benjamin (1738–1820) US painter, resident in Britain from 1763. He was appointed historical painter to George III in 1769 and became the second president of the Royal Academy on Joshua Reynolds's death in 1792. His picture *The Death of General Wolfe* (1771) depicted its subject in contemporary rather than classical dress, signifying a new departure in English historical painting.

West, Mae (1892–1980) US actress and dramatist. She made her name on Broadway appearing in her own comedies *Sex* (1926) and *Diamond Lil* (1928), which were memorable for their frank and spirited approach to sexual matters; the former resulted in a short period of imprisonment for alleged obscenity. In the early 1930s West began her long and successful Hollywood career; major films included *She Done Him Wrong* (1933) and *Klondike Annie* (1936). She is also noted for the autobiography *Goodness Had Nothing to Do with It* (1959). The inflatable life-jacket used by the RAF in World War II was nicknamed the Mae West in tribute to her curvaceous figure.

West, Dame Rebecca (born Cicily Isabel Fairfield) (1892–1983) British writer and feminist, born in Ireland. From 1911 she wrote journalistic articles in support of women's suffrage, adopting 'Rebecca West' as her pseudonym after one of Ibsen's heroines. She was sent to report on Yugoslavia in 1937, publishing her observations in the *Black Lamb and Grey Falcon* (1942) in two volumes. Her other works include *The Meaning of Treason* (1949), a study of the psychology of traitors, and *A Train of Power* (1955), a critique of the Nuremberg war trials. West's many novels include *The Fountain Overflows* (1957).

West Bank A region west of the River Jordan and north-west of the Dead Sea, which became part of

Jordan in 1948 and was occupied by Israel in the Six-Day War of 1967; area 5,879 sq km (2,270 sq miles); pop. (1994) 1,122,900. Its chief town is Jericho and 97 per cent of its people are Palestinian Arabs. In the Camp David agreement of 1978, proposals were accepted to set up a self-governing Palestinian state in the area. In 1988 Jordan relinquished its claims to the area and the Palestine Liberation Organization declared it a Palestinian state. In 1993 Israel agreed to withdraw troops and the Palestinian National Authority, under Yassir ARAFAT, assumed control in 1994–95.

West Bengal A state in eastern India to the south of Sikkim and Bhutan, formed in 1947 from the Hindu area of former Bengal; area 87,853 sq km (33,933 sq miles); pop. (1991) 67,982,730; capital, Calcutta. Its chief products are coal, rice, oilseeds, wheat, jute, fish, and tea.

westerlies Winds blowing from the west, most often occurring in mid-latitudes. In the northern hemisphere they are usually more variable in force and direction than in the southern hemisphere. See ROARING FORTIES.

Western Film genre dealing with various aspects of the opening up of the American West in the 19th century. In view of the substantial US contribution to the early development of the cinema, it is hardly surprising that US film-makers quickly made use of the vast store of history and legend readily available. The Western was the first film genre to emerge, beginning with *The Great Train Robbery* (1903). GRIFFITH and Thomas Ince (1882–1924) made a number of short Westerns, the latter introducing the Western's first star, William S. Hart (1870–1946). By the 1920s DEMILLE, FORD, and other major directors were making Westerns, and sound increased their appeal. Westerns reached their heyday in the 1940s and 1950s, the advent of colour being particularly felicitous for them. Classics, such as *Stagecoach* (1939), *High Noon* (1952), and *Shane* (1953), achieved resonances well beyond their immediate subject-matter. In the late 1960s a variant appeared in Europe, the Italian 'spaghetti' Western. However, the popularity of the genre declined during the 1970s and 1980s. A revival of interest in the Western was signalled in the 1990s by the great success of the US film *Unforgiven* (1992) and the US television series *Lonesome Dove* (1995).

Western Australia A state comprising the western part of Australia; area 2,525,500 sq km (975,473 sq miles); pop. (1991) 1,650,600; capital, Perth. It was first settled by the British in 1826 and 1829, and was federated with the other states of Australia in 1901. Iron ore, nickel, bauxite, and gold are amongst its chief mineral resources. Sheep, wheat, and fruit are the principal agricultural products.

Western Cape A province of South Africa created in 1994 from part of the former Cape Province; pop. (1995) 3,721,200. Its capital is Cape Town.

Western European Union (WEU) A West European defence organization founded in 1955 by Belgium, France, the UK, Luxembourg, the Netherlands, West Germany, and Italy. The WEU came into being as a successor to the Brussels Treaty organization, after France had refused to ratify the treaty providing for a European Defence Community; its primary function was to supervise the rearmament and accession to NATO of West Germany. The Union formally ended the occupation of West Germany and Italy by the Allies. The social and cultural activities initially envisaged by its founders were transferred to the COUNCIL OF EUROPE in 1960, leaving the Union with the task of improving defence cooperation among the countries of Western Europe. Reactivated in 1984, it was involved from 1987 in arms control, and was joined by Spain and Portugal in 1989 and by the former East Germany after German reunification in 1990. The WEU helped to coordinate Europe's contribution to the anti-Iraq coalition in the Gulf War in 1991. In 1993, the Eurocorps rapid reaction unit was founded, comprising land-based forces from France, Germany, and Belgium. In 1994, several former Soviet satellite states of Eastern Europe (e.g. Bulgaria, Poland, Romania) were granted associate member status. The MAASTRICHT TREATY (1992) envisaged it as the defence component of the European Union.

Western Ghats See GHATS.

Western Isles ▶**1** The Hebridean islands off the west coast of Scotland; ▶**2** An administrative islands area of Scotland consisting of the Outer Hebrides; area 2,898 sq km (1,119 sq miles); pop. (1991) 29,110; administrative centre, Stornoway.

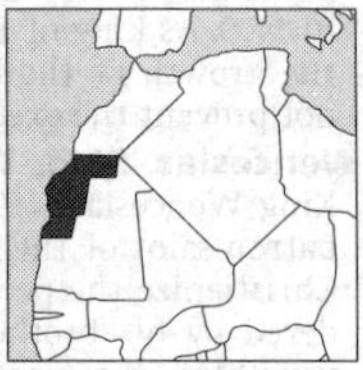

Western Sahara A former Spanish colony (Spanish Sahara) on the Atlantic coast of north-west Africa; area 252,126 sq km (97,383 sq miles); pop. (est. 1989) 186,500 (within the area controlled by Morocco); capital, La'youn (El Aaiún). It has the world's largest deposits of phosphate rock. Annexed by Morocco and Mauritania in 1976 after it had ceased to become a Spanish province, Mauritania withdrew from the territory in 1979 and Morocco extended its control over the entire region. A liberation movement (*Frente Polisario*), which launched a guerrilla war against the Spanish in 1973, has continued its struggle against Morocco in an attempt to establish an independent Saharawi Arab Democratic Republic.

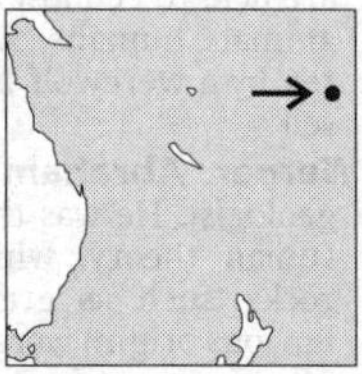

Western Samoa A country consisting of a group of nine islands in the south-west Pacific, which forms part of SAMOA.

Physical. The country's two major islands, Upolu and Savai'i, are both volcanic and are fringed by coral reefs. The islands have tall, evergreen rain forests and swamps, with 16 species of bird that are unique to the area.

Economy. The economy of Western Samoa is based on agriculture. The main exports are cocoa, copra, and bananas, but tropical fruits and timber are also exported. There is a little industry, based around food-processing. Tourism is expanding.

History. The Samoan archipelago was first settled in about 1000 BC and was the centre of Polynesian migrations eastwards. Although sighted by the Dutch in 1722, the first European to set foot on the islands was Louis-Antoine de Bougainville in 1768. Germany, Britain, and the USA competed for control of the archipelago until 1899 when Western Samoa passed to Germany and the eastern islands became AMERICAN SAMOA. Western Samoa remained a German protectorate until 1914; thereafter it was administered by New Zealand, initially (1920–46) under a League of Nations Mandate and then as a UN Trust Territory, until it gained full independence in 1962. Western Samoa joined the COMMONWEALTH OF NATIONS in 1970. Susuga Malietoa Tanumafili II became head of state in 1963. He is a constitutional monarch with the power to dissolve the legislative assembly, which is known as the Fono.

Capital: Apia
Area: 2831 sq km (1093 sq mi)
Population: 166,000 (1995)
Currency: 1 tala = 100 sene
Religions: Congregational 47.2%; Roman Catholic 22.3%; Methodist 15%
Ethnic Groups: Samoan 88%; Euronesian 10%; European 2%
Languages: Samoan; English
International Organizations: UN; Commonwealth; South Pacific Forum

Western Somalia See OGADEN.

Western Wall (or **Wailing Wall**) A high wall in Jerusalem, originally part of the Temple mount (the platform upon which the Jewish Temple was built by King Solomon in 950 BC). It has formed the western wall of the sanctuary enclosing the Dome of the Rock and other buildings, the third most holy place to Muslims after Mecca and Medina. Jews have been accustomed, probably since the Middle Ages, to lament at this wall the destruction of the Temple and the Holy City in 70 AD and to pray for its restoration.

West Glamorgan A former county of South Wales, created in 1974 from part of Glamorgan; its administrative centre was Swansea. In 1996 it was abolished and replaced by the new county of Swansea and the county borough of Neath and Port Talbot.

West Indian music See CALYPSO; CARIBBEAN MUSIC; STEEL BAND.

West Indies The islands of the CARIBBEAN. COLUMBUS, who in 1492 was the first European to reach the islands, called them the West Indies because he believed he had arrived near India by travelling westward. The islands were opened up by the Spanish in the 16th century and thereafter were the theatre of rivalry between the European colonial powers. Cultivation of sugar was introduced and the population was transformed by the mass importation of West African slaves to work the agricultural plantations; their descendants form the largest group in the population.

Westinghouse, George (1846–1914) US engineer. His achievements were wide and he held over 400 patents, but he is best known for developing vacuum-operated safety brakes and electrically controlled railway signals. He was concerned with the generation and transmission of electric power; he championed the use of alternating current (making use of the work of Nikola TESLA), and built up a huge company to manufacture his products. Westinghouse also pioneered the use of natural gas and compressed air, and installed water turbines to generate electric power at Niagara Falls.

Westmeath A county of the Irish Republic, in the province of Leinster, north-east of the River Shannon; area 1,764 sq km (681 sq miles); pop. (1991) 61,880; county town, Mullingar.

West Midlands A metropolitan county of central England; area 899 sq km (347 sq miles); pop. (1991) 2,500,400; county town, Birmingham. It is divided into seven districts.

Westminster (in full **City of Westminster**) An inner borough of London, England, containing the Houses of Parliament and many government offices, etc.; pop. (1991) 181,500. It also includes London's West End, associated with its many department stores, clubs, restaurants, and theatres.

Westminster, Palace of A palace originally built for Edward the Confessor on the site now occupied by the Houses of Parliament in London. It was damaged by fire in 1512 and ceased to be a royal residence, but a great part of it remained. The Houses of Lords and Commons for a long time sat in its buildings, until these were destroyed by fire in 1834.

Westminster, Statute of (1931) Legislation on the status of British DOMINIONS. At the 1926 and 1930 Imperial Conferences pressure was exerted by the dominions of Canada, New Zealand, the Commonwealth of Australia, the Union of South Africa, Eire, and Newfoundland for full autonomy within the British COMMONWEALTH. The result was the Statute of Westminster, accepted by each dominion Parliament, which recognized the right of each dominion to control its own domestic and foreign affairs, to establish a diplomatic corps, and to be represented at the League of Nations. It still left unresolved certain legal and constitutional questions – not least the status of the British crown. The Consequential Provisions Act (1949) allowed republics such as India to remain members of the Commonwealth.

Westminster Abbey The collegiate church of St Peter in Westminster, London, originally the abbey church of a Benedictine monastery. The present building, begun by Henry III in 1245 and altered and added to by successive rulers, replaced an earlier church built by Edward the Confessor. Nearly all the kings and queens of Britain have been crowned in Westminster Abbey; it is also the burial place of many of Britain's monarchs (up to George II) and of the nation's leading statesmen, poets (in the section called Poet's Corner), and other celebrities, and of the Unknown Warrior.

Westmorland A former county of north-west England. In 1974 it was united with Cumberland and northern parts of Lancashire to form the county of Cumbria.

Westphalia A former province of north-west Germany, which from 1815 formed part of Prussia, now part of the German state of North Rhine-Westphalia; capital, Düsseldorf. The Peace of Westphalia (1648) ended the Thirty Years War.

West Point (in full **West Point Academy**) The US Military Academy, founded in 1802, located on the site of a former strategic fort on the west bank of the Hudson River in New York State.

West Sussex A county of south-east England; area 1,989 sq km (768 sq miles); pop. (1991) 692,800; county town, Chichester. It is divided into seven districts.

West Virginia A state of the USA, to the west of Virginia; area 62,759 sq km (24,231 sq miles); pop. (1990) 1,793,480; capital, Charleston. It is also known as the Mountain State. It separated from Virginia during the American Civil War (1861), and became the 35th state of the USA in 1863. Its industries produce coal, gas, steel, aluminium, glass, timber, and chemicals and amongst its chief landmarks are the New River Gorge and Harpers Ferry.

West Yorkshire A metropolitan county of northern England; area 2,036 sq km (786 sq miles); pop. (1991) 1,984,700; county town, Wakefield. It is divided into five districts.

wetland Bogs, fens, swamps and marshes, where the water-table is at or near the surface of the soil for much of the year. Wetlands often contain unique COMMUNITIES and are frequently highly productive, providing food for a large range of organisms. They may also act as breeding sites for mosquitoes and other disease carriers. Depending upon the nutrient status of the soil and water, wetlands can be classified as acidic, neutral, or base-rich. These chemical factors influence the SUCCES-

SION of wetlands and, unless maintained by regular catastrophic clearance, most wetlands will ultimately revert to dry land. As a habitat, wetlands have suffered great reduction in total area, either through reclamation for agricultural land, or drainage to eradicate disease organisms. Conservation measures include making some wetlands nature reserves, and in a few instances (notably in Switzerland) transplanting small wetland areas to new sites, where the water and nutrient regime can be maintained.

Wexford ▶**1** A county in south-east Ireland, in the province of Leinster to the south of the Wicklow Mountains; area 2,352 sq km (908 sq miles); pop. (1991) 102,040. ▶**2** Its county town, at the mouth of the River Slaney; pop. (1991) 9,540.

Weyden, Rogier van der (French name Rogier de la Pasture) (*c.*1400–64) Flemish painter. He was based in Brussels from about 1435, when he was appointed official painter to the city. His work, mostly portraits and religious paintings, became widely known in Europe during his lifetime; he was particularly influential in the development of portrait painting. Major works include *The Last Judgement* and *The Deposition* (both *c.*1450).

Weygand, Maxime (1867–1965) French general. He was FOCH's chief of staff in World War I, and in 1920 was sent by the French government to aid the Poles in their ultimately successful defence against the advancing Soviet RED ARMY. In the military crisis of May 1940 Weygand was recalled to assume command of the French armies attempting to stem the German BLITZKRIEG attack. Advising capitulation, he later commanded the VICHY forces in North Africa, was dismissed at the request of the Germans, arrested by the Gestapo, and then freed by the Allies. He was tried and acquitted under the DE GAULLE regime on a charge of collaboration with the Germans.

whale An aquatic mammal of the order Cetacea; they are divided into the WHALEBONE WHALES and the TOOTHED WHALES. Their specializations for life in water are greater than those of any other mammals, and their entire lives are spent in water. Adaptations to aquatic life are noticeable in the shape of the animal. The most obvious difference from a typical fish shape is the horizontally placed tail flukes, which move up and down to provide the propulsive thrust. The hind-limbs have been completely lost except for small internal traces. The forelimbs are reduced to small, paddle-like flippers.

Like all mammals, whales breathe air, and their respiratory system shows special developments. The nose or blow-hole is high on the head and has valves for closing the nostrils during diving. Air is inhaled and exhaled through the blowhole, which connects directly with the lungs. This allows whales to feed while submerged in water without the possibility of water entering the lungs. Their spouts of water-laden air have characteristic forms, so that whales can be recognized at considerable distances. Sounds are emitted for such purposes as the attraction of females by males, communication between mother and offspring, and for the avoidance of obstacles in the dark. Some whales produce clicks, while others, like the HUMPBACKED WHALE, have a song. These animals display elaborate behaviour involving social life, cooperation between individuals, communication and learning. Many species migrate and some orientate and navigate by following the shape of the sea-bed. Whales include the largest known animals, either fossil or recent. Many species are endangered and conservation is needed. See also WHALING.

Whale See CETUS.

whalebone whale (or **baleen whale**) A WHALE that comprises the suborder Mysticetae. Whalebone whales, which include the largest known animal, the BLUE WHALE, are usually larger than the TOOTHED WHALES. They are characterized by a series of plates, baleen or whalebone, which take the place of teeth in the upper jaws. The frayed inner edges of the whalebone allow small planktonic crustacea, such as krill, to be filtered from the water. Most of these whales have a dorsal fin and a series of parallel grooves running longitudinally below the throat, except in the right whales. Other whalebone whales include RORQUALS and the GREY WHALE.

whale-headed stork (or **shoe-bill**) A bird, *Balaeniceps rex*, native to central Africa and in a family of its own, Balaeniciptidae. It stands about 1.3 m (4 feet) high and is grey with black wings and tail. Its most distinctive feature is its enormous, broad beak with a hook at the end with which it catches fish and amphibians. It makes a nest of reeds in swamps, raising one or two young.

whale shark The largest living fish, *Rhincodon typus*, which attains a length of 18 m (60 feet). It occurs in all tropical seas and is usually seen close to the surface, where it feeds on planktonic animals and small fishes. It is thought to give birth to live young, each about 50 cm (20 inches) long. It is frequently found with schools of tuna, probably because they are attracted to plankton-rich areas. The whale shark is now rare over much of its range.

whaling The pursuit and slaughter of WHALES. In the early 19th century, whales were pursued by six-man rowing boats armed with hand harpoons and lances. Carcasses were dismembered alongside the mother ship and the blubber was rendered (melted down) in brick ovens. The resulting whale oil was used for lighting and lubrication and in the manufacture of varnish, linoleum, leather, and pharmaceuticals. Baleen (whalebone) was used for corsets, knife handles, umbrella ribs, and brushes. Whaling activity lessened in the 1850s due to dwindling stocks of suitable animals and to the replacement of whale oil and spermaceti by petroleum products.

Modern whaling techniques were introduced in about 1870, when steam-powered whale catchers replaced the traditional rowing boats. Increased demand for SOAPS and MARGARINE in the early 20th century led to the development of self-contained factory fleets. A factory ship has a slipway at the stern for easy loading of the catch. Its power butchering machinery and pressure cookers can deal with a 100-tonne whale within one hour. The whaling industry declined in the 1960s, when no large concentrations of whales remained; alternatives to whale products were generally established. Since 1986 there has been an international moratorium on commercial whaling, although Japan and Iceland continue to catch whales for research, and Norway has continued whaling commercially.

Wharton, Edith (Newbold) (1862–1937) US novelist and short-story writer, resident in France from 1907. She established her reputation with the novel *The House of Mirth* (1905). Her novels, many of them set in New York high society, show the influence of Henry James and are chiefly preoccupied with the often tragic conflict between social and individual fulfilment. They include *Ethan Frome* (1911) and *The Age of Innocence* (1920), which won a Pulitzer Prize.

wheat A cereal species of the genus *Triticum* that have been cultivated for at least 10,000 years. Einkorn and emmer were the earliest domesticated species, the former probably being one of the ancestors of all cultivated wheats. Emmer was once widely grown, and has been found preserved in Egyptian tombs; it was the chief cereal in the Graeco-Roman period. Both types had fairly small grains and were difficult to thresh. They were eventually replaced by bread wheat, *T. aestivum*, a hybrid between emmer and a grass called goat-face grass, *T. tauschii*. Durum wheat, *T. durum*, is closely related to emmer and is grown in the Mediterranean region to provide the flour for macaroni, spaghetti, and other pasta.

Bread wheat is the major cereal of the world in terms of the amount produced. It contains the protein gluten and, depending on the characteristics of this gluten, the grain is used for bread or biscuit manufacture. Bread-making requires a high-grade gluten wheat known as 'hard wheat', since the gluten makes the dough elastic and enables light, airy bread to be produced. It is grown in Russia, North and South America, Europe, and Australia, and it exists in two forms, depending on the time of sowing. Spring wheats are suitable for areas with cold winters, and so dominate production in the northern wheat belt of the USA and Canada. The slower-growing but higher-yielding winter wheats are characteristic of the southern wheat belt of the USA.

wheatear A member of the thrush family that belongs to the genus *Oenanthe*. There are about 19 species, most of which are found in Europe, western Asia, and Africa, though one species, the common wheatear, *Oenanthe oenanthe*, spreads all the way across eastern Asia and over the Bering Straits into Alaska. Like many of the other species, including those that breed in Alaska, the common wheatear spends the winter in Africa. Wheatears inhabit open country, including deserts and rocky hillsides, nesting in holes in the ground. They are insectivorous.

Wheatstone, Sir Charles (1802–75) British physicist and pioneer of electric TELEGRAPHY. From 1834 he was Professor of Experimental Physics at King's College, London, where his research included work on the speed of light. In 1837, with COOKE, he patented an electric telegraph, and to exploit this interest commercially they became business partners. In 1843 he invented the **Wheatstone bridge**, a device for measuring electrical resistance. He also developed an interest in acoustics and binocular vision.

wheel A circular revolving disc or frame used on a vehicle to reduce resistance to motion and for a variety of purposes in mechanisms and industry. Its earliest use was probably in the quern, consisting of two circular stones, for grinding cereals, and in the potter's wheel. However, the most significant application of the wheel is for road transport. It is thought likely that wheels for carts and chariots were invented about 6,000 years ago. The earliest evidence of a wheeled vehicle is an illustration of a cart from the Tigris-Euphrates valley, *c.*3000 BC. The earliest wheels were solid wood or made from three planks, but spoked wheels are known from around 2000 BC as far apart as Scandinavia, China, and Mesopotamia. On these early vehicles the wheels either turned on an axle, or were rigidly fastened to an axle that revolved in a housing on the vehicle body. Lightweight wire-spoked wheels were devised by CAYLEY in about 1808; they were developed for the BICYCLE by James Starley in 1870. Originally the spokes ran radially out from the hub, but in 1874 Starley patented tangential spoking, in which spokes run diagonally from wheel to hub in a cross-over pattern, improving the wheel's strength. The invention of the steam locomotive led to the development of wrought-iron wheels. Motor vehicles now generally use pressed-steel or cast-aluminium wheels.

wheel animalcule See ROTIFER.

Wheeler, John Archibald (1911–) US theoretical physicist. Wheeler was involved in early work with Niels Bohr on nuclear fission, and joined the team to develop the hydrogen bomb at Los Alamos in 1949–50. He became professor of physics at Princeton in 1947 and at Texas in 1976. Wheeler worked on the search for a unified field theory, and collaborated with Richard Feynman on problems concerning the retarded effects of action at a distance. He was the first to use the term *black hole*, in 1968.

wheel-lock See FIREARM.

whelk A large, predatory SNAIL of the family Buccinidae, found on the sea-shore and responsible for the neat, round holes so often drilled through other molluscs' shells. The whelks rasp the hole using their ribbon of stout teeth, aided by a special acidic secretion, and then eat the shell contents. Some whelks also smother their victims with their large flat foot. Whelk shells are often encrusted with other animals, such as polyps, bryozoans, and barnacles, and when empty they sometimes form the chosen homes of hermit crabs. Masses of papery whelk egg-cases are also a frequent sight along the sea-shore.

Whig A member of the British political party traditionally opposed to the Tories. The Whigs owed their name, like the Tories, to the exclusion crisis of Charles II's reign. Those who petitioned for the recall of Parliament in 1679 were named Whigs (Scottish Covenanting brigands) by their Tory opponents. The Whigs suffered defeat in Charles's reign, but joined with the Tories in inviting WILLIAM of Orange to England, and they alternated with the Tories in power until 1714. Their principles were to maintain the power and privileges of Parliament, to show sympathy with religious dissent, keeping links between Church and state to a minimum, and to play an active role in Europe.

From the accession of GEORGE I the Hanoverian kings placed their trust in the Whigs, and there followed the long period of Whig supremacy. From the mid-1720s there were Whigs in opposition to WALPOLE and the development of factions within the party became increasingly acute by the mid-century, bringing political instability in the 1760s. The Rockingham faction, which formed the core of FOX's followers, became the basis of the new Whig party in the late 18th century. The changed political and social conditions of the 19th century caused the break-up of the Whig party. Many of its members, however, formed the core of the LIBERAL PARTY.

whimbrel See CURLEW.

whip-poor-Will See NIGHTJAR.

whirlpool A fierce, almost circular eddy of water in rivers or the sea usually occurring when fast flows of water from different directions meet. In rivers, whirlpools can form in the plunge-pool at the foot of waterfalls, or where tributary channels meet the main flow. In the sea, they occur in narrow channels, where winds and tides are moving in different directions, or where strong currents meet each other.

whirlwind A revolving column of air that arises in conditions of atmospheric instability. On land the larger whirlwinds are usually called TORNADOES and on lakes or at sea WATERSPOUTS. When they occur in deserts, the sand and other rock particles lifted by the updraught can be carried many miles. Smaller eddies are also sometimes seen when the surface is very hot.

whistler See THICKHEAD.

Whistler, James (Abbott) McNeill (1834–1903) US painter and etcher. In 1855 he went to Paris, where he was influenced by the realist painter Gustave Courbet. Based mainly in London from 1859, Whistler retained his contact with Paris and shared the admiration of contemporary French painters for Japanese prints; his work reflected this in the attention he gave to the composition of subtle patterns of light. Whistler mainly painted in one or two colours, and sought to achieve harmony of colour and tone, as in the portrait *Arrangement in Grey and Black: The Artist's Mother* (1872) and the landscape *Old Battersea Bridge: Nocturne – Blue and Gold* (*c.*1872–75).

whistling swan *Cygnus columbianus columbianus*, the New World cousin of BEWICK'S SWAN, *Cygnus columbianus bewickii*, but differing in the yellow patch on its beak, which is reduced to a small spot. They are numerous and common winter visitors to Atlantic and Pacific coasts of North America, migrating there from the Arctic, where they nest.

Whitby A resort town and former whaling port on the North Sea coast of North Yorkshire, England, at the mouth of the River Esk; pop. (1991) 13,640. There are remains of a 13th-century abbey built on the site of a former abbey destroyed by Danes in the 9th century. A conference, known as the **Synod of Whitby**, held here in 664 chiefly to settle the method of calculating the date of Easter, resulted in England severing its connections with the Irish Church.

white A butterfly of the family Pieridae, which also includes the yellows, brimstones, orange-tips, and wood-whites. The family occurs worldwide, with most of the 1,100 species in the tropics; unlike many butterflies, all pierids have three pairs of normal legs used for walking. In almost all, the scales contain white or yellow pigments derived from a waste product, uric acid. CABBAGE WHITES, familiar in many countries, are typical of the group, as is the green-veined white, *Pieris napi*, found in meadow and woodland throughout Europe, across Asia to Japan, in North Africa, and in North America. Its caterpillars feed on cruciferous plants, such as hedge mustard, but not on cabbages.

White, Gilbert (1720–93) British clergyman and naturalist. He spent most of his life in his native village of Selborne, Hampshire, becoming curate there in 1784. White is best known for the many letters he wrote to friends, sharing his acute observations on all aspects of natural history, especially ornithology; these were published in 1789 as *The Natural History and Antiquities of Selborne*, which has remained in print ever since. He was the first to identify the harvest mouse and the noctule bat.

White, Patrick (Victor Martindale) (1912–90) Australian novelist, born in Britain. White's international reputation is based on his two novels *The Tree of Man* (1955) and *Voss* (1957); the latter relates the doomed attempt made in 1845 by a German explorer to cross the Australian continent. He was awarded the Nobel Prize for literature in 1973.

White, T(erence) H(anbury) (1906–64) British novelist, born in India. White first won recognition with *England Have My Bones* (1936). He is best known for the tetralogy *The Once and Future King*, his highly original reworking of the Arthurian legend that began with *The Sword in the Stone* (1937). This was adapted as the Broadway musical *Camelot* (1959), which brought him considerable fame and financial success.

white admiral A blackish-brown BRUSH-FOOTED BUTTERFLY of the genus *Ladoga*, with a white band across fore- and hind-wings. A number of species are found in woodlands in Europe, Asia, India, and North America. The European white admiral, *L. camilla*, has powerful, gliding flight; its caterpillars are green with two rows of brown spines, and feed on honeysuckle.

white ant See TERMITE.

whitebait The young of HERRINGS and SPRATS. Both species spawn offshore, but their young drift inshore, entering estuaries in late summer and forming large, mixed schools. They are about 5 cm (2 inches) long, and are caught for sale.

white dwarf A hot star (typically 30,000 K) with low luminosity and very high density (100,000 to 100 million times that of water). A white dwarf has exhausted its nuclear fuel and is composed of degenerate matter, so that the only remaining source for the energy radiated is the star's residual heat. The diameter of a typical white dwarf is similar to that of the Earth, but the mass is about that of the Sun; the upper limit is the CHANDRASEKHAR limit of 1.44 times the Sun's mass.

white-eye A member of the family Zosteropidae, containing about 96 species of birds that occur throughout the warmer areas of the Old World, though most species are found in south-east Asia. They are small, 10–13 cm (4–5 inches) in length, and fairly uniform in appearance, greyish or yellowish-green with pale or yellow underparts. The striking feature of most species is the white ring around the eye, which gives them their name. They spend much of their time in small flocks and feed primarily on fruits, nectar, and insects.

whitefly A tiny, plant-sucking BUG of the family Aleyrodidae, related to cicadas and aphids. The wings of adults, which rarely exceed 3 mm (0.1 inch) in length, are covered with white, waxy powder. Adults and young pierce individual plant cells and suck out the sap; they excrete unwanted sugars as honeydew. Newly hatched larvae are active, but after one moult they secrete a scale which covers their body, within which development proceeds, and they become sessile. They are primarily tropical, and are pests of crops throughout the world.

Whitehall A street in Westminster, London, in which many important government offices are located. The name is taken from the former royal palace of White Hall, originally a residence of Cardinal Wolsey confiscated by Henry VIII. The Cenotaph stands in the middle of Whitehall.

Whitehead, A(lfred) N(orth) (1861–1947) British philosopher and mathematician. Whitehead is remembered chiefly for *Principia Mathematica* (1910–13), in which he and his former pupil Bertrand Russell attempted to express all of mathematics in formal logical terms. He was also concerned to explain more generally the connections between mathematics, theoretical science, and ordinary experience. Whitehead's work on geometry led to an interest in the philosophy of science; he proposed an alternative to Einstein's theories of relativity, and later developed a general and systematic metaphysical view.

white hole A theoretical region of space in which matter is created and ejected into the universe. This is in contrast to a BLACK HOLE, which drags matter in its vicinity out of existence from the universe. It has been speculated that, in a manner not at all understood, a black hole and a white hole, connected by a tunnel, may act as a means of transporting matter from one point in our universe to another.

Whitehorse The capital (since 1953) of Yukon Territory in north-west Canada, situated on the Yukon River at the junction of the Alaska and Klondike highways; pop. (1991) 21,650. Established as a rail terminus by gold prospectors following the 1897 gold-rush, Whitehorse was linked by ore-carrying sternwheelers to the territory's former capital Dawson which lay down river.

White House The official residence of the US President in Washington, DC. It was built in 1792–99 of greyish-white limestone from designs of the Irish-born architect James Hoban (1762–1831) on a site chosen by George Washington; President John Adams took up residence there in 1800. The building was restored in 1814 after being burnt by British troops, the smoke-stained walls being painted white. Although known informally as the White House from the early 19th century, it was not formally so designated until the time of Theodore Roosevelt (1902).

white lead The common name for a type of lead carbonate, $Pb_3(OH)_2(CO_3)_2$. It is prepared commercially by the action of air, carbon dioxide, and ethanoic acid vapour on LEAD. It is widely used as a PIGMENT in PAINT, but has the disadvantages of both toxicity and blackening in the presence of hydrogen sulphide, due to the formation of lead sulphide.

White Nile (Arabic **Bahr el Ablad**) That part of the upper Nile River that flows from Uganda through southern Sudan before meeting the Blue Nile at Khartoum.

White Paper See BILL.

White Russia See BELARUS, REPUBLIC OF.

White Russians Those who fought against the Soviet RED ARMY in the RUSSIAN CIVIL WAR (1918–21). The name was derived from the royalist opponents of the French Revolution, known as Whites, because they adopted the white flag of the French Bourbon dynasty. The White Army, though smaller than the Red, was better equipped and had an abundance of Tsarist officers, some of whom offered to serve as ordinary soldiers. Its two main bases were in the south, where the army was successively led by Kornilov, Denikin, and Wrangel, and in Siberia where Kolchak was nominally head of a provisional government at Omsk. The White Russians were ultimately defeated by their own internal quarrels and by their refusal to grant land reforms in the areas under their control.

whiting A fish, *Merlangius merlangius*, of the COD family who, like its relatives, has three dorsal and two anal fins, although it lacks a chin barbel. The whiting is conspicuously silvery in colour. It is an abundant fish in inshore waters of the northern Atlantic, and lives mainly in mid-water and just above the sea-bed. Small fishes live close inshore, but at a length of 3–5 cm (1–2 inches) they often take shelter among the tentacles of jellyfish. They eat small fishes and crustaceans. The whiting is a valuable food-fish, which can grow to a length of 40 cm (16 inches). In North America the name whiting is used for members of the genus *Merluccius*, known as HAKE elsewhere.

Whitlam, (Edward) Gough (1916–) Australian Labor statesman, Prime Minister 1972–75. While in office he ended compulsory military service in Australia and relaxed the laws for Asian and African immigrants. When, in 1975, the opposition blocked finance bills in the Senate, he refused to call a general election and was dismissed by the Governor-General Sir John Kerr, the first occasion in 200 years that the British Crown had removed an elected Prime Minister. Whitlam remained leader of the Labor Party until 1977.

Whitman, Walt (1819–92) US poet. Inspired partly by the writings of EMERSON and the Transcendentalists, he published in 1855 and 1856 the first and second editions of *Leaves of Grass*, including the poems later entitled 'Song of Myself', 'Crossing Brooklyn Ferry', and 'Out of the Cradle Endlessly Rocking'. Six further expanded editions appeared in his lifetime. During the American Civil War he worked as a volunteer nurse and produced the moving collection *Drum Taps* (1865), later incorporated in *Leaves of Grass*. Whitman pioneered the use of FREE VERSE and created a distinctive American voice in poetry.

Whitney, Eli (1765–1825) US inventor. He devised the mechanical cotton-gin (patented 1794), as well as conceiving the idea of mass-producing interchangeable parts. This he applied in his fulfilment of a US government contract (1797) to supply muskets; Whitney manufactured these in standardized parts for reassembly, meaning that for the first time worn parts could be replaced by spares rather than requiring special replacements to be made.

Whittier, John Greenleaf (1807–92) US Quaker poet and abolitionist. From the early 1840s he edited various periodicals and wrote poetry for the abolitionist cause. He is best known for his poems on rural themes, especially 'Snow-Bound' (1866), and for his epic of the Civil War 'Barbara Frietchie' (1863).

Whittington, Sir Richard (known as 'Dick') (died 1423) English merchant and Lord Mayor of London. Whittington was a London mercer who became Lord Mayor three times (1397–98; 1406–07; 1419–20). He left legacies for rebuilding Newgate Prison and for establishing a city library. The popular legend of Dick Whittington's early life as an orphan from a lowly background, his only possession a cat, is first recorded in 1605.

Whittle, Sir Frank (1907–96) British aeronautical engineer, test pilot, and inventor of the jet aircraft engine. He took out the first patent for a turbojet engine in 1930, while still a student. A Gloster aircraft made the first British flight using Whittle's jet engine in May 1941 (two years after the first German jet aircraft), and similar machines later entered service with the RAF. He took up a post at the US Naval Academy in Maryland in 1977.

Whitworth, Sir Joseph (1803–87) British engineer who won international acclaim as a machine-tool maker. After working as a mechanic, he joined Henry Maudslay (inventor of the metal lathe) in 1825 and had a rigorous training in the use of sophisticated machine-tools. In 1833 he opened his own business in Manchester, setting standards of precision never before attempted in toolmaking. Aware of the need for standardization, he devised the British Standard Whitworth (BSW) thread for screws, which is still widely used in the USA. In the

1870s he extended his interests to armaments and shipbuilding.

WHO See WORLD HEALTH ORGANIZATION.

whooper swan A bird, *Cygnus cygnus*, which resembles the MUTE SWAN, but its bill is yellow and black, and it swims with its neck held erect. In flight it utters loud whooping calls. Breeding in Iceland, northern Europe, and Asia, whooper swans migrate south in winter, visiting Britain regularly.

whooping cough An infection of the air passages by the bacterium *Bordetella pertussis*, causing a distressing and sometimes dangerous illness. The organism adheres to the living cells, and prevents the normal clearance of mucus. The first symptoms, which appear seven to ten days after infection, are those common to any other mild respiratory infection. Then a dry, hacking cough appears and may be followed by the characteristic whoop, produced by forced intake of breath through a partially closed part of the vocal cords. Vaccination can prevent infection, or severely reduce its effects.

whydah bird (or **indigobird**) A bird of the genus *Vidua*, related to the WEAVERBIRD. All 15 species live in Africa in open, grassy country. They are the size of small sparrows, but the males of some species have extremely long tails, giving them a total length of 60 cm (2 feet). The males display in groups to which the females come for mating. The females lay their eggs in the nests of waxbills.

Whymper, Edward (1840–1911) British mountaineer. In 1860 he was commissioned to make drawings of the Alps, and in the following year he returned to attempt to climb the Matterhorn. After seven attempts he finally succeeded in 1865, at the age of 25. On the way down four of his fellow climbers fell to their deaths, raising contemporary public doubts about the sport.

Wichita A commercial and industrial city in southern Kansas, USA, on the Arkansas River; pop. (1990) 304,010. Founded in 1868 on the site of a Wichita Indian village. It expanded as a centre of the wheat trade and with the discovery of oil to become the largest city in Kansas. It has a large aircraft industry, oil refineries, and meat-packing plants, and manufactures oil-field equipment.

Wick A town on the north-east coast of Scotland, formerly administrative headquarters of Caithness District, Highland Region (abolished 1996); pop. (1981) 7,900.

Wicklow ▶**1** A county of eastern Ireland, in the province of Leinster; area 2,025 sq km (782 sq miles); pop. (1991) 97,290. ▶**2** Its county town, a resort on the Irish Sea to the south of Dublin; pop. (1991) 5,850.

wide-bodied aircraft A modern commercial transport AIRLINER having a passenger cabin wide enough to allow three groups of seats, one central and the other two on either side of the aircraft, with two aisles between them, i.e. more than 4.7 m (15.5 feet) wide. The (US) Boeing 747 jumbo jet and the European Airbus A-320 are wide-bodied aircraft.

Wiener, Norbert (1894–1964) US mathematician. He is best known for establishing the science of cybernetics in the late 1940s. Wiener spent most of his working life at the Massachusetts Institute of Technology, making major contributions to the study of stochastic processes, integral equations, harmonic analysis, and related fields.

Wiesbaden The capital of the state of Hesse in western Germany, situated on the River Rhine at the foot of the Taunus Mountains; pop. (1991) 264,020. Founded as a Celtic settlement, it became a popular Roman spa known as Aquae Mattiacorum. In 1806 it was made capital of Nassau and in 1866 it passed to Prussia. It is now an important spa and conference centre with industries producing chemicals, textiles, and metal goods.

Wiesel, Elie(zer) (1928–) Romanian-born US human-rights campaigner, novelist, and academic. A survivor of Auschwitz and Buchenwald concentration camps, he emigrated to the USA in 1956 and subsequently pursued a career as a humanities lecturer. Wiesel emerged as a leading authority on the Holocaust, documenting and publicizing Nazi war crimes perpetrated against Jews and others during World War II. Genocide, violence, and racism were also the subjects of several acclaimed novels and short-story collections. Wiesel was awarded the Nobel Peace Prize in 1986.

Wiesenthal, Simon (1908–) Austrian Jewish investigator of Nazi war crimes. After spending 1942 to 1945 in Nazi labour and concentration camps he began his long campaign to bring Nazi war criminals to justice. Enlisting the help of West German, Israeli, and other government agents, he traced some 1,000 unprosecuted criminals, including Adolf Eichmann. In 1961 he opened the Jewish Documentation Centre, also known as the Wiesenthal Centre, in Vienna and continued to track down Nazi criminals when other countries had ceased to pursue their cases.

Wigan A town in the Greater Manchester metropolitan county, north-west England; pop. (1991) 85,819. On the site of a Roman fort, it was a market town in medieval times before being transformed by the Industrial Revolution into a textile, engineering, and coal-mining centre. It is now a centre of light industries.

wigeon Any of three species of dabbling DUCK: the European wigeon, *Anas penelope*, American wigeon, *A. americana*, and chiloe, *A. sibilatrix*, of South America. The drake of the European wigeon displays a patterned plumage of chestnut, blue, grey, white, and black, and utters a distinctive whistling call. The European species is mainly herbivorous, and notably gregarious.

Wigtownshire A former county of south-west Scotland. It became part of the region of Dumfries and Galloway in 1975.

Wilberforce, William (1759–1833) British politician and social reformer. An MP and close associate of Pitt the Younger, he was a prominent campaigner for the abolition of the slave trade, successfully promoting a bill outlawing its practice in the British West Indies (1807). Later he pushed for the abolition of slavery throughout the British Empire, his efforts resulting in the 1833 Slavery Abolition Act.

wild boar See BOAR.

wild cat Any of various species of the genus *Felis*, in the CAT family. There are 28 species of small wild cats found in all types of terrain from thick jungle to desert, and present in the Old and New Worlds. The majority are slightly larger than the domestic cat but all are similar in shape. One of the best known is the European wild cat, *Felis sylvestris sylvestris*, the head and body of which is about 63 cm (25 inches) long and the tail 35 cm (14 inches) long. The coat is yellowish-grey or grey broken up by darker stripes. The tail is heavy and blunt-ended, with black rings. It lives in areas of heavy cover and the lair is a crevice in the rocks. About a month after mating two to four kittens are born, fully furred but blind for the first ten days.

Other species include the LYNX, *F. lynx*, ocelot, *F. pardalis*, bobcat, *F. rufus*, and serval, *F. serval*.

Wilde, Oscar (Fingal O'Flahertie Wills) (1854–1900) Irish-born dramatist and poet. A disciple of the essayist and critic PATER and of the cult of 'art for art's sake', he attracted attention with his flamboyant aestheticism. His early publications include *Poems* (1881), *The Happy Prince and Other Tales* (1888), written for his sons, and his only novel *The Picture of Dorian Gray* (1891), a Gothic melodrama. His brilliant comedies for the stage include *Lady Windermere's Fan* (1892), and his masterpiece, *The Importance of Being Earnest* (1895), in which he exposes Victorian hypocrisies. The Marquis of Queensberry, father of Lord Alfred Douglas, disapproved of his son's homosexual friendship with Wilde and brought about Wilde's imprisonment in 1895 for homosexuality. In *De Profundis* (1905) Wilde apologized for his conduct and claimed to have stood 'in symbolic relation to the art and culture' of his age. *The Ballad of Reading Gaol* (published anonymously in 1898) was inspired by his prison experiences.

wildebeest See GNU.

Wilder, Billy (born Samuel Wilder) (1906–) US film director and screenwriter, born in Austria. After emigrating to the USA in 1934, he wrote screenplays for a number of Hollywood films before earning recognition as a writer-director with *Double Indemnity* (1944); written with Raymond Chandler, it is regarded as a *film noir* classic. He subsequently co-wrote and directed *Sunset Boulevard* (1950), *Some Like It Hot* (1959), and *The Apartment* (1960); the latter won Oscars for best script, director, and picture.

Wilder, Thornton (Niven) (1897–1975) US novelist and dramatist. His work is especially concerned with the universality of human experience, irrespective of time or place. He established his reputation as a novelist with *The Bridge of San Luis Rey* (1927), for which he won a Pulitzer Prize. His plays, often experimental in form, include *Our Town* (1938) and *The Skin of Our Teeth* (1942), both of which received Pulitzer Prizes. His comic drama *The Matchmaker* (1954) provided the basis for the musical *Hello, Dolly!* (1964).

wild ox See AUROCHS.

Wilhelm I (1797–1888) King of Prussia 1861–88 and emperor of Germany 1871–88. His reign saw the unification of Germany, the driving force behind which was Bismarck, his chief minister. He became the first emperor of Germany after Prussia's victory against France in 1871. The latter part of his reign was marked by the rise of German socialism, to which he responded with harsh repressive measures.

Wilhelm II (known as **Kaiser Wilhelm**) (1859–1941) Emperor of Germany 1888–1918, grandson of Queen Victoria. After forcing his chief minister, Bismarck, to resign in 1890 he proved unable to exercise a strong or consistent influence over German policies, which became increasingly militaristic in foreign affairs. He was unable to prevent the outbreak of World War I (1914), and was vilified by Allied propaganda as the author of the conflict. In 1918 he went into exile in Holland and abdicated his throne.

Wilhelmina (1880–1962) Queen of the Netherlands 1890–1948. She became queen as a child, with her mother as regent until 1898. During World War II she maintained a government in exile in London, and through frequent radio broadcasts became a symbol of resistance to the Dutch people. She returned to the Netherlands in 1945, but three years later abdicated in favour of her daughter Juliana.

Wilkie, Sir David (1785–1841) Scottish painter. He made his name with the painting *Village Politicians* (1806); influenced by 17th-century Dutch and Flemish genre painters, it defined Wilkie's style for the next 20 years. Wilkie's paintings were popular and contributed to the growing prestige of genre painting in Britain.

Wilkins, Sir (George) Hubert (1888–1958) Australian polar explorer who flew 3,400 km (over 2,100 miles) across the Arctic, from Alaska to Spitsbergen, in 1928. He returned there in 1931, trying to reach the North Pole by submarine. In 1933–39 he managed the ELLSWORTH Antarctic expeditions, and in World War II he was Arctic adviser to the US Army. After his death his ashes were scattered at the North Pole.

Wilkins, Maurice Hugh Frederick (1916–) New Zealand-born British biochemist and molecular biologist. Studying the structure of the DNA molecule by means of X-ray diffraction analysis, he and his colleague Rosalind Franklin provided the evidence for and confirmed the double helix structure proposed by Francis Crick and James Watson in 1953. Wilkins, Crick, and Watson shared a Nobel Prize for their work on DNA in 1962.

will (in law) A document setting out the intentions of a person (the testator) regarding the disposal of his or her property after death. In England, this must be signed by the testator and the making of the signature verified by two witnesses. In other countries, it is possible to create a will by other methods, including oral declaration before several witnesses, declaration before a public official, and signed writing by the testator alone. A will is revocable at any time before death, and in some cases is automatically revoked by the divorce or marriage of the testator. On the testator's death, an executor is appointed who, after obtaining PROBATE, distributes the property in accordance with the will.

Willard, Emma (1787–1870) US educational reformer. A pioneer of women's education, she founded a boarding-school in Vermont (1814) to teach subjects not then available to women (such as mathematics and philosophy). Willard moved the school to Troy, New York (1821), where it became known as the Troy Female Seminary; the college education that it offered served as a model for subsequent women's colleges in the USA and Europe.

Willemstadt The capital of the Netherlands Antilles, situated on the south-west coast of the island of Curaçao, pop. (1986) 50,000. It is a centre of oil refining. The Mikve Israel-Emanuel synagogue, which dates from 1732, is said to be the oldest in the Western Hemisphere.

William Two kings of England, and two of Great Britain and Ireland. **William I** (known as William the Conqueror) (*c.*1027–87) reigned 1066–87, the first Norman king of England. He was the illegitimate son of Robert, Duke of Normandy, and claimed the English throne on the death of Edward the Confessor, stating that Edward had promised it to him. He landed in England at the head of an invasion force, defeated Harold II at the Battle of Hastings (1066), and was crowned king. Having repressed a series of uprisings, he imposed his rule on England, introducing Norman institutions and customs (including feudalism and administrative and legal practices). He also instigated the property survey of England known as the Domesday Book.

William II (known as William Rufus, 'red-faced') (*c.*1060–1100), son of William I, reigned 1087–1100. His succession was challenged by a group of Norman barons in England who wanted William's elder brother Robert Curthose (*c.*1054–1134), Duke of Normandy, to rule England instead. However, William's forces crushed their rebellions in 1088 and 1095. William also campaigned against his brother Robert in Normandy (1089–96), ultimately acquiring the duchy in 1096 when Robert mortgaged it to William before leaving to go on the First Crusade. In the north of England William secured the frontier against the Scots along a line from the Solway Firth to the Tweed. He was killed by an arrow while out hunting; whether he was assassinated or whether his death was an accident remains unclear. **William III** (known as William of Orange) (1650–1702), grandson of Charles I, reigned 1689–1702. Son of the Prince of Orange and Mary, daughter of Charles I, William was stadtholder (chief magistrate) of the Netherlands from 1672 and married Mary, daughter of the future James II, in 1677. In 1688 he landed in England at the invitation of disaffected politicians, deposed James II, and, having accepted the Declaration of Rights (which was designed to ensure that the Crown would not act without Parliament's consent), was crowned along with his wife the following year. He defeated James's supporters in Scotland and Ireland (1689–90), and thereafter devoted most of his energies towards opposing the territorial ambitions of Louis XIV of France. **William IV** (known as 'the Sailor King') (1765–1837), son of George III, reigned 1830–37. He served in the Royal Navy from 1779, rising to Lord High Admiral in 1827, and came to the throne after the death of his brother George IV. Although an opponent of the first Reform Bill (1832), William reluctantly agreed to create 50 new peers to overcome opposition to it in the House of Lords. In 1834 he intervened in political affairs by imposing his own choice of Prime Minister (the Conservative Robert Peel), despite a Whig majority in Parliament.

William I (known as **William the Lion**) (1143–1214) grandson of David I, king of Scotland 1165–1214. He attempted to reassert Scottish independence but was forced to pay homage to Henry II of England after being captured by him in 1174.

William-and-Mary style A style in English interior decoration and design roughly coinciding with the reign of William (of Orange) and Mary (1689–1702). Although William was Dutch by birth, the period marked an increase in French influence compared with the RESTORATION style. This was partly because of the dominance of Versailles and partly because of an influx of Huguenot (Protestant) refugees from France. In general, the William-and-Mary style was lighter, more elegant, and more domestic than the Restoration style, although there was no sharp break between the two.

William of Ockham (or **Occam**) (*c.*1290–*c.*1347) English theologian and scholastic philosopher. He was a Franciscan friar who developed an anti-papal theory of the state, denying the pope secular authority and was excommunicated in 1328, living thereafter in Munich under Emperor Louis IV's protection. His form of nominalist philosophy saw God as beyond human powers of reasoning, and things as provable only by experience or by (unprovable) scriptural authority. Hence his famous maxim, 'Ockham's razor', that the fewest possible assumptions should be made in explaining a thing (see ONTOLOGY).

William of Orange William III of Great Britain and Ireland. See WILLIAM.

William Rufus William II of England. See WILLIAM.

Williams, Hank (born Hiram King Williams) (1923–53) US country singer and songwriter. A performer since boyhood, Williams had the first of many country hits, 'Lovesick Blues', in 1949, and that year joined the *Grand Ole Opry* TV programme. He soon began to cross over into the mainstream pop market, many of his songs being successfully recorded by other artists.

Williams, John (Christopher) (1941–) Australian guitarist and composer. He studied with Andrés Segovia before making his London début in 1958. Based in Britain, he became much in demand as a recitalist, noted for both classical and popular music. In 1979 he founded the pop group Sky, playing with them until 1984.

Williams, J(ohn) P(eter) R(hys) (1949–) Welsh Rugby Union player. A former junior Wimbledon tennis champion (1966), he made his rugby début for Wales in 1969 and became one of the leading full-backs of the 1970s. Williams played 63 times for his country (1969–81), as well as for the British Lions (1971–77). In 1981 he retired from rugby to pursue a career in orthopaedic medicine.

Williams, Tennessee (born Thomas Lanier Williams) (1911–83) US dramatist. He was brought up in the South, the setting for many of his plays. He achieved success with the semi-autobiographical *The Glass Menagerie* (1944) and *A Streetcar Named Desire* (1947), plays that deal with the tragedy of vulnerable heroines living in fragile fantasy worlds. Williams's later plays, while still dealing with strong passions and family tensions, increasingly feature Gothic and macabre elements; they include *Cat on a Hot Tin Roof* (1955), *Suddenly Last Summer* (1958), and *The Night of the Iguana* (1962).

Williams, William Carlos (1883–1963) US poet, novelist, short-story writer, and essayist. While practising as a doctor in New Jersey, he wrote poetry, first in the manner of the Imagists, later in a style he called Objectivism ('no ideas but in things'), which attempted to present objects without interpretation or emotion. He favoured a lean, vigorous, vernacular American poetry, and fiercely opposed the Europeanizing influence of T. S. Eliot. His answer to *The Waste Land* was *Paterson* (1946–51, 1958), a long poem about a New Jersey city and a semi-mythic protagonist, incorporating much non-poetic material. The lyrics can be found in *Collected Later Poems* (1950) and *Collected Earlier Poems* (1951).

Williamsburg A historic colonial town in south-east Virginia, USA, between the James and York rivers; pop. (1990) 11,530. First settled in 1633 and originally known as Middle Plantation, it was chosen as the site of the William and Mary College in 1693. It was the state capital of Virginia 1699–1779 and was renamed in honour of William III. A large section of the early colonial town has been restored to its 18th-century appearance.

Williamson, Henry (1895–1977) British novelist. He is best known for *Tarka the Otter* (1927), one of several wildlife tales. His pro-Hitler views damaged his later literary reputation, although he continued with a sequence of 15 autobiographical novels, *A Chronicle of Ancient Sunlight* (1951–69).

William the Conqueror William I of England. See WILLIAM.

willow A tree belonging to the genus *Salix*, of which there are about 300 species. Willows belong to the same family as poplars, Salicaceae, and vary from large trees, such as the European white willow, *S. alba*, to tiny creeping shrubs, such as the dwarf willow, *S. herbacea*. All willows have deciduous, simple leaves and small catkins, often with long hairy bracts, familiar in the pussy willow. All willow catkins are erect, unlike poplars, and they have nectaries, which attract insect pollinators.

Willows are found throughout the world, except in Australasia, but are most abundant in the Northern Hemisphere. Dwarf willows are particularly important in mountain vegetation and in taiga and tundra zones. In other regions, willows are principally found beside rivers or streams, or on marshy ground. Shrubby species, such as sallows, *S. caprea* and *S. cinerea*, can tolerate drier soils and are often scrub species in woodland edges. Osiers are willows with long, narrow leaves, grown in 'osier beds' for their pliable young shoots. These are used for making baskets and hurdles.

Willows are propagated by cuttings and are famous for the rapid production of roots from them. Most familiar in gardens is the weeping willow, perhaps a hybrid between *S. alba* and *S. babylonica*.

willow grouse See RED GROUSE.

willowherb A perennial, herbaceous plant of the genera *Epilobium* or *Chamaenerion*, related to fuchsias, clarkias, and evening primroses in the family Onagraceae. About 160 species are known, widely distributed in the temperate and alpine regions of the world. The flowers are produced in the axils of the leaves or in terminal spikes and the petals are usually rose-purple or white. Rosebay willowherb or fireweed, *C. angustifolium*, with its handsome purple flower spikes and downy, wind-blown seeds, is one of the first colonizers of waste ground.

willow warbler A species of Old World WARBLER, *Phylloscopus trochilus*. It is closely related and very similar in appearance to the chiffchaff, but with a much more melodious song. It breeds over a wide area of Europe and the northern parts of Asia, migrating to Africa for the winter. It lives in woodland, nesting on the ground.

Wills, William John (1834–61) British explorer. Having emigrated to Australia, in 1860 he was a member, with two others, of Robert Burke's expedition to cross the continent from south to north. They became the first white people to make this journey, but Wills, Burke, and one of their companions died of starvation on the return journey.

Willstatter, Richard (1872–1942) German chemist who developed a method for separating chemicals, now called CHROMATOGRAPHY. He succeeded in showing that green plants contain two chlorophyll pigments by passing a solution of chlorophyll through a column containing chalk. He received the 1915 Nobel Prize for chemistry for this work. It is also recognized that the Russian botanist Mikhail Tswett worked independently on identifying the constituents of chlorophyll and developed similar analytical techniques.

Wilson, Charles Thomson Rees (1869–1959) British physicist of Scottish extraction who invented the **Wilson cloud chamber** – a device that reveals the tracks of charged particles by radioactive atoms. The particles pass through a cold vapour, leaving trails similar to those seen behind high-flying aircraft. He shared the Nobel Prize for physics in 1927 with Arthur COMPTON.

Wilson, Edmund (1895–1972) US literary critic and essayist. A leading man of letters, he is best known for his works of literary criticism: *Axel's Castle* (1931), a study of the SYMBOLIST tradition; *Patriotic Gore* (1962), on the literature of the American Civil War; and the more miscellaneous *The Triple Thinkers* (1938, 1948) and *The Wound and the Bow* (1941). He also wrote novels, plays, and *To the Finland Station* (1940), a study of European socialist thought.

Wilson, (James) Harold, Baron Wilson of Rievaulx (1916–95) British Labour statesman, Prime Minister 1964–70 and 1974–76. In both terms of office he faced severe economic problems; repeated sterling crises led to devaluation in 1967, while he attempted unsuccessfully to deal with high inflation in 1974–76 by seeking an agreement with trade unions over limiting pay increases. His government introduced a number of social reforms, including reducing the voting age to 18, liberalizing the laws on divorce, homosexuality, and abortion, and introducing comprehensive schooling. Overseas, he was unable to persuade the regime of Ian Smith in Rhodesia (Zimbabwe) to back down over its declaration of independence (1965), and therefore introduced economic sanctions against Rhodesia. In 1974 Wilson renegotiated Britain's terms of entry into the European Economic Community, confirming British membership after a referendum in 1975. He resigned as leader of the Labour Party the following year and was replaced as Prime Minister by James Callaghan.

Wilson, (Thomas) Woodrow (1856–1924) US Democratic statesman, 28th President of the USA 1913–21. He was a prominent academic in the field of law and political economy prior to his election victory. As President he carried out a series of successful administrative and fiscal reforms. He initially kept the USA out of World War I, but, following the German reintroduction of unrestricted submarine warfare, entered the war on the Allied side in April 1917. Wilson's conditions for a peace treaty, as set out in his 'Fourteen Points' speech (1918), and his plan for the formation of the League of Nations were crucial in the international negotiations surrounding the end of the war, and he was awarded the Nobel Peace Prize in 1919. However, he was unable to obtain the Senate's ratification of the Treaty of Versailles, his health collapsed, and he lost the presidential election.

Wiltshire A county of south-west England; area 3,479 sq km (1,344 sq miles); pop. (1991) 553,300; county town, Trowbridge. It is divided into five districts.

Wimbledon A residential suburb of London, containing the headquarters of the All England Lawn Tennis and Croquet Club, scene of the 'Lawn Tennis Championships on Grass', the oldest tournament of this kind, since 1877.

Wimshurst machine An early, manually operated electrostatic generator, invented by James Wimshurst in 1883. It consists of two wheels, under 30 cm (1 foot) in diameter, mounted on the same axis. These are made to rotate in opposite directions by turning a handle. The wheels are arranged to brush each other, and this action generates static electricity.

Winchester The county town of Hampshire in southern England, a city on the River Itchen; pop. (1991) 36,121. Known to the Romans as Venta Belgarum, it became capital of the Anglo-Saxon kingdom of Wessex (519) and later capital of England under Alfred the Great (827). Its 11th-century cathedral, is the second-longest in Europe. Winchester College, founded by William Wykeham in 1382, is one of the oldest public schools in England.

King Arthur's so-called Round Table hangs in the 13th-century Great Hall of the castle. The *Domesday Book* was compiled in Winchester.

Winchester disk See HARD DISK.

Winckelmann, Johann (Joachim) (1717–68) German archaeologist and art historian, born in Prussia. In 1755 he was appointed librarian to a cardinal in Rome; there he took part in the excavations at Pompeii and Herculaneum and was instrumental in enforcing professional archaeological standards. Winckelmann became superintendent of Roman antiquities in 1763. His best-known work, *History of the Art of Antiquity* (1764), was a seminal text in the neoclassical movement.

wind Air in natural motion. It is produced around the Earth by differences in atmospheric PRESSURE from one place to another, called pressure gradients. On a global scale, however, it never blows directly from an area of high pressure to one of low pressure, but is deflected by the CORIOLIS FORCE. Planetary winds change direction: winds blowing polewards from subtropical highs become WESTERLIES, while those blowing towards the Equator become the easterly TRADE WINDS. Those high in the atmosphere, which are determined solely by the pressure gradient and Coriolis force, are called geostrophic winds. Nearer the ground, the airflow pattern is more complicated, being influenced not only by local heating and cooling (and therefore by changing pressure gradients) but also by the distribution of land and sea and variations in land relief. The secondary wind systems that result include those of the MONSOONS, the winds of various strengths associated with anticyclones and depressions, the sea-land and land-sea breezes, and those, such as the CHINOOK, which arise as a consequence of particular landforms. Local winds on land or sea are classified in the BEAUFORT SCALE. Often they pursue a circular path, as in tropical revolving storms. Winds may be dry or rain-bearing. They also carry dust in suspension, which makes them agents of EROSION.

Windaus, Adolf (1876–1959) German organic chemist. He did pioneering work on the chemistry and structure of steroids and their derivatives, notably cholesterol. He also investigated the D vitamins and vitamin B_1, and discovered the important substance histamine. Windaus was awarded the Nobel Prize for chemistry in 1928.

Windermere (or **Lake Windermere**) A lake in Cumbria, in the south-east part of the Lake District of north-west England. At about 17 km (10 miles) in length, it is the largest lake in England. It is linked to Morecambe Bay by the River Leven and the town of Windermere lies on its eastern shore.

Windhoek The capital of Namibia, situated at an altitude of 1,650 m (5,410 ft) 300 km (190 miles) east of Walvis Bay; pop. (1992) 58,600. Originally the seat of a Namaqualand chief, it was made capital of the German colony of South West Africa in 1892 and capital of the independent state of Namibia in 1990. It retains some German influence in its cultural life and buildings. Industries include meat canning, brewing, the making of bone meal, and dressing of lamb skins.

wind instruments Conventionally all those musical instruments sounded by human breath, thus excluding ORGANS and AEOLIAN HARPS. There are two basic divisions, WOODWIND (comprised of flutes and reed instruments) and BRASS INSTRUMENTS.

windmill A structure designed to extract energy from the wind. Although windmills were used 2,500 years ago in India, the first detailed account is in a Persian manuscript of about 900 AD, and windmills were common there by the 7th century. The ancient mills were of the vertical-axis type, with a curved wall to direct the wind, and the shaft connected directly to a millstone. European mills, developed in the 12th century from the design of Roman water-mills, adopted a horizontal shaft driving through right-angled gears. In the early postmills, the entire body containing all the machinery was mounted on a vertical post and could be rotated manually into the wind by means of a slanting tailpole. Fixed stone or wooden towers

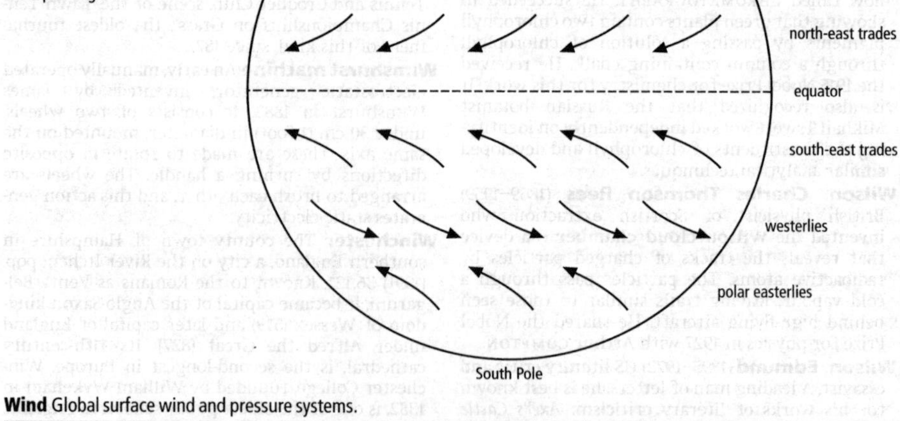

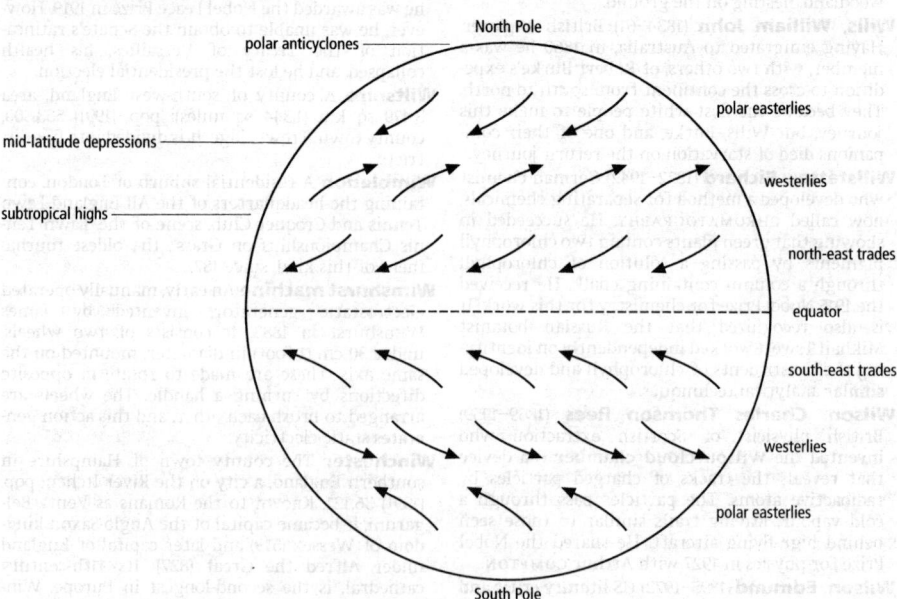

Wind Global surface wind and pressure systems.

appeared in the 15th century, with sails mounted on a cap, which could be rotated. Automatic rotation was achieved with the fantail (1745), a set of vanes at right angles to the sails, geared to wheels on a circular track. From the 15th century the Dutch used windmills for land drainage. Other uses included flour-milling, oil-pressing, paper-pulping, and sawing timber, and by the 18th century tens of thousands of mills were operating throughout Europe and North America, with power outputs as high as 50 kW. These large mills were gradually replaced by steam-power, but from the 1850s there were increasing numbers of small multi-bladed machines, producing about half a kilowatt of power to pump water. Over six million were built in the USA, an estimated 100,000 remaining in use today. Similar windmills are also used for water pumping in India, South Africa, Australia, and many other countries.

The main development of the 20th century has been the use of WIND POWER for electricity, with traditional windmills replaced by modern aero-generators.

wind power Electric power generated by wind machines. These have the advantage of being relatively safe and a pollution-free method of providing power. It is estimated that wind generators could satisfy up to a fifth of the demand for electric power in many countries, but in 1990 the highest proportion of demand met by wind generation was 1 per cent, in Denmark. The first wind generator was built in 1890, also in Denmark, starting a 30-year programme there which produced over 100 machines. In the years between the two World Wars cheap fuel everywhere gave little incentive for development of large-scale systems, but thousands of 1 kW machines were built for farms and remote communities. With a generator mounted behind the propeller, these no longer needed the vertical shaft and gearing of earlier machines. The 1940s saw new interest in generators in the 10-100 kW range, while the Putnam machine in Vermont, USA, 50 m (160 feet) in diameter, produced up to 1,250 kW for a few years. No larger machine was built until the 1970s oil crises, which encouraged the development of many two-bladed and three-bladed horizontal-axis turbines, with output from 10 to 3,000 kW. This period also saw the introduction of vertical-axis wind turbines. First proposed in 1931, these have the advantage of direct drive to a ground-level generator and an independence of wind direction.

In spite of concern about their unsightliness, in 1993 19 UK **wind farms** (groups of up to several hundred wind generators at one site) have generated sufficient current for 150,000 homes. Similar wind farms exist in the USA.

Windscale See SELLAFIELD.

wind scorpion See SUN SPIDER.

Windsor A town in Berkshire, southern England, on the River Thames opposite Eton; pop. (1991) 30,136. Its castle, which is a royal residence, was built by William the Conqueror; St George's Chapel contains the tombs of English kings including Henry VIII, Charles I, and Edward VII, and in the Home Park stands the Frogmore Mausoleum, the burial place of Queen Victoria and Prince Albert.

Windsor, Duke of The title conferred on EDWARD VIII on his abdication in 1936.

Windsor, House of The official designation of the British royal family since 1917. Anti-German feeling during World War I was sufficiently strong for George V to feel that it would be an appropriate gesture to remove all references to the German titles of Saxe-Coburg, derived originally from the marriage of Queen Victoria to Prince Albert of Saxe-Coburg-Gotha. 'Windsor' was adopted because Windsor Castle, Berkshire, has long been a home of British monarchs.

windsurfing The sport of offshore sailing on a surfboard. As opposed to surfing, which requires specific wave conditions, windsurfing needs a relatively calm sea and light winds. The mast is usually clipped into the board, and the sailor uses a horizontal crossbar to manœuvre the sail and catch the wind.

wind-tunnel An apparatus designed to produce a controlled air-stream, used for studying the AERODYNAMICS of aeroplanes, ships, buildings, and other shapes. It comprises a duct containing a scale or full-size model, connected to instruments that electrically measure the forces acting upon the model. Early tunnels were open-ended, with a small-bore test section in which the air was accelerated, but more recent designs use a closed circuit in which the temperature, pressure, and humidity of the air can be precisely controlled. Air-speeds in wind-tunnels vary from a few kilometres per hour up to hypersonic speeds of 16,000 km/h (10,000 mph) or more. At hypersonic speeds the test air must be at extremely high temperatures in order to simulate flight conditions: such tunnels are operated in pulses of only a few milliseconds.

Windward Islands A group of islands in the eastern Caribbean that constitute the southern part of the Lesser Antilles. The largest are Dominica, Martinique, St Lucia, and Barbados. They are nearest to the direction of the prevailing easterly winds, hence their name.

wine An alcoholic drink made from fermented grape or other fruit juice; wine-making is known to have been practised for over 5,000 years. Juice is extracted from grapes either by pressing them or by piling the grapes in a container with a false bottom and draining off the juice (free-run juice). For white wines, the juice and skins are then separated, and the juice may be settled or centrifuged to remove cloud. For red wines the skins, seeds, and juice are fermented together. The grape juice (must) is now fermented: the yeasts used in FERMENTATION may be those naturally present on the skins of the grapes, or a pure yeast culture that is added to the must. Temperature control during fermentation is essential for the production of wine with good colour and flavour. Fermentation usually ends after 10 to 30 days, when the sugar concentration in the must has fallen low. The wine is then 'racked' or drawn off to separate the lees (sedimentary material, including the majority of yeast cells) from the wine. It may be clarified at this stage (for example, with isinglass, a form of gelatine obtained from fish) to remove remaining suspended material. Wine is usually aged in oak or redwood casks: for red wines the ageing may be two to three years; but white wines need less time, and some are not casked. Before bottling, wines are often blended, and preservatives may be used to limit further microbial action. Better red wines improve from ageing in the bottle: some may mature for up to 20 years.

Wingate, Orde Charles (1903–44) British major-general. A brilliant exponent of guerrilla warfare, in the 1930s he helped to establish and train Jewish irregular forces operating against Arabs in Palestine, and in 1941 he organized Sudanese and Abyssinian irregulars to fight the Italian occupiers and restore Emperor Haile Selassie to the throne. He created and led the *chindits*, a Burmese guerrilla group that operated behind Japanese lines. He died in an air crash in 1944 at the outset of his second, and greatly enlarged, *chindit* operation.

winkle (or **periwinkle**) A SNAIL of the family Littorinidae found worldwide on sea-shores. Winkles show a phenomenon known as zonation: the occurrence of different species at successive shore heights. Some small species, highly resistant to desiccation, live in cliff crevices rarely even splashed by waves; other forms occur between tide levels amongst algae and in rock-pools, where they are fully aquatic. Winkles thus show a great range of colour and shape, yet all are herbivores and most species are grazers of seaweeds. They are collected as food by birds or by man.

Winnipeg The capital of Manitoba, and the largest city of the prairie provinces of central Canada; pop. (1991) 652,350 (metropolitan area). Established as a trading post in 1821–22 by the Hudson's Bay Company, it is situated at the junction of the Assiniboine and Red rivers which together formed the main route followed by early fur traders. In 1882 it became an important stop and outlet for grain on the east–west Canadian Pacific railroad and in the years prior to World War I it attracted large numbers of European immigrants. It has two universities including the University of Manitoba, which was founded here in 1877, a ballet company, and symphony orchestra. It is one of the world's largest grain markets and has grain elevators, flour mills, and food-processing plants.

Winnipeg, Lake A large lake in Manitoba, Canada, north of the city of Winnipeg; area 24,387 sq km (9,416 sq miles). A remnant of the glacial Lake Agassiz, it is the third-largest lake in Canada. It receives the Red, Saskatchewan, and Winnipeg rivers and is drained by the Nelson River, which flows northeastwards to Hudson Bay.

Winsor, Frederick Albert (or **Winzer**) (1763–1830) German-born British pioneer of the coal-gas industry. Visiting Paris in 1802, he witnessed a demonstration of GAS LIGHTING by Lebon. Two years later, in London, he embarked on an intensive campaign to arouse public interest in gas lighting. This led to the foundation of the Gas Light and Coke Company in 1812, which grew to be the largest gas undertaking in the UK.

wintergreen ▶**1** A creeping evergreen plant of the family Pyrolaceae, of the northern temperate zone, which includes some 20 species in the genus *Pyrola*. ▶**2** The plant from which **oil of wintergreen** is derived: *Gaultheria procumbens* of North America, a member of the heather family and closely related to the cranberry. The oil is rich in salicylic acid, a type of antiseptic, and is used as an effective linament for bruises and pulled muscles.

Winterhalter, Franz Xavier (1806–73) German painter based in Paris for most of his career. He painted many portraits of European royalty and aristocracy. His subjects included Napoleon III, the emperor Franz Josef, and Queen Victoria and her family.

wireworm See CLICK BEETLE.

Wirral, the The name given to the narrow peninsula to the north of Chester, which separates the mouth of the River Dee from the Mersey estuary.

Wisconsin A state in the northern USA to the east of the Mississippi River, bordering on Lakes Superior and Michigan; area 145,436 sq km (56,153 sq miles); pop. (1990) 4,891,770; capital, Madison. The largest cities are Milwaukee and Madison. It is also known as the Badger State. Dairy farming and the manufacture of automobiles, machinery, paper, and beer are among its chief industries. Ceded to Britain by the French in 1763 and acquired by the USA in 1783, it became the 30th state of the USA in 1848. Its chief landmarks are the Apostle Islands, the Ice Age National Scientific Reserve, and the St Croix National Scenic Riverway.

Wisden, John (1826–84) English cricketer. He is remembered as the publisher of *Wisden Cricketers' Almanack*, an annual publication, which first appeared in 1864.

wisteria A deciduous climber of the genus *Wisteria*, native to the eastern USA and northeast Asia. They are members of the pea family and have divided leaves and trusses of white or pale lilac-blue pea flowers. Most familiar is *W. sinensis* from central China, a beautiful climber for house walls, sometimes used in bonsai in Japan.

witan (from Old English *witenagemot*, 'moot', or meeting, of the king's councillors) The council summoned by the Anglo-Saxon kings. The meetings of the witan in the 10th and 11th centuries were a formalization of the primitive councils that existed in the early Saxon kingdoms of the 7th century. These formal gatherings of ALDERMEN, THANES, and bishops discussed royal grants of land, church benefices, charters, aspects of taxation, defence and foreign policy, customary law, and the prosecution of traitors. The succession of a king had usually to be acknowledged by the witan.

witchcraft The malevolent exercise of supposed supernatural powers, especially by women, attributed to a connection with the devil or evil spirits. The witch's male counterpart is wizard, sorcerer, or warlock. There are accounts of witchcraft in ancient Greek and Roman texts, for example Medea, who uses sorcery to help JASON win the Golden Fleece. In the Old Testament King Saul consults the Witch of Endor. In the early Middle Ages popular superstition began to associate witchcraft with demonic possession and the rejection of God. By the late 13th century the INQUISITION dealt with cases of witchcraft involving heresy, and secular courts, especially in Germany, punished these supposed crimes with characteristic cruelty. Mass persecutions began to take place in the 15th century, and the publication of *Malleus Maleficarum* ('Hammer of Witches') in 1487, describing witches' sabbaths, night-flying, intercourse with the devil, transformation into animals, and malicious spells cast on men and cattle, greatly increased superstition and persecution. Witches were popularly depicted with a black cat (the 'familiar') and a broomstick. The 16th-century Reformers further contributed to the persecution of witches, as did the unrest stirred up by the religious wars. The last trials for witchcraft in England were in 1712, and on the Continent (in Prussia) in 1793. In America the belief in witchcraft was rife but the SALEM witch trials (1692) caused a general revulsion. In the 17th century better education led to rejection of belief in witchcraft, but popular superstition survived much longer. In the 20th century, in Europe and the USA, a new kind of witchcraft claiming to be a revival of pre-Christian pagan religion, has been practised by a small number of adherents and has at times been associated with allegations of animal sacrifice and CHILD SEXUAL ABUSE.

witchetty grub See GOAT MOTH.

witch hazel A small deciduous tree or shrub of the genus *Hamamelis*, with strap-shaped petals in fours. The four or five species are members of the family Hamamelidaceae. Most widely seen are the forms of Chinese witch hazel, *H. mollis*, from western China, which produce their scented flowers in midwinter. The popular remedy, witch hazel, is derived from extracts of the leaves and bark of the common witch hazel, *H. virginiana*, native to the eastern USA and flowering in autumn. The leaves resemble those of hazel trees and the twigs were used by early settlers in North America for water divining; hence the popular name.

Withering, William (1741–99) British physician and botanist. The son of an apothecary, he qualified in medicine in Edinburgh and later set up a medical practice in Birmingham. In 1785, he published a treatise on the treatment of dropsy (oedema, or accumulation of water in the body tissues) with foxgloves, the active principle of which (digitalis) is still widely prescribed for certain forms of heart disease.

Wittgenstein, Ludwig (Josef Johann) (1889–1951) Austrian-born philosopher. He went to England in 1911 and studied mathematical logic at Cambridge under Bertrand Russell (1912–13). He then turned to the study of language and its relationship to the world, and in the *Tractatus Logico-philosophicus* (1921) contended that language achieves meaning by 'picturing' things by established conventions. He also pointed out that logical truths are tautologous because they are necessarily true within their own system and argued that metaphysical speculation is meaningless, theories which influenced the development of logical positivism. He returned to Cambridge in 1929, where he was professor of philosophy (1939–47); he became a British citizen in 1938. Principal among his later posthumous works is *Philosophical Investigations* (1953). In this he argues that words take on different roles according to the different human activities in which they are used, and that they do not have definite intrinsic meanings. He showed that some philosophical problems are simply a result of a misunderstanding of the nature of language, as for example the assumption by some earlier philosophers that individual human beings have a private language in which their thoughts as well as their utterances are composed.

Witwatersrand A series of parallel ridges forming a watershed between the Vaal and Olifant rivers in northern South Africa. The Witwatersrand or Rand area is South Africa's chief centre of gold-mining. Its Afrikaans name means 'ridge of white waters'.

woad A biennial or short-lived perennial herb, *Isatis tinctoria*, native to central and southern Europe, which belongs to the mustard family, Cruciferae. It has a tap root system, bluish-green leaves, and stems of small, yellow flowers. A blue DYE can be produced from the leaves, which was formerly much used to colour fabrics.

Wodehouse, Sir P(elham) G(renville) (1881–1975) British humorous writer. In a writing career that spanned more than 70 years his output included over 120 volumes, and he became Broadway's leading writer of musical comedy lyrics. After 1955 he held both US and UK citizenship. His best-known characters include the valet Jeeves and his youthful employer Bertie Wooster. Wodehouse's stories describe life in 1920s upper-class English society.

Woden See ODIN.

Wöhler, Friedrich (1800–82) German chemist who succeeded in preparing urea, $CO(NH_2)_2$, from ammonium cyanate, NH_4CNO. Historically this was important since it represented the first laboratory synthesis of a naturally occurring compound. His collaboration with LIEBIG led to the idea of the FUNCTIONAL GROUP. He also isolated aluminium and beryllium and discovered calcium carbide, from which he obtained ethyne (acetylene).

wolf A carnivore of the dog family, Canidae. The grey wolf, *Canis lupus*, once ranged over the entire Northern Hemisphere, even into Arctic regions, the exception being extreme desert areas: it is now more restricted. It is 90 cm (3 feet) tall at the shoulders, the head is wide and the ears fairly short, the jaws are long, and it has a long bushy tail. Its coat varies from almost black to near white. A pack of wolves usually consists of a dozen animals, including the parents and young together with adult relatives. Their family ties are strong since male and female mate for life. The male will help to excavate an underground den and tunnel leading to it, often near a hilltop and with an unobstructed view of the surrounding country. Four to 14 pups are born two months after mating, usually in spring. Besides the grey wolf there is also the red wolf, *C. rufus*, once found in the southeast USA, but now thought to be extinct in the wild.

Wolf, Hugo (Philipp Jakob) (1860–1903) Austrian composer. He is chiefly known as a composer of lieder and from about 1883 onwards produced some 300 songs. His early songs are settings of German poets, especially Goethe and Heinrich Heine. He turned to translations of Spanish and Italian verse for the three volumes of his *Spanish Songbook* (1891) and the two volumes of his *Italian Songbook* (1892–96). He also wrote an opera, *Der Corregidor* (1895). His career was cut short by mental illness resulting from syphilis, and his last years were spent in an asylum.

Wolfe, James (1727–59) British general. As one of the leaders of the expedition sent to seize French Canada, he played a vital role in the capture of Louisbourg on Cape Breton Island in 1758. The following year he commanded the attack on the French capital, the city of Quebec. He was fatally wounded while leading his troops to victory on the Plains of Abraham, the scene of the battle that was to lead to British control of Canada.

Wolfe, Thomas (Clayton) (1900–38) US novelist. He gave up his teaching post at New York University after the success of his first, autobiographical novel *Look Homeward Angel* (1929). His intense, romantic works dwell idealistically on the USA. Many, including the short-story collection *The Hills Beyond* (1941), were published posthumously, following his death from a brain tumour.

Wolfe, Tom (full name Thomas Kennerley Wolfe Jr.) (1931–) US writer. He was a news reporter for the *Washington Post* (1959–62) and the *Herald Tribune* (1962–66), and became known for his advocacy of the New Journalism and his treatment of contemporary US culture in books, such as *The Electric Kool-Aid Acid Test* (1968). His novel *The Bonfire of the Vanities* (1988) was immensely successful.

Wolff, Caspar Friedrich (1733–94) German embryologist. He advanced the theory of epigenesis, which postulated (quite correctly) that the development of an embryo involves the gradual and progressive growth of body organs and tissues. The view held prior to Wolff's theory was that a miniature of the animal or plant was present inside the sperm, egg, or seed.

wolfram The principal ore of tungsten. It has the chemical formula (Fe, Mn)WO_4. Correctly known as wolframite, it is found in PEGMATITE and other veins as tabular crystals or in red-brown masses.

Wolfson, Sir Isaac (1897–1991) Scottish businessman and philanthropist. He was appointed managing director of Great Universal Stores in 1934, later becoming its chairman (1946) and honorary life president (1987). In 1955 he established the Wolfson Foundation for promoting and funding medical research and education. In 1966 Wolfson endowed the Oxford college that now bears his name; University College, Cambridge, changed its name to Wolfson College in 1973 in recognition of grants received from the foundation.

wolf spider (or **hunting spider**) A ground-dwelling spider of the family Lycosidae, with highly developed eyes for detecting prey, usually small insects, which it kills with quick-acting poisons. A few species have venom which can cause spreading ulceration in humans. These spiders are generally quite small and cryptically coloured, often rather hairy. Some females signal receptiveness to mating by releasing a special scent (pheromone) to attract males. This occurs at night, when males of some species often lull their potential mates by a song produced by scraping two parts of the leg together. Female wolf spiders often carry their eggs around in a coloured silken sac and the young are carried on the mothers' backs after hatching, clinging on to special knobbed hairs.

Wollaston, William Hyde (1766–1828) British metallurgist. In his scientific research he was attracted particularly by the relatively abundant, but very intractable metal PLATINUM, which had defeated all attempts to produce it in malleable form. He succeeded by developing a new technique of powder metallurgy (1804) in which grains of the metal were made to cohere by compression, heating, and forging. The product was very expensive but in considerable demand – from SULPHURIC ACID manufacturers and others – because of its high resistance to corrosion.

Wollongong A port and industrial city to the south of Sydney on the Illawarra Coast of New South Wales, Australia, situated around Port Kembla Harbour; pop. (1991) 211,420. Steel is produced and grain and coal are exported. It became the chief port of the southern Wollongong–Lithgow–Newcastle coalfield area in the 1890s.

Wollstonecraft, Mary (1759–97) British writer and feminist, of Irish descent. She was associated with a radical circle known as the 'English Jacobins', whose members included Thomas Paine and William Godwin. In 1790 she published *A Vindication of the Rights of Man* in reply to Edmund Burke's *Reflections on the Revolution in France*. Her best-known work, *A Vindication of the Rights of Woman* (1792), defied Jean-Jacques Rousseau's assumptions about male supremacy and championed educational equality for women. In 1797 she married Godwin and died shortly after giving birth to their daughter Mary Shelley.

Wolsey, Thomas (known as **Cardinal Wolsey**) (*c.*1474–1530) English prelate and statesman. Favoured by Henry VIII, he dominated foreign and domestic policy in the early part of Henry's reign and held positions as Archbishop of York (1514–30), cardinal (1515–30), and Lord Chancellor (1515–29). His main interest was foreign politics, in which he sought to increase England's influence in European affairs by holding the balance of power between the Holy Roman Empire and France. Wolsey incurred royal displeasure through his failure to secure the papal dispensation for Henry's divorce from Catherine of Aragon; he was arrested on a charge of treason and died on his way to trial in London. See also HAMPTON COURT.

Wolverhampton An industrial city in the west Midlands of England, north-west of Birmingham; pop. (1991) 239,800. The city is named after Wulfruna, sister of Edgar II, who endowed the first collegiate church here in 994. Engineering and the manufacture of chemicals, aircraft parts, and metal goods are among its chief industries. The University of Wolverhampton (formerly Wolverhampton Polytechnic) was established in 1992.

wolverine A member of the family Mustelidae, *Gulo gulo*, also known as glutton because of its supposed insatiable appetite. It inhabits the tundra and northern forests of North America and Eurasia. Weighing up to 30 kg (66 pounds), it is by far the largest relative of the weasel, and is also a fearless predator, often driving wolves and bears from their kills. It is capable of killing animals up to the size of deer, but is mainly a scavenger. It also feeds on grubs and birds' eggs. Wolverines are solitary, but there are social attachments between a male and several females.

womb See UTERUS.

wombat Any of three species of MARSUPIAL in the family Vombatidae, found in coastal regions and hills of southeastern Australia, Tasmania, and Flinders Island. They are large, burrowing, tail-less animals with rodent-like grinding teeth. In some respects they are equivalent to badgers, using their sturdy limbs and claws to dig burrows up to 30 m (100 feet) long with a nest chamber at the end. Wombats are nocturnal, remaining in their burrows by day, emerging in darkness to feed upon grasses, roots, and the inner bark of trees. They are solitary except at mating time; a single young is born, which is then carried in the mother's pouch.

women's liberation See FEMINISM.

women's movement See FEMINISM.

women's suffrage The right of women to take part in political life and to vote in an election. Women's suffrage was advocated by Mary WOLLSTONECRAFT in *A Vindication of the Rights of Woman* (1792), and throughout the 19th century, in Britain and the USA, calls were made for voting rights for women. These were first attained at a national level in New Zealand (1893). The state of Wyoming, USA, introduced women's suffrage in 1869 and by 1920 all women over 21 were given the vote in the USA. The first European nation to grant female suffrage was Finland in 1906, with Norway following in 1913, and Germany in 1919. In Britain, as a result of agitation by the Women's Social and Political Union, led by Emmeline Pankhurst and her daughter Christabel (see SUFFRAGETTES), the vote was granted in 1918 to those over 30 and in 1928 to women over 21. In the years following World War I, women were granted the vote in many countries, including Germany, Poland, Austria, and Sweden (1919), and the USA (1920). The Roman Catholic Church was reluctant to support women's suffrage and in many Catholic countries it was not gained until after World War II; in France it was granted in 1944, in Belgium in 1948, while in Switzerland not until 1971. In Russia women gained the right to vote with the Revolution (1917), and women's suffrage was extended to the Soviet Union from 1922. In developing countries, women's suffrage was usually obtained with independence, and in most Muslim countries women now have the vote. Women still do not have the vote in certain absolute monarchies, such as Saudi Arabia and Kuwait (where all suffrage is restricted). See also FEMINISM.

Wonder, Stevie (born Steveland Judkins Morris)

(1950–) US singer, songwriter, and musician. He was blind from birth, but his musical gifts were recognized at an early age and he became a recording artist with Motown in 1961. Although he was at first a soul singer, from the 1970s his repertoire has broadened to include rock, funk, and romantic ballads. Among his albums are *Innervisions* (1973) and *Songs in the Key of Life* (1976).

wood The tissue beneath the BARK of trees, used for fuel, timber, paper and other products. In DICOTYLEDONS and CONIFERS it is composed of dead cells that conduct water from the roots for TRANSPIRATION; other elongated, thick-walled cells that give strength; and several kinds of thin-walled cells. In PALMS, wood consists of bundles of conducting cells embedded in hard, fibrous tissue. There is a seasonal production of wood from the cambium of trees giving patterns of annual rings which enable us to age trees and date timbers (see DATING SYSTEMS). In most trees only the younger sapwood conducts water: the heartwood becomes blocked by tannins which have preservative properties, and it then serves only a mechanical function. Wood from conifers is called softwood, and that from other trees hardwood, irrespective of the hardness of the tissue. Timber merchants and forensic biologists identify woods by the arrangement of the cells and their wall sculpturing.

Wood, Mrs Henry (née Ellen Price) (1814–87) British novelist. She had immense success with her first novel, *East Lynne* (1861), and went on to write nearly 40 books. Her ingenious and sensational plots about murders, thefts, and forgeries, in works such as *Elster's Folly* (1866) and *Roland Yorke* (1869), make her one of the forerunners of the modern detective novelist.

Wood, Sir Henry (Joseph) (1869–1944) British conductor. In 1895 he instituted the first of the Promenade Concerts at the Queen's Hall in London, and conducted these every year until he died. During this time he introduced music by composers, such as Schoenberg, Janáček, and Scriabin to British audiences. He made many orchestral transcriptions and arranged the *Fantasia on British Sea Songs* (including 'Rule, Britannia'), which has become a regular feature of the last night of each year's promenade concert season.

Wood, John (known as **John Wood the Elder**) (1704–54) British architect, active mainly in his native Bath, which he was largely responsible for transforming into the finest Georgian town in England. From 1729 his career was devoted largely to creating splendid new streets of houses in Bath, conceived as unified compositions in a dignified Palladian style. The most original and magnificent part of his scheme is The Circus, begun in the year of his death and completed by his son, **John Wood the Younger** (1728–81). It is a vast circular space completely surrounded by regular housing.

Wood, Natalie (1938–81) US actress. On joining Warner Brothers in 1955 Wood immediately attracted serious attention as the vulnerable adolescent heroine of *Rebel Without A Cause* (1955). She continued to play similar film roles in productions such as *Cry in the Night* (1956), *West Side Story* (1961), and *Inside Daisy Clover* (1966). She drowned in an accident in 1981.

wood-block printing Printing from a relief image carved from a block of wood. Wooden blocks were first used for printing in the Far East in about the 8th century, and in Europe, by monks, in the 14th century. After the invention of metal type in the 15th century, the use of wood-blocks was principally for illustrations (woodcuts). They were the chief form of printed illustration in the 16th and 17th centuries, but later copper ENGRAVING began to displace woodcuts. The development of fine wood engraving by the British engraver Thomas Bewick (1753–1828) extended the use of wood-blocks until the late 19th century, when the cheaper process engraving prevailed. However, the process is still used by some illustrators, and for printing on textiles.

woodcarving The art of cutting or incising wood. The great variety in the colour of woods available, from the almost ivory paleness of sycamore to the rich black satin of walnut and ebony, can be exploited to stunning effect. Woodcarving is a widespread art, the richest traditions today being in Africa and Oceania. In Europe little woodcarving has survived from the ancient world, but the late Middle Ages saw a great flowering of the art. Inside medieval churches the skills of the woodcarver were displayed in choir-stalls, screens, pulpits, lecterns, and misericords. Woodcarving was also used to decorate secular interiors, as in the work of Grinling GIBBONS. In Africa one of the most ubiquitous pieces of furniture is the low wooden stool; artistic elegance reaches its climax in the caryatid stools of the Democratic Republic of Congo, showing a female figure with ornate hair-styles and an intricate pattern of body scars, supporting the seat of the stool. Woodcarving has also been used to decorate ritual and ceremonial objects, such as masks, ancestor figures, and royal stools in Africa, and the totem-poles of North American Indian art. Wooden musical instruments have often been carved, some of the finest being the drums of the Aztec culture of Central America. In most societies statues have been carved of wood, and these were mostly painted in European art until the 20th century. The present century has seen a flowering of abstract wood sculpture in the work of BRANCUSI, HEPWORTH, and MOORE.

woodchuck (or **groundhog**) A MARMOT, *Marmota monax*, of North America. Like all marmots, the woodchuck has a thickset body and short tail and lives in underground colonies on mountain slopes, coming out by day to feed on surface vegetation. It spends the winter in deep hibernation.

woodcock Any of six species of WADING BIRD belonging to the genus *Scolopax*, which are found over much of Eurasia and North America. They live on the forest floor and, like their relative the snipe, are beautifully concealed by their leaf-like coloration of mottled browns and blacks. They are solidly built, long-beaked birds up to 35 cm (14 inches) in length, which probe into soft soil for worms and similar animals. The European woodcock, *S. rusticola*, and American woodcock, *S. minor*, are valued as sporting birds.

woodcreeper A bird of the family Dendrocolaptidae, which is confined to forests of Central and South America. Remarkably like TREECREEPERS, except for their size, they can be as large as a crow, and are speckled, or mottled, brown birds with stiffened tails. They climb up tree trunks in their search for food which is primarily insects. Their beak shape varies markedly among the 46 species, from medium length and straight to long and strongly curved.

wood hoopoe A bird of the family Phoeniculidae, containing some five species of *Phoeniculus* found in central and southern Africa, where they live in wooded country. They have a body about the size of a small thrush, and a long tail. They are glossy blue-black or greenish-black, with white spots at the tips of the tail feathers and white marks in the wing. The beak is usually red, long, and markedly curved in some species. They feed primarily on insects, and nest in holes in trees.

woodlouse A CRUSTACEAN of the order Isopoda, common in most terrestrial habitats. Woodlice have no waterproof covering, and their life revolves around avoiding desiccation. To this end, they congregate in humid spots, only being active at night when humidity is usually higher. Some species, such as pill bugs, resemble tiny armadillos, and can curl into a ball for protection. Most species of woodlice feed on decaying vegetation or rotten wood and protect their young in a special pouch after birth.

wood mouse (or **field mouse**) A small MOUSE of the genus *Apodemus*, widely distributed throughout Europe and non-tropical Asia in a variety of habitats from grasslands to woodlands. There are some 13 species, two of which occur in Britain – the wood mouse, *Apodemus sylvaticus*, and the yellow-necked mouse, *A. flavicollis*, which are distinguished by their large, beady eyes and prominent ears, as well as by their long tails. Their food consists of seeds, berries, roots, and insects. They are of economic importance because they kill tree seedlings, and are of great ecological significance as seed-dispersers and as food for avian and mammalian predators. They are nocturnal, spending the day in burrows, in which they also rear their young. One female is capable of rearing up to six litters in her one year of life. They do not hibernate, even in the coldest winters, but some store food in the summer for winter use.

The equivalent mice of the New World are the deer mice or white-footed mice, some 49 species in the genus *Peromyscus*, distributed from the Arctic to northern South America.

woodpecker A bird of the family Picidae, containing about 200 species. Their distribution is worldwide within wooded habitats, though they are absent from Australasia and most oceanic islands. They range in size from 9–55 cm (3.5–22 inches) and in colour from green and yellow to spotted black and brown. Most climb vertical trunks using their strong feet and stiffened tail feathers for support. They feed on seeds and insects, and extract many of the latter from timber by drilling holes with their powerful beaks and retrieving their prey by means of their very long tongues. Most also use their beaks to excavate nesting cavities in trees, but a few nest in banks or termite mounds. American sapsuckers of the genus *Sphyrapicus* drill rows of small holes in trees, drink the exuding sap and eat the insects attracted by it. The acorn woodpecker, *Melanerpes formicivorus*, drills rows of holes in the bark of a single tree and stores an acorn in each; these enormous stores are guarded by family parties of birds. The family includes the wrynecks and the flickers (*Colaptes* species) of North America. Many have distinctive calls which carry far, the European green woodpecker, *Picus viridis*, being known in some areas as the 'yaffle', supposedly mimicking its call.

woodpigeon (or **ring-dove**) A PIGEON, *Columba palumbus*, which occurs over much of Europe and western Asia. It is a large, pale, bluish-grey bird, 40 cm (16 inches) in length, with a wine-red throat, and a white band across the wings which is visible only in flight. A white patch on either side of the neck looks as if the bird has a ring around its neck and so gives rise to the name ring dove, which is more properly applied to the Barbary dove. It lives in wooded areas for much of the year, but feeds readily in fields, where it can cause serious damage to crops such as cabbages and sprouts.

wood-pulp See PAPER MANUFACTURE.

woodruff Any of several species of plants of the genera *Asperula* and *Galium*, related to bedstraws in the family Rubiaceae. They are slender, perennial plants with creeping rootstocks, whorls of narrow leaves, and terminal clusters of small white or blue flowers. Growing in woodlands and hedgerows, they are widely distributed throughout Europe, Italy, and North Africa. The common woodruff, *A. odorata*, is a fragrant herb which is used as an ingredient of perfumed snuffs and was once in great demand as a medicinal plant.

wood swallow A bird of the family Artamidae, of which there are 11 species native to India, south-east Asia, Australia, and some Pacific islands. They live in open wooded country, often near water, and are about the size of a sparrow, primarily greyish or brownish, with a stoutish beak. Most species catch flying insects by fluttering and swooping like true swallows, or by darting out from a perch.

wood warbler **▶1** Any of the birds comprising the New World family Parulidae (see WARBLER). **▶2** A species of Old World WARBLER, *Phylloscopus sibilatrix*, a bird closely related to the willow warbler and chiffchaff. It differs from these in being a little larger, 12.5 cm (5 inches) in length, with a yellow throat and a white belly. It breeds in Europe and spends the winter in Africa, living in woodland which has little ground cover. It has a trilling song which accelerates towards the end.

Woodward, Robert Burns (1917–79) US organic chemist. He was the first to synthesize a wide range of complex organic compounds, including quinine, cholesterol, cortisone, strychnine, chlorophyll, and vitamin B_{12}. In 1965, with the Polish-born US chemist Roald Hoffmann (1937–), he devised the symmetry-based rules that govern the course of concerted rearrangement reactions involving cyclic intermediates. He was awarded the Nobel Prize for chemistry in 1965.

woodwasp Any of various species of large SAWFLY, the adults of which are orange and black or uniformly blue, and the females have a long ovipositor. They fly with a loud buzz and insert their eggs into the wood of conifers, where the larvae bore damaging tunnels. Often confused with true wasps, they cannot sting.

woodwind Musical instruments that include the orchestral FLUTES and REEDS. All were originally wooden except SAXOPHONES, which, because their reed and mouthpiece are similar to those of CLARINETS, are nevertheless regarded as woodwind. Ivory has occasionally been used for FLUTES since the 16th century, for OBOES in the 18th century, and for clarinets in the 19th, and glass was fashionable for flutes early in the 19th century. Metal was used for all woodwind from the mid-19th century, often for military bands and ships' orchestras. The woodwind section in the symphony ORCHESTRA, was established by Beethoven, with two each of flutes, oboes, clarinets, and BASSOONS. In their early works, Haydn and Mozart often scored for oboes only. Oboes were sometimes scored in the outer movements and flutes in the quieter slow movement. The woodwind section was enlarged by Berlioz and Wagner to three or more of each instrument. A flautist was expected to play PICCOLO, and later alto flute, an oboist to play COR ANGLAIS, a clarinettist to play high or low clarinets, and a bassoonist to play contrabassoon.

wool A fibre obtained from the domesticated

sheep, used to make fabrics since antiquity. Before YARN was spun, garments were made from woollen FELT. Wool is a protein fibre, similar to cotton in diameter but much longer. The length depends on the breed of sheep and on the part of its body from which the wool is taken. Long fibres are spun into worsted YARN; shorter fibres are used for felting or for woollen yarns. All wool fibres are naturally wavy and, in addition, have an outer layer of very fine scales. These two features render the fibres mutually cohesive in a way that reduces the amount of twist needed in SPINNING and makes true felting possible. At the same time, the crimp and scales are not wholly desirable because they give wool its propensity to shrink when washed. Wool is damaged by alkaline liquors, but is resistant to acids and can readily be dyed to good fast colours using acid DYES. Wool is often blended with synthetic fibres, such as NYLON, POLYESTER, or ACRYLIC FIBRES to make clothes that are harder wearing.

Woolf, (Adeline) Virginia (née Stephen) (1882–1941) British novelist, essayist, and critic. From 1904 her family's London house became the centre of the Bloomsbury Group, among whose members was **Leonard Woolf** (1880–1969), whom she married in 1912. She and her husband founded the Hogarth Press in 1917. She gained recognition with her third novel, *Jacob's Room* (1922); subsequent novels, such as *Mrs Dalloway* (1925), *To the Lighthouse* (1927), and *The Waves* (1931), characterized by their stream-of-consciousness technique and poetic impressionism, established her as a principal exponent of modernism. Her non-fiction includes *A Room of One's Own* (1929), a major work of the women's movement. She suffered from severe depression throughout her life, and drowned herself shortly after completing her final and most experimental novel, *Between the Acts* (published posthumously in 1941).

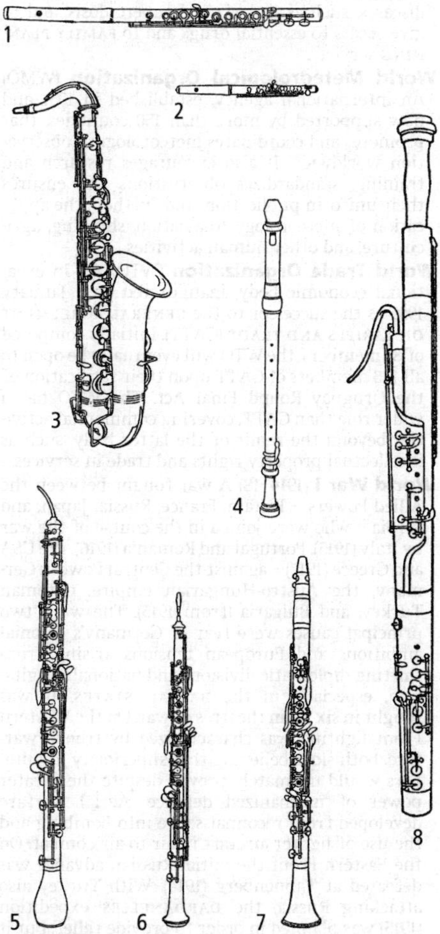

Woodwind instruments (1) Flute. (2) Piccolo. (3) Saxophone. (4) Tenor recorder. (5) Cor anglais. (6) Oboe. (7) Clarinet. (8) Bassoon.

Woolley, Sir (Charles) Leonard (1880–1960) British archaeologist. Between 1922 and 1934 he was director of a joint British–US archaeological expedition to excavate the Sumerian city of Ur (in what is now southern Iraq). His discoveries included rich royal tombs and thousands of clay tablets providing valuable information on everyday life of the period.

woolly rhinoceros An extinct type of Pleistocene mammal, which once roamed over much of Eurasia. It stood about 2 m (6.5 feet) high, had two horns, and was well protected from the icy climate of that time by a thick, black coat covered with reddish hairs. Early man hunted it and portrayed it extensively in cave paintings.

Woolwich A district of east London, south-east England, on the south bank of the River Thames in the borough of Greenwich. It was the site of the Royal Dockyard in which famous ships such as Henry VIII's *Great Harry* were built, and of the Royal Arsenal (now being redeveloped). The University of Greenwich (formerly Thames Polytechnic) was founded here in 1992.

Woolworth, Frank Winfield (1852–1919) US businessman. He opened his first shop selling low-priced goods in 1879. He gradually built up a large chain of US stores selling a wide variety of items, and the business later became an international retail organization.

Worcester A city in the county of Hereford and Worcester, England, on the River Severn; pop. (1991) 81,800. Its cathedral is the burial place of King John and Worcester was the scene of a battle (1651) in which Cromwell defeated a Scottish army under Charles II. The city shares with Hereford and Gloucester the annual Three Choirs Festival.

word processor (WP) A computer program or complete computer system designed to enable the user to manipulate text on screen and produce letters, documents, or other written material for printing. Text is entered using the keyboard, and displayed and edited under computer control. The edited document may then be stored on a FLOPPY DISK or HARD DISK for future use, or printed out on paper (hard copy). Using WP facilities, a block of text may, for example, be added, deleted, or moved from one location in a file (document) to another, or copied into a second file. After insertions or deletions, the text can be rearranged to re-form paragraphs, or as required, using the word-wrap facility. A document may be entirely reformatted by changing the margins, tabulation, justification, line spacing, number of lines per page, or highlighting. Some word processors also incorporate a spelling checker. Word processors also allow the frequent change or update of documents. Largely repetitive items may be quickly created and, with merge facilities, personalized letters, for example, are easily generated from a single basic form. For reproduction purposes word processors are capable of outputting print-quality images of an acceptable typographic standard, for both editing and printing purposes. This is more commonly the field of DESK-TOP PUBLISHING.

Wordsworth, Dorothy (1771–1855) British diarist. She was William Wordsworth's sister and devoted companion. Her detailed diaries (such as her *Grasmere Journal*, 1800–03), in addition to providing a biographical perspective on her brother, document her intense response to nature and mingle the sublime with the matter-of-fact. In 1835 she began to suffer from a form of dementia from which she never recovered.

Wordsworth, William (1770–1850) British poet. He was born in the Lake District and much of his work was inspired by the landscape of this region. He spent some time in France (1790–91) and became an enthusiastic supporter of the French Revolution, although he later became disillusioned by the excesses of the Terror and in later life assumed a more conservative stance. From 1795 to 1799 he lived in Somerset, where, with Coleridge, he composed the *Lyrical Ballads* (1798), a landmark in the history of English romantic poetry, containing in particular his poem 'Tintern Abbey'. In 1799 he returned to the Lake District, settling in Grasmere with his sister Dorothy; his wife joined them after their marriage in 1802. Among his many poems are the ode 'Intimations of Immortality' (1807), sonnets, such as 'Surprised by Joy' and 'I Wandered Lonely as a Cloud' (both 1815), and the posthumously published, autobiographical *The Prelude* (1850). He was appointed Poet Laureate in 1843.

work (in physics) The process of a transfer of ENERGY. As with all forms of energy, the SI UNIT of work is the joule. Work is the scalar product of the force and displacement vectors. The work done by a force is the product of that force and the distance over which it is applied in the direction in which it acts. One joule of work is done when one newton is applied over one metre.

workhouse A public institution in which people unable to support themselves were housed and (if able-bodied) made to work. The 1601 POOR LAW Act made parishes responsible for their own workhouses, but often they were hard to distinguish from the houses of correction, set up to discipline vagrants. The 1723 Workhouse Act denied relief to able-bodied paupers who refused to enter workhouses.

World Bank The popular name of the International Bank for Reconstruction and Development. It was set up by the United Nations in 1945 to promote the economic development of member-nations by facilitating the investment of capital for productive purposes, encouraging private foreign investment, and if necessary lending money from its own funds. Its headquarters are in Washington, DC.

World Council of Churches An inter-denominational organization of Christian Churches, created in 1948. Apart from the ROMAN CATHOLIC CHURCH and the Unitarians, the Council includes all the major and many minor denominations and nearly all the Eastern Orthodox Churches. Since 1961 the Roman Catholic Church has sent accredited observers. The World Council of Churches is the most important of a number of ecumenical movements advocating greater unity amongst the Christian Churches. Most of the work of the Council is advisory, but it also has a number of administrative units; the largest of these is the division of Inter-Church Aid, Refugee, and World Service.

World Health Organization (WHO) A UNITED NATIONS specialized agency established in 1948 with the broad aim of attaining the highest level of health for all people, and supported by about 160 countries. Its head office is in Geneva, Switzerland. WHO does not conduct its own research but promotes biomedical and health research in some 500 collaborating centres worldwide, arranging international medical conferences and the exchange and training of research workers. WHO compiles the *International Pharmacopœia*, monitors epidemics, evaluates new drugs, and advises on biological standards. It publishes quarterly an international journal of health development (*World Health Forum*) in Arabic, Chinese, English, French, Russian, and Spanish. A notable success of WHO has been the eradication of smallpox throughout the world.

WHO advocates a number of PUBLIC HEALTH measures to provide safe drinking water and adequate sanitation, the IMMUNIZATION of all children against major COMMUNICABLE DISEASES, and the reduction of malnutrition. In addition, it has intensified efforts to prevent and combat endemic diseases, such as malaria and tuberculosis, and to give access to essential drugs and to FAMILY PLANNING services.

World Meteorological Organization (WMO) An international agency, established in 1951 and now supported by more than 150 countries, that promotes and coordinates meteorological observation worldwide. It also encourages research and training; standardizes observations and ensures their uniform publication; and furthers the application of meteorology to aviation, shipping, agriculture, and other human activities.

World Trade Organization (WTO) An international economic body, inaugurated on 1 January 1995 as the successor to the GENERAL AGREEMENT ON TARIFFS AND TRADE (GATT). Initially composed of 81 members, the WTO will eventually be open to all 125 members of GATT upon their ratification of the Uruguay Round Final Act. The WTO has a wider role than GATT, covering commercial activities beyond the remit of the latter body, such as intellectual property rights and trade in services.

World War I (1914–18) A war fought between the Allied Powers – Britain, France, Russia, Japan, and Serbia – who were joined in the course of the war by Italy (1915), Portugal and Romania (1916), the USA and Greece (1917) – against the Central Powers: Germany, the Austro-Hungarian empire, Ottoman Turkey, and Bulgaria (from 1915). The war's two principal causes were fear of Germany's colonial ambitions and European tensions arising from shifting diplomatic divisions and nationalist agitation, especially in the BALKAN STATES. It was fought in six main theatres of war. On the Western Front fighting was characterized by trench warfare, both sides believing that superiority in numbers would ultimately prevail despite the greater power of mechanized defence. Aerial warfare developed from reconnaissance into bombing and the use of fighter aircraft in air-to-air combat. On the Eastern Front the initial Russian advance was defeated at Tannenberg (1914). With Turkey also attacking Russia, the DARDANELLES expedition (1915) was planned in order to provide relief, but it failed. Temporary Russian success against Austria-Hungary was followed (1917) by military disaster and the RUSSIAN REVOLUTION. The Mesopotamian Campaign was prompted by Britain's desire to protect oil installations and to conquer outlying parts of the Ottoman empire. A British advance in 1917 against the Turks in Palestine, aided by an Arab revolt, succeeded. In north-east Italy a long and disastrous campaign after Italy had joined the Allies was waged against Austria-Hungary, with success only coming late in 1918. Campaigns against Germany's colonial possessions in Africa and the Pacific were less demanding. At sea there was only one major encounter, the inconclusive Battle of JUTLAND (1916). A conservative estimate of casualties of the war gives 10 million killed and 20 million wounded. An armistice was signed and peace terms agreed in the VERSAILLES PEACE SETTLEMENT.

World War II (1939–45) A war fought between the AXIS POWERS and the Allies, including Britain, the Soviet Union, and the USA. Having secretly rearmed Germany, HITLER occupied (1936) the Rhineland, in contravention of the VERSAILLES PEACE SETTLEMENT. In the same year the Italian fascist dictator, Benito MUSSOLINI, joined Hitler in a Berlin-Rome axis, and in 1937 Italy pledged support for the ANTI-COMINTERN PACT between Germany and Japan. In the 1938 ANSCHLUSS, Germany annexed Austria into the THIRD REICH, and in the same year invaded Czechoslovak SUDETENLAND. Hitler, having secured the MUNICH PACT with CHAMBERLAIN in 1938, signed the Nazi–Soviet Pact with STALIN in August 1939. Germany then felt free to invade the POLISH CORRIDOR and divide Poland between itself and the Soviet Union. Britain, which until 1939 had followed a policy of APPEASEMENT, now declared war (3 September) on Germany, and in 1940 Winston CHURCHILL became head of a coalition government. The Soviet Union occupied the Baltic States and attacked Finland. Denmark, parts of Norway, Belgium, the Netherlands, and three-fifths of France fell to Germany in rapid succession, while the rest of France was established as a neutral state with its government at VICHY. A massive BOMBING OFFENSIVE was launched against Britain, but the planned invasion of the country was postponed indefinitely after Germany failed to gain air superiority in the Battle of BRITAIN. Pro-Nazi governments in Hungary, Romania, Bulgaria and Slovakia now joined the Axis Powers, and Greece and Yugoslavia were overrun in March–April 1941. Hitler, breaking his pact with Stalin, invaded the Soviet Union, where his forces reached the outskirts of Moscow. Without declaring war, Japan attacked the US fleet at PEARL HARBOR in December 1941, provoking the USA to enter into the war on the side of Britain. In 1942 the first Allied counter-offensive began against ROMMEL in North Africa (see NORTH AFRICAN CAMPAIGNS), and in 1943 Allied troops began an invasion of the Italian mainland, resulting in the overthrow of Mussolini's government a month later. On the Eastern Front the decisive battles around KURSK and STALINGRAD broke the German hold. The Allied invasion of western Europe was launched in the NORMANDY CAMPAIGN in June 1944 and Germany surrendered, after Hitler's suicide in Berlin, in May 1945. The Pacific Campaigns had eliminated the Japanese navy, and the heavy strategic bombing of Japan by the USA, culminating in the atomic bombing of Hiroshima and Nagasaki on 6 and 9 August 1945, induced Japan's surrender a month later.

The dead in World War II have been estimated at 15 million military, of which up to 2 million were Soviet prisoners-of-war. An estimated 35 million civilians died, with some 6 million Jews perishing in CONCENTRATION CAMPS in mass murders in Eastern Europe. Refugees from the Soviet Union and Eastern Europe numbered many millions. The long-term results of the war in Europe were the division of Germany, the restoration to the Soviet Union of lands lost in 1919–21, together with the creation of communist buffer-states along the Soviet frontier. Britain had accumulated a $20 billion debt, while in the Far East nationalist resistance forces were to ensure the decolonization of south-east Asian countries. The USA and the Soviet Union emerged from the war as the two largest global powers. Their war-time alliance collapsed within three years and each embarked on a programme of rearmament with nuclear capability, as the COLD WAR developed.

World Wide Web See INTERNET.

worm An invertebrate with a long, thin, soft, and generally pinkish-brown body, which lacks a hardened outer covering. Worms specifically belong to the phylum Annelida (see ANNELID), but many disparate groups are called worms, particularly the parasitic ROUNDWORMS and TAPEWORMS. The Annelida include the familiar EARTHWORMS, BRISTLEWORMS, and FANWORMS.

A worm-shaped body is very suitable in shape for burrowing, sinuous wriggling, or swimming. It is particularly useful to parasites, which inhabit the guts of other animals or live inside plants. It is, however, a poor design for terrestrial life, so worms are at best only semi-terrestrial. Only the WALKING WORMS of the species *Peripatus* possess simple legs, which allow them to move over hard terrain without too much friction.

Worms An industrial town on the Rhine in the Rhineland Palatinate of western Germany; pop. (1991) 77,430. At the **Diet of Worms** (the Imperial Diet of Charles V) in 1521 Martin Luther committed himself to the cause of Protestant reform. On the last day of the Diet his teaching was formally condemned in the Edict of Worms. It is a centre of wine production and the manufacture of chemicals and metal goods.

wormwood See ARTEMISIA.

worsted See WOOL.

Worth, Charles Frederick (1825–95) British couturier, resident in France from 1845. He opened his own establishment in Paris in 1858, and soon gained the patronage of the Empress Eugénie, wife of Napoleon III. Regarded as the founder of Parisian *haute couture*, he is noted for designing gowns with crinolines, making extensive use of rich fabrics, and for introducing the bustle.

wrasse A member of a large family of BONY FISHES, Labridae, which are most abundant in tropical seas but also extend into temperate waters. About 400 species are known. In some species females change sex into functional males as they age. Like the related PARROT FISHES, they have well-developed teeth. Several wrasses feed on external parasites infesting other fishes, and most sleep at night by burrowing into sand or hiding under cover. Many species are brilliantly coloured.

wren Any of about 75 species of bird in the family Troglodytidae, which occur primarily in South and Central America, though about ten species extend into North America, and one, the common wren, *Troglodytes troglodytes*, is widespread in Europe and Asia. Generally small, they range up to the size of a thrush. Most are greyish or brownish, usually heavily streaked or barred. They live in a wide variety of habitats, from forest to cactus desert, and build domed nests of twigs and leaves.

Wren, Sir Christopher (1632–1723) English architect. He turned to architecture in the 1660s after an academic career as a scientist. Following the Great Fire of London (1666) he submitted plans for the rebuilding of the city; although these were never realized, Wren was appointed Surveyor-General of the King's Works in 1669 and was responsible for the design of the new St Paul's Cathedral (1675–1711) and many of the city's churches. The influence of the Baroque, seen in elements of St Paul's, is particularly apparent in his Greenwich Hospital (begun 1696). Among Wren's other works are Greenwich Observatory (1675) and a partial rebuilding of Hampton Court (1689–94). He was a founder member (1660) and later president of the Royal Society (1680–82).

wren thrush A bird, *Zeledonia coronata*, that belongs to the family Parulidae. It is restricted to dense montane forests above about 1,500 m (5,000 feet) in Panama and Costa Rica. Wren thrushes are about 11 cm (4 inches) in length, olive-grey above and grey below, except for an orange crown. They are primarily insectivorous.

wrestling The ancient sport of hand-to-hand grappling, practised worldwide according to a variety of disciplines. Two styles, Greco-Roman and all-in or freestyle, are contested at the OLYMPIC GAMES. There are ten classes, ranging from 48 kg (106 pounds) to 130 kg (286 pounds). Contestants wear leotards and light boots, and bouts last for three three-minute rounds unless previously decided by a fall or disqualification. In Greco-Roman wrestling, no holds are allowed below the waist, and the legs may not be used to grip an opponent. Freestyle is faster and permits any fair hold, throw, or trip. Bouts are won on points or by a fall, pinning the opponent's shoulders to the mat for one second. Sumo wrestling, which requires both bulk and speed, is practised at the highest level only in Japan. Victory goes to the wrestler who forces his opponent to the mat or across the rope in a circular ring.

Wright, Billy (full name William Ambrose Wright) (1924–94) British footballer. A wing-half and latterly a defender, Wright spent his entire professional career with Wolverhampton Wanderers, with whom he won three league championships. He won 105 England caps (90 as captain), and was the first player to make more than 100 appearances for his country. After his retirement in 1959 he managed Arsenal 1962–66 and then worked as an executive in television sport.

Wright, Frank Lloyd (1869–1959) US architect. His early work, with its use of new building materials and cubic forms, was particularly significant for the development of modernist architecture, in particular the international style. His 'prairie-style' houses in Chicago revolutionized US domestic architecture in the first decade of the 20th century with their long low horizontal lines and intercommunicating interior spaces. He advocated an 'organic' architecture, characterized by a close relationship between building and landscape and the nature of the materials used, as can be seen in the Kaufmann House (known as 'Falling Water') in Pennsylvania (1935–39), which incorporates natural features such as a waterfall into its design. Other notable buildings include the Johnson Wax office block in Racine, Wisconsin (1936), and the Guggenheim Museum of Art in New York (1956–59).

Wright, Orville (1871–1948) US aviation pioneer, who with his brother **Wilbur** (1867–1912) made the first powered aircraft flight. The Wright brothers were mostly self-taught as engineers; they began by designing and building printing machinery, and later designed and manufactured bicycles. They became interested in aeronautics in 1896, when Wilbur read an account of the gliding experiments of LILIENTHAL. Between 1899 and 1903 they undertook an extensive programme of research and development: it involved a period of serious theoretical study, experimentation with models and kites, exhaustive tests of full-sized gliders (both in a home-built wind-tunnel and in more than 1,000 open-air flights), and the design and building of an efficient propeller and a suitable engine. They made their first sustained, powered human flight, lasting 12 seconds, in 1903 at Kitty Hawk, North Carolina, USA. Their first practical aeroplane was the Flyer III (1905), which could stay airborne for over half an hour. Improved Wright machines appeared until 1911, but later, European designs became dominant.

writing A system of inscribed signs replacing or recording spoken LANGUAGE. Various writing systems worldwide have developed independently. Writing is closely associated with the appearance of civilization, since in simple societies speech and memory were sufficient and there was no need for writing. It was essential, however, for the administration on which civilized states depend. The simplest form was the *quipus* of the INCAS, which were bundles of variously knotted strings; these served the purposes of accounting but lacked the flexibility of all other writing systems, whether carved, painted, scratched, impressed, handwritten, or printed.

The earliest forms of writing are non-phonological; that is, they do not represent the sounds of a language. The first pictogram system (direct representations of simple objects and notions) was that of the SUMERIANS in *c.*3400 BC. Pictographic writing evolved into ideographic. Ideograms depict more abstract concepts, ideas, and expressions. Egyptian HIEROGLYPHS are an example of ideographic writing, which typically is a mixture of pictograms, ideograms, and representations of certain sounds of the language (phonograms). In logographic writing systems, such as Chinese, logograms represent words or their parts (morphemes) and usually include SEMANTIC and PHONETIC components. There are two purely phonological writing systems: syllabaries, (e.g. in the linear scripts of MINOAN Crete and modern Japanese) in which the symbols correspond to the syllables of words; and alphabetic systems, in which the symbols directly correspond to individual sounds (phonemes). See ALPHABET.

wryneck Either of two species of WOODPECKERS that live in open woodland. They are about the size of a sparrow, finely patterned in greys, buffs, and browns with a shortish, sharply pointed beak. The Eurasian wryneck, *Jynx torquilla*, breeds across large areas of Europe and Asia, but spends the winter in Africa, where the red-breasted wryneck, *J. ruficollis*, occurs. They nest in holes in trees and eat mainly ants. They get their name from the way in which they twist their heads.

Wuhan (formerly **Hankow**) A port, commercial, and industrial city on the Yangtze River, capital of Hubei province in eastern China; pop. (1990) 3,710,000. Formerly a fishing village, it developed on being designated a treaty port after the 19th-century Opium Wars, with the arrival of the railway, and with the establishment of China's first modern iron and steel manufacturing complex (1891). It is made up of the cities of Wuchang, Hankow, and Hanyang, and is one of the most important industrial centres in China with iron and steel, paper-making, textiles, and cement industries. The Yangtze is crossed here by a mile-long road and rail bridge. Although 970 km (600 miles) from the sea, the port handles ocean-going ships.

Wundt, Wilhelm (1832–1920) German psychologist. Working in Leipzig, he was the founder of psychology as a separate discipline, establishing a laboratory devoted to its study. He felt that the major task of the psychologist was to analyse human consciousness, which could be broken down into simpler fundamental units. Wundt required subjects to report their sensory impressions under controlled conditions, and although this method of inquiry was later rejected, his legacy includes the rigorous methodology upon which he insisted.

Wuppertal An industrial city of western Germany, on the River Wupper in North Rhine-Westphalia; pop. (1991) 385,460. It was formed in 1929 by the merger of Barmen, Elberfeld, Vohwinkel, and smaller towns. It is a major textiles centre.

Wurtz, Charles-Adolphe (1817–84) French chemist noted for his research on organic nitrogen compounds, hydrocarbons, and glycols. He developed a method for preparing aliphatic hydrocarbons by the reaction of an ethereal solution of a halocarbon with sodium. Together with Marcellin BERTHELOT he succeeded in making the Sorbonne one of Europe's leading centres of tuition in chemistry.

Würzburg An industrial city in southern Germany on the River Main; pop. (1991) 128,500. The 11th-century cathedral was damaged in World War II but later restored. It is a cultural and wine-growing centre.

Wyatt, James (1746–1813) British architect. Following a six-year stay in Italy he returned to England, where he built the neoclassical Pantheon in London (1772), later destroyed by fire. Although he continued to build in a neoclassical style Wyatt became a leading figure in the Gothic revival, most notably with his design for Fonthill Abbey in Wiltshire (1796–1807). He was also involved in the restoration of several English medieval cathedrals, work which was later strongly criticized by Pugin.

Wyatt, Sir Thomas (1503–42) English poet. He held various diplomatic posts in the service of Henry VIII, one of which took him to Italy (1527), a visit which probably stimulated him to translate and imitate the poems of Petrarch. His work includes sonnets, rondeaux, songs for the lute, and satires. His son, **Sir Thomas Wyatt** (*c.*1521–54), was executed after leading the unsuccessful WYATT'S REBELLION.

Wyatt's Rebellion (February 1554) A protest in England against MARY I's projected marriage to the future PHILIP II of Spain. Its leader was a Kentish landowner, Sir Thomas WYATT. Convinced that the marriage would turn England into 'a cockleboat towed by a Spanish galleon', he led 3,000 Kentishmen in a march on London. The rebellion's ultimate aims are uncertain, as is the involvement of Mary's half-sister, Princess Elizabeth, but it led to the execution of Lady Jane GREY. Wyatt found most Londoners' loyalty to Mary stronger than their antipathy to Spain. He surrendered, and was executed with 100 others.

Wycherley, William (*c.*1640–1716) English dramatist. His Restoration comedies are characterized by their acute social criticism, particularly of sexual morality and marriage conventions. They include *The Gentleman Dancing-Master* (1672), *The Country Wife* (1675), and *The Plain-Dealer* (1676).

Wyclif, John (or **Wycliffe**) (*c.*1330–84) English religious reformer. He was a lecturer at Oxford (1361–82) and a prolific writer, whose attacks on medieval theocracy are regarded as precursors of the Reformation. He criticized the wealth and power of the Church, upheld the Bible as the sole guide for doctrine, and questioned the scriptural basis of the papacy; his teachings were disseminated by itinerant preachers. In accordance with his belief that such texts should be accessible to ordinary people, he instituted the first English translation of the complete Bible. He was compelled to retire from Oxford after his attack on the doctrine of transubstantiation and after the Peasants' Revolt (1381), which was blamed on his teaching. The followers of Wyclif were known as Lollards.

Wyndham, John (pseudonym of John Wyndham Parkes Lucas Beynon Harris) (1903–69) British writer of science fiction. He is noted for several novels, including *The Day of the Triffids* (1951), *The Chrysalids* (1955), and *The Midwich Cuckoos* (1957). His fiction often deals with a sudden invasion of catastrophe, usually fantastic rather than technological in nature, and analyses its psychological impact.

Wyndham Lewis, Percy See LEWIS, (PERCY) WYNDHAM.

Wynette, Tammy (born Tammy Wynette Pugh) (1942–98) US country singer. She started singing to pay the medical bills for her last child, who suffered from spinal meningitis. Her first success came in 1966 with 'Apartment No. 9' and continued with songs such as 'Stand by Your Man' (1968). Her unique lamenting voice made her one of the most popular country singers, her *Greatest Hits* album (1969) remaining in the bestseller charts for more than a year.

Wyoming A Rocky Mountain state in the western central USA, the smallest state by population; area 253,326 sq km (97,809 sq miles); pop. (1990) 453,590; capital, Cheyenne. It is also known as the Equality State. Wyoming is a leading producer of oil, gas, sodium bicarbonate, bentonite, uranium, and wool. Acquired as part of the Louisiana Purchase in 1803, it became the 44th state of the USA in 1890. Its chief landmarks are Yellowstone and Grand Teton national parks, Fossil Butte National Monument, and Fort Laramie National Historic Site.

X

Xanthippe (or **Xantippe**) (5th century BC) Wife of the philosopher Socrates. Her bad-tempered behaviour towards her husband has made her a proverbial shrew.

Xavier, **St Francis** (known as 'the Apostle of the Indies') (1506–52) Spanish missionary. While studying in Paris in 1529 he met St Ignatius Loyola and five years later became with him one of the original seven Jesuits. He was ordained in 1537, and from 1540 onwards made a series of missionary journeys to southern India, Malacca, the Moluccas, Sri Lanka, and Japan, during which he made many thousands of converts. He died while on his way to China. Feast day, 3 December.

X-chromosome See CHROMOSOME.

Xenakis, **Iannis** (1922–) French composer and architect, of Greek descent. Born in Romania, he later moved to Greece, where he studied engineering, and settled in Paris in 1947. He became a French citizen and worked for 12 years for the architect Le Corbusier, during which time he began to compose music. He evolved a stochastic style of composition, in which a random sequence of notes is produced according to mathematical probabilities, as in *Pithoprakta* (1955–56). His music also makes use of computer-aided calculations and electronic instruments.

xenon (symbol Xe, at. no. 54, r.a.m. 131.30) One of the NOBLE GASES, discovered in 1898 as a result of the fractional distillation of liquid air. It constitutes one part in 20 million of the atmosphere. Formerly xenon was thought to be totally inert, but various xenon compounds have now been prepared, particularly with fluorine, for example XeF_2 and XeF_4. The ionic compound $Xe^+PtF_6^-$ was the first noble-gas compound to be discovered. Commercially xenon is obtained from liquid air; it is used in special lamps and discharge tubes and in the control of nuclear FISSION chain reactions.

Xenophanes (*c*.570–*c*.480 BC) Greek philosopher. He was a member of the Eleatic school of philosophers and a critic of the belief that the gods resembled human beings, whether in conduct, physical appearance, or understanding. He was a proponent of a form of monotheism, arguing that there is a single eternal self-sufficient Consciousness, which influences the universe (with which it is identical) through thought.

Xenophon (*c*.435–*c*.354 BC) Greek historian, writer, and military leader. He was born in Athens and became a disciple and friend of Socrates. In 401 he joined the campaign of the Persian prince CYRUS THE YOUNGER against Artaxerxes II; when Cyrus was killed north of Babylon, Xenophon led an army of 10,000 Greek mercenaries in their retreat to the Black Sea, a journey of about 1,500 km (900 miles). His historical works include the *Anabasis*, an account of the campaign with Cyrus and its aftermath, and the *Hellenica*, a history of Greece. Among his other writings are three works concerning the life and teachings of Socrates, and the *Cyropaedia*, a historical romance about the education of Cyrus the Younger.

Xenopus A genus comprising the African clawed frogs. These frogs are totally aquatic and have a smooth, slippery skin. They have a short head with a semi-elliptical outline, long, pointed fingers and large, fully webbed feet with sharp, black claws on the three inner toes; they are therefore well adapted to an aquatic life. The best-known species, *Xenopus laevis*, feeds on worms, fishes, or other small animals. African clawed frogs are native to tropical and southern Africa and belong to a family, Pipidae, of tongueless frogs. Unlike most frogs, they spend virtually all of their lives under water.

xerography See PHOTOCOPIER.

xerophyte (or **xerophile**) A plant able to grow in very dry conditions because it has adapted to restrict water loss by shedding leaves at the beginning of the dry season or by growing waxy leaves or dense hairs.

Xerxes I (known as **Xerxes the Great**) Ruler of the Achaemenid Persian empire 486–465 BC. He personally led the great expedition against Greece, but after watching his fleet being defeated at SALAMIS in 480 BC, he withdrew, leaving behind Mardonius under whose command the army was defeated at Plataea in 479. The subsequent activities of the DELIAN LEAGUE deprived him of many Greek cities in Asia Minor. The latter part of his reign was marked by intrigues, one of which led to his murder.

Xhosa A branch of the Bantu people of the Cape region of South Africa. Their language is similar to Zulu.

Xian (formerly **Changan**, **Siking**, or **Sian**) An industrial city of northern China, capital of Shaanxi province; pop. (1990) 2,911,000. It was the capital of China under several ruling dynasties. The Qin emperor Shi Huangdi (*c*.259–210 BC) is buried here in an elaborate tomb complex, guarded by 10,000 life-size pottery soldiers and horses, the 'terracotta army', discovered in 1974. The city was called Siking when it was the western capital of the Tang dynasty, but since the Ming dynasty has been known by its present name. Its industries manufacture steel, fertilizers, textiles, machine tools, and irrigation equipment.

Ximenes de Cisneros See JIMÉNEZ DE CISNEROS.

Xingú A South American river that rises in the

Mato Grosso of west Brazil and flows northwards for a distance of 1,979 km (1,230 miles) to join the River Amazon at the head of the Amazon delta. A proposal to dam the Xingu River and flood adjacent land focused international attention on the plight of the Amerindians of the Brazilian rainforest.

Xinjiang (formerly **Sinkiang**) An autonomous region of north-west China; area 1,646,800 sq km (636,075 sq miles); pop. (1990) 15,156,000; capital, Urumqi. Occupying one-sixth of China, the region includes the Tien Shan mountain range, the Taklimakan Desert, and the Turfan Depression. It is rich in mineral resources, such as oil, nickel, lead, copper, and manganese, which have been exploited since the 1950s. Nomadic herding has been the traditional way of life for non-Chinese ethnic groups, but for reasons of security in this strategic area, and to increase economic development, there has been large-scale compulsory Chinese settlement.

Xiongnu Nomad horsemen who began harrying northern Chinese states *c.*300 BC. Their homelands were in southern Siberia and Mongolia. It was to fend off their incursions that some Chinese states built walls, later joined together to form the GREAT WALL OF CHINA. The most serious attacks came under the early HAN, after the Xiongnu had formed a league under their Shan Yu (Heavenly Ruler). In the confusion following the Han's collapse, claiming descent from Chinese princesses, they set up ephemeral dynasties in northern China. Thereafter Chinese records make no reference to them. The Eastern Turks, who submitted to the Tang emperor TAIZONG, are thought to be their descendants.

Xiuhtecuhtli The Aztec fire-god, also known as Huehueteotl (Nahuati, 'old god'), ruler of the Sun of the present universe, to whom human sacrifices were made. As the leader of souls, Xiuhtecuhtli helped the spirits of the dead to be absorbed into the earth.

Xizang The Chinese name for the autonomous region of TIBET.

X-ray astronomy The study of space and celestial bodies by means of the X-rays they emit. As X-rays are absorbed by the Earth's atmosphere, these studies have to be carried out by rocket or satellite. In 1970 the first of a series of X-ray satellites was launched carrying X-RAY TELESCOPES. These satellites have revealed that in addition to many individual sources in the Universe, there seems to be a faint background of X-radiation, the source of which is unknown.

X-ray burster See BURSTER.

X-ray crystallography A technique for determining the arrangement of ATOMS within crystalline materials. A beam of X-RAYS is passed through a crystal, and the interference pattern caused by the interaction of the X-rays with the regular arrangement of atoms within the crystal is recorded on a photographic plate. The position and intensity of the spots in this pattern can be analysed to reveal the arrangement of the atoms in the crystal. At the start of the 20th century, this technique was first used to discover the arrangement of atoms in simple ionic solids, such as sodium chloride. The availability of computing power has enabled the technique to be applied in research institutions throughout the world to complex biological molecules and has revealed the structure of proteins and DNA.

X-rays A form of ELECTROMAGNETIC RADIATION with a much greater energy than light because of their shorter wavelengths (10^{-9} to 10^{-11} m). Only extremely hot sources, such as some stars, emit them naturally, and any that reach the Earth's atmosphere are generally absorbed by it. They arise from electronic rearrangements in the inner ELECTRON shells of atoms. Their powers of penetration, however, are great. Produced by allowing a beam of high-energy electrons to strike a metal target anode (for example, copper) inside an evacuated tube, they can penetrate some distance into most materials and have many uses. Differing extents of penetration and their ability to affect photographic plates is used to obtain X-ray 'photographs', which reveal abnormalities within the body, such as fractures, infection, and the presence of foreign objects. Substances opaque to X-rays (radiopaque) may also be administered in order to visualize body organs; barium sulphate is used in the diagnosis of gastro-intestinal disorders (see diagnostic RADIOLOGY). X-rays may also be used in the treatment of diseases (RADIOTHERAPY), such as CANCER, in which high-energy X-rays are used to destroy tumour cells. X-rays can be used also to examine the structure of a crystal, in a process known as X-RAY CRYSTALLOGRAPHY. X-rays were discovered in Germany (1895) by Wilhelm RÖNTGEN.

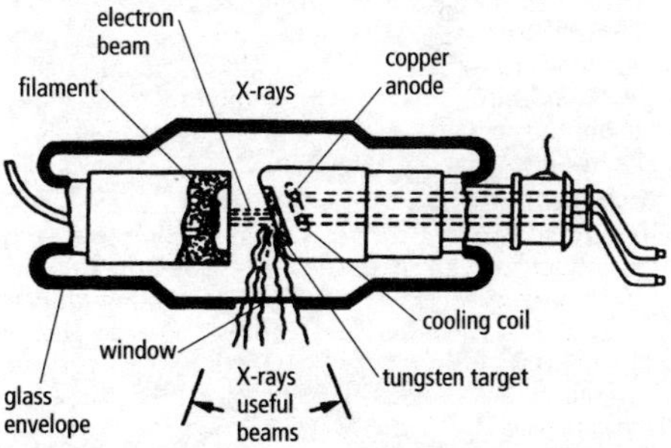

X-rays An X-ray beam is produced by allowing a beam of high-energy electrons to strike a tungsten target attached to a water-cooled copper anode within an evacuated glass envelope.

X-ray telescope A device used in XUV ASTRONOMY for detecting and measuring X-rays from distant sources and for determining the positions of those sources. The extreme penetrating power of X-rays makes it difficult to design telescope-like apparatus but techniques have been developed in recent years utilizing coincidence detectors, collimators, and occultation devices. X-rays are focused by reflecting them at very small angles. In some telescopes the X-rays are collected through a honeycomb of metal tubes and the field of view depends on the length and diameter of the tubes. X-ray telescopes have been flown in an X-ray satellite to map out the X-ray universe, that is, the distribution of sources in the sky that emit radiation in the X-ray region of the spectrum.

Xuchang A city in Henan province, east-central China, south of Zhengzhou; pop. (1986) 254,000.

Xun Zi See CONFUCIANISM.

XUV astronomy Astronomy using instruments capable of detecting that region of the electromagnetic spectrum involving ultraviolet and X-rays. This recently developed field of astronomy is mapping the number of sources in the universe emitting such radiation. In particular, the artificial Earth satellite ROSAT (Roentgen satellite), which came into operation in January 1991, has pinpointed a number of SEYFERT GALAXIES as strong X-ray emitters. During its first year of operation ROSAT detected over a thousand XUV sources.

Xuzhou (formerly **Suchow**) An industrial city in north-west Jiangsu province, eastern China, on the Fei Huang River; pop. (1990) 910,000. It was known as Tongshan 1912–45. It is the centre of a rich coal-mining area and has machinery and textiles industries.

xylem A tissue that transports water and dissolved mineral nutrients in plants. In angiosperms it consists of hollow vessels joined end to end to form a series of tubes. The walls of xylem vessels are strengthened with a complex polymer called lignin; in trees and shrubs this accumulates to form WOOD.

xylophone A percussion musical instrument consisting of a series of wooden bars, each tuned to a different pitch. It is known in south-east Asia, as well as Africa, Mexico, and Guatemala. The modern European instrument derives from the African variety, which was recreated by African slaves in Central America. It had bars lashed to a wooden frame with gourd or horn resonators below the bars. The modern version is laid out like a piano keyboard with tubular resonators below the bars.

XYZ Affair An episode (1797–98) in US–French diplomatic relations. A three-man mission was sent to France to resolve a dispute caused by the USA's unwillingness to aid France in the French Revolutionary wars in spite of treaty obligations made in 1778. TALLEYRAND refused to see the delegation and indirect suggestions of loans and bribes to France came through Mme de Villette, a friend of Talleyrand. Negotiations were carried on through her with X (Jean Conrad Hottinguer), Y (a Mr Bellamy, a US banker in Hamburg), and Z (Lucien Hauteval). A proposal that the Americans should pay Talleyrand $250,000 created outrage in the USA. President ADAMS, however, ignored calls for war and reached agreement with the French at the Convention of Mortefontaine (30 September 1800).

Y

yacht Originally, a small fighting or dispatch vessel, which later developed into a vessel used by royalty and the rich, both for transport and for sport. More recently any sail or power boat used for pleasure has been called a yacht. An early English yacht was the *Mary* (100 tonnes), presented by the Dutch to Charles II in 1660 for his own use. Before World War I many yachts were large and crewed by paid hands, but many people subsequently began to find pleasure in handling their own craft for racing and occasional long voyages. Since the early 1950s the use of FIBRE-REINFORCED PLASTIC for hulls and synthetic fibres for sails and ropes has made yachts cheaper to build, and thus brought them to a much wider market.

Yacoub, Sir Magdi (Habib) (1935–) Egyptian-born British heart surgeon. After studying in Cairo, he came to London in 1962, becoming a consultant cardiac surgeon at the National Heart Hospital (1973–89) and Harefield Hospital (1989–). He was a pioneer of heart-lung transplantation surgery, heart-valve repairs, and the surgical treatment of ischaemic heart disease.

yaffle See WOODPECKER.

Yagi, Hidetsugu (1886–1976) Japanese electrical engineer. He graduated in electrical engineering at Tokyo University in 1909, and in 1919 he was appointed professor at Tohoku Imperial University. He is remembered particularly for the VHF Yagi directional ANTENNA (patented in 1926), a simple directional antenna, often used for domestic radio and television receivers, which is more selective and less prone to interference than the basic DIPOLE antenna.

Yahweh (YHWH) The Tetragrammaton (four-letter name) for the God of Israel. Traditionally standing for the omnipotent tautology 'I am that I am', it has always been considered by Jews too sacred to pronounce, except by the High Priest in the Holy of Holies (the shrine of the Tabernacle and later of the first Temple of Jerusalem) on the Day of Atonement. On all other occasions Jews refer to God as *Hashem* (Hebrew, 'The Name') or *adonai* (Lord). Christians have erroneously, according to the Jews, pronounced the Tetragrammaton 'Jehovah' when it appears in biblical contexts.

Yājūj and Mājūj In Islamic belief, the two hostile forces that will ravage the Earth at the end of time. The Muslim counterpart of the biblical Gog and Magog, they are mentioned in the Koran in connection with Dhu'l-Qarnayn (Alexander the Great), who, in response to a request made by people being terrorized by these forces, is said to have built a wall of iron and brass between two mountains to keep them out.

yak A species of large mammal of the family Bovidae, *Bos grunniens*, unsurpassed among cattle for its capacity to survive under the bleakest mountain conditions at heights of up to 6,000 m (20,000 feet) in the Tibetan highlands. It has a rounded forehead with smooth, round horns curving upwards, outwards, and forwards, and a hump over the shoulders. It is covered with long, dark brown hair with a fringe of long black hair on the flanks. Large bulls can be nearly 1.82 m (6 feet) tall at the shoulder. In the summer, cows and calves will collect together in herds of 10–100.

Yakut A people of Siberia who speak a Turkic language and who settled in the Lena basin during the 13th–15th centuries.

Yakutia (official name **The Republic of Sakha**) A republic of the Russian Federation in north-east Siberia, stretching southwards from the Laptev and East Siberian seas to the Stanovoy Range; area 3,103,200 sq km (1,198,610 sq miles); pop. (1989) 1,081,000; capital, Yakutsk. It is the largest of the republics of Russia, with 40 per cent of its territory lying to the north of the Arctic Circle. Absorbed into the Russian empire during the 17th century, the territory was an autonomous republic of the former Soviet Union from 1922 until 1991 after which it continued as a republic of the Russian Federation. Its principal industries are the production of timber and the mining of diamonds, gold, silver, lead, coal, mica, and tin.

Yakutsk The capital of Yakutia (The Republic of Sakha) in Siberian Russia, a port on the River Lena; pop. (1990) 187,000.

Yale University A US university, now non-sectarian, originally a 'collegiate school' founded in 1701 at Killingworth and Saybrook, Connecticut, by a group of Congregational ministers. In 1716 it moved to its present site at New Haven and soon afterwards was renamed Yale College after Elihu Yale, a notable benefactor. In 1887 it became Yale University.

Yalta A port and health resort on the Black Sea near the southern tip of the Crimean peninsula, southern Ukraine, site of the **Yalta Conference** in February 1945 between the Allied leaders Churchill, Roosevelt, and Stalin, who met to plan the final stages of World War II and to agree the subsequent territorial division of Europe. In spite of the friendship displayed at the time the scene was set for the ensuing Cold War between East and West. Its mild 'Mediterranean' climate has led to the development of Yalta as a health and tourist resort.

yam A plant of the genus *Dioscorea*, grown for their starch-rich edible underground tubers. They are found throughout the wetter tropics, especially in West Africa. There are around 60 cultivated species, but only 11 are important crop species, differing in their climatic requirements. They form part of the monocotyledonous family Dioscoreaceae, which comprises some 630 species. The Chinese yam, grown in temperate regions, is unusual in this largely tropical family. All are broad-leaved, climbing plants between 3 and 12 m (9.75 and 39 feet) tall. The greater yam of south-east Asia gives the largest yield of tubers, but the white yam of West Africa accounts for most of the world production. Its tubers may reach 3 m (9.75 feet) in length and 60 kg (150 pounds) in weight, but weights of between 5 and 10 kg (12 and 25 pounds) are more usual. The lesser yam, cultivated mainly in Asia and the Pacific, produces a cluster of 5–20 small, round or ovoid tubers. Less fibrous than some of the other types, they are more palatable but do not store well, for they bruise easily. Yams have been independently cultivated from wild species throughout south-east Asia, South and Central America, and West Africa. This makes them the most cosmopolitan of food crops used by man. The tubers are eaten after peeling and either boiling or roasting. In the USA the SWEET POTATO is sometimes wrongly called a yam.

Yama In Hindu mythology, the first man to die, becoming lord of the dead. Later considered as god of death, Yama is usually depicted carrying a club representing authority and punishment, and a noose with which he seizes the souls of his victims. His mount is a buffalo.

Yamamoto, Isoroku (1884–1943) Japanese admiral. Although he initially opposed his country's involvement in World War II, as Commander-in-Chief of the Combined Fleet (air and naval forces) from 1939, he was responsible for planning the successful Japanese attack on the US naval base at Pearl Harbor (1941). He then directed his forces in Japanese operations to gain control of the Pacific, but was thwarted by the defeat of his fleet at the Battle of Midway (1942). He was killed when the Allies shot down his plane over the Solomon Islands.

Yamasaki, Minoru (1912–86) US architect. He designed the St Louis Municipal Airport Terminal (1956), a barrel-vaulted building that influenced much subsequent US air-terminal design. Other notable designs include the World Trade Center in New York (1972), a skyscraper consisting of twin towers 110 storeys high.

Yamato The clan from which all the emperors of Japan are descended. Claiming the Sun-goddess as ancestress, they had their chief shrine at Ise. Gradually they established control over rival clans and by the 5th century AD much of Japan was subject to them. They were influenced by Chinese culture, initially learning of China through southern Korea. BUDDHISM and the study of Chinese language and literature were introduced in the 7th century and Prince Shotuku produced administrative systems based on SUI China. The Yamato chief assumed the title emperor and built capitals based on TANG Chinese designs first at Nara then at Kyoto. By the 9th century the Fujiwara family controlled the imperial court and during the period of the shoguns the imperial family had little power.

Yamoussoukro The capital-designate (since 1983) of the Côte d'Ivoire (Ivory Coast), originally a small village at the heartland of the Baoulé tribe; pop. (1986) 120,000. It was the home of former President Félix Houphouët-Boigny (1905–1993).

Yangchow See YANGZHOU.

yangqin A musical instrument, the Chinese DULCIMER, deriving from the Persian *santūr*, with thin brass or steel strings struck with very light bamboo beaters. The resonator is a lacquered trapezoid box, the sloping sides usually being curved, with a small, central drawer to store the beaters and a heavy brass tuning hammer, and a lift-off lid. There are two bridges, the left-hand about one-third of the way across the soundboard, and the right-hand a quarter of the way. The yangqin is an important instrument in much Chinese ensemble music.

Yangshao An ancient civilization of northern China during the 3rd millennium BC, characterized by painted pottery with naturalistic designs of fish and human faces, and abstract patterns of triangles, spirals, arcs, and dots.

Yangtze River (Chinese **Chang Jiang**; formerly also **Yangtse-Kiang**) The principal river of China, which rises in Tibet and flows 6,276 km (3,900 miles) generally eastwards through central China to the East China Sea. On the frontier between the provinces of Sichuan and Hubei it emerges from its upper reaches onto the fertile lowland basin, passing through the **Yangtze Gorges** and hydroelectric schemes that include the immense Gezhouba Dam. A major waterway for many centuries and the third-longest river in the world, its entire length was first navigated in 1986 by a Chinese expedition. In 1994 work began on the Three Gorges Dam, the world's largest hydroelectric power project.

Yangzhou (formerly **Yangchow**) A city in the province of Jiangsu, eastern China, on the Grand Canal; pop. (1988) 400,000. A capital of the Sui dynasty and later an important cultural and religious centre of the Tang dynasty, it was a seat of Nestorian Christianity governed by Marco Polo 1282–85. The site of a major system of water control, it has a long tradition of craftsmanship and storytelling.

Yanomami An Amerindian people of the Amazon rain forest believed to be the world's oldest surviving isolated Indian tribe. Numbering 9,000 in 1990, they were the focus of international attention in 1987 when rich mineral deposits were discovered and large numbers of miners (*garimpeiros*) invaded their tribal lands.

Yaoundé The capital of Cameroon, situated east of the coastal plain to the south of the Sanaga River; pop. (est. 1992) 800,000. Founded by German traders in 1888, it was made capital of French Cameroon in 1921 and capital of the independent Republic of Cameroon in 1960. The city is an agricultural centre trading in sugar, coffee, and cacao.

Yap An island group comprising four islands and 13 coral atolls in the western Pacific, one of the four Federated States of Micronesia; area 119 sq km (46 sq miles); pop. (est. 1990) 13,900; capital, Kolonia (on Pohnpei). Held by Germany from 1899 until World War I, Yap was mandated to Japan from 1920 until its capture by US forces in 1945.

yarn FIBRE prepared for use in weaving (see LOOM), KNITTING, and other processes. Textile yarns are of two basic types: those made from fibres of relatively short length (staple fibres), such as cotton, wool, or linen, and those made from long, effectively continuous filaments, such as silk. SYNTHETIC FIBRES may be in either staple or filament form and are used in both types of yarn. Staple fibre is converted into yarns by first parallelizing the fibres by CARDING MACHINES, then SPINNING them together to form a compact, coherent, twisted structure. Fibres of different types may be used together to form blended yarns, such as wool and acrylic or polyester and cotton. Continuous-filament materials may be directly converted into yarns by twisting, texturing, or intermingling parallel filaments. The fineness or coarseness of yarns is expressed as the length of yarn for a given weight or as weight of yarn for a given length. The most universal unit is the tex, defined as the weight in grams of one kilometre of yarn. Yarns used in women's stockings and tights may be finer than 1 tex, while yarns used in carpets are 500 tex or more. Industrial applications, such as reinforcements in tyres, drive-belts, and conveyors, often require very much heavier and stronger yarns.

Yaroslavl An industrial river port and rail junction of western Russia, on the Volga north-east of Moscow; pop. (1990) 636,000. Formerly the capital of an independent principality, it developed as a textile centre on the trade route between Moscow and Archangel and was Moscow's Volga River port until the building of the Moscow–Volga Canal in 1937.

yawl A rig for a small sailing boat or YACHT in which the mizen (rear) mast, which is smaller than that of a KETCH, is stepped behind the rudder head. Boats with a yawl rig were often used as SHIPS' boats, and the rig was also common on fishing vessels.

yaws An infectious tropical disease caused by the spirochaete *Treponema pertenue*. It is transmitted by direct contact with infected persons. The spirochaete enters through skin abrasions causing fever, pains, and itching followed by small tumours on the face, hands, and legs, which deteriorate into deep ulcers. It responds well to treatment with antibiotics.

Y-chromosome See CHROMOSOME.

Yeager, Charles E(lwood) (known as 'Chuck') (1923–) US pilot. Yeager was a veteran World War II pilot who, in 1947, became the first person to break the sound barrier when he piloted the Bell X-1 rocket research aircraft to a level-flight speed of 670 mph. He also set a world speed record in 1953 when he flew the Bell X-1A rocket plane at 1,650 mph.

year The time required for the Earth to complete one orbital revolution about the Sun. Depending on how the measurement of this revolution is made, four astronomical definitions of the year are possible.

The **sidereal year** is the Earth's orbital period with respect to the stellar background.

The **tropical year** (also known as the **astronomical, equinoctial**, or **mean solar year**) is the interval between two successive vernal EQUINOXES. However, because of PRECESSION the equinoxes are not fixed in the CELESTIAL SPHERE and so the tropical year differs slightly from the sidereal year.

The **anomalistic year** is the interval from one perihelion to the next. This definition is necessary when the perturbations of the other planets on the Earth's orbit are taken into account.

Finally, the **eclipse year** is defined as the interval between successive passages of the Sun through the same node of the Moon's orbit. This interval, which differs significantly from the others, indicates the times when ECLIPSES are likely to occur.

The **calendar year** is that used most commonly for the reckoning of time in civil matters. Based on a calendar, it contains either 365 or 366 days. The occurrence of leap years is arranged so that the average length of the year is as close as possible to the tropical year. Minor corrections to the length of the calendar year are needed from time to time to take account of changes in tide patterns and bulk movements in the Earth's interior, each of which has an effect on the relative periods of axial rotation and of orbit about the Sun. A LUNAR CALENDAR is based on the **lunar year**, which is usually taken to be 12 synodic months (354 days). It is therefore related to the motion of the Moon about the Earth rather than the Earth about the Sun.

yeast A unicellular FUNGUS that grows in the form of microscopic single cells or as chains or colonies of cells, which multiply by budding and by the formation of spores. There are several different types; for example, the shadow yeasts, which live as SAPROPHYTES on leaves and fruit (bloom), others that are parasites on man, causing the disease THRUSH, and the yeast used in brewing and baking. Brewers' yeast ferments sugar, producing alcohol and carbon dioxide. It is this gas that makes dough rise when yeast and sugar are added to it.

Yeats, W(illiam) B(utler) (1865–1939) Irish poet and dramatist. He spent a large part of his life in London, but maintained his interest in Irish culture. He was a co-founder of the Irish National Theatre Company (later based at the Abbey Theatre in Dublin) and his play *The Countess Cathleen* (1892) began the Irish theatrical revival. He was also prominent in Ireland's cultural and literary revival, which takes its name from his collection of stories, *The Celtic Twilight* (1893). In his poetry, the elaborate style of his earlier work was influenced by the Pre-Raphaelites, while his later work used a sparser, more lyrical, style and was influenced by his interest in mysticism and the occult. His best-known collections from this later period are *The Tower* (1928), including the poems 'Sailing to Byzantium' and 'Leda and the Swan', and *The Winding Stair* (1929). Yeats served as a senator of the Irish Free State (1922–28) and was awarded the Nobel Prize for literature in 1923. His younger brother **Jack Butler Yeats** (1871–1934) was a notable Irish painter. Brought up in Ireland, he went to London to study, but his Expressionist paintings largely reflected everyday Irish life as well as Celtic myth, contributing to the nationalist feeling in the arts, inspired by the movement for Irish independence.

Yekaterinburg An industrial city in central Russia, in the eastern foothills of the Urals; pop. (1990) 1,372,000. Founded in 1821 as a military post and trading centre, it was known as Sverdlovsk 1924–91. Tsar Nicholas II and his family were murdered here by Russian revolutionaries in 1918.

yellow (or **sulphur**) A butterfly belonging to the family Pieridae, together with whites, brimstones, and orange-tips. Many, such as the clouded yellow, *Colias croceus*, have black margins around the wings, or black wingtips. In brimstones and many others, females are much paler, almost white. Like other pierids they lay spindle-shaped, ribbed eggs; the caterpillars are usually slender, green, and not very hairy; and the pupae are attached to a silken pad at the tail end and supported by a silken girdle. Some, including the African migrant butterfly, *Catopsilia florella*, are wide-ranging migrants.

yellow fever A dangerous virus infection, confined to tropical Africa and Central America. It is spread by mosquitoes and typically causes JAUNDICE due to liver damage. It also causes damage to the kidneys and often proves fatal if untreated. A vaccine gives good protection.

yellowhammer (or **yellow bunting**) A species of BUNTING, *Emberiza citrinella*, which is found over wide areas of Europe and western Asia. This bird lives in open woodland and is common in European hedgerows. The male is streaky brown above with a rufous rump, while the head and much of the underparts are yellow streaked with brown. The female is not as brightly coloured as the male but is otherwise similar.

Yellowknife The capital of the Northwest Territories of Canada, on the north shore of the Great Slave Lake; pop. (1991) 15,180. Founded in 1935 as a gold-mining town, Yellowknife was named after the copper knives used by local Indians. It became capital of the Northwest Territories in 1967.

Yellow River (Chinese **Huang He**) The second-largest river in China. Rising in the Kunlun Mountains of west Qinghai province in central China, it flows in a great circle for a distance of about 4,630 km (2,877 miles) before entering the Bo Hai Gulf. The name refers to its large silt content. Its tendency to frequent disastrous flooding, which gave it the nickname 'China's Sorrow', has been greatly reduced by dyking and damming.

Yellowstone An area of Wyoming, Idaho, and Montana in the USA, reserved as the **Yellowstone National Park**, since 1872. It is famous for its scenery, geysers, and wildlife, and was the first national park to be designated in the USA.

yellowtail A fish that belongs to the genus *Seriola* of the family Carangidae; it is slender and streamlined, with a deeply forked tail. Yellowtails occur in coastal waters adjacent to the open ocean in tropical areas and migrate in huge schools, feeding principally on fishes, squids, and crustaceans. They are important food fishes and fine game-fish wherever they occur.

Yeltsin, Boris (Nikolaevich) (1931–) Russian statesman, President of the Russian Federation since 1991. At first a supporter of Mikhail Gorbachev's reform programme, he soon became its leading radical opponent. In 1990 Yeltsin was elected President of the Russian Soviet Federative Socialist Republic; shortly afterwards he and his supporters resigned from the Communist Party. He emerged with new stature after an attempted coup in 1991, during which he rallied support for Gorbachev; on the breakup of the USSR at the end of that year he became President of the independent Russian Federation. He survived another attempted coup in 1993. Despite criticism over his handling of the conflict in Chechnya, a heart attack in 1995, and a subsequent coronary bypass operation, he was re-elected in the presidential elections of 1996. Concern over his health continues.

Yemen, Republic of A country in the south of the peninsula of Arabia, bordering on Saudi Arabia and Oman on the north.

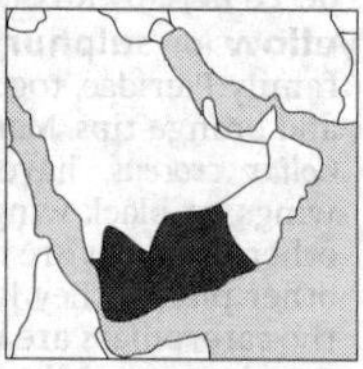

Physical. Behind the western, Red Sea, coast are high mountains. Here light summer rains provide for the growth of cotton and coffee; and camels, goats, and sheep graze on coarse grass high in the hills. The lower-lying eastern part has a coast on the Gulf of Aden. Here it is very arid, mostly hot desert, though these are areas where cotton can be grown.

Economy. In the north, agriculture, mainly sheep- and goat-raising, cotton, coffee, the narcotic *qat*, and other food crops, was the mainstay of the economy until oil production began in 1986. However, further oil exploration is jeopardized by a border dispute with Saudi Arabia. In the south, which was formerly a one-party communist republic with a centrally planned economy heavily dependent on Soviet aid, agriculture is the principal economic activity. Production of the chief crops (cotton, millet, and wheat) is limited by lack of arable land and irrigation. Other than the oil refinery in the south, industry is limited to food-processing. Yemen is heavily dependent on the remittances of migrant workers, and the economy was severely affected by Saudi Arabia's repatriation of a large number of Yemeni workers following Yemen's neutral stance in the 1991 Gulf War.

History. From *c.*950 to 115 BC Yemen was a flourishing region called Saba – the site of the kingdom of the biblical queen of Sheba. Because of its summer rains it was known to Rome as Arabia Felix ('Happy Arabia'), but it declined with its irrigation system around the 6th century AD. It was converted to ISLAM in the 7th century and came under the rule of the Muslim caliphate. Much of it was under the rule of the Ottomans (1517–1918), although the British established the colony of ADEN in 1839. In 1918, with British support, the territory (excluding Aden) was proclaimed a kingdom under Imam Yahya, its borders with both Aden and Saudi Arabia for long being matters of dispute. Yahya was assassinated in 1948, and his son Ahmad ruled until 1962. On his death the army under General Abdullah al-Sallal proclaimed the Yemen Arab Republic (North Yemen), backed by both Egypt and Syria. Saudi Arabia supported those tribes who gave their loyalty to Ahmad's son Imam Muhammad al-Badr. Civil war lasted until 1967, when Nasser withdrew Egyptian troops, after the defeat of the Six-Day War. Sallal resigned and a more moderate government was formed. In April 1970 there was a general pacification, but in 1979 a month-long war broke out with the neighbouring People's Republic of Yemen (South Yemen, formed from Aden and neighbouring emirates when British rule ended in 1967). Intermittent talks to unify North Yemen and South Yemen followed, with a draft constitution agreed in December 1989. The unified state was proclaimed in May 1990, its political capital being Sana'a and commercial capital Aden. A five-member Council was headed by President Ali Abdullah Saleh. The new republic was welcomed to the UN and found itself a member of the Security Council at the time of the Gulf Crisis, when its decision to oppose the US-dominated intervention, leading to the GULF WAR, had strong popular support. Yet it resulted in economic reprisals by the Gulf States, by Europe, and by the USA, while some 800,000 migrant workers were expelled from Saudi Arabia. The latter also gave 'substantial financial support' to anti-government Islamic fundamentalists, who had a strong following among the conservative tribes of the interior. Political tensions, focusing on the distribution of oil revenues, culminated in the southern Yemeni leaders declaring secession, which prompted a three-month civil war in 1994. The war ended when forces from northern Yemen captured Aden. A peace settlement was made and the constitution was amended, the ruling Council being replaced by a directly elected President.

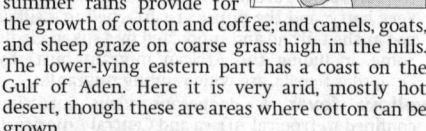

Capital: San'a (political) Aden (economic)
Area: 472,099 sq km (182,336 sq mi)
Population: 11,058,000 (1995)
Currency: 1 Yemeni dinar = 1,000 fils; 1 Yemeni rial = 100 fils
Religions: Sunni Muslim 53.0%; Shi'i Muslim (mainly in north) 46.9%
Ethnic Groups: Arab 97.0%; Indian and Pakistani 1.5%; Somali 1.5%
Languages: Arabic (official)
International Organizations: UN; Arab league

Yenisei (or **Yenisey**) A river of Siberian Russia whose headwaters rise in the east Sayan Mountains on the frontier with Mongolia. It flows 3,487 km (2,195 miles) northwards to join the Yenisei Gulf, an inlet of the Kara Sea, but from the source of its chief headwater, the Angara River, it has a total length of 4,989 km (3,100 miles). It is navigable for most of its length although frozen in sections throughout much of the year.

yeoman A person in late Medieval England qualified by possessing free land of an annual value of 40 shillings to serve on juries, vote for knights of the shire, and exercise other rights. In the 13th and 14th centuries yeomen in England were freehold peasants, but by 1400, as many peasants became richer, all prosperous peasants, whether freeholders or not, as well as franklins (freehold farmers), were called yeomen. In the 15th century some yeoman farmers, leasehold as well as freehold, entered the ranks of the gentry.

Yerevan (or **Erivan**) The capital of the Republic of Armenia, on the Razdan River in the southern Caucasus; pop. (1990) 1,202,000. Its main industries include chemicals, tyres, metals, machinery, electrical equipment, foodstuffs, and wine-making.

Yerkes Observatory An OBSERVATORY on the northern shores of Lake Geneva, at Williams Bay, Wisconsin and now part of the University of Chicago. It was founded in 1892 by the financier Charles Tyson Yerkes to create a telescope that was bigger than that at the Lick Observatory. With a 40-inch (1.02 m) achromatic doublet lens, the telescope is still the largest REFRACTING TELESCOPE in the world.

yeti (or **Abominable Snowman**) A creature said to frequent the Himalayas, the only evidence for which are huge footprints in the snow. There have been no authenticated sightings of this creature, which is described by hearsay evidence as large, hairy, and resembling a human.

Yevtushenko, Yevgeny (Aleksandrovich) (1933–) Russian poet and novelist of the post-Stalinist generation. His poem 'Babiy Yar' (1961), commemorating the Nazi massacre of Ukrainian Jews, was interpreted as a criticism of Soviet anti-Semitism, and he fell into official disfavour, although he received considerable popular acclaim. The publication of his *Precocious Autobiography* (1963) was also well received, as was his *Farewell to the Red Banner* (1992).

yew Any of eight or nine species of tree of the genus *Taxus*, found in the more humid regions of the northern temperate zone, but reaching as far south as Sulawesi in Indonesia. GYMNOSPERMS allied to the conifers, they are sometimes included with them. Yews are evergreen, slow-growing trees casting dense shade and bearing male and female flowers on different trees. The seeds are enclosed in a fleshy type of covering called an aril, which is attractive to birds, but the seed itself, like the rest of the tree, is very poisonous. The common yew, *T. baccata*, is native to Europe, North Africa, and western Asia and is the longest-lived of all European trees, probably living well over 1,000 years. The tree is widely used for hedging, but is often associated with churchyards and considered a symbol of sadness. Formerly it was the most important wood for the construction of bows in England.

Yggdrasil (Old Norse **Mimameidr**) The cosmic ash tree of Norse and Germanic mythology. The tree supports the universe: its roots reach down to Jötunheim, land of the giants; to Niflheim, abode of the dragon monster Nidhogg; and to Asgard, home of the gods. At its base are three wells: Urdarbrunnr, the Well of Fate, from which the tree is watered by the Norns or Fates; Hvergelmir, the Roaring Water Pot, in which the Nidhogg dwells, gnawing at the tree's roots; and Mímisbrunnr, the Well of Mimir, source of Wisdom. Its branches overhang the world, and reach up beyond the heavens. The god Odin discovered the secret of runic wisdom by sacrificing himself to the tree, remaining suspended in it for nine days and nine nights. After the terrible Battle of Ragnarök, the cosmic tree, though badly harmed, will be the source of new life.

Yiddish (from German *Jüdisch*, 'Jewish') A language spoken by ASHKENAZI Jews in central and eastern Europe. It developed in the 9th century from German, but soon acquired a distinctive character of its own. It is now written in the Hebrew alphabet. Many words have been borrowed from Slavic, as well as from Hebrew–Aramaic (see SEMITIC LANGUAGES). Western Yiddish (dialects of Germany and Holland) was the medium of spoken communication between European Jews until the 18th century, when it was replaced by a new literary language based on Eastern Yiddish from the Baltic and Slavic lands. There is a continuous literary tradition (both religious and secular) from the 12th century to the present. Modern Standard Yiddish is based on the East European dialect. Before World War II there were 11 million speakers in Europe; now the number of speakers worldwide is estimated at under 5 million, mainly Jews living in North America, Latin America, Israel, and the republics of the former Soviet Union, for most of whom it is a second language. However, a number of Yiddish words have entered the English language, especially in New York.

Yijing (or **I Ching**; Chinese, 'Classic of Changes') An ancient Chinese text, forming part of the five classic texts of CONFUCIANISM. Originally it was a book of divination, but during the Han Dynasty (206–20 AD) the original meaning of the book was expanded and a comprehensive system of cosmology was developed in a series of appendices or 'wings'. It stresses constant change and transformation, occasioned by the interaction of YIN AND YANG. It is still used as a practical means of solving everyday problems, in both China and the West.

Yima In ancient Iranian belief, the son of the Sun, the first man, king and founder of civilization, replaced by Gayomart in Zoroastrianism. According to one legend, Yima refused Ahura Mazda's request to act as his prophet and became instead a king under whose rule man and beast prospered and multiplied so much that Yima had to enlarge the world. According to another, warned of destruction by a great winter, he and the best of men, women, and beasts survived in an underground cavern. Under the name of Jamshid, Yima is the subject of many tales known throughout the Islamic and Hindu world.

yin and yang (Japanese **in-yō**) Two opposing forces whose complementary interaction forms and sustains the Universe according to Eastern thought. Originally yin described the cold, northern side of a mountain, and yang the hot, southern slope. By the 3rd century BC, yin, the passive force, was taken in China to represent the Earth, darkness, and all that is feminine and receptive, while yang, the active force, represents light, the sky, and all that is masculine and penetrating. The common symbol of yin and yang resembles the light and dark halves of a circle, curving one into the other.

Yin and yang The symbol represents the opposing but complementary forces of light (yin) and dark (yang).

Each holds a small particle of the other in it. This balance between yin and yang applies to all human affairs as well as to all physical processes.

Yinchuan The capital of the Ningxia autonomous region of north-east China, an industrial city producing textiles, rubber goods, chemicals, and machine tools; pop. (1986) 658,000.

ylang ylang The aromatic oil extracted from the flowers of the tree *Cananga odorata*, which belongs to the family Annonaceae and is distributed from tropical Asia to northern Australia. The oil is used in perfume, and is also known as macassar oil or cananga oil.

yoga (Sanskrit, 'yoking', 'union') Any form of religious activity, particularly within HINDUISM, designed to harness the practitioner to the knowledge of the divine. In particular, yoga is one of the six orthodox systems of Hindu philosophy, based on the yoga Sutras (doctrinal works) of Patañjali. The highest yogic form, Rāja yoga, aims at the spiritual purification of the practitioner through a series of eight stages, requiring expert teaching and guidance. The first four teach restraint and religious observance, followed by physical preparations involving postures (*āsanas*, such as the Lotus position) and breathing exercises (*prāṇāyāma*). The next stages involve the withdrawal of the senses, concentration of the mind, and meditation, until the final stage, *samādhi*, or union with the divine, is achieved. In Western countries, the first four stages (the basis of Hatha Yoga) have become popular as a form of exercise and relaxation, and the control of breathing and the use of postures in particular have been adapted to numerous fitness courses. In a wider sense, yoga refers to the different paths leading to a spiritual liberation (*moksha*); as well as Rāja yoga, these include karma yoga (selfless action), *bhakti*-yoga, devotion to a personal deity, and *jñāna*-yoga, the way of intellectual knowledge. Yoga is not limited to Hindu practice and may be found within other religions, such as TIBETAN BUDDHISM.

Yogyakarta (or **Jogjakarta**) A city of south-central Java, Indonesia, situated at the foot of Mount Merapi; pop. (1990) 412,000. The modern city was founded in 1755 near the site of the former capital of the Mataram kingdom. Its chief landmarks are the Grand Mosque and the Kraton palace. It is a centre of Javanese culture and its many handicrafts include batik textiles, shadow puppets, and silverware.

Yokohama A seaport and cultural city to the south of Tokyo on Honshu Island, Japan, capital of Kanagawa prefecture; pop. (1990) 3,220,000. Originally a fishing village, it developed into Japan's second-largest city after 1858, when it became the first port open to foreign trade. It is a centre of shipbuilding, oil refining, engineering, and the manufacture of goods such as glass, textiles, and furniture. It has four universities. It was rebuilt after being virtually destroyed by an earthquake in 1923 and bombing during World War II.

Yom Kippur (Hebrew, 'Day of Atonement') The holiest day in the Jewish year, a time for MEDITATION and for the expiation of sins, marked by abstention from food, drink, and sexual relations. It is celebrated from the evening of the ninth day of the lunar month of Tishri. Referred to as the Sabbath of Sabbaths, it is the day on which observant Jews attend the SYNAGOGUE, confessing collective and personal guilt, and asking for absolution. Prayers are said for God's forgiveness for those who have died in the past year. The Book of Jonah is read.

Yom Kippur War (1973) The Israeli name for the Arab–Israeli war called by the Arabs the October War. The war began on 6 October, the Feast of YOM KIPPUR, Israel's most important holy day, when Egyptian forces crossed the Suez Canal and breached the Israeli Bar Lev Line. Syrian troops threw back Israeli forces on the Golan Heights, occupied by the latter since the SIX-DAY WAR. The war lasted three weeks, in which time Israel pushed Syrian forces back into Syria and crossed the Canal, encircling an Egyptian army. In the aftermath, disengagement agreements were signed by Israel with Syria in 1974 and with Egypt in 1974 and 1975. The Israeli withdrawal from Sinai was completed in 1982 after the 1978 Israeli–Egyptian peace treaty.

York A historic walled city in North Yorkshire, England, on the River Ouse; pop. (1991) 100,600. Founded as a Roman provincial capital (Eboracum) in 71 AD, it became in turn an Anglo-Saxon capital, a Danish settlement (Jorvik), and seat of the archbishop, Primate of England. It gave its name to the English royal **House of York**, which ruled England from 1461 until 1485 (see YORKIST). Its principal landmarks are the medieval gates, York Minster with its beautiful medieval stained-glass windows, and its many old buildings. It has a university founded in 1963. York is a commercial and market centre with a large confectionery industry.

York, Duke of The title often given in the UK to the second son of the monarch. George VI was Duke of York, and the present Queen Mother was the Duchess, before George VI became king. Prince ANDREW, the second son of Elizabeth II, is the present Duke of York.

York, Richard Plantagenet, 3rd Duke of (1411–60) The son of Richard, Earl of Cambridge, and Anne Mortimer, who until 1453 was heir to the throne of England. He led the opposition to HENRY VI, especially after the death of Humphrey, Duke of Gloucester in 1447, and in 1455 he captured Henry at the first Battle of ST ALBANS and became Protector of the kingdom. In October 1460 he claimed the English throne, but two months later he was defeated and killed by LANCASTRIAN forces in the Battle of WAKEFIELD. The YORKIST party survived him, and triumphed at the second Battle of ST ALBANS.

Yorkist A descendant, or a supporter of the descendants, of Edmund of Langley (1341–1402), fifth son of Edward III and (from 1385) 1st Duke of York. Adherents of his grandson Richard, 3rd Duke of YORK, adopted a white rose as their badge. Despite Richard's death at the Battle of WAKEFIELD (1460), his party was soon afterwards successful against the LANCASTRIANS and his son Edward became king as EDWARD IV. The House of York continued on the throne with EDWARD V, and then with Edward IV's younger brother, RICHARD III, until HENRY VII began the TUDOR dynasty after his victory at BOSWORTH FIELD in 1485. Henry prudently married the Yorkist heiress, Edward IV's eldest daughter, Elizabeth of York.

Yorkshire A former county of northern England, divided administratively into East, West, and North Ridings. In 1974 it was divided into the new counties of North, West, and South Yorkshire, while part of the East Riding went to Humberside and part of the North Riding became Cleveland. When Humberside and Cleveland were abolished in 1996, the East Riding was reinstated as a unitary authority.

Yorkshire Dales The valleys of the Pennine Chain in the former English county of Yorkshire, most of which are formed by tributaries of the River Ouse. They include Airedale, Nidderdale, Swaledale, Teesdale, Wensleydale, and Wharfedale.

Yoruba A people in the coastal region (Yorubaland) of West Africa, especially in Nigeria where they are the largest ethnic group with their own culture, speaking a tonal language of the Niger-Congo language group. Many Yoruba were taken as slaves to Brazil, Hispaniola, and Cuba.

Yoshkar-Ola The capital city of the Republic of Mari El in east-central European Russia, on the Kokshaga River; pop. (1990) 246,000. It manufactures agricultural machinery and pharmaceuticals.

Young, Brigham (1801–77) US MORMON leader. After Joseph SMITH's death in Illinois in 1844, Young became the dominant figure of Mormonism, leading the migration west to Salt Lake City, ruling over the new community with autocratic firmness, and turning a desert waste into a flourishing and expanding city.

Young, Neil (Percival) (1945–) Canadian singer, songwriter, and guitarist. After early success with the group Buffalo Springfield (1966–68) Young embarked on a long and productive solo career, in which he has combined plaintive country-influenced acoustic material with his distinctively distorted electric-guitar playing. Young's greatest commercial success remains *Harvest* (1972); later albums include *Sleeps with Angels* (1994).

Young, Thomas (1773–1829) British physicist, physician, and Egyptologist. Young learned 13 languages while still a child, and pursued diverse interests in his career. His major work in physics concerned the wave theory of light, which he supported with the help of advanced experiments in optical interference. His work on the elasticity of materials led to the ratio of stress to strain being known as **Young's Modulus**. He also investigated the optics of the human eye, and played a major part in the deciphering of the Rosetta Stone.

Young England A British political movement of young Tory aristocrats in the early 1840s. It aimed at ending the political dominance of the middle classes by an alliance between the aristocracy and the working classes, which would carry out all necessary social reforms. The romantic ideas of its members were given some substance by Benjamin DISRAELI, who defined its principles in his novel *Coningsby* (1844). The movement broke up in 1845 over the issue of FREE TRADE and the disputed grant to Maynooth College, the principal institution in Ireland for training Roman Catholic clergy.

Young Ireland An Irish nationalist movement of the 1840s. Led by young Protestants, including Smith O'Brien (1803–64) and John Mitchel (1815–75), who, inspired by Mazzini's YOUNG ITALY, set up their own newspaper, the *Nation*. It called for a revival of Ireland's cultural heritage. At first the members of Young Ireland were associated with Daniel O'CONNELL in his campaign to repeal the Act of UNION, but later they turned to more radical solutions. In 1848 they attempted a rebellion, which was easily suppressed, O'Brien and Mitchel being sentenced to transportation.

Young Italy An Italian patriotic society. Formed in 1831 by Giuseppe MAZZINI and 40 other Italian exiles in Marseilles, it set out to replace earlier secret societies, such as the CARBONARI as a prime force in the RISORGIMENTO. Its significance lay in the kindling of national consciousness and thus contributed towards Italian unification.

Young Pretender, the See STUART, CHARLES EDWARD.

Young Turks A number of late 19th- and early 20th-century reformers in the OTTOMAN EMPIRE who carried out the Revolution of 1908. The most prominent party was the Committee of Union and Progress, which seized power in 1913 and under the triumvirate of ENVER, Talat, and Jamal Pasha ruled the Ottoman empire until 1918, supporting the Central Powers in World War I.

Ypres (Flemish **Ieper**) A town in the province of West Flanders, Belgium, on the River Ieper near the French frontier; pop. (1990) 35,235. During the Middle Ages it was a major cloth-making centre. It was the scene of some of the bitterest fighting on the Western Front during World War I, commemorated by the Menin Gate (Menenpoort).

ytterbium (symbol Yb, at. no. 70, r.a.m. 173.04) A silvery LANTHANIDE element discovered in 1878 by J. D. G. Marignac and named after the Swedish village of Ytterby. It occurs in gadolinite and monazite and is used in small quantities in special steels.

yttrium (symbol Y, at. no. 39, r.a.m. 88.91) A LANTHANIDE element discovered in 1828 by F. Wöhler. It is used in making europium phosphors, which give the red colour in television tubes. Analysis of lunar rock from the Apollo 11 mission indicated an unusually high yttrium content.

Yuan A Mongol dynasty of emperors in China founded in 1271 by Kublai Khan. Described by Marco Polo, the elaborate court of the Yuan Dynasty lasted until it was overthrown in 1368 and replaced by the Ming Dynasty.

Yuan Jiang The Chinese name for the RED RIVER.

Yucatán The peninsula of eastern Mexico, and the state forming the northern part. The peninsula projects north-eastward from Central America for some 640 km (400 miles) between the Gulf of Mexico and the Caribbean Sea. Its northern part is a low, stony plain that shows signs of past changes in sea-level, while the land gently rises southward to about 150 m (500 feet). In places the surface is swampy and covered with jungle. The underlying limestone has been attacked by weathering to form rounded pits called 'cenotes'.

In prehistory it was the northern area of MAYA civilization, including several long-occupied, powerful cities, some being occupied as early as *c.*750 BC. From *c.*800 AD many Maya migrated from the Southern Lowlands (Guatemala) into the Northern Lowlands of the peninsula and founded new states at Chichén Itzá, Izamal, Mayapán, and Uxmal, linked by political alliances and trade. At first Chichén Itzá dominated, then Mayapán, and 17 small principalities were formed in the late 15th century. Fernández de Córdoba explored the coast in 1516–17 sighting several cities, but resistance to conquest was strong and they were not fully subdued until the 1540s.

yucca A perennial shrub or medium-sized tree of

the genus *Yucca*, with some 40 species native to Central America and the southern USA. The evergreen, sword-shaped leaves, borne in terminal whorls, are tough, leathery, and often tipped with a sharp spine like that of their other relatives in the family Agavaceae (see AGAVE), the sisal hemp and agaves. The white, bell-shaped flowers in dense spikes up to 2 m (6.5 feet) in length, have remarkable symbiotic associations with the YUCCA MOTH.

yucca moth A moth of the genus *Pronuba*, found in North America and Mexico, which has a symbiotic relationship with yucca plants. A female moth collects yucca pollen and uses this to pollinate another flower in the ovary of which she lays eggs. Caterpillars eat some of the developing seeds, but not all; without the moth no seeds are set. These small moths are closely related to the LONGHORN MOTHS.

Yugoslavia Formerly, a country in south-east Europe. At the end of World War I it was formed as the Kingdom of the Serbs, Croats, and Slovenes, from the former Slavic provinces of AUSTRIA-HUNGARY (Slovenia, Croatia, Bosnia and Hercegovina), together with Serbia and Montenegro, and with Macedonian lands ceded from Bulgaria. The monarch of Serbia, Peter I, was to rule the new kingdom and was succeeded by his son ALEXANDER I. At first the Serbian Premier Nikola Pasic (1921–26) held the rival nations together, but after his death political turmoil caused the new king to establish a royal dictatorship, renaming the country Yugoslavia (January 1929). Moves towards democracy ended with his assassination (1934). During World War II Yugoslavia was overrun by German forces (1941), aided by Bulgarian, Hungarian, and Italian armies. The king fled to London and dismemberment of the country followed, with thousands of Serbs being massacred and the puppet state of CROATIA established under Ante Pavelić. A guerrilla war began, waged by two groups, supporters of the Chetnik MIHAILOVICH and TITO's Communist partisans. In 1945 Tito, supported by the Soviet Union, proclaimed the Socialist Federal Republic of Yugoslavia consisting of the republics of BOSNIA-HERCEGOVINA, CROATIA, MACEDONIA, MONTENEGRO, SERBIA, and SLOVENIA, and two autonomous Serbian provinces, KOSOVO and Vojvodina. Expelled by Stalin from the Soviet bloc in 1948, Yugoslavia became a leader of the non-aligned nations and the champion of 'positive neutrality'. Improved relations with the West followed and, after Stalin's death, diplomatic and economic ties with the Soviet Union were renewed (1955).

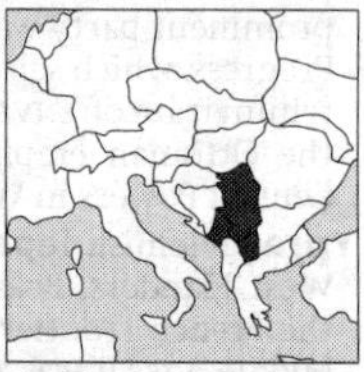

On Tito's death in 1980 his presidency was replaced by an eight-man Collective State Presidency, with the office of President rotating annually. In 1989, multi-party systems were introduced in Croatia and Slovenia, and demands for independence soon followed. In 1990 a rebellion by Croatia's 12 per cent Serb population was supported by Serbia, while in the same year Serbia, under its President, Slobodan Milosevic, brutally suppressed the 90 per cent Albanian majority in the province of Kosovo. Croatia and Slovenia declared independence in 1991, provoking a full-scale military conflict with the Serb-led Yugoslav army. Atrocities were committed by both Croatian and Serb forces, creating large-scale refugee problems. The Belgrade leadership having failed to crush nationalism in Croatia and Slovenia, both states were recognized as independent in January 1991. Bosnia-Hercegovina was also recognized as independent but erupted into fierce civil war between ethnic Serbs (aided by the Belgrade government), Muslims, and Croats. By the end of 1992, after brutal and extensive 'ethnic cleansing', more than two-thirds of Bosnia-Hercegovina was under Serb control. Sanctions were imposed on Serbia by the international community, and a UN force was sent to Bosnia to attempt to keep humanitarian relief lines open. After a long period of political indecision in the West, NATO forces finally launched air raids on Serb positions around Sarajevo in 1995. At the end of the year the presidents of Serbia, Croatia, and Bosnia-Hercegovina accepted the US-brokered Dayton Accord, a peace plan for the region, and a cease-fire came into force. In Serbia, sanctions and general economic collapse left 40 per cent of the population unemployed and the country suffering from hyper-inflation. The new Federal Republic of Yugoslavia, proclaimed by the Belgrade government in 1992 and comprising Serbia and Montenegro, has so far received little international recognition. The independence of Macedonia was generally recognized in 1993, and in 1996 relations between Serbia-Montenegro and Macedonia were normalized. This may lead to international recognition of the new Yugoslav republic by the EU and other countries; Austria extended recognition in April 1996. However, in 1998 Serbian aggression against secessionists in Kosovo provoked widespread condemnation in the EU and USA.

Yukawa, Hideki (1907–81) Japanese physicist who received the 1949 Nobel Prize for physics for predicting the existence of the MESON. He was professor of physics at Kyoto University, 1939 to 1970, where he developed his theories of forces in elementary particles.

Yukon A river of North America 3,185 km (2,004 miles) long, rising in Lake Tagish on the northern frontier of British Columbia, Canada. It flows north and north-west through Yukon Territory before entering Alaska where it takes a south-westerly course before entering Norton Sound, an inlet of the Bering Sea. The upper 1,149 km (723 miles) of the river lies within Canada. It takes its name from an Indian word meaning 'great river' and was the chief migration route followed by the original settlers of North America.

Yukon Territory A territory of north-west Canada, largely comprising a subarctic plateau that slopes down towards the Beaufort Sea and is isolated by mountains; area 482,515 sq km (186,661 sq miles); pop. (1991) 27,800. Associated with the Klondike gold-rush of 1896, its economy is based on tourism, fishing, and the mining of gold, zinc, lead, and copper.

Yunnan A province of southern China on the frontier with Vietnam, Laos, and Burma; area 436,200 sq km (168,482 sq miles); pop. (1990) 36,973,000; capital, Kunming. It is a mountainous area, rich in plant species many of which have been introduced into Europe and North America. Agricultural crops include rice, maize, wheat, tobacco, sugar cane, coffee, tea, rubber, and bananas. It has vast mineral resources, especially tin, iron, coal, lead, zinc, copper, mercury, and antimony. Many of China's minority nationalities live in the province.

Z

Zacharias (or **Zachariah**) In the Bible and Koran (as Zakariya), a temple priest and father of John the Baptist. In the New Testament Zacharias is struck dumb until his son's circumcision because he disbelieves the angel Gabriel's message that his aged and barren wife Elizabeth will bear a child. In the Koranic account, Zakariya is also the guardian of the Virgin Mary.

Zagreb The capital of the Republic of Croatia, on the River Sava; pop. (1991) 706,700. Known as Agram from 1526 to 1918. It has several Gothic and Baroque churches and palaces. Its industries include electrical machinery and appliances, chemicals, cement, pharmaceuticals, and other light industries.

Zagros Mountains A range of mountains in western Iran comprising a series of ridges separated by fertile valleys that produce tobacco, cotton, and fruit. Most of Iran's oilfields lie along the western foothills of the central Zagros Mountains. There are many peaks over 2,750 m (9,000 ft), the highest of which is Zard Kuh which rises to 4,548 m (14,921 ft) west of Isfahan.

zaibatsu Japanese business conglomerates. The zaibatsu (literally 'financial clique') were large business concerns, with ownership concentrated in the hands of a single family, which grew up in the industrialization of late 19th-century Japan. They had their origins in the activities of the seisho ('political merchants'), who made their fortunes by exploiting business links with the newly restored Meiji government. The five major zaibatsu (Mitsubishi, Mitsui, Okura, Sumitomo, Yasuda) controlled much of Japanese industry and trade up to World War II. In 1948 a decree limited the influence of the traditional zaibatsu families, and prevented members of these families from continuing to hold official positions in zaibatsu companies. The influence of the zaibatsu therefore declined. They are now more usually known in Japan as keiretsu.

Zaïre The former name (1971–97) of the Democratic Republic of CONGO.

Zambezi (or **Zambesi**) An African river that rises in north-west Zambia and flows 2,575 km (1,600 miles) south through eastern Angola, then generally eastwards along the Zambia–Zimbabwe frontier, and across central Mozambique where it empties into the Mozambique Channel of the Indian Ocean. It is dammed at Cabora Bassa and Kariba where hydroelectric power is generated, and the Victoria Falls are one of Africa's leading landmarks.

Zambia A landlocked country lying on a plateau in central Africa, surrounded by Angola, the Democratic Republic of Congo, Tanzania, Malawi, Mozambique, Zimbabwe, and Namibia (the Caprivi Strip).

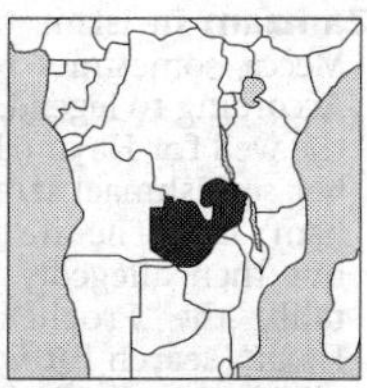

Physical. The Zambezi and its tributaries the Kafue and Luangwa run through Zambia, while in the north the Chambeshi drains into swampy areas round Lake Bangweulu. These river valleys are very warm and wet; but the rolling plateaux surrounding them are high, drier, and less hot. In the south-west there are forests of teak.

Economy. With the fourth largest copper reserves in the world, Zambia has rich mineral resources, including coal, lead, zinc, manganese, cobalt, and gemstones; copper accounts for 91 per cent of exports, followed by cobalt and zinc. However, economic development has been restricted by fluctuating world commodity prices, lack of investment in infrastructure, especially in the mining sector, a large foreign debt, and drought. Industry includes vehicle assembly, petroleum-refining, cement, and chemicals. Neglect of agriculture has led to a decline in the importance of tobacco, sugar cane, and other cash crops and dependence on food imports; staple crops include maize, cassava and millet, and cattle-rearing is also important.

History. Zambia was settled by Nguni people in flight from Zululand in 1835, but was also subject throughout much of the 19th century to Arab slave-traders. Agents from Cecil RHODES entered the country (known at this time as Barotseland) in 1890. Rhodes's British South Africa Company had been granted responsibility for it in its charter of 1889 and it began to open up the rich deposits of Broken Hill from 1902. The country was named Northern Rhodesia in 1911. It became a British protectorate in 1924 and between 1953 and 1963 was federated with Southern Rhodesia and Nyasaland, before becoming the independent republic of Zambia under President Kenneth KAUNDA in 1964. Dependent on its large copper-mining industry, Zambia has experienced persistent economic difficulties due to its lack of a coastline and port facilities and to low copper prices. It suffered from economic sanctions against Rhodesia (1965–80), but was assisted by the construction of the Tan-Zam railway. It gave refuge to political exiles from its neighbours Rhodesia (Zimbabwe), Angola, Namibia, and Mozambique, as well as from the ANC. In September 1990 Kaunda yielded to pressure to hold a referendum on the introduction of a multi-party system, and in November 1991 Frederick Chiluba, an ex-trade union leader, was elected President. He inherited both severe economic problems and an inefficient and corrupt civil service, but was helped by promises that Zambia's international debt-loan would be eased. Chiluba's programme of economic reform was hampered by the drought that swept southern Africa in 1992–93. Also, alleged high-level corruption in government led to the dismissal of a number of ministers.

Capital: Lusaka
Area: 752,614 sq km (290,586 sq mi)
Population: 9,456,000 (1995)
Currency: 1 Zambian kwacha = 100 ngwee
Religions: Protestant 34.2%; Roman Catholic 26.2%; African Christian 8.3%; traditional beliefs 27.0%; Muslim 0.3%
Ethnic Groups: Bemba 36.2%; Nyanja 15%; Tonga 19%; Mambwe 8.0%; Barotze 7.0%
Languages: English (official); Bemba; Tonga; local languages
International Organizations: UN; Commonwealth; SADC; OAU

Zamzam In Islam, the sacred well in the city of Mecca, sometimes referred to as Ishmael's Well. According to legend, the archangel Gabriel opened the well for Hajar (Hagar), desperate for water for her son Ishmael after their expulsion from Abraham's land. The site of the well was later forgotten but then allegedly rediscovered by Abd al-Muttalib, the Prophet Muhammad's grandfather. Hajar's search for water is commemorated in the pilgrimage (*hajj*) rites, and pilgrims take water from Zamzam back to their countries, often dipping their shrouds in it before leaving.

zander See PIKE-PERCH.

Zanuck, **Darryl F(rancis)** (1902–79) US film producer. In 1933 Zanuck co-founded Twentieth Century pictures. After the company's merger with the Fox Company two years later Zanuck remained controlling executive of Twentieth Century-Fox, and was president from 1965 until his retirement in 1971. Among his many successful productions are *The Grapes of Wrath* (1940), *The Longest Day* (1962), and *The Sound of Music* (1965).

Zanzibar An island off the coast of East Africa, part of Tanzania; area 1,554 sq km (600 sq miles); pop. (1988) 641,000 (with Pemba); capital, Zanzibar. Coming under Omani Arab rule in the 17th century Zanzibar was developed as a major ivory-and slave-trading port of the Indian Ocean. It became (together with the islands of Pemba and Latham) a sultanate from 1856 before being annexed by Germany in 1885 and then handed over to Britain in exchange for Heligoland in 1890. Zanzibar remained a British protectorate until it gained independence as a member state of the Commonwealth in 1963. In the following year the Sultan's government was overthrown and the country became a republic, uniting with Tanganyika to form the United Republic of Tanzania. In 1993 there were moves to dissolve the union. In the 19th century the port of Zanzibar was used by the British navy in its suppression of the slave-trade and as the base for European explorers, traders, and missionaries. Its chief products are cloves and there is a considerable fishing industry.

Zàojūn (Chinese, 'Lord of the Stove or Hearth') A Daoist household deity, protector of the family, and an important figure in Chinese folk belief. The picture of Zàojūn surrounded by children is placed above the hearth and venerated by the family on days of the full and new Moon.

Zapata, **Emiliano** (1879–1919) Mexican revolutionary. In 1911 he participated in the revolution led by Francisco Madero (1873–1913); when Madero failed to redistribute land to the peasants, Zapata intitiated his own programme of agrarian reform and attempted to implement this by means of guerrilla warfare. He later joined forces with Pancho Villa and others, overthrowing General Huerta (1854–1916) in 1914; from 1914 to 1919 he and Villa fought against the regime of Venustiano Carranza (1859–1920). Zapata was ambushed and killed by Carranza's soldiers in 1919.

Zapotec A Mesoamerican civilization of the Classic Period (300–900 AD), whose culture was centred on the cities of Monte Alban and Mitla in the state of Oaxaca, south-west Mexico.

Zappa, **Frank** (1940–93) US rock singer, musician, and songwriter. In 1965 he formed the Mothers of Invention, who released their first album, *Freak-Out!*, in 1966. They played psychedelic rock with elements of jazz, satire, and parodies of 1950s pop, while their stage performances set out to shock. Zappa later pursued a solo career, in which he frequently combined flowing guitar improvisations with scatological humour; he also became a respected composer of avant-garde orchestral and electronic music.

Zaragoza See SARAGOSSA.

Zarathustra (or **Zoroaster**) (7th–6th century BC) Persian religious reformer, the founder of ZOROASTRIANISM. Born in an aristocratic family, and probably a priest, he is said to have received a vision from Ahura Mazda ('the Wise Lord'), one of many gods then worshipped, urging belief in one god. After King Vishtaspa's conversion (*c.*588 BC) the religion spread. It is difficult to distinguish between his actual teachings and later legends, for the details of his life cannot be reconstructed with accuracy. He brought Ahura Mazda, the creator, to the centre of worship as the principle of 'good', but retained the ancient fire cult, while abolishing orgiastic sacrificial practices. The *Gathas* (hymns) contain his teachings, but they are unauthenticated.

Zatopek, **Emil** (1922–) Czech long-distance runner. During his career he set world records for nine different distances and in the 1952 Olympic Games won gold medals in the 5,000 metres, 10,000 metres, and the marathon.

Zealand (Danish **Sjaelland**) The principal island of Denmark, situated between the Jutland peninsula and the south tip of Sweden. Its chief city is Copenhagen, capital of Denmark.

Zealots The party of revolt among the Jews of Roman Palestine known for their fanaticism. Also known as Canaans after the early inhabitants of Palestine, they have been identified with the 'Daggermen' ('Sicarii') of the Jewish Revolt of 66–70 AD and the defenders of MASADA. Simon, one of the disciples of JESUS CHRIST, was also known as 'the Zealot', meaning either that he was a member of the party, or equally likely, that he was of a 'zealous' disposition.

zebra Any of three species of HORSE found in eastern and southern Africa. They have a long head with large ears, and an erect mane. The largest and most elegant is Grevy's zebra, *Equus grevyi*, 1.5 m (5 feet) tall at the shoulders, the mare and stallion being of similar size. This is an inhabitant of semi-deserts and bush-covered plains of northern Kenya and southern Ethiopia. Most numerous is the plains zebra, *E. burchelli*, standing 1.3 m (4.2 feet) at the shoulder, found on open plains and hills, and in lightly forested country. The smallest is the mountain zebra, *E. zebra*, 1.2 m (4 feet) at the shoulders, and confined to the mountains of southern Africa. Plains and mountain zebras move in large herds, which are loose gatherings of family units, each unit consisting of a stallion and about six mares with their foals. When alarmed, a zebra will emit a yelping bark, which sets the whole herd galloping.

zebu (or **Brahman**) Domesticated cattle, *Bos indicus*, of Asia and India. With long horns and a distinctive hump over the shoulder, zebu have been crossbred with other cattle to preserve their tolerance of heat and resistance to insects. The zebu is used as a draught animal and is regarded by some Hindus as sacred.

Zeebrugge A seaport on the coast of Belgium, linked by canal to Bruges and by ferry to Hull and Dover in England.

Zeeman effect A discovery in 1896 by the Dutch physicist Pieter Zeeman (1865–1943). Analysing the light from hot sodium vapour, he found that the lines in its spectrum were split if the gas was in a strong magnetic field. According to the QUANTUM THEORY, light is emitted when an electron drops to a lower energy level in an atom. Identical energy changes in many atoms give light of the same wavelength and produce one spectral line. A magnetic field splits each line because electrons, which previously had the same energy take on different energies depending on their orientation. By measuring the degree of POLARIZATION and the splitting of spectral lines from a cosmic source, astronomers can estimate the strength of the magnetic field within the source. For the discovery of this effect, Zeeman shared the 1902 Nobel Prize for physics with Hendrik LORENTZ, who offered the theoretical explanation.

Zeffirelli, Franco (born Gianfranco Corsi) (1923–) Italian film and theatre director. He began to direct his own operatic productions in the early 1950s, becoming known for the opulence of his sets and costumes, and working in many of the world's leading opera houses. He began his film career working as Visconti's assistant, and made his directorial début in the late 1960s. Among his films are *Romeo and Juliet* (1968) *Brother Sun, Sister Moon* (1973), and a film version of the opera *La Traviata* (1983).

Zeiss, Carl (1816–88) German manufacturer of optical instruments. After qualifying in medicine, he began the manufacture of optical instruments, which he knew would be in increasing demand as science and medicine advanced. He spent seven years in the workshops of various European instrument-makers before establishing his own business in 1846 in Jena. There he took ABBE into partnership and recruited Schott, an established glass manufacturer. The firm of Carl Zeiss, Jena, quickly gained an international reputation for a wide range of instruments of superb quality. After World War II a separate Zeiss company was formed in West Germany, producing microscopes, lenses, binoculars, and cameras; following German reunification, the two companies merged and the original site at Jena was closed down.

Zen (from Chinese *ch'an*, from Sanskrit *dhyāna*, 'meditation') A BUDDHIST sect of major importance in Japan. Strongly influenced by DAOISM, it originated in China in the 7th century and spread to Japan during the KAMAKURA period (12th century). In sharp contrast to popular sects, it seeks salvation through enlightenment. Enlightenment is not achieved through scriptural texts or ritual worship, but through *satori*, a sudden enlightenment experience, which is usually achieved under the guidance of a teacher. Meditation under a master, intellectual exercises, and physical endurance are stressed. Different branches of Zen teach different methods of achieving enlightenment, such as MEDITATION on paradoxical statements *kōans*), and seating posture (*zazen*). With its strict discipline it appealed to the SAMURAI. It flowered under the Ashikaga, when its masters, emphasizing harmony with nature, had much influence on aesthetics. It was associated with such refinements as the tea ceremony, which emerged under the Ashikaga.

zenith The point on the CELESTIAL SPHERE directly above the observer. This is the geometrical zenith obtained by intersecting the celestial sphere by a line drawn from the Earth's centre through the observer's position. It is 90 degrees away from the HORIZON and is in the direction opposite to the NADIR. Strictly speaking, because the Earth is not spherical, the plumb-bob zenith, that is, the direction opposite to which a suspended plumb-bob would hang, rarely coincides with the geometrical zenith.

Zenobia (3rd century AD) Queen of Palmyra *c.*267–272. She succeeded her murdered husband as ruler and then conquered Egypt and much of Asia Minor. When she proclaimed her son emperor, the Roman emperor Aurelian marched against her and eventually defeated and captured her. She was later given a pension and a villa in Italy.

Zeno of Citium (*c.*335–*c.*262 BC) Greek philosopher. He was the founder of the STOICS. He attended the ACADEMY in Athens, devoting himself first to the Cynic philosophy and then to the Socratic method of enquiry. The school of thought which he originated included a theory of knowledge, ethics, and physics, and a new system of logic. He taught that virtue, the one true good, is the only important thing, the virtue of a wise man cannot be destroyed, and that the vicissitudes of life are irrelevant to a man's happiness.

Zeno of Elea (born *c.*490 BC) Greek philosopher. He was a pupil of Parmenides and a keen advocate of his theory of monism (the theory that there is only a single ultimate principle or kind of being). He wrote a famous work that drew pairs of contradictory conclusions from the presuppositions of his rivals. This led ARISTOTLE to credit him with the invention of dialectic. His most renowned paradox is that of Achilles and the tortoise, by which it is shown that once Achilles has given the tortoise a start he can never overtake it, since by the time he arrives where it was it has already moved on.

zeolite Any one of a group of mineral aluminosilicates of sodium, potassium, calcium, and barium that occur chiefly in igneous rocks. They have a light, open-framework structure, with an overall negative charge, into which gases, water, and positive ions can diffuse. These characteristics enable them to be used as molecular sieves, by absorption of molecules of a specific size into the pores of the lattice. They can also act as ion exchangers, notably for WATER SOFTENING. Permutit is a synthetic zeolite containing sodium, the calcium ions in the water being replaced by the soluble sodium ions. The permutit is regenerated by treatment with concentrated sodium chloride solution.

Zeppelin, Ferdinand (Adolf August Heinrich), Count von (1838–1917) German aviation pioneer. An army officer until his retirement in 1890, he devoted the rest of his life to the development of the dirigible airship, known as the Zeppelin. After his airship's maiden flight in 1900, Zeppelin continued to develop and produce airships at his factory at Friedrichshafen; one of his craft achieved the first 24-hour flight in 1906.

zero-point energy The residual energy possessed by a particle at ABSOLUTE ZERO, −273.15°C

(−459.67°F). The properties of matter on an atomic scale are described by the laws of QUANTUM MECHANICS, which state that the energy of atoms and molecules can take only certain definite values. The lowest energy level is called the ground state and all higher levels are called excited states. As the temperature of a substance is lowered, molecules in higher states fall to lower states and, finally, to the ground state. At the lowest possible temperature, absolute zero, all molecules would be in the ground state. For certain types of molecular motion, such as rotation, the ground state is one of no energy at all. On the other hand, chemical bonds vibrate, and the vibrational ground state involves the molecules retaining a small residual energy. This is the zero-point energy.

Zeus In Greek mythology, the son of Cronus, whom he overthrew and succeeded as the supreme god. The greatest of the gods and ruler of the universe, he was married to his sister Hera, and was consort of a number of goddesses and lover of mortal women. The latter legends may be accounted for in some cases by the claim of royal houses to be descended from him. Zeus was the giver of laws; he saw that justice was done and liberty maintained. Supreme among gods, his power was limited only by the mysterious dictates of the Fates.

Zeuxis (fl. late 5th century BC) Greek painter. None of his works survive, but ancient writers describe him as one of the greatest Greek painters, and one of the stories about his powers of imitation tells that he painted some grapes so naturalistically that birds pecked at them. He is said to have specialized in panel paintings, and there are also references to his works in clay.

Zhejiang (formerly **Chekiang**) A mountainous province of eastern China to the south of the Yangtze River; area 101,800 sq km (39,320 sq miles); pop. (1990) 41,446,000; capital, Hangzhou. It is China's smallest mainland province. Chief among its products are rice, rapeseed, silkworm cocoons, bamboo, and tea.

Zhengzhou (formerly **Chengchow**) The capital of Henan province in north-east-central China, situated on the Yellow River; pop. (1990) 1,943,000. It is a major rail centre with textile and food industries.

Zhou A dynasty of emperors in early China, ruling territory to the north of the Yangtze River from 1122–221 BC. Their capital moved from Hao to Luoyang *c.*700 BC and during the Zhou Dynasty multiplication tables and iron casting were developed.

Zhou Enlai (or **Chou En-lai**) (1898–1976) Chinese Communist statesman, Prime Minister of China 1949–76. One of the founders of the Chinese Communist Party, he joined SUN YAT-SEN in 1924. In 1927 he organized a Communist workers' revolt in Shanghai in support of the Kuomintang forces surrounding the city. In the early 1930s he formed a partnership with Mao Zedong, supporting his rise to power within the Communist Party in 1935. On the formation of the People's Republic of China in 1949 Zhou became Premier and also served as Foreign Minister (1949–58). During the 1960s he continued to keep open communication channels with the USA, and he presided over the moves towards détente in 1972–73. He was also a moderating influence during the Cultural Revolution.

Zhoukoudian (or **Choukoutien**) A cave complex south-west of Beijing, made famous by fossils of PEKING MAN. The fossils are believed to represent a Chinese variant of HOMO ERECTUS (*Homo erectus pekinensis*). More than 40 male and female *Homo erectus* individuals are now known from the caves. Added to this hominid collection are many tens of thousands of simple flaked stone tools as well as fossilized bones of more than 100 animal species and so-called ash layers that were once interpreted as cooking hearths. The caves were occupied by Peking Man from about 500,000 to 250,000 years ago.

Zhuangzi (or **Chuang-tzu**) A classic text of DAOISM, much of which was written by Zhuangzi (*c.*369–286 BC), a Chinese philosopher from the state of Meng on the border of present-day Shandong. Although Zhuangzi's philosophy differs from that found in the DAODEJING, an earlier Daoist work ascribed to Laozi, his concept of *Dao* was a further naturalization of Laozi's concept. To him all things change at all moments and though they are different and conflicting, *Dao* transforms and unites them into a harmonious whole. The ideal person does not interfere with the Way of Nature but is at one with it. Thus the mystical and metaphysical features of Daoist thought are ultimately vehicles for addressing human problems.

Zhukov, Georgi (Konstantinovich) (1896–1974) Soviet military leader, born in Russia. He was responsible for much of the planning of the Soviet Union's campaigns in World War II. He defeated the Germans at Stalingrad (1943), lifted the Siege of Leningrad (1944), led the final assault on Germany and the capture of Berlin (1945), and became commander of the Soviet zone in occupied Germany after the war.

Zhu Xi See CONFUCIANISM.

Zia ul-Haq, Muhammad (1924–88) Pakistani general and statesman, President 1978–88. As Chief of Staff he led the bloodless coup which deposed President Zulfikar Bhutto in 1977. After being sworn in as President in 1978, he banned all political parties and began to introduce strict Islamic laws. Reappointed President in 1984, Zia ul-Haq lifted martial law but continued to maintain strict political control. He died in an air crash, possibly as the result of sabotage.

Ziegfeld, Florenz (1869–1932) US theatre manager. In 1907 he produced the first of a series of revues in New York, based on those of the Folies-Bergère, entitled the *Ziegfeld Follies*. These continued annually until his death, being staged intermittently thereafter until 1957. Among the many famous performers promoted by Ziegfeld were W. C. Fields and Fred Astaire.

Ziegler, Karl (1898–1973) German organic chemist. He was Director of the Kaiser Wilhelm (subsequently Max Planck) Institute for Coal Research at Mülheim from 1943 to 1969. There he researched in the fields of organic free radicals, organic compounds of aluminium and alkali metals, and polymerization. In the last of these he made a major technical advance with the invention of a low-temperature, low-pressure process for manufacturing POLYTHENE, which revolutionized the plastics industry. NATTA later developed the process for the manufacture of POLYPROPYLENE, and shared with Ziegler the 1963 Nobel Prize for chemistry.

ziggurat A step pyramid of sun-baked brick in ancient Babylonia and Assyria, which stood like a shrine to a god. The ziggurat at Babylon may have been the biblical Tower of Babel.

Zimbabwe A landlocked country in southern Africa. It is surrounded by Zambia, Mozambique, South Africa, and Botswana.

Physical. On the north-west boundary of Zim-

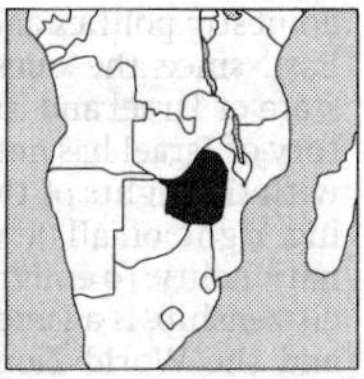

babwe with Zambia are the Victoria Falls and Lake Kariba on the Zambezi, and on the boundary with South Africa is the Limpopo. The country stands mainly on a plateau drained by tributaries of these and other rivers. The height of the plateau modifies the heat; cattle thrive, and crops can be grown.

Economy. The main exports are tobacco, gold, metal alloys, and cotton. Mineral resources include gold, nickel, copper, tin, chrome, gems, and coal. The main cash crops are tobacco, maize (the main staple), cotton, coffee, and sugar. Beef production is also important. Agriculture has substantially recovered from the devastation of the liberation war, despite recurrent drought. Fluctuations in international commodity prices have restricted the foreign-exchange investment necessary to expand industry, which concentrates on food-processing, metal-refining, chemicals, and textiles.

History. Zimbabwe is named after the ancient palace city of Great Zimbabwe, a 24-ha (64-acre) site, that dates from the 11th to the 15th centuries. Gold and copper were exported from more than 1,000 mines by the 10th century AD, the trade passing through Sofala, in Mozambique, to Arab hands. In the early 15th century the region's riches enabled the rise of the Shona (Karanga) empire, with the stone-built city as its capital. The sovereign had an elaborate court and constitution, and trade links with both sides of Africa; but after Portuguese incursions in the 16th century, Zimbabwe's fortunes steadily declined. In 1629 an attempt to expel the Portuguese resulted in the installation of a puppet ruler. After 1693 the territory was absorbed by the Rozvi empire. In the early 19th century, the Ndebele, under their leader MZILIKAZI, invaded the country from the south. He created a kingdom of Matabeleland, which for the next 50 years was to be in a state of permanent tension with the Shona to the north, in what came to be called Mashonaland. When Mzilikazi died he had obtained a peace treaty with the new Transvaal Republic, and he was succeeded by his son Lobengula. In 1889 the British South Africa Company of Cecil RHODES was founded, and in 1890 his Pioneer Column marched into Mashonaland. Following the Jameson Raid and the Matabele War of 1893, Mashonaland and Matabeleland were united. Rebellion erupted in 1896–97, but it was ruthlessly suppressed. Rapid economic development followed, the country becoming the crown colony of Southern Rhodesia in 1911 and a self-governing colony in 1923.

After the victory of the right-wing Rhodesian Front in 1962, the colony sought independence but refused British demands for black political participation in government and, under Prime Minister Ian Smith, issued the Unilateral Declaration of Independence (UDI) in 1965, renouncing colonial status and declaring Rhodesian independence. Subsequent British-sponsored attempts at negotiating a political compromise failed and nationalist forces waged an increasingly successful guerrilla campaign. Military pressure finally forced Smith to concede the principle of black majority rule, but the regime of the moderate Bishop Muzorewa could not come to an accommodation with the guerrilla leaders of the Patriotic Front, Robert MUGABE and Joshua NKOMO. Following the Lancaster House Conference (1979) Robert Mugabe was elected Prime Minister, and Rhodesia became the republic of Zimbabwe in 1980.

The decade of the 1980s saw a revival of tension between Shona and Ndebele, personified by Mugabe and Nkomo. The new constitution of 1987 not only eased this, by merging the two parties of which Mugabe and Nkomo were leaders, but also ended racial representation and created the office of executive President. With internal domestic tensions eased, Zimbabwe played a leading role in the politics of southern Africa, while its five-year plan (1986–90) did much to expand the economy. The state of emergency of 1965 was finally ended in July 1990. Since that date the country has suffered grievously from an unprecedentedly severe drought. Controversial land redistribution plans were enacted during 1993–94, with productive farms owned by whites and by black opposition leaders being seized by the government. In April 1995, the Zimbabwe African National Union-Patriotic Front (ZANU-PF), which had ruled the country since the inception of black majority rule, won its fourth successive election victory with an increased majority. The leader of the only opposition party to win seats, the Rev. Ndabaningi Sithole of ZANU-Ndonga, was arrested on charges of conspiracy to assassinate President Mugabe later the same year. In March 1996 Mugabe was re-elected as President; turnout at the polls was lower than 40% of the electorate.

Capital: Harare
Area: 390,759 sq km (150,873 sq mi)
Population: 11,261,000 (1995)
Currency: 1 Zimbabwe dollar = 100 cents
Religions: Protestant 17.5%; African indigenous 13.6%; Roman Catholic 11.7%; traditional beliefs 40.0%
Ethnic Groups: Shona 70.8%; Ndebele Nguni 15.8%; Nyanja 5.0%; European 2.0%; Asian 0.1%
Languages: English (official); Shona; Ndebele
International Organizations: UN; Commonwealth; OAU; SADC; Non-Aligned Movement

zinc (symbol Zn, at. no. 30, r.a.m. 65.38) A soft, white TRANSITION METAL that quickly tarnishes to a blue-grey appearance. The main ores are the sulphide (ZnS), known as zinc blende and the carbonate ($ZnCO_2$) known as smithsonite. Zinc is used widely in the manufacture of dry BATTERIES and in the production of alloys such as BRASS and solder. It is alloyed with ALUMINIUM to give the aluminium properties suitable for DIE CASTING. Zinc is also used for GALVANIZING OF SHERARDIZING iron. Zinc oxide is used as a white paint pigment that does not blacken in hydrogen sulphide, as a filler for automobile tyres and other rubber goods, and in medicinal ointments for skin irritations. Zinc chloride can serve as a FLUX for soldering and as a wood preservative. Zinc sulphate is used in the production of the white paint pigment lithopone. Zinc is an essential TRACE ELEMENT in the growth of human beings and animals.

zinc oxide (or **flowers of zinc**, ZnO) A white powder obtained by roasting zinc or zinc blende. It is used as a pigment in paints, as a filler in plastics and rubber, and in zinc ointment and cosmetics.

zinc sulphate ($ZnSO_4$) Once known as white vitriol, a white crystalline compound made by dissolving the metal in sulphuric acid and allowing the resulting solution to evaporate. It is used in the manufacture of agricultural sprays.

zinc sulphide (ZnS) A compound that occurs naturally as the ore zinc blende (sphalerite) from which zinc is extracted. The most important deposits occur in Belgium, New South Wales, Australia, and the USA. It is used extensively in the white pigment lithopone, a mixture of zinc sulphide and barium sulphate. It is phosphorescent and is used in making fluorescent tubes, luminous paints, and television screens.

Zinjanthropus An East African AUSTRALOPITHECINE fossil from OLDUVAI GORGE, Tanzania, from about 1.8 million years ago; it is now usually called *Australopithecus boisei*. An almost complete skull of this species has been popularly known as 'Nutcracker Man', because of the very rugged build of its teeth and jaw-bone.

Zinnemann, Fred (1907–97) Austrian-born US film director. He studied law in Vienna before becoming a cinematographer and then emigrating to the USA in 1929. In 1937 he joined MGM as a director of shorts, winning an Oscar for *That Mothers Might Live* (1938). His features, which are noted for their meticulous realism, include *High Noon* (1952) and the Oscar-winning films *From Here to Eternity* (1953) and *A Man for All Seasons* (1966).

zinnia Any of some 15 species of plant of the genus *Zinnia*, belonging to the sunflower family, mostly native to Mexico. *Z. elegans*, a species with a good deal of natural variation, has been exploited by selective breeding to produce a wide variety of decorative summer-flowering annuals.

Zinoviev, Grigori Yevseyevich (1883–1936) Soviet communist leader. Despite originally opposing the RUSSIAN REVOLUTION, he became chairman of the COMINTERN (1919–26). In 1924 a letter, apparently signed by him (known as the **Zinoviev letter**) was sent by the COMINTERN to the British Communist Party, urging revolutionary activity within the army and in Ireland. Published in British Conservative newspapers four days before the general election, it may have swung the middle-class vote away from the Labour Party, who claimed that it was a forgery. On LENIN's death Zinoviev, with STALIN and Kamenev, formed a triumvirate, but he lost power and was executed after Stalin's first show trial.

Zion The Jebusite hilltop fortress captured by David, identified with Ophel in modern Jerusalem. In the Bible, Zion is used to mean Jerusalem and by Christians to mean the Christian Church or the Kingdom of Heaven. For Jews Zion also symbolizes their return to the Promised Land.

Zionism A movement advocating the return of Jews to PALESTINE founded in 1897 under the leadership of Theodore HERZL. Originally a secular movement, Zionism has its foundation in the MILLENARIAN belief that the Jews, the chosen people of God, will be reunited from diaspora (dispersion or exile) in their rightful homeland. After the Russian POGROMS of 1881, Leo Pinsker wrote a pamphlet, *Auto-Emanzipation*, appealing for the establishment of a Jewish colony in Palestine. Zionism assumed a political character, notably through Herzl's *Der Judenstaat* (1896). The issue of the BALFOUR Declaration in 1917 and the grant of a mandate for Palestine to Britain gave impetus to the movement. During the mandate period (1920–48) under Chaim WEIZMANN the World Zionist Organization played a major part in the development of the Jewish community in Palestine by facilitating immigration, by investment (especially in land), and through the Jewish Agency. The movement was further strengthened by the persecution and annihilation of the Jewish people in World War II (the HOLOCAUST). Zionist activities in the USA were influential in winning the support of Congress and the Presidency in 1946–48 for the creation of the state of Israel.

Zionism remains an important issue in Israeli domestic politics and in the politics of the Middle East, since the question of the existence of the state of Israel and its claim to all the biblical territory of Israel has not been satisfactorily reconciled with the rights of the PALESTINIANS. The continuing right of all Jews worldwide, whatever their nationality, to emigrate to Israel and to take Israeli citizenship, is a fundamental principle of Zionism, and the World Zionist Congress, an independent body, exists to support Jewish emigration to Israel.

zip A device for fastening together the edges of garments and other textile articles. Zips provide a more rapid way of fastening than buttons, hooks-and-eyes, etc. The concept was patented in 1893 by Whitcombe Judson, an engineer from Chicago. The design for the modern zip was patented in 1913 by Gideon Sundbach (Sweden). The fastener consists of two tapes sewn on to the edges of the garment to be closed or opened. Each tape carries a row of fine teeth, which interlock when the zip is closed. The zip is opened or closed by the sliding of a simple clip mechanism. Zips gained widespread acceptance in the 1920s.

zircon A mineral consisting of zirconium silicate, $ZrSiO_4$, that commonly occurs in very small amounts in igneous, sedimentary, and metamorphic rock. Very hard and with a high refractive index, its transparent varieties are used as gems.

zirconia (or **zirconium oxide**, ZrO_2) An important CERAMIC that can occur in a number of different crystal structures, stabilized by different alloying additions to form a solid solution. It can be much less brittle than conventional ceramics due to its property of changing its crystal structure when stressed (transformation toughening). This gives it properties that are valuable in engineering. Zirconia is an important artificial gemstone in single-crystal form. It is also an electrical conductor at high temperature: in this conducting form it is used as a sensor of oxygen concentration.

zirconium (symbol Zr, at. no. 40, r.a.m. 91.22) A silvery metal found in acid igneous rocks. The main ores are zircon (containing $ZrSiO_4$) and baddeleyite (containing ZIRCONIA). Zirconium ores contain traces of the rare metal hafnium, which is highly neutron absorbent, and is used in NUCLEAR REACTOR control rods. Hafnium-free zirconium has low neutron absorbency and is used in cladding for NUCLEAR FUELS. The metal is also used as a lining for jet engines. Zirconium is added to steel as a toughening agent. Zirconium dioxide is an excellent REFRACTORY material. In a modified crystallographic form, zirconium is a substitute for DIAMONDS in jewellery.

zither A plucked stringed folk instrument of Austria and Bavaria, in its present most common form comprising a shallow wooden soundbox over which are stretched five melody strings and accompanying strings tuned to form chords. In the modern ethnomusicological sense it covers a far wider range of instruments, with strings running parallel with the resonator, which may be a tube, trough, stick, raft, bar, or board. Very commonly, especially in Europe, the board is the upper surface of a box. Such instruments are usually plucked (PSALTERIES) or hammered (DULCIMERS), but some are bowed (the HURDY-GURDY with a wheel, others with a bow), and a few are blown (AEOLIAN HARPS).

zodiac A band of the heavens close to the Sun's apparent annual path through the CELESTIAL SPHERE, as viewed from Earth, and including about 8 degrees on each side of the ECLIPTIC. This band is divided into 12 equal parts, the **signs of the zodiac**, each named after a prominent constellation situated in it. The Sun appears to move through these signs at the approximate rate of one per month.

The zodiac, comprising stars immensely distant, appeared from Earth to be immutable. All the seven moving stars or planets known before modern times – the Sun, Moon, Mercury, Venus, Mars, Jupiter, and Saturn – moved within the zodiacal band, constantly changing their positions in relation to the Earth and each other, and these movements formed the basis of ASTROLOGY. Each sign was supposed to govern a different part of the body, and a planet's influence changed as it moved from one sign to another. The constellations are no longer located in the zodiacal signs named after them, a consequence of the fact that the Earth is not a perfect sphere and the polar axis changes slightly each year by PRECESSION.

Zoffany, Johann (1733–1810) German-born painter, resident in England from 1758. Many of his earlier paintings depict scenes from the contemporary theatre, and feature the actor David Garrick (for example *The Farmer's Return*, 1762). Zoffany received the patronage of George III and painted several portraits of the royal family. The king also paid for Zoffany to visit Italy (1772–79), where he painted one of his best-known works, *The Tribuna of the Uffizi* (1772–78).

Zog I (full name Ahmed Bey Zogu) (1895–1961) Albanian statesman and ruler, Prime Minister 1922–24, President 1925–28, and king 1928–39. A leader of the reformist Popular Party, he headed a republican government as Premier and later President, ultimately proclaiming himself king in 1928. Zog's autocratic rule resulted in a period of relative political stability, but the close links he had cultivated with Italy from 1925 onwards led to increasing Italian domination of Albania, and when the country was invaded by Italy in 1939, Zog went into exile. He abdicated in 1946 after Albania became a Communist state, and died in France.

Zola, Émile (Édouard Charles Antoine) (1840–1902) French novelist and critic. Between 1871 and 1893 he published a series of 20 novels collectively entitled *Les Rougon-Macquart*; it includes *Nana* (1880), *Germinal* (1885), and *La Terre* (1887). The series chronicles in great detail the lives of the Rougon and Macquart families over several generations, and sets out to show how human behaviour is determined by environment and heredity. His collection of essays *Le Roman expérimental* (1880), which establishes an analogy between the novelist's aims and practices and those of the scientist, is regarded as the manifesto of naturalism. Zola is also remembered for his outspoken support of Alfred DREYFUS, most notably for his open letter *J'accuse* (1898) after which he fled to England. He was welcomed back to France as a hero after Dreyfus had been cleared.

Zollverein (German, 'customs union') A customs union to abolish trade and economic barriers between the German states. The Prussian Zollverein was founded in 1833 by merging the North German Zollverein with smaller customs unions, thus increasing Prussian influence. After the Austro-Prussian War (1866) the newly formed North German Confederation entered the Zollverein, and by 1888 the union, which excluded Austria, had largely achieved the economic unification of Germany.

zombi In the Voodoo cult of Haiti, a soulless body and the slave of a magician. A zombi can be a living person whose soul has been removed by magic, or a revived corpse whose soul has been separated

Aries, the Ram ♈ 21 March
Taurus, the Bull ♉ 20 April
Gemini, the Twins ♊ 21 May
Cancer, the Crab ♋ 21 June
Leo, the Lion ♌ 23 July
Virgo, the Virgin ♍ 23 August
Libra, the Balance ♎ 23 September
Scorpio, the Scorpion ♏ 23 October
Sagittarius, the Archer ♐ 22 November
Capricorn, the Goat ♑ 22 December
Aquarius, the Water-Carrier ♒ 20 January
Pisces, the Fishes ♓ 19 February

Signs of the zodiac

from it by death. It is believed that the Ghede, the top-hatted death spirits, have the power to re-animate corpses as zombis.

zone refining A method of purifying crystalline materials. A bar of the solid substance is moved progressively through a furnace in such a way that a small molten zone traverses its length. Impurities tend to remain in the molten zone and are moved along the bar. Repeating the operation many times causes the impurities to become concentrated in one end of the bar, which is then cut off. This technique is used to produce very pure SILICON and GERMANIUM needed by the electronics industry for making SEMICONDUCTOR DEVICES.

zoo (or **zoological garden**) A place in which wild and domesticated animals are exhibited in enclosures. Many of the more eminent zoos are run by scientific societies, whose primary aims are to initiate research, to help with the conservation and breeding of rare species (see ENDANGERED SPECIES), to provide an educational centre for the study of animals, and to give children an opportunity they would not otherwise have of seeing a wide variety of wild animals. Zoos began with private collections of animals and were first recorded in Egypt about 1500 BC, when one zoo held monkeys, leopards, and a giraffe. An English royal collection was housed in the Tower of London from the 13th century until 1834, when the last animals were moved to a new zoo in Regent's Park.

zoogeography See BIOGEOGRAPHY.

zoology The study of animals, which has been a popular science since the early Greek civilization. Particular groups of animals are studied in smaller divisions, such as entomology (insects), ornithology (birds), and so on. Modern zoology deals with all aspects of the biology of animals, from BIOCHEMISTRY to ECOLOGY. Subjects peculiar to zoology include animal mechanics, which investigates how animals move; neurology; animal behaviour; and the study of animal social groups.

The concepts and mechanisms derived from zoological research are invaluable to the advancement of modern society. Virtually every technological advance that man 'invents' has some natural parallel. Bats were using 'radar' long before man appeared on Earth, and insects had evolved hovering flight virtually before any terrestial animal existed. A sobering lesson to be learned from zoology is that man is a part of the animal kingdom.

zorilla See POLECAT.

Zoroaster See ZARATHUSTRA.

Zoroastrianism A monotheistic religion of ancient Iran founded by ZARATHUSTRA (or Zoroaster) in the 6th century BC. According to Zoroastrian mythology the supreme god, Ahura Mazda, created twin spirits, one of which chose truth and light, the other untruth and darkness. Later formulations pit Ahura Mazda (now called Ormazd) against his own evil twin (Ahriman). Zoroastrianism survives today in isolated areas of Iran and in India, where followers are known as Parsees. The Zendavesta are the sacred scriptures of the faith.

Zsigmondy, Richard Adolph (1865–1929) Austrian-born German chemist. His research began with a study of the colours of glass, which developed into his main work on colloids. He investigated the properties of various colloidal solutions, especially of gold in glass or water, and invented the ultramicroscope for counting colloidal particles. Zsigmondy was awarded the Nobel Prize for chemistry in 1925.

Zuiderzee A shallow inlet of the North Sea in The Netherlands, about 5,000 sq km (2,000 sq mi) in extent. From about 400 AD the Fresian inhabitants built extensive dykes and *terpen* mounds to stem the high waters, creating a mixture of lowlands and freshwater lakes which lasted until the 13th century when further flooding created the Zuiderzee proper. In 1927–32 a 30-km (19-mile) long dam was built across the Zuiderzee, separating it into the outer Waddenzee, open to the North Sea, and the inner Lake IJSSEL (IJsselmeer). By the 1990s much of the IJsselmeer had been reclaimed for agriculture, and its waters become fresh.

Zulu A South African Bantu people inhabiting the north-eastern part of Natal and speaking a language of the Niger-Congo group of languages.

Zulu Inkatha Movement See INKATHA.

Zululand See KWAZULU-NATAL.

Zulu War (1879) A war fought between Britain and Zululand. Until he occupied the Transvaal in 1877, the policy of the Natal Secretary for Native Affairs, Theophilus Shepstone, had been to protect the Zulu empire of CETSHWAYO against Afrikaner aggression. After the annexation, he reversed this policy to placate the Afrikaner population, and a scheme was prepared to seize Zululand. Frontier incidents provided opportunities, and the British High Commissioner ordered the disbandment of the Zulu army within 30 days. However CETSHWAYO did not comply, and war began on 11 January 1879. On 22 January the British suffered disaster at Isandhlwana, but with reinforcements the Zulu capital, Ulundi, was burnt, Cetshwayo was captured (28 August), and the war ceased on 1 September.

Zurbarán, Francisco de (1598–1664) Spanish painter. In 1628 he became official painter to the town of Seville, where he spent much of his life; he also carried out commissions for many churches and for Philip IV, for whom he painted a series of mythological pictures *The Labours of Hercules* (1634) and a historical scene *The Defence of Cadiz* (1634). His work reflects the influence of Caravaggio and much of his subject-matter is religious, including narrative series of scenes from the lives of the saints, painted with simple colour and form in a realistic style.

Zurich (or **Zürich**) The largest city in Switzerland, situated at the foot of the Alps on Lake Zurich; pop. (1990) 342,860. It is capital of Zurich canton and a major tourist and European financial centre with an international airport (Kloten) to the north of the city. It was a lakeside settlement before the Romans visited the area in the 1st century BC. Ulrich ZWINGLI founded Swiss Protestantism here in 1523.

Zweig, Stefan (1881–1942) German poet, short-story writer, and dramatist. Of Jewish decent, his work was deeply influenced by the psychology of Sigmund Freud, notably the stories *First Experience* (1911), *Amok* (1922), *Conflicts* (1925), and *The Royal Game* (1942). Zweig wrote several plays, including *Jeremias* (1917), and provided Richard STRAUSS with the libretto for *The Silent Woman* (1935). He is also the author of the longer biographical study *Triumph and Tragedy of Erasmus of Rotterdam* (1935). After emigrating to Brazil to escape the Nazis, he and his wife committed suicide.

Zwingli, Ulrich (1484–1531) Swiss Protestant reformer, the principal figure of the Swiss Reformation. He was minister of Zurich from 1518, where he sought to carry through his political and religious reforms and met with strong local support. From 1522 he published articles advocating the liberation of believers from the control of the papacy and bishops, and upholding the Gospel as the sole basis of truth. He attacked the idea of purgatory, the invocation of saints, monasticism, and other orthodox doctrines. His beliefs differed most markedly from Martin Luther's in his rejection of the latter's doctrine of consubstantiation. The spread of Zwingli's ideas in Switzerland met with fierce resistance and Zwingli was killed in the resulting civil war.

zwitterion (in chemistry) An electrically neutral ION that carries both a positive and a negative charge. Zwitterions occur when a compound contains both an acidic and a basic group. Amino acids under normal conditions exist almost entirely in this state; the positive and negative groups are equally ionized. For example, the amino acid glycine exists as the zwitterion $^{+}H_3N.CH_2.COO^{-}$.

Zwolle A market town on the Zwartewater River, east Netherlands, capital of the province of Overijssel; pop. (1991) 95,570. It has shipbuilding, iron, and chemical industries.

Zworykin, Vladimir (Kuzmich) (1889–1982) Russian-born US physicist and television pioneer. He invented an electronic television input device, which incorporated a screen scanned by an electron beam and sent an electric signal to a cathode-ray tube adapted to reproduce the image. This had been developed into the first practical television camera (the iconoscope) by about 1929. Zworykin continued to be involved in television development, introducing photomultipliers to make cameras more sensitive.

zygote See FERTILIZATION.

Quick Reference

SI UNITS

Base and Supplementary SI Units

Physical quantity	*SI unit*	*Symbol*
length	metre	m
mass	kilogram	kg
time	second	s
electric current	ampere	A
thermodynamic temperature	kelvin	K
luminous intensity	candela	cd
amount of substance	mole	mol
plane angle (supplementary unit)	radian	rad
solid angle (supplementary unit)	steradian	sr

Derived SI Units with Special Names

Physical quantity	*SI unit*	*Symbol*
frequency	hertz	Hz
energy	joule	J
force	newton	N
power	watt	W
pressure	pascal	Pa
electric charge	coulomb	C
electric potential difference	volt	V
electric resistance	ohm	Ω
electric conductance	siemens	S
electric capacitance	farad	F
magnetic flux	weber	Wb
inductance	henry	H
magnetic flux density (magnetic induction)	tesla	T
luminous flux	lumen	lm
illuminance	lux	lx
absorbed dose	gray	Gy
activity	becquerel	Bq
dose equivalent	sievert	Sv

Decimal Multiples and Submultiples used with SI Units

Submultiple	*Prefix*	*Symbol*	*Multiple*	*Prefix*	*Symbol*
10^{-1}	deci-	d	10	deca-	da
10^{-2}	cent-	c	10^{2}	hecto-	h
10^{-3}	milli-	m	10^{3}	kilo-	k
10^{-6}	micro-	μ	10^{6}	mega-	M
10^{-9}	nano-	n	10^{9}	giga-	G
10^{-12}	pico-	p	10^{12}	tera-	T
10^{-15}	femto-	f	10^{15}	peta-	P
10^{-18}	atto-	a	10^{18}	exa-	E
10^{-21}	zepto-	z	10^{21}	zetta-	Z
10^{-24}	yocto-	y	10^{24}	yotta	Y

UNIT CONVERSION TABLES

Length

	metre	*centimetre*	*inch*	*foot*	*yard*
1 metre	1	100	39.3701	3.28084	1.09361
1 centimetre	0.01	1	0.393701	0.0328084	0.0109361
1 inch	0.0254	2.54	1	0.0833333	0.0277778
1 foot	0.3048	30.48	12	1	0.333333
1 yard	0.9144	91.44	36	3	1

	kilometre	*mile*	*nautical mile*
1 kilometre	1	0.621371	0.539957
1 mile	1.60934	1	0.868976
1 nautical mile	1.85200	1.15078	1

Area

	m^2	cm^2	in^2	ft^2
1 square metre	1	10^4	1550	10.7639
1 square centimetre	10^{-4}	1	0.155	1.07639×10^{-3}
1 square inch	6.4516×10^{-4}	6.4516	1	6.94444×10^{-3}
1 square foot	9.2903×10^{-2}	929.03	144	1

	m^2	km^2	yd^2	mi^2	*acre*
1 square metre	1	10^{-6}	1.19599	3.86019×10^{-7}	2.47105×10^{-4}
1 square kilometre	10^6	1	1.19599×10^6	0.386019	247.105
1 square yard	0.836127	8.36127×10^{-7}	1	3.22831×10^{-7}	2.06612×10^{-4}
1 square mile	2.58999×10^6	2.58999	3.0976×10^6	1	640
1 acre	4.04686×10^3	4.04686×10^{-3}	4840	1.5625×10^{-3}	1

Volume

	m^3	cm^3	in^3	ft^3	*gallons*
1 cubic metre	1	10^6	6.10236×10^4	35.3146	219.969
1 cubic centimetre	10^{-6}	1	0.0610236	3.53146×10^{-5}	2.19969×10^{-4}
1 cubic inch	1.63871×10^{-5}	16.3871	1	5.78704×10^{-4}	3.60464×10^{-3}
1 cubic foot	0.0283168	28316.8	1728	1	6.22882
1 gallon (UK)	4.54609×10^{-3}	4546.09	277.42	0.160544	1

Speed

	m/sec	*km/hr*	*mi/hr*	*ft/sec*
1 metre per second	1	3.6	2.23694	3.28084
1 kilometre per hour	0.277778	1	0.621371	0.911346
1 mile per hour	0.44704	1.609344	1	1.46667
1 foot per second	0.3048	1.09728	0.681817	1

Mass

	kg	*g*	*lb*
1 kilogram	1	1000	2.20462
1 gram	10^{-3}	1	2.20462×10^{-3}
1 pound	0.453592	453.592	1

Density

	kg/m^3	g/m^3	lb/ft^3
1 kilogram per cubic metre	1	10^{-3}	0.062428
1 gram per cubic centimetre	1000	1	62.428
1 pound per cubic foot	16.0185	0.0160185	1

Force

	N	*kg*	*dyne*	*poundal*	*lb*
1 newton	1	0.101972	10^5	7.23300	0.224809
1 kilogram force	9.80665	1	9.80665×10^5	70.9316	2.20462
1 dyne	10^{-5}	1.01972×10^{-6}	1	7.23300×10^{-5}	2.4809×10^{-6}
1 poundal	0.138255	1.40981×10^{-2}	1.38255×10^4	1	0.031081
1 pound force	4.44822	0.453592	4.44823×10^5	32.174	1

Pressure

	$N/m^2(Pa)$	kg/cm^2	lb/in^2	*atmos*
1 newton per square metre (pascal)	1	1.01972×10^{-5}	1.45038×10^{-4}	9.86923×10^{-6}
1 kilogram per square centimetre	980.665×10^2	1	14.2234	0.967841
1 pound per square inch	6.89476×10^3	0.0703068	1	0.068046
1 atmosphere	1.01325×10^5	1.03323	14.6959	1

Work and Energy

	J	cal_{IT}	*kWhr*	btu_{IT}
1 joule	1	0.238846	2.77778×10^{-7}	9.47813×10^{-4}
1 calorie (IT)	4.1868	1	1.16300×10^{-6}	3.96831×10^{-3}
1 kilowatt hour	3.6×10^6	8.59845×10^5	1	3412.14
1 British Thermal Unit (IT)	1055.06	251.997	2.93071×10^{-4}	1

PERIODIC TABLE

Group

Period	1	2	3	4	5	6	7	8	9	10	11	12	13	14	15	16	17	18
1	1 **H**																	2 **He**
2	3 **Li**	4 **Be**											5 **B**	6 **C**	7 **N**	8 **O**	9 **F**	10 **Ne**
3	11 **Na**	12 **Mg**											13 **Al**	14 **Si**	15 **P**	16 **S**	17 **Cl**	18 **Ar**
4	19 **K**	20 **Ca**	21 **Sc**	22 **Ti**	23 **V**	24 **Cr**	25 **Mn**	26 **Fe**	27 **Co**	28 **Ni**	29 **Cu**	30 **Zn**	31 **Ga**	32 **Ge**	33 **As**	34 **Se**	35 **Br**	36 **Kr**
5	37 **Rb**	38 **Sr**	39 **Y**	40 **Zr**	41 **Nb**	42 **Mo**	43 **Tc**	44 **Ru**	45 **Rh**	46 **Pd**	47 **Ag**	48 **Cd**	49 **In**	50 **Sn**	51 **Sb**	52 **Te**	53 **I**	54 **Xe**
6	55 **Cs**	56 **Ba**	57–71 **La–Lu**	72 **Hf**	73 **Ta**	74 **W**	75 **Re**	76 **Os**	77 **Ir**	78 **Pt**	79 **Au**	80 **Hg**	81 **Tl**	82 **Pb**	83 **Bi**	84 **Po**	85 **At**	86 **Rn**
	87 **Fr**	88 **Ra**	89–103 **Ac–Lr**															

6	Lanthanides	57 **La**	58 **Ce**	59 **Pr**	60 **Nd**	61 **Pm**	62 **Sm**	63 **Eu**	64 **Gd**	65 **Tb**	66 **Dy**	67 **Ho**	68 **Er**	69 **Tm**	70 **Yb**	71 **Lu**
7	Actinides	89 **Ac**	90 **Th**	91 **Pa**	92 **U**	93 **Np**	94 **Pu**	95 **Am**	96 **Cm**	97 **Bk**	98 **Cf**	99 **Es**	100 **Fm**	101 **Md**	102 **No**	103 **Lr**

Correspondence of recommended group designations to other designations in recent use

IUPAC 1990 recommendations	1	2	3	4	5	6	7	8	9	10	11	12	13	14	15	16	17	18
Usual European convention	IA	IIA	IIIA	IVA	VA	VIA	VIIA	VIII (or VIIIA)			IB	IIB	IIIB	IVB	VB	VIB	VIIB	0 (or VIIIB)
Usual N. American convention	IA	IIA	IIIB	IVB	VB	VIB	VIIB	VIII (or VIIIB)			IB	IIB	IIIA	IVA	VA	VIA	VIIA	VIIIA (or 0)

CLASSIFICATION OF THE ANIMAL KINGDOM

(including only major phyla and classes)

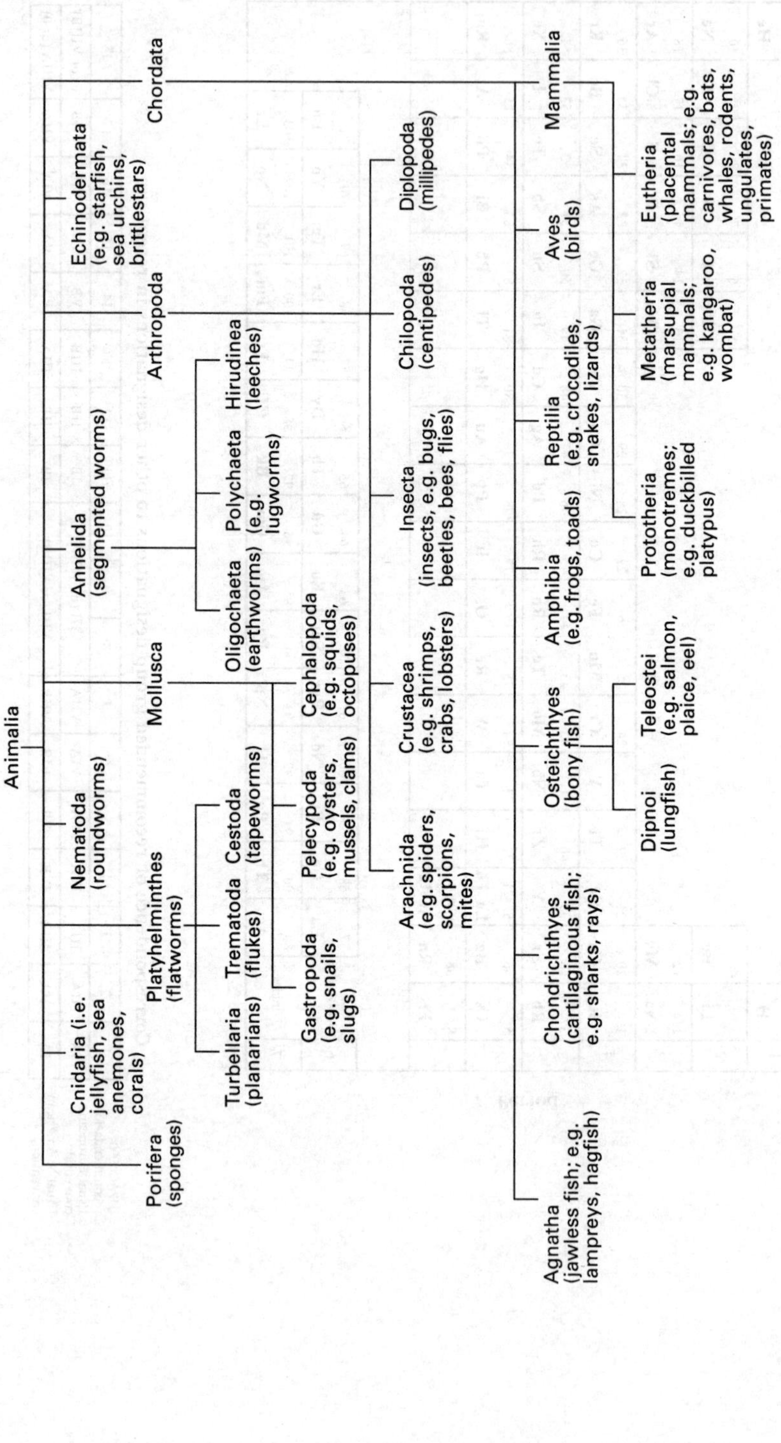

CLASSIFICATION OF THE PLANT KINGDOM

(excluding extinct and mostly extinct groups)

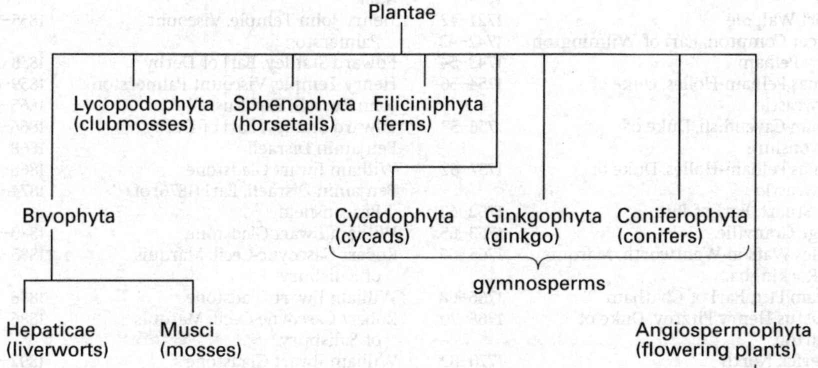

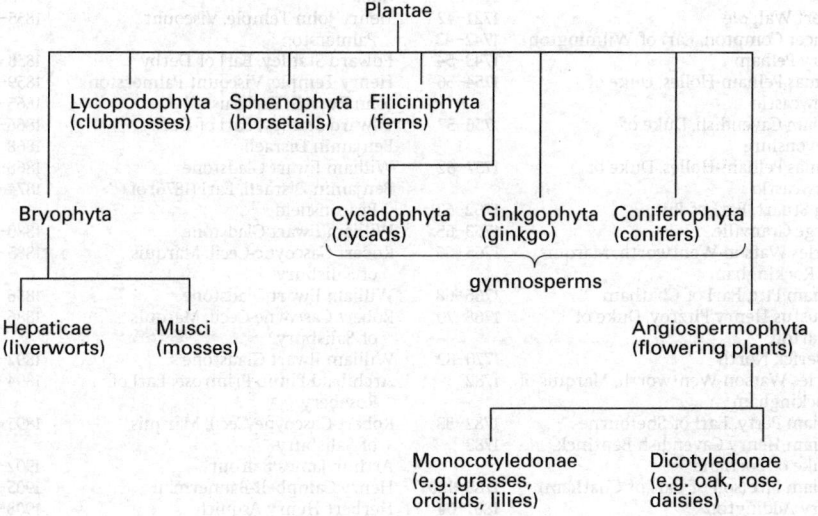

BOOKS OF THE BIBLE

Old Testament

Genesis
Exodus
Leviticus
Numbers
Deuteronomy
Joshua
Judges
Ruth
1 Samuel
2 Samuel
1 Kings
2 Kings
1 Chronicles
2 Chronicles
Ezra
Nehemiah
Esther
Job
Psalms
Proverbs
Ecclesiastes
Song of Solomon
Isaiah
Jeremiah
Lamentations
Ezekiel
Daniel
Hosea
Joel
Amos
Obadiah
Jonah
Micah
Nahum
Habakkuk
Zephaniah
Haggai
Zechariah
Malachi

New Testament

Matthew
Mark
Luke
John
The Acts
Romans
1 Corinthians
2 Corinthians
Galatians
Ephesians
Philippians
Colossians
1 Thessalonians
2 Thessalonians
1 Timothy
2 Timothy
Titus
Philemon
Hebrews
James
1 Peter
2 Peter
1 John
2 John
3 John
Jude
Revelation

PRIME MINISTERS

Great Britain (from 1721)

Name	Term
Robert Walpole	1721–42
Spencer Compton, Earl of Wilmington	1742–43
Henry Pelham	1743–54
Thomas Pelham-Holles, Duke of Newcastle	1754–56
William Cavendish, Duke of Devonshire	1756–57
Thomas Pelham-Holles, Duke of Newcastle	1757–62
John Stuart, Earl of Bute	1762–63
George Granville	1763–65
Charles Watson-Wentworth, Marquis of Rockingham	1765–66
William Pitt, Earl of Chatham	1766–68
Augustus Henry Fitzroy, Duke of Grafton	1768–70
Frederick North	1770–82
Charles Watson-Wentworth, Marquis of Rockingham	1782
William Petty, Earl of Shelburne	1782–83
William Henry Cavendish Bentinck, Duke of Portland	1783
William Pitt (son of Earl of Chatham)	1783–1801
Henry Addington	1801–04
William Pitt	1804–06
William Wyndham Grenville, Baron Grenville	1806–07
William Bentinck, Duke of Portland	1807–09
Spencer Perceval	1809–12
Robert Banks Jenkinson, Earl of Liverpool	1812–27
George Canning	1827
Frederick John Robinson, Viscount Goderich	1827–28
Arthur Wellesley, Duke of Wellington	1828–30
Charles Grey, Earl Grey	1830–34
William Lamb, Viscount Melbourne	1834
Robert Peel	1834–35
William Lamb, Viscount Melbourne	1835–41
Robert Peel	1841–46
John Russell	1846–52
Edward George Geoffrey Smith Stanley, Earl of Derby	1852
George Hamilton Gordon, Earl of Aberdeen	1852–55
Henry John Temple, Viscount Palmerston	1855–58
Edward Stanley, Earl of Derby	1858–59
Henry Temple, Viscount Palmerston	1859–65
John Russell, Earl Russell	1865–66
Edward Stanley, Earl of Derby	1866–68
Benjamin Disraeli	1868
William Ewart Gladstone	1868–74
Benjamin Disraeli, Earl (1876) of Beaconsfield	1874–80
William Ewart Gladstone	1880–85
Robert Gascoyne-Cecil, Marquis of Salisbury	1885–86
William Ewart Gladstone	1886
Robert Gascoyne-Cecil, Marquis of Salisbury	1886–92
William Ewart Gladstone	1892–94
Archibald Philip Primrose, Earl of Rosebery	1894–95
Robert Gascoyne-Cecil, Marquis of Salisbury	1895–1902
Arthur James Balfour	1902–05
Henry Campbell-Bannerman	1905–08
Herbert Henry Asquith	1908–16
David Lloyd George	1916–22
Andrew Bonar Law	1922–23
Stanley Baldwin	1923–24
James Ramsay MacDonald	1924
Stanley Baldwin	1924–29
James Ramsay MacDonald	1929–35
Stanley Baldwin	1935–37
Neville Chamberlain	1937–40
Winston Churchill	1940–45
Clement Richard Attlee	1945–51
Winston Churchill	1951–55
Anthony Eden	1955–57
Harold Macmillan	1957–63
Alec Douglas-Home	1963–64
Harold Wilson	1964–70
Edward Heath	1970–74
Harold Wilson	1974–76
James Callaghan	1976–79
Margaret Thatcher	1979–90
John Major	1990–97
Tony Blair	1997–

Irish Free State, Éire, and the Republic of Ireland

Name	Term
William Thomas Cosgrave	1923–32
Eamon De Valera	1932–48
John A. Costello	1948–51
Eamon De Valera	1951–54
John A. Costello	1954–57
Eamon De Valera	1957–59
Sean F. Lemass	1959–66
Jack M. Lynch	1966–73
Liam Cosgrave	1973–77
Jack M. Lynch	1977–79
Charles J. Haughey	1979–81
Garrett Fitzgerald	1981–82
Charles J. Haughey	1982
Garrett Fitzgerald	1982–87
Charles J. Haughey	1987–92
Albert Reynolds	1992–94
John Bruton	1994–97
Bertie Ahern	1997–

Australia

Name	Term	Name	Term
Edmund Barion	1901–03	Robert Gordon-Menzies	1939–41
Alfred Deakin	1903–04	Arthur William Fadden	1941
John C. Watson	1904	John Curtin	1941–45
George Houstoun Reid	1904–05	Joseph Benedict Chifley	1945–49
Alfred Deakin	1905–08	Robert Gordon Menzies	1949–66
Andrew Fisher	1908–09	Harold Edward Holt	1966–67
Alfred Deakin	1909–10	John Grey Gorton	1968–71
Andrew Fisher	1910–13	William McMahon	1971–72
Joseph Cook	1913–14	Gough Whitlam	1972–75
Andrew Fisher	1914–15	J. Malcolm Fraser	1975–83
William M. Hughes	1915–23	Robert Hawke	1983–91
Stanley M. Bruce	1923–29	Paul Keating	1991–96
James H. Scullin	1929–31	John Howard	1996–
Joseph A. Lyons	1932–39		

Canada

Name	Term	Name	Term
John A. Macdonald	1867–73	Richard B. Bennett	1930–35
Alexander Mackenzie	1873–78	W. L. Mackenzie King	1935–48
John A. Macdonald	1878–91	Louis Stephen St. Laurent	1948–57
John J. C. Abbott	1891–92	John George Diefenbaker	1957–63
John S. D. Thompson	1892–94	Lester B. Pearson	1963–68
Mackenzie Bowell	1894–96	Pierre Elliott Trudeau	1968–79
Charles Tupper	1896	Joseph Clark	1979–80
Wilfrid Laurier	1896–1911	Pierre Elliott Trudeau	1980–84
Robert L. Borden	1911–20	John Turner	1984
Arthur Meighen	1920–21	Brian Mulroney	1984–93
W. L. Mackenzie King	1921–26	Kim Campbell	1993
Arthur Meighen	1926	Jean Chrétien	1993–
W. L. Mackenzie King	1926–30		

New Zealand

Name	Term	Name	Term
Henry Sewell	1856	John Ballance	1891–93
William Fox	1856	Richard John Seddon	1893–1906
Edward William Stafford	1856–61	William Hall-Jones	1906
William Fox	1861–62	Joseph George Ward	1906–12
Alfred Domett	1862–63	Thomas Mackenzie	1912
Frederick Whitaker	1863–64	William Ferguson Massey	1912–25
Frederick Aloysius Weld	1864–65	Francis Henry Dillon Bell	1925
Edward William Stafford	1865–69	Joseph Gordon Coates	1925–28
William Fox	1869–72	Joseph George Ward	1928–30
Edward William Stafford	1872	George William Forbes	1930–35
George Marsden Waterhouse	1872–73	Michael J. Savage	1935–40
William Fox	1873	Peter Fraser	1940–49
Julius Vogel	1873–75	Sidney G. Holland	1949–57
Daniel Pollen	1875–76	Walter Nash	1957–60
Julius Vogel	1876	Keith J. Holyoake	1960–72
Harry Albert Atkinson	1876–77	John R. Marshall	1972
George Grey	1877–79	Norman Kirk	1972–74
John Hall	1879–82	Wallace Rowling	1974–75
Frederick Whitaker	1882–83	Robert D. Muldoon	1975–84
Harry Albert Atkinson	1883–84	David Lange	1984–89
Robert Stout	1884	Geoffrey Palmer	1989–90
Harry Albert Atkinson	1884	Michael Moore	1990
Robert Stout	1884–87	James Bolger	1990–97
Harry Albert Atkinson	1887–91	Jenny Shipley	1997–

Prime Ministers (1910–84) and Presidents* (1984–) of South Africa

Name	Term	Name	Term
Louis Botha	1910–19	P(ieter) W(illem) Botha	1978–84
Jan (Christian) Smuts	1919–24	P(ieter) W(illem) Botha	1984–89
James Barry Munnik Hertzog	1924–39	F(rederik) W(illem) de Klerk	1989–94
Jan (Christian) Smuts	1939–48	Nelson (Rolihlahla) Mandela	1994–
Daniel F(rançois) Malan	1948–54		
Johannes Gerhardus Strijdom	1954–58		
Hendrik Frensch Verwoerd	1958–66		
Balthazar Johannes Vorster	1966–78		

*The office of president was created as an honorific title when South Africa became a republic in 1961; the 1983 constitution made the president pre-eminent in power.

PRESIDENTS OF THE UNITED STATES OF AMERICA

Name	*Term*	*Name*	*Term*
George Washington	1789–97	Grover Cleveland	1885–89
John Adams	1797–1801	Benjamin Harrison	1889–93
Thomas Jefferson	1801–09	Grover Cleveland	1893–97
James Madison	1809–17	William McKinley	1897–1901
James Monroe	1817–25	Theodore Roosevelt	1901–09
John Quincy Adams	1825–29	William Howard Taft	1909–13
Andrew Jackson	1829–37	Woodrow Wilson	1913–21
Martin Van Buren	1837–41	Warren Gamaliel Harding	1921–23
William Henry Harrison	1841	Calvin Coolidge	1923–29
John Tyler	1841–45	Herbert Clark Hoover	1929–33
James Knox Polk	1845–49	Franklin Delano Roosevelt	1933–45
Zachary Taylor	1849–50	Harry S. Truman	1945–53
Millard Fillmore	1850–53	Dwight David Eisenhower	1953–61
Franklin Pierce	1853–57	John Fitzgerald Kennedy	1961–63
James Buchanan	1857–61	Lyndon Baines Johnson	1963–69
Abraham Lincoln	1861–65	Richard Milhous Nixon	1969–74
Andrew Johnson	1865–69	Gerald Rudolph Ford	1974–77
Ulysses Simpson Grant	1869–77	James Earl Carter	1977–81
Rutherford Hayes	1877–81	Ronald Wilson Reagan	1981–89
James Abram Garfield	1881	George Herbert Walker Bush	1989–93
Chester Alan Arthur	1881–85	William Jefferson Clinton	1993–

THE BRITISH MONARCHY

Kings and Queens of England

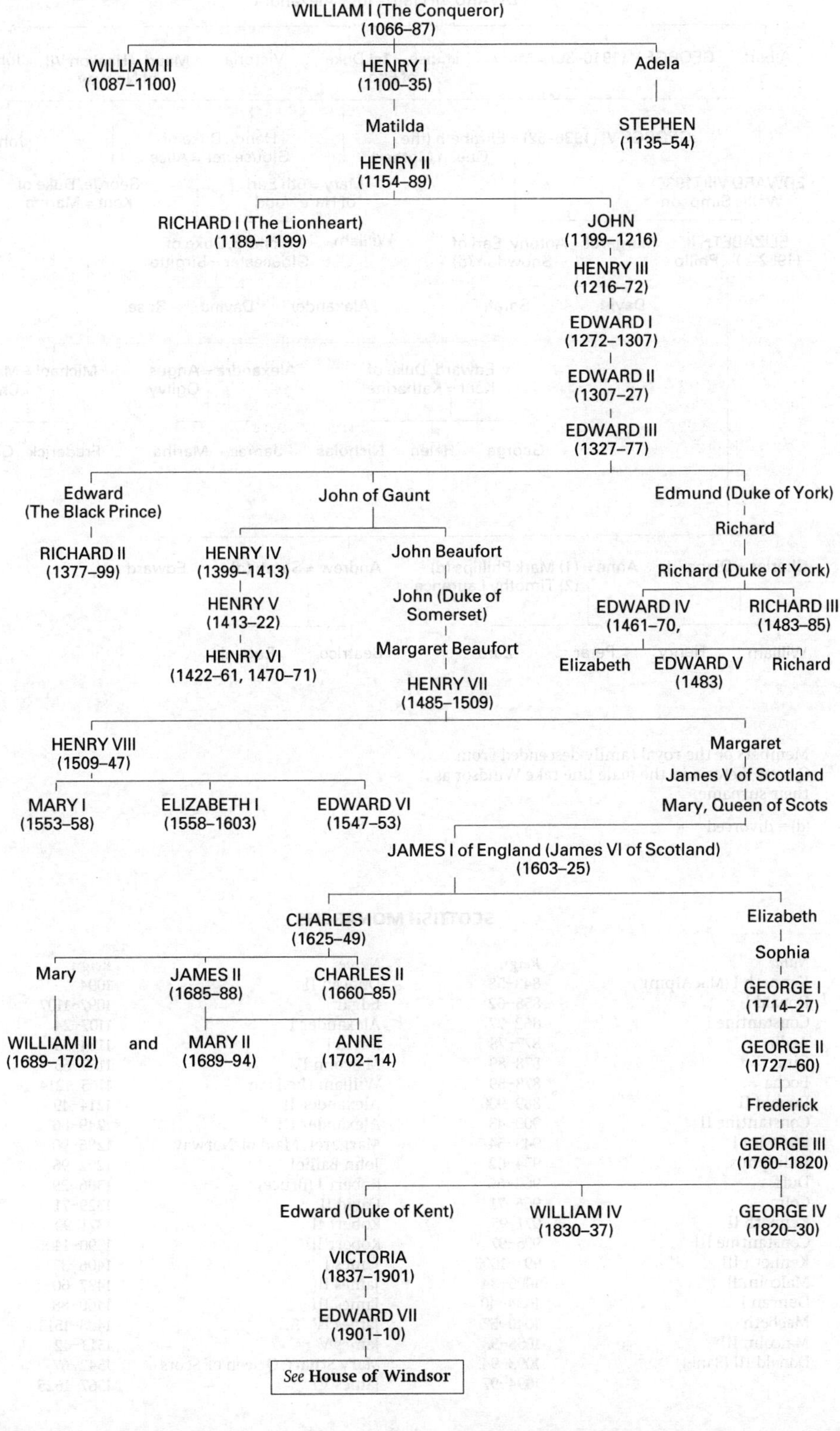
WILLIAM I (The Conqueror)
(1066–87)
WILLIAM II
(1087–1100)
HENRY I
(1100–35)
Adela
Matilda
STEPHEN
(1135–54)
HENRY II
(1154–89)
RICHARD I (The Lionheart)
(1189–1199)
JOHN
(1199–1216)
HENRY III
(1216–72)
EDWARD I
(1272–1307)
EDWARD II
(1307–27)
EDWARD III
(1327–77)
Edward
(The Black Prince)
John of Gaunt
Edmund (Duke of York)
RICHARD II
(1377–99)
HENRY IV
(1399–1413)
John Beaufort
Richard
HENRY V
(1413–22)
John (Duke of
Somerset)
Richard (Duke of York)
HENRY VI
(1422–61, 1470–71)
Margaret Beaufort
EDWARD IV
1461–70,
RICHARD III
(1483–85)
HENRY VII
(1485–1509)
Elizabeth
EDWARD V
(1483)
Richard
HENRY VIII
(1509–47)
Margaret
James V of Scotland
Mary, Queen of Scots
MARY I
(1553–58)
ELIZABETH I
(1558–1603)
EDWARD VI
(1547–53)
JAMES I of England (James VI of Scotland)
(1603–25)
CHARLES I
(1625–49)
Elizabeth
Sophia
Mary
JAMES II
(1685–88)
CHARLES II
(1660–85)
GEORGE I
(1714–27)
WILLIAM III
(1689–1702)
and
MARY II
(1689–94)
ANNE
(1702–14)
GEORGE II
(1727–60)
Frederick
GEORGE III
(1760–1820)
Edward (Duke of Kent)
WILLIAM IV
(1830–37)
GEORGE IV
(1820–30)
VICTORIA
(1837–1901)
EDWARD VII
(1901–10)
See House of Windsor

House of Windsor

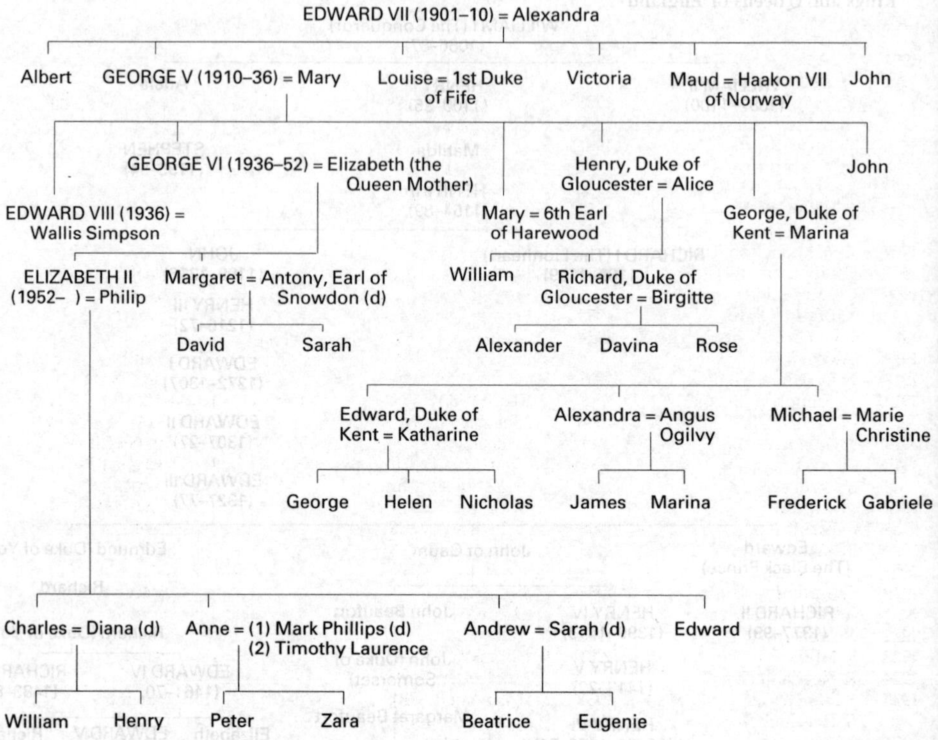

Members of the royal family descended from Queen Victoria in the male line take Windsor as their surname.

(d) = divorced

SCOTTISH MONARCHS

Name	*Reign*	*Name*	*Reign*
Kenneth I (MacAlpin)	843–58	Duncan II	1094
Donald I	858–62	Edgar	1097–1107
Constantine I	862–77	Alexander I	1107–24
Aedh	877–78	David I	1124–53
Girac	878–89	Malcolm IV	1153–65
Eocha	878–89	William the Lion	1165–1214
Donald II	889–900	Alexander II	1214–49
Constantine II	900–43	Alexander III	1249–86
Malcolm I	943–54	Margaret, Maid of Norway	1286–90
Indulphus	954–62	John Balliol	1292–96
Duff	962–66	Robert I (Bruce)	1306–29
Colin	966–71	David II	1329–71
Kenneth II	971–95	Robert II	1371–90
Constantine III	995–97	Robert III	1390–1406
Kenneth III	997–1005	James I	1406–37
Malcolm II	1005–34	James II	1437–60
Duncan I	1034–40	James III	1460–88
Macbeth	1040–57	James IV	1488–1513
Malcolm III	1058–93	James V	1513–42
Donald III (Bane)	1093–94, 1094–97	Mary Stuart, Queen of Scots	1542–67
		James VI	1567–1625

NOBEL PRIZE WINNERS

Physics

Year	*Name*
1901	W. Röntgen (Ger)
1902	H. Antoon Lorentz (Neth)
	P. Zeeman (Neth)
1903	A. Becquerel (Fr)
	P. Curie (Fr)
	M. Curie (Fr)
1904	Lord Rayleigh (UK)
1905	P. Lenard (Ger)
1906	Sir J. J. Thomson (UK)
1907	A. A. Michelson (USA)
1908	G. Lippmann (Fr)
1909	G. Marconi (It)
	K. Braun (Ger)
1910	J. Van Der Waals (Neth)
1911	W. Wien (Ger)
1912	N. G. Dalen (Swed)
1913	H. Kamerlingh Onnes (Neth)
1914	M. Von Laue (Ger)
1915	Sir W. Bragg (UK)
	Sir L. Bragg (UK)
1916	no award
1917	C. Barkla (UK)
1918	M. Planck (Ger)
1919	J. Stark (Ger)
1920	C. Guillaume (Swtz)
1921	A. Einstein (Switz)
1922	N. Bohr (Den)
1923	R. Millikan (USA)
1924	K. Siegbahn (Swed)
1925	J. Franck (Ger)
	G. Hertz (Ger)
1926	J. Perrin (Fr)
1927	A. H. Compton (USA)
	C. Wilson (UK)
1928	Sir O. Richardson (UK)
1929	Prince L. de Broglie (Fr)
1930	Sir C. Raman (India)
1931	no award
1932	W. Heisenberg (Ger)
1933	P. A. M. Dirac (UK)
	E. Schrödinger (Austria)
1934	no award
1935	Sir J. Chadwick (UK)
1936	V. Hess (Austria)
	C. Anderson (USA)
1937	C. Davisson (USA)
	Sir G. P. Thomson (UK)
1938	E. Fermi (It)
1939	E. Lawrence (USA)
1940	no award
1941	no award
1942	no award

Year	*Name*
1943	O. Stern (USA)
1944	I. Rabi (USA)
1945	W. Pauli (Austria)
1946	P. Bridgman (USA)
1947	Sir E. Appleton (UK)
1948	P. Blackett (UK)
1949	H. Yukawa (Jap)
1950	C. Powell (UK)
1951	Sir J. Cockcroft (UK)
	E. Walton (Ire)
1952	F. Bloch (USA)
	E. Purcell (USA)
1953	F. Zernike (Neth)
1954	M. Born (UK)
	W. Bothe (Ger)
1955	W. Lamb, Jr. (USA)
	P. Kusch (USA)
1956	W. Shockley (USA)
	J. Bardeen (USA)
	W. Brattain (USA)
1957	Tsung-Dao Lee (China)
	C. N. Yang (China)
1958	P. A. Cherenkov (USSR)
	I. M. Frank (USSR)
	I. Y. Tamm (USSR)
1959	E. Segrè (USA)
	O. Chamberlain (USA)
1960	D. Glaser (USA)
1961	R. Hofstadter (USA)
	R. Mössbauer (Ger)
1962	L. D. Landau (USSR)
1963	J. H. D. Jensen (Ger)
	M. G. Mayer (USA)
	E. P. Wigner (USA)
1964	C. H. Townes (USA)
	N. G. Basov (USSR)
	A. M. Prokhorov (USSR)
1965	J. S. Schwinger (USA)
	R. P. Feynman (USA)
	S. Tomonaga (Jap)
1966	A. Kastler (Fr)
1967	H. A. Bethe (USA)
1968	L. W. Alvarez (USA)
1969	M. Gell-Mann (USA)
1970	H. Alvén (Swed)
	L. Néel (Fr)
1971	D. Gabor (UK)
1972	J. Bardeen (USA)
	L. N. Cooper (USA)
	J. R. Schrieffer (USA)
1973	L. Esaki (Jap)
	I. Giaever (USA)
	B. Josephson (UK)

Year	*Name*
1974	Sir M. Ryle (UK)
	A. Hewish (UK)
1975	J. Rainwater (USA)
	A. Bohr (Den)
	B. Mottelson (Den)
1976	B. Richter (USA)
	S. Ting (USA)
1977	P. W. Anderson (USA)
	Sir N. F. Mott (UK)
	J. H. van Vleck (USA)
1978	P. L. Kapitsa (USSR)
	A. A. Penzias (USA)
	R. W. Wilson (USA)
1979	S. L. Glashow (USA)
	A. Salam (Pak)
	S. Weinberg (USA)
1980	J. Cronin (USA)
	V. Fitch (USA)
1981	K. Siegbahn (Swed)
	N. Bloembergen (USA)
	A. Schawlow (USA)
1982	K. G. Wilson (USA)
1983	S. Chandrasekhar (USA)
	W. Fowler (USA)
1984	C. Rubbia (It)
	S. van der Meer (Neth)
1985	K. von Klitzing (Ger)
1986	E. Ruska (Ger)
	G. Binnig (Ger)
	H. Rohrer (Switz)
1987	A. Müller (Switz)
	G. Bednorz (Ger)
1988	L. M. Lederman (USA)
	M. Schwartz (USA)
	J. Steinberger (Ger)
1989	H. Dehmelt (USA)
	W. Paulm (Ger)
	N. Ramsey (USA)
1990	J. Friedman (USA)
	H. Kendall (USA)
	R. Taylor (Can)
1991	P. De Gennes (Fr)
1992	G. Charpak
1993	R. Hulse (USA)
	J. Taylor (USA)
1994	B. Brockhoue (Can)
	C. Shull (USA)
1995	M. Perl (USA)
	F. Reines (USA)
1996	D. M. Lee (USA)
	D. D. Oscherof (USA)
	R. C. Richardson (USA)
1997	S. Chu (USA)

Chemistry

Year	*Name*
1901	J. V. Hoff (Neth)
1902	E. Fischer (Ger)
1903	S. Arrhenius (Swed)
1904	Sir W. Ramsay (UK)
1905	A. von Baeyer (Ger)
1906	H. Moissan (Fr)
1907	E. Buchner (Ger)
1908	Lord Rutherford (UK)
1909	W. Ostwald (Ger)
1910	O. Wallach (Ger)
1911	M. Curie (Fr)
1912	V. Grignard (Fr)
	P. Sabatier (Fr)

Year	*Name*
1913	A. Werner (Switz)
1914	T. Richards (USA)
1915	R. Willstätter (Ger)
1916	no award
1917	no award
1918	F. Haber (Ger)
1919	no award
1920	W. Nernst (Ger)
1921	F. Soddy (UK)
1922	F. Aston (UK)
1923	F. Pregl (Austria)
1924	no award
1925	R. Zsigmondy (Austria)

Year	*Name*
1926	T. Svedberg (Swed)
1927	H. Wieland (Ger)
1928	A. Windaus (Ger)
1929	Sir A. Harden (UK)
	H. von Euler-Chelpin (Swed)
1930	H. Fischer (Ger)
1931	K. Bosch (Ger)
	F. Bergius (Ger)
1932	I. Langmuir (USA)
1933	no award
1934	H. Urey (USA)
1935	F. Joliot-Curie (Fr)

Year	Name
	I. Joliot-Curie (Fr)
1936	P. Debye (Neth)
1937	Sir W. Haworth (UK)
	P. Karrer (Switz)
1938	R. Kuhn (Ger)
1939	A. Butenandt (Ger)
	L. Ruzicka (Switz)
1940	no award
1941	no award
1942	no award
1943	G. de Hevesy (Hung)
1944	O. Hahn (Ger)
1945	A. Virtanen (Fin)
1946	J. Sumner (USA)
	J. Northrop (USA)
	W. Stanley (USA)
1947	Sir R. Robinson (UK)
1948	A. Tiselius (Swed)
1949	W. Giauque (USA)
1950	O. Diels (Ger)
	K. Alder (Ger)
1951	E. McMillan (USA)
	G. Seaborg (USA)
1952	A. Martin (UK)
	R. Synge (UK)
1953	H. Staudinger (Ger)
1954	L. C. Pauling (USA)
1955	V. du Vigneaud (USA)
1956	N. Semyonov (USSR)
	Sir C. Hinshelwood (UK)
1957	Sir A. Todd (UK)
1958	F. Sanger (UK)
1959	J. Heyrovsky (Czech)
1960	W. Libby (USA)
1961	M. Calvin (USA)
1962	J. C. Kendrew (UK)
	M. F. Perutz (UK)
1963	G. Natta (It)
	K. Ziegler (Ger)
1964	D. M. C. Hodgkin (UK)
1965	R. B. Woodward (USA)
1966	R. S. Mulliken (USA)
1967	M. Eigen (Ger)
	R. G. W. Norrish (UK)
	G. Porter (UK)
1968	L. Onsager (USA)
1969	D. H. R. Barton (UK)
	O. Hassel (Nor)
1970	L. F. Leloir (Arg)
1971	G. Herzberg (Can)
1972	C. B. Anfinsen (USA)
	S. Moore (USA)
	W. H. Stein (USA)
1973	E. Fischer (Ger)
	G. Wilkinson (UK)
1974	P. J. Flory (USA)
1975	J. W. Cornfort (Austral)
	V. Prelog (Switz)
1976	W. M. Lipscomb (USA)
1977	I. Prigogine (Belg)
1978	P. Mitchell (UK)
1979	H. C. Brown (USA)
	G. Wittig (Ger)
1980	P. Berg (USA)
	W. Gilbert (USA)
	F. Sanger (UK)
1981	K. Fukui (Jap)
	R. Hoffmann (Pol)
1982	A. Klug (UK)
1983	H. Taube (USA)
1984	R. B. Merrifield (USA)
1985	H. Hauptman (USA)
	J. Karle (USA)
1986	D. Herschbach (USA)
	Y. Tseh Lee (USA)
	J. Polanyi (Can)
1987	D. Cram (USA)
	J. Lehn (Fr)
	C. Pedersen (USA)
1988	J. Diesenhofer (Ger)
	R. Huber (Ger)
	H. Michel (Ger)
1989	S. Altman (USA)
	T. Cech (USA)
1990	E. Cory (USA)
1991	R. Ernst (Switz)
1992	R. Marcus (Can)
1993	K. Mullis (USA)
	M. Smith (USA)
1994	G. Olah (USA)
1995	P. Crutzen (Neth)
	M. Molina (Mex)
	F. Rowland (USA)
1996	H. Kroto (UK)
	R. Curl (USA)
	R. Smalley (USA)
1997	P. D. Boyer (USA)
	J. E. Walker (UK)
	J. C. Skou (Den)

Physiology or Medicine

Year	Name
1901	E. von Behring (Ger)
1902	Sir R. Ross (UK)
1903	N. R. Finsen (Den)
1904	I. Pavlov (Russia)
1905	R. Koch (Ger)
1906	C. Golgi (It)
	S. Ramón y Cajal (Sp)
1907	A. Laveran (Fr)
1908	P. Ehrlich (Ger)
	I. Mechnikov (Russia)
1909	E. Kocher (Switz)
1910	A. Kossel (Ger)
1911	A. Gullstrand (Swed)
1912	A. Carrel (Fr)
1913	C. Richet (Fr)
1914	R. Bárány (Austria)
1915	no award
1916	no award
1917	no award
1918	no award
1919	J. Bordet (Belg)
1920	A. Krogh (Den)
1921	no award
1922	A. V. Hill (UK)
	O. Meyerhof (Ger)
1923	Sir F. G. Banting (Can)
	J. J. R. MacLeod (UK)
1924	W. Einthoven (Neth)
1925	no award
1926	J. Fibiger (Den)
1927	J. Wagner von Jauregg (Austria)
1928	C. Nicolle (Fr)
1929	C. Eijkman (Neth)
	Sir F. Hopkins (UK)
1930	K. Landsteiner (USA)
1931	O. Warburg (Ger)
1932	E. D. Adrian (UK)
	Sir C. Sherrington (UK)
1933	T. H. Morgan (USA)
1934	G. R. Minot (USA)
	W. P. Murphy (USA)
	G. H. Whipple (USA)
1935	H. Spemann (Ger)
1936	Sir H. H. Dale (UK)
	O. Loewi (Ger)
1937	A. Szent-Györgyi (Hung)
1938	C. Heymans (Belg)
1939	G. Domagk (Ger)
1940	no award
1941	no award
1942	no award
1943	H. Dam (Den)
	E. A. Doisy (USA)
1944	J. Erlanger (USA)
	H. S. Gasser (USA)
1945	Sir A. Fleming (UK)
	E. B. Chain (UK)
	Lord Florey (Austral)
1946	H. J. Muller (USA)
1947	C. F. Cori (USA)
	G. T. Cori (USA)
	B. Houssay (Arg)
1948	P. Müller (Switz)
1949	W. R. Hess (Switz)
	A. E. Moniz (Port)
1950	P. S. Hench (USA)
	E. C. Kendall (USA)
	T. Reichstein (Switz)
1951	M. Theiler (S Af)
1952	S. A. Waksman (USA)
1953	F. A. Lipmann (USA)
	Sir H. A. Krebs (UK)
1954	J. F. Enders (USA)
	T. H. Weller (USA)
	F. Robbins (USA)
1955	A. H. Theorell (Swed)
1956	W. Forssmann (Ger)
	D. Richards (USA)
	A. F. Cournand (USA)
1957	D. Bovet (It)
1958	G. W. Beadle (USA)
	E. L. Tatum (USA)
	J. Lederberg (USA)
1959	S. Ochoa (USA)
	A. Kornberg (USA)
1960	Sir F. MacFarlane Burnet (Austral)
	P. B. Medawar (UK)
1961	G. von Békésy (USA)
1962	F. H. C. Crick (UK)
	J. D. Watson (USA)
	M. Wilkins (UK)
1963	Sir J. C. Eccles (Austral)
	A. L. Hodgkin (UK)
	A. F. Huxley (UK)
1964	K. Bloch (USA)
	F. Lynen (Ger)
1965	F. Jacob (Fr)
	A. Lwoff (Fr)
	J. Monod (Fr)
1966	C. B. Huggins (USA)
	F. P. Rous (USA)
1967	H. K. Hartline (USA)
	G. Wald (USA)
	R. A. Granit (Swed)
1968	R. W. Holley (USA)
	H. G. Khorana (USA)

Year	Name
	M. W. Nirenberg (USA)
1969	M. Delbrück (USA)
	A. D. Hershey (USA)
	S. E. Luria (USA)
1970	J. Axelrod (USA)
	Sir B. Katz (UK)
	U. von Euler (Swed)
1971	E. W. Sutherland, Jr. (USA)
1972	G. M. Edelman (USA)
	R. R. Porter (UK)
1973	K. von Frisch (Ger)
	K. Lorenz (Ger)
	N. Tinbergen (Neth)
1974	A. Claude (USA)
	C. de Duve (Belg)
	G. E. Palade (Belg)
1975	D. Baltimore (USA)
	R. Dulbecco (USA)
	H. M. Temin (USA)
1976	B. S. Blumberg (USA)
	D. G. Gajdusek (USA)
1977	R. S. Yalow (USA)
	R. Guillemin (USA)
	A. V. Schally (USA)
1978	W. Arber (Switz)
	D. Nathans (USA)
	H. Smith (USA)
1979	A. M. Cormack (USA)
	G. N. Hounsfield (UK)
1980	G. Snell (USA)
	J. Dausset (Fr)
	B. Benacerraf (USA)
1981	R. Sperry (USA)
	D. Hubel (USA)
	T. Wiesel (Swed)
1982	S. K. Bergstrom (Swed)
	B. I. Samuelson (Swed)
	J. R. Vane (UK)
1983	B. McClintock (USA)
1984	N. K. Jerne (Den)
	G. J. F. Köhler (Ger)
	C. Milstein (UK)
1985	J. Goldstein (USA)
	M. Brown (USA)
1986	S. Cohen (USA)
	R. Levi-Montalcini (It)
1987	S. Tonegawa (Jap)
1988	J. W. Black (UK)
	G. B. Elion (USA)
	G. H. Hitchings (USA)
1989	M. Bishop (USA)
	H. Varmus (USA)
1990	J. Murray (USA)
	E. Thomas (USA)
1991	E. Neher (Ger)
	B. Sakmann (Ger)
1992	E. Fischer (USA)
	E. Krebs (USA)
1993	R. Roberts (USA)
	P. Sharp (USA)
1994	A. Gilman (USA)
	M. Rodbell (USA)
1995	E. Lewis (USA)
	C. Nüesslein-Volhard (Ger)
	E. Wieschaus (USA)
1996	P. Doherty (Austral)
	R. Zinkernagel (Switz)
1997	S. B. Prusiner (USA)

Literature

Year	Name
1901	S. Prudhomme (Fr)
1902	T. Mommsen (Ger)
1903	B. Bjørnson (Nor)
1904	F. Mistral (Fr)
	J. Echegaray y Eizaguirre (Sp)
1905	H. Sienkiewicz (Pol)
1906	G. Carducci (It)
1907	R. Kipling (UK)
1908	R. Eucken (Ger)
1909	S. Lagerlöf (Swed)
1910	P. von Heyse (Ger)
1911	M. Maeterlinck (Belg)
1912	G. Hauptmann (Ger)
1913	Sir R. Tagore (India)
1914	no award
1915	R. Rolland (Fr)
1916	V. von Heidenstam (Swed)
1917	K. Gjellerup (Den)
	H. Pontoppidan (Den)
1918	no award
1919	C. Spitteler (Switz)
1920	K. Hamsun (Nor)
1921	A. France (Fr)
1922	J. Benavente y Martinez (Sp)
1923	W. B. Yeats (Ire)
1924	W. S. Reymont (Pol)
1925	G. B. Shaw (Ire)
1926	G. Deledda (It)
1927	H. Bergson (Fr)
1928	S. Undset (Nor)
1929	T. Mann (Ger)
1930	S. Lewis (USA)
1931	E. A. Karlfeldt (Swed)
1932	J. Galsworthy (UK)
1933	I. Bunin (USSR)
1934	L. Pirandello (It)
1935	no award
1936	E. O'Neill (USA)
1937	R. M. du Gard (Fr)
1938	P. Buck (USA)
1939	F. E. Sillanpää (Fin)
1940	no award
1941	no award
1942	no award
1943	no award
1944	J. V. Jensen (Den)
1945	G. Mistral (Chile)
1946	H. Hesse (Switz)
1947	A. Gide (Fr)
1948	T. S. Eliot (UK)
1949	W. Faulkner (USA)
1950	B. Russell (UK)
1951	P. F. Lagerkvist (Swed)
1952	F. Mauriac (Fr)
1953	Sir Winston Churchill (UK)
1954	E. Hemingway (USA)
1955	H. K. Laxness (Ice)
1956	J. R. Jiménez (Sp)
1957	A. Camus (Fr)
1958	B. L. Pasternak (declined award) (USSR)
1959	S. Quasimodo (It)
1960	S. J. Perse (Fr)
1961	I. Andrić (Yugos)
1962	J. Steinbeck (USA)
1963	G. Seferis (Greece)
1964	J. P. Sartre (declined award) (Fr)
1965	M. Sholokhov (USSR)
1966	S. Y. Agnon (Isr)
	N. Sachs (Swed)
1967	M. A. Asturias (Guat)
1968	K. Yasunari (Jap)
1969	S. Beckett (Ire)
1970	A. I. Solzhenitsyn (USSR)
1971	P. Neruda (Chile)
1972	H. Böll (Ger)
1973	P. White (Austral)
1974	E. Johnson (Swed)
	H. Martinson (Swed)
1975	E. Montale (It)
1976	S. Bellow (USA)
1977	S. Aleixandre (Sp)
1978	I. B. Singer (USA)
1979	O. Alepoudellis (Greece)
1980	C. Milosz (USA)
1981	E. Canetti (Bulg)
1982	G. Garcia Marquez (Colombia)
1983	W. Golding (UK)
1984	J. Seifert (Czech)
1985	C. Simon (Fr)
1986	W. Soyinka (Nigeria)
1987	J. Brodsky (USA)
1988	N. Mahfouz (Egypt)
1989	C. José Cela (Sp)
1990	O. Paz (Mex)
1991	N. Gordimer (S Af)
1992	D. Walcott (W Indies)
1993	T. Morrison (USA)
1994	Kensaburo Oë (Jap)
1995	S. Heaney (Ire)
1996	W. Szymborska (Pol)
1997	D. Foe (It)

Peace

Year	Name
1901	J. H. Dunant (Switz)
	F. Passy (Fr)
1902	E. Ducommun (Switz)
	C. A. Gobat (Switz)
1903	Sir W. Cremer (UK)
1904	Institute of International Law
1905	Baroness Von Suttner (Austria)
1906	T. Roosevelt (USA)
1907	E. Teodoro Moneta (It)
	L. Renault (Fr)
1908	K. P. Arnoldson (Swed)
1909	Baron d'Estournelles de Constant (Fr)
	A. Beernaert (Belg)
1910	International Peace Bureau
1911	T. Asser (Neth)
	A. Fried (Austria)
1912	E. Root (USA)
1913	H. Lafontaine (Belg)
1914	no award
1915	no award
1916	no award
1917	International Red Cross Committee
1918	no award
1919	W. Wilson (USA)
1920	L. Bourgeois (Fr)
1921	K. Branting (Swed)
	C. L. Lange (Nor)
1922	F. Nansen (Nor)
1923	no award
1924	no award
1925	Sir A. Chamberlain (UK)
	C. G. Dawes (USA)
1926	A. Briand (Fr)
	G. Stresemann (Ger)
1927	F. Buisson (Fr)
	L. Quidde (Ger)
1928	no award
1929	F. B. Kellogg (USA)
1930	N. Söderblom (Swed)
1931	J. Addams (USA)
	N. M. Butler (USA)
1932	no award
1933	Sir N. Angell (UK)
1934	A. Henderson (UK)
1935	C. von Ossietzky (Ger)
1936	C. S. Lamas (Arg)
1937	Viscount Cecil of Chelwood (UK)
1938	Nansen International Office for Refugees
1939	no award
1940	no award
1941	no award
1942	no award
1943	no award
1944	International Red Cross Committee
1945	C. Hull (USA)
1946	E. G. Balch (USA)
	J. R. Mott (USA)
1947	American Friends' Service Committee (USA)
	Friends' Service Council (London)
1948	no award
1949	Lord Boyd-Orr (UK)
1950	R. Bunche (USA)
1951	L. Jouhaux (Fr)
1952	A. Schweitzer (Fr)
1953	G. C. Marshall (USA)
1954	Office of the United Nations High Commission for Refugees
1955	no award
1956	no award
1957	L. B. Pearson (Can)
1958	D. G. Pire (Belg)
1959	P. J. Noel-Baker (UK)
1960	A. J. Luthuli (S Af)
1961	D. Hammarskjöld (Swed)
1962	L. C. Pauling (USA)
1963	International Red Cross Committee
	League of Red Cross Societies (Geneva)
1964	M. Luther King, Jr. (USA)
1965	United Nations Children's Fund
1966	no award
1967	no award
1968	R. Cassin (Fr)
1969	International Labour Organization
1970	N. E. Borlaug (USA)
1971	W. Brandt (Ger)
1972	no award
1973	H. Kissinger (USA)
	Le Duc Tho (declined award) (N Viet)
1974	S. MacBride (Ire)
	E. Sato (Jap)
1975	A. S. Sakharov (USSR)
1976	Mrs. B. Williams (N Ire)
	Miss M. Corrigan (N Ire)
1977	Amnesty International
1978	A. Sadat (Egypt)
	M. Begin (Isr)
1979	Mother Teresa (Yugos)
1980	A. P. Esquivel (Arg)
1981	Office of the United Nations High Commission for Refugees
1982	A. Garcia Robles (Mex)
	Mrs. A. Myrdal (Swed)
1983	L. Walesa (Pol)
1984	Bishop D. Tutu (S Af)
1985	International Physicians for the Prevention of Nuclear War
1986	E. Wiesel (USA)
1987	Oscar Arias Sánchez (Costa Rica)
1988	The United Nations peacekeeping forces
1989	Dalai Lama (Tibet)
1990	M. Gorbachov (Russia)
1991	A. San Suu Kyi (Burma)
1992	R. Menchu (Guat)
1993	F. W. de Klerk (S Af)
	N. Mandela (S Af)
1994	Y. Arafat (Palestine)
	S. Peres (Isr)
	Y. Rabin (Isr)
1995	J. Rotblat (UK)
1996	J. Ramos-Horta (E Timor)
	C. Belo (E Timor)
1997	The International Campaign to Ban Landmines (headed by J. Williams, a co-recipient of the prize)

Economics

Year	Name
1969	R. Frisch (Nor)
	J. Tinbergen (Neth)
1970	P. A. Samuelson (USA)
1971	S. Kuznets (USA)
1972	R. Hicks (UK)
	K. J. Arrow (USA)
1973	W. Leontief (USA)
1974	G. Myrdal (Swed)
	F. A. von Hayek (UK)
1975	L. Kantorovich (USSR)
	T. C. Koopmans (USA)
1976	M. Friedman (USA)
1977	B. Ohlin (Swed)
	J. E. Meade (UK)
1978	H. A. Simon (USA)
1979	T. W. Schultz (USA)
	A. Lewis (UK)
1980	L. R. Klein (USA)
1981	J. Tobin (USA)
1982	G. J. Stigler (USA)
1983	G. Debreu (USA)
1984	R. Stone (UK)
1985	F. Modigliani (USA)
1986	J. M. Buchanan, Jr. (USA)
1987	R. M. Solow (USA)
1988	M. Allais (Fr)
1989	T. Haavelmo (Nor)
1990	H. Markowitz (USA)
	W. F. Sharpe (USA)
	M. Miller (USA)
1991	R. H. Coase (UK)
1992	G. S. Becker (USA)
1993	R. Fogel (USA)
	D. North (USA)
1994	J. Harsanyi (USA)
	J. Nash (USA)
	R. Selton (Ger)
1995	R. Lucas (USA)
1996	J. Mirrlees (UK)
	W. Vickrey (Can)
1997	R. C. Merton (USA)
	M. S. Scholes (USA)

ACADEMY AWARD WINNERS

	Best Picture	Best Director	Best Actor	Best Actress
1927–28	*Wings*	Frank Borzage *Seventh Heaven*; Lewis Milestone *Two Arabian Knights*	Emil Jannings *The Last Command, The Way of All Flesh*	Janet Gaynor *Seventh Heaven, Street Angel, Sunrise*
1928–29	*The Broadway Melody*	Frank Lloyd *The Divine Lady*	Warner Baxter *In Old Arizona*	Mary Pickford *Coquette*
1929–30	*All Quiet on the Western Front*	Lewis Milestone *All Quiet on the Western Front*	George Arliss *Disraeli*	Norma Shearer *The Divorcee*
1930–31	*Cimarron*	Norman Taurog *Skippy*	Lionel Barrymore *A Free Soul*	Marie Dressler *Min and Bill*
1931–32	*Grand Hotel*	Frank Borzage *Bad Girl*	Wallace Beery *The Champ*; Fredric March *Dr. Jekyll and Mr. Hyde*	Helen Hayes *The Sin of Madelon Claudet*
1932–33	*Cavalcade*	Frank Lloyd *Cavalcade*	Charles Laughton *The Private Life of Henry VIII*	Katharine Hepburn *Morning Glory*
1934	*It Happened One Night*	Frank Capra *It Happened One Night*	Clark Gable *It Happened One Night*	Claudette Colbert *It Happened One Night*
1935	*Mutiny on the Bounty*	John Ford *The Informer*	Victor McLaglen *The Informer*	Bette Davis *Dangerous*
1936	*The Great Ziegfeld*	Frank Capra *Mr Deeds Goes to Town*	Paul Muni *The Story of Louis Pasteur*	Luise Rainer *The Great Ziegfeld*
1937	*The Life of Emile Zola*	Leo McCarey *The Awful Truth*	Spencer Tracy *Captains Courageous*	Luise Rainer *The Good Earth*
1938	*You Can't Take It With You*	Frank Capra *You Can't Take It With You*	Spencer Tracy *Boys Town*	Bette Davis *Jezebel*
1939	*Gone With the Wind*	Victor Fleming *Gone With the Wind*	Robert Donat *Goodbye, Mr. Chips*	Vivien Leigh *Gone With the Wind*
1940	*Rebecca*	John Ford *The Grapes of Wrath*	James Stewart *The Philadelphia Story*	Ginger Rogers *Kitty Foyle*
1941	*How Green Was My Valley*	John Ford *How Green Was My Valley*	Gary Cooper *Sergeant York*	Joan Fontaine *Suspicion*
1942	*Mrs. Miniver*	William Wyler *Mrs Miniver*	James Cagney *Yankee Doodle Dandy*	Greer Garson *Mrs. Miniver*
1943	*Casablanca*	Michael Curtiz *Casablanca*	Paul Lukas *Watch on the Rhine*	Jennifer Jones *The Song of Bernadette*
1944	*Going My Way*	Leo McCarey *Going My Way*	Bing Crosby *Going My Way*	Ingrid Bergman *Gaslight*
1945	*The Lost Weekend*	Billy Wilder *The Lost Weekend*	Ray Milland *The Lost Weekend*	Joan Crawford *Mildred Pierce*
1946	*The Best Years of Our Lives*	William Wyler *The Best Years of Our Lives*	Fredric March *The Best Years of Our Lives*	Olivia de Havilland *To Each His Own*
1947	*Gentleman's Agreement*	Elia Kazan *Gentleman's Agreement*	Ronald Colman *A Double Life*	Loretta Young *The Farmer's Daughter*
1948	*Hamlet*	John Huston *The Treasure of the Sierra Madre*	Laurence Olivier *Hamlet*	Jane Wyman *Johnny Belinda*
1949	*All the King's Men*	Joseph L. Mankiewicz *A Letter to Three Wives*	Broderick Crawford *All the King's Men*	Olivia de Havilland *The Heiress*
1950	*All About Eve*	Joseph L. Mankiewicz *All About Eve*	José Ferrer *Cyrano de Bergerac*	Judy Holliday *Born Yesterday*
1951	*An American in Paris*	George Stevens *A Place in the Sun*	Humphrey Bogart *The African Queen*	Vivien Leigh *A Streetcar Named Desire*
1952	*The Greatest Show on Earth*	John Ford *The Quiet Man*	Gary Cooper *High Noon*	Shirley Booth *Come Back, Little Sheba*
1953	*From Here to Eternity*	Fred Zinnemann *From Here to Eternity*	William Holden *Stalag 17*	Audrey Hepburn *Roman Holiday*
1954	*On the Waterfront*	Elia Kazan *On the Waterfront*	Marlon Brando *On the Waterfront*	Grace Kelly *The Country Girl*
1955	*Marty*	Delbert Mann *Marty*	Ernest Borgnine *Marty*	Anna Magnani *The Rose Tattoo*
1956	*Around the World in 80 Days*	George Stevens *Giant*	Yul Brynner *The King and I*	Ingrid Bergman *Anastasia*
1957	*The Bridge on the River Kwai*	David Lean *The Bridge on the River Kwai*	Alec Guinness *The Bridge on the River Kwai*	Joanne Woodward *The Three Faces of Eve*
1958	*Gigi*	Vincente Minnelli *Gigi*	David Niven *Separate Tables*	Susan Hayward *I Want to Live*

	Best Picture	Best Director	Best Actor	Best Actress
1959	*Ben-Hur*	William Wyler *Ben-Hur*	Charlton Heston *Ben-Hur*	Simone Signoret *Room at the Top*
1960	*The Apartment*	Billy Wilder *The Apartment*	Burt Lancaster *Elmer Gantry*	Elizabeth Taylor *Butterfield 8*
1961	*West Side Story*	Jerome Robbins and Robert Wise *West Side Story*	Maximilian Schell *Judgment at Nuremberg*	Sophia Loren *Two Women*
1962	*Lawrence of Arabia*	David Lean *Lawrence of Arabia*	Gregory Peck *To Kill a Mockingbird*	Anne Bancroft *The Miracle Worker*
1963	*Tom Jones*	Tony Richardson *Tom Jones*	Sidney Poitier *Lilies of the Field*	Patricia Neal *Hud*
1964	*My Fair Lady*	George Cukor *My Fair Lady*	Rex Harrison *My Fair Lady*	Julie Andrews *Mary Poppins*
1965	*The Sound of Music*	Robert Wise *The Sound of Music*	Lee Marvin *Cat Ballou*	Julie Christie *Darling*
1966	*A Man for All Seasons*	Fred Zinnemann *A Man for All Seasons*	Paul Scofield *A Man for All Seasons*	Elizabeth Taylor *Who's Afraid of Virginia Woolf?*
1967	*In the Heat of the Night*	Mike Nichols *The Graduate*	Rod Steiger *In the Heat of the Night*	Katharine Hepburn *Guess Who's Coming to Dinner*
1968	*Oliver!*	Sir Carol Reed *Oliver!*	Cliff Robertson *Charly*	Katharine Hepburn *The Lion in Winter*; Barbra Streisand *Funny Girl*
1969	*Midnight Cowboy*	John Schlesinger *Midnight Cowboy*	John Wayne *True Grit*	Maggie Smith *The Prime of Miss Jean Brodie*
1970	*Patton*	Franklin J. Schaffner *Patton*	George C. Scott *Patton*	Glenda Jackson *Women in Love*
1971	*The French Connection*	William Friedkin *The French Connection*	Gene Hackman *The French Connection*	Jane Fonda *Klute*
1972	*The Godfather*	Bob Fosse *Cabaret*	Marlon Brando *The Godfather*	Liza Minnelli *Cabaret*
1973	*The Sting*	George Roy Hill *The Sting*	Jack Lemmon *Save the Tiger*	Glenda Jackson *A Touch of Class*
1974	*The Godfather Part II*	Francis Ford Coppola *The Godfather Part II*	Art Carney *Harry and Tonto*	Ellen Burstyn *Alice Doesn't Live Here Anymore*
1975	*One Flew Over the Cuckoo's Nest*	Milos Forman *One Flew Over the Cuckoo's Nest*	Jack Nicholson *One Flew Over the Cuckoo's Nest*	Louise Fletcher *One Flew Over the Cuckoo's Nest*
1976	*Rocky*	John G. Avildsen *Rocky*	Peter Finch *Network*	Faye Dunaway *Network*
1977	*Annie Hall*	Woody Allen *Annie Hall*	Richard Dreyfuss *The Goodbye Girl*	Diane Keaton *Annie Hall*
1978	*The Deer Hunter*	Michael Cimino *The Deer Hunter*	Jon Voight *Coming Home*	Jane Fonda *Coming Home*
1979	*Kramer vs. Kramer*	Robert Benton *Kramer vs. Kramer*	Dustin Hoffman *Kramer vs. Kramer*	Sally Field *Norma Rae*
1980	*Ordinary People*	Robert Redford *Ordinary People*	Robert De Niro *Raging Bull*	Sissy Spacek *Coal Miner's Daughter*
1981	*Chariots of Fire*	Warren Beatty *Reds*	Henry Fonda *On Golden Pond*	Katharine Hepburn *On Golden Pond*
1982	*Gandhi*	Richard Attenborough *Gandhi*	Ben Kingsley *Gandhi*	Meryl Streep *Sophie's Choice*
1983	*Terms of Endearment*	James L. Brooks *Terms of Endearment*	Robert Duvall *Tender Mercies*	Shirley MacLaine *Terms of Endearment*
1984	*Amadeus*	Milos Forman *Amadeus*	F. Murray Abraham *Amadeus*	Sally Field *Places in the Heart*
1985	*Out of Africa*	Sydney Pollack *Out of Africa*	William Hurt *Kiss of the Spider Woman*	Geraldine Page *The Trip to Bountiful*
1986	*Platoon*	Oliver Stone *Platoon*	Paul Newman *The Color of Money*	Marlee Matlin *Children of a Lesser God*
1987	*The Last Emperor*	Bernardo Bertolucci *The Last Emperor*	Michael Douglas *Wall Street*	Cher *Moonstruck*
1988	*Rain Man*	Barry Levinson *Rain Man*	Dustin Hoffman *Rain Man*	Jodie Foster *The Accused*
1989	*Driving Miss Daisy*	Oliver Stone *Born on the Fourth of July*	Daniel Day-Lewis *My Left Foot*	Jessica Tandy *Driving Miss Daisy*
1990	*Dances with Wolves*	Kevin Costner *Dances with Wolves*	Jeremy Irons *Reversal of Fortune*	Kathy Bates *Misery*

	Best Picture	Best Director	Best Actor	Best Actress
1991	*The Silence of the Lambs*	Jonathan Demme *The Silence of the Lambs*	Anthony Hopkins *The Silence of the Lambs*	Jodie Foster *The Silence of the Lambs*
1992	*Unforgiven*	Clint Eastwood *Unforgiven*	Clint Eastwood *Unforgiven*	Emma Thompson *Howards End*
1993	*Schindler's List*	Steven Spielberg *Schindler's List*	Tom Hanks *Philadelphia*	Holly Hunter *The Piano*
1994	*Forrest Gump*	Robert Zemeckis *Forrest Gump*	Tom Hanks *Forrest Gump*	Jessica Lange *Blue Sky*
1995	*Braveheart*	Mel Gibson *Braveheart*	Nicolas Cage *Leaving Las Vegas*	Susan Sarandon *Dead Man Walking*
1996	*The English Patient*	Anthony Minghella *The English Patient*	Geoffrey Rush *Shine*	Frances McDormand *Fargo*
1997	*Titanic*	James Cameron *Titanic*	Jack Nicholson *As Good as It Gets*	Helen Hunt *As Good as It Gets*

	Best Supporting Actor	Best Supporting Actress	Best Foreign Language Film
1936	Walter Brennan *Come and Get It!*	Gale Sondergaard *Anthony Adverse*	
1937	Joseph Schildkraut *The Life of Emile Zola*	Alice Brady *In Old Chicago*	
1938	Walter Brennan *Kentucky*	Fay Bainter *Jezebel*	
1939	Thomas Mitchell *Stagecoach*	Hattie McDaniel *Gone With the Wind*	
1940	Walter Brennan *The Westerner*	Jane Darwell *The Grapes of Wrath*	
1941	Donald Crisp *How Green Was My Valley*	Mary Astor *The Great Lie*	
1942	Van Heflin *Johnny Eager*	Teresa Wright *Mrs. Miniver*	
1943	Charles Coburn *The More the Merrier*	Katina Paxinou *For Whom the Bell Tolls*	
1944	Barry Fitzgerald *Going My Way*	Ethel Barrymore *None but the Lonely Heart*	
1945	James Dunn *A Tree Grows in Brooklyn*	Anne Revere *National Velvet*	
1946	Harold Russell *The Best Years of Our Lives*	Anne Baxter *The Razor's Edge*	
1947	Edmund Gwenn *Miracle on 34th Street*	Celeste Holm *Gentleman's Agreement*	*Shoe Shine* (It)
1948	Walter Huston *The Treasure of The Sierra Madre*	Claire Trevor *Key Largo*	*Monsieur Vincent* (Fr)
1949	Dean Jagger *Twelve O'Clock High*	Mercedes McCambridge *All the King's Men*	*The Bicycle Thief* (It)
1950	George Sanders *All About Eve*	Josephine Hull *Harvey*	*The Walls of Malapaga* (Fr/It)
1951	Karl Malden *A Streetcar Named Desire*	Kim Hunter *A Streetcar Named Desire*	*Rashomon* (Jap)
1952	Anthony Quinn *Viva Zapata!*	Gloria Grahame *The Bad and the Beautiful*	*Forbidden Games* (Fr)
1953	Frank Sinatra *From Here to Eternity*	Donna Reed *From Here to Eternity*	No Award
1954	Edmond O'Brien *The Barefoot Contessa*	Eva Maria Saint *On the Waterfront*	*Gate of Hell* (Jap)
1955	Jack Lemmon *Mister Roberts*	Jo Van Fleet *East of Eden*	*Samurai* (Jap)
1956	Anthony Quinn *Lust for Life*	Dorothy Malone *Written on the Wind*	*La Strada* (It)
1957	Red Buttons *Sayonara*	Miyoshi Umeki *Sayonara*	*The Nights of Cabiria* (It)
1958	Burl Ives *The Big Country*	Wendy Hiller *Separate Tables*	*Mon Oncle* (Fr)
1959	Hugh Griffith *Ben-Hur*	Shelley Winters *The Diary of Anne Frank*	*Black Orpheus* (Fr, filmed in Braz)
1960	Peter Ustinov *Spartacus*	Shirley Jones *Elmer Gantry*	*The Virgin Spring* (Swed)
1961	George Chakiris *West Side Story*	Rita Moreno *West Side Story*	*Through a Glass Darkly* (Swed)
1962	Ed Begley *Sweet Bird of Youth*	Patty Duke *The Miracle Worker*	*Sundays and Cybele* (Fr)
1963	Melvyn Douglas *Hud*	Margaret Rutherford *The V.I.P.s*	*8½* (It)
1964	Peter Ustinov *Topkapi*	Lila Kedrova *Zorba the Greek*	*Yesterday, Today, and Tomorrow* (It)
1965	Martin Balsam *A Thousand Clowns*	Shelley Winters *A Patch of Blue*	*The Shop on Main Street* (Czech)
1966	Walter Matthau *The Fortune Cookie*	Sandy Dennis *Who's Afraid of Virginia Woolf?*	*A Man and a Woman* (Fr)
1967	George Kennedy *Cool Hand Luke*	Estelle Parsons *Bonnie and Clyde*	*Closely Watched Trains* (Czech)
1968	Jack Albertson *The Subject Was Roses*	Ruth Gordon *Rosemary's Baby*	*War and Peace* (USSR)

	Best Supporting Actor	Best Supporting Actress	Best Foreign Language Film
1969	Gig Young *They Shoot Horses Don't They?*	Goldie Hawn *Cactus Flower*	Z (Fr/Alg)
1970	John Mills *Ryan's Daughter*	Helen Hayes *Airport*	*Investigation of a Citizen Above Suspicion* (It)
1971	Ben Johnson *The Last Picture Show*	Cloris Leachman *The Last Picture Show*	*The Garden of the Finzi-Continis* (It)
1972	Joel Grey *Cabaret*	Eileen Heckart *Butterflies are Free*	*The Discreet Charm of the Bourgeoise* (Fr)
1973	John Houseman *The Paper Chase*	Tatum O'Neal *Paper Moon*	*Day for Night* (Fr)
1974	Robert De Niro *Godfather Part II*	Ingrid Bergman *Murder on the Orient Express*	*Amarcord* (It)
1975	George Burns *The Sunshine Boys*	Lee Grant *Shampoo*	*Dersu Uzala* (Jap/USSR)
1976	Jason Robards *All the President's Men*	Beatrice Straight *Network*	*Black and White in Color* (Ivory Coast/Fr)
1977	Jason Robards *Julia*	Vanessa Redgrave *Julia*	*Madame Rosa* (Fr)
1978	Christopher Walken *The Deer Hunter*	Maggie Smith *California Suite*	*Get Out Your Handkerchiefs* (Fr)
1979	Melvyn Douglas *Being There*	Meryl Streep *Kramer vs. Kramer*	*The Tin Drum* (W Ger)
1980	Timothy Hutton *Ordinary People*	Mary Steenburgen *Melvin and Howard*	*Moscow Does Not Believe in Tears* (USSR)
1981	John Gielgud *Arthur*	Maureen Stapleton *Reds*	*Mephisto* (Hung)
1982	Louis Gossett, Jr. *An Officer and a Gentleman*	Jessica Lange *Tootsie*	*Volver a Empezar/ To Begin Again* (Sp)
1983	Jack Nicholson *Terms of Endearment*	Linda Hunt *The Year of Living Dangerously*	*Fanny & Alexander* (Swed)
1984	Haing S. Ngor *The Killing Fields*	Peggy Ashcroft *A Passage to India*	*Dangerous Moves* (Switz)
1985	Don Ameche *Cocoon*	Anjelica Huston *Prizzi's Honor*	*The Official Story* (Arg)
1986	Michael Caine *Hannah and Her Sisters*	Dianne Wiest *Hannah and Her Sisters*	*The Assault* (Neth)
1987	Sean Connery *The Untouchables*	Olympia Dukakis *Moonstruck*	*Babette's Feast* (Den)
1988	Kevin Kline *A Fish Called Wanda*	Geena Davis *The Accidental Tourist*	*Pelle the Conqueror* (Den)
1989	Denzel Washington *Glory*	Brenda Fricker *My Left Foot*	*Cinema Paradiso* (It)
1990	Joe Pesci *Goodfellas*	Whoopi Goldberg *Ghost*	*Journey of Hope* (Switz)
1991	Jack Palance *City Slickers*	Mercedes Ruehl *The Fisher King*	*Mediterraneo* (It)
1992	Gene Hackman *Unforgiven*	Marisa Tomei *My Cousin Vinny*	*Indochine* (Fr)
1993	Tommy Lee Jones *The Fugitive*	Anna Paquin *The Piano*	*Belle Epoque* (Sp)
1994	Martin Landau *Ed Wood*	Diane Wiest *Bullets over Broadway*	*Burnt by the Sun* (CIS)
1995	Kevin Spacey *The Usual Suspects*	Mira Sorvino *Mighty Aphrodite*	*Antonia's Line* (Neth)
1996	Cuba Gooding, Jr. *Jerry Maguire*	Juliette Binoche *The English Patient*	*Kolya* (Czech Rep)
1997	Robin Williams *Good Will Hunting*	Kim Basinger *L. A. Confidential*	*Character* (Neth)

BOOKER PRIZE WINNERS

1969	P H Newby *Something to Answer For*	1984	Anita Brookner *Hotel du Lac*
1970	Bernice Rubens *The Elected Member*	1985	Keri Hulme *The Bone People*
1971	V S Naipaul *In a Free State*	1986	Kingsley Amis *The Old Devils*
1972	John Berger *G*	1987	Penelope Lively *Moon Tiger*
1973	J G Farrell *The Siege of Krishnapur*	1988	Peter Carey *Oscar and Lucinda*
1974	Nadine Gordimer *The Conservationist* Stanley Middleton *Holiday*	1989	Kazuo Ishiguro *The Remains of the Day*
		1990	A S Byatt *Possession*
1975	Ruth Prawer Jhabvala *Heat and Dust*	1991	Ben Okri *The Famished Road*
1976	David Storey *Saville*	1992	Michael Ondaatje *The English Patient* Barry Unsworth *Sacred Hunger*
1977	Paul Scott *Staying On*		
1978	Iris Murdoch *The Sea, The Sea*	1993	Roddy Doyle *Paddy Clarke Ha Ha Ha*
1979	Penelope Fitzgerald *Offshore*	1994	James Kelman *How Late It Was, How Late*
1980	William Golding *Rites of Passage*	1995	Pat Barker *The Ghost Road*
1981	Salman Rushdie *Midnight's Children**	1996	Graham Swift *Last Orders*
1982	Thomas Keneally *Schindler's Ark*	1997	Arundhati Roy *The God of Small Things*
1983	J M Coetzee *Life & Times of Michael K*		

*Winner of the 1993 Booker of Bookers

THE OLYMPIC GAMES: VENUES

I	Athens, Greece	1896
II	Paris, France	1900
III	St Louis, USA	1904
	Athens[1]	1906
IV	London, Great Britain	1908
V	Stockholm, Sweden	1912
VI[2]	Berlin, Germany	1916
VII	Antwerp, Belgium	1920
VIII	Paris, France	1924
IX	Amsterdam, Netherlands	1928
X	Los Angeles, USA	1932
XI	Berlin, Germany	1936
XII[2]	Tokyo, Japan & Helsinki, Finland	1940
XIII[2]	London, Great Britain	1944
XIV	London, Great Britain	1948
XV	Helsinki, Finland	1952
XVI[3]	Melbourne, Australia	1956
XVII	Rome, Italy	1960
XVIII	Tokyo, Japan	1964
XIX	Mexico City, Mexico	1968
XX	Munich, West Germany	1972
XXI	Montreal, Canada	1976
XXII	Moscow, USSR	1980
XXIII	Los Angeles, USA	1984
XXIV	Seoul, South Korea	1988
XXV	Barcelona, Spain	1992
XXVI	Atlanta, USA	1996
XXVII	Sydney, Australia	2000
XXVIII	Athens, Greece	2004

Winter Olympic Games

I	Chamonix, France	1924
II	St Moritz, Switzerland	1928
III	Lake Placid, USA	1932
IV	Garmisch-Partenkirchen, Germany	1936
V	St Moritz, Switzerland	1948
VI	Oslo, Norway	1952
VII	Cortina d'Ampezzo, Italy	1956
VIII	Squaw Valley, USA	1960
IX	Innsbruck, Austria	1964
X	Grenoble, France	1968
XI	Sapporo, Japan	1972
XII	Innsbruck, Austria	1976
XIII	Lake Placid, USA	1980
XIV	Sarajevo, Yugoslavia	1984
XV	Calgary, Canada	1988
XVI	Albertville, France	1992
XVII	Lillehammer, Norway	1994
XVIII	Nagano, Japan	1998
XIX	Salt Lake City, USA	2002

[1] The 'Intercalated' Games.

[2] Games scheduled but cancelled due to World Wars.

[3] Equestrian events held in Stockholm, Sweden.

ASSOCIATION FOOTBALL: FIFA WORLD CUP

	Venue	*Winner*
1930	Uruguay	Uruguay
1934	Italy	Italy
1938	France	Italy
1950	Brazil	Uruguay
1954	Switzerland	West Germany
1958	Sweden	Brazil
1962	Chile	Brazil
1966	England	England
1970	Mexico	Brazil
1974	West Germany	West Germany
1978	Argentina	Argentina
1982	Spain	Italy
1986	Mexico	Argentina
1990	Italy	West Germany
1994	USA	Brazil
1998	France	
2002	Japan & Korea	

RUGBY UNION

International Test Matches (1871–Aug 1996)[1]

	England			Scotland			Ireland			Wales			British Lions[3]		
	W	D	L[2]	W	D	L	W	D	L	W	D	L	W	D	L
England *vs*	–	–	–	57	17	39	63	8	38	42	12	48	–	–	–
Scotland *vs*	39	17	57	–	–	–	57	1	45	44	2	54	–	–	–
Ireland *vs*	38	8	63	45	1	57	–	–	–	36	6	58	–	–	–
Wales *vs*	48	12	42	54	2	44	58	6	36	–	–	–	–	–	–
British Lions[3] *vs*	–	–	–	–	–	–	–	–	–	–	–	–	–	–	–
South Africa *vs*	8	1	4	6	0	3	8	1	1	8	1	0	20	6	14
New Zealand *vs*	14	0	4	18	2	0	12	1	0	13	0	3	24	3	5
Australia *vs*	12	0	7	7	0	8	11	0	6	11	0	8	3	0	14
France *vs*	26	7	39	33	2	32	40	5	25	29	3	38	0	0	0

	South Africa			New Zealand			Australia			France		
	W	D	L	W	D	L	W	D	L	W	D	L
England *vs*	4	1	8	4	0	14	7	0	12	39	7	26
Scotland *vs*	3	0	6	0	2	18	8	0	7	32	2	33
Ireland *vs*	1	1	8	0	1	12	6	0	11	25	5	40
Wales *vs*	0	1	8	3	0	13	8	0	11	38	3	29
British Lions[3] *vs*	14	6	20	5	3	24	14	0	3	0	0	0
South Africa *vs*	–	–	–	22	3	22	24	0	11	16	5	5
New Zealand *vs*	22	3	22	–	–	–	72	5	27	24	0	8
Australia *vs*	11	0	24	27	5	72	–	–	–	10	2	13
France *vs*	5	5	16	8	0	24	13	2	10	–	–	–

[1] Read table from left to right: for example, England have won 57, drawn 17, and lost 39 matches against Scotland.

[2] W = wins, D = draws, L = losses.

[3] The "British Lions" (official name: British Isles) is a team drawn from the four "Home Unions" (England, Scotland, Ireland, and Wales).

Five Nations Championship Winners

1947	England, Wales
1948	Ireland[3]
1949	Ireland[1]
1950	Wales[3]
1951	Ireland
1952	Wales[3]
1953	England
1954	England[1], France, Wales
1955	France, Wales
1956	Wales
1957	England[3]
1958	England
1959	France
1960	England[1], France
1961	France
1962	France
1963	England
1964	Scotland, Wales
1965	Wales[1]
1966	Wales
1967	France
1968	France[2]
1969	Wales[1]
1970	France, Wales
1971	Wales[3]
1972	competition incomplete
1973	five-way tie
1974	Ireland
1975	Wales
1976	Wales[3]
1977	France[2] *
1978	Wales[3]
1979	Wales[1]
1980	England[3]
1981	France[2]
1982	Ireland[1]
1983	France, Ireland
1984	Scotland[3]
1985	Ireland[3]
1986	France, Scotland
1987	France[2]
1988	Wales[3]
1989	France
1990	Scotland[2]
1991	England[2]
1992	England[2]
1993	France
1994	Wales
1995	England[2]
1996	England
1997	France

[1] Triple Crown (winning all three "Home Unions" matches, i.e. excluding France).

[2] Grand Slam (winning all four matches).

[3] Triple Crown and Grand Slam.

* Triple Crown won by Wales.

World Cup

	Venue	*Winner*
1987	New Zealand & Australia	New Zealand
1991	England, Scotland, Ireland, Wales, & France	Australia
1995	South Africa	South Africa
1999	Wales	

CRICKET

First-Class Test Matches (to Sept. 1996)[1]

	England			Australia			South Africa			West Indies			New Zealand		
	W	D	L[2]	W	D	L	W	D	L	W	D	L	W	D	L
England *vs*	–	–	–	90	81	108	47	43	20	27	40	48	34	37	4
Australia *vs*	108	81	90	–	–	–	31	15	13	32	22	27	13	11	7
South Africa *vs*	20	43	47	13	15	31	–	–	–	0	0	1	22	6	3
West Indies *vs*	48	40	27	27	22	32	1	0	0	–	–	–	10	14	4
New Zealand *vs*	4	37	34	7	11	13	3	6	22	4	13	9	–	–	–
India *vs*	6	14	38	31	8	18	24	0	3	1	7	31	27	13	16
Pakistan *vs*	9	32	14	11	15	14	0	0	1	7	12	12	17	16	4
Sri Lanka *vs*	1	1	3	0	3	7	0	2	1	0	1	0	4	7	4
Zimbabwe *vs*	0	0	0	0	0	0	0	0	1	0	0	0	0	3	1

	India			Pakistan			Sri Lanka			Zimbabwe		
	W	D	L	W	D	L	W	D	L	W	D	L
England *vs*	31	38	14	14	32	9	3	1	1	0	0	0
Australia *vs*	24	18	8	14	15	11	7	3	0	0	0	0
South Africa *vs*	1	3	0	1	0	0	1	2	0	1	0	0
West Indies *vs*	27	31	7	12	12	7	0	1	0	0	0	0
New Zealand *vs*	6	16	13	4	16	17	4	7	2	1	3	0
India *vs*	–	–	–	4	33	7	8	4	1	1	1	0
Pakistan *vs*	7	33	4	–	–	–	9	5	3	4	1	1
Sri Lanka *vs*	1	4	8	3	5	9	–	–	–	2	3	0
Zimbabwe *vs*	0	1	1	1	1	4	0	3	2	–	–	–

[1] Read table from left to right: for example, England have won 90, drawn 81, and lost 108 matches against Australia.

[2] W = wins, D = draws, L = losses.

World Cup

	Venue	*Winner*
1975	England	West Indies
1979	England	West Indies
1983	England	India
1987	India & Pakistan	Australia
1992	Australia	Pakistan
1996	India, Pakistan, & Sri Lanka	Sri Lanka
1999	England	
2003	South Africa & Zimbabwe	

TENNIS: GRAND SLAM CHAMPIONSHIPS – SINGLES

All-England (Wimbledon) Championships

	Men	*Women*
1877	S. W. Gore (UK)	
1878	P. F. Hadow (UK)	
1879	J. T. Hartley (UK)	
1880	J. T. Hartley (UK)	
1881	W. Renshaw (UK)	
1882	W. Renshaw (UK)	
1883	W. Renshaw (UK)	
1884	W. Renshaw (UK)	M. Watson (UK)
1885	W. Renshaw (UK)	M. Watson (UK)
1886	W. Renshaw (UK)	B. Bingley (UK)
1887	H. F. Lawford (UK)	L. Dod (UK)
1888	E. Renshaw (UK)	L. Dod (UK)
1889	W. Renshaw (UK)	B. Bingley Hillyard (UK)
1890	W. J. Hamilton (UK)	L. Rice (UK)
1891	W. Baddeley (UK)	L. Dod (UK)
1892	W. Baddeley (UK)	L. Dod (UK)
1893	J. Pim (UK)	L. Dod (UK)
1894	J. Pim (UK)	B. Hillyard (UK)
1895	W. Baddeley (UK)	C. Cooper (UK)
1896	H. Mahony (UK)	C. Cooper (UK)
1897	R. Doherty (UK)	B. Hillyard (UK)
1898	R. Doherty (UK)	C. Cooper (UK)
1899	R. Doherty (UK)	B. Hillyard (UK)
1900	R. Doherty (UK)	B. Hillyard (UK)
1901	A. W. Gore (UK)	C. Cooper Sterry (UK)
1902	L. Doherty (UK)	M. E. Robb (UK)
1903	L. Doherty (UK)	D. Douglass (UK)
1904	L. Doherty (UK)	D. Douglass (UK)
1905	L. Doherty (UK)	M. Sutton (USA)
1906	L. Doherty (UK)	D. Douglass (UK)
1907	N. Brookes (Austral)	M. Sutton (USA)
1908	A. W. Gore (UK)	C. Sterry (UK)
1909	A. W. Gore (UK)	D. Boothby (UK)
1910	T. Wilding (NZ)	D. Douglass Lambert Chambers (UK)
1911	T. Wilding (NZ)	D. Lambert Chambers (UK)
1912	T. Wilding (NZ)	E. W. Larcombe (UK)
1913	T. Wilding (NZ)	D. Lambert Chambers (UK)
1914	N. Brookes (Austral)	D. Lambert Chambers (UK)
1915–18		no competition
1919	G. Patterson (Austral)	S. Lenglen (Fr)
1920	B. Tilden (USA)	S. Lenglen (Fr)
1921	B. Tilden (USA)	S. Lenglen (Fr)
1922	G. Patterson (Austral)	S. Lenglen (Fr)
1923	B. Johnston (USA)	S. Lenglen (Fr)
1924	J. Borotra (Fr)	K. McKane (UK)
1925	R. Lacoste (Fr)	S. Lenglen (Fr)
1926	J. Borotra (Fr)	K. McKane Godfree (UK)
1927	H. Cochet (Fr)	H. Wills (USA)
1928	R. Lacoste (Fr)	H. Wills (USA)
1929	H. Cochet (Fr)	H. Wills (USA)
1930	B. Tilden (USA)	H. Wills Moody (USA)
1931	S. Wood (USA)	C. Aussem (Ger)
1932	E. Vines (USA)	H. Wills Moody (USA)
1933	J. Crawford (Austral)	H. Wills Moody (USA)
1934	F. Perry (UK)	D. Round (UK)
1935	F. Perry (UK)	H. Wills Moody (USA)
1936	F. Perry (UK)	H. Jacobs (USA)
1937	D. Budge (USA)	D. Round (UK)
1938	D. Budge (USA)	H. Wills Moody (USA)
1939	B. Riggs (USA)	A. Marble (USA)
1940–45		no competition
1946	Y. Petra (Fr)	P. Betz (USA)
1947	J. Kramer (USA)	M. Osborne (USA)
1948	B. Falkenburg (USA)	L. Brough (USA)
1949	T. Schroeder (USA)	L. Brough (USA)
1950	B. Patty (USA)	L. Brough (USA)
1951	D. Savitt (USA)	D. Hart (USA)
1952	F. Sedgman (Austral)	M. Connolly (USA)
1953	V. Seixas (USA)	M. Connolly (USA)
1954	J. Drobny (Czech)	M. Connolly (USA)
1955	T. Trabert (USA)	L. Brough (USA)
1956	L. Hoad (Austral)	S. Fry (USA)
1957	L. Hoad (Austral)	A. Gibson (USA)
1958	A. Cooper (Austral)	A. Gibson (USA)
1959	A. Olmedo (Peru)	M. Bueno (Braz)
1960	N. Fraser (Austral)	M. Bueno (Braz)
1961	R. Laver (Austral)	A. Mortimer (UK)
1962	R. Laver (Austral)	K. Susman (USA)
1963	C. McKinley (USA)	M. Smith (Austral)
1964	R. Emerson (Austral)	M. Bueno (Braz)
1965	R. Emerson (Austral)	M. Smith (Austral)
1966	M. Santana (Sp)	B. J. King (USA)
1967	J. Newcombe (Austral)	B. J. King (USA)
1968*	R. Laver (Austral)	B. J. King (USA)
1969	R. Laver (Austral)	A. Jones (UK)
1970	J. Newcombe (Austral)	M. Smith Court (Austral)
1971	J. Newcombe (Austral)	E. Goolagong (Austral)
1972	S. Smith (USA)	B. J. King (USA)
1973	J. Kodeš (Czech)	B. J. King (USA)
1974	J. Connors (USA)	C. Evert (USA)
1975	A. Ashe (USA)	B. J. King (USA)
1976	B. Borg (Swed)	C. Evert (USA)
1977	B. Borg (Swed)	V. Wade (UK)
1978	B. Borg (Swed)	M. Navratilova (Czech)
1979	B. Borg (Swed)	M. Navratilova (USA)
1980	B. Borg (Swed)	E. Goolagong Cawley (Austral)
1981	J. McEnroe (USA)	C. Evert Lloyd (USA)
1982	J. Connors (USA)	M. Navratilova (USA)
1983	J. McEnroe (USA)	M. Navratilova (USA)
1984	J. McEnroe (USA)	M. Navratilova (USA)
1985	B. Becker (W Ger)	M. Navratilova (USA)
1986	B. Becker (W Ger)	M. Navratilova (USA)
1987	P. Cash (Austral)	M. Navratilova (USA)
1988	S. Edberg (Swed)	S. Graf (W Ger)
1989	B. Becker (W Ger)	S. Graf (W Ger)
1990	S. Edberg (Swed)	M. Navratilova (USA)
1991	M. Stich (Ger)	S. Graf (Ger)
1992	A. Agassi (USA)	S. Graf (Ger)
1993	P. Sampras (USA)	S. Graf (Ger)
1994	P. Sampras (USA)	C. Martinez (Sp)
1995	P. Sampras (USA)	S. Graf (Ger)
1996	R. Krajicek (Neth)	S. Graf (Ger)
1997	P. Sampras (USA)	M. Hingis (Switz)

*Became Open Championships (amateurs and professionals) in 1968.

United States Open Championships

Year	*Men*	*Women*
1881	D. Sears (USA)	
1882	D. Sears (USA)	
1883	D. Sears (USA)	
1884	D. Sears (USA)	
1885	D. Sears (USA)	
1886	D. Sears (USA)	
1887	D. Sears (USA)	E. Hansell (USA)
1888	H. Slocum (USA)	B. Townsend (USA)
1889	H. Slocum (USA)	B. Townsend (USA)
1890	O. Campbell (USA)	E. Roosevelt (USA)
1891	O. Campbell (USA)	M. Cahill (USA)
1892	O. Campbell (USA)	M. Cahill (USA)
1893	R. Wrenn (USA)	A. Terry (USA)
1894	R. Wrenn (USA)	H. Helwig (USA)
1895	F. Hovey (USA)	J. Atkinson (USA)
1896	R. Wrenn (USA)	E. Moore (USA)
1897	R. Wrenn (USA)	J. Atkinson (USA)
1898	M. D. Whitman (USA)	J. Atkinson (USA)
1899	M. D. Whitman (USA)	M. Jones (USA)
1900	M. D. Whitman (USA)	M. AcAteer (USA)
1901	W. A. Larned (USA)	E. Moore (USA)
1902	W. A. Larned (USA)	M. Jones (USA)
1903	L. Doherty (UK)	E. Moore (USA)
1904	H. Ward (USA)	M. Sutton (USA)
1905	B. Wright (USA)	E. Moore (USA)
1906	W. J. Clothier (USA)	H. Homans (USA)
1907	W. A. Larned (USA)	E. Sears (USA)
1908	W. A. Larned (USA)	M. Bargar-Wallach (USA)
1909	W. A. Larned (USA)	H. Hotchkiss (USA)
1910	W. A. Larned (USA)	H. Hotchkiss (USA)
1911	W. A. Larned (USA)	H. Hotchkiss (USA)
1912	M. McLoughlin (USA)	M. K. Browne (USA)
1913	M. McLoughlin (USA)	M. K. Browne (USA)
1914	D. Williams (USA)	M. K. Browne (USA)
1915	B. Johnston (USA)	M. Bjurstedt (Nor)
1916	D. Williams (USA)	M. Bjurstedt (Nor)
1917	R. L. Murray (USA)	M. Bjurstedt (Nor)
1918	R. L. Murray (USA)	M. Bjurstedt (Nor)
1919	B. Johnston (USA)	H. Hotchkiss Wightman (USA)
1920	B. Tilden (USA)	M. Bjurstedt Mallory (USA)
1921	B. Tilden (USA)	M. Mallory (USA)
1922	B. Tilden (USA)	M. Mallory (USA)
1923	B. Tilden (USA)	H. Wills (USA)
1924	B. Tilden (USA)	H. Wills (USA)
1925	B. Tilden (USA)	H. Wills (USA)
1926	R. Lacoste (Fr)	M. Mallory (USA)
1927	R. Lacoste (Fr)	H. Wills (USA)
1928	H. Cochet (Fr)	H. Wills (USA)
1929	B. Tilden (USA)	H. Wills (USA)
1930	J. Doeg (USA)	B. Nuthall (UK)
1931	E. Vines (USA)	H. Wills Moody (USA)
1932	E. Vines (USA)	H. Jacobs (USA)
1933	F. Perry (UK)	H. Jacobs (USA)
1934	F. Perry (UK)	H. Jacobs (USA)
1935	W. Allison (USA)	H. Jacobs (USA)
1936	F. Perry (UK)	A. Marble (USA)
1937	D. Budge (USA)	A. Lizana (Chile)
1938	D. Budge (USA)	A. Marble (USA)
1939	B. Riggs (USA)	A. Marble (USA)
1940	D. McNeill (USA)	A. Marble (USA)
1941	B. Riggs (USA)	S. Palfrey Cooke (USA)
1942	T. Schroeder (USA)	P. Betz (USA)
1943	J. R. Hunt (USA)	P. Betz (USA)
1944	F. Parker (USA)	P. Betz (USA)
1945	F. Parker (USA)	S. Palfrey Cooke (USA)
1946	J. Kramer (USA)	P. Betz (USA)
1947	J. Kramer (USA)	L. Brough (USA)
1948	P. Gonzales (USA)	M. du Pont (USA)
1949	P. Gonzales (USA)	M. du Pont (USA)
1950	A. Larsen (USA)	M. du Pont (USA)
1951	F. Sedgman (Austral)	M. Connolly (USA)
1952	F. Sedgman (Austral)	M. Connolly (USA)
1953	T. Trabert (USA)	M. Connolly (USA)
1954	V. Seixas (USA)	D. Hart (USA)
1955	T. Trabert (USA)	D. Hart (USA)
1956	K. Rosewall (Austral)	S. Fry (USA)
1957	M. Anderson (Austral)	A. Gibson (USA)
1958	A. Cooper (Austral)	A. Gibson (USA)
1959	N. Fraser (Austral)	M. Bueno (Braz)
1960	N. Fraser (Austral)	D. Hard (USA)
1961	R. Emerson (Austral)	D. Hard (USA)
1962	R. Laver (Austral)	M. Smith (Austral)
1963	R. Osuna (Mex)	M. Bueno (Braz)
1964	R. Merson (Austral)	M. Bueno (Braz)
1965	M. Santana (Sp)	M. Smith (Austral)
1966	F. Stolle (Austral)	M. Bueno (Braz)
1967	J. Newcombe (Austral)	B. J. King (USA)
1968*	A. Ashe (USA)	V. Wade (UK)
	A. Ashe (USA)	M. Smith Court (Austral)
1969*	R. Laver (Austral)	M. Court (Austral)
	R. Smith (USA)	M. Court (Austral)
1970	K. Rosewall (Austral)	M. Court (Austral)
1971	S. Smith (USA)	B. J. King (USA)
1972	I. Nastase (Rom)	B. J. King (USA)
1973	J. Newcombe (Austral)	M. Court (Austral)
1974	J. Connors (USA)	B. J. King (USA)
1975	M. Orantes (Sp)	C. Evert (USA)
1976	J. Connors (USA)	C. Evert (USA)
1977	G. Vilas (Arg)	C. Evert (USA)
1978	J. Connors (USA)	C. Evert (USA)
1979	J. McEnroe (USA)	T. Austin (USA)
1980	J. McEnroe (USA)	C. Evert Lloyd (USA)
1981	J. McEnroe (USA)	T. Austin (USA)
1982	J. Connors (USA)	C. Evert Lloyd (USA)
1983	J. Connors (USA)	M. Navratilova (USA)
1984	J. McEnroe (USA)	M. Navratilova (USA)
1985	I. Lendl (Czech)	H. Mandikova (Czech)
1986	I. Lendl (Czech)	M. Navratilova (USA)
1987	I. Lendl (Czech)	M. Navratilova (USA)
1988	M. Wilander (Swed)	S. Graf (W Ger)
1989	B. Becker (W Ger)	S. Graf (W Ger)
1990	P. Sampras (USA)	G. Sabatini (Arg)
1991	S. Edberg (Swed)	M. Seles (Yugos)
1992	S. Edberg (Swed)	M. Seles (Yugos)
1993	P. Sampras (USA)	S. Graf (Ger)
1994	A. Agassi (USA)	A. Sánchez Vicario (Sp)
1995	P. Sampras (USA)	S. Graf (Ger)
1996	P. Sampras (USA)	S. Graf (Ger)
1997	P. Rafter (Austral)	M. Hingis (Switz)

*Both amateur and open championships took place in 1968 and 1969: the Open winner appears first. In 1970 the championships became exclusively open (amateurs and professionals).

Australian Open Championships

	Men	Women
1905	R. Heath (Austral)	
1906	T. Wilding (NZ)	
1907	H. Rice (Austral)	
1908	F. Alexander (USA)	
1909	T. Wilding (NZ)	
1910	R. Heath (Austral)	
1911	N. Brookes (Austral)	
1912	J. C. Parke (UK)	
1913	E. F. Parker (Austral)	
1914	P. O'Hara Wood (Austral)	
1915	F. G Lowe (UK)	
1916–18		no competition
1919	A. R. F. Kingscote (UK)	
1920	P. O'Hara Wood (Austral)	
1921	R. Gemmell (Austral)	
1922	J. Anderson (Austral)	M. Molesworth (Austral)
1923	P. O'Hara Wood (Austral)	M. Molesworth (Austral)
1924	J. Anderson (Austral)	S. Lance (Austral)
1925	J. Anderson (Austral)	D. Akhurst (Austral)
1926	J. Hawkes (Austral)	D. Akhurst (Austral)
1927	G. Patterson (Austral)	E. Boyd (Austral)
1928	J. Borotra (Fr)	D. Akhurst (Austral)
1929	J. C. Gregory (UK)	D. Akhurst (Austral)
1930	E. F. Moon (Austral)	D. Akhurst (Austral)
1931	J. Crawford (Austral)	C. Buttsworth (Austral)
1932	J. Crawford (Austral)	C. Buttsworth (Austral)
1933	J. Crawford (Austral)	J. Hartigan (Austral)
1934	F. Perry (UK)	J. Hartigan (Austral)
1935	J. Crawford (Austral)	D. Round (UK)
1936	A. Quist (Austral)	J. Hartigan (Austral)
1937	V. McGrath (Austral)	N. Wynne (Austral)
1938	D. Budge (USA)	D. Bundy (USA)
1939	J. Bromwich (Austral)	E. Westacott (Austral)
1940	A. Quist (Austral)	N. Wynne (Austral)
1941–45		no competition
1946	J. Bromwich (Austral)	N. Wynne Bolton (Austral)
1947	D. Pails (Austral)	N. Bolton (Austral)
1948	A. Quist (Austral)	N. Bolton (Austral)
1949	F. Sedgman (Austral)	D. Hart (USA)
1950	F. Sedgman (Austral)	L. Brough (USA)
1951	D. Savitt (USA)	N. Bolton (Austral)
1952	K. McGregor (Austral)	T. Long (Austral)
1953	K. Rosewall (Austral)	M. C. Connolly (USA)
1954	M. Rose (Austral)	T. Long (Austral)
1955	K. Rosewall (Austral)	B. Penrose (Austral)
1956	L. Hoad (Austral)	M. Carter (Austral)
1957	A. Cooper (Austral)	S. Fry (USA)
1958	A. Cooper (Austral)	A. Mortimer (UK)
1959	A. Olmedo (Peru)	M. Carter Reitano (Austral)
1960	R. Laver (Austral)	M. Smith (Austral)
1961	R. Emerson (Austral)	M. Smith (Austral)
1962	R. Laver (Austral)	M. Smith (Austral)
1963	R. Emerson (Austral)	M. Smith (Austral)
1964	R. Emerson (Austral)	M. Smith (Austral)
1965	R. Emerson (Austral)	M. Smith (Austral)
1966	R. Emerson (Austral)	M. Smith (Austral)
1967	R. Emerson (Austral)	N. Richey (USA)
1968	B. Bowrey (Austral)	B. J. King (USA)
1969	R. Laver (Austral)	M. Smith Court (Austral)
1970	A. Ashe (USA)	M. Court (Austral)
1971	K. Rosewall (Austral)	M. Court (Austral)
1972	K. Rosewall (Austral)	V. Wade (UK)
1973	J. Newcombe (Austral)	M. Court (Austral)
1974	J. Connors (USA)	E. Goolagong (Austral)
1975	J. Newcombe (Austral)	E. Goolagong (Austral)
1976	M. Edmondson (Austral)	E. Goolagong Cawley (Austral)
1977	R. Tanner (USA)	K. Reid (Austral)
1978	V. Gerulaitis (USA)	E. Cawley (Austral)
1979	G. Vilas (Arg)	C. O'Neill (Austral)
1980	G. Vilas (Arg)	B. Jordan (USA)
1981	B. Teacher (USA)	H. Mandlikova (Czech)
1982	J. Kriek (S. Af)	M. Navratilova (USA)
1983	J. Kriek (S. Af)	C. Evert Lloyd (USA)
1984	M. Wilander (Swed)	M. Navratilova (USA)
1985	M. Wilander (Swed)	C. Evert Lloyd (USA)
1986	S. Edberg (Swed)	M. Navratilova (USA)
1987	S. Edberg (Swed)	H. Mandlikova (Czech)
1988	M. Wilander (Swed)	S. Graf (W Ger)
1989	I. Lendl (Czech)	S. Graf (W Ger)
1990	I. Lendl (Czech)	S. Graf (W Ger)
1991	B. Becker (Ger)	M. Seles (Yugos)
1992	J. Courier (USA)	M. Seles (Yugos)
1993	J. Courier (USA)	M. Seles (Yugos)
1994	P. Sampras (USA)	S. Graf (Ger)
1995	A. Agassi (USA)	M. Pierce (Fr)
1996	B. Becker (Ger)	M. Seles (USA)
1997	P. Sampras (USA)	M. Hingis (Switz)

French Open Championship

	Men	Women
1891	J. Briggs	
1892	J. Schopfer	
1893	L. Riboulet	
1894	A. Vacherot	
1895	A. Vacherot	
1896	A. Vacherot	
1897	P. Aymé	C. Masson
1898	P. Aymé	C. Masson
1899	P. Aymé	C. Masson
1900	P. Aymé	C. Prévost
1901	A. Vacherot	P. Girod
1902	A. Vacherot	C. Masson
1903	M. Decugis	C. Masson
1904	M. Decugis	K. Gillou
1905	M. Germot	K. Gillou
1906	M. Germot	K. Fenwick
1907	M. Decugis	M. de Kermel
1908	M. Decugis	K. Fenwick
1909	M. Decugis	J. Mattey
1910	M. Germot	J. Mattey
1911	A. Gobert	J. Mattey
1912	M. Decugis	J. Mattey
1913	M. Decugis	M. Broquedis
1914	M. Decugis	M. Broquedis
1915–19	no competition	
1920	A. Gobert	S. Lenglen
1921	J. Samazeuilh	S. Lenglen
1922	H. Cochet	S. Lenglen
1923	P. Blanchy	S. Lenglen
1924	J. Borotra	S. Lenglen
1925*	R. Lacoste (Fr)	S. Lenglen (Fr)
1926	H. Cochet (Fr)	S. Lenglen (Fr)
1927	R. Lacoste (Fr)	K. Bouman (Neth)
1928	H. Cochet (Fr)	H. Wills (USA)
1929	R. Lacoste (Fr)	H. Wills (USA)
1930	H. Cochet (Fr)	H. Wills Moody (USA)
1931	J. Borotra (Fr)	C. Aussem (Ger)
1932	H. Cochet (Fr)	H. Wills Moody (USA)

	Men	Women
1933	J. Crawford (Austral)	M. Scriven (UK)
1934	G. von Cramm (Ger)	M. Scriven (UK)
1935	F. Perry (UK)	H. Sperling (Den)
1936	G. von Cramm (Ger)	H. Sperling (Den)
1937	H. Henkel (Ger)	H. Sperling (Den)
1938	D. Budge (USA)	S. Mathieu (Fr)
1939	D. McNeill (USA)	S. Mathieu (Fr)
1940–45		no competition
1946	M. Bernard (Fr)	M. Osborne (USA)
1947	J. Asboth (Hung)	P. Todd (USA)
1948	F. Parker (USA)	N. Landry (Belg)
1949	F. Parker (USA)	M. Osborne du Pont (USA)
1950	B. Patty (USA)	D. Hart (USA)
1951	J. Drobny (Czech)	S. Fry (USA)
1952	J. Drobny (Czech)	D. Hart (USA)
1953	K. Rosewall (Austral)	M. Connolly (USA)
1954	T. Trabert (USA)	M. Connolly (USA)
1955	T. Trabert (USA)	A. Mortimer (UK)
1956	L. Hoad (Austral)	A. Gibson (USA)
1957	S. Davidson (Swed)	S. Bloomer (UK)
1958	M. Rose (Austral)	S. Kormoczi (Hung)
1959	N. Pietrangeli (It)	C. Truman (UK)
1960	N. Pietrangeli (It)	D. Hard (USA)
1961	M. Santana (Sp)	A. Haydon (UK)
1962	R. Laver (Austral)	M. Smith (Austral)
1963	R. Emerson (Austral)	L. Turner (Austral)
1964	M. Santana (Sp)	M. Smith (Austral)
1965	F. Stolle (Austral)	L. Turner (Austral)
1966	T. Roche (Austral)	A. Haydon Jones (UK)
1967	R. Emerson (Austral)	F. Durr (Fr)
1968	K. Rosewall (Austral)	N. Richey (USA)

	Men	Women
1969	R. Laver (Austral)	M. Smith Court (Austral)
1970	J. Kodeš (Czech)	M. Court (Austral)
1971	J. Kodeš (Czech)	E. Goolagong (Austral)
1972	A. Gimeno (Sp)	B. J. King (USA)
1973	I. Nastase (Rom)	M. Court (Austral)
1974	B. Borg (Swed)	C. Evert (USA)
1975	B. Borg (Swed)	C. Evert (USA)
1976	A. Panatta (It)	S. Barker (UK)
1977	G. Vilas (Arg)	M. Jausovec (Yugos)
1978	B. Borg (Swed)	V. Ruzici (Rom)
1979	B. Borg (Swed)	C. Evert Lloyd (USA)
1980	B. Borg (Swed)	C. Evert Lloyd (USA)
1981	B. Borg (Swed)	H. Mandlikova (Czech)
1982	M. Wilander (Swed)	M. Navratilova (USA)
1983	Y. Noah (Fr)	C. Evert Lloyd (USA)
1984	I. Lendl (Czech)	M. Navratilova (USA)
1985	M. Wilander (Swed)	C. Evert Lloyd (USA)
1986	I. Lendl (Czech)	C. Evert Lloyd (USA)
1987	I. Lendl (Czech)	S. Graf (W Ger)
1988	M. Wilander (Swed)	S. Graf (W Ger)
1989	M. Chang (USA)	A. Sánchez Vicario (Sp)
1990	A. Gómez (Ecuador)	M. Seles (Yugos)
1991	J. Courier (USA)	M. Seles (Yugos)
1992	J. Courier (USA)	M. Seles (Yugos)
1993	S. Bruguera (Sp)	S. Graf (Ger)
1994	S. Bruguera (Sp)	A. Sánchez Vicario (Sp)
1995	T. Muster (Austria)	S. Graf (Ger)
1996	Yo Kafelnikov (Russia)	S. Graf (Ger)
1997	G. Kuerten (Braz)	I. Majoli (Croatia)

*Opened to non-French competitors in 1925.

TENNIS: INTERNATIONAL TEAM COMPETITIONS

Davis Cup Winners (men)

1900	USA	1927	France	1956	Australia	1980	Czechoslovakia
1901	no competition	1928	France	1957	Australia	1981	USA
1902	USA	1929	France	1958	USA	1982	USA
1903	British Isles[1]	1930	France	1959	Australia	1983	Australia
1904	British Isles	1931	France	1960	Australia	1984	Sweden
1905	British Isles	1932	France	1961	Australia	1985	Sweden
1906	British Isles	1933	UK	1962	Australia	1986	Australia
1907	Australasia[2]	1934	UK	1963	USA	1987	Sweden
1908	Australasia	1935	UK	1964	Australia	1988	West Germany
1909	Australasia	1936	UK	1965	Australia	1989	West Germany
1910	no competition	1937	USA	1966	Australia	1990	USA
1911	Australasia	1938	USA	1967	Australia	1991	France
1912	British Isles	1939	Australia	1968	USA	1992	USA
1913	USA	1940–45	no competition	1969	USA	1993	Germany
1914	Australasia	1946	USA	1970	USA	1994	Sweden
1915–18	no competition	1947	USA	1971	USA	1995	USA
1919	Australasia	1948	USA	1972	USA	1996	France
1920	USA	1949	USA	1973	Australia	1997	Sweden
1921	USA	1950	Australia	1974	South Africa		
1922	USA	1951	Australia	1975	Sweden		
1923	USA	1952	Australia	1976	Italy		
1924	USA	1953	Australia	1977	Australia		
1925	USA	1954	USA	1978	USA		
1926	USA	1955	Australia	1979	USA		

[1] Included Ireland until 1922.

[2] Included New Zealand until 1923.

Federation Cup Winners (women)

1963	USA	1972	South Africa	1981	USA	1990	USA
1964	Australia	1973	Australia	1982	USA	1991	Spain
1965	Australia	1974	Australia	1983	Czechoslovakia	1992	Germany
1966	USA	1975	Czechoslovakia	1984	Czechoslovakia	1993	Spain
1967	USA	1976	USA	1985	Czechoslovakia	1994	Spain
1968	Australia	1977	USA	1986	USA	1995	Spain
1969	USA	1978	USA	1987	West Germany	1996	USA
1970	Australia	1979	USA	1988	West Germany	1997	France
1971	Australia	1980	USA	1989	West Germany		

MOTOR RACING: FORMULA ONE WORLD CHAMPIONSHIP OF DRIVERS

	Winner	*Car**
1950	G. Farina (It)	Alfa Romeo
1951	J. Fangio (Arg)	Alfa Romeo
1952	A. Ascari (It)	Ferrari
1953	A. Ascari (It)	Ferrari
1954	J. Fangio (Arg)	Mercedes & Maserati
1955	J. Fangio (Arg)	Mercedes
1956	J. Fangio (Arg)	Lancia–Ferrari
1957	J. Fangio (Arg)	Maserati
1958	M. Hawthorn (UK)	Ferrari
1959	J. Brabham (Austral)	Cooper–Climax
1960	J. Brabham (Austral)	Cooper–Climax
1961	P. Hill (USA)	Ferrari
1962	G. Hill (UK)	BRM
1963	J. Clark (UK)	Lotus–Climax
1964	J. Surtees (UK)	Ferrari
1965	J. Clark (UK)	Lotus–Climax
1966	J. Brabham (Austral)	Brabham–Repco
1967	D. Hulme (NZ)	Brabham–Repco
1968	G. Hill (UK)	Lotus–Ford
1969	J. Stewart (UK)	Matra–Ford
1970	J. Rindt (Austria)	Lotus–Ford
1971	J. Stewart (UK)	Tyrrell–Ford
1972	E. Fittipaldi (Braz)	John Player Special–Ford
1973	J. Stewart (UK)	Tyrrell–Ford
1974	E. Fittipaldi (Braz)	McLaren–Ford
1975	N. Lauda (Austria)	Ferrari
1976	J. Hunt (UK)	McLaren–Ford
1977	N. Lauda (Austria)	Ferrari
1978	M. Andretti (USA)	Lotus
1979	J. Scheckter (S Af)	Ferrari
1980	A. Jones (Austral)	Williams
1981	N. Piquet (Braz)	Brabham
1982	K. Rosberg (Fin)	Williams
1983	N. Piquet (Braz)	Brabham
1984	N. Lauda (Austria)	McLaren–Porsche/TAG
1985	A. Prost (Fr)	McLaren–Porsche/TAG
1986	A. Prost (Fr)	McLaren–Porsche/TAG
1987	N. Piquet (Braz)	Williams–Honda
1988	A. Senna (Braz)	McLaren
1989	A. Prost (Braz)	McLaren
1990	A. Senna (Braz)	McLaren
1991	A. Senna (Braz)	McLaren
1992	N. Mansell (UK)	Williams–Renault
1993	A. Prost (Braz)	Williams–Renault
1994	M. Schumacher (Ger)	Benetton–Ford
1995	M. Schumacher (Ger)	Benetton–Renault
1996	D. Hill (UK)	Williams–Renault
1997	J. Villeneuve (Can)	Williams–Renault

*Where chassis and engine are made by different companies, the chassis manufacturer appears first and is separated from the engine manufacturer by a dash.